Food & Beverage Market Place

Volume 1

2021
Twentieth Edition

Food & Beverage Market Place

Volume 1

- Food & Beverage Manufacturers
- Product Categories
- Company Profiles

AMENIA, NY 12501

PRESIDENT: Richard Gottlieb
PUBLISHER: Leslie Mackenzie
EDITORIAL DIRECTOR: Laura Mars

PRODUCTION MANAGER: Kristen Hayes
RESEARCH ASSISTANTS: Olivia Parsonson; Sarah Reside
COMPOSITION: David Garoogian

MARKETING DIRECTOR: Jessica Moody

Grey House Publishing, Inc.
4919 Route 22
Amenia, NY 12501
518.789.8700
FAX 845.373.6390
www.greyhouse.com
e-mail: books @greyhouse.com

While every effort has been made to ensure the reliability of the information presented in this publication, Grey House Publishing neither guarantees the accuracy of the data contained herein nor assumes any responsibility for errors, omissions or discrepancies. Grey House accepts no payment for listing; inclusion in the publication of any organization, agency, institution, publication, service or individual does not imply endorsement of the editors or publisher.

Errors brought to the attention of the publisher and verified to the satisfaction of the publisher will be corrected in future editions.

Except by express prior written permission of the Copyright Proprietor no part of this work may be copied by any means of publication or communication now known or developed hereafter including, but not limited to, use in any directory or compilation or other print publication, in any information storage and retrieval system, in any other electronic device, or in any visual or audio-visual device or product.

This publication is an original and creative work, copyrighted by Grey House Publishing, Inc. and is fully protected by all applicable copyright laws, as well as by laws covering misappropriation, trade secrets and unfair competition.

Grey House has added value to the underlying factual material through one or more of the following efforts: unique and original selection; expression; arrangement; coordination; and classification.

Grey House Publishing, Inc. will defend its rights in this publication.

Copyright © 2020 Grey House Publishing, Inc.
All rights reserved
First edition published 2001
Twentieth edition published 2020
Printed in Canada

Food & beverage market place. — 20th ed. (2021) —
   3 v. ; 27.5 cm. Annual
  Includes index.
  ISSN: 1554-6334

1. Food industry and trade—United States—Directories. 2. Food industry and trade—Canada—Directories. 3. Beverage industry—United States—Directories. 4. Beverage industry—Canada—Directories. I. Grey House Publishing, Inc. II. Title: Food & beverage market place.

HD9003.T48
338-dc21

3-Volume Set	ISBN: 978-1-64265-464-6
Volume 1	**ISBN: 978-1-64265-465-3**
Volume 2	ISBN: 978-1-64265-466-0
Volume 3	ISBN: 978-1-64265-467-7

Table of Contents

VOLUME 1

Introduction	vii
Summary of Best Practices for Retail Food Stores, Restaurants, and Food Pick-Up/Delivery Services During the COVID-19 Pandemic	ix
The Impact of COVID-19 on Shopping Behavior	xi
Food & Beverage Manufacturers User Guide	2
Food & Beverage Product Category List	5
Food & Beverage Product Categories	27
Food & Beverage Manufacturer Profiles	453
Brand Name Index	1259
Ethnic Food Index	1311
Geographic Index	1317
Parent Company Index	1357

VOLUME 2

Introduction
Equipment, Supplies & Services User Guide
Equipment, Supplies & Services Product Category List
Equipment, Supplies & Services Product Categories
Equipment, Supplies & Services Company Profiles
Brand Name Index
Geographic Index

VOLUME 3

Introduction
Broker Companies User Guide
Broker Company Profiles
Broker Market Index
Brokered Product Index

Importers/Exporters User Guide
Importers/Exporters Company Profiles
Export Region Index
Import Region Index

Transportation Firms User Guide
Transportation Firm Profiles
Transportation Region Index
Transportation Type Index

Warehouse Companies User Guide
Warehouse Company Profiles
Warehouse Region Index
Warehouse Type and Service Index

Wholesalers/Distributors User Guide
Wholesalers/Distributors Company Profiles
Wholesale Product Type Index

ALL BRANDS INDEX
ALL COMPANIES INDEX

Introduction

This 2021 edition of *Food & Beverage Market Place* represents the largest, most comprehensive resource of food and beverage manufacturers and service suppliers on the market today. These three volumes include over 45,000 company profiles that address all sectors of the industry—finished goods and ingredients manufacturers, equipment manufacturers, and third-party logistics providers, including transportation, warehousing, wholesalers, brokers, importers and exporters.

While the food and beverage industry generally continues to grow, the reality of the COVID-19 pandemic has presented many challenges to this truly essential industry. At the time of this writing, out of home consumption, with its high margin of profit, has been reduced nearly to a standstill for several months. Mandated quarantines have disrupted supply chains. Consumers are shifing to digital shopping and home delivery. The industry is redefining its work force and finding new ways to connect with customers.

One segment has found a silver lining in the cloud of COVID-19, and that is meal-kit companies. As consumers adapt to cooking and eating at home, meal kits, delivered to your door with conveniently packaged food and easy-to-follow recipes, have a huge appeal. Time will tell if they can sustain and build on the momentum created by the current quarantine.

Another interesting consequence of the current environment is the kinds of foods that people are eating. While certain long-standing food trends are well entrenched in our society, especially now, including natural and organic food, like those with antioxidants for healthy aging, and foods with good bacteria that promote digestive health, there is a significant uptick in online searches for cinammon roll and hot cross buns recipes, and a shortage of yeast on supermarket shelves. The growth in plant-based food is significant and, experts say, a trend that is likely to continue. While that would be a good thing, hopefully another trend—quarantine snacking—is temporary, as people start to spend less time around the house. In addition, following this Introduction in Volume 1 are two items that offer more information related to COVID-19 and the food and beverage industry: *Best Practices for Retail Food Stores, Restaurants & Food Pick Up and Delivery Services;* and *The Impact of COVID-19 on Shopping Behavior.*

Other industry trends are likely to continue, as consumers focus on foods that encourage sustainability, foods that are convenient and healthy, foods that are processed in secure and safe environments, and foods with complex world flavors.

As food and beverage consumers' needs evolve, *Food & Beverage Market Place* continues to keep pace. The research for this edition focused on ingredient, nutrition and health food manufacturers. You'll find packaging that is mindful of the environment, and processing systems that are safe and secure. Whatever slice of the market you cater to, you will find your buyers, sellers, and users in this comprehensive, three-volume reference tool containing the complete coverage our subscribers have come to expect. Our extensive indexing makes quick work of locating exactly the company, product or service you are looking for.

Data Statistics

Each of the eight chapters in *Food & Beverage Market Place* reflects a massive update effort. This 2021 edition includes hundreds of new company profiles and thousands of updates throughout the three volumes. You will find 83,214 key executives, 22,668 web sites, and 15,869 e-mails. The volumes break down as follows:

Volume 1   Food, Beverage & Ingredient Manufacturers - 14,086

Volume 2   Equipment, Supply & Service Providers - 13,465

Volume 3   Third Party Logistics
                 Brokers - 1,287
                 Importers & Exporters - 8,818
                 Transportation Firms - 707
                 Warehouse Companies - 1,044
                 Wholesalers & Distributors - 5,904

Introduction

Arrangement

The product category sections for both food and beverage products in Volume 1 and equipment and supplies in Volume 2 begin with Product Category Lists. These include over 6,000 alphabetical terms for everything from Abalone to Zinc Citrate, from Adhesive Tapes to Zipper Application Systems. Use the detailed cross-references to find the full entry in the Product Category sections that immediately follow. Here you will find up to three levels of detail, for example—*Fish & Seafood: Fish: Abalone* or *Ingredients, Flavors & Additives: Vitamins & Supplements: Zinc Citrate*—with the name, location, phone number and packaging format of companies who manufacturer/process the product you are looking for. Organic and Gluten-Free categories make it easy to locate those manufacturers who focus on these food types.

In addition to company profiles, this edition has 17 indexes, 15 chapter-specific, arranged by geographic region, product or company type, and two—All Brands and All Companies—that comprise all three volumes. See the Table of Contents for a complete list of specific indexes. Plus, chapters include User Guides that help you navigate chapter-specific data.

We are confident that this reference is the foremost research tool in the food and beverage industry. It will prove invaluable to manufacturers, buyers, specifiers, market researchers, consultants, and anyone working in food and beverage—one of the largest industries in the country.

Praise for previous editions:

> *"...This set can be used to find basic information or to track trends in a dynamic industry.... Recommended for large public or academic libraries."*

> *"...Each volume contains helpful user guides and key that describes the field of data that appear in that chapter.... This publication is essential for researchers in the food industry, and large academic and public libraries."*

—American Reference Books Annual

Online Database & Mailing Lists

Food & Beverage Market Place is also available for subscription on https://gold.greyhouse.com for even faster, easier access to this wealth of information. Subscribers can search by product category, state, sales volume, employee size, personnel name, title and much more. Plus, users can print out prospect sheets or download data into their own spreadsheet or database. This database is a must for anyone marketing a product or service to this vast industry. Visit the site, or call 800-562-2139 for a free trial.

Summary of Best Practices for Retail Food Stores, Restaurants, and Food Pick-Up/Delivery Services During the COVID-19 Pandemic

FDA | U.S. FOOD & DRUG ADMINISTRATION

BE HEALTHY, BE CLEAN

- Employees - Stay home or leave work if sick; consult doctor if sick, and contact supervisor
- Employers - Instruct sick employees to stay home and send home immediately if sick
- Employers - Pre-screen employees exposed to COVID-19 for temperature and other symptoms

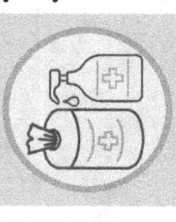

- Wash your hands often with soap and water for at least 20 seconds
- If soap and water are not available, use a 60% alcohol-based hand sanitizer per CDC
- Avoid touching your eyes, nose, and mouth with unwashed hands
- Wear mask/face covering per CDC & FDA

- Never touch Ready-to-Eat foods with bare hands
- Use single service gloves, deli tissue, or suitable utensils
- Wrap food containers to prevent cross contamination
- Follow 4 steps to food safety Clean, Separate, Cook, and Chill

CLEAN & DISINFECT

- Train employees on cleaning and disinfecting procedures, and protective measures, per CDC and FDA
- Have and use cleaning products and supplies
- Follow protective measures

- Disinfect high-touch surfaces frequently
- Use EPA-registered disinfectant
- Ensure food containers and utensils are cleaned and sanitized

- Prepare and use sanitizers according to label instructions
- Offer sanitizers and wipes to customers to clean grocery cart/basket handles, or utilize store personnel to conduct cleaning/sanitizing

SOCIAL DISTANCE

- Help educate employees and customers on importance of social distancing:
  - Signs
  - Audio messages
  - Consider using every other check-out lane to aid in distancing

- Avoid displays that may result in customer gatherings; discontinue self-serve buffets and salad bars; discourage employee gatherings
- Place floor markings and signs to encourage social distancing

- Shorten customer time in store by encouraging them to:
  - Use shopping lists
  - Order ahead of time, if offered
- Set up designated pick-up areas inside or outside retail establishments

PICK-UP & DELIVERY

- If offering delivery options:
  - Ensure coolers and transport containers are cleaned and sanitized
  - Maintain time and temperature controls
  - Avoid cross contamination; for example, wrap food during transport

- Encourage customers to use "no touch" deliveries
- Notify customers as the delivery is arriving by text message or phone call

- Establish designated pick-up zones for customers
- Offer curb-side pick-up
- Practice social distancing by offering to place orders in vehicle trunks

April 2020

For more information, see Best Practices for Retail Food Stores, Restaurants, and Food Pick-Up/Delivery Services During the COVID-19 Pandemic

introduction

At the onset of the coronavirus pandemic in the U.S., we saw grocery shopping behavior change seemingly overnight. With social distancing and safety in mind, many have turned to online grocery and click-and-collect to fulfill their shopping needs. Others have continued to rely on trips to physical grocery stores, often struggling to navigate the disruption in that experience brought on by the crisis. With these shifting dynamics in mind, the question for many retailers and manufacturers is how the current crisis, and the changes it has brought, will impact future shopping behavior once the country returns to a new normal.

From April 4–5, 2020, Blue Chip fielded a national survey among 500 primary grocery shoppers across the U.S. to better understand how their grocery shopping behavior has changed due to the coronavirus pandemic, what their impressions are of the new shopping environment, and what they predict their shopping behavior will be like in the future. The results paint a picture of what retailers and brands should be thinking about now to win with shoppers later.

© 2020 blue chip. All rights reserved.

FROM emotion to transaction
in-store

The coronavirus crisis has highlighted the central importance of the in-store grocery shopping experience in modern American lives.

Even as the virus spread through the U.S. in March, 9 out of 10 shoppers still chose to get their groceries in a physical store. Three times as many people still shopped in a physical store compared to online.

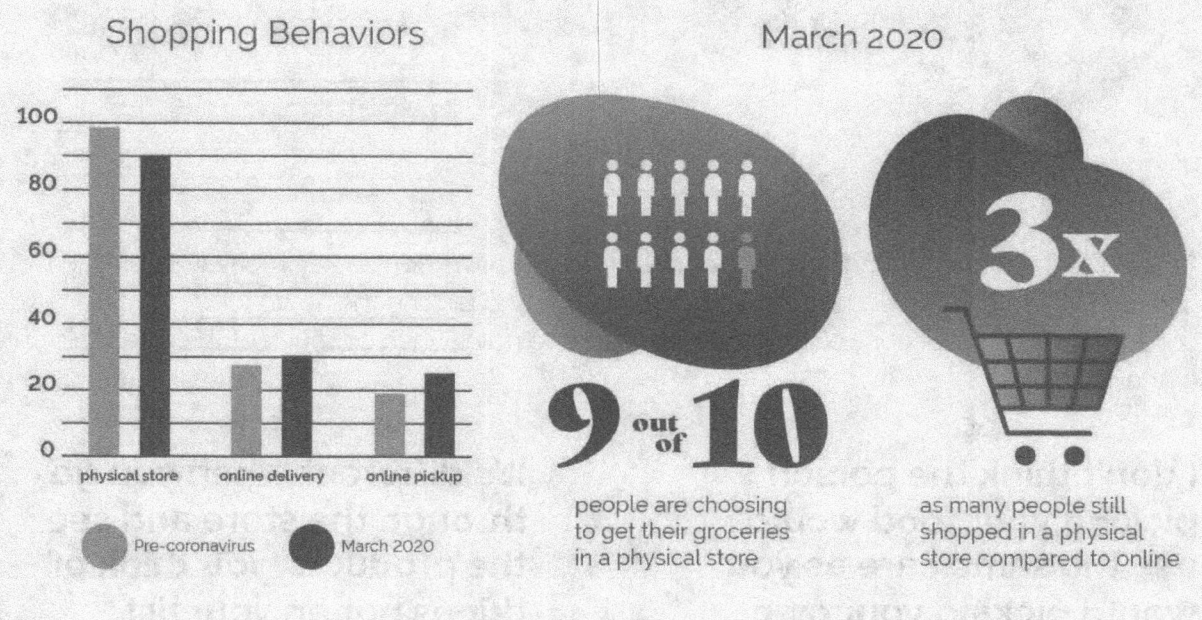

Shopping Behaviors — physical store, online delivery, online pickup (Pre-coronavirus vs. March 2020)

March 2020: 9 out of 10 people are choosing to get their groceries in a physical store

3x as many people still shopped in a physical store compared to online

© 2020 blue chip. All rights reserved.

FROM emotion to transaction in-store

What do you enjoy about shopping in-store?

Key drivers for choosing to shop in-store: DISCOVERY, INDEPENDENCE, EXPLORATION

- **83%** picking from products that are on sale
- **69%** broad selection of products
- **69%** ability to discover new products
- **64%** comparing prices
- **20%** interaction with store personnel
- **20%** seeing friends or neighbors

Source: Blue Chip survey of 500 U.S. grocery shoppers conducted from April 4 – 5, 2020

Respondents noted **discovery, independence** and **exploration** as key motivators driving this choice. The experience of going into a grocery store and picking their own foods gives consumers a sense of control. This is even more true now, when so much of their life feels out of their control.

> "I don't think the person picking your food would use the same care as you would picking your own."

> "It's different when you go through the store and see the products, you think of things not on your list."

© 2020 blue chip. All rights reserved.

THE changing in-store experience

Although 90% of surveyed shoppers still make in-store trips, those shopping experiences are nearly unrecognizable compared to pre-pandemic times. Everything from social distancing measures to one-way aisles, capacity limits to inventory challenges—it is entirely unfamiliar. Self-serve areas of the store, such as sampling areas, hot bars, bakeries and delis, have closed. Prepared foods in many stores are likewise on temporary hiatus. The in-store experience that retailers spent years building has begun dissolving, and the pendulum has swung back toward a fundamentally transactional experience. Shoppers are being retrained to treat the visit as such.

from browsing to sprinting

Shoppers are going through stores with *purpose*, planning with clear intention to get in and out with what they need quickly, in order to limit exposure. This has been compounded by retailers managing shopper traffic flow in their stores with measures like traffic-controlled checkout queues, one-way aisle flow, one-in-one-out policies and more.

Walmart recently implemented a one-in-one-out policy.

Source: Field Agent

THE changing in-store experience

In this environment, shoppers appear to be forming strategies for their limited stock-up trips, driven by the simple goal of acquiring each item on their list. There is less browsing, less consideration between brands and less discovery.

Adding to that, brands and grocery merchandisers have reduced in-store promotions, which, pre-pandemic, would have affected in-store shopping behaviors. Given that shopping is more mission driven today, pre-store planning and list-making are more important than ever, providing opportunities for both retailers and brands to reach shoppers. Going forward, it will be important to observe the nature and behaviors of the in-store trip that endure as shoppers adapt to a new normal, which may be driven more by efficiency and offer fewer experiences, like sampling.

from "my brand" to "any brand"

Brands in commodity categories that shoppers consider essential have been in high demand and susceptible to frantic buying and out-of-stocks. As a result, these brands have faced difficult challenges in maintaining inventories—a fact that will affect their brand strategies during the crisis and beyond. Shoppers now make purchase decisions based upon what is available and whether they need to stock up.

Leading brands in essential categories like toilet paper had, up until recently, loyal shoppers that led on differentiated positioning, but out-of-stock issues have forced shoppers to try competitors that they may be unfamiliar with. Those less familiar brands will now forever be in shopper consideration sets in future trips after the crisis has passed. Once we reach that new normal, leading brands in essential categories will need to reestablish their dominance in the shopper consideration set and potentially reevaluate their value proposition.

© 2020 blue chip. All rights reserved.

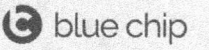

THE changing in-store experience

Once we reach that new normal, leading brands in essential categories will need to reestablish their dominance in the shopper consideration set. On the flip side, those brands gaining trial due to their availability should think about how to stay top-of-mind and turn new triers into future buyers.

looking ahead

Once the pandemic subsides and Americans once again feel safe and welcome shopping in-store, the experience may still be fundamentally different. Learned shopping behaviors are likely to stay. A heightened concern over cleanliness and sanitation will certainly remain, potentially disrupting long-held practices of food and beverage sampling. The store, the aisle and the category will be shopped differently.

So what should brands and retailers be thinking about *now* to have real impact *later*?

implications

- Sampling—once a key discovery and trial driver for food and beverage—will not come back immediately, if at all. Rethink in-store sampling strategy (e.g., individually wrapped, single serve packages).

- While in-store activity has stalled, price and promotion will play a big part in brands getting back in front of shoppers and easing the squeeze felt during the pandemic period.

- Brands will need to rebuild loyalty with consumers who may have temporarily switched to other brands. Premium brands will need to lean into their value proposition and rebuild those relationships.

- Retailers will need to reevaluate how to bring back experience elements within the boundaries of the new normal.

© 2020 blue chip. All rights reserved.

The Impact of COVID-19 on Shopping Behavior

From transaction to emotion online

Facing the new reality of social distancing and the potential health risks of going to the grocery store, many consumers turned to e-commerce solutions to fulfill their needs. While 90% of shoppers were making in-store trips, online and click-and-collect increased 32% during March 2020 compared to before the pandemic. Additionally, our survey showed that half of people who haven't shopped online yet are open to doing so in the future.

Why shop online?

Pre-coronavirus
- 86% convenience
- 79% good prices
- 75% saves me time

March 2020
- 89% minimize exposure to health risk
- 85% convenience
- 84% reduces stress

Placing an online order inspired feelings of "safety, gratitude, comfort and relief."

50% of people who haven't shopped online yet plan to/are open to do so in the future

Source: Blue Chip survey of 500 U.S. grocery shoppers conducted from April 4 – 5, 2020.

Before the coronavirus pandemic, consumers valued e-commerce because it was convenient, saving them time and money. However, as external motivators pushed people online, there was a shift in the value equation. Safety, convenience and stress reduction emerged as key factors to shop online. "Reducing stress" increased 20 points alone during this time period. Online grocery shopping inspired feelings of safety, relief, comfort and gratitude.

© 2020 blue chip. All rights reserved.

THE spectrum of satisfaction

While heightened emotions surround the e-commerce experience, only 4 in 10 surveyed noted they were "very satisfied" with the actual online shopping experience itself.

Those who were satisfied with the experience noted emotional associations of safety, relief and comfort, along with a new recognition of the practical aspects of convenience and time-saving.

> **It makes my life easier. I feel safer being at home instead of having to go our and shop.**

> **I am less intimidated by the process; the ease and convenience of it was a revelation.**

For others, out-of-stock items, product substitutions, lengthy delivery windows and inflated prices soured the experience.

> **Prices were extremely marked up. They would substitute store brand when possible, but the price was the same as name brand.**

> **Not always having what I need in stock and not finding out until after I attempt to place an order.**

© 2020 blue chip. All rights reserved.

THE spectrum of satisfaction

the missing link

Until now, online grocery shopping has, for most shoppers, been largely functional and transactional. The convenience it provides rises to the top of shopper needs and imparts a higher-level benefit of control over one's time, which is critical for many. But for many others, it hasn't risen to the level of true *shopping*. It lacks the *feel* of shopping, the *visceral reward* of shopping, the *personal touch* of shopping. It has been the red-haired stepchild of *real shopping*. It lacks the feelings of trust, humanity and control that are inherent in the in-store experience.

Looking ahead, when going to the grocery store is no longer a life or death situation and the heightened emotions around health and safety subside, the pre-crisis e-commerce selling points of convenience and time-saving alone will not be enough to keep some shoppers in the e-commerce environment.

How can retailers and brands evolve the online experience on the other end of this crisis to fill the emotional voids of trust, humanity and control in the current online grocery environment?

> "I need to feel that they care about my money and my family."

> "I need to trust the person selecting my order."

© 2020 blue chip. All rights reserved.

THE Spectrum of Satisfaction

immediate implications

- Brands and retailers should implement shopper offers to entice repeat purchase online.

- Surprise and delight in delivery orders to keep margins but 'sweeten the deal' on some of the price disparity. Brands can also consider incentives to help offset delivery fees.

- Brands must show up meaningfully and consistently online. If you don't already have an e-commerce strategy in place, plan for it now. Invest in e-commerce but as a brand equity builder.

- Take the time now to reevaluate your e-commerce content to not only ensure there are guideposts for size comparison and product variations but to inspire further exploration and discovery.

longer term

- Online customer service for brand and retailers will be more important than ever. It will no longer be about just providing technical support; it will require human interaction, advice and guidance.

- In the e-commerce space, retailers must examine how to translate those distinct elements of brand personality cultivated in the in-store environment via associates, atmosphere, interaction and selection that shoppers *trust*.

- Humanizing the person fulfilling the order will build trust and affirm that they care about the order as much the shopper who placed it.

- Additionally, show the precautionary measures they use to handle their order with care.

© 2020 blue chip. All rights reserved.

finding the balance

Shopping as we know it has most likely changed forever. At the end of this pandemic, the pendulum may fall back to rest in the middle (or slightly left or right of center) for in-store and online shopping. In all likelihood, the in-store experience won't fully return to what shoppers once considered normal, given the new level of purpose and intention they have brought to the experience and their learned behaviors around "sprint" shopping and heightened safety. At the same time, many who shifted at least some of their shopping to e-commerce, motivated by emotional drivers that emerged in the crisis, may continue to shop more frequently online—especially if retailers and brands deliver emotions that transform the experience from one that is strictly transactional to one that is about building ongoing relationships with shoppers.

Further, as the crisis subsides, we may see the emergence of a Brave New Shopper in the U.S. One with new adaptability, a sharpened set of shopping skills and higher expectations for their shopping experience. To incite discovery and rebuild loyalty in-store, brands will need to reteach shoppers how to navigate categories and find ways to encourage them to shop the aisles. In e-commerce, retailers must develop a richer shopping experience. By instilling emotions like trust, control and humanity into online shopping, they can boost the consumer-retailer relationship and inspire online loyalty.

In the end, the coronavirus crisis has accelerated the appearance of a new omnichannel reality born of uncertainty but fed by the need for action and a spirit of adaptability. This new reality defines a bright, promising future for the brands and retailers who choose to embrace it.

© 2020 blue chip. All rights reserved.

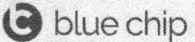

"The impact of COVID-19 on shopping behavior." Blue Chip, 2020. Reprinted with permission, May 2020. The full report can be found online: https://www2.smartbrief.com/rest/lp-proxy/landing-pages/ce9cde09-910e-42db-a5e3-5baa26fb454f.

MANUFACTURERS

User Guide
Product Category List
Product Categories
Company Profiles
Brand Name Index
Ethnic Food Index
Geographic Index
Parent/Child Index

Manufacturer User Guide

The **Food & Beverage Manufacturers Chapter** of *Food & Beverage Market Place* includes companies that manufacture food and beverage products, both finished goods and ingredients. The chapter begins with a **Product Category Listing** of food and beverage products that are manufactured by companies in this chapter. This category list is followed by a **Product Category Index**, organized by product. Each company listing includes packaging type, city and phone number.

Following the **Product Category Index** are the descriptive listings, which are organized alphabetically. Following the A – Z Food and Beverage Manufacturers listings are four indexes: **Brand Index**, which lists food and beverage brand names; **Ethnic Food Index**, which lists companies by ethnic type of food they manufacture; **Geographic Index**, which lists all companies by state, and **Parent Company Index**; which lists companies by their corporate parent. These Indexes refers to listing numbers, not page numbers.

Below is a sample listing illustrating the kind of information that is or might be included in a Food and Beverage Manufacturer listing. Each numbered item of information is described in the User Key on the following page.

---

1 → 100000

2 → **(HQ) AFF Specialties**

3 → 555 Maplewood Drive

Cordova, TN 38016

4 → 001-381-3222

5 → 001-381-3223

6 → 888-381-324

7 → info@AFF.com

8 → www.AFF.com

9 → Manufacturer of Italian cheese and dried pasta and cooking oils. Exporter of olive oil.

10 → President: Brian Miller
CFO: Philip George
COO: Blakeny Pinschell
Vice President: Kristin Rolls
Marketing: Melissa Backwith

11 → *Estimated Sales*: $65 Million

12 → *Number Employees*: 80

13 → *Sq. Footage*: 30000

14 → *Parent Co.*: Associated Foods

15 → *Type of Packaging:* Consumer, Food Service, Bulk

16 → *Company is also listed in the following section(s)*: Exporter

17 → *Other Locations*: AFF Specialties, Atlanta, GA

18 → *Brands:* Unique, Fiesta, Baking Rite, Carruso, Golden Dairy

Manufacturer User Key

1 → **Record Number:** Entries are listed alphabetically within each category and numbered sequentially. The entry number, rather than the page number, is used in the indexes to refer to listings.

2 → **Company Name:** Formal name of company. HQ indicates headquarter location. If names are completely capitalized, the listing will appear at the beginning of the alphabetized section.

3 → **Address:** Location or permanent address of the company. If the mailing address differs from the street address, it will appear second. Companies are indexed by state.

4 → **Phone Number:** The listed phone number is usually for the main office, but may also be for the sales, marketing, or public relations office as provided.

5 → **Fax Number:** This is listed when provided by the company.

6 → **Toll-Free Number:** This is listed when provided by the company.

7 → **E-Mail:** This is listed when provided, and is generally the main office e-mail.

8 → **Web Site:** This is listed when provided by the company and is also referred to as an URL address. These web sites are accessed through the Internet by typing http:// before the URL address.

9 → **Description**: This paragraph contains a brief description of the food and beverages manufactured by the company, as well as other services they provide. Companies are indexed by the ethnic food they manufacture.

10 → **Key Personnel:** Names and titles of company executives.

11 → **Estimated Sales:** This is listed when provided by the company.

12 → **Number of Employees:** Total number of employees within the company.

13 → **Sq. Footage:** Size of facility.

14 → **Parent Co.:** If the listing is a division of another company, the parent is listed here. Companies are indexed by the ethnic foods they manufacture.

15 → **Type of Packaging:** Indicates the market that the food or beverage products are packaged for.

16 → Indicates what other section in *Food & Beverage Market Place* this company is listed: Volume 1: Manufacturers. Volume 2: Equipment, Supplies & Services; Transportation; Warehouse; Wholesalers/Distributors. Volume 3: Brokers; Importers/Exporters.

17 → **Other locations:** Indicates other company locations.

18 → **Brands:** Listing of brand names that the company manufactures. Companies are indexed by brand names.

Product Category List

A

Abalone Fish *See Fish & Seafood: Fish: Abalone*
Arborio Rice *See Cereals, Grains, Rice & Flour: Rice: Aborio*
Acacia Gum *See Ingredients, Flavors & Additives: Gums: Acacia Gum*
Acetic Acidulants *See Ingredients, Flavors & Additives: Acidulants: Acetic*
Acidophilus Cultures *See Ingredients, Flavors & Additives: Cultures & Yeasts: Acidophilus Cultures*
Acids *See Ingredients, Flavors & Additives: Acids*
Acidulants *See Ingredients, Flavors & Additives: Acidulants*
Acorn Squash *See Fruits & Vegetables: Squash: Acorn*
Active Salt *See Spices, Seasonings & Seeds: Salt: Active*
Additives *See Ingredients, Flavors & Additives: Additives*
Additives Enzymes *See Ingredients, Flavors & Additives: Enzymes: Additives*
Ade Juices *See Beverages: Juices: Ade*
Adipic Acids *See Ingredients, Flavors & Additives: Acids: Adipic*
Adjuncts *See Ingredients, Flavors & Additives: Adjuncts*
Adobo Powders *See Ingredients, Flavors & Additives: Powders: Adobo*
Adzuki Beans *See Fruits & Vegetables: Beans: Adzuki*
Agar-Agar *See Ingredients, Flavors & Additives: Gums: Agar-Agar*
Agents *See Ingredients, Flavors & Additives: Agents*
Agnolotti *See Pasta & Noodles: Agnolotti*
Albacore Tuna Fish *See Fish & Seafood: Fish: Tuna: Albacore*
Albumen Solids *See Eggs & Egg Products: Solids: Albumen*
Alcoholic Beverages *See Beverages: Alcoholic Beverages*
Alcohols *See Ingredients, Flavors & Additives: Alcohols*
Alfalfa *See Cereals, Grains, Rice & Flour: Alfalfa*
Alfalfa Seeds *See Spices, Seasonings & Seeds: Seeds: Alfalfa*
Alfalfa Sprouts *See Fruits & Vegetables: Sprouts: Alfalfa*
Alfredo Sauces *See Sauces, Dips & Dressings: Sauces: Alfredo*
Algae *See Fruits & Vegetables: Algae*
Algin & Alginates *See Ingredients, Flavors & Additives: Gums: Algin & Alginates*
All Purpose Flour *See Cereals, Grains, Rice & Flour: Flour: All Purpose*
All Purpose Herbs Blends *See Ingredients, Flavors & Additives: Blends: Herbs: All Purpose*
Alligator Game *See Meats & Meat Products: Game: Alligator*
Allspice *See Spices, Seasonings & Seeds: Spices: Allspice*
Almond Biscotti *See Baked Goods: Cookies & Bars: Biscotti: Almond*
Almond Cookies *See Baked Goods: Cookies & Bars: Almond Cookies*
Almond Flavors *See Ingredients, Flavors & Additives: Flavors: Almond*
Almond Flour *See Cereals, Grains, Rice & Flour: Flour: Almond*
Almond Nut Butters *See Nuts & Nut Butters: Nut Butters: Almond*
Almond Nut Pastes *See Nuts & Nut Butters: Nut Pastes: Almond*
Almond Oils *See Oils, Shortening & Fats: Oils: Almond*
Almond Pastes *See Ingredients, Flavors & Additives: Pastes: Almond*
Almonds *See Nuts & Nut Butters: Nuts: Almonds*
Aloe Juices *See Beverages: Juices: Aloe*
Aloe Vera *See Fruits & Vegetables: Aloe Vera*
Amaranth *See Cereals, Grains, Rice & Flour: Grains: Amaranth*
Amaretto Cookies *See Baked Goods: Cookies & Bars: Amaretto Cookies*
Amaretto Flavors *See Ingredients, Flavors & Additives: Flavors: Amaretto*
Amaretto Liqueurs & Cordials *See Beverages: Spirits & Liqueurs: Liqueurs & Cordials: Amaretto*
Amber Ale *See Beverages: Beers: American & British Ale: Amber Ale*
Amber Jack *See Fish & Seafood: Fish: Amber Jack*
Amber Lager *See Beverages: Beers: Lager: Amber Lager*
American & British Ale *See Beverages: Beers: American & British Ale*
American Cheese *See Cheese & Cheese Products: Cheese: American*
American Cheese Imitations *See Cheese & Cheese Products: Imitation Cheeses & Substitutes: Imitation: American*
American Cheese Powders *See Ingredients, Flavors & Additives: Powders: Cheese: American*
American Cheese Substitutes *See Cheese & Cheese Products: Imitation Cheeses & Substitutes: Substitutes: American*
American/Skim Milk Cheese, Sliced Blend *See Cheese & Cheese Products: Cheese: Blend - American/Skim Milk: Sliced*
Aminoacetic Acids *See Ingredients, Flavors & Additives: Acids: Aminoacetic*
Ammonium Carbonate *See Ingredients, Flavors & Additives: Ammonium Carbonate*
Ammonium Phosphates *See Ingredients, Flavors & Additives: Ammonium Phosphates*
Analogs *See Ingredients, Flavors & Additives: Analogs*
Ancho Ground Chile Pepper *See Spices, Seasonings & Seeds: Spices: Chile Pepper: Ancho Ground*
Ancho Peppers *See Fruits & Vegetables: Peppers: Ancho*
Anchovies *See Fish & Seafood: Fish: Anchovies*
Anchovies Paste *See Fish & Seafood: Fish: Anchovies: Paste*
Andouille Sausage Seasonings *See Spices, Seasonings & Seeds: Seasonings: Sausage: Andouille*
Andouille Sausages *See Meats & Meat Products: Smoked, Cured & Deli Meats: Sausages: Andouille*
Angel Food Cake *See Baked Goods: Cakes & Pastries: Angel Food Cake*
Angel Hair *See Pasta & Noodles: Angel Hair*
Animal Crackers *See Baked Goods: Cookies & Bars: Animal Crackers*
Anise Flavors *See Ingredients, Flavors & Additives: Flavors: Anise; See also Spices/Anise Seed*
Anise Liqueur *See Beverages: Spirits & Liqueurs: Liqueurs & Cordials: Anise Liqueur*
Anise or Aniseed Oils *See Oils, Shortening & Fats: Oils: Anise or Aniseed*
Anise or Aniseed Seeds *See Spices, Seasonings & Seeds: Seeds: Anise or Aniseed*
Anise, Star *See Spices, Seasonings & Seeds: Spices: Anise - Star*
Annatto Colors *See Ingredients, Flavors & Additives: Colors: Annatto*
Annatto Natural Colors *See Ingredients, Flavors & Additives: Colors: Natural: Annatto*
Annatto Seeds *See Spices, Seasonings & Seeds: Seeds: Annatto*
Anthocyanins Grape Skin *See Ingredients, Flavors & Additives: Colors: Natural: Anthocyanins Grape Skin*
Anticaking Additives *See Ingredients, Flavors & Additives: Additives: Anticaking*
Anticaking Agents *See Ingredients, Flavors & Additives: Agents: Anticaking*
Antimicrobial Agents *See Ingredients, Flavors & Additives: Agents: Antimicrobial*
Antioxidants *See Specialty & Organic Foods: Organic Foods: Natural: Antioxidants; See also Organic Foods; See also Ingredients, Flavors & Additives: Antioxidants*
Antipasto *See Prepared Foods: Antipasto*
Antipasto Salads *See Prepared Foods: Prepared Salads: Antipasto*
Appaloosa Beans *See Fruits & Vegetables: Beans: Appaloosa*
Appetizers *See Prepared Foods: Appetizers; See also Prepared Foods: Appetizers: Fresh, Canned & Frozen*
Apple *See Fruits & Vegetables: Apple*
Apple Boysin Berry Juices *See Beverages: Juices: Apple Boysin Berry*
Apple Butter *See Jams, Jellies & Spreads: Spreads: Apple Butter*
Apple Cider Juices *See Beverages: Juices: Apple Cider*
Apple Cider Vinegar *See Sauces, Dips & Dressings: Vinegar: Apple Cider*
Apple Cobbler *See Baked Goods: Cakes & Pastries: Apple Cobbler*
Apple Cranberry Juices *See Beverages: Juices: Apple Cranberry*
Apple Flavors *See Ingredients, Flavors & Additives: Flavors: Apple*
Apple Grape Juices *See Beverages: Juices: Apple Grape*
Apple Juices *See Beverages: Juices: Apple*
Apple Pectins *See Ingredients, Flavors & Additives: Pectins: Apple*
Apple Pies *See Baked Goods: Pies: Apple*
Apple Rings *See Fruits & Vegetables: Apple: Rings*
Apple Sauces *See Fruits & Vegetables: Sauces: Apple*
Apple Sauces with Other Fruit or Spices *See Fruits & Vegetables: Sauces: Apple: with Other Fruit or Spices*
Apple Slices *See Fruits & Vegetables: Apple: Slices*
Apricot *See Fruits & Vegetables: Apricot*
Apricot Jams *See Jams, Jellies & Spreads: Jams: Apricot*
Apricot Juices *See Beverages: Juices: Apricot*
Apricot Kernals *See Fruits & Vegetables: Apricot: Kernals*
Aquaculture *See Specialty & Organic Foods: Aquaculture; See also Organic Foods*
Arabic *See Ingredients, Flavors & Additives: Gums: Arabic*
Arctic Charr *See Fish & Seafood: Fish: Arctic Charr*
Ardouille Sausage *See Meats & Meat Products: Pork & Pork Products: Sausage: Ardouille*
Aroma Chemicals & Materials *See Ingredients, Flavors & Additives: Aroma Chemicals & Materials; See also Ingredients, Flavors & Additives: Aroma Chemicals; See also See Ingredients, Flavors & Additives: Aroma Chemicals & Materials: Materials*
Arrowroot Flour *See Cereals, Grains, Rice & Flour: Flour: Arrowroot*
Arrowroot Starches *See Ingredients, Flavors & Additives: Starches: Arrowroot*
Arrowroot Thickening Agents *See Ingredients, Flavors & Additives: Agents: Thickening: Arrowroot*
Artichoke *See Fruits & Vegetables: Artichoke*
Artificial Flavors *See Ingredients, Flavors & Additives: Flavors: Artificial*
Artificial Sweeteners *See Sugars, Syrups & Sweeteners: Artificial*
Ascorbic Acid *See Ingredients, Flavors & Additives: Antioxidants: Ascorbic Acid; See also Flavors & Additives: Vitamins & Supplements: C: Ascorbic Acid*
Aseptic Packed Capsicums Peppers *See Fruits & Vegetables: Peppers: Capsicums: Aseptic Packed*
Asiago Cheese *See Cheese & Cheese Products: Cheese: Asiago*
Asian *See Ethnic Foods: Asian*
Asian Pear *See Fruits & Vegetables: Pear: Asian*
Asparagus *See Fruits & Vegetables: Asparagus*
Aspartame *See Sugars, Syrups & Sweeteners: Sugar Substitutes: Aspartame*
Au Gratin Potatoes *See Fruits & Vegetables: Potatoes: Au Gratin*
Autolysates Yeast *See Ingredients, Flavors & Additives: Cultures & Yeasts: Yeast: Autolysates*
Avocado *See Fruits & Vegetables: Avocado*
Avocado Oils *See Oils, Shortening & Fats: Oils: Avocado*
Avocado Products *See Fruits & Vegetables: Avocado: Avocado Products*

B

Babka *See Baked Goods: Cakes & Pastries: Babka*
Baby Carrot *See Fruits & Vegetables: Carrot: Baby*
Baby Spinach *See Fruits & Vegetables: Spinach: Baby*
Bacillus Cultures *See Ingredients, Flavors & Additives: Cultures & Yeasts: Bacillus*
Bacon *See Meats & Meat Products: Smoked, Cured & Deli Meats: Bacon*
Bacon Pork Rinds *See Snack Foods: Pork Rinds: Bacon*
Bacon Slices *See Meats & Meat Products: Smoked, Cured & Deli Meats: Bacon: Slices*
Bacteria *See Ingredients, Flavors & Additives: Cultures & Yeasts: Bacteria*
Bacterial Cultures, Starter Media & Culture Replacements *See Ingredients, Flavors & Additives: Cultures & Yeasts: Bacterial Cultures, Starter Media & Culture Replacements*
Bacteriological Cultures & Yeasts *See Ingredients, Flavors & Additives: Cultures & Yeasts: Bacteriological*
Bagel Chips *See Snack Foods: Chips: Bagel Chips*
Bagels *See Baked Goods: Breads: Bagels*
Bagged Parboiled Rice *See Cereals, Grains, Rice & Flour: Rice: Parboiled: Bagged*
Bagged Specialty-Packaged Candy *See Candy & Confectionery: Specialty-Packaged Candy: Bagged*
Bagged Wheat *See Cereals, Grains, Rice & Flour: Wheat: Bagged*
Baguettes *See Baked Goods: Breads: Baguettes*
Baita Fruli Cheese *See Cheese & Cheese Products: Cheese: Baita Fruli*
Baked & Stuffed Potatoes *See Fruits & Vegetables: Potatoes: Baked & Stuffed*

EXAMPLE: **Canadian Style Bacon** *See Meats & Meat Products: Smoked, Cured & Deli Meats: Bacon: Canadian Style*

1. Product or Service you are looking for
2. Main Category, in alphabetical order, located in the page headers starting on page 27
3. Category Description, located in black bars and in page headers
4. Product Category, located in gray bars
5. Product Type, located under gray bars, centered in bold

Product Category List

Baked Beans *See Prepared Foods: Baked Beans (see also Pork & Beans); See also Fruits & Vegetables: Beans: Baked*
Baked Chips *See Snack Foods: Chips: Baked*
Baked Goods *See Baked Goods*
Baked Potato Chips *See Snack Foods: Chips: Potato: Baked*
Bakers Active Yeast *See Ingredients, Flavors & Additives: Cultures & Yeasts: Yeast: Bakers Active*
Bakers Cheese Powders *See Ingredients, Flavors & Additives: Powders: Cheese: Bakers*
Bakers' & Confectioners' Supplies *See Ingredients, Flavors & Additives: Confectionery: Bakers' & Confectioners' Supplies*
Bakers' Yeast *See Ingredients, Flavors & Additives: Cultures & Yeasts: Yeast: Bakers'*
Bakery Ingredients *See Ingredients, Flavors & Additives: Ingredients: Bakery*
Bakery Mix Flour *See Cereals, Grains, Rice & Flour: Flour: Bakery Mix*
Baking Bits *See Ingredients, Flavors & Additives: Bits: Baking*
Baking Chocolate *See Candy & Confectionery: Chocolate Products: Baking Chocolate*
Baking Decorations *See Candy & Confectionery: Decorations & Icings: Decorations: Baking*
Baking Doughs *See Doughs, Mixes & Fillings: Doughs: Baking*
Baking Fillings *See Doughs, Mixes & Fillings: Fillings: Baking*
Baking Mixes *See Doughs, Mixes & Fillings: Mixes: Baking*
Baking Mixes Flour *See Cereals, Grains, Rice & Flour: Flour: Baking Mixes*
Baking Powders *See Ingredients, Flavors & Additives: Powders: Baking*
Baking Seasonings *See Spices, Seasonings & Seeds: Seasonings: Baking*
Baking Shells *See Baked Goods: Pies: Baking Shells*
Baking Soda *See Ingredients, Flavors & Additives: Leaveners: Baking Soda*
Baklava *See Baked Goods: Cakes & Pastries: Baklava*
Balsamic Vinegar *See Sauces, Dips & Dressings: Vinegar: Balsamic*
Balsamic Vinegar Salad Dressings *See Sauces, Dips & Dressings: Salad Dressings: Balsamic Vinegar*
Bamboo Shoots *See Fruits & Vegetables: Bamboo Shoots*
Banana *See Fruits & Vegetables: Banana*
Banana Chips *See Snack Foods: Chips: Banana*
Banana Flakes *See Ingredients, Flavors & Additives: Flakes: Banana*
Banana Flavors *See Ingredients, Flavors & Additives: Flavors: Banana*
Banana Peppers *See Fruits & Vegetables: Peppers: Banana*
Banana Products *See Fruits & Vegetables: Banana: Banana Products*
Bar Mixers *See Beverages: Mixers: Bar Mixers*
Bar Syrups *See Sugars, Syrups & Sweeteners: Syrups: Bar*
Barbecue Potato Chips *See Snack Foods: Chips: Potato: Barbecue*
Barbecue Products *See Specialty Processed Foods: Barbecue Products (See also Specific Foods)*
Barbecue Sauces *See Sauces, Dips & Dressings: Sauces: Barbecue*
Barbecue Seasonings *See Spices, Seasonings & Seeds: Seasonings: Barbecue*
Barbecued Beef *See Meats & Meat Products: Beef & Beef Products: Barbecued*
Barbecued Chicken *See Meats & Meat Products: Poultry: Chicken: Barbecued*
Barbecued Chicken, Frozen *See Meats & Meat Products: Poultry: Chicken: Barbecued Frozen*
Barbecued Pork *See Meats & Meat Products: Pork & Pork Products: Barbecued*
Barley *See Cereals, Grains, Rice & Flour: Barley*
Barley Bran Fiber *See Cereals, Grains, Rice & Flour: Fiber: Barley Bran*
Barley Flour *See Cereals, Grains, Rice & Flour: Flour: Barley*
Bars, Cereal *See Cereals, Grains, Rice & Flour: Cereal: Bars*
Bars, Cookies *See Baked Goods: Cookies & Bars: Bars*
Bartlett Pear *See Fruits & Vegetables: Pear: Bartlett*
Bases *See Ingredients, Flavors & Additives: Bases*
Bases, Ice Cream *See Dairy Products: Ice Cream: Bases*
Basil Leaf *See Spices, Seasonings & Seeds: Spices: Basil Leaf*
Basil Spices *See Spices, Seasonings & Seeds: Spices: Basil*
Basmati Rice *See Cereals, Grains, Rice & Flour: Rice: Basmati*
Bass *See Fish & Seafood: Fish: Bass*
Batters *See Doughs, Mixes & Fillings: Batters*

Bay Leaves *See Spices, Seasonings & Seeds: Spices: Bay Leaves*
Bean Dips *See Sauces, Dips & Dressings: Dips: Bean*
Bean Flour *See Cereals, Grains, Rice & Flour: Flour: Bean*
Bean Oils *See Oils, Shortening & Fats: Oils: Bean*
Bean Sprouts *See Fruits & Vegetables: Sprouts: Bean*
Beans *See Fruits & Vegetables: Beans*
Bearnaise Sauces *See Sauces, Dips & Dressings: Sauces: Bearnaise*
Bee Pollen & Propolis *See Sugars, Syrups & Sweeteners: Honey: Bee Pollen & Propolis*
Beech Mushrooms *See Fruits & Vegetables: Mushrooms: Beech*
Beef & Beef Products *See Meats & Meat Products: Beef & Beef Products*
Beef & Beef Products, Sliced *See Meats & Meat Products: Beef & Beef Products: Sliced*
Beef & Beef Products, Special Trim *See Meats & Meat Products: Beef & Beef Products: Special Trim*
Beef Bases *See Ingredients, Flavors & Additives: Bases: Beef*
Beef Bouillon *See Ingredients, Flavors & Additives: Bases: Bouillon: Beef*
Beef Casings *See Meats & Meat Products: Smoked, Cured & Deli Meats: Sausages: Casings: Sausage, Pork, Beef*
Beef Certified Organic *See Specialty & Organic Foods: Organic Foods: Certified: Beef; See also Organic Foods*
Beef Dinners *See Meats & Meat Products: Beef & Beef Products: Dinners*
Beef Dinners, Prepared Meals *See Prepared Foods: Prepared Meals: Beef Dinner*
Beef Extracts *See Ingredients, Flavors & Additives: Extracts: Beef*
Beef Frankfurters *See Meats & Meat Products: Frankfurters: Beef*
Beef Jerky *See Meats & Meat Products: Smoked, Cured & Deli Meats: Beef Jerky*
Beef Marinades *See Sauces, Dips & Dressings: Marinades: Beef*
Beef Soup *See Prepared Foods: Soups & Stews: Beef Soup*
Beef Stew *See Meats & Meat Products: Beef & Beef Products: Stew; See also See Prepared Foods: Soups & Stews: Beef Stew*
Beef Stock Powders *See Ingredients, Flavors & Additives: Powders: Beef Stock*
Beef, Frozen Rolls *See Meats & Meat Products: Beef & Beef Products: Rolls - Frozen*
Beer Flavors *See Ingredients, Flavors & Additives: Flavors: Beer*
Beers *See Beverages: Beers*
Bees Wax *See Sugars, Syrups & Sweeteners: Honey: Bees Wax*
Beet Jellies *See Jams, Jellies & Spreads: Jellies: Beets*
Beet Juices *See Beverages: Juices: Beet*
Beet Powder *See Fruits & Vegetables: Dried & Dehydrated Vegetables: Beet Powder*
Beet Relishes *See Relishes & Pickled Products: Relishes: Beets*
Beets *See Fruits & Vegetables: Beets*
Belgian & French Ale *See Beverages: Beers: Belgian & French Ale*
Bell Peppers *See Fruits & Vegetables: Peppers: Bell*
Bell Peppers, Dehydrated *See Fruits & Vegetables: Dried & Dehydrated Vegetables: Bell Peppers*
Benzoate of Soda *See Ingredients, Flavors & Additives: Benzoate of Soda*
Benzoic Acids *See Ingredients, Flavors & Additives: Acids: Benzoic*
Berries *See Fruits & Vegetables: Berries*
Berries, Frozen *See Fruits & Vegetables: Frozen Fruit: Berries*
Beta Carotene *See Ingredients, Flavors & Additives: Vitamins & Supplements: Beta Carotene*
Betaine Beet *See Ingredients, Flavors & Additives: Colors: Natural: Betaine Beet*
Beverage Bases *See Ingredients, Flavors & Additives: Bases: Beverage*
Beverage Extracts *See Ingredients, Flavors & Additives: Extracts: Beverages*
Beverage Flavors *See Ingredients, Flavors & Additives: Flavors: Beverage*
Beverage Mixes *See Doughs, Mixes & Fillings: Mixes: Beverage*
Beverage Powders *See Ingredients, Flavors & Additives: Powders: Beverage*
Beverage Syrups *See Sugars, Syrups & Sweeteners: Syrups: Beverages*
Beverages *See Beverages*
Bialys *See Baked Goods: Breads: Bialys*
Binders *See Ingredients, Flavors & Additives: Binders*
Binders for Meat Products *See Ingredients, Flavors & Additives: Binders: for Meat Products*

Bing Cherries *See Fruits & Vegetables: Cherries: Bing*
Bioflavinoids *See Ingredients, Flavors & Additives: Bioflavinoids*
Biopolymers *See Ingredients, Flavors & Additives: Biopolymers*
Biotin *See Ingredients, Flavors & Additives: Vitamins & Supplements: Biotin*
Biscotti *See Baked Goods: Cookies & Bars: Biscotti*
Biscuit Mixes *See Doughs, Mixes & Fillings: Mixes: Biscuit*
Biscuits *See Baked Goods: Breads: Biscuits*
Bits *See Ingredients, Flavors & Additives: Bits*
Bits, Imitation Bacon *See Meats & Meat Products: Smoked, Cured & Deli Meats: Bacon: Bits Imitation*
Bits, Real Bacon *See Meats & Meat Products: Smoked, Cured & Deli Meats: Bacon: Bits Real*
Bitters *See Beverages: Bitters*
Black & Tan Ale *See Beverages: Beers: American & British Ale: Black & Tan*
Black Bean Sauces *See Sauces, Dips & Dressings: Sauces: Black Bean*
Black Beans *See Fruits & Vegetables: Beans: Black*
Black Cod Fish *See Fish & Seafood: Fish: Cod: Black*
Black Currant Tea *See Beverages: Coffee & Tea: Tea: Black Currant*
Black Forest Ham *See Meats & Meat Products: Smoked, Cured & Deli Meats: Ham: Black Forest*
Black Olives *See Fruits & Vegetables: Olives: Black*
Black Pepper *See Spices, Seasonings & Seeds: Spices: Pepper: Black - White - Red; See also See Spices, Seasonings & Seeds: Spices: Black Pepper - Ground*
Black Pepper Oils *See Oils, Shortening & Fats: Oils: Black Pepper*
Black Puinoa Rice *See Cereals, Grains, Rice & Flour: Rice: Black Puinoa*
Black Sesame Seeds *See Spices, Seasonings & Seeds: Seeds: Sesame: Black*
Black Sliced Truffles *See Fruits & Vegetables: Mushrooms: Truffles: Black Sliced*
Black Tea *See Beverages: Coffee & Tea: Tea: Black*
Black Thai Rice *See Cereals, Grains, Rice & Flour: Rice: Black Thai*
Black Tiger Shrimp *See Fish & Seafood: Shellfish: Shrimp: Black Tiger*
Black Trumpet Mushrooms *See Fruits & Vegetables: Mushrooms: Black Trumpet*
Black Trumpet Mushrooms, Dehydrated *See Fruits & Vegetables: Dried & Dehydrated Vegetables: Mushrooms: Black Trumpets*
Black Walnuts *See Nuts & Nut Butters: Nuts: Walnuts: Black*
Black Whole Truffles *See Fruits & Vegetables: Mushrooms: Truffles: Black Whole*
Black-eyed Peas *See Fruits & Vegetables: Peas: Black-eyed*
Blackberry *See Fruits & Vegetables: Berries: Blackberry*
Blackberry Flavors *See Ingredients, Flavors & Additives: Flavors: Blackberry*
Blackening Seasonings *See Spices, Seasonings & Seeds: Seasonings: Blackening*
Blackeye Beans *See Fruits & Vegetables: Beans: Blackeye (Cowpeas)*
Blended Scotch Whiskey *See Beverages: Spirits & Liqueurs: Scotch Whiskey: Blended*
Blends *See Ingredients, Flavors & Additives: Blends*
Blends, Butter *See Dairy Products: Butter: Blends*
Blends, Corn Syrups *See Sugars, Syrups & Sweeteners: Syrups: Corn: Blends*
Blintzes *See Baked Goods: Cakes & Pastries: Blintzes*
Blood Orange *See Fruits & Vegetables: Orange: Blood*
Blood Orange Juice *See Beverages: Juices: Orange: Blood*
Blood Sausages *See Meats & Meat Products: Smoked, Cured & Deli Meats: Sausages: Blood*
Blue Cheese *See Cheese & Cheese Products: Cheese: Blue*
Blue Cheese Salad Dressings *See Sauces, Dips & Dressings: Salad Dressings: Blue Cheese*
Blue Cheese Salad Dressings, Mixes *See Sauces, Dips & Dressings: Salad Dressings: Mixes: Blue Cheese*
Blue Crab *See Fish & Seafood: Shellfish: Crab: Blue*
Blue Lake Beans *See Fruits & Vegetables: Beans: Blue Lake*
Blueberry *See Fruits & Vegetables: Berries: Blueberry*
Blueberry Flavors *See Ingredients, Flavors & Additives: Flavors: Blueberry*
Blueberry Juices *See Beverages: Juices: Blueberry*
Blueberry Pies *See Baked Goods: Pies: Blueberry*
Bluefish *See Fish & Seafood: Fish: Bluefish*
Boar *See Meats & Meat Products: Game: Boar*
Bock Lager *See Beverages: Beers: Lager: Bock*
Bockwurst Sausages *See Meats & Meat Products: Smoked, Cured & Deli Meats: Sausages: Bockwurst*
Boiled Eggs *See Eggs & Egg Products: Boiled*

Product Category List

Bok Choy Cabbage *See Fruits & Vegetables: Cabbage: Bok Choy*
Boletes Mushrooms *See Fruits & Vegetables: Mushrooms: Boletes*
Bologna Smoked, Cured & Deli Meats *See Meats & Meat Products: Smoked, Cured & Deli Meats: Bologna*
Bon Bons *See Candy & Confectionery: Candy: Bon Bons*
Boned Herring *See Fish & Seafood: Fish: Herring: Boned*
Borage Oils *See Oils, Shortening & Fats: Oils: Borage*
Bordeaux Vinegar *See Sauces, Dips & Dressings: Vinegar: Bordeaux*
Boric/Boracic Acids *See Ingredients, Flavors & Additives: Acids: Boric/Boracic*
Borscht *See Prepared Foods: Soups & Stews: Borscht*
Bosc Pear *See Fruits & Vegetables: Pear: Bosc*
Boston Butterhead Lettuce *See Fruits & Vegetables: Lettuce: Butterhead: Boston*
Botanical Extracts *See Ingredients, Flavors & Additives: Extracts: Botanical*
Bottled Apple Juices *See Beverages: Juices: Apple: Bottled*
Bottled Beers *See Beverages: Beers: Bottled*
Bottled Cherry Juices *See Beverages: Juices: Cherry: Bottled*
Bottled Cranberry Juices *See Beverages: Juices: Cranberry: Bottled*
Bottled Fruit & Vegetable Juices *See Beverages: Juices: Fruit & Vegetable: Bottled*
Bottled Fruit Juices *See Beverages: Juices: Fruit: Bottled*
Bottled Grape Juices *See Beverages: Juices: Grape: Bottled*
Bottled Grapefruit Juices *See Beverages: Juices: Grapefruit: Bottled*
Bottled Lemon Juices *See Beverages: Juices: Lemon: Bottled*
Bottled Water *See Beverages: Water: Bottled*
Bottomfish *See Fish & Seafood: Fish: Bottomfish*
Boudin Sausages *See Meats & Meat Products: Smoked, Cured & Deli Meats: Sausages: Boudin*
Bouillon Bases *See Ingredients, Flavors & Additives: Bases: Bouillon*
Bourbon Whiskey *See Beverages: Spirits & Liqueurs: Whiskey, American: Bourbon*
Bows *See Pasta & Noodles: Bows*
Boxed Apple Juices *See Beverages: Juices: Apple: Boxed*
Boxed Cherry Juices *See Beverages: Juices: Cherry: Boxed*
Boxed Chocolate *See Candy & Confectionery: Chocolate Products: Boxed Chocolate*
Boxed Cranberry Juices *See Beverages: Juices: Cranberry: Boxed*
Boxed Grape Juices *See Beverages: Juices: Grape: Boxed*
Boxed Grapefruit Juices *See Beverages: Juices: Grapefruit: Boxed*
Boxed Pineapple Juices *See Beverages: Juices: Pineapple: Boxed*
Boxed Specialty-Packaged Candy *See Candy & Confectionery: Specialty-Packaged Candy: Boxed*
Boxed Specialty-Packaged Candy, Non-Chocolate *See Candy & Confectionery: Specialty-Packaged Candy: Non-Chocolate - Boxed*
Boxed Tomato Juices *See Beverages: Juices: Tomato: Boxed*
Boysenberry *See Fruits & Vegetables: Berries: Boysenberry*
Bra Cheese *See Cheese & Cheese Products: Cheese: Bra*
Bran *See Cereals, Grains, Rice & Flour: Bran*
Brandied Fruits *See Fruits & Vegetables: Brandied Fruits*
Brandy *See Beverages: Spirits & Liqueurs: Brandy*
Brandy Liqueur *See Beverages: Spirits & Liqueurs: Liqueurs & Cordials: Brandy Liqueur*
Bratwurst *See Meats & Meat Products: Smoked, Cured & Deli Meats: Bratwurst*
Bratwurst Sausages *See Meats & Meat Products: Smoked, Cured & Deli Meats: Sausages: Bratwurst*
Braunschweiger Sausages *See Meats & Meat Products: Smoked, Cured & Deli Meats: Sausages: Braunschweiger*
Brazil Nuts *See Nuts & Nut Butters: Nuts: Brazil*
Bread Crumbs & Croutons *See Baked Goods: Bread Crumbs & Croutons; See also Baked Goods: Bread Crumbs & Croutons: Bread Crumbs*
Bread Doughs *See Doughs, Mixes & Fillings: Doughs: Bread*
Bread Mixes *See Doughs, Mixes & Fillings: Mixes: Bread*
Bread Sticks *See Baked Goods: Bread Sticks*
Bread Stuffing *See Baked Goods: Stuffing: Bread*
Bread, Wheat *See Cereals, Grains, Rice & Flour: Wheat: Bread*

Breaded Chicken *See Meats & Meat Products: Poultry: Chicken: Breaded*
Breaded Clam Strips *See Fish & Seafood: Shellfish: Clam: Breaded Strips*
Breaded Frozen Veal *See Meats & Meat Products: Beef & Beef Products: Veal: Breaded Frozen*
Breaded Pork *See Meats & Meat Products: Pork & Pork Products: Breaded*
Breaded Shrimp *See Fish & Seafood: Shellfish: Shrimp: Breaded*
Breaded Vegetables *See Prepared Foods: Breaded Vegetables*
Breading *See Doughs, Mixes & Fillings: Breading*
Breading Batters *See Doughs, Mixes & Fillings: Batters: Breading*
Breading Mixes *See Doughs, Mixes & Fillings: Mixes: Breading*
Breads *See Baked Goods: Breads*
Breakfast Cereal *See Cereals, Grains, Rice & Flour: Cereal: Breakfast*
Breakfast, Instant *See Prepared Foods: Breakfast Foods: Instant*
Breakfast, Prepared Meals *See Prepared Foods: Prepared Meals: Breakfast*
Breast Turkey *See Meats & Meat Products: Poultry: Turkey: Breast*
Breath Tablets *See Candy & Confectionery: Candy: Breath Tablets*
Brewers' Active Yeast *See Ingredients, Flavors & Additives: Cultures & Yeasts: Yeast: Brewers Active*
Brewers' Rice *See Cereals, Grains, Rice & Flour: Rice: Brewers'*
Brewers' Yeast *See Ingredients, Flavors & Additives: Cultures & Yeasts: Yeast: Brewers'*
Brewing Adjuncts *See Ingredients, Flavors & Additives: Adjuncts: Brewing*
Brie *See Cheese & Cheese Products: Cheese: Brie*
Brisket of Beef *See Meats & Meat Products: Beef & Beef Products: Brisket*
Brittles *See Candy & Confectionery: Candy: Brittles*
Broad Beans *See Fruits & Vegetables: Beans: Broad*
Broccoli *See Fruits & Vegetables: Broccoli*
Broccoli & Cauliflower Mixed Vegetables *See Fruits & Vegetables: Vegetables Mixed: Broccoli & Cauliflower*
Broccoli, Dried *See Fruits & Vegetables: Dried & Dehydrated Vegetables: Broccoli*
Broccoli, Peas & Carrots Mixed Vegetables *See Fruits & Vegetables: Vegetables Mixed: Broccoli, Peas & Carrots*
Broilers *See Meats & Meat Products: Poultry: Chicken: Broilers*
Brook Trout *See Fish & Seafood: Fish: Trout: Brook*
Broth *See Prepared Foods: Broth*
Broth Powders *See Ingredients, Flavors & Additives: Powders: Broth*
Brown Bettys *See Baked Goods: Cakes & Pastries: Brown Bettys*
Brown Breads *See Baked Goods: Breads: Brown*
Brown Mustard *See Sauces, Dips & Dressings: Mustard: Brown*
Brown Rice *See Cereals, Grains, Rice & Flour: Rice: Brown*
Brown Rice Crisps *See Cereals, Grains, Rice & Flour: Crisps: Brown Rice*
Brown Sugar *See Sugars, Syrups & Sweeteners: Sugar: Brown*
Brownie Mixes *See Doughs, Mixes & Fillings: Mixes: Brownie*
Brownie Pies *See Baked Goods: Pies: Brownie*
Brownies with Nuts *See Baked Goods: Cookies & Bars: Brownies: with Nuts*
Brownies, Baking Mixes *See Doughs, Mixes & Fillings: Mixes: Baking: Brownies*
Brownies, Cookies & Bars *See Baked Goods: Cookies & Bars: Brownies*
Brussel Sprouts *See Fruits & Vegetables: Brussel Sprouts*
Buckwheat Flour *See Cereals, Grains, Rice & Flour: Flour: Buckwheat*
Buffalo *See Meats & Meat Products: Game: Buffalo*
Bulgar Wheat *See Cereals, Grains, Rice & Flour: Wheat: Bulgar*
Bulk Wines *See Beverages: Wines: Bulk*
Bulking Additives *See Ingredients, Flavors & Additives: Additives: Bulking*
Bulking Agents *See Ingredients, Flavors & Additives: Agents: Bulking*
Buns *See Baked Goods: Breads: Buns*

Burgers, Veal *See Meats & Meat Products: Beef & Beef Products: Veal: Burgers*
Burgers, Vegetarian *See Specialty & Organic Foods: Vegetarian Products: Burgers; See also Organic Foods*
Burnt Sugar Colors *See Ingredients, Flavors & Additives: Colors: Burnt Sugar*
Burritos *See Ethnic Foods: Burritos*
Burritos, Prepared Meals *See Prepared Foods: Prepared Meals: Burritos*
Butter *See Dairy Products: Butter*
Butter & Cheese Colors *See Ingredients, Flavors & Additives: Colors: Butter & Cheese*
Butter Beans *See Fruits & Vegetables: Beans: Butter*
Butter, Flavors *See Ingredients, Flavors & Additives: Flavors: Butter*
Butter, Honey *See Sugars, Syrups & Sweeteners: Honey: Butter*
Butter, Maple Flavors *See Ingredients, Flavors & Additives: Flavors: Maple: Butter*
Butter, Maple Sugar *See Sugars, Syrups & Sweeteners: Sugar: Maple: Butter*
Butter, Milk Flavors *See Ingredients, Flavors & Additives: Flavors: Milk: Butter*
Butter, Snack Seasonings *See Spices, Seasonings & Seeds: Seasonings: Snack: Butter*
Butter, Toffee Rum Flavors *See Ingredients, Flavors & Additives: Flavors: Rum: Butter Toffee*
Butterfish *See Fish & Seafood: Fish: Butterfish*
Butterhead Lettuce *See Fruits & Vegetables: Lettuce: Butterhead*
Buttermilk *See Dairy Products: Buttermilk & Buttermilk Products: Buttermilk*
Buttermilk & Buttermilk Products *See Dairy Products: Buttermilk & Buttermilk Products*
Buttermilk Bacteria *See Ingredients, Flavors & Additives: Cultures & Yeasts: Bacteria: Buttermilk*
Buttermilk Flavors *See Ingredients, Flavors & Additives: Flavors: Buttermilk*
Buttermilk Powders *See Ingredients, Flavors & Additives: Powders: Buttermilk*
Buttermilk Products *See Dairy Products: Buttermilk & Buttermilk Products: Buttermilk Products*
Butterscotch Candy *See Candy & Confectionery: Candy: Butterscotch*
Butterscotch Flavors *See Ingredients, Flavors & Additives: Flavors: Butterscotch*

C

Cabbage *See Fruits & Vegetables: Cabbage*
Cabbage Flakes *See Fruits & Vegetables: Dried & Dehydrated Vegetables: Cabbage Flakes*
Cabbage Seeds *See Spices, Seasonings & Seeds: Seeds: Cabbage*
Cabernet Sauvignon *See Beverages: Wines: Red Grape Wines: Cabernet Sauvignon*
Cacciatore Sausages *See Meats & Meat Products: Smoked, Cured & Deli Meats: Sausages: Cacciatore*
Caciotta Cheese *See Cheese & Cheese Products: Cheese: Caciotta*
Cactus *See Fruits & Vegetables: Cactus*
Caffeine *See Ingredients, Flavors & Additives: Caffeine*
Cajeta Flavors *See Ingredients, Flavors & Additives: Flavors: Cajeta*
Cajun Fried Porkskins *See Prepared Foods: Porkskins: Fried: Cajun*
Cajun Sausages *See Meats & Meat Products: Smoked, Cured & Deli Meats: Sausages: Cajun*
Cajun Spice Snack Seasonings *See Spices, Seasonings & Seeds: Seasonings: Snack: Cajun Spice*
Cajun Style Seasonings *See Spices, Seasonings & Seeds: Seasonings: Cajun Style*
Cake Batters *See Doughs, Mixes & Fillings: Batters: Cake*
Cake Decorations *See Candy & Confectionery: Decorations & Icings: Decorations: Cake*
Cake Fillings *See Doughs, Mixes & Fillings: Fillings: Cake*
Cake Flour *See Cereals, Grains, Rice & Flour: Flour: Cake*
Cake Icings *See Candy & Confectionery: Decorations & Icings: Icings: Cake*
Cake Mixes *See Doughs, Mixes & Fillings: Mixes: Cake*
Cakes *See Baked Goods: Cakes & Pastries: Cakes*
Cakes & Donut Toppings *See Ingredients, Flavors & Additives: Toppings: Cakes & Donuts*
Cakes & Pastries *See Baked Goods: Cakes & Pastries*
Cakes, Crab *See Fish & Seafood: Shellfish: Crab: Cakes*
Cakes, Fish *See Fish & Seafood: Fish: Cakes*

EXAMPLE: **Canadian Style Bacon** *See Meats & Meat Products: Smoked, Cured & Deli Meats: Bacon: Canadian Style*

1. Product or Service you are looking for
2. Main Category, in alphabetical order, located in the page headers starting on page 27
3. Category Description, located in black bars and in page headers
4. Product Category, located in gray bars
5. Product Type, located under gray bars, centered in bold

Product Category List

Cakes, Frozen Crab *See Fish & Seafood: Shellfish: Crab: Cakes Frozen*
Calcium *See Ingredients, Flavors & Additives: Vitamins & Supplements: Calcium*
Calcium & Nutritionally Fortified Pellets *See Ingredients, Flavors & Additives: Half-Products: Calcium & Nutritionally Fortified Pellets*
Calcium Phosphate *See Ingredients, Flavors & Additives: Phosphates: Calcium Phosphate*
Camembert *See Cheese & Cheese Products: Cheese: Camembert*
Canadian Style Bacon *See Meats & Meat Products: Smoked, Cured & Deli Meats: Bacon: Canadian Style*
Candied Fruits *See Fruits & Vegetables: Candied Fruits*
Candy *See Candy & Confectionery: Candy*
Candy Bars *See Candy & Confectionery: Candy: Candy Bars*
Candy Canes *See Candy & Confectionery: Candy: Canes*
Candy Coatings *See Candy & Confectionery: Candy Coatings*
Candy Makers' Waxes *See Ingredients, Flavors & Additives: Waxes: Candy Makers'*
Cane Sugar *See Sugars, Syrups & Sweeteners: Sugar: Cane*
Cane Syrup *See Sugars, Syrups & Sweeteners: Syrups: Cane*
Caneberries *See Fruits & Vegetables: Caneberries*
Canned & Frozen Chili *See Prepared Foods: Chili: Canned & Frozen*
Canned & Frozen Collard Greens *See Fruits & Vegetables: Collard Greens: Canned & Frozen*
Canned & Frozen Corn *See Fruits & Vegetables: Corn: Canned & Frozen*
Canned & Frozen Enchiladas *See Ethnic Foods: Enchiladas: Canned & Frozen*
Canned & Frozen Guava *See Fruits & Vegetables: Guava: Canned & Frozen*
Canned & Frozen Hash *See Prepared Foods: Hash: Canned & Frozen*
Canned & Frozen Mustard Greens *See Fruits & Vegetables: Mustard: Greens: Canned & Frozen*
Canned & Frozen Tomato Pastes *See Ingredients, Flavors & Additives: Pastes: Tomato: Canned & Frozen*
Canned Anchovies *See Fish & Seafood: Fish: Anchovies: Canned*
Canned Apple *See Fruits & Vegetables: Apple: Canned*
Canned Apple Juices *See Beverages: Juices: Apple: Canned*
Canned Apple Sauces *See Fruits & Vegetables: Sauces: Apple: Canned*
Canned Apple Slices *See Fruits & Vegetables: Apple: Slices: Canned*
Canned Apricot *See Fruits & Vegetables: Apricot: Canned*
Canned Apricot Juices *See Beverages: Juices: Apricot: Canned*
Canned Artichoke *See Fruits & Vegetables: Artichoke: Canned*
Canned Asparagus *See Fruits & Vegetables: Asparagus: Canned*
Canned Baked Beans *See Prepared Foods: Baked Beans (see also Pork & Beans): Canned*
Canned Beans *See Fruits & Vegetables: Beans: Canned*
Canned Beef with Natural Juices *See Meats & Meat Products: Beef & Beef Products: Canned with Natural Juices*
Canned Beers *See Beverages: Beers: Canned*
Canned Beets *See Fruits & Vegetables: Beets: Canned*
Canned Berries *See Fruits & Vegetables: Berries: Canned*
Canned Black-eyed Peas *See Fruits & Vegetables: Peas: Black-eyed: Canned*
Canned Blue Lake Beans *See Fruits & Vegetables: Beans: Blue Lake: Canned*
Canned Blueberry *See Fruits & Vegetables: Berries: Blueberry: Canned*
Canned Boned Chicken *See Meats & Meat Products: Poultry: Chicken: Canned Boned*
Canned Boysenberry *See Fruits & Vegetables: Berries: Boysenberry: Canned*
Canned Broth *See Prepared Foods: Broth: Canned, Frozen, Powdered*
Canned Brussel Sprouts *See Fruits & Vegetables: Brussel Sprouts: Canned*
Canned Butter Beans *See Fruits & Vegetables: Beans: Butter: Canned*
Canned Cabbage *See Fruits & Vegetables: Cabbage: Canned*
Canned Carrot *See Fruits & Vegetables: Carrot: Canned*
Canned Cauliflower *See Fruits & Vegetables: Cauliflower: Canned*
Canned Celery *See Fruits & Vegetables: Celery: Canned*
Canned Cherries *See Fruits & Vegetables: Cherries: Canned*

Canned Cherry Juices *See Beverages: Juices: Cherry: Canned*
Canned Chili *See Prepared Foods: Chili: Canned*
Canned Chop Suey *See Ethnic Foods: Chop Suey: Canned*
Canned Clam *See Fish & Seafood: Shellfish: Clam: Canned*
Canned Corn *See Fruits & Vegetables: Corn: Canned*
Canned Crab *See Fish & Seafood: Shellfish: Crab: Canned*
Canned Crab Meat *See Fish & Seafood: Shellfish: Crab: Meat Canned*
Canned Cranberry *See Fruits & Vegetables: Berries: Cranberry: Canned*
Canned Cranberry Juices *See Beverages: Juices: Cranberry: Canned*
Canned Dry Beans *See Fruits & Vegetables: Beans: Dry: Canned*
Canned Figs *See Fruits & Vegetables: Figs: Canned*
Canned Fish *See Fish & Seafood: Fish: Canned*
Canned Fish Cakes *See Fish & Seafood: Fish: Cakes: Canned*
Canned French Fries *See Prepared Foods: French Fries: Canned*
Canned Fruit & Vegetable Juices *See Beverages: Juices: Fruit & Vegetable: Canned*
Canned Fruit Juices *See Beverages: Juices: Fruit: Canned*
Canned Fruits *See Fruits & Vegetables: Canned Fruits*
Canned Grape Juices *See Beverages: Juices: Grape: Canned*
Canned Grapefruit Juices *See Beverages: Juices: Grapefruit: Canned*
Canned Greek Beans *See Fruits & Vegetables: Beans: Greek: Canned*
Canned Green Beans *See Fruits & Vegetables: Beans: Green: Canned*
Canned Ham *See Meats & Meat Products: Smoked, Cured & Deli Meats: Ham: Canned*
Canned Hominy *See Cereals, Grains, Rice & Flour: Hominy: Canned*
Canned Kidney Beans *See Fruits & Vegetables: Beans: Kidney: Canned*
Canned Lemon Juices *See Beverages: Juices: Lemon: Canned*
Canned Lentil Beans *See Fruits & Vegetables: Beans: Lentil: Canned*
Canned Lima Beans *See Fruits & Vegetables: Beans: Lima: Canned*
Canned Luncheon Meat *See Meats & Meat Products: Smoked, Cured & Deli Meats: Luncheon Meat: Canned*
Canned Mandarin Orange *See Fruits & Vegetables: Orange: Mandarin: Canned*
Canned Meat Balls *See Prepared Foods: Meat Balls: Canned*
Canned Mushrooms *See Fruits & Vegetables: Mushrooms: Canned*
Canned Navy Beans *See Fruits & Vegetables: Beans: Navy: Canned*
Canned Nectar *See Fruits & Vegetables: Nectar: Canned*
Canned Noodles *See Pasta & Noodles: Noodles: Canned*
Canned Okra *See Fruits & Vegetables: Okra: Canned*
Canned Onion *See Fruits & Vegetables: Onion: Canned*
Canned Orange Sections *See Fruits & Vegetables: Orange: Sections: Canned*
Canned Oriental Vegetables *See Fruits & Vegetables: Oriental Vegetables: Canned*
Canned Oysters *See Fish & Seafood: Shellfish: Oysters: Canned*
Canned Pasta *See Pasta & Noodles: Canned*
Canned Peach *See Fruits & Vegetables: Peach: Canned; See also Fruits & Vegetables: Peach: Klingstone: Canned - Sliced & Diced*
Canned Pear *See Fruits & Vegetables: Pear: Canned*
Canned Peas *See Fruits & Vegetables: Peas: Canned*
Canned Peas & Carrots *See Fruits & Vegetables: Vegetables Mixed: Peas & Carrots: Canned*
Canned Peppers *See Fruits & Vegetables: Peppers: Canned*
Canned Pigs' Feet *See Meats & Meat Products: Pork & Pork Products: Pigs' Feet: Canned*
Canned Pineapple *See Fruits & Vegetables: Pineapple: Canned*
Canned Pineapple Chunks *See Fruits & Vegetables: Pineapple: Canned: Chunks*
Canned Pineapple Juices *See Beverages: Juices: Pineapple: Canned*
Canned Plums *See Fruits & Vegetables: Plums: Canned*
Canned Pork & Beans *See Prepared Foods: Pork & Beans (see also Baked Beans): Canned*
Canned Pork with Natural Juices *See Meats & Meat Products: Pork & Pork Products: Canned with Natural Juices*
Canned Potatoes *See Fruits & Vegetables: Potatoes: Canned*
Canned Prepared Meals *See Prepared Foods: Prepared Meals: Canned*

Canned Prunes *See Fruits & Vegetables: Prunes: Canned*
Canned Pumpkin *See Fruits & Vegetables: Pumpkin: Canned*
Canned Ravioli *See Pasta & Noodles: Ravioli: Canned*
Canned Refried Beans *See Fruits & Vegetables: Beans: Refried: Canned*
Canned Rhubarb *See Fruits & Vegetables: Rhubarb: Canned*
Canned Rutabaga *See Fruits & Vegetables: Rutabaga: Canned*
Canned Salsa *See Sauces, Dips & Dressings: Salsa: Canned*
Canned Sardines *See Fish & Seafood: Fish: Sardines: Canned*
Canned Seafood *See Fish & Seafood: Seafood: Canned*
Canned Shellfish *See Fish & Seafood: Shellfish: Canned*
Canned Shrimp *See Fish & Seafood: Shellfish: Shrimp: Canned*
Canned Soup *See Prepared Foods: Soups & Stews: Canned Soup*
Canned Spaghetti *See Prepared Foods: Prepared Meals: Spaghetti: Canned; See also Pasta & Noodles: Spaghetti: Canned*
Canned Spanish Rice *See Cereals, Grains, Rice & Flour: Rice: Spanish: Canned*
Canned Spinach *See Fruits & Vegetables: Spinach: Canned*
Canned Squash *See Fruits & Vegetables: Squash: Canned*
Canned Stew *See Prepared Foods: Soups & Stews: Canned Stew*
Canned Strawberry *See Fruits & Vegetables: Berries: Strawberry: Canned*
Canned Succotash *See Fruits & Vegetables: Succotash: Canned*
Canned Tomato *See Fruits & Vegetables: Tomato: Canned*
Canned Tomato Juices *See Beverages: Juices: Tomato: Canned*
Canned Tomato Pulps & Purees *See Fruits & Vegetables: Pulps & Purees: Tomato: Canned*
Canned Tomato Sauces *See Sauces, Dips & Dressings: Sauces: Tomato: Canned*
Canned Tuna *See Fish & Seafood: Fish: Tuna: Canned*
Canned Tuna - Chunk Light in Oil *See Fish & Seafood: Fish: Tuna: Canned - Chunk Light in Oil*
Canned Tuna - Chunk Light in Water *See Fish & Seafood: Fish: Tuna: Canned - Chunk Light in Water*
Canned Tuna - Chunk Solid in Oil *See Fish & Seafood: Fish: Tuna: Canned - Chunk Solid in Oil*
Canned Tuna - Chunk Solid in Water *See Fish & Seafood: Fish: Tuna: Canned - Chunk Solid in Water*
Canned Turkey *See Meats & Meat Products: Poultry: Turkey: Canned*
Canned Turnip *See Fruits & Vegetables: Turnip: Canned*
Canned Vegetables *See Fruits & Vegetables: Canned Vegetables*
Canned Vegetables, Mixed *See Fruits & Vegetables: Vegetables Mixed: Canned*
Canned Venison *See Meats & Meat Products: Game: Venison: Canned*
Canned Water Pack Cherries *See Fruits & Vegetables: Cherries: Water Pack: Canned*
Canned Wax Beans *See Fruits & Vegetables: Beans: Wax: Canned*
Canned Yams *See Fruits & Vegetables: Yams: Canned*
Cannellini Beans *See Fruits & Vegetables: Beans: Cannellini*
Cannelloni *See Pasta & Noodles: Cannelloni*
Cannoli *See Baked Goods: Cakes & Pastries: Cannoli*
Canola Oils *See Oils, Shortening & Fats: Oils: Canola*
Cantaloupe *See Fruits & Vegetables: Melon: Cantaloupe*
Capellini *See Pasta & Noodles: Capellini*
Capers *See Spices, Seasonings & Seeds: Spices: Capers*
Capon Chicken *See Meats & Meat Products: Poultry: Chicken: Capon*
Cappuccino *See Beverages: Coffee & Tea: Cappuccino; See also Beverages: Coffee & Tea: Coffee: Cappuccino*
Cappuccino Mixes *See Doughs, Mixes & Fillings: Mixes: Cappuccino*
Cappuccino Powders *See Ingredients, Flavors & Additives: Powders: Cappuccino*
Capsicums Peppers *See Fruits & Vegetables: Peppers: Capsicums*
Caramel Apple *See Fruits & Vegetables: Apple: Caramel*
Caramel Burnt Sugar Colors *See Ingredients, Flavors & Additives: Colors: Burnt Sugar: Caramel*
Caramel Candy *See Candy & Confectionery: Candy: Caramel*
Caramel Colors *See Ingredients, Flavors & Additives: Colors: Caramel*
Caramel Covered Apple *See Fruits & Vegetables: Apple: Covered: Caramel*
Caramel Flavors *See Ingredients, Flavors & Additives: Flavors: Caramel*
Caraway Oils *See Oils, Shortening & Fats: Oils: Caraway*

Product Category List

Caraway Seeds *See* Spices, Seasonings & Seeds: Caraway
Carboxymethylcellulose *See* Ingredients, Flavors & Additives: Gums: Carboxymethylcellulose
Cardamom Oils *See* Oils, Shortening & Fats: Oils: Cardamom
Cardamom Seeds *See* Spices, Seasonings & Seeds: Seeds: Cardamom
Cardamom Spices *See* Spices, Seasonings & Seeds: Spices: Cardamom
Caribou *See* Meats & Meat Products: Game: Caribou
Carmine *See* Ingredients, Flavors & Additives: Colors: Natural: Carmine
Carob Candy *See* Candy & Confectionery: Candy: Carob
Carob Candy Coatings *See* Candy & Confectionery: Candy Coatings: Carob
Carob Ingredients *See* Candy & Confectionery: Chocolate Products: Carob Ingredients
Carob Powder Spices *See* Spices, Seasonings & Seeds: Spices: Carob Powder
Carob Powders *See* Ingredients, Flavors & Additives: Powders: Carob
Carotenoids *See* Ingredients, Flavors & Additives: Colors: Natural: Carotenoids
Carp *See* Fish & Seafood: Fish: Carp
Carrageenan *See* Ingredients, Flavors & Additives: Gums: Carrageenan
Carrot *See* Fruits & Vegetables: Carrot
Carrot Cake *See* Baked Goods: Cakes & Pastries: Carrot Cake
Carrot Juices *See* Beverages: Juices: Carrot
Cascabel Peppers *See* Fruits & Vegetables: Peppers: Cascabel
Casein *See* Ingredients, Flavors & Additives: Casein & Caseinates; *See also* Ingredients, Flavors & Additives: Casein & Caseinates: Casein
Cashews *See* Nuts & Nut Butters: Nuts: Cashews
Casings *See* Meats & Meat Products: Smoked, Cured & Deli Meats: Sausages: Casings: Sausage, Pork, Beef
Cassava Chips *See* Snack Foods: Chips: Cassava
Cassava Powders *See* Ingredients, Flavors & Additives: Powders: Cassava
Cassava Starches *See* Ingredients, Flavors & Additives: Starches: Cassava
Cassava Tapioca *See* Cereals, Grains, Rice & Flour: Tapioca: Cassava
Casseroles, Prepared Meals *See* Prepared Foods: Prepared Meals: Casseroles
Cassia *See* Spices, Seasonings & Seeds: Spices: Cassia (Cinnamon); *See also* Spices, Seasonings & Seeds: Spices: Cinnamon: Cassia
Cassia Oils *See* Oils, Shortening & Fats: Oils: Cassia
Castor Oils *See* Oils, Shortening & Fats: Oils: Castor
Catfish *See* Fish & Seafood: Fish: Catfish
Cauliflower *See* Fruits & Vegetables: Cauliflower
Cauliflower, Pickled *See* Relishes & Pickled Products: Pickled Products: Cauliflower
Cavatappi *See* Pasta & Noodles: Cavatappi
Cavatelli *See* Pasta & Noodles: Cavatelli
Caviar *See* Fish & Seafood: Caviar (Roe)
Cayenne Pepper *See* Spices, Seasonings & Seeds: Spices: Cayenne Pepper
Cayenne Spices *See* Spices, Seasonings & Seeds: Spices: Cayenne
Ceasar Salad Dressings *See* Sauces, Dips & Dressings: Salad Dressings: Ceasar
Ceasar Salad Dressings, Mixes *See* Sauces, Dips & Dressings: Salad Dressings: Mixes: Ceasar
Celery *See* Fruits & Vegetables: Celery
Celery Flakes *See* Fruits & Vegetables: Dried & Dehydrated Vegetables: Celery Flakes; *See also* Spices, Seasonings & Seeds: Spices: Celery Flakes
Celery Oils *See* Oils, Shortening & Fats: Oils: Celery
Celery Powders *See* Ingredients, Flavors & Additives: Powders: Celery
Celery Salt *See* Spices, Seasonings & Seeds: Salt: Celery
Celery Seeds *See* Spices, Seasonings & Seeds: Seeds: Celery
Celery Sticks *See* Fruits & Vegetables: Celery: Sticks
Cellulose Fiber *See* Cereals, Grains, Rice & Flour: Fiber: Cellulose
Cellulose Gel *See* Ingredients, Flavors & Additives: Cellulose Gel
Cereal *See* Cereals, Grains, Rice & Flour: Cereal
Cereal Bars *See* Cereals, Grains, Rice & Flour: Cereal: Bars

Cereal Binders *See* Ingredients, Flavors & Additives: Binders: Cereal
Cereal Crisps *See* Cereals, Grains, Rice & Flour: Crisps: Cereal
Cereal Solids Hydrolyzed Anticaking Agents *See* Ingredients, Flavors & Additives: Agents: Anticaking: Cereal Solids Hydrolyzed
Cereal Solids Hydrolyzed Products *See* Ingredients, Flavors & Additives: Hydrolyzed Products: Cereal Solids
Certified Dyes *See* Ingredients, Flavors & Additives: Colors: Dyes: Certified
Certified Organic Foods *See* Specialty & Organic Foods: Organic Foods: Certified; *See also* Organic Foods
Chai Tea *See* Beverages: Coffee & Tea: Tea: Chai
Challah *See* Baked Goods: Breads: Challah
Chalupa Shells *See* Ethnic Foods: Shells: Chalupa
Chamomile Tea *See* Beverages: Coffee & Tea: Tea: Chamomile
Champagne *See* Beverages: Wines: French: Champagne
Champagne Vinegar *See* Sauces, Dips & Dressings: Vinegar: Champagne
Chanterelle *See* Fruits & Vegetables: Mushrooms: Chanterelle
Chardonnay *See* Beverages: Wines: White Grape Varieties: Chardonnay
Cheddar Cheese *See* Cheese & Cheese Products: Cheese: Cheddar
Cheddar Cheese, Imitation *See* Cheese & Cheese Products: Imitation Cheeses & Substitutes: Imitation: Cheddar
Cheddar Cheese, Powders *See* Ingredients, Flavors & Additives: Powders: Cheese: Cheddar
Cheddar Snack Seasonings *See* Spices, Seasonings & Seeds: Seasonings: Snack: Cheddar
Cheese *See* Cheese & Cheese Products; *See also* Cheese & Cheese Products: Cheese
Cheese Bacteria *See* Ingredients, Flavors & Additives: Cultures & Yeasts: Bacteria: Cheese
Cheese Blends *See* Ingredients, Flavors & Additives: Blends: Cheese
Cheese Cake *See* Baked Goods: Cakes & Pastries: Cheese Cake
Cheese Curls *See* Snack Foods: Cheese Curls
Cheese Dips *See* Sauces, Dips & Dressings: Dips: Cheese
Cheese Flavors *See* Ingredients, Flavors & Additives: Flavors: Cheese
Cheese Foods & Substitutes *See* Cheese & Cheese Products: Imitation Cheeses & Substitutes: Cheese Foods & Substitutes
Cheese Loaves, Yellow Process *See* Cheese & Cheese Products: Cheese: Process Loaves: Yellow
Cheese Pizza *See* Prepared Foods: Pizza & Pizza Products: Pizza: Cheese
Cheese Powders *See* Ingredients, Flavors & Additives: Powders: Cheese
Cheese Ravioli *See* Pasta & Noodles: Ravioli: Cheese
Cheese Sauces *See* Sauces, Dips & Dressings: Sauces: Cheese
Cheese Seasonings *See* Spices, Seasonings & Seeds: Seasonings: Cheese
Cheese Starter Media *See* Ingredients, Flavors & Additives: Starter Media: Cheese
Cheese Substitutes *See* Cheese & Cheese Products: Imitation Cheeses & Substitutes: Substitutes
Cheese Twists *See* Snack Foods: Cheese Twists
Cheese, Blend - American/Skim Milk *See* Cheese & Cheese Products: Cheese: Blend - American/Skim Milk
Cheese, No-Fat *See* Cheese & Cheese Products: Cheese: No-Fat
Cheese, White/Yellow Process Sliced *See* Cheese & Cheese Products: Cheese: Process Sliced: White/Yellow
Cheesecake Flavors *See* Ingredients, Flavors & Additives: Flavors: Cheesecake
Chelating Agents *See* Ingredients, Flavors & Additives: Chelating Agents
Chemicals *See* Ingredients, Flavors & Additives: Chemicals
Chemicals, Aroma *See* Ingredients, Flavors & Additives: Aroma Chemicals & Materials: Chemicals
Cherries *See* Fruits & Vegetables: Cherries
Cherry Flavors *See* Ingredients, Flavors & Additives: Flavors: Cherry
Cherry Juices *See* Beverages: Juices: Cherry
Cherry Peppers *See* Fruits & Vegetables: Peppers: Cherry
Cherry Pies *See* Baked Goods: Pies: Cherry
Cherry Tomato *See* Fruits & Vegetables: Tomato: Cherry
Chervil *See* Spices, Seasonings & Seeds: Spices: Chervil

Chestnut Flower Flour *See* Cereals, Grains, Rice & Flour: Flour: Chestnut Flower
Chestnuts *See* Nuts & Nut Butters: Nuts: Chestnuts
Chewing Gum *See* Candy & Confectionery: Candy: Chewing Gum
Chianti *See* Beverages: Wines: Italian: Chianti
Chick Beans *See* Fruits & Vegetables: Beans: Chick
Chicken *See* Meats & Meat Products: Poultry: Chicken
Chicken & Dumplings Soups & Stews *See* Prepared Foods: Soups & Stews: Chicken & Dumplings
Chicken & Noodles Soups & Stews *See* Prepared Foods: Soups & Stews: Chicken & Noodles
Chicken Bases *See* Ingredients, Flavors & Additives: Bases: Chicken
Chicken Broth *See* Prepared Foods: Broth: Chicken
Chicken Bulk *See* Meats & Meat Products: Poultry: Chicken: Bulk (Leg Quarters, Legs, Thighs)
Chicken Extenders *See* Ingredients, Flavors & Additives: Extenders: Chicken
Chicken Extracts *See* Ingredients, Flavors & Additives: Extracts: Chicken
Chicken Fats & Lard *See* Oils, Shortening & Fats: Fats & Lard: Chicken
Chicken Frankfurters *See* Meats & Meat Products: Frankfurters: Chicken
Chicken Marinades *See* Sauces, Dips & Dressings: Marinades: Chicken
Chicken Nuggets *See* Meats & Meat Products: Poultry: Chicken: Nuggets
Chicken Sausages *See* Meats & Meat Products: Smoked, Cured & Deli Meats: Sausages: Chicken
Chicken, Cut-Up Frozen *See* Meats & Meat Products: Poultry: Chicken: Cut-Up Frozen
Chicken, Cut-Up IQF *See* Meats & Meat Products: Poultry: Chicken: Cut-Up IQF (Individually Quick Frozen)
Chicken, Prepared Meals *See* Prepared Foods: Prepared Meals: Chicken
Chicken, Prepared Salads *See* Prepared Foods: Prepared Salads: Chicken
Chicks Hatcheries *See* Eggs & Egg Products: Hatcheries: Chicks
Chicory *See* Fruits & Vegetables: Chicory
Chile Pepper Spices *See* Spices, Seasonings & Seeds: Spices: Chile Pepper
Chile Peppers *See* Fruits & Vegetables: Peppers: Chile
Chili *See* Prepared Foods: Chili
Chili Beans *See* Fruits & Vegetables: Beans: Chili
Chili Crush *See* Spices, Seasonings & Seeds: Spices: Chili Crush
Chili Dips *See* Sauces, Dips & Dressings: Dips: Chili
Chili Mixes *See* Doughs, Mixes & Fillings: Mixes: Chili
Chili Pods *See* Spices, Seasonings & Seeds: Spices: Chili Pods
Chili Powder *See* Spices, Seasonings & Seeds: Spices: Chili Powder; *See also* Ingredients, Flavors & Additives: Powders: Chili
Chili Sauces *See* Sauces, Dips & Dressings: Sauces: Chili
Chili with Cheese *See* Prepared Foods: Chili: with Cheese
Chilled Apple Juices *See* Beverages: Juices: Apple: Chilled
Chilled Cherry Juices *See* Beverages: Juices: Cherry: Chilled
Chilled Grape Juices *See* Beverages: Juices: Grape: Chilled
Chimichangas *See* Prepared Foods: Prepared Meals: Burritos: Chimichangas
Chinese *See* Ethnic Foods: Chinese
Chinese Black Rice *See* Cereals, Grains, Rice & Flour: Rice: Chinese Black
Chinese Cabbage *See* Fruits & Vegetables: Cabbage: Chinese
Chinese Spices *See* Spices, Seasonings & Seeds: Spices: Chinese
Chinese Style Seasonings *See* Spices, Seasonings & Seeds: Seasonings: Chinese Style
Chip Dips *See* Sauces, Dips & Dressings: Dips: Chip
Chipotle Peppers *See* Fruits & Vegetables: Peppers: Chipotle
Chipped Beef *See* Meats & Meat Products: Beef & Beef Products: Chipped
Chips *See* Snack Foods: Chips
Chives *See* Spices, Seasonings & Seeds: Spices: Chives; *See also* Fruits & Vegetables: Chives
Chlorophyll *See* Ingredients, Flavors & Additives: Chlorophyll

---

EXAMPLE: **Canadian Style Bacon** *See* Meats & Meat Products: Smoked, Cured & Deli Meats: Bacon: Canadian Style

1. Product or Service you are looking for
2. Main Category, in alphabetical order, located in the page headers starting on page 27
3. Category Description, located in black bars and in page headers
4. Product Category, located in gray bars
5. Product Type, located under gray bars, centered in bold

Product Category List

Chocolate Almond Biscotti See Baked Goods: Cookies & Bars: Biscotti: Chocolate Almond
Chocolate Bars See Candy & Confectionery: Chocolate Products: Chocolate Bars
Chocolate Bases See Ingredients, Flavors & Additives: Bases: Chocolate
Chocolate Candy See Candy & Confectionery: Chocolate Products: Chocolate Candy
Chocolate Candy Coatings See Candy & Confectionery: Candy Coatings: Chocolate
Chocolate Cherries See Candy & Confectionery: Chocolate Products: Chocolate Cherries
Chocolate Chip Compound for Ice Cream See Ingredients, Flavors & Additives: Chocolate Products: Chocolate Chip Compound for Ice Cream
Chocolate Chip Cookies See Baked Goods: Cookies & Bars: Chocolate Chip Cookies
Chocolate Chips See Candy & Confectionery: Chocolate Products: Chocolate Chips; See also Snack Foods: Chips: Chocolate
Chocolate Chunks See Candy & Confectionery: Chocolate Products: Chocolate Chunks
Chocolate Coated Nuts See Nuts & Nut Butters: Nuts: Coated: Chocolate
Chocolate Coated Raisins See Fruits & Vegetables: Raisins: Chocolate Coated
Chocolate Covered Apple See Fruits & Vegetables: Apple: Covered: Chocolate
Chocolate Dessert Fillings See Doughs, Mixes & Fillings: Fillings: Dessert: Chocolate
Chocolate Dipped Biscotti See Baked Goods: Cookies & Bars: Biscotti: Chocolate Dipped
Chocolate Drinks See Beverages: Cocoa & Chocolate Drinks: Chocolate Drinks
Chocolate Fillings See Doughs, Mixes & Fillings: Fillings: Chocolate
Chocolate Flavors See Ingredients, Flavors & Additives: Flavors: Chocolate
Chocolate Liqueur See Beverages: Spirits & Liqueurs: Liqueurs & Cordials: Chocolate Liqueur
Chocolate Milk See Dairy Products: Milk & Milk Products: Milk: Chocolate
Chocolate Products See Candy & Confectionery: Chocolate Products; See also Ingredients, Flavors & Additives: Chocolate Products
Chocolate Pudding See Dairy Products: Pudding: Chocolate
Chop Suey See Ethnic Foods: Chop Suey
Chopped Broccoli See Fruits & Vegetables: Broccoli: Chopped
Chopped Broccoli, Dehydrated See Fruits & Vegetables: Dried & Dehydrated Vegetables: Broccoli: Chopped
Chopped Celery See Fruits & Vegetables: Celery: Chopped
Chopped Clam See Fish & Seafood: Shellfish: Clam: Chopped
Chopped Garlic See Spices, Seasonings & Seeds: Spices: Garlic: Chopped
Chopped Onion See Spices, Seasonings & Seeds: Spices: Onion: Chopped
Chopped Shellfish See Fish & Seafood: Shellfish: Chopped
Chorizo Sausages See Meats & Meat Products: Smoked, Cured & Deli Meats: Sausages: Chorizo
Chourico Sausages See Meats & Meat Products: Smoked, Cured & Deli Meats: Sausages: Chourico
Chow Chow See Ethnic Foods: Chow Chow
Chow Fun Noodles See Pasta & Noodles: Noodles: Chow Fun
Chow Mein See Ethnic Foods: Chow Mein
Chow Mein Noodles See Pasta & Noodles: Noodles: Chow Mein
Chowder See Fish & Seafood: Fish: Chowder; See also Prepared Foods: Soups & Stews: Chowder; See also Prepared Foods: Chowder
Christmas Specialty-Packaged Candy See Candy & Confectionery: Specialty-Packaged Candy: Christmas
Chub See Fish & Seafood: Fish: Chub
Chum Salmon See Fish & Seafood: Fish: Salmon: Chum
Chunky Salsa See Sauces, Dips & Dressings: Salsa: Chunky
Churros See Baked Goods: Cakes & Pastries: Churros
Chutney See Prepared Foods: Chutney
Cider & Vinegar Colors See Ingredients, Flavors & Additives: Colors: Cider & Vinegar
Cinnamon Flavors See Ingredients, Flavors & Additives: Flavors: Cinnamon
Cinnamon Leaf & Bark Oils See Oils, Shortening & Fats: Oils: Cinnamon - Leaf & Bark
Cinnamon Rolls See Baked Goods: Breads: Rolls: Cinnamon
Cinnamon Spices See Spices, Seasonings & Seeds: Spices: Cinnamon
Cinnamon Toast See Baked Goods: Breads: Cinnamon Toast

Cinnamon Toast, Snack Seasonings See Spices, Seasonings & Seeds: Seasonings: Snack: Cinnamon Toast
Citric Acidulants See Ingredients, Flavors & Additives: Acidulants: Citric
Citron See Spices, Seasonings & Seeds: Spices: Citron
Citrus Blends Juices See Beverages: Juices: Citrus Blends
Citrus Flavors See Ingredients, Flavors & Additives: Flavors: Citrus
Citrus Fruits See Fruits & Vegetables: Citrus Fruits
Citrus Oils See Oils, Shortening & Fats: Oils: Citrus
Citrus Pectins See Ingredients, Flavors & Additives: Pectins: Citrus
Citrus Peel Products See Fruits & Vegetables: Citrus Peel Products
Citrus Pulps & Purees See Fruits & Vegetables: Pulps & Purees: Citrus
Clam See Fish & Seafood: Shellfish: Clam
Clam & Fish Chowder See Prepared Foods: Chowder: Clam & Fish
Clam Juice See Fish & Seafood: Shellfish: Clam: Juice
Clam Sauces See Sauces, Dips & Dressings: Sauces: Clam
Clarifying Agents See Ingredients, Flavors & Additives: Agents: Clarifying
Cloudear Mushrooms See Fruits & Vegetables: Mushrooms: Cloudear
Clove Oils See Oils, Shortening & Fats: Oils: Clove
Cloves See Spices, Seasonings & Seeds: Spices: Cloves
Club Soda See Beverages: Soft Drinks & Sodas: Club Soda
Coagulants See Ingredients, Flavors & Additives: Coagulants
Coarse Frozen Ground Beef See Meats & Meat Products: Beef & Beef Products: Ground: Coarse Frozen
Coated Candy Bars See Candy & Confectionery: Candy: Candy Bars: Coated
Coated Nuts See Nuts & Nut Butters: Nuts: Coated
Coated Popcorn See Snack Foods: Popcorn: Coated
Coatings See Ingredients, Flavors & Additives: Coatings
Cocktail Fruit See Fruits & Vegetables: Fruit: Cocktail
Cocktail Mixes See Doughs, Mixes & Fillings: Mixes: Cocktail
Cocktail Onion See Fruits & Vegetables: Onion: Cocktail
Cocktail Sauces See Sauces, Dips & Dressings: Sauces: Cocktail
Cocktail Seafood See Fish & Seafood: Seafood: Cocktail
Cocktail Shrimp See Fish & Seafood: Shellfish: Shrimp: Cocktail
Cocktail Tomato See Fruits & Vegetables: Tomato: Cocktail
Cocktail Tomato Juices See Beverages: Juices: Tomato: Cocktail
Cocoa & Chocolate Drinks See Beverages: Cocoa & Chocolate Drinks
Cocoa & Cocoa Products See Candy & Confectionery: Chocolate Products: Cocoa & Cocoa Products
Cocoa & Rice Pellets See Ingredients, Flavors & Additives: Half-Products: Cocoa & Rice Pellets
Cocoa Butter See Ingredients, Flavors & Additives: Cocoa Butter
Cocoa Flavors See Ingredients, Flavors & Additives: Flavors: Cocoa
Cocoa Powders See Ingredients, Flavors & Additives: Powders: Cocoa
Cocoa Replacers See Ingredients, Flavors & Additives: Replacers: Cocoa
Cocoa Rice Crisps See Cereals, Grains, Rice & Flour: Crisps: Cocoa Rice
Cocoa Soy Crisps See Cereals, Grains, Rice & Flour: Crisps: Cocoa Soy
Coconut & Coconut Products See Fruits & Vegetables: Coconut & Coconut Products
Coconut Candy See Candy & Confectionery: Candy: Coconut
Coconut Flavors See Ingredients, Flavors & Additives: Flavors: Coconut
Coconut Juices See Beverages: Juices: Coconut
Coconut Oils See Oils, Shortening & Fats: Oils: Coconut
Cod See Fish & Seafood: Fish: Cod
Cod Liver Oils See Oils, Shortening & Fats: Oils: Cod Liver
Coffee See Beverages: Coffee & Tea; See also Beverages: Coffee & Tea: Coffee
Coffee Cake See Baked Goods: Cakes & Pastries: Coffee Cake
Coffee Creamers See Dairy Products: Creamers: Coffee
Coffee Extenders See Ingredients, Flavors & Additives: Extenders: Coffee
Coffee Extracts See Ingredients, Flavors & Additives: Extracts: Coffee
Coffee Flavors See Ingredients, Flavors & Additives: Flavors: Coffee
Coffee Liqueur See Beverages: Spirits & Liqueurs: Liqueurs & Cordials: Coffee Liqueur
Coho Salmon See Fish & Seafood: Fish: Salmon: Coho

Cola Soft Drinks See Beverages: Soft Drinks & Sodas: Soft Drinks: Cola
Colby See Cheese & Cheese Products: Cheese: Colby
Cold Smoked Seafood See Fish & Seafood: Seafood: Smoked: Cold
Cole Slaw See Prepared Foods: Prepared Salads: Cole Slaw
Collard Greens See Fruits & Vegetables: Collard Greens
Colloids Stabilizers See Ingredients, Flavors & Additives: Stabilizers: Colloids
Colored Crisps See Cereals, Grains, Rice & Flour: Crisps: Colored
Colored Pellets See Ingredients, Flavors & Additives: Half-Products: Colored Pellets
Colored Starch Bits See Ingredients, Flavors & Additives: Toppings: Colored Starch Bits; See also Ingredients, Flavors & Additives: Bits: Colored Starch
Colors See Ingredients, Flavors & Additives: Colors
Compacting Agents See Ingredients, Flavors & Additives: Agents: Compacting
Compound Coatings See Ingredients, Flavors & Additives: Coatings: Compound
Compounds See Ingredients, Flavors & Additives: Compounds
Concentrate Ade Juices See Beverages: Juices: Ade: Concentrate
Concentrate Apple Juices See Beverages: Juices: Apple: Concentrate
Concentrate Apricot Juices See Beverages: Juices: Apricot: Concentrate
Concentrate Cherry Juices See Beverages: Juices: Cherry: Concentrate
Concentrate Cranberry Juices See Beverages: Juices: Cranberry: Concentrate
Concentrate Drink Juices See Beverages: Juices: Drink: Concentrate
Concentrate Fruit & Vegetable Juices See Beverages: Juices: Fruit & Vegetable: Concentrate
Concentrate Fruit Juices See Beverages: Juices: Fruit: Concentrate
Concentrate Fruit Punch Juices See Beverages: Juices: Fruit Punch: Concentrate
Concentrate Fruit Puree Juices See Beverages: Juices: Vegetable: Concentrates - Fruit Puree
Concentrate Grape Juices See Beverages: Juices: Grape: Concentrate
Concentrate Grapefruit Juices See Beverages: Juices: Grapefruit: Concentrate
Concentrate Lemon Juices See Beverages: Juices: Lemon: Concentrate
Concentrate Lemonade Juices See Beverages: Juices: Lemonade: Concentrate
Concentrate Orange Juices See Beverages: Juices: Orange: Concentrate
Concentrate Orange Juices, Frozen See Beverages: Juices: Orange: Concentrate - Frozen
Concentrate Pineapple Juices See Beverages: Juices: Pineapple: Concentrate
Concentrate Soy Protein See Fruits & Vegetables: Soy: Soy Protein: Concentrate
Concentrates See Ingredients, Flavors & Additives: Concentrates
Conch Fish See Fish & Seafood: Fish: Conch
Conch Shellfish See Fish & Seafood: Shellfish: Conch
Conchigite Rigate See Pasta & Noodles: Conchigite Rigate
Condensed Buttermilk See Dairy Products: Buttermilk & Buttermilk Products: Buttermilk Products: Condensed
Condensed Milk See Dairy Products: Milk & Milk Products: Milk: Condensed
Condensed Milk, Bulk Only See Dairy Products: Milk & Milk Products: Milk: Condensed - Bulk Only
Condiments See Sauces, Dips & Dressings: Condiments
Cones See Baked Goods: Cones
Confectioners Crunch See Candy & Confectionery: Confectionery: Confectioners Crunch
Confectioners Dipping Fruit See Fruits & Vegetables: Dipping Fruit: Confectioners'
Confectionery See Candy & Confectionery: Confectionery; See also Candy & Confectionery: Confectionery; See also Ingredients, Flavors & Additives: Confectionery
Confectionery Candy Coatings See Candy & Confectionery: Candy Coatings: Confectionery
Confectionery Toppings See Ingredients, Flavors & Additives: Toppings: Confectionery
Convenience Food See Prepared Foods: Convenience Food
Convenience Prepared Meals See Prepared Foods: Prepared Meals: Convenience
Cooked See Eggs & Egg Products: Cooked
Cooked Chicken, Breaded - Frozen See Meats & Meat Products: Poultry: Chicken: Cooked - Breaded - Frozen
Cooked Corn-on-the-Cob See Fruits & Vegetables: Corn: Corn-on-the-Cob: Cooked

Product Category List

Cooked Crab See Fish & Seafood: Shellfish: Crab: Cooked
Cooked Frozen Hamburger See Meats & Meat Products: Beef & Beef Products: Hamburger: Cooked Frozen
Cooked Frozen Patties See Meats & Meat Products: Beef & Beef Products: Patties: Cooked Frozen
Cooked Ham, Water-added Chilled See Meats & Meat Products: Smoked, Cured & Deli Meats: Ham: Cooked - Water-added Chilled
Cooked Oysters See Fish & Seafood: Shellfish: Oysters: Cooked
Cooked Shrimp See Fish & Seafood: Shellfish: Shrimp: Cooked
Cookie Batters See Doughs, Mixes & Fillings: Batters: Cookie
Cookie Bits See Ingredients, Flavors & Additives: Bits: Cookie
Cookie Doughs See Doughs, Mixes & Fillings: Doughs: Cookie
Cookie Fillings See Doughs, Mixes & Fillings: Fillings: Cookie
Cookie Mixes See Doughs, Mixes & Fillings: Mixes: Cookie
Cookies See Baked Goods: Cookies & Bars: Cookies
Cookies & Bars See Baked Goods: Cookies & Bars
Cookies & Biscuits See Baked Goods: Cookies & Bars: Cookies & Biscuits
Cookies Bars See Baked Goods: Cookies & Bars: Bars
Cooking Compounds See Ingredients, Flavors & Additives: Compounds: Cooking
Cooking Compounds, Fats & Lard See Oils, Shortening & Fats: Fats & Lard: Lard: Cooking Compounds
Cooking Oils See Oils, Shortening & Fats: Oils: Cooking
Cooking Wines See Beverages: Wines: Cooking
Coriander See Spices, Seasonings & Seeds: Spices: Coriander (Cilantro)
Coriander Seed Oils See Oils, Shortening & Fats: Oils: Coriander Seed
Coriander Seeds See Spices, Seasonings & Seeds: Seeds: Coriander
Corn See Fruits & Vegetables: Corn
Corn Bran Fiber See Cereals, Grains, Rice & Flour: Fiber: Corn Bran
Corn Breads See Baked Goods: Breads: Corn
Corn Candy See Candy & Confectionery: Candy: Corn
Corn Chips See Snack Foods: Chips: Corn
Corn Dogs See Meats & Meat Products: Frankfurters: Corn Dogs
Corn Flour See Cereals, Grains, Rice & Flour: Flour: Corn
Corn Fritters See Prepared Foods: Prepared Meals: Corn Fritters
Corn Meal See Cereals, Grains, Rice & Flour: Corn Meal
Corn Nuts See Snack Foods: Corn Nuts
Corn Oils See Oils, Shortening & Fats: Oils: Corn
Corn Starches See Ingredients, Flavors & Additives: Starches: Corn
Corn Syrups See Sugars, Syrups & Sweeteners: Syrups: Corn
Corn-Based Cereal See Cereals, Grains, Rice & Flour: Cereal: Corn-Based
Corn-on-the-Cob See Fruits & Vegetables: Corn: Corn-on-the-Cob
Corned Beef See Meats & Meat Products: Smoked, Cured & Deli Meats: Corned Beef
Cornish Game Hens See Meats & Meat Products: Poultry: Cornish Game Hens
Corsignano See Cheese & Cheese Products: Cheese: Corsignano
Cottage Cheese See Cheese & Cheese Products: Cheese: Cottage
Cotton Candy See Candy & Confectionery: Candy: Cotton
Cottonseed Oils See Oils, Shortening & Fats: Oils: Cottonseed
Couscous See Ethnic Foods: Couscous
Covered Apple See Fruits & Vegetables: Apple: Covered
Crab See Fish & Seafood: Shellfish: Crab; See also Prepared Foods: Prepared Meals: Crab
Crab Extracts See Ingredients, Flavors & Additives: Extracts: Crab
Crab Meat See Fish & Seafood: Shellfish: Crab: Meat
Crackers See Baked Goods: Crackers; See also Baked Goods: Crackers: Crackers
Cranberry See Fruits & Vegetables: Berries: Cranberry
Cranberry Juices See Beverages: Juices: Cranberry
Cranberry Orange Biscotti See Baked Goods: Cookies & Bars: Biscotti: Cranberry Orange
Cranberry Sauces See Fruits & Vegetables: Sauces: Cranberry

Crayfish See Fish & Seafood: Shellfish: Crayfish
Cream See Dairy Products: Cream
Cream Ale See Beverages: Beers: American & British Ale: Cream Ale
Cream Cheese See Cheese & Cheese Products: Cheese: Cream
Cream Cheese Powders See Ingredients, Flavors & Additives: Powders: Cheese: Cream
Cream Dessert Fillings See Doughs, Mixes & Fillings: Fillings: Dessert: Cream
Cream from Milk See Dairy Products: Cream: from Milk
Cream of Broccoli Soups & Stews See Prepared Foods: Soups & Stews: Cream of Broccoli
Cream of Mushroom Soups & Stews See Prepared Foods: Soups & Stews: Cream of Mushroom
Cream of Potato Soups & Stews See Prepared Foods: Soups & Stews: Cream of Potato
Cream of Tartar See Spices, Seasonings & Seeds: Spices: Tartar: Cream
Cream Puff See Baked Goods: Cakes & Pastries: Cream Puff
Cream Soda See Beverages: Soft Drinks & Sodas: Soft Drinks: Cream Soda - Vanilla; See also Beverages: Soft Drinks & Sodas: Soft Drinks: Cream Soda
Creamers See Dairy Products: Creamers
Creamy Dijon Salad Dressings See Sauces, Dips & Dressings: Salad Dressings: Mixes: Creamy Dijon; See also Sauces, Dips & Dressings: Salad Dressings: Creamy Dijon
Creme Fillings See Doughs, Mixes & Fillings: Fillings: Creme
Cremes Candy See Candy & Confectionery: Candy: Cremes
Creole Chicken See Prepared Foods: Prepared Meals: Chicken: Creole
Crepes See Prepared Foods: Crepes
Criminis Mushrooms See Fruits & Vegetables: Mushrooms: Criminis
Crisp Rice Toppings See Ingredients, Flavors & Additives: Toppings: Crisp Rice
Crisped Bran Crisps See Cereals, Grains, Rice & Flour: Crisps: Crisped Bran
Crisped Corn Crisps See Cereals, Grains, Rice & Flour: Crisps: Crisped Corn
Crisped Oat Crisps See Cereals, Grains, Rice & Flour: Crisps: Crisped Oat
Crisped Rice Crisps See Cereals, Grains, Rice & Flour: Crisps: Crisped Rice
Crisped Soy Crisps See Cereals, Grains, Rice & Flour: Crisps: Crisped Soy
Crisped Wheat Crisps See Cereals, Grains, Rice & Flour: Crisps: Crisped Wheat
Crisps See Cereals, Grains, Rice & Flour: Crisps
Criterion Apple See Fruits & Vegetables: Apple: Criterion
Croaker See Fish & Seafood: Fish: Croaker
Croissant Sesame Crackers See Baked Goods: Crackers: Croissant Sesame Crackers
Croissants See Baked Goods: Breads: Croissants
Croquettes See Prepared Foods: Croquettes
Croutons See Baked Goods: Bread Crumbs & Croutons; See also Baked Goods: Bread Crumbs & Croutons: Crumbs
Crumpets See Baked Goods: Cakes & Pastries: Crumpets
Crunch Toppings See Ingredients, Flavors & Additives: Toppings: Crunch
Crunches See Baked Goods: Crunches
Crunchy Peanut Butter See Nuts & Nut Butters: Nut Butters: Peanut Butter: Crunchy
Crushed Canned Tomato See Fruits & Vegetables: Tomato: Canned: Crushed
Crushed Fruits & Vegetables See Fruits & Vegetables: Crushed
Crushed Onion See Fruits & Vegetables: Onion: Crushed
Crushed Red Pepper See Spices, Seasonings & Seeds: Spices: Red Pepper: Crushed
Crysanthemums See Fruits & Vegetables: Crysanthemums
Crystalline Fructose See Sugars, Syrups & Sweeteners: Fructose: Crystalline
Crystallized Ginger See Spices, Seasonings & Seeds: Spices: Ginger: Crystallized; See also Fruits & Vegetables: Ginger: Crystallized
Crystallized, Glace Candied Fruits See Fruits & Vegetables: Candied Fruits: Crystallized, Glace
Cucumber See Fruits & Vegetables: Cucumber
Cucumber for Pickling See Fruits & Vegetables: Cucumber: for Pickling

Cultured Flavors See Ingredients, Flavors & Additives: Flavors: Cultured
Cultures See Ingredients, Flavors & Additives: Cultures & Yeasts: Cultures
Cultures & Yeasts See Ingredients, Flavors & Additives: Cultures & Yeasts
Cumin Seeds See Spices, Seasonings & Seeds: Seeds: Cumin
Cumin Spices See Spices, Seasonings & Seeds: Spices: Cumin
Cupcake See Baked Goods: Cakes & Pastries: Cupcakes
Curd Seasonings See Spices, Seasonings & Seeds: Seasonings: Curd
Cured Smoked Seafood See Fish & Seafood: Seafood: Smoked: Cured
Curing Preparations See Ingredients, Flavors & Additives: Curing Preparations
Currants Berries See Fruits & Vegetables: Berries: Currants
Curry Powder See Spices, Seasonings & Seeds: Spices: Curry Powder; See also Ingredients, Flavors & Additives: Powders: Curry
Curry Sauces See Sauces, Dips & Dressings: Sauces: Curry
Cusk See Fish & Seafood: Fish: Cusk
Custard See Dairy Products: Custard
Custard Dessert Fillings See Doughs, Mixes & Fillings: Fillings: Dessert: Custard
Custard Powders See Ingredients, Flavors & Additives: Powders: Custard
Custom Blends See Ingredients, Flavors & Additives: Blends: Custom
Custom Designed Colloid Stabilizers See Ingredients, Flavors & Additives: Stabilizers: Colloids: Custom Designed

D

D'Anjou/Bosc Pear See Fruits & Vegetables: Pear: D'Anjou/Bosc
Dairy Bases See Ingredients, Flavors & Additives: Bases: Dairy
Dairy Butter See Dairy Products: Butter: Dairy
Dairy Coagulants See Ingredients, Flavors & Additives: Coagulants: Dairy
Dairy Drinks See Dairy Products: Dairy Drinks
Dairy Flavors See Ingredients, Flavors & Additives: Flavors: Dairy
Dairy Ingredients See Ingredients, Flavors & Additives: Ingredients: Dairy
Dairy Products See Dairy Products
Dairy Seasonings See Spices, Seasonings & Seeds: Seasonings: Dairy Products
Dairy Whipped Toppings See Ingredients, Flavors & Additives: Toppings: Whipped: Dairy
Danish See Baked Goods: Cakes & Pastries: Danish
Darjeeling Tea See Beverages: Coffee & Tea: Tea: Darjeeling
Dark Green Zucchini See Fruits & Vegetables: Zucchini: Dark Green
Dark Red Kidney Beans See Fruits & Vegetables: Beans: Kidney: Dark Red
Dark Rum See Beverages: Spirits & Liqueurs: Rum: Dark
DarkLager/Dunkel Lager See Beverages: Beers: Lager: DarkLager/Dunkel
Dates See Fruits & Vegetables: Dates
De Arbol Peppers See Fruits & Vegetables: Peppers: De Arbol
Decaffeinated Coffee See Beverages: Coffee & Tea: Coffee: Decaffeinated
Decaffeinated Coffee, Naturally See Beverages: Coffee & Tea: Coffee: Decaffeinated Naturally
Decaffeinated Espresso See Beverages: Coffee & Tea: Espresso: Decaffeinated
Decaffeinated Tea See Beverages: Coffee & Tea: Tea: Decaffeinated
Decorations See Candy & Confectionery: Decorations & Icings; See also Candy & Confectionery: Decorations & Icings: Decorations
Decorative Items See Ingredients, Flavors & Additives: Decorative Items
Defatted Wheat Germ See Cereals, Grains, Rice & Flour: Wheat: Germ: Defatted
Defoamers See Ingredients, Flavors & Additives: Defoamers
Dehydrated Capsicums Peppers See Fruits & Vegetables: Peppers: Capsicums: Dehydrated

Product Category List

Dehydrated Carrot *See Fruits & Vegetables: Carrot: Dehydrated*
Dehydrated Celery *See Fruits & Vegetables: Celery: Dehydrated*
Dehydrated Egg *See Eggs & Egg Products: Dehydrated*
Dehydrated Food *See Specialty Processed Foods: Dehydrated Food (See also Specific Foods)*
Dehydrated Fruit *See Fruits & Vegetables: Dried & Dehydrated Fruits: Dehydrated Fruit; See also Fruits & Vegetables: Dehydrated*
Dehydrated Mushrooms *See Fruits & Vegetables: Mushrooms: Dehydrated*
Dehydrated Onion *See Fruits & Vegetables: Dried & Dehydrated Vegetables: Onion: Dehydrated*
Dehydrated Parsley *See Spices, Seasonings & Seeds: Spices: Parsley: Dehydrated*
Dehydrated Potatoes *See Fruits & Vegetables: Potatoes: Dehydrated*
Dehydrated Shellfish *See Fish & Seafood: Shellfish: Dehydrated*
Dehydrated Soup *See Prepared Foods: Soups & Stews: Dehydrated Soup*
Dehydrated Vegetables *See Fruits & Vegetables: Dried & Dehydrated Vegetables: Dehydrated Vegetables; See also Fruits & Vegetables: Dehydrated*
Deli Foods *See Meats & Meat Products: Smoked, Cured & Deli Meats: Deli Foods*
Deli Meats *See Meats & Meat Products: Smoked, Cured & Deli Meats: Deli Meats*
Deli Meats, Fresh Turkey Breast *See Meats & Meat Products: Smoked, Cured & Deli Meats: Turkey: Deli Breast - Fresh*
Deli Meats, Frozen Turkey Breast *See Meats & Meat Products: Smoked, Cured & Deli Meats: Turkey: Deli Breast - Frozen*
Deli Meats, Smoked Turkey Breast *See Meats & Meat Products: Smoked, Cured & Deli Meats: Turkey: Deli Breast - Smoked*
Desiccated & Shredded Coconut *See Fruits & Vegetables: Coconut & Coconut Products: Desiccated & Shredded*
Desiccated Egg *See Eggs & Egg Products: Dried: Desiccated*
Desiccated Fruit *See Fruits & Vegetables: Dried & Dehydrated Fruits: Desiccated Fruit*
Desiccated Vegetables *See Fruits & Vegetables: Dried & Dehydrated Vegetables: Desiccated Vegetables*
Dessert Fillings *See Doughs, Mixes & Fillings: Fillings: Dessert*
Dessert Mixes *See Doughs, Mixes & Fillings: Mixes: Dessert*
Dessert Mixes, Frozen *See Doughs, Mixes & Fillings: Mixes: Frozen: Dessert*
Dessert Sauces *See Sauces, Dips & Dressings: Sauces: Dessert*
Dessert Tarts *See Baked Goods: Cakes & Pastries: Dessert Tarts*
Dessert Toppings *See Ingredients, Flavors & Additives: Toppings: Dessert*
Desserts *See Baked Goods: Desserts*
Dextrin Starches *See Ingredients, Flavors & Additives: Starches: Dextrin*
Dextrose Corn Syrups *See Sugars, Syrups & Sweeteners: Syrups: Corn: Dextrose*
Dextrose Sweeteners *See Ingredients, Flavors & Additives: Sweeteners: Dextrose*
Diced & Cooked Chicken *See Meats & Meat Products: Poultry: Chicken: Diced & Cooked*
Diced Canned Pear *See Fruits & Vegetables: Pear: Canned: Diced*
Diced Frozen Chicken *See Meats & Meat Products: Poultry: Chicken: Diced Frozen*
Diced Tomato *See Fruits & Vegetables: Tomato: Diced*
Diet & Weight Loss Aids *See Specialty & Organic Foods: Dietary Products: Diet & Weight Loss Aids; See also Organic Foods*
Dietary Products *See Specialty & Organic Foods: Dietary Products; See also Organic Foods*
Dietary Supplements *See Specialty & Organic Foods: Dietary Products: Dietary Supplements; See also Organic Foods*
Dietetic Candy *See Candy & Confectionery: Candy: Dietetic*
Dietetic Juices *See Beverages: Juices: Dietetic*
Digestive Aids *See Ingredients, Flavors & Additives: Digestive Aids*
Dijon Mixes *See Sauces, Dips & Dressings: Salad Dressings: Mixes: Dijon*
Dill Pickles *See Relishes & Pickled Products: Pickled Products: Pickles: Dill*
Dill Seeds *See Spices, Seasonings & Seeds: Seeds: Dill*
Dill Spices *See Spices, Seasonings & Seeds: Spices: Dill*

Dill Weed Spices *See Spices, Seasonings & Seeds: Spices: Dill Weed*
Dillweed Oils *See Oils, Shortening & Fats: Oils: Dillweed*
Dim Sum *See Ethnic Foods: Dim Sum*
Dip Mixes *See Doughs, Mixes & Fillings: Mixes: Dip*
Dipping Fruit *See Fruits & Vegetables: Dipping Fruit*
Dips *See Sauces, Dips & Dressings: Dips*
Distilled Water *See Beverages: Water: Distilled*
Divinity Candy *See Candy & Confectionery: Candy: Divinity*
Dogfish *See Fish & Seafood: Fish: Dogfish*
Dolcetto *See Beverages: Wines: Red Grape Wines: Dolcetto*
Dolphin *See Fish & Seafood: Fish: Dolphin*
Donut Mixes *See Doughs, Mixes & Fillings: Mixes: Donut*
Doughnut Doughs *See Doughs, Mixes & Fillings: Doughs: Doughnuts*
Doughnut Fillings *See Doughs, Mixes & Fillings: Fillings: Doughnuts*
Doughnuts *See Baked Goods: Cakes & Pastries: Doughnuts*
Doughs *See Doughs, Mixes & Fillings: Doughs*
Dressing Flavors *See Ingredients, Flavors & Additives: Flavors: Flavors: Dressing*
Dried & Dehydrated Fruits *See Fruits & Vegetables: Dried & Dehydrated Fruits*
Dried & Dehydrated Vegetables *See Fruits & Vegetables: Dried & Dehydrated Vegetables*
Dried Apple *See Fruits & Vegetables: Apple: Dried*
Dried Apricot *See Fruits & Vegetables: Apricot: Dried*
Dried Banana *See Fruits & Vegetables: Banana: Dried*
Dried Beans *See Fruits & Vegetables: Beans: Dried*
Dried Beet Pulp *See Fruits & Vegetables: Pulps & Purees: Pulp: Dried Beet*
Dried Blueberry *See Fruits & Vegetables: Berries: Blueberry: Dried*
Dried Cantaloupe *See Fruits & Vegetables: Melon: Cantaloupe: Dried*
Dried Cayenne Pepper *See Spices, Seasonings & Seeds: Spices: Cayenne Pepper: Dried*
Dried Cherries *See Fruits & Vegetables: Cherries: Dried*
Dried Chicken Fats *See Oils, Shortening & Fats: Fats & Lard: Chicken: Dried*
Dried Chile Peppers *See Fruits & Vegetables: Peppers: Chile: Dried Pods*
Dried Chives *See Fruits & Vegetables: Dried & Dehydrated Vegetables: Dried Chives*
Dried Coconut *See Fruits & Vegetables: Coconut & Coconut Products: Dried*
Dried Cranberry *See Fruits & Vegetables: Berries: Cranberry: Dried*
Dried Cream *See Dairy Products: Cream: Dried*
Dried Egg *See Eggs & Egg Products: Dried*
Dried Fruit *See Fruits & Vegetables: Dried & Dehydrated Fruits: Dried Fruit*
Dried Honey *See Sugars, Syrups & Sweeteners: Honey: Dried*
Dried Mango *See Fruits & Vegetables: Mango: Dried*
Dried Molasses *See Sugars, Syrups & Sweeteners: Molasses: Dried*
Dried Papaya *See Fruits & Vegetables: Papaya: Dried*
Dried Peach *See Fruits & Vegetables: Peach: Dried*
Dried Pear *See Fruits & Vegetables: Pear: Dried*
Dried Pineapple *See Fruits & Vegetables: Pineapple: Dried*
Dried Plums *See Fruits & Vegetables: Plums: Dried*
Dried Prunes *See Fruits & Vegetables: Prunes: Dried*
Dried Raisins *See Fruits & Vegetables: Raisins: Dried*
Dried Refried Beans *See Fruits & Vegetables: Beans: Refried: Dried*
Dried Sliced Beef *See Meats & Meat Products: Beef & Beef Products: Sliced: Dried*
Dried Spices *See Spices, Seasonings & Seeds: Spices: Dried*
Dried Strawberry *See Fruits & Vegetables: Berries: Strawberry: Dried*
Dried Tomato *See Fruits & Vegetables: Tomato: Dried*
Drink Mixes *See Doughs, Mixes & Fillings: Mixes: Drink*
Dry Beans *See Fruits & Vegetables: Beans: Dry*
Dry Buttermilk *See Dairy Products: Buttermilk & Buttermilk Products: Buttermilk Products: Dry*
Dry Malt *See Cereals, Grains, Rice & Flour: Malt: Dry*
Dry Pancake Batters *See Doughs, Mixes & Fillings: Batters: Pancake: Dry*
Dry Peas *See Fruits & Vegetables: Peas: Dry*
Dry Raisin Juice *See Ingredients, Flavors & Additives: Replacers: Raisin Juice: Dry*
Dry Sweetcream Buttermilk *See Dairy Products: Buttermilk & Buttermilk Products: Buttermilk Products: Dry Sweetcream*
Duck *See Meats & Meat Products: Poultry: Duck*
Duck Sauces *See Sauces, Dips & Dressings: Sauces: Duck*
Dumpling Mixes *See Doughs, Mixes & Fillings: Mixes: Dumplings*
Dumplings *See Baked Goods: Cakes & Pastries: Dumplings*

Dungeness Crab *See Fish & Seafood: Shellfish: Crab: Dungeness*
Dusting Starches *See Ingredients, Flavors & Additives: Starches: Dusting*
Dutch *See Ethnic Foods: Dutch*
Dyes *See Ingredients, Flavors & Additives: Colors: Dyes*

E

E - Tocopherol *See Ingredients, Flavors & Additives: Vitamins & Supplements: E - Tocopherol*
Earl Grey Tea *See Beverages: Coffee & Tea: Tea: Earl Grey*
Earl Grey Tea, Decaffeinated *See Beverages: Coffee & Tea: Tea: Earl Grey Decaffeinated*
Easter Specialty-Packaged Candy *See Candy & Confectionery: Specialty-Packaged Candy: Easter*
Eastern Oregon Dry Bulb Onion *See Fruits & Vegetables: Onion: Eastern Oregon Dry Bulb Onion*
Echinacea Purpurea Powders *See Ingredients, Flavors & Additives: Powders: Echinacea Purpurea*
Eclairs *See Baked Goods: Cakes & Pastries: Eclairs*
Edam *See Cheese & Cheese Products: Cheese: Edam*
Edible Coatings *See Ingredients, Flavors & Additives: Coatings: Edible*
Edible Dry Beans *See Fruits & Vegetables: Beans: Dry: Edible*
Edible Oils *See Oils, Shortening & Fats: Oils: Edible*
Edible Release, Grease Agents *See Ingredients, Flavors & Additives: Agents: Release,Grease: Edible*
Eel *See Fish & Seafood: Fish: Eel*
Egg Drop Soup *See Prepared Foods: Soups & Stews: Egg Drop Soup*
Egg Nog *See Dairy Products: Egg Nog*
Egg Noodles *See Pasta & Noodles: Noodles: Egg*
Egg Powders *See Ingredients, Flavors & Additives: Powders: Egg*
Egg Replacers *See Ingredients, Flavors & Additives: Replacers: Egg*
Egg Rolls *See Ethnic Foods: Egg Rolls*
Egg Substitutes *See Eggs & Egg Products: Substitutes*
Egg Tomato *See Fruits & Vegetables: Tomato: Roma (Egg)*
Eggplant *See Fruits & Vegetables: Eggplant*
Eggplant Parmigiana *See Prepared Foods: Prepared Meals: Eggplant Parmigiana*
Eggplant, Dried & Dehydrated *See Fruits & Vegetables: Dried & Dehydrated Vegetables: Eggplant*
Eggs & Egg Products *See Eggs & Egg Products*
Eggs, Pickled Products *See Relishes & Pickled Products: Pickled Products: Eggs*
Eggs, Prepared Meals *See Prepared Foods: Prepared Meals: Eggs*
Elbow Macaroni *See Pasta & Noodles: Elbow Macaroni*
Emu *See Meats & Meat Products: Game: Emu*
Emulsifiers *See Ingredients, Flavors & Additives: Emulsifiers*
Enchiladas *See Ethnic Foods: Enchiladas*
Endive *See Spices, Seasonings & Seeds: Spices: Endive*
Energy Bars *See Specialty & Organic Foods: Health & Dietary: Energy Bars; See also Organic Foods*
English Breakfast Tea *See Beverages: Coffee & Tea: Tea: English Breakfast*
English Breakfast Tea, Decaffeinated *See Beverages: Coffee & Tea: Tea: English Breakfast Decaffeinated*
English Muffins *See Baked Goods: Breads: English Muffins*
English Style B Ale *See Beverages: Beers: American & British Ale: English Style B*
Enhancers *See Ingredients, Flavors & Additives: Enhancers*
Enokis Mushrooms *See Fruits & Vegetables: Mushrooms: Enokis*
Enrichment & Nutrient Additives *See Ingredients, Flavors & Additives: Additives: Enrichment & Nutrient*
Enrichment Blends *See Ingredients, Flavors & Additives: Blends: Enrichment*
Entrees Prepared Meals *See Prepared Foods: Prepared Meals: Entrees*
Enzymes *See Ingredients, Flavors & Additives: Enzymes*
Enzymes Additives *See Ingredients, Flavors & Additives: Additives: Enzymes*
Epazote Herb *See Spices, Seasonings & Seeds: Spices: Epazote Herb*
Escargot *See Prepared Foods: Prepared Meals: Escargot*
Escarole *See Spices, Seasonings & Seeds: Spices: Escarole*
Espresso *See Beverages: Coffee & Tea: Espresso*
Essential Fatty Acids *See Ingredients, Flavors & Additives: Fatty Acids: Essential*
Essential Oils *See Oils, Shortening & Fats: Oils: Essential*
Ethnic Foods *See Ethnic Foods*
Ethyleneamines *See Ingredients, Flavors & Additives: Ethyleneamines*
Etoufee *See Prepared Foods: Prepared Meals: Etoufee*

Product Category List

Evaporated Milk *See Dairy Products: Milk & Milk Products: Milk: Evaporated*
Extenders *See Ingredients, Flavors & Additives: Extenders*
Extra Virgin Olive Oils *See Oils, Shortening & Fats: Oils: Olive: Extra Virgin*
Extract Flavors *See Ingredients, Flavors & Additives: Flavors: Extract*
Extracts *See Ingredients, Flavors & Additives: Extracts*
Extracts, Spices *See Spices, Seasonings & Seeds: Spices: Extracts*
Extracts, Yeast *See Ingredients, Flavors & Additives: Cultures & Yeasts: Yeast: Extracts*

F

Fair-Trade Tea *See Beverages: Coffee & Tea: Tea: Fair-Trade*
Fajita Chicken Strips *See Meats & Meat Products: Poultry: Chicken: Fajita Strips*
Fajita Marinades *See Sauces, Dips & Dressings: Marinades: Fajita*
Fajita Seasonings *See Spices, Seasonings & Seeds: Seasonings: Fajita*
Farfalle *See Pasta & Noodles: Farfalle*
Farina Cereal *See Cereals, Grains, Rice & Flour: Cereal: Farina*
Farm-Raised Game *See Meats & Meat Products: Game: Farm-Raised*
Fat & Cholesterol Free *See Eggs & Egg Products: Fat & Cholesterol Free*
Fat Flavors *See Ingredients, Flavors & Additives: Flavors: Fat*
Fat Replacers *See Ingredients, Flavors & Additives: Replacers: Fat*
Fat-Free Ice Cream *See Dairy Products: Ice Cream: Fat-Free*
Fat-Free Milk *See Dairy Products: Milk & Milk Products: Milk: Fat-Free*
Fats *See Oils, Shortening & Fats*
Fats & Lard *See Oils, Shortening & Fats: Fats & Lard*
Fatty Acids *See Ingredients, Flavors & Additives: Fatty Acids*
Fava Beans *See Fruits & Vegetables: Beans: Fava*
Fennel Seeds *See Spices, Seasonings & Seeds: Seeds: Fennel*
Fennel Spices *See Spices, Seasonings & Seeds: Spices: Fennel*
Fenugreek Seeds *See Spices, Seasonings & Seeds: Seeds: Fenugreek*
Fenugreek Spices *See Spices, Seasonings & Seeds: Spices: Fenugreek*
Fermented Products *See Specialty Processed Foods: Fermented Products (See also Specific Foods)*
Feta Cheese *See Cheese & Cheese Products: Cheese: Feta*
Fettuccine *See Pasta & Noodles: Fettuccine*
Feverfew Powders *See Ingredients, Flavors & Additives: Powders: Feverfew*
Fiber *See Cereals, Grains, Rice & Flour: Fiber*
Fig Pastes *See Ingredients, Flavors & Additives: Pastes: Fig*
Fig, Dried *See Fruits & Vegetables: Dried & Dehydrated Fruits: Fig*
Figs *See Fruits & Vegetables: Figs*
Filberts *See Nuts & Nut Butters: Nuts: Filberts*
Filet Mignon *See Meats & Meat Products: Beef & Beef Products: Filet Mignon*
Filled Candy *See Candy & Confectionery: Candy: Filled*
Filled Doughnuts *See Baked Goods: Cakes & Pastries: Doughnuts: Filled*
Fillers *See Ingredients, Flavors & Additives: Fillers*
Fillets, Chicken *See Meats & Meat Products: Poultry: Chicken: Fillets*
Fillets, Fish *See Fish & Seafood: Fish: Fillets*
Fillets, Herring *See Fish & Seafood: Fish: Herring: Fillets*
Fillets, Turkey *See Meats & Meat Products: Poultry: Turkey: Fillets*
Fillings *See Doughs, Mixes & Fillings: Fillings*
Finfish *See Fish & Seafood: Fish: Finfish*
Fire Roasted Vegetables *See Fruits & Vegetables: Fire Roasted Vegetables*
Firming Agents *See Ingredients, Flavors & Additives: Agents: Firming*
Fish *See Fish & Seafood: Fish; See also Prepared Foods: Prepared Meals: Fish*
Fish & Chips *See Prepared Foods: Prepared Meals: Fish & Chips*
Fish Oils *See Oils, Shortening & Fats: Oils: Fish*

Fish Paste *See Fish & Seafood: Fish: Paste*
Fish Patties *See Prepared Foods: Prepared Meals: Fish Patties*
Fish Powders *See Ingredients, Flavors & Additives: Powders: Fish*
Fish Sauces *See Sauces, Dips & Dressings: Sauces: Fish*
Fish Steaks *See Fish & Seafood: Fish: Steaks*
Fish Sticks *See Prepared Foods: Prepared Meals: Fish Sticks; See also See Fish & Seafood: Fish: Sticks*
Flakes *See Ingredients, Flavors & Additives: Flakes*
Flat Breads *See Baked Goods: Breads: Flat*
Flavor Bases *See Ingredients, Flavors & Additives: Bases: Flavor*
Flavor Bits *See Ingredients, Flavors & Additives: Bits: Flavor*
Flavor Enhancers *See Ingredients, Flavors & Additives: Flavors: Enhancers; See also See Ingredients, Flavors & Additives: Flavor Enhancers*
Flavored Cheese Cake *See Baked Goods: Cakes & Pastries: Cheese Cake: Flavored*
Flavored Coffee *See Beverages: Coffee & Tea: Coffee: Flavored*
Flavored Ice Cream *See Dairy Products: Ice Cream: Flavored*
Flavored Liquid Vinegar *See Sauces, Dips & Dressings: Vinegar: Liquid: Flavored*
Flavored Milk *See Dairy Products: Milk & Milk Products: Milk: Flavored*
Flavored Pellets *See Ingredients, Flavors & Additives: Half-Products: Flavored Pellets*
Flavored Popcorn *See Snack Foods: Popcorn: Flavored*
Flavored Pretzels *See Snack Foods: Pretzels: Flavored*
Flavored Stout *See Beverages: Beers: Stout & Porter: Flavored Stout*
Flavored Sugar Bits *See Ingredients, Flavors & Additives: Bits: Flavored Sugar*
Flavored Tea *See Beverages: Coffee & Tea: Tea: Flavored*
Flavored Water *See Beverages: Water: Flavored*
Flavored Wraps *See Baked Goods: Wraps: Flavored*
Flavoring Extracts *See Ingredients, Flavors & Additives: Extracts: Flavoring*
Flavors *See Ingredients, Flavors & Additives: Flavors; See also Ingredients, Flavors & Additives: Flavors*
Flax Crisps *See Cereals, Grains, Rice & Flour: Crisps: Flax*
Flax Seeds *See Spices, Seasonings & Seeds: Seeds: Flax*
Flounder *See Fish & Seafood: Fish: Flounder*
Flour *See Cereals, Grains, Rice & Flour: Flour*
Flour, Rice Starch, Organic *See Specialty & Organic Foods: Organic Foods: Rice Starch: Flour; See also Organic Foods*
Flowers, Edible *See Fruits & Vegetables: Flowers - Edible*
Fluid Shortening *See Oils, Shortening & Fats: Shortening: Fluid*
Fluke *See Fish & Seafood: Fish: Fluke*
Foaming & Whipping Agents *See Ingredients, Flavors & Additives: Agents: Foaming & Whipping*
Focaccia *See Baked Goods: Breads: Focaccia*
Foie Gras *See Meats & Meat Products: Pates & Foie Gras: Foie Gras*
Fondant *See Sugars, Syrups & Sweeteners: Sugar: Fondant*
Fondants *See Candy & Confectionery: Candy: Fondants*
Fontina Cheese *See Cheese & Cheese Products: Cheese: Fontina*
Food Bases *See Ingredients, Flavors & Additives: Bases: Food*
Food Ingredients *See Ingredients, Flavors & Additives: Ingredients: Food*
Food Preservatives *See Ingredients, Flavors & Additives: Preservatives: Food*
Food Releases *See Ingredients, Flavors & Additives: Releases: Food*
Foodservice, Individual Packets *See Prepared Foods: Individual Packets: Foodservice*
Formula *See Baby Foods: Formula*
Fortification Protein *See Ingredients, Flavors & Additives: Vitamins & Supplements: Protein Supplements: Fortification Protein*
Fortified Refined Vegetable Oils *See Oils, Shortening & Fats: Oils: Vegetable: Fortified Refined*
Fortune Cookies *See Baked Goods: Cookies & Bars: Fortune Cookies*
Fra Diavolo Sauces *See Sauces, Dips & Dressings: Sauces: Fra Diavolo*
Fragrances *See Ingredients, Flavors & Additives: Aroma Chemicals & Materials: Fragrances*
Frankfurters *See Meats & Meat Products: Frankfurters*

Frankfurters, Mini *See Meats & Meat Products: Frankfurters: Mini*
Free Flow Additives *See Ingredients, Flavors & Additives: Additives: Free Flow*
Freeze-Dried Food *See Specialty Processed Foods: Freeze Dried Food (See also Specific Foods)*
Freeze-Dried Fruits & Vegetables *See Fruits & Vegetables: Dehydrated: Freeze Dried; See also Fruits & Vegetables: Dried & Dehydrated Fruits: Freeze Dried; See also Fruits & Vegetables: Dried & Dehydrated Vegetables: Freeze Dried*
Freeze-Dried Mushrooms *See Fruits & Vegetables: Dried & Dehydrated Vegetables: Mushrooms: Freeze Dried*
Freeze-Dried Seafood *See Fish & Seafood: Seafood: Freeze-Dried*
French Breads *See Baked Goods: Breads: French*
French Fries *See Prepared Foods: French Fries*
French Salad Dressings *See Sauces, Dips & Dressings: Salad Dressings: French; See also See Sauces, Dips & Dressings: Salad Dressings: Mixes: French*
French Toast *See Prepared Foods: French Toast*
French Wines *See Beverages: Wines: French*
Fresh Apple *See Fruits & Vegetables: Apple: Fresh*
Fresh Bagels *See Baked Goods: Breads: Bagels: Fresh*
Fresh Bakes Goods *See Baked Goods: Fresh*
Fresh Beef *See Meats & Meat Products: Beef & Beef Products: Fresh*
Fresh Biscuits *See Baked Goods: Breads: Biscuits: Fresh*
Fresh Breads *See Baked Goods: Breads: Fresh*
Fresh Chicken *See Meats & Meat Products: Poultry: Chicken: Fresh*
Fresh Clam *See Fish & Seafood: Shellfish: Clam: Fresh*
Fresh Crab *See Fish & Seafood: Shellfish: Crab: Fresh*
Fresh Cream *See Dairy Products: Cream: Fresh*
Fresh Eggs *See Eggs & Egg Products: Fresh*
Fresh Fish *See Fish & Seafood: Fish: Fresh*
Fresh Fish Cakes *See Fish & Seafood: Fish: Cakes: Fresh*
Fresh Fruit *See Fruits & Vegetables: Fresh Fruit*
Fresh Ham *See Meats & Meat Products: Smoked, Cured & Deli Meats: Ham: Fresh*
Fresh Herring *See Fish & Seafood: Fish: Herring: Fresh*
Fresh Lamb *See Meats & Meat Products: Lamb: Fresh*
Fresh Lobster *See Fish & Seafood: Shellfish: Lobster: Fresh*
Fresh Milk *See Dairy Products: Milk & Milk Products: Milk: Fresh*
Fresh Mushrooms *See Fruits & Vegetables: Mushrooms: Fresh*
Fresh Oysters *See Fish & Seafood: Shellfish: Oysters: Fresh*
Fresh Peas *See Fruits & Vegetables: Peas: Fresh*
Fresh Pies *See Baked Goods: Pies: Fresh*
Fresh Pork *See Meats & Meat Products: Pork & Pork Products: Fresh*
Fresh Potatoes *See Fruits & Vegetables: Potatoes: Fresh*
Fresh Prepared Foods *See Prepared Foods: Fresh*
Fresh Rolls *See Baked Goods: Breads: Rolls: Fresh*
Fresh Sardines *See Fish & Seafood: Fish: Sardines: Fresh*
Fresh Seafood *See Fish & Seafood: Seafood: Fresh*
Fresh Shellfish *See Fish & Seafood: Shellfish: Fresh*
Fresh Shrimp *See Fish & Seafood: Shellfish: Shrimp: Fresh*
Fresh Soy *See Fruits & Vegetables: Soy: Fresh*
Fresh Stew *See Prepared Foods: Soups & Stews: Fresh Stew*
Fresh Succotash *See Fruits & Vegetables: Succotash: Fresh*
Fresh Tomato *See Fruits & Vegetables: Tomato: Fresh*
Fresh Turkey *See Meats & Meat Products: Poultry: Turkey: Fresh*
Fresh Veal *See Meats & Meat Products: Beef & Beef Products: Veal: Fresh*
Fresh Vegetables *See Fruits & Vegetables: Fresh Vegetables*
Fresh Yeast *See Ingredients, Flavors & Additives: Cultures & Yeasts: Yeast: Fresh*
Freshwater Fish *See Fish & Seafood: Fish: Freshwater*
Fried Chips *See Snack Foods: Chips: Fried*
Fried Oysters *See Fish & Seafood: Shellfish: Oysters: Fried*
Fried Porkskins *See Prepared Foods: Porkskins: Fried*
Fried Rice, Prepared Meals *See Prepared Foods: Prepared Meals: Fried Rice*
Fried Rice, Seasonings *See Spices, Seasonings & Seeds: Seasonings: Fried Rice*
Frozen Appetizers *See Prepared Foods: Appetizers: Frozen*
Frozen Apple *See Fruits & Vegetables: Apple: Frozen*
Frozen Apple Juices *See Beverages: Juices: Apple: Frozen*
Frozen Apricot *See Fruits & Vegetables: Apricot: Frozen*
Frozen Apricot Juices *See Beverages: Juices: Apricot: Frozen*

EXAMPLE: **Canadian Style Bacon** *See Meats & Meat Products: Smoked, Cured & Deli Meats: Bacon: Canadian Style*

1. Product or Service you are looking for
2. Main Category, in alphabetical order, located in the page headers starting on page 27
3. Category Description, located in black bars and in page headers
4. Product Category, located in gray bars
5. Product Type, located under gray bars, centered in bold

Product Category List

Frozen Artichoke See Fruits & Vegetables: Artichoke: Frozen
Frozen Asparagus See Fruits & Vegetables: Asparagus: Frozen
Frozen Au Gratin Potatoes See Fruits & Vegetables: Potatoes: Au Gratin: Frozen
Frozen Bagels See Baked Goods: Breads: Bagels: Frozen
Frozen Baked & Stuffed Potatoes See Fruits & Vegetables: Potatoes: Baked & Stuffed: Frozen
Frozen Baked Goods See Baked Goods: Frozen
Frozen Baking Doughs See Doughs, Mixes & Fillings: Doughs: Baking: Frozen
Frozen Barbecued Beef See Meats & Meat Products: Beef & Beef Products: Barbecued: Frozen
Frozen Barbecued Pork See Meats & Meat Products: Pork & Pork Products: Barbecued: Frozen
Frozen Beans See Fruits & Vegetables: Beans: Frozen
Frozen Beef & Beef Products See Meats & Meat Products: Beef & Beef Products: Frozen
Frozen Beef Stew See Meats & Meat Products: Beef & Beef Products: Stew: Frozen
Frozen Beets See Fruits & Vegetables: Beets: Frozen
Frozen Berries See Fruits & Vegetables: Berries: Frozen
Frozen Beverage Mixes See Doughs, Mixes & Fillings: Mixes: Beverage: Frozen
Frozen Biscuits See Baked Goods: Breads: Biscuits: Frozen
Frozen Black-eyed Peas See Fruits & Vegetables: Peas: Black-eyed: Frozen
Frozen Blackberry See Fruits & Vegetables: Berries: Blackberry: Frozen
Frozen Blintzes See Baked Goods: Cakes & Pastries: Blintzes: Frozen
Frozen Blue Lake Beans See Fruits & Vegetables: Beans: Blue Lake: Frozen
Frozen Blueberry See Fruits & Vegetables: Berries: Blueberry: Frozen
Frozen Boysenberry See Fruits & Vegetables: Berries: Boysenberry: Frozen
Frozen Breads See Baked Goods: Breads: Frozen
Frozen Broccoli See Fruits & Vegetables: Broccoli: Frozen
Frozen Broth See Prepared Foods: Broth: Frozen
Frozen Brussel Sprouts See Fruits & Vegetables: Brussel Sprouts: Frozen
Frozen Buns See Baked Goods: Breads: Buns: Frozen
Frozen Butter Beans See Fruits & Vegetables: Beans: Butter: Frozen
Frozen Cabbage See Fruits & Vegetables: Cabbage: Frozen
Frozen Cake Batters See Doughs, Mixes & Fillings: Batters: Cake: Frozen
Frozen Cakes See Baked Goods: Cakes & Pastries: Frozen Cakes
Frozen Cappuccino Mixes See Doughs, Mixes & Fillings: Mixes: Cappuccino: Frozen
Frozen Capsicums Peppers See Fruits & Vegetables: Peppers: Capsicums: Frozen
Frozen Carrot See Fruits & Vegetables: Carrot: Frozen
Frozen Cauliflower See Fruits & Vegetables: Cauliflower: Frozen
Frozen Celery See Fruits & Vegetables: Celery: Frozen
Frozen Cheese Cake See Baked Goods: Cakes & Pastries: Cheese Cake: Frozen
Frozen Cherries See Fruits & Vegetables: Cherries: Frozen
Frozen Cherry Juices See Beverages: Juices: Cherry: Frozen
Frozen Chicken See Meats & Meat Products: Poultry: Chicken: Frozen
Frozen Chicken Fats & Lard See Oils, Shortening & Fats: Fats & Lard: Chicken: Frozen
Frozen Chili See Prepared Foods: Chili: Frozen
Frozen Chop Suey See Ethnic Foods: Chop Suey: Frozen
Frozen Clam See Fish & Seafood: Shellfish: Clam: Frozen
Frozen Clam Strips See Fish & Seafood: Shellfish: Clam: Frozen Strips
Frozen Coconut & Coconut Products See Fruits & Vegetables: Coconut & Coconut Products: Frozen
Frozen Convenience Food See Prepared Foods: Convenience Food: Frozen
Frozen Cookies See Baked Goods: Cookies & Bars: Frozen Cookies
Frozen Corn See Fruits & Vegetables: Corn: Frozen
Frozen Corn-on-the-Cob See Fruits & Vegetables: Corn: Corn-on-the-Cob: Frozen
Frozen Crab See Fish & Seafood: Shellfish: Crab: Frozen; See also See Prepared Foods: Prepared Meals: Crab: Frozen
Frozen Crab Meat See Fish & Seafood: Shellfish: Crab: Meat Frozen
Frozen Cranberry See Fruits & Vegetables: Berries: Cranberry: Frozen
Frozen Cranberry Juices See Beverages: Juices: Cranberry: Frozen

Frozen Crayfish See Fish & Seafood: Shellfish: Crayfish: Frozen
Frozen Crepes See Prepared Foods: Crepes: Frozen
Frozen Dehydrated Potatoes See Fruits & Vegetables: Potatoes: Dehydrated: Frozen
Frozen Doughnuts See Baked Goods: Cakes & Pastries: Doughnuts: Frozen
Frozen Doughs See Doughs, Mixes & Fillings: Doughs: Frozen
Frozen Eggs See Eggs & Egg Products: Frozen
Frozen Enchiladas See Ethnic Foods: Enchiladas: Frozen
Frozen Entrees See Prepared Foods: Prepared Meals: Entrees: Frozen
Frozen Figs See Fruits & Vegetables: Figs: Frozen
Frozen Fish See Fish & Seafood: Fish: Frozen
Frozen Fish Cakes See Fish & Seafood: Fish: Cakes: Frozen
Frozen Fish Sticks See Prepared Foods: Prepared Meals: Fish Sticks: Frozen
Frozen Foods See Specialty Processed Foods: Frozen Foods (See also Specific Foods)
Frozen French Fries See Prepared Foods: French Fries: Frozen
Frozen French Toast See Prepared Foods: French Toast: Frozen
Frozen Fruit See Fruits & Vegetables: Frozen Fruit
Frozen Fruit & Vegetable Juices See Beverages: Juices: Fruit & Vegetable: Frozen
Frozen Fruit Juices See Beverages: Juices: Fruit: Frozen
Frozen Fruit Pies See Baked Goods: Pies: Fruit: Frozen
Frozen Garlic Breads See Baked Goods: Breads: Garlic: Frozen
Frozen Gnocchi See Pasta & Noodles: Gnocchi: Frozen
Frozen Grape Juices See Beverages: Juices: Grape: Frozen
Frozen Grapefruit Juices See Beverages: Juices: Grapefruit: Frozen
Frozen Green Beans See Fruits & Vegetables: Beans: Green: Frozen
Frozen Ground Beef & Beef Products See Meats & Meat Products: Beef & Beef Products: Ground: Frozen
Frozen Ham See Meats & Meat Products: Smoked, Cured & Deli Meats: Ham: Frozen
Frozen Herring See Fish & Seafood: Fish: Herring: Frozen
Frozen Kale See Fruits & Vegetables: Kale: Frozen
Frozen Kidney Beans See Fruits & Vegetables: Beans: Kidney: Frozen
Frozen Lamb See Meats & Meat Products: Lamb: Frozen
Frozen Lasagna See Pasta & Noodles: Lasagna: Frozen
Frozen Lemon Juices See Beverages: Juices: Lemon: Frozen
Frozen Lima Beans See Fruits & Vegetables: Beans: Lima: Frozen
Frozen Lobster See Fish & Seafood: Shellfish: Lobster: Frozen
Frozen Mashed Sweet Potatoes See Fruits & Vegetables: Sweet Potatoes: Mashed: Frozen
Frozen Meat Balls See Prepared Foods: Meat Balls: Frozen
Frozen Meat Pies See Baked Goods: Pies: Meat: Frozen
Frozen Melon Balls See Fruits & Vegetables: Melon: Balls: Frozen
Frozen Mixes See Doughs, Mixes & Fillings: Mixes: Frozen
Frozen Mozzarella Cheese, Lite Shredded See Cheese & Cheese Products: Cheese: Mozzarella: Lite Shredded - Frozen
Frozen Muffins See Baked Goods: Cakes & Pastries: Muffins: Frozen
Frozen Mushrooms See Fruits & Vegetables: Mushrooms: Frozen
Frozen Non-Dairy Desserts See Baked Goods: Desserts: Non-Dairy: Frozen
Frozen Non-Fruit Pies See Baked Goods: Pies: Non-Fruit: Frozen
Frozen Okra See Fruits & Vegetables: Okra: Frozen
Frozen Onion See Fruits & Vegetables: Onion: Frozen
Frozen Onion Rings See Prepared Foods: Onion Rings: Frozen
Frozen Oven Type Potatoes See Fruits & Vegetables: Potatoes: Oven Type: Frozen
Frozen Oysters See Fish & Seafood: Shellfish: Oysters: Frozen
Frozen Pancakes See Prepared Foods: Pancakes: Frozen
Frozen Pasta See Pasta & Noodles: Pasta: Frozen
Frozen Patties Beef & Beef Products See Meats & Meat Products: Beef & Beef Products: Patties: Frozen
Frozen Peach See Fruits & Vegetables: Peach: Frozen
Frozen Pear See Fruits & Vegetables: Pear: Frozen
Frozen Peas See Fruits & Vegetables: Peas: Frozen
Frozen Peas & Carrots See Fruits & Vegetables: Vegetables Mixed: Peas & Carrots: Frozen
Frozen Peppers See Fruits & Vegetables: Peppers: Frozen

Frozen Pineapple See Fruits & Vegetables: Pineapple: Frozen
Frozen Pineapple Juices See Beverages: Juices: Pineapple: Frozen
Frozen Pizza See Prepared Foods: Pizza & Pizza Products: Pizza: Frozen
Frozen Pizza Doughs See Doughs, Mixes & Fillings: Doughs: Pizza: Frozen
Frozen Pizza Shells See Prepared Foods: Pizza & Pizza Products: Shells: Frozen
Frozen Plums See Fruits & Vegetables: Plums: Frozen
Frozen Pork & Pork Products See Meats & Meat Products: Pork & Pork Products: Frozen
Frozen Potato Rounds See Fruits & Vegetables: Potatoes: Frozen: Rounds
Frozen Potatoes See Fruits & Vegetables: Potatoes: Frozen
Frozen Prepared Foods See Prepared Foods: Frozen
Frozen Prepared Meals See Prepared Foods: Prepared Meals: Frozen
Frozen Prepared Pork & Pork Products See Meats & Meat Products: Pork & Pork Products: Prepared: Frozen
Frozen Prunes See Fruits & Vegetables: Prunes: Frozen
Frozen Pumpkin See Fruits & Vegetables: Pumpkin: Frozen
Frozen Rabbit See Meats & Meat Products: Game: Rabbit: Frozen
Frozen Raspberries See Fruits & Vegetables: Berries: Raspberries: Frozen
Frozen Ravioli See Pasta & Noodles: Ravioli: Frozen
Frozen Rhubarb See Fruits & Vegetables: Rhubarb: Frozen
Frozen Rice See Cereals, Grains, Rice & Flour: Rice: Frozen
Frozen Rolls See Baked Goods: Breads: Rolls: Frozen
Frozen Rutabaga See Fruits & Vegetables: Rutabaga: Frozen
Frozen Sauces See Sauces, Dips & Dressings: Sauces: Frozen
Frozen Scampi See Fish & Seafood: Shellfish: Scampi: Frozen
Frozen Seafood See Fish & Seafood: Seafood: Frozen
Frozen Shellfish See Fish & Seafood: Shellfish: Frozen
Frozen Shrimp See Fish & Seafood: Shellfish: Shrimp: Frozen
Frozen Sliced Beef & Beef Products See Meats & Meat Products: Beef & Beef Products: Sliced: Frozen
Frozen Slices Apple See Fruits & Vegetables: Apple: Slices: Frozen
Frozen Soup See Prepared Foods: Soups & Stews: Frozen Soup
Frozen Spaghetti See Pasta & Noodles: Spaghetti: Frozen
Frozen Special Trim Beef & Beef Products See Meats & Meat Products: Beef & Beef Products: Special Trim: Frozen
Frozen Spinach See Fruits & Vegetables: Spinach: Frozen
Frozen Squash See Fruits & Vegetables: Squash: Frozen
Frozen Stew See Prepared Foods: Soups & Stews: Frozen Stew
Frozen Strawberry See Fruits & Vegetables: Berries: Strawberry: Frozen
Frozen Stuffed Cabbage See Prepared Foods: Prepared Meals: Stuffed Cabbage: Frozen
Frozen Substitutes See Eggs & Egg Products: Substitutes: Frozen
Frozen Succotash See Fruits & Vegetables: Succotash: Frozen
Frozen Sweet Potatoes See Fruits & Vegetables: Sweet Potatoes: Frozen
Frozen Tamales See Ethnic Foods: Tamales: Frozen
Frozen Tomato See Fruits & Vegetables: Tomato: Frozen
Frozen Tomato Juices See Beverages: Juices: Tomato: Frozen
Frozen Tomato Sauces See Sauces, Dips & Dressings: Sauces: Tomato: Frozen
Frozen Tuna See Fish & Seafood: Fish: Tuna: Frozen
Frozen Turkey See Meats & Meat Products: Poultry: Turkey: Frozen
Frozen Turnip See Fruits & Vegetables: Turnip: Frozen
Frozen Veal See Meats & Meat Products: Beef & Beef Products: Veal: Frozen
Frozen Vegetables See Fruits & Vegetables: Frozen Vegetables
Frozen Vegetables Mixed See Fruits & Vegetables: Vegetables Mixed: Frozen
Frozen Venison See Meats & Meat Products: Game: Venison: Frozen
Frozen Waffles See Baked Goods: Waffles: Frozen
Frozen Wax Beans See Fruits & Vegetables: Beans: Wax: Frozen
Frozen Yams See Fruits & Vegetables: Yams: Frozen
Frozen Yogurt See Dairy Products: Yogurt: Frozen
Frozen Yogurt Powders See Ingredients, Flavors & Additives: Powders: Yogurt: Frozen
Fructose See Sugars, Syrups & Sweeteners: Fructose

Product Category List

Fruit *See Fruits & Vegetables: Fruit*
Fruit & Vegetable Coating Waxes *See Ingredients, Flavors & Additives: Waxes: Fruit & Vegetable Coating*
Fruit & Vegetable Juices *See Beverages: Juices: Fruit & Vegetable*
Fruit & Vegetable Pulps & Purees *See Fruits & Vegetables: Pulps & Purees: Fruit & Vegetable*
Fruit & Vegetable Puree *See Fruits & Vegetables: Pulps & Purees: Puree: Fruit & Vegetable*
Fruit Bases *See Ingredients, Flavors & Additives: Bases: Fruit*
Fruit Butter Spreads *See Jams, Jellies & Spreads: Spreads: Fruit Butter*
Fruit Cake *See Baked Goods: Cakes & Pastries: Fruit Cake*
Fruit Cobbler *See Baked Goods: Cakes & Pastries: Fruit Cobbler*
Fruit Cocktail *See Fruits & Vegetables: Fruit Cocktail*
Fruit Concentrates *See Ingredients, Flavors & Additives: Concentrates: Fruit*
Fruit Extracts *See Ingredients, Flavors & Additives: Extracts: Fruit*
Fruit Fillings *See Doughs, Mixes & Fillings: Fillings: Fruit*
Fruit Flavors *See Ingredients, Flavors & Additives: Flavors: Fruit*
Fruit Juices *See Beverages: Juices: Fruit*
Fruit Oils *See Oils, Shortening & Fats: Oils: Fruit*
Fruit Pastes *See Ingredients, Flavors & Additives: Pastes: Fruit*
Fruit Pectins *See Ingredients, Flavors & Additives: Pectins: Fruit*
Fruit Pies *See Baked Goods: Pies: Fruit*
Fruit Powders *See Ingredients, Flavors & Additives: Powders: Fruit*
Fruit Pulp *See Fruits & Vegetables: Pulps & Purees: Pulp: Fruit*
Fruit Pulps & Purees *See Fruits & Vegetables: Pulps & Purees: Fruit*
Fruit Punch Juices *See Beverages: Juices: Fruit Punch*
Fruit Puree *See Fruits & Vegetables: Pulps & Purees: Puree: Fruit*
Fruit Puree Concentrates *See Ingredients, Flavors & Additives: Concentrates: Fruit Puree*
Fruit Salad *See Fruits & Vegetables: Fruit: Salad*
Fruit Syrups *See Sugars, Syrups & Sweeteners: Syrups: Fruit*
Fruit Toppings *See Ingredients, Flavors & Additives: Toppings: Fruit*
Fruit, Certified Organic *See Specialty & Organic Foods: Organic Foods: Certified: Fruit; See also Organic Foods*
Fruits & Vegetables *See Fruits & Vegetables*
Fruits, Organic *See Specialty & Organic Foods: Organic Foods: Fruits; See also Organic Foods*
Fryer Rabbit *See Meats & Meat Products: Game: Rabbit: Fryer*
Fudge Candy *See Candy & Confectionery: Candy: Fudge*
Fudge Chocolate Products *See Candy & Confectionery: Chocolate Products: Fudge*
Fudge Sauces *See Sauces, Dips & Dressings: Sauces: Fudge*
Fudgesicles *See Dairy Products: Ice Cream: Fudgesicles*
Fumaric Acidulants *See Ingredients, Flavors & Additives: Acidulants: Fumaric*
Fund Raising Specialty-Packaged Candy *See Candy & Confectionery: Specialty-Packaged Candy: Fund Raising*
Funnel Cake *See Baked Goods: Cakes & Pastries: Funnel Cake*

G

Galangal *See Fruits & Vegetables: Galangal*
Game Meat & Poultry *See Meats & Meat Products: Game: Meat & Poultry; See also See Meats & Meat Products: Game*
Garbanzo Beans *See Fruits & Vegetables: Beans: Garbanzo*
Garlic *See Fruits & Vegetables: Garlic*
Garlic Bread Sticks *See Baked Goods: Bread Sticks: Garlic*
Garlic Breads *See Baked Goods: Breads: Garlic*
Garlic Juices *See Beverages: Juices: Garlic*
Garlic Oils *See Oils, Shortening & Fats: Oils: Garlic*
Garlic Powders *See Ingredients, Flavors & Additives: Powders: Garlic (See also Spices/Garlic Powder)*
Garlic Salt *See Spices, Seasonings & Seeds: Salt: Garlic; See also See Spices, Seasonings & Seeds: Spices: Garlic Salt*
Garlic Sauces *See Sauces, Dips & Dressings: Sauces: Garlic*

Garlic Spices *See Spices, Seasonings & Seeds: Spices: Garlic*
Gefilte Fish *See Fish & Seafood: Fish: Gefilte*
Gelatin Thickeners *See Ingredients, Flavors & Additives: Thickeners: Gelatin*
Gelato *See Dairy Products: Ice Cream: Gelato*
Gellan *See Ingredients, Flavors & Additives: Gums: Gellan*
General Grocery *See General Grocery*
Geoduck Clams *See Fish & Seafood: Shellfish: Geoduck Clams*
Gewurztraminer *See Beverages: Wines: White Grape Varieties: Gewurztraminer*
Ghatti *See Ingredients, Flavors & Additives: Gums: Ghatti*
Gherkins Pickles *See Relishes & Pickled Products: Pickled Products: Pickles: Gherkins*
Giardiniera *See Prepared Foods: Giardiniera*
Gin *See Beverages: Spirits & Liqueurs: Gin*
Ginger *See Fruits & Vegetables: Ginger*
Ginger Ale *See Beverages: Soft Drinks & Sodas: Soft Drinks: Ginger Ale*
Ginger Oils *See Oils, Shortening & Fats: Oils: Ginger*
Ginger Pieces *See Spices, Seasonings & Seeds: Spices: Ginger: Pieces*
Ginger Sauces *See Sauces, Dips & Dressings: Sauces: Ginger*
Ginger Snaps *See Baked Goods: Cookies & Bars: Ginger Snaps*
Ginger Spices *See Spices, Seasonings & Seeds: Spices: Ginger*
Gingko Powders *See Ingredients, Flavors & Additives: Powders: Gingko*
Ginseng Powders *See Ingredients, Flavors & Additives: Powders: Ginseng*
Ginseng Spices *See Spices, Seasonings & Seeds: Spices: Ginseng*
Glace *See Fruits & Vegetables: Glace*
Glandulars *See Ingredients, Flavors & Additives: Glandulars*
Glass-Packed Apple Juices *See Beverages: Juices: Apple: Glass-Packed*
Glass-Packed Apricot Juices *See Beverages: Juices: Apricot: Glass-Packed*
Glass-Packed Cherry Juices *See Beverages: Juices: Cherry: Glass-Packed*
Glass-Packed Chilled Tomato Juices *See Beverages: Juices: Tomato: Glass-Packed Chilled*
Glass-Packed Cranberry Juices *See Beverages: Juices: Cranberry: Glass-Packed*
Glass-Packed Fish *See Fish & Seafood: Fish: Packed: Glass*
Glass-Packed Fruit & Vegetable Juices *See Beverages: Juices: Fruit & Vegetable: Glass-Packed*
Glass-Packed Fruit Juices *See Beverages: Juices: Fruit: Glass-Packed*
Glass-Packed Grape Juices *See Beverages: Juices: Grape: Glass-Packed*
Glass-Packed Grapefruit Juices *See Beverages: Juices: Grapefruit: Glass-Packed*
Glass-Packed Lemon Juices *See Beverages: Juices: Lemon: Glass-Packed*
Glass-Packed Pineapple Juices *See Beverages: Juices: Pineapple: Glass-Packed*
Glazed & Coated Nuts *See Nuts & Nut Butters: Nuts: Glazed & Coated*
Glazes *See Sauces, Dips & Dressings: Glazes*
Gluconates *See Ingredients, Flavors & Additives: Flavor Enhancers: Gluconates*
Gluconic Acids (Gluconolactone) *See Ingredients, Flavors & Additives: Acids: Gluconic (Gluconolactone)*
Glucose *See Sugars, Syrups & Sweeteners: Syrups: Corn: Glucose - Etc.*
Glutamic Acids *See Ingredients, Flavors & Additives: Acids: Glutamic*
Gluten Flour *See Cereals, Grains, Rice & Flour: Flour: Gluten*
Gluten Wheat *See Cereals, Grains, Rice & Flour: Wheat: Gluten*
Glycine *See Ingredients, Flavors & Additives: Glycine*
Gnocchi *See Pasta & Noodles: Gnocchi*
Goat *See Meats & Meat Products: Goat*
Goat Milk *See Dairy Products: Milk & Milk Products: Milk: Goat*
Goat's Cheese *See Cheese & Cheese Products: Cheese: Goat's*
Gold Kiwi *See Fruits & Vegetables: Kiwi: Gold*

Golden Delicious Apple *See Fruits & Vegetables: Apple: Golden Delicious*
Golden Scallopino Squash *See Fruits & Vegetables: Squash: Golden Scallopino*
Golden Trout *See Fish & Seafood: Fish: Trout: Golden*
Goose Berries *See Fruits & Vegetables: Berries: Goose*
Goose Poultry *See Meats & Meat Products: Poultry: Goose*
Gorgonzola Cheese *See Cheese & Cheese Products: Cheese: Gorgonzola*
Gotu Kola Powders *See Ingredients, Flavors & Additives: Powders: Gotu Kola*
Gouda Cheese *See Cheese & Cheese Products: Cheese: Gouda*
Gourmet & Specialty Foods *See Specialty & Organic Foods: Gourmet & Specialty Foods; See also Organic Foods major cateory; See also Specialty & Organic Foods: Gourmet & Specialty Foods: Gourmet & Specialty Foods*
Gourmet Flavored Lollypops *See Candy & Confectionery: Candy: Lollypops: Gourmet Flavored*
Gourmet Potato Chips *See Snack Foods: Chips: Potato: Gourmet*
Gourmet Salad Dressings *See Sauces, Dips & Dressings: Salad Dressings: Gourmet*
Graham Toppings *See Ingredients, Flavors & Additives: Toppings: Graham*
Grain Flavors *See Ingredients, Flavors & Additives: Flavors: Grain*
Grain-Based Ingredients *See Ingredients, Flavors & Additives: Grain-Based*
Grains *See Cereals, Grains, Rice & Flour: Grains*
Granita Ice Cream *See Dairy Products: Ice Cream: Granita*
Granita Mixes *See Doughs, Mixes & Fillings: Mixes: Granita*
Granny Smith Apple *See Fruits & Vegetables: Apple: Granny Smith*
Granola *See Cereals, Grains, Rice & Flour: Granola*
Granola Toppings *See Ingredients, Flavors & Additives: Toppings: Granola*
Granulated Garlic *See Fruits & Vegetables: Garlic: Granulated; See also Spices, Seasonings & Seeds: Spices: Garlic: Granulated*
Granulated Onion *See Fruits & Vegetables: Dried & Dehydrated Vegetables: Onion: Granulated; See also Spices, Seasonings & Seeds: Spices: Onion: Granulated*
Granulated Peanuts *See Nuts & Nut Butters: Nuts: Peanuts: Granulated*
Granulated Starch Pearl Tapioca *See Cereals, Grains, Rice & Flour: Tapioca: Pearl: Granulated, Starch*
Granulated Sugar *See Sugars, Syrups & Sweeteners: Sugar: Granulated*
Granules Honey *See Sugars, Syrups & Sweeteners: Honey: Granules*
Grape *See Fruits & Vegetables: Grape*
Grape Ade Juices *See Beverages: Juices: Ade: Grape*
Grape Jams *See Jams, Jellies & Spreads: Jams: Grape*
Grape Juices *See Beverages: Juices: Grape*
Grape Leaves *See Fruits & Vegetables: Grape: Leaves*
Grape Skin Extract Color *See Ingredients, Flavors & Additives: Colors: Grape Skin Extract Color*
Grapefruit *See Fruits & Vegetables: Grapefruit*
Grapefruit Juices *See Beverages: Juices: Grapefruit*
Grapefruit Oils *See Oils, Shortening & Fats: Oils: Grapefruit*
Grapeseed Oils *See Oils, Shortening & Fats: Oils: Grapeseed*
Grated Cheese *See Cheese & Cheese Products: Cheese: Grated*
Gravy *See Sauces, Dips & Dressings: Gravy*
Gravy Bases *See Ingredients, Flavors & Additives: Bases: Gravy*
Gravy Mixes *See Doughs, Mixes & Fillings: Mixes: Gravy*
Great Northern Beans *See Fruits & Vegetables: Beans: Great Northern*
Greek Beans *See Fruits & Vegetables: Beans: Greek*
Greek Olives *See Fruits & Vegetables: Olives: Greek*
Greek Oregano *See Spices, Seasonings & Seeds: Spices: Oregano: Greek*
Greek Style Seasonings *See Spices, Seasonings & Seeds: Seasonings: Greek Style*
Green & Yellow Split Peas, Dried *See Fruits & Vegetables: Peas: Green & Yellow Split - Dried*
Green Beans *See Fruits & Vegetables: Beans: Green*
Green Bell Peppers, Dried *See Fruits & Vegetables: Dried & Dehydrated Vegetables: Bell Peppers: Green*

EXAMPLE: **Canadian Style Bacon** *See Meats & Meat Products: Smoked, Cured & Deli Meats: Bacon: Canadian Style*
(1) (2) (3) (4) (5)

1. Product or Service you are looking for
2. Main Category, in alphabetical order, located in the page headers starting on page 27
3. Category Description, located in black bars and in page headers
4. Product Category, located in gray bars
5. Product Type, located under gray bars, centered in bold

Product Category List

Green Cabbage See Fruits & Vegetables: Cabbage: Green
Green Kiwi See Fruits & Vegetables: Kiwi: Green
Green Looseleaf Lettuce See Fruits & Vegetables: Lettuce: Looseleaf: Green
Green Mung Beans See Fruits & Vegetables: Beans: Green Mung; See also Fruits & Vegetables: Beans: Mung: Green
Green Olives See Fruits & Vegetables: Olives: Green
Green Olives with Pimiento See Fruits & Vegetables: Olives: Green: with Pimiento
Green Onion See Fruits & Vegetables: Onion: Green
Green Peas See Fruits & Vegetables: Peas: Green
Green Tea See Beverages: Coffee & Tea: Tea: Green
Greens Mustard See Fruits & Vegetables: Mustard: Greens
Grilled Patties Chicken See Meats & Meat Products: Poultry: Chicken: Grilled Patties
Grits See Cereals, Grains, Rice & Flour: Grits; See also Cereals, Grains, Rice & Flour: Grits: Corn White & Yellow
Groats See Cereals, Grains, Rice & Flour: Oats & Oat Products: Groats
Ground Allspice See Spices, Seasonings & Seeds: Spices: Allspice: Ground
Ground Bay Leaves See Spices, Seasonings & Seeds: Spices: Bay Leaves: Ground
Ground Beef & Beef Products See Meats & Meat Products: Beef & Beef Products: Ground
Ground Cardamom See Spices, Seasonings & Seeds: Spices: Cardamom: Ground
Ground Cayenne Pepper See Spices, Seasonings & Seeds: Spices: Cayenne Pepper: Ground
Ground Celery Seeds See Spices, Seasonings & Seeds: Seeds: Celery: Ground
Ground Cinnamon See Spices, Seasonings & Seeds: Spices: Cinnamon: Ground
Ground Cloves See Spices, Seasonings & Seeds: Spices: Cloves: Ground
Ground Coriander Seeds See Spices, Seasonings & Seeds: Seeds: Coriander: Ground
Ground Fennel Seeds See Spices, Seasonings & Seeds: Seeds: Fennel: Ground
Ground Ginger See Spices, Seasonings & Seeds: Spices: Ginger: Ground
Ground Mace See Spices, Seasonings & Seeds: Spices: Mace (See also Nutmeg): Ground
Ground Nutmeg See Spices, Seasonings & Seeds: Spices: Nutmeg (See also Mace): Ground
Ground Peppercorns See Spices, Seasonings & Seeds: Spices: Peppercorns: Ground
Ground Rosemary See Spices, Seasonings & Seeds: Spices: Rosemary: Ground
Ground Star Anise See Spices, Seasonings & Seeds: Spices: Anise - Star: Ground
Ground Thyme See Spices, Seasonings & Seeds: Spices: Thyme: Ground
Ground Turkey See Meats & Meat Products: Poultry: Turkey: Ground
Ground Turmeric See Spices, Seasonings & Seeds: Spices: Turmeric: Ground
Ground Veal See Meats & Meat Products: Beef & Beef Products: Veal: Ground
Ground White Pepper See Spices, Seasonings & Seeds: Spices: White Pepper: Ground
Grouper See Fish & Seafood: Fish: Grouper
Gruyere A1802 See Cheese & Cheese Products: Cheese: Gruyere
Guacamole See Ethnic Foods: Guacamole
Guacamole Dips See Sauces, Dips & Dressings: Dips: Guacamole
Guajillo Peppers See Fruits & Vegetables: Peppers: Guajillo
Guar Gum See Ingredients, Flavors & Additives: Gums: Guar Gum
Guava See Fruits & Vegetables: Guava
Guava Juices See Beverages: Juices: Guava
Guinea Hen See Meats & Meat Products: Game: Guinea Hen
Gumbo See Prepared Foods: Soups & Stews: Gumbo
Gums See Ingredients, Flavors & Additives: Gums
Gums & Jellies See Candy & Confectionery: Candy: Gums & Jellies
Gyros See Prepared Foods: Prepared Meals: Gyros

H

Habanero Peppers See Fruits & Vegetables: Peppers: Habanero
Habanero Sauces See Sauces, Dips & Dressings: Sauces: Habanero
Haddock See Fish & Seafood: Fish: Haddock
Hake See Fish & Seafood: Fish: Hake
Halal Foods See Ethnic Foods: Halal Foods
Half & Half See Dairy Products: Milk & Milk Products: Milk: Half & Half
Half & Half Flavors See Ingredients, Flavors & Additives: Flavors: Half & Half
Half-Products See Ingredients, Flavors & Additives: Half-Products
Half-Products, Calcium & Nutritionally Fortified Pellets See Ingredients, Flavors & Additives: Half-Products: Calcium & Nutritionally Fortified Pellets
Half-Products, Cocoa & Rice Pellets See Ingredients, Flavors & Additives: Half-Products: Cocoa & Rice Pellets
Half-Products, Colored Pellets See Ingredients, Flavors & Additives: Half-Products: Colored Pellets
Half-Products, Organic Pellets See Ingredients, Flavors & Additives: Half-Products: Organic Pellets; See also Organic Foods
Half-Products, Veggie & Rice Pellets See Ingredients, Flavors & Additives: Half-Products: Veggie & Rice Pellets
Half_Products, Flavored Pellets See Ingredients, Flavors & Additives: Half-Products: Flavored Pellets
Halibut See Fish & Seafood: Fish: Halibut
Halloween Specialty-Packaged Candy See Candy & Confectionery: Specialty-Packaged Candy: Halloween
Ham See Meats & Meat Products: Smoked, Cured & Deli Meats: Ham
Ham Steak See Meats & Meat Products: Smoked, Cured & Deli Meats: Ham: Steak
Hamburger See Meats & Meat Products: Beef & Beef Products: Hamburger
Hard Candy See Candy & Confectionery: Candy: Hard
Hard-Boiled Eggs See Eggs & Egg Products: Hard-Boiled
Hash See Prepared Foods: Hash
Hash Browned Potatoes See Prepared Foods: Potato Products: Hash Browned Potatoes
Hatcheries See Eggs & Egg Products: Hatcheries
Hatcheries, Turkey Chicks See Eggs & Egg Products: Hatcheries: Chicks: Turkey
Havarti Cheese See Cheese & Cheese Products: Cheese: Havarti
Hazelnut Biscotti See Baked Goods: Cookies & Bars: Biscotti: Hazelnut
Hazelnut Flavors See Ingredients, Flavors & Additives: Flavors: Hazelnut
Hazelnut Flour See Cereals, Grains, Rice & Flour: Flour: Hazelnut
Hazelnut Nut Butters See Nuts & Nut Butters: Nut Butters: Hazelnut
Hazelnut Oils See Oils, Shortening & Fats: Oils: Hazelnut
Hazelnuts See Nuts & Nut Butters: Nuts: Hazelnuts
Head Cheese See Meats & Meat Products: Smoked, Cured & Deli Meats: Head Cheese
Health & Dietary See Specialty & Organic Foods: Health & Dietary; See also Organic Foods
Health Products See Specialty & Organic Foods: Dietary Products: Health Products; See also Organic Foods
Hearts Artichoke See Fruits & Vegetables: Artichoke: Hearts
Heat Stable Flavors See Ingredients, Flavors & Additives: Flavors: Heat Stable
Heather See Spices, Seasonings & Seeds: Spices: Heather
Hemp Nut Oils See Oils, Shortening & Fats: Oils: Hemp Nut
Herbal Supplements See Spices, Seasonings & Seeds: Herbs: Herbal Supplements
Herbal Tea See Beverages: Coffee & Tea: Tea: Herbal
Herbes de Provence See Spices, Seasonings & Seeds: Spices: Herbes de Provence
Herbs See Spices, Seasonings & Seeds: Herbs
Herbs & Spices Blends See Ingredients, Flavors & Additives: Blends: Herbs & Spices
Herbs Blends See Ingredients, Flavors & Additives: Blends: Herbs
Herbs for Beef See Spices, Seasonings & Seeds: Herbs: for Beef
Herbs for Pork See Spices, Seasonings & Seeds: Herbs: for Pork
Herbs for Poultry See Spices, Seasonings & Seeds: Herbs: for Poultry
Herbs for Seafood See Spices, Seasonings & Seeds: Herbs: for Seafood
Herring See Fish & Seafood: Fish: Herring
Herring Caviar See Fish & Seafood: Caviar (Roe): Herring
Hickory Smoke Oil Flavors See Ingredients, Flavors & Additives: Flavors: Hickory Smoke Oil
High Amylose Starches See Ingredients, Flavors & Additives: Starches: High Amylose
High Bush Blueberry See Fruits & Vegetables: Berries: Blueberry: High Bush
High Fructose Corn Syrups See Sugars, Syrups & Sweeteners: Syrups: Corn: High Fructose
Hoisin Sauces See Sauces, Dips & Dressings: Sauces: Hoisin
Hoki See Fish & Seafood: Fish: Hoki
Hollandaise See Sauces, Dips & Dressings: Sauces: Hollandaise
Hominy See Cereals, Grains, Rice & Flour: Hominy
Honey See Sugars, Syrups & Sweeteners: Honey
Honeydew See Fruits & Vegetables: Melon: Honeydew
Hops See Cereals, Grains, Rice & Flour: Hops
Horse See Meats & Meat Products: Horse
Horseradish See Spices, Seasonings & Seeds: Spices: Horseradish; See also Sauces, Dips & Dressings: Sauces: Horseradish
Hot Chili Powders See Ingredients, Flavors & Additives: Powders: Chili: Hot
Hot Chocolate See Beverages: Cocoa & Chocolate Drinks: Hot Chocolate
Hot Chocolate Mixes See Doughs, Mixes & Fillings: Mixes: Hot Chocolate
Hot Cocoa See Beverages: Cocoa & Chocolate Drinks: Hot Cocoa
Hot Cocoa with Marshmallows See Beverages: Cocoa & Chocolate Drinks: Hot Cocoa: with Marshmallows
Hot Cross Buns See Baked Goods: Breads: Buns: Hot Cross
Hot Curry Powders See Ingredients, Flavors & Additives: Powders: Curry: Hot
Hot Dogs See Meats & Meat Products: Frankfurters: Hot Dogs
Hot Italian Sausage Seasonings See Spices, Seasonings & Seeds: Seasonings: Sausage: Hot Italian
Hot Italian Sausages See Meats & Meat Products: Smoked, Cured & Deli Meats: Sausages: Hot Italian
Hot Pepper Sauces See Sauces, Dips & Dressings: Sauces: Pepper: Hot
Hot Salami See Meats & Meat Products: Smoked, Cured & Deli Meats: Salami: Hot
Hot Sauces See Sauces, Dips & Dressings: Sauces: Hot
Hot Sausages See Meats & Meat Products: Smoked, Cured & Deli Meats: Sausages: Hot
Hulled Sesame Seeds See Spices, Seasonings & Seeds: Seeds: Sesame: Hulled
Hulls Rice See Cereals, Grains, Rice & Flour: Rice: Hulls
Humectants See Ingredients, Flavors & Additives: Humectants
Hummus See Cereals, Grains, Rice & Flour: Hummus
Hush Puppies See Prepared Foods: Hush Puppies
Hush Puppies, Frozen & Mixes See Prepared Foods: Hush Puppies: Frozen & Mixes
Husks Corn See Fruits & Vegetables: Corn: Husks
Hydrocolloids See Ingredients, Flavors & Additives: Hydrocolloids
Hydrogenated Fats & Lard See Oils, Shortening & Fats: Fats & Lard: Hydrogenated
Hydrolyzed Products See Ingredients, Flavors & Additives: Hydrolyzed Products
Hydroxypropyl Methylcellulose See Ingredients, Flavors & Additives: Gums: Hydroxypropyl Methylcellulose

I

Ice Cream See Dairy Products: Ice Cream
Ice Cream Bases See Dairy Products: Ice Cream: Bases
Ice Cream Mixes See Doughs, Mixes & Fillings: Mixes: Ice Cream
Ice Cream Powders See Ingredients, Flavors & Additives: Powders: Ice Cream
Ice Cream, Ribbons See Dairy Products: Ice Cream: Ribbons
Ice Cream, Roll See Dairy Products: Ice Cream: Roll
Ice Milk See Dairy Products: Ice Cream: Ice Milk
Iceberg Lettuce Based Prepared Salads See Prepared Foods: Prepared Salads: Iceberg Lettuce Based
Iced Coffee See Beverages: Coffee & Tea: Coffee: Iced
Iced Tea See Beverages: Coffee & Tea: Tea: Iced
Ices See Dairy Products: Ice Cream: Ices
Icing Sugar See Sugars, Syrups & Sweeteners: Sugar: Icing
Icings See Candy & Confectionery: Decorations & Icings: Icings
Imitation Cheeses & Substitutes See Cheese & Cheese Products: Imitation Cheeses & Substitutes; See also Cheese & Cheese Products: Imitation Cheeses & Substitutes: Imitation
Imitation Crab See Fish & Seafood: Shellfish: Crab: Imitation
Imitation Fish See Fish & Seafood: Fish: Imitation
Improvers Doughs See Doughs, Mixes & Fillings: Doughs: Improvers
Inclusions See Ingredients, Flavors & Additives: Inclusions
India Pale Ale See Beverages: Beers: American & British Ale: India Pale Ale
Individual Packets See Prepared Foods: Individual Packets
Individual Quick Frozen Food See Prepared Foods: Individual Quick Frozen Food

Product Category List

Individually Packaged Cookies & Bars See Baked Goods: Cookies & Bars: Individually Packaged
Ingredients See Ingredients, Flavors & Additives: Ingredients; See also Baked Goods: Ingredients
Ingredients, Flavors & Additives See Ingredients, Flavors & Additives
Ingredients, Flavors & Additives, Almond Pastes See Ingredients, Flavors & Additives: Pastes: Almond
Ingredients, Organic Foods See Specialty & Organic Foods: Organic Foods: Ingredients; See also Organic Foods
Ink Squid See Fish & Seafood: Shellfish: Squid: Ink
Inositol See Ingredients, Flavors & Additives: Vitamins & Supplements: Inositol
Instant Cereal See Cereals, Grains, Rice & Flour: Cereal: Instant
Instant Coffee See Beverages: Coffee & Tea: Coffee: Instant
Instant Coffee, Decaffeinated See Beverages: Coffee & Tea: Coffee: Instant - Decaffeinated
Instant Potatoes See Fruits & Vegetables: Potatoes: Instant
Instant Rice See Cereals, Grains, Rice & Flour: Rice: Instant
Instant Tea See Beverages: Coffee & Tea: Tea: Instant
Instantized Flour See Cereals, Grains, Rice & Flour: Flour: Instantized
Invert Sugar See Sugars, Syrups & Sweeteners: Sugar: Invert
IQF Frozen Cherries See Fruits & Vegetables: Cherries: Frozen: IQF (Individually Quick Frozen)
IQF Rice See Cereals, Grains, Rice & Flour: Rice: IQF (Individual Quick Frozen)
IQF Vegetables See Fruits & Vegetables: Vegetables: IQF (Individual Quick Frozen)
Irish Breakfast Tea See Beverages: Coffee & Tea: Tea: Irish Breakfast
Irish Creme Flavors See Ingredients, Flavors & Additives: Flavors: Irish Creme
Irish Whiskey See Beverages: Spirits & Liqueurs: Irish Whiskey
Isolate Soy Protein See Fruits & Vegetables: Soy: Soy Protein: Isolate
Italian See Ethnic Foods: Italian
Italian Beans See Fruits & Vegetables: Beans: Italian
Italian Beef & Beef Products See Meats & Meat Products: Beef & Beef Products: Italian
Italian Breads See Baked Goods: Breads: Italian
Italian Herbs Seasonings See Spices, Seasonings & Seeds: Seasonings: Italian Herbs
Italian Olives See Fruits & Vegetables: Olives: Italian
Italian Style Salad Dressings See Sauces, Dips & Dressings: Salad Dressings: Italian Style
Italian Style Salad Dressings, Mixes See Sauces, Dips & Dressings: Salad Dressings: Mixes: Italian Style
Italian Style Seasonings See Spices, Seasonings & Seeds: Seasonings: Italian Style
Italian Wines See Beverages: Wines: Italian

J

Jalapeno & Chiles Peppers See Fruits & Vegetables: Peppers: Jalapeno & Chiles
Jalapeno Peppers See Fruits & Vegetables: Peppers: Jalapeno
Jamacain Beef Patties See Meats & Meat Products: Beef & Beef Products: Patties: Jamacain
Jambalaya See Ethnic Foods: Jambalaya
Jambalaya Mixes See Doughs, Mixes & Fillings: Mixes: Jambalaya
Jams See Jams, Jellies & Spreads: Jams
Japanese See Ethnic Foods: Japanese
Japanese Wines See Beverages: Wines: Japanese
Japones Peppers See Fruits & Vegetables: Peppers: Japones
Jarred or Cupped Fruit See Fruits & Vegetables: Fruit: Jarred or Cupped
Jasmati Rice See Cereals, Grains, Rice & Flour: Rice: Jasmati
Jasmine Rice See Cereals, Grains, Rice & Flour: Rice: Jasmine
Jasmine Tea See Beverages: Coffee & Tea: Tea: Jasmine
Jellied Cranberry Sauces See Fruits & Vegetables: Sauces: Cranberry: Jellied
Jellies See Jams, Jellies & Spreads: Jellies
Jelly Beans See Candy & Confectionery: Candy: Jelly Beans

Jelly Powders See Ingredients, Flavors & Additives: Powders: Jelly
Jerk Sauces See Sauces, Dips & Dressings: Sauces: Jerk
Juice Bases See Ingredients, Flavors & Additives: Bases: Juice
Juice Concentrates See Beverages: Juices: Concentrates
Juice Drinks See Beverages: Juices: Drink
Juice, Tropical Fruit See Beverages: Juices: Tropical Fruits
Juices See Beverages: Juices
Juniper Berries See Fruits & Vegetables: Berries: Juniper; See also Spices, Seasonings & Seeds: Spices: Juniper Berries

K

Kale See Fruits & Vegetables: Kale
Karaya Gum See Ingredients, Flavors & Additives: Gums: Karaya Gum
Kasmati Rice See Cereals, Grains, Rice & Flour: Rice: Kasmati
Kefir See Dairy Products: Milk & Milk Products: Kefir
Kegged Beers See Beverages: Beers: Kegged
Kelp Products See Fruits & Vegetables: Kelp Products
Ketchup See Sauces, Dips & Dressings: Ketchup
Key Lime Juices See Beverages: Juices: Key Lime
Key Lime Pies See Baked Goods: Pies: Key Lime
Kidney Beans See Fruits & Vegetables: Beans: Kidney
Kielbasa Sausage Seasonings See Spices, Seasonings & Seeds: Seasonings: Sausage: Kielbasa
Kielbasa Sausages See Meats & Meat Products: Smoked, Cured & Deli Meats: Sausages: Kielbasa
Kiev Chicken See Prepared Foods: Prepared Meals: Chicken: Kiev
King Cod See Fish & Seafood: Fish: King Cod
King Crab See Fish & Seafood: Shellfish: Crab: King
King Salmon See Fish & Seafood: Fish: Salmon: King
Kingfish See Fish & Seafood: Fish: Kingfish
Kisses See Candy & Confectionery: Candy: Kisses
Kiwi See Fruits & Vegetables: Kiwi
Klingstone Peach See Fruits & Vegetables: Peach: Klingstone
Knishes See Prepared Foods: Knishes
Knockwurst See Meats & Meat Products: Smoked, Cured & Deli Meats: Knockwurst
Knockwurst Sausages See Meats & Meat Products: Smoked, Cured & Deli Meats: Sausages: Knockwurst
Kohlrabi See Fruits & Vegetables: Kohlrabi
Kolsch Belgian & French Ale See Beverages: Beers: Belgian & French Ale: Kolsch
Kosher Foods See Ethnic Foods: Kosher Foods
Kosher Frankfurters See Meats & Meat Products: Frankfurters: Kosher
Kosher Pickles See Relishes & Pickled Products: Pickled Products: Pickles: Kosher
Kumquat See Fruits & Vegetables: Kumquat

L

Lactic Acidulants See Ingredients, Flavors & Additives: Acidulants: Lactic
Lactobacillus Acidophilus See Ingredients, Flavors & Additives: Cultures & Yeasts: Lactobacillus Acidophilus
Lactoferrin See Ingredients, Flavors & Additives: Lactoferrin
Lactose Sweeteners See Ingredients, Flavors & Additives: Sweeteners: Lactose
Lactose-Free Milk See Dairy Products: Milk & Milk Products: Milk: Lactose-Free
Lady Fingers See Baked Goods: Cookies & Bars: Lady Fingers; See also Baked Goods: Cakes & Pastries: Ladyfingers
Lager Beers See Beverages: Beers: Lager
Lamb See Meats & Meat Products: Lamb
Lamb Marinades See Sauces, Dips & Dressings: Marinades: Lamb
Langostinos See Fish & Seafood: Shellfish: Langostinos
Lard See Oils, Shortening & Fats: Fats & Lard: Lard
Lasagna See Pasta & Noodles: Lasagna; See also Prepared Foods: Prepared Meals: Lasagna
Latte Coffee See Beverages: Coffee & Tea: Coffee: Latte
Lavender See Spices, Seasonings & Seeds: Spices: Lavender
Lavender Flowers See Spices, Seasonings & Seeds: Spices: Lavender Flowers
Leaveners See Ingredients, Flavors & Additives: Leaveners

Lecithin Emulsifiers See Ingredients, Flavors & Additives: Emulsifiers: Lecithin
Lecithinated Stabilizers See Ingredients, Flavors & Additives: Stabilizers: Lecithinated
Leek See Fruits & Vegetables: Leek
Leeks, Chopped Dried See Fruits & Vegetables: Dried & Dehydrated Vegetables: Leeks - Chopped
Leg of Lamb See Meats & Meat Products: Lamb: Leg of
Lemon See Fruits & Vegetables: Lemon
Lemon & Basil Seasonings See Spices, Seasonings & Seeds: Seasonings: Lemon & Basil
Lemon & Dill Seasonings See Spices, Seasonings & Seeds: Seasonings: Lemon & Dill
Lemon Ade Juices See Beverages: Juices: Ade: Lemon
Lemon Flavors See Ingredients, Flavors & Additives: Flavors: Lemon
Lemon Grass Oils See Oils, Shortening & Fats: Oils: Lemon Grass
Lemon Grass Spices See Spices, Seasonings & Seeds: Spices: Lemon Grass
Lemon Juices See Beverages: Juices: Lemon
Lemon Oils See Oils, Shortening & Fats: Oils: Lemon
Lemon Peel See Spices, Seasonings & Seeds: Spices: Lemon Peel
Lemon Pepper Seasonings See Spices, Seasonings & Seeds: Seasonings: Lemon Pepper
Lemon Sauces See Sauces, Dips & Dressings: Sauces: Lemon
Lemon Tea See Beverages: Coffee & Tea: Tea: Lemon
Lemon-Lime Soda See Beverages: Soft Drinks & Sodas: Soft Drinks: Lemon-Lime Soda
Lemon-Meringue Pies See Baked Goods: Pies: Lemon-Meringue
Lemonade Juices See Beverages: Juices: Lemonade
Lentil Beans See Fruits & Vegetables: Beans: Lentil; See also Fruits & Vegetables: Beans: Dried: Lentil Blend
Lentil Soup See Prepared Foods: Soups & Stews: Lentil Soup
Lettuce See Fruits & Vegetables: Lettuce
Licorice Candy See Candy & Confectionery: Candy: Licorice
Licorice Flavors See Ingredients, Flavors & Additives: Flavors: Licorice
Light Red Kidney Beans See Fruits & Vegetables: Beans: Kidney: Light Red
Lima Beans See Fruits & Vegetables: Beans: Lima
Limburger Cheese See Cheese & Cheese Products: Cheese: Limburger
Lime See Fruits & Vegetables: Lime
Lime Flavors See Ingredients, Flavors & Additives: Flavors: Lime
Lime Juices See Beverages: Juices: Lime
Lime Oils See Oils, Shortening & Fats: Oils: Lime
Lingonberries See Fruits & Vegetables: Berries: Lingonberries
Linguica Sausages See Meats & Meat Products: Smoked, Cured & Deli Meats: Sausages: Linguica
Link Sausages See Meats & Meat Products: Smoked, Cured & Deli Meats: Sausages: Link
Liqueur Cake See Baked Goods: Cakes & Pastries: Liqueur Cake
Liqueur Flavors See Ingredients, Flavors & Additives: Flavors: Liqueur
Liqueurs & Cordials See Beverages: Spirits & Liqueurs: Liqueurs & Cordials
Liquid See Eggs & Egg Products: Liquid
Liquid & Granulated Sugar See Sugars, Syrups & Sweeteners: Sugar: Liquid & Granulated
Liquid Beverage Mixes See Doughs, Mixes & Fillings: Mixes: Beverage: Liquid
Liquid Chicken Fats & Lard See Oils, Shortening & Fats: Fats & Lard: Chicken: Liquid
Liquid Egg Whites See Eggs & Egg Products: Liquid: Whites
Liquid Honey See Sugars, Syrups & Sweeteners: Honey: Liquid
Liquid Mixes See Doughs, Mixes & Fillings: Mixes: Liquid
Liquid Spices See Spices, Seasonings & Seeds: Spices: Liquid
Liquid Sugar See Sugars, Syrups & Sweeteners: Sugar: Liquid
Liquid Vegetable Shortening See Oils, Shortening & Fats: Shortening: Vegetable: Liquid
Liquid Vinegar See Sauces, Dips & Dressings: Vinegar: Liquid
Live Crab See Fish & Seafood: Shellfish: Crab: Live

EXAMPLE: **Canadian Style Bacon** See Meats & Meat Products: Smoked, Cured & Deli Meats: Bacon: Canadian Style
(1) (2) (3) (4) (5)

1. Product or Service you are looking for
2. Main Category, in alphabetical order, located in the page headers starting on page 27
3. Category Description, located in black bars and in page headers
4. Product Category, located in gray bars
5. Product Type, located under gray bars, centered in bold

Product Category List

Live Crayfish *See Fish & Seafood: Shellfish: Crayfish: Live*
Live Lobster *See Fish & Seafood: Shellfish: Lobster: Live*
Live Shellfish *See Fish & Seafood: Shellfish: Live*
Liver *See Meats & Meat Products: Beef & Beef Products: Liver*
Liver Extracts *See Ingredients, Flavors & Additives: Extracts: Liver*
Liverwurst *See Meats & Meat Products: Smoked, Cured & Deli Meats: Liverwurst*
Lobster *See Fish & Seafood: Shellfish: Lobster*
Lobster Meat *See Fish & Seafood: Shellfish: Lobster: Meat*
Lobster Mushrooms *See Fruits & Vegetables: Mushrooms: Lobster*
Lobster Tails *See Fish & Seafood: Shellfish: Lobster: Tails*
Locust Bean Gum *See Ingredients, Flavors & Additives: Gums: Locust Bean Gum*
Loganberries *See Fruits & Vegetables: Loganberries*
Loin Chop, Lamb *See Meats & Meat Products: Lamb: Loin Chop*
Loin Chop, Pork *See Meats & Meat Products: Pork & Pork Products: Loin Chop; See also Meats & Meat Products: Pork & Pork Products: Loins*
Loin Chop, Veal *See Meats & Meat Products: Beef & Beef Products: Veal: Loin Chop*
Lollypops *See Candy & Confectionery: Candy: Lollypops*
London Broil *See Meats & Meat Products: Beef & Beef Products: London Broil*
Loose Leaf Tea *See Beverages: Coffee & Tea: Tea: Loose Leaf*
Looseleaf Lettuce *See Fruits & Vegetables: Lettuce: Looseleaf*
Low Carb Bread Mixes *See Doughs, Mixes & Fillings: Mixes: Bread: Low Carb*
Low Carb Dessert Mixes *See Doughs, Mixes & Fillings: Mixes: Dessert: Low Carb*
Low Carb Desserts *See Baked Goods: Desserts: Low Carb*
Low Carb Ice Cream Mixes *See Doughs, Mixes & Fillings: Mixes: Ice Cream: Low Carb*
Low Fat Butter *See Dairy Products: Butter: Low Fat*
Low Moisture Part Skim Mozzarella Cheese *See Cheese & Cheese Products: Cheese: Mozzarella: Low Moisture Part Skim*
Low Moisture Part Skim Mozzarella Cheese, Shredded - Frozen *See Cheese & Cheese Products: Cheese: Mozzarella: Low Moisture Part Skim Shredded - Frozen*
Low-Calorie Desserts *See Specialty & Organic Foods: Dietary Products: Low-Calorie Desserts; See also Organic Foods; See also Baked Goods: Desserts: Low-Calorie*
Low-Calorie Non-Dairy Ice Cream *See Dairy Products: Ice Cream: Non-Dairy: Low-Calorie*
Low-Fat Cheese *See Cheese & Cheese Products: Cheese: Low-Fat*
Low-Fat Ice Cream *See Dairy Products: Ice Cream: Low-Fat*
Low-Fat Milk *See Dairy Products: Milk & Milk Products: Milk: Low-Fat*
Low-Fat Potato Chips *See Snack Foods: Chips: Potato: Low-Fat*
Low-Fat Yogurt *See Dairy Products: Yogurt: Low-Fat*
Lox Smoked Seafood *See Fish & Seafood: Seafood: Smoked: Lox*
Lozenges Candy *See Candy & Confectionery: Candy: Lozenges*
Lumpfish *See Fish & Seafood: Fish: Lumpfish*
Luncheon Meat *See Meats & Meat Products: Smoked, Cured & Deli Meats: Luncheon Meat*
Lupini Beans *See Fruits & Vegetables: Beans: Lupini*
Luxury Cognac Brandy *See Beverages: Spirits & Liqueurs: Brandy: Luxury Cognac*

M

Macadamia Flavors *See Ingredients, Flavors & Additives: Flavors: Macadamia*
Macadamia Nuts *See Nuts & Nut Butters: Nuts: Macadamia*
Macaroni, Prepared Meals *See Prepared Foods: Prepared Meals: Macaroni*
Macaroni, Prepared Salads *See Prepared Foods: Prepared Salads: Macaroni*
Macaroons *See Baked Goods: Cookies & Bars: Macaroons*
Mace Spices *See Spices, Seasonings & Seeds: Spices: Mace (See also Nutmeg)*
Mackerel *See Fish & Seafood: Fish: Mackerel*
Mahi-Mahi *See Fish & Seafood: Fish: Mahi-Mahi*
Maitakes *See Fruits & Vegetables: Mushrooms: Maitakes*
Malic Acidulants *See Ingredients, Flavors & Additives: Acidulants: Malic*
Malt *See Cereals, Grains, Rice & Flour: Malt*
Malt Extract Syrups *See Sugars, Syrups & Sweeteners: Syrups: Malt Extract*
Malt Liquor *See Beverages: Beers: Lager: Malt Liquor*
Malt Vinegar *See Sauces, Dips & Dressings: Vinegar: Malt*
Maltodextrin *See Ingredients, Flavors & Additives: Maltodextrin*
Mandarin Orange *See Fruits & Vegetables: Orange: Mandarin*
Mango *See Fruits & Vegetables: Mango*
Mango Juices *See Beverages: Juices: Mango*
Manhattan Chowder *See Prepared Foods: Soups & Stews: Chowder: Manhattan*
Maple Candy *See Candy & Confectionery: Candy: Maple*
Maple Flavors *See Ingredients, Flavors & Additives: Flavors: Maple*
Maple Sugar *See Sugars, Syrups & Sweeteners: Sugar: Maple*
Maple Syrups *See Sugars, Syrups & Sweeteners: Syrups: Maple*
Maraschino Cherries *See Fruits & Vegetables: Cherries: Maraschino*
Margarine *See Oils, Shortening & Fats: Margarine*
Marinades *See Sauces, Dips & Dressings: Marinades*
Marinara Sauces *See Sauces, Dips & Dressings: Sauces: Marinara*
Marinated Shellfish *See Fish & Seafood: Shellfish: Marinated*
Marinated Tomato *See Fruits & Vegetables: Tomato: Marinated*
Marjoram Spices *See Spices, Seasonings & Seeds: Spices: Marjoram*
Marlin *See Fish & Seafood: Fish: Marlin*
Marmalades & Preserves *See Jams, Jellies & Spreads: Marmalades & Preserves*
Marsala Cooking Wines *See Beverages: Wines: Cooking: Marsala*
Marshmallow Candy *See Candy & Confectionery: Candy: Marshmallow*
Marshmallow Creme Candy *See Candy & Confectionery: Candy: Marshmallow Creme*
Marshmallows *See Candy & Confectionery: Candy: Marshmallows*
Marzipan *See Candy & Confectionery: Candy: Marzipan*
Masa Flour *See Cereals, Grains, Rice & Flour: Flour: Masa*
Mascarpone Cheese *See Cheese & Cheese Products: Cheese: Mascarpone*
Mashed Sweet Potatoes *See Fruits & Vegetables: Sweet Potatoes: Mashed*
Masking Flavors *See Ingredients, Flavors & Additives: Flavors: Masking*
Mature Rabbit *See Meats & Meat Products: Game: Rabbit: Mature*
Matzo *See Ethnic Foods: Matzo*
Matzo Meal *See Ethnic Foods: Matzo: Meal*
Mayonnaise *See Sauces, Dips & Dressings: Mayonnaise*
Meal *See Fish & Seafood: Fish: Meal*
Meal Crackers *See Baked Goods: Crackers: Meal*
Meal Fillers *See Ingredients, Flavors & Additives: Fillers: Meal*
Meat Analogs *See Ingredients, Flavors & Additives: Analogs: Meat*
Meat Balls *See Prepared Foods: Meat Balls*
Meat Curing Preparations *See Ingredients, Flavors & Additives: Curing Preparations: Meat*
Meat Extenders *See Ingredients, Flavors & Additives: Extenders: Meat*
Meat Flavors *See Ingredients, Flavors & Additives: Flavors: Meat*
Meat Loaf *See Prepared Foods: Meat Loaf*
Meat Marinades *See Sauces, Dips & Dressings: Marinades: Meat*
Meat Meal *See Meats & Meat Products: Meat Meal*
Meat Pies *See Baked Goods: Pies: Meat*
Meat Powders *See Ingredients, Flavors & Additives: Powders: Meat*
Meat Products Seasonings *See Spices, Seasonings & Seeds: Seasonings: Meat Products*
Meat Ravioli *See Pasta & Noodles: Ravioli: Meat*
Meat Sauces *See Sauces, Dips & Dressings: Sauces: Meat*
Meat Spaghetti Sauces *See Sauces, Dips & Dressings: Sauces: Spaghetti: Meat*
Meat Stock Powders *See Ingredients, Flavors & Additives: Powders: Meat Stock*
Meat Stuffing *See Prepared Foods: Stuffing: Meat*
Meat Tenderizers *See Ingredients, Flavors & Additives: Tenderizers: Meat*
Meatless Spaghetti Sauces *See Sauces, Dips & Dressings: Sauces: Spaghetti: Meatless*
Meats & Meat Products *See Meats & Meat Products*
Medical Nutritionals *See Ingredients, Flavors & Additives: Vitamins & Supplements: Medical Nutritionals*
Mediterranean Sauces *See Sauces, Dips & Dressings: Sauces: Mediterranean*
Melba Toast *See Baked Goods: Breads: Melba Toast*
Melon *See Fruits & Vegetables: Melon*
Melon Balls *See Fruits & Vegetables: Melon: Balls*
Meringue Dessert Fillings *See Doughs, Mixes & Fillings: Fillings: Dessert: Meringue*
Meringue Powders *See Ingredients, Flavors & Additives: Powders: Meringue*
Meringue Toppings *See Ingredients, Flavors & Additives: Toppings: Meringue*
Merlot *See Beverages: Wines: Red Grape Wines: Merlot*
Mesquite BBQ Snack Seasonings *See Spices, Seasonings & Seeds: Seasonings: Snack: Mesquite BBQ*
Methoxypolyethylene Glycols *See Ingredients, Flavors & Additives: Methoxypolyethylene Glycols*
Methyl Salicylate *See Ingredients, Flavors & Additives: Aroma Chemicals & Materials: Chemicals: Methyl Salicylate*
Methylcellulose *See Ingredients, Flavors & Additives: Gums: Methylcellulose*
Mexican *See Ethnic Foods: Mexican*
Mexican Food Sauces *See Sauces, Dips & Dressings: Sauces: Mexican Food*
Mexican Oregano *See Spices, Seasonings & Seeds: Spices: Oregano: Mexican*
Mexican Style Seasonings *See Spices, Seasonings & Seeds: Seasonings: Mexican Style*
Microwavable Entrees *See Prepared Foods: Prepared Meals: Entrees: Microwavable*
Microwave Flavors *See Ingredients, Flavors & Additives: Flavors: Microwave*
Milano Salami *See Meats & Meat Products: Smoked, Cured & Deli Meats: Salami: Milano*
Mild Salsa *See Sauces, Dips & Dressings: Salsa: Mild*
Milk *See Dairy Products: Milk & Milk Products: Milk*
Milk & Milk Products *See Dairy Products: Milk & Milk Products*
Milk Calcium *See Ingredients, Flavors & Additives: Milk Calcium*
Milk Coconut *See Fruits & Vegetables: Coconut & Coconut Products: Milk*
Milk Enzyme *See Dairy Products: Milk & Milk Products: Milk Products: Milk & Milk Fat: Enzyme*
Milk Flavors *See Ingredients, Flavors & Additives: Flavors: Milk*
Milk Powders *See Ingredients, Flavors & Additives: Powders: Milk*
Milk Productss *See Dairy Products: Milk & Milk Products: Milk Products*
Milk Proteins *See Ingredients, Flavors & Additives: Hydrolyzed Products: Milk Proteins; See also Dairy Products: Milk & Milk Products: Milk Products: Milk Proteins*
Milk Rice Powders *See Ingredients, Flavors & Additives: Powders: Rice: Milk*
Milk Solids *See Dairy Products: Milk & Milk Products: Milk Solids*
Milk, Modified - Dry Blends *See Dairy Products: Milk & Milk Products: Milk Products: Modified - Dry Blends*
Milled Rice *See Cereals, Grains, Rice & Flour: Rice: Milled*
Millet *See Cereals, Grains, Rice & Flour: Millet*
Millet Flour *See Cereals, Grains, Rice & Flour: Flour: Millet*
Milo *See Beverages: Cocoa & Chocolate Drinks: Milo*
Minced Clam *See Fish & Seafood: Shellfish: Clam: Minced*
Minced Garlic *See Spices, Seasonings & Seeds: Spices: Garlic: Minced*
Minced Onion *See Fruits & Vegetables: Dried & Dehydrated Vegetables: Onion: Minced; See also Spices, Seasonings & Seeds: Spices: Onion: Minced; See also Fruits & Vegetables: Onion: Minced*
Mineral Blends *See Ingredients, Flavors & Additives: Vitamins & Supplements: Mineral Blends*
Mineral Supplements *See Ingredients, Flavors & Additives: Vitamins & Supplements: Supplements: Minerals; See also Ingredients, Flavors & Additives: Vitamins & Supplements: Minerals*
Mineral Water *See Beverages: Water: Mineral*
Miners Lettuce *See Fruits & Vegetables: Lettuce: Miners*
Mini Frankfurters *See Meats & Meat Products: Frankfurters: Mini*
Mint Herb Tea *See Beverages: Coffee & Tea: Tea: Mint Herb*
Mint Leaves *See Spices, Seasonings & Seeds: Spices: Mint Leaves*
Mint Sauces *See Sauces, Dips & Dressings: Sauces: Mint*
Mint Spices *See Spices, Seasonings & Seeds: Spices: Mint*
Mint Tea *See Beverages: Coffee & Tea: Tea: Mint*
Mints Candy *See Candy & Confectionery: Candy: Mints*
Miso *See Fruits & Vegetables: Miso*
Mix *See Eggs & Egg Products: Mix*

Product Category List

Mixed Nuts *See Nuts & Nut Butters: Nuts: Mixed Nuts*
Mixers *See Beverages: Mixers*
Mixes *See Doughs, Mixes & Fillings: Mixes*
Mixes, Salad Dressings *See Sauces, Dips & Dressings: Salad Dressings: Mixes*
Mixes, Sauces *See Sauces, Dips & Dressings: Sauces: Mixes*
Mocha Biscotti *See Baked Goods: Cookies & Bars: Biscotti: Mocha*
Mocha Coffee & Tea *See Beverages: Coffee & Tea: Mocha*
Modified Food Starches *See Ingredients, Flavors & Additives: Agents: Anticaking: Modified Food Starch*
Modified Rice Starches *See Ingredients, Flavors & Additives: Starches: Rice: Modified*
Modified Starches *See Ingredients, Flavors & Additives: Starches: Modified*
Modifiers Agents *See Ingredients, Flavors & Additives: Agents: Modifiers*
Molasses *See Sugars, Syrups & Sweeteners: Molasses*
Molasses Flakes *See Ingredients, Flavors & Additives: Flakes: Molasses*
Molasses Powders *See Ingredients, Flavors & Additives: Powders: Molasses*
Molding Starches *See Ingredients, Flavors & Additives: Starches: Molding*
Mole Sauces *See Sauces, Dips & Dressings: Sauces: Mole*
Monkfish *See Fish & Seafood: Fish: Monkfish*
Montasio *See Cheese & Cheese Products: Cheese: Montasio*
Monte Veronese *See Cheese & Cheese Products: Cheese: Monte Veronese*
Monterey Jack *See Cheese & Cheese Products: Cheese: Monterey Jack*
Morel Mushrooms *See Fruits & Vegetables: Mushrooms: Morel; See also Fruits & Vegetables: Dried & Dehydrated Vegetables: Mushrooms: Morels Whole*
Mortadella Sausages *See Meats & Meat Products: Smoked, Cured & Deli Meats: Sausages: Mortadella*
Mousse Candy *See Candy & Confectionery: Candy: Mousse*
Mousseron *See Fruits & Vegetables: Mushrooms: Mousseron*
Mozzarella *See Cheese & Cheese Products: Cheese: Mozzarella*
Mozzarella Cheese, Low Moisture Part Skim *See Cheese & Cheese Products: Cheese: Mozzarella: Low Moisture Part Skim*
Mozzarella Cheese, Low Moisture Part Skim, Shredded - Frozen *See Cheese & Cheese Products: Cheese: Mozzarella: Low Moisture Part Skim Shredded - Frozen*
Mozzarella Sticks *See Prepared Foods: Prepared Meals: Mozzarella Sticks*
Mozzarella, Imitation *See Cheese & Cheese Products: Imitation Cheeses & Substitutes: Imitation: Mozzarella*
MSG & Salt Mixture *See Spices, Seasonings & Seeds: Salt: MSG & Salt Mixture*
Muenster *See Cheese & Cheese Products: Cheese: Muenster*
Muesli Cereal *See Cereals, Grains, Rice & Flour: Cereal: Muesli*
Muffin Batters *See Doughs, Mixes & Fillings: Batters: Muffin*
Muffin Loaves *See Baked Goods: Cakes & Pastries: Muffin Loaves*
Muffin Mixes *See Doughs, Mixes & Fillings: Mixes: Muffin*
Muffins *See Baked Goods: Cakes & Pastries: Muffins*
Mulato Peppers *See Fruits & Vegetables: Peppers: Mulato*
Mulberries *See Fruits & Vegetables: Berries: Mulberries*
Mulled Wine Spice *See Spices, Seasonings & Seeds: Spices: Mulled Wine Spice*
Mullet *See Fish & Seafood: Fish: Mullet*
Mulling *See Spices, Seasonings & Seeds: Spices: Mulling*
Multi-Grain Breads *See Baked Goods: Breads: Multi-Grain*
Multi-Packs Specialty-Packaged Candy *See Candy & Confectionery: Specialty-Packaged Candy: Multi-Packs*
Mung Bean Noodles *See Pasta & Noodles: Noodles: Mung Bean*
Mung Bean Sprouts *See Fruits & Vegetables: Sprouts: Mung Bean*
Mung Beans *See Fruits & Vegetables: Beans: Mung*
Muscovy Duck *See Meats & Meat Products: Game: Muscovy Duck*
Mushroom Sauces *See Sauces, Dips & Dressings: Sauces: Mushroom*
Mushrooms *See Fruits & Vegetables: Dried & Dehydrated Vegetables: Mushrooms; See also Fruits & Vegetables: Mushrooms*
Muskox *See Meats & Meat Products: Game: Muskox*
Mussels *See Fish & Seafood: Shellfish: Mussels*
Mustard *See Sauces, Dips & Dressings: Mustard; See also Fruits & Vegetables: Mustard*
Mustard Bran *See Cereals, Grains, Rice & Flour: Bran: Mustard*
Mustard Flour *See Cereals, Grains, Rice & Flour: Flour: Mustard*
Mustard Oils *See Oils, Shortening & Fats: Oils: Mustard*
Mustard Powder *See Spices, Seasonings & Seeds: Spices: Mustard Powder; See also Ingredients, Flavors & Additives: Powders: Mustard*
Mustard Seeds *See Spices, Seasonings & Seeds: Seeds: Mustard*
Mustard Spices *See Spices, Seasonings & Seeds: Spices: Mustards; See also Spices, Seasonings & Seeds: Spices: Mustard*
Mustard Spices, Dry - Prepared *See Spices, Seasonings & Seeds: Spices: Mustard: Dry - Prepared*
Mutton *See Meats & Meat Products: Mutton*

N

Nacho Cheese Sauces *See Sauces, Dips & Dressings: Sauces: Cheese: Nacho*
Nacho Cheese Snack Seasonings *See Spices, Seasonings & Seeds: Seasonings: Snack: Nacho Cheese*
Nacho Chips *See Snack Foods: Chips: Nacho*
Napoli Salami *See Meats & Meat Products: Smoked, Cured & Deli Meats: Salami: Napoli*
Natural Chemicals *See Ingredients, Flavors & Additives: Chemicals: Natural*
Natural Colors *See Ingredients, Flavors & Additives: Colors: Natural; See also See Ingredients, Flavors & Additives: Colors: Natural: Others*
Natural Flavorings Spices *See Spices, Seasonings & Seeds: Spices: Natural Flavorings*
Natural Granules Honey *See Sugars, Syrups & Sweeteners: Honey: Granules: Natural*
Natural Gums *See Ingredients, Flavors & Additives: Gums: Natural*
Natural Organic Foods *See Specialty & Organic Foods: Organic Foods: Natural; See also Organic Foods*
Natural Sweeteners *See Sugars, Syrups & Sweeteners: Natural Sweeteners*
Naval Orange *See Fruits & Vegetables: Orange: Naval*
Navy Beans *See Fruits & Vegetables: Beans: Navy*
Nectar *See Fruits & Vegetables: Nectar*
Nectarines *See Fruits & Vegetables: Nectarines*
Neutral Spirits & Liqueurs *See Beverages: Spirits & Liqueurs: Neutral*
New England Chowder *See Prepared Foods: Soups & Stews: Chowder: New England*
New York Style Cheese Cake *See Baked Goods: Cakes & Pastries: Cheese Cake: New York Style*
Niacin *See Ingredients, Flavors & Additives: Vitamins & Supplements: Niacin*
No Salt Potato Chips *See Snack Foods: Chips: Potato: No Salt*
No-Fat Cheese *See Cheese & Cheese Products: Cheese: No-Fat*
No-Fat Yogurt *See Dairy Products: Yogurt: No-Fat*
Non-Alcoholic Beers *See Beverages: Beers: Non-Alcoholic*
Non-Alcoholic Beverages *See Beverages: Non-Alcoholic Beverages*
Non-Alcoholic Wines *See Beverages: Wines: Non-Alcoholic*
Non-Dairy & Imitation Dairy Bases *See Ingredients, Flavors & Additives: Bases: Dairy: Non-Dairy & Imitation*
Non-Dairy Coffee Creamers *See Dairy Products: Creamers: Coffee: Non-Dairy*
Non-Dairy Cream *See Dairy Products: Cream: Non-Dairy*
Non-Dairy Desserts *See Baked Goods: Desserts: Non-Dairy*
Non-Dairy Ice Cream *See Dairy Products: Ice Cream: Non-Dairy*
Non-Dairy Whipped Toppings *See Ingredients, Flavors & Additives: Toppings: Whipped: Non-Dairy*
Non-Fat Cheese Cake *See Baked Goods: Cakes & Pastries: Cheese Cake: Non-Fat*
Non-Fat Milk Solids *See Dairy Products: Milk & Milk Products: Milk Solids: Non-Fat*
Non-Fat Salad Dressings *See Sauces, Dips & Dressings: Salad Dressings: Non-Fat*
Non-Fruit Pies *See Baked Goods: Pies: Non-Fruit*
Non-Fruit Toppings *See Ingredients, Flavors & Additives: Toppings: Non-Fruit*
Non-Stick Coatings *See Ingredients, Flavors & Additives: Coatings: Non-Stick*
Nonpareils *See Candy & Confectionery: Candy: Nonpareils*
Noodles *See Pasta & Noodles: Noodles*
Nougats *See Candy & Confectionery: Candy: Nougats*
Novelties, Candy *See Candy & Confectionery: Candy: Novelties*
Novelties, Ice Cream *See Dairy Products: Ice Cream: Novelties*
Nut Breads *See Baked Goods: Breads: Nut*
Nut Butters *See Nuts & Nut Butters: Nut Butters*
Nut Flavors *See Ingredients, Flavors & Additives: Flavors: Nut*
Nut Flour *See Cereals, Grains, Rice & Flour: Flour: Nut*
Nut Meats *See Nuts & Nut Butters: Nuts: Nut Meats*
Nut Pastes *See Nuts & Nut Butters: Nut Pastes*
Nutmeg Spices *See Spices, Seasonings & Seeds: Spices: Nutmeg (See also Mace)*
Nutmeg Oils *See Oils, Shortening & Fats: Oils: Nutmeg*
Nutraceuticals *See Ingredients, Flavors & Additives: Vitamins & Supplements: Nutraceuticals*
Nutritional Supplements *See Ingredients, Flavors & Additives: Vitamins & Supplements: Nutritional Supplements*
Nuts *See Nuts & Nut Butters: Nuts*
NY Strip Steak *See Meats & Meat Products: Beef & Beef Products: NY Strip Steak*

O

Oat Bran *See Cereals, Grains, Rice & Flour: Oats & Oat Products: Oat Bran*
Oat Bran Fiber *See Cereals, Grains, Rice & Flour: Fiber: Oat Bran*
Oat Fiber Crisps *See Cereals, Grains, Rice & Flour: Crisps: Oat Fiber*
Oat Flour *See Cereals, Grains, Rice & Flour: Flour: Oat*
Oatmeal *See Cereals, Grains, Rice & Flour: Oats & Oat Products: Oatmeal*
Oatmeal & Chocolate Chip Cookies *See Baked Goods: Cookies & Bars: Oatmeal & Chocolate Chip Cookies*
Oatmeal Cereal *See Cereals, Grains, Rice & Flour: Cereal: Oatmeal*
Oatmeal Cookies *See Baked Goods: Cookies & Bars: Oatmeal Cookies*
Oatmeal Raisin Cookies *See Baked Goods: Cookies & Bars: Oatmeal Raisin Cookies*
Oats & Oat Products *See Cereals, Grains, Rice & Flour: Oats & Oat Products*
Oats Fiber *See Cereals, Grains, Rice & Flour: Fiber: Oats*
Oats Flakes *See Ingredients, Flavors & Additives: Flakes: Oats*
Ocean Perch *See Fish & Seafood: Fish: Perch: Ocean*
Octopus *See Fish & Seafood: Shellfish: Octopus*
Oil & Vinegar Salad Dressings *See Sauces, Dips & Dressings: Salad Dressings: Oil & Vinegar*
Oil & Vinegar Salad Dressings, Mixes *See Sauces, Dips & Dressings: Salad Dressings: Mixes: Oil & Vinegar*
Oils *See Oils, Shortening & Fats; See also See Oils, Shortening & Fats: Oils*
Okra *See Fruits & Vegetables: Okra*
Olive Loaf *See Meats & Meat Products: Smoked, Cured & Deli Meats: Olive Loaf*
Olive Oil Anchovies *See Fish & Seafood: Fish: Anchovies: Olive Oil*
Olive Oil Bread Sticks *See Baked Goods: Bread Sticks: Olive Oil*
Olive Oils *See Oils, Shortening & Fats: Oils: Olive*
Olive Spreads *See Jams, Jellies & Spreads: Spreads: Olive*
Olives *See Fruits & Vegetables: Olives*
One Percent Milk *See Dairy Products: Milk & Milk Products: Milk: 1 Percent*
Onion *See Fruits & Vegetables: Onion*
Onion Bread Sticks *See Baked Goods: Bread Sticks: Onion*
Onion for Dehydration *See Fruits & Vegetables: Dried & Dehydrated Vegetables: Onion: for Dehydration*
Onion Juices *See Beverages: Juices: Onion*
Onion Oils *See Oils, Shortening & Fats: Oils: Onion*
Onion Powders *See Ingredients, Flavors & Additives: Powders: Onion (See also Spices/Onion Powder)*
Onion Rings *See Prepared Foods: Onion Rings*
Onion Salt *See Spices, Seasonings & Seeds: Salt: Onion*
Onion Spices *See Spices, Seasonings & Seeds: Spices: Onion*
Onion, Dried & Dehydrated *See Fruits & Vegetables: Dried & Dehydrated Vegetables: Onion*

EXAMPLE: **Canadian Style Bacon** [1] *See* Meats & Meat Products[2]: Smoked, Cured & Deli Meats[3]: Bacon[4]: Canadian Style[5]

1. Product or Service you are looking for
2. Main Category, in alphabetical order, located in the page headers starting on page 27
3. Category Description, located in black bars and in page headers
4. Product Category, located in gray bars
5. Product Type, located under gray bars, centered in bold

Product Category List

Oolong Tea *See Beverages: Coffee & Tea: Tea: Oolong*
Orange *See Fruits & Vegetables: Orange*
Orange Ade Juices *See Beverages: Juices: Ade: Orange*
Orange Flavors *See Ingredients, Flavors & Additives: Flavors: Orange*
Orange Juices *See Beverages: Juices: Orange*
Orange Juices, Not Concentrated *See Beverages: Juices: Orange: Not Concentrated*
Orange Oils *See Oils, Shortening & Fats: Oils: Orange*
Orange Peel Pieces *See Fruits & Vegetables: Orange: Peels: Pieces*
Orange Pekoe Tea *See Beverages: Coffee & Tea: Tea: Orange Pekoe*
Orange Puree *See Fruits & Vegetables: Pulps & Purees: Puree: Orange*
Orange Roughy *See Fish & Seafood: Fish: Orange Roughy*
Orange Sauces *See Sauces, Dips & Dressings: Sauces: Orange*
Orange Sections *See Fruits & Vegetables: Orange: Sections*
Oregano Spices *See Spices, Seasonings & Seeds: Spices: Oregano*
Organic *See Baby Foods: Organic; See also Organic Foods*
Organic Carrot *See Fruits & Vegetables: Carrot: Organic; See also Organic Foods*
Organic Foods *See also Specialty & Organic Foods: Organic Foods*
Organic Pellets *See Ingredients, Flavors & Additives: Half-Products: Organic Pellets; See also Organic Foods*
Organic Rice *See Cereals, Grains, Rice & Flour: Rice: Organic; See also Organic Foods*
Organic Sauces *See Sauces, Dips & Dressings: Sauces: Organic; See also Organic Foods*
Oriental *See Ethnic Foods: Oriental*
Oriental Mustard *See Sauces, Dips & Dressings: Mustard: Oriental*
Oriental Noodles *See Pasta & Noodles: Noodles: Oriental*
Oriental Vegetables *See Fruits & Vegetables: Oriental Vegetables*
Orzo Pasta *See Pasta & Noodles: Pasta: Orzo*
Osaka Purple Mustard *See Fruits & Vegetables: Mustard: Osaka Purple*
Ostrich *See Meats & Meat Products: Game: Ostrich*
Oven Type Potatoes *See Fruits & Vegetables: Potatoes: Oven Type*
Oyster Mushrooms *See Fruits & Vegetables: Mushrooms: Oyster*
Oyster Mushrooms, Dried *See Fruits & Vegetables: Dried & Dehydrated Vegetables: Mushrooms: Oyster*
Oyster Sauces *See Sauces, Dips & Dressings: Sauces: Oyster*
Oysters *See Fish & Seafood: Shellfish: Oysters*

P

Packaged Meats *See Meats & Meat Products: Packaged*
Packed Fish *See Fish & Seafood: Fish: Packed*
Paella *See Ethnic Foods: Paella*
Pale Ale *See Beverages: Beers: American & British Ale: Pale Ale*
Palm Kernel Oils *See Oils, Shortening & Fats: Oils: Palm: Kernel*
Palm Oils *See Oils, Shortening & Fats: Oils: Palm*
Pan Coatings & Sprays *See Oils, Shortening & Fats: Pan Coatings & Sprays*
Pancake Batters *See Doughs, Mixes & Fillings: Batters: Pancake*
Pancake Flour *See Cereals, Grains, Rice & Flour: Flour: Pancake*
Pancake Mixes *See Doughs, Mixes & Fillings: Mixes: Pancake*
Pancake Syrups *See Sugars, Syrups & Sweeteners: Syrups: Pancake*
Pancakes *See Prepared Foods: Pancakes*
Pancakes with Fruit *See Prepared Foods: Pancakes: with Fruit*
Panettones *See Baked Goods: Cakes & Pastries: Panettones*
Pantothenic Acid *See Ingredients, Flavors & Additives: Vitamins & Supplements: Pantothenic Acid*
Papaya *See Fruits & Vegetables: Papaya*
Papaya Juices *See Beverages: Juices: Papaya*
Paprika *See Spices, Seasonings & Seeds: Spices: Paprika*
Paraffin Waxes *See Ingredients, Flavors & Additives: Waxes: Paraffin*
Parboiled Rice *See Cereals, Grains, Rice & Flour: Rice: Parboiled*
Parmesan Cheese *See Cheese & Cheese Products: Cheese: Parmesan*
Parmesan Cheese, Imitation *See Cheese & Cheese Products: Imitation Cheeses & Substitutes: Imitation: Parmesan*
Parmesan Salad Dressing Mixes *See Sauces, Dips & Dressings: Salad Dressings: Mixes: Parmesan*
Parsley Spices *See Spices, Seasonings & Seeds: Spices: Parsley*
Particulates *See Ingredients, Flavors & Additives: Particulates*
Partridge *See Meats & Meat Products: Game: Partridge*
Parve Foods *See Ethnic Foods: Parve Foods*
Passion Fruit Flavors *See Ingredients, Flavors & Additives: Flavors: Passion Fruit*
Passion Fruit Juices *See Beverages: Juices: Passion Fruit*
Pasta *See Pasta & Noodles: Pasta*
Pasta & Noodle Dishes *See Prepared Foods: Prepared Meals: Pasta & Noodle Dishes*
Pasta & Noodles *See Pasta & Noodles*
Pasta Prepared Salads *See Prepared Foods: Prepared Salads: Pasta*
Pasta Sauces *See Sauces, Dips & Dressings: Sauces: Pasta*
Pastes *See Ingredients, Flavors & Additives: Pastes*
Pastrami *See Meats & Meat Products: Smoked, Cured & Deli Meats: Pastrami*
Pastries *See Baked Goods: Cakes & Pastries: Pastries*
Pastry Flour *See Cereals, Grains, Rice & Flour: Flour: Pastry*
Pates *See Meats & Meat Products: Pates & Foie Gras: Pates*
Pates & Foie Gras *See Meats & Meat Products: Pates & Foie Gras*
Patti Sausages *See Meats & Meat Products: Smoked, Cured & Deli Meats: Sausages: Patti*
Patties, Beef *See Meats & Meat Products: Beef & Beef Products: Patties*
Patties, Breaded Chicken *See Meats & Meat Products: Poultry: Chicken: Patties Breaded*
Patties, Chicken *See Meats & Meat Products: Poultry: Chicken: Patties*
Patties, Fish *See Fish & Seafood: Fish: Patties*
Patties, Vegetarian *See Specialty & Organic Foods: Vegetarian Products: Patties; See also Organic Foods*
Pau D'Arco Bark Powders *See Ingredients, Flavors & Additives: Powders: Pau D'Arco Bark*
Peach *See Fruits & Vegetables: Peach*
Peach Flavors *See Ingredients, Flavors & Additives: Flavors: Peach*
Peach Juices *See Beverages: Juices: Peach*
Peach Pies *See Baked Goods: Pies: Peach*
Peaches, Sliced *See Fruits & Vegetables: Peach: Sliced*
Peanut Brittle *See Candy & Confectionery: Candy: Peanut Brittle*
Peanut Butter *See Nuts & Nut Butters: Nut Butters: Peanut Butter*
Peanut Butter Chips *See Snack Foods: Chips: Peanut Butter*
Peanut Butter, No Additives *See Nuts & Nut Butters: Nut Butters: Peanut Butter: No Additives*
Peanut Butter, Smooth *See Nuts & Nut Butters: Nut Butters: Peanut Butter: Smooth*
Peanut Flour *See Cereals, Grains, Rice & Flour: Flour: Peanut*
Peanut Oils *See Oils, Shortening & Fats: Oils: Peanut*
Peanut Sauces *See Sauces, Dips & Dressings: Sauces: Peanut*
Peanut Seeds *See Spices, Seasonings & Seeds: Seeds: Peanut*
Peanuts *See Nuts & Nut Butters: Nuts: Peanuts*
Pear *See Fruits & Vegetables: Pear*
Pear Flavors *See Ingredients, Flavors & Additives: Flavors: Pear*
Pear Juices *See Beverages: Juices: Pear*
Pear, Canned Halves *See Fruits & Vegetables: Pear: Canned: Halves*
Pearl & Cocktail Onions *See Fruits & Vegetables: Onion: Pearl & Cocktail Onions*
Pearl Tapioca *See Cereals, Grains, Rice & Flour: Tapioca: Pearl*
Peas *See Fruits & Vegetables: Peas*
Peas & Carrots *See Fruits & Vegetables: Vegetables Mixed: Peas & Carrots*
Peas, Air-dried *See Fruits & Vegetables: Dried & Dehydrated Vegetables: Peas - Air-dried*
Pecan Butter Flavors *See Ingredients, Flavors & Additives: Flavors: Butter: Pecan*
Pecan Log *See Baked Goods: Cakes & Pastries: Pecan Log*
Pecan Nuts *See Nuts & Nut Butters: Nuts: Pecan*
Pecorino *See Cheese & Cheese Products: Cheese: Pecorino*
Pectin Gums *See Ingredients, Flavors & Additives: Gums: Pectin*
Pectins *See Ingredients, Flavors & Additives: Pectins*
Peeled Carrot *See Fruits & Vegetables: Carrot: Peeled*
Peeled Eggs *See Eggs & Egg Products: Peeled*
Peeled Shrimp *See Fish & Seafood: Shellfish: Shrimp: Peeled*
Peels, Citrus Fruits *See Fruits & Vegetables: Citrus Fruits: Peels*
Peels, Lemon *See Fruits & Vegetables: Lemon: Peels*
Peels, Orange *See Fruits & Vegetables: Orange: Peels*
Peking Duck *See Meats & Meat Products: Game: Peking Duck*
Penne *See Pasta & Noodles: Penne*
Pentanol *See Ingredients, Flavors & Additives: Alcohols: Pentanol*
Pepatello *See Cheese & Cheese Products: Cheese: Pepatello*
Pepper *See Spices, Seasonings & Seeds: Spices: Pepper*
Pepper Blends *See Ingredients, Flavors & Additives: Blends: Pepper*
Pepper Mash *See Spices, Seasonings & Seeds: Spices: Pepper Mash*
Pepper Oils *See Oils, Shortening & Fats: Oils: Pepper*
Pepper Sauces *See Sauces, Dips & Dressings: Sauces: Pepper*
Peppercorn Salad Dressing Mixes *See Sauces, Dips & Dressings: Salad Dressings: Mixes: Peppercorn*
Peppercorns *See Spices, Seasonings & Seeds: Spices: Peppercorns*
Peppermint *See Spices, Seasonings & Seeds: Spices: Peppermint*
Peppermint Flavors *See Ingredients, Flavors & Additives: Flavors: Peppermint*
Peppermint Leaf Tea *See Beverages: Coffee & Tea: Tea: Peppermint Leaf*
Peppermint Oils *See Oils, Shortening & Fats: Oils: Peppermint*
Pepperoncini Peppers *See Fruits & Vegetables: Peppers: Pepperoncini*
Pepperoni *See Meats & Meat Products: Smoked, Cured & Deli Meats: Pepperoni*
Pepperoni Salami *See Meats & Meat Products: Smoked, Cured & Deli Meats: Salami: Pepperoni*
Peppers *See Fruits & Vegetables: Peppers*
Peppers, Pickled *See Relishes & Pickled Products: Pickled Products: Peppers*
Perch *See Fish & Seafood: Fish: Perch*
Persimmons *See Fruits & Vegetables: Persimmons*
Pesto Sauces *See Sauces, Dips & Dressings: Sauces: Pesto*
Petit Fours *See Baked Goods: Cakes & Pastries: Petit Fours*
Pheasant *See Meats & Meat Products: Game: Pheasant*
Phosphates *See Ingredients, Flavors & Additives: Phosphates*
Phosphoric Acidulants *See Ingredients, Flavors & Additives: Acidulants: Phosphoric*
Picante Salsa *See Sauces, Dips & Dressings: Salsa: Picante*
Pickerel *See Fish & Seafood: Fish: Pickerel*
Pickled Ginger *See Fruits & Vegetables: Ginger: Pickled*
Pickled Meat Products *See Relishes & Pickled Products: Pickled Products: Meats*
Pickled Products *See Relishes & Pickled Products: Pickled Products*
Pickles *See Relishes & Pickled Products: Pickled Products: Pickles*
Pickling Spices *See Spices, Seasonings & Seeds: Spices: Pickling Spices*
Pie Crust Mixes *See Doughs, Mixes & Fillings: Mixes: Pie Crust*
Pie Fillings *See Doughs, Mixes & Fillings: Fillings: Pie*
Pierogies *See Prepared Foods: Pierogies*
Pies *See Baked Goods: Pies*
Pignolias Nuts *See Nuts & Nut Butters: Nuts: Pignolias*
Pigs' Feet *See Meats & Meat Products: Pork & Pork Products: Pigs' Feet*
Pike *See Fish & Seafood: Fish: Pike*
Pilsner Lager *See Beverages: Beers: Lager: Pilsner*
Pimiento Oils *See Oils, Shortening & Fats: Oils: Pimiento*
Pimientos *See Fruits & Vegetables: Pimientos*
Pine Nuts *See Nuts & Nut Butters: Nuts: Pine*
Pineapple *See Fruits & Vegetables: Pineapple*
Pineapple Flavors *See Ingredients, Flavors & Additives: Flavors: Pineapple*
Pineapple Juices *See Beverages: Juices: Pineapple*
Pink Beans *See Fruits & Vegetables: Beans: Pink*
Pink Grapefruit *See Fruits & Vegetables: Grapefruit: Pink*
Pink Salmon *See Fish & Seafood: Fish: Salmon: Pink*
Pinot Blanc *See Beverages: Wines: White Grape Varieties: Pinot Blanc*
Pinot Gris *See Beverages: Wines: White Grape Varieties: Pinot Gris*
Pinot Noir *See Beverages: Wines: Red Grape Wines: Pinot Noir*
Pinto Beans *See Fruits & Vegetables: Beans: Pinto*
Pistachio Nuts *See Nuts & Nut Butters: Nuts: Pistachio*
Pita Breads *See Baked Goods: Breads: Pita*

Product Category List

Pita Chips *See Snack Foods: Chips: Pita*
Pizelle *See Prepared Foods: Pizelle*
Pizza *See Prepared Foods: Pizza & Pizza Products: Pizza*
Pizza & Pizza Products *See Prepared Foods: Pizza & Pizza Products*
Pizza Bagels *See Prepared Foods: Pizza & Pizza Products: Pizza Bagels*
Pizza Crust *See Prepared Foods: Pizza & Pizza Products: Pizza: Crust*
Pizza Doughs *See Doughs, Mixes & Fillings: Doughs: Pizza*
Pizza Sauces *See Sauces, Dips & Dressings: Sauces: Pizza*
Pizza Seasonings *See Spices, Seasonings & Seeds: Seasonings: Pizza*
Pizza Shells *See Prepared Foods: Pizza & Pizza Products: Shells*
Pizza Toppings *See Prepared Foods: Pizza & Pizza Products: Pizza Toppings*
Plantain Chips *See Snack Foods: Chips: Plantain*
Plantains *See Fruits & Vegetables: Banana: Plantain*
Plum Pudding *See Dairy Products: Pudding: Plum*
Plum Sauces *See Sauces, Dips & Dressings: Sauces: Plum*
Plum Tomato *See Fruits & Vegetables: Tomato: Plum*
Plums *See Fruits & Vegetables: Plums*
Pocket Sandwiches *See Prepared Foods: Prepared Meals: Sandwiches: Pocket*
Poi *See Cereals, Grains, Rice & Flour: Poi*
Polenta *See Pasta & Noodles: Pasta: Polenta*
Polish Sausages *See Meats & Meat Products: Smoked, Cured & Deli Meats: Sausages: Polish*
Pollack *See Fish & Seafood: Fish: Pollack*
Polythylene Glycols *See Ingredients, Flavors & Additives: Polythylene Glycols*
Pomace Apple *See Fruits & Vegetables: Apple: Pomace*
Pomace Olive Oils *See Oils, Shortening & Fats: Oils: Olive: Pomace*
Pomegranate *See Fruits & Vegetables: Pomegranate*
Pompano *See Fish & Seafood: Fish: Pompano*
Popcorn *See Snack Foods: Popcorn*
Popcorn Specialties *See Candy & Confectionery: Candy: Popcorn Specialties*
Popping Corn Oils *See Oils, Shortening & Fats: Oils: Popping Corn*
Poppy & Sesame Crackers *See Baked Goods: Crackers: Poppy & Sesame Crackers*
Poppy Seed Oils *See Oils, Shortening & Fats: Oils: Poppy Seed*
Poppy Seeds *See Spices, Seasonings & Seeds: Seeds: Poppy*
Popsicles *See Dairy Products: Ice Cream: Popsicles*
Porcini Mushrooms *See Fruits & Vegetables: Mushrooms: Porcini*
Porcini Mushrooms, Dried *See Fruits & Vegetables: Dried & Dehydrated Vegetables: Mushrooms: Porcini*
Pork & Beans *See Prepared Foods: Pork & Beans (see also Baked Beans)*
Pork & Pork Products *See Meats & Meat Products: Pork & Pork Products*
Pork Casings *See Meats & Meat Products: Smoked, Cured & Deli Meats: Sausages: Casings: Sausage, Pork, Beef*
Pork Frankfurters *See Meats & Meat Products: Frankfurters: Pork*
Pork Rinds *See Snack Foods: Pork Rinds*
Pork Sausages *See Meats & Meat Products: Smoked, Cured & Deli Meats: Sausages: Pork*
Porkskins *See Prepared Foods: Porkskins*
Porter *See Beverages: Beers: Stout & Porter: Porter*
Porterhouse Beef *See Meats & Meat Products: Beef & Beef Products: Porterhouse*
Portion Contol & Packaged Foods *See Prepared Foods: Portion Contol & Packaged Foods*
Portioned Juices *See Beverages: Juices: Portioned*
Portobello Mushrooms *See Fruits & Vegetables: Mushrooms: Portobello*
Portuguese Port Wines *See Beverages: Wines: Portuguese: Port*
Portuguese Wines *See Beverages: Wines: Portuguese*
Pot Pies *See Prepared Foods: Pot Pies*
Pot Roast *See Meats & Meat Products: Beef & Beef Products: Pot Roast*
Pot Stickers *See Prepared Foods: Pot Stickers*
Potassium Bitartrate *See Ingredients, Flavors & Additives: Potassium Bitartrate (Cream of Tartar)*
Potassium Bromate *See Ingredients, Flavors & Additives: Potassium Bromate*
Potassium Citrate *See Ingredients, Flavors & Additives: Potassium Citrate*

Potassium Lactate *See Ingredients, Flavors & Additives: Potassium Lactate*
Potassium Sorbate *See Ingredients, Flavors & Additives: Potassium Sorbate*
Potato Chips *See Snack Foods: Chips: Potato*
Potato Chips, No Salt *See Snack Foods: Chips: Potato: No Salt*
Potato Flakes *See Ingredients, Flavors & Additives: Flakes: Potato*
Potato Flour *See Cereals, Grains, Rice & Flour: Flour: Potato*
Potato Products *See Prepared Foods: Potato Products*
Potato Puffs, Frozen Products *See Prepared Foods: Potato Products: Puffs - Frozen*
Potato Starches *See Ingredients, Flavors & Additives: Starches: Potato*
Potato Sticks *See Snack Foods: Potato Sticks*
Potato, Prepared Salads *See Prepared Foods: Prepared Salads: Potato*
Potatoes *See Fruits & Vegetables: Potatoes; See also See Fruits & Vegetables: Potatoes: Potatoes*
Potatoes, Frozen Wedges *See Fruits & Vegetables: Potatoes: Frozen: Wedges*
Pouch-Packed Fish *See Fish & Seafood: Fish: Packed: Pouch*
Pouch-Packed Tuna Fish *See Fish & Seafood: Fish: Tuna: Pouch-Packed*
Poultry *See Meats & Meat Products: Poultry*
Poultry & Game *See Meats & Meat Products: Smoked, Cured & Deli Meats: Smoked Meat: Poultry & Game*
Poultry Flavors *See Ingredients, Flavors & Additives: Flavors: Poultry*
Poultry, Certified Organic *See Specialty & Organic Foods: Organic Foods: Certified: Poultry; See also Organic Foods*
Pound Cake *See Baked Goods: Cakes & Pastries: Pound Cake*
Powdered Broth *See Prepared Foods: Broth: Powdered*
Powdered Chicken Fats & Lard *See Oils, Shortening & Fats: Fats & Lard: Chicken: Powdered*
Powdered Fruit Juices *See Beverages: Juices: Powdered Fruit*
Powdered Garlic *See Spices, Seasonings & Seeds: Spices: Garlic: Powdered*
Powdered Mixes *See Doughs, Mixes & Fillings: Mixes: Powdered*
Powdered Sugar *See Sugars, Syrups & Sweeteners: Sugar: Powdered*
Powdered Vegetables *See Ingredients, Flavors & Additives: Powdered Vegetables*
Powders *See Ingredients, Flavors & Additives: Powders*
Powders Prepared for Further Processing *See Ingredients, Flavors & Additives: Powders: Prepared for Further Processing*
Pralines *See Nuts & Nut Butters: Nuts: Pralines (See also Confectionery)*
Prawns *See Fish & Seafood: Shellfish: Prawns*
Precooked Rice *See Cereals, Grains, Rice & Flour: Rice: Precooked*
Preformed Snack Pellets *See Snack Foods: Snack Pellets: Preformed*
Pregelatinized Powders *See Ingredients, Flavors & Additives: Powders: Pregelatinized*
Pregelatinized Starches *See Ingredients, Flavors & Additives: Starches: Pregelatinized*
Prepared Bases *See Ingredients, Flavors & Additives: Bases: Prepared*
Prepared Chicken *See Meats & Meat Products: Poultry: Chicken: Prepared*
Prepared Cocktail Mixes *See Beverages: Mixers: Prepared Cocktail Mixes*
Prepared Eggs *See Eggs & Egg Products: Eggs: Prepared*
Prepared Foods *See Prepared Foods*
Prepared Frozen Chicken *See Meats & Meat Products: Poultry: Chicken: Prepared Frozen*
Prepared Gravy *See Sauces, Dips & Dressings: Gravy: Prepared*
Prepared Meals *See Prepared Foods: Prepared Meals*
Prepared Mustard *See Spices, Seasonings & Seeds: Spices: Mustard: Prepared*
Prepared Pork & Pork Products *See Meats & Meat Products: Pork & Pork Products: Prepared*
Prepared Salads *See Prepared Foods: Prepared Salads*
Prepared Yams *See Fruits & Vegetables: Yams: Prepared*
Preservatives *See Ingredients, Flavors & Additives: Preservatives*

Pressed Dextrose Candy *See Candy & Confectionery: Candy: Pressed Dextrose*
Pretzels *See Snack Foods: Pretzels*
Pretzels, Sticks or Rods *See Snack Foods: Pretzels: Sticks or Rods*
Primary Dried Yeast *See Ingredients, Flavors & Additives: Cultures & Yeasts: Yeast: Primary Dried*
Primavera Sauces *See Sauces, Dips & Dressings: Sauces: Primavera*
Process Cheese Loaves *See Cheese & Cheese Products: Cheese: Process Loaves*
Process Sliced Cheese *See Cheese & Cheese Products: Cheese: Process Sliced*
Processed American Cheese *See Cheese & Cheese Products: Cheese: Processed American*
Processed Beef & Beef Products *See Meats & Meat Products: Beef & Beef Products: Processed*
Processed Coconut & Coconut Products *See Fruits & Vegetables: Coconut & Coconut Products: Processed*
Processed Swiss Cheese *See Cheese & Cheese Products: Cheese: Processed Swiss*
Processed Tomato *See Fruits & Vegetables: Tomato: Processed*
Produce *See Fruits & Vegetables: Produce*
Produce, Certified Organic *See Specialty & Organic Foods: Organic Foods: Certified: Produce; See also Organic Foods*
Products, Beef *See Meats & Meat Products: Beef & Beef Products: Products*
Products, Cranberry *See Fruits & Vegetables: Berries: Cranberry: Products*
Products, Tomato *See Fruits & Vegetables: Tomato: Products*
Propanol Alcohols *See Ingredients, Flavors & Additives: Alcohols: Propanol*
Propylene Glycols *See Ingredients, Flavors & Additives: Alcohols: Propylene Glycols*
Prosciutto *See Meats & Meat Products: Smoked, Cured & Deli Meats: Prosciutto*
Protein Clusters Toppings *See Ingredients, Flavors & Additives: Toppings: Protein Clusters*
Protein Powders *See Ingredients, Flavors & Additives: Powders: Protein*
Protein Supplements *See Ingredients, Flavors & Additives: Vitamins & Supplements: Protein Supplements*
Protein, Rice *See Cereals, Grains, Rice & Flour: Rice: Protein*
Protein, Soy *See Fruits & Vegetables: Soy: Protein*
Proteins *See Ingredients, Flavors & Additives: Proteins*
Provolone *See Cheese & Cheese Products: Cheese: Provolone*
Prune Juices *See Beverages: Juices: Prune*
Prunes *See Fruits & Vegetables: Prunes*
Pudding *See Dairy Products: Pudding*
Puff Pastry *See Baked Goods: Cakes & Pastries: Puff Pastry*
Puff Pastry Doughs *See Doughs, Mixes & Fillings: Doughs: Puff Pastry*
Pulp *See Fruits & Vegetables: Pulps & Purees: Pulp*
Pulps & Purees *See Fruits & Vegetables: Pulps & Purees*
Pumpernickel *See Baked Goods: Breads: Pumpernickel*
Pumpkin *See Fruits & Vegetables: Pumpkin*
Pumpkin Seed Oils *See Oils, Shortening & Fats: Oils: Pumpkin Seed*
Pumpkin Seeds *See Spices, Seasonings & Seeds: Seeds: Pumpkin*
Punch Mixes *See Doughs, Mixes & Fillings: Mixes: Punch*
Punch Powders *See Ingredients, Flavors & Additives: Powders: Punch*
Puree *See Fruits & Vegetables: Pulps & Purees: Puree*
Purple Sticky Rice *See Cereals, Grains, Rice & Flour: Rice: Purple Sticky*
Puttanesca Sauces *See Sauces, Dips & Dressings: Sauces: Puttanesca*

Q

Quail *See Meats & Meat Products: Game: Quail (See also Eggs: Quail)*
Quail Eggs *See Eggs & Egg Products: Eggs: Quail*
Quiche *See Prepared Foods: Quiche*
Quince *See Fruits & Vegetables: Quince*
Quinoa *See Cereals, Grains, Rice & Flour: Quinoa*

EXAMPLE: **Canadian Style Bacon** *See Meats & Meat Products: Smoked, Cured & Deli Meats: Bacon: Canadian Style*
(1) (2) (3) (4) (5)

1. Product or Service you are looking for
2. Main Category, in alphabetical order, located in the page headers starting on page 27
3. Category Description, located in black bars and in page headers
4. Product Category, located in gray bars
5. Product Type, located under gray bars, centered in bold

Product Category List

R

Rabbit *See Meats & Meat Products: Game: Rabbit*
Radish *See Fruits & Vegetables: Radish*
Rainbow Trout *See Fish & Seafood: Fish: Trout: Rainbow*
Raisin Breads *See Baked Goods: Breads: Raisin*
Raisin Juice Replacers *See Ingredients, Flavors & Additives: Replacers: Raisin Juice*
Raisin Juices *See Beverages: Juices: Raisin*
Raisins *See Fruits & Vegetables: Raisins*
Ramen Noodles *See Pasta & Noodles: Noodles: Ramen*
Ranch Salad Dressing *See Sauces, Dips & Dressings: Salad Dressings: Ranch*
Ranch Salad Dressing Mixes *See Sauces, Dips & Dressings: Salad Dressings: Mixes: Ranch*
Ranch Snack Seasonings *See Spices, Seasonings & Seeds: Seasonings: Snack: Ranch*
Rape Seeds *See Spices, Seasonings & Seeds: Seeds: Rape*
Raschera *See Cheese & Cheese Products: Cheese: Raschera*
Raspberries *See Fruits & Vegetables: Berries: Raspberries*
Raspberry Flavors *See Ingredients, Flavors & Additives: Flavors: Raspberry*
Raspberry Juices *See Beverages: Juices: Raspberry*
Raspberry Vinegar *See Sauces, Dips & Dressings: Vinegar: Raspberry*
Raspberry Vinegrette Salad Dressing *See Sauces, Dips & Dressings: Salad Dressings: Raspberry Vinegrette*
Raspberry Vinegrette Salad Dressing Mixes *See Sauces, Dips & Dressings: Salad Dressings: Mixes: Raspberry Vinegrette*
Ravioli *See Pasta & Noodles: Ravioli*
Raw & Shelled Peanuts *See Nuts & Nut Butters: Nuts: Peanuts: Raw & Shelled*
Raw Beef & Beef Products *See Meats & Meat Products: Beef & Beef Products: Raw*
Raw Chicken *See Meats & Meat Products: Poultry: Chicken: Raw*
Raw Crayfish *See Fish & Seafood: Shellfish: Crayfish: Raw*
Raw Peanuts *See Nuts & Nut Butters: Nuts: Peanuts: Raw*
Raw Pork & Pork Products *See Meats & Meat Products: Pork & Pork Products: Raw*
Raw Turkey *See Meats & Meat Products: Poultry: Turkey: Raw*
Raw Veal *See Meats & Meat Products: Beef & Beef Products: Veal: Raw*
Ready to Use Icings *See Candy & Confectionery: Decorations & Icings: Icings: Ready to Use*
Red Bell Peppers, Dried *See Fruits & Vegetables: Dried & Dehydrated Vegetables: Bell Peppers: Red*
Red Bordeaux *See Beverages: Wines: French: Red Bordeaux*
Red Burgundy *See Beverages: Wines: French: Red Burgundy*
Red Cabbage *See Fruits & Vegetables: Cabbage: Red*
Red Currants *See Fruits & Vegetables: Berries: Currants: Red*
Red Delicious Apple *See Fruits & Vegetables: Apple: Red Delicious*
Red Grape Wines *See Beverages: Wines: Red Grape Wines; See also Beverages: Wines: Red Grapes*
Red Looseleaf Lettuce *See Fruits & Vegetables: Lettuce: Looseleaf: Red*
Red Meritage/Bordeaux *See Beverages: Wines: Red Grape Wines: Red Meritage/Bordeaux*
Red Onion *See Fruits & Vegetables: Onion: Red*
Red Pear *See Fruits & Vegetables: Pear: Red*
Red Pepper *See Spices, Seasonings & Seeds: Spices: Red Pepper; See also See Spices, Seasonings & Seeds: Pepper: Black - White - Red*
Red Potatoes *See Fruits & Vegetables: Potatoes: Red*
Reduced-Calorie Beer *See Beverages: Beers: Specialty & Cider: Reduced Calorie Beer*
Reduced-Calorie Salad Dressing Mixes *See Sauces, Dips & Dressings: Salad Dressings: Mixes: Reduced-Calorie*
Reduced-Fat Cheddar Cheese *See Cheese & Cheese Products: Cheese: Cheddar: Reduced Fat*
Reduced-Fat Milk *See Dairy Products: Milk & Milk Products: Milk: Reduced-Fat*
Reduced-Fat Shredded Cheddar Cheese *See Cheese & Cheese Products: Cheese: Cheddar: Reduced Fat - Shredded*
Refried Beans *See Fruits & Vegetables: Beans: Refried*
Refrigerated Appetizers *See Prepared Foods: Appetizers: Refrigerated*
Refrigerated Apple Juices *See Beverages: Juices: Apple: Refrigerated*
Refrigerated Apricot Juices *See Beverages: Juices: Apricot: Refrigerated*
Refrigerated Buns *See Baked Goods: Breads: Buns: Refrigerated*
Refrigerated Cherry Juices *See Beverages: Juices: Cherry: Refrigerated*
Refrigerated Cranberry Juices *See Beverages: Juices: Cranberry: Refrigerated*
Refrigerated Egg Substitutes *See Eggs & Egg Products: Substitutes: Refrigerated*
Refrigerated Fruit Juices *See Beverages: Juices: Fruit: Refrigerated*
Refrigerated Grape Juices *See Beverages: Juices: Grape: Refrigerated*
Refrigerated Grapefruit Juices *See Beverages: Juices: Grapefruit: Refrigerated*
Refrigerated Juices *See Beverages: Juices: Refrigerated*
Refrigerated Lemon Juices *See Beverages: Juices: Lemon: Refrigerated*
Refrigerated Pancakes *See Prepared Foods: Pancakes: Refrigerated*
Refrigerated Pineapple Juices *See Beverages: Juices: Pineapple: Refrigerated*
Regular & Lowfat Bakery Mix *See Cereals, Grains, Rice & Flour: Flour: Bakery Mix: Regular & Lowfat*
Regular Chili Powders *See Ingredients, Flavors & Additives: Powders: Chili: Regular*
Release, Grease Agents *See Ingredients, Flavors & Additives: Agents: Release, Grease*
Releases *See Ingredients, Flavors & Additives: Releases*
Relishes *See Relishes & Pickled Products: Relishes*
Relishes & Condiments *See Relishes & Pickled Products: Relishes: Relishes & Condiments*
Replacers *See Ingredients, Flavors & Additives: Replacers*
Replacers, Milk Solids *See Dairy Products: Milk & Milk Products: Milk Solids: Replacers*
Resistant Starch Fiber *See Cereals, Grains, Rice & Flour: Fiber: Resistant Starch*
Rhubarb *See Fruits & Vegetables: Rhubarb*
Rhubarb Pie *See Baked Goods: Pies: Rhubarb Pie*
Rib Center Cut Pork *See Meats & Meat Products: Pork & Pork Products: Rib Center Cut*
Rib Chop Lamb *See Meats & Meat Products: Lamb: Rib Chop*
Rib Chop Veal *See Meats & Meat Products: Beef & Beef Products: Veal: Rib Chop*
Rib Eye Roast Beef *See Meats & Meat Products: Beef & Beef Products: Rib Eye Roast*
Rib Eye Steak *See Meats & Meat Products: Beef & Beef Products: Rib Eye Steak*
Rib Rub Seasonings *See Spices, Seasonings & Seeds: Seasonings: Rib Rub*
Rib Steak *See Meats & Meat Products: Beef & Beef Products: Rib Steak*
Rice *See Cereals, Grains, Rice & Flour: Rice*
Rice Bran *See Cereals, Grains, Rice & Flour: Bran: Rice*
Rice Bran Oils *See Oils, Shortening & Fats: Oils: Rice Bran*
Rice Cakes *See Snack Foods: Rice Cakes*
Rice Crisps *See Cereals, Grains, Rice & Flour: Crisps: Rice*
Rice Flour *See Cereals, Grains, Rice & Flour: Flour: Rice*
Rice Mixes *See Doughs, Mixes & Fillings: Mixes: Rice*
Rice Pilaf *See Cereals, Grains, Rice & Flour: Rice: Pilaf*
Rice Powders *See Ingredients, Flavors & Additives: Powders: Rice*
Rice Pudding *See Dairy Products: Pudding: Rice*
Rice Starches *See Ingredients, Flavors & Additives: Starches: Rice*
Rice Starches, Organic *See Specialty & Organic Foods: Organic Foods: Rice Starch; See also Organic Foods*
Rice, Bagged Parboiled *See Cereals, Grains, Rice & Flour: Rice: Parboiled: Bagged*
Rice, Parboiled, US #1 Long Grain *See Cereals, Grains, Rice & Flour: Rice: Parboiled: US #1 Long Grain*
Rice, Prepared Meals *See Prepared Foods: Prepared Meals: Rice*
Rice-Based Cereal *See Cereals, Grains, Rice & Flour: Cereal: Rice-Based*
Ricotta *See Cheese & Cheese Products: Cheese: Ricotta*
Riesling *See Beverages: Wines: White Grape Varieties: Riesling*
Rigatoni *See Pasta & Noodles: Rigatoni*
Riso *See Pasta & Noodles: Riso*
Risotto Rice *See Cereals, Grains, Rice & Flour: Rice: Risotto*
Roast Beef *See Meats & Meat Products: Beef & Beef Products: Roast Beef*
Roast Pork Tenderloin *See Meats & Meat Products: Pork & Pork Products: Tenderloin Roast*
Roasted Coffee *See Beverages: Coffee & Tea: Coffee: Roasted*
Roasted Garlic & Herb Crackers *See Baked Goods: Crackers: Roasted Garlic & Herb Crackers*
Roasted Nuts *See Nuts & Nut Butters: Nuts: Roasted*
Roasted Peanuts *See Nuts & Nut Butters: Nuts: Peanuts: Roasted*
Roasted Peppers *See Fruits & Vegetables: Peppers: Roasted*
Roasted Vegetables *See Fruits & Vegetables: Roasted Vegetables*
Rock Candy *See Candy & Confectionery: Candy: Rock*
Rock Fish *See Fish & Seafood: Fish: Rock Fish*
Rock Salt *See Spices, Seasonings & Seeds: Salt: Rock*
Rolled Oats *See Cereals, Grains, Rice & Flour: Oats & Oat Products: Rolled*
Rolls *See Baked Goods: Breads: Rolls*
Roma Tomato *See Fruits & Vegetables: Tomato: Roma (Egg)*
Romaine Lettuce *See Fruits & Vegetables: Lettuce: Romaine*
Romano *See Cheese & Cheese Products: Cheese: Romano*
Rome Beauty *See Fruits & Vegetables: Apple: Rome Beauty*
Root Beer Extracts *See Ingredients, Flavors & Additives: Extracts: Root Beer*
Root Beer Flavors *See Ingredients, Flavors & Additives: Flavors: Root Beer*
Roots & Tubers *See Fruits & Vegetables: Roots & Tubers*
Roquefort *See Cheese & Cheese Products: Cheese: Roquefort*
Rosellino *See Cheese & Cheese Products: Cheese: Rosellino*
Rosemary *See Spices, Seasonings & Seeds: Spices: Rosemary*
Rosemary Spices, Cut *See Spices, Seasonings & Seeds: Spices: Rosemary: Cut*
Rotelle *See Pasta & Noodles: Rotelle*
Rotini *See Pasta & Noodles: Rotini*
Royal Jellies *See Jams, Jellies & Spreads: Jellies: Royal*
Rubbed Sage *See Spices, Seasonings & Seeds: Spices: Sage: Rubbed*
Rugulach *See Baked Goods: Cakes & Pastries: Rugulach*
Rum *See Beverages: Spirits & Liqueurs: Rum*
Rum Cake *See Baked Goods: Cakes & Pastries: Rum Cake*
Rum Flavors *See Ingredients, Flavors & Additives: Flavors: Rum*
Rusk *See Baked Goods: Cakes & Pastries: Rusk*
Russet Potatoes, Fresh *See Fruits & Vegetables: Potatoes: Fresh: Russet*
Rutabaga *See Fruits & Vegetables: Rutabaga*
Rye *See Cereals, Grains, Rice & Flour: Rye*
Rye Breads *See Baked Goods: Breads: Rye*
Rye Flour *See Cereals, Grains, Rice & Flour: Flour: Rye*

S

Sablefish *See Fish & Seafood: Fish: Sablefish*
Saccharin *See Sugars, Syrups & Sweeteners: Sugar Substitutes: Saccharin*
Safflower Oils *See Oils, Shortening & Fats: Oils: Safflower*
Saffron *See Spices, Seasonings & Seeds: Spices: Saffron*
Sage *See Spices, Seasonings & Seeds: Spices: Sage*
Sage Leaves *See Spices, Seasonings & Seeds: Spices: Sage: Leaves*
Sage Oils *See Oils, Shortening & Fats: Oils: Sage*
Sake *See Beverages: Wines: Japanese: Sake*
Salad Dressings *See Sauces, Dips & Dressings: Salad Dressings*
Salad Greens *See Fruits & Vegetables: Salad Greens*
Salad Oils *See Oils, Shortening & Fats: Oils: Salad*
Salad, Prepared Meals *See Prepared Foods: Prepared Meals: Salad*
Salami *See Meats & Meat Products: Smoked, Cured & Deli Meats: Salami*
Salmon *See Fish & Seafood: Fish: Salmon*
Salmon Caviar *See Fish & Seafood: Caviar (Roe): Salmon*
Salmon Sausages *See Meats & Meat Products: Smoked, Cured & Deli Meats: Sausages: Salmon*
Salmon Steak *See Fish & Seafood: Fish: Salmon: Steak*
Salmon, Prepared Salads *See Prepared Foods: Prepared Salads: Salmon*
Salsa *See Sauces, Dips & Dressings: Salsa*
Salsa Dips *See Sauces, Dips & Dressings: Dips: Salsa*
Salsa with Cheese *See Sauces, Dips & Dressings: Salsa: with Cheese*
Salt *See Spices, Seasonings & Seeds: Salt*
Salt Anchovies *See Fish & Seafood: Fish: Anchovies: Salt*
Salt Substitutes *See Spices, Seasonings & Seeds: Salt: Substitutes*
Salt-free Chili Powders *See Ingredients, Flavors & Additives: Powders: Chili: Salt-free*
Salted & Marinated Herring *See Fish & Seafood: Fish: Herring: Salted & Marinated*
Salted Almonds *See Nuts & Nut Butters: Nuts: Almonds: Salted*
Salted Butter *See Dairy Products: Butter: Salted*
Salted Fish *See Fish & Seafood: Fish: Salted*
Salted Peanuts *See Nuts & Nut Butters: Nuts: Peanuts: Salted*
Salted Pecans *See Nuts & Nut Butters: Nuts: Pecan: Salted*

Product Category List

Salted Potato Chips *See Snack Foods: Chips: Potato: Salted*
Sandwich Creme Cookies *See Baked Goods: Cookies & Bars: Sandwich Creme Cookies*
Sandwiches, Prepared Meals *See Prepared Foods: Prepared Meals: Sandwiches*
Sangiovese *See Beverages: Wines: Red Grape Wines: Sangiovese*
Sardines *See Fish & Seafood: Fish: Sardines*
Sarsaparilla *See Beverages: Soft Drinks & Sodas: Soft Drinks: Sarsaparilla*
Sassafras Oils *See Oils, Shortening & Fats: Oils: Sassafras*
Sauce Bases *See Ingredients, Flavors & Additives: Bases: Sauce*
Sauces *See Fruits & Vegetables: Sauces; See also Sauces, Dips & Dressings: Sauces*
Sauerkraut *See Relishes & Pickled Products: Sauerkraut*
Sauerkraut Juice *See Relishes & Pickled Products: Sauerkraut: Juice*
Sausage Binders *See Ingredients, Flavors & Additives: Binders: Sausage*
Sausage Casings *See Meats & Meat Products: Smoked, Cured & Deli Meats: Sausages: Casings: Sausage, Pork, Beef*
Sausage Seasonings *See Spices, Seasonings & Seeds: Seasonings: Sausage*
Sausage, Pork *See Meats & Meat Products: Pork & Pork Products: Sausage*
Sausage, Smoked *See Meats & Meat Products: Smoked, Cured & Deli Meats: Sausages*
Sausage, Turkey *See Meats & Meat Products: Poultry: Turkey: Sausage*
Sauvignon Blanc *See Beverages: Wines: White Grape Varieties: Sauvignon Blanc*
Savory *See Spices, Seasonings & Seeds: Spices: Savory*
Saw Palmetto Berry Powders *See Ingredients, Flavors & Additives: Powders: Saw Palmetto Berry*
Scallions *See Fruits & Vegetables: Scallions*
Scallops *See Fish & Seafood: Shellfish: Scallops*
Scampi *See Fish & Seafood: Shellfish: Scampi*
Scampi, Prepared Meals *See Prepared Foods: Prepared Meals: Scampi*
Schnapps Liqueur *See Beverages: Spirits & Liqueurs: Liqueurs & Cordials: Schnapps Liqueur*
Scones *See Baked Goods: Breads: Scones*
Scotch Whiskey *See Beverages: Spirits & Liqueurs: Scotch Whiskey*
Scrapple *See Meats & Meat Products: Pork & Pork Products: Scrapple*
Sea Bass *See Fish & Seafood: Fish: Sea Bass*
Sea Salt *See Spices, Seasonings & Seeds: Salt: Sea*
Sea Trout *See Fish & Seafood: Fish: Sea Trout*
Seafood *See Fish & Seafood: Seafood*
Seafood Bases *See Ingredients, Flavors & Additives: Bases: Seafood*
Seafood Extracts *See Ingredients, Flavors & Additives: Extracts: Seafood*
Seafood Flavors *See Ingredients, Flavors & Additives: Flavors: Seafood*
Seafood Powders *See Ingredients, Flavors & Additives: Powders: Seafood*
Seafood Ravioli *See Pasta & Noodles: Ravioli: Seafood*
Seafood Salad *See Fish & Seafood: Seafood: Salad*
Seafood Sauces *See Sauces, Dips & Dressings: Sauces: Seafood*
Seafood Soup Bases *See Ingredients, Flavors & Additives: Bases: Soup: Seafood*
Seafood, Prepared Meals *See Prepared Foods: Prepared Meals: Seafood*
Seafood, Prepared Salads *See Prepared Foods: Prepared Salads: Seafood*
Seasoning Powders *See Ingredients, Flavors & Additives: Powders: Seasoning*
Seasonings *See Spices, Seasonings & Seeds: Seasonings*
Seasonings for Corned Beef *See Spices, Seasonings & Seeds: Seasonings: for Corned Beef*
Seasonings for Tacos *See Spices, Seasonings & Seeds: Seasonings: for Tacos*
Seaweeds & Sea Vegetables *See Fruits & Vegetables: Seaweeds & Sea Vegetables*
Seedless Watermelon *See Fruits & Vegetables: Melon: Watermelon: Seedless*
Seeds *See Spices, Seasonings & Seeds: Seeds*
Self-Rising Flour *See Cereals, Grains, Rice & Flour: Flour: Self-Rising*
Semolina *See Pasta & Noodles: Semolina*

Semolina Flour *See Cereals, Grains, Rice & Flour: Flour: Semolina*
Serrano Peppers *See Fruits & Vegetables: Peppers: Serrano*
Sesame Bread Sticks *See Baked Goods: Bread Sticks: Sesame*
Sesame Oils *See Oils, Shortening & Fats: Oils: Sesame*
Sesame Seeds *See Spices, Seasonings & Seeds: Seeds: Sesame*
Shad *See Fish & Seafood: Fish: Shad*
Shad Caviar *See Fish & Seafood: Caviar (Roe): Shad*
Shallot *See Fruits & Vegetables: Shallot*
Shallots *See Spices, Seasonings & Seeds: Spices: Shallots*
Shallots, Freeze-Dried *See Fruits & Vegetables: Dried & Dehydrated Vegetables: Shallots - Freeze Dried*
Shark *See Fish & Seafood: Fish: Shark*
Sheephead *See Fish & Seafood: Fish: Sheephead*
Shelf Stable Entrees *See Prepared Foods: Prepared Meals: Entrees: Shelf Stable*
Shelled Nuts *See Nuts & Nut Butters: Nuts: Shelled*
Shellfish *See Fish & Seafood: Shellfish: Shellfish; See also Fish & Seafood: Shellfish*
Shells *See Ethnic Foods: Shells; See also Pasta & Noodles: Shells*
Sherbet *See Dairy Products: Ice Cream: Sherbet*
Sherry *See Beverages: Wines: Spanish: Sherry*
Sherry Vinegar *See Sauces, Dips & Dressings: Vinegar: Sherry*
Shiitake *See Fruits & Vegetables: Mushrooms: Shiitake; See also Fruits & Vegetables: Dried & Dehydrated Vegetables: Mushrooms: Shiitake Whole*
Shoestring French Fries *See Prepared Foods: French Fries: Shoestring*
Shoofly Mixes *See Doughs, Mixes & Fillings: Mixes: Shoofly*
Shoofly Pie *See Baked Goods: Pies: Shoofly Pie*
Short Breads *See Baked Goods: Breads: Short*
Shortening *See Oils, Shortening & Fats; See also See Oils, Shortening & Fats: Shortening*
Shredded Cheddar Cheese *See Cheese & Cheese Products: Cheese: Cheddar: Shredded*
Shrimp *See Fish & Seafood: Shellfish: Shrimp*
Shrimp, Frozen Scampi *See Prepared Foods: Prepared Meals: Scampi: Shrimp Frozen*
Sicilian Style Sausages *See Meats & Meat Products: Smoked, Cured & Deli Meats: Sausages: Sicilian Style (with Cheese)*
Siciliano Salami *See Meats & Meat Products: Smoked, Cured & Deli Meats: Salami: Siciliano*
Single & Blended Enrichment & Nutrient Additives *See Ingredients, Flavors & Additives: Additives: Enrichment & Nutrient: Single & Blended*
Sirloin Cubes *See Meats & Meat Products: Beef & Beef Products: Sirloin Cubes*
Skim Milk *See Dairy Products: Milk & Milk Products: Milk: Skim*
Sliced Beef & Beef Products *See Meats & Meat Products: Beef & Beef Products: Sliced*
Sliced Blend, American/Skim Milk Cheese *See Cheese & Cheese Products: Cheese: Blend - American/Skim Milk: Sliced*
Sliced Peaches *See Fruits & Vegetables: Peach: Sliced*
Slushes *See Dairy Products: Ice Cream: Slushes*
Small Red Beans *See Fruits & Vegetables: Beans: Small Red*
Smelt *See Fish & Seafood: Fish: Smelt*
Smoke Flavors *See Ingredients, Flavors & Additives: Flavors: Smoke*
Smoked & Cured Fish *See Fish & Seafood: Fish: Smoked & Cured*
Smoked Ham *See Meats & Meat Products: Smoked, Cured & Deli Meats: Ham: Smoked*
Smoked Meat *See Meats & Meat Products: Smoked, Cured & Deli Meats: Smoked Meat*
Smoked Salmon *See Fish & Seafood: Fish: Salmon: Smoked*
Smoked Sausages *See Meats & Meat Products: Smoked, Cured & Deli Meats: Sausages: Smoked*
Smoked Seafood *See Fish & Seafood: Seafood: Smoked*
Smoked Shellfish *See Fish & Seafood: Shellfish: Smoked*
Smoked Turkey *See Meats & Meat Products: Smoked, Cured & Deli Meats: Turkey: Smoked*
Smoked, Cured & Deli Meats *See Meats & Meat Products: Smoked, Cured & Deli Meats*
Smooth Peanut Butter *See Nuts & Nut Butters: Nut Butters: Peanut Butter: Smooth*

Smoothie Powder Mixes *See Doughs, Mixes & Fillings: Mixes: Smoothie Powder*
Smoothie Powders *See Ingredients, Flavors & Additives: Powders: Smoothie*
Smoothies *See Beverages: Smoothies*
Snack Foods *See Snack Foods*
Snack Pellets *See Snack Foods: Snack Pellets*
Snack Seasonings *See Spices, Seasonings & Seeds: Seasonings: Snack*
Snails *See Fish & Seafood: Shellfish: Snails*
Snake Beans *See Fruits & Vegetables: Beans: Snake*
Snap Peas *See Fruits & Vegetables: Peas: Snap*
Snapper *See Fish & Seafood: Fish: Snapper*
Snow Crab *See Fish & Seafood: Shellfish: Crab: Snow*
Sockeye Salmon *See Fish & Seafood: Fish: Salmon: Sockeye*
Soda Water *See Beverages: Soft Drinks & Sodas: Soda Water*
Sodium *See Ingredients, Flavors & Additives: Sodium*
Sodium Alginates *See Ingredients, Flavors & Additives: Sodium Alginates*
Sodium Benzoate *See Ingredients, Flavors & Additives: Sodium Benzoate*
Sodium Citrate *See Ingredients, Flavors & Additives: Sodium Citrate*
Sodium Phosphate *See Ingredients, Flavors & Additives: Phosphates: Sodium Phosphate*
Soft Cookies *See Baked Goods: Cookies & Bars: Soft Cookies*
Soft Drinks & Sodas *See Beverages: Soft Drinks & Sodas; See also Beverages: Soft Drinks & Sodas: Soft Drinks*
Soft Pretzels *See Snack Foods: Pretzels: Soft*
Soft Shell Crab *See Fish & Seafood: Shellfish: Crab: Soft Shell*
Sole *See Fish & Seafood: Fish: Sole*
Solids *See Eggs & Egg Products: Solids*
Solubilizers *See Ingredients, Flavors & Additives: Surfactants & Solubilizers: Solubilizers*
Sorbet *See Dairy Products: Ice Cream: Sorbet*
Sorbic Acidulants *See Ingredients, Flavors & Additives: Acidulants: Sorbic*
Sorbitol *See Ingredients, Flavors & Additives: Sweeteners: Sorbitol*
Sorghum *See Cereals, Grains, Rice & Flour: Sorghum*
Sorrel *See Spices, Seasonings & Seeds: Spices: Sorrel*
Soup Bases *See Ingredients, Flavors & Additives: Bases: Soup*
Soup Blend *See Fruits & Vegetables: Dried & Dehydrated Vegetables: Soup Blend*
Soup Mixes *See Doughs, Mixes & Fillings: Mixes: Soup*
Soups & Stews *See Prepared Foods: Soups & Stews*
Sour Cream *See Dairy Products: Sour Cream*
Sour Cream & Onion Potato Chips *See Snack Foods: Chips: Potato: Sour Cream & Onion*
Sour Cream & Onion Snack Seasonings *See Spices, Seasonings & Seeds: Seasonings: Snack: Sour Cream & Onion*
Sour Cream Flavors *See Ingredients, Flavors & Additives: Flavors: Sour: Cream*
Sour Flavors *See Ingredients, Flavors & Additives: Flavors: Sour*
Sourdough Breads *See Baked Goods: Breads: Sourdough*
Southern Peas *See Fruits & Vegetables: Peas: Southern*
Southwest Seasonings *See Spices, Seasonings & Seeds: Seasonings: Southwest*
Soy *See Fruits & Vegetables: Soy*
Soy Bean *See Fruits & Vegetables: Soy: Soy Bean*
Soy Bean Meal *See Cereals, Grains, Rice & Flour: Soy Bean Meal*
Soy Bran Fiber *See Cereals, Grains, Rice & Flour: Fiber: Soy Bran*
Soy Crisps *See Cereals, Grains, Rice & Flour: Crisps: Soy*
Soy Crumbs Toppings *See Ingredients, Flavors & Additives: Toppings: Soy Crumbs*
Soy Flakes *See Ingredients, Flavors & Additives: Flakes: Soy*
Soy Frankfurters *See Meats & Meat Products: Frankfurters: Soy*
Soy Milk *See Fruits & Vegetables: Soy: Soy Milk*
Soy Milk Powders *See Ingredients, Flavors & Additives: Powders: Soy Milk*
Soy Nuts *See Nuts & Nut Butters: Nuts: Soy*
Soy Powders *See Ingredients, Flavors & Additives: Powders: Soy*
Soy Protein *See Fruits & Vegetables: Soy: Soy Protein*

EXAMPLE: **Canadian Style Bacon** *See Meats & Meat Products: Smoked, Cured & Deli Meats: Bacon: Canadian Style*
(1) (2) (3) (4) (5)

1. Product or Service you are looking for
2. Main Category, in alphabetical order, located in the page headers starting on page 27
3. Category Description, located in black bars and in page headers
4. Product Category, located in gray bars
5. Product Type, located under gray bars, centered in bold

Product Category List

Soy Protein Flour See Cereals, Grains, Rice & Flour: Flour: Soy Protein
Soy Sauces See Sauces, Dips & Dressings: Sauces: Soy
Soybean Flour See Cereals, Grains, Rice & Flour: Flour: Soybean
Soybean Oils See Oils, Shortening & Fats: Oils: Soybean
Spaghetti See Pasta & Noodles: Spaghetti
Spaghetti Sauces See Sauces, Dips & Dressings: Sauces: Spaghetti
Spaghetti with Meatballs See Prepared Foods: Prepared Meals: Spaghetti: with Meatballs
Spaghetti, Prepared Meals See Prepared Foods: Prepared Meals: Spaghetti
Spanish Onion See Fruits & Vegetables: Onion: Spanish
Spanish Rice See Cereals, Grains, Rice & Flour: Rice: Spanish
Spanish Wines See Beverages: Wines: Spanish
Spareribs See Meats & Meat Products: Pork & Pork Products: Spareribs
Sparkling Apple Boysenberry Juices See Beverages: Juices: Apple Boysenberry: Sparkling
Sparkling Apple Cider Juices See Beverages: Juices: Apple Cider: Sparkling
Sparkling Apple Cranberry Juices See Beverages: Juices: Apple Cranberry: Sparkling
Sparkling Apple Grape Juices See Beverages: Juices: Apple Grape: Sparkling
Sparkling Apple Juices See Beverages: Juices: Apple: Sparkling
Sparkling Water See Beverages: Soft Drinks & Sodas: Sparkling Water
Sparkling Wines See Beverages: Wines: Sparkling (See also French/Champagne)
Spearmint See Spices, Seasonings & Seeds: Spices: Spearmint
Spearmint Flavors See Ingredients, Flavors & Additives: Flavors: Spearmint
Spearmint Leaves See Spices, Seasonings & Seeds: Spices: Mint Leaves: Spearmint
Specialty & Cider Beers See Beverages: Beers: Specialty & Cider
Specialty Bread Crumbs See Ingredients, Flavors & Additives: Toppings: Specialty Bread Crumbs
Specialty-Packaged Candy See Candy & Confectionery: Specialty-Packaged Candy
Specialty-Packaged Candy, Bagged See Candy & Confectionery: Specialty-Packaged Candy: Bagged
Specialty-Packaged Candy, Boxed See Candy & Confectionery: Specialty-Packaged Candy: Boxed
Specialty-Packaged Candy, Boxed Non-Chocolate See Candy & Confectionery: Specialty-Packaged Candy: Non-Chocolate - Boxed
Specialty-Packaged Candy, Christmas See Candy & Confectionery: Specialty-Packaged Candy: Christmas
Specialty-Packaged Candy, Easter See Candy & Confectionery: Specialty-Packaged Candy: Easter
Specialty-Packaged Candy, Fund-Raising See Candy & Confectionery: Specialty-Packaged Candy: Fund Raising
Specialty-Packaged Candy, Halloween See Candy & Confectionery: Specialty-Packaged Candy: Halloween
Specialty-Packaged Candy, Multi-Packs See Candy & Confectionery: Specialty-Packaged Candy: Multi-Packs
Specialty-Packaged Candy, Packaged for Racks See Candy & Confectionery: Specialty-Packaged Candy: Packaged for Racks
Specialty-Packaged Candy, Packaged for Theaters See Candy & Confectionery: Specialty-Packaged Candy: Packaged for Theaters
Specialty-Packaged Candy, Valentine See Candy & Confectionery: Specialty-Packaged Candy: Valentine
Specialty-Packaged Candy, Vending See Candy & Confectionery: Specialty-Packaged Candy: Vending
Spelt See Pasta & Noodles: Spelt
Spelt Flour See Cereals, Grains, Rice & Flour: Flour: Spelt
Spice Seeds See Spices, Seasonings & Seeds: Seeds: Spice
Spiced Herring See Fish & Seafood: Fish: Herring: Spiced
Spices See Spices, Seasonings & Seeds: Spices
Spinach See Fruits & Vegetables: Spinach
Spinach Pasta See Pasta & Noodles: Spinach
Spinach Powder See Fruits & Vegetables: Dried & Dehydrated Vegetables: Spinach Powder
Spirits & Liqueurs See Beverages: Spirits & Liqueurs
Spirulina See Ingredients, Flavors & Additives: Spirulina
Sponge Cake See Baked Goods: Cakes & Pastries: Sponge Cake
Sponge Gourd See Fruits & Vegetables: Sponge Gourd
Sports Drinks See Beverages: Sports Drinks
Spray Cooking Oils See Oils, Shortening & Fats: Oils: Cooking: Spray
Spreads See Jams, Jellies & Spreads: Spreads
Spring Rolls See Ethnic Foods: Egg Rolls: Spring Rolls
Spring Water See Beverages: Water: Spring

Spring Wheat See Cereals, Grains, Rice & Flour: Wheat: Spring
Sprinkles See Ingredients, Flavors & Additives: Toppings: Sprinkles
Sprouts See Fruits & Vegetables: Sprouts
Squab See Meats & Meat Products: Game: Squab
Squash See Fruits & Vegetables: Squash
Squid See Fish & Seafood: Shellfish: Squid
St. John's Wort See Ingredients, Flavors & Additives: Powders: St. John's Wort
Stabilizers See Ingredients, Flavors & Additives: Stabilizers
Star Anise See Spices, Seasonings & Seeds: Spices: Star Anise; See also See Spices, Seasonings & Seeds: Spices: Anise - Star
Star Fruit See Fruits & Vegetables: Star Fruit
Starches See Ingredients, Flavors & Additives: Starches
Starter Media See Ingredients, Flavors & Additives: Starter Media
Steak See Meats & Meat Products: Beef & Beef Products: Steak
Steak Sauces See Sauces, Dips & Dressings: Sauces: Steak
Steaks See Meats & Meat Products: Steaks
Stewed Tomato See Fruits & Vegetables: Tomato: Stewed
Sticky Buns See Baked Goods: Breads: Buns: Sticky
Stir-Fry Sauces See Sauces, Dips & Dressings: Sauces: Stir-Fry
Stone Crab See Fish & Seafood: Shellfish: Crab: Stone
Stone Crab Claws See Fish & Seafood: Shellfish: Crab: Claws Stone
Stored Corn See Fruits & Vegetables: Corn: Stored
Stout & Porter Beers See Beverages: Beers: Stout & Porter
Strawberry See Fruits & Vegetables: Berries: Strawberry
Strawberry Flavors See Ingredients, Flavors & Additives: Flavors: Strawberry
Strawberry Jams See Jams, Jellies & Spreads: Jams: Strawberry
Strawberry Juices See Beverages: Juices: Strawberry
Strawberry Milk See Dairy Products: Milk & Milk Products: Milk: Strawberry
Strawberry Shortcake See Baked Goods: Cakes & Pastries: Strawberry Shortcake
String Cheese See Cheese & Cheese Products: Cheese: String
Striped Bass See Fish & Seafood: Fish: Bass: Striped
Strudel See Baked Goods: Cakes & Pastries: Strudel
Stuffed Cabbage, Prepared Meals See Prepared Foods: Prepared Meals: Stuffed Cabbage
Stuffed Crab See Fish & Seafood: Shellfish: Crab: Stuffed
Stuffed Crab, Prepared Meals See Prepared Foods: Prepared Meals: Crab: Stuffed
Stuffed Fish, Prepared Meals See Prepared Foods: Prepared Meals: Fish: Stuffed
Stuffed Peppers, Prepared Meals See Prepared Foods: Prepared Meals: Stuffed Peppers
Stuffed Shells See Pasta & Noodles: Stuffed Shells
Stuffed Shells Prepared Meals See Prepared Foods: Prepared Meals: Stuffed Shells
Stuffing See Baked Goods: Stuffing; See also Prepared Foods: Stuffing
Stuffing for Meat See Baked Goods: Stuffing: for Meat
Stuffing for Poultry See Baked Goods: Stuffing: for Poultry
Sturgeon See Fish & Seafood: Fish: Sturgeon
Substitutes, Cheese See Cheese & Cheese Products: Imitation Cheeses & Substitutes: Substitutes
Substitutes, Egg See Eggs & Egg Products: Substitutes
Substitutes, Salt See Spices, Seasonings & Seeds: Salt: Substitutes
Succotash See Fruits & Vegetables: Succotash
Sucrose See Sugars, Syrups & Sweeteners: Sucrose
Sugar See Sugars, Syrups & Sweeteners: Sugar
Sugar Alternatives See Sugars, Syrups & Sweeteners: Sugar Substitutes: Sugar Alternatives
Sugar Beets See Fruits & Vegetables: Beets: Sugar
Sugar Cookies See Baked Goods: Cookies & Bars: Sugar Cookies
Sugar Substitutes See Sugars, Syrups & Sweeteners: Sugar Substitutes
Sugar Wafers See Baked Goods: Cookies & Bars: Wafers: Sugar
Sugar-Free Foods See Specialty & Organic Foods: Dietary Products: Sugar-Free Foods; See also Organic Foods
Sugars, Syrups & Sweeteners See Sugars, Syrups & Sweeteners
Sumac Berries See Spices, Seasonings & Seeds: Spices: Sumac Berries
Sun Tea See Beverages: Coffee & Tea: Tea: Sun
Sun-Dried Fruit See Fruits & Vegetables: Sun Dried Fruit
Sun-Dried Tomato See Fruits & Vegetables: Tomato: Sun-Dried
Sundae Toppings See Sugars, Syrups & Sweeteners: Syrups: Toppings: Sundae

Sunflower See Fruits & Vegetables: Sunflower
Sunflower Oils See Oils, Shortening & Fats: Oils: Sunflower
Sunflower Seeds See Spices, Seasonings & Seeds: Seeds: Sunflower
Supplements See Ingredients, Flavors & Additives: Vitamins & Supplements: Supplements
Supplements, Fiber See Cereals, Grains, Rice & Flour: Fiber: Supplements
Surfactants & Solubilizers See Ingredients, Flavors & Additives: Surfactants & Solubilizers
Survival Foods See Specialty & Organic Foods: Survival Foods; See also Organic Foods
Sushi See Fish & Seafood: Sushi
Swamp Cabbage See Fruits & Vegetables: Cabbage: Swamp
Swedish Meat Balls See Prepared Foods: Meat Balls: Swedish
Sweet & Sour Sauces See Sauces, Dips & Dressings: Sauces: Sweet & Sour
Sweet Cherries See Fruits & Vegetables: Cherries: Sweet
Sweet Corn See Fruits & Vegetables: Corn: Sweet
Sweet Italian Sausage Seasonings See Spices, Seasonings & Seeds: Seasonings: Sausage: Sweet Italian
Sweet Italian Sausages See Meats & Meat Products: Smoked, Cured & Deli Meats: Sausages: Sweet Italian
Sweet Peppers See Fruits & Vegetables: Peppers: Sweet
Sweet Pickles See Relishes & Pickled Products: Pickled Products: Pickles: Sweet
Sweet Potatoes See Fruits & Vegetables: Sweet Potatoes
Sweet Processed Corn See Fruits & Vegetables: Corn: Sweet Processed
Sweet Rolls See Baked Goods: Breads: Rolls: Sweet
Sweet Salami See Meats & Meat Products: Smoked, Cured & Deli Meats: Salami: Sweet
Sweet Sausages See Meats & Meat Products: Smoked, Cured & Deli Meats: Sausages: Sweet
Sweet Stout See Beverages: Beers: Stout & Porter: Sweet Stout
Sweetened & Condensed Milk See Dairy Products: Milk & Milk Products: Milk: Sweetened & Condensed
Sweetened Milk See Dairy Products: Milk & Milk Products: Milk: Sweetened
Sweeteners See Ingredients, Flavors & Additives: Sweeteners
Swiss Cheese See Cheese & Cheese Products: Cheese: Swiss
Swordfish See Fish & Seafood: Fish: Swordfish
Synthetic Glycerine See Ingredients, Flavors & Additives: Synthetic Glycerine
Syrah Red Grape Wines See Beverages: Wines: Red Grape Wines: Syrah
Syrup Malt See Cereals, Grains, Rice & Flour: Malt: Syrup
Syrups See Sugars, Syrups & Sweeteners: Syrups
Szechuan Sauces See Sauces, Dips & Dressings: Sauces: Szechuan

T

Tabbouleh See Ethnic Foods: Tabbouleh
Table Grape See Fruits & Vegetables: Grape: Table
Tabletizing Compacting Agents See Ingredients, Flavors & Additives: Agents: Compacting: Tabletizing
Taco Chips See Snack Foods: Chips: Taco
Taco Fillings See Ethnic Foods: Tacos: Fillings
Taco Sauces See Sauces, Dips & Dressings: Sauces: Taco
Taco Shells See Ethnic Foods: Shells: Taco
Tacos See Ethnic Foods: Tacos
Taffy See Candy & Confectionery: Candy: Taffy
Tagliatelle See Pasta & Noodles: Tagliatelle
Tahini Sauces See Sauces, Dips & Dressings: Sauces: Tahini
Taleggio See Cheese & Cheese Products: Cheese: Taleggio
Tamales See Ethnic Foods: Tamales
Tamarind See Fruits & Vegetables: Tamarind
Tandoori See Spices, Seasonings & Seeds: Spices: Tandoori
Tangelos See Fruits & Vegetables: Tangelos
Tangerine Juices See Beverages: Juices: Tangerine
Tangerine Oils See Oils, Shortening & Fats: Oils: Tangerine
Tangerines See Fruits & Vegetables: Tangerines
Tapioca See Cereals, Grains, Rice & Flour: Tapioca
Tapioca Flour See Cereals, Grains, Rice & Flour: Flour: Tapioca
Tapioca Pudding See Dairy Products: Pudding: Tapioca
Tapioca Starches See Ingredients, Flavors & Additives: Starches: Tapioca
Taquitos See Ethnic Foods: Taquitos
Tara See Ingredients, Flavors & Additives: Gums: Tara
Taro See Fruits & Vegetables: Taro
Tarragon See Spices, Seasonings & Seeds: Spices: Tarragon

Product Category List

Tart Cherries See Fruits & Vegetables: Cherries: Tart
Tartar See Spices, Seasonings & Seeds: Spices: Tartar
Tartar Sauces See Sauces, Dips & Dressings: Sauces: Tartar
Tartaric Acidulants See Ingredients, Flavors & Additives: Acidulants: Tartaric
Tarts See Baked Goods: Cakes & Pastries: Tarts
Tartufo See Fruits & Vegetables: Tartufo
Tasso See Meats & Meat Products: Smoked, Cured & Deli Meats: Tasso
Tater Tots See Prepared Foods: French Fries: Tater Tots
Tea See Beverages: Coffee & Tea: Tea
Tea Bags See Beverages: Coffee & Tea: Tea: Bags
Tea Cookies See Baked Goods: Cookies & Bars: Tea Cookies
Tea Extracts See Ingredients, Flavors & Additives: Extracts: Tea
Tea Flavors See Ingredients, Flavors & Additives: Flavors: Tea
Tea, Fair-Trade See Beverages: Coffee & Tea: Tea: Fair-Trade
Teas See Spices, Seasonings & Seeds: Spices: Teas
Tempeh See Ethnic Foods: Tempeh
Tenderizers See Ingredients, Flavors & Additives: Tenderizers
Tenderizing Compounds See Ingredients, Flavors & Additives: Compounds: Tenderizing
Tequila and Mezcal See Beverages: Spirits & Liqueurs: Tequila and Mezcal
Teriyaki Sauces See Sauces, Dips & Dressings: Sauces: Teriyaki
Texture Modifiers Agents See Ingredients, Flavors & Additives: Modifiers: Texture
Textured Vegetable Protein See Fruits & Vegetables: Textured Vegetable Protein
Texturized Soy Protein See Fruits & Vegetables: Soy: Protein: Texturized; See also Fruits & Vegetables: Soy: Soy Protein: Texturized
Thick Bacon Slices See Meats & Meat Products: Smoked, Cured & Deli Meats: Bacon: Slices Thick
Thickeners See Ingredients, Flavors & Additives: Thickeners
Thickening Agents See Ingredients, Flavors & Additives: Agents: Thickening
Thin Boiling Starches See Ingredients, Flavors & Additives: Starches: Thin Boiling
Thousand Island Salad Dressing See Sauces, Dips & Dressings: Salad Dressings: Thousand Island
Thousand Island Salad Dressing Mixes See Sauces, Dips & Dressings: Salad Dressings: Mixes: Thousand Island
Thyme See Spices, Seasonings & Seeds: Spices: Thyme
Thyme Oils See Oils, Shortening & Fats: Oils: Thyme
Tilapia See Fish & Seafood: Fish: Tilapia
Tiramisu See Baked Goods: Cakes & Pastries: Tiramisu
Toasted Breads See Baked Goods: Breads: Toasted
Toffee See Candy & Confectionery: Candy: Toffee
Tofu Powders See Ingredients, Flavors & Additives: Powders: Tofu
Tomatillos See Fruits & Vegetables: Tomatillos
Tomato See Fruits & Vegetables: Tomato
Tomato Concentrates See Ingredients, Flavors & Additives: Concentrates: Tomato
Tomato Juices See Beverages: Juices: Tomato
Tomato Pastes See Ingredients, Flavors & Additives: Pastes: Tomato
Tomato Pesto Seasonings See Spices, Seasonings & Seeds: Seasonings: Tomato Pesto
Tomato Powder See Fruits & Vegetables: Dried & Dehydrated Vegetables: Tomatoes: Tomato Powder; See also Ingredients, Flavors & Additives: Powders: Tomato
Tomato Pulps & Purees See Fruits & Vegetables: Pulps & Purees: Tomato; See also Fruits & Vegetables: Pulps & Purees: Puree: Tomato
Tomato Sauce with Spices See Sauces, Dips & Dressings: Sauces: Tomato: with Spices
Tomato Sauces See Sauces, Dips & Dressings: Sauces: Tomato
Tomatoes, Dried See Fruits & Vegetables: Dried & Dehydrated Vegetables: Tomatoes
Tomatoes, Dried Halves See Fruits & Vegetables: Dried & Dehydrated Vegetables: Tomatoes: Halves
Tongue See Meats & Meat Products: Beef & Beef Products: Tongue
Toppings See Sugars, Syrups & Sweeteners: Syrups: Toppings; See also Ingredients, Flavors & Additives: Toppings

Tortellini See Pasta & Noodles: Tortellini
Tortes See Baked Goods: Cakes & Pastries: Tortes
Tortilla & Tortilla Products See Ethnic Foods: Tortilla & Tortilla Products
Tortilla Chips See Snack Foods: Chips: Tortilla
Tortillas See Ethnic Foods: Tortilla & Tortilla Products: Tortillas
Tortoni See Dairy Products: Ice Cream: Tortoni
Torula See Ingredients, Flavors & Additives: Cultures & Yeasts: Yeast: Torula Dried
Toscano Salami See Meats & Meat Products: Smoked, Cured & Deli Meats: Salami: Toscano
Tostadas See Ethnic Foods: Tostadas
Tragacanth See Ingredients, Flavors & Additives: Gums: Tragacanth
Trail Mix See Snack Foods: Trail Mix
Trail Mixes See Doughs, Mixes & Fillings: Mixes: Trail
Tricalcium Phosphate See Ingredients, Flavors & Additives: Agents: Anticaking: Tricalcium Phosphate
Tripe See Meats & Meat Products: Tripe
Tropical & Exotic Fruit See Fruits & Vegetables: Tropical & Exotic Fruit
Tropical Fruit Juices See Beverages: Juices: Tropical Fruits
Trout See Fish & Seafood: Fish: Trout
Truffles, Candy See Candy & Confectionery: Candy: Truffles
Truffles, Mushrooms See Fruits & Vegetables: Mushrooms: Truffles
Tubetti See Pasta & Noodles: Tubetti
Tuffoli See Pasta & Noodles: Tuffoli
Tuna See Fish & Seafood: Fish: Tuna
Tuna, Prepared Salads See Prepared Foods: Prepared Salads: Tuna
Turbot See Fish & Seafood: Fish: Turbot
Turkey See Meats & Meat Products: Poultry: Turkey
Turkey Dinner, Prepared Meals See Prepared Foods: Prepared Meals: Turkey Dinner
Turkey Frankfurters See Meats & Meat Products: Frankfurters: Turkey
Turkey Leg See Meats & Meat Products: Poultry: Turkey: Leg
Turkey Sausages See Meats & Meat Products: Smoked, Cured & Deli Meats: Sausages: Turkey
Turkey, Game See Meats & Meat Products: Game: Turkey
Turkey, Prepared Salads See Prepared Foods: Prepared Salads: Turkey
Turkey, Smoked See Meats & Meat Products: Smoked, Cured & Deli Meats: Turkey
Turmeric Natural Colors See Ingredients, Flavors & Additives: Colors: Natural: Turmeric
Turmeric Spices See Spices, Seasonings & Seeds: Spices: Turmeric
Turnip See Fruits & Vegetables: Turnip
Turnip Greens See Fruits & Vegetables: Turnip: Turnip Greens: Canned
Turnovers See Baked Goods: Cakes & Pastries: Turnovers
Turtle Seafood See Fish & Seafood: Seafood: Turtle
Twists Pretzels See Snack Foods: Pretzels: Twists
Two Percent Milk See Dairy Products: Milk & Milk Products: Milk: 2 Percent

U

Uncompounded Aroma Materials See Ingredients, Flavors & Additives: Aroma Chemicals & Materials: Materials: Uncompounded
Uncooked Frozen Hamburger See Meats & Meat Products: Beef & Beef Products: Hamburger: Uncooked Frozen
Unsalted Butter See Dairy Products: Butter: Unsalted

V

V.S. Cognac Three Star Brandy See Beverages: Spirits & Liqueurs: Brandy: V.S. Cognac Three Star
V.S.O.P. Cognac Brandy See Beverages: Spirits & Liqueurs: Brandy: V.S.O.P. Cognac
Vacuum Packed Coffee See Beverages: Coffee & Tea: Coffee: Vacuum Packed
Valencia Orange See Fruits & Vegetables: Orange: Valencia
Valentine Specialty-Packaged Candy See Candy & Confectionery: Specialty-Packaged Candy: Valentine
Valerian Root Powders See Ingredients, Flavors & Additives: Powders: Valerian Root

Vanilla Beans See Spices, Seasonings & Seeds: Spices: Vanilla Beans
Vanilla Butter Flavors See Ingredients, Flavors & Additives: Flavors: Butter: Vanilla
Vanilla Extracts See Ingredients, Flavors & Additives: Extracts: Vanilla
Vanilla Flavors See Ingredients, Flavors & Additives: Flavors: Vanilla
Vanilla Powders See Ingredients, Flavors & Additives: Powders: Vanilla
Vanilla Pudding See Dairy Products: Pudding: Vanilla
Vanilla Spices See Spices, Seasonings & Seeds: Spices: Vanilla
Vanillin Flavors See Ingredients, Flavors & Additives: Flavors: Vanillin
Variegates Flavors See Ingredients, Flavors & Additives: Flavors: Variegates
Veal See Meats & Meat Products: Beef & Beef Products: Veal
Veal Cutlet See Meats & Meat Products: Beef & Beef Products: Veal: Cutlet
Veal Sausages See Meats & Meat Products: Smoked, Cured & Deli Meats: Sausages: Veal
Vegetable Bases See Ingredients, Flavors & Additives: Bases: Vegetable
Vegetable Colors See Ingredients, Flavors & Additives: Colors: Vegetable
Vegetable Concentrates See Ingredients, Flavors & Additives: Concentrates: Vegetable
Vegetable Extracts See Ingredients, Flavors & Additives: Extracts: Vegetable
Vegetable Flavors See Ingredients, Flavors & Additives: Flavors: Vegetable
Vegetable Gum See Ingredients, Flavors & Additives: Gums: Vegetable Gum
Vegetable Juices See Beverages: Juices: Vegetable
Vegetable Mixes See Doughs, Mixes & Fillings: Mixes: Vegetable
Vegetable Oils See Oils, Shortening & Fats: Oils: Vegetable
Vegetable Proteins See Ingredients, Flavors & Additives: Hydrolyzed Products: Vegetable Proteins
Vegetable Pulp See Fruits & Vegetables: Pulps & Purees: Pulp: Vegetable
Vegetable Puree See Fruits & Vegetables: Pulps & Purees: Puree: Vegetable
Vegetable Ravioli See Pasta & Noodles: Ravioli: Vegetable
Vegetable Seeds See Spices, Seasonings & Seeds: Seeds: Vegetable
Vegetable Shortening See Oils, Shortening & Fats: Shortening: Vegetable
Vegetable Stuffing See Prepared Foods: Stuffing: Vegetable
Vegetables See Fruits & Vegetables: Vegetables
Vegetables, Mixed See Fruits & Vegetables: Vegetables Mixed
Vegetables, Organic See Specialty & Organic Foods: Organic Foods: Vegetables; See also Organic Foods
Vegetables, Pickled See Relishes & Pickled Products: Pickled Products: Vegetables
Vegetarian Products See Specialty & Organic Foods: Vegetarian Products; See also Organic Foods
Vegetarian, Prepared Meals See Prepared Foods: Prepared Meals: Vegetarian
Veggie & Rice Pellets See Ingredients, Flavors & Additives: Half-Products: Veggie & Rice Pellets
Vending Specialty-Packaged Candy See Candy & Confectionery: Specialty-Packaged Candy: Vending
Venison See Meats & Meat Products: Game: Venison
Venison Sausages See Meats & Meat Products: Smoked, Cured & Deli Meats: Sausages: Venison
Vermicelli See Pasta & Noodles: Vermicelli
Vinegar See Sauces, Dips & Dressings: Vinegar
Viognier See Beverages: Wines: White Grape Varieties: Viognier
Vitamin A See Ingredients, Flavors & Additives: Vitamins & Supplements: A
Vitamin C See Ingredients, Flavors & Additives: Vitamins & Supplements: C
Vitamin E See Ingredients, Flavors & Additives: Vitamins & Supplements: E - Tocopherol
Vitamin Oils See Oils, Shortening & Fats: Oils: Vitamin
Vitamins & Supplements See Ingredients, Flavors & Additives: Vitamins & Supplements; See also Ingredients, Flavors & Additives: Vitamins & Supplements: Supplements: Vitamins; See also Ingredients, Flavors & Additives: Vitamins & Supplements: Vit
Vodka See Beverages: Spirits & Liqueurs: Vodka

EXAMPLE: **Canadian Style Bacon** See Meats & Meat Products: Smoked, Cured & Deli Meats: Bacon: Canadian Style
(1) (2) (3) (4) (5)

1. Product or Service you are looking for
2. Main Category, in alphabetical order, located in the page headers starting on page 27
3. Category Description, located in black bars and in page headers
4. Product Category, located in gray bars
5. Product Type, located under gray bars, centered in bold

Product Category List

Volpino Salami *See Meats & Meat Products: Smoked, Cured & Deli Meats: Salami: Volpino*

W

Wafers *See Baked Goods: Cookies & Bars: Wafers*
Waffle Mixes *See Doughs, Mixes & Fillings: Mixes: Waffle*
Waffle Syrups *See Sugars, Syrups & Sweeteners: Syrups: Waffle*
Waffles *See Baked Goods: Waffles*
Walnut Oils *See Oils, Shortening & Fats: Oils: Walnut*
Walnuts Nuts *See Nuts & Nut Butters: Nuts: Walnuts*
Wasabi *See Spices, Seasonings & Seeds: Spices: Wasabi*
Water *See Beverages: Water*
Water Chestnuts *See Fruits & Vegetables: Water Chestnuts*
Water Pack Cherries *See Fruits & Vegetables: Cherries: Water Pack*
Watercress *See Fruits & Vegetables: Watercress*
Watermelon *See Fruits & Vegetables: Melon: Watermelon*
Watermelon, Seedless *See Fruits & Vegetables: Melon: Watermelon: Seedless*
Wax Beans *See Fruits & Vegetables: Beans: Wax*
Waxes *See Ingredients, Flavors & Additives: Waxes*
Waxy Maize Starches *See Ingredients, Flavors & Additives: Starches: Waxy Maize*
Waxy Starches *See Ingredients, Flavors & Additives: Starches: Waxy*
Wehani Rice *See Cereals, Grains, Rice & Flour: Rice: Wehani*
Wheat *See Cereals, Grains, Rice & Flour: Wheat*
Wheat Ale *See Beverages: Beers: Wheat: Wheat Ale*
Wheat Beers *See Beverages: Beers: Wheat*
Wheat Bran *See Cereals, Grains, Rice & Flour: Bran: Wheat*
Wheat Bran Fiber *See Cereals, Grains, Rice & Flour: Fiber: Wheat Bran*
Wheat Breads *See Baked Goods: Breads: Wheat*
Wheat Flakes *See Cereals, Grains, Rice & Flour: Wheat: Flakes*
Wheat Flour *See Cereals, Grains, Rice & Flour: Flour: Wheat*
Wheat Germ *See Cereals, Grains, Rice & Flour: Wheat: Germ*
Wheat Germ Oils *See Oils, Shortening & Fats: Oils: Wheat Germ*
Wheat Starches *See Ingredients, Flavors & Additives: Starches: Wheat*
Wheat, Bagged *See Cereals, Grains, Rice & Flour: Wheat: Bagged*
Wheat-Based Cereal *See Cereals, Grains, Rice & Flour: Cereal: Wheat-Based*
Whey & Whey Products *See Cereals, Grains, Rice & Flour: Whey & Whey Products*
Whey Crisps *See Cereals, Grains, Rice & Flour: Crisps: Whey*
Whey Protein Concentrates & Isolates *See Ingredients, Flavors & Additives: Concentrates: Whey Protein Concentrates & Isolates*
Whipped Cream *See Dairy Products: Cream: Whipped*
Whipped Toppings *See Ingredients, Flavors & Additives: Toppings: Whipped*
Whiskey, American *See Beverages: Spirits & Liqueurs: Whiskey, American*
Whiskey, Canadian *See Beverages: Spirits & Liqueurs: Whiskey, Canadian*
White Breads *See Baked Goods: Breads: White*
White Burgundy *See Beverages: Wines: French: White Burgundy*
White Chocolate Dipped Biscotti *See Baked Goods: Cookies & Bars: Biscotti: White Chocolate Dipped*
White Distilled Vinegar *See Sauces, Dips & Dressings: Vinegar: White Distilled*
White Fresh Potatoes *See Fruits & Vegetables: Potatoes: Fresh: White*
White Grape Wines *See Beverages: Wines: White Grape Varieties; See also See Beverages: Wines: White Grapes*
White Grapefruit *See Fruits & Vegetables: Grapefruit: White*
White Ground Pepper *See Spices, Seasonings & Seeds: Spices: Pepper: White Ground*
White Mushrooms *See Fruits & Vegetables: Mushrooms: White*
White Pepper *See Spices, Seasonings & Seeds: Spices: White Pepper; See also See Spices, Seasonings & Seeds: Spices: Pepper: Black - White - Red*
White Rice *See Cereals, Grains, Rice & Flour: Rice: White*
White Sesame Seeds *See Spices, Seasonings & Seeds: Seeds: Sesame: White*
White Silver Rum *See Beverages: Spirits & Liqueurs: Rum: White Silver*
White Unbleached Flour *See Cereals, Grains, Rice & Flour: Flour: White Unbleached*
White Whole Truffles *See Fruits & Vegetables: Mushrooms: Truffles: White Whole*
White/Yellow Process Sliced Cheese *See Cheese & Cheese Products: Cheese: Process Sliced: White/Yellow*
Whitefish *See Fish & Seafood: Fish: Whitefish*
Whiting *See Fish & Seafood: Fish: Whiting*
Whole & Dried Chili Pods *See Spices, Seasonings & Seeds: Spices: Chili Pods: Whole & Dried*
Whole Allspice *See Spices, Seasonings & Seeds: Spices: Allspice: Whole*
Whole Black Olives *See Fruits & Vegetables: Olives: Black: Whole*
Whole Broccoli *See Fruits & Vegetables: Broccoli: Whole*
Whole Cayenne Pepper *See Spices, Seasonings & Seeds: Spices: Cayenne Pepper: Whole*
Whole Cinnamon *See Spices, Seasonings & Seeds: Spices: Cinnamon: Whole*
Whole Clam *See Fish & Seafood: Shellfish: Clam: Whole*
Whole Coriander Seeds *See Spices, Seasonings & Seeds: Seeds: Coriander: Whole*
Whole Corn *See Fruits & Vegetables: Corn: Whole*
Whole Egg Solids *See Eggs & Egg Products: Solids: Whole Egg*
Whole Frozen Turkey *See Meats & Meat Products: Poultry: Turkey: Whole Frozen*
Whole Grain Muffins *See Baked Goods: Cakes & Pastries: Muffins: Whole Grain*
Whole Maraschino Cherries *See Fruits & Vegetables: Cherries: Maraschino: Whole*
Whole Milk *See Dairy Products: Milk & Milk Products: Milk: Whole*
Whole Milk Solids *See Dairy Products: Milk & Milk Products: Milk Solids: Whole*
Whole Nutmeg Spices *See Spices, Seasonings & Seeds: Spices: Nutmeg (See also Mace): Whole*
Whole Shiitake Mushrooms *See Fruits & Vegetables: Mushrooms: Shiitake: Whole*
Whole Threads Saffron *See Spices, Seasonings & Seeds: Spices: Saffron: Whole Threads*
Whole Wheat Bread Sticks *See Baked Goods: Bread Sticks: Whole Wheat*
Whole Wheat Flour *See Cereals, Grains, Rice & Flour: Flour: Whole wheat*
Whole wheat Pastry Flour *See Cereals, Grains, Rice & Flour: Flour: Whole wheat: Pastry*
Whole Yellow Mustard Seeds *See Spices, Seasonings & Seeds: Seeds: Mustard: Whole Yellow*
Wild Game *See Meats & Meat Products: Game: Wild*
Wild Mushrooms *See Fruits & Vegetables: Mushrooms: Wild*
Wild Rice *See Cereals, Grains, Rice & Flour: Rice: Wild*
Wild Turkey *See Meats & Meat Products: Game: Turkey: Wild*
Wine Flavors *See Ingredients, Flavors & Additives: Flavors: Wine*
Wine Grape *See Fruits & Vegetables: Grape: Wine*
Wine Vinegar *See Sauces, Dips & Dressings: Vinegar: Wine*
Wine Yeast *See Ingredients, Flavors & Additives: Cultures & Yeasts: Yeast: Wine*
Wines *See Beverages: Wines*
Winter Squash Pumpkin *See Fruits & Vegetables: Pumpkin: Winter Squash*
Winter Wheat *See Cereals, Grains, Rice & Flour: Wheat: Winter*
Wonton Chips *See Ethnic Foods: Wonton Chips*
Wonton Soup *See Prepared Foods: Soups & Stews: Wonton Soup*
Wontons *See Ethnic Foods: Wontons*
Wood Ear Mushrooms *See Fruits & Vegetables: Mushrooms: Wood Ear*
Wood Ear Mushrooms, Dried *See Fruits & Vegetables: Dried & Dehydrated Vegetables: Mushrooms: Wood Ears*
Wood Pigeon *See Meats & Meat Products: Game: Wood Pigeon*
Worcestershire Sauces *See Sauces, Dips & Dressings: Sauces: Worcestershire*
Wrappers, Egg Roll *See Ethnic Foods: Egg Rolls: Wrappers*
Wraps *See Baked Goods: Wraps*

X

X.O. Cognac Brandy *See Beverages: Spirits & Liqueurs: Brandy: X.O. Cognac*
Xanthan Gum *See Ingredients, Flavors & Additives: Gums: Xanthan Gum*

Y

Yams *See Fruits & Vegetables: Yams*
Yeast *See Ingredients, Flavors & Additives: Cultures & Yeasts: Yeast*
Yeast Extracts *See Ingredients, Flavors & Additives: Extracts: Yeast*
Yellow Cherry Tomato *See Fruits & Vegetables: Tomato: Yellow Cherry*
Yellow Mustard *See Sauces, Dips & Dressings: Mustard: Yellow*
Yellow Process Cheese Loaves *See Cheese & Cheese Products: Cheese: Process Loaves: Yellow*
Yellow Split Peas *See Fruits & Vegetables: Peas: Yellow Split*
Yellowfin Tuna *See Fish & Seafood: Fish: Tuna: Yellowfin*
Yogurt *See Dairy Products: Yogurt*
Yogurt Bacteria *See Ingredients, Flavors & Additives: Cultures & Yeasts: Bacteria: Yogurt*
Yogurt Bases *See Ingredients, Flavors & Additives: Bases: Yogurt*
Yogurt Bases, Flavors, Stabilizers *See Dairy Products: Yogurt: Bases, Flavors, Stabilizers*
Yogurt Coated Nuts *See Nuts & Nut Butters: Nuts: Coated: Yogurt*
Yogurt Coated Raisins *See Fruits & Vegetables: Raisins: Yogurt Coated*
Yogurt Cultures *See Ingredients, Flavors & Additives: Cultures & Yeasts: Yogurt*
Yogurt Flavors *See Ingredients, Flavors & Additives: Flavors: Yogurt*
Yogurt Powder Mixes *See Doughs, Mixes & Fillings: Mixes: Yogurt Powder*
Yogurt Powders *See Ingredients, Flavors & Additives: Powders: Yogurt*
Yogurt Stabilizers *See Ingredients, Flavors & Additives: Stabilizers: Yogurt*
Yogurt with Fruit *See Dairy Products: Yogurt: with Fruit*
Yogurt, No-Fat *See Dairy Products: Yogurt: No-Fat*
Yolk *See Eggs & Egg Products: Yolk*

Z

Zinc Citrate *See Ingredients, Flavors & Additives: Vitamins & Supplements: Zinc Citrate*
Zinfandel, Red *See Beverages: Wines: Red Grape Wines: Zinfandel*
Zucchini *See Fruits & Vegetables: Zucchini*

Baby Foods

Cereal

Gerber Products Co
   Arlington, VA 800-284-9488
Hain Celestial Group Inc
   Lake Success, NY 800-434-4246
Happy Family
   New York, NY 855-644-2779
Healthy Times Baby Food
   San Diego, CA 858-513-1550

Formula

Abbott Laboratories
   Abbott Park, IL 847-938-3887
Gerber Products Co
   Arlington, VA 800-284-9488
Hain Celestial Group Inc
   Lake Success, NY 800-434-4246

Organic

Amara Organic Baby Food
   San Francisco, CA 267-981-6411
Ella's Kitchen
   New Castle, DE 800-685-7799
Fresh Bellies
   White Plains, NY 866-888-0467
Gerber Products Co
   Arlington, VA 800-284-9488
Hain Celestial Group Inc
   Lake Success, NY 800-434-4246
Happy Family
   New York, NY 855-644-2779
Healthy Times Baby Food
   San Diego, CA 858-513-1550
J M Swank Co
   North Liberty, IA 800-593-6375
Little Duck Organics
   New York, NY 877-458-1321
Oh Baby Foods, Inc.
   Fayetteville, AR 800-788-1451
Plum Organics
   Emeryville, CA 877-914-7586
Sprout Nutrition
   Montvale, NJ 877-704-8777
Square One Organics
   River Forest, IL 866-771-7138
Stonyfield Organic
   Londonderry, NH 800-776-2697
Tastybaby
   Malibu, CA 866-588-8278

Puree

Gerber Products Co
   Arlington, VA 800-284-9488
Hain Celestial Group Inc
   Lake Success, NY 800-434-4246
Happy Family
   New York, NY 855-644-2779
Little Duck Organics
   New York, NY 877-458-1321
Oh Baby Foods, Inc.
   Fayetteville, AR 800-788-1451
Once Upon a Farm
   San Diego, CA 888-983-1606
Square One Organics
   River Forest, IL 866-771-7138

Whole

Gerber Products Co
   Arlington, VA 800-284-9488
Hain Celestial Group Inc
   Lake Success, NY 800-434-4246
Happy Family
   New York, NY 855-644-2779

Baked Goods

General

A Southern Season
  Hillsborough, NC 800-253-3663
Adam Matthews Inc
  Jeffersontown, KY 502-499-1244
Adams Foods & Milling
  Dothan, AL 334-983-4233
Ak Mak Bakeries
  Sanger, CA 559-875-5511
Aladdin Bakers
  Brooklyn, NY 718-499-1818
Alati-Caserta Desserts
  Montr,al, QC 877-377-5680
Alfred & Sam's Italian Bakery
  Lancaster, PA 717-392-6311
Allegria Italian Bakers
  Sunnyvale, CA 800-467-8648
Alois J Binder Bakery
  New Orleans, LA 504-947-1111
Alpha Baking Company
  South Bend, IN 773-261-6000
Amalfitano's Italian Bakery
  New Castle, DE 302-324-9005
Amcan Industries
  Elmsford, NY 914-347-4838
American Copak Corporation
  Chatsworth, CA 818-576-1000
Ames International Inc
  Fife, WA 888-469-2637
Amoroso's Baking Co
  Bellmawr, NJ 215-471-4740
Andre-Boudin Bakeries
  San Francisco, CA 415-882-1849
Anthony & Sons Italian Bakery
  Fairfield, NJ 973-575-5865
April Hill Inc
  Grand Rapids, MI 616-245-0595
Arturo's Spinella's Bakery
  Waterbury, CT 203-754-3056
Artuso Pastry
  Bronx, NY 718-367-2515
Aryzta
  Los Angeles, CA 855-427-9982
Athens Baking Company
  Fresno, CA 800-775-2867
Athens Foods Inc
  Brookpark, OH 843-916-2000
Atkinson Milling Co.
  Selma, NC 800-948-5707
Atlanta Bread Co.
  Smyrna, GA 800-398-3728
August Foods LTD
  Lubbock, TX 806-744-1918
Aunt Gussie Cookies & Crackers
  Garfield, NJ 800-422-6654
Aunt Heddy's Bakery
  Brooklyn, NY 718-782-0582
Aunt Millie's Bakeries
  Fort Wayne, IN 855-755-2253
Automatic Rolls Of New Jersey
  Edison, NJ 877-222-2867
Award Baking Intl
  New Germany, MN 800-333-3523
Awrey Bakeries
  Livonia, MI 800-950-2253
Azteca Foods Inc
  Chicago, IL 708-563-6600
B&A Bakery
  Toronto, ON 800-263-2878
Bagel Guys
  Brooklyn, NY 718-222-4361
Bagels By Bell
  Brooklyn, NY 718-272-2780
Bake City
  Atlanta, GA 855-336-4777
Bake Rite Rolls Inc
  Bensalem, PA 800-949-5623
BakeMark USA
  Schaumburg, IL 847-519-3135
Baker Boy Bake Shop Inc
  Dickinson, ND 800-437-2008
Baker Boys
  Calgary, AB 877-246-6036
Baker's Dozen & Cafe
  Herkimer, NY 315-866-6770

Bakerhaus Veit Limited
  Woodbridge, ON 800-387-8860
Bakers of Paris
  Brisbane, CA 415-468-9100
BakeryCorp
  Miami, FL 305-623-3838
Baking Leidenheimer
  New Orleans, LA 800-259-9099
Baldinger Baking Co
  St Paul, MN 651-224-5761
Balticshop.Com LLC
  Glastonbury, CT 800-506-2312
Bama Foods LTD
  Tulsa, OK 800-756-2262
Banquet Schusters Bakery
  Pueblo, CO 719-544-1062
Baptista's Bakery
  Franklin, WI 414-409-2000
Barbara's Bakery
  Lakeville, MN 800-343-0590
Barbero Bakery, Inc.
  Trenton, NJ 609-394-5122
Barker System Bakery
  Mt Carmel, PA 570-339-3380
Base Culture
  Clearwater, FL
Basque French Bakery
  Fresno, CA 559-268-7088
Bays English Muffin Corporation
  Chicago, IL 800-367-2297
BBU Bakeries
  Horsham, PA 800-984-0989
Beanitos
  Austin, TX 512-609-8017
Beatrice Bakery Co
  Beatrice, NE 800-228-4030
Beck's Waffles of Oklahoma
  Shawnee, OK 800-646-6254
Beckmann's Old World Bakery
  Santa Cruz, CA 831-423-9242
Bella-Napoli Italian Bakery
  Troy, NY 888-800-0103
Berkshire Mountain Bakery
  Housatonic, MA 866-274-6124
Berlin Natural Bakery
  Berlin, OH 800-686-5334
Best Harvest Bakeries
  Kansas City, KS 800-811-5715
Best Maid Cookie Co
  River Falls, WI 888-444-0322
Beth's Fine Desserts
  Mill Valley, CA 415-383-3991
Better Bagel Bakery
  Sarasota, FL 941-924-0393
Better Bites Bakery
  Austin, TX
Betty Lou's
  McMinnville, OR 800-242-5205
Bien Cuit
  Brooklyn, NY 718-852-0200
Bindi North America
  Kearny, NJ 973-812-8118
Birkholm's Solvang Bakery
  Solvang, CA 800-377-4253
Bite Size Bakery
  Rio Rancho, NM 505-994-3093
Blue Dog Bakery
  Seattle, WA 888-749-7229
Blue Planet Foods
  Collegedale, TN 877-396-3145
Bluepoint Bakery
  Denver, CO 303-298-1100
Boboli Intl. Inc.
  Stockton, CA 209-473-3507
Bodacious Foods
  Jasper, GA 800-391-1979
Bonert's Pies Inc
  Santa Ana, CA 714-540-3535
Bonnie Baking Company
  La Porte, IN 219-362-4561
Borinquen Biscuit Corporation
  Yauco, PR 787-856-3030
Boudreaux's Foods
  New Orleans, LA 504-733-8440
BP Gourmet
  Hauppauge, NY 631-234-8200

Bread Box Cafe
  Astoria, NY 718-389-9703
Breadworks
  Charlottesville, VA 434-296-4663
Brooklyn Bagel Company
  Staten Island, NY 800-349-3055
Brooklyn Baking Company
  Waterbury, CT 203-574-9198
Brookshire Grocery Company
  Tyler, TX 888-937-3776
Bruce Baking Company
  New Rochelle, NY 914-636-0808
Bubbles Baking Co
  Van Nuys, CA 800-777-4970
Bunny Bread
  Evansville, IN
Buns & Roses Organic Wholegrain Bakery
  Edmonton, AB 780-438-0098
Buonitalia
  New York, NY 212-633-9090
Burnham & Morrill Co
  Portland, ME 800-813-2165
Busken Bakery
  Cincinnati, OH 513-871-2114
Byrnes & Kiefer Co
  Callery, PA 724-538-5200
C W Resources Inc
  New Britain, CT 860-229-7700
Calgary Italian Bakery
  Calgary, AB 800-661-6868
California Smart Foods
  San Francisco, CA 415-826-0449
Calise & Sons Bakery Inc
  Lincoln, RI 800-225-4737
Calmar Bakery
  Calmar, AB 780-985-3583
Campbell Soup Co.
  Camden, NJ 800-257-8443
Canada Bread Co, Ltd
  Etobicoke, ON 800-465-5515
Canaf Foods International
  Bolton, ON 905-362-0524
Caribbean Food Delights Inc
  Tappan, NY 845-398-3000
Carmine's Bakery
  Sanford, FL 407-328-4141
Carole's Cheesecake Company
  Toronto, ON 416-256-0000
Carolina Foods Inc
  Charlotte, NC 800-234-0441
Case Side Holdings Company
  Kensington, PE 902-836-4214
Casino Bakery
  Tampa, FL 813-242-0311
Catania Bakery
  Washington, DC 202-332-5135
Cateraid Inc
  Howell, MI 800-508-8217
CBC Foods
  Little River, KS 800-276-4770
Cedarlane Foods
  Carson, CA 800-826-3322
Celebrity Cheesecake
  Davie, FL 877-986-2253
Cellone Bakery Inc
  Pittsburgh, PA 800-334-8438
Central Bakery
  Fall River, MA 508-675-7620
Charlie's Specialties Inc
  Hermitage, PA 724-346-2350
Chattanooga Bakery Inc
  Chattanooga, TN 800-251-3404
Cheesecake Etc Desserts
  Miami Springs, FL 305-887-0258
Cheesecake Factory Inc.
  Calabasas Hills, CA 818-871-3000
Chella's Dutch Delicacies
  Lake Oswego, OR 800-458-3331
Chelsea Flower Market
  New York, NY 888-727-7887
Cheri's Desert Harvest
  Tucson, AZ 800-743-1141
Chewys Rugulach
  San Diego, CA 800-241-3456
Chex Finer Foods Inc
  Mansfield, MA 800-227-8114

Product Categories / Baked Goods: General

Chicago Pastry
   Bloomingdale, IL 630-529-6391
Chisholm Bakery
   Chisholm, MN 218-254-4006
Chmura's Bakery
   Indian Orchard, MA 413-543-2521
Chocolate Chix
   Waxahachie, TX 214-744-2442
Chudleigh's
   Milton, ON 800-387-4028
Cinderella Cheese Cake Co
   Riverside, NJ 800-521-1171
City Cafe & Bakery
   Fayetteville, GA 770-461-6800
Clarkson Scottish Bakery
   Mississauga, ON 905-823-1500
Claxton Bakery Inc
   Claxton, GA 800-841-4211
Clement's Pastry Shops Inc
   Hyattsville, MD 301-277-6300
Cloverhill Bakery-Vend Corporation
   Chicago, IL 773-745-9800
Clyde's Delicious Donuts
   Addison, IL 630-628-6555
Coby's Cookies
   Toronto, ON 416-633-1567
Cohen's Bakery
   Ellenville, NY 845-647-2200
Colchester Bakery
   Colchester, CT 860-537-2415
Cold Spring Bakery Inc
   Cold Spring, MN 320-685-8681
Cole's Quality Foods
   Grand Rapids, MI 616-975-0081
Collin Street Bakery
   Corsicana, TX 800-267-4657
Colombo Bakery
   Sacramento, CA 916-648-1011
Colonial Cookies, Ltd
   Kitchener, ON 800-265-6508
Colors Gourmet Pizza
   Vista, CA. 760-597-1400
Community Bakeries
   Downers Grove, IL 800-952-5754
Community Orchards
   Fort Dodge, IA 888-573-8212
Cookie Factory
   Bronx, NY 718-379-6223
Cookie Kingdom
   Oglesby, IL 815-883-3331
Cookie Specialties Inc
   Wheeling, IL 847-537-3888
Cookie Tree Bakeries
   Salt Lake City, UT 801-268-2253
Cookies United
   Islip, NY 631-581-4000
Cookiezen, LLC
   Falls Church, VA. 703-389-9274
Corfu Foods Inc
   Bensenville, IL 630-595-2510
Cotton Baking Company
   Alexandria, LA 318-448-6600
Cougar Mountain Baking Co
   Seattle, WA 877-328-2622
Country Club Bakery
   Fairmont, WV 304-363-5690
Creative Spices
   Union City, CA 510-471-4956
Creme Curls
   Hudsonville, MI 800-466-1219
Crum Creek Mils
   Springfield, PA 888-607-3500
Crusty Bakery Inc
   New York, NY 917-733-6396
Culinar Canada
   Baie-Comeau, QC. 418-296-4395
Culinary Masters Corporation
   Alpharetta, GA 800-261-5261
Cupoladua Oven
   Wexford, PA 412-592-5378
Cusano's Baking Company
   Hallandale, FL 954-458-1010
Cutie Pie Corp
   Salt Lake City, UT 800-453-4575
Dairy State Foods Inc
   Milwaukee, WI 800-435-4499
Dakota Brands Intl
   Jamestown, ND 800-844-5073
Dancing Deer Baking Company
   Boston, MA. 888-699-3337
Daniel's Bagel & Baguette Corporation
   Calgary, AB. 403-243-3207

Davis Bakery & Delicatessen
   Cleveland, OH 216-292-3060
Davis Bread & Desserts
   Davis, CA 530-220-4375
DeBeukelaer Cookie Co
   Madison, MS. 601-856-7454
Deerfield Bakery
   Buffalo Grove, IL 847-520-0068
Del's Pastry
   Toronto, ON 800-461-0663
Delia's Food Co
   Cincinnati, OH 513-221-4322
Delicious Frookie
   Des Plaines, IL 847-699-3200
Denny's 5th Avenue Bakery
   Bloomington, MN. 952-881-4445
Desserts by David Glass
   South Windsor, CT 860-462-7520
Desserts Of Distinction
   Tigard, OR 503-654-8370
Desserts On Us Inc
   Arcata, CA 707-822-0160
Dewey's Bakery
   Winston-Salem, NC 877-339-3974
Di Camillo Baking Co
   Niagara Falls, NY 800-634-4363
Dimitria Delights Baking Co
   North Grafton, MA 800-763-1113
Dimpflmeier Bakery
   Toronto, ON 800-268-2421
Dinkel's Bakery Inc
   Chicago, IL 800-822-8817
Dipaolo Baking Co Inc
   Rochester, NY. 585-232-3510
Divine Foods
   Elizabethtown, NC 910-862-2576
Dong Kee Company
   Chicago, IL 312-225-6340
Doral International
   Bayside, NY 718-224-7413
Dough-To-Go
   Santa Clara, CA 408-727-4094
Drader Manufacturing Industries
   Edmonton, AB 800-661-4122
Dufflet Pastries
   Toronto, ON 866-238-0899
Dunford Bakers
   West Jordan, UT 800-748-4335
Dunkin' Brands Inc.
   Canton, MA 800-859-5339
Dutch Ann Foods Company
   Natchez, MS 601-445-5566
Dutch Girl Donut Co
   Detroit, MI 313-368-3020
Dutchess Bakery
   Charleston, WV 304-346-4237
DWC Specialities
   Horicon, WI 800-383-8808
Dynamic Foods
   Lubbock, TX 806-723-5600
Eddy's Bakery
   Boise, ID 208-377-8100
Edelweiss Patisserie
   Medford, MN 781-628-0225
Eden Vineyards Winery
   Alva, FL 239-728-9463
Edner Corporation
   Hayward, CA 510-441-8504
Edwards Baking Company
   Marshall, MN 866-739-2328
El Charro Mexican Food Ind
   Roswell, NM. 575-622-8590
El Peto Products
   Cambridge, ON 800-387-4064
Elegant Desserts
   Lyndhurst, NJ 201-933-0770
Eli's Cheesecake
   Chicago, IL 800-354-2253
Ellison Bakery, Inc.
   Fort Wayne, IN
Elmwood Pastry Shop
   West Hartford, CT. 860-233-2029
Ener-G Foods
   Seattle, WA 800-331-5222
Engel's Bakeries
   Calgary, AB. 403-250-9560
Entenmann's
   Totowa, NJ 973-785-7601
Erba Food Products
   Brooklyn, NY 718-272-7700
Ericas Rugelach & Baking Co
   Brooklyn, NY 718-965-3657

Esco Foods Inc
   San Francisco, CA 415-864-2147
Euroam Importers Inc
   Auburn, WA 888-839-2702
European Bakers
   Tucker, GA 770-723-6180
European Style Bakery
   Beverly Hills, CA 818-368-6876
Falcone's Cookie Land LTD
   Brooklyn, NY 718-236-4200
Fancy Lebanese Bakery
   Halifax, NS 902-429-0400
Fantasia
   Sedalia, MO 660-827-1172
Fantasy Cookie Company
   Sylmar, CA 800-354-4488
Fantini Baking Co Inc
   Haverhill, MA 800-343-2110
Fantis Foods Inc
   Carlstadt, NJ 201-933-6200
Farrell Baking Company
   West Middlesex, PA 724-342-7906
Father Sam's Bakery
   Buffalo, NY. 800-521-6719
Fayes Bakery Products
   Dexter, MO 573-624-4920
Fazio's Bakery
   St Louis, MO. 314-645-6239
Federal Pretzel Baking Company
   Bridgeport, NJ 215-467-0505
Felix Roma & Son Inc
   Endicott, NY 607-748-3336
Ferrara Bakery & Cafe
   New York, NY 212-226-6150
Field's Pies
   Pauls Valley, OK 800-286-7501
Fiera Foods
   Toronto, ON 800-675-6356
Finkemeier Bakery
   Kansas City, KS 913-831-3103
Firehook Bakery & Coffeehouse
   Chantilly, VA. 703-263-2253
Fireside Kitchen
   Halifax, NS 902-454-7387
Flamin' Red's Woodfired
   Pawlet, VT 802-325-3641
Flax4Life
   Bellingham, WA 877-352-9487
Fleischer's Bagels
   Macedon, NY 315-986-9999
Flowers Baking Co
   Birmingham, AL 205-252-1161
Flowers Baking Co
   Tuscaloosa, AL 205-752-5586
Flowers Baking Co
   El Paso, TX 800-328-6111
Flowers Foods Inc.
   Thomasville, GA. 229-226-9110
Food Mill
   Oakland, CA 510-482-3848
Food of Our Own Design
   Maplewood, NJ 973-762-0985
Fortella Fortune Cookies
   Chicago, IL 312-567-9000
Fortune Cookie Factory
   Oakland, CA 510-832-5552
Forty Second Street Bagel Cafe
   Upland, CA 909-949-7334
Foxtail Foods
   Fairfield, OH 800-487-2253
France Delices
   Montreal, QC 800-663-1365
Franklin Baking Company
   Kinston, NC 800-248-7494
Frankly Natural Bakers
   San Diego, CA 800-727-7229
Franz Bakery Outlet Store
   Portland, OR 503-232-2191
Freedman's Bakery
   Belmar, NJ. 732-681-2334
Freedom Foods LLC
   Randolph, VM 802-728-0070
Fresh Start Bakeries
   Brea, CA 714-256-8900
Frisco Baking Co Inc
   Los Angeles, CA. 323-225-6111
Future Bakery & Cafe
   Toronto, ON 416-231-1491
G Debbas Chocolatier
   Fresno, CA 559-294-2071
Gabila's Knishes
   Copiague, NY 631-789-2220

Product Categories / Baked Goods: General

Gadoua Bakery
  Napierville, QC 800-661-7246
GAF Seelig Inc
  Flushing, NY 718-899-5000
Galasso's Bakery
  Mira Loma, CA 951-360-1211
Gambino's Bakeries Inc
  Kenner, LA 504-712-0809
Gardner Pie Co
  Akron, OH 330-245-2030
Gartner Studios Inc
  Stillwater, MN 651-351-7700
George's Candy Shop Inc
  Mobile, AL 800-633-1306
Georgia Fruitcake Co
  Claxton, GA 912-739-2683
German Bakery at Village Corner
  Stone Mountain, GA 866-476-6443
GH Bent Company
  Milton, MA 617-322-9287
Giant Food
  Landover, MD 888-469-4426
Ginny Bakes
  Miami, FL 305-638-5103
Glamorgan Bakery
  Calgary, AB 403-232-2800
Global Bakeries Inc
  Pacoima, CA 818-896-0525
Glutino
  Laval, QC 800-363-3438
Gold Coast Bakeries
  Santa Ana, CA 714-545-2253
Gold Coast Baking Co Inc
  Santa Ana, CA 714-545-2253
Gold Crust Baking Co Inc
  Landover, MD 301-364-3320
Gold Medal Bakery Inc
  Fall River, MA 508-674-5766
Gold Standard Baking Inc
  Chicago, IL 800-648-7904
Golden Brown Bakery Inc
  South Haven, MI 269-637-3418
Golden Edibles LLC
  Davie, FL 866-779-7781
Goldilocks USA
  Hayward, CA 510-476-0700
Goll's Bakery
  Havre De Grace, MD 410-939-4321
Good Old Days Foods
  Little Rock, AR 501-565-1257
Gould's Maple Sugarhouse
  Shelburne Falls, MA 413-625-6170
Gourmet Croissant
  Brooklyn, NY 718-499-4911
Grandma Beth's Cookies
  Alliance, NE 308-762-8433
Granello Bakery
  Las Vegas, NV 702-361-0311
Granny Roddy's LLC
  Annandale, VA 703-503-3431
Grebe's Bakery
  Milwaukee, WI 800-833-3158
Grecian Delight Foods Inc
  Elk Grove Village, IL 800-621-4387
Greenhills Irish Bakery
  Dorchester Ctr, MA 617-825-8187
Gregory's Foods, Inc.
  St Paul, MN 800-231-4734
Greyston Bakery Inc
  Yonkers, NY 800-289-2253
Grossingers Home Bakery
  New York, NY 800-479-6996
Guttenplan's Frozen Dough
  Middletown, NJ 888-422-4357
GWB Foods Corporation
  Brooklyn, NY 877-977-7610
H Cantin
  Beauport, QC 800-463-5268
H&S Bakery
  Baltimore, MD 800-959-7655
H-E-B Grocery Co. LP
  San Antonio, TX 800-432-3113
Haby's Alsatian Bakery
  Castroville, TX 830-538-2118
Hafner USA
  Stone Mountain, GA 888-725-4605
Hahn's Old Fashioned Cake Co
  Farmingdale, NY 631-249-3456
Handy Pax
  Randolph, MA 781-963-8300
Harbar LLC
  Canton, MA 800-881-7040

Harlan Bakeries
  Avon, IN 800-435-2738
Harold Food Company
  Charlotte, NC 704-588-8061
Harting's Bakery
  Bowmansville, PA 717-445-5644
Harvest Bakery
  Central Islip, NY 631-232-1709
Harvest Valley Bakery Inc
  La Salle, IL 815-224-9030
Havi Food Services Worldwide
  Oak Park, IL 708-445-1700
Hawaii Candy Inc
  Honolulu, HI 800-303-2507
Hawaii Star Bakery
  Honolulu, HI 808-841-3602
Hawaiian Bagel
  Honolulu, HI 808-596-0638
Health Valley Company
  Irwindale, CA 800-334-3204
Heidi's Gourmet Desserts
  Tucker, GA 800-241-4166
Heltzman Bakery
  Louisville, KY 502-447-3515
Herman's Bakery
  Cambridge, MN 763-689-1515
Heyerly Bakery
  Ossian, IN 260-622-4196
Highlandville Packing
  Highlandville, MO 417-443-3365
Holsum Bakery Inc
  Phoenix, AZ 602-252-2351
Holt's Bakery Inc
  Douglas, GA 912-384-2202
Home Bakery
  Rochester, MI 248-651-4830
Home Maid Bakery
  Wailuku, HI 808-244-7015
Home Style Bakery Of Grand Junction
  Grand Junction, CO 970-243-1233
Homestead Baking Co
  Rumford, MI 800-556-7216
Homestyle Bread Bakery
  Phoenix, AZ 602-268-0676
Horizon Snack Foods
  Livermore, CA 800-229-2552
Hostess Brands
  Kansas City, MO 816-701-4600
Hunt Country Foods Inc
  Marshall, VA 540-364-2622
Hye Quality Bakery
  Fresno, CA 877-445-1778
Il Gelato
  Astoria, NY 800-899-9299
Il Giardino Del Dolce Inc
  Chicago, IL 773-889-2388
Immaculate Consumption
  Columbia, SC 888-826-6567
Independent Bakers Association
  Washington, DC 202-333-8190
Ingles Markets
  Black Mountain, NC 828-669-2941
Interbake Foods
  Richmond, VA 800-221-1002
International Brownie
  East Weymouth, MA 800-230-1588
Irresistible Cookie Jar
  Hayden Lake, ID 208-664-1261
Italian Bakery of Virginia
  Virginia, MN 218-741-3464
Italian Peoples Bakery Inc
  Ewing, NJ 609-771-1369
J & J Wall Bakery Co
  Sacramento, CA 916-381-1410
J J Gandy's Pies Inc
  Palm Harbor, FL 727-938-7437
J M Swank Co
  North Liberty, IA 800-593-6375
J.P. Sunrise Bakery
  Edmonton, AB 780-454-5797
Jacques Pastries
  Suncook, NH 603-485-4035
Jacquet Bakery
  New York, NY
Jamae Natural Foods
  Los Angeles, CA 800-343-0052
James Skinner Company
  Omaha, NE 800-358-7428
Jerabek's New Bohemian Coffee House
  Saint Paul, MN 651-228-1245
Jerusalem House
  Eugene, OR 541-485-1012

Jewel Bakery
  Melrose Park, IL 708-531-6000
Jim's Cheese Pantry
  Waterloo, WI 800-345-3571
Jimmys Cookies
  Clifton, NJ 973-779-8500
Joey's Fine Foods
  Newark, NJ 973-482-1400
John J. Nissen Baking Company
  Brewer, ME 207-989-7654
John W Macy's Cheesesticks Inc
  Elmwood Park, NJ 800-643-0573
Jon Donaire Desserts
  Santa Fe Springs, CA 877-366-2473
Jonathan Lord Cheesecakes
  Bohemia, NY 800-814-7517
Jubelt Variety Bakeries
  Litchfield, IL 217-324-5314
Jubilations
  West Point, MS 800-530-7808
Julian's Recipe
  Brooklyn, NY 888-640-8880
Just Desserts
  Fairfield, CA 415-780-6860
Just Off Melrose
  Palm Springs, CA 760-320-7414
K & S Cakes
  Leesburg, VA 910-265-6779
Kangaroo Brands
  Omaha, NE 877-266-2472
Kapaa Bakery
  Kapaa, HI 808-821-0060
Keebler Company
  Battlecreek, MI 800-962-1413
Keller's Bakery
  Lafayette, LA 337-235-1568
Kemach Food Products
  Brooklyn, NY 718-272-5655
Keystone Pretzel Bakery
  Lititz, PA 888-572-4500
Kids Kookie Company
  San Clemente, CA 800-350-7577
Kim & Scott's Gourmet Pretzels
  Chicago, IL 800-578-9478
Kim and Jake's
  Boulder, CO 303-499-9126
King's Hawaiian Holding Co Inc.
  Torrance, CA 877-695-4227
Koffee Kup Bakery
  Burlington, VT 802-863-2696
Kollar Cookies
  Long Branch, NJ 732-343-4217
Korbs Baking Company
  Pawtucket, RI 401-726-4422
Kosher French Baguettes
  Brooklyn, NY 718-633-4994
Kossar's Bagels & Bialys
  New York, NY 877-424-2597
Krispy Kreme Doughnuts Inc
  Charlotte, NC
Kroger Bakery
  Clackamas, OR 503-650-2000
Kupris Home Bakery
  Bolton, CT 860-649-4746
Kyger Bakery Products
  Lafayette, IN 765-447-1252
L & M Bakery
  Riverside, NJ 888-887-1335
LA Boulangerie
  San Diego, CA 858-578-4040
La Brea Bakery Inc
  San Leandro, CA 855-427-9982
La Buena Mexican Foods Products
  Tucson, AZ 520-624-1796
La Moderna
  Toluca, MX
LA Patisserie Bakery
  Cupertino, CA 408-446-4744
La Piccolina
  Decatur, GA 800-626-1624
La Tempesta
  S San Francisco, CA 800-762-8330
LA Torilla Factory
  Santa Rosa, CA 800-446-1516
Lake States Yeast
  Rhinelander, WI 715-369-4949
Lakeview Bakery
  Calgary, AB 403-246-6127
Lamonaca Bakery
  Windber, PA 814-467-4909
Landolfi's Food Products
  Trenton, NJ 609-392-1830

Product Categories / Baked Goods: General

Lanthier Bakery
   Alexandria, ON...............613-525-2435
Lark Fine Foods
   Essex, MA......................978-768-0012
Laronga Bakery
   Somerville, MA................617-625-8600
Larosa Bakery Inc
   Shrewsbury, NJ...............800-527-6722
Latonia Bakery
   Covington, KY.................859-491-8855
Laura's French Baking Co
   Los Angeles, CA..............888-353-5144
Lavash Corp
   Los Angeles, CA..............323-663-5249
Lavoi Corporation
   Atlanta, GA....................404-325-1016
Lax & Mandel Bakery
   South Euclid, OH..............216-382-8877
Le Chic French Bakery
   Miami Beach, FL..............305-673-5522
Le Donne Brothers Bakery
   Roseto, PA.....................610-588-0423
Lefse House
   Camrose, AB..................780-672-7555
Leidenheimer Baking Co
   New Orleans, LA..............800-259-9099
Lenchner Bakery
   Concord, ON..................905-738-8811
Leo's Bakery
   Marshfield, MA................781-837-3300
Lepage Bakeries
   Auburn, ME....................207-783-9161
Lewis Bakeries Inc
   Evansville, IN..................812-425-4642
Linden Cookies Inc
   Congers, NY...................845-268-5050
Livermore Falls Baking Company
   Livermore Falls, ME..........207-897-3442
Loafin' Around
   Madison, AL...................301-570-4513
Loghouse Foods
   Minneapolis, MN..............763-546-8395
Lombardi's Bakery
   Torrington, CT.................860-489-4766
Lone Star Bakery
   Round Rock, TX..............512-255-7268
Longo's Bakery Inc
   Hazleton, PA..................570-454-5825
Lotus Bakery
   Santa Rosa, CA...............800-875-6887
Louis Swiss Pastry
   Aspen, CO.....................970-925-8592
Love Quiches Desserts
   Freeport, NY..................516-623-8800
Love's Bakery
   Honolulu, HI...................808-841-0397
Lowcountry Produce
   Raleigh, NC....................800-935-2792
Lucerne Foods
   Pleasanton, CA...............877-232-4271
Lucy's Sweet Surrender
   Beachwood, OH..............216-752-0828
Ludwick's Frozen Donuts
   Grand Rapids, MI.............800-366-8816
Luna's Tortillas
   Dallas, TX......................214-747-2661
Lupi-Marchigiano Bakery
   New Haven, CT...............203-562-9491
Mac Farms Of Hawaii Inc
   Captain Cook, HI.............808-328-2435
Mac's Donut Shop
   Aliquippa, PA..................724-375-6776
Maggiora Baking Co
   Richmond, CA................510-235-0274
Magna Foods Corporation
   City of Industry, CA...........800-995-4394
Main Street Gourmet
   Cuyahoga Falls, OH.........800-678-6246
Mancuso Cheese Co
   Joliet, IL.........................815-722-2475
Manderfield's Home Bakery
   Menasha, WI..................920-882-6500
Maple Leaf Bakery
   Montreal, QC..................800-268-3708
Marika's Kitchen
   Hancock, ME..................800-694-9400
Marin Food Specialties
   Byron, CA......................925-634-6126
Marshall's Biscuit Company
   Westerville, OH................251-679-6226
Martino's Bakery
   Burbank, CA..................818-842-0715

Mary Ann's Baking Co Inc
   Sacramento, CA..............916-681-7444
Mary of Puddin Hill
   Palestine, TX..................800-545-8889
Matthew's Bakery
   Stamford, CT..................203-316-9392
Maui Bagel
   Kahului, HI....................808-270-7561
Mayer's Cider Mill
   Webster, NY..................800-543-0043
Mazelle's Cheesecakes Concoctions Creations
   Dallas, TX......................214-328-9102
McKee Foods Corp.
   Collegedale, TN...............800-522-4499
Mediterranean Gyro Products
   Long Island City, NY.........718-786-3399
Mehaffies Pies
   Dayton, OH....................800-289-7437
Meijer Inc
   Grand Rapids, MI.............616-453-6711
Mememe Inc
   Toronto, ON...................416-972-0973
Metropolitan Baking Co
   Hamtramck, MI................313-875-7246
Meyer's Bakeries
   Casa Grande, AZ............800-528-5770
Michel's Bakery
   Philadelphia, PA..............267-345-7914
Mikawaya LLC
   Vernon, CA....................323-587-5504
Mikey's
   Scottsdale, AZ
Milano Bakery Inc
   Joliet, IL.........................815-727-2253
Millie's Pierogi
   Chicopee Falls, MA..........800-743-7641
Modern Italian Bakery of West Babylon
   Oakdale, NY..................631-589-7300
Molinaro's Fine Italian Foods Ltd.
   Mississauga, ON.............905-281-0352
Mom's Bakery
   Sherman, TX..................903-893-7585
Mom's Famous
   Boca Raton, FL...............561-750-1903
Monaco Baking Company
   Santa Fe Springs, CA.......800-569-4640
Monastery Fruitcake
   Martinsburg, WV.............304-596-2024
Monks' Specialty Bakery
   Piffard, NY
Monster Cone
   Montreal, QC..................800-542-9801
Montione's Biscotti & Baked Goods
   Norton, MA....................800-559-1010
Moon Rabbit Foods
   Savannah, NY................828-273-6649
Morabito Baking Co Inc
   Norristown, PA................800-525-7747
Morrison Meat Pies
   West Valley, UT...............801-977-0181
Mozzicato De Pasquale Bakery
   Hartford, CT...................860-296-0426
Mrs Baird's
   Horsham, PA..................800-984-0989
Mrs. Fly's Bakery
   Collegeville, PA...............610-489-7288
Mt. View Bakery
   Mountain View, HI............808-968-6353
Multi Marques
   Montreal, QC..................514-934-1866
My Cup of Cake™
   Port Washington, NY........516-767-5137
My Grandma's Coffee Cake
   Hyde Park, MA................800-847-2636
Nabisco
   Parsippany, NJ................973-682-5000
Naji's Pita Gourmet Restaurant
   Birmingham, AL..............205-945-6001
Najla's Specialty Foods Inc
   Louisville, KY..................877-962-5527
Naleway Foods
   Winnipeg, MB.................800-665-7448
Nancy's Specialty Foods
   Newark, CA....................510-494-1100
Nardi Breads
   South Windsor, CT..........860-289-5458
Natural Food Mill
   Corona, CA....................800-797-5090
Naturally Delicious Inc
   Oakland Park, FL............888-221-7352
Nature's Hilights
   Chico, CA......................800-313-6454

Nature's Path Foods
   Blaine, WA.....................888-808-9505
Ne-Mo's Bakery Inc
   Escondido, CA...............800-325-2692
Neuman Bakery Specialties
   Addison, IL....................800-253-5298
Nevada Baking Company
   Las Vegas, NV...............702-384-8950
New Bakery Company of Ohio
   Zanesville, OH................800-848-9845
New England Country Bakers
   Watertown, CT...............800-225-3779
New England Muffin Co Inc
   Fall River, MA.................508-675-2833
New Horizons Baking Co
   Fremont, IN....................260-495-7055
New Salem Tea-Bread Company
   New Salem, MA..............800-897-5910
New York Bakeries Inc
   Hialeah, FL.....................305-883-0790
New York Frozen Foods Inc
   Bedford, OH...................216-292-5655
New York Intl Bread Co
   Orlando, FL....................407-843-9744
Nicole's Divine Crackers
   Chicago, IL.....................312-640-8883
Nikki's Cookies
   Milwaukee, WI................800-776-7107
Nikola's Foods
   Bloomington, MN.............888-645-6527
Nonni's Foods LLC
   Tulsa, OK.......................877-295-9604
North American Enterprises
   Tucson, AZ....................800-817-8666
Northeast Foods Inc
   Baltimore, MD.................800-769-2867
Northside Bakery
   Brooklyn, NY..................718-782-2700
Northwoods Candy Emporium
   Branson, MO..................417-332-1010
Notre Dame Bakery
   Conception Harbour, NL...709-535-2738
Nustef Foods
   Mississauga, ON.............877-306-7562
Nutri-Bake Inc
   Laval, QC......................450-933-5936
Nutrilicious Natural Bakery
   Countryside, IL................800-835-8097
O'Doughs
   Toronto, ON...................855-636-8447
Oak State Products Inc
   Wenona, IL....................815-853-4348
Oakhurst Industries
   Commerce, CA...............818-502-1400
Oakrun Farm Bakery
   Ancaster, ON.................800-263-6422
OH Chocolate
   Seattle, WA....................206-329-8777
Ohta Wafer Factory
   Honolulu, HI...................808-949-2775
Old Country Bakery
   North Hollywood, CA.......818-838-2302
Old Fashioned Kitchen Inc
   Lakewood, NJ................732-364-4100
Olivia's Croutons
   New Haven, VT..............888-425-3080
Orange Bakery
   Irvine, CA.......................949-863-1377
Orwasher's Bakery
   New York, NY................212-288-6569
Otis Spunkmeyer
   Brockport, NY.................855-427-9982
Ottenberg's Bakers
   Sykesville, MD................800-334-7264
Our Farms To You, LLC
   Middletown, VA...............703-507-7604
Outer Aisle
   Galeta, CA.....................805-242-9265
Oven Fresh Baking Company
   Chicago, IL.....................773-638-1234
Ozark Empire
   Rogers, AR....................479-636-3313
Ozery Bakery Inc
   Vaughan, ON.................905-265-1143
PDEQ
   Fresno, CA....................559-490-4412
P&H Milling Group
   Cambridge, ON...............519-650-6400
Pacific Ocean Produce
   Santa Cruz, CA...............831-423-2654
Palermo Bakery
   Seaside, CA...................831-394-8212

31

Product Categories / Baked Goods: General

Pan Pepin
  Bayamon, PR 787-787-1717
Pan-O-Gold Baking Co.
  St. Cloud, MN 800-444-7005
Panera Bread
  Saint Louis, MO 314-984-1000
Pantry Shelf/Mixxm
  Hutchinson, KS 800-968-3346
Paris Pastry
  Van Nuys, CA 805-487-2227
Park Avenue Bakery
  Helena, MT 406-449-8424
Pasta Shoppe
  Nashville, TN 800-247-0188
Pastry Chef
  Pawtucket, RI 800-639-8606
Pati-Petite Cookies Inc
  Bridgeville, PA 800-253-5805
Patisserie Wawel
  Montreal, QC 614-524-3348
Peggy Lawton Kitchens
  East Walpole, MA 800-843-7325
Peking Noodle Co Inc
  Los Angeles, CA 323-223-0897
Pellman Foods Inc
  New Holland, PA 717-354-8070
Pete & Joy's Bakery
  Little Falls, MN 320-632-6388
Petrofsky's Bakery Products
  Chesterfield, MO 636-519-1613
Phipps Desserts
  North York, ON 416-391-5800
Piantedosi Baking Co Inc
  Malden, MA 800-339-0080
Pie Piper Products
  Wheeling, IL 800-621-8183
Piemonte Bakery Co
  Rockford, IL 815-962-4833
Pierre's French Bakery
  Portland, OR 503-233-8871
Pioneer Frozen Foods
  Duncanville, TX 972-298-4281
Pita King Bakery
  Everett, WA 425-258-4040
Pittsfield Rye Bakery
  Pittsfield, MA 413-443-9141
Plaidberry Company
  Vista, CA 760-727-5403
Plehn's Bakery Inc
  Louisville, KY 502-896-4438
Pocono Cheesecake Factory
  Swiftwater, PA 570-839-6844
Pollman's Bake Shop
  Mobile, AL 251-438-1511
Poppies International
  Battleboro, NC 252-442-4309
Portuguese Baking Company
  Newark, NJ 973-589-8875
Positively 3rd St Bakery
  Duluth, MN 218-724-8619
Powers Baking Company
  Miami, FL 305-381-7000
President's Choice
  Brampton, ON 888-495-5111
Priester's Pecans
  Fort Deposit, AL 866-477-4736
Primos Northgate
  Flowood, MS 601-936-3398
Prince of Peace
  Hayward, CA 800-732-2328
Productos Del Plata
  Miami, FL 786-357-8261
Protano's Bakery
  Hollywood, FL 954-925-3474
Publix Super Market
  Lakeland, FL 800-242-1227
Pure's Food Specialties
  Broadview, IL 708-344-8884
Purity Factories
  St. John's, NL 800-563-3411
Quality Bakery
  Invermere, BC 888-681-9977
Quality Bakery Products
  Houston, TX 866-449-4977
Quality Croutons
  Chicago, IL 800-334-2796
Quality Naturally Foods
  City Of Industry, CA 888-498-6986
Quinzani Bakery
  Boston, MA 800-999-1062
R.M. Palmer Co.
  West Reading, PA 610-372-8971

R.W. Frookies
  Sag Harbor, NY 800-913-3663
Ranaldi Bros. Frozen Food Products
  Warwick, RI 401-737-5130
Ranieri Fine Foods
  Brooklyn, NY 718-599-9520
Real Food Marketing
  Kansas City, MO 816-221-4100
Real Torino
  Brookside, NJ 973-895-5420
Red Plate Foods
  Bend, OR 541-550-7676
Rich Products Corp
  Buffalo, NY 800-828-2021
Rich's Ice Cream Co Inc
  West Palm Beach, FL 561-833-7585
Richmond Baking Co
  Richmond, IN 765-962-8535
Rising Dough Bakery
  Sacramento, CA 916-387-9700
Robert's Bakery
  Minnetonka, MN 612-473-9719
Rockland Bakery
  Nanuet, NY 800-734-4376
Rolling Pin Bakery
  Bow Island, AB 403-545-2434
Rolling Pin Bakery
  Great Bend, KS 620-793-5381
Roma & Ray's Italian Bakery
  Valley Stream, NY 516-825-7610
Roma Bakeries
  Rockford, IL 815-964-6737
Romero's Food Products Inc
  Santa Fe Springs, CA 800-719-2690
Rondo Specialty Foods LTD
  New Castle, DE 800-724-6636
Rosemark Bakery
  St Paul, MN 651-698-3838
Rotella's Italian Bakery Inc.
  La Vista, NE 402-592-6600
Rothbury Farms
  Grand Rapids, MI 877-684-2879
Rovira Biscuit Corporation
  Ponce, PR 787-844-8585
Rowena
  Norfolk, VA 800-627-8699
Royal Home Bakery
  Newmarket, ON 905-715-7044
Rubschlager Baking Corp
  800-661-7246
Rudolph's Specialty Bakery
  Toronto, ON 800-268-1589
Ruiz Flour Tortillas
  Riverside, CA 909-947-7811
Run-A-Ton Group Inc
  Chester, NJ 800-247-6580
Russell & Kohne Inc
  Newport Beach, CA 949-645-8441
Ruth Ashbrook Bakery
  Portland, OR 503-240-7437
Ryals Bakery
  Milledgeville, GA 478-452-0321
Ryke's Bakery
  Muskegon, MI 231-726-2253
S & M Communion Bread Co
  Nashville, TN 615-292-1969
Sacramento Baking Co
  Sacramento, CA 916-361-2000
Salem Baking Company
  Winston Salem, NC 800-274-2994
San Anselmo's Cookies & Biscotti
  San Anselmo, CA 800-229-1249
San Francisco Fine Bakery
  Redwood City, CA 650-369-8573
San Francisco French Bread
  Oakland, CA 510-729-6232
San-J International Inc
  Henrico, VA 800-446-5500
Sanborn Sourdough Bakery
  Las Vegas, NV 702-795-1030
Sandors Bakeries
  Miami, FL 305-642-8484
Sanitary Bakery
  Nanticoke, PA 570-735-6630
Sara Lee Frozen Bakery
  Kings Mountain, NC 800-323-7117
Sarabeth's Office
  Bronx, NY 800-773-7378
SASIB Biscuits and Snacks Division
  Hudson, OH 330-656-3317
Saxby Foods
  Edmonton, AB 780-440-4179

Schadel's Bakery
  Silver City, NM 505-538-3031
Schaller's Bakery Inc
  Greensburg, PA 800-241-1777
Schat's Dutch Bakeries
  Bishop, CA 866-323-5854
Schulze & Burch Biscuit Co
  Chicago, IL 773-927-6622
Schwan's Food Service Inc.
  Marshall, MN 877-302-7426
Schwebel Baking Co.
  Youngstown, OH 800-860-2867
Scialo Brothers Bakery
  Providence, RI 877-421-0986
Scotty Wotty's Creamy Cheesecake
  Hillsborough, NJ 908-281-9720
Seaver's Bakery
  Kingsport, TN 423-245-2441
Sedona Baking Company
  Gardena, CA 323-770-2674
Shamrock Foods Co
  Phoenix, AZ 800-289-3663
Shashy's Bakery & Fine Foods
  Montgomery, AL 334-263-7341
Shaw Baking Company
  Thunder Bay, ON 807-345-7327
Sheila's Select Gourmet Recipe
  Heber City, UT 800-516-7286
Sheryl's Chocolate Creations
  Hicksville, NY 888-882-2462
Siljans Crispy Cup Company
  Calgary, AB 403-275-0135
Silver Tray Cookies
  Fort Lauderdale, FL 305-883-0800
Simit + Smith
  Ridgefield, NJ 201-699-0320
Simon Hubig Company
  New Orleans, LA 504-945-2181
Sinbad Sweets
  Madera, CA 866-746-2232
SJR Foods
  New Bedford, MA 617-500-4516
Slingshot Foods
  San Francisco, CA 415-423-2444
Smart Baking Co.
  Sanford, FL 407-915-5519
Smith's Bakery
  Hattiesburg, MS 601-288-7000
Smoak's Bakery & Catering Service
  Augusta, GA 706-738-1792
Solana Beach Baking Company
  Carlsbad, CA 760-444-9800
Soloman Baking Company
  Denver, CO 303-371-2777
Sophia Foods
  Brooklyn, NY 718-272-1110
Southern Season
  Chapel Hill, NC 877-929-7133
Southwest Foods
  Tyler, TX 888-937-3776
Spanish Gardens Food Manufacturing
  Kansas City, KS 913-831-4242
Specialty Bakers
  Marysville, PA 800-233-0778
Specialty Food Association
  New York, NY 646-878-0301
Spilke's Baking Company
  Moosic, PA 570-457-2400
Spohrers Bakeries
  Collingdale, PA 610-532-9959
Spring Glen Fresh Foods
  Ephrata, PA 800-641-2853
St Armands Baking Co
  Bradenton, FL 941-753-7494
St-Germain Bakery
  Honolulu, HI 808-847-5396
St. Amour Inc/French Cookies
  Costa Mesa, CA 714-754-1900
Stacy's Pita Chip Co
  Randolph, MA 888-332-4477
Standard Bakery Inc
  Kealakekua, HI 808-322-3688
Stangl's Bakery
  Ambridge, PA 724-266-5675
Starbucks
  Seattle, WA 800-782-7282
Stauffer's
  Cuba, NY 585-968-2700
Stella D'oro
  Charlotte, NC 800-995-2623
Sterling Foods LLC
  San Antonio, TX 210-490-1669

Product Categories / Baked Goods: Bread Crumbs & Croutons

Steve's Authentic Key Lime Pies
  Brooklyn, NY 888-450-5463
Steve's Mom
  Bronx, NY 800-362-4545
Sticky Fingers Bakeries
  Spokane, WA 800-458-5826
Strauss Bakery
  Brooklyn, NY 718-851-7728
Strossner's Bakery & Cafe
  Greenville, SC 864-233-2990
Sugar Bowl Bakery
  Hayward, CA 888-688-1380
Summerfield Foods
  Santa Rosa, CA 707-579-3938
Sun Pac Foods
  Brampton, ON 905-792-2700
Sunset Specialty Foods
  Lake Arrowhead, CA 909-337-7643
Super Mom's LLC
  St Paul Park, MN 800-944-7276
Superior Bakery Inc
  N Grosvenordale, CT 860-923-9555
Superior Cake Products
  Southbridge, MA 508-764-3276
Svenhard's Swedish Bakery Inc
  Oakland, CA 800-705-3379
Swatt Baking Co
  Olean, NY 800-370-6656
Sweet Endings Inc
  West Palm Beach, FL 888-635-1177
Sweet Gallery Exclusive Pastry
  Toronto, ON 416-766-0289
Sweet Life Enterprises
  Santa Ana, CA 714-256-8900
Sweet Sams Baking Corp
  Bronx, NY 718-822-0599
Sweetery
  Anderson, SC 800-752-1188
T. Marzetti Company
  Westerville, OH 800-999-1835
Table De France
  Ontario, CA 909-923-5205
Tasty Mix Quality Foods
  Brooklyn, NY 718-855-7680
Teeny Foods Inc
  Portland, OR 503-252-3006
Tennessee Bun Company
  Nashville, TN 888-486-2867
Terranettis Italian Bakery
  Mechanicsburg, PA 717-697-5434
Teti Bakery
  Etobicoke, ON 800-465-0123
Texas Crumb & Food Products
  Farmers Branch, TX 800-522-7862
The Great San Saba River Pecan Company
  San Saba, TX 800-621-8121
The Konery
  Brooklyn, NY 917-750-4147
The Pillsbury Company
  Chelsea, MA 800-370-7834
Thyme Garden Herb Co
  Alsea, OR 800-482-4372
Tom Cat Bakery Inc
  Queens, NY 718-786-7659
Tomanetti Food Products Inc
  Oakmont, PA 800-875-3040
Tomaro's Bakery
  Clarksburg, WV 304-622-0691
Traditional Baking Inc
  Bloomington, CA 909-877-8471
Treasure Foods
  West Valley, UT 801-974-0911
Tripoli Bakery Inc
  Lawrence, MA 978-682-7754
Troppers
  Santa Barbara, CA 805-969-4054
Trumps Food Interest
  Vancouver, BC 604-732-8473
Turano Baking
  Berwyn, IL 708-788-9220
Turnbull Bakeries
  New Orleans, LA 504-581-5383
Tuscan Bakery
  Portland, OR 800-887-2261
Twin City Bagels
  South St Paul, MN 651-554-0200
Twin Marquis
  Brooklyn, NY 800-367-6868
Two Chefs on a Roll
  Carson, CA 800-842-3025
ULDO USA
  Lexington, MA 781-860-7800

Ultimate Biscotti
  Eugene, OR 541-344-8220
Uncle Andy's Cafe
  South Portland, ME 207-799-7199
Uncle Ralph's Cookies
  Frederick, MD 800-422-0626
United Noodle Manufacturing Company
  Salt Lake City, UT 801-485-0951
United Pies Of Elkhart Inc
  Elkhart, IN 574-294-3419
Upper Crust Bakery USA
  Phoenix, AZ 602-255-0464
Upper Crust Biscotti
  Pismo Beach, CA 866-972-6879
Uptown Bakers
  Hyattsville, MD 301-864-1500
Valley Bakery
  Burnaby, BC 604-291-0674
Valley Lahvosh
  Fresno, CA 800-480-2704
Vallos Baking Co
  Bethlehem, PA 610-866-1012
Van de Kamps
  Peoria, IL 800-798-3318
Vande Walle's Candies Inc
  Appleton, WI 800-738-1020
Venus Wafers Inc
  Hingham, MA 800-545-4538
Verdant Kitchen
  Norcross, GA 912-349-2958
Vie De France Yamazaki Inc
  Vienna, VA 800-446-4404
Vigneri Chocolate Inc.
  Rochester, NY 877-844-6374
Vocatura Bakery Inc
  Norwich, CT 860-887-2220
Wally Biscotti
  Denver, CO 866-659-2559
Wedding Cake Studio
  Williamsfield, OH 440-667-1765
Wedemeyer's Bakery
  S San Francisco, CA 650-873-1000
Wegmans Food Markets Inc.
  Rochester, NY 800-934-6267
WEIS Markets Inc.
  Sunbury, PA 866-999-9347
Wendysue & Tobey's
  Gardena, CA 310-516-9705
Wenger's Bakery
  Reading, PA 610-372-6545
Wenner Bakery
  Bayport, NY 800-869-6262
Wenzel's Bakery
  Tamaqua, PA 570-668-2360
Weston Foods
  Etobicoke, ON 416-252-7323
Wheat Montana Farms Inc
  Three Forks, MT 800-535-2798
Whole Earth Bakery
  New York, NY 212-677-7597
Wick's Pies Inc
  Winchester, IN 800-642-5880
Widoffs Modern Bakery
  Worcester, MA 508-752-7200
William Poll Inc
  New York, NY 800-993-7655
Williamsburg Chocolatier
  Williamsburg, VA 757-253-1474
Willmar Cookie & Nut Company
  Willmar, MN 800-426-7845
Willmark Sales Company
  Brooklyn, NY 718-388-7141
Wisconsin Cheeseman
  Madison, WI 800-693-0834
Wolferman's
  Medford, OR 800-798-6241
Wonton Food
  Brooklyn, NY 800-776-8889
Woodie Pie Company
  Artesia, NM 575-746-2132
World Of Chantilly
  Brooklyn, NY 718-859-1110
Wow! Factor Desserts
  Sherwood Park, AB 800-604-2253
Wuollet Bakery
  Minneapolis, MN 612-922-4341
Y Z Enterprises Inc
  Maumee, OH 800-736-8779
Ya-Hoo Baking Co
  Sherman, TX 888-869-2466
Young's Bakery
  Uniontown, PA 724-437-6361

Zoelsmann's Bakery & Deli
  Pueblo, CO 719-543-0407

Bread Crumbs & Croutons

H&S Edible Products Corporation
  Mount Vernon, NY 800-253-3364
Just Off Melrose
  Palm Springs, CA 760-320-7414
Lecoq Cuisine Corp
  Bridgeport, CT 203-334-1010
Lesley Stowe Fine Foods
  Richmond, BC 604-238-2180
Mignardise
  Chambly, QC 450-447-0777
Olivia's Croutons
  New Haven, VT 888-425-3080
Quality Bakery Products
  Houston, TX 866-449-4977
Quality Croutons
  Chicago, IL 800-334-2796
Rothbury Farms
  Grand Rapids, MI 877-684-2879
Sugar Foods Corp
  New York, NY
Sun Pac Foods
  Brampton, ON 905-792-2700

Bread Crumbs

4C Foods Corp
  Brooklyn, NY 718-272-4242
Colonna Brothers Inc
  North Bergen, NJ 201-864-1115
Duval Bakery Products
  Jacksonville, FL 904-354-7878
Lakeview Bakery
  Calgary, AB 403-246-6127
Newly Weds Foods Inc
  Chicago, IL 800-621-7521
Quality Bakery Products
  Houston, TX 866-449-4977
Richmond Baking Co
  Richmond, IN 765-962-8535
Sun Pac Foods
  Brampton, ON 905-792-2700
Texas Crumb & Food Products
  Farmers Branch, TX 800-522-7862
Turnbull Bakeries
  New Orleans, LA 504-581-5383
Vigo Importing Co
  Tampa, FL 800-282-4130

Croutons

Ace Bakery
  North York, ON 800-443-7929
Aladdin Bakers
  Brooklyn, NY 718-499-1818
Eco-Planet Cookies
  Santa Monica, CA 310-829-9050
Icco Cheese Co
  Orangeburg, NY 845-680-2436
Just Off Melrose
  Palm Springs, CA 760-320-7414
Lakeview Bakery
  Calgary, AB 403-246-6127
Live A Little Gourmet Foods
  Oakland, CA 888-744-2300
Natural Food Mill
  Corona, CA 800-797-5090
Olivia's Croutons
  New Haven, VT 888-425-3080
Progresso Quality Foods
  Vineland, NJ 856-691-1565
Quality Bakery Products
  Houston, TX 866-449-4977
Quality Croutons
  Chicago, IL 800-334-2796
Rothbury Farms
  Grand Rapids, MI 877-684-2879
San Francisco French Bread
  Oakland, CA 510-729-6232
Sugar Foods Corp
  Sun Valley, CA 818-768-7900
Sun Pac Foods
  Brampton, ON 905-792-2700

Crumbs

Aladdin Bakers
  Brooklyn, NY 718-499-1818
Eco-Planet Cookies
  Santa Monica, CA 310-829-9050

Product Categories / Baked Goods: Bread Sticks

Icco Cheese Co
  Orangeburg, NY 845-680-2436
Newly Weds Foods Inc
  Chicago, IL 800-621-7521
Progresso Quality Foods
  Vineland, NJ 856-691-1565
Quality Bakery Products
  Houston, TX 866-449-4977
Richmond Baking Co
  Richmond, IN 765-962-8535
Sun Pac Foods
  Brampton, ON 905-792-2700
Texas Crumb & Food Products
  Farmers Branch, TX 800-522-7862
Vigo Importing Co
  Tampa, FL 800-282-4130

Bread Sticks

Andre-Boudin Bakeries
  San Francisco, CA 415-882-1849
Bake Crafters Food Company
  McDonald, TN 423-396-3392
Clown Global Brands
  Northbrook, IL 800-323-5778
Colonna Brothers Inc
  North Bergen, NJ 201-864-1115
Dwayne Keith Brooks Company
  Orangevale, CA 916-988-1030
Falcone's Cookie Land LTD
  Brooklyn, NY 718-236-4200
Good Groceries
  Brooklyn, NY 347-853-7462
John W Macy's Cheesesticks Inc
  Elmwood Park, NJ 800-643-0573
Kemach Food Products
  Brooklyn, NY 718-272-5655
La Piccolina
  Decatur, GA 800-626-1624
Nature's Hilights
  Chico, CA 800-313-6454
Real Food Marketing
  Kansas City, MO 816-221-4100
Stella D'oro
  Charlotte, NC 800-995-2623
Teeny Foods Inc
  Portland, OR 503-252-3006
Tomanetti Food Products
  Oakmont, PA 800-875-3040
Tropical Nut Fruit & Bulk Cndy
  Lithia Springs, GA 800-544-3762
Turnbull Bakeries
  New Orleans, LA 504-581-5383

Garlic

Djerdan Burek Corp
  South Hackensack, NJ 888-462-8735

Sesame

Nature's Legacy Inc.
  Hudson, MI 517-448-2050

Breads

Angelic Bakehouse
  Cudahy, WI
Arctic Beverages
  Winnipeg, MB 866-503-1270
Aunt Millie's Bakeries
  Fort Wayne, IN 855-755-2253
Bake Crafters Food Company
  McDonald, TN 423-396-3392
BakeMark Ingredients Canada
  Richmond, BC 800-665-9441
BakeryCorp
  Miami, FL 305-623-3838
Bakkavor USA
  Charlotte, NC 800-842-3025
Barely Bread
Beckmann's Old World Bakery
  Santa Cruz, CA 831-423-9242
Beer Bakers Inc.
  Nashville, TN 615-775-3329
Bella Chi-Cha Products
  Santa Cruz, CA 831-423-1851
Berkshire Mountain Bakery
  Housatonic, MA 866-274-6124
Bien Cuit
  Brooklyn, NY 718-852-0200
Bimbo Bakeries USA Inc.
  Horsham, PA 800-984-0989

Bluepoint Bakery
  Denver, CO 303-298-1100
Boboli Intl. Inc.
  Stockton, CA 209-473-3507
Brazi Bites
  Portland, OR 503-303-2272
Butter Krust Baking Company
  Thomasville, GA 800-282-8093
California Lavash
  Gilroy, CA 408-846-7705
Chatila's
  Salem, NH 603-898-5459
Chella's Dutch Delicacies
  Lake Oswego, OR 800-458-3331
Clarmil Manufacturing Corp
  Hayward, CA 888-252-7645
Colchester Bakery
  Colchester, CT 860-537-2415
Cotton Baking Company
  Alexandria, LA 318-448-6600
Cyrils Bakery
  Fort Lauderdale, FL 800-929-7457
Dole & Bailey Inc
  Woburn, MA 781-935-1234
East Balt Commissary Inc
  Chicago, IL 800-621-8555
Essential Baking Co, The
  Seattle, WA 206-545-3804
Flowers Baking Co
  El Paso, TX 800-328-6111
Flowers Foods Inc.
  Thomasville, GA 229-226-9110
Food for Life Baking
  Corona, CA 800-797-5090
Franklin Baking Co.
  Goldsboro, NC 919-735-0344
French Meadow Bakery & Cafe
  Minneapolis, MN 612-870-7855
Frisco Baking Co Inc
  Los Angeles, CA 323-225-6111
Fullbloom Baking Co
  Newark, CA 800-201-9909
GAF Seelig Inc
  Flushing, NY 718-899-5000
Gold Coast Baking Co Inc
  Santa Ana, CA 714-545-2253
Goldilocks USA
  Hayward, CA 510-476-0700
Grace Baking Company
  Richmond, CA 510-231-7200
Granello Bakery
  Las Vegas, NV 702-361-0311
Greenhills Irish Bakery
  Dorchester Ctr, MA 617-825-8187
H&S Bakery
  Baltimore, MD 800-959-7655
Haby's Alsatian Bakery
  Castroville, TX 830-538-2118
Happy Campers
  Portland, OR
Holsum Bakery Inc
  Phoenix, AZ 602-252-2351
Hybread
  Marina del Ray, CA 310-312-1200
Jacquet Bakery
  New York, NY
Julian Bakery
  Oceanside, CA 760-721-5200
Kim and Jake's
  Boulder, CO 303-499-9126
King's Hawaiian Holding Co Inc.
  Torrance, CA 877-695-4227
Klosterman Baking Co.
  Cincinnati, OH 877-301-1004
Koffee Kup Bakery
  Burlington, VT 802-863-2696
La Brea Bakery Inc
  San Leandro, CA 855-427-9982
Lakeview Bakery
  Calgary, AB 403-246-6127
Lavoi Corporation
  Atlanta, GA 404-325-1016
Love's Bakery
  Honolulu, HI 808-841-0397
Martins Famous Pastry Shoppe
  Chambersburg, PA 800-548-1200
Metropolitan Bakery
  Philadelphia, PA 877-412-7323
Metropolitan Baking Co
  Hamtramck, MI 313-875-7246
Mikey's
  480-696-2483

Morabito Baking Co Inc
  Norristown, PA 800-525-7747
Morse's Sauerkraut
  Waldoboro, ME 866-832-5569
Mrs Baird's
  Horsham, PA 800-984-0989
Natural Food Mill
  Corona, CA 800-797-5090
Natural Ovens Bakery Inc
  Manitowoc, WI 800-558-3535
Naturally Delicious Inc
  Oakland Park, FL 888-221-7352
Nature's Hilights
  Chico, CA 800-313-6454
Nema Food Distribution
  Fairfield, NJ 973-256-4415
Neuman Bakery Specialties
  Addison, IL 800-253-5298
New Horizon Foods
  Union City, CA 510-489-8600
O'Doughs
  Toronto, ON 855-636-8447
Oasis Breads
  Escondido, CA 760-747-7390
Old World Bakery
  Cincinnati, OH 513-931-1411
One Degree Organic Foods
  Abbotsford, BC 855-834-2642
Orlando Baking Co
  Cleveland, OH 800-362-5504
Orwasher's Bakery
  New York, NY 212-288-6569
Pepperidge Farm Inc.
  Norwalk, CT 888-737-7374
Plehn's Bakery Inc
  Louisville, KY 502-896-4438
Rockland Bakery
  Nanuet, NY 800-734-4376
Royal Caribbean Bakery
  Mt Vernon, NY 888-818-0971
Sanborn Sourdough Bakery
  Las Vegas, NV 702-795-1030
Sandors Bakeries
  Miami, FL 305-642-8484
Simit + Smith
  Ridgefield, NJ 201-699-0320
Southern Baking
  Greer, SC 864-627-1380
Spelt Right Foods, LLC
  Brooklyn, NY 877-773-5801
Sterling Foods LLC
  San Antonio, TX 210-490-1669
Superior Baking Co
  Brockton, MA 800-696-2253
T. Marzetti Company
  Westerville, OH 800-999-1835
Taste Maker Foods
  Memphis, TN 800-467-1407
The Lancaster Food Company
  Lancaster, PA
The Perfect Pita
  Springfield, VA 703-644-0004
Turano Baking
  Berwyn, IL 708-788-9220
Upper Crust Bakery USA
  Phoenix, AZ 602-255-0464
Vermont Bread Co
  Brattleboro, VT 802-254-4600
Vie De France Yamazaki Inc
  Vienna, VA 800-446-4404
Whipped Pastry Boutique
  Brooklyn, NY 718-858-8088
Wuollet Bakery
  Minneapolis, MN 612-922-4341

Bagels

Ace Bakery
  North York, ON 800-443-7929
Aladdin Bakers
  Brooklyn, NY 718-499-1818
Alpha Baking Company
  South Bend, IN 773-261-6000
Amoroso's Baking Co
  Bellmawr, NJ 215-471-4740
Andre-Boudin Bakeries
  San Francisco, CA 415-882-1849
Awrey Bakeries
  Livonia, MI 800-950-2253
Bagel Factory
  Los Angeles, CA 310-836-9865
Bagel Guys
  Brooklyn, NY 718-222-4361

Product Categories / Baked Goods: Breads

Bagelworks
   New York, NY 212-744-6444
Bake Crafters Food Company
   McDonald, TN 423-396-3392
Barely Bread
BBU Bakeries
   Horsham, PA 800-984-0989
Better Bagel Bakery
   Sarasota, FL 941-924-0393
Boca Bagelworks
   Boca Raton, FL 561-852-8992
Brooklyn Bagel Company
   Staten Island, NY 800-349-3055
Buckhead Gourmet
   Atlanta, GA 800-673-6338
Bylada Foods
   Moonachie, NJ 201-933-7474
California Smart Foods
   San Francisco, CA 415-826-0449
Century Blends LLC
   Hunt Valley, MD 410-771-6606
Chatila's
   Salem, NH 603-898-5459
Dakota Brands Intl
   Jamestown, ND 800-844-5073
Enjoy Life Foods
   Chicago, IL 888-503-6569
Felix Roma & Son Inc
   Endicott, NY 607-748-3336
Fleischer's Bagels
   Macedon, NY 315-986-9999
French Meadow Bakery & Cafe
   Minneapolis, MN 612-870-7855
Global Bakeries Inc
   Pacoima, CA 818-896-0525
Greater Knead, The
   Bensalem, PA 267-522-8523
H&S Bakery
   Baltimore, MD 800-959-7655
Harlan Bakeries
   Avon, IN 800-435-2738
Lakeview Bakery
   Calgary, AB 403-246-6127
Lenchner Bakery
   Concord, ON 905-738-8811
Maui Bagel
   Kahului, HI 808-270-7561
O'Doughs
   Toronto, ON 855-636-8447
Otis Spunkmeyer
   Brockport, NY 855-427-9982
Ottenberg's Bakers
   Sykesville, MD 800-334-7264
Pan-O-Gold Baking Co.
   St. Cloud, MN 800-444-7005
Petrofsky's Bakery Products
   Chesterfield, MO 636-519-1613
Positively 3rd St Bakery
   Duluth, MN 218-724-8619
Prairie Malt
   Biggar, SK 306-948-3500
Quality Naturally Foods
   City Of Industry, CA 888-498-6986
Rudi's Organic Bakery
   Boulder, CO 877-293-0876
Schwebel Baking Co.
   Youngstown, OH 800-860-2867
SJR Foods
   New Bedford, MA 617-500-4516
Spelt Right Foods, LLC
   Brooklyn, NY 877-773-5801
Twin City Bagels
   South St Paul, MN 651-554-0200
Ultimate Bagel
   Santa Barbara, CA 805-845-2511
Wenner Bakery
   Bayport, NY 800-869-6262
Western Bagel Baking Corp
   Van Nuys, CA 818-786-5847

Fresh

Bagel Guys
   Brooklyn, NY 718-222-4361
Bantam Bagels
   New York, NY 646-852-6320
Felix Roma & Son Inc
   Endicott, NY 607-748-3336
Fleischer's Bagels
   Macedon, NY 315-986-9999
Harlan Bakeries
   Avon, IN 800-435-2738

Rockland Bakery
   Nanuet, NY 800-734-4376
Russ & Daughters
   New York, NY 800-787-7229
Western Bagel Baking Corp
   Van Nuys, CA 818-786-5847

Frozen

Aladdin Bakers
   Brooklyn, NY 718-499-1818
Andre-Boudin Bakeries
   San Francisco, CA 415-882-1849
Awrey Bakeries
   Livonia, MI 800-950-2253
Brooklyn Bagel Company
   Staten Island, NY 800-349-3055
Bylada Foods
   Moonachie, NJ 201-933-7474
Fleischer's Bagels
   Macedon, NY 315-986-9999
Guttenplan's Frozen Dough
   Middletown, NJ 888-422-4357
Harlan Bakeries
   Avon, IN 800-435-2738
Petrofsky's Bakery Products
   Chesterfield, MO 636-519-1613
Quality Naturally Foods
   City Of Industry, CA 888-498-6986
Wenner Bakery
   Bayport, NY 800-869-6262
Western Bagel Baking Corp
   Van Nuys, CA 818-786-5847

Baguettes

Ace Bakery
   North York, ON 800-443-7929
Epi De France Bakery
   Atlanta, GA 800-325-1014
Frisco Baking Co Inc
   Los Angeles, CA 323-225-6111
Julian's Recipe
   Brooklyn, NY 888-640-8880
Kosher French Baguettes
   Brooklyn, NY 718-633-4994
Lavoi Corporation
   Atlanta, GA 404-325-1016
Tom Cat Bakery Inc
   Queens, NY 718-786-7659

Bialys

Harlan Bakeries
   Avon, IN 800-435-2738
Russ & Daughters
   New York, NY 800-787-7229

Biscuits

American Vintage Wine Biscuits
   Long Island City, NY 718-361-1003
Awrey Bakeries
   Livonia, MI 800-950-2253
Bake Crafters Food Company
   McDonald, TN 423-396-3392
Baker Boy Bake Shop Inc
   Dickinson, ND 800-437-2008
Bama Foods LTD
   Tulsa, OK 800-756-2262
Bluechip Group
   Salt Lake City, UT 800-878-0099
Borinquen Biscuit Corporation
   Yauco, PR 787-856-3030
Bremner Biscuit Company
   Denver, CO 866-972-6879
Bridgford Foods Corp
   Anaheim, CA 800-527-2105
Buonitalia
   New York, NY 212-633-9090
Byrd Cookie
   Savannah, GA 800-291-2973
Callie's Charleston Biscuits
   North Charleston, SC 843-577-1198
Chelsea Flower Market
   New York, NY 888-727-7887
Chelsea Milling Co.
   Chelsea, MI 800-727-2460
Chex Finer Foods Inc
   Mansfield, MA 800-227-8114
Damascus Bakery
   Brooklyn, NY 718-855-1456
Del's Pastry
   Toronto, ON 800-461-0663

Di Camillo Baking Co
   Niagara Falls, NY 800-634-4363
Ener-G Foods
   Seattle, WA 800-331-5222
Falcone's Cookie Land LTD
   Brooklyn, NY 718-236-4200
Fresh Start Bakeries
   Brea, CA 714-256-8900
Frisco Baking Co Inc
   Los Angeles, CA 323-225-6111
Grebe's Bakery
   Milwaukee, WI 800-833-3158
GWB Foods Corporation
   Brooklyn, NY 877-977-7610
Heltzman Bakery
   Louisville, KY 502-447-3515
Hostess Brands
   Kansas City, MO 816-701-4600
Keebler Company
   Battlecreek, MI 800-962-1413
Le Chef Bakery
   Montebello, CA 323-888-2929
Lone Star Bakery
   Round Rock, TX 512-255-7268
Mason Dixie Biscuit Co.
   Washington, DC 202-880-2315
Merlino Italian Baking Company
   Kent, WA 800-800-9490
Mom's Bakery
   Sherman, TX 903-893-7585
Pacific Ocean Produce
   Santa Cruz, CA 831-423-2654
Pett Spice Products Inc
   Atlanta, GA 404-691-5235
Pioneer Frozen Foods
   Duncanville, TX 972-298-4281
Purity Factories
   St. John's, NL 800-563-3411
Quality Naturally Foods
   City Of Industry, CA 888-498-6986
Rovira Biscuit Corporation
   Ponce, PR 787-844-8585
Royal Home Bakery
   Newmarket, ON 905-715-7044
Schulze & Burch Biscuit Co
   Chicago, IL 773-927-6622
Stella D'oro
   Charlotte, NC 800-995-2623
Sterling Foods LLC
   San Antonio, TX 210-490-1669
Superior Bakery Inc
   N Grosvenordale, CT 860-923-9555
Ultimate Biscotti
   Eugene, OR 541-344-8220
Wedemeyer's Bakery
   S San Francisco, CA 650-873-1000
Y Z Enterprises Inc
   Maumee, OH 800-736-8779

Fresh

Automatic Rolls Of New Jersey
   Edison, NJ 877-222-2867
Ener-G Foods
   Seattle, WA 800-331-5222
Mrs. Kavanagh's English Muffins
   Rumford, RI 800-556-7216
New Bakery Company of Ohio
   Zanesville, OH 800-848-9845
Quinzani Bakery
   Boston, MA 800-999-1062

Frozen

Awrey Bakeries
   Livonia, MI 800-950-2253
Bake Crafters Food Company
   McDonald, TN 423-396-3392
Bama Foods LTD
   Tulsa, OK 800-756-2262
Callie's Charleston Biscuits
   North Charleston, SC 843-577-1198
Dynamic Foods
   Lubbock, TX 806-723-5600
Fresh Start Bakeries
   Brea, CA 714-256-8900
Lone Star Bakery
   Round Rock, TX 512-255-7268
Pacific Ocean Produce
   Santa Cruz, CA 831-423-2654

Product Categories / Baked Goods: Breads

Brown

Burnham & Morrill Co
　Portland, ME................800-813-2165
Naji's Pita Gourmet Restaurant
　Birmingham, AL..............205-945-6001
Terranettis Italian Bakery
　Mechanicsburg, PA...........717-697-5434

Buns

Ace Bakery
　North York, ON..............800-443-7929
Alois J Binder Bakery
　New Orleans, LA.............504-947-1111
Aryzta
　Los Angeles, CA.............855-427-9982
Athens Baking Company
　Fresno, CA..................800-775-2867
Aunt Millie's Bakeries
　Fort Wayne, IN..............855-755-2253
Baldinger Baking Co
　St Paul, MN.................651-224-5761
Best Harvest Bakeries
　Kansas City, KS.............800-811-5715
Bimbo Bakeries USA Inc.
　Horsham, PA.................800-984-0989
Bread Box Cafe
　Astoria, NY.................718-389-9703
Calgary Italian Bakery
　Calgary, AB.................800-661-6868
Caribbean Food Delights Inc
　Tappan, NY..................845-398-3000
Colombo Bakery
　Sacramento, CA..............916-648-1011
Country Club Bakery
　Fairmont, WV................304-363-5690
Dimpflmeier Bakery
　Toronto, ON.................800-268-2421
El Peto Products
　Cambridge, ON...............800-387-4064
European Bakers
　Tucker, GA..................770-723-6180
Fancy Lebanese Bakery
　Halifax, NS.................902-429-0400
Flowers Baking Co
　Birmingham, AL..............205-252-1161
Flowers Baking Co
　Tuscaloosa, AL..............205-752-5586
Food for Life Baking
　Corona, CA..................800-797-5090
Frisco Baking Co Inc
　Los Angeles, CA.............323-225-6111
Gadoua Bakery
　Napierville, QC.............800-661-7246
Gold Coast Bakeries
　Santa Ana, CA...............714-545-2253
Gold Coast Baking Co Inc
　Santa Ana, CA...............714-545-2253
H&S Bakery
　Baltimore, MD...............800-959-7655
Harting's Bakery
　Bowmansville, PA............717-445-5644
Holsum Bakery Inc
　Phoenix, AZ.................602-252-2351
Hostess Brands
　Kansas City, MO.............816-701-4600
J.P. Sunrise Bakery
　Edmonton, AB................780-454-5797
Kim and Jake's
　Boulder, CO.................303-499-9126
Klosterman Baking Co.
　Cincinnati, OH..............877-301-1004
Lakeview Bakery
　Calgary, AB.................403-246-6127
Lavoi Corporation
　Atlanta, GA.................404-325-1016
Metropolitan Baking Co
　Hamtramck, MI...............313-875-7246
Mrs Baird's
　Horsham, PA.................800-984-0989
Nardi Breads
　South Windsor, CT...........860-289-5458
Natural Food Mill
　Corona, CA..................800-797-5090
New Horizons Baking Co
　Fremont, IN.................260-495-7055
O'Doughs
　Toronto, ON.................855-636-8447
Ottenberg's Bakers
　Sykesville, MD..............800-334-7264
Ozark Empire
　Rogers, AR..................479-636-3313
Ozery Bakery
　Vaughan, ON.................888-556-5560
Pan-O-Gold Baking Co.
　St. Cloud, MN...............800-444-7005
Pepperidge Farm Inc.
　Norwalk, CT.................888-737-7374
Red Plate Foods
　Bend, OR....................541-550-7676
Rotella's Italian Bakery Inc.
　La Vista, NE................402-592-6600
Royal Home Bakery
　Newmarket, ON...............905-715-7044
Rudi's Organic Bakery
　Boulder, CO.................877-293-0876
Schwan's Food Service Inc.
　Marshall, MN................877-302-7426
Schwebel Baking Co.
　Youngstown, OH..............800-860-2867
Smart Baking Co.
　Sanford, FL.................407-915-5519
Tennessee Bun Company
　Nashville, TN...............888-486-2867
Twin Marquis
　Brooklyn, NY................800-367-6868
Wenger's Bakery
　Reading, PA.................610-372-6545

Sticky

Bluepoint Bakery
　Denver, CO..................303-298-1100
Cinnamon Bakery
　Braintree, MA...............800-886-2867
Keller's Bakery
　Lafayette, LA...............337-235-1568

Challah

Atlanta Bread Co.
　Smyrna, GA..................800-398-3728
Orwasher's Bakery
　New York, NY................212-288-6569

Cinnamon Toast

Happy Campers
　Portland, OR
Loghouse Foods
　Minneapolis, MN.............763-546-8395

Corn

Bake Crafters Food Company
　McDonald, TN................423-396-3392
Dynamic Foods
　Lubbock, TX.................806-723-5600
Legacy Bakehouse
　Waukesha, WI................800-967-2447
Sara Lee Frozen Bakery
　Kings Mountain, NC..........800-323-7117
Tova Industries LLC
　Louisville, KY..............888-532-8682

Croissants

Andre-Boudin Bakeries
　San Francisco, CA...........415-882-1849
Bake Crafters Food Company
　McDonald, TN................423-396-3392
BakeMark Canada
　Laval, QC...................800-361-4998
Bluepoint Bakery
　Denver, CO..................303-298-1100
California Smart Foods
　San Francisco, CA...........415-826-0449
Edner Corporation
　Hayward, CA.................510-441-8504
GAF Seelig Inc
　Flushing, NY................718-899-5000
Galaxy Desserts
　Richmond, CA................800-225-3523
Global Bakeries Inc
　Pacoima, CA.................818-896-0525
Nikola's Foods
　Bloomington, MN.............888-645-6527
Sara Lee Frozen Bakery
　Kings Mountain, NC..........800-323-7117
Vie De France Yamazaki Inc
　Vienna, VA..................800-446-4404

English Muffins

Aryzta
　Los Angeles, CA.............855-427-9982
Aunt Millie's Bakeries
　Fort Wayne, IN..............855-755-2253
Bimbo Bakeries USA Inc.
　Horsham, PA.................800-984-0989
Food for Life Baking
　Corona, CA..................800-797-5090
Fresh Start Bakeries
　Brea, CA....................714-256-8900
H&S Bakery
　Baltimore, MD...............800-959-7655
Homestead Baking Co
　Rumford, RI.................800-556-7216
Meyer's Bakeries
　Casa Grande, AZ.............800-528-5770
Mikey's
　Scottsdale, AZ
Mikey's
　............................480-696-2483
Mrs. Kavanagh's English Muffins
　Rumford, RI.................800-556-7216
Natural Food Mill
　Corona, CA..................800-797-5090
New Horizons Baking Co
　Fremont, IN.................260-495-7055
Oakrun Farm Bakery
　Ancaster, ON................800-263-6422
Ottenberg's Bakers
　Sykesville, MD..............800-334-7264
Rudi's Organic Bakery
　Boulder, CO.................877-293-0876
Weston Foods
　Etobicoke, ON...............416-252-7323
Wolferman's
　Medford, OR.................800-798-6241

Flat

Ak Mak Bakeries
　Sanger, CA..................559-875-5511
Aladdin Bakers
　Brooklyn, NY................718-499-1818
American Flatbread
　Pittsfield, NH..............603-435-5119
California Lavash
　Gilroy, CA..................408-846-7705
Di Camillo Baking Co
　Niagara Falls, NY...........800-634-4363
Falcone's Cookie Land LTD
　Brooklyn, NY................718-236-4200
Flatout Inc
　Saline, MI..................866-944-5445
Good Wives
　Wilmington, MA..............800-521-8160
Just Off Melrose
　Palm Springs, CA............760-320-7414
Kemach Food Products
　Brooklyn, NY................718-272-5655
Klosterman Baking Co.
　Cincinnati, OH..............877-301-1004
Kronos
　Glendale Heights, IL........800-621-0099
Molinaro's Fine Italian Foods Ltd.
　Mississauga, ON.............905-281-0352
Nita Crisp Crackers LLC
　Fort Collins, CO............866-493-4609
Nu-World Amaranth Inc
　Naperville, IL..............630-369-6851
O'Doughs
　Toronto, ON.................855-636-8447
Old London Foods
　Yadkinville, NC
Real Food Marketing
　Kansas City, MO.............816-221-4100
Rudolph's Specialty Bakery
　Toronto, ON.................800-268-1589
Rustic Bakery Inc.
　San Rafael, CA..............415-479-5600
Rustic Crust Inc
　Pittsfield, NH..............603-435-5119
Schwebel Baking Co.
　Youngstown, OH..............800-860-2867
Sonoma Flatbreads
　Columbus, OH
Teeny Foods Inc
　Portland, OR................503-252-3006
Teti Bakery
　Etobicoke, ON...............800-465-0123
Valley Lahvosh
　Fresno, CA..................800-480-2704
Vicky's Artisan Bakery
　Markham, ON.................905-944-0940

Product Categories / Baked Goods: Breads

Focaccia

Atlanta Bread Co.
   Smyrna, GA 800-398-3728
Clarmil Manufacturing Corp
   Hayward, CA 888-252-7645
Colors Gourmet Pizza
   Vista, CA 760-597-1400
Epi De France Bakery
   Atlanta, GA 800-325-1014
Molinaro's Fine Italian Foods Ltd.
   Mississauga, ON 905-281-0352
Real Food Marketing
   Kansas City, MO 816-221-4100
Teeny Foods Inc
   Portland, OR 503-252-3006
Tomanetti Food Products Inc
   Oakmont, PA 800-875-3040

French

Atlanta Bread Co.
   Smyrna, GA 800-398-3728
Frisco Baking Co Inc
   Los Angeles, CA 323-225-6111
Galasso's Bakery
   Mira Loma, CA 951-360-1211
Gold Coast Bakeries
   Santa Ana, CA 714-545-2253
Hawaii Star Bakery
   Honolulu, HI 808-841-3602
Le Donne Brothers Bakery
   Roseto, PA. 610-588-0423
Leidenheimer Baking Co
   New Orleans, LA 800-259-9099
Metropolitan Baking Co
   Hamtramck, MI. 313-875-7246
Orlando Baking Co
   Cleveland, OH 800-362-5504
Piemonte Bakery Co
   Rockford, IL 815-962-4833
Quinzani Bakery
   Boston, MA. 800-999-1062
The Pillsbury Company
   Chelsea, MA 800-370-7834
Tom Cat Bakery Inc
   Queens, NY. 718-786-7659

Fresh

Ace Bakery
   North York, ON. 800-443-7929
Alfred & Sam's Italian Bakery
   Lancaster, PA. 717-392-6311
Alois J Binder Bakery
   New Orleans, LA. 504-947-1111
Alpha Baking Company
   South Bend, IN 773-261-6000
Amoroso's Baking Co
   Bellmawr, NJ. 215-471-4740
Andre-Boudin Bakeries
   San Francisco, CA 415-882-1849
Baldinger Baking Co
   St Paul, MN. 651-224-5761
Brooklyn Baking Company
   Waterbury, CT. 203-574-9198
Casino Bakery
   Tampa, FL. 813-242-0311
Chicago Pastry
   Bloomingdale, IL 630-529-6391
Cole's Quality Foods
   Grand Rapids, MI 616-975-0081
Colombo Bakery
   Sacramento, CA 916-648-1011
Ener-G Foods
   Seattle, WA 800-331-5222
Epi De France Bakery
   Atlanta, GA 800-325-1014
Father Sam's Bakery
   Buffalo, NY. 800-521-6719
Felix Roma & Son Inc
   Endicott, NY 607-748-3336
Galasso's Bakery
   Mira Loma, CA 951-360-1211
Glamorgan Bakery
   Calgary, AB. 403-232-2800
Gold Coast Bakeries
   Santa Ana, CA 714-545-2253
Gold Standard Baking Inc
   Chicago, IL 800-648-7904
Gonnella Baking Company
   Schamburg, IL. 800-322-8829
Harlan Bakeries
   Avon, IN 800-435-2738

Highlandville Packing
   Highlandville, MO 417-443-3365
Homestead Baking Co
   Rumford, RI 800-556-7216
Jubelt Variety Bakeries
   Litchfield, IL. 217-324-5314
Kosher French Baguettes
   Brooklyn, NY 718-633-4994
L & M Bakery
   Riverside, NJ. 888-887-1335
Landolfi's Food Products
   Trenton, NJ 609-392-1830
Lanthier Bakery
   Alexandria, ON 613-525-2435
Leidenheimer Baking Co
   New Orleans, LA 800-259-9099
Lucerne Foods
   Pleasanton, CA 877-232-4271
Multi Marques
   Montreal, QC 514-934-1866
Naji's Pita Gourmet Restaurant
   Birmingham, AL. 205-945-6001
Natural Food Mill
   Corona, CA 800-797-5090
Natural Ovens Bakery Inc
   Manitowoc, WI 800-558-3535
Nevada Baking Company
   Las Vegas, NV 702-384-8950
Ottenberg's Bakers
   Sykesville, MD 800-334-7264
Piantedosi Baking Co Inc
   Malden, MA 800-339-0080
Piemonte Bakery Co
   Rockford, IL 815-962-4833
Pittsfield Rye Bakery
   Pittsfield, MA 413-443-9141
Positively 3rd St Bakery
   Duluth, MN. 218-724-8619
Quinzani Bakery
   Boston, MA. 800-999-1062
Real Food Marketing
   Kansas City, MO 816-221-4100
Rudi's Organic Bakery
   Boulder, CO 877-293-0876
San Francisco French Bread
   Oakland, CA. 510-729-6232
Schwebel Baking Co.
   Youngstown, OH. 800-860-2867
Shaw Baking Company
   Thunder Bay, ON 807-345-7327
St Armands Baking Co
   Bradenton, FL. 941-753-7494
Superior Bakery Inc
   N Grosvenordale, CT 860-923-9555
Swatt Baking Co
   Olean, NY. 800-370-6656
Teeny Foods Inc
   Portland, OR 503-252-3006
Terranettis Italian Bakery
   Mechanicsburg, PA. 717-697-5434
Weston Foods
   Etobicoke, ON 416-252-7323
Wolferman's
   Medford, OR. 800-798-6241

Frozen

Ace Bakery
   North York, ON. 800-443-7929
Alpha Baking Company
   South Bend, IN 773-261-6000
American Flatbread
   Pittsfield, NH 603-435-5119
Andre-Boudin Bakeries
   San Francisco, CA 415-882-1849
Awrey Bakeries
   Livonia, MI. 800-950-2253
Caribbean Food Delights Inc
   Tappan, NY. 845-398-3000
Cedarlane Foods
   Carson, CA 800-826-3322
Cole's Quality Foods
   Grand Rapids, MI 616-975-0081
Epi De France Bakery
   Atlanta, GA 800-325-1014
Guttenplan's Frozen Dough
   Middletown, NJ 888-422-4357
Harlan Bakeries
   Avon, IN 800-435-2738
Leidenheimer Baking Co
   New Orleans, LA 800-259-9099
New York Frozen Foods Inc
   Bedford, OH 216-292-5655

Piantedosi Baking Co Inc
   Malden, MA 800-339-0080
Positively 3rd St Bakery
   Duluth, MN. 218-724-8619
Real Food Marketing
   Kansas City, MO 816-221-4100
Rhodes International Inc
   Salt Lake City, UT 800-876-7333
Rubschlager Baking Corp
    800-661-7246
Rudi's Organic Bakery
   Boulder, CO 877-293-0876
The Pillsbury Company
   Chelsea, MA 800-370-7834
Wenner Bakery
   Bayport, NY 800-869-6262
Wolferman's
   Medford, OR. 800-798-6241

Garlic

Cole's Quality Foods
   Grand Rapids, MI 616-975-0081
Dabruzzi's Italian Foods
   Hudson, WI 715-386-3653
Landolfi's Food Products
   Trenton, NJ 609-392-1830
Piemonte Bakery Co
   Rockford, IL 815-962-4833
Real Food Marketing
   Kansas City, MO 816-221-4100

Frozen

Better Baked Foods Inc
   North East, PA. 814-725-8778

Honey Buns

Maple Donuts
   York, PA. 800-627-5348

Italian

Armanino Foods of Distinction
   Hayward, CA 800-255-8588
Butter Krust Baking Company
   Thomasville, GA 800-282-8093
Cusano's Baking Company
   Hallandale, FL 954-458-1010
Epi De France Bakery
   Atlanta, GA 800-325-1014
Frisco Baking Co Inc
   Los Angeles, CA 323-225-6111
Le Donne Brothers Bakery
   Roseto, PA. 610-588-0423
Metropolitan Baking Co
   Hamtramck, MI. 313-875-7246
Milano Bakery Inc
   Joliet, IL 815-727-2253
Orlando Baking Co
   Cleveland, OH 800-362-5504
Piemonte Bakery Co
   Rockford, IL 815-962-4833
Quinzani Bakery
   Boston, MA. 800-999-1062
Schwebel Baking Co.
   Youngstown, OH. 800-860-2867
Scialo Brothers Bakery
   Providence, RI 877-421-0986
Teeny Foods Inc
   Portland, OR 503-252-3006
Tom Cat Bakery Inc
   Queens, NY. 718-786-7659
Wenner Bakery
   Bayport, NY 800-869-6262

Melba Toast

Old London Foods
   Yadkinville, NC
Turnbull Bakeries
   New Orleans, LA 504-581-5383
Turnbull Cone Baking Company
   Chattanooga, TN. 423-265-4551

Multi-Grain

Beckmann's Old World Bakery
   Santa Cruz, CA 831-423-9242
French Meadow Bakery & Cafe
   Minneapolis, MN 612-870-7855
Harvest Innovations
   Indianola, IA 515-962-5063
Mother Nature's Goodies
   Yucaipa, CA 909-795-6018

Product Categories / Baked Goods: Breads

Multigrains Bread Co
 Lawrence, MA 978-691-6100
Natural Food Mill
 Corona, CA 800-797-5090
Rudi's Organic Bakery
 Boulder, CO 877-293-0876

Nut

L & M Bakery
 Riverside, NJ 888-887-1335

Pita

Bake Crafters Food Company
 McDonald, TN 423-396-3392
Byblos Bakery
 Calgary, AB 403-250-3711
Corfu Foods Inc
 Bensenville, IL 630-595-2510
Fancy Lebanese Bakery
 Halifax, NS 902-429-0400
Father Sam's Bakery
 Buffalo, NY 800-521-6719
Food for Life Baking
 Corona, CA 800-797-5090
Global Bakeries Inc
 Pacoima, CA 818-896-0525
Kangaroo Brands
 Omaha, NE 877-266-2472
Klosterman Baking Co.
 Cincinnati, OH 877-301-1004
Konto's Foods
 Patterson, NJ 973-278-2800
Kronos
 Glendale Heights, IL 800-621-0099
Mediterranean Gyro Products
 Long Island City, NY 718-786-3399
Mediterranean Pita Bakery
 Edmonton, AB 780-476-6666
Naji's Pita Gourmet Restaurant
 Birmingham, AL 205-945-6001
Ozery Bakery
 Vaughan, ON 888-556-5560
Pita King Bakery
 Everett, WA 425-258-4040
Pita Products
 Farmington Hills, MI 800-600-7482
Schwebel Baking Co.
 Youngstown, OH 800-860-2867
Soloman Baking Company
 Denver, CO 303-371-2777
Stacy's Pita Chip Co
 Randolph, MA 888-332-4477
Teeny Foods Inc
 Portland, OR 503-252-3006
The Perfect Pita
 Springfield, VA 703-644-0004
Toufayan Bakeries
 Ridgefield, NJ 201-861-4131

Pumpernickel

Atlanta Bread Co.
 Smyrna, GA 800-398-3728
Colchester Bakery
 Colchester, CT 860-537-2415
Dimpflmeier Bakery
 Toronto, ON 800-268-2421
Orwasher's Bakery
 New York, NY 212-288-6569

Raisin

Clarmil Manufacturing Corp
 Hayward, CA 888-252-7645
French Meadow Bakery & Cafe
 Minneapolis, MN 612-870-7855
Natural Food Mill
 Corona, CA 800-797-5090
Nature's Path Foods
 Blaine, WA 888-808-9505
Orwasher's Bakery
 New York, NY 212-288-6569
Ottenberg's Bakers
 Sykesville, MD 800-334-7264
Schwebel Baking Co.
 Youngstown, OH 800-860-2867

Reduced-Fat

Schwebel Baking Co.
 Youngstown, OH 800-860-2867

Rolls

Ace Bakery
 North York, ON 800-443-7929
Alois J Binder Bakery
 New Orleans, LA 504-947-1111
Alpha Baking Company
 South Bend, IN 773-261-6000
Amoroso's Baking Co
 Bellmawr, NJ 215-471-4740
April Hill Inc
 Grand Rapids, MI 616-245-0595
Atlanta Bread Co.
 Smyrna, GA 800-398-3728
Aunt Millie's Bakeries
 Fort Wayne, IN 855-755-2253
Automatic Rolls Of New Jersey
 Edison, NJ 877-222-2867
Awrey Bakeries
 Livonia, MI 800-950-2253
B&A Bakery
 Toronto, ON 800-263-2878
Bake Rite Rolls Inc
 Bensalem, PA 800-949-5623
Baker Boy Bake Shop Inc
 Dickinson, ND 800-437-2008
Baker's Dozen & Cafe
 Herkimer, NY 315-866-6770
Bakers of Paris
 Brisbane, CA 415-468-9100
BakeryCorp
 Miami, FL 305-623-3838
Baking Leidenheimer
 New Orleans, LA 800-259-9099
Baldinger Baking Co
 St Paul, MN 651-224-5761
Basque French Bakery
 Fresno, CA 559-268-7088
Beckmann's Old World Bakery
 Santa Cruz, CA 831-423-9242
Berlin Natural Bakery
 Berlin, OH 800-686-5334
Best Harvest Bakeries
 Kansas City, KS 800-811-5715
Better Bagel Bakery
 Sarasota, FL 941-924-0393
Bluepoint Bakery
 Denver, CO 303-298-1100
Bonnie Baking Company
 La Porte, IN 219-362-4561
Busken Bakery
 Cincinnati, OH 513-871-2114
Butter Krust Baking Company
 Thomasville, GA 800-282-8093
California Smart Foods
 San Francisco, CA 415-826-0449
Cellone Bakery Inc
 Pittsburgh, PA 800-334-8438
Clarmil Manufacturing Corp
 Hayward, CA 888-252-7645
Clyde's Delicious Donuts
 Addison, IL 630-628-6555
Cohen's Bakery
 Ellenville, NY 845-647-2200
Colombo Bakery
 Sacramento, CA 916-648-1011
Country Club Bakery
 Fairmont, WV 304-363-5690
Dakota Brands Intl
 Jamestown, ND 800-844-5073
Dimpflmeier Bakery
 Toronto, ON 800-268-2421
Dipaolo Baking Co Inc
 Rochester, NY 585-232-3510
Eden Vineyards Winery
 Alva, FL 239-728-9463
Egypt Star Bakery Inc
 Allentown, PA 610-434-8516
Ener-G Foods
 Seattle, WA 800-331-5222
Epi De France Bakery
 Atlanta, GA 800-325-1014
Felix Roma & Son Inc
 Endicott, NY 607-748-3336
Flowers Baking Co
 Tuscaloosa, AL 205-752-5586
Forty Second Street Bagel Cafe
 Upland, CA 909-949-7334
French Meadow Bakery & Cafe
 Minneapolis, MN 612-870-7855
Fresh Start Bakeries
 Brea, CA 714-256-8900

Galasso's Bakery
 Mira Loma, CA 951-360-1211
German Bakery at Village Corner
 Stone Mountain, GA 866-476-6443
Giant Food
 Landover, MD 888-469-4426
Global Bakeries Inc
 Pacoima, CA 818-896-0525
Gold Coast Bakeries
 Santa Ana, CA 714-545-2253
Gold Medal Bakery Inc
 Fall River, MA 508-674-5766
Golden Brown Bakery Inc
 South Haven, MI 269-637-3418
Grebe's Bakery
 Milwaukee, WI 800-833-3158
Guttenplan's Frozen Dough
 Middletown, NJ 888-422-4357
H&S Bakery
 Baltimore, MD 800-959-7655
Havi Food Services Worldwide
 Oak Park, IL 708-445-1700
Hawaii Star Bakery
 Honolulu, HI 808-841-3602
Heltzman Bakery
 Louisville, KY 502-447-3515
Holsum Bakery Inc
 Phoenix, AZ 602-252-2351
Homestead Baking Co
 Rumford, RI 800-556-7216
Hostess Brands
 Kansas City, MO 816-701-4600
James Skinner Company
 Omaha, NE 800-358-7428
John J. Nissen Baking Company
 Brewer, ME 207-989-7654
Julian's Recipe
 Brooklyn, NY 888-640-8880
Kim and Jake's
 Boulder, CO 303-499-9126
King's Hawaiian Holding Co Inc.
 Torrance, CA 877-695-4227
Klosterman Baking Co.
 Cincinnati, OH 877-301-1004
Koffee Kup Bakery
 Burlington, VT 802-863-2696
Lake States Yeast
 Rhinelander, WI 715-369-4949
Lanthier Bakery
 Alexandria, ON 613-525-2435
Lavoi Corporation
 Atlanta, GA 404-325-1016
Leidenheimer Baking Co
 New Orleans, LA 800-259-9099
Lepage Bakeries
 Auburn, ME 207-783-9161
Livermore Falls Baking Company
 Livermore Falls, ME 207-897-3442
Longo's Bakery Inc
 Hazleton, PA 570-454-5825
Lucerne Foods
 Pleasanton, CA 877-232-4271
Maggiora Baking Co
 Richmond, CA 510-235-0274
Marshall's Biscuit Company
 Westerville, OH 251-679-6226
Martins Famous Pastry Shoppe
 Chambersburg, PA 800-548-1200
Mary Ann's Baking Co Inc
 Sacramento, CA 916-681-7444
Maui Bagel
 Kahului, HI 808-270-7561
Metropolitan Baking Co
 Hamtramck, MI 313-875-7246
Milano Bakery Inc
 Joliet, IL 815-727-2253
Morabito Baking Co Inc
 Norristown, PA 800-525-7747
Mrs Baird's
 Horsham, PA 800-984-0989
Mrs. Kavanagh's English Muffins
 Rumford, RI 800-556-7216
Mt. View Bakery
 Mountain View, HI 808-968-6353
Multi Marques
 Montreal, QC 514-934-1866
Nevada Baking Company
 Las Vegas, NV 702-384-8950
New Bakery Company of Ohio
 Zanesville, OH 800-848-9845
New York Bakeries Inc
 Hialeah, FL 305-883-0790

Product Categories / Baked Goods: Breads

New York Frozen Foods Inc
  Bedford, OH 216-292-5655
Orlando Baking Co
  Cleveland, OH 800-362-5504
Orwasher's Bakery
  New York, NY 212-288-6569
Oven Ready Products
  Guelph, ON 519-767-2415
Pan-O-Gold Baking Co.
  St. Cloud, MN 800-444-7005
Pepperidge Farm Inc.
  Norwalk, CT 888-737-7374
Piemonte Bakery Co
  Rockford, IL 815-962-4833
Pittsfield Rye Bakery
  Pittsfield, MA 413-443-9141
Portuguese Baking Company
  Newark, NJ 973-589-8875
Powers Baking Company
  Miami, FL 305-381-7000
Quinzani Bakery
  Boston, MA 800-999-1062
Roma Bakeries
  Rockford, IL 815-964-6737
Rudi's Organic Bakery
  Boulder, CO 877-293-0876
Ryals Bakery
  Milledgeville, GA 478-452-0321
San Francisco French Bread
  Oakland, CA 510-729-6232
Schwebel Baking Co.
  Youngstown, OH. 800-860-2867
Shaw Baking Company
  Thunder Bay, ON 807-345-7327
Simon Hubig Company
  New Orleans, LA 504-945-2181
St Armands Baking Co
  Bradenton, FL 941-753-7494
St-Germain Bakery
  Honolulu, HI 808-847-5396
Sterling Foods LLC
  San Antonio, TX 210-490-1669
Superior Bakery Inc
  N Grosvenordale, CT 860-923-9555
Swatt Baking Co
  Olean, NY 800-370-6656
Terranettis Italian Bakery
  Mechanicsburg, PA 717-697-5434
Tom Cat Bakery Inc
  Queens, NY 718-786-7659
Tomaro's Bakery
  Clarksburg, WV 304-622-0691
Tripoli Bakery Inc
  Lawrence, MA 978-682-7754
Turano Baking
  Berwyn, IL 708-788-9220
Upper Crust Bakery USA
  Phoenix, AZ 602-255-0464
Valley Bakery
  Burnaby, BC 604-291-0674
Vallos Baking Co
  Bethlehem, PA 610-866-1012
Wedemeyer's Bakery
  S San Francisco, CA 650-873-1000
Wenner Bakery
  Bayport, NY 800-869-6262
Weston Foods
  Etobicoke, ON 416-252-7323
Zoelsmann's Bakery & Deli
  Pueblo, CO 719-543-0407

Cinnamon

Chef's Pride Gifts LLC
  Taylor, MI 800-878-1800
Cinnamon Bakery
  Braintree, MA 800-886-2867
Clarmil Manufacturing Corp
  Hayward, CA 888-252-7645
James Skinner Company
  Omaha, NE 800-358-7428
Lone Star Bakery
  Round Rock, TX 512-255-7268
Lone Star Consolidated Foods Inc.
  Dallas, TX 800-658-5637
Maple Donuts
  York, PA 800-627-5348
Mrs Baird's
  Horsham, PA 800-984-0989
Pacific Ocean Produce
  Santa Cruz, CA 831-423-2654
Sara Lee Frozen Bakery
  Kings Mountain, NC 800-323-7117

Schwan's Food Service Inc.
  Marshall, MN 877-302-7426
Svenhard's Swedish Bakery Inc
  Oakland, CA 800-705-3379

Fresh

Best Harvest Bakeries
  Kansas City, KS 800-811-5715
Felix Roma & Son Inc
  Endicott, NY 607-748-3336
Galasso's Bakery
  Mira Loma, CA 951-360-1211
Homestead Baking Co
  Rumford, RI 800-556-7216
Lanthier Bakery
  Alexandria, ON 613-525-2435
Leidenheimer Baking Co
  New Orleans, LA 800-259-9099
Lucerne Foods
  Pleasanton, CA 877-232-4271
Multi Marques
  Montreal, QC 514-934-1866
New York Frozen Foods Inc
  Bedford, OH 216-292-5655
Ottenberg's Bakers
  Sykesville, MD 800-334-7264
Quinzani Bakery
  Boston, MA 800-999-1062
Schwebel Baking Co.
  Youngstown, OH. 800-860-2867
Shaw Baking Company
  Thunder Bay, ON 807-345-7327
Terranettis Italian Bakery
  Mechanicsburg, PA 717-697-5434
Weston Foods
  Etobicoke, ON 416-252-7323

Frozen

Awrey Bakeries
  Livonia, MI 800-950-2253
Bake Crafters Food Company
  McDonald, TN 423-396-3392
Dwayne Keith Brooks Company
  Orangevale, CA 916-988-1030
Dynamic Foods
  Lubbock, TX 806-723-5600
Fresh Start Bakeries
  Brea, CA 714-256-8900
Guttenplan's Frozen Dough
  Middletown, NJ 888-422-4357
J & J Wall Bakery Co
  Sacramento, CA 916-381-1410
James Skinner Company
  Omaha, NE 800-358-7428
Leidenheimer Baking Co
  New Orleans, LA 800-259-9099
Lone Star Bakery
  Round Rock, TX 512-255-7268
Pacific Ocean Produce
  Santa Cruz, CA 831-423-2654

Sweet

Awrey Bakeries
  Livonia, MI 800-950-2253
Baker Boy Bake Shop Inc
  Dickinson, ND 800-437-2008
Clyde's Delicious Donuts
  Addison, IL 630-628-6555
King's Hawaiian Holding Co Inc.
  Torrance, CA 877-695-4227
Lone Star Consolidated Foods Inc.
  Dallas, TX 800-658-5637
McKee Foods Corp.
  Collegedale, TN 800-522-4499
St Armands Baking Co
  Bradenton, FL 941-753-7494
Zoelsmann's Bakery & Deli
  Pueblo, CO 719-543-0407

Rye

Alfred & Sam's Italian Bakery
  Lancaster, PA 717-392-6311
Alpha Baking Company
  South Bend, IN 773-261-6000
Amest Food
  Stony Point, NY 718-360-0886
Amoroso's Baking Co
  Bellmawr, NJ 215-471-4740
Atlanta Bread Co.
  Smyrna, GA 800-398-3728

Chicago Pastry
  Bloomingdale, IL 630-529-6391
Chmura's Bakery
  Indian Orchard, MA 413-543-2521
Colchester Bakery
  Colchester, CT 860-537-2415
Cybros
  Waukesha, WI. 800-876-2253
Dimpflmeier Bakery
  Toronto, ON 800-268-2421
French Meadow Bakery & Cafe
  Minneapolis, MN 612-870-7855
Hawaii Star Bakery
  Honolulu, HI 808-841-3602
Highlandville Packing
  Highlandville, MO 417-443-3365
Metropolitan Baking Co
  Hamtramck, MI. 313-875-7246
Orlando Baking Co
  Cleveland, OH 800-362-5504
Orwasher's Bakery
  New York, NY 212-288-6569
Patisserie Wawel
  Montreal, QC 614-524-3348
Piemonte Bakery Co
  Rockford, IL 815-962-4833
Pyrenees French Bakery
  Bakersfield, CA 888-898-7159
Quality Bakery
  Invermere, BC 888-681-9977
Rubschlager Baking Corp
  800-661-7246
Rudi's Organic Bakery
  Boulder, CO 877-293-0876
Rudolph's Specialty Bakery
  Toronto, ON 800-268-1589
Terranettis Italian Bakery
  Mechanicsburg, PA 717-697-5434
Tribeca Oven
  Carlstadt, NJ 201-935-8800

Scones

Bette's Oceanview Diner
  Berkeley, CA 510-644-3230
Bluepoint Bakery
  Denver, CO 303-298-1100
Butter Baked Goods
  Vancouver, BC 604-221-4333
California Smart Foods
  San Francisco, CA 415-826-0449
Case Side Holdings Company
  Kensington, PE 902-836-4214
Conifer Foods
  Medina, WA 800-588-9160
Davis Bread & Desserts
  Davis, CA 530-220-4375
Dere Street
  Danbury, CT 203-797-9386
Immaculate Consumption
  Columbia, SC 888-826-6567
Moon Rabbit Foods
  Savannah, NY 828-273-6649
Nikola's Foods
  Bloomington, MN 888-645-6527
Sticky Fingers Bakeries
  Spokane, WA. 800-458-5826
Treasure Foods
  West Valley, UT. 801-974-0911
Uptown Bakers
  Hyattsville, MD 301-864-1500

Short

Biscottea
  Issaquah, WA 425-313-1993
Merlino Italian Baking Company
  Kent, WA 800-800-9490
R.M. Palmer Co.
  West Reading, PA 610-372-8971
Vermont Chocolatiers
  Northfield, VT 877-485-4226
Walkers Shortbread
  Hauppauge, NY 800-521-0141

Soda

Greenhills Irish Bakery
  Dorchester Ctr, MA 617-825-8187

Sourdough

Atlanta Bread Co.
  Smyrna, GA 800-398-3728

Product Categories / Baked Goods: Cakes & Pastries

Beckmann's Old World Bakery
   Santa Cruz, CA 831-423-9242
Berkshire Mountain Bakery
   Housatonic, MA 866-274-6124
French Meadow Bakery & Cafe
   Minneapolis, MN 612-870-7855
Frisco Baking Co Inc
   Los Angeles, CA 323-225-6111
Gold Coast Bakeries
   Santa Ana, CA 714-545-2253
Gold Coast Baking Co Inc
   Santa Ana, CA 714-545-2253
H&S Bakery
   Baltimore, MD 800-959-7655
Hawaii Star Bakery
   Honolulu, HI 808-841-3602
Kim and Jake's
   Boulder, CO 303-499-9126
Morabito Baking Co Inc
   Norristown, PA 800-525-7747
Orwasher's Bakery
   New York, NY 212-288-6569
Ottenberg's Bakers
   Sykesville, MD 800-334-7264
Rudi's Organic Bakery
   Boulder, CO 877-293-0876
Schwebel Baking Co.
   Youngstown, OH 800-860-2867

Wheat

Alpha Baking Company
   South Bend, IN 773-261-6000
Atlanta Bread Co.
   Smyrna, GA 800-398-3728
Beckmann's Old World Bakery
   Santa Cruz, CA 831-423-9242
Butter Krust Baking Company
   Thomasville, GA 800-282-8093
Highlandville Packing
   Highlandville, MO 417-443-3365
Klosterman Baking Co.
   Cincinnati, OH 877-301-1004
Metropolitan Baking Co
   Hamtramck, MI 313-875-7246
Naji's Pita Gourmet Restaurant
   Birmingham, AL 205-945-6001
Orlando Baking Co
   Cleveland, OH 800-362-5504
Orwasher's Bakery
   New York, NY 212-288-6569
Pyrenees French Bakery
   Bakersfield, CA 888-898-7159
Rudi's Organic Bakery
   Boulder, CO 877-293-0876
Schwebel Baking Co.
   Youngstown, OH 800-860-2867
Shaw Baking Company
   Thunder Bay, ON 807-345-7327
Tribeca Oven
   Carlstadt, NJ 201-935-8800

White

Alpha Baking Company
   South Bend, IN 773-261-6000
Arctic Beverages
   Winnipeg, MB 866-503-1270
Beckmann's Old World Bakery
   Santa Cruz, CA 831-423-9242
Highlandville Packing
   Highlandville, MO 417-443-3365
Klosterman Baking Co.
   Cincinnati, OH 877-301-1004
Metropolitan Baking Co
   Hamtramck, MI 313-875-7246
Orwasher's Bakery
   New York, NY 212-288-6569
Pan-O-Gold Baking Co.
   St. Cloud, MN 800-444-7005
Pyrenees French Bakery
   Bakersfield, CA 888-898-7159
Rudi's Organic Bakery
   Boulder, CO 877-293-0876
Schwebel Baking Co.
   Youngstown, OH 800-860-2867
Shaw Baking Company
   Thunder Bay, ON 807-345-7327
Terranettis Italian Bakery
   Mechanicsburg, PA 717-697-5434

Cakes & Pastries

BakeMark Canada
   Laval, QC 800-361-4998

Angel Food Cake

Kyger Bakery Products
   Lafayette, IN 765-447-1252
Specialty Bakers
   Marysville, PA 800-233-0778

Babka

Aunt Heddy's Bakery
   Brooklyn, NY 718-782-0582
Morse's Sauerkraut
   Waldoboro, ME 866-832-5569

Baklava

Athens Baking Company
   Fresno, CA 800-775-2867
Athens Foods Inc
   Brookpark, OH 843-916-2000
Fillo Factory, The
   Northvale, NJ 800-653-4556
Marika's Kitchen
   Hancock, ME 800-694-9400
Sinbad Sweets
   Madera, CA 866-746-2232

Blintzes

Frozen

Echo Lake Foods, Inc.
   Burlington, WI 262-763-9551
Old Fashioned Kitchen Inc
   Lakewood, NJ 732-364-4100

Brown Bettys

Euro Chocolate Fountain
   San Diego, CA 800-423-9303

Cakes

Adams Foods & Milling
   Dothan, AL 334-983-4233
Alati-Caserta Desserts
   Montr,al, QC 877-377-5680
Angel's Bakeries
   Brooklyn, NY 718-389-1400
Aryzta
   Los Angeles, CA 855-427-9982
Atkins Elegant Desserts
   Fishers, IN 800-887-8808
Awrey Bakeries
   Livonia, MI 800-950-2253
BakeMark Canada
   Laval, QC 800-361-4998
Baker Boy Bake Shop Inc
   Dickinson, ND 800-437-2008
BakeryCorp
   Miami, FL 305-623-3838
Balboa Dessert Co Inc
   Santa Ana, CA 800-974-9699
Banquet Schusters Bakery
   Pueblo, CO 719-544-1062
Bauducco Foods Inc.
   Miami, FL 305-477-9270
BBU Bakeries
   Horsham, PA 800-984-0989
Beatrice Bakery Co
   Beatrice, NE 800-228-4030
Berke-Blake Fancy Foods, Inc.
   Longwood, FL 888-386-2253
Big Fatty's Flaming Foods
   Valley View, TX 888-248-6332
Bimbo Bakeries USA Inc.
   Horsham, PA 800-984-0989
Birkholm's Solvang Bakery
   Solvang, CA 800-377-4253
Bittersweet Pastries
   Norwood, NJ 800-217-2938
Bluepoint Bakery
   Denver, CO 303-298-1100
Breadworks
   Charlottesville, VA 434-296-4663
Brownie Baker Inc
   Fresno, CA 800-598-6501
Busken Bakery
   Cincinnati, OH 513-871-2114
C'est Gourmet
   Framingham, MA 508-877-0000

Cal-Java International Inc
   Northridge, CA 800-207-2750
Calamondin Cafe
   Fort Myers, FL 239-288-5535
California Smart Foods
   San Francisco, CA 415-826-0449
Calmar Bakery
   Calmar, AB 780-985-3583
Caribbean Food Delights Inc
   Tappan, NY 845-398-3000
Carole's Cheesecake Company
   Toronto, ON 416-256-0000
Carolina Foods Inc
   Charlotte, NC 800-234-0441
Case Side Holdings Company
   Kensington, PE 902-836-4214
Cateraid Inc
   Howell, MI 800-508-8217
Celebrity Cheesecake
   Davie, FL 877-986-2253
Chattanooga Bakery Inc
   Chattanooga, TN 800-251-3404
Cheesecake Etc Desserts
   Miami Springs, FL 305-887-0258
Cheesecake Factory Inc.
   Calabasas Hills, CA 818-871-3000
Cheryl's Cookies
   Westerville, OH 800-443-8124
Chocolate Chix
   Waxahachie, TX 214-744-2442
Cinderella Cheese Cake Co
   Riverside, NJ 800-521-1171
City Bakery Cafe
   Asheville, NC 877-328-3687
Clarmil Manufacturing Corp
   Hayward, CA 888-252-7645
Cloverhill Bakery-Vend Corporation
   Chicago, IL 773-745-9800
Clyde's Delicious Donuts
   Addison, IL 630-628-6555
Collin Street Bakery
   Corsicana, TX 800-267-4657
Comanzo & Company Specialty Bakers
   Smithfield, RI 888-352-5455
Cookie Factory
   Bronx, NY 718-379-6223
Crane's Pie Pantry Restaurant
   Fennville, MI 269-561-2297
Culinar Canada
   Baie-Comeau, QC 418-296-4395
Dancing Deer Baking Company
   Boston, MA 888-699-3337
David's Cookies
   Cedar Grove, NJ 800-500-2800
Davis Bakery & Delicatessen
   Cleveland, OH 216-292-3060
Decadent Desserts
   Calgary, AB 403-245-5535
Deerfield Bakery
   Buffalo Grove, IL 847-520-0068
Del's Pastry
   Toronto, ON 800-461-0663
Denny's 5th Avenue Bakery
   Bloomington, MN 952-881-4445
Desserts by David Glass
   South Windsor, CT 860-462-7520
Di Camillo Baking Co
   Niagara Falls, NY 800-634-4363
Dinkel's Bakery Inc
   Chicago, IL 800-822-8817
Dr. Cookie
   Seattle, WA 206-389-9321
Dufflet Pastries
   Toronto, ON 866-238-0899
Dutch Kitchen Bake Shop & Deli
   Fitchburg, MA 978-345-1393
DWC Specialities
   Horicon, WI 800-383-8808
Dynamic Foods
   Lubbock, TX 806-723-5600
Eddy's Bakery
   Boise, ID 208-377-8100
Edelweiss Patisserie
   Medford, MA 781-628-0225
Effies Homemade
   Hyde Park, MA 617-364-9300
Eilenberger Bakeries
   Palestine, TX 800-831-2544
El Peto Products
   Cambridge, ON 800-387-4064
Elmwood Pastry Shop
   West Hartford, CT 860-233-2029

Product Categories / Baked Goods: Cakes & Pastries

Entenmann's
　Totowa, NJ 973-785-7601
European Style Bakery
　Beverly Hills, CA 818-368-6876
Fantasia
　Sedalia, MO 660-827-1172
Farm & Oven Snacks
　Boulder, CO
Ferrara Bakery & Cafe
　New York, NY 212-226-6150
Firehook Bakery & Coffeehouse
　Chantilly, VA 703-263-2253
Fireside Kitchen
　Halifax, NS 902-454-7387
Flowers Baking Co
　El Paso, TX 800-328-6111
Flowers Foods Inc.
　Thomasville, GA 229-226-9110
Food of Our Own Design
　Maplewood, NJ 973-762-0985
Foxtail Foods
　Fairfield, OH 800-487-2253
France Delices
　Montreal, QC 800-663-1365
Franklin Baking Co.
　Goldsboro, NC 919-735-0344
Fruit of the Boot
　Gaineswillve, FL 352-376-3643
Future Bakery & Cafe
　Toronto, ON 416-231-1491
Georgia Fruitcake Co
　Claxton, GA 912-739-2683
Giant Food
　Landover, MD 888-469-4426
Golden Brown Bakery Inc
　South Haven, MI 269-637-3418
Golden Kernel Pecan Co
　Cameron, SC 803-823-2311
Golden Walnut Specialty Foods
　Wayzata, MN 800-843-3645
Goldilocks USA
　Hayward, CA 510-476-0700
Gourmet Treats
　Torrance, CA 800-444-9549
Great Western Co LLC
　Hollywood, AL 256-259-3578
Grebe's Bakery
　Milwaukee, WI 800-833-3158
Greyston Bakery Inc
　Yonkers, NY 800-289-2253
Grossingers Home Bakery
　New York, NY 800-479-6996
GWB Foods Corporation
　Brooklyn, NY 877-977-7610
Haby's Alsatian Bakery
　Castroville, TX 830-538-2118
Hahn's Old Fashioned Cake Co
　Farmingdale, NY 631-249-3456
Harrington's of Vermont
　Richmond, VT
Hawaii Candy Inc
　Honolulu, HI 800-303-2507
Haydel's Bakery
　New Orleans, LA 800-442-1342
Heidi's Gourmet Desserts
　Tucker, GA 800-241-4166
Heltzman Bakery
　Louisville, KY 502-447-3515
Holton Food Products
　La Grange, IL 708-352-5599
Hot Cakes-Molten Chocolate
　Seattle, WA 206-453-3792
Hudson River Foods
　Castleton, NY 888-417-9343
Hunt Country Foods Inc
　Marshall, VA 540-364-2622
Ivy Cottage Scone Mixes
　S Pasadena, CA 626-441-2761
Jacquet Bakery
　New York, NY
James Skinner Company
　Omaha, NE 800-358-7428
JC's Pie Pops
　Chatsworth, CA 818-349-1880
Jennies Gluten-Free Bakery
　Moosic, PA 570-457-2400
Joey's Fine Foods
　Newark, NJ 973-482-1400
John J. Nissen Baking Company
　Brewer, ME 207-989-7654
Jon Donaire Desserts
　Santa Fe Springs, CA 877-366-2473

Just Desserts
　Fairfield, CA 415-780-6860
K & S Cakes
　Leesburg, VA 910-265-6779
Keller's Bakery
　Lafayette, LA 337-235-1568
Kennedy Gourmet
　Glendale Heights, IL 800-729-8116
Kyger Bakery Products
　Lafayette, IN 765-447-1252
L & M Bakery
　Riverside, NJ 888-887-1335
Laura's French Baking Co
　Los Angeles, CA 888-353-5144
Lax & Mandel Bakery
　South Euclid, OH 216-382-8877
Le Chef Bakery
　Montebello, CA 323-888-2929
Little Miss Muffin
　Chicago, IL 800-456-9328
Lone Star Bakery
　Round Rock, TX 512-255-7268
Lone Star Consolidated Foods Inc.
　Dallas, TX 800-658-5637
Love Quiches Desserts
　Freeport, NY 516-623-8800
M/S Smears
　Chadbourn, NC 910-654-5163
Mac's Donut Shop
　Aliquippa, PA 724-375-6776
Martino's Bakery
　Burbank, CA 818-842-0715
Mary of Puddin Hill
　Palestine, TX 800-545-8889
Matthews 1812 House
　Cornwall Bridge, CT 800-662-1812
Maurice French Pastries
　Metairie, LA 888-285-8261
McKee Foods Corp.
　Collegedale, TN 800-522-4499
Mehaffies Pies
　Dayton, OH 800-289-7437
Michel's Bakery
　Philadelphia, PA 267-345-7914
Mid-Atlantic Foods Inc
　Easton, MD 800-922-4688
Milano Bakery Inc
　Joliet, IL 815-727-2253
Moon Rabbit Foods
　Savannah, NY 828-273-6649
Moravian Cookies Shop
　Winston Salem, NC 800-274-2994
Mortgage Apple Cake
　Teaneck, NJ 201-692-9538
Mozzicato De Pasquale Bakery
　Hartford, CT 860-296-0426
Multi Marques
　Montreal, QC 514-934-1866
My Cup of Cake™
　Port Washington, NY 516-767-5137
My Daddy's Cheesecake
　Cape Girardeau, MO 800-735-6765
My Grandma's Coffee Cake
　Hyde Park, MA 800-847-2636
Naturally Delicious Inc
　Oakland Park, FL 888-221-7352
New Glarus Bakery & Tea Room
　New Glarus, WI 866-805-5536
New York Bakeries Inc
　Hialeah, FL 305-883-0790
Northside Bakery
　Brooklyn, NY 718-782-2700
O & H Danish Bakery Inc
　Racine, WI 262-637-8895
Ohta Wafer Factory
　Honolulu, HI 808-949-2775
Old Country Bakery
　North Hollywood, CA 818-838-2302
Our Lady of Guadalupe Trappist Abbey
　Carlton, OR 503-852-0103
Pacific Ocean Produce
　Santa Cruz, CA 831-423-2654
Pastry Chef
　Pawtucket, RI 800-639-8606
Patti's Plum Puddings
　Lawndale, CA 310-376-1463
Pearl River Pastry & Chocolate
　Pearl River, NY 800-632-2639
Pellman Foods Inc
　New Holland, PA 717-354-8070
Pepperidge Farm Inc.
　Norwalk, CT 888-737-7374

Pie Piper Products
　Wheeling, IL 800-621-8183
Plaza Sweets Bakery
　Mamaroneck, NY 800-816-8416
Plehn's Bakery Inc
　Louisville, KY 502-896-4438
Pocono Cheesecake Factory
　Swiftwater, PA 570-839-6844
Quality Bakery Products
　Houston, TX 866-449-4977
Real Food Marketing
　Kansas City, MO 816-221-4100
Rich's Ice Cream Co Inc
　West Palm Beach, FL 561-833-7585
Rising Dough Bakery
　Sacramento, CA 916-387-9700
Rockland Bakery
　Nanuet, NY 800-734-4376
Rolling Pin Bakery
　Bow Island, AB 403-545-2434
Rowena
　Norfolk, VA 800-627-8699
Royal Caribbean Bakery
　Mt Vernon, NY 888-818-0971
Royal Home Bakery
　Newmarket, ON 905-715-7044
Rudolph's Specialty Bakery
　Toronto, ON 800-268-1589
Ruth Ashbrook Bakery
　Portland, OR 503-240-7437
Ryals Bakery
　Milledgeville, GA 478-452-0321
Ryke's Bakery
　Muskegon, MI 231-726-2253
Sacramento Baking Co
　Sacramento, CA 916-361-2000
Safeway Inc.
　Pleasanton, CA 877-723-3929
Samadi Sweets Cafe
　Falls Church, VA 703-578-0606
Sara Lee Frozen Bakery
　Kings Mountain, NC 800-323-7117
Saxby Foods
　Edmonton, AB 780-440-4179
Scialo Brothers Bakery
　Providence, RI 877-421-0986
Silver Tray Cookies
　Fort Lauderdale, FL 305-883-0800
Silverland Bakery
　Forest Park, IL 708-488-0800
Smart Baking Co.
　Sanford, FL 407-915-5519
Smoak's Bakery & Catering Service
　Augusta, GA 706-738-1792
Southeast Dairy Processors Inc
　Tampa, FL 813-620-1516
Specialty Bakers
　Marysville, PA 800-233-0778
Spilke's Baking Company
　Moosic, PA 570-457-2400
Standard Bakery Inc
　Kealakekua, HI 808-322-3688
Sterling Foods LLC
　San Antonio, TX 210-490-1669
Steve's Mom
　Bronx, NY 800-362-4545
Strossner's Bakery & Cafe
　Greenville, SC 864-233-2990
Sugar Plum LLC
　Houma, LA 985-872-9524
Superior Cake Products
　Southbridge, MA 508-764-3276
Swagger Foods Corp
　Vernon Hills, IL 847-913-1200
Sweet Endings Inc
　West Palm Beach, FL 888-635-1177
Sweet Gallery Exclusive Pastry
　Toronto, ON 416-766-0289
Sweet Lady Jane
　Los Angeles, CA 323-653-7145
Tasty Baking Company
　Philadelphia, PA 800-248-2789
The Great San Saba River Pecan Company
　San Saba, TX 800-621-8121
Trumps Food Interest
　Vancouver, BC 604-732-8473
Two Chicks and a Ladle
　New York, NY 212-251-0025
Uncle Ralph's Cookies
　Frederick, MD 800-422-0626
Uniquely Together
　Chicago, IL 800-613-7276

Product Categories / Baked Goods: Cakes & Pastries

Upper Crust Bakery USA
 Phoenix, AZ....................602-255-0464
Uptown Bakers
 Hyattsville, MD..................301-864-1500
Vickey's Vittles
 North Hills, CA...................818-841-1944
Vigneri Chocolate Inc.
 Rochester, NY....................877-844-6374
Warwick Ice Cream
 Warwick, RI......................401-821-8403
Wedding Cake Studio
 Williamsfield, OH.................440-667-1765
Weiss Homemade Kosher Bakery
 Brooklyn, NY.....................800-498-3477
Wenger's Bakery
 Reading, PA......................610-372-6545
Whipped Pastry Boutique
 Brooklyn, NY.....................718-858-8088
White Oak Farms Inc
 Sandown, NH.....................800-473-8869
Wholesome Bakery
 San Francisco, CA.................415-343-5414
Williamsburg Chocolatier
 Williamsburg, VA..................757-253-1474
World Of Chantilly
 Brooklyn, NY.....................718-859-1110
Wow! Factor Desserts
 Sherwood Park, AB................800-604-2253
Ya-Hoo Baking Co
 Sherman, TX.....................888-869-2466
Young's Bakery
 Uniontown, PA....................724-437-6361
Zoelsmann's Bakery & Deli
 Pueblo, CO.......................719-543-0407

Cannoli
Artuso Pastry
 Bronx, NY........................718-367-2515
Golden Cannoli
 Chelsea, MA.....................617-868-2826

Carrot Cake
Clarmil Manufacturing Corp
 Hayward, CA.....................888-252-7645
Eli's Cheesecake
 Chicago, IL.......................800-354-2253
Nush Foods
 Salt Lake City, UT.................801-953-1370

Cheese Cake
American Quality Foods
 Mills River, NC....................828-890-8344
Aryzta
 Los Angeles, CA..................855-427-9982
Atkins Elegant Desserts
 Fishers, IN.......................800-887-8808
Balboa Dessert Co Inc
 Santa Ana, CA....................800-974-9699
Berke-Blake Fancy Foods, Inc.
 Longwood, FL....................888-386-2253
Bindi North America
 Kearny, NJ.......................973-812-8118
Brownie Baker Inc
 Fresno, CA.......................800-598-6501
California Smart Foods
 San Francisco, CA.................415-826-0449
Carole's Cheesecake Company
 Toronto, ON.....................416-256-0000
Cateraid Inc
 Howell, MI.......................800-508-8217
Celebrity Cheesecake
 Davie, FL........................877-986-2253
Chatila's
 Salem, NH.......................603-898-5459
Cheesecake Etc Desserts
 Miami Springs, FL................305-887-0258
Cheesecake Factory Inc.
 Calabasas Hills, CA...............818-871-3000
Cheesecake Momma
 Ukiah, CA.......................707-462-2253
Cinderella Cheese Cake Co
 Riverside, NJ.....................800-521-1171
Collin Street Bakery
 Corsicana, TX....................800-267-4657
D-Liteful Baking Company
 Medley, FL......................305-883-6449
Desserts by David Glass
 South Windsor, CT................860-462-7520
Eli's Cheesecake
 Chicago, IL.......................800-354-2253

Future Bakery & Cafe
 Toronto, ON.....................416-231-1491
Golden Walnut Specialty Foods
 Wayzata, MN....................800-843-3645
Heidi's Gourmet Desserts
 Tucker, GA......................800-241-4166
Hoff's Bakery
 Medford, MA....................888-871-5100
Holey Moses Cheesecake
 Westhampton Beach, NY.........800-225-2253
Jon Donaire Desserts
 Santa Fe Springs, CA.............877-366-2473
Jubilations
 West Point, MS..................800-530-7808
Love Quiches Desserts
 Freeport, NY....................516-623-8800
Mazelle's Cheesecakes Concoctions Creations
 Dallas, TX.......................214-328-9102
Mehaffies Pies
 Dayton, OH.....................800-289-7437
New England Country Bakers
 Watertown, CT..................800-225-3779
Pellman Foods Inc
 New Holland, PA.................717-354-8070
Pie Piper Products
 Wheeling, IL.....................800-621-8183
Pocono Cheesecake Factory
 Swiftwater, PA...................570-839-6844
Scotty Wotty's Creamy Cheesecake
 Hillsborough, NJ..................908-281-9720
Steve's Mom
 Bronx, NY.......................800-362-4545
Sweet Lady Jane
 Los Angeles, CA.................323-653-7145
Tolteca Foodservice
 Norcross, GA....................800-541-6835
Trumps Food Interest
 Vancouver, BC..................604-732-8473
Two Chicks and a Ladle
 New York, NY...................212-251-0025
Wow! Factor Desserts
 Sherwood Park, AB..............800-604-2253

Flavored
Jon Donaire Desserts
 Santa Fe Springs, CA.............877-366-2473
Junior's Cheesecake
 Maspeth, NY....................800-458-6467
Pellman Foods Inc
 New Holland, PA.................717-354-8070
Sugarplum Desserts
 Langley, BC.....................604-534-2282

Frozen
Balboa Dessert Co Inc
 Santa Ana, CA...................800-974-9699
Cateraid Inc
 Howell, MI......................800-508-8217
Cinderella Cheese Cake Co
 Riverside, NJ....................800-521-1171
Desserts Of Distinction
 Tigard, OR......................503-654-8370
Galaxy Desserts
 Richmond, CA...................800-225-3523
Heidi's Gourmet Desserts
 Tucker, GA......................800-241-4166
Lawler Foods LTD
 Humble, TX.....................800-541-8285
Love Quiches Desserts
 Freeport, NY....................516-623-8800
Mehaffies Pies
 Dayton, OH.....................800-289-7437
Pellman Foods Inc
 New Holland, PA.................717-354-8070
Sugarplum Desserts
 Langley, BC.....................604-534-2282

Low-Fat
American Quality Foods
 Mills River, NC...................828-890-8344

NewYork Style
Cannoli Factory
 Wyandanch, NY..................631-643-2700

Non-Fat
Two Chicks and a Ladle
 New York, NY...................212-251-0025

Churros
Tolteca Foodservice
 Norcross, GA....................800-541-6835

Coffee Cake
Awrey Bakeries
 Livonia, MI......................800-950-2253
Boston Coffee Cake
 North Andover, MA..............800-434-0500
Clyde's Delicious Donuts
 Addison, IL......................630-628-6555
DWC Specialities
 Horicon, WI.....................800-383-8808
Homefree LLC
 Windham, NH...................800-552-7172
James Skinner Company
 Omaha, NE.....................800-358-7428
L & M Bakery
 Riverside, NJ....................888-887-1335
Nikola's Foods
 Bloomington, MN...............888-645-6527
Sedona Baking Company
 Gardena, CA...................323-770-2674
Wholesome Bakery
 San Francisco, CA...............415-343-5414

Cream Puff
Boboli Intl. Inc.
 Stockton, CA...................209-473-3507
Creme Curls
 Hudsonville, MI................800-466-1219
Hafner USA
 Stone Mountain, GA............888-725-4605
Irene's Bakery & Gourmet
 Bensalem, PA..................215-244-6200
McKee Foods Corp.
 Collegedale, TN................800-522-4499
Rich's Ice Cream Co Inc
 West Palm Beach, FL...........561-833-7585

Crumpets
Aryzta
 Los Angeles, CA................855-427-9982
Wolferman's
 Medford, OR...................800-798-6241

Cupcakes
Better Bites Bakery
 Austin, TX
Butter Baked Goods
 Vancouver, BC.................604-221-4333
Crumbs Bake Shop
 New York, NY..................877-278-6270
Lucky Spoon Bakery LLC
 Salt Lake City, UT...............801-824-0624
Magnolia Bakery
 New York, NY..................855-622-5379
Mrs Baird's
 Horsham, PA..................800-984-0989
Red Plate Foods
 Bend, OR......................541-550-7676
Sweet Lady Jane
 Los Angeles, CA...............323-653-7145
Tasty Baking Company
 Philadelphia, PA...............800-248-2789
Veronica's Treats
 Middleboro, MA...............866-576-1122
Wholesome Bakery
 San Francisco, CA.............415-343-5414

Danish
Aryzta
 Los Angeles, CA...............855-427-9982
Atlanta Bread Co.
 Smyrna, GA...................800-398-3728
Awrey Bakeries
 Livonia, MI.....................800-950-2253
BakeMark Canada
 Laval, QC......................800-361-4998
Brownie Baker Inc
 Fresno, CA.....................800-598-6501
California Smart Foods
 San Francisco, CA.............415-826-0449
Chicago Pastry
 Bloomingdale, IL..............630-529-6391
Clyde's Delicious Donuts
 Addison, IL....................630-628-6555
Davis Bread & Desserts
 Davis, CA......................530-220-4375

Product Categories / Baked Goods: Cakes & Pastries

Del's Pastry
  Toronto, ON 800-461-0663
Dimitria Delights Baking Co
  North Grafton, MA 800-763-1113
Entenmann's
  Totowa, NJ 973-785-7601
Fiera Foods
  Toronto, ON 800-675-6356
Gourmet Croissant
  Brooklyn, NY 718-499-4911
Heltzman Bakery
  Louisville, KY 502-447-3515
James Skinner Company
  Omaha, NE 800-358-7428
Joey's Fine Foods
  Newark, NJ 973-482-1400
Laura's French Baking Co
  Los Angeles, CA 888-353-5144
Mary Ann's Baking Co Inc
  Sacramento, CA 916-681-7444
Michel's Bakery
  Philadelphia, PA 267-345-7914
Roma Bakeries
  Rockford, IL 815-964-6737
Shaw Baking Company
  Thunder Bay, ON 807-345-7327
Strossner's Bakery & Cafe
  Greenville, SC 864-233-2990
Svenhard's Swedish Bakery Inc
  Oakland, CA 800-705-3379
Uptown Bakers
  Hyattsville, MD 301-864-1500
Vie De France Yamazaki Inc
  Vienna, VA 800-446-4404

Dessert Tarts

Birkholm's Solvang Bakery
  Solvang, CA 800-377-4253

Doughnuts

All Round Foods Bakery Prod
  Westbury, NY 800-428-8802
Annette's Donuts Ltd.
  Toronto, ON 888-839-7857
Awrey Bakeries
  Livonia, MI 800-950-2253
Bake Crafters Food Company
  McDonald, TN 423-396-3392
Baker Boy Bake Shop Inc
  Dickinson, ND 800-437-2008
Baker's Dozen & Cafe
  Herkimer, NY 315-866-6770
BBU Bakeries
  Horsham, PA 800-984-0989
Busken Bakery
  Cincinnati, OH 513-871-2114
Butter Krust Baking Company
  Thomasville, GA 800-282-8093
California Smart Foods
  San Francisco, CA 415-826-0449
Carolina Foods Inc
  Charlotte, NC 800-234-0441
Case Side Holdings Company
  Kensington, PE 902-836-4214
Chatila's
  Salem, NH 603-898-5459
Cloverhill Bakery-Vend Corporation
  Chicago, IL 773-745-9800
Clyde's Delicious Donuts
  Addison, IL 630-628-6555
Davis Bakery & Delicatessen
  Cleveland, OH 216-292-3060
Denny's 5th Avenue Bakery
  Bloomington, MN 952-881-4445
Donut Farm
  Oakland, CA 510-338-6319
Dunford Bakers
  West Jordan, UT 800-748-4335
Dutch Girl Donut Co
  Detroit, MI 313-368-3020
Elmwood Pastry Shop
  West Hartford, CT 860-233-2029
Entenmann's
  Totowa, NJ 973-785-7601
Giant Food
  Landover, MD 888-469-4426
Grebe's Bakery
  Milwaukee, WI 800-833-3158
Harting's Bakery
  Bowmansville, PA 717-445-5644
Heltzman Bakery
  Louisville, KY 502-447-3515
Jubelt Variety Bakeries
  Litchfield, IL 217-324-5314
Keller's Bakery
  Lafayette, LA 337-235-1568
Koffee Kup Bakery
  Burlington, VT 802-863-2696
Lepage Bakeries
  Auburn, ME 207-783-9161
Lone Star Consolidated Foods Inc.
  Dallas, TX 800-658-5637
Ludwick's Frozen Donuts
  Grand Rapids, MI 800-366-8816
Mac's Donut Shop
  Aliquippa, PA 724-375-6776
Madysen's Marshmallows
  Heber City, UT 435-315-0045
Maple Donuts
  York, PA 800-627-5348
Maui Bagel
  Kahului, HI 808-270-7561
Mrs. Willman's Baking
  Burnaby, BC 604-434-0027
Mt. View Bakery
  Mountain View, HI 808-968-6353
Nutrilicious Natural Bakery
  Countryside, IL 800-835-8097
Pan-O-Gold Baking Co.
  St. Cloud, MN 800-444-7005
Parmenter's Northville Cider Mill
  Northville, MI 248-349-3181
Plehn's Bakery Inc
  Louisville, KY 502-896-4438
Quality Naturally Foods
  City Of Industry, CA 888-498-6986
Rolling Pin Bakery
  Bow Island, AB 403-545-2434
Ruth Ashbrook Bakery
  Portland, OR 503-240-7437
Sara Lee Frozen Bakery
  Kings Mountain, NC 800-323-7117
Shaw Baking Company
  Thunder Bay, ON 807-345-7327
Steve's Doughnut Shop
  Somerset, MA 508-672-0865
Vallos Baking Co
  Bethlehem, PA 610-866-1012
Yum Yum Donut Shops Inc
  City Of Industry, CA 626-964-1478

Frozen

All Round Foods Bakery Prod
  Westbury, NY 800-428-8802
Awrey Bakeries
  Livonia, MI 800-950-2253
Bake Crafters Food Company
  McDonald, TN 423-396-3392
Carolina Foods Inc
  Charlotte, NC 800-234-0441
Clyde's Delicious Donuts
  Addison, IL 630-628-6555
Ludwick's Frozen Donuts
  Grand Rapids, MI 800-366-8816
Mel-O-Cream Donuts Intl
  Springfield, IL 217-483-7272

Dumplings

Atkinson Milling Co.
  Selma, NC 800-948-5707
Byrnes & Kiefer Co
  Callery, PA 724-538-5200
Chang Food Company
  Garden Grove, CA 714-265-9990
Chateau Food Products Inc
  Cicero, IL 708-863-4207
Chinese Spaghetti Factory
  Boston, MA 617-445-7714
Community Orchards
  Fort Dodge, IA 888-573-8212
Dimitria Delights Baking Co
  North Grafton, MA 800-763-1113
Harvest Food Products Co Inc
  Hayward, CA 510-675-0383
Harvest Time Foods
  Ayden, NC 252-746-6675
Jewel Date Co
  Thermal, CA 760-399-4474
La Tang Cuisine Manufacturing
  Houston, TX 713-780-4876
Mando Inc
  Englewood, NJ 201-568-9337
Mayfield Farms and Nursery
  Athens, TN 423-746-9859
Millie's Pierogi
  Chicopee Falls, MA 800-743-7641
Naleway Foods
  Winnipeg, MB 800-665-7448
Prime Food Processing Corp
  Brooklyn, NY 718-963-2323
Shine Foods Inc
  Torrance, CA 310-533-6010
Sweet Sue Kitchens
  Athens, AL 256-216-0500
Twin Marquis
  Brooklyn, NY 800-367-6868
Wei-Chuan USA Inc
  Bell Gardens, CA 562-372-2020

Eclairs

Boboli Intl. Inc.
  Stockton, CA 209-473-3507
Creme Curls
  Hudsonville, MI 800-466-1219
Rich's Ice Cream Co Inc
  West Palm Beach, FL 561-833-7585

Frozen Cakes

Alati-Caserta Desserts
  Montr,al, QC 877-377-5680
Andros Foods North America
  Mount Jackson, VA 844-426-3767
Awrey Bakeries
  Livonia, MI 800-950-2253
Bodega Chocolates
  Fountain Valley, CA 888-326-3342
Carolina Foods Inc
  Charlotte, NC 800-234-0441
Carousel Cakes
  Nanuet, NY 800-659-2253
Cinderella Cheese Cake Co
  Riverside, NJ 800-521-1171
Dynamic Foods
  Lubbock, TX 806-723-5600
Fantasia
  Sedalia, MO 660-827-1172
French Patisserie
  Pacifica, CA 800-300-2253
Grossingers Home Bakery
  New York, NY 800-479-6996
Heidi's Gourmet Desserts
  Tucker, GA 800-241-4166
James Skinner Company
  Omaha, NE 800-358-7428
Kyger Bakery Products
  Lafayette, IN 765-447-1252
Little Miss Muffin
  Chicago, IL 800-456-9328
Lone Star Bakery
  Round Rock, TX 512-255-7268
Love Quiches Desserts
  Freeport, NY 516-623-8800
McCain Foods Ltd.
  Toronto, ON 416-955-1700
Mehaffies Pies
  Dayton, OH 800-289-7437
My Grandma's Coffee Cake
  Hyde Park, MA 800-847-2636
Pacific Ocean Produce
  Santa Cruz, CA 831-423-2654
Pastry Chef
  Pawtucket, RI 800-639-8606
Pellman Foods Inc
  New Holland, PA 717-354-8070
Real Food Marketing
  Kansas City, MO 816-221-4100
Rowena
  Norfolk, VA 800-627-8699
Saxby Foods
  Edmonton, AB 780-440-4179
Schwan's Company
  Marshall, MN 800-533-5290
The Daphne Baking Company, LLC
  New York, NY 212-517-7626
Uncle Ralph's Cookies
  Frederick, MD 800-422-0626
Warwick Ice Cream
  Warwick, RI 401-821-8403

Product Categories / Baked Goods: Cakes & Pastries

Fruit Cake

Beatrice Bakery Co
   Beatrice, NE.................800-228-4030
Caribbean Food Delights Inc
   Tappan, NY...................845-398-3000
Claxton Bakery Inc
   Claxton, GA..................800-841-4211
Collin Street Bakery
   Corsicana, TX................800-267-4657
Fireside Kitchen
   Halifax, NS..................902-454-7387
Milano Bakery Inc
   Joliet, IL...................815-727-2253
Multi Marques
   Montreal, QC.................514-934-1866
Neuman Bakery Specialties
   Addison, IL..................800-253-5298
Old Cavendish Products
   Cavendish, VT................800-536-7899

Fruit Cobbler

Good Old Days Foods
   Little Rock, AR..............501-565-1257
Harold Food Company
   Charlotte, NC................704-588-8061
Lone Star Bakery
   Round Rock, TX...............512-255-7268
Pacific Ocean Produce
   Santa Cruz, CA...............831-423-2654
Quality Bakery Products
   Houston, TX..................866-449-4977
Spring Glen Fresh Foods
   Ephrata, PA..................800-641-2853
Ya-Hoo Baking Co
   Sherman, TX..................888-869-2466

Ladyfingers

Specialty Bakers
   Marysville, PA...............800-233-0778

Liqueur Cake

Beatrice Bakery Co
   Beatrice, NE.................800-228-4030
Dinkel's Bakery Inc
   Chicago, IL..................800-822-8817

Muffins

Abe's Vegan Muffins
   NY...........................845-735-5100
American Quality Foods
   Mills River, NC..............828-890-8344
Andre-Boudin Bakeries
   San Francisco, CA............415-882-1849
Angel's Bakeries
   Brooklyn, NY.................718-389-1400
Aryzta
   Los Angeles, CA..............855-427-9982
Atlanta Bread Co.
   Smyrna, GA...................800-398-3728
Awrey Bakeries
   Livonia, MI..................800-950-2253
Bake Crafters Food Company
   McDonald, TN.................423-396-3392
Bake Rite Rolls Inc
   Bensalem, PA.................800-949-5623
BakeMark Canada
   Laval, QC....................800-361-4998
BakeMark Ingredients Canada
   Richmond, BC.................800-665-9441
Baker Boy Bake Shop Inc
   Dickinson, ND................800-437-2008
BakeryCorp
   Miami, FL....................305-623-3838
BBU Bakeries
   Horsham, PA..................800-984-0989
Bluepoint Bakery
   Denver, CO...................303-298-1100
Brownie Baker Inc
   Fresno, CA...................800-598-6501
Busken Bakery
   Cincinnati, OH...............513-871-2114
Calgary Italian Bakery
   Calgary, AB..................800-661-6868
California Smart Foods
   San Francisco, CA............415-826-0449
Case Side Holdings Company
   Kensington, PE...............902-836-4214
Central Bakery
   Fall River, MA...............508-675-7620
Chatila's
   Salem, NH....................603-898-5459
Cloverhill Bakery-Vend Corporation
   Chicago, IL..................773-745-9800
Community Bakeries
   Downers Grove, IL............800-952-5754
Continental Mills Inc
   Tukwila, WA..................206-816-7000
Del's Pastry
   Toronto, ON..................800-461-0663
Denny's 5th Avenue Bakery
   Bloomington, MN..............952-881-4445
DWC Specialities
   Horicon, WI..................800-383-8808
Edelweiss Patisserie
   Medford, MA..................781-628-0225
Edner Corporation
   Hayward, CA..................510-441-8504
El Peto Products
   Cambridge, ON................800-387-4064
Entenmann's
   Totowa, NJ...................973-785-7601
Enterprises Pates et Croutes
   Boucherville, QC.............800-265-7790
Farm & Oven Snacks
   Boulder, CO
Fireside Kitchen
   Halifax, NS..................902-454-7387
Foxtail Foods
   Fairfield, OH................800-487-2253
Fresh Start Bakeries
   Brea, CA.....................714-256-8900
Gourmet Croissant
   Brooklyn, NY.................718-499-4911
Greyston Bakery Inc
   Yonkers, NY..................800-289-2253
Hawaii Star Bakery
   Honolulu, HI.................808-841-3602
Heltzman Bakery
   Louisville, KY...............502-447-3515
Homestead Baking Co
   Rumford, RI..................800-556-7216
Hudson River Foods
   Castleton, NY................888-417-9343
International Brownie
   East Weymouth, MA............800-230-1588
Irresistible Cookie Jar
   Hayden Lake, ID..............208-664-1261
James Skinner Company
   Omaha, NE....................800-358-7428
Joey's Fine Foods
   Newark, NJ...................973-482-1400
Lavoi Corporation
   Atlanta, GA..................404-325-1016
Lenny & Larry's
   Panorama City, CA
Lone Star Bakery
   Round Rock, TX...............512-255-7268
Lucky Spoon Bakery LLC
   Salt Lake City, UT...........801-824-0624
Mac's Donut Shop
   Aliquippa, PA................724-375-6776
Magnificent Muffin
   Farmingdale, NY..............631-454-8022
Main Street Gourmet
   Cuyahoga Falls, OH...........800-678-6246
Meyer's Bakeries
   Casa Grande, AZ..............800-528-5770
Michel's Bakery
   Philadelphia, PA.............267-345-7914
Mikey's
  480-696-2483
Mt. View Bakery
   Mountain View, HI............808-968-6353
Muffin Revolution
   Richmond, CA.................510-859-7655
New England Muffin Co Inc
   Fall River, MA...............508-675-2833
New Horizons Baking Co
   Fremont, IN..................260-495-7055
Nikola's Foods
   Bloomington, MN..............888-645-6527
North Coast Farms
   Santa Cruz, CA...............831-426-3733
Notre Dame Bakery
   Conception Harbour, NL.......709-535-2738
Oakrun Farm Bakery
   Ancaster, ON.................800-263-6422
Otis Spunkmeyer
   Norcross, GA.................855-427-9982
Oven Fresh Baking Company
   Chicago, IL..................773-638-1234
Pacific Ocean Produce
   Santa Cruz, CA...............831-423-2654
Pan-O-Gold Baking Co.
   St. Cloud, MN................800-444-7005
Plaidberry Company
   Vista, CA....................760-727-5403
Red Plate Foods
   Bend, OR.....................541-550-7676
Rising Dough Bakery
   Sacramento, CA...............916-387-9700
Sara Lee Frozen Bakery
   Kings Mountain, NC...........800-323-7117
Shaw Baking Company
   Thunder Bay, ON..............807-345-7327
Soozy's Grain-Free
   New York, NY
Sterling Foods LLC
   San Antonio, TX..............210-490-1669
Upper Crust Bakery USA
   Phoenix, AZ..................602-255-0464
Uptown Bakers
   Hyattsville, MD..............301-864-1500
Vitalicious
   New York, NY.................877-848-2877
Weston Foods
   Etobicoke, ON................416-252-7323

Frozen

Dynamic Foods
   Lubbock, TX..................806-723-5600
Main Street Gourmet
   Cuyahoga Falls, OH...........800-678-6246

Whole Grain

Main Street Gourmet
   Cuyahoga Falls, OH...........800-678-6246

Panettones

Vigneri Chocolate Inc.
   Rochester, NY................877-844-6374

Pastries

Alessi Bakery
   Tampa, FL....................813-879-4544
Artuso Pastry
   Bronx, NY....................718-367-2515
Aryzta
   Los Angeles, CA..............855-427-9982
Athens Foods Inc
   Brookpark, OH................843-916-2000
Atlanta Bread Co.
   Smyrna, GA...................800-398-3728
BakeryCorp
   Miami, FL....................305-623-3838
Banquet Schusters Bakery
   Pueblo, CO...................719-544-1062
Big Fatty's Flaming Foods
   Valley View, TX..............888-248-6332
Bimbo Bakeries USA Inc.
   Horsham, PA..................800-984-0989
Boboli Intl. Inc.
   Stockton, CA.................209-473-3507
Bodega Chocolates
   Fountain Valley, CA..........888-326-3342
Byrnes & Kiefer Co
   Callery, PA..................724-538-5200
Calgary Italian Bakery
   Calgary, AB..................800-661-6868
Caribbean Food Delights Inc
   Tappan, NY...................845-398-3000
Case Side Holdings Company
   Kensington, PE...............902-836-4214
Castella Imports Inc
   Brentwood, NY................631-231-5500
Chatila's
   Salem, NH....................603-898-5459
Chella's Dutch Delicacies
   Lake Oswego, OR..............800-458-3331
Chicago Pastry
   Bloomingdale, IL.............630-529-6391
Clarkson Scottish Bakery
   Mississauga, ON..............905-823-1500
Clement's Pastry Shops Inc
   Hyattsville, MD..............301-277-6300
Cohen's Bakery
   Ellenville, NY...............845-647-2200
Cookie Factory
   Bronx, NY....................718-379-6223
Creme Curls
   Hudsonville, MI..............800-466-1219

Product Categories / Baked Goods: Cakes & Pastries

Crepini & The Crepe Team
  Brooklyn, NY 718-372-0505
Cyrils Bakery
  Fort Lauderdale, FL 800-929-7457
Denny's 5th Avenue Bakery
  Bloomington, MN 952-881-4445
Dimitria Delights Baking Co
  North Grafton, MA 800-763-1113
Dipaolo Baking Co Inc
  Rochester, NY 585-232-3510
Dufour Pastry Kitchens Inc
  Bronx, NY 800-439-1282
Edelweiss Patisserie
  Medford, MA 781-628-0225
Elegant Desserts
  Lyndhurst, NJ 201-933-0770
Ferrara Bakery & Cafe
  New York, NY 212-226-6150
Fiera Foods
  Toronto, ON 800-675-6356
Fillo Factory, The
  Northvale, NJ 800-653-4556
Food of Our Own Design
  Maplewood, NJ 973-762-0985
Future Bakery & Cafe
  Toronto, ON 416-231-1491
Glamorgan Bakery
  Calgary, AB 403-232-2800
Hafner USA
  Stone Mountain, GA 888-725-4605
Holt's Bakery Inc
  Douglas, GA 912-384-2202
James Skinner Company
  Omaha, NE 800-358-7428
John J. Nissen Baking Company
  Brewer, ME 207-989-7654
Just Desserts
  Fairfield, CA 415-780-6860
Keller's Bakery
  Lafayette, LA 337-235-1568
Laura's French Baking Co
  Los Angeles, CA 888-353-5144
Lax & Mandel Bakery
  South Euclid, OH 216-382-8877
Lenchner Bakery
  Concord, ON 905-738-8811
Let Them Eat Cake
  Tampa, FL 813-837-6888
Little Miss Muffin
  Chicago, IL 800-456-9328
Lucy's Sweet Surrender
  Beachwood, OH 216-752-0828
Mac's Donut Shop
  Aliquippa, PA 724-375-6776
Mary Ann's Baking Co Inc
  Sacramento, CA 916-681-7444
Michel's Bakery
  Philadelphia, PA 267-345-7914
Mikawaya LLC
  Vernon, CA 323-587-5504
Moravian Cookies Shop
  Winston Salem, NC 800-274-2994
Morse's Sauerkraut
  Waldoboro, ME 866-832-5569
Mrs. Willman's Baking
  Burnaby, BC 604-434-0027
Nancy's Specialty Foods
  Newark, CA 510-494-1100
Northside Bakery
  Brooklyn, NY 718-782-2700
Oakrun Farm Bakery
  Ancaster, ON 800-263-6422
Old Country Bakery
  North Hollywood, CA 818-838-2302
Pauline's Pastries
  Vaughan, ON 877-292-6826
Pepperidge Farm Inc
  Norwalk, CT 888-737-7374
Poppies International
  Battleboro, NC 252-442-4309
Prime Pastries
  Concord, ON 905-669-5883
Quaker Bonnet
  Buffalo, NY 800-283-2447
Quality Naturally Foods
  City Of Industry, CA 888-498-6986
Ranaldi Bros. Frozen Food Products
  Warwick, RI 401-737-5130
Ravico USA
  Riderwood, MD 443-921-8025
Rockland Bakery
  Nanuet, NY 800-734-4376
Rolling Pin Bakery
  Bow Island, AB 403-545-2434
Royal Caribbean Bakery
  Mt Vernon, NY 888-818-0971
Ryke's Bakery
  Muskegon, MI 231-726-2253
Scialo Brothers Bakery
  Providence, RI 877-421-0986
Shaw Baking Company
  Thunder Bay, ON 807-345-7327
Simit + Smith
  Ridgefield, NJ 201-699-0320
Solana Beach Baking Company
  Carlsbad, CA 760-444-9800
Spohrers Bakeries
  Collingdale, PA 610-532-9959
St-Germain Bakery
  Honolulu, HI 808-847-5396
Standard Bakery Inc
  Kealakekua, HI 808-322-3688
Strossner's Bakery & Cafe
  Greenville, SC 864-233-2990
Svenhard's Swedish Bakery Inc
  Oakland, CA 800-705-3379
Sweet Gallery Exclusive Pastry
  Toronto, ON 416-766-0289
Taste It Presents Inc
  Kenilworth, NJ 908-241-0672
Tasty Baking Company
  Philadelphia, PA 800-248-2789
Turano Baking
  Berwyn, IL 708-788-9220
Uptown Bakers
  Hyattsville, MD 301-864-1500
Valley Bakery
  Burnaby, BC 604-291-0674
Vie De France Yamazaki Inc
  Vienna, VA 800-446-4404
Vienna Bakery
  Barrington, RI 401-245-2355
Vigneri Chocolate Inc.
  Rochester, NY 877-844-6374
Weiss Homemade Kosher Bakery
  Brooklyn, NY 800-498-3477
Wenger's Bakery
  Reading, PA 610-372-6545

Pecan Log
Golden Kernel Pecan Co
  Cameron, SC 803-823-2311

Petit Fours
Cookies United
  Islip, NY 631-581-4000
Ferrara Bakery & Cafe
  New York, NY 212-226-6150
Mazelle's Cheesecakes Concoctions Creations
  Dallas, TX 214-328-9102

Pound Cake
Abe's Vegan Muffins
  NY 845-735-5100
Adams Foods & Milling
  Dothan, AL 334-983-4233
Brownie Baker Inc
  Fresno, CA 800-598-6501
Clarmil Manufacturing Corp
  Hayward, CA 888-252-7645
McDuffies Bakery
  Clarence, NY 800-875-1598
New England Country Bakers
  Watertown, CT 800-225-3779
Rowena
  Norfolk, VA 800-627-8699
Silver Tray Cookies
  Fort Lauderdale, FL 305-883-0800

Pudding Cake
Sticky Toffee Pudding Company
  Austin, TX 512-472-0039

Puff Pastry
Aryzta
  Los Angeles, CA 855-427-9982
BakeMark USA
  Schaumburg, IL 847-519-3135
Dutchland Frozen Foods
  Lester, IA 888-497-7243

Rugulach
Byrnes & Kiefer Co
  Callery, PA 724-538-5200
Chewys Rugulach
  San Diego, CA 800-241-3456
Ericas Rugelach & Baking Co
  Brooklyn, NY 718-965-3657
Morse's Sauerkraut
  Waldoboro, ME 866-832-5569
Neuman Bakery Specialties
  Addison, IL 800-253-5298
Steve's Mom
  Bronx, NY 800-362-4545
Suzanne's Sweets
  Katonah, NY

Rum Cake
Cassandra's Gourmet Classics/Island Treasures Gourmet
  Manassas, VA 703-590-7900

Sponge Cake
Clarmil Manufacturing Corp
  Hayward, CA 888-252-7645
Multi Marques
  Montreal, QC 514-934-1866
Patisserie Wawel
  Montreal, QC 614-524-3348
Specialty Bakers
  Marysville, PA 800-233-0778
Sticky Toffee Pudding Company
  Austin, TX 512-472-0039
Sweet Gallery Exclusive Pastry
  Toronto, ON 416-766-0289

Strudel
Aryzta
  Los Angeles, CA 855-427-9982
Athens Foods Inc
  Brookpark, OH 843-916-2000
Creme Curls
  Hudsonville, MI 800-466-1219
Culinary Institute Lenotre
  Houston, TX 888-536-6873
Dimitria Delights Baking Co
  North Grafton, MA 800-763-1113
Fillo Factory, The
  Northvale, NJ 800-653-4556
Rising Dough Bakery
  Sacramento, CA 916-387-9700
Sinbad Sweets
  Madera, CA 866-746-2232
Svenhard's Swedish Bakery Inc
  Oakland, CA 800-705-3379

Tarts
Bluepoint Bakery
  Denver, CO 303-298-1100
California Smart Foods
  San Francisco, CA 415-826-0449
City Bakery
  New York, NY 212-366-1414
Clarmil Manufacturing Corp
  Hayward, CA 888-252-7645
Denny's 5th Avenue Bakery
  Bloomington, MN 952-881-4445
Dufflet Pastries
  Toronto, ON 866-238-0899
Dufour Pastry Kitchens Inc
  Bronx, NY 800-439-1282
Elegant Desserts
  Lyndhurst, NJ 201-933-0770
Firehook Bakery & Coffeehouse
  Chantilly, VA 703-263-2253
Galaxy Desserts
  Richmond, CA 800-225-3523
Granello Bakery
  Las Vegas, NV 702-361-0311
Greyston Bakery Inc
  Yonkers, NY 800-289-2253
Hail Merry
  Dallas, TX 214-905-5005
Health Valley Company
  Irwindale, CA 800-334-3204
J.P. Sunrise Bakery
  Edmonton, AB 780-454-5797
Joey's Fine Foods
  Newark, NJ 973-482-1400
Love Quiches Desserts
  Freeport, NY 516-623-8800

Product Categories / Baked Goods: Cones

Royal Home Bakery
  Newmarket, ON 905-715-7044
Sinbad Sweets
  Madera, CA 866-746-2232
Sweet Lady Jane
  Los Angeles, CA 323-653-7145
The Daphne Baking Company, LLC
  New York, NY 212-517-7626
Trumps Food Interest
  Vancouver, BC 604-732-8473

Tiramisu

Bindi North America
  Kearny, NJ 973-812-8118
Vigneri Chocolate Inc.
  Rochester, NY 877-844-6374

Tortes

Alessi Bakery
  Tampa, FL 813-879-4544
Aryzta
  Los Angeles, CA 855-427-9982
Balboa Dessert Co Inc
  Santa Ana, CA 800-974-9699
Dufflet Pastries
  Toronto, ON 866-238-0899
Heidi's Gourmet Desserts
  Tucker, GA 800-241-4166
Hoff's Bakery
  Medford, MA 888-871-5100
Strossner's Bakery & Cafe
  Greenville, SC 864-233-2990
Sweet Endings Inc
  West Palm Beach, FL 888-635-1177
Sweet Gallery Exclusive Pastry
  Toronto, ON 416-766-0289
Vigneri Chocolate Inc.
  Rochester, NY 877-844-6374

Turnovers

BakeMark Canada
  Laval, QC 800-361-4998
BakeMark USA
  Schaumburg, IL 847-519-3135
Creme Curls
  Hudsonville, MI 800-466-1219
Del's Pastry
  Toronto, ON 800-461-0663
Fiera Foods
  Toronto, ON 800-675-6356
Oven Ready Products
  Guelph, ON 519-767-2415

Cones

Great Western Co LLC
  Hollywood, AL 256-259-3578
Joy Cone Co
  Hermitage, PA 724-962-5747
Kemach Food Products
  Brooklyn, NY 718-272-5655
Monster Cone
  Montreal, QC 800-542-9801
O'Boyle's Ice Cream Company
  Bristol, PA 215-788-3882
Olde Tyme Food Corporation
  East Longmeadow, MA 800-356-6533
Ono Cones of Hawaii LLC
  Pearl City, HI 808-487-8690
Table De France
  Ontario, CA 909-923-5205
Turnbull Cone Baking Company
  Chattanooga, TN 423-265-4551

Cookies & Bars

Almond Cookies

Andre-Boudin Bakeries
  San Francisco, CA 415-882-1849
Balticshop.Com LLC
  Glastonbury, CT 800-506-2312
Bindi North America
  Kearny, NJ 973-812-8118
Dong Kee Company
  Chicago, IL 312-225-6340
Erba Food Products
  Brooklyn, NY 718-272-7700
Fortella Fortune Cookies
  Chicago, IL 312-567-9000
Mamma Says
  Butler, NJ 877-283-6282

Y Z Enterprises Inc
  Maumee, OH 800-736-8779

Animal Crackers

Good Zebra
  512-698-7907
Old Colony Baking Co Inc
  Northbrook, IL 847-498-5434

Bars

18 Rabbits Inc.
  San Francisco, CA 415-922-6006
AMT Labs Inc
  North Salt Lake, UT 801-294-3126
Aryzta
  Los Angeles, CA 855-427-9982
Bake Crafters Food Company
  McDonald, TN 423-396-3392
Bakeology
  Torrance, CA
Barbara's Bakery
  Lakeville, MN 800-343-0590
Betty Lou's
  McMinnville, OR 800-242-5205
Big Spoon Roasters
  Durham, NC 919-309-9100
California Smart Foods
  San Francisco, CA 415-826-0449
Cambridge Food
  Monterey, CA 800-433-2584
Carrie's Chocolates
  Edmonton, AB 877-778-2462
Chase & Poe Candy Co
  St Joseph, MO 800-786-1625
CHS Sunprairie
  Minot, ND 800-556-6807
Cream Of The West
  Harlowton, MT 800-477-2383
Edner Corporation
  Hayward, CA 510-441-8504
Ethel's Baking Co.
  St. Clair Shores, MI 586-552-5110
Fieldbrook Foods Corp.
  Dunkirk, NY 800-333-0805
Food of Our Own Design
  Maplewood, NJ 973-762-0985
Frankly Natural Bakers
  San Diego, CA 800-727-7229
Frozfruit Corporation
  Gardena, CA 310-217-1034
Fullbloom Baking Co
  Newark, CA 800-201-9909
Genisoy
  San Francisco, CA 866-972-6879
Global Health Laboratories
  Amityville, NY 631-777-2134
Govadinas Fitness Foods
  San Diego, CA 800-900-0108
Hain Celestial Group Inc
  Lake Success, NY 800-434-4246
Health Valley Company
  Irwindale, CA 800-334-3204
Jamae Natural Foods
  Los Angeles, CA 800-343-0052
JSL Foods
  Los Angeles, CA 800-745-3236
Kashi Company
  Solana Beach, CA 877-747-2467
L & M Bakery
  Riverside, NJ 888-887-1335
Lotus Bakery
  Santa Rosa, CA 800-875-6887
Magnolia Bakery
  New York, NY 855-622-5379
Marin Food Specialties
  Byron, CA 925-634-6126
Matt's Cookies
  Wheeling, IL 847-537-3888
Merlino Italian Baking Company
  Kent, WA 800-800-9490
Nana's Cookie Co.
  San Diego, CA 800-836-7534
Naturally Clean Eats
  Manhattan Beach, CA
Nature's Bakery
  Reno, NV
Nature's Plus
  Melville, NY 800-645-9500
Nellson Candies Inc
  Irwindale, CA 626-334-4508

No Cow
  Denver, CO
Nothin' But Foods
  Elmwood Park, NJ 203-557-8637
Oberweis Dairy Inc
  North Aurora, IL 866-623-7934
Oven Arts
  Hackensack, NJ 855-354-4070
Premier Protein
  Emeryville, CA 888-836-8977
Redd Superfood Energy Bars
  Portland, ME 207-370-4433
Sam Mills USA
  Boynton Beach, FL 561-572-0510
Santa Barbara Bar
  Santa Barbara, CA 855-722-2701
Schulze & Burch Biscuit Co
  Chicago, IL 773-927-6622
Sheffa Foods
  New York, NY 800-494-1956
Sucesores de Pedro Cortes
  Hato Rey, PR 787-754-7040
Sweety Novelty
  Monterey Park, CA 626-282-4482
Tate's Bake Shop
  Southampton, NY 631-283-9830
That's It Nutrition
  Los Angeles, CA 888-862-5235
Thinkthin, LLC
  Los Angeles, CA 866-988-4465
Tram Bar LLC
  Victor, ID 208-354-4790
Tribe 9 Foods
  Madison, WI 608-257-7216
Ultimate Nutrition
  Farmington, CT 860-409-7100
Wai Lana Snacks
  Sacramento, CA 888-924-5262
Weaver Nut Co. Inc.
  Ephrata, PA 800-473-2688
Wella Bar
  East Lockhart, TX 877-725-7289
Wholesome Bakery
  San Francisco, CA 415-343-5414
Your Bar Factory
  LaSalle, QC 888-366-0258
Zego Foods
  San Francisco, CA 415-706-8094

Big Cookies

Buff Bake
  Santa Ana, CA 949-274-9464

Biscotti

Award Baking Intl
  New Germany, MN 800-333-3523
Be-Bop Biscotti
  Bend, OR 888-545-7487
Bernadette Baking Company
  Medford, MA 781-393-8700
Big Island Candies Inc
  Hilo, HI 800-935-5510
Biscoti Di Suzy
  Oakland, CA 800-211-5903
Biscotti Goddess
  Richmond, VA 804-745-9490
Di Camillo Baking Co
  Niagara Falls, NY 800-634-4363
Elliott Bay Baking Co.
  Seattle, WA 206-545-3804
Euro Cafe
  Rochester, NY 800-298-9410
Ferrara Bakery & Cafe
  New York, NY 212-226-6150
G Debbas Chocolatier
  Fresno, CA 559-294-2071
Grain-Free JK Gourmet, Inc.
  Toronto, ON 800-608-0465
Healing Home Foods
  Pound Ridge, NY 914-764-1303
Immaculate Consumption
  Columbia, SC 888-826-6567
Irene's Bakery & Gourmet
  Bensalem, PA 215-244-6200
Just Off Melrose
  Palm Springs, CA 760-320-7414
La Tempesta
  S San Francisco, CA 800-762-8330
Larosa Bakery Inc
  Shrewsbury, NJ 800-527-6722

Product Categories / Baked Goods: Cookies & Bars

Mamma Says
   Butler, NJ 877-283-6282
Merlino Italian Baking Company
   Kent, WA 800-800-9490
Mikaela's Simply Divine
   Dover, NJ 866-659-1553
Montione's Biscotti & Baked Goods
   Norton, MA 800-559-1010
Moon Dance Baking
   Rohnert Park, CA 707-588-0800
My Boy's Baking LLC
   Allentown, PA 610-759-4552
Nikola's Foods
   Bloomington, MN 888-645-6527
Nonni's Foods LLC
   Tulsa, OK 877-295-9604
North American Enterprises
   Tucson, AZ 800-817-8666
Spring Street Bake Shop
   Pottstown, PA 484-624-8201
Sweet Mavens, LLC
   Glastonbury, CT 860-490-1407
The Bites Company
   Westport, CT 203-296-2482
Thyme Garden Herb Co
   Alsea, OR 800-482-4372
Touche Bakery
   London, ON 518-455-0044
Tuscan Bakery
   Portland, OR 800-887-2261
Tutti Gourmet
   Hudson, QC 450-458-0911
Ultimate Biscotti
   Eugene, OR 541-344-8220
Upper Crust Biscotti
   Pismo Beach, CA 866-972-6879
Wally Biscotti
   Denver, CO 866-659-2559

Almond

Sweet Mavens, LLC
   Glastonbury, CT 860-490-1407

Chocolate Almond

Nonni's Foods LLC
   Tulsa, OK 877-295-9604

Chocolate Dipped

Sweet Mavens, LLC
   Glastonbury, CT 860-490-1407

Brownies

American Quality Foods
   Mills River, NC 828-890-8344
Andre-Boudin Bakeries
   San Francisco, CA 415-882-1849
Bake Crafters Food Company
   McDonald, TN 423-396-3392
BakeMark Canada
   Laval, QC 800-361-4998
Bakers Breakfast Cookie
   Bellingham, WA 877-889-1090
Better Bites Bakery
   Austin, TX
Big Island Candies Inc
   Hilo, HI 800-935-5510
Boca Bons East
   Greenacres, FL 800-314-2835
Brownie Baker Inc
   Fresno, CA 800-598-6501
Browniepops LLC
   Leawood, KS 816-797-0715
Byrnes & Kiefer Co
   Callery, PA 724-538-5200
Cheryl's Cookies
   Westerville, OH 800-443-8124
Chris's Cookies
   Teterboro, NJ 201-288-8881
Christie Cookie
   Nashville, TN 800-458-2447
Cisse Trading Co
   Mamaroneck, NY 914-381-5555
Coby's Cookies
   Toronto, ON 416-633-1567
Dufflet Pastries
   Toronto, ON 866-238-0899
DWC Specialities
   Horicon, WI 800-383-8808
Dynamic Foods
   Lubbock, TX 806-723-5600

Eilenberger Bakeries
   Palestine, TX 800-831-2544
Fairytale Brownies
   Phoenix, AZ 800-324-7982
Farm & Oven Snacks
   Boulder, CO
Food of Our Own Design
   Maplewood, NJ 973-762-0985
Frankly Natural Bakers
   San Diego, CA 800-727-7229
Handy Pax
   Randolph, MA 781-963-8300
Harvest Valley Bakery Inc
   La Salle, IL 815-224-9030
Heavenscent Edibles
   New York, NY 212-369-0310
Heidi's Gourmet Desserts
   Tucker, GA 800-241-4166
Hudson River Foods
   Castleton, NY 888-417-9343
Lavoi Corporation
   Atlanta, GA 404-325-1016
Lawler Foods LTD
   Humble, TX 800-541-8285
Lone Star Bakery
   Round Rock, TX 512-255-7268
Mac's Donut Shop
   Aliquippa, PA 724-375-6776
Magnolia Bakery
   New York, NY 855-622-5379
Mari's New York
   New York, NY
McDuffies Bakery
   Clarence, NY 800-875-1598
Michel's Bakery
   Philadelphia, PA 267-345-7914
Mrs Sullivan's Pies
   Jackson, TN 731-427-2101
Mrs. Fields Original Cookies
   Bloomfield, CO 800-266-2547
Otis Spunkmeyer
   Norcross, GA 855-427-9982
Oven Arts
   Hackensack, NJ 855-354-4070
Pacific Ocean Produce
   Santa Cruz, CA 831-423-2654
Peggy Lawton Kitchens
   East Walpole, MA 800-843-7325
Pie Piper Products
   Wheeling, IL 800-621-8183
Rule Breaker
   Brooklyn, NY 646-820-8074
Salt of the Earth Bakery
   Brooklyn, NY 646-330-5089
Selma's Cookies
   Apopka, FL 800-992-6654
Sheila G Brands LLC
   West Palm Beach, FL 561-688-1890
Sheila Gs Brownie Brittle Co
   West Palm Beach, FL 561-557-1178
Silverland Bakery
   Forest Park, IL 708-488-0800
Sterling Foods LLC
   San Antonio, TX 210-490-1669
Sweet Lady Jane
   Los Angeles, CA 323-653-7145
Tasty Baking Company
   Philadelphia, PA 800-248-2789
Veronica's Treats
   Middleboro, MA 866-576-1122
Vitalicious
   New York, NY 877-848-2877
Wholesome Bakery
   San Francisco, CA 415-343-5414
William Poll Inc
   New York, NY 800-993-7655

Individually Wrapped

French Meadow Bakery & Cafe
   Minneapolis, MN 612-870-7855
Lenny & Larry's
   Panorama City, CA
Nature's Bakery
   Reno, NV

with Nuts

Dinkel's Bakery Inc
   Chicago, IL 800-822-8817

Chocolate Chip Cookies

Abimar Foods Inc
   Abilene, TX 325-691-5425
Belgian Boys
   Farmingdale, NY
Carve Nutrition
   Marina Del Rey, CA 310-905-8100
Chris's Cookies
   Teterboro, NJ 201-288-8881
Christie Cookie
   Nashville, TN 800-458-2447
Country Choice Organic
   Eden Prairie, MN 952-829-8824
Dinkel's Bakery Inc
   Chicago, IL 800-822-8817
Erba Food Products
   Brooklyn, NY 718-272-7700
Homefree LLC
   Windham, NH 800-552-7172
Linden Cookies Inc
   Congers, NY 845-268-5050
Mary's Gone Crackers
   Gridley, CA 888-258-1250
Mississippi Cheese Straw
   Yazoo City, MS 800-530-7496
Peggy Lawton Kitchens
   East Walpole, MA 800-843-7325
Sugar & Plumm
   New York, NY 212-787-8778
Sunset Specialty Foods
   Lake Arrowhead, CA 909-337-7643

Cookies

A La Carte
   Chicago, IL 800-722-2370
A Southern Season
   Hillsborough, NC 800-253-3663
Abimar Foods Inc
   Abilene, TX 325-691-5425
Abraham's Natural Foods
   Long Branch, NJ 800-327-9903
Alessi Bakery
   Tampa, FL 813-879-4544
All Wrapped Up
   Plantation, FL 800-891-2194
Alpendough
Ames International Inc
   Fife, WA 888-469-2637
Andre-Boudin Bakeries
   San Francisco, CA 415-882-1849
Angel's Bakeries
   Brooklyn, NY 718-389-1400
Arcor USA
   Coral Gables, FL 800-572-7267
Arturo's Spinella's Bakery
   Waterbury, CT 203-754-3056
Aunt Gussie Cookies & Crackers
   Garfield, NJ 800-422-6654
Austin Special Foods Company
   Austin, TX 512-372-8665
Authentic Marotti Biscotti
   Lewisville, TX 972-221-7295
Back to Nature Foods
   855-346-2225
Bake Crafters Food Company
   McDonald, TN 423-396-3392
BakeMark Canada
   Laval, QC 800-361-4998
BakeMark Ingredients Canada
   Richmond, BC 800-665-9441
BakeMark USA
   Schaumburg, IL 847-519-3135
Baker Boy Bake Shop Inc
   Dickinson, ND 800-437-2008
Bakers Breakfast Cookie
   Bellingham, WA 877-889-1090
Bama Foods LTD
   Tulsa, OK 800-756-2262
Barbara's Bakery
   Lakeville, MN 800-343-0590
Bavarian Specialty Foods, LLC
   Los Angeles, CA 626-856-3188
Beckmann's Old World Bakery
   Santa Cruz, CA 831-423-9242
Berkshire Mountain Bakery
   Housatonic, MA 866-274-6124
Best Maid Cookie Co
   River Falls, WI 888-444-0322
Beth's Fine Desserts
   Mill Valley, CA 415-383-3991

Product Categories / Baked Goods: Cookies & Bars

Betty Lou's
  McMinnville, OR 800-242-5205
Big Fatty's Flaming Foods
  Valley View, TX 888-248-6332
Big Island Candies Inc
  Hilo, HI 800-935-5510
Biscomerica Corporation
  Rialto, CA 909-877-5997
Biscotti & Co.
  White Plains, NY 914-682-2165
Bite Size Bakery
  Rio Rancho, NM 505-994-3093
Bitsy's Brainfood
  New York, NY 212-461-1572
Bloomfield Bakers
  Los Alamitos, CA 800-594-4111
Blue Chip Cookies
  Milford, OH 800-888-9866
Bluechip Group
  Salt Lake City, UT 800-878-0099
Bluepoint Bakery
  Denver, CO 303-298-1100
Borinquen Biscuit Corporation
  Yauco, PR 787-856-3030
Boston America Corporation
  Woburn, MA 781-933-3535
Botanical Bakery, LLC
  Napa, CA 707-344-8103
BP Gourmet
  Hauppauge, NY 631-234-8200
Brimhall Foods
  Bartlett, TN 800-628-6559
Brooklyn Baking Company
  Waterbury, CT 203-574-9198
Brooklyn Cookie Company
  Brooklyn, NY 347-973-0568
Brownie Baker Inc
  Fresno, CA 800-598-6501
Buckeye Pretzel Company
  Williamsport, PA 800-257-6029
Buonitalia
  New York, NY 212-633-9090
Busken Bakery
  Cincinnati, OH 513-871-2114
Byrd Cookie
  Savannah, GA 800-291-2973
Byrnes & Kiefer Co
  Callery, PA 724-538-5200
California Smart Foods
  San Francisco, CA 415-826-0449
Carolina Cookie Co
  Greensboro, NC 800-447-5797
Case Side Holdings Company
  Kensington, PE 902-836-4214
Charlie's Specialties Inc
  Hermitage, PA 724-346-2350
Chatila's
  Salem, NH 603-898-5459
Chelsea Flower Market
  New York, NY 888-727-7887
Chip'n Dipped Cookie Co
  Huntington, NY 631-470-2579
Chocoholics Divine Desserts
  Linden, CA 800-760-2462
Chocolate Chix
  Waxahachie, TX 214-744-2442
Chocolate Moon
  Asheville, NC 800-723-1236
Chocolates a La Carte
  Valencia, CA 800-818-2462
Chris's Cookies
  Teterboro, NJ 201-288-8881
Christie Cookie
  Nashville, TN 800-458-2447
City Bakery
  New York, NY 212-366-1414
Clarmil Manufacturing Corp
  Hayward, CA 888-252-7645
Collin Street Bakery
  Corsicana, TX 800-267-4657
Colonial Cookies, Ltd
  Kitchener, ON 800-265-6508
Commercial Bakeries
  Toronto, ON 416-247-5478
Consolidated Biscuit Company
  McComb, OH
Cookie Factory
  Bronx, NY 718-379-6223
Cookie Kingdom
  Oglesby, IL 815-883-3331
Cookie Specialties Inc
  Wheeling, IL 847-537-3888

Cookie Tree Bakeries
  Salt Lake City, UT 801-268-2253
Cookies United
  Islip, NY 631-581-4000
Cooperstown Cookie Company
  Cooperstown, NY 888-269-7315
Country Choice Organic
  Eden Prairie, MN 952-829-8824
Cybele's Free To Eat
  Los Angeles, CA 877-895-3729
Cybros
  Waukesha, WI 800-876-2253
Dainty Confections
  Windsor, ON 800-268-0222
Dairy State Foods Inc
  Milwaukee, WI 800-435-4499
Dancing Deer Baking Company
  Boston, MA 888-699-3337
Dare Foods
  Spartanburg, SC 800-668-3273
Dare Foods Incorporated
  Kitchener, ON 800-668-3273
David's Cookies
  Cedar Grove, NJ 800-500-2800
DeBeukelaer Cookie Co
  Madison, MS 601-856-7454
Delicious Frookie
  Des Plaines, IL 847-699-3200
DeLuscious Cookies
  Los Angeles, CA 323-460-2370
Di Camillo Baking Co
  Niagara Falls, NY 800-634-4363
Diamond Bakery Co LTD
  Honolulu, HI 808-847-3551
DiBella Baking Company
  Oceanside, CA 888-857-6151
Dinkel's Bakery Inc
  Chicago, IL 800-822-8817
DO, Cookie Dough Confections
  New York, NY 646-892-3600
Dong Kee Company
  Chicago, IL 312-225-6340
Donsuemor Madeleines
  Alameda, CA 888-420-4441
Dr. Lucy's LLC
  Norfolk, VA 757-233-9495
Dufflet Pastries
  Toronto, ON 866-238-0899
Dutchess Bakery
  Charleston, WV 304-346-4237
Eco-Planet Cookies
  Santa Monica, CA 310-829-9050
Edelweiss Patisserie
  Medford, MA 781-628-0225
Eleni's Cookies
  New York, NY 888-435-3647
Elliott Bay Baking Co.
  Seattle, WA 206-545-3804
Ellison Bakery, Inc.
  Fort Wayne, IN
Elmwood Pastry Shop
  West Hartford, CT 860-233-2029
Ener-G Foods
  Seattle, WA 800-331-5222
Enjoy Life Foods
  Chicago, IL 888-503-6569
Entenmann's
  Totowa, NJ 973-785-7601
Erba Food Products
  Brooklyn, NY 718-272-7700
Ericas Rugelach & Baking Co
  Brooklyn, NY 718-965-3657
Ethel's Baking Co.
  St. Clair Shores, MI 586-552-5110
Ethnic Edibles
  New York, NY 718-320-0147
Falcone's Cookie Land LTD
  Brooklyn, NY 718-236-4200
Fancypants Bakery
  Walpole, MA 508-660-1140
Fantasy Cookie Company
  Sylmar, CA 800-354-4488
Fantis Foods Inc
  Carlstadt, NJ 201-933-6200
Federal Pretzel Baking Company
  Bridgeport, NJ 215-467-0505
Fernando C Pujals & Bros
  Guaynabo, PR 787-792-3080
Ferrara Bakery & Cafe
  New York, NY 212-226-6150
Firefly Fandango
  Seattle, WA 206-760-3700

Fireside Kitchen
  Halifax, NS 902-454-7387
Flathau's Fine Foods
  Hattiesburg, MS 888-263-1299
FNI Group LLC
  Sherborn, MA 508-655-4175
Food Mill
  Oakland, CA 510-482-3848
Fortella Fortune Cookies
  Chicago, IL 312-567-9000
Fortunate Cookie
  Stowe, VT 866-266-5337
Fortune Cookie Factory
  Oakland, CA 510-832-5552
Foxtail Foods
  Fairfield, OH 800-487-2253
Frankly Natural Bakers
  San Diego, CA 800-727-7229
GH Bent Company
  Milton, MA 617-322-9287
Giant Food
  Landover, MD 888-469-4426
Ginny Bakes
  Miami, FL 305-638-5103
Gladder's Gourmet Cookies
  Lockhart, TX 888-398-4523
Glennys
  Brooklyn, NY 888-864-1243
Glow Gluten Free
  New York, NY 800-497-7434
Glutino
  Laval, QC 800-363-3438
Golden Kernel Pecan Co
  Cameron, SC 803-823-2311
Golden Walnut Specialty Foods
  Wayzata, MN 800-843-3645
Goodie Girl
  Ridgefield, NJ
Gourmet Treats
  Torrance, CA 800-444-9549
Grandma Beth's Cookies
  Alliance, NE 308-762-8433
Granello Bakery
  Las Vegas, NV 702-361-0311
Grey Ghost Bakery
  Charleston, SC 803-238-1123
Greyston Bakery Inc
  Yonkers, NY 800-289-2253
GWB Foods Corporation
  Brooklyn, NY 877-977-7610
H-E-B Grocery Co. LP
  San Antonio, TX 800-432-3113
H.B. Trading
  Totowa, NJ 973-812-1022
Haby's Alsatian Bakery
  Castroville, TX 830-538-2118
Handy Pax
  Randolph, MA 781-963-8300
Hannah Max Baking
  Gardena, CA 310-324-9871
Harvest Valley Bakery Inc
  La Salle, IL 815-224-9030
Hawaii Candy Inc
  Honolulu, HI 800-303-2507
Hawaiian King Candies
  Honolulu, HI 800-570-1902
Health Valley Company
  Irwindale, CA 800-334-3204
Heavenscent Edibles
  New York, NY 212-369-0310
Heltzman Bakery
  Louisville, KY 502-447-3515
HempNut
  Henderson, NV 707-576-7050
Heritage Short Bread
  Hilton Head Isle, SC 843-422-3458
Heyerly Bakery
  Ossian, IN 260-622-4196
Hollandia Bakeries Limited
  Mt Brydges, ON 800-265-3480
Holt's Bakery Inc
  Douglas, GA 912-384-2202
Holton Food Products
  La Grange, IL 708-352-5599
Homefree LLC
  Windham, NH 800-552-7172
Hudson River Foods
  Castleton, NY 888-417-9343
Hunt Country Foods Inc
  Marshall, VA 540-364-2622
Immaculate Baking Company
  Wakefield, MA 888-826-6567

Product Categories / Baked Goods: Cookies & Bars

Immaculate Consumption
  Columbia, SC 888-826-6567
Indianola Pecan House Inc
  Indianola, MS 800-541-6252
Interbake Foods
  Richmond, VA 800-221-1002
Irene's Bakery & Gourmet
  Bensalem, PA 215-244-6200
Irresistible Cookie Jar
  Hayden Lake, ID 208-664-1261
J & M Foods Inc
  Little Rock, AR 800-264-2278
Jamae Natural Foods
  Los Angeles, CA 800-343-0052
Jimmys Cookies
  Clifton, NJ 973-779-8500
Joey's Fine Foods
  Newark, NJ 973-482-1400
Joseph's Lite Cookies
  Deming, NM 800-373-3726
Jovial Foods
  North Stonington, CT 877-642-0644
JSL Foods
  Los Angeles, CA 800-745-3236
Jubelt Variety Bakeries
  Litchfield, IL 217-324-5314
Just Desserts
  Fairfield, CA 415-780-6860
K & F Select Fine Coffees
  Portland, OR 800-558-7788
Kashi Company
  Solana Beach, CA 877-747-2467
Kauai Kookie
  Eleele, HI 800-361-1126
Keebler Company
  Battlecreek, MI 800-962-1413
Keller's Bakery
  Lafayette, LA 337-235-1568
Kelsen, Inc.
  Melville, NY 888-253-5736
Kemach Food Products
  Brooklyn, NY 718-272-5655
Kerri Kreations
  Santa Cruz, CA 831-429-5129
Kids Kookie Company
  San Clemente, CA. 800-350-7577
Kim and Jake's
  Boulder, CO 303-499-9126
Klara's Gourmet Cookies
  Lee, MA 413-243-3370
Kollar Cookies
  Long Branch, NJ. 732-343-4217
LA Boulangerie
  San Diego, CA 858-578-4040
Larosa Bakery Inc
  Shrewsbury, NJ. 800-527-6722
Lavoi Corporation
  Atlanta, GA. 404-325-1016
Lazzaroni USA
  Saddle Brook, NJ 201-368-1240
Lenny & Larry's
  Panorama City, CA
Leo's Bakery & Deli
  East Rochester, NY. 585-249-1000
Linden Cookies Inc
  Congers, NY 845-268-5050
Liz Lovely Inc
  Waitsfield, VT. 802-496-6390
Lotte USA Inc
  Battle Creek, MI 269-963-6664
Lotus Bakery
  Santa Rosa, CA 800-875-6887
Lovin Oven Cakery
  Round Lake Beach, IL 888-775-0099
Lucky Spoon Bakery LLC
  Salt Lake City, UT 801-824-0624
Ludwick's Frozen Donuts
  Grand Rapids, MI 800-366-8816
Luv Yu Bakery
  Louisville, KY. 502-451-4511
LWC Brands Inc.
  Dallas, TX. 800-552-8006
Mac Farms Of Hawaii Inc
  Captain Cook, HI 808-328-2435
Mac's Donut Shop
  Aliquippa, PA 724-375-6776
Madrona Specialty Foods LLC
  Seattle, WA 425-656-2997
Magna Foods Corporation
  City of Industry, CA 800-995-4394
Magnolia Bakery
  New York, NY 855-622-5379

Mamma Says
  Butler, NJ 877-283-6282
Marin Food Specialties
  Byron, CA. 925-634-6126
Mary's Gone Crackers
  Gridley, CA. 888-258-1250
Matt's Cookies
  Wheeling, IL 847-537-3888
Maxine's Heavenly
  Los Angeles, CA
McDuffies Bakery
  Clarence, NY. 800-875-1598
McKee Foods Corp.
  Collegedale, TN 800-522-4499
Mctavish Shortbread
  Portland, OR. 800-256-9844
Merlino Italian Baking Company
  Kent, WA. 800-800-9490
Michael's Cookies
  Clear Lake, IA. 800-822-5384
Miss Meringue
  San Marcos, CA 800-561-6516
Monaco Baking Company
  Santa Fe Springs, CA 800-569-4640
Moon Dance Baking
  Rohnert Park, CA 707-588-0800
Moon Rabbit Foods
  Savannah, NY. 828-273-6649
Moravian Cookies Shop
  Winston Salem, NC. 800-274-2994
Mozzicato De Pasquale Bakery
  Hartford, CT 860-296-0426
Mrs. Denson's Cookie Company
  Ukiah, CA. 800-219-3199
Mrs. Fields Original Cookies
  Bloomfield, CO. 800-266-2547
Mt. View Bakery
  Mountain View, HI 808-968-6353
My Boy's Baking LLC
  Allentown, PA. 610-759-4552
Nabisco
  Parsippany, NJ. 973-682-5000
Nana's Cookie Co.
  San Diego, CA 800-836-7534
Natural Nectar
  Huntington, NY 631-367-7280
Nikki's Cookies
  Milwaukee, WI 800-776-7107
Northwoods Candy Emporium
  Branson, MO 417-332-1010
Nothin' But Foods
  Elmwood Park, NJ 203-557-8637
Notre Dame Bakery
  Conception Harbour, NL 709-535-2738
Nui Foods
  Anaheim, CA
Nustef Foods
  Mississauga, ON 877-306-7562
Nutrilicious Natural Bakery
  Countryside, IL. 800-835-8097
Oak State Products Inc
  Wenona, IL 815-853-4348
Oh, Sugar! LLC
  Roswell, GA 866-557-8427
Old Colony Baking Co Inc
  Northbrook, IL. 847-498-5434
Olde Colony Bakery
  Mt Pleasant, SC. 800-722-9932
Otis Spunkmeyer
  Norcross, GA 855-427-9982
Our Cookie
  Miami, FL 877-885-2715
Oven Arts
  Hackensack, NJ. 855-354-4070
Pamela's Products
  Ukiah, CA. 707-462-6605
Paris Pastry
  Van Nuys, CA 805-487-2227
Partners: A Tasteful Choice
  Kent, WA. 800-632-7477
Pati-Petite Cookies Inc
  Bridgeville, PA 800-253-5805
Peggy Lawton Kitchens
  East Walpole, MA. 800-843-7325
Peking Noodle Co Inc
  Los Angeles, CA. 323-223-0897
Pepperidge Farm Inc.
  Norwalk, CT 888-737-7374
Plehn's Bakery Inc
  Louisville, KY. 502-896-4438
Poppie's Dough
  Chicago, IL. 888-767-7431

Poppies International
  Battleboro, NC 252-442-4309
Positively 3rd St Bakery
  Duluth, MN 218-724-8619
Pure Batch
  Hillsborough, NJ 609-373-2015
Pure's Food Specialties
  Broadview, IL 708-344-8884
Quaker Bonnet
  Buffalo, NY. 800-283-2447
Quality Naturally Foods
  City Of Industry, CA 888-498-6986
R.W. Frookies
  Sag Harbor, NY 800-913-3663
Real Cookies
  Merrick, NY 800-822-5113
Rene Rey Chocolates Ltd
  North Vancouver, BC 888-985-0949
Richmond Baking Co
  Richmond, IN 765-962-8535
Rip Van
  Brooklyn, NY 415-529-5403
Rose Randolph Cookies, LLC
  Wappingers Falls, NY 917-834-2310
Rustic Bakery Inc.
  San Rafael, CA 415-479-5600
Ryke's Bakery
  Muskegon, MI 231-726-2253
Sacramento Cookie Factory
  Sacramento, CA 877-877-2646
Salem Baking Company
  Winston Salem, NC. 800-274-2994
Salt of the Earth Bakery
  Brooklyn, NY 646-330-5089
San Anselmo's Cookies & Biscotti
  San Anselmo, CA 800-229-1249
Sandusky Filling & Brittle
  Sandusky, OH 800-274-8853
Sanitary Bakery
  Nanticoke, PA 570-735-6630
Sara Snacker Cookie Company
  Rye, NY. 914-305-6363
Schulze & Burch Biscuit Co
  Chicago, IL 773-927-6622
Scialo Brothers Bakery
  Providence, RI 877-421-0986
Sejoyia Foods
  Louisville, CO. 855-293-5577
Selma Good Company
  Selma, AL 334-412-4214
Selma's Cookies
  Apopka, FL 800-992-6654
Shepherdsfield Bakery
  Fulton, MO 573-642-0009
Sherwood Brands
  New Brunswick, NJ 973-249-8200
Sheryl's Chocolate Creations
  Hicksville, NY 888-882-2462
Shur-Good Biscuit Co.
  Cincinnati, OH 513-458-6200
Silver Tray Cookies
  Fort Lauderdale, FL 305-883-0800
Simit + Smith
  Ridgefield, NJ 201-699-0320
Simple Mills
  Chicago, IL 312-600-6196
Simply Gourmet Confections
  Irvine, CA 714-505-3955
Simply Shari's Gluten Free
  Thousand Oaks, CA 805-241-5676
Sister's Gourmet
  Winder, GA 877-338-1388
Skipping Stone Productions
  Paso Robles, CA. 805-226-2998
Smoak's Bakery & Catering Service
  Augusta, GA. 706-738-1792
Snyder's-Lance Inc.
  Charlotte, NC 800-438-1880
Sorbee Intl.
  Philadelphia, PA 800-654-3997
Soupergirl
  Washington, DC 202-609-7177
Spilke's Baking Company
  Moosic, PA 570-457-2400
Sporting Colors LLC
  St. Louis, MO 888-394-2292
Spring Street Bake Shop
  Pottstown, PA 484-624-8201
Spruce Foods
  San Clemente, CA. 800-326-3612
Sprucewood Handmade Cookie Company
  Warkworth, ON 877-632-1300

Product Categories / Baked Goods: Cookies & Bars

St. Amour Inc/French Cookies
   Costa Mesa, CA 714-754-1900
Stauffer Biscuit Co
   York, PA 888-480-1988
Stauffer's
   Cuba, NY 585-968-2700
Stella D'oro
   Charlotte, NC 800-995-2623
Sterling Foods LLC
   San Antonio, TX. 210-490-1669
Steve & Andy's Organics
   Brooklyn, NY 718-499-7933
Steve's Mom
   Bronx, NY 800-362-4545
Sucre
   New Orleans, LA 504-708-4366
Sugar & Plumm
   New York, NY 212-787-8778
Suity Confections Co
   Miami, FL 305-639-3300
Sunset Specialty Foods
   Lake Arrowhead, CA 909-337-7643
Susie's Smart Cookie
   Katonah, NY 914-740-1007
Sweet Loren's
   New York, NY 646-257-5700
Sweet Pillar
   Newport Beach, CA 310-913-7261
Table De France
   Ontario, CA. 909-923-5205
Taste of Nature Inc.
   Santa Monica, CA. 310-396-4433
Tasty Baking Company
   Philadelphia, PA 800-248-2789
Tasty Brand Inc
   Calabasas, CA. 818-225-9000
Tate's Bake Shop
   Southampton, NY. 631-283-9830
Tea Aura
   Toronto, ON 416-225-8868
That's How We Roll, LLC
   Fairfield, NJ 973-602-3011
Thyme Garden Herb Co
   Alsea, OR 800-482-4372
Todd's
   Vernon, CA. 800-938-6337
Torn Ranch
   Novato, CA. 707-796-7800
Touche Bakery
   London, ON 518-455-0044
Tribe 9 Foods
   Madison, WI 608-257-7216
Trumps Food Interest
   Vancouver, BC 604-732-8473
Turkey Hill Sugarbush
   Waterloo, QC 450-539-4822
Uncle Ralph's Cookies
   Frederick, MD. 800-422-0626
United Noodle Manufacturing Company
   Salt Lake City, UT 801-485-0951
Unna Bakery
   New York, NY 917-543-8133
Uptown Bakers
   Hyattsville, MD 301-864-1500
V L Foods
   White Plains, NY 914-697-4851
Valley Bakery
   Burnaby, BC 604-291-0674
Veronica's Treats
   Middleboro, MA. 866-576-1122
Vickey's Vittles
   North Hills, CA. 818-841-1944
Voortman Bakery
   Burlington, ON 800-808-5950
Wackym's Kitchen
   Dallas, TX. 214-327-7667
Walkers Shortbread
   Hauppauge, NY 800-521-0141
Wenger's Bakery
   Reading, PA 610-372-6545
Westbrae Natural Foods
   Melville, NY. 800-434-4246
Whipped Pastry Boutique
   Brooklyn, NY 718-858-8088
Wholesome Bakery
   San Francisco, CA 415-343-5414
Wildlife Cookies Co
   St Charles, IL 630-377-6196
Williams & Bennett
   Orlando, FL. 561-276-9007
Willmar Cookie & Nut Company
   Willmar, MN. 800-426-7845

Wonton Food
   Brooklyn, NY 800-776-8889
Y Z Enterprises Inc
   Maumee, OH 800-736-8779
Ya-Hoo Baking Co
   Sherman, TX 888-869-2466
Yohay Baking Co
   Lindenhurst, NY 631-225-0300
Young's Bakery
   Uniontown, PA 724-437-6361
Zazi Baking Company
   Petaluma, CA 707-778-1635

Cookies & Biscuits

A Southern Season
   Hillsborough, NC 800-253-3663
Abimar Foods Inc
   Abilene, TX. 325-691-5425
Ames International Inc
   Fife, WA 888-469-2637
Arcor USA
   Coral Gables, FL. 800-572-7267
Arturo's Spinella's Bakery
   Waterbury, CT. 203-754-3056
Aunt Gussie Cookies & Crackers
   Garfield, NJ. 800-422-6654
Bama Foods LTD
   Tulsa, OK 800-756-2262
Barbara's Bakery
   Lakeville, MN. 800-343-0590
Best Maid Cookie Co
   River Falls, WI 888-444-0322
Betty Lou's
   McMinnville, OR 800-242-5205
Bite Size Bakery
   Rio Rancho, NM 505-994-3093
Blendco Inc
   Hattiesburg, MS 888-253-6326
Blue Dog Bakery
   Seattle, WA 888-749-7229
Bluechip Group
   Salt Lake City, UT 800-878-0099
Borinquen Biscuit Corporation
   Yauco, PR 787-856-3030
Bremner Biscuit Company
   Denver, CO. 866-972-6879
Brimhall Foods
   Bartlett, TN. 800-628-6559
Brooklyn Baking Company
   Waterbury, CT. 203-574-9198
Buckeye Pretzel Company
   Williamsport, PA 800-257-6029
Buonitalia
   New York, NY 212-633-9090
Busken Bakery
   Cincinnati, OH 513-871-2114
Byrd Cookie
   Savannah, GA. 800-291-2973
Case Side Holdings Company
   Kensington, PE 902-836-4214
Charlie's Specialties Inc
   Hermitage, PA. 724-346-2350
Chelsea Flower Market
   New York, NY 888-727-7887
Chicago Pastry
   Bloomingdale, IL 630-529-6391
Chocolate Chix
   Waxahachie, TX 214-744-2442
Colonial Cookies, Ltd
   Kitchener, ON 800-265-6508
Cookie Factory
   Bronx, NY. 718-379-6223
Cookie Specialties Inc
   Wheeling, IL 847-537-3888
Cookie Tree Bakeries
   Salt Lake City, UT 801-268-2253
Cooper Street Cookies
   Birmingham, MI 248-283-7700
Dairy State Foods Inc
   Milwaukee, WI 800-435-4499
Dancing Deer Baking Company
   Boston, MA. 888-699-3337
Dare Foods
   Spartanburg, SC 800-668-3273
DeBeukelaer Cookie Co
   Madison, MS. 601-856-7454
Di Camillo Baking Co
   Niagara Falls, NY 800-634-4363
Diamond Bakery Co LTD
   Honolulu, HI 808-847-3551
Dinkel's Bakery Inc
   Chicago, IL 800-822-8817

Dong Kee Company
   Chicago, IL 312-225-6340
Dufflet Pastries
   Toronto, ON 866-238-0899
Dutchess Bakery
   Charleston, WV 304-346-4237
DWC Specialities
   Horicon, WI 800-383-8808
Edelweiss Patisserie
   Medford, MA 781-628-0225
Edward & Sons Trading Co
   Carpinteria, CA 805-684-8500
Ellison Bakery, Inc.
   Fort Wayne, IN
Elmwood Pastry Shop
   West Hartford, CT. 860-233-2029
Erba Food Products
   Brooklyn, NY 718-272-7700
Ericas Rugelach & Baking Co
   Brooklyn, NY 718-965-3657
Falcone's Cookie Land LTD
   Brooklyn, NY 718-236-4200
Fantasy Cookie Company
   Sylmar, CA 800-354-4488
Federal Pretzel Baking Company
   Bridgeport, NJ. 215-467-0505
Fernando C Pujals & Bros
   Guaynabo, PR 787-792-3080
Ferrara Bakery & Cafe
   New York, NY 212-226-6150
Fireside Kitchen
   Halifax, NS 902-454-7387
Food Mill
   Oakland, CA 510-482-3848
Forever Green Food Inc.
   Commerce, CA. 323-721-9928
Fortella Fortune Cookies
   Chicago, IL 312-567-9000
Fortune Cookie Factory
   Oakland, CA 510-832-5552
Foxtail Foods
   Fairfield, OH. 800-487-2253
Frankly Natural Bakers
   San Diego, CA 800-727-7229
G Debbas Chocolatier
   Fresno, CA 559-294-2071
GH Bent Company
   Milton, MA 617-322-9287
Giant Food
   Landover, MD. 888-469-4426
Grandma Beth's Cookies
   Alliance, NE 308-762-8433
Granowska's
   Toronto, ON 416-533-7755
Greyston Bakery Inc
   Yonkers, NY 800-289-2253
GWB Foods Corporation
   Brooklyn, NY 877-977-7610
H-E-B Grocery Co. LP
   San Antonio, TX. 800-432-3113
Hain Celestial Group Inc
   Lake Success, NY. 800-434-4246
Handy Pax
   Randolph, MA 781-963-8300
Harvest Valley Bakery Inc
   La Salle, IL 815-224-9030
Hawaii Candy Inc
   Honolulu, HI 800-303-2507
Health Valley Company
   Irwindale, CA 800-334-3204
Heyerly Bakery
   Ossian, IN 260-622-4196
Holt's Bakery Inc
   Douglas, GA 912-384-2202
Hunt Country Foods Inc
   Marshall, VA 540-364-2622
Hye Quality Bakery
   Fresno, CA 877-445-1778
Immaculate Consumption
   Columbia, SC 888-826-6567
Interbake Foods
   Richmond, VA. 800-221-1002
Irresistible Cookie Jar
   Hayden Lake, ID 208-664-1261
Jamae Natural Foods
   Los Angeles, CA. 800-343-0052
James Candy Company
   Atlantic City, NJ 800-441-1404
Jim's Cheese Pantry
   Waterloo, WI. 800-345-3571
Joey's Fine Foods
   Newark, NJ 973-482-1400

Product Categories / Baked Goods: Cookies & Bars

Jubelt Variety Bakeries
   Litchfield, IL 217-324-5314
Just Desserts
   Fairfield, CA 415-780-6860
Kedem
   Bayonne, NJ 718-369-4600
Keebler Company
   Battlecreek, MI 800-962-1413
Kemach Food Products
   Brooklyn, NY 718-272-5655
Kids Kookie Company
   San Clemente, CA 800-350-7577
Kinnikinnick Foods
   Edmonton, AB 877-503-4466
Kollar Cookies
   Long Branch, NJ 732-343-4217
LA Boulangerie
   San Diego, CA 858-578-4040
Larosa Bakery Inc
   Shrewsbury, NJ 800-527-6722
Le Chef Bakery
   Montebello, CA 323-888-2929
Linden Cookies Inc
   Congers, NY 845-268-5050
Loc Maria Biscuits
   Philadelphia, PA
Loghouse Foods
   Minneapolis, MN 763-546-8395
Lotus Bakery
   Santa Rosa, CA 800-875-6887
Ludwick's Frozen Donuts
   Grand Rapids, MI 800-366-8816
Mac Farms Of Hawaii Inc
   Captain Cook, HI 808-328-2435
Mac's Donut Shop
   Aliquippa, PA 724-375-6776
Magna Foods Corporation
   City of Industry, CA 800-995-4394
Marin Food Specialties
   Byron, CA 925-634-6126
Merlino Italian Baking Company
   Kent, WA 800-800-9490
Mozzicato De Pasquale Bakery
   Hartford, CT 860-296-0426
Mt. View Bakery
   Mountain View, HI 808-968-6353
Nabisco
   Parsippany, NJ 973-682-5000
Nicole's Divine Crackers
   Chicago, IL 312-640-8883
Nikki's Cookies
   Milwaukee, WI 800-776-7107
Northwoods Candy Emporium
   Branson, MO 417-332-1010
Notre Dame Bakery
   Conception Harbour, NL 709-535-2738
Nustef Foods
   Mississauga, ON 877-306-7562
Nutrilicious Natural Bakery
   Countryside, IL 800-835-8097
Oak State Products Inc
   Wenona, IL 815-853-4348
Ohta Wafer Factory
   Honolulu, HI 808-949-2775
Paris Pastry
   Van Nuys, CA 805-487-2227
Pati-Petite Cookies Inc
   Bridgeville, PA 800-253-5805
Peggy Lawton Kitchens
   East Walpole, MA 800-843-7325
Peking Noodle Co Inc
   Los Angeles, CA 323-223-0897
Pioneer Frozen Foods
   Duncanville, TX 972-298-4281
Positively 3rd St Bakery
   Duluth, MN 218-724-8619
Pure's Food Specialties
   Broadview, IL 708-344-8884
Purity Factories
   St. John's, NL 800-563-3411
R.M. Palmer Co.
   West Reading, PA 610-372-8971
R.W. Frookies
   Sag Harbor, NY 800-913-3663
Richmond Baking Co
   Richmond, IN 765-962-8535
Rose Randolph Cookies, LLC
   Wappingers Falls, NY 917-834-2310
Rovira Biscuit Corporation
   Ponce, PR 787-844-8585
Ryke's Bakery
   Muskegon, MI 231-726-2253

S & M Communion Bread Co
   Nashville, TN 615-292-1969
Salem Baking Company
   Winston Salem, NC 800-274-2994
San Anselmo's Cookies & Biscotti
   San Anselmo, CA 800-229-1249
Sandusky Filling & Brittle
   Sandusky, OH 800-274-8853
Sanitary Bakery
   Nanticoke, PA 570-735-6630
Schulze & Burch Biscuit Co
   Chicago, IL 773-927-6622
Scialo Brothers Bakery
   Providence, RI 877-421-0986
Sheryl's Chocolate Creations
   Hicksville, NY 888-882-2462
Silver Tray Cookies
   Fort Lauderdale, FL 305-883-0800
Smoak's Bakery & Catering Service
   Augusta, GA 706-738-1792
Snyder's-Lance Inc.
   Charlotte, NC 800-438-1880
Spilke's Baking Company
   Moosic, PA 570-457-2400
Sporting Colors LLC
   St. Louis, MO 888-394-2292
St. Amour Inc/French Cookies
   Costa Mesa, CA 714-754-1900
Stauffer's
   Cuba, NY 585-968-2700
Stella D'oro
   Charlotte, NC 800-995-2623
Sunset Specialty Foods
   Lake Arrowhead, CA 909-337-7643
Table De France
   Ontario, CA 909-923-5205
Thyme Garden Herb Co
   Alsea, OR 800-482-4372
Treasure Foods
   West Valley, UT 801-974-0911
Triple-C
   Hamilton, ON 800-263-9105
Turnbull Cone Baking Company
   Chattanooga, TN 423-265-4551
Tuscan Bakery
   Portland, OR 800-887-2261
Ultimate Biscotti
   Eugene, OR 541-344-8220
Uncle Ralph's Cookies
   Frederick, MD 800-422-0626
United Noodle Manufacturing Company
   Salt Lake City, UT 801-485-0951
Uptown Bakers
   Hyattsville, MD 301-864-1500
UTZ Quality Foods Inc.
   Hanover, PA 800-367-7629
V L Foods
   White Plains, NY 914-697-4851
Venus Wafers Inc
   Hingham, MA 800-545-4538
Wenger's Bakery
   Reading, PA 610-372-6545
Westbrae Natural Foods
   Melville, NY 800-434-4246
Willmar Cookie & Nut Company
   Willmar, MN 800-426-7845
Wonton Food
   Brooklyn, NY 800-776-8889
Y Z Enterprises Inc
   Maumee, OH 800-736-8779
Ya-Hoo Baking Co
   Sherman, TX 888-869-2466
Young's Bakery
   Uniontown, PA 724-437-6361

Fortune Cookies

Dong Kee Company
   Chicago, IL 312-225-6340
Fortella Fortune Cookies
   Chicago, IL 312-567-9000
Fortune Cookie Factory
   Oakland, CA 510-832-5552
Hawaii Candy Inc
   Honolulu, HI 800-303-2507
Ohta Wafer Factory
   Honolulu, HI 808-949-2775
Peking Noodle Co Inc
   Los Angeles, CA 323-223-0897
United Noodle Manufacturing Company
   Salt Lake City, UT 801-485-0951
Wings Foods of Alberta Ltd
   Edmonton, AB 780-433-6406

Wonton Food
   Brooklyn, NY 800-776-8889

Frozen Cookies

Bama Foods LTD
   Tulsa, OK 800-756-2262
GWB Foods Corporation
   Brooklyn, NY 877-977-7610
Orange Bakery
   Irvine, CA 949-863-1377
RoRo's Baking Company
   Dallas, TX 972-897-2315
Sugarplum Desserts
   Langley, BC 604-534-2282
Sunset Specialty Foods
   Lake Arrowhead, CA 909-337-7643

Ginger Snaps

Country Choice Organic
   Eden Prairie, MN 952-829-8824
Mary's Gone Crackers
   Gridley, CA 888-258-1250

Individually Packaged

Biscomerica Corporation
   Rialto, CA 909-877-5997
Boulder Cookie
   Boulder, CO
Munk Pack
   Greenwich, CT
No Cow
   Denver, CO
Paleo Prime Foods
   Chicago, IL 312-659-6596

Macaroons

Abimar Foods Inc
   Abilene, TX 325-691-5425
Duverger
   Oxnard, CA
Emmy's Organics
   Ithaca, NY 855-463-6697
Erba Food Products
   Brooklyn, NY 718-272-7700
Jennies Gluten-Free Bakery
   Moosic, PA 570-457-2400
L & M Bakery
   Riverside, NJ 888-887-1335
Macaron Paris LLC
   New York, NY 212-465-0510
Northern Valley Baking Co
   Dumont, NJ 201-338-2812
Poppies International
   Battleboro, NC 252-442-4309
St. Julien Macaroons
   Sandown, NH 800-473-8869
Steve's Mom
   Bronx, NY 800-362-4545
Sucre
   New Orleans, LA 504-708-4366
Sugar & Plumm
   New York, NY 212-787-8778

Mini Cookies

Bakeology
   Torrance, CA
Bauducco Foods Inc.
   Miami, FL 305-477-9270
Biscomerica Corporation
   Rialto, CA 909-877-5997
Ginny Bakes
   Miami, FL 305-638-5103

Oatmeal & Chocolate Chip Cookies

Klara's Gourmet Cookies
   Lee, MA 413-243-3370
Olivia's Kitchen
   New York, NY 917-374-0077
Sweet Street Desserts
   Reading, PA 800-793-3897

Oatmeal Cookies

Abimar Foods Inc
   Abilene, TX 325-691-5425
Country Choice Organic
   Eden Prairie, MN 952-829-8824
Homefree LLC
   Windham, NH 800-552-7172

Product Categories / Baked Goods: Crackers

Kashi Company
  Solana Beach, CA 877-747-2467
Mississippi Cheese Straw
  Yazoo City, MS 800-530-7496
Olivia's Kitchen
  New York, NY 917-374-0077
Peggy Lawton Kitchens
  East Walpole, MA 800-843-7325

Oatmeal Raisin Cookies

Linden Cookies Inc
  Congers, NY 845-268-5050

Sandwich Creme Cookies

Abimar Foods Inc
  Abilene, TX 325-691-5425
Biscomerica Corporation
  Rialto, CA 909-877-5997
Country Choice Organic
  Eden Prairie, MN 952-829-8824
Tasty Brand Inc
  Calabasas, CA 818-225-9000

Soft Cookies

Biscomerica Corporation
  Rialto, CA 909-877-5997
Jack's Paleo Kitchen
  Ferndale, WA
Oak State Products Inc
  Wenona, IL 815-853-4348

Sugar Cookies

Falcone's Cookie Land LTD
  Brooklyn, NY 718-236-4200
Young's Bakery
  Uniontown, PA 724-437-6361

Tea Cookies

Botanical Bakery, LLC
  Napa, CA 707-344-8103
Hawaii Candy Inc
  Honolulu, HI 800-303-2507
J & M Foods Inc
  Little Rock, AR 800-264-2278
Klara's Gourmet Cookies
  Lee, MA 413-243-3370
Ohta Wafer Factory
  Honolulu, HI 808-949-2775
Simply Scruptious Confections
  Irvine, CA 714-505-3955

Wafers

Arcor USA
  Coral Gables, FL 800-572-7267
Castella Imports Inc
  Brentwood, NY 631-231-5500
DeBeukelaer Corp
  Madison, MS 601-856-7454
Fernando C Pujals & Bros
  Guaynabo, PR 787-792-3080
Functional Foods
  Roseville, MI 877-372-0550
Honey Wafer Baking Co
  Crestwood, IL 800-977-9012
Kitchen Table
  Syosset, NY 800-486-4582
Loacker USA
  New York, NY 212-742-8510
Pez Candy Inc
  Orange, CT 203-795-0531
Q Bell Foods
  Nyack, NY 845-358-1475
Ruger LLC
  Bethesda, MD 301-675-2398
Smarties
  Union, NJ 800-631-7968
Snyder's-Lance Inc.
  Charlotte, NC 800-438-1880
Table De France
  Ontario, CA 909-923-5205
V L Foods
  White Plains, NY 914-697-4851
Yohay Baking Co
  Lindenhurst, NY 631-225-0300

Sugar

ADM Wild Flavors & Specialty
  Erlanger, KY 859-342-3600

Alfred L. Wolff, Inc.
  Park Ridge, IL 847-759-8888
American Culinary Garden
  Springfield, MO 888-831-2433
Annie's Frozen Yogurt
  Minneapolis, MN 800-969-9648
BakeMark Canada
  Laval, QC 800-361-4998
Bouchard Family Farm
  Fort Kent, ME 800-239-3237
Brookside Foods
  Abbotsford, BC 800-468-1714
Calico Cottage
  Amityville, NY 800-645-5345
California Cereal Products
  Oakland, CA 510-452-4500
Canada Bread Co, Ltd
  Etobicoke, ON 800-465-5515
Chelsea Milling Co.
  Chelsea, MI 800-727-2460
Country Choice Organic
  Eden Prairie, MN 952-829-8824
Crown Processing Company
  Cerritos, CA 562-865-0293
Dutch Ann Foods Company
  Natchez, MS 601-445-5566
Ellison Milling Company
  Lethbridge, AB 403-328-6622
Embassy Flavours Ltd.
  Brampton, ON 800-334-3371
Flavormatic Industries
  Wappingers Falls, NY 845-297-9100
Foley's Chocolates & Candies
  Richmond, BC 888-236-5397
Great Recipes
  Beaverton, OR 800-273-2331
Gregory's Foods, Inc.
  St Paul, MN 800-231-4734
GWB Foods Corporation
  Brooklyn, NY 877-977-7610
JER Creative Food Concepts, Inc.
  Commerce, CA 800-350-2462
La Cookie
  Burbank, CA 818-495-5732
Marie Callender's Gourmet Products/Goldrush Products
  San Jose, CA 800-729-5428
Martha Olson's Great Foo
  Sutter Creek, CA 800-973-3966
Mimac Glaze
  Brampton, ON 877-990-9975
Natrium Products Inc
  Cortland, NY 800-962-4203
Ottens Flavors
  Philadelphia, PA 800-523-0767
Paradise Island Foods
  Nanaimo, BC 800-889-3370
Petra International
  Mississauga, ON 800-261-7226
Pillsbury
  Minneapolis, MN 800-775-4777
Produits Alimentaire
  St Lambert De Lauzon, QC 800-463-1787
Sanford Milling Co Inc
  Henderson, NC 866-438-4526
Southern Brown Rice
  Weiner, AR 800-421-7423
Southern Style Nuts
  Denison, TX 903-463-3161
Sugar Flowers Plus
  Glendale, CA 800-972-2935
Tasty Selections
  Concord, ON 905-760-2353
Teff Co
  Nampa, ID 888-822-2221
Westco-BakeMark
  Pico Rivera, CA 562-949-1054
Yorktown Baking Company
  Yorktown Heights, NY 800-235-3961

Crackers

Crackers

34-Degrees
  Denver, CO 303-861-4818
Abimar Foods Inc
  Abilene, TX 325-691-5425
American Vintage Wine Biscuits
  Long Island City, NY 718-361-1003
Aunt Gussie Cookies & Crackers
  Garfield, NJ 800-422-6654
Back to Nature Foods
   855-346-2225

Bake Crafters Food Company
  McDonald, TN 423-396-3392
Bama Foods LTD
  Tulsa, OK 800-756-2262
Bespoke Provisions
  Boulder, CO 646-963-1245
Bite Size Bakery
  Rio Rancho, NM 505-994-3093
Bitsy's Brainfood
  New York, NY 212-461-1572
Blue Dog Bakery
  Seattle, WA 888-749-7229
Borinquen Biscuit Corporation
  Yauco, PR 787-856-3030
Christie-Brown
  East Hanover, NJ 973-503-4000
Consolidated Biscuit Company
  McComb, OH
Dairyfood USA Inc
  Blue Mounds, WI 800-236-3300
Dan-D Foods Ltd
  Richmond, BC 800-633-4788
Dare Foods Incorporated
  Kitchener, ON 800-668-3273
Delicious Frookie
  Des Plaines, IL 847-699-3200
Diamond Bakery Co LTD
  Honolulu, HI 808-847-3551
Earth Balance
  Boulder, CO 866-234-6429
Ella's Flats
  Naples, FL
Falcone's Cookie Land LTD
  Brooklyn, NY 718-236-4200
Flackers
  Minneapolis, MN
Flax4Life
  Bellingham, WA 877-352-9487
Foods Alive
  Angola, IN 260-488-4497
Fortitude Brands LLC
  Coral Gables, FL 305-661-8198
Gilda Industries Inc
  Hialeah, FL 305-887-8286
Glutino
  Laval, QC 800-363-3438
Good Groceries
  Brooklyn, NY 347-853-7462
Grains of Health LLC
  Fremont, CA 510-516-2556
GWB Foods Corporation
  Brooklyn, NY 877-977-7610
Handy Pax
  Randolph, MA 781-963-8300
Healing Home Foods
  Pound Ridge, NY 914-764-1303
Health Valley Company
  Irwindale, CA 800-334-3204
Hye Quality Bakery
  Fresno, CA 877-445-1778
Interbake Foods
  Richmond, VA 800-221-1002
J & M Foods Inc
  Little Rock, AR 800-264-2278
Jilz Gluten Free
  Ventura, CA 805-585-5297
Jim's Cheese Pantry
  Waterloo, WI 800-345-3571
Jovial Foods
  North Stonington, CT 877-642-0644
Kameda USA Inc.
  Torrance, CA 310-944-9639
Kapow Now!
  North Vancouver, BC 604-726-6391
Kashi Company
  Solana Beach, CA 877-747-2467
Keebler Company
  Battlecreek, MI 800-962-1413
Kemach Food Products
  Brooklyn, NY 718-272-5655
La Piccolina
  Decatur, GA 800-626-1624
Legacy Bakehouse
  Waukesha, WI 800-967-2447
Magna Foods Corporation
  City of Industry, CA 800-995-4394
Manischewitz Co
  Newark, NJ 201-553-1100
Mary's Gone Crackers
  Gridley, CA 888-258-1250
Nabisco
  Parsippany, NJ 973-682-5000

Product Categories / Baked Goods: Crunches

Nicole's Divine Crackers
   Chicago, IL 312-640-8883
Nonni's Foods LLC
   Tulsa, OK 877-295-9604
Oberweis Dairy Inc
   North Aurora, IL 866-623-7934
Panorama Foods Inc.
   Braintree, MA 781-592-1069
Partners: A Tasteful Choice
   Kent, WA. 800-632-7477
Pepperidge Farm Inc.
   Norwalk, CT .888-737-7374
Richmond Baking Co
   Richmond, IN 765-962-8535
Rovira Biscuit Corporation
   Ponce, PR 787-844-8585
San-J International Inc
   Henrico, VA .800-446-5500
Schulze & Burch Biscuit Co
   Chicago, IL 773-927-6622
Simple Mills
   Chicago, IL 312-600-6196
Small Planet Foods
   Minneapolis, MN 800-624-4123
Snyder's-Lance Inc.
   Charlotte, NC 800-438-1880
Stauffer Biscuit Co
   York, PA 888-480-1988
TH Foods, Inc.
   Loves Park, IL. 815-636-9500
That's How We Roll, LLC
   Fairfield, NJ .973-602-3011
Urban Accents
   Chicago, IL 877-872-7742
Urban Oven
   Chandler, AZ. 866-770-6836
Venus Wafers Inc
   Hingham, MA. 800-545-4538
Vision Pack Brands
   El Segundo, CA 877-477-8500
Way Better Snacks
   Minneapolis, MN 612-314-2060
Willmar Cookie & Nut Company
   Willmar, MN. 800-426-7845

Meal

Newly Weds Foods Inc
   Chicago, IL 800-621-7521
Richmond Baking Co
   Richmond, IN 765-962-8535
Sugar Foods Corp
   New York, NY

Oyster Crackers

Panorama Foods Inc.
   Braintree, MA 781-592-1069

Poppy & Sesame Crackers

Ella's Flats
   Naples, FL

Saltines

Abimar Foods Inc
   Abilene, TX. .325-691-5425

Crunches

Rustic Bakery Inc.
   San Rafael, CA 415-479-5600
Sweet Street Desserts
   Reading, PA .800-793-3897

Desserts

Adams Foods & Milling
   Dothan, AL. .334-983-4233
Aglamesis Bros Ice Cream
   Cincinnati, OH 513-531-5196
Agropur
   Granby, QC .800-363-5686
Al Gelato Bornay
   Franklin Park, IL. 847-455-5355
Alati-Caserta Desserts
   Montr,al, QC 877-377-5680
Alexian Pâtés
   Neptune, NJ .800-927-9473
Alpenrose Dairy
   Portland, OR 503-244-1133
American Classic Ice Cream Company
   Bay Shore, NY 800-736-4100

Andre-Boudin Bakeries
   San Francisco, CA 415-882-1849
Aryzta
   Los Angeles, CA. 855-427-9982
ASK Foods Inc
   Palmyra, PA. 800-879-4275
Athens Foods Inc
   Brookpark, OH 843-916-2000
Awrey Bakeries
   Livonia, MI .800-950-2253
BakeryCorp
   Miami, FL. 305-623-3838
Balboa Dessert Co Inc
   Santa Ana, CA 800-974-9699
Bama Foods LTD
   Tulsa, OK 800-756-2262
Banquet Schusters Bakery
   Pueblo, CO .719-544-1062
Barnes Ice Cream Company
   Manchester, ME 207-622-0827
Baskin-Robbins LLC
   Canton, MA .800-859-5339
BBU Bakeries
   Horsham, PA 800-984-0989
Beatrice Bakery Co
   Beatrice, NE .800-228-4030
Best Maid Cookie Co
   River Falls, WI 888-444-0322
Beth's Fine Desserts
   Mill Valley, CA 415-383-3991
Birdsall Ice Cream Company
   Mason City, IA 641-423-5365
Birkholm's Solvang Bakery
   Solvang, CA .800-377-4253
Bittersweet Pastries
   Norwood, NJ 800-217-2938
Black's Barbecue
   Lockhart, TX 888-632-8225
Blue Bell Creameries LP
   Brenham, TX. 800-327-8135
Bluepoint Bakery
   Denver, CO .303-298-1100
Boboli Intl. Inc.
   Stockton, CA. 209-473-3507
Bonnie Doon LLC
   Elkhart, IN. 574-264-3390
Brighams
   Arlington, MA 800-242-2423
Brown's Ice Cream Co
   Minneapolis, MN 612-378-1075
Brownie Brittle, LLC
   West Palm Beach, FL 561-688-1890
Browns' Ice Cream Company
   Minneapolis, MN 612-378-1075
Bubbies Homemade Ice Cream
   Aiea, HI. 808-487-7218
Buck's Spumoni Company
   Milford, CT .888-222-8257
Busken Bakery
   Cincinnati, OH 513-871-2114
Calmar Bakery
   Calmar, AB. .780-985-3583
Cannoli Factory
   Wyandanch, NY 631-643-2700
Caprine Estates
   Bellbrook, OH. 937-848-7406
Caribbean Food Delights Inc
   Tappan, NY .845-398-3000
Carole's Cheesecake Company
   Toronto, ON 416-256-0000
Carolina Foods Inc
   Charlotte, NC 800-234-0441
Carousel Cakes
   Nanuet, NY .800-659-2253
Cascadian Farm Inc
   Sedro Woolley, WA. 360-855-0542
Case Side Holdings Company
   Kensington, PE 902-836-4214
Cateraid Inc
   Howell, MI .800-508-8217
CBC Foods
   Little River, KS 800-276-4770
Cedar Crest Specialties
   Cedarburg, WI. 800-877-8341
Celebrity Cheesecake
   Davie, FL 877-986-2253
Centreside Dairy
   Renfrew, ON 800-889-9974
Chattanooga Bakery Inc
   Chattanooga, TN 800-251-3404
Cheesecake Etc Desserts
   Miami Springs, FL 305-887-0258

Cheesecake Factory Inc.
   Calabasas Hills, CA 818-871-3000
Chef Hans' Gourmet Foods
   Monroe, LA. 800-890-4267
Chef's Pride Gifts LLC
   Taylor, MI 800-878-1800
Chella's Dutch Delicacies
   Lake Oswego, OR. 800-458-3331
Chelsea Milling Co.
   Chelsea, MI. .800-727-2460
Chewys Rugulach
   San Diego, CA 800-241-3456
Chicago Pastry
   Bloomingdale, IL 630-529-6391
Chocolaterie Bernard Callebaut
   Calgary, AB. .800-661-8367
Chudleigh's
   Milton, ON .800-387-4028
Ciao Bella Gelato Company
   Irvington, NJ 800-435-2863
Clarkson Scottish Bakery
   Mississauga, ON 905-823-1500
Claxton Bakery Inc
   Claxton, GA .800-841-4211
Clement's Pastry Shops Inc
   Hyattsville, MD 301-277-6300
Cloverhill Bakery-Vend Corporation
   Chicago, IL 773-745-9800
Clyde's Delicious Donuts
   Addison, IL. .630-628-6555
Coby's Cookies
   Toronto, ON 416-633-1567
Cold Fusion Foods
   West Hollywood, CA 310-287-3244
Collin Street Bakery
   Corsicana, TX 800-267-4657
Community Orchards
   Fort Dodge, IA 888-573-8212
Conifer Specialties Inc
   Woodinville, WA. 800-588-9160
Cookie Factory
   Bronx, NY. 718-379-6223
Country Choice Organic
   Eden Prairie, MN 952-829-8824
Creme Curls
   Hudsonville, MI 800-466-1219
Crystal Creamery
   Modesto, CA. 866-225-4821
Culinar Canada
   Baie-Comeau, QC 418-296-4395
Cummings Studio Chocolates
   Salt Lake City, UT 800-537-3957
Dancing Deer Baking Company
   Boston, MA. .888-699-3337
Dannon Yo Cream
   Portland, OR 800-962-7326
David's Cookies
   Cedar Grove, NJ 800-500-2800
Davis Bakery & Delicatessen
   Cleveland, OH 216-292-3060
Davis Bread & Desserts
   Davis, CA 530-220-4375
Deep Foods Inc
   Union, NJ 908-810-7500
Deerfield Bakery
   Buffalo Grove, IL 847-520-0068
Del's Pastry
   Toronto, ON 800-461-0663
Delicious Desserts
   Brooklyn, NY 718-680-1156
Desserts by David Glass
   South Windsor, CT 860-462-7520
Desserts Of Distinction
   Tigard, OR 503-654-8370
Di Camillo Baking Co
   Niagara Falls, NY 800-634-4363
Dimitria Delights Baking Co
   North Grafton, MA 800-763-1113
Dinkel's Bakery Inc
   Chicago, IL 800-822-8817
Dipaolo Baking Co Inc
   Rochester, NY 585-232-3510
Divine Delights
   Petaluma, CA 800-443-2836
Don's Food Products
   Schwenksville, PA 888-321-3667
Dufflet Pastries
   Toronto, ON 866-238-0899
DWC Specialities
   Horicon, WI .800-383-8808
Dynamic Foods
   Lubbock, TX. 806-723-5600

Product Categories / Baked Goods: Desserts

Eddy's Bakery
 Boise, ID 208-377-8100
Edelweiss Patisserie
 Medford, MA 781-628-0225
Edwards Baking Company
 Marshall, MN 866-739-2328
Elegant Desserts
 Lyndhurst, NJ 201-933-0770
Eli's Cheesecake
 Chicago, IL 800-354-2253
Elmwood Pastry Shop
 West Hartford, CT 860-233-2029
European Style Bakery
 Beverly Hills, CA 818-368-6876
Fairview Dairy Inc
 Latrobe, PA 724-537-7111
Fantasia
 Sedalia, MO 660-827-1172
Farr Candy Company
 Idaho Falls, ID 208-522-8215
Fendall Ice Cream Company
 Salt Lake City, UT 801-355-3583
Field's Pies
 Pauls Valley, OK 800-286-7501
Fieldbrook Foods Corp.
 Dunkirk, NY 800-333-0805
Fiera Foods
 Toronto, ON 800-675-6356
Fillo Factory, The
 Northvale, NJ 800-653-4556
Fireside Kitchen
 Halifax, NS 902-454-7387
Flavor Right Foods Group
 St Phoenix, AZ 888-464-3734
Flavors from Florida
 Bartow, FL 800-888-0409
Flowers Baking Co
 El Paso, TX 800-328-6111
FNI Group LLC
 Sherborn, MA 508-655-4175
Food of Our Own Design
 Maplewood, NJ 973-762-0985
Foxtail Foods
 Fairfield, OH 800-487-2253
France Delices
 Montreal, QC 800-663-1365
Frankly Natural Bakers
 San Diego, CA 800-727-7229
French Patisserie
 Pacifica, CA 800-300-2253
Frozfruit Corporation
 Gardena, CA 310-217-1034
FrutStix
 Santa Barbara, CA 805-965-1656
Future Bakery & Cafe
 Toronto, ON 416-231-1491
Galliker Dairy Co
 Johnstown, PA 800-477-6455
Garber Ice Cream Co Inc
 Winchester, VA 800-662-5422
Gardner Pie Co
 Akron, OH 330-245-2030
Gelato Fresco
 Toronto, ON 416-785-5415
Georgia Fruitcake Co
 Claxton, GA 912-739-2683
GH Bent Company
 Milton, MA 617-322-9287
Giant Food
 Landover, MD 888-469-4426
Gifford's Ice Cream
 Skowhegan, ME 800-950-2604
Gimbals Fine Candies
 S San Francisco, CA 800-344-6225
Glover's Ice Cream Inc
 Frankfort, IN 800-686-5163
GoBio!
 Action, ON 519-853-2958
Golden Brown Bakery Inc
 South Haven, MI 269-637-3418
Good Old Days Foods
 Little Rock, AR 501-565-1257
Gourmet Croissant
 Brooklyn, NY 718-499-4911
Govatos Chocolates
 Wilmington, DE 888-799-5252
Grace Baking Company
 Richmond, CA 510-231-7200
Grainaissance
 Emeryville, CA 800-472-4697
Granowska's
 Toronto, ON 416-533-7755

Great American Dessert Co
 Flushing, NY 800-458-6467
Great Northern Maple Products
 Saint Honor, De Shenley, QC ... 418-485-7777
Grebe's Bakery
 Milwaukee, WI 800-833-3158
Grecian Delight Foods Inc
 Elk Grove Village, IL 800-621-4387
Greyston Bakery Inc
 Yonkers, NY 800-289-2253
Grossingers Home Bakery
 New York, NY 800-479-6996
Gumpert's Canada
 Mississauga, ON 800-387-9324
H-E-B Grocery Co. LP
 San Antonio, TX 800-432-3113
Haby's Alsatian Bakery
 Castroville, TX 830-538-2118
Hafner USA
 Stone Mountain, GA 888-725-4605
Hahn's Old Fashioned Cake Co
 Farmingdale, NY 631-249-3456
Handy Pax
 Randolph, MA 781-963-8300
Hanover Foods Corp
 Hanover, PA 717-632-6000
Happy & Healthy Products Inc
 Boca Raton, FL 561-367-0739
Harold Food Company
 Charlotte, NC 704-588-8061
Harry & David
 Medford, OR 877-322-1200
Harvest Foods
 Central Islip, NY 631-232-1709
Harvest Valley Bakery Inc
 La Salle, IL 815-224-9030
Health Valley Company
 Irwindale, CA 800-334-3204
Hearthy Foods
 Los Angeles, CA 213-372-5093
Heidi's Gourmet Desserts
 Tucker, GA 800-241-4166
Heltzman Bakery
 Louisville, KY 502-447-3515
HFI Foods
 Redmond, WA 425-883-1320
Holt's Bakery Inc
 Douglas, GA 912-384-2202
Holton Food Products
 La Grange, IL 708-352-5599
Homer's Ice Cream
 Wilmette, IL 847-251-0477
Hormel Foods Corp.
 Austin, MN 507-437-5611
Hostess Brands
 Kansas City, MO 816-701-4600
Hunt Country Foods Inc
 Marshall, VA 540-364-2622
Hunter Farms - High Point Division
 High Point, NC 800-446-8035
Ice Cream Bowl
 Zanesville, OH 740-452-5267
Ice Cream Club Inc
 Boynton Beach, FL 800-535-7711
Ice Cream Specialties Inc
 St Louis, MO 800-662-7550
Il Gelato
 Astoria, NY 800-899-9299
Incredible Cheesecake
 San Diego, CA 619-563-9722
It's It Ice Cream Co
 Burlingame, CA 800-345-1928
Italian Bakery of Virginia
 Virginia, MN 218-741-3464
J.A.M.B. Low Carb Distributor
 Pompano Beach, FL 800-708-6738
J.P. Sunrise Bakery
 Edmonton, AB 780-454-5797
J.W. Haywood & Sons Dairy
 Louisville, KY 502-774-2311
Jack & Jill Ice Cream
 Moorestown, NJ 856-813-2300
James Skinner Company
 Omaha, NE 800-358-7428
Jaxon's Ice Cream Parlor
 Dania Beach, FL 954-923-4445
Joey's Fine Foods
 Newark, NJ 973-482-1400
John J. Nissen Baking Company
 Brewer, ME 207-989-7654
Johnson's Real Ice Cream
 Columbus, OH 614-231-0014

Jon Donaire Desserts
 Santa Fe Springs, CA 877-366-2473
Josh & John's Ice Cream
 Colorado Springs, CO 800-530-2855
Joyva Corp
 Brooklyn, NY 718-497-0170
Jubelt Variety Bakeries
 Litchfield, IL 217-324-5314
Just Desserts
 Fairfield, CA 415-780-6860
Kan-Pak
 Arkansas City, KS 800-378-1265
Kapaa Poi Factory
 Kapaa, HI 808-822-5426
Katrina's Tartufo
 Port Jeffrsn Sta, NY 800-480-8836
Klinke Brothers Ice Cream Co
 Memphis, TN 901-322-6640
KOZY Shack Enterprises Inc
 St Paul, MN 855-716-1555
Kyger Bakery Products
 Lafayette, IN 765-447-1252
L & M Bakery
 Riverside, NJ 888-887-1335
Larosa Bakery Inc
 Shrewsbury, NJ 800-527-6722
Lax & Mandel Bakery
 South Euclid, OH 216-382-8877
Leader Candies
 Brooklyn, NY 718-366-6900
Lenchner Bakery
 Concord, ON 905-738-8811
Lone Star Bakery
 Round Rock, TX 512-255-7268
Love Quiches Desserts
 Freeport, NY 516-623-8800
Lucy's Sweet Surrender
 Beachwood, OH 216-752-0828
M&L Gourmet Ice Cream
 Baltimore, MD 410-276-4880
Mac's Donut Shop
 Aliquippa, PA 724-375-6776
Mack's Bill Ice Cream
 Dover, PA 717-292-1931
Mackie International, Inc.
 Riverside, CA 800-733-9762
Maple Island
 Saint Paul, MN 800-369-1022
Mar-Key Foods
 Vidalia, GA 912-537-4204
Marie Callender's
 Mission Viejo, CA 800-776-7437
Mario's Gelati
 Vancouver, BC 604-879-9411
Martino's Bakery
 Burbank, CA 818-842-0715
Mary Ann's Baking Co Inc
 Sacramento, CA 916-681-7444
Matador Processors
 Blanchard, OK 800-847-0797
Mayer's Cider Mill
 Webster, NY 800-543-0043
Mazelle's Cheesecakes Concoctions Creations
 Dallas, TX 214-328-9102
McCain Foods Ltd.
 Toronto, ON 416-955-1700
McConnell's Fine Ice Cream
 Santa Barbara, CA 805-963-8813
Meadows Country Products
 Hollidaysburg, PA 888-499-1001
Mehaffies Pies
 Dayton, OH 800-289-7437
Mia Products
 Scranton, PA 570-207-5328
Michel's Bakery
 Philadelphia, PA 267-345-7914
Michele's Family Bakery
 York, PA 717-741-2027
Michelle Chocolatiers
 Colorado Springs, CO 888-447-3654
Michigan Dairy LLC
 Livonia, MI 734-367-5390
Mikawaya LLC
 Vernon, CA 323-587-5504
Miles of Chocolate
 Austin, TX
Millie's Pierogi
 Chicopee Falls, MA 800-743-7641
Mississippi Cheese Straw
 Yazoo City, MS 800-530-7496
Mister Cookie Face
 Dunkirk, NY 800-333-0305

Product Categories / Baked Goods: Desserts

Model Dairy LLC
  Reno, NV 800-433-2030
Monaco Baking Company
  Santa Fe Springs, CA 800-569-4640
Moonlight Gourmet
  Tyler, TX 903-581-1228
Mozzicato De Pasquale Bakery
  Hartford, CT 860-296-0426
Mrs Baird's
  Horsham, PA 800-984-0989
Mrs Sullivan's Pies
  Jackson, TN 731-427-2101
Mt. View Bakery
  Mountain View, HI 808-968-6353
Multi Marques
  Montreal, QC 514-934-1866
Multiflex Company
  Hawthorne, NJ 973-636-9700
My Daddy's Cheesecake
  Cape Girardeau, MO 800-735-6765
My Grandma's Coffee Cake
  Hyde Park, MA 800-847-2636
Najila's
  Binghamton, NY 607-722-4287
Natural Fruit Corp
  Hialeah, FL 305-887-7525
Naturally Delicious Inc
  Oakland Park, FL 888-221-7352
Nature's Hilights
  Chico, CA 800-313-6454
New York Bakeries Inc
  Hialeah, FL 305-883-0790
Nikki's Cookies
  Milwaukee, WI 800-776-7107
Northside Bakery
  Brooklyn, NY 718-782-2700
Notre Dame Bakery
  Conception Harbour, NL 709-535-2738
O'Boyle's Ice Cream Company
  Bristol, PA 215-788-3882
Oak Leaf Confections
  877-261-7887
OH Chocolate
  Seattle, WA 206-329-8777
Old Country Bakery
  North Hollywood, CA 818-838-2302
Old Fashioned Kitchen Inc
  Lakewood, NJ 732-364-4100
Omaha Steaks Inc
  800-960-8400
Out of a Flower
  Lancaster, TX 800-743-4696
Pacific Ocean Produce
  Santa Cruz, CA 831-423-2654
Parker Products
  Fort Worth, TX 817-336-7441
Pasta Factory
  Melrose Park, IL 800-615-6951
Pastry Chef
  Pawtucket, RI 800-639-8606
Patisserie Wawel
  Montreal, QC 614-524-3348
Pearl River Pastry & Chocolate
  Pearl River, NY 800-632-2639
Peggy Lawton Kitchens
  East Walpole, MA 800-843-7325
Pellman Foods Inc
  New Holland, PA 717-354-8070
Perry's Ice Cream Co Inc
  Akron, NY 800-873-7797
Petersen Ice Cream Company
  Oak Park, IL 708-386-6130
Phipps Desserts
  North York, ON 416-391-5800
Pie Piper Products
  Wheeling, IL 800-621-8183
Piedmont Candy Co
  Lexington, NC 336-248-2477
Pinocchio Italian Ice Cream Company
  Edmonton, AB 780-455-1905
Platte Valley Creamery
  Scottsbluff, NE 308-632-4225
Plehn's Bakery Inc
  Louisville, KY 502-896-4438
Pocono Cheesecake Factory
  Swiftwater, PA 570-839-6844
Poppies International
  Battleboro, NC 252-442-4309
Price Co
  Yakima, WA 509-966-4110
Pride Dairies
  Bottineau, ND 701-228-2216

Priester's Pecans
  Fort Deposit, AL. 866-477-4736
Puritan/ATZ Ice Cream
  Kendallville, IN 260-347-2700
Purity Dairies LLC
  Nashville, TN 615-244-1900
Purity Ice Cream Co
  Ithaca, NY 607-272-1545
Quality Naturally Foods
  City Of Industry, CA 888-498-6986
Real Food Marketing
  Kansas City, MO 816-221-4100
Reinhold Ice Cream Company
  Pittsburgh, PA 412-321-7600
Reiter Dairy
  Newport, KY 800-544-6455
Reiter Dairy LLC
  Springfield, OH 937-323-5777
Rhino Foods Inc
  Burlington, VT 802-862-0252
Rich's Ice Cream Co Inc
  West Palm Beach, FL 561-833-7585
Rising Dough Bakery
  Sacramento, CA 916-387-9700
Rolling Pin Bakery
  Bow Island, AB 403-545-2434
Roma Bakeries
  Rockford, IL 815-964-6737
Rosati Italian Water Ice
  Clifton Heights, PA 855-476-7284
Roselani Tropics Ice Cream
  Wailuku, HI 808-244-7951
Rowena
  Norfolk, VA 800-627-8699
Royal Home Bakery
  Newmarket, ON 905-715-7044
RW Delights
  Millington, NJ 866-892-1096
Ryals Bakery
  Milledgeville, GA 478-452-0321
Ryke's Bakery
  Muskegon, MI 231-726-2253
Sacramento Baking Co
  Sacramento, CA 916-361-2000
Sara Lee Frozen Bakery
  Kings Mountain, NC 800-323-7117
Sarabeth's Office
  Bronx, NY 800-773-7378
Savino's Italian Ices
  Deerfield Beach, FL 954-426-4119
Saxby Bakery
  Edmonton, AB 780-440-4179
Schneider's Dairy Inc
  Pittsburgh, PA 412-881-3525
Schneider-Valley Farms Inc
  Williamsport, PA 570-326-2021
Schwan's Food Service Inc.
  Marshall, MN 877-302-7426
Scialo Brothers Bakery
  Providence, RI 877-421-0986
Scotty Wotty's Creamy Cheesecake
  Hillsborough, NJ 908-281-9720
Seaver's Bakery
  Kingsport, TN 423-245-2441
Serv-Agen Corporation
  Cherry Hill, NJ 856-663-6966
Shaw Baking Company
  Thunder Bay, ON 807-345-7327
Silver Tray Cookies
  Fort Lauderdale, FL 305-883-0800
Sinbad Sweets
  Madera, CA 866-746-2232
Sisler's Ice & Ice Cream
  Ohio, IL 888-891-3856
Smoak's Bakery & Catering Service
  Augusta, GA 706-738-1792
Snelgrove Ice Cream Company
  Salt Lake City, UT 800-569-0005
So Delicious Dairy Free
  Springfield, OR 866-388-7853
Solana Beach Baking Company
  Carlsbad, CA 760-444-9800
Southern Ice Cream Specialties
  Marietta, GA 770-428-0452
Specialty Bakers
  Marysville, PA 800-233-0778
Spilke's Baking Company
  Moosic, PA 570-457-2400
Spohrers Bakeries
  Collingdale, PA 610-532-9959
Spring Glen Fresh Foods
  Ephrata, PA 800-641-2853

Standard Bakery Inc
  Kealakekua, HI 808-322-3688
Stewart's Shops Corp
  Ballston Spa, NY 518-581-1200
Stone's Home Made Candy Shop
  Oswego, NY 888-223-3928
Strossner's Bakery & Cafe
  Greenville, SC 864-233-2990
SugarCreek
  Cincinnati, OH 800-445-2715
Super Stores Industries
  Turlock, CA 209-668-2100
Superior Cake Products
  Southbridge, MA 508-764-3276
Svenhard's Swedish Bakery Inc
  Oakland, CA 800-705-3379
Sweenors Chocolates
  Wakefield, RI 800-834-3123
Sweet Endings Inc
  West Palm Beach, FL 888-635-1177
Sweet Gallery Exclusive Pastry
  Toronto, ON 416-766-0289
Sweet Lady Jane
  Los Angeles, CA 323-653-7145
Sweet Street Desserts
  Reading, PA 800-793-3897
Sweetaly
  Oceanside, CA 760-539-2196
Sweety Novelty
  Monterey Park, CA 626-282-4482
Table De France
  Ontario, CA 909-923-5205
Taste It Presents Inc
  Kenilworth, NJ 908-241-0672
Tasty Baking Company
  Philadelphia, PA 800-248-2789
Tebay Dairy Company
  Parkersburg, WV 304-863-3705
Terrapin Ridge
  Clearwater, FL 800-999-4052
The Great San Saba River Pecan Company
  San Saba, TX 800-621-8121
The Piping Gourmets
  786-233-8660
The Valpo Velvet Shoppe
  Valparaiso, IN 219-464-4141
Tillamook County Creamery Association
  Tillamook, OR 503-842-4481
Tipiak Inc
  Stamford, CT 203-961-9117
Tirawisu
  Sherman Oaks, CA 818-906-2640
Toft Dairy Inc
  Sandusky, OH 800-521-4606
Tofutti Brands Inc
  Cranford, NJ 908-272-2400
Tony's Ice Cream Co
  Gastonia, NC 704-867-7085
Top Hat Co Inc
  Wilmette, IL 847-256-6565
Treat Ice Cream Co
  San Jose, CA 408-292-9321
Tropical Treets
  North York, ON 888-424-8229
Turkey Hill Dairy Inc
  Conestoga, PA 800-693-2479
Two Chefs on a Roll
  Carson, CA 800-842-3025
Two Chicks and a Ladle
  New York, NY 212-251-0025
TyRy Inc
  Rocklin, CA 800-322-6325
Umpqua Dairy
  Roseburg, OR 888-672-6455
Uncle Ralph's Cookies
  Frederick, MD 800-422-0626
United Pies of Elkhart Inc
  Elkhart, IN 574-294-3419
Uptown Bakers
  Hyattsville, MD 301-864-1500
Van de Kamps
  Peoria, IL 800-798-3318
Varda Chocolatier
  Elizabeth, NJ 800-448-2732
Vickey's Vittles
  North Hills, CA 818-841-1944
Vie De France Yamazaki Inc
  Vienna, VA 800-446-4404
Vigneri Chocolate Inc.
  Rochester, NY 877-844-6374
VIP Foods
  Flushing, NY 718-821-5330

Vitamilk Dairy
Bellingham, WA 206-529-4128
Warwick Ice Cream
Warwick, RI 401-821-8403
Wedding Cake Studio
Williamsfield, OH................. 440-667-1765
Welch Foods Inc.
Concord, MA 800-340-6870
Weldon Ice Cream Co
Millersport, OH................... 740-467-2400
Welsh Farms
Clifton, NJ....................... 973-772-2388
Wenger's Bakery
Reading, PA 610-372-6545
White Coffee Corporation
Long Island City, NY 800-221-0140
Whitey's Ice Cream Inc
Moline, IL....................... 888-594-4839
Wick's Pies Inc
Winchester, IN 800-642-5880
Williamsburg Chocolatier
Williamsburg, VA 757-253-1474
Winmix/Natural Care Products
Englewood, FL 941-475-7432
Woodie Pie Company
Artesia, NM...................... 575-746-2132
Wright's Ice Cream Co
Cayuga, IN 800-686-9561
Wuollet Bakery
Minneapolis, MN 612-922-4341
Ya-Hoo Baking Co
Sherman, TX..................... 888-869-2466
Young's Bakery
Uniontown, PA 724-437-6361
Zoelsmann's Bakery & Deli
Pueblo, CO 719-543-0407

Low Carb

Real Food Marketing
Kansas City, MO.................. 816-221-4100

Low-Calorie

Cedar Crest Specialties
Cedarburg, WI.................... 800-877-8341
Fendall Ice Cream Company
Salt Lake City, UT 801-355-3583
Health Valley Company
Irwindale, CA 800-334-3204
Jaxon's Ice Cream Parlor
Dania Beach, FL.................. 954-923-4445
Master Mix
Placentia, CA 714-524-1698
O'Boyle's Ice Cream Company
Bristol, PA....................... 215-788-3882
Price Co
Yakima, WA 509-966-4110
Real Food Marketing
Kansas City, MO.................. 816-221-4100
Tova Industries LLC
Louisville, KY 888-532-8682

Fresh

Botanical Bakery, LLC
Napa, CA........................ 707-344-8103
Fresh Start Bakeries
Brea, CA 714-256-8900
Super Mom's LLC
St Paul Park, MN 800-944-7276

Frozen

Aladdin Bakers
Brooklyn, NY 718-499-1818
Alati-Caserta Desserts
Montr,al, QC..................... 877-377-5680
All Round Foods Bakery Prod
Westbury, NY 800-428-8802
Andre-Boudin Bakeries
San Francisco, CA 415-882-1849
Aphrodite Divine Confections
Garland, TX 972-485-1005
Athens Foods Inc
Brookpark, OH 843-916-2000
Atkins Elegant Desserts
Fishers, IN....................... 800-887-8808
Awrey Bakeries
Livonia, MI...................... 800-950-2253
Bake Crafters Food Company
McDonald, TN 423-396-3392
Baker Boy Bake Shop Inc
Dickinson, ND 800-437-2008
Bama Foods LTD
Tulsa, OK 800-756-2262
Beck's Waffles of Oklahoma
Shawnee, OK 800-646-6254
Best Maid Cookie Co
River Falls, WI 888-444-0322
Boboli Intl. Inc.
Stockton, CA..................... 209-473-3507
Bodega Chocolates
Fountain Valley, CA 888-326-3342
Brooklyn Bagel Company
Staten Island, NY 800-349-3055
Caribbean Food Delights Inc
Tappan, NY...................... 845-398-3000
Carolina Foods Inc
Charlotte, NC 800-234-0441
CBC Foods
Little River, KS................... 800-276-4770
Cedarlane Foods
Carson, CA 800-826-3322
Chewys Rugulach
San Diego, CA 800-241-3456
Cinderella Cheese Cake Co
Riverside, NJ..................... 800-521-1171
Cole's Quality Foods
Grand Rapids, MI 616-975-0081
Cookie Tree Bakeries
Salt Lake City, UT 801-268-2253
Culinary Institute Lenotre
Houston, TX 888-536-6873
Desserts Of Distinction
Tigard, OR 503-654-8370
Dimitria Delights Baking Co
North Grafton, MA 800-763-1113
Dutch Ann Foods Company
Natchez, MS 601-445-5566
Dynamic Foods
Lubbock, TX..................... 806-723-5600
Edner Corporation
Hayward, CA 510-441-8504
Edwards Baking Company
Marshall, MN 866-739-2328
Eli's Cheesecake
Chicago, IL...................... 800-354-2253
Engel's Bakeries
Calgary, AB...................... 403-250-9560
English Bay Batter Us Inc
Columbus, OH 800-253-6844
Fantasia
Sedalia, MO 660-827-1172
Fantis Foods Inc
Carlstadt, NJ 201-933-6200
Field's Pies
Pauls Valley, OK.................. 800-286-7501
Fiera Foods
Toronto, ON 800-675-6356
Fleischer's Bagels
Macedon, NY 315-986-9999
France Delices
Montreal, QC 800-663-1365
Fresh Start Bakeries
Brea, CA 714-256-8900
Gabila's Knishes
Copiague, NY 631-789-2220
Gardner Pie Co
Akron, OH....................... 330-245-2030
Good Old Days Foods
Little Rock, AR................... 501-565-1257
Gourmet Croissant
Brooklyn, NY 718-499-4911
Grecian Delight Foods Inc
Elk Grove Village, IL 800-621-4387
Gregory's Foods, Inc.
St Paul, MN...................... 800-231-4734
Grossingers Home Bakery
New York, NY 800-479-6996
Guttenplan's Frozen Dough
Middletown, NJ 888-422-4357
GWB Foods Corporation
Brooklyn, NY 877-977-7610
Harlan Bakeries
Avon, IN 800-435-2738
Harold Food Company
Charlotte, NC 704-588-8061
J & J Wall Bakery Co
Sacramento, CA 916-381-1410
James Skinner Company
Omaha, NE 800-358-7428
Kyger Bakery Products
Lafayette, IN..................... 765-447-1252
Leidenheimer Baking Co
New Orleans, LA 800-259-9099
Lenchner Bakery
Concord, ON..................... 905-738-8811
Lone Star Bakery
Round Rock, TX.................. 512-255-7268
Love Quiches Desserts
Freeport, NY..................... 516-623-8800
Ludwick's Frozen Donuts
Grand Rapids, MI 800-366-8816
Main Street Gourmet
Cuyahoga Falls, OH 800-678-6246
Mehaffies Pies
Dayton, OH...................... 800-289-7437
Mother Nature's Goodies
Yucaipa, CA 909-795-6018
Mrs Sullivan's Pies
Jackson, TN 731-427-2101
Mrs. Kavanagh's English Muffins
Rumford, RI 800-556-7216
My Grandma's Coffee Cake
Hyde Park, MA................... 800-847-2636
Naleway Foods
Winnipeg, MB.................... 800-665-7448
Nancy's Specialty Foods
Newark, CA 510-494-1100
New England Muffin Co Inc
Fall River, MA 508-675-2833
Old Fashioned Kitchen Inc
Lakewood, NJ 732-364-4100
Orange Bakery
Irvine, CA 949-863-1377
PDEQ
Fresno, CA 559-490-4412
Pacific Ocean Produce
Santa Cruz, CA 831-423-2654
Pastry Chef
Pawtucket, RI 800-639-8606
Pellman Foods Inc
New Holland, PA 717-354-8070
Petrofsky's Bakery Products
Chesterfield, MO 636-519-1613
Poppies International
Battleboro, NC 252-442-4309
Positively 3rd St Bakery
Duluth, MN...................... 218-724-8619
Prairie City Bakery
Vernon Hills, IL 800-338-5122
Ramona's Mexican Foods
Gardena, CA..................... 310-323-1950
Ranaldi Bros. Frozen Food Products
Warwick, RI 401-737-5130
Real Food Marketing
Kansas City, MO.................. 816-221-4100
Rhodes International Inc
Salt Lake City, UT 800-876-7333
Rich Products Corp
Buffalo, NY...................... 800-828-2021
RoRo's Baking Company
Dallas, TX....................... 972-897-2315
Rowena
Norfolk, VA...................... 800-627-8699
Sara Lee Frozen Bakery
Kings Mountain, NC............... 800-323-7117
Saxby Foods
Edmonton, AB 780-440-4179
Spelt Right Foods, LLC
Brooklyn, NY 877-773-5801
Sunset Specialty Foods
Lake Arrowhead, CA 909-337-7643
Super Mom's LLC
St Paul Park, MN 800-944-7276
Table De France
Ontario, CA...................... 909-923-5205
Tasty Mix Quality Foods
Brooklyn, NY 718-855-7680
The Pillsbury Company
Chelsea, MA 800-370-7834
Two Chefs on a Roll
Carson, CA 800-842-3025
Uncle Ralph's Cookies
Frederick, MD.................... 800-422-0626
Wenner Bakery
Bayport, NY 800-869-6262
Wick's Pies Inc
Winchester, IN 800-642-5880
Wolferman's
Medford, OR..................... 800-798-6241

Ingredients

1-2-3 Gluten Free
Chagrin Falls, OH................. 216-378-9233
Al-Rite Fruits & Syrups Co
Miami, FL....................... 305-652-2540

Product Categories / Baked Goods: Pies

AnaCon Foods Company
  Atchison, KS................800-328-0291
BakeMark USA
  Pico Rivera, CA.............866-232-8575
Brolite Products Inc
  Streamwood, IL..............888-276-5483
California Blending Co
  El Monte, CA................626-448-1918
Castella Imports Inc
  Brentwood, NY...............631-231-5500
Caulipower
  Encino, CA..................844-422-8544
Cherrybrook Kitchen
  Burlington, MA..............866-458-8225
Clara Foods
  San Francisco, CA
Clofine Dairy Products Inc
  Linwood, NJ.................609-653-1000
Creme Curls
  Hudsonville, MI.............800-466-1219
Deer Creek Honey Farms LTD
  London, OH..................740-852-0899
Dorothy Dawson Food Products
  Jackson, MI.................517-788-9830
Dufour Pastry Kitchens Inc
  Bronx, NY...................800-439-1282
Eden Processing
  Poplar Grove, IL............815-765-2000
Flavorchem Corp
  Downers Grove, IL...........800-435-2867
Fleischmann's Yeast
  Chesterfield, MO............800-777-4959
GAF Seelig Inc
  Flushing, NY................718-899-5000
Holton Food Products
  La Grange, IL...............708-352-5599
Hulman & Co
  Terre Haute, IN.............812-232-9446
Indiana Sugars
  Lemont, IL..................630-986-9150
Lake States Yeast
  Rhinelander, WI.............715-369-4949
Lucas Meyer
  Decatur, IL.................800-769-3660
Lyoferm & Vivolac Cultures
  Indianapolis, IN............317-356-8460
Main Street Ingredients
  La Crosse, WI...............800-359-2345
Meli's Monster Cookies
  Austin, TX
Pacific Westcoast Foods
  Beaverton, OR...............800-874-9333
Roland Machinery
  Springfield, IL.............800-325-1183
Watson Inc
  West Haven, CT..............800-388-3481

Pies

American Quality Foods
  Mills River, NC.............828-890-8344
Bake Crafters Food Company
  McDonald, TN................423-396-3392
Bear Creek Smokehouse Inc
  Marshall, TX................800-950-2327
Beckmann's Old World Bakery
  Santa Cruz, CA..............831-423-9242
Berke-Blake Fancy Foods, Inc.
  Longwood, FL................888-386-2253
Bluepoint Bakery
  Denver, CO..................303-298-1100
Bonert's Pies Inc
  Santa Ana, CA...............714-540-3535
Chatila's
  Salem, NH...................603-898-5459
Chattanooga Bakery Inc
  Chattanooga, TN.............800-251-3404
Cheryl's Cookies
  Westerville, OH.............800-443-8124
Clarmil Manufacturing Corp
  Hayward, CA.................888-252-7645
Collin Street Bakery
  Corsicana, TX...............800-267-4657
Davis Bread & Desserts
  Davis, CA...................530-220-4375
Entenmann's
  Totowa, NJ..................973-785-7601
Golden Kernel Pecan Co
  Cameron, SC.................803-823-2311
Goldilocks USA
  Hayward, CA.................510-476-0700
Granello Bakery
  Las Vegas, NV...............702-361-0311
JC's Pie Pops
  Chatsworth, CA..............818-349-1880
Keller's Bakery
  Lafayette, LA...............337-235-1568
Lowcountry Produce
  Raleigh, NC.................800-935-2792
Moon Rabbit Foods
  Savannah, NY................828-273-6649
Mrs Baird's
  Horsham, PA.................800-984-0989
Primos Northgate
  Flowood, MS.................601-936-3398
Rockland Bakery
  Nanuet, NY..................800-734-4376
Shawnee Canning Co
  Cross Junction, VA..........800-713-1414
Sweet Lady Jane
  Los Angeles, CA.............323-653-7145
Table Talk Pies Inc
  Worcester, MA...............508-798-8811
Tasty Baking Company
  Philadelphia, PA............800-248-2789
Willamette Valley Pie Co
  Salem, OR...................503-362-8857

Apple

Bama Foods LTD
  Tulsa, OK...................800-756-2262
Cheryl's Cookies
  Westerville, OH.............800-443-8124
Davis Bread & Desserts
  Davis, CA...................530-220-4375
Gould's Maple Sugarhouse
  Shelburne Falls, MA.........413-625-6170
Mayer's Cider Mill
  Webster, NY.................800-543-0043
Mehaffies Pies
  Dayton, OH..................800-289-7437

Baking Shells

American Quality Foods
  Mills River, NC.............828-890-8344
Bama Foods LTD
  Tulsa, OK...................800-756-2262
Calise & Sons Bakery Inc
  Lincoln, RI.................800-225-4737
Canada Bread Co, Ltd
  Etobicoke, ON...............800-465-5515
Dessert Innovations Inc
  Atlanta, GA.................800-359-7351
Dufour Pastry Kitchens Inc
  Bronx, NY...................800-439-1282
Dutch Ann Foods Company
  Natchez, MS.................601-445-5566
Father Sam's Bakery
  Buffalo, NY.................800-521-6719
Hafner USA
  Stone Mountain, GA..........888-725-4605
Hong Kong Noodle Company
  Chicago, IL.................312-842-0480
Lamonaca Bakery
  Windber, PA.................814-467-4909
Livermore Falls Baking Company
  Livermore Falls, ME.........207-897-3442
Lone Star Bakery
  Round Rock, TX..............512-255-7268
Maple Donuts
  York, PA....................800-627-5348
Molinaro's Fine Italian Foods Ltd.
  Mississauga, ON.............905-281-0352
Pacific Ocean Produce
  Santa Cruz, CA..............831-423-2654
Pasta Factory
  Melrose Park, IL............800-615-6951
Richmond Baking Co
  Richmond, IN................765-962-8535
Specialty Bakers
  Marysville, PA..............800-233-0778
Tomaro's Bakery
  Clarksburg, WV..............304-622-0691
Wick's Pies Inc
  Winchester, IN..............800-642-5880

Blueberry

Mehaffies Pies
  Dayton, OH..................800-289-7437

Brownie

Bama Foods LTD
  Tulsa, OK...................800-756-2262
Sweet Street Desserts
  Reading, PA.................800-793-3897

Cherry

Bama Foods LTD
  Tulsa, OK...................800-756-2262
Davis Bread & Desserts
  Davis, CA...................530-220-4375
Mehaffies Pies
  Dayton, OH..................800-289-7437

Fresh

Aryzta
  Los Angeles, CA.............855-427-9982
August Foods LTD
  Lubbock, TX.................806-744-1918
Banquet Schusters Bakery
  Pueblo, CO..................719-544-1062
BBU Bakeries
  Horsham, PA.................800-984-0989
Busken Bakery
  Cincinnati, OH..............513-871-2114
Carole's Cheesecake Company
  Toronto, ON.................416-256-0000
Case Side Holdings Company
  Kensington, PE..............902-836-4214
Celebrity Cheesecake
  Davie, FL...................877-986-2253
Clarkson Scottish Bakery
  Mississauga, ON.............905-823-1500
Del's Pastry
  Toronto, ON.................800-461-0663
Dufflet Pastries
  Toronto, ON.................866-238-0899
El Peto Products
  Cambridge, ON...............800-387-4064
Foxtail Foods
  Fairfield, OH...............800-487-2253
Giant Food
  Landover, MD................888-469-4426
Greyston Bakery Inc
  Yonkers, NY.................800-289-2253
Horizon Snack Foods
  Livermore, CA...............800-229-2552
Italian Bakery of Virginia
  Virginia, MN................218-741-3464
L & M Bakery
  Riverside, NJ...............888-887-1335
Love Quiches Desserts
  Freeport, NY................516-623-8800
Mehaffies Pies
  Dayton, OH..................800-289-7437
Michel's Bakery
  Philadelphia, PA............267-345-7914
Mrs Sullivan's Pies
  Jackson, TN.................731-427-2101
Mt. View Bakery
  Mountain View, HI...........808-968-6353
New England Country Bakers
  Watertown, CT...............800-225-3779
Northside Bakery
  Brooklyn, NY................718-782-2700
Notre Dame Bakery
  Conception Harbour, NL......709-535-2738
Plaidberry Company
  Vista, CA...................760-727-5403
Priester's Pecans
  Fort Deposit, AL............866-477-4736
Rising Dough Bakery
  Sacramento, CA..............916-387-9700
Roma Bakeries
  Rockford, IL................815-964-6737
Ryke's Bakery
  Muskegon, MI................231-726-2253
Scialo Brothers Bakery
  Providence, RI..............877-421-0986
Seaver's Bakery
  Kingsport, TN...............423-245-2441
Sinbad Sweets
  Madera, CA..................866-746-2232
Spring Glen Fresh Foods
  Ephrata, PA.................800-641-2853
Standard Bakery Inc
  Kealakekua, HI..............808-322-3688
Sweet Endings Inc
  West Palm Beach, FL.........888-635-1177
The Great San Saba River Pecan Company
  San Saba, TX................800-621-8121
United Pies Of Elkhart Inc
  Elkhart, IN.................574-294-3419

Product Categories / Baked Goods: Stuffing

Van de Kamps
  Peoria, IL 800-798-3318
Wenger's Bakery
  Reading, PA 610-372-6545
Zoelsmann's Bakery & Deli
  Pueblo, CO 719-543-0407

Fruit

Bonert's Pies Inc
  Santa Ana, CA 714-540-3535
Table Talk Pies Inc
  Worcester, MA 508-798-8811

Frozen

Bama Foods LTD
  Tulsa, OK 800-756-2262
Cutie Pie Corp
  Salt Lake City, UT 800-453-4575
Dynamic Foods
  Lubbock, TX 806-723-5600
Edwards Baking Company
  Marshall, MN 866-739-2328
Field's Pies
  Pauls Valley, OK 800-286-7501
Gardner Pie Co
  Akron, OH 330-245-2030
Harold Food Company
  Charlotte, NC 704-588-8061
Mehaffies Pies
  Dayton, OH 800-289-7437
Pastry Chef
  Pawtucket, RI 800-639-8606

Key Lime

Cheesecake Etc Desserts
  Miami Springs, FL 305-887-0258

Lemon-Meringue

D-Liteful Baking Company
  Medley, FL 305-883-6449
Kyger Bakery Products
  Lafayette, IN 765-447-1252
Mehaffies Pies
  Dayton, OH 800-289-7437

Meat

Goldilocks USA
  Hayward, CA 510-476-0700
Mexi-Frost Specialties Company
  Brooklyn, NY 718-625-3324
Morrison Lamothe
  Toronto, ON 877-677-6533
Mortimer's Fine Foods
  Burlington, ON 905-336-0000
The Van Cleve Seafood Company
  Spotsylvania, VA 800-628-5202

Frozen

Mexi-Frost Specialties Company
  Brooklyn, NY 718-625-3324

Non-Fruit

Le Donne Brothers Bakery
  Roseto, PA 610-588-0423
MacEwan's Meats
  Calgary, AB 403-228-9999
Snyder Foods
  Port Perry, ON 905-985-7373

Frozen

Bama Foods LTD
  Tulsa, OK 800-756-2262
Dimitria Delights Baking Co
  North Grafton, MA 800-763-1113
Dynamic Foods
  Lubbock, TX 806-723-5600
Edwards Baking Company
  Marshall, MN 866-739-2328
Field's Pies
  Pauls Valley, OK 800-286-7501
Gardner Pie Co
  Akron, OH 330-245-2030
Kyger Bakery Products
  Lafayette, IN 765-447-1252
Nancy's Specialty Foods
  Newark, CA 510-494-1100
Pastry Chef
  Pawtucket, RI 800-639-8606
Wick's Pies Inc
  Winchester, IN 800-642-5880

Peach

Bama Foods LTD
  Tulsa, OK 800-756-2262
Davis Bread & Desserts
  Davis, CA 530-220-4375
Mehaffies Pies
  Dayton, OH 800-289-7437

Rhubarb Pie

Bear Stewart Corp
  Chicago, IL 800-697-2327

Stuffing

Amalgamated Produce
  Bridgeport, CT 800-358-3808
Bodin Foods
  New Iberia, LA 337-367-1344
Coastal Seafoods
  Ridgefield, CT 203-431-0453
Good Old Days Foods
  Little Rock, AR 501-565-1257
Quality Bakery Products
  Houston, TX 866-449-4977
Rothbury Farms
  Grand Rapids, MI 877-684-2879
Texas Crumb & Food Products
  Farmers Branch, TX 800-522-7862

for Meat

Bluechip Group
  Salt Lake City, UT 800-878-0099
Leelanau Fruit Co
  Peshawbestown, MI 231-271-3514
Savoie's Sausage and Food Products
  Opelousas, LA 337-942-7241
Texas Crumb & Food Products
  Farmers Branch, TX 800-522-7862
World Flavors Inc
  Warminster, PA 215-672-4400

for Poultry

Leelanau Fruit Co
  Peshawbestown, MI 231-271-3514
Savoie's Sausage and Food Products
  Opelousas, LA 337-942-7241

World Flavors Inc
  Warminster, PA 215-672-4400

Waffles

Augustin's Waffles
  Long Valley, NJ 908-684-0830
Bake Crafters Food Company
  McDonald, TN 423-396-3392
Continental Mills Inc
  Tukwila, WA 206-816-7000
Eat Dutch Waffles, LLC
  Orem, UT 801-319-4788
Food for Life Baking
  Corona, CA 800-797-5090
Jacquet Bakery
  New York, NY
Julian's Recipe
  Brooklyn, NY 888-640-8880
Kloss Manufacturing Co Inc
  Allentown, PA 800-445-7100
Natural Food Mill
  Corona, CA 800-797-5090
Nature's Path Foods
  Blaine, WA 888-808-9505
Poppies International
  Battleboro, NC 252-442-4309
Shepherdsfield Bakery
  Fulton, MO 573-642-0009
Swapples
  Washington, DC
The Stroopie
  Lancaster, PA 717-875-3426
Van's International Foods
  Torrance, CA 310-320-8611
WaffleWaffle
  Nutley, NJ 201-559-1286

Frozen

Bake Crafters Food Company
  McDonald, TN 423-396-3392
Beck's Waffles of Oklahoma
  Shawnee, OK 800-646-6254
Continental Mills Inc
  Tukwila, WA 206-816-7000
Echo Lake Foods, Inc.
  Burlington, WI 262-763-9551
Van's International Foods
  Torrance, CA 310-320-8611

Wraps

LA Torilla Factory
  Santa Rosa, CA 800-446-1516
Maria and Ricardo's
  Canton, MA 800-881-7040
Nanka Seimen Company
  Vernon, CA 323-585-9967
Scott Adams Foods
  Newton, NJ 973-300-2091
Valley Lahvosh
  Fresno, CA 800-480-2704
Wrawp
  Pomona, CA 855-972-9748

Flavored

LA Torilla Factory
  Santa Rosa, CA 800-446-1516

Beverages

General

A Hill of Beans Coffee Roasters
  Omaha, NE 402-333-6048
A. Lassonde Inc.
  Rougemont, QC 866-552-7643
ABC Tea House
  Baldwin Park, CA 888-220-3988
Abita Brewing Co
  Covington, LA 800-737-2311
Absopure Water Company
  Plymouth, MI 800-422-7678
Abunda Life
  Asbury Park, NJ 732-775-9338
Acacia Vineyard
  Napa, CA 877-226-1700
Ace Farm USA Inc
  Bronx, NY 718-991-3816
Acqua Blox LLC
  Santa Fe Springs, CA 562-693-9599
Adirondack Beverages Inc
  Scotia, NY 800-316-6096
Admiral Beverage Corp
  Worland, WY 307-347-4201
Agri-Mark Inc
  West Springfield, MA 978-552-5500
Aimonetto and Sons
  Renton, WA 866-823-2777
Ajiri Tea Company
  Upper Black Eddy, PA 610-982-5075
Al-Rite Fruits & Syrups Co
  Miami, FL 305-652-2540
Alacer Corp
  Carlisle, PA 888-425-2362
Alfer Laboratories
  Chatsworth, CA 818-709-0737
All American Foods Inc
  Mankato, MN 800-833-2661
All Juice Food & Beverage
  Ankeny, IA 800-736-5674
Allegro Coffee Co
  Thornton, CO 800-666-4869
Aloe Farms Inc
  Harlingen, TX 800-262-6771
Aloe Laboratories
  Harlingen, TX 800-258-5380
Aloha Distillers
  Honolulu, HI 808-841-5787
Alpenglow Beverage Company
  Linden, VA 540-635-2118
Alpine Valley Water
  Harvey, IL 708-333-3910
Alternative Health & Herbs
  Albany, OR 800-345-4152
Ambootia Tea Estate
  Chicago, IL 312-661-1550
Amcan Beverages Inc
  American Canyon, CA 800-972-5962
Amcan Industries
  Elmsford, NY 914-347-4838
American Soy Products Inc
  Saline, MI 734-429-2310
Andalusia Distributing Co Inc
  Andalusia, AL 334-222-3671
Andrew Peller Limited
  Grimsby, ON 905-643-4131
Apple & Eve LLC
  Port Washington, NY 800-969-8018
Aqua Clara Bottling & Distribution
  Clearwater, FL 727-446-2999
Arbuckle Coffee Roasters
  Tucson, AZ 800-533-8278
Arcadian Estate Winery
  Rock Stream, NY 800-298-1346
Ariel Vineyards
  Napa, CA 800-456-9472
Arizona Beverage Company
  Cincinnati, OH 800-832-3775
Asiamerica Ingredients
  Westwood, NJ 201-497-5531
Aspire
  Chicago, OH
Atlanta Coffee Roasters
  Atlanta, GA 800-252-8211
August Schell Brewing Co
  New Ulm, MN 800-770-5020
Austrian Trade Commission
  New York, NY 212-421-5250
B.M. Lawrence & Company
  San Francisco, CA 415-981-2926
Bacardi Canada, Inc.
  Toronto, ON 905-451-6100
Barrows Tea Company
  New Bedford, MA 800-832-5024
Batavia Wine Cellars
  Canandaigua, NY 585-396-7600
Baywood Cellars
  Lodi, CA 800-214-0445
BCGA Concept Corporation
  New York, NY 212-488-0661
Bean Forge
  Coos Bay, OR 888-292-1632
Beckmen Vineyards
  Los Olivos, CA 805-688-8664
Belton Foods Inc
  Dayton, OH 800-443-2266
Benmarl Wine Co
  Marlboro, NY 845-236-4265
Berkeley Farms
  Hayward, CA 800-395-7004
Best Foods
  Englewood Cliffs, NJ 201-894-4000
Bevco Sales International Inc.
  Surrey, BC 800-663-0090
Beverage Capital Corporation
  Baltimore, MD 410-242-7404
Bianchi Winery
  Paso Robles, CA 805-226-9922
Big Red Bottling
  Austin, TX 254-772-7791
Birdseye Dairy-Morning Glory
  Green Bay, WI 920-494-5388
Black Prince Distillery Inc
  Clifton, NJ 973-365-2050
Blk Enterprises
  New York, NY 212-764-3331
Blossom Water, LLC
  Westwood, MA 855-325-5777
Blue Sky Beverage Company
  Corona, CA 800-426-7367
Bolt House Farms-Shipping Dept
  Bakersfield, CA 800-467-4683
Borden Dairy
  Dallas, TX 855-311-1583
Boston's Best Coffee Roasters
  South Easton, MA 800-898-8393
Boulder Beer
  Boulder, CO 303-444-8448
Brander Vineyard
  Santa Ynez, CA 800-970-9979
Brick Brewery
  Kitchener, ON 800-505-8971
Brimstone Hill Vineyard
  Pine Bush, NY 845-744-2231
British Aisles, LTD.
  Nashua, NH 800-520-8565
Brookshire Grocery Company
  Tyler, TX 888-937-3776
Buckmaster Coffee Co
  Hillsboro, OR 800-962-9148
Buena Vista Historic Tstng Rm
  Sonoma, CA 800-926-1266
Buffalo Trace Distillery
  Frankfort, KY 800-654-8471
Bully Hill Vineyards
  Hammondsport, NY 607-868-3610
Cadillac Coffee Co
  Ft. Wayne, IN 800-438-6900
Cafe Altura
  Santa Paula, CA 800-526-8328
Cafe Du Monde Coffee Stand
  New Orleans, LA 800-772-2927
Cafe Yaucono/Jimenez & Fernandez
  San Juan, PR 787-721-3337
California Natural Products
  Lathrop, CA 209-858-2525
Callaway Vineyards & Winery
  Temecula, CA 800-472-2377
Canadian Mist Distillers
  Collingwood, ON 705-445-4690
Canoe Ridge Vineyard
  Walla Walla, WA 509-527-0885
Cappo Drinks
  Baldwin Park, CA 626-813-1006
Capri Sun
  Granite City, IL
Caracolillo Coffee Mills
  Tampa, FL 800-682-0023
Caravan Company
  Worcester, MA 508-752-3777
Carmenet Winery
  Sonoma, CA 707-996-3526
Carolina Products
  Tampa, FL 813-313-1800
Carolina Treet
  Wilmington, NC 800-616-6344
Cascade Mountain Winery
  Amenia, NY 845-373-9021
Cass-Clay Creamery
  Fargo, ND 701-293-6455
Castello di Borghese Vineyard
  Cutchogue, NY 631-734-5111
Cawy Bottling Co
  Miami, FL 877-917-2299
CB Beverage Corporation
  Hopkins, MN 952-935-9905
Cecchetti Sebastiani Cellar
  Sonoma, CA 707-933-3230
Cedar Creek Winery
  Cedarburg, WI 800-827-8020
Cedar Lake Foods
  Cedar Lake, MI 800-246-5039
Central Dairies
  St Johns, NL 800-563-6455
Chalone Vineyard
  Soledad, CA 831-678-1717
Chase Brothers Dairy
  Oxnard, CA 800-438-6455
Chateau des Charmes Wines
  St. Davids, ON 800-263-2541
Chateau Julien Winery
  Carmel, CA 831-624-2600
Chateau St Jean Winery
  Kenwood, CA 707-833-4134
Cheribundi
  Geneva, NY 800-699-0460
Chestnut Mountain Winery
  Hoschton, GA 770-867-6914
Chicago Coffee Roastery
  Huntley, IL 800-762-5402
Chicama Vineyards
  West Tisbury, MA 888-244-2262
Chimere Winery
  Santa Maria, CA 805-928-5611
Chocolat
  Bellevue, WA 800-808-2462
Chouinard Vineyards & Winery
  Castro Valley, CA 510-582-9900
Christine Woods Winery
  Philo, CA 707-895-2115
Christopher Creek Winery
  Healdsburg, CA 707-433-2001
Cienega Valley Winery/DeRose
  Hollister, CA 831-636-9143
Cimarron Cellars
  Caney, OK 580-889-5997
Cinnabar Winery
  Saratoga, CA 408-867-1010
Citrosuco North America Inc
  Lake Wales, FL 800-356-4592
Citrus International
  Winter Park, FL 407-629-8037
Citrus Service
  Winter Garden, FL 407-656-4999
City Bean
  Los Angeles, CA 888-248-9232
City Brewing Company
  La Crosse, WI 608-785-4200
Claiborne & Churchill Vintners
  San Luis Obispo, CA 805-544-4066
Classic Tea
  Libertyville, IL 630-680-9934
Clayton Coffee & Tea
  Modesto, CA 209-576-1120
Clear Creek Distillery
  Portland, OR 503-248-9470
Clear Mountain Coffee Company
  Silver Spring, MD 301-587-2233

Product Categories / Beverages: General

Clearwater Coffee Company
Lake Zurich, IL 847-540-7711
Cline Cellars
Sonoma, CA 800-543-2070
Clinton Vineyards Inc
Clinton Corners, NY 845-266-5372
Clos Du Bois Winery
Geyserville, CA 800-222-3189
Clos Du Lac Cellars
Ione, CA 209-274-2238
Clos Du Val Co LTD
Napa, CA. 707-261-5200
Clos Pegase Winery
Calistoga, CA 800-866-8583
Cloudstone Vineyards
Los Altos Hills, CA 650-948-8621
Clover Hill Vineyards & Winery
Breinigsville, PA. 800-256-8374
Coastal Goods
Barnstable, MA. 508-375-1050
Coastlog Industries
Novi, MI 248-344-9556
Cobraz Brazilian Coffee
New York, NY 212-759-7700
Coca-Cola Beverages Northeast
Bedford, NH 844-619-3388
Cocolalla Winery
Cocolalla, ID. 208-263-3774
Coffee Associates
Edgewater, NJ. 201-945-1060
Coffee Barrel
Holt, MI. 517-694-9000
Coffee Bean
Englewood, CO. 303-922-1238
Coffee Bean & Tea Leaf
Bloomington, MN. 952-853-1148
Coffee Bean Intl
Portland, OR 800-877-0474
Coffee Bean of Leesburg
Leesburg, VA 800-232-6872
Coffee Beanery LTD
Flushing, MI 800-441-2255
Coffee Butler Service
Alexandria, VA 703-823-0028
Coffee Culture-A House
Lincoln, NE. 402-438-8456
Coffee Holding Co Inc
Staten Island, NY 800-458-2233
Coffee Masters
Spring Grove, IL. 800-334-6485
Coffee Mill Roastery
Elon, NC. 800-729-1727
Coffee Millers & Roasting
Cape Coral, FL 239-573-6800
Coffee People
Beaverton, OR 800-354-5282
Coffee Process
Houston, TX 713-695-8483
Coffee Reserve
Phoenix, AZ 888-755-6789
Coffee Roasters Inc
Oakland, NJ 800-285-2445
Coffee Roasters Of New Orleans
Kenner, LA 800-737-5464
Coffee Roasters of New Orleans
New Orleans, LA 800-737-5464
Coffee Up
Chicago, IL 847-288-9330
Coffee Works
Sacramento, CA 800-275-3335
Cold Hollow Cider Mill
Waterbury Center, VT. 800-327-7537
College Coffee Roaster
Mountville, PA 717-285-9561
Coloma Frozen Foods Inc
Coloma, MI. 800-642-2723
Colonial Coffee Roasters Inc
Miami, FL. 305-638-0885
Colorado Cellars
Palisade, CO 970-464-7921
Colorado Spice Co
Boulder, CO 800-677-7423
Columbia Winery
Woodinville, WA. 425-488-2776
Commodities Marketing Inc
Clarksburg, NJ 732-516-0700
Community Coffee Co.
Baton Rouge, LA 800-884-5282
Concannon Vineyard
Livermore, CA 800-258-9866
Conneaut Cellars Winery LLC
Conneaut Lake, PA 877-229-9463
Conrotto A. Winery
Gilroy, CA. 408-847-2233
Continental Coffee Products Company
Houston, TX 800-323-6178
Cool
Richardson, TX. 972-437-9352
Coon Creek Winery
St Helena, CA. 800-793-7960
Cooper Mountain Vineyards
Beaverton, OR 503-649-0027
Corim Industries Inc
Brick, NJ. 800-942-4201
Cosentino Winery
Napa, CA. 800-764-1220
Cotswold Cottage Foods
Arvada, CO 800-208-1977
Country Pure Foods Inc
Akron, OH. 877-995-8423
Cowie Wine Cellars & Vineyards
Paris, AR. 479-963-3990
Crescini Wines
Soquel, CA 831-462-1466
Cristom Vineyards
Salem, OR. 503-375-3068
Criveller California Corp
Healdsburg, CA 888-849-2266
Cronin Vineyards
Woodside, CA. 650-851-1452
Crown Regal Wine Cellars
Brooklyn, NY 718-604-1430
Cruse Vineyards
Chester, SC 803-377-3944
Crystal & Vigor Beverages
Kearny, NJ. 201-991-2342
Crystal Springs Bottled Water
Lakeland, FL. 800-728-5508
Crystal Springs Water Company
Lakeland, FL. 800-728-5508
CTL Foods
Colfax, WI. 800-962-5227
Culligan International Company
Rosemont, IL. 847-205-6000
Cuneo Cellars
Amity, OR. 503-835-2782
Cutrale Citrus Juices
Auburndale, FL. 863-965-5000
Cutting Edge Beverages
Boca Raton, FL. 561-347-5860
Cuvaison Winery
Calistoga, CA 707-942-6266
Cygnet Cellars
Hollister, CA. 831-637-7559
Dairy Fresh Foods Inc
Taylor, MI 313-299-0735
Dairy Maid Dairy LLC
Frederick, MD. 301-663-5114
Dalla Valle Vineyards
Napa, CA. 707-944-2676
Dallis Brothers
Long Island City, NY 718-845-3010
Damron Corp
Chicago, IL 800-333-1860
David Rio
San Francisco, CA 800-454-9605
Davis Bynum Winery
Healdsburg, CA 800-826-1073
Daybreak Coffee Roasters
Glastonbury, CT 800-882-5282
Daymar Select Fine Coffees
El Cajon, CA. 800-466-7590
De Coty Coffee Co
San Angelo, TX 800-588-8001
Deaver Vineyards
Plymouth, CA 209-245-4099
Deer Park Spring Water Co
Chesapeake, VA 800-832-0271
Del's Lemonade & Refreshments
Cranston, RI 401-463-6190
Delicato Family Vineyards
Napa, CA. 707-265-1700
DeLima Coffee
Liverpool, NY. 800-962-8864
Deloach Vineyards
Santa Rosa, CA. 707-755-3300
Delorimier Winery
Geyserville, CA 800-546-7718
Denatale Vineyards
Healdsburg, CA 707-431-8460
Denning's Point Distillery, LLC
Beacon, NY. 845-476-8413
Destileria Serralles Inc
Mercedita, PR 787-840-1000
Devansoy Farms
Carroll, IA. 800-747-8605
Devine Foods
Elwyn, PA 888-338-4631
Devlin Wine Cellars
Soquel, CA 831-476-7288
DG Yuengling & Son, Inc.
Pottsville, PA. 570-628-4890
Diageo Canada Inc.
Toronto, ON 416-626-2000
Diamond Creek Vineyards
Calistoga, CA 707-942-6926
Diamond Water Bottling Fclty
Hot Springs, AR 501-623-1251
Diehl Food Ingredients
Defiance, OH 800-251-3033
Digrazia Vineyards
Brookfield, CT 800-230-8853
Distant Lands Coffee Roaster
Renton, WA. 800-758-4437
Distillata
Cleveland, OH 800-999-2906
Divine Foods
Elizabethtown, NC 910-862-2576
DMH Ingredients Inc
Libertyville, IL 847-362-9977
Domaine Chandon
Yountville, CA 888-242-6366
Domaine St George Winery
Healdsburg, CA 707-433-5508
Don Hilario Estate Coffee
Oldsmar, FL 800-799-1903
Don Jose Foods
Scottsdale, AZ. 480-443-1000
Donatoni Winery
Inglewood, CA 310-645-5445
Door Peninsula Winery
Sturgeon Bay, WI 800-551-5049
Douwe Egberts
Worthington, OH 800-582-6617
Downeast Coffee Roasters
Pawtucket, RI 800-345-2007
Dr Konstantin Frank's Vinifera
Hammondsport, NY 800-320-0735
Dream Foods Intl
Santa Monica, CA. 310-315-5739
DreamPak LLC
Alexandria, VA 877-687-4662
Dreyer Sonoma
Woodside, CA. 650-851-9448
Droubi's Imports
Houston, TX 713-334-1829
Dry Creek Vineyard
Healdsburg, CA 800-864-9463
DS Services of America
Lakeland, FL. 800-728-5508
Duck Pond Cellars
Dundee, OR. 800-437-3213
Duckhorn Vineyards
St Helena, CA. 888-354-8885
Duncan Peak Vineyards
Lafayette, CA 925-283-3632
Dundee Wine Company
Dundee, OR. 888-427-4953
Dunn Vineyards
Angwin, CA 707-965-3642
Duplin Wine Cellars
Rose Hill, NC 800-774-9634
Dutch Henry Winery
Calistoga, CA 888-224-5879
E & J Gallo Winery
Modesto, CA. 877-687-9463
E L K Run Vineyards
Mt Airy, MD 800-414-2513
Eagle Coffee Co Inc
Baltimore, MD 410-685-5893
Eagle Crest Vineyards LLC
Conesus, NY 800-977-7117
Easley Winery
Indianapolis, IN 317-636-4516
East Side Winery/Oak Ridge Vineyards
Lodi, CA 209-369-4758
Eastern Tea Corp
Monroe Twp, NJ 800-221-0865
Eastrise Trading Corp.
Baldwin Park, CA
Eberle Winery
Paso Robles, CA. 805-238-9607
Ed Oliveira Winery
Arcata, CA 707-822-3023
Eden Foods Inc
Clinton, MI 888-424-3336

Product Categories / Beverages: General

Edgewood Estate Winery
  Napa, CA 800-755-2374
Edmunds St. John
  Berkeley, CA 510-981-1510
Edna Valley Vineyard
  San Luis Obispo, CA 866-979-8477
Eight O'Clock Coffee Company
  North Bergen, NJ 800-299-2739
El Paso Winery
  Ulster Park, NY 845-331-8642
Eldorado Artesian Springs Inc
  Louisville, CO 303-499-1316
Elk Cove Vineyards
  Gaston, OR 877-355-2683
Ellis Coffee Co
  Philadelphia, PA 800-822-3984
Elliston Vineyards
  Sunol, CA 925-862-2377
Elmhurst Milked
  Elma, NY 888-356-1925
Empire Tea Svc
  Columbus, IN 800-790-0246
Empresas La Famosa
  Toa Baja, PR 787-251-0060
Ener-G Foods
  Seattle, WA 800-331-5222
Enz Vineyards
  Hollister, CA 831-637-6443
Eola Hills Wine Cellars
  Rickreall, OR 800-291-6730
EOS Estate Winery
  Paso Robles, CA 800-249-9463
Erath Vineyards Winery
  Dundee, OR 800-539-5463
Erba Food Products
  Brooklyn, NY 718-272-7700
Espresso Vivace
  Seattle, WA 206-860-5869
Essentia Water
  Bothell, WA 877-293-2239
Eureka Water Co
  Oklahoma City, OK 800-310-8474
Eurobubblies
  Ashland, MA 800-273-0750
European Coffee
  Clearwater, FL 888-635-4882
European Roasterie
  Le Center, MN 888-588-5282
Evensen Vineyards
  Oakville, CA 707-944-2396
Everfresh Beverages
  Warren, MI 800-323-3416
Ex Drinks
  Henderson, NV 866-753-4929
Eyrie Vineyards
  Mcminnville, OR 888-440-4970
Fall Creek Vineyards
  Austin, TX 512-476-4477
Far Niente Winery
  Oakville, CA 707-944-2861
Farella-Park Vineyards
  Napa, CA 707-254-9489
Farfelu Vineyards
  Flint Hill, VA 540-364-2930
Farmland Dairies
  Wallington, NJ 888-727-6252
Fee Brothers
  Rochester, NY 800-961-3337
Fenestra Winery
  Livermore, CA 800-789-9463
Fenn Valley Vineyards
  Fennville, MI 269-561-2396
Fenn Valley Vineyards
  Fennville, MI 800-432-6265
Ferolito Vultaggio & Sons
  Woodbury, NY 800-832-3775
Ferrante Winery & Ristorante
  Geneva, OH 440-466-6046
Ferrara Bakery & Cafe
  New York, NY 212-226-6150
Ferrara Winery
  Escondido, CA 760-745-7632
Ferrari-Carano
  Healdsburg, CA 800-831-0381
Ferrigno Vineyards & Wine
  St James, MO 573-265-7742
Fess Parker Winery
  Los Olivos, CA 800-841-1104
Ficklin Vineyards Winery
  Madera, CA 559-674-4598
Fidalgo Bay Roasting Co
  Burlington, WA 800-310-5540
Field Coffee
  Norcross, GA 844-343-5326
Field Stone Winery
  Healdsburg, CA 800-544-7273
Fieldbrook Valley Winery
  Mckinleyville, CA 707-839-4140
Fife Vineyards
  Redwood Valley, CA 707-485-0323
Filsinger Vineyards & Winery
  Temecula, CA 951-302-6363
Finlay Extracts & Ingredients USA, Inc.
  Florham Park, NJ 800-288-6272
Fiore Winery
  Pylesville, MD 410-452-0132
Firelands Winery
  Sandusky, OH 800-548-9463
Firestone Vineyard
  Los Olivos, CA 805-688-3940
First Colony Coffee & Tea Company
  Norfolk, VA 800-446-8555
First Roasters of Central Florida
  Longwood, FL 407-699-6364
Fisher Ridge Wine Co Inc
  Charleston, WV 304-342-8702
Fisher Vineyards
  Santa Rosa, CA 707-539-7511
Fitzpatrick Winery & Lodge
  Somerset, CA 800-245-9166
Fizz-O Water Co
  Tulsa, OK 918-834-3691
Flavouressence Products
  Mississauga, ON 866-209-7778
Flora Springs Winery
  St Helena, CA 707-963-5711
Florida Caribbean Distillers
  Lake Alfred, FL 863-956-2002
Florida Food Products Inc
  Eustis, FL 800-874-2331
Florida Fruit Juices
  Chicago, IL 773-586-6200
Florida Key West
  Fort Myers, FL 239-694-8787
Flynn Vineyards Winery
  Rickreall, OR 888-427-4953
Fmali Herb
  Santa Cruz, CA 831-423-7913
Foley Estates Vineyard
  Lompoc, CA 805-737-6222
Folgers Coffee Co
  Orrville, OH 800-937-9745
Folie _ Deux Winery
  Oakville, CA 800-535-6400
Folklore Foods
  Selby, SD 605-649-1144
Foppiano Vineyards
  Healdsburg, CA 707-433-7272
Foris Vineyards
  Cave Junction, OR 541-592-3752
Forman Vineyard
  St Helena, CA 707-963-3900
Fortino Winery
  Gilroy, CA 888-617-6606
Fortuna Cellars
  Davis, CA 530-756-6686
Fortunes International Teas
  Mc Kees Rocks, PA 412-771-7767
Four Chimneys Farm Winery Trust
  Himrod, NY 607-243-7502
Four Sisters Winery
  Belvidere, NJ 908-475-3671
Fox Vineyards & Winery
  Social Circle, GA 770-787-5402
Foxen Foxen 7200
  Santa Maria, CA 805-937-4251
Franco's Cocktail Mixes
  Pompano Beach, FL 800-782-4508
Frank Family Vineyards
  Calistoga, CA 880-574-9463
Frank-Lin Distributors
  Fairfield, CA 800-922-9363
Franklin Hill Vineyards
  Bangor, PA 888-887-2839
Franzia Winery
  Ripon, CA 209-599-4111
Fratelli Perata
  Paso Robles, CA 805-238-2809
Frederick Wildman & Sons LTD
  New York, NY 800-733-9463
Freed, Teller & Freed
  South San Francisco, CA 800-370-7371
Freemark Abbey Winery
  St Helena, CA 800-963-9698
Freixenet USA Inc
  Sonoma, CA 707-996-4981
Frey Vineyards
  Redwood Valley, CA 800-760-3739
Frick Winery
  Geyserville, CA 707-857-1980
Frisinger Cellars
  Napa, CA 707-255-3749
Frog's Leap Winery
  Rutherford, CA 800-959-4704
Frontenac Point Vineyard
  Trumansburg, NY 607-387-9619
Gadsden Coffee/Caffe
  Arivaca, AZ 888-514-5282
Gainey Vineyard
  Santa Ynez, CA 805-688-0558
Galante Vineyards
  Carmel Valley, CA 800-425-2683
Galena Cellars Winery
  Galena, IL 800-397-9463
Galleano Winery
  Mira Loma, CA 951-685-5376
Galliker Dairy Co
  Johnstown, PA 800-477-6455
Gary Farrell Vineyards-Winery
  Healdsburg, CA 866-277-9463
Gehl Foods, Inc.
  Germantown, WI 800-521-2873
George A Dickel & Company
  Tullahoma, TN 888-342-5352
Georgia Wines Inc
  Ringgold, GA 706-937-2177
Georis Winery
  Carmel Valley, CA 831-659-1050
Germanton Winery
  Germanton, NC 800-322-2894
Ginseng Up Corp
  Worcester, MA 800-446-7364
Girard Spring Water
  North Providence, RI 800-477-9287
Girardet Wine Cellar
  Roseburg, OR 541-679-7252
Glen Summit Springs Water Company
  Mountain Top, PA 800-621-7596
Glenora Wine Cellars
  Dundee, NY 800-243-5513
Global Beverage Company
  Rochester, NY 585-381-3560
Global Food Industries
  Townville, SC 800-225-4152
Global Health Laboratories
  Amityville, NY 631-777-2134
Globus Coffee LLC
  Manhasset, NY 516-304-5780
Gloria Ferrer Champagne
  Sonoma, CA 707-933-1917
Gloria Jean's Gourmet Coffees
  Irvine, CA 877-320-5282
Gloria Winery & Vineyard
  Springfield, MO 417-926-6263
Glunz Family Winery & Cellars
  Grayslake, IL 847-548-9463
Golden Moon Tea
  Bristow, VA 877-327-5473
Golden Town Apple Products
  Rougemont, QC 866-552-7643
Good Earth Company
  New Providence, NJ 888-625-8227
Good Harbor Vineyards & Winery
  Lake Leelanau, MI 231-256-7165
Good-O-Beverages Inc
  Bronx, NY 718-328-6400
Goodson Brothers Coffee
  Knoxville, TN 800-737-1519
Goosecross Cellars Inc
  Yountville, CA 800-276-9210
Gourmet Mondiale
  Ste-Catherine, QC 450-638-6380
Goya Foods Inc.
  Jersey City, NJ 201-348-4900
Grace Tea Co
  Acton, MA 978-635-9500
Grainaissance
  Emeryville, CA 800-472-4697
Grand River Cellars
  Madison, OH 440-298-9838
Grande River Vineyards
  Palisade, CO 800-264-7696
Granite Springs Winery
  Somerset, CA 800-638-6041
Great Eastern Sun Trading Co
  Asheville, NC 800-334-5809

61

Product Categories / Beverages: General

Great Western Juice Co
 Maple Heights, OH 800-321-9180
Green Mountain Chocolate Inc
 Franklin, MA 508-520-7160
Green Mountain Cidery
 Middlebury, VT 802-388-0700
Green Spot Packaging
 Claremont, CA 800-456-3210
Greenfield Wine Company
 Vallejo, CA 707-552-5199
Greenwood Ridge Vineyards
 Philo, CA 707-895-2002
Groth Vineyards & Winery
 Oakville, CA 707-944-0290
Groupe Paul Masson
 Longueuil, QC 514-878-3050
Gruet Winery
 Albuquerque, NM 888-857-9463
Guenoc & Langtry Estate
 Middletown, CA 707-995-7501
Guglielmo Winery
 Morgan Hill, CA 408-779-2145
Guilliams Winery
 St Helena, CA 707-963-9059
Guinness Import Co
 Stamford, CT 800-521-1591
Gundlach-Bundschu Winery
 Sonoma, CA 707-939-3015
GWB Foods Corporation
 Brooklyn, NY 877-977-7610
H & H Products Co
 Orlando, FL 800-678-8448
H Coturri & Sons Winery
 Glen Ellen, CA 866-268-8774
H R Nicholson Co
 Baltimore, MD 800-638-3514
Habersham Vineyards & Winery
 Helen, GA 706-878-9463
Hafner Vineyard
 Healdsburg, CA 707-433-4606
Hahn Family Wines
 Soledad, CA 831-678-4555
Haight Brown Vineyard
 Litchfield, CT 800-577-9463
Hallcrest Vineyards
 Felton, CA 831-335-4441
Handley Cellars
 Philo, CA 800-733-3151
Hanks Beverage Co
 Feasterville-Trevose, PA 800-289-4722
Hanover Foods Corp
 Hanover, PA 717-632-6000
Hanzell Vineyards
 Sonoma, CA 707-996-3860
Harbor Winery
 West Sacramento, CA 916-371-6776
Harmony Bay Coffee
 North Andover, MA 800-514-3663
Harmony Cellars
 Harmony, CA 800-432-9239
Harney & Sons Tea Co.
 Millerton, NY 800-832-8463
Harold L King & Co Inc
 Redwood City, CA 888-368-2233
Harpersfield Vineyard
 Geneva, OH 440-466-4739
Harrisburg Dairies Inc
 Harrisburg, PA 800-692-7429
Hart Winery
 Temecula, CA 877-638-8788
Hartford Family Winery
 Forestville, CA 707-887-8030
Has Beans Coffee & Tea Co
 Chico, CA 800-427-2326
Hastings Co-Op Creamery-Dairy
 Hastings, MN 651-437-9414
Hathaway Coffee Co Inc
 Summit Argo, IL 708-458-7666
Hawaii Coffee Company
 Honolulu, HI 800-338-8353
Hawaiian Isles Kona Coffee Co
 Honolulu, HI 800-657-7716
Hawaiian Natural Water Company
 Pearl City, HI 808-483-0520
Haydenergy Health
 Valley Stream, NY 800-255-1660
Hazlitt 1852 Vineyards
 Hector, NY 888-750-0494
Health-Ade LLC
 Los Angeles, CA 844-337-6368
Heartland Vinyards
 Westlake, OH 440-871-0701

Heaven Hill Distilleries Inc.
 Bardstown, KY 502-337-1000
Heck Cellars
 Arvin, CA 661-854-6120
Hecker Pass Winery
 Gilroy, CA 408-842-8755
Hegy's South Hills Vineyard & Winery
 Twin Falls, ID 208-599-0074
Heineman Winery
 Put In Bay, OH 419-285-2811
Heitz Wine Cellars
 St Helena, CA 707-963-3542
Helena View/Johnston Vineyard
 Calistoga, CA 707-942-4956
Heller Estates
 Carmel Valley, CA 800-625-8466
Hells Canyon Winery
 Caldwell, ID 800-318-7873
Henry Estate Winery
 Umpqua, OR 800-782-2686
Henry Hill & Co
 Napa, CA 707-253-1663
Heritage Books & Gifts
 Virginia Beach, VA 800-862-2923
Heritage Coffee Co & Cafe
 Juneau, AK 800-478-5282
Heritage Farms Dairy
 Murfreesboro, TN 615-895-2790
Heritage Wine Cellars
 North East, PA 800-747-0083
Hermann J. Wiemer Vineyard
 Dundee, NY 800-371-7971
Hermannhof Vineyards
 Hermann, MO 800-393-0100
Heron Hill Winery
 Hammondsport, NY 800-441-4241
Hess Collection
 Napa, CA 707-255-1144
Hi-Country Foods Corporation
 Selah, WA 509-697-7292
HiBix Corporation
 Pleasanton, CA 925-225-0800
High Grade Beverage
 Monmouth Jct, NJ 887-327-4277
High Rise Coffee Roasters
 Colorado Springs, CO 719-633-1833
Highland Manor Winery
 Jamestown, TN 931-879-9519
Highwood Distillers
 High River, AB 403-652-3202
Hiland Dairy Foods Co
 Springfield, MO 800-492-4022
Hillcrest Vineyards
 Roseburg, OR 541-673-3709
Hillsboro Coffee Company
 Tampa, FL 813-877-2126
Hinckley Springs Bottled Water
 800-201-6218
Hinzerling Winery
 Prosser, WA 800-727-6702
Home Roast Coffee
 Lutz, FL 813-949-0807
Homewood Winery
 Sonoma, CA 707-996-6353
Honest Tea Inc
 Atlanta, GA 800-520-2653
Honeywood Winery
 Salem, OR 800-726-4101
Honig Vineyard and Winery
 Rutherford, CA 800-929-2217
Hood River Coffee Co
 Hood River, OR 800-336-2954
Hood River Distillers Inc
 Hood River, OR 541-386-1588
Hood River Vineyards and Winery
 Hood River, OR 541-386-3772
Hoodsport Winery
 Hoodsport, WA 800-580-9894
Hop Kiln Winery
 Healdsburg, CA 707-433-6491
Hopkins Vineyard
 Warren, CT 860-868-7954
Horizon Cellars Winery
 Siler City, NC 919-742-1404
House of Coffee Beans
 Houston, TX 800-422-1799
Hubers Orchard Winery-Vineyards
 Borden, IN 800-345-9463
Hudson Valley Brewery
 Beacon, NY 845-218-9156
Hudson Valley Farmhouse Cider
 Staatsburg, NY 845-266-3979

Hudson Valley Fruit Juice
 Highland, NY 845-691-8061
Hunter Farms - High Point Division
 High Point, NC 800-446-8035
Husch Vineyards & Winery
 Philo, CA 800-554-8724
Hyde Park Brewing Company
 Hyde Park, NY 845-229-8277
Hygeia Dairy Company
 Corpus Christi, TX 361-854-4561
Ideal Distributing Company
 Bothell, WA 425-488-6121
ILHWA American Corporation
 Belleville, NJ 800-446-7364
Imperial Foods, Inc.
 Long Island City, NY 718-784-3400
Indian Hollow Farms
 Richland Center, WI 800-236-3944
Indian Rock Vineyards
 Murphys, CA 209-728-8514
Indian Springs Vineyards
 Penn Vally, CA 800-375-9311
Indigo Coffee Roasters
 Florence, MA 800-447-5450
Inglenook
 Rutherford, CA 707-968-1100
Ingleside Vineyards
 Colonial Beach, VA 804-224-8687
Inn Foods Inc
 Watsonville, CA 800-708-7836
Inniskillin Wines
 Niagara-On-The-Lake, ON 888-466-4754
Intense Milk
 Buffalo, NY 716-892-3156
Inter-American Products
 Cincinnati, OH 800-645-2233
Inter-Continental Imports Company
 Newington, CT 800-424-4422
Iron Horse Vineyards
 Sebastopol, CA 707-887-1507
Ironstone Vineyards
 Murphys, CA 209-728-1251
Island Sweetwater Beverage Company
 Bryn Mawr, PA 610-525-7444
J Filippi Winery
 Rancho Cucamonga, CA 909-899-5755
J. Fritz Winery
 Cloverdale, CA 800-418-9463
J. Stonestreet & Sons Vineyard
 Healdsburg, CA 800-355-8008
J.B. Peel Coffee Roasters
 Red Hook, NY 800-231-7372
J.G. British Imports
 Bradenton, FL 888-965-1700
Jack Daniel Distillery
 Lynchburg, TN 888-551-5225
Jamaica John Inc
 Franklin Park, IL 847-451-1730
Java Sun Coffee Roasters
 Marblehead, MA 781-631-7788
Jayone Foods Inc
 Paramount, CA 562-633-7400
Jenny's Country Kitchen
 Dover, MN 800-357-3497
Jeremiah's Pick Coffee Co
 San Francisco, CA 877-537-3642
Jodar Vineyard & Winery
 Placerville, CA 530-644-3474
Jodyana Corporation
 Miami, FL 888-563-5282
Jogue Inc
 Northville, MI 800-531-3888
Johlin Century Winery
 Oregon, OH 419-693-6288
John A Vassilaros & Son Inc
 Flushing, NY 718-886-4140
John Conti Coffee Co
 Louisville, KY 800-928-5282
Johnson Estate Winery
 Westfield, NY 800-374-6569
Johnston's Winery Inc
 Ballston Spa, NY 518-882-6310
Jones Brewing Company
 Smithton, PA 724-483-2400
Joseph Phelps Vineyards
 St Helena, CA 800-707-5789
Joseph Swan Vineyards
 Forestville, CA 707-573-3747
Josuma Coffee Co
 Menlo Park, CA 650-366-5453
Joullian Vineyards
 Carmel Valley, CA 866-659-8101

Product Categories / Beverages: General

Juice Mart
　West Hills, CA 877-888-1011
Juicy Whip Inc
　La Verne, CA 909-392-7500
Justin Vineyards & Winery LLC
　Paso Robles, CA 800-237-4152
Kaffe Magnum Opus
　Millville, NJ 800-652-5282
Kalin Cellars
　Novato, CA 415-883-3543
Kan-Pak
　Arkansas City, KS 800-378-1265
Kate's Vineyard
　Napa, CA 707-255-2644
Kathryn Kennedy Winery
　Saratoga, CA 408-867-4170
Kauai Coffee Co Inc
　Kalaheo, HI 800-545-8605
Kava King
　Ormond Beach, FL 800-638-0082
Kelley's Island Wine Company
　Kelleys Island, OH 419-746-2678
Kemach Food Products
　Brooklyn, NY 718-272-5655
Kendall-Jackson
　Fulton, CA 866-287-9818
Kenwood Vineyards
　Kenwood, CA 707-833-5891
KeVita
　Oxnard, CA 888-310-6106
Kicking Horse Coffee
　Invermere, BC 888-287-5282
King Brewing Company
　Pontiac, MI 248-745-5900
King Estate Winery
　Eugene, OR 800-884-4441
King Juice Co
　Milwaukee, WI 414-482-0303
Kiona Vineyards Winery
　Benton City, WA 509-588-6716
Kirigin Cellars
　Gilroy, CA 408-847-8827
Kistler Vineyards
　Sebastopol, CA 707-823-5603
Kittling Ridge Estate Wines & Spirits
　Vaughan, ON 800-461-9463
Kittridge & Fredrickson LTD
　Portland, OR 800-558-7788
Klingshirn Winery
　Avon Lake, OH 440-933-6666
Knapp Vineyards
　Romulus, NY 800-869-9271
Knouse Foods Co-Op Inc.
　Peach Glen, PA 717-677-8181
Kobricks Coffee Company
　Jersey City, NJ 800-562-7491
Kona Coffee Council
　Kealakekua, HI 808-323-2911
Koryo Winery Company
　Gardena, CA 310-532-9616
Kramer Vineyards
　Gaston, OR 800-619-4637
Krier Foods
　Random Lake, WI 920-994-2469
Kunde Estate Winery
　Kenwood, CA 707-833-5501
Kusmi Tea
　New York, NY 646-346-1756
L.A. Libations
　El Segundo, CA
La Abra Farm & Winery
　Lovingston, VA 434-263-5392
LA Buena Vida Vineyards
　Grapevine, TX 817-481-9463
LA Chiripada Winery
　Dixon, NM 800-528-7801
LA Costa Coffee Roasting Co
　Carlsbad, CA 760-438-8160
LA Jota Vineyard Co
　Angwin, CA 877-222-0292
LA Rocca Vineyards & Winery
　Forest Ranch, CA 800-808-9463
La Rochelle Winery
　Livermore, CA 888-647-7768
La Vans Coffee Company
　Bordentown, NJ 609-298-0688
LA Vina Winery
　Anthony, NM 575-882-7632
Labatt Brewing Company
　Toronto, ON 800-268-2337
Lacas Coffee Co Inc
　Pennsauken, NJ 800-220-1133

Laetitia Vineyard & Winery
　Arroyo Grande, CA 888-809-8463
Lafollette Vineyard & Winery
　Sebastopol, CA 707-395-3902
Laird & Company
　Scobeyville, NJ 877-438-5247
Lake Sonoma Winery
　Glen Ellen, CA 877-586-2796
Lakeridge Winery & Vineyards
　Clermont, FL 800-768-9463
Lakeshore Winery
　Romulus, NY 315-549-7075
Lakewood Juice Co.
　Miami, FL 866-324-5900
Lakewood Vineyards Inc
　Watkins Glen, NY 877-535-9252
Lambert Bridge Winery
　Healdsburg, CA 800-975-0555
Lamoreaux Landing Wine Cellars
　Lodi, NY 607-582-6011
Lancaster County Winery LTD
　Willow Street, PA 717-464-3555
Land O'Lakes Inc
　Arden Hills, MN 800-328-9680
Landmark Vineyards
　Kenwood, CA 707-833-0053
Lange Estate Winery & Vineyard
　Dundee, OR 503-538-6476
Larry's Vineyards & Winery
　Altamont, NY 518-355-7365
Latah Creek Wine Cellar
　Spokane Valley, WA 509-926-0164
Latcham Vineyards
　Somerset, CA 800-750-5591
Laurel Glen Vineyard
　Glen Ellen, CA 707-933-9877
Lava Cap Winery
　Placerville, CA 800-475-0175
Lavazza Premium Coffees
　New York, NY 800-466-3287
Layman Distributing
　Salem, VA 800-237-1319
Lazy Creek Vineyards
　Philo, CA 888-529-9275
Le Bleu Corp
　Advance, NC 800-854-4471
Leaves Pure Teas
　Scottsdale, AZ 800-242-8807
Leelanau Cellars
　Omena, MI 800-782-8128
Leeward Winery
　Oxnard, CA 805-656-5054
Leidenfrost Vineyards
　Hector, NY 607-546-2800
Lemon Creek Winery
　Berrien Springs, MI 269-471-1321
Lemon-X Corporation
　Huntington Station, NY 800-220-1061
Lenox-Martell Inc
　Boston, MA 877-325-2489
Leonetti Cellar
　Walla Walla, WA 509-525-1670
Leroy Hill Coffee Co Inc
　Mobile, AL 800-866-5282
Les Bourgeois Vineyards
　Rocheport, MO 800-690-1830
Les Mouts De P.O.M.
　Sain-Francois-Xavier, QC 819-845-5555
Lewis Cellars
　Napa, CA 707-255-3400
Lexington Coffee & Tea
　Lexington, KY 859-277-1102
LiDestri Food & Drink
　Fairport, NY 585-377-7700
Lifeway
　Morton Grove, IL 877-281-3874
Light Rock Beverage Company
　Danbury, CT 203-743-3410
Lincourt Vineyards
　Solvang, CA 805-688-8554
Lindsay's Teas
　Petaluma, CA 800-624-7031
Lingle Brothers Coffee
　Bell Gardens, CA 562-927-3317
Lion Brewery Inc
　Wilkes Barre, PA 888-295-2337
Lipsey Mountain Spring Water
　Norcross, GA 770-449-0001
Little Amana Winery
　Amana, IA 319-668-9664
Live Oaks Winery
　Gilroy, CA 408-842-2401

Lockcoffee
　Larchmont, NY 914-273-7838
Lola Savannah
　Houston, TX 888-663-9166
Lorina, Inc.
　Coral Gables, FL 305-779-3085
Lost Trail Root Beer
　Louisburg, KS 800-748-7765
Louis Dreyfus Company Citrus Inc
　Winter Garden, FL 407-656-1000
Louis Dreyfus Company LLC
　Wilton, CT 203-761-2000
Louisburg Cider Mill
　Louisburg, KS 800-748-7765
Love Creek Orchards
　Medina, TX 800-449-0882
Lowcountry Produce
　Raleigh, NC 800-935-2792
Lucas Vineyards & Winery
　Interlaken, NY 800-682-9463
Lucas Winery
　Lodi, CA 209-368-2006
Lucerne Foods
　Pleasanton, CA 877-232-4271
Luxco Inc
　St Louis, MO 314-772-2626
Lynfred Winery Inc
　Roselle, IL 630-529-9463
Lyons Magnus
　Fresno, CA 800-344-7130
M S Walker Inc
　Somerville, MA 617-776-6700
M.E. Swing Company
　Alexandria, VA 800-485-4019
Mackie International, Inc.
　Riverside, CA 800-733-9762
MacKinlay Teas
　Ann Arbor, MI 734-846-0966
Maddalena Restaurant-Sn
　Los Angeles, CA 800-626-7722
Madison Foods
　Saint Paul, MN 651-265-8212
Madys Company
　San Francisco, CA 415-822-2227
Magnetic Springs
　Columbus, OH 800-572-2990
Magnum Coffee Roastery
　Nunica, MI 888-937-5282
Majestic Coffee & Tea Inc
　San Carlos, CA 650-591-5678
Makana Beverages Inc.
　Oxnard, CA
Manhattan Special Bottling
　Brooklyn, NY 718-388-4144
Mar-Key Foods
　Vidalia, GA 912-537-4204
Marie Brizard Wines & Spirits
　St. Helena, CA 800-878-1123
Markham Vineyards
　St Helena, CA 707-963-5292
Martin Ray Winery
　Santa Rosa, CA 707-823-2404
Marva Maid Dairy
　Newport News, VA 800-768-6243
Masala Chai Company
　Santa Cruz, CA 831-475-8881
Master Brew
　Northbrook, IL 847-564-3600
Matilija Water Company
　Santa Barbara, CA 805-963-7873
Maui Gold Pineapple Company
　Pukalani, HI 808-877-3805
Maxwell House & Post
　Rye Brook, NY 914-335-2500
Mayacamas Vineyards & Winery
　Napa, CA 707-224-4030
Mayer Bros
　Buffalo, NY 800-696-2928
Mayer's Cider Mill
　Webster, NY 800-543-0043
Mayfield Farms and Nursery
　Athens, TN 423-746-9859
McArthur Dairy LLC
　Miami, FL 561-659-4811
Mccutcheon Apple Products
　Frederick, MD 800-888-7537
Mcgregor Vineyard Winery
　Dundee, NY 800-272-0192
McSteven's
　Vancouver, WA 800-838-1056
Meadow Brook Dairy Co
　Erie, PA 800-352-4010

Product Categories / Beverages: General

Meier's Wine Cellars Inc
  Cincinnati, OH 800-346-2941
Melitta USA Inc
  Clearwater, FL 888-635-4880
Meramec Vineyards
  St James, MO 877-216-9463
Merci Spring Water
  Maryland Heights, MO 314-872-9323
Meridian Beverage Company
  Atlanta, GA 800-728-1481
Merlinos
  Canon City, CO 719-275-5558
Merritt Estate Winery Inc
  Forestville, NY 888-965-4800
Michigan Dairy LLC
  Livonia, MI 734-367-5390
Mike's Beverage Company
  Toronto, ON 647-428-3123
Milsolv Corporation
  Butler, WI 800-558-8501
Minnehaha Spring Water Company
  Cleveland, OH 216-431-0243
Mogen David Wine Corp
  Westfield, NY 716-326-3151
Monarch Beverage Company
  Atlanta, GA 800-241-3732
Mondial Foods Company
  Los Angeles, CA 213-383-3531
Monster Beverage Corp.
  Corona, CA 800-426-7367
Mother Parker's Tea & Coffee
  Mississauga, ON 800-387-9398
Mount Olympus Waters
   800-782-5508
Mountain Valley Products Inc
  Sunnyside, WA 509-837-8084
Mountain Valley Spring Water
  Asheville, NC 800-627-1062
Murray Cider Co Inc
  Roanoke, VA 540-977-9000
Music Mountain Water Company
  Shreveport, LA 800-349-6555
Natalie's Orchid Island Juice Co.
  Ft. Pierce, FL 800-373-7444
Natrel
  St. Laurent, QC 800-501-1150
Natural Spring Water Company
  Johnson City, TN 423-926-7905
Nature's Plus
  Melville, NY 800-645-9500
Neenah Springs
  Oxford, WI 608-586-5696
Nehalem Bay Winery
  Nehalem, OR 888-368-9463
Nestle USA Inc
  Glendale, CA 800-225-2270
New Age Beverages
  Denver, CO 303-289-8655
Niche W&S
  Cedar Knolls, NJ 973-993-8450
North Country Natural Spring Water
  Port Kent, NY 518-834-9400
Northland Cranberries
  Jackson, WI 866-719-5215
Northwest Naturals LLC
  Bothell, WA 425-881-2200
Northwestern Coffee Mills
  Washburn, WI 800-243-5283
Northwestern Foods
  Arden Hills, MN 800-236-4937
Ntc Marketing
  Williamsville, NY 800-333-1637
Nutritional Counselors of America
  Spencer, TN 931-946-3600
O-At-Ka Milk Prods Co-Op Inc.
  Batavia, NY 800-828-8152
Ocean Spray International
  Lakeville-Middleboro, MA 800-662-3263
Octavia Tea LLC
  Batavia, IL 866-505-6387
Office General des Eaux Minerales
  Montreal, QC 514-482-7221
Old Dutch Mustard Company
  Great Neck, NY 516-466-0522
Old Fashioned Natural Products
  Santa Ana, CA 800-552-9045
Old Orchard Brands, LLC
  Sparta, MI 800-330-2173
Omar Coffee Co
  Newington, CT 800-394-6627
One World Enterprises
  Los Angeles, CA 888-663-2626
Opa! Originals
  Rochester, NY 585-368-5623
Orchid Island Juice Co
  Fort Pierce, FL 800-373-7444
Organic Gemini
  Brooklyn, NY 347-662-2900
Orientex Foods
  Pittsburg, CA 800-660-0962
Ormand Peugeog Corporation
  Miami, FL 305-624-6834
Pappy's Sassafras Tea
  Columbus Grove, OH 877-659-5110
Paramount Distillers
  Cleveland, OH 800-821-2989
Parducci Wine Cellars
  Ukiah, CA 888-362-9463
Partners Coffee LLC
  Atlanta, GA 800-341-5282
Pearl Coffee Co
  Akron, OH 800-822-5282
Peerless Coffee & Tea
  Oakland, CA 800-310-5662
Perfect Foods Inc
  Goshen, NY 800-933-3288
Pernod Ricard USA
  New York, NY 212-372-5400
Perricone Juices
  Beaumont, CA 951-769-7171
Perry Creek Winery
  Somerset, MO 800-880-4026
Personal Edge Nutrition
  Ballwin, MO 514-636-4512
Pete's Brewing Company
  San Antonio, TX 800-877-7383
Pfefferkorn's Coffee Inc
  Baltimore, MD 800-682-4665
Phamous Phloyd's Barbecue
  Denver, CO 800-497-3281
Phillips Beverage Company
  Minneapolis, MN 612-362-7500
Phillips Syrup Corp
  Cleveland, OH 800-350-8443
Pleasant Valley Wine Co
  Hammondsport, NY 607-569-6111
Pleasant View Dairy
  Highland, IN 219-838-0155
Polar Beverages Inc.
  Worcester, MA 800-734-9800
Polar Water Company
  Carnegie, PA 412-429-5550
Pontiac Coffee Break
  Waterford, MI 248-332-6333
Porto Rico Importing
  New York, NY 212-477-5421
Post Familie Vineyards
  Altus, AR 800-275-8423
Postum
  Charlotte, NC 704-221-5587
Powell & Mahoney Ltd.
  Salem, MA 978-745-4332
Premier Juices
  Clearwater, FL 727-533-8200
Premium Water
  Kansas City, MO 800-332-3332
Pride Dairies
  Bottineau, ND 701-228-2216
Prince of Peace
  Hayward, CA 800-732-2328
Productos Del Plata
  Miami, FL 786-357-8261
Progenix Corporation
  Wausau, WI 800-233-3356
Promised Land Dairy
  Colorado Springs, CO 877-520-2479
Purity Dairies LLC
  Nashville, TN 615-244-1900
Q.E. Tea
  Bridgeville, PA 800-622-8327
Quality Kitchen Corporation
  Wyoming, DE 302-697-3118
Quality Naturally Foods
  City Of Industry, CA 888-498-6986
R.J. Corr Naturals
  Posen, IL 708-389-4200
RC Bottling Company
  Evenasville, IN 812-424-7978
REBBL
  Emeryville, CA 855-732-2500
Rebound
  Newburgh, NY 845-562-5400
Red Diamond Coffee & Tea
  Moody, AL 800-292-4651
Reggie's Roast
  Linden, NJ 908-862-3700
Rejuvila
  Boulder, CO 877-480-4402
Renault Winery
  Egg Harbor City, NJ 609-965-2111
Revive Kombucha
  Petaluma, CA 707-536-1193
Richland Beverage Association
  Carrollton, TX 214-357-0248
Robert Keenan Winery
  St Helena, CA 707-963-9177
Robert Mondavi Winery
  Oakville, CA 888-766-6328
Rondo Specialty Foods LTD
  New Castle, DE 800-724-6636
Roos Foods
  Kenton, DE 800-343-3642
Roselani Tropics Ice Cream
  Wailuku, HI 808-244-7951
Rosenberger's Dairies
  Hatfield, PA 800-355-9074
Royal Cup Coffee
  Birmingham, AL 800-366-5836
Russo Farms
  Vineland, NJ 856-692-5942
Rutherford Hill Winery
  Rutherford, CA 707-963-1871
Safeway Milk Plant
  Tempe, AZ 480-894-4391
San Francisco Bay Coffee
  Lincoln, CA 800-829-1300
San-Ei Gen FFI
  New York, NY 212-315-7850
Sandstone Winery
  Amana, IA 319-622-3081
Sara Lee Foodservice
  Peoria, IL 800-641-4025
Saranac Brewery
  Utica, NY 800-765-6288
Saratoga Spring Water Co
  Saratoga Springs, NY 888-426-8642
Sazerac Company, Inc.
  Metairie, LA 866-729-3722
Schirf Brewing Company
  Park City, UT 435-649-0900
Schneider's Dairy Inc
  Pittsburgh, PA 412-881-3525
Schramsberg Vineyards
  Calistoga, CA 800-877-3623
Scotian Gold
  Coldbrook, NS 888-726-8426
Sea Breeze Fruit Flavors
  Towaco, NJ 800-732-2733
Sesinco Foods
  New York, NY 212-243-1306
Shasta Beverages Inc
  Baltimore, MS 800-834-9980
Sherbrooke OEM Ltd
  Sherbrooke, QC 866-851-2579
Silvan Ridge Winery
  Eugene, OR 541-345-1945
Silver Springs Citrus Inc
  Howey-in-the-Hills, FL 800-940-2277
Simi Winery
  Healdsburg, CA 707-433-3686
Simpson & Vail
  Brookfield, CT 800-282-8327
Skjodt-Barrett Foods
  Brampton, ON 877-600-1200
Smeltzer Orchard Co
  Frankfort, MI 231-882-4421
Smith Dairy
  Orrville, OH 800-776-7076
SnowBird Corporation
  Bayonne, NJ 800-576-1616
Solana Gold Organics
  Sebastopol, CA 800-459-1121
Somerset Syrup & Concessions
  Edison, NJ 800-526-8865
Southern Beverage Packers Inc
  Appling, GA 800-326-2469
Spangler Vineyards
  Roseburg, OR 541-679-9654
Specialty Coffee Roasters
  Delray Beach, FL 800-253-9363
SPI West Port, Inc
  South San Fancisco, CA
Spoetzl Brewery
  Shiner, TX 361-594-3383
St Arnold Brewing Co
  Houston, TX 800-801-6402

Product Categories / Beverages: Alcoholic Beverages

St Julian Winery
  Paw Paw, MI 800-732-6002
Stash Tea Co
  Portland, OR 800-547-1514
STE Michelle Wine Estates
  Woodinville, WA 800-267-6793
Sterling Vineyards
  Calistoga, CA 707-942-3344
Stevens Point Brewery
  Stevens Point, WI 800-369-4911
Stevens Tropical Plantation
  West Palm Beach, FL 561-683-4701
Stewart's Private Blend Foods
  Chicago, IL 800-654-2862
Stockton Graham & Co
  Raleigh, NC 800-835-5943
Stone Hill Winery
  Hermann, MO 573-486-2221
Stop & Shop Manufacturing
  Readville, MA 508-977-5132
Straub Brewery Inc
  St Marys, PA 814-834-2875
Sturm Foods Inc
  Manawa, WI 800-347-8876
Summit Brewing Company
  Saint Paul, MN 651-265-7800
Sun Orchard INC
  Haines City, FL 877-875-8423
Sun Pac Foods
  Brampton, ON 905-792-2700
Sunlike Juice
  Rougemont, QC 866-552-7643
Sunshine Farms
  Portage, WI 608-742-2016
Sunsweet Growers Inc.
  Yuba City, CA 800-417-2253
Suntory International
  New York, NY 212-891-6600
Super Stores Industries
  Turlock, CA 209-668-2100
Superbrand Dairies
  Miami, FL 305-769-6600
Sutter Home Winery
  St Helena, CA 800-967-4663
SVB Food & Beverage Company
  Martinsburg, WV 304-267-8500
Swiss Premium Dairy Inc
  Lebanon, PA 800-222-2129
SYFO Beverage Company of Florida
  Ponte Vedra Beach, FL 904-381-9002
Tamarack Farms Dairy
  Newark, OH 866-221-4141
Tatra Herb Co
  Morrisville, PA 888-828-7248
Taylor Wine Company
  Hammondsport, NY 607-868-3245
Templar Food Products
  New Providence, NJ 800-883-6752
Terrace At J Vineyards
  Healdsburg, CA 800-885-9463
Tetley USA
  Marietta, GA 770-428-5555
Tetley USA
  Edison, NJ 800-728-0084
Texas Coffee Co
  Beaumont, TX 800-259-3400
Texas Coffee Traders Inc
  Austin, TX 800-343-4875
The Humphrey Co
  Lockport, NY 716-597-1974
The Kroger Co.
  Murray, KY 800-632-6900
The Water Kefir People
  Bend, OR
Thomas Canning/Maidstone
  Maidstone, ON 519-737-1531
Thomas Kruse Winery
  Gilroy, CA 408-842-7016
Three Lakes Winery
  Three Lakes, WI 800-944-5434
Todhunter Foods
  Lake Alfred, FL 863-956-1116
Toft Dairy Inc
  Sandusky, OH 800-521-4606
Tone Products Inc
  Melrose Park, IL 800-536-8663
Traditional Medicinals Inc
  Sebastopol, CA 800-543-4372
Tree Top Inc
  Selah, WA 509-697-7251
Trefethen Family Vineyards
  Napa, CA 707-255-7700

Trigo Corporation
  Toa Baja, PR 787-794-1300
Triple Springs Spring Water Co
  Meriden, CT 203-235-8374
Tropicana Products Inc.
  Chicago, IL 800-237-7799
TruBrain
  Santa Monica, CA 650-241-8372
True Organic Product Inc
  Helm, CA 800-487-0379
Tumericalive Healing Enterprise
  New York, NY 347-559-6760
Turkey Hill Dairy Inc
  Conestoga, PA 800-693-2479
Turkey Hill Sugarbush
  Waterloo, QC 450-539-4822
United Dairy Inc.
  Martins Ferry, OH 800-252-1542
United Dairymen of Arizona
  Tempe, AZ 480-966-7211
Universal Impex Corporation
  Toronto, ON 416-743-7778
Up Mountain Switchel
  Brooklyn, NY 315-939-3085
Uptime Energy, Inc.
  Canoga Park, CA
V Sattui Winery
  St Helena, CA 707-963-7774
Valley Fig Growers
  Fresno, CA 559-237-3893
Valley View Packing Co
  Yuba City, CA 530-673-7356
Van Roy Coffee Co
  Cleveland, OH 877-826-7669
Vancouver Island Brewing Company
  Victoria, BC 800-663-6383
Varni Brothers/7-Up Bottling
  Modesto, CA 209-521-1777
Vegetable Juices Inc
  Chicago, IL 888-776-9752
Ventura Coastal LLC
  Ventura, CA 805-653-7000
Venture Vineyards
  Lodi, NY 888-635-6277
Vie-Del Co
  Fresno, CA 559-834-2525
Viking Distillery
  Albany, GA 866-729-3722
Villa Mt. Eden Winery
  Saint Helena, CA 866-931-1624
Vincor Canada
  Mississauga, ON 800-265-9463
Vintage Wine Estates
  Santa Rosa, CA 877-289-9463
Vita Food Products Inc
  Chicago, IL 800-989-8482
Vitamilk Dairy
  Bellingham, WA 206-529-4128
Von Stiehl Winery
  Algoma, WI 800-955-5208
W.J. Stearns & Sons/Mountain Dairy
  Storrs Mansfield, CT 860-423-9289
Wagner Vineyards
  Lodi, NY 866-924-6378
Wah Yet Group
  Hayward, CA 800-229-3392
Water Concepts
  East Dundee, IL 847-699-9797
Wayne Dairy Products Inc
  Richmond, IN 765-935-7521
Weaver Nut Co. Inc.
  Ephrata, PA 800-473-2688
Wechsler Coffee Corporation
  Teterboro, NJ 800-800-2633
WEIS Markets Inc.
  Sunbury, PA 866-999-9347
Welch Foods Inc
  Concord, MA 800-340-6870
Welch Foods Inc.
  Concord, MA 800-340-6870
Welsh Farms
  Wallington, NJ 800-221-0663
Westbrae Natural Foods
  Melville, NY 800-434-4246
Wheeling Coffee & Spice Co
  Wheeling, WV 800-500-0141
Whitaker & Assoc Architects
  Atlanta, GA 404-266-1265
White Coffee Corporation
  Long Island City, NY 800-221-0140
White Rock Products Corp
  Flushing, NY 800-969-7625

WhiteWave Foods
  Denver, CO 800-488-9283
Whole Herb Co
  Sonoma, CA 707-935-1077
Widmers Wine Cellars
  Canandaigua, NY 585-374-6311
Wild Aseptics, LLC
  Erlanger, KY 877-787-7221
Winchester Farms Dairy
  Winchester, KY 859-745-5500
Windmill Water Inc
  Edgewood, NM 505-281-9287
Winmix/Natural Care Products
  Englewood, FL 941-475-7432
Woodbury Vineyards
  Fredonia, NY 866-691-9463
World Citrus West
  Fullerton, CA 714-870-6171
Yakima Craft Brewing Company
  Yakima, WA 509-654-7357
Yoder Dairies
  Chesapeake, VA 757-482-4068
Yoo-Hoo Chocolate Beverage Company
  Carlstadt, NJ 201-933-0070
York Mountain Winery
  Templeton, CA 805-237-7575
Young Winfield
  Hamilton, ON 905-893-2536
Zd Wines
  Napa, CA 800-487-7757
Zeigler's
  Lansdale, PA 215-855-5161
Zephyrhills Bottled Water Company
  Tampa, FL 800-950-9398

Alcoholic Beverages

A. Nonini Winery
  Fresno, CA 559-275-1936
A. Rafanelli Winery
  Healdsburg, CA 707-433-1385
Abita Brewing Co
  Covington, LA 800-737-2311
Acacia Vineyard
  Napa, CA 877-226-1700
Ackerman Winery
  Amana, IA 319-622-3379
Adair Vineyards
  New Paltz, NY 845-255-1377
Adam Puchta Winery
  Hermann, MO 573-486-5596
Adams County Winery
  Orrtanna, PA 877-601-7936
Adelaida Cellars Inc
  Paso Robles, CA 800-676-1232
Adelsheim Vineyard
  Newberg, OR 503-538-3652
Adler Fels Winery
  Santa Rosa, CA 707-539-3123
Afton Mountain Vineyards Inc
  Afton, VA 540-456-8667
Ahlgren Vineyard
  Boulder Creek, CA 800-338-6071
Airlie Winery
  Monmouth, OR 503-838-6013
Alba Vineyard & Winery
  Milford, NJ 908-995-7800
Alexis Bailly Vineyard
  Hastings, MN 651-437-1413
Allegro Winery & Vineyards
  Brogue, PA 717-927-9148
Almarla Vineyards & Winery
  Shubuta, MS 601-687-5548
Aloha Distillers
  Honolulu, HI 808-841-5787
Alpen Cellars
  Trinity Center, CA 530-266-9513
Alpine Vineyards
  Monroe, OR 541-424-5851
Alta Vineyard Cellar
  Calistoga, CA 707-942-6708
Altamura Winery
  Napa, CA 707-253-2000
Alto Vineyards & Winery
  Alto Pass, IL 618-893-4898
Amador Foothill Winery
  Plymouth, CA 800-778-9463
Amalthea Cellars Farm Winery
  Atco, NJ 856-768-8585
Amberg Wine Cellars
  Clifton Springs, NY 315-462-3455
Americana Vineyards & Winery
  Interlaken, NY 888-600-8067

Product Categories / Beverages: Alcoholic Beverages

Amity Vineyards
   Amity, OR 888-264-8966
Amizetta Vineyards
   St Helena, CA 707-963-1460
Amwell Valley Vineyard
   Ringoes, NJ 908-788-5852
Anchor Brewing Company
   San Francisco, CA 415-863-8350
Ancient Peaks Winery
   Santa Margarita, CA 805-365-7045
Anderson Valley Brewing Co
   Boonville, CA 800-207-2237
Anderson's Conn Valley Vineyards
   St Helena, CA 800-946-3497
Andrew Peller Limited
   Grimsby, ON 905-643-4131
Angry Orchard Cider Company, LLC
   Walden, NY 888-845-3311
Annapolis Winery
   Annapolis, CA 707-886-5460
Antelope Valley Winery
   Lancaster, CA 800-282-8332
Anthony Road Wine Co
   Penn Yan, NY 800-559-2182
Applewood Winery
   Warwick, NY 845-988-9292
Arbor Crest Wine Cellars
   Spokane, WA 509-927-9463
Arbor Hill Grapery & Winery
   Naples, NY 800-554-7553
Argyle Winery
   Dundee, OR 888-427-4953
Arizona Vineyards
   Nogales, AZ 520-287-7972
Arns Winery
   St Helena, CA 707-963-3429
Arrowood Winery
   Glen Ellen, CA 800-938-5170
Artesa Vineyards & Winery
   Napa, CA 707-224-1668
Ashland Vineyards & Winery
   Ashland, OR 541-488-0088
ASV Wines
   Delano, CA 661-792-3159
Au Bon Climat Winery
   Los Olivos, CA 805-937-9801
August Schell Brewing Co
   New Ulm, MN 800-770-5020
Augusta Winery
   Augusta, MO 888-667-9463
Autumn Wind Vineyard
   Newberg, OR 503-538-6931
B R Cohn Winery & Olive Oil Co
   Glen Ellen, CA 800-330-4064
Babcock Winery & Vineyards
   Lompoc, CA 805-736-1455
Bacardi Canada, Inc.
   Toronto, ON 905-451-6100
Bacardi USA Inc
   Coral Gables, FL 800-222-2734
Bad Seed Cider Company, LLC
   Highland, NY 845-236-0956
Bagley's
   Hector, NY 607-582-6421
Baileyana Winery
   San Luis Obispo, CA 805-544-9080
Baily Vineyard & Winery
   Temecula, CA 951-676-9463
Balagna Winery Company
   Los Alamos, NM 505-672-3678
Baldwin Vineyards
   Pine Bush, NY 845-744-2226
Balic Winery
   Mays Landing, NJ 609-625-2166
Banfi Vintners
   Old Brookville, NY 800-645-6511
Barca Wine Cellars
   Roseville, CA 916-786-0770
Bargetto Winery
   Soquel, CA 800-422-7438
Baron Vineyards
   Paso Robles, CA 805-239-3313
Basignani Winery
   Sparks Glencoe, MD 410-472-0703
Baxters Vineyards & Winery
   Nauvoo, IL 800-854-1396
Baywood Cellars
   Lodi, CA 800-214-0445
Beachaven Vineyards & Winery
   Clarksville, TN 931-645-8867
Beam Suntory
   Chicago, IL 312-964-6999

Bear Creek Winery
   Cave Junction, OR 877-273-4843
Beaucanon Estate Wines
   Napa, CA 800-660-3520
Beckmen Vineyards
   Los Olivos, CA 805-688-8664
Bedell Northfork LLC
   Cutchogue, NY 631-734-7537
Bell Mountain Vineyards
   Willow City, TX 830-685-3297
Bellerose Vineyard
   Healdsburg, CA 707-433-1637
Benziger Family Winery
   Glen Ellen, CA 888-490-2739
Bernardo Winery
   San Diego, CA 858-487-1866
Bernardus Winery Tasting Rm
   Carmel Valley, CA 800-223-2533
Bernheim Distilling Company
   Louisville, KY 800-303-0053
Berryessa Gap Tasting Room
   Winters, CA 530-795-3201
Bethel Heights Vineyard
   Salem, OR 503-399-9588
Bianchi Winery
   Paso Robles, CA 805-226-9922
Bias Vineyards & Winery
   Berger, MO 800-905-2427
Bidwell Vineyard
   Cutchogue, NY 631-734-5200
Biltmore Estate Wine Company
   Asheville, NC 800-411-3812
Binns Vineyards & Winery
   Las Cruces, NM 575-526-6738
Bishop Farms Winery
   Cheshire, CT 203-272-8243
Bittermilk LLC
   Charleston, SC 843-641-0455
Black Mesa Winery
   Velarde, NM 800-852-6372
Black Prince Distillery Inc
   Clifton, NJ 973-365-2050
Black Sheep Vintners
   Murphys, CA 209-728-2157
Blumenhof Vineyards-Winery
   Dutzow, MO 800-419-2245
Boeger Winery
   Placerville, CA 530-622-8094
Bogle Vineyards Inc
   Clarksburg, CA 916-744-1030
Bohemian Brewery
   Midvale, UT 801-566-5474
Boisset Family Estates
   St Helena, CA 800-878-1123
Bonny Doon Vineyard
   Santa Cruz, CA 888-819-6789
Boordy Vineyards Inc
   Hydes, MD 410-592-5015
Bordoni Vineyards
   Vallejo, CA 707-642-1504
Boskydel Vineyard
   Lake Leelanau, MI 231-256-7272
Bouchaine Vineyards
   Napa, CA 800-654-9463
Boulder Beer
   Boulder, CO 303-444-8448
Brander Vineyard
   Santa Ynez, CA 800-970-9979
Braren Pauli Winery
   Redwood Valley, CA 800-423-6519
Braswell's Winery
   Dora, AL 205-648-8335
Bravard Vineyards & Winery
   Hopkinsville, KY 270-269-2583
Breitenbach Wine Cellars
   Dover, OH 330-343-3603
Briceland Vineyards
   Redway, CA 707-923-2429
Brick Brewery
   Kitchener, ON 800-505-8971
Brimstone Hill Vineyard
   Pine Bush, NY 845-744-2231
Bristle Ridge Vineyards
   Knob Noster, MO 800-994-9463
Broad Run Vineyards
   Louisville, KY 502-231-0372
Broadhead Brewing Co
   Orl,ans, ON 613-830-3944
Broadley Vineyards
   Monroe, OR 541-847-5934
Bronco Wine Co
   Ceres, CA 855-874-2394

Brooklyn Cider House
   Brooklyn, NY 347-295-0308
Brookmere Wine & Vineyard
   Belleville, PA 717-935-5380
Brotherhood Winery
   Washingtonville, NY 845-496-3661
Brown County Winery
   Nashville, IN 888-298-2984
Brutocao Cellars
   Hopland, CA 800-433-3689
Bryant Vineyard
   Talladega, AL 256-268-2638
Buccia Vineyard
   Conneaut, OH 440-593-5976
Buckingham Valley Vineyards
   Buckingham, PA 215-794-7188
Buehler Vineyards
   St Helena, CA 707-963-2155
Bull and Barrel Brewpub
   Brewster, NY 845-278-2855
Burnley Vineyards
   Barboursville, VA 540-832-2828
Butler Winery
   Bloomington, IN 812-332-6660
Butterfly Creek Winery
   Mariposa, CA 209-742-4567
Buttonwood Farm Winery & Vineyard
   Solvang, CA 800-715-1404
Byington Vineyard & Winery
   Los Gatos, CA 408-354-1111
Byron Vineyard & Winery
   Santa Maria, CA 805-938-7365
Cache Cellars
   Davis, CA 530-756-6068
Cain Vineyard & Winery
   St Helena, CA 707-963-1616
Cakebread Cellars
   Rutherford, CA 800-588-0298
Calafia Cellars
   St Helena, CA 707-963-0114
Calera Wine Co
   Hollister, CA 831-637-9170
Callaway Vineyards & Winery
   Temecula, CA 800-472-2377
Camas Prairie Winery
   Moscow, ID 800-616-0214
Cambria Winery
   Santa Maria, CA 888-339-9463
Campari
   New York, NY 212-891-3600
Canoe Ridge Vineyard
   Walla Walla, WA 509-527-0885
Caparone Winery LLC
   Paso Robles, CA 805-610-5308
Caporale Winery
   Napa, CA 707-253-9230
Caprock Winery Inc
   Lubbock, TX 800-546-9463
Cardinale Winery
   Oakville, CA 800-588-0279
Carlson Vineyards Winery
   Palisade, CO 888-464-5554
Carmenet Winery
   Sonoma, CA 707-996-3526
Carneros Creek Winery
   Napa, CA 707-253-9464
Carrousel Cellars
   Gilroy, CA 408-847-2060
Casa Larga Vineyards
   Fairport, NY 585-223-4210
Casa Nuestra Winery & Vineyard
   St Helena, CA 866-844-9463
Castello di Borghese Vineyard
   Cutchogue, NY 631-734-5111
Catoctin Vineyards
   Brookeville, MD 301-774-2310
Catskill Distilling Company
   Bethel, NY 845-583-3141
Cavender Castle Winery
   Atlanta, GA 706-864-4759
Caymus Vineyards
   Rutherford, CA 707-967-3010
Cayuga Ridge Estate Winery
   Ovid, NY 800-598-9463
Cedar Creek Winery
   Cedarburg, WI 800-827-8020
Cedar Mountain Winery
   Livermore, CA 925-373-6636
Chacewater Winery and Olive Mill
   Kelseyville, CA 707-279-2995
Chaddsford Winery
   Chadds Ford, PA 610-388-6221

Product Categories / Beverages: Alcoholic Beverages

Chalet Debonne Vineyards
   Madison, OH...................440-466-3485
Chalk Hill Estate Winery
   Healdsburg, CA................707-657-4839
Chalone Vineyard
   Soledad, CA...................831-678-1717
Chambord
   Louisville, KY.................800-523-3811
Champoeg Wine Cellars Inc
   Aurora, OR....................503-678-2144
Channing Rudd Cellars
   Middletown, CA................707-987-2209
Chappellet Winery
   St Helena, CA.................800-494-6379
Charles B. Mitchell Vineyards
   Somerset, CA..................800-704-9463
Charles Spinetta Winery
   Plymouth, CA..................209-245-3384
Chateau Anne Marie
   Carlton, OR...................503-864-2991
Chateau Boswell Winery
   St Helena, CA.................707-963-5472
Chateau Chevre Winery
   Napa, CA......................707-944-2184
Chateau des Charmes Wines
   St. Davids, ON................800-263-2541
Chateau Diana Winery
   Healdsburg, CA................707-433-6992
Chateau Grand Traverse Winery
   Traverse City, MI.............231-938-6120
Chateau Julien Winery
   Carmel, CA....................831-624-2600
Chateau LA Fayette Reneau
   Hector, NY....................800-469-9463
Chateau Montelena Winery
   Calistoga, CA.................707-942-5105
Chateau Morrisette Winery
   Floyd, VA.....................540-593-2865
Chateau Potelle Winery
   St Helena, CA.................707-255-9440
Chateau Ra-Ha
   Jerseyville, IL...............866-639-4832
Chateau Souverain
   Cloverdale, CA................877-687-9463
Chateau St Jean Winery
   Kenwood, CA...................707-833-4134
Chatom Vineyards Inc
   San Andreas, CA...............800-435-8852
Chestnut Mountain Winery
   Hoschton, GA..................770-867-6914
Chicama Vineyards
   West Tisbury, MA..............888-244-2262
Chimere Winery
   Santa Maria, CA...............805-928-5611
Chouinard Vineyards & Winery
   Castro Valley, CA.............510-582-9900
Christine Woods Winery
   Philo, CA.....................707-895-2115
Christopher Creek Winery
   Healdsburg, CA................707-433-2001
Cienega Valley Winery/DeRose
   Hollister, CA.................831-636-9143
Cimarron Cellars
   Caney, OK.....................580-889-5997
Cinnabar Winery
   Saratoga, CA..................408-867-1010
City Brewing Company
   La Crosse, WI.................608-785-4200
Claiborne & Churchill Vintners
   San Luis Obispo, CA...........805-544-4066
Clear Creek Distillery
   Portland, OR..................503-248-9470
Cline Cellars
   Sonoma, CA....................800-543-2070
Clos Du Bois Winery
   Geyserville, CA...............800-222-3189
Clos Du Lac Cellars
   Ione, CA......................209-274-2238
Clos Du Val Co LTD
   Napa, CA......................707-261-5200
Clos Pegase Winery
   Calistoga, CA.................800-866-8583
Cloudstone Vineyards
   Los Altos Hills, CA...........650-948-8621
Clover Hill Vineyards & Winery
   Breinigsville, PA.............800-256-8374
Cocktail Kits 2 Go LLC
   New York, NY..................917-750-3998
Cocolalla Winery
   Cocolalla, ID.................208-263-3774
Colorado Cellars
   Palisade, CO..................970-464-7921

Columbia Winery
   Woodinville, WA...............425-488-2776
Concannon Vineyard
   Livermore, CA.................800-258-9866
Conneaut Cellars Winery LLC
   Conneaut Lake, PA.............877-229-9463
Conrotto A. Winery
   Gilroy, CA....................408-847-2233
Coon Creek Winery
   St Helena, CA.................800-793-7960
Cooper Mountain Vineyards
   Beaverton, OR.................503-649-0027
Corby Distilleries
   Toronto, ON...................800-367-9079
Cosentino Winery
   Napa, CA......................800-764-1220
Cowie Wine Cellars & Vineyards
   Paris, AR.....................479-963-3990
Crescini Wines
   Soquel, CA....................831-462-1466
Cribari Vineyard Inc
   Fresno, CA....................800-277-9095
Cristom Vineyards
   Salem, OR.....................503-375-3068
Criveller California Corp
   Healdsburg, CA................888-849-2266
Cronin Vineyards
   Woodside, CA..................650-851-1452
Crooked Vine/Stony Ridge Wnry
   Livermore, CA.................925-449-0458
Crossings Winery
   Glenns Ferry, ID..............208-366-2539
Crown Regal Wine Cellars
   Brooklyn, NY..................718-604-1430
Cruse Winery
   Chester, SC...................803-377-3944
Cuneo Cellars
   Amity, OR.....................503-835-2782
Cuvaison Winery
   Calistoga, CA.................707-942-6266
Cygnet Cellars
   Hollister, CA.................831-637-7559
Dalla Valle Vineyards
   Napa, CA......................707-944-2676
Davis Bynum Winery
   Healdsburg, CA................800-826-1073
Deaver Vineyards
   Plymouth, CA..................209-245-4099
Deloach Vineyards
   Santa Rosa, CA................707-755-3300
Delorimier Winery
   Geyserville, CA...............800-546-7718
Denatale Vineyards
   Healdsburg, CA................707-431-8460
Denning's Point Distillery, LLC
   Beacon, NY....................845-476-8413
Devlin Wine Cellars
   Soquel, CA....................831-476-7288
DG Yuengling & Son, Inc.
   Pottsville, PA................570-628-4890
Diageo Canada Inc.
   Toronto, ON...................416-626-2000
Diageo North America Inc
   Norwalk, CT...................203-229-2100
Diamond Creek Vineyards
   Calistoga, CA.................707-942-6926
Diamond Water Bottling Fclty
   Hot Springs, AR...............501-623-1251
Digrazia Vineyards
   Brookfield, CT................800-230-8853
Domaine St George Winery
   Healdsburg, CA................707-433-5508
Donatoni Winery
   Inglewood, CA.................310-645-5445
Door Peninsula Winery
   Sturgeon Bay, WI..............800-551-5049
Dreyer Sonoma
   Woodside, CA..................650-851-9448
Dry Creek Vineyard
   Healdsburg, CA................800-864-9463
Duck Pond Cellars
   Dundee, OR....................800-437-3213
Duckhorn Vineyards
   St Helena, CA.................888-354-8885
Duncan Peak Vineyards
   Lafayette, CA.................925-283-3632
Dundee Wine Company
   Dundee, OR....................888-427-4953
Dunn Vineyards
   Angwin, CA....................707-965-3642
Duplin Wine Cellars
   Rose Hill, NC.................800-774-9634

Dutch Henry Winery
   Calistoga, CA.................888-224-5879
E L K Run Vineyards
   Mt Airy, MD...................800-414-2513
Eagle Crest Vineyards LLC
   Conesus, NY...................800-977-7117
East Side Winery/Oak Ridge Vineyards
   Lodi, CA......................209-369-4758
Eberle Winery
   Paso Robles, CA...............805-238-9607
Ed Oliveira Winery
   Arcata, CA....................707-822-3023
Edgewood Estate Winery
   Napa, CA......................800-755-2374
Edmunds St. John
   Berkeley, CA..................510-981-1510
Edna Valley Vineyard
   San Luis Obispo, CA...........866-979-8477
El Molino Winery
   St Helena, CA.................707-963-3632
Elk Cove Vineyards
   Gaston, OR....................877-355-2683
Elliston Vineyards
   Sunol, CA.....................925-862-2377
Enz Vineyards
   Hollister, CA.................831-637-6443
Eola Hills Wine Cellars
   Rickreall, OR.................800-291-6730
EOS Estate Winery
   Paso Robles, CA...............800-249-9463
Erath Vineyards Winery
   Dundee, OR....................800-539-5463
Esterlina Vineyard & Winery
   Healdsburg, CA................888-474-7456
Evensen Vineyards
   Oakville, CA..................707-944-2396
Eyrie Vineyards
   Mcminnville, OR...............888-440-4970
Fall Creek Vineyards
   Austin, TX....................512-476-4477
Far Niente Winery
   Oakville, CA..................707-944-2861
Farella-Park Vineyards
   Napa, CA......................707-254-9489
Farfelu Vineyards
   Flint Hill, VA................540-364-2930
Farmstead At Long Meadow Ranch
   St Helena, CA.................877-627-2645
Fenestra Winery
   Livermore, CA.................800-789-9463
Fenn Valley Vineyards
   Fennville, MI.................800-432-6265
Ferrante Winery & Ristorante
   Geneva, OH....................440-466-6046
Ferrara Winery
   Escondido, CA.................760-745-7632
Ferrari-Carano
   Healdsburg, CA................800-831-0381
Ferrigno Vineyards & Wine
   St James, MO..................573-265-7742
Fess Parker Winery
   Los Olivos, CA................800-841-1104
Ficklin Vineyards Winery
   Madera, CA....................559-674-4598
Field Stone Winery
   Healdsburg, CA................800-544-7273
Fieldbrook Valley Winery
   Mckinleyville, CA.............707-839-4140
Fife Vineyards
   Redwood Valley, CA............707-485-0323
Filsinger Vineyards & Winery
   Temecula, CA..................951-302-6363
Fiore Winery
   Pylesville, MD................410-452-0132
Firelands Winery
   Sandusky, OH..................800-548-9463
Firestone Vineyard
   Los Olivos, CA................805-688-3940
Fisher Ridge Wine Co Inc
   Charleston, WV................304-342-8702
Fisher Vineyards
   Santa Rosa, CA................707-539-7511
Fitzpatrick Winery & Lodge
   Somerset, CA..................800-245-9166
Flora Springs Winery
   St Helena, CA.................707-963-5711
Florida Caribbean Distillers
   Lake Alfred, FL...............863-956-2002
Flying Embers
   Ventura, CA
Flynn Vineyards Winery
   Rickreall, OR.................888-427-4953

Product Categories / Beverages: Alcoholic Beverages

Foley Estates Vineyard
   Lompoc, CA 805-737-6222
Folie _ Deux Winery
   Oakville, CA 800-535-6400
Foris Vineyards
   Cave Junction, OR 541-592-3752
Forman Vineyard
   St Helena, CA 707-963-3900
Fortino Winery
   Gilroy, CA 888-617-6606
Fortuna Cellars
   Davis, CA 530-756-6686
Four Sisters Winery
   Belvidere, NJ 908-475-3671
Fox Vineyards & Winery
   Social Circle, GA 770-787-5402
Foxen Foxen 7200
   Santa Maria, CA 805-937-4251
Frank Family Vineyards
   Calistoga, CA 880-574-9463
Frank-Lin Distributors
   Fairfield, CA 800-922-9363
Franklin Hill Vineyards
   Bangor, PA 888-887-2839
Franzia Winery
   Ripon, CA 209-599-4111
Fratelli Perata
   Paso Robles, CA 805-238-2809
Frederick Wildman & Sons LTD
   New York, NY 800-733-9463
Freemark Abbey Winery
   St Helena, CA 800-963-9698
Freixenet USA Inc
   Sonoma, CA 707-996-4981
Frey Vineyards
   Redwood Valley, CA. 800-760-3739
Frick Winery
   Geyserville, CA 707-857-1980
Frisinger Cellars
   Napa, CA 707-255-3749
Frog's Leap Winery
   Rutherford, CA 800-959-4704
Frontenac Point Vineyard
   Trumansburg, NY 607-387-9619
Gainey Vineyard
   Santa Ynez, CA. 805-688-0558
Galante Vineyards
   Carmel Valley, CA 800-425-2683
Galena Cellars Winery
   Galena, IL 800-397-9463
Gallup Sales Company
   Gallup, NM 505-863-5241
Gary Farrell Vineyards-Winery
   Healdsburg, CA 866-277-9463
George A Dickel & Company
   Tullahoma, TN 888-342-5352
Georgia Wines Inc
   Ringgold, GA 706-937-2177
Georis Winery
   Carmel Valley, CA 831-659-1050
Germanton Winery
   Germanton, NC 800-322-2894
Girardet Wine Cellar
   Roseburg, OR 541-679-7252
Gloria Ferrer Champagne
   Sonoma, CA 707-933-1917
Gloria Winery & Vineyard
   Springfield, MO 417-926-6263
Glunz Family Winery & Cellars
   Grayslake, IL. 847-548-9463
Golden City Brewery
   Golden, CO 303-279-8092
Good Harbor Vineyards & Winery
   Lake Leelanau, MI 231-256-7165
Goodson Brothers Coffee
   Knoxville, TN 800-737-1519
Grand River Cellars
   Madison, OH 440-298-9838
Grand Teton Brewing Co
   Victor, ID. 888-899-1656
Grande River Vineyards
   Palisade, CO 800-264-7696
Granite Springs Winery
   Somerset, CA 800-638-6041
Great Divide Brewing Co
   Denver, CO 303-296-9460
Greenfield Wine Company
   Vallejo, CA 707-552-5199
Greenwood Ridge Vineyards
   Philo, CA 707-895-2002
Groth Vineyards & Winery
   Oakville, CA. 707-944-0290

Groupe Paul Masson
   Longueuil, QC 514-878-3050
Gruet Winery
   Albuquerque, NM. 888-857-9463
Guenoc & Langtry Estate
   Middletown, CA 707-995-7501
Guglielmo Winery
   Morgan Hill, CA. 408-779-2145
Guilliams Winery
   St Helena, CA 707-963-9059
Gundlach-Bundschu Winery
   Sonoma, CA 707-939-3015
H Coturri & Sons Winery
   Glen Ellen, CA 866-268-8774
Habersham Vineyards & Winery
   Helen, GA 706-878-9463
Hafner Vineyard
   Healdsburg, CA 707-433-4606
Hahn Family Wines
   Soledad, CA 831-678-4555
Haight Brown Vineyard
   Litchfield, CT 800-577-9463
Hallcrest Vineyards
   Felton, CA 831-335-4441
Handley Cellars
   Philo, CA 800-733-3151
Hanzell Vineyards
   Sonoma, CA 707-996-3860
Harbor Winery
   West Sacramento, CA 916-371-6776
Harmony Cellars
   Harmony, CA 800-432-9239
Harpersfield Vineyard
   Geneva, OH. 440-466-4739
Hart Winery
   Temecula, CA 877-638-8788
Hartford Family Winery
   Forestville, CA 707-887-8030
Hazlitt 1852 Vineyards
   Hector, NY 888-750-0494
Heartland Vinyards
   Westlake, OH 440-871-0701
Heck Cellars
   Arvin, CA. 661-854-6120
Hecker Pass Winery
   Gilroy, CA 408-842-8755
Hegy's South Hills Vineyard & Winery
   Twin Falls, ID 208-599-0074
Heineman Winery
   Put In Bay, OH 419-285-2811
Helena View/Johnston Vineyard
   Calistoga, CA 707-942-4956
Hells Canyon Winery
   Caldwell, ID 800-318-7873
Henry Estate Winery
   Umpqua, OR. 800-782-2686
Henry Hill & Co
   Napa, CA. 707-253-1663
Heritage Wine Cellars
   North East, PA. 800-747-0083
Hermann J. Wiemer Vineyard
   Dundee, NY 800-371-7971
Hermannhof Vineyards
   Hermann, MO 800-393-0100
Heron Hill Winery
   Hammondsport, NY 800-441-4241
Hess Collection
   Napa, CA 707-255-1144
Hidden Mountain Ranch Winery
   Paso Robles, CA 805-226-9907
Highland Manor Winery
   Jamestown, TN 931-879-9519
Highwood Distillers
   High River, AB 403-652-3202
Hillcrest Vineyards
   Roseburg, OR 541-673-3709
Hinzerling Winery
   Prosser, WA 800-727-6702
Hiram Walker & Sons
   Windsor, ON 519-254-5171
Homewood Winery
   Sonoma, CA 707-996-6353
Honeywood Winery
   Salem, OR 800-726-4101
Honig Vineyard and Winery
   Rutherford, CA 800-929-2217
Hood River Distillers Inc
   Hood River, OR 541-386-1588
Hood River Vineyards and Winery
   Hood River, OR 541-386-3772
Hoodsport Winery
   Hoodsport, WA 800-580-9894

Hop Kiln Winery
   Healdsburg, CA 707-433-6491
Hopkins Vineyard
   Warren, CT 860-868-7954
Horizon Cellars Winery
   Siler City, NC 919-742-1404
Hubers Orchard Winery-Vineyards
   Borden, IN. 800-345-9463
Hudson Valley Brewery
   Beacon, NY 845-218-9156
Hudson Valley Farmhouse Cider
   Staatsburg, NY 845-266-3979
Hunt Country Vineyards
   Branchport, NY. 800-946-3289
Husch Vineyards & Winery
   Philo, CA. 800-554-8724
Hyde Park Brewing Company
   Hyde Park, NY 845-229-8277
Ingleside Vineyards
   Colonial Beach, VA 804-224-8687
Inniskillin Wines
   Niagara-On-The-Lake, ON. 888-466-4754
Ipswich Ale Brewery
   Ipswich, MA 978-356-3329
Iron Horse Vineyards
   Sebastopol, CA. 707-887-1507
Ironstone Vineyards
   Murphys, CA. 209-728-1251
J Filippi Winery
   Rancho Cucamonga, CA 909-899-5755
J Lohr Vineyards & Wines
   San Jose, CA 408-288-5057
J. Fritz Winery
   Cloverdale, CA 800-418-9463
J. Stonestreet & Sons Vineyard
   Healdsburg, CA 800-355-8008
Jack Daniel Distillery
   Lynchburg, TN 888-551-5225
Jodar Vineyard & Winery
   Placerville, CA 530-644-3474
Johlin Century Winery
   Oregon, OH. 419-693-6288
Johnson's Alexander Valley Wines
   Healdsburg, CA 800-888-5532
Johnston's Winery Inc
   Ballston Spa, NY 518-882-6310
Jones Brewing Company
   Smithton, PA 724-483-2400
Joseph Swan Vineyards
   Forestville, CA 707-573-3747
Joullian Vineyards
   Carmel Valley, CA 866-659-8101
Justin Vineyards & Winery LLC
   Paso Robles, CA. 800-237-4152
Kalin Cellars
   Novato, CA 415-883-3543
Kate's Vineyard
   Napa, CA. 707-255-2644
Kathryn Kennedy Winery
   Saratoga, CA 408-867-4170
Kelley's Island Wine Company
   Kelleys Island, OH 419-746-2678
Kelson Creek Winery
   Plymouth, CA 209-245-4700
Kendall-Jackson
   Fulton, CA 866-287-9818
King Brewing Company
   Pontiac, MI 248-745-5900
King Estate Winery
   Eugene, OR. 800-884-4441
Kiona Vineyards Winery
   Benton City, WA 509-588-6716
Kirigin Cellars
   Gilroy, CA 408-847-8827
Kistler Vineyards
   Sebastopol, CA 707-823-5603
Kittling Ridge Estate Wines & Spirits
   Vaughan, ON. 800-461-9463
Klingshirn Winery
   Avon Lake, OH 440-933-6666
Knapp Vineyards
   Romulus, NY 800-869-9271
Koryo Winery Company
   Gardena, CA 310-532-9616
Kramer Vineyards
   Gaston, OR 800-619-4637
Kunde Estate Winery
   Kenwood, CA 707-833-5501
L Mawby Vineyards
   Peshawbestown, MI 231-271-3522
La Abra Farm & Winery
   Lovingston, VA. 434-263-5392

Product Categories / Beverages: Alcoholic Beverages

LA Buena Vida Vineyards
  Grapevine, TX 817-481-9463
LA Chiripada Winery
  Dixon, NM 800-528-7801
LA Rocca Vineyards & Winery
  Forest Ranch, CA 800-808-9463
LA Vina Winery
  Anthony, NM 575-882-7632
Labatt Brewing Company
  Toronto, ON 800-268-2337
Laetitia Vineyard & Winery
  Arroyo Grande, CA 888-809-8463
Lafollette Vineyard & Winery
  Sebastopol, CA 707-395-3902
Laird & Company
  Scobeyville, NJ 877-438-5247
Lake Sonoma Winery
  Glen Ellen, CA 877-586-2796
Lakeridge Winery & Vineyards
  Clermont, FL 800-768-9463
Lakeshore Winery
  Romulus, NY 315-549-7075
Lakewood Vineyards Inc
  Watkins Glen, NY 877-535-9252
Lambert Bridge Winery
  Healdsburg, CA 800-975-0555
Lamoreaux Landing Wine Cellars
  Lodi, NY 607-582-6011
Lancaster County Winery LTD
  Willow Street, PA 717-464-3555
Landmark Vineyards
  Kenwood, CA 707-833-0053
Lange Estate Winery & Vineyard
  Dundee, OR. 503-538-6476
Larry's Vineyards & Winery
  Altamont, NY 518-355-7365
Latah Creek Wine Cellar
  Spokane Valley, WA 509-926-0164
Latcham Vineyards
  Somerset, CA 800-750-5591
Laurel Glen Vineyard
  Glen Ellen, CA 707-933-9877
Lava Cap Winery
  Placerville, CA 800-475-0175
Lazy Creek Vineyards
  Philo, CA. 888-529-9275
Le Vigne Winery
  Paso Robles, CA 800-891-6055
Leelanau Cellars
  Omena, MI 800-782-8128
Leidenfrost Vineyards
  Hector, NY 607-546-2800
Lemon Creek Winery
  Berrien Springs, MI 269-471-1321
Leonetti Cellar
  Walla Walla, WA 509-525-1670
Les Bourgeois Vineyards
  Rocheport, MO 800-690-1830
Lewis Cellars
  Napa, CA. 707-255-3400
Lincourt Vineyards
  Solvang, CA 805-688-8554
Little Amana Winery
  Amana, IA. 319-668-9664
Little Hills Winery
  St Charles, MO 877-584-4557
Live Oaks Winery
  Gilroy, CA 408-842-2401
Livermore Valley Cellars
  Livermore, CA 925-454-9463
Livingston Moffett Winery
  Saint Helena, CA 800-788-0370
Llano Estacado Winery
  Lubbock, TX 800-634-3854
Lockwood Vineyards
  St. Helena, CA 707-963-6925
Loew Vineyards
  Mt Airy, MD 301-831-5464
Lolonis Winery
  Walnut Creek, CA. 925-938-8066
Long Vineyards
  St Helena, CA 707-963-2496
Lost Mountain Winery
  Sequim, WA 888-683-5229
Louis M Martini Winery
  St Helena, CA 800-321-9463
Lucas Winery
  Lodi, CA 209-368-2006
Luxco Inc
  St Louis, MO. 314-772-2626
Lve & Raymond Vineyards
  St Helena, CA 800-525-2659

Lynfred Winery Inc
  Roselle, IL. 630-529-9463
M S Walker Inc
  Somerville, MA 617-776-6700
Madison Foods
  Saint Paul, MN 651-265-8212
Madison Vineyard
  Ribera, NM 575-421-8028
Madonna Estate Winery
  Napa, CA. 866-724-2993
Madrona Vineyards
  Camino, CA 530-644-5948
Magnanini Farm Winery
  Wallkill, NY 845-895-2767
Magnotta Winery Corporation
  Vaughan, ON. 800-461-9463
Mama Rap's & Winery
  Gilroy, CA. 800-842-6262
Marie Brizard Wines & Spirits
  St. Helena, CA 800-878-1123
Marietta Cellars
  Geyservill, CA 707-433-2747
Marimar Torres Estates
  Sebastopol, CA 707-823-4365
Marin Brewing Co
  Larkspur, CA. 415-461-4677
Markham Vineyards
  St Helena, CA 707-963-5292
Markko Vineyard
  Conneaut, OH. 800-252-3197
Marlow Wine Cellars
  Monteagle, TN 931-924-2120
Martin & Weyrich Winery
  Templeton, CA 805-239-1640
Mastantuono Winery
  Templeton, CA 805-238-0676
Matanzas Creek Winery
  Santa Rosa, CA. 800-500-6464
Matson Vineyards
  Redding, CA 530-222-2833
Maui Wine
  Kula, HI. 877-878-6058
Maurice Carrie Winery
  Temecula, CA. 800-716-1711
Mayacamas Vineyards & Winery
  Napa, CA. 707-224-4030
Mazzocco Vineyards
  Healdsburg, CA 800-501-8466
McCormick Distilling Co
  Weston, MO 888-640-3082
McDowell Valley Vineyards & Cellars
  Hopland, CA 707-744-1774
McHenry Vineyard
  Davis, CA 530-756-3202
McIntosh's Ohio Valley Wines
  Bethel, OH 937-379-1159
Menghini Winery
  Julian, CA 760-765-2072
Meredyth Vineyard
  Middleburg, VA 540-687-6277
Meridian Vineyards
  Napa, CA. 800-226-7133
Merryvale Vineyards
  St Helena, CA 800-326-6069
Messina Hof Winery & Resort
  Bryan, TX 979-778-9463
Michael David Winery
  Lodi, CA 888-707-9463
Michel-Schlumberger Wine Est
  Healdsburg, CA 800-447-3060
Mike's Beverage Company
  Toronto, ON 647-428-3123
Milat Vineyards Winery
  St Helena, CA 800-546-4528
Mill Creek Vineyards
  Healdsburg, CA 877-349-2121
Millbrook Vineyards
  Millbrook, NY 800-662-9463
Milliaire Winery
  Murphys, CA. 209-728-1658
Mission Mountain Winery
  Dayton, MT 406-849-5524
Mon Ami Restaurant
  Port Clinton, OH 800-777-4266
Montelle Winery
  Augusta, MO. 888-595-9463
Monterey Winery
  Gonzales, CA 831-675-4000
Montevina Winery
  Plymouth, CA 209-245-6942
Montmorenci Vineyards
  Aiken, SC 803-649-4870

Moonlight Brewing Company
  Windsor, CA. 707-528-2537
Moss Creek Winery
  Napa, CA. 707-252-1295
Mount Palomar Winery
  Temecula, CA 800-854-5177
Mt Bethel Winery
  Altus, AR 479-468-2444
Mt Eden Vineyards
  Saratoga, CA 408-867-9587
Mt Nittany Vineyard & Winery
  Centre Hall, PA 814-466-6373
Mt Pleasant Winery
  Branson, MO. 800-467-9463
Murphy Goode Estate Winery
  Geyserville, CA 707-431-7644
Nahmias et Fils
  Yonkers, NY 914-294-0055
Naked Mountain Winery Vineyard
  Markham, VA 540-364-1609
Nalle Winery
  Healdsburg, CA 707-433-1040
Nantucket Vineyard
  Nantucket, MA 508-228-9235
Napa Cellars
  Napa, CA. 800-535-6400
Napa Wine Company
  Oakville, CA. 800-848-9630
Nashoba Valley Winery
  Bolton, MA 978-779-5521
National Wine & Spirits
  Indianapolis, IN
Navarro Vineyards
  Philo, CA. 707-895-3686
Naylor Wine Cellars Inc
  Stewartstown, PA 800-292-3370
Nevada City Winery
  Nevada City, CA 800-203-9463
Nevada County Wine Guild
  Nevada City, CA 855-494-7025
New Belgium Brewing Co
  Fort Collins, CO 888-622-4044
New Hope Winery
  New Hope, PA. 800-592-9463
New Land Vineyard
  Geneva, NY 315-585-4432
Newport Vineyards & Winery
  Middletown, RI. 401-848-5161
Newton Vineyard
  St Helena, CA 707-204-7423
Nicasio Vineyards
  Soquel, CA 831-423-1073
Niche W&S
  Cedar Knolls, NJ 973-993-8450
Nichelini Family Winery Inc
  St Helena, CA 707-963-0717
Niebaum-Coppola Estate Winery
  Rutherford, CA 800-782-4266
Nissley Vineyards & Winery
  Bainbridge, PA 800-522-2387
Nordman Of California
  Sanger, CA 559-638-9923
Northern Lights Brewing Company
  Airway Heights, WA 509-242-2739
Northern Vineyards Winery
  Stillwater, MN 651-430-1032
Northville Winery & Brewing Co
  Northville, MI 248-320-6507
Nutmeg Vineyard
  Andover, CT 860-742-8402
Oak Grove Orchards Winery
  Rickreall, OR 541-364-7052
Oak Knoll Winery
  Hillsboro, OR. 800-625-5665
Oak Ridge Winery LLC
  Lodi, CA 209-369-4758
Oak Spring Winery
  Altoona, PA 814-946-3799
Oasis Winery
  Hume, VA 800-304-7656
Obester Winery
  Half Moon Bay, CA 650-726-9463
Ocena Wineary & Vineyards
  New Era, MI 231-861-4657
Ogeki Sake USA Inc
  Hollister, CA 831-637-9217
Ojai Vineyard
  Oak View, CA 805-649-1674
Old Creek Ranch Winery
  Ventura, CA 805-649-4132
Old Mill Winery
  Geneva, OH. 440-466-5560

Product Categories / Beverages: Alcoholic Beverages

Old Rip Van Winkle Distillery
   Frankfort, KY 502-897-9113
Old South Winery
   Natchez, MS 601-445-9924
Old Wine Cellar
   Amana, IA 319-622-3116
Olde Heurich Brewing Company
   Washington, DC 202-333-2313
Olympic Cellars
   Port Angeles, WA 360-452-0160
One Vineyard and Winery
   Saint Helena, CA 707-963-1123
Optima Wine Cellars
   Healdsburg, CA 707-431-8222
Opus One
   Oakville, CA 800-292-6787
Orange County Distillery
   Goshen, NY 845-651-2929
Orchard Heights Winery
   Salem, OR 503-391-7308
Orfila Vineyards
   Escondido, CA 760-738-6500
Organic Wine Co Inc
   San Francisco, CA 888-326-9463
Ormand Peugeog Corporation
   Miami, FL 305-624-6834
Orr Mountain Winery
   Madisonville, TN 423-442-5340
Pabst Brewing Company
   San Antonio, TX 800-947-2278
Pacheco Ranch Winery
   Novato, CA 415-883-5583
Pacific Echo Cellars
   Philo, CA 707-895-2065
Pacific Hop Exchange Brewing Company
   Novato, CA 415-884-2820
Page Mill Winery
   Livermore, CA 925-456-7676
Pahlmeyer Winery
   St Helena, CA 707-255-2321
Pahrump Valley Winery
   Pahrump, NV 800-368-9463
Palmer Vineyards Inc
   Riverhead, NY 800-901-8783
Panther Creek Cellars
   Dundee, OR. 503-472-8080
Pantry Shelf/Mixxm
   Hutchinson, KS 800-968-3346
Paper City Brewery
   Holyoke, MA 413-535-1588
Paradise Valley Vineyards
   Phoenix, AZ 602-233-8727
Paraiso Vineyards
   Soledad, CA 831-678-0300
Pastori Winery
   Cloverdale, CA 707-857-3418
Paumanok Vineyards
   Aquebogue, NY 631-722-8800
Peaceful Bend Winery
   Steelville, MO 573-775-3000
Peconic Bay Winery
   Cutchogue, NY 631-734-7361
Pedrizzetti Winery
   Morgan Hill, CA 408-779-7389
Pedroncelli J Winery
   Geyserville, CA 800-836-3894
Peju Province Winery
   Rutherford, CA 800-446-7358
Pellegrini Wine Co
   Santa Rosa, CA 800-891-0244
Penn Shore Winery Vineyards
   North East, PA 814-725-8688
Pennsylvania Renaissance Faire
   Manheim, PA 717-664-0476
Pernod Ricard USA
   New York, NY 212-372-5400
Perry Creek Winery
   Somerset, CA 800-880-4026
Pete's Brewing Company
   San Antonio, TX 800-877-7383
Peter Michael Winery
   Calistoga, CA 800-354-4459
Peterson & Sons Winery
   Kalamazoo, MI 269-626-9755
Pharmco Aaper
   Brookfield, CT 203-740-3471
Pheasant Ridge Winery
   Lubbock, TX 806-746-6033
Philip Togni Vineyard
   St Helena, CA 707-963-3731
Phillips Beverage Company
   Minneapolis, MN 612-362-7500

Piedmont Vineyards & Winery
   Middleburg, VA 540-687-5528
Piedra Creek Winery
   San Luis Obispo, CA 805-541-1281
Pikes Peak Vineyards
   Colorado Springs, CO. 719-576-0075
Pindar Vineyards
   Peconic, NY 631-734-6200
Pine Ridge Vineyards
   Napa, CA. 800-575-9777
Plainfield Winery & Tasting Rm
   Plainfield, IN. 888-761-9463
Plam Vineyards & Winery
   La Quinta, CA 760-972-4465
Plum Creek Winery
   Palisade, CO. 970-464-7586
Plymouth Colony Winery
   Plymouth, MA. 508-747-3334
Pommeraie Winery
   Sebastopol, CA 707-823-9463
Ponderosa Valley Vineyard
   Ponderosa, NM 800-946-3657
Ponzi Vineyards
   Sherwood, OR. 503-628-1227
Porter Creek Vineyards
   Healdsburg, CA 707-433-6321
Prager Winery & Port Works
   St Helena, CA 800-969-7678
Presque Isle Wine Cellars
   North East, PA. 800-488-7492
Preston Premium Wines
   Pasco, WA 509-545-1990
Preston Vineyards & Winery
   Healdsburg, CA 800-305-9707
Prince Michel
   Leon, VA 800-869-8242
Prohibition Distillery, LLC
   Roscoe, NY 917-685-8989
Quady Winery
   Madera, CA 800-733-8068
Quail Ridge Cellars & Vineyards
   Saint Helena, CA 800-706-9463
Quilceda Creek Vintners
   Snohomish, WA 360-568-2389
Quivira Vineyards & Winery
   Healdsburg, CA 800-292-8339
R.H. Phillips
   Esparto, CA 530-662-3504
Rabbit Ridge Winery
   Paso Robles, CA 805-467-3331
Radanovich Vineyards & Winery
   Mariposa, CA 209-966-3187
Rainbow Hills Vineyards
   Newcomerstown, OH 740-545-9305
Rancho De Philo Winery
   Rancho Cucamonga, CA 909-987-4208
Rancho Sisquoc Winery
   Santa Maria, CA 805-934-4332
Rapazzini Winery
   Gilroy, CA. 800-842-6262
Ravenswood Winery
   Sonoma, CA 866-568-3946
Rebec Vineyards
   Amherst, VA 434-946-5168
Redhawk Vineyard & Winery
   Salem, OR. 503-362-1596
Reeve Wines
   Healdsburg, CA 707-235-6345
Refresco Beverages US Inc.
   Tampa, FL. 888-260-3776
Renaissance Vineyard & Winery
   Oregon House, CA 800-655-3277
Renault Winery
   Egg Harbor City, NJ 609-965-2111
Renwood Winery
   Plymouth, CA 800-348-8466
Retzlaff Vineyards
   Livermore, CA 925-447-8941
Richard L. Graeser Winery
   Calistoga, CA 707-942-4437
Richardson Vineyards
   Sonoma, CA 707-938-2610
Richland Beverage Association
   Carrollton, TX. 214-357-0248
Ridge Vineyards Inc
   Cupertino, CA 408-867-3233
Ritchie Creek Vineyard
   St Helena, CA 707-963-4661
River Run Vintners
   Watsonville, CA 831-726-3112
Roberian Vineyards
   Forestville, NY 716-679-1620

Robert F Pliska & Company Winery
   Purgitsville, WV 877-747-2737
Robert Keenan Winery
   St Helena, CA 707-963-9177
Robert Mondavi Winery
   Oakville, CA 888-766-6328
Robert Mueller Cellars
   Windsor, CA 707-837-7399
Robert Pecota Winery
   Calistoga, CA 707-479-7770
Robert Sinskey Vineyards Inc
   Napa, CA. 800-869-2030
Robller Vineyard Winery
   New Haven, MO 573-237-3986
Roche Caneros Estate Winery
   Sonoma, CA 800-825-9475
Rodney Strong Vineyards
   Healdsburg, CA 800-474-9463
Rogue Ales Brewery
   Newport, OR 541-265-3188
Rombauer Vineyards
   St Helena, CA 800-622-2206
Rose Creek Vineyards
   Hagerman, ID 208-837-4353
Rosenblum Cellars
   Alameda, CA 510-865-7007
Roudon-Smith Vineyards
   Saratoga, CA 831-438-1244
Round Hill Vineyards
   St Helena, CA 800-778-0424
Rudd Winery
   Oakville, CA 707-944-8577
Rutherford Hill Winery
   Rutherford, CA 707-963-1871
Saddleback Cellars
   Oakville, CA 707-944-1305
Sainte Genevieve Winery
   Ste Genevieve, MO 800-398-1298
Saintsbury
   Napa, CA. 707-252-0592
Sakeone Corp
   Forest Grove, OR 800-550-7253
Salamandre Wine Cellars
   Aptos, CA 831-685-0321
Salishan Vineyards
   La Center, WA. 360-263-2713
San Dominique Winery
   Camp Verde, AZ 480-945-8583
Sand Castle Winery
   Erwinna, PA 800-722-9463
Sandia Shadows Vineyard & Winery
   Albuquerque, NM. 505-856-1006
Sanford Winery
   Lompoc, CA 800-426-9463
Santa Barbara Winery
   Santa Barbara, CA 805-963-3633
Santa Cruz Mountain Vineyard
   Felton, CA. 831-426-6209
Santa Fe Vineyards
   Espanola, NM 505-753-8100
Santa Ynez Wine Corp
   Los Olivos, CA 800-824-8584
Sarah's Vineyard
   Gilroy, CA. 408-842-4278
Saranac Brewery
   Utica, NY 800-765-6288
Satiety Winery & Cafe
   Davis, CA 530-757-2699
Saucilito Canyon Vineyard
   San Luis Obispo, CA 805-543-2111
Sausal Winery
   Healdsburg, CA 800-500-2285
Savannah Chanelle Vineyards
   Saratoga, CA 408-741-2934
Sawtooth Winery
   Nampa, ID. 208-467-1200
Sazerac Co Inc
   New Orleans, LA 504-831-9450
Sazerac Company, Inc.
   Metairie, LA 866-729-3722
Scenic Valley Winery
   Lanesboro, MN 507-259-4981
Schirf Brewing Company
   Park City, UT 435-649-0900
Schloss Doepken Winery
   Ripley, NY 716-326-3636
Schoppaul Hill Winery atIvanhoe
   Denton, TX 940-380-9463
Schramsberg Vineyards
   Calistoga, CA 800-877-3623
Schug Carneros Estate Winery
   Sonoma, CA 800-966-9365

Product Categories / Beverages: Alcoholic Beverages

Sea Ridge Winery
  Occidental, CA 800-692-5780
Seavey Vineyard
  St Helena, CA 707-963-8339
Seghesio Family Vineyards
  Healdsburg, CA 707-433-0545
Sequoia Grove
  Napa, CA 800-851-7841
Serendipity Cellars
  Monmouth, OR 503-838-4284
Seven Hills Winery
  Walla Walla, WA 877-777-7870
Seven Lakes Vineyard & Winery
  Fenton, MI 810-373-6081
Shafer Vineyards
  Napa, CA 707-944-2877
Shallon Winery
  Astoria, OR 503-325-5978
Sharon Mill Winery
  Manchester, MI 734-971-6337
Shenandoah Vineyards
  Plymouth, CA 209-245-4455
Sierra Vista Winery
  Placerville, CA 800-946-3916
Signore Winery
  Brooktondale, NY 607-539-7935
Signorello Vineyards
  Napa, CA 707-255-5990
Silvan Ridge Winery
  Eugene, OR 541-345-1945
Silver Creek Distillers
  Rigby, ID 208-754-0042
Silver Fox Vineyards
  Mariposa, CA 209-966-4800
Silver Mountain Vineyards
  Santa Cruz, CA 408-353-2278
Silverado Vineyards Inc
  Napa, CA 800-997-1770
Simi Winery
  Healdsburg, CA 707-433-3686
Simon Levi Cellars
  Kenwood, CA 888-315-0040
Six Mile Creek Vineyard
  Ithaca, NY 800-260-0612
Sky Vineyards
  Glen Ellen, CA 707-935-1391
Slate Quarry Winery
  Nazareth, PA 610-746-3900
Smith Vineyard & Winery
  Grass Valley, CA 530-273-7032
Smith-Madrone Vineyards & Winery
  St Helena, CA 707-963-2283
Smothers Brothers Tasting Room
  Glen Ellen, CA 800-795-9463
Sobon Estate
  Plymouth, CA 209-333-6275
Sokol Blosser Winery
  Dayton, OR 800-582-6668
Solis Winery
  Gilroy, CA 888-838-6427
Sonoita Vineyards
  Elgin, AZ 520-455-5893
Sonoma Wine Services
  Vineburg, CA 707-996-9773
Sonoma-Cutrer Vineyards
  Windsor, CA 707-528-1181
Southern California Brewing Company
  Los Angeles, CA 213-622-1261
Sow's Ear Winery
  Brooksville, ME 207-326-4649
Spangler Vineyards
  Roseburg, OR 541-679-9654
Spoetzl Brewery
  Shiner, TX 361-594-3383
Spottswoode
  St Helena, CA 707-963-0134
Spring Mountain Vineyard
  St Helena, CA 877-769-4637
Springhill Cellars
  Albany, OR 541-928-1009
Spurgeon Vineyards & Winery
  Highland, WI 800-236-5555
St Arnold Brewing Co
  Houston, TX 800-801-6402
St Francis Winery & Vineyards
  Santa Rosa, CA 707-833-4668
St Innocent Winery
  Salem, OR 503-378-1526
St Julian Winery
  Paw Paw, MI 800-732-6002
St. James Winery
  Saint James, MO 800-280-9463

Stags' Leap Winery
  Napa, CA 707-944-1303
Starr & Brown
  Portland, OR 503-287-1775
Starr Hill Winery & Vineyard
  Curwensville, PA 814-236-0910
Ste Chapelle Winery
  Caldwell, ID 877-783-2427
Stearns Wharf Vintners
  Santa Barbara, CA 805-966-6624
Steltzner Vineyards
  Napa, CA 800-707-9463
Sterling Vineyards
  Calistoga, CA 707-942-3344
Steuk's Country Market & Winery
  Sandusky, OH 419-625-8324
Stevenot Winery
  Murphys, CA 209-728-3485
Stevens Point Brewery
  Stevens Point, WI 800-369-4911
Stone Hill Winery
  Hermann, MO 573-486-2221
Stonegate
  St Helena, CA 707-603-2203
Stoneridge Winery
  Sutter Creek, CA 209-223-1761
Stonington Vineyards
  Stonington, CT 800-421-9463
Stony Hill Vineyard
  St Helena, CA 707-963-2636
Stonybrook Mountain Winery
  Calistoga, CA 707-942-5282
Storrs Winery
  Santa Cruz, CA 831-458-5030
Story Winery
  Plymouth, CA 800-712-6390
Stoutridge Vineyard
  Marlboro, NY
Straub Brewery Inc
  St Marys, PA 814-834-2875
Streblow Vineyards
  Saint Helena, CA 707-963-5892
Stryker Sonoma
  Geyserville, CA 800-433-1944
Sudwerk Privatbrauerei Hubsch
  Davis, CA 530-758-8700
Sugar Creek Winery
  Defiance, MO 636-987-2400
Sullivan Vineyards
  St Helena, CA 877-244-7337
Summit Brewing Company
  Saint Paul, MN 651-265-7800
Summit Lake Vineyards
  Angwin, CA 707-965-2488
Sunrise Winery
  San Jose, CA 408-741-1310
Sutter Home Winery
  St Helena, CA 800-967-4663
Sweet Traders
  Huntington Beach, CA 714-903-6800
Sycamore Creek
  Saint Helena, CA 800-963-9698
Takara Sake USA Inc
  Berkeley, CA 510-540-8250
Talbott Vineyards
  Salinas, CA 831-675-3000
Talley Vineyards
  Arroyo Grande, CA 805-489-2508
Tamuzza Vineyards
  Hope, NJ 856-896-0619
Taos Brewing Supply
  El Prado, NM 575-779-0449
Tarara Winery
  Leesburg, VA 703-771-7100
Taylor Wine Company
  Hammondsport, NY 607-868-3245
Terrace At J Vineyards
  Healdsburg, CA 800-885-9463
The Boisset Collection
  St. Helena, CA 707-967-7667
The Meeker Vineyard
  Healdsburg, CA 707-431-2148
The Rubin Family of Wines
  Sebastopol, CA 707-887-8130
Thoma Vineyards
  Dallas, OR 800-884-1927
Thomas Fogarty Winery
  Woodside, CA 800-247-4163
Thomas Kruse Winery
  Gilroy, CA 408-842-7016
Thornton Winery
  Temecula, CA 951-699-0099

Thorpe Vineyard
  Wolcott, NY 315-594-2502
Three Meadows Spirits LLC
  Millerton, NY 845-702-3903
Tkc Vineyards
  Plymouth, CA 888-627-2356
Tomaselli Winery
  Hammonton, NJ 800-666-9463
Topolos at Russian River Vine
  Forestville, CA 707-887-3344
Transamerica Wine Corporation
  Brooklyn, NY 718-875-4017
Trefethen Family Vineyards
  Napa, CA 707-255-7700
Trentadue Winery
  Geyserville, CA 888-332-3032
Triple Rock Brewing Co Brkly
  Berkeley, CA 510-843-2739
Truchard Vineyards
  Napa, CA 707-253-7153
Truckee River Winery
  Truckee, CA 530-587-4626
Tucker Cellars
  Sunnyside, WA 509-837-8701
Tudal Winery
  St Helena, CA 707-963-3947
Tularosa Vineyards
  Tularosa, NM 800-687-4467
Tuthilltown Spirits
  Gardiner, NY 845-255-1527
Tyee Wine Cellars
  Corvallis, OR 541-753-8754
Uinta Brewing Co
  Salt Lake City, UT 801-467-0909
US Distilled Products Co
  Princeton, MN 763-389-4903
Val Verde Winery
  Del Rio, TX 830-775-9714
Valhalla Winery
  Veneta, OR 541-935-9711
Valley of the Moon Winery
  Glen Ellen, CA 707-996-6941
Valley View Winery
  Jacksonville, OR 800-781-9463
Van Der Heyden Vineyards
  Napa, CA 800-948-9463
Vancouver Island Brewing Company
  Victoria, BC 800-663-6383
Varni Brothers/7-Up Bottling
  Modesto, CA 209-521-1777
Ventana Vineyards Winery
  Monterey, CA 800-237-8846
Vetter Vineyards Winery
  Westfield, NY 716-326-3100
Via Della Chiesa Vineyards
  Raynham, MA 508-822-7775
Viader Vineyards & Winery
  Deer Park, CA 707-963-3816
Viano Vineyards
  Martinez, CA 925-228-6465
Viansa Winery
  Sonoma, CA 800-995-4740
Vie-Del Co
  Fresno, CA 559-834-2525
Villa Helena/Arger-Martucci Winery
  St Helena, CA 707-963-4334
Villa Milan Vineyard
  Milan, IN 812-654-3419
Villa Mt. Eden Winery
  Saint Helena, CA 866-931-1624
Villar Vintners of Valdese
  Valdese, NC 828-879-3202
Vincent Arroyo Winery
  Calistoga, CA 707-942-6995
Vincor Canada
  Mississauga, ON 800-265-9463
Vinoklet Winery
  Cincinnati, OH 513-385-9309
Von Stiehl Winery
  Algoma, WI 800-955-5208
Von Strasser
  Calistoga, CA 888-359-9463
Vynecrest Winery
  Breinigsville, PA 800-361-0725
Wachusett Brewing Co
  Westminster, MA 978-874-9965
Warner Vineyards
  Paw Paw, MI 800-756-5357
Warwick Valley Winery & Distillery
  Warwick, NY 845-258-4858
Wasson Brothers Winery
  Sandy, OR 503-668-3124

Product Categories / Beverages: Beers

Weibel Vineyards
  Lodi, CA 800-932-9463
Wente Family Estates
  Livermore, CA 925-456-2305
Wermuth Winery
  Calistoga, CA 707-942-5924
West Park Wine Cellars
  West Park, NY 845-384-6709
Westbend Vinyards
  Lewisville, NC 866-901-5032
Westport Rivers Vineyard
  Westport, MA 800-993-9695
Westwood Winery
  Sonoma, CA 707-933-7837
Whaler Vineyard
  Ukiah, CA 707-462-6355
Whitcraft Winery
  Santa Barbara, CA 805-730-1086
White Oak Vineyards & Winery
  Healdsburg, CA 707-433-8429
White Rock Vineyards
  Napa, CA 707-257-7922
Whitecliff Vineyard & Winery
  Gardiner, NY 845-255-4613
Whitehall Lane Winery
  St Helena, CA 707-963-9454
Whitford Cellars
  Napa, CA 707-942-0840
Widmers Wine Cellars
  Canandaigua, NY 585-374-6311
Wiederkehr Wine Cellars Inc
  Altus, AR 800-622-9463
Wild Hog Vineyard
  Cazadero, CA 707-847-3687
Wild Horse Winery & Vineyards
  Templeton, CA 805-434-2541
Wildhurst Vineyards
  Kelseyville, CA 800-595-9463
William Grant & Sons
  Irvine, CA
William Harrison Winery LLC
  St Helena, CA 707-963-8762
William Hill Estate Winery
  Napa, CA 707-265-3024
Williams Selyem Winery
  Healdsburg, CA 707-433-6425
Williamsburg Winery LTD
  Williamsburg, VA 757-229-0999
Wimberley Valley Winery
  Driftwood, TX 512-847-2592
Windwalker Vineyards & Winery
  Somerset, CA 530-620-4054
Witness Tree Vineyard LTD
  Salem, OR 888-478-8766
Wolf Creek Winery
  Barberton, OH 800-436-0426
Wollersheim Winery
  Prairie Du Sac, WI 800-847-9463
Wooden Valley Winery
  Fairfield, CA 707-864-0730
Woodside Vineyards
  Menlo Park, CA 650-851-3144
Woodward Canyon
  Touchet, WA 509-525-4129
Worden
  Spokane, WA 509-455-7835
Wyandotte Winery LLC
  Gahanna, OH 877-906-7464
Yakima Craft Brewing Company
  Yakima, WA 509-654-7357
Yakima River Winery
  Prosser, WA 509-786-2805
Yamhill Valley Vineyards
  Mcminnville, OR 800-825-4845
York Mountain Winery
  Templeton, CA 805-237-7575
Zaca Mesa Winery
  Los Olivos, CA 800-350-7972
Zayante Vineyards
  Felton, CA 831-335-7992
Zd Wines
  Napa, CA 800-487-7757

Beers

AB InBev
  St. Louis, MO 314-577-7427
Abita Brewing Co
  Covington, LA 800-737-2311
Alaskan Brewing Company
  Juneau, AK 907-780-5866
AleSmith Brewing Company
  San Diego, CA 858-549-9888
Alley Kat Brewing Co, Ltd
  Edmonton, AB 780-436-8922
Amstell Holding
  New Bedford, MA 508-995-6100
Amsterdam Brewing Company
  Toronto, ON 416-504-6882
Anchor Brewing Company
  San Francisco, CA 415-863-8350
Anderson Valley Brewing Co
  Boonville, CA 800-207-2237
Andrews Brewing Co
  Andrews, NC 828-321-2006
Anheuser-Busch
  St. Louis, MO 800-342-5283
Apani Southwest
  Abilene, TX 325-690-1550
Arnold Foods Company
  Horsham, PA 800-984-0989
Assets Grille & Southwest Brewing Company
  Albuquerque, NM 505-889-6400
Atwater Block Brewing Company
  Detroit, MI 313-877-9205
August Schell Brewing Co
  New Ulm, MN. 800-770-5020
Avery Brewing Company
  Boulder, CO 877-844-5679
Bad Frog Brewery Co
  St Augustine, FL 888-223-3764
Baltimore Brewing Company
  Baltimore, MD 410-837-5000
Bar Harbor Brewing Company
  Bar Harbor, ME. 207-288-4592
Bay Hawk Ales
  Irvine, CA 949-442-7565
Beaver Street Brewery
  Flagstaff, AZ 928-779-0079
Bell's Brewery Inc
  Kalamazoo, MI 269-382-2338
Belmont Brewing Co
  Long Beach, CA 562-433-3891
Berghoff Brewery
  Chicago, IL 608-358-4992
Berkshire Brewing Co Inc
  South Deerfield, MA 877-222-7468
Big Bucks Brewery & Steakhouse
  Gaylord, MI. 989-731-0401
Big Rock Brewery
  Calgary, AB. 800-242-3107
Big Sky Brewing Co
  Missoula, MT 800-559-2774
Bison Brewing Company
  Berkeley, CA. 510-697-1537
BJ's Restaurants Inc.
  Huntington Beach, CA 714-500-2400
Bloomington Brewing Co
  Bloomington, IN 812-323-2112
Blue Point Brewing Co
  Patchogue, NY 631-475-6944
Bluegrass Brewing Company
  Louisville, KY 502-899-7070
Bohemian Brewery
  Midvale, UT 801-566-5474
Boston Beer Co Inc.
  Boston, MA. 888-661-2337
Boston Stoker
  Vandalia, OH. 937-890-6401
Boulder Beer
  Boulder, CO 303-444-8448
Boulder Creek Brewing Company
  Boulder Creek, CA 831-338-7882
Boulevard Brewing
  Kansas City, MO 816-474-7095
Bow Valley Brewing Company
  Canmore, AB 403-678-2739
Brasserie Brasal Brewery
  Lasalle, QC 800-463-2728
Breckenridge Brewery
  Denver, CO 800-328-6723
Brewers Association
  Boulder, CO 888-822-6273
Brewery Ommegang
  Cooperstown, NY 800-544-1809
Brick Brewery
  Kitchener, ON 800-505-8971
Bristol Brewing Co
  Colorado Springs, CO. 719-368-6120
Broadhead Brewing Co
  Orl,ans, ON 613-830-3944
Broken Bow Brewery
  Tuckahoe, NY 914-268-0900
Brooklyn Brew Shop
  Brooklyn, NY 718-874-0119
Brooklyn Brewery
  Brooklyn, NY 718-486-7422
Browns Brewing Co
  Troy, NY 518-273-2337
Buffalo Bill Brewing Company
  Hayward, CA 510-886-9823
Bull and Barrel Brewpub
  Brewster, NY 845-278-2855
Calapooia Brewing Co
  Albany, OR 541-928-1931
Capalbo's Fruit Baskets
  Clifton, NJ. 800-252-6262
Capital Brewery & Beer Garden
  Middleton, WI. 608-836-7100
Captain Lawrence Brewing Co
  Elmsford, NY 914-741-2337
Carolina Brewery
  Chapel Hill, NC 919-942-1800
Carta Blanca
  El Paso, TX. 915-544-6367
Catskill Brewery
  Livingston Manor, NY 845-439-1232
Champion Beverages
  Darien, CT 203-655-9026
Christopher Joseph Brewing Company
  Paradise Valley, AZ. 480-948-7882
Cisco Brewers
  Nantucket, MA 508-325-5929
City Brewing Company
  La Crosse, WI 608-785-4200
Clemson Bros. Brewery
  Middletown, NY 845-775-4638
Clipper City Brewing
  Halethorpe, MD 410-247-7822
Columbus Brewing Co
  Columbus, OH 614-464-2739
Copper Tank Brewing Company
  Austin, TX. 512-854-9380
Craft Brew Alliance
  Portland, OR 503-331-7270
Creemore Springs Brewery
  Creemore, ON 800-267-2240
Criveller California Corp
  Healdsburg, CA 888-849-2266
Crooked River Brewing Company
  Cleveland, OH 216-771-2337
Crowley Beverage Corporation
  Wayland, MA 800-997-3337
Dempsey's Restaurant & Brewery
  Petaluma, CA 707-765-9694
Deschutes Brewery
  Bend, OR. 541-385-8606
DG Yuengling & Son, Inc.
  Pottsville, PA. 570-628-4890
Dl Geary Brewing
  Portland, ME. 207-878-2337
Dogfish Head Craft Brewery
  Lewes, DE. 888-834-3474
Dogwood Brewing Company
  Atlanta, GA 404-367-0500
Drakes Brewing Co
  San Leandro, CA 510-568-2739
Durango Brewing Co
  Durango, CO. 970-247-3396
Eastern Brewing Corporation
  Hammonton, NJ 609-561-2700
El Toro Brew Pub
  Morgan Hill, CA. 408-782-2739
Etna Brewing Co
  Etna, CA 530-467-5277
Falla Imports
  Greenville, ME 609-476-4106
Flagstaff Brewing Co
  Flagstaff, AZ. 928-773-1442
Florida Brewery
  Auburndale, FL 863-965-1825
Flying Dog Brewery
  Frederick, MD. 301-694-7899
Fort Garry Brewing Company
  Winnipeg, MB. 204-487-3678
Fox N Hare Brewing Co.
  Port Jervis, NY 845-672-0100
French's Coffee
  Walnut Creek, CA. 925-932-5901
Full Sail Brewing Co
  Hood River, OR 888-244-2337
Gambrinus Co
  San Antonio, TX 210-490-9128
Garrison Brewing
  Halifax, NS 902-453-5343
Genesee Brewing Company
  Rochester, NY. 585-263-9200

Product Categories / Beverages: Beers

Gentle Ben's Brewing Co
　Tucson, AZ 520-624-4177
Golden City Brewery
　Golden, CO 303-279-8092
Goose Island Beer Co
　Chicago, IL 800-466-7363
Gordon Biersch Brewery Restaurant
　San Jose, CA 408-278-1008
Grain Belt
　New Ulm, MN. 800-770-5020
Grand Teton Brewing Co
　Victor, ID 888-899-1656
Gray's Brewing Co
　Janesville, WI 608-752-3552
Great Divide Brewing Co
　Denver, CO 303-296-9460
Great Lakes Brewing Co.
　Cleveland, OH 216-771-4404
Great Lakes Wine & Spirits
　Highland Park, MI 313-453-2200
Great Northern Brewing Co
　Whitefish, MT 406-863-1000
Great Western Brewing Company
　Saskatoon, SK. 800-764-4492
Guinness Import Co
　Stamford, CT 800-521-1591
Hair Of The Dog Brewing
　Portland, OR 503-232-6585
Hale's Brewery
　Seattle, WA 206-782-0737
Harpoon Brewery
　Boston, MA 800-427-7666
Heartland Brewery
　New York, NY 212-400-2300
Hog Haus Brewing Company
　Fayetteville, AR 479-521-2739
Hogtown Brewing Company
　Mississauga, ON. 905-855-9065
Hornell Brewing Company
　New Hyde Park, NY 516-812-0300
Humboldt Brews LLC
　Arcata, CA 707-826-2739
Hyde Park Brewing Company
　Hyde Park, NY 845-229-8277
Ipswich Ale Brewery
　Ipswich, MA 978-356-3329
Jacob Leinenkugel Brewing Co
　Chippewa Falls, WI 715-723-5557
Jones Brewing Company
　Smithton, PA. 724-483-2400
Karl Strauss Brewing Co
　San Diego, CA 858-273-2739
Keegan Ales
　Kingston, NY 845-331-2739
Kevton Gourmet Tea
　Streetman, TX. 888-538-8668
Kirin Brewery
　Los Angeles, CA. 310-381-3040
Kona Brewing
　Kailua Kona, HI 808-334-1133
Krinos Foods
　Bronx, NY. 718-729-9000
La Brasserie McAuslan Brewing
　Montreal, QC 514-939-3060
Labatt Brewing Company
　Toronto, ON 800-268-2337
Lafayette Brewing Co
　Lafayette, IN. 765-742-2591
Laguna Beach Brewing Company
　Laguna Beach, CA 949-497-3381
Lakefront Brewery Inc
　Milwaukee, WI. 414-372-8800
Lakeport Brewing Corporation
　Moncton, NB 800-268-2337
Lang Creek Brewery
　Marion, MT. 406-858-2200
Left Hand Brewing Co
　Longmont, CO 303-772-0258
Legend Brewing Co
　Richmond, VA. 804-232-8871
Leinenkugel's
　Chippewa Falls, WI 888-534-6437
Les Brasseurs Du Nord
　Blainville, QC 800-378-3733
Les Brasseurs GMT
　Montreal, QC 888-253-8330
Lion Brewery Inc
　Wilkes Barre, PA. 888-295-2337
Long Trail Brewing Co Inc
　Bridgewater Cors, VT. 802-672-5011
Los Gatos Brewing Company
　Los Gatos, CA. 408-395-9929

Lost Coast Brewery
　Eureka, CA 707-267-9651
M J Barleyhoppers Sports Bar
　Lewiston, ID. 800-232-6730
Magnotta Winery Corporation
　Vaughan, ON. 800-461-9463
Manhattan Beach Brewing Company
　Manhattan Beach, CA. 310-798-2744
Marin Brewing Co
　Larkspur, CA. 415-461-4677
Maritime Pacific Brewing Co
　Seattle, WA 206-782-6181
Mayer's Cider Mill
　Webster, NY 800-543-0043
Mendocino Brewing Co Inc
　Ukiah, CA. 707-463-2627
Mike's Beverage Company
　Toronto, ON 647-428-3123
Millrose Restaurant
　South Barrington, IL. 800-464-5576
Millstream Brewing Co
　Amana, IA. 319-622-3672
Mishawaka Brewing Company
　Granger, IN. 574-256-9993
Moet Hennessy USA
　New York, NY 212-251-8200
Molson Coors Beverage Company
　Chicago, IL 800-645-5376
Molson Coors North America
　Chicago, IL 800-645-5376
Moonlight Brewing Company
　Windsor, CA 707-528-2537
Moosehead Breweries Ltd.
　St. John, NB
Mountain Sun Pubs & Breweries
　Boulder, CO 303-546-0886
Nevada City Brewing
　Nevada City, CA. 530-265-2446
New Belgium Brewing Co
　Fort Collins, CO 888-622-4044
New Glarus Brewing CompaNy
　New Glarus, WI 608-527-5850
New Holland Brewing Co
　Holland, MI. 616-355-6422
Newburgh Brewing Company
　Newburgh, NY 845-569-2337
North American Breweries Inc.
　Rochester, NY. 585-546-1030
Northampton Brewing Company
　Northampton, MA. 413-584-9903
Northern Breweries
　Marie, ON 514-908-7545
Northern Lights Brewing Company
　Airway Heights, WA. 509-242-2739
Northville Winery & Brewing Co
　Northville, MI. 248-320-6507
Nutfield Brewing Company
　Derry, NH 603-434-9678
Oak Creek Brewing Company
　Sedona, AZ. 928-204-1300
Odell Brewing Co
　Fort Collins, CO 970-498-9070
Okanagan Spring Brewery
　Vernon, BC 800-652-0755
Oland Breweries
　Halifax, NS 800-268-2337
Old Credit Brewing Co. Ltd.
　Toronto, ON 416-494-2766
Olde Heurich Brewing Company
　Washington, DC 202-333-2313
Onalaska Brewing
　Onalaska, WA. 360-978-4253
Oskar Blues Brewery
　Longmont, CO 303-776-1914
Pabst Brewing Company
　San Antonio, TX. 800-947-2278
Pacific Coast Brewing
　Oakland, CA 510-836-2739
Pacific Hop Exchange Brewing Company
　Novato, CA 415-884-2820
Pacific Western Brewing Company
　Prince George, BC 250-562-2424
Palmetto Brewing Co
　Charleston, SC 843-937-0903
Paper City Brewery
　Holyoke, MA 413-535-1588
Peekskill Brewery
　Peekskill, N7. 914-734-2337
Pennsylvania Brewing Company
　Pittsburgh, PA. 412-237-9400
Pete's Brewing Company
　San Antonio, TX. 800-877-7383

Pike Brewing Co
　Seattle, WA 206-622-6044
Pittsburgh Brewing Co
　Pittsburgh, PA. 412-682-7400
Prescott Brewing Co
　Prescott, AZ 928-771-2795
Pyramid Alehouse-Seattle
　Seattle, WA 206-682-3377
Red Brick Brewing Company
　Atlanta, GA 800-475-5417
Red White & Brew
　Redding, CA 530-222-5891
Redhook Brewery
　Portland, OR 503-331-7270
Remarkable Liquids
　Altamont, NY 518-861-5351
Richland Beverage Association
　Carrollton, TX. 214-357-0248
River Market Brewing Company
　Kansas City, MO. 816-471-6300
Rock Bottom Restaurant & Brewery
　Denver, CO 303-534-7616
Rogue Ales Brewery
　Newport, OR. 541-265-3188
Rohrbach Brewing Co
　Rochester, NY. 585-594-9800
Russell Breweries, Inc.
　Surrey, BC 604-599-1190
Santa Cruz Mountain Brewing
　Santa Cruz, CA 831-425-4900
Santa Fe Brewing Co
　Santa Fe, NM 505-424-3333
Sapporo USA, Inc.
　New York, NY 212-922-9165
Saranac Brewery
　Utica, NY 800-765-6288
Schirf Brewing Company
　Park City, UT 435-649-0900
Schlafly Tap Room
　St Louis, MO. 314-241-2337
Sea Dog Brewing Company
　Topsham, ME 207-725-0162
Sequoia Brewing Co
　Fresno, CA 559-264-5521
Seven Barrel Brewery
　West Lebanon, NH 603-298-5566
Shipyard Brewing Co
　Portland, ME. 207-761-0807
Shipyard Brewing Co
　Portland, ME. 800-789-0684
Short's Brewing Co
　Bellaire, MI 231-498-2300
Sierra Nevada Taproom & Rstrnt
　Chico, CA 530-893-3520
Sleeman Breweries, Ltd.
　Guelph, ON. 800-268-8537
Smuttynose Brewing Co
　Portsmouth, NH 603-436-4026
Snake River Brewing Company
　Jackson, WY 307-739-2337
Southern California Brewing Company
　Los Angeles, CA. 213-622-1261
Spoetzl Brewery
　Shiner, TX. 361-594-3383
Sprecher Brewing Co
　Milwaukee, WI. 888-650-2739
St Arnold Brewing Co
　Houston, TX. 800-801-6402
St. Croix Beer Company
　Saint Paul, MN 651-387-0708
St. Stan's Brewing Company
　Modesto, CA. 209-284-0170
Stevens Point Brewery
　Stevens Point, WI 800-369-4911
Stone Brewing
　Escondido, CA 760-294-7899
StoneHammer Brewing
　Guelph, ON. 519-824-1194
Stoudt Brewing Co
　Adamstown, PA 717-484-4386
Straub Brewery Inc
　St Marys, PA 814-834-2875
Stroh Brewery
　Detroit, MI 313-446-2000
Stroh's Beer
　Detroit, MI
Sudwerk Privatbrauerei Hubsch
　Davis, CA. 530-758-8700
Summit Brewing Company
　Saint Paul, MN 651-265-7800
Sweet Water Brewing Co
　Atlanta, GA 404-691-2537

Product Categories / Beverages: Beers

Taos Brewing Supply
  El Prado, NM 575-779-0449
Taos Mesa Brewing Co
  El Prado, NM 575-758-1900
The Roscoe NY Beer Company, Inc.
  Roscoe, NY. 607-290-5002
Tin Whistle Brewing Co
  Penticton, BC 250-770-1122
Trafalgar Brewing Company
  Oakville, ON. 905-337-0133
Triple Rock Brewing Co Brkly
  Berkeley, CA. 510-843-2739
Triumph Brewing Co
  Princeton, NJ 609-924-7855
Uinta Brewing Co
  Salt Lake City, UT 801-467-0909
Unibroue/Unibrew
  Chambly, QC. 450-658-7658
Vancouver Island Brewing Company
  Victoria, BC 800-663-6383
Vino's Brew Pub
  Little Rock, AR. 501-375-8466
Wachusett Brewing Co
  Westminster, MA 978-874-9965
Wagner Vineyards
  Lodi, NY. 866-924-6378
Wellington Brewery
  Guelph, ON. 800-576-3853
Westtown Brew Works
  Westtown, NY
What's Brewing
  San Antonio, TX. 877-262-7311
Whistler Brewing Company
  Whistler, BC 604-731-2900
Whistler Brewing Company
  Whistler, BC 604-962-8889
Yakima Craft Brewing Company
  Yakima, WA 509-654-7357
Yonkers Brewing Company LLC
  Yonkers, NY 914-226-8327

American & British Ale

Amber Ale

Alaskan Brewing Company
  Juneau, AK 907-780-5866
Bull and Barrel Brewpub
  Brewster, NY 845-278-2855
Genesee Brewing Company
  Rochester, NY. 585-263-9200
Grand Teton Brewing Co
  Victor, ID. 888-899-1656
Keegan Ales
  Kingston, NY 845-331-2739
Pete's Brewing Company
  San Antonio, TX. 800-877-7383
St Arnold Brewing Co
  Houston, TX. 800-801-6402
Unibroue/Unibrew
  Chambly, QC. 450-658-7658

American Ale

Bull and Barrel Brewpub
  Brewster, NY 845-278-2855
Fox N Hare Brewing Co.
  Port Jervis, NY 845-672-0100
Newburgh Brewing Company
  Newburgh, NY 845-569-2337
Westtown Brew Works
  Westtown, NY
Yonkers Brewing Company LLC
  Yonkers, NY 914-226-8327

Black & Tan

DG Yuengling & Son, Inc.
  Pottsville, PA. 570-628-4890
Stevens Point Brewery
  Stevens Point, WI 800-369-4911

Cream Ale

Genesee Brewing Company
  Rochester, NY. 585-263-9200
Northern Lights Brewing Company
  Airway Heights, WA. 509-242-2739

India Pale Ale

Broken Bow Brewery
  Tuckahoe, NY. 914-268-0900
Bull and Barrel Brewpub
  Brewster, NY 845-278-2855

Catskill Brewery
  Livingston Manor, NY 845-439-1232
Clemson Bros. Brewery
  Middletown, NY 845-775-4638
Fox N Hare Brewing Co.
  Port Jervis, NY 845-672-0100
Golden City Brewery
  Golden, CO 303-279-8092
Hudson Valley Brewery
  Beacon, NY. 845-218-9156
Keegan Ales
  Kingston, NY 845-331-2739
Newburgh Brewing Company
  Newburgh, NY 845-569-2337
Peekskill Brewery
  Peekskill, N7. 914-734-2337
St Arnold Brewing Co
  Houston, TX. 800-801-6402
The Roscoe NY Beer Company, Inc.
  Roscoe, NY. 607-290-5002
Yonkers Brewing Company LLC
  Yonkers, NY 914-226-8327

Mild Ale

Hudson Valley Brewery
  Beacon, NY. 845-218-9156

Pale Ale

Clemson Bros. Brewery
  Middletown, NY 845-775-4638
Deschutes Brewery
  Bend, OR. 541-385-8606
DG Yuengling & Son, Inc.
  Pottsville, PA. 570-628-4890
Northern Lights Brewing Company
  Airway Heights, WA. 509-242-2739
Pete's Brewing Company
  San Antonio, TX. 800-877-7383
Stevens Point Brewery
  Stevens Point, WI 800-369-4911

Scottish Style

Genesee Brewing Company
  Rochester, NY. 585-263-9200

Belgian & French Ale

Belgian Style Blo

Newburgh Brewing Company
  Newburgh, NY 845-569-2337

Kolsch

St Arnold Brewing Co
  Houston, TX. 800-801-6402

Bottled

Alaskan Brewing Company
  Juneau, AK 907-780-5866
Arizona Beverage Company
  Cincinnati, OH 800-832-3775
August Schell Brewing Co
  New Ulm, MN. 800-770-5020
Big Rock Brewery
  Calgary, AB. 800-242-3107
Brooklyn Brewery
  Brooklyn, NY. 718-486-7422
Buffalo Bill Brewing Company
  Hayward, CA 510-886-9823
DG Yuengling & Son, Inc.
  Pottsville, PA. 570-628-4890
Jones Brewing Company
  Smithton, PA. 724-483-2400
Spaten North America Inc
  Little Neck, NY. 718-281-1912
Stevens Point Brewery
  Stevens Point, WI 800-369-4911
Straub Brewery Inc
  St Marys, PA 814-834-2875

Canned

Arizona Beverage Company
  Cincinnati, OH 800-832-3775
Jones Brewing Company
  Smithton, PA. 724-483-2400
Patagonia Provisions
  Sausalito, CA 888-221-8208
Stevens Point Brewery
  Stevens Point, WI 800-369-4911

Kegged

Bohemian Brewery
  Midvale, UT 801-566-5474
DG Yuengling & Son, Inc.
  Pottsville, PA. 570-628-4890
Golden City Brewery
  Golden, CO 303-279-8092
Jones Brewing Company
  Smithton, PA. 724-483-2400

Lager

Amber Lager

Broken Bow Brewery
  Tuckahoe, NY. 914-268-0900
Catskill Brewery
  Livingston Manor, NY 845-439-1232
DG Yuengling & Son, Inc.
  Pottsville, PA. 570-628-4890
Grain Belt
  New Ulm, MN. 800-770-5020
Hyde Park Brewing Company
  Hyde Park, NY 845-229-8277
Karl Strauss Brewing Co
  San Diego, CA 858-273-2739
Stevens Point Brewery
  Stevens Point, WI 800-369-4911
Unibroue/Unibrew
  Chambly, QC. 450-658-7658
Yonkers Brewing Company LLC
  Yonkers, NY 914-226-8327

Black Beer

Brooklyn Brewery
  Brooklyn, NY. 718-486-7422
Hyde Park Brewing Company
  Hyde Park, NY 845-229-8277

Bock

St Arnold Brewing Co
  Houston, TX. 800-801-6402

DarkLager/Dunkel

Brick Brewery
  Kitchener, ON 800-505-8971

Malt Liquor

Bad Frog Brewery Co
  St Augustine, FL 888-223-3764
Jones Brewing Company
  Smithton, PA. 724-483-2400
Mike's Beverage Company
  Toronto, ON 647-428-3123

PaleLager

Deschutes Brewery
  Bend, OR. 541-385-8606
Hyde Park Brewing Company
  Hyde Park, NY 845-229-8277

Pilsner

Anderson Valley Brewing Co
  Boonville, CA 800-207-2237
Big Rock Brewery
  Calgary, AB. 800-242-3107
Catskill Brewery
  Livingston Manor, NY 845-439-1232
Hyde Park Brewing Company
  Hyde Park, NY 845-229-8277
St Arnold Brewing Co
  Houston, TX. 800-801-6402

Non-Alcoholic

Athletic Brewing Co.
  Stratford, CT 203-273-0422
B.M. Lawrence & Company
  San Francisco, CA 415-981-2926
Jones Brewing Company
  Smithton, PA. 724-483-2400
Lion Brewery Inc
  Wilkes Barre, PA. 888-295-2337
Richland Beverage Association
  Carrollton, TX. 214-357-0248

Product Categories / Beverages: Bitters

Specialty & Cider

Draft Cider
Angry Orchard Cider Company, LLC
 Walden, NY...................888-845-3311
Applewood Winery
 Warwick, NY..................845-988-9292
Bad Seed Cider Company, LLC
 Highland, NY..................845-236-0956
Brooklyn Cider House
 Brooklyn, NY..................347-295-0308
Graft Cider
 Newburgh, NY.................410-967-1926
Gravity Ciders, Inc.
 Sydney, NY
Hudson Valley Farmhouse Cider
 Staatsburg, NY.................845-266-3979
Northville Winery & Brewing Co
 Northville, MI..................248-320-6507
Warwick Valley Winery & Distillery
 Warwick, NY..................845-258-4858

Fruit Beer
Brooklyn Brewery
 Brooklyn, NY..................718-486-7422
Buffalo Bill Brewing Company
 Hayward, CA..................510-886-9823
Clemson Bros. Brewery
 Middletown, NY................845-775-4638
Downeast Cider House
 East Boston, MA...............857-301-8881
Hudson Valley Brewery
 Beacon, NY....................845-218-9156
Unibroue/Unibrew
 Chambly, QC..................450-658-7658

Herb & Spice Beer
Remarkable Liquids
 Altamont, NY..................518-861-5451

Reduced Calorie Beer
DG Yuengling & Son, Inc.
 Pottsville, PA..................570-628-4890

Stout & Porter

Dry Stout
Alaskan Brewing Company
 Juneau, AK....................907-780-5866
Catskill Brewery
 Livingston Manor, NY..........845-439-1232
Keegan Ales
 Kingston, NY..................845-331-2739
Newburgh Brewing Company
 Newburgh, NY.................845-569-2337
The Roscoe NY Beer Company, Inc.
 Roscoe, NY....................607-290-5002

Flavored Porter
Deschutes Brewery
 Bend, OR......................541-385-8606
Westtown Brew Works
 Westtown, NY

Flavored Stout
Broken Bow Brewery
 Tuckahoe, NY.................914-268-0900
Brooklyn Brewery
 Brooklyn, NY..................718-486-7422
Buffalo Bill Brewing Company
 Hayward, CA..................510-886-9823
Deschutes Brewery
 Bend, OR......................541-385-8606
Hyde Park Brewing Company
 Hyde Park, NY.................845-229-8277
St Arnold Brewing Co
 Houston, TX...................800-801-6402

Imperial Stout
Clemson Bros. Brewery
 Middletown, NY................845-775-4638

Porter
Brooklyn Brewery
 Brooklyn, NY..................718-486-7422
Clemson Bros. Brewery
 Middletown, NY................845-775-4638

DG Yuengling & Son, Inc.
 Pottsville, PA..................570-628-4890
Hyde Park Brewing Company
 Hyde Park, NY.................845-229-8277

Sweet Stout
Pete's Brewing Company
 San Antonio, TX...............800-877-7383

Wheat

Flavored Wheat
Broken Bow Brewery
 Tuckahoe, NY.................914-268-0900
Clemson Bros. Brewery
 Middletown, NY................845-775-4638

Wheat Ale
Alley Kat Brewing Co, Ltd
 Edmonton, AB................780-436-8922
Grand Teton Brewing Co
 Victor, ID......................888-899-1656
Hudson Valley Brewery
 Beacon, NY....................845-218-9156
Yonkers Brewing Company LLC
 Yonkers, NY..................914-226-8327

Bitters
Fee Brothers
 Rochester, NY.................800-961-3337
Flora Inc
 Lynden, WA...................800-446-2110
Hella Cocktail
 Long Island City, NY..........646-854-8004
Improper Goods
 Portland, OR..................503-662-7147
King Floyd's
 Novato, CA...................415-475-7811
Kittling Ridge Estate Wines & Spirits
 Vaughan, ON.................800-461-9463
Stirrings
 New Bedford, MA.............866-646-4266

Cocoa & Chocolate Drinks

Chocolate Drinks
B&D Food Corporation
 New York, NY................212-937-8456
Cacoco
Coca-Cola Beverages Northeast
 Bedford, NH...................844-619-3388
Fermalife
North American Beverage Co
 Ocean City, NJ................609-399-1486
Richard's Gourmet Coffee
 West Bridgewater, MA.........800-370-2633
Sucre
 New Orleans, LA..............504-708-4366
Yoo-Hoo Chocolate Beverage Company
 Carlstadt, NJ..................201-933-0070

Hot Chocolate
City Bakery
 New York, NY................212-366-1414
Gourmet du Village
 Morin-Heights, QC............800-668-2314
Know Brainer
 Lafayette, CO.................303-475-0456
Lacas Coffee Co Inc
 Pennsauken, NJ...............800-220-1133
Madrona Specialty Foods LLC
 Seattle, WA...................425-656-2997
Mars Inc.
 McLean, VA..................703-821-4900
Tea Room
 San Leandro, CA.............510-567-8868

Hot Cocoa
Blue Marble Brands
 Providence, RI.................888-534-0246
Caffe D'Amore Gourmet Beverages
 Pittsburgh, PA.................800-999-0171
Chatz Roasting Co
 Ceres, CA....................209-541-1100
Chicago Coffee Roastery
 Huntley, IL....................800-762-5402
Cisse Trading Co
 Mamaroneck, NY.............914-381-5555

Coffee Masters
 Spring Grove, IL...............800-334-6485
Conifer Foods
 Medina, WA..................800-588-9160
Country Choice Organic
 Eden Prairie, MN..............952-829-8824
Gloria Jean's Gourmet Coffees
 Irvine, CA.....................877-320-5282
Indulgent Foods
 Farmington, UT...............801-939-9100
Jenny's Country Kitchen
 Dover, MN...................800-357-3497
Keurig, Inc
 Reading, MA.................866-901-2739
Kittridge & Fredrickson LTD
 Portland, OR..................800-558-7788
Nantucket Tea Traders
 Nantucket, MA...............508-325-0203
Neighbors Coffee
 Oklahoma City, OK...........800-299-9016
Northwestern Foods
 Arden Hills, MN..............800-236-4937
Omanhene Cocoa Bean Co
 Milwaukee, WI..............800-588-2462
Swagger Foods Corp
 Vernon Hills, IL...............847-913-1200
Utah Coffee Roasters
 South Salt Lake, UT..........888-486-3334
White Coffee Corporation
 Long Island City, NY........800-221-0140

with Marshmallows
Todd's
 Des Moines, IA..............800-247-5363

Coffee & Tea
Ajiri Tea Company
 Upper Black Eddy, PA.......610-982-5075
Alvita
 Amherst, NY.................833-258-4821
Amelia Bay
 Suwanee, GA................770-772-6360
Aroma Coffee Company
 Forest Park, IL................708-488-8340
Atlanta Bread Co
 Smyrna, GA.................800-398-3728
Bellocq
 Brooklyn, NY................347-463-9231
Bhakti
 Boulder, CO.................303-484-8770
Burke Brands
 Miami, FL....................877-436-7225
Captain Cook Coffee Company
 Kealakekua, HI..............650-766-9149
Fairwinds Gourmet Coffee
 Lincoln, CA..................800-829-1300
Farmer Brothers Company
 Northlake, TX................682-549-6600
GH Ford Tea Company
 Shokan, NY..................845-464-6755
Groundwork Coffee Co.
 North Hollywood, CA........818-506-6020
Ingenuity Beverages
 Brooklyn, NY................800-611-7434
Javo Beverage Co., Inc.
 Vista, CA.....................760-330-1141
JFG Coffee
 New Orleans, LA.............800-535-1961
Kohana Coffee
 Austin, TX...................512-904-1174
La Crema Coffee Company
 West Chester, OH............513-779-6278
Lowcountry Produce
 Raleigh, NC..................800-935-2792
North River Roasters
 Poughkeepsie, NY...........845-418-2739
Onnit Labs
 Austin, TX...................855-666-4899
Orinoco Coffee & Tea
 Jessup, MD..................410-312-5292
Point Group
 Satellite Beach, FL............888-272-1249
Queen City Coffee Company
 West Chester, OH............800-487-7460
Sara Lee Coffee & Tea
 Suffolk, VA..................757-538-8083
Southern Season
 Chapel Hill, NC..............877-929-7133
Stevens Creative Enterprises, Inc.
 New York, NY................646-558-6336

75

Product Categories / Beverages: Coffee & Tea

Stonewall Kitchen
   York, ME..................800-826-1752
Sun Opta Inc.
   Mississauga, ON............952-820-2518
Teeccino
   Carpinteria, CA.............800-498-3434
Tetley Tea
   New Providence, NJ.........800-728-0084
Texas Spice Co
   Round Rock, TX.............800-880-8007
TMI Trading Co
   Brooklyn, NY...............718-821-5052
Torke Coffee Co
   Sheboygan, WI..............800-242-7671
TreeHouse Foods, Inc.
   Oak Brook, IL..............708-483-1300
UBF Food Solutions
   Lisle, IL..................630-955-5394
Zephyr Hills
   Tampa, FL..................800-950-9398

Cappuccino

Agropur
   Granby, QC.................800-363-5686
Aloe'Ha Drink Products
   Houston, TX................713-978-6359
American Instants Inc
   Flanders, NJ...............973-584-8811
Arcadia Dairy Farms Inc
   Arden, NC..................828-684-3556
Arctic Beverages
   Winnipeg, MB...............866-503-1270
Baltimore Brewing Company
   Baltimore, MD..............410-837-5000
Beacon Drive Inn
   Spartanburg, SC............864-585-9387
Beaver Street Brewery
   Flagstaff, AZ..............928-779-0079
Belmar Spring Water
   Glen Rock, NJ..............201-444-1010
Better Beverages Inc
   Cerritos, CA...............800-344-5219
Bigelow Tea
   Fairfield, CT..............888-244-3569
Blenheim Bottling Company
   Hamer, SC..................800-270-9344
Bluechip Group
   Salt Lake City, UT.........800-878-0099
Boissons Miami Pomor
   Longueuil, QC..............877-977-3744
Bottle Green Drinks Company
   Mississauga, ON............905-273-6137
Bow Valley Brewing Company
   Canmore, AB................403-678-2739
Brasserie Brasel Brewery
   Lasalle, QC................800-463-2728
Caffe D'Oro
   Chino, CA..................800-200-5005
Caffe D'Vita
   Chino, CA..................800-200-5005
Campbell Soup Co.
   Camden, NJ.................800-257-8443
Chicago Coffee Roastery
   Huntley, IL................800-762-5402
Clipper City Brewing
   Halethorpe, MD.............410-247-7822
Creemore Springs Brewery
   Creemore, ON...............800-267-2240
Creme D'Lite
   Irving, TX.................972-255-7255
De Coty Coffee Co
   San Angelo, TX.............800-588-8001
Dogfish Head Craft Brewery
   Lewes, DE..................888-834-3474
Ensemble Beverages
   Montgomery, AL.............334-324-7719
Faygo Beverages Inc
   Detroit, MI................313-925-1600
Finlays
   Lincoln, RI................800-288-6272
Flora Inc
   Lynden, WA.................800-446-2110
Florida Natural Flavors
   Casselberry, FL............800-872-5979
Florida's Natural Growers
   Lake Wales, FL.............888-657-6600
Fresh Juice Delivery
   Beverly Hills, CA..........310-271-7373
Fresh Samantha
   Saco, ME...................800-658-4635
Gedney Foods Co
   Sun Valley, CA.............888-244-0653

Great Lakes Brewing Co.
   Cleveland, OH..............216-771-4404
Great Northern Brewing Co
   Whitefish, MT..............406-863-1000
Great Western Brewing Company
   Saskatoon, SK..............800-764-4492
Halifax Group
   Washington, DC.............202-530-8300
Healthmate Products
   Highland Park, IL..........847-579-1051
Hobarama Corporation
   Miami, FL..................880-439-2295
Hogtown Brewing Company
   Mississauga, ON............905-855-9065
Honickman Affiliates
   Pennsauken, NJ.............800-573-7745
Ideal Dairy Farms
   Hudson Falls, NY...........518-747-5059
Indian River Select® LLC
   Stuart, FL.................888-373-7426
Indulgent Foods
   Farmington, UT.............801-939-9100
Jianlibao America
   New York, NY...............800-526-1688
Key Colony Red Parrot Juice
   Lemont, IL.................844-783-8572
King Cupboard
   Red Lodge, MT..............800-962-6555
Kola
   New York, NY...............212-688-1895
Lake Country Foods Inc
   Oconomowoc, WI.............262-567-5521
Lakefront Brewery Inc
   Milwaukee, WI..............414-372-8800
Left Hand Brewing Co
   Longmont, CO...............303-772-0258
Magic Valley Quality Milk
   Jerome, ID.................208-324-7519
Martin Coffee Co
   Jacksonville, FL...........904-355-9661
Mendocino Brewing Co Inc
   Ukiah, CA..................707-463-2627
Millstream Brewing Co
   Amana, IA..................319-622-3672
Monticello Vineyards-Corley
   Napa, CA...................707-253-2802
Moosehead Breweries Ltd.
   St. John, NB
Mrs Clark's Foods
   Ankeny, IA.................800-736-5674
Nature's First Inc
   Orange, CT.................800-523-3752
Neighbors Coffee
   Oklahoma City, OK..........800-299-9016
Noel Corp
   Yakima, WA.................509-248-1313
North American Breweries Inc.
   Rochester, NY..............585-546-1030
Northumberland Dairy
   Miramichi, NB..............800-501-1150
Northwestern Foods
   Arden Hills, MN............800-236-4937
Oak Farms
   El Paso, TX................800-395-7004
Ojai Cook
   Los Angeles, CA............886-571-1551
Olympic Foods
   Spokane, WA................509-455-8059
Pennsylvania Brewing Company
   Pittsburgh, PA.............412-237-9400
Quality Naturally Foods
   City Of Industry, CA.......888-498-6986
Reiter Dairy
   Newport, KY................800-544-6455
Richard's Gourmet Coffee
   West Bridgewater, MA.......800-370-2633
Royale Brands
   Davenport, IA..............563-386-5222
San Marco Coffee, Inc.
   Charlotte, NC..............800-715-9298
Santa Cruz Mountain Brewing
   Santa Cruz, CA.............831-425-4900
Sebastiani Vineyards
   Sonoma, CA.................855-232-2338
Shipyard Brewing Co
   Portland, ME...............800-789-0684
Southern Gardens Citrus
   Clewiston, FL..............863-983-3030
Southern Heritage Coffee Company
   Indianapolis, IN...........800-486-1198
Stewart's Beverages
   rye Brook, NY..............800-762-7753

Swiss Dairy
   Riverside, CA..............951-898-9427
Taos Brewing Supply
   El Prado, NM...............575-779-0449
Thyme Garden Herb Co
   Alsea, OR..................800-482-4372
Tonex
   Wallington, NJ.............973-773-5135
Tova Industries LLC
   Louisville, KY.............888-532-8682
Triple H Food Processors Inc
   Riverside, CA..............951-352-5700
True Beverages
   O Fallon, MO...............800-325-6152
Ultra Seal
   New Paltz, NY..............845-255-2490
Unilever Canada
   Toronto, ON................416-415-3000
Virgil's Root Beer
   Norwalk, CT................800-997-3337
Warren Laboratories LLC
   Abbott, TX.................800-421-2563
Whistler Brewing Company
   Whistler, BC...............604-962-8889

Coffee

A Hill of Beans Coffee Roasters
   Omaha, NE..................402-333-6048
Afineur
   Brooklyn, NY...............617-480-1340
Ajiri Tea Company
   Upper Black Eddy, PA.......610-982-5075
Alakef Coffee Roasters Inc
   Duluth, MN.................800-438-9228
All Goode Organics
   Santa Barbara, CA..........805-683-3370
Allann Brothers Coffee Roasters
   Albany, OR.................800-926-6886
Allegro Coffee Co
   Thornton, CO...............800-666-4869
Alpen Sierra Coffee Company
   Minden, NV.................800-531-1405
Alpine Coffee Roasters
   Leavenworth, WA............800-246-2761
Amcan Beverages Inc
   American Canyon, CA........800-972-5962
Ancora Coffee Roasters
   Madison, WI................800-260-0217
Arbuckle Coffee Roasters
   Tucson, AZ.................800-533-8278
ARCO Coffee
   Superior, WI...............800-283-2726
Armenia Coffee Corporation
   Purchase, NY...............914-694-6100
Armeno Coffee Roasters LTD
   Northborough, MA...........508-393-2821
Aroma Coffee Roasters Inc
   Hoboken, NJ................201-792-1730
Aroma Ridge
   Marietta, GA...............800-528-2123
Artist Coffee
   Londonderry, NH............866-440-4511
Atlanta Coffee & Tea Co
  800-426-4781
Atlanta Coffee Roasters
   Atlanta, GA................800-252-8211
Atlantic Natural Foods
   Nashville, NC..............888-491-0524
Austin Chase Coffee
   Seattle, WA................888-502-2333
Avalon Organic Coffees
   Albuquerque, NM............800-662-2575
B&D Food Corporation
   New York, NY...............212-937-8456
B&K Coffee
   Oneonta, NY................800-432-1499
B.B. Bean, Coffee
   Monument, CO...............719-481-1170
Baby's Coffee
   Key West, FL...............800-523-2326
Back Bay Trading
   Alpharetta, GA.............800-650-8327
Baltimore Coffee & Tea Co Inc
   Lutherville, MD............800-823-1408
Barefoot Contessa Pantry
   York, ME...................800-826-1752
Barnie's Coffee and Tea
   Orlando, FL................800-284-1416
Barrie House Gourmet Coffee
   Elmsford, NY...............800-876-2233
Barrington Coffee Roasting
   Lee, MA....................800-528-0998

Product Categories / Beverages: Coffee & Tea

Batdorf & Bronson
Olympia, WA 800-955-5282
Bay View Farm
Honaunau, HI 800-662-5880
Bean Forge
Coos Bay, OR 888-292-1632
Benbow's Coffee Roasters
Bar Harbor, ME 207-288-2552
Berardi's Fresh Roast
Cleveland, OH 800-876-9109
Big Shoulders Coffee
Chicago, IL 312-846-1883
Big Train Inc
Lake Forest, CA 800-244-8724
Big Watt Coffee
Minneapolis, MN
Blackbear Coffee Company
Hendersonville, NC 828-692-6333
Boston's Best Coffee Roasters
South Easton, MA 800-898-8393
Bountiful Pantry
Nantucket, MA 617-487-8019
Boyd's Coffee Co
Portland, OR 800-735-2878
Boyer's Coffee
Denver, CO 800-452-5282
Bridgetown Coffee
Portland, OR 800-726-0320
Brisk Coffee Co
Tampa, FL 800-899-5282
Brooklyn Bean Roastery
Brooklyn, NY 908-205-0018
Brown & Jenkins Trading Company
Cambridge, VT 800-456-5282
Bruce Coffee Svc Plan USA
Hartford, CT 800-227-6638
Buckmaster Coffee Co
Hillsboro, OR 800-962-9148
Buywell Coffee
Colorado Springs, CO 877-294-6246
Cadillac Coffee Co
Ft. Wayne, IN 800-438-6900
Cafe Altura
Santa Paula, CA 800-526-8328
Cafe Bustelo
Miami, FL 800-990-9039
Cafe Cartago
Denver, CO 800-443-8666
Cafe Del Mundo
Anchorage, AK 800-770-2326
Cafe Descafeinado de Chiapas
Doral, FL 305-499-9775
Cafe Du Monde Coffee Stand
New Orleans, LA 800-772-2927
Cafe Kreyol
Manassas, VA
Cafe La Semeuse
Brooklyn, NY 800-242-6333
Cafe Moak
Rockford, MI 616-866-7625
Cafe Moto
San Diego, CA 800-818-3363
Cafe Society Coffee Company
Dallas, TX 800-717-6000
Cafe Yaucono/Jimenez & Fernandez
San Juan, PR 787-721-3337
Caffe Appassionato Coffee
Seattle, WA 888-502-2333
Caffe D'Oro
Chino, CA 800-200-5005
Caffe Darte
Federal Way, WA 800-999-5334
Caffe Ibis Gallery Deli
Logan, UT 888-740-4777
Caffe Luca Coffee Roaste
Seattle, WA 800-728-9116
Caffe Trieste
San Francisco, CA 415-550-1107
Cajun Creole Products Inc
New Iberia, LA 800-946-8688
Cape Cod Coffee Roasters
Mashpee, MA 508-477-2400
Cappuccine
Corona, CA 800-511-3127
Capricorn Coffees Inc
San Francisco, CA 800-541-0758
Captain Cook Coffee Company
Kealakekua, HI 650-766-9149
Caracolillo Coffee Mills
Tampa, FL 800-682-0023
Caravan Company
Worcester, MA 508-752-3777

Caribbean Coffee Co
Goleta, CA 800-932-5282
Caribou Coffee Co Inc
Minneapolis, MN 888-227-4268
Carrabassett Coffee Roasters
Kingfield, ME 888-292-2326
Cascade Coffee
Everett, WA 800-995-9655
Chatz Roasting Co
Ceres, CA 209-541-1100
Chauvin Coffee Corporation
Saint Louis, MO 800-455-5282
Chicago Coffee Roastery
Huntley, IL 800-762-5402
Chock Full O'Nuts
.... 888-246-2598
City Bean
Los Angeles, CA 888-248-9232
Clayton Coffee & Tea
Modesto, CA 209-576-1120
Clear Mountain Coffee Company
Silver Spring, MD 301-587-2233
Clearwater Coffee Company
Lake Zurich, IL 847-540-7711
Cobraz Brazilian Coffee
New York, NY 212-759-7700
Coffee Associates
Edgewater, NJ 201-945-1060
Coffee Barrel
Holt, MI 517-694-9000
Coffee Bean
Englewood, CO 303-922-1238
Coffee Bean & Tea Leaf
Bloomington, MN 952-853-1148
Coffee Bean Intl
Portland, OR 800-877-0474
Coffee Bean of Leesburg
Leesburg, VA 800-232-6872
Coffee Beanery LTD
Flushing, MI 800-441-2255
Coffee Brothers Inc
Colton, CA 888-443-5282
Coffee Butler Service
Alexandria, VA 703-823-0028
Coffee Culture-A House
Lincoln, NE 402-438-8456
Coffee Exchange
Providence, RI 877-263-3334
Coffee Express Roasting Co
Plymouth, MI 800-466-9000
Coffee Holding Co Inc
Staten Island, NY 800-458-2233
Coffee Masters
Spring Grove, IL 800-334-6485
Coffee Mill Roastery
Elon, NC 800-729-1727
Coffee Mill Roasting Company
Sudbury, ON 705-525-2700
Coffee Millers & Roasting
Cape Coral, FL 239-573-6800
Coffee People
Beaverton, OR 800-354-5282
Coffee Process
Houston, TX 713-695-8483
Coffee Reserve
Phoenix, AZ 888-755-6789
Coffee Roasters Inc
Oakland, NJ 800-285-2445
Coffee Roasters Of New Orleans
Kenner, LA 800-737-5464
Coffee Roasters of New Orleans
New Orleans, LA 800-737-5464
Coffee Up
Chicago, IL 847-288-9330
Coffee Works
Sacramento, CA 800-275-3335
College Coffee Roaster
Mountville, PA 717-285-9561
Colonial Coffee Roasters Inc
Miami, FL 305-638-0885
Community Coffee Co.
Baton Rouge, LA 800-884-5282
Continental Coffee Products Company
Houston, TX 800-323-6178
Copper Moon Coffee LLC
Lafayette, IN 317-541-9000
Corim Industries Inc
Brick, NJ 800-942-4201
Counter Culture Coffee
Durham, NC 888-238-5282
Cupper's Coffee Company
Lethbridge, AB 403-380-4555

Custom Coffee Plan
Torrance, CA 800-841-5949
Dallis Brothers
Long Island City, NY 718-845-3010
David Rio
San Francisco, CA 800-454-9605
Daybreak Coffee Roasters
Glastonbury, CT 800-882-5282
Daymar Select Fine Coffees
El Cajon, CA 800-466-7590
Dazbog Coffee Co
Denver, CO 303-892-9999
De Coty Coffee Co
San Angelo, TX 800-588-8001
Dean & De Luca Inc
Honolulu, HI 808-729-9720
Deep Valley
New York, NY 917-673-5121
DeLima Coffee
Liverpool, NY 800-962-8864
Diedrich Coffee
Irvine, CA 800-354-5282
Dillanos Coffee Roasters
Sumner, WA 800-234-5282
Distant Lands Coffee Roaster
Renton, WA 800-758-4437
DMH Ingredients Inc
Libertyville, IL 847-362-9977
Don Hilario Estate Coffee
Oldsmar, FL 800-799-1903
Downeast Coffee Roasters
Pawtucket, RI 800-345-2007
Droubi's Imports
Houston, TX 713-334-1829
Dunkin' Brands Inc.
Canton, MA 800-859-5339
Eagle Coffee Co Inc
Baltimore, MD 410-685-5893
East Indies Coffee & Tea Co
Lebanon, PA 800-220-2326
ECOM Agroindustrial Corporation Ltd
Pully,
Eight O'Clock Coffee Company
North Bergen, NJ 800-299-2739
Eldorado Coffee Distributors
Flushing, NY 800-635-2566
Ellis Coffee Co
Philadelphia, PA 800-822-3984
Equal Exchange Inc
West Bridgewater, MA 774-776-7400
Erba Food Products
Brooklyn, NY 718-272-7700
Espresso Vivace
Seattle, WA 206-860-5869
European Coffee
Clearwater, FL 888-635-4882
European Roasterie
Le Center, MN 888-588-5282
F. Gavina & Sons
Vernon, CA 800-428-4627
Fama Sales Co
New York, NY 800-682-0425
Fenn Valley Vineyards
Fennville, MI 269-561-2396
Ferrara Bakery & Cafe
New York, NY 212-226-6150
Fidalgo Bay Roasting Co
Burlington, WA 800-310-5540
Field Coffee
Norcross, GA 844-343-5326
Finlays
Lincoln, RI 800-288-6272
First Colony Coffee & Tea Company
Norfolk, VA 800-446-8555
First Roasters of Central Florida
Longwood, FL 407-699-6364
Flat Tire Bike Shop
Cave Creek, AZ 480-488-5261
Folgers Coffee Co
Orrville, OH 800-937-9745
Four Sigmatic
Venice, CA
Fratello Coffee Roasters
Calgary, AB 800-465-7227
Freed, Teller & Freed
South San Francisco, CA 800-370-7371
French Market Coffee
New Orleans, LA 800-535-1961
Gadsden Coffee/Caffe
Arivaca, AZ 888-514-5282
Gardner's Gourmet
Fremont, CA 800-676-8558

77

Product Categories / Beverages: Coffee & Tea

Gerhart Coffee Co
 Lancaster, PA 800-536-4310
Global Food Industries
 Townville, SC 800-225-4152
Globus Coffee LLC
 Manhasset, NY 516-304-5780
Gloria Jean's Gourmet Coffees
 Irvine, CA 877-320-5282
GoBio!
 Action, ON 519-853-2958
Godiva Chocolatier
 New York, NY 800-946-3482
Green Mountain Chocolate Inc
 Franklin, MA 508-520-7160
Greene Brothers Specialty Coffee Roaster
 Hackettstown, NJ 908-979-0022
Greenwell Farms Inc
 Kealakekua, HI 888-592-5662
Grounds for Change
 Poulsbo, WA 800-796-6820
Harmony Bay Coffee
 North Andover, MA 800-514-3663
Harold L King & Co Inc
 Redwood City, CA 888-368-2233
Has Beans Coffee & Tea Co
 Chico, CA 800-427-2326
Hathaway Coffee Co Inc
 Summit Argo, IL 708-458-7666
Hawaii Coffee Company
 Honolulu, HI 800-338-8353
Hawaiian Isles Kona Coffee Co
 Honolulu, HI 800-657-7716
Heartland Sweeteners
 Carmel, IN. 317-566-9750
Hena Inc
 Brooklyn, NY 718-272-8237
Heritage Coffee Co & Cafe
 Juneau, AK 800-478-5282
Heyday Beverage Co.
 Austin, TX. 512-443-9876
High Brew Coffee
 Austin, TX
High Rise Coffee Roasters
 Colorado Springs, CO. 719-633-1833
Hillsboro Coffee Company
 Tampa, FL. 813-877-2126
Home Roast Coffee
 Lutz, FL. 813-949-0807
Hood River Coffee Co
 Hood River, OR 800-336-2954
House of Coffee Beans
 Houston, TX 800-422-1799
House of Tsang
 San Francisco, CA 415-282-9952
Humboldt Bay Coffee Co.
 Eureka, CA 707-444-3969
Ideal Distributing Company
 Bothell, WA. 425-488-6121
Immordl
 San Clemente, CA. 844-466-6735
Indigo Coffee Roasters
 Florence, MA 800-447-5450
Innovative Beverage Concepts
 Irvine, CA. 949-831-8656
Instant Products of America
 Columbus, IN 812-372-9100
Inter-American Products
 Cincinnati, OH 800-645-2233
Inter-Continental Imports Company
 Newington, CT 800-424-4422
Ito En USA Inc
 Brooklyn, NY 808-847-4477
J.B. Peel Coffee Roasters
 Red Hook, NY 800-231-7372
J.M. Smucker Co.
 Orrville, OH 888-550-9555
Jaguar Yerba Company
 Ashland, OR 800-839-0775
Jamaica John Inc
 Franklin Park, IL. 847-451-1730
Jamaican Gourmet Coffee Company
 Philadelphia, PA 800-261-2859
Jasper Products Corp
 Joplin, MO 417-206-3877
Java Beans and Joe Coffee
 Petaluma, CA 800-624-7031
Java Cabana
 Miami, FL. 305-592-7302
Java Sun Coffee Roasters
 Marblehead, MA. 781-631-7788
Java-Gourmet/Keuka Lake Coffee Roaster
 Penn Yan, NY 888-478-2739

Javalution Coffee Company
 Chula Vista, CA 800-982-3197
Javo Beverage Co., Inc.
 Vista, CA. 760-330-1141
Jelks Coffee Roasters
 Shreveport, LA 800-235-7361
Jenny's Country Kitchen
 Dover, MN 800-357-3497
Jeremiah's Pick Coffee Co
 San Francisco, CA 877-537-3642
Jodyana Corporation
 Miami, FL. 888-563-5282
John A Vassilaros & Son Inc
 Flushing, NY. 718-886-4140
John Conti Coffee Co
 Louisville, KY 800-928-5282
Josuma Coffee Co
 Menlo Park, CA 650-366-5453
Juice Tyme, Inc.
 Chicago, IL 800-236-5823
Kaffe Magnum Opus
 Millville, NJ 800-652-5282
Kauai Coffee Co Inc
 Kalaheo, HI 800-545-8605
Keurig Dr Pepper
 Plano, TX 800-696-5891
Keurig, Inc
 Reading, MA. 866-901-2739
Keystone Coffee Co
 San Jose, CA. 408-998-2221
Kicking Horse Coffee
 Invermere, BC. 888-287-5282
Kittridge & Fredrickson LTD
 Portland, OR 800-558-7788
Kobricks Coffee Company
 Jersey City, NJ 800-562-7491
Kohana Coffee
 Austin, TX. 512-904-1174
Kona Coffee Council
 Kealakekua, HI 808-323-2911
Kona Premium Coffee Company
 Holualoa, HI 888-322-9550
Kraft Heinz Canada
 North York, ON. 416-441-5000
LA Costa Coffee Roasting Co
 Carlsbad, CA. 760-438-8160
La Societe
 Montreal, QC 514-507-9223
La Vans Coffee Company
 Bordentown, NJ 609-298-0688
Lacas Coffee Co Inc
 Pennsauken, NJ 800-220-1133
Laird Superfood
 Sisters, OR 888-670-6796
Larry's Beans
 Raleigh, NC 919-828-1234
Lavazza Premium Coffees
 New York, NY 800-466-3287
Leavenworth Coffee Roast
 Leavenworth, WA. 800-246-2761
Lenson Coffee & Tea Company
 Pleasantville, NJ 609-646-3003
Leona's Restaurante
 Chimayo, NM 888-561-5569
Leroy Hill Coffee Co Inc
 Mobile, AL 800-866-5282
Lexington Coffee & Tea
 Lexington, KY 859-277-1102
Limitless
 Chicago, IL
Lindsay's Teas
 Petaluma, CA 800-624-7031
Lingle Brothers Coffee
 Bell Gardens, CA 562-927-3317
Lockcoffee
 Larchmont, NY. 914-273-7838
Lola Savannah
 Houston, TX 888-663-9166
Longbottom Coffee & Tea Inc
 Hillsboro, OR 800-288-1271
Lost Coast Roast
 Arcata, CA
Louis Dreyfus Company LLC
 Wilton, CT 203-761-2000
Love Creek Orchards
 Medina, TX. 800-449-0882
Lowcountry Produce
 Raleigh, NC 800-935-2792
Lowery's Premium Roast Gourmet Coffee
 Snohomish, WA. 800-767-1783
M.E. Swing Company
 Alexandria, VA 800-485-4019

Madrinas Coffee
 St. Louis, MO
Magnum Coffee Roastery
 Nunica, MI 888-937-5282
Majestic Coffee & Tea Inc
 San Carlos, CA 650-591-5678
Massimo Zanetti Beverage USA
 Suffolk, VA 888-246-2598
Master Brew
 Northbrook, IL 847-564-3600
Maui Coffee Roasters Wholesale
 Kahului, HI 800-645-2877
Maxwell House & Post
 Rye Brook, NY 914-335-2500
Mayorga Coffee
 Rockville, MD 877-526-3322
Mccullagh Coffee Roasters
 Buffalo, NY. 800-753-3473
Melitta USA Inc
 Clearwater, FL 888-635-4880
Mercon Coffee Group.ÿ
 Miami, FL. 786-254-2300
Michael's Gourmet Coffee
 Ft. Lauderdale, FL 888-346-4646
Mills Coffee Roasting Co
 Providence, RI 888-781-5282
Milone Brothers Coffee Co
 Modesto, CA. 800-974-8500
Mokk-a
 Rotterdam,
Monarch Beverage Company
 Atlanta, GA. 800-241-3732
Montana Coffee Traders
 Whitefish, MT. 800-345-5282
MorningStar Coffee Company
 West Chester, PA. 888-854-2233
Mother Parker's Tea & Coffee
 Mississauga, ON 800-387-9398
Mountain City Coffee Roasters
 Enka, NC 888-730-0869
Mountanos Family Coffee & Tea Co.
 Petaluma, CA 800-624-7031
Moutanos Brothers Coffee Company
 South San Francisco, CA 800-624-7031
Mr Espresso
 Oakland, CA. 510-287-5200
Muqui Coffee Company
 San Jose, CA. 408-272-8471
Mystic Coffee Roasters
 Mystic, CT 860-536-2999
Nantucket Tea Traders
 Nantucket, MA 508-325-0203
Native American Herbal Tea
 Aberdeen, SD 888-291-8517
Nature's First Inc
 Orange, CT 800-523-3752
NeuRoast
 New York, NY
New Barn Organics
 Rohnert Park, CA 888-635-7102
New England Tea & Coffee Co
 Malden, MA 800-225-3537
New Harmony Coffee & Tea Co.
 New Harmony, IN. 812-682-4563
New Jamaican Gold
 Hayward, CA 800-672-9956
Nobletree Coffee
 Brooklyn, NY 718-643-6080
North American Coffees
 Morriston, NJ 973-359-0300
Northwest Naturals LLC
 Bothell, WA. 425-881-2200
Northwestern Coffee Mills
 Washburn, WI. 800-243-5283
NuZee, Inc.
 Vista, CA. 844-696-8933
O'Neill Coffee Co
 West Middlesex, PA 724-528-2244
Oasis Coffee Co Inc
 Norwalk, CT 203-847-0554
Olam Spices
 Fresno, CA 559-447-1390
Olympic Coffee & Roasting
 Bellevue, WA 888-244-8313
Omar Coffee Co
 Newington, CT 800-394-6627
Oskri Corporation
 Lake Mills, WI 920-648-8300
Pan American Coffee Co
 Hoboken, NJ 800-229-1883
Paramount Coffee
 Lansing, MI. 800-968-1222

Product Categories / Beverages: Coffee & Tea

Partners Coffee LLC
  Atlanta, GA 800-341-5282
Pascal Coffee
  Yonkers, NY 914-969-7933
Peaberry's Coffee & Tea
  Oakland, CA 510-653-0450
Pear's Coffee
  Bellevue, NE 800-828-7688
Pearl Coffee Co
  Akron, OH 800-822-5282
Peerless Coffee & Tea
  Oakland, CA 800-310-5662
Peet's Coffee
  Berkeley, CA 800-999-2132
PepsiCo.
  Purchase, NY 914-253-2000
Pfefferkorn's Coffee Inc
  Baltimore, MD 800-682-4665
Picnik
  Austin, TX
PJ's Coffee & Tea
  Covington, LA 800-527-1055
Plaza House Coffee
  Staten Island, NY 718-979-9555
Polly's Gourmet Coffee
  Long Beach, CA 562-433-2996
Pontiac Coffee Break
  Waterford, MI 248-332-6333
Pontiac Foods
  Columbia, SC 803-699-1600
Porto Rico Importing
  New York, NY 212-477-5421
Puroast Coffee Co Inc
  Woodland, CA 877-569-2243
Q.E. Tea
  Bridgeville, PA 800-622-8327
Queen Anne Coffee Roaster
  Seattle, WA 206-284-2530
Reading Coffee Roasters
  Birdsboro, PA 800-331-6713
Red Diamond Coffee & Tea
  Moody, AL 800-292-4651
Rethemeyer Coffee Company
  St Louis, MO 314-231-0990
Richard's Gourmet Coffee
  West Bridgewater, MA 800-370-2633
Riffel's Coffee Company
  Wichita, KS 888-399-4567
RISE Brewing Co.
  Cos Cob, CT
River Road Coffee
  Lake Clear, NY 315-769-9941
Roasterie Inc
  Kansas City, MO 800-376-0245
Rocky Mountain Coffee Roasters
  Jasper, Alberta T0E 1E0, AB 800-666-3465
Rodda Coffee Company
  Yachats, OR 541-547-4132
Ronnoco Coffee Co
  St Louis, MO 800-428-2287
Rostov's Coffee & Tea Co
  Richmond, VA 800-637-6772
Rowland Coffee Roasters Inc.
  Miami, FL 866-318-0422
Royal Cup Coffee
  Birmingham, AL 800-366-5836
S & D Coffee Inc
  Concord, NC 800-933-2210
Sahara Coffee
  Reno, NV 775-825-5033
Sambets Cajun Deli
  Austin, TX 800-472-6238
San Francisco Bay Coffee
  Lincoln, CA 800-829-1300
San Francisco Bay Coffee Company
  Lincoln, CA 800-829-1300
San Jose Apartments
  San Jose, CA 408-347-8209
San Juan Coffee Roasting Co
  Friday Harbor, WA 800-624-4119
San Marco Coffee, Inc.
  Charlotte, NC 800-715-9298
SANGARIA USA
  Torrance, CA 310-530-2202
Santa Barbara Roasting Co
  Santa Barbara, CA 800-321-5282
Santa Elena Coffee Company
  Hutto, TX 512-846-2908
Sappore Coffee Co Of Alaska
  Anchorage, AK 907-333-3626
Schuil Coffee Co
  Grand Rapids, MI 616-956-6815

Seattle's Best Coffee
  Seattle, WA 800-611-7793
Seven Hills Coffee Co
  Blue Ash, OH 513-489-5220
Shamrock Foods Co
  Phoenix, AZ 800-289-3663
Shelburne Falls Coffee Roaster
  Shelburne Falls, MA 413-625-2123
Sierra Madre Coffee
  Denver, CO 303-446-0050
Simpson & Vail
  Brookfield, CT 800-282-8327
Sivetz Coffee
  Corvallis, OR 541-753-9713
Slo Roasted Coffee
  Los Osos, CA 800-382-6837
South Beach Coffee Company
  Miami Beach, FL 305-576-9696
Southern Heritage Coffee Company
  Indianapolis, IN 800-486-1198
Specialty Coffee Roasters
  Delray Beach, FL 800-253-9363
Specialty Food Association
  New York, NY 646-878-0301
Spices of Life Gourmet Coffee
  Fort Myers, FL 239-334-8004
Spinelli Coffee Company
  Seattle, WA 415-821-7100
Starbucks
  Seattle, WA 800-782-7282
Stasero International
  Kent, WA 888-929-2378
Steep & Brew
  Monona, WI 800-876-1986
Stevens Creative Enterprises, Inc.
  New York, NY 646-558-6336
Stewart's Private Blend Foods
  Chicago, IL 800-654-2862
Stockton Graham & Co
  Raleigh, NC 800-835-5943
Sugai Kona Coffee
  Holualoa, HI 808-322-7717
Sunup Green Coffee
  New York, NY 212-842-9767
Sweeney's Gourmet Coffee Roast
  Henderson, NV 702-558-0505
Tadin Herb & Tea Co
  Vernon, CA 800-838-2346
Teeccino
  Carpinteria, CA 800-498-3434
Texas Coffee Co
  Beaumont, TX 800-259-3400
Texas Coffee Traders Inc
  Austin, TX 800-343-4875
Thanksgiving Coffee Co
  Fort Bragg, CA 800-462-1999
The Coffee Bean & Tea Leaf
  Los Angeles, CA 877-653-1963
Thrive Farmers
  Roswell, GA 855-553-2763
Tierra Farm
  Valatie, NY 519-392-8300
TMI Trading Co
  Brooklyn, NY 718-821-5052
Toddy Products Inc
  Midland, TX 713-225-2066
Tom & Dave's Coffee
  San Rafael, CA 800-249-5050
Torke Coffee Co
  Sheboygan, WI 800-242-7671
Torrefazione Italia
  Seattle, WA 800-827-2333
Torreo Coffee Company
  Philadelphia, PA 888-286-7736
Tradewinds Coffee Company
  Raleigh, NC 800-457-0406
Tristao Trading
  New York, NY 212-285-8120
Uncommon Grounds Coffee
  Berkeley, CA 800-567-9183
United Intratrade
  Houston, TX 713-827-7799
Utah Coffee Roasters
  South Salt Lake, UT 888-486-3334
Valley Tea & Coffee
  Alhambra, CA 626-281-5799
Van Roy Coffee Co
  Cleveland, OH 877-826-7669
Vermont Coffee Co
  Middlebury, VT 888-308-5099
Victor Allen Coffee Company
  Albuquerque, NM 800-662-2575

Victor Allen's Coffee and Tea
  Little Chute, WI 800-394-5282
Village Roaster
  Lakewood, CO 800-237-3822
Wallingford Coffee Co Inc
  Cincinnati, OH 800-533-3690
Walsh's Coffee Roasters
  San Mateo, CA 650-347-5112
Wandering Bear Coffee
  New York, NY 929-251-3752
Weaver Nut Co. Inc.
  Ephrata, PA 800-473-2688
Wechsler Coffee Corporation
  Teterboro, NJ 800-800-2633
West Coast Specialty Coffee
  Campbell, CA 650-259-9308
What's Brewing
  San Antonio, TX 877-262-7311
Wheeling Coffee & Spice Co
  Wheeling, WV 800-500-0141
White Cloud Coffee
  Boise, ID 888-229-3249
White Coffee Corporation
  Long Island City, NY 800-221-0140
Willoughby's Coffee & Tea
  Branford, CT 800-388-8400
World Cup Coffee & Tea
  Portland, OR 503-228-5503
World Of Coffee
  Stirling, NJ 800-543-0062
Young Winfield
  Hamilton, ON 905-893-2536

Americano

NeuRoast
  New York, NY

Cappuccino

B&D Food Corporation
  New York, NY 212-937-8456
Caffe D'Amore
  Beloit, WI 800-999-0171
Caffe D'Amore Gourmet Beverages
  Pittsburgh, PA 800-999-0171
High Brew Coffee
  Austin, TX
Instant Products of America
  Columbus, IN 812-372-9100
Sherwood Brands
  New Brunswick, NJ 973-249-8200
Wild Aseptics, LLC
  Erlanger, KY 877-787-7221

Decaffeinated

Arbuckle Coffee Roasters
  Tucson, AZ 800-533-8278
Atlanta Coffee & Tea Co
  800-426-4781
Caffe Darte
  Federal Way, WA 800-999-5334
Caffe Luca Coffee Roaste
  Seattle, WA 800-728-9116
Chock Full O'Nuts
  888-246-2598
Coffee Exchange
  Providence, RI 877-263-3334
Coffee Roasters Of New Orleans
  Kenner, LA 800-737-5464
Folgers Coffee Co
  Orrville, OH 800-937-9745
French Market Coffee
  New Orleans, LA 800-535-1961
Grounds For Change
  Poulsbo, WA 800-796-6820
Hawaii Coffee Company
  Honolulu, HI 800-338-8353
Heritage Coffee Co & Cafe
  Juneau, AK 800-478-5282
Jelks Coffee Roasters
  Shreveport, LA 800-235-7361
Kaffe Magnum Opus
  Millville, NJ 800-652-5282
Kohana Coffee
  Austin, TX 512-904-1174
Mccullagh Coffee Roasters
  Buffalo, NY 800-753-3473
Puroast Coffee Co Inc
  Woodland, CA 877-569-2243
San Francisco Bay Coffee Company
  Lincoln, CA 800-829-1300

Product Categories / Beverages: Coffee & Tea

Stewart's Private Blend Foods
  Chicago, IL 800-654-2862
Thanksgiving Coffee Co
  Fort Bragg, CA 800-462-1999
Utah Coffee Roasters
  South Salt Lake, UT 888-486-3334
Van Roy Coffee Co
  Cleveland, OH 877-826-7669
Weaver Nut Co. Inc.
  Ephrata, PA 800-473-2688
Wechsler Coffee Corporation
  Teterboro, NJ 800-800-2633

Flavored

A Hill of Beans Coffee Roasters
  Omaha, NE 402-333-6048
Arbuckle Coffee Roasters
  Tucson, AZ 800-533-8278
ARCO Coffee
  Superior, WI 800-283-2726
Aroma Coffee Company
  Forest Park, IL 708-488-8340
Atlanta Coffee & Tea Co
  800-426-4781
Cafe Society Coffee Company
  Dallas, TX 800-717-6000
Coffee Roasters Of New Orleans
  Kenner, LA 800-737-5464
Daymar Select Fine Coffees
  El Cajon, CA 800-466-7590
De Coty Coffee Co
  San Angelo, TX 800-588-8001
Distant Lands Coffee Roaster
  Renton, WA 800-758-4437
East Indies Coffee & Tea Co
  Lebanon, PA 800-220-2326
Empire Coffee Company
  Port Chester, NY 800-642-1100
Folgers Coffee Co
  Orrville, OH 800-937-9745
Forto Coffee
  New York, NY 844-450-7575
French Market Coffee
  New Orleans, LA 800-535-1961
Greene Brothers Specialty Coffee Roaster
  Hackettstown, NJ 908-979-0022
Harold L King & Co Inc
  Redwood City, CA 888-368-2233
Hawaii Coffee Company
  Honolulu, HI 800-338-8353
Heritage Coffee Co & Cafe
  Juneau, AK 800-478-5282
Java Beans and Joe Coffee
  Petaluma, CA 800-624-7031
Jelks Coffee Roasters
  Shreveport, LA 800-235-7361
Jodyana Corporation
  Miami, FL 888-563-5282
Kaffe Magnum Opus
  Millville, NJ 800-652-5282
Kauai Coffee Co Inc
  Kalaheo, HI 800-545-8605
Lexington Coffee & Tea
  Lexington, KY 859-277-1102
Longbottom Coffee & Tea Inc
  Hillsboro, OR 800-288-1271
Love Creek Orchards
  Medina, TX 800-449-0882
Lowery's Premium Roast Gourmet Coffee
  Snohomish, WA 800-767-1783
Magnum Coffee Roastery
  Nunica, MI 888-937-5282
Mccullagh Coffee Roasters
  Buffalo, NY 800-753-3473
New Age Beverages
  Denver, CO 303-289-8655
Pearl Coffee Co
  Akron, OH 800-822-5282
Puroast Coffee Co Inc
  Woodland, CA 877-569-2243
Riffel's Coffee Company
  Wichita, KS 888-399-4567
San Francisco Bay Coffee Company
  Lincoln, CA 800-829-1300
San Juan Coffee Roasting Co
  Friday Harbor, WA 800-624-4119
Stewart's Private Blend Foods
  Chicago, IL 800-654-2862
Thanksgiving Coffee Co
  Fort Bragg, CA 800-462-1999
Utah Coffee Roasters
  South Salt Lake, UT 888-486-3334

Weaver Nut Co. Inc.
  Ephrata, PA 800-473-2688
Wechsler Coffee Corporation
  Teterboro, NJ 800-800-2633

Iced

Arizona Beverage Company
  Cincinnati, OH 800-832-3775
Bossen
  Hayward, CA 510-324-0168
Cold Brew EvyTea
  Boston, MA 617-429-5229
Grady's Cold Brew
  Bronx, NY 718-860-1600
Kohana Coffee
  Austin, TX 512-904-1174

Instant

Alpine Start Foods
  Boulder, CO
Chameleon Cold Brew
  Austin, TX
Chock Full O'Nuts
  888-246-2598
Coffee Globe LLC
  Huntington Beach, CA 587-966-1171
Coffee Holding Co Inc
  Staten Island, NY 800-458-2233
Daymar Select Fine Coffees
  El Cajon, CA 800-466-7590
Folgers Coffee Co
  Orrville, OH 800-937-9745
Instant Products of America
  Columbus, IN 812-372-9100
Know Brainer
  Lafayette, CO 303-475-0456
Kuju Coffee
  San Francisco, CA 415-634-5858
LonoLife
  Oceanside, CA 855-843-8566
NeuRoast
  New York, NY
Tonex
  Wallington, NJ 973-773-5135

Instant - Decaffeinated

Swagger Foods Corp
  Vernon Hills, IL 847-913-1200

Latte

Navitas Naturals
  Novato, CA 888-645-4282
NeuRoast
  New York, NY
Pop & Bottle Inc.
  San Francisco, CA

Roasted

A Hill of Beans Coffee Roasters
  Omaha, NE 402-333-6048
Alakef Coffee Roasters Inc
  Duluth, MN 800-438-9228
Allegro Coffee Co
  Thornton, CO 800-666-4869
Arbuckle Coffee Roasters
  Tucson, AZ 800-533-8278
Armeno Coffee Roasters LTD
  Northborough, MA 508-393-2821
Atlanta Coffee & Tea Co
  800-426-4781
Boyd's Coffee Co
  Portland, OR 800-735-2878
Brisk Coffee Co
  Tampa, FL 800-899-5282
Buckmaster Coffee Co
  Hillsboro, OR 800-962-9148
Cafe Bustelo
  Miami, FL 800-990-9039
Cafe Grumpy
  Brooklyn, NY 718-383-0748
Cafe Moto
  San Diego, CA 800-818-3363
Caffe Darte
  Federal Way, WA 800-999-5334
Caffe Ibis Gallery Deli
  Logan, UT 888-740-4777
Captain Cook Coffee Company
  Kealakekua, HI 650-766-9149
Clear Mountain Coffee Company
  Silver Spring, MD 301-587-2233

Coffee Bean Intl
  Portland, OR 800-877-0474
Coffee Reserve
  Phoenix, AZ 888-755-6789
Colonial Coffee Roasters Inc
  Miami, FL 305-638-0885
Daymar Select Fine Coffees
  El Cajon, CA 800-466-7590
Di Lusso & Be Bop Baskote LLC
  Redmond, OR 888-545-7487
Distant Lands Coffee Roaster
  Renton, WA 800-758-4437
Eldorado Coffee Distributors
  Flushing, NY 800-635-2566
Ethical Bean Coffee
  Vancouver, BC 877-431-3830
Finger Lakes Coffee Roasters
  Victor, NY 800-420-6154
Folgers Coffee Co
  Orrville, OH 800-937-9745
Generous Coffee
  Denver, CO
Grounds for Change
  Poulsbo, WA 800-796-6820
Grounds For Thought
  Bowling Green, OH 419-354-3266
Heritage Coffee Co & Cafe
  Juneau, AK 800-478-5282
House of Coffee Beans
  Houston, TX 800-422-1799
Indigo Coffee Roasters
  Florence, MA 800-447-5450
Jeremiah's Pick Coffee Co
  San Francisco, CA 877-537-3642
Kauai Coffee Co Inc
  Kalaheo, HI 800-545-8605
Kohana Coffee
  Austin, TX 512-904-1174
KonaRed Corp.
  Carlsbad, CA 949-682-4700
Lexington Coffee & Tea
  Lexington, KY 859-277-1102
Lola Savannah
  Houston, TX 888-663-9166
Lucile's
  Boulder, CO 800-727-3653
M.E. Swing Company
  Alexandria, VA 800-485-4019
Magnum Coffee Roastery
  Nunica, MI 888-937-5282
Maui Coffee Roasters Wholesale
  Kahului, HI 800-645-2877
Mccullagh Coffee Roasters
  Buffalo, NY 800-753-3473
Milone Brothers Coffee Co
  Modesto, CA 800-974-8500
Montana Coffee Traders
  Whitefish, MT. 800-345-5282
MorningStar Coffee Company
  West Chester, PA 888-854-2233
New Harmony Coffee & Tea Co.
  New Harmony, IN 812-682-4563
North River Roasters
  Poughkeepsie, NY 845-418-2739
Oasis Coffee Co Inc
  Norwalk, CT 203-847-0554
Olympic Coffee & Roasting
  Bellevue, WA 888-244-8313
Pan American Coffee Co
  Hoboken, NJ 800-229-1883
Pfefferkorn's Coffee Inc
  Baltimore, MD 800-682-4665
Puroast Coffee Co Inc
  Woodland, CA 877-569-2243
San Francisco Bay Coffee
  Lincoln, CA 800-829-1300
San Juan Coffee Roasting Co
  Friday Harbor, WA 800-624-4119
Sara Lee Foodservice
  Peoria, IL 800-641-4025
Southern Heritage Coffee Company
  Indianapolis, IN 800-486-1198
Steep & Brew
  Monona, WI 800-876-1986
Stewart's Private Blend Foods
  Chicago, IL 800-654-2862
Texas Coffee Co
  Beaumont, TX 800-259-3400
Torke Coffee Co
  Sheboygan, WI 800-242-7671
U Roast Em Inc
  Hayward, WI 715-634-6255

Product Categories / Beverages: Coffee & Tea

Utah Coffee Roasters
   South Salt Lake, UT 888-486-3334
Van Roy Coffee Co
   Cleveland, OH 877-826-7669
Weaver Nut Co. Inc.
   Ephrata, PA 800-473-2688
Wheeling Coffee & Spice Co
   Wheeling, WV 800-500-0141
White Cloud Coffee
   Boise, ID 888-229-3249
Young Winfield
   Hamilton, ON 905-893-2536

Vacuum Packed

Folgers Coffee Co
   Orrville, OH 800-937-9745

Espresso

A Hill of Beans Coffee Roasters
   Omaha, NE 402-333-6048
Arel Group Wine & Spirits Inc
   Atlanta, GA 404-869-4387
Aroma Coffee Company
   Forest Park, IL 708-488-8340
B&K Coffee
   Oneonta, NY 800-432-1499
Bluechip Group
   Salt Lake City, UT 800-878-0099
Caffe Darte
   Federal Way, WA 800-999-5334
Caffe Luca Coffee Roaste
   Seattle, WA 800-728-9116
Chock Full O'Nuts
    888-246-2598
Dallis Brothers
   Long Island City, NY 718-845-3010
Distant Lands Coffee Roaster
   Renton, WA 800-758-4437
Fama Sales Co
   New York, NY 800-682-0425
Folklore Foods
   Selby, SD 605-649-1144
Fratelli Mantova
   Naperville, IL 630-904-0002
Heritage Coffee Co & Cafe
   Juneau, AK 800-478-5282
High Brew Coffee
   Austin, TX
Ideal Dairy Farms
   Hudson Falls, NY 518-747-5059
Kobricks Coffee Company
   Jersey City, NJ 800-562-7491
Martin Coffee Co
   Jacksonville, FL 904-355-9661
Monticello Vineyards-Corley
   Napa, CA 707-253-2802
Oak Farms
   El Paso, TX 800-395-7004
Puroast Coffee Co Inc
   Woodland, CA. 877-569-2243
Reiter Dairy
   Newport, KY 800-544-6455
San Marco Coffee, Inc.
   Charlotte, NC 800-715-9298
Sebastiani Vineyards
   Sonoma, CA 855-232-2338
Sopralco
   Plantation, FL 954-584-2225
Southern Heritage Coffee Company
   Indianapolis, IN 800-486-1198
Ultra Seal
   New Paltz, NY 845-255-2490
Unilever Canada
   Toronto, ON 416-415-3000

Mocha

Jones Brewing Company
   Smithton, PA 724-483-2400
REBBL
   Emeryville, CA 855-732-2500

Tea

8th Wonder
   Denver, CO 303-868-6296
Abunda Life
   Asbury Park, NJ 732-775-9338
Ahmad Tea
   Deer Park, TX 800-637-7704
Ajiri Tea Company
   Upper Black Eddy, PA 610-982-5075

Al-Rite Fruits & Syrups Co
   Miami, FL 305-652-2540
Alaska Herb & Tea Co
   Anchorage, AK 800-654-2764
Alexander Gourmet Beverages
   Bolton, ON 800-265-5081
Allen Flavors Inc
   Edison, NJ 908-561-5995
Alpine Pure USA
   Falls River, MA 888-332-3392
Alternative Health & Herbs
   Albany, OR 800-345-4152
Amazon Trading, Ltd.
   Colombo,
Amcan Beverages Inc
   American Canyon, CA 800-972-5962
American Instants Inc
   Flanders, NJ 973-584-8811
American Soy Products Inc
   Saline, MI 734-429-2310
Argo Tea
   Chicago, IL 612-553-1550
Artist Coffee
   Londonderry, NH 866-440-4511
Atlanta Coffee & Tea Co
    800-426-4781
B&K Coffee
   Oneonta, NY 800-432-1499
Bagai Tea Company
   San Marcos, CA 760-591-3084
Baily Tea USA Inc
   Rockville, MD 301-704-1739
Barnes & Watson Fine Teas
   Seattle, WA 800-447-8832
Barrows Tea Company
   New Bedford, MA 800-832-5024
Beacon Drive Inn
   Spartanburg, SC 864-585-9387
Bellocq
   Brooklyn, NY 347-463-9231
Bhakti
   Boulder, CO 303-484-8770
Bigelow Tea
   Fairfield, CT 888-244-3569
Blue Willow Tea Co
   Berkeley, CA 800-328-0353
Boston Tea Company
   Hackensack, NJ 800-495-9026
Bountiful Pantry
   Nantucket, MA 617-487-8019
Boyd's Coffee Co
   Portland, OR 800-735-2878
Bread & Chocolate Inc
   Wells River, VT 800-524-6715
Brew Dr. Kombucha
   Portland, OR 760-487-8895
Bruce Tea
Buddha Teas
   Carlsbad, CA 800-642-3754
Busy Bee Yerba Mate
Cadillac Coffee Co
   Ft. Wayne, IN 800-438-6900
Caribbean Coffee Co
   Goleta, CA 800-932-5282
Carolina Treet
   Wilmington, NC 800-616-6344
Celebrity Tea, LLC
   Tampa, FL 813-600-3317
Cham Cold Brew Tea
   New York, NY 646-926-0206
Charleston Tea Plantation
   Wadmalaw Island, SC 800-443-5987
Chartreuse Organic Tea
   Trenton, MI 866-315-7832
Chicago Coffee Roastery
   Huntley, IL 800-762-5402
China Mist Brands
   Scottsdale, AZ 800-242-8807
Choice Organic Teas
   Seattle, WA 866-972-6879
City Bean
   Los Angeles, CA 888-248-9232
Clayton Coffee & Tea
   Modesto, CA 209-576-1120
Clear Mountain Coffee Company
   Silver Spring, MD 301-587-2233
Clearly Kombucha
   San Francisco, CA
Coca-Cola Beverages Northeast
   Bedford, NH 844-619-3388
Coffee Bean & Tea Leaf
   Bloomington, MN 952-853-1148

Coffee Bean Intl
   Portland, OR 800-877-0474
Coffee Beanery LTD
   Flushing, MI 800-441-2255
Coffee Mill Roastery
   Elon, NC 800-729-1727
Coffee Roasters Of New Orleans
   Kenner, LA 800-737-5464
Colorado Spice Co
   Boulder, CO 800-677-7423
Community Coffee Co.
   Baton Rouge, LA 800-884-5282
Company of a Philadelphia Gentleman
   Philadelphia, PA 215-427-2827
Continental Coffee Products Company
   Houston, TX 800-323-6178
Cora Italian Specialties
   Countryside, IL 800-696-2672
Cotswold Cottage Foods
   Arvada, CO 800-208-1977
Custom Coffee Plan
   Torrance, CA 800-841-5949
Damron Corp
   Chicago, IL 800-333-1860
David Rio
   San Francisco, CA 800-454-9605
Davidson's Organics
   Reno, NV 800-882-5888
Davinci Gourmet LTD
   Seattle, WA 800-640-6779
De Coty Coffee Co
   San Angelo, TX 800-588-8001
DMH Ingredients Inc
   Libertyville, IL 847-362-9977
Dried Ingredients, LLC.
   Miami, FL 786-999-8499
Droubi's Imports
   Houston, TX 713-334-1829
East Indies Coffee & Tea Co
   Lebanon, PA 800-220-2326
Eastern Tea Corp
   Monroe Twp, NJ 800-221-0865
Eastrise Trading Corp.
   Baldwin Park, CA
Eden Foods Inc
   Clinton, MI 888-424-3336
Empire Tea Svc
   Columbus, IN 800-790-0246
Equal Exchange Inc
   West Bridgewater, MA 774-776-7400
Evy Tea
   Boston, MA
Farmtrue
   North Stonington, CT 860-495-2231
Fat Snax
   Brooklyn, NY 347-496-5834
Father's Country Hams
   Bremen, KY 270-525-3554
Fee Brothers
   Rochester, NY 800-961-3337
Field Coffee
   Norcross, GA 844-343-5326
Finlay Extracts & Ingredients USA, Inc.
   Florham Park, NJ 800-288-6272
Finlays
   Lincoln, RI 800-288-6272
Flora Inc
   Lynden, WA. 800-446-2110
Flying Embers
   Ventura, CA
Fmali Herb
   Santa Cruz, CA 831-423-7913
Fortunes International Teas
   Mc Kees Rocks, PA 412-771-7767
Generation Tea
   Monsey, NY 866-742-5668
GH Ford Tea Company
   Shokan, NY 845-464-6755
Gloria Jean's Gourmet Coffees
   Irvine, CA 877-320-5282
Golden Moon Tea
   Bristow, VA 877-327-5473
Good Earth Company
   New Providence, NJ 888-625-8227
Grace Tea Co
   Acton, MA 978-635-9500
Great Eastern Sun Trading Co
   Asheville, NC 800-334-5809
H & H Products Co
   Orlando, FL 800-678-8448
Hain Celestial Group Inc
   Lake Success, NY 800-434-4246

Product Categories / Beverages: Coffee & Tea

Harney & Sons Tea Co.
  Millerton, NY 800-832-8463
Harris Tea Company
  Moorestown, NJ 856-793-0290
Has Beans Coffee & Tea Co
  Chico, CA 800-427-2326
Herbs Etc
  Santa Fe, NM 888-694-3727
Heritage Books & Gifts
  Virginia Beach, VA 800-862-2923
Holy Kombucha
  Dallas, TX 855-694-6595
House of Coffee Beans
  Houston, TX 800-422-1799
Humm Kombucha
  Bend, OR. 541-306-6329
Ideal Distributing Company
  Bothell, WA. 425-488-6121
IGZU
ILHWA American Corporation
  Belleville, NJ 800-446-7364
Ineeka Inc
  Chicago, IL 312-733-8327
Innovative Beverage Concepts
  Irvine, CA 949-831-8656
International Tea Importers
  Pico Rivera, CA 877-832-5263
J.G. British Imports
  Bradenton, FL 888-965-1700
Javo Beverage Co., Inc.
  Vista, CA 760-330-1141
John A Vassilaros & Son Inc
  Flushing, NY 718-886-4140
Juice Tyme, Inc.
  Chicago, IL 800-236-5823
Kasira
  Buena Park, CA 800-220-6131
Keurig, Inc
  Reading, MA. 866-901-2739
KeVita
  Oxnard, CA. 888-310-6106
Kobricks Coffee Company
  Jersey City, NJ 800-562-7491
KOE Organic Kombucha
  Vernon, CA
Kombucha Wonder Drink
  Portland, OR 877-224-7331
Kuli Kuli, Inc.
  Oakland, CA. 510-350-8325
LA Lifestyle Nutritional Products
  Santa Ana, CA 800-387-4786
Lacas Coffee Co Inc
  Pennsauken, NJ. 800-220-1133
Leaves Pure Teas
  Scottsdale, AZ. 800-242-8807
Lexington Coffee & Tea
  Lexington, KY 859-277-1102
LIVE Soda
  Austin, TX
Lowcountry Produce
  Raleigh, NC 800-935-2792
Lyons Magnus
  Fresno, CA 800-344-7130
MacKinlay Teas
  Ann Arbor, MI 734-846-0966
Madys Company
  San Francisco, CA 415-822-2277
Marin Kombucha
  Novato, CA. 415-496-5441
Mars Inc.
  McLean, VA 703-821-4900
Martin Bauer Group
  Sacaucus, NJ. 201-659-3100
Masala Chai Company
  Santa Cruz, CA 831-475-8881
Master Brew
  Northbrook, IL 847-564-3600
Metropolitan Tea Company
  Cheektowaga, NY. 800-388-0351
Mighty Leaf Tea
  San Rafael, CA 877-698-5323
MindFull, Inc.
  Hutto, TX
Miracle Tree
  Miami, FL. 888-590-1555
Miss Tea Brooklyn Inc
  Brooklyn, NY 718-389-9090
Montana Coffee Traders
  Whitefish, MT. 800-345-5282
Mother Parker's Tea & Coffee
  Mississauga, ON 800-387-9398

Mountanos Family Coffee & Tea Co.
  Petaluma, CA 800-624-7031
Mr. Mak's
  New York, NY 888-953-9209
New Age Beverages
  Denver, CO 303-289-8655
Newby Teas
  East Lansing, MI. 517-999-0590
Nirwana Foods
  Jersey City, NJ 201-659-2200
Northwestern Foods
  Arden Hills, MN 800-236-4937
Numi Organic Tea
  Oakland, CA. 888-404-6864
O'Neil's Distributors
  Goodland, IN 219-297-4521
O'Neill Coffee Co
  West Middlesex, PA 724-528-2244
Pappy's Sassafras Tea
  Columbus Grove, OH 877-659-5110
PepsiCo.
  Purchase, NY 914-253-2000
Piper & Leaf
  Huntsville, AL 256-929-9404
Pocas International
  South Hackensack, NJ. 201-941-7900
Prince of Peace
  Hayward, CA 800-732-2328
Progenix Corporation
  Wausau, WI. 800-233-3356
Q.E. Tea
  Bridgeville, PA 800-622-8327
Refresco Beverages US Inc.
  Tampa, FL. 888-260-3776
Republic of Tea
  Novato, CA. 800-298-4832
Richard's Gourmet Coffee
  West Bridgewater, MA. 800-370-2633
Rooibee Red Tea
  Louisville, KY 502-749-0800
Royal Pacific Coffee Co
  Scottsdale, AZ. 480-951-8251
S & D Coffee Inc
  Concord, NC 800-933-2210
Sampac Enterprises
  S San Francisco, CA. 650-876-0808
Schneider's Dairy Inc
  Pittsburgh, PA. 412-881-3525
Secret Tea Garden
  Vancouver, BC 604-261-3070
Serendipitea
  Manhasset, NY 888-832-5433
Sherwood Brands
  New Brunswick, NJ 973-249-8200
Simpson & Vail
  Brookfield, CT 800-282-8327
SpecialTeas
  Norwalk, CT 888-365-6983
Starbucks
  Seattle, WA 800-782-7282
Stevens Creative Enterprises, Inc.
  New York, NY 646-558-6336
Stewart's Private Blend Foods
  Chicago, IL. 800-654-2862
Sturm Foods Inc
  Manawa, WI. 800-347-8876
Sunfood
  El Cajon, CA. 888-729-3663
Sunlike Juice
  Rougemont, QC 866-552-7643
Takeiya USA
  Huntington Beach, CA 714-374-9900
Tata Tea
  Plant City, FL. 813-754-2602
Tatra Herb Co
  Morrisville, PA. 888-828-7248
Tazo Tea
  Kent, WA. 855-829-6832
Tea Beyond
  West Caldwell, NJ. 973-226-0327
Tea Forte
  Concord, MA 978-369-1598
Tea Needs Inc
  Boca Raton, FL. 877-832-8289
Tea Room
  San Leandro, CA. 510-567-8868
Teeccino
  Carpinteria, CA. 800-498-3434
Templar Food Products
  New Providence, NJ. 800-883-6752
Ten Ren Tea & Ginseng Co Inc
  New York, NY 800-292-2049

Tetley USA
  Marietta, GA. 770-428-5555
Tetley USA
  Edison, NJ. 800-728-0084
The Tea Spot, Inc.
  Boulder, CO 303-444-8324
Thirs-Tea Corp
  Boca Raton, FL. 561-948-5600
Thrive Farmers
  Roswell, GA 855-553-2763
Thyme Garden Herb Co
  Alsea, OR. 800-482-4372
TMI Trading Co
  Brooklyn, NY 718-821-5052
Traditional Medicinals Inc
  Sebastopol, CA. 800-543-4372
Two Leaves & A Bud Inc
  Basalt, CO. 866-631-7973
U Roast Em Inc
  Hayward, WI. 715-634-6255
Ultra Seal
  New Paltz, NY 845-255-2490
Uncle Lee's Tea Inc
  South El Monte, CA 800-732-8830
Unilever Canada
  Toronto, ON 416-415-3000
Unilever Food Solutions
  Englewood Cliffs, NJ
Van Roy Coffee Co
  Cleveland, OH 877-826-7669
VIP Foods
  Flushing, NY 718-821-5330
Weaver Nut Co. Inc.
  Ephrata, PA 800-473-2688
Wechsler Coffee Corporation
  Teterboro, NJ. 800-800-2633
White Coffee Corporation
  Long Island City, NY 800-221-0140
White Rock Products Corp
  Flushing, NY 800-969-7625
Whole Herb Co
  Sonoma, CA 707-935-1077
Wild Hibiscus Flower Company
  Richford, VT 800-499-8490
Wild Zora Foods
  Loveland, CO 970-541-9672
Wise Mouth
  Warren, RI
World Ginseng Ctr Inc
  San Francisco, CA. 800-747-8808
Yaupon Tea
  Savannah, GA 912-596-1506
Yellow Emperor Inc
  Eugene, OR 877-485-6664
Yogi® Tea
  Springfield, OR. 800-964-4832
Zest Tea LLC
  Baltimore, MD 636-579-1809
Zhena's Gypsy Tea
  Commerce, CA 800-448-0803

Bags

ABC Tea House
  Baldwin Park, CA. 888-220-3988
Barrows Tea Company
  New Bedford, MA 800-832-5024
Blue Ridge Tea & Herb Co
  Brooklyn, NY 718-625-3100
Carrington Tea Co.
  Closter, NJ. 800-505-9546
Choice Organic Teas
  Seattle, WA 866-972-6879
Eastern Shore Tea
  Lutherville, MD 800-823-1408
Eastern Tea Corp
  Monroe Twp, NJ. 800-221-0865
Empire Tea Svc
  Columbus, IN 800-790-0246
Modern Tea Packers
  Brooklyn, NY 718-417-1060
Newby Teas
  East Lansing, MI. 517-999-0590
Numi Organic Tea
  Oakland, CA. 888-404-6864
Tetley Tea
  New Providence, NJ. 800-728-0084

Black

Alpine Pure USA
  Falls River, MA 888-332-3392

Product Categories / Beverages: Coffee & Tea

Atlanta Coffee & Tea Co 800-426-4781
Bellocq
  Brooklyn, NY 347-463-9231
Frontier Co-op
  Norway, IA 844-550-6200
GH Ford Tea Company
  Shokan, NY 845-464-6755
Harney & Sons Tea Co.
  Millerton, NY 800-832-8463
Harris Tea Company
  Moorestown, NJ 856-793-0290
MindFull, Inc.
  Hutto, TX
Nourishtea
  Toronto, ON 416-539-9299
SpecialTeas
  Norwalk, CT 888-365-6983
Stash Tea Co
  Portland, OR 800-547-1514
Talbott Teas
  Emeryville, CA 855-850-6309

Chai

Alpine Pure USA
  Falls River, MA 888-332-3392
Bhakti
  Boulder, CO 303-484-8770
Chai Diaries
  Mission Viejo, CA 917-460-6828
Choice Organic Teas
  Seattle, WA 866-972-6879
David Rio
  San Francisco, CA 800-454-9605
Davinci Gourmet LTD
  Seattle, WA 800-640-6779
Father's Country Hams
  Bremen, KY 270-525-3554
Gray Duck
  Minneapolis, MN
Harris Tea Company
  Moorestown, NJ 856-793-0290
Know Brainer
  Lafayette, CO 303-475-0456
Masala Chai Company
  Santa Cruz, CA 831-475-8881
Nature's Guru
  Cerritos, CA 949-478-4878
Oregon Chai
  Portland, OR 888-874-2424
Pacific Chai
  Farmington, UT 888-882-4248
Sattwa Chai
  Newberg, OR 503-538-4715
Stash Tea Co
  Portland, OR 800-547-1514
Templar Food Products
  New Providence, NJ 800-883-6752
Third Street Inc
  Louisville, CO 800-636-3790
Toddy Products Inc
  Midland, TX 713-225-2066

Chamomile

Castella Imports Inc
  Brentwood, NY 631-231-5500
Cham Cold Brew Tea
  New York, NY 646-926-0206
Choice Organic Teas
  Seattle, WA 866-972-6879
The Poseidon Group
  New York, NY 646-926-0206

Darjeeling

Choice Organic Teas
  Seattle, WA 866-972-6879
GH Ford Tea Company
  Shokan, NY 845-464-6755

Decaffeinated

Alexander Gourmet Beverages
  Bolton, ON 800-265-5081
Ancora Coffee Roasters
  Madison, WI 800-260-0217
Boston Tea Company
  Hackensack, NJ 800-495-9026
Castella Imports Inc
  Brentwood, NY 631-231-5500
Choice Organic Teas
  Seattle, WA 866-972-6879

GH Ford Tea Company
  Shokan, NY 845-464-6755
Harney & Sons Tea Co.
  Millerton, NY 800-832-8463
Martin Bauer Group
  Sacaucus, NJ 201-659-3100
Masala Chai Company
  Santa Cruz, CA 831-475-8881
Mother Parker's Tea & Coffee
  Mississauga, ON 800-387-9398
SpecialTeas
  Norwalk, CT 888-365-6983
Weaver Nut Co. Inc.
  Ephrata, PA 800-473-2688

Earl Grey

Alpine Pure USA
  Falls River, MA 888-332-3392
Blue Willow Tea Co
  Berkeley, CA 800-328-0353
Choice Organic Teas
  Seattle, WA 866-972-6879
GH Ford Tea Company
  Shokan, NY 845-464-6755
Harris Tea Company
  Moorestown, NJ 856-793-0290

Earl Grey Decaffeinated

Choice Organic Teas
  Seattle, WA 866-972-6879

English Breakfast

Choice Organic Teas
  Seattle, WA 866-972-6879
Harris Tea Company
  Moorestown, NJ 856-793-0290

Fair-Trade

Flying Bird Botanicals LLC
  Bellingham, WA 360-366-8013
North River Roasters
  Poughkeepsie, NY 845-418-2739

Flavored

Alaska Herb & Tea Co
  Anchorage, AK 800-654-2764
Aqua Vie Beverage Corporation
  Ketchum, ID 800-744-7500
Arbuckle Coffee Roasters
  Tucson, AZ 800-533-8278
Belmar Spring Water
  Glen Rock, NJ 201-444-1010
Best Foods
  Englewood Cliffs, NJ 201-894-4000
Boston Tea Company
  Hackensack, NJ 800-495-9026
Cafe Society Coffee Company
  Dallas, TX 800-717-6000
Celebrity Tea, LLC
  Tampa, FL 813-600-3317
Choice Organic Teas
  Seattle, WA 866-972-6879
Coca-Cola Beverages Northeast
  Bedford, NH 844-619-3388
Daymar Select Fine Coffees
  El Cajon, CA 800-466-7590
Dr. B's Beverages, LLC
  Inwood, WV 304-283-2257
East Indies Coffee & Tea Co
  Lebanon, PA 800-220-2326
Empire Tea Svc
  Columbus, IN 800-790-0246
Father's Country Hams
  Bremen, KY 270-525-3554
First Colony Coffee & Tea Company
  Norfolk, VA 800-446-8555
Fortunes International Teas
  Mc Kees Rocks, PA 412-771-7767
Harney & Sons Tea Co.
  Millerton, NY 800-832-8463
Harris Tea Company
  Moorestown, NJ 856-793-0290
Houston Tea & Beverage
  Houston, TX 800-585-4549
LemonKind
  New York, NY 954-678-1700
Martin Bauer Group
  Sacaucus, NJ 201-659-3100
Masala Chai Company
  Santa Cruz, CA 831-475-8881

Mother Parker's Tea & Coffee
  Mississauga, ON 800-387-9398
Pappy's Sassafras Tea
  Columbus Grove, OH 877-659-5110
Rooibee Red Tea
  Louisville, KY 502-749-0800
San Francisco Bay Coffee Company
  Lincoln, CA 800-829-1300
SpecialTeas
  Norwalk, CT 888-365-6983
Stewart's Private Blend Foods
  Chicago, IL 800-654-2862
Weaver Nut Co. Inc.
  Ephrata, PA 800-473-2688

Green

360 Nutrition
  Los Angeles, CA 213-805-3015
Aiya America Inc
  Torrance, CA 310-212-1395
Alexander Gourmet Beverages
  Bolton, ON 800-265-5081
Alpine Pure USA
  Falls River, MA 888-332-3392
Ancora Coffee Roasters
  Madison, WI 800-260-0217
AOI Tea Company
  Huntington Beach, CA 877-264-0877
Baycliff Co Inc
  Garwood, NJ 866-772-7569
Bellocq
  Brooklyn, NY 347-463-9231
Boston Tea Company
  Hackensack, NJ 800-495-9026
China Mist Brands
  Scottsdale, AZ 800-242-8807
Choice Organic Teas
  Seattle, WA 866-972-6879
Davinci Gourmet LTD
  Seattle, WA 800-640-6779
Eden Foods Inc
  Clinton, MI 888-424-3336
Empire Tea Svc
  Columbus, IN 800-790-0246
Fmali Herb
  Santa Cruz, CA 831-423-7913
Fortunes International Teas
  Mc Kees Rocks, PA 412-771-7767
Frontier Co-op
  Norway, IA 844-550-6200
Fuzz East Coast
  Englewood Cliffs, NJ 866-438-3893
GH Ford Tea Company
  Shokan, NY 845-464-6755
Harney & Sons Tea Co.
  Millerton, NY 800-832-8463
Harris Tea Company
  Moorestown, NJ 856-793-0290
Healthy Beverage LLC
  Doylestown, PA 800-295-1388
Jade Leaf Matcha
  San Francisco, CA
Limitless
  Chicago, IL
Martin Bauer Group
  Sacaucus, NJ 201-659-3100
MindFull, Inc.
  Hutto, TX
Motto
  Milton, MA 617-848-9248
Nourishtea
  Toronto, ON 416-539-9299
Nu Naturals Inc
  Eugene, OR 800-753-4372
REBBL
  Emeryville, CA 855-732-2500
RFi Ingredients
  Blauvelt, NY 800-962-7663
Sencha Naturals
  Los Angeles, CA 888-473-6242
SpecialTeas
  Norwalk, CT 888-365-6983
Stash Tea Co
  Portland, OR 800-547-1514
Talbott Teas
  Emeryville, CA 855-850-6309
Teapigs
  Brooklyn, NY 212-705-8723
Templar Food Products
  New Providence, NJ 800-883-6752
The Healthy Beverage Company
  Doylestown, PA 800-295-1388

Product Categories / Beverages: Coffee & Tea

The Long Life Beverage Company
  Mission Hills, CA 800-848-7331

Herbal

Abunda Life
  Asbury Park, NJ 732-775-9338
Algonquin Tea
  Eganville, ON 800-292-6671
Alternative Health & Herbs
  Albany, OR 800-345-4152
Ancora Coffee Roasters
  Madison, WI 800-260-0217
Bellocq
  Brooklyn, NY 347-463-9231
Berardi's Fresh Roast
  Cleveland, OH 800-876-9109
Best Foods
  Englewood Cliffs, NJ 201-894-4000
Body Breakthrough Inc
  Deer Park, NY 800-924-3343
Boston Spice & Tea Company
  Boston, VA 800-966-4372
Boston Tea Company
  Hackensack, NJ 800-495-9026
Chartreuse Organic Tea
  Trenton, MI 866-315-7832
China Mist Brands
  Scottsdale, AZ 800-242-8807
Choice Organic Teas
  Seattle, WA 866-972-6879
Coffee Bean Intl
  Portland, OR 800-877-0474
Common Folk Farm
  Naples, ME 207-787-2764
Empire Tea Svc
  Columbus, IN 800-790-0246
Fmali Herb
  Santa Cruz, CA 831-423-7913
Fortunes International Teas
  Mc Kees Rocks, PA 412-771-7767
Frontier Co-op
  Norway, IA 844-550-6200
GH Ford Tea Company
  Shokan, NY 845-464-6755
Harris Tea Company
  Moorestown, NJ 856-793-0290
Health & Wholeness Store
  Fairfield, IA 800-255-8332
Herb Tea Company
  Oxnard, CA 805-486-6477
HerbaSway Laboratories
  Wallingford, CT 800-672-7322
Heritage Books & Gifts
  Virginia Beach, VA 800-862-2923
Hobe Laboratories Inc
  Tempe, AZ 800-528-4482
ILHWA American Corporation
  Belleville, NJ 800-446-7364
Madys Company
  San Francisco, CA 415-822-2227
Martin Bauer Group
  Sacaucus, NJ 201-659-3100
Montana Tea & Spice Trading
  Missoula, MT 406-721-4882
Mother Parker's Tea & Coffee
  Mississauga, ON 800-387-9398
Native Scents
  Taos, NM 800-645-3471
Nourishtea
  Toronto, ON 416-539-9299
NOW Foods
  Bloomingdale, IL 888-669-3663
Nutritional Counselors of America
  Spencer, TN 931-946-3600
Old Fashioned Natural Products
  Santa Ana, CA 800-552-9045
Organic India USA
  Boulder, CO 888-550-8332
P C Teas Co
  Burlingame, CA 800-423-8728
Progenix Corporation
  Wausau, WI 800-233-3356
San Francisco Bay Coffee Company
  Lincoln, CA 800-829-1300
Stash Tea Co
  Portland, OR 800-547-1514
Sugai Kona Coffee
  Holualoa, HI 808-322-7717
Tatra Herb Co
  Morrisville, PA 888-828-7248
Templar Food Products
  New Providence, NJ 800-883-6752

Traditional Medicinals Inc
  Sebastopol, CA 800-543-4372
Triple Leaf Tea Inc
  S San Francisco, CA 800-552-7448
Vermont Liberty Tea
  Waterbury, VT 802-244-6102
Wah Yet Group
  Hayward, CA 800-229-3392
Whole Herb Co
  Sonoma, CA 707-935-1077

Iced

4C Foods Corp
  Brooklyn, NY 718-272-4242
Al-Rite Fruits & Syrups Co
  Miami, FL 305-652-2540
Amcan Beverages Inc
  American Canyon, CA 800-972-5962
Arizona Beverage Company
  Cincinnati, OH 800-832-3775
Arteasans Beverages LLC
  North Miami Beach, FL 305-363-5410
Bay Pac Beverages
  Walnut Creek, CA 925-279-0800
Best Foods
  Englewood Cliffs, NJ 201-894-4000
Better Beverages Inc
  Cerritos, CA 800-344-5219
Bhakti
  Boulder, CO 303-484-8770
Bigelow Tea
  Fairfield, CT 888-244-3569
Boyd's Coffee Co
  Portland, OR 800-735-2878
China Mist Brands
  Scottsdale, AZ 800-242-8807
Clover Farms Dairy Co Inc
  Reading, PA 800-323-0123
Coca-Cola Beverages Northeast
  Bedford, NH 844-619-3388
Dr. B's Beverages, LLC
  Inwood, WV 304-283-2257
Droubi's Imports
  Houston, TX 713-334-1829
Ensemble Beverages
  Montgomery, AL 334-324-7719
Farmland Dairies
  Wallington, NJ 888-727-6252
Galliker Dairy Co
  Johnstown, PA 800-477-6455
Global Beverage Company
  Rochester, NY 585-381-3560
Good-O-Beverages Inc
  Bronx, NY 718-328-6400
Harney & Sons Tea Co.
  Millerton, NY 800-832-8463
Harris Tea Company
  Moorestown, NJ 856-793-0290
Hearttea Inc.
  Brooklyn, NY 917-725-3164
Honest Tea Inc
  Atlanta, GA 800-520-2653
Inko's Tea
  Willowbrook, IL
Ito En USA Inc
  Brooklyn, NY 808-847-4477
Joe Tea and Joe Chips
  Upper Montclair, NJ 973-744-7502
Keurig Dr Pepper
  Plano, TX 800-696-5891
Lassonde Pappas & Company, Inc.
  Carneys Point, NJ 800-257-7019
Leroy Hill Coffee Co Inc
  Mobile, AL 800-866-5282
Marburger Farm Dairy
  Evans City, PA 800-331-1295
Moonshine Sweet Tea
  Austin, TX 888-793-3883
Motto
  Milton, MA 617-848-9248
Northwestern Foods
  Arden Hills, MN 800-236-4937
PR Bar
  Chandler, AZ 800-397-5556
Purity Organic
  Oakland, CA 415-440-7777
Rosenberger's Dairies
  Hatfield, PA 800-355-9074
Schneider's Dairy Inc
  Pittsburgh, PA 412-881-3525
Schneider-Valley Farms Inc
  Williamsport, PA 570-326-2021

Serengeti Tea Co
  Gardena, CA 888-604-2040
Stash Tea Co
  Portland, OR 800-547-1514
Sturm Foods Inc
  Manawa, WI 800-347-8876
Sunlike Juice
  Rougemont, QC 866-552-7643
Sweet Leaf Tea Company
  Austin, TX 512-328-7775
Swiss Premium Dairy Inc
  Lebanon, PA 800-222-2129
The Healthy Beverage Company
  Doylestown, PA 800-295-1388
Third Street Inc
  Louisville, CO 800-636-3790
Tradewinds
  Austin, TX
Turkey Hill Dairy Inc
  Conestoga, PA 800-693-2479
United Dairy Inc.
  Martins Ferry, OH 800-252-1542
White Rock Products Corp
  Flushing, NY 800-969-7625
Zeigler's
  Lansdale, PA 215-855-5161

Instant

American Instants Inc
  Flanders, NJ 973-584-8811
Best Foods
  Englewood Cliffs, NJ 201-894-4000
Castella Imports Inc
  Brentwood, NY 631-231-5500
Cusa Tea
  Boulder, CO
Daymar Select Fine Coffees
  El Cajon, CA 800-466-7590
Finlay Extracts & Ingredients USA, Inc.
  Florham Park, NJ 800-288-6272
Harris Tea Company
  Moorestown, NJ 856-793-0290
Martin Bauer Group
  Sacaucus, NJ 201-659-3100
Northwestern Foods
  Arden Hills, MN 800-236-4937
Pappy's Sassafras Tea
  Columbus Grove, OH 877-659-5110
Prince of Peace
  Hayward, CA 800-732-2328
VIP Foods
  Flushing, NY 718-821-5330
Weaver Nut Co. Inc.
  Ephrata, PA 800-473-2688
Whole Herb Co
  Sonoma, CA 707-935-1077

Irish Breakfast

Choice Organic Teas
  Seattle, WA 866-972-6879
Harris Tea Company
  Moorestown, NJ 856-793-0290

Jasmine

Alpine Pure USA
  Falls River, MA 888-332-3392
Blue Willow Tea Co
  Berkeley, CA 800-328-0353
Choice Organic Teas
  Seattle, WA 866-972-6879

Lemon

Davinci Gourmet LTD
  Seattle, WA 800-640-6779
Father's Country Hams
  Bremen, KY 270-525-3554

Loose Leaf

Bigelow Tea
  Fairfield, CT 888-244-3569
Choice Organic Teas
  Seattle, WA 866-972-6879
David Rio
  San Francisco, CA 800-454-9605
Great Lakes Tea & Spice
  Glen Arbor, MI 877-645-9363
Newby Teas
  East Lansing, MI 517-999-0590
Numi Organic Tea
  Oakland, CA 888-404-6864

Product Categories / Beverages: Juices

Rishi Tea
   Milwaukee, WI 866-747-4483
Takeiya USA
   Huntington Beach, CA 714-374-9900
Tea Room
   San Leandro, CA. 510-567-8868
The Tao of Tea
   Portland, OR 503-736-0119
Thrive Farmers
   Roswell, GA 855-553-2763
Tiesta Tea
   Chicago, IL 312-202-6800
Vermont Tea & Trading Co Inc
   Middlebury, VT. 888-255-9327
Wild Leaf Active Tea
   Sparta, NJ 888-605-7564

Mint

Choice Organic Teas
   Seattle, WA. 866-972-6879
Father's Country Hams
   Bremen, KY 270-525-3554
GH Ford Tea Company
   Shokan, NY. 845-464-6755
Harris Tea Company
   Moorestown, NJ 856-793-0290

Mint Herb

Choice Organic Teas
   Seattle, WA. 866-972-6879
REBBL
   Emeryville, CA. 855-732-2500

Oolong

Astral Extracts
   Syosset, NY. 516-496-2505
Bellocq
   Brooklyn, NY 347-463-9231
Choice Organic Teas
   Seattle, WA. 866-972-6879
Harney & Sons Tea Co.
   Millerton, NY 800-832-8463
Martin Bauer Group
   Sacaucus, NJ 201-659-3100
SpecialTeas
   Norwalk, CT 888-365-6983
Stash Tea Co
   Portland, OR 800-547-1514
Templar Food Products
   New Providence, NJ. 800-883-6752
Whole Herb Co
   Sonoma, CA 707-935-1077

Orange Pekoe

Choice Organic Teas
   Seattle, WA. 866-972-6879

Peppermint Leaf

Choice Organic Teas
   Seattle, WA. 866-972-6879
Martin Bauer Group
   Sacaucus, NJ 201-659-3100
Whole Herb Co
   Sonoma, CA 707-935-1077

Sun

American Instants Inc
   Flanders, NJ 973-584-8811
Atlanta Coffee & Tea Co
   800-426-4781
Thirs-Tea Corp
   Boca Raton, FL. 561-948-5600
Unilever Canada
   Toronto, ON 416-415-3000

Juices

Alamance Foods
   Burlington, NC
Alfer Laboratories
   Chatsworth, CA 818-709-0737
All Juice Food & Beverage
   Ankeny, IA 800-736-5674
Aloe Farms Inc
   Harlingen, TX. 800-262-6771
Aloe Laboratories
   Harlingen, TX. 800-258-5380
Amcan Beverages Inc
   American Canyon, CA 800-972-5962
Amcan Industries
   Elmsford, NY 914-347-4838
American Soy Products Inc
   Saline, MI 734-429-2310
Arctic Beverages
   Winnipeg, MB. 866-503-1270
Aseltine Cider Company
   Comstock Park, MI 616-784-6615
Back to Nature Foods
   855-346-2225
Berkeley Farms
   Hayward, CA 800-395-7004
Beverage Capital Corporation
   Baltimore, MD 410-242-7404
Birdseye Dairy-Morning Glory
   Green Bay, WI. 920-494-5388
Bully Hill Vineyards
   Hammondsport, NY 607-868-3610
Cadbury Beverages Canada
   Mississauga, ON. 905-712-4121
California Custom Fruits
   Baldwin Park, CA. 877-558-0056
Carolina Products
   Tampa, FL. 813-313-1800
Cascadian Farm Inc
   Sedro Woolley, WA. 360-855-0542
Cell-Nique
   Norwalk, CT 888-417-9343
Chase Brothers Dairy
   Oxnard, CA 800-438-6455
Citrosuco North America Inc
   Lake Wales, FL. 800-356-4592
Citrus International
   Winter Park, FL. 407-629-8037
Citrus Service
   Winter Garden, FL 407-656-4999
Clover Farms Dairy Co Inc
   Reading, PA 800-323-0123
Coastlog Industries
   Novi, MI 248-344-9556
Coca-Cola Bottling Co. Consolidated
   Charlotte, NC 800-866-2653
Coca-Cola Bottling Company UNITED, Inc.
   Birmingham, AB. 800-844-2653
Coca-Cola Co.
   Atlanta, GA. 800-438-2653
Coca-Cola European Partners
   Uxbridge, Middx. 800-418-4223
Cold Hollow Cider Mill
   Waterbury Center, VT. 800-327-7537
Commodities Marketing Inc
   Clarksburg, NJ 732-516-0700
Conoley Citrus Packers Inc
   Winter Garden, FL 407-656-3300
Country Life
   Hauppauge, NY 800-645-5768
Country Pure Foods Inc
   Akron, OH. 877-995-8423
Crown Regal Wine Cellars
   Brooklyn, NY 718-604-1430
Cumberland Dairy
   Rosenhayn, NJ 800-257-8484
Cutting Edge Beverages
   Boca Raton, FL. 561-347-5860
Cyclone Enterprises Inc
   Houston, TX. 281-872-0087
Daily Greens LLC
   Austin, TX. 512-524-1500
Dairy Maid Dairy LLC
   Frederick, MD. 301-663-5114
Damon Industries
   Sparks, NV 800-225-3046
Del Monte Fresh Produce Inc.
   Coral Gables, FL. 800-950-3683
Del's Lemonade & Refreshments
   Cranston, RI 401-463-6190
Empresa La Famosa
   Toa Baja, PR 787-251-0060
Empresas La Famosa
   Toa Baja, PR 787-251-0060
Everfresh Beverages
   Warren, MI 800-323-3416
Farmland Dairies
   Wallington, NJ 888-727-6252
Flavouressence Products
   Mississauga, ON. 866-209-7778
Florida Key West
   Fort Myers, FL 239-694-8787
Four Chimneys Farm Winery Trust
   Himrod, NY 607-243-7502
Fuzz East Coast
   Englewood Cliffs, NJ 866-438-3893
GLCC Co
   Paw Paw, MI. 269-657-3167
Global Beverage Company
   Rochester, NY 585-381-3560
Good-O-Beverages Inc
   Bronx, NY. 718-328-6400
Green Spot Packaging
   Claremont, CA 800-456-3210
Hallcrest Vineyards
   Felton, CA. 831-335-4441
Happy Planet Foods
   Burnaby, BC 800-811-3213
Harrisburg Dairies Inc
   Harrisburg, PA 800-692-7429
Heck Cellars
   Arvin, CA 661-854-6120
Helthe Brands
   Austin, TX. 888-311-2157
Heritage Farms Dairy
   Murfreesboro, TN 615-895-2790
Hi-Country Foods Corporation
   Selah, WA 509-697-7292
Honest Tea Inc
   Atlanta, GA. 800-520-2653
Howard Foods Inc
   Danvers, MA. 978-774-6207
Hudson Valley Fruit Juice
   Highland, NY 845-691-8061
Hygeia Dairy Company
   Corpus Christi, TX 361-854-4561
Inn Foods Inc
   Watsonville, CA 800-708-7836
IQ Juice
   Bayville, NY 516-864-0034
Island Aseptics
   Byesville, OH 740-685-2548
IZZE Beverage
   Boulder, CO 877-476-7380
Jin+Ja
   New York, NY 215-690-1470
Johanna Foods Inc.
   Flemington, NJ 800-727-6700
Juice Mart
   West Hills, CA 877-888-1011
Juice Tyme, Inc.
   Chicago, IL 800-236-5823
Juicy Whip Inc
   La Verne, CA 909-392-7500
Kan-Pak
   Arkansas City, KS. 800-378-1265
Kemach Food Products
   Brooklyn, NY 718-272-5655
Keurig Dr Pepper
   Plano, TX 800-696-5891
KidsLuv
   San Francisco, CA 855-543-7588
King Juice Co
   Milwaukee, WI 414-482-0303
Kleinpeter Farms Dairy LLC
   Baton Rouge, LA 225-753-2121
Knouse Foods Co-Op Inc.
   Peach Glen, PA 717-677-8181
Kobu Beverages, LLC,
   Brooklyn, NY 718-566-2739
Krier Foods
   Random Lake, WI. 920-994-2469
Lakewood Juice Company
   Miami, FL 866-324-5900
Legacy Juice Works
   Saratoga Springs, NY 518-583-1108
Lemon-X Corporation
   Huntington Station, NY 800-220-1061
Lenox-Martell Inc
   Boston, MA. 877-325-2489
Louis Dreyfus Company Citrus Inc
   Winter Garden, FL 407-656-1000
Lyons Magnus
   Fresno, CA 800-344-7130
M & B Products Inc
   Tampa, FL. 800-899-7255
Magnotta Winery Corporation
   Vaughan, ON. 800-461-9463
Mamma Chia
   Carlsbad, CA. 855-588-2442
Marburger Farm Dairy
   Evans City, PA 800-331-1295
Marquis
   Los Angeles, CA. 213-250-7414
Marva Maid Dairy
   Newport News, VA 800-768-6243
Maui Gold Pineapple Company
   Pukalani, HI 808-877-3805

Product Categories / Beverages: Juices

Mayer Bros
Buffalo, NY............................800-696-2928
Mayer's Cider Mill
Webster, NY............................800-543-0043
Mayfield Dairy Farms LLC
Athens, TN.............................800-362-9546
Mayfield Farms and Nursery
Athens, TN.............................423-746-9859
Mccutcheon Apple Products
Frederick, MD..........................800-888-7537
Meduri Farms
Dallas, OR.............................877-388-8800
Meier's Wine Cellars Inc
Cincinnati, OH.........................800-346-2941
Meramec Vineyards
St James, MO..........................877-216-9463
Misfit Juicery
Washington, DC........................703-465-5355
Mott's
Plano, TX.............................800-426-4891
Mott's LLP
Plano, TX.............................800-426-4891
Mountain Valley Products Inc
Sunnyside, WA.........................509-837-8084
Naked Juice Company
Monrovia, CA..........................877-858-4237
Nana Mae's Organics
Sebastopol, CA........................707-829-7359
Natalie's Orchid Island Juice Co.
Ft. Pierce, FL.........................800-373-7444
National Grape Co-Op
Westfield, NY..........................800-340-6870
Nootra Life
Northland Cranberries
Jackson, WI............................866-719-5215
Northland Juices
Port Washington, NY...................866-719-5215
Northwest Naturals LLC
Bothell, WA............................425-881-2200
Oakhurst Dairy
Portland, ME...........................800-482-0718
Oberweis Dairy Inc
North Aurora, IL.......................866-623-7934
Odwalla
Sugar Land, TX........................800-639-2552
Patience Fruit & Co.
Villeroy, QC
Peace Mountain Natural Beverages
Springfield, MA........................413-567-4942
Perfect Foods Inc
Goshen, NY............................800-933-3288
Pilgrim Foods
Great Neck, NY........................516-466-0522
POM Wonderful LLC
Los Angeles, CA......................866-976-6999
Premier Juices
Clearwater, FL........................727-533-8200
Pressery
Denver, CO
Purity Dairies LLC
Nashville, TN..........................615-244-1900
Purity Organic
Oakland, CA...........................415-440-7777
Pyramid Juice Company
Ashland, OR...........................541-482-2292
R.J. Corr Naturals
Posen, IL..............................708-389-4200
Rapunzel Pure Organics
Bloomfield, NJ........................800-225-1449
Refresco Beverages US Inc.
Tampa, FL.............................888-260-3776
Reiter Dairy LLC
Springfield, OH........................937-323-5777
SANGARIA USA
Torrance, CA..........................310-530-2202
Saratoga Spring Water Co
Saratoga Springs, NY.................888-426-8642
Scally's Imperial Importing Company Inc
Staten Island, NY.....................718-983-1938
Schneider's Dairy Inc
Pittsburgh, PA........................412-881-3525
Schneider-Valley Farms Inc
Williamsport, PA......................570-326-2021
Sherrill Orchards
Arvin, CA.............................661-858-2035
Shonan USA Inc
Grandview, WA........................509-882-5583
Silver Springs Citrus Inc
Howey-in-the-Hills, FL...............800-940-2277
Sir Real Foods
White Plains, NY......................914-948-9342

Skimpy Cocktails LLC
Carrollton, TX.........................469-892-7988
Smeltzer Orchard Co
Frankfort, MI..........................231-882-4421
SoBe Beverages
Norwalk, CT...........................800-588-0548
Solana Gold Organics
Sebastopol, CA........................800-459-1121
St Julian Winery
Paw Paw, MI..........................800-732-6002
St. James Winery
Saint James, MO.....................800-280-9463
Starbucks
Seattle, WA...........................800-782-7282
Stevens Tropical Plantation
West Palm Beach, FL................561-683-4701
Stop & Shop Manufacturing
Readville, MA.........................508-977-5132
Suja Juice
Oceanside, CA........................855-879-7852
Sun Orchard Inc
Miami, FL.............................800-505-8423
Sun Pac Foods
Brampton, ON........................905-792-2700
Sun Tropics Inc
San Ramon, CA......................925-380-6324
Sunco & Frenchie
Clifton, NJ............................973-478-1011
Sundance Industries
Newburgh, NY........................845-565-6065
Sunfresh Beverages Inc.
Birmingham, AL......................706-324-0040
Sunlike Juice
Rougemont, QC......................866-552-7643
Sunny Avocado
Jamul, CA............................800-999-2862
Sunny Delight Beverage Company
Cincinnati, OH
Super Stores Industries
Turlock, CA...........................209-668-2100
Superbrand Dairies
Miami, FL.............................305-769-6600
Switch Beverage
Darien, CT............................203-202-7383
Tamarack Farms Dairy
Newark, OH..........................866-221-4141
Tazo Tea
Kent, WA.............................855-829-6832
Thomas Canning/Maidstone
Maidstone, ON.......................519-737-1531
Titusville Dairy Products Co
Titusville, PA.........................800-352-0101
Todhunter Foods
Lake Alfred, FL.......................863-956-1116
Toft Dairy Inc
Sandusky, OH.......................800-521-4606
Tradewinds
Austin, TX
Trailblazer Foods
Portland, OR.........................800-777-7179
Tree Top Inc
Selah, WA............................509-697-7251
Treesweet Products
Houston, TX..........................281-876-3759
Tri-Boro Fruit Co
Fresno, CA...........................559-486-4141
Triple D Orchards Inc
Empire, MI............................231-326-5174
True Organic Product Inc
Helm, CA.............................800-487-0379
Uncle Matt's Organic
Clermont, FL.........................833-729-8625
United Juice Companies of America
Vero Beach, FL......................772-562-5442
Valley Fig Growers
Fresno, CA...........................559-237-3893
Valley View Packing Co
Yuba City, CA........................530-673-7356
Vegetable Juices Inc
Chicago, IL...........................888-776-9752
Ventura Coastal LLC
Ventura, CA..........................805-653-7000
Veryfine Products Inc
Mason, OH
Vive Organic
Venice, CA...........................877-774-9291
Washington State Juice
Pacoima, CA.........................818-899-1195
Welch Foods Inc.
Concord, MA.........................800-340-6870
Welsh Farms
Wallington, NJ........................800-221-0663

White House Foods
Winchester, VA.......................540-662-3401
White Rock Products Corp
Flushing, NY..........................800-969-7625
Winmix/Natural Care Products
Englewood, FL.......................941-475-7432
Yoder Dairies
Chesapeake, VA.....................757-482-4068

Ade

Honest Tea Inc
Atlanta, GA...........................800-520-2653
Optimal Nutrients
Foster City, CA.......................707-528-1800
PepsiCo.
Purchase, NY.........................914-253-2000
Sunfresh Beverages Inc.
Birmingham, AL......................706-324-0040

Concentrate

California Custom Fruits
Baldwin Park, CA....................877-558-0056
Garden of Flavor LLC
Cleveland, OH........................216-702-7991
Wild Aseptics, LLC
Erlanger, KY..........................877-787-7221

Grape

Arizona Beverage Company
Cincinnati, OH........................800-832-3775

Lemon

Arizona Beverage Company
Cincinnati, OH........................800-832-3775
Borden Dairy
Dallas, TX.............................855-311-1583
Natalie's Orchid Island Juice Co.
Ft. Pierce, FL.........................800-373-7444
Perricone Juices
Beaumont, CA........................951-769-7171
Sun Orchard INC
Haines City, FL.......................877-875-8423
Sunfresh Beverages Inc.
Birmingham, AL......................706-324-0040

Orange

Arizona Beverage Company
Cincinnati, OH........................800-832-3775
Sunfresh Beverages Inc.
Birmingham, AL......................706-324-0040

Aloe

Alfer Laboratories
Chatsworth, CA......................818-709-0737
Aloe Farms Inc
Harlingen, TX.........................800-262-6771
Aloe Laboratories
Harlingen, TX.........................800-258-5380
Detoxwater
Brooklyn, NY.........................888-887-4318
Emerling International Foods
Buffalo, NY...........................716-833-7381
JJ Martin Group
Newark, NJ..........................862-240-1813
Lakewood Juice Co.
Miami, FL.............................866-324-5900
Pocas International
South Hackensack, NJ.............201-941-7900
Superbrand Dairies
Miami, FL.............................305-769-6600
Vink & Beri
Montgomeryville, PA...............215-654-5252

Apple

All Juice Food & Beverage
Ankeny, IA...........................800-736-5674
Apple & Eve LLC
Port Washington, NY..............800-969-8018
Aseltine Cider Company
Comstock Park, MI................616-784-6615
Birdseye Dairy-Morning Glory
Green Bay, WI.......................920-494-5388
Cal India Foods Inc
Chino, CA............................909-613-1660
Carolina Products
Tampa, FL...........................813-313-1800
Cherry Central Cooperative, Inc.
Traverse City, MI...................231-946-1860

Product Categories / Beverages: Juices

Citrosuco North America Inc
  Lake Wales, FL 800-356-4592
Cold Hollow Cider Mill
  Waterbury Center, VT. 800-327-7537
Coloma Frozen Foods Inc
  Coloma, MI. 800-642-2723
Country Pure Foods Inc
  Akron, OH. 877-995-8423
Erba Food Products
  Brooklyn, NY 718-272-7700
Florida Fruit Juices
  Chicago, IL 773-586-6200
Golden Town Apple Products
  Rougemont, QC 866-552-7643
Green Spot Packaging
  Claremont, CA 800-456-3210
Hazel Creek Orchards
  Mt Airy, GA 706-754-4899
Heritage Farms Dairy
  Murfreesboro, TN 615-895-2790
Hi-Country Foods Corporation
  Selah, WA 509-697-7292
Knouse Foods Co-Op Inc.
  Peach Glen, PA 717-677-8181
Lakewood Juice Co.
  Miami, FL 866-324-5900
Lassonde Pappas & Company, Inc.
  Carneys Point, NJ 800-257-7019
Legacy Juice Works
  Saratoga Springs, NY 518-583-1108
M & B Products Inc
  Tampa, FL. 800-899-7255
Madera Enterprises Inc
  Madera, CA. 800-507-9555
Materne North America
  New York, NY 212-675-7881
Mayer Bros
  Buffalo, NY. 800-696-2928
Mayfield Farms and Nursery
  Athens, TN 423-746-9859
Mccutcheon Apple Products
  Frederick, MD. 800-888-7537
Merlinos
  Canon City, CO 719-275-5558
Mott's
  Plano, TX 800-426-4891
Mott's LLP
  Plano, TX 800-426-4891
Mountain Valley Products Inc
  Sunnyside, WA 509-837-8084
Murray Cider Co Inc
  Roanoke, VA 540-977-9000
Nana Mae's Organics
  Sebastopol, CA 707-829-7359
Nestle USA Inc
  Glendale, CA 800-225-2270
Old Dutch Mustard Company
  Great Neck, NY 516-466-0522
Old Orchard Brands, LLC
  Sparta, MI 800-330-2173
Perricone Juices
  Beaumont, CA. 951-769-7171
Rosenberger's Dairies
  Hatfield, PA 800-355-9074
Smeltzer Orchard Co
  Frankfort, MI 231-882-4421
Solana Gold Organics
  Sebastopol, CA 800-459-1121
Sunlike Juice
  Rougemont, QC 866-552-7643
Tree Top Inc
  Selah, WA 509-697-7251
Triple D Orchards Inc
  Empire, MI 231-326-5174
True Organic Product Inc
  Helm, CA 800-487-0379
Valley View Packing Co
  Yuba City, CA 530-673-7356
White House Foods
  Winchester, VA 540-662-3401
Yoder Dairies
  Chesapeake, VA 757-482-4068

Bottled

Apple & Eve LLC
  Port Washington, NY 800-969-8018
Aseltine Cider Company
  Comstock Park, MI. 616-784-6615
Broughton Foods LLC
  El Paso, TX 800-395-7004
Carolina Products
  Tampa, FL. 813-313-1800
Northland Juices
  Port Washington, NY 866-719-5215

Boxed

Cloverland/Green Spring Dairy
  Baltimore, MD 800-876-6455
Emerling International Foods
  Buffalo, NY. 716-833-7381

Canned

Emerling International Foods
  Buffalo, NY. 716-833-7381
Florida's Natural Growers
  Lake Wales, FL 888-657-6600
Greenwood Associates
  Niles, IL 847-579-5500
Langer Juice Co Inc
  City of Industry, CA 626-336-3100
Manzana Products Co.
  Sebastopol, CA 707-823-5313
Mason County Fruit Packers Cooperative
  Hart, MI. 231-873-7504
Mccutcheon Apple Products
  Frederick, MD 800-888-7537
Mrs Clark's Foods
  Ankeny, IA 800-736-5674
Noel Corp
  Yakima, WA 509-248-1313
Old Dutch Mustard Company
  Great Neck, NY 516-466-0522
Sunlike Juice
  Rougemont, QC 866-552-7643
Triple D Orchards Inc
  Empire, MI 231-326-5174

Chilled

Emerling International Foods
  Buffalo, NY. 716-833-7381

Concentrate

Citrosuco North America Inc
  Lake Wales, FL 800-356-4592
GLCC Co
  Paw Paw, MI 269-657-3167
Green Spot Packaging
  Claremont, CA 800-456-3210
Mountain Valley Products Inc
  Sunnyside, WA 509-837-8084
Pacific Coast Fruit Co
  Portland, OR 503-234-6411
Small Planet Foods
  Minneapolis, MN 800-624-4123
Sun Pac Foods
  Brampton, ON. 905-792-2700
Tree Top Inc
  Selah, WA 509-697-7251
Valley View Packing Co
  Yuba City, CA 530-673-7356

Frozen

Greenwood Associates
  Niles, IL 847-579-5500
Old Dutch Mustard Company
  Great Neck, NY 516-466-0522
Old Orchard Brands, LLC
  Sparta, MI 800-330-2173
Smeltzer Orchard Co
  Frankfort, MI 231-882-4421
Triple D Orchards Inc
  Empire, MI 231-326-5174

Glass-Packed

Emerling International Foods
  Buffalo, NY. 716-833-7381

Apple Cider

CideRoad, LLC
  Mendham, NJ 973-543-9003
Five Star Foodies
  Cincinnati, OH
Lassonde Pappas & Company, Inc.
  Carneys Point, NJ 800-257-7019
Lost Trail Root Beer
  Louisburg, KS 800-748-7765
Parmenter's Northville Cider Mill
  Northville, MI. 248-349-3181
Shawnee Canning Co
  Cross Junction, VA 800-713-1414
Shire City Herbals
  Pittsfield, MA 413-213-6702
Spotted Tavern Winery & Dodd's Cider Mill
  Hartwood, VA 540-752-4453
Talbott Farms
  Palisade, CO 970-464-5656
Wild Aseptics, LLC
  Erlanger, KY 877-787-7221
Zeigler's
  Lansdale, PA 215-855-5161

Sparkling

Clos Saint-Denis
  Richelieu, QC 450-645-9777
Lost Trail Root Beer
  Louisburg, KS 800-748-7765

Apricot

Valley View Packing Co
  Yuba City, CA 530-673-7356

Canned

Emerling International Foods
  Buffalo, NY. 716-833-7381
Greenwood Associates
  Niles, IL 847-579-5500

Concentrate

Valley View Packing Co
  Yuba City, CA 530-673-7356

Frozen

Greenwood Associates
  Niles, IL 847-579-5500

Glass-Packed

Emerling International Foods
  Buffalo, NY. 716-833-7381
Greenwood Associates
  Niles, IL 847-579-5500

Beet

Emerling International Foods
  Buffalo, NY. 716-833-7381
Legacy Juice Works
  Saratoga Springs, NY 518-583-1108
Vegetable Juices Inc
  Chicago, IL 888-776-9752

Blueberry

Blueberry Store
  Grand Junction, MI 877-654-2400
Hazel Creek Orchards
  Mt Airy, GA 706-754-4899
Jasper Wyman & Son
  Topsfield, MA 978-887-7472
Lakewood Juice Co.
  Miami, FL 866-324-5900
Lassonde Pappas & Company, Inc.
  Carneys Point, NJ 800-257-7019
Patience Fruit & Co.
  Villeroy, QC

Carrot

Emerling International Foods
  Buffalo, NY. 716-833-7381
Lakewood Juice Co.
  Miami, FL 866-324-5900
Post Familie Vineyards
  Altus, AR 800-275-8423
Vegetable Juices Inc
  Chicago, IL 888-776-9752

Cherry

Erba Food Products
  Brooklyn, NY 718-272-7700
Greenwood Associates
  Niles, IL 847-579-5500
Hazel Creek Orchards
  Mt Airy, GA 706-754-4899
Lakewood Juice Co.
  Miami, FL 866-324-5900
Langer Juice Co Inc
  City of Industry, CA 626-336-3100
M & B Fruit Juice Co
  Akron, OH. 330-253-7465
Manzana Products Co.
  Sebastopol, CA 707-823-5313

Product Categories / Beverages: Juices

Merlinos
  Canon City, CO 719-275-5558
Sunlike Juice
  Rougemont, QC 866-552-7643

Canned

Emerling International Foods
  Buffalo, NY 716-833-7381

Concentrate

GLCC Co
  Paw Paw, MI 269-657-3167

Frozen

Emerling International Foods
  Buffalo, NY 716-833-7381
Milne Fruit Products Inc
  Prosser, WA 509-786-2611

Glass-Packed

Emerling International Foods
  Buffalo, NY 716-833-7381
Greenwood Associates
  Niles, IL 847-579-5500
Minute Maid Company
  Atlanta, GA 800-520-2653

Citrus Blends

Apac Chemical Corporation
  Arcadia, CA 866-849-2722
Apple & Eve LLC
  Port Washington, NY 800-969-8018
Citrus International
  Winter Park, FL 407-629-8037
Citrus Service
  Winter Garden, FL 407-656-4999
Conoley Citrus Packers Inc
  Winter Garden, FL 407-656-3300
Emerling International Foods
  Buffalo, NY 716-833-7381
Florida's Natural Growers
  Lake Wales, FL 888-657-6600
Fresh Juice Delivery
  Beverly Hills, CA 310-271-7373
Galliker Dairy Co
  Johnstown, PA 800-477-6455
Green Spot Packaging
  Claremont, CA 800-456-3210
Island Aseptics
  Byesville, OH 740-685-2548
Johanna Foods Inc.
  Flemington, NJ 800-727-6700
Kennesaw Fruit & Juice
  Pompano Beach, FL 800-949-0371
Key Colony Red Parrot Juice
  Lemont, IL 844-783-8572
Minute Maid Company
  Atlanta, GA 800-520-2653
Sales USA
  Salado, TX 800-766-7344
Saratoga Spring Water Co
  Saratoga Springs, NY 888-426-8642
Silver Springs Citrus Inc
  Howey-in-the-Hills, FL 800-940-2277
Southern Gardens Citrus
  Clewiston, FL 863-983-3030
Sun Orchard INC
  Haines City, FL 877-875-8423
Sunlike Juice
  Rougemont, QC 866-552-7643
Superbrand Dairies
  Miami, FL 305-769-6600
T G Lee Dairy
  Orlando, FL 800-432-4872
Ventura Coastal LLC
  Ventura, CA 805-653-7000
World Citrus West
  Fullerton, CA 714-870-6171

Coconut

Amy & Brian Naturals
  Buena Park, CA
Buddha Brands
  Montreal, QC 514-382-3805
C2O Pure Coconut Water
  Long Beach, CA 877-295-0873
Coco Lopez Inc
  Miramar, FL 800-341-2242
Commodities Marketing Inc
  Clarksburg, NJ 732-516-0700
Genius Juice
  Torrance, CA 800-682-7790
Lakewood Juice Co.
  Miami, FL 866-324-5900
Pocas International
  South Hackensack, NJ 201-941-7900
Pure Life Organic Foods
  Las Vegas, NV 708-990-5817
Vink & Beri
  Montgomeryville, PA 215-654-5252

Concentrates

Chase Brothers Dairy
  Oxnard, CA 800-438-6455
Citrosuco North America Inc
  Lake Wales, FL 800-356-4592
Citrus Service
  Winter Garden, FL 407-656-4999
Del's Lemonade & Refreshments
  Cranston, RI 401-463-6190
Delano Growers Grape Products
  Delano, CA 661-725-3255
Fee Brothers
  Rochester, NY 800-961-3337
GLCC Co
  Paw Paw, MI 269-657-3167
Green Spot Packaging
  Claremont, CA 800-456-3210
Imperial Flavors Beverage Co
  Milwaukee, WI 414-536-7788
Juice Tyme, Inc.
  Chicago, IL 800-236-5823
KERR Concentrates Inc
  Salem, OR 800-910-5377
Lemon-X Corporation
  Huntington Station, NY 800-220-1061
Louis Dreyfus Company Citrus Inc
  Winter Garden, FL 407-656-1000
Main Squeeze
  Columbia, MO 573-817-5616
Maui Gold Pineapple Company
  Pukalani, HI 808-877-3805
Merci Spring Water
  Maryland Heights, MO 314-872-9323
Minute Maid Company
  Atlanta, GA 800-520-2653
Mountain Valley Products Inc
  Sunnyside, WA 509-837-8084
Northwest Naturals LLC
  Bothell, WA. 425-881-2200
Ntc Marketing
  Williamsville, NY 800-333-1637
Orange Bang Inc
  Sylmar, CA 818-833-1000
Pacific Coast Fruit Co
  Portland, OR 503-234-6411
RFi Ingredients
  Blauvelt, NY 800-962-7663
Rocket Products Company
  Fenton, MO 800-325-9567
Sea Breeze Fruit Flavors
  Towaco, NJ 800-732-2733
Silver Springs Citrus Inc
  Howey-in-the-Hills, FL 800-940-2277
Sun Pac Foods
  Brampton, ON 905-792-2700
Sunsweet Growers Inc.
  Yuba City, CA. 800-417-2253
Tastepoint
  Philadelphia, PA 800-363-5286
Tone Products Inc
  Melrose Park, IL 800-536-8663
Tova Industries LLC
  Louisville, KY 888-532-8682
Tropicana Products Inc.
  Chicago, IL 800-237-7799
Valley Fig Growers
  Fresno, CA 559-237-3893
Valley View Packing Co
  Yuba City, CA 530-673-7356
Vegetable Juices Inc
  Chicago, IL 888-776-9752
Vie-Del Co
  Fresno, CA 559-834-2525
Welch Foods Inc
  Concord, MA 800-340-6870
Welch Foods Inc.
  Concord, MA 800-340-6870

Cranberry

Apple & Eve LLC
  Port Washington, NY 800-969-8018
Atoka Cranberries, Inc.
  Manseau, Quebec, QC 819-356-2001
Delectable Gourmet LLC
  Deer Park, NY 800-696-1350
Erba Food Products
  Brooklyn, NY 718-272-7700
Key Colony Red Parrot Juice
  Lemont, IL 844-783-8572
Lakewood Juice Co.
  Miami, FL 866-324-5900
Langer Juice Co Inc
  City of Industry, CA 626-336-3100
Lassonde Pappas & Company, Inc.
  Carneys Point, NJ 800-257-7019
Mccutcheon Apple Products
  Frederick, MD 800-888-7537
Northland Juices
  Port Washington, NY 866-719-5215
Old Orchard Brands, LLC
  Sparta, MI 800-330-2173
Patience Fruit & Co.
  Villeroy, QC
Sunlike Juice
  Rougemont, QC 866-552-7643
Welch Foods Inc.
  Concord, MA 800-340-6870

Bottled

Apple & Eve LLC
  Port Washington, NY 800-969-8018
Northland Juices
  Port Washington, NY 866-719-5215

Boxed

Emerling International Foods
  Buffalo, NY 716-833-7381

Canned

Emerling International Foods
  Buffalo, NY 716-833-7381
Mccutcheon Apple Products
  Frederick, MD 800-888-7537

Concentrate

GLCC Co
  Paw Paw, MI 269-657-3167
Pacific Coast Fruit Co
  Portland, OR 503-234-6411
Sea Breeze Fruit Flavors
  Towaco, NJ 800-732-2733
Simply Incredible Foods
  Port Edwards, WI 715-697-6232
Small Planet Foods
  Minneapolis, MN 800-624-4123

Frozen

Milne Fruit Products Inc
  Prosser, WA 509-786-2611
Old Orchard Brands, LLC
  Sparta, MI 800-330-2173

Glass-Packed

Emerling International Foods
  Buffalo, NY 716-833-7381

Dietetic

Boissons Miami Pomor
  Longueuil, QC 877-977-3744
Florida Natural Flavors
  Casselberry, FL 800-872-5979
Healthmate Products
  Highland Park, IL 847-579-1051
Southern Gardens Citrus
  Clewiston, FL 863-983-3030

Drink

Concentrate

Beverage Flavors Intl
  Chicago, IL 773-248-3860
Commodities Marketing Inc
  Clarksburg, NJ 732-516-0700
Wild Aseptics, LLC
  Erlanger, KY 877-787-7221

Product Categories / Beverages: Juices

Fruit

3V Company
   Brooklyn, NY 718-858-7333
A. Lassonde Inc.
   Rougemont, QC 866-552-7643
Alca Trading Co.
   Miami, FL. 305-265-8331
All American Seasonings
   Denver, CO 303-623-2320
All Juice Food & Beverage
   Ankeny, IA 800-736-5674
ALO Drink
   South San Francisco, CA 650-616-7777
Amcan Beverages Inc
   American Canyon, CA 800-972-5962
Andros Foods North America
   Mount Jackson, VA. 844-426-3767
Apple & Eve LLC
   Port Washington, NY 800-969-8018
Aseltine Cider Company
   Comstock Park, MI 616-784-6615
B.M. Lawrence & Company
   San Francisco, CA 415-981-2926
Batavia Wine Cellars
   Canandaigua, NY 585-396-7600
Birdseye Dairy-Morning Glory
   Green Bay, WI. 920-494-5388
Brothers International Food Corporation
   Rochester, NY. 585-343-3007
Bully Hill Vineyards
   Hammondsport, NY 607-868-3610
Cal India Foods Inc
   Chino, CA. 909-613-1660
Carolina Products
   Tampa, FL. 813-313-1800
Century Foods Intl LLC
   Sparta, WI. 800-269-1901
Ceres Fruit Juices
   San Diego, CA 800-778-6498
Chase Brothers Dairy
   Oxnard, CA 800-438-6455
Chiquita Brands LLC.
   Fort Lauderdale, FL 954-924-5700
Citrosuco North America Inc
   Lake Wales, FL. 800-356-4592
Cold Hollow Cider Mill
   Waterbury Center, VT. 800-327-7537
Country Pure Foods Inc
   Akron, OH. 877-995-8423
Crown Regal Wine Cellars
   Brooklyn, NY 718-604-1430
Cutrale Citrus Juices
   Auburndale, FL. 863-965-5000
Del's Lemonade & Refreshments
   Cranston, RI 401-463-6190
Erba Food Products
   Brooklyn, NY 718-272-7700
Everfresh Beverages
   Warren, MI 800-323-3416
Faribault Foods, Inc.
   Fairbault, MN 507-331-1400
Fizzy Lizzy
   Jersey City, NJ 800-203-9336
Florida Fruit Juices
   Chicago, IL 773-586-6200
Florida Key West
   Fort Myers, FL 239-694-8787
Four Chimneys Farm Winery Trust
   Himrod, NY 607-243-7502
Fruigees
   Los Angeles, CA
Galliker Dairy Co
   Johnstown, PA. 800-477-6455
Global Beverage Company
   Rochester, NY. 585-381-3560
Golden Town Apple Products
   Rougemont, QC 866-552-7643
Great Western Juice Co
   Maple Heights, OH. 800-321-9180
Hale Indian River Groves
   Vero Beach, FL. 800-562-4502
Harrisburg Dairies Inc
   Harrisburg, PA 800-692-7429
Healthee
   Arcadia, CA 626-574-1719
Heck Cellars
   Arvin, CA 661-854-6120
Heineman Winery
   Put In Bay, OH 419-285-2811
Heritage Farms Dairy
   Murfreesboro, TN. 615-895-2790

Hi-Country Foods Corporation
   Selah, WA 509-697-7292
Hudson Valley Fruit Juice
   Highland, NY 845-691-8061
Hygeia Dairy Company
   Corpus Christi, TX 361-854-4561
Inn Foods Inc
   Watsonville, CA 800-708-7836
IQ Juice
   Bayville, NY 516-864-0034
Island Aseptics
   Byesville, OH 740-685-2548
Lakewood Juice Co.
   Miami, FL 866-324-5900
Leeward Resources
   Baltimore, MD 410-837-9003
Leonard Fountain Specialties
   Detroit, MI 313-891-4141
Louis Dreyfus Company Citrus Inc
   Winter Garden, FL 407-656-1000
Ludfords
   Riverside, CA 951-823-0306
Madera Enterprises Inc
   Madera, CA. 800-507-9555
Malibu Beach Beverage
   Roswell, GA 877-825-0655
Mamma Chia
   Carlsbad, CA. 855-588-2442
Maui Gold Pineapple Company
   Pukalani, HI 808-877-3805
Mayer Bros
   Buffalo, NY 800-696-2928
Mayer's Cider Mill
   Webster, NY 800-543-0043
Mayfield Farms and Nursery
   Athens, TN 423-746-9859
Mccutcheon Apple Products
   Frederick, MD. 800-888-7537
Meduri Farms
   Dallas, OR. 877-388-8800
Meramec Vineyards
   St James, MO 877-216-9463
Merlinos
   Canon City, CO 719-275-5558
Monarch Beverage Company
   Atlanta, GA 800-241-3732
Mott's LLP
   Plano, TX 800-426-4891
Mountain Valley Products Inc
   Sunnyside, WA 509-837-8084
Mrs. Denson's Cookie Company
   Ukiah, CA 800-219-3199
Murray Cider Co Inc
   Roanoke, VA. 540-977-9000
Nana Mae's Organics
   Sebastopol, CA 707-829-7359
Natalie's Orchid Island Juice Co.
   Ft. Pierce, FL. 800-373-7444
National Grape Co-Op
   Westfield, NY. 800-340-6870
Nectar Island
   St Paul, MN 651-292-9963
Northland Cranberries
   Jackson, WI. 866-719-5215
Northland Juices
   Port Washington, NY 866-719-5215
Northwest Naturals LLC
   Bothell, WA. 425-881-2200
Ntc Marketing
   Williamsville, NY 800-333-1637
Oatworks
   New York, NY 646-624-2400
Old Orchard Brands, LLC
   Sparta, MI 800-330-2173
PepsiCo.
   Purchase, NY 914-253-2000
Point Group
   Satellite Beach, FL 888-272-1249
Prairie Farms Dairy Inc.
   Edwardsville, IL 618-659-5700
Premier Juices
   Clearwater, FL 727-533-8200
Purity Dairies LLC
   Nashville, TN 615-244-1900
Quality Kitchen Corporation
   Wyoming, DE 302-697-3118
R.J. Corr Naturals
   Posen, IL. 708-389-4200
Reiter Dairy LLC
   Springfield, OH. 937-323-5777
River Hills Harvest
   Minneapolis, MN 855-662-3779

Rosenberger's Dairies
   Hatfield, PA. 800-355-9074
Sambazon
   San Clemente, CA. 877-726-2296
SANGARIA USA
   Torrance, CA. 310-530-2202
Saratoga Spring Water Co
   Saratoga Springs, NY 888-426-8642
Schneider's Dairy Inc
   Pittsburgh, PA 412-881-3525
Schneider-Valley Farms Inc
   Williamsport, PA 570-326-2021
Shoreline Fruit
   Traverse City, MI 800-836-3972
Silver Springs Citrus Inc
   Howey-in-the-Hills, FL 800-940-2277
Smart Juice
   Whitehall, PA 610-443-1506
Smeltzer Orchard Co
   Frankfort, MI 231-882-4421
Smith Dairy
   Orrville, OH 800-776-7076
Solana Gold Organics
   Sebastopol, CA 800-459-1121
St Julian Winery
   Paw Paw, MI 800-732-6002
St. James Winery
   Saint James, MO 800-280-9463
Stevens Tropical Plantation
   West Palm Beach, FL 561-683-4701
Stone Hill Winery
   Hermann, MO 573-486-2221
Sun Opta Inc.
   Mississauga, ON 952-820-2518
Sun Pac Foods
   Brampton, ON. 905-792-2700
Sun Tropics Inc
   San Ramon, CA 925-380-6324
Sunlike Juice
   Rougemont, QC 866-552-7643
Sunny Avocado
   Jamul, CA 800-999-2862
Sunsweet Growers Inc.
   Yuba City, CA. 800-417-2253
Super Stores Industries
   Turlock, CA 209-668-2100
Superbrand Dairies
   Miami, FL 305-769-6600
Swiss Premium Dairy Inc
   Lebanon, PA 800-222-2129
Tamarack Farms Dairy
   Newark, OH 866-221-4141
Titusville Dairy Products Co
   Titusville, PA 800-352-0101
Todhunter Foods
   Lake Alfred, FL 863-956-1116
Toft Dairy Inc
   Sandusky, OH 800-521-4606
Tree Top Inc
   Selah, WA 509-697-7251
Treesweet Products
   Houston, TX 281-876-3759
Tri-Boro Fruit Co
   Fresno, CA 559-486-4141
Triple D Orchards Inc
   Empire, MI 231-326-5174
True Organic Product Inc
   Helm, CA 800-487-0379
Valley Fig Growers
   Fresno, CA 559-237-3893
Valley View Packing Co
   Yuba City, CA. 530-673-7356
Ventura Coastal LLC
   Ventura, CA 805-653-7000
Venture Vineyards
   Lodi, NY. 888-635-6277
Veryfine Products Inc
   Mason, OH
Welch Foods Inc
   Concord, MA 800-340-6870
Welch Foods Inc.
   Concord, MA 800-340-6870
White Rock Products Corp
   Flushing, NY. 800-969-7625
Wild Poppy
   Los Angeles, CA. 310-384-1004
Winmix/Natural Care Products
   Englewood, FL 941-475-7432
World Citrus West
   Fullerton, CA 714-870-6171
Yoder Dairies
   Chesapeake, VA 757-482-4068

Product Categories / Beverages: Juices

Bottled

Apple & Eve LLC
  Port Washington, NY 800-969-8018
Aseltine Cider Company
  Comstock Park, MI 616-784-6615
Bully Hill Vineyards
  Hammondsport, NY 607-868-3610
Carolina Products
  Tampa, FL 813-313-1800
Lakewood Juice Co.
  Miami, FL 866-324-5900

Canned

B.M. Lawrence & Company
  San Francisco, CA 415-981-2926
Blue Monkey
  Long Beach, CA
Mccutcheon Apple Products
  Frederick, MD 800-888-7537
Northland Cranberries
  Jackson, WI. 866-719-5215
SANGARIA USA
  Torrance, CA 310-530-2202
Silver Springs Citrus Inc
  Howey-in-the-Hills, FL 800-940-2277
Sun Pac Foods
  Brampton, ON 905-792-2700
Triple D Orchards Inc
  Empire, MI 231-326-5174

Concentrate

American Fruits & Flavors
  Pacoima, CA 818-899-9574
Citrosuco North America Inc
  Lake Wales, FL 800-356-4592
Felbro Food Products
  Los Angeles, CA 323-936-5266
GLCC Co
  Paw Paw, MI 269-657-3167
Green Spot Packaging
  Claremont, CA 800-456-3210
Lakewood Juice Co.
  Miami, FL 866-324-5900
Louis Dreyfus Company Citrus Inc
  Winter Garden, FL 407-656-1000
Mountain Valley Products Inc
  Sunnyside, WA 509-837-8084
Pacific Coast Fruit Co
  Portland, OR 503-234-6411
Sea Breeze Fruit Flavors
  Towaco, NJ 800-732-2733
Shoreline Fruit
  Traverse City, MI 800-836-3972
Tree Top Inc
  Selah, WA 509-697-7251
Valley Fig Growers
  Fresno, CA 559-237-3893
Valley View Packing Co
  Yuba City, CA 530-673-7356
Ventura Coastal LLC
  Ventura, CA 805-653-7000

Frozen

Citrosuco North America Inc
  Lake Wales, FL 800-356-4592
Del's Lemonade & Refreshments
  Cranston, RI 401-463-6190
Emerling International Foods
  Buffalo, NY 716-833-7381
Florida Natural Flavors
  Casselberry, FL 800-872-5979
Florida's Natural Growers
  Lake Wales, FL 888-657-6600
Greenwood Associates
  Niles, IL 847-579-5500
Harrisburg Dairies Inc
  Harrisburg, PA 800-692-7429
Inn Foods Inc
  Watsonville, CA 800-708-7836
Lt Blender's Frozen Concoctions
  Galveston, TX 409-765-5666
Minute Maid Company
  Atlanta, GA 800-520-2653
Old Orchard Brands, LLC
  Sparta, MI 800-330-2173
Saratoga Spring Water Co
  Saratoga Springs, NY 888-426-8642
Smeltzer Orchard Co
  Frankfort, MI 231-882-4421

Triple D Orchards Inc
  Empire, MI 231-326-5174
Unique Ingredients LLC
  Gold Canyon, AZ 480-983-2498
Wild Fruitz Beverages
  Ambler, PA 888-688-7632

Glass-Packed

Lakewood Juice Co.
  Miami, FL 866-324-5900
Lorina, Inc.
  Coral Gables, FL 305-779-3085
Northland Cranberries
  Jackson, WI 866-719-5215

Refrigerated

Silver Springs Citrus Inc
  Howey-in-the-Hills, FL 800-940-2277

Fruit & Vegetable

Aileen Quirk & Sons Inc
  Kansas City, MO 816-471-4580
Apple & Eve LLC
  Port Washington, NY 800-969-8018
Arcadia Dairy Farms Inc
  Arden, NC 828-684-3556
Astral Extracts
  Syosset, NY 516-496-2505
Barsotti Family Juice Co.
  Camino, CA 530-622-4629
Beckman & Gast Co
  St Henry, OH 419-678-4195
Bevco Sales International Inc.
  Surrey, BC 800-663-0090
Beverage Capital Corporation
  Baltimore, MD 410-242-7404
Blue Moon Foods
  White River Junction, VT 802-295-1165
Cal-Tex Citrus Juice LP
  Houston, TX 800-231-0133
Campbell Soup Co.
  Camden, NJ 800-257-8443
Citrosuco North America Inc
  Lake Wales, FL 800-356-4592
Community Orchards
  Fort Dodge, IA 888-573-8212
Florida's Natural Growers
  Lake Wales, FL 888-657-6600
Fresh Juice Delivery
  Beverly Hills, CA 310-271-7373
Fresh Samantha
  Saco, ME 800-658-4635
Great Western Juice Co
  Maple Heights, OH 800-321-9180
Greenwood Associates
  Niles, IL 847-579-5500
H R Nicholson Co
  Baltimore, MD 800-638-3514
Hanover Foods Corp
  Hanover, PA 717-632-6000
Hudson Valley Fruit Juice
  Highland, NY 845-691-8061
Indian River Select® LLC
  Stuart, FL 888-373-7426
Island Aseptics
  Byesville, OH 740-685-2548
Jel Sert
  West Chicago, IL 800-323-2592
Key Colony Red Parrot Juice
  Lemont, IL 844-783-8572
Lakewood Juice Co.
  Miami, FL 866-324-5900
Lakewood Juice Company
  Miami, FL 866-324-5900
Lane's Dairy
  El Paso, TX 915-772-6700
Langer Juice Co Inc
  City of Industry, CA 626-336-3100
Lenox-Martell Inc
  Boston, MA 877-325-2489
M & B Fruit Juice Co
  Akron, OH 330-253-7465
Manzana Products Co.
  Sebastopol, CA 707-823-5313
Mayfield Farms and Nursery
  Athens, TN 423-746-9859
Meier's Wine Cellars Inc
  Cincinnati, OH 800-346-2941
Minute Maid Company
  Atlanta, GA 800-520-2653

Mrs Clark's Foods
  Ankeny, IA 800-736-5674
Noel Corp
  Yakima, WA 509-248-1313
Ocean Spray International
  Lakeville-Middleboro, MA 800-662-3263
Old Dutch Mustard Company
  Great Neck, NY 516-466-0522
Olympic Foods
  Spokane, WA 509-455-8059
Paw Paw Grape Juice Company
  Paw Paw, MI 800-756-5357
Plaidberry Company
  Vista, CA 760-727-5403
Post Familie Vineyards
  Altus, AR 800-275-8423
Reiter Dairy
  Newport, KY 800-544-6455
RFi Ingredients
  Blauvelt, NY 800-962-7663
Sales USA
  Salado, TX 800-766-7344
Schepps Dairy
  Dallas, TX 800-395-7004
Seneca Juice
  Marion, NY 315-926-3228
Southern Gardens Citrus
  Clewiston, FL 863-983-3030
Tamarack Farms Dairy
  Newark, OH 866-221-4141
Ultra Seal
  New Paltz, NY 845-255-2490
Unique Ingredients LLC
  Gold Canyon, AZ 480-983-2498
Vegetable Juices Inc
  Chicago, IL 888-776-9752

Bottled

Apple & Eve LLC
  Port Washington, NY 800-969-8018
Beverage Capital Corporation
  Baltimore, MD 410-242-7404
Lassonde Pappas & Company, Inc.
  Carneys Point, NJ 800-257-7019
Polar Beverages Inc.
  Worcester, MA 800-734-9800

Canned

B.M. Lawrence & Company
  San Francisco, CA 415-981-2926
Beverage Capital Corporation
  Baltimore, MD 410-242-7404
Polar Beverages Inc.
  Worcester, MA 800-734-9800

Concentrate

Astral Extracts
  Syosset, NY 516-496-2505
Citrosuco North America Inc
  Lake Wales, FL 800-356-4592
Emerling International Foods
  Buffalo, NY 716-833-7381
Wild Aseptics, LLC
  Erlanger, KY 877-787-7221

Frozen

Citrosuco North America Inc
  Lake Wales, FL 800-356-4592
Ludfords
  Riverside, CA 951-823-0306

Refrigerated

Lakewood Juice Co.
  Miami, FL 866-324-5900

Fruit Punch

Arizona Beverage Company
  Cincinnati, OH 800-832-3775
Borden Dairy
  Dallas, TX 855-311-1583
Erba Food Products
  Brooklyn, NY 718-272-7700
Reilly Dairy & Food Company
  Tampa, FL 813-839-8458
Rocket Products Company
  Fenton, MO 800-325-9567
Sunfresh Beverages Inc.
  Birmingham, AL 706-324-0040
Sunlike Juice
  Rougemont, QC 866-552-7643

Product Categories / Beverages: Juices

Trailblazer Foods
   Portland, OR 800-777-7179
Triple H Food Processors Inc
   Riverside, CA 951-352-5700
United Dairy Inc.
   Martins Ferry, OH 800-252-1542

Concentrate

Better Beverages Inc
   Cerritos, CA 800-344-5219
Mayer Bros
   Buffalo, NY 800-696-2928

Garlic

Emerling International Foods
   Buffalo, NY 716-833-7381
Howard Foods Inc
   Danvers, MA 978-774-6207
Vegetable Juices Inc
   Chicago, IL 888-776-9752

Grape

A.W. Jantzi & Sons
   Wellesley, ON 519-656-2400
Arcadia Dairy Farms Inc
   Arden, NC 828-684-3556
Bully Hill Vineyards
   Hammondsport, NY 607-868-3610
Country Pure Foods Inc
   Akron, OH. 877-995-8423
Crown Regal Wine Cellars
   Brooklyn, NY 718-604-1430
Everfresh Beverages
   Warren, MI 800-323-3416
Florida Fruit Juices
   Chicago, IL 773-586-6200
Florida's Natural Growers
   Lake Wales, FL 888-657-6600
Four Chimneys Farm Winery Trust
   Himrod, NY 607-243-7502
Green Spot Packaging
   Claremont, CA 800-456-3210
Greenwood Associates
   Niles, IL 847-579-5500
Growers Cooperative Juice Co
   Westfield, NY 716-326-3161
Hillcrest Orchard
   Lake Placid, FL 865-397-5273
Kayco
   Bayonne, NJ 718-369-4600
Kedem
   Bayonne, NJ 718-369-4600
Lakewood Juice Co.
   Miami, FL 866-324-5900
Langer Juice Co Inc
   City of Industry, CA 626-336-3100
Lassonde Pappas & Company, Inc.
   Carneys Point, NJ 800-257-7019
M & B Fruit Juice Co
   Akron, OH. 330-253-7465
Madera Enterprises Inc
   Madera, CA. 800-507-9555
Manzana Products Co.
   Sebastopol, CA 707-823-5313
Mayer Bros
   Buffalo, NY 800-696-2928
Mayer's Cider Mill
   Webster, NY 800-543-0043
Mccutcheon Apple Products
   Frederick, MD 800-888-7537
Meier's Wine Cellars Inc
   Cincinnati, OH 800-346-2941
Meramec Vineyards
   St James, MO 877-216-9463
Merlinos
   Canon City, CO. 719-275-5558
Minute Maid Company
   Atlanta, GA. 800-520-2653
Paklab Products
   Boucherville, QC 888-946-3233
Post Familie Vineyards
   Altus, AR 800-275-8423
Royal Wine Corp
   Bayonne, NJ 718-384-2400
St Julian Winery
   Paw Paw, MI 800-732-6002
St. James Winery
   Saint James, MO 800-280-9463
Sunlike Juice
   Rougemont, QC 866-552-7643

Tree Top Inc
   Selah, WA 509-697-7251
True Organic Product Inc
   Helm, CA 800-487-0379
Venture Vineyards
   Lodi, NY 888-635-6277
Welch Foods Inc.
   Concord, MA 800-340-6870

Bottled

Broughton Foods LLC
   El Paso, TX 800-395-7004
Manischewitz Co
   Newark, NJ 201-553-1100
Northland Juices
   Port Washington, NY 866-719-5215
Sunlike Juice
   Rougemont, QC 866-552-7643

Boxed

Cloverland/Green Spring Dairy
   Baltimore, MD 800-876-6455
Wild Aseptics, LLC
   Erlanger, KY 877-787-7221

Canned

Emerling International Foods
   Buffalo, NY 716-833-7381
Growers Cooperative Juice Co
   Westfield, NY 716-326-3161
Mccutcheon Apple Products
   Frederick, MD 800-888-7537
Unique Ingredients LLC
   Gold Canyon, AZ 480-983-2498
Wild Aseptics, LLC
   Erlanger, KY 877-787-7221

Chilled

Emerling International Foods
   Buffalo, NY 716-833-7381
Wild Aseptics, LLC
   Erlanger, KY 877-787-7221

Concentrate

GLCC Co
   Paw Paw, MI 269-657-3167
Green Spot Packaging
   Claremont, CA 800-456-3210
Louis Dreyfus Company Citrus Inc
   Winter Garden, FL 407-656-1000
Mayer Bros
   Buffalo, NY 800-696-2928
Mountain Valley Products Inc
   Sunnyside, WA 509-837-8084
Paklab Products
   Boucherville, QC 888-946-3233
Small Planet Foods
   Minneapolis, MN 800-624-4123
Sun Pac Foods
   Brampton, ON 905-792-2700
Tree Top Inc
   Selah, WA 509-697-7251
Welch's Global Ingredients Group
   Concord, MA 978-371-3692

Frozen

Emerling International Foods
   Buffalo, NY 716-833-7381
Growers Cooperative Juice Co
   Westfield, NY 716-326-3161
Louis Dreyfus Company Citrus Inc
   Winter Garden, FL 407-656-1000
Milne Fruit Products Inc
   Prosser, WA 509-786-2611
Wild Aseptics, LLC
   Erlanger, KY 877-787-7221

Glass-Packed

Emerling International Foods
   Buffalo, NY 716-833-7381
Growers Cooperative Juice Co
   Westfield, NY 716-326-3161
Unique Ingredients LLC
   Gold Canyon, AZ 480-983-2498
Wild Aseptics, LLC
   Erlanger, KY 877-787-7221

Grapefruit

Cutrale Citrus Juices
   Auburndale, FL. 863-965-5000
Florida Fruit Juices
   Chicago, IL 773-586-6200
Gene's Citrus Ranch
   Palmetto, FL 888-723-2006
Greenwood Associates
   Niles, IL 847-579-5500
Indian River Select® LLC
   Stuart, FL 888-373-7426
Kennesaw Fruit & Juice
   Pompano Beach, FL 800-949-0371
Lakewood Juice Co.
   Miami, FL 866-324-5900
Lassonde Pappas & Company, Inc.
   Carneys Point, NJ 800-257-7019
Louis Dreyfus Company Citrus Inc
   Winter Garden, FL 407-656-1000
Mayer Bros
   Buffalo, NY 800-696-2928
Minute Maid Company
   Atlanta, GA 800-520-2653
Natalie's Orchid Island Juice Co.
   Ft. Pierce, FL. 800-373-7444
Ocean Spray International
   Lakeville-Middleboro, MA 800-662-3263
Perricone Juices
   Beaumont, CA. 951-769-7171
Quality Kitchen Corporation
   Wyoming, DE 302-697-3118
Saratoga Spring Water Co
   Saratoga Springs, NY 888-426-8642
Silver Springs Citrus Inc
   Howey-in-the-Hills, FL 800-940-2277
Sun Orchard INC
   Haines City, FL 877-875-8423
Sun Orchard Inc
   Miami, FL 800-505-8423
Sunlike Juice
   Rougemont, QC 866-552-7643
Superbrand Dairies
   Miami, FL 305-769-6600
Tropicana Products Inc.
   Chicago, IL 800-237-7799
United Juice Companies of America
   Vero Beach, FL 772-562-5442
World Citrus West
   Fullerton, CA. 714-870-6171
Yoder Dairies
   Chesapeake, VA 757-482-4068

Bottled

Northland Juices
   Port Washington, NY 866-719-5215

Boxed

Emerling International Foods
   Buffalo, NY 716-833-7381
Wild Aseptics, LLC
   Erlanger, KY 877-787-7221

Canned

Emerling International Foods
   Buffalo, NY 716-833-7381
Ocean Spray International
   Lakeville-Middleboro, MA 800-662-3263
Wild Aseptics, LLC
   Erlanger, KY 877-787-7221

Concentrate

Sea Breeze Fruit Flavors
   Towaco, NJ 800-732-2733
Sun Pac Foods
   Brampton, ON. 905-792-2700

Frozen

Emerling International Foods
   Buffalo, NY 716-833-7381
Ocean Spray International
   Lakeville-Middleboro, MA 800-662-3263
Wild Aseptics, LLC
   Erlanger, KY 877-787-7221

Glass-Packed

Emerling International Foods
   Buffalo, NY 716-833-7381
Ocean Spray International
   Lakeville-Middleboro, MA 800-662-3263

Product Categories / Beverages: Juices

Wild Aseptics, LLC
Erlanger, KY 877-787-7221

Refrigerated

Ocean Spray International
Lakeville-Middleboro, MA 800-662-3263
Wild Aseptics, LLC
Erlanger, KY 877-787-7221

Guava

Stevens Tropical Plantation
West Palm Beach, FL 561-683-4701

Key Lime

Florida Key West
Fort Myers, FL 239-694-8787

Lemon

Agrocan
Ville St Laurent, QC 877-247-6226
Castella Imports Inc
Brentwood, NY 631-231-5500
Erba Food Products
Brooklyn, NY 718-272-7700
Florida Key West
Fort Myers, FL 239-694-8787
Greenwood Associates
Niles, IL 847-579-5500
Jus-Made
Dallas, TX 800-969-3746
Lakewood Juice Co.
Miami, FL 866-324-5900
Lassonde Pappas & Company, Inc.
Carneys Point, NJ 800-257-7019
Louis Dreyfus Company Citrus Inc
Winter Garden, FL 407-656-1000
Minute Maid Company
Atlanta, GA 800-520-2653
Natalie's Orchid Island Juice Co.
Ft. Pierce, FL 800-373-7444
Nielsen Citrus Products Inc
Huntington Beach, CA 714-892-5586
Perricone Juices
Beaumont, CA 951-769-7171
Sophia Foods
Brooklyn, NY 718-272-1110
Sun Orchard Inc
Miami, FL 800-505-8423
Wild Aseptics, LLC
Erlanger, KY 877-787-7221

Canned

Emerling International Foods
Buffalo, NY 716-833-7381
Wild Aseptics, LLC
Erlanger, KY 877-787-7221

Concentrate

Citrico
Northbrook, IL 800-445-2171
Citromax Flavors Inc
Carlstadt, NJ 201-933-8405
Louis Dreyfus Company Citrus Inc
Winter Garden, FL 407-656-1000

Frozen

Emerling International Foods
Buffalo, NY 716-833-7381
Louis Dreyfus Company Citrus Inc
Winter Garden, FL 407-656-1000
Nielsen Citrus Products Inc
Huntington Beach, CA 714-892-5586
Wild Aseptics, LLC
Erlanger, KY 877-787-7221

Glass-Packed

Emerling International Foods
Buffalo, NY 716-833-7381
Wild Aseptics, LLC
Erlanger, KY 877-787-7221

Refrigerated

Wild Aseptics, LLC
Erlanger, KY 877-787-7221

Lemonade

4Pure
ME 207-831-1030
Anderson Erickson Dairy
Des Moines, IA 515-265-2521
Anderson Erickson Dairy
Kansas City, KS 913-621-4801
Calvert's
El Paso, TX 888-472-5727
Del's Lemonade & Refreshments
Cranston, RI 401-463-6190
Fermenting Fairy
Santa Monica, CA
Happy Planet Foods
Burnaby, BC 800-811-3213
Hubert's Lemonade
Tustin, CA 877-265-3286
Joe Tea and Joe Chips
Upper Montclair, NJ 973-744-7502
Jones Soda Company
Seattle, WA 800-656-6050
Lakewood Juice Co.
Miami, FL 866-324-5900
Lassonde Pappas & Company, Inc.
Carneys Point, NJ 800-257-7019
Lorina, Inc.
Coral Gables, FL 305-779-3085
M & B Fruit Juice Co
Akron, OH 330-253-7465
Me & the Bees Lemonade
Austin, TX
Natrel
St. Laurent, QC 800-501-1150
Newman's Own
Westport, CT 203-222-0136
Poppilu
Chicago, IL
Rocket Products Company
Fenton, MO 800-325-9567
Sunlike Juice
Rougemont, QC 866-552-7643
Sweet Leaf Tea Company
Austin, TX 512-328-7775
Third Street Inc
Louisville, CO 800-636-3790
United Juice Companies of America
Vero Beach, FL 772-562-5442
Zeigler's
Lansdale, PA 215-855-5161

Concentrate

Baltimore Brewing Company
Baltimore, MD 410-837-5000
Beaulieu Vineyard
Rutherford, CA 707-257-5749
Beaver Street Brewery
Flagstaff, AZ 928-779-0079
Bow Valley Brewing Company
Canmore, AB 403-678-2739
Brasserie Brasel Brewery
Lasalle, QC 800-463-2728
Bravard Vineyards & Winery
Hopkinsville, KY 270-269-2583
Clipper City Brewing
Halethorpe, MD 410-247-7822
Creemore Springs Brewery
Creemore, ON 800-267-2240
Dogfish Head Craft Brewery
Lewes, DE 888-834-3474
Great Lakes Brewing Co.
Cleveland, OH 216-771-4404
Great Northern Brewing Co
Whitefish, MT 406-863-1000
Great Western Brewing Company
Saskatoon, SK 800-764-4492
Hogtown Brewing Company
Mississauga, ON 905-855-9065
Lakefront Brewery Inc
Milwaukee, WI 414-372-8800
Left Hand Brewing Co
Longmont, CO 303-772-0258
Mayer Bros
Buffalo, NY 800-696-2928
Mendocino Brewing Co Inc
Ukiah, CA 707-463-2627
Millstream Brewing Co
Amana, IA 319-622-3672
Minute Maid Company
Atlanta, GA 800-520-2653
Monticello Vineyards-Corley
Napa, CA 707-253-2802
Moosehead Breweries Ltd.
St. John, NB
Pennsylvania Brewing Company
Pittsburgh, PA 412-237-9400
Santa Cruz Mountain Brewing
Santa Cruz, CA 831-425-4900
Sebastiani Vineyards
Sonoma, CA 855-232-2338
Shipyard Brewing Co
Portland, ME 800-789-0684
Small Planet Foods
Minneapolis, MN 800-624-4123
Whistler Brewing Company
Whistler, BC 604-962-8889

Lime

Castella Imports Inc
Brentwood, NY 631-231-5500
Emerling International Foods
Buffalo, NY 716-833-7381
Florida's Natural Growers
Lake Wales, FL 888-657-6600
Greenwood Associates
Niles, IL 847-579-5500
Lassonde Pappas & Company, Inc.
Carneys Point, NJ 800-257-7019
M & B Fruit Juice Co
Akron, OH 330-253-7465
Mott's LLP
Plano, TX 800-426-4891
Natalie's Orchid Island Juice Co.
Ft. Pierce, FL 800-373-7444
Nielsen Citrus Products Inc
Huntington Beach, CA 714-892-5586
Perricone Juices
Beaumont, CA 951-769-7171
Sun Orchard Inc
Miami, FL 800-505-8423
Sunfresh Beverages Inc.
Birmingham, AL 706-324-0040
True Organic Product Inc
Helm, CA 800-487-0379
United Juice Companies of America
Vero Beach, FL 772-562-5442
Wild Aseptics, LLC
Erlanger, KY 877-787-7221

Mango

Lakewood Juice Co.
Miami, FL 866-324-5900
Stevens Tropical Plantation
West Palm Beach, FL 561-683-4701
Sunlike Juice
Rougemont, QC 866-552-7643

Onion

Emerling International Foods
Buffalo, NY 716-833-7381
Howard Foods Inc
Danvers, MA 978-774-6207
Vegetable Juices Inc
Chicago, IL 888-776-9752

Orange

Alta Dena Certified Dairy LLC
City Of Industry, CA 800-535-1369
Anderson Erickson Dairy
Des Moines, IA 515-265-2521
Anderson Erickson Dairy
Kansas City, KS 913-621-4801
Arcadia Dairy Farms Inc
Arden, NC 828-684-3556
Birdseye Dairy-Morning Glory
Green Bay, WI 920-494-5388
Borden Dairy
Dallas, TX 855-311-1583
Broughton Foods LLC
El Paso, TX 800-395-7004
Byrne Dairy, Inc.
Syracuse, NY 800-899-1535
Cass-Clay Creamery
Fargo, ND 701-293-6455
Chase Brothers Dairy
Oxnard, CA 800-438-6455
Citrosuco North America Inc
Lake Wales, FL 800-356-4592
Cloverland/Green Spring Dairy
Baltimore, MD 800-876-6455
Country Pure Foods Inc
Akron, OH 877-995-8423
Cutrale Citrus Juices
Auburndale, FL 863-965-5000
Emerling International Foods
Buffalo, NY 716-833-7381

Product Categories / Beverages: Juices

Erba Food Products
  Brooklyn, NY 718-272-7700
Everfresh Beverages
  Warren, MI 800-323-3416
Evolution Fresh
  Seattle, WA 800-794-9986
Florida Fruit Juices
  Chicago, IL 773-586-6200
Florida's Natural Growers
  Lake Wales, FL 888-657-6600
Galliker Dairy Co
  Johnstown, PA 800-477-6455
Gene's Citrus Ranch
  Palmetto, FL 888-723-2006
Green Spot Packaging
  Claremont, CA 800-456-3210
Greenwood Associates
  Niles, IL 847-579-5500
Harrisburg Dairies Inc
  Harrisburg, PA 800-692-7429
Heritage Farms Dairy
  Murfreesboro, TN 615-895-2790
Hygeia Dairy Company
  Corpus Christi, TX 361-854-4561
Indian River Select® LLC
  Stuart, FL 888-373-7426
Inn Foods Inc
  Watsonville, CA 800-708-7836
Jus-Made
  Dallas, TX 800-969-3746
Key Colony Red Parrot Juice
  Lemont, IL 844-783-8572
Lakewood Juice Co.
  Miami, FL 866-324-5900
Lassonde Pappas & Company, Inc.
  Carneys Point, NJ 800-257-7019
Leonard Fountain Specialties
  Detroit, MI 313-891-4141
Lorina, Inc.
  Coral Gables, FL 305-779-3085
Louis Dreyfus Company Citrus Inc
  Winter Garden, FL 407-656-1000
M & B Fruit Juice Co
  Akron, OH 330-253-7465
M & B Products Inc
  Tampa, FL 800-899-7255
Marva Maid Dairy
  Newport News, VA 800-768-6243
Mayer Bros
  Buffalo, NY 800-696-2928
Minute Maid Company
  Atlanta, GA 800-520-2653
Natalie's Orchid Island Juice Co.
  Ft. Pierce, FL 800-373-7444
Noel Corp
  Yakima, WA 509-248-1313
Northland Juices
  Port Washington, NY 866-719-5215
Perricone Juices
  Beaumont, CA 951-769-7171
Prairie Farms Dairy Inc.
  Edwardsville, IL 618-659-5700
Quality Kitchen Corporation
  Wyoming, DE 302-697-3118
Reilly Dairy & Food Company
  Tampa, FL 813-839-8458
Reiter Dairy
  Newport, KY 800-544-6455
Reiter Dairy LLC
  Springfield, OH 937-323-5777
Rocket Products Company
  Fenton, MO 800-325-9567
Saratoga Spring Water Co
  Saratoga Springs, NY 888-426-8642
Sun Orchard INC
  Haines City, FL 877-875-8423
Sun Orchard Inc
  Miami, FL 800-505-8423
Sunlike Juice
  Rougemont, QC 866-552-7643
Super Stores Industries
  Turlock, CA 209-668-2100
Superbrand Dairies
  Miami, FL 305-769-6600
Swiss Premium Dairy Inc
  Lebanon, PA 800-222-2129
Toft Dairy Inc
  Sandusky, OH 800-521-4606
Treesweet Products
  Houston, TX 281-876-3759
Tropicana Products Inc.
  Chicago, IL 800-237-7799

True Organic Product Inc
  Helm, CA 800-487-0379
United Dairy Farmers Inc.
  Cincinnati, OH 866-837-4833
United Dairy Inc.
  Martins Ferry, OH 800-252-1542
United Juice Companies of America
  Vero Beach, FL 772-562-5442
US Sugar Company
  Clewiston, FL 863-983-8121
Wild Aseptics, LLC
  Erlanger, KY 877-787-7221
World Citrus West
  Fullerton, CA 714-870-6171
Yoder Dairies
  Chesapeake, VA 757-482-4068

Concentrate

California Citrus Producers
  Lindsay, CA 559-562-5169
Chase Brothers Dairy
  Oxnard, CA 800-438-6455
Country Pure Foods Inc
  Ellington, CT 877-995-8423
Green Spot Packaging
  Claremont, CA 800-456-3210
Greenwood Associates
  Niles, IL 847-579-5500
Louis Dreyfus Company Citrus Inc
  Winter Garden, FL 407-656-1000
Mayer Bros
  Buffalo, NY 800-696-2928
Minute Maid Company
  Atlanta, GA 800-520-2653
Sea Breeze Fruit Flavors
  Towaco, NJ 800-732-2733
Small Planet Foods
  Minneapolis, MN 800-624-4123
Sun Pac Foods
  Brampton, ON 905-792-2700

Concentrate - Frozen

Louis Dreyfus Company Citrus Inc
  Winter Garden, FL 407-656-1000

Not Concentrated

Broughton Foods LLC
  El Paso, TX 800-395-7004
Citrosuco North America Inc
  Lake Wales, FL 800-356-4592
Greenwood Associates
  Niles, IL 847-579-5500
Minute Maid Company
  Atlanta, GA 800-520-2653
Silver Springs Citrus Inc
  Howey-in-the-Hills, FL 800-940-2277

Papaya

Lakewood Juice Co.
  Miami, FL 866-324-5900
Stevens Tropical Plantation
  West Palm Beach, FL 561-683-4701
Sunlike Juice
  Rougemont, QC 866-552-7643

Peach

Green Spot Packaging
  Claremont, CA 800-456-3210
Hazel Creek Orchards
  Mt Airy, GA 706-754-4899
Sunlike Juice
  Rougemont, QC 866-552-7643
Valley View Packing Co
  Yuba City, CA 530-673-7356

Pear

Valley View Packing Co
  Yuba City, CA 530-673-7356

Pineapple

Cal India Foods Inc
  Chino, CA 909-613-1660
Commodities Marketing Inc
  Clarksburg, NJ 732-516-0700
Country Pure Foods Inc
  Akron, OH 877-995-8423
Emerling International Foods
  Buffalo, NY 716-833-7381

Florida Fruit Juices
  Chicago, IL 773-586-6200
Greenwood Associates
  Niles, IL 847-579-5500
Lakewood Juice Co.
  Miami, FL 866-324-5900
Langer Juice Co Inc
  City of Industry, CA 626-336-3100
Lassonde Pappas & Company, Inc.
  Carneys Point, NJ 800-257-7019
M & B Products Inc
  Tampa, FL 800-899-7255
Maui Gold Pineapple Company
  Pukalani, HI 808-877-3805
Mondial Foods Company
  Los Angeles, CA 213-383-3531
Ntc Marketing
  Williamsville, NY 800-333-1637
Sunlike Juice
  Rougemont, QC 866-552-7643
True Organic Product Inc
  Helm, CA 800-487-0379
Wild Aseptics, LLC
  Erlanger, KY 877-787-7221

Boxed

Wild Aseptics, LLC
  Erlanger, KY 877-787-7221

Canned

Ntc Marketing
  Williamsville, NY 800-333-1637
Wild Aseptics, LLC
  Erlanger, KY 877-787-7221

Concentrate

Maui Gold Pineapple Company
  Pukalani, HI 808-877-3805
Pacific Coast Fruit Co
  Portland, OR 503-234-6411
Sun Pac Foods
  Brampton, ON 905-792-2700
Transpacific Foods Inc
  Irvine, CA 949-975-9900

Frozen

Wild Aseptics, LLC
  Erlanger, KY 877-787-7221

Glass-Packed

Wild Aseptics, LLC
  Erlanger, KY 877-787-7221

Refrigerated

Wild Aseptics, LLC
  Erlanger, KY 877-787-7221

Portioned

Arcadia Dairy Farms Inc
  Arden, NC 828-684-3556

Powdered Fruit

American Fruits & Flavors
  Pacoima, CA 818-899-9574
Energy Foods Intl
  Miami, FL 844-772-6622

Prune

Emerling International Foods
  Buffalo, NY 716-833-7381
Erba Food Products
  Brooklyn, NY 718-272-7700
Lakewood Juice Co.
  Miami, FL 866-324-5900
Lassonde Pappas & Company, Inc.
  Carneys Point, NJ 800-257-7019
Madera Enterprises Inc
  Madera, CA 800-507-9555
Sunsweet Growers Inc.
  Yuba City, CA 800-417-2253
Valley View Packing Co
  Yuba City, CA 530-673-7356
Wild Aseptics, LLC
  Erlanger, KY 877-787-7221

Raisin

Lion Raisins Inc
  Selma, CA 559-834-6677

Product Categories / Beverages: Mixers

Victor Packing
   Madera, CA 559-673-5908

Raspberry
Hazel Creek Orchards
   Mt Airy, GA 706-754-4899
Meduri Farms
   Dallas, OR 877-388-8800
Merlinos
   Canon City, CO 719-275-5558
Stone Hill Winery
   Hermann, MO 573-486-2221

Refrigerated
Apple & Eve LLC
   Port Washington, NY 800-969-8018
Perfect Foods Inc
   Goshen, NY 800-933-3288
Swiss Premium Dairy Inc
   Lebanon, PA 800-222-2129
World Citrus West
   Fullerton, CA 714-870-6171

Strawberry
Green Spot Packaging
   Claremont, CA 800-456-3210
Madera Enterprises Inc
   Madera, CA 800-507-9555
Merlinos
   Canon City, CO 719-275-5558

Tangerine
Emerling International Foods
   Buffalo, NY 716-833-7381
Greenwood Associates
   Niles, IL 847-579-5500
Louis Dreyfus Company Citrus Inc
   Winter Garden, FL 407-656-1000
Minute Maid Company
   Atlanta, GA 800-520-2653
Perricone Juices
   Beaumont, CA 951-769-7171
True Organic Product Inc
   Helm, CA 800-487-0379
United Juice Companies of America
   Vero Beach, FL 772-562-5442
Wild Aseptics, LLC
   Erlanger, KY 877-787-7221

Tomato
Alimentaire Whyte's Inc
   Laval, QC 866-420-9520
Beckman & Gast Co
   St Henry, OH 419-678-4195
Cal-Tex Citrus Juice LP
   Houston, TX 800-231-0133
Dei Fratelli
   Toledo, OH 800-837-1631
Erba Food Products
   Brooklyn, NY 718-272-7700
Natalie's Orchid Island Juice Co.
   Ft. Pierce, FL 800-373-7444
Ocean Spray International
   Lakeville-Middleboro, MA ... 800-662-3263
Sun Pac Foods
   Brampton, ON 905-792-2700
Thomas Canning/Maidstone
   Maidstone, ON 519-737-1531
Welch Foods Inc.
   Concord, MA 800-340-6870
Wild Aseptics, LLC
   Erlanger, KY 877-787-7221

Boxed
Wild Aseptics, LLC
   Erlanger, KY 877-787-7221

Canned
Agrocan
   Ville St Laurent, QC 877-247-6226
Emerling International Foods
   Buffalo, NY 716-833-7381
Hirzel Canning Co & Farms
   Luckey, OH 419-419-7525
Wild Aseptics, LLC
   Erlanger, KY 877-787-7221

Cocktail
Emerling International Foods
   Buffalo, NY 716-833-7381
Vegetable Juices Inc
   Chicago, IL 888-776-9752

Frozen
Vegetable Juices Inc
   Chicago, IL 888-776-9752
Wild Aseptics, LLC
   Erlanger, KY 877-787-7221

Glass-Packed Chilled
Emerling International Foods
   Buffalo, NY 716-833-7381
Wild Aseptics, LLC
   Erlanger, KY 877-787-7221

Tropical Fruits
Care Foods International
   Long Island, NY 718-392-3355
Emerling International Foods
   Buffalo, NY 716-833-7381
Green Spot Packaging
   Claremont, CA 800-456-3210
Hawaiian Sun Products
   Honolulu, HI 808-845-3211
Healthmate Products
   Highland Park, IL 847-579-1051
International Trade Impact Inc
   Lawrenceville, NJ 800-223-5484
Lakewood Juice Co.
   Miami, FL 866-324-5900
Langer Juice Co Inc
   City of Industry, CA 626-336-3100
Lassonde Pappas & Company, Inc.
   Carneys Point, NJ 800-257-7019
Mondial Foods Company
   Los Angeles, CA 213-383-3531
Rubicon Food Products
   Richmond Hill, ON 905-883-1112
Stevens Tropical Plantation
   West Palm Beach, FL 561-683-4701
Sunlike Juice
   Rougemont, QC 866-552-7643
True Organic Product Inc
   Helm, CA 800-487-0379
Wild Aseptics, LLC
   Erlanger, KY 877-787-7221

Vegetable
Apple & Eve LLC
   Port Washington, NY 800-969-8018
B.M. Lawrence & Company
   San Francisco, CA 415-981-2926
Beckman & Gast Co
   St Henry, OH 419-678-4195
Campbell Soup Co.
   Camden, NJ 800-257-8443
Century Foods Intl LLC
   Sparta, WI 800-269-1901
Evolution Fresh
   Seattle, WA 800-794-9986
Florida Food Products Inc
   Eustis, FL 800-874-2331
Greenwood Associates
   Niles, IL 847-579-5500
Howard Foods Inc
   Danvers, MA 978-774-6207
Hudson Valley Fruit Juice
   Highland, NY 845-691-8061
Island Aseptics
   Byesville, OH 740-685-2548
Ludfords
   Riverside, CA 951-823-0306
Rapunzel Pure Organics
   Bloomfield, NJ 800-225-1449
RFi Ingredients
   Blauvelt, NY 800-962-7663
Tamarack Farms Dairy
   Newark, OH 866-221-4141
Thomas Canning/Maidstone
   Maidstone, ON 519-737-1531
Vegetable Juices Inc
   Chicago, IL 888-776-9752

Concentrates - Fruit Puree
GLCC Co
   Paw Paw, MI 269-657-3167

Greenwood Associates
   Niles, IL 847-579-5500
RFi Ingredients
   Blauvelt, NY 800-962-7663

Mixers

Bar Mixers
Better Beverages Inc
   Cerritos, CA 800-344-5219
Callie's Charleston Biscuits
   North Charleston, SC 843-577-1198
Coastal Promotions, Inc.
   Destin, FL 850-460-2328
Davis & Davis Gourmet Foods
   Allison Park, PA 412-487-7770
Hella Cocktail
   Long Island City, NY 646-854-8004
Improper Goods
   Portland, OR 503-662-7147
LA Jota Vineyard Co
   Angwin, CA 877-222-0292
Mixallogy
   Ponte Vedra Beach, FL
Nimble Nectar
   951-775-9543
Panorama Foods Inc.
   Braintree, MA 781-592-1069
Q Mixers
   Brooklyn, NY 718-398-6642
Refresco Beverages US Inc.
   Tampa, FL 888-260-3776
Regatta Craft Mixers
   Locust Valley, NY
Stirrings
   New Bedford, MA 866-646-4266
The Murphs Famous Inc.
   Henrietta, NY 888-281-6400
United Juice Companies of America
   Vero Beach, FL 772-562-5442

Prepared Cocktail Mixes
A.C. Calderoni
   Brisbane, CA 866-468-1897
Al-Rite Fruits & Syrups Co
   Miami, FL 305-652-2540
American Beverage Marketers
   New Albany, IN 812-944-3585
Bacardi Canada, Inc.
   Toronto, ON 905-451-6100
Bacardi USA Inc
   Coral Gables, FL 800-222-2734
Bartush Schnitzius Foods Co
   Lewisville, TX 972-219-1270
Beam Suntory
   Chicago, IL 312-964-6999
Blue Crab Bay
   Melfa, VA 800-221-2722
Callie's Charleston Biscuits
   North Charleston, SC 843-577-1198
Carolina Treet
   Wilmington, NC 800-616-6344
Century Blends LLC
   Hunt Valley, MD 410-771-6606
Circle B Ranch
   Seymour, MO 417-683-0271
Coastal Cocktails
   Irvine, CA 949-250-8951
Cocktail Crate
   Long Island City, NY 718-316-2033
Commodities Marketing Inc
   Clarksburg, NJ 732-516-0700
Davis & Davis Gourmet Foods
   Allison Park, PA 412-487-7770
Demitri's Bloody Mary Seasonings
   Seattle, WA 800-627-9649
Fee Brothers
   Rochester, NY 800-961-3337
Fentimans North America
   Burnaby, BC 877-326-3248
Ficks & Co.
   San Francisco, CA
Finest Call
   New Albany, IN 812-944-3585
Flavouressence Products
   Mississauga, ON 866-209-7778
Franco's Cocktail Mixes
   Pompano Beach, FL 800-782-4508
Frank & Dean's Cocktail Mixes
   Pasadena, CA 626-351-4272

Product Categories / Beverages: Non-Alcoholic Beverages

Glossop's Syrup
   Los Angeles, CA 424-832-7266
Great Western Juice Co
   Maple Heights, OH 800-321-9180
Hella Cocktail
   Long Island City, NY 646-854-8004
Island Aseptics
   Byesville, OH 740-685-2548
Island Oasis Frozen Cocktail
   Beloit, WI 800-777-4752
Jus-Made
   Dallas, TX 800-969-3746
Key Colony Red Parrot Juice
   Lemont, IL 844-783-8572
Kittling Ridge Estate Wines & Spirits
   Vaughan, ON 800-461-9463
LA Paz Products Inc
   Brea, CA 714-990-0982
Lemate Of New England Inc
   Foxboro, MA 508-543-9035
Lemon-X Corporation
   Huntington Station, NY 800-220-1061
Main Squeeze
   Columbia, MO 573-817-5616
Margarita Man
   San Antonio, TX 800-950-8149
Mele-Koi Farms
   Newport Beach, CA 949-660-9000
Miramar Fruit Trading Company
   Doral, FL 305-883-4774
Misty's Restaurant & Lounge
   Lincoln, NE 402-466-7222
Morris Kitchen
   Brooklyn, NY 347-457-6994
Mott's LLP
   Plano, TX 800-426-4891
Mr. C's
   Kent, WA 888-929-2378
Owl's Brew
   New York, NY 212-564-0218
Prima Foods International
   Silver Springs, FL 800-774-8751
Royale Brands
   Davenport, IA 563-386-5222
Ruffner's
   Wayne, PA 610-687-9800
Sea Breeze Fruit Flavors
   Towaco, NJ 800-732-2733
Sirocco Enterprises Inc
   New Orleans, LA 504-834-1549
Skinny Mixes LLC
   Clearwater, FL 727-826-0306
Southern Twist Cocktail
   Folly Beach, SC 843-343-9577
St Julian Winery
   Paw Paw, MI 800-732-6002
Stirrings
   New Bedford, MA 866-646-4266
Stonewall Kitchen
   York, ME 800-826-1752
SuckerPunch Gourmet
   Bridgeview, IL 708-784-3000
Texas Beach
   Richmond, VA 757-403-3598
Trader Vic's Food Products
   Emeryville, CA 877-762-4824
Tree Ripe Products
   Whippany, NJ 800-873-3747
Tropical Illusions
   Trenton, MO 660-359-5422
Ubons Sauce LLC
   Yazoo City, MS 662-716-7100
Uncle Dougie's
   Chicago, IL
Vegetable Juices Inc
   Chicago, IL 888-776-9752
Wagner Excello Food Products
   Broadview, IL 708-338-4488
Wild Aseptics, LLC
   Erlanger, KY 877-787-7221

Non-Alcoholic Beverages

American Instants Inc
   Flanders, NJ 973-584-8811
Ariel Vineyards
   Napa, CA 800-456-9472
Atlanta Coffee & Tea Co
    800-426-4781
B.M. Lawrence & Company
   San Francisco, CA 415-981-2926
Ex Drinks
   Henderson, NV 866-753-4929

Fee Brothers
   Rochester, NY 800-961-3337
Finlays
   Lincoln, RI 800-288-6272
Florida Caribbean Distillers
   Lake Alfred, FL 863-956-2002
Franco's Cocktail Mixes
   Pompano Beach, FL 800-782-4508
Ipswich Ale Brewery
   Ipswich, MA 978-356-3329
Kristian Regale
   Hudson, WI 715-386-8388
Lion Brewery Inc
   Wilkes Barre, PA 888-295-2337
Martin Coffee Co
   Jacksonville, FL 904-355-9661
Meier's Wine Cellars Inc
   Cincinnati, OH 800-346-2941
Natural Group
   Oxnard, CA 805-485-3420
Pok Pok Som
   Portland, OR 503-235-0004
Richland Beverage Association
   Carrollton, TX 214-357-0248
Skimpy Cocktails LLC
   Carrollton, TX 469-892-7988
Sweet Traders
   Huntington Beach, CA 714-903-6800
TOST Beverages LLC
   Red Hook, NY

Smoothies

Blendtopia
   Nashville, TN
Bluechip Group
   Salt Lake City, UT 800-878-0099
Bright Greens
   Portland, OR 760-487-8895
Broughton Foods LLC
   El Paso, TX 800-395-7004
Caffe D'Amore Gourmet Beverages
   Pittsburgh, PA 800-999-0171
Cascade Fresh
   Seattle, WA 800-511-0057
Dr. Smoothie Brands
   Fullerton, CA 888-466-9941
Essential Living Foods
   Torrance, CA 310-319-1555
Evolution Fresh
   Seattle, WA 800-794-9986
Foods Alive
   Angola, IN 260-488-4497
Gardner's Gourmet
   Fremont, CA 800-676-8558
Genius Juice
   Torrance, CA 800-682-7790
GPI USA LLC
   Mokena, IL 800-929-4248
Hain Celestial Group Inc
   Lake Success, NY 800-434-4246
Happy Family
   New York, NY 855-644-2779
Happy Planet Foods
   Burnaby, BC 800-811-3213
Hunter Farms - High Point Division
   High Point, NC 800-446-8035
Ideal Dairy Farms
   Hudson Falls, NY 518-747-5059
Jus-Made
   Dallas, TX 800-969-3746
K & F Select Fine Coffees
   Portland, OR 800-558-7788
Lane's Dairy
   El Paso, TX 915-772-6700
Maola Milk & Ice Cream Co.
    844-287-1970
Navitas Naturals
   Novato, CA 888-645-4282
NOKA
   Pacific Palisades, CA
Oak Farms
   El Paso, TX 800-395-7004
Odwalla
   Sugar Land, TX 800-639-2552
Saratoga Spring Water Co
   Saratoga Springs, NY 888-426-8642
Scally's Imperial Importing Company Inc
   Staten Island, NY 718-983-1938
Sheila's Select Gourmet Recipe
   Heber City, UT 800-516-7286
Soylent
   Los Angeles, CA

Stonyfield Organic
   Londonderry, NH 800-776-2697
Sunshine Dairy Foods Inc
   Portland, OR 503-234-7526
Victor Packing
   Madera, CA 559-673-5908

Soft Drinks & Sodas

51 Fifty Enterprises
   Livingston, CA 855-513-4389
Arctic Beverages
   Winnipeg, MB 866-503-1270
Beverage Capital Corporation
   Baltimore, MD 410-242-7404
Big Red Bottling
   Austin, TX 254-772-7791
BN Soda
   Brookline, MA 617-782-7888
Cadbury Beverages Canada
   Mississauga, ON 905-712-4121
Cawston Press
   Pittsburgh, PA
Cool
   Richardson, TX 972-437-9352
Fentimans North America
   Burnaby, BC 877-326-3248
Grand Teton Brewing Co
   Victor, ID 888-899-1656
Grown-up Soda
   New York, NY 212-355-7454
High Grade Beverage
   Monmouth Jct, NJ 887-327-4277
Honest Tea Inc
   Atlanta, GA 800-520-2653
Ipswich Ale Brewery
   Ipswich, MA 978-356-3329
J.M. Smucker Co.
   Orrville, OH 888-550-9555
Jones Soda Company
   Seattle, WA 800-656-6050
PepsiCo.
   Purchase, NY 914-253-2000
Reed's, Inc.
   Los Angeles, CA
Refresco Beverages US Inc.
   Tampa, FL 888-260-3776
Safeway Inc.
   Pleasanton, CA 877-723-3929
Sipp
   Stamford, CT 866-222-4735
Smith & Salmon
   Burlington, VT 802-578-8242
Snow Beverages
   New York, NY 212-353-3270
Stevens Point Brewery
   Stevens Point, WI 800-369-4911
Tincture Distillers
   Arlington, VA 888-658-6899
Universal Impex Corporation
   Toronto, ON 416-743-7778
Zevia
   Culver City, CA 855-469-3842

Club Soda

Ipswich Ale Brewery
   Ipswich, MA 978-356-3329
Joia All Natural Soda
   Minneapolis, MN 612-308-2056
Regatta Craft Mixers
   Locust Valley, NY

Soda Water

Coca-Cola Beverages Northeast
   Bedford, NH 844-619-3388

Soft Drinks

1642
   Montreal, QC 800-774-4907
A-Treat Bottling Co
   Allentown, PA 800-220-1531
Abita Brewing Co
   Covington, LA 800-737-2311
Admiral Beverage Corp
   Worland, WY 307-347-4201
Arctic Beverages
   Winnipeg, MB 866-503-1270
Aspire
   Chicago, OH
B.M. Lawrence & Company
   San Francisco, CA 415-981-2926

Product Categories / Beverages: Soft Drinks & Sodas

Beverage Capital Corporation
  Baltimore, MD 410-242-7404
Blue Sky Beverage Company
  Corona, CA 800-426-7367
BN Soda
  Brookline, MA 617-782-7888
Catawissa Bottling Co
  Catawissa, PA 800-892-4419
Cawy Bottling Co
  Miami, FL 877-917-2299
Coca-Cola Beverages Northeast
  Bedford, NH 844-619-3388
Coca-Cola Co.
  Atlanta, GA 800-438-2653
Cool Mountain Beverages Inc
  Des Plaines, IL 888-838-7632
Crystal & Vigor Beverages
  Kearny, NJ 201-991-2342
CTL Foods
  Colfax, WI 800-962-5227
Everfresh Beverages
  Warren, MI 800-323-3416
Ginseng Up Corp
  Worcester, MA 800-446-7364
Global Beverage Company
  Rochester, NY 585-381-3560
Good-O-Beverages Inc
  Bronx, NY 718-328-6400
Hanks Beverage Co
  Feasterville-Trevose, PA 800-289-4722
Haydenergy Health
  Valley Stream, NY 800-255-1660
Island Sweetwater Beverage Company
  Bryn Mawr, PA 610-525-7444
Krier Foods
  Random Lake, WI 920-994-2469
Lenox-Martell Inc
  Boston, MA 877-325-2489
Leonard Fountain Specialties
  Detroit, MI 313-891-4141
Lost Trail Root Beer
  Louisburg, KS 800-748-7765
Manhattan Special Bottling
  Brooklyn, NY 718-388-4144
Mar-Key Foods
  Vidalia, GA 912-537-4204
Monarch Beverage Company
  Atlanta, GA 800-241-3732
Moon Shot Energy
  Austin, TX 512-387-4703
Mt Claire Beverages
  Torrington, CT 888-525-2473
National Beverage Corporation
  Fort Lauderdale, FL 877-622-3499
Original American Beverage Company
  North Stonington, CT 800-625-3767
Polar Beverages Inc.
  Worcester, MA 800-734-9800
Q Drinks
  Brooklyn, NY 718-398-6642
R.J. Corr Naturals
  Posen, IL 708-389-4200
RC Bottling Company
  Evensaville, IN 812-424-7978
Roselani Tropics Ice Cream
  Wailuku, HI 808-244-7951
SANGARIA USA
  Torrance, CA 310-530-2202
Saranac Brewery
  Utica, NY 800-765-6288
Shasta Beverages Inc
  Baltimore, MS 800-834-9980
Signature Beverage
  Merrick, NY 800-277-2755
Soho Beverages
  Vienna, VA 703-689-2800
Southern Beverage Packers Inc
  Appling, GA 800-326-2469
Stop & Shop Manufacturing
  Readville, MA 508-977-5132
The Veri Soda Company
  New York, NY 203-409-3995
Todhunter Foods
  Lake Alfred, FL 863-956-1116
Varni Brothers/7-Up Bottling
  Modesto, CA 209-521-1777
Vermont Sweetwater Bottling Co
  Poultney, VT 800-974-9877
Wet Planet Beverage
  Monachie, NJ 201-288-1999
White Label Yerba Mate Soda
  New York, NY
White Rock Products Corp
  Flushing, NY 800-969-7625
Wild Poppy
  Los Angeles, CA 310-384-1004
Zevia
  Culver City, CA 855-469-3842

Cola

1642
  Montreal, QC 800-774-4907
A-Treat Bottling Co
  Allentown, PA 800-220-1531
Adirondack Beverages Inc
  Scotia, NY 800-316-6096
Al's Beverage Company
  East Windsor, CT 888-257-7632
Aloe'Ha Drink Products
  Houston, TX 713-978-6359
American Bottling & Beverage
  Walterboro, SC 843-538-7937
Bar Harbor Brewing Company
  Bar Harbor, ME 207-288-4592
Better Beverages Inc
  Cerritos, CA 800-344-5219
Beverage America
  Holland, MI 616-396-1281
Beverage House Inc
  Cartersville, GA 888-367-8327
Boylan Bottling Company
  Haledon, NJ 800-289-7978
Cable Car Beverage Corporation
  Denver, CO 303-298-9038
Castle Beverages Inc
  Ansonia, CT 203-734-0883
Catawissa Bottling Co
  Catawissa, PA 800-892-4419
Champion Beverages
  Darien, CT 203-655-9026
Coca-Cola Beverages Northeast
  Bedford, NH 844-619-3388
Coca-Cola Bottling Co. Consolidated
  Charlotte, NC 800-866-2653
Coca-Cola Bottling Company UNITED, Inc.
  Birmingham, AB 800-844-2653
Coca-Cola Co.
  Atlanta, GA 800-438-2653
Coca-Cola European Partners
  Uxbridge, Middx, ... 800-418-4223
Cornell Beverages Inc
  Brooklyn, NY 718-381-3000
Crowley Beverage Corporation
  Wayland, MA 800-997-3377
Double-Cola Company
  Chattanooga, TN 423-267-5691
Dr Pepper Snapple Group
  Plano, TX 800-696-5891
Egg Cream America Inc
  Northbrook, IL 847-559-2703
Faygo Beverages Inc
  Detroit, MI 313-925-1600
Gulf States Canners Inc
  Clinton, MS 601-924-0511
Hampton Associates & Sons
  Fairfax, VA 703-968-5847
Honickman Affiliates
  Pennsauken, NJ 800-573-7745
Hosmer Mountain Bottling Co
  Willimantic, CT 800-763-2445
Jones Soda Company
  Seattle, WA 800-656-6050
Kennebec Fruit Company
  Lisbon Falls, ME 207-353-8173
Keurig Dr Pepper
  Plano, TX 800-696-5891
Kola
  New York, NY 212-688-1895
Lenox-Martell Inc
  Boston, MA 877-325-2489
Leonard Fountain Specialties
  Detroit, MI 313-891-4141
Millstream Brewing Co
  Amana, IA 319-622-3672
Moceri South Western
  San Diego, CA 619-297-7900
New York Bottling Co Inc
  Bronx, NY 718-842-7416
Noel Corp
  Yakima, WA 509-248-1313
North Shore Bottling Co
  Brooklyn, NY 718-272-8900
Northern Neck
  Montross, VA 804-493-8051
Pennsylvania Dutch: Birch Beer
  Doylestown, PA 856-662-1869
Pocono Mountain Bottling Company
  Wilkes Barre, PA 570-822-7695
Premier Beverages
  Plano, TX 972-547-6295
REED'S Inc
  Los Angeles, CA 800-997-3337
Rivella USA
  Boca Raton, FL 561-417-5810
Sarum Tea Company
  Lakeville, CT 860-435-2086
Shabazz Fruit Cola Company
  Newark, NJ 973-230-4641
Shasta Beverages Inc
  Baltimore, MS 800-834-9980
SoBe Beverages
  Norwalk, CT 800-588-0548
Stewart's Beverages
  rye Brook, NY 800-762-7753
Sun State Beverage
  Atlanta, GA 770-451-3990
Thomas Kemper Soda Company
  Austin, TX 206-381-8712
Triple XXX Root Beer Co.
  West Lafayette, IN 765-743-5373
USA Beverage
  Warrenton, MO 636-456-5468
Virgil's Root Beer
  Norwalk, CT 800-997-3337

Cream Soda

Catawissa Bottling Co
  Catawissa, PA 800-892-4419
Coca-Cola Beverages Northeast
  Bedford, NH 844-619-3388
Cool Mountain Beverages Inc
  Des Plaines, IL 888-838-7632
Dr Pepper Snapple Group
  Plano, TX 800-696-5891
Ipswich Ale Brewery
  Ipswich, MA 978-356-3329
Jones Soda Company
  Seattle, WA 800-656-6050
Keurig Dr Pepper
  Plano, TX 800-696-5891
Signature Beverage
  Merrick, NY 800-277-2755

Cream Soda - Vanilla

Thomas Kemper Soda Company
  Austin, TX 206-381-8712

Ginger Ale

1642
  Montreal, QC 800-774-4907
Adirondack Beverages Inc
  Scotia, NY 800-316-6096
Bruce Cost Ginger Ale
  Brooklyn, NY 212-488-0661
Bull's Head
  Richmond, QC 819-212-1583
Coca-Cola Beverages Northeast
  Bedford, NH 844-619-3388
Cool Mountain Beverages Inc
  Des Plaines, IL 888-838-7632
Dr Pepper Snapple Group
  Plano, TX 800-696-5891
Grand Teton Brewing Co
  Victor, ID. 888-899-1656
Keurig Dr Pepper
  Plano, TX 800-696-5891
Leonard Fountain Specialties
  Detroit, MI 313-891-4141
Regatta Craft Mixers
  Locust Valley, NY
Thomas Kemper Soda Company
  Austin, TX 206-381-8712
Verdant Kitchen
  Norcross, GA 912-349-2958

Lemon-Lime Soda

Cool Mountain Beverages Inc
  Des Plaines, IL 888-838-7632
Ipswich Ale Brewery
  Ipswich, MA 978-356-3329
Manhattan Special Bottling
  Brooklyn, NY 718-388-4144
Shasta Beverages Inc
  Baltimore, MS 800-834-9980

Product Categories / Beverages: Spirits & Liqueurs

Sarsaparilla

Manhattan Special Bottling
Brooklyn, NY 718-388-4144

Sparkling Water

Arctic Beverages
Winnipeg, MB 866-503-1270
Bevco Sales International Inc.
Surrey, BC 800-663-0090
Blue Sky Beverage Company
Corona, CA 800-426-7367
Coca-Cola Bottling Co. Consolidated
Charlotte, NC 800-866-2653
Coca-Cola Bottling Company UNITED, Inc.
Birmingham, AB 800-844-2653
Coca-Cola European Partners
Uxbridge, Middx 800-418-4223
Crystal Geyser Water Co.
Burlingame, CA 800-443-9737
Crystal Rock LLC
Watertown, CT 800-525-0070
Dr Pepper Snapple Group
Plano, TX 800-696-5891
DRY Soda Co.
Seattle, WA 888-379-7632
Eternal Water
Walnut Creek, CA 877-854-5494
Hinckley Springs Bottled Water
. . . . 800-201-6218
Kalena
Chicago, IL
Keurig Dr Pepper
Plano, TX 800-696-5891
LaCroix
Ft. Lauderdale, FL 888-241-7360
Make It Simple
Woodbury, MN
Matilija Water Company
Santa Barbara, CA 805-963-7873
Mount Olympus Waters
. . . . 800-782-5508
Polar Beverages Inc.
Worcester, MA 800-734-9800
Polar Water Company
Carnegie, PA 412-429-5550
R.J. Corr Naturals
Posen, IL 708-389-4200
Saratoga Spring Water Co
Saratoga Springs, NY 888-426-8642
Signature Beverage
Merrick, NY 800-277-2755
Southern Beverage Packers Inc
Appling, GA 800-326-2469
Sparkletts
Lakeland, FL 800-728-5508
Spindrift Beverage
Waltham, MA 617-391-0356
Sweet Earth Foods
Moss Landing, CA 800-737-3311
Topo Chico Mineral Water
Plano, TX 888-456-4357
TOST Beverages LLC
Red Hook, NY
Universal Beverages Inc
Ponte Vedra Bch, FL 904-280-7795

Tonic Water

1642
Montreal, QC 800-774-4907
Regatta Craft Mixers
Locust Valley, NY

Spirits & Liqueurs

Brandy

Corby Distilleries
Toronto, ON 800-367-9079
Craft Distillers
Ukiah, CA 800-782-8145
Denning's Point Distillery, LLC
Beacon, NY 845-476-8413
E & J Gallo Winery
Modesto, CA 877-687-9463
Heaven Hill Distilleries Inc.
Bardstown, KY 502-337-1000
Heck Cellars
Arvin, CA 661-854-6120
Hood River Distillers Inc
Hood River, OR 541-386-1588

Ironstone Vineyards
Murphys, CA 209-728-1251
Kittling Ridge Estate Wines & Spirits
Vaughan, ON 800-461-9463
Laird & Company
Scobeyville, NJ 877-438-5247
M S Walker Inc
Somerville, MA 617-776-6700
Marie Brizard Wines & Spirits
St. Helena, CA 800-878-1123
Pernod Ricard USA
New York, NY 212-372-5400
Stoutridge Vineyard
Marlboro, NY
Todhunter Foods
West Palm Beach, FL 800-336-9463
US Distilled Products Co
Princeton, MN 763-389-4903
Vie-Del Co
Fresno, CA 559-834-2525

Grappa

Catskill Distilling Company
Bethel, NY 845-583-3141

Luxury Cognac

Heaven Hill Distilleries Inc.
Bardstown, KY 502-337-1000

V.S. Cognac Three Star

Corby Distilleries
Toronto, ON 800-367-9079

V.S.O.P. Cognac

Corby Distilleries
Toronto, ON 800-367-9079

X.O. Cognac

Corby Distilleries
Toronto, ON 800-367-9079

Gin

A. Smith Bowman Distillery
Fredericksburg, VA 540-373-4555
Beam Suntory
Chicago, IL 312-964-6999
Catskill Distilling Company
Bethel, NY 845-583-3141
Corby Distilleries
Toronto, ON 800-367-9079
Denning's Point Distillery, LLC
Beacon, NY 845-476-8413
Destileria Serralles Inc
Mercedita, PR 787-840-1000
Diageo Canada Inc.
Toronto, ON 416-626-2000
E & J Gallo Winery
Modesto, CA 877-687-9463
Heaven Hill Distilleries Inc.
Bardstown, KY 502-337-1000
Hiram Walker & Sons
Windsor, ON 519-254-5171
Hood River Distillers Inc
Hood River, OR 541-386-1588
Laird & Company
Scobeyville, NJ 877-438-5247
Marie Brizard Wines & Spirits
St. Helena, CA 800-878-1123
Orange County Distillery
Goshen, NY 845-651-2929
Pernod Ricard USA
New York, NY 212-372-5400
Prohibition Distillery, LLC
Roscoe, NY 917-685-8989
Stoutridge Vineyard
Marlboro, NY
Tuthilltown Spirits
Gardiner, NY 845-255-1527
Union Square Wines & Spirits
New York, NY 212-675-8100
Viking Distillery
Albany, GA 866-729-3722
Vincor Canada
Mississauga, ON 800-265-9463
Warwick Valley Winery & Distillery
Warwick, NY 845-258-4858

Irish Whiskey

Beam Suntory
Chicago, IL 312-964-6999
Corby Distilleries
Toronto, ON 800-367-9079
George A Dickel & Company
Tullahoma, TN 888-342-5352
Heaven Hill Distilleries Inc.
Bardstown, KY 502-337-1000
Hiram Walker & Sons
Windsor, ON 519-254-5171
Jack Daniel Distillery
Lynchburg, TN 888-551-5225
Kittling Ridge Estate Wines & Spirits
Vaughan, ON 800-461-9463
Laird & Company
Scobeyville, NJ 877-438-5247
Pernod Ricard USA
New York, NY 212-372-5400

Liqueurs & Cordials

Aloha Distillers
Honolulu, HI 808-841-5787
Bacardi Canada, Inc.
Toronto, ON 905-451-6100
Beam Suntory
Chicago, IL 312-964-6999
Black Prince Distillery Inc
Clifton, NJ 973-365-2050
Chambord
Louisville, KY 800-523-3811
Clear Creek Distillery
Portland, OR 503-248-9470
Destileria Serralles Inc
Mercedita, PR 787-840-1000
Diageo North America Inc
Norwalk, CT 203-229-2100
Florida Caribbean Distillers
Lake Alfred, FL 863-956-2002
Heaven Hill Distilleries Inc.
Bardstown, KY 502-337-1000
Highwood Distillers
High River, AB 403-652-3202
Hiram Walker & Sons
Windsor, ON 519-254-5171
Kittling Ridge Estate Wines & Spirits
Vaughan, ON 800-461-9463
M S Walker Inc
Somerville, MA 617-776-6700
Marie Brizard Wines & Spirits
St. Helena, CA 800-878-1123
Paramount Distillers
Cleveland, OH 800-821-2989
Pernod Ricard USA
New York, NY 212-372-5400
Phillips Beverage Company
Minneapolis, MN 612-362-7500
Renault Winery
Egg Harbor City, NJ 609-965-2111
Sakeone Distillery
Forest Grove, OR 800-550-7253
Todhunter Foods
West Palm Beach, FL 800-336-9463
Union Square Wines & Spirits
New York, NY 212-675-8100
US Distilled Products Co
Princeton, MN 763-389-4903

Amaretto

Heaven Hill Distilleries Inc.
Bardstown, KY 502-337-1000

Anise Liqueur

Pernod Ricard USA
New York, NY 212-372-5400

Chocolate Liqueur

Aloha Distillers
Honolulu, HI 808-841-5787

Coffee Liqueur

Aloha Distillers
Honolulu, HI 808-841-5787
Heaven Hill Distilleries Inc.
Bardstown, KY 502-337-1000

Fruit Liqueur

KAS Spirits
Mahopac, NY 845-750-6000

Product Categories / Beverages: Spirits & Liqueurs

Nahmias et Fils
  Yonkers, NY 914-294-0055
Warwick Valley Winery & Distillery
  Warwick, NY 845-258-4858

Herbal Liqueur

KAS Spirits
  Mahopac, NY 845-750-6000
Tuthilltown Spirits
  Gardiner, NY. 845-255-1527

Schnapps Liqueuer

Marie Brizard Wines & Spirits
  St. Helena, CA 800-878-1123

Neutral

Buffalo Trace Distillery
  Frankfort, KY 800-654-8471
M S Walker Inc
  Somerville, MA 617-776-6700
Paramount Distillers
  Cleveland, OH 800-821-2989
Royal Wine Corp
  Bayonne, NJ 718-384-2400

Rum

A. Smith Bowman Distillery
  Fredericksburg, VA 540-373-4555
Bacardi Canada, Inc.
  Toronto, ON 905-451-6100
Bacardi USA Inc
  Coral Gables, FL. 800-222-2734
Beam Suntory
  Chicago, IL 312-964-6999
Buffalo Trace Distillery
  Frankfort, KY 800-654-8471
Corby Distilleries
  Toronto, ON 800-367-9079
Destileria Serralles Inc
  Mercedita, PR 787-840-1000
Florida Caribbean Distillers
  Lake Alfred, FL 863-956-2002
Heaven Hill Distilleries Inc.
  Bardstown, KY 502-337-1000
Highwood Distillers
  High River, AB 403-652-3202
Hiram Walker & Sons
  Windsor, ON. 519-254-5171
Hood River Distillers Inc
  Hood River, OR 541-386-1588
Kittling Ridge Estate Wines & Spirits
  Vaughan, ON. 800-461-9463
Marie Brizard Wines & Spirits
  St. Helena, CA 800-878-1123
Terressentia Corp.
  Ladson, SC 843-225-3100
Trigo Corporation
  Toa Baja, PR 787-794-1300
Union Square Wines & Spirits
  New York, NY 212-675-8100

Dark

Bacardi Canada, Inc.
  Toronto, ON 905-451-6100
Corby Distilleries
  Toronto, ON 800-367-9079

White Silver

Corby Distilleries
  Toronto, ON 800-367-9079

Scotch Whiskey

A. Smith Bowman Distillery
  Fredericksburg, VA 540-373-4555
Bacardi Canada, Inc.
  Toronto, ON 905-451-6100
Beam Suntory
  Chicago, IL 312-964-6999
Brown-Forman Corp
  Louisville, KY. 502-585-1100
Canadian Mist Distillers
  Collingwood, ON 705-445-4690
George A Dickel & Company
  Tullahoma, TN 888-342-5352
Heaven Hill Distilleries Inc.
  Bardstown, KY 502-337-1000
Hiram Walker & Sons
  Windsor, ON. 519-254-5171

Hood River Distillers Inc
  Hood River, OR 541-386-1588
Jack Daniel Distillery
  Lynchburg, TN 888-551-5225
Kittling Ridge Estate Wines & Spirits
  Vaughan, ON. 800-461-9463
Laird & Company
  Scobeyville, NJ 877-438-5247
Maker's Mark Distillery Inc
  Loretto, KY. 270-865-2881
Marie Brizard Wines & Spirits
  St. Helena, CA 800-878-1123
Pernod Ricard USA
  New York, NY 212-372-5400

Blended

Maker's Mark Distillery Inc
  Loretto, KY. 270-865-2881

Highland Malt

Maker's Mark Distillery Inc
  Loretto, KY. 270-865-2881

Tequila and Mezcal

A. Smith Bowman Distillery
  Fredericksburg, VA 540-373-4555
Beam Suntory
  Chicago, IL 312-964-6999
Brown-Forman Corp
  Louisville, KY. 502-585-1100
Corby Distilleries
  Toronto, ON 800-367-9079
Heaven Hill Distilleries Inc.
  Bardstown, KY 502-337-1000
Highwood Distillers
  High River, AB 403-652-3202
Hood River Distillers Inc
  Hood River, OR 541-386-1588
Luxco Inc
  St Louis, MO 314-772-2626
Marie Brizard Wines & Spirits
  St. Helena, CA 800-878-1123
McCormick Distilling Co
  Weston, MO 888-640-3082
Union Square Wines & Spirits
  New York, NY 212-675-8100
Vincor Canada
  Mississauga, ON 800-265-9463

Vodka

A. Smith Bowman Distillery
  Fredericksburg, VA 540-373-4555
Bacardi Canada, Inc.
  Toronto, ON 905-451-6100
Bacardi USA Inc
  Coral Gables, FL. 800-222-2734
Barber's Farm Distillery LLC
  Middleburgh, NY
Beam Suntory
  Chicago, IL 312-964-6999
Boisset Family Estates
  St Helena, CA 800-878-1123
Brown-Forman Corp
  Louisville, KY. 502-585-1100
Capalbo's Fruit Baskets
  Clifton, NJ. 800-252-6262
Catskill Distilling Company
  Bethel, NY 845-583-3141
Corby Distilleries
  Toronto, ON 800-367-9079
Crillon Importers LTD
  Paramus, NJ. 201-368-8878
Denning's Point Distillery, LLC
  Beacon, NY. 845-476-8413
Destileria Serralles Inc
  Mercedita, PR 787-840-1000
Florida Caribbean Distillers
  Lake Alfred, FL 863-956-2002
Heaven Hill Distilleries Inc.
  Bardstown, KY 502-337-1000
Highwood Distillers
  High River, AB 403-652-3202
Hiram Walker & Sons
  Windsor, ON. 519-254-5171
Hood River Distillers Inc
  Hood River, OR 541-386-1588
Kittling Ridge Estate Wines & Spirits
  Vaughan, ON. 800-461-9463
Laird & Company
  Scobeyville, NJ 877-438-5247

Luxco Inc
  St Louis, MO. 314-772-2626
Marie Brizard Wines & Spirits
  St. Helena, CA 800-878-1123
McCormick Distilling Co
  Weston, MO 888-640-3082
Orange County Distillery
  Goshen, NY. 845-651-2929
Pernod Ricard USA
  New York, NY 212-372-5400
Prohibition Distillery, LLC
  Roscoe, NY. 917-685-8989
R&A Imports
  Pacific Palisades, CA 310-454-2247
Stoutridge Vineyard
  Marlboro, NY.
Terressentia Corp.
  Ladson, SC 843-225-3100
Three Meadows Spirits LLC
  Millerton, NY 845-702-3903
Trigo Corporation
  Toa Baja, PR 787-794-1300
Tuthilltown Spirits
  Gardiner, NY. 845-255-1527
Union Square Wines & Spirits
  New York, NY 212-675-8100
Viking Distillery
  Albany, GA 866-729-3722
Vincor Canada
  Mississauga, ON 800-265-9463

Whiskey, American

Beam Suntory
  Chicago, IL 312-964-6999
Catskill Distilling Company
  Bethel, NY 845-583-3141
Corby Distilleries
  Toronto, ON 800-367-9079
Denning's Point Distillery, LLC
  Beacon, NY. 845-476-8413
Florida Caribbean Distillers
  Lake Alfred, FL 863-956-2002
George A Dickel & Company
  Tullahoma, TN 888-342-5352
Heaven Hill Distilleries Inc.
  Bardstown, KY 502-337-1000
Hiram Walker & Sons
  Windsor, ON. 519-254-5171
Jack Daniel Distillery
  Lynchburg, TN 888-551-5225
Kittling Ridge Estate Wines & Spirits
  Vaughan, ON. 800-461-9463
Laird & Company
  Scobeyville, NJ 877-438-5247
McCormick Distilling Co
  Weston, MO 888-640-3082
Nahmias et Fils
  Yonkers, NY 914-294-0055
Prohibition Distillery, LLC
  Roscoe, NY. 917-685-8989
Sazerac Company, Inc.
  Metairie, LA 866-729-3722
Stoutridge Vineyard
  Marlboro, NY
US Distilled Products Co
  Princeton, MN. 763-389-4903

Bourbon

A. Smith Bowman Distillery
  Fredericksburg, VA 540-373-4555
Brown-Forman Corp
  Louisville, KY. 502-585-1100
Buffalo Trace Distillery
  Frankfort, KY 800-654-8471
Catskill Distilling Company
  Bethel, NY 845-583-3141
Corby Distilleries
  Toronto, ON 800-367-9079
Heaven Hill Distilleries Inc.
  Bardstown, KY 502-337-1000
Laird & Company
  Scobeyville, NJ 877-438-5247
Marie Brizard Wines & Spirits
  St. Helena, CA 800-878-1123
Old Rip Van Winkle Distillery
  Frankfort, KY 502-897-9113
Orange County Distillery
  Goshen, NY. 845-651-2929
Pernod Ricard USA
  New York, NY 212-372-5400

Product Categories / Beverages: Sports Drinks

Sazerac Company, Inc.
  Metairie, LA 866-729-3722
Tuthilltown Spirits
  Gardiner, NY 845-255-1527
Viking Distillery
  Albany, GA 866-729-3722

Rye Whiskey

Catskill Distilling Company
  Bethel, NY 845-583-3141
Tuthilltown Spirits
  Gardiner, NY 845-255-1527

Tennessee Whiskey

Brown-Forman Corp
  Louisville, KY 502-585-1100

Whiskey, Canadian

Beam Suntory
  Chicago, IL 312-964-6999
Brown-Forman Corp
  Louisville, KY 502-585-1100
Corby Distilleries
  Toronto, ON 800-367-9079

Sports Drinks

Asiamerica Ingredients
  Westwood, NJ 201-497-5531
Berri Pro
  Santa Monica, CA
Bonk Breaker
  Santa Monica, CA 310-315-4129
Captiva Limited Inc
  Augusta, NJ 973-579-7883
Cell-Nique
  Norwalk, CT 888-417-9343
Celsius
  Boca Raton, FL 866-423-5748
Century Foods Intl LLC
  Sparta, WI 800-269-1901
Coca-Cola Beverages Northeast
  Bedford, NH 844-619-3388
Cool
  Richardson, TX 972-437-9352
Crystal Star Herbal Nutrition
  Salinas, CA 831-422-7500
GREEN Energy
  Kailua, HI 808-396-9454
Hiball, Inc.
  San Francisco, CA 833-442-2553
I Rice & Co Inc
  Philadelphia, PA 800-232-6022
Ito En USA Inc
  Brooklyn, NY 808-847-4477
Kill Cliff
  Atlanta, GA 855-552-5433
Lassonde Pappas & Company, Inc.
  Carneys Point, NJ 800-257-7019
LifeAID
  Santa Cruz, CA 888-558-1113
Masala Chai Company
  Santa Cruz, CA 831-475-8881
MODe Sports Nutrition
  Costa Mesa, CA 949-274-9948
Monarch Beverage Company
  Atlanta, GA 800-241-3732
Nature's Best Inc
  Hauppauge, NY 800-345-2378
Nhs Labs Inc
  Star, ID 888-546-8694
Nutrisciences Labs
  Farmingdale, NY 855-492-7388
Nutriwest
  Douglas, WY 800-443-3333
Nuun Active Hydration
  Seattle, WA 855-426-6886
Optimum Nutrition
  Aurora, IL 800-763-3444
Pitbull Energy Products
  Carson, CA 800-686-3697
PowerBar
  Kings Mountain, NC 800-587-6937
Pyure Brands
  Naples, FL 305-509-5096
Queen of America
  Belleview, FL 352-245-3600
Refresco Beverages US Inc.
  Tampa, FL 888-260-3776
Sherbrooke OEM Ltd
  Sherbrooke, QC 866-851-2579
The Pickle Juice Company
  Mesquite, TX 972-755-0289
Tigo+
  FL 786-207-4772
Tova Industries LLC
  Louisville, KY 888-532-8682
Ultima Health Products Inc.
  Cortland, OH 888-663-8584
Uptime Energy, Inc.
  Canoga Park, CA
Wild Aseptics, LLC
  Erlanger, KY 877-787-7221

Water

3 Springs Water Co
  Laurel Run, PA 800-332-7873
3 Water
  Huntington, NY 877-371-8704
Absopure Water Company
  Plymouth, MI 800-422-7678
Acqua Blox LLC
  Santa Fe Springs, CA 562-693-9599
Adobe Springs
  Patterson, CA 408-897-3023
Alamance Foods
  Burlington, NC
Alpine Valley Water
  Harvey, IL 708-333-3910
Aqua Clara Bottling & Distribution
  Clearwater, FL 727-446-2999
Arbor Springs Water Co
  Ferndale, MI 248-543-7151
Ax Water
  Fargo, ND
Blossom Water, LLC
  Westwood, MA 855-325-5777
Blue Hills Spring Water Company
  Quincy, MA 614-715-3900
Blue Sky Beverage Company
  Corona, CA 800-426-7367
Captiva Limited Inc
  Augusta, NJ 973-579-7883
Cascade Clear Water
  Portland, OR 800-888-3879
Clearly Canadian Beverage Corporation
  Vanghan, ON 866-414-2326
Crystal Springs
  Mississauga, ON 800-822-5889
Crystal Springs Bottled Water
  Lakeland, FL 800-728-5508
Crystal Springs Water Company
  Lakeland, FL 800-728-5508
Culligan International Company
  Rosemont, IL 847-205-6000
Distillata
  Cleveland, OH 800-999-2906
DS Services of America
  Lakeland, FL 800-728-5508
Eldorado Artesian Springs Inc
  Louisville, CO 303-499-1316
Essentia Water
  Bothell, WA 877-293-2239
Eureka Water Co
  Oklahoma City, OK 800-310-8474
Fantis Foods Inc
  Carlstadt, NJ 201-933-6200
Fizz-O Water Co
  Tulsa, OK 918-834-3691
Fizzy Lizzy
  Jersey City, NJ 800-203-9336
Girard Spring Water
  North Providence, RI 800-477-9287
Glen Summit Springs Water Company
  Mountain Top, PA 800-621-7596
Global Beverage Company
  Rochester, NY 585-381-3560
Green-Go Cactus Water
  Oakville, CA 707-944-2039
GWB Foods Corporation
  Brooklyn, NY 877-977-7610
Harrisburg Dairies Inc
  Harrisburg, PA 800-692-7429
Hawaiian Natural Water Company
  Pearl City, HI 808-483-0520
Heck Cellars
  Arvin, CA 661-854-6120
Herbal Water, Inc.
  Yuba City, CA 610-668-4000
Holly Camp Springs Inc
  Hudgins, VA 804-795-2096
Island Sweetwater Beverage Company
  Bryn Mawr, PA 610-525-7444
Kentwood Springs
  Lakeland, FL 800-728-5508
Le Bleu Corp
  Advance, NC 800-854-4471
Light Rock Beverage Company
  Danbury, CT 203-743-3410
Lipsey Mountain Spring Water
  Norcross, GA 770-449-0001
Lynn Springs Water LLC
  Tucker, GA 770-572-5928
Maverick Brands, LLC
  Palo Alto, CA 424-571-7230
Mayer Bros
  Buffalo, NY 800-696-2928
Metro Mint
  San Francisco, CA 415-979-0781
Minnehaha Spring Water Company
  Cleveland, OH 216-431-0243
Monarch Beverage Company
  Atlanta, GA 800-241-3732
Mountain Valley Spring Company
  Hot Springs, AR 800-643-1501
Mountain Valley Spring Water
  Asheville, NC 800-627-1062
Mt Claire Beverages
  Torrington, CT 888-525-2473
Music Mountain Water Company
  Shreveport, LA 800-349-6555
Nantze Springs Inc
  Dothan, AL 800-239-7873
Natural Group
  Oxnard, CA 805-485-3420
Natural Spring Water Company
  Johnson City, TN 423-926-7905
Naya
  Montreal, QC 450-562-7911
Neenah Springs
  Oxford, WI 608-586-5696
North American Water Group
  Overland Park, KS 913-469-1156
North Country Natural Spring Water
  Port Kent, NY 518-834-9400
Northern Falls
  Rockford, MI 616-915-0970
Oakhurst Dairy
  Portland, ME 800-482-0718
Office General des Eaux Minerales
  Montreal, QC 514-482-7221
Ozarka Drinking Water
  Dallas, TX 817-354-9526
Peace Mountain Natural Beverages
  Springfield, MA 413-567-4942
Penta Water
  Colton, CA 800-531-5088
Pocono Spring Company
  Mt Pocono, PA 800-634-4584
Premium Water
  Kansas City, MO 800-332-3332
Primo Water Corporation
  Winston-Salem, NC 844-237-7466
Private Spring Water
  San Martin, CA 877-664-1500
Pure Flo Water Co
  Santee, CA 800-787-3356
Q Mixers
  Brooklyn, NY 718-398-6642
Quibell Spring Water Beverage
  Martinsville, VA 540-632-0100
R.J. Corr Naturals
  Posen, IL 708-389-4200
Rebound
  Newburgh, NY 845-562-5400
Refresco Beverages US Inc.
  Tampa, FL 888-260-3776
Sand Springs
  Williamstown, MA 413-458-8281
Saratoga Spring Water Co
  Saratoga Springs, NY 888-426-8642
Schneider's Dairy Inc
  Pittsburgh, PA 412-881-3525
SnowBird Corporation
  Bayonne, NJ 800-576-1616
Something Natural LLC
  Boston, MA 617-315-7169
St. Clair Industries
  Ft Lauderdale, FL 954-491-0400
Talking Rain Beverage Co
  Preston, WA 800-734-0748
TRC Corp
  Tulsa, OK 800-258-5028
Triple Springs Spring Water Co
  Meriden, CT 203-235-8374

Product Categories / Beverages: Water

Universal Beverages Inc
  Leesburg, FL...................352-315-1010
Varni Brothers/7-Up Bottling
  Modesto, CA....................209-521-1777
Vichy Springs Mineral Water
  Ukiah, CA......................707-462-9515
Water Concepts
  East Dundee, IL................847-699-9797
White Rock Products Corp
  Flushing, NY...................800-969-7625
Windmill Water Inc
  Edgewood, NM...................505-281-9287
Winterbrook Beverage Group
  Greendale, IN..................812-537-7348
Zephyrhills Bottled Water Company
  Tampa, FL......................800-950-9398

Bottled

Absopure Water Company
  Plymouth, MI...................800-422-7678
Alamance Foods
  Burlington, NC
Alpine Valley Water
  Harvey, IL.....................708-333-3910
Aqua Clara Bottling & Distribution
  Clearwater, FL.................727-446-2999
Arbor Springs Water Co
  Ferndale, MI...................248-543-7151
Arctic Beverages
  Winnipeg, MB...................866-503-1270
Asarasi
  Danbury, CT
Belmar Spring Water
  Glen Rock, NJ..................201-444-1010
Bevco Sales International Inc.
  Surrey, BC.....................800-663-0090
Bio-Hydration Research Lab
  Carlsbad, CA...................800-531-5088
Brands Within Reach
  Mamaroneck, NY.................847-720-9090
Broughton Foods LLC
  El Paso, TX....................800-395-7004
Calcium Springs Water Company
  Park City, UT..................435-615-7600
Captiva Limited Inc
  Augusta, NJ....................973-579-7883
Clark Spring Water Co
  Pueblo, CO.....................719-543-1594
Coca-Cola Beverages Northeast
  Bedford, NH....................844-619-3388
Coca-Cola Co.
  Atlanta, GA....................800-438-2653
Country Pure Foods Inc
  Akron, OH......................877-995-8423
Crystal Rock LLC
  Watertown, CT..................800-525-0070
Crystal Springs
  Mississauga, ON................800-822-5889
Crystal Springs Bottled Water
  Lakeland, FL...................800-728-5508
Crystal Springs Water Company
  Lakeland, FL...................800-728-5508
Deer Park Spring Water Co
  Chesapeake, VA.................800-832-0271
Distillata
  Cleveland, OH..................800-999-2906
DS Services of America
  Lakeland, FL...................800-728-5508
Eldorado Artesian Springs Inc
  Louisville, CO.................303-499-1316
Eureka Water Co
  Oklahoma City, OK..............800-310-8474
Figuerola Laboratories
  Santa Ynez, CA.................800-219-1147
Fiji Water Co LLC
  Los Angeles, CA................888-426-3454
Girard Spring Water
  North Providence, RI...........800-477-9287
Glen Summit Springs Water Company
  Mountain Top, PA...............800-621-7596
Global Beverage Company
  Rochester, NY..................585-381-3560
GWB Foods Corporation
  Brooklyn, NY...................877-977-7610
H3O
  Beckley, WV....................888-436-9287
Hawaiian Natural Water Company
  Pearl City, HI.................808-483-0520
Heck Cellars
  Arvin, CA......................661-854-6120
Hi-Country Foods Corporation
  Selah, WA......................509-697-7292
Hinckley Springs Bottled Water
 800-201-6218
Holly Camp Springs Inc
  Hudgins, VA....................804-795-2096
Island Sweetwater Beverage Company
  Bryn Mawr, PA..................610-525-7444
Le Bleu Corp
  Advance, NC....................800-854-4471
Light Rock Beverage Company
  Danbury, CT....................203-743-3410
Lipsey Mountain Spring Water
  Norcross, GA...................770-449-0001
Matilija Water Company
  Santa Barbara, CA..............805-963-7873
Merci Spring Water
  Maryland Heights, MO...........314-872-9323
Mount Olympus Waters
 800-782-5508
Mountain Valley Spring Company
  Hot Springs, AR................800-643-1501
Mountain Valley Spring Water
  Asheville, NC..................800-627-1062
Music Mountain Water Company
  Shreveport, LA.................800-349-6555
Natural Spring Water Company
  Johnson City, TN...............423-926-7905
Naya
  Montreal, QC...................450-562-7911
Neo North America Inc.
  San Francisco, CA..............800-604-7051
New Age Beverages
  Denver, CO.....................303-289-8655
Nirvana Natural Spring Water
  Forestport, NY.................888-463-5675
North American Water Group
  Overland Park, KS..............913-469-1156
Peace Mountain Natural Beverages
  Springfield, MA................413-567-4942
Pocono Mountain Bottling Company
  Wilkes Barre, PA...............570-822-7695
Pocono Spring Company
  Mt Pocono, PA..................800-634-4584
Polar Beverages Inc.
  Worcester, MA..................800-734-9800
Polar Water Company
  Carnegie, PA...................412-429-5550
Premium Water
  Kansas City, MO................800-332-3332
Primo Water Corporation
  Winston-Salem, NC..............844-237-7466
Private Spring Water
  San Martin, CA.................877-664-1500
Pure Flo Water Co
  Santee, CA.....................800-787-3356
Quibell Spring Water Beverage
  Martinsville, VA...............540-632-0100
SnowBird Corporation
  Bayonne, NJ....................800-576-1616
Southern Beverage Packers Inc
  Appling, GA....................800-326-2469
Sparkletts
  Lakeland, FL...................800-728-5508
Tanzamaji USA
  Fairview, TX
Titusville Dairy Products Co
  Titusville, PA.................800-352-0101
Universal Beverages Inc
  Leesburg, FL...................352-315-1010
Universal Beverages Inc
  Ponte Vedra Bch, FL............904-280-7795
Varni Brothers/7-Up Bottling
  Modesto, CA....................209-521-1777
Vichy Springs Mineral Water
  Ukiah, CA......................707-462-9515
Virginia Artesian Bottling Company
  Mechanicsville, VA.............804-779-7500
Water Concepts
  East Dundee, IL................847-699-9797
Windmill Water Inc
  Edgewood, NM...................505-281-9287
Winterbrook Beverage Group
  Greendale, IN..................812-537-7348
Zephyrhills Bottled Water Company
  Tampa, FL......................800-950-9398

Distilled

Alacer Corp
  Carlisle, PA...................888-425-2362
Alpine Valley Water
  Harvey, IL.....................708-333-3910
Arcadia Dairy Farms Inc
  Arden, NC......................828-684-3556
Belmar Spring Water
  Glen Rock, NJ..................201-444-1010
Bevco Sales International Inc.
  Surrey, BC.....................800-663-0090
Broughton Foods LLC
  El Paso, TX....................800-395-7004
Clark Spring Water Co
  Pueblo, CO.....................719-543-1594
Crystal Rock LLC
  Watertown, CT..................800-525-0070
Crystal Springs Water Company
  Lakeland, FL...................800-728-5508
Deer Park Spring Water Co
  Chesapeake, VA.................800-832-0271
Distillata
  Cleveland, OH..................800-999-2906
Energy Brands/Haute Source
  Flushing, NY...................800-746-0087
Fizz-O Water Co
  Tulsa, OK......................918-834-3691
Hinckley Springs Bottled Water
 800-201-6218
Le Bleu Corp
  Advance, NC....................800-854-4471
Matilija Water Company
  Santa Barbara, CA..............805-963-7873
Merci Spring Water
  Maryland Heights, MO...........314-872-9323
Mount Olympus Waters
 800-782-5508
Mountain Valley Spring Company
  Hot Springs, AR................800-643-1501
Polar Beverages Inc.
  Worcester, MA..................800-734-9800
Polar Water Company
  Carnegie, PA...................412-429-5550
Premium Water
  Kansas City, MO................800-332-3332
Reiter Dairy
  Newport, KY....................800-544-6455
SnowBird Corporation
  Bayonne, NJ....................800-576-1616
Southern Beverage Packers Inc
  Appling, GA....................800-326-2469
Sparkletts
  Lakeland, FL...................800-728-5508
Zephyr Hills
  Tampa, FL......................800-950-9398

Flavored

Avitae
  Cleveland, OH..................888-228-4823
Bitter Love
  Portland, ME
Blossom Water, LLC
  Westwood, MA...................855-325-5777
Blume Honey Water
  Pittsburgh, PA.................412-406-7391
Captiva Limited Inc
  Augusta, NJ....................973-579-7883
Clearly Canadian Beverage Corporation
  Vaghan, ON.....................866-414-2326
Ex Drinks
  Henderson, NV..................866-753-4929
Flurowater, Inc.
  Los Angeles, CA
Harmless Harvest
  San Francisco, CA
Heritage Short Bread
  Hilton Head Isle, SC...........843-422-3458
Hiball, Inc.
  San Francisco, CA..............833-442-2553
Hinckley Springs Bottled Water
 800-201-6218
Hint Water
  San Francisco, CA..............415-513-4050
Hubble
  Manhattan Beach, CA
Keurig Dr Pepper
  Plano, TX......................800-696-5891
KidsLuv
  San Francisco, CA..............855-543-7588
Northern Falls
  Rockford, MI...................616-915-0970
Pervida
  Blacksburg, VA.................540-808-0800
Sapp Birch Water
  Chicago, IL....................708-351-7777
Saratoga Spring Water Co
  Saratoga Springs, NY...........888-426-8642
Sun Opta Inc.
  Mississauga, ON................952-820-2518

Product Categories / Beverages: Wines

Treo Brands
  Harrison, NY 914-341-1850
True Nopal Cactus Water
  Scottsdale, AZ 480-636-8044
Tu Me Beverage Company
  CA 818-237-5105
Unique Beverage Company
  Everett, WA 425-267-0959
Varni Brothers/7-Up Bottling
  Modesto, CA 209-521-1777
Verday
  New York, NY
Watermark Innovation
  Southampton, NY 631-259-2329

Mineral

3 Springs Water Co
  Laurel Run, PA 800-332-7873
Adobe Springs
  Patterson, CA 408-897-3023
Beaulieu Vineyard
  Rutherford, CA 707-257-5749
Clearly Canadian Beverage Corporation
  Vanghan, ON 866-414-2326
Matilija Water Company
  Santa Barbara, CA 805-963-7873
Monticello Vineyards-Corley
  Napa, CA 707-253-2802
Office General des Eaux Minerales
  Montreal, QC 514-482-7221
R.J. Corr Naturals
  Posen, IL 708-389-4200
SD Watersboten
  Ardmore, PA 610-645-7572
Seawater Food & Beverage
  Dallas, TX 214-537-5070
Sebastiani Vineyards
  Sonoma, CA 855-232-2338

Spring

Amanda Hills Spring Water
  Etna, OH 800-375-0885
Arizona Beverage Company
  Cincinnati, OH 800-832-3775
Belmar Spring Water
  Glen Rock, NJ 201-444-1010
Bevco Sales International Inc.
  Surrey, BC 800-663-0090
Clark Spring Water Co
  Pueblo, CO 719-543-1594
Country Pure Foods Inc
  Akron, OH 877-995-8423
Crystal Geyser Water Co.
  Burlingame, CA 800-443-9737
Crystal Rock LLC
  Watertown, CT 800-525-0070
Crystal Springs Water Company
  Lakeland, FL 800-728-5508
Deer Park Spring Water Co
  Chesapeake, VA 800-832-0271
Eternal Water
  Walnut Creek, CA 877-854-5494
Fizz-O Water Co
  Tulsa, OK 918-834-3691
Garelick Farms
  Dallas, TX 800-343-4982
Girard Spring Water
  North Providence, RI 800-477-9287
Glen Summit Springs Water Company
  Mountain Top, PA 800-621-7596
Harford Glen Water
  Harford, NY 866-844-8351
Harrisburg Dairies Inc
  Harrisburg, PA 800-692-7429
Hawaiian Natural Water Company
  Pearl City, HI 808-483-0520
Hinckley Springs Bottled Water
 800-201-6218
Holly Camp Springs Inc
  Hudgins, VA 804-795-2096
Kentwood Springs
  Lakeland, FL 800-728-5508
Matilija Water Company
  Santa Barbara, CA 805-963-7873
Mayer Bros
  Buffalo, NY 800-696-2928
Merci Spring Water
  Maryland Heights, MO 314-872-9323
Meridian Beverage Company
  Atlanta, GA 800-728-1481

Minnehaha Spring Water Company
  Cleveland, OH 216-431-0243
Mount Olympus Waters
 800-782-5508
Mountain Valley Spring Company
  Hot Springs, AR 800-643-1501
Music Mountain Water Company
  Shreveport, LA 800-349-6555
National Beverage Corporation
  Fort Lauderdale, FL 877-622-3499
Natural Spring Water Company
  Johnson City, TN 423-926-7905
Naya
  Montreal, QC 450-562-7911
North Country Natural Spring Water
  Port Kent, NY 518-834-9400
Northern Falls
  Rockford, MI 616-915-0970
Polar Beverages Inc.
  Worcester, MA 800-734-9800
Polar Water Company
  Carnegie, PA 412-429-5550
Premium Water
  Kansas City, MO 800-332-3332
Private Spring Water
  San Martin, CA 877-664-1500
Sand Springs
  Williamstown, MA 413-458-8281
Saratoga Spring Water Co
  Saratoga Springs, NY 888-426-8642
Signature Beverage
  Merrick, NY 800-277-2755
SnowBird Corporation
  Bayonne, NJ 800-576-1616
Southern Beverage Packers Inc
  Appling, GA 800-326-2469
Triple Springs Spring Water Co
  Meriden, CT 203-235-8374
Tumai Water
  Martinsburg, WV 866-948-8624
Varni Brothers/7-Up Bottling
  Modesto, CA 209-521-1777
White Rock Products Corp
  Flushing, NY 800-969-7625
Windmill Water Inc
  Edgewood, NM 505-281-9287
Yoder Dairies
  Chesapeake, VA 757-482-4068
Zephyr Hills
  Tampa, FL 800-950-9398

Wines

A to Z Wineworks
  Newburg, OR 800-739-4455
A. Nonini Winery
  Fresno, CA 559-275-1936
A. Rafanelli Winery
  Healdsburg, CA 707-433-1385
Abingdon Vineyard & Winery
  Abingdon, VA 276-623-1255
Acacia Vineyard
  Napa, CA 877-226-1700
Ackerman Winery
  Amana, IA 319-622-3379
Adair Vineyards
  New Paltz, NY 845-255-1377
Adam Puchta Winery
  Hermann, MO 573-486-5596
Adams County Winery
  Orrtanna, PA 877-601-7936
Adelaida Cellars Inc
  Paso Robles, CA 800-676-1232
Adelsheim Vineyard
  Newberg, OR 503-538-3652
Adler Fels Winery
  Santa Rosa, CA 707-539-3123
Afton Mountain Vineyards Inc
  Afton, VA 540-456-8667
Ahlgren Vineyard
  Boulder Creek, CA 800-338-6071
Airlie Winery
  Monmouth, OR 503-838-6013
Alba Vineyard & Winery
  Milford, NJ 908-995-7800
Alexis Bailly Vineyard
  Hastings, MN 651-437-1413
Allegro Winery & Vineyards
  Brogue, PA 717-927-9148
Allied Wine Corporation
  Ellenville, NY 800-796-4100
Almarla Vineyards & Winery
  Shubuta, MS 601-687-5548

Alpen Cellars
  Trinity Center, CA 530-266-9513
Alpine Vineyards
  Monroe, OR 541-424-5851
Alta Vineyard Cellar
  Calistoga, CA 707-942-6708
Altamura Winery
  Napa, CA 707-253-2000
Alto Vineyards & Winery
  Alto Pass, IL 618-893-4898
Amador Foothill Winery
  Plymouth, CA 800-778-9463
Amalthea Cellars Farm Winery
  Atco, NJ 856-768-8585
Amavi Cellars
  Walla Walla, WA 509-525-3541
Amberg Wine Cellars
  Clifton Springs, NY 315-462-3455
AmByth Estate
  Templeton, CA 805-319-6967
Americana Vineyards & Winery
  Interlaken, NY 888-600-8067
Amity Vineyards
  Amity, OR 888-264-8966
Amizetta Vineyards
  St Helena, CA 707-963-1460
Amrhein's Wine Cellars
  Bent Mountain, VA 540-929-4632
Amwell Valley Vineyard
  Ringoes, NJ 908-788-5852
Anchor Brewing Company
  San Francisco, CA 415-863-8350
Ancient Peaks Winery
  Santa Margarita, CA 805-365-7045
Anderson's Conn Valley Vineyards
  St Helena, CA 800-946-3497
Andrew Peller Limited
  Grimsby, ON 905-643-4131
Annapolis Winery
  Annapolis, CA 707-886-5460
Antelope Valley Winery
  Lancaster, CA 800-282-8332
Anthony Road Wine Co
  Penn Yan, NY 800-559-2182
Arbor Crest Wine Cellars
  Spokane, WA 509-927-9463
Arbor Hill Grapery & Winery
  Naples, NY 800-554-7553
Arbor Mist Winery
  Canandaigua, NY 866-396-7394
Arcadian Estate Winery
  Rock Stream, NY 800-298-1346
Arel Group Wine & Spirits Inc
  Atlanta, GA 404-869-4387
Argyle Winery
  Dundee, OR 888-427-4953
Ariel Vineyards
  Napa, CA 800-456-9472
Arizona Vineyards
  Nogales, AZ 520-287-7972
Arns Winery
  St Helena, CA 707-963-3429
Arrowood Winery
  Glen Ellen, CA 800-938-5170
Artesa Vineyards & Winery
  Napa, CA 707-224-1668
Ashland Vineyards & Winery
  Ashland, OR 541-488-0088
ASV Wines
  Delano, CA 661-792-3159
Atlas Peak Vineyards
  Napa, CA 707-252-7971
Atwater Block Brewing Company
  Detroit, MI 313-877-9205
Au Bon Climat Winery
  Los Olivos, CA 805-937-9801
Augusta Winery
  Augusta, MO 888-667-9463
Autumn Hill Vineyards/Blue Ridge Wine
  Stanardsville, VA 434-985-6100
Autumn Wind Vineyard
  Newberg, OR 503-538-6931
Avalon Organic Coffees
  Albuquerque, NM 800-662-2575
B R Cohn Winery & Olive Oil Co
  Glen Ellen, CA 800-330-4064
Babcock Winery & Vineyards
  Lompoc, CA 805-736-1455
Bagley's
  Hector, NY 607-582-6421
Baileyana Winery
  San Luis Obispo, CA 805-544-9080

Product Categories / Beverages: Wines

Baily Vineyard & Winery
 Temecula, CA 951-676-9463
Balagna Winery Company
 Los Alamos, NM. 505-672-3678
Baldwin Vineyards
 Pine Bush, NY 845-744-2226
Balic Winery
 Mays Landing, NJ 609-625-2166
Banfi Vintners
 Old Brookville, NY. 800-645-6511
Barboursville Vineyards
 Barboursville, VA. 540-832-3824
Barca Wine Cellars
 Roseville, CA 916-786-0770
Bargetto Winery
 Soquel, CA .800-422-7438
Baron Vineyards
 Paso Robles, CA 805-239-3313
Basignani Winery
 Sparks Glencoe, MD. 410-472-0703
Batavia Wine Cellars
 Canandaigua, NY 585-396-7600
Baxters Vineyards & Winery
 Nauvoo, IL .800-854-1396
Baywood Cellars
 Lodi, CA 800-214-0445
Beachaven Vineyards & Winery
 Clarksville, TN 931-645-8867
Bear Creek Winery
 Cave Junction, OR 877-273-4843
Beaucanon Estate Wines
 Napa, CA. .800-660-3520
Beaulieu Vineyard
 Rutherford, CA 707-257-5749
Beckmen Vineyards
 Los Olivos, CA 805-688-8664
Bedell Northfork LLC
 Cutchogue, NY 631-734-7537
Bell Mountain Vineyards
 Willow City, TX 830-685-3297
Bellerose Vineyard
 Healdsburg, CA 707-433-1637
Benmarl Wine Co
 Marlboro, NY 845-236-4265
Benziger Family Winery
 Glen Ellen, CA 888-490-2739
Bernardo Winery
 San Diego, CA 858-487-1866
Bernardus Winery Tasting Rm
 Carmel Valley, CA 800-223-2533
Berryessa Gap Tasting Room
 Winters, CA. 530-795-3201
Bethel Heights Vineyard
 Salem, OR. 503-399-9588
Bianchi Winery
 Paso Robles, CA 805-226-9922
Bias Vineyards & Winery
 Berger, MO 800-905-2427
Bidwell Vineyard
 Cutchogue, NY 631-734-5200
Biltmore Estate Wine Company
 Asheville, NC 800-411-3812
Binns Vineyards & Winery
 Las Cruces, NM 575-526-6738
Bishop Farms Winery
 Cheshire, CT. 203-272-8243
Black Bear Farm Winery
 Chenango Forks, NY 607-656-9863
Black Mesa Winery
 Velarde, NM 800-852-6372
Black Sheep Vintners
 Murphys, CA. 209-728-2157
Blalock Seafood & Specialty
 Orange Beach, AL 251-974-5811
Blue Hills Spring Water Company
 Quincy, MA. 614-715-3900
Blue Mountain Vineyards
 New Tripoli, PA 610-298-3068
Blumenhof Vineyards-Winery
 Dutzow, MO 800-419-2245
Boeger Winery
 Placerville, CA 800-655-2634
Bogle Vineyards Inc
 Clarksburg, CA. 916-744-1030
Boisset Family Estates
 St Helena, CA 800-878-1123
Bonny Doon Vineyard
 Santa Cruz, CA 888-819-6789
Bonterra Vineyard
 Hopland, CA 707-744-7575
Boordy Vineyards Inc
 Hydes, MD 410-592-5015

Bordoni Vineyards
 Vallejo, CA 707-642-1504
Borra Vineyards
 Lodi, CA 209-368-2446
Boskydel Vineyard
 Lake Leelanau, MI 231-256-7272
Bouchaine Vineyards
 Napa, CA .800-654-9463
Brandborg Cellars
 Elkton, OR 510-215-9553
Brander Vineyard
 Santa Ynez, CA 800-970-9979
Braren Pauli Winery
 Redwood Valley, CA 800-423-6519
Braswell's Winery
 Dora, AL 205-648-8335
Bravard Vineyards & Winery
 Hopkinsville, KY 270-269-2583
Breaux Vineyards
 Purcellville, VA. 800-492-9961
Breitenbach Wine Cellars
 Dover, OH .330-343-3603
Briceland Vineyards
 Redway, CA 707-923-2429
Bridgeview Vineyards Winery
 Cave Junction, OR 877-273-4843
Brimstone Hill Vineyard
 Pine Bush, NY 845-744-2231
Bristle Ridge Vineyards
 Knob Noster, MO 800-994-9463
Broad Run Vineyards
 Louisville, KY 502-231-0372
Broadley Vineyards
 Monroe, OR 541-847-5934
Bronco Wine Co
 Ceres, CA .855-874-2394
Brookmere Wine & Vineyard
 Belleville, PA 717-935-5380
Brotherhood Winery
 Washingtonville, NY 845-496-3661
Brothers International Food Corporation
 Rochester, NY 585-343-3007
Brown County Winery
 Nashville, IN. 888-298-2984
Brown-Forman Corp
 Louisville, KY 502-585-1100
Brutocao Cellars
 Hopland, CA. 800-433-3689
Bryant Vineyard
 Talladega, AL 256-268-2638
Buccia Vineyard
 Conneaut, OH 440-593-5976
Buckingham Valley Vineyards
 Buckingham, PA 215-794-7188
Buehler Vineyards
 St Helena, CA 707-963-2155
Buena Vista Historic Tstng Rm
 Sonoma, CA 800-926-1266
Buffalo Trace Distillery
 Frankfort, KY 800-654-8471
Bully Hill Vineyards
 Hammondsport, NY 607-868-3610
Burnley Vineyards
 Barboursville, VA 540-832-2828
Butler Winery
 Bloomington, IN 812-332-6660
Butterfly Creek Winery
 Mariposa, CA 209-742-4567
Buttonwood Farm Winery & Vineyard
 Solvang, CA 800-715-1404
Byington Vineyard & Winery
 Los Gatos, CA 408-354-1111
Byron Vineyard & Winery
 Santa Maria, CA 805-938-7365
Cache Cellars
 Davis, CA .530-756-6068
Cain Vineyard & Winery
 St Helena, CA 707-963-1616
Cakebread Cellars
 Rutherford, CA 800-588-0298
Calafia Cellars
 St Helena, CA 707-963-0114
Calera Wine Co
 Hollister, CA. 831-637-9170
California Olive Oil Council
 Berkeley, CA. 888-718-9830
Callaway Vineyards & Winery
 Temecula, CA 800-472-2377
Camas Prairie Winery
 Moscow, ID. 800-616-0214
Cambria Winery
 Santa Maria, CA 888-339-9463

Campagana Winery
 Redwood Valley, CA. 707-485-1221
Campari
 New York, NY 212-891-3600
Canoe Ridge Vineyard
 Walla Walla, WA. 509-527-0885
Capalbo's Fruit Baskets
 Clifton, NJ. 800-252-6262
Caparone Winery LLC
 Paso Robles, CA 805-610-5308
Caporale Winery
 Napa, CA. 707-253-9230
Caprock Winery Inc
 Lubbock, TX 800-546-9463
Cardinale Winery
 Oakville, CA 800-588-0279
Carlson Vineyards Winery
 Palisade, CO 888-464-5554
Carmenet Winery
 Sonoma, CA 707-996-3526
Carneros Creek Winery
 Napa, CA .707-253-9464
Carrousel Cellars
 Gilroy, CA. 408-847-2060
Casa Larga Vineyards
 Fairport, NY 585-223-4210
Casa Nuestra Winery & Vineyard
 St Helena, CA 866-844-9463
Cascade Mountain Winery
 Amenia, NY 845-373-9021
Castello di Borghese Vineyard
 Cutchogue, NY 631-734-5111
Catoctin Vineyards
 Brookeville, MD 301-774-2310
Cavender Castle Winery
 Atlanta, GA 706-864-4759
Caymus Vineyards
 Rutherford, CA 707-967-3010
Cayuga Ridge Estate Winery
 Ovid, NY 800-598-9463
Cecchetti Sebastiani Cellar
 Sonoma, CA 707-933-3230
Cedar Creek Winery
 Cedarburg, WI. 800-827-8020
Cedar Mountain Winery
 Livermore, CA 925-373-6636
Chacewater Winery and Olive Mill
 Kelseyville, CA. 707-279-2995
Chaddsford Winery
 Chadds Ford, PA 610-388-6221
Chalet Debonne Vineyards
 Madison, OH. 440-466-3485
Chalk Hill Estate Winery
 Healdsburg, CA 707-657-4839
Chalone Vineyard
 Soledad, CA 831-678-1717
Chambord
 Louisville, KY 800-523-3811
Champoeg Wine Cellars Inc
 Aurora, OR 503-678-2144
Channing Rudd Cellars
 Middletown, CA 707-987-2209
Chappellet Winery
 St Helena, CA 800-494-6379
Charles B. Mitchell Vineyards
 Somerset, CA 800-704-9463
Charles Krug Winery
 St Helena, CA 707-967-2200
Charles Spinetta Winery
 Plymouth, CA. 209-245-3384
Chateau Anne Marie
 Carlton, OR. 503-864-2991
Chateau Boswell Winery
 St Helena, CA 707-963-5472
Chateau Chevre Winery
 Napa, CA. 707-944-2184
Chateau des Charmes Wines
 St. Davids, ON 800-263-2541
Chateau Diana Winery
 Healdsburg, CA 707-433-6992
Chateau Grand Traverse Winery
 Traverse City, MI 231-938-6120
Chateau Julien Winery
 Carmel, CA. 831-624-2600
Chateau LA Fayette Reneau
 Hector, NY 800-469-9463
Chateau Montelena Winery
 Calistoga, CA 707-942-5105
Chateau Morrisette Winery
 Floyd, VA .540-593-2865
Chateau Potelle Winery
 St Helena, CA 707-255-9440

Product Categories / Beverages: Wines

Chateau Ra-Ha
  Jerseyville, IL 866-639-4832
Chateau Souverain
  Cloverdale, CA 877-687-9463
Chateau St Jean Winery
  Kenwood, CA 707-833-4134
Chatom Vineyards Inc
  San Andreas, CA 800-435-8852
Chestnut Mountain Winery
  Hoschton, GA 770-867-6914
Chicama Vineyards
  West Tisbury, MA 888-244-2262
Chimere Winery
  Santa Maria, CA 805-928-5611
Chouinard Vineyards & Winery
  Castro Valley, CA 510-582-9900
Christensen Ridge Winery
  Madison, VA 540-923-4800
Christine Woods Winery
  Philo, CA 707-895-2115
Christopher Creek Winery
  Healdsburg, CA 707-433-2001
Cienega Valley Winery/DeRose
  Hollister, CA 831-636-9143
Cimarron Cellars
  Caney, OK 580-889-5997
Cinnabar Winery
  Saratoga, CA 408-867-1010
Claiborne & Churchill Vintners
  San Luis Obispo, CA 805-544-4066
Clear Creek Distillery
  Portland, OR 503-248-9470
Cliff Lede Vineyards
  Yountville, CA 800-428-2259
Cline Cellars
  Sonoma, CA 800-543-2070
Clinton Vineyards Inc
  Clinton Corners, NY 845-266-5372
Clos Du Bois Winery
  Geyserville, CA 800-222-3189
Clos Du Lac Cellars
  Ione, CA 209-274-2238
Clos Du Val Co LTD
  Napa, CA 707-261-5200
Clos Pegase Winery
  Calistoga, CA 800-866-8583
Cloudstone Vineyards
  Los Altos Hills, CA 650-948-8621
Clover Hill Vineyards & Winery
  Breinigsville, PA 800-256-8374
Cocolalla Winery
  Cocolalla, ID 208-263-3774
Colorado Cellars
  Palisade, CO 970-464-7921
Columbia Winery
  Woodinville, WA 425-488-2776
Concannon Vineyard
  Livermore, CA 800-258-9866
Conneaut Cellars Winery LLC
  Conneaut Lake, PA 877-229-9463
Conrotto A. Winery
  Gilroy, CA 408-847-2233
Coon Creek Winery
  St Helena, CA 800-793-7960
Cooper Mountain Vineyards
  Beaverton, OR 503-649-0027
Cooper Vineyards
  Louisa, VA 540-894-5474
Cosentino Winery
  Napa, CA 800-764-1220
Country Life
  Hauppauge, NY 800-645-5768
Cowie Wine Cellars & Vineyards
  Paris, AR 479-963-3990
Crescini Wines
  Soquel, CA 831-462-1466
Cribari Vineyard Inc
  Fresno, CA 800-277-9095
Cristom Vineyards
  Salem, OR 503-375-3068
Cronin Vineyards
  Woodside, CA 650-851-1452
Crooked Vine/Stony Ridge Wnry
  Livermore, CA 925-449-0458
Crossings Winery
  Glenns Ferry, ID 208-366-2539
Crown Regal Wine Cellars
  Brooklyn, NY 718-604-1430
Cruse Vineyards
  Chester, SC 803-377-3944
Cuneo Cellars
  Amity, OR 503-835-2782
Cuvaison Winery
  Calistoga, CA 707-942-6266
Cygnet Cellars
  Hollister, CA 831-637-7559
Dalla Valle Vineyards
  Napa, CA 707-944-2676
Damiani Wine Cellars LLC
  Burdett, NY 607-546-5557
Davis Bynum Winery
  Healdsburg, CA 800-826-1073
Deaver Vineyards
  Plymouth, CA 209-245-4099
Delicato Family Vineyards
  Napa, CA 707-265-1700
Deloach Vineyards
  Santa Rosa, CA 707-755-3300
Delorimier Winery
  Geyserville, CA 800-546-7718
Denatale Vineyards
  Healdsburg, CA 707-431-8460
Destileria Serralles Inc
  Mercedita, PR 787-840-1000
Devlin Wine Cellars
  Soquel, CA 831-476-7288
Diageo Canada Inc.
  Toronto, ON 416-626-2000
Diageo North America Inc
  Norwalk, CT 203-229-2100
Diamond Creek Vineyards
  Calistoga, CA 707-942-6926
Diamond Water Bottling Fclty
  Hot Springs, AR 501-623-1251
Digrazia Vineyards
  Brookfield, CT 800-230-8853
Domaine Chandon
  Yountville, CA 888-242-6366
Domaine St George Winery
  Healdsburg, CA 707-433-5508
Dominion Wine Cellars
  Culpeper, VA 540-825-8772
Don Sebastiani & Sons
  Sonoma, CA 707-224-0410
Donatoni Winery
  Inglewood, CA 310-645-5445
Door Peninsula Winery
  Sturgeon Bay, WI 800-551-5049
Douknie Winery
  Purcellville, VA 540-668-6464
Dr Konstantin Frank's Vinifera
  Hammondsport, NY 800-320-0735
Dreyer Sonoma
  Woodside, CA 650-851-9448
Dry Creek Vineyard
  Healdsburg, CA 800-864-9463
Duck Pond Cellars
  Dundee, OR 800-437-3213
Duckhorn Vineyards
  St Helena, CA 888-354-8885
Duncan Peak Vineyards
  Lafayette, CA 925-283-3632
Dundee Wine Company
  Dundee, OR 888-427-4953
Dunn Vineyards
  Angwin, CA 707-965-3642
Duplin Wine Cellars
  Rose Hill, NC 800-774-9634
Dutch Henry Winery
  Calistoga, CA 888-224-5879
E & J Gallo Winery
  Modesto, CA 877-687-9463
E L K Run Vineyards
  Mt Airy, MD 800-414-2513
Eagle Crest Vineyards LLC
  Conesus, NY 800-977-7117
Easley Winery
  Indianapolis, IN 317-636-4516
East Side Winery/Oak Ridge Vineyards
  Lodi, CA 209-369-4758
Ed Oliveira Winery
  Arcata, CA 707-822-3023
Edgewood Estate Winery
  Napa, CA 800-755-2374
Edmunds St. John
  Berkeley, CA 510-981-1510
Edna Valley Vineyard
  San Luis Obispo, CA 866-979-8477
El Molino Winery
  St Helena, CA 707-963-3632
El Paso Winery
  Ulster Park, NY 845-331-8642
Elk Cove Vineyards
  Gaston, OR 877-355-2683
Elliston Vineyards
  Sunol, CA 925-862-2377
Enz Vineyards
  Hollister, CA 831-637-6443
Eola Hills Wine Cellars
  Rickreall, OR 800-291-6730
EOS Estate Winery
  Paso Robles, CA 800-249-9463
Erath Vineyards Winery
  Dundee, OR 800-539-5463
Esterlina Vineyard & Winery
  Healdsburg, CA 888-474-7456
Evensen Vineyards
  Oakville, CA 707-944-2396
Evergreen Juices Inc.
  Don Mills, ON 877-915-8423
Eyrie Vineyards
  Mcminnville, OR 888-440-4970
Fall Creek Vineyards
  Austin, TX 512-476-4477
Fantis Foods Inc
  Carlstadt, NJ 201-933-6200
Far Niente Winery
  Oakville, CA 707-944-2861
Farella-Park Vineyards
  Napa, CA 707-254-9489
Farfelu Vineyards
  Flint Hill, VA 540-364-2930
Farmstead At Long Meadow Ranch
  St Helena, CA 877-627-2645
Fenestra Winery
  Livermore, CA 800-789-9463
Fenn Valley Vineyards
  Fennville, MI 800-432-6265
Ferrante Winery & Ristorante
  Geneva, OH 440-466-6046
Ferrara Winery
  Escondido, CA 760-745-7632
Ferrari-Carano
  Healdsburg, CA 800-831-0381
Ferrigno Vineyards & Wine
  St James, MO 573-265-7742
Fess Parker Winery
  Los Olivos, CA 800-841-1104
Fetzer Vineyards
  Hopland, CA 707-744-1250
Ficklin Vineyards Winery
  Madera, CA 559-674-4598
Field Stone Winery
  Healdsburg, CA 800-544-7273
Fieldbrook Valley Winery
  Mckinleyville, CA 707-839-4140
Fife Vineyards
  Redwood Valley, CA 707-485-0323
Filsinger Vineyards & Winery
  Temecula, CA 951-302-6363
Fiore Winery
  Pylesville, MD 410-452-0132
Firelands Winery
  Sandusky, OH 800-548-9463
Firestone Vineyard
  Los Olivos, CA 805-688-3940
First Colony Winery
  Charlottesville, VA 877-979-7105
Fisher Ridge Wine Co Inc
  Charleston, WV 304-342-8702
Fisher Vineyards
  Santa Rosa, CA 707-539-7511
Fitzpatrick Winery & Lodge
  Somerset, CA 800-245-9166
Flora Springs Winery
  St Helena, CA 707-963-5711
Flynn Vineyards Winery
  Rickreall, OR 888-427-4953
Foley Estates Vineyard
  Lompoc, CA 805-737-6222
Folie _ Deux Winery
  Oakville, CA 800-535-6400
Foppiano Vineyards
  Healdsburg, CA 707-433-7272
Foris Vineyards
  Cave Junction, OR 541-592-3752
Forman Vineyard
  St Helena, CA 707-963-3900
Fortino Winery
  Gilroy, CA 888-617-6606
Fortuna Cellars
  Davis, CA 530-756-6686
Four Sisters Winery
  Belvidere, NJ 908-475-3671
Fox Run Vineyards
  Penn Yan, NY 800-636-9786

Product Categories / Beverages: Wines

Fox Vineyards & Winery
Social Circle, GA 770-787-5402
Foxen Foxen 7200
Santa Maria, CA 805-937-4251
Franciscan Estate
St. Helena, CA 707-967-3830
Frank Family Vineyards
Calistoga, CA 880-574-9463
Franklin Hill Vineyards
Bangor, PA 888-887-2839
Franzia Winery
Ripon, CA 209-599-4111
Fratelli Perata
Paso Robles, CA 805-238-2809
Frederick Wildman & Sons LTD
New York, NY 800-733-9463
Freemark Abbey Winery
St Helena, CA 800-963-9698
Freixenet USA Inc
Sonoma, CA 707-996-4981
Frey Vineyards
Redwood Valley, CA 800-760-3739
Frick Winery
Geyserville, CA 707-857-1980
Frisinger Cellars
Napa, CA 707-255-3749
Frog's Leap Winery
Rutherford, CA 800-959-4704
Frontenac Point Vineyard
Trumansburg, NY 607-387-9619
Gainey Vineyard
Santa Ynez, CA 805-688-0558
Galante Vineyards
Carmel Valley, CA 800-425-2683
Galena Cellars Winery
Galena, IL 800-397-9463
Galleano Winery
Mira Loma, CA 951-685-5376
Gary Farrell Vineyards-Winery
Healdsburg, CA 866-277-9463
Georgia Wines Inc
Ringgold, GA 706-937-2177
Georis Winery
Carmel Valley, CA 831-659-1050
Germanton Winery
Germanton, NC 800-322-2894
Geyser Peak Winery
Healdsburg, CA 800-255-9463
Girardet Wine Cellar
Roseburg, OR 541-679-7252
Glenora Wine Cellars
Dundee, NY 800-243-5513
Gloria Ferrer Champagne
Sonoma, CA 707-933-1917
Gloria Winery & Vineyard
Springfield, MO 417-926-6263
Glunz Family Winery & Cellars
Grayslake, IL 847-548-9463
Gold Digger Cellars
Oroville, WA 509-476-4887
Good Harbor Vineyards & Winery
Lake Leelanau, MI 231-256-7165
Goodson Brothers Coffee
Knoxville, TN 800-737-1519
Goosecross Cellars Inc
Yountville, CA 800-276-9210
Grand River Cellars
Madison, OH 440-298-9838
Grand View Winery
East Calais, VT 802-456-7012
Grande River Vineyards
Palisade, CO 800-264-7696
Granite Springs Winery
Somerset, CA 800-638-6041
Great Lakes Wine & Spirits
Highland Park, MI 313-453-2200
Greenfield Wine Company
Vallejo, CA 707-552-5199
Greenwood Ridge Vineyards
Philo, CA 707-895-2002
Groth Vineyards & Winery
Oakville, CA 707-944-0290
Groupe Paul Masson
Longueuil, QC 514-878-3050
Gruet Winery
Albuquerque, NM 888-857-9463
Guenoc & Langtry Estate
Middletown, CA 707-995-7501
Guglielmo Winery
Morgan Hill, CA 408-779-2145
Guilliams Winery
St Helena, CA 707-963-9059
Gundlach-Bundschu Winery
Sonoma, CA 707-939-3015
H Coturri & Sons Winery
Glen Ellen, CA 866-268-8774
Habersham Vineyards & Winery
Helen, GA 706-878-9463
Hafner Vineyard
Healdsburg, CA 707-433-4606
Hahn Family Wines
Soledad, CA 831-678-4555
Haight Brown Vineyard
Litchfield, CT 800-577-9463
Hallcrest Vineyards
Felton, CA 831-335-4441
Handley Cellars
Philo, CA 800-733-3151
Hanzell Vineyards
Sonoma, CA 707-996-3860
Harbor Winery
West Sacramento, CA 916-371-6776
Harmony Cellars
Harmony, CA 800-432-9239
Harpersfield Vineyard
Geneva, OH 440-466-4739
Hart Winery
Temecula, CA 877-638-8788
Hartford Family Winery
Forestville, CA 707-887-8030
Hazlitt 1852 Vineyards
Hector, NY 888-750-0494
Heartland Vinyards
Westlake, OH 440-871-0701
Heaven Hill Distilleries Inc.
Bardstown, KY 502-337-1000
Heck Cellars
Arvin, CA 661-854-6120
Hecker Pass Winery
Gilroy, CA 408-842-8755
Hegy's South Hills Vineyard & Winery
Twin Falls, ID 208-599-0074
Heineman Winery
Put In Bay, OH 419-285-2811
Heitz Wine Cellars
St Helena, CA 707-963-3542
Helena View/Johnston Vineyard
Calistoga, CA 707-942-4956
Heller Estates
Carmel Valley, CA 800-625-8466
Hells Canyon Winery
Caldwell, ID 800-318-7873
Henry Estate Winery
Umpqua, OR 800-782-2686
Henry Hill & Co
Napa, CA 707-253-1663
Heritage Wine Cellars
North East, PA 800-747-0083
Hermann J. Wiemer Vineyard
Dundee, NY 800-371-7971
Hermannhof Vineyards
Hermann, MO 800-393-0100
Heron Hill Winery
Hammondsport, NY 800-441-4241
Hess Collection
Napa, CA 707-255-1144
Hickory Farms
Maumee, OH 800-753-8558
Hidden Mountain Ranch Winery
Paso Robles, CA 805-226-9907
Highland Manor Winery
Jamestown, TN 931-879-9519
Hill Top Berry Farm & Winery
Nellysford, VA 434-361-1266
Hillcrest Vineyards
Roseburg, OR 541-673-3709
Hinzerling Winery
Prosser, WA 800-727-6702
Homewood Winery
Sonoma, CA 707-996-6353
Honeywood Winery
Salem, OR 800-726-4101
Honig Vineyard and Winery
Rutherford, CA 800-929-2217
Hood River Vineyards and Winery
Hood River, OR 541-386-3772
Hoodsport Winery
Hoodsport, WA 800-580-9894
Hop Kiln Winery
Healdsburg, CA 707-433-6491
Hopkins Vineyard
Warren, CT 860-868-7954
Horizon Cellars Winery
Siler City, NC 919-742-1404
Horton Vineyards
Gordonsville, VA 800-829-4633
Houdini Inc
Fullerton, CA 714-525-0325
Hubers Orchard Winery-Vineyards
Borden, IN 800-345-9463
Hunt Country Vineyards
Branchport, NY 800-946-3289
Husch Vineyards & Winery
Philo, CA 800-554-8724
Indian Rock Vineyards
Murphys, CA 209-728-8514
Indian Springs Vineyards
Penn Vally, CA 800-375-9311
Inglenook
Rutherford, CA 707-968-1100
Ingleside Vineyards
Colonial Beach, VA 804-224-8687
Inniskillin Wines
Niagara-On-The-Lake, ON 888-466-4754
Iron Horse Vineyards
Sebastopol, CA 707-887-1507
Ironstone Vineyards
Murphys, CA 209-728-1251
J Filippi Winery
Rancho Cucamonga, CA 909-899-5755
J Lohr Vineyards & Wines
San Jose, CA 408-288-5057
J. Fritz Winery
Cloverdale, CA 800-418-9463
J. Stonestreet & Sons Vineyard
Healdsburg, CA 800-355-8008
Jamaican Gourmet Coffee Company
Philadelphia, PA 800-261-2859
Jefferson Vineyards
Charlottesville, VA 800-272-3042
Jodar Vineyard & Winery
Placerville, CA 530-644-3474
Johlin Century Winery
Oregon, OH 419-693-6288
Johnson Estate Winery
Westfield, NY 800-374-6569
Johnson's Alexander Valley Wines
Healdsburg, CA 800-888-5532
Johnston's Winery Inc
Ballston Spa, NY 518-882-6310
Joseph Phelps Vineyards
St Helena, CA 800-707-5789
Joseph Swan Vineyards
Forestville, CA 707-573-3747
Joullian Vineyards
Carmel Valley, CA 866-659-8101
Justin Vineyards & Winery LLC
Paso Robles, CA 800-237-4152
Kalin Cellars
Novato, CA 415-883-3543
Kate's Vineyard
Napa, CA 707-255-2644
Kathryn Kennedy Winery
Saratoga, CA 408-867-4170
Kelley's Island Wine Company
Kelleys Island, OH 419-746-2678
Kelson Creek Winery
Plymouth, CA 209-245-4700
Kendall-Jackson
Fulton, CA 866-287-9818
Kenwood Vineyards
Kenwood, CA 707-833-5891
King Brewing Company
Pontiac, MI 248-745-5900
King Estate Winery
Eugene, OR 800-884-4441
Kiona Vineyards Winery
Benton City, WA 509-588-6716
Kirigin Cellars
Gilroy, CA 408-847-8827
Kistler Vineyards
Sebastopol, CA 707-823-5603
Kittling Ridge Estate Wines & Spirits
Vaughan, ON 800-461-9463
Klingshirn Winery
Avon Lake, OH 440-933-6666
Knapp Vineyards
Romulus, NY 800-869-9271
Konzelmann Estate Winery
Niagara on the Lake, ON 905-935-2866
Koryo Winery Company
Gardena, CA 310-532-9616
Kramer Vineyards
Gaston, OR 800-619-4637
Krinos Foods
Bronx, NY 718-729-9000

Product Categories / Beverages: Wines

Kristin Hill Winery
  Amity, OR 503-835-4012
Kunde Estate Winery
  Kenwood, CA 707-833-5501
L Mawby Vineyards
  Peshawbestown, MI 231-271-3522
La Abra Farm & Winery
  Lovingston, VA 434-263-5392
LA Buena Vida Vineyards
  Grapevine, TX 817-481-9463
LA Chiripada Winery
  Dixon, NM 800-528-7801
LA Jota Vineyard Co
  Angwin, CA 877-222-0292
LA Rocca Vineyards & Winery
  Forest Ranch, CA 800-808-9463
La Rochelle Winery
  Livermore, CA 888-647-7768
LA Vina Winery
  Anthony, NM 575-882-7632
Laetitia Vineyard & Winery
  Arroyo Grande, CA 888-809-8463
Lafollette Vineyard & Winery
  Sebastopol, CA 707-395-3902
Laird & Company
  Scobeyville, NJ 877-438-5247
Lake Sonoma Winery
  Glen Ellen, CA 877-586-2796
Lakeridge Winery & Vineyards
  Clermont, FL 800-768-9463
Lakeshore Winery
  Romulus, NY 315-549-7075
Lakewood Vineyards Inc
  Watkins Glen, NY 877-535-9252
Lambert Bridge Winery
  Healdsburg, CA 800-975-0555
Lamoreaux Landing Wine Cellars
  Lodi, NY 607-582-6011
Lancaster County Winery LTD
  Willow Street, PA 717-464-3555
Landmark Vineyards
  Kenwood, CA 707-833-0053
Lange Estate Winery & Vineyard
  Dundee, OR 503-538-6476
Larry's Vineyards & Winery
  Altamont, NY 518-355-7365
Latah Creek Wine Cellar
  Spokane Valley, WA 509-926-0164
Latcham Vineyards
  Somerset, CA 800-750-5591
Laurel Glen Vineyard
  Glen Ellen, CA 707-933-9877
Lava Cap Winery
  Placerville, CA 800-475-0175
Lazy Creek Vineyards
  Philo, CA 888-529-9275
Le Vigne Winery
  Paso Robles, CA 800-891-6055
Leelanau Cellars
  Omena, MI 800-782-8128
Leeward Winery
  Oxnard, CA 805-656-5054
Leidenfrost Vineyards
  Hector, NY 607-546-2800
Lemon Creek Winery
  Berrien Springs, MI 269-471-1321
Leonetti Cellar
  Walla Walla, WA 509-525-1670
Les Bourgeois Vineyards
  Rocheport, MO 800-690-1830
Lewis Cellars
  Napa, CA 707-255-3400
Life Force Specialty Foods
  Moscow, ID 877-657-9471
Lincourt Vineyards
  Solvang, CA 805-688-8554
Little Amana Winery
  Amana, IA 319-668-9664
Little Hills Winery
  St Charles, MO 877-584-4557
Live Oaks Winery
  Gilroy, CA 408-842-2401
Livermore Valley Cellars
  Livermore, CA 925-454-9463
Livingston Moffett Winery
  Saint Helena, CA 800-788-0370
Llano Estacado Winery
  Lubbock, TX 800-634-3854
Lockwood Vineyards
  St Helena, CA 707-963-6925
Loew Vineyards
  Mt Airy, MD 301-831-5464

Lolonis Winery
  Walnut Creek, CA 925-938-8066
Long Vineyards
  St Helena, CA 707-963-2496
Lost Mountain Winery
  Sequim, WA 888-683-5229
Louis M Martini Winery
  St Helena, CA 800-321-9463
Lucas Vineyards & Winery
  Interlaken, NY 800-682-9463
Lucas Winery
  Lodi, CA 209-368-2006
Luxco Inc
  St Louis, MO 314-772-2626
Lve & Raymond Vineyards
  St Helena, CA 800-525-2659
Lynfred Winery Inc
  Roselle, IL 630-529-9463
M S Walker Inc
  Somerville, MA 617-776-6700
Maddalena Restaurant-Sn
  Los Angeles, CA 800-626-7722
Madison Foods
  Saint Paul, MN 651-265-8212
Madison Vineyard
  Ribera, NM 575-421-8028
Madonna Estate Winery
  Napa, CA 866-724-2993
Madrona Vineyards
  Camino, CA 530-644-5948
Magnanini Farm Winery
  Wallkill, NY 845-895-2767
Mama Rap's & Winery
  Gilroy, CA 800-842-6262
Manischewitz Wine Co.
  Brooklyn, NY 718-339-0547
Marie Brizard Wines & Spirits
  St. Helena, CA 800-878-1123
Marietta Cellars
  Geyservill, CA 707-433-2747
Marimar Torres Estates
  Sebastopol, CA 707-823-4365
Markham Vineyards
  St Helena, CA 707-963-5292
Markko Vineyard
  Conneaut, OH 800-252-3197
Marlow Wine Cellars
  Monteagle, TN 931-924-2120
Martin & Weyrich Winery
  Templeton, CA 805-239-1640
Martin Ray Winery
  Santa Rosa, CA 707-823-2404
Mastantuono Winery
  Templeton, CA 805-238-0676
Matanzas Creek Winery
  Santa Rosa, CA 800-500-6464
Matson Vineyards
  Redding, CA 530-222-2833
Maui Wine
  Kula, HI 877-878-6058
Maurice Carrie Winery
  Temecula, CA 800-716-1711
Mayacamas Vineyards & Winery
  Napa, CA 707-224-4030
Mazzocco Vineyards
  Healdsburg, CA 800-501-8466
McDowell Valley Vineyards & Cellars
  Hopland, CA 707-744-1774
Mcgregor Vineyard Winery
  Dundee, NY 800-272-0192
McHenry Vineyard
  Davis, CA 530-756-3202
McIntosh's Ohio Valley Wines
  Bethel, OH 937-379-1159
Meier's Wine Cellars Inc
  Cincinnati, OH 800-346-2941
Menghini Winery
  Julian, CA 760-765-2072
Meredyth Vineyard
  Middleburg, VA 540-687-6277
Meridian Vineyards
  Napa, CA 800-226-7133
Merritt Estate Winery Inc
  Forestville, NY 888-965-4800
Merryvale Vineyards
  St Helena, CA 800-326-6069
Messina Hof Winery & Resort
  Bryan, TX 979-778-9463
Michael David Winery
  Lodi, CA 888-707-9463
Michel-Schlumberger Wine Est
  Healdsburg, CA 800-447-3060

Milat Vineyards Winery
  St Helena, CA 800-546-4528
Milea Estate Vineyard
  Staatsburg, NY 845-264-0403
Mill Creek Vineyards
  Healdsburg, CA 877-349-2121
Millbrook Vineyards
  Millbrook, NY 800-662-9463
Milliaire Winery
  Murphys, CA 209-728-1658
Mission Mountain Winery
  Dayton, MT 406-849-5524
Mogen David Wine Corp
  Westfield, NY 716-326-3151
Montelle Winery
  Augusta, MO 888-595-9463
Monterey Vineyard
  Gonzales, CA 831-675-4000
Montevina Winery
  Plymouth, CA 209-245-6942
Monticello Vineyards-Corley
  Napa, CA 707-253-2802
Montmorenci Vineyards
  Aiken, SC 803-649-4870
Morgan Winery
  Salinas, CA 831-751-7777
Mosby Winery
  Buellton, CA 800-706-6729
Moss Creek Winery
  Napa, CA 707-252-1295
Mosti Mondiale/Gourmet Mondiale
  Ste-Catherine, QC 450-638-6380
Mount Palomar Winery
  Temecula, CA 800-854-5177
Mountain Cove Vineyards
  Lovingston, VA 434-263-5392
Mt Baker Vineyards
  Everson, WA 360-592-2300
Mt Bethel Winery
  Altus, AR 479-468-2444
Mt Eden Vineyards
  Saratoga, CA 408-867-9587
Mt Nittany Vineyard & Winery
  Centre Hall, PA 814-466-6373
Mt Pleasant Winery
  Branson, MO 800-467-9463
Murphy Goode Estate Winery
  Geyserville, CA 707-431-7644
Naked Mountain Winery Vineyard
  Markham, VA 540-364-1609
Nalle Winery
  Healdsburg, CA 707-433-1040
Nantucket Vineyard
  Nantucket, MA 508-228-9235
Napa Cellars
  Napa, CA 800-535-6400
Napa Wine Company
  Oakville, CA 800-848-9630
Nashoba Valley Winery
  Bolton, MA 978-779-5521
National Wine & Spirits
  Indianapolis, IN
Navarro Vineyards
  Philo, CA 707-895-3686
Naylor Wine Cellars Inc
  Stewartstown, PA 800-292-3370
Nevada City Winery
  Nevada City, CA 800-203-9463
Nevada County Wine Guild
  Nevada City, CA 855-494-7025
New Hope Winery
  New Hope, PA 800-592-9463
New Land Vineyard
  Geneva, NY 315-585-4432
Newman's Own
  Westport, CT 203-222-0136
Newport Vineyards & Winery
  Middletown, RI 401-848-5161
Newton Vineyard
  St Helena, CA 707-204-7423
Nicasio Vineyards
  Soquel, CA 831-423-1073
Niche W&S
  Cedar Knolls, NJ 973-993-8450
Nichelini Family Winery Inc
  St Helena, CA 707-963-0717
Niebaum-Coppola Estate Winery
  Rutherford, CA 800-782-4266
Nissley Vineyards & Winery
  Bainbridge, PA 800-522-2387
Nordman Of California
  Sanger, CA 559-638-9923

Product Categories / Beverages: Wines

Northern Vineyards Winery
  Stillwater, MN 651-430-1032
Northville Winery & Brewing Co
  Northville, MI 248-320-6507
Nutmeg Vineyard
  Andover, CT 860-742-8402
Oak Grove Orchards Winery
  Rickreall, OR 541-364-7052
Oak Knoll Winery
  Hillsboro, OR 800-625-5665
Oak Ridge Winery LLC
  Lodi, CA 209-369-4758
Oak Spring Winery
  Altoona, PA 814-946-3799
Oasis Winery
  Hume, VA 800-304-7656
Obester Winery
  Half Moon Bay, CA 650-726-9463
Ocena Wineary & Vineyards
  New Era, MI 231-861-4657
Ojai Vineyard
  Oak View, CA 805-649-1674
Old Creek Ranch Winery
  Ventura, CA 805-649-4132
Old Firehouse Winery
  Geneva, OH 800-362-6751
Old House Vineyards
  Culpeper, VA 540-423-1032
Old Mill Winery
  Geneva, OH 440-466-5560
Old South Winery
  Natchez, MS 601-445-9924
Old Wine Cellar
  Amana, IA 319-622-3116
Oliver Winery
  Bloomington, IN 800-258-2783
Olympic Cellars
  Port Angeles, WA 360-452-0160
One Vineyard and Winery
  Saint Helena, CA 707-963-1123
Optima Wine Cellars
  Healdsburg, CA 707-431-8222
Opus One
  Oakville, CA 800-292-6787
Orchard Heights Winery
  Salem, OR 503-391-7308
Orfila Vineyards
  Escondido, CA 760-738-6500
Organic Wine Co Inc
  San Francisco, CA 888-326-9463
Ormand Peugeog Corporation
  Miami, FL 305-624-6834
Orr Mountain Winery
  Madisonville, TN 423-442-5340
Pacheco Ranch Winery
  Novato, CA 415-883-5583
Pacific Echo Cellars
  Philo, CA 707-895-2065
Page Mill Winery
  Livermore, CA 925-456-7676
Pahlmeyer Winery
  St Helena, CA 707-255-2321
Pahrump Valley Winery
  Pahrump, NV 800-368-9463
Palmer Vineyards Inc
  Riverhead, NY 800-901-8783
Panther Creek Cellars
  Dundee, OR 503-472-8080
Paradise Valley Vineyards
  Phoenix, AZ 602-233-8727
Paraiso Vineyards
  Soledad, CA 831-678-0300
Parducci Wine Cellars
  Ukiah, CA 888-362-9463
Pastori Winery
  Cloverdale, CA 707-857-3418
Paumanok Vineyards
  Aquebogue, NY 631-722-8800
Pazdar Winery
  Scotchtown Branch, NY 845-695-1903
Peaceful Bend Winery
  Steelville, MO 573-775-3000
Peconic Bay Winery
  Cutchogue, NY 631-734-7361
Pedrizzetti Winery
  Morgan Hill, CA 408-779-7389
Pedroncelli J Winery
  Geyserville, CA 800-836-3894
Peju Province Winery
  Rutherford, CA 800-446-7358
Pellegrini Wine Co
  Santa Rosa, CA 800-891-0244

Penn Shore Winery Vineyards
  North East, PA 814-725-8688
Pennsylvania Renaissance Faire
  Manheim, PA 717-664-0476
Pernod Ricard USA
  New York, NY 212-372-5400
Perry Creek Winery
  Somerset, CA 800-880-4026
Peter Michael Winery
  Calistoga, CA 800-354-4459
Peterson & Sons Winery
  Kalamazoo, MI 269-626-9755
Pheasant Ridge Winery
  Lubbock, TX 806-746-6033
Philip Togni Vineyard
  St Helena, CA 707-963-3731
Piedmont Vineyards & Winery
  Middleburg, VA 540-687-5528
Piedra Creek Winery
  San Luis Obispo, CA 805-541-1281
Pikes Peak Vineyards
  Colorado Springs, CO 719-576-0075
Pindar Vineyards
  Peconic, NY 631-734-6200
Pine Ridge Vineyards
  Napa, CA 800-575-9777
Plainfield Winery & Tasting Rm
  Plainfield, IN 888-761-9463
Plam Vineyards & Winery
  La Quinta, CA 760-972-4465
Pleasant Valley Wine Co
  Hammondsport, NY 607-569-6111
Plum Creek Winery
  Palisade, CO 970-464-7586
Plymouth Colony Winery
  Plymouth, MA 508-747-3334
Pommeraie Winery
  Sebastopol, CA 707-823-9463
Ponderosa Valley Vineyard
  Ponderosa, NM 800-946-3657
Ponzi Vineyards
  Sherwood, OR 503-628-1227
Porter Creek Vineyards
  Healdsburg, CA 707-433-6321
Post Familie Vineyards
  Altus, AR 800-275-8423
Prager Winery & Port Works
  St Helena, CA 800-969-7678
Presque Isle Wine Cellars
  North East, PA 800-488-7492
Preston Premium Wines
  Pasco, WA 509-545-1990
Preston Vineyards & Winery
  Healdsburg, CA 800-305-9707
Prince Michel
  Leon, VA 800-869-8242
Quady Winery
  Madera, CA 800-733-8068
Quail Ridge Cellars & Vineyards
  Saint Helena, CA 800-706-9463
Quilceda Creek Vintners
  Snohomish, WA 360-568-2389
Quivira Vineyards & Winery
  Healdsburg, CA 800-292-8339
R.H. Phillips
  Esparto, CA 530-662-3504
Rabbit Ridge Winery
  Paso Robles, CA 805-467-3331
Radanovich Vineyards & Winery
  Mariposa, CA 209-966-3187
Rainbow Hills Vineyards
  Newcomerstown, OH 740-545-9305
Rancho De Philo Winery
  Rancho Cucamonga, CA 909-987-4208
Rancho Sisquoc Winery
  Santa Maria, CA 805-934-4332
Rapazzini Winery
  Gilroy, CA 800-842-6262
Rebec Vineyards
  Amherst, VA 434-946-5168
Redhawk Vineyard & Winery
  Salem, OR 503-362-1596
Reeve Wines
  Healdsburg, CA 707-235-6345
Renaissance Vineyard & Winery
  Oregon House, CA 800-655-3277
Renault Winery
  Egg Harbor City, NJ 609-965-2111
Renwood Winery
  Plymouth, CA 800-348-8466
Retzlaff Vineyards
  Livermore, CA 925-447-8941

Richard L. Graeser Winery
  Calistoga, CA 707-942-4437
Richardson Vineyards
  Sonoma, CA 707-938-2610
Ridge Vineyards Inc
  Cupertino, CA 408-867-3233
Ritchie Creek Vineyard
  St Helena, CA 707-963-4661
River Run Vintners
  Watsonville, CA 831-726-3112
Roberian Vineyards
  Forestville, NY 716-679-1620
Robert F Pliska & Company Winery
  Purgitsville, WV 877-747-2737
Robert Keenan Winery
  St Helena, CA 707-963-9177
Robert Mondavi Winery
  Oakville, CA 888-766-6328
Robert Mueller Cellars
  Windsor, CA 707-837-7399
Robert Pecota Winery
  Calistoga, CA 707-479-7770
Robert Sinskey Vineyards Inc
  Napa, CA 800-869-2030
Robller Vineyard Winery
  New Haven, MO 573-237-3986
Roche Caneros Estate Winery
  Sonoma, CA 800-825-9475
Rockbridge Vineyard
  Raphine, VA 540-377-6204
Rodney Strong Vineyards
  Healdsburg, CA 800-474-9463
Rogue Ales Brewery
  Newport, OR 541-265-3188
Rombauer Vineyards
  St Helena, CA 800-622-2206
Rose Creek Vineyards
  Hagerman, ID 208-837-4353
Rosenblum Cellars
  Alameda, CA 510-865-7007
Roudon-Smith Vineyards
  Saratoga, CA 831-438-1244
Round Hill Vineyards
  St Helena, CA 800-778-0424
Royal Wine Corp
  Bayonne, NJ 718-384-2400
Rudd Winery
  Oakville, CA 707-944-8577
Rutherford Hill Winery
  Rutherford, CA 707-963-1871
Saddleback Cellars
  Oakville, CA 707-944-1305
Sainte Genevieve Winery
  Ste Genevieve, MO 800-398-1298
Saintsbury
  Napa, CA 707-252-0592
Salamandre Wine Cellars
  Aptos, CA 831-685-0321
Salishan Vineyards
  La Center, WA 360-263-2713
San Dominique Winery
  Camp Verde, AZ 480-945-8583
Sand Castle Winery
  Erwinna, PA 800-722-9463
Sandia Shadows Vineyard & Winery
  Albuquerque, NM 505-856-1006
Sandstone Winery
  Amana, IA 319-622-3081
Sanford Winery
  Lompoc, CA 800-426-9463
Santa Barbara Winery
  Santa Barbara, CA 805-963-3633
Santa Cruz Mountain Vineyard
  Felton, CA 831-426-6209
Santa Fe Vineyards
  Espanola, NM 505-753-8100
Santa Ynez Wine Corp
  Los Olivos, CA 800-824-8584
Sarah's Vineyard
  Gilroy, CA 408-842-4278
Satiety Winery & Cafe
  Davis, CA 530-757-2699
Saucilito Canyon Vineyard
  San Luis Obispo, CA 805-543-2111
Sausal Winery
  Healdsburg, CA 800-500-2285
Savannah Chanelle Vineyards
  Saratoga, CA 408-741-2934
Sawtooth Winery
  Nampa, ID 208-467-1200
Scenic Valley Winery
  Lanesboro, MN 507-259-4981

Product Categories / Beverages: Wines

Schloss Doepken Winery
  Ripley, NY 716-326-3636
Schoppaul Hill Winery at Ivanhoe
  Denton, TX 940-380-9463
Schramsberg Vineyards
  Calistoga, CA 800-877-3623
Schug Carneros Estate Winery
  Sonoma, CA 800-966-9365
Sea Ridge Winery
  Occidental, CA 800-692-5780
Seavey Vineyard
  St Helena, CA 707-963-8339
Sebastiani Vineyards
  Sonoma, CA 855-232-2338
Seghesio Family Vineyards
  Healdsburg, CA 707-433-0545
Sequoia Grove
  Napa, CA 800-851-7841
Serendipity Cellars
  Monmouth, OR 503-838-4284
Seven Hills Winery
  Walla Walla, WA 877-777-7870
Seven Lakes Vineyard & Winery
  Fenton, MI 810-373-6081
Shafer Vineyards
  Napa, CA 707-944-2877
Shallon Winery
  Astoria, OR 503-325-5978
Sharon Mill Winery
  Manchester, MI 734-971-6337
Sharp Rock Farm B & B
  Sperryville, VA 540-987-8020
Shenandoah Vineyards
  Plymouth, CA 209-245-4455
Sierra Vista Winery
  Placerville, CA 800-946-3916
Signore Winery
  Brooktondale, NY 607-539-7935
Signorello Vineyards
  Napa, CA 707-255-5990
Silvan Ridge Winery
  Eugene, OR 541-345-1945
Silver Fox Vineyards
  Mariposa, CA 209-966-4800
Silver Mountain Vineyards
  Santa Cruz, CA 408-353-2278
Silverado Vineyards Inc
  Napa, CA 800-997-1770
Simi Winery
  Healdsburg, CA 707-433-3686
Simon Levi Cellars
  Kenwood, CA 888-315-0040
Six Mile Creek Vineyard
  Ithaca, NY 800-260-0612
Sky Vineyards
  Glen Ellen, CA 707-935-1391
Slate Quarry Winery
  Nazareth, PA 610-746-3900
Smith Vineyard & Winery
  Grass Valley, CA 530-273-7032
Smith-Madrone Vineyards & Winery
  St Helena, CA 707-963-2283
Smokehouse Winery
  Sperryville, VA 540-987-3194
Smothers Brothers Tasting Room
  Glen Ellen, CA 800-795-9463
Sobon Estate
  Plymouth, CA 209-333-6275
Sokol Blosser Winery
  Dayton, OR 800-582-6668
Solis Winery
  Gilroy, CA 888-838-6427
Sonoita Vineyards
  Elgin, AZ 520-455-5893
Sonoma Wine Services
  Vineburg, CA 707-996-9773
Sonoma-Cutrer Vineyards
  Windsor, CA 707-528-1181
Sow's Ear Winery
  Brooksville, ME 207-326-4649
Spangler Vineyards
  Roseburg, OR 541-679-9654
Spottswoode
  St Helena, CA 707-963-0134
Spring Mountain Vineyard
  St Helena, CA 877-769-4637
Springhill Cellars
  Albany, OR 541-928-1009
Spurgeon Vineyards & Winery
  Highland, WI 800-236-5555
St Francis Winery & Vineyards
  Santa Rosa, CA 707-833-4668

St Innocent Winery
  Salem, OR 503-378-1526
St Julian Winery
  Paw Paw, MI 800-732-6002
St. James Winery
  Saint James, MO 800-280-9463
Stags' Leap Winery
  Napa, CA 707-944-1303
Starr & Brown
  Portland, OR 503-287-1775
Starr Hill Winery & Vineyard
  Curwensville, PA 814-236-0910
Ste Chapelle Winery
  Caldwell, ID 877-783-2427
STE Michelle Wine Estates
  Woodinville, WA 800-267-6793
Stearns Wharf Vintners
  Santa Barbara, CA 805-966-6624
Steltzner Vineyards
  Napa, CA 800-707-9463
Sterling Vineyards
  Calistoga, CA 707-942-3344
Steuk's Country Market & Winery
  Sandusky, OH 419-625-8324
Stevenot Winery
  Murphys, CA 209-728-3485
Stone Hill Winery
  Hermann, MO 573-486-2221
Stonegate
  St Helena, CA 707-603-2203
Stoneridge Winery
  Sutter Creek, CA 209-223-1761
Stonington Vineyards
  Stonington, CT 800-421-9463
Stony Hill Vineyard
  St Helena, CA 707-963-2636
Stonybrook Mountain Winery
  Calistoga, CA 707-942-5282
Storrs Winery
  Santa Cruz, CA 831-458-5030
Story Winery
  Plymouth, CA 800-712-6390
Stoutridge Vineyard
  Marlboro, NY
Streblow Vineyards
  Saint Helena, CA 707-963-5892
Stryker Sonoma
  Geyserville, CA 800-433-1944
Sugar Creek Winery
  Defiance, MO 636-987-2400
Sullivan Vineyards
  St Helena, CA 877-244-7337
Summit Lake Vineyards
  Angwin, CA 707-965-2488
Sunrise Winery
  San Jose, CA 408-741-1310
Sunstone Vineyards & Winery
  Santa Ynez, CA 800-313-9463
Susquehanna Valley Winery
  Danville, PA 570-275-2364
Sutter Home Winery
  St Helena, CA 800-967-4663
Swanson Vineyards & Winery
  Rutherford, CA 800-942-0809
Swedish Hill Vineyard & Winery
  Romulus, NY 888-549-9463
Sweet Traders
  Huntington Beach, CA 714-903-6800
Sycamore Vineyards
  Saint Helena, CA 800-963-9698
Sylvin Farms Winery
  Egg Harbor City, NJ 609-965-1548
Tabor Hill Winery & Restaurant
  Buchanan, MI 800-283-3363
Talbott Vineyards
  Salinas, CA 831-675-3000
Talley Vineyards
  Arroyo Grande, CA 805-489-2508
Tamuzza Vineyards
  Hope, NJ 856-896-0619
Tarara Winery
  Leesburg, VA 703-771-7100
Taylor Wine Company
  Hammondsport, NY 607-868-3245
Terrace At J Vineyards
  Healdsburg, CA 800-885-9463
The Boisset Collection
  St. Helena, CA 707-967-7667
The Meeker Vineyard
  Healdsburg, CA 707-431-2148
The Rubin Family of Wines
  Sebastopol, CA 707-887-8130

Thoma Vineyards
  Dallas, OR 800-884-1927
Thomas Fogarty Winery
  Woodside, CA 800-247-4163
Thomas Kruse Winery
  Gilroy, CA 408-842-7016
Thornton Winery
  Temecula, CA 951-699-0099
Thorpe Vineyard
  Wolcott, NY 315-594-2502
Three Lakes Winery
  Three Lakes, WI 800-944-5434
Tkc Vineyards
  Plymouth, CA 888-627-2356
Todhunter Foods
  West Palm Beach, FL 800-336-9463
Todhunter Foods
  Lake Alfred, FL 863-956-1116
Tomasello Winery
  Hammonton, NJ 800-666-9463
Topolos at Russian River Vine
  Forestville, CA 707-887-3344
Transamerica Wine Corporation
  Brooklyn, NY 718-875-4017
Treasury Wine Estates
  Napa, CA 707-259-4500
Trefethen Family Vineyards
  Napa, CA 707-255-7700
Trentadue Winery
  Geyserville, CA 888-332-3032
Trigo Corporation
  Toa Baja, PR 787-794-1300
Truchard Vineyards
  Napa, CA 707-253-7153
Truckee River Winery
  Truckee, CA 530-587-4626
Tucker Cellars
  Sunnyside, WA 509-837-8701
Tudal Winery
  St Helena, CA 707-963-3947
Tularosa Vineyards
  Tularosa, NM 800-687-4467
Twenty Rows
  Napa, CA 800-620-7697
Tyee Wine Cellars
  Corvallis, OR 541-753-8754
Union Square Wines & Spirits
  New York, NY 212-675-8100
Union Wine Co
  Tualatin, OR
V Sattui Winery
  St Helena, CA 707-963-7774
Val Verde Winery
  Del Rio, TX 830-775-9714
Valhalla Winery
  Veneta, OR 541-935-9711
Valley of the Moon Winery
  Glen Ellen, CA 707-996-6941
Valley View Winery
  Jacksonville, OR 800-781-9463
Van Der Heyden Vineyards
  Napa, CA 800-948-9463
Ventana Vineyards Winery
  Monterey, CA 800-237-8846
Veramar Vineyard
  Berryville, VA 540-955-5510
Vetter Vineyards Winery
  Westfield, NY 716-326-3100
Via Della Chiesa Vineyards
  Raynham, MA 508-822-7775
Viader Vineyards & Winery
  Deer Park, CA 707-963-3816
Viano Vineyards
  Martinez, CA 925-228-6465
Viansa Winery
  Sonoma, CA 800-995-4740
Vie-Del Co
  Fresno, CA 559-834-2525
Villa Helena/Arger-Martucci Winery
  St Helena, CA 707-963-4334
Villa Milan Vineyard
  Milan, IN 812-654-3419
Villa Mt. Eden Winery
  Saint Helena, CA 866-931-1624
Villar Vintners of Valdese
  Valdese, NC 828-879-3202
Vincent Arroyo Winery
  Calistoga, CA 707-942-6995
Vinoklet Winery
  Cincinnati, OH 513-385-9309
Vintage Wine Estates
  Santa Rosa, CA 877-289-9463

Product Categories / Beverages: Wines

Vista D'Oro Farms
  Langley, BC 855-514-3539
Von Stiehl Winery
  Algoma, WI. 800-955-5208
Von Strasser
  Calistoga, CA 888-359-9463
Vynecrest Winery
  Breinigsville, PA 800-361-0725
Wagner Vineyards
  Lodi, NY. 866-924-6378
Wagshal's Imports
  Washington, DC 202-363-5698
Warner Vineyards
  Paw Paw, MI. 800-756-5357
Wasson Brothers Winery
  Sandy, OR 503-668-3124
Weibel Vineyards
  Lodi, CA 800-932-9463
Wente Family Estates
  Livermore, CA 925-456-2305
Wermuth Winery
  Calistoga, CA 707-942-5924
West Park Wine Cellars
  West Park, NY. 845-384-6709
Westbend Vinyards
  Lewisville, NC 866-901-5032
Westport Rivers Vineyard
  Westport, MA 800-993-9695
Westwood Winery
  Sonoma, CA 707-933-7837
Whaler Vineyard
  Ukiah, CA 707-462-6355
Whitcraft Winery
  Santa Barbara, CA 805-730-1086
White Hall Vineyards
  Crozet, VA. 434-823-8615
White Oak Vineyards & Winery
  Healdsburg, CA 707-433-8429
White Rock Vineyards
  Napa, CA. 707-257-7922
Whitecliff Vineyard & Winery
  Gardiner, NY. 845-255-4613
Whitehall Lane Winery
  St Helena, CA 707-963-9454
Whitford Cellars
  Napa, CA. 707-942-0840
Widmers Wine Cellars
  Canandaigua, NY 585-374-6311
Wiederkehr Wine Cellars Inc
  Altus, AR 800-622-9463
Wild Hog Vineyard
  Cazadero, CA 707-847-3687
Wild Horse Winery & Vineyards
  Templeton, CA 805-434-2541
Wildhurst Vineyards
  Kelseyville, CA. 800-595-9463
William Grant & Sons
  Irvine, CA
William Harrison Winery LLC
  St Helena, CA 707-963-8762
William Hill Estate Winery
  Napa, CA. 707-265-3024
Williams Selyem Winery
  Healdsburg, CA 707-433-6425
Williamsburg Winery LTD
  Williamsburg, VA. 757-229-0999
Willowcroft Farm Vineyards
  Leesburg, VA 703-777-8161
Wimberley Valley Winery
  Driftwood, TX 512-847-2592
Windwalker Vineyards & Winery
  Somerset, CA 530-620-4054
Wine Group
  San Francisco, CA 415-986-8700
Wine-A-Rita
  Texarkana, TX. 903-832-7309
Wintergreen Winery
  Nellysford, VA 434-361-2519
Wishnev Wine Management
  Walnut Creek, CA. 925-930-6374
Witness Tree Vineyard LTD
  Salem, OR. 888-478-8766
Wolf Creek Winery
  Barberton, OH. 800-436-0426
Wollersheim Winery
  Prairie Du Sac, WI 800-847-9463
Woodbury Vineyards
  Fredonia, NY 866-691-9463
Wooden Valley Winery
  Fairfield, CA 707-864-0730
Woodside Vineyards
  Menlo Park, CA 650-851-3144

Woodward Canyon
  Touchet, WA. 509-525-4129
Worden
  Spokane, WA. 509-455-7835
Wyandotte Winery LLC
  Gahanna, OH. 877-906-7464
Yakima River Winery
  Prosser, WA. 509-786-2805
Yamhill Valley Vineyards
  Mcminnville, OR 800-825-4845
York Mountain Winery
  Templeton, CA 805-237-7575
Zaca Mesa Winery
  Los Olivos, CA 800-350-7972
Zayante Vineyards
  Felton, CA. 831-335-7992
Zd Wines
  Napa, CA. 800-487-7757

Bulk

Brothers International Food Corporation
  Rochester, NY. 585-343-3007
Cribari Vineyard Inc
  Fresno, CA 800-277-9095

Cooking

Batavia Wine Cellars
  Canandaigua, NY 585-396-7600
California Olive Oil Council
  Berkeley, CA. 888-718-9830
Cribari Vineyard Inc
  Fresno, CA 800-277-9095
Emerling International Foods
  Buffalo, NY 716-833-7381
Four Chimneys Farm Winery Trust
  Himrod, NY 607-243-7502
KARI-Out Co
  White Plains, NY. 800-433-8799
Mizkan Americas Inc
  Mount Prospect, IL 800-323-4358
Rapazzini Winery
  Gilroy, CA. 800-842-6262
Todhunter Foods
  West Palm Beach, FL 800-336-9463
Todhunter Foods
  Lake Alfred, FL. 863-956-1116

Marsala

Cribari Vineyard Inc
  Fresno, CA 800-277-9095
Pernod Ricard USA
  New York, NY 212-372-5400

French

Beaulieu Vineyard
  Rutherford, CA 707-257-5749
Boisset Family Estates
  St Helena, CA 800-878-1123

Champagne

Briceland Vineyards
  Redway, CA 707-923-2429
Brimstone Hill Vineyard
  Pine Bush, NY 845-744-2231
Brotherhood Winery
  Washingtonville, NY 845-496-3661
Buena Vista Historic Tstng Rm
  Sonoma, CA 800-926-1266
Bully Hill Vineyards
  Hammondsport, NY 607-868-3610
Chateau des Charmes Wines
  St. Davids, ON 800-263-2541
Chicama Vineyards
  West Tisbury, MA 888-244-2262
Chouinard Vineyards & Winery
  Castro Valley, CA 510-582-9900
Clinton Vineyards Inc
  Clinton Corners, NY. 845-266-5372
Domaine Chandon
  Yountville, CA 888-242-6366
Dr Konstantin Frank's Vinifera
  Hammondsport, NY 800-320-0735
Fenn Valley Vineyards
  Fennville, MI 800-432-6265
Frontenac Point Vineyard
  Trumansburg, NY 607-387-9619
Glenora Wine Cellars
  Dundee, NY 800-243-5513
Marie Brizard Wines & Spirits
  St. Helena, CA 800-878-1123

Meier's Wine Cellars Inc
  Cincinnati, OH 800-346-2941
Mon Ami Restaurant
  Port Clinton, OH. 800-777-4266
Schramsberg Vineyards
  Calistoga, CA 800-877-3623
St Julian Winery
  Paw Paw, MI 800-732-6002
Stone Hill Winery
  Hermann, MO 573-486-2221
Thornton Winery
  Temecula, CA. 951-699-0099
Vintage Wine Estates
  Santa Rosa, CA 877-289-9463
Westport Rivers Vineyard
  Westport, MA 800-993-9695
Woodbury Vineyards
  Fredonia, NY 866-691-9463
York Mountain Winery
  Templeton, CA 805-237-7575

Red

Callaway Vineyards & Winery
  Temecula, CA. 800-472-2377
Union Square Wines & Spirits
  New York, NY 212-675-8100
Warwick Valley Winery & Distillery
  Warwick, NY 845-258-4858
Whitecliff Vineyard & Winery
  Gardiner, NY. 845-255-4613

Red Bordeaux

Babcock Winery & Vineyards
  Lompoc, CA 805-736-1455
Pahlmeyer Winery
  St Helena, CA. 707-255-2321

Red Burgundy

Bristle Ridge Vineyards
  Knob Noster, MO 800-994-9463
Cribari Vineyard Inc
  Fresno, CA 800-277-9095
Heineman Winery
  Put In Bay, OH 419-285-2811

White

Firelands Winery
  Sandusky, OH 800-548-9463
Frey Vineyards
  Redwood Valley, CA. 800-760-3739
Warwick Valley Winery & Distillery
  Warwick, NY 845-258-4858
Whitecliff Vineyard & Winery
  Gardiner, NY. 845-255-4613

White Burgundy

Buena Vista Historic Tstng Rm
  Sonoma, CA 800-926-1266

Italian

Boisset Family Estates
  St Helena, CA 800-878-1123
Buena Vista Historic Tstng Rm
  Sonoma, CA 800-926-1266
E & J Gallo Winery
  Modesto, CA. 877-687-9463
V Sattui Winery
  St Helena, CA 707-963-7774

Chianti

E & J Gallo Winery
  Modesto, CA. 877-687-9463

Moscato d' Asti

Fetzer Vineyards
  Hopland, CA 707-744-1250

Red

E & J Gallo Winery
  Modesto, CA. 877-687-9463
Frey Vineyards
  Redwood Valley, CA. 800-760-3739
Seghesio Family Vineyards
  Healdsburg, CA 707-433-0545

White

Callaway Vineyards & Winery
  Temecula, CA. 800-472-2377

Product Categories / Beverages: Wines

Seghesio Family Vineyards
  Healdsburg, CA 707-433-0545

Japanese
Sake

Ogeki Sake USA Inc
  Hollister, CA 831-637-9217
Takara Sake USA Inc
  Berkeley, CA 510-540-8250

Non-Alcoholic

Ariel Vineyards
  Napa, CA 800-456-9472
Black Bear Farm Winery
  Chenango Forks, NY 607-656-9863
Cedar Creek Winery
  Cedarburg, WI 800-827-8020
Kedem
  Bayonne, NJ 718-369-4600
Royal Wine Corp
  Bayonne, NJ 718-384-2400
Tabor Hill Winery & Restaurant
  Buchanan, MI 800-283-3363
Wiederkehr Wine Cellars Inc
  Altus, AR 800-622-9463

Portuguese
Port

Alto Vineyards & Winery
  Alto Pass, IL 618-893-4898
Chateau Grand Traverse Winery
  Traverse City, MI 231-938-6120
Chouinard Vineyards & Winery
  Castro Valley, CA 510-582-9900
Cienega Valley Winery/DeRose
  Hollister, CA 831-636-9143
Fenestra Winery
  Livermore, CA 800-789-9463
Fenn Valley Vineyards
  Fennville, MI 800-432-6265
Ficklin Vineyards Winery
  Madera, CA 559-674-4598

Red Grape Wines

Hazlitt 1852 Vineyards
  Hector, NY 888-750-0494
Hermannhof Vineyards
  Hermann, MO 800-393-0100
Heron Hill Winery
  Hammondsport, NY 800-441-4241

Cabernet Sauvignon

A. Rafanelli Winery
  Healdsburg, CA 707-433-1385
Amrhein's Wine Cellars
  Bent Mountain, VA 540-929-4632
Applewood Winery
  Warwick, NY 845-988-9292
Autumn Hill Vineyards/Blue Ridge Wine
  Stanardsville, VA 434-985-6100
Babcock Winery & Vineyards
  Lompoc, CA 805-736-1455
Barboursville Vineyards
  Barboursville, VA 540-832-3824
Black Mesa Winery
  Velarde, NM 800-852-6372
Breaux Vineyards
  Purcellville, VA 800-492-9961
Burnley Vineyards
  Barboursville, VA 540-832-2828
Cardinale Winery
  Oakville, CA 800-588-0279
Catoctin Vineyards
  Brookeville, MD 301-774-2310
Cedar Creek Winery
  Cedarburg, WI 800-827-8020
Chateau Morrisette Winery
  Floyd, VA 540-593-2865
Chatom Vineyards Inc
  San Andreas, CA 800-435-8852
Chicama Vineyards
  West Tisbury, MA 888-244-2262
Chouinard Vineyards & Winery
  Castro Valley, CA 510-582-9900
Cienega Valley Winery/DeRose
  Hollister, CA 831-636-9143
Columbia Winery
  Woodinville, WA 425-488-2776
Cooper Vineyards
  Louisa, VA 540-894-5474
Cosentino Winery
  Napa, CA 800-764-1220
Cribari Vineyard Inc
  Fresno, CA 800-277-9095
Cuvaison Winery
  Calistoga, CA 707-942-6266
Delicato Family Vineyards
  Napa, CA 707-265-1700
Douknie Winery
  Purcellville, VA 540-668-6464
E & J Gallo Winery
  Modesto, CA 877-687-9463
Farfelu Vineyards
  Flint Hill, VA 540-364-2930
Fenestra Winery
  Livermore, CA 800-789-9463
Fetzer Vineyards
  Hopland, CA 707-744-1250
Ficklin Vineyards Winery
  Madera, CA 559-674-4598
First Colony Winery
  Charlottesville, VA 877-979-7105
Foris Vineyards
  Cave Junction, OR 541-592-3752
Freemark Abbey Winery
  St Helena, CA 800-963-9698
Frog's Leap Winery
  Rutherford, CA 800-959-4704
Georgia Wines Inc
  Ringgold, GA 706-937-2177
Greenwood Ridge Vineyards
  Philo, CA 707-895-2002
Groth Vineyards & Winery
  Oakville, CA 707-944-0290
Hahn Family Wines
  Soledad, CA 831-678-4555
Hazlitt 1852 Vineyards
  Hector, NY 888-750-0494
Heineman Winery
  Put In Bay, OH 419-285-2811
Honig Vineyard and Winery
  Rutherford, CA 800-929-2217
Le Vigne Winery
  Paso Robles, CA 800-891-6055
Mayacamas Vineyards & Winery
  Napa, CA 707-224-4030
Oasis Winery
  Hume, VA 800-304-7656
Obester Winery
  Half Moon Bay, CA 650-726-9463
Old House Vineyards
  Culpeper, VA 540-423-1032
Pahlmeyer Winery
  St Helena, CA 707-255-2321
Piedmont Vineyards & Winery
  Middleburg, VA 540-687-5528
Plum Creek Winery
  Palisade, CO 970-464-7586
Retzlaff Vineyards
  Livermore, CA 925-447-8941
Ritchie Creek Vineyard
  St Helena, CA 707-963-4661
Robert Pecota Winery
  Calistoga, CA 707-479-7770
Rodney Strong Vineyards
  Healdsburg, CA 800-474-9463
Seven Hills Winery
  Walla Walla, WA 877-777-7870
Shafer Vineyards
  Napa, CA 707-944-2877
Signorello Vineyards
  Napa, CA 707-255-5990
Silver Fox Vineyards
  Mariposa, CA 209-966-4800
Silver Oak
  Oakville, CA 707-944-8808
Smith Vineyard & Winery
  Grass Valley, CA 530-273-7032
Smothers Brothers Tasting Room
  Glen Ellen, CA 800-795-9463
Sonoita Vineyards
  Elgin, AZ 520-455-5893
Spottswoode
  St Helena, CA 707-963-0134
Stone Mountain Vineyards
  Dyke, VA 434-990-9463
Sycamore Vineyards
  Saint Helena, CA 800-963-9698
Tularosa Vineyards
  Tularosa, NM 800-687-4467
Veramar Vineyard
  Berryville, VA 540-955-5510
Veritas Vineyard
  Afton, VA 540-456-8000
Vincent Arroyo Winery
  Calistoga, CA 707-942-6995
Von Stiehl Winery
  Algoma, WI 800-955-5208
Wente Family Estates
  Livermore, CA 925-456-2305
Westbend Vinyards
  Lewisville, NC 866-901-5032
White Hall Vineyards
  Crozet, VA 434-823-8615
White Oak Vineyards & Winery
  Healdsburg, CA 707-433-8429
Whitehall Lane Winery
  St Helena, CA 707-963-9454
Willowcroft Farm Vineyards
  Leesburg, VA 703-777-8161
Wintergreen Winery
  Nellysford, VA 434-361-2519
Woodside Vineyards
  Menlo Park, CA 650-851-3144
York Mountain Winery
  Templeton, CA 805-237-7575
Zd Wines
  Napa, CA 800-487-7757

Dolcetto

Cosentino Winery
  Napa, CA 800-764-1220
Firelands Winery
  Sandusky, OH 800-548-9463
Witness Tree Vineyard LTD
  Salem, OR 888-478-8766

Malbec

Brotherhood Winery
  Washingtonville, NY 845-496-3661
E & J Gallo Winery
  Modesto, CA 877-687-9463

Merlot

A. Rafanelli Winery
  Healdsburg, CA 707-433-1385
Applewood Winery
  Warwick, NY 845-988-9292
Autumn Hill Vineyards/Blue Ridge Wine
  Stanardsville, VA 434-985-6100
Babcock Winery & Vineyards
  Lompoc, CA 805-736-1455
Barboursville Vineyards
  Barboursville, VA 540-832-3824
Breaux Vineyards
  Purcellville, VA 800-492-9961
Brotherhood Winery
  Washingtonville, NY 845-496-3661
Cain Vineyard & Winery
  St Helena, CA 707-963-1616
Chateau Grand Traverse Winery
  Traverse City, MI 231-938-6120
Chateau Morrisette Winery
  Floyd, VA 540-593-2865
Chateau Souverain
  Cloverdale, CA 877-687-9463
Chicama Vineyards
  West Tisbury, MA 888-244-2262
Cienega Valley Winery/DeRose
  Hollister, CA 831-636-9143
Columbia Winery
  Woodinville, WA 425-488-2776
Cooper Vineyards
  Louisa, VA 540-894-5474
Cosentino Winery
  Napa, CA 800-764-1220
Cribari Vineyard Inc
  Fresno, CA 800-277-9095
Cuvaison Winery
  Calistoga, CA 707-942-6266
Delicato Family Vineyards
  Napa, CA 707-265-1700
Douknie Winery
  Purcellville, VA 540-668-6464
E & J Gallo Winery
  Modesto, CA 877-687-9463
Fenestra Winery
  Livermore, CA 800-789-9463
Fetzer Vineyards
  Hopland, CA 707-744-1250

Product Categories / Beverages: Wines

Firelands Winery
  Sandusky, OH 800-548-9463
First Colony Winery
  Charlottesville, VA 877-979-7105
Foris Vineyards
  Cave Junction, OR 541-592-3752
Frog's Leap Winery
  Rutherford, CA 800-959-4704
Gainey Vineyard
  Santa Ynez, CA 805-688-0558
Georgia Wines Inc
  Ringgold, GA 706-937-2177
Greenwood Ridge Vineyards
  Philo, CA 707-895-2002
Groth Vineyards & Winery
  Oakville, CA 707-944-0290
Gundlach-Bundschu Winery
  Sonoma, CA 707-939-3015
Hahn Family Wines
  Soledad, CA 831-678-4555
Hazlitt 1852 Vineyards
  Hector, NY 888-750-0494
Henry Estate Winery
  Umpqua, OR 800-782-2686
Heron Hill Winery
  Hammondsport, NY 800-441-4241
Jefferson Vineyards
  Charlottesville, VA 800-272-3042
Le Vigne Winery
  Paso Robles, CA 800-891-6055
Nevada City Winery
  Nevada City, CA 800-203-9463
Oasis Winery
  Hume, VA 800-304-7656
Old House Vineyards
  Culpeper, VA 540-423-1032
Plum Creek Winery
  Palisade, CO 970-464-7586
Retzlaff Vineyards
  Livermore, CA 925-447-8941
Robert Pecota Winery
  Calistoga, CA 707-479-7770
Rodney Strong Vineyards
  Healdsburg, CA 800-474-9463
Seven Hills Winery
  Walla Walla, WA 877-777-7870
Shafer Vineyards
  Napa, CA 707-944-2877
Signorello Vineyards
  Napa, CA 707-255-5990
Silver Fox Vineyards
  Mariposa, CA 209-966-4800
Smith Vineyard & Winery
  Grass Valley, CA 530-273-7032
Smothers Brothers Tasting Room
  Glen Ellen, CA 800-795-9463
Sycamore Vineyards
  Saint Helena, CA 800-963-9698
Tularosa Vineyards
  Tularosa, NM 800-687-4467
Veritas Vineyard
  Afton, VA 540-456-8000
Vincent Arroyo Winery
  Calistoga, CA 707-942-6995
Von Stiehl Winery
  Algoma, WI 800-955-5208
Westbend Vinyards
  Lewisville, NC 866-901-5032
White Hall Vineyards
  Crozet, VA 434-823-8615
White Oak Vineyards & Winery
  Healdsburg, CA 707-433-8429
Whitehall Lane Winery
  St Helena, CA 707-963-9454
York Mountain Winery
  Templeton, CA 805-237-7575

Pinot Noir

A to Z Wineworks
  Newburg, OR 800-739-4455
Babcock Winery & Vineyards
  Lompoc, CA 805-736-1455
Barboursville Vineyards
  Barboursville, VA 540-832-3824
Brotherhood Winery
  Washingtonville, NY 845-496-3661
Buena Vista Historic Tstng Rm
  Sonoma, CA 800-926-1266
Byron Vineyard & Winery
  Santa Maria, CA 805-938-7365
Cambria Winery
  Santa Maria, CA 888-339-9463
Chateau Grand Traverse Winery
  Traverse City, MI 231-938-6120
Columbia Winery
  Woodinville, WA 425-488-2776
Cosentino Winery
  Napa, CA 800-764-1220
Cristom Vineyards
  Salem, OR 503-375-3068
Cuvaison Winery
  Calistoga, CA 707-942-6266
E & J Gallo Winery
  Modesto, CA 877-687-9463
Edna Valley Vineyard
  San Luis Obispo, CA 866-979-8477
Fenestra Winery
  Livermore, CA 800-789-9463
Fess Parker Winery
  Los Olivos, CA 800-841-1104
Fetzer Vineyards
  Hopland, CA 707-744-1250
Firelands Winery
  Sandusky, OH 800-548-9463
Flynn Vineyards Winery
  Rickreall, OR 888-427-4953
Foris Vineyards
  Cave Junction, OR 541-592-3752
Fox Run Vineyards
  Penn Yan, NY 800-636-9786
Frontenac Point Vineyard
  Trumansburg, NY 607-387-9619
Gainey Vineyard
  Santa Ynez, CA 805-688-0558
Greenwood Ridge Vineyards
  Philo, CA 707-895-2002
Gundlach-Bundschu Winery
  Sonoma, CA 707-939-3015
Hahn Family Wines
  Soledad, CA 831-678-4555
Handley Cellars
  Philo, CA 800-733-3151
Hanzell Vineyards
  Sonoma, CA 707-996-3860
Hartford Family Winery
  Forestville, CA 707-887-8030
Henry Estate Winery
  Umpqua, OR 800-782-2686
Hermann J. Wiemer Vineyard
  Dundee, NY 800-371-7971
Heron Hill Winery
  Hammondsport, NY 800-441-4241
Mark West Wines
  Forestville, CA 707-544-4813
Mayacamas Vineyards & Winery
  Napa, CA 707-224-4030
Mcgregor Vineyard Winery
  Dundee, NY 800-272-0192
Milea Estate Vineyard
  Staatsburg, NY 845-264-0403
Nalle Winery
  Healdsburg, CA 707-433-1040
Nehalem Bay Winery
  Nehalem, OR. 888-368-9463
Pahlmeyer Winery
  St Helena, CA 707-255-2321
Ritchie Creek Vineyard
  St Helena, CA 707-963-4661
Rodney Strong Vineyards
  Healdsburg, CA 800-474-9463
Sonoma-Cutrer Vineyards
  Windsor, CA 707-528-1181
Taste Wine Co
  New York, NY 212-461-1708
Tualatin Estate Vineyards
  Forest Grove, OR 503-357-5005
Westwood Winery
  Sonoma, CA 707-933-7837
Whitford Cellars
  Napa, CA 707-942-0840
Williams Selyem Winery
  Healdsburg, CA 707-433-6425
Witness Tree Vineyard LTD
  Salem, OR 888-478-8766
Woodside Vineyards
  Menlo Park, CA 650-851-3144
York Mountain Winery
  Templeton, CA 805-237-7575
Zd Wines
  Napa, CA 800-487-7757

Red Meritage/Bordeaux

Fenn Valley Vineyards
  Fennville, MI 800-432-6265

Sangiovese

Babcock Winery & Vineyards
  Lompoc, CA 805-736-1455
Columbia Winery
  Woodinville, WA 425-488-2776
Cosentino Winery
  Napa, CA 800-764-1220
E & J Gallo Winery
  Modesto, CA 877-687-9463
Fenestra Winery
  Livermore, CA 800-789-9463
Le Vigne Winery
  Paso Robles, CA 800-891-6055
Nevada City Winery
  Nevada City, CA 800-203-9463
Plum Creek Winery
  Palisade, CO 970-464-7586
Tularosa Vineyards
  Tularosa, NM 800-687-4467
Vincent Arroyo Winery
  Calistoga, CA 707-942-6995

Syrah

Babcock Winery & Vineyards
  Lompoc, CA 805-736-1455
Black Mesa Winery
  Velarde, NM 800-852-6372
Brotherhood Winery
  Washingtonville, NY 845-496-3661
Cambria Winery
  Santa Maria, CA 888-339-9463
Cedar Creek Winery
  Cedarburg, WI 800-827-8020
Chouinard Vineyards & Winery
  Castro Valley, CA 510-582-9900
Columbia Winery
  Woodinville, WA 425-488-2776
Cooper Vineyards
  Louisa, VA 540-894-5474
Cosentino Winery
  Napa, CA 800-764-1220
Cuvaison Winery
  Calistoga, CA 707-942-6266
Fenestra Winery
  Livermore, CA 800-789-9463
Fess Parker Winery
  Los Olivos, CA 800-841-1104
Gainey Vineyard
  Santa Ynez, CA 805-688-0558
Handley Cellars
  Philo, CA 800-733-3151
Le Vigne Winery
  Paso Robles, CA 800-891-6055
Nevada City Winery
  Nevada City, CA 800-203-9463
Plum Creek Winery
  Palisade, CO 970-464-7586
Signorello Vineyards
  Napa, CA 707-255-5990
Sky Vineyards
  Glen Ellen, CA 707-935-1391
Tularosa Vineyards
  Tularosa, NM 800-687-4467
Westwood Winery
  Sonoma, CA 707-933-7837
Whitford Cellars
  Napa, CA 707-942-0840

Zinfandel

A. Nonini Winery
  Fresno, CA 559-275-1936
A. Rafanelli Winery
  Healdsburg, CA 707-433-1385
Brotherhood Winery
  Washingtonville, NY 845-496-3661
Chateau Souverain
  Cloverdale, CA 877-687-9463
Chatom Vineyards Inc
  San Andreas, CA 800-435-8852
Chouinard Vineyards & Winery
  Castro Valley, CA 510-582-9900
Cienega Valley Winery/DeRose
  Hollister, CA 831-636-9143
Columbia Winery
  Woodinville, WA 425-488-2776
Cosentino Winery
  Napa, CA 800-764-1220
Cribari Vineyard Inc
  Fresno, CA 800-277-9095
Cuvaison Winery
  Calistoga, CA 707-942-6266

Product Categories / Beverages: Wines

Delicato Family Vineyards
  Napa, CA...................707-265-1700
E & J Gallo Winery
  Modesto, CA.................877-687-9463
Fenestra Winery
  Livermore, CA...............800-789-9463
Fess Parker Winery
  Los Olivos, CA..............800-841-1104
Fetzer Vineyards
  Hopland, CA.................707-744-1250
Frog's Leap Winery
  Rutherford, CA..............800-959-4704
Gundlach-Bundschu Winery
  Sonoma, CA..................707-939-3015
Handley Cellars
  Philo, CA...................800-733-3151
Hartford Family Winery
  Forestville, CA.............707-887-8030
Le Vigne Winery
  Paso Robles, CA.............800-891-6055
Livermore Valley Cellars
  Livermore, CA...............925-454-9463
Nalle Winery
  Healdsburg, CA..............707-433-1040
Nevada City Winery
  Nevada City, CA.............800-203-9463
Old Wine Cellar
  Amana, IA...................319-622-3116
Ravenswood Winery
  Sonoma, CA..................866-568-3946
Rodney Strong Vineyards
  Healdsburg, CA..............800-474-9463
Seghesio Family Vineyards
  Healdsburg, CA..............707-433-0545
Silver Fox Vineyards
  Mariposa, CA................209-966-4800
Sky Vineyards
  Glen Ellen, CA..............707-935-1391
Stonybrook Mountain Winery
  Calistoga, CA...............707-942-5282
Vincent Arroyo Winery
  Calistoga, CA...............707-942-6995
Von Stiehl Winery
  Algoma, WI..................800-955-5208
Wente Family Estates
  Livermore, CA...............925-456-2305
White Oak Vineyards & Winery
  Healdsburg, CA..............707-433-8429
Williams Selyem Winery
  Healdsburg, CA..............707-433-6425
Woodside Vineyards
  Menlo Park, CA..............650-851-3144
York Mountain Winery
  Templeton, CA...............805-237-7575

Red Grapes

Alto Vineyards & Winery
  Alto Pass, IL...............618-893-4898
Babcock Winery & Vineyards
  Lompoc, CA..................805-736-1455
Chateau Grand Traverse Winery
  Traverse City, MI...........231-938-6120
Chicama Vineyards
  West Tisbury, MA............888-244-2262
Chouinard Vineyards & Winery
  Castro Valley, CA...........510-582-9900
Cienega Valley Winery/DeRose
  Hollister, CA...............831-636-9143
Columbia Winery
  Woodinville, WA.............425-488-2776
Cosentino Winery
  Napa, CA....................800-764-1220
Cribari Vineyard Inc
  Fresno, CA..................800-277-9095
E & J Gallo Winery
  Modesto, CA.................877-687-9463
Fess Parker Winery
  Los Olivos, CA..............800-841-1104
Galleano Winery
  Mira Loma, CA...............951-685-5376
Heineman Winery
  Put In Bay, OH..............419-285-2811
Mt Baker Vineyards
  Everson, WA.................360-592-2300
Newport Vineyards & Winery
  Middletown, RI..............401-848-5161
Oliver Winery
  Bloomington, IN.............800-258-2783
Ravenswood Winery
  Sonoma, CA..................866-568-3946
Steltzner Vineyards
  Napa, CA....................800-707-9463

Swedish Hill Vineyard & Winery
  Romulus, NY.................888-549-9463
Tabor Hill Winery & Restaurant
  Buchanan, MI................800-283-3363
Wiederkehr Wine Cellars Inc
  Altus, AR...................800-622-9463
Wild Horse Winery & Vineyards
  Templeton, CA...............805-434-2541
Wildhurst Vineyards
  Kelseyville, CA.............800-595-9463
Wooden Valley Winery
  Fairfield, CA...............707-864-0730

Spanish

Sherry

Brotherhood Winery
  Washingtonville, NY.........845-496-3661
Cribari Vineyard Inc
  Fresno, CA..................800-277-9095
Pleasant Valley Wine Co
  Hammondsport, NY............607-569-6111

Sparkling (See also French/Champagne)

A to Z Wineworks
  Newburg, OR.................800-739-4455
Brimstone Hill Vineyard
  Pine Bush, NY...............845-744-2231
Brown-Forman Corp
  Louisville, KY..............502-585-1100
Buena Vista Historic Tstng Rm
  Sonoma, CA..................800-926-1266
Bully Hill Vineyards
  Hammondsport, NY............607-868-3610
Clinton Vineyards Inc
  Clinton Corners, NY.........845-266-5372
Diamond Water Bottling Fclty
  Hot Springs, AR.............501-623-1251
Domaine Chandon
  Yountville, CA..............888-242-6366
Dr Konstantin Frank's Vinifera
  Hammondsport, NY............800-320-0735
E & J Gallo Winery
  Modesto, CA.................877-687-9463
Glenora Wine Cellars
  Dundee, NY..................800-243-5513
Gloria Ferrer Champagne
  Sonoma, CA..................707-933-1917
Hazlitt 1852 Vineyards
  Hector, NY..................888-750-0494
Hermannhof Vineyards
  Hermann, MO.................800-393-0100
Heron Hill Winery
  Hammondsport, NY............800-441-4241
La Rochelle Winery
  Livermore, CA...............888-647-7768
Meier's Wine Cellars Inc
  Cincinnati, OH..............800-346-2941
Milea Estate Vineyard
  Staatsburg, NY..............845-264-0403
Mon Ami Restaurant
  Port Clinton, OH............800-777-4266
Mt Baker Vineyards
  Everson, WA.................360-592-2300
Oliver Winery
  Bloomington, IN.............800-258-2783
Schramsberg Vineyards
  Calistoga, CA...............800-877-3623
St Innocent Winery
  Salem, OR...................503-378-1526
Swedish Hill Vineyard & Winery
  Romulus, NY.................888-549-9463
Tabor Hill Winery & Restaurant
  Buchanan, MI................800-283-3363
Tualatin Estate Vineyards
  Forest Grove, OR............503-357-5005
V Sattui Winery
  St Helena, CA...............707-963-7774
Vintage Wine Estates
  Santa Rosa, CA..............877-289-9463
Wiederkehr Wine Cellars Inc
  Altus, AR...................800-622-9463
Woodbury Vineyards
  Fredonia, NY................866-691-9463

White Grape Varieties

Alto Vineyards & Winery
  Alto Pass, IL...............618-893-4898
Babcock Winery & Vineyards
  Lompoc, CA..................805-736-1455

Cienega Valley Winery/DeRose
  Hollister, CA...............831-636-9143
Hazlitt 1852 Vineyards
  Hector, NY..................888-750-0494
Hermannhof Vineyards
  Hermann, MO.................800-393-0100
Heron Hill Winery
  Hammondsport, NY............800-441-4241

Chardonnay

A to Z Wineworks
  Newburg, OR.................800-739-4455
Amrhein's Wine Cellars
  Bent Mountain, VA...........540-929-4632
Applewood Winery
  Warwick, NY.................845-988-9292
Autumn Hill Vineyards/Blue Ridge Wine
  Stanardsville, VA...........434-985-6100
Babcock Winery & Vineyards
  Lompoc, CA..................805-736-1455
Barboursville Vineyards
  Barboursville, VA...........540-832-3824
Benmarl Wine Co
  Marlboro, NY................845-236-4265
Breaux Vineyards
  Purcellville, VA............800-492-9961
Brotherhood Winery
  Washingtonville, NY.........845-496-3661
Buena Vista Historic Tstng Rm
  Sonoma, CA..................800-926-1266
Burnley Vineyards
  Barboursville, VA...........540-832-2828
Byron Vineyard & Winery
  Santa Maria, CA.............805-938-7365
Cambria Winery
  Santa Maria, CA.............888-339-9463
Catoctin Vineyards
  Brookeville, MD.............301-774-2310
Cedar Creek Winery
  Cedarburg, WI...............800-827-8020
Chateau Grand Traverse Winery
  Traverse City, MI...........231-938-6120
Chateau Morrisette Winery
  Floyd, VA...................540-593-2865
Chateau Souverain
  Cloverdale, CA..............877-687-9463
Chicama Vineyards
  West Tisbury, MA............888-244-2262
Chouinard Vineyards & Winery
  Castro Valley, CA...........510-582-9900
Cienega Valley Winery/DeRose
  Hollister, CA...............831-636-9143
Columbia Winery
  Woodinville, WA.............425-488-2776
Cooper Vineyards
  Louisa, VA..................540-894-5474
Cosentino Winery
  Napa, CA....................800-764-1220
Cribari Vineyard Inc
  Fresno, CA..................800-277-9095
Cristom Vineyards
  Salem, OR...................503-375-3068
Cuvaison Winery
  Calistoga, CA...............707-942-6266
Delicato Family Vineyards
  Napa, CA....................707-265-1700
Douknie Winery
  Purcellville, VA............540-668-6464
E & J Gallo Winery
  Modesto, CA.................877-687-9463
Edna Valley Vineyard
  San Luis Obispo, CA.........866-979-8477
Fenestra Winery
  Livermore, CA...............800-789-9463
Fenn Valley Vineyards
  Fennville, MI...............800-432-6265
Fess Parker Winery
  Los Olivos, CA..............800-841-1104
Fetzer Vineyards
  Hopland, CA.................707-744-1250
Firelands Winery
  Sandusky, OH................800-548-9463
First Colony Winery
  Charlottesville, VA.........877-979-7105
Flynn Vineyards Winery
  Rickreall, OR...............888-427-4953
Foris Vineyards
  Cave Junction, OR...........541-592-3752
Fox Run Vineyards
  Penn Yan, NY................800-636-9786
Freemark Abbey Winery
  St Helena, CA...............800-963-9698

111

Product Categories / Beverages: Wines

Frog's Leap Winery
  Rutherford, CA. 800-959-4704
Frontenac Point Vineyard
  Trumansburg, NY 607-387-9619
Gainey Vineyard
  Santa Ynez, CA. 805-688-0558
Georgia Wines Inc
  Ringgold, GA 706-937-2177
Groth Vineyards & Winery
  Oakville, CA. 707-944-0290
Gundlach-Bundschu Winery
  Sonoma, CA 707-939-3015
Hahn Family Wines
  Soledad, CA. 831-678-4555
Handley Cellars
  Philo, CA. 800-733-3151
Hanzell Vineyards
  Sonoma, CA 707-996-3860
Hartford Family Winery
  Forestville, CA 707-887-8030
Hazlitt 1852 Vineyards
  Hector, NY 888-750-0494
Heineman Winery
  Put In Bay, OH 419-285-2811
Hermann J. Wiemer Vineyard
  Dundee, NY 800-371-7971
Heron Hill Winery
  Hammondsport, NY 800-441-4241
Kistler Vineyards
  Sebastopol, CA 707-823-5603
Le Vigne Winery
  Paso Robles, CA 800-891-6055
Maui Wine
  Kula, HI. 877-878-6058
Mayacamas Vineyards & Winery
  Napa, CA. 707-224-4030
Mcgregor Vineyard Winery
  Dundee, NY 800-272-0192
Milea Estate Vineyard
  Staatsburg, NY 845-264-0403
Nalle Winery
  Healdsburg, CA 707-433-1040
Nehalem Bay Winery
  Nehalem, OR. 888-368-9463
Nevada City Winery
  Nevada City, CA. 800-203-9463
Oasis Winery
  Hume, VA 800-304-7656
Obester Winery
  Half Moon Bay, CA 650-726-9463
Old House Vineyards
  Culpeper, VA. 540-423-1032
Pahlmeyer Winery
  St Helena, CA 707-255-2321
Plum Creek Winery
  Palisade, CO 970-464-7586
Retzlaff Vineyards
  Livermore, CA 925-447-8941
Rodney Strong Vineyards
  Healdsburg, CA 800-474-9463
Shafer Vineyards
  Napa, CA. 707-944-2877
Signorello Vineyards
  Napa, CA. 707-255-5990
Sky Vineyards
  Glen Ellen, CA 707-935-1391
Smith Vineyard & Winery
  Grass Valley, CA 530-273-7032
Sonoma-Cutrer Vineyards
  Windsor, CA 707-528-1181
Stone Mountain Vineyards
  Dyke, VA. 434-990-9463
Stonington Vineyards
  Stonington, CT 800-421-9463
Tularosa Vineyards
  Tularosa, NM 800-687-4467
Veramar Vineyard
  Berryville, VA. 540-955-5510
Veritas Vineyard
  Afton, VA. 540-456-8000
Vincent Arroyo Winery
  Calistoga, CA 707-942-6995
Wente Family Estates
  Livermore, CA 925-456-2305
White Hall Vineyards
  Crozet, VA. 434-823-8615
White Oak Vineyards & Winery
  Healdsburg, CA 707-433-8429
Whitehall Lane Winery
  St Helena, CA 707-963-9454
Whitford Cellars
  Napa, CA. 707-942-0840

Williams Selyem Winery
  Healdsburg, CA 707-433-6425
Willowcroft Farm Vineyards
  Leesburg, VA. 703-777-8161
Wintergreen Winery
  Nellysford, VA 434-361-2519
Witness Tree Vineyard LTD
  Salem, OR. 888-478-8766
Woodside Vineyards
  Menlo Park, CA 650-851-3144
Zd Wines
  Napa, CA. 800-487-7757

Gewurztraminer

Babcock Winery & Vineyards
  Lompoc, CA 805-736-1455
Chouinard Vineyards & Winery
  Castro Valley, CA 510-582-9900
Columbia Winery
  Woodinville, WA. 425-488-2776
Cosentino Winery
  Napa, CA. 800-764-1220
Fenn Valley Vineyards
  Fennville, MI 800-432-6265
Fetzer Vineyards
  Hopland, CA 707-744-1250
Foris Vineyards
  Cave Junction, OR 541-592-3752
Fox Run Vineyards
  Penn Yan, NY 800-636-9786
Gundlach-Bundschu Winery
  Sonoma, CA 707-939-3015
Hazlitt 1852 Vineyards
  Hector, NY 888-750-0494
Mcgregor Vineyard Winery
  Dundee, NY 800-272-0192
Nevada City Winery
  Nevada City, CA. 800-203-9463
Stonington Vineyards
  Stonington, CT 800-421-9463
Tualatin Estate Vineyards
  Forest Grove, OR 503-357-5005
White Hall Vineyards
  Crozet, VA. 434-823-8615

Pinot Blanc

Foris Vineyards
  Cave Junction, OR 541-592-3752
Handley Cellars
  Philo, CA. 800-733-3151
Nehalem Bay Winery
  Nehalem, OR. 888-368-9463
Tualatin Estate Vineyards
  Forest Grove, OR 503-357-5005
Witness Tree Vineyard LTD
  Salem, OR. 888-478-8766

Pinot Gris

A to Z Wineworks
  Newburg, OR 800-739-4455
Babcock Winery & Vineyards
  Lompoc, CA 805-736-1455
Cambria Winery
  Santa Maria, CA 888-339-9463
Columbia Winery
  Woodinville, WA. 425-488-2776
Cosentino Winery
  Napa, CA. 800-764-1220
Cristom Vineyards
  Salem, OR. 503-375-3068
Flynn Vineyards Winery
  Rickreall, OR 888-427-4953
Foris Vineyards
  Cave Junction, OR 541-592-3752
Hahn Family Wines
  Soledad, CA. 831-678-4555
Handley Cellars
  Philo, CA. 800-733-3151
Hazlitt 1852 Vineyards
  Hector, NY 888-750-0494
Heineman Winery
  Put In Bay, OH 419-285-2811
Henry Estate Winery
  Umpqua, OR. 800-782-2686
Jefferson Vineyards
  Charlottesville, VA 800-272-3042
Kistler Vineyards
  Sebastopol, CA 707-823-5603
Seven Hills Winery
  Walla Walla, WA. 877-777-7870

White Hall Vineyards
  Crozet, VA. 434-823-8615

Riesling

A to Z Wineworks
  Newburg, OR 800-739-4455
Abingdon Vineyard & Winery
  Abingdon, VA. 276-623-1255
Applewood Winery
  Warwick, NY 845-988-9292
Autumn Hill Vineyards/Blue Ridge Wine
  Stanardsville, VA 434-985-6100
Barboursville Vineyards
  Barboursville, VA. 540-832-3824
Brotherhood Winery
  Washingtonville, NY 845-496-3661
Catoctin Vineyards
  Brookeville, MD 301-774-2310
Chateau Grand Traverse Winery
  Traverse City, MI 231-938-6120
Chouinard Vineyards & Winery
  Castro Valley, CA 510-582-9900
Columbia Winery
  Woodinville, WA. 425-488-2776
Douknie Winery
  Purcellville, VA. 540-668-6464
E & J Gallo Winery
  Modesto, CA 877-687-9463
Fenestra Winery
  Livermore, CA 800-789-9463
Fenn Valley Vineyards
  Fennville, MI 800-432-6265
Fess Parker Winery
  Los Olivos, CA 800-841-1104
Fetzer Vineyards
  Hopland, CA 707-744-1250
Firelands Winery
  Sandusky, OH 800-548-9463
Fox Run Vineyards
  Penn Yan, NY 800-636-9786
Freemark Abbey Winery
  St Helena, CA 800-963-9698
Frontenac Point Vineyard
  Trumansburg, NY 607-387-9619
Greenwood Ridge Vineyards
  Philo, CA. 707-895-2002
Gundlach-Bundschu Winery
  Sonoma, CA 707-939-3015
Handley Cellars
  Philo, CA. 800-733-3151
Hazlitt 1852 Vineyards
  Hector, NY 888-750-0494
Heineman Winery
  Put In Bay, OH 419-285-2811
Hermann J. Wiemer Vineyard
  Dundee, NY 800-371-7971
Heron Hill Winery
  Hammondsport, NY 800-441-4241
Jefferson Vineyards
  Charlottesville, VA 800-272-3042
Mcgregor Vineyard Winery
  Dundee, NY 800-272-0192
Milea Estate Vineyard
  Staatsburg, NY 845-264-0403
Oasis Winery
  Hume, VA 800-304-7656
Obester Winery
  Half Moon Bay, CA 650-726-9463
Plum Creek Winery
  Palisade, CO 970-464-7586
Seven Hills Winery
  Walla Walla, WA. 877-777-7870
Tualatin Estate Vineyards
  Forest Grove, OR 503-357-5005
Veramar Vineyard
  Berryville, VA. 540-955-5510
Westbend Vinyards
  Lewisville, NC 866-901-5032
Willowcroft Farm Vineyards
  Leesburg, VA. 703-777-8161
Wintergreen Winery
  Nellysford, VA 434-361-2519

Sauvignon Blanc

Babcock Winery & Vineyards
  Lompoc, CA 805-736-1455
Brotherhood Winery
  Washingtonville, NY 845-496-3661
Chateau Souverain
  Cloverdale, CA 877-687-9463

Product Categories / Beverages: Wines

Chicama Vineyards
  West Tisbury, MA 888-244-2262
Chouinard Vineyards & Winery
  Castro Valley, CA 510-582-9900
Cosentino Winery
  Napa, CA 800-764-1220
Delicato Family Vineyards
  Napa, CA 707-265-1700
E & J Gallo Winery
  Modesto, CA 877-687-9463
Fenestra Winery
  Livermore, CA 800-789-9463
Fetzer Vineyards
  Hopland, CA 707-744-1250
Frog's Leap Winery
  Rutherford, CA 800-959-4704
Gainey Vineyard
  Santa Ynez, CA 805-688-0558
Groth Vineyards & Winery
  Oakville, CA 707-944-0290
Handley Cellars
  Philo, CA 800-733-3151
Honig Vineyard and Winery
  Rutherford, CA 800-929-2217
Mayacamas Vineyards & Winery
  Napa, CA 707-224-4030
Nalle Winery
  Healdsburg, CA 707-433-1040
Nevada City Winery
  Nevada City, CA 800-203-9463
Plum Creek Winery
  Palisade, CO 970-464-7586
Retzlaff Vineyards
  Livermore, CA 925-447-8941
Rodney Strong Vineyards
  Healdsburg, CA 800-474-9463
Signorello Vineyards
  Napa, CA 707-255-5990
Spottswoode
  St Helena, CA 707-963-0134
Wente Family Estates
  Livermore, CA 925-456-2305
Westbend Vinyards
  Lewisville, NC 866-901-5032
White Oak Vineyards & Winery
  Healdsburg, CA 707-433-8429
Whitehall Lane Winery
  St Helena, CA 707-963-9454

Viognier

Amrhein's Wine Cellars
  Bent Mountain, VA 540-929-4632
Breaux Vineyards
  Purcellville, VA 800-492-9961
Brotherhood Winery
  Washingtonville, NY 845-496-3661
Cambria Winery
  Santa Maria, CA 888-339-9463
Chicama Vineyards
  West Tisbury, MA 888-244-2262
Cienega Valley Winery/DeRose
  Hollister, CA 831-636-9143
Columbia Winery
  Woodinville, WA 425-488-2776
Cosentino Winery
  Napa, CA 800-764-1220
Cristom Vineyards
  Salem, OR 503-375-3068
Fenestra Winery
  Livermore, CA 800-789-9463
Fess Parker Winery
  Los Olivos, CA 800-841-1104
Seven Hills Winery
  Walla Walla, WA 877-777-7870
Signorello Vineyards
  Napa, CA 707-255-5990
Tularosa Vineyards
  Tularosa, NM 800-687-4467
Witness Tree Vineyard LTD
  Salem, OR 888-478-8766

White Grapes

Chateau Grand Traverse Winery
  Traverse City, MI 231-938-6120
Chicama Vineyards
  West Tisbury, MA 888-244-2262
Chouinard Vineyards & Winery
  Castro Valley, CA 510-582-9900
Columbia Winery
  Woodinville, WA 425-488-2776
Cribari Vineyard Inc
  Fresno, CA 800-277-9095
Galleano Winery
  Mira Loma, CA 951-685-5376
Heineman Winery
  Put In Bay, OH 419-285-2811
Maui Wine
  Kula, HI 877-878-6058
Mt Baker Vineyards
  Everson, WA 360-592-2300
Newport Vineyards & Winery
  Middletown, RI 401-848-5161
Oliver Winery
  Bloomington, IN 800-258-2783
Steltzner Vineyards
  Napa, CA 707-707-9463
Swedish Hill Vineyard & Winery
  Romulus, NY 888-549-9463
Tabor Hill Winery & Restaurant
  Buchanan, MI 800-283-3363
V Sattui Winery
  St Helena, CA 707-963-7774
Wiederkehr Wine Cellars Inc
  Altus, AR 800-622-9463
Wild Horse Winery & Vineyards
  Templeton, CA 805-434-2541
Wildhurst Vineyards
  Kelseyville, CA 800-595-9463
Wooden Valley Winery
  Fairfield, CA 707-864-0730

Candy & Confectionery

Candy

21st Century Snack Foods
  Ronkonkoma, NY 631-588-8000
A La Carte
  Chicago, IL 800-722-2370
A Southern Season
  Hillsborough, NC 800-253-3663
Abbott's Candy Shop
  Hagerstown, IN 877-801-1200
Abdallah Candies & Gifts
  Burnsville, MN 952-890-0859
Across Foods, LLC
  New Hope, PA 215-693-6274
Adirondack Maple Farms
  Fonda, NY 518-853-4022
Aglamesis Bros Ice Cream
  Cincinnati, OH 513-531-5196
Alaska Jacks
  Anchorage, AK 888-660-2257
All Wrapped Up
  Plantation, FL 800-891-2194
Ameri-Suisse Group
  South Plainfield, NJ 908-222-1001
American Food Products Inc
  Methuen, MA 978-682-1855
American Licorice
  La Porte, IL 866-442-2783
American Mint
  New York, NY 800-401-6468
American Specialty Confections
  Saint Paul, MN 800-776-2085
AmeriGift
  Oxnard, CA 800-421-9039
Amy's Candy Bar
  Chicago, IL 773-942-6386
Andre Prost Inc
  Old Saybrook, CT 800-243-0897
Andre's Confiserie Suisse
  Kansas City, MO 800-892-1234
Ann Hemyng Candy Inc
  Trumbauersville, PA 800-779-7004
Annabelle Candy Co Inc
  Hayward, CA 510-783-2900
Arcor USA
  Coral Gables, FL 800-572-7267
Arizona Cowboy
  Phoenix, AZ 800-529-8627
Art CoCo Chocolate Company
  Geneva, IL 877-232-9901
Artesian Honey Producers
  Artesian, SD 605-527-2423
Artisan Confections
  Hershey, PA 866-237-0152
Arway Confections Inc
  Chicago, IL 800-695-0612
Asher's Chocolates
  Kulpsville, PA 855-827-4377
Asti Holdings Ltd
  New Westminster, BC 604-523-6866
Atkinson Candy Co
  Lufkin, TX 936-639-2333
Aunt Aggie De's Pralines
  Sinton, TX 800-333-9354
Aunt Sally's Praline Shops
  New Orleans, LA 800-642-7257
Aurora Products
  Orange, CT 800-398-1048
Azar Nut Co
  El Paso, TX 800-351-8178
B & R Classics LLC
  Huntington, NY 631-427-5675
B. Nutty
  Oakland, CA 510-374-4658
Bacci Chocolate Design
  Swampscott, MA 888-725-2877
Baker Candy Company
  Snohomish, WA 425-422-6331
Baker Maid Products, Inc.
  New Orleans, LA 800-664-7882
Baker's Candies Factory Store
  Greenwood, NE 800-804-7330
Balticshop.Com LLC
  Glastonbury, CT 800-506-2312
Banner Candy Manufacturing Company
  Brooklyn, NY 718-647-4747

Barcelona Nut Co
  Baltimore, MD 800-296-6887
Bari & Gail
  Walpole, MA 800-828-9318
Bazaar Inc
  River Grove, IL 800-736-1888
Bee International
  Chula Vista, CA 800-421-6465
Beehive Botanicals
  Hayward, WI 800-233-4483
Belly Treats, Inc.
  Toronto, ON 416-418-3285
Ben Heggy's Candy Co
  Canton, OH 330-455-7703
Bergen Marzipan & Chocolate
  Bergenfield, NJ 201-385-8343
Betty Jane Homemade Candy
  Dubuque, IA 800-642-1254
Betty Lou's
  McMinnville, OR 800-242-5205
Bidwell Candies
  Mattoon, IL 217-234-3858
Birnn Chocolates of Vermont
  South Burlington, VT 800-338-3141
Biscomerica Corporation
  Rialto, CA 909-877-5997
Bissinger's Handcrafted Chocolatier
  St. Louis, MO 314-615-2400
Black Forest Organic
  Oakbrook Terrace, IL 800-323-1768
Black Hound New York
  Brooklyn, NY 800-344-4417
Blanton's
  Frankfort, KY 502-223-9874
Blommer Chocolate Co
  Chicago, IL 800-621-1606
Blommer Chocolate Co
  East Greenville, PA 800-825-8181
Bluebird Restaurant
  Logan, UT 435-752-3155
Boca Bons East
  Greenacres, FL 800-314-2835
Boston America Corporation
  Woburn, MA 781-933-3535
Boston Fruit Slice & Confectionery Corporation
  Lawrence, MA 978-686-2699
Bread & Chocolate Inc
  Wells River, VT 800-524-6715
British Aisles, LTD.
  Nashua, NH 800-520-8565
Brittle Kittle
  Tigard, OR 800-447-2128
Buonitalia
  New York, NY 212-633-9090
Burke Candy Ingredients Inc
  Milwaukee, WI 888-287-5350
Butterfields
  Nashville, NC 800-945-5957
C Howard Co
  Bellport, NY 631-286-7940
Cadbury Adams
  Toronto, ON 416-590-5000
Cadbury Trebor Allan
  Granby, QC 800-387-3267
Calif Snack Foods
  South El Monte, CA 626-454-4099
Cambridge Brands Inc
  Cambridge, MA 617-491-2500
Cameo Confections
  Bay Village, OH 440-871-5732
Cameron Birch Syrup & Confections
  Wasilla, AK 800-962-4724
Campbell Soup Co.
  Camden, NJ 800-257-8443
Candy Bouquet of Elko
  Elko, NV 888-855-3391
Candy Central
  East Hanover, NJ
Candy Mountain Sweets & Treats
  Atlanta, GA 800-621-1954
Canelake's Candy
  Virginia, MN 888-928-8889
Capco Enterprises
  East Hanover, NJ 800-252-1011
Cape Cod Sweets, LLC
  Pocasset, MA 508-564-5840

Caprine Estates
  Bellbrook, OH 937-848-7406
Caribbean Cookie Company
  Virginia Beach, VA 800-326-5200
Carolyn's Gourmet
  Concord, MA 800-656-2940
Carrie's Chocolates
  Edmonton, AB 877-778-2462
Catoris Candies Inc
  New Kensington, PA 724-335-4371
Charlotte's Confections
  Millbrae, CA 800-798-2427
Chase & Poe Candy Co
  St Joseph, MO 800-786-1625
Cheese Straws & More
  Monroe, LA 800-997-1921
Cheri's Desert Harvest
  Tucson, AZ 800-743-1141
Chevalier Chocolates
  Enfield, CT 860-741-3330
Chex Finer Foods Inc
  Mansfield, MA 800-227-8114
Chocoholics Divine Desserts
  Linden, CA 800-760-2462
Chocolat Belge Heyez
  St-Lazare-De-Bellechasse, QC 450-653-5616
Chocolat Jean Talon
  Montreal, QC 888-333-8540
Chocolat Michel Cluizel
  New York, NY 646-415-9126
Chocolate By Design Inc
  Ronkonkoma, NY 631-737-0082
Chocolate Moon
  Asheville, NC 800-723-1236
Chocolate Smith
  Santa Fe, NM 505-473-2111
Chocolate Soup
  Steamboat Springs, CO 970-870-0224
Chocolate Street of Hartville
  Hartville, OH 888-853-5904
Chocolate Studio
  Norristown, PA 610-272-3872
Chocolaterie Stam
  Des Moines, IA 877-782-6246
Chocolates by Mark
  Houston, TX 832-736-2626
Chocolates By Mr Roberts
  Boca Raton, FL 561-392-3007
Chocolati Handmade Chocolates
  Seattle, WA 206-784-5212
Chocolatier
  Exeter, NH 888-246-5528
Chris Candies Inc
  Pittsburgh, PA 412-322-9400
Clasen Quality Chocolate
  Madison, WI 877-459-4500
Classic Confectionery
  Fort Worth, TX 800-674-4435
Clear-Vu Industries
  Ashland, MA 508-881-9100
Cloud Nine
  Claremont, CA 909-624-3147
CNS Confectionery Products
  Bayonne, NJ 888-823-4330
Cocomels by JJ's Sweets
  Boulder, CO 303-800-6492
Colts Chocolates
  Nashville, TN 615-251-0100
Confectionately Yours LTD
  Buffalo Grove, IL 800-875-6978
ConSup North America
  Lincoln Park, NJ 973-628-7330
Cowgirl Chocolates
  Moscow, ID 888-882-4098
Cranberry Sweets Co
  Coos Bay, OR 800-527-5748
Creative Cotton
  Northbrook, IL 847-291-4128
Creme Curls
  Hudsonville, MI 800-466-1219
Croft's Crackers
  Monroe, WI 608-325-1223
Crown Candy Corp
  Macon, GA 800-241-3529
Crystal Temptations
  North Arlington, NJ 201-246-7990

Product Categories / Candy & Confectionery: Candy

CTC Manufacturing
 Calgary, AB 800-668-7677
Cummings Studio Chocolates
 Salt Lake City, UT 800-537-3957
Cupid Candies
 Chicago, IL 773-925-8191
Custom Confections & More
 Algonquin, IL 832-420-5944
Cyclone Enterprises Inc
 Houston, TX 281-872-0087
Daprano & Company
 Charlotte, NC 877-365-2337
Dare Foods
 Spartanburg, SC 800-668-3273
Das Foods
 Chicago, IL 312-224-8590
David Bradley Chocolatier
 Windsor, NJ 877-289-7933
Day Spring Enterprises
 Cheektowaga, NY 800-879-7677
Daymar Select Fine Coffees
 El Cajon, CA 800-466-7590
Dayton Nut Specialties
 Springboro, OH 937-743-4377
Debrand Chocolatier
 Fort Wayne, IN 260-969-8333
Decko Products Inc
 Sandusky, OH 800-537-6143
Delancey Dessert Company
 New York, NY 800-254-5254
Dessert Innovations Inc
 Atlanta, GA 800-359-7351
Di Camillo Baking Co
 Niagara Falls, NY 800-634-4363
Dilettante Chocolates
 Kent, WA 800-800-9490
Dillon Candy Co
 Boston, GA 800-382-8338
Dipasa USA Inc
 Brownsville, TX 956-831-4072
Divine Delights
 Petaluma, CA 800-443-2836
Donaldson's Finer Chocolates
 Lebanon, IN 800-975-7236
Donells Candies
 Casper, WY 877-461-2009
Donna & Company
 Cranford, NJ 908-272-4380
Donnelly Fine Chocolates
 Santa Cruz, CA 888-685-1871
Dorothy Timberlake Candies
 Madison, NH 603-447-2221
Doscher's Candies Co.
 Cincinnati, OH 513-381-8656
Doumak Inc
 Elk Grove Village, IL 800-323-0318
Downeast Candies
 Boothbay Harbor, ME 207-633-5178
Dundee Brandied Fruit Co
 Dundee, OR 503-537-2500
Dundee Candy Shop
 Louisville, KY 866-877-9266
Dundee Groves
 Dundee, FL 800-294-2266
Dynamic Confections
 Salt Lake City, UT 801-355-4422
Eclat Chocolate
 West Chester, PA 610-692-5206
EcoNatural Solutions
 Boulder, CO 303-357-5682
Ed & Don's Of Hawaii Inc
 Honolulu, HI 808-423-8200
Eda's Sugar Free
 Philadelphia, PA 215-324-3412
Edner Corporation
 Hayward, CA 510-441-8504
Elaine's Toffee Co.
 Clayton, CA 800-883-3050
Elegant Edibles
 Houston, TX 800-227-3226
Elmer Chocolate®
 Ponchatoula, LA 800-843-9537
Emmy's Candy from Belgium
 Charlotte, NC 866-879-1901
Enstrom Candies, Inc.
 Grand Junction, CO 800-367-8766
Esther Price Candies & Gifts
 Dayton, OH 855-337-8437
Euphoria Chocolate Company
 Eugene, OR 541-344-4914
Evans Creole Candy
 New Orleans, LA 800-637-6675

F B Washburn Candy Corp
 Brockton, MA 508-588-0820
Fabio Imports
 Oceanside, CA 760-726-7040
Family Sweets Candy Company
 Elk Grove Village, IL 800-334-1607
Faroh Candies
 Middleburg Heights, OH 440-888-9866
Farr Candy Company
 Idaho Falls, ID 208-522-8215
Fernando C Pujals & Bros
 Guaynabo, PR 787-792-3080
Ferrara Bakery & Cafe
 New York, NY 212-226-6150
Ferrara Candy Co Inc
 Chicago, IL 800-323-1768
Ficon
 St Louis, MO 888-569-4099
Fieldbrook Foods Corp.
 Dunkirk, NY 800-333-0805
Fitzkee's Candies Inc
 York, PA 717-741-1031
Flix Candy
 Niles, IL 847-647-1370
Foley's Chocolates & Candies
 Richmond, BC 888-236-5397
Forbes Candies
 Virginia Beach, VA 800-626-5898
Foreign Candy Company
 Hull, IA 800-831-8541
Fralinger's
 Atlantic City, NJ 800-938-2339
Frankford Candy & Chocolate Co
 Philadelphia, PA 800-523-9090
Freed, Teller & Freed
 South San Francisco, CA 800-370-7371
G Debbas Chocolatier
 Fresno, CA 559-294-2071
G Scaccianoce & Co
 Bronx, NY 718-991-4462
Gardners Candies Inc
 Tyrone, PA 800-242-2639
Gearharts Fine Chocolates
 Charlottesville, VA 800-625-0595
Gene & Boots Candies Inc
 Perryopolis, PA 800-864-4222
Georgia Nut Co
 Skokie, IL 877-674-2993
Germack Pistachio Co
 Detroit, MI 800-872-4006
Gia Michaels Confections Inc
 Elmont, NY 516-354-3905
Gifford's Ice Cream & Candy Co
 Silver Spring, MA 800-708-1938
Gimbals Fine Candies
 S San Francisco, CA 800-344-6225
Gingerhaus, LLC
 Norfolk, VA 757-348-4274
GKI Foods
 Brighton, MI 248-486-0055
Glee Gum
 Providence, RI 401-351-6415
GNS Foods
 Arlington, TX 817-795-4671
Godiva Chocolatier
 New York, NY 800-946-3482
Goetze's Candy Co
 Baltimore, MD 410-342-2010
Golden Edibles LLC
 Davie, FL 866-779-7781
Golden Fluff Popcorn Co
 Lakewood, NJ 732-367-5448
Goodart Candy Inc
 Lubbock, TX 806-747-2600
Govadinas Fitness Foods
 San Diego, CA 800-900-0108
Govatos Chocolates
 Wilmington, DE 888-799-5252
Graeter's Mfg. Co.
 Cincinnati, OH 800-721-3323
Grandpops Lollipops
 Kansas City, MO 800-255-7873
Gray & Company
 Hart, MI 800-551-6009
Great Expectations Confectionery Gourmet Foods
 Chicago, IL 773-525-4865
Green County Foods
 Monroe, WI 800-233-3564
Green Mountain Chocolate Inc
 Franklin, MA 508-520-7160
Greenwell Farms Inc
 Kealakekua, HI 888-592-5662

Groovy Candies
 Cleveland, OH 888-729-1960
Gurley's Foods
 Willmar, MN 800-426-7845
GWB Foods Corporation
 Brooklyn, NY 877-977-7610
H.B. Trading
 Totowa, NJ 973-812-1022
Haby's Alsatian Bakery
 Castroville, TX 830-538-2118
Happy Goat
 Boston, MA 617-549-2776
Hauser Chocolates
 Westerly, RI 888-599-8231
Haven's Candies
 Westbrook, ME 800-639-6309
Hawaii Candy Inc
 Honolulu, HI 800-303-2507
Hawaiian Host Inc
 Honolulu, HI 888-414-4678
Healthy Food Brands LLC
 Brooklyn, NY 212-444-9909
Heavenly Organics, LLC
 Longmont, CO 641-636-2095
Hebert Candies
 Shrewsbury, MA 866-609-6533
Helms Candy Co., Inc
 Bristol, VA 276-669-2533
Hernan
 Del Rio, TX 646-263-3598
Hershey Co.
 Hershey, PA 800-468-1714
Hialeah Products Co
 Hollywood, FL 800-923-3379
Hickory Farms
 Maumee, OH 800-753-8558
Hickory Harvest Foods
 Akron, OH 800-448-6887
Holistic Products Corporation
 Englewood, NJ 800-221-0308
Hospitality Mints LLC
 Boone, NC 800-334-5181
House of Spices
 Flushing, NY 718-507-4600
Humphrey Co
 Cleveland, OH 800-486-3739
Hyde Candy Company
 Seattle, WA 206-322-5743
Imani Chimani Chocolate
 Brooklyn, NY 718-484-1011
Imperial Nougat Co
 Santa Fe Springs, CA 562-693-8423
Indianola Pecan House Inc
 Indianola, MS 800-541-6252
International Home Foods
 Parsippany, NJ 973-359-9920
Issimo Food Group
 La Jolla, CA 619-260-1900
Jakeman's Maple Products
 Beachville, ON 800-382-9795
James Candy Company
 Atlantic City, NJ 800-441-1404
Jason & Son Specialty Foods
 Rancho Cordova, CA 800-810-9093
Jed's Maple Products
 Derby, VT 802-766-2700
Jerry's Nut House
 Denver, CO 303-861-2262
Jeryl's Jems
 Tappan, NY 201-236-8372
Jo's Candies
 Torrance, CA 800-770-1946
Joe Clark Fund Raising Candies
 Tarentum, PA 888-459-9520
Joray Candy
 Brooklyn, NY 718-871-6300
Josh Early Candies
 Allentown, PA 610-395-4321
Joyva Corp
 Brooklyn, NY 718-497-0170
Judy's Cream Caramels
 Sherwood, OR 503-625-7161
Just Born Inc
 Bethlehem, PA 800-445-5787
K & F Select Fine Coffees
 Portland, OR 800-558-7788
Kara Chocolates
 Orem, UT 800-284-5272
Kastner's Pastry Shop & Grocery
 Surfside, FL 305-866-6993
Kate Latter Candy Company
 New Orleans, LA 800-825-5359

Product Categories / Candy & Confectionery: Candy

Kateri Foods
   Hopkins, MN 800-330-8351
Kehr's candies
   Milwaukee, WI 414-344-4305
Kemach Food Products
   Brooklyn, NY 718-272-5655
Kencraft, Inc.
   Alpine, UT 800-377-4368
Kenny's Candy & Confections
   Perham, MN
Kerr Brothers
   Toronto, ON 416-252-7341
Key III Candies
   Fort Wayne, IN 800-752-2382
Kidsmania
   Santa Fe Springs, CA 562-946-8822
King Nut Co
   Solon, OH 800-860-5464
Kloss Manufacturing Co Inc
   Allentown, PA. 800-445-7100
Knudsen Candy
   Hayward, CA 800-736-6887
Koeze Company
   Grand Rapids, MI 800-555-9688
Koppers Chocolate
   Cranford, NJ 800-325-0026
Krema Nut Co
   Columbus, OH 800-222-4132
L C Good Candy Company
   Allentown, PA 610-432-3290
Lagomarcino's Confectionery
   Moline, IL 309-764-1814
Lake Champlain Chocolates
   Burlington, VT 800-634-8105
Lammes Candies
   Austin, TX. 800-252-1885
Lanco
   Hauppauge, NY 800-938-4500
Landies Candies Co
   Buffalo, NY. 800-955-2634
Larosa Bakery Inc
   Shrewsbury, NJ 800-527-6722
Laura Paige Candy Company
   Newburgh, NY 845-566-4209
Layman Distributing
   Salem, VA 800-237-1319
Le Grand Confectionary
   Sacramento, CA 888-361-2125
Leader Candies
   Brooklyn, NY 718-366-6900
Len Libby Chocolatier-Maine
   Scarborough, ME 207-883-4897
Lerro Candy Company
   Darby, PA 610-461-8886
Loghouse Foods
   Minneapolis, MN 763-546-8395
Long Grove Confectionary
   Buffalo Grove, IL 800-373-3102
Longford-Hamilton Company
   Beaverton, OR 503-642-5661
Loretta's Authentic Pralines
   New Orleans, LA 504-529-6170
Lotte USA Inc
   Battle Creek, MI 269-963-6664
Lou-Retta's Custom Chocolates
   Buffalo, NY. 716-833-7111
Louis J Rheb Candy Co
   Baltimore, MD 800-514-8293
Lowery's Home Made Candies
   Muncie, IN 800-541-3340
Lucille's Own Make Candies
   Manahawkin, NJ. 800-426-9168
Lucky You
   San Diego, CA 619-450-6700
Ludo LLC
   Solon, OH 440-542-6000
Ludwick's Frozen Donuts
   Grand Rapids, MI 800-366-8816
Lukas Confections
   York, PA 717-843-0921
Lynard Company
   Stamford, CT. 203-323-0231
Mac Farms Of Hawaii Inc
   Captain Cook, HI 808-328-2435
Madrona Specialty Foods LLC
   Seattle, WA 425-656-2997
Magna Foods Corporation
   City of Industry, CA 800-995-4394
Manhattan Food Brands, LLC
   Metuchen, NJ 732-906-2168
Maple Grove Farms Of Vermont
   St Johnsbury, VT. 802-748-5141

Mari's Candy
   Chicago, IL. 773-254-3351
Marich Confectionery
   Hollister, CA. 800-624-7055
Maries Candies
   West Liberty, OH 866-465-5781
Marin Food Specialties
   Byron, CA 925-634-6126
Marlow Candy & Nut Co
   Englewood, NJ 201-569-3725
Mars Inc.
   McLean, VA 703-821-4900
Mary of Puddin Hill
   Palestine, TX. 800-545-8889
MarySue.com
   Baltimore, MD 800-662-2639
Marzipan Specialties Inc
   Nashville, TN 615-226-4800
Matangos Candies
   Harrisburg, PA 717-234-0882
Maxfield Candy
   Salt Lake City, UT 800-288-8002
Menehune Mac
   Honolulu, HI 808-841-3344
Merb's Candies
   St Louis, MO 314-832-7117
Merlin Candies
   Harahan, LA 800-899-1549
Michelle Chocolatiers
   Colorado Springs, CO. 888-447-3654
Midwest Nut Co
   Minneapolis, MN 800-328-5502
Miesse Candies
   Lancaster, PA. 717-392-6011
Mister Snacks Inc
   Amherst, NY. 800-333-6393
Mitch Chocolate
   Melville, NY 631-777-2400
Mom N' Pops Inc
   New Windsor, NY. 845-567-0640
Monastery Fruitcake
   Martinsburg, WV 304-596-2024
Monterrey Products
   San Antonio, TX. 210-435-2872
Moo Chocolate/Organic Children's Chocolate LLC
   Cos Cob, CT 203-561-8864
Moonlight Gourmet
   Tyler, TX 903-581-1228
Moore's Candies
   Baltimore, MD 410-836-8840
Mother Nature's Goodies
   Yucaipa, CA 909-795-6018
Mount Franklin Foods
   El Paso, TX 800-351-8178
Mrs Annie's Peanut Patch
   Floresville, TX 830-393-7845
Multiflex Company
   Hawthorne, NJ 973-636-9700
Munson's Chocolates
   Bolton, CT 888-686-7667
Muth's Candy Store
   Louisville, KY 502-582-2639
Naron Mary Sue Candies
   Baltimore, MD 800-662-2639
Nassau Candy Distributors
   Hicksville, NY 516-433-7100
National Importers
   Richmond, BC 888-894-6464
Natural Foods Inc
   Toledo, OH 419-537-1711
Natural Rush
   San Francisco, CA 415-863-2503
Nature's Candy
   Fredericksburg, TX. 800-729-0085
Naylor Candies Inc
   Mt Wolf, PA 717-266-2706
Neal's Chocolates
   Salt Lake City, UT 801-521-6500
New Century Snacks
   City of Commerce, CA 800-688-6887
Newton Candy Company
   Houston, TX. 713-691-6969
Niagara Chocolates
   Buffalo, NY. 877-261-7887
Nora's Candy Shop
   Rome, NY 888-544-8224
Northwest Chocolate Factory
   Salem, OR. 503-362-1340
Northwoods Candy Emporium
   Branson, MO. 417-332-1010
Nutty Bavarian
   Sanford, FL 800-382-4788

Oak Leaf Confections
   877-261-7887
OH Chocolate
   Seattle, WA 206-329-8777
Oh, Sugar! LLC
   Roswell, GA 866-557-8427
Old Dominion Peanut Corp
   Norfolk, VA. 800-368-6887
Old Monmouth Candies
   Freehold, NJ 732-462-1311
Old Time Candy Co
   Lagrange, OH 440-355-4345
Olde Tyme Food Corporation
   East Longmeadow, MA 800-356-6533
Olde Tyme Mercantile
   Arroyo Grande, CA. 805-489-7991
Ole Smoky Candy Kitchen
   Gatlinburg, TN 865-436-4716
Olivier's Candies
   Calgary, AB. 403-266-6028
Ooh La La Candy
   855-817-1896
Pacific Gold Marketing
   Arlington, TX. 817-795-4671
Palmer Candy Co
   Sioux City, IA 800-831-0828
Pangburn Candy Company
   Fort Worth, TX 817-332-8856
Pantry Shelf/Mixxm
   Hutchinson, KS. 800-968-3346
Papas Chris A & Son Co
   Covington, KY 859-431-0499
Parker Products
   Fort Worth, TX 817-336-7441
Parkside Candy Co
   Buffalo, NY. 716-833-7540
Patsy's Candy
   Colorado Springs, CO. 866-372-8797
Paul's Candy Factory
   Salt Lake City, UT 800-825-9912
Paulaur Corp
   Cranbury, NJ 609-395-8844
Peanut Patch Gift Shop
   Courtland, VA. 800-544-0896
Pearl River Pastry & Chocolate
   Pearl River, NY 800-632-2639
Pearson Candy Co
   St Paul, MN. 651-698-0356
Pease's Candy
   Springfield, IL. 217-523-3721
Pecan Deluxe Candy Co
   Dallas, TX. 800-733-3589
Perfetti Van Melle USA Inc
   Erlanger, KY 859-283-1234
Pez Candy Inc
   Orange, CT 203-795-0531
Pfizer
   New York, NY 800-879-3477
Phillip's Candy House
   Dorchester, MA. 617-282-2090
Phillips Candies
   Seaside, OR. 503-738-5402
Piedmont Candy Co
   Lexington, NC 336-248-2477
Pine River Pre-Pack Inc
   Newton, WI. 920-726-4216
Pippin Snack Pecans
   Albany, GA 800-554-6887
Plantation Candies
   Telford, PA 888-678-6468
Plyley's Candy
   Lagrange, IN. 877-665-2778
Popcorn Connection
   North Hollywood, CA 800-852-2676
Poppers Supply Company
   Allentown, PA. 800-457-9810
Poppingfun Inc
   Neenah, WI 920-486-7210
Priester's Pecans
   Fort Deposit, AL 866-477-4736
Prifti Candy Company
   Worcester, MA 800-447-7438
Primrose Candy Co
   Chicago, IL. 800-268-9522
Prince of Peace
   Hayward, CA 800-732-2328
Produits Alimentaire
   St Lambert De Lauzon, QC 800-463-1787
Project 7
   San Clemente, CA. 949-891-0729
Promotion in Motion Companies
   Closter, NJ. 800-369-7391

Product Categories / Candy & Confectionery: Candy

Pulakos 926 Chocolate
 Erie, PA 814-452-4026
Pure Dark
 Hackettstown, NJ 973-856-1899
Purity Candy Co
 Lewisburg, PA 800-821-4748
Quality Candy Company
 Walnut, CA 909-444-1025
Queen Bee Gardens
 Lovell, WY 800-225-7553
Queensway Foods Company
 Burlingame, CA 650-871-7770
Quigley Industries Inc
 Farmington, MI 800-367-2441
Quintessential Chocolates
 Fredericksburg, TX 800-842-3382
R.L. Albert & Son
 Stamford, CT 203-622-8655
R.M. Palmer Co.
 West Reading, PA 610-372-8971
Ragold Confections
 Wilton Manors, FL 954-566-9092
Realsalt
 Heber City, UT 800-367-7258
Rebecca-Ruth Candy Factory
 Frankfort, KY 800-444-3866
Red Rocker Candy
 Troy, VA 434-589-2011
Republica Del Cacao LLC
 Long Beach, CA 932-256-1320
Richards Maple Products
 Chardon, OH 800-352-4052
Richardson Brands Co
 Canajoharie, NY 518-673-3553
Ricos Candy Snack & Bakery
 Hialeah, FL 305-885-7392
Riddles' Sweet Impressions
 Edmonton, AB 780-465-8085
Rigoni Di Asiago
 Miami, FL 305-470-7583
Rito Mints
 Trois Rivieres, QC 819-379-1449
Rivard Popcorn Products
 Lancaster, PA 717-898-7131
Riverdale Fine Foods
 Dayton, OH 800-548-1304
Rosalind Candy Castle Inc
 New Brighton, PA 724-843-1144
Rosetti's Fine Foods Biscotti
 Clovis, CA 559-323-6450
Ross Fine Candies
 Waterford, MI 248-682-5640
Ruger LLC
 Bethesda, MD 301-675-2398
Runk Candy Company
 Cincinnati, OH 800-641-8551
Russell Stover Candies Inc.
 Kansas City, MO 800-777-4004
Ruth Hunt Candy Co
 Mt Sterling, KY 800-927-0302
S P Enterprises
 Las Vegas, NV 800-746-4774
S Zitner Co
 Philadelphia, PA 215-229-9828
S.L. Kaye Company
 New York, NY 212-683-5600
Sahagian & Associates
 Oak Park, IL 800-327-9273
Salem Old Fashioned Candies
 Salem, MA 978-744-3242
Sally Lane's Candy Farm
 Paris, TN 731-642-5801
Sambets Cajun Deli
 Austin, TX 800-472-6238
Sanders Candy Inc
 Clinton Twp, MI 800-852-2253
Sandy Candy
 Chester Springs, PA 800-386-7263
Sconza Candy Co
 Oakdale, CA 877-568-8137
Scott's Candy
 Glennville, GA 800-356-2100
Scott-Bathgate
 Winnipeg, MB 800-216-2990
Scripture Candy
 Birmingham, AL 888-317-7333
Seattle Bar Company
 Seattle, WA 206-601-4301
Seattle Gourmet Foods
 Tukwila, WA 800-800-9490
See's Candies
 Carson, CA 800-347-7337
Senor Murphy Candymaker
 Santa Fe, NM 877-988-4311
Shaker Country Meadowsweets
 Hillside, NJ 800-524-1304
Shane Candy Co
 Philadelphia, PA 215-922-1048
Sherbrooke OEM Ltd
 Sherbrooke, QC 866-851-2579
Sherm Edwards Candies
 Trafford, PA 800-436-5424
Sifers Valomilk Candy Co
 Shawnee, KS 913-722-0991
Silver Sweet Candies
 Lawrence, MA 978-688-0474
Silverland Bakery
 Forest Park, IL 708-488-0800
Simply Scruptious Confections
 Irvine, CA 714-505-3955
SmartSweets
 Vancouver, BC
Snackerz
 Commerce, CA 888-576-2253
Sole Grano LLC
 Fair Lawn, NJ 201-797-7100
Sorbee Intl.
 Philadelphia, PA 800-654-3997
South Beach Novelties & Confectionery
 Staten Island, NY 718-727-4500
Southern Style Nuts
 Denison, TX 903-463-3161
Spangler Candy Co
 Bryan, OH 888-636-4221
Specialty Food Association
 New York, NY 646-878-0301
Spokandy
 Spokane, WA 509-624-1969
Squirrel Brand Company
 McKinney, TX 800-624-8242
St Laurent Brothers
 Bay City, MI 800-289-7688
Standard Functional Foods Grp
 Nashville, TN 800-226-4340
Star Kay White Inc
 Congers, NY 800-874-8518
Stark Candy Company
 Revere, MA 800-225-5508
Startupcandy Co
 Provo, UT 801-373-8673
Stevens Creative Enterprises, Inc.
 New York, NY 646-558-6336
Stewart Candies
 Waycross, GA 912-283-1970
Stichler Products Inc
 Reading, PA 610-921-0211
Stone's Home Made Candy Shop
 Oswego, NY 888-223-3928
Storck Canada
 Mississauga, ON 905-272-4480
Storck U.S.A.
 Chicago, IL 800-852-5542
Stutz Candy Company
 Philadelphia, PA 888-692-2639
Sucesores de Pedro Cortes
 Hato Rey, PR 787-754-7040
Sugar Plum LLC
 Houma, LA 985-872-9524
Sunridge Farms
 Royal Oaks, CA 831-786-7000
Sweenors Chocolates
 Wakefield, RI 800-834-3123
Sweet Candy Company
 Salt Lake City, UT 855-772-7720
Sweet City Supply
 Virginia Beach, VA 888-793-3824
Sweet Sensations
 Labrador City, NL 709-944-2660
Sweetcraft Candies
 Timonium, MD 410-252-0684
SweetWorks Inc
 Buffalo, NY 716-634-0880
Tastee Apple
 Newcomerstown, OH 800-262-7753
Tasty Brand Inc
 Calabasas, CA 818-225-9000
Temo Candy
 Akron, OH 330-376-7229
Terri Lynn Inc
 Elgin, IL 800-323-0775
Testamints Sales-Distribution
 Hopatcong, NJ 888-879-0400
Texas Coffee Traders Inc
 Austin, TX 800-343-4875
Texas Toffee
 Odessa, TX 800-599-2133
The Great San Saba River Pecan Company
 San Saba, TX 800-621-8121
Todd's
 Vernon, CA 800-938-6337
Toffee Co
 Houston, TX 713-688-5531
Tom & Sally's Handmade Chocolates
 Brattleboro, VT 800-827-0800
Tony Vitrano Company
 Jessup, MD 800-481-3784
Tootsie Roll Industries Inc.
 Chicago, IL 866-972-6879
Torie & Howard LLC
 New Milford, CT 860-799-7772
Torn & Glasser
 Los Angeles, CA 800-282-6887
Totally Chocolate
 Blaine, WA 800-255-5506
Toucan Chocolates
 Waban, MA 617-964-8696
Trappistine Quality Candy
 Wrentham, MA 866-549-8929
Tremblay's Sweet Shop
 Hayward, WI 715-634-2785
Triple-C
 Hamilton, ON 800-263-9105
Tropical Foods
 Charlotte, NC 800-438-4470
Tropical Foods
 Lithia Springs, GA 800-544-3762
Tropical Nut & Fruit Co
 Orlando, FL 800-749-8869
Tropical Nut Fruit & Bulk Cndy
 Lithia Springs, GA 800-544-3762
Truan's Candies
 Detroit, MI 800-584-3004
Truffle Treasures
 Ottawa, ON 613-761-3859
Turkey Hill Sugarbush
 Waterloo, QC 450-539-4822
Twenty First Century Snacks
 Ronkonkoma, NY 800-975-2883
Tyler Candy Co LLC
 Tyler, TX 903-561-3046
Ultimate Nut & Candy Company
 Los Angeles, CA 800-767-5259
Valhrona
 Los Angeles, CA 310-277-0401
Van Leer Chocolate Corporation
 Chicago, IL 800-225-1418
Van Otis Chocolates
 Manchester, NH 800-826-6847
Vande Walle's Candies Inc
 Appleton, WI 800-738-1020
Varda Chocolatier
 Elizabeth, NJ 800-448-2732
Vaughn-Russell Candy Kitchen
 Greenville, SC 864-271-7786
Velatis
 Silver Spring, MD 888-483-5284
Velvet Creme Popcorn Co
 Westwood, KS 888-553-6708
Verdant Kitchen
 Norcross, GA 912-349-2958
Vigneri Chocolate Inc.
 Rochester, NY 877-844-6374
Vitality Life Choice
 Carson City, NV 800-423-8365
Warner-Lambert Confections
 Cambridge, MA 617-491-2500
Warrell Corp
 Camp Hill, PA 800-233-7082
Warrell Corp
 Camp Hill, PA 844-234-3217
Waymouth Farms Inc
 Minneapolis, MN 800-527-0094
Weaver Nut Co. Inc.
 Ephrata, PA 800-473-2688
Webb's Candy
 Davenport, FL 800-289-9322
Wedding Cake Studio
 Williamsfield, OH 440-667-1765
Westbrae Natural Foods
 Melville, NY 800-434-4246
Westdale Foods Company
 Orland Park, IL 708-458-7774
Whetstone Candy Company
 St. Augustine, FL 904-825-1700
White-Stokes Company
 Chicago, IL 800-978-6537

Product Categories / Candy & Confectionery: Candy

Whitley Peanut Factory Inc
   Hayes, VA 800-470-2244
Widman's Candy Shop
   Crookston, MN 218-281-1487
Wilkinson-Spitz
   Yonkers, NY 914-237-5000
Williams & Bennett
   Orlando, FL 561-276-9007
Williams Candy Co
   Chesapeake, VA 757-545-9311
Williams Candy Company
   Somerville, MA 617-776-0814
Williamsburg Chocolatier
   Williamsburg, VA 757-253-1474
Wilson Candy Co
   Jeannette, PA 724-523-3151
Wilson's Fantastic Candy
   Memphis, TN 901-767-1900
Winans Chocolates & Coffees
   Piqua, OH 937-381-0247
Windmill Candies
   Granite Falls, MN 877-771-8892
Windsor Confections
   Oakland, CA 800-860-0021
Winfrey Fudge & Candy
   Rowley, MA 888-946-3739
Wisconsin Dairyland Fudge Company
   Wisconsin Dells, WI 608-254-7771
Wisteria Candy Cottage
   Boulevard, CA 800-458-8246
Woodstock Farms Manufacturing
   Edison, NJ 800-526-4349
World Confections Inc
   South Orange, NJ 718-768-8100
Wright's Ice Cream Co
   Cayuga, IN 800-686-9561
Wrigley
   Chicago, IL 312-794-6000
Yost Candy Co Inc
   Dalton, OH 800-750-1976
Z Specialty Food, LLC
   Woodland, CA 800-678-1226
Zachary Confections Inc
   Frankfort, IN 800-445-4222

Bon Bons

Delaviuda USA Inc
   Coral Gables, FL 786-599-9814
Ferrara Bakery & Cafe
   New York, NY 212-226-6150
Kerr Brothers
   Toronto, ON 416-252-7341
Knudsen Candy
   Hayward, CA 800-736-6887
Tony Vitrano Company
   Jessup, MD 800-481-3784

Breath Tablets

Ferrero USA Inc
   Somerset, NJ 800-337-7376
Hershey Co.
   Hershey, PA 800-468-1714
Liberty Natural Products Inc
   Oregon City, OR 800-289-8427
Pfizer
   New York, NY 800-879-3477
Sherbrooke OEM Ltd
   Sherbrooke, QC 866-851-2579

Brittles

Arway Confections Inc
   Chicago, IL 800-695-0612
B & B Pecan Processors
   Turkey, NC 866-328-7322
Bazzini Holdings LLC
   Allentown, PA 610-366-1606
Brittle Kittle
   Tigard, OR 800-447-2128
Buddy Squirrel LLC
   St Francis, WI 800-972-2658
Charlotte's Confections
   Millbrae, CA 800-798-2427
Chase & Poe Candy Co
   St Joseph, MO 800-786-1625
Cheese Straws & More
   Monroe, LA 800-997-1921
Claeys Candy Inc
   South Bend, IN 574-287-1818
Crickle Company
   Thomasville, GA 800-237-8689

Crown Candy Corp
   Macon, GA 800-241-3529
Dillon Candy Co
   Boston, GA 800-382-8338
Elegant Edibles
   Houston, TX 800-227-3226
Enstrom Candies, Inc.
   Grand Junction, CO 800-367-8766
Georgia Nut Co
   Skokie, IL 877-674-2993
GKI Foods
   Brighton, MI 248-486-0055
GNS Foods
   Arlington, TX 817-795-4671
Gurley's Foods
   Willmar, MN 800-426-7845
Hialeah Products Co
   Hollywood, FL 800-923-3379
Idaho Candy Co
   Boise, ID 800-898-6986
Kay Foods Co
   Detroit, MI 313-393-1100
La Piccolina
   Decatur, GA 800-626-1624
Layman Distributing
   Salem, VA 800-237-1319
Maries Candies
   West Liberty, OH 866-465-5781
Michele's Chocolate Truffles
   Clackamas, OR 800-656-7112
Mrs Annie's Peanut Patch
   Floresville, TX 830-393-7845
Muth's Candy Store
   Louisville, KY 502-582-2639
Old Dominion Peanut Corp
   Norfolk, VA 800-368-6887
Olde Tyme Mercantile
   Arroyo Grande, CA 805-489-7991
Olivier's Candies
   Calgary, AB 403-266-6028
Palmer Candy Co
   Sioux City, IA 800-831-0828
Patsy's Candy
   Colorado Springs, CO 866-372-8797
Roger's Recipe
   Glover, VT 802-525-3050
Sally Lane's Candy Farm
   Paris, TN 731-642-5801
Sconza Candy Co
   Oakdale, CA 877-568-8137
Snackerz
   Commerce, CA 888-576-2253
Squirrel Brand Company
   McKinney, TX 800-624-8242
St. Jacobs Candy Co.
   Waterloo, ON 519-884-3505
Susie's South Forty Confection
   Midland, TX 800-221-4442
Sweet Jubilee Gourmet
   Mechanicsburg, PA 877-691-9732
Trophy Nut Co
   Tipp City, OH 800-219-9004
Vande Walle's Candies Inc
   Appleton, WI 800-738-1020
Warrell Corp
   Camp Hill, PA 800-233-7082

Butterscotch

Ferrara Candy Co Inc
   Chicago, IL 800-323-1768
Sole Grano LLC
   Fair Lawn, NJ 201-797-7100
Weaver Nut Co. Inc.
   Ephrata, PA 800-473-2688

Candy Bars

Alcove Chocolate
   Los Angeles, CA 323-284-2229
Ameri Candy
   Louisville, KY 502-583-1776
Ann Hemyng Candy Inc
   Trumbauersville, PA 800-779-7004
Arctic Beverages
   Winnipeg, MB 866-503-1270
Bertie County Peanuts
   Windsor, NC 800-457-0005
Blommer Chocolate Co
   Chicago, IL 800-621-1606
Cambridge Brands Inc
   Cambridge, MA 617-491-2500

Carrie's Chocolates
   Edmonton, AB 877-778-2462
Chase & Poe Candy Co
   St Joseph, MO 800-786-1625
Chocolate Street of Hartville
   Hartville, OH 888-853-5904
Chris Candies Inc
   Pittsburgh, PA 412-322-9400
Cloud Nine
   Claremont, CA 909-624-3147
Doscher's Candies Co.
   Cincinnati, OH 513-381-8656
Eda's Sugar Free
   Philadelphia, PA 215-324-3412
Edner Corporation
   Hayward, CA 510-441-8504
Ferrara Bakery & Cafe
   New York, NY 212-226-6150
G Debbas Chocolatier
   Fresno, CA 559-294-2071
Gardners Candies Inc
   Tyrone, PA 800-242-2639
Go Max Go Foods
Good Stuff Cacao
   Metamora, MI 248-690-5114
Hershey Co.
   Hershey, PA 800-468-1714
Joyva Corp
   Brooklyn, NY 718-497-0170
Long Grove Confectionary
   Buffalo Grove, IL 800-373-3102
Lukas Confections
   York, PA 717-843-0921
Mars Inc.
   McLean, VA 703-821-4900
Niagara Chocolates
   Buffalo, NY 877-261-7887
Nikki's Coconut Butter
   Hudson, WI
NuGo Nutrition
   Oakmont, PA 888-421-2032
Papas Chris A & Son Co
   Covington, KY 859-431-0499
Raaka Chocolate
   Brooklyn, NY 855-255-3354
Ruth Hunt Candy Co
   Mt Sterling, KY 800-927-0302
RXBAR
   Chicago, IL 312-624-8200
Sucesores de Pedro Cortes
   Hato Rey, PR 787-754-7040
Vande Walle's Candies Inc
   Appleton, WI 800-738-1020
Weaver Nut Co. Inc.
   Ephrata, PA 800-473-2688
World Confections Inc
   South Orange, NJ 718-768-8100

Coated

Alcove Chocolate
   Los Angeles, CA 323-284-2229

Caramel

Amella
   El Segundo, CA 800-205-0080
Asti Holdings Ltd
   New Westminster, BC 604-523-6866
Becky's Blissful Bakery
   Pewaukee, WI 262-327-4111
Bequet Confections
   Bozeman, MT 877-423-7838
Big Picture Farm LLC
   Townshend, VT 802-221-0547
Cambridge Brands Inc
   Cambridge, MA 617-491-2500
Carousel Candies
   Geneva, IL 888-656-1552
Charlotte's Confections
   Millbrae, CA 800-798-2427
Chocolate Signatures LP
   Toronto, ON 416-234-8528
Cocomels by JJ's Sweets
   Boulder, CO 303-800-6492
Das Foods
   Chicago, IL 312-224-8590
Davinci Gourmet LTD
   Seattle, WA 800-640-6779
Double Premium Confections
   McLean, VA 202-495-1884
Ferrara Candy Co Inc
   Chicago, IL 800-323-1768

Product Categories / Candy & Confectionery: Candy

Gene & Boots Candies Inc
 Perryopolis, PA 800-864-4222
GKI Foods
 Brighton, MI 248-486-0055
Goetze's Candy Co
 Baltimore, MD 410-342-2010
J Morgan's Confections
 Ogden, UT 801-399-3007
Jason & Son Specialty Foods
 Rancho Cordova, CA 800-810-9093
Judy's Cream Caramels
 Sherwood, OR 503-625-7161
Key III Candies
 Fort Wayne, IN 800-752-2382
Knudsen Candy
 Hayward, CA 800-736-6887
Kohler Original Recipe Chocolates
 Kohler, WI 920-208-4930
Leader Candies
 Brooklyn, NY 718-366-6900
Lowery's Home Made Candies
 Muncie, IN 800-541-3340
Lukas Confections
 York, PA 717-843-0921
Matangos Candies
 Harrisburg, PA 717-234-0882
Mccreas Candies
 Hyde Park, MA 617-276-3388
Moonstruck Chocolate Co
 Portland, OR 800-557-6666
Moore's Candies
 Baltimore, MD 410-836-8840
Mrs Prindables
 Niles, IL 888-215-1100
Muth's Candy Store
 Louisville, KY 502-582-2639
Nunes Farms Marketing
 Gustine, CA 209-862-3033
Ruth Hunt Candy Co
 Mt Sterling, KY 800-927-0302
S Zitner Co
 Philadelphia, PA 215-229-9828
St. Jacobs Candy Co.
 Waterloo, ON 519-884-3505
Suss Sweets
 Nashua, NH 603-864-8563
Sweet Designs Chocolatier Inc
 Lakewood, OH 216-226-4888
Tahana Confections LLC
 Portsmouth, NH 603-498-6246
Tastee Apple
 Newcomerstown, OH 800-262-7753
The Lovely Candy Company LLC
 Woodstock, IL 801-824-0624
Tropical Nut Fruit & Bulk Cndy
 Lithia Springs, GA 800-544-3762
Vande Walle's Candies Inc
 Appleton, WI 800-738-1020
Weaver Nut Co. Inc.
 Ephrata, PA 800-473-2688
White-Stokes Company
 Chicago, IL 800-978-6537
World Confections Inc
 South Orange, NJ 718-768-8100

Carob

Clasen Quality Chocolate
 Madison, WI 877-459-4500
Famarco Limited
 Virginia Beach, VA 757-460-3573
GKI Foods
 Brighton, MI 248-486-0055
Setton International Foods
 Commack, NY 800-227-4397

Chewing Gum

Adams USA Inc.
 Cookeville, TN 800-251-6857
American Food Products Inc
 Methuen, MA 978-682-1855
Arcor USA
 Coral Gables, FL 800-572-7267
Beehive Botanicals
 Hayward, WI 800-233-4483
C Howard Co
 Bellport, NY 631-286-7940
Candyrific
 Louisville, KY 502-893-3626
Fernando C Pujals & Bros
 Guaynabo, PR 787-792-3080

Ford Gum & Mach Co Inc
 Akron, NY 716-542-4561
Foreign Candy Company
 Hull, IA 800-831-8541
Glee Gum
 Providence, RI 401-351-6415
Golden Fluff Popcorn Co
 Lakewood, NJ 732-367-5448
Hershey Co.
 Hershey, PA 800-468-1714
Lotte USA Inc
 Battle Creek, MI 269-963-6664
Mars Inc.
 McLean, VA 703-821-4900
Oak Leaf Confections
 877-261-7887
Perfetti Van Melle USA Inc
 Erlanger, KY 859-283-1234
Pfizer
 New York, NY 800-879-3477
Simply Gum
 New York, NY
SP Enterprises, Inc.
 Las Vegas, NV 800-746-4774
Sweet Breath
 New York, NY 877-673-9777
SweetWorks Inc
 Buffalo, NY 716-634-0880
Whetstone Chocolates
 St Augustine, FL 877-261-7887
World Confections Inc
 South Orange, NJ 718-768-8100
Wrigley
 Chicago, IL 312-794-6000

Chocolate Substitutes

Blommer Chocolate Co
 Chicago, IL 800-621-1606

Cocoa Drops

Blommer Chocolate Co
 Chicago, IL 800-621-1606
Hershey Co.
 Hershey, PA 800-468-1714

Coconut

Chase & Poe Candy Co
 St Joseph, MO 800-786-1625
Crown Candy Corp
 Macon, GA 800-241-3529
David Bradley Chocolatier
 Windsor, NJ 877-289-7933
Dundee Groves
 Dundee, FL 800-294-2266
GKI Foods
 Brighton, MI 248-486-0055
Island Delights, Inc.
 Seville, OH 866-877-4100
Mari's Candy
 Chicago, IL 773-254-3351
Olde Tyme Mercantile
 Arroyo Grande, CA 805-489-7991
Papas Chris A & Son Co
 Covington, KY 859-431-0499
Sally Lane's Candy Farm
 Paris, TN 731-642-5801

Corn

American Food Products Inc
 Methuen, MA 978-682-1855
El Brands
 Ozark, AL 334-445-2828
Fernando C Pujals & Bros
 Guaynabo, PR 787-792-3080
Frankford Candy & Chocolate Co
 Philadelphia, PA 800-523-9090
Gurley's Foods
 Willmar, MN 800-426-7845
Hyde & Hyde Inc
 Corona, CA 951-279-5239
Jelly Belly Candy Co.
 Fairfield, CA 800-522-3267
New Century Snacks
 City of Commerce, CA 800-688-6887
Rogers' Chocolates Ltd
 Victoria, BC 800-663-2220
Seattle Bar Company
 Seattle, WA 206-601-4301
Setton International Foods
 Commack, NY 800-227-4397

Snackerz
 Commerce, CA 888-576-2253
Sweet Candy Company
 Salt Lake City, UT 855-772-7720
Sweet City Supply
 Virginia Beach, VA 888-793-3824
Todd's
 Vernon, CA 800-938-6337
Triple-C
 Hamilton, ON 800-263-9105
Trophy Nut Co
 Tipp City, OH 800-219-9004

Cotton

Barcelona Nut Co
 Baltimore, MD 800-296-6887
Brennan Snacks Manufacturing
 Bogalusa, LA 800-290-7486
Fare Foods Corp
 Du Quoin, IL 618-542-2155
Great Western Co LLC
 Hollywood, AL 256-259-3578
Kloss Manufacturing Co Inc
 Allentown, PA 800-445-7100
Olde Tyme Food Corporation
 East Longmeadow, MA 800-356-6533
Taste of Nature Inc.
 Santa Monica, CA 310-396-4433

Cremes

Blommer Chocolate Co
 Chicago, IL 800-621-1606
Brown & Haley
 Fife, WA 800-426-8400
Chocolates a La Carte
 Valencia, CA 800-818-2462
De Fluri's Fine Chocolate
 Martinsburg, WV 304-264-3698
Fannie May Fine Chocolate
 Oakdale, MN 800-999-3629
Fernando C Pujals & Bros
 Guaynabo, PR 787-792-3080
Goetze's Candy Co
 Baltimore, MD 410-342-2010
Lammes Candies
 Austin, TX 800-252-1885
Layman Distributing
 Salem, VA 800-237-1319
Lowery's Home Made Candies
 Muncie, IN 800-541-3340
Maramor Chocolates
 Columbus, OH 800-843-7722
Moore's Candies
 Baltimore, MD 410-836-8840
New Century Snacks
 City of Commerce, CA 800-688-6887
Palmer Candy Co
 Sioux City, IA 800-831-0828
Patsy's Candy
 Colorado Springs, CO 866-372-8797
Rene Rey Chocolates Ltd
 North Vancouver, BC 888-985-0949
Sanders Candy Inc
 Clinton Twp, MI 800-852-2253
Sweet City Supply
 Virginia Beach, VA 888-793-3824
V L Foods
 White Plains, NY 914-697-4851
Z Specialty Food, LLC
 Woodland, CA 800-678-1226

Dietetic

Balanced Health Products
 New York, NY 212-794-9878
Bidwell Candies
 Mattoon, IL 217-234-3858
GKI Foods
 Brighton, MI 248-486-0055
Hillside Candy Co
 Hillside, NJ 800-524-1304
Lowery's Home Made Candies
 Muncie, IN 800-541-3340
Lukas Confections
 York, PA 717-843-0921
Olde Tyme Mercantile
 Arroyo Grande, CA 805-489-7991
Sally Lane's Candy Farm
 Paris, TN 731-642-5801
Setton International Foods
 Commack, NY 800-227-4397

Product Categories / Candy & Confectionery: Candy

Divinity

Ludwick's Frozen Donuts
  Grand Rapids, MI 800-366-8816

Filled

American Food Products Inc
  Methuen, MA 978-682-1855
Andre's Confiserie Suisse
  Kansas City, MO 800-892-1234
Arcor USA
  Coral Gables, FL 800-572-7267
Bissinger's Handcrafted Chocolatier
  St. Louis, MO 314-615-2400
Brockmann's Chocolates
  Delta, BC 888-494-2270
Brown & Haley
  Fife, WA 800-426-8400
Cadbury Trebor Allan
  Granby, QC 800-387-3267
Chocolate By Design Inc
  Ronkonkoma, NY 800-536-3618
Chocolate House
  Milwaukee, WI 800-236-2022
Chocolates a La Carte
  Valencia, CA 800-818-2462
Chocolove
  Boulder, CO 888-246-2656
Double Play Foods
  New York, NY 212-682-4611
El Brands
  Ozark, AL 334-445-2828
Empress Chocolate Company
  Brooklyn, NY 800-793-3809
Fannie May Fine Chocolate
  Oakdale, MN 800-999-3629
Fernando C Pujals & Bros
  Guaynabo, PR 787-792-3080
Ferrero USA Inc
  Somerset, NJ 800-337-7376
Frankford Candy & Chocolate Co
  Philadelphia, PA 800-523-9090
Goetze's Candy Co
  Baltimore, MD 410-342-2010
Hagensborg Chocolates LTD.
  Burnaby, BC 877-554-7763
Harbor Sweets
  Salem, MA 800-243-2115
Hyde & Hyde Inc
  Corona, CA 951-279-5239
Idaho Candy Co
  Boise, ID 800-898-6986
Knudsen Candy
  Hayward, CA 800-736-6887
Leader Candies
  Brooklyn, NY 718-366-6900
Lowery's Home Made Candies
  Muncie, IN 800-541-3340
Nature's Candy
  Fredericksburg, TX 800-729-0085
New Century Snacks
  City of Commerce, CA 800-688-6887
Plantation Candies
  Telford, PA 888-678-6468
Primrose Candy Co
  Chicago, IL 800-268-9522
Rebecca-Ruth Candy Factory
  Frankfort, KY 800-444-3866
Richardson Brands Co
  Canajoharie, NY 518-673-3553
Setton International Foods
  Commack, NY 800-227-4397
Snackerz
  Commerce, CA 888-576-2253
Sweet Candy Company
  Salt Lake City, UT 855-772-7720
Todd's
  Vernon, CA 800-938-6337
V L Foods
  White Plains, NY 914-697-4851
Warner Candy
  El Paso, TX 847-928-7200
Webb's Candy
  Davenport, FL 800-289-9322

Fudge

Amcan Industries
  Elmsford, NY 914-347-4838
Bear Creek Smokehouse Inc
  Marshall, TX 800-950-2327
Betty Lou's
  McMinnville, OR 800-242-5205
Blommer Chocolate Co
  Chicago, IL 800-621-1606
Bodega Chocolates
  Fountain Valley, CA 888-326-3342
Calico Cottage
  Amityville, NY 800-645-5345
Cambridge Brands Inc
  Cambridge, MA 617-491-2500
Charlotte's Confections
  Millbrae, CA 800-798-2427
Country Fresh Food & Confections, Inc.
  Oliver Springs, TN 800-545-8782
Crown Candy Corp
  Macon, GA 800-241-3529
Donells Candies
  Casper, WY 877-461-2009
Downeast Candies
  Boothbay Harbor, ME 207-633-5178
Enstrom Candies, Inc.
  Grand Junction, CO 800-367-8766
Fieldbrook Foods Corp.
  Dunkirk, NY 800-333-0805
Fudge Fatale
  Studio City, CA 800-809-8298
Gene & Boots Candies Inc
  Perryopolis, PA 800-864-4222
Giambri's Quality Sweets Inc
  Clementon, NJ 866-238-0169
Haven's Candies
  Westbrook, ME 800-639-6309
Hershey Co.
  Hershey, PA 800-468-1714
J Morgan's Confections
  Ogden, UT 801-399-3007
James Candy Company
  Atlantic City, NJ 800-441-1404
JER Creative Food Concepts, Inc.
  Commerce, CA 800-350-2462
Kelly's Candies
  Pooler, GA 800-523-3051
Layman Distributing
  Salem, VA 800-237-1319
Maple Leaf Cheesemakers
  New Glarus, WI 888-624-1234
McJak Candy Company LLC
  Medina, OH 800-424-2942
Nancy's Candy
  Meadows Of Dan, VA 800-328-3834
Olde Tyme Mercantile
  Arroyo Grande, CA 805-489-7991
Phenomenal Fudge Inc
  Shoreham, VT 800-430-5442
Phillip's Candy House
  Dorchester, MA 617-282-2090
Rocky Top Country Store
  Sevierville, TN 866-260-0670
St. Jacobs Candy Co.
  Waterloo, ON 519-884-3505
Sweenors Chocolates
  Wakefield, RI 800-834-3123
The Lovely Candy Company LLC
  Woodstock, IL 801-824-0624
Tony Vitrano Company
  Jessup, MD 800-481-3784
Vande Walle's Candies Inc
  Appleton, WI 800-738-1020
Webb's Candy
  Davenport, FL 800-289-9322

Gums & Jellies

Albanese Confectionery Group
  Merrillville, IN 800-536-0581
Amazing Candy Craft Company
  Hollis, NY 800-429-9368
American Food Products Inc
  Methuen, MA 978-682-1855
Andros Foods North America
  Mount Jackson, VA 844-426-3767
Arcor USA
  Coral Gables, FL 800-572-7267
Au'some Candies
  Monmouth Junction, NJ 877-287-6649
Barcelona Nut Co
  Baltimore, MD 800-296-6887
Beehive Botanicals
  Hayward, WI 800-233-4483
Boston Fruit Slice & Confectionery Corporation
  Lawrence, MA 978-686-2699
C Howard Co
  Bellport, NY 631-286-7940
Cadbury Trebor Allan
  Granby, QC 800-387-3267
Cambridge Brands Inc
  Cambridge, MA 617-491-2500
Diamond Foods
  Santa Cruz, CA 831-457-3200
El Brands
  Ozark, AL 334-445-2828
Extreme Creations
  El Dorado Hills, CA 916-941-0444
Fannie May Fine Chocolate
  Oakdale, MN 800-999-3629
Fernando C Pujals & Bros
  Guaynabo, PR 787-792-3080
Ferrara Candy Co Inc
  Chicago, IL 800-323-1768
Foreign Candy Company
  Hull, IA 800-831-8541
Frankford Candy & Chocolate Co
  Philadelphia, PA 800-523-9090
Ganong Bros Ltd
  St. Stephen, NB 888-270-8222
Gene & Boots Candies Inc
  Perryopolis, PA 800-864-4222
GNS Foods
  Arlington, TX 817-795-4671
Golden Fluff Popcorn Co
  Lakewood, NJ 732-367-5448
Gurley's Foods
  Willmar, MN 800-426-7845
Haribo of America
  Baltimore, MD 847-260-0580
Healthy Food Brands LLC
  Brooklyn, NY 212-444-9909
Hershey Co.
  Hershey, PA 800-468-1714
Hyde & Hyde Inc
  Corona, CA 951-279-5239
Island Snacks
  Buena Park, CA 714-994-1228
Jelly Belly Candy Co.
  Fairfield, CA 800-522-3267
Joyva Corp
  Brooklyn, NY 718-497-0170
Kenny's Candy & Confections
  Perham, MN
Kolatin Real Kosher Gelatin
  Lakewood, NJ 732-364-8700
Koppers Chocolate
  Cranford, NJ 800-325-0026
Leader Candies
  Brooklyn, NY 718-366-6900
Liberty Orchards Co Inc
  Cashmere, WA 800-231-3242
Little I
  Blaine, WA 360-332-3258
Mt Franklin Foods
  El Paso, TX 800-685-1475
New Century Snacks
  City of Commerce, CA 800-688-6887
Oak Leaf Confections
  877-261-7887
Original Foods
  Dunnville, ON 888-440-8880
Palmer Candy Co
  Sioux City, IA 800-831-0828
Richardson Brands Co
  Canajoharie, NY 518-673-3553
Roseville Corporation
  Mountain View, CA 888-247-9338
Ruger LLC
  Bethesda, MD 301-675-2398
SmartSweets
  Vancouver, BC
Snackerz
  Commerce, CA 888-576-2253
Sole Grano LLC
  Fair Lawn, NJ 201-797-7100
Sorbee Intl.
  Philadelphia, PA 800-654-3997
Standard Functional Foods Grp
  Nashville, TN 800-226-4340
Stevens Creative Enterprises, Inc.
  New York, NY 646-558-6336
Suity Confections Co
  Miami, FL 305-639-3300
Sweet Blessings
  Malibu, CA 310-317-1172
Sweet City Supply
  Virginia Beach, VA 888-793-3824
SWELL Philadelphia Chewing Gum Corporation
  Havertown, PA 610-449-1700
Taste of Nature Inc.
  Santa Monica, CA 310-396-4433

Product Categories / Candy & Confectionery: Candy

Tasty Brand Inc
  Calabasas, CA 818-225-9000
The Pur Company
  Toronto, ON 416-941-7557
Toe-Food Chocolates and Candy
  Berkeley, CA 888-863-3663
Triple-C
  Hamilton, ON 800-263-9105
Trophy Nut Co
  Tipp City, OH 800-219-9004
Warner Candy
  El Paso, TX 847-928-7200
Weaver Nut Co. Inc.
  Ephrata, PA 800-473-2688
World Confections Inc
  South Orange, NJ 718-768-8100

Hard

A La Carte
  Chicago, IL 800-722-2370
Adams & Brooks Inc
  Los Angeles, CA 213-749-3226
American Food Products Inc
  Methuen, MA 978-682-1855
Anastasia Confections Inc
  Orlando, FL 800-329-7100
Arcor USA
  Coral Gables, FL 800-572-7267
Artek USA
  Westlake Village, CA 866-278-3501
Baker Candy Company
  Snohomish, WA 425-422-6331
Barcelona Nut Co
  Baltimore, MD 800-296-6887
Bidwell Candies
  Mattoon, IL 217-234-3858
Blanton's
  Frankfort, KY 502-223-9874
Brother's Trading LLC
  San Gabriel, CA 626-378-9323
Butterfields
  Nashville, NC 800-945-5957
C Howard Co
  Bellport, NY 631-286-7940
Cadbury Trebor Allan
  Granby, QC 800-387-3267
Cambridge Brands Inc
  Cambridge, MA 617-491-2500
Cap Candy
  Napa, CA 707-251-9321
Claeys Candy Inc
  South Bend, IN 574-287-1818
Cloud Nine
  Claremont, CA 909-624-3147
Day Spring Enterprises
  Cheektowaga, NY 800-879-7677
Doscher's Candies Co.
  Cincinnati, OH 513-381-8656
Eda's Sugar Free
  Philadelphia, PA 215-324-3412
El Brands
  Ozark, AL 334-445-2828
Enstrom Candies, Inc.
  Grand Junction, CO 800-367-8766
F B Washburn Candy Corp
  Brockton, MA 508-588-0820
Fannie May Fine Chocolate
  Oakdale, MN 800-999-3629
Fernando C Pujals & Bros
  Guaynabo, PR 787-792-3080
Ferrara Candy Co Inc
  Chicago, IL 800-323-1768
Foreign Candy Company
  Hull, IA 800-831-8541
Frankford Candy & Chocolate Co
  Philadelphia, PA 800-523-9090
Giambri's Quality Sweets Inc
  Clementon, NJ 866-238-0169
Gimbals Fine Candies
  S San Francisco, CA 800-344-6225
Grumpe's Specialties
  Baird, TX 866-854-1106
Gurley's Foods
  Willmar, MN 800-426-7845
Hawaii Candy Inc
  Honolulu, HI 800-303-2507
Helms Candy Co., Inc
  Bristol, VA 276-669-2533
Hillside Candy Co
  Hillside, NJ 800-524-1304
Hyde & Hyde Inc
  Corona, CA 951-279-5239

Ice Chips Candy
  Olympia, WA 866-202-6623
Idaho Candy Co
  Boise, ID 800-898-6986
Karma Candy
  Hamilton, ON 905-527-6222
Kencraft, Inc.
  Alpine, UT 800-377-4368
Kerr Brothers
  Toronto, ON 416-252-7341
Leader Candies
  Brooklyn, NY 718-366-6900
Lotte USA Inc
  Battle Creek, MI 269-963-6664
Mitch Chocolate
  Melville, NY 631-777-2400
Moore's Candies
  Baltimore, MD 410-836-8840
Mt Franklin Foods
  El Paso, TX 800-685-1475
Nassau Candy Distributors
  Hicksville, NY 516-433-7100
New Century Snacks
  City of Commerce, CA 800-688-6887
New Hope Natural Media
  Boulder, CO 303-939-8440
Oak Leaf Confections
  877-261-7887
Old Dominion Peanut Corp
  Norfolk, VA 800-368-6887
Olivier's Candies
  Calgary, AB 403-266-6028
Original Foods
  Dunnville, ON 888-440-8880
Palmer Candy Co
  Sioux City, IA 800-831-0828
Perfetti Van Melle USA Inc
  Erlanger, KY 859-283-1234
Pez Candy Inc
  Orange, CT 203-795-0531
Piedmont Candy Co
  Lexington, NC 336-248-2477
Plantation Candies
  Telford, PA 888-678-6468
Primrose Candy Co
  Chicago, IL 800-268-9522
Produits Alimentaire
  St Lambert De Lauzon, QC 800-463-1787
Quigley Industries Inc
  Farmington, MI 800-367-2441
Rainbow Pops
  Cheektowaga, NY 800-879-7677
Richardson Brands Co
  Canajoharie, NY 518-673-3553
Ricos Candy Snack & Bakery
  Hialeah, FL 305-885-7392
Salem Old Fashioned Candies
  Salem, MA 978-744-3242
Sconza Candy Co
  Oakdale, CA 877-568-8137
Scripture Candy
  Birmingham, AL 888-317-7333
Setton International Foods
  Commack, NY 800-227-4397
Smarties
  Union, NJ 800-631-7968
Snackerz
  Commerce, CA 888-576-2253
SP Enterprises, Inc.
  Las Vegas, NV 800-746-4774
Spangler Candy Co
  Bryan, OH 888-636-4221
St. Jacobs Candy Co.
  Waterloo, ON 519-884-3505
Sweenors Chocolates
  Wakefield, RI 800-834-3123
Sweet Candy Company
  Salt Lake City, UT 855-772-7720
Sweet City Supply
  Virginia Beach, VA 888-793-3824
SWELL Philadelphia Chewing Gum Corporation
  Havertown, PA 610-449-1700
Todd's
  Vernon, CA 800-938-6337
Tootsie Roll Industries Inc.
  Chicago, IL 866-972-6879
Torie & Howard LLC
  New Milford, CT 860-799-7772
Trophy Nut Co
  Tipp City, OH 800-219-9004
Turkey Hill Sugarbush
  Waterloo, QC 450-539-4822

V L Foods
  White Plains, NY 914-697-4851
Warner Candy
  El Paso, TX 847-928-7200
Weaver Nut Co. Inc.
  Ephrata, PA 800-473-2688
Webb's Candy
  Davenport, FL 800-289-9322
Williams Candy Co
  Chesapeake, VA 757-545-9311
Wrigley
  Chicago, IL 312-794-6000

Jelly Beans

American Food Products Inc
  Methuen, MA 978-682-1855
Arcor USA
  Coral Gables, FL 800-572-7267
Cambridge Brands Inc
  Cambridge, MA 617-491-2500
Cap Candy
  Napa, CA 707-251-9321
El Brands
  Ozark, AL 334-445-2828
Fannie May Fine Chocolate
  Oakdale, MN 800-999-3629
Fernando C Pujals & Bros
  Guaynabo, PR 787-792-3080
Ferrara Candy Co Inc
  Chicago, IL 800-323-1768
Ganong Bros Ltd
  St. Stephen, NB 888-270-8222
Gimbals Fine Candies
  S San Francisco, CA 800-344-6225
GNS Foods
  Arlington, TX 817-795-4671
Gurley's Foods
  Willmar, MN 800-426-7845
Jelly Belly Candy Co.
  Fairfield, CA 800-522-3267
Just Born Inc
  Bethlehem, PA 800-445-5787
Leader Candies
  Brooklyn, NY 718-366-6900
Mt Franklin Foods
  El Paso, TX 800-685-1475
New Century Snacks
  City of Commerce, CA 800-688-6887
Palmer Candy Co
  Sioux City, IA 800-831-0828
Setton International Foods
  Commack, NY 800-227-4397
Snackerz
  Commerce, CA 888-576-2253
Stevens Creative Enterprises, Inc.
  New York, NY 646-558-6336
Sweet Candy Company
  Salt Lake City, UT 855-772-7720
Sweet City Supply
  Virginia Beach, VA 888-793-3824
Todd's
  Vernon, CA 800-938-6337
Triple-C
  Hamilton, ON 800-263-9105
Warner Candy
  El Paso, TX 847-928-7200
Weaver Nut Co. Inc.
  Ephrata, PA 800-473-2688

Kisses

Cadbury Trebor Allan
  Granby, QC 800-387-3267
Setton International Foods
  Commack, NY 800-227-4397

Licorice

American Food Products Inc
  Methuen, MA 978-682-1855
American Licorice
  La Porte, IL 866-442-2783
Andros Foods North America
  Mount Jackson, VA 844-426-3767
Buddy Squirrel LLC
  St Francis, WI 800-972-2658
Cadbury Trebor Allan
  Granby, QC 800-387-3267
Cambridge Brands Inc
  Cambridge, MA 617-491-2500
Capco Enterprises
  East Hanover, NJ 800-252-1011

Product Categories / Candy & Confectionery: Candy

El Brands
   Ozark, AL....................334-445-2828
Fannie May Fine Chocolate
   Oakdale, MN..................800-999-3629
Ferrara Candy Co Inc
   Chicago, IL...................800-323-1768
Fiesta Candy Company
   Rochester, NH.................800-285-9735
Foreign Candy Company
   Hull, IA......................800-831-8541
G Scaccianoce & Co
   Bronx, NY.....................718-991-4462
Ganong Bros Ltd
   St. Stephen, NB...............888-270-8222
Gimbals Fine Candies
   S San Francisco, CA...........800-344-6225
Groovy Candies
   Cleveland, OH.................888-729-1960
Gurley's Foods
   Willmar, MN...................800-426-7845
Haribo of America
   Baltimore, MD.................847-260-0580
Jelly Belly Candy Co.
   Fairfield, CA.................800-522-3267
Kenny's Candy & Confections
   Perham, MN
Kookaburra
   Monroe, WA....................360-805-6858
Morre-Tec Ind Inc
   Union, NJ.....................908-686-0307
Morris National
   Azusa, CA.....................626-385-2000
New Century Snacks
   City of Commerce, CA..........800-688-6887
Palmer Candy Co
   Sioux City, IA................800-831-0828
Patsy's Candy
   Colorado Springs, CO..........866-372-8797
Sahagian & Associates
   Oak Park, IL..................800-327-9273
Snackerz
   Commerce, CA..................888-576-2253
Sorbee Intl.
   Philadelphia, PA..............800-654-3997
Sweet Candy Company
   Salt Lake City, UT............855-772-7720
Sweet City Supply
   Virginia Beach, VA............888-793-3824
The Lovely Candy Company LLC
   Woodstock, IL.................801-824-0624
Todd's
   Vernon, CA....................800-938-6337
Triple-C
   Hamilton, ON..................800-263-9105
Warner Candy
   El Paso, TX...................847-928-7200
Westbrae Natural Foods
   Melville, NY..................800-434-4246

Lollypops

Adams & Brooks Inc
   Los Angeles, CA...............213-749-3226
Amazing Candy Craft Company
   Hollis, NY....................800-429-9368
American Food Products Inc
   Methuen, MA...................978-682-1855
Andros Foods North America
   Mount Jackson, VA.............844-426-3767
Ann Hemyng Candy Inc
   Trumbauersville, PA...........800-779-7004
Arcor USA
   Coral Gables, FL..............800-572-7267
Artek USA
   Westlake Village, CA..........866-278-3501
Au'some Candies
   Monmouth Junction, NJ.........877-287-6649
Baraboo Candy Co LLC
   Baraboo, WI...................800-967-1690
Browniepops LLC
   Leawood, KS...................816-797-0715
Cadbury Trebor Allan
   Granby, QC....................800-387-3267
Cap Candy
   Napa, CA......................707-251-9321
Carrie's Chocolates
   Edmonton, AB..................877-778-2462
CTC Manufacturing
   Calgary, AB...................800-668-7677
Das Foods
   Chicago, IL...................312-224-8590
David Bradley Chocolatier
   Windsor, NJ...................877-289-7933

Day Spring Enterprises
   Cheektowaga, NY...............800-879-7677
El Brands
   Ozark, AL.....................334-445-2828
Extreme Creations
   El Dorado Hills, CA...........916-941-0444
Fernando C Pujals & Bros
   Guaynabo, PR..................787-792-3080
Ferrara Candy Co Inc
   Chicago, IL...................800-323-1768
Foreign Candy Company
   Hull, IA......................800-831-8541
Frankford Candy & Chocolate Co
   Philadelphia, PA..............800-523-9090
Fun Factory
   Milwaukee, WI.................877-894-6767
Glennys
   Brooklyn, NY..................888-864-1243
Groovy Candies
   Cleveland, OH.................888-729-1960
Grumpe's Specialties
   Baird, TX.....................866-854-1106
Gurley's Foods
   Willmar, MN...................800-426-7845
Hand Made Lollies
   Maitland, FL..................877-784-2724
Helms Candy Co., Inc
   Bristol, VA...................276-669-2533
Impact Confections
   Janesville, WI................800-535-4401
James Candy Company
   Atlantic City, NJ.............800-441-1404
Jed's Maple Products
   Derby, VT.....................802-766-2700
Kencraft, Inc.
   Alpine, UT....................800-377-4368
Kendon Candies Inc
   San Jose, CA..................800-332-2639
Kerr Brothers
   Toronto, ON...................416-252-7341
Laura Paige Candy Company
   Newburgh, NY..................845-566-4209
Leader Candies
   Brooklyn, NY..................718-366-6900
Light Vision Confections
   Cincinnati, OH................513-351-9444
Linda's Lollies Company
   Mahwah, NJ....................800-347-1545
McIlhenny Company
   Avery Island, LA..............800-634-9599
McJak Candy Company LLC
   Medina, OH....................800-424-2942
Melville Candy Corp
   Weymouth, MA..................781-331-2005
Mitch Chocolate
   Melville, NY..................631-777-2400
Mom N' Pops Inc
   New Windsor, NY...............845-567-0640
Multiflex Company
   Hawthorne, NJ.................973-636-9700
New Century Snacks
   City of Commerce, CA..........800-688-6887
Original Foods
   Dunnville, ON.................888-440-8880
Original Gourmet Food Co
   Salem, NH.....................603-894-1200
Parkside Candy Co
   Buffalo, NY...................716-833-7540
Perfetti Van Melle USA Inc
   Erlanger, KY..................859-283-1234
Plymouth Lollipop Company
   Westford, MA..................800-777-0115
Primrose Candy Co
   Chicago, IL...................800-268-9522
Produits Alimentaire
   St Lambert De Lauzon, QC......800-463-1787
Rainbow Pops
   Cheektowaga, NY...............800-879-7677
Richardson Brands Co
   Canajoharie, NY...............518-673-3553
Riddles' Sweet Impressions
   Edmonton, AB..................780-465-8085
Roseville Corporation
   Mountain View, CA.............888-247-9338
Salem Old Fashioned Candies
   Salem, MA.....................978-744-3242
Scripture Candy
   Birmingham, AL................888-317-7333
Setton International Foods
   Commack, NY...................800-227-4397
Smarties
   Union, NJ.....................800-631-7968

Sorbee Intl.
   Philadelphia, PA..............800-654-3997
SP Enterprises, Inc.
   Las Vegas, NV.................800-746-4774
Spangler Candy Co
   Bryan, OH.....................888-636-4221
Strawberry Hill Grand Delights
   Everett, MA...................617-319-3557
Suity Confections Co
   Miami, FL.....................305-639-3300
Tom & Sally's Handmade Chocolates
   Brattleboro, VT...............800-827-0800
Tootsie Roll Industries Inc.
   Chicago, IL...................866-972-6879
Triple-C
   Hamilton, ON..................800-263-9105
Turkey Hill Sugarbush
   Waterloo, QC..................450-539-4822
Williamsburg Chocolatier
   Williamsburg, VA..............757-253-1474
World Confections Inc
   South Orange, NJ..............718-768-8100
Wrigley
   Chicago, IL...................312-794-6000
Yost Candy Co Inc
   Dalton, OH....................800-750-1976

Gourmet Flavored

Das Foods
   Chicago, IL...................312-224-8590
Hand Made Lollies
   Maitland, FL..................877-784-2724
Kendon Candies Inc
   San Jose, CA..................800-332-2639

Lozenges

Adams USA Inc.
   Cookeville, TN................800-251-6857
Bestco Inc
   Mooresville, NC...............704-664-4300
Cadbury Trebor Allan
   Granby, QC....................800-387-3267
Ganong Bros Ltd
   St. Stephen, NB...............888-270-8222
Holistic Products Corporation
   Englewood, NJ.................800-221-0308
Kerr Brothers
   Toronto, ON...................416-252-7341
MYNTZ!
   Kent, WA......................800-800-9490
Rito Mints
   Trois Rivieres, QC............819-379-1449
Snackerz
   Commerce, CA..................888-576-2253
Sorbee Intl.
   Philadelphia, PA..............800-654-3997

Maple

Butternut Mountain Farm
   Morrisville, VT...............800-828-2376
D & D Sugarwoods Farm
   Glover, VT....................800-245-3718
Finding Home Farms
   Middletown, NY................845-355-4335
Jed's Maple Products
   Derby, VT.....................802-766-2700
Key III Candies
   Fort Wayne, IN................800-752-2382
Maple Grove Farms Of Vermont
   St Johnsbury, VT..............802-748-5141
Maple Valley Cooperative
   Cashton, WI...................608-654-7319
Nature's Candy
   Fredericksburg, TX............800-729-0085
Richards Maple Products
   Chardon, OH...................800-352-4052
Swisser Sweet Maple
   Castorland, NY................315-346-1034

Marshmallow

Charlotte's Confections
   Millbrae, CA..................800-798-2427
Clown Global Brands
   Northbrook, IL................800-323-5778
Doumak Inc
   Elk Grove Village, IL.........800-323-0318
Durkee-Mower
   Lynn, MA......................781-593-8007
EIWA America Inc.
   Torrance, CA..................310-327-7222

Product Categories / Candy & Confectionery: Candy

Gimbals Fine Candies
  S San Francisco, CA 800-344-6225
Glatech Productions LLC
  Lakewood, NJ 732-364-8700
Golden Fluff Popcorn Co
  Lakewood, NJ 732-367-5448
Kolatin Real Kosher Gelatin
  Lakewood, NJ 732-364-8700
Madyson's Marshmallows
  Heber City, UT 435-315-0045
Philadelphia Candies Inc
  Hermitage, PA 724-981-6341
Plush Puffs Marshmallows
  Burbank, CA 818-784-2931
S Zitner Co
  Philadelphia, PA 215-229-9828
Solo Foods
  Countryside, IL 800-328-7656
The Crispery
  Portsmouth, VA 501-224-8947
White-Stokes Company
  Chicago, IL 800-978-6537

Marshmallow Creme

Solo Foods
  Countryside, IL 800-328-7656

Marshmallows

Annabelle Candy Co Inc
  Hayward, CA 510-783-2900
Charlotte's Confections
  Millbrae, CA 800-798-2427
Chicago Vegan Foods
  Lombard, IL 630-629-9667
David Bradley Chocolatier
  Windsor, NJ 877-289-7933
Doumak Inc
  Elk Grove Village, IL 800-323-0318
Ferrara Candy Co Inc
  Chicago, IL 800-323-1768
Frankford Candy & Chocolate Co
  Philadelphia, PA 800-523-9090
Ganong Bros Ltd
  St. Stephen, NB 888-270-8222
Golden Fluff Popcorn Co
  Lakewood, NJ 732-367-5448
Joyva Corp
  Brooklyn, NY 718-497-0170
Just Born Inc
  Bethlehem, PA 800-445-5787
Michele's Chocolate Truffles
  Clackamas, OR 800-656-7112
Papas Chris A & Son Co
  Covington, KY 859-431-0499
Patsy's Candy
  Colorado Springs, CO 866-372-8797
Richardson Brands Co
  Canajoharie, NY 518-673-3553
Roseville Corporation
  Mountain View, CA 888-247-9338
S Zitner Co
  Philadelphia, PA 215-229-9828
Smashmallow
  Sonoma, CA 707-512-0605
Spangler Candy Co
  Bryan, OH 888-636-4221
Strawberry Hill Grand Delights
  Everett, MA 617-319-3557
Sucre
  New Orleans, LA 504-708-4366
Suity Confections Co
  Miami, FL 305-639-3300
Sweet City Supply
  Virginia Beach, VA 888-793-3824
Warrell Corp
  Camp Hill, PA 800-233-7082

Marzipan

American Almond Products Co
  Brooklyn, NY 800-825-6663
Amoretti
  Oxnard, CA 800-266-7388
B. Nutty
  Oakland, CA 510-374-4658
Snackerz
  Commerce, CA 888-576-2253
Sweet Swiss Confections Inc
  Spokane, WA 509-838-1334

Miniatures

Foreign Candy Company
  Hull, IA 800-831-8541
Hershey Co.
  Hershey, PA 800-468-1714

Mints

Adams USA Inc.
  Cookeville, TN 800-251-6857
Ameri Candy
  Louisville, KY 502-583-1776
American Mint
  New York, NY 800-401-6468
Art CoCo Chocolate Company
  Geneva, IL 877-232-9901
Big Sky Brands
  Mississauga, ON 416-599-5415
Boston America Corporation
  Woburn, MA 781-933-3535
Brown & Haley
  Fife, WA 800-426-8400
Cadbury Trebor Allan
  Granby, QC 800-387-3267
Chocolati Handmade Chocolates
  Seattle, WA 206-784-5212
Cloud Nine
  Claremont, CA 909-624-3147
Cracked Candy LLC
  Brooklyn, NY 646-543-1405
Ferrara Candy Co Inc
  Chicago, IL 800-323-1768
Foley's Chocolates & Candies
  Richmond, BC 888-236-5397
Ford Gum & Mach Co Inc
  Akron, NY 716-542-4561
Fun Factory
  Milwaukee, WI 877-894-6767
G Scaccianoce & Co
  Bronx, NY 718-991-4462
Helms Candy Co., Inc
  Bristol, VA 276-669-2533
Hillside Candy Co
  Hillside, NJ 800-524-1304
Hint Mint
  Los Angeles, CA 800-991-6468
Hospitality Mints LLC
  Boone, NC 800-334-5181
IFive Brands
  Seattle, WA 800-882-5615
Joe Clark Fund Raising Candies
  Tarentum, PA 888-459-9520
Kerr Brothers
  Toronto, ON 416-252-7341
Koppers Chocolate
  Cranford, NJ 800-325-0026
Landies Candies Co
  Buffalo, NY 800-955-2634
Little I
  Blaine, WA 360-332-3258
Marich Confectionery
  Hollister, CA 800-624-7055
Matangos Candies
  Harrisburg, PA 717-234-0882
Maxfield Candy
  Salt Lake City, UT 800-288-8002
MYNTZ!
  Kent, WA 800-800-9490
Naylor Candies Inc
  Mt Wolf, PA 717-266-2706
New Century Snacks
  City of Commerce, CA 800-688-6887
Palmer Candy Co
  Sioux City, IA 800-831-0828
Perfetti Van Melle USA Inc
  Erlanger, KY 859-283-1234
Pfizer
  New York, NY 800-879-3477
Piedmont Candy Co
  Lexington, NC 336-248-2477
Plantation Candies
  Telford, PA 888-678-6468
Rebecca-Ruth Candy Factory
  Frankfort, KY 800-444-3866
Reutter Candy & Chocolates
  Baltimore, MD 800-392-0870
Rito Mints
  Trois Rivieres, QC 819-379-1449
Salem Old Fashioned Candies
  Salem, MA 978-744-3242
Schuster Marketing Corporation
  Milwaukee, WI 888-254-8948
Scripture Candy
  Birmingham, AL 888-317-7333
Sencha Naturals
  Los Angeles, CA 888-473-6242
Setton International Foods
  Commack, NY 800-227-4397
Sherbrooke OEM Ltd
  Sherbrooke, QC 866-851-2579
SP Enterprises, Inc.
  Las Vegas, NV 800-746-4774
Sweenors Chocolates
  Wakefield, RI 800-834-3123
Sweet Breath
  New York, NY 877-673-9777
Todd's
  Vernon, CA 800-938-6337
Tootsie Roll Industries Inc
  Chicago, IL 866-972-6879
Unica
  Glen Ellyn, IL 630-790-8107
VerMints Inc.
  Braintree, VT 800-367-4442
VitaThinQ Inc.
  Davie, FL
Weaver Nut Co. Inc.
  Ephrata, PA 800-473-2688
Webb's Candy
  Davenport, FL 800-289-9322
Wrench Mints
  Chicago, IL 312-496-3690
Wrigley
  Chicago, IL 312-794-6000

Mousse

Abel & Schafer Inc
  Ronkonkoma, NY 800-443-1260
Alati-Caserta Desserts
  Montr,al, QC 877-377-5680
Alexian Pâtés
  Neptune, NJ 800-927-9473
Blommer Chocolate Co
  Chicago, IL 800-621-1606
Century Blends Inc
  Hunt Valley, MD 410-771-6606
Desserts by David Glass
  South Windsor, CT 860-462-7520
Granowska's
  Toronto, ON 416-533-7755
HFI Foods
  Redmond, WA 425-883-1320
Hormel Foods Corp.
  Austin, MN 507-437-5611
Jon Donaire Desserts
  Santa Fe Springs, CA 877-366-2473
Love Quiches Desserts
  Freeport, NY 516-623-8800
Paris Pastry
  Van Nuys, CA 805-487-2227
Tova Industries LLC
  Louisville, KY 888-532-8682
World Of Chantilly
  Brooklyn, NY 718-859-1110

Nougats

Asti Holdings Ltd
  New Westminster, BC 604-523-6866
Ferrara Bakery & Cafe
  New York, NY 212-226-6150
Ferrara Candy Co Inc
  Chicago, IL 800-323-1768
Joe Clark Fund Raising Candies
  Tarentum, PA 888-459-9520
Lukas Confections
  York, PA 717-843-0921
Webb's Candy
  Davenport, FL 800-289-9322
White-Stokes Company
  Chicago, IL 800-978-6537

Novelties

Ann Hemyng Candy Inc
  Trumbauersville, PA 800-779-7004
Carrie's Chocolates
  Edmonton, AB 877-778-2462
Chocolate Street of Hartville
  Hartville, OH 888-853-5904
Chocolates by Mark
  Houston, TX 832-736-2626
Chris Candies Inc
  Pittsburgh, PA 412-322-9400

Product Categories / Candy & Confectionery: Candy

David Bradley Chocolatier
  Windsor, NJ 877-289-7933
Doscher's Candies Co.
  Cincinnati, OH 513-381-8656
Ferrara Bakery & Cafe
  New York, NY 212-226-6150
Gourmet du Village
  Morin-Heights, QC 800-668-2314
Hershey Co.
  Hershey, PA 800-468-1714
Laura Paige Candy Company
  Newburgh, NY 845-566-4209
Leader Candies
  Brooklyn, NY 718-366-6900
Long Grove Confectionary
  Buffalo Grove, IL 800-373-3102
Maxfield Candy
  Salt Lake City, UT 800-288-8002
Merb's Candies
  St Louis, MO 314-832-7117
Merlin Candies
  Harahan, LA 800-899-1549
Niagara Chocolates
  Buffalo, NY 877-261-7887
Papas Chris A & Son Co
  Covington, KY 859-431-0499
Sherbrooke OEM Ltd
  Sherbrooke, QC 866-851-2579
Stichler Products Inc
  Reading, PA 610-921-0211
Weaver Nut Co. Inc.
  Ephrata, PA 800-473-2688
World Confections Inc
  South Orange, NJ 718-768-8100
Yost Candy Co Inc
  Dalton, OH 800-750-1976
Zachary Confections Inc
  Frankfort, IN 800-445-4222

Peanut Brittle

B & B Pecan Processors
  Turkey, NC 866-328-7322
Maxwell's Gourmet Food
  Raleigh, NC 800-952-6887
Moore's Candies
  Baltimore, MD 410-836-8840
Muth's Candy Store
  Louisville, KY 502-582-2639
Sally Lane's Candy Farm
  Paris, TN 731-642-5801
Virginia Diner Inc
  Wakefield, VA 888-823-4637

Popcorn Specialties

Cloud Nine
  Claremont, CA 909-624-3147
Eda's Sugar Free
  Philadelphia, PA 215-324-3412
Faroh Candies
  Middleburg Heights, OH 440-888-9866
Fun City Popcorn
  Las Vegas, NV 800-423-1710
GKI Foods
  Brighton, MI 248-486-0055
Golden Kernel Pecan Co
  Cameron, SC 803-823-2311
Humphrey Co
  Cleveland, OH 800-486-3739
Kenny's Candy & Confections
  Perham, MN
Koeze Company
  Grand Rapids, MI 800-555-9688
Midwest Nut Co
  Minneapolis, MN 800-328-5502
Olympia Candies
  Strongsville, OH 800-574-7747
Pop Art Snacks
  Salt Lake City, UT 801-983-7470
Popcorn Connection
  North Hollywood, CA 800-852-2676
Poppers Supply Company
  Allentown, PA 800-457-9810
Popsalot
  Beverly Hills, CA 213-761-0156
Rygmyr Foods
  South Saint Paul, MN 800-545-3903
Vande Walle's Candies Inc
  Appleton, WI 800-738-1020
Weaver Popcorn Co Inc
  Van Buren, IN

Rock

Salem Old Fashioned Candies
  Salem, MA 978-744-3242
Setton International Foods
  Commack, NY 800-227-4397

Taffy

Adams & Brooks Inc
  Los Angeles, CA 213-749-3226
Alaska Jacks
  Anchorage, AK 888-660-2257
Anastasia Confections Inc
  Orlando, FL 800-329-7100
Annabelle Candy Co Inc
  Hayward, CA 510-783-2900
Bidwell Candies
  Mattoon, IL 217-234-3858
Cadbury Trebor Allan
  Granby, QC 800-387-3267
Charlotte's Confections
  Millbrae, CA 800-798-2427
Downeast Candies
  Boothbay Harbor, ME 207-633-5178
El Brands
  Ozark, AL 334-445-2828
Ferrara Candy Co Inc
  Chicago, IL 800-323-1768
Forbes Candies
  Virginia Beach, VA 800-626-5898
Foreign Candy Company
  Hull, IA 800-831-8541
Gurley's Foods
  Willmar, MN 800-426-7845
Haven's Candies
  Westbrook, ME 800-639-6309
Humphrey Co
  Cleveland, OH 800-486-3739
James Candy Company
  Atlantic City, NJ 800-441-1404
Jelly Belly Candy Co.
  Fairfield, CA 800-522-3267
Kencraft, Inc.
  Alpine, UT 800-377-4368
Lammes Candies
  Austin, TX 800-252-1885
Layman Distributing
  Salem, OR 800-237-1319
Lowery's Home Made Candies
  Muncie, IN 800-541-3340
Lukas Confections
  York, PA 717-843-0921
Maxfield Candy
  Salt Lake City, UT 800-288-8002
Merb's Candies
  St Louis, MO 314-832-7117
New Century Snacks
  City of Commerce, CA 800-688-6887
Original Foods
  Dunnville, ON 888-440-8880
Patsy's Candy
  Colorado Springs, CO 866-372-8797
Phillip's Candy House
  Dorchester, MA 617-282-2090
Primrose Candy Co
  Chicago, IL 800-268-9522
Queen Bee Gardens
  Lovell, WY 800-225-7553
Sahagian & Associates
  Oak Park, IL 800-327-9273
Salem Old Fashioned Candies
  Salem, MA 978-744-3242
Salty Road
  Brooklyn, NY 929-250-2615
Seattle Gourmet Foods
  Tukwila, WA 800-800-9490
Setton International Foods
  Commack, NY 800-227-4397
Snackerz
  Commerce, CA 888-576-2253
Squirrel Brand Company
  McKinney, TX 800-624-8242
St. Jacobs Candy Co.
  Waterloo, ON 519-884-3505
Sweet Candy Company
  Salt Lake City, UT 855-772-7720
Sweet City Supply
  Virginia Beach, VA 888-793-3824
Taffy Town Inc
  Salt Lake City, UT 800-765-4770
Todd's
  Vernon, CA 800-938-6337
Warrell Corp
  Camp Hill, PA 800-233-7082
Webb's Candy
  Davenport, FL 800-289-9322

Toffee

Blissfully Better
  Chester, NJ
Bt. McElrath Chocolatier
  Minneapolis, MN 612-331-8800
Cadbury Trebor Allan
  Granby, QC 800-387-3267
Cary's of Oregon
  Grants Pass, OR 888-822-9300
Chocolate Signatures LP
  Toronto, ON 416-234-8528
Columbine Confections LLC
  Windsor, CO 970-377-2293
Confectionately Yours LTD
  Buffalo Grove, IL 800-875-6978
Creative Cotton
  Northbrook, IL 847-291-4128
Double Premium Confections
  McLean, VA 202-495-1884
Elegant Edibles
  Houston, TX 800-227-3226
Enstrom Candies, Inc.
  Grand Junction, CO 800-367-8766
Fancy's Candy's
  Rougemont, NC 888-403-2629
Ferncreek Confections LLC
  Fort Collins, CO 970-377-2293
Ferrara Candy Co Inc
  Chicago, IL 800-323-1768
Georgia Nut Co
  Skokie, IL 877-674-2993
Kohler Original Recipe Chocolates
  Kohler, WI 920-208-4930
Landies Candies Co
  Buffalo, NY 800-955-2634
Laurie & Sons
  New York, NY 212-866-6600
Leader Candies
  Brooklyn, NY 718-366-6900
Lukas Confections
  York, PA 717-843-0921
Madrona Specialty Foods LLC
  Seattle, WA 425-656-2997
Manhattan Food Brands, LLC
  Metuchen, NJ 732-906-2168
Marich Confectionery
  Hollister, CA 800-624-7055
Maries Candies
  West Liberty, OH 866-465-5781
Moonstruck Chocolate Co
  Portland, OR 800-557-6666
Northern Flair Foods
  Mound, MN 888-530-4453
Nunes Farms Marketing
  Gustine, CA 209-862-3033
Old Dominion Peanut Corp
  Norfolk, VA 800-368-6887
Pecan Deluxe Candy Co
  Dallas, TX 800-733-3589
Perfetti Van Melle USA Inc
  Erlanger, KY 859-283-1234
Poco Dolce
  San Francisco, CA 415-255-1443
Praim Co
  Salem, MA 800-970-9646
Quigley Industries Inc
  Farmington, MI 800-367-2441
Sticky Toffee Pudding Company
  Austin, TX 512-472-0039
Sweet Shop USA
  Mt Pleasant, TX 888-957-9338
Tall Grass Toffee Co
  Lenexa, KS 877-344-0442
Texas Toffee
  Odessa, TX 800-599-2133
Toffee Boutique
  Rancho Cordova, CA 916-638-8462
Toffee Co
  Houston, TX 713-688-5531
Vande Walle's Candies Inc
  Appleton, WI 800-738-1020
Weaver Nut Co. Inc.
  Ephrata, PA 800-473-2688
Webb's Candy
  Davenport, FL 800-289-9322

Product Categories / Candy & Confectionery: Candy Coatings

Truffles

Anette's Chocolate & Ice Cream
  Napa, CA.................707-252-4228
Birnn Chocolates of Vermont
  South Burlington, VT..........800-338-3141
Boca Bons East
  Greenacres, FL................800-314-2835
Bodega Chocolates
  Fountain Valley, CA...........888-326-3342
Bt. McElrath Chocolatier
  Minneapolis, MN...............612-331-8800
Candy Basket Inc
  Portland, OR..................800-864-1924
Chocoholics Divine Desserts
  Linden, CA....................800-760-2462
Chocolate Signatures LP
  Toronto, ON...................416-234-8528
Chocolati Handmade Chocolates
  Seattle, WA...................206-784-5212
De Fluri's Fine Chocolate
  Martinsburg, WV...............304-264-3698
Double Premium Confections
  McLean, VA....................202-495-1884
Fine & Raw Chocolate
  Brooklyn, NY..................718-366-3633
G Debbas Chocolatier
  Fresno, CA....................559-294-2071
GKI Foods
  Brighton, MI..................248-486-0055
J Morgan's Confections
  Ogden, UT.....................801-399-3007
Just Truffles
  St Paul, MN...................877-977-9177
Kohler Original Recipe Chocolates
  Kohler, WI....................920-208-4930
Moonstruck Chocolate Co
  Portland, OR..................800-557-6666
Moore's Candies
  Baltimore, MD.................410-836-8840
Morris National
  Azusa, CA.....................626-385-2000
No Whey Foods
  Lakewood, NJ..................732-806-5218
Noble Chocolates NV
  Veurne,
Poco Dolce
  San Francisco, CA.............415-255-1443
Praim Co
  Salem, MA.....................800-970-9646
Premium Chocolatiers LLC
  Lakewood, NJ..................732-806-5218
Sabatino Truffles USA
  West Haven, CT................888-444-9971
Sugar & Plumm
  New York, NY..................212-787-8778
Sweet Designs Chocolatier Inc
  Lakewood, OH..................216-226-4888
Sweet Shop USA
  Mt Pleasant, TX...............888-957-9338
Tea Room
  San Leandro, CA...............510-567-8868
Two Friends Chocolates
  Boxborough, MA................978-264-1949
Veritas Chocolatier
  Glenview, IL..................800-555-8331
Vosges Haut-Chocolat
  Chicago, IL...................888-301-9866

Candy Coatings

Caramel

Abdallah Candies & Gifts
  Burnsville, MN................952-890-0859
Calico Cottage
  Amityville, NY................800-645-5345
Sapore della Vita
  Sarasota, FL..................941-914-4256
Sweet Shop USA
  Mt Pleasant, TX...............888-957-9338
The Ardent Homesteader
  Arden, NY

Carob

Clasen Quality Chocolate
  Madison, WI...................877-459-4500

Chocolate

Anette's Chocolate & Ice Cream
  Napa, CA......................707-252-4228

Blommer Chocolate Co
  Chicago, IL...................800-621-1606
Clasen Quality Chocolate
  Madison, WI...................877-459-4500
Laurie & Sons
  New York, NY..................212-866-6600
Madyson's Marshmallows
  Heber City, UT................435-315-0045
Michael Mootz Candies
  Hanover Twp, PA...............570-823-8272
Pacific Gold Marketing
  Arlington, TX.................817-795-4671
Sole Grano LLC
  Fair Lawn, NJ.................201-797-7100
Sucesores de Pedro Cortes
  Hato Rey, PR..................787-754-7040
Sweet Pillar
  Newport Beach, CA.............310-913-7261
US Chocolate Corp
  Brooklyn, NY..................718-788-8555
Williams & Bennett
  Orlando, FL...................561-276-9007

Confectionery

Cache Creek Foods LLC
  Woodland, CA..................530-662-1764
Paulsen Foods
  Atlanta, GA...................404-873-1804

Chocolate Products

A La Carte
  Chicago, IL...................800-722-2370
Abdallah Candies & Gifts
  Burnsville, MN................952-890-0859
Adams & Brooks Inc
  Los Angeles, CA...............213-749-3226
Aglamesis Bros Ice Cream
  Cincinnati, OH................513-531-5196
Al Richard's Chocolates
  Bayonne, NJ...................888-777-6964
Al-Rite Fruits & Syrups Co
  Miami, FL.....................305-652-2540
Alaska Jacks
  Anchorage, AK.................888-660-2257
Alati-Caserta Desserts
  Montr,al, QC..................877-377-5680
Albanese Confectionery Group
  Merrillville, IN..............800-536-0581
Alcove Chocolate
  Los Angeles, CA...............323-284-2229
Ameri Candy
  Louisville, KY................502-583-1776
American Nut & Chocolate Co
  Boston, MA....................800-797-6887
Ames International Inc
  Fife, WA......................888-469-2637
Andre-Boudin Bakeries
  San Francisco, CA.............415-882-1849
Baker Candy Company
  Snohomish, WA.................425-422-6331
Barkeater Chocolates
  North Creek, NY...............518-251-4438
Barkthins Snacking Chocolate
  Congers, NY...................845-770-5802
Barry Callebaut USA
  Chicago, IL...................866-443-0460
Betty Lou's
  McMinnville, OR...............800-242-5205
Big Island Candies Inc
  Hilo, HI......................800-935-5510
Bissinger's Handcrafted Chocolatier
  St. Louis, MO.................314-615-2400
Bixby & Co., LLC
  Rockland, ME..................207-691-1778
Blackberry Patch
  Thomasville, GA...............800-853-5598
Blanton's
  Frankfort, KY.................502-223-9874
Blommer Chocolate Co
  Chicago, IL...................800-621-1606
Blommer Chocolate Co
  East Greenville, PA...........800-825-8181
Bloomsberry LLC
  Salem, MA.....................800-745-5154
Bridge Brands Chocolate
  San Francisco, CA.............888-732-4626
Brighams
  Arlington, MA.................800-242-2423
Brix Chocolates
  Youngstown, OH................866-613-2749

Cacao Prieto
  Brooklyn, NY..................347-225-0130
Cachafaz US
  Miami, FL.....................305-779-6340
Calico Cottage
  Amityville, NY................800-645-5345
Campbell Soup Co.
  Camden, NJ....................800-257-8443
Candy Cottage Company
  Huntingdon Valley, PA.........215-953-8288
Canelake's Candy
  Virginia, MN..................888-928-8889
Cape Cod Provisions
  Pocasset, MA..................508-564-5840
Charles Chocolates
  San Francisco, CA
Chase & Poe Candy Co
  St Joseph, MO.................800-786-1625
Chelsea Milling Co.
  Chelsea, MI...................800-727-2460
Cherry Moon Farms
  San Diego, CA.................800-580-2913
Chic Naturals
  Lahaina, HI...................808-463-7878
Chip'n Dipped Cookie Co
  Huntington, NY................631-470-2579
Choclatique
  Los Angeles, CA...............310-479-3849
Chocolat Michel Cluizel
  New York, NY..................646-415-9126
Chocolat Moderne, LLC.
  New York, NY..................212-229-4797
Chocolate Chocolate Chocolate
  St Louis, MO..................314-338-3501
Chocolate Fantasies
  Burr Ridge, IL................630-572-0045
Chocolate Works
  Freeport, NY
ChocoME US LLC
  Laguna Hills, CA..............949-500-8837
Chocomize
  Long Island City, NY..........800-621-3294
Chocopologie By Knipschildt
  Norwalk, CT...................203-854-4754
Chris Candies Inc
  Pittsburgh, PA................412-322-9400
Chuao Chocolatier
  Carlsbad, CA..................888-635-1444
Chukar Cherries
  Prosser, WA...................800-624-9544
Claeys Candy Inc
  South Bend, IN................574-287-1818
Clasen Quality Chocolate
  Madison, WI...................877-459-4500
Clear Mountain Coffee Company
  Silver Spring, MD.............301-587-2233
Coca-Cola Beverages Northeast
  Bedford, NH...................844-619-3388
Cocomira Confections
  Toronto, ON...................866-413-9049
Colorado Nut Co
  Denver, CO....................800-876-1625
Columbine Confections LLC
  Windsor, CO...................970-377-2293
Confection Art Inc
  Portland, OR..................503-505-0481
Crown Candy Corp
  Macon, GA.....................800-241-3529
Cummings Studio Chocolates
  Salt Lake City, UT............800-537-3957
Dandelion Chocolate
  San Francisco, CA.............800-785-2301
Davinci Gourmet LTD
  Seattle, WA...................800-640-6779
Daymar Select Fine Coffees
  El Cajon, CA..................800-466-7590
Dessert Innovations Inc
  Atlanta, GA...................800-359-7351
Desserts by David Glass
  South Windsor, CT.............860-462-7520
Dipasa USA Inc
  Brownsville, TX...............956-831-4072
Donaldson's Finer Chocolates
  Lebanon, IN...................800-975-7236
Droga Chocolates
  Fort Lauderdale, FL...........800-213-0754
East Shore Specialty Foods
  Hartland, WI..................800-236-1069
Eda's Sugar Free
  Philadelphia, PA..............215-324-3412
Edward Marc Brands
  Pittsburgh, PA................877-488-1808

Product Categories / Candy & Confectionery: Chocolate Products

Elmer Chocolate®
 Ponchatoula, LA 800-843-9537
Enstrom Candies, Inc.
 Grand Junction, CO 800-367-8766
Euro Chocolate Fountain
 San Diego, CA 800-423-9303
Fabio Imports
 Oceanside, CA 760-726-7040
Faroh Candies
 Middleburg Heights, OH 440-888-9866
Figamajigs
 San Mateo, CA 650-227-3830
Fitzkee's Candies Inc
 York, PA 717-741-1031
Fran's Chocolates
 Seattle, WA 800-422-3726
Free2b Foods
 Boulder, CO
Gardners Candies Inc
 Tyrone, PA 800-242-2639
GEM Berry Products
 Orofino, ID 888-231-1699
Gene & Boots Candies Inc
 Perryopolis, PA 800-864-4222
Gertrude Hawk Chocolates
 Dunmore, PA. 800-822-2032
GH Bent Company
 Milton, MA 617-322-9287
Ghirardelli Chocolate Co
 San Leandro, CA 800-877-9338
Gloria Jean's Gourmet Coffees
 Irvine, CA 877-320-5282
Golden Moon Tea
 Bristow, VA 877-327-5473
Gorant Chocolatier
 Youngstown, OH. 330-726-8821
Gourmedas Inc
 Quebec, QC. 418-210-3703
Gourmet Nut
 Brooklyn, NY 347-413-5180
Govadinas Fitness Foods
 San Diego, CA 800-900-0108
Gray & Company
 Hart, MI. 800-551-6009
Green & Black's Organic Chocolate
 Plano, TX 877-299-1254
Green Mountain Chocolate Inc
 Franklin, MA 508-520-7160
H B Taylor Co
 Chicago, IL 773-254-4805
H Fox & Co Inc
 Brooklyn, NY 718-385-4600
Haven's Candies
 Westbrook, ME 800-639-6309
Hershey Co.
 Hershey, PA. 800-468-1714
Hialeah Products Co
 Hollywood, FL 800-923-3379
Hickory Farms
 Maumee, OH. 800-753-8558
Hnina Gourmet
 Los Angeles, CA. 323-876-2609
Home Bakery
 Rochester, MI 248-651-4830
Hope Foods
 Boulder, CO 303-248-7019
Humboldt Chocolate
 Eureka, CA 707-630-5355
Hunt Country Foods Inc
 Marshall, VA 540-364-2622
Imani Chimani Chocolate
 Brooklyn, NY 718-484-1011
Island Princess
 Honolulu, HI 866-872-8601
Jason & Son Specialty Foods
 Rancho Cordova, CA 800-810-9093
Jer's Chocolates
 Solana Beach, CA. 800-540-7265
Joe Clark Fund Raising Candies
 Tarentum, PA. 888-459-9520
John Kelly Chocolates
 Los Angeles, CA. 800-609-4243
Jomart Chocolates
 Brooklyn, NY 718-375-1277
Justin's Nut Butter
 Boulder, CO 844-448-0302
Kamish Food Products
 Chicago, IL 773-725-6959
Karma Candy
 Hamilton, ON 905-527-6222
Kemach Food Products
 Brooklyn, NY 718-272-5655

Key III Candies
 Fort Wayne, IN 800-752-2382
Knudsen Candy
 Hayward, CA 800-736-6887
Koeze Company
 Grand Rapids, MI 800-555-9688
Kohler Original Recipe Chocolates
 Kohler, WI. 920-208-4930
Koppers Chocolate
 Cranford, NJ 800-325-0026
KOZY Shack Enterprises Inc
 St Paul, MN. 855-716-1555
La Cure Gourmande USA
 New York, NY 646-935-9329
Landies Candies Co
 Buffalo, NY. 800-955-2634
Layman Distributing
 Salem, VA 800-237-1319
Lerro Candy Company
 Darby, PA 610-461-8886
Lily's Sweets
 Boulder, CO 877-587-0557
Loghouse Foods
 Minneapolis, MN 763-546-8395
Long Grove Confectionary
 Buffalo Grove, IL 800-373-3102
Lou-Retta's Custom Chocolates
 Buffalo, NY. 716-833-7111
Louis J Rheb Candy Co
 Baltimore, MD 800-514-8293
Lowery's Home Made Candies
 Muncie, IN 800-541-3340
Lukas Confections
 York, PA 717-843-0921
Lynch Foods
 North York, ON. 416-449-5464
Lyons Magnus
 Fresno, CA 800-344-7130
Maple Leaf Cheesemakers
 New Glarus, WI 888-624-1234
MarySue.com
 Baltimore, MD 800-662-2639
Matangos Candies
 Harrisburg, PA 717-234-0882
Maxfield Candy
 Salt Lake City, UT 800-288-8002
Merb's Candies
 St Louis, MO 314-832-7117
Mont Blanc Gourmet
 Denver, CO 800-877-3811
Morse's Sauerkraut
 Waldoboro, ME. 866-832-5569
Munson's Chocolates
 Bolton, CT 888-686-7667
My Sweet
 Brooklyn, NY 347-689-4402
NibMor
 Kennebunk, ME 207-502-7541
No Whey Foods
 Lakewood, NJ 732-806-5218
Noble Chocolates NV
 Veurne,
Northwest Chocolate Factory
 Salem, OR. 503-362-1340
Northwestern Foods
 Arden Hills, MN. 800-236-4937
Oak Leaf Confections
 877-261-7887
Old Time Candy Co
 Lagrange, OH 440-355-4345
Olde Tyme Mercantile
 Arroyo Grande, CA. 805-489-7991
Organic Nectars LLC
 Malden On Hudson, NY. 845-246-0506
Pacari Organic Chocolate
 Boca Raton, FL
Parkside Candy Co
 Buffalo, NY. 716-833-7540
Pascha Chocolate
 Toronto, Ontario, ... 855-472-7242
Paulaur Corp
 Cranbury, NJ 609-395-8844
Pecan Deluxe Candy Co
 Dallas, TX 800-733-3589
Pez Candy Inc
 Orange, CT 203-795-0531
Philadelphia Candies Inc
 Hermitage, PA. 724-981-6341
Phillip's Candy House
 Dorchester, MA. 617-282-2090
Phillips Syrup Corp
 Cleveland, OH 800-350-8443

Pied-Mont/Dora
 Anne Des Plaines, QC 800-363-8003
Plantation Candies
 Telford, PA 888-678-6468
Praim Co
 Salem, MA 800-970-9646
Premium Chocolatiers LLC
 Lakewood, NJ 732-806-5218
Pretzel Perfection
 Vancouver, WA 360-635-3886
Priester's Pecans
 Fort Deposit, AL 866-477-4736
Prince of Peace
 Hayward, CA 800-732-2328
Pulakos 926 Chocolate
 Erie, PA. 814-452-4026
Puratos Canada
 Mississauga, ON. 905-362-3668
Q Bell Foods
 Nyack, NY 845-358-1475
Rapunzel Pure Organics
 Bloomfield, NJ 800-225-1449
Ravico USA
 Riderwood, MD 443-921-8025
Raw Rev
 Hawthorne, NY 914-326-4095
Rawmantic Chocolate
 New York, NY 212-247-2229
Rich's Ice Cream Co Inc
 West Palm Beach, FL 561-833-7585
Ripple Brand Collective
 Congers, NY 845-353-1251
Rocky Mountain Chocolate Factory
 Durango, CO 888-525-2462
Roland Machinery
 Springfield, IL 800-325-1183
Rosalind Candy Castle Inc
 New Brighton, PA. 724-843-1144
S Zitner Co
 Philadelphia, PA 215-229-9828
SAPNA Foods
 Atlanta, GA 404-589-0977
Sapore della Vita
 Sarasota, FL 941-914-4256
Saxon Chocolates
 Toronto, ON 416-675-6363
Scharffen Berger Chocolate Maker
 San Francisco, CA 866-608-6944
Scott's Candy
 Glennville, GA 800-356-2100
Sea Breeze Fruit Flavors
 Towaco, NJ 800-732-2733
See's Candies
 Carson, CA 800-347-7337
Seth Ellis Chocolatier
 Boulder, CO 720-565-2462
Shakespeare's
 Davenport, IA 800-664-4114
Shane Candy Co
 Philadelphia, PA 215-922-1048
Sherwood Brands
 New Brunswick, NJ 973-249-8200
Shoreline Chocolates
 Alburg, VT 800-310-3730
Sibu Sura Chocolates, LLC
 Myersville, MD 877-642-7872
Sjaak's Organic Chocolates
 Petaluma, CA 707-775-2434
Snack Works/Metrovox Snacks
 Orange, CA 800-783-9870
Sole Grano LLC
 Fair Lawn, NJ 201-797-7100
Somebody's Mother's Chocolate
 Houston, TX 713-627-3055
Southern Season
 Chapel Hill, NC 877-929-7133
Spice Rack Chocolates
 Fredericksburg, VA. 540-847-2063
Strawberry Hill Grand Delights
 Everett, MA. 617-319-3557
Stutz Candy Company
 Philadelphia, PA 888-692-2639
Sucesores de Pedro Cortes
 Hato Rey, PR. 787-754-7040
Sucre
 New Orleans, LA 504-708-4366
Sugar & Plumm
 New York, NY 212-787-8778
Sulpice Chocolate
 Barrington, IL 630-301-2345
Sunridge Farms
 Royal Oaks, CA 831-786-7000

Product Categories / Candy & Confectionery: Chocolate Products

Sweet Designs Chocolatier Inc
  Lakewood, OH 216-226-4888
Sweet Traders
  Huntington Beach, CA 714-903-6800
Swerseys Chocolate
  Brooklyn, NY 718-497-8800
Taza Chocolate
  Somerville, MA 617-623-0804
TCHO Ventures
  San Francisco, CA 415-981-0189
Tea Room
  San Leandro, CA 510-567-8868
Terri Lynn Inc
  Elgin, IL 800-323-0775
Texas Coffee Traders Inc
  Austin, TX 800-343-4875
Theo Chocolate
  Seattle, WA 206-632-5100
Tonex
  Wallington, NJ 973-773-5135
Tropical Nut & Fruit Co
  Orlando, FL 800-749-8869
Tumbador Chocolate
  Brooklyn, NY 718-788-0200
UnReal Brands
  Boston, MA
US Chocolate Corp
  Brooklyn, NY 718-788-8555
V Chocolates
  Salt Lake City, UT 801-269-8444
Valley View Blueberries
  Vancouver, WA 360-892-2839
Vermont Confectionery
  Bennington, VT 800-545-9243
Vigneri Chocolate Inc.
  Rochester, NY 877-844-6374
Vintage Plantations Chocolates
  Newark, NJ 800-207-7058
Vivoo
  Verona,
Weaver Nut Co. Inc.
  Ephrata, PA 800-473-2688
Webb's Candy
  Davenport, FL 800-289-9322
Western Syrup Company
  Santa Fe Springs, CA 562-921-4485
Wild Things Snacks
  Seattle, WA 720-231-9196
William Bounds
  Torrance, CA 800-473-0504
Wilson Candy Co
  Jeannette, PA 724-523-3151
Windy City Organics
  Northbrook, IL 800-925-0577
World Confections Inc
  South Orange, NJ 718-768-8100
World's Finest Chocolate Inc
  Chicago, IL 888-821-8452
Yoo-Hoo Chocolate Beverage Company
  Carlstadt, NJ 201-933-0070
Z Specialty Food, LLC
  Woodland, CA 800-678-1226
Zachary Confections Inc
  Frankfort, IN 800-445-4222
Zotter Chocolates
  Cape Coral, FL 239-214-7883

Baking Chocolate

Artisan Kettle
  833-605-6929
Blommer Chocolate Co
  Chicago, IL 800-621-1606
Ghirardelli Chocolate Co
  San Leandro, CA 800-877-9338
Hershey Co.
  Hershey, PA 800-468-1714
Jomart Chocolates
  Brooklyn, NY 718-375-1277
King Arthur Flour
  Norwich, VT 800-827-6836
Taza Chocolate
  Somerville, MA 617-623-0804

Boxed Chocolate

Abdallah Candies & Gifts
  Burnsville, MN 952-890-0859
Ameri Candy
  Louisville, KY 502-583-1776
Ann Hemyng Candy Inc
  Trumbauersville, PA 800-779-7004
Astor Chocolate Corp
  Lakewood, NJ 732-901-1001
Berkshire Bark Inc
  Sheffield, MA 413-229-8120
Bissinger's Handcrafted Chocolatier
  St Louis, MO 800-325-8881
Blommer Chocolate Co
  Chicago, IL 800-621-1606
Boca Bons East
  Greenacres, FL 800-314-2835
Brockmann's Chocolates
  Delta, BC 888-494-2270
Brown & Haley
  Fife, WA 800-426-8400
Buddy Squirrel LLC
  St Francis, WI 800-972-2658
Charlotte's Confections
  Millbrae, CA 800-798-2427
Chocolates a La Carte
  Valencia, CA 800-818-2462
Chocolates by Mark
  Houston, TX 832-736-2626
Chocolates Turin
  Plano, TX 972-731-6771
Claudia B Chocolates
  San Antonio, TX 800-725-4602
Daniel Le Chocolat Belge
  Vancouver, BC 604-879-7782
David Bradley Chocolatier
  Windsor, NJ 877-289-7933
Davinci Gourmet LTD
  Seattle, WA 800-640-6779
Double Premium Confections
  McLean, VA 202-495-1884
Elmer Chocolate®
  Ponchatoula, LA 800-843-9537
Empress Chocolate Company
  Brooklyn, NY 800-793-3809
Fannie May Fine Chocolate
  Oakdale, MN 800-999-3629
Faroh Candies
  Middleburg Heights, OH 440-888-9866
Fenton & Lee Chocolatiers
  Eugene, OR 800-336-8661
Frankford Candy & Chocolate Co
  Philadelphia, PA 800-523-9090
Functional Foods
  Roseville, CA 877-372-0550
Ganong Bros Ltd
  St. Stephen, NB 888-270-8222
Godiva Chocolatier
  New York, NY 800-946-3482
Gorant Chocolatier
  Youngstown, OH 330-726-8821
Guylian USA Inc.
  Englewood Cliffs, NJ 201-871-4144
Hagensborg Chocolates LTD.
  Burnaby, BC 877-554-7763
Harbor Sweets
  Salem, MA 800-243-2115
Harry London Candies Inc
  Melrose Park, IL 800-333-3629
Hawaiian King Candies
  Honolulu, HI 800-570-1902
Hibiscus Aloha Corporation
  Honolulu, HI 808-591-8826
Imagine Chocolate
  Burnank, CA 916-837-5772
Jer's Chocolates
  Solana Beach, CA 800-540-7265
Joe Clark Fund Raising Candies
  Tarentum, PA 888-459-9520
Joyva Corp
  Brooklyn, NY 718-497-0170
Koeze Company
  Grand Rapids, MI 800-555-9688
Kohler Original Recipe Chocolates
  Kohler, WI 920-208-4930
Lammes Candies
  Austin, TX 800-252-1885
Liberty Orchards Co Inc
  Cashmere, WA 800-231-3242
Lindt & Sprungli USA
  Stratham, NH 603-778-8100
Long Grove Confectionary
  Buffalo Grove, IL 800-373-3102
Maggie Lyon Chocolatiers
  Norcross, GA 800-969-3500
Maramor Chocolates
  Columbus, OH 800-843-7722
MarySue.com
  Baltimore, MD 800-662-2639
Maxfield Candy
  Salt Lake City, UT 800-288-8002
Michele's Chocolate Truffles
  Clackamas, OR 800-656-7112
Munson's Chocolates
  Bolton, CT 888-686-7667
Niagara Chocolates
  Buffalo, NY 877-261-7887
NibMor
  Kennebunk, ME 207-502-7541
Papas Chris A & Son Co
  Covington, KY 859-431-0499
Patsy's Candy
  Colorado Springs, CO 866-372-8797
Peanut Patch
  Yuma, AZ 800-872-7688
Piedmont Candy Co
  Lexington, NC 336-248-2477
Queen Bee Gardens
  Lovell, WY 800-225-7553
R.M. Palmer Co.
  West Reading, PA 610-372-8971
Rene Rey Chocolates Ltd
  North Vancouver, BC 888-985-0949
Reutter Candy & Chocolates
  Baltimore, MD 800-392-0870
Rogers' Chocolates Ltd
  Victoria, BC 800-663-2220
Russell Stover Candies Inc.
  Kansas City, MO 800-777-4004
Ruth Hunt Candy Co
  Mt Sterling, KY 800-927-0302
S Zitner Co
  Philadelphia, PA 215-229-9828
Sanders Candy Inc
  Clinton Twp, MI 800-852-2253
Scott's Candy
  Glennville, GA 800-356-2100
Seattle Chocolates
  Tukwila, WA 800-334-3600
Sjaak's Organic Chocolates
  Petaluma, CA 707-775-2434
Stutz Candy Company
  Philadelphia, PA 888-692-2639
Sugar & Plumm
  New York, NY 212-787-8778
Susie's South Forty Confection
  Midland, TX 800-221-4442
Sweet Blessings
  Malibu, CA 310-317-1172
Sweet Designs Chocolatier Inc
  Lakewood, OH 216-226-4888
Sweet Shop USA
  Mt Pleasant, TX 888-957-9338
Swerseys Chocolate
  Brooklyn, NY 718-497-8800
Tootsie Roll Industries Inc.
  Chicago, IL 866-972-6879
Trophy Nut Co
  Tipp City, OH 800-219-9004
Vande Walle's Candies Inc
  Appleton, WI 800-738-1020
Whetstone Chocolates
  St Augustine, FL 877-261-7887
Wilson Candy Co
  Jeannette, PA 724-523-3151
World Confections Inc
  South Orange, NJ 718-768-8100

Candy & Confectionery: Chocolate Products: White

Candy Basket Inc
  Portland, OR 800-864-1924
Sjaak's Organic Chocolates
  Petaluma, CA 707-775-2434

Chocolate Bars

Amano Artisan Chocolate
  Orem, UT 801-655-1996
B. Nutty
  Oakland, CA 510-374-4658
Blommer Chocolate Co
  Chicago, IL 800-621-1606
Chocomize
  Long Island City, NY 800-621-3294
Chris Candies Inc
  Pittsburgh, PA 412-322-9400
Dina's Organic Chocolate
  Mt Kisco, NY 888-625-2008
Divine Chocolate
  Washington, DC 202-332-8913

Product Categories / Candy & Confectionery: Chocolate Products

Earth Source Organics
  Vista, CA....................760-734-1867
Eating Evolved
  Setauket, NY.................631-675-2440
Eda's Sugar Free
  Philadelphia, PA.............215-324-3412
Elements Truffles
  Kearny, NJ...................917-836-2819
Equal Exchange Inc
  West Bridgewater, MA.........774-776-7400
Fine & Raw Chocolate
  Brooklyn, NY.................718-366-3633
Funkychunky Inc.
  Edina, MN....................888-473-8659
Good Stuff Cacao
  Metamora, MI.................248-690-5114
Greenwell Farms Inc
  Kealakekua, HI...............888-592-5662
Gutsii
  Los Angeles, CA
Hershey Co.
  Hershey, PA..................800-468-1714
Honey Acres
  Neosho, WI...................920-474-4411
Hu Kitchen
  New York, NY.................212-510-8919
Jer's Chocolates
  Solana Beach, CA.............800-540-7265
JoJo's Chocolate
  Mesa, AZ.....................805-395-6567
Jomart Chocolates
  Brooklyn, NY.................718-375-1277
Joyfuls
  Fairfield, NJ................888-989-9050
Justin's Nut Butter
  Boulder, CO..................844-448-0302
Kiss My Keto
  Los Angeles, CA..............310-765-1553
Kohler Original Recipe Chocolates
  Kohler, WI...................920-208-4930
Lily's Sweets
  Boulder, CO..................877-587-0557
Loacker USA
  New York, NY.................212-742-8510
Madecasse
  Brooklyn, NY.................917-382-2020
Malie Kai Hawaiian Chocolates
  Honolulu, HI.................808-599-8600
MilkBoy Swiss Chocolate
  Brooklyn, NY
Moonstruck Chocolate Co
  Portland, OR.................800-557-6666
Munson's Chocolates
  Bolton, CT...................888-686-7667
Olive & Sinclair Chocolate Co
  Nashville, TN................615-262-3007
Pascha Chocolate
  Toronto, Ontario,............855-472-7242
Poco Dolce
  San Francisco, CA............415-255-1443
Praim Co
  Salem, MA....................800-970-9646
Pure7 Chocolate
  Lynn, MA.....................844-547-8737
Raaka Chocolate
  Brooklyn, NY.................855-255-3354
Rawmantic Chocolate
  New York, NY.................212-247-2229
Sjaak's Organic Chocolates
  Petaluma, CA.................707-775-2434
Sucre
  New Orleans, LA..............504-708-4366
Sulpice Chocolate
  Barrington, IL...............630-301-2345
Sweet Designs Chocolatier Inc
  Lakewood, OH.................216-226-4888
Taza Chocolate
  Somerville, MA...............617-623-0804
Tony's Chocolonely
  Portland, OR.................503-388-5990
Travel Chocolate
  New York, NY.................718-841-7030
Videri Chocolate Factory
  Raleigh, NC..................919-755-5053
Vivra Chocolate
  Walpole, MA..................800-359-8950
Zazubean
  Vancouver, BC................604-801-5488

Chocolate Candy

21st Century Snack Foods
  Ronkonkoma, NY...............631-588-8000
Abbott's Candy Shop
  Hagerstown, IN...............877-801-1200
Aglamesis Bros Ice Cream
  Cincinnati, OH...............513-531-5196
Alexandra & Nicolay Chocolate Company
  Portland, PA.................570-897-6223
All American Snacks
  Midland, TX..................800-840-2455
All Wrapped Up
  Plantation, FL...............800-891-2194
Ameri-Suisse Group
  South Plainfield, NJ.........908-222-1001
American Nut & Chocolate Co
  Boston, MA...................800-797-6887
AmeriGift
  Oxnard, CA...................800-421-9039
Andre Prost Inc
  Old Saybrook, CT.............800-243-0897
Andre's Confiserie Suisse
  Kansas City, MO..............800-892-1234
Ann Hemyng Candy Inc
  Trumbauersville, PA..........800-779-7004
Anthony Thomas Candy Co
  Columbus, OH.................877-226-3921
Art CoCo Chocolate Company
  Geneva, IL...................877-232-9901
Artisan Confections
  Hershey, PA..................866-237-0152
Aunt Sally's Praline Shops
  New Orleans, LA..............800-642-7257
B & B Pecan Processors
  Turkey, NC...................866-328-7322
Baker Candy Company
  Snohomish, WA................425-422-6331
Baker Maid Products, Inc.
  New Orleans, LA..............800-664-7882
Baker's Candies Factory Store
  Greenwood, NE................800-804-7330
Banner Candy Manufacturing Company
  Brooklyn, NY.................718-647-4747
Baraboo Candy Co LLC
  Baraboo, WI..................800-967-1690
Bari & Gail
  Walpole, MA..................800-828-9318
Bee International
  Chula Vista, CA..............800-421-6465
Ben Heggy's Candy Co
  Canton, OH...................330-455-7703
Bergen Marzipan & Chocolate
  Bergenfield, NJ..............201-385-8343
Best Chocolate In Town
  Indianapolis, IN.............888-294-2378
Bidwell Candies
  Mattoon, IL..................217-234-3858
Birnn Chocolates of Vermont
  South Burlington, VT.........800-338-3141
Biscomerica Corporation
  Rialto, CA...................909-877-5997
Bissinger's Handcrafted Chocolatier
  St. Louis, MO................314-615-2400
Black Hound New York
  Brooklyn, NY.................800-344-4417
Blanton's
  Frankfort, KY................502-223-9874
Blommer Chocolate Co
  Chicago, IL..................800-621-1606
Blommer Chocolate Co
  East Greenville, PA..........800-825-8181
Bluebird Restaurant
  Logan, UT....................435-752-3155
Boca Bons East
  Greenacres, FL...............800-314-2835
Boyer Candy Co Inc
  Altoona, PA..................814-944-9401
Bread & Chocolate Inc
  Wells River, VT..............800-524-6715
Brockmann's Chocolates
  Delta, BC....................888-494-2270
Bt. McElrath Chocolatier
  Minneapolis, MN..............612-331-8800
Buddy Squirrel LLC
  St Francis, WI...............800-972-2658
Byrne & Carlson
  Portsmouth, NH...............888-559-9778
Cambridge Brands Inc
  Cambridge, MA................617-491-2500
Cameo Confections
  Bay Village, OH..............440-871-5732
Campbell Soup Co.
  Camden, NJ...................800-257-8443
Candy Central
  East Hanover, NJ
Candy Flowers
  Mentor, OH...................440-974-1333
Canelake's Candy
  Virginia, MN.................888-928-8889
Caribbean Cookie Company
  Virginia Beach, VA...........800-326-5200
Carousel Candies
  Geneva, IL...................888-656-1552
Carrie's Chocolates
  Edmonton, AB.................877-778-2462
Charlotte's Confections
  Millbrae, CA.................800-798-2427
Chase & Poe Candy Co
  St Joseph, MO................800-786-1625
Chevalier Chocolates
  Enfield, CT..................860-741-3330
Chocoholics Divine Desserts
  Linden, CA...................800-760-2462
Chocolat Belge Heyez
  St-Lazare-De-Bellechasse, QC.450-653-5616
Chocolat Jean Talon
  Montreal, QC.................888-333-8540
Chocolate By Design Inc
  Ronkonkoma, NY...............631-737-0082
Chocolate Chocolate Chocolate
  St Louis, MO.................314-338-3501
Chocolate Creations
  Monaca, PA...................724-774-7675
Chocolate House
  Milwaukee, WI................800-236-2022
Chocolate Moon
  Asheville, NC................800-723-1236
Chocolate Smith
  Santa Fe, NM.................505-473-2111
Chocolate Street of Hartville
  Hartville, OH................888-853-5904
Chocolate Studio
  Norristown, PA...............610-272-3872
Chocolaterie Bernard Callebaut
  Calgary, AB..................800-661-8367
Chocolaterie Stam
  Des Moines, IA...............877-782-6246
Chocolates a La Carte
  Valencia, CA.................800-818-2462
Chocolates by Mark
  Houston, TX..................832-736-2626
Chocolates By Mr Roberts
  Boca Raton, FL...............561-392-3007
Chocolates El Rey, Inc
  Houston, TX..................800-357-3999
Chocolati Handmade Chocolates
  Seattle, WA..................206-784-5212
Chocolatier
  Exeter, NH...................888-246-5528
Chocolove
  Boulder, CO..................888-246-2656
Chris Candies Inc
  Pittsburgh, PA...............412-322-9400
Christopher Norman Chocolates
  Hudson, NY...................518-822-0300
Clasen Quality Chocolate
  Madison, WI..................877-459-4500
Classic Confectionery
  Fort Worth, TX...............800-674-4435
Clear-Vu Industries
  Ashland, MA..................508-881-9100
Cloud Nine
  Claremont, CA................909-624-3147
CNS Confectionery Products
  Bayonne, NJ..................888-823-4330
Colts Chocolates
  Nashville, TN................615-251-0100
ConSup North America
  Lincoln Park, NJ.............973-628-7330
Cora Italian Specialties
  Countryside, IL..............800-696-2672
Cowgirl Chocolates
  Moscow, ID...................888-882-4098
Creative Cotton
  Northbrook, IL...............847-291-4128
Criterion Chocolates Inc
  Eatontown, NJ................800-804-6060
Croft's Crackers
  Monroe, WI...................608-325-1223
Crown Candy Corp
  Macon, GA....................800-241-3529
Cummings Studio Chocolates
  Salt Lake City, UT...........800-537-3957
DAGOBA Organic Chocolate
  Ashland, OR..................866-972-6879
Dairy Management Inc
  Rosemont, IL.................800-853-2479

Product Categories / Candy & Confectionery: Chocolate Products

Daprano & Company
   Charlotte, NC 877-365-2337
David Bradley Chocolatier
   Windsor, NJ 877-289-7933
Daymar Select Fine Coffees
   El Cajon, CA 800-466-7590
Dayton Nut Specialties
   Springboro, OH 937-743-4377
Delancey Dessert Company
   New York, NY 800-254-5254
Dessert Innovations Inc
   Atlanta, GA 800-359-7351
DGZ Chocolate
   Houston, TX 877-949-9444
Dilettante Chocolates
   Kent, WA 800-800-9490
Dipasa USA Inc
   Brownsville, TX 956-831-4072
Divine Delights
   Petaluma, CA 800-443-2836
Dolphin Natural Chocolates
   Cambria, CA 800-236-5744
Donaldson's Finer Chocolates
   Lebanon, IN 800-975-7236
Donells Candies
   Casper, WY 877-461-2009
Donnelly Fine Chocolates
   Santa Cruz, CA 888-685-1871
Doscher's Candies Co.
   Cincinnati, OH 513-381-8656
Double Play Foods
   New York, NY 212-682-4611
Dundee Brandied Fruit Co
   Dundee, OR 503-537-2500
Dundee Candy Shop
   Louisville, KY 866-877-9266
Dundee Groves
   Dundee, FL 800-294-2266
Ed & Don's Of Hawaii Inc
   Honolulu, HI 808-423-8200
Eda's Sugar Free
   Philadelphia, PA 215-324-3412
Emmy's Candy from Belgium
   Charlotte, NC 866-879-1901
Endangered Species Chocolate
   Indianapolis, IN 800-293-0160
Esther Price Candies & Gifts
   Dayton, OH 855-337-8437
Ethel M Chocolates
   Henderson, NV 800-438-4356
Euphoria Chocolate Company
   Eugene, OR 541-344-4914
Euro Cafe
   Rochester, NY 800-298-9410
Evans Creole Candy
   New Orleans, LA 800-637-6675
Fairytale Brownies
   Phoenix, AZ 800-324-7982
Fancy's Candy's
   Rougemont, NC 888-403-2629
Fantasy Chocolates
   Boynton Beach, FL 800-804-4962
Faroh Candies
   Middleburg Heights, OH 440-888-9866
Fenton & Lee Chocolatiers
   Eugene, OR 800-336-8661
Ferrara Candy Co Inc
   Chicago, IL 800-323-1768
Ferrero USA Inc
   Somerset, NJ 800-337-7376
Ficon
   St Louis, MO 888-569-4099
Fitzkee's Candies Inc
   York, PA 717-741-1031
Foley's Chocolates & Candies
   Richmond, BC 888-236-5397
Fralinger's
   Atlantic City, NJ 800-938-2339
Frankford Candy & Chocolate Co
   Philadelphia, PA 800-523-9090
Functional Foods
   Roseville, MI 877-372-0550
G Debbas Chocolatier
   Fresno, CA 559-294-2071
Ganong Bros Ltd
   St. Stephen, NB 888-270-8222
Gardners Candies Inc
   Tyrone, PA 800-242-2639
Gene & Boots Candies Inc
   Perryopolis, PA 800-864-4222
Georgia Nut Co
   Skokie, IL 877-674-2993

Germack Pistachio Co
   Detroit, MI 800-872-4006
Ghirardelli Chocolate Co
   San Leandro, CA 800-877-9338
Ghyslain Chocolatier
   Union City, IN 866-449-7524
GKI Foods
   Brighton, MI 248-486-0055
Godiva Chocolatier
   New York, NY 800-946-3482
Goldenberg's Peanut Chews
   Bethlehem, PA 888-645-3453
Gorant Chocolatier
   Youngstown, OH 330-726-8821
Govatos Chocolates
   Wilmington, DE 888-799-5252
Great Expectations Confectionery Gourmet Foods
   Chicago, IL 773-525-4865
Green County Foods
   Monroe, WI 800-233-3564
Green Mountain Chocolate Inc
   Franklin, MA 508-520-7160
Greenwell Farms Inc
   Kealakekua, HI 888-592-5662
Gurley's Foods
   Willmar, MN 800-426-7845
Hagensborg Chocolates LTD.
   Burnaby, BC 877-554-7763
Harbor Sweets
   Salem, MA 800-243-2115
Hauser Chocolates
   Westerly, RI 888-599-8231
Haven's Candies
   Westbrook, ME 800-639-6309
Hawaiian Host Inc
   Honolulu, HI 888-414-4678
Hawaiian King Candies
   Honolulu, HI 800-570-1902
Healthy Food Brands LLC
   Brooklyn, NY 212-444-9909
Hebert Candies
   Shrewsbury, MA 866-609-6533
Helms Candy Co., Inc
   Bristol, VA 276-669-2533
Hershey Co.
   Hershey, PA 800-468-1714
Hialeah Products Co
   Hollywood, FL 800-923-3379
Hibiscus Aloha Corporation
   Honolulu, HI 808-591-8826
Huppen Bakery
   Los Angeles, CA 323-656-7501
Hyde Candy Company
   Seattle, WA 206-322-5743
Idaho Candy Co
   Boise, ID 800-898-6986
Imperial Nougat Co
   Santa Fe Springs, CA 562-693-8423
Issimo Food Group
   La Jolla, CA 619-260-1900
Jason & Son Specialty Foods
   Rancho Cordova, CA 800-810-9093
Jeryl's Jems
   Tappan, NY 201-236-8372
Jo's Candies
   Torrance, CA 800-770-1946
Joe Clark Fund Raising Candies
   Tarentum, PA 888-459-9520
Josh Early Candies
   Allentown, PA 610-395-4321
Just Born Inc
   Bethlehem, PA 800-445-5787
Kara Chocolates
   Orem, UT 800-284-5272
Kastner's Pastry Shop & Grocery
   Surfside, FL 305-866-6993
Kate Latter Candy Company
   New Orleans, LA 800-825-5359
Kelly's Candies
   Pooler, GA 800-523-3051
Kemach Food Products
   Brooklyn, NY 718-272-5655
Kennedy Gourmet
   Glendale Heights, IL 800-729-8116
Key III Candies
   Fort Wayne, IN 800-752-2382
Knudsen Candy
   Hayward, CA 800-736-6887
Koeze Company
   Grand Rapids, MI 800-555-9688
Koppers Chocolate
   Cranford, NJ 800-325-0026

L C Good Candy Company
   Allentown, PA 610-432-3290
Lake Champlain Chocolates
   Burlington, VT 800-634-8105
Lanco
   Hauppauge, NY 800-938-4500
Landies Candies Co
   Buffalo, NY 800-955-2634
Lang's Chocolates
   Williamsport, PA 570-323-6320
Layman Distributing
   Salem, VA 800-237-1319
Lazzaroni USA
   Saddle Brook, NJ 201-368-1240
Len Libby Chocolatier-Maine
   Scarborough, ME 207-883-4897
Les Chocolats Vadeboncoeur Inc.
   Montreal, QC 800-276-8504
Lindt & Sprungli USA
   Stratham, NH 603-778-8100
Long Grove Confectionary
   Buffalo Grove, IL 800-373-3102
Longford-Hamilton Company
   Beaverton, OR 503-642-5661
Loretta's Authentic Pralines
   New Orleans, LA 504-529-6170
Lou-Retta's Custom Chocolates
   Buffalo, NY 716-833-7111
Louis J Rheb Candy Co
   Baltimore, MD 800-514-8293
Lowery's Home Made Candies
   Muncie, IN 800-541-3340
Lucille's Own Make Candies
   Manahawkin, NJ 800-426-9168
Lukas Confections
   York, PA 717-843-0921
Lynard Company
   Stamford, CT 203-323-0231
Madelaine Chocolate Company
   Rockaway Beach, NY 800-322-1505
Madrona Specialty Foods LLC
   Seattle, WA 425-656-2997
Maggie Lyon Chocolatiers
   Norcross, GA 800-969-3500
Maramor Chocolates
   Columbus, OH 800-843-7722
Marich Confectionery
   Hollister, CA 800-624-7055
Marlow Candy & Nut Co
   Englewood, NJ 201-569-3725
Mary of Puddin Hill
   Palestine, TX 800-545-8889
MarySue.com
   Baltimore, MD 800-662-2639
Maxfield Candy
   Salt Lake City, UT 800-288-8002
Menehune Mac
   Honolulu, HI 808-841-3344
Merb's Candies
   St Louis, MO 314-832-7117
Merlin Candies
   Harahan, LA 800-899-1549
Michele's Chocolate Truffles
   Clackamas, OR 800-656-7112
Michelle Chocolatiers
   Colorado Springs, CO 888-447-3654
Miesse Candies
   Lancaster, PA 717-392-6011
Mom N' Pops Inc
   New Windsor, NY 845-567-0640
Mona Lisa Foods
   Chicago, IL 866-443-0460
Moore's Candies
   Baltimore, MD 410-836-8840
Munson's Chocolates
   Bolton, CT 888-686-7667
Muth's Candy Store
   Louisville, KY 502-582-2639
Nancy's Candy
   Meadows Of Dan, VA 800-328-3834
Naron Mary Sue Candies
   Baltimore, MD 800-662-2639
Nassau Candy Distributors
   Hicksville, NY 516-433-7100
Natural Rush
   San Francisco, CA 415-863-2503
Neal's Chocolates
   Salt Lake City, UT 801-521-6500
Neuchatel Chocolatier
   Oxford, PA 800-597-0759
Newton Candy Company
   Houston, TX 713-691-6969

Product Categories / Candy & Confectionery: Chocolate Products

Niagara Chocolates
  Buffalo, NY 877-261-7887
Nora's Candy Shop
  Rome, NY 888-544-8224
Northern Flair Foods
  Mound, MN 888-530-4453
Northwest Chocolate Factory
  Salem, OR 503-362-1340
Nunes Farms Marketing
  Gustine, CA 209-862-3033
OH Chocolate
  Seattle, WA 206-329-8777
Old Dominion Peanut Corp
  Norfolk, VA 800-368-6887
Old Monmouth Candies
  Freehold, NJ 732-462-1311
Old Time Candy Co
  Lagrange, OH 440-355-4345
Olde Tyme Mercantile
  Arroyo Grande, CA 805-489-7991
Olivier's Candies
  Calgary, AB 403-266-6028
Omanhene Cocoa Bean Co
  Milwaukee, WI 800-588-2462
Oregon Bark
  Portland, OR
Pacific Gold Marketing
  Arlington, TX 817-795-4671
Palmer Candy Co
  Sioux City, IA 800-831-0828
Pangburn Candy Company
  Fort Worth, TX 817-332-8856
Papas Chris A & Son Co
  Covington, KY 859-431-0499
Patsy's Candy
  Colorado Springs, CO 866-372-8797
Paul's Candy Factory
  Salt Lake City, UT 800-825-9912
Paulaur Corp
  Cranbury, NJ 609-395-8844
Peanut Patch
  Yuma, AZ 800-872-7688
Pearl River Pastry & Chocolate
  Pearl River, NY 800-632-2639
Pease's Candy
  Springfield, IL 217-523-3721
Pecan Deluxe Candy Co
  Dallas, TX 800-733-3589
Phillip's Candy House
  Dorchester, MA 617-282-2090
Pine River Pre-Pack Inc
  Newton, WI 920-726-4216
Pippin Snack Pecans
  Albany, GA 800-554-6587
Plantation Candies
  Telford, PA 888-678-6468
Plyley's Candy
  Lagrange, IN 877-665-2778
Prifti Candy Company
  Worcester, MA 800-447-7438
Prince of Peace
  Hayward, CA 800-732-2328
Pulakos 926 Chocolate
  Erie, PA 814-452-4026
Purity Candy Co
  Lewisburg, PA 800-821-4748
Queen Bee Gardens
  Lovell, WY 800-225-7553
Quintessential Chocolates
  Fredericksburg, TX 800-842-3382
R.L. Albert & Son
  Stamford, CT 203-622-8655
Ragold Confections
  Wilton Manors, FL 954-566-9092
Rebecca-Ruth Candy Factory
  Frankfort, KY 800-444-3866
Rene Rey Chocolates Ltd
  North Vancouver, BC 888-985-0949
Reutter Candy & Chocolates
  Baltimore, MD 800-392-0870
Riddles' Sweet Impressions
  Edmonton, AB 780-465-8085
Riverdale Fine Foods
  Dayton, OH 800-548-1304
Rogers' Chocolates Ltd
  Victoria, BC 800-663-2220
Rosalind Candy Castle Inc
  New Brighton, PA 724-843-1144
Rosetti's Fine Foods Biscotti
  Clovis, CA 559-323-6450
Roseville Corporation
  Mountain View, CA 888-247-9338

Royal Baltic LTD
  Brooklyn, NY 718-385-8300
Runk Candy Company
  Cincinnati, OH 800-641-8551
S P Enterprises
  Las Vegas, NV 800-746-4774
S Zitner Co
  Philadelphia, PA 215-229-9828
S.L. Kaye Company
  New York, NY 212-683-5600
Sahagian & Associates
  Oak Park, IL 800-327-9273
Sanders Candy Inc
  Clinton Twp, MI 800-852-2253
Scott's Candy
  Glennville, GA 800-356-2100
Seattle Bar Company
  Seattle, WA 206-601-4301
Seattle Chocolates
  Tukwila, WA 800-334-3600
Seattle Gourmet Foods
  Tukwila, WA 800-800-9490
Setton International Foods
  Commack, NY 800-227-4397
Shakespeare's
  Davenport, IA 800-664-4114
Shane Candy Co
  Philadelphia, PA 215-922-1048
Sherm Edwards Candies
  Trafford, PA 800-436-5424
Sherwood Brands of Rhode Island Inc
  Rumford, RI 401-726-4500
Sifers Valomilk Candy Co
  Shawnee, KS 913-722-0991
Silver Sweet Candies
  Lawrence, MA 978-688-0474
Silverland Bakery
  Forest Park, IL 708-488-0800
Sjaak's Organic Chocolates
  Petaluma, CA 707-775-2434
Sorbee Intl.
  Philadelphia, PA 800-654-3997
South Beach Novelties & Confectionery
  Staten Island, NY 718-727-4500
South Bend Chocolate Co
  South Bend, IN 800-301-4961
SP Enterprises, Inc.
  Las Vegas, NV 800-746-4774
Spangler Candy Co
  Bryan, OH 888-636-4221
Spokandy
  Spokane, WA 509-624-1969
Sporting Colors LLC
  St. Louis, MO 888-394-2292
Squirrel Brand Company
  McKinney, TX 800-624-8242
St. Jacobs Candy Co.
  Waterloo, ON 519-884-3505
Stanchfield Farms
  Milo, ME 207-732-5173
Standard Functional Foods Grp
  Nashville, TN 800-226-4340
Stewart Candies
  Waycross, GA 912-283-1970
Stutz Candy Company
  Philadelphia, PA 888-692-2639
Sucesores de Pedro Cortes
  Hato Rey, PR 787-754-7040
Sucre
  New Orleans, LA 504-708-4366
Suity Confections Co
  Miami, FL 305-639-3300
Sun Empire Foods
  Kerman, CA 800-252-4786
Supreme Chocolatier
  Staten Island, NY 718-761-9600
Susie's South Forty Confection
  Midland, TX 800-221-4442
Sweenors Chocolates
  Wakefield, RI 800-834-3123
Sweet Blessings
  Malibu, CA 310-317-1172
Sweet Candy Company
  Salt Lake City, UT 855-772-7720
Testamints Sales-Distribution
  Hopatcong, NJ 888-879-0400
Toe-Food Chocolates and Candy
  Berkeley, CA 888-863-3663
Tom & Sally's Handmade Chocolates
  Brattleboro, VT 800-827-0800
Tootsie Roll Industries Inc.
  Chicago, IL 866-972-6879

Totally Chocolate
  Blaine, WA 800-255-5506
Toucan Chocolates
  Waban, MA 617-964-8696
Trappistine Quality Candy
  Wrentham, MA 866-549-8929
Tremblay's Sweet Shop
  Hayward, WI 715-634-2785
Triple-C
  Hamilton, ON 800-263-9105
Trophy Nut Co
  Tipp City, OH 800-219-9004
Tropical Nut & Fruit Co
  Orlando, FL 800-749-8869
Truan's Candies
  Detroit, MI 800-584-3004
Ultimate Nut & Candy Company
  Los Angeles, CA 800-767-5259
US Chocolate Corp
  Brooklyn, NY 718-788-8555
V L Foods
  White Plains, NY 914-697-4851
Valhrona
  Los Angeles, CA 310-277-0401
Van Leer Chocolate Corporation
  Chicago, IL 800-225-1418
Van Otis Chocolates
  Manchester, NH 800-826-6847
Vande Walle's Candies Inc
  Appleton, WI 800-738-1020
Varda Chocolatier
  Elizabeth, NJ 800-448-2732
Vaughn-Russell Candy Kitchen
  Greenville, SC 864-271-7786
Vermont Nut Free Chocolates
  Grand Isle, VT 888-468-8373
Vigneri Chocolate Inc.
  Rochester, NY 877-844-6374
Vitality Life Choice
  Carson City, NV 800-423-8365
Warner-Lambert Confections
  Cambridge, MA 617-491-2500
Warrell Corp
  Camp Hill, PA 800-233-7082
Weaver Nut Co. Inc.
  Ephrata, PA 800-473-2688
Webb's Candy
  Davenport, FL 800-289-9322
Westdale Foods Company
  Orland Park, IL 708-458-7774
Whetstone Candy Company
  St. Augustine, FL 904-825-1700
Whetstone Chocolates
  St Augustine, FL 877-261-7887
Widman's Candy Shop
  Crookston, MN 218-281-1487
Wilbur Chocolate Candy
  Lititz, PA 888-294-5287
Wilkinson-Spitz
  Yonkers, NY 914-237-5000
Williams Candy Co
  Chesapeake, VA 757-545-9311
Williams Candy Company
  Somerville, MA 617-776-0814
Williamsburg Chocolatier
  Williamsburg, VA 757-253-1474
Wilson Candy Co
  Jeannette, PA 724-523-3151
Windmill Candies
  Granite Falls, MN 877-771-8892
Windsor Confections
  Oakland, CA 800-860-0021
Winfrey Fudge & Candy
  Rowley, MA 888-946-3739
Wisconsin Dairyland Fudge Company
  Wisconsin Dells, WI 608-254-7771
Wisteria Candy Cottage
  Boulevard, CA 800-458-8246
World Confections Inc
  South Orange, NJ 718-768-8100
Yamate Chocolatier
  Highland Park, NJ 800-433-2462
Z Specialty Food, LLC
  Woodland, CA 800-678-1226
Zenobia Co
  Bronx, NY 866-936-6242

Chocolate Cherries

Bissinger's Handcrafted Chocolatier
  St. Louis, MO 314-615-2400
Cambridge Brands Inc
  Cambridge, MA 617-491-2500

Product Categories / Candy & Confectionery: Chocolate Products

Faroh Candies
  Middleburg Heights, OH 440-888-9866
Farr Candy Company
  Idaho Falls, ID 208-522-8215
GKI Foods
  Brighton, MI 248-486-0055
Godiva Chocolatier
  New York, NY 800-946-3482
Gray & Company
  Hart, MI 800-551-6009
Hialeah Products Co
  Hollywood, FL 800-923-3379
Lerro Candy Company
  Darby, PA 610-461-8886
Lowery's Home Made Candies
  Muncie, IN 800-541-3340
Marich Confectionery
  Hollister, CA 800-624-7055
Maxfield Candy
  Salt Lake City, UT 800-288-8002
Moore's Candies
  Baltimore, MD 410-836-8840
Papas Chris A & Son Co
  Covington, KY 859-431-0499
Terri Lynn Inc
  Elgin, IL 800-323-0775
Truan's Candies
  Detroit, MI 800-584-3004

Chocolate Chips

Blommer Chocolate Co
  Chicago, IL 800-621-1606
Hershey Co.
  Hershey, PA 800-468-1714
Homefree LLC
  Windham, NH 800-552-7172
King Arthur Flour
  Norwich, VT 800-827-6836
Lily's Sweets
  Boulder, CO 877-587-0557
Loghouse Foods
  Minneapolis, MN 763-546-8395
Pascha Chocolate
  Toronto, Ontario 855-472-7242
Setton International Foods
  Commack, NY 800-227-4397
Tea Room
  San Leandro, CA 510-567-8868

Chocolate Chunks

Blommer Chocolate Co
  Chicago, IL 800-621-1606
Chocomize
  Long Island City, NY 800-621-3294
Fine & Raw Chocolate
  Brooklyn, NY 718-366-3633
JC's Pie Pops
  Chatsworth, CA 818-349-1880
Michael Mootz Candies
  Hanover Twp, PA 570-823-8272

Cocoa & Cocoa Products

Al-Rite Fruits & Syrups Co
  Miami, FL 305-652-2540
Alaska Herb & Tea Co
  Anchorage, AK 800-654-2764
Alexander Gourmet Beverages
  Bolton, ON 800-265-5081
American Key Food Products Inc
  Closter, NJ 877-263-7539
American Nut & Chocolate Co
  Boston, MA 800-797-6887
American Yeast
  Memphis, TN 866-920-9885
Andre's Confiserie Suisse
  Kansas City, MO 800-892-1234
Andre-Boudin Bakeries
  San Francisco, CA 415-882-1849
Ann Hemyng Candy Inc
  Trumbauersville, PA 800-779-7004
Aunt Aggie De's Pralines
  Sinton, TX 800-333-9354
BakeMark Canada
  Laval, QC 800-361-4998
Barkeater Chocolates
  North Creek, NY 518-251-4438
Barry Callebaut USA
  Chicago, IL 866-443-0460
Blommer Chocolate Co
  Chicago, IL 800-621-1606

Blommer Chocolate Co
  East Greenville, PA 800-825-8181
Blue Marble Brands
  Providence, RI 888-534-0246
Boyd's Coffee Co
  Portland, OR 800-735-2878
Bread & Chocolate Inc
  Wells River, VT 800-524-6715
Brookema Company
  West Chicago, IL 630-562-2290
Calico Cottage
  Amityville, NY 800-645-5345
Cambridge Brands Inc
  Cambridge, MA 617-491-2500
Campbell Soup Co.
  Camden, NJ 800-257-8443
Caprine Estates
  Bellbrook, OH 937-848-7406
Carrie's Chocolates
  Edmonton, AB 877-778-2462
Chatz Roasting Co
  Ceres, CA 209-541-1100
Chocolat Belge Heyez
  St-Lazare-De-Bellechasse, QC 450-653-5616
Chocolat Jean Talon
  Montreal, QC 888-333-8540
Chocolate Street of Hartville
  Hartville, OH 888-853-5904
Chocolaterie Bernard Callebaut
  Calgary, AB 800-661-8367
Chocolates by Mark
  Houston, TX 832-736-2626
Cloud Nine
  Claremont, CA 909-624-3147
CocoaPlanet Inc.
  Sonoma, CA 650-454-0757
Consolidated Mills Inc
  Houston, TX 713-896-4196
Creative Cotton
  Northbrook, IL 847-291-4128
Crown Candy Corp
  Macon, GA 800-241-3529
Davidson's Organics
  Reno, NV 800-882-5888
Donells Candies
  Casper, WY 877-461-2009
Doscher's Candies Co.
  Cincinnati, OH 513-381-8656
ECOM Agroindustrial Corporation Ltd
  Pully,
Equal Exchange Inc
  West Bridgewater, MA 774-776-7400
Erba Food Products
  Brooklyn, NJ 718-272-7700
Foley's Chocolates & Candies
  Richmond, BC 888-236-5397
Forbes Chocolate BP
  Broadview Hts, OH 440-838-4400
G Debbas Chocolatier
  Fresno, CA 559-294-2071
Gel Spice Co LLC
  Bayonne, NJ 800-922-0230
Georgia Nut Co
  Skokie, IL 877-674-2993
Germack Pistachio Co
  Detroit, MI 800-872-4006
Ghirardelli Chocolate Co
  San Leandro, CA 800-877-9338
GKI Foods
  Brighton, MI 248-486-0055
Godiva Chocolatier
  New York, NY 800-946-3482
Govatos Chocolates
  Wilmington, DE 888-799-5252
Hauser Chocolates
  Westerly, RI 888-599-8231
Hebert Candies
  Shrewsbury, MA 866-609-6533
Herb Patch of Vermont
  Bellows Falls, VT 800-282-4372
Hershey Co.
  Hershey, PA 800-468-1714
Hialeah Products Co
  Hollywood, FL 800-923-3379
Home Bakery
  Rochester, MI 248-651-4830
Homefree LLC
  Windham, NH 800-552-7172
Jason & Son Specialty Foods
  Rancho Cordova, CA 800-810-9093
Jenny's Country Kitchen
  Dover, MN 800-357-3497

JER Creative Food Concepts, Inc.
  Commerce, CA 800-350-2462
King Arthur Flour
  Norwich, VT 800-827-6836
King Cupboard
  Red Lodge, MT 800-962-6555
Koeze Company
  Grand Rapids, MI 800-555-9688
Loghouse Foods
  Minneapolis, MN 763-546-8395
Magna Foods Corporation
  City of Industry, CA 800-995-4394
Marich Confectionery
  Hollister, CA 800-624-7055
Martha Olson's Great Foo
  Sutter Creek, CA 800-973-3966
Mc Steven's Coca Factory Store
  Vancouver, WA 800-547-2803
Merlin Candies
  Harahan, LA 800-899-1549
Michelle Chocolatiers
  Colorado Springs, CO 888-447-3654
Monster Cone
  Montreal, QC 800-542-9801
Nantucket Tea Traders
  Nantucket, MA 508-325-0203
Natra US
  Chula Vista, CA 800-262-6216
New Organics
  Kenwood, CA 734-677-5570
Niagara Chocolates
  Buffalo, NY 877-261-7887
Nora's Candy Shop
  Rome, NY 888-544-8224
OH Chocolate
  Seattle, WA 206-329-8777
Olam Spices
  Fresno, CA 559-447-1390
Olivier's Candies
  Calgary, AB 403-266-6028
Paulaur Corp
  Cranbury, NJ 609-395-8844
Phillips Syrup Corp
  Cleveland, OH 800-350-8443
Pine River Pre-Pack Inc
  Newton, WI 920-726-4216
Plantation Candies
  Telford, PA 888-678-6468
Quality Naturally Foods
  City Of Industry, CA 888-498-6986
R.M. Palmer Co.
  West Reading, PA 610-372-8971
Rapunzel Pure Organics
  Bloomfield, NJ 800-225-1449
Riddles' Sweet Impressions
  Edmonton, AB 780-465-8085
Service Packing Company
  Vancouver, BC 604-681-0264
Setton International Foods
  Commack, NY 800-227-4397
Stevens Creative Enterprises, Inc.
  New York, NY 646-558-6336
Sturm Foods Inc
  Manawa, WI 800-347-8876
Sucesores de Pedro Cortes
  Hato Rey, PR 787-754-7040
Sweenors Chocolates
  Wakefield, RI 800-834-3123
Taza Chocolate
  Somerville, MA 617-623-0804
Terri Lynn Inc
  Elgin, IL 800-323-0775
Timber Peaks Gourmet
  Parker, CO 800-982-7687
Tom & Sally's Handmade Chocolates
  Brattleboro, VT 800-827-0800
Top Hat Co Inc
  Wilmette, IL 847-256-6565
Tova Industries LLC
  Louisville, KY 888-532-8682
Vande Walle's Candies Inc
  Appleton, WI 800-738-1020
Varda Chocolatier
  Elizabeth, NJ 800-448-2732
Vigneri Chocolate Inc.
  Rochester, NY 877-844-6374
White Coffee Corporation
  Long Island City, NY 800-221-0140
Wilbur Chocolate Candy
  Lititz, PA 888-294-5287
Williamsburg Chocolatier
  Williamsburg, VA 757-253-1474

Product Categories / Candy & Confectionery: Confectionery

Wisconsin Cheeseman
   Madison, WI 800-693-0834

Cocoa Bean

Blommer Chocolate Co
   Chicago, IL 800-621-1606
Ghirardelli Chocolate Co
   San Leandro, CA 800-877-9338

Fudge

BakeMark Ingredients Canada
   Richmond, BC 800-665-9441
Blommer Chocolate Co
   Chicago, IL 800-621-1606
Calico Cottage
   Amityville, NY 800-645-5345
Original Herkimer Cheese
   Ilion, NY 315-895-7428
Solo Foods
   Countryside, IL 800-328-7656

Confectionery

Confectioners Crunch

Bon Courage Gourmet
   Durham, NC 888-865-5841
Cocomira Confections
   Toronto, ON 866-413-9049
Island Princess
   Honolulu, HI 866-872-8601
Plush Puffs Marshmallows
   Burbank, CA 818-784-2931

Confectionery

1000 Islands River Rat Cheese
   Clayton, NY 800-752-1341
Aglamesis Bros Ice Cream
   Cincinnati, OH 513-531-5196
Amcan Industries
   Elmsford, NY 914-347-4838
American Almond Products Co
   Brooklyn, NY 800-825-6663
American Food Products Inc
   Methuen, MA 978-682-1855
American Key Food Products Inc
   Closter, NJ 877-263-7539
American Licorice
   La Porte, IL 866-442-2783
Ames International Inc
   Fife, WA 888-469-2637
Andre's Confiserie Suisse
   Kansas City, MO 800-892-1234
Andrews Caramel Apples
   Chicago, IL 800-305-3004
Andros Foods North America
   Mount Jackson, VA 844-426-3767
Ann Hemyng Candy Inc
   Trumbauersville, PA 800-779-7004
Arway Confections Inc
   Chicago, IL 800-695-0612
Aunt Aggie De's Pralines
   Sinton, TX 800-333-9354
Baker Candy Company
   Snohomish, WA 425-422-6331
Bazzini Holdings LLC
   Allentown, PA 610-366-1606
Beehive Botanicals
   Hayward, WI 800-233-4483
Bestco Inc
   Mooresville, NC 704-664-4300
Betty Jane Homemade Candy
   Dubuque, IA 800-642-1254
Betty Lou's
   McMinnville, OR 800-242-5205
Bissinger's Handcrafted Chocolatier
   St. Louis, MO 314-615-2400
Blanton's
   Frankfort, KY 502-223-9874
Blommer Chocolate Co
   East Greenville, PA 800-825-8181
Boca Bons East
   Greenacres, FL 800-314-2835
Bodega Chocolates
   Fountain Valley, CA 888-326-3342
Brennan Snacks Manufacturing
   Bogalusa, LA 800-290-7486
Brittle Kittle
   Tigard, OR 800-447-2128
Brookside Foods
   Abbotsford, BC 800-468-1714

Burke Candy Ingredients Inc
   Milwaukee, WI 888-287-5350
Byrne & Carlson
   Portsmouth, NH 888-559-9778
Byrnes & Kiefer Company
   Callery, PA 724-538-5200
C Howard Co
   Bellport, NY 631-286-7940
Cambridge Brands Inc
   Cambridge, MA 617-491-2500
Campbell Soup Co.
   Camden, NJ 800-257-8443
Canelake's Candy
   Virginia, MN 888-928-8889
Caprine Estates
   Bellbrook, OH 937-848-7406
Carrie's Chocolates
   Edmonton, AB 877-778-2462
Casani Candy Company
   Pennsauken, NJ 856-488-0045
Catoris Candies Inc
   New Kensington, PA 724-335-4371
Charlotte's Confections
   Millbrae, CA 800-798-2427
Chase & Poe Candy Co
   St Joseph, MO 800-786-1625
Cheese Straws & More
   Monroe, LA 800-997-1921
Chex Finer Foods Inc
   Mansfield, MA 800-227-8114
Chocolat Belge Heyez
   St-Lazare-De-Bellechasse, QC 450-653-5616
Chocolat Jean Talon
   Montreal, QC 888-333-8540
Chocolate Street of Hartville
   Hartville, OH 888-853-5904
Chocolates by Mark
   Houston, TX 832-736-2626
Chocolati Handmade Chocolates
   Seattle, WA 206-784-5212
Chris Candies Inc
   Pittsburgh, PA 412-322-9400
Christopher Norman Chocolates
   Hudson, NY 518-822-0300
Clasen Quality Chocolate
   Madison, WI 877-459-4500
Cloud Nine
   Claremont, CA 909-624-3147
Concord Foods, LLC
   Brockton, MA 508-580-1700
Confectionately Yours LTD
   Buffalo Grove, IL 800-875-6978
Creative Cotton
   Northbrook, IL 847-291-4128
Creme Curls
   Hudsonville, MI 800-466-1219
Creole Delicacies Gourmet Shop
   New Orleans, LA 504-525-9508
Crown Candy Corp
   Macon, GA 800-241-3529
CTC Manufacturing
   Calgary, AB 800-668-7677
Cummings Studio Chocolates
   Salt Lake City, UT 800-537-3957
Cupid Candies
   Chicago, IL 773-925-8191
David Bradley Chocolatier
   Windsor, NJ 877-289-7933
Day Spring Enterprises
   Cheektowaga, NY 800-879-7677
Daymar Select Fine Coffees
   El Cajon, CA 800-466-7590
Decko Products Inc
   Sandusky, OH 800-537-6143
Dessert Innovations Inc
   Atlanta, GA 800-359-7351
Dillon Candy Co
   Boston, GA 800-382-8338
Dipasa USA Inc
   Brownsville, TX 956-831-4072
DMH Ingredients Inc
   Libertyville, IL 847-362-9977
Dolphin Natural Chocolates
   Cambria, CA 800-236-5744
Donaldson's Finer Chocolates
   Lebanon, IN 800-975-7236
Donells Candies
   Casper, WY 877-461-2009
Doscher's Candies Co.
   Cincinnati, OH 513-381-8656
Doumak Inc
   Elk Grove Village, IL 800-323-0318

Downeast Candies
   Boothbay Harbor, ME 207-633-5178
Dyna Tabs LLC
   Brooklyn, NY 718-376-6084
EcoNatural Solutions
   Boulder, CO 303-357-5682
Eda's Sugar Free
   Philadelphia, PA 215-324-3412
Edison Grainery
   Benicia, CA 510-382-0202
Edward & Sons Trading Co
   Carpinteria, CA 805-684-8500
El Brands
   Ozark, AL 334-445-2828
Elmer Chocolate®
   Ponchatoula, LA 800-843-9537
Enstrom Candies, Inc.
   Grand Junction, CO 800-367-8766
Fantazzmo Fun Stuff
   Schaumburg, IL 847-413-4036
Faroh Candies
   Middleburg Heights, OH 440-888-9866
Farr Candy Company
   Idaho Falls, ID 208-522-8215
Fernando C Pujals & Bros
   Guaynabo, PR 787-792-3080
Ferrara Bakery & Cafe
   New York, NY 212-226-6150
Ferrara Candy Co Inc
   Chicago, IL 800-323-1768
Fitzkee's Candies Inc
   York, PA 717-741-1031
FNI Group LLC
   Sherborn, MA 508-655-4175
Forbes Candies
   Virginia Beach, VA 800-626-5898
Frankford Candy & Chocolate Co
   Philadelphia, PA 800-523-9090
FrutStix
   Santa Barbara, CA 805-965-1656
Fudge Farms
   Buchanan, MI 800-874-0261
G Debbas Chocolatier
   Fresno, CA 559-294-2071
G Scaccianoce & Co
   Bronx, NY 718-991-4462
Gardners Candies Inc
   Tyrone, PA 800-242-2639
Gene & Boots Candies Inc
   Perryopolis, PA 800-864-4222
Georgia Nut Co
   Skokie, IL 877-674-2993
Germack Pistachio Co
   Detroit, MI 800-872-4006
Gimbals Fine Candies
   S San Francisco, CA 800-344-6225
GKI Foods
   Brighton, MI 248-486-0055
Godiva Chocolatier
   New York, NY 800-946-3482
Golden Fluff Popcorn Co
   Lakewood, NJ 732-367-5448
Goodart Candy Inc
   Lubbock, TX 806-747-2600
Govatos Chocolates
   Wilmington, DE 888-799-5252
Gray & Company
   Hart, MI 800-551-6009
Green Mountain Chocolate Inc
   Franklin, MA 508-520-7160
Greenwell Farms Inc
   Kealakekua, HI 888-592-5662
Groovy Candies
   Cleveland, OH 888-729-1960
Gurley's Foods
   Willmar, MN 800-426-7845
GWB Foods Corporation
   Brooklyn, NY 877-977-7610
H.B. Trading
   Totowa, NJ 973-812-1022
Haby's Alsatian Bakery
   Castroville, TX 830-538-2118
Happy Hive
   Dearborn Heights, MI 313-562-3707
Harlow House Company
   Atlanta, GA 404-325-1270
Hauser Chocolates
   Westerly, RI 888-599-8231
Haven's Candies
   Westbrook, ME 800-639-6309
Hawaii Candy Inc
   Honolulu, HI 800-303-2507

Hebert Candies
Shrewsbury, MA 866-609-6533
Hershey Co.
Hershey, PA...................... 800-468-1714
Hialeah Products Co
Hollywood, FL 800-923-3379
Hillside Candy Co
Hillside, NJ 800-524-1304
Holistic Products Corporation
Englewood, NJ 800-221-0308
Hospitality Mints LLC
Boone, NC........................ 800-334-5181
Imuraya USA
Irvine, CA........................ 949-251-9205
J.A.M.B. Low Carb Distributor
Pompano Beach, FL 800-708-6738
James Candy Company
Atlantic City, NJ 800-441-1404
Jason & Son Specialty Foods
Rancho Cordova, CA 800-810-9093
JER Creative Food Concepts, Inc.
Commerce, CA 800-350-2462
Joe Clark Fund Raising Candies
Tarentum, PA..................... 888-459-9520
Jomart Chocolates
Brooklyn, NY 718-375-1277
Joyva Corp
Brooklyn, NY 718-497-0170
Judy's Cream Caramels
Sherwood, OR.................... 503-625-7161
Kay Foods Co
Detroit, MI 313-393-1100
Kemach Food Products
Brooklyn, NY 718-272-5655
Key III Candies
Fort Wayne, IN 800-752-2382
Kloss Manufacturing Co Inc
Allentown, PA.................... 800-445-7100
Knudsen Candy
Hayward, CA 800-736-6887
Koeze Company
Grand Rapids, MI 800-555-9688
Kolatin Real Kosher Gelatin
Lakewood, NJ..................... 732-364-8700
Koppers Chocolate
Cranford, NJ 800-325-0026
Lanco
Hauppauge, NY 800-938-4500
Landies Candies Co
Buffalo, NY....................... 800-955-2634
Lang's Chocolates
Williamsport, PA.................. 570-323-6320
Laura Paige Candy Company
Newburgh, NY 845-566-4209
Layman Distributing
Salem, VA 800-237-1319
Leader Candies
Brooklyn, NY 718-366-6900
Lerro Candy Company
Darby, PA 610-461-8886
Loghouse Foods
Minneapolis, MN 763-546-8395
Long Grove Confectionary
Buffalo Grove, IL 800-373-3102
Lou-Retta's Custom Chocolates
Buffalo, NY....................... 716-833-7111
Louis J Rheb Candy Co
Baltimore, MD 800-514-8293
Lowery's Home Made Candies
Muncie, IN 800-541-3340
Lukas Confections
York, PA 717-843-0921
Mac Farms Of Hawaii Inc
Captain Cook, HI 808-328-2435
Magna Foods Corporation
City of Industry, CA 800-995-4394
Manhattan Food Brands, LLC
Metuchen, NJ 732-906-2168
Maple Grove Farms Of Vermont
St Johnsbury, VT.................. 802-748-5141
Mari's Candy
Chicago, IL....................... 773-254-3351
Marich Confectionery
Hollister, CA...................... 800-624-7055
Maries Candies
West Liberty, OH 866-465-5781
Mary of Puddin Hill
Palestine, TX...................... 800-545-8889
MarySue.com
Baltimore, MD 800-662-2639
Marzipan Specialties Inc
Nashville, TN 615-226-4800

Matangos Candies
Harrisburg, PA 717-234-0882
Maxfield Candy
Salt Lake City, UT 800-288-8002
Merb's Candies
St Louis, MO...................... 314-832-7117
Merlin Candies
Harahan, LA 800-899-1549
Michael Mootz Candies
Hanover Twp, PA 570-823-8272
Michelle Chocolatiers
Colorado Springs, CO............. 888-447-3654
Midwest Nut Co
Minneapolis, MN 800-328-5502
Milsolv Corporation
Butler, WI 800-558-8501
Milton A. Klein Company
New York, NY 800-221-0248
Mitch Chocolate
Melville, NY...................... 631-777-2400
Mitsubishi Chemical Holdings
New York, NY 212-672-9400
Moore's Candies
Baltimore, MD 410-836-8840
Mrs Annie's Peanut Patch
Floresville, TX 830-393-7845
Multiflex Company
Hawthorne, NJ 973-636-9700
Munson's Chocolates
Bolton, CT 888-686-7667
Muth's Candy Store
Louisville, KY 502-582-2639
My Daddy's Cheesecake
Cape Girardeau, MO............... 800-735-6765
MYNTZ!
Kent, WA......................... 800-800-9490
Nature's Candy
Fredericksburg, TX................ 800-729-0085
Naylor Candies Inc
Mt Wolf, PA 717-266-2706
New Century Snacks
City of Commerce, CA............. 800-688-6887
Niagara Chocolates
Buffalo, NY....................... 877-261-7887
Nora's Candy Shop
Rome, NY........................ 888-544-8224
Northwest Chocolate Factory
Salem, OR........................ 503-362-1340
Northwoods Candy Emporium
Branson, MO...................... 417-332-1010
Nunes Farms Marketing
Gustine, CA 209-862-3033
OCG Cacao
Whitinsville, MA 888-482-2226
OH Chocolate
Seattle, WA 206-329-8777
Old Time Candy Co
Lagrange, OH 440-355-4345
Olde Tyme Food Corporation
East Longmeadow, MA 800-356-6533
Olde Tyme Mercantile
Arroyo Grande, CA................ 805-489-7991
Ole Smoky Candy Kitchen
Gatlinburg, TN 865-436-4716
Olivier's Candies
Calgary, AB....................... 403-266-6028
Palmer Candy Co
Sioux City, IA 800-831-0828
Parker Products
Fort Worth, TX 817-336-7441
Parkside Candy Co
Buffalo, NY....................... 716-833-7540
Paulaur Corp
Cranbury, NJ...................... 609-395-8844
Peanut Patch Gift Shop
Courtland, VA..................... 800-544-0896
Pecan Deluxe Candy Co
Dallas, TX........................ 800-733-3589
Pez Candy Inc
Orange, CT 203-795-0531
Pfizer
New York, NY 800-879-3477
Philadelphia Candies Inc
Hermitage, PA..................... 724-981-6341
Phillip's Candy House
Dorchester, MA.................... 617-282-2090
Pine River Pre-Pack Inc
Newton, WI....................... 920-726-4216
Pioneer Marketing International
Los Gatos, CA..................... 408-356-4990
Plaidberry Company
Vista, CA......................... 760-727-5403

Plantation Candies
Telford, PA 888-678-6468
Popcorn Connection
North Hollywood, CA 800-852-2676
Poppers Supply Company
Allentown, PA..................... 800-457-9810
Priester's Pecans
Fort Deposit, AL................... 866-477-4736
Prince of Peace
Hayward, CA 800-732-2328
Produits Alimentaire
St Lambert De Lauzon, QC 800-463-1787
Pulakos 926 Chocolate
Erie, PA.......................... 814-452-4026
Quigley Industries Inc
Farmington, MI.................... 800-367-2441
R.M. Palmer Co.
West Reading, PA 610-372-8971
Rebecca-Ruth Candy Factory
Frankfort, KY 800-444-3866
Richards Maple Products
Chardon, OH...................... 800-352-4052
Ricos Candy Snack & Bakery
Hialeah, FL....................... 305-885-7392
Riddles' Sweet Impressions
Edmonton, AB 780-465-8085
Rito Mints
Trois Rivieres, QC 819-379-1449
Rivard Popcorn Products
Lancaster, PA 717-898-7131
Rosalind Candy Castle Inc
New Brighton, PA.................. 724-843-1144
Ross Fine Candies
Waterford, MI 248-682-5640
Ruth Hunt Candy Co
Mt Sterling, KY 800-927-0302
S Zitner Co
Philadelphia, PA 215-229-9828
Salem Old Fashioned Candies
Salem, MA 978-744-3242
Sally Lane's Candy Farm
Paris, TN......................... 731-642-5801
Scott's Candy
Glennville, GA 800-356-2100
See's Candies
Carson, CA 800-347-7337
Senor Murphy Candymaker
Santa Fe, NM 877-988-4311
Sensational Sweets
Lewisburg, PA..................... 570-524-4361
Shane Candy Co
Philadelphia, PA 215-922-1048
Sherm Edwards Candies
Trafford, PA 800-436-5424
Signature Brands LLC
Ocala, FL......................... 800-456-9573
Simply Gourmet Confections
Irvine, CA 714-505-3955
Smarties
Union, NJ 800-631-7968
Snackerz
Commerce, CA..................... 888-576-2253
Somerset Syrup & Concessions
Edison, NJ........................ 800-526-8865
Southern Style Nuts
Denison, TX 903-463-3161
Splendid Specialties
Petaluma, CA 707-796-7800
Star Kay White Inc
Congers, NY 800-874-8518
Stark Candy Company
Revere, MA........................ 800-225-5508
Startupcandy Co
Provo, UT 801-373-8673
Stichler Products Inc
Reading, PA....................... 610-921-0211
Stone's Home Made Candy Shop
Oswego, NY 888-223-3928
Stutz Candy Company
Philadelphia, PA 888-692-2639
Sucesores de Pedro Cortes
Hato Rey, PR...................... 787-754-7040
Sweenors Chocolates
Wakefield, RI 800-834-3123
Sweet City Supply
Virginia Beach, VA................ 888-793-3824
Taste of Nature Inc.
Santa Monica, CA.................. 310-396-4433
Taste Teasers
Dallas, TX........................ 800-526-1840
Temo Candy
Akron, OH........................ 330-376-7229

Product Categories / Candy & Confectionery: Decorations & Icings

Texas Toffee
  Odessa, TX 800-599-2133
Todd's
  Vernon, CA 800-938-6337
Tom & Sally's Handmade Chocolates
  Brattleboro, VT 800-827-0800
Torn & Glasser
  Los Angeles, CA 800-282-6887
Torn Ranch
  Novato, CA 707-796-7800
Tropical Foods
  Charlotte, NC 800-438-4470
Tropical Foods
  Lithia Springs, GA 800-544-3762
Tropical Nut & Fruit Co
  Orlando, FL 800-749-8869
Tropical Nut Fruit & Bulk Cndy
  Lithia Springs, GA 800-544-3762
Vande Walle's Candies Inc
  Appleton, WI 800-738-1020
Varda Chocolatier
  Elizabeth, NJ 800-448-2732
Vigneri Chocolate Inc.
  Rochester, NY 877-844-6374
Virginia Diner Inc
  Wakefield, VA 888-823-4637
Warner Candy
  El Paso, TX 847-928-7200
Warrell Corp
  Camp Hill, PA 844-234-3217
Weaver Nut Co. Inc.
  Ephrata, PA 800-473-2688
Weaver Popcorn Co Inc
  Van Buren, IN
Webb's Candy
  Davenport, FL 800-289-9322
Wedding Cake Studio
  Williamsfield, OH 440-667-1765
Westbrae Natural Foods
  Melville, NY 800-434-4246
Whetstone Chocolates
  St Augustine, FL 877-261-7887
White-Stokes Company
  Chicago, IL 800-978-6537
Wilbur Chocolate Candy
  Lititz, PA 888-294-5287
Williamsburg Chocolatier
  Williamsburg, VA 757-253-1474
Wilson Candy Co
  Jeannette, PA 724-523-3151
Wilson's Fantastic Candy
  Memphis, TN 901-767-1900
Winans Chocolates & Coffees
  Piqua, OH 937-381-0247
Wisconsin Cheeseman
  Madison, WI 800-693-0834
World Confections Inc
  South Orange, NJ 718-768-8100
Wright's Ice Cream Co
  Cayuga, IN 800-686-9561
Yamate Chocolatier
  Highland Park, NJ 800-433-2462
Yost Candy Co Inc
  Dalton, OH 800-750-1976
Z Specialty Food, LLC
  Woodland, CA 800-678-1226

Decorations & Icings

Decorations

Baking

Byrnes & Kiefer Company
  Callery, PA 724-538-5200
Jomart Chocolates
  Brooklyn, NY 718-375-1277
King Arthur Flour
  Norwich, VT 800-827-6836
L&M Bakers Supply Company
  Toronto, ON 800-465-7361
Satin Fine Foods
  Chester, NY
Signature Brands LLC
  Ocala, FL 800-456-9573

Cake

Adams Foods & Milling
  Dothan, AL 334-983-4233
American Key Food Products Inc
  Closter, NJ 877-263-7539

BakeMark Canada
  Laval, QC 800-361-4998
Byrnes & Kiefer Company
  Callery, PA 724-538-5200
Decko Products Inc
  Sandusky, OH 800-537-6143
Erba Food Products
  Brooklyn, NY 718-272-7700
Jomart Chocolates
  Brooklyn, NY 718-375-1277
King Arthur Flour
  Norwich, VT 800-827-6836
L&M Bakers Supply Company
  Toronto, ON 800-465-7361
Multiflex Company
  Hawthorne, NJ 973-636-9700
Paulaur Corp
  Cranbury, NJ 609-395-8844
Petra International
  Mississauga, ON 800-261-7226
Signature Brands LLC
  Ocala, FL 800-456-9573
Sugar Flowers Plus
  Glendale, CA 800-972-2935

Icings

BakeMark Canada
  Laval, QC 800-361-4998
BakeMark Ingredients Canada
  Richmond, BC 800-665-9441
Byrnes & Kiefer Company
  Callery, PA 724-538-5200
Chelsea Milling Co.
  Chelsea, MI 800-727-2460
Creme Unlimited
  Matteson, IL 800-227-3637
Erba Food Products
  Brooklyn, NY 718-272-7700
Lawrence Foods Inc
  Elk Grove Village, IL 847-437-2400
Louisiana Gourmet Enterprises
  Houma, LA 800-328-5586
Mimac Glaze
  Brampton, ON 877-990-9975
Newport Flavours & Fragrances
  Orange, CA 714-744-3700
Parrish's Cake Decorating
  Gardena, CA 800-736-8443
Quality Naturally Foods
  City Of Industry, CA 888-498-6986
Ribus Inc.
  St. Louis, MO 314-727-4287
Snelgrove Ice Cream Company
  Salt Lake City, UT 800-569-0005
Solo Foods
  Countryside, IL 800-328-7656
Warwick Ice Cream
  Warwick, RI 401-821-8403
Westco-BakeMark
  Pico Rivera, CA 562-949-1054

Ready to Use

Presto Avoset Group
  Claremont, CA 909-399-0062

Specialty-Packaged Candy

Bagged

American Licorice
  La Porte, IL 866-442-2783
Ann Hemyng Candy Inc
  Trumbauersville, PA 800-779-7004
Blommer Chocolate Co
  Chicago, IL 800-621-1606
Cambridge Brands Inc
  Cambridge, MA 617-491-2500
Chase & Poe Candy Co
  St Joseph, MO 800-786-1625
Crown Candy Corp
  Macon, GA 800-241-3529
David Bradley Chocolatier
  Windsor, NJ 877-289-7933
Eda's Sugar Free
  Philadelphia, PA 215-324-3412
Ganong Bros Ltd
  Moncton, NB 506-389-7898
GKI Foods
  Brighton, MI 248-486-0055
Hialeah Products Co
  Hollywood, FL 800-923-3379

Hillside Candy Co
  Hillside, NJ 800-524-1304
Joyva Corp
  Brooklyn, NY 718-497-0170
Kerr Brothers
  Toronto, ON 416-252-7341
Leader Candies
  Brooklyn, NY 718-366-6900
Ludwick's Frozen Donuts
  Grand Rapids, MI 800-366-8816
Lukas Confections
  York, PA 717-843-0921
Olde Tyme Mercantile
  Arroyo Grande, CA 805-489-7991
Papas Chris A & Son Co
  Covington, KY 859-431-0499
Piedmont Candy Co
  Lexington, NC 336-248-2477
Quigley Industries Inc
  Farmington, MI 800-367-2441
Salem Old Fashioned Candies
  Salem, MA 978-744-3242
Suity Confections Co
  Miami, FL 305-639-3300
Weaver Nut Co. Inc.
  Ephrata, PA 800-473-2688
Webb's Candy
  Davenport, FL 800-289-9322
World Confections Inc
  South Orange, NJ 718-768-8100
Yost Candy Co Inc
  Dalton, OH 800-750-1976

Boxed

Anastasia Confections Inc
  Orlando, FL 800-329-7100
Anthony Thomas Candy Co
  Columbus, OH 877-226-3921
Arcor USA
  Coral Gables, FL 800-572-7267
Astor Chocolate Corp
  Lakewood, NJ 732-901-1001
Baraboo Candy Co LLC
  Baraboo, WI 800-967-1690
Best Chocolate In Town
  Indianapolis, IN 888-294-2378
Blanton's
  Frankfort, KY 502-223-9874
Blommer Chocolate Co
  East Greenville, PA 800-825-8181
Boyer Candy Co Inc
  Altoona, PA 814-944-9401
Calico Cottage
  Amityville, NY 800-645-5345
Chocolate House
  Milwaukee, WI 800-236-2022
Ghirardelli Chocolate Co
  San Leandro, CA 800-877-9338
GKI Foods
  Brighton, MI 248-486-0055
MarySue.com
  Baltimore, MD 800-662-2639
Ruth Hunt Candy Co
  Mt Sterling, KY 800-927-0302
Scott's Candy
  Glennville, GA 800-356-2100
Terri Lynn Inc
  Elgin, IL 800-323-0775

Christmas

Bee International
  Chula Vista, CA 800-421-6465
Blanton's
  Frankfort, KY 502-223-9874
Charlotte's Confections
  Millbrae, CA 800-798-2427
Chase & Poe Candy Co
  St Joseph, MO 800-786-1625
Chocolat Jean Talon
  Montreal, QC 888-333-8540
David Bradley Chocolatier
  Windsor, NJ 877-289-7933
Day Spring Enterprises
  Cheektowaga, NY 800-879-7677
Doscher's Candies Co.
  Cincinnati, OH 513-381-8656
Ferrara Bakery & Cafe
  New York, NY 212-226-6150
Gimbals Fine Candies
  S San Francisco, CA 800-344-6225

Product Categories / Candy & Confectionery: Specialty-Packaged Candy

GKI Foods
   Brighton, MI 248-486-0055
Groovy Candies
   Cleveland, OH .888-729-1960
Haven's Candies
   Westbrook, ME 800-639-6309
Kerr Brothers
   Toronto, ON 416-252-7341
Landies Candies Co
   Buffalo, NY 800-955-2634
Leader Candies
   Brooklyn, NY 718-366-6900
Lukas Confections
   York, PA 717-843-0921
Madrona Specialty Foods LLC
   Seattle, WA 425-656-2997
Old Dominion Peanut Corp
   Norfolk, VA. 800-368-6887
Papas Chris A & Son Co
   Covington, KY .859-431-0499
Piedmont Candy Co
   Lexington, NC .336-248-2477
R.M. Palmer Co.
   West Reading, PA 610-372-8971
Setton International Foods
   Commack, NY .800-227-4397
Shane Candy Co
   Philadelphia, PA 215-922-1048
World Confections Inc
   South Orange, NJ 718-768-8100
Zachary Confections Inc
   Frankfort, IN 800-445-4222

Easter

Bee International
   Chula Vista, CA 800-421-6465
Blanton's
   Frankfort, KY 502-223-9874
Charlotte's Confections
   Millbrae, CA. 800-798-2427
Chase & Poe Candy Co
   St Joseph, MO. .800-786-1625
Chocolat Jean Talon
   Montreal, QC 888-333-8540
David Bradley Chocolatier
   Windsor, NJ. 877-289-7933
Day Spring Enterprises
   Cheektowaga, NY. 800-879-7677
Doscher's Candies Co.
   Cincinnati, OH .513-381-8656
Ferrara Bakery & Cafe
   New York, NY .212-226-6150
Gimbals Fine Candies
   S San Francisco, CA 800-344-6225
GKI Foods
   Brighton, MI 248-486-0055
Golden Fluff Popcorn Co
   Lakewood, NJ .732-367-5448
Groovy Candies
   Cleveland, OH .888-729-1960
Leader Candies
   Brooklyn, NY 718-366-6900
Madrona Specialty Foods LLC
   Seattle, WA 425-656-2997
Multiflex Company
   Hawthorne, NJ .973-636-9700
Papas Chris A & Son Co
   Covington, KY .859-431-0499
Piedmont Candy Co
   Lexington, NC .336-248-2477
R.M. Palmer Co.
   West Reading, PA 610-372-8971
S Zitner Co
   Philadelphia, PA 215-229-9828
Vande Walle's Candies Inc
   Appleton, WI 800-738-1020
Vigneri Chocolate Inc.
   Rochester, NY .877-844-6374
World Confections Inc
   South Orange, NJ 718-768-8100
Zachary Confections Inc
   Frankfort, IN 800-445-4222

Fund Raising

Chase & Poe Candy Co
   St Joseph, MO. .800-786-1625
David Bradley Chocolatier
   Windsor, NJ. 877-289-7933
Hillside Candy Co
   Hillside, NJ. 800-524-1304
Joe Clark Fund Raising Candies
   Tarentum, PA. .888-459-9520
Joyva Corp
   Brooklyn, NY 718-497-0170
Koeze Company
   Grand Rapids, MI 800-555-9688
Leader Candies
   Brooklyn, NY 718-366-6900
Lukas Confections
   York, PA 717-843-0921
Old Dominion Peanut Corp
   Norfolk, VA. 800-368-6887
Papas Chris A & Son Co
   Covington, KY .859-431-0499
Quigley Industries Inc
   Farmington, MI. 800-367-2441
Terri Lynn Inc
   Elgin, IL 800-323-0775
Vande Walle's Candies Inc
   Appleton, WI 800-738-1020

Halloween

Astor Chocolate Corp
   Lakewood, NJ .732-901-1001
Bee International
   Chula Vista, CA 800-421-6465
Blanton's
   Frankfort, KY 502-223-9874
Charlotte's Confections
   Millbrae, CA. 800-798-2427
Chase & Poe Candy Co
   St Joseph, MO. .800-786-1625
Chocolat Jean Talon
   Montreal, QC 888-333-8540
David Bradley Chocolatier
   Windsor, NJ. 877-289-7933
Day Spring Enterprises
   Cheektowaga, NY. 800-879-7677
Ferrara Bakery & Cafe
   New York, NY .212-226-6150
Gimbals Fine Candies
   S San Francisco, CA 800-344-6225
GKI Foods
   Brighton, MI 248-486-0055
Groovy Candies
   Cleveland, OH .888-729-1960
Joyva Corp
   Brooklyn, NY 718-497-0170
Kerr Brothers
   Toronto, ON 416-252-7341
Leader Candies
   Brooklyn, NY 718-366-6900
Lukas Confections
   York, PA 717-843-0921
Madrona Specialty Foods LLC
   Seattle, WA 425-656-2997
Piedmont Candy Co
   Lexington, NC .336-248-2477
R.M. Palmer Co.
   West Reading, PA 610-372-8971
Shane Candy Co
   Philadelphia, PA 215-922-1048
World Confections Inc
   South Orange, NJ 718-768-8100
Yost Candy Co Inc
   Dalton, OH 800-750-1976
Zachary Confections Inc
   Frankfort, IN 800-445-4222

Multi-Packs

World Confections Inc
   South Orange, NJ 718-768-8100

Non-Chocolate - Boxed

Hillside Candy Co
   Hillside, NJ. 800-524-1304

Leader Candies
   Brooklyn, NY 718-366-6900
Moore's Candies
   Baltimore, MD .410-836-8840
Ozone Confectioners & Bakers Supplies
   Elmwood Park, NJ 201-791-4444
Webb's Candy
   Davenport, FL. .800-289-9322

Packaged for Racks

American Licorice
   La Porte, IL 866-442-2783
David Bradley Chocolatier
   Windsor, NJ. 877-289-7933
Jason & Son Specialty Foods
   Rancho Cordova, CA 800-810-9093
Joyva Corp
   Brooklyn, NY 718-497-0170
Setton International Foods
   Commack, NY .800-227-4397
Sherbrooke OEM Ltd
   Sherbrooke, QC 866-851-2579
Weaver Nut Co. Inc.
   Ephrata, PA 800-473-2688

Packaged for Theaters

American Licorice
   La Porte, IL 866-442-2783
Joyva Corp
   Brooklyn, NY 718-497-0170

Valentine

Arway Confections Inc
   Chicago, IL 800-695-0612
Astor Chocolate Corp
   Lakewood, NJ .732-901-1001
Bee International
   Chula Vista, CA 800-421-6465
Blanton's
   Frankfort, KY 502-223-9874
Charlotte's Confections
   Millbrae, CA. 800-798-2427
Chase & Poe Candy Co
   St Joseph, MO. .800-786-1625
David Bradley Chocolatier
   Windsor, NJ. 877-289-7933
Day Spring Enterprises
   Cheektowaga, NY. 800-879-7677
Ferrara Bakery & Cafe
   New York, NY .212-226-6150
Gimbals Fine Candies
   S San Francisco, CA 800-344-6225
Groovy Candies
   Cleveland, OH .888-729-1960
Leader Candies
   Brooklyn, NY 718-366-6900
R.M. Palmer Co.
   West Reading, PA 610-372-8971
Rito Mints
   Trois Rivieres, QC 819-379-1449
Shane Candy Co
   Philadelphia, PA 215-922-1048
Vande Walle's Candies Inc
   Appleton, WI 800-738-1020
World Confections Inc
   South Orange, NJ 718-768-8100
Zachary Confections Inc
   Frankfort, IN 800-445-4222

Vending

Chase & Poe Candy Co
   St Joseph, MO. .800-786-1625
GKI Foods
   Brighton, MI 248-486-0055
Joyva Corp
   Brooklyn, NY 718-497-0170
Lukas Confections
   York, PA 717-843-0921
Papas Chris A & Son Co
   Covington, KY .859-431-0499
Sherbrooke OEM Ltd
   Sherbrooke, QC 866-851-2579

Cereals, Grains, Rice & Flour

Alfalfa

Christopher's Herb Shop
  Springville, UT 888-372-4372
Enray, Inc
  Livermore, CA 800-288-3637
International Specialty Supply
  Cookeville, TN 931-526-1106
Julie Anne's
  Las Vegas, NV 702-767-4765
New Organics
  Kenwood, CA 734-677-5570
S & E Organic Farms Inc
  Bakersfield, CA 661-325-2644
Verhoff Alfalfa Mill Inc
  Ottawa, OH 800-834-8563

Barley

Agricore United
  St Louis Park, MN 877-509-5865
Christopher's Herb Shop
  Springville, UT 888-372-4372
Ferris Organic Farms
  Eaton Rapids, MI 800-628-8736
Fizzle Flat Farm, L.L.C.
  Yale, IL 618-793-2060
Grain Millers Inc
  Eden Prairie, MN 800-232-6287
Graysmarsh Berry Farm
  Sequim, WA 800-683-4367
Great River Organic Milling
  Arcadia, WI. 608-687-9580
Green Foods Corp.
  Oxnard, CA. 800-777-4430
J M Swank Co
  North Liberty, IA 800-593-6375
La Crosse Milling Company
  Cochrane, WI 800-441-5411
Natural Way Mills Inc
  Middle River, MN. 218-222-3677
Ottawa Valley Grain Products
  Renfrew, ON 613-432-3614
Pines International
  Lawrence, KS 800-697-4637
Prairie Malt
  Biggar, SK. 306-948-3500
Raymond-Hadley Corporation
  Spencer, NY 800-252-5220
T.S. Smith & Sons
  Bridgeville, DE 302-337-8271
Terra Ingredients
  Minneapolis, MN 888-497-3308
Timeless Seeds
  Ulm, MT 406-866-3340
Wallace Grain & Pea Company
  Pullman, WA. 509-878-1561

Bran

Bluechip Group
  Salt Lake City, UT 800-878-0099
Bunge North America Inc.
  Chesterfield, MO 314-292-2000
Canadian Harvest-U.S.A.
  Edina, MN. 888-689-5800
Cereal Food Processors Inc
  Mcpherson, KS 800-835-2067
Chef Hans' Gourmet Foods
  Monroe, LA. 800-890-4267
Great Grains Milling Company
  Scobey, MT. 406-783-5581
GS Dunn & Company
  Hamilton, ON 905-522-0833
Healthy Food Ingredients
  Fargo, ND 844-275-3443
J M Swank Co
  North Liberty, IA 800-593-6375
J.R. Short Canadian Mills
  Toronto, ON 416-421-3463
Kerry Foodservice
  Mansfield, OH 800-533-2722
Knappen Milling Co
  Augusta, MI 800-562-7736
New Organics
  Kenwood, CA 734-677-5570
Ohta Wafer Factory
  Honolulu, HI 808-949-2775
Raymond-Hadley Corporation
  Spencer, NY 800-252-5220
Ricex Company
  El Dorado Hills, CA 916-933-3000
Riviana Foods Inc.
  Houston, TX 713-529-3251
SJH Enterprises
  Middleton, WI. 888-745-3845
Southern Brown Rice
  Weiner, AR 800-421-7423
Star of the West Milling Co.
  Frankenmuth, MI 989-652-9971

Mustard

GS Dunn & Company
  Hamilton, ON 905-522-0833

Rice

Beaumont Rice Mills
  Beaumont, TX. 409-832-2521
Bunge North America Inc.
  Chesterfield, MO 314-292-2000
Farmers Rice Milling Co
  Lake Charles, LA 337-433-5205
Louis Dreyfus Corporation
  Rotterdam,
RiceBran Technologies
  Scottsdale, AZ. 602-522-3000
Ricex Company
  El Dorado Hills, CA 916-933-3000
Riviana Foods Inc.
  Houston, TX 713-529-3251
Sahara Natural Foods
  San Leandro, CA. 510-352-5111
Southern Brown Rice
  Weiner, AR 800-421-7423

Wheat

Bluechip Group
  Salt Lake City, UT 800-878-0099
Canadian Harvest-U.S.A.
  Edina, MN. 888-689-5800
Cereal Food Processors Inc
  Mcpherson, KS 800-835-2067
New Organics
  Kenwood, CA 734-677-5570

Cereal

Amcan Industries
  Elmsford, NY 914-347-4838
B & G Foods Inc.
  Parsippany, NJ. 973-401-6500
Back to Nature Foods
   855-346-2225
Barbara's Bakery
  Lakeville, MN. 800-343-0590
Batory Foods
  Des Plaines, IL 847-299-1999
Bob's Red Mill Natural Foods
  Milwaukie, OR 800-349-2173
Cambridge Food
  Monterey, CA 800-433-2584
Clara Foods
  Clara City, MN 888-844-8518
Coach's Oats
  Yorba Linda, CA 714-692-6885
Continental Mills Inc
  Tukwila, WA. 206-816-7000
Earnest Eats
  Solana Beach, CA. 858-299-4238
Earth Song Whole Foods
  Fair Oaks, CA 877-327-8476
Edison Grainery
  Benicia, CA. 510-382-0202
Fiddlers Green Farm
  North Vassalboro, ME 800-729-7935
Freekehlicious
  Norwood, NJ. 201-297-7957
Grain Place Foods Inc
  Marquette, NE. 888-714-7246
Grain Process Enterprises Ltd.
  Scarborough, ON 800-387-5292
Great River Organic Milling
  Arcadia, WI. 608-687-9580
Hain Celestial Group Inc
  Lake Success, NY 800-434-4246
Harvest Innovations
  Indianola, IA 515-962-5063
Hearthside Food Solutions
  Downers Grove, IL 630-967-3600
InfraReady Products Ltd.
  Saskatoon, SK 800-510-1828
Ingles Markets
  Black Mountain, NC. 828-669-2941
Inn Maid Food
  Lenox, MA 413-637-2732
Kashi Company
  Solana Beach, CA. 877-747-2467
Kay's Naturals, Inc.
  Clara City, MN 866-873-5499
KAYS Processing LLC
  Clara City, MN 320-847-3220
Kemach Food Products
  Brooklyn, NY. 718-272-5655
McKee Foods Corp.
  Collegedale, TN 800-522-4499
Meijer Inc
  Grand Rapids, MI 616-453-6711
Nature's Path Foods
  Blaine, WA 888-808-9505
Newman's Own
  Westport, CT. 203-222-0136
Nu-World Amaranth Inc
  Naperville, IL 630-369-6851
Prairie Mills Products LLC
  Rochester, IN 574-223-3177
Publix Super Market
  Lakeland, FL. 800-242-1227
Raymond-Hadley Corporation
  Spencer, NY 800-252-5220
SBK Preserves
  Bronx, NY. 800-773-7378
Specialty Food Association
  New York, NY 646-878-0301
Sunridge Farms
  Royal Oaks, CA 831-786-7000
Sunridge Farms Inc
  Salinas, CA. 831-755-1530
TMI Trading Co
  Brooklyn, NY. 718-821-5052
Two Moms In The Raw
  Longmont, CO 720-221-8555
Wegmans Food Markets Inc.
  Rochester, NY. 800-934-6267
WEIS Markets Inc.
  Sunbury, PA. 866-999-9347
Wildtime Foods
  Eugene, OR. 800-356-4458
Winn-Dixie Stores
  Jacksonville, FL. 800-967-9105

Bars

Bobo's Oat Bars
  Boulder, CO 303-938-1977
Budi Products LLC
  Marblehead, MA. 781-990-3411
Coco International
  Wayne, NJ 973-694-1200
Don't Go Nuts
  Salida, CO. 855-666-8826
Earnest Eats
  Solana Beach, CA. 858-299-4238
FreeYumm
  Vancouver, BC
Kashi Company
  Solana Beach, CA. 877-747-2467
Kellogg Canada Inc.
  Mississauga, ON 888-876-3750
Kuli Kuli, Inc.
  Oakland, CA 510-350-8325
Quaker Oats Company
  Chicago, IL 312-821-1000
The Good Bean
  Berkeley, CA. 561-243-7773
Two Moms In The Raw
  Longmont, CO 720-221-8555

Product Categories / Cereals, Grains, Rice & Flour: Corn Germ

Breakfast

Back to the Roots
 Oakland, CA 510-922-9758
Bake Crafters Food Company
 McDonald, TN 423-396-3392
Barbara's Bakery
 Lakeville, MN 800-343-0590
Bede Inc
 Haledon, NJ 866-239-6565
Birkett Mills
 Penn Yan, NY 315-536-3311
Black Ranch Organic Grains
 Etna, CA 916-467-3387
Blue Marble Brands
 Providence, RI 888-534-0246
Blue Planet Foods
 Collegedale, TN 877-396-3145
Bluechip Group
 Salt Lake City, UT 800-878-0099
Bob's Red Mill Natural Foods
 Milwaukie, OR 800-349-2173
C H Guenther & Son Inc
 San Antonio, TX 210-227-1401
California Cereal Products
 Oakland, CA 510-452-4500
Carlisle Cereal Company
 Bismarck, ND 800-809-6018
Christine & Rob's Inc
 Stayton, OR 503-769-2993
CHS Sunprairie
 Minot, ND 800-556-6807
Cook Natural Products
 Lafayette, CA 800-537-7589
Cook-In-The-Kitchen
 Hampden, ME 207-848-4900
Country Choice Organic
 Eden Prairie, MN 952-829-8824
Cream Of The West
 Harlowton, MT 800-477-2383
Dakota Specialty Milling, Inc.
 Fargo, ND 844-633-2746
Edwards Mill
 Hollister, MO 800-222-0525
Efco Products Inc
 Poughkeepsie, NY 800-284-3326
Ener-G Foods
 Seattle, WA 800-331-5222
Fry Krisp Food Products
 Jackson, MI 877-854-5440
General Mills
 Minneapolis, MN 800-248-7310
GFA Brands Inc
 Paramus, NJ 201-568-9300
Gilster-Mary Lee Corp
 Chester, IL 618-826-2361
GKI Foods
 Brighton, MI 248-486-0055
Grain Craft
 Chattanooga, TN 423-265-2313
Grain Process Enterprises Ltd.
 Scarborough, ON 800-387-5292
Health Valley Company
 Irwindale, CA 800-334-3204
Hodgson Mill Inc
 Effingham, IL 800-347-0198
Homestead Mills
 Cook, MN 800-652-5233
I Heart Keenwah
 Chicago, IL
Indiana Grain Company
 Baltimore, MD 410-685-6410
International Home Foods
 Parsippany, NJ 973-359-9920
Julian Bakery
 Oceanside, CA 760-721-5200
Kashi Company
 Solana Beach, CA 877-747-2467
Kellogg Canada Inc.
 Mississauga, ON 888-876-3750
Kellogg Co.
 Battle Creek, MI 800-962-1413
Knappen Milling Co
 Augusta, MI 800-562-7736
Lima Grain Cereal Seeds LLC
 Fort Collins, CO 970-498-2200
Little Crow Foods
 Warsaw, IN 800-288-2769
Luban International
 Doral, FL 305-629-8730
Lundberg Family Farms
 Richvale, CA 530-538-3500
Martha Olson's Great Foo
 Sutter Creek, CA 800-973-3966
Mills Brothers Intl
 Seattle, WA 206-575-3000
Mixes by Danielle
 Warren, OH 800-537-6499
Morrison Milling Co
 Denton, TX 800-531-7912
Native State Foods
 Santa Monica, CA 866-647-2291
Natural Food Mill
 Corona, CA 800-797-5090
Natural Way Mills Inc
 Middle River, MN 218-222-3677
Nestle USA Inc
 Glendale, CA 800-225-2270
Nutri Base
 Phoenix, AZ 877-223-5459
One Degree Organic Foods
 Abbotsford, BC 855-834-2642
Organic Milling
 San Dimas, CA 909-599-0961
Pacific Ethanol Inc.
 Sacramento, CA 916-403-2123
Patagonia Provisions
 Sausalito, CA 888-221-8208
PepsiCo.
 Purchase, NY 914-253-2000
Post Consumer Brands
 Lakeville, MN 800-431-7678
Quaker Oats Company
 Chicago, IL 312-821-1000
Quaker Oats Company
 Peterborough, ON 800-267-6287
Senor Pinos de Santa Fe
 Santa Fe, NM 505-473-3437
Silver Palate Kitchens
 Cresskill, NJ 201-568-0110
Small Planet Foods
 Minneapolis, MN 800-624-4123
Stafford County Flour Mills Company
 Hudson, KS 800-530-5640
Star of the West Milling Co.
 Frankenmuth, MI 989-652-9971
Sturm Foods Inc
 Manawa, WI 800-347-8876
Teeccino
 Carpinteria, CA 800-498-3434
The Soulfull Project
 Camden, NJ
TyRy Inc
 Rocklin, CA 800-322-6325
US Mills
 Bala Cynwyd, PA 800-422-1125
Wanda's Nature Farm
 Lincoln, NE 800-735-6828
Weetabix Canada
 Cobourg, ON 888-933-8249
Weetabix Food Co.
 Marlborough, MA 800-343-0590

Corn-Based

Kellogg Canada Inc.
 Mississauga, ON 888-876-3750
Terra Ingredients
 Minneapolis, MN 888-497-3308

Farina

Bob's Red Mill Natural Foods
 Milwaukie, OR 800-349-2173
Sturm Foods Inc
 Manawa, WI 800-347-8876

Instant

Nature's Legacy Inc.
 Hudson, MI 517-448-2050
Quaker Oats Company
 Chicago, IL 312-821-1000
San Francisco Spice Co.
 Woodland, CA 866-972-6879
TMI Trading Co
 Brooklyn, NY 718-821-5052

Muesli

Bliss Gourmet Foods
 St. Paul, MN
Bob's Red Mill Natural Foods
 Milwaukie, OR 800-349-2173
GrandyOats
 Hiram, ME 207-935-7415
Seven Sundays, LLC
 Minneapolis, MN 612-562-5316
Zego Foods
 San Francisco, CA 415-706-8094

Mueslix

Hodgson Mill Inc
 Effingham, IL 800-347-0198
Kellogg Canada Inc.
 Mississauga, ON 888-876-3750

Oatmeal

Bob's Red Mill Natural Foods
 Milwaukie, OR 800-349-2173
Earnest Eats
 Solana Beach, CA 858-299-4238
Inviting Foods
 Chicago, IL 844-782-5374
Maker Oats
 844-782-5374
MUSH Foods
 Vista, CA
Mylk Labs
 City of Industry, CA
Natierra
 Van Nuys, CA 310-559-0259
New Organics
 Kenwood, CA 734-677-5570
Quaker Oats Company
 Chicago, IL 312-821-1000
Sturm Foods Inc
 Manawa, WI 800-347-8876

Rice-Based

Bob's Red Mill Natural Foods
 Milwaukie, OR 800-349-2173
Fantastic World Foods
 Providence, RI
Kashi Company
 Solana Beach, CA 877-747-2467
Kellogg Canada Inc.
 Mississauga, ON 888-876-3750
Lundberg Family Farms
 Richvale, CA 530-538-3500
Post Consumer Brands
 Lakeville, MN 800-431-7678

Rolled Oats

Bob's Red Mill Natural Foods
 Milwaukie, OR 800-349-2173
GF Harvest
 Powell, WY 888-941-9922
GloryBee
 Eugene, OR 800-456-7923
Hodgson Mill Inc
 Effingham, IL 800-347-0198
Innovative Beverage Concepts
 Irvine, CA 949-831-8656
La Crosse Milling Company
 Cochrane, WI 800-441-5411
New Organics
 Kenwood, CA 734-677-5570
Terra Ingredients
 Minneapolis, MN 888-497-3308
Umpqua Oats
 Henderson, NV 877-303-8107
Zego Foods
 San Francisco, CA 415-706-8094

Wheat-Based

Bob's Red Mill Natural Foods
 Milwaukie, OR 800-349-2173
H Fox & Co Inc
 Brooklyn, NY 718-385-4600
Hodgson Mill Inc
 Effingham, IL 800-347-0198
Weetabix Canada
 Cobourg, ON 888-933-8249

Corn Germ

Aussie Crunch
 Nashville, TN 800-401-6534
Kreher Family Farms
 Clarence, NY 716-759-6802

Corn Meal

Adluh Flour
 Columbia, SC 800-692-3584

Product Categories / Cereals, Grains, Rice & Flour: Crisps

Agricor Inc
  Marion, IN. 765-662-0606
American Key Food Products Inc
  Closter, NJ. 877-263-7539
Ashland Milling
  Ashland, VA 888-897-3336
Atkinson Milling Co.
  Selma, NC 800-948-5707
Bob's Red Mill Natural Foods
  Milwaukie, OR 800-349-2173
Bunge
  Chesterfield, MO 314-292-2000
California Oils Corp
  Richmond, CA 800-225-6457
Hodgson Mill Inc
  Effingham, IL 800-347-0198
Homestead Mills
  Cook, MN 800-652-5233
Hoople Country Kitchen Inc
  Rockport, IN 877-466-7537
House-Autry Mills Inc
  Four Oaks, NC 800-849-0802
J P Green Milling Co
  Mocksville, NC 336-751-2126
King Arthur Flour
  Norwich, VT 800-827-6836
Lakeside Mills
  Rutherfordton, NC 828-286-4866
Maysville Milling Company
  Maysville, NC. 606-759-8789
Mills Brothers Intl
  Seattle, WA 206-575-3000
Nustef Foods
  Mississauga, ON 877-306-7562
Renwood Mills
  Newton, NC 828-464-1611
Scott's Auburn Mills
  Russellville, KY 270-726-2080
Shawnee Milling Co
  Shawnee, OK 405-273-7000
Shenandoah Mills
  Lebanon, TN 615-444-0841
SJH Enterprises
  Middleton, WI. 888-745-3845
Southeastern Mills Inc
  Rome, GA 800-334-4468
UNOI Grainmill
  Seaford, DE. 302-629-4083
War Eagle Mill
  Rogers, AR 866-492-7324
Wilkins Rogers Inc
  Ellicott City, MD. 410-465-5800

Crisps

Bran
Ace Bakery
  North York, ON. 800-443-7929
Flat Cracker Inc.
  Lawrence, NY. 347-223-2587

Cereal
Kii Naturals Inc
  Vaughan, ON. 905-738-8887
Post Consumer Brands
  Lakeville, MN. 800-431-7678

Flax
Harvest Innovations
  Indianola, IA. 515-962-5063
Terra Ingredients
  Minneapolis, MN 888-497-3308

Rice
Kameda USA Inc.
  Torrance, CA. 310-944-9639
Victoria Amory & Co LLC
  Greenwich, CT 203-220-6454

Fiber
Alfred L. Wolff, Inc.
  Park Ridge, IL. 847-759-8888
Batory Foods
  Des Plaines, IL 847-299-1999
Brenntag North America
  Reading, PA 610-926-6100
Bunge Loders Croklaan
  Channahon, IL. 800-621-4710
Canadian Harvest-U.S.A.
  Edina, MN. 888-689-5800

Cereal Ingredients, Inc.
  Leavenworth, KS 913-727-3434
Crea Fill Fibers Corp
  Chestertown, MD 800-832-4662
Eckhart Corporation
  Novato, CA. 800-200-4201
Functional Foods
  Englishtown, NJ 800-442-9524
Garuda International
  Exeter, CA. 559-594-4380
Grain Millers Inc
  Eden Prairie, MN 800-232-6287
Great Grains Milling Company
  Scobey, MT. 406-783-5581
Gum Technology Corporation
  Tucson, AZ. 800-369-4867
Healthy Food Ingredients
  Fargo, ND 844-275-3443
N D Labs
  Lynbrook, NY. 888-263-5227
Nellson Nutraceutical LLC
  Anaheim, CA. 844-635-5766
Ricex Company
  El Dorado Hills, CA 916-933-3000
San-Ei Gen FFI
  New York, NY 212-315-7850
Solvaira Specialties
  North Tonawanda, NY 888-698-1936
Southern Brown Rice
  Weiner, AR 800-421-7423
TIC Gums
  Belcamp, MD 800-899-3953
Unique Ingredients LLC
  Gold Canyon, AZ 480-983-2498
Weetabix Canada
  Cobourg, ON. 888-933-8249
World Flavors Inc
  Warminster, PA 215-672-4400
Yerba Prima
  Ashland, OR 800-488-4339

Cellulose
Gum Technology Corporation
  Tucson, AZ. 800-369-4867

Corn Bran
Canadian Harvest-U.S.A.
  Edina, MN. 888-689-5800

Nuts
Post Consumer Brands
  Lakeville, MN. 800-431-7678

Oat Bran
Canadian Harvest-U.S.A.
  Edina, MN. 888-689-5800
La Crosse Milling Company
  Cochrane, WI 800-441-5411
New Organics
  Kenwood, CA 734-677-5570

Oats
Canadian Harvest-U.S.A.
  Edina, MN. 888-689-5800
La Crosse Milling Company
  Cochrane, WI 800-441-5411
New Organics
  Kenwood, CA 734-677-5570
Organic Planet
  San Francisco, CA 415-765-5590

Pea Bran
Best Cooking Pulses, Inc.
  Portage la Prairie, MB 204-857-4451

Psyllium
Psyllium Labs
  Schaumburg, IL. 888-851-6667

Soy Bran
Fibred
  Cumberland, MD 800-598-8894

Supplements
Abunda Life
  Asbury Park, NJ 732-775-9338
Southern Brown Rice
  Weiner, AR 800-421-7423

Wheat Bran
Canadian Harvest-U.S.A.
  Edina, MN. 888-689-5800
Cereal Ingredients, Inc.
  Leavenworth, KS 913-727-3434

Flour
Adluh Flour
  Columbia, SC 800-692-3584
AG Processing Inc
  Omaha, NE 800-247-1345
Agri-Dairy Products
  Purchase, NY 914-697-9580
Agricore United
  St Louis Park, MN 877-509-5865
American Almond Products Co
  Brooklyn, NY 800-825-6663
Arcadia Biosciences
  Davis, CA 530-756-7077
Ardent Mills Corp
  Denver, CO. 800-851-9618
Ashland Milling
  Ashland, VA 888-897-3336
Atlantic Seasonings
  Kinston, NC 800-433-5261
Attala Development Corporation
  Kosciusko, MS 662-289-2981
Azteca Milling
  Irving, TX 800-364-0040
Bakery Essentials Inc
  Vernon Hills, IL 847-573-0844
Bartlett Milling Co.
  Statesville, NC 800-438-6016
Bay State Milling Co.
  Quincy, MA. 800-553-5687
Beta Pure Foods
  Santa Cruz, CA 831-685-6565
Big J Milling Co
  Brigham City, UT 435-723-3459
Birkett Mills
  Penn Yan, NY 315-536-3311
Blend Pak Inc
  Bloomfield, KY 502-252-8000
Bluechip Group
  Salt Lake City, UT 800-878-0099
Bob's Red Mill Natural Foods
  Milwaukie, OR 800-349-2173
Bouchard Family Farm
  Fort Kent, ME 800-239-3237
Brandt Mills
  Mifflinville, PA 570-752-4271
Byrd Mill Co
  Ashland, VA 888-897-3336
California Cereal Products
  Oakland, CA 510-452-4500
Centennial Mills
  Cheney, WA 509-235-6216
Central Milling Co
  Logan, UT 435-752-6625
Cereal Food Processors
  Salt Lake City, UT 801-355-2981
Cereal Food Processors Inc
  Mcpherson, KS 800-835-2067
Cereal Food Processors Inc
  Mission Woods, KS 913-890-6300
Champlain Valley Milling Corp
  Westport, NY. 518-962-4711
CHS Inc.
  Inver Grove Hts., MN 800-328-6539
CHS Sunprairie
  Minot, ND. 800-556-6807
Clofine Dairy Products Inc
  Linwood, NJ 609-653-1000
Community Mill & Bean
  Savannah, NY 800-755-0554
Continental Grain Company
  New York, NY 212-207-5100
Cup 4 Cup LLC
  Yountville, CA 833-287-4287
Dakota Specialty Milling, Inc.
  Fargo, ND 844-633-2746
Devansoy Farms
  Carroll, IA. 800-747-8605
Dillman Farm Inc
  Bloomington, IN. 800-359-1362
Dipasa USA Inc
  Brownsville, TX 956-831-4072
Eden Foods Inc
  Clinton, MI 888-424-3336
Edison Grainery
  Benicia, CA. 510-382-0202

Product Categories / Cereals, Grains, Rice & Flour: Flour

El Peto Products
  Cambridge, ON 800-387-4064
Ellison Milling Company
  Lethbridge, AB 403-328-6622
Ener-G Foods
  Seattle, WA 800-331-5222
Erba Food Products
  Brooklyn, NY 718-272-7700
Fairhaven Cooperative Flour Mill
  Bellingham, WA 360-757-9947
Farmers Way
Food & Vine Inc.
  Napa, CA 707-251-3900
Fresh Hemp Foods
  Winnipeg, NB 800-665-4367
Gilt Edge Flour Mills
  Richmond, UT 435-258-2425
Giusto's Specialty Foods Inc
  S San Francisco, CA 650-873-6566
Glean, LLC
  Snow Hill, NC
Grain Process Enterprises Ltd.
  Scarborough, ON 800-387-5292
Great Grains Milling Company
  Scobey, MT 406-783-5581
Great River Organic Milling
  Arcadia, WI. 608-687-9580
Greenfield Mills
  North Howe, IN 260-367-2394
GS Dunn & Company
  Hamilton, ON 905-522-0833
H Nagel & Son Co
  Cincinnati, OH 513-665-4550
Healthy Food Ingredients
  Fargo, ND 844-275-3443
Heartland Mills Shipping
  Marienthal, KS 800-232-8533
Hialeah Products Co
  Hollywood, FL 800-923-3379
Hodgson Mill Inc
  Effingham, IL 800-347-0198
Homestead Mills
  Cook, MN 800-652-5233
Hudson Valley Hops
  Beacon, NY 845-202-2398
Idaho Frank Association Inc
  Pleasant Hill, CA 925-609-8458
Idaho Pacific Holdings Inc
  Rigby, ID. 800-238-5503
Inca Gold Organics
  Scarborough, ON 416-264-4622
Iya Foods LLC
  North Aurora, IL 630-854-7107
J P Green Milling Co
  Mocksville, NC 336-751-2126
J.M. Smucker Co.
  Orrville, OH 888-550-9555
J.R. Short Canadian Mills
  Toronto, ON 416-421-3463
Jovial Foods
  North Stonington, CT 877-642-0644
Kemach Food Products
  Brooklyn, NY 718-272-5655
King Arthur Flour
  Norwich, VT 800-827-6836
King Milling Co Inc
  Lowell, MI 616-897-9264
Knappen Milling Co
  Augusta, MI 800-562-7736
Lacey Milling Company
  Hanford, CA 559-584-6634
Lehi Mills
  Lehi, UT 877-311-3566
Lucas Meyer
  Decatur, IL 800-769-3660
Mennel Milling Company
  Fostoria, OH 800-688-8151
Mex America Foods LLC
  St Marys, PA 814-781-1447
Mills Brothers Intl
  Seattle, WA 206-575-3000
Minn-Dak Growers LTD
  Grand Forks, ND. 701-746-7453
Montana Flour & Grains
  Fort Benton, MT 800-622-5790
Morris J Golombeck Inc
  Brooklyn, NY 718-284-3505
Mother Earth Enterprises
  New York, NY 866-436-7688
Natural Products Inc
  Grinnell, IA 641-236-0852

Natural Way Mills Inc
  Middle River, MN 218-222-3677
Nature's Legacy Inc.
  Hudson, MI 517-448-2050
New Hope Mills Mfg Inc
  Auburn, NY 315-252-2676
New Organics
  Kenwood, CA 734-677-5570
Newly Weds Foods Inc
  Chicago, IL 800-621-7521
North Dakota Mill & Elevator Assn.
  Grand Forks, ND 800-538-7721
Northwestern Foods
  Arden Hills, MN 800-236-4937
NutraSun
  Regina, SK 306-751-2040
Old Dutch Mustard Company
  Great Neck, NY 516-466-0522
One Degree Organic Foods
  Abbotsford, BC 855-834-2642
Oregon Potato Co
  Boardman, OR 800-336-6311
Organic Gemini
  Brooklyn, NY 347-662-2900
Orlinda Milling Company
  Orlinda, TN. 615-654-3633
Pacific Grain & Foods
  Fresno, CA 559-276-2580
Panhandle Milling
  Dawn, TX 800-897-5226
Particle Control
  Albertville, MN. 763-497-3075
Pillsbury
  Minneapolis, MN 800-775-4777
Prairie Mills Products LLC
  Rochester, IN 574-223-3177
Produits Alimentaire
  St Lambert De Lauzon, QC 800-463-1787
Quality Naturally Foods
  City Of Industry, CA. 888-498-6986
R&J Farms
  West Salem, OH 419-846-3179
Raymond-Hadley Corporation
  Spencer, NY 800-252-5220
Renwood Mills
  Newton, NC 828-464-1611
Research Products Co
  Salina, KS 800-234-7174
Sanford Milling Co Inc
  Henderson, NC 866-438-4526
Scott's Auburn Mills
  Russellville, KY 270-726-2080
SFP Food Products
  Conway, AR 800-654-5329
Shawnee Milling Co
  Shawnee, OK 405-273-7000
Shawnee Milling Co
  Shawnee, OK 800-654-2600
Shepherdsfield Bakery
  Fulton, MO 573-642-0009
SJH Enterprises
  Middleton, WI. 888-745-3845
Solnuts
  Hudson, IA 800-648-3503
Southeastern Mills Inc
  Rome, GA. 800-334-4468
Southern Brown Rice
  Weiner, AR 800-421-7423
Star of the West Milling Co.
  Frankenmuth, MI 989-652-9971
Teff Co
  Nampa, ID 888-822-2221
To Your Health Sprouted Flour Co., Inc.
  Floyd, VA 540-283-9589
Uhlmann Co
  Kansas City, MO 866-866-8627
War Eagle Mill
  Rogers, AR 866-492-7324
Wheat Montana Farms Inc
  Three Forks, MT 800-535-2798
Wilkins Rogers Inc
  Ellicott City, MD 410-465-5800

All Purpose

Ardent Mills Corp
  Denver, CO 800-851-9618
Bob's Red Mill Natural Foods
  Milwaukie, OR 800-349-2173
Cereal Food Processors Inc
  Mcpherson, KS 800-835-2067
King Arthur Flour
  Norwich, VT 800-827-6836

Orlinda Milling Company
  Orlinda, TN. 615-654-3633
Uhlmann Co
  Kansas City, MO 866-866-8627
UNOI Grainmill
  Seaford, DE. 302-629-4083

Almond

Bob's Red Mill Natural Foods
  Milwaukie, OR 800-349-2173
NOW Foods
  Bloomingdale, IL 888-669-3663

Amaranth

Bob's Red Mill Natural Foods
  Milwaukie, OR 800-349-2173

Arrowroot

American Key Food Products Inc
  Closter, NJ. 877-263-7539

Bakery Mix

Regular & Lowfat

1-2-3 Gluten Free
  Chagrin Falls, OH 216-378-9233
Mennel Milling Company
  Fostoria, OH 800-688-8151

Baking Mixes

1-2-3 Gluten Free
  Chagrin Falls, OH 216-378-9233
Cereal Food Processors Inc
  Mcpherson, KS 800-835-2067
Cup 4 Cup LLC
  Yountville, CA 833-287-4287
Harvest Innovations
  Indianola, IA 515-962-5063
Hodgson Mill Inc
  Effingham, IL 800-347-0198
Homefree LLC
  Windham, NH 800-552-7172
Hudson River Foods
  Castleton, NY 888-417-9343
NOW Foods
  Bloomingdale, IL 888-669-3663
Shawnee Milling Co
  Shawnee, OK 800-654-2600
Southern Culture Foods
  Peachtree Corners, GA

Barley

Bob's Red Mill Natural Foods
  Milwaukie, OR 800-349-2173
CHS Inc.
  Inver Grove Hts., MN 800-328-6539
Eden Foods Inc
  Clinton, MI 888-424-3336
Ettlinger Corp
  Lincolnwood, IL 847-564-5020
Grain Millers Inc
  Eden Prairie, MN 800-232-6287
Great River Organic Milling
  Arcadia, WI. 608-687-9580
Heartland Mills Shipping
  Marienthal, KS 800-232-8533
Hodgson Mill Inc
  Effingham, IL 800-347-0198
Homefree LLC
  Windham, NH 800-552-7172
Homestead Mills
  Cook, MN 800-652-5233
La Crosse Milling Company
  Cochrane, WI 800-441-5411
New Organics
  Kenwood, CA 734-677-5570
SJH Enterprises
  Middleton, WI. 888-745-3845

Bean

Besco Grain Ltd
  Brunkild, MB 204-736-3570
Bob's Red Mill Natural Foods
  Milwaukie, OR 800-349-2173
BRAMI Snacks
  New York, NY 917-291-1945
Love Grown Foods
  Denver, CO 855-328-5683

Product Categories / Cereals, Grains, Rice & Flour: Flour

Bleached
Hodgson Mill Inc
  Effingham, IL 800-347-0198

Buckwheat
Bob's Red Mill Natural Foods
  Milwaukie, OR 800-349-2173
Bouchard Family Farm
  Fort Kent, ME 800-239-3237
Byrd Mill Co
  Ashland, VA 888-897-3336
Eden Foods Inc
  Clinton, MI 888-424-3336
Ener-G Foods
  Seattle, WA 800-331-5222
Fairhaven Cooperative Flour Mill
  Bellingham, WA 360-757-9947
Great River Organic Milling
  Arcadia, WI 608-687-9580
Greenfield Mills
  North Howe, IN 260-367-2394
Homestead Mills
  Cook, MN 800-652-5233
King Arthur Flour
  Norwich, VT 800-827-6836
Minn-Dak Growers LTD
  Grand Forks, ND 701-746-7453
New Hope Mills Mfg Inc
  Auburn, NY 315-252-2676
New Organics
  Kenwood, CA 734-677-5570
Terra Ingredients
  Minneapolis, MN 888-497-3308
UNOI Grainmill
  Seaford, DE 302-629-4083

Cake
Byrd Mill Co
  Ashland, VA 888-897-3336
Cereal Food Processors Inc
  Mission Woods, KS 913-890-6300
H Nagel & Son Co
  Cincinnati, OH 513-665-4550
King Arthur Flour
  Norwich, VT 800-827-6836
Pillsbury
  Minneapolis, MN 800-775-4777

Cassava
Otto's Naturals
  Clinton, NJ 732-654-6886

Corn
Adluh Flour
  Columbia, SC 800-692-3584
Agricor Inc
  Marion, IN. 765-662-0606
Ardent Mills Corp
  Denver, CO 800-851-9618
Attala Development Corporation
  Kosciusko, MS 662-289-2981
Azteca Milling
  Irving, TX 800-364-0040
Bob's Red Mill Natural Foods
  Milwaukie, OR 800-349-2173
Byrd Mill Co
  Ashland, VA 888-897-3336
Ener-G Foods
  Seattle, WA 800-331-5222
Fairhaven Cooperative Flour Mill
  Bellingham, WA 360-757-9947
Great River Organic Milling
  Arcadia, WI 608-687-9580
Mex America Foods LLC
  St Marys, PA 814-781-1447
Mills Brothers Intl
  Seattle, WA 206-575-3000
Minsa Corp
  Lubbock, TX 800-852-8291
Shenandoah Mills
  Lebanon, TN 615-444-0841
Tom Farms
  Leesburg, IN 574-453-3300

Masa
Bob's Red Mill Natural Foods
  Milwaukie, OR 800-349-2173

Gluten
Bluechip Group
  Salt Lake City, UT 800-878-0099
Clofine Dairy Products Inc
  Linwood, NJ 609-653-1000
North Dakota Mill & Elevator Assn.
  Grand Forks, ND 800-538-7721
NOW Foods
  Bloomingdale, IL 888-669-3663
Organic Planet
  San Francisco, CA 415-765-5590
SJH Enterprises
  Middleton, WI. 888-745-3845

Graham
Bob's Red Mill Natural Foods
  Milwaukie, OR 800-349-2173
Great River Organic Milling
  Arcadia, WI 608-687-9580

Hazelnut
Bob's Red Mill Natural Foods
  Milwaukie, OR 800-349-2173
King Arthur Flour
  Norwich, VT 800-827-6836

Instantized
TyRy Inc
  Rocklin, CA 800-322-6325

Millet
Bob's Red Mill Natural Foods
  Milwaukie, OR 800-349-2173
Heartland Mills Shipping
  Marienthal, KS 800-232-8533
New Organics
  Kenwood, CA 734-677-5570

Mustard
GS Dunn & Company
  Hamilton, ON 905-522-0833
Harvest Innovations
  Indianola, IA 515-962-5063
Minn-Dak Growers LTD
  Grand Forks, ND 701-746-7453
Montana Specialty Mills LLC
  Great Falls, MT. 800-332-2024
Tova Industries LLC
  Louisville, KY 888-532-8682

Nut
American Almond Products Co
  Brooklyn, NY 800-825-6663
Amoretti
  Oxnard, CA 800-266-7388
Harvest Innovations
  Indianola, IA 515-962-5063
Hialeah Products Co
  Hollywood, FL 800-923-3379
Mother Earth Enterprises
  New York, NY 866-436-7688
Santa Barbara Pistachio Co
  Maricopa, CA 800-896-1044

Oat
Ardent Mills Corp
  Denver, CO 800-851-9618
Bob's Red Mill Natural Foods
  Milwaukie, OR 800-349-2173
Eden Foods Inc
  Clinton, MI 888-424-3336
GF Harvest
  Powell, WY 888-941-9922
Grain Millers Inc
  Eden Prairie, MN 800-232-6287
Healthy Food Ingredients
  Fargo, ND 844-275-3443
Heartland Mills Shipping
  Marienthal, KS 800-232-8533
Homefree LLC
  Windham, NH 800-552-7172
La Crosse Milling Company
  Cochrane, WI 800-441-5411
New Organics
  Kenwood, CA 734-677-5570
Particle Control
  Albertville, MN. 763-497-3075

SJH Enterprises
  Middleton, WI. 888-745-3845

Pancake
Bette's Oceanview Diner
  Berkeley, CA 510-644-3230
Bouchard Family Farm
  Fort Kent, ME. 800-239-3237
Byrd Mill Co
  Ashland, VA 888-897-3336
Carbon's Golden Malted
  South Bend, IN 800-253-0590
Champlain Valley Milling Corp
  Westport, NY 518-962-4711
Foxtail Foods
  Fairfield, OH. 800-487-2253
Great River Organic Milling
  Arcadia, WI 608-687-9580
Gust John Foods & Products
  Batavia, IL. 800-756-5886
Homestead Mills
  Cook, MN 800-652-5233
Little Crow Foods
  Warsaw, IN 800-288-2769
Marie Callender's Gourmet Products/Goldrush Products
  San Jose, CA 800-729-5428
Martha Olson's Great Foo
  Sutter Creek, CA 800-973-3966
New Hope Mills Mfg Inc
  Auburn, NY 315-252-2676
Northwestern Foods
  Arden Hills, MN 800-236-4937
Quality Naturally Foods
  City Of Industry, CA. 888-498-6986
SFP Food Products
  Conway, AR 800-654-5329
Shenandoah Mills
  Lebanon, TN 615-444-0841
Southern Culture Foods
  Peachtree Corners, GA
Wanda's Nature Farm
  Lincoln, NE. 800-735-6828

Pastry
Bob's Red Mill Natural Foods
  Milwaukie, OR 800-349-2173
Brandt Mills
  Mifflinville, PA 570-752-4271
Cereal Food Processors Inc
  Mission Woods, KS 913-890-6300
Champlain Valley Milling Corp
  Westport, NY 518-962-4711
Eden Foods Inc
  Clinton, MI 888-424-3336
Ellison Milling Company
  Lethbridge, AB 403-328-6622
H Nagel & Son Co
  Cincinnati, OH 513-665-4550
King Arthur Flour
  Norwich, VT 800-827-6836
Natural Way Mills Inc
  Middle River, MN. 218-222-3677
New Organics
  Kenwood, CA 734-677-5570
SJH Enterprises
  Middleton, WI. 888-745-3845

Pea
Best Cooking Pulses, Inc.
  Portage la Prairie, MB 204-857-4451

Potato
AgraWest Foods
  Prince Edward Island, NS. 877-687-1400
Ardent Mills Corp
  Denver, CO 800-851-9618
Bob's Red Mill Natural Foods
  Milwaukie, OR 800-349-2173
Emerling International Foods
  Buffalo, NY. 716-833-7381
Ener-G Foods
  Seattle, WA 800-331-5222
Ettlinger Corp
  Lincolnshire, IL 847-564-5020
Hodgson Mill Inc
  Effingham, IL 800-347-0198
Idaho Pacific Holdings Inc
  Rigby, ID. 800-238-5503
King Arthur Flour
  Norwich, VT 800-827-6836

Product Categories / Cereals, Grains, Rice & Flour: Grains

Oregon Potato Co
Boardman, OR 800-336-6311

Pancake

Linda's Gourmet Latkes
Los Angeles, CA 888-452-8537

Quinoa

Ardent Mills Corp
Denver, CO 800-851-9618
Bob's Red Mill Natural Foods
Milwaukie, OR 800-349-2173
Inca Gold Organics
Scarborough, ON 416-264-4622

Rice

Affiliated Rice Milling
Alvin, TX 281-331-6176
Ardent Mills Corp
Denver, CO 800-851-9618
Axiom Foods, Inc.
Los Angeles, CA 800-711-3587
Bob's Red Mill Natural Foods
Milwaukie, OR 800-349-2173
California Cereal Products
Oakland, CA 510-452-4500
Eden Foods Inc
Clinton, MI 888-424-3336
Ener-G Foods
Seattle, WA 800-331-5222
Far West Rice Inc
Nelson, CA 530-891-1339
Harvest Innovations
Indianola, IA 515-962-5063
J M Swank Co
North Liberty, IA 800-593-6375
King Arthur Flour
Norwich, VT 800-827-6836
KODA Farms Inc
South Dos Palos, CA 209-392-2191
Lundberg Family Farms
Richvale, CA 530-538-3500
Sage V Foods
Boulder, CO 303-449-5626

Rye

Ardent Mills Corp
Denver, CO 800-851-9618
Bob's Red Mill Natural Foods
Milwaukie, OR 800-349-2173
Champlain Valley Milling Corp
Westport, NY 518-962-4711
Ellison Milling Company
Lethbridge, AB 403-328-6622
Fairhaven Cooperative Flour Mill
Bellingham, WA 360-757-9947
Great River Organic Milling
Arcadia, WI 608-687-9580
Heartland Mills Shipping
Marienthal, KS 800-232-8533
Homestead Mills
Cook, MN 800-652-5233
King Arthur Flour
Norwich, VT 800-827-6836
SJH Enterprises
Middleton, WI 888-745-3845

Self-Rising

Cereal Food Processors Inc
Mcpherson, KS 800-835-2067
Orlinda Milling Company
Orlinda, TN 615-654-3633

Semolina

Bob's Red Mill Natural Foods
Milwaukie, OR 800-349-2173
CHS Inc.
Inver Grove Hts., MN 800-328-6539
Heartland Mills Shipping
Marienthal, KS 800-232-8533
Howson Mills
Blyth, ON 866-422-7522
King Arthur Flour
Norwich, VT 800-827-6836
North Dakota Mill & Elevator Assn.
Grand Forks, ND 800-538-7721

Sorghum

Bob's Red Mill Natural Foods
Milwaukie, OR 800-349-2173

Soy Protein

Champlain Valley Milling Corp
Westport, NY 518-962-4711

Soybean

Acatris USA
Edina, MN 952-920-7700
AG Processing Inc
Omaha, NE 800-247-1345
Besco Grain Ltd
Brunkild, MB 204-736-3570
Bob's Red Mill Natural Foods
Milwaukie, OR 800-349-2173
Clofine Dairy Products Inc
Linwood, NJ 609-653-1000
Devansoy Farms
Carroll, IA 800-747-8605
Healthy Food Ingredients
Fargo, ND 844-275-3443
IOM Grain
Portland, IN 877-283-8882
Lucas Meyer
Decatur, IL 800-769-3660
Modern Macaroni Co LTD
Honolulu, HI 808-845-6841
New Organics
Kenwood, CA 734-677-5570
Solnuts
Hudson, IA 800-648-3503
Spectrum Foods Inc
Springfield, IL 217-528-5301
Tom Farms
Leesburg, IN 574-453-3300

Spelt

Bob's Red Mill Natural Foods
Milwaukie, OR 800-349-2173
Heartland Mills Shipping
Marienthal, KS 800-232-8533
King Arthur Flour
Norwich, VT 800-827-6836
Nature's Legacy Inc.
Hudson, MI 517-448-2050

Tapioca

American Key Food Products Inc
Closter, NJ 877-263-7539
Bob's Red Mill Natural Foods
Milwaukie, OR 800-349-2173
Ener-G Foods
Seattle, WA 800-331-5222
Kinnikinnick Foods
Edmonton, AB 877-503-4466
NOW Foods
Bloomingdale, IL 888-669-3663
Tipiak Inc
Stamford, CT 203-961-9117

Triticale

Bob's Red Mill Natural Foods
Milwaukie, OR 800-349-2173

Wheat

Arcadia Biosciences
Davis, CA 530-756-7077
King Milling Co Inc
Lowell, MI 616-897-9264
New Organics
Kenwood, CA 734-677-5570
Shawnee Milling Co
Shawnee, OK 800-654-2600
Siemer Milling Co
Teutopolis, IL 800-826-1065

White Unbleached

Bob's Red Mill Natural Foods
Milwaukie, OR 800-349-2173
Champlain Valley Milling Corp
Westport, NY 518-962-4711
Ener-G Foods
Seattle, WA 800-331-5222
Great Grains Milling Company
Scobey, MT 406-783-5581
Heartland Mills Shipping
Marienthal, KS 800-232-8533
King Arthur Flour
Norwich, VT 800-827-6836
King Milling Co Inc
Lowell, MI 616-897-9264
Lehi Mills
Lehi, UT 877-311-3566
Natural Way Mills Inc
Middle River, MN 218-222-3677
Tolteca Foodservice
Norcross, GA 800-541-6835
Uhlmann Co
Kansas City, MO 866-866-8627

Whole wheat

Brandt Mills
Mifflinville, PA 570-752-4271
Cereal Food Processors Inc
Mission Woods, KS 913-890-6300
Great Grains Milling Company
Scobey, MT 406-783-5581
Great River Organic Milling
Arcadia, WI 608-687-9580
Hodgson Mill Inc
Effingham, IL 800-347-0198
Homestead Mills
Cook, MN 800-652-5233
Keynes Brothers Inc
Logan, OH 800-282-5627
King Arthur Flour
Norwich, VT 800-827-6836
Lehi Mills
Lehi, UT 877-311-3566
Montana Specialty Mills LLC
Great Falls, MT 800-332-2024
New Organics
Kenwood, CA 734-677-5570
Panhandle Milling
Dawn, TX 800-897-5226
Siemer Milling Co
Teutopolis, IL 800-826-1065
SJH Enterprises
Middleton, WI 888-745-3845
Terra Botanica Products
Dahlonega, GA 770-718-9340
Uhlmann Co
Kansas City, MO 866-866-8627
War Eagle Mill
Rogers, AR 866-492-7324

Pastry

Brandt Mills
Mifflinville, PA 570-752-4271
George's Candy Shop Inc
Mobile, AL 800-633-1306
New Organics
Kenwood, CA 734-677-5570
SJH Enterprises
Middleton, WI 888-745-3845

Grains

Acharice Specialties
Greenville, MS 800-432-4901
Agfinity Inc
Eaton, CO 800-433-4688
Aliments Trigone
St-Francois-De-La-Rivier, QC 877-259-7491
Ancient Harvest
Boulder, CO 310-217-8125
Ardent Mills Corp
Denver, CO 800-851-9618
Attala Development Corporation
Kosciusko, MS 662-289-2981
Azteca Milling
Irving, TX 800-364-0040
Bakery Essentials Inc
Vernon Hills, IL 847-573-0844
Baptista's Bakery
Franklin, WI 414-409-2000
Beaumont Rice Mills
Beaumont, TX 409-832-2521
Besco Grain Ltd
Brunkild, MB 204-736-3570
Beta Pure Foods
Santa Cruz, CA 831-685-6565
Big J Milling Co
Brigham City, UT 435-723-3459
Black Ranch Organic Grains
Etna, CA 916-467-3387

Product Categories / Cereals, Grains, Rice & Flour: Granola

Blue Planet Foods
  Collegedale, TN 877-396-3145
Briess Malt & Ingredients Co.
  Chilton, WI 800-657-0806
Bunge North America Inc.
  Chesterfield, MO 314-292-2000
California Cereal Products
  Oakland, CA 510-452-4500
Canadian Harvest-U.S.A.
  Edina, MN. 888-689-5800
Caribbean Food Delights Inc
  Tappan, NY. 845-398-3000
Cayuga Pure Organics
  Brooktondale, NY 607-273-2621
Central Milling Co
  Logan, UT. 435-752-6625
Champlain Valley Milling Corp
  Westport, NY. 518-962-4711
Chef Hans' Gourmet Foods
  Monroe, LA. 800-890-4267
CHS Inc.
  Inver Grove Hts., MN. 800-328-6539
CHS Sunflower
  Grandin, ND 701-484-5313
Cinnabar Specialty Foods Inc
  Prescott, AZ 866-293-6433
Coach's Oats
  Yorba Linda, CA. 714-692-6885
Conrad Rice Mill Inc
  New Iberia, LA. 800-551-3245
Continental Grain Company
  New York, NY 212-207-5100
Cormier Rice Milling Co Inc
  De Witt, AR 870-946-3561
Dakota Specialty Milling, Inc.
  Fargo, ND 844-633-2746
Devansoy Farms
  Carroll, IA. 800-747-8605
DMH Ingredients Inc
  Libertyville, IL. 847-362-9977
Ellison Milling Company
  Lethbridge, AB. 403-328-6622
Everspring Farms
  Seaforth, ON. 519-527-0990
Fairhaven Cooperative Flour Mill
  Bellingham, WA 360-757-9947
Falcon Rice Mill Inc
  Crowley, LA. 800-738-7423
Fall River Wild Rice
  Fall River Mills, CA. 800-626-4366
Farmer Direct Organic
  Regina, SK 306-563-7815
Farmers Rice Milling Co
  Lake Charles, LA. 337-433-5205
Farmers Way
Ferris Organic Farms
  Eaton Rapids, MI 800-628-8736
Fizzle Flat Farm, L.L.C.
  Yale, IL. 618-793-2060
Freeland Bean & Grain Inc
  Freeland, MI. 800-447-9131
Fresh Ideas
  Las Vegas, NV 702-701-4272
Garber Farms
  Iota, LA. 800-824-2284
Grain Place Foods Inc
  Marquette, NE. 888-714-7246
Grain Process Enterprises Ltd.
  Scarborough, ON. 800-387-5292
Great Western Malting Co
  Vancouver, WA 360-693-3661
Grey Owl Foods
  Grand Rapids, MN 800-527-0172
Hall Grain Company
  Akron, CO. 970-345-2206
Harvest Innovations
  Indianola, IA. 515-962-5063
HealthBest
  San Marcos, CA 760-752-5230
Healthy Food Ingredients
  Fargo, ND 844-275-3443
Heartland Gourmet LLC
  Lincoln, NE. 800-735-6828
Heartland Mills Shipping
  Marienthal, KS 800-232-8533
High Quality Organics
  Reno, NV 775-971-8550
Highland Family Farms
  Mapleton, MN. 507-524-3797
Homegrown Naturals
  Napa, CA. 800-288-1089

Homestead Mills
  Cook, MN 800-652-5233
Honeyville Grain Inc
  Brigham City, UT 435-494-4200
In Harvest Inc
  Bemidji, MN. 800-346-7032
Inn Maid Food
  Lenox, MA 413-637-2732
J & L Grain Processing
  Riceville, IA. 800-244-9211
J M Swank Co
  North Liberty, IA 800-593-6375
J. R. Simplot Co.
  Boise, ID 208-336-2110
J.R. Short Canadian Mills
  Toronto, ON 416-421-3463
Kashi Company
  Solana Beach, CA. 877-747-2467
Knappen Milling Co
  Augusta, MI 800-562-7736
La Crosse Milling Company
  Cochrane, WI 800-441-5411
LaCrosse Milling Company
  Cochrane, WI 800-441-5411
Landreth Wild Rice
  Norman, OK 800-333-3533
Leech Lake Wild Rice
  Cass Lake, MN 218-335-8200
Legumex Walker, Inc.
  Winnipeg, MB. 204-808-0448
Lone Pine Enterprise Inc
  Carlisle, AR 870-552-3217
Louisiana Rice Mill
  Crowley, LA. 337-783-9777
Lowell Farms
  El Campo, TX. 888-484-9213
Luxor California Exports Corp.
  San Diego, CA 619-465-7777
Maple Leaf Foods International
  North York, ON. 800-268-3708
Marubeni America Corp.
  New York, NY 212-450-0100
McKnight Milling Company
  Hickory Ridge, AR. 800-287-2383
Mid Kansas Co-Op Assn
  Moundridge, KS 800-864-4428
Mille Lacs Wild Rice Corp
  Aitkin, MN 800-626-3809
Mills Brothers Intl
  Seattle, WA 206-575-3000
Minn-Dak Growers LTD
  Grand Forks, ND. 701-746-7453
Minnestalgia Foods LLC
  Mcgregor, MN 800-328-6731
Montana Flour & Grains
  Fort Benton, MT 800-622-5790
Montana Specialty Mills LLC
  Great Falls, MT. 800-332-2024
Mosher Products Inc
  Cheyenne, WY 307-632-1492
Mountain High Organics
  New Milford, CT 860-210-7805
Mustard Seed
  Central, SC 877-621-2591
Natural Food Mill
  Corona, CA. 800-797-5090
Natural Way Mills Inc
  Middle River, MN 218-222-3677
Nature's Legacy Inc.
  Hudson, MI 517-448-2050
New Organics
  Kenwood, CA 734-677-5570
Northwestern Extract
  Germantown, WI. 800-466-3034
Olam Spices
  Fresno, CA 559-447-1390
Osowski Farms
  Minto, ND. 701-248-3341
Ottawa Valley Grain Products
  Renfrew, ON. 613-432-3614
Perfect Foods Inc
  Goshen, NY. 800-933-3288
Pines International
  Lawrence, KS 800-697-4637
Pizzey's Milling & Baking Company
  Twin Falls, ID 208-733-7555
Pleasant Grove Farms
  Pleasant Grove, CA 916-655-3391
R&J Farms
  West Salem, OH 419-846-3179
Raymond-Hadley Corporation
  Spencer, NY 800-252-5220

Rice Hull Specialty Products
  Stuttgart, AR. 870-673-8507
Riviana Foods Inc.
  Houston, TX 713-529-3251
Roberts Seed
  Axtell, NE. 308-743-2565
S & E Organic Farms Inc
  Bakersfield, CA 661-325-2644
Scott's Auburn Mills
  Russellville, KY 270-726-2080
SJH Enterprises
  Middleton, WI. 888-745-3845
Sole Grano LLC
  Fair Lawn, NJ 201-797-7100
Sorrenti Family Farms
  Escalon, CA 888-435-9490
Southeastern Mills Inc
  Rome, GA 800-334-4468
Southern Brown Rice
  Weiner, AR 800-421-7423
Specialty Commodities Inc
  Fargo, ND. 701-282-8222
Specialty Rice Inc
  Brinkley, AR. 800-467-1233
Stan-Mark Food Products Inc
  Chicago, IL 800-651-0994
Star of the West Milling Co.
  Frankenmuth, MI 989-652-9971
Stengel Seed & Grain Co
  Milbank, SD 605-432-6030
Sun West Foods
  Davis, CA 530-758-8550
Sunnyland Mills
  Fresno, CA 800-501-8017
SunWest Foods, Inc.
  Davis, CA 530-758-8550
T.S. Smith & Sons
  Bridgeville, DE. 302-337-8271
Teff Co
  Nampa, ID. 888-822-2221
Terra Ingredients LLC
  Minneapolis, MN 855-497-3308
Timeless Seeds
  Ulm, MT. 406-866-3340
Trinidad Benham Corporation
  Denver, CO 303-220-1400
Tundra Wild Rice
  Pine Falls, NB 204-367-8651
TyRy Inc
  Rocklin, CA 800-322-6325
Uhlmann Co
  Kansas City, MO. 866-866-8627
Vitamins
  Chicago, IL 312-861-0700
Wagner Gourmet Foods
  Lenexa, KS 913-469-5411
Weisenberger Mills
  Midway, KY 800-643-8678
WG Thompson & Sons
  Blenheim, ON. 800-265-5225
Wheat Montana Farms Inc
  Three Forks, MT. 800-535-2798
Wild Rice Exchange
  Woodland, CA. 800-223-7423
World Nutrition, Inc.
  Scottsdale, AZ. 800-548-2710

Granola

18 Rabbits Inc.
  San Francisco, CA 415-922-6006
Ace Bakery
  North York, ON. 800-443-7929
Alvarado Street Bakery
  Petaluma, CA 707-789-6700
Ambrosial Granola
  Brooklyn, NY 718-491-1335
Barbara's Bakery
  Lakeville, MN. 800-343-0590
Bear Naked, Inc.
  Solana Beach, CA. 866-374-4442
Beaujolais Panforte
  Santa Rosa, CA 800-776-1778
Big Boss Baking Co
  High Point, NC 336-861-1212
Bliss Gourmet Foods
  St. Paul, MN
Blue Planet Foods
  Collegedale, TN 877-396-3145
Bob's Red Mill Natural Foods
  Milwaukie, OR 800-349-2173
Boulder Granola
  Boulder, CO 303-443-1136

Product Categories / Cereals, Grains, Rice & Flour: Grits

Chappaqua Crunch
   Marblehead, MA 781-631-8118
Cream Of The West
   Harlowton, MT 800-477-2383
Edner Corporation
   Hayward, CA 510-441-8504
EFFi Foods
   Los Angeles, CA 310-582-5938
Enjoy Life Foods
   Chicago, IL 888-503-6569
GKI Foods
   Brighton, MI 248-486-0055
Grain Process Enterprises Ltd.
   Scarborough, ON 800-387-5292
Grain-Free JK Gourmet, Inc.
   Toronto, ON 800-608-0465
Grandma Emily
   Montreal, QC 877-943-3661
GrandyOats
   Hiram, ME 207-935-7415
Healing Home Foods
   Pound Ridge, NY 914-764-1303
Health Valley Company
   Irwindale, CA 800-334-3204
Hialeah Products Co
   Hollywood, FL 800-923-3379
Hudson Henry Baking Co.
   Palmyra, VA 817-733-0709
Inn Maid Food
   Lenox, MA 413-637-2732
Julie's Real
   Dallas, TX 877-659-4375
Lehi Valley Trading Company
   Mesa, AZ 480-684-1402
Lola Granola Bar Corporation
   Croton Falls, NY 914-617-8833
Lowcountry Produce
   Raleigh, NC 800-935-2792
McKee Foods Corp.
   Collegedale, TN 800-522-4499
Michaelene's Gourmet Granola
   Clarkston, MI 248-625-0156
Mother Nature's Goodies
   Yucaipa, CA 909-795-6018
Nature's Habit Brand. Inc.
   Washago, ON 707-712-2826
Nature's Path Foods
   Blaine, WA 888-808-9505
New Century Snacks
   City of Commerce, CA 800-688-6887
New England Natural Bakers
   Greenfield, MA 800-910-2884
Nuts About Granola
   York, PA 717-814-9648
Orchard Pond
   Tallahassee, FL 850-894-0154
Organic Milling
   San Dimas, CA 909-599-0961
Partners: A Tasteful Choice
   Kent, WA 800-632-7477
Poppa's Granola
   Perkinsville, VT 802-263-5342
Positively 3rd St Bakery
   Duluth, MN 218-724-8619
Purely Pecans
   Valdosta, GA 800-627-6630
Red Rose Trading Company
   Lancaster, PA 717-293-7833
Riverside Natural Foods
   Vaughan, ON 416-360-8200
San Franola Granola
   San Francisco, CA 415-506-9582
SBK Preserves
   Bronx, NY 800-773-7378
Schulze & Burch Biscuit Co
   Chicago, IL 773-927-6622
Small Batch Organics
   Manchester Center, VT 802-367-1054
Small Planet Foods
   Minneapolis, MN 800-624-4123
Snackerz
   Commerce, CA 888-576-2253
Sole Grano LLC
   Fair Lawn, NJ 201-797-7100
The Safe + Fair Food Company
   Chicago, IL
The Toasted Oat Bakehouse
   Columbus, OH
Torn & Glasser
   Los Angeles, CA 800-282-6887
Two Moms In The Raw
   Longmont, CO 720-221-8555

Udi's Granola
   Denver, CO 303-657-6366
US Mills
   Bala Cynwyd, PA 800-422-1125
Vikis Foods
   Bethpage, NY 516-767-8700
Viktoria's Gourmet Foods, LLC
   Bethpage, NY 516-767-8700
Well Dressed Food Company
   Tupper Lake, NY 518-359-5280
WholeMe
   Minneapolis, MN 612-247-9728
Wildway
   San Antonio, TX 512-677-9965

Grits

Callie's Charleston Biscuits
   North Charleston, SC 843-577-1198
Healthy Food Ingredients
   Fargo, ND 844-275-3443
J P Green Milling Co
   Mocksville, NC 336-751-2126
Minn-Dak Growers LTD
   Grand Forks, ND 701-746-7453
Natural Products Inc
   Grinnell, IA 641-236-0852
Natural Way Mills Inc
   Middle River, MN 218-222-3677
Sturm Foods Inc
   Manawa, WI 800-347-8876

Corn White & Yellow

Agricor Inc
   Marion, IN 765-662-0606
House-Autry Mills Inc
   Four Oaks, NC 800-849-0802
Mills Brothers Intl
   Seattle, WA 206-575-3000

Hominy

Cateraid Inc
   Howell, MI 800-508-8217
Juanita's Foods
   Wilmington, CA 800-303-2965

Canned

Juanita's Foods
   Wilmington, CA 800-303-2965

Hops

Andean Naturals LLC
   Foster City, CA 650-303-1780
Hops Extract Corporation of America
   Yakima, WA 800-339-8410
Hudson Valley Hops
   Beacon, NY 845-202-2398
John I. Haas
   Washington, DC
Northwestern Extract
   Germantown, WI 800-466-3034
S S Steiner Inc
   New York, NY 212-838-8901
Watson Inc
   West Haven, CT 800-388-3481
Yakima Chief-Hopunion LLC
   Yakima, WA 509-453-4792

Hummus

Banzos
   Denver, CO 303-447-2133
Haig's Delicacies
   Hayward, CA 510-782-6285
Helen's Pure Foods
   Cheltenham, PA 215-379-6433
Hope Foods
   Boulder, CO 303-248-7019
Hungry Sultan
   Lake Forest, CA 949-215-0000
Ithaca Craft Hummus
   Escondido, CA 855-979-6751
Pita Pal
   Houston, TX 713-777-7482
Quong Hop & Company
   S San Francisco, CA 650-553-9900
Tribe Mediterranean
   Taunton, MA 800-848-6687

Malt

Briess Malt & Ingredients Co.
   Chilton, WI 800-657-0806
Great Western Malting Co
   Vancouver, WA 360-693-3661
Hudson Valley Malt
   Germantown, NY 845-489-3450
Jones Brewing Company
   Smithton, PA 724-483-2400
Lake Country Foods Inc
   Oconomowoc, WI 262-567-5521
Lion Brewery Inc
   Wilkes Barre, PA 888-295-2337
Malt Diastase Co
   Saddle Brook, NJ 800-526-0180
Malteurop North America
   Milwaukee, WI 414-671-1166
Northwestern Extract
   Germantown, WI 800-466-3034
Prairie Malt
   Biggar, SK 306-948-3500
Premier Malt Products Inc
   Warren, MI 800-521-1057
Rahr Malting Co
   Shakopee, MN 952-445-1431
United Canadian Malt
   Peterborough, ON 800-461-6400
Watson Inc
   West Haven, CT 800-388-3481

Syrup

Briess Malt & Ingredients Co.
   Chilton, WI 800-657-0806
Malt Diastase Co
   Garfield, NJ 800-772-0416
Schiff Food Products Co Inc
   Totowa, NJ 973-237-1990
United Canadian Malt
   Peterborough, ON 800-461-6400

Millet

American Key Food Products Inc
   Closter, NJ 877-263-7539
CHS Sunflower
   Grandin, ND 701-484-5313
Great River Organic Milling
   Arcadia, WI 608-687-9580
Healthy Food Ingredients
   Fargo, ND 844-275-3443
Hialeah Products Co
   Hollywood, FL 800-923-3379
Mills Brothers Intl
   Seattle, WA 206-575-3000
Natural Way Mills Inc
   Middle River, MN 218-222-3677
Organic Planet
   San Francisco, CA 415-765-5590
Red River Commodities Inc
   Fargo, ND 800-437-5539

Oats & Oat Products

Agricore United
   St Louis Park, MN 877-509-5865
Anna's Oatcakes
   Weston, VT 802-824-3535
Avena Foods Ltd.
   Regina, SK 306-757-3663
Barbara's Bakery
   Lakeville, MN 800-343-0590
Blue Planet Foods
   Collegedale, TN 877-396-3145
Fizzle Flat Farm, L.L.C.
   Yale, IL 618-793-2060
GF Harvest
   Powell, WY 888-941-9922
Giusto's Specialty Foods Inc
   S San Francisco, CA 650-873-6566
Grain Millers Inc
   Eden Prairie, MN 800-232-6287
Healthy Food Ingredients
   Fargo, ND 844-275-3443
Heartland Mills Shipping
   Marienthal, KS 800-232-8533
Honeyville Grain Inc
   Brigham City, UT 435-494-4200
J M Swank Co
   North Liberty, IA 800-593-6375
Oatworks
   New York, NY 646-624-2400

Product Categories / Cereals, Grains, Rice & Flour: Poi

Particle Control
   Albertville, MN............763-497-3075
Richardson International
   Winnipeg, MB............866-217-6211
SJH Enterprises
   Middleton, WI............888-745-3845
West Thomas Partners, LLC
   Grand Rapids, MI............616-755-8432

Oat Bran

Foley's Chocolates & Candies
   Richmond, BC............888-236-5397
Grain Millers Inc
   Eden Prairie, MN............800-232-6287
Natural Foods Inc
   Toledo, OH............419-537-1711
SJH Enterprises
   Middleton, WI............888-745-3845

Oatmeal

Grain Millers Inc
   Eden Prairie, MN............800-232-6287
Honeyville Grain Inc
   Brigham City, UT............435-494-4200
LaCrosse Milling Company
   Cochrane, WI............800-441-5411
Nature's Path Foods
   Blaine, WA............888-808-9505
Oats Overnight
   Tempe, AZ
Silver Palate Kitchens
   Cresskill, NJ............201-568-0110
The Kroger Co.
   Murray, KY............800-632-6900

Quick

Modern Oats
   Irvine, CA............888-662-2334

Rolled

Grain Millers Inc
   Eden Prairie, MN............800-232-6287
Heartland Mills Shipping
   Marienthal, KS............800-232-8533
Honeyville Grain Inc
   Brigham City, UT............435-494-4200

Steel Cut

King Arthur Flour
   Norwich, VT............800-827-6836

Poi

Aloha Poi Factory Inc
   Wailuku, HI............808-244-3536
Puueo Poi Shop
   Hilo, HI............808-935-8435

Quinoa

Alter Eco
   San Francisco, CA............415-701-1214
EatKeenwa, Inc.
   Jersey City, NJ............855-453-3692
Highland Farm Foods
   Rock Hill, SC............803-396-1439
I Heart Keenwah
   Chicago, IL
Nature's Earthly Choice
   Eagle, ID............208-898-4004
Terra Ingredients
   Minneapolis, MN............888-497-3308
Tiny Hero Foods
   San Francisco, CA............855-778-4662
Top Tier Foods Inc.
   Vancouver, BC............778-628-0015

Rice

Acharice Specialties
   Greenville, MS............800-432-4901
Affiliated Rice Milling
   Alvin, TX............281-331-6176
Agrusa
   Leonia, NJ............201-592-5950
Ankeny Lake Wild Rice
   Salem, OR............800-555-5380
Baycliff Co Inc
   Garwood, NJ............866-772-7569
Beaumont Rice Mills
   Beaumont, TX............409-832-2521

Berberian Nut Company
   Chico, CA............530-981-4900
Bgreen Food
   San Diego, CA............619-825-9330
Bluechip Group
   Salt Lake City, UT............800-878-0099
Bunge
   Chesterfield, MO............314-292-2000
Bunge North America Inc.
   Chesterfield, MO............314-292-2000
Buonitalia
   New York, NY............212-633-9090
California Cereal Products
   Oakland, CA............510-452-4500
California Natural Products
   Lathrop, CA............209-858-2525
Caribbean Food Delights Inc
   Tappan, NY............845-398-3000
Castor River Farms
   Dexter, MO
Chef Hans' Gourmet Foods
   Monroe, LA............800-890-4267
Chef Merito Inc
   Van Nuys, CA............800-637-4861
Chieftain Wild Rice
   Spooner, WI............800-262-6368
Cinnabar Specialty Foods Inc
   Prescott, AZ............866-293-6433
Commodities Marketing Inc
   Clarksburg, NJ............732-516-0700
Conrad Rice Mill Inc
   New Iberia, LA............800-551-3245
Cormier Rice Milling Co Inc
   De Witt, AR............870-946-3561
Country Cupboard
   Lewisburg, PA............570-523-3211
Crunchy Rollers
   Dallas, TX
Dalian Xinfeng International Industry & Trade Co.
   Golden Valley, MN............612-964-7391
Deerwood Rice & Grain Procng
   Deerwood, MN............218-534-3762
Dixie Rice
   Gueydan, LA............337-536-9276
Eden Foods Inc
   Clinton, MI............888-424-3336
Falcon Rice Mill Inc
   Crowley, LA............800-738-7423
Fall River Wild Rice
   Fall River Mills, CA............800-626-4366
Fantastic World Foods
   Providence, RI
Farmers Rice Milling Co
   Lake Charles, LA............337-433-5205
Garber Farms
   Iota, LA............800-824-2284
Genki USA
   Torrance, CA
Giusto's Specialty Foods Inc
   S San Francisco, CA............650-873-6566
Gourmet House
   Allentown, PA............800-226-9522
Goya Foods Inc.
   Jersey City, NJ............201-348-4900
Green Valley Foods
   Salem, OR............844-588-3535
Grey Owl Foods
   Grand Rapids, MN............800-527-0172
Hung's Noodle House
   Calgary, AB............403-250-1663
In Harvest Inc
   Bemidji, MN............800-346-7032
Kalustyan
   New York, NY............800-352-3451
KODA Farms Inc
   South Dos Palos, CA............209-392-2191
Kohinoor Foods
   Edison, NJ............888-440-7423
Landreth Wild Rice
   Norman, OK............800-333-3533
Leech Lake Wild Rice
   Cass Lake, MN............218-335-8200
Lone Pine Enterprise Inc
   Carlisle, AR............870-552-3217
Lotus Foods
   Richmond, CA............510-525-3137
Louis Dreyfus Corporation
   Rotterdam,
Louisiana Gourmet Enterprises
   Houma, LA............800-328-5586
Louisiana Rice Mill
   Crowley, LA............337-783-9777

Lowell Farms
   El Campo, TX............888-484-9213
Lundberg Family Farms
   Richvale, CA............530-538-3500
McKnight Milling Company
   Hickory Ridge, AR............800-287-2383
Mermaid Spice Corporation
   Fort Myers, FL............239-693-1986
Mille Lacs Wild Rice Corp
   Aitkin, MN............800-626-3809
Mills Brothers Intl
   Seattle, WA............206-575-3000
Minnestalgia Foods LLC
   Mcgregor, MN............800-328-6731
Miracle Noodle
   Los Angeles, CA............800-948-4205
Mountain High Organics
   New Milford, CT............860-210-7805
Natural Way Mills Inc
   Middle River, MN............218-222-3677
North Bay Trading Co
   Brule, WI............800-348-0164
Oak Grove Smoke House Inc
   Prairieville, LA............225-673-6857
Olam Spices
   Fresno, CA............559-447-1390
Pleasant Grove Farms
   Pleasant Grove, CA............916-655-3391
Primo Foods
   Toronto, ON............800-377-6945
Producers Rice Mill Inc.
   Stuttgart, AR............870-673-4444
Raymond-Hadley Corporation
   Spencer, NY............800-252-5220
Ribus Inc.
   St. Louis, MO............314-727-4287
Rice Company
   Fair Oaks, CA............916-784-7745
Rice Foods
   Mount Vernon, IL............618-242-0026
Rice Hull Specialty Products
   Stuttgart, AR............870-673-8507
Riceland Foods Inc.
   Stuttgart, AR............855-742-3929
Ricetec
   Alvin, TX............800-580-7423
Riviana Foods Inc.
   Houston, TX............713-529-3251
Royal Caribbean Bakery
   Mt Vernon, NY............888-818-0971
Sage V Foods
   Boulder, CO............303-449-5626
Shah Trading Company
   Scarborough, ON............416-292-6927
Sorrenti Family Farms
   Escalon, CA............888-435-9490
Southern Brown Rice
   Weiner, AR............800-421-7423
Specialty Rice Inc
   Brinkley, AR............800-467-1233
Sun West
   Torrance, CA............310-320-4000
SunWest Foods, Inc.
   Davis, CA............530-758-8550
SunWest Organics
   Davis, CA............530-758-8550
Tipiak Inc
   Stamford, CT............203-961-9117
Torn & Glasser
   Los Angeles, CA............800-282-6887
Trinidad Benham Corporation
   Denver, CO............303-220-1400
Tropical Foods
   Lithia Springs, GA............800-544-3762
Tundra Wild Rice
   Pine Falls, NB............204-367-8651
Vigo Importing Co
   Tampa, FL............800-282-4130
Wagner Gourmet Foods
   Lenexa, KS............913-469-5411
Wild Rice Exchange
   Woodland, CA............800-223-7423
Wildly Organic
   Silver Bay, MN............800-945-3801
Willow Foods
   Beaverton, OR............800-338-3609
Wysong Corp
   Midland, MI............800-748-0188

Arborio

Gourmet House
   Allentown, PA............800-226-9522

Product Categories / Cereals, Grains, Rice & Flour: Rye

Lundberg Family Farms
  Richvale, CA 530-538-3500

Basmati

Commodities Marketing Inc
  Clarksburg, NJ 732-516-0700
Gourmet House
  Allentown, PA 800-226-9522
In Harvest Inc
  Bemidji, MN 800-346-7032
Kalustyan
  New York, NY 800-352-3451
Lone Pine Enterprise Inc
  Carlisle, AR 870-552-3217
Lundberg Family Farms
  Richvale, CA 530-538-3500
McKnight Milling Company
  Hickory Ridge, AR 800-287-2383
New Organics
  Kenwood, CA 734-677-5570
Ricetec
  Alvin, TX 800-580-7423
Southern Brown Rice
  Weiner, AR 800-421-7423
Specialty Rice Inc
  Brinkley, AR 800-467-1233
Wild Rice Exchange
  Woodland, CA 800-223-7423

Brewers'

Beaumont Rice Mills
  Beaumont, TX 409-832-2521
Commodities Marketing Inc
  Clarksburg, NJ 732-516-0700

Brown

Bunge North America Inc.
  Chesterfield, MO 314-292-2000
California Natural Products
  Lathrop, CA 209-858-2525
Castor River Farms
  Dexter, MO
Cormier Rice Milling Co Inc
  De Witt, AR 870-946-3561
Gourmet House
  Allentown, PA 800-226-9522
Healthee
  Arcadia, CA 626-574-1719
Lone Pine Enterprise Inc
  Carlisle, AR 870-552-3217
Louisiana Rice Mill
  Crowley, LA 337-783-9777
Lundberg Family Farms
  Richvale, CA 530-538-3500
McKnight Milling Company
  Hickory Ridge, AR 800-287-2383
New Organics
  Kenwood, CA 734-677-5570
Ricetec
  Alvin, TX 800-580-7423
Sobaya
  Cowansville, QC 800-319-8808
Southern Brown Rice
  Weiner, AR 800-421-7423
Wild Rice Exchange
  Woodland, CA 800-223-7423

Frozen

Sage V Foods
  Boulder, CO 303-449-5626

Hulls

Farmers Rice Milling Co
  Lake Charles, LA 337-433-5205
Rice Hull Specialty Products
  Stuttgart, AR 870-673-8507

IQF (Individual Quick Frozen)

Emerling International Foods
  Buffalo, NY 716-833-7381
Sage V Foods
  Boulder, CO 303-449-5626

Instant

Mars Inc.
  McLean, VA 703-821-4900
Sage V Foods
  Boulder, CO 303-449-5626

Jasmine

Commodities Marketing Inc
  Clarksburg, NJ 732-516-0700
Falcon Rice Mill Inc
  Crowley, LA 800-738-7423
Gourmet House
  Allentown, PA 800-226-9522
In Harvest Inc
  Bemidji, MN 800-346-7032
KP USA Trading
  Los Angeles, CA 323-881-9871
Lowell Farms
  El Campo, TX 888-484-9213
Lundberg Family Farms
  Richvale, CA 530-538-3500
New Organics
  Kenwood, CA 734-677-5570
Ricetec
  Alvin, TX 800-580-7423

Milled

Besco Grain Ltd
  Brunkild, MB 204-736-3570
Cormier Rice Milling Co Inc
  De Witt, AR 870-946-3561
Farmers Rice Milling Co
  Lake Charles, LA 337-433-5205

Organic

Gourmet House
  Allentown, PA 800-226-9522
Koda Farms
  South Dos Palos, CA 209-392-2191
Sage V Foods
  Boulder, CO 303-449-5626

Parboiled

US #1 Long Grain

McKnight Milling Company
  Hickory Ridge, AR 800-287-2383

Pilaf

Chef Hans' Gourmet Foods
  Monroe, LA 800-890-4267
Country Cupboard
  Lewisburg, PA 570-523-3211
Kashi Company
  Solana Beach, CA 877-747-2467
Lundberg Family Farms
  Richvale, CA 530-538-3500
Wild Rice Exchange
  Woodland, CA 800-223-7423

Precooked

Riviana Foods Inc.
  Houston, TX 713-529-3251
Sage V Foods
  Boulder, CO 303-449-5626

Risotto

Agrusa
  Leonia, NJ 201-592-5950
Italian Foods Corporation
  Raleigh, NC 888-516-7262
Lundberg Family Farms
  Richvale, CA 530-538-3500

Spanish

Country Cupboard
  Lewisburg, PA 570-523-3211

Canned

Conrad Rice Mill Inc
  New Iberia, LA 800-551-3245

Wehani

Lundberg Family Farms
  Richvale, CA 530-538-3500

White

Castor River Farms
  Dexter, MO
Falcon Rice Mill Inc
  Crowley, LA 800-738-7423
Gourmet House
  Allentown, PA 800-226-9522

Wild

Ankeny Lake Wild Rice
  Salem, OR 800-555-5380
Chef Hans' Gourmet Foods
  Monroe, LA 800-890-4267
Chieftain Wild Rice
  Spooner, WI 800-262-6368
Conrad Rice Mill Inc
  New Iberia, LA 800-551-3245
Country Cupboard
  Lewisburg, PA 570-523-3211
Deerwood Rice & Grain Procng
  Deerwood, MN 218-534-3762
Fall River Wild Rice
  Fall River Mills, CA 800-626-4366
Floating Leaf Fine Foods
  Winnipeg, MB 866-989-7696
Gourmet House
  Allentown, PA 800-226-9522
Grey Owl Foods
  Grand Rapids, MN 800-527-0172
In Harvest Inc
  Bemidji, MN 800-346-7032
Landreth Wild Rice
  Norman, OK 800-333-3533
Leech Lake Wild Rice
  Cass Lake, MN 218-335-8200
Lundberg Family Farms
  Richvale, CA 530-538-3500
Mille Lacs Wild Rice Corp
  Aitkin, MN 800-626-3809
Minnestalgia Foods LLC
  Mcgregor, MN 800-328-6731
North Bay Trading Co
  Brule, WI 800-348-0164
Secret Garden
  Park Rapids, MN 800-950-4409
Sorrenti Family Farms
  Escalon, CA 888-435-9490
Southern Brown Rice
  Weiner, AR 800-421-7423
Sun West Foods
  Davis, CA 530-758-8550
SunWest Foods, Inc.
  Davis, CA 530-758-8550
Tundra Wild Rice
  Pine Falls, NB 204-367-8651
Wild Rice Exchange
  Woodland, CA 800-223-7423

Rye

Alfred & Sam's Italian Bakery
  Lancaster, PA 717-392-6311
Fizzle Flat Farm, L.L.C.
  Yale, IL 618-793-2060
Healthy Food Ingredients
  Fargo, ND 844-275-3443
Montana Specialty Mills LLC
  Great Falls, MT 800-332-2024
Natural Way Mills Inc
  Middle River, MN 218-222-3677

Sorghum

DuPont Pioneer
  Johnston, IA 515-535-5954
Healthy Food Ingredients
  Fargo, ND 844-275-3443
Nu Life Market
  Scott City, KS 866-962-5236
Webbpak Inc
  Trussville, AL 800-655-3500

Bagged & Bulk

Nu Life Market
  Scott City, KS 866-962-5236

Grain

Nu Life Market
  Scott City, KS 866-962-5236

Soy Bean Meal

Clofine Dairy Products Inc
  Linwood, NJ 609-653-1000
International Service Group
  Alpharetta, GA 770-518-0988

Product Categories / Cereals, Grains, Rice & Flour: Tapioca

Tapioca

American Key Food Products Inc
  Closter, NJ 877-263-7539
Commodities Marketing Inc
  Clarksburg, NJ 732-516-0700
Heartline Foods
  Westport, CT 203-222-0381
Organic Planet
  San Francisco, CA 415-765-5590

Wheat

Agri-Dairy Products
  Purchase, NY 914-697-9580
Agricore United
  St Louis Park, MN 877-509-5865
Aliments Trigone
  St-Francois-De-La-Rivier, QC 877-259-7491
Bakery Essentials Inc
  Vernon Hills, IL 847-573-0844
Bluechip Group
  Salt Lake City, UT 800-878-0099
Briess Malt & Ingredients Co.
  Chilton, WI 800-657-0806
Bunge
  Chesterfield, MO 314-292-2000
DuPont Pioneer
  Johnston, IA 515-535-5954
El Peto Products
  Cambridge, ON 800-387-4064
Ferris Organic Farms
  Eaton Rapids, MI 800-628-8736
Fizzle Flat Farm, L.L.C.
  Yale, IL 618-793-2060
Florence Macaroni Manufacturing
  Chicago, IL 800-647-2782
Healthy Food Ingredients
  Fargo, ND 844-275-3443
Knappen Milling Co
  Augusta, MI 800-562-7736
Knight Seed Company
  Burnsville, MN 800-328-2999
Kreher Family Farms
  Clarence, NY 716-759-6802
Lone Pine Enterprise Inc
  Carlisle, AR 870-552-3217
Louis Dreyfus Corporation
  Rotterdam,
Manildra Milling Corporation
  Fairway, KS 800-323-8435
Montana Specialty Mills LLC
  Great Falls, MT 800-332-2024
Natural Way Mills Inc
  Middle River, MN 218-222-3677
Nature's Legacy Inc.
  Hudson, MI 517-448-2050
New Organics
  Kenwood, CA 734-677-5570
Perfect Foods Inc
  Goshen, NY 800-933-3288
Pines International
  Lawrence, KS 800-697-4637
Pleasant Grove Farms
  Pleasant Grove, CA 916-655-3391
Roberts Seed
  Axtell, NE 308-743-2565
SJH Enterprises
  Middleton, WI 888-745-3845
Sunnyland Mills
  Fresno, CA 800-501-8017

T.S. Smith & Sons
  Bridgeville, DE 302-337-8271
Viterra, Inc
  Regina, SK 866-647-4090
Wysong Corp
  Midland, MI 800-748-0188
Zinda Products
  Candiac, QC 888-867-6664

Bread

Chicago Pastry
  Bloomingdale, IL 630-529-6391

Flakes

Attala Development Corporation
  Kosciusko, MS 662-289-2981
King Arthur Flour
  Norwich, VT 800-827-6836

Germ

Ardent Mills Corp
  Denver, CO 800-851-9618
Canadian Harvest-U.S.A.
  Edina, MN 888-689-5800
Garuda International
  Exeter, CA 559-594-4380
Green Foods Corp.
  Oxnard, CA 800-777-4430
New Organics
  Kenwood, CA 734-677-5570
Norac Technologies
  Edmonton, AB 780-414-9595
Star of the West Milling Co.
  Frankenmuth, MI 989-652-9971
Viobin USA
  Monticello, IL 888-473-9645
Vitamins
  Chicago, IL 312-861-0700

Defatted

Vitamins
  Chicago, IL 312-861-0700

Gluten

Ardent Mills Corp
  Denver, CO 800-851-9618
Bluechip Group
  Salt Lake City, UT 800-878-0099
Clofine Dairy Products Inc
  Linwood, NJ 609-653-1000
El Peto Products
  Cambridge, ON 800-387-4064
Manildra Milling Corporation
  Fairway, KS 800-323-8435

Winter

Natural Way Mills Inc
  Middle River, MN 218-222-3677

Whey & Whey Products

Agri-Dairy Products
  Purchase, NY 914-697-9580
Anderson Custom Processing
  New Ulm, MN 877-588-4950
Berkshire Dairy
  Wyomissing, PA 877-696-6455

Blossom Farm Products
  Ridgewood, NJ 800-729-1818
Bongard's Creameries
  Chanhassen, MN 952-277-5500
Brewster Dairy Inc
  Brewster, OH 800-874-8874
Calpro Ingredients
  Corona, CA 909-493-4890
Century Foods Intl LLC
  Sparta, WI 800-269-1901
Clofine Dairy Products Inc
  Linwood, NJ 609-653-1000
Con Yeager Spice Co
  Zelienople, PA 800-222-2460
CP Kelco
  Atlanta, GA 800-535-2687
Crest Foods Inc
  Ashton, IL 877-273-7893
Davisco Foods International
  Eden Prairie, MN 800-757-7611
Farmdale Creamery Inc
  San Bernardino, CA 800-346-7306
First District Association
  Litchfield, MN 320-693-3236
Grande Cheese Company
  Fond du Lac, WI 800-678-3122
Grande Custom Ingredients Group
  Fond du Lac, WI 800-772-3210
Great Lakes Cheese Company, Inc.
  Hiram, OH 440-834-2500
Hilmar Cheese Company
  Hilmar, CA 800-577-5772
Holmes Cheese Co
  Millersburg, OH 330-674-6451
Honeyville Grain Inc
  Brigham City, UT 435-494-4200
Kantner Group
  Wapakoneta, OH 877-738-3448
Lactalis USA Inc
  Belmont, WI 608-762-5136
Land O'Lakes Inc
  Arden Hills, MN 800-328-9680
Leprino Foods Co.
  Denver, CO 800-537-7466
Main Street Ingredients
  La Crosse, WI 800-359-2345
Minerva Cheese Factory
  Minerva, OH 330-868-4196
Mt Capra Products
  Chehalis, WA 800-574-1961
Particle Control
  Albertville, MN 763-497-3075
Plainview Milk Products
  Plainview, MN 800-356-5606
Quality Ingredients
  Burnsville, MN 952-898-4002
Saputo Cheese USA Inc.
  Lincolnshire, IL 847-267-1100
Tillamook County Creamery Association
  Tillamook, OR 503-842-4481
Valley Queen Cheese Factory
  Milbank, SD 605-432-4563
Westin Foods
  Omaha, NE 800-228-6098

Cheese & Cheese Products

General

Advanced Food Products LLC
  New Holland, PA 800-732-5373
Agri-Mark Inc
  West Springfield, MA 978-552-5500
Agropur
  Appleton, WI 920-687-2489
Asiago PDO & Speck Alto Adige PGI
  New York, NY 646-624-2885
Austrian Trade Commission
  New York, NY 212-421-5250
Bletsoe's Cheese Inc
  Marathon, WI 715-443-2526
Blue Marble Brands
  Providence, RI 888-534-0246
Brazos Valley Cheese
  Waco, TX 254-230-2535
Brookshire Grocery Company
  Tyler, TX 888-937-3776
Capalbo's Fruit Baskets
  Clifton, NJ 800-252-6262
Caputo Cheese
  Melrose Park, IL 708-450-0074
Cheese Merchants of America
  Carol Stream, IL 630-768-0317
Comte Cheese Association
  New York, NY 646-515-9209
Couturier Na Inc
  Hudson, NY 518-851-2570
Dairiconcepts
  Springfield, MO 877-596-4374
Dairyfood USA Inc
  Blue Mounds, WI 800-236-3300
Di Bruno Bros
  Philadelphia, PA 215-922-2876
Farms For City Kids Foundation, Inc.
  Reading, VT 802-484-1236
GAF Seelig Inc
  Flushing, NY 718-899-5000
Golden Valley Dairy Products
  Tulare, CA 559-687-1188
Good PLANeT Foods
  Bellevue, WA 425-449-8134
Green Dirt Farm
  Weston, MO 816-386-2156
Hilmar Ingredients
  Hilmar, CA 888-300-4465
Hormel Foods Corp.
  Austin, MN 507-437-5611
Ingles Markets
  Black Mountain, NC 828-669-2941
J & M Foods Inc
  Little Rock, AR 800-264-2278
Kantner Group
  Wapakoneta, OH 877-738-3448
Liuzzi Angeloni Cheese
  Hamden, CT 203-287-8477
Maplebrook Farm
  Bennington, VT 802-440-9950
Marwood Sales, Inc
  Overland Park, KS 800-745-2881
Meijer Inc
  Grand Rapids, MI 616-453-6711
Minerva Dairy Inc
  Minerva, OH 330-868-4196
Old Tavern Food Products Inc
  Waukesha, WI 888-542-5317
Parmela Creamery
  Torrance, CA 310-584-7541
Point Reyes Farmstead Cheese Co.
  Point Reyes Station, CA 800-591-6787
Pondini Imports
  Somerset, NJ 732-545-1255
Publix Super Market
  Lakeland, FL 800-242-1227
Reilly Dairy & Food Company
  Tampa, FL 813-839-8458
Rogue Creamery
  Central Point, OR 866-396-4704
Shaker Valley Foods
  Cleveland, OH 216-961-8600
Swiss Heritage Cheese Inc
  Monticello, WI 608-938-4455
T. Marzetti Company
  Westerville, OH 800-999-1835
Twin County Dairy
  Kalona, IA 319-656-2776
Tyson Foods Inc.
  Springdale, AR 479-290-4000
Wegmans Food Markets Inc.
  Rochester, NY 800-934-6267
WEIS Markets Inc.
  Sunbury, PA 866-999-9347
Winn-Dixie Stores
  Jacksonville, FL 800-967-9105

Cheese

1000 Islands River Rat Cheese
  Clayton, NY 800-752-1341
350 Cheese Straws
  Beaufort, NC 252-838-9080
4C Foods Corp
  Brooklyn, NY 718-272-4242
Advanced Food Products LLC
  New Holland, PA 800-732-5373
Agri-Dairy Products
  Purchase, NY 914-697-9580
Agropur
  Granby, QC 800-363-5686
Agropur
  Appleton, WI 920-687-2489
AgSource Milk Analysis Laboratory
  Bonduel, WI 715-758-2178
Al Pete Meats
  Muncie, IN 765-288-8817
Alberta Cheese Company
  Calgary, AB 403-279-4353
Alpine Cheese Company
  Winesburg, OH 330-359-6291
Alta Dena Certified Dairy LLC
  City Of Industry, CA 800-535-1369
Ambrosi Cheese USA
  Maspeth, NY
American Cheesemen
  Clear Lake, IA 641-357-7176
Anchor Appetizer Group
  Appleton, WI 920-997-2200
Anco Foods
  Miami, FL 866-343-1108
Annie's Homegrown
  Berkeley, CA 800-288-1089
Applegate Farms
  Bridgewater, NJ 866-587-5858
Ardmore Cheese Company
  Ardmore, TN 931-427-2191
Ariza Cheese Co
  Paramount, CA 800-762-4736
Arla Foods Inc
  Concord, ON 905-669-9393
Associated Milk Producers Inc.
  New Ulm, MN. 800-533-3580
Astro Dairy Products
  Toronto, ON 416-622-2811
Atwood Cheese Company
  Atwood, ON 519-356-2271
Avanti Foods Co
  Walnut, IL 800-243-3739
B & D Foods
  Boise, ID 208-344-1183
Bang & Soderlund Inc
  Bonita Springs, FL 239-498-0600
Bartlett Dairy & Food Service
  Jamaica, NY 718-658-2299
Bass Lake Cheese Factory
  Somerset, WI 800-368-2437
Beecher's Handmade Cheese
  Seattle, WA 206-956-1964
Bel Brands USA
  Chicago, IL 312-462-1500
Bel Cheese USA
  Leitchfield, KY 270-259-4071
BelGioioso Cheese Inc.
  Green Bay, WI 920-863-2123
Belle Plaine Cheese Factory
  Shawano, WI 866-245-5924
Bellwether Farms
  Valley Ford, CA 707-478-8067
Berner Food & Beverage LLC
  Dakota, IL 800-819-8199
Biazzo Dairy Products Inc
  Ridgefield, NJ 201-941-6800
Bieri's Jackson Cheese
  Jackson, WI 800-321-6077
Biery Cheese Co
  Louisville, OH 330-875-3381
Big Picture Farm LLC
  Townshend, VT 802-221-0547
Big Russ Beer Cheese
  Beaver Dam, KY 270-485-6544
Blakely Freezer Locker
  Blakeley, GA 229-723-3622
Blaser's USA, Inc.
  Comstock, WI 866-570-2439
Bletsoe's Cheese Inc
  Marathon, WI 715-443-2526
Blue Harbour Cheese
  Halifax, NS 902-240-0305
Boar's Head
  Sarasota, FL 800-352-6277
Bongard's Creameries
  Chanhassen, MN 952-277-5500
Borden Dairy
  Dallas, TX 855-311-1583
Boulder Vegans LLC
  Morrison, CO 303-667-5628
Brewster Dairy Inc
  Brewster, OH 800-874-8874
Brunkow Cheese Of Wisconsin
  Darlington, WI 608-776-3716
Brunnett Dairy Co-Op
  Grantsburg, WI 715-689-2748
Bunker Hill Cheese Co Inc
  Millersburg, OH 800-253-6636
Buonitalia
  New York, NY 212-633-9090
Byrne Dairy, Inc.
  Syracuse, NY 800-899-1535
CA Fortune & Company
  Bloomingdale, IL 630-539-3100
Cabot Creamery Co-Op
  Waitsfield, VT 888-792-2268
Cady Cheese Factory
  Wilson, WI 715-772-4218
Calabro Cheese Corp
  East Haven, CT 203-469-1311
Callie's Charleston Biscuits
  North Charleston, SC 843-577-1198
Capalbo's Fruit Baskets
  Clifton, NJ 800-252-6262
Caprine Estates
  Bellbrook, OH 937-848-7406
Carr Cheese Factory/GileCheese Company
  Cuba City, WI 608-744-8455
Carr Valley Cheese
  Fennimore, WI 800-462-7258
Carr Valley Cheese Company
  La Valle, WI 800-462-7258
Cascade Cheese Co
  Cascade, WI 920-528-8221
Castle Cheese
  Slippery Rock, PA 800-252-4373
Caves Of Faribault/SwissValley
  Faribault, MN 507-334-5260
Cedar Grove Cheese Inc
  Plain, WI 800-200-6020
Cedar Valley Cheese Store
  Belgium, WI 920-994-9500
Chalet Cheese Co-Op
  Monroe, WI 608-325-4343
Cheddar Box Cheese House
  Shawano, WI 715-526-5411
Cheese Factory
  Buffalo, NY 716-828-0178
CheeseLand
  Seattle, WA 206-709-1220
Chicago 58 Food Products
  Woodbridge, ON 416-603-4244
Chicopee Provision Co Inc
  Chicopee, MA 800-924-6328
Churny Company
  Waupaca, WI 715-258-4040
Churny Company
  Glenview, IL 847-646-5500
Clofine Dairy Products Inc
  Linwood, NJ 609-653-1000
Clover Leaf Cheese
  Calgary, AB 888-835-0126

147

Clover Stornetta Farms Inc
Petaluma, CA 800-237-3315
Cobb Hill Cheese
Hartland, VT 802-436-4360
Colonna Brothers Inc
North Bergen, NJ 201-864-1115
Colony Brands Inc
Monroe, WI 800-544-9036
Commercial Creamery Co
Spokane, WA 509-747-4131
Cooper Lake Farm LLC
Bearsville, NY 845-679-7822
Corfu Foods Inc
Bensenville, IL 630-595-2510
Creamland Dairies Inc
Albuquerque, NM 505-247-0721
Crowley Cheese Inc
Mt Holly, VT 800-683-2606
Crystal Farms Dairy Company
Minnetonka, MN 800-672-8260
Curran's Cheese Plant Inc
Browntown, WI 608-966-3361
Cyclone Enterprises Inc
Houston, TX 281-872-0087
Cypress Grove
Arcata, CA 707-825-1100
Dairy Farmers Of America
Kansas City, KS 888-332-6455
Dairy Fresh Foods Inc
Taylor, MI 313-299-0735
Dairy Group
Jericho, NY 516-433-0080
Dan Carter
Richfield, WI 800-782-0741
Dean Foods Co.
Dallas, TX 800-395-7004
Deca & Otto Farms
Miami, FL 305-629-9335
Decatur Dairy
Brodhead, WI 608-897-8661
Deppeler Cheese Factory
Monroe, WI 608-325-6311
Deseret Dairy Products
Salt Lake City, UT 801-240-7350
Dexpa
Cumming, GA 770-887-7412
Dimock Dairy Products
Dimock, SD 605-928-3833
Dole & Bailey Inc
Woburn, MA 781-935-1234
Drangle Foods
Gilman, WI 715-447-8241
Dulce de Leche Delcampo Products
Miami, FL 877-472-9408
Dupont Cheese
Marion, WI 800-895-2873
Dutch Cheese Makers Corp
Garden City, NY 631-533-9202
Dutch Farms Inc
Chicago, IL 800-637-3447
Eatem Foods Co
Vineland, NJ 800-683-2836
Eau Galle Cheese Factory Shop
Durand, WI 715-283-4211
Ellsworth Cooperative Creamery
Ellsworth, WI 715-273-4311
Elm City Cheese Co Inc
Hamden, CT 203-865-5768
Emkay Trading Corporation
Elmsford, NY 914-592-9000
F & A Dairy Products Inc
Dresser, WI 800-657-8582
Fairview Swiss Cheese
Fredonia, PA 724-475-4154
Fantis Foods Inc
Carlstadt, NJ 201-933-6200
Farmdale Creamery Inc
San Bernardino, CA 800-346-7306
Farmers Cooperative Dairy
Saint-Hubert, QC 800-501-1150
Farmgate Cheese LLC
Los Angelse, CA 310-733-6853
Father's Country Hams
Bremen, KY 270-525-3554
Finlandia Cheese
Parsippany, NJ 973-316-6609
First District Association
Litchfield, MN 320-693-3236
Fleur De Lait Foods Inc
New Holland, PA 800-322-2743
Floron Food Services
Edmonton, AB 780-438-9300
Food Matters Again
Brooklyn, NY 718-361-3183
Foremost Farms USA
Baraboo, WI 800-362-9196
Frank Brunckhorst Company
Sarasota, FL 804-722-4100
Frankfort Cheese
Edgar, WI 715-352-2345
Franklin's Cheese
Los Banos, CA 209-826-6259
Fried Provisions Company
Evans City, PA 724-538-3160
Friendship Dairies LLC
Friendship, NY 800-854-3243
Frog City Cheese
Plymouth Notch, VT 802-672-3650
Froma-Dar
St. Boniface, QC 819-535-3946
Fry Foods Inc
Tiffin, OH 800-626-2294
Gad Cheese Retail Store
Medford, WI 715-748-4273
GAF Seelig Inc
Flushing, NY 718-899-5000
Galaxy Dairy Products
Ramsey, NJ 201-818-2030
GFA Brands Inc
Paramus, NJ 201-568-9300
Gibbsville Cheese Company
Sheboygan Falls, WI 920-564-3242
Gile Cheese Store
Cuba City, WI 608-744-3456
Gossner Foods Inc.
Logan, UT 800-944-0454
GPI USA LLC.
Mokena, IL 800-929-4248
Grafton Village Cheese Co LLC
Brattleboro, VT 800-472-3866
Graham Cheese Corporation
Elnora, IN 800-472-9178
Grande Cheese Company
Fond du Lac, WI 800-678-3122
Great American Appetizers
Nampa, ID 800-282-4834
Great Lakes Cheese Company
Wausau, WI 715-842-3214
Great Lakes Cheese Company, Inc.
Hiram, OH 440-834-2500
Green Bay Cheese
Lincolnshire, IL 800-824-3373
Green Valley Food Corp
Dallas, TX 800-853-8399
Greenberg Cheese Co
Commerce, CA 800-301-4507
Guggisberg Cheese
Millersburg, OH 800-262-2505
H B Taylor Co
Chicago, IL 773-254-4805
H-E-B Grocery Co. LP
San Antonio, TX 800-432-3113
Harrington's of Vermont
Richmond, VT
Heluva Good Cheese
Lynnfield, MA 800-644-5473
Henning Cheese Factory
Kiel, WI 920-894-3032
Heritage Farms Dairy
Murfreesboro, TN 615-895-2790
Hickory Farms
Maumee, OH 800-753-8558
Hidden Villa Ranch
Fullerton, CA 800-326-3220
High Ridge Foods LLC
White Plains, NY 914-761-2900
Hiland Dairy Foods Co
Springfield, MO 800-492-4022
Hilmar Cheese Company
Hilmar, CA 800-577-5772
Hilmar Ingredients
Hilmar, CA 888-300-4465
Hollow Road Farms
Stuyvesant, NY 518-758-1881
Holmes Cheese Co
Millersburg, OH 330-674-6451
Hooks Cheese Co
Mineral Point, WI 608-987-3259
Icco Cheese Co
Orangeburg, NY 845-680-2436
Idaho Milk Products
Jerome, ID 208-644-2882
IMAC
Oklahoma City, OK 888-878-7827
Imperial Foods, Inc.
Long Island City, NY 718-784-3400
Inter-American Products
Cincinnati, OH 800-645-2233
International Cheese Company
Toronto, ON 416-769-3547
International Trading Company
Houston, TX 713-224-5901
Ito Cariani Sausage Company
Hayward, CA 510-887-0882
Ivanhoe Cheese Inc
Madoc, ON 613-473-4269
J B & Son LTD
Yonkers, NY 914-963-5192
J G Noble Cheese Company
Etiwanda, CA 909-899-2603
Jim's Cheese Pantry
Waterloo, WI 800-345-3571
John Koller & Son Inc
Fredonia, PA 724-475-4154
Joseph Farms
Atwater, CA 209-394-7984
JVM Sales Corp.
Linden, NJ 908-862-4866
Kantner Group
Wapakoneta, OH 877-738-3448
Karoun Dairies Inc
San Fernando, CA 888-767-0778
Keller's Creamery
Kansas City, MO 800-535-5371
Kirby Holloway Provision Co
Harrington, DE 800-995-4729
Klondike Cheese Factory
Monroe, WI 608-325-3021
Kolb-Lena Bresse Bleu Inc
Lena, IL 815-369-4577
Kraemer Wisconsin Cheese LTD
Watertown, WI 800-236-8033
LA Grander Hillside Dairy Inc
Stanley, WI 715-644-2275
Lactalis American Group Inc
Buffalo, NY 877-522-8254
Lactalis Ingredients Inc
Buffalo, NY
Lactalis USA Inc
Belmont, WI 608-762-5136
Lake Erie Frozen Foods Co
Ashland, OH 800-766-8501
Lakeview Banquit Cheese
Salt Lake City, UT 801-364-3607
Lamagna Cheese Co
Verona, PA 412-828-6112
Land O'Lakes Inc
Arden Hills, MN 800-328-9680
Laura Chenel's Chevre
Sonoma, CA 707-996-1252
Layman Distributing
Salem, VA 800-237-1319
Le Sueur Cheese Co
Le Sueur, MN 800-757-7611
Lebanon Cheese Co
Lebanon, NJ 908-236-2611
Lengacher's Cheese House
Kinzers, PA 717-355-6490
Leprino Foods Co.
Denver, CO 800-537-7466
Leraysville Cheese Factory
Le Raysville, PA 800-595-5196
LFI Inc
Fairfield, NJ 973-882-0550
Lifeline Food Company, Inc.
Seaside, CA 831-899-5040
Lifeway
Morton Grove, IL 877-281-3874
Linden Cheese Factory
Linden, WI 800-660-5051
Lioni Latticini Inc
Union, NJ 908-624-9450
Lisanatti Foods
Oregon City, OR 866-864-3922
Liuzzi Angeloni Cheese
Hamden, CT 203-287-8477
Los Altos Food Products
City Of Industry, CA 626-330-6555
Lynn Dairy Inc
Granton, WI 715-238-7129
M.H. Greenebaum
Airmont, NY 973-538-9200
Mahoning Swiss Cheese Cooperative
Smicksburg, PA 814-257-8884
Maison Riviera
Varennes, QC 800-363-0092

Product Categories / Cheese & Cheese Products: Cheese

Mancuso Cheese Co
Joliet, IL 815-722-2475
Maple Leaf Cheesemakers
New Glarus, WI 888-624-1234
Maplehill Creamery
Stuyvesant, NY 518-758-7777
Marathon Cheese
Medford, WI 715-748-4500
Marathon Cheese Corp
Marathon, WI 715-443-2211
Marin French Cheese Co
Petaluma, CA 800-292-6001
Marshallville Packing Co
Marshallville, OH 330-855-2871
Marva Maid Dairy
Newport News, VA 800-768-6243
Marwood Sales, Inc
Overland Park, KS 800-745-2881
Masters Gallery Foods Inc
Plymouth, WI 800-236-8431
Matador Processors
Blanchard, OK 800-847-0797
Mccadam Cheese Co Inc
Chateaugay, NY 800-639-4031
Meister Cheese Company
Muscoda, WI 800-634-7837
Michael Granese & Company
Norristown, PA 610-272-5099
Michigan Dairy LLC
Livonia, MI 734-367-5390
Michigan Farm Cheese Dairy
Fountain, MI 877-624-3373
Middlebury Cheese Company
Middlebury, IN 800-262-2505
Middlefield Cheese House
Middlefield, OH 800-327-9477
Mille Lacs Gourmet Foods
Madison, WI 800-843-1381
Miller's Cheese Corp
Brooklyn, NY 718-965-1840
Milsolv Corporation
Butler, WI 800-558-8501
Minerva Cheese Factory
Minerva, OH 330-868-4196
Morningland Dairy Cheese Company
Mountain View, MO 417-855-0588
Mossholder's Farm Cheese Factory
Appleton, WI 920-734-7575
Mozzarella Co
Dallas, TX 800-798-2954
Mt Sterling Cheese Co-Op Creamery
Highland, WI 866-289-4628
Nasonville Dairy
Marshfield, WI 715-676-2177
Nema Food Distribution
Fairfield, NJ 973-256-4415
Network Food Brokers
Haverford, PA 610-649-7210
Newburg Corners Cheese Factory
Bangor, WI 608-452-3636
Nodine's Smokehouse Inc
Torrington, CT 800-222-2059
Noon Hour Food Products Inc
Chicago, IL 800-621-6636
Nor-Tech Dairy Advisors
Sioux Falls, SD 605-338-2404
Northern Utah Manufacturing
Wellsville, UT 435-245-4542
Northern WIS Produce Co
Manitowoc, WI 920-684-4461
Old Chatham Sheepherding Co
Old Chatham, NY 888-743-3760
Old Country Cheese
Cashton, WI 888-320-9469
Old Europe Cheese Inc
Benton Harbor, MI 269-925-5003
Old Fashioned Foods
Mayville, WI 920-387-7924
Old Wisconsin Food Products
Homewood, IL 888-633-5684
Olde Tyme Food Corporation
East Longmeadow, MA 800-356-6533
ORB Weaver Farm
New Haven, VT 802-877-3755
Original Herkimer Cheese
Ilion, NY 315-895-7428
Oscar's Wholesale Meats
Ogden, UT 801-621-5655
Oshkosh Cold Storage
Oshkosh, WI 800-580-4680
Pacific Cheese Co
Hayward, CA 510-784-8800

Park Cheese Company Inc
Fond Du Lac, WI 800-752-7275
Parker Farm
Minneapolis, MN 800-869-6685
Parkers Farm
Coon Rapids, MN 800-869-6685
Parmalat Canada
Toronto, ON 800-563-1515
Pastorelli Food Products
Chicago, IL 800-767-2829
Pearl Valley Cheese Inc
Fresno, OH 740-545-6002
Pecoraro Dairy Products
Brooklyn, NY 718-388-2379
Penn Cheese
Winfield, PA 570-524-7700
Pine River Cheese & Butter Company
Ripley, ON 800-265-1175
Pine River Pre-Pack Inc
Newton, WI 920-726-4216
Plumrose USA
Chicago, IL 800-526-4909
Plymouth Cheese Counter
Plymouth, WI 888-607-9477
Pollio Dairy Products
Campbell, NY 607-527-3621
Prairie Farms Dairy Inc.
Edwardsville, IL 618-659-5700
Prima Kase
Monticello, WI 608-938-4227
Providence Cheese
Johnston, RI 401-421-5653
Purity Dairies LLC
Nashville, TN 615-244-1900
Queensboro Farm Products
Canastota, NY 315-687-6133
Queensboro Farm Products
Jamica, NY 718-658-5000
Ragersville Swiss Cheese
Sugarcreek, OH 330-897-3055
Raven Creamery Company
Portland, OR 503-288-5101
REDCLAY Gourmet
Winston-Salem, NC 336-575-3360
Redwood Hill Farm
Sebastopol, CA 877-238-3543
Regez Cheese & Paper Supply
Monroe, WI 608-325-3417
Renard's Cheese
Algoma, WI 920-487-2825
RM Heagy Foods
Lancaster, PA 717-569-1032
Roberto A Cheese Factory
East Canton, OH 330-488-1551
Rochester Cheese
Rochester, MN 888-288-6678
Roelli Cheese Co
Shullsburg, WI 800-575-4372
Rogue Creamery
Central Point, OR 866-396-4704
Ron's Wisconsin Cheese LLC
Luxemburg, WI 920-845-5330
Roos Foods
Kenton, DE 800-343-3642
Rosenberger's Dairies
Hatfield, PA 800-355-9074
Roth Cheese USA
Fitchburg, WI 608-285-9800
Royal Baltic LTD
Brooklyn, NY 718-385-8300
Rumiano Cheese Co.
Crescent City, CA 866-328-2433
Rumiano Cheese Factory
Willows, CA 866-328-2433
Safeway Inc.
Pleasanton, CA 877-723-3929
Salemville Cheese
Cambria, WI 920-394-3431
Salmans & Assoc
Chicago, IL 312-226-1820
Saputo Cheese USA Inc.
Lincolnshire, IL 847-267-1100
Saputo Inc.
Montreal, QC 800-672-8866
Sardinia Cheese
Seymour, CT 203-735-3374
Sargento Foods Inc
Plymouth, WI 800-243-3737
Sartori Co
Plymouth, WI 920-893-6061
Saxon Creamery
Cleveland, WI 920-693-8500

Schneider Cheese
Waldo, WI 920-467-3351
Schneider's Dairy Inc
Pittsburgh, PA 412-881-3525
Schobert's Cottage Cheese Corporation
Akron, OH 216-733-6876
Schreiber Foods Inc.
Green Bay, WI 920-437-7601
Schuman Cheese
Fairfield, NJ 800-888-2433
Scott's of Wisconsin
Sun Prairie, WI 800-693-0834
Scray's Cheese
De Pere, WI 920-336-8359
Sea Stars Goat Cheese
Santa Cruz, CA 831-423-7200
Sequoia Specialty Cheese Company
Visalia, CA 559-752-4106
Shenk's Foods
Lancaster, PA 717-393-4240
Sierra Cheese Mfg Co
Compton, CA 800-266-4270
Sierra Nevada Cheese Co.
Willows, CA 530-934-8660
Silani Sweet Cheese
Woodbridge, ON 905-792-3811
Simon's Specialty Cheese
Appleton, WI 800-444-0374
Sini Fulvi U.S.A.
Newark, NJ 973-274-0822
Sisler's Ice & Ice Cream
Ohio, IL 888-891-3856
Sofo Foods
Toledo, OH 800-447-4211
Sommer Maid Creamery Inc
Pipersville, PA 215-345-6160
Sonoma Creamery
Sonoma, CA 707-996-1000
Sparboe Foods Corp
New Hampton, IA 641-394-3040
Spaulding & Assoc
Brighton, MI 810-229-4166
Specialities Importers & Distributers
Millington, NJ 800-899-6689
Specialty Cheese Co Inc
Reeseville, WI 800-367-1711
Spring Grove Foods
Miamisburg, OH 937-866-4311
Springbank Cheese Company
Woodstock, ON 800-265-1973
Springdale Cheese Factory
Richland Center, WI 608-538-3213
Sprout Creek Farm
Poughkeepsie, NY 845-485-8432
St. Maurice Laurent
St-Bruno-Lac-St-Jean, QC 418-343-3655
Stallings Head Cheese Co
Houston, TX 713-523-1751
State Of Maine Cheese Co
Rockport, ME 800-762-8895
Steiner Cheese
Baltic, OH 888-897-5505
Stella Foods
Hinesburg, VT 802-482-2121
Stella Reedsburg
Reedsburg, WI 608-524-8244
Stremick's Heritage Foods
Santa Ana, CA 800-371-9010
Sugarbush Farm
Woodstock, VT 800-281-1757
Sun States
Charlotte, NC 704-821-0615
Sun-Re Cheese Co
Sunbury, PA 570-286-1511
Sunnyrose Cheese
Diamond City, AB 403-381-4024
Sunshine Farms
Portage, WI 608-742-2016
Super Stores Industries
Turlock, CA 209-668-2100
Suprema Specialties
Manteca, CA 209-858-9696
Supreme Artisan Foods
San Diego, CA 844-278-3663
Supreme Dairy Farms Co
Warwick, RI 401-739-8180
Swiss American Inc
St Louis, MO 800-325-8150
Swiss Way Cheese
Berne, IN 260-589-3531
T Sterling Assoc
Jamestown, NY 716-483-0769

Product Categories / Cheese & Cheese Products: Cheese

Taftsville Country Store
  Taftsville, VT 800-854-0013
Tall Talk Dairy
  Canby, OR. 503-266-1644
Taylor Cheese Corp
  Weyauwega, WI 920-867-2337
The Worlds Best Cheese
  Armonk, NY 800-922-4337
Thiel Cheese & Ingredients
  Hilbert, WI 920-989-1440
Tholstrup Cheese
  Muskegon, MI. 800-426-0938
Tillamook County Creamery Association
  Tillamook, OR 503-842-4481
Timber Lake Cheese Company
  Timber Lake, SD. 605-865-3605
Tomanetti Food Products Inc
  Oakmont, PA 800-875-3040
Torkelson Cheese Co
  Lena, IL. 815-369-4265
Trega Foods
  Weyauwega, WI 920-867-2137
Tropical Cheese
  Perth Amboy, NJ 888-874-4928
Twin County Dairy
  Kalona, IA. 319-656-2776
Umpqua Dairy
  Roseburg, OR 888-672-6455
V & V Supremo
  Chicago, IL 888-887-8773
Valley Grain Products
  Fresno, CA 559-675-3400
Valley Queen Cheese Factory
  Milbank, SD 605-432-4563
Valley View Cheese Co Inc
  Conewango Valley, NY. 716-296-5821
Vella Cheese Co
  Sonoma, CA 800-848-0505
Vermont Creamery
  Websterville, VT. 800-884-6287
Vern's Cheese
  Chilton, WI 920-849-7717
VOD Gourmet
  Greenwich, CT 203-531-5172
Wagshal's Imports
  Washington, DC 202-363-5698
Wapsie Creamery
  Independence, IA 319-334-7193
Weaver Brothers
  Berne, IN 219-589-2869
Wenger Spring Brook Cheese Inc
  Davis, IL 815-865-5612
West Point Dairy Products
  West Point, NE 402-372-5551
Western Creamery
  Brampton, ON. 800-265-3230
Weyauwega Star Dairy
  Weyauwega, WI 888-813-9720
Whitehall Specialties Inc
  Whitehall, WI 888-755-9900
WhiteWave Foods
  Denver, CO. 800-488-9283
Widmer's Cheese Cellars Inc
  Theresa, WI. 888-878-1107
Williams-R J
  Linwood, MI. 800-968-4462
Williams-R J
  Linwood, MI. 800-968-4492
Winger Cheese
  Towner, ND. 701-537-5463
Winona Foods
  Green Bay, WI. 920-662-2184
Wisconsin Cheeseman
  Madison, WI. 800-693-0834
Wisconsin Farmers Union
  Chippewa Falls, WI. 800-272-5531
Wisconsin Milk Mktng Board Inc
  Madison, WI. 800-589-5127
Wohlt Cheese Corp
  New London, WI 920-982-9000
Woolwich Dairy
  Orangeville, ON 877-438-3499
World Cheese Inc
  Brooklyn, NY 718-965-1700
Yerba Santa Goat Dairy
  Lakeport, CA 707-263-8131
Zimmerman Cheese Inc
  South Wayne, WI 608-968-3414

American

Crystal Farms Dairy Company
  Minnetonka, MN. 800-672-8260
Reilly Dairy & Food Company
  Tampa, FL. 813-839-8458
Sargento Foods Inc
  Plymouth, WI 800-243-3737

Asiago

BelGioioso Cheese Inc.
  Green Bay, WI. 920-863-2123
JVM Sales Corp.
  Linden, NJ. 908-862-4866
Kantner Group
  Wapakoneta, OH 877-738-3448
Lactalis American Group Inc
  Buffalo, NY. 877-522-8254
Park Cheese Company Inc
  Fond Du Lac, WI 800-752-7275
Sargento Foods Inc
  Plymouth, WI 800-243-3737
Sartori Co
  Plymouth, WI 920-893-6061
Vella Cheese Co
  Sonoma, CA 800-848-0505
Weyauwega Star Dairy
  Weyauwega, WI 888-813-9720

Blend - American/Skim Milk

Sliced

Kantner Group
  Wapakoneta, OH 877-738-3448

Blue

Bletsoe's Cheese Inc
  Marathon, WI 715-443-2526
Clofine Dairy Products Inc
  Linwood, NJ 609-653-1000
Great Hill Dairy Inc
  Marion, MA 888-748-2208
Lactalis American Group Inc
  Buffalo, NY. 877-522-8254
Marathon Cheese Corp
  Marathon, WI 715-443-2211
Reilly Dairy & Food Company
  Tampa, FL. 813-839-8458
Roth Cheese USA
  Fitchburg, WI 608-285-9800
Sargento Foods Inc
  Plymouth, WI 800-243-3737

Brie

Daphne's Creamery
   707-762-1760
Kolb-Lena Bresse Bleu Inc
  Lena, IL. 815-369-4577
Lactalis American Group Inc
  Buffalo, NY. 877-522-8254
Marin French Cheese Co
  Petaluma, CA 800-292-6001
Old Europe Cheese Inc
  Benton Harbor, MI 269-925-5003
Reilly Dairy & Food Company
  Tampa, FL. 813-839-8458
Supreme Artisan Foods
  San Diego, CA 844-278-3663
Woolwich Dairy
  Orangeville, ON 877-438-3499

Camembert

Kolb-Lena Bresse Bleu Inc
  Lena, IL. 815-369-4577
Lakeview Banquit Cheese
  Salt Lake City, UT 801-364-3607
Marin French Cheese Co
  Petaluma, CA 800-292-6001
Old Europe Cheese Inc
  Benton Harbor, MI 269-925-5003
Reilly Dairy & Food Company
  Tampa, FL. 813-839-8458

Cheddar

Advanced Food Products LLC
  New Holland, PA 800-732-5373
Alberta Cheese Company
  Calgary, AB. 403-279-4353
Alta Dena Certified Dairy LLC
  City Of Industry, CA. 800-535-1369
Ardmore Cheese Company
  Ardmore, TN. 931-427-2191
Bass Lake Cheese Factory
  Somerset, WI. 800-368-2437
Bletsoe's Cheese Inc
  Marathon, WI 715-443-2526
Cady Cheese Factory
  Wilson, WI 715-772-4218
Crystal Farms Dairy Company
  Minnetonka, MN. 800-672-8260
Daphne's Creamery
   707-762-1760
Father's Country Hams
  Bremen, KY 270-525-3554
Foremost Farms USA
  Baraboo, WI 800-362-9196
Golden Valley Dairy Products
  Tulare, CA. 559-687-1188
Guggisberg Cheese
  Millersburg, OH 800-262-2505
Hilmar Cheese Company
  Hilmar, CA 800-577-5772
Kantner Group
  Wapakoneta, OH 877-738-3448
Kraft Heinz Canada
  North York, ON 416-441-5000
Lactalis USA Inc
  Belmont, WI 608-762-5136
Reilly Dairy & Food Company
  Tampa, FL. 813-839-8458
Saputo Cheese USA Inc.
  Lincolnshire, IL. 847-267-1100
Sargento Foods Inc
  Plymouth, WI 800-243-3737
Trega Foods
  Weyauwega, WI 920-867-2137
Twin County Dairy
  Kalona, IA. 319-656-2776

Reduced Fat

Kantner Group
  Wapakoneta, OH 877-738-3448
Whitehall Specialties Inc
  Whitehall, WI 888-755-9900

Reduced Fat - Shredded

Crowley Cheese Inc
  Mt Holly, VT. 800-683-2606
Kantner Group
  Wapakoneta, OH 877-738-3448

Shredded

Horizon Organic Dairy
  Broomfield, CO 888-494-3020
Kantner Group
  Wapakoneta, OH 877-738-3448
WhiteWave Foods
  Denver, CO. 800-488-9283

Colby

Bass Lake Cheese Factory
  Somerset, WI. 800-368-2437
Belle Plaine Cheese Factory
  Shawano, WI. 866-245-5924
Bletsoe's Cheese Inc
  Marathon, WI 715-443-2526
Brunkow Cheese Of Wisconsin
  Darlington, WI 608-776-3716
Brunnett Dairy Co-Op
  Grantsburg, WI 715-689-2748
Cady Cheese Factory
  Wilson, WI 715-772-4218
Dupont Cheese
  Marion, WI 800-895-2873
Finlandia Cheese
  Parsippany, NJ. 973-316-6609
Graham Cheese Corporation
  Elnora, IN 800-472-9178
Guggisberg Cheese
  Millersburg, OH 800-262-2505
Heluva Good Cheese
  Lynnfield, MA 800-644-5473
Henning Cheese Factory
  Kiel, WI. 920-894-3032
Middlebury Cheese Company
  Middlebury, IN 800-262-2505
Pine River Cheese & Butter Company
  Ripley, ON. 800-265-1175
Reilly Dairy & Food Company
  Tampa, FL. 813-839-8458
Reiter Dairy
  Newport, KY 800-544-6455

Product Categories / Cheese & Cheese Products: Cheese

Saputo Cheese USA Inc.
  Lincolnshire, IL. 847-267-1100
Sargento Foods Inc
  Plymouth, WI .800-243-3737
Swiss American Inc
  St Louis, MO. .800-325-8150
Wapsie Creamery
  Independence, IA 319-334-7193
Widmer's Cheese Cellars Inc
  Theresa, WI. 888-878-1107

Cottage

Aimonetto and Sons
  Renton, WA. 866-823-2777
Alpina
  Batavia, NY. 855-886-1914
Alta Dena Certified Dairy LLC
  City Of Industry, CA. 800-535-1369
Anderson Dairy Inc
  Las Vegas, NV 702-642-7507
Anderson Erickson Dairy
  Des Moines, IA. 515-265-2521
Anderson Erickson Dairy
  Kansas City, KS 913-621-4801
Astro Dairy Products
  Toronto, ON 416-622-2811
Berkeley Farms
  Hayward, CA .800-395-7004
Borden Dairy
  Dallas, TX. 855-311-1583
Broughton Foods LLC
  El Paso, TX. 800-395-7004
Byrne Dairy, Inc.
  Syracuse, NY .800-899-1535
Clofine Dairy Products Inc
  Linwood, NJ 609-653-1000
Cloverland/Green Spring Dairy
  Baltimore, MD. 800-876-6455
Darigold
  Seattle, WA 800-333-6455
Friendship Dairies LLC
  Friendship, NY 800-854-3243
GAF Seelig Inc
  Flushing, NY. .718-899-5000
Good Culture
  Irvine, CA. 844-899-8884
H-E-B Grocery Co. LP
  San Antonio, TX. 800-432-3113
Heritage Farms Dairy
  Murfreesboro, TN 615-895-2790
Hiland Dairy Foods Co
  Springfield, MO 800-492-4022
Horizon Organic Dairy
  Broomfield, CO 888-494-3020
HP Hood LLC
  Lynnfield, MA 800-343-6592
Kemps LLC
  St Paul, MN
Marva Maid Dairy
  Newport News, VA 800-768-6243
Michigan Dairy LLC
  Livonia, MI. 734-367-5390
Nancy's Probiotic Foods
  Eugene, OR
Oakhurst Dairy
  Portland, ME. 800-482-0718
Old Home Foods Inc
  New Brighton, MN 651-312-8900
Plains Dairy Products
  Amarillo, TX. .800-365-5608
Prairie Farms Dairy Inc.
  Edwardsville, IL 618-659-5700
Purity Dairies LLC
  Nashville, TN 615-244-1900
Queensboro Farm Products
  Canastota, NY 315-687-6133
Queensboro Farm Products
  Jamica, NY. 718-658-5000
Reilly Dairy & Food Company
  Tampa, FL. 813-839-8458
Rockview Farms
  Downey, CA .800-423-2479
Schepps Dairy
  Dallas, TX. 800-395-7004
Sisler's Ice & Ice Cream
  Ohio, IL. 888-891-3856
Smith Dairy
  Orrville, OH 800-776-7076
Springfield Creamery Inc
  Eugene, OR. .541-689-2911
Super Stores Industries
  Turlock, CA 209-668-2100

Umpqua Dairy
  Roseburg, OR 888-672-6455
WhiteWave Foods
  Denver, CO .800-488-9283

Cream

Alouette Cheese USA
  New Holland, PA 800-322-2743
Astro Dairy Products
  Toronto, ON .416-622-2811
Clofine Dairy Products Inc
  Linwood, NJ .609-653-1000
Don's Food Products
  Schwenksville, PA 888-321-3667
Emkay Trading Corporation
  Elmsford, NY 914-592-9000
Franklin Foods
  Enosburg Falls, VT 800-933-6114
GAF Seelig Inc
  Flushing, NY. 718-899-5000
Horizon Organic Dairy
  Broomfield, CO 888-494-3020
Kite Hill
  Hayward, CA 888-588-0994
Kraft Heinz Canada
  North York, ON. 416-441-5000
Marburger Farm Dairy
  Evans City, PA 800-331-1295
Original Herkimer Cheese
  Ilion, NY. 315-895-7428
Queensboro Farm Products
  Jamica, NY. 718-658-5000
Rachael's Smoked Fish
  Springfield, MA 800-327-3412
Reilly Dairy & Food Company
  Tampa, FL. 813-839-8458
Schepps Dairy
  Dallas, TX. 800-395-7004
Schneider's Dairy Inc
  Pittsburgh, PA 412-881-3525
Schreiber Foods Inc.
  Green Bay, WI. 920-437-7601
Sierra Nevada Cheese Co.
  Willows, CA .530-934-8660
Springfield Creamery Inc
  Eugene, OR. .541-689-2911
Tofutti Brands Inc
  Cranford, NJ .908-272-2400
WhiteWave Foods
  Denver, CO .800-488-9283
Woolwich Dairy
  Orangeville, ON 877-438-3499

Edam

Old Europe Cheese Inc
  Benton Harbor, MI 269-925-5003
Saputo Cheese USA Inc.
  Lincolnshire, IL. 847-267-1100

Feta

Advanced Food Products LLC
  New Holland, PA 800-732-5373
Alberta Cheese Company
  Calgary, AB. .403-279-4353
Atwood Cheese Company
  Atwood, ON 519-356-2271
Blue Marble Brands
  Providence, RI 888-534-0246
Castella Imports Inc
  Brentwood, NY 631-231-5500
FAGE USA Dairy Ind Inc
  Johnstown, NY 866-962-5912
Kolb-Lena Bresse Bleu Inc
  Lena, IL. 815-369-4577
Lactalis American Group Inc
  Buffalo, NY. .877-522-8254
Lamagna Cheese Co
  Verona, PA. .412-828-6112
Michigan Farm Cheese Dairy
  Fountain, MI 877-624-3373
Mt Capra Products
  Chehalis, WA 800-574-1961
Mt Sterling Co-Op Creamery
  Highland, WI 866-289-4628
Pecoraro Dairy Products
  Brooklyn, NY 718-388-2379
Reilly Dairy & Food Company
  Tampa, FL. 813-839-8458
Sierra Cheese Mfg Co
  Compton, CA 800-266-4270

Stickney Hill Dairy Inc
  Kimball, MN. 320-398-5360
Trega Foods
  Weyauwega, WI 920-867-2137
Vermont Creamery
  Websterville, VT 800-884-6287
Woolwich Dairy
  Orangeville, ON 877-438-3499

Fontina

Atwood Cheese Company
  Atwood, ON 519-356-2271
BelGioioso Cheese Inc.
  Green Bay, WI. 920-863-2123
Lactalis American Group Inc
  Buffalo, NY. .877-522-8254
Old Europe Cheese Inc
  Benton Harbor, MI 269-925-5003
Park Cheese Company Inc
  Fond Du Lac, WI 800-752-7275
Prima Kase
  Monticello, WI 608-938-4227
Sartori Co
  Plymouth, WI 920-893-6061

Goat's

Alta Dena Certified Dairy LLC
  City Of Industry, CA. 800-535-1369
Bass Lake Cheese Factory
  Somerset, WI. 800-368-2437
Daphne's Creamery
 707-762-1760
Epic Source Food
  Frisco, TX 214-407-7154
Lactalis American Group Inc
  Buffalo, NY. .877-522-8254
Laura Chenel's Chevre
  Sonoma, CA 707-996-1252
Mackenzie Creamery
  Hiram, OH 330-569-3368
Montchevre-Betin, Inc
  Rolling Hills Estates, CA 310-541-3520
Mozzarella Co
  Dallas, TX. 800-798-2954
Mt Capra Products
  Chehalis, WA 800-574-1961
Mt Sterling Co-Op Creamery
  Highland, WI 866-289-4628
Quillisascut Cheese Co
  Rice, WA 509-738-2011
Rollingstone Chevre
  Parma, ID 208-722-6460
Sierra Nevada Cheese Co.
  Willows, CA .530-934-8660
Sprout Creek Farm
  Poughkeepsie, NY 845-485-8432
Stickney Hill Dairy Inc
  Kimball, MN. 320-398-5360
Swiss American Inc
  St Louis, MO. 800-325-8150
Vermont Creamery
  Websterville, VT 800-884-6287
Vermont Creamery
  Websterville, VT 802-479-9371
Westfield Farm
  Hubbardston, MA 877-777-3900

Gorgonzola

BelGioioso Cheese Inc.
  Green Bay, WI. 920-863-2123
Lactalis American Group Inc
  Buffalo, NY. .877-522-8254
Reilly Dairy & Food Company
  Tampa, FL. 813-839-8458

Gouda

Bass Lake Cheese Factory
  Somerset, WI. 800-368-2437
Bel Brands USA
  Chicago, IL. .312-462-1500
Cady Cheese Factory
  Wilson, WI. .715-772-4218
Finlandia Cheese
  Parsippany, NJ. 973-316-6609
Old Europe Cheese Inc
  Benton Harbor, MI 269-925-5003
Prima Kase
  Monticello, WI 608-938-4227
Roth Cheese USA
  Fitchburg, WI 608-285-9800

Product Categories / Cheese & Cheese Products: Cheese

Winchester Cheese Company
  Winchester, CA..................951-926-4239
Woolwich Dairy
  Orangeville, ON..................877-438-3499

Grated

Calabro Cheese Corp
  East Haven, CT..................203-469-1311
Clofine Dairy Products Inc
  Linwood, NJ..................609-653-1000
Colonna Brothers Inc
  North Bergen, NJ..................201-864-1115
Elm City Cheese Co Inc
  Hamden, CT..................203-865-5768
Icco Cheese Co
  Orangeburg, NY..................845-680-2436
JVM Sales Corp.
  Linden, NJ..................908-862-4866
Kantner Group
  Wapakoneta, OH..................877-738-3448
Mancuso Cheese Co
  Joliet, IL..................815-722-2475
Park Cheese Company Inc
  Fond Du Lac, WI..................800-752-7275
Pastene Co LTD
  Canton, MA..................781-298-3397
Sargento Foods Inc
  Plymouth, WI..................800-243-3737
Sun-Re Cheese Co
  Sunbury, PA..................570-286-1511

Gruyere

Castella Imports Inc
  Brentwood, NY..................631-231-5500
Roth Cheese USA
  Fitchburg, WI..................608-285-9800

Havarti

Finlandia Cheese
  Parsippany, NJ..................973-316-6609
Prima Kase
  Monticello, WI..................608-938-4227
Roth Cheese USA
  Fitchburg, WI..................608-285-9800

Low-Fat

Cabot Creamery Co-Op
  Waitsfield, VT..................888-792-2268
Froma-Dar
  St. Boniface, QC..................819-535-3946
Lactalis American Group Inc
  Buffalo, NY..................877-522-8254
Le Sueur Cheese Co
  Le Sueur, MN..................800-757-7611

Mascarpone

BelGioioso Cheese Inc.
  Green Bay, WI..................920-863-2123
GAF Seelig Inc
  Flushing, NY..................718-899-5000
Lactalis American Group Inc
  Buffalo, NY..................877-522-8254
Miceli Dairy Products Co
  Cleveland, OH..................216-791-6222
Pecoraro Dairy Products
  Brooklyn, NY..................718-388-2379
Reilly Dairy & Food Company
  Tampa, FL..................813-839-8458
Vermont Creamery
  Websterville, VT..................800-884-6287
Vermont Creamery
  Websterville, VT..................802-479-9371

Monterey Jack

Alberta Cheese Company
  Calgary, AB..................403-279-4353
Alta Dena Certified Dairy LLC
  City Of Industry, CA..................800-535-1369
Avanti Foods Co
  Walnut, IL..................800-243-3739
Bass Lake Cheese Factory
  Somerset, WI..................800-368-2437
Belle Plaine Cheese Factory
  Shawano, WI..................866-245-5924
Bletsoe's Cheese Inc
  Marathon, WI..................715-443-2526
Brunkow Cheese Of Wisconsin
  Darlington, WI..................608-776-3716
Cabot Creamery Co-Op
  Waitsfield, VT..................888-792-2268
Cady Cheese Factory
  Wilson, WI..................715-772-4218
Henning Cheese Factory
  Kiel, WI..................920-894-3032
Hilmar Cheese Company
  Hilmar, CA..................800-577-5772
Horizon Organic Dairy
  Broomfield, CO..................888-494-3020
Lakeview Banquit Cheese
  Salt Lake City, UT..................801-364-3607
Pine River Cheese & Butter Company
  Ripley, ON..................800-265-1175
Reilly Dairy & Food Company
  Tampa, FL..................813-839-8458
Rumiano Cheese Factory
  Willows, CA..................866-328-2433
Sargento Foods Inc
  Plymouth, WI..................800-243-3737
Suprema Specialties
  Manteca, CA..................209-858-9696
Swiss American Inc
  St Louis, MO..................800-325-8150
Vella Cheese Co
  Sonoma, CA..................800-848-0505
Wapsie Creamery
  Independence, IA..................319-334-7193
WhiteWave Foods
  Denver, CO..................800-488-9283

Mozzarella

Angelo & Franco U.S.A.
  Hawthorne, CA..................310-263-0506
Antonio Mozzarella Factory
  Springfield, NJ..................973-379-0033
Atwood Cheese Company
  Atwood, ON..................519-356-2271
B & D Foods
  Boise, ID..................208-344-1183
BelGioioso Cheese Inc.
  Green Bay, WI..................920-863-2123
Biazzo Dairy Products Inc
  Ridgefield, NJ..................201-941-6800
Bletsoe's Cheese Inc
  Marathon, WI..................715-443-2526
Brunnett Dairy Co-Op
  Grantsburg, WI..................715-689-2748
Cacique
  Monrovia, CA..................800-521-6987
Calabro Cheese Corp
  East Haven, CT..................203-469-1311
Clofine Dairy Products Inc
  Linwood, NJ..................609-653-1000
Crystal Farms Dairy Company
  Minnetonka, MN..................800-672-8260
Daphne's Creamery
 707-762-1760
Deca & Otto Farms
  Miami, FL..................305-629-9335
Floron Food Services
  Edmonton, AB..................780-438-9300
Foremost Farms USA
  Baraboo, WI..................800-362-9196
Fry Foods Inc
  Tiffin, OH..................800-626-2294
Golden Valley Dairy Products
  Tulare, CA..................559-687-1188
Great Lakes Cheese Company, Inc.
  Hiram, OH..................440-834-2500
Henning Cheese Factory
  Kiel, WI..................920-894-3032
J B & Son LTD
  Yonkers, NY..................914-963-5192
Kantner Group
  Wapakoneta, OH..................877-738-3448
Lactalis American Group Inc
  Buffalo, NY..................877-522-8254
Lactalis USA Inc
  Belmont, WI..................608-762-5136
Lakeview Banquit Cheese
  Salt Lake City, UT..................801-364-3607
Lamagna Cheese Co
  Verona, PA..................412-828-6112
Leprino Foods Co.
  Denver, CO..................800-537-7466
Liuzzi Angeloni Cheese
  Hamden, CT..................203-287-8477
Mancuso Cheese Co
  Joliet, IL..................815-722-2475
Marathon Cheese Corp
  Marathon, WI..................715-443-2211
Miceli Dairy Products Co
  Cleveland, OH..................216-791-6222
Michael Granese & Company
  Norristown, PA..................610-272-5099
Mozzarella Co
  Dallas, TX..................800-798-2954
Pecoraro Dairy Products
  Brooklyn, NY..................718-388-2379
Pine River Cheese & Butter Company
  Ripley, ON..................800-265-1175
Pollio Dairy Products
  Campbell, NY..................607-527-3621
Reilly Dairy & Food Company
  Tampa, FL..................813-839-8458
Sargento Foods Inc
  Plymouth, WI..................800-243-3737
Sierra Cheese Mfg Co
  Compton, CA..................800-266-4270
Sun-Re Cheese Co
  Sunbury, PA..................570-286-1511
Suprema Specialties
  Manteca, CA..................209-858-9696
Supreme Dairy Farms Co
  Warwick, RI..................401-739-8180
Trega Foods
  Weyauwega, WI..................920-867-2137
WhiteWave Foods
  Denver, CO..................800-488-9283
Wisconsin Milk Mktng Board Inc
  Madison, WI..................800-589-5127
Woolwich Dairy
  Orangeville, ON..................877-438-3499

Lite Shredded - Frozen

Kantner Group
  Wapakoneta, OH..................877-738-3448

Low Moisture Part Skim

Kantner Group
  Wapakoneta, OH..................877-738-3448

Low Moisture Part Skim Shredded - Frozen

Kantner Group
  Wapakoneta, OH..................877-738-3448

Muenster

Finlandia Cheese
  Parsippany, NJ..................973-316-6609
Heluva Good Cheese
  Lynnfield, MA..................800-644-5473
Reilly Dairy & Food Company
  Tampa, FL..................813-839-8458
Roth Cheese USA
  Fitchburg, WI..................608-285-9800
Sargento Foods Inc
  Plymouth, WI..................800-243-3737
Springdale Cheese Factory
  Richland Center, WI..................608-538-3213
Wenger Spring Brook Cheese Inc
  Davis, IL..................815-865-5612

Natural American

Barrel

Arla Foods Inc
  Concord, ON..................905-669-9393

No-Fat

Le Sueur Cheese Co
  Le Sueur, MN..................800-757-7611
Shenk's Foods
  Lancaster, PA..................717-393-4240

Parmesan

Atwood Cheese Company
  Atwood, ON..................519-356-2271
BelGioioso Cheese Inc.
  Green Bay, WI..................920-863-2123
Castella Imports Inc
  Brentwood, NY..................631-231-5500
Cheese Merchants of America
  Carol Stream, IL..................630-768-0317
Clofine Dairy Products Inc
  Linwood, NJ..................609-653-1000
Colonna Brothers Inc
  North Bergen, NJ..................201-864-1115
Crystal Farms Dairy Company
  Minnetonka, MN..................800-672-8260

Product Categories / Cheese & Cheese Products: Imitation Cheeses & Substitutes

Icco Cheese Co
  Orangeburg, NY 845-680-2436
JVM Sales Corp.
  Linden, NJ 908-862-4866
Kantner Group
  Wapakoneta, OH 877-738-3448
Lactalis American Group Inc
  Buffalo, NY 877-522-8254
Mancuso Cheese Co
  Joliet, IL 815-722-2475
Miceli Dairy Products Co
  Cleveland, OH 216-791-6222
Park Cheese Company Inc
  Fond Du Lac, WI 800-752-7275
Parmx
  Calgary, AB 403-237-0707
Reilly Dairy & Food Company
  Tampa, FL 813-839-8458
Sargento Foods Inc
  Plymouth, WI 800-243-3737
Sartori Co
  Plymouth, WI 920-893-6061
Suprema Specialties
  Manteca, CA 209-858-9696
Valley Grain Products
  Fresno, CA 559-675-3400
Weyauwega Star Dairy
  Weyauwega, WI 888-813-9720

Pecorino
Kantner Group
  Wapakoneta, OH 877-738-3448

Pepatello
Rumiano Cheese Factory
  Willows, CA 866-328-2433

Process Loaves

Yellow
Arla Foods Inc
  Concord, ON 905-669-9393
Kantner Group
  Wapakoneta, OH 877-738-3448
Wohlt Cheese Corp
  New London, WI 920-982-9000

Process Sliced

White/Yellow
Kantner Group
  Wapakoneta, OH 877-738-3448
Kraft Heinz Canada
  North York, ON 416-441-5000

Processed American
Finlandia Cheese
  Parsippany, NJ 973-316-6609
Kantner Group
  Wapakoneta, OH 877-738-3448
Schreiber Foods Inc.
  Green Bay, WI 920-437-7601
Welcome Dairy Inc
  Colby, WI 715-223-2874
Wohlt Cheese Corp
  New London, WI 920-982-9000

Processed Swiss
Finlandia Cheese
  Parsippany, NJ 973-316-6609

Provolone
Alberta Cheese Company
  Calgary, AB 403-279-4353
BelGioioso Cheese Inc.
  Green Bay, WI 920-863-2123
Brunnett Dairy Co-Op
  Grantsburg, WI 715-689-2748
Crystal Farms Dairy Company
  Minnetonka, MN 800-672-8260
Golden Valley Dairy Products
  Tulare, CA 559-687-1188
Kantner Group
  Wapakoneta, OH 877-738-3448
Lactalis American Group Inc
  Buffalo, NY 877-522-8254
Lamagna Cheese Co
  Verona, PA 412-828-6112
Mancuso Cheese Co
  Joliet, IL 815-722-2475
Park Cheese Company Inc
  Fond Du Lac, WI 800-752-7275
Reilly Dairy & Food Company
  Tampa, FL 813-839-8458
Sargento Foods Inc
  Plymouth, WI 800-243-3737
Trega Foods
  Weyauwega, WI 920-867-2137

Ricotta
Alberta Cheese Company
  Calgary, AB 403-279-4353
BelGioioso Cheese Inc.
  Green Bay, WI 920-863-2123
Biazzo Dairy Products Inc
  Ridgefield, NJ 201-941-6800
Calabro Cheese Corp
  East Haven, CT 203-469-1311
Castella Imports Inc
  Brentwood, NY 631-231-5500
Crystal Farms Dairy Company
  Minnetonka, MN 800-672-8260
J B & Son LTD
  Yonkers, NY 914-963-5192
Kantner Group
  Wapakoneta, OH 877-738-3448
Kite Hill
  Hayward, CA 888-588-0994
Lactalis American Group Inc
  Buffalo, NY 877-522-8254
Lamagna Cheese Co
  Verona, PA 412-828-6112
Liuzzi Angeloni Cheese
  Hamden, CT 203-287-8477
Losurdo Creamery
  Hackensack, NJ 888-567-8736
Mancuso Cheese Co
  Joliet, IL 815-722-2475
Miceli Dairy Products Co
  Cleveland, OH 216-791-6222
Michael Granese & Company
  Norristown, PA 610-272-5099
Pecoraro Dairy Products
  Brooklyn, NY 718-388-2379
Pollio Dairy Products
  Campbell, NY 607-527-3621
Reilly Dairy & Food Company
  Tampa, FL 813-839-8458
Sargento Foods Inc
  Plymouth, WI 800-243-3737
Schneider's Dairy Inc
  Pittsburgh, PA 412-881-3525
Sierra Cheese Mfg Co
  Compton, CA 800-266-4270
Sun-Re Cheese Co
  Sunbury, PA 570-286-1511
Supreme Dairy Farms Co
  Warwick, RI 401-739-8180
Tofutti Brands Inc
  Cranford, NJ 908-272-2400

Romano
Advanced Food Products LLC
  New Holland, PA 800-732-5373
BelGioioso Cheese Inc.
  Green Bay, WI 920-863-2123
Brunnett Dairy Co-Op
  Grantsburg, WI 715-689-2748
Castella Imports Inc
  Brentwood, NY 631-231-5500
Clofine Dairy Products Inc
  Linwood, NJ 609-653-1000
Colonna Brothers Inc
  North Bergen, NJ 201-864-1115
JVM Sales Corp.
  Linden, NJ 908-862-4866
Kantner Group
  Wapakoneta, OH 877-738-3448
Mancuso Cheese Co
  Joliet, IL 815-722-2475
Miceli Dairy Products Co
  Cleveland, OH 216-791-6222
Park Cheese Company Inc
  Fond Du Lac, WI 800-752-7275
Reilly Dairy & Food Company
  Tampa, FL 813-839-8458
Sargento Foods Inc
  Plymouth, WI 800-243-3737
Sartori Co
  Plymouth, WI 920-893-6061
Suprema Specialties
  Manteca, CA 209-858-9696
Valley Grain Products
  Fresno, CA 559-675-3400
Weyauwega Star Dairy
  Weyauwega, WI 888-813-9720

String
Aunt Lizzie's Inc
  Memphis, TN 800-993-7788
Baker Cheese Factory Inc
  St Cloud, WI 920-477-7871
Bletsoe's Cheese Inc
  Marathon, WI 715-443-2526
Horizon Organic Dairy
  Broomfield, CO 888-494-3020
Parmalat Canada
  Toronto, ON 800-563-1515
Weyauwega Star Dairy
  Weyauwega, WI 888-813-9720
WhiteWave Foods
  Denver, CO 800-488-9283

Swiss
Bletsoe's Cheese Inc
  Marathon, WI 715-443-2526
Brewster Dairy Inc
  Brewster, OH 800-874-8874
Clofine Dairy Products Inc
  Linwood, NJ 609-653-1000
Crystal Farms Dairy Company
  Minnetonka, MN 800-672-8260
Emmi Roth USA
  Monroe, WI 608-845-5796
Finlandia Cheese
  Parsippany, NJ 973-316-6609
Guggisberg Cheese
  Millersburg, OH 800-262-2505
Heluva Good Cheese
  Lynnfield, MA 800-644-5473
Holmes Cheese Co
  Millersburg, OH 330-674-6451
Kolb-Lena Bresse Bleu Inc
  Lena, IL 815-369-4577
Los Altos Food Products
  City Of Industry, CA 626-330-6555
Marathon Cheese Corp
  Marathon, WI 715-443-2211
Middlebury Cheese Company
  Middlebury, IN 800-262-2505
Middlefield Cheese House
  Middlefield, OH 800-327-9477
Penn Cheese
  Winfield, PA 570-524-7700
Ragersville Swiss Cheese
  Sugarcreek, OH 330-897-3055
Sargento Foods Inc
  Plymouth, WI 800-243-3737
Steiner Cheese
  Baltic, OH 888-897-5505
Wenger Spring Brook Cheese Inc
  Davis, IL 815-865-5612

Imitation Cheeses & Substitutes

Cheese Foods & Substitutes
A Southern Season
  Hillsborough, NC 800-253-3663
Al Pete Meats
  Muncie, IN 765-288-8817
Arla Foods Inc
  Concord, ON 905-669-9393
B & D Foods
  Boise, ID 208-344-1183
Baker Cheese Factory Inc
  St Cloud, WI 920-477-7871
Bel Brands USA
  Chicago, IL 312-462-1500
Bernardi Italian Foods Company
  Bloomsburg, PA 570-389-5500
Castle Cheese
  Slippery Rock, PA 800-252-4373
Century Foods Intl LLC
  Sparta, WI 800-269-1901
Cheese Straws & More
  Monroe, LA 800-997-1921
Clofine Dairy Products Inc
  Linwood, NJ 609-653-1000

153

Product Categories / Cheese & Cheese Products: Imitation Cheeses & Substitutes

Earth Island
   Chatsworth, CA .888-394-3949
Galaxy Nutritional Foods Inc
   North Kingstown, RI 800-441-9419
Great American Appetizers
   Nampa, ID. 800-282-4834
Hormel Foods Corp.
   Austin, MN 507-437-5611
Ingretec
   Lebanon, PA .717-273-0711
John W Macy's Cheesesticks Inc
   Elmwood Park, NJ 800-643-0573
Kantner Group
   Wapakoneta, OH. 877-738-3448
Matador Processors
   Blanchard, OK 800-847-0797
Mehaffies Pies
   Dayton, OH. .800-289-7437
Nuts For Cheese
   London, ON .519-601-5070
Parkers Farm
   Coon Rapids, MN 800-869-6685
Parmela Creamery
   Torrance, CA. 310-584-7541
Pine River Pre-Pack Inc
   Newton, WI. .920-726-4216
Pocono Cheesecake Factory
   Swiftwater, PA 570-839-6844
Sierra Cheese Mfg Co
   Compton, CA 800-266-4270
Texas Heat
   San Antonio, TX 800-656-5916
Tomanetti Food Products Inc
   Oakmont, PA. 800-875-3040
Vtopian Artisan Cheeses
   Portland, OR
Whitehall Specialties Inc
   Whitehall, WI 888-755-9900
Wisconsin Milk Mktng Board Inc
   Madison, WI. 800-589-5127

Imitation

American

Kantner Group
   Wapakoneta, OH. 877-738-3448

Cheddar

Kantner Group
   Wapakoneta, OH. 877-738-3448

Mozzarella

Kantner Group
   Wapakoneta, OH. 877-738-3448

Parmesan

Kantner Group
   Wapakoneta, OH. 877-738-3448

Substitutes

Chicago Vegan Foods
   Lombard, IL .630-629-9667
Earth Island
   Chatsworth, CA 888-394-3949
Hormel Foods Corp.
   Austin, MN 507-437-5611
Kantner Group
   Wapakoneta, OH. 877-738-3448
Parmela Creamery
   Torrance, CA. 310-584-7541

American

Kantner Group
   Wapakoneta, OH. 877-738-3448

Dairy Products

Butter

Agri-Mark Inc
  West Springfield, MA 978-552-5500
Ahara Ghee
  Portland, OR 503-997-5050
Allfresh Food Products
  Evanston, IL 847-869-3100
American Almond Products Co
  Brooklyn, NY 800-825-6663
Ancient Organics
  Berkeley, CA 510-280-5043
Associated Milk Producers Inc.
  New Ulm, MN. 800-533-3580
Bartlett Dairy & Food Service
  Jamaica, NY 718-658-2299
Borden Dairy
  Dallas, TX. 855-311-1583
Butterball Farms
  Grand Rapids, MI 888-828-8837
Byrne Dairy, Inc.
  Syracuse, NY 800-899-1535
California Dairies Inc.
  Visalia, CA 559-625-2200
Carr Valley Cheese Company
  La Valle, WI 800-462-7258
Cass-Clay Creamery
  Fargo, ND 701-293-6455
Challenge Dairy Products, Inc.
  Dublin, CA 800-733-2479
Chef Shamy Gourmet
  Salt Lake City, UT
Clover Sonoma
  Petaluma, CA 800-237-3315
Cloverland Dairy
  Saint Clairsville, OH. 740-699-0509
Crush Foods Service
  Westlake Village, CA 818-699-6381
Crystal Farms Dairy Company
  Minnetonka, MN. 800-672-8260
Dairy Farmers Of America
  Kansas City, KS 888-332-6455
Daphne's Creamery
   707-762-1760
Darigold
  Seattle, WA 800-333-6455
Epicurean Butter
  Federal Heights, CO 303-427-5527
Farmdale Creamery Inc
  San Bernardino, CA 800-346-7306
Farmtrue
  North Stonington, CT 860-495-2231
Foothills Creamery
  Calgary, AB. 800-661-4909
Foremost Farms USA
  Baraboo, WI 800-362-9196
GAF Seelig Inc
  Flushing, NY. 718-899-5000
Gossner Foods Inc.
  Logan, UT. 800-944-0454
Gourmet Ghee
  Lynbrook, NY 516-744-0770
Graf Creamery Co
  Bonduel, WI 715-758-2137
Grassland Dairy Products Inc
  Greenwood, WI. 800-428-8837
Green River Chocolates
  Hinesburg, VT. 802-482-6727
Grouse Hunt Farm Inc
  Tamaqua, PA 570-467-2850
H B Taylor Co
  Chicago, IL 773-254-4805
Hidden Villa Ranch
  Fullerton, CA 800-326-3220
Hope Creamery
  Hope, MN 507-451-2029
Horizon Organic Dairy
  Broomfield, CO 888-494-3020
Houlton Farms Dairy
  Houlton, ME 207-532-3170
J M Swank Co
  North Liberty, IA 800-593-6375
Kozlowski Farms
  Forestville, CA 800-473-2767
Land O'Lakes Inc
  Arden Hills, MN 800-328-9680
Lost Trail Root Beer
  Louisburg, KS 800-748-7765
Maison Riviera
  Varennes, QC 800-363-0092
Marburger Farm Dairy
  Evans City, PA 800-331-1295
Maryland & Virginia Milk Producers Cooperative
  Reston, VA 703-742-6800
Minerva Cheese Factory
  Minerva, OH. 330-868-4196
Minerva Dairy Inc
  Minerva, OH 330-868-4196
Natrel
  St. Laurent, QC 800-501-1150
O-At-Ka Milk Prods Co-Op Inc.
  Batavia, NY. 800-828-8152
Oakhurst Dairy
  Portland, ME 800-482-0718
Oasis Food Co
  Hillside, NJ 800-275-0477
OMGhee
  Cedar Grove, NJ 973-931-3476
Plainview Milk Products
  Plainview, MN. 800-356-5606
Prairie Farms Dairy Inc.
  Edwardsville, IL 618-659-5700
Pride Dairies
  Bottineau, ND 701-228-2216
Producers Dairy Foods Inc
  Fresno, CA 559-264-6583
Pure Indian
  Princeton Jct., NJ 877-588-4433
Purity Farms
  La Farge, WI 877-211-4819
Queensboro Farm Products
  Canastota, NY. 315-687-6133
Reilly Dairy & Food Company
  Tampa, FL. 813-839-8458
Rockview Farms
  Downey, CA 800-423-2479
Schepps Dairy
  Dallas, TX. 800-395-7004
Schneider's Dairy Inc
  Pittsburgh, PA 412-881-3525
Shenk's Foods
  Lancaster, PA 717-393-4240
Sisler's Ice & Ice Cream
  Ohio, IL. 888-891-3856
Sommer Maid Creamery Inc
  Pipersville, PA. 215-345-6160
Sparboe Foods Corp
  New Hampton, IA 641-394-3040
Tin Star Foods
  Austin, TX
Turner & Pease Company
  Seattle, WA 206-282-9535
Umpqua Dairy
  Roseburg, OR 888-672-6455
United Dairymen of Arizona
  Tempe, AZ. 480-966-7211
Ventura Foods LLC
  Brea, CA 800-421-6257
Vermont Creamery
  Webstervile, VT. 800-884-6287
Westin Foods
  Omaha, NE 800-228-6098
WhiteWave Foods
  Denver, CO 800-488-9283
Whitewave Foods Company
  Broomfield, CO 303-635-4000
Century Foods Intl LLC
  Sparta, WI. 800-269-1901
Clofine Dairy Products Inc
  Linwood, NJ 609-653-1000
Crystal Creamery
  Modesto, CA. 866-225-4821
Danish Maid Butter Co
  Chicago, IL 773-731-8787
F C C
  Mcminnville, OR 503-472-2157
Grassland Dairy Products Inc
  Greenwood, WI. 800-428-8837
Keller's Creamery
  Kansas City, MO. 800-535-5371
Larosa Bakery Inc
  Shrewsbury, NJ 800-527-6722
Mt Sterling Co-Op Creamery
  Highland, WI 866-289-4628
St. Maurice Laurent
  St-Bruno-Lac-St-Jean, QC 418-343-3655
Swagger Foods Corp
  Vernon Hills, IL 847-913-1200
Tillamook County Creamery Association
  Tillamook, OR 503-842-4481
United Dairymen of Arizona
  Tempe, AZ. 480-966-7211
Vermont Creamery
  Webstervile, VT. 800-884-6287
WhiteWave Foods
  Denver, CO 800-488-9283

Low Fat

Dixie USA
  Tomball, TX 800-233-3668

Salted

Grassland Dairy Products Inc
  Greenwood, WI. 800-428-8837
Reilly Dairy & Food Company
  Tampa, FL. 813-839-8458

Unsalted

Grassland Dairy Products Inc
  Greenwood, WI. 800-428-8837
Keller's Creamery
  Kansas City, MO. 800-535-5371
Reilly Dairy & Food Company
  Tampa, FL. 813-839-8458

Buttermilk & Buttermilk Products

Buttermilk

Agri-Dairy Products
  Purchase, NY 914-697-9580
Alta Dena Certified Dairy LLC
  City Of Industry, CA. 800-535-1369
Anderson Dairy Inc
  Las Vegas, NV 702-642-7507
Associated Milk Producers Inc.
  New Ulm, MN. 800-533-3580
Barber Dairies
  Birmingham, AL. 205-942-2351
Borden Dairy
  Dallas, TX. 855-311-1583
Broughton Foods LLC
  El Paso, TX 800-395-7004
California Dairies Inc.
  Visalia, CA 559-625-2200
Century Foods Intl LLC
  Sparta, WI. 800-269-1901
Chase Brothers Dairy
  Oxnard, CA. 800-438-6455
Clofine Dairy Products Inc
  Linwood, NJ 609-653-1000
Cloverland Dairy
  Saint Clairsville, OH. 740-699-0509
Dairy Maid Dairy LLC
  Frederick, MD 301-663-5114
Friendship Dairies LLC
  Friendship, NY 800-854-3243
Graf Creamery Co
  Bonduel, WI 715-758-2137
J M Swank Co
  North Liberty, IA 800-593-6375

Blends

Chef Shamy Gourmet
  Salt Lake City, UT
Medlee Foods
  Chicago, IL 312-442-0406

Dairy

Agropur
  Granby, QC 800-363-5686
Allfresh Food Products
  Evanston, IL 847-869-3100
Alliston Creamery
  Alliston, ON 705-435-6751

Product Categories / Dairy Products: Cream

Kleinpeter Farms Dairy LLC
  Baton Rouge, LA 225-753-2121
Ludwig Dairy Product
  Elk Grove Vlg, IL 847-860-8646
Marburger Farm Dairy
  Evans City, PA 800-331-1295
McArthur Dairy LLC
  Miami, FL 561-659-4811
Mom's Bakery
  Sherman, TX 903-893-7585
Plains Dairy Products
  Amarillo, TX 800-365-5608
Plainview Milk Products
  Plainview, MN 800-356-5606
Pleasant View Dairy
  Highland, IN 219-838-0155
Promised Land Dairy
  Colorado Springs, CO. 877-520-2479
Queensboro Farm Products
  Jamica, NY 718-658-5000
Reilly Dairy & Food Company
  Tampa, FL 813-839-8458
Schepps Dairy
  Dallas, TX. 800-395-7004
Schneider-Valley Farms Inc
  Williamsport, PA. 570-326-2021
United Dairy Farmers Inc.
  Cincinnati, OH 866-837-4833
Welsh Farms
  Wallington, NJ 800-221-0663
Winchester Farms Dairy
  Winchester, KY 859-745-5500
Yoder Dairies
  Chesapeake, VA 757-482-4068

Buttermilk Products

Graf Creamery Co
  Bonduel, WI 715-758-2137

Condensed

Graf Creamery Co
  Bonduel, WI 715-758-2137

Dry

Kantner Group
  Wapakoneta, OH. 877-738-3448

Dry Sweetcream

Kantner Group
  Wapakoneta, OH. 877-738-3448

Cream

Alta Dena Certified Dairy LLC
  City Of Industry, CA. 800-535-1369
Anastasia Confections Inc
  Orlando, FL. 800-329-7100
Anderson Dairy Inc
  Las Vegas, NV 702-642-7507
Arcor USA
  Coral Gables, FL. 800-572-7267
Barber Dairies
  Birmingham, AL. 205-942-2351
Bartlett Dairy & Food Service
  Jamaica, NY 718-658-2299
Berkeley Farms
  Hayward, CA 800-395-7004
Berkshire Dairy
  Wyomissing, PA. 877-696-6455
Bluechip Group
  Salt Lake City, UT 800-878-0099
Broughton Foods LLC
  El Paso, TX. 800-395-7004
Byrne Dairy, Inc.
  Syracuse, NY 800-899-1535
C F Burger Creamery Co
  Detroit, MI 313-584-4040
Cass-Clay Creamery
  Fargo, ND 701-293-6455
Clover Farms Dairy Co Inc
  Reading, PA 800-323-0123
Clover Sonoma
  Petaluma, CA 800-237-3315
Clover Stornetta Farms Inc
  Petaluma, CA 800-237-3315
Country Fresh
  Grand Rapids, MI 616-243-0171
D & D Sugarwoods Farm
  Glover, VT 800-245-3718
Fairlife
  Chicago, IL
Farmdale Creamery Inc
  San Bernardino, CA 800-346-7306
First District Association
  Litchfield, MN 320-693-3236
GAF Seelig Inc
  Flushing, NY. 718-899-5000
GPI USA LLC.
  Mokena, IL 800-929-4248
H B Taylor Co
  Chicago, IL 773-254-4805
Horizon Organic Dairy
  Broomfield, CO 888-494-3020
HP Hood LLC
  Lynnfield, MA 800-343-6592
Ideal Dairy Farms
  Hudson Falls, NY 518-747-5059
Jasper Products Corp
  Joplin, MO 417-206-3877
Kleinpeter Farms Dairy LLC
  Baton Rouge, LA 225-753-2121
Marburger Farm Dairy
  Evans City, PA 800-331-1295
Maryland & Virginia Milk Producers Cooperative
  Reston, VA 703-742-6800
Muller-Pinehurst Dairy
  Rockford, IL 815-968-0441
Natural By Nature
  Newark, DE. 302-455-1261
Oak Farms
  El Paso, TX. 800-395-7004
Oakhurst Dairy
  Portland, ME. 800-482-0718
Pioneer Dairy
  Southwick, MA. 413-569-6132
Plains Dairy Products
  Amarillo, TX. 800-365-5608
Price's Creameries
  El Paso, TX. 915-565-2711
Producers Dairy Foods Inc
  Fresno, CA 559-264-6583
Purity Dairies LLC
  Nashville, TN 615-244-1900
Queensboro Farm Products
  Jamica, NY 718-658-5000
Reilly Dairy & Food Company
  Tampa, FL. 813-839-8458
Reiter Dairy LLC
  Springfield, OH. 937-323-5777
Rosenberger's Dairies
  Hatfield, PA. 800-355-9074
Sabatino Truffles USA
  West Haven, CT 888-444-9971
Saint Albans Cooperative Creamery
  Saint Albans, VT. 802-524-6581
Schepps Dairy
  Dallas, TX. 800-395-7004
Schneider's Dairy Inc
  Pittsburgh, PA. 412-881-3525
Stonyfield Organic
  Londonderry, NH 800-776-2697
Turner Dairy Farms Inc
  Pittsburgh, PA. 800-892-1039
United Dairy Inc.
  Martins Ferry, OH. 800-252-1542
Velda Farms
  Orlando, FL. 800-795-4649
Vermont Creamery
  Websterville, VT. 800-884-6287
W.J. Stearns & Sons/Mountain Dairy
  Storrs Mansfield, CT 860-423-9289
WhiteWave Foods
  Denver, CO. 800-488-9283

Dried

Agri-Dairy Products
  Purchase, NY 914-697-9580
Batory Foods
  Des Plaines, IL. 847-299-1999
Blossom Farm Products
  Ridgewood, NJ. 800-729-1818
Century Foods Intl LLC
  Sparta, WI. 800-269-1901
Clofine Dairy Products Inc
  Linwood, NJ. 609-653-1000
Kantner Group
  Wapakoneta, OH. 877-738-3448
Quality Ingredients
  Burnsville, MN 952-898-4002

Fresh

Agri-Dairy Products
  Purchase, NY 914-697-9580
Agropur
  Granby, QC. 800-363-5686
Auburn Dairy Products Inc
  Auburn, WA 800-950-9264
Brum's Dairy
  Pembroke, ON. 613-735-2325
Clofine Dairy Products Inc
  Linwood, NJ. 609-653-1000
Larosa Bakery Inc
  Shrewsbury, NJ. 800-527-6722
Northumberland Dairy
  Miramichi, NB 800-501-1150
O-At-Ka Milk Prods Co-Op Inc.
  Batavia, NY. 800-828-8152
Stremick's Heritage Foods
  Santa Ana, CA 800-371-9010

Non-Dairy

Bay Valley Foods
  El Paso, TX 800-236-1119
New Barn Organics
  Rohnert Park, CA 888-635-7102
Nutpods
  Bellevue, WA 800-977-6094
Siggi's Dairy
   855-860-6683
Sugar Foods Corp
  Sun Valley, CA 818-768-7900

Whipped

Alamance Foods
  Burlington, NC
Berkeley Farms
  Hayward, CA 800-395-7004
Brighams
  Arlington, MA 800-242-2423
Broughton Foods LLC
  El Paso, TX. 800-395-7004
C F Burger Creamery Co
  Detroit, MI 313-584-4040
Cass-Clay Creamery
  Fargo, ND 701-293-6455
Caughman's Meat Plant
  Lexington, SC 803-356-0076
Clofine Dairy Products Inc
  Linwood, NJ. 609-653-1000
Crave Natural Foods
  Los Angeles, CA. 877-425-2599
Crystal Farms Dairy Company
  Minnetonka, MN. 800-672-8260
Erba Food Products
  Brooklyn, NY 718-272-7700
Jasper Products Corp
  Joplin, MO 417-206-3877
Marva Maid Dairy
  Newport News, VA 800-768-6243
Mayfield Dairy Farms LLC
  Athens, TN 800-362-9546
Prairie Farms Dairy Inc.
  Edwardsville, IL 618-659-5700
Schepps Dairy
  Dallas, TX. 800-395-7004
Schneider's Dairy Inc
  Pittsburgh, PA. 412-881-3525
Tiller Foods Company
  Dayton, OH 937-435-4601
Yoder Dairies
  Chesapeake, VA 757-482-4068

from Milk

Auburn Dairy Products Inc
  Auburn, WA 800-950-9264
DairyPure
  El Paso, TX. 800-395-7004
Trickling Springs Creamery
  Chambersburg, PA 717-709-0711

Creamers

Auburn Dairy Products Inc
  Auburn, WA 800-950-9264
Broughton Foods LLC
  El Paso, TX. 800-395-7004
DairyPure
  El Paso, TX. 800-395-7004
H B Taylor Co
  Chicago, IL 773-254-4805

Product Categories / Dairy Products: Custard

Kan-Pak
  Arkansas City, KS 800-378-1265
Mccullagh Coffee Roasters
  Buffalo, NY 800-753-3473
Nature's First Inc
  Orange, CT 800-523-3752
Nulaid Foods Inc
  Ripon, CA 209-599-2121
Promised Land Dairy
  Colorado Springs, CO 877-520-2479
Schepps Dairy
  Dallas, TX 800-395-7004
Schneider's Dairy Inc
  Pittsburgh, PA 412-881-3525
Smith Dairy
  Orrville, OH 800-776-7076
Tiller Foods Company
  Dayton, OH 937-435-4601
Utah Coffee Roasters
  South Salt Lake, UT 888-486-3334
W.J. Stearns & Sons/Mountain Dairy
  Storrs Mansfield, CT 860-423-9289

Coffee

Agri-Dairy Products
  Purchase, NY 914-697-9580
Baldwin Richardson Foods
  Oakbrook Terrace, IL 866-644-2732
Boston's Best Coffee Roasters
  South Easton, MA 800-898-8393
Byrne Dairy, Inc.
  Syracuse, NY 800-899-1535
C F Burger Creamery Co
  Detroit, MI 313-584-4040
Califia Farms
  Pasadena, CA 844-237-4779
Danone North America
  Broomfield, CO 303-635-4000
H B Taylor Co
  Chicago, IL 773-254-4805
Hanan Products Co
  Hicksville, NY 516-938-1000
Kiss My Keto
  Los Angeles, CA 310-765-1553
Know Brainer
  Lafayette, CO 303-475-0456
Natural Bliss
  800-637-8534
Safeway Milk Plant
  Tempe, AZ 480-894-4391
Tova Industries LLC
  Louisville, KY 888-532-8682
WhiteWave Foods
  Denver, CO 800-488-9283

Non-Dairy

Bay Valley Foods
  El Paso, TX 800-236-1119
Broughton Foods LLC
  El Paso, TX 800-395-7004
Diehl Food Ingredients
  Defiance, OH 800-251-3033
Erba Food Products
  Brooklyn, NY 718-272-7700
Golden 100
  Deland, FL 386-734-0113
Laird Superfood
  Sisters, OR 888-670-6796
Lake City Foods
  Mississauga, ON 905-625-8244
Leaner Creamer
  Beverly Hills, CA 866-739-2298
Mccullagh Coffee Roasters
  Buffalo, NY 800-753-3473
NeuRoast
  New York, NY
New Barn Organics
  Rohnert Park, CA 888-635-7102
Oatly
  New York, NY
Quality Ingredients
  Burnsville, MN 952-898-4002
Stickney & Poor Company
  Peterborough, NH 603-924-2259
Tiller Foods Company
  Dayton, OH 937-435-4601
Tonex
  Wallington, NJ 973-773-5135

Custard

Artuso Pastry
  Bronx, NY 718-367-2515
BakeMark Ingredients Canada
  Richmond, BC 800-665-9441
Dreyer's Grand Ice Cream Inc.
  Oakland, CA 877-437-3937
Schoep's Ice Cream
  Madison, WI 800-236-4050

Dairy

1000 Islands River Rat Cheese
  Clayton, NY 800-752-1341
A B Munroe Dairy Inc
  East Providence, RI 401-438-4450
Abbott Laboratories
  Abbott Park, IL 847-938-3887
Advanced Food Products LLC
  New Holland, PA 800-732-5373
Aglamesis Bros Ice Cream
  Cincinnati, OH 513-531-5196
Agri-Dairy Products
  Purchase, NY 914-697-9580
Agri-Mark Inc
  West Springfield, MA 978-552-5500
Agropur
  Granby, QC 800-363-5686
Al Gelato Bornay
  Franklin Park, IL 847-455-5355
Al Pete Meats
  Muncie, IN 765-288-8817
Al's Beverage Company
  East Windsor, CT 888-257-7632
All American Foods Inc
  Mankato, MN 800-833-2661
Allfresh Food Products
  Evanston, IL 847-869-3100
Alliston Creamery
  Alliston, ON 705-435-6751
Alpenrose Dairy
  Portland, OR 503-244-1133
Alpina
  Batavia, NY 855-886-1914
American Classic Ice Cream Company
  Bay Shore, NY 800-736-4100
American Lecithin Company
  Oxford, CT 800-364-4416
Ammerland America
  Hallandale Beach, FL 954-350-0325
Anderson Dairy Inc
  Las Vegas, NV 702-642-7507
Anderson Erickson Dairy
  Des Moines, IA 515-265-2521
Anderson Erickson Dairy
  Kansas City, KS 913-621-4801
APC Inc
  Ankeny, IA 800-369-2672
Ariza Cheese Co
  Paramount, CA 800-762-4736
Arla Foods Inc
  Concord, ON 905-669-9393
Astro Dairy Products
  Toronto, ON 416-622-2811
Atwood Cheese Company
  Atwood, ON 519-356-2271
Auburn Dairy Products Inc
  Auburn, WA 800-950-9264
Avanti Foods Co
  Walnut, IL 800-243-3739
B & D Foods
  Boise, ID 208-344-1183
Baird Dairy LLC
  Clarksville, IN 812-283-3345
Baker Cheese Factory Inc
  St Cloud, WI 920-477-7871
Barber Dairies
  Birmingham, AL 205-942-2351
Barnes Ice Cream Company
  Manchester, ME 207-622-0827
Bartlett Dairy & Food Service
  Jamaica, NY 718-658-2299
Bartolini Ice Cream
  Bronx, NY 718-589-5151
BCFoods
  Santa Rosa, CA 707-547-1776
Bel Brands USA
  Chicago, IL 312-462-1500
Belle Plaine Cheese Factory
  Shawano, WI 866-245-5924
Berkeley Farms
  Hayward, CA 800-395-7004

Bernardi Italian Foods Company
  Bloomsburg, PA 570-389-5500
Berner Food & Beverage LLC
  Dakota, IL 800-819-8199
Bernie's Foods
  Brooklyn, NY 718-417-6677
Biazzo Dairy Products Inc
  Ridgefield, NJ 201-941-6800
Bio-K + International Inc.
  Laval, QC 800-593-2465
Birdsall Ice Cream Company
  Mason City, IA 641-423-5365
Bliss Brothers Dairy, Inc.
  Attleboro, MA 800-622-8789
Bloomfield Bakers
  Los Alamitos, CA 800-594-4111
Blossom Farm Products
  Ridgewood, NJ 800-729-1818
Blue Bell Creameries LP
  Brenham, TX 800-327-8135
Blue Ribbon Farm Dairy Fresh
  Exeter, PA 570-655-5579
Bluechip Group
  Salt Lake City, UT 800-878-0099
Bongard's Creameries
  Chanhassen, MN 952-277-5500
Bonnie Doon LLC
  Elkhart, IN 574-264-3390
Borden Dairy
  Dallas, TX 855-311-1583
Boston's Best Coffee Roasters
  South Easton, MA 800-898-8393
Braum's Inc
  Oklahoma City, OK 800-327-6455
Brewster Dairy Inc
  Brewster, OH 800-874-8874
Brighams
  Arlington, MA 800-242-2423
Brookshire Grocery Company
  Tyler, TX 888-937-3776
Brookside Foods
  Abbotsford, BC 800-468-1714
Brown Dairy Inc
  Coalville, UT 435-336-5952
Brown Produce Company
  Farina, IL 618-245-3301
Brown's Ice Cream Co
  Minneapolis, MN 612-378-1075
Browns' Ice Cream Company
  Minneapolis, MN 612-378-1075
Brum's Dairy
  Pembroke, ON 613-735-2325
Brunkow Cheese Of Wisconsin
  Darlington, WI 608-776-3716
Bubbies Homemade Ice Cream
  Aiea, HI 808-487-7218
Buck's Spumoni Company
  Milford, CT 888-222-8257
Bunker Hill Cheese Co Inc
  Millersburg, OH 800-253-6636
Buonitalia
  New York, NY 212-633-9090
Bush Brothers Provision Co
  West Palm Beach, FL 800-327-1345
Butter Buds Food Ingredients
  Racine, WI 800-426-1119
Butterball Farms
  Grand Rapids, MI 888-828-8837
Byrne Dairy, Inc.
  Syracuse, NY 800-899-1535
Cabot Creamery Co-Op
  Waitsfield, VT 888-792-2268
Calabro Cheese Corp
  East Haven, CT 203-469-1311
California Dairies Inc.
  Visalia, CA 559-625-2200
Calpro Ingredients
  Corona, CA 909-493-4890
Caprine Estates
  Bellbrook, OH 937-848-7406
Cascade Fresh
  Seattle, WA 800-511-0057
Casper's Ice Cream
  Richmond, UT 800-772-4182
Cass-Clay Creamery
  Fargo, ND 701-293-6455
Castle Cheese
  Slippery Rock, PA 800-252-4373
Cedar Crest Specialties
  Cedarburg, WI 800-877-8341
Central Dairies
  St Johns, NL 800-563-6455

Product Categories / Dairy Products: Dairy

Central Dairy
 Jefferson City, MO 573-635-6148
Centreside Dairy
 Renfrew, ON 800-889-9974
Century Foods Intl LLC
 Sparta, WI 800-269-1901
Challenge Dairy Products, Inc.
 Dublin, CA 800-733-2479
Chase Brothers Dairy
 Oxnard, CA 800-438-6455
Cheese Straws & More
 Monroe, LA 800-997-1921
Chester Dairy Co
 Chester, IL 618-826-2394
Chicago 58 Food Products
 Woodbridge, ON 416-603-4244
Chocolaterie Bernard Callebaut
 Calgary, AB 800-661-8367
Chozen Ice Cream
 New York, NY 212-675-4191
Churny Company
 Waupaca, WI 715-258-4040
Ciao Bella Gelato Company
 Irvington, NJ 800-435-2863
Circus Man Ice Cream Corporation
 Farmingdale, NY 516-249-4400
Clofine Dairy Products Inc
 Linwood, NJ 609-653-1000
Clover Farms Dairy Co Inc
 Reading, PA 800-323-0123
Clover Sonoma
 Petaluma, CA 800-237-3315
Clover Stornetta Farms Inc
 Petaluma, CA 800-237-3315
Cloverland Dairy
 Saint Clairsville, OH 740-699-0509
Cloverland/Green Spring Dairy
 Baltimore, MD 800-876-6455
Coastlog Industries
 Novi, MI 248-344-9556
Colchester Foods
 Bozrah, CT 800-243-0469
Colonna Brothers Inc
 North Bergen, NJ 201-864-1115
Colteryahn Dairy
 Pittsburgh, PA 412-881-1408
Compton Dairy
 Shelbyville, IN 317-398-8621
Cordon Bleu International
 Anjou, QC 800-363-1182
Corfu Foods Inc
 Bensenville, IL 630-595-2510
Country Delite Farms LLC
 Nashville, TN 800-232-4791
Cream Crock Distributors
 Sterling, MA 800-423-2736
Creamland Dairies Inc
 Albuquerque, NM 505-247-0721
Crescent Ridge Dairy
 Sharon, MA 800-660-2740
Crowley Cheese Inc
 Mt Holly, VT 800-683-2606
Crystal Creamery
 Modesto, CA 866-225-4821
Crystal Farms Dairy Company
 Minnetonka, MN 800-672-8260
Crystal Lake LLC
 Warsaw, IN 574-858-2514
Culture Systems Inc
 Mishawaka, IN 574-258-0602
Cumberland Dairy
 Rosenhayn, NJ 800-257-8484
Cyclone Enterprises Inc
 Houston, TX 281-872-0087
Czepiel Millers Dairy
 Ludlow, MA 413-589-0828
D F Ingredients Inc
 Washington, MO 888-583-0802
Dairy Fresh Foods Inc
 Taylor, MI 313-299-0735
Dairy King Milk Farms/Foodservice
 Whitter, CA 800-900-6455
Dairy Maid Dairy LLC
 Frederick, MD 301-663-5114
Dairy-Mix Inc
 St Petersburg, FL 800-955-6101
Dairytown Products Ltd
 Sussex, NB 800-561-5598
Daisy Brand
 Dallas, TX 877-292-9830
Danish Maid Butter Co
 Chicago, IL 773-731-8787

Dannon Yo Cream
 Portland, OR 800-962-7326
Danone North America
 Broomfield, CO 303-635-4000
Darifair Foods
 Jacksonville, FL 904-268-9916
Daybreak Foods Inc
 Long Prairie, MN 320-732-2966
Dean Foods Co.
 Dallas, TX 800-395-7004
Debel Food Products
 Elizabeth, NJ 800-421-3447
Deep Foods Inc
 Union, NJ 908-810-7500
Deseret Dairy Products
 Salt Lake City, UT 801-240-7350
Dimock Dairy Products
 Dimock, SD 605-928-3833
Dixie Egg Co
 Jacksonville, FL 800-394-3447
Double B Foods Inc
 Arlington, TX 800-679-0349
Driftwood Dairy
 El Monte, CA 626-444-9591
Dupont Cheese
 Marion, WI 800-895-2873
Dutch Farms Inc
 Chicago, IL 800-637-3447
Eagle Family Foods
 Richfield, OH 888-656-3245
Eatem Foods Co
 Vineland, NJ 800-683-2836
Eberhard Creamery
 Redmond, OR 541-548-5181
Echo Spring Dairy
 Eugene, OR 541-342-1291
Eggland's Best Eggs
 Malvern, PA 800-922-3447
Elm City Cheese Co Inc
 Hamden, CT 203-865-5768
Emkay Trading Corporation
 Elmsford, NY 914-592-9000
Erie Foods Intl Inc
 Erie, IL 309-659-2233
Erivan Dairy
 Oreland, PA 215-887-2009
Everything Yogurt
 Washington, DC 202-842-2990
F C C
 Mcminnville, OR 503-472-2157
Fairview Dairy Inc
 Latrobe, PA 724-537-7111
Fairview Swiss Cheese
 Fredonia, PA 724-475-4154
Farbest-Tallman Foods Corp
 Montvale, NJ 201-573-4900
Farmdale Creamery Inc
 San Bernardino, CA 800-346-7306
Farmer's Hen House
 Kalona, IA 319-683-2206
Farmers Dairies
 El Paso, TX 915-772-2736
Farmers Seafood Co Wholesale
 Shreveport, LA 800-874-0203
Farmland Dairies
 Wallington, NJ 888-727-6252
Farmland Fresh Dairies
 Newark, NJ 973-961-2500
Farr Candy Company
 Idaho Falls, ID 208-522-8215
Feature Foods
 Brampton, ON 905-452-7741
Fendall Ice Cream Company
 Salt Lake City, UT 801-355-3583
Fieldbrook Foods Corp.
 Dunkirk, NY 800-333-0805
First District Association
 Litchfield, MN 320-693-3236
Flavors from Florida
 Bartow, FL 800-888-0409
Fleur De Lait Foods Inc
 New Holland, PA 800-322-2743
Foothills Creamery
 Calgary, AB 800-661-4909
Foremost Farms USA
 Baraboo, WI 800-362-9196
Freeman Industries
 Tuckahoe, NY 800-666-6454
Fried Provisions Company
 Evans City, PA 724-538-3160
Friendship Dairies LLC
 Friendship, NY 800-854-3243

Frog City Cheese
 Plymouth Notch, VT 802-672-3650
Froma-Dar
 St. Boniface, QC 819-535-3946
Frozfruit Corporation
 Gardena, CA 310-217-1034
Gad Cheese Retail Store
 Medford, WI 715-748-4273
GAF Seelig Inc
 Flushing, NY 718-899-5000
Galliker Dairy Co
 Johnstown, PA 800-477-6455
Gamay Flavors
 New Berlin, WI 888-345-4560
Garber Ice Cream Co Inc
 Winchester, VA 800-662-5422
Gelato Fresco
 Toronto, ON 416-785-5415
GFA Brands Inc
 Paramus, NJ 201-568-9300
Gibbsville Cheese Company
 Sheboygan Falls, WI 920-564-3242
Gifford's Ice Cream
 Skowhegan, ME 800-950-2604
Global Food Industries
 Townville, SC 800-225-4152
Glover's Ice Cream Inc
 Frankfort, IN 800-686-5163
Golden Valley Dairy Products
 Tulare, CA 559-687-1188
Grace Foods International
 Astoria, NY 718-433-4789
Graf Creamery Co
 Bonduel, WI 715-758-2137
Graham Cheese Corporation
 Elnora, IN 800-472-9178
Grande Cheese Company
 Fond du Lac, WI 800-678-3122
Grassland Dairy Products Inc
 Greenwood, WI 800-428-8837
Great American Appetizers
 Nampa, ID 800-282-4834
Great Lakes Cheese Company, Inc.
 Hiram, OH 440-834-2500
Great Valley Mills
 Barto, PA 800-688-6455
Green Dirt Farm
 Weston, MO 816-386-2156
Grossingers Home Bakery
 New York, NY 800-479-6996
Guers Dairy
 Tamaqua, PA 570-277-6611
Guida's Dairy
 New Britain, CT 800-832-8929
H B Taylor Co
 Chicago, IL 773-254-4805
H-E-B Grocery Co. LP
 San Antonio, TX 800-432-3113
Harrisburg Dairies Inc
 Harrisburg, PA 800-692-7429
Harvest Direct
 Norwell, MA 800-733-2106
Hastings Co-Op Creamery-Dairy
 Hastings, MN 651-437-9414
Heartland Farms Dairy & Food Products, LLC
 St. Louis, MO 888-633-6455
Heartland Ingredients LLC
 Troy, MO 800-557-2621
Heluva Good Cheese
 Lynnfield, MA 800-644-5473
HempNut
 Henderson, NV 707-576-7050
Henning Cheese Factory
 Kiel, WI 920-894-3032
Henningsen Foods Inc
 Omaha, NE 800-228-2769
Heritage's Dairy Stores
 West Deptford, NJ 856-845-2855
High Road Craft Ice Cream, Inc.
 Atlanta, GA 678-701-7623
Highland Dairies
 Wichita, KS 800-336-0765
Hiland Dairy Foods Co
 Springfield, MO 800-492-4022
Hillandale
 Lake City, FL 386-397-1300
Holmes Cheese Co
 Millersburg, OH 330-674-6451
Holton Food Products
 La Grange, IL 708-352-5599
Homer's Ice Cream
 Wilmette, IL 847-251-0477

Product Categories / Dairy Products: Dairy

Homestead Dairy
  Plymouth, IN......................574-936-6126
Honeyville Grain Inc
  Brigham City, UT..................435-494-4200
Hope Creamery
  Hope, MN..........................507-451-2029
Horizon Organic Dairy
  Broomfield, CO....................888-494-3020
Hormel Foods Corp.
  Austin, MN........................507-437-5611
Houlton Farms Dairy
  Houlton, ME.......................207-532-3170
Hudsonville Ice Cream
  Holland, MI.......................616-546-4005
Humboldt Creamery
  Modesto, CA.......................888-316-6064
Hunter Farms - High Point Division
  High Point, NC....................800-446-8035
Hygeia Dairy Company
  Corpus Christi, TX................361-854-4561
Icco Cheese Co
  Orangeburg, NY....................845-680-2436
Ice Cream Bowl
  Zanesville, OH....................740-452-5267
Ice Cream Club Inc
  Boynton Beach, FL.................800-535-7711
Ice Cream Specialties Inc
  St Louis, MO......................800-662-7550
Ideal Dairy Farms
  Hudson Falls, NY..................518-747-5059
IMAC
  Oklahoma City, OK.................888-878-7827
Imperial Foods, Inc.
  Long Island City, NY..............718-784-3400
Independent Dairy Inc
  Monroe, MI........................734-241-6016
Ingles Markets
  Black Mountain, NC................828-669-2941
Ingredia Inc
  Wapakoneta, OH....................419-738-4060
Ingretec
  Lebanon, PA.......................717-273-0711
Instantwhip Foods Inc
  Columbus, OH......................800-544-9447
International Cheese Company
  Toronto, ON.......................416-769-3547
International Farmers Market
  Chamblee, GA......................770-455-1777
International Food Products
  Fenton, MO........................800-227-8427
Inverness Dairy
  Cheboygan, MI.....................231-627-4655
Ise America Inc
  Galena, MD........................410-755-6300
Island Farms Dairies Cooperative Association
  Victoria, BC......................250-360-5200
It's It Ice Cream Co
  Burlingame, CA....................800-345-1928
Ito Cariani Sausage Company
  Hayward, CA.......................510-887-0882
J B & Son LTD
  Yonkers, NY.......................914-963-5192
J M Swank Co
  North Liberty, IA.................800-593-6375
J.W. Haywood & Sons Dairy
  Louisville, KY....................502-774-2311
Jack & Jill Ice Cream
  Moorestown, NJ....................856-813-2300
Jaxon's Ice Cream Parlor
  Dania Beach, FL...................954-923-4445
Jim's Cheese Pantry
  Waterloo, WI......................800-345-3571
John W Macy's Cheesesticks Inc
  Elmwood Park, NJ..................800-643-0573
Johnson's Real Ice Cream
  Columbus, OH......................614-231-0014
Johnson, Nash & Sons Farms
  Warsaw, NC........................910-289-6842
Joseph Farms
  Atwater, CA.......................209-394-7984
Josh & John's Ice Cream
  Colorado Springs, CO..............800-530-2855
Kalamazoo Creamery
  Kalamazoo, MI.....................616-343-2558
Kan-Pak
  Arkansas City, KS.................800-378-1265
Katrina's Tartufo
  Port Jeffrsn Sta, NY..............800-480-8836
Kauai Producers
  Lihue, HI.........................800-262-1400
Keller's Creamery
  Kansas City, MO...................800-535-5371

Kemps LLC
  St Paul, MN
Kent Foods Inc
  Gonzales, TX......................830-672-7993
Kentucky Beer Cheese
  Nicholasville, KY.................859-887-1645
Kirby Holloway Provision Co
  Harrington, DE....................800-995-4729
Kleinpeter Farms Dairy LLC
  Baton Rouge, LA...................225-753-2121
Klinke Brothers Ice Cream Co
  Memphis, TN.......................901-322-6640
Klondike Cheese Factory
  Monroe, WI........................608-325-3021
Kolb-Lena Bresse Bleu Inc
  Lena, IL..........................815-369-4577
LA Grander Hillside Dairy Inc
  Stanley, WI.......................715-644-2275
Lake Country Foods Inc
  Oconomowoc, WI....................262-567-5521
Lake Erie Frozen Foods Co
  Ashland, OH.......................800-766-8501
Lakeview Banquet Cheese
  Salt Lake City, UT................801-364-3607
Lakeview Farms
  Delphos, OH.......................800-755-9925
Lancaster Packing Company
  Myerstown, PA.....................717-397-9727
Land O'Lakes Inc
  Arden Hills, MN...................800-328-9680
Lane's Dairy
  El Paso, TX.......................915-772-6700
Larkin Cold Storage
  Long Island City, NY..............718-937-2007
Larosa Bakery Inc
  Shrewsbury, NJ....................800-527-6722
Layman Distributing
  Salem, VA.........................800-237-1319
Leprino Foods Co.
  Denver, CO........................800-537-7466
Lewes Dairy Inc
  Lewes, DE.........................302-645-6281
Lifeway
  Morton Grove, IL..................877-281-3874
Longacres Modern Dairy Inc
  Barto, PA.........................610-845-7551
Lowell-Paul Dairy
  Greeley, CO.......................970-353-0278
Lubbers Family Farm
  Grand Rapids, MI..................616-453-4257
Ludwig Dairy Product
  Elk Grove Vlg, IL.................847-860-8646
Lyoferm & Vivolac Cultures
  Indianapolis, IN..................317-356-8460
M.E. Franks Inc.
  Wayne, PA.........................610-989-9688
Mack's Bill Ice Cream
  Dover, PA.........................717-292-1931
Magic Valley Quality Milk
  Jerome, ID........................208-324-7519
Main Street Ingredients
  La Crosse, WI.....................800-359-2345
Mancuso Cheese Co
  Joliet, IL........................815-722-2475
Maola Milk & Ice Cream Co.
 844-287-1970
Maple Hill Farms
  Bloomfield, CT....................800-842-7304
Maple Leaf Foods International
  North York, ON....................800-268-3708
Marantha Natural Foods
  San Francisco, CA.................866-972-6879
Marathon Cheese Corp
  Marathon, NJ......................715-443-2211
Marburger Farm Dairy
  Evans City, PA....................800-331-1295
Marin French Cheese Co
  Petaluma, CA......................800-292-6001
Mario's Gelati
  Vancouver, BC.....................604-879-9411
Marshallville Packing Co
  Marshallville, OH.................330-855-2871
Marva Maid Dairy
  Newport News, VA..................800-768-6243
Marwood Sales, Inc
  Overland Park, KS.................800-745-2881
Master Mix
  Placentia, CA.....................714-524-1698
Matador Processors
  Blanchard, OK.....................800-847-0797
Mayfield Dairy Farms LLC
  Athens, TN........................800-362-9546

Maytag Dairy Farms Inc
  Newton, IA........................800-247-2458
McAnally Enterprises
  Lakeview, CA......................800-726-2002
McArthur Dairy LLC
  Miami, FL.........................561-659-4811
Mccadam Cheese Co Inc
  Chateaugay, NY....................800-639-4031
McConnell's Fine Ice Cream
  Santa Barbara, CA.................805-963-8813
Meadow Brook Dairy Co
  Erie, PA..........................800-352-4010
Meadowbrook Farm
  Bronx, NY.........................718-828-6400
Meijer Inc
  Grand Rapids, MI..................616-453-6711
Mercer's Dairy
  Boonville, NY.....................866-637-2377
Meyer Brothers Dairy
  Maple Plain, MN...................952-473-7343
Micalizzi Italian Ice
  Bridgeport, CT....................203-366-2353
Michael Granese & Company
  Norristown, PA....................610-272-5099
Michele's Family Bakery
  York, PA..........................717-741-2027
Michelle Chocolatiers
  Colorado Springs, CO..............888-447-3654
Michigan Dairy LLC
  Livonia, MI.......................734-367-5390
Michigan Farm Cheese Dairy
  Fountain, MI......................877-624-3373
Michigan Milk Producers Assn
  Novi, MI..........................248-474-6672
Mikawaya LLC
  Vernon, CA........................323-587-5504
Milk Specialties Global
  Eden Prairie, MN..................952-942-7310
Milky Way Jersey Farm Inc
  Starr, SC.........................864-352-2014
Miller's Cheese Corp
  Brooklyn, NY......................718-965-1840
Milnot Company
  Orrville, OH......................888-656-3245
Milsolv Corporation
  Butler, WI........................800-558-8501
Minerva Cheese Factory
  Minerva, OH.......................330-868-4196
Minerva Dairy Inc
  Minerva, OH.......................330-868-4196
Mister Cookie Face
  Dunkirk, NY.......................800-333-0305
Mitchel Dairies
  Bronx, NY.........................718-994-6655
Model Dairy LLC
  Reno, NV..........................800-433-2030
Monument Farms Dairy
  Middlebury, VT....................802-545-2119
Mooresville Ice Cream Co
  Mooresville, NC...................800-304-7172
Morning Star Foods
  East Brunswick, NJ................800-237-5320
Morningland Dairy Cheese Company
  Mountain View, MO.................417-855-0588
Mountain High Yogurt
  Minneapolis, MN...................866-964-4878
Mountainside Farms Inc
  Roxbury, NY.......................607-326-4161
Mt Sterling Co-Op Creamery
  Highland, WI......................866-289-4628
Muller-Pinehurst Dairy
  Rockford, IL......................815-968-0441
Mulligan Sales
  City of Industry, CA..............626-968-9621
Murdock Farm Dairy
  Winchendon, MA....................978-297-2196
Mystic Lake Dairy
  Sammamish, WA.....................425-868-2029
Natrel
  St. Laurent, QC...................800-501-1150
Natural By Nature
  Newark, DE........................302-455-1261
Natural Fruit Corp
  Hialeah, FL.......................305-887-7525
Nature's Dairy
  Roswell, NM.......................575-623-9640
Ninth Avenue Foods
  CA................................626-364-8722
Nodine's Smokehouse Inc
  Torrington, CT....................800-222-2059
Noon Hour Food Products Inc
  Chicago, IL.......................800-621-6636

Product Categories / Dairy Products: Dairy

Nor-Tech Dairy Advisors
Sioux Falls, SD 605-338-2404
Northumberland Dairy
Miramichi, NB 800-501-1150
Norwalk Dairy
Santa Fe Springs, CA 562-921-5712
O'Boyle's Ice Cream Company
Bristol, PA 215-788-3882
O-At-Ka Milk Prods Co-Op Inc.
Batavia, NY 800-828-8152
Oak Farm's Dairy
Waco, TX 254-756-5421
Oak Farms
El Paso, TX 800-395-7004
Oak Grove Dairy
Clintonville, WI 715-823-6226
Oakhurst Dairy
Portland, ME 800-482-0718
Oberweis Dairy
North Aurora, IL 866-623-7934
OCG Cacao
Whitinsville, MA 888-482-2226
Old Home Foods Inc
New Brighton, MN 651-312-8900
Olde Tyme Food Corporation
East Longmeadow, MA 800-356-6533
Oregon Hill Farms
St Helens, OR 800-243-4541
Organic Pastures
Fresno, CA 877-729-6455
Orientex Foods
Pittsburg, PA 800-660-0962
Oskaloosa Food Products
Oskaloosa, IA 800-477-7239
Out of a Flower
Lancaster, TX 800-743-4696
Park Cheese Company Inc
Fond Du Lac, WI 800-752-7275
Parkers Farm
Coon Rapids, MN 800-869-6685
Pascobel Inc
Longueuil, QC 450-677-2443
Pastorelli Food Products
Chicago, IL 800-767-2829
Pearl Valley Cheese Inc
Fresno, OH 740-545-6002
Pecoraro Dairy Products
Brooklyn, NY 718-388-2379
Penn Cheese
Winfield, PA 570-524-7700
Perry's Ice Cream Co Inc
Akron, NY 800-873-7797
PET Dairy
Winston Salem, NC 800-735-2050
Petersen Ice Cream Company
Oak Park, IL 708-386-6130
Philip R's Frozen Desserts
Winchester, MA 781-721-6330
Pierz Cooperative Association
Pierz, MN 320-468-6655
Pine River Cheese & Butter Company
Ripley, ON 800-265-1175
Pine River Pre-Pack Inc
Newton, WI 920-726-4216
Pioneer Dairy
Southwick, MA 413-569-6132
Plains Dairy Products
Amarillo, TX 800-365-5608
Plainview Milk Products
Plainview, MN 800-356-5606
Platte Valley Creamery
Scottsbluff, NE 308-632-4225
Pleasant View Dairy
Highland, IN 219-838-0155
Plehn's Bakery Inc
Louisville, KY 502-896-4438
Plymouth Cheese Counter
Plymouth, WI 888-607-9477
Pocono Cheesecake Factory
Swiftwater, PA 570-839-6844
Pollio Dairy Products
Campbell, NY 607-527-3621
Pon Food Corp
Ponchatoula, LA 985-386-6941
Potomac Farms Dairy Inc
Cumberland, MD 301-722-4410
Potter Siding Creamery Company
Tripoli, IA 319-882-4444
Prairie Farms Dairy Inc.
Edwardsville, IL 618-659-5700
Prestige Proteins
Boca Raton, FL 561-997-8770

Price's Creameries
El Paso, TX 915-565-2711
Pride Dairies
Bottineau, ND 701-228-2216
Primo Foods
Oceanside, CA 760-439-8711
Producers Dairy Foods Inc
Fresno, CA 559-264-6583
Promised Land Dairy
Colorado Springs, CO. 877-520-2479
Protient
St Paul, MN 800-328-9680
Publix Super Market
Lakeland, FL 800-242-1227
Pure Gourmet
Glenside, PA 215-609-4219
Puritan/ATZ Ice Cream
Kendallville, IN 260-347-2700
Purity Dairies LLC
Nashville, TN 615-244-1900
Purity Farms
La Farge, WI 877-211-4819
Purity Ice Cream Co
Ithaca, NY 607-272-1545
Quality Dairy Co
East Lansing, MI 517-319-4114
Quality Ingredients
Burnsville, MN 952-898-4002
Queensboro Farm Products
Canastota, NY 315-687-6133
Queensboro Farm Products
Jamica, NY 718-658-5000
Rachael's Smoked Fish
Springfield, MA 800-327-3412
Ragersville Swiss Cheese
Sugarcreek, OH 330-897-3055
Ramsen Inc
Lakeville, MN 952-431-0400
Ranieri Fine Foods
Brooklyn, NY 718-599-9520
Ratners Retail Foods
New York, NY 212-677-5588
Red Smith Foods Inc
Davie, FL 954-581-1996
Rehemond Farm Inc
Minot, ME 207-345-5611
Reinhold Ice Cream Company
Pittsburgh, PA 412-321-7600
Reiter Dairy
Newport, KY 800-544-6455
Reiter Dairy LLC
Springfield, OH 937-323-5777
Rich's Ice Cream Co Inc
West Palm Beach, FL 561-833-7585
Ritchey's Dairy
Martinsburg, PA 800-296-2157
RM Heagy Foods
Lancaster, PA 717-569-1032
Rockview Farms
Downey, CA 800-423-2479
Rocky Top Farms
Ellsworth, MI 800-862-9303
Ronny Brook Farm Dairy
Ancramdale, NY 800-772-6455
Ronzoni
Largo, FL 800-730-5957
Roos Foods
Kenton, DE 800-343-3642
Rosa Brothers Milk Co Inc
Hanford, CA 559-685-8825
Rose Acre Farms
Wolcott, IN 765-258-4015
Rosebud Creamery
Plattsburgh, NY 518-561-5160
Roselani Tropics Ice Cream
Wailuku, HI 808-244-7951
Rosenberger's Dairies
Hatfield, PA. 800-355-9074
Royal Crest Dairy
Denver, CO 888-226-6455
Rutter's Dairy
York, PA 800-840-1664
S.T. Jerrell Company
Bessemer, AL 205-426-8930
Safeway Milk Plant
Tempe, AZ 480-894-4391
Saint Albans Cooperative Creamery
Saint Albans, VT 802-524-6581
Sapore della Vita
Sarasota, FL 941-914-4256
Saputo Cheese USA Inc.
Lincolnshire, IL 847-267-1100

Saputo Dairy Division (Canada)
Saint-Laurent, QC 800-672-8866
Schepps Dairy
Dallas, TX 800-395-7004
Schneider's Dairy Inc
Pittsburgh, PA 412-881-3525
Schneider-Valley Farms Inc
Williamsport, PA 570-326-2021
Seger Egg Corporation
Farina, IL 618-245-3301
Sequoia Specialty Cheese Company
Visalia, CA 559-752-4106
Sesinco Foods
New York, NY 212-243-1306
Shenk's Foods
Lancaster, PA 717-393-4240
Siegel Egg Co
North Billerica, MA 978-528-2010
Sierra Cheese Mfg Co
Compton, CA 800-266-4270
Siggi's Dairy
. . . . 855-860-6683
Silani Sweet Cheese
Woodbridge, ON 905-792-3811
Sisler's Ice & Ice Cream
Ohio, IL 888-891-3856
Skim Delux Mendenhall Laboratories
Paris, TN 800-642-9321
Skinners' Dairy
Ponte Vedra Beach, FL 904-733-5440
Smith Dairy
Orrville, OH 800-776-7076
Smith Packing Regional Meat
Utica, NY 315-732-5125
Snelgrove Ice Cream Company
Salt Lake City, UT 800-569-0005
Snow Dairy Inc
Springville, UT 801-489-6081
Sommer Maid Creamery Inc
Pipersville, PA 215-345-6160
Source Food Technology
Durham, NC 866-277-3849
Southeast Dairy Processors Inc
Tampa, FL 813-620-1516
Southern Ice Cream Specialties
Marietta, GA 770-428-0452
Sparboe Foods Corp
New Hampton, IA 641-394-3040
Specialty Food Association
New York, NY 646-878-0301
Specialty Ingredients
Buffalo Grove, IL 847-419-9595
Spring Grove Foods
Miamisburg, OH 937-866-4311
Spring Hill Pure Water
Haverhill, MA 978-373-3481
Springbank Cheese Company
Woodstock, ON 800-265-1973
Springdale Cheese Factory
Richland Center, WI 608-538-3213
Springfield Creamery Inc
Eugene, OR 541-689-2911
St. Maurice Laurent
St-Bruno-Lac-St-Jean, QC 418-343-3655
Steiner Cheese
Baltic, OH 888-897-5505
Stewart's Shops Corp
Ballston Spa, NY 518-581-1200
Stone's Home Made Candy Shop
Oswego, NY 888-223-3928
Stop & Shop Manufacturing
Readville, MA 508-977-5132
Straus Family Creamery
Petaluma, CA 800-572-7783
Stremick's Heritage Foods
Santa Ana, CA 800-371-9010
Sturm Foods Inc
Manawa, WI 800-347-8876
SugarCreek
Cincinnati, OH 800-445-2715
Sunny Fresh Foods
Monticello, MN 800-872-3447
Sunshine Dairy
Middletown, CT 860-346-6644
Sunshine Dairy Foods Inc
Portland, OR 503-234-7526
Sunshine Farms
Portage, WI 608-742-2016
Super Stores Industries
Turlock, CA 209-668-2100
Superbrand Dairies
Miami, FL 305-769-6600

Product Categories / Dairy Products: Dairy Alternatives

Superior Dairy
  Wauseon, OH 419-335-3553
Supreme Dairy Farms Co
  Warwick, RI 401-739-8180
Swagger Foods Corp
  Vernon Hills, IL 847-913-1200
Sweety Novelty
  Monterey Park, CA 626-282-4482
Swiss American Inc
  St Louis, MO 800-325-8150
Swiss Dairy
  Riverside, CA 951-898-9427
Swiss Premium Dairy Inc
  Lebanon, PA 800-222-2129
T. Marzetti Company
  Westerville, OH 800-999-1835
Tamarack Farms Dairy
  Newark, OH 866-221-4141
Tanglewood Farms
  Warsaw, VA 804-394-4505
Tebay Dairy Company
  Parkersburg, WV 304-863-3705
Texas Heat
  San Antonio, TX 800-656-5916
The Valpo Velvet Shoppe
  Valparaiso, IN 219-464-4141
Thomas Dairy
  Rutland, VT 802-773-6788
Thornton Foods Company
  Eden Prairie, MN 952-944-1735
Tillamook County Creamery Association
  Tillamook, OR 503-842-4481
Tiller Foods Company
  Dayton, OH 937-435-4601
Titusville Dairy Products Co
  Titusville, PA 800-352-0101
Toft Dairy Inc
  Sandusky, OH 800-521-4606
Tolteca Foodservice
  Norcross, GA 800-541-6835
Tomanetti Food Products Inc
  Oakmont, PA 800-875-3040
Tony's Ice Cream Co
  Gastonia, NC 704-867-7085
Trickling Springs Creamery
  Chambersburg, PA 717-709-0711
Tropical Treets
  North York, ON 888-424-8229
Turner & Pease Company
  Seattle, WA 206-282-9535
Turner Dairy Farms Inc
  Pittsburgh, PA 800-892-1039
Twin County Dairy
  Kalona, IA 319-656-2776
Umpqua Dairy
  Roseburg, OR 888-672-6455
United Dairy Farmers Inc.
  Cincinnati, OH 866-837-4833
United Dairy Inc.
  Martins Ferry, OH 800-252-1542
United Dairymen of Arizona
  Tempe, AZ 480-966-7211
United Valley Bell Dairy
  Charleston, WV 304-344-2511
Upstate Farms
  Buffalo, NY 716-896-3156
Upstate Niagara Co-Op Inc.
  Buffalo, NY 716-892-3156
US Foods & Pharmaceuticals Inc
  Madison, WI 800-362-8294
Valley Grain Products
  Fresno, CA 559-675-3400
Valley Milk Products
  Strasburg, VA 540-465-5113
Valley Queen Cheese Factory
  Milbank, SD 605-432-4563
Van Peenans Dairy
  Wayne, NJ 973-694-2551
Vance's Foods
  San Francisco, CA 415-621-1171
Velda Farms
  Orlando, FL 800-795-4649
Vella Cheese Co
  Sonoma, CA 800-848-0505
Velvet Ice Cream Co Inc
  Utica, OH 800-589-5000
Vermont Creamery
  Websterville, VT 800-884-6287
Vita Plus Corp
  Madison, WI 608-256-1988
Vitamilk Dairy
  Bellingham, WA 206-529-4128

Vitarich Ice Cream
  Fortuna, CA 707-725-6182
W.J. Stearns & Sons/Mountain Dairy
  Storrs Mansfield, CT 860-423-9289
Wabash Valley Produce Inc
  Dubois, IN 812-678-3131
Wapsie Creamery
  Independence, IA 319-334-7193
Warwick Ice Cream
  Warwick, RI 401-821-8403
Waugh Foods Inc
  East Peoria, IL 309-427-8000
Wawa Inc
  Wawa, PA 800-444-9292
Wayne Dairy Products Inc
  Richmond, IN 765-935-7521
Wegmans Food Markets Inc.
  Rochester, NY 800-934-6267
WEIS Markets Inc.
  Sunbury, PA 866-999-9347
Weldon Ice Cream Co
  Millersport, OH 740-467-2400
Welsh Farms
  Wallington, NJ 800-221-0663
Welsh Farms
  Clifton, NJ 973-772-2388
Wenger Spring Brook Cheese Inc
  Davis, IL 815-865-5612
Wenk Foods Inc
  Madison, SD 605-256-4569
Wessanan
  Minneapolis, MN 612-331-3775
Westin Foods
  Omaha, NE 800-228-6098
WhiteWave Foods
  Denver, CO 800-488-9283
Whitewave Foods Company
  Broomfield, CO 303-635-4000
Whitey's Ice Cream Inc
  Moline, IL 888-594-4839
Whitney Foods Inc
  Jamaica, NY 718-291-3333
Widmer's Cheese Cellars Inc
  Theresa, WI 888-878-1107
Winchester Farms Dairy
  Winchester, KY 859-745-5500
Winmix/Natural Care Products
  Englewood, FL 941-475-7432
Winn-Dixie Stores
  Jacksonville, FL 800-967-9105
Winsor SB Dairy
  Johnston, RI 401-231-7832
Wisconsin Milk Mktng Board Inc
  Madison, WI 800-589-5127
Wolf Canyon Foods
  Carmel, CA 831-626-1323
Woolwich Dairy
  Orangeville, ON 877-438-3499
World Cheese Inc
  Brooklyn, NY 718-965-1700
Wright's Ice Cream Co
  Cayuga, IN 800-686-9561
Wurth Dairy
  Caseyville, IL 217-271-7580
Yoder Dairies
  Chesapeake, VA 757-482-4068
Yoplait
  Mississauga, ON 800-516-7780
Young's Jersey Dairy
  Yellow Springs, OH 937-325-0629
Ziegenfelder Ice Cream Co
  Wheeling, WV 800-322-3642
Zuccaro Produce
  Columbia Heights, MN 612-333-1122

Dehydrated

Cheeses, Buttermilk, Milk

Associated Milk Producers Inc.
  New Ulm, MN 800-533-3580
Fleur De Lait Foods Inc
  New Holland, PA 800-322-2743
Florence Pasta & Cheese
  Marshall, MN 800-533-5290
Tolteca Foodservice
  Norcross, GA 800-541-6835

Dairy Alternatives

Annabella
  Longmont, CO

CO YO
  Albuquerque, NM 505-247-0012
Culina
  Austin, TX
Danone North America
  Broomfield, CO 303-635-4000
Elmhurst Milked
  Elma, NY 888-356-1925
Fora Foods
  Brooklyn, NY
Forager Project
  San Francisco, CA
Galaxy Nutritional Foods Inc
  North Kingstown, RI 800-441-9419
Global Gardens Group Inc.
  Richmond, BC 855-409-4365
Goat Partners Intl.
  Rolling Meadows, IL 833-872-4628
Good Karma Foods
  Boulder, CO 800-550-6731
Good PLANeT Foods
  Bellevue, WA 425-449-8134
Happy Planet Foods
  Burnaby, BC 800-811-3213
Jasper Products Corp
  Joplin, MO 417-206-3877
Killer Creamery
  Boise, ID
LAVVA
  Warwick, NY
Leaner Creamer
  Beverly Hills, CA 866-739-2298
MALK Organics
  Houston, TX 281-974-3251
Mooala
  Dallas, TX 214-206-1902
New Barn
  888-635-7102
New Barn Organics
  Rohnert Park, CA 888-635-7102
Oatly
  New York, NY
Planet Oat
  Lynnfield, MA 800-242-2423
Ripple
  Berkeley, CA
Three Trees Almondmilk
  San Mateo, CA 855-863-8733
Violife
  Thessaloniki,
Vixen Kitchen
  Santa Cruz, CA 707-223-5627
WhiteWave Foods
  Denver, CO 800-488-9283

Dairy Drinks

Alpina
  Batavia, NY 855-886-1914
Baskin-Robbins LLC
  Canton, MA 800-859-5339
Dahlicious
  Leominster, MA
Danone North America
  Broomfield, CO 303-635-4000
McArthur Dairy LLC
  Miami, FL 561-659-4811
Ninth Avenue Foods
  CA 626-364-8722
PowerBar
  Kings Mountain, NC 800-587-6937
Smith Dairy
  Orrville, OH 800-776-7076

Egg Nog

Alta Dena Certified Dairy LLC
  City Of Industry, CA 800-535-1369
Anderson Dairy Inc
  Las Vegas, NV 702-642-7507
Broughton Foods LLC
  El Paso, TX 800-395-7004
C F Burger Creamery Co
  Detroit, MI 313-584-4040
Cass-Clay Creamery
  Fargo, ND 701-293-6455
Chase Brothers Dairy
  Oxnard, CA 800-438-6455
HP Hood LLC
  Lynnfield, MA 800-343-6592
Kleinpeter Farms Dairy LLC
  Baton Rouge, LA 225-753-2121

Product Categories / Dairy Products: Ice Cream

Plains Dairy Products
 Amarillo, TX..................800-365-5608
Rockview Farms
 Downey, CA...................800-423-2479
Smith Dairy
 Orrville, OH..................800-776-7076
United Dairy Inc
 Martins Ferry, OH.............800-252-1542
WhiteWave Foods
 Denver, CO....................800-488-9283
Yoder Dairies
 Chesapeake, VA................757-482-4068

Ice Cream

Agave Dream
 La Canada, CA.................310-619-1575
Aglamesis Bros Ice Cream
 Cincinnati, OH................513-531-5196
Agropur
 Granby, QC....................800-363-5686
Al Gelato Bornay
 Franklin Park, IL.............847-455-5355
Al-Rite Fruits & Syrups Co
 Miami, FL.....................305-652-2540
Alpenrose Dairy
 Portland, OR..................503-244-1133
American Classic Ice Cream Company
 Bay Shore, NY.................800-736-4100
Anderson Dairy Inc
 Las Vegas, NV.................702-642-7507
Anderson Erickson Dairy
 Des Moines, IA................515-265-2521
Anderson Erickson Dairy
 Kansas City, KS...............913-621-4801
Archibald Frozen Desserts
 New Albany, IN................812-941-8267
Arctic Beverages
 Winnipeg, MB..................866-503-1270
Arctic Ice Cream Co
 Ewing, NJ.....................800-858-8966
Arctic Zero
 San Diego, CA.................888-272-1715
Asael Farr & Sons Co
 Salt Lake City, UT............877-553-2777
B&M Enterprises
 Greenfield, WI................414-399-7402
Barnes Ice Cream Company
 Manchester, ME................207-622-0827
Bartolini Ice Cream
 Bronx, NY.....................718-589-5151
Baskin-Robbins LLC
 Canton, MA....................800-859-5339
Bassett's
 Philadelphia, PA..............888-999-6314
Beck's Ice Cream
 York, PA......................717-764-4585
Ben & Jerry's Homemade Inc
 South Burlington, VT..........866-258-6877
Berkeley Farms
 Hayward, CA...................800-395-7004
Bernie's Foods
 Brooklyn, NY..................718-417-6677
Birdsall Ice Cream Company
 Mason City, IA................641-423-5365
Black Market Gelato
 North Hollywood, CA...........818-983-6040
Blue Bell Creameries LP
 Brenham, TX...................800-327-8135
Bonnie Doon LLC
 Elkhart, IN...................574-264-3390
Bonnie's Ice Cream
 Paradise, PA..................717-687-9301
Boulder Homemade Inc
 Boulder, CO...................800-691-5002
Brighams
 Arlington, MA.................800-242-2423
Brookside Foods
 Abbotsford, BC................800-468-1714
Brothers Desserts
 Santa Ana, CA.................949-655-0080
Brothers International Desserts
 Santa Ana, CA.................949-655-0080
Broughton Foods LLC
 El Paso, TX...................800-395-7004
Brown's Ice Cream Co
 Minneapolis, MN...............612-378-1075
Browns' Ice Cream Company
 Minneapolis, MN...............612-378-1075
Bubbies Homemade Ice Cream
 Aiea, HI......................808-487-7218
Buck's Spumoni Company
 Milford, CT...................888-222-8257

Byrne Dairy, Inc.
 Syracuse, NY..................800-899-1535
Casper's Ice Cream
 Richmond, UT..................800-772-4182
Cass-Clay Creamery
 Fargo, ND.....................701-293-6455
Cedar Crest Specialties
 Cedarburg, WI.................800-877-8341
Central Dairy
 Jefferson City, MO............573-635-6148
Centreside Dairy
 Renfrew, ON...................800-889-9974
Chino Valley Dairy
 Chino, CA.....................800-324-7948
Chocolate Shoppe Ice Cream Co
 Madison, WI...................800-466-8043
Chocolaterie Bernard Callebaut
 Calgary, AB...................800-661-8367
Choctal
 Pasadena, CA..................626-798-1351
Circus Man Ice Cream Corporation
 Farmingdale, NY...............516-249-4400
Clemmy's
 Randcho Mirage, CA............877-253-6698
Clover Sonoma
 Petaluma, CA..................800-237-3315
Cookie Kingdom
 Oglesby, IL...................815-883-3331
Cool Brands International
 Ronkonkoma, NY................631-737-9700
Coolhaus
 Culver City, CA...............310-853-8995
Country Clubs Famous Desserts
 Feasterville Trevose, PA......800-843-2253
Country Fresh
 Grand Rapids, MI..............616-243-0173
Crave Natural Foods
 Los Angeles, CA...............877-425-2599
Creamland Dairies Inc
 Albuquerque, NM...............505-247-0721
Crystal Creamery
 Modesto, CA...................866-225-4821
Culture Republick
 Englewood Cliffs, NJ..........800-662-0348
Dannon Yo Cream
 Portland, OR..................800-962-7326
Deconna Ice Cream
 Reddick, FL...................800-824-8254
Dippin' Dots LLC
 Paducah, KY...................270-443-8994
Dolci Gelati
 Washington, DC................202-257-5323
Double Rainbow Gourmet Ice Cream
 San Francisco, CA.............800-489-3580
Dreyer's Grand Ice Cream Inc.
 Oakland, CA...................877-437-3937
Dunkin' Brands Inc.
 Canton, MA....................800-859-5339
Eagle Ice Cream Company
 Cleveland, OH.................440-232-0085
Eden Creamery
 Los Angeles, CA
Elgin Dairy Foods
 Chicago, IL...................800-786-9900
Enlightened
 Bronx, NY.....................212-888-1120
Fairview Dairy Inc
 Latrobe, PA...................724-537-7111
Farmers Cooperative Dairy
 Saint-Hubert, QC..............800-501-1150
Farmland Dairies
 Wallington, NJ................888-727-6252
Farr Candy Company
 Idaho Falls, ID...............208-522-8215
Feeding the Turkeys, Inc.
 Boston, MA....................207-712-4034
Fendall Ice Cream Company
 Salt Lake City, UT............801-355-3583
Fieldbrook Foods Corp.
 Dunkirk, NY...................800-333-0805
Flavors from Florida
 Bartow, FL....................800-888-0409
Foothills Creamery
 Calgary, AB...................800-661-4909
Fosselman's Ice Cream Co
 Alhambra, CA..................626-282-6533
Frozfruit Corporation
 Gardena, CA...................310-217-1034
Galliker Dairy Co
 Johnstown, PA.................800-477-6455
Garber Ice Cream Co Inc
 Winchester, VA................800-662-5422

Gelato Fresco
 Toronto, ON...................416-785-5415
Getchell Brothers Inc
 Brewer, ME....................800-949-4423
Gifford's Ice Cream
 Skowhegan, ME.................800-950-2604
Gifford's Ice Cream & Candy Co
 Silver Spring, MA.............800-708-1938
Glover's Ice Cream Inc
 Frankfort, IN.................800-686-5163
Good Humor-Breyers Ice Cream
 Englewood Cliffs, NJ..........800-931-2854
Gossner Foods Inc
 Logan, UT.....................800-944-0454
Graeter's Mfg. Co.
 Cincinnati, OH................800-721-3323
Grays Ice Cream
 Tiverton, RI..................401-624-4500
Green Dirt Farm
 Weston, MO....................816-386-2156
Green River Chocolates
 Hinesburg, VT.................802-482-6727
Greenwood Ice Cream Co
 Atlanta, GA...................800-678-6166
Haagen-Dazs
 Wilkes-Barre, PA..............800-767-0120
Herrell's Ice Cream
 Northampton, MA...............413-586-9700
Hershey Creamery Co
 Harrisburg, PA................888-240-1905
Homer's Ice Cream
 Wilmette, IL..................847-251-0477
Honey Hut
 Brecksville, OH...............440-526-0606
Hood Home Service
 Burlington, VT................802-864-0941
Houlton Farms Dairy
 Houlton, ME...................207-532-3170
House of Flavors Inc
 Ludington, MI.................800-930-7740
House of Spices
 Flushing, NY..................718-507-4600
HP Hood LLC
 Lynnfield, MA.................800-343-6592
Hudsonville Ice Cream
 Holland, MI...................616-546-4005
Humboldt Creamery
 Modesto, CA...................888-316-6064
Humphry Slocombe
 San Francisco, CA.............415-550-6971
Hunt-Wesson Foods
 Chicago, IL...................877-266-2472
Hunter Farms - High Point Division
 High Point, NC................800-446-8035
Ice Cream Bowl
 Zanesville, OH................740-452-5267
Ice Cream Club Inc
 Boynton Beach, FL.............800-535-7711
Ice Cream Specialties Inc
 St Louis, MO..................800-662-7550
Ideal Dairy Farms
 Hudson Falls, NY..............518-747-5059
Il Gelato
 Astoria, NY...................800-899-9299
Independent Dairy Inc
 Monroe, MI....................734-241-6016
It's It Ice Cream Co
 Burlingame, CA................800-345-1928
J.W. Haywood & Sons Dairy
 Louisville, KY................502-774-2311
Jack & Jill Ice Cream
 Moorestown, NJ................856-813-2300
Jaxon's Ice Cream Parlor
 Dania Beach, FL...............954-923-4445
Jeni's Splendid Ice Creams
 Columbus, OH..................614-488-3224
Johnson's Real Ice Cream
 Columbus, OH..................614-231-0014
Josh & John's Ice Cream
 Colorado Springs, CO..........800-530-2855
Kan-Pak
 Arkansas City, KS.............800-378-1265
Katies Korner Inc
 Girard, OH....................330-539-4140
Katrina's Tartufo
 Port Jeffrsn Sta, NY..........800-480-8836
Kemps LLC
 St Paul, MN
Killer Creamery
 Boise, ID
Kith Treats
 New York, NY..................646-648-6285

162

Product Categories / Dairy Products: Ice Cream

Klinke Brothers Ice Cream Co
  Memphis, TN 901-322-6640
Lee's Ice Cream
  Scottsdale, AZ 888-669-5337
Leiby's Premium Ice Cream
  Tamaqua, PA 877-453-4297
Living Harvest Foods
  Portland, OR 888-690-3958
Louis Sherry Premium Chocolate and Tins
  Chicago, IL 212-849-2862
Lucerne Foods
  Pleasanton, CA 877-232-4271
M&L Gourmet Ice Cream
  Baltimore, MD 410-276-4880
Mack's Bill Ice Cream
  Dover, PA 717-292-1931
Mack's Homemade Ice Cream
  York, PA 717-741-2027
MacKay's Cochrane Ice Cream
  Cochrane, AB 403-932-2455
Mama Tish's Italian Specialties
  Chicago, IL 708-929-2023
Mammoth Creameries
  Austin, TX
Maola Milk & Ice Cream Co
  New Bern, NC 800-476-1021
Maola Milk & Ice Cream Co.
  844-287-1970
Maple Island
  Saint Paul, MN 800-369-1022
Mario's Gelati
  Vancouver, BC 604-879-9411
Mayfield Dairy Farms LLC
  Athens, TN 800-362-9546
McConnell's Fine Ice Cream
  Santa Barbara, CA 805-963-8813
Micalizzi Italian Ice
  Bridgeport, CT 203-366-2353
Michele's Family Bakery
  York, PA 717-741-2027
Michelle Chocolatiers
  Colorado Springs, CO 888-447-3654
Michigan Dairy LLC
  Livonia, MI 734-367-5390
Mikawaya LLC
  Vernon, CA 323-587-5504
Minus the Moo
  Dorchester, MA 703-999-7183
Mister Cookie Face
  Dunkirk, NY 800-333-0305
Model Dairy LLC
  Reno, NV 800-433-2030
Mooresville Ice Cream Co
  Mooresville, NC 800-304-7172
Mozzicato De Pasquale Bakery
  Hartford, CT 860-296-0426
Mr. Green Tea Ice Cream
  Keyport, NJ 732-446-9800
Muller-Pinehurst Dairy
  Rockford, IL 815-968-0441
My/Mo Mochi Ice Cream
  Vernon, CA 323-587-5504
Natural Fruit Corp
  Hialeah, FL 305-887-7525
Nelson Ice Cream
  Stillwater, MN 651-430-1103
Nestle USA Inc
  Glendale, CA 800-225-2270
New Direction Foods
  Huntington Beach, CA 888-393-5590
New Horizon Foods
  Union City, CA 510-489-8600
O'Boyle's Ice Cream Company
  Bristol, PA 215-788-3882
O'Danny Boy Ice Cream
  Trotwood, OH 937-837-2100
Oberweis Dairy Inc
  North Aurora, IL 866-623-7934
Oregon Ice Cream Co.
  Vancouver, WA 360-713-6800
Out of a Flower
  Lancaster, TX 800-743-4696
Perry's Ice Cream Co Inc
  Akron, NY 800-873-7797
Petersen Ice Cream Company
  Oak Park, IL 708-386-6130
Phin & Phebes
  Brooklyn, NY 718-383-4300
Pierre's French Ice Cream Inc
  Cleveland, OH 800-837-7342
Platte Valley Creamery
  Scottsbluff, NE 308-632-4225

Plehn's Bakery Inc
  Louisville, KY 502-896-4438
Pony Boy Ice Cream
  Acushnet, MA 508-994-4422
Prairie Farms Dairy Inc.
  Edwardsville, IL 618-659-5700
Price's Creameries
  El Paso, TX 915-565-2711
Pride Dairies
  Bottineau, ND 701-228-2216
Producers Dairy Foods Inc
  Fresno, CA 559-264-6583
Puritan/ATZ Ice Cream
  Kendallville, IN 260-347-2700
Purity Dairies LLC
  Nashville, TN 615-244-1900
Purity Ice Cream Co
  Ithaca, NY 607-272-1545
Reinhold Ice Cream Company
  Pittsburgh, PA 412-321-7600
Reiter Dairy
  Newport, KY 800-544-6455
Reiter Dairy LLC
  Springfield, OH 937-323-5777
Rhino Foods Inc
  Burlington, VT 802-862-0252
Rich's Ice Cream Co Inc
  West Palm Beach, FL 561-833-7585
Richardson's Ice Cream
  Middleton, MA 978-774-5450
Ronny Brook Farm Dairy
  Ancramdale, NY 800-772-6455
Roselani Tropics Ice Cream
  Wailuku, HI 808-244-7951
Safeway Inc.
  Pleasanton, CA 877-723-3929
San Bernardo Ice Cream
  Miramar, FL 954-322-2668
Schneider's Dairy Inc
  Pittsburgh, PA 412-881-3525
Schneider-Valley Farms Inc
  Williamsport, PA 570-326-2021
Schoep's Ice Cream
  Madison, WI 800-236-4050
Scotsburn Ice Cream Co.
  Saint-Hubert, QC 800-501-1150
Seaside Ice Cream
  Pelham, NY 914-636-2751
Sebastiano's
  Toledo, OH 419-382-0615
Shaner's Family Restaurant
  South Paris, ME 207-743-6367
Sisler's Ice & Ice Cream
  Ohio, IL 888-891-3856
Smith Dairy
  Orrville, OH 800-776-7076
Snelgrove Ice Cream Company
  Salt Lake City, UT 800-569-0005
Snow Monkey
  Santa Monica, CA
Snow's Ice Cream Co Inc
  Greenfield, MA 413-774-7438
South County Creamery
  Great Barrington, MA 413-528-8400
Southern Ice Cream Specialties
  Marietta, GA 770-428-0452
Springdale Ice Cream & Bev
  Cincinnati, OH 513-671-2790
St Clair Ice Cream Co
  Norwalk, CT 203-853-4774
Steve's Ice Cream, Craft Collective
  Brooklyn, NY 888-782-7688
Stewart's Shops Corp
  Ballston Spa, NY 518-581-1200
Stone's Home Made Candy Shop
  Oswego, NY 888-223-3928
SugarCreek
  Cincinnati, OH 800-445-2715
Super Stores Industries
  Turlock, CA 209-668-2100
Sweet Mountain Magic
  Chicago, IL 773-755-4539
Sweety Novelty
  Monterey Park, CA 626-282-4482
Tearrific Ice Cream
  Bridgeport, CT 203-354-9805
Tebay Dairy Company
  Parkersburg, WV 304-863-3705
Ted Drewes Frozen Custard
  St Louis, MO 314-481-2652
The Valpo Velvet Shoppe
  Valparaiso, IN 219-464-4141

Three Twins Ice Cream
  Petaluma, CA 707-763-8946
Tillamook County Creamery Association
  Tillamook, OR 503-842-4481
Toft Dairy Inc
  Sandusky, OH 800-521-4606
Tony's Ice Cream Co
  Gastonia, NC 704-867-7085
Too Cool Chix
  New York, NY 929-244-3022
Treat Ice Cream Co
  San Jose, CA 408-292-9321
Tropical Treets
  North York, ON 888-424-8229
Turkey Hill Dairy Inc
  Conestoga, PA 800-693-2479
Umpqua Dairy
  Roseburg, OR 888-672-6455
Unilever US
  Englewood Cliffs, NJ 800-298-5018
United Dairy Farmers Inc.
  Cincinnati, OH 866-837-4833
United Dairy Inc.
  Martins Ferry, OH 800-252-1542
Van Dyke Ice Cream
  Ridgewood, NJ 201-444-1429
Van Leeuwen
  Brooklyn, NY 718-701-1630
Velda Farms
  Orlando, FL 800-795-4649
Velvet Ice Cream Co Inc
  Utica, OH 800-589-5000
Vitamilk Dairy
  Bellingham, WA 206-529-4128
Vitarich Ice Cream
  Fortuna, CA 707-725-6182
Warwick Ice Cream
  Warwick, RI 401-821-8403
Wayne Dairy Products Inc
  Richmond, IN 765-935-7521
Weldon Ice Cream Co
  Millersport, OH 740-467-2400
Wells Enterprises Inc.
  Le Mars, IA 712-546-4000
Welsh Farms
  Wallington, NJ 800-221-0663
Welsh Farms
  Clifton, NJ 973-772-2388
Whitey's Ice Cream Inc
  Moline, IL 888-594-4839
Winmix/Natural Care Products
  Englewood, FL 941-475-7432
World's Greatest Ice Cream
  Miami Beach, FL 305-538-0207
Wright's Ice Cream Co
  Cayuga, IN 800-686-9561
WSU Creamery
  Pullman, WA 800-457-5442
Ziegenfelder Ice Cream Co
  Wheeling, WV 800-322-3642
Zurheide Ice Cream Company
  Sheboygan, WI 920-458-4581

Bases

Boulder Homemade Inc
  Boulder, CO 800-691-5002
GPI USA LLC.
  Mokena, IL 800-929-4248
Solo Foods
  Countryside, IL 800-328-7656
Turner Dairy Farms Inc
  Pittsburgh, PA 800-892-1039

Cones

Sugar

Kith Treats
  New York, NY 646-648-6285
Three Twins Ice Cream
  Petaluma, CA 707-763-8946

Wafer

Foothills Creamery
  Calgary, AB 800-661-4909
Kith Treats
  New York, NY 646-648-6285

Fat-Free

Cedar Crest Specialties
  Cedarburg, WI 800-877-8341

Product Categories / Dairy Products: Ice Cream

Clay Center Locker Plant
  Clay Center, KS 800-466-5543
Perry's Ice Cream Co Inc
  Akron, NY 800-873-7797

Flavored

Boulder Homemade Inc
  Boulder, CO 800-691-5002
Byrne Dairy, Inc.
  Syracuse, NY 800-899-1535
DF Mavens
  Astoria, NY 347-813-4705
Hershey Creamery Co
  Harrisburg, PA 888-240-1905
Mack's Bill Ice Cream
  Dover, PA 717-292-1931
Penny Lick Ice Cream Company
  Hastings, NY 914-525-1580
Petersen Ice Cream Company
  Oak Park, IL 708-386-6130
San Bernardo Ice Cream
  Miramar, FL 954-322-2668

Gelato

Boulder Homemade Inc
  Boulder, CO 800-691-5002
Casper's Ice Cream
  Richmond, UT 800-772-4182
Ciao Bella Gelato Company
  Irvington, NJ 800-435-2863
Forte Gelato
  Greens Farms, CT 203-764-1826
Gelateria Naia
  Hercules, CA 510-724-2479
Gelato Fiasco
  Brunswick, ME 207-607-4262
Gelato Giuliana
  New Haven, CT 203-772-0607
Good Humor-Breyers Ice Cream
  Englewood Cliffs, NJ 800-931-2854
Graeter's Mfg. Co.
  Cincinnati, OH 800-721-3323
Maple's Organics
  Yarmouth, ME 207-846-1000
Revel, Gelato
  Huntington Beach, CA 866-203-9145
Snelgrove Ice Cream Company
  Salt Lake City, UT 800-569-0005
Talenti Gelato e Sorbetto
  Dallas, TX
Unilever US
  Englewood Cliffs, NJ 800-298-5018
Weldon Ice Cream Co
  Millersport, OH. 740-467-2400

Granita

Folklore Foods
  Selby, SD 605-649-1144

Ice Milk

Kith Treats
  New York, NY 646-648-6285
Perry's Ice Cream Co Inc
  Akron, NY 800-873-7797
Whitey's Ice Cream Inc
  Moline, IL 888-594-4839

Ices

Cappola Foods
  Toronto, ON 416-633-0389
Chill & Moore
  Fort Worth, TX 800-676-3055
Dippin' Dots LLC
  Paducah, KY 270-443-8994
Gelato Fresco
  Toronto, ON 416-785-5415
Helados Mexico
  Chino, CA
Kemach Food Products
  Brooklyn, NY 718-272-5655
Mackie International, Inc.
  Riverside, CA 800-733-9762
Mama Tish's Italian Specialties
  Chicago, IL 708-929-2023
Mar-Key Foods
  Vidalia, GA 912-537-4204
Rosati Italian Water Ice
  Clifton Heights, PA 855-476-7284
Tova Industries LLC
  Louisville, KY 888-532-8682

Low-Fat

Eden Creamery
  Los Angeles, CA
Good Humor-Breyers Ice Cream
  Englewood Cliffs, NJ 800-931-2854
Hudsonville Ice Cream
  Holland, MI 616-546-4005
Mayfield Dairy Farms LLC
  Athens, TN 800-362-9546
Perry's Ice Cream Co Inc
  Akron, NY 800-873-7797
Stewart's Shops Corp
  Ballston Spa, NY 518-581-1200
Vitarich Ice Cream
  Fortuna, CA 707-725-6182
Wink Frozen Desserts
  Stamford, CT. 516-323-5283

Non-Dairy

Low-Calorie

Chicago Vegan Foods
  Lombard, IL 630-629-9667
Coconut Bliss
  Eugene, OR 844-305-5441
Eden Creamery
  Los Angeles, CA
Hakuna Banana
  Los Angeles, CA 323-736-1630
Luna & Larry's Coconut Bliss
  Eugene, OR 541-345-0020
NadaMoo
  Austin, TX
New Barn Organics
  Rohnert Park, CA 888-635-7102
Vixen Kitchen
  Santa Cruz, CA 707-223-5627
Wink Frozen Desserts
  Stamford, CT. 516-323-5283

Novelties

Broughton Foods LLC
  El Paso, TX 800-395-7004
Country Fresh
  Grand Rapids, MI 616-243-0173
Del's Lemonade & Refreshments
  Cranston, RI 401-463-6190
Dreyer's Grand Ice Cream Inc.
  Oakland, CA 877-437-3937
Fieldbrook Foods Corp.
  Dunkirk, NY 800-333-0805
Foothills Creamery
  Calgary, AB 800-661-4909
Frozfruit Corporation
  Gardena, CA 310-217-1034
Glover's Ice Cream Inc
  Frankfort, IN 800-686-5163
Grossingers Home Bakery
  New York, NY 800-479-6996
Hershey Creamery Co
  Harrisburg, PA 888-240-1905
Ice Cream Specialties Inc
  St Louis, MO. 800-662-7550
It's It Ice Cream Co
  Burlingame, CA 800-345-1928
Natural Fruit Corp
  Hialeah, FL 305-887-7525
Nestle USA Inc
  Glendale, CA 800-225-2270
Perry's Ice Cream Co Inc
  Akron, NY 800-873-7797
Schneider's Dairy Inc
  Pittsburgh, PA 412-881-3525
Schoep's Ice Cream
  Madison, WI 800-236-4050
Southern Ice Cream Specialties
  Marietta, GA 770-428-0452
Sweety Novelty
  Monterey Park, CA 626-282-4482
Unilever US
  Englewood Cliffs, NJ 800-298-5018
Vitarich Ice Cream
  Fortuna, CA 707-725-6182
Weldon Ice Cream Co
  Millersport, OH. 740-467-2400
Wells Enterprises Inc.
  Le Mars, IA 712-546-4000
Whitey's Ice Cream Inc
  Moline, IL 888-594-4839
Wright's Ice Cream Co
  Cayuga, IN 800-686-9561

Ziegenfelder Ice Cream Co
  Wheeling, WV 800-322-3642

Popsicles

Brewla Inc.
  Brooklyn, NY 855-543-7677
Broughton Foods LLC
  El Paso, TX 800-395-7004
Chill Pop
  Cleveland, OH
Chloe's Fruit
  New York, NY 646-442-8000
DeeBee's Organics
  Victoria, BC 855-515-8327
Hershey Co.
  Hershey, PA 800-468-1714
Hershey Creamery Co
  Harrisburg, PA 888-240-1905
Ice Cream Specialties Inc
  St Louis, MO. 800-662-7550
Iris Brands
  St. Louis Park, MN
JonnyPops
  Minneapolis, MN 651-243-0705
Leader Candies
  Brooklyn, NY 718-366-6900
Mackie International, Inc.
  Riverside, CA 800-733-9762
Mar-Key Foods
  Vidalia, GA 912-537-4204
Modern Pop
  Laguna Beach, CA
Natural Ice Fruits
  Orlando, FL 407-270-9194
Ruby Rockets
  New York, NY 855-543-7677
Scotsburn Ice Cream Co.
  Saint-Hubert, QC 800-501-1150
Unilever US
  Englewood Cliffs, NJ 800-298-5018
Welch Foods Inc.
  Concord, MA 800-340-6870
Ziegenfelder Ice Cream Co
  Wheeling, WV 800-322-3642

Ribbons

Solo Foods
  Countryside, IL. 800-328-7656

Roll

Grossingers Home Bakery
  New York, NY 800-479-6996

Sherbet

Byrne Dairy, Inc.
  Syracuse, NY 800-899-1535
Cedar Crest Specialties
  Cedarburg, WI. 800-877-8341
Dippin' Dots LLC
  Paducah, KY 270-443-8994
Fieldbrook Foods Corp.
  Dunkirk, NY 800-333-0805
Flavors from Florida
  Bartow, FL 800-888-0409
Gelato Fresco
  Toronto, ON 416-785-5415
Hudsonville Ice Cream
  Holland, MI 616-546-4005
Jel Sert
  West Chicago, IL 800-323-2592
Johnson's Real Ice Cream
  Columbus, OH 614-231-0014
Mayfield Dairy Farms LLC
  Athens, TN 800-362-9546
Perry's Ice Cream Co Inc
  Akron, NY 800-873-7797
Pierre's French Ice Cream Inc
  Cleveland, OH 800-837-7342
Schneider-Valley Farms Inc
  Williamsport, PA. 570-326-2021
Schoep's Ice Cream
  Madison, WI 800-236-4050
The Valpo Velvet Shoppe
  Valparaiso, IN 219-464-4141
Tova Industries LLC
  Louisville, KY 888-532-8682
Wayne Dairy Products Inc
  Richmond, IN 765-935-7521

Product Categories / Dairy Products: Milk & Milk Products

Slushes

Al-Rite Fruits & Syrups Co
   Miami, FL 305-652-2540
Fee Brothers
   Rochester, NY 800-961-3337
Flavouressence Products
   Mississauga, ON 866-209-7778
Royale Brands
   Davenport, IA 563-386-5222
Tropical Illusions
   Trenton, MO 660-359-5422
Wayne Dairy Products Inc
   Richmond, IN 765-935-7521

Sorbet

Açaí Roots
   San Diego, CA 866-401-2224
Agave Dream
   La Canada, CA 310-619-1575
Ben & Jerry's Homemade Inc
   South Burlington, VT 866-258-6877
Bernie's Foods
   Brooklyn, NY 718-417-6677
Boulder Homemade Inc
   Boulder, CO 800-691-5002
Brothers Desserts
   Santa Ana, CA 949-655-0080
Ciao Bella Gelato Company
   Irvington, NJ 800-435-2863
Coolhaus
   Culver City, CA 310-853-8995
Dannon Yo Cream
   Portland, OR 800-962-7326
Fieldbrook Foods Corp.
   Dunkirk, NY 800-333-0805
Gelateria Naia
   Hercules, CA 510-724-2479
Gelati Celesti
   Redondo Beach, CA 800-550-7550
Gelato Fresco
   Toronto, ON 416-785-5415
GoodPop
   Austin, TX 888-840-0188
Gourmet Sorbet Corporation
   New York, NY 646-243-9868
Graeter's Mfg. Co.
   Cincinnati, OH 800-721-3323
Green Dirt Farm
   Weston, MO 816-386-2156
Homer's Ice Cream
   Wilmette, IL 847-251-0477
Jolly Llama
   Richmond, UT
MacKay's Cochrane Ice Cream
   Cochrane, AB 403-932-2455
Mama Tish's Italian Specialties
   Chicago, IL 708-929-2023
Penny Lick Ice Cream Company
   Hastings, NY 914-525-1580
Pierre's French Ice Cream Inc
   Cleveland, OH 800-837-7342
Royal Ice Cream Co
   Manchester, CT 800-246-2958
Sun Tropics Inc
   San Ramon, CA 925-380-6324
Talenti Gelato e Sorbetto
   Dallas, TX
Twenty-Two Desserts
   Brooklyn, NY 917-979-3438
Unilever US
   Englewood Cliffs, NJ 800-298-5018
Winmix/Natural Care Products
   Englewood, FL 941-475-7432

Tortoni

Royal Ice Cream Co
   Manchester, CT 800-246-2958

Milk & Milk Products

Ingredia Inc
   Wapakoneta, OH 419-738-4060

Kefir

Clover Sonoma
   Petaluma, CA 800-237-3315
Clover Stornetta Farms Inc
   Petaluma, CA 800-237-3315
Emerling International Foods
   Buffalo, NY 716-833-7381
Fermenting Fairy
   Santa Monica, CA
Jamieson Laboratories
   Windsor, ON 800-265-5088
Latta USA
   Fair Lawn, NJ 201-512-8400
Lifeway
   Morton Grove, IL 877-281-3874
Nancy's Probiotic Foods
   Eugene, OR
Redwood Hill Farm
   Sebastopol, CA 877-238-3543
Wallaby Yogurt Co
   Broomfield, CO 855-925-4636

Milk

A2 Milk Company
   Boulder, CO 844-422-6455
Agri-Mark Inc
   West Springfield, MA 978-552-5500
Aimonetto and Sons
   Renton, WA 866-823-2777
All American Foods Inc
   Mankato, MN 800-833-2661
Alpenrose Dairy
   Portland, OR 503-244-1133
Alta Dena Certified Dairy LLC
   City Of Industry, CA 800-535-1369
Anderson Dairy Inc
   Las Vegas, NV 702-642-7507
Anderson Erickson Dairy
   Des Moines, IA 515-265-2521
Anderson Erickson Dairy
   Kansas City, KS 913-621-4801
Aurora Organic Dairy
   Boulder, CO 303-284-3313
Barber Dairies
   Birmingham, AL 205-942-2351
Berkeley Farms
   Hayward, CA 800-395-7004
Borden Dairy
   Dallas, TX 855-311-1583
Broughton Foods LLC
   El Paso, TX 800-395-7004
Byrne Dairy, Inc.
   Syracuse, NY 800-899-1535
Cass-Clay Creamery
   Fargo, ND 701-293-6455
Cedar Lake Foods
   Cedar Lake, MI 800-246-5039
Chase Brothers Dairy
   Oxnard, CA 800-438-6455
Chino Valley Dairy
   Chino, CA 800-324-7948
Clover Sonoma
   Petaluma, CA 800-237-3315
Coastlog Industries
   Novi, MI 248-344-9556
Country Fresh
   Grand Rapids, MI 616-243-0173
Cumberland Dairy
   Rosenhayn, NJ 800-257-8484
Dairy Farmers Of America
   Kansas City, KS 888-332-6455
Dairy Maid Dairy LLC
   Frederick, MD 301-663-5114
DairyAmerica
   Fresno, CA 800-722-3110
DairyPure
   El Paso, TX 800-395-7004
Darigold
   Seattle, WA 800-333-6455
Devansoy Farms
   Carroll, IA 800-747-8605
Fairlife
   Chicago, IL
Farmland Dairies
   Wallington, NJ 888-727-6252
Five Acre Farms
   Brooklyn, NY 718-522-3819
Fonterra Co-operative Group Limited
   Chicago, IL 888-869-6455
Foremost Farms USA
   Baraboo, WI 800-362-9196
GAF Seelig Inc
   Flushing, NY 718-899-5000
Galliker Dairy Co
   Johnstown, PA 800-477-6455
Garelick Farms
   Dallas, TX 800-343-4982
Gossner Foods Inc.
   Logan, UT 800-944-0454
GPI USA LLC.
   Mokena, IL 800-929-4248
Green Dirt Farm
   Weston, MO 816-386-2156
H-E-B Grocery Co. LP
   San Antonio, TX 800-432-3113
Happy Planet Foods
   Burnaby, BC 800-811-3213
Harrisburg Dairies Inc
   Harrisburg, PA 800-692-7429
Hastings Co-Op Creamery-Dairy
   Hastings, MN 651-437-9414
Heritage Farms Dairy
   Murfreesboro, TN 615-895-2790
Hiland Dairy Foods Co
   Springfield, MO 800-492-4022
Horizon Organic Dairy
   Broomfield, CO 888-494-3020
HP Hood LLC
   Lynnfield, MA 800-343-6592
Hygeia Dairy Company
   Corpus Christi, TX 361-854-4561
Ingredia Inc
   Wapakoneta, OH 419-738-4060
Intense Milk
   Buffalo, NY 716-892-3156
J M Swank Co
   North Liberty, IA 800-593-6375
Jasper Products Corp
   Joplin, MO 417-206-3877
Keller's Creamery
   Kansas City, MO 800-535-5371
Lafleur Dairy Products,
   New Orleans, LA 504-729-3330
Land O'Lakes Inc
   Arden Hills, MN 800-328-9680
Marva Maid Dairy
   Newport News, VA 800-768-6243
Maryland & Virginia Milk Producers Cooperative
   Reston, VA 703-742-6800
Mayfield Dairy Farms LLC
   Athens, TN 800-362-9546
McArthur Dairy LLC
   Miami, FL 561-659-4811
Mead Johnson Nutrition
   Chicago, IL 312-466-5800
Meadow Brook Dairy Co
   Erie, PA 800-352-4010
Meijer Inc
   Grand Rapids, MI 616-453-6711
Michigan Dairy LLC
   Livonia, MI 734-367-5390
Milnot Company
   Orrville, OH 888-656-3245
Muller-Pinehurst Dairy
   Rockford, IL 815-968-0441
Natrel
   St. Laurent, QC 800-501-1150
Natural By Nature
   Newark, DE 302-455-1261
Ninth Avenue Foods
   CA 626-364-8722
Norwalk Dairy
   Santa Fe Springs, CA 562-921-5712
Oakhurst Dairy
   Portland, ME 800-482-0718
Olam Spices
   Fresno, CA 559-447-1390
Parmalat Canada
   Toronto, ON 800-563-1515
Plains Dairy Products
   Amarillo, TX 800-365-5608
Pleasant View Dairy
   Highland, IN 219-838-0155
Prairie Farms Dairy Inc.
   Edwardsville, IL 618-659-5700
Price's Creameries
   El Paso, TX 915-565-2711
Pride Dairies
   Bottineau, ND 701-228-2216
Promised Land Dairy
   Colorado Springs, CO 877-520-2479
Purity Dairies LLC
   Nashville, TN 615-244-1900
Queensboro Farm Products
   Canastota, NY 315-687-6133
Queensboro Farm Products
   Jamica, NY 718-658-5000
Reilly Dairy & Food Company
   Tampa, FL 813-839-8458
Reiter Dairy LLC
   Springfield, OH 937-323-5777

Product Categories / Dairy Products: Milk & Milk Products

Roland Machinery
   Springfield, IL 800-325-1183
Rosa Brothers Milk Co Inc
   Hanford, CA 559-685-8825
Rosenberger's Dairies
   Hatfield, PA 800-355-9074
Rye Fresh
   Piscataway, NJ 732-855-0008
Safeway Inc.
   Pleasanton, CA 877-723-3929
Safeway Milk Plant
   Tempe, AZ 480-894-4391
Santini Foods
   San Lorenzo, CA 800-835-6888
Saputo Inc.
   Montreal, QC 800-672-8866
Schepps Dairy
   Dallas, TX 800-395-7004
Schneider's Dairy Inc
   Pittsburgh, PA 412-881-3525
Schneider-Valley Farms Inc
   Williamsport, PA 570-326-2021
Smith Dairy
   Orrville, OH 800-776-7076
Stewart's Shops Corp
   Ballston Spa, NY 518-581-1200
Stonyfield Organic
   Londonderry, NH 800-776-2697
Stop & Shop Manufacturing
   Readville, MA 508-977-5132
Sunshine Farms
   Portage, WI 608-742-2016
Super Stores Industries
   Turlock, CA 209-668-2100
Superbrand Dairies
   Miami, FL 305-769-6600
Swiss Premium Dairy Inc
   Lebanon, PA 800-222-2129
Swissland Milk
   Berne, IN 260-589-2761
Tamarack Farms Dairy
   Newark, OH 866-221-4141
Toft Dairy Inc
   Sandusky, OH 800-521-4606
Trickling Springs Creamery
   Chambersburg, PA 717-709-0711
Turkey Hill Dairy Inc
   Conestoga, PA 800-693-2479
Umpqua Dairy
   Roseburg, OR 888-672-6455
United Dairy Inc.
   Martins Ferry, OH 800-252-1542
United Dairymen of Arizona
   Tempe, AZ. 480-966-7211
Valley Farms LLC
   Williamsport, PA 570-326-2021
Velda Farms
   Orlando, FL 800-795-4649
Vitamilk Dairy
   Bellingham, WA 206-529-4128
W.J. Stearns & Sons/Mountain Dairy
   Storrs Mansfield, CT 860-423-9289
Wayne Dairy Products Inc
   Richmond, IN 765-935-7521
Welsh Farms
   Wallington, NJ 800-221-0663
WhiteWave Foods
   Denver, CO 800-488-9283
Whitewave Foods Company
   Broomfield, CO 303-635-4000
Winchester Farms Dairy
   Winchester, KY 859-745-5500
Yoder Dairies
   Chesapeake, VA 757-482-4068

1 Percent

A2 Milk Company
   Boulder, CO 844-422-6455
Alta Dena Certified Dairy LLC
   City Of Industry, CA. 800-535-1369
Berkeley Farms
   Hayward, CA 800-395-7004
Borden Dairy
   Dallas, TX 855-311-1583
Broughton Foods LLC
   El Paso, TX 800-395-7004
Chase Brothers Dairy
   Oxnard, CA 800-438-6455
Cumberland Dairy
   Rosenhayn, NJ 800-257-8484
Dairy Maid Dairy LLC
   Frederick, MD 301-663-5114
Meadow Brook Dairy Co
   Erie, PA 800-352-4010
Pleasant View Dairy
   Highland, IN 219-838-0155
Promised Land Dairy
   Colorado Springs, CO. 877-520-2479
Safeway Milk Plant
   Tempe, AZ 480-894-4391
Schneider's Dairy Inc
   Pittsburgh, PA 412-881-3525
Valley Farms LLC
   Williamsport, PA 570-326-2021
Yoder Dairies
   Chesapeake, VA 757-482-4068

2 Percent

A2 Milk Company
   Boulder, CO 844-422-6455
Alta Dena Certified Dairy LLC
   City Of Industry, CA. 800-535-1369
Berkeley Farms
   Hayward, CA 800-395-7004
Borden Dairy
   Dallas, TX 855-311-1583
Broughton Foods LLC
   El Paso, TX 800-395-7004
Cumberland Dairy
   Rosenhayn, NJ 800-257-8484
Dairy Maid Dairy LLC
   Frederick, MD 301-663-5114
Meadow Brook Dairy Co
   Erie, PA 800-352-4010
Oak Knoll Dairy, Inc.
   Windsor, VT 802-674-5426
Pleasant View Dairy
   Highland, IN 219-838-0155
Promised Land Dairy
   Colorado Springs, CO. 877-520-2479
Safeway Milk Plant
   Tempe, AZ 480-894-4391
Schneider's Dairy Inc
   Pittsburgh, PA 412-881-3525
Stewart's Shops Corp
   Ballston Spa, NY 518-581-1200
Swiss Premium Dairy Inc
   Lebanon, PA 800-222-2129
T G Lee Dairy
   Orlando, FL. 800-432-4872
Valley Farms LLC
   Williamsport, PA 570-326-2021
Winchester Farms Dairy
   Winchester, KY 859-745-5500

Chocolate

A2 Milk Company
   Boulder, CO 844-422-6455
Alta Dena Certified Dairy LLC
   City Of Industry, CA. 800-535-1369
Barber Dairies
   Birmingham, AL 205-942-2351
Berkeley Farms
   Hayward, CA 800-395-7004
Borden Dairy
   Dallas, TX 855-311-1583
Broughton Foods LLC
   El Paso, TX 800-395-7004
Chase Brothers Dairy
   Oxnard, CA 800-438-6455
Clover Sonoma
   Petaluma, CA 800-237-3315
Cloverland/Green Spring Dairy
   Baltimore, MD 800-876-6455
Cocoa Metro
   St. George, UT 888-676-1527
Happy Planet Foods
   Burnaby, BC 800-811-3213
Harrisburg Dairies Inc
   Harrisburg, PA 800-692-7429
Hygeia Dairy Company
   Corpus Christi, TX 361-854-4561
Intense Milk
   Buffalo, NY 716-892-3156
Kleinpeter Farms Dairy LLC
   Baton Rouge, LA 225-753-2121
Marburger Farm Dairy
   Evans City, PA 800-331-1295
McArthur Dairy LLC
   Miami, FL 561-659-4811
Natrel
   St. Laurent, QC 800-501-1150
Norwalk Dairy
   Santa Fe Springs, CA 562-921-5712
Oak Knoll Dairy, Inc.
   Windsor, VT 802-674-5426
Plains Dairy Products
   Amarillo, TX 800-365-5608
Promised Land Dairy
   Colorado Springs, CO. 877-520-2479
Swiss Dairy
   Riverside, CA 951-898-9427
TruMoo
   El Paso, TX 800-395-7004
Valley Farms LLC
   Williamsport, PA 570-326-2021
Winchester Farms Dairy
   Winchester, KY 859-745-5500
Yoder Dairies
   Chesapeake, VA 757-482-4068
Yoo-Hoo Chocolate Beverage Company
   Carlstadt, NJ 201-933-0070

Condensed

Abbott Laboratories
   Abbott Park, IL 847-938-3887
Agri-Mark Inc
   West Springfield, MA. 978-552-5500
All American Foods Inc
   Mankato, MN 800-833-2661
Berkshire Dairy
   Wyomissing, PA 877-696-6455
Blossom Farm Products
   Ridgewood, NJ 800-729-1818
Eagle Family Foods
   Richfield, OH 888-656-3245
Galloway Co
   Neenah, WI 800-722-8903
Graf Creamery Co
   Bonduel, WI 715-758-2137
J.M. Smucker Co.
   Orrville, OH 888-550-9555
Milnot Company
   Orrville, OH 888-656-3245
O-At-Ka Milk Prods Co-Op Inc.
   Batavia, NY 800-828-8152
Queensboro Farm Products
   Jamica, NY 718-658-5000
Ronzoni
   Largo, FL 800-730-5957
Saint Albans Cooperative Creamery
   Saint Albans, VT 802-524-6581

Condensed - Bulk Only

Agri-Dairy Products
   Purchase, NY 914-697-9580
Clofine Dairy Products Inc
   Linwood, NJ 609-653-1000
Maryland & Virginia Milk Producers Cooperative
   Reston, VA 703-742-6800

Evaporated

Abbott Laboratories
   Abbott Park, IL 847-938-3887
Agri-Dairy Products
   Purchase, NY 914-697-9580
Clofine Dairy Products Inc
   Linwood, NJ 609-653-1000
Meyenberg Goat Milk
   Turlock, CA 800-891-4628
Milnot Company
   Orrville, OH 888-656-3245

Fat-Free

Agri-Mark Inc
   West Springfield, MA. 978-552-5500
Alta Dena Certified Dairy LLC
   City Of Industry, CA. 800-535-1369
Berkeley Farms
   Hayward, CA 800-395-7004
Broughton Foods LLC
   El Paso, TX 800-395-7004
California Dairies Inc.
   Visalia, CA 559-625-2200
Chase Brothers Dairy
   Oxnard, CA 800-438-6455
Clofine Dairy Products Inc
   Linwood, NJ 609-653-1000
First District Association
   Litchfield, MN 320-693-3236
Humboldt Creamery
   Modesto, CA 888-316-6064

Product Categories / Dairy Products: Milk & Milk Products

IMAC
  Oklahoma City, OK 888-878-7827
Main Street Ingredients
  La Crosse, WI 800-359-2345
Meadow Brook Dairy Co
  Erie, PA 800-352-4010
Norwalk Dairy
  Santa Fe Springs, CA 562-921-5712
Plainview Milk Products
  Plainview, MN 800-356-5606
Promised Land Dairy
  Colorado Springs, CO 877-520-2479
Quality Ingredients
  Burnsville, MN 952-898-4002
Ramsen Inc
  Lakeville, MN 952-431-0400
Saint Albans Cooperative Creamery
  Saint Albans, VT 802-524-6581
Schneider's Dairy Inc
  Pittsburgh, PA 412-881-3525
Swiss Dairy
  Riverside, CA 951-898-9427
Valley Farms LLC
  Williamsport, PA 570-326-2021

Flavored

Berkeley Farms
  Hayward, CA 800-395-7004
Borden Dairy
  Dallas, TX 855-311-1583
Broughton Foods LLC
  El Paso, TX 800-395-7004
Chase Brothers Dairy
  Oxnard, CA 800-438-6455
Coco Lopez Inc
  Miramar, FL 800-341-2242
Country Fresh
  Grand Rapids, MI 616-243-0173
Fairlife
  Chicago, IL
Intense Milk
  Buffalo, NY 716-892-3156
Marburger Farm Dairy
  Evans City, PA 800-331-1295
Norwalk Dairy
  Santa Fe Springs, CA 562-921-5712
Schepps Dairy
  Dallas, TX 800-395-7004
Schneider's Dairy Inc
  Pittsburgh, PA 412-881-3525
Schneider-Valley Farms Inc
  Williamsport, PA 570-326-2021
TruMoo
  El Paso, TX 800-395-7004
Winchester Farms Dairy
  Winchester, KY 859-745-5500

Fresh

A B Munroe Dairy Inc
  East Providence, RI 401-438-4450
Agropur
  Granby, QC 800-363-5686
Al's Beverage Company
  East Windsor, CT 888-257-7632
Alpenrose Dairy
  Portland, OR 503-244-1133
Anderson Dairy Inc
  Las Vegas, NV 702-642-7507
Bartlett Dairy & Food Service
  Jamaica, NY 718-658-2299
Berkeley Farms
  Hayward, CA 800-395-7004
Bliss Brothers Dairy, Inc.
  Attleboro, MA 800-622-8789
Blue Ribbon Farm Dairy Fresh
  Exeter, PA 570-655-5579
Borden Dairy
  Dallas, TX 855-311-1583
Braum's Inc
  Oklahoma City, OK 800-327-6455
Brown Dairy Inc
  Coalville, UT 435-336-5952
Brum's Dairy
  Pembroke, ON 613-735-2325
Caprine Estates
  Bellbrook, OH 937-848-7406
Central Dairy
  Jefferson City, MO 573-635-6148
Chase Brothers Dairy
  Oxnard, CA 800-438-6455

Chester Dairy Co
  Chester, IL 618-826-2394
Clover Farms Dairy Co Inc
  Reading, PA 800-323-0123
Clover Stornetta Farms Inc
  Petaluma, CA 800-237-3315
Cloverland/Green Spring Dairy
  Baltimore, MD 800-876-6455
Coastlog Industries
  Novi, MI 248-344-9556
Colteryahn Dairy
  Pittsburgh, PA 412-881-1408
Compton Dairy
  Shelbyville, IN 317-398-8621
Country Delite Farms LLC
  Nashville, TN 800-232-4791
Cream Crock Distributors
  Sterling, MA 800-423-2736
Crescent Ridge Dairy
  Sharon, MA 800-660-2740
Cumberland Creamery
  Antioch, TN 615-641-1027
Czepiel Millers Dairy
  Ludlow, MA 413-589-0828
Dairy Management Inc
  Rosemont, IL 800-853-2479
Darifair Foods
  Jacksonville, FL 904-268-9916
Daybreak Foods Inc
  Long Prairie, MN 320-732-2966
Dean Foods Co.
  Dallas, TX 800-395-7004
Deseret Dairy Products
  Salt Lake City, UT 801-240-7350
Eagle Family Foods
  Richfield, OH 888-656-3245
Everything Yogurt
  Washington, DC 202-842-2990
Farmers Dairies
  El Paso, TX 915-772-2736
Farmland Dairies
  Wallington, NJ 888-727-6252
Gandy's Dairies LLC
  Lubbock, TX 800-338-6841
Garelick Farms
  Lynn, MA 781-599-1300
Guers Dairy
  Tamaqua, PA 570-277-6611
H-E-B Grocery Co. LP
  San Antonio, TX 800-432-3113
Harrisburg Dairies Inc
  Harrisburg, PA 800-692-7429
Hastings Co-Op Creamery-Dairy
  Hastings, MN 651-437-9414
Heritage Farms Dairy
  Murfreesboro, TN 615-895-2790
Heritage's Dairy Stores
  West Deptford, NJ 856-845-2855
Highland Dairies
  Wichita, KS 800-336-0765
Homestead Dairy
  Plymouth, IN 574-936-6126
Hood Sterile Division
  Oneida, NY 315-363-3870
Houlton Farms Dairy
  Houlton, ME 207-532-3170
Humboldt Creamery
  Modesto, CA 888-316-6064
Hygeia Dairy Company
  Corpus Christi, TX 361-854-4561
Inverness Dairy
  Cheboygan, MI 231-627-4655
Kalamazoo Creamery
  Kalamazoo, MI 616-343-2558
Kemps LLC
  St Paul, MN
Kleinpeter Farms Dairy LLC
  Baton Rouge, LA 225-753-2121
Land O'Lakes Inc
  Arden Hills, MN 800-328-9680
Land-O-Sun Dairies Inc
  O Fallon, IL 314-436-6820
Lehigh Valley Dairy Farms
  Lansdale, PA 800-395-7004
Longacres Modern Dairy Inc
  Barto, PA 610-845-7551
Louisville Dairy
  Louisville, KY 502-451-9111
Lowell-Paul Dairy
  Greeley, CO 970-353-0278
Lubbers Family Farm
  Grand Rapids, MI 616-453-4257

Ludwig Dairy Product
  Elk Grove Vlg, IL 847-860-8646
Magic Valley Quality Milk
  Jerome, ID 208-324-7519
Maple Hill Farms
  Bloomfield, CT 800-842-7304
Maplehurst Farms
  Rochelle, IL 815-562-8723
Marburger Farm Dairy
  Evans City, PA 800-331-1295
McArthur Dairy LLC
  Miami, FL 561-659-4811
Meadow Brook Dairy Co
  Erie, PA 800-352-4010
Meadowbrook Farm
  Bronx, NY 718-828-6400
Meyenberg Goat Milk
  Turlock, CA 800-891-4628
Meyer Brothers Dairy
  Maple Plain, MN 952-473-7343
Michigan Milk Producers Assn
  Novi, MI 248-474-6672
Milky Way Jersey Farm Inc
  Starr, SC 864-352-2014
Mitchel Dairies
  Bronx, NY 718-994-6655
Monument Farms Dairy
  Middlebury, VT 802-545-2119
Morning Glory Dairy
  De Pere, WI 920-336-4206
Morning Star Foods
  East Brunswick, NJ 800-237-5320
Mountainside Farms Inc
  Roxbury, NY 607-326-4161
Muller-Pinehurst Dairy
  Rockford, IL 815-968-0441
Murdock Farm Dairy
  Winchendon, MA 978-297-2196
Mystic Lake Dairy
  Sammamish, WA 425-868-2029
Nature's Dairy
  Roswell, NM 575-623-9640
Northern Dairy
  Franklin Park, IL 847-671-2697
Northumberland Dairy
  Miramichi, NB 800-501-1150
Norwalk Dairy
  Santa Fe Springs, CA 562-921-5712
Oak Farm's Dairy
  Waco, TX 254-756-5421
Oak Grove Dairy
  Clintonville, WI 715-823-6226
Oberweis Dairy Inc
  North Aurora, IL 866-623-7934
Peeler's Jersey Farms
  Athens, GA 706-543-7383
Pierz Cooperative Association
  Pierz, MN 320-468-6655
Pioneer Dairy
  Southwick, MA 413-569-6132
Potomac Farms Dairy Inc
  Cumberland, MD 301-722-4410
Potter Siding Creamery Company
  Tripoli, IA 319-882-4444
Producers Dairy Foods Inc
  Fresno, CA 559-264-6583
Pure Milk & Ice Cream Company
  Austin, TX 512-837-2685
Purity Dairies LLC
  Nashville, TN 615-244-1900
Quality Dairy Co
  East Lansing, MI 517-319-4114
Queensboro Farm Products
  Jamica, NY 718-658-5000
Rehemond Farm Inc
  Minot, ME 207-345-5611
Reiter Dairy LLC
  Springfield, OH 937-323-5777
Richardson's Ice Cream
  Middleton, MA 978-774-5450
Ritchey's Dairy
  Martinsburg, PA 800-296-2157
Rockview Farms
  Downey, CA 800-423-2479
Ronny Brook Farm Dairy
  Ancramdale, NY 800-772-6455
Rosebud Creamery
  Plattsburgh, NY 518-561-5160
Royal Crest Dairy
  Denver, CO 888-226-6455
Rutter's Dairy
  York, PA 800-840-1664

Product Categories / Dairy Products: Milk & Milk Products

S.T. Jerrell Company
   Bessemer, AL 205-426-8930
Safeway Milk Plant
   Tempe, AZ 480-894-4391
Saint Albans Cooperative Creamery
   Saint Albans, VT 802-524-6581
Santini Foods
   San Lorenzo, CA 800-835-6888
Schneider's Dairy Inc
   Pittsburgh, PA 412-881-3525
Seger Egg Corporation
   Farina, IL 618-245-3301
Shedd Food Products
   Dallas, TX 214-374-4751
Skinners' Dairy
   Ponte Vedra Beach, FL 904-733-5440
Snow Dairy Inc
   Springville, UT 801-489-6081
Southeast Dairy Processors Inc
   Tampa, FL 813-620-1516
Spring Hill Pure Water
   Haverhill, MA 978-373-3481
Stop & Shop Manufacturing
   Readville, MA 508-977-5132
Stremick's Heritage Foods
   Santa Ana, CA 800-371-9010
Suiza Dairy Corporation
   San Juan, PR 787-707-6500
Sunshine Dairy
   Middletown, CT 860-346-6644
Sunshine Dairy Foods Inc
   Portland, OR 503-234-7526
Super Stores Industries
   Turlock, CA 209-668-2100
Superbrand Dairies
   Miami, FL 305-769-6600
Swiss Dairy
   Riverside, CA 951-898-9427
Swiss Premium Dairy Inc
   Lebanon, PA 800-222-2129
Tamarack Farms Dairy
   Newark, OH 866-221-4141
Tanglewood Farms
   Warsaw, VA 804-394-4505
Thomas Dairy
   Rutland, VT 802-773-6788
Toft Dairy Inc
   Sandusky, OH 800-521-4606
Tri-State Dairy
   Fort Wayne, IN 256-534-8464
Turner Dairy Farms Inc
   Pittsburgh, PA 800-892-1039
Ultra Dairy
   Delhi, NY 607-746-2141
Umpqua Dairy
   Roseburg, OR 888-672-6455
United Dairy Farmers Inc.
   Cincinnati, OH 866-837-4833
United Dairymen of Arizona
   Tempe, AZ 480-966-7211
United Valley Bell Dairy
   Charleston, WV 304-344-2511
Valley Milk Products
   Strasburg, VA 540-465-5113
Van Peenans Dairy
   Wayne, NJ 973-694-2551
Verifine Dairy
   Sheboygan, WI 920-457-7733
Vitamilk Dairy
   Bellingham, WA 206-529-4128
W.J. Stearns & Sons/Mountain Dairy
   Storrs Mansfield, CT 860-423-9289
Wawa Inc
   Wawa, PA 800-444-9292
Wessanan
   Minneapolis, MN 612-331-3775
Whitney Foods Inc
   Jamaica, NY 718-291-3333
Winchester Farms Dairy
   Winchester, KY 859-745-5500
Winsor SB Dairy
   Johnston, RI 401-231-7832
Wurth Dairy
   Caseyville, IL 217-271-7580
Young's Jersey Dairy
   Yellow Springs, OH 937-325-0629

Goat

Abunda Life
   Asbury Park, NJ 732-775-9338
C F Burger Creamery Co
   Detroit, MI 313-584-4040
Coach Farm Enterprises
   Pine Plains, NY 800-999-4628
Fat Toad Farm
   Brookfield, VT 802-279-0098
Maison Riviera
   Varennes, QC 800-363-0092
Meyenberg Goat Milk
   Turlock, CA 800-891-4628
Oak Knoll Dairy, Inc.
   Windsor, VT 802-674-5426
Sunshine Farms
   Portage, WI 608-742-2016
Woolwich Dairy
   Orangeville, ON 877-438-3499

Half & Half

C F Burger Creamery Co
   Detroit, MI 313-584-4040
Cass-Clay Creamery
   Fargo, ND 701-293-6455
Central Dairy
   Jefferson City, MO 573-635-6148
Chase Brothers Dairy
   Oxnard, CA 800-438-6455
Clover Farms Dairy Co Inc
   Reading, PA 800-323-0123
Horizon Organic Dairy
   Broomfield, CO 888-494-3020
Oak Knoll Dairy, Inc.
   Windsor, VT 802-674-5426
Prairie Farms Dairy Inc.
   Edwardsville, IL 618-659-5700
Rockview Farms
   Downey, CA 800-423-2479
Safeway Milk Plant
   Tempe, AZ 480-894-4391
Stonyfield Organic
   Londonderry, NH 800-776-2697
Tiller Foods Company
   Dayton, OH 937-435-4601
WhiteWave Foods
   Denver, CO 800-488-9283
Whitewave Foods Company
   Broomfield, CO 303-635-4000
Yoder Dairies
   Chesapeake, VA 757-482-4068

Lactose-Free

DairyPure
   El Paso, TX 800-395-7004

Low-Fat

Anderson Erickson Dairy
   Des Moines, IA 515-265-2521
Anderson Erickson Dairy
   Kansas City, KS 913-621-4801
Berkeley Farms
   Hayward, CA 800-395-7004
Borden Dairy
   Dallas, TX 855-311-1583
Chase Brothers Dairy
   Oxnard, CA 800-438-6455
Cloverland/Green Spring Dairy
   Baltimore, MD 800-876-6455
Country Fresh Farms
   Salt Lake City, UT 800-878-0099
Dairy Maid Dairy LLC
   Frederick, MD 301-663-5114
DairyPure
   El Paso, TX 800-395-7004
Humboldt Creamery
   Modesto, CA 888-316-6064
Intense Milk
   Buffalo, NY 716-892-3156
Marva Maid Dairy
   Newport News, VA 800-768-6243
McArthur Dairy LLC
   Miami, FL 561-659-4811
Meadow Brook Dairy Co
   Erie, PA 800-352-4010
Pleasant View Dairy
   Highland, IN 219-838-0155
Safeway Milk Plant
   Tempe, AZ 480-894-4391
Schneider's Dairy Inc
   Pittsburgh, PA 412-881-3525
Schneider-Valley Farms Inc
   Williamsport, PA 570-326-2021
Swiss Dairy
   Riverside, CA 951-898-9427
Swiss Premium Dairy Inc
   Lebanon, PA 800-222-2129
T G Lee Dairy
   Orlando, FL 800-432-4872
Valley Farms LLC
   Williamsport, PA 570-326-2021
Winchester Farms Dairy
   Winchester, KY 859-745-5500
Yoder Dairies
   Chesapeake, VA 757-482-4068

Reduced-Fat

Berkeley Farms
   Hayward, CA 800-395-7004
Borden Dairy
   Dallas, TX 855-311-1583
Dairy Maid Dairy LLC
   Frederick, MD 301-663-5114
Humboldt Creamery
   Modesto, CA 888-316-6064
Marva Maid Dairy
   Newport News, VA 800-768-6243
McArthur Dairy LLC
   Miami, FL 561-659-4811
Meadow Brook Dairy Co
   Erie, PA 800-352-4010
Norwalk Dairy
   Santa Fe Springs, CA 562-921-5712
Pleasant View Dairy
   Highland, IN 219-838-0155
Safeway Milk Plant
   Tempe, AZ 480-894-4391
Schneider's Dairy Inc
   Pittsburgh, PA 412-881-3525
Schneider-Valley Farms Inc
   Williamsport, PA 570-326-2021
Swiss Dairy
   Riverside, CA 951-898-9427
Swiss Premium Dairy Inc
   Lebanon, PA 800-222-2129
WhiteWave Foods
   Denver, CO 800-488-9283
Winchester Farms Dairy
   Winchester, KY 859-745-5500
Yoder Dairies
   Chesapeake, VA 757-482-4068

Skim

Agri-Mark Inc
   West Springfield, MA 978-552-5500
Berkeley Farms
   Hayward, CA 800-395-7004
Borden Dairy
   Dallas, TX 855-311-1583
Chase Brothers Dairy
   Oxnard, CA 800-438-6455
Cloverland/Green Spring Dairy
   Baltimore, MD 800-876-6455
Country Fresh Farms
   Salt Lake City, UT 800-878-0099
Cumberland Dairy
   Rosenhayn, NJ 800-257-8484
Dairy Maid Dairy LLC
   Frederick, MD 301-663-5114
IMAC
   Oklahoma City, OK 888-878-7827
Kleinpeter Farms Dairy LLC
   Baton Rouge, LA 225-753-2121
Marva Maid Dairy
   Newport News, VA 800-768-6243
McArthur Dairy LLC
   Miami, FL 561-659-4811
Meadow Brook Dairy Co
   Erie, PA 800-352-4010
Pleasant View Dairy
   Highland, IN 219-838-0155
Safeway Milk Plant
   Tempe, AZ 480-894-4391
Saint Albans Cooperative Creamery
   Saint Albans, VT 802-524-6581
Schneider's Dairy Inc
   Pittsburgh, PA 412-881-3525
Schneider-Valley Farms Inc
   Williamsport, PA 570-326-2021
Stewart's Shops Corp
   Ballston Spa, NY 518-581-1200
Swiss Premium Dairy Inc
   Lebanon, PA 800-222-2129
Valley Farms LLC
   Williamsport, PA 570-326-2021

Product Categories / Dairy Products: Pudding

WhiteWave Foods
  Denver, CO 800-488-9283
Winchester Farms Dairy
  Winchester, KY 859-745-5500
Yoder Dairies
  Chesapeake, VA 757-482-4068

Strawberry

Berkeley Farms
  Hayward, CA 800-395-7004
DairyPure
  El Paso, TX 800-395-7004
Hygeia Dairy Company
  Corpus Christi, TX 361-854-4561
Intense Milk
  Buffalo, NY 716-892-3156
Kleinpeter Farms Dairy LLC
  Baton Rouge, LA 225-753-2121
TruMoo
  El Paso, TX 800-395-7004

Sweetened

All American Foods Inc
  Mankato, MN 800-833-2661
Gateway Food Products Co
  Dupo, IL 877-220-1963
Milnot Company
  Orrville, OH 888-656-3245

Sweetened & Condensed

Arnhem Group
  Cranford, NJ 800-851-1052
Reilly Dairy & Food Company
  Tampa, FL 813-839-8458
Suprema Specialties
  Manteca, CA 209-858-9696

Vanilla Flavored

Intense Milk
  Buffalo, NY 716-892-3156

Whole

A2 Milk Company
  Boulder, CO 844-422-6455
Berkeley Farms
  Hayward, CA 800-395-7004
Borden Dairy
  Dallas, TX 855-311-1583
Cloverland/Green Spring Dairy
  Baltimore, MD 800-876-6455
Cumberland Dairy
  Rosenhayn, NJ 800-257-8484
DairyAmerica
  Fresno, CA 800-722-3110
GAF Seelig Inc
  Flushing, NY 718-899-5000
Happy Planet Foods
  Burnaby, BC 800-811-3213
Kleinpeter Farms Dairy LLC
  Baton Rouge, LA 225-753-2121
Marva Maid Dairy
  Newport News, VA 800-768-6243
McArthur Dairy LLC
  Miami, FL 561-659-4811
Meadow Brook Dairy Co
  Erie, PA 800-352-4010
Plainview Milk Products
  Plainview, MN 800-356-5606
Pleasant View Dairy
  Highland, IN 219-838-0155
Safeway Milk Plant
  Tempe, AZ 480-894-4391
Saint Albans Cooperative Creamery
  Saint Albans, VT 802-524-6581
Schneider's Dairy Inc
  Pittsburgh, PA 412-881-3525
Schneider-Valley Farms Inc
  Williamsport, PA 570-326-2021
Stewart's Shops Corp
  Ballston Spa, NY 518-581-1200
T G Lee Dairy
  Orlando, FL 800-432-4872
Trickling Springs Creamery
  Chambersburg, PA 717-709-0711
WhiteWave Foods
  Denver, CO 800-488-9283
Winchester Farms Dairy
  Winchester, KY 859-745-5500
Yoder Dairies
  Chesapeake, VA 757-482-4068

Milk Products

Milk & Milk Fat: Enzyme

Brown's Dairy
  New Orleans, LA 800-680-6455
Farmers Cooperative Dairy
  Saint-Hubert, QC 800-501-1150
Garden Spot Distributors
  New Holland, PA 800-829-5100
Idaho Milk Products
  Jerome, ID 208-644-2882
Maple Island
  Saint Paul, MN 800-369-1022

Milk Proteins

Austrade
  Palm Beach Gdns, FL 561-209-2447
Clofine Dairy Products Inc
  Linwood, NJ 609-653-1000
Erie Foods Intl Inc
  Erie, IL 309-659-2233
Kantner Group
  Wapakoneta, OH 877-738-3448
Lactalis USA Inc
  Belmont, WI 608-762-5136
Main Street Ingredients
  La Crosse, WI 800-359-2345
Rosa Brothers Milk Co Inc
  Hanford, CA 559-685-8825

Modified - Dry Blends

Kantner Group
  Wapakoneta, OH 877-738-3448
King Arthur Flour
  Norwich, VT 800-827-6836

Non-Dairy Milk - Imitation

Ripple
  Berkeley, CA

Milk Solids

Non-Fat

California Dairies Inc.
  Visalia, CA 559-625-2200
Kantner Group
  Wapakoneta, OH 877-738-3448
Main Street Ingredients
  La Crosse, WI 800-359-2345
Ramsen Inc
  Lakeville, MN 952-431-0400

Replacers

APC Inc
  Ankeny, IA 800-369-2672
Kantner Group
  Wapakoneta, OH 877-738-3448

Whole

Kantner Group
  Wapakoneta, OH 877-738-3448
Lactalis USA Inc
  Belmont, WI 608-762-5136
Meyenberg Goat Milk
  Turlock, CA 800-891-4628

Pudding

Advanced Food Products LLC
  New Holland, PA 800-732-5373
Aryzta
  Los Angeles, CA 855-427-9982
Dufflet Pastries
  Toronto, ON 866-238-0899
Echo Farms Puddings
  Hinsdale, NH 866-488-3246
Gehl Foods, Inc.
  Germantown, WI. 800-521-2873
Good Old Days Foods
  Little Rock, AR. 501-565-1257
GPI USA LLC.
  Mokena, IL 800-929-4248
Grainaissance
  Emeryville, CA. 800-472-4697
Hormel Foods Corp.
  Austin, MN. 507-437-5611
Hudson River Foods
  Castleton, NY 888-417-9343
Inter-American Products
  Cincinnati, OH 800-645-2233
Kosto Food Products Co
  Wauconda, IL 847-487-2600
KOZY Shack Enterprises Inc
  St Paul, MN. 855-716-1555
Michigan Desserts
  Oak Park, MI. 800-328-8632
Rodgers' Puddings
  Chesapeake, VA 757-543-9290
Serv-Agen Corporation
  Cherry Hill, NJ 856-663-6966
Spring Glen Fresh Foods
  Ephrata, PA. 800-641-2853
Terrapin Ridge
  Clearwater, FL 800-999-4052

Chocolate

EJZ Foods
  Winston-Salem, NC
Knouse Foods Co-Op Inc.
  Peach Glen, PA 717-677-8181
KOZY Shack Enterprises Inc
  St Paul, MN. 855-716-1555

Plum

Patti's Plum Puddings
  Lawndale, CA 310-376-1463

Rice

Knouse Foods Co-Op Inc.
  Peach Glen, PA 717-677-8181
KOZY Shack Enterprises Inc
  St Paul, MN. 855-716-1555
Lakeview Farms
  Delphos, OH 800-755-9925
Petit Pot
  Emeryville, CA 650-488-7432

Tapioca

Knouse Foods Co-Op Inc.
  Peach Glen, PA 717-677-8181
KOZY Shack Enterprises Inc
  St Paul, MN. 855-716-1555

Vanilla

Knouse Foods Co-Op Inc.
  Peach Glen, PA 717-677-8181
KOZY Shack Enterprises Inc
  St Paul, MN. 855-716-1555

Sour Cream

Aimonetto and Sons
  Renton, WA. 866-823-2777
Alta Dena Certified Dairy LLC
  City Of Industry, CA. 800-535-1369
Anderson Erickson Dairy
  Des Moines, IA 515-265-2521
Anderson Erickson Dairy
  Kansas City, KS 913-621-4801
Astro Dairy Products
  Toronto, ON 416-622-2811
Auburn Dairy Products Inc
  Auburn, WA. 800-950-9264
Berkeley Farms
  Hayward, CA 800-395-7004
Bison Foods
  Buffalo, NY 716-892-3156
Borden Dairy
  Dallas, TX. 855-311-1583
Broughton Foods LLC
  El Paso, TX. 800-395-7004
Byrne Dairy, Inc.
  Syracuse, NY 800-899-1535
Campbell Soup Co.
  Camden, NJ. 800-257-8443
Cascade Fresh
  Seattle, WA. 800-511-0057
Central Dairy
  Jefferson City, MO 573-635-6148
Chino Valley Dairy
  Chino, CA 800-324-7948
Clofine Dairy Products Inc
  Linwood, NJ 609-653-1000
Clover Farms Dairy Co Inc
  Reading, PA 800-323-0123
Clover Sonoma
  Petaluma, CA 800-237-3315

Product Categories / Dairy Products: Yogurt

Clover Stornetta Farms Inc
  Petaluma, CA 800-237-3315
Cloverland/Green Spring Dairy
  Baltimore, MD 800-876-6455
Country Fresh
  Grand Rapids, MI 616-243-0173
Creamland Dairies Inc
  Albuquerque, NM 505-247-0721
Dairy Maid Dairy LLC
  Frederick, MD 301-663-5114
DairyPure
  El Paso, TX 800-395-7004
Daisy Brand
  Dallas, TX 877-292-9830
Darigold
  Seattle, WA 800-333-6455
Elgin Dairy Foods
  Chicago, IL 800-786-9900
Farmers Cooperative Dairy
  Saint-Hubert, QC 800-501-1150
Foremost Farms USA
  Baraboo, WI 800-362-9196
Friendship Dairies LLC
  Friendship, NY 800-854-3243
GAF Seelig Inc
  Flushing, NY 718-899-5000
Good Culture
  Irvine, CA 844-899-8884
HP Hood LLC
  Lynnfield, MA 800-343-6592
Hunter Farms - High Point Division
  High Point, NC 800-446-8035
Kemps LLC
  St Paul, MN
Lakeview Farms
  Delphos, OH 800-755-9925
Ludwig Dairy Product
  Elk Grove Vlg, IL 847-860-8646
Marburger Farm Dairy
  Evans City, PA 800-331-1295
Marquez Brothers International
  Hanford, CA 800-858-1119
Marva Maid Dairy
  Newport News, VA 800-768-6243
Mayfield Dairy Farms LLC
  Athens, TN 800-362-9546
Nancy's Probiotic Foods
  Eugene, OR
Natural By Nature
  Newark, DE 302-455-1261
Oakhurst Dairy
  Portland, ME 800-482-0718
Old Home Foods Inc
  New Brighton, MN 651-312-8900
Parmalat Canada
  Toronto, ON 800-563-1515
Plains Dairy Products
  Amarillo, TX 800-365-5608
Pleasant View Dairy
  Highland, IN 219-838-0155
Prairie Farms Dairy Inc.
  Edwardsville, IL 618-659-5700
Purity Dairies LLC
  Nashville, TN 615-244-1900
Queensboro Farm Products
  Canastota, NY 315-687-6133
Queensboro Farm Products
  Jamica, NY 718-658-5000
Reilly Dairy & Food Company
  Tampa, FL 813-839-8458
Roos Foods
  Kenton, DE 800-343-3642
Rosenberger's Dairies
  Hatfield, PA 800-355-9074
Schepps Dairy
  Dallas, TX 800-395-7004
Schneider-Valley Farms Inc
  Williamsport, PA 570-326-2021
Sisler's Ice & Ice Cream
  Ohio, IL 888-891-3856
Smith Dairy
  Orrville, OH 800-776-7076
Springfield Creamery Inc
  Eugene, OR 541-689-2911
Sterzing Food Co
  Burlington, IA 800-754-8467
Tiller Foods Company
  Dayton, OH 937-435-4601
Umpqua Dairy
  Roseburg, OR 888-672-6455
United Dairy Inc.
  Martins Ferry, OH 800-252-1581

Upstate Farms
  Buffalo, NY 716-896-3156
Upstate Niagara Co-Op Inc.
  Buffalo, NY 716-892-3156
Vitamilk Dairy
  Bellingham, WA 206-529-4128
Wallaby Yogurt Co
  Broomfield, CO 855-925-4636

Yogurt

Agro Farma Inc.
  New Berlin, NY 877-847-6181
Aimonetto and Sons
  Renton, WA 866-823-2777
Alta Dena Certified Dairy LLC
  City Of Industry, CA 800-535-1369
Anderson Erickson Dairy
  Des Moines, IA 515-265-2521
Anderson Erickson Dairy
  Kansas City, KS 913-621-4801
Anita's Yogurt
  Brooklyn, NY
Astro Dairy Products
  Toronto, ON 416-622-2811
Auburn Dairy Products Inc
  Auburn, WA 800-950-9264
Bartlett Dairy & Food Service
  Jamaica, NY 718-658-2299
Ben & Jerry's Homemade Inc
  South Burlington, VT 866-258-6877
Berkeley Farms
  Hayward, CA 800-395-7004
Blue Hill Yogurt
  Pocantico Hills, NY 914-366-9600
Broughton Foods LLC
  El Paso, TX 800-395-7004
Brown Cow Farm
  Londonderry, NH 888-429-5459
Byrne Dairy, Inc.
  Syracuse, NY 800-899-1535
Cascade Fresh
  Seattle, WA 800-511-0057
Cass-Clay Creamery
  Fargo, ND 701-293-6455
Cedar Crest Specialties
  Cedarburg, WI. 800-877-8341
Chino Valley Dairy
  Chino, CA 800-324-7948
Chobani, Inc.
  Norwich, NY
Clio Snacks
  Roselle, NJ
Clofine Dairy Products Inc
  Linwood, NJ 609-653-1000
Clover Sonoma
  Petaluma, CA 800-237-3315
Clover Stornetta Farms Inc
  Petaluma, CA 800-237-3315
Cloverland/Green Spring Dairy
  Baltimore, MD 800-876-6455
CO YO
  Albuquerque, NM 505-247-0012
Coach Farm Enterprises
  Pine Plains, NY 800-999-4628
Coconut Collaborative
Continental Yogurt
  Glendale, CA 818-240-7400
Culina
  Austin, TX
Culture
  New York, NY 718-499-0207
Dairy Maid Dairy LLC
  Frederick, MD 301-663-5114
Dannon Company
  Allentown, PA. 877-326-6668
Danone North America
  Broomfield, CO 303-635-4000
Darigold
  Seattle, WA 800-333-6455
Deca & Otto Farms
  Miami, FL 305-629-9335
Dreaming Cow
  GA
Ellenos
  Seattle, WA 206-535-7562
FAGE USA Dairy Ind Inc
  Johnstown, NY 866-962-5912
Farmers Cooperative Dairy
  Saint-Hubert, QC 800-501-1150
Farmland Dairies
  Wallington, NJ 888-727-6252

Fieldbrook Foods Corp.
  Dunkirk, NY 800-333-0805
Franklin Foods
  Enosburg Falls, VT 800-933-6114
General Mills
  Minneapolis, MN 800-248-7310
Glover's Ice Cream Inc
  Frankfort, IN 800-686-5163
GPI USA LLC.
  Mokena, IL 800-929-4248
Green Dirt Farm
  Weston, MO 816-386-2156
Green Mountain Creamery
  Brattleboro, VT 855-996-4946
Heritage Farms Dairy
  Murfreesboro, TN 615-895-2790
Horizon Organic Dairy
  Broomfield, CO 888-494-3020
Hudson River Foods
  Castleton, NY 888-417-9343
Icelandic Milk and Skyr Corporation
  New York, NY 212-966-6950
Icelandic Provisions
  New York, NY 866-991-7597
Imperial Foods, Inc.
  Long Island City, NY 718-784-3400
Jason & Son Specialty Foods
  Rancho Cordova, CA 800-810-9093
Jaxon's Ice Cream Parlor
  Dania Beach, FL 954-923-4445
Katies Korner Inc
  Girard, OH 330-539-4140
Kemps LLC
  St Paul, MN
Kite Hill
  Hayward, CA 888-588-0994
Klinke Brothers Ice Cream Co
  Memphis, TN 901-322-6640
Krinos Foods
  Bronx, NY 718-729-9000
LAVVA
  Warwick, NY
Lifeway
  Morton Grove, IL 877-281-3874
Ludwig Dairy Product
  Elk Grove Vlg, IL 847-860-8646
Lyo-San
  Lachute, QC 800-363-3697
Maison Riviera
  Varennes, QC 800-363-0092
Maple Hill Creamery
  Kinderhook, NY 518-758-7777
Maplehill Creamery
  Stuyvesant, NY 518-758-7777
Marburger Farm Dairy
  Evans City, PA 800-331-1295
Master Mix
  Placentia, CA 714-524-1698
Michigan Dairy LLC
  Livonia, MI 734-367-5390
Mister Snacks Inc
  Amherst, NY. 800-333-6393
Mountain High Yogurt
  Minneapolis, MN 866-964-4878
Nancy's Probiotic Foods
  Eugene, OR
Natural By Nature
  Newark, DE 302-455-1261
Old Chatham Sheepherding Co
  Old Chatham, NY 888-743-3760
Old Home Foods Inc
  New Brighton, MN 651-312-8900
Parmalat Canada
  Toronto, ON 800-563-1515
Pavel's Yogurt
  San Leandro, CA 510-352-1474
Pecoraro Dairy Products
  Brooklyn, NY 718-388-2379
Pioneer Dairy
  Southwick, MA 413-569-6132
Plains Dairy Products
  Amarillo, TX 800-365-5608
Powerful Foods
  Miami, FL 305-779-2449
Prairie Farms Dairy Inc.
  Edwardsville, IL 618-659-5700
Purity Dairies LLC
  Nashville, TN 615-244-1900
Queensboro Farm Products
  Jamica, NY 718-658-5000
Redwood Hill Farm
  Sebastopol, CA 877-238-3543

Product Categories / Dairy Products: Yogurt

Reilly Dairy & Food Company
  Tampa, FL 813-839-8458
Restaurant Systems International
  Staten Island, NY 718-494-8888
Rockview Farms
  Downey, CA 800-423-2479
Schreiber Foods Inc.
  Green Bay, WI 920-437-7601
Siggi's Dairy
  New York, NY 212-966-6950
Siggi's Dairy
  855-860-6683
Springfield Creamery Inc
  Eugene, OR 541-689-2911
Stonyfield Organic
  Londonderry, NH 800-776-2697
Super Stores Industries
  Turlock, CA 209-668-2100
The Valpo Velvet Shoppe
  Valparaiso, IN 219-464-4141
Toft Dairy Inc
  Sandusky, OH 800-521-4606
Tropical Illusions
  Trenton, MO 660-359-5422
United Dairy Farmers Inc.
  Cincinnati, OH 866-837-4833
Upstate Farms
  Buffalo, NY 716-896-3156
Wallaby Yogurt Co
  Broomfield, CO 855-925-4636
WhiteWave Foods
  Denver, CO 800-488-9283
Yoplait
  Mississauga, ON 800-516-7780

Bases, Flavors, Stabilizers

California Custom Fruits
  Baldwin Park, CA 877-558-0056
Chobani, Inc.
  Norwich, NY
Idaho Milk Products
  Jerome, ID 208-644-2882
Nature's Godfather
  Lexington, MA 339-970-9888

Frozen

Brighams
  Arlington, MA 800-242-2423
Byrne Dairy, Inc.
  Syracuse, NY 800-899-1535
Cedar Crest Specialties
  Cedarburg, WI 800-877-8341
Chino Valley Dairy
  Chino, CA 800-324-7948
Cloud Top
  Pasadena, CA 888-263-1778
Dannon Yo Cream
  Portland, OR 800-962-7326
Elgin Dairy Foods
  Chicago, IL 800-786-9900

Fieldbrook Foods Corp.
  Dunkirk, NY 800-333-0805
Foothills Creamery
  Calgary, AB 800-661-4909
Glover's Ice Cream Inc
  Frankfort, IN 800-686-5163
Hudsonville Ice Cream
  Holland, MI 616-546-4005
Jack & Jill Ice Cream
  Moorestown, NJ 856-813-2300
Jaxon's Ice Cream Parlor
  Dania Beach, FL 954-923-4445
Kemps LLC
  St Paul, MN
Klinke Brothers Ice Cream Co
  Memphis, TN 901-322-6640
Lafleur Dairy Products,
  New Orleans, LA 504-729-3330
MacKay's Cochrane Ice Cream
  Cochrane, AB 403-932-2455
Mayfield Dairy Farms LLC
  Athens, TN 800-362-9546
O'Boyle's Ice Cream Company
  Bristol, PA 215-788-3882
Perry's Ice Cream Co Inc
  Akron, NY 800-873-7797
Petersen Ice Cream Company
  Oak Park, IL 708-386-6130
Rainbow Valley Frozen Yogurt
  White Lake, MI 800-979-8669
Reinhold Ice Cream Company
  Pittsburgh, PA 412-321-7600
Restaurant Systems International
  Staten Island, NY 718-494-8888
Stonyfield Organic
  Londonderry, NH 800-776-2697
The Valpo Velvet Shoppe
  Valparaiso, IN 219-464-4141
Toft Dairy Inc
  Sandusky, OH 800-521-4606
Turkey Hill Dairy Inc
  Conestoga, PA 800-693-2479
Vitarich Ice Cream
  Fortuna, CA 707-725-6182
Welsh Farms
  Clifton, NJ 973-772-2388
Whitey's Ice Cream Inc
  Moline, IL 888-594-4839

Low-Fat

Alta Dena Certified Dairy LLC
  City Of Industry, CA 800-535-1369
Auburn Dairy Products Inc
  Auburn, WA 800-950-9264
Broughton Foods LLC
  El Paso, TX 800-395-7004
Bunker Hill Cheese Co Inc
  Millersburg, OH 800-253-6636
Cascade Fresh
  Seattle, WA 800-511-0057

Dannon Company
  Allentown, PA 877-326-6668
FAGE USA Dairy Ind Inc
  Johnstown, NY 866-962-5912
Natren Inc
  Thousand Oaks, CA 800-992-3323
Perry's Ice Cream Co Inc
  Akron, NY 800-873-7797
Siggi's Dairy
  855-860-6683
Upstate Niagara Co-Op Inc.
  Buffalo, NY 716-892-3156
Vitarich Ice Cream
  Fortuna, CA 707-725-6182
Wunder Creamery
  New York, NY 844-986-3371

No-Fat

Agro Farma Inc.
  New Berlin, NY 877-847-6181
Broughton Foods LLC
  El Paso, TX 800-395-7004
Cascade Fresh
  Seattle, WA 800-511-0057
Cedar Crest Specialties
  Cedarburg, WI 800-877-8341
FAGE USA Dairy Ind Inc
  Johnstown, NY 866-962-5912
Gifford's Ice Cream
  Skowhegan, ME 800-950-2604
O'Boyle's Ice Cream Company
  Bristol, PA 215-788-3882
Perry's Ice Cream Co Inc
  Akron, NY 800-873-7797
Vitarich Ice Cream
  Fortuna, CA 707-725-6182

with Fruit

Alpina
  Batavia, NY 855-886-1914
Broughton Foods LLC
  El Paso, TX 800-395-7004
Byrne Dairy, Inc.
  Syracuse, NY 800-899-1535
Chobani, Inc.
  Norwich, NY
Dannon Company
  Allentown, PA 877-326-6668
Green Mountain Creamery
  Brattleboro, VT 855-996-4946
Noosa Yoghurt
  Bellvue, CO 844-800-4329
Petersen Ice Cream Company
  Oak Park, IL 708-386-6130
Stonyfield Organic
  Londonderry, NH 800-776-2697
Yoplait
  Mississauga, ON 800-516-7780

Doughs, Mixes & Fillings

Batters

Breading

Beneficial Blends
  Tampa, FL 800-230-5952
Blend Pak Inc
  Bloomfield, KY 502-252-8000
Chef Merito Inc
  Van Nuys, CA 800-637-4861
Concord Foods, LLC
  Brockton, MA 508-580-1700
Dorothy Dawson Food Products
  Jackson, MI 517-788-9830
Drum Rock Specialty Co Inc
  Warwick, RI 401-737-5165
Fry Krisp Food Products
  Jackson, MI 877-854-5440
Griffith Foods Inc.
  Alsip, IL 708-371-0900
Hydroblend Limited
  Nampa, ID 208-467-7441
Louisiana Fish Fry Products
  Baton Rouge, LA 800-356-2905
Quality Naturally Foods
  City Of Industry, CA 888-498-6986
Richmond Baking Co
  Richmond, IN 765-962-8535
Richmond Baking Co
  Alma, GA 912-632-7213
Shenandoah Mills
  Lebanon, TN 615-444-0841
Specialty Products
  Gloucester, MA 800-222-6846
Texas Crumb & Food Products
  Farmers Branch, TX 800-522-7862
Tova Industries LLC
  Louisville, KY 888-532-8682
UFL Foods
  Mississauga, ON 905-670-7776
Wilkins Rogers Inc
  Ellicott City, MD 410-465-5800
World Flavors Inc
  Warminster, PA 215-672-4400
Yorktown Baking Company
  Yorktown Heights, NY 800-235-3961

Cake

Frozen

BakeMark USA
  Schaumburg, IL 847-519-3135

Cookie

BakeMark USA
  Schaumburg, IL 847-519-3135
French Meadow Bakery & Cafe
  Minneapolis, MN 612-870-7855

Muffin

Bagelworks
  New York, NY 212-744-6444
BakeMark USA
  Schaumburg, IL 847-519-3135
Coby's Cookies
  Toronto, ON 416-633-1567

Tempora

Andy's Seasoning
  St Louis, MO 800-305-3004

Breading

Andy's Seasoning
  St Louis, MO 800-305-3004
Atkinson Milling Co.
  Selma, NC 800-948-5707
Blend Pak Inc
  Bloomfield, KY 502-252-8000
Blendex Co
  Louisville, KY 800-626-6325
Chef Hans' Gourmet Foods
  Monroe, LA 800-890-4267
Colonna Brothers Inc
  North Bergen, NJ 201-864-1115

Dorothy Dawson Food Products
  Jackson, MI 517-788-9830
Drum Rock Specialty Co Inc
  Warwick, RI 401-737-5165
Drusilla Seafood
  Baton Rouge, LA 800-364-8844
Griffith Foods Inc.
  Alsip, IL 708-371-0900
House-Autry Mills Inc
  Four Oaks, NC 800-849-0802
Hydroblend Limited
  Nampa, ID 208-467-7441
Lakeside Mills
  Rutherfordton, NC 828-286-4866
Louisiana Fish Fry Products
  Baton Rouge, LA 800-356-2905
Newly Weds Foods Inc
  Chicago, IL 800-621-7521
Oak Grove Smoke House Inc
  Prairieville, LA 225-673-6857
Quality Bakery Products
  Houston, TX 866-449-4977
Richmond Baking Co
  Richmond, IN 765-962-8535
Roland Machinery
  Springfield, IL 800-325-1183
Shenandoah Mills
  Lebanon, TN 615-444-0841
Southeastern Mills Inc
  Rome, GA 800-334-4468
Specialty Products
  Gloucester, MA 800-222-6846
Taste Maker Foods
  Memphis, TN 800-467-1407
Texas Crumb & Food Products
  Farmers Branch, TX 800-522-7862
Tova Industries LLC
  Louisville, KY 888-532-8682
United Supermarkets
  Lubbock, TX 806-745-9667
Wilkins Rogers Inc
  Ellicott City, MD 410-465-5800
World Flavors Inc
  Warminster, PA 215-672-4400

Doughs

American Ingredients Co
  Lenexa, KS 800-669-4092
Athens Baking Company
  Fresno, CA 800-775-2867
Athens Foods Inc
  Brookpark, OH 843-916-2000
Batory Foods
  Des Plaines, IL 847-299-1999
Bridgford Foods Corp
  Anaheim, CA 800-527-2105
Carolina Foods Inc
  Charlotte, NC 800-234-0441
Cohen's Bakery
  Ellenville, NY 845-647-2200
Creme Curls
  Hudsonville, MI 800-466-1219
D I Mfg LLC
  Omaha, NE 402-330-5650
Dimitria Delights Baking Co
  North Grafton, MA 800-763-1113
EFCO Products Inc
  Poughkeepsie, NY 800-284-3326
Fillo Factory, The
  Northvale, NJ 800-653-4556
Lentia Enterprises Ltd.
  Surrey, BC 888-768-7368
Leon's Bakery
  North Haven, CT 800-223-6844
Northwestern Foods
  Arden Hills, MN 800-236-4937
Ranaldi Bros. Frozen Food Products
  Warwick, RI 401-737-5130
Rhodes International Inc
  Salt Lake City, UT 800-876-7333
Spelt Right Foods, LLC
  Brooklyn, NY 877-773-5801
Teeny Foods Inc
  Portland, OR 503-252-3006
TNT Crust
  Green Bay, WI 920-431-7240

Baking

Bridgford Foods Corp
  Anaheim, CA 800-527-2105
Clofine Dairy Products Inc
  Linwood, NJ 609-653-1000
Creme Curls
  Hudsonville, MI 800-466-1219
Dufour Pastry Kitchens Inc
  Bronx, NY 800-439-1282
EFCO Products Inc
  Poughkeepsie, NY 800-284-3326
Northwestern Foods
  Arden Hills, MN 800-236-4937

Frozen

Callie's Charleston Biscuits
  North Charleston, SC 843-577-1198
Creme Curls
  Hudsonville, MI 800-466-1219
Dufour Pastry Kitchens Inc
  Bronx, NY 800-439-1282
Sugarplum Desserts
  Langley, BC 604-534-2282

Bread

Baker Boy Bake Shop Inc
  Dickinson, ND 800-437-2008
Country Home Bakers
  Atlanta, GA 800-241-6445
J & J Wall Bakery Co
  Sacramento, CA 916-381-1410
Lone Star Bakery
  Round Rock, TX 512-255-7268
Lora Brody Products Inc
  Waltham, MA 781-899-3910
Pacific Ocean Produce
  Santa Cruz, CA 831-423-2654
Pyrenees French Bakery
  Bakersfield, CA 888-898-7159
Rhodes International Inc
  Salt Lake City, UT 800-876-7333
Senape's Bakery Inc
  Hazleton, PA 570-454-0839
Spelt Right Foods, LLC
  Brooklyn, NY 877-773-5801

Cookie

Austin Special Foods Company
  Austin, TX 512-372-8665
Best Maid Cookie Co
  River Falls, WI 888-444-0322
Cappello's
  Denver, CO 844-353-2863
CBC Foods
  Little River, KS 800-276-4770
Coby's Cookies
  Toronto, ON 416-633-1567
David's Cookies
  Cedar Grove, NJ 800-500-2800
Edoughble
  Los Angeles, CA
Gladder's Gourmet Cookies
  Lockhart, TX 888-398-4523
JUST Inc
  San Francisco, CA 844-423-6637
Lone Star Bakery
  Round Rock, TX 512-255-7268
Michael's Cookies
  Clear Lake, IA 800-822-5384
Otis Spunkmeyer
  Brockport, NY 855-427-9982
Pacific Ocean Produce
  Santa Cruz, CA 831-423-2654
The Cookie Dough Cafe
  Bloomington, IL 309-539-4585
Touche Bakery
  London, ON 519-455-0044

Doughnuts

BakeMark Canada
  Laval, QC 800-361-4998
Baker Boy Bake Shop Inc
  Dickinson, ND 800-437-2008

Product Categories / Doughs, Mixes & Fillings: Fillings

Country Home Bakers
   Atlanta, GA 800-241-6445
EFCO Products Inc
   Poughkeepsie, NY 800-284-3326

Frozen

Annie's Frozen Yogurt
   Minneapolis, MN 800-969-9648
Austin Special Foods Company
   Austin, TX 512-372-8665
Baker Boy Bake Shop Inc
   Dickinson, ND 800-437-2008
Best Maid Cookie Co
   River Falls, WI 888-444-0322
Bridgford Foods Corp
   Anaheim, CA 800-527-2105
Carolina Foods Inc
   Charlotte, NC 800-234-0441
Coby's Cookies
   Toronto, ON 416-633-1567
Cookie Tree Bakeries
   Salt Lake City, UT 801-268-2253
Country Home Bakers
   Atlanta, GA 800-241-6445
Creme Curls
   Hudsonville, MI 800-466-1219
Dakota Brands Intl
   Jamestown, ND 800-844-5073
De Iorio's Foods Inc
   Utica, NY 800-649-7612
Dimitria Delights Baking Co
   North Grafton, MA 800-763-1113
Dough-To-Go
   Santa Clara, CA 408-727-4094
Dufour Pastry Kitchens Inc
   Bronx, NY 800-439-1282
English Bay Batter Us Inc
   Columbus, OH 800-253-6844
Enterprises Pates et Croutes
   Boucherville, QC 800-265-7790
Famous Specialties Co
   Island Park, NY 800-894-9218
Gonnella Baking Company
   Schamburg, IL 800-322-8829
Guttenplan's Frozen Dough
   Middletown, NJ 888-422-4357
Harlan Bakeries
   Avon, IN 800-435-2738
J & J Wall Bakery Co
   Sacramento, CA 916-381-1410
La Cookie
   Burbank, CA 818-495-5732
Leon's Bakery
   North Haven, CT 800-223-6844
Lone Star Bakery
   Round Rock, TX 512-255-7268
Mel-O-Cream Donuts Intl
   Springfield, IL 217-483-7272
Michael's Cookies
   Clear Lake, IA 800-822-5384
Morrison Meat Pies
   West Valley, UT 801-977-0181
Orange Bakery
   Irvine, CA 949-863-1377
Otis Spunkmeyer
   Brockport, NY 855-427-9982
Quality Naturally Foods
   City Of Industry, CA 888-498-6986
Ranaldi Bros. Frozen Food Products
   Warwick, RI 401-737-5130
Rhodes International Inc
   Salt Lake City, UT 800-876-7333
Rich Products Corp
   Buffalo, NY 800-828-2021
Sinbad Sweets
   Madera, CA 866-746-2232
Tasty Mix Quality Foods
   Brooklyn, NY 718-855-7680
TNT Crust
   Green Bay, WI 920-431-7240
Ya-Hoo Baking Co
   Sherman, TX 888-869-2466

Improvers

California Blending Co
   El Monte, CA 626-448-1918

Pizza

A Tavola Together
   Stockton, CA 209-608-5455

Baker Boy Bake Shop Inc
   Dickinson, ND 800-437-2008
BBU Bakeries
   Horsham, PA 800-984-0989
Cohen's Bakery
   Ellenville, NY 845-647-2200
De Iorio's Foods Inc
   Utica, NY 800-649-7612
French Meadow Bakery & Cafe
   Minneapolis, MN 612-870-7855
Northwestern Foods
   Arden Hills, MN 800-236-4937
Senape's Bakery Inc
   Hazleton, PA 570-454-0839
Spelt Right Foods, LLC
   Brooklyn, NY 877-773-5801
TNT Crust
   Green Bay, WI 920-431-7240
Weisenberger Mills
   Midway, KY 800-643-8678

Frozen

TNT Crust
   Green Bay, WI 920-431-7240

Puff Pastry

Dufour Pastry Kitchens Inc
   Bronx, NY 800-439-1282
Fillo Factory, The
   Northvale, NJ 800-653-4556
VLR Food Corporation
   Vaughan, ON 800-387-7437

Fillings

Abel & Schafer Inc
   Ronkonkoma, NY 800-443-1260
Bake N Joy Foods
   North Andover, MA 800-666-4937
Calico Cottage
   Amityville, NY 800-645-5345
Frank Korinek & Co
   Cicero, IL 708-652-2870
Lyons Magnus
   Fresno, CA 800-344-7130
Newport Flavours & Fragrances
   Orange, CA 714-744-3700
Pacific Westcoast Foods
   Beaverton, OR 800-874-9333
Patisserie Wawel
   Montreal, QC 614-524-3348
Puratos Canada
   Mississauga, ON 905-362-3668
Skjodt-Barrett Foods
   Brampton, ON 877-600-1200
Ya-Hoo Baking Co
   Sherman, TX 888-869-2466

Baking

Bear Stewart Corp
   Chicago, IL 800-697-2327
Century Blends LLC
   Hunt Valley, MD 410-771-6606
Clements Foods Co
   Oklahoma City, OK 800-654-8355

Cake

Abel & Schafer Inc
   Ronkonkoma, NY 800-443-1260
American Key Food Products Inc
   Closter, NJ 877-263-7539
Bear Stewart Corp
   Chicago, IL 800-697-2327
Belcolade
   Pennsauken, NJ 856-661-9123
Brookside Foods
   Abbotsford, BC 800-468-1714
California Custom Fruits
   Baldwin Park, CA 877-558-0056
Erba Food Products
   Brooklyn, NY 718-272-7700
Golden West Fruit Company
   Commerce, CA 323-726-9419
JER Creative Food Concepts, Inc.
   Commerce, CA 800-350-2462
Lawrence Foods Inc
   Elk Grove Village, IL 847-437-2400
Pacific Westcoast Foods
   Beaverton, OR 800-874-9333
Plaidberry Company
   Vista, CA 760-727-5403

Quality Naturally Foods
   City Of Industry, CA 888-498-6986
Skjodt-Barrett Foods
   Brampton, ON 877-600-1200
Solo Foods
   Countryside, IL 800-328-7656
Westco-BakeMark
   Pico Rivera, CA 562-949-1054
Ya-Hoo Baking Co
   Sherman, TX 888-869-2466

Chocolate

Erba Food Products
   Brooklyn, NY 718-272-7700

Creme

Galaxy Desserts
   Richmond, CA 800-225-3523

Dessert

Chocolate

Century Blends LLC
   Hunt Valley, MD 410-771-6606

Cream

Flavor Right Foods Group
   St Phoenix, AZ 888-464-3734

Meringue

Bear Stewart Corp
   Chicago, IL 800-697-2327

Doughnuts

BakeMark USA
   Schaumburg, IL 847-519-3135
Pamlico Packing Company
   Grantsboro, NC 800-682-1113
Skjodt-Barrett Foods
   Brampton, ON 877-600-1200

Fruit

EFCO Products Inc
   Poughkeepsie, NY 800-284-3326

Meringue

Jada Foods LLC
   Hallandale Beach, FL 855-936-3746
Sweet Whispers
   Mclean, VA 954-328-5079

Pie

Abel & Schafer Inc
   Ronkonkoma, NY 800-443-1260
American Almond Products Co
   Brooklyn, NY 800-825-6663
American Key Food Products Inc
   Closter, NJ 877-263-7539
BakeMark Canada
   Laval, QC 800-361-4998
BakeMark Ingredients Canada
   Richmond, BC 800-665-9441
Baldwin Richardson Foods
   Oakbrook Terrace, IL 866-644-2732
Bear Stewart Corp
   Chicago, IL 800-697-2327
Brookside Foods
   Abbotsford, BC 800-468-1714
California Custom Fruits
   Baldwin Park, CA 877-558-0056
Carriere Foods Inc
   Saint-Denis-Sur-Richelie, QC 450-787-3411
Clements Foods Co
   Oklahoma City, OK 800-654-8355
Country Cupboard
   Lewisburg, PA 570-523-3211
Eden Processing
   Poplar Grove, IL 815-765-2000
Erba Food Products
   Brooklyn, NY 718-272-7700
Frank Korinek & Co
   Cicero, IL 708-652-2870
Fruit Fillings Inc
   Fresno, CA 800-995-4514
Golden West Fruit Company
   Commerce, CA 323-726-9419
Grandma Hoerner's Inc
   Alma, KS 785-765-2300

Product Categories / Doughs, Mixes & Fillings: Mixes

H Cantin
  Beauport, QC 800-463-5268
Indian Bay Frozen Foods
  Centreville, NL 709-678-2844
JER Creative Food Concepts, Inc.
  Commerce, CA 800-350-2462
Knouse Foods Co-Op Inc.
  Peach Glen, PA 717-677-8181
Lawrence Foods Inc
  Elk Grove Village, IL 847-437-2400
Leahy Orchards
  Franklin Centre, QC 800-667-7380
Lynch Foods
  North York, ON 416-449-5464
Michigan Desserts
  Oak Park, MI 800-328-8632
Nation Wide Canning Ltd.
  Cottam, ON 519-839-4831
Pacific Westcoast Foods
  Beaverton, OR 800-874-9333
Pearson's Berry Farm
  Bowden, AB 403-224-3011
Pied-Mont/Dora
  Anne Des Plaines, QC 800-363-8003
Plaidberry Company
  Vista, CA 760-727-5403
Reinhart Foods
  Toronto, ON 416-645-4910
Schmidt Bros Inc
  Swanton, OH 800-200-7318
Skjodt-Barrett Foods
  Brampton, ON 877-600-1200
Steel's Gourmet Foods, Ltd.
  Bridgeport, PA 800-678-3357
Steve's Authentic Key Lime Pies
  Brooklyn, NY 888-450-5463
Valley View Blueberries
  Vancouver, WA 360-892-2839
White-Stokes Company
  Chicago, IL 800-978-6537
Ya-Hoo Baking Co
  Sherman, TX 888-869-2466

Mixes

1-2-3 Gluten Free
  Chagrin Falls, OH 216-378-9233
Bountiful Pantry
  Nantucket, MA 617-487-8019
Boyd's Coffee Co
  Portland, OR 800-735-2878
Calico Cottage
  Amityville, NY 800-645-5345
Cherryvale Farms
  310-910-1124
De Iorio's Foods Inc
  Utica, NY 800-649-7612
Gluten-Free Heaven
  Pleasant Grove, UT 801-380-6478
Golden Malted
  South Bend, IN 888-596-4040
Lehi Mills
  Lehi, UT 877-311-3566
Ontario Foods
  Guelph, ON 888-466-2372
Paradigm Foodworks Inc
  Lake Oswego, OR. 800-234-0250
Phoenix Foods
  Canton, TX 903-287-9166
Shawnee Canning Co
  Cross Junction, VA 800-713-1414
Sister's Gourmet
  Winder, GA 770-338-1388
Smart Flour Foods, LLC
  Austin, TX. 512-706-1775
VCPB Transportation
  Secaucus, NJ 201-770-0070

Baking

1-2-3 Gluten Free
  Chagrin Falls, OH 216-378-9233
Abel & Schafer Inc
  Ronkonkoma, NY 800-443-1260
Advanced Food Services
  Lenexa, KS 913-888-8088
Adventure Foods
  Whittier, NC 828-497-4113
America's Classic Foods
  Cambria, CA 805-927-0745
Annie's Frozen Yogurt
  Minneapolis, MN 800-969-9648
Arnel's Originals, Inc
  Ventura, CA. 805-322-6900
Bake N Joy Foods
  North Andover, MA 800-666-4937
BakeMark Ingredients Canada
  Richmond, BC 800-665-9441
Bear Stewart Corp
  Chicago, IL 800-697-2327
Bernard Food Industries Inc
  Evanston, IL 800-323-3663
Beth's Fine Desserts
  Mill Valley, CA 415-383-3991
Bette's Oceanview Diner
  Berkeley, CA. 510-644-3230
Big Steer
  Houston, TX 800-421-4951
Blend Pak Inc
  Bloomfield, KY 502-252-8000
Bluechip Group
  Salt Lake City, UT 800-878-0099
Bob's Red Mill Natural Foods
  Milwaukie, OR 800-349-2173
Brass Ladle Products
  Concordville, PA. 800-955-2353
Brookema Company
  West Chicago, IL 630-562-2290
Byrd Mill Co
  Ashland, VA 888-897-3336
Byrnes & Kiefer Company
  Callery, PA 724-538-5200
C W Resources Inc
  New Britain, CT 860-229-7700
Cafe Du Monde Coffee Stand
  New Orleans, LA 800-772-2927
Calhoun Bend Mill
  Libuse, LA 800-519-6455
Calico Cottage
  Amityville, NY 800-645-5345
Carol Lee Donuts
  Salina, KS 785-827-2402
Century Foods Intl LLC
  Sparta, WI 800-269-1901
Cereal Food Processors Inc
  Mcpherson, KS 800-835-2067
Chelsea Milling Co.
  Chelsea, MI 800-727-2460
Chimayo To Go / Cibolo Junction
  Albuquerque, NM 800-683-9628
Choice Food Distributors LLC
  Nashville, TN 615-350-6070
Chukar Cherries
  Prosser, WA. 800-624-9544
Cinnabar Specialty Foods Inc
  Prescott, AZ 866-293-6433
Cisse Trading Co
  Mamaroneck, NY 914-381-5555
Clabber Girl Corporation
  Terre Haute, IN 812-232-9446
CMA Global Partners/German Foods LLC
  NW Washington, DC 800-881-6419
Commodities Marketing Inc
  Clarksburg, NJ 732-516-0700
Continental Mills Inc
  Tukwila, WA 206-816-7000
Cook-In-The-Kitchen
  Hampden, ME 207-848-4900
Cotswold Cottage Foods
  Arvada, CO 800-208-1977
Country Home Creations Inc
  Flint, MI 800-457-3477
Cowboy Food & Drink
  Chagrin Falls, OH 800-759-5489
Cream Of The West
  Harlowton, MT 800-477-2383
Creation Nation
  Calabasas, CA 424-234-5800
Crown Maple Syrup
  Dover Plains, NY 845-877-0640
Crum Creek Mils
  Springfield, PA 888-607-3500
Dakota Specialty Milling, Inc.
  Fargo, ND 844-633-2746
Dawn Food Products, Inc
  Jackson, MI 800-248-1144
De Iorio's Foods Inc
  Utica, NY 800-649-7612
Dorothy Dawson Food Products
  Jackson, MI. 517-788-9830
Dowd & Rogers
  San Clemente, CA. 800-232-8619
Dr. Pete's
  Savannah, GA 912-233-3035
Drusilla Seafood
  Baton Rouge, LA 800-364-8844
EFCO Products Inc
  Poughkeepsie, NY 800-284-3326
El Peto Products
  Cambridge, ON. 800-387-4064
Ellison Milling Company
  Lethbridge, AB 403-328-6622
Embassy Flavours Ltd.
  Brampton, ON. 800-334-3371
Ener-G Foods
  Seattle, WA 800-331-5222
English Bay Batter Us Inc
  Columbus, OH 800-253-6844
Fiera Foods
  Toronto, ON 800-675-6356
Food Concentrate Corporation
  Oklahoma City, OK 405-840-5633
Foodstirs
  Santa Monica, CA 844-250-3332
Frank Korinek & Co
  Cicero, IL 708-652-2870
French Feast Inc.
  Englewood, NJ 201-731-3102
Fry Krisp Food Products
  Jackson, MI 877-854-5440
Galloway Co
  Neenah, WI 800-722-8903
Gilster-Mary Lee Corp
  Chester, IL 618-826-2361
Global Food Industries
  Townville, SC 800-225-4152
Good Food Inc
  Honey Brook, PA 800-327-4406
Grain Millers Inc
  Eden Prairie, MN 800-232-6287
Grain Process Enterprises Ltd.
  Scarborough, ON 800-387-5292
Great Grains Milling Company
  Scobey, MT 406-783-5581
Great Recipes
  Beaverton, OR 800-273-2331
Gregory's Foods, Inc.
  St Paul, MN. 800-231-4734
Gust John Foods & Products
  Batavia, IL. 800-756-5886
H Nagel & Son Co
  Cincinnati, OH 513-665-4550
HC Brill Company
  Tucker, GA 800-241-8526
Heartland Food Products
  Westwood, KS. 866-571-0222
Heidi's Gourmet Desserts
  Tucker, GA 800-241-4166
Highland Sugarworks
  Websterville, VT 800-452-4012
Hodgson Mill Inc
  Effingham, IL 800-347-0198
Hollman Foods
  Des Moines, IA 888-926-2879
Homestead Mills
  Cook, MN 800-652-5233
House-Autry Mills Inc
  Four Oaks, NC 800-849-0802
Inn Maid Food
  Lenox, MA 413-637-2732
Iveta Gourmet Inc
  Santa Cruz, CA 831-423-5149
J.M. Smucker Co.
  Orrville, OH 888-550-9555
Johnson's Food Products
  Dorchester, MA 617-265-3400
Kamish Food Products
  Chicago, IL 773-725-6959
Little Crow Foods
  Warsaw, IN 800-288-2769
Louisiana Gourmet Enterprises
  Houma, LA 800-328-5586
Lynch Foods
  North York, ON 416-449-5464
Manischewitz Co
  Newark, NJ 201-553-1100
Maple Grove Farms Of Vermont
  St Johnsbury, VT. 802-748-5141
Marie Callender's Gourmet Products/Goldrush Products
  San Jose, CA 800-729-5428
Martha Olson's Great Foo
  Sutter Creek, CA. 800-973-3966
Minnestalgia Foods LLC
  Mcgregor, MN 800-328-6731
Miss Jones Baking Co.
  Emeryville, CA

Product Categories / Doughs, Mixes & Fillings: Mixes

Modern Products Inc
  Mequon, WI 800-877-8935
Nantucket Tea Traders
  Nantucket, MA 508-325-0203
New Hope Mills Mfg Inc
  Auburn, NY 315-252-2676
No Pudge! Foods
  Wolfeboro Falls, NH 888-667-8343
Northwestern Foods
  Arden Hills, MN 800-236-4937
Old Tyme Mill Company
  Chicago, IL 773-521-9484
Paradise Island Foods
  Nanaimo, BC 800-889-3370
Pelican Bay Ltd.
  Dunedin, FL 800-826-8982
Pett Spice Products Inc
  Atlanta, GA 404-691-5235
Pillsbury
  Minneapolis, MN 800-775-4777
Puratos Canada
  Mississauga, ON 905-362-3668
Quality Naturally Foods
  City Of Industry, CA 888-498-6986
Real Cookies
  Merrick, NY 800-822-5113
Red Rose Trading Company
  Lancaster, PA 717-293-7833
Reimann Food Classics
  Palatine, IL 847-991-1366
Renwood Mills
  Newton, NC 828-464-1611
Richmond Baking Co
  Alma, GA 912-632-7213
Roland Machinery
  Springfield, IL 800-325-1183
Rose Randolph Cookies, LLC
  Wappingers Falls, NY 917-834-2310
Rothbury Farms
  Grand Rapids, MI 877-684-2879
S&N Food Company
  Mesquite, TX 972-222-1184
Sells Best
  Mishawaka, IN 800-837-8368
SFP Food Products
  Conway, AR 800-654-5329
Shenandoah Mills
  Lebanon, TN 615-444-0841
Sister's Gourmet
  Winder, GA 770-338-1388
Sofo Foods
  Toledo, OH 800-447-4211
SOUPerior Bean & Spice Company
  Vancouver, WA 800-878-7687
Southeastern Mills Inc
  Rome, GA 800-334-4468
Stevens Creative Enterprises, Inc.
  New York, NY 646-558-6336
Strossner's Bakery & Cafe
  Greenville, SC 864-233-2990
Subco Foods Inc
  Sheboygan, WI 800-473-0757
Sundial Herb Garden
  Higganum, CT 860-345-4290
Swagger Foods Corp
  Vernon Hills, IL 847-913-1200
Sweetstacks LLC
  San Diego, CA 619-997-1097
Tait Farm Foods
  Centre Hall, PA 800-787-2716
Tarazi Specialty Foods
  Chino, CA 909-628-3601
Taste Maker Foods
  Memphis, TN 800-467-1407
Taste of Gourmet
  Indianola, MS 800-833-7731
Tasty Mix Quality Foods
  Brooklyn, NY 718-855-7680
Tasty Selections
  Concord, ON 905-760-2353
Texas Crumb & Food Products
  Farmers Branch, TX 800-522-7862
The Invisible Chef
  Canton, OH 330-880-5223
The Lollipop Tree, Inc
  Auburn, NY 800-842-6691
Timber Peaks Gourmet
  Parker, CO 800-982-7687
Tova Industries LLC
  Louisville, KY 888-532-8682
Valley View Blueberries
  Vancouver, WA 360-892-2839
VIP Foods
  Flushing, NY 718-821-5330
Wanda's Nature Farm
  Lincoln, NE 800-735-6828
War Eagle Mill
  Rogers, AR 866-492-7324
Weisenberger Mills
  Midway, KY 800-643-8678
West Pac
  Idaho Falls, ID 800-973-7407
Westco-BakeMark
  Pico Rivera, CA 562-949-1054
Wilkins Rogers Inc
  Ellicott City, MD 410-465-5800
Wisconsin Wilderness Food Products
  Lake Bluff, IL 800-359-3039
World Flavors Inc
  Warminster, PA 215-672-4400
Yorktown Baking Company
  Yorktown Heights, NY 800-235-3961

Brownies

Bluechip Group
  Salt Lake City, UT 800-878-0099
Chelsea Milling Co.
  Chelsea, MI 800-727-2460
Hodgson Mill Inc
  Effingham, IL 800-347-0198
Sister's Gourmet
  Winder, GA 770-338-1388
Sisters' Gourmet
  Dacula, GA 216-292-7700

Beverage

Abunda Life
  Asbury Park, NJ 732-775-9338
Al-Rite Fruits & Syrups Co
  Miami, FL 305-652-2540
Alexander International (USA)
  Brightwaters, NY 866-965-0143
Alkinco
  New York, NY 800-424-7118
Atlantic Seasonings
  Kinston, NC 800-433-5261
Bacardi Canada, Inc.
  Toronto, ON 905-451-6100
Bainbridge Festive Foods
  Farmington, TN 800-545-9205
Baldwin Richardson Foods
  Oakbrook Terrace, IL 866-644-2732
Bartush Schnitzius Foods Co
  Lewisville, TX 972-219-1270
Bede Inc
  Haledon, NJ 866-239-6565
Best Foods
  Englewood Cliffs, NJ 201-894-4000
Blue Crab Bay
  Melfa, VA 800-221-2722
Boissons Miami Pomor
  Longueuil, QC 877-977-3744
Boyd's Coffee Co
  Portland, OR 800-735-2878
Brookema Company
  West Chicago, IL 630-562-2290
Cappuccine
  Corona, CA 800-511-3127
Carborator Rental Svc
  Philadelphia, PA 800-220-3556
Carolina Treet
  Wilmington, NC 800-616-6344
Century Blends LLC
  Hunt Valley, MD 410-771-6606
Century Foods Intl LLC
  Sparta, WI 800-269-1901
Chase Brothers Dairy
  Oxnard, CA 800-438-6455
Citrus Service
  Winter Garden, FL 407-656-4999
Consolidated Mills Inc
  Houston, TX 713-896-4196
Creative Foodworks Inc
  San Antonio, TX 210-212-4761
Dairy-Mix Inc
  St Petersburg, FL 800-955-6101
Devansoy Farms
  Carroll, IA 800-747-8605
Diamond Crystal Brands Inc
  Savannah, GA 800-654-5115
Erba Food Products
  Brooklyn, NY 718-272-7700
Fair Scones
  Medina, WA 800-588-9160
Fine Foods Intl
  St Louis, MO 314-842-4473
Finest Call
  New Albany, IN 812-944-3585
Finlays
  Lincoln, RI 800-288-6272
Flavor Systems Intl.
  Cincinnati, OH 800-498-2783
Fountain Shakes/MS Foods
  Minnetonka, MN 952-988-6940
Four Percent Company
  Highland Park, MI 313-345-5880
Franco's Cocktail Mixes
  Pompano Beach, FL 800-782-4508
Frank & Dean's Cocktail Mixes
  Pasadena, CA 626-351-4272
Genisoy
  San Francisco, CA 866-972-6879
Gilly's Hot Vanilla
  Lenox, MA 413-637-1515
Gilster-Mary Lee Corp
  Chester, IL 618-826-2361
GLCC Co
  Paw Paw, MI 269-657-3167
Great Western Juice Co
  Maple Heights, OH 800-321-9180
Green Foods Corp.
  Oxnard, CA 800-777-4430
H Fox & Co Inc
  Brooklyn, NY 718-385-4600
Hena Inc
  Brooklyn, NY 718-272-8237
Highwood Distillers
  High River, AB 403-652-3202
Instant Products of America
  Columbus, IN 812-372-9100
J. Crow Company
  New Ipswich, NH 800-878-1965
Jel Sert
  West Chicago, IL 800-323-2592
Jogue Inc
  Northville, MI 800-531-3888
Jus-Made
  Dallas, TX 800-969-3746
K & F Select Fine Coffees
  Portland, OR 800-558-7788
Kemach Food Products
  Brooklyn, NY 718-272-5655
Kittling Ridge Estate Wines & Spirits
  Vaughan, ON 800-461-9463
LA Paz Products Inc
  Brea, CA 714-990-0982
Lake City Foods
  Mississauga, ON 905-625-8244
Land O'Lakes Inc
  Arden Hills, MN 800-328-9680
Lasco Foods Inc
  St Louis, MO 314-832-1906
Lemate Of New England Inc
  Foxboro, MA 508-543-9035
Lynch Foods
  North York, ON 416-449-5464
Main Street Ingredients
  La Crosse, WI 800-359-2345
Mar-Key Foods
  Vidalia, GA 912-537-4204
Margarita Man
  San Antonio, TX 800-950-8149
Mc Steven's Coca Factory Store
  Vancouver, WA 800-547-2803
Mccullagh Coffee Roasters
  Buffalo, NY 800-753-3473
Melchers Flavors of America
  Indianapolis, IN 800-235-2867
Mele-Koi Farms
  Newport Beach, CA 949-660-9000
Mingo Bay Beverages
  Myrtle Beach, SC 843-448-5320
Minute Maid Company
  Atlanta, GA 800-520-2653
Natural Formulas
  Hayward, CA 510-372-1800
Northwestern Foods
  Arden Hills, MN 800-236-4937
Paca Foods Inc
  Tampa, FL 800-388-7419
Phillips Syrup Corp
  Cleveland, OH 800-350-8443
Pied-Mont/Dora
  Anne Des Plaines, QC 800-363-8003

Product Categories / Doughs, Mixes & Fillings: Mixes

Plainview Milk Products
  Plainview, MN 800-356-5606
PR Bar
  Chandler, AZ 800-397-5556
Pro Form Labs
  Orinda, CA 707-752-9010
Quality Instant Teas
  Morristown, NJ 888-283-8327
Quality Naturally Foods
  City Of Industry, CA 888-498-6986
Robertet Flavors
  Piscataway, NJ 732-981-8300
Roos Foods
  Kenton, DE 800-343-3642
Ruffner's
  Wayne, PA 610-687-9800
Schlotterbeck & Foss Company
  Portland, ME 800-777-4666
Sea Breeze Fruit Flavors
  Towaco, NJ 800-732-2733
Skim Delux Mendenhall Laboratories
  Paris, TN 800-642-9321
Skinny Mixes LLC
  Clearwater, FL 727-826-0306
Southern Gardens Citrus
  Clewiston, FL 863-983-3030
Sturm Foods Inc
  Manawa, WI 800-347-8876
Subco Foods Inc
  Sheboygan, WI 800-473-0757
SugarCreek
  Cincinnati, OH 800-445-2715
Swagger Foods Corp
  Vernon Hills, IL 847-913-1200
Tex-Mex Gourmet
  Brenham, TX 888-345-8467
The Peanut Butter Shop of Williamsburg
  Toano, VA 800-831-1828
Thirs-Tea Corp
  Boca Raton, FL 561-948-5600
Tova Industries LLC
  Louisville, KY 888-532-8682
Trader Vic's Food Products
  Emeryville, CA 877-762-4824
Tree Ripe Products
  Whippany, NJ 800-873-3747
Ultra Seal
  New Paltz, NY 845-255-2490
United Citrus
  Norwood, MA 800-229-7300
VIP Foods
  Flushing, NY 718-821-5330
Wayne Dairy Products Inc
  Richmond, IN 765-935-7521
Webbpak Inc
  Trussville, AL 800-655-3500
Wechsler Coffee Corporation
  Teterboro, NJ 800-800-2633
Welsh Farms
  Wallington, NJ 800-221-0663
World Flavors Inc
  Warminster, PA 215-672-4400

Frozen

Al-Rite Fruits & Syrups Co
  Miami, FL 305-652-2540
Baldwin Richardson Foods
  Oakbrook Terrace, IL 866-644-2732
J. Crow Company
  New Ipswich, NH 800-878-1965
Jogue Inc
  Northville, MI 800-531-3888

Liquid

Baldwin Richardson Foods
  Oakbrook Terrace, IL 866-644-2732
Hummingbird Kitchens
  Whitehouse, TX 800-921-9470
J. Crow Company
  New Ipswich, NH 800-878-1965
Jogue Inc
  Northville, MI 800-531-3888
Pestano Foods
  New Rochelle, NY

Biscuit

Atkinson Milling Co.
  Selma, NC 800-948-5707
Blackberry Patch
  Thomasville, GA 800-853-5598

Bob's Red Mill Natural Foods
  Milwaukie, OR 800-349-2173
Bountiful Pantry
  Nantucket, MA 617-487-8019
Byrd Mill Co
  Ashland, VA 888-897-3336
Country Cupboard
  Lewisburg, PA 570-523-3211
Father's Country Hams
  Bremen, KY 270-525-3554
House-Autry Mills Inc
  Four Oaks, NC 800-849-0802
Iveta Gourmet Inc
  Santa Cruz, CA 831-423-5149
J.M. Smucker Co.
  Orrville, OH 888-550-9555
Mennel Milling Company
  Fostoria, OH 800-688-8151
Weisenberger Mills
  Midway, KY 800-643-8678

Bread

Abel & Schafer Inc
  Ronkonkoma, NY 800-443-1260
Aunt Millie's Bakeries
  Fort Wayne, IN 855-755-2253
BakeMark USA
  Schaumburg, IL 847-519-3135
Bob's Red Mill Natural Foods
  Milwaukie, OR 800-349-2173
Bountiful Pantry
  Nantucket, MA 617-487-8019
Byrd Mill Co
  Ashland, VA 888-897-3336
Chester's International, LLC
  Mountain Brook, AL 800-288-1555
Chimayo To Go / Cibolo Junction
  Albuquerque, NM 800-683-9628
Cotswold Cottage Foods
  Arvada, CO 800-208-1977
Drusilla Seafood
  Baton Rouge, LA 800-364-8844
Grain Process Enterprises Ltd.
  Scarborough, ON 800-387-5292
Hollman Foods
  Des Moines, IA 888-926-2879
Kokopelli's Kitchen
  Phoenix, AZ 888-943-9802
Lehi Mills
  Lehi, UT 877-311-3566
Lentia Enterprises Ltd.
  Surrey, BC 888-768-7368
Leonard Mountain Inc
  Bixby, OK 800-822-7700
Marie Callender's
  Mission Viejo, CA 800-776-7437
Old Tyme Mill Company
  Chicago, IL 773-521-9484
Pamela's Products
  Ukiah, CA 707-462-6605
Pett Spice Products Inc
  Atlanta, GA 404-691-5235
Phoenix Foods
  Canton, TX 903-287-9166
Puratos Canada
  Mississauga, ON 905-362-3668
Rabbit Creek
  Louisburg, KS 800-837-3073
Rill Specialty Foods
  Thorp, WA 509-964-2520
Sambets Cajun Deli
  Austin, TX 800-472-6238
Sassafras Enterprises Inc
  Chicago, IL 800-537-4941
Sells Best
  Mishawaka, IN 800-837-8368
Smart Flour Foods, LLC
  Austin, TX 512-706-1775
SOUPerior Bean & Spice Company
  Vancouver, WA 800-878-7687
Southeastern Mills Inc
  Rome, GA 800-334-4468
Strossner's Bakery & Cafe
  Greenville, SC 864-233-2990
The Lollipop Tree, Inc
  Auburn, NY 800-842-6691
Timber Peaks Gourmet
  Parker, CO 800-982-7687
Valley View Blueberries
  Vancouver, WA 360-892-2839

Low Carb

Dixie USA
  Tomball, TX 800-233-3668

Breading

Blend Pak Inc
  Bloomfield, KY 502-252-8000
Chef Hans' Gourmet Foods
  Monroe, LA 800-890-4267
Dorothy Dawson Food Products
  Jackson, MI 517-788-9830
Griffith Foods Inc.
  Alsip, IL 708-371-0900
Newly Weds Foods Inc
  Chicago, IL 800-621-7521
Roland Machinery
  Springfield, IL 800-325-1183
Specialty Products
  Gloucester, MA 800-222-6846
Texas Crumb & Food Products
  Farmers Branch, TX 800-522-7862

Brownie

BakeMark USA
  Schaumburg, IL 847-519-3135
Cherryvale Farms
  310-910-1124
Country Cupboard
  Lewisburg, PA 570-523-3211
Dawn Food Products, Inc
  Jackson, MI 800-248-1144
Lehi Mills
  Lehi, UT 877-311-3566
No Pudge! Foods
  Wolfeboro Falls, NH 888-667-8343
Pamela's Products
  Ukiah, CA 707-462-6605
Rabbit Creek
  Louisburg, KS 800-837-3073
Touche Bakery
  London, ON 519-455-0044

Cake

Abel & Schafer Inc
  Ronkonkoma, NY 800-443-1260
Atkinson Milling Co.
  Selma, NC 800-948-5707
BakeMark Ingredients Canada
  Richmond, BC 800-665-9441
BakeMark USA
  Schaumburg, IL 847-519-3135
Bear Stewart Corp
  Chicago, IL 800-697-2327
Beth's Fine Desserts
  Mill Valley, CA 415-383-3991
Brass Ladle Products
  Concordville, PA 800-955-2353
Brookema Company
  West Chicago, IL 630-562-2290
Butternut Mountain Farm
  Morrisville, VT 800-828-2376
Byrd Mill Co
  Ashland, VA 888-897-3336
Byrnes & Kiefer Company
  Callery, PA 724-538-5200
Chelsea Milling Co.
  Chelsea, MI 800-727-2460
Country Cupboard
  Lewisburg, PA 570-523-3211
Dawn Food Products, Inc
  Jackson, MI 800-248-1144
Dr. Oetker Canada Ltd.
  Mississauga, ON 800-387-6939
Embassy Flavours Ltd.
  Brampton, ON 800-334-3371
Good Food Inc
  Honey Brook, PA 800-327-4406
Halladay's Harvest Barn
  Bellows Falls, VT 802-463-3471
Kiki's Gluten-Free
  Park Ridge, IL
Kingly Heirs
  Elkhart, IN 574-596-3763
Kodiak Cakes
  Park City, UT 801-328-4067
Little Crow Foods
  Warsaw, IN 800-288-2769
Louisiana Gourmet Enterprises
  Houma, LA 800-328-5586

Product Categories / Doughs, Mixes & Fillings: Mixes

Martha Olson's Great Foo
   Sutter Creek, CA 800-973-3966
Meadowvale Inc
   Yorkville, IL 800-953-0201
Northwestern Foods
   Arden Hills, MN 800-236-4937
Pillsbury
   Minneapolis, MN 800-775-4777
Quality Naturally Foods
   City Of Industry, CA 888-498-6986
Royal Resources
   New Orleans, LA 800-888-9932
Sells Best
   Mishawaka, IN 800-837-8368
Sundial Herb Garden
   Higganum, CT. 860-345-4290
Tasty Selections
   Concord, ON. 905-760-2353
Tova Industries LLC
   Louisville, KY 888-532-8682
VIP Foods
   Flushing, NY. 718-821-5330
Wanda's Nature Farm
   Lincoln, NE. 800-735-6828
West Pac
   Idaho Falls, ID 800-973-7407

Cappuccino

Mc Steven's Coca Factory Store
   Vancouver, WA 800-547-2803
Mont Blanc Gourmet
   Denver, CO 800-877-3811
Utah Coffee Roasters
   South Salt Lake, UT 888-486-3334

Chili

Chili Dude
   Dallas, TX. 214-354-9906
Fernandez Chili Co
   Alamosa, CO. 719-589-6043
Monterrey Products
   San Antonio, TX. 210-435-2872
Red Lion Spicy Foods Company
   Red Lion, PA. 717-309-8303
Texas Heat
   San Antonio, TX. 800-656-5916
Tova Industries LLC
   Louisville, KY 888-532-8682
Westfield Foods
   Greenville, RI 401-949-3558

Cocktail

Al-Rite Fruits & Syrups Co
   Miami, FL. 305-652-2540
Bacardi USA Inc
   Coral Gables, FL. 800-222-2734
Demitri's Bloody Mary Seasonings
   Seattle, WA 800-627-9649
Franco's Cocktail Mixes
   Pompano Beach, FL 800-782-4508
Frank & Dean's Cocktail Mixes
   Pasadena, CA 626-351-4272
Great Western Juice Co
   Maple Heights, OH 800-321-9180
Island Aseptics
   Byesville, OH 740-685-2548
LA Paz Products Inc
   Brea, CA 714-990-0982
Lemon-X Corporation
   Huntington Station, NY 800-220-1061
Leonard Fountain Specialties
   Detroit, MI 313-891-4141
Main Squeeze
   Columbia, MO 573-817-5616
Natural Fruit Corp
   Hialeah, FL. 305-887-7525
Ruffner's
   Wayne, PA. 610-687-9800
Skinny Mixes LLC
   Clearwater, FL. 727-826-0306
Tree Ripe Products
   Whippany, NJ 800-873-3747
Wagner Excello Food Products
   Broadview, IL 708-338-4488

Cookie

BakeMark USA
   Schaumburg, IL. 847-519-3135
Big Dipper Dough Co.
   Traverse City, MI 231-883-6035

Cherryvale Farms
   310-910-1124
FatBoy's Cookie Company
   Fair Lawn, NJ 888-328-2690
FlapJacked
   Westminster, CO 720-476-4758
Jimmys Cookies
   Clifton, NJ 973-779-8500
Lehi Mills
   Lehi, UT 877-311-3566
Zemas Madhouse Foods Inc.
   Highland Park, IL 847-910-4512

Dessert

Abel & Schafer Inc
   Ronkonkoma, NY. 800-443-1260
All American Seasonings
   Denver, CO 303-623-2320
American Key Food Products Inc
   Closter, NJ. 877-263-7539
Baird Dairy LLC
   Clarksville, IN. 812-283-3345
Bear Stewart Corp
   Chicago, IL 800-697-2327
Blend Pak Inc
   Bloomfield, KY 502-252-8000
Brass Ladle Products
   Concordville, PA. 800-955-2353
Byrd Mill Co
   Ashland, VA 888-897-3336
Byrnes & Kiefer Company
   Callery, PA 724-538-5200
Calico Cottage
   Amityville, NY 800-645-5345
California Custom Fruits
   Baldwin Park, CA. 877-558-0056
Carolina Foods Inc
   Charlotte, NC 800-234-0441
Century Blends LLC
   Hunt Valley, MD. 410-771-6606
Chelsea Milling Co.
   Chelsea, MI. 800-727-2460
Clofine Dairy Products Inc
   Linwood, NJ 609-653-1000
Creme Curls
   Hudsonville, MI 800-466-1219
Dairy-Mix Inc
   St Petersburg, FL 800-955-6101
Dutch Ann Foods Company
   Natchez, MS 601-445-5566
Embassy Flavours Ltd.
   Brampton, ON. 800-334-3371
Famous Specialties Co
   Island Park, NY 800-894-9218
First Food Co
   Dallas, TX. 800-527-1866
Galliker Dairy Co
   Johnstown, PA. 800-477-6455
Galloway Co
   Neenah, WI 800-722-8903
Golden Fluff Popcorn Co
   Lakewood, NJ 732-367-5448
Great Recipes
   Beaverton, OR 800-273-2331
Gumpert's Canada
   Mississauga, ON 800-387-9324
Heidi's Gourmet Desserts
   Tucker, GA 800-241-4166
Kent Precision Foods Group Inc
   Muscatine, IA 800-442-5242
Kosto Food Products Co
   Wauconda, IL 847-487-2600
Limpert Bros Inc
   Vineland, NJ 800-691-1353
Lloyd's
   Exton, PA 610-647-3144
Louisiana Gourmet Enterprises
   Houma, LA 800-328-5586
Lynch Foods
   North York, ON. 416-449-5464
Maple Island
   Saint Paul, MN 800-369-1022
Master Mix
   Placentia, CA 714-524-1698
Meadowvale Inc
   Yorkville, IL 800-953-0201
Mennel Milling Company
   Fostoria, OH 800-688-8151
Michigan Desserts
   Oak Park, MI. 800-328-8632
Nanci's Frozen Yogurt
   Mesa, AZ. 800-788-0808

Natrel
   St. Laurent, QC 800-501-1150
Nature's Hand Inc
Nog Incorporated
   Dunkirk, NY. 800-332-2664
Northwestern Foods
   Arden Hills, MN. 800-236-4937
Pasta Factory
   Melrose Park, IL 800-615-6951
Paulaur Corp
   Cranbury, NJ 609-395-8844
Quality Naturally Foods
   City Of Industry, CA 888-498-6986
Rio Syrup Co
   St Louis, MO. 800-325-7666
S&N Food Company
   Mesquite, TX 972-222-1184
Schneider's Dairy Inc
   Pittsburgh, PA. 412-881-3525
Sells Best
   Mishawaka, IN 800-837-8368
Serv-Agen Corporation
   Cherry Hill, NJ 856-663-6966
Sno Shack Inc
   Rexburg, ID. 888-766-7425
Specialty Bakers
   Marysville, PA 800-233-0778
SugarCreek
   Cincinnati, OH 800-445-2715
Swagger Foods Corp
   Vernon Hills, IL 847-913-1200
Timber Peaks Gourmet
   Parker, CO. 800-982-7687
Tova Industries LLC
   Louisville, KY 888-532-8682
Tropical Illusions
   Trenton, MO 660-359-5422
VIP Foods
   Flushing, NY. 718-821-5330
Welch Foods Inc.
   Concord, MA 800-340-6870
Wisconsin Wilderness Food Products
   Lake Bluff, IL 800-359-3039

Low Carb

Dixie USA
   Tomball, TX 800-233-3668

Dip

Advanced Food Products LLC
   New Holland, PA 800-732-5373
Amberland Foods
   Harvey, ND. 800-950-4558
Au Printemps Gourmet
   Saint-Jerome, QC 800-438-6676
Big Steer
   Houston, TX 800-421-4951
C W Resources Inc
   New Britain, CT 860-229-7700
Chugwater Chili
   Chugwater, WY 800-972-4454
Country Home Creations Inc
   Flint, MI 800-457-3477
Erba Food Products
   Brooklyn, NY 718-272-7700
Fountain Valley Foods
   Colorado Springs, CO 719-573-6012
Heluva Good Cheese
   Lynnfield, MA 800-644-5473
Hollman Foods
   Des Moines, IA 888-926-2879
Jodie's Kitchen
   Pinellas Park, FL. 800-728-3704
Just Delicious Gourmet Foods
   Seal Beach, CA 800-871-6085
Lesley Elizabeth Inc
   Lapeer, MI. 800-684-3300
Limited Edition
   Midland, TX 432-686-2008
Olde Tyme Food Corporation
   East Longmeadow, MA 800-356-6533
Rabbit Creek
   Louisburg, KS. 800-837-3073
Spice Hunter Inc
   Richmond, VA. 800-444-3061
Swagger Foods Corp
   Vernon Hills, IL 847-913-1200
The Pantry Club
   Clearwater, FL. 877-335-8842

Product Categories / Doughs, Mixes & Fillings: Mixes

Donut
BakeMark USA
  Schaumburg, IL 847-519-3135

Drink
American Instants Inc
  Flanders, NJ 973-584-8811
Bread & Chocolate Inc
  Wells River, VT 800-524-6715
Desert Pepper Trading Co
  El Paso, TX 888-472-5727
Frontera Foods
  Chicago, IL 800-509-4441
Granny Blossom Specialty Foods
  Wells, VT 802-645-0507
Leonard Mountain Inc
  Bixby, OK 800-822-7700
Nature's Hand Inc

Dumplings
Tova Industries LLC
  Louisville, KY 888-532-8682

Frozen
Bama Frozen Dough
  Tulsa, OK 800-756-2262
Best Foods
  Englewood Cliffs, NJ 201-894-4000
Pro Form Labs
  Orinda, CA 707-752-9010

Granita
Nanci's Frozen Yogurt
  Mesa, AZ 800-788-0808

Gravy
Dorothy Dawson Food Products
  Jackson, MI 517-788-9830
Griffith Foods Inc.
  Alsip, IL 708-371-0900
Lawry's Foods
  Hunt Valley, MD 800-952-9797
Morgan Foods Inc
  Austin, IN 888-430-1780
R C Fine Foods Inc
  Hillsborough, NJ 800-526-3953

Hot Chocolate
Mrs. Field's Hot Cocoas
  Farmington, UT 800-845-2400
Utah Coffee Roasters
  South Salt Lake, UT 888-486-3334

Ice Cream
Agri-Dairy Products
  Purchase, NY 914-697-9580
Al-Rite Fruits & Syrups Co
  Miami, FL 305-652-2540
America's Classic Foods
  Cambria, CA 805-927-0745
Baird Dairy LLC
  Clarksville, IN 812-283-3345
Blue Bell Creameries LP
  Brenham, TX 800-327-8135
Clofine Dairy Products Inc
  Linwood, NJ 609-653-1000
Cumberland Dairy
  Rosenhayn, NJ 800-257-8484
Dairy-Mix Inc
  St Petersburg, FL 800-955-6101
Galliker Dairy Co
  Johnstown, PA 800-477-6455
Kosto Food Products Co
  Wauconda, IL 847-487-2600
Leiby's Premium Ice Cream
  Tamaqua, PA 877-453-4297
Master Mix
  Placentia, CA 714-524-1698
Natrel
  St. Laurent, QC 800-501-1150
Nog Incorporated
  Dunkirk, NY 800-332-2664
Quality Naturally Foods
  City Of Industry, CA 888-498-6986
Queensboro Farm Products
  Canastota, NY 315-687-6133
Queensboro Farm Products
  Jamica, NY 718-658-5000

Reiter Dairy LLC
  Springfield, OH 937-323-5777
Schneider's Dairy Inc
  Pittsburgh, PA 412-881-3525
Titusville Dairy Products Co
  Titusville, PA 800-352-0101
Tova Industries LLC
  Louisville, KY 888-532-8682
Vitarich Ice Cream
  Fortuna, CA 707-725-6182

Jambalaya
Reggie Balls Cajun Foods
  Lake Charles, LA 337-436-0291

Liquid
Best Foods
  Englewood Cliffs, NJ 201-894-4000
National Fruit Flavor Co Inc
  New Orleans, LA 800-966-1123
Pro Form Labs
  Orinda, CA 707-752-9010

Muffin
Abel & Schafer Inc
  Ronkonkoma, NY 800-443-1260
Atkinson Milling Co.
  Selma, NC 800-948-5707
Aunt Millie's Bakeries
  Fort Wayne, IN 855-755-2253
Bake N Joy Foods
  North Andover, MA 800-666-4937
Dr. Oetker Canada Ltd.
  Mississauga, ON 800-387-6939
EFCO Products Inc
  Poughkeepsie, NY 800-284-3326
Fiera Foods
  Toronto, ON 800-675-6356
FlapJacked
  Westminster, CO 720-476-4758
Food Concentrate Corporation
  Oklahoma City, OK 405-840-5633
Grain Process Enterprises Ltd.
  Scarborough, ON 800-387-5292
Gust John Foods & Products
  Batavia, IL 800-756-5886
Hodgson Mill Inc
  Effingham, IL 800-347-0198
Iveta Gourmet Inc
  Santa Cruz, CA 831-423-5149
J.M. Smucker Co.
  Orrville, OH 888-550-9555
Kodiak Cakes
  Park City, UT 801-328-4067
Kokopelli's Kitchen
  Phoenix, AZ 888-943-9802
Marie Callender's
  Mission Viejo, CA 800-776-7437
Mennel Milling Company
  Fostoria, OH 800-688-8151
Pemberton's Foods Inc
  Gray, ME 800-255-8401
Rill Specialty Foods
  Thorp, WA 509-964-2520
Sells Best
  Mishawaka, IN 800-837-8368
Shepherdsfield Bakery
  Fulton, MO 573-642-0009
Sorrenti Family Farms
  Escalon, CA 888-435-9490

Pancake
Atkinson Milling Co.
  Selma, NC 800-948-5707
Bette's Oceanview Diner
  Berkeley, CA 510-644-3230
Birch Benders
  Denver, CO 855-572-6225
Blackberry Patch
  Thomasville, GA 800-853-5598
Bob's Red Mill Natural Foods
  Milwaukie, OR 800-349-2173
Byrd Mill Co
  Ashland, VA 888-897-3336
Casually Gourmet
  New Haven, VT 800-639-7604
Cereal Food Processors Inc
  Mcpherson, KS 800-835-2067
CHS Sunprairie
  Minot, ND 800-556-6807

Country Cupboard
  Lewisburg, PA 570-523-3211
Cream Of The West
  Harlowton, MT 800-477-2383
D & D Sugarwoods Farm
  Glover, VT 800-245-3718
FlapJacked
  Westminster, CO 720-476-4758
Golden Malted
  South Bend, IN 888-596-4040
Greenfield Mills
  North Howe, IN 260-367-2394
Gust John Foods & Products
  Batavia, IL 800-756-5886
Heartland Food Products
  Westwood, KS 866-571-0222
Highland Sugarworks
  Websterville, VT 800-452-4012
Hodgson Mill Inc
  Effingham, IL 800-347-0198
Homestead Mills
  Cook, MN 800-652-5233
Inn Maid Food
  Lenox, MA 413-637-2732
J.M. Smucker Co.
  Orrville, OH 888-550-9555
Kamish Food Products
  Chicago, IL 773-725-6959
Kodiak Cakes
  Park City, UT 801-328-4067
Kokopelli's Kitchen
  Phoenix, AZ 888-943-9802
Lehi Mills
  Lehi, UT 877-311-3566
Little Crow Foods
  Warsaw, IN 800-288-2769
Maple Grove Farms Of Vermont
  St Johnsbury, VT 802-748-5141
Mennel Milling Company
  Fostoria, OH 800-688-8151
Minnestalgia Foods LLC
  Mcgregor, MN 800-328-6731
Nature's Path Foods
  Blaine, WA 888-808-9505
North Coast Farms
  Santa Cruz, CA 831-426-3733
Northwestern Foods
  Arden Hills, MN 800-236-4937
Old Tyme Mill Company
  Chicago, IL 773-521-9484
Pemberton's Foods Inc
  Gray, ME 800-255-8401
Reimann Food Classics
  Palatine, IL 847-991-1366
SFP Food Products
  Conway, AR 800-654-5329
Smart Flour Foods, LLC
  Austin, TX 512-706-1775
Sweetstacks LLC
  San Diego, CA 619-997-1097
Tait Farm Foods
  Centre Hall, PA 800-787-2716
Turkey Hill Sugarbush
  Waterloo, QC 450-539-4822
Valley View Blueberries
  Vancouver, WA 360-892-2839
Weisenberger Mills
  Midway, KY 800-643-8678

Pie Crust
Country Cupboard
  Lewisburg, PA 570-523-3211
Smart Flour Foods, LLC
  Austin, TX 512-706-1775

Powdered
1-2-3 Gluten Free
  Chagrin Falls, OH 216-378-9233
Crystal Star Herbal Nutrition
  Salinas, CA 831-422-7500
Northwestern Foods
  Arden Hills, MN 800-236-4937
Pro Form Labs
  Orinda, CA 707-752-9010

Punch
Four Percent Company
  Highland Park, MI 313-345-5880
Quality Naturally Foods
  City Of Industry, CA 888-498-6986

Product Categories / Doughs, Mixes & Fillings: Mixes

Tova Industries LLC
   Louisville, KY 888-532-8682

Rice
Manischewitz Co
   Newark, NJ 201-553-1100

Shoofly
Good Food Inc
   Honey Brook, PA 800-327-4406

Smoothie Powder
Farmers Way
Monin Inc.
   Clearwater, FL 855-352-8671
Nanci's Frozen Yogurt
   Mesa, AZ 800-788-0808

Soup
Amalgamated Produce
   Bridgeport, CT 800-358-3808
Amberland Foods
   Harvey, ND 800-950-4558
Bernard Food Industries Inc
   Evanston, IL 800-323-3663
Best Foods
   Englewood Cliffs, NJ 201-894-4000
Bob's Red Mill Natural Foods
   Milwaukie, OR 800-349-2173
Boston Spice & Tea Company
   Boston, VA 800-966-4372
Bountiful Pantry
   Nantucket, MA 617-487-8019
Brookema Company
   West Chicago, IL 630-562-2290
Campbell Soup Co.
   Camden, NJ 800-257-8443
Commodities Marketing Inc
   Clarksburg, NJ 732-516-0700
Cook-In-The-Kitchen
   Hampden, ME 207-848-4900
Country Home Creations Inc
   Flint, MI 800-457-3477
Crazy Jerrys Inc Kahuna-Sauces
   Woodstock, GA 800-347-2823
Diamond Crystal Brands Inc
   Savannah, GA 800-654-5115
Dismat Corporation
   Toledo, OH 419-531-8963
Dorothy Dawson Food Products
   Jackson, MI 517-788-9830
Edward & Sons Trading Co
   Carpinteria, CA 805-684-8500
Fair Scones
   Medina, WA 800-588-9160
Flavor House, Inc.
   Adelanto, CA 760-246-9131
Halladay's Harvest Barn
   Bellows Falls, VT 802-463-3471
High Country Gourmet
   Orem, UT 801-426-4383
Hummingbird Kitchens
   Whitehouse, TX 800-921-9470
Idaho Pacific Holdings Inc
   Rigby, ID 800-238-5503
Kemach Food Products
   Brooklyn, NY 718-272-5655
Kent Precision Foods Group Inc
   Muscatine, IA 800-442-5242

Lake City Foods
   Mississauga, ON 905-625-8244
Lynch Foods
   North York, ON 416-449-5464
Magic Seasoning Blends
   New Orleans, LA 800-457-2857
Nor-Cliff Farms
   Port Colborne, ON 905-835-0808
North Bay Trading Co
   Brule, WI. 800-348-0164
R C Fine Foods Inc
   Hillsborough, NJ 800-526-3953
Rabbit Creek
   Louisburg, KS 800-837-3073
Rill Specialty Foods
   Thorp, WA 509-964-2520
Sheila's Select Gourmet Recipe
   Heber City, UT 800-516-7286
Sorrenti Family Farms
   Escalon, CA 888-435-9490
Spice Hunter Inc
   Richmond, VA. 800-444-3061
Swagger Foods Corp
   Vernon Hills, IL 847-913-1200
Tova Industries LLC
   Louisville, KY 888-532-8682
Tropical Nut Fruit & Bulk Cndy
   Lithia Springs, GA 800-544-3762
Vogue Cuisine Foods
   Sunnyvale, CA 888-236-4144
Westfield Foods
   Greenville, RI 401-949-3558
White Coffee Corporation
   Long Island City, NY 800-221-0140

Trail
Aurora Products
   Orange, CT 800-398-1048
Bazzini Holdings LLC
   Allentown, PA 610-366-1606
Chukar Cherries
   Prosser, WA 800-624-9544
Dave's Gourmet
   San Rafael, CA 800-758-0372
Durey-Libby Edible Nuts
   Carlstadt, NJ 800-332-6887
Hialeah Products Co
   Hollywood, FL 800-923-3379
Inn Maid Food
   Lenox, MA 413-637-2732
Jason & Son Specialty Foods
   Rancho Cordova, CA 800-810-9093
King Nut Co
   Solon, OH 800-860-5464
Marantha Natural Foods
   San Francisco, CA 866-972-6879
Midwest Nut Co
   Minneapolis, MN 800-328-5502
Nature Kist Snacks
   Commerce, CA 323-278-9578
New England Natural Bakers
   Greenfield, MA 800-910-2884
Nspired Natural Foods
   Boulder, CO 800-434-4246
Nut Factory
   Spokane Valley, WA 888-239-5288
Sonne
   Wahpeton, ND. 800-727-6663
Sunridge Farms
   Royal Oaks, CA 831-786-7000

Superior Nut & Candy
   Chicago, IL 800-843-2238
Timber Peaks Gourmet
   Parker, CO 800-982-7687
Tova Industries LLC
   Louisville, KY 888-532-8682
Tropical Foods
   Charlotte, NC 800-438-4470
Valley View Blueberries
   Vancouver, WA 360-892-2839
Waymouth Farms Inc
   Minneapolis, MN 800-527-0094
Weaver Nut Co. Inc.
   Ephrata, PA 800-473-2688
Wysong Corp
   Midland, MI 800-748-0188

Waffle
Bountiful Pantry
   Nantucket, MA 617-487-8019
Byrd Mill Co
   Ashland, VA 888-897-3336
Cereal Food Processors Inc
   Mcpherson, KS 800-835-2067
Country Cupboard
   Lewisburg, PA 570-523-3211
Cream Of The West
   Harlowton, MT 800-477-2383
Eat My Waffles
   Cardiff By The Sea, CA
Golden Malted
   South Bend, IN 888-596-4040
Great Grains Milling Company
   Scobey, MT 406-783-5581
Gust John Foods & Products
   Batavia, IL 800-756-5886
Heartland Food Products
   Westwood, KS 866-571-0222
Inn Maid Food
   Lenox, MA 413-637-2732
J.M. Smucker Co.
   Orrville, OH 888-550-9555
Kamish Food Products
   Chicago, IL 773-725-6959
Kodiak Cakes
   Park City, UT 801-328-4067
Maple Grove Farms Of Vermont
   St Johnsbury, VT 802-748-5141
Mennel Milling Company
   Fostoria, OH 800-688-8151
North Coast Farms
   Santa Cruz, CA 831-426-3733
Old Tyme Mill Company
   Chicago, IL 773-521-9484
Reimann Food Classics
   Palatine, IL 847-991-1366
SFP Food Products
   Conway, AR 800-654-5329
Smart Flour Foods, LLC
   Austin, TX 512-706-1775
WaffleWaffle
   Nutley, NJ 201-559-1286

Yogurt Powder
Kantner Group
   Wapakoneta, OH 877-738-3448

Eggs & Egg Products

General

Almark Foods
  Gainesville, GA 800-849-3447
Alta Dena Certified Dairy LLC
  City Of Industry, CA. 800-535-1369
Bartolini Ice Cream
  Bronx, NY. 718-589-5151
Brookshire Grocery Company
  Tyler, TX. 888-937-3776
Brown Produce Company
  Farina, IL. 618-245-3301
Burn Brae Farms
  Mississauga, ON. 905-624-3600
Cal-Maine Foods Inc.
  Jackson, MS. 601-948-6813
Cargill Kitchen Solutions Inc.
  Wayzata, MN. 833-535-5205
Cordon Bleu International
  Anjou, QC. 800-363-1182
Creighton Brothers
  Warsaw, IN. 574-267-3101
Crystal Lake LLC
  Warsaw, IN. 574-858-2514
Davidson's Safest Choice Eggs
  Lansing, IL. 800-410-7619
Debel Food Products
  Elizabeth, NJ. 800-421-3447
Dutch Farms Inc
  Chicago, IL. 800-637-3447
Eggland's Best Eggs
  Malvern, PA. 800-922-3447
Farbest-Tallman Foods Corp
  Montvale, NJ. 201-573-4900
Golden Valley Foods Ltd.
  Abbotsford, BC. 888-299-8855
Henningsen Foods Inc
  Omaha, NE 800-228-2769
Hidden Villa Ranch
  Fullerton, CA. 800-326-3220
Hillandale
  Lake City, FL. 386-397-1300
Hormel Foods Corp.
  Austin, MN. 507-437-5611
Ingles Markets
  Black Mountain, NC. 828-669-2941
J M Swank Co
  North Liberty, IA. 800-593-6375
Kreher Family Farms
  Clarence, NY. 716-759-6802
Lubbers Family Farm
  Grand Rapids, MI. 616-453-4257
Meijer Inc
  Grand Rapids, MI. 616-453-6711
MFI Food Canada
  Winnipeg, MB. 204-992-8200
National Food Corporation
  Everett, WA. 425-349-4257
NestFresh
  Denver, CO. 877-241-8385
Nulaid Foods Inc
  Ripon, CA. 209-599-2121
Oliver Egg Products
  Crewe, VA. 800-525-3447
Publix Super Market
  Lakeland, FL. 800-242-1227
Rembrandt Foods
  Spirit Lake, IA. 877-344-4055
Rose Acre Farms
  Wolcott, IN. 765-258-4015
Rosenberger's Dairies
  Hatfield, PA. 800-355-9074
Sauder's Eggs
  Lititz, PA. 800-233-0413
Smith Packing Regional Meat
  Utica, NY. 315-732-5125
T. Marzetti Company
  Westerville, OH. 800-999-1835
Turner Dairy Farms Inc
  Pittsburgh, PA. 800-892-1039
Vital Farms
  Austin, TX. 877-455-3063
Wegmans Food Markets Inc.
  Rochester, NY. 800-934-6267
WEIS Markets Inc.
  Sunbury, PA. 866-999-9347
Wenk Foods Inc
  Madison, SD. 605-256-4569
WhiteWave Foods
  Denver, CO. 800-488-9283
Wilcox Farms
  Roy, WA. 360-458-7774
Winn-Dixie Stores
  Jacksonville, FL. 800-967-9105
Yoder Dairies
  Chesapeake, VA. 757-482-4068

Boiled

Agri-Dairy Products
  Purchase, NY 914-697-9580

Cooked

Cargill Kitchen Solutions Inc.
  Wayzata, MN 833-535-5205
Crystal Lake LLC
  Warsaw, IN. 574-858-2514
Egg Low Farms
  Sherburne, NY. 607-674-4653

Dehydrated

Ballas Egg Products Corp
  Zanesville, OH. 740-453-0386
Oskaloosa Food Products
  Oskaloosa, IA. 800-477-7239

Dried

Ballas Egg Products Corp
  Zanesville, OH. 740-453-0386
Century Blends LLC
  Hunt Valley, MD. 410-771-6606
Double B Foods Inc
  Arlington, TX. 800-679-0349
Henningsen Foods Inc
  Omaha, NE. 800-228-2769
Kelly Flour Company
  Addison, IL. 630-678-5300
King Arthur Flour
  Norwich, VT. 800-827-6836
MFI Food Canada
  Winnipeg, MB. 204-992-8200
Oskaloosa Food Products
  Oskaloosa, IA. 800-477-7239
Wenk Foods Inc
  Madison, SD. 605-256-4569

Desiccated

Agri-Dairy Products
  Purchase, NY. 914-697-9580
Clofine Dairy Products Inc
  Linwood, NJ. 609-653-1000
New Organics
  Kenwood, CA. 734-677-5570

Fat & Cholesterol Free

Cargill Kitchen Solutions Inc.
  Wayzata, MN. 833-535-5205
Hormel Foods Corp.
  Austin, MN. 507-437-5611
Tofutti Brands Inc
  Cranford, NJ. 908-272-2400

Fresh

Agri-Dairy Products
  Purchase, NY. 914-697-9580
Broughton Foods LLC
  El Paso, TX. 800-395-7004
Byrne Dairy, Inc.
  Syracuse, NY. 800-899-1535
Creighton Brothers
  Warsaw, IN. 574-267-3101
Davidson's Safest Choice Eggs
  Lansing, IL. 800-410-7619
Dixie Egg Co
  Jacksonville, FL. 800-394-3447
Egg Innovations
  Warsaw, IN. 800-337-1951
Egg Low Farms
  Sherburne, NY. 607-674-4653
Feature Foods
  Brampton, ON. 905-452-7741
Golden Valley Foods Ltd.
  Abbotsford, BC. 888-299-8855
Great Valley Mills
  Barto, PA. 800-688-6455
Happy Egg Dealers
  Tampa, FL. 813-248-2362
Horizon Organic Dairy
  Broomfield, CO. 888-494-3020
Ise America Inc
  Galena, MD. 410-755-6300
Mountainside Farms Inc
  Roxbury, NY. 607-326-4161
National Food Corporation
  Everett, WA. 425-349-4257
Oskaloosa Food Products
  Oskaloosa, IA. 800-477-7239
Pete and Gerry's Organic Eggs
  Monroe, NH. 800-210-6657
Radlo Foods
  Watertown, MA. 800-370-1439
Rose Acre Farms Inc
  Seymour, IN. 800-356-3447
Schepps Dairy
  Dallas, TX. 800-395-7004
Siegel Egg Co
  North Billerica, MA. 978-528-2010
Sommer Maid Creamery Inc
  Pipersville, PA. 215-345-6160
Sparboe Foods Corp
  New Hampton, IA. 641-394-3040
Sunny Fresh Foods
  Monticello, MN. 800-872-3447
Suter Co Inc
  Sycamore, IL. 800-435-6942

Frozen

Agri-Dairy Products
  Purchase, NY. 914-697-9580
Almark Foods
  Gainesville, GA. 800-849-3447
Ballas Egg Products Corp
  Zanesville, OH. 740-453-0386
Brown Produce Company
  Farina, IL. 618-245-3301
Cargill Kitchen Solutions Inc.
  Wayzata, MN. 833-535-5205
Century Blends LLC
  Hunt Valley, MD. 410-771-6606
Creighton Brothers
  Warsaw, IN. 574-267-3101
Crystal Lake LLC
  Warsaw, IN. 574-858-2514
Dixie Egg Co
  Jacksonville, FL. 800-394-3447
Global Egg Corporation
  Toronto, ON. 416-231-2309
Great Valley Mills
  Barto, PA. 800-688-6455
Ise America Inc
  Galena, MD. 410-755-6300
Kent Foods Inc
  Gonzales, TX. 830-672-7993
Land O'Lakes Inc
  Arden Hills, MN. 800-328-9680
McAnally Enterprises
  Lakeview, CA. 800-726-2002
MFI Food Canada
  Winnipeg, MB. 204-992-8200
Michael Foods, Inc.
  Minnetonka, MN. 952-258-4000
Oliver Egg Products
  Crewe, VA. 800-525-3447
Oskaloosa Food Products
  Oskaloosa, IA. 800-477-7239
Siegel Egg Co
  North Billerica, MA. 978-528-2010
Sparboe Foods Corp
  New Hampton, IA. 641-394-3040
Wenk Foods Inc
  Madison, SD. 605-256-4569

Product Categories / Eggs & Egg Products: Hard-Boiled

Hard-Boiled
Almark Foods
  Gainesville, GA 800-849-3447
Cargill Kitchen Solutions Inc.
  Wayzata, MN 833-535-5205
Creighton Brothers
  Warsaw, IN 574-267-3101
Dixie Egg Co
  Jacksonville, FL 800-394-3447
Eggland's Best Eggs
  Malvern, PA 800-922-3447
Feature Foods
  Brampton, ON 905-452-7741
Ise America Inc
  Galena, MD 410-755-6300
Pete and Gerry's Organic Eggs
  Monroe, NH 800-210-6657
Radlo Foods
  Watertown, MA 800-370-1439
Sunny Fresh Foods
  Monticello, MN 800-872-3447
Suter Co Inc
  Sycamore, IL 800-435-6942

Hatcheries
Amick Farms LLC
  Batesburg, SC 800-926-4257
Hickory Baked Ham Co
  Castle Rock, CO 303-688-2633
Norfolk Hatchery
  Norfolk, NE 800-345-2449

Chicks

Turkey
Hickory Baked Ham Co
  Castle Rock, CO 303-688-2633

Liquid
Ballas Egg Products Corp
  Zanesville, OH 740-453-0386
Brown Produce Company
  Farina, IL 618-245-3301
Cargill Kitchen Solutions Inc.
  Wayzata, MN 833-535-5205
Crystal Lake LLC
  Warsaw, IN 574-858-2514
Eggology
  Canoga Park, CA 818-610-2222
Global Egg Corporation
  Toronto, ON 416-231-2309
Golden Valley Foods Ltd.
  Abbotsford, BC 888-299-8855
Kent Foods Inc
  Gonzales, TX 830-672-7993
McAnally Enterprises
  Lakeview, CA 800-726-2002
MFI Food Canada
  Winnipeg, MB 204-992-8200
Michael Foods, Inc.
  Minnetonka, MN 952-258-4000
National Food Corporation
  Everett, WA 425-349-4257
Nulaid Foods Inc
  Ripon, CA 209-599-2121
Oskaloosa Food Products
  Oskaloosa, IA 800-477-7239
Primer Foods Corporation
  Cameron, WI 800-365-2409
Sunny Fresh Foods
  Monticello, MN 800-872-3447
Wilcox Farms
  Roy, WA 360-458-7774

Whites
Eggland's Best Eggs
  Malvern, PA 800-922-3447
Eggology
  Canoga Park, CA 818-610-2222
Golden Valley Foods Ltd.
  Abbotsford, BC 888-299-8855
Horizon Organic Dairy
  Broomfield, CO 888-494-3020
MFI Food Canada
  Winnipeg, MB 204-992-8200
Michael Foods, Inc.
  Minnetonka, MN 952-258-4000
National Food Corporation
  Everett, WA 425-349-4257
Pete and Gerry's Organic Eggs
  Monroe, NH 800-210-6657
WhiteWave Foods
  Denver, CO 800-488-9283

Whole
Golden Valley Foods Ltd.
  Abbotsford, BC 888-299-8855
Michael Foods, Inc.
  Minnetonka, MN 952-258-4000
National Food Corporation
  Everett, WA 425-349-4257

Yolk
Golden Valley Foods Ltd.
  Abbotsford, BC 888-299-8855
Michael Foods, Inc.
  Minnetonka, MN 952-258-4000
National Food Corporation
  Everett, WA 425-349-4257

Low-Cholesterol
Cargill Kitchen Solutions Inc.
  Wayzata, MN 833-535-5205

Mix
Cargill Kitchen Solutions Inc.
  Wayzata, MN 833-535-5205
National Food Corporation
  Everett, WA 425-349-4257
Oliver Egg Products
  Crewe, VA 800-525-3447
Primer Foods Corporation
  Cameron, WI 800-365-2409
Sunny Fresh Foods
  Monticello, MN 800-872-3447

Peeled
Agri-Dairy Products
  Purchase, NY 914-697-9580
Dixie Egg Co
  Jacksonville, FL 800-394-3447
Eggland's Best Eggs
  Malvern, PA 800-922-3447
Feature Foods
  Brampton, ON 905-452-7741
Great Valley Mills
  Barto, PA 800-688-6455
Ise America Inc
  Galena, MD 410-755-6300
MFI Food Canada
  Winnipeg, MB 204-992-8200

Prepared
Agri-Dairy Products
  Purchase, NY 914-697-9580
Almark Foods
  Gainesville, GA 800-849-3447
Cargill Kitchen Solutions Inc.
  Wayzata, MN 833-535-5205
Clofine Dairy Products Inc
  Linwood, NJ 609-653-1000
Eggland's Best Eggs
  Malvern, PA 800-922-3447
Primer Foods Corporation
  Cameron, WI 800-365-2409

Quail
Squab Producers of California
  Modesto, CA 209-537-4744

Solids

Albumen
Brown Produce Company
  Farina, IL 618-245-3301
Holton Food Products
  La Grange, IL 708-352-5599
Wabash Valley Produce Inc
  Dubois, IN 812-678-3131

Whole Egg
Oliver Egg Products
  Crewe, VA 800-525-3447
Primer Foods Corporation
  Cameron, WI 800-365-2409

Fortified
Cargill Kitchen Solutions Inc.
  Wayzata, MN 833-535-5205

Substitutes
Bay Valley Foods
  El Paso, TX 800-236-1119
Cargill Kitchen Solutions Inc.
  Wayzata, MN 833-535-5205
JUST Inc
  San Francisco, CA 844-423-6637
Michael Foods, Inc.
  Minnetonka, MN 952-258-4000

Frozen
Cargill Kitchen Solutions Inc.
  Wayzata, MN 833-535-5205
Clofine Dairy Products Inc
  Linwood, NJ 609-653-1000

Refrigerated
Cargill Kitchen Solutions Inc.
  Wayzata, MN 833-535-5205
Clofine Dairy Products Inc
  Linwood, NJ 609-653-1000
Michael Foods, Inc.
  Minnetonka, MN 952-258-4000

Yolk
Clofine Dairy Products Inc
  Linwood, NJ 609-653-1000
Global Egg Corporation
  Toronto, ON 416-231-2309
MFI Food Canada
  Winnipeg, MB 204-992-8200
Michael Foods, Inc.
  Minnetonka, MN 952-258-4000
National Food Corporation
  Everett, WA 425-349-4257
Norac Technologies
  Edmonton, AB 780-414-9595
Wabash Valley Produce Inc
  Dubois, IN 812-678-3131

Ethnic Foods

General

Afia Foods
  Austin, TX 512-698-8448
Amy's Kitchen Inc
  Santa Rosa, CA 707-781-6600
Ayara Products
  Los Angeles, CA 310-410-8848
Bayou Crab
  Grand Bay, AL 251-824-2076
Blansh International
  Turlock, CA 209-250-1237
Blue Marble Brands
  Providence, RI 888-534-0246
British Aisles, LTD.
  Nashua, NH 800-520-8565
Bruce Foods Corporation
  Lafayette, LA 800-299-9082
Burke Corp
  Nevada, IA 800-654-1152
C&J Trading
  San Francisco, CA 415-822-8910
Calidad Foods
  Grand Prairie, TX 214-521-7999
Casablanca Market
  Newark, CA 650-964-3000
Chong Mei Trading
  East Point, GA 404-768-3838
CJ Omni
  South Gate, CA 323-567-8171
Cocina De Mino
  Oklahoma City, OK 405-632-1036
Corfu Foods Inc
  Bensenville, IL 800-874-9767
Deluxe Delight
  Lost Angeles, CA 424-230-3664
Discovery Foods
  Hayward, CA 510-780-9238
Don Jose Foods
  Scottsdale, AZ 480-443-1000
El Perico Charro
  Garden City, KS 620-275-6454
Elena's Food Specialties
  S San Francisco, CA 800-376-5368
Ethnic Gourmet Foods
  Boulder, CO 800-434-4246
Falafel Republic
  Needham Heights, MA 781-878-6027
Frontera Foods
  Chicago, IL 800-509-4441
Gharana Foods
  Edison, NJ 732-985-9331
Goldilocks USA
  Hayward, CA 510-476-0700
Gringo Jack's
  Manchester Ctr, VT 802-362-0836
H & W Foods
  Kapolei, HI 808-682-8300
Hong Kong Supermarket
  Norcross, GA 770-582-6800
Houston Calco, Inc
  Houston, TX 713-236-8668
India's Rasoi
  St Louis, MO 314-361-6911
JaynRoss Creations LLC
  Whitmore Lake, MI 734-657-5852
Juanita's Foods
  Wilmington, CA 800-303-2965
Kyong Hae Kim Company
  Honolulu, HI 808-926-8720
LA Mexicana Tortilla
  Seattle, WA 206-763-1488
M&M Food Distributors/Oriental Pride
  Virginia Beach, VA 757-499-5676
Manischewitz Co
  Newark, NJ 201-553-1100
Maria & Son
  St Louis, MO 866-481-9009
Marjie's Plantain Foods, Inc.
  New York, NY 908-627-5627
Marukai Market
  Gardena, CA 310-660-6300
Marukan Vinegar USA Inc.
  Paramount, CA 562-630-6060
Marukome USA Inc.
  Irvine, CA 949-863-0110
Maya Kaimal
  Rhinebeck, NY 845-876-8200
Mayakaimal Fine Indian Foods
  Rhinebeck, NY 845-876-8200
Mercado Latino
  City Of Industry, CA 800-432-7266
Mishrun
  Edison, NJ 347-495-4320
Mission Foods Corp.
  Irving, TX 214-583-5113
Monsoon Kitchens
  Shrewsbury, MA 508-842-0070
Morii Foods, Inc.
  Tualatin, OR 503-691-7007
My Own Meals Inc
  Deerfield, IL 847-948-1118
National Importers
  Richmond, BC 888-894-6464
Natural Quick Foods
  Seattle, WA 206-365-5757
Oriental Foods
  Alhambra, CA 626-293-1994
Preferred Brands Inc
  Stamford, CT 800-827-8900
Rancho Sierra
  Salinas, CA 800-398-2929
Rico Foods Inc
  Paterson, NJ 973-278-0589
Rokeach Food Corp
  Newark, NJ 973-589-1472
Rothman's Food Inc
  St Louis, MO 314-367-5448
Salonika Imports Inc
  Pittsburgh, PA 800-794-2256
Sanchez Distributors
  San Antonio, TX 210-341-1682
Santini Foods
  San Lorenzo, CA 800-835-6888
Shell Ridge Jalapeno Project
  Rockport, TX 512-790-8028
Snapdragon Foods
  Oakland, CA 877-881-7627
Squair Food Company
  Los Angeles, CA 213-749-7041
Steve Mendez
  Woodland, CA 530-662-0512
Sukhi's Gourmet Indian Food
  Hayward, CA 888-478-5447
Sun Sun Food Products
  Edmonton, AB 780-454-4261
T. Marzetti Company
  Westerville, OH 800-999-1835
Taj Gourmet Foods
  Boulder, CO 800-434-4246
Tamashiro Market Inc
  Honolulu, HI 808-841-8047
Taqueria El Milagro
  Chicago, IL 773-579-2410
Tekita House Foods
  El Paso, TX 915-779-2181
Tropical Cheese
  Perth Amboy, NJ 888-874-4928
Universal Impex Corporation
  Toronto, ON 416-743-7778
VIP Sales Company
  Hayward, CA 866-536-8008
Wing Seafood Company
  Chicago, IL 312-421-8686
Wing Sing Chong Company
  S San Francisco, CA 415-552-1234
Wong Wing
  Florenceville-Bristol, NB 866-622-2461
Y.M.C. Corp.
  Chicago, IL 312-842-4900
Yamasho Inc
  Elk Grove Village, IL 847-981-9342
Ying Leong Look Funn Factory
  Honolulu, HI 808-537-4304
Zippy's Inc
  Honolulu, HI 808-973-0880

Asian

99 Ranch Market
  Hacienda Heights, CA 626-839-2899
Ajinomoto Foods North America, Inc.
  Ontario, CA 909-477-4700
Ajinomoto Frozen Foods USA, Inc.
  Ontario, CA 866-536-8008
Amy Food Inc
  Houston, TX 713-910-5860
Asian Foods Inc
  St Paul, MN 651-558-2400
Chungs Gourmet Foods
  Houston, TX 713-741-2118
CJ Foods
  La Palma, CA 714-367-7200
CJ Omni
  South Gate, CA 323-567-8171
Discovery Foods
  Hayward, CA 510-780-9238
Feel Good Foods
  Brooklyn, NY 800-638-8949
House of Tsang
  San Francisco, CA 415-282-9952
JMAC Trading, Inc.
  Torrance, CA 877-566-4569
Kahiki Foods Inc
  Columbus, OH 855-524-4540
Lucky Foods
  Tualatin, OR 503-612-1300
McCormick & Company
  Hunt Valley, MD 410-527-6189
Naughty Noah's
  La Jolla, CA
San-J International Inc
  Henrico, VA 800-446-5500
Sempio Foods
  Cerritos, CA 562-207-9540
Snapdragon Foods
  Oakland, CA 877-881-7627
Star Anise Foods
  San Francisco, CA
Suji's Korean Cuisine
  Seattle, WA 206-985-6640
Superior Foods
  Watsonville, CA 831-728-3691
We Rub You
  Brooklyn, NY 718-387-9797
Yai's Thai
  Denver, CO
Ying's Kitchen
  Lake Villa, IL 847-403-7078

Burritos

Baja Foods LLC
  Chicago, IL 773-376-9030
Bakkavor USA
  Charlotte, NC 800-842-3025
Camino Real Foods Inc
  Vernon, CA 800-421-6201
Cedarlane Foods
  Carson, CA 800-826-3322
Elena's Food Specialties
  S San Francisco, CA 800-376-5368
La Tang Cuisine Manufacturing
  Houston, TX 713-780-4876
Manuel's Odessa Tortilla
  Odessa, TX 800-753-2445
Mexi-Frost Specialties Company
  Brooklyn, NY 718-625-3324
Pepe's Mexican Restaurant
  Anaheim, CA 714-952-9410
Queen International Foods
  Monterey Park, CA 800-423-4414
Ramona's Mexican Foods
  Gardena, CA 310-323-1950
Ruiz Food Products Inc.
  Dinuba, CA 800-477-6474
Supreme Frozen Products
  Chicago, IL 773-622-3777
Sweet Earth Foods
  Moss Landing, CA 800-737-3311
The Food Collective
  Irvine, CA 866-328-8638

Chinese

Amy Food Inc
  Houston, TX 713-910-5860
Asian Foods Inc
  St Paul, MN 651-558-2400

Product Categories / Ethnic Foods: Chop Suey

First Oriental Market
  Decatur, GA 404-377-6950
Hong Kong Supermarket
  Norcross, GA 770-582-6800
La Choy
  Chicago, IL 312-549-5000
National Importers
  Richmond, BC 888-894-6464
P & S Food & Liquor
  Chicago, IL 773-685-0088
Wei-Chuan USA Inc
  Bell Gardens, CA 562-372-2020
Wong Wing
  Florenceville-Bristol, NB 866-622-2461

Chop Suey

Canned

Young's Noodle Factory Inc
  Honolulu, HI 808-533-6478

Frozen

Nanka Seimen Company
  Vernon, CA 323-585-9967

Chow Chow

Golding Farms Foods
  Winston Salem, NC 336-766-6161
Lancaster Packing Company
  Myerstown, PA 717-397-9727
United Pickles
  Bronx, NY 718-933-6060

Chow Mein

C&J Trading
  San Francisco, CA 415-822-8910
Willow Foods
  Beaverton, OR 800-338-3609
Y.M.C. Corp.
  Chicago, IL 312-842-4900

Couscous

Bob's Red Mill Natural Foods
  Milwaukie, OR 800-349-2173
Hodgson Mill Inc
  Effingham, IL 800-347-0198
Lundberg Family Farms
  Richvale, CA 530-538-3500
Organic Planet
  San Francisco, CA 415-765-5590
Setton International Foods
  Commack, NY 800-227-4397

Dim Sum

Calco of Calgary
  Calgary, AB 403-295-3578
Fine Choice Foods
  Richmond, BC 866-760-0888
Shine Foods Inc
  Torrance, CA 310-533-6010

Egg Rolls

Amy Food Inc
  Houston, TX 713-910-5860
Asian Foods Inc
  St Paul, MN 651-558-2400
Cathay Foods Corporation
  Boston, MA 617-427-1507
Chang Food Company
  Garden Grove, CA 714-265-9990
Chinese Spaghetti Factory
  Boston, MA 617-445-7714
Chungs Gourmet Foods
  Houston, TX 713-741-2118
Dong Kee Company
  Chicago, IL 312-225-6340
Egg Roll Fantasy
  Auburn, CA 530-887-9197
Fine Choice Foods
  Richmond, BC 866-760-0888
Frozen Specialties Inc
  Perrysburg, OH 419-867-2005
Harvest Food Products Co Inc
  Hayward, CA 510-675-0383
Health is Wealth Foods
  Moonachie, NJ 201-933-7474
Kubla Khan Food Company
  Portland, OR 503-234-7494

La Tang Cuisine Manufacturing
  Houston, TX 713-780-4876
Mexi-Frost Specialties Company
  Brooklyn, NY 718-625-3324
Nanka Seimen Company
  Vernon, CA 323-585-9967
Passport Food Group
  Ontario, CA 310-463-0954
Peking Noodle Co Inc
  Los Angeles, CA 323-223-0897
Prime Food Processing Corp
  Brooklyn, NY 718-963-2323
Shine Foods Inc
  Torrance, CA 310-533-6010
Spring Kitchen
  Houston, TX 713-222-0598
Valdez Food Inc
  Philadelphia, PA 215-634-6106
Wei-Chuan USA Inc
  Bell Gardens, CA 562-372-2020
Willow Foods
  Beaverton, OR 800-338-3609
Wong Wing
  Florenceville-Bristol, NB 866-622-2461
Wonton Food
  Brooklyn, NY 800-776-8889

Spring Rolls

Calco of Calgary
  Calgary, AB 403-295-3578
Chang Food Company
  Garden Grove, CA 714-265-9990
Chungs Gourmet Foods
  Houston, TX 713-741-2118
Clarmil Manufacturing Corp
  Hayward, CA 888-252-7645
Health is Wealth Foods
  Moonachie, NJ 201-933-7474
Spring Kitchen
  Houston, TX 713-222-0598
Willow Foods
  Beaverton, OR 800-338-3609

Wrappers

Delta Food Products
  Edmonton, AB 780-424-3636
International Noodle Co
  Madison Heights, MI 248-583-2479
Mandarin Noodle Manufacturing Company
  Calgary, AB 403-265-1383
Wing's Food Products
  Toronto, ON 416-259-2662

Enchiladas

Canned & Frozen

Baja Foods LLC
  Chicago, IL 773-376-9030
Queen International Foods
  Monterey Park, CA 800-423-4414

Frozen

Cedarlane Foods
  Carson, CA 800-826-3322
Elena's Food Specialties
  S San Francisco, CA 800-376-5368
Ruiz Food Products Inc.
  Dinuba, CA 800-477-6474

Filafel

Kronos
  Glendale Heights, IL 800-621-0099

Guacamole

Avo-King Internatl
  Orange, CA 800-286-5464
Diversified Avocado Products
  Mission Viejo, CA 800-879-2555
Frontera Foods
  Chicago, IL 800-509-4441
Sunny Avocado
  Jamul, CA 800-999-2862

Halal Foods

Al Safa Halal
  New York City, NY 800-268-8147
Burke Corp
  Nevada, IA 800-654-1152

Butterball Farms
  Grand Rapids, MI 888-828-8837
Crescent Foods
  Chicago, IL 800-939-6268
Foremost Farms USA
  Baraboo, WI 800-362-9196
Global Food Industries
  Townville, SC 800-225-4152
Halal Fine Foods
  Toronto, ON 416-679-8000
J&M Food Products Co
  Deerfield, IL 847-948-1290
Javed & Sons
  Houston, TX 713-835-6850
Madani Halal
  Ozone Park, NY 718-323-9732
Midamar
  Cedar Rapids, IA 800-362-3711
My Own Meals Inc
  Deerfield, IL 847-948-1118
National Fruit Flavor Co Inc
  New Orleans, LA 800-966-1123
Nema Food Distribution
  Fairfield, NJ 973-256-4415
Northwestern Foods
  Arden Hills, MN 800-236-4937
Saad Wholesale Meats
  Detroit, MI 313-831-8126
Salwa Foods
  Lawrenceville, GA 770-263-8207
Zabiha Halal Meat Processors
  Addison, IL 630-620-5000

Italian

Amanida USA Corp
  Coral Gables, FL
Boscoli Foods Inc
  Kenner, LA 504-469-5500
Fratelli Mantova
  Naperville, IL 630-904-0002
Italian Connection
  Dumont, NJ 201-385-2226
Joe Fazio's Famous Italian
  Charleston, WV 304-344-3071
Marconi Italian Specialty Foods
  Chicago, IL 312-421-0485
Sapore della Vita
  Sarasota, FL 941-914-4256
Shamrock Foods Co
  Phoenix, AZ 800-289-3663
Sidari's Italian Foods
  Cleveland, OH 216-431-3344
Stella D'oro
  Charlotte, NC 800-995-2623
Superior Foods
  Watsonville, CA 831-728-3691

Jambalaya

Chef Hans' Gourmet Foods
  Monroe, LA 800-890-4267
Mama Amy's Quality Foods
  Mississauga, ON 905-456-0056

Japanese

Ajinomoto Frozen Foods USA, Inc.
  Ontario, CA 866-536-8008
Genki USA
  Torrance, CA
House Foods America Corp
  Garden Grove, CA 877-333-7077
Imuraya USA
  Irvine, CA 949-251-9205
Japan Gold USA
  Poway, CA 858-486-1707
Marukai Market
  Gardena, CA 310-660-6300
Marukome USA Inc.
  Irvine, CA 949-863-0110
Otafuku Foods
  Santa Fe Springs, CA 562-404-4700
Sun Noodle
  Honolulu, HI 808-841-5808
Yamasho Inc
  Elk Grove Village, IL 847-981-9342

Kosher Foods

A-1 Eastern-Homemade Pickle Co
  Los Angeles, CA 323-223-1141
Abraham's Natural Foods
  Long Branch, NJ 800-327-9903

Product Categories / Ethnic Foods: Kosher Foods

Adrienne's Gourmet Foods
  Santa Barbara, CA 800-937-7010
Al-Rite Fruits & Syrups Co
  Miami, FL 305-652-2540
All American Foods Inc
  Mankato, MN 800-833-2661
Alle Processing Corp
  Flushing, NY 718-894-2000
Allied Wine Corporation
  Ellenville, NY 800-796-4100
Alta Dena Certified Dairy LLC
  City Of Industry, CA 800-535-1369
Annie Chun's
  Los Angeles, CA 415-479-8272
Arbre Farms Inc
  Walkerville, MI 231-873-3337
Aunt Gussie Cookies & Crackers
  Garfield, NJ 800-422-6654
Avatar Corp
  University Park, IL 800-255-3181
Bake Crafters Food Company
  McDonald, TN 423-396-3392
Bascom Family Farms Inc
  Brattleboro, VT 888-266-6271
Beatrice Bakery Co
  Beatrice, NE 800-228-4030
Bella Viva Orchards
  Hughson, CA 800-552-8218
Benson's Gourmet Seasonings
  Azusa, CA 800-325-5619
Bernie's Foods
  Brooklyn, NY 718-417-6677
Biazzo Dairy Products Inc
  Ridgefield, NJ 201-941-6800
Blue Planet Foods
  Collegedale, TN 877-396-3145
Bluechip Group
  Salt Lake City, UT 800-878-0099
Boca Bons East
  Greenacres, FL 800-314-2835
Briess Malt & Ingredients Co.
  Chilton, WI 800-657-0806
Bruno Specialty Foods
  West Sayville, NY 631-589-1700
Butterball Farms
  Grand Rapids, MI 888-828-8837
Cache Creek Foods LLC
  Woodland, CA 530-662-1764
Calhoun Bend Mill
  Libuse, LA 800-519-6455
California Custom Fruits
  Baldwin Park, CA 877-558-0056
Campbell Soup Co.
  Camden, NJ 800-257-8443
Capalbo's Fruit Baskets
  Clifton, NJ 800-252-6262
Carmi Flavor & Fragrance Company
  Commerce, CA 800-421-9647
Casa Visco
  Schenectady, NY 888-607-2823
Catch Up Logistics
  Pittsburgh, PA 412-441-9512
Champlain Valley Milling Corp
  Westport, NY 518-962-4711
Chewys Rugulach
  San Diego, CA 800-241-3456
Chris Candies Inc
  Pittsburgh, PA 412-322-9400
Christopher's Herb Shop
  Springville, UT 888-372-4372
Coach's Oats
  Yorba Linda, CA 714-692-6885
Coffee Masters
  Spring Grove, IL 800-334-6485
Commissariat Imports
  Los Angeles, CA 310-475-5628
Cookies United
  Islip, NY 631-581-4000
Country Choice Organic
  Eden Prairie, MN 952-829-8824
Crosby Molasses Company
  Saint John, NB 800-561-2206
Deer Creek Honey Farms LTD
  London, OH 740-852-0899
Delicious Frookie
  Des Plaines, IL 847-699-3200
Dr Praeger's Sensible Foods
  Elmwood Park, NJ 877-772-3437
Dynamic Health Laboratories Inc.
  Brooklyn, NY 800-396-2114
Eatem Foods Co
  Vineland, NJ 800-683-2836

Ed Roller Inc
  Rochester, NY 585-458-8020
Eggology
  Canoga Park, CA 818-610-2222
Elan Vanilla Co
  Newark, NJ 973-344-8014
Enrico's/Ventre Packing
  Syracuse, NY 888-472-8237
Erba Food Products
  Brooklyn, NY 718-272-7700
FNI Group LLC
  Sherborn, MA 508-655-4175
Foremost Farms USA
  Baraboo, WI 800-362-9196
Fratelli Beretta USA
  Mount Olive, NJ 201-438-0723
Freeda Vitamins Inc
  Long Island City, NY 800-777-3737
Fresh Roasted Almond Company
  Warren, MI 877-478-6887
Georgia Spice Company
  Atlanta, GA 800-453-9997
Gerber Products Co
  Arlington, VA 800-284-9488
Gimbals Fine Candies
  S San Francisco, CA 800-344-6225
GKI Foods
  Brighton, MI 248-486-0055
GoBio!
  Action, ON 519-853-2958
Gold Pure Food Products Co. Inc.
  Hempstead, NY 800-422-4681
Golden Fluff Popcorn Co
  Lakewood, NJ 732-367-5448
Hanan Products Co
  Hicksville, NY 516-938-1000
Happy & Healthy Products Inc
  Boca Raton, FL 561-367-0739
Harbar LLC
  Canton, MA 800-881-7040
Harvest Valley Bakery Inc
  La Salle, IL 815-224-9030
Hausbeck Pickle Co
  Saginaw, MI 866-754-4721
Helen's Pure Foods
  Cheltenham, PA 215-379-6433
Hermann Pickle Co
  Garrettsville, OH 800-245-2696
Hialeah Products Inc
  Hollywood, FL 800-923-3379
Honey Run Winery
  Chico, CA 530-345-6405
Honeywood Winery
  Salem, OR 800-726-4101
House of Flavors Inc
  Ludington, MI 800-930-7740
Imagine Foods
  Boulder, CO 800-434-4246
International Glatt Kosher
  Brooklyn, NY 718-630-5555
Joe Jurgielwicz & Sons
  Hamburg, PA 800-543-8257
Joyva Corp
  Brooklyn, NY 718-497-0170
Kaplan & Zubrin
  Camden, NJ 856-964-1083
Kayco
  Bayonne, NJ 718-369-4600
KD Canners Inc
  Mississauga, ON 905-602-1825
Kedem
  Bayonne, NJ 718-369-4600
Kemach Food Products
  Brooklyn, NY 718-272-5655
Klein's Kosher Pickles
  Phoenix, AZ 800-437-4255
L & S Packing Co
  Farmingdale, NY 800-286-6487
Lee Kum Kee USA Inc
  City Of Industry, CA 800-654-5082
Lenchner Bakery
  Concord, ON 905-738-8811
Lifeway
  Morton Grove, IL 877-281-3874
Loriva Culinary Oils
  San Francisco, CA 866-972-6879
Losurdo Creamery
  Hackensack, NJ 888-567-8736
M&L Gourmet Ice Cream
  Baltimore, MD 410-276-4880
Macabee Foods
  West Nyack, NY 845-623-1300

Mada'n Kosher Foods
  Dania, FL 954-925-0077
Magic Seasoning Blends
  New Orleans, LA 800-457-2857
Main Street Gourmet
  Cuyahoga Falls, OH 800-678-6246
Mancini Packing Co
  Zolfo Springs, FL 800-741-1778
Manischewitz Co
  Newark, NJ 201-553-1100
Maple Products
  Sherbrooke, QC 819-569-5161
Marie Callender's Gourmet Products/Goldrush Products
  San Jose, CA 800-729-5428
Marion-Kay Spice Co
  Brownstown, IN 800-627-7423
Martin Farms
  Brockport, NY 877-838-7369
Marukan Vinegar USA Inc.
  Paramount, CA 562-630-6060
Mendocino Mustard
  Fort Bragg, CA 800-964-2270
Mille Lacs Wild Rice Corp
  Aitkin, MN 800-626-3809
Miller's Cheese Corp
  Brooklyn, NY 718-965-1840
Milmar Food Group
  Goshen, NY 845-294-5400
Mogen David Wine Corp
  Westfield, NY 716-326-3151
Mona Lisa Foods
  Chicago, IL 866-443-0460
Mrs. Leeper's Pasta
  Excelsior Springs, MO 800-848-5266
Mushroom Co
  Cambridge, MD 410-221-8971
Musicon Deer Farm
  Goshen, NY 845-294-6378
My Brother Bobby's Salsa
  Poughkeepsie, NY 845-462-6227
My Grandma's Coffee Cake
  Hyde Park, MA 800-847-2636
National Fruit Flavor Co Inc
  New Orleans, LA 800-966-1123
Nature's Products Inc
  Sunrise, FL 800-752-7873
Navarro Pecan Co
  Corsicana, TX 800-333-9507
Northwestern Foods
  Arden Hills, MN 800-236-4937
Norwalk Dairy
  Santa Fe Springs, CA 562-921-5712
Nu-World Amaranth Inc
  Naperville, IL 630-369-6851
Old Fashioned Kitchen Inc
  Lakewood, NJ 732-364-4100
Pacific Salmon Company
  Edmonds, WA 425-774-1315
Palmieri Food Products
  New Haven, CT 800-845-5447
Preferred Brands Inc
  Stamford, CT 800-827-8900
Price Co
  Yakima, WA 509-966-4110
Primo Foods
  Oceanside, CA 760-439-8711
Quality Naturally Foods
  City Of Industry, CA 888-498-6986
Rachael's Smoked Fish
  Springfield, MA 800-327-3412
Ranaldi Bros. Frozen Food Products
  Warwick, RI 401-737-5130
Real Kosher Sausage Company
  Newark, NJ 973-690-5394
Redmond Minerals Inc
  Heber City, UT 866-312-7258
Rogers Sugar Inc.
  Montreal, QC 514-527-8686
Royal Palate Foods
  Inglewood, CA 310-330-7701
Russian Chef
  New York, NY 212-249-1550
Sandt's Honey Co
  Easton, PA 800-935-3960
Seabrook Brothers & Sons
  Seabrook, NJ 856-455-8080
Setton International Foods
  Commack, NY 800-227-4397
Simply Divine
  New York, NY 212-541-7300
Solana Gold Organics
  Sebastopol, CA 800-459-1121

Product Categories / Ethnic Foods: Matzo

Spilke's Baking Company
  Moosic, PA 570-457-2400
Steve's Mom
  Bronx, NY 800-362-4545
Strub Pickles
  Brantford, ON 519-751-1717
Sun Harvest Foods Inc
  San Diego, CA 619-661-0909
Sunergia Soyfoods
  Charlottesville, VA 800-693-5134
Sure-Fresh Produce Inc
  Santa Maria, CA 888-423-5379
Thomas Canning/Maidstone
  Maidstone, ON 519-737-1531
Todhunter Foods
  West Palm Beach, FL 800-336-9463
Top Hat Co Inc
  Wilmette, IL 847-256-6565
Touche Bakery
  London, ON 518-455-0044
Tova Industries LLC
  Louisville, KY 888-532-8682
Umanoff & Parsons
  Bronx, NY 800-248-9993
US Chocolate Corp
  Brooklyn, NY 718-788-8555
Vacaville Fruit Co
  Vacaville, CA 707-447-1085
Vermont Country Naturals
  Charlotte, VT 800-528-7021
Weaver Nut Co. Inc.
  Ephrata, PA 800-473-2688
Weinberg Foods
  Kirkland, WA 800-866-3447
Weiss Homemade Kosher Bakery
  Brooklyn, NY 800-498-3477
Wenner Bakery
  Bayport, NY 800-869-6262
World Cheese Inc
  Brooklyn, NY 718-965-1700
World Harbors
  Auburn, ME 800-355-6221
World Of Chantilly
  Brooklyn, NY 718-859-1110
World's Finest Chocolate Inc
  Chicago, IL 888-821-8452
Y Z Enterprises Inc
  Maumee, OH 800-736-8779
Your Bar Factory
  LaSalle, QC 888-366-0258

Matzo

Erba Food Products
  Brooklyn, NY 718-272-7700
Manischewitz Co
  Newark, NJ 201-553-1100
Streit's
  Orangeburg, NY 845-359-9203

Meal

Manischewitz Co
  Newark, NJ 201-553-1100

Mexican

Alamo Tamale Corporation
  Houston, TX 800-252-0586
Amy Food Inc
  Houston, TX 713-910-5860
Art's Mexican Products
  Kansas City, KS 913-371-2163
Cacique
  Monrovia, CA 800-521-6987
Feel Good Foods
  Brooklyn, NY 800-638-8949
Fiesta Mexican Foods
  Brawley, CA 760-344-3580
Flying Burrito Co
  Fayetteville, AR 479-527-0400
Fresca Mexican Foods LLC
  Boise, ID 208-376-6922
Frontera Foods
  Chicago, IL 800-509-4441
Gladstone Food Products Company
  Kansas City, MO 816-436-1255
Intermex Products USA LTD
  Grand Prairie, TX 972-660-2071
J & J Snack Foods Corp
  Pennsauken, NJ 800-486-9533
JJ's Tamales & Barbacoa
  San Antonio, TX 210-737-1300

LA Chapalita Inc
  South El Monte, CA 626-443-8556
La Preferida, Inc.
  Chicago, IL 773-254-7200
Leona's Restaurante
  Chimayo, NM 888-561-5569
Los Pericos Food Products
  Pomona, CA 909-623-5625
McCormick & Company
  Hunt Valley, MD 410-527-6189
Mission Foodservice
  Oldsmar, FL 800-443-7994
Molli
  Dallas, TX
National Importers
  Richmond, BC 888-894-6464
Palacios & Sons
  Irving, TX 469-449-2060
Patricia Quintana
  Los Angeles, CA
PepsiCo.
  Purchase, NY 914-253-2000
Red's All Natural
  North Sioux City, SD 605-956-7337
Sabor Mexicano
  Berkeley, CA
San Antonio Farms
  Platteville, WI 800-236-1119
Shamrock Foods Co
  Phoenix, AZ 800-289-3663
Superior Foods
  Watsonville, CA 831-728-3691
T.W. Garner Food Company
  Winston Salem, NC 800-476-7383
Teasdale Quality Foods Inc
  Atwater, CA 209-358-5616
Truco Enterprises
  Carrollton, TX 972-869-4600
Tyson Foods Inc.
  Springdale, AR 479-290-4000

Oriental

Cafe Spice
  New Windsor, NY 845-863-0910
Hanmi Inc
  Chicago, IL 773-271-0730
Koha Food
  Honolulu, HI 808-845-4232
M&M Food Distributors/Oriental Pride
  Virginia Beach, VA 757-499-5676
Mah Chena Company
  Chicago, IL 312-226-5100

Paella

Conrad Rice Mill Inc
  New Iberia, LA 800-551-3245
Cuizina Food Company
  Woodinville, WA 425-486-7000

Parve Foods

Bruno Specialty Foods
  West Sayville, NY 631-589-1700
Coach's Oats
  Yorba Linda, CA 714-692-6885
Country Choice Organic
  Eden Prairie, MN 952-829-8824
Delicious Frookie
  Des Plaines, IL 847-699-3200
Dr Praeger's Sensible Foods
  Elmwood Park, NJ 877-772-3437
Dynamic Health Laboratories Inc.
  Brooklyn, NY 800-396-2114
Eggology
  Canoga Park, CA 818-610-2222
Enrico's/Ventre Packing
  Syracuse, NY 888-472-8237
FNI Group LLC
  Sherborn, MA 508-655-4175
GoBio!
  Action, ON 519-853-2958
Happy & Healthy Products Inc
  Boca Raton, FL 561-367-0739
Honey Run Winery
  Chico, CA 530-345-6405
KD Canners Inc
  Mississauga, ON 905-602-1825
Marukan Vinegar USA Inc.
  Paramount, CA 562-630-6060
Mrs. Leeper's Pasta
  Excelsior Springs, MO 800-848-5266

New World Pasta Co
  Harrisburg, PA 800-730-5957
Northwestern Foods
  Arden Hills, MN 800-236-4937
Touche Bakery
  London, ON 518-455-0044
US Chocolate Corp
  Brooklyn, NY 718-788-8555
Y Z Enterprises Inc
  Maumee, OH 800-736-8779

Shells

Chalupa

Rudy's Tortillas
  Carrollton, TX 800-878-2401

Taco

Abuelita Mexican Foods
  Manassas Park, VA 703-369-0232
Amigos Canning Company
  San Antonio, TX 210-798-5360
Anita's Mexican Foods Corporation
  San Bernardino, CA 909-884-8706
Azteca Foods Inc
  Chicago, IL 708-563-6600
El Rancho Tortilla
  San Antonio, TX 210-922-8411
La Buena Mexican Foods Products
  Tucson, AZ 520-624-1796
La Preferida, Inc.
  Chicago, IL 773-254-7200
Las Cruces Brand Products
  El Paso, TX 915-779-5709
Las Cruces Foods
  Las Cruces, NM 575-526-2352
Li'l Guy Foods
  Kansas City, MO 800-886-8226
Luna's Tortillas
  Dallas, TX 214-747-2661
Manuel's Odessa Tortilla
  Odessa, TX 800-753-2445
Mission Foodservice
  Oldsmar, FL 800-443-7994
Perez Food Products
  Kansas City, MO 816-931-8761
Puebla Foods Inc
  Passaic, NJ 973-473-0201
Rudy's Tortillas
  Carrollton, TX 800-878-2401
Sam's Leon Mexican Food
  Omaha, NE 402-733-3809
Spanish Gardens Food Manufacturing
  Kansas City, KS 913-831-4242

Tabbouleh

Bishop Brothers
  Bristow, OK 800-859-8304
Tarazi Specialty Foods
  Chino, CA 909-628-3601

Tacos

Amigos Canning Company
  San Antonio, TX 210-798-5360
Flying Burrito Co
  Fayetteville, AR 479-527-0400
La Preferida, Inc.
  Chicago, IL 773-254-7200
Mission Foods Corp.
  Irving, TX 214-583-5113
Queen International Foods
  Monterey Park, CA 800-423-4414
R & S Mexican Food
  Glendale, AZ 602-272-2727
Ruiz Food Products Inc.
  Dinuba, CA 800-477-6474

Fillings

Burke Corp
  Nevada, IA 800-654-1152
First Original Texas Chili Company
  Fort Worth, TX 800-507-0009
Ready Foods Inc
  Denver, CO 800-748-1218
Texas Chili Co
  Fort Worth, TX 800-507-0009

Product Categories / Ethnic Foods: Tamales

Tamales

Abuelita Mexican Foods
  Manassas Park, VA 703-369-0232
Alamo Tamale Corporation
  Houston, TX 800-252-0586
Art's Tamales
  Metamora, IL 309-367-2850
Baja Foods LLC
  Chicago, IL 773-376-9030
Comanche Tortilla Factory
  Fort Stockton, TX 432-336-3245
El Rey Cooked Meats
  St Louis, MO 314-521-3113
Grande Tortilla Factory
  Tucson, AZ 520-622-8338
Kelly Foods
  Jackson, TN 731-424-2255
La Buena Mexican Foods Products
  Tucson, AZ 520-624-1796
Luna's Tortillas
  Dallas, TX 214-747-2661
Mama Maria's Tortillas
  Midvale, UT 801-566-5150
Manuel's Odessa Tortilla
  Odessa, TX 800-753-2445
Mexi-Frost Specialties Company
  Brooklyn, NY 718-625-3324
Mi Ranchito Foods
  Phoenix, AZ 602-272-3949
Mr Jay's Tamales & Chili
  Lynwood, CA 310-537-3932
R & S Mexican Food
  Glendale, AZ 602-272-2727
Ramona's Mexican Foods
  Gardena, CA 310-323-1950
Ruiz Food Products Inc.
  Dinuba, CA 800-477-6474
Supreme Frozen Products
  Chicago, IL 773-622-3777
Supreme Frozen Products
  Elk Grove Village, IL 847-979-8480
Texas Tamale Co
  Houston, TX 713-795-5500
Tom Tom Tamale & Bakery Co
  Chicago, IL 773-523-5675

Frozen

Art's Tamales
  Metamora, IL 309-367-2850
Baja Foods LLC
  Chicago, IL 773-376-9030
Edmond's Chile Co
  St Louis, MO 314-772-1499
El Rey Cooked Meats
  St Louis, MO 314-521-3113
Mexi-Frost Specialties Company
  Brooklyn, NY 718-625-3324
Mi Ranchito Foods
  Phoenix, AZ 602-272-3949
Ramona's Mexican Foods
  Gardena, CA 310-323-1950
Ruiz Food Products Inc.
  Dinuba, CA 800-477-6474
Tom Tom Tamale & Bakery Co
  Chicago, IL 773-523-5675

Taquitos

Queen International Foods
  Monterey Park, CA 800-423-4414
Ruiz Food Products Inc.
  Dinuba, CA 800-477-6474

Tempeh

Twenty-First Century Foods
  Jamaica Plain, MA 617-522-7595

Tortilla & Tortilla Products

Anita's Mexican Foods Corporation
  San Bernardino, CA 909-884-8706
Cabo Chips
  Cypress, CA
Calidad Foods
  Grand Prairie, TX 214-521-7999
Comanche Tortilla Factory
  Fort Stockton, TX 432-336-3245
El Matador Foods
  Baytown, TX 800-470-2447
Fresca Mexican Foods LLC
  Boise, ID 208-376-6922
Frontera Foods
  Chicago, IL 800-509-4441
Good Wives
  Wilmington, MA 800-521-8160
Harbar LLC
  Canton, MA 800-881-7040
La Bonita Ole Inc
  Tampa, FL 800-522-6648
La Preferida, Inc.
  Chicago, IL 773-254-7200
LA Torilla Factory
  Santa Rosa, CA 800-446-1516
Los Pericos Food Products
  Pomona, CA 909-623-5625
Mama Maria's Tortillas
  Midvale, UT 801-566-5150
Maria and Ricardo's
  Canton, MA 800-881-7040
Masienda
  Los Angeles, CA
Mi Rancho
  San Leandro, CA 510-553-0444
Mission Foods
  Tempe, AZ 480-491-2511
Mission Foods Corp.
  Irving, TX 214-583-5113
Mrs Rios Corn Products
  San Angelo, TX 325-653-5640
One Degree Organic Foods
  Abbotsford, BC 855-834-2642
Rudolph's Specialty Bakery
  Toronto, ON 800-268-1589
Siete Family Foods
  Austin, TX
Tolteca Foodservice
  Norcross, GA 800-541-6835

Tortillas

Abuelita Mexican Foods
  Manassas Park, VA 703-369-0232
Azteca Foods Inc
  Chicago, IL 708-563-6600
Azteca Milling
  Irving, TX 800-364-0040
Bien Padre Foods Inc
  Eureka, CA 707-442-4585
Blue Marble Brands
  Providence, RI 888-534-0246
Bueno Foods
  Albuquerque, NM 800-888-7336
Casa Valdez Inc
  Caldwell, ID 208-459-6461
Cedarlane Foods
  Carson, CA 800-826-3322
Comanche Tortilla Factory
  Fort Stockton, TX 432-336-3245
Custom Ingredients Inc
  New Braunfels, TX 800-457-8935
Delicious Popcorn
  Waupaca, WI 715-258-7683
El Charro Mexican Food Ind
  Roswell, NM 575-622-8590
El Milagro
  Chicago, IL 773-579-6120
El Rancho Tortilla
  San Antonio, TX 210-922-8411
Father Sam's Bakery
  Buffalo, NY 800-521-6719
Fiesta Mexican Foods
  Brawley, CA 760-344-3580
Flowers Foods Inc.
  Thomasville, GA 229-226-9110
Food Products Corporation
  Phoenix, AZ 602-273-7139
French Meadow Bakery & Cafe
  Minneapolis, MN 612-870-7855
Frontera Foods
  Chicago, IL 800-509-4441
Grande Tortilla Factory
  Tucson, AZ 520-622-8338
Great Western Tortilla
  Denver, CO 303-298-0705
Harbar LLC
  Canton, MA 800-881-7040
La Buena Mexican Foods Products
  Tucson, AZ 520-624-1796
LA Canasta Mexican Foods
  Phoenix, AZ 855-269-7721
LA Chapalita Inc
  South El Monte, CA 626-443-8556
La Chiquita Tortilla Manufacturing
  Atlanta, GA 800-486-3942
LA Colonial
  San Jose, CA 408-436-5551
LA Mexicana Tortilla Factory
  Duncanville, TX 214-943-7770
LA Reina Inc
  Los Angeles, CA 800-367-7522
LA Tapatia Tortilleria Inc
  Fresno, CA 559-441-1030
LA Torilla Factory
  Santa Rosa, CA 800-446-1516
La Tortilla Factory
  Santa Rosa, CA 800-446-1516
Lago Tortillas International
  Austin, TX 800-369-9017
Laredo Tortilleria & Mexican
  Fort Wayne, IN 800-252-7336
Las Cruces Brand Products
  El Paso, TX 915-779-5709
Las Cruces Foods
  Las Cruces, NM 575-526-2352
Li'l Guy Foods
  Kansas City, MO 800-886-8226
Lone Star Bakery
  Round Rock, TX 512-255-7268
Los Amigo Tortilla Mfg Co
  Atlanta, GA 800-969-8226
Luna's Tortillas
  Dallas, TX 214-747-2661
Manuel's Mexican-American Fine Foods
  Salt Lake City, UT 800-748-5072
Manuel's Odessa Tortilla
  Odessa, TX 800-753-2445
Metzger Popcorn Co
  Delphos, OH 800-819-6072
Mexi-Frost Specialties Company
  Brooklyn, NY 718-625-3324
Mexican Accent
  New Berlin, WI 262-784-4422
Mi Mama's Tortilla Factory Inc
  Omaha, NE 402-345-2099
Mi Ranchito Foods
  Phoenix, AZ 602-272-3949
Mikey's 480-696-2483
Mission Foods Corp.
  Irving, TX 214-583-5113
Mission Foodservice
  Oldsmar, FL 800-443-7994
Natural Food Mill
  Corona, CA 800-797-5090
Ozuna Food Products Corporation
  Sunnyvale, CA 408-400-0495
Pacific Ocean Produce
  Santa Cruz, CA 831-423-2654
Pepe's Mexican Restaurant
  Anaheim, CA 714-952-9410
Perez Food Products
  Kansas City, MO 816-931-8761
Puebla Foods Inc
  Passaic, NJ 973-473-0201
R & S Mexican Food
  Glendale, AZ 602-272-2727
Ramona's Mexican Foods
  Gardena, CA 310-323-1950
Ready Foods Inc
  Denver, CO 800-748-1218
Rudi's Organic Bakery
  Boulder, CO 877-293-0876
Rudolph's Specialty Bakery
  Toronto, ON 800-268-1589
Rudy's Tortillas
  Carrollton, TX 800-878-2401
Ruiz Flour Tortillas
  Riverside, CA 909-947-7811
Ruiz Food Products Inc.
  Dinuba, CA 800-477-6474
Sabor Mexicano
  Berkeley, CA
Sam's Leon Mexican Food
  Omaha, NE 402-733-3809
Sanitary Tortilla Manufacturing Company
  San Antonio, TX 210-226-9209
Selecto Sausage Co
  Houston, TX 713-926-1626
Severance Foods Inc
  Hartford, CT 860-724-7063
Shirley Foods
  Shirley, IN 800-560-2908
Soloman Baking Company
  Denver, CO 303-371-2777
Spanish Gardens Food Manufacturing
  Kansas City, KS 913-831-4242

Product Categories / Ethnic Foods: Tostadas

Sweet Corn Products Co
  Bloomfield, NE 877-628-6115
Tolteca Foodservice
  Norcross, GA 800-541-6835
Tortillas Inc
  North Las Vegas, NV 702-399-3300
Vermont Tortilla Company
  Shelburne, VT 802-999-4823

Tostadas

Delicious Popcorn
  Waupaca, WI 715-258-7683
El Rancho Tortilla
  San Antonio, TX 210-922-8411
Happy's Potato Chip Co
  Minneapolis, MN 612-781-3121
La Buena Mexican Foods Products
  Tucson, AZ 520-624-1796
LA Tapatia Tortilleria Inc
  Fresno, CA 559-441-1030
Las Cruces Brand Products
  El Paso, TX 915-779-5709
Luna's Tortillas
  Dallas, TX 214-747-2661
Manuel's Mexican-American Fine Foods
  Salt Lake City, UT 800-748-5072
Mission Foodservice
  Oldsmar, FL 800-443-7994
Rudy's Tortillas
  Carrollton, TX 800-878-2401

Wonton Chips

Maebo Noodle Factory Inc
  Hilo, HI 877-663-8667

Wontons

Chang Food Company
  Garden Grove, CA 714-265-9990
Delta Food Products
  Edmonton, AB 780-424-3636
Harvest Food Products Co Inc
  Hayward, CA 510-675-0383
La Tang Cuisine Manufacturing
  Houston, TX 713-780-4876
Mandarin Noodle Manufacturing Company
  Calgary, AB 403-265-1383
Montreal Chop Suey Company
  Montreal, QC 514-522-3134
Nanka Seimen Company
  Vernon, CA 323-585-9967
Passport Food Group
  Ontario, CA 310-463-0954
Peking Noodle Co Inc
  Los Angeles, CA 323-223-0897
Wan Hua Foods
  Seattle, WA 206-622-8417
Wonton Food
  Brooklyn, NY 800-776-8889

Fish & Seafood

Canned

American Tuna
  Bonita, CA 866-817-0497
Crusoe Seafood LLC
  Sun Valley, CA 866-343-7629
King Oscar
  San Diego, CA
Season Brand
  Newark, NJ 201-553-1100
Vital Choice
  Bellingham, WA 800-608-4825

General

Lamex Foods Inc.
  Bloomington, MN 952-844-0585
Omega Pure
  Irvine, CA 562-429-3335
Sofina Foods Inc
  Markham, ON 855-763-4621

Caviar (Roe)

Angy's Food Products Inc
  Westfield, MA 413-572-1010
Black River Caviar
  Breckenridge, CO 888-315-0575
Calvisius Caviar
  New York, NY 212-207-8222
Castella Imports Inc
  Brentwood, NY 631-231-5500
Ferroclad Fishery
  Batchawana Bay, ON 705-882-2295
Fine Foods Trading Company
  Union City, NJ 973-772-2221
Fulton Fish Market
  New York, NY 718-842-8908
High Liner Foods Inc.
  Lunenburg, NS 902-634-8811
Kelley's Katch Caviar
  Savannah, TN 888-681-8565
Newell Lobsters
  Yarmouth, NS 902-742-6272
Notre Dame Seafoods Inc.
  Comfort Cove, NL 709-244-5511
Paramount Caviar
  Long Island City, NY 800-992-2842
Produits Belle Baie
  Caraquet, NB 506-727-4414
Raffield Fisheries Inc
  Port St Joe, FL 850-229-8494
Royal Caviar Inc
  Glendale, CA 818-546-5858
Royal Gourmet Caviar
  Lynbrook, NY 516-612-7407
Russ & Daughters
  New York, NY 800-787-7229
Russian Chef
  New York, NY 212-249-1550
Sterling Caviar LLC
  Sacramento, CA 800-525-0333
Warbucks Seafood
  Brooklyn, NY 718-998-4900

Herring

Cowart Seafood Corp
  Lottsburg, VA 804-529-6101

Salmon

Captain Little Seafood
  Queens County, NS 902-947-2087
Crown Prince Inc
  City Of Industry, CA 626-912-3700
Haines Packing Company
  Haines, AK 907-766-2883
Johns Cove Fisheries
  Yarmouth, NS 902-742-8691
Vital Choice
  Bellingham, WA 800-608-4825

Shad

Calise & Sons Bakery Inc
  Lincoln, RI 800-225-4737
Flowers Baking Co
  El Paso, TX 800-328-6111

Fish

A&C Quinlin Fisheries
  Centreville, NS 902-745-2742
Ace Development
  Bruneau, ID 208-845-2487
Acme Smoked Fish Corporation
  Brooklyn, NY 718-383-8585
Acme Steak & Seafood
  Youngstown, OH 800-686-2263
Acushnet Fish Corporation
  Fairhaven, MA 508-997-7482
Agger Fish Corp
  Brooklyn, NY 718-855-1717
Al Safa Halal
  New York City, NY 800-268-8147
Alaska Sausage & Seafood
  Anchorage, AK 800-798-3636
Alaskan Gourmet Seafoods
  Anchorage, AK 800-288-3740
Alpine Butcher
  Lowell, MA 978-256-7771
Amano Fish Cake Factory
  Hilo, HI 808-935-5555
Amcan Industries
  Elmsford, NY 914-347-4838
Annabelle Lee
  Kennebunkport, ME 207-967-4611
Aquatec Seafoods Ltd.
  Comox, BC 250-339-6412
Arrowac Fisheries
  Seattle, WA 206-282-5655
Asian Foods Inc
  St Paul, MN 651-558-2400
Atlantic Capes Fisheries
  Cape May, NJ 609-884-3000
Atlantic Fish Specialties
  Charlottetown, PE 902-894-7005
Atlantic Sea Pride
  Boston, MA 617-269-7700
B.M. Lawrence & Company
  San Francisco, CA 415-981-2926
Baensch Food Products Co
  Milwaukee, WI 414-562-4643
Bakalars Sausage Co
  La Crosse, WI 608-784-0384
Baker's Point Fisheries
  Oyster Pond Jeddore, NS 902-845-2347
Basin Crawfish Processors
  Breaux Bridge, LA 337-332-6655
Bay Haven Lobster Pound
  York, ME 207-363-5265
Bayou Food Distributors
  Kenner, LA 800-516-8283
Bayou Land Seafood
  Breaux Bridge, LA 337-667-6118
Beaver Street Fisheries
  Jacksonville, FL 800-874-6426
Becker Foods
  Westminster, CA 714-891-9474
Belle River Enterprises
  Belle River, PE 902-962-2248
Billingsgate Fish Company
  Calgary, AB 403-571-7700
Birch Street Seafoods
  Digby, NS 902-245-6551
Blalock Seafood & Specialty
  Orange Beach, AL 251-974-5811
Blue Harvest Foods
  New Bedford, MA 508-993-5700
Blue Lakes Trout Farm
  Jerome, ID 208-734-7151
BlueWater Seafoods
  Gloucester, MA 888-560-2539
Bornstein Seafoods
  Bellingham, WA 360-734-7990
Bos Smoked Fish Inc
  Woodstock, ON 519-537-5000
Boston Seafarms
  Boston, MA 617-784-4777
Boundary Fish Company
  Blaine, WA 360-332-6715
Boutique Seafood Brokers
  Atlanta, GA 404-752-8852
Breakwater Fisheries
  St John's, NL 709-754-1999

Brookshire Grocery Company
  Tyler, TX 888-937-3776
Brucepac
  Woodburn, OR 800-899-3629
Burleigh Brothers Seafoods
  Ellerslie, PE 902-831-2349
Caito Fisheries Inc
  Fort Bragg, CA 707-964-6368
Caleb Haley & Co LLC
  Bronx, NY 718-617-7474
California Shellfish Company
  San Francisco, CA 415-923-7400
Canadian Fish Exporters
  Auburndale, MA 800-225-4215
Captain Alex Seafoods
  Niles, IL 847-803-8833
Carrington Foods Co Inc
  Saraland, AL 251-675-9700
Certi Fresh Foods Inc
  Wilmington, CA 310-221-6262
Channel Fish Processing
  Gloucester, MA 800-457-0054
Channel Fish Processing Co Inc
  Boston, MA 800-536-3474
Charlton Charters
  Warrenton, OR 503-338-0569
Chicago Food Market
  Chicago, IL 312-842-4361
Chicken Of The Sea
  El Segundo, CA 844-267-8862
Chuck's Seafoods
  Charleston, OR 541-888-5525
Clear Springs Foods Inc.
  Buhl, ID 800-635-8211
Connors Aquaculture
  Eastport, ME 207-853-6081
Consolidated Sea Products
  Mobile, AL 251-433-3240
Cook Inlet Processing
  Anchorage, AK 907-243-1166
Cooke Aguaculture
  Blacks Harbour, NB 506-456-6600
Cowart Seafood Corp
  Lottsburg, VA 804-529-6101
Crest International Corporation
  San Diego, CA 800-548-1232
Crown Prince Inc
  City Of Industry, CA 626-912-3700
Cuizina Food Company
  Woodinville, WA 425-486-7000
Culver Fish Farm
  Mcpherson, KS 800-241-5205
Cushner Seafoods Inc
  Baltimore, MD 410-358-5564
Dave's Gourmet Albacore
  Watsonville, CA 206-999-5517
Deep Creek Custom Packing
  Ninilchik, AK 800-764-0078
Delaware Valley Fish Co
  Norristown, PA 610-277-4900
Delta Pride Catfish
  Indianola, MS 800-228-3474
Dixon's Fisheries
  East Peoria, IL 800-373-1457
Dole & Bailey Inc
  Woburn, MA 781-935-1234
Dressel Collins Fish Company
  Seattle, WA 206-725-0121
Dynamic Foods
  Lubbock, TX 806-723-5600
Ed's Kasilof Seafoods
  Kasilof, AK 800-982-2377
Edelman Meats Inc
  Antigo, WI 715-623-7686
Emery Smith Fisheries Limited
  Shag Harbour, NS 902-723-2115
Erba Food Products
  Brooklyn, NY 718-272-7700
Feature Foods
  Brampton, ON 905-452-7741
Ferroclad Fishery
  Batchawana Bay, ON 705-882-2295
Finestkind Fish Market
  York, ME 800-288-8154
First Oriental Market
  Decatur, GA 404-377-6950

Product Categories / Fish & Seafood: Fish

Fish Brothers
   Blue Lake, CA 800-244-0583
Fishermens Net
   Portland, ME 207-772-3565
Fishpeople
   Portland, OR 503-342-2424
Flavor House, Inc.
   Adelanto, CA 760-246-9131
Fleet Fisheries Inc
   New Bedford, MA 508-910-2100
Fresh Island Fish
   Kahului, HI 808-871-1111
Freshwater Fish Market
   Winnipeg, MB 800-345-3113
Fulton Fish Market
   New York, NY 718-842-8908
Garden & Valley Isle Seafood
   Honolulu, HI 800-689-2733
George Robberecht Seafood
   Montross, VA 804-472-3556
Giovanni's Appetizing Food Co
   Richmond, MI 586-727-9355
Glenn Sales Company
   Atlanta, GA 770-952-9292
Gold Star Smoked Fish Inc
   Brooklyn, NY 718-522-1545
Gorton's Inc.
   Gloucester, MA 800-222-6846
Great Glacier Salmon
   Prince Rupert, BC 250-627-4955
Great Northern Products Inc
   Cranston, RI 401-490-4590
Hallmark Fisheries
   Charleston, OR 541-888-3253
Hamilos Bros Inspected Meat
   Madison, IL 618-876-3710
Handy International Inc
   Salisbury, MD 800-426-3977
Harbor Fish Market
   Portland, ME 800-370-1790
Harbor Seafood
   New Hyde Park, NY 800-645-2211
Harbour Lobster Ltd
   Shag Harbour, NS 902-723-2500
Hawaii International Seafood
   Kailua, HI 808-839-5010
Henry Davis Company
   Gary, IN 219-949-8555
HFI Foods
   Redmond, WA 425-883-1320
High Liner Foods Inc.
   Lunenburg, NS 902-634-8811
Homer's Wharf Seafood Company
   New Bedford, MA 508-997-0766
Idaho Trout Company
   Buhl, ID 866-878-7688
Independent Packers Corporation
   Seattle, WA 206-285-6000
Indian Bay Frozen Foods
   Centreville, NL 709-678-2844
Indian Valley Meats
   Indian, AK 907-653-7511
Ingles Markets
   Black Mountain, NC 828-669-2941
Inshore Fisheries
   Middle West Pubnico, NS 902-762-2522
International Seafoods - Alaska
   Kodiak, AK 907-486-4768
Isaacson & Stein Fish Company
   Chicago, IL 312-421-2444
Island Marine Products
   Clarks Harbour, NS 902-745-2222
J Deluca Fish Co Inc
   San Pedro, CA 310-684-5180
J Moniz Co Inc
   Fall River, MA 508-674-8451
J Turner Seafood
   Gloucester, MA 978-281-8535
J. Matassini & Sons Fish Company
   Tampa, FL 813-229-0829
J.S. McMillan Fisheries
   North Vancouver, BC 604-981-4000
James L. Mood Fisheries
   Nova Scotia, NS 902-723-2360
Jessie's Ilwaco Fish Company
   San Francisco, CA 360-642-3773
Joe Patti's Seafood Co
   Pensacola, FL 800-500-9929
John B. Wright Fish Company
   Gloucester, MA 978-283-4205
K&N Fisheries
   Upper Port La Tour, NS 902-768-2478

Key Largo Fisheries
   Key Largo, FL 800-432-4358
King Fish Restaurants
   Louisville, KY 502-339-0565
Kodiak Salmon Packers
   Larsen Bay, AK 907-847-2250
Kwikpak Fisheries
   Anchorage, AK 800-509-3332
L&M Evans
   Conyers, GA 770-483-9373
LEF McLean Brothers International
   Wheatley, ON 519-825-4656
Leo G. Atkinson Fisheries
   Clarks Harbor, NS 902-745-3047
Les Trois Petits Cochons
   Brooklyn, NY 800-537-7283
LLJ's Sea Products
   Round Pond, ME 207-529-4224
Lougheed Fisheries
   Owen Sound, ON 519-376-1586
Lowland Seafood
   Lowland, NC 252-745-3751
Lund's Fisheries
   Cape May, NJ 609-884-7600
Mada'n Kosher Foods
   Dania, FL 954-925-0077
Manischewitz Co
   Newark, NJ 201-553-1100
Mariner Seafood LLC
   New Bedford, MA 774-202-4121
Martin Brothers Seafood Co
   Westwego, LA 504-341-2251
Maxim's Import Corporation
   Miami, FL 800-331-6652
Meijer Inc
   Grand Rapids, MI 616-453-6711
Menemsha Fish Market
   Chilmark, MA 508-645-2282
Mid-South Fish Company
   Aubrey, AR 870-295-5600
Mill Cove Lobster Pound
   Trevett, ME 207-633-3340
Millen Fish
   Millen, GA 478-982-4988
Minor Fisheries
   Port Colborne, ON 905-834-9232
Mutual Fish Co
   Seattle, WA 206-322-4368
Nelson Crab Inc
   Tokeland, WA 800-262-0069
Neptune Foods
   Vernon, CA 323-232-8300
Nodine's Smokehouse Inc
   Torrington, CT 800-222-2059
Noon Hour Food Products Inc
   Chicago, IL 800-621-6636
Nordic Group Inc
   Boston, MA 800-486-4002
North Atlantic Inc
   Portland, ME 207-774-6025
North Atlantic Seafood
   Portland, ME 800-774-6025
Northern Products Corporation
   Seattle, WA 888-599-6290
Notre Dame Seafoods Inc.
   Comfort Cove, NL 709-244-5511
Ocean Beauty Seafoods Inc
   Seattle, WA 800-365-8950
Ocean Fresh Seafoods
   Seattle, WA 206-285-2412
Okuhara Foods Inc
   Honolulu, HI 808-848-0581
Omaha Steaks Inc
    800-960-8400
Ore-Cal Corp
   Los Angeles, CA 800-827-7474
Pacific American Fish Co Inc
   Vernon, CA 800-625-2525
Pacific Salmon Company
   Edmonds, WA 425-774-1315
Pacific Seafoods International
   Port Hardy, BC 250-949-8781
Paramount Caviar
   Long Island City, NY 800-992-2842
Park 100 Foods Inc
   Tipton, IN 800-854-6504
Paul Piazza & Son Inc
   New Orleans, LA 800-969-6011
Penguin Frozen Foods Inc
   Northbrook, IL 800-323-1485
Peter Pan Seafoods Inc.
   Bellevue, WA 206-728-6000

Premier Smoked Fish Company
   Bensalem, PA 800-654-6682
Proacec USA
   Santa Monica, CA 310-996-7770
Produits Belle Baie
   Caraquet, NB 506-727-4414
Protica Inc
   Whitehall, PA 800-776-8422
Publix Super Market
   Lakeland, FL 800-242-1227
QualiGourmet
   Boisbriand, QC 514-287-3530
Quinault Pride
   Taholah, WA 360-276-4431
Rachael's Smoked Fish
   Springfield, MA 800-327-3412
Raffield Fisheries Inc
   Port St Joe, FL 850-229-8494
Rego Smoked Fish Company
   Flushing, NY 718-894-1400
Roland Seafood Co
   Atlantic Beach, FL 904-246-9443
Roman Sausage Company
   Santa Clara, CA 800-497-7462
Royal Seafood Inc
   Brooklyn, NY 718-769-1517
Russian Chef
   New York, NY 212-249-1550
S.A.S. Foods
   Norcross, GA 770-263-9312
Salmon River Smokehouse
   Gustavus, AK 907-697-2330
Salt River Lobster Inc
   Boothbay, ME 207-633-5357
Santa Monica Seafood Co.
   Rancho Dominguez, CA 800-969-8862
Sau-Sea Foods
   Tarrytown, NY 914-631-1717
SC Enterprises
   Owen Sound, ON 519-371-0456
Scandia Seafood Company
   Rockland, ME 207-596-7102
Schafer Fisheries Inc
   Thomson, IL 800-291-3474
Sea Bear Smokehouse
   Anacortes, WA 800-645-3474
Sea Best Corporation
   Ipswich, MA 978-768-7475
Sea Farm & Farm Fresh Importing Company
   Monterey Park, CA 323-265-7075
Sea Fresh USA Inc
   North Kingstown, RI 401-583-0200
Sea Horse Wharf
   Phippsburg, ME 207-389-2312
Sea Lyons
   Spanish Fort, AL 251-626-2841
Sea Safari
   Belhaven, NC 800-688-6174
Sea-Fresh Seafood Market
   Mobile, AL 251-634-8650
Seabreeze Fish
   Bakersfield, CA 661-323-7936
Seafood Connection
   Honolulu, HI 808-591-8550
Seafood Express
   Brunswick, ME 207-729-0887
Seafood Hawaii Inc
   Honolulu, HI 808-597-1971
Seafood International
   Henderson, LA 337-228-7568
Seafood Packaging Inc
   New Orleans, LA 800-949-9656
Seafood Plus Corporation
   Orland Park, IL 708-795-4820
Seafood Producers Co-Op
   Bellingham, WA 360-733-0120
Seafood Services
   Newburyport, MA 508-999-6785
Seaway Company
   Fairhaven, MA 508-992-1221
Seven Seas Seafoods
   Alhambra, CA 626-570-9129
Sewell's Seafood & Fish Market
   Rogersville, AL 256-247-1378
Seymour & Sons Seafoods Inc
   Diberville, MS 228-392-4020
Sharkco's
   Venice, LA 504-534-9577
Shore Trading Co
   Alpharetta, GA 770-998-0566
Shuckman's Fish Co & Smokery
   Louisville, KY 502-775-6478

Product Categories / Fish & Seafood: Fish

Silver Streak Bass Co
  El Campo, TX 979-543-6343
SOPAKCO Foods
  Mullins, SC 800-276-9678
Sorrento Lobster
  Sorrento, ME 207-422-9082
South Shores Seafood
  Anaheim, CA 714-956-2722
Southern Fish & Oyster Company
  Mobile, AL 251-438-2408
Southern Pride Catfish Company
  Seattle, WA 800-343-8046
Spence & Company
  Brockton, MA 508-427-5577
Sportsman's Paradise Whites Ranch
  Paradise, UT 435-245-3053
Sportsmen's Cannery & Smokehouse
  Winchester Bay, OR 800-457-8048
Sportsmens Seafoods
  San Diego, CA 619-224-3551
St. Simons Seafood
  Brunswick, GA 912-265-5225
State Fish Distributors
  Chicago, IL 312-451-0800
Stavis Seafoods
  Boston, MA 800-390-5103
Sterling Caviar LLC
  Elverta, CA 800-525-0333
Stoller Fisheries
  Spirit Lake, IA 800-831-5174
Strub Pickles
  Brantford, ON 519-751-1717
Sunshine Food Sales
  Miami, FL 305-696-2885
Sunshine Seafood
  Stonington, ME 207-367-2955
Super Snooty Sea Food Corporation
  Boston, MA 617-426-6390
Superior Seafood
  New Orleans, LA 504-293-3474
Sweet Water Seafood
  Carlstadt, NJ 201-939-6622
Taku Smokehouse
  Juneau, AK 800-582-5122
Tampa Maid Foods Inc
  Lakeland, FL 800-237-7637
Tempest Fisheries LTD
  New Bedford, MA 508-997-0720
Tenth & M Seafoods
  Anchorage, AK 800-770-2722
Thompson Seafood
  Darien, GA 912-437-4649
Three Rivers Fish Company
  Simmesport, LA 318-941-2467
Tichon Sea Food Corp
  New Bedford, MA 508-999-5607
Trident Seafoods Corp
  Wrangell, AK 907-874-3346
Tropic Fish Hawaii LLC
  Honolulu, HI 808-591-2936
True World Foods LLC
  Rockleigh, NJ 201-750-0024
Ungars Food
  Elmwood Park, NJ 201-773-6846
Union Fisheries Corp
  Chicago, IL 773-738-0448
United Fishing Agency LTD
  Honolulu, HI 808-536-2148
Valdez Food Inc
  Philadelphia, PA 215-634-6106
Van de Kamps
  Peoria, IL 800-798-3318
Viking Seafoods Inc
  Malden, MA 800-225-3020
Vinalhaven Fishermens Co-op
  Camden, ME 207-236-0092
Virginia Trout Co
  Monterey, VA 540-468-2280
Vita Food Products Inc
  Chicago, IL 800-989-8482
Wabash Seafood Co
  Chicago, IL 312-733-5070
Wanchese Fish Co Inc
  Suffolk, VA 757-673-4500
Waterfield Farms
  Amherst, MA 413-549-3558
Wegmans Food Markets Inc.
  Rochester, NY 800-934-6267
West Coast Seafood Processors Association
  Portland, OR 503-227-5076
Weyand's Fishery
  Wyandotte, MI 800-521-9815

White Cap Fish Market
  Islip, NY 631-277-6577
Yamasa Fish Cake Co
  Los Angeles, CA 213-626-2211

Abalone
Crown Prince Inc
  City Of Industry, CA 626-912-3700
North Pacific Seafoods Inc
  Seattle, WA 206-726-9900

Amber Jack
Griffin's Seafood
  Golden Meadow, LA 985-396-2453

Anchovies
Chicken Of The Sea
  El Segundo, CA 844-267-8862
Crown Prince Inc
  City Of Industry, CA 626-912-3700
Northwest Wild Products
  Astoria, OR 503-791-1907

Canned
Ron Son Foods Inc
  Swedesboro, NJ 856-241-7333
Vital Choice
  Bellingham, WA 800-608-4825

Olive Oil
Castella Imports Inc
  Brentwood, NY 631-231-5500

Paste
Giovanni's Appetizing Food Co
  Richmond, MI 586-727-9355

Arctic Charr
Fumoir Grizzly
  St Augustin, QC 418-878-8941

Bass
Culver Fish Farm
  Mcpherson, KS 800-241-5205
Louisiana Seafood Exchange
  Jefferson, LA 800-969-9394
Minor Fisheries
  Port Colborne, ON 905-834-9232
North Atlantic Seafood
  Portland, ME 800-774-6025
Wanchese Fish Co Inc
  Suffolk, VA 757-673-4500

Striped
Advanced Aquaculture Systems
  Brandon, FL 800-994-7599

Bluefish
Menemsha Fish Market
  Chilmark, MA 508-645-2282
Raffield Fisheries Inc
  Port St Joe, FL 850-229-8494

Bottomfish
Charlton Charters
  Warrenton, OR 503-338-0569

Butterfish
Atlantic Capes Fisheries
  Cape May, NJ 609-884-3000
Okuhara Foods Inc
  Honolulu, HI 808-848-0581
Raffield Fisheries Inc
  Port St Joe, FL 850-229-8494

Cakes
Amano Fish Cake Factory
  Hilo, HI 808-935-5555
LA Monica Fine Foods
  Millville, NJ
Valdez Food Inc
  Philadelphia, PA 215-634-6106
Viking Seafoods Inc
  Malden, MA 800-225-3020
Yamasa Fish Cake Co
  Los Angeles, CA 213-626-2211

Canned
Cuizina Food Company
  Woodinville, WA 425-486-7000
LA Monica Fine Foods
  Millville, NJ

Fresh
Cuizina Food Company
  Woodinville, WA 425-486-7000
Valdez Food Inc
  Philadelphia, PA 215-634-6106
Yamasa Fish Cake Co
  Los Angeles, CA 213-626-2211

Frozen
Amano Fish Cake Factory
  Hilo, HI 808-935-5555
Cuizina Food Company
  Woodinville, WA 425-486-7000
Gorton's Inc.
  Gloucester, MA 800-222-6846
Viking Seafoods Inc
  Malden, MA 800-225-3020
Yamasa Fish Cake Co
  Los Angeles, CA 213-626-2211

Canned
Alaskan Gourmet Seafoods
  Anchorage, AK 800-288-3740
Amano Fish Cake Factory
  Hilo, HI 808-935-5555
B.M. Lawrence & Company
  San Francisco, CA 415-981-2926
Chicken Of The Sea
  El Segundo, CA 844-267-8862
Chuck's Seafoods
  Charleston, OR 541-888-5525
Cook Inlet Processing
  Anchorage, AK 907-243-1166
Cowart Seafood Corp
  Lottsburg, VA 804-529-6101
Deep Creek Custom Packing
  Ninilchik, AK 800-764-0078
Dressel Collins Fish Company
  Seattle, WA 206-725-0121
Fishhawk Fisheries
  Astoria, OR 503-325-5252
IMO Foods
  Yarmouth, NS 902-742-3519
Indian Valley Meats
  Indian, AK 907-653-7511
J Moniz Co Inc
  Fall River, MA 508-674-8451
J Turner Seafood
  Gloucester, MA 978-281-8535
J.S. McMillan Fisheries
  North Vancouver, BC 604-981-4000
Kodiak Salmon Packers
  Larsen Bay, AK 907-847-2250
LLJ's Sea Products
  Round Pond, ME 207-529-4224
Monterey Fish Company
  Salinas, CA 831-771-9221
Nelson Crab Inc
  Tokeland, WA 800-262-0069
Noon Hour Food Products Inc
  Chicago, IL 800-621-6636
Notre Dame Seafoods Inc.
  Comfort Cove, NL 709-244-5511
Ocean Fresh Seafoods
  Seattle, WA 206-285-2412
Pacific Salmon Company
  Edmonds, WA 425-774-1315
Pastene Co LTD
  Canton, MA 781-298-3397
Quinault Pride
  Taholah, WA 360-276-4431
Ron Son Foods Inc
  Swedesboro, NJ 856-241-7333
S&D Bait Company
  Morgan City, LA 504-252-3500
Shafer-Haggart
  Vancouver, BC 604-669-5512
Sportsman's Paradise Whites Ranch
  Paradise, UT 435-245-3053
Sportsmen's Cannery & Smokehouse
  Winchester Bay, OR 800-457-8048
Sportsmens Seafoods
  San Diego, CA 619-224-3551

190

Product Categories / Fish & Seafood: Fish

Trident Seafoods Corp
  Wrangell, AK 907-874-3346

Carp

Culver Fish Farm
  Mcpherson, KS 800-241-5205
Stoller Fisheries
  Spirit Lake, IA 800-831-5174

Catfish

America's Catch
  Itta Bena, MS 800-242-0041
Carolina Classics Catfish Inc
  Ayden, NC 252-746-2818
Catfish Wholesale
  Abbeville, LA 800-334-7292
Channel Fish Processing
  Gloucester, MA 800-457-0054
CJ's Seafood
  Des Allemands, LA 985-758-1237
Consolidated Catfish Co LLC
  Isola, MS 662-962-3101
Culver Fish Farm
  Mcpherson, KS 800-241-5205
Delta Catfish Products
  Eudora, AR 870-355-4192
Delta Pride Catfish
  Indianola, MS 800-228-3474
Fish Breeders of Idaho
  Hagerman, ID 208-837-6114
Great American Foods Commissary
  Hughes Springs, TX 903-639-1482
Guidry's Catfish Inc
  Breaux Bridge, LA 337-228-7546
Haring Catfish
  Wisner, LA 800-467-3474
Harvest Select
  Northport, AL 800-816-7426
Inshore Fisheries
  Middle West Pubnico, NS 902-762-2522
J. Matassini & Sons Fish Company
  Tampa, FL 813-229-0829
New Orleans Fish House II LLC
  New Orleans, LA 800-839-3474
Pickwick Catfish Farm
  Counce, TN 731-689-3805
Pond Pure Catfish
  Moulton, AL 256-974-6698
Roadrunner Seafood Inc
  Colquitt, GA 229-758-6098
Roy Dick Company
  Griffin, GA 770-227-3916
Seymour & Sons Seafoods Inc
  Diberville, MS 228-392-4020
Southern Farms Fish Processors
  Kansas City, MO 800-264-2594
Southern Pride Catfish Company
  Seattle, WA 800-343-8046

Chowder

LA Monica Fine Foods
  Millville, NJ

Chub

Raffield Fisheries Inc
  Port St Joe, FL 850-229-8494
Russ & Daughters
  New York, NY 800-787-7229

Cod

Alaska Pacific Seafoods
  Kodiak, AK 907-486-3234
Angy's Food Products Inc
  Westfield, MA 413-572-1010
Arrowac Fisheries
  Seattle, WA 206-282-5655
BlueWater Seafoods
  Gloucester, MA 888-560-2539
Breakwater Fisheries
  St John's, NL 709-754-1999
C.L. Deveau & Son
  Salmon River, NS 902-649-2812
Canadian Fish Exporters
  Auburndale, MA 800-225-4215
Castella Imports Inc
  Brentwood, NY 631-231-5500
Ceilidh Fisherman's Cooperative
  Port Hood, NS 902-787-2666
Certi Fresh Foods Inc
  Wilmington, CA 310-221-6262

Channel Fish Processing
  Gloucester, MA 800-457-0054
D Waybret & Sons Fisheries
  Shelburne, NS 902-745-3477
Davis Strait Fisheries
  Halifax, NS 902-450-5115
DB Kenney Fisheries
  Westport, NS 902-839-2023
Deep Creek Custom Packing
  Ninilchik, AK 800-764-0078
Dorset Fisheries
  St Josephs, NL 709-739-7147
Felix Custom Smoking
  Monroe, WA 425-485-2439
Harbor Seafood
  New Hyde Park, NY 800-645-2211
Helshiron Fisheries
  Grand Manan, NB 506-662-3696
High Liner Foods Inc.
  Lunenburg, NS 902-634-8811
Independent Packers Corporation
  Seattle, WA 206-285-6000
Inshore Fisheries
  Middle West Pubnico, NS 902-762-2522
K&N Fisheries
  Upper Port La Tour, NS 902-768-2478
La Have Seafoods
  La Have, NS 902-688-2773
Lund's Fisheries
  Cape May, NJ 609-884-7600
Menemsha Fish Market
  Chilmark, MA 508-645-2282
MG Fisheries
  Grand Manan, NB 506-662-3471
Mutual Fish Co
  Seattle, WA 206-322-4368
Neptune Foods
  Vernon, CA 323-232-8300
Nordic Group Inc
  Boston, MA 800-486-4002
North Atlantic Seafood
  Portland, ME 800-774-6025
Northern Products Corporation
  Seattle, WA 888-599-6290
Northwest Fisheries
  Hubbards, NS 902-228-2232
Northwest Wild Products
  Astoria, OR 503-791-1907
Notre Dame Seafoods Inc.
  Comfort Cove, NL 709-244-5511
Ocean Pride Fisheries
  Lower Wedgeport, NS 902-663-4579
Paul Piazza & Son Inc
  New Orleans, LA 800-969-6011
Peter Pan Seafoods Inc.
  Bellevue, WA 206-728-6000
Produits Belle Baie
  Caraquet, NB 506-727-4414
Royal Seafood Inc
  Brooklyn, NY 718-769-1517
Seafood Producers Co-Op
  Bellingham, WA 360-733-0120
Spruce Lane Investments
  Stratford, PE 902-892-2600
Taku Smokehouse
  Juneau, AK 800-582-5122
Tampa Bay Fisheries Inc
  Dover, FL 800-732-3663
Viking Seafoods Inc
  Malden, MA 800-225-3020
Vital Choice
  Bellingham, WA 800-608-4825

Black

Alaska Pacific Seafoods
  Kodiak, AK 907-486-3234
Dragnet Fisheries
  Anchorage, AK 907-276-4551
Fishhawk Fisheries
  Astoria, OR 503-325-5252
North Pacific Seafoods Inc
  Seattle, WA 206-726-9900
Pacific Salmon Company
  Edmonds, WA 425-774-1315
Royal Seafood Inc
  Brooklyn, NY 718-769-1517
Seafood Producers Co-Op
  Bellingham, WA 360-733-0120

Conch

Anchor Frozen Foods
  Westbury, NY 800-566-3474
Roadrunner Seafood Inc
  Colquitt, GA 229-758-6098

Croaker

Glenn Sales Company
  Atlanta, GA 770-952-9292
Griffin's Seafood
  Golden Meadow, LA 985-396-2453
Raffield Fisheries Inc
  Port St Joe, FL 850-229-8494
Roadrunner Seafood Inc
  Colquitt, GA 229-758-6098

Cusk

Canadian Fish Exporters
  Auburndale, MA 800-225-4215

Dehydrated

Oregon Freeze Dry, Inc.
  Albany, OR 541-926-6001

Eel

George Robberecht Seafood
  Montross, VA 804-472-3556
Ocean Union Company
  Lawrenceville, GA 770-995-1957

Fillets

Arrowac Fisheries
  Seattle, WA 206-282-5655
Barry Group
  Corner Brook, NL 709-785-7387
Bayou Food Distributors
  Kenner, LA 800-516-8283
Cozy Harbor Seafood Inc
  Portland, ME 800-225-2586
Ducktrap River Of Maine
  Belfast, ME 800-434-8727
Erba Food Products
  Brooklyn, NY 718-272-7700
Good Harbor Fillet Company
  New Bedford, MA 800-343-8046
Jessie's Ilwaco Fish Company
  San Francisco, CA 360-642-3773
Neptune Foods
  Vernon, CA 323-232-8300
Nordic Group Inc
  Boston, MA 800-486-4002
Ocean Beauty Seafoods Inc
  Seattle, WA 800-365-8950
Pacific American Fish Co Inc
  Vernon, CA 800-625-2525
Pacific Seafoods International
  Port Hardy, BC 250-949-8781
Penguin Frozen Foods Inc
  Northbrook, IL 800-323-1485
Roman Sausage Company
  Santa Clara, CA 800-497-7462
Super Snooty Sea Food Corporation
  Boston, MA 617-426-6390
Taku Smokehouse
  Juneau, AK 800-582-5122
Ungars Food
  Elmwood Park, NJ 201-773-6846

Finfish

Arrowac Fisheries
  Seattle, WA 206-282-5655
Bold Coast Smokehouse
  Lubec, ME 888-733-0807
Highland Fisheries
  Glace Bay, NS 902-849-6016

Flounder

Bon Secour Fisheries Inc
  Bon Secour, AL 251-949-7411
Carrington Foods Co Inc
  Saraland, AL 251-675-9700
Catfish Wholesale
  Abbeville, LA 800-334-7292
Glenn Sales Company
  Atlanta, GA 770-952-9292
Gorton's Inc.
  Gloucester, MA 800-222-6846

Product Categories / Fish & Seafood: Fish

Griffin's Seafood
   Golden Meadow, LA 985-396-2453
Gulf City Marine Supply
   Bayou La Batre, AL 251-824-2516
Inshore Fisheries
   Middle West Pubnico, NS 902-762-2522
Lund's Fisheries
   Cape May, NJ 609-884-7600
Menemsha Fish Market
   Chilmark, MA 508-645-2282
Mirasco
   Atlanta, GA 770-956-1945
North Atlantic Seafood
   Portland, ME 800-774-6025
Northern Products Corporation
   Seattle, WA 888-599-6290
Pamlico Packing Company
   Grantsboro, NC 800-682-1113
Roadrunner Seafood Inc
   Colquitt, GA 229-758-6098
Royal Seafood Inc
   Brooklyn, NY 718-769-1517
Tampa Maid Foods Inc
   Lakeland, FL 800-237-7637
Thompson Seafood
   Darien, GA 912-437-4649
Wanchese Fish Co Inc
   Suffolk, VA 757-673-4500

Fluke

Agger Fish Corp
   Brooklyn, NY 718-855-1717

Fresh

Arrowac Fisheries
   Seattle, WA 206-282-5655
Atlantic Salmon of Maine
   Belfast, ME 800-508-7861
Baker's Point Fisheries
   Oyster Pond Jeddore, NS 902-845-2347
Bama Fish Atlanta
   East Point, GA 404-765-9896
Bayou Land Seafood
   Breaux Bridge, LA 337-667-6118
Birch Street Seafoods
   Digby, NS 902-245-6551
Blue Circle Foods
   Washington, DC 202-232-5282
Bon Secour Fisheries Inc
   Bon Secour, AL 251-949-7411
Cleanfish Inc
   San Francisco, CA 415-626-3500
Cook Inlet Processing
   Anchorage, AK 907-243-1166
Crest International Corporation
   San Diego, CA 800-548-1232
Deep Creek Custom Packing
   Ninilchik, AK 800-764-0078
Ferroclad Fishery
   Batchawana Bay, ON 705-882-2295
Galilean Seafood Inc
   Bristol, RI 401-253-3030
Harbor Fish Market
   Portland, ME 800-370-1790
HFI Foods
   Redmond, WA 425-883-1320
High Liner Foods Inc.
   Lunenburg, NS 902-634-8811
Inshore Fisheries
   Middle West Pubnico, NS 902-762-2522
International Seafoods - Alaska
   Kodiak, AK 907-486-4768
Island Marine Products
   Clarks Harbour, NS 902-745-2222
J. Matassini & Sons Fish Company
   Tampa, FL 813-229-0829
Jessie's Ilwaco Fish Company
   San Francisco, CA 360-642-3773
King Food Service
   Rock Island, IL 309-787-4488
Kyler's Catch Seafood Market
   New Bedford, MA 888-859-5377
LA Monica Fine Foods
   Millville, NJ
Lougheed Fisheries
   Owen Sound, ON 519-376-1586
Mac Knight Smoke House Inc
   Miami, FL 305-651-3323
Mariner Seafood LLC
   New Bedford, MA 774-202-4121
Menemsha Fish Market
   Chilmark, MA 508-645-2282
Minor Fisheries
   Port Colborne, ON 905-834-9232
Morey's Seafood Intl LLC
   Motley, MN 800-808-3474
Mutual Fish Co
   Seattle, WA 206-322-4368
North Atlantic Seafood
   Portland, ME 800-774-6025
Ocean Beauty Seafoods Inc
   Seattle, WA 800-365-8950
Ocean Fresh Seafoods
   Seattle, WA 206-285-2412
Pacific American Fish Co Inc
   Vernon, CA 800-625-2525
Pacific Seafoods International
   Port Hardy, BC 250-949-8781
Paul Piazza & Son Inc
   New Orleans, LA 800-969-6011
QualiGourmet
   Boisbriand, QC 514-287-3530
Royal Seafood Inc
   Brooklyn, NY 718-769-1517
Sportsman's Paradise Whites Ranch
   Paradise, UT 435-245-3053
Sunshine Food Sales
   Miami, FL 305-696-2885
Tampa Bay Fisheries Inc
   Dover, FL 800-732-3663
Trident Seafoods Corp
   Wrangell, AK 907-874-3346
Union Fisheries Corp
   Chicago, IL 773-738-0448
Virginia Trout Co
   Monterey, VA 540-468-2280
Wanchese Fish Co Inc
   Suffolk, VA 757-673-4500
Weyand's Fishery
   Wyandotte, MI 800-521-9815
Yamasa Fish Cake Co
   Los Angeles, CA 213-626-2211

Freshwater

Hamilos Bros Inspected Meat
   Madison, IL 618-876-3710

Frozen

Alaskan Gourmet Seafoods
   Anchorage, AK 800-288-3740
Alpine Butcher
   Lowell, MA 978-256-7771
Amano Fish Cake Factory
   Hilo, HI 808-935-5555
Arrowac Fisheries
   Seattle, WA 206-282-5655
Baker's Point Fisheries
   Oyster Pond Jeddore, NS 902-845-2347
Bama Fish Atlanta
   East Point, GA 404-765-9896
Barry Group
   Corner Brook, NL 709-785-7387
Bayou Land Seafood
   Breaux Bridge, LA 337-667-6118
Beaver Street Fisheries
   Jacksonville, FL 800-874-6426
Big Al's Seafood
   Bozman, MD 410-745-2637
Birch Street Seafoods
   Digby, NS 902-245-6551
Birdie Pak Products
   Chicago, IL 773-247-5293
Blue Circle Foods
   Washington, DC 202-232-5282
Bon Secour Fisheries Inc
   Bon Secour, AL 251-949-7411
Breakwater Fisheries
   St John's, NL 709-754-1999
Buedel Food Products
   Bridgeview, IL 708-496-3500
Carrington Foods Co Inc
   Saraland, AL 251-675-9700
Certi Fresh Foods Inc
   Wilmington, CA 310-221-6262
Channel Fish Processing
   Gloucester, MA 800-457-0054
Clear Springs Foods Inc.
   Buhl, ID 800-635-8211
Cook Inlet Processing
   Anchorage, AK 907-243-1166

Cozy Harbor Seafood Inc
   Portland, ME 800-225-2586
Crest International Corporation
   San Diego, CA 800-548-1232
Cuizina Food Company
   Woodinville, WA 425-486-7000
DB Kenney Fisheries
   Westport, NS 902-839-2023
Deep Creek Custom Packing
   Ninilchik, AK 800-764-0078
Delta Pride Catfish
   Indianola, MS 800-228-3474
Ferroclad Fishery
   Batchawana Bay, ON 705-882-2295
George Robberecht Seafood
   Montross, VA 804-472-3556
Glacier Fish Company
   Seattle, WA 206-298-1200
Great Glacier Salmon
   Prince Rupert, BC 250-627-4955
Great Northern Products Inc
   Cranston, RI 401-490-4590
Hamilos Bros Inspected Meat
   Madison, IL 618-876-3710
Handy International Inc
   Salisbury, MD 800-426-3977
HFI Foods
   Redmond, WA 425-883-1320
High Liner Foods Inc.
   Lunenburg, NS 902-634-8811
Hook Line and Savor
   Gloucester, MA 833-457-2867
Independent Packers Corporation
   Seattle, WA 206-285-6000
Inshore Fisheries
   Middle West Pubnico, NS 902-762-2522
International Seafoods - Alaska
   Kodiak, AK 907-486-4768
Island Marine Products
   Clarks Harbour, NS 902-745-2222
J. Matassini & Sons Fish Company
   Tampa, FL 813-229-0829
Jessie's Ilwaco Fish Company
   San Francisco, CA 360-642-3773
Key Largo Fisheries
   Key Largo, FL 800-432-4358
Kodiak Salmon Packers
   Larsen Bay, AK 907-847-2250
Kyler's Catch Seafood Market
   New Bedford, MA 888-859-5377
Lougheed Fisheries
   Owen Sound, ON 519-376-1586
Lund's Fisheries
   Cape May, NJ 609-884-7600
Mada'n Kosher Foods
   Dania, FL 954-925-0077
Martin Brothers Seafood Co
   Westwego, LA 504-341-2251
Menemsha Fish Market
   Chilmark, MA 508-645-2282
Mill Cove Lobster Pound
   Trevett, ME 207-633-3340
Minor Fisheries
   Port Colborne, ON 905-834-9232
Monterey Fish Company
   Salinas, CA 831-771-9221
Morey's Seafood Intl LLC
   Motley, MN 800-808-3474
Mutual Fish Co
   Seattle, WA 206-322-4368
Nelson Crab Inc
   Tokeland, WA 800-262-0069
Nordic Group Inc
   Boston, MA 800-486-4002
North Atlantic Seafood
   Portland, ME 800-774-6025
Notre Dame Seafoods Inc.
   Comfort Cove, NL 709-244-5511
Ocean Beauty Seafoods Inc
   Seattle, WA 800-365-8950
Ocean Fresh Seafoods
   Seattle, WA 206-285-2412
Okuhara Foods Inc
   Honolulu, HI 808-848-0581
Pacific American Fish Co Inc
   Vernon, CA 800-625-2525
Pacific Salmon Company
   Edmonds, WA 425-774-1315
Pacific Seafoods International
   Port Hardy, BC 250-949-8781
Pamlico Packing Company
   Grantsboro, NC 800-682-1113

Product Categories / Fish & Seafood: Fish

Paul Piazza & Son Inc
   New Orleans, LA 800-969-6011
Penguin Frozen Foods Inc
   Northbrook, IL 800-323-1485
Peter Pan Seafoods Inc.
   Bellevue, WA 206-728-6000
Quinault Pride
   Taholah, WA 360-276-4431
Royal Seafood Inc
   Brooklyn, NY 718-769-1517
Santa Monica Seafood Co.
   Rancho Dominguez, CA 800-969-8862
Sea Safari
   Belhaven, NC 800-688-6174
Seymour & Sons Seafoods Inc
   Diberville, MS 228-392-4020
Spruce Lane Investments
   Stratford, PE 902-892-2600
Sterling Caviar LLC
   Elverta, CA 800-525-0333
Sunshine Food Sales
   Miami, FL 305-696-2885
Super Snooty Sea Food Corporation
   Boston, MA 617-426-6390
Taku Smokehouse
   Juneau, AK 800-582-5122
Tampa Bay Fisheries Inc
   Dover, FL 800-732-3663
Tampa Maid Foods Inc
   Lakeland, FL 800-237-7637
Tichon Sea Food Corp
   New Bedford, MA 508-999-5607
Trident Seafoods Corp
   Wrangell, AK 907-874-3346
Union Fisheries Corp
   Chicago, IL 773-738-0448
Viking Seafoods Inc
   Malden, MA 800-225-3020
Virginia Trout Co
   Monterey, VA 540-468-2280
Wanchese Fish Co Inc
   Suffolk, VA 757-673-4500
Weyand's Fishery
   Wyandotte, MI 800-521-9815
White Cap Fish Market
   Islip, NY 631-277-6577
Yamasa Fish Cake Co
   Los Angeles, CA 213-626-2211

Gefilte

Erba Food Products
   Brooklyn, NY 718-272-7700
Manischewitz Co
   Newark, NJ 201-553-1100

Grouper

Griffin's Seafood
   Golden Meadow, LA 985-396-2453
Mirasco
   Atlanta, GA 770-956-1945
North Atlantic Seafood
   Portland, ME 800-774-6025
Ocean Union Company
   Lawrenceville, GA 770-995-1957
Poseidon Enterprises
   Charlotte, NC 800-863-7886

Haddock

Adams Fisheries Ltd
   Shag Harbour, NS 902-723-2435
BlueWater Seafoods
   Gloucester, MA .888-560-2539
Canadian Fish Exporters
   Auburndale, MA 800-225-4215
Davis Strait Fisheries
   Halifax, NS 902-450-5115
DB Kenney Fisheries
   Westport, NS 902-839-2023
High Liner Foods Inc.
   Lunenburg, NS .902-634-8811
I. Deveau Fisheries LTD
   Barrington Passage, NS 902-745-2877
Inshore Fisheries
   Middle West Pubnico, NS 902-762-2522
Island Marine Products
   Clarks Harbour, NS 902-745-2222
La Have Seafoods
   La Have, NS 902-688-2773
Leo G. Atkinson Fisheries
   Clarks Harbor, NS 902-745-3047

Menemsha Fish Market
   Chilmark, MA 508-645-2282
MG Fisheries
   Grand Manan, NB 506-662-3471
Nordic Group Inc
   Boston, MA 800-486-4002
North Atlantic Seafood
   Portland, ME 800-774-6025
Ocean Pride Fisheries
   Lower Wedgeport, NS 902-663-4579
W.A. Beans & Sons
   Bangor, ME 800-649-1958

Hake

Canadian Fish Exporters
   Auburndale, MA 800-225-4215
Helshiron Fisheries
   Grand Manan, NB 506-662-3696
Mirasco
   Atlanta, GA 770-956-1945
North Atlantic Seafood
   Portland, ME 800-774-6025

Halibut

Alaska Pacific Seafoods
   Kodiak, AK 907-486-3234
Alaskan Gourmet Seafoods
   Anchorage, AK .800-288-3740
Angy's Food Products Inc
   Westfield, MA 413-572-1010
Arrowac Fisheries
   Seattle, WA 206-282-5655
Boundary Fish Company
   Blaine, WA 360-332-6715
California Shellfish Company
   San Francisco, CA 415-923-7400
Calkins & Burke
   Vancouver, BC .800-669-7992
Captain Little Seafood
   Queens County, NS 902-947-2087
Certi Fresh Foods Inc
   Wilmington, CA 310-221-6262
Channel Fish Processing
   Gloucester, MA .800-457-0054
Charlton Charters
   Warrenton, OR .503-338-0569
D Waybret & Sons Fisher ies
   Shelburne, NS .902-745-3477
Deep Creek Custom Packing
   Ninilchik, AK 800-764-0078
Felix Custom Smoking
   Monroe, WA 425-485-2439
Fishhawk Fisheries
   Astoria, OR 503-325-5252
Glacier Fish Company
   Seattle, WA 206-298-1200
Haines Packing Company
   Haines, AK 907-766-2883
High Liner Foods Inc.
   Lunenburg, NS .902-634-8811
Independent Packers Corporation
   Seattle, WA 206-285-6000
Indian Valley Meats
   Indian, AK 907-653-7511
Island Marine Products
   Clarks Harbour, NS 902-745-2222
Menemsha Fish Market
   Chilmark, MA 508-645-2282
Neptune Foods
   Vernon, CA 323-232-8300
North Atlantic Seafood
   Portland, ME 800-774-6025
North Pacific Seafoods Inc
   Seattle, WA 206-726-9900
Northwest Fisheries
   Hubbards, NS 902-228-2232
Northwest Wild Products
   Astoria, OR 503-791-1907
Ocean Beauty Seafoods Inc
   Seattle, WA 800-365-8950
Pacific Salmon Company
   Edmonds, WA .425-774-1315
Peter Pan Seafoods Inc.
   Bellevue, WA 206-728-6000
Santa Monica Seafood Co.
   Rancho Dominguez, CA 800-969-8862
Seafood Producers Co-Op
   Bellingham, WA 360-733-0120
Taku Smokehouse
   Juneau, AK 800-582-5122

Tampa Bay Fisheries Inc
   Dover, FL 800-732-3663
Tenth & M Seafoods
   Anchorage, AK .800-770-2722
Trident Seafoods Corp
   Wrangell, AK 907-874-3346
Viking Seafoods Inc
   Malden, MA 800-225-3020
Vital Choice
   Bellingham, WA 800-608-4825

Herring

Acme Smoked Fish Corporation
   Brooklyn, NY 718-383-8585
Alimentaire Whyte's Inc
   Laval, QC 866-420-9520
Angy's Food Products Inc
   Westfield, MA 413-572-1010
Baensch Food Products Co
   Milwaukee, WI .414-562-4643
Barry Group
   Corner Brook, NL 709-785-7387
Bos Smoked Fish Inc
   Woodstock, ON 519-537-5000
Breakwater Fisheries
   St John's, NL 709-754-1999
Canadian Fish Exporters
   Auburndale, MA 800-225-4215
Castella Imports Inc
   Brentwood, NY .631-231-5500
Chicago 58 Food Products
   Woodbridge, ON 416-603-4244
Comeau's Seafoods
   Saulnierville, NS 902-769-2101
Cowart Seafood Corp
   Lottsburg, VA 804-529-6101
Delta Pacific Seafoods
   Delta, BC 604-946-5160
Dragnet Fisheries
   Anchorage, AK .907-276-4551
Duguay Fish Packers
   Cap-Pele, NB 506-577-2287
Feature Foods
   Brampton, ON .905-452-7741
Ferroclad Fishery
   Batchawana Bay, ON 705-882-2295
Flaum Appetizing
   Brooklyn, NY 718-821-1970
Gaudet & Ouellette
   Cap-Pele, NB 506-577-4016
Great Northern Products Inc
   Cranston, RI 401-490-4590
Island Marine Products
   Clarks Harbour, NS 902-745-2222
Leslie Leger & Sons
   Cap-Pele, NB 506-577-4730
Lund's Fisheries
   Cape May, NJ .609-884-7600
Menemsha Fish Market
   Chilmark, MA 508-645-2282
Newell Lobsters
   Yarmouth, NS 902-742-6272
North Pacific Seafoods Inc
   Seattle, WA 206-726-9900
Premier Smoked Fish Company
   Bensalem, PA 800-654-6682
Produits Belle Baie
   Caraquet, NB 506-727-4414
Rachael's Smoked Fish
   Springfield, MA 800-327-3412
Raffield Fisheries Inc
   Port St Joe, FL .850-229-8494
Royal Seafood Inc
   Brooklyn, NY 718-769-1517
Russ & Daughters
   New York, NY .800-787-7229
Salmolux Inc
   Federal Way, WA 253-874-6570
Spruce Lane Investments
   Stratford, PE 902-892-2600
Strub Pickles
   Brantford, ON 519-751-1717
Trident Seafoods Corp
   Wrangell, AK 907-874-3346
Vita Food Products Inc
   Chicago, IL 800-989-8482

Boned

Feature Foods
   Brampton, ON .905-452-7741

Product Categories / Fish & Seafood: Fish

Fillets

Angy's Food Products Inc
   Westfield, MA......................413-572-1010

Fresh

Angy's Food Products Inc
   Westfield, MA......................413-572-1010
Bella Coola Fisheries
   Surrey, BC..........................604-541-0339
Feature Foods
   Brampton, ON......................905-452-7741
Ferroclad Fishery
   Batchawana Bay, ON.............705-882-2295
Royal Seafood Inc
   Brooklyn, NY.......................718-769-1517
Trident Seafoods Corp
   Wrangell, AK.......................907-874-3346

Frozen

Angy's Food Products Inc
   Westfield, MA......................413-572-1010
Bella Coola Fisheries
   Surrey, BC..........................604-541-0339
Breakwater Fisheries
   St John's, NL......................709-754-1999
Ferroclad Fishery
   Batchawana Bay, ON.............705-882-2295
Great Northern Products Inc
   Cranston, RI.......................401-490-4590
Island Marine Products
   Clarks Harbour, NS..............902-745-2222
Lund's Fisheries
   Cape May, NJ.....................609-884-7600
Menemsha Fish Market
   Chilmark, MA......................508-645-2282
Peter Pan Seafoods Inc.
   Bellevue, WA......................206-728-6000
Royal Seafood Inc
   Brooklyn, NY.......................718-769-1517
Trident Seafoods Corp
   Wrangell, AK.......................907-874-3346

Salted & Marinated

Feature Foods
   Brampton, ON......................905-452-7741
High Liner Foods Inc.
   Lunenburg, NS....................902-634-8811
Island Marine Products
   Clarks Harbour, NS..............902-745-2222

Spiced

Baensch Food Products Co
   Milwaukee, WI.....................414-562-4643
Feature Foods
   Brampton, ON......................905-452-7741

Imitation

Flavor House, Inc.
   Adelanto, CA......................760-246-9131
HFI Foods
   Redmond, WA.....................425-883-1320
Ocean Food Co. Ltd.
   Toronto, ON.......................416-285-6487
Peter Pan Seafoods Inc.
   Bellevue, WA......................206-728-6000
Shining Ocean Inc
   Sumner, WA.......................800-935-6464
Trans-Ocean Products Inc
   Bellingham, WA...................800-290-2722

King Cod

Deep Creek Custom Packing
   Ninilchik, AK.......................800-764-0078
Minor Fisheries
   Port Colborne, ON...............905-834-9232

Kingfish

Sunshine Food Sales
   Miami, FL...........................305-696-2885

Lumpfish

Notre Dame Seafoods Inc.
   Comfort Cove, NL................709-244-5511
Russian Chef
   New York, NY.....................212-249-1550

Mackerel

Atlantic Capes Fisheries
   Cape May, NJ.....................609-884-3000
Atlantic Fish Specialties
   Charlottetown, PE................902-894-7005
Bold Coast Smokehouse
   Lubec, ME..........................888-733-0807
Bos Smoked Fish Inc
   Woodstock, ON...................519-537-5000
Breakwater Fisheries
   St John's, NL.....................709-754-1999
Canadian Fish Exporters
   Auburndale, MA..................800-225-4215
Castella Imports Inc
   Brentwood, NY....................631-231-5500
Chicken Of The Sea
   El Segundo, CA..................844-267-8862
Crown Prince Inc
   City Of Industry, CA.............626-912-3700
Ducktrap River Of Maine
   Belfast, ME.........................800-434-8727
Erba Food Products
   Brooklyn, NY.......................718-272-7700
Griffin's Seafood
   Golden Meadow, LA............985-396-2453
J Deluca Fish Co Inc
   San Pedro, CA...................310-684-5180
Lund's Fisheries
   Cape May, NJ.....................609-884-7600
Menemsha Fish Market
   Chilmark, MA......................508-645-2282
Northwest Wild Products
   Astoria, OR........................503-791-1907
Notre Dame Seafoods Inc.
   Comfort Cove, NL................709-244-5511
Ocean Union Company
   Lawrenceville, GA...............770-995-1957
Royal Seafood Inc
   Brooklyn, NY.......................718-769-1517
Russ & Daughters
   New York, NY.....................800-787-7229
Spruce Lane Investments
   Stratford, PE......................902-892-2600
Sunshine Food Sales
   Miami, FL...........................305-696-2885
Vital Choice
   Bellingham, WA...................800-608-4825

Mahi-Mahi

Griffin's Seafood
   Golden Meadow, LA............985-396-2453
North Atlantic Seafood
   Portland, ME.......................800-774-6025
Ocean Beauty Seafoods Inc
   Seattle, WA........................800-365-8950
Omega Foods
   Mississauga, ON.................877-212-9484
Peter Pan Seafoods Inc.
   Bellevue, WA......................206-728-6000

Marlin

Mid-Pacific Hawaii Fishery
   Hilo, HI..............................808-935-6110
Sportsmens Seafoods
   San Diego, CA...................619-224-3551

Meal

Acatris USA
   Edina, MN..........................952-920-7700
Barry Group
   Corner Brook, NL.................709-785-7387

Monkfish

Agger Fish Corp
   Brooklyn, NY.......................718-855-1717
Atlantic Capes Fisheries
   Cape May, NJ.....................609-884-3000
North Atlantic Seafood
   Portland, ME.......................800-774-6025

Mullet

Griffin's Seafood
   Golden Meadow, LA............985-396-2453
Raffield Fisheries Inc
   Port St Joe, FL...................850-229-8494
Roadrunner Seafood Inc
   Colquitt, GA........................229-758-6098

Orange Roughy

Neptune Foods
   Vernon, CA.........................323-232-8300

Packed

Ore-Cal Corp
   Los Angeles, CA.................800-827-7474

Glass

Indian Valley Meats
   Indian, AK..........................907-653-7511
Noon Hour Food Products Inc
   Chicago, IL.........................800-621-6636

Pouch

Cook Inlet Processing
   Anchorage, AK...................907-243-1166
Haines Packing Company
   Haines, AK.........................907-766-2883
Indian Valley Meats
   Indian, AK..........................907-653-7511
Noon Hour Food Products Inc
   Chicago, IL.........................800-621-6636
Seajoy
   Miami, FL...........................877-537-1717

Paste

Giovanni's Appetizing Food Co
   Richmond, MI.....................586-727-9355

Patties

CBS Food Products Corporation
   Franklin, TN.......................800-216-9605
Roman Sausage Company
   Santa Clara, CA.................800-497-7462

Perch

A&A Marine & Drydock Company
   Blenheim, ON.....................519-676-2030
High Liner Foods Inc.
   Lunenburg, NS....................902-634-8811
Inshore Fisheries
   Middle West Pubnico, NS.....902-762-2522
Kingsville Fisherman's Company
   Kingsville, ON.....................519-733-6534
Minor Fisheries
   Port Colborne, ON...............905-834-9232
Mutual Fish Co
   Seattle, WA........................206-322-4368
North Atlantic Seafood
   Portland, ME.......................800-774-6025
Paul Piazza & Son Inc
   New Orleans, LA................800-969-6011
Royal Seafood Inc
   Brooklyn, NY.......................718-769-1517
Viking Seafoods Inc
   Malden, MA........................800-225-3020

Ocean

DB Kenney Fisheries
   Westport, NS......................902-839-2023
Mill Cove Lobster Pound
   Trevett, ME........................207-633-3340

Pickerel

A&A Marine & Drydock Company
   Blenheim, ON.....................519-676-2030
Kingsville Fisherman's Company
   Kingsville, ON.....................519-733-6534
Minor Fisheries
   Port Colborne, ON...............905-834-9232

Pollack

Alaska Pacific Seafoods
   Kodiak, AK.........................907-486-3234
BlueWater Seafoods
   Gloucester, MA...................888-560-2539
Glacier Fish Company
   Seattle, WA........................206-298-1200
Glenn Sales Company
   Atlanta, GA........................770-952-9292
Harbor Seafood
   New Hyde Park, NY.............800-645-2211
Inshore Fisheries
   Middle West Pubnico, NS.....902-762-2522
K&N Fisheries
   Upper Port La Tour, NS........902-768-2478

Product Categories / Fish & Seafood: Fish

Neptune Foods
  Vernon, CA 323-232-8300
North Atlantic Seafood
  Portland, ME 800-774-6025
Peter Pan Seafoods Inc.
  Bellevue, WA 206-728-6000

Pompano

Griffin's Seafood
  Golden Meadow, LA 985-396-2453

Red Snapper

Northwest Wild Products
  Astoria, OR 503-791-1907

Rock Fish

Deep Creek Custom Packing
  Ninilchik, AK 800-764-0078
North Pacific Seafoods Inc
  Seattle, WA 206-726-9900
Seafood Producers Co-Op
  Bellingham, WA 360-733-0120
Vital Choice
  Bellingham, WA 800-608-4825

Sablefish

Rego Smoked Fish Company
  Flushing, NY 718-894-1400
Russ & Daughters
  New York, NY 800-787-7229
Vital Choice
  Bellingham, WA 800-608-4825

Salmon

Alaska General Seafoods
  Kenmore, WA 425-485-7755
Alaska Pacific Seafoods
  Kodiak, AK 907-486-3234
Alaskan Gourmet Seafoods
  Anchorage, AK 800-288-3740
Alaskan Smoked Salmon & Seafood
  Anchorage, AK 907-349-8234
Alder Springs Smoked Salmon
  Sequim, WA 360-683-2829
Angy's Food Products Inc
  Westfield, MA 413-572-1010
Aquatec Seafoods Ltd.
  Comox, BC 250-339-6412
Arrowac Fisheries
  Seattle, WA 206-282-5655
Atlantic Salmon of Maine
  Belfast, ME 800-508-7861
Barry Group
  Corner Brook, NL 709-785-7387
Bella Coola Fisheries
  Surrey, BC 604-541-0339
Bering Sea Fisheries
  Snohomish, WA 425-334-1498
Blue Marble Brands
  Providence, RI 888-534-0246
BlueWater Seafoods
  Gloucester, MA 888-560-2539
Blundell Seafoods
  Richmond, BC 604-270-3300
Bos Smoked Fish Inc
  Woodstock, ON 519-537-5000
Brucepac
  Woodburn, OR 800-899-3629
Caito Fisheries Inc
  Fort Bragg, CA 707-964-6368
California Shellfish Company
  San Francisco, CA 415-923-7400
Calkins & Burke
  Vancouver, BC 800-669-7992
Casey Fisheries
  Digby, NS 902-245-5801
Certi Fresh Foods Inc
  Wilmington, CA 310-221-6262
Charlton Charters
  Warrenton, OR 503-338-0569
Chicken Of The Sea
  El Segundo, CA 844-267-8862
Chuck's Seafoods
  Charleston, OR 541-888-5525
Dave's Gourmet Albacore
  Watsonville, CA 206-999-5517
Dear North
  Juneau, AK 907-789-8500
Deep Creek Custom Packing
  Ninilchik, AK 800-764-0078

Delta Pacific Seafoods
  Delta, BC 604-946-5160
Dragnet Fisheries
  Anchorage, AK 907-276-4551
Dressel Collins Fish Company
  Seattle, WA 206-725-0121
Ducktrap River Of Maine
  Belfast, ME 800-434-8727
FDI Inc
  Berkeley, IL 708-544-1880
Fiddlers Green Farm
  North Vassalboro, ME 800-729-7935
Fishhawk Fisheries
  Astoria, OR 503-325-5252
Giovanni's Appetizing Food Co
  Richmond, MI 586-727-9355
Glacier Fish Company
  Seattle, WA 206-298-1200
Great Glacier Salmon
  Prince Rupert, BC 250-627-4955
Great Pacific Seafoods
  Seattle, WA 206-764-7180
Haines Packing Company
  Haines, AK 907-766-2883
Handy International Inc
  Salisbury, MD 800-426-3977
Heritage Salmon Company
  Richmond, BC 604-277-3093
High Liner Foods Inc.
  Lunenburg, NS 902-634-8811
High Tide Seafoods Inc
  Port Angeles, WA 360-452-8488
Independent Packers Corporation
  Seattle, WA 206-285-6000
Indian Valley Meats
  Indian, AK 907-653-7511
J.S. McMillan Fisheries
  North Vancouver, BC 604-981-4000
Jessie's Ilwaco Fish Company
  San Francisco, CA 360-642-3773
Kodiak Salmon Packers
  Larsen Bay, AK 907-847-2250
Maine Coast Nordic
  Mahiasport, ME 207-255-6714
Menemsha Fish Market
  Chilmark, MA 508-645-2282
Morey's Seafood Intl LLC
  Motley, MN 800-808-3474
Mutual Fish Co
  Seattle, WA 206-322-4368
Nelson Crab Inc
  Tokeland, WA 800-262-0069
Neptune Foods
  Vernon, CA 323-232-8300
Nordic Group Inc
  Boston, MA 800-486-4002
North Atlantic Seafood
  Portland, ME 800-774-6025
North Pacific Seafoods Inc
  Seattle, WA 206-726-9900
Northern Products Corporation
  Seattle, WA 888-599-6290
Northwest Wild Products
  Astoria, OR 503-791-1907
Ocean Beauty Seafoods Inc
  Seattle, WA 800-365-8950
Ocean Food Co. Ltd.
  Toronto, ON 416-285-6487
Okuhara Foods Inc
  Honolulu, HI 808-848-0581
Omega Foods
  Mississauga, ON 877-212-9484
Pacific Salmon Company
  Edmonds, WA 425-774-1315
Pacific Seafoods International
  Port Hardy, BC 250-949-8781
Paramount Caviar
  Long Island City, NY 800-992-2842
Patagonia Provisions
  Sausalito, CA 888-221-8208
Perona Farms
  Andover, NJ 800-750-6190
Peter Pan Seafoods Inc.
  Bellevue, WA 206-728-6000
Poseidon Enterprises
  Charlotte, NC 800-863-7886
Premier Smoked Fish Company
  Bensalem, PA 800-654-6682
QualiGourmet
  Boisbriand, QC 514-287-3530
Quinault Pride
  Taholah, WA 360-276-4431

Rachael's Smoked Fish
  Springfield, MA 800-327-3412
Rego Smoked Fish Company
  Flushing, NY 718-894-1400
Roman Sausage Company
  Santa Clara, CA 800-497-7462
Royal Seafood Inc
  Brooklyn, NY 718-769-1517
Russian Chef
  New York, NY 212-249-1550
Salmolux Inc
  Federal Way, WA 253-874-6570
Salty Girl Seafood
  Santa Barbara, CA 805-699-5025
Santa Monica Seafood Co.
  Rancho Dominguez, CA 800-969-8862
Seafood Producers Co-Op
  Bellingham, WA 360-733-0120
Shafer-Haggart
  Vancouver, BC 604-669-5512
Splendid Spreads
  Eagan, MN 877-773-2374
Sportsmen's Cannery & Smokehouse
  Winchester Bay, OR 800-457-8048
Taku Smokehouse
  Juneau, AK 800-582-5122
Tampa Bay Fisheries Inc
  Dover, FL 800-732-3663
Tenth & M Seafoods
  Anchorage, AK 800-770-2722
Trident Seafoods Corp
  Wrangell, AK 907-874-3346
Verlasso
  FL 786-522-8418
Vita Food Products Inc
  Chicago, IL 800-989-8482
Vital Choice
  Bellingham, WA 800-608-4825
Walcan Seafood
  Heroit Bay, BC 250-285-3361
Woodsmoke Provisions
  Atlanta, GA 404-355-5125

Chum

Haines Packing Company
  Haines, AK 907-766-2883

Coho

Haines Packing Company
  Haines, AK 907-766-2883

King

Haines Packing Company
  Haines, AK 907-766-2883

Pink

Chicken Of The Sea
  El Segundo, CA 844-267-8862
Crown Prince Inc
  City Of Industry, CA 626-912-3700
Haines Packing Company
  Haines, AK 907-766-2883

Smoked

Alaska Bounty Seafoods & Smokery
  Sitka, AK 907-747-3730
Alaska Jacks
  Anchorage, AK 888-660-2257
Alaska Seafood Co
  Juneau, AK 800-451-1400
Alaska Smokehouse
  Woodinville, WA 800-422-0852
Alaskan Gourmet Seafoods
  Anchorage, AK 800-288-3740
Alaskan Smoked Salmon & Seafood
  Anchorage, AK 907-349-8234
Alder Springs Smoked Salmon
  Sequim, WA 360-683-2829
Bold Coast Smokehouse
  Lubec, ME 888-733-0807
California Shellfish Company
  San Francisco, CA 415-923-7400
Comeau's Seafoods
  Saulnierville, NS 902-769-2101
Dollar Food Manufacturing
  Vancouver, BC 604-253-1422
Dressel Collins Fish Company
  Seattle, WA 206-725-0121
E-Fish-Ent Fish Company
  Sooke, BC 250-642-4007

Product Categories / Fish & Seafood: Fish

Felix Custom Smoking
  Monroe, WA 425-485-2439
Fish Brothers
  Blue Lake, CA 800-244-0583
Fish King Processors
  Brunswick, GA 800-841-0205
Fumoir Grizzly
  St Augustin, QC 418-878-8941
Giovanni's Appetizing Food Co
  Richmond, MI 586-727-9355
Haines Packing Company
  Haines, AK 907-766-2883
Homarus Inc
  Long Island City, NY 917-832-0333
Imperial Salmon House
  Vancouver, BC 604-251-1114
Jensen's Old Fashioned Smokehouse
  Seattle, WA 206-364-5569
Kasilof Fish Company
  Everett, WA 800-322-7552
Katy's Smokehouse
  Trinidad, CA 707-677-0151
Nordic Group Inc
  Boston, MA 800-486-4002
Ocean Pride Fisheries
  Lower Wedgeport, NS 902-663-4579
Oceanfood Sales
  Vancouver, BC 877-255-1414
Oven Head Salmon Smokers
  Bethel, NB 877-955-2507
Pacific Seafoods International
  Port Hardy, BC 250-949-8781
Paramount Caviar
  Long Island City, NY 800-992-2842
Pickwick Catfish Farm
  Counce, TN 731-689-3805
Portier Fine Foods
  Mamaroneck, NY 800-272-9463
Premier Smoked Fish Company
  Bensalem, PA 800-654-6682
Rego Smoked Fish Company
  Flushing, NY 718-894-1400
Rier Smoked Salmon
  Lubec, ME 888-733-0807
Russ & Daughters
  New York, NY 800-787-7229
Russian Chef
  New York, NY 212-249-1550
SeaBear Wild Salmon
  Anacortes, WA 800-645-3474
Sullivan Harbor Farm
  Hancock Village, ME 800-422-4014

Sockeye

Alaska Smokehouse
  Woodinville, WA 800-422-0852
Haines Packing Company
  Haines, AK 907-766-2883

Steak

Arrowac Fisheries
  Seattle, WA 206-282-5655
Nelson Crab Inc
  Tokeland, WA 800-262-0069
Neptune Foods
  Vernon, CA 323-232-8300

Salted

Canadian Fish Exporters
  Auburndale, MA 800-225-4215
DB Kenney Fisheries
  Westport, NS 902-839-2023
Island Marine Products
  Clarks Harbour, NS 902-745-2222
Taku Smokehouse
  Juneau, AK 800-582-5122

Sardines

Castella Imports Inc
  Brentwood, NY 631-231-5500
Crown Prince Inc
  City Of Industry, CA 626-912-3700
Erba Food Products
  Brooklyn, NY 718-272-7700
J Deluca Fish Co Inc
  San Pedro, CA 310-684-5180
Jessie's Ilwaco Fish Company
  San Francisco, CA 360-642-3773
Northwest Wild Products
  Astoria, OR 503-791-1907

Raffield Fisheries Inc
  Port St Joe, FL 850-229-8494

Canned

Ardy Fisher
  877-699-5066
Blue Marble Brands
  Providence, RI 888-534-0246
Chicken Of The Sea
  El Segundo, CA 844-267-8862
Crown Prince Inc
  City Of Industry, CA 626-912-3700
Pastene Co LTD
  Canton, MA 781-298-3397
Season Brand
  Newark, NJ 201-553-1100
Vital Choice
  Bellingham, WA 800-608-4825

Fresh

Jessie's Ilwaco Fish Company
  San Francisco, CA 360-642-3773

Sea Bass

Arrowac Fisheries
  Seattle, WA 206-282-5655
North Atlantic Seafood
  Portland, ME 800-774-6025
Ocean Beauty Seafoods Inc
  Seattle, WA 800-365-8950
Santa Monica Seafood Co.
  Rancho Dominguez, CA 800-969-8862
Tampa Bay Fisheries Inc
  Dover, FL 800-732-3663

Sea Trout

Glenn Sales Company
  Atlanta, GA 770-952-9292

Shad

Fishhawk Fisheries
  Astoria, OR 503-325-5252
Lund's Fisheries
  Cape May, NJ 609-884-7600
Nelson Crab Inc
  Tokeland, WA 800-262-0069

Shark

Agger Fish Corp
  Brooklyn, NY 718-855-1717
Arrowac Fisheries
  Seattle, WA 206-282-5655
Caito Fisheries Inc
  Fort Bragg, CA 707-964-6368
Louisiana Seafood Exchange
  Jefferson, LA 800-969-9394
Mid-Pacific Hawaii Fishery
  Hilo, HI 808-935-6110
New Orleans Fish House II LLC
  New Orleans, LA 800-839-3474
Ocean Beauty Seafoods Inc
  Seattle, WA 800-365-8950
Pacific Salmon Company
  Edmonds, WA 425-774-1315
Scandinavian Laboratories
  Belvidere, PA 866-623-2650

Sheephead

Griffin's Seafood
  Golden Meadow, LA 985-396-2453
New Orleans Fish House II LLC
  New Orleans, LA 800-839-3474
Stoller Fisheries
  Spirit Lake, IA 800-831-5174

Smelt

Burleigh Brothers Seafoods
  Ellerslie, PE 902-831-2349
Certi Fresh Foods Inc
  Wilmington, CA 310-221-6262
Channel Fish Processing
  Gloucester, MA 800-457-0054
Fishhawk Fisheries
  Astoria, OR 503-325-5252
Jessie's Ilwaco Fish Company
  San Francisco, CA 360-642-3773
Minor Fisheries
  Port Colborne, ON 905-834-9232

Pacific Salmon Company
  Edmonds, WA 425-774-1315

Smoked & Cured

Acme Smoked Fish Corporation
  Brooklyn, NY 718-383-8585
Alaska Jacks
  Anchorage, AK 888-660-2257
Alaska Sausage & Seafood
  Anchorage, AK 800-798-3636
Alaskan Gourmet Seafoods
  Anchorage, AK 800-288-3740
Bos Smoked Fish Inc
  Woodstock, ON 519-537-5000
Buedel Food Products
  Bridgeview, IL 708-496-3500
California Shellfish Company
  San Francisco, CA 415-923-7400
Chuck's Seafoods
  Charleston, OR 541-888-5525
Deep Creek Custom Packing
  Ninilchik, AK 800-764-0078
Dressel Collins Fish Company
  Seattle, WA 206-725-0121
Ducktrap River Of Maine
  Belfast, ME 800-434-8727
Fish Brothers
  Blue Lake, CA 800-244-0583
Gold Star Smoked Fish Inc
  Brooklyn, NY 718-522-1545
High Liner Foods Inc.
  Lunenburg, NS 902-634-8811
Homarus Inc
  Long Island City, NY 917-832-0333
J Moniz Co Inc
  Fall River, MA 508-674-8451
J Turner Seafood
  Gloucester, MA 978-281-8535
Mac Knight Smoke House Inc
  Miami, FL 305-651-3323
Menemsha Fish Market
  Chilmark, MA 508-645-2282
Mutual Fish Co
  Seattle, WA 206-322-4368
Nelson Crab Inc
  Tokeland, WA 800-262-0069
Nordic Group Inc
  Boston, MA 800-486-4002
Ocean Fresh Seafoods
  Seattle, WA 206-285-2412
Paramount Caviar
  Long Island City, NY 800-992-2842
Premier Smoked Fish Company
  Bensalem, PA 800-654-6682
Quinault Pride
  Taholah, WA 360-276-4431
Rego Smoked Fish Company
  Flushing, NY 718-894-1400
Russ & Daughters
  New York, NY 800-787-7229
Russian Chef
  New York, NY 212-249-1550
Sea Bear Smokehouse
  Anacortes, WA 800-645-3474
Sterling Caviar LLC
  Elverta, CA 800-525-0333
Taku Smokehouse
  Juneau, AK 800-582-5122

Snapper

Bon Secour Fisheries Inc
  Bon Secour, AL 251-949-7411
California Shellfish Company
  San Francisco, CA 415-923-7400
Griffin's Seafood
  Golden Meadow, LA 985-396-2453
North Atlantic Seafood
  Portland, ME 800-774-6025
Northern Products Corporation
  Seattle, WA 888-599-6290
Ocean Union Company
  Lawrenceville, GA 770-995-1957
Poseidon Enterprises
  Charlotte, NC 800-863-7886

Sole

BlueWater Seafoods
  Gloucester, MA 888-560-2539
DB Kenney Fisheries
  Westport, NS 902-839-2023

Product Categories / Fish & Seafood: Fish

Gorton's Inc.
  Gloucester, MA 800-222-6846
High Liner Foods Inc.
  Lunenburg, NS 902-634-8811
Northwest Wild Products
  Astoria, OR 503-791-1907
Penguin Frozen Foods Inc
  Northbrook, IL 800-323-1485
Royal Seafood Inc
  Brooklyn, NY 718-769-1517
Vital Choice
  Bellingham, WA 800-608-4825

Steaks
Ocean Beauty Seafoods Inc
  Seattle, WA 800-365-8950

Sticks
High Liner Foods Inc.
  Lunenburg, NS 902-634-8811
Viking Seafoods Inc
  Malden, MA 800-225-3020

Sturgeon
Charlton Charters
  Warrenton, OR 503-338-0569
Fiddlers Green Farm
  North Vassalboro, ME 800-729-7935
Fish Breeders of Idaho
  Hagerman, ID 208-837-6114
Fish Brothers
  Blue Lake, CA 800-244-0583
Fishhawk Fisheries
  Astoria, OR 503-325-5252
Great Northern Products Inc
  Cranston, RI 401-490-4590
Homarus Inc
  Long Island City, NY 917-832-0333
Jessie's Ilwaco Fish Company
  San Francisco, CA 360-642-3773
Lund's Fisheries
  Cape May, NJ 609-884-7600
Menemsha Fish Market
  Chilmark, MA 508-645-2282
Northwest Wild Products
  Astoria, OR 503-791-1907
Rego Smoked Fish Company
  Flushing, NY 718-894-1400
Russ & Daughters
  New York, NY 800-787-7229
Russian Chef
  New York, NY 212-249-1550
Sportsmen's Cannery & Smokehouse
  Winchester Bay, OR 800-457-8048
Sterling Caviar LLC
  Elverta, CA 800-525-0333

Swordfish
Arrowac Fisheries
  Seattle, WA 206-282-5655
Caito Fisheries Inc
  Fort Bragg, CA 707-964-6368
Griffin's Seafood
  Golden Meadow, LA 985-396-2453
James L. Mood Fisheries
  Nova Scotia, NS 902-723-2360
Menemsha Fish Market
  Chilmark, MA 508-645-2282
North Atlantic Seafood
  Portland, ME 800-774-6025
Ocean Beauty Seafoods Inc
  Seattle, WA 800-365-8950
Peter Pan Seafoods Inc.
  Bellevue, WA 206-728-6000
Poseidon Enterprises
  Charlotte, NC 800-863-7886
Santa Monica Seafood Co.
  Rancho Dominguez, CA 800-969-8862
Tampa Bay Fisheries Inc
  Dover, FL 800-732-3663

Steak
North Atlantic Seafood
  Portland, ME 800-774-6025

Tilapia
BlueWater Seafoods
  Gloucester, MA 888-560-2539
Fish Breeders of Idaho
  Hagerman, ID 208-837-6114

North Atlantic Seafood
  Portland, ME 800-774-6025
Pots de Creme
  Lexington, KY 859-299-2254
Vince's Seafoods
  Gretna, LA 504-368-1544
Waterfield Farms
  Amherst, MA 413-549-3558

Trout
Alleghany's Fish Farm
  Saint Philemon, QC 418-469-2823
Atlantic Fish Specialties
  Charlottetown, PE 902-894-7005
Blue Lakes Trout Farm
  Jerome, ID 208-734-7151
Bold Coast Smokehouse
  Lubec, ME 888-733-0807
Bos Smoked Fish Inc
  Woodstock, ON 519-537-5000
Burleigh Brothers Seafoods
  Ellerslie, PE 902-831-2349
Caito Fisheries Inc
  Fort Bragg, CA 707-964-6368
Catfish Wholesale
  Abbeville, LA 800-334-7292
Certi Fresh Foods Inc
  Wilmington, CA 310-221-6262
Culver Fish Farm
  Mcpherson, KS 800-241-5205
Dave's Gourmet Albacore
  Watsonville, CA 206-999-5517
Ducktrap River Of Maine
  Belfast, ME 800-434-8727
Ferroclad Fishery
  Batchawana Bay, ON 705-882-2295
Fiddlers Green Farm
  North Vassalboro, ME 800-729-7935
Fish Breeders of Idaho
  Hagerman, ID 208-837-6114
Fish Brothers
  Blue Lake, CA 800-244-0583
Fumoir Grizzly
  St Augustin, QC 418-878-8941
Griffin's Seafood
  Golden Meadow, LA 985-396-2453
Homarus Inc
  Long Island City, NY 917-832-0333
Idaho Trout Company
  Buhl, ID 866-878-7688
J. Matassini & Sons Fish Company
  Tampa, FL 813-229-0829
Lenny's Bee Productions
  Bearsville, NY 845-679-4514
Louisiana Seafood Exchange
  Jefferson, LA 800-969-9394
Morey's Seafood Intl LLC
  Motley, MN 800-808-3474
Pamlico Packing Company
  Grantsboro, NC 800-682-1113
Portier Fine Foods
  Mamaroneck, NY 800-272-9463
Pots de Creme
  Lexington, KY 859-299-2254
Rego Smoked Fish Company
  Flushing, NY 718-894-1400
Russian Chef
  New York, NY 212-249-1550
SC Enterprises
  Owen Sound, ON 519-371-0456
Sunburst Trout Farms
  Waynesville, NC 800-673-3051
Thompson Seafood
  Darien, GA 912-437-4649
Vince's Seafoods
  Gretna, LA 504-368-1544
Virginia Trout Co
  Monterey, VA 540-468-2280
Wanchese Fish Co Inc
  Suffolk, VA 757-673-4500
Woodsmoke Provisions
  Atlanta, GA 404-355-5125

Brook
Russ & Daughters
  New York, NY 800-787-7229

Golden
Idaho Trout Company
  Buhl, ID 866-878-7688

Rainbow
Blue Lakes Trout Farm
  Jerome, ID 208-734-7151
Clear Springs Foods Inc.
  Buhl, ID 800-635-8211
Dave's Gourmet Albacore
  Watsonville, CA 206-999-5517
Idaho Trout Company
  Buhl, ID 866-878-7688
Sportsman's Paradise Whites Ranch
  Paradise, UT 435-245-3053

Tuna
Brucepac
  Woodburn, OR 800-899-3629
Captain Little Seafood
  Queens County, NS 902-947-2087
Charlton Charters
  Warrenton, OR 503-338-0569
Chicken Of The Sea
  El Segundo, CA 844-267-8862
Chuck's Seafoods
  Charleston, OR 541-888-5525
Crown Prince Inc
  City Of Industry, CA 626-912-3700
Dave's Gourmet Albacore
  Watsonville, CA 206-999-5517
Erba Food Products
  Brooklyn, NY 718-272-7700
Great Northern Products Inc
  Cranston, RI 401-490-4590
Griffin's Seafood
  Golden Meadow, LA 985-396-2453
Hallmark Fisheries
  Charleston, OR 541-888-3253
Homarus Inc
  Long Island City, NY 917-832-0333
Independent Packers Corporation
  Seattle, WA 206-285-6000
Island Marine Products
  Clarks Harbour, NS 902-745-2222
James L. Mood Fisheries
  Nova Scotia, NS 902-723-2360
Jessie's Ilwaco Fish Company
  San Francisco, CA 360-642-3773
Lund's Fisheries
  Cape May, NJ 609-884-7600
Menemsha Fish Market
  Chilmark, MA 508-645-2282
Mid-Pacific Hawaii Fishery
  Hilo, HI 808-935-6110
Neptune Foods
  Vernon, CA 323-232-8300
New Orleans Fish House II LLC
  New Orleans, LA 800-839-3474
North Atlantic Seafood
  Portland, ME 800-774-6025
Northwest Wild Products
  Astoria, OR 503-791-1907
Ocean Beauty Seafoods Inc
  Seattle, WA 800-365-8950
Ocean Union Company
  Lawrenceville, GA 770-995-1957
Omega Foods
  Mississauga, ON 877-212-9484
Pastene Co LTD
  Canton, MA 781-298-3397
Peter Pan Seafoods Inc.
  Bellevue, WA 206-728-6000
Poseidon Enterprises
  Charlotte, NC 800-863-7886
Roman Sausage Company
  Santa Clara, CA 800-497-7462
Royal Seafood Inc
  Brooklyn, NY 718-769-1517
Russ & Daughters
  New York, NY 800-787-7229
Russian Chef
  New York, NY 212-249-1550
Sportsmen's Cannery & Smokehouse
  Winchester Bay, OR 800-457-8048
Sportsmens Seafoods
  San Diego, CA 619-224-3551
Stavis Seafoods
  Boston, MA 800-390-5103
Triangle Seafood
  Louisville, KY 502-561-0055
Tuna Fresh
  Gretna, LA 504-363-2744
Vince's Seafoods
  Gretna, LA 504-368-1544

Product Categories / Fish & Seafood: Seafood

Vital Choice
 Bellingham, WA 800-608-4825
Wanchese Fish Co Inc
 Suffolk, VA 757-673-4500
White Cap Fish Market
 Islip, NY 631-277-6577

Albacore

Caito Fisheries Inc
 Fort Bragg, CA 707-964-6368
Chicken Of The Sea
 El Segundo, CA 844-267-8862
Crown Prince Inc
 City Of Industry, CA. 626-912-3700
Dave's Gourmet Albacore
 Watsonville, CA 206-999-5517
Fish Brothers
 Blue Lake, CA 800-244-0583
Royal Seafood Inc
 Brooklyn, NY 718-769-1517
Sportsmens Seafoods
 San Diego, CA 619-224-3551

Canned

Blue Marble Brands
 Providence, RI 888-534-0246
Bumble Bee
 San Diego, CA 858-715-4000
Chicken Of The Sea
 El Segundo, CA 844-267-8862
Chuck's Seafoods
 Charleston, OR 541-888-5525
Crown Prince Inc
 City Of Industry, CA. 626-912-3700
Hallmark Fisheries
 Charleston, OR 541-888-3253
Safe Catch
 Sausalito, CA 888-568-4211
Season Brand
 Newark, NJ 201-553-1100
Shafer-Haggart
 Vancouver, BC 604-669-5512
Sportsmen's Cannery & Smokehouse
 Winchester Bay, OR 800-457-8048
Sportsmens Seafoods
 San Diego, CA 619-224-3551
Starkist Co
 Pittsburgh, PA 412-231-0361
Vital Choice
 Bellingham, WA 800-608-4825

Canned - Chunk Light in Oil

Chicken Of The Sea
 El Segundo, CA 844-267-8862

Canned - Chunk Light in Water

Chicken Of The Sea
 El Segundo, CA 844-267-8862

Canned - Chunk Solid in Oil

Chicken Of The Sea
 El Segundo, CA 844-267-8862

Canned - Chunk Solid in Water

Chicken Of The Sea
 El Segundo, CA 844-267-8862

Frozen

Cuizina Food Company
 Woodinville, WA................. 425-486-7000
Great Northern Products Inc
 Cranston, RI 401-490-4590
Hallmark Fisheries
 Charleston, OR 541-888-3253
Independent Packers Corporation
 Seattle, WA 206-285-6000
Jessie's Ilwaco Fish Company
 San Francisco, CA 360-642-3773
Lund's Fisheries
 Cape May, NJ 609-884-7600
Menemsha Fish Market
 Chilmark, MA.................... 508-645-2282
Royal Seafood Inc
 Brooklyn, NY 718-769-1517
Wanchese Fish Co Inc
 Suffolk, VA 757-673-4500
White Cap Fish Market
 Islip, NY 631-277-6577

Pouch-Packed

Chicken Of The Sea
 El Segundo, CA 844-267-8862
Safe Catch
 Sausalito, CA 888-568-4211
Season Brand
 Newark, NJ 201-553-1100

Yellowfin

Russ & Daughters
 New York, NY 800-787-7229

Turbot

Breakwater Fisheries
 St John's, NL.................... 709-754-1999
North Atlantic Seafood
 Portland, ME.................... 800-774-6025
Notre Dame Seafoods Inc.
 Comfort Cove, NL 709-244-5511
Penguin Frozen Foods Inc
 Northbrook, IL 800-323-1485
Spruce Lane Investments
 Stratford, PE 902-892-2600
Stavis Seafoods
 Boston, MA...................... 800-390-5103

Whitefish

Bos Smoked Fish Inc
 Woodstock, ON.................. 519-537-5000
Ferroclad Fishery
 Batchawana Bay, ON 705-882-2295
Flaum Appetizing
 Brooklyn, NY 718-821-1970
Homarus Inc
 Long Island City, NY 917-832-0333
Minor Fisheries
 Port Colborne, ON 905-834-9232
Rachael's Smoked Fish
 Springfield, MA 800-327-3412
Rego Smoked Fish Company
 Flushing, NY..................... 718-894-1400
Russ & Daughters
 New York, NY 800-787-7229
Russian Chef
 New York, NY 212-249-1550

Whiting

Arrowac Fisheries
 Seattle, WA 206-282-5655
Bon Secour Fisheries Inc
 Bon Secour, AL.................. 251-949-7411
Certi Fresh Foods Inc
 Wilmington, CA 310-221-6262
Channel Fish Processing
 Gloucester, MA.................. 800-457-0054
Glenn Sales Company
 Atlanta, GA 770-952-9292
Jessie's Ilwaco Fish Company
 San Francisco, CA 360-642-3773
Mirasco
 Atlanta, GA 770-956-1945
Morey's Seafood Intl LLC
 Motley, MN..................... 800-808-3474
Pamlico Packing Company
 Grantsboro, NC 800-682-1113
Stavis Seafoods
 Boston, MA...................... 800-390-5103

Seafood

A&C Quinlin Fisheries
 Centreville, NS 902-745-2742
Acadian Fine Foods
 New Orleans, LA 504-581-2355
Acme Steak & Seafood
 Youngstown, OH................. 800-686-2263
Agger Fish Corp
 Brooklyn, NY 718-855-1717
Ah Dor Kosher Fish Corporation
 Monsey, NY 845-425-2060
Alabama Gulf Seafood
 Bayou La Batre, AL 251-824-4396
Alaska Aquafarms
 Moose Pass, AK 907-288-3667
Alaska General Seafoods
 Kenmore, WA 425-485-7755
Alaska Ocean Trading
 Anchorage, AK 907-243-4399
Alaska Pacific Seafoods
 Kodiak, AK...................... 907-486-3234

Alaska Sausage & Seafood
 Anchorage, AK.................. 800-798-3636
Alaskan Gourmet Seafoods
 Anchorage, AK.................. 800-288-3740
Alaskan Leader Fisheries
 Lynden, WA 360-318-1280
Aliotti Wholesale Fish Company
 Monterey, CA 408-722-4597
Alyeska Seafoods
 Unalaska, AK 907-581-1211
Amcan Industries
 Elmsford, NY 914-347-4838
American Canadian Fisheries
 Bellingham, WA 800-344-7942
American Seafoods
 Seattle, WA 206-448-0300
Ameripure Processing Co
 Franklin, LA 800-328-6729
Anchor Frozen Foods
 Westbury, NY 800-566-3474
Annette Island Packing Company
 Metlakatla, AK 907-886-4441
AquaCuisine
 Portland, OR.................... 208-323-2782
Aquatec Seafoods Ltd.
 Comox, BC 250-339-6412
Aquatech
 Anchorage, AK.................. 877-938-2722
Arista Industries Inc
 Wilton, CT 800-255-6457
Arizona Sunland Foods
 Tucson, AZ 520-624-7068
Arrowac Fisheries
 Seattle, WA 206-282-5655
ASC Seafood Inc
 Largo, FL 800-876-3474
Atka Pride Seafoods Inc
 Juneau, AK 888-927-4232
Atlanta Fish Market
 Atlanta, GA 404-262-3165
Atlantic Aqua Farms
 Orwell Cove, PE 902-651-2563
Atlantic Foods
 Scotch Plains, NJ 908-889-8182
Atlantic Mussel Growers Corporation
 Murray Harbour, PE 800-838-3106
Atlantic Sea Pride
 Boston, MA..................... 617-269-7700
Atlantic Seacove Inc
 Boston, MA..................... 617-442-6206
Atlantic Seafood Direct
 Portland, ME.................... 800-774-6025
Aurora Alaska Premium Smoked Salmon & Seafood
 Anchorage, AK.................. 800-653-3474
Axelsson & Johnson Fish Company
 Cape May, NJ 609-884-8426
B & C Riverside
 Vacherie, LA 225-265-8356
B & J Seafood
 New Bern, NC 252-637-0483
B G Smith & Sons Oyster Co
 Sharps, VA 877-483-8279
B&M Fisheries
 Georgetown, MA 978-352-6663
B.C. Fisheries
 Hancock, ME 207-422-8205
B.M. Lawrence & Company
 San Francisco, CA 415-981-2926
Baensch Food Products Co
 Milwaukee, WI 414-562-4643
Bailey's Basin Seafood
 Morgan City, LA 985-384-4926
Bakalars Sausage Co
 La Crosse, WI 608-784-0384
Bandon Bay Fisheries
 Bandon, OR 541-347-4454
Basin Crawfish Processors
 Breaux Bridge, LA 337-332-6655
Bay Hundred Seafood Inc
 St Michaels, MD 410-745-9329
Bay Oceans Sea Foods
 Garibaldi, OR 503-322-3316
Bayley's Lobster Pound
 Scarborough, ME 800-932-6456
Bayou Crab
 Grand Bay, AL 251-824-2076
Bayou Food Distributors
 Kenner, LA 800-516-8283
Bayou Land Seafood
 Breaux Bridge, LA 337-667-6118
Beaver Street Fisheries
 Jacksonville, FL 800-874-6426

Product Categories / Fish & Seafood: Seafood

Becker Foods
  Westminster, CA 714-891-9474
Belle River Enterprises
  Belle River, PE 902-962-2248
Benton's Seafood Ctr
  Tifton, GA 229-382-4976
Big Easy Foods
  Lake Charles, LA 855-477-9296
Big Island Seafood, LLC
  Atlanta, GA 404-366-8943
Bill's Seafood
  Baltimore, MD 410-256-9520
Billingsgate Fish Company
  Calgary, AB 403-571-7700
Billy's Seafood Inc
  Bon Secour, AL 888-424-5597
Biloxi Freezing Processing Inc.
  Biloxi, MS 228-436-0017
Blakely Freezer Locker
  Blakeley, GA 229-723-3622
Blalock Seafood & Specialty
  Orange Beach, AL 251-974-5811
Blau Oyster Co Inc
  Bow, WA 360-766-6171
Blount Fine Foods
  Fall River, MA 774-888-1300
Blue Star Food Products
  Doral, FL 305-836-6858
BlueWater Seafoods
  Gloucester, MA 888-560-2539
Bodin Foods
  New Iberia, LA 337-367-1344
Bon Secour Fisheries Inc
  Bon Secour, AL 251-949-7411
Bornstein Seafoods
  Bellingham, WA 360-734-7990
Boston Seafarms
  Boston, MA 617-784-4777
Boundary Fish Company
  Blaine, WA 360-332-6715
Boutique Seafood Brokers
  Atlanta, GA 404-752-8852
Bradye P. Todd & Son
  Cambridge, MD 410-228-8633
Braun Seafood Co
  Cutchogue, NY 631-734-6700
Breakwater Fisheries
  St John's, NL 709-754-1999
Breakwater Seafoods & Chowder
  Aberdeen, WA 360-532-5693
Byrd's Seafood Inc
  Crisfield, MD 410-968-0990
C C Conway Seafoods
  Wicomico, VA 804-642-2853
C F Gollott & Son Seafood
  Diberville, MS 228-392-2747
C. Gould Seafoods
  Scottsdale, AZ 480-314-9250
C.E. Fish Company
  Jonesboro, ME 207-434-2631
Cajun Crawfish Distributors
  Branch, LA 888-254-8626
Cajun Seafood Enterprises
  Murrayville, GA 706-864-9688
Caleb Haley & Co LLC
  Bronx, NY 718-617-7474
California Shellfish Company
  San Francisco, CA 415-923-7400
Callis Seafood
  Lancaster, VA 804-462-7634
Cameron Seafood Processors
  Cameron, LA 318-775-5510
Can Am Seafood
  Lubec, ME 207-733-2267
Canadian Fish Exporters
  Auburndale, MA 800-225-4215
Cantrell's Seafood
  Bath, ME 207-442-7261
Cape Ann Seafood
  Gloucester, MA 978-283-0687
Capt Collier Seafood
  Coden, AL 251-824-4925
Captain Alex Seafoods
  Niles, IL 847-803-8833
Captain's Choice
  Federal Way, WA 253-941-1184
Carrington Foods Co Inc
  Saraland, AL 251-675-9700
Cathay Foods Corporation
  Boston, MA 617-427-1507
Cedar Valley Fish Market
  Waterloo, IA 319-236-2965

Centennial Food Corporation
  Calgary, AB 403-214-0044
Central Coast Seafood
  Atascadero, CA 800-273-4741
Certi Fresh Foods Inc
  Wilmington, CA 310-221-6262
Certi-Fresh Foods, Inc
  Wilmington, CA 910-221-6262
Channel Fish Processing
  Gloucester, MA 800-457-0054
Channel Fish Processing Co Inc
  Boston, MA 800-536-3474
Charles H. Parks & Company
  Fishing Creek, MD 410-397-3400
Charlton Charters
  Warrenton, OR 503-338-0569
Chases Lobster Pound
  Port Howe, NS 902-243-2408
Chef Hans' Gourmet Foods
  Monroe, LA 800-890-4267
Cherbogue Fisheries
  Yarmouth, NS 902-742-9157
Chester W. Howeth & Brother
  Crisfield, MD 410-968-1398
Chris Hansen Seafood
  Port Sulphur, LA 504-564-2888
Chuck's Seafoods
  Charleston, OR 541-888-5525
City Market
  Brunswick, GA 912-265-4430
Clarke J F Corp
  Franklin Square, NY 800-229-7474
Clayton's Crab Co
  Rockledge, FL 321-636-6673
Clearwater Fine Foods
  Bedford, NS 902-443-0550
Clem's Seafood & Specialties
  Buckner, KY 502-222-7571
Coast Seafoods Company
  Bellevue, WA 800-423-2303
Coastal Seafood Partners
  Chicago, IL 773-235-4000
Coastal Seafood Processors
  Harahan, LA 504-734-9444
Cobscook Bay Seafood
  Perry, ME 207-853-2890
Cohen's Original Tasty Coddie
  Baltimore, MD 410-539-0111
Coldwater Fish Farms
  Lisco, NE 800-658-4450
Collins Cavier Co
  Michigan City, IN 219-809-8100
Comeaux's
  Lafayette, LA 888-264-5460
Conroy Foods
  Pittsburgh, PA 412-781-0977
Consolidated Catfish Co LLC
  Isola, MS 662-962-3101
Cowart Seafood Corp
  Lottsburg, VA 804-529-6101
Cozy Harbor Seafood Inc
  Portland, ME 800-225-2586
Craby's Fish Market
  Blackwood, NJ 856-227-9743
Cranberry Isles Fisherman's
  Islesford, ME 207-244-5438
Craven Crab Company
  New Bern, NC 252-637-3562
Crest International Corporation
  San Diego, CA 800-548-1232
Crevettes Du Nord
  Gaspe, QC 418-368-1414
Cuizina Food Company
  Woodinville, WA 425-486-7000
Cushner Seafoods Inc
  Baltimore, MD 410-358-5564
Custom House Seafoods
  Portland, ME 207-773-2778
D Seafood
  Chicago, IL 312-808-1086
D&M Seafood
  Honolulu, HI 808-531-0687
Dave's Gourmet Albacore
  Watsonville, CA 206-999-5517
Davis Street Fish Market
  Evanston, IL 847-869-3474
DB Kenney Fisheries
  Westport, NS 902-839-2023
De Maria's Seafood
  Newport News, VA 757-930-3474
Deep Creek Custom Packing
  Ninilchik, AK 800-764-0078

Del's Seaway Shrimp & Oyster Company
  Biloxi, MS 228-432-2604
Denzer's Food Products
  Baltimore, MD 410-889-1500
Di Cola's Seafood
  Chicago, IL 773-238-7071
Diamond Seafood
  Wood Dale, IL 630-787-1100
DIP Seafood Mudbugs
  Mobile, AL 251-479-0123
Dixon's Fisheries
  East Peoria, IL 800-373-1457
Don's Dock Seafood Market
  Des Plaines, IL 847-827-1817
Door County Fish Market
  Northbrook, IL 847-559-9229
Dorchester Crab Co
  Wingate, MD 410-397-8103
Doug Hardy Company
  Deer Isle, ME 207-348-6604
Dow Distribution
  Honolulu, HI 808-836-3511
Down East Specialty Products/Cape Bald Packers
  Portland, ME 800-369-6327
Dressel Collins Fish Company
  Seattle, WA 206-725-0121
Drusilla Seafood
  Baton Rouge, LA 800-364-8844
Dubois Seafood
  Houma, LA 985-876-2514
Ducktrap River Of Maine
  Belfast, ME 800-434-8727
Duxbury Mussel & Seafood Corporation
  Kingston, MA 781-585-5517
E. Gagnon & Fils
  St Therese-De-Gaspe, QC 418-385-3011
Eagle Seafood Producers
  Brooklyn, NY 718-963-0939
East Point Seafood Company
  Raymond, WA 888-317-8459
Eastern Fish Company
  Teaneck, NJ 800-526-9066
Eastern Sea Products
  Scoudouc, NB 800-565-6364
Eastern Seafood Co
  Chicago, IL 312-243-2090
Eastside Seafood
  Macon, GA 478-743-1888
Ed's Kasilof Seafoods
  Kasilof, AK 800-982-2377
Eldorado Seafood Inc
  Burlington, MA 800-416-5656
Elliott Seafood Company
  Cushing, ME 207-354-2533
Emery Smith Fisheries Limited
  Shag Harbour, NS 902-723-2115
Errol's Cajun Foods
  Belle Rose, LA 866-746-6003
Eschete's Seafood
  Houma, LA 985-872-4120
Eskimo Candy Inc
  Kihei, HI 808-879-5686
Faidley Seafood
  Baltimore, MD 410-727-4898
Fantis Foods Inc
  Carlstadt, NJ 201-933-6200
Farm 2 Market
  San Francisco, CA 800-447-2967
Farmers Seafood Co Wholesale
  Shreveport, LA 800-874-0203
Feature Foods
  Brampton, ON 905-452-7741
Ferme Ostreicole Dugas
  Caraquet, NB 506-727-3226
Fine Line Seafood
  Newtown, PA 215-598-3359
First Oriental Market
  Decatur, GA 404-377-6950
Fish Breeders of Idaho
  Hagerman, ID 208-837-6114
Fish Brothers
  Blue Lake, CA 800-244-0583
Fish Express
  Lihue, HI 808-245-9918
Fish King
  Glendale, CA 818-244-2161
Fish Market Inc
  Louisville, KY 502-587-7474
Fishermens Net
  Portland, ME 207-772-3565
Fishhawk Fisheries
  Astoria, OR 503-325-5252

Product Categories / Fish & Seafood: Seafood

Fishland Market
  Honolulu, HI 808-523-6902
Flavor House, Inc.
  Adelanto, CA 760-246-9131
Fleet Fisheries Inc
  New Bedford, MA 508-910-2100
Fortune Seas
  Gloucester, MA 978-281-6666
Fournier R & Sons Seafood
  Biloxi, MS 228-392-4293
Frank Mattes & Sons Reliable Seafood
  Bel Air, MD 410-879-5444
Frank Pagano Company
  Lockport, IL 815-838-0303
French Market Foods
  Lake Charles, LA 337-477-9296
French Quarter Seafood
  Chalmette, LA 504-277-1679
Fresh Island Fish
  Kahului, HI 808-871-1111
Fresh Pack Seafood
  Waldoboro, ME 207-832-7720
Fresh Seafood Distrib
  Daphne, AL 251-626-1106
Freshwater Farms Of Ohio
  Urbana, OH 800-634-7434
Friendship International
  Rockland, ME 207-594-1111
Frozen Specialties Inc
  Perrysburg, OH 419-867-2005
Fulcher's Point Pride Seafood
  Oriental, NC 252-249-0123
Fulton Fish Market
  New York, NY 718-842-8908
FW Thurston
  Bernard, ME 207-244-3320
G & J Land & Marine Food Distr
  Morgan City, LA 800-256-9187
Galilean Seafood Inc
  Bristol, RI 401-253-3030
Garden & Valley Isle Seafood
  Honolulu, HI 800-689-2733
George Robberecht Seafood
  Montross, VA 804-472-3556
Georgia Seafood Wholesale
  Chamblee, GA 770-936-0483
Gerard & Dominique Seafoods
  Harbor, OR 800-858-0449
Gesco ENR
  Gaspe, QC 418-368-1414
Gilmore's Seafoods
  Bath, ME 800-849-9667
Giovanni's Appetizing Food Co
  Richmond, MI 586-727-9355
Glenn Sales Company
  Atlanta, GA 770-952-9292
Gold Star Seafoods
  Chicago, IL 773-376-8080
Golden Alaska Seafoods LLC
  Seattle, WA 206-441-1990
Golden Eye Seafood
  Tall Timbers, MD 301-994-2274
Golden Gulf Coast Packing Co
  Biloxi, MS 228-374-6121
Good Harbor Fillet Company
  New Bedford, MA 800-343-8046
Gorton's Inc.
  Gloucester, MA 800-222-6846
Graham & Rollins Inc
  Hampton, VA 800-272-2728
Graham Fisheries
  Bayou La Batre, AL 251-824-7370
Great American Seafood Company
  Champaigne, IL 217-352-0986
Great American Smokehouse & Seafood Company
  Brookings, OR 800-828-3474
Great Glacier Salmon
  Prince Rupert, BC 250-627-4955
Great Midwest Seafood Company
  Davenport, IA 563-388-4770
Great Northern Products Inc
  Cranston, RI 401-490-4590
Green Turtle Cannery & Seafood
  Islamorada, FL 305-664-9595
Griffin's Seafood
  Golden Meadow, LA 985-396-2453
Gulf Atlantic Freezers
  Gretna, LA 504-392-3590
Gulf Central Seafood
  Biloxi, MS 228-436-6346
Gulf Crown Seafood Co
  Delcambre, LA 337-685-4722

Gulf Food Products Co Inc
  New Orleans, LA 504-733-1516
Gulf Marine & Industrial Supplies Inc
  Houston, TX 800-886-6252
Gulf Pride Enterprises
  Biloxi, MS 888-689-0560
Gulf Shrimp, Inc.
  Fort Myers Beach, FL 239-463-8788
H&H Fisheries Limited
  Eastern Passage, NS 866-773-4400
H.Gass Seafood
  Hollywood, MD 301-373-6882
Hallmark Fisheries
  Charleston, OR 541-888-3253
Hama Hama Oyster® Company
  Lilliwaup, WA 888-877-5844
Hamilton Marine
  Rockland, ME 207-594-8181
Handy International Inc
  Salisbury, MD 800-426-3977
Hansen Caviar Company
  Kingston, NY 800-735-0441
Harbor Fish Market
  Portland, ME 800-370-1790
Harbor Seafood
  New Hyde Park, NY 800-645-2211
Harbour Lobster Ltd
  Shag Harbour, NS 902-723-2500
Haring Catfish
  Wisner, LA 800-467-3474
Harlon's LA Fish
  Kenner, LA 504-467-3809
Harpers Seafood Market
  Thomasville, GA 229-226-7525
Harvard Seafood Company
  Grand Bay, AL 251-865-0558
Hawaii International Seafood
  Kailua, HI 808-839-5010
Heritage Salmon
  Eastport, ME 877-407-5577
HFI Foods
  Redmond, WA 425-883-1320
Higgins Seafood
  Lafitte, LA 504-689-3577
High Liner Foods Inc.
  Lunenburg, NS 902-634-8811
Hillard Bloom Packing Co Inc
  Port Norris, NJ 856-785-0120
Hillmans Shrimp & Oyster
  Port Lavaca, TX 800-582-4416
Hilo Fish Company
  Hilo, HI 808-961-0877
Homer's Wharf Seafood Company
  New Bedford, MA 508-997-0766
Hong Kong Supermarket
  Norcross, GA 770-582-6800
Honolulu Fish Company
  Honolulu, HI 808-833-1123
Horst Seafood
  Juneau, AK 877-518-4300
Hosford & Wood Fresh Seafood Providers
  Tucson, AZ 520-795-1920
Huck's Seafood
  Easton, MD 410-770-9211
Hue's Seafood
  Baton Rouge, LA 225-383-0809
Idaho Trout Company
  Buhl, ID 866-878-7688
Imaex Trading Company
  Suwanee, GA 678-541-0234
Independent Packers Corporation
  Seattle, WA 206-285-6000
Indian Bay Frozen Foods
  Centreville, NL 709-678-2844
Indian Ridge Shrimp Co
  Chauvin, LA 800-594-0920
Indian Valley Meats
  Indian, AK 907-653-7511
Inland Seafood Inc
  Atlanta, GA 800-883-3474
Inlet Salmon
  Fort Lauderdale, FL 954-525-9777
Inny's Wholesale
  Honolulu, HI 808-841-3172
Inshore Fisheries
  Middle West Pubnico, NS 902-762-2522
Interior Alaska Fish Processors
  Fairbanks, AK 800-478-3885
International Seafoods - Alaska
  Kodiak, AK 907-486-4768
International Seafoods of Chicago
  Chicago, IL 312-243-2330

Ipswich Maritime Product Company
  Ipswich, MA 978-356-9866
Ipswich Shellfish Co Inc
  Ipswich, MA 800-477-9424
ISF Trading
  Portland, ME 207-879-1575
Island Marine Products
  Clarks Harbour, NS 902-745-2222
Island Scallops
  Qualicum Beach, BC 250-757-9811
Island Seafood
  Eliot, ME 207-439-8508
Island Seafoods
  Kodiak, AK 800-355-8575
J & B Seafood
  Coden, AL 251-824-4512
J & L Seafood
  Bayou La Batre, AL 251-824-2371
J Bernard Seafood
  Cottonport, LA 318-876-2716
J Deluca Fish Co Inc
  San Pedro, CA 310-684-5180
J M Clayton Co
  Cambridge, MD 800-652-6931
J Moniz Co Inc
  Fall River, MA 508-674-8451
J P's Shellfish Co
  Eliot, ME 207-439-6018
J Turner Seafood
  Gloucester, MA 978-281-8535
J&R Fisheries
  Seward, AK 907-224-5584
J. Matassini & Sons Fish Company
  Tampa, FL 813-229-0829
J.R. Fish Company
  Wrangell, AK 907-874-2399
J.R.'s Seafood
  Oak Lawn, IL 708-422-4555
J.S. McMillan Fisheries
  North Vancouver, BC 604-981-4000
Ja-Ca Seafood Products
  Boston, MA 978-281-8848
James L. Mood Fisheries
  Nova Scotia, NS 902-723-2360
Janes Family Foods
  Mississauga, ON 800-565-2637
JBS Packing Inc
  Port Arthur, TX 409-982-3216
Jessie's Ilwaco Fish Company
  San Francisco, CA 360-642-3773
Jim Foley Company
  Marietta, GA 770-427-5102
Joe Fazio's Famous Italian
  Charleston, WV 304-344-3071
Joe Patti's Seafood Co
  Pensacola, FL 800-500-9929
John B. Wright Fish Company
  Gloucester, MA 978-283-4205
Johns Cove Fisheries
  Yarmouth, NS 902-742-8691
Johnson Sea Products Inc
  AL 251-824-2693
Jubilee Foods
  Bayou La Batre, AL 251-824-2110
K Horton Specialty Foods
  Portland, ME 207-228-2056
K.S.M. Seafood Corporation
  Baton Rouge, LA 225-383-1517
Kachemak Bay Seafood
  Homer, AK 907-235-2799
Karla's Smokehouse
  Rockaway Beach, OR 503-355-2362
Kent's Wharf
  Swans Island, ME 207-526-4186
Kettle Master
  Hillsville, VA 276-728-7571
Key Largo Fisheries
  Key Largo, FL 800-432-4358
Keys Fisheries Market & Marina
  Marathon, FL 866-743-4353
Keyser Brothers
  Lottsburg, VA 804-529-6837
Kibun Foods
  Seattle, WA 206-467-6287
King & Prince Seafood
  Brunswick, GA 888-391-5223
King & Prince Seafood Corp
  Brunswick, GA 800-841-0205
Kings Seafood Co
  Costa Mesa, CA 800-269-8425
Kitchens Seafood
  Plant City, FL 800-327-0132

Product Categories / Fish & Seafood: Seafood

Kodiak Salmon Packers
　Larsen Bay, AK 907-847-2250
Kona Fish Co Inc
　Kailua Kona, HI 808-326-7708
KOOL Ice & Seafood Co
　Cambridge, MD 800-437-2417
L & M Lockers
　Belt, MT 406-277-3522
L&C Fisheries
　Kensington, PE 902-886-2770
L&M Evans
　Conyers, GA 770-483-9373
L.H. Rodriguez Wholesale Seafood
　Tucson, AZ 520-623-1931
LA Monica Fine Foods
　Millville, NJ
Lady Gale Seafood
　Baldwin, LA 337-923-2060
Landlocked Seafoods
　Carroll, IA 712-792-9599
Larry J. Williams Company
　Jesup, GA 912-427-7729
Lartigue Seafood
　Orange Beach, AL 251-948-2644
Leblanc Seafood
　Lafitte, LA 504-689-2631
LEF McLean Brothers International
　Wheatley, ON 519-825-4656
Les Trois Petits Cochons
　Brooklyn, NY 800-537-7283
Lisbon Seafood Co
　Fall River, MA 508-672-3617
Little River Seafood Inc
　Reedville, VA 804-453-3670
Livingston's Bulls Bay Seafood
　Mc Clellanville, SC 843-887-3519
LLJ's Sea Products
　Round Pond, ME 207-529-4224
Lombardi's Seafood
　Winter Park, FL 800-879-8411
Lombardi's Seafood Inc
　Winter Park, FL 407-628-3474
Long Food Industries
　Fripp Island, SC 843-838-3205
Los Angeles Smoking & Curing Company
　Seattle, WA 213-628-1246
Louisiana Oyster Processors
　Baton Rouge, LA 225-291-6923
Louisiana Packing Company
　Westwego, LA 800-666-1293
Louisiana Pride Seafood
　New Orleans, LA 504-286-8736
Louisiana Seafoods
　New Orleans, LA 504-286-8736
Lowcountry Shellfish Inc
　Charleston, SC 800-999-2503
Lowland Seafood
　Lowland, NC 252-745-3751
Lucky Seafood Corporation
　Morrow, GA 770-960-9889
Lumar Lobster
　Lawrence, NY 516-371-0083
Lund's Fisheries
　Cape May, NJ 609-884-7600
Lusty Lobster
　Portland, ME 207-773-2829
Luxury Crab
　St John's, NL 709-739-6668
MacGregors Meat & Seafood
　Toronto, ON 888-383-3663
Machias Bay Seafood
　Machias, ME 207-255-8671
Maloney Seafood Corporation
　Quincy, MA 800-566-2837
Manchac Seafood Market
　Ponchatoula, LA 985-370-7070
Maple Leaf Foods International
　North York, ON 800-268-3708
Marine MacHines
　Bar Harbor, ME 207-288-0107
Market Fisheries
　Chicago, IL 773-483-3233
Martin Brothers Seafood Co
　Westwego, LA 504-341-2251
Martin Seafood Company
　Jessup, MD 410-799-5822
Maxim's Import Corporation
　Miami, FL 800-331-6652
Mazzetta Company
　Highland Park, IL 847-433-1150
McCoy Matt Frontier International
　Pismo Beach, CA 805-773-2994

Mcfarling Foods Inc
　Indianapolis, IN 317-635-2633
Mclaughlin Seafood
　Bangor, ME 800-222-9107
McNasby's Seafood Market
　Annapolis, MD 410-295-9022
Meat & Fish Fellas
　Glendale, AZ 623-931-6190
Menemsha Fish Market
　Chilmark, MA 508-645-2282
Meredith & Meredith
　Toddville, MD 410-397-8151
Merrill Seafood Center
　Jacksonville, FL 904-744-3132
Metafoods LLC
　Brookhaven, GA 404-843-2400
Metompkin Bay Oyster Company, Inc
　Crisfield, MD 410-968-0662
Mid-Atlantic Foods Inc
　Easton, MD 800-922-4688
Midwest Seafood
　Indianapolis, IN 317-466-1027
Mill Cove Lobster Pound
　Trevett, ME 207-633-3340
Miller Johnson Seafood
　Coden, AL 251-873-4444
Mills Seafood Ltd.
　Bouctouche, NB 506-743-2444
Milsolv Corporation
　Butler, WI 800-558-8501
Mister Fish Inc.
　Baltimore, MD 410-288-2722
Misty Islands Seafoods
　Dipper Harbour, NB 506-659-2781
Mobile Bay Seafood
　Coden, AL 251-973-0410
Mobile Processing
　Mobile, AL 251-438-6944
Mohn's Fisheries
　Harpers Ferry, IA 563-586-2269
Monarch Seafoods Inc
　Honolulu, HI 808-841-7877
Moon's Seafood Company
　Melbourne, FL 800-526-5624
Morey's Seafood Intl LLC
　Motley, MN 800-808-3474
Morgan Mill
　Cherokee, NC 828-497-9227
Mortillaro Lobster Company
　Gloucester, MA 978-282-4621
Mutual Fish Co
　Seattle, WA 206-322-4368
N.B.J. Enterprises
　Mobile, AL 251-661-2285
N.Y.K. Line (North America)
　Lombard, IL 888-695-7447
Nagasako Fish
　Wailuku, HI 808-242-4073
Nan Sea Enterprises of Wisconsin
　Waukesha, WI 262-542-8841
Nancy's Shellfish
　Falmouth, ME 207-774-3411
National Fish & Seafood Inc
　Gloucester, MA 800-229-1750
National Fish & Seafood Inc
　Gloucester, MA 800-229-1750
Nelson Crab Inc
　Tokeland, WA 800-262-0069
Neptune Fisheries
　Newport News, VA 800-545-7474
New Ocean
　Doraville, GA 770-458-5235
New Orleans Gulf Seafood
　New Orleans, LA 504-733-1516
New Wave Cuisine
　Mount Holly, NJ 800-486-0276
Newfound Resources
　St Josephs, NL 709-579-7676
Newmeadows Lobster Inc
　Portland, ME 800-668-1612
Nisbet Oyster Company
　Bay Center, WA 888-875-6629
Noon Hour Food Products Inc
　Chicago, IL 800-621-6636
Nordic Group Inc
　Boston, MA 800-486-4002
Norpac Fisheries Inc
　Honolulu, HI 808-528-3474
North Atlantic Inc
　Portland, ME 207-774-6025
North Atlantic Products
　South Thomaston, ME 207-596-0331

North Atlantic Seafood
　Portland, ME 800-774-6025
North Pacific Seafoods Inc
　Seattle, WA 206-726-9900
Northern Discovery Seafoods
　Grapeview, WA 800-843-6921
Northern Keta Caviar
　Juneau, AK 907-586-6095
Northern Ocean Marine
　Gloucester, MA 978-283-0222
Northern Products Corporation
　Seattle, WA 888-599-6290
Northern Wind Inc
　New Bedford, MA 888-525-2525
Northwest Natural Foods
　Olympia, WA 360-866-9661
Notre Dame Seafoods Inc.
　Comfort Cove, NL 709-244-5511
Ntc Marketing
　Williamsville, NY 800-333-1637
O'Donnell-Usen
　Tampa, FL 813-241-9200
O'Hara Corp
　Rockland, ME 207-594-4444
Oak Island Seafood Company
　Portland, ME 207-594-9250
Ocean Beauty Seafoods Inc
　Seattle, WA 800-365-8950
Ocean Crest Seafoods
　Gloucester, MA 800-259-4769
Ocean Food Co. Ltd.
　Toronto, ON 416-285-6487
Ocean Fresh Seafoods
　Seattle, WA 206-285-2412
Ocean King International
　Alhambra, CA 626-289-9399
Ocean Select Seafood
　Delcambre, LA 337-685-5315
Ocean Springs Seafood
　Ocean Springs, MS 228-875-0104
Ocean Union Company
　Lawrenceville, GA 770-995-1957
Oceanledge Seafoods
　Rockland, ME 207-594-4955
Oceans Prome Distributing
　Glenview, IL 847-998-5813
Offshore Seafood Co
　St Petersburg, FL 727-329-8848
Offshore Systems Inc
　Dutch Harbor, AK 907-581-1827
Ohana Seafood, LLC
　Honolulu, HI 808-843-1844
Okuhara Foods Inc
　Honolulu, HI 808-848-0581
Olsen Fish Co
　Minneapolis, MN 800-882-0212
Orca Bay Foods
　Seattle, WA 800-932-6722
Oregon Seafoods
　Coos Bay, OR 541-267-3474
Oversea Fishery & Investment
　Honolulu, HI 808-847-2500
P & J Oyster Co
　New Orleans, LA 504-523-2651
P & T Flannery Seafood Inc
　San Francisco, CA 415-346-1303
P&E Foods
　Honolulu, HI 808-839-9094
P&L Seafood of Venice
　Gretna, LA 504-363-2744
P. Janes & Sons
　Hant's Harbor, NL 709-586-2252
P.J. Markos Seafood Company
　Ipswich, MA 978-356-4347
P.J. Merrill Seafood Inc
　Portland, ME 207-773-1321
P.M. Innis Lobster Company
　Biddeford Pool, ME 207-284-5000
P.T. Fish
　Portland, ME 207-772-0239
Pacific American Fish Co Inc
　Vernon, CA 800-625-2525
Pacific Gourmet Seafood
　Bakersfield, CA 661-533-1260
Pacific Salmon Company
　Edmonds, WA 425-774-1315
Pacific Seafoods International
　Port Hardy, BC 250-949-8781
Pacific Valley Foods Inc
　Bellevue, WA 425-643-1805
Pacsea Corporation
　Aiea, HI 808-836-8888

Product Categories / Fish & Seafood: Seafood

Pamlico Packing Company
  Grantsboro, NC 800-682-1113
Parker Fish Company
  Wrightsville, GA 478-864-3406
Paul Piazza & Son Inc
  New Orleans, LA 800-969-6011
PEI Mussel King
  Morrell, PE 800-673-2767
Pelican Seafoods
  Pelican, AK 907-735-2211
Pemaquid Seafood
  Pemaquid, ME 866-864-2897
Penguin Frozen Foods Inc
  Northbrook, IL 800-323-1485
Perino's Inc
  Marrero, LA 504-347-5410
Perona Farms
  Andover, NJ 800-750-6190
Peter Pan Seafoods Inc.
  Bellevue, WA 206-728-6000
Phillips Foods
  Baltimore, MD 888-234-2722
Phillips Seafood
  Townsend, GA 912-832-4423
Piazza's Seafood World LLC
  St Rose, LA 504-602-5050
Pilot Meat & Sea Food Company
  Galena, IL 319-556-0760
Pine Point Seafood
  Scarborough, ME 207-883-4701
Pioneer Live Shrimp
  Oak Brook, IL 630-789-1133
Point Judith Fisherman's Company
  Narragansett, RI 401-782-1500
Point Saint George Fisheries
  Santa Rosa, CA 707-542-9490
Pon Food Corp
  Ponchatoula, LA 985-386-6941
Pond Pure Catfish
  Moulton, AL 256-974-6698
Pontchartrain Blue Crab
  Slidell, LA 985-649-6645
POP Fishing & Marine
  Honolulu, HI 808-537-2905
Port Royal Seafood
  St. Helena, SC 843-812-0257
Portland Shellfish Company
  Portland, ME 207-799-9290
Portland Specialty Seafoods
  Portland, ME 207-775-5765
Portsmouth Chowder Co
  Portsmouth, NH 877-616-7631
Poseidon Enterprises
  Charlotte, NC 800-863-7886
Poteet Seafood Co
  Brunswick, GA 912-264-5340
Premier Pacific Seafoods Inc
  Seattle, WA 206-286-8584
Premiere Seafood
  Lexington, KY 606-259-3474
Price Seafood
  Havre De Grace, MD 410-939-2782
Prime Cut Meat & Seafood Company
  Phoenix, AZ 800-277-1054
Primo Foods
  Oceanside, CA 760-439-8711
Produits Belle Baie
  Caraquet, NB 506-727-4414
Quality Crab Co Inc
  Elizabeth City, NC 252-338-0808
Quality Fisheries
  Niota, IL 217-448-4241
Quality Meats & Seafood
  West Fargo, ND 800-342-4250
Quality Seafood
  Apalachicola, FL 850-653-9696
R & R Seafood
  Tybee Island, GA 912-786-5504
R&J Seafoods
  Ninilchik, AK 907-567-3222
Raffield Fisheries Inc
  Port St Joe, FL 850-229-8494
Rainbow Seafood Market
  Baldwin Park, CA 626-962-6888
Rainbow Seafoods
  Topsfield, MA 978-887-9121
Red Chamber Co
  Vernon, CA 323-234-9000
Registry Steak & Seafood
  Bridgeview, IL 708-458-3100
Rego Smoked Fish Company
  Flushing, NY 718-894-1400

Reilly's Sea Products
  South Bristol, ME 207-644-1400
Resource Trading Company
  Portland, ME 207-772-2299
Rippons Seafood
  Ocean City, MD 410-723-0056
Roadrunner Seafood Inc
  Colquitt, GA 229-758-6098
Robin & Cohn Seafood Distributors
  Chalmette, LA 504-277-1679
Rock Point Oyster Company
  Quilcene, WA 360-765-3765
Rockport Lobster Co
  Gloucester, MA 978-281-0225
Rocky Point Shrimp Association
  Phoenix, AZ 602-254-8041
Roland Seafood Co
  Atlantic Beach, FL 904-246-9443
Rose Hill Seafood
  Columbus, GA 706-322-1269
Roy Dick Company
  Griffin, GA 770-227-3916
Royal Atlantic Seafood
  Gloucester, MA 978-281-6373
Royal Baltic LTD
  Brooklyn, NY 718-385-8300
Royal Lagoon Seafood Inc
  Theodore, AL 800-844-6972
Royal Pacific Fisheries
  Kenai, AK 907-283-9370
Royal Seafood Inc
  Brooklyn, NY 718-769-1517
Ruark & Ashton
  Woolford, MD 800-725-5032
Rubino's Seafood Company
  Chicago, IL 312-258-0020
Ruggiero Seafood
  Newark, NJ 866-225-2627
Russo's Seafood
  Savannah, GA 866-234-5196
Rymer Seafood
  Chicago, IL 312-236-3266
S S Lobster LTD
  Fitchburg, MA 978-342-6135
Sahalee of Alaska
  Anchorage, AK 800-349-4151
Salamatof Seafoods
  Kenai, AK 907-283-7000
Salmolux Inc
  Federal Way, WA 253-874-6570
Santa Monica Seafood Co.
  Rancho Dominguez, CA 800-969-8862
SC Enterprises
  Owen Sound, ON 519-371-0456
Sea Bear Smokehouse
  Anacortes, WA 800-645-3474
Sea Fresh USA Inc
  North Kingstown, RI 401-583-0200
Sea Pac Of Idaho Inc
  Filer, ID 208-326-3100
Sea Pearl Seafood
  Bayou La Batre, AL 800-872-8804
Sea Safari
  Belhaven, NC 800-688-6174
Sea Snack Foods Inc
  Los Angeles, CA 213-622-2204
Sea View Fillet Company
  New Bedford, MA 508-984-1406
Sea Watch Intl
  Easton, MD 410-822-7500
Seafare Market Wholesale
  Moody, ME 207-646-5160
Seafood Merchants LTD
  Vernon Hills, IL 847-634-0900
Seafood Producers Co-Op
  Bellingham, WA 360-733-0120
Seafood Specialties
  Anna, IL 618-833-6083
Sealaska Corp
  Juneau, AK 907-586-1512
SeaPerfect Atlantic Farms
  Charleston, SC 800-728-0099
SeaSpecialties
  Miami, FL 800-654-6682
Seatech Corporation
  Lynnwood, WA 425-487-3231
Seatrade Corporation
  Hoboken, NJ 201-963-5700
Seaview Lobster Co
  Kittery, ME 800-245-4997
Seymour & Sons Seafoods Inc
  Diberville, MS 228-392-4020

Shamrock Foods Co
  Phoenix, AZ 800-289-3663
Shaw's Southern Belle Frozen, Inc.
  Jacksonville, FL 888-742-9701
Shawmut Fishing Company
  Anchorage, AK 709-334-2559
Shemper Seafood Co
  Biloxi, MS 228-435-2703
Shining Ocean Inc
  Sumner, WA 800-935-6464
Shore Seafood Distr
  Saxis, VA 757-824-5517
Signature Seafoods Inc
  Seattle, WA 206-285-2815
Silver Lining Seafood
  Seattle, WA 800-426-5490
Silverston Fisheries
  Superior, WI 715-392-5551
Singleton Seafood Company
  Plant City, FL 813-241-1500
Sonoma Seafoods
  Sonoma, CA 800-411-2123
Southern Pride Catfish Company
  Seattle, WA 800-343-8046
Southern Shell Fish Company
  Harvey, LA 504-341-5631
Southern Shellfish
  Savannah, GA 912-897-3650
Southside Seafood Inc
  Scranton, PA 570-969-9726
Spinney Creek Shellfish
  Eliot, ME 877-778-6727
Sportsmen's Cannery
  Winchester Bay, OR 800-457-8048
Sportsmen's Cannery & Smokehouse
  Winchester Bay, OR 800-457-8048
Sportsmens Seafoods
  San Diego, CA 619-224-3551
St. Ours & Company
  East Weymouth, MA 781-331-8520
St. Simons Seafood
  Brunswick, GA 912-265-5225
Stacey's Famous Foods
  Hayden, ID 800-782-2395
Stanley's Best Seafood
  Coden, AL 251-824-2801
Star Seafood
  Bayou La Batre, AL 251-824-3110
Starich
  Daphne, AL 251-626-5037
Steve Connolly Seafood Co Inc
  Boston, MA 800-225-5595
Stewarts Seafood
  Coden, AL 251-824-7368
Stone Crabs Inc
  Miami Beach, FL 800-260-2722
Straub's
  Clayton, MO 888-725-2121
Sunshine Food Sales
  Miami, FL 305-696-2885
Sunshine Seafood
  Stonington, ME 207-367-2955
Super Snooty Sea Food Corporation
  Boston, MA 617-426-6390
Superior Ocean Produce
  Chicago, IL 773-283-8400
Superior Seafood & Meat Company
  South Bend, IN 574-289-0511
T&T Seafood
  Baker, LA 225-261-5438
T.B. Seafood
  Portland, ME 207-871-2420
T.J. Kraft
  Honolulu, HI 808-842-3474
Taku Smokehouse
  Juneau, AK 800-582-5122
Tampa Maid Foods Inc
  Lakeland, FL 800-237-7637
Tempest Fisheries LTD
  New Bedford, MA 508-997-0720
Terry Brothers, Inc
  Willis Wharf, VA 757-442-6251
Tex-Mex Cold Storage
  Brownsville, TX 956-831-9433
Tichon Sea Food Corp
  New Bedford, MA 508-999-5607
Tideland Seafood Company
  Dulac, LA 985-563-4516
Tony's Seafood LTD
  Baton Rouge, LA 800-356-2905
Triangle Seafood
  Louisville, KY 502-561-0055

Product Categories / Fish & Seafood: Seafood

Trident Seafoods Corp
   Seattle, WA 800-426-5490
Trident Seafoods Corp
   Wrangell, AK 907-874-3346
Triton Seafood Co
   Medley, FL 305-888-0051
Tsar Nicoulai Caviar LLC
   San Francisco, CA 800-952-2842
Turk Brothers Custom Meats Inc
   Ashland, OH 800-789-1051
Union Fisheries Corp
   Chicago, IL 773-738-0448
Union Seafoods
   Phoenix, AZ 602-254-4114
United Provision Meat Company
   Columbus, OH 614-252-1126
Upcountry Fisheries
   Makawao, HI 808-871-8484
Val's Seafood
   Mobile, AL 251-639-2570
Valdez Food Inc
   Philadelphia, PA 215-634-6106
Van de Kamps
   Peoria, IL 800-798-3318
Viking Seafoods Inc
   Malden, MA 800-225-3020
Viking Trading
   Atlanta, GA 770-455-8630
Vinalhaven Fishermens Co-op
   Camden, ME 207-236-0092
Vince's Seafoods
   Gretna, LA 504-368-1544
Vincent Piazza Jr & Sons
   Harahan, LA 800-259-5016
Virginia Trout Co
   Monterey, VA 540-468-2280
Vision Seafood Partners
   Kingston, MA 781-585-2000
W. Forrest Haywood Seafood Company
   Poquoson, VA 757-868-6748
W.O. Sasser
   Savannah, GA 912-897-1154
W.T. Ruark & Company
   Fishing Creek, MD 410-397-3133
Wabash Seafood Co
   Chicago, IL 312-733-5070
Wabi Fishing Company
   Marysville, WA 888-536-7696
Wagner Seafood
   Oak Lawn, IL 708-636-2646
Wagshal's Imports
   Washington, DC 202-363-5698
Wainani Kai Seafood
   Honolulu, HI 808-847-7435
Walden Foods
   Winchester, VA 800-648-7688
Walker Meats
   Carrollton, GA 800-741-3601
Walker's Seafood
   Jonesboro, AR 870-932-0375
Wallace Fisheries
   Gulf Shores, AL 251-986-7211
Wallace Plant Company
   Bath, ME 207-443-2640
Walsh's Seafood
   Gouldsboro, ME 207-963-2578
Wanchese Fish Co Inc
   Suffolk, VA 757-673-4500
Waterfront Seafood
   Bayou La Batre, AL 251-824-2185
Waterfront Seafood Market
   West Des Moines, IA 515-223-5106
WEIS Markets Inc.
   Sunbury, PA. 866-999-9347
West Bay Fishing
   Gouldsboro, ME 207-963-2392
Weyand's Fishery
   Wyandotte, MI 800-521-9815
Wharton Seafood Sales
   Paauilo, HI 800-352-8507
White Cap Fish Market
   Islip, NY 631-277-6577
Wichita Fish Co
   Wichita, KS 316-265-3474
Wiegardt Brothers
   Nahcotta, WA 360-665-4111
Wild Planet Foods
   McKinleyville, CA 800-998-9945
Winn-Dixie Stores
   Jacksonville, FL 800-967-9105
Winter Harbor Co-Op Inc
   Winter Harbor, ME 207-963-5857

WK Eckerd & Sons
   Brunswick, GA 912-265-0332
Wolverton Seafood
   Houlton, ME 506-276-4629
Woodfield Fish & Oyster Company
   Galesville, MD 410-897-1093
World Flavors Inc
   Warminster, PA 215-672-4400
Wright Brand Oysters
   Coden, AL 251-824-7880
Y&W Shellfish
   Woodbine, GA 912-729-4814
Yarmer Boys Catfish International
   Beaumont, TX 409-842-1962
Yeomen Seafoods Inc
   Gloucester, MA 978-283-7422
Zabiha Halal Meat Processors
   Addison, IL 630-620-5000

Canned

Alaska Pacific Seafoods
   Kodiak, AK 907-486-3234
Charles H. Parks & Company
   Fishing Creek, MD 410-397-3400
Chuck's Seafoods
   Charleston, OR 541-888-5525
Cowart Seafood Corp
   Lottsburg, VA 804-529-6101
Crown Prince Inc
   City Of Industry, CA 626-912-3700
Dressel Collins Fish Company
   Seattle, WA 206-725-0121
J Moniz Co Inc
   Fall River, MA 508-674-8451
J Turner Seafood
   Gloucester, MA 978-281-8535
Kodiak Salmon Packers
   Larsen Bay, AK 907-847-2250
LA Monica Fine Foods
   Millville, NJ
LLJ's Sea Products
   Round Pond, ME 207-529-4224
Mid-Atlantic Foods Inc
   Easton, MD 800-922-4688
Noon Hour Food Products Inc
   Chicago, IL 800-621-6636
Notre Dame Seafoods Inc.
   Comfort Cove, NL 709-244-5511
Ocean Fresh Seafoods
   Seattle, WA 206-285-2412
Safe Catch
   Sausalito, CA 888-568-4211
Sea Watch Intl
   Easton, MD 410-822-7500
Seatech Corporation
   Lynnwood, WA 425-487-3231
Southern Shell Fish Company
   Harvey, LA 504-341-5631
Sportsmens Seafoods
   San Diego, CA 619-224-3551
Tideland Seafood Company
   Dulac, LA 985-563-4516
Trident Seafoods Corp
   Wrangell, AK 907-874-3346

Cocktail

Sea Snack Foods Inc
   Los Angeles, CA. 213-622-2204

Freeze-Dried

Haines Packing Company
   Haines, AK 907-766-2883
Wolf Canyon Foods
   Carmel, CA 831-626-1323

Fresh

Anderson Seafood
   Anaheim, CA 714-777-7100
Aquatec Seafoods Ltd.
   Comox, BC 250-339-6412
Arrowac Fisheries
   Seattle, WA 206-282-5655
Atlantic Capes Fisheries
   Cape May, NJ 609-884-3000
Atlantic Sea Pride
   Boston, MA 617-269-7700
Atlantic Seacove Inc
   Boston, MA 617-442-6206
B G Smith & Sons Oyster Co
   Sharps, VA 877-483-8279

Bayou Land Seafood
   Breaux Bridge, LA 337-667-6118
BlueWater Seafoods
   Gloucester, MA. 888-560-2539
Boundary Fish Company
   Blaine, WA 360-332-6715
Briney Sea Delicaseas
   Tumwater, WA 888-772-5666
Buzzards Bay Trading Company
   Fairhaven, MA 508-996-0242
Caraquet Ice Company
   Caraquet, NB 506-727-7211
Carolina Classics Catfish Inc
   Ayden, NC 252-746-2818
Charles H. Parks & Company
   Fishing Creek, MD 410-397-3400
Coast Seafoods Company
   Bellevue, WA 800-423-2303
Cowart Seafood Corp
   Lottsburg, VA 804-529-6101
Cozy Harbor Seafood Inc
   Portland, ME 800-225-2586
Crest International Corporation
   San Diego, CA 800-548-1232
DB Kenney Fisheries
   Westport, NS 902-839-2023
French Creek Seafood
   Parksville, BC 250-248-7100
Granville Gates & Sons
   Hubbards, NS 902-228-2559
Great Atlantic Trading Company
   Brentwood, TN 888-268-8780
Gulf Crown Seafood Co
   Delcambre, LA 337-685-4722
Hallmark Fisheries
   Charleston, OR 541-888-3253
Harbor Fish Market
   Portland, ME 800-370-1790
Hillard Bloom Packing Co Inc
   Port Norris, NJ 856-785-0120
Hillmans Shrimp & Oyster
   Port Lavaca, TX 800-582-4416
Hilo Fish Company
   Hilo, HI 808-961-0877
Independent Packers Corporation
   Seattle, WA 206-285-6000
International Seafoods - Alaska
   Kodiak, AK 907-486-4768
Island Marine Products
   Clarks Harbour, NS 902-745-2222
J. Matassini & Sons Fish Company
   Tampa, FL 813-229-0829
Jessie's Ilwaco Fish Company
   San Francisco, CA 360-642-3773
Keyser Brothers
   Lottsburg, VA 804-529-6837
LA Monica Fine Foods
   Millville, NJ
Little River Seafood Inc
   Reedville, VA 804-453-3670
Menemsha Fish Market
   Chilmark, MA 508-645-2282
Minterbrook Oyster Co
   Gig Harbor, WA 253-857-5251
National Fish & Oyster
   Olympia, WA 360-491-5550
Nordic Group Inc
   Boston, MA 800-486-4002
North Pacific Seafoods Inc
   Seattle, WA 206-726-9900
Ocean Beauty Seafoods Inc
   Seattle, WA 800-365-8950
Ocean Fresh Seafoods
   Seattle, WA 206-285-2412
Pacific American Fish Co Inc
   Vernon, CA 800-625-2525
Pacific Salmon Company
   Edmonds, WA 425-774-1315
Pacific Seafoods International
   Port Hardy, BC 250-949-8781
Pamlico Packing Company
   Grantsboro, NC 800-682-1113
Paul Piazza & Son Inc
   New Orleans, LA 800-969-6011
Portland Shellfish Company
   Portland, ME 207-799-9290
Quality Seafood
   Apalachicola, FL 850-653-9696
Red Chamber Co
   Vernon, CA 323-234-9000
Rippons Seafood
   Ocean City, MD 410-723-0056

Product Categories / Fish & Seafood: Seafood

Royal Seafood Inc
  Brooklyn, NY 718-769-1517
Ruggiero Seafood
  Newark, NJ 866-225-2627
Stone Crabs Inc
  Miami Beach, FL 800-260-2722
Sunshine Food Sales
  Miami, FL 305-696-2885
Tampa Bay Fisheries Inc
  Dover, FL 800-732-3663
Taylor Shellfish Farms
  Shelton, WA 360-426-6178
Terry Brothers, Inc
  Willis Wharf, VA 757-442-6251
Trident Seafoods Corp
  Wrangell, AK 907-874-3346
Ultimate Foods
  Linden, NJ 908-486-0800
Union Fisheries Corp
  Chicago, IL 773-738-0448
Wanchese Fish Co Inc
  Suffolk, VA 757-673-4500
Weyand's Fishery
  Wyandotte, MI 800-521-9815
Wiegardt Brothers
  Nahcotta, WA 360-665-4111

Frozen

Acme Steak & Seafood
  Youngstown, OH 800-686-2263
Alaskan Gourmet Seafoods
  Anchorage, AK 800-288-3740
Aliotti Wholesale Fish Company
  Monterey, CA 408-722-4597
American Seafoods
  Seattle, WA 206-448-0300
Anderson Seafood
  Anaheim, CA 714-777-7100
Aquatec Seafoods Ltd.
  Comox, BC 250-339-6412
Arista Industries Inc
  Wilton, CT 800-255-6457
Arrowac Fisheries
  Seattle, WA 206-282-5655
ASC Seafood Inc
  Largo, FL 800-876-3474
Atlantic Capes Fisheries
  Cape May, NJ 609-884-3000
Azuma Foods Intl Inc USA
  Hayward, CA 510-782-1112
B G Smith & Sons Oyster Co
  Sharps, VA 877-483-8279
Bandon Bay Fisheries
  Bandon, OR 541-347-4454
Bay Oceans Sea Foods
  Garibaldi, OR 503-322-3316
Bayou Land Seafood
  Breaux Bridge, LA 337-667-6118
Beaver Street Fisheries
  Jacksonville, FL 800-874-6426
Biloxi Freezing Processing Inc.
  Biloxi, MS 228-436-0017
Blount Fine Foods
  Fall River, MA 774-888-1300
BlueWater Seafoods
  Gloucester, MA 888-560-2539
Bon Secour Fisheries Inc
  Bon Secour, AL 251-949-7411
Boundary Fish Company
  Blaine, WA 360-332-6715
Buzzards Bay Trading Company
  Fairhaven, MA 508-996-0242
C F Gollott & Son Seafood
  Diberville, MS 228-392-2747
Callis Seafood
  Lancaster, VA 804-462-7634
Caraquet Ice Company
  Caraquet, NB 506-727-7211
Carolina Atlantic Seafood Enterprises
  Beaufort, NC 252-504-2663
Carolina Classics Catfish Inc
  Ayden, NC 252-746-2818
Carrington Foods Co Inc
  Saraland, AL 251-675-9700
Cathay Foods Corporation
  Boston, MA 617-427-1507
Certi Fresh Foods Inc
  Wilmington, CA 310-221-6262
Channel Fish Processing
  Gloucester, MA 800-457-0054
Chases Lobster Pound
  Port Howe, NS 902-243-2408

Cherbogue Fisheries
  Yarmouth, NS 902-742-9157
Chester W. Howeth & Brother
  Crisfield, MD 410-968-1398
Clearwater Fine Foods
  Bedford, NS 902-443-0550
Cowart Seafood Corp
  Lottsburg, VA 804-529-6101
Cozy Harbor Seafood Inc
  Portland, ME 800-225-2586
Crest International Corporation
  San Diego, CA 800-548-1232
Crevettes Du Nord
  Gaspe, QC 418-368-1414
Cuizina Food Company
  Woodinville, WA 425-486-7000
Czimer's Game & Seafoods
  Homer Glen, IL 888-294-6377
DB Kenney Fisheries
  Westport, NS 902-839-2023
Deep Creek Custom Packing
  Ninilchik, AK 800-764-0078
Del's Seaway Shrimp & Oyster Company
  Biloxi, MS 228-432-2604
E. Gagnon & Fils
  St Therese-De-Gaspe, QC 418-385-3011
Eastern Fish Company
  Teaneck, NJ 800-526-9066
F W Bryce Inc
  Gloucester, MA 978-283-7080
Fish Breeders of Idaho
  Hagerman, ID 208-837-6114
Fish King
  Glendale, CA 818-244-2161
Fish Market Inc
  Louisville, KY 502-587-7474
French Creek Seafood
  Parksville, BC 250-248-7100
Frozen Specialties Inc
  Perrysburg, OH 419-867-2005
Galilean Seafood Inc
  Bristol, RI 401-253-3030
George Robberecht Seafood
  Montross, VA 804-472-3556
Gerard & Dominique Seafoods
  Harbor, OR 800-858-0449
Gesco ENR
  Gaspe, QC 418-368-1414
Golden Gulf Coast Packing Co
  Biloxi, MS 228-374-6121
Good Harbor Fillet Company
  New Bedford, MA 800-343-8046
Gorton's Inc.
  Gloucester, MA 800-222-6846
Great Atlantic Trading Company
  Brentwood, TN 888-268-8780
Great Glacier Salmon
  Prince Rupert, BC 250-627-4955
Great Northern Products Inc
  Cranston, RI 401-490-4590
Gulf Pride Enterprises
  Biloxi, MS 888-689-0560
H&H Fisheries Limited
  Eastern Passage, NS 866-773-4400
Hallmark Fisheries
  Charleston, OR 541-888-3253
Handy International Inc
  Salisbury, MD 800-426-3977
HFI Foods
  Redmond, WA 425-883-1320
Higgins Seafood
  Lafitte, LA 504-689-3577
High Liner Foods Inc.
  Lunenburg, NS 902-634-8811
Hillard Bloom Packing Co Inc
  Port Norris, NJ 856-785-0120
Hillmans Shrimp & Oyster
  Port Lavaca, TX 800-582-4416
Hilo Fish Company
  Hilo, HI 808-961-0877
Independent Packers Corporation
  Seattle, WA 206-285-6000
Indian Ridge Shrimp Co
  Chauvin, LA 800-594-0920
International Seafoods - Alaska
  Kodiak, AK 907-486-4768
Island Marine Products
  Clarks Harbour, NS 902-745-2222
Island Scallops
  Qualicum Beach, BC 250-757-9811
J. Matassini & Sons Fish Company
  Tampa, FL 813-229-0829

Janes Family Foods
  Mississauga, ON 800-565-2637
JBS Packing Inc
  Port Arthur, TX 409-982-3216
Jessie's Ilwaco Fish Company
  San Francisco, CA 360-642-3773
Jubilee Foods
  Bayou La Batre, AL 251-824-2110
Key Largo Fisheries
  Key Largo, FL 800-432-4358
Keyser Brothers
  Lottsburg, VA 804-529-6837
Kitchens Seafood
  Plant City, FL 800-327-0132
Kodiak Salmon Packers
  Larsen Bay, AK 907-847-2250
L&C Fisheries
  Kensington, PE 902-886-2770
LA Monica Fine Foods
  Millville, NJ
Lady Gale Seafood
  Baldwin, LA 337-923-2060
Lombardi's Seafood
  Winter Park, FL 800-879-8411
Louisiana Packing Company
  Westwego, LA 800-666-1293
Lund's Fisheries
  Cape May, NJ 609-884-7600
Luxury Crab
  St John's, NL 709-739-6668
Maple Leaf Foods International
  North York, ON 800-268-3708
Martin Seafood Company
  Jessup, MD 410-799-5822
Maxim's Import Corporation
  Miami, FL 800-331-6652
Menemsha Fish Market
  Chilmark, MA 508-645-2282
Mid-Atlantic Foods Inc
  Easton, MD 800-922-4688
Minterbrook Oyster Co
  Gig Harbor, WA 253-857-5251
Mobile Processing
  Mobile, AL 251-438-6944
Morey's Seafood Intl LLC
  Motley, MN 800-808-3474
Mutual Fish Co
  Seattle, WA 206-322-4368
Nan Sea Enterprises of Wisconsin
  Waukesha, WI 262-542-8841
National Fish & Oyster
  Olympia, WA 360-491-5550
Nelson Crab Inc
  Tokeland, WA 800-262-0069
Neptune Fisheries
  Newport News, VA 800-545-7474
Newfound Resources
  St Josephs, NL 709-579-7676
Nordic Group Inc
  Boston, MA 800-486-4002
North Pacific Seafoods Inc
  Seattle, WA 206-726-9900
Northern Wind Inc
  New Bedford, MA 888-525-2525
Notre Dame Seafoods Inc.
  Comfort Cove, NL 709-244-5511
Ocean Beauty Seafoods Inc
  Seattle, WA 800-365-8950
Ocean Food Co. Ltd.
  Toronto, ON 416-285-6487
Ocean Fresh Seafoods
  Seattle, WA 206-285-2412
Ocean Springs Seafood
  Ocean Springs, MS 228-875-0104
Okuhara Foods Inc
  Honolulu, HI 808-848-0581
Orca Bay Foods
  Seattle, WA 800-932-6722
P. Janes & Sons
  Hant's Harbor, NL 709-586-2252
Pacific American Fish Co Inc
  Vernon, CA 800-625-2525
Pacific Seafoods International
  Port Hardy, BC 250-949-8781
Pacific Valley Foods Inc
  Bellevue, WA 425-643-1805
Pamlico Packing Company
  Grantsboro, NC 800-682-1113
Paul Piazza & Son Inc
  New Orleans, LA 800-969-6011
PEI Mussel King
  Morrell, PE 800-673-2767

Product Categories / Fish & Seafood: Shellfish

Peter Pan Seafoods Inc.
  Bellevue, WA 206-728-6000
Portland Shellfish Company
  Portland, ME 207-799-9290
Prairie Cajun Wholesale
  Eunice, LA 337-546-6195
Quality Seafood
  Apalachicola, FL 850-653-9696
Resource Trading Company
  Portland, ME 207-772-2299
Royal Seafood Inc
  Brooklyn, NY 718-769-1517
Ruggiero Seafood
  Newark, NJ 866-225-2627
Santa Monica Seafood Co.
  Rancho Dominguez, CA 800-969-8862
Sea Pearl Seafood
  Bayou La Batre, AL 800-872-8804
Sea Safari
  Belhaven, NC 800-688-6174
Sea Snack Foods Inc
  Los Angeles, CA 213-622-2204
Sea Watch Intl
  Easton, MD 410-822-7500
Seafood Producers Co-Op
  Bellingham, WA 360-733-0120
Seajoy
  Miami, FL 877-537-1717
Seatech Corporation
  Lynnwood, WA 425-487-3231
Seymour & Sons Seafoods Inc
  Diberville, MS 228-392-4020
Shawmut Fishing Company
  Anchorage, AK 709-334-2559
Silver Lining Seafood
  Seattle, WA 800-426-5490
Spruce Lane Investments
  Stratford, PE 902-892-2600
St. Ours & Company
  East Weymouth, MA 781-331-8520
Stacey's Famous Foods
  Hayden, ID 800-782-2395
Stone Crabs Inc
  Miami Beach, FL 800-260-2722
Sunshine Food Sales
  Miami, FL 305-696-2885
Super Snooty Sea Food Corporation
  Boston, MA 617-426-6390
Sweet Water Seafood
  Carlstadt, NJ 201-939-6622
Taku Smokehouse
  Juneau, AK 800-582-5122
Tampa Bay Fisheries Inc
  Dover, FL 800-732-3663
Tampa Maid Foods Inc
  Lakeland, FL 800-237-7637
Taylor Shellfish Farms
  Shelton, WA 360-426-6178
Tex-Mex Cold Storage
  Brownsville, TX 956-831-9433
Tichon Sea Food Corp
  New Bedford, MA 508-999-5607
Trident Seafoods Corp
  Wrangell, AK 907-874-3346
Triton Seafood Co
  Medley, FL 305-888-0051
Ultimate Foods
  Linden, NJ 908-486-0800
Union Fisheries Corp
  Chicago, IL 773-738-0448
Viking Seafoods Inc
  Malden, MA 800-225-3020
Vince's Seafoods
  Gretna, LA 504-368-1544
Vincent Piazza Jr & Sons
  Harahan, LA 800-259-5016
Virginia Trout Co
  Monterey, VA 540-468-2280
Wanchese Fish Co Inc
  Suffolk, VA 757-673-4500
Weyand's Fishery
  Wyandotte, MI 800-521-9815
White Cap Fish Market
  Islip, NY 631-277-6577

Smoked

Anderson Seafood
  Anaheim, CA 714-777-7100
Blount Fine Foods
  Fall River, MA 774-888-1300
Cooke Aquaculture
  Blacks Harbour, NB 506-456-6600

Dressel Collins Fish Company
  Seattle, WA 206-725-0121
Indian Valley Meats
  Indian, AK 907-653-7511
Salmolux Inc
  Federal Way, WA 253-874-6570
Sea Bear Smokehouse
  Anacortes, WA 800-645-3474

Cold

Tonex
  Wallington, NJ 973-773-5135

Cured

J Moniz Co Inc
  Fall River, MA 508-674-8451
J Turner Seafood
  Gloucester, MA 978-281-8535
Ocean Fresh Seafoods
  Seattle, WA 206-285-2412
Tideland Seafood Company
  Dulac, LA 985-563-4516

Lox

Bold Coast Smokehouse
  Lubec, ME 888-733-0807
Homarus Inc
  Long Island City, NY 917-832-0333
Vita Food Products Inc
  Chicago, IL 800-989-8482

Nova Style

Vita Food Products Inc
  Chicago, IL 800-989-8482
Vital Choice
  Bellingham, WA 800-608-4825

Turtle

Bayou Land Seafood
  Breaux Bridge, LA 337-667-6118

Shellfish

Canned

Channel Fish Processing
  Gloucester, MA 800-457-0054
Charles H. Parks & Company
  Fishing Creek, MD 410-397-3400
Chicken Of The Sea
  El Segundo, CA 844-267-8862
Chuck's Seafoods
  Charleston, OR 541-888-5525
Crown Prince Inc
  City Of Industry, CA 626-912-3700
Cuizina Food Company
  Woodinville, WA 425-486-7000
Gulf City Marine Supply
  Bayou La Batre, AL 251-824-2516
Hallmark Fisheries
  Charleston, OR 541-888-3253
Mid-Atlantic Foods Inc
  Easton, MD 800-922-4688
Nelson Crab Inc
  Tokeland, WA 800-262-0069
Notre Dame Seafoods Inc.
  Comfort Cove, NL 709-244-5511
Ntc Marketing
  Williamsville, NY 800-333-1637
Pacific Salmon Company
  Edmonds, WA 425-774-1315
Peter Pan Seafoods Inc.
  Bellevue, WA 206-728-6000
Sea Safari
  Belhaven, NC 800-688-6174
Southern Shell Fish Company
  Harvey, LA 504-341-5631
Sweet Water Seafood
  Carlstadt, NJ 201-939-6622
Trident Seafoods Corp
  Wrangell, AK 907-874-3346

Chopped

S & M Fisheries Inc
  Kennebunkport, ME 207-985-3456

Clam

Atlantic Aqua Farms
  Orwell Cove, PE 902-651-2563

Atlantic Capes Fisheries
  Cape May, NJ 609-884-3000
Big Al's Seafood
  Bozman, MD 410-745-2637
Biloxi Freezing Processing Inc.
  Biloxi, MS 228-436-0017
Blount Fine Foods
  Fall River, MA 774-888-1300
Bon Secour Fisheries Inc
  Bon Secour, AL 251-949-7411
C.E. Fish Company
  Jonesboro, ME 207-434-2631
Caito Fisheries Inc
  Fort Bragg, CA 707-964-6368
Cajun Crawfish Distributors
  Branch, LA 888-254-8626
Certi Fresh Foods Inc
  Wilmington, CA 310-221-6262
Chases Lobster Pound
  Port Howe, NS 902-243-2408
Chester River Clam Co
  Centreville, MD 410-758-3810
Chuck's Seafoods
  Charleston, OR 541-888-5525
Clearwater Fine Foods
  Bedford, NS 902-443-0550
Coast Seafoods Company
  Bellevue, WA 800-423-2303
Comeaux's
  Lafayette, LA 888-264-5460
Crevettes Du Nord
  Gaspe, QC 418-368-1414
Crown Prince Inc
  City Of Industry, CA 626-912-3700
Cuizina Food Company
  Woodinville, WA 425-486-7000
Davis Strait Fisheries
  Halifax, NS 902-450-5115
Del's Seaway Shrimp & Oyster Company
  Biloxi, MS 228-432-2604
E. Gagnon & Fils
  St Therese-De-Gaspe, QC 418-385-3011
Frozen Specialties Inc
  Perrysburg, OH 419-867-2005
Fulton Fish Market
  New York, NY 718-842-8908
Gerard & Dominique Seafoods
  Harbor, OR 800-858-0449
Gesco ENR
  Gaspe, QC 418-368-1414
Gulf Pride Enterprises
  Biloxi, MS 888-689-0560
H&H Fisheries Limited
  Eastern Passage, NS 866-773-4400
Hillard Bloom Packing Co Inc
  Port Norris, NJ 856-785-0120
Hillmans Shrimp & Oyster
  Port Lavaca, TX 800-582-4416
Huck's Seafood
  Easton, MD 410-770-9211
Innovative Fishery Products
  Belliveau Cove, NS 902-837-5163
International Enterprises
  Herring Neck, NL 709-628-7406
Island Scallops
  Qualicum Beach, BC 250-757-9811
JBS Packing Inc
  Port Arthur, TX 409-982-3216
Jubilee Foods
  Bayou La Batre, AL 251-824-2110
L&C Fisheries
  Kensington, PE 902-886-2770
L&M Evans
  Conyers, GA 770-483-9373
LA Monica Fine Foods
  Millville, NJ
Lady Gale Seafood
  Baldwin, LA 337-923-2060
Louisiana Packing Company
  Westwego, LA 800-666-1293
Menemsha Fish Market
  Chilmark, MA 508-645-2282
Mid-Atlantic Foods Inc
  Easton, MD 800-922-4688
Mill Cove Lobster Pound
  Trevett, ME 207-633-3340
Mobile Processing
  Mobile, AL 251-438-6944
Mutual Fish Co
  Seattle, WA 206-322-4368
Nan Sea Enterprises of Wisconsin
  Waukesha, WI 262-542-8841

Product Categories / Fish & Seafood: Shellfish

New Orleans Fish House II LLC
   New Orleans, LA 800-839-3474
Newfound Resources
   St Josephs, NL 709-579-7676
North Atlantic Seafood
   Portland, ME 800-774-6025
Northern Wind Inc
   New Bedford, MA 888-525-2525
Northwest Wild Products
   Astoria, OR 503-791-1907
Ocean Springs Seafood
   Ocean Springs, MS 228-875-0104
PEI Mussel King
   Morrell, PE 800-673-2767
Pine Point Seafood
   Scarborough, ME 207-883-4701
Price Seafood
   Havre De Grace, MD 410-939-2782
Resource Trading Company
   Portland, ME 207-772-2299
SeaPerfect Atlantic Farms
   Charleston, SC 800-728-0099
Shawmut Fishing Company
   Anchorage, AK 709-334-2559
St. Ours & Company
   East Weymouth, MA 781-331-8520
Stavis Seafoods
   Boston, MA 800-390-5103
Tampa Bay Fisheries Inc
   Dover, FL 800-732-3663
Terry Brothers, Inc
   Willis Wharf, VA 757-442-6251
Vincent Piazza Jr & Sons
   Harahan, LA 800-259-5016
Vital Choice
   Bellingham, WA 800-608-4825
Young's Lobster Pound
   Belfast, ME 207-338-1160

Breaded Strips

LA Monica Fine Foods
   Millville, NJ

Canned

Blount Fine Foods
   Fall River, MA 774-888-1300
Chicken Of The Sea
   El Segundo, CA 844-267-8862
Chuck's Seafoods
   Charleston, OR 541-888-5525
Cuizina Food Company
   Woodinville, WA 425-486-7000
LA Monica Fine Foods
   Millville, NJ
Mid-Atlantic Foods Inc
   Easton, MD 800-922-4688
Mutual Fish Co
   Seattle, WA 206-322-4368
New Orleans Food Co-op
   New Orleans, LA 800-628-4900
Stavis Seafoods
   Boston, MA 800-390-5103

Chopped

LA Monica Fine Foods
   Millville, NJ

Fresh

Coast Seafoods Company
   Bellevue, WA 800-423-2303
Cuizina Food Company
   Woodinville, WA 425-486-7000
LA Monica Fine Foods
   Millville, NJ
Menemsha Fish Market
   Chilmark, MA 508-645-2282
Mutual Fish Co
   Seattle, WA 206-322-4368
Sweet Water Seafood
   Carlstadt, NJ 201-939-6622
Taylor Shellfish Farms
   Shelton, WA 360-426-6178
Terry Brothers, Inc
   Willis Wharf, VA 757-442-6251

Frozen

Cedar Key Aquaculture Farms
   Riverview, FL 888-252-6735
Certi Fresh Foods Inc
   Wilmington, CA 310-221-6262
Clearwater Fine Foods
   Bedford, NS 902-443-0550
Cuizina Food Company
   Woodinville, WA 425-486-7000
Gorton's Inc.
   Gloucester, MA 800-222-6846
Harbor Seafood
   New Hyde Park, NY 800-645-2211
Hillard Bloom Packing Co Inc
   Port Norris, NJ 856-785-0120
LA Monica Fine Foods
   Millville, NJ
Menemsha Fish Market
   Chilmark, MA 508-645-2282
Mid-Atlantic Foods Inc
   Easton, MD 800-922-4688
Minterbrook Oyster Co
   Gig Harbor, WA 253-857-5251
Mutual Fish Co
   Seattle, WA 206-322-4368
St. Ours & Company
   East Weymouth, MA 781-331-8520
Taylor Shellfish Farms
   Shelton, WA 360-426-6178

Frozen Strips

LA Monica Fine Foods
   Millville, NJ

Juice

Chincoteague Seafood Co Inc
   Parsonsburg, MD 443-260-4800
Crown Prince Inc
   City Of Industry, CA 626-912-3700
Flavor House, Inc.
   Adelanto, CA 760-246-9131

Minced

LA Monica Fine Foods
   Millville, NJ

Whole

LA Monica Fine Foods
   Millville, NJ

Conch

Denzer's Food Products
   Baltimore, MD 410-889-1500
Fulton Fish Market
   New York, NY 718-842-8908
Harbor Seafood
   New Hyde Park, NY 800-645-2211
LA Monica Fine Foods
   Millville, NJ
Sweet Water Seafood
   Carlstadt, NJ 201-939-6622
Triton Seafood Co
   Medley, FL 305-888-0051

Crab

Arrowac Fisheries
   Seattle, WA 206-282-5655
Bandon Bay Fisheries
   Bandon, OR 541-347-4454
Barry Group
   Corner Brook, NL 709-785-7387
Bay Hundred Seafood Inc
   St Michaels, MD 410-745-9329
Bayou Food Distributors
   Kenner, LA 800-516-8283
Bayou Land Seafood
   Breaux Bridge, LA 337-667-6118
Beaver Street Fisheries
   Jacksonville, FL 800-874-6426
Big Al's Seafood
   Bozman, MD 410-745-2637
Blue Star Food Products
   Doral, FL 305-836-6858
Bradye P. Todd & Son
   Cambridge, MD 410-228-8633
Caito Fisheries Inc
   Fort Bragg, CA 707-964-6368
California Shellfish Company
   San Francisco, CA 415-923-7400
Callis Seafood
   Lancaster, VA 804-462-7634
Captain Little Seafood
   Queens County, NS 902-947-2087
Carrington Foods Co Inc
   Saraland, AL 251-675-9700
Catfish Wholesale
   Abbeville, LA 800-334-7292
Cathay Foods Corporation
   Boston, MA 617-427-1507
Ceilidh Fisherman's Cooperative
   Port Hood, NS 902-787-2666
Certi Fresh Foods Inc
   Wilmington, CA 310-221-6262
Charles H. Parks & Company
   Fishing Creek, MD 410-397-3400
Clearwater Fine Foods
   Bedford, NS 902-443-0550
Crab Quarters
   Baltimore, MD 410-686-2222
Crown Prince Inc
   City Of Industry, CA 626-912-3700
Cuizina Food Company
   Woodinville, WA 425-486-7000
Dave's Gourmet Albacore
   Watsonville, CA 206-999-5517
Dorchester Crab Co
   Wingate, MD 410-397-8103
Fisherman's Market International
   Halifax, NS 902-445-3474
Fishhawk Fisheries
   Astoria, OR 503-325-5252
Fulton Fish Market
   New York, NY 718-842-8908
Goldcoast Salads
   Naples, FL 239-513-0430
Great Northern Products Inc
   Cranston, RI 401-490-4590
Gulf Stream Crab Company
   Bayou La Batre, AL 251-824-4717
H.Gass Seafood
   Hollywood, MD 301-373-6882
Hallmark Fisheries
   Charleston, OR 541-888-3253
Handy International Inc
   Salisbury, MD 800-426-3977
Harris Crab House
   Grasonville, MD 410-827-9500
Huck's Seafood
   Easton, MD 410-770-9211
Independent Packers Corporation
   Seattle, WA 206-285-6000
J. Matassini & Sons Fish Company
   Tampa, FL 813-229-0829
JBS Packing Inc
   Port Arthur, TX 409-982-3216
Jessie's Ilwaco Fish Company
   San Francisco, CA 360-642-3773
Keyser Brothers
   Lottsburg, VA 804-529-6837
Kitchens Seafood
   Plant City, FL 800-327-0132
LA Monica Fine Foods
   Millville, NJ
Larry J. Williams Company
   Jesup, GA 912-427-7729
Little River Seafood Inc
   Reedville, VA 804-453-3670
Lowland Seafood
   Lowland, NC 252-745-3751
Luxury Crab
   St John's, NL 709-739-6668
Martin Brothers Seafood Co
   Westwego, LA 504-341-2251
McGraw Seafood
   Tracadie Sheila, NB 506-395-3374
Menemsha Fish Market
   Chilmark, MA 508-645-2282
Mercer Processing
   Modesto, CA 209-529-0150
Mutual Fish Co
   Seattle, WA 206-322-4368
Nelson Crab Inc
   Tokeland, WA 800-262-0069
New Orleans Fish House II LLC
   New Orleans, LA 800-839-3474
North Atlantic Seafood
   Portland, ME 800-774-6025
Northwest Wild Products
   Astoria, OR 503-791-1907
Notre Dame Seafoods Inc.
   Comfort Cove, NL 709-244-5511
Ocean Food Co. Ltd.
   Toronto, ON 416-285-6487
Ocean Union Company
   Lawrenceville, GA 770-995-1957
Pamlico Packing Company
   Grantsboro, NC 800-682-1113

Product Categories / Fish & Seafood: Shellfish

Peter Pan Seafoods Inc.
  Bellevue, WA 206-728-6000
Phillips Foods
  Baltimore, MD 888-234-2722
Price Seafood
  Havre De Grace, MD 410-939-2782
Produits Belle Baie
  Caraquet, NB 506-727-4414
Red Chamber Co
  Vernon, CA 323-234-9000
Rippons Seafood
  Ocean City, MD 410-723-0056
Sea Safari
  Belhaven, NC 800-688-6174
Sea Watch Intl
  Easton, MD 410-822-7500
Silver Lining Seafood
  Seattle, WA 800-426-5490
Southern Shell Fish Company
  Harvey, LA 504-341-5631
St. Ours & Company
  East Weymouth, MA 781-331-8520
Stone Crabs Inc
  Miami Beach, FL 800-260-2722
Sunshine Food Sales
  Miami, FL 305-696-2885
Taku Smokehouse
  Juneau, AK 800-582-5122
Trident Seafoods Corp
  Wrangell, AK 907-874-3346
Vince's Seafoods
  Gretna, LA 504-368-1544
Vital Choice
  Bellingham, WA 800-608-4825
W.T. Ruark & Company
  Fishing Creek, MD 410-397-3133
Waverly Crabs
  Baltimore, MD 410-243-1181
Young's Lobster Pound
  Belfast, ME 207-338-1160

Blue

Casey's Seafood Inc
  Newport News, VA 757-928-1979
J M Clayton Co
  Cambridge, MD 800-652-6931
Little River Seafood Inc
  Reedville, VA 804-453-3670
Price Seafood
  Havre De Grace, MD 410-939-2782
Sea Safari
  Belhaven, NC 800-688-6174

Cakes

Bradley Creek Seafood
  Savannah, GA 912-484-3510
Casey's Seafood Inc
  Newport News, VA 757-928-1979
Chesapeake Bay Crab Cakes & More
  Owings Mills, MD 800-282-2722
Handy International Inc
  Salisbury, MD 800-426-3977
J. Matassini & Sons Fish Company
  Tampa, FL 813-229-0829
LA Monica Fine Foods
  Millville, NJ
Tampa Bay Fisheries Inc
  Dover, FL 800-732-3663
The Van Cleve Seafood Company
  Spotsylvania, VA 800-628-5202

Cakes Frozen

Chincoteague Seafood Co Inc
  Parsonsburg, MD 443-260-4800
Coastal Seafoods
  Ridgefield, CT 203-431-0453
Cuizina Food Company
  Woodinville, WA 425-486-7000
Handy International Inc
  Salisbury, MD 800-426-3977
J. Matassini & Sons Fish Company
  Tampa, FL 813-229-0829

Canned

Cathay Foods Corporation
  Boston, MA 617-427-1507
Charles H. Parks & Company
  Fishing Creek, MD 410-397-3400
Chicken Of The Sea
  El Segundo, CA 844-267-8862

Cuizina Food Company
  Woodinville, WA 425-486-7000
Mutual Fish Co
  Seattle, WA 206-322-4368
Sea Safari
  Belhaven, NC 800-688-6174
Southern Shell Fish Company
  Harvey, LA 504-341-5631
Trident Seafoods Corp
  Wrangell, AK 907-874-3346
Vital Choice
  Bellingham, WA 800-608-4825

Claws Stone

Luxury Crab
  St John's, NL 709-739-6668

Cooked

Bayou Food Distributors
  Kenner, LA 800-516-8283

Dungeness

Arrowac Fisheries
  Seattle, WA 206-282-5655
Dave's Gourmet Albacore
  Watsonville, CA 206-999-5517
Glacier Fish Company
  Seattle, WA 206-298-1200
Jessie's Ilwaco Fish Company
  San Francisco, CA 360-642-3773

Fresh

Arrowac Fisheries
  Seattle, WA 206-282-5655
Bayou Land Seafood
  Breaux Bridge, LA 337-667-6118
Cathay Foods Corporation
  Boston, MA 617-427-1507
Charles H. Parks & Company
  Fishing Creek, MD 410-397-3400
Cuizina Food Company
  Woodinville, WA 425-486-7000
Daley Brothers ltd.
  St John's, NL 709-364-8844
Dave's Gourmet Albacore
  Watsonville, CA 206-999-5517
J. Matassini & Sons Fish Company
  Tampa, FL 813-229-0829
Jessie's Ilwaco Fish Company
  San Francisco, CA 360-642-3773
Keyser Brothers
  Lottsburg, VA 804-529-6837
Little River Seafood Inc
  Reedville, VA 804-453-3670
Lowland Seafood
  Lowland, NC 252-745-3751
Menemsha Fish Market
  Chilmark, MA 508-645-2282
Mutual Fish Co
  Seattle, WA 206-322-4368
Nelson Crab Inc
  Tokeland, WA 800-262-0069
Phillips Foods
  Baltimore, MD 888-234-2722
Portland Shellfish Company
  Portland, ME 207-799-9290
Rippons Seafood
  Ocean City, MD 410-723-0056
Sea Watch Intl
  Easton, MD 410-822-7500
Stone Crabs Inc
  Miami Beach, FL 800-260-2722
Sunshine Food Sales
  Miami, FL 305-696-2885
Taylor Shellfish Farms
  Shelton, WA 360-426-6178
Trident Seafoods Corp
  Wrangell, AK 907-874-3346

Frozen

Arrowac Fisheries
  Seattle, WA 206-282-5655
Bandon Bay Fisheries
  Bandon, OR 541-347-4454
Bayou Land Seafood
  Breaux Bridge, LA 337-667-6118
Beaver Street Fisheries
  Jacksonville, FL 800-874-6426
Callis Seafood
  Lancaster, VA 804-462-7634

Carrington Foods Co Inc
  Saraland, AL 251-675-9700
Cathay Foods Corporation
  Boston, MA 617-427-1507
Certi Fresh Foods Inc
  Wilmington, CA 310-221-6262
Clearwater Fine Foods
  Bedford, NS 902-443-0550
Cowart Seafood Corp
  Lottsburg, VA 804-529-6101
Cuizina Food Company
  Woodinville, WA 425-486-7000
Daley Brothers ltd.
  St John's, NL 709-364-8844
Dave's Gourmet Albacore
  Watsonville, CA 206-999-5517
Fogo Island Cooperative Society
  Seldom Fogo Island, NL 709-627-3452
Great Northern Products Inc
  Cranston, RI 401-490-4590
Higgins Seafood
  Lafitte, LA 504-689-3577
Independent Packers Corporation
  Seattle, WA 206-285-6000
J. Matassini & Sons Fish Company
  Tampa, FL 813-229-0829
Jessie's Ilwaco Fish Company
  San Francisco, CA 360-642-3773
Keyser Brothers
  Lottsburg, VA 804-529-6837
Kitchens Seafood
  Plant City, FL 800-327-0132
Luxury Crab
  St John's, NL 709-739-6668
Menemsha Fish Market
  Chilmark, MA 508-645-2282
Mutual Fish Co
  Seattle, WA 206-322-4368
Notre Dame Seafoods Inc.
  Comfort Cove, NL 709-244-5511
Pamlico Packing Company
  Grantsboro, NC 800-682-1113
Portland Shellfish Company
  Portland, ME 207-799-9290
Sea Safari
  Belhaven, NC 800-688-6174
Sea Watch Intl
  Easton, MD 410-822-7500
Silver Lining Seafood
  Seattle, WA 800-426-5490
Spruce Lane Investments
  Stratford, PE 902-892-2600
St. Ours & Company
  East Weymouth, MA 781-331-8520
Stone Crabs Inc
  Miami Beach, FL 800-260-2722
Sunshine Food Sales
  Miami, FL 305-696-2885
Taku Smokehouse
  Juneau, AK 800-582-5122
Taylor Shellfish Farms
  Shelton, WA 360-426-6178
Trident Seafoods Corp
  Wrangell, AK 907-874-3346

Imitation

Harbor Seafood
  New Hyde Park, NY 800-645-2211

King

Arrowac Fisheries
  Seattle, WA 206-282-5655
Harbor Seafood
  New Hyde Park, NY 800-645-2211
New Ocean
  Doraville, GA 770-458-5235
North Pacific Seafoods Inc
  Seattle, WA 206-726-9900
Tenth & M Seafoods
  Anchorage, AK 800-770-2722

Live

Dorchester Crab Co
  Wingate, MD 410-397-8103

Meat

Bandon Bay Fisheries
  Bandon, OR 541-347-4454
Bay Hundred Seafood Inc
  St Michaels, MD 410-745-9329

Product Categories / Fish & Seafood: Shellfish

Bayou Food Distributors
  Kenner, LA 800-516-8283
Bayou Land Seafood
  Breaux Bridge, LA 337-667-6118
Beaver Street Fisheries
  Jacksonville, FL 800-874-6426
Blalock Seafood & Specialty
  Orange Beach, AL 251-974-5811
Blue Crab Bay
  Melfa, VA 800-221-2722
Boja's Foods Inc
  Bayou La Batre, AL 251-824-4186
Certi Fresh Foods Inc
  Wilmington, CA 310-221-6262
Charles H. Parks & Company
  Fishing Creek, MD 410-397-3400
Dave's Gourmet Albacore
  Watsonville, CA 206-999-5517
Dorchester Crab Co
  Wingate, MD 410-397-8103
Hallmark Fisheries
  Charleston, OR 541-888-3253
Harmon's Original Clam Cakes
  Kennebunkport, ME 207-967-4100
Harvest Time Seafood Inc
  Abbeville, LA 337-893-9029
Keyser Brothers
  Lottsburg, VA 804-529-6837
Little River Seafood Inc
  Reedville, VA 804-453-3670
Luxury Crab
  St John's, NL 709-739-6668
Martin Brothers Seafood Co
  Westwego, LA 504-341-2251
Nelson Crab Inc
  Tokeland, WA 800-262-0069
Pamlico Packing Company
  Grantsboro, NC 800-682-1113
Penguin Frozen Foods Inc
  Northbrook, IL 800-323-1485
Peter Pan Seafoods Inc.
  Bellevue, WA 206-728-6000
Phillips Foods
  Baltimore, MD 888-234-2722
Rippons Seafood
  Ocean City, MD 410-723-0056
Sea Safari
  Belhaven, NC 800-688-6174
Sea Watch Intl
  Easton, MD 410-822-7500
Southern Shell Fish Company
  Harvey, LA 504-341-5631
W.T. Ruark & Company
  Fishing Creek, MD 410-397-3133

Meat Canned

Bayou Land Seafood
  Breaux Bridge, LA 337-667-6118
Cathay Foods Corporation
  Boston, MA 617-427-1507
Charles H. Parks & Company
  Fishing Creek, MD 410-397-3400
Martin Brothers Seafood Co
  Westwego, LA 504-341-2251
Miami Crab Corporation
  Miami, FL 800-269-8395
New Orleans Food Co-op
  New Orleans, LA 800-628-4900
Peter Pan Seafoods Inc.
  Bellevue, WA 206-728-6000
Phillips Foods
  Baltimore, MD 888-234-2722
Sea Safari
  Belhaven, NC 800-688-6174
Southern Shell Fish Company
  Harvey, LA 504-341-5631

Meat Frozen

Alpine Butcher
  Lowell, MA 978-256-7771
Bandon Bay Fisheries
  Bandon, OR 541-347-4454
Bayou Land Seafood
  Breaux Bridge, LA 337-667-6118
Beaver Street Fisheries
  Jacksonville, FL 800-874-6426
Cathay Foods Corporation
  Boston, MA 617-427-1507
Certi Fresh Foods Inc
  Wilmington, CA 310-221-6262

Harvest Time Seafood Inc
  Abbeville, LA 337-893-9029
Keyser Brothers
  Lottsburg, VA 804-529-6837
Luxury Crab
  St John's, NL 709-739-6668
Martin Brothers Seafood Co
  Westwego, LA 504-341-2251
Miami Crab Corporation
  Miami, FL 800-269-8395
Nelson Crab Inc
  Tokeland, WA 800-262-0069
Penguin Frozen Foods Inc
  Northbrook, IL 800-323-1485
Peter Pan Seafoods Inc.
  Bellevue, WA 206-728-6000
Phillips Foods
  Baltimore, MD 888-234-2722

Snow

Arrowac Fisheries
  Seattle, WA 206-282-5655
Breakwater Fisheries
  St John's, NL 709-754-1999
Harbor Seafood
  New Hyde Park, NY 800-645-2211
New Ocean
  Doraville, GA 770-458-5235
North Pacific Seafoods Inc
  Seattle, WA 206-726-9900
Spruce Lane Investments
  Stratford, PE 902-892-2600
Taku Smokehouse
  Juneau, AK 800-582-5122

Soft Shell

Bayou Food Distributors
  Kenner, LA 800-516-8283
Cowart Seafood Corp
  Lottsburg, VA 804-529-6101
Handy International Inc
  Salisbury, MD 800-426-3977
Rippons Seafood
  Ocean City, MD 410-723-0056
W.T. Ruark & Company
  Fishing Creek, MD 410-397-3133

Stone

Stone Crabs Inc
  Miami Beach, FL 800-260-2722

Stuffed

Belle River Enterprises
  Belle River, PE 902-962-2248
Bon Secour Fisheries Inc
  Bon Secour, AL 251-949-7411
Clayton's Crab Co
  Rockledge, FL 321-636-6673
Dave's Gourmet Albacore
  Watsonville, CA 206-999-5517
E. Gagnon & Fils
  St Therese-De-Gaspe, QC 418-385-3011
Gerard & Dominique Seafoods
  Harbor, OR 800-858-0449
Handy International Inc
  Salisbury, MD 800-426-3977
Lowland Seafood
  Lowland, NC 252-745-3751
Menemsha Fish Market
  Chilmark, MA 508-645-2282
Nan Sea Enterprises of Wisconsin
  Waukesha, WI 262-542-8841
Pamlico Packing Company
  Grantsboro, NC 800-682-1113
Rippons Seafood
  Ocean City, MD 410-723-0056
Shawmut Fishing Company
  Anchorage, AK 709-334-2559

Crayfish

Basin Crawfish Processors
  Breaux Bridge, LA 337-332-6655
Bayou Land Seafood
  Breaux Bridge, LA 337-667-6118
Gulf Marine
  Westwego, LA 504-436-2682
Natchitoches Crawfish Company
  Natchitoches, LA 318-352-2194
Northwest Wild Products
  Astoria, OR 503-791-1907

Ocean Pride Seafood
  Delcambre, LA 337-685-2336
Raffield Fisheries Inc
  Port St Joe, FL 850-229-8494
Vince's Seafoods
  Gretna, LA 504-368-1544

Frozen

Bayou Land Seafood
  Breaux Bridge, LA 337-667-6118

Live

Belle River Enterprises
  Belle River, PE 902-962-2248

Raw

Bayou Land Seafood
  Breaux Bridge, LA 337-667-6118

Dehydrated

Mercer Processing
  Modesto, CA 209-529-0150

Fresh

Acme Steak & Seafood
  Youngstown, OH 800-686-2263
Arrowac Fisheries
  Seattle, WA 206-282-5655
B G Smith & Sons Oyster Co
  Sharps, VA 877-483-8279
Bay Oceans Sea Foods
  Garibaldi, OR 503-322-3316
Bayou Land Seafood
  Breaux Bridge, LA 337-667-6118
Blount Fine Foods
  Fall River, MA 774-888-1300
BlueWater Seafoods
  Gloucester, MA 888-560-2539
Bon Secour Fisheries Inc
  Bon Secour, AL 251-949-7411
C F Gollott & Son Seafood
  Diberville, MS 228-392-2747
Channel Fish Processing
  Gloucester, MA 800-457-0054
Charles H. Parks & Company
  Fishing Creek, MD 410-397-3400
Coast Seafoods Company
  Bellevue, WA 800-423-2303
Cowart Seafood Corp
  Lottsburg, VA 804-529-6101
Cozy Harbor Seafood Inc
  Portland, ME 800-225-2586
Delaware Valley Fish Co
  Norristown, PA 610-277-4900
Fisherman's Market International
  Halifax, NS 902-445-3474
Gulf City Marine Supply
  Bayou La Batre, AL 251-824-2516
Gulf Pride Enterprises
  Biloxi, MS 888-689-0560
Hallmark Fisheries
  Charleston, OR 541-888-3253
Hillard Bloom Packing Co Inc
  Port Norris, NJ 856-785-0120
Hillmans Shrimp & Oyster
  Port Lavaca, TX 800-582-4416
Independent Packers Corporation
  Seattle, WA 206-285-6000
Intervest Trading Company Inc.
  Halifax, NS 902-425-2018
IOE Atlanta
  Galena, MD 410-755-6300
Island Marine Products
  Clarks Harbour, NS 902-745-2222
J. Matassini & Sons Fish Company
  Tampa, FL 813-229-0829
Jessie's Ilwaco Fish Company
  San Francisco, CA 360-642-3773
Keyser Brothers
  Lottsburg, VA 804-529-6837
LA Monica Fine Foods
  Millville, NJ
Little River Seafood Inc
  Reedville, VA 804-453-3670
Minterbrook Oyster Co
  Gig Harbor, WA 253-857-5251
National Fish & Oyster
  Olympia, WA 360-491-5550
Nelson Crab Inc
  Tokeland, WA 800-262-0069

Product Categories / Fish & Seafood: Shellfish

Pacific Salmon Company
   Edmonds, WA 425-774-1315
Paul Piazza & Son Inc
   New Orleans, LA 800-969-6011
Peter Pan Seafoods Inc.
   Bellevue, WA 206-728-6000
Portland Shellfish Company
   Portland, ME 207-799-9290
Quality Seafood
   Apalachicola, FL 850-653-9696
Rippons Seafood
   Ocean City, MD 410-723-0056
Royal Seafood Inc
   Brooklyn, NY 718-769-1517
Ruggiero Seafood
   Newark, NJ 866-225-2627
Seafood Producers Co-Op
   Bellingham, WA 360-733-0120
Sportsmen's Cannery & Smokehouse
   Winchester Bay, OR 800-457-8048
Stone Crabs Inc
   Miami Beach, FL 800-260-2722
Sweet Water Seafood
   Carlstadt, NJ 201-939-6622
Taylor Shellfish Farms
   Shelton, WA 360-426-6178
Terry Brothers, Inc
   Willis Wharf, VA 757-442-6251
Tichon Sea Food Corp
   New Bedford, MA 508-999-5607
Trident Seafoods Corp
   Wrangell, AK 907-874-3346
Wanchese Fish Co Inc
   Suffolk, VA 757-673-4500
Wiegardt Brothers
   Nahcotta, WA 360-665-4111
Young's Lobster Pound
   Belfast, ME 207-338-1160

Frozen

A.C. Inc.
   Beals, ME 207-497-2261
Arista Industries Inc
   Wilton, CT 800-255-6457
Arrowac Fisheries
   Seattle, WA 206-282-5655
B G Smith & Sons Oyster Co
   Sharps, VA 877-483-8279
Bandon Bay Fisheries
   Bandon, OR 541-347-4454
Bayou Land Seafood
   Breaux Bridge, LA 337-667-6118
Beaver Street Fisheries
   Jacksonville, FL 800-874-6426
Bon Secour Fisheries Inc
   Bon Secour, AL 251-949-7411
Breakwater Fisheries
   St John's, NL 709-754-1999
Callis Seafood
   Lancaster, VA 804-462-7634
Carrington Foods Co Inc
   Saraland, AL 251-675-9700
Cathay Foods Corporation
   Boston, MA 617-427-1507
Certi Fresh Foods Inc
   Wilmington, CA 310-221-6262
Channel Fish Processing
   Gloucester, MA 800-457-0054
Clearwater Fine Foods
   Bedford, NS 902-443-0550
Cowart Seafood Corp
   Lottsburg, VA 804-529-6101
Cozy Harbor Seafood Inc
   Portland, ME 800-225-2586
Cuizina Food Company
   Woodinville, WA 425-486-7000
Eastern Fish Company
   Teaneck, NJ 800-526-9066
Fish King
   Glendale, CA 818-244-2161
Glacier Fish Company
   Seattle, WA 206-298-1200
Golden Gulf Coast Packing Co
   Biloxi, MS 228-374-6121
Great Northern Products Inc
   Cranston, RI 401-490-4590
Gulf City Marine Supply
   Bayou La Batre, AL 251-824-2516
Hallmark Fisheries
   Charleston, OR 541-888-3253
Handy International Inc
   Salisbury, MD 800-426-3977

Hillard Bloom Packing Co Inc
   Port Norris, NJ 856-785-0120
Hillmans Shrimp & Oyster
   Port Lavaca, TX 800-582-4416
Independent Packers Corporation
   Seattle, WA 206-285-6000
Indian Ridge Shrimp Co
   Chauvin, LA 800-594-0920
Intervest Trading Company Inc.
   Halifax, NS 902-425-2018
Island Marine Products
   Clarks Harbour, NS 902-745-2222
J. Matassini & Sons Fish Company
   Tampa, FL 813-229-0829
Janes Family Foods
   Mississauga, ON 800-565-2637
Jessie's Ilwaco Fish Company
   San Francisco, CA 360-642-3773
Key Largo Fisheries
   Key Largo, FL 800-432-4358
Keyser Brothers
   Lottsburg, VA 804-529-6837
Lund's Fisheries
   Cape May, NJ 609-884-7600
Luxury Crab
   St John's, NL 709-739-6668
Maxim's Import Corporation
   Miami, FL 800-331-6652
Menemsha Fish Market
   Chilmark, MA 508-645-2282
Mid-Atlantic Foods Inc
   Easton, MD 800-922-4688
Minterbrook Oyster Co
   Gig Harbor, WA 253-857-5251
National Fish & Oyster
   Olympia, WA 360-491-5550
Nelson Crab Inc
   Tokeland, WA 800-262-0069
Neptune Fisheries
   Newport News, VA 800-545-7474
O'Hara Corp
   Rockland, ME 207-594-4444
Okuhara Foods Inc
   Honolulu, HI 808-848-0581
Pacific American Fish Co Inc
   Vernon, CA 800-625-2525
Pacific Salmon Company
   Edmonds, WA 425-774-1315
Paul Piazza & Son Inc
   New Orleans, LA 800-969-6011
Penguin Frozen Foods Inc
   Northbrook, IL 800-323-1485
Portland Shellfish Company
   Portland, ME 207-799-9290
Quality Seafood
   Apalachicola, FL 850-653-9696
Royal Seafood Inc
   Brooklyn, NY 718-769-1517
Ruggiero Seafood
   Newark, NJ 866-225-2627
Sea Pearl Seafood
   Bayou La Batre, AL 800-872-8804
Sea Snack Foods Inc
   Los Angeles, CA 213-622-2204
Seafood Producers Co-Op
   Bellingham, WA 360-733-0120
Seymour & Sons Seafoods Inc
   Diberville, MS 228-392-4020
Silver Lining Seafood
   Seattle, WA 800-426-5490
Spruce Lane Investments
   Stratford, PE 902-892-2600
St. Ours & Company
   East Weymouth, MA 781-331-8520
Stone Crabs Inc
   Miami Beach, FL 800-260-2722
Taku Smokehouse
   Juneau, AK 800-582-5122
Tampa Maid Foods Inc
   Lakeland, FL 800-237-7637
Taylor Shellfish Farms
   Shelton, WA 360-426-6178
Tichon Sea Food Corp
   New Bedford, MA 508-999-5607
Trident Seafoods Corp
   Wrangell, AK 907-874-3346
Triton Seafood Co
   Medley, FL 305-888-0051
Viking Seafoods Inc
   Malden, MA 800-225-3020
Vince's Seafoods
   Gretna, LA 504-368-1544

Wanchese Fish Co Inc
   Suffolk, VA 757-673-4500
Young's Lobster Pound
   Belfast, ME 207-338-1160

Geoduck Clams

Peter Pan Seafoods Inc.
   Bellevue, WA 206-728-6000

Langostinos

Kitchens Seafood
   Plant City, FL 800-327-0132

Live

A.C. Inc.
   Beals, ME 207-497-2261

Lobster

Acme Steak & Seafood
   Youngstown, OH 800-686-2263
Adams Fisheries Ltd
   Shag Harbour, NS 902-723-2435
Arista Industries Inc
   Wilton, CT 800-255-6457
Barry Group
   Corner Brook, NL 709-785-7387
Bay Haven Lobster Pound
   York, ME 207-363-5265
Bay Shore Chowders & Bisques
   Fall River, MA 888-675-6892
BBS Lobster Co
   Machiasport, ME 207-255-8888
Beal's Lobster Pier
   SW Harbor, ME 800-244-7178
Bickford Daniel Lobster Company
   Vinalhaven, ME 207-863-4688
Blount Fine Foods
   Fall River, MA 774-888-1300
Bon Secour Fisheries Inc
   Bon Secour, AL 251-949-7411
Boothbay Lobster Wharf
   Boothbay Harbor, ME 207-633-4900
Boston Direct Lobsters
   Jefferson, LA 504-834-6404
C.B.S. Lobster Company
   Portland, ME 207-775-2917
Captain Little Seafood
   Queens County, NS 902-947-2087
Castle Hill Lobster
   Ipswich, MA 978-356-3947
Ceilidh Fisherman's Cooperative
   Port Hood, NS 902-787-2666
Certi Fresh Foods Inc
   Wilmington, CA 310-221-6262
Chases Lobster Pound
   Port Howe, NS 902-243-2408
Clearwater Fine Foods
   Bedford, NS 902-443-0550
Coastside Lobster Company
   Stonington, ME 207-367-2297
Corea Lobster Cooperative
   Corea, ME 207-963-7936
Cranberry Isles Fisherman's
   Islesford, ME 207-244-5438
D Waybret & Sons Fisheries
   Shelburne, NS 902-745-3477
DB Kenney Fisheries
   Westport, NS 902-839-2023
Dorset Fisheries
   St Josephs, NL 709-739-7147
Dunham's Lobster Pot
   Avon, ME 207-639-2815
Fisherman's Market International
   Halifax, NS 902-445-3474
Fulton Fish Market
   New York, NY 718-842-8908
FW Thurston
   Bernard, ME 207-244-3320
Gerard & Dominique Seafoods
   Harbor, OR 800-858-0449
Giovanni's Appetizing Food Co
   Richmond, MI 586-727-9355
Goldcoast Salads
   Naples, FL 239-513-0430
Gouldsboro Enterprises
   Gouldsboro, ME 207-963-2203
Graffam Brothers
   Rockport, ME 800-535-5358
Great Northern Products Inc
   Cranston, RI 401-490-4590

Product Categories / Fish & Seafood: Shellfish

Greg's Lobster Company
  Harwich Port, MA 508-432-8080
H&H Fisheries Limited
  Eastern Passage, NS 866-773-4400
Hancock Gourmet Lobster Co
  Topsham, ME 207-725-1855
Harbor Seafood
  New Hyde Park, NY 800-645-2211
Howard Turner & Son
  Marie Joseph, NS 902-347-2616
I. Deveau Fisheries LTD
  Barrington Passage, NS 902-745-2877
Innovative Fishery Products
  Belliveau Cove, NS 902-837-5163
International Enterprises
  Herring Neck, NL 709-628-7406
Island Lobster
  Matinicus, ME 207-366-3937
Island Marine Products
  Clarks Harbour, NS 902-745-2222
J. Matassini & Sons Fish Company
  Tampa, FL 813-229-0829
Kitchens Seafood
  Plant City, FL 800-327-0132
Kona Cold Lobsters
  Kailua Kona, HI 808-329-4332
L&C Fisheries
  Kensington, PE 902-886-2770
Little River Lobster Company
  East Boothbay, ME 207-633-2648
Lobster Gram
  Chicago, IL 800-548-3562
Look Lobster Co
  Jonesport, ME 207-497-2353
Lusty Lobster
  Portland, ME 207-773-2829
Luxury Crab
  St John's, NL 709-739-6668
Maine Lobster Outlet
  York, ME 207-363-4449
McGraw Seafood
  Tracadie Sheila, NB 506-395-3374
Menemsha Fish Market
  Chilmark, MA 508-645-2282
Mill Cove Lobster Pound
  Trevett, ME 207-633-3340
Nan Sea Enterprises of Wisconsin
  Waukesha, WI 262-542-8841
New Harbor Fisherman's Cooperative
  New Harbor, ME 866-883-2922
Newell Lobsters
  Yarmouth, NS 902-742-6272
North Atlantic Seafood
  Portland, ME 800-774-6025
North Lake Fish Cooperative
  Elmira, PE 902-357-2572
Northern Wind Inc
  New Bedford, MA 888-525-2525
Northwest Wild Products
  Astoria, OR 503-791-1907
Notre Dame Seafoods Inc.
  Comfort Cove, NL 709-244-5511
P.M. Innis Lobster Company
  Biddeford Pool, ME 207-284-5000
Paul Piazza & Son Inc
  New Orleans, LA 800-969-6011
Paul Stevens Lobster
  Hingham, MA 781-740-8001
Penguin Frozen Foods Inc
  Northbrook, IL 800-323-1485
Pine Point Seafood
  Scarborough, ME 207-883-4701
Point Lobster Co
  Point Pleasant Beach, NJ 732-892-1729
Port Lobster Co Inc
  Kennebunkport, ME 800-486-7029
Produits Belle Baie
  Caraquet, NB 506-727-4414
Red Chamber Co
  Vernon, CA 323-234-9000
Resource Trading Company
  Portland, ME 207-772-2299
Rockport Lobster Co
  Gloucester, MA 978-281-0225
Sealand Lobster Corporation
  Tenants Harbor, ME 207-372-6247
Seymour & Sons Seafoods Inc
  Diberville, MS 228-392-4020
St. Ours & Company
  East Weymouth, MA 781-331-8520
Stavis Seafoods
  Boston, MA 800-390-5103

Stone Crabs Inc
  Miami Beach, FL 800-260-2722
Stonington Lobster Co-Op
  Stonington, ME 207-367-2286
Straub's
  Clayton, MO 888-725-2121
Sunshine Food Sales
  Miami, FL 305-696-2885
Taylor Lobster Co
  Kittery, ME 207-439-1350
Thomas Lobster Co
  Islesford, ME 207-244-5876
Three Rivers Fish Company
  Simmesport, LA 318-941-2467
Trenton Bridge Lobster Pound
  Trenton, ME 207-667-2977
Vital Choice
  Bellingham, WA 800-608-4825
West Brothers Lobster
  Steuben, ME 207-546-3622
Young's Lobster Pound
  Belfast, ME 207-338-1160

Fresh

Capt Joe & Sons Inc
  Gloucester, MA 978-283-1454
Clearwater Fine Foods
  Bedford, NS 902-443-0550
J. Matassini & Sons Fish Company
  Tampa, FL 813-229-0829
Menemsha Fish Market
  Chilmark, MA 508-645-2282
Paul Piazza & Son Inc
  New Orleans, LA 800-969-6011
Portland Shellfish Company
  Portland, ME 207-799-9290
Poseidon Enterprises
  Charlotte, NC 800-863-7886
St. Ours & Company
  East Weymouth, MA 781-331-8520
Stone Crabs Inc
  Miami Beach, FL 800-260-2722
Sunshine Food Sales
  Miami, FL 305-696-2885

Frozen

Acme Steak & Seafood
  Youngstown, OH 800-686-2263
Arista Industries Inc
  Wilton, CT 800-255-6457
Certi Fresh Foods Inc
  Wilmington, CA 310-221-6262
Great Northern Products Inc
  Cranston, RI 401-490-4590
Island Marine Products
  Clarks Harbour, NS 902-745-2222
J. Matassini & Sons Fish Company
  Tampa, FL 813-229-0829
Kitchens Seafood
  Plant City, FL 800-327-0132
Luxury Crab
  St John's, NL 709-739-6668
Menemsha Fish Market
  Chilmark, MA 508-645-2282
North Bay Fisherman's Cooperative
  Ballantyne's Cove, NS 902-863-4988
Notre Dame Seafoods Inc.
  Comfort Cove, NL 709-244-5511
Paul Piazza & Son Inc
  New Orleans, LA 800-969-6011
Penguin Frozen Foods Inc
  Northbrook, IL 800-323-1485
Portland Shellfish Company
  Portland, ME 207-799-9290
Seymour & Sons Seafoods Inc
  Diberville, MS 228-392-4020
Stone Crabs Inc
  Miami Beach, FL 800-260-2722
Sunshine Food Sales
  Miami, FL 305-696-2885

Live

Bay Shore Chowders & Bisques
  Fall River, MA 888-675-6892
Chases Lobster Pound
  Port Howe, NS 902-243-2408
DB Kenney Fisheries
  Westport, NS 902-839-2023
H&H Fisheries Limited
  Eastern Passage, NS 866-773-4400

Harbour Lobster Ltd
  Shag Harbour, NS 902-723-2500
Island Marine Products
  Clarks Harbour, NS 902-745-2222
James L. Mood Fisheries
  Nova Scotia, NS 902-723-2360
Johns Cove Fisheries
  Yarmouth, NS 902-742-8691
Lumar Lobster
  Lawrence, NY 516-371-0083
Menemsha Fish Market
  Chilmark, MA 508-645-2282

Meat

Acme Steak & Seafood
  Youngstown, OH 800-686-2263
Island Marine Products
  Clarks Harbour, NS 902-745-2222
Luxury Crab
  St John's, NL 709-739-6668

Tails

Anchor Frozen Foods
  Westbury, NY 800-566-3474
Arista Industries Inc
  Wilton, CT 800-255-6457
King & Prince Seafood Corp
  Brunswick, GA 800-841-0205
Neptune Fisheries
  Newport News, VA 800-545-7474
New Ocean
  Doraville, GA 770-458-5235
Stone Crabs Inc
  Miami Beach, FL 800-260-2722
Tampa Bay Fisheries Inc
  Dover, FL 800-732-3663

Mussels

Atlantic Aqua Farms
  Orwell Cove, PE 902-651-2563
Atlantic Mussel Growers Corporation
  Murray Harbour, PE 800-838-3106
Bay Shore Chowders & Bisques
  Fall River, MA 888-675-6892
Blount Fine Foods
  Fall River, MA 774-888-1300
Harbor Seafood
  New Hyde Park, NY 800-645-2211
Hillmans Shrimp & Oyster
  Port Lavaca, TX 800-582-4416
L&C Fisheries
  Kensington, PE 902-886-2770
Minterbrook Oyster Co
  Gig Harbor, WA 253-857-5251
North Atlantic Seafood
  Portland, ME 800-774-6025
Northwest Wild Products
  Astoria, OR 503-791-1907
Olympia Oyster Co
  Shelton, WA 877-427-3193
Patagonia Provisions
  Sausalito, CA 888-221-8208
PEI Mussel King
  Morrell, PE 800-673-2767
Stavis Seafoods
  Boston, MA 800-390-5103
Sweet Water Seafood
  Carlstadt, NJ 201-939-6622
Tampa Bay Fisheries Inc
  Dover, FL 800-732-3663
Taylor Shellfish Farms
  Shelton, WA 360-426-6178
Vital Choice
  Bellingham, WA 800-608-4825

Octopus

Anchor Frozen Foods
  Westbury, NY 800-566-3474
Arista Industries Inc
  Wilton, CT 800-255-6457
Fish King
  Glendale, CA 818-244-2161
Fulton Fish Market
  New York, NY 718-842-8908

Oysters

Ameripure Processing Co
  Franklin, LA 800-328-6729
Aquatec Seafoods Ltd.
  Comox, BC 250-339-6412

Product Categories / Fish & Seafood: Shellfish

Atlantic Aqua Farms
   Orwell Cove, PE 902-651-2563
Atlantic Capes Fisheries
   Cape May, NJ 609-884-3000
B G Smith & Sons Oyster Co
   Sharps, VA 877-483-8279
Barry Group
   Corner Brook, NL 709-785-7387
Bay Hundred Seafood Inc
   St Michaels, MD 410-745-9329
Blalock Seafood & Specialty
   Orange Beach, AL 251-974-5811
Blau Oyster Co Inc
   Bow, WA 360-766-6171
Bon Secour Fisheries Inc
   Bon Secour, AL 251-949-7411
Callis Seafood
   Lancaster, VA 804-462-7634
Canoe Lagoon Oyster Company
   Coffman Cove, AK 907-329-2253
Coast Seafoods Company
   Bellevue, WA 800-423-2303
Cowart Seafood Corp
   Lottsburg, VA 804-529-6101
Crown Prince Inc
   City Of Industry, CA 626-912-3700
Dave's Gourmet Albacore
   Watsonville, CA 206-999-5517
Farm 2 Market
   San Francisco, CA 800-447-2967
Ferme Ostreicole Dugas
   Caraquet, NB 506-727-3226
Fish Breeders of Idaho
   Hagerman, ID 208-837-6114
Great Northern Products Inc
   Cranston, RI 401-490-4590
Gulf City Marine Supply
   Bayou La Batre, AL 251-824-2516
H.Gass Seafood
   Hollywood, MD 301-373-6882
Harpers Seafood Market
   Thomasville, GA 229-226-7525
Harris Crab House
   Grasonville, MD 410-827-9500
Higgins Seafood
   Lafitte, LA 504-689-3577
Hillard Bloom Packing Co Inc
   Port Norris, NJ 856-785-0120
Hillmans Shrimp & Oyster
   Port Lavaca, TX 800-582-4416
Huck's Seafood
   Easton, MD 410-770-9211
J. Matassini & Sons Fish Company
   Tampa, FL 813-229-0829
Louisiana Oyster Processors
   Baton Rouge, LA 225-291-6923
McGraw Seafood
   Tracadie Sheila, NB 506-395-3374
Mill Cove Lobster Pound
   Trevett, ME 207-633-3340
Neptune Foods
   Vernon, CA 323-232-8300
New Orleans Fish House II LLC
   New Orleans, LA 800-839-3474
Nisbet Oyster Company
   Bay Center, WA 888-875-6629
North Atlantic Seafood
   Portland, ME 800-774-6025
Northwest Wild Products
   Astoria, OR 503-791-1907
Pamlico Packing Company
   Grantsboro, NC 800-682-1113
PEI Mussel King
   Morrell, PE 800-673-2767
Rippons Seafood
   Ocean City, MD 410-723-0056
Roadrunner Seafood Inc
   Colquitt, GA 229-758-6098
Roy Dick Company
   Griffin, GA 770-227-3916
Sea Pearl Seafood
   Bayou La Batre, AL 800-872-8804
Southern Shell Fish Company
   Harvey, LA 504-341-5631
Tampa Bay Fisheries Inc
   Dover, FL 800-732-3663
Tampa Maid Foods Inc
   Lakeland, FL 800-237-7637
Terry Brothers, Inc
   Willis Wharf, VA 757-442-6251
Vital Choice
   Bellingham, WA 800-608-4825

W.T. Ruark & Company
   Fishing Creek, MD 410-397-3133
Wiegardt Brothers
   Nahcotta, WA 360-665-4111
Wilsons Oysters
   Houma, LA 985-857-8855

Canned

Chicken Of The Sea
   El Segundo, CA 844-267-8862
New Orleans Food Co-op
   New Orleans, LA 800-628-4900
Olympia Oyster Co
   Shelton, WA 877-427-3193
Southern Shell Fish Company
   Harvey, LA 504-341-5631

Fresh

B G Smith & Sons Oyster Co
   Sharps, VA 877-483-8279
Blau Oyster Co Inc
   Bow, WA 360-766-6171
Boquet's Oyster House
   Chauvin, LA 504-594-5574
Coast Seafoods Company
   Bellevue, WA 800-423-2303
Cowart Seafood Corp
   Lottsburg, VA 804-529-6101
Great Northern Products Inc
   Cranston, RI 401-490-4590
Hillmans Shrimp & Oyster
   Port Lavaca, TX 800-582-4416
J. Matassini & Sons Fish Company
   Tampa, FL 813-229-0829
Mac's Oysters
   Fanny Bay, BC 250-335-2233
Minterbrook Oyster Co
   Gig Harbor, WA 253-857-5251
National Fish & Oyster
   Olympia, WA 360-491-5550
Olympia Oyster Co
   Shelton, WA 877-427-3193
Rippons Seafood
   Ocean City, MD 410-723-0056
Taylor Shellfish Farms
   Shelton, WA 360-426-6178
Terry Brothers, Inc
   Willis Wharf, VA 757-442-6251
Wiegardt Brothers
   Nahcotta, WA 360-665-4111

Fried

J. Matassini & Sons Fish Company
   Tampa, FL 813-229-0829

Frozen

B G Smith & Sons Oyster Co
   Sharps, VA 877-483-8279
Big Al's Seafood
   Bozman, MD 410-745-2637
Bon Secour Fisheries Inc
   Bon Secour, AL 251-949-7411
Boquet's Oyster House
   Chauvin, LA 504-594-5574
Callis Seafood
   Lancaster, VA 804-462-7634
Cowart Seafood Corp
   Lottsburg, VA 804-529-6101
Dave's Gourmet Albacore
   Watsonville, CA 206-999-5517
Great Northern Products Inc
   Cranston, RI 401-490-4590
Hillard Bloom Packing Co Inc
   Port Norris, NJ 856-785-0120
Hillmans Shrimp & Oyster
   Port Lavaca, TX 800-582-4416
Minterbrook Oyster Co
   Gig Harbor, WA 253-857-5251
National Fish & Oyster
   Olympia, WA 360-491-5550
Olympia Oyster Co
   Shelton, WA 877-427-3193
Pamlico Packing Company
   Grantsboro, NC 800-682-1113
Sea Pearl Seafood
   Bayou La Batre, AL 800-872-8804
Tampa Maid Foods Inc
   Lakeland, FL 800-237-7637

Prawns

Caito Fisheries Inc
   Fort Bragg, CA 707-964-6368
Pots de Creme
   Lexington, KY 859-299-2254
Vital Choice
   Bellingham, WA 800-608-4825

Scallops

Arista Industries Inc
   Wilton, CT 800-255-6457
Atlantic Capes Fisheries
   Cape May, NJ 609-884-3000
Blue Harvest Foods
   New Bedford, MA 508-993-5700
Bold Coast Smokehouse
   Lubec, ME 888-733-0807
Bon Secour Fisheries Inc
   Bon Secour, AL 251-949-7411
Captain Little Seafood
   Queens County, NS 902-947-2087
Casey Fisheries
   Digby, NS 902-245-5801
Centennial Food Corporation
   Calgary, AB 403-214-0044
Certi Fresh Foods Inc
   Wilmington, CA 310-221-6262
Clearwater Fine Foods
   Bedford, NS 902-443-0550
DB Kenney Fisheries
   Westport, NS 902-839-2023
Ducktrap River Of Maine
   Belfast, ME 800-434-8727
Farm 2 Market
   San Francisco, CA 800-447-2967
Fish King
   Glendale, CA 818-244-2161
Fulton Fish Market
   New York, NY 718-842-8908
Georgia Seafood Wholesale
   Chamblee, GA 770-936-0483
Great Northern Products Inc
   Cranston, RI 401-490-4590
Hillmans Shrimp & Oyster
   Port Lavaca, TX 800-582-4416
Homarus Inc
   Long Island City, NY 917-832-0333
Innovative Fishery Products
   Belliveau Cove, NS 902-837-5163
Island Scallops
   Qualicum Beach, BC 250-757-9811
J. Matassini & Sons Fish Company
   Tampa, FL 813-229-0829
LA Monica Fine Foods
   Millville, NJ
Lowland Seafood
   Lowland, NC 252-745-3751
Menemsha Fish Market
   Chilmark, MA 508-645-2282
Mill Cove Lobster Pound
   Trevett, ME 207-633-3340
Mills Seafood Ltd.
   Bouctouche, NB 506-743-2444
Neptune Fisheries
   Newport News, VA 800-545-7474
Neptune Foods
   Vernon, CA 323-232-8300
New Ocean
   Doraville, GA 770-458-5235
North Bay Fisherman's Cooperative
   Ballantyne's Cove, NS 902-863-4988
North Lake Fish Cooperative
   Elmira, PE 902-357-2572
Northern Wind Inc
   New Bedford, MA 888-525-2525
Northwest Wild Products
   Astoria, OR 503-791-1907
O'Hara Corp
   Rockland, ME 207-594-4444
Pamlico Packing Company
   Grantsboro, NC 800-682-1113
Portier Fine Foods
   Mamaroneck, NY 800-272-9463
Resource Trading Company
   Portland, ME 207-772-2299
Tampa Bay Fisheries Inc
   Dover, FL 800-732-3663
Tampa Maid Foods Inc
   Lakeland, FL 800-237-7637
Taylor Shellfish Farms
   Shelton, WA 360-426-6178

Product Categories / Fish & Seafood: Shellfish

Tenth & M Seafoods
   Anchorage, AK 800-770-2722
Tichon Sea Food Corp
   New Bedford, MA 508-999-5607
Viking Seafoods Inc
   Malden, MA 800-225-3020
Vital Choice
   Bellingham, WA 800-608-4825
Wanchese Fish Co Inc
   Suffolk, VA 757-673-4500
Young's Lobster Pound
   Belfast, ME 207-338-1160

Sea Cucumber

Captain Little Seafood
   Queens County, NS 902-947-2087

Shellfish

Acme Steak & Seafood
   Youngstown, OH 800-686-2263
Anglo American Trading
   Harvey, LA 504-341-5631
Aquatec Seafoods Ltd.
   Comox, BC 250-339-6412
Arista Industries Inc
   Wilton, CT 800-255-6457
Arrowac Fisheries
   Seattle, WA 206-282-5655
B G Smith & Sons Oyster Co
   Sharps, VA 877-483-8279
Badger Island Shell-Fish & Lobster
   Kittery, ME 207-703-0431
Bandon Bay Fisheries
   Bandon, OR 541-347-4454
Bay Hundred Seafood Inc
   St Michaels, MD 410-745-9329
Bay Oceans Sea Foods
   Garibaldi, OR 503-322-3316
Bayou Food Distributors
   Kenner, LA 800-516-8283
Bayou Land Seafood
   Breaux Bridge, LA 337-667-6118
Beaver Street Fisheries
   Jacksonville, FL 800-874-6426
Blount Fine Foods
   Fall River, MA 774-888-1300
BlueWater Seafoods
   Gloucester, MA 888-560-2539
Boyton Shellfish
   Ellsworth, ME 207-667-8580
Bradye P. Todd & Son
   Cambridge, MD 410-228-8633
Breakwater Fisheries
   St John's, NL 709-754-1999
C F Gollott & Son Seafood
   Diberville, MS 228-392-2747
Caleb Haley & Co LLC
   Bronx, NY 718-617-7474
California Shellfish Company
   San Francisco, CA 415-923-7400
Callis Seafood
   Lancaster, VA 804-462-7634
Carrington Foods Co Inc
   Saraland, AL 251-675-9700
Cathay Foods Corporation
   Boston, MA 617-427-1507
Centennial Food Corporation
   Calgary, AB 403-214-0044
Certi Fresh Foods Inc
   Wilmington, CA 310-221-6262
Charles H. Parks & Company
   Fishing Creek, MD 410-397-3400
Chuck's Seafoods
   Charleston, OR 541-888-5525
Clearwater Fine Foods
   Bedford, NS 902-443-0550
Coast Seafoods Company
   Bellevue, WA 800-423-2303
Cooke Aguaculture
   Blacks Harbour, NB 506-456-6600
Cowart Seafood Corp
   Lottsburg, VA 804-529-6101
Cozy Harbor Seafood Inc
   Portland, ME 800-225-2586
Crown Prince Inc
   City Of Industry, CA 626-912-3700
Cuizina Food Company
   Woodinville, WA 425-486-7000
Dave's Gourmet Albacore
   Watsonville, CA 206-999-5517

DB Kenney Fisheries
   Westport, NS 902-839-2023
Denzer's Food Products
   Baltimore, MD 410-889-1500
Dorchester Crab Co
   Wingate, MD 410-397-8103
Ducktrap River Of Maine
   Belfast, ME 800-434-8727
Eastern Fish Company
   Teaneck, NJ 800-526-9066
Fish King
   Glendale, CA 818-244-2161
Fishhawk Fisheries
   Astoria, OR 503-325-5252
French Market Foods
   Lake Charles, LA 337-477-9296
Frozen Specialties Inc
   Perrysburg, OH 419-867-2005
Golden Gulf Coast Packing Co
   Biloxi, MS 228-374-6121
Gorton's Inc.
   Gloucester, MA 800-222-6846
Great Northern Products Inc
   Cranston, RI 401-490-4590
Gulf Pride Enterprises
   Biloxi, MS 888-689-0560
H.B. Dawe
   Cupids, NL 709-528-4347
H.Gass Seafood
   Hollywood, MD 301-373-6882
Handy International Inc
   Salisbury, MD 800-426-3977
Henry H. Misner Ltd.
   Simcoe, ON 519-426-5546
Hillard Bloom Packing Co Inc
   Port Norris, NJ 856-785-0120
Hillmans Shrimp & Oyster
   Port Lavaca, TX 800-582-4416
Huck's Seafood
   Easton, MD 410-770-9211
Independent Packers Corporation
   Seattle, WA 206-285-6000
Indian Ridge Shrimp Co
   Chauvin, LA 800-594-0920
Island Marine Products
   Clarks Harbour, NS 902-745-2222
J M Clayton Co
   Cambridge, MD 800-652-6931
J. Matassini & Sons Fish Company
   Tampa, FL 813-229-0829
Jessie's Ilwaco Fish Company
   San Francisco, CA 360-642-3773
Key Largo Fisheries
   Key Largo, FL 800-432-4358
Keyser Brothers
   Lottsburg, VA 804-529-6837
King & Prince Seafood Corp
   Brunswick, GA 800-841-0205
Kitchens Seafood
   Plant City, FL 800-327-0132
LA Monica Fine Foods
   Millville, NJ
Little River Seafood Inc
   Reedville, VA 804-453-3670
Long Food Industries
   Fripp Island, SC 843-838-3205
Lowland Seafood
   Lowland, NC 252-745-3751
Lund's Fisheries
   Cape May, NJ 609-884-7600
Luxury Crab
   St John's, NL 709-739-6668
Maine Mahogony Shellfish
   Addison, ME 207-483-2865
Martin Brothers Seafood Co
   Westwego, LA 504-341-2251
Maxim's Import Corporation
   Miami, FL 800-331-6652
Menemsha Fish Market
   Chilmark, MA 508-645-2282
Mercer Processing
   Modesto, CA 209-529-0150
Mid-Atlantic Foods Inc
   Easton, MD 800-922-4688
Nancy's Shellfish
   Falmouth, ME 207-774-3411
Neptune Fisheries
   Newport News, VA 800-545-7474
Notre Dame Seafoods Inc.
   Comfort Cove, NL 709-244-5511
Ntc Marketing
   Williamsville, NY 800-333-1637

Ocean Harvest
   Dennysville, ME 207-726-0609
Okuhara Foods Inc
   Honolulu, HI 808-848-0581
Pacific American Fish Co Inc
   Vernon, CA 800-625-2525
Pacific Salmon Company
   Edmonds, WA 425-774-1315
Pamlico Packing Company
   Grantsboro, NC 800-682-1113
Paul Piazza & Son Inc
   New Orleans, LA 800-969-6011
Penguin Frozen Foods Inc
   Northbrook, IL 800-323-1485
Produits Belle Baie
   Caraquet, NB 506-727-4414
Quality Seafood
   Apalachicola, FL 850-653-9696
Raffield Fisheries Inc
   Port St Joe, FL 850-229-8494
Rippons Seafood
   Ocean City, MD 410-723-0056
Roland Seafood Co
   Atlantic Beach, FL 904-246-9443
Royal Seafood Inc
   Brooklyn, NY 718-769-1517
Ruggiero Seafood
   Newark, NJ 866-225-2627
Sea Pearl Seafood
   Bayou La Batre, AL 800-872-8804
Sea Safari
   Belhaven, NC 800-688-6174
Sea Snack Foods Inc
   Los Angeles, CA 213-622-2204
SeaPerfect Atlantic Farms
   Charleston, SC 800-728-0099
Seymour & Sons Seafoods Inc
   Diberville, MS 228-392-4020
Silver Lining Seafood
   Seattle, WA 800-426-5490
Southern Shell Fish Company
   Harvey, LA 504-341-5631
Sportsmen's Cannery & Smokehouse
   Winchester Bay, OR 800-457-8048
St. Ours & Company
   East Weymouth, MA 781-331-8520
Stone Crabs Inc
   Miami Beach, FL 800-260-2722
Sunshine Food Sales
   Miami, FL 305-696-2885
Sunshine Seafood
   Stonington, ME 207-367-2955
Taku Smokehouse
   Juneau, AK 800-582-5122
Tampa Maid Foods Inc
   Lakeland, FL 800-237-7637
Terry Brothers, Inc
   Willis Wharf, VA 757-442-6251
Thompson Seafood
   Darien, GA 912-437-4649
Trident Seafoods Corp
   Wrangell, AK 907-874-3346
Triton Seafood Co
   Medley, FL 305-888-0051
Valdez Food Inc
   Philadelphia, PA 215-634-6106
Viking Seafoods Inc
   Malden, MA 800-225-3020
Vince's Seafoods
   Gretna, LA 504-368-1544
W.T. Ruark & Company
   Fishing Creek, MD 410-397-3133
Wanchese Fish Co Inc
   Suffolk, VA 757-673-4500
Wiegardt Brothers
   Nahcotta, WA 360-665-4111

Shrimp

Anchor Frozen Foods
   Westbury, NY 800-566-3474
Arista Industries Inc
   Wilton, CT 800-255-6457
Bandon Bay Fisheries
   Bandon, OR 541-347-4454
Barry Group
   Corner Brook, NL 709-785-7387
Bay Oceans Sea Foods
   Garibaldi, OR 503-322-3316
Bayou Food Distributors
   Kenner, LA 800-516-8283
Bayou Land Seafood
   Breaux Bridge, LA 337-667-6118

Product Categories / Fish & Seafood: Shellfish

Beaver Street Fisheries
  Jacksonville, FL 800-874-6426
Big Easy Foods
  Lake Charles, LA 855-477-9296
Biloxi Freezing Processing Inc.
  Biloxi, MS 228-436-0017
Blalock Seafood & Specialty
  Orange Beach, AL 251-974-5811
BlueWater Seafoods
  Gloucester, MA 888-560-2539
Bon Secour Fisheries Inc
  Bon Secour, AL 251-949-7411
Breakwater Fisheries
  St John's, NL 709-754-1999
C F Gollott & Son Seafood
  Diberville, MS 228-392-2747
Callis Seafood
  Lancaster, VA 804-462-7634
Captain Little Seafood
  Queens County, NS 902-947-2087
Carrington Foods Co Inc
  Saraland, AL 251-675-9700
Catfish Wholesale
  Abbeville, LA 800-334-7292
Certi Fresh Foods Inc
  Wilmington, CA 310-221-6262
Channel Fish Processing
  Gloucester, MA 800-457-0054
Chuck's Seafoods
  Charleston, OR 541-888-5525
Clearwater Fine Foods
  Bedford, NS 902-443-0550
Cozy Harbor Seafood Inc
  Portland, ME 800-225-2586
Crevettes Du Nord
  Gaspe, QC 418-368-1414
Crown Prince Inc
  City Of Industry, CA 626-912-3700
Del's Seaway Shrimp & Oyster Company
  Biloxi, MS 228-432-2604
Diazteca Inc
  Rio Rico, AZ 520-761-4621
Ducktrap River Of Maine
  Belfast, ME 800-434-8727
Eastern Fish Company
  Teaneck, NJ 800-526-9066
Eldorado Seafood Inc
  Burlington, MA 800-416-5656
Farm 2 Market
  San Francisco, CA 800-447-2967
Fish Breeders of Idaho
  Hagerman, ID 208-837-6114
Fish King
  Glendale, CA 818-244-2161
Fishhawk Fisheries
  Astoria, OR 503-325-5252
French Market Foods
  Lake Charles, LA 337-477-9296
Georgia Seafood Wholesale
  Chamblee, GA 770-936-0483
Gerard & Dominique Seafoods
  Harbor, OR 800-858-0449
Gesco ENR
  Gaspe, QC 418-368-1414
Golden Gulf Coast Packing Co
  Biloxi, MS 228-374-6121
Great Northern Products Inc
  Cranston, RI 401-490-4590
Gulf City Marine Supply
  Bayou La Batre, AL 251-824-2516
Gulf Crown Seafood Co
  Delcambre, LA 337-685-4722
Gulf Marine
  Westwego, LA 504-436-2682
Gulf Pride Enterprises
  Biloxi, MS 888-689-0560
Hallmark Fisheries
  Charleston, OR 541-888-3253
Harbor Seafood
  New Hyde Park, NY 800-645-2211
Hi Seas
  Dulac, LA 985-563-7155
Homarus Inc
  Long Island City, NY 917-832-0333
Imaex Trading Company
  Suwanee, GA 678-541-0234
Indian Ridge Shrimp Co
  Chauvin, LA 800-594-0920
J. Matassini & Sons Fish Company
  Tampa, FL 813-229-0829
JBS Packing Inc
  Port Arthur, TX 409-982-3216
Jessie's Ilwaco Fish Company
  San Francisco, CA 360-642-3773
Joe Patti's Seafood Co
  Pensacola, FL 800-500-9929
Jubilee Foods
  Bayou La Batre, AL 251-824-2110
King & Prince Seafood Corp
  Brunswick, GA 800-841-0205
Kitchens Seafood
  Plant City, FL 800-327-0132
LA Monica Fine Foods
  Millville, NJ
Lady Gale Seafood
  Baldwin, LA 337-923-2060
Larry J. Williams Company
  Jesup, GA 912-427-7729
Louisiana Packing Company
  Westwego, LA 800-666-1293
Louisiana Seafood Promotion & Marketing Board
  Baton Rouge, LA 225-342-0552
Lowland Seafood
  Lowland, NC 252-745-3751
Luxury Crab
  St John's, NL 709-739-6668
Maxim's Import Corporation
  Miami, FL 800-331-6652
Mill Cove Lobster Pound
  Trevett, ME 207-633-3340
Mobile Processing
  Mobile, AL 251-438-6944
Nelson Crab Inc
  Tokeland, WA 800-262-0069
Neptune Fisheries
  Newport News, VA 800-545-7474
Neptune Foods
  Vernon, CA 323-232-8300
New Ocean
  Doraville, GA 770-458-5235
New Orleans Fish House II LLC
  New Orleans, LA 800-839-3474
Newfound Resources
  St Josephs, NL 709-579-7676
Northwest Wild Products
  Astoria, OR 503-791-1907
Ntc Marketing
  Williamsville, NY 800-333-1637
Ocean Pride Seafood
  Delcambre, LA 337-685-2336
Ocean Springs Seafood
  Ocean Springs, MS 228-875-0104
Ore-Cal Corp
  Los Angeles, CA 800-827-7474
Pacific American Fish Co Inc
  Vernon, CA 800-625-2525
Pamlico Packing Company
  Grantsboro, NC 800-682-1113
Paul Piazza & Son Inc
  New Orleans, LA 800-969-6011
Penguin Frozen Foods Inc
  Northbrook, IL 800-323-1485
Pioneer Live Seafood
  Oak Brook, IL 630-789-1133
Price Seafood
  Havre De Grace, MD 410-939-2782
Produits Belle Baie
  Caraquet, NB 506-727-4414
Quality Seafood
  Apalachicola, FL 850-653-9696
Red Chamber Co
  Vernon, CA 323-234-9000
Resource Trading Company
  Portland, ME 207-772-2299
Rocky Point Shrimp Association
  Phoenix, AZ 602-254-8041
Roland Seafood Co
  Atlantic Beach, FL 904-246-9443
Roy Dick Company
  Griffin, GA 770-227-3916
Sau-Sea Foods
  Tarrytown, NY 914-631-1717
Sea Pearl Seafood
  Bayou La Batre, AL 800-872-8804
Sea Snack Foods Inc
  Los Angeles, CA 213-622-2204
Seafood Producers Co-Op
  Bellingham, WA 360-733-0120
Seajoy
  Miami, FL 877-537-1717
Singleton Seafood
  Tampa, FL 800-732-3663
Smith & Sons Seafood
  Darien, GA 912-437-6471
Southern Shell Fish Company
  Harvey, LA 504-341-5631
Stavis Seafoods
  Boston, MA 800-390-5103
Tampa Bay Fisheries Inc
  Dover, FL 800-732-3663
Tampa Maid Foods Inc
  Lakeland, FL 800-237-7637
Tenth & M Seafoods
  Anchorage, AK 800-770-2722
Tex-Mex Cold Storage
  Brownsville, TX 956-831-9433
Thompson Seafood
  Darien, GA 912-437-4649
Tideland Seafood Company
  Dulac, LA 985-563-4516
Trident Seafoods Corp
  Wrangell, AK 907-874-3346
Valdez Food Inc
  Philadelphia, PA 215-634-6106
Viking Seafoods Inc
  Malden, MA 800-225-3020
Vincent Piazza Jr & Sons
  Harahan, LA 800-259-5016
Vital Choice
  Bellingham, WA 800-608-4825
Wayne Estay Shrimp Company
  Grand Isle, LA 877-787-2166
Young's Lobster Pound
  Belfast, ME 207-338-1160

Black Tiger

Bay Oceans Sea Foods
  Garibaldi, OR 503-322-3316
Biloxi Freezing Processing Inc.
  Biloxi, MS 228-436-0017
BlueWater Seafoods
  Gloucester, MA 888-560-2539
Crevettes Du Nord
  Gaspe, QC 418-368-1414
Del's Seaway Shrimp & Oyster Company
  Biloxi, MS 228-432-2604
Gerard & Dominique Seafoods
  Harbor, OR 800-858-0449
Gesco ENR
  Gaspe, QC 418-368-1414
Gulf Pride Enterprises
  Biloxi, MS 888-689-0560
JBS Packing Inc
  Port Arthur, TX 409-982-3216
Jubilee Foods
  Bayou La Batre, AL 251-824-2110
Lady Gale Seafood
  Baldwin, LA 337-923-2060
Louisiana Packing Company
  Westwego, LA 800-666-1293
Mobile Processing
  Mobile, AL 251-438-6944
Newfound Resources
  St Josephs, NL 709-579-7676
Ocean Springs Seafood
  Ocean Springs, MS 228-875-0104
Price Seafood
  Havre De Grace, MD 410-939-2782
Resource Trading Company
  Portland, ME 207-772-2299
Stavis Seafoods
  Boston, MA 800-390-5103
Vincent Piazza Jr & Sons
  Harahan, LA 800-259-5016

Breaded

Eldorado Seafood Inc
  Burlington, MA 800-416-5656
Fish King
  Glendale, CA 818-244-2161
Golden Gulf Coast Packing Co
  Biloxi, MS 228-374-6121
J. Matassini & Sons Fish Company
  Tampa, FL 813-229-0829
King & Prince Seafood Corp
  Brunswick, GA 800-841-0205
LA Monica Fine Foods
  Millville, NJ
Neptune Foods
  Vernon, CA 323-232-8300
Ocean Springs Seafood
  Ocean Springs, MS 228-875-0104
Pacific American Fish Co Inc
  Vernon, CA 800-625-2525

Product Categories / Fish & Seafood: Sushi

Penguin Frozen Foods Inc
  Northbrook, IL 800-323-1485
Sea Pearl Seafood
  Bayou La Batre, AL 800-872-8804
Seajoy
  Miami, FL 877-537-1717
Tampa Bay Fisheries Inc
  Dover, FL 800-732-3663
Tampa Maid Foods Inc
  Lakeland, FL 800-237-7637

Canned

Bayou Land Seafood
  Breaux Bridge, LA 337-667-6118
Channel Fish Processing
  Gloucester, MA 800-457-0054
Chicken Of The Sea
  El Segundo, CA 844-267-8862
Chuck's Seafoods
  Charleston, OR 541-888-5525
Nelson Crab Inc
  Tokeland, WA 800-262-0069
New Orleans Food Co-op
  New Orleans, LA 800-628-4900
Ntc Marketing
  Williamsville, NY 800-333-1637
Ore-Cal Corp
  Los Angeles, CA 800-827-7474
Seafood Producers Co-Op
  Bellingham, WA 360-733-0120
Southern Shell Fish Company
  Harvey, LA 504-341-5631
Trident Seafoods Corp
  Wrangell, AK 907-874-3346
Vital Choice
  Bellingham, WA 800-608-4825

Cooked

King & Prince Seafood Corp
  Brunswick, GA 800-841-0205
Neptune Fisheries
  Newport News, VA 800-545-7474
Neptune Foods
  Vernon, CA 323-232-8300
Pacific American Fish Co Inc
  Vernon, CA 800-625-2525
Tampa Bay Fisheries Inc
  Dover, FL 800-732-3663

Fresh

Cozy Harbor Seafood Inc
  Portland, ME 800-225-2586
Davis Strait Fisheries
  Halifax, NS 902-450-5115
Great Northern Products Inc
  Cranston, RI 401-490-4590
J. Matassini & Sons Fish Company
  Tampa, FL 813-229-0829
Jessie's Ilwaco Fish Company
  San Francisco, CA 360-642-3773
Nelson Crab Inc
  Tokeland, WA 800-262-0069
Paul Piazza & Son Inc
  New Orleans, LA 800-969-6011
Quality Seafood
  Apalachicola, FL 850-653-9696
Trident Seafoods Corp
  Wrangell, AK 907-874-3346

Frozen

Alpine Butcher
  Lowell, MA 978-256-7771
Arista Industries Inc
  Wilton, CT 800-255-6457
Bandon Bay Fisheries
  Bandon, OR 541-347-4454
Bayou Land Seafood
  Breaux Bridge, LA 337-667-6118
Beaver Street Fisheries
  Jacksonville, FL 800-874-6426
Bon Secour Fisheries Inc
  Bon Secour, AL 251-949-7411
Breakwater Fisheries
  St John's, NL 709-754-1999

C F Gollott & Son Seafood
  Diberville, MS 228-392-2747
Callis Seafood
  Lancaster, VA 804-462-7634
Carrington Foods Co Inc
  Saraland, AL 251-675-9700
Certi Fresh Foods Inc
  Wilmington, CA 310-221-6262
Channel Fish Processing
  Gloucester, MA 800-457-0054
Clearwater Fine Foods
  Bedford, NS 902-443-0550
Cozy Harbor Seafood Inc
  Portland, ME 800-225-2586
Eastern Fish Company
  Teaneck, NJ 800-526-9066
Fisherman's Reef Shrimp Company
  Beaumont, TX 409-842-9520
Golden Gulf Coast Packing Co
  Biloxi, MS 228-374-6121
Great Northern Products Inc
  Cranston, RI 401-490-4590
Indian Ridge Shrimp Co
  Chauvin, LA 800-594-0920
J. Matassini & Sons Fish Company
  Tampa, FL 813-229-0829
Jessie's Ilwaco Fish Company
  San Francisco, CA 360-642-3773
Kitchens Seafood
  Plant City, FL 800-327-0132
Luxury Crab
  St John's, NL 709-739-6668
Maxim's Import Corporation
  Miami, FL 800-331-6652
Neptune Fisheries
  Newport News, VA 800-545-7474
Pacific American Fish Co Inc
  Vernon, CA 800-625-2525
Paul Piazza & Son Inc
  New Orleans, LA 800-969-6011
Penguin Frozen Foods Inc
  Northbrook, IL 800-323-1485
Portland Shellfish Company
  Portland, ME 207-799-9290
Quality Seafood
  Apalachicola, FL 850-653-9696
Sea Pearl Seafood
  Bayou La Batre, AL 800-872-8804
Sea Snack Foods Inc
  Los Angeles, CA 213-622-2204
Seafood Producers Co-Op
  Bellingham, WA 360-733-0120
Spruce Lane Investments
  Stratford, PE 902-892-2600
Suram Trading Corporation
  Coral Gables, FL 305-448-7165
Tampa Maid Foods Inc
  Lakeland, FL 800-237-7637
Tex-Mex Cold Storage
  Brownsville, TX 956-831-9433
Trident Seafoods Corp
  Wrangell, AK 907-874-3346
Viking Seafoods Inc
  Malden, MA 800-225-3020

Jumbo

Davis Strait Fisheries
  Halifax, NS 902-450-5115

Peeled

Bayou Food Distributors
  Kenner, LA 800-516-8283
Neptune Fisheries
  Newport News, VA 800-545-7474
Seajoy
  Miami, FL 877-537-1717
Tampa Bay Fisheries Inc
  Dover, FL 800-732-3663
Tampa Maid Foods Inc
  Lakeland, FL 800-237-7637

Rock

Caito Fisheries Inc
  Fort Bragg, CA 707-964-6368

Davis Strait Fisheries
  Halifax, NS 902-450-5115

Smoked

Menemsha Fish Market
  Chilmark, MA 508-645-2282

Squid

Aliotti Wholesale Fish Company
  Monterey, CA 408-722-4597
Anchor Frozen Foods
  Westbury, NY 800-566-3474
Atlantic Capes Fisheries
  Cape May, NJ 609-884-3000
Blue Gold Mussels
  New Bedford, MA 508-993-2635
Breakwater Fisheries
  St John's, NL 709-754-1999
Caito Fisheries Inc
  Fort Bragg, CA 707-964-6368
Channel Fish Processing
  Gloucester, MA 800-457-0054
Fulton Fish Market
  New York, NY 718-842-8908
Great Northern Products Inc
  Cranston, RI 401-490-4590
Harbor Seafood
  New Hyde Park, NY 800-645-2211
J Deluca Fish Co Inc
  San Pedro, CA 310-684-5180
LA Monica Fine Foods
  Millville, NJ
Lund's Fisheries
  Cape May, NJ 609-884-7600
Menemsha Fish Market
  Chilmark, MA 508-645-2282
Northwest Wild Products
  Astoria, OR 503-791-1907
Notre Dame Seafoods Inc.
  Comfort Cove, NL 709-244-5511
Pacific American Fish Co Inc
  Vernon, CA 800-625-2525
Pacific Salmon Company
  Edmonds, WA 425-774-1315
Royal Seafood Inc
  Brooklyn, NY 718-769-1517
Ruggiero Seafood
  Newark, NJ 866-225-2627
Sea Watch Intl
  Easton, MD 410-822-7500
Spruce Lane Investments
  Stratford, PE 902-892-2600
Stavis Seafoods
  Boston, MA 800-390-5103
Sweet Water Seafood
  Carlstadt, NJ 201-939-6622
Tampa Bay Fisheries Inc
  Dover, FL 800-732-3663
Tichon Sea Food Corp
  New Bedford, MA 508-999-5607
Vital Choice
  Bellingham, WA 800-608-4825

Urchins

Captain Little Seafood
  Queens County, NS 902-947-2087

Whelk

Captain Little Seafood
  Queens County, NS 902-947-2087

Sushi

Azuma Foods Intl Inc USA
  Hayward, CA 510-782-1112
Baycliff Company
  New York, NY 212-772-6078
IOE Atlanta
  Galena, MD 410-755-6300

Fruits & Vegetables

General

Alfred Louie Inc
　Bakersfield, CA 661-831-2520
Arbre Farms Inc
　Walkerville, MI 231-873-3337
Black's Barbecue
　Lockhart, TX 888-632-8225
Brooklyn Whatever LLC
　Brooklyn, NY 917-669-5525
Brookshire Grocery Company
　Tyler, TX 888-937-3776
Capalbo's Fruit Baskets
　Clifton, NJ 800-252-6262
Coco Lopez Inc
　Miramar, FL 800-341-2242
Colavita USA
　Edison, NJ 888-265-2848
Country Fresh Inc
　Spring, TX 281-453-3300
Crop One
　Oakland, CA
Diazteca Inc
　Rio Rico, AZ 520-761-4621
Duda Farm Fresh Foods Inc
　Oviedo, FL 407-365-2111
Farm Fresh to You
　Anaheim, CA 800-796-6009
Five Ponds Farm
　Lineville, AL 256-396-5217
Five Star Home Foods, Inc.
　King of Prussia, PA 800-246-5405
Four Seasons Produce Inc
　Ephrata, PA 800-422-8384
Fresh Origins
　San Marcos, CA 760-736-4072
Frieda's Inc
　Los Alamitos, CA 714-826-6100
Fruvemex
　Calexico, CA 760-203-1896
G. Banis Company
　Wilmington, DE 617-516-9092
GAF Seelig Inc
　Flushing, NY 718-899-5000
Grace & I
　Los Angeles, CA 800-584-1736
Gulf Pecan Company
　Mobile, AL 251-661-2931
Highland Family Farms
　Mapleton, MN 507-524-3797
Ingles Markets
　Black Mountain, NC 828-669-2941
J M Swank Co
　North Liberty, IA 800-593-6375
Jain Americas Inc
　Columbus, OH 888-473-7539
Kingsburg Orchards
　Kingsburg, CA 559-897-5132
La Morena
　Huamantla, ... 222-211-0515
Lamex Foods Inc.
　Bloomington, MN 952-844-0585
Local Roots Farms
　Burt, NY 716-946-3198
Made In Nature
　Boulder, CO 800-906-7426
Manassero Farms
　Irvine, CA 949-554-5103
Meijer Inc
　Grand Rapids, MI 616-453-6711
NAR
　Nashua, NH 603-888-5420
North Bay Produce Inc
　Traverse City, MI 231-946-1941
Oak Hill Farm
　Glen Ellen, CA 800-878-7808
Oberweis Dairy Inc
　North Aurora, IL 866-623-7934
Oneonta Starr Ranch Growers
　Wenatchee, WA 509-663-2191
ORB Weaver Farm
　New Haven, VT 802-877-3755
Patsy's Italian Restaurant
　New York, NY 212-247-3491
Peterson Farms Inc
　Shelby, MI 231-861-0119
Plenty
　San Francisco, CA 650-735-3737
Prairie Thyme LTD
　Santa Fe, NM 800-869-0009
Primo Foods
　Oceanside, CA 760-439-8711
Publix Super Market
　Lakeland, FL 800-242-1227
Root Cellar Preserves
　Wellesley, MA 781-864-7440
Safeway Inc.
　Pleasanton, CA 877-723-3929
Seneca Foods Corp
　Marion, NY 315-926-8100
Shamrock Foods Co
　Phoenix, AZ 800-289-3663
Smirk's
　Fort Morgan, CO 970-762-0202
Steckel Produce
　Jerseyville, IL 618-498-4274
The Power of Fruit
　Lebanon, NJ 908-450-9806
Tolteca Foodservice
　Norcross, GA 800-541-6835
Tropical Açaí LLC
　Pompano Beach, FL 855-550-2224
Tru Fru, LLC
　Salt Lake City, UT 888-437-2497
Veggie Grill
　Irvine, CA
Wegmans Food Markets Inc.
　Rochester, NY 800-934-6267
WEIS Markets Inc.
　Sunbury, PA 866-999-9347
Western Pacific Produce
　Santa Barbara, CA 800-963-4451
Winn-Dixie Stores
　Jacksonville, FL 800-967-9105
Wish Farms
　Plant City, FL 813-752-5111
Wonderful Citrus
　Mission, TX 956-205-7300
Z&S Distributing
　Fresno, CA 800-467-0788

Algae

New Earth
　Klamath Falls, OR 541-882-5406
Sea Veggies
　Commerce, CA 323-728-4762
Vitarich Laboratories
　Naples, FL 800-817-9999

Aloe Vera

Alfer Laboratories
　Chatsworth, CA 818-709-0737
Aloe Commodities International
　Carrollton, TX 800-701-2563
Aloe Farms Inc
　Harlingen, TX 800-262-6771
Aloe Laboratories
　Harlingen, TX 800-258-5380
Christopher's Herb Shop
　Springville, UT 888-372-4372
Emerling International Foods
　Buffalo, NY 716-833-7381
Florida Food Products Inc
　Eustis, FL 800-874-2331
Real Aloe Company
　Las Vegas, NV 800-541-7809
Russo Farms
　Vineland, NJ 856-692-5942
Universal Preservachem Inc
　Somerset, NJ 732-568-1266
Warren Laboratories LLC
　Abbott, TX 800-421-2563
Winning Solutions Inc
　Irving, TX 800-899-2563

Apple

A. Gagliano Co Inc
　Milwaukee, WI 800-272-1516
AgroCepia
　Miami, FL 305-704-3488
Agvest
　Cleveland, OH 216-464-3737
Allan Bros. Inc.
　Naches, WA 509-653-2625
Apple Acres
　La Fayette, NY 603-893-8596
Applewood Orchards Inc
　Deerfield, MI 800-447-3854
Baker Produce
　Kennewick, WA 800-624-7553
Ballantine Produce Company
　Reedley, CA 559-875-2583
Belleharvest Sales Inc
　Belding, MI 800-452-7753
Ben B. Schwartz & Sons
　Detroit, MI 313-841-8300
Bennett's Apples & Cider
　Ancaster, ON 905-648-6878
Bridenbaugh Orchards
　Martinsburg, PA 814-793-2364
Brothers International Food Corporation
　Rochester, NY 585-343-3007
Burnette Foods
　Elk Rapids, MI 231-264-8116
Cahoon Farms
　Wolcott, NY 315-594-9610
Cal Harvest Marketing Inc
　Hanford, CA 559-582-4494
Chazy Orchards
　Chazy, NY 518-846-7171
Chelan Fresh Marketing
　Chelan, WA 509-682-2591
Chief Wenatchee
　Wenatchee, WA 509-662-5197
Citrosuco North America Inc
　Lake Wales, FL 800-356-4592
Clements Foods Co
　Oklahoma City, OK 800-654-8355
Coloma Frozen Foods Inc
　Coloma, MI 800-642-2723
Congdon Orchards Inc.
　Yakima, WA 509-966-4440
Country Fresh Inc
　Spring, TX 281-453-3300
Crane & Crane Inc
　Brewster, WA 509-689-3447
Del Mar Food Products Corp
　Watsonville, CA 831-722-3516
Diamond Fruit Growers
　Hood River, OR 541-354-5300
Earthbound Farm
　San Jn Bautista, CA 800-690-3200
Ever Fresh Fruit Co
　Boring, OR 800-239-8026
Flippin-Seaman Inc
　Tyro, VA 434-277-5828
Fowler Farms
　Wolcott, NY 800-836-9537
Fruit Growers Supply Company
　Valencia, CA 888-997-4855
George W Saulpaugh & Son
　Germantown, NY 518-537-6500
Giumarra Companies
　Los Angeles, CA 213-627-2900
Golden Town Apple Products
　Rougemont, QC 866-552-7643
Harner Farms
　State College, PA 814-237-7919
Hazel Creek Orchards
　Mt Airy, GA 706-754-4899
Henggeler Packing Company
　Fruitland, ID 208-452-4212
HH Dobbins Inc
　Lyndonville, NY 877-362-2467
Hillcrest Orchard
　Lake Placid, FL 865-397-5273
Indian Hollow Farms
　Richland Center, WI 800-236-3944
International Home Foods
　Parsippany, NJ 973-359-9920
J C Watson Co
　Parma, ID 208-722-5141
Knight's Appleden Fruit LTD
　Colborne, ON 905-349-2521
Kozlowski Farms
　Forestville, CA 800-473-2767

Product Categories / Fruits & Vegetables: Apple

Leroux Creek
  Hotchkiss, CO 877-970-5670
Love Creek Orchards
  Medina, TX 800-449-0882
Mariani Packing Co.
  Vacaville, CA 707-452-2800
Marley Orchards Corporation
  Yakima, WA 509-248-5231
Mason County Fruit Packers Cooperative
  Hart, MI 231-873-7504
Matson Fruit Co
  Selah, WA 509-697-7100
Mayer's Cider Mill
  Webster, NY 800-543-0043
Mayfield Farms and Nursery
  Athens, TN 423-746-9859
Mrs Prindables
  Niles, IL 888-215-1100
Naraghi Group
  Escalon, CA 209-579-5253
National Fruit Product Co Inc
  Winchester, VA 540-723-9614
Natural Foods Inc
  Toledo, OH 419-537-1711
Naumes, Inc.
  Medford, OR 541-772-6268
New Era Canning Company
  New Era, MI 231-861-2151
New Organics
  Kenwood, CA 734-677-5570
New York Apple Sales Inc
  Glenmont, NY 888-477-6770
Niagara Foods
  Middleport, NY 716-735-7722
North Bay Produce Inc
  Traverse City, MI 231-946-1941
Northern Orchard Co Inc
  Peru, NY 518-643-2367
Nuchief Sales Inc
  Wenatchee, WA 888-269-4638
Oneonta Starr Ranch Growers
  Wenatchee, WA 509-663-2191
P R Farms Inc
  Clovis, CA 559-299-0201
Pacific Coast Fruit Co
  Portland, OR 503-234-6411
Pandol Brothers Inc
  Delano, CA 661-725-3755
Park 100 Foods Inc
  Tipton, IN 800-854-6504
Pastor Chuck Orchards
  Portland, ME 207-773-1314
Pavero Cold Storage
  Highland, NY 800-435-2994
Peterson Farms Inc
  Shelby, MI 231-861-0119
Reinhart Foods
  Toronto, ON 416-645-4910
Rice Fruit Co
  Gardners, PA 800-627-3359
Roche Fruit LLC
  Yakima, WA 509-248-7200
S Zitner Co
  Philadelphia, PA 215-229-9828
Scotian Gold
  Coldbrook, NS 888-726-8426
Shafer Lake Fruit Inc
  Hartford, MI 269-621-3194
Shawnee Canning Co
  Cross Junction, VA 800-713-1414
Smeltzer Orchard Co
  Frankfort, MI 231-882-4421
Snowcrest Packer
  Abbotsford, BC 800-265-3686
Solana Gold Organics
  Sebastopol, CA 800-459-1121
Stadelman Fruit LLC
  Zillah, WA 509-829-5145
Stanley Orchards Sales, Inc.
  Modena, NY 845-883-7351
Sunshine Farm & Garden
  Renick, WV 304-497-2208
Symms Fruit Ranch Inc
  Caldwell, ID 208-459-4821
T.S. Smith & Sons
  Bridgeville, DE 302-337-8271
Tastee Apple
  Newcomerstown, OH 800-262-7753
Timber Crest Farms
  Healdsburg, CA 888-766-4233
Tom Ringhausen Orchards
  Hardin, IL 800-258-6645

Tony Vitrano Company
  Jessup, MD 800-481-3784
Trinity Fruit Sale Co
  Fresno, CA 559-433-3777
Triple D Orchards Inc
  Empire, MI 231-326-5174
United Apple Sales
  New Paltz, NY 585-765-2460
Vermont Village
  Barre, VT
Viva Tierra
  Mt Vernon, WA 360-855-0566
White House Foods
  Winchester, VA 540-662-3401
Wiards Orchards Inc
  Ypsilanti, MI 734-390-9211
Yakima Fresh
  Yakima, WA 509-248-5770

Canned
Burnette Foods
  Elk Rapids, MI 231-264-8116
Emerling International Foods
  Buffalo, NY 716-833-7381
New Era Canning Company
  New Era, MI 231-861-2151
New Organics
  Kenwood, CA 734-677-5570
Setton International Foods
  Commack, NY 800-227-4397
Terri Lynn Inc
  Elgin, IL 800-323-0775
Unique Ingredients LLC
  Gold Canyon, AZ 480-983-2498

Caramel
Andrews Caramel Apples
  Chicago, IL 800-305-3004
S Zitner Co
  Philadelphia, PA 215-229-9828
Tastee Apple
  Newcomerstown, OH 800-262-7753

Covered

Candied
Calif Snack Foods
  South El Monte, CA 626-454-4099

Caramel
Carousel Candies
  Geneva, IL 888-656-1552
DGZ Chocolate
  Houston, TX 877-949-9444
Parmenter's Northville Cider Mill
  Northville, MI 248-349-3181
S Zitner Co
  Philadelphia, PA 215-229-9828

Criterion
Natural Foods Inc
  Toledo, OH 419-537-1711
Weaver Nut Co. Inc.
  Ephrata, PA 800-473-2688

Dried
AgroCepia
  Miami, FL 305-704-3488
American Importing Co.
  Minneapolis, MN 855-273-0466
Atwater Foods
  Lyndonville Orleans, NY 585-765-2639
Bedemco Inc
  White Plains, NY 914-683-1119
Emerling International Foods
  Buffalo, NY 716-833-7381
Golden Town Apple Products
  Rougemont, QC 866-552-7643
Golden Valley Natural
  Shelley, ID 888-270-7147
Green Earth Orchards
  Salt Lake City, UT 801-888-7161
Just Tomatoes
  Westley, CA 800-537-1985
Kozlowski Farms
  Forestville, CA 800-473-2767
Leroux Creek
  Hotchkiss, CO 877-970-5670

Made In Nature
  Boulder, CO 800-906-7426
Mariani Packing Co.
  Vacaville, CA 707-452-2800
Mayfield Farms and Nursery
  Athens, TN 423-746-9859
New Organics
  Kenwood, CA 734-677-5570
Niagara Foods
  Middleport, NY 716-735-7722
Setton International Foods
  Commack, NY 800-227-4397
Solana Gold Organics
  Sebastopol, CA 800-459-1121
Terri Lynn Inc
  Elgin, IL 800-323-0775
ThreeWorks Snacks
  259 Niagara St., ON
Timber Crest Farms
  Healdsburg, CA 888-766-4233
Unique Ingredients LLC
  Gold Canyon, AZ 480-983-2498

Fresh
Belleharvest Sales Inc
  Belding, MI 800-452-7753
Bridenbaugh Orchards
  Martinsburg, PA 814-793-2364
Chazy Orchards
  Chazy, NY 518-846-7171
Ever Fresh Fruit Co
  Boring, OR 800-239-8026
Golden Town Apple Products
  Rougemont, QC 866-552-7643
Naraghi Group
  Escalon, CA 209-579-5253
Peterson Farms Inc
  Shelby, MI 231-861-0119
Price Co
  Yakima, WA 509-966-4110
Unique Ingredients LLC
  Gold Canyon, AZ 480-983-2498

Frozen
Agvest
  Cleveland, OH 216-464-3737
Cahoon Farms
  Wolcott, NY 315-594-9610
Citrosuco North America Inc
  Lake Wales, FL 800-356-4592
Emerling International Foods
  Buffalo, NY 716-833-7381
Ever Fresh Fruit Co
  Boring, OR 800-239-8026
Mason County Fruit Packers Cooperative
  Hart, MI 231-873-7504
New Organics
  Kenwood, CA 734-677-5570
Pacific Coast Fruit Co
  Portland, OR 503-234-6411
Paris Foods Corporation
  Trappe, MD 410-200-9595
Peterson Farms Inc
  Shelby, MI 231-861-0119
Setton International Foods
  Commack, NY 800-227-4397
Smeltzer Orchard Co
  Frankfort, MI 231-882-4421
Snowcrest Packer
  Abbotsford, BC 800-265-3686
Terri Lynn Inc
  Elgin, IL 800-323-0775
Triple D Orchards Inc
  Empire, MI 231-326-5174
Unique Ingredients LLC
  Gold Canyon, AZ 480-983-2498

Golden Delicious
Allan Bros. Inc.
  Naches, WA 509-653-2625
Baker Produce
  Kennewick, WA 800-624-7553
Belleharvest Sales Inc
  Belding, MI 800-452-7753

Pomace
Emerling International Foods
  Buffalo, NY 716-833-7381
Unique Ingredients LLC
  Gold Canyon, AZ 480-983-2498

Product Categories / Fruits & Vegetables: Apricot

Red Delicious
Allan Bros. Inc.
   Naches, WA 509-653-2625
Baker Produce
   Kennewick, WA 800-624-7553
Belleharvest Sales Inc
   Belding, MI 800-452-7753

Rings
AgroCepia
   Miami, FL 305-704-3488
Timber Crest Farms
   Healdsburg, CA 888-766-4233

Slices
Boskovich Farms Inc
   Oxnard, CA 805-487-2299
Bridenbaugh Orchards
   Martinsburg, PA 814-793-2364
Chiquita Brands LLC.
   Fort Lauderdale, FL 954-924-5700
Ever Fresh Fruit Co
   Boring, OR 800-239-8026
Golden Town Apple Products
   Rougemont, QC 866-552-7643
Mayfield Farms and Nursery
   Athens, TN 423-746-9859
Naraghi Group
   Escalon, CA 209-579-5253
National Fruit Product Co Inc
   Winchester, VA 540-723-9614
New Era Canning Company
   New Era, MI 231-861-2151
White House Foods
   Winchester, VA 540-662-3401

Canned
Mayfield Farms and Nursery
   Athens, TN 423-746-9859
New Era Canning Company
   New Era, MI 231-861-2151

Frozen
Ever Fresh Fruit Co
   Boring, OR 800-239-8026
Mayfield Farms and Nursery
   Athens, TN 423-746-9859

Apricot
American Key Food Products Inc
   Closter, NJ 877-263-7539
Ballantine Produce Company
   Reedley, CA 559-875-2583
Brandt Farms Inc
   Reedley, CA 559-638-6961
California Fruit
   San Diego, CA 877-378-4811
Copper Hills Fruit Sales
   Fresno, CA 559-432-5400
Custom Produce Sales
   Parlier, CA 559-254-5800
Del Mar Food Products Corp
   Watsonville, CA 831-722-3516
Fowler Packing Co
   Fresno, CA 559-834-5911
HMC Farms
   Kingsburg, CA 559-897-1025
Kalustyan
   New York, NY 800-352-3451
Kings Canyon
   Reedley, CA 559-638-3571
Miss Scarlett's Flowers
   Juneau, AK 800-345-6734
Muirhead Canning Co
   The Dalles, OR 541-298-1660
Natural Foods Inc
   Toledo, OH 419-537-1711
P R Farms Inc
   Clovis, CA 559-299-0201
Patterson Vegetable Company
   Patterson, CA 209-892-2611
Prima® Wawona
   Fresno, CA 559-787-8780
Sunfood
   El Cajon, CA 888-729-3663
Sunsweet Growers Inc.
   Yuba City, CA 800-417-2253
Terri Lynn Inc
   Elgin, IL 800-323-0775

Trinity Fruit Sale Co
   Fresno, CA 559-433-3777
Tufts Ranch
   Winters, CA 530-795-4144
Unique Ingredients LLC
   Gold Canyon, AZ 480-983-2498
Viva Tierra
   Mt Vernon, WA 360-855-0566
Z&S Distributing
   Fresno, CA 800-467-0788

Canned
Emerling International Foods
   Buffalo, NY 716-833-7381

Dried
American Importing Co.
   Minneapolis, MN 855-273-0466
Bedemco Inc
   White Plains, NY 914-683-1119
California Fruit
   San Diego, CA 877-378-4811
Central California Raisin Packing Co, Inc.
   Del Rey, CA 559-888-2195
Green Earth Orchards
   Salt Lake City, UT 801-888-7161
Kalustyan
   New York, NY 800-352-3451
King Arthur Flour
   Norwich, VT 800-827-6836
Made In Nature
   Boulder, CO 800-906-7426
Mariani Packing Co.
   Vacaville, CA 707-452-2800
Natural Foods Inc
   Toledo, OH 419-537-1711
Setton International Foods
   Commack, NY 800-227-4397
Sunridge Farms
   Royal Oaks, CA 831-786-7000
Sunsweet Growers Inc.
   Yuba City, CA 800-417-2253
Timber Crest Farms
   Healdsburg, CA 888-766-4233
Weaver Nut Co. Inc.
   Ephrata, PA 800-473-2688

Frozen
Emerling International Foods
   Buffalo, NY 716-833-7381

Kernals
Emerling International Foods
   Buffalo, NY 716-833-7381

Artichoke
Fayter Farms Produce
   Bradley, CA 831-385-8515
Ocean Mist Farms
   Castroville, CA 831-633-2144
Orleans Packing Co
   Hyde Park, MA 617-361-6611
SupHerb Farms
   Turlock, CA 800-787-4372
Vegetable Juices Inc
   Chicago, IL 888-776-9752

Canned
Agrocan
   Ville St Laurent, QC 877-247-6226
Emerling International Foods
   Buffalo, NY 716-833-7381
Ron Son Foods Inc
   Swedesboro, NJ 856-241-7333

Frozen
Emerling International Foods
   Buffalo, NY 716-833-7381
SupHerb Farms
   Turlock, CA 800-787-4372
Vegetable Juices Inc
   Chicago, IL 888-776-9752

Hearts
Castella Imports Inc
   Brentwood, NY 631-231-5500
Colonna Brothers Inc
   North Bergen, NJ 201-864-1115

SupHerb Farms
   Turlock, CA 800-787-4372

Arugula
80 Acres Farms
   Hamilton, OH 888-574-1569
AeroFarms
   Newark, NJ 973-242-2495
Bowery Farming Inc.
   New York, NY
BrightFarms
   Irvington, NY 866-857-8745
Earthbound Farm
   San Jn Bautista, CA 800-690-3200
Plenty
   San Francisco, CA 650-735-3737

Asparagus
Arbre Farms Inc
   Walkerville, MI 231-873-3337
Boskovich Farms Inc
   Oxnard, CA 805-487-2299
Brock Seed Company
   Finley, TN 731-286-2430
Burnette Foods
   Elk Rapids, MI 231-264-8116
Cal Harvest Marketing Inc
   Hanford, CA 559-582-4494
Coloma Frozen Foods Inc
   Coloma, MI 800-642-2723
Delta Packing
   Lodi, CA 209-334-1023
Di Mare Fresh Inc
   Fort Worth, TX 817-385-3000
Earthbound Farm
   San Jn Bautista, CA 800-690-3200
Foster Family Farm
   South Windsor, CT 860-648-9366
George W Saulpaugh & Son
   Germantown, NY 518-537-6500
Giumarra Companies
   Los Angeles, CA 213-627-2900
Heartland Strawberry Farm
   Waterloo, IA 888-747-7423
Lakeside Foods Inc.
   Manitowoc, WI 800-466-3834
Metzger Specialty Brands
   New York, NY 212-957-0055
Michigan Freeze Pack
   Hart, MI 231-873-2175
Miss Scarlett's Flowers
   Juneau, AK 800-345-6734
New Era Canning Company
   New Era, MI 231-861-2151
North Bay Produce Inc
   Traverse City, MI 231-946-1941
Ocean Mist Farms
   Castroville, CA 831-633-2144
Pictsweet Co
   Bells, TN 731-663-7600
Sedlock Farm
   Lynn Center, IL 309-521-8284
Shafer Lake Fruit Inc
   Hartford, MI 269-621-3194
Smeltzer Orchard Co
   Frankfort, MI 231-882-4421
Snowcrest Packer
   Abbotsford, BC 800-265-3686
Symms Fruit Ranch Inc
   Caldwell, ID 208-459-4821
T.S. Smith & Sons
   Bridgeville, DE 302-337-8271
Weil's Food Processing
   Wheatley, ON 519-825-4572

Canned
Carriere Foods Inc
   Saint-Denis-Sur-Richelie, QC 450-787-3411
Emerling International Foods
   Buffalo, NY 716-833-7381
Fruit Belt Canning Inc
   Lawrence, MI 269-674-3939
Unique Ingredients LLC
   Gold Canyon, AZ 480-983-2498

Frozen
Emerling International Foods
   Buffalo, NY 716-833-7381
Fruit Belt Canning Inc
   Lawrence, MI 269-674-3939

Product Categories / Fruits & Vegetables: Avocado

Paris Foods Corporation
  Trappe, MD. 410-200-9595
Unique Ingredients LLC
  Gold Canyon, AZ 480-983-2498

Avocado

Brooks Tropicals Inc
  Homestead, FL 800-327-4833
Calavo Growers
  Santa Paula, CA 805-525-1245
Castellini Group
  Newport, KY. 800-233-8560
Del Monte Fresh Produce Inc.
  Coral Gables, FL. 800-950-3683
Diversified Avocado Products
  Mission Viejo, CA 800-879-2555
Earthbound Farm
  San Jn Bautista, CA 800-690-3200
Emerling International Foods
  Buffalo, NY. 716-833-7381
Giumarra Companies
  Los Angeles, CA. 213-627-2900
J. R. Simplot Co.
  Boise, ID 208-336-2110
McDaniel Fruit
  Fallbrook, CA 760-728-8438
Prime Produce
  Orange, CA 714-771-0718
Reed Lang Farms
  Rio Hondo, TX 956-748-2354
Simpatica
  Camarillo, CA. 310-286-2236
West Pak Avocado Inc
  Murrieta, CA. 800-266-4414

Bamboo Shoots

Dong Kee Company
  Chicago, IL 312-225-6340
Emerling International Foods
  Buffalo, NY. 716-833-7381
Lee's Food Products
  Toronto, ON 416-465-2407
SupHerb Farms
  Turlock, CA 800-787-4372

Banana

A. Gagliano Co Inc
  Milwaukee, WI 800-272-1516
Chiquita Brands LLC.
  Fort Lauderdale, FL 954-924-5700
Del Monte Fresh Produce Inc.
  Coral Gables, FL. 800-950-3683
Emerling International Foods
  Buffalo, NY. 716-833-7381
Organics Unlimited
  San Diego, CA 619-710-0658
Paris Foods Corporation
  Trappe, MD. 410-200-9595
Santanna Banana Company
  Harrisburg, PA 717-238-8321
Surface Banana Company
  Parkersburg, WV. 304-485-2400
Unique Ingredients LLC
  Gold Canyon, AZ 480-983-2498

Banana Products

Banana Distributing Company
  San Antonio, TX. 210-227-8285
Confoco USA, Inc.
  Elizabeth, NJ. 908-659-0566
KOZY Shack Enterprises Inc
  St Paul, MN. 855-716-1555
Spreda Group
  Louisville, KY. 502-426-9411

Dried

Barnana
  Santa Monica, CA. 858-480-1543
Bedemco Inc
  White Plains, NY 914-683-1119
Fine Dried Foods Intl
  Santa Cruz, CA. 831-426-1413
Made In Nature
  Boulder, CO 800-906-7426
Mariani Packing Co.
  Vacaville, CA 707-452-2800
Setton International Foods
  Commack, NY 800-227-4397
Sunridge Farms
  Royal Oaks, CA 831-786-7000

Plantain

MIC Foods
  Miami, FL. 800-788-9335
Organics Unlimited
  San Diego, CA 619-710-0658
Tantos Foods International
  Markham, ON 905-943-9993

Beans

A. Lassonde Inc.
  Rougemont, QC 866-552-7643
Abbott & Cobb Inc
  Feasterville, PA. 800-345-7333
Agricore United
  St Louis Park, MN 877-509-5865
Amigos Canning Company
  San Antonio, TX 210-798-5360
B & G Foods Inc.
  Parsippany, NJ. 973-401-6500
Beckman & Gast Co
  St Henry, OH 419-678-4195
Buckhead Gourmet
  Atlanta, GA. 800-673-6338
Burnette Foods
  Elk Rapids, MI 231-264-8116
Burnham & Morrill Co
  Portland, ME. 800-813-2165
Buxton Foods
  Buxton, ND. 800-726-8057
Cajun Boy's Louisiana Products
  Church Point, LA 800-880-9575
California Fruit and Tomato Kitchens
  Modesto, CA. 209-574-9407
California Garden Products
  San Juan Capistrano, CA 949-215-0000
Camellia Beans
  Harahan, LA 504-733-8480
Campbell Soup Co.
  Camden, NJ. 800-257-8443
Capco Enterprises
  East Hanover, NJ. 800-252-1011
Castella Imports Inc
  Brentwood, NY. 631-231-5500
Chef Merito Inc
  Van Nuys, CA 800-637-4861
Cooperative Elevator Co
  Pigeon, MI 800-968-0601
Country Cupboard
  Lewisburg, PA. 570-523-3211
Crookston Bean
  Crookston, MN 218-281-2567
Eckroat Seed Company
  Oklahoma City, OK 800-331-7333
Eden Foods Inc
  Clinton, MI 888-424-3336
Everspring Farms
  Seaforth, ON 519-527-0990
Faribault Foods, Inc.
  Fairbault, MN 507-331-1400
Foster Family Farm
  South Windsor, CT 860-648-9366
Furmano's Foods
  Northumberland, PA 800-952-1111
Goya Foods Inc.
  Jersey City, NJ 201-348-4900
Grandma Browns Beans Inc
  Mexico, NY 315-963-7221
Green Valley Foods
  Salem, OR. 844-588-3535
Hanover Foods Corp
  Hanover, PA 717-632-6000
HealthBest
  San Marcos, CA 760-752-5230
Heartline Foods
  Westport, CT 203-222-0381
Hoopeston Foods Inc
  Burnsville, MN 952-854-0903
Hormel Foods Corp.
  Austin, MN 507-437-5611
Houston Calco, Inc
  Houston, TX. 713-236-8668
HP Schmid
  San Francisco, CA 415-765-5925
In Harvest Inc
  Bemidji, MN. 800-346-7032
Inland Empire Foods
  Riverside, CA 888-452-3267
Inter-American Products
  Cincinnati, OH 800-645-2233
International Home Foods
  Parsippany, NJ. 973-359-9920

Kalustyan
  New York, NY 800-352-3451
Knight Seed Company
  Burnsville, MN 800-328-2999
Krinos Foods
  Bronx, NY. 718-729-9000
L & S Packing Co
  Farmingdale, NY 800-286-6487
Lakeside Foods Inc.
  Plainview, MN 507-534-3141
Les Aliments Ramico Foods
  St. Leonard, QC 514-329-1844
Louis Dreyfus Corporation
  Rotterdam,
Meridian Foods New Inc
  Eaton, IN 765-396-3344
Mills Brothers Intl
  Seattle, WA 206-575-3000
Miramar Fruit Trading Company
  Doral, FL. 305-883-4774
Miyako Oriental Foods Inc
  Baldwin Park, CA. 877-788-6476
Morgan Foods Inc
  Austin, IN 888-430-1780
Nation Wide Canning Ltd.
  Cottam, ON. 519-839-4831
National Frozen Foods Corp
  Seattle, WA 206-322-8900
Natural Foods Inc
  Toledo, OH 419-537-1711
New Era Canning Company
  New Era, MI 231-861-2151
New Harvest Foods
  Washington, DC 920-822-2578
NORPAC Foods Inc
  Salem, OR
North Bay Trading Co
  Brule, WI. 800-348-0164
Northern Feed & Bean Company
  Lucerne, CO 800-316-2326
Osowski Farms
  Minto, ND. 701-248-3341
Pacific Collier Fresh Company
  Immokalee, FL 800-226-7274
Paisano Food Products
  Elk Grove Village, IL 800-672-4726
Pictsweet Co
  Bells, TN 731-663-7600
Pleasant Grove Farms
  Pleasant Grove, CA 916-655-3391
Producers Cooperative
  Bryan, TX 979-778-6000
Produits Ronald
  St. Damase, QC 800-465-0118
Purity Foods Inc
  Hudson, MI 800-997-7358
Quetzal Internet Cafe
  San Francisco, CA 888-673-8181
R&J Farms
  West Salem, OH 419-846-3179
Randall Food Products
  Cincinnati, OH 513-793-6525
Raymond-Hadley Corporation
  Spencer, NY 800-252-5220
Red River Commodities Inc
  Fargo, ND 800-437-5539
Rice Company
  Fair Oaks, CA 916-784-7745
Riceland Foods Inc.
  Stuttgart, AR. 855-742-3929
Roberts Seed
  Axtell, NE. 308-743-2565
Sambets Cajun Deli
  Austin, TX. 800-472-6238
Seabrook Brothers & Sons
  Seabrook, NJ. 856-455-8080
Seapoint Farms
  Huntington Beach, CA 714-374-9831
Smith Frozen Foods Inc
  Weston, OR. 541-566-3515
Snowcrest Packer
  Abbotsford, BC. 800-265-3686
Sole Grano LLC
  Fair Lawn, NJ 201-797-7100
SOPAKCO Foods
  Mullins, SC 800-276-9678
Spokane Seed Co
  Spokane Valley, WA 800-359-8478
Sprague Foods
  Belleville, ON 613-966-1200
Sugai Kona Coffee
  Holualoa, HI 808-322-7717

Product Categories / Fruits & Vegetables: Beans

Talley Farms
   Arroyo Grande, CA 805-489-5400
Tipiak Inc
   Stamford, CT 203-961-9117
Torn & Glasser
   Los Angeles, CA 800-282-6887
Torrefazione Barzula & Import
   Mississauga, ON 866-358-5488
Trinidad Benham Corporation
   Denver, CO 303-220-1400
Twin City Foods Inc.
   Stanwood, WA 206-515-2400
United Intertrade Corporation
   Houston, TX 800-969-2233
Vegetarian Traveler
   Woodbury, MN
Veronica Foods Inc
   Oakland, CA 800-370-5554
Vincent Formusa Company
   Des Plaines, IL 847-813-6040
Weaver Nut Co. Inc.
   Ephrata, PA 800-473-2688
Webster Farms
   Cambridge, NS 800-507-8844
WG Thompson & Sons
   Blenheim, ON 800-265-5225
Wicklund Farms
   Springfield, OR 541-747-5998
Wildcat Produce
   McGrew, NE 308-783-2438
Z&S Distributing
   Fresno, CA 800-467-0788
Zarda Bar-B-Q & Catering Company
   Blue Springs, MO 800-776-7427

Adzuki

Bob's Red Mill Natural Foods
   Milwaukie, OR 800-349-2173
Emerling International Foods
   Buffalo, NY 716-833-7381
New Organics
   Kenwood, CA 734-677-5570
Organic Planet
   San Francisco, CA 415-765-5590

Baked

A. Lassonde Inc.
   Rougemont, QC 866-552-7643
Burnham & Morrill Co
   Portland, ME 800-813-2165
California Garden Products
   San Juan Capistrano, CA 949-215-0000
Capco Enterprises
   East Hanover, NJ 800-252-1011
Captain Ken's Foods Inc
   St Paul, MN 800-510-3811
Grandma Browns Beans Inc
   Mexico, NY 315-963-7221
Hanover Foods Corp
   Hanover, PA 717-632-6000
Produits Ronald
   St. Damase, QC 800-465-0118
TyRy Inc
   Rocklin, CA 800-322-6325
Wornick Company
   Cincinnati, OH 800-860-4555
Zarda Bar-B-Q & Catering Company
   Blue Springs, MO 800-776-7427

Beans: Snap Blue Lake

Arbre Farms Inc
   Walkerville, MI 231-873-3337

Black

Agricore United
   St Louis Park, MN 877-509-5865
Buckhead Gourmet
   Atlanta, GA 800-673-6338
Country Cupboard
   Lewisburg, PA 570-523-3211
Miyako Oriental Foods Inc
   Baldwin Park, CA 877-788-6476
Teasdale Quality Foods Inc
   Atwater, CA 209-358-5616

Blackeye (Cowpeas)

Hanover Foods Corp
   Hanover, PA 717-632-6000
Trinidad Benham Corporation
   Denver, CO 303-220-1400

Blue Lake

Canned

Emerling International Foods
   Buffalo, NY 716-833-7381
New Era Canning Company
   New Era, MI 231-861-2151
NORPAC Foods Inc
   Salem, OR

Frozen

Emerling International Foods
   Buffalo, NY 716-833-7381
NORPAC Foods Inc
   Salem, OR
Pictsweet Co
   Bells, TN 731-663-7600
Seabrook Brothers & Sons
   Seabrook, NJ 856-455-8080
Twin City Foods Inc.
   Stanwood, WA 206-515-2400

Broad

Park 100 Foods Inc
   Tipton, IN 800-854-6504

Butter

Canned

Emerling International Foods
   Buffalo, NY 716-833-7381

Frozen

Emerling International Foods
   Buffalo, NY 716-833-7381

Canned

Bush Brothers & Co
   800-590-3797
California Garden Products
   San Juan Capistrano, CA 949-215-0000
Carriere Foods Inc
   Saint-Denis-Sur-Richelie, QC ... 450-787-3411
Pastene Co LTD
   Canton, MA 781-298-3397
Seneca Foods Corp
   Marion, NY 315-926-8100
Teasdale Quality Foods Inc
   Atwater, CA 209-358-5616

Cannellini

Bob's Red Mill Natural Foods
   Milwaukie, OR 800-349-2173
Emerling International Foods
   Buffalo, NY 716-833-7381
New Organics
   Kenwood, CA 734-677-5570
Organic Planet
   San Francisco, CA 415-765-5590

Chick

Agrocan
   Ville St Laurent, QC 877-247-6226
Emerling International Foods
   Buffalo, NY 716-833-7381
New Organics
   Kenwood, CA 734-677-5570
Organic Planet
   San Francisco, CA 415-765-5590
Saffron Road
   Stamford, CT 877-425-2587
The Amazing Chickpea
   St. Louis Park, MN 612-548-1099
Timeless Seeds
   Ulm, MT 406-866-3340

Chili

Emerling International Foods
   Buffalo, NY 716-833-7381
Faribault Foods, Inc.
   Faribault, MN 507-331-1400
Hanover Foods Corp
   Hanover, PA 717-632-6000
Milnot Company
   Litchfield, IL 800-877-6455
Organic Planet
   San Francisco, CA 415-765-5590

SOPAKCO Foods
   Mullins, SC 800-276-9678

Dried

Bland

Kelley Bean Co Inc
   Scottsbluff, NE 308-635-6438

Dry

Agfinity Inc
   Eaton, CO 800-433-4688
Basic American Foods
   Walnut Creek, CA 925-472-4000
Berberian Nut Company
   Chico, CA 530-981-4900
Burnette Foods
   Elk Rapids, MI 231-264-8116
C & F Foods Inc
   City Of Industry, CA 626-723-1000
Camellia Beans
   Harahan, LA 504-733-8480
Central Bean Co
   Quincy, WA 509-787-1544
Commodities Marketing Inc
   Clarksburg, NJ 732-516-0700
Cooperative Elevator Co
   Pigeon, MI 800-968-0601
Crookston Bean
   Crookston, MN 218-281-2567
Eckhart Seed Company
   Salinas, CA 831-758-0925
Eckroat Seed Company
   Oklahoma City, OK 800-331-7333
Emerling International Foods
   Buffalo, NY 716-833-7381
Farmers Cooperative Grain Co
   Kinde, MI 989-874-4200
Freeland Bean & Grain Inc
   Freeland, MI 800-447-9131
H.K. Canning
   Ventura, CA 805-652-1392
High Country Elevators Inc
   Dove Creek, CO 970-677-2251
Hoopeston Foods Inc
   Burnsville, MN 952-854-0903
HP Schmid
   San Francisco, CA 415-765-5925
Jack's Bean Co LLC
   Holyoke, CO 970-854-3702
Kalustyan
   New York, NY 800-352-3451
Knight Seed Company
   Burnsville, MN 800-328-2999
Luxor California Exports Corp.
   San Diego, CA 619-465-7777
Meridian Foods New Inc
   Eaton, IN 765-396-3344
Mills Brothers Intl
   Seattle, WA 206-575-3000
Morrison Farms
   Clearwater, NE 402-887-5335
Nature's Legacy Inc.
   Hudson, MI 517-448-2050
New Organics
   Kenwood, CA 734-677-5570
Nk Hurst Co Inc
   Indianapolis, IN 800-426-2336
Northern Feed & Bean Company
   Lucerne, CO 800-316-2326
Northwest Pea & Bean Co
   Spokane Valley, WA 509-534-3821
Oakland Bean Cleaning & Storage
   Knights Landing, CA ... 530-735-6203
Organic Planet
   San Francisco, CA 415-765-5590
Osowski Farms
   Minto, ND 701-248-3341
Paisano Food Products
   Elk Grove Village, IL .. 800-672-4726
Producers Cooperative
   Bryan, TX 979-778-6000
R&J Farms
   West Salem, OH 419-846-3179
Randall Food Products
   Cincinnati, OH 513-793-6525
Red River Commodities Inc
   Fargo, ND 800-437-5539
Rhodes Bean & Supply Co-Op
   Tracy, CA 209-835-1284

Product Categories / Fruits & Vegetables: Beans

Roberts Seed
  Axtell, NE 308-743-2565
Russell E. Womack, Inc.
  Lubbock, TX 877-787-3559
S & E Organic Farms Inc
  Bakersfield, CA 661-325-2644
Seed Enterprises Inc
  West Point, NE 888-440-7333
Smith Frozen Foods Inc
  Weston, OR 541-566-3515
Sprague Foods
  Belleville, ON 613-966-1200
Terra Ingredients LLC
  Minneapolis, MN 855-497-3308
Trinidad Benham Company
  Bridgeport, NE 308-262-1361
Trinidad Benham Corporation
  Denver, CO 303-220-1400
Vege-Cool
  Newman, CA 209-862-2360
Webster Farms
  Cambridge, NS 800-507-8844
Westbrae Natural Foods
  Melville, NY 800-434-4246
WG Thompson & Sons
  Blenheim, ON 800-265-5225

Canned

Carriere Foods Inc
  Saint-Denis-Sur-Richelie, QC . . . 450-787-3411
Emerling International Foods
  Buffalo, NY 716-833-7381

Edible

Agfinity Inc
  Eaton, CO 800-433-4688
Russell E. Womack, Inc.
  Lubbock, TX 877-787-3559

Fava

Bob's Red Mill Natural Foods
  Milwaukie, OR 800-349-2173
Emerling International Foods
  Buffalo, NY 716-833-7381
Kalustyan
  New York, NY 800-352-3451
Organic Planet
  San Francisco, CA 415-765-5590
Tarazi Specialty Foods
  Chino, CA 909-628-3601

Frozen

Agfinity Inc
  Eaton, CO 800-433-4688
Amigos Canning Company
  San Antonio, TX 210-798-5360
Buxton Foods
  Buxton, ND 800-726-8057
Campbell Soup Co.
  Camden, NJ 800-257-8443
Captain Ken's Foods Inc
  St Paul, MN 800-510-3811
Diversified Foods & Seasonings
  Covington, LA 800-914-2382
Emerling International Foods
  Buffalo, NY 716-833-7381
Hanover Foods Corp
  Hanover, PA 717-632-6000
Lakeside Foods Inc.
  Plainview, MN 507-534-3141
Lakeside Foods Inc.
  Manitowoc, WI 800-466-3834
Meridian Foods New Inc
  Eaton, IN 765-396-3344
National Frozen Foods Corp
  Seattle, WA 206-322-8900
NORPAC Foods Inc
  Salem, OR
Pictsweet Co
  Bells, TN 731-663-7600
Seabrook Brothers & Sons
  Seabrook, NJ 856-455-8080
Smith Frozen Foods Inc
  Weston, OR 541-566-3515
Snowcrest Packer
  Abbotsford, BC 800-265-3686
Twin City Foods Inc.
  Stanwood, WA 206-515-2400

Garbanzo

Bob's Red Mill Natural Foods
  Milwaukie, OR 800-349-2173
Buckhead Gourmet
  Atlanta, GA 800-673-6338
California Fruit and Tomato Kitchens
  Modesto, CA 209-574-9407
Capco Enterprises
  East Hanover, NJ 800-252-1011
Emerling International Foods
  Buffalo, NY 716-833-7381
In Harvest Inc
  Bemidji, MN 800-346-7032
Kalustyan
  New York, NY 800-352-3451
New Organics
  Kenwood, CA 734-677-5570
Northwest Pea & Bean Co
  Spokane Valley, WA 509-534-3821
Organic Planet
  San Francisco, CA 415-765-5590
Sprague Foods
  Belleville, ON 613-966-1200
Teasdale Quality Foods Inc
  Atwater, CA 209-358-5616
Vana Life Foods
  Seattle, WA 347-446-6504

Great Northern

Agricore United
  St Louis Park, MN 877-509-5865
Bob's Red Mill Natural Foods
  Milwaukie, OR 800-349-2173
Emerling International Foods
  Buffalo, NY 716-833-7381
Hanover Foods Corp
  Hanover, PA 717-632-6000
Jack's Bean Co LLC
  Holyoke, CO 970-854-3702
New Organics
  Kenwood, CA 734-677-5570
Organic Planet
  San Francisco, CA 415-765-5590
Randall Food Products
  Cincinnati, OH 513-793-6525

Greek

Canned

Agrocan
  Ville St Laurent, QC 877-247-6226

Green

Beckman & Gast Co
  St Henry, OH 419-678-4195
Burnette Foods
  Elk Rapids, MI 231-264-8116
Faribault Foods, Inc.
  Fairbault, MN 507-331-1400
Hanover Foods Corp
  Hanover, PA 717-632-6000
Miss Scarlett's Flowers
  Juneau, AK 800-345-6734
National Frozen Foods Corp
  Seattle, WA 206-322-8900
New Era Canning Company
  New Era, MI 231-861-2151
New Harvest Foods
  Washington, DC 920-822-2578
NORPAC Foods Inc
  Salem, OR
Patterson Frozen Foods
  Patterson, CA 209-892-2611
Pictsweet Co
  Bells, TN 731-663-7600
Seabrook Brothers & Sons
  Seabrook, NJ 856-455-8080
Seneca Foods Corp
  Princeville, IL 309-385-4301
Twin City Foods Inc.
  Stanwood, WA 206-515-2400
Veronica Foods Inc
  Oakland, CA 800-370-5554
Wicklund Farms
  Springfield, OR 541-747-5998
Wildcat Produce
  McGrew, NE 308-783-2438

Canned

Beckman & Gast Co
  St Henry, OH 419-678-4195
Burnette Foods
  Elk Rapids, MI 231-264-8116
Carriere Foods Inc
  Saint-Denis-Sur-Richelie, QC 450-787-3411
Commodities Marketing Inc
  Clarksburg, NJ 732-516-0700
Emerling International Foods
  Buffalo, NY 716-833-7381
Faribault Foods, Inc.
  Fairbault, MN 507-331-1400
New Era Canning Company
  New Era, MI 231-861-2151
New Harvest Foods
  Washington, DC 920-822-2578
NORPAC Foods Inc
  Salem, OR
Seneca Foods Corp
  Princeville, IL 309-385-4301
Truitt Bros Inc
  Salem, OR 800-547-8712

Frozen

Lisa's Organics
  Carnelian Bay, CA 877-584-5711
National Frozen Foods Corp
  Seattle, WA 206-322-8900
NORPAC Foods Inc
  Salem, OR
Paris Foods Corporation
  Trappe, MD 410-200-9595
Pictsweet Co
  Bells, TN 731-663-7600
Seabrook Brothers & Sons
  Seabrook, NJ 856-455-8080
Twin City Foods Inc.
  Stanwood, WA 206-515-2400

Green Mung

New Organics
  Kenwood, CA 734-677-5570
Organic Planet
  San Francisco, CA 415-765-5590

Italian

National Frozen Foods Corp
  Seattle, WA 206-322-8900
Pictsweet Co
  Bells, TN 731-663-7600

Kidney

Agfinity Inc
  Eaton, CO 800-433-4688
Bob's Red Mill Natural Foods
  Milwaukie, OR 800-349-2173
Burnette Foods
  Elk Rapids, MI 231-264-8116
California Garden Products
  San Juan Capistrano, CA 949-215-0000
Cordon Bleu International
  Anjou, QC 800-363-1182
Hanover Foods Corp
  Hanover, PA 717-632-6000
International Home Foods
  Parsippany, NJ 973-359-9920
Jack's Bean Co LLC
  Holyoke, CO 970-854-3702
Nation Wide Canning Ltd.
  Cottam, ON 519-839-4831
New Era Canning Company
  New Era, MI 231-861-2151
Oakland Bean Cleaning & Storage
  Knights Landing, CA 530-735-6203
Pleasant Grove Farms
  Pleasant Grove, CA 916-655-3391
Red River Commodities Inc
  Fargo, ND 800-437-5539
Sprague Foods
  Belleville, ON 613-966-1200
Teasdale Quality Foods Inc
  Atwater, CA 209-358-5616
WG Thompson & Sons
  Blenheim, ON 800-265-5225

Canned

Burnette Foods
  Elk Rapids, MI 231-264-8116

Product Categories / Fruits & Vegetables: Beans

Cordon Bleu International
  Anjou, QC 800-363-1182
Emerling International Foods
  Buffalo, NY 716-833-7381
International Home Foods
  Parsippany, NJ 973-359-9920
Nation Wide Canning Ltd.
  Cottam, ON 519-839-4831
New Era Canning Company
  New Era, MI 231-861-2151
Red River Commodities Inc
  Fargo, ND 800-437-5539
Vegetable Juices Inc
  Chicago, IL 888-776-9752

Dark Red

Agrocan
  Ville St Laurent, QC 877-247-6226
Cordon Bleu International
  Anjou, QC 800-363-1182
Red River Commodities Inc
  Fargo, ND 800-437-5539
Sprague Foods
  Belleville, ON 613-966-1200

Frozen

Emerling International Foods
  Buffalo, NY 716-833-7381
Vegetable Juices Inc
  Chicago, IL 888-776-9752

Light Red

Jack's Bean Co LLC
  Holyoke, CO 970-854-3702
Red River Commodities Inc
  Fargo, ND 800-437-5539

Lentil

Agricore United
  St Louis Park, MN 877-509-5865
Bob's Red Mill Natural Foods
  Milwaukie, OR 800-349-2173
C & F Foods Inc
  City Of Industry, CA 626-723-1000
Camellia Beans
  Harahan, LA 504-733-8480
Emerling International Foods
  Buffalo, NY 716-833-7381
Farmer Direct Organic
  Regina, SK 306-563-7815
Garden Valley Corp
  Sutherlin, OR 541-459-9565
HP Schmid
  San Francisco, CA 415-765-5925
In Harvest Inc
  Bemidji, MN 800-346-7032
Inland Empire Foods
  Riverside, CA 888-452-3267
Kalustyan
  New York, NY 800-352-3451
Mezza
  Lake Forest, IL 888-206-6054
Mills Brothers Intl
  Seattle, WA 206-575-3000
New Organics
  Kenwood, CA 734-677-5570
Northwest Pea & Bean Co
  Spokane Valley, WA 509-534-3821
Primo Foods
  Toronto, ON 800-377-6945
Shah Trading Company
  Scarborough, ON 416-292-6927
Spokane Seed Co
  Spokane Valley, WA 800-359-8478
Timeless Seeds
  Ulm, MT 406-866-3340
United Pulse Trading Inc
  Bismarck, ND 701-751-1623
Wallace Grain & Pea Company
  Pullman, WA 509-878-1561

Canned

Organic Planet
  San Francisco, CA 415-765-5590

Lima

Bob's Red Mill Natural Foods
  Milwaukie, OR 800-349-2173
California Fruit and Tomato Kitchens
  Modesto, CA 209-574-9407

Country Cupboard
  Lewisburg, PA 570-523-3211
Hanover Foods Corp
  Hanover, PA 717-632-6000
In Harvest Inc
  Bemidji, MN 800-346-7032
Lakeside Foods Inc.
  Plainview, MN 507-534-3141
National Frozen Foods Corp
  Seattle, WA 206-322-8900
Patterson Frozen Foods
  Patterson, CA 209-892-2611
Pictsweet Co
  Bells, TN 731-663-7600
Seabrook Brothers & Sons
  Seabrook, NJ 856-455-8080
Smith Frozen Foods Inc
  Weston, OR 541-566-3515
Trinidad Benham Corporation
  Denver, CO 303-220-1400
Vege-Cool
  Newman, CA 209-862-2360

Canned

Emerling International Foods
  Buffalo, NY 716-833-7381
Hanover Foods Corp
  Hanover, PA 717-632-6000
Lakeside Foods Inc.
  Plainview, MN 507-534-3141

Frozen

Hanover Foods Corp
  Hanover, PA 717-632-6000
National Frozen Foods Corp
  Seattle, WA 206-322-8900
Paris Foods Corporation
  Trappe, MD 410-200-9595
Pictsweet Co
  Bells, TN 731-663-7600
Seabrook Brothers & Sons
  Seabrook, NJ 856-455-8080
Smith Frozen Foods Inc
  Weston, OR 541-566-3515

Lupini

Castella Imports Inc
  Brentwood, NY 631-231-5500
Emerling International Foods
  Buffalo, NY 716-833-7381
L & S Packing Co
  Farmingdale, NY 800-286-6487

Mung

Green

Bob's Red Mill Natural Foods
  Milwaukie, OR 800-349-2173
Commodities Marketing Inc
  Clarksburg, NJ 732-516-0700
Eckroat Seed Company
  Oklahoma City, OK 800-331-7333
Emerling International Foods
  Buffalo, NY 716-833-7381
Jonathan's Sprouts
  Rochester, MA 508-763-2577
Kalustyan
  New York, NY 800-352-3451

Navy

Bob's Red Mill Natural Foods
  Milwaukie, OR 800-349-2173
Central Bean Co
  Quincy, WA 509-787-1544
Jack's Bean Co LLC
  Holyoke, CO 970-854-3702
New Era Canning Company
  New Era, MI 231-861-2151
Sprague Foods
  Belleville, ON 613-966-1200

Canned

Emerling International Foods
  Buffalo, NY 716-833-7381
New Era Canning Company
  New Era, MI 231-861-2151

Pink

Central Bean Co
  Quincy, WA 509-787-1544
Oakland Bean Cleaning & Storage
  Knights Landing, CA 530-735-6203

Pinto

Agfinity Inc
  Eaton, CO 800-433-4688
Agricore United
  St Louis Park, MN 877-509-5865
Buxton Foods
  Buxton, ND 800-726-8057
Central Bean Co
  Quincy, WA 509-787-1544
Crookston Bean
  Crookston, MN 218-281-2567
Emerling International Foods
  Buffalo, NY 716-833-7381
Hanover Foods Corp
  Hanover, PA 717-632-6000
International Home Foods
  Parsippany, NJ 973-359-9920
Jack's Bean Co LLC
  Holyoke, CO 970-854-3702
New Organics
  Kenwood, CA 734-677-5570
Northern Feed & Bean Company
  Lucerne, CO 800-316-2326
Organic Planet
  San Francisco, CA 415-765-5590
Producers Cooperative
  Bryan, TX 979-778-6000
Randall Food Products
  Cincinnati, OH 513-793-6525
Russell E. Womack, Inc.
  Lubbock, TX 877-787-3559
Teasdale Quality Foods Inc
  Atwater, CA 209-358-5616
Trinidad Benham Corporation
  Denver, CO 303-220-1400
Vegetable Juices Inc
  Chicago, IL 888-776-9752

Refried

Amigos Canning Company
  San Antonio, TX 210-798-5360
Hormel Foods Corp.
  Austin, MN 507-437-5611
Teasdale Quality Foods Inc
  Atwater, CA 209-358-5616

Canned

Amigos Canning Company
  San Antonio, TX 210-798-5360
Morgan Foods Inc
  Austin, IN 888-430-1780

Shoots

Houston Calco, Inc
  Houston, TX 713-236-8668

Small Red

Central Bean Co
  Quincy, WA 509-787-1544

Snap Green

Arbre Farms Inc
  Walkerville, MI 231-873-3337
Boskovich Farms Inc
  Oxnard, CA 805-487-2299

Snap Wax

Arbre Farms Inc
  Walkerville, MI 231-873-3337

Wax

Hanover Foods Corp
  Hanover, PA 717-632-6000
National Frozen Foods Corp
  Seattle, WA 206-322-8900
New Era Canning Company
  New Era, MI 231-861-2151
NORPAC Foods Inc
  Salem, OR
Pictsweet Co
  Bells, TN 731-663-7600

Product Categories / Fruits & Vegetables: Beets

Seabrook Brothers & Sons
  Seabrook, NJ....................856-455-8080
Twin City Foods Inc.
  Stanwood, WA...................206-515-2400

Canned

Arbre Farms Inc
  Walkerville, MI..................231-873-3337
Carriere Foods Inc
  Saint-Denis-Sur-Richelie, QC........450-787-3411
Emerling International Foods
  Buffalo, NY.....................716-833-7381
New Era Canning Company
  New Era, MI....................231-861-2151
NORPAC Foods Inc
  Salem, OR

Frozen

Arbre Farms Inc
  Walkerville, MI..................231-873-3337
Emerling International Foods
  Buffalo, NY.....................716-833-7381
National Frozen Foods Corp
  Seattle, WA.....................206-322-8900
NORPAC Foods Inc
  Salem, OR
Pictsweet Co
  Bells, TN.......................731-663-7600
Seabrook Brothers & Sons
  Seabrook, NJ....................856-455-8080
Twin City Foods Inc.
  Stanwood, WA...................206-515-2400

Beets

Boskovich Farms Inc
  Oxnard, CA.....................805-487-2299
Dehydrates Inc
  Hewlett, NY....................800-983-4443
Earthbound Farm
  San Jn Bautista, CA..............800-690-3200
Gouw Quality Onions
  Taber, AB......................403-223-1440
Local Roots Farms
  Burt, NY.......................716-946-3198
Love Beets
  Bala Cynwyd, PA................856-692-1740
Old Country Packers
  Duryea, PA.....................570-655-9608
Osowski Farms
  Minto, ND......................701-248-3341
Plenty
  San Francisco, CA...............650-735-3737
Sargent and Greenleaf
  Nicholasville, KY................800-826-7652
Schiff Food Products Co Inc
  Totowa, NJ.....................973-237-1990
Vegetable Juices Inc
  Chicago, IL.....................888-776-9752

Canned

Emerling International Foods
  Buffalo, NY.....................716-833-7381

Frozen

Emerling International Foods
  Buffalo, NY.....................716-833-7381
Vegetable Juices Inc
  Chicago, IL.....................888-776-9752

Sugar

Agri-Dairy Products
  Purchase, NY...................914-697-9580
Michigan Sugar Company
  Bay City, MI....................989-686-0161
Nyssa-Nampa Beet Growers
  Nyssa, OR.....................541-372-2904
Osowski Farms
  Minto, ND......................701-248-3341
Western Sugar Cooperative
  Denver, CO....................800-523-7497

Berries

Abbotsford Growers Ltd.
  Abbotsford, BC.................604-864-0022
Allen's Blueberry Freezer Inc
  Ellsworth, ME..................207-667-5561
Atlantic Blueberry
  Hammonton, NJ................609-561-8600

Behm Blueberry Farms
  Grand Haven, MI...............616-846-1650
Bluechip Group
  Salt Lake City, UT...............800-878-0099
Carolina Blueberry Co-Op Assn
  Garland, NC...................910-588-4220
Cherry Central Cooperative, Inc.
  Traverse City, MI...............231-946-1860
Coastal Classics
  Duxbury, MA...................508-746-6058
Country Fresh Inc
  Spring, TX.....................281-453-3300
Crop Pharms, LLC
  Staatsburg, NY.................845-266-8999
Custom Produce Sales
  Parlier, CA.....................559-254-5800
Decas Cranberry Sales Inc
  Carver, MA....................800-649-9811
Del Mar Food Products Corp
  Watsonville, CA.................831-722-3516
E.W. Bowker Company
  Pemberton, NJ.................609-894-9508
Earth Circle Organics
  Auburn, CA....................877-922-3663
Firestone Pacific Foods Co
  Vancouver, WA.................360-695-9484
From Oregon
  Springfield, OR.................541-747-4222
Giumarra Companies
  Los Angeles, CA................213-627-2900
Graysmarsh Berry Farm
  Sequim, WA...................800-683-4367
Grow-Pac
  Cornelius, OR..................503-357-9691
J H Verbridge & Son Inc
  Williamson, NY.................315-589-2366
Jersey Fruit Co-Op
  Glassboro, NJ..................856-863-9100
K.B. Hall Ranch
  Ojai, CA.......................805-525-5875
KERR Concentrates Inc
  Salem, OR.....................800-910-5377
Krupka's Blueberries
  Fennville, MI...................269-857-4278
Leelanau Fruit Co
  Peshawbestown, MI............231-271-3514
Macrie Brothers
  Hammonton, NJ................609-561-6822
Meduri Farms
  Dallas, OR.....................877-388-8800
Midwest Blueberry Farms
  Holland, MI....................616-399-2133
Norm's Farms
  Purdy, MO.....................417-522-1375
North American Blueberry Council
  Folsom, CA....................800-824-6395
Oregon Raspberry & Blackberry Commission
  Corvallis, OR...................541-758-4043
Organic Nectars LLC
  Malden On Hudson, NY........845-246-0506
Oxford Frozen Foods
  Oxford, NS....................902-447-2100
Pamlico Packing Company
  Grantsboro, NC................800-682-1113
Peterson Farms Inc
  Shelby, MI.....................231-861-0119
Plaidberry Company
  Vista, CA......................760-727-5403
R M Lawton Cranberries Inc
  Middleboro, MA................508-947-7465
Ragold Confections
  Wilton Manors, FL..............954-566-9092
Reiter Affiliated Companies
  Oxnard, CA...................805-483-1000
Scenic Fruit Co
  Gresham, OR..................877-927-3434
Setton International Foods
  Commack, NY.................800-227-4397
Smeltzer Orchard Co
  Frankfort, MI..................231-882-4421
Snowcrest Packer
  Abbotsford, BC................800-265-3686
Sunfood
  El Cajon, CA..................888-729-3663
Terri Lynn Inc
  Elgin, IL......................800-323-0775
Timber Crest Farms
  Healdsburg, CA...............888-766-4233
Tom Ringhausen Orchards
  Hardin, IL....................800-258-6645
Topaz Farm
  Portland, OR.................503-708-0008

Tru-Blu Cooperative Associates
  New Lisbon, NJ...............609-894-8717
True Blue Farms
  Grand Junction, MI...........877-654-2400
Valley View Blueberries
  Vancouver, WA..............360-892-2839
Vilore Foods Co Inc
  Laredo, TX..................956-722-7190
Well-Pict Inc
  Watsonville, CA.............831-722-3871
Wetherby Cranberry Company
  Warrens, WI................608-378-4813
Wilhelm Foods
  Newberg, OR..............503-538-2929
Wish Farms
  Plant City, FL..............813-752-5111

Canned & Frozen

Abbotsford Growers Ltd.
  Abbotsford, BC.............604-864-0022
Allen's Blueberry Freezer Inc
  Ellsworth, ME..............207-667-5561
Atlantic Blueberry
  Hammonton, NJ...........609-561-8600
Carolina Blueberry Co-Op Assn
  Garland, NC...............910-588-4220
Cherry Central Cooperative, Inc.
  Traverse City, MI..........231-946-1860
E.W. Bowker Company
  Pemberton, NJ............609-894-9508
G M Allen & Son Inc
  Orland, ME...............207-469-7060
Grow-Pac
  Cornelius, OR............503-357-9691
J H Verbridge & Son Inc
  Williamson, NY...........315-589-2366
KERR Concentrates Inc
  Salem, OR................800-910-5377
Leelanau Fruit Co
  Peshawbestown, MI.....231-271-3514
Oxford Frozen Foods
  Oxford, NS...............902-447-2100
Plaidberry Company
  Vista, CA.................760-727-5403
Scenic Fruit Co
  Gresham, OR............877-927-3434
Snowcrest Packer
  Abbotsford, BC..........800-265-3686
Tru-Blu Cooperative Associates
  New Lisbon, NJ.........609-894-8717
True Blue Farms
  Grand Junction, MI.....877-654-2400
Unique Ingredients LLC
  Gold Canyon, AZ.......480-983-2498
Wawona Frozen Foods Inc
  Clovis, CA...............559-299-2901

Blackberry

Coloma Frozen Foods Inc
  Coloma, MI.............800-642-2723
Driscoll Strawberry Assoc Inc
  Watsonville, CA........831-424-0506
Grow-Pac
  Cornelius, OR..........503-357-9691
KERR Concentrates Inc
  Salem, OR.............800-910-5377
North Bay Produce Inc
  Traverse City, MI......231-946-1941
Oregon Fruit Products Co
  Salem, OR.............800-394-9333
Rainsweet Inc
  Salem, OR.............800-363-4293
Reiter Affiliated Companies
  Oxnard, CA...........805-483-1000
Sand Hill Berries
  Mt Pleasant, PA.......724-547-4760
Symons Frozen Foods
  Centralia, WA.........360-736-1321
Tom Ringhausen Orchards
  Hardin, IL.............800-258-6645
Unique Ingredients LLC
  Gold Canyon, AZ.....480-983-2498
Venture Vineyards
  Lodi, NY..............888-635-6277
Wish Farms
  Plant City, FL.........813-752-5111

Frozen

Coloma Frozen Foods Inc
  Coloma, MI..........800-642-2723

Product Categories / Fruits & Vegetables: Berries

Emerling International Foods
　Buffalo, NY......................716-833-7381
Grow-Pac
　Cornelius, OR...................503-357-9691
KERR Concentrates Inc
　Salem, OR.......................800-910-5377
Merrill's Blueberry Farms
　Ellsworth, ME...................800-711-6551
Oregon Fruit Products Co
　Salem, OR.......................800-394-9333
Overlake Foods
　Olympia, WA.....................800-683-1078
Paris Foods Corporation
　Trappe, MD......................410-200-9595
Rainsweet Inc
　Salem, OR.......................800-363-4293
Symons Frozen Foods
　Centralia, WA...................360-736-1321
Townsend Farms Inc
　Fairview, OR....................503-666-1780
Unique Ingredients LLC
　Gold Canyon, AZ.................480-983-2498

Blueberry

Agvest
　Cleveland, OH...................216-464-3737
Allen's Blueberry Freezer Inc
　Ellsworth, ME...................207-667-5561
Blueberry Store
　Grand Junction, MI..............877-654-2400
Christy Wild Blueberry Farms
　Amherst, NS.....................902-667-3013
Coloma Frozen Foods Inc
　Coloma, MI......................800-642-2723
Custom Produce Sales
　Parlier, CA.....................559-254-5800
Diamond Blueberry Inc
　Hammonton, NJ...................609-561-3661
Driscoll Strawberry Assoc Inc
　Watsonville, CA.................831-424-0506
E.W. Bowker Company
　Pemberton, NJ...................609-894-9508
Earthbound Farm
　San Jn Bautista, CA.............800-690-3200
Enfield Farms Inc
　Lynden, WA......................360-354-2919
Fruit d'Or
　Villeroy, QC....................819-385-1126
G M Allen & Son Inc
　Orland, ME......................207-469-7060
Hawkins Farm
　Bristol, WI....................262-857-2616
Hialeah Products Co
　Hollywood, FL...................800-923-3379
Honee Bear Canning
　Lawton, MI.....................800-626-2327
Indian Bay Frozen Foods
　Centreville, NL................709-678-2844
Just Tomatoes
　Westley, CA....................800-537-1985
Krupka's Blueberries
　Fennville, MI..................269-857-4278
Maberry & Maberry Berry Associates
　Lynden, WA.....................360-354-7708
Macrie Brothers
　Hammonton, NJ..................609-561-6822
Maine Wild Blueberry Company
　Cherryfield, ME................800-243-4005
Meduri Farms
　Dallas, OR.....................877-388-8800
Merrill's Blueberry Farms
　Ellsworth, ME..................800-711-6551
Midwest Blueberry Farms
　Holland, MI....................616-399-2133
New England Cranberry
　Lynn, MA.......................800-410-2892
Niagara Foods
　Middleport, NY.................716-735-7722
North American Blueberry Council
　Folsom, CA.....................800-824-6395
North Bay Produce Inc
　Traverse City, MI..............231-946-1941
Oregon Fruit Products Co
　Salem, OR......................800-394-9333
Pacific Coast Fruit Co
　Portland, OR...................503-234-6411
Pandol Brothers Inc
　Delano, CA.....................661-725-3755
Peterson Farms Inc
　Shelby, MI.....................231-861-0119
Producer Marketing Overlake
　Olympia, WA....................360-352-9096

Rainsweet Inc
　Salem, OR......................800-363-4293
Reiter Affiliated Companies
　Oxnard, CA.....................805-483-1000
Royal Ridge Fruits
　Royal City, WA.................509-346-1520
Smeltzer Orchard Co
　Frankfort, MI..................231-882-4421
Snowcrest Packer
　Abbotsford, BC.................800-265-3686
Symons Frozen Foods
　Centralia, WA..................360-736-1321
Terri Lynn Inc
　Elgin, IL......................800-323-0775
Timber Crest Farms
　Healdsburg, CA.................888-766-4233
Townsend Farms Inc
　Fairview, OR...................503-666-1780
Unique Ingredients LLC
　Gold Canyon, AZ................480-983-2498
Valley View Blueberries
　Vancouver, WA..................360-892-2839
Venture Vineyards
　Lodi, NY.......................888-635-6277
Wild Blueberries
　Old Town, ME...................207-570-3535
Wish Farms
　Plant City, FL.................813-752-5111

Canned

Honee Bear Canning
　Lawton, MI.....................800-626-2327
Maine Wild Blueberry Company
　Cherryfield, ME................800-243-4005
Merrill's Blueberry Farms
　Ellsworth, ME..................800-711-6551
Oregon Fruit Products Co
　Salem, OR......................800-394-9333

Dried

Atwater Foods
　Lyndonville Orleans, NY........585-765-2639
Bedemco Inc
　White Plains, NY...............914-683-1119
Golden Valley Natural
　Shelley, ID....................888-270-7147
Hodgson Mill Inc
　Effingham, IL..................800-347-0198
Setton International Foods
　Commack, NY....................800-227-4397

Frozen

Agvest
　Cleveland, OH..................216-464-3737
Allen's Blueberry Freezer Inc
　Ellsworth, ME..................207-667-5561
Bleuet Nordic
　Dolbeau-Mistassini, QC.........418-239-1001
Blueberry Store
　Grand Junction, MI.............877-654-2400
Christy Wild Blueberry Farms
　Amherst, NS....................902-667-3013
Diamond Blueberry Inc
　Hammonton, NJ..................609-561-3661
E.W. Bowker Company
　Pemberton, NJ..................609-894-9508
Earthbound Farm
　San Jn Bautista, CA............800-690-3200
Emerling International Foods
　Buffalo, NY....................716-833-7381
Enfield Farms Inc
　Lynden, WA.....................360-354-2919
Fruit d'Or
　Villeroy, QC...................819-385-1126
G M Allen & Son Inc
　Orland, ME.....................207-469-7060
Maberry & Maberry Berry Associates
　Lynden, WA.....................360-354-7708
Maine Wild Blueberry Company
　Cherryfield, ME................800-243-4005
Oregon Fruit Products Co
　Salem, OR......................800-394-9333
Overlake Foods
　Olympia, WA....................800-683-1078
Pacific Coast Fruit Co
　Portland, OR...................503-234-6411
Paris Foods Corporation
　Trappe, MD....................410-200-9595
Rainsweet Inc
　Salem, OR......................800-363-4293

Snowcrest Packer
　Abbotsford, BC.................800-265-3686
Townsend Farms Inc
　Fairview, OR...................503-666-1780
Unique Ingredients LLC
　Gold Canyon, AZ................480-983-2498

High Bush

Victor Packing
　Madera, CA.....................559-673-5908

Boysenberry

KERR Concentrates Inc
　Salem, OR......................800-910-5377
Oregon Fruit Products Co
　Salem, OR......................800-394-9333
Rainsweet Inc
　Salem, OR......................800-363-4293

Canned

Oregon Fruit Products Co
　Salem, OR......................800-394-9333

Frozen

Emerling International Foods
　Buffalo, NY....................716-833-7381
KERR Concentrates Inc
　Salem, OR......................800-910-5377
Oregon Fruit Products Co
　Salem, OR......................800-394-9333
Rainsweet Inc
　Salem, OR......................800-363-4293
Townsend Farms Inc
　Fairview, OR...................503-666-1780

Canned

Emerling International Foods
　Buffalo, NY....................716-833-7381
Maine Wild Blueberry Company
　Cherryfield, ME................800-243-4005
Plaidberry Company
　Vista, CA......................760-727-5403

Cranberry

Agvest
　Cleveland, OH..................216-464-3737
Coastal Classics
　Duxbury, MA....................508-746-6058
Decas Cranberry Sales Inc
　Carver, MA.....................800-649-9811
E.W. Bowker Company
　Pemberton, NJ..................609-894-9508
Fruit d'Or
　Villeroy, QC...................819-385-1126
Hialeah Products Co
　Hollywood, FL..................800-923-3379
Joseph J. White
　Browns Mills, NJ...............609-893-2332
New England Cranberry
　Lynn, MA.......................800-410-2892
Niagara Foods
　Middleport, NY.................716-735-7722
Pacific Coast Fruit Co
　Portland, OR...................503-234-6411
R M Lawton Cranberries Inc
　Middleboro, MA.................508-947-7465
Setton International Foods
　Commack, NY....................800-227-4397
Smeltzer Orchard Co
　Frankfort, MI..................231-882-4421
Snowcrest Packer
　Abbotsford, BC.................800-265-3686
Terri Lynn Inc
　Elgin, IL......................800-323-0775
Timber Crest Farms
　Healdsburg, CA.................888-766-4233
Unique Ingredients LLC
　Gold Canyon, AZ................480-983-2498
Wetherby Cranberry Company
　Warrens, WI....................608-378-4813

Dried

American Importing Co.
　Minneapolis, MN................855-273-0466
Atwater Foods
　Lyndonville Orleans, NY........585-765-2639
Bedemco Inc
　White Plains, NY...............914-683-1119

223

Product Categories / Fruits & Vegetables: Berries

Fruit d'Or
  Villeroy, QC 819-385-1126
King Arthur Flour
  Norwich, VT 800-827-6836
Mariani Packing Co.
  Vacaville, CA 707-452-2800
Patience Fruit & Co.
  Villeroy, QC
Simply Incredible Foods
  Port Edwards, WI 715-697-6232
Sunridge Farms
  Royal Oaks, CA 831-786-7000

Frozen

Agvest
  Cleveland, OH 216-464-3737
E.W. Bowker Company
  Pemberton, NJ 609-894-9508
Fruit d'Or
  Villeroy, QC 819-385-1126
Niagara Foods
  Middleport, NY 716-735-7722
Pacific Coast Fruit Co
  Portland, OR 503-234-6411
Simply Incredible Foods
  Port Edwards, WI 715-697-6232
Snowcrest Packer
  Abbotsford, BC 800-265-3686

Products

Emerling International Foods
  Buffalo, NY 716-833-7381
Simply Incredible Foods
  Port Edwards, WI 715-697-6232
Unique Ingredients LLC
  Gold Canyon, AZ 480-983-2498

Whole

Patience Fruit & Co.
  Villeroy, QC
Simply Incredible Foods
  Port Edwards, WI 715-697-6232

Currants

Crop Pharms, LLC
  Staatsburg, NY 845-266-8999
Emerling International Foods
  Buffalo, NY 716-833-7381
Milne Fruit Products Inc
  Prosser, WA 509-786-2611
Pacific Coast Fruit Co
  Portland, OR 503-234-6411
Setton International Foods
  Commack, NY 800-227-4397

Red

Pacific Coast Fruit Co
  Portland, OR 503-234-6411

Frozen

Abbotsford Growers Ltd.
  Abbotsford, BC 604-864-0022
Agvest
  Cleveland, OH 216-464-3737
Christy Wild Blueberry Farms
  Amherst, NS 902-667-3013
Coloma Frozen Foods Inc
  Coloma, MI 800-642-2723
Diamond Blueberry Inc
  Hammonton, NJ 609-561-3661
E.W. Bowker Company
  Pemberton, NJ 609-894-9508
Earthbound Farm
  San Jn Bautista, CA 800-690-3200
Emerling International Foods
  Buffalo, NY 716-833-7381
Enfield Farms Inc
  Lynden, WA 360-354-2919
G M Allen & Son Inc
  Orland, ME 207-469-7060
Grow-Pac
  Cornelius, OR 503-357-9691
J H Verbridge & Son Inc
  Williamson, NY 315-589-2366
Maberry & Maberry Berry Associates
  Lynden, WA 360-354-7708
Maine Wild Blueberry Company
  Cherryfield, ME 800-243-4005
Niagara Foods
  Middleport, NY 716-735-7722

Ocean Spray International
  Lakeville-Middleboro, MA 800-662-3263
Oregon Fruit Products Co
  Salem, OR 800-394-9333
Overlake Foods
  Olympia, WA 800-683-1078
Pacific Coast Fruit Co
  Portland, OR 503-234-6411
Prairie Berries Inc.
  Keeler, SK 306-788-2018
Rainsweet Inc
  Salem, OR 800-363-4293
Snowcrest Packer
  Abbotsford, BC 800-265-3686
Sunrise Growers
  Placentia, CA 714-630-6292
Symons Frozen Foods
  Centralia, WA 360-736-1321
Webster Farms
  Cambridge, NS 800-507-8844

Goose

Oregon Fruit Products Co
  Salem, OR 800-394-9333

Juniper

Schiff Food Products Co Inc
  Totowa, NJ 973-237-1990

Lingonberries

Indian Bay Frozen Foods
  Centreville, NL 709-678-2844

Mulberries

Kalustyan
  New York, NY 800-352-3451

Raspberries

Bridenbaugh Orchards
  Martinsburg, PA 814-793-2364
Coloma Frozen Foods Inc
  Coloma, MI 800-642-2723
Decker Farms Inc
  Hillsboro, OR 503-628-1532
Driscoll Strawberry Assoc Inc
  Watsonville, CA 831-424-0506
Enfield Farms Inc
  Lynden, WA 360-354-2919
Graysmarsh Berry Farm
  Sequim, WA 800-683-4367
Heartland Strawberry Farm
  Waterloo, IA 888-747-7423
Just Tomatoes
  Westley, CA. 800-537-1985
KERR Concentrates Inc
  Salem, OR. 800-910-5377
Mike & Jean's Berry Farm
  Mt Vernon, WA 360-424-7220
Oregon Fruit Products Co
  Salem, OR 800-394-9333
Pacific Coast Fruit Co
  Portland, OR 503-234-6411
Rainsweet Inc
  Salem, OR 800-363-4293
Reiter Affiliated Companies
  Oxnard, CA 805-483-1000
Royal Ridge Fruits
  Royal City, WA 509-346-1520
Sand Hill Berries
  Mt Pleasant, PA 724-547-4760
Snowcrest Packer
  Abbotsford, BC 800-265-3686
Strebin Farms
  Troutdale, OR 503-665-8328
Symons Frozen Foods
  Centralia, WA 360-736-1321
Terri Lynn Inc
  Elgin, IL 800-323-0775
Townsend Farms Inc
  Fairview, OR 503-666-1780
Unique Ingredients LLC
  Gold Canyon, AZ 480-983-2498
Venture Vineyards
  Lodi, NY 888-635-6277
Wish Farms
  Plant City, FL 813-752-5111

Frozen

Abbotsford Growers Ltd.
  Abbotsford, BC 604-864-0022

Coloma Frozen Foods Inc
  Coloma, MI 800-642-2723
Earthbound Farm
  San Jn Bautista, CA 800-690-3200
Emerling International Foods
  Buffalo, NY 716-833-7381
Enfield Farms Inc
  Lynden, WA 360-354-2919
KERR Concentrates Inc
  Salem, OR 800-910-5377
Oregon Fruit Products Co
  Salem, OR 800-394-9333
Overlake Foods
  Olympia, WA 800-683-1078
Pacific Coast Fruit Co
  Portland, OR 503-234-6411
Rainsweet Inc
  Salem, OR 800-363-4293
Snowcrest Packer
  Abbotsford, BC 800-265-3686
Strebin Farms
  Troutdale, OR 503-665-8328
Symons Frozen Foods
  Centralia, WA 360-736-1321
Townsend Farms Inc
  Fairview, OR 503-666-1780
Unique Ingredients LLC
  Gold Canyon, AZ 480-983-2498

Strawberry

Bluechip Group
  Salt Lake City, UT 800-878-0099
Boskovich Farms Inc
  Oxnard, CA 805-487-2299
Bridenbaugh Orchards
  Martinsburg, PA 814-793-2364
Clofine Dairy Products Inc
  Linwood, NJ 609-653-1000
Coloma Frozen Foods Inc
  Coloma, MI 800-642-2723
Decker Farms Inc
  Hillsboro, OR 503-628-1532
Del Mar Food Products Corp
  Watsonville, CA 831-722-3516
Driscoll Strawberry Assoc Inc
  Watsonville, CA 831-424-0506
Etchandy Farms
  Anaheim, CA
Grow-Pac
  Cornelius, OR 503-357-9691
Hialeah Products Co
  Hollywood, FL 800-923-3379
J H Verbridge & Son Inc
  Williamson, NY 315-589-2366
KERR Concentrates Inc
  Salem, OR 800-910-5377
Mike & Jean's Berry Farm
  Mt Vernon, WA 360-424-7220
Niagara Foods
  Middleport, NY 716-735-7722
Oregon Fruit Products Co
  Salem, OR 800-394-9333
Pacific Coast Fruit Co
  Portland, OR 503-234-6411
Paradise Inc
  Plant City, FL 813-752-1155
Producer Marketing Overlake
  Olympia, WA 360-352-9096
Rainsweet Inc
  Salem, OR 800-363-4293
Reiter Affiliated Companies
  Oxnard, CA 805-483-1000
Smeltzer Orchard Co
  Frankfort, MI 231-882-4421
Snowcrest Packer
  Abbotsford, BC 800-265-3686
Sunrise Growers
  Placentia, CA 714-630-6292
T.S. Smith & Sons
  Bridgeville, DE 302-337-8271
Terri Lynn Inc
  Elgin, IL 800-323-0775
Townsend Farms Inc
  Fairview, OR 503-666-1780
Unique Ingredients LLC
  Gold Canyon, AZ 480-983-2498
Valley View Blueberries
  Vancouver, WA 360-892-2839
Webster Farms
  Cambridge, NS 800-507-8844
Well-Pict Inc
  Watsonville, CA 831-722-3871

Product Categories / Fruits & Vegetables: Brandied Fruits

Wish Farms
   Plant City, FL 813-752-5111

Canned

Emerling International Foods
   Buffalo, NY. 716-833-7381
Oregon Fruit Products Co
   Salem, OR. 800-394-9333
Overlake Foods
   Olympia, WA 800-683-1078
Unique Ingredients LLC
   Gold Canyon, AZ 480-983-2498

Dried

Atwater Foods
   Lyndonville Orleans, NY 585-765-2639
Bedemco Inc
   White Plains, NY 914-683-1119

Frozen

Coloma Frozen Foods Inc
   Coloma, MI. 800-642-2723
Earthbound Farm
   San Jn Bautista, CA 800-690-3200
Emerling International Foods
   Buffalo, NY. 716-833-7381
Fruit Belt Canning Inc
   Lawrence, MI 269-674-3939
Grow-Pac
   Cornelius, OR 503-357-9691
J H Verbridge & Son Inc
   Williamson, NY 315-589-2366
KERR Concentrates Inc
   Salem, OR. 800-910-5377
Niagara Foods
   Middleport, NY. 716-735-7722
Overlake Foods
   Olympia, WA 800-683-1078
Pacific Coast Fruit Co
   Portland, OR 503-234-6411
Rainsweet Inc
   Salem, OR. 800-363-4293
Snowcrest Packer
   Abbotsford, BC. 800-265-3686
Sunrise Growers
   Placentia, CA 714-630-6292
Townsend Farms Inc
   Fairview, OR. 503-666-1780
Webster Farms
   Cambridge, NS 800-507-8844

Brandied Fruits

Au Printemps Gourmet
   Saint-Jerome, QC 800-438-6676
Dundee Brandied Fruit Co
   Dundee, OR. 503-537-2500
Hurd Orchards
   Holley, NY 585-638-8838
Jubilee Gourmet Creations
   Manchester, NH 603-625-0654
Silver Palate Kitchens
   Cresskill, NJ 201-568-0110

Broccoli

Boskovich Farms Inc
   Oxnard, CA. 805-487-2299
Cal Harvest Marketing Inc
   Hanford, CA 559-582-4494
D'Arrigo Brothers Company of California
   Salinas, CA. 831-455-4500
Dehydrates Inc
   Hewlett, NY 800-983-4443
Earthbound Farm
   San Jn Bautista, CA 800-690-3200
Great American Appetizers
   Nampa, ID. 800-282-4834
Hanover Foods Corp
   Hanover, PA 717-632-6000
Kuhlmann's Market Gardens & Greenhouses
   Edmonton, AB 780-475-7500
Mann Packing Co
   Salinas, CA. 800-285-1002
Michigan Freeze Pack
   Hart, MI. 231-873-2175
Patterson Frozen Foods
   Patterson, CA 209-892-2611
Patterson Vegetable Company
   Patterson, CA 209-892-2611
Pictsweet Co
   Bells, TN. 731-663-7600
Snowcrest Packer
   Abbotsford, BC. 800-265-3686
Talley Farms
   Arroyo Grande, CA. 805-489-5400
Tanimura Antle Inc
   Salinas, CA. 800-772-4542
Teixeira Farms, Inc.
   Santa Maria, CA 805-928-3801
Titan Farms
   Ridge Spring, SC 803-685-5381
Vegetable Juices Inc
   Chicago, IL 888-776-9752
Western Pacific Produce
   Santa Barbara, CA 800-963-4451

Chopped

80 Acres Farms
   Hamilton, OH 888-574-1569
Pictsweet Co
   Bells, TN. 731-663-7600

Frozen

Emerling International Foods
   Buffalo, NY. 716-833-7381
Great American Appetizers
   Nampa, ID. 800-282-4834
Lisa's Organics
   Carnelian Bay, CA 877-584-5711
Paris Foods Corporation
   Trappe, MD. 410-200-9595
Pictsweet Co
   Bells, TN. 731-663-7600
Snowcrest Packer
   Abbotsford, BC. 800-265-3686
Sun Harvest Foods Inc
   San Diego, CA 619-661-0909
Sure-Fresh Produce Inc
   Santa Maria, CA 888-423-5379
Unique Ingredients LLC
   Gold Canyon, AZ 480-983-2498
Vegetable Juices Inc
   Chicago, IL 888-776-9752

Brussel Sprouts

Boskovich Farms Inc
   Oxnard, CA. 805-487-2299
Miss Scarlett's Flowers
   Juneau, AK 800-345-6734
Patterson Frozen Foods
   Patterson, CA 209-892-2611
Pictsweet Co
   Bells, TN. 731-663-7600
Snowcrest Packer
   Abbotsford, BC. 800-265-3686
Star Fine Foods
   Fresno, CA 559-498-2900

Frozen

Emerling International Foods
   Buffalo, NY. 716-833-7381
Paris Foods Corporation
   Trappe, MD. 410-200-9595
Pictsweet Co
   Bells, TN. 731-663-7600
Snowcrest Packer
   Abbotsford, BC. 800-265-3686

Cabbage

Boskovich Farms Inc
   Oxnard, CA. 805-487-2299
Carando Gourmet Frozen Foods
   Agawam, MA. 888-227-2636
Club Chef LLC
   Covington, KY. 859-578-3100
Dehydrates Inc
   Hewlett, NY 800-983-4443
Eckert Cold Storage
   Manteca, CA 209-823-3181
Exeter Produce
   Exeter, ON. 519-235-0141
F & S Produce Co Inc
   Vineland, NJ 800-886-3316
HH Dobbins Inc
   Lyndonville, NY 877-362-2467
Kuhlmann's Market Gardens & Greenhouses
   Edmonton, AB 780-475-7500
Pacific Collier Fresh Company
   Immokalee, FL 800-226-7274
R.C. McEntire & Company
   Columbia, SC 803-799-3388
Russo Farms
   Vineland, NJ 856-692-5942
Sales USA
   Salado, TX 800-766-7344
Sure-Fresh Produce Inc
   Santa Maria, CA 888-423-5379
Teixeira Farms, Inc.
   Santa Maria, CA 805-928-3801
Vegetable Juices Inc
   Chicago, IL 888-776-9752
Vessey & Co Inc
   Holtville, CA. 760-356-0130

Bok Choy

AeroFarms
   Newark, NJ. 973-242-2495
Boskovich Farms Inc
   Oxnard, CA. 805-487-2299
Eckert Cold Storage
   Manteca, CA 209-823-3181
Sure-Fresh Produce Inc
   Santa Maria, CA 888-423-5379
Talley Farms
   Arroyo Grande, CA. 805-489-5400
Vessey & Co Inc
   Holtville, CA. 760-356-0130

Canned

Emerling International Foods
   Buffalo, NY. 716-833-7381
Sure-Fresh Produce Inc
   Santa Maria, CA 888-423-5379

Chinese

Pioneer Growers
   Belle Glade, FL. 229-243-9306

Frozen

Carando Gourmet Frozen Foods
   Agawam, MA. 888-227-2636
Eckert Cold Storage
   Manteca, CA 209-823-3181
Emerling International Foods
   Buffalo, NY. 716-833-7381
Ripon Pickle Co Inc
   Ripon, WI 920-748-7110
Sure-Fresh Produce Inc
   Santa Maria, CA 888-423-5379
Vegetable Juices Inc
   Chicago, IL 888-776-9752

Green

Seneca Foods Corp
   Princeville, IL 309-385-4301
Vessey & Co Inc
   Holtville, CA. 760-356-0130

Processed

Mama O's Premium Kimchi
   Brooklyn, NY 917-326-1557

Red

F & S Produce Co Inc
   Vineland, NJ 800-886-3316
Vessey & Co Inc
   Holtville, CA. 760-356-0130

Cactus

D'Arrigo Brothers Company of California
   Salinas, CA. 831-455-4500
True Nopal Cactus Water
   Scottsdale, AZ. 480-636-8044

Candied Fruits

Crystallized, Glace

American Key Food Products Inc
   Closter, NJ. 877-263-7539
California Custom Fruits
   Baldwin Park, CA. 877-558-0056
Emerling International Foods
   Buffalo, NY. 716-833-7381
Gray & Company
   Hart, MI. 800-551-6009
Hialeah Products Co
   Hollywood, FL 800-923-3379
King Arthur Flour
   Norwich, VT 800-827-6836

Product Categories / Fruits & Vegetables: Canned Fruits

Limpert Bros Inc
   Vineland, NJ 800-691-1353
Olde Tyme Food Corporation
   East Longmeadow, MA 800-356-6533
Paradise Inc
   Plant City, FL 813-752-1155
Reinhart Foods
   Toronto, ON 416-645-4910
Scala-Wisell International Inc.
   Floral Park, NY 516-437-8600
Setton International Foods
   Commack, NY 800-227-4397
Unique Ingredients LLC
   Gold Canyon, AZ 480-983-2498
Weaver Nut Co. Inc.
   Ephrata, PA 800-473-2688

Canned Fruits

Agrocan
   Ville St Laurent, QC 877-247-6226
B.M. Lawrence & Company
   San Francisco, CA 415-981-2926
BGS Jourdan & Sons
   Darlington, MD. 410-457-4904
Bob Gordon & Associates
   Oak Park, IL 708-524-9611
Burnette Foods
   Elk Rapids, MI 231-264-8116
Coco Lopez Inc
   Miramar, FL 800-341-2242
Curtice Burns Foods
   Shortsville, NY 585-289-4414
Del Monte Foods Inc.
   Walnut Creek, CA
Derco Foods Intl
   Fresno, CA 559-435-2664
Emerling International Foods
   Buffalo, NY. 716-833-7381
Florida Citrus
   Bartow, FL 863-537-3999
Hurd Orchards
   Holley, NY 585-638-8838
International Home Foods
   Parsippany, NJ. 973-359-9920
Knouse Foods Co-Op Inc.
   Peach Glen, PA 717-677-8181
L & S Packing Co
   Farmingdale, NY 800-286-6487
Lancaster Packing Company
   Myerstown, PA 717-397-9727
Maine Wild Blueberry Company
   Cherryfield, ME 800-243-4005
Majestic Foods
   Huntington, NY 631-424-9444
Manzana Products Co.
   Sebastopol, CA 707-823-5313
Maui Gold Pineapple Company
   Pukalani, HI 808-877-3805
Neil Jones Food Company
   Vancouver, WA 800-291-3862
New Era Canning Company
   New Era, MI 231-861-2151
Ntc Marketing
   Williamsville, NY 800-333-1637
Oregon Cherry Growers Inc
   Salem, OR
Oregon Fruit Products Co
   Salem, OR. 800-394-9333
Pacific Coast Producers
   Lodi, CA 877-618-4776
Patterson Frozen Foods
   Patterson, CA 209-892-2611
Plaidberry Company
   Vista, CA. 760-727-5403
Snokist Growers
   Yakima, WA 800-377-2857
Triple D Orchards Inc
   Empire, MI 231-326-5174
Truitt Bros Inc
   Salem, OR. 800-547-8712

Canned Vegetables

A. Lassonde Inc.
   Rougemont, QC 866-552-7643
Appleton Produce Company
   Weiser, ID 208-414-3352
B.M. Lawrence & Company
   San Francisco, CA 415-981-2926
BGS Jourdan & Sons
   Darlington, MD. 410-457-4904

Bob Gordon & Associates
   Oak Park, IL 708-524-9611
Border Foods
   New Hope, MN. 763-559-7338
Burnette Foods
   Elk Rapids, MI 231-264-8116
Capitol Foods
   Memphis, TN 662-781-9021
Carriere Foods Inc
   Saint-Denis-Sur-Richelie, QC 450-787-3411
Coco Lopez Inc
   Miramar, FL 800-341-2242
Cordon Bleu International
   Anjou, QC. 800-363-1182
Curtice Burns Foods
   Shortsville, NY 585-289-4414
Deep Foods Inc
   Union, NJ 908-810-7500
Del Monte Foods Inc.
   Walnut Creek, CA
Dong Kee Company
   Chicago, IL 312-225-6340
Ebro Foods
   Chicago, IL 773-696-0150
Emerling International Foods
   Buffalo, NY. 716-833-7381
Escalon Premier Brand
   Escalon, CA 209-838-7341
Fiesta Canning Co
   Phoenix, AZ 602-212-2424
Ful-Flav-R Foods
   Alamo, CA 925-838-0300
Gl Mezzetta Inc
   American Canyon, CA 800-941-7044
Green Valley Foods
   Salem, OR. 844-588-3535
GWB Foods Corporation
   Brooklyn, NY 877-977-7610
Hanover Foods Corp
   Hanover, PA 717-632-6000
Hermann Pickle Co
   Garrettsville, OH. 800-245-2696
International Home Foods
   Parsippany, NJ. 973-359-9920
John N Wright Jr Inc
   Federalsburg, MD. 410-754-9044
Juanita's Foods
   Wilmington, CA 800-303-2965
L & S Packing Co
   Farmingdale, NY 800-286-6487
Lakeside Foods Inc.
   Plainview, MN 507-534-3141
Lakeside Foods Inc.
   Manitowoc, WI 800-466-3834
Lakeside Packing Company
   Harrow, ON. 519-738-2314
Lodi Canning Co
   Lodi, WI 608-592-4236
Majestic Foods
   Huntington, NY 631-424-9444
Mccall Farms
   Effingham, SC. 800-277-2012
Meridian Foods New Inc
   Eaton, IN. 765-396-3344
Miami Purveyors Inc
   Miami, FL. 800-966-6328
Milroy Canning Company
   Milroy, IN 765-629-2221
Monterey Mushrooms Inc
   Watsonville, CA 800-333-6874
Monticello Canning Company
   Crossville, TN
Musco Family Olive Co
   Tracy, CA 800-523-9828
Nation Wide Canning Ltd.
   Cottam, ON. 519-839-4831
Neil Jones Food Company
   Vancouver, WA 800-291-3862
New Era Canning Company
   New Era, MI 231-861-2151
New Harvest Foods
   Washington, DC 920-822-2578
Nickabood's Inc
   Los Angeles, CA. 213-746-1541
NORPAC Foods Inc
   Salem, OR
Northwest Packing Co
   Vancouver, WA 800-543-4356
Pacific Coast Producers
   Lodi, CA 877-618-4776
Paradise Products Corporation
   Boca Raton, FL 800-826-1235

Pastene Co LTD
   Canton, MA 781-298-3397
Patterson Frozen Foods
   Patterson, CA 209-892-2611
Produits Ronald
   St. Damase, QC. 800-465-0118
Pure Food Ingredients
   Verona, WI 800-355-9601
Ralph Sechler & Son Inc
   St Joe, IN. 800-332-5461
Red Gold Inc.
   Elwood, IN 866-729-7187
Red River Commodities Inc
   Fargo, ND 800-437-5539
Ron Son Foods Inc
   Swedesboro, NJ 856-241-7333
San Antonio Farms
   Platteville, WI 800-236-1119
Seneca Foods Corp
   Marion, NY 315-926-8100
Simplot Food Group
   Boise, ID 800-572-7783
Sun Harvest Foods Inc
   San Diego, CA 619-661-0909
Sun-Brite Canning
   Kingsville, ON 519-326-9033
Thomas Canning/Maidstone
   Maidstone, ON 519-737-1531
Tolteca Foodservice
   Norcross, GA 800-541-6835
Truitt Bros Inc
   Salem, OR. 800-547-8712
Unilever Food Solutions
   Englewood Cliffs, NJ
United Canning Corporation
   North Lima, OH 216-549-9807
Weil's Food Processing
   Wheatley, ON 519-825-4572
Wornick Company
   Cincinnati, OH 800-860-4555

Carrot

Boskovich Farms Inc
   Oxnard, CA 805-487-2299
De Bruyn Produce Company
   Ponpano Beach, FL. 800-733-9177
Dehydrates Inc
   Hewlett, NY 800-983-4443
Del Monte Fresh Produce Inc.
   Coral Gables, FL. 800-950-3683
Earthbound Farm
   San Jn Bautista, CA 800-690-3200
Exeter Produce
   Exeter, ON. 519-235-0141
F & S Produce Co Inc
   Vineland, NJ 800-886-3316
Fresh Express, Inc.
   Salinas, CA 800-242-5472
Grimmway Farms
   Bakersfield, CA 800-301-3101
Hanover Foods Corp
   Hanover, PA 717-632-6000
JES Foods
   Cleveland, OH 216-883-8987
Just Tomatoes
   Westley, CA. 800-537-1985
KERN Ridge Growers LLC
   Arvin, CA 661-854-3141
Kuhlmann's Market Gardens & Greenhouses
   Edmonton, AB 780-475-7500
Local Roots Farms
   Burt, NY 716-946-3198
Miss Scarlett's Flowers
   Juneau, AK 800-345-6734
National Frozen Foods Corp
   Seattle, WA 206-322-8900
New Harvest Foods
   Washington, DC 920-822-2578
Patterson Frozen Foods
   Patterson, CA 209-892-2611
Pictsweet Co
   Bells, TN. 731-663-7600
Pioneer Growers
   Belle Glade, FL. 229-243-9306
R.C. McEntire & Company
   Columbia, SC 803-799-3388
Ripon Pickle Co Inc
   Ripon, WI 920-748-7110
Rousseau Farming Co
   Phoenix, AZ 623-936-7100
Smith Frozen Foods Inc
   Weston, OR 541-566-3515

Product Categories / Fruits & Vegetables: Cauliflower

Strathroy Foods
   Strathroy, ON 519-245-4600
Twin City Foods Inc.
   Stanwood, WA 206-515-2400
Vegetable Juices Inc
   Chicago, IL 888-776-9752

Baby
Sales USA
   Salado, TX 800-766-7344

Canned
Arbre Farms Inc
   Walkerville, MI 231-873-3337
Emerling International Foods
   Buffalo, NY 716-833-7381
Hanover Foods Corp
   Hanover, PA 717-632-6000
New Harvest Foods
   Washington, DC 920-822-2578

Dehydrated
Advanced Spice & Trading
   Carrollton, TX 800-872-7811
Tova Industries LLC
   Louisville, KY 888-532-8682

Frozen
Arbre Farms Inc
   Walkerville, MI 231-873-3337
Emerling International Foods
   Buffalo, NY 716-833-7381
Hanover Foods Corp
   Hanover, PA 717-632-6000
National Frozen Foods Corp
   Seattle, WA 206-322-8900
Paris Foods Corporation
   Trappe, MD 410-200-9595
Pictsweet Co
   Bells, TN 731-663-7600
Smith Frozen Foods Inc
   Weston, OR 541-566-3515
Strathroy Foods
   Strathroy, ON 519-245-4600
Twin City Foods Inc.
   Stanwood, WA 206-515-2400
Vegetable Juices Inc
   Chicago, IL 888-776-9752

Organic
Seneca Foods Corp
   Princeville, IL 309-385-4301

Peeled
Chiquita Brands LLC.
   Fort Lauderdale, FL 954-924-5700
Rousseau Farming Co
   Phoenix, AZ 623-936-7100

with Greens
Boskovich Farms Inc
   Oxnard, CA 805-487-2299

Cauliflower
Al Pete Meats
   Muncie, IN 765-288-8817
Crown Packing Company
   Salinas, CA 831-424-2067
Earthbound Farm
   San Jn Bautista, CA 800-690-3200
EDCO Food Products Inc
   Hobart, WI 800-255-3768
Exeter Produce
   Exeter, ON 519-235-0141
F & S Produce Co Inc
   Vineland, NJ 800-886-3316
Great American Appetizers
   Nampa, ID 800-282-4834
Lake Erie Frozen Foods Co
   Ashland, OH 800-766-8501
Long Island Cauliflower Assn
   Riverhead, NY 631-727-2212
Mike & Jean's Berry Farm
   Mt Vernon, WA 360-424-7220
Paradise Products Corporation
   Boca Raton, FL 800-826-1235
Patterson Frozen Foods
   Patterson, CA 209-892-2611

Pictsweet Co
   Bells, TN 731-663-7600
Ripon Pickle Co Inc
   Ripon, WI 920-748-7110
Sargent and Greenleaf
   Nicholasville, KY 800-826-7652
Snowcrest Packer
   Abbotsford, BC 800-265-3686
Tanimura Antle Inc
   Salinas, CA 800-772-4542
Vegetable Juices Inc
   Chicago, IL 888-776-9752

Canned
Emerling International Foods
   Buffalo, NY 716-833-7381
Paradise Products Corporation
   Boca Raton, FL 800-826-1235
Seneca Foods Corp
   Marion, NY 315-926-8100

Frozen
Al Pete Meats
   Muncie, IN 765-288-8817
Emerling International Foods
   Buffalo, NY 716-833-7381
Great American Appetizers
   Nampa, ID 800-282-4834
Paris Foods Corporation
   Trappe, MD 410-200-9595
Pictsweet Co
   Bells, TN 731-663-7600
Snowcrest Packer
   Abbotsford, BC 800-265-3686

Celery
Boskovich Farms Inc
   Oxnard, CA 805-487-2299
Crown Packing Company
   Salinas, CA 831-424-2067
Dehydrates Inc
   Hewlett, NY 800-983-4443
Earthbound Farm
   San Jn Bautista, CA 800-690-3200
F & S Produce Co Inc
   Vineland, NJ 800-886-3316
JES Foods
   Cleveland, OH 216-883-8987
Leach Farms Inc
   Berlin, WI 920-361-1880
Michigan Celery Cooperative
   Hudsonville, MI 616-669-1250
Michigan Freeze Pack
   Hart, MI 231-873-2175
Nature Quality
   San Martin, CA 408-683-2182
Pioneer Growers
   Belle Glade, FL 229-243-9306
R.C. McEntire & Company
   Columbia, SC 803-799-3388
State Garden Inc.
   Chelsea, MA
Sure-Fresh Produce Inc
   Santa Maria, CA 888-423-5379
Tanimura Antle Inc
   Salinas, CA 800-772-4542
Teixeira Farms, Inc.
   Santa Maria, CA 805-928-3801
Tri-Counties Packing Company
   Salinas, CA 831-422-7841

Canned
Emerling International Foods
   Buffalo, NY 716-833-7381
Sure-Fresh Produce Inc
   Santa Maria, CA 888-423-5379

Dehydrated
Advanced Spice & Trading
   Carrollton, TX 800-872-7811
Emerling International Foods
   Buffalo, NY 716-833-7381
Tova Industries LLC
   Louisville, KY 888-532-8682
Unique Ingredients LLC
   Gold Canyon, AZ 480-983-2498

Frozen
Emerling International Foods
   Buffalo, NY 716-833-7381
Nature Quality
   San Martin, CA 408-683-2182
Paris Foods Corporation
   Trappe, MD 410-200-9595
Sure-Fresh Produce Inc
   Santa Maria, CA 888-423-5379
Vegetable Juices Inc
   Chicago, IL 888-776-9752

Sticks
R.C. McEntire & Company
   Columbia, SC 803-799-3388

Cherries
Agvest
   Cleveland, OH 216-464-3737
Bob Gordon & Associates
   Oak Park, IL 708-524-9611
Bridenbaugh Orchards
   Martinsburg, PA 814-793-2364
Brothers International Food Corporation
   Rochester, NY 585-343-3007
Burnette Foods
   Elk Rapids, MI 231-264-8116
Cahoon Farms
   Wolcott, NY 315-594-9610
Cal Harvest Marketing Inc
   Hanford, CA 559-582-4494
California Fruit Processors
   Stockton, CA 209-931-1760
Castella Imports Inc
   Brentwood, NY 631-231-5500
Chelan Fresh Marketing
   Chelan, WA 509-682-2591
Cherry Central Cooperative, Inc.
   Traverse City, MI 231-946-1860
Cherry Hill Orchards
   Lancaster, PA 717-872-9311
Cherry Hut
   Traverse City, MI 888-882-4431
Cherry Lane Frozen Fruits
   Vineland Station, ON 877-243-7796
Chief Wenatchee
   Wenatchee, WA 509-662-5197
Christopher Ranch LLC
   Gilroy, CA 408-847-1100
Chukar Cherries
   Prosser, WA 800-624-9544
Coloma Frozen Foods Inc
   Coloma, MI 800-642-2723
Delta Packing
   Lodi, CA 209-334-1023
Diamond Fruit Growers
   Hood River, OR 541-354-5300
Earthbound Farm
   San Jn Bautista, CA 800-690-3200
Fruit Acres Farm Market and U-Pick
   Coloma, MI 269-208-3591
Giumarra Companies
   Los Angeles, CA 213-627-2900
Gl Mezzetta Inc
   American Canyon, CA 800-941-7044
Gray & Company
   Hart, MI 800-551-6009
Harner Farms
   State College, PA 814-237-7919
Honee Bear Canning
   Lawton, MI 800-626-2327
J H Verbridge & Son Inc
   Williamson, NY 315-589-2366
Just Tomatoes
   Westley, CA 800-537-1985
Kalustyan
   New York, NY 800-352-3451
L & S Packing Co
   Farmingdale, NY 800-286-6487
Leroux Creek
   Hotchkiss, CO 877-970-5670
Mason County Fruit Packers Cooperative
   Hart, MI 231-873-7504
Meduri Farms
   Dallas, OR 877-388-8800
Miss Scarlett's Flowers
   Juneau, AK 800-345-6734
Natural Foods Inc
   Toledo, OH 419-537-1711
Niagara Foods
   Middleport, NY 716-735-7722

Product Categories / Fruits & Vegetables: Chicory

North Bay Produce Inc
   Traverse City, MI 231-946-1941
Oneonta Starr Ranch Growers
   Wenatchee, WA. 509-663-2191
Oregon Cherry Growers Inc
   Salem, OR
Oregon Fruit Products Co
   Salem, OR 800-394-9333
Pandol Brothers Inc
   Delano, CA 661-725-3755
Paradise Inc
   Plant City, FL 813-752-1155
Paradise Products Corporation
   Boca Raton, FL. 800-826-1235
Peterson Farms Inc
   Shelby, MI 231-861-0119
Price Co
   Yakima, WA 509-966-4110
Purity Products
   Plainview, NY 800-256-6102
Reinhart Foods
   Toronto, ON 416-645-4910
Smeltzer Orchard Co
   Frankfort, MI 231-882-4421
Snowcrest Packer
   Abbotsford, BC. 800-265-3686
Stadelman Fruit LLC
   Zillah, WA 509-829-5145
Symms Fruit Ranch Inc
   Caldwell, ID 208-459-4821
Terri Lynn Inc
   Elgin, IL 800-323-0775
Timber Crest Farms
   Healdsburg, CA 888-766-4233
Trinity Fruit Sale Co
   Fresno, CA 559-433-3777
Triple D Orchards Inc
   Empire, MI 231-326-5174
Unique Ingredients LLC
   Gold Canyon, AZ 480-983-2498
Yakima Fresh
   Yakima, WA 509-248-5770

Canned

Arbre Farms Inc
   Walkerville, MI 231-873-3337
Bob Gordon & Associates
   Oak Park, IL 708-524-9611
Burnette Foods
   Elk Rapids, MI 231-264-8116
Emerling International Foods
   Buffalo, NY. 716-833-7381
Honee Bear Canning
   Lawton, MI 800-626-2327
L & S Packing Co
   Farmingdale, NY 800-286-6487
Oregon Cherry Growers Inc
   Salem, OR
Oregon Fruit Products Co
   Salem, OR 800-394-9333
Paradise Products Corporation
   Boca Raton, FL. 800-826-1235
Triple D Orchards Inc
   Empire, MI 231-326-5174
Truitt Bros Inc
   Salem, OR. 800-547-8712
Unique Ingredients LLC
   Gold Canyon, AZ 480-983-2498

Dried

American Importing Co.
   Minneapolis, MN 855-273-0466
Atwater Foods
   Lyndonville Orleans, NY 585-765-2639
Bedemco Inc
   White Plains, NY 914-683-1119
King Arthur Flour
   Norwich, VT. 800-827-6836
Setton International Foods
   Commack, NY 800-227-4397
South Bend Chocolate Co
   South Bend, IN 800-301-4961

Frozen

Agvest
   Cleveland, OH 216-464-3737
Arbre Farms Inc
   Walkerville, MI 231-873-3337
Cahoon Farms
   Wolcott, NY 315-594-9610
Cherry Lane Frozen Fruits
   Vineland Station, ON 877-243-7796
Coloma Frozen Foods Inc
   Coloma, MI. 800-642-2723
Emerling International Foods
   Buffalo, NY. 716-833-7381
Fruithill Inc
   Yamhill, OR 503-662-3926
Great Lakes Packing Co
   Kewadin, MI. 231-264-5561
Honee Bear Canning
   Lawton, MI 800-626-2327
J H Verbridge & Son Inc
   Williamson, NY 315-589-2366
Leelanau Fruit Co
   Peshawbestown, MI 231-271-3514
Mason County Fruit Packers Cooperative
   Hart, MI 231-873-7504
Muir Copper Canyon Farms
   Salt Lake City, UT 800-564-0949
Niagara Foods
   Middleport, NY 716-735-7722
Norfood Cherry Growers
   Simcoe, ON. 519-426-5784
Oregon Cherry Growers Inc
   Salem, OR
Oregon Fruit Products Co
   Salem, OR 800-394-9333
Smeltzer Orchard Co
   Frankfort, MI 231-882-4421
Snowcrest Packer
   Abbotsford, BC. 800-265-3686
Townsend Farms Inc
   Fairview, OR 503-666-1780
Triple D Orchards Inc
   Empire, MI 231-326-5174
Unique Ingredients LLC
   Gold Canyon, AZ 480-983-2498

Maraschino

Bells Foods International
   Gervais, OR. 503-390-1425
Bob Gordon & Associates
   Oak Park, IL 708-524-9611
Eden Processing
   Poplar Grove, IL 815-765-2000
Emerling International Foods
   Buffalo, NY. 716-833-7381
Gl Mezzetta Inc
   American Canyon, CA 800-941-7044
Gray & Company
   Hart, MI. 800-551-6009
Johnson Foods, Inc. - Cannery Plant
   Sunnyside, WA 509-837-4188
L & S Packing Co
   Farmingdale, NY 800-286-6487
Metzger Specialty Brands
   New York, NY 212-957-0055
Oregon Cherry Growers Inc
   Salem, OR
Pacific Choice Brands
   Fresno, CA 559-476-3581
Paradise Products Corporation
   Boca Raton, FL. 800-826-1235
Purity Products
   Plainview, NY 800-256-6102
Reinhart Foods
   Toronto, ON 416-645-4910
Seneca Foods Corp
   Marion, NY 315-926-8100
Unique Ingredients LLC
   Gold Canyon, AZ 480-983-2498

Sweet

Peterson Farms Inc
   Shelby, MI 231-861-0119
Royal Ridge Fruits
   Royal City, WA 509-346-1520

Tart

Cherry Hill Orchards
   Lancaster, PA. 717-872-9311
Fruit Belt Canning Inc
   Lawrence, MI 269-674-3939
Royal Ridge Fruits
   Royal City, WA 509-346-1520
South Bend Chocolate Co
   South Bend, IN 800-301-4961

Chicory

Whole Herb Co
   Sonoma, CA 707-935-1077

Chives

SupHerb Farms
   Turlock, CA 800-787-4372
Vegetable Juices Inc
   Chicago, IL 888-776-9752

Citrus Fruits

Armistead Citrus Company
   Mesa, AZ. 480-830-2491
Brooks Tropicals Inc
   Homestead, FL 800-327-4833
Brothers International Food Corporation
   Rochester, NY. 585-343-3007
Conoley Citrus Packers Inc
   Winter Garden, FL 407-656-3300
Corona College Heights
   Riverside, CA 951-351-7880
Crown Processing Company
   Cerritos, CA 562-865-0293
Del Monte Fresh Produce Inc.
   Coral Gables, FL. 800-950-3683
Di Mare Fresh Inc
   Fort Worth, TX 817-385-3000
DNE World Fruit Sales
   Fort Pierce, FL 800-327-6676
Dundee Citrus Growers Assn
   Dundee, FL. 800-447-1574
Dundee Groves
   Dundee, FL. 800-294-2266
Evans Properties
   Vero Beach, FL 772-234-2410
Fillmore Piru Citrus
   Piru, CA 805-521-1781
Golden River Fruit Company
   Vero Beach, FL 772-562-8610
Haines City Citrus Growers
   Haines City, FL. 800-327-6676
Heller Brothers Packing Corp
   Winter Garden, FL 855-543-5537
Hunt Brothers Cooperative
   Lake Wales, FL 863-676-1411
Magnolia Citrus Assn
   Porterville, CA 559-784-4455
Mixon Fruit Farms Inc
   Bradenton, FL. 800-608-2525
North Bay Produce Inc
   Traverse City, MI 231-946-1941
Oneonta Starr Ranch Growers
   Wenatchee, WA. 509-663-2191
Orange Cove-Sanger Citrus
   Orange Cove, CA 559-626-4453
P R Farms Inc
   Clovis, CA 559-299-0201
Reed Lang Farms
   Rio Hondo, TX 956-748-2354
Shields Date Garden
   Indio, CA. 800-414-2555
Sun Groves Inc
   Safety Harbor, FL 800-672-6438
Sun Pacific
   Pasadena, CA 213-612-9957
Tony Vitrano Company
   Jessup, MD 800-481-3784
Visalia Citrus Packing Group
   Woodlake, CA. 559-564-3351
Wileman Brothers & Elliott Inc
   Cutler, CA. 559-528-4772
Wonderful Citrus
   Mission, TX 956-205-7300
Yokohl Packing Co
   Lindsay, CA 559-562-1327

Peels

Con Yeager Spice Co
   Zelienople, PA. 800-222-2460
Crown Processing Company
   Cerritos, CA 562-865-0293
Paradise Inc
   Plant City, FL 813-752-1155
Vita-Pakt Citrus Products Co
   Covina, CA 888-684-8272

Citrus Peel Products

Eden Processing
   Poplar Grove, IL 815-765-2000

Product Categories / Fruits & Vegetables: Coconut & Coconut Products

Fmali Herb
  Santa Cruz, CA 831-423-7913
Vita-Pakt Citrus Products Co
  Covina, CA 888-684-8272

Coconut & Coconut Products

Alpha Health
  Burnaby, BC 888-826-9625
American Key Food Products Inc
  Closter, NJ 877-263-7539
Baker's Coconut
  East Hanover, NJ 855-535-5648
Blue Marble Brands
  Providence, RI 888-534-0246
Coconut Beach
  Bonita, CA
Commodities Marketing Inc
  Clarksburg, NJ 732-516-0700
Eden Processing
  Poplar Grove, IL 815-765-2000
Emerling International Foods
  Buffalo, NY 716-833-7381
Hawaii Candy Inc
  Honolulu, HI 800-303-2507
Hearty Naturals
  West McLean, VA 513-443-2789
Hialeah Products Co
  Hollywood, FL 800-923-3379
L & M Bakery
  Riverside, NJ 888-887-1335
Marx Brothers Inc
  Birmingham, AL 800-633-6376
Maverick Brands, LLC
  Palo Alto, CA 424-571-7230
Mehaffies Pies
  Dayton, OH 800-289-7437
Miramar Fruit Trading Company
  Doral, FL 305-883-4774
Munkijo
  Irvine, CA 949-861-2798
Olde Tyme Mercantile
  Arroyo Grande, CA 805-489-7991
Organics Unlimited
  San Diego, CA 619-710-0658
Premier Organics
  Oakland, CA 866-237-8688
Red V Foods
  Buford, GA 770-729-8983
Reinhart Foods
  Toronto, ON 416-645-4910
Rv Industries
  Buford, GA 770-729-8983
Sally Lane's Candy Farm
  Paris, TN 731-642-5801
Spicy Sense
  Kearny, NJ 718-790-0070
White-Stokes Company
  Chicago, IL 800-978-6537
Wildly Organic
  Silver Bay, MN 800-945-3801

Desiccated & Shredded

Commodities Marketing Inc
  Clarksburg, NJ 732-516-0700
Emerling International Foods
  Buffalo, NY 716-833-7381
International Coconut Corp
  Elizabeth, NJ 908-289-1555
King Arthur Flour
  Norwich, VT 800-827-6836
Loghouse Foods
  Minneapolis, MN 763-546-8395
Organic Planet
  San Francisco, CA 415-765-5590
Rv Industries
  Buford, GA 770-729-8983
Service Packing Company
  Vancouver, BC 604-681-0264
Setton International Foods
  Commack, NY 800-227-4397

Dried

Bedemco Inc
  White Plains, NY 914-683-1119
Hialeah Products Co
  Hollywood, FL 800-923-3379
King Arthur Flour
  Norwich, VT 800-827-6836
To Your Health Sprouted Flour Co., Inc.
  Floyd, VA 540-283-9589

Frozen

Emerling International Foods
  Buffalo, NY 716-833-7381

Processed

Hialeah Products Co
  Hollywood, FL 800-923-3379

Collard Greens

Earthbound Farm
  San Jn Bautista, CA 800-690-3200
Emerling International Foods
  Buffalo, NY 716-833-7381
Oxford Frozen Foods
  Oxford, NS 902-447-2100
Pictsweet Co
  Bells, TN 731-663-7600
Seabrook Brothers & Sons
  Seabrook, NJ 856-455-8080

Canned & Frozen

Paris Foods Corporation
  Trappe, MD 410-200-9595
Pictsweet Co
  Bells, TN 731-663-7600
Seabrook Brothers & Sons
  Seabrook, NJ 856-455-8080
Walter P Rawl & Sons Inc
  Pelion, SC 803-894-1900

Corn

A. Lassonde Inc.
  Rougemont, QC 866-552-7643
Abbott & Cobb Inc
  Feasterville, PA 800-345-7333
Christopher Ranch LLC
  Gilroy, CA 408-847-1100
Coutts Specialty Foods Inc
  Boxborough, MA 800-919-2952
Dehydrates Inc
  Hewlett, NY 800-983-4443
Didion Milling Inc
  Johnson Creek, WI 920-348-6816
DuPont Pioneer
  Johnston, IA 515-535-5954
F & S Produce Co Inc
  Vineland, NJ 800-886-3316
Fruit Acres Farm Market and U-Pick
  Coloma, MI 269-208-3591
Furmano's Foods
  Northumberland, PA 800-952-1111
John Copes Food Products
  Hanover, PA 800-888-4646
Just Tomatoes
  Westley, CA 800-537-1985
Lakeside Foods Inc.
  Plainview, MN 507-534-3141
Miss Scarlett's Flowers
  Juneau, AK 800-345-6734
National Frozen Foods Corp
  Seattle, WA 206-322-8900
Natural Way Mills Inc
  Middle River, MN 218-222-3677
New Harvest Foods
  Washington, DC 920-822-2578
NSG Transport Inc
  Gothenburg, NE 308-537-7191
Paradise Products Corporation
  Boca Raton, FL 800-826-1235
Pioneer Growers
  Belle Glade, FL 229-243-9306
Pop Art Snacks
  Salt Lake City, UT 801-983-7470
Produits Ronald
  St. Damase, QC 800-465-0118
Roberts Seed
  Axtell, NE 308-743-2565
Smith Frozen Foods Inc
  Weston, OR 541-566-3515
Sno-Pac Foods Inc
  Caledonia, MN 800-533-2215
Snowcrest Packer
  Abbotsford, BC 800-265-3686
Sonne
  Wahpeton, ND 800-727-6663
Subco Foods Inc
  Sheboygan, WI 800-473-0757
Symons Frozen Foods
  Centralia, WA 360-736-1321
Twin City Foods Inc.
  Stanwood, WA 206-515-2400
Unique Ingredients LLC
  Gold Canyon, AZ 480-983-2498
Vegetable Juices Inc
  Chicago, IL 888-776-9752
Veronica Foods Inc
  Oakland, CA 800-370-5554
Z&S Distributing
  Fresno, CA 800-467-0788

Canned

A. Lassonde Inc.
  Rougemont, QC 866-552-7643
Carriere Foods Inc
  Saint-Denis-Sur-Richelie, QC 450-787-3411
Emerling International Foods
  Buffalo, NY 716-833-7381
Lakeside Foods Inc.
  Plainview, MN 507-534-3141
Lakeside Foods Inc.
  Manitowoc, WI 800-466-3834
Lodi Canning Co
  Lodi, WI 608-592-4236
New Harvest Foods
  Washington, DC 920-822-2578
Paradise Products Corporation
  Boca Raton, FL 800-826-1235
Produits Ronald
  St. Damase, QC 800-465-0118
SEW Friel
  Queenstown, MD 410-827-8841

Canned & Frozen

Seneca Foods Corp
  Princeville, IL 309-385-4301

Corn-on-the-Cob

A. Lassonde Inc.
  Rougemont, QC 866-552-7643
AgriNorthwest
  Kennewick, WA 509-734-1195
Emerling International Foods
  Buffalo, NY 716-833-7381
National Frozen Foods Corp
  Seattle, WA 206-322-8900
Pictsweet Co
  Bells, TN 731-663-7600
Produits Ronald
  St. Damase, QC 800-465-0118
Smith Frozen Foods Inc
  Weston, OR 541-566-3515
Twin City Foods Inc.
  Stanwood, WA 206-515-2400

Frozen

Bennett's Apples & Cider
  Ancaster, ON 905-648-6878
National Frozen Foods Corp
  Seattle, WA 206-322-8900
Pictsweet Co
  Bells, TN 731-663-7600
Smith Frozen Foods Inc
  Weston, OR 541-566-3515
Twin City Foods Inc.
  Stanwood, WA 206-515-2400
Vessey & Co Inc
  Holtville, CA 760-356-0130

Frozen

Lakeside Foods Inc.
  Plainview, MN 507-534-3141
Lakeside Foods Inc.
  Manitowoc, WI 800-466-3834
Lisa's Organics
  Carnelian Bay, CA 877-584-5711
Lodi Canning Co
  Lodi, WI 608-592-4236
Ocean Mist Farms
  Castroville, CA 831-633-2144
Paris Foods Corporation
  Trappe, MD 410-200-9595
Smith Frozen Foods Inc
  Weston, OR 541-566-3515
Snowcrest Packer
  Abbotsford, BC 800-265-3686
Symons Frozen Foods
  Centralia, WA 360-736-1321
Zuccaro Produce
  Columbia Heights, MN 612-333-1122

Product Categories / Fruits & Vegetables: Cranberries

Stored
Acme Steak & Seafood
  Youngstown, OH 800-686-2263
Seneca Foods Corp
  Marion, NY 315-926-8100

Sweet
Christopher Ranch LLC
  Gilroy, CA 408-847-1100
New Harvest Foods
  Washington, DC 920-822-2578
T.S. Smith & Sons
  Bridgeville, DE 302-337-8271

Cranberries
Rainsweet Inc
  Salem, OR 800-363-4293

Crushed
Baldwin Richardson Foods
  Oakbrook Terrace, IL 866-644-2732
Clofine Dairy Products Inc
  Linwood, NJ 609-653-1000
Emerling International Foods
  Buffalo, NY 716-833-7381

Crysanthemums
Heritage Farms Dairy
  Murfreesboro, TN 615-895-2790

Cucumber
Abbott & Cobb Inc
  Feasterville, PA 800-345-7333
Ben B. Schwartz & Sons
  Detroit, MI 313-841-8300
Carson City Pickle Company
  Carson City, MI 989-584-3148
Cates Addis Company
  Parkton, NC 800-423-1883
Earthbound Farm
  San Jn Bautista, CA 800-690-3200
F & S Produce Co Inc
  Vineland, NJ 800-886-3316
Giumarra Companies
  Los Angeles, CA 213-627-2900
Nash Produce
  Nashville, NC 800-334-3032
Pacific Collier Fresh Company
  Immokalee, FL 800-226-7274
Rene Produce Dist
  Rio Rico, AZ 520-281-0806
Russo Farms
  Vineland, NJ 856-692-5942
United Pickles
  Bronx, NY 718-933-6060
United With Earth
  Berkeley, CA 510-210-4359
Vegetable Juices Inc
  Chicago, IL 888-776-9752
Wholesum Family Farms
  Nogales, AZ 520-281-9233
Wildcat Produce
  McGrew, NE 308-783-2438
Z&S Distributing
  Fresno, CA 800-467-0788

for Pickling
Bissett Produce Company
  Spring Hope, NC 800-849-5073
Rick's Picks
  Brooklyn, NY 212-358-0428

Dates
Alya Foods
  North Brunswick, NJ 917-495-0815
American Importing Co.
  Minneapolis, MN 855-273-0466
Amport Foods
  St. Paul, MN 800-236-1119
Bard Valley Medjool Date Growers
  Yuma, AZ 928-726-0901
Bautista Family Organic Date
  Mecca, CA 760-396-2337
Date Lady Inc.
  Springfield, MO 417-414-2282
Desert Valley Date
  Coachella, CA 760-398-0999
Double Date Packing
  Coachella, CA 760-398-8900
Emerling International Foods
  Buffalo, NY 716-833-7381
Hadley's Date Gardens
  Thermal, CA 760-399-5191
Kalustyan
  New York, NY 800-352-3451
Lee Andersons
  Coachella, CA 760-398-3441
Marin Food Specialties
  Byron, CA 925-634-6126
New Organics
  Kenwood, CA 734-677-5570
Noour Inc.
  Huntington Beach, CA 800-621-1378
Nut Factory
  Spokane Valley, WA 888-239-5288
Peter Rabbit Farms
  Coachella, CA 760-398-0136
Reinhart Foods
  Toronto, ON 416-645-4910
Royal Medjool Date Gardens
  Bard, CA 760-572-0524
Sahara Date Company
  Vienna, VA 703-745-7463
Service Packing Company
  Vancouver, BC 604-681-0264
Setton International Foods
  Commack, NY 800-227-4397
Shields Date Garden
  Indio, CA 800-414-2555
Sunfood
  El Cajon, CA 888-729-3663
Sweet Pillar
  Newport Beach, CA 310-913-7261
Terri Lynn Inc
  Elgin, IL 800-323-0775
Timber Crest Farms
  Healdsburg, CA 888-766-4233
To Your Health Sprouted Flour Co., Inc.
  Floyd, VA 540-283-9589
United With Earth
  Berkeley, CA 510-210-4359

Dehydrated
Abbotsford Growers Ltd.
  Abbotsford, BC 604-864-0022
Advanced Spice & Trading
  Carrollton, TX 800-872-7811
Agvest
  Cleveland, OH 216-464-3737
Amport Foods
  St. Paul, MN 800-236-1119
Associated Fruit Company
  Phoenix, OR 541-535-1787
Atlantic Blueberry
  Hammonton, NJ 609-561-8600
Bay Cities Produce Co Inc
  San Leandro, CA 510-346-4943
California Fruit and Tomato Kitchens
  Modesto, CA 209-574-9407
Caltex Foods
  Canoga Park, CA 800-522-5839
Carolina Blueberry Co-Op Assn
  Garland, NC 910-588-4220
Century Blends LLC
  Hunt Valley, MD 410-771-6606
Chazy Orchards
  Chazy, NY 518-846-7171
Cherry Central Cooperative, Inc.
  Traverse City, MI 231-946-1860
Cherry Hill Orchards
  Lancaster, PA 717-872-9311
Chooljian Bros Packing Co
  Sanger, CA 559-875-5501
Chukar Cherries
  Prosser, WA 800-624-9544
Congdon Orchards Inc.
  Yakima, WA 509-966-4440
Cooperative Elevator Co
  Pigeon, MI 800-968-0601
Crane & Crane Inc
  Brewster, WA 509-689-3447
Del Rey Packing
  Del Rey, CA 559-888-2031
Fig Garden Packing Inc
  Fresno, CA 559-271-9000
Fine Dried Foods Intl
  Santa Cruz, CA 831-426-1413
Hialeah Products Co
  Hollywood, FL 800-923-3579
Larsen Farms
  Hamer, ID 208-374-5592
Made In Nature
  Boulder, CO 800-906-7426
Mayfield Farms and Nursery
  Athens, TN 423-746-9859
Mercer Processing
  Modesto, CA 209-529-0150
Oxford Frozen Foods
  Oxford, NS 902-447-2100
Paisano Food Products
  Elk Grove Village, IL 800-672-4726
Powder Pure
  The Dalles, OR 541-298-4800
Red River Foods Inc
  Richmond, VA 804-320-1800
Reinhart Foods
  Toronto, ON 416-645-4910
RFi Ingredients
  Blauvelt, NY 800-962-7663
Serv-Agen Corporation
  Cherry Hill, NJ 856-663-6966
Shields Date Garden
  Indio, CA 800-414-2555
Smeltzer Orchard Co
  Frankfort, MI 231-882-4421
Solana Gold Organics
  Sebastopol, CA 800-459-1121
Terri Lynn Inc
  Elgin, IL 800-323-0775
Timber Crest Farms
  Healdsburg, CA 888-766-4233
Tova Industries LLC
  Louisville, KY 888-532-8682
Tru-Blu Cooperative Associates
  New Lisbon, NJ 609-894-8717
True Blue Farms
  Grand Junction, MI 877-654-2400
Ursula's Island Farms Company
  Seattle, WA 206-762-3113
Valley View Packing Co
  Yuba City, CA 530-673-7356
Washington Potato Company
  Pasco, WA 800-897-2726
Wenda America Inc
  Naperville, IL 844-999-3632
White Oaks Frozen Foods
  Merced, CA 209-725-9492
Zuccaro Produce
  Columbia Heights, MN 612-333-1122

Freeze Dried
Advanced Spice & Trading
  Carrollton, TX 800-872-7811
Oregon Freeze Dry, Inc.
  Albany, OR 541-926-6001
RFi Ingredients
  Blauvelt, NY 800-962-7663
Setton International Foods
  Commack, NY 800-227-4397
SupHerb Farms
  Turlock, CA 800-787-4372
Unique Ingredients LLC
  Gold Canyon, AZ 480-983-2498
Van Drunen Farms
  Momence, IL 815-472-3100

Dipping Fruit

Confectioners'
Baldwin Richardson Foods
  Oakbrook Terrace, IL 866-644-2732
Bella Viva Orchards
  Hughson, CA 800-552-8218
Terri Lynn Inc
  Elgin, IL 800-323-0775

Dried & Dehydrated Fruits

Dehydrated Fruit
Agvest
  Cleveland, OH 216-464-3737
American Nut & Chocolate Co
  Boston, MA 800-797-6887
Amport Foods
  St. Paul, MN 800-236-1119
Bautista Family Organic Date
  Mecca, CA 760-396-2337
Casados Farms
  Ohkay Owingeh, NM 505-852-2433

Product Categories / Fruits & Vegetables: Dried & Dehydrated Fruits

Century Blends LLC
   Hunt Valley, MD 410-771-6606
Chaucer Foods, Inc. USA
   Forest Grove, OR
Cherry Central Cooperative, Inc.
   Traverse City, MI 231-946-1860
Chukar Cherries
   Prosser, WA 800-624-9544
Clic International Inc
   Laval, QC 450-669-2663
Desert Valley Date
   Coachella, CA 760-398-0999
Fig Garden Packing Inc
   Fresno, CA 559-271-9000
Fine Dried Foods Intl
   Santa Cruz, CA 831-426-1413
Freeman Industries
   Tuckahoe, NY 800-666-6454
Fruition Northwest LLC
   North Plains, OR. 503-880-5193
Golden Town Apple Products
   Rougemont, QC 866-552-7643
Gulf Pecan Company
   Mobile, AL 251-661-2931
Hialeah Products Co
   Hollywood, FL 800-923-3379
Hurd Orchards
   Holley, NY 585-638-8838
Kamish Food Products
   Chicago, IL 773-725-6959
Kozlowski Farms
   Forestville, CA 800-473-2767
Leroux Creek
   Hotchkiss, CO. 877-970-5670
Made In Nature
   Boulder, CO 800-906-7426
Maine Wild Blueberry Company
   Cherryfield, ME 800-243-4005
Mariani Packing Co.
   Vacaville, CA 707-452-2800
Marshall Ingredients
   Wolcott, NY 800-796-9353
Mercer Processing
   Modesto, CA. 209-529-0150
Niagara Foods
   Middleport, NY. 716-735-7722
Organic Planet
   San Francisco, CA 415-765-5590
Ramos Orchards
   Winters, CA 530-795-4748
Red River Foods Inc
   Richmond, VA. 804-320-1800
S&P Marketing, Inc.
   Maple Grove, MN. 763-559-0436
Sensible Foods LLC
   Santa Rosa, CA. 888-222-0170
Shields Date Garden
   Indio, CA. 800-414-2555
Silva International
   Momence, IL. 815-472-3535
Specialty Ingredients
   Buffalo Grove, IL 847-419-9595
Spice King Corporation
   Beverly Hills, CA 310-836-7770
Spreda Group
   Louisville, KY. 502-426-9411
Sunridge Farms
   Royal Oaks, CA 831-786-7000
Timber Crest Farms
   Healdsburg, CA 888-766-4233
Torn & Glasser
   Los Angeles, CA. 800-282-6887
Torn Ranch
   Novato, CA. 707-796-7800
Ursula's Island Farms Company
   Seattle, WA. 206-762-3113
Valley View Packing Co
   Yuba City, CA 530-673-7356
Van Drunen Farms
   Momence, IL. 815-472-3100
World Nutrition, Inc.
   Scottsdale, AZ. 800-548-2710
Yogavive
   Tiburon, CA. 415-366-6226

Desiccated Fruit

Fig Garden Packing Inc
   Fresno, CA 559-271-9000
Hialeah Products Co
   Hollywood, FL 800-923-3379
Kozlowski Farms
   Forestville, CA 800-473-2767

Leroux Creek
   Hotchkiss, CO. 877-970-5670
Maine Wild Blueberry Company
   Cherryfield, ME 800-243-4005
Ramos Orchards
   Winters, CA 530-795-4748
San Joaquin Figs Inc
   Fresno, CA 559-224-4963
Spreda Group
   Louisville, KY. 502-426-9411

Dried Fruit

Agrexco USA
   Jamaica, NY 718-481-8700
Amalgamated Produce
   Bridgeport, CT 800-358-3808
American Food Ingredients Inc
   Oceanside, CA 760-967-6287
American Importing Co.
   Minneapolis, MN 855-273-0466
American Key Food Products Inc
   Closter, NJ. 877-263-7539
American Nuts Inc.
   Sylmar, CA 818-364-8855
American Spoon Foods Inc
   Petoskey, MI 888-735-6700
Amphora International
   Lake Forest, IL 888-380-4808
Amport Foods
   St. Paul, MN 800-236-1119
Ann's House of Nuts, Inc.
   Columbia, MD 410-309-6887
Atwater Foods
   Lyndonville Orleans, NY 585-765-2639
Aurora Products
   Orange, CT 800-398-1048
Azar Nut Co
   El Paso, TX 800-351-8178
Bazzini Holdings LLC
   Allentown, PA 610-366-1606
Bella Viva Orchards
   Hughson, CA 800-552-8218
Blueberry Store
   Grand Junction, MI. 877-654-2400
Boghosian Raisin Packing Co
   Fowler, CA 559-834-5348
Buchanan Hollow Nut Co
   Le Grand, CA 800-532-1500
Cal Ranch
   Concord, CA. 925-429-2900
California Fruit
   San Diego, CA 877-378-4811
California Fruit & Nut
   Gustine, CA. 888-747-8224
California Packing Company
   Olivehurst, CA 530-740-1040
Casados Farms
   Ohkay Owingeh, NM 505-852-2433
Christy Wild Blueberry Farms
   Amherst, NS 902-667-3013
Chukar Cherries
   Prosser, WA 800-624-9544
Cibo Vita
   Totowa, NJ 862-238-8020
Colorado Nut Co
   Denver, CO 800-876-1625
Creative Snacks Co LLC
   Greensboro, NC 336-668-4151
Dan-D Foods Ltd
   Richmond, BC 800-633-4788
Dardimans California
   Panorama City, CA 818-849-5770
Derco Foods Intl
   Fresno, CA 559-435-2664
Desert Valley Date
   Coachella, CA 760-398-0999
Diamond Foods
   Santa Cruz, CA 831-457-3200
Fannie May Fine Chocolate
   Oakdale, MN. 800-999-3629
Fine Dried Foods Intl
   Santa Cruz, CA 831-426-1413
Frontier Co-op
   Norway, IA 844-550-6200
Fruit d'Or
   Villeroy, QC 819-385-1126
Ganong Bros Ltd
   St. Stephen, NB. 888-270-8222
GNS Foods
   Arlington, TX. 817-795-4671
Gold Pure Food Products Co. Inc.
   Hempstead, NY. 800-422-4681

Golden Town Apple Products
   Rougemont, QC 866-552-7643
Hadley's Date Gardens
   Thermal, CA 760-399-5191
HealthBest
   San Marcos, CA 760-752-5230
Healthco Canada Enterprises
   Victoria, BC 877-468-2875
Heartland Ingredients LLC
   Troy, MO. 800-557-2621
Hialeah Products Co
   Hollywood, FL 800-923-3379
Hickory Harvest Foods
   Akron, OH. 800-448-6887
HP Schmid
   San Francisco, CA 415-765-5925
International Harvest Inc
   Mt Vernon, NY 800-277-4268
JF Braun & Sons Inc.
   Elizabeth, NJ 800-997-7177
Just Tomatoes
   Westley, CA. 800-537-1985
Kalustyan
   New York, NY 800-352-3451
Kamish Food Products
   Chicago, IL 773-725-6959
Kendall Frozen Fruits, Inc.
   Beverly Hills, CA 310-288-9920
King Nut Co
   Solon, OH 800-860-5464
Kiwi Kiss
   Boca Raton, FL
Kozlowski Farms
   Forestville, CA 800-473-2767
Krispy Kernels
   Quebec, QC. 877-791-9986
Leroux Creek
   Hotchkiss, CO. 877-970-5670
Made In Nature
   Boulder, CO 800-906-7426
Maine Wild Blueberry Company
   Cherryfield, ME 800-243-4005
Majestic Foods
   Huntington, NY 631-424-9444
Mariani Packing Co.
   Vacaville, CA 707-452-2800
Marx Brothers Inc
   Birmingham, AL. 800-633-6376
Mavuno Harvest
   Philadelphia, PA
Meduri Farms
   Dallas, OR. 877-388-8800
Mezza
   Lake Forest, IL 888-206-6054
Midwest Nut Co
   Minneapolis, MN 800-328-5502
Mountain High Organics
   New Milford, CT 860-210-7805
Natural Food Source
   Bethlehem, PA 610-997-0500
Natural Foods Inc
   Toledo, OH 419-537-1711
Natural Sins
   New York, NY
Nature's Bandits
   Riverside, CT 203-571-2040
Navitas Naturals
   Novato, CA 888-645-4282
New Century Snacks
   City of Commerce, CA. 800-688-6887
New Organics
   Kenwood, CA. 734-677-5570
Newtown Foods USA Inc
   Newtown, PA 215-579-2120
Niagara Foods
   Middleport, NY. 716-735-7722
Nimeks Organics
   Bethlehem, PA 610-997-0500
Nothing But The Fruit
   Concord, MA 978-341-1221
Nspired Natural Foods
   Boulder, CO 800-434-4246
Nut Factory
   Spokane Valley, WA 888-239-5288
Organically Grown Co
   Eugene, OR. 800-937-9677
Osage Pecan Co
   Butler, MO 800-748-8305
Pacific Fruit Processors
   Suite 600, CA 952-820-2518
Pacific Gold Marketing
   Arlington, TX. 817-795-4671

Product Categories / Fruits & Vegetables: Dried & Dehydrated Vegetables

Paradise Fruits NA
 Norwood, MA.....781-769-4900
Patsy's Candy
 Colorado Springs, CO.....866-372-8797
Primex International Trading
 Los Angeles, CA.....310-410-7100
Ramos Orchards
 Winters, CA.....530-795-4748
Raymond-Hadley Corporation
 Spencer, NY.....800-252-5220
Red River Foods Inc
 Richmond, VA.....804-320-1800
Regal Health Food
 Chicago, IL.....773-252-1044
Reinhart Foods
 Toronto, ON.....416-645-4910
Royal Ridge Fruits
 Royal City, WA.....509-346-1520
Service Packing Company
 Vancouver, BC.....604-681-0264
Setton Farms
 Terra Bella, CA.....559-535-6050
Setton International Foods
 Commack, NY.....800-227-4397
Shields Date Garden
 Indio, CA.....800-414-2555
Shoei Foods USA Inc
 Olivehurst, CA.....530-237-1295
Shoreline Fruit
 Traverse City, MI.....800-836-3972
Sigona's
 San Carlos, CA.....650-368-6992
Smeltzer Orchard Co
 Frankfort, MI.....231-882-4421
Snackerz
 Commerce, CA.....888-576-2253
Society Hill Snacks
 Philadelphia, PA.....800-595-0050
Solana Gold Organics
 Sebastopol, CA.....800-459-1121
Sole Grano LLC
 Fair Lawn, NJ.....201-797-7100
Specialty Commodities Inc
 Fargo, ND.....701-282-8222
Spreda Group
 Louisville, KY.....502-426-9411
Star Snacks
 Jersey City, NJ.....888-782-7688
Stretch Island Fruit
 Solana Beach, CA.....800-700-9687
Sun Empire Foods
 Kerman, CA.....800-252-4786
Sun-Maid Growers of California
 Kingsburg, CA.....559-896-8000
Sunridge Farms
 Royal Oaks, CA.....831-786-7000
Sunridge Farms Inc
 Salinas, CA.....831-755-1530
Sunsweet Growers Inc.
 Yuba City, CA.....800-417-2253
Swerseys Chocolate
 Brooklyn, NY.....718-497-8800
Terri Lynn Inc
 Elgin, IL.....800-323-0775
Timber Crest Farms
 Healdsburg, CA.....888-766-4233
Todd's
 Vernon, CA.....800-938-6337
Torn & Glasser
 Los Angeles, CA.....800-282-6887
Traina Foods Inc
 Patterson, CA.....209-892-5472
Trophy Nut Co
 Tipp City, OH.....800-219-9004
Tropical Foods
 Charlotte, NC.....800-438-4470
Tropical Foods
 Lithia Springs, GA.....800-544-3762
Tropical Nut Fruit & Bulk Cndy
 Lithia Springs, GA.....800-544-3762
Twenty First Century Snacks
 Ronkonkoma, NY.....800-975-2883
TyRy Inc
 Rocklin, CA.....800-322-6325
Unique Ingredients LLC
 Gold Canyon, AZ.....480-983-2498
Ursula's Island Farms Company
 Seattle, WA.....206-762-3113
Vacaville Fruit Co
 Vacaville, CA.....707-447-1085
Valley View Blueberries
 Vancouver, WA.....360-892-2839
Valley View Packing Co
 Yuba City, CA.....530-673-7356
Van Drunen Farms
 Momence, IL.....815-472-3100
Waymouth Farms Inc
 Minneapolis, MN.....800-527-0094
Weaver Nut Co. Inc.
 Ephrata, PA.....800-473-2688
Z Foods Inc
 Madera, CA.....888-400-1015

Fig

Fig Garden Packing Inc
 Fresno, CA.....559-271-9000
Kalustyan
 New York, NY.....800-352-3451
Natural Foods Inc
 Toledo, OH.....419-537-1711
Nut Factory
 Spokane Valley, WA.....888-239-5288
San Joaquin Figs Inc
 Fresno, CA.....559-224-4963
Timber Crest Farms
 Healdsburg, CA.....888-766-4233
Unique Ingredients LLC
 Gold Canyon, AZ.....480-983-2498

Freeze Dried

BCFoods
 Santa Rosa, CA.....707-547-1776
Brothers All Natural
 Rochester, NY.....877-842-7477
Chaucer Consumer Solutions
 Calabasas, CA
Crispy Green Inc.
 Fairfield, NJ.....973-679-4515
Homegrown Organic Farms
 Porterville, CA.....559-306-1750
Mercer Foods
 Modesto, CA.....209-529-0150
Oregon Freeze Dry, Inc.
 Albany, OR.....541-926-6001
Paradise Fruits NA
 Norwood, MA.....781-769-4900
Wolf Canyon Foods
 Carmel, CA.....831-626-1323

Dried & Dehydrated Vegetables

AgroCepia
 Miami, FL.....305-704-3488
Bautista Family Organic Date
 Mecca, CA.....760-396-2337
Emerling International Foods
 Buffalo, NY.....716-833-7381
Frontier Co-op
 Norway, IA.....844-550-6200
Healthco Canada Enterprises
 Victoria, BC.....877-468-2875
Hialeah Products Co
 Hollywood, FL.....800-923-3379
High Quality Organics
 Reno, NV.....775-971-8550
International Harvest Inc
 Mt Vernon, NY.....800-277-4268
Jain Americas Inc
 Columbus, OH.....888-473-7539
Just Tomatoes
 Westley, CA.....800-537-1985
Made In Nature
 Boulder, CO.....800-906-7426
Maine Coast Sea Vegetables
 Franklin, ME.....207-565-2907
Mills Brothers Intl
 Seattle, WA.....206-575-3000
Nimeks Organics
 Bethlehem, PA.....610-997-0500
RFi Ingredients
 Blauvelt, NY.....800-962-7663
Sensible Foods LLC
 Santa Rosa, CA.....888-222-0170
Specialty Ingredients
 Buffalo Grove, IL.....847-419-9595
Sun Ray International
 Davis, CA.....530-297-1688
Sunco & Frenchie
 Clifton, NJ.....973-478-1011
SupHerb Farms
 Turlock, CA.....800-787-4372
Traina Foods Inc
 Patterson, CA.....209-892-5472
Van Eeghen International Inc
 St Laurent, QC.....514-332-6455

Beet Powder

RFi Ingredients
 Blauvelt, NY.....800-962-7663
Seneca Foods Corp
 Marion, NY.....315-926-8100

Bell Peppers

Green

RFi Ingredients
 Blauvelt, NY.....800-962-7663

Red

RFi Ingredients
 Blauvelt, NY.....800-962-7663

Broccoli

Chopped

RFi Ingredients
 Blauvelt, NY.....800-962-7663

Cabbage Flakes

RFi Ingredients
 Blauvelt, NY.....800-962-7663

Celery Flakes

RFi Ingredients
 Blauvelt, NY.....800-962-7663

Dehydrated Vegetables

AgroCepia
 Miami, FL.....305-704-3488
American Food Ingredients Inc
 Oceanside, CA.....760-967-6287
Caltex Foods
 Canoga Park, CA.....800-522-5839
Dehydrates Inc
 Hewlett, NY.....800-983-4443
Freeman Industries
 Tuckahoe, NY.....800-666-6454
Garden Valley Corp
 Sutherlin, OR.....541-459-9565
Inland Empire Foods
 Riverside, CA.....888-452-3267
Larsen Farms
 Hamer, ID.....208-374-5592
Mercer Processing
 Modesto, CA.....209-529-0150
New Season Foods Inc
 Forest Grove, OR.....503-357-7124
Oregon Potato Co
 Boardman, OR.....800-336-6311
Paisano Food Products
 Elk Grove Village, IL.....800-672-4726
Sarant International Cmmdts
 Stony Brook, NY.....631-675-2875
Schiff Food Products Co Inc
 Totowa, NJ.....973-237-1990
Serv-Agen Corporation
 Cherry Hill, NJ.....856-663-6966
Silva International
 Momence, IL.....815-472-3535
South Mill
 Kennett Square, PA.....610-444-4800
Spice King Corporation
 Beverly Hills, CA.....310-836-7770
Two Guys Spice Company
 Jacksonville, FL.....800-874-5656
Unified Food Ingredients
 San Marcos, CA.....760-744-7225
Vauxhall Foods
 Vauxhall, AB.....403-654-2771
Washington Potato Company
 Pasco, WA.....800-897-2726
World Spice
 Roselle, NJ.....800-234-1060

Dried Chives

SupHerb Farms
 Turlock, CA.....800-787-4372

Eggplant

Setton International Foods
 Commack, NY.....800-227-4397

Product Categories / Fruits & Vegetables: Eggplant

Freeze Dried
American Food Ingredients Inc
  Oceanside, CA 760-967-6287
BCFoods
  Santa Rosa, CA 707-547-1776
Hanover Foods Corp
  Hanover, PA 717-632-6000
Ocean Mist Farms
  Castroville, CA 831-633-2144
Oregon Freeze Dry, Inc.
  Albany, OR 541-926-6001
RFi Ingredients
  Blauvelt, NY 800-962-7663
SupHerb Farms
  Turlock, CA 800-787-4372
Wolf Canyon Foods
  Carmel, CA 831-626-1323
Zuccaro Produce
  Columbia Heights, MN 612-333-1122

Leeks - Chopped
RFi Ingredients
  Blauvelt, NY 800-962-7663

Mushrooms
North American Reishi/Nammex
  Gibsons, BC 604-886-7799
South Mill
  Kennett Square, PA 610-444-4800

Mushroom Powder
Mushroom Harvest
  Athens, OH 740-448-7376

Onion

Dehydrated
Advanced Spice & Trading
  Carrollton, TX 800-872-7811
American Key Food Products Inc
  Closter, NJ 877-263-7539
Emerling International Foods
  Buffalo, NY 716-833-7381
Jain Americas Inc
  Columbus, OH 888-473-7539
Schiff Food Products Co Inc
  Totowa, NJ 973-237-1990
Swagger Foods Corp
  Vernon Hills, IL 847-913-1200

Granulated
Acme Steak & Seafood
  Youngstown, OH 800-686-2263
Basic American Foods
  Walnut Creek, CA 925-472-4000
Bottom Line Foods
  Pembroke Pines, FL 954-843-0562
Bryant Preserving Company
  Alma, AR 800-634-2413
Burnham & Morrill Co
  Portland, ME 800-813-2165
H.K. Canning
  Ventura, CA 805-652-1392
Hye Cuisine
  Del Rey, CA 559-834-3000
Les Aliments Livabec Foods
  Sherrington, QC 450-454-7971
Nor-Cliff Farms
  Port Colborne, ON 905-835-0808
Oxford Frozen Foods
  Oxford, NS 902-447-2100
Pacific Valley Foods Inc
  Bellevue, WA 425-643-1805
Seneca Foods Corp
  Princeville, IL 309-385-4301
Seneca Foods Corp
  Marion, NY 315-926-8100
Supreme Dairy Farms Co
  Warwick, RI 401-739-8180

for Dehydration
Ful-Flav-R Foods
  Alamo, CA 925-838-0300

Peas - Air-dried
Bryant Preserving Company
  Alma, AR 800-634-2413

Oxford Frozen Foods
  Oxford, NS 902-447-2100

Shallots - Freeze Dried
Oxford Frozen Foods
  Oxford, NS 902-447-2100
RFi Ingredients
  Blauvelt, NY 800-962-7663
SupHerb Farms
  Turlock, CA 800-787-4372

Soup Blend
Sentry Seasonings
  Elmhurst, IL 630-530-5370

Spinach Powder
RFi Ingredients
  Blauvelt, NY 800-962-7663

Tomatoes

Halves
Bryant Preserving Company
  Alma, AR 800-634-2413
Oxford Frozen Foods
  Oxford, NS 902-447-2100
Zuccaro Produce
  Columbia Heights, MN 612-333-1122

Tomato Powder
Bryant Preserving Company
  Alma, AR 800-634-2413

Eggplant
Buona Vita Inc
  Bridgeton, NJ 856-453-7972
Castella Imports Inc
  Brentwood, NY 631-231-5500
Dolce Nonna
  Whitestone, NY 718-767-3501
Dominex
  St Augustine, FL 904-810-2132
Giumarra Companies
  Los Angeles, CA 213-627-2900
L & S Packing Co
  Farmingdale, NY 800-286-6487
Michigan Freeze Pack
  Hart, MI 231-873-2175
Miss Scarlett's Flowers
  Juneau, AK 800-345-6734
Ocean Mist Farms
  Castroville, CA 831-633-2144
Peter Rabbit Farms
  Coachella, CA 760-398-0136
Rene Produce Dist
  Rio Rico, AZ 520-281-0806
Russo Farms
  Vineland, NJ 856-692-5942
Turri's Italian Foods
  Roseville, MI 586-773-6010
Vegetable Juices Inc
  Chicago, IL 888-776-9752
Wholesum Family Farms
  Nogales, AZ 520-281-9233
Z&S Distributing
  Fresno, CA 800-467-0788

Figs
Fig Garden Packing Inc
  Fresno, CA 559-271-9000
Figamajigs
  San Mateo, CA 650-227-3830
Hadley's Date Gardens
  Thermal, CA 760-399-5191
Kalustyan
  New York, NY 800-352-3451
Made In Nature
  Boulder, CO 800-906-7426
Natural Foods Inc
  Toledo, OH 419-537-1711
New Organics
  Kenwood, CA 734-677-5570
North Bay Produce Inc
  Traverse City, MI 231-946-1941
Prima® Wawona
  Fresno, CA 559-787-8780
Service Packing Company
  Vancouver, BC 604-681-0264

Setton International Foods
  Commack, NY 800-227-4397
Sunfood
  El Cajon, CA 888-729-3663
Terri Lynn Inc
  Elgin, IL 800-323-0775
Timber Crest Farms
  Healdsburg, CA 888-766-4233
To Your Health Sprouted Flour Co., Inc.
  Floyd, VA 540-283-9589
United With Earth
  Berkeley, CA 510-210-4359
Valley Fig Growers
  Fresno, CA 559-237-3893

Frozen
FDI Inc
  Berkeley, IL 708-544-1880

Fire Roasted Vegetables
SupHerb Farms
  Turlock, CA 800-787-4372

Flowers - Edible
Fmali Herb
  Santa Cruz, CA 831-423-7913
Wild Hibiscus Flower Company
  Richford, VT 800-499-8490

Fresh Fruit
Bay Cities Produce Co Inc
  San Leandro, CA 510-346-4943
Belleharvest Sales Inc
  Belding, MI 800-452-7753
Cherry Hill Orchards
  Lancaster, PA 717-872-9311
Diamond Blueberry Inc
  Hammonton, NJ 609-561-3661
Dole Food Company, Inc.
  Thousand Oaks, CA 800-356-3111
Family Tree Farms
  Reedley, CA 866-352-8671
Florida Citrus
  Bartow, FL 863-537-3999
Glacier Foods
  Houston, TX 832-375-6300
Golden Town Apple Products
  Rougemont, QC 866-552-7643
Homegrown Organic Farms
  Porterville, CA 559-306-1750
Limehouse Produce Co
  North Charleston, SC 843-556-3400
Maui Gold Pineapple Company
  Pukalani, HI 808-877-3805
Muir Copper Canyon Farms
  Salt Lake City, UT 800-564-0949
Silver Creek Farms
  Twin Falls, ID 208-736-0829
Snokist Growers
  Yakima, WA 800-377-2857
Sun Rich Fresh Foods USA Inc
  Corona, CA 800-735-3801
Townsend Farms Inc
  Fairview, OR 503-666-1780
Washington Fruit & Produce Company
  Yakima, WA 509-457-6177

Fresh Vegetables
Bay Cities Produce Co Inc
  San Leandro, CA 510-346-4943
Boskovich Farms Inc
  Oxnard, CA 805-487-2299
Dole Food Company, Inc.
  Thousand Oaks, CA 800-356-3111
Glacier Foods
  Houston, TX 832-375-6300
Hanover Foods Corp
  Hanover, PA 717-632-6000
International Specialty Supply
  Cookeville, TN 931-526-1106
Lennox Farm
  Shelburne, ON 519-925-6444
Limehouse Produce Co
  North Charleston, SC 843-556-3400
Monterey Mushrooms Inc
  Watsonville, CA 800-333-6874
Muir Copper Canyon Farms
  Salt Lake City, UT 800-564-0949
Musco Family Olive Co
  Tracy, CA 800-523-9828

Product Categories / Fruits & Vegetables: Frozen Fruit

R.C. McEntire & Company
  Columbia, SC 803-799-3388
Silver Creek Farms
  Twin Falls, ID 208-736-0829
Western Pacific Produce
  Santa Barbara, CA 800-963-4451

Prepared

DNO Inc
  Columbus, OH 614-231-3601
Dole Food Company, Inc.
  Thousand Oaks, CA 800-356-3111
Risvold's Inc.
  Gardena, CA 323-770-2674

Frozen Fruit

Abbotsford Growers Ltd.
  Abbotsford, BC 604-864-0022
Agvest
  Cleveland, OH 216-464-3737
Bay Cities Produce Co Inc
  San Leandro, CA 510-346-4943
BCFoods
  Santa Rosa, CA 707-547-1776
Beta Pure Foods
  Santa Cruz, CA 831-685-6565
Blue Marble Brands
  Providence, RI 888-534-0246
Bonduelle North America
  Quebec, ON 450-787-3411
Cahoon Farms
  Wolcott, NY 315-594-9610
Carriere Foods Inc
  Saint-Denis-Sur-Richelie, QC 450-787-3411
Cherry Lane Frozen Fruits
  Vineland Station, ON 877-243-7796
Christy Wild Blueberry Farms
  Amherst, NS 902-667-3013
Clofine Dairy Products Inc
  Linwood, NJ 609-653-1000
Coloma Frozen Foods Inc
  Coloma, MI 800-642-2723
Decker Farms Inc
  Hillsboro, OR 503-628-1532
Diamond Blueberry Inc
  Hammonton, NJ 609-561-3661
E.W. Bowker Company
  Pemberton, NJ 609-894-9508
Eckert Cold Storage
  Manteca, CA 209-823-3181
Emerling International Foods
  Buffalo, NY 716-833-7381
Enfield Farms Inc
  Lynden, WA 360-354-2919
Ever Fresh Fruit Co
  Boring, OR 800-239-8026
Froozer
  Denver, CO 720-446-0145
Frozfruit Corporation
  Gardena, CA 310-217-1034
Fru-V
  Stouffville, ON
Fruit Belt Canning Inc
  Lawrence, MI 269-674-3939
Glacier Foods
  Houston, TX 832-375-6300
Golden Town Apple Products
  Rougemont, QC 866-552-7643
Grow-Pac
  Cornelius, OR 503-357-9691
Hartog Rahal Foods
  Norwood, NJ 201-750-0500
Inn Foods Inc
  Watsonville, CA 800-708-7836
Interfrost
  East Rochester, NY 585-381-0320
J H Verbridge & Son Inc
  Williamson, NY 315-589-2366
Kendall Frozen Fruits, Inc.
  Beverly Hills, CA 310-288-9920
KERR Concentrates Inc
  Salem, OR 800-910-5377
Maine Wild Blueberry Company
  Cherryfield, ME 800-243-4005
Majestic Foods
  Huntington, NY 631-424-9444
Mason County Fruit Packers Cooperative
  Hart, MI. 231-873-7504
Midwest Frozen Foods, Inc.
  Hanover Park, IL. 866-784-0123

Milne Fruit Products Inc
  Prosser, WA 509-786-2611
National Frozen Foods Corp
  Seattle, WA 206-322-8900
Natural Food Source
  Bethlehem, PA 610-997-0500
Nature's Touch
  Saint-Laurent, QC
Niagara Foods
  Middleport, NY 716-735-7722
Ocean Spray International
  Lakeville-Middleboro, MA 800-662-3263
Oregon Cherry Growers Inc
  Salem, OR
Oregon Fruit Products Co
  Salem, OR 800-394-9333
Overlake Foods
  Olympia, WA 800-683-1078
Pacific Coast Fruit Co
  Portland, OR 503-234-6411
Paris Foods Corporation
  Trappe, MD. 410-200-9595
Patterson Frozen Foods
  Patterson, CA 209-892-2611
Rainsweet Inc
  Salem, OR 800-363-4293
Small Planet Foods
  Minneapolis, MN 800-624-4123
Smeltzer Orchard Co
  Frankfort, MI 231-882-4421
Snowcrest Packer
  Abbotsford, BC 800-265-3686
Sparboe Foods Corp
  New Hampton, IA 641-394-3040
Stahlbush Island Farms Inc
  Corvallis, OR 541-757-1497
Sunrise Growers
  Placentia, CA 714-630-6292
Superior Foods
  Watsonville, CA 831-728-3691
Symons Frozen Foods
  Centralia, WA 360-736-1321
Tatangelo's Wholesale Fruit & Vegetables
  Woodbridge, ON 877-328-8503
Townsend Farms Inc
  Fairview, OR 503-666-1780
Triple D Orchards Inc
  Empire, MI 231-326-5174
Unique Ingredients LLC
  Gold Canyon, AZ 480-983-2498
VIP Sales Company
  Hayward, CA 866-536-8008
Webster Farms
  Cambridge, NS 800-507-8844
Willamette Valley Pie Co
  Salem, OR 503-362-8857

Berries

Cherry Central Cooperative, Inc.
  Traverse City, MI 231-946-1860
Froozer
  Denver, CO 720-446-0145
Royal Ridge Fruits
  Royal City, WA 509-346-1520
Small Planet Foods
  Minneapolis, MN 800-624-4123
Stahlbush Island Farms Inc
  Corvallis, OR 541-757-1497

Frozen Vegetables

Al Pete Meats
  Muncie, IN 765-288-8817
Appleton Produce Company
  Weiser, ID 208-414-3352
BCFoods
  Santa Rosa, CA 707-547-1776
Beta Pure Foods
  Santa Cruz, CA 831-685-6565
Bonduelle North America
  Quebec, ON 450-787-3411
Boskovich Farms Inc
  Oxnard, CA 805-487-2299
Bright Harvest Sweet Potato Co
  Clarksville, AR 800-793-7440
Carando Gourmet Frozen Foods
  Agawam, MA 888-227-2636
Carriere Foods Inc
  Saint-Denis-Sur-Richelie, QC 450-787-3411
Coloma Frozen Foods Inc
  Coloma, MI 800-642-2723

Dairy King Milk Farms/Foodservice
  Whitter, CA 800-900-6455
Deep Foods Inc
  Union, NJ 908-810-7500
Dickinson Frozen Foods
  Eagle, ID 800-886-4326
Eckert Cold Storage
  Manteca, CA 209-823-3181
Fresh Frozen Foods
  Jefferson, GA 800-277-9851
Froozer
  Denver, CO 720-446-0145
Fru-V
  Stouffville, ON
Fruit Belt Canning Inc
  Lawrence, MI 269-674-3939
GC Farms
  Morgan Hill, CA 408-778-0562
Glacier Foods
  Houston, TX 832-375-6300
Great American Appetizers
  Nampa, ID 800-282-4834
Hanover Foods Corp
  Hanover, PA 717-632-6000
Hermann Pickle Co
  Garrettsville, OH 800-245-2696
Inn Foods Inc
  Watsonville, CA 800-708-7836
Interfrost
  East Rochester, NY 585-381-0320
International Specialty Supply
  Cookeville, TN 931-526-1106
J G Townsend Jr & Co
  Georgetown, DE 302-856-2525
John Copes Food Products
  Hanover, PA 800-888-4646
Juanita's Foods
  Wilmington, CA 800-303-2965
Lakeside Foods Inc.
  Plainview, MN 507-534-3141
Lakeside Foods Inc.
  Manitowoc, WI 800-466-3834
Lennox Farm
  Shelburne, ON 519-925-6444
Lodi Canning Co
  Lodi, WI 608-592-4236
Meridian Foods New Inc
  Eaton, IN 765-396-3344
Miami Purveyors Inc
  Miami, FL 800-966-6328
Midwest Frozen Foods, Inc.
  Hanover Park, IL 866-784-0123
Milroy Canning Company
  Milroy, IN 765-629-2221
Monticello Canning Company
  Crossville, TN
National Frozen Foods Corp
  Seattle, WA 206-322-8900
Natural Food Source
  Bethlehem, PA 610-997-0500
Nature Quality
  San Martin, CA 408-683-2182
Niagara Foods
  Middleport, NY 716-735-7722
NORPAC Foods Inc
  Salem, OR
Oregon Potato Co
  Boardman, OR 800-336-6311
Paris Foods Corporation
  Trappe, MD 410-200-9595
Patterson Frozen Foods
  Patterson, CA 209-892-2611
Pictsweet Co
  Bells, TN 731-663-7600
Rainsweet Inc
  Salem, OR 800-363-4293
Red Gold Inc.
  Elwood, IN 866-729-7187
RFS Limited
  Roswell, GA 770-993-0030
San Antonio Farms
  Platteville, WI 800-236-1119
Seabrook Brothers & Sons
  Seabrook, NJ 856-455-8080
Seenergy Foods
  Woodbridge, ON 800-609-7674
Simplot Food Group
  Boise, ID 800-572-7783
Small Planet Foods
  Minneapolis, MN 800-624-4123
Smeltzer Orchard Co
  Frankfort, MI 231-882-4421

Product Categories / Fruits & Vegetables: Fruit

Smith Frozen Foods Inc
  Weston, OR 541-566-3515
Snowcrest Packer
  Abbotsford, BC 800-265-3686
Stahlbush Island Farms Inc
  Corvallis, OR 541-757-1497
Strathroy Foods
  Strathroy, ON 519-245-4600
Superior Foods
  Watsonville, CA 831-728-3691
SupHerb Farms
  Turlock, CA 800-787-4372
Symons Frozen Foods
  Centralia, WA 360-736-1321
Tatangelo's Wholesale Fruit & Vegetables
  Woodbridge, ON 877-328-8503
Trans Pecos Foods
  San Antonio, TX 210-228-0896
Twin City Foods Inc.
  Stanwood, WA 206-515-2400
Unique Ingredients LLC
  Gold Canyon, AZ 480-983-2498
VIP Sales Company
  Hayward, CA 866-536-8008
Washington Potato Company
  Pasco, WA 800-897-2726
Washington Rhubarb Grower Assn
  Sumner, WA 800-435-9911
Webster Farms
  Cambridge, NS 800-507-8844
Westin Foods
  Omaha, NE 800-228-6098
Wornick Company
  Cincinnati, OH 800-860-4555

Fruit

A. Gagliano Co Inc
  Milwaukee, WI 800-272-1516
Adobe Creek Packing Co Inc
  Kelseyville, CA 707-279-4204
Agvest
  Cleveland, OH 216-464-3737
American Yeast
  Memphis, TN 866-920-9885
Amport Foods
  St. Paul, MN 800-236-1119
Anastasia Confections Inc
  Orlando, FL 800-329-7100
Andros Foods North America
  Mount Jackson, VA 844-426-3767
Applewood Orchards Inc
  Deerfield, MI 800-447-3854
Arcor USA
  Coral Gables, FL 800-572-7267
Ariel Natural Foods
  Bellevue, WA 425-637-3345
Atlanta Bread Co.
  Smyrna, GA 800-398-3728
BCFoods
  Santa Rosa, CA 707-547-1776
Ben B. Schwartz & Sons
  Detroit, MI 313-841-8300
Bilgore's Groves
  Clearwater, FL 727-442-2171
Bissinger's Handcrafted Chocolatier
  St. Louis, MO 314-615-2400
Bob Gordon & Associates
  Oak Park, IL 708-524-9611
Bridenbaugh Orchards
  Martinsburg, PA 814-793-2364
Burnette Foods
  Elk Rapids, MI 231-264-8116
Cahoon Farms
  Wolcott, NY 315-594-9610
Casados Farms
  Ohkay Owingeh, NM 505-852-2433
Cascadian Farm Inc
  Sedro Woolley, WA 360-855-0542
Castellini Group
  Newport, KY 800-233-8560
Cherry Lane Frozen Fruits
  Vineland Station, ON 877-243-7796
Christy Wild Blueberry Farms
  Amherst, NS 902-667-3013
Chudleigh's
  Milton, ON 800-387-4028
Chukar Cherries
  Prosser, WA 800-624-9544
Cinnabar Specialty Foods Inc
  Prescott, AZ 866-293-6433
Citrosuco North America Inc
  Lake Wales, FL 800-356-4592

Classic Commissary
  Binghamton, NY 800-929-3486
Clements Foods Co
  Oklahoma City, OK 800-654-8355
Concannon Vineyard
  Livermore, CA 800-258-9866
Concord Foods, LLC
  Brockton, MA 508-580-1700
Country Fresh Inc
  Spring, TX 281-453-3300
Decas Cranberry Sales Inc
  Carver, MA 800-649-9811
Del Mar Food Products Corp
  Watsonville, CA 831-722-3516
Del Monte Fresh Produce Inc.
  Coral Gables, FL 800-950-3683
Delta Packing
  Lodi, CA 209-334-1023
Desert Valley Date
  Coachella, CA 760-398-0999
Diamond Blueberry Inc
  Hammonton, NJ 609-561-3661
Diamond Fruit Growers
  Hood River, OR 541-354-5300
DMH Ingredients Inc
  Libertyville, IL 847-362-9977
DNO Inc
  Columbus, OH 614-231-3601
E Waldo Ward & Son Marmalades
  Sierra Madre, CA 800-355-9273
E.D. Smith Foods Ltd
  Hamilton, ON 905-573-1207
E.W. Bowker Company
  Pemberton, NJ 609-894-9508
Earth Circle Organics
  Auburn, CA 877-922-3663
East Coast Fresh Cuts Inc
  Laurel, MD
Eckert Cold Storage
  Manteca, CA 209-823-3181
El Brands
  Ozark, AL 334-445-2828
Enfield Farms Inc
  Lynden, WA 360-354-2919
Ever Fresh Fruit Co
  Boring, OR 800-239-8026
Family Tree Farms
  Reedley, CA 866-352-8671
Fannie May Fine Chocolate
  Oakdale, MN 800-999-3629
Fernando C Pujals & Bros
  Guaynabo, PR 787-792-3080
Fillmore Piru Citrus
  Piru, CA 805-521-1781
Fine Dried Foods Intl
  Santa Cruz, CA 831-426-1413
Firestone Pacific Foods Co
  Vancouver, WA 360-695-9484
Flippin-Seaman Inc
  Tyro, VA 434-277-5828
Frieda's Inc
  Los Alamitos, CA 714-826-6100
Frozfruit Corporation
  Gardena, CA 310-217-1034
Fruit Fillings Inc
  Fresno, CA 800-995-4514
Ganong Bros Ltd
  St. Stephen, NB 888-270-8222
Gene Belk Briners
  Bloomington, CA 909-877-1819
Gl Mezzetta Inc
  American Canyon, CA 800-941-7044
Glacier Foods
  Houston, TX 832-375-6300
Graceland Fruit Inc
  Frankfort, MI 800-352-7181
Gray & Company
  Hart, MI 800-551-6009
Graysmarsh Berry Farm
  Sequim, WA 800-683-4367
Grouse Hunt Farm Inc
  Tamaqua, PA 570-467-2850
Grow-Pac
  Cornelius, OR 503-357-9691
Gurley's Foods
  Willmar, MN 800-426-7845
Hallcrest Vineyards
  Felton, CA 831-335-4441
Harris Farms Inc
  Coalinga, CA 800-311-6211
Harry & David
  Medford, OR 877-322-1200

Hartog Rahal Foods
  Norwood, NJ 201-750-0500
Heller Brothers Packing Corp
  Winter Garden, FL 855-543-5537
Henggeler Packing Company
  Fruitland, ID 208-452-4212
HH Dobbins Inc
  Lyndonville, NY 877-362-2467
Hialeah Products Co
  Hollywood, FL 800-923-3379
Hickory Farms
  Maumee, OH 800-753-8558
Indian Bay Frozen Foods
  Centreville, NL 709-678-2844
Indian Hollow Farms
  Richland Center, WI 800-236-3944
International Home Foods
  Parsippany, NJ 973-359-9920
J C Watson Co
  Parma, ID 208-722-5141
J H Verbridge & Son Inc
  Williamson, NY 315-589-2366
J. R. Simplot Co.
  Boise, ID 208-336-2110
Jersey Fruit Co-Op
  Glassboro, NJ 856-863-9100
JES Foods
  Cleveland, OH 216-883-8987
JF Braun & Sons Inc.
  Elizabeth, NJ 800-997-7177
Johnson Foods, Inc.
  Sunnyside, WA 509-837-4214
Joseph J. White
  Browns Mills, NJ 609-893-2332
K.B. Hall Ranch
  Ojai, CA 805-525-5875
Kalustyan
  New York, NY 800-352-3451
Kiona Vineyards Winery
  Benton City, WA 509-588-6716
Knight's Appleden Fruit LTD
  Colborne, ON 905-349-2521
Knouse Foods Co-Op Inc.
  Peach Glen, PA 717-677-8181
Kozlowski Farms
  Forestville, CA 800-473-2767
Krupka's Blueberries
  Fennville, MI 269-857-4278
L & S Packing Co
  Farmingdale, NY 800-286-6487
La Vigne Enterprises
  Fallbrook, CA 760-723-9997
Lee Andersons
  Coachella, CA 760-398-3441
Leroux Creek
  Hotchkiss, CO 877-970-5670
Liberty Orchards Co Inc
  Cashmere, WA 800-231-3242
Macrie Brothers
  Hammonton, NJ 609-561-6822
Made In Nature
  Boulder, CO 800-906-7426
Maine Wild Blueberry Company
  Cherryfield, ME 800-243-4005
Majestic Foods
  Huntington, NY 631-424-9444
Mange
  Somerville, MA 917-880-2104
Mariani Packing Co.
  Vacaville, CA 707-452-2800
Mason County Fruit Packers Cooperative
  Hart, MI 231-873-7504
Maui Gold Pineapple Company
  Pukalani, HI 808-877-3805
Mayer's Cider Mill
  Webster, NY 800-543-0043
Mayfield Farms and Nursery
  Athens, TN 423-746-9859
Mccartney Produce Co
  Paris, TN 731-642-2362
Mercer Processing
  Modesto, CA 209-529-0150
Midwest Blueberry Farms
  Holland, MI 616-399-2133
Mira International Foods
  East Brunswick, NJ 800-818-6472
Miramar Fruit Trading Company
  Doral, FL 305-883-4774
Moonlight Co
  Reedley, CA 559-638-7799
Naraghi Group
  Escalon, CA 209-579-5253

Product Categories / Fruits & Vegetables: Galangal

Nassau Candy Distributors
  Hicksville, NY 516-433-7100
National Flavors
  Kalamazoo, MI 800-525-2431
Natural Fruit Corp
  Hialeah, FL 305-887-7525
Nekta
  Auckland, ... 649-250-2789
New Century Snacks
  City of Commerce, CA 800-688-6887
New Era Canning Company
  New Era, MI 231-861-2151
New York Apple Sales Inc
  Glenmont, NY 888-477-6770
North American Blueberry Council
  Folsom, CA 800-824-6395
Northern Orcharad Co Inc
  Peru, NY 518-643-2367
Nutri Fruit
  Gresham, OR. 503-663-2680
Oneonta Starr Ranch Growers
  Wenatchee, WA. 509-663-2191
Orange Bang Inc
  Sylmar, CA 818-833-1000
Orange Cove-Sanger Citrus
  Orange Cove, CA 559-626-4453
Oregon Cherry Growers Inc
  Salem, OR
Oregon Fruit Products Co
  Salem, OR. 800-394-9333
Organically Grown Co
  Eugene, OR. 800-937-9677
Ouhlala Gourmet
  Coral Gables, FL. 305-774-7332
Pacific Coast Fruit Co
  Portland, OR. 503-234-6411
Pacific Trellis
  Reedley, CA 559-638-5100
Pacific Westcoast Foods
  Beaverton, OR. 800-874-9333
Palmer Candy Co
  Sioux City, IA 800-831-0828
Paradise Products Corporation
  Boca Raton, FL. 800-826-1235
Pavero Cold Storage
  Highland, NY 800-435-2994
Peaceful Fruits
  330-356-8515
Plaidberry Company
  Vista, CA 760-727-5403
Purity Products
  Plainview, NY. 800-256-6102
R M Lawton Cranberries Inc
  Middleboro, MA. 508-947-7465
Rainsweet Inc
  Salem, OR. 800-363-4293
Ramos Orchards
  Winters, CA 530-795-4748
Reed Lang Farms
  Rio Hondo, TX 956-748-2354
Regal Health Food
  Chicago, IL. 773-252-1044
Reinhart Foods
  Toronto, ON 416-645-4910
Reter Fruit
  Medford, OR. 541-772-9560
Rice Fruit Co
  Gardners, PA 800-627-3359
Russo Farms
  Vineland, NJ 856-692-5942
S A Carlson Inc
  Yakima, WA 509-965-8333
S Zitner Co
  Philadelphia, PA 215-229-9828
Sand Hill Berries
  Mt Pleasant, PA. 724-547-4760
Santanna Banana Company
  Harrisburg, PA 717-238-8321
SAPNA Foods
  Atlanta, GA. 404-589-0977
Satiety Winery & Cafe
  Davis, CA 530-757-2699
Scotian Gold
  Coldbrook, NS 888-726-8426
Shafer Lake Fruit Inc
  Hartford, MI 269-621-3194
Shields Date Garden
  Indio, CA. 800-414-2555
Signature Fruit
  Bloomingdale, IL 630-980-2481
Silver Palate Kitchens
  Cresskill, NJ 201-568-0110

Smeltzer Orchard Co
  Frankfort, MI 231-882-4421
Snackerz
  Commerce, CA 888-576-2253
Snowcrest Packer
  Abbotsford, BC. 800-265-3686
Solana Gold Organics
  Sebastopol, CA. 800-459-1121
SOPAKCO Foods
  Mullins, SC 800-276-9678
Southern Okie
  Edmond, OK 405-657-7765
Sparboe Foods Corp
  New Hampton, IA 641-394-3040
Specialty Food Association
  New York, NY 646-878-0301
Spreda Group
  Louisville, KY. 502-426-9411
Spring Ledge Farm Stand
  New London, NH 603-526-6253
Sun Groves Inc
  Safety Harbor, FL. 800-672-6438
Sundia Corp
  Oakland, CA 415-762-0600
Sunrise Growers
  Placentia, CA 714-630-6292
Sunsweet Growers Inc.
  Yuba City, CA. 800-417-2253
Surface Banana Company
  Parkersburg, WV. 304-485-2400
Sweet Candy Company
  Salt Lake City, UT 855-772-7720
T.S. Smith & Sons
  Bridgeville, DE. 302-337-8271
Tastee Apple
  Newcomerstown, OH 800-262-7753
Taylor Farms
  Salinas, CA 831-754-0471
Taylor Farms Pacific
  Tracy, CA 209-830-1086
Tejon Ranch Co
  Lebec, CA 661-248-3000
Tom Ringhausen Orchards
  Hardin, IL 800-258-6645
Tony Vitrano Company
  Jessup, MD. 800-481-3784
Trailblazer Foods
  Portland, OR. 800-777-7179
Trefethen Family Vineyards
  Napa, CA. 707-255-7700
Tri-Boro Fruit Co
  Fresno, CA 559-486-4141
Triple D Orchards Inc
  Empire, MI 231-326-5174
Trophy Nut Co
  Tipp City, OH 800-219-9004
Truitt Bros Inc
  Salem, OR. 800-547-8712
Tuscarora Organic Growers Cooperative
  Hustontown, PA 814-448-2173
United Marketing Exchange
  Delta, CO 970-874-3332
Ursula's Island Farms Company
  Seattle, WA. 206-762-3113
Valley Fig Growers
  Fresno, CA 559-237-3893
Valley View Blueberries
  Vancouver, WA. 360-892-2839
Valley View Packing Co
  Yuba City, CA. 530-673-7356
Varet Street Market
  Brooklyn, NY 718-302-0560
Vilore Foods Co Inc
  Laredo, TX 956-722-7190
Visalia Produce Sales
  Kingsburg, CA 559-897-6652
Warner Candy
  El Paso, TX 847-928-7200
Washington Fruit & Produce Company
  Yakima, WA 509-457-6177
Webster Farms
  Cambridge, NS 800-507-8844
Well-Pict Inc
  Watsonville, CA 831-722-3871
Wetherby Cranberry Company
  Warrens, WI 608-378-4813
Wiards Orchards Inc
  Ypsilanti, MI 734-390-9211
World Nutrition, Inc.
  Scottsdale, AZ. 800-548-2710
Yakima Fresh
  Yakima, WA 509-248-5770

Yokohl Packing Co
  Lindsay, CA 559-562-1327

Aseptic Packaged

Cherry Moon Farms
  San Diego, CA 800-580-2913

Cocktail

Emerling International Foods
  Buffalo, NY. 716-833-7381

Jarred or Cupped

Emerling International Foods
  Buffalo, NY. 716-833-7381
Keep Moving Inc.
  New York, NY
Kurtz Orchards Farms
  Niagra-on-the-Lake, ON. 905-468-2937

Salad

Risvold's Inc.
  Gardena, CA 323-770-2674

Galangal

Nickabood's Inc
  Los Angeles, CA. 213-746-1541

Garlic

Black Garlic
  Hayward, CA. 888-811-9065
California Garlic Co
  San Diego, CA 951-506-8883
Colonna Brothers Inc
  North Bergen, NJ 201-864-1115
Country Cupboard
  Lewisburg, PA 570-523-3211
Earthbound Farm
  San Jn Bautista, CA 800-690-3200
Emerling International Foods
  Buffalo, NY. 716-833-7381
Garlic Co
  Bakersfield, CA 661-393-4212
Miss Scarlett's Flowers
  Juneau, AK 800-345-6734
Obis One
  Blacksburg, VA. 609-202-9766
Stinking Rose, The
  San Francisco, CA 800-995-7674
Sunny Dell Foods Inc
  Oxford, PA 610-932-5164
SupHerb Farms
  Turlock, CA 800-787-4372
Vegetable Juices Inc
  Chicago, IL. 888-776-9752

Dehydrated

Bedemco Inc
  White Plains, NY 914-683-1119

Granulated

American Key Food Products Inc
  Closter, NJ. 877-263-7539
Emerling International Foods
  Buffalo, NY. 716-833-7381
Vegetable Juices Inc
  Chicago, IL. 888-776-9752

Ginger

Christopher Ranch LLC
  Gilroy, CA 408-847-1100
Christopher's Herb Shop
  Springville, UT 888-372-4372
Con Yeager Spice Co
  Zelienople, PA. 800-222-2460
Emerling International Foods
  Buffalo, NY. 716-833-7381
Ful-Flav-R Foods
  Alamo, CA 925-838-0300
Ginger People, The
  Marina, CA. 800-551-5284
International Glace
  Spokane, WA. 800-884-5041
Morris J Golombeck Inc
  Brooklyn, NY 718-284-3505
Paradise Inc
  Plant City, FL 813-752-1155
Schiff Food Products Co Inc
  Totowa, NJ 973-237-1990

Product Categories / Fruits & Vegetables: Glace

SupHerb Farms
  Turlock, CA 800-787-4372
Texas Coffee Co
  Beaumont, TX 800-259-3400
Triple Leaf Tea Inc
  S San Francisco, CA 800-552-7448
Ungerer & Co
  Lincoln Park, NJ 973-706-7381
Vegetable Juices Inc
  Chicago, IL 888-776-9752

Crystallized

Emerling International Foods
  Buffalo, NY 716-833-7381
King Arthur Flour
  Norwich, VT 800-827-6836
Organic Planet
  San Francisco, CA 415-765-5590
Setton International Foods
  Commack, NY 800-227-4397
Verdant Kitchen
  Norcross, GA 912-349-2958

Pickled

Paradise Inc
  Plant City, FL 813-752-1155

Glace

Dixie Dew Prods Co
  Erlanger, KY 800-867-8548
Fruit Fillings Inc
  Fresno, CA 800-995-4514
International Glace
  Spokane, WA 800-884-5041

Grape

Ballantine Produce Company
  Reedley, CA 559-875-2583
Brothers International Food Corporation
  Rochester, NY 585-343-3007
Cal Harvest Marketing Inc
  Hanford, CA 559-582-4494
Concannon Vineyard
  Livermore, CA 800-258-9866
Custom Produce Sales
  Parlier, CA 559-254-5800
Delta Packing
  Lodi, CA 209-334-1023
Fowler Packing Co
  Fresno, CA 559-834-5911
George W Saulpaugh & Son
  Germantown, NY 518-537-6500
Giumarra Companies
  Los Angeles, CA 213-627-2900
Hallcrest Vineyards
  Felton, CA 831-335-4441
Hillcrest Orchard
  Lake Placid, FL 865-397-5273
Jasmine Vineyards, Inc.
  Delano, CA 661-792-2141
Moonlight Co
  Reedley, CA 559-638-7799
Naraghi Group
  Escalon, CA 209-579-5253
Oneonta Starr Ranch Growers
  Wenatchee, WA 509-663-2191
Pacific Trellis
  Reedley, CA 559-638-5100
Pandol Brothers Inc
  Delano, CA 661-725-3755
Prima® Wawona
  Fresno, CA 559-787-8780
Royal Vista Marketing Inc
  Visalia, CA 559-636-9198
Satiety Winery & Cafe
  Davis, CA 530-757-2699
Spiech Farms Fruit & Floral
  Paw Paw, MI 269-657-1980
Spring Ledge Farm Stand
  New London, NH 603-526-6253
Tejon Ranch Co
  Lebec, CA 661-248-3000
Trefethen Family Vineyards
  Napa, CA 707-255-7700
Venture Vineyards
  Lodi, NY 888-635-6277
Z&S Distributing
  Fresno, CA 800-467-0788

Leaves

Castella Imports Inc
  Brentwood, NY 631-231-5500
Corfu Foods Inc
  Bensenville, IL 630-595-2510
Grecian Delight Foods Inc
  Elk Grove Village, IL 800-621-4387
Hye Cuisine
  Del Rey, CA 559-834-3000
Pacific Choice Brands
  Fresno, CA 559-476-3581
Setton International Foods
  Commack, NY 800-227-4397
Yergat Packing Co
  Fresno, CA 559-276-9180

Table

Anton Caratan & Son
  Bakersfield, CA 661-725-2575
Corrin Produce Sales
  Dinuba, CA 559-596-0517
Lucich Santos Farms
  Patterson, CA 209-892-6500
Peter Rabbit Farms
  Coachella, CA 760-398-0136
Richard Bagdasarian Inc
  Mecca, CA 760-396-2168
Satiety Winery & Cafe
  Davis, CA 530-757-2699
Sun Pacific
  Pasadena, CA 213-612-9957
Vincent B Zaninovich & Sons
  Richgrove, CA 661-725-2497
Z&S Distributing
  Fresno, CA 800-467-0788

Wine

Delta Packing
  Lodi, CA 209-334-1023
Galleano Winery
  Mira Loma, CA 951-685-5376
Kiona Vineyards Winery
  Benton City, WA 509-588-6716
Satiety Winery & Cafe
  Davis, CA 530-757-2699
Symms Fruit Ranch Inc
  Caldwell, ID 208-459-4821
Talbott Farms
  Palisade, CO 970-464-5656
Tejon Ranch Co
  Lebec, CA 661-248-3000
The Wine RayZyn Company
  Napa, CA 707-251-1600
Trefethen Family Vineyards
  Napa, CA 707-255-7700

Grapefruit

Agrexco USA
  Jamaica, NY 718-481-8700
Bautista Family Organic Date
  Mecca, CA 760-396-2337
Corona College Heights
  Riverside, CA 951-351-7880
DNE World Fruit Sales
  Fort Pierce, FL 800-327-6676
Dundee Groves
  Dundee, FL 800-294-2266
Gene's Citrus Ranch
  Palmetto, FL 888-723-2006
Golden River Fruit Company
  Vero Beach, FL 772-562-8610
Haines City Citrus Growers
  Haines City, FL 800-327-6676
Hale Indian River Groves
  Vero Beach, FL 800-562-4502
Heller Brothers Packing Corp
  Winter Garden, FL 855-543-5537
Hunt Brothers Cooperative
  Lake Wales, FL 863-676-1411
Lane Southern Orchards
  Fort Valley, GA 800-277-3224
Leroy Smith Inc
  Vero Beach, FL 772-569-2059
Reed Lang Farms
  Rio Hondo, TX 956-748-2354
Seald Sweet
  Vero Beach, FL 559-636-4400
Wonderful Citrus
  Mission, TX 956-205-7300

Pink

DNE World Fruit Sales
  Fort Pierce, FL 800-327-6676

White

DNE World Fruit Sales
  Fort Pierce, FL 800-327-6676

Guava

Brooks Tropicals Inc
  Homestead, FL 800-327-4833
Unique Ingredients LLC
  Gold Canyon, AZ 480-983-2498

Canned & Frozen

Emerling International Foods
  Buffalo, NY 716-833-7381
Unique Ingredients LLC
  Gold Canyon, AZ 480-983-2498

Kale

AeroFarms
  Newark, NJ 973-242-2495
Alive and Radiant
  Needham, MA 800-385-1417
Bowery Farming Inc.
  New York, NY
BrightFarms
  Irvington, NY 866-857-8745
Earthbound Farm
  San Jn Bautista, CA 800-690-3200
Emerling International Foods
  Buffalo, NY 716-833-7381
Plenty
  San Francisco, CA 650-735-3737
Rhythm Superfoods
  Austin, TX 512-441-5667
Seabrook Brothers & Sons
  Seabrook, NJ 856-455-8080

Fresh

80 Acres Farms
  Hamilton, OH 888-574-1569
Boskovich Farms Inc
  Oxnard, CA 805-487-2299

Frozen

Paris Foods Corporation
  Trappe, MD 410-200-9595
Vegetable Juices Inc
  Chicago, IL 888-776-9752

Kelp Products

Acadian Seaplants
  Dartmouth, NS 800-575-9100
Atlantic Laboratories Inc
  Waldoboro, ME 888-662-5357
Gum Technology Corporation
  Tucson, AZ 800-369-4867
Maine Coast Sea Vegetables
  Franklin, ME 207-565-2907
Silver Fern Chemical Inc
  Seattle, WA 866-282-3384

Kiwi

Giumarra Companies
  Los Angeles, CA 213-627-2900
Nekta
  Auckland, ... 649-250-2789
Oneonta Starr Ranch Growers
  Wenatchee, WA 509-663-2191
Royal Vista Marketing Inc
  Visalia, CA 559-636-9198
Setton International Foods
  Commack, NY 800-227-4397
Sun Pacific
  Pasadena, CA 213-612-9957
Unique Ingredients LLC
  Gold Canyon, AZ 480-983-2498
Viva Tierra
  Mt Vernon, WA 360-855-0566

Gold

Brandt Farms Inc
  Reedley, CA 559-638-6961

Product Categories / Fruits & Vegetables: Kohlrabi

Kohlrabi
Seneca Foods Corp
  Princeville, IL 309-385-4301

Kumquat
Paradise Products Corporation
  Boca Raton, FL 800-826-1235
Setton International Foods
  Commack, NY 800-227-4397
West Pak Avocado Inc
  Murrieta, CA 800-266-4414

Leek
Calif Watercress Inc
  Fillmore, CA 805-524-4808
SupHerb Farms
  Turlock, CA 800-787-4372
Sure-Fresh Produce Inc
  Santa Maria, CA 888-423-5379
VCPB Transportation
  Secaucus, NJ 201-770-0070
Vegetable Juices Inc
  Chicago, IL 888-776-9752

Lemon
Corona College Heights
  Riverside, CA 951-351-7880
Di Mare Fresh Inc
  Fort Worth, TX 817-385-3000
DNE World Fruit Sales
  Fort Pierce, FL 800-327-6676
Oneonta Starr Ranch Growers
  Wenatchee, WA 509-663-2191
Paradise Inc
  Plant City, FL 813-752-1155
Seald Sweet
  Vero Beach, FL 559-636-4400
Wonderful Citrus
  Mission, TX 956-205-7300
Z&S Distributing
  Fresno, CA 800-467-0788

Peels
Fmali Herb
  Santa Cruz, CA 831-423-7913

Lettuce
Ben B. Schwartz & Sons
  Detroit, MI 313-841-8300
Boskovich Farms Inc
  Oxnard, CA 805-487-2299
BrightFarms
  Irvington, NY 866-857-8745
Cal Harvest Marketing Inc
  Hanford, CA 559-582-4494
Club Chef LLC
  Covington, KY 859-578-3100
Crop One
  Oakland, CA
Crown Packing Company
  Salinas, CA 831-424-2067
Del Monte Fresh Produce Inc.
  Coral Gables, FL 800-950-3683
Earthbound Farm
  San Jn Bautista, CA 800-690-3200
F & S Produce Co Inc
  Vineland, NJ 800-886-3316
Fresh Express, Inc.
  Salinas, CA 800-242-5472
Hari Om Farms
  Eagleville, TN 615-368-7778
Live Gourmet
  Carpinteria, CA
R.C. McEntire & Company
  Columbia, SC 803-799-3388
Ready Pac Foods Inc
  Irwindale, CA 800-800-4088
Sales USA
  Salado, TX 800-766-7344
State Garden Inc.
  Chelsea, MA
Talley Farms
  Arroyo Grande, CA. 805-489-5400
Tanimura Antle Inc
  Salinas, CA 800-772-4542
Teixeira Farms, Inc.
  Santa Maria, CA 805-928-3801
Vegetable Juices Inc
  Chicago, IL 888-776-9752

Butterhead
Boston
Tanimura Antle Inc
  Salinas, CA 800-772-4542

Looseleaf
Green
80 Acres Farms
  Hamilton, OH 888-574-1569
Bowery Farming Inc.
  New York, NY
BrightFarms
  Irvington, NY 866-857-8745
Tanimura Antle Inc
  Salinas, CA 800-772-4542

Red
80 Acres Farms
  Hamilton, OH 888-574-1569
Bowery Farming Inc.
  New York, NY
Tanimura Antle Inc
  Salinas, CA 800-772-4542

Romaine
80 Acres Farms
  Hamilton, OH 888-574-1569
Bowery Farming Inc.
  New York, NY
Royce C. Bone Farms
  Nashville, NC 252-443-3773
Talley Farms
  Arroyo Grande, CA. 805-489-5400
Tanimura Antle Inc
  Salinas, CA 800-772-4542

Lime
Agri-Dairy Products
  Purchase, NY 914-697-9580
Brooks Tropicals Inc
  Homestead, FL 800-327-4833
DNE World Fruit Sales
  Fort Pierce, FL 800-327-6676
Hunt Brothers Cooperative
  Lake Wales, FL 863-676-1411
Key West Key Lime Pie Co
  Big Pine Key, FL. 877-882-7437
Shanley Farms
  Morro Bay, CA 805-323-6525
Wonderful Citrus
  Mission, TX 956-205-7300

Loganberries
KERR Concentrates Inc
  Salem, OR 800-910-5377

Mango
Brooks Tropicals Inc
  Homestead, FL 800-327-4833
Clofine Dairy Products Inc
  Linwood, NJ 609-653-1000
Commodities Marketing Inc
  Clarksburg, NJ 732-516-0700
Couture Farms
  Kettleman City, CA 559-386-9865
Earthbound Farm
  San Jn Bautista, CA 800-690-3200
Eckert Cold Storage
  Manteca, CA 209-823-3181
Just Tomatoes
  Westley, CA. 800-537-1985
Natural Foods Inc
  Toledo, OH 419-537-1711
North Bay Produce Inc
  Traverse City, MI 231-946-1941
Organic Planet
  San Francisco, CA 415-765-5590
Setton International Foods
  Commack, NY 800-227-4397
Simply Panache
  Hampton, VA 800-313-5613
Townsend Farms Inc
  Fairview, OR 503-666-1780
Unique Ingredients LLC
  Gold Canyon, AZ 480-983-2498

Dried
American Importing Co.
  Minneapolis, MN 855-273-0466
Bedemco Inc
  White Plains, NY 914-683-1119
Fine Dried Foods Intl
  Santa Cruz, CA 831-426-1413
Made In Nature
  Boulder, CO 800-906-7426
Mariani Packing Co.
  Vacaville, CA 707-452-2800
Sunfood
  El Cajon, CA. 888-729-3663
Sunridge Farms
  Royal Oaks, CA 831-786-7000

Melon
Del Monte Fresh Produce Inc.
  Coral Gables, FL 800-950-3683
Emerling International Foods
  Buffalo, NY. 716-833-7381
Giumarra Companies
  Los Angeles, CA. 213-627-2900

Balls
Frozen
Emerling International Foods
  Buffalo, NY. 716-833-7381

Cantaloupe
Couture Farms
  Kettleman City, CA. 559-386-9865
Earthbound Farm
  San Jn Bautista, CA 800-690-3200
F & S Produce Co Inc
  Vineland, NJ 800-886-3316
Hialeah Products Co
  Hollywood, FL 800-923-3379
Vessey & Co Inc
  Holtville, CA. 760-356-0130
Zuccaro Produce
  Columbia Heights, MN. 612-333-1122

Dried
Setton International Foods
  Commack, NY 800-227-4397

Honeydew
Couture Farms
  Kettleman City, CA. 559-386-9865
Turlock Fruit Co
  Turlock, CA 209-634-7207
Zuccaro Produce
  Columbia Heights, MN. 612-333-1122

Watermelon
Bryant Preserving Company
  Alma, AR 800-634-2413
F & S Produce Co Inc
  Vineland, NJ 800-886-3316
Zuccaro Produce
  Columbia Heights, MN. 612-333-1122

Seedless
Bissett Produce Company
  Spring Hope, NC. 800-849-5073

Miso
Great Eastern Sun Trading Co
  Asheville, NC 800-334-5809
Miyako Oriental Foods Inc
  Baldwin Park, CA 877-788-6476
Organic Gourmet
  Sherman Oaks, CA 800-400-7772

Mushrooms
Al Pete Meats
  Muncie, IN 765-288-8817
Alimentaire Whyte's Inc
  Laval, QC 866-420-9520
Basciani Foods Inc
  Avondale, PA 610-268-3610
Bob Gordon & Associates
  Oak Park, IL 708-524-9611
Buonitalia
  New York, NY 212-633-9090

Product Categories / Fruits & Vegetables: Mushrooms

Colonna Brothers Inc
  North Bergen, NJ 201-864-1115
Country Fresh Mushroom Co
  Toughkenamon, PA 610-268-3033
Crazy Jerrys Inc Kahuna-Sauces
  Woodstock, GA 800-347-2823
Cutone Specialty Foods
  Chelsea, MA 617-889-1122
Dong Kee Company
  Chicago, IL 312-225-6340
Emerling International Foods
  Buffalo, NY 716-833-7381
Flavor House, Inc.
  Adelanto, CA 760-246-9131
Fungus Among Us
  Snohomish, WA 360-568-3403
Giorgio Foods
  Temple, PA 800-220-2139
Giovanni's Appetizing Food Co
  Richmond, MI 586-727-9355
Gourmet's Finest
  Avondale, PA 610-268-6910
Great American Appetizers
  Nampa, ID 800-282-4834
Great Lakes Foods
  Menominee, MI 800-800-7492
H.K. Canning
  Ventura, CA 805-652-1392
Hanover Foods Corp
  Hanover, PA 717-632-6000
Health Concerns
  Oakland, CA 800-233-9355
Kitchen Pride Mushrooms Farm
  Gonzales, TX 830-540-4528
L & S Packing Co
  Farmingdale, NY 800-286-6487
L F Lambert Spawn Co
  Coatesville, PA 610-384-5031
L K Bowman
  Nottingham, PA 800-853-1919
Lake Erie Frozen Foods Co
  Ashland, OH 800-766-8501
Lee's Food Products
  Toronto, ON 416-465-2407
Les Aliments Livabec Foods
  Sherrington, QC 450-454-7971
Matador Processors
  Blanchard, OK 800-847-0797
Miss Scarlett's Flowers
  Juneau, AK 800-345-6734
Money's Mushrooms
  Vancouver, BC 800-669-7992
Monterey Mushrooms Inc
  Watsonville, CA 800-333-6874
Mushroom Co
  Cambridge, MD 410-221-8971
Nation Wide Canning Ltd.
  Cottam, ON 519-839-4831
North American Reishi/Nammex
  Gibsons, BC 604-886-7799
Ntc Marketing
  Williamsville, NY 800-333-1637
Om Mushrooms
  Carlsbad, CA 866-740-6874
Ostrom Mushrooms
  Olympia, WA 360-491-1410
Paradise Products Corporation
  Boca Raton, FL 800-826-1235
Phillips Gourmet Inc
  Kennett Square, PA 610-925-0520
Prairie Mushrooms
  Ardrossan, AB 780-467-3555
Rainsweet Inc
  Salem, OR 800-363-4293
Ron Son Foods Inc
  Swedesboro, NJ 856-241-7333
S.D. Mushrooms
  Avondale, PA 610-268-8082
Sabatino Truffles USA
  West Haven, CT 888-444-9971
Setton International Foods
  Commack, NY 800-227-4397
South Mill
  Kennett Square, PA 610-444-4800
Star Fine Foods
  Fresno, CA 559-498-2900
Sunny Dell Foods Inc
  Oxford, PA 610-932-5164
Superior Mushroom Farms
  Ardrossan, AB 866-687-2242
SupHerb Farms
  Turlock, CA 800-787-4372
Tiger Mushroom Farm
  Nanton, AB 403-646-2578
Unique Foods
  Raleigh, NC 919-779-5600
United Canning Corporation
  North Lima, OH 216-549-9807
VCPB Transportation
  Secaucus, NJ 201-770-0070
Vegetable Juices Inc
  Chicago, IL 888-776-9752

Beech

Country Fresh Mushroom Co
  Toughkenamon, PA 610-268-3033
Monterey Mushrooms Inc
  Watsonville, CA 800-333-6874
Phillips Gourmet Inc
  Kennett Square, PA 610-925-0520

Canned

Agrocan
  Ville St Laurent, QC 877-247-6226
Bob Gordon & Associates
  Oak Park, IL 708-524-9611
Dong Kee Company
  Chicago, IL 312-225-6340
Giorgio Foods
  Temple, PA 800-220-2139
Great Lakes Foods
  Menominee, MI 800-800-7492
Lee's Food Products
  Toronto, ON 416-465-2407
Money's Mushrooms
  Vancouver, BC 800-669-7992
Monterey Mushrooms Inc
  Watsonville, CA 800-333-6874
Mushroom Co
  Cambridge, MD 410-221-8971
Nation Wide Canning Ltd.
  Cottam, ON 519-839-4831
Ntc Marketing
  Williamsville, NY 800-333-1637
Paradise Products Corporation
  Boca Raton, FL 800-826-1235
Ron Son Foods Inc
  Swedesboro, NJ 856-241-7333
Shafer-Haggart
  Vancouver, BC 604-669-5512
Sunny Dell Foods Inc
  Oxford, PA 610-932-5164
Unique Foods
  Raleigh, NC 919-779-5600
United Canning Corporation
  North Lima, OH 216-549-9807

Chanterelle

Country Fresh Mushroom Co
  Toughkenamon, PA 610-268-3033
Emerling International Foods
  Buffalo, NY 716-833-7381

Criminis

Country Fresh Mushroom Co
  Toughkenamon, PA 610-268-3033
Giorgio Foods
  Temple, PA 800-220-2139
Ostrom Mushrooms
  Olympia, WA 360-491-1410
Phillips Gourmet Inc
  Kennett Square, PA 610-925-0520

Dehydrated

Emerling International Foods
  Buffalo, NY 716-833-7381
Nikken Foods
  St Louis, MO 314-881-5818
South Mill
  Kennett Square, PA 610-444-4800
Unique Ingredients LLC
  Gold Canyon, AZ 480-983-2498

Enokis

Country Fresh Mushroom Co
  Toughkenamon, PA 610-268-3033
Giorgio Foods
  Temple, PA 800-220-2139
Ostrom Mushrooms
  Olympia, WA 360-491-1410
Phillips Gourmet Inc
  Kennett Square, PA 610-925-0520

Fresh

Country Fresh Mushroom Co
  Toughkenamon, PA 610-268-3033
Giorgio Foods
  Temple, PA 800-220-2139

Frozen

Al Pete Meats
  Muncie, IN 765-288-8817
Giorgio Foods
  Temple, PA 800-220-2139
Great American Appetizers
  Nampa, ID 800-282-4834
Hanover Foods Corp
  Hanover, PA 717-632-6000
Lake Erie Frozen Foods Co
  Ashland, OH 800-766-8501
Matador Processors
  Blanchard, OK 800-847-0797
Monterey Mushrooms Inc
  Watsonville, CA 800-333-6874
Mushroom Co
  Cambridge, MD 410-221-8971
Paris Foods Corporation
  Trappe, MD 410-200-9595
Rainsweet Inc
  Salem, OR 800-363-4293

Lobster

Country Fresh Mushroom Co
  Toughkenamon, PA 610-268-3033

Maitakes

Country Fresh Mushroom Co
  Toughkenamon, PA 610-268-3033
Hardscrabble Enterprises
  Franklin, WV 304-358-2921
Phillips Gourmet Inc
  Kennett Square, PA 610-925-0520

Morel

Country Fresh Mushroom Co
  Toughkenamon, PA 610-268-3033
Emerling International Foods
  Buffalo, NY 716-833-7381

Oyster

Concord Farms
  Union City, CA 510-429-8855
Country Fresh Mushroom Co
  Toughkenamon, PA 610-268-3033
Emerling International Foods
  Buffalo, NY 716-833-7381
Giorgio Foods
  Temple, PA 800-220-2139
Ostrom Mushrooms
  Olympia, WA 360-491-1410
Phillips Gourmet Inc
  Kennett Square, PA 610-925-0520

Porcini

Country Fresh Mushroom Co
  Toughkenamon, PA 610-268-3033
Emerling International Foods
  Buffalo, NY 716-833-7381

Portobello

Country Fresh Mushroom Co
  Toughkenamon, PA 610-268-3033
Giorgio Foods
  Temple, PA 800-220-2139
Ostrom Mushrooms
  Olympia, WA 360-491-1410
Phillips Gourmet Inc
  Kennett Square, PA 610-925-0520

Shiitake

Baycliff Co Inc
  Garwood, NJ 866-772-7569
Concord Farms
  Union City, CA 510-429-8855
Country Fresh Mushroom Co
  Toughkenamon, PA 610-268-3033
Emerling International Foods
  Buffalo, NY 716-833-7381

Product Categories / Fruits & Vegetables: Mustard

Hardscrabble Enterprises
 Franklin, WV 304-358-2921
Monterey Mushrooms Inc
 Watsonville, CA 800-333-6874
Ostrom Mushrooms
 Olympia, WA 360-491-1410
Phillips Gourmet Inc
 Kennett Square, PA 610-925-0520
SupHerb Farms
 Turlock, CA 800-787-4372

Truffles

Buonitalia
 New York, NY 212-633-9090
Garland Truffles, Inc.
 Hillsborough, NC 919-732-3041

White

Country Fresh Mushroom Co
 Toughkenamon, PA 610-268-3033
Giorgio Foods
 Temple, PA 800-220-2139
Monterey Mushrooms Inc
 Watsonville, CA 800-333-6874
Ostrom Mushrooms
 Olympia, WA 360-491-1410
Phillips Gourmet Inc
 Kennett Square, PA 610-925-0520

Wild

Country Fresh Mushroom Co
 Toughkenamon, PA 610-268-3033
Grapevine Trading Company
 Santa Rosa, CA 800-469-6478

Wood Ear

Country Fresh Mushroom Co
 Toughkenamon, PA 610-268-3033

Mustard

Arbor Hill Grapery & Winery
 Naples, NY 800-554-7553
Ashman Manufacturing & Distributing Company
 Virginia Beach, VA 800-641-9924
Bauer's Mustard
 Flushing, NY 718-821-3570
Baumer Foods Inc
 Metairie, LA 504-482-5761
Beaverton Foods Inc
 Hillsboro, OR 800-223-8076
Boetje Foods Inc
 Rock Island, IL 877-726-3853
Booneway Farms
 Berea, KY 859-986-2636
Boston Spice & Tea Company
 Boston, VA 800-966-4372
Brad's Taste of New York
 Floral Park, NY 516-354-9004
Bread & Chocolate Inc
 Wells River, VT 800-524-6715
Buonitalia
 New York, NY 212-633-9090
Casa Visco
 Schenectady, NY 888-607-2823
Casually Gourmet
 New Haven, VT 800-639-7604
Cedarvale Food Products
 Toronto, ON 416-656-3330
Cherchies
 Malvern, PA 800-644-1980
Ciro Foods
 Pittsburgh, PA 412-771-9018
Clements Foods Co
 Oklahoma City, OK 800-654-8355
Coastal Classics
 Duxbury, MA 508-746-6058
Delicae Gourmet
 Tarpon Springs, FL 800-942-2502
Dorina So-Good Inc
 Union, IL 815-923-2144
East Shore Specialty Foods
 Hartland, WI 800-236-1069
Erba Food Products
 Brooklyn, NY 718-272-7700
Fischer & Wieser Spec Foods
 Fredericksburg, TX 877-861-0260
Ford's Gourmet Foods
 Raleigh, NC 800-446-0947
Fox Hollow
 Crestwood, KY 502-241-8621

G.E. Barbour
 Sussex, NB 506-432-2300
Garden Complements Inc
 Kansas City, MO 800-966-1091
Garlic Festival Foods
 Hollister, CA 888-427-5423
Gold Pure Food Products Co. Inc.
 Hempstead, NY 800-422-4681
Golden State Foods Corp
 Irvine, CA 949-247-8000
Grapevine Trading Company
 Santa Rosa, CA 800-469-6478
Grouse Hunt Farm Inc
 Tamaqua, PA 570-467-2850
GS Dunn & Company
 Hamilton, ON 905-522-0833
Heinz Portion Control
 Jacksonville, FL 904-695-1300
Hot Licks
 Spring Valley, CA 888-766-6468
International Home Foods
 Parsippany, NJ 973-359-9920
J.N. Bech
 Elk Rapids, MI 800-232-4583
KARI-Out Co
 White Plains, NY 800-433-8799
Kathy's Gourmet Specialties
 Mendocino, CA 707-937-1383
Kelchner's Horseradish
 Allentown, PA 800-424-1952
Knese Enterprise
 Bellerose, NY 516-354-9004
Koloa Rum Corp
 Kalaheo, HI 808-332-9333
Kozlowski Farms
 Forestville, CA 800-473-2767
Lounsbury Foods
 Toronto, ON 416-656-6330
Mad Will's Food Company
 Auburn, CA 888-275-9455
Mccutcheon Apple Products
 Frederick, MD 800-888-7537
Mizkan Americas Inc
 Kansas City, MO 800-323-4358
Morehouse Foods Inc
 City Of Industry, CA 888-297-9800
Mother's Mountain Pantry
 Falmouth, ME 800-440-9891
Mountainbrook of Vermont
 Jeffersonville, VT 802-644-1988
Mucky Duck Mustard Company
 Ferndale, MI 248-544-4610
Mutchler's Dakota Gold Mustard
 Spearfish, SD 605-642-8166
New Canaan Farms
 Dripping Springs, TX 800-727-5267
Northeast Kingdom Mustard Company
 Derby, VT 866-478-7388
Old Cavendish Products
 Cavendish, VT 800-536-7899
Olde Tyme Mercantile
 Arroyo Grande, CA 805-489-7991
Olds Products Co
 Pleasant Prairie, WI 262-947-3500
Paris Foods Corporation
 Trappe, MD 410-200-9595
Pemberton's Foods Inc
 Gray, ME 800-255-8401
Pictsweet Co
 Bells, TN 731-663-7600
Piknik Products Company
 Montgomery, AL 334-240-2218
Pilgrim Foods
 Great Neck, NY 516-466-0522
Plochman Inc
 Manteno, IL 800-843-4566
Purity Products
 Plainview, NY 800-256-6102
Quality Foods
 Qualicum Beach, BC 877-833-7890
Rapazzini Winery
 Gilroy, CA 800-842-6262
Red Pelican Food Products
 Detroit, MI 313-881-4095
Restaurant Lulu Gourmet Products
 San Francisco, CA 888-693-5800
REX Pure Products
 New Orleans, LA 800-344-8314
Riba Foods
 Houston, TX 800-327-7422
Rising Sun Farms
 Phoenix, OR 800-888-0795

Robert Rothschild Farm
 Cincinnati, OH 800-222-9966
Schlotterbeck & Foss Company
 Portland, ME 800-777-4666
Scott-Bathgate
 Winnipeg, MB 800-216-2990
Select Food Products
 Toronto, ON 800-699-8016
Silver Palate Kitchens
 Cresskill, NJ 201-568-0110
Stello Foods Inc
 Punxsutawney, PA 800-849-4599
TexaFrance
 Round Rock, TX 800-776-8937
Tropical Foods
 Charlotte, NC 800-438-4470
UFL Foods
 Mississauga, ON 905-670-7776
Ultra Seal
 New Paltz, NY 845-255-2490
Uncle Fred's Fine Foods
 Rockport, TX 361-729-8320
Westport Rivers Vineyard
 Westport, MA 800-993-9695
Wild Thymes Farm Inc
 Greenville, NY 845-266-8387
William Poll Inc
 New York, NY 800-993-7655
Wing Nien Food
 Hayward, CA 510-487-8877
Wing's Food Products
 Toronto, ON 416-259-2662
Wisconsin Spice Inc
 Berlin, WI 920-361-3555
Woeber Mustard Mfg Co
 Springfield, OH 800-548-2929
Wood Brothers Inc
 West Columbia, SC 803-796-5146

Cress

Koppert Cress USA
 Cutchogue, NY 631-734-8500

Greens

Canned & Frozen

Barhyte Specialty Foods Inc
 Pendleton, OR 800-227-4983
Bauer's Mustard
 Flushing, NY 718-821-3570
Heintz & Weber Co
 Buffalo, NY 716-852-7171
Mendocino Mustard
 Fort Bragg, CA 800-964-2270
Montana Specialty Mills LLC
 Great Falls, MT 800-332-2024
Mrs. Dog's Products
 Grand Rapids, MI 800-267-7364
Seabrook Brothers & Sons
 Seabrook, NJ 856-455-8080
Terrapin Ridge
 Clearwater, FL 800-999-4052
Wisconsin Wilderness Food Products
 Lake Bluff, IL 800-359-3039

Osaka Purple

Alfred L. Wolff, Inc.
 Park Ridge, IL 847-759-8888

Nectar

Mira International Foods
 East Brunswick, NJ 800-818-6472
WCC Honey Marketing
 City Of Industry, CA 626-855-3086

Canned

Healthmate Products
 Highland Park, IL 847-579-1051

Nectarines

Ballantine Produce Company
 Reedley, CA 559-875-2583
Brandt Farms Inc
 Reedley, CA 559-638-6961
California Fruit
 San Diego, CA 877-378-4811
Cherry Hill Orchards
 Lancaster, PA 717-872-9311

Product Categories / Fruits & Vegetables: Okra

Copper Hills Fruit Sales
   Fresno, CA 559-432-5400
Corrin Produce Sales
   Dinuba, CA 559-596-0517
Custom Produce Sales
   Parlier, CA 559-254-5800
Earthbound Farm
   San Jn Bautista, CA 800-690-3200
Fowler Packing Co
   Fresno, CA 559-834-5911
HMC Farms
   Kingsburg, CA 559-897-1025
Mountain View Fruit Sales
   Reedley, CA 559-637-9933
Oneonta Starr Ranch Growers
   Wenatchee, WA 509-663-2191
P R Farms Inc
   Clovis, CA 559-299-0201
Pandol Brothers Inc
   Delano, CA 661-725-3755
Prima® Wawona
   Fresno, CA 559-787-8780
Stadelman Fruit LLC
   Zillah, WA 509-829-5145
Sun Valley Packing
   Reedley, CA 559-591-1515
Symms Fruit Ranch Inc
   Caldwell, ID 208-459-4821
T.S. Smith & Sons
   Bridgeville, DE 302-337-8271
Tom Ringhausen Orchards
   Hardin, IL 800-258-6645
Trinity Fruit Sale Co
   Fresno, CA 559-433-3777
Unique Ingredients LLC
   Gold Canyon, AZ 480-983-2498
Z&S Distributing
   Fresno, CA 800-467-0788

Okra

Boskovich Farms Inc
   Oxnard, CA 805-487-2299
Miss Scarlett's Flowers
   Juneau, AK 800-345-6734
Pictsweet Co
   Bells, TN 731-663-7600
Talk O'Texas Brands Inc
   San Angelo, TX 800-749-6572
Trappey's Fine Foods Inc
   New Iberia, LA 337-365-8281

Canned

Emerling International Foods
   Buffalo, NY 716-833-7381

Frozen

Emerling International Foods
   Buffalo, NY 716-833-7381
Paris Foods Corporation
   Trappe, MD 410-200-9595
Pictsweet Co
   Bells, TN 731-663-7600

Olives

Aceitunas Losada
   Carmona, Sevilla,
Adams Olive Ranch
   Lindsay, CA 888-216-5483
Agrocan
   Ville St Laurent, QC 877-247-6226
Alimentaire Whyte's Inc
   Laval, QC 866-420-9520
Alive & Well Olives
   Ponte Vedra Beach, FL
Bahama Specialty Foods
   Durham, NC 919-471-4051
Bari Olive Oil Co
   Dinuba, CA 877-638-3626
Bell-Carter Foods Inc
   Walnut Creek, CA 800-252-3557
Blue Marble Brands
   Providence, RI 888-534-0246
Bob Gordon & Associates
   Oak Park, IL 708-524-9611
C.C. Graber Company
   Ontario, CA 800-996-5483
California Olive Growers
   Fresno, CA 888-965-4837
Caltex Foods
   Canoga Park, CA 800-522-5839
Castella Imports Inc
   Brentwood, NY 631-231-5500
Corfu Foods Inc
   Bensenville, IL 630-595-2510
Cormier Rice Milling Co Inc
   De Witt, AR 870-946-3561
Cosmo Food Products
   West Haven, CT 800-942-6766
Country Cupboard
   Lewisburg, PA 570-523-3211
Crazy Jerrys Inc Kahuna-Sauces
   Woodstock, GA 800-347-2823
DeLallo Italian Foods
   Jeannette, PA 800-433-9100
E Waldo Ward & Son Marmalades
   Sierra Madre, CA 800-355-9273
Emerling International Foods
   Buffalo, NY 716-833-7381
Fantis Foods Inc
   Carlstadt, NJ 201-933-6200
FoodMatch Inc
   New York, NY 800-350-3411
Gl Mezzetta Inc
   American Canyon, CA 800-941-7044
Grainaissance
   Emeryville, CA 800-472-4697
Jeff's Garden
   American Canyon, CA 707-266-7444
Kaiser Pickles
   Cincinnati, OH 888-291-0608
Krinos Foods
   Bronx, NY 718-729-9000
L & S Packing Co
   Farmingdale, NY 800-286-6487
Lakeside Packing Company
   Harrow, ON 519-738-2314
Leonard Mountain Inc
   Bixby, OK 800-822-7700
M & CP FARMS
   Orland, CA 530-865-9810
Mancuso Cheese Co
   Joliet, IL 815-722-2475
Manhattan Food Brands, LLC
   Metuchen, NJ 732-906-2168
Mario Camancho Foods
   Plant City, FL 800-293-9783
Musco Family Olive Co
   Tracy, CA 800-523-9828
Nature Quality
   San Martin, CA 408-683-2182
Ntc Marketing
   Williamsville, NY 800-333-1637
Oil & Olives Company
   Miami, FL 305-670-0979
Olde Tyme Mercantile
   Arroyo Grande, CA 805-489-7991
Orleans Packing Co
   Hyde Park, MA 617-361-6611
Pacific Choice Brands
   Fresno, CA 559-476-3581
Paradise Products Corporation
   Boca Raton, FL 800-826-1235
Pastene Co LTD
   Canton, MA 781-298-3397
Picklesmith Inc
   Taft, TX 800-499-3401
Price Co
   Yakima, WA 509-966-4110
Proacec USA
   Santa Monica, CA 310-996-7770
Pure Food Ingredients
   Verona, WI 800-355-9601
Ron Son Foods Inc
   Swedesboro, NJ 856-241-7333
San Marzano Imports
   Howell, NJ 732-364-1724
Sandt's Honey Co
   Easton, PA 800-935-3960
Santa Barbara Olive Company
   Santa Barbara, CA 800-624-4896
Sargent and Greenleaf
   Nicholasville, KY 800-826-7652
Sieco USA Corporation
   Houston, TX 713-464-1726
Silverleaf International Corp
   Rosharon, TX 800-442-7542
Spruce Foods
   San Clemente, CA 800-326-3612
Stinking Rose, The
   San Francisco, CA 800-995-7674
Sunfood
   El Cajon, CA 888-729-3663
Sutter Buttes Olive Oil
   Sutter, CA 530-763-7921
Tee Pee Olives, Inc.
   Rye, NY 800-431-1529
Trattore Farms
   Geyserville, CA 707-431-7200
Vegetable Juices Inc
   Chicago, IL 888-776-9752
Veronica Foods Inc
   Oakland, CA 800-370-5554
Vincent Formusa Company
   Des Plaines, IL 847-813-6040
West Coast Products
   Orland, CA 800-382-3072
Woodlake Ranch
   Woodlake, CA 559-564-2161

Black

Agrocan
   Ville St Laurent, QC 877-247-6226
Bell-Carter Foods Inc
   Walnut Creek, CA 800-252-3557
Bob Gordon & Associates
   Oak Park, IL 708-524-9611
Musco Family Olive Co
   Tracy, CA 800-523-9828

Whole

Adams Olive Ranch
   Lindsay, CA 888-216-5483

Greek

Adams Olive Ranch
   Lindsay, CA 888-216-5483
Castella Imports Inc
   Brentwood, NY 631-231-5500
Taziki's Cafe
   Birmingham, AL

Green

Agrocan
   Ville St Laurent, QC 877-247-6226
Bob Gordon & Associates
   Oak Park, IL 708-524-9611
Musco Family Olive Co
   Tracy, CA 800-523-9828
Ron Son Foods Inc
   Swedesboro, NJ 856-241-7333
Woodlake Ranch
   Woodlake, CA 559-564-2161

with Pimiento

Bell-Carter Foods Inc
   Walnut Creek, CA 800-252-3557
Musco Family Olive Co
   Tracy, CA 800-523-9828

Italian

Adams Olive Ranch
   Lindsay, CA 888-216-5483
Bono USA
   Fairfield, NJ 862-485-8729
Castella Imports Inc
   Brentwood, NY 631-231-5500

Onion

Agri-Pack
   Pasco, WA 509-545-6181
Alsum Farms & Produce
   Cambria, WI 800-236-5127
Appleton Produce Company
   Weiser, ID 208-414-3352
Baker Produce
   Kennewick, WA 800-624-7553
Boardman Foods Inc
   Boardman, OR 541-481-3000
Bob Gordon & Associates
   Oak Park, IL 708-524-9611
Boskovich Farms Inc
   Oxnard, CA 805-487-2299
Cascade Specialties, Inc.
   Boardman, OR 541-481-2522
Castella Imports Inc
   Brentwood, NY 631-231-5500
Christopher Ranch LLC
   Gilroy, CA 408-847-1100
Club Chef LLC
   Covington, KY 859-578-3100

Product Categories / Fruits & Vegetables: Orange

Coulter Giufre & Co Inc
  Chittenango, NY 315-687-6510
De Bruyn Produce Company
  Ponpano Beach, FL 800-733-9177
Del Monte Fresh Produce Inc.
  Coral Gables, FL 800-950-3683
Delta Packing
  Lodi, CA 209-334-1023
Dickinson Frozen Foods
  Eagle, ID 800-886-4326
Earthbound Farm
  San Jn Bautista, CA 800-690-3200
Exeter Produce
  Exeter, ON 519-235-0141
F & S Produce Co Inc
  Vineland, NJ 800-886-3316
Fiesta Farms
  Toronto, ON 416-537-1235
Fresh Express, Inc.
  Salinas, CA 800-242-5472
Ful-Flav-R Foods
  Alamo, CA 925-838-0300
Gill's Onions LLC
  Oxnard, CA 800-348-2255
Gl Mezzetta Inc
  American Canyon, CA 800-941-7044
Gouw Quality Onions
  Taber, AB 403-223-1440
Haliburton International Inc
  Ontario, CA 877-980-4295
Harris Farms Inc
  Coalinga, CA 800-311-6211
Isadore A. Rapasadi & Son
  Canastota, NY 800-828-7277
J C Watson Co
  Parma, ID 208-722-5141
JES Foods
  Cleveland, OH 216-883-8987
L & S Packing Co
  Farmingdale, NY 800-286-6487
Magic Valley Growers
  Wendell, ID 208-536-6693
Miss Scarlett's Flowers
  Juneau, AK 800-345-6734
Muir Copper Canyon Farms
  Salt Lake City, UT 800-564-0949
Murakami Farms
  Ontario, OR 800-421-8814
National Frozen Foods Corp
  Seattle, WA 206-322-8900
Nature Quality
  San Martin, CA 408-683-2182
Oneonta Starr Ranch Growers
  Wenatchee, WA 509-663-2191
Ontario Produce Company
  Ontario, OR 541-889-6485
Paradise Products Corporation
  Boca Raton, FL 800-826-1235
Peri & Sons Farms
  Yerington, NV 775-463-4444
POG
  Grand Bend, ON 519-238-5704
R.C. McEntire & Company
  Columbia, SC 803-799-3388
Rainsweet Inc
  Salem, OR 800-363-4293
Sargent and Greenleaf
  Nicholasville, KY 800-826-7652
Schiff Food Products Co Inc
  Totowa, NJ 973-237-1990
Seald Sweet
  Vero Beach, FL 559-636-4400
Superior Nutrition Corporation
  Wilmington, DE 302-655-5762
SupHerb Farms
  Turlock, CA 800-787-4372
Swagger Foods Corp
  Vernon Hills, IL 847-913-1200
Symms Fruit Ranch Inc
  Caldwell, ID 208-459-4821
Tanimura Antle Inc
  Salinas, CA 800-772-4542
United Marketing Exchange
  Delta, CO 970-874-3332
Vegetable Juices Inc
  Chicago, IL 888-776-9752
Vessey & Co Inc
  Holtville, CA 760-356-0130
Viva Tierra
  Mt Vernon, WA 360-855-0566
Wildcat Produce
  McGrew, NE 308-783-2438

Z&S Distributing
  Fresno, CA 800-467-0788

Canned

Appleton Produce Company
  Weiser, ID 208-414-3352
Bob Gordon & Associates
  Oak Park, IL 708-524-9611
Ful-Flav-R Foods
  Alamo, CA 925-838-0300
Gl Mezzetta Inc
  American Canyon, CA 800-941-7044
L & S Packing Co
  Farmingdale, NY 800-286-6487
Paradise Products Corporation
  Boca Raton, FL 800-826-1235
Reckitt Benckiser LLC
  Parsippany, NJ 973-404-2600

Cocktail

Castella Imports Inc
  Brentwood, NY 631-231-5500

Crushed

Schiff Food Products Co Inc
  Totowa, NJ 973-237-1990

Frozen

Appleton Produce Company
  Weiser, ID 208-414-3352
Dickinson Frozen Foods
  Eagle, ID 800-886-4326
National Frozen Foods Corp
  Seattle, WA 206-322-8900
Nature Quality
  San Martin, CA 408-683-2182
Paris Foods Corporation
  Trappe, MD 410-200-9595
POG
  Grand Bend, ON 519-238-5704
Rainsweet Inc
  Salem, OR 800-363-4293
SupHerb Farms
  Turlock, CA 800-787-4372
Vegetable Juices Inc
  Chicago, IL 888-776-9752

Green

Di Mare Fresh Inc
  Fort Worth, TX 817-385-3000
Russo Farms
  Vineland, NJ 856-692-5942
SupHerb Farms
  Turlock, CA 800-787-4372
Tanimura Antle Inc
  Salinas, CA 800-772-4542
Walter P Rawl & Sons Inc
  Pelion, SC 803-894-1900

Minced

Swagger Foods Corp
  Vernon Hills, IL 847-913-1200

Pearl & Cocktail Onions

Kingston Fresh
  Idaho Falls, ID 208-522-2365
L & S Packing Co
  Farmingdale, NY 800-286-6487
Magic Valley Growers
  Wendell, ID 208-536-6693
National Frozen Foods Corp
  Seattle, WA 206-322-8900
POG
  Grand Bend, ON 519-238-5704
Weiser River Packing
  Weiser, ID 208-549-0200

Red

Baker Produce
  Kennewick, WA 800-624-7553
Pawelski Farm
  Goshen, NY 845-772-2600
Peri & Sons Farms
  Yerington, NV 775-463-4444
SupHerb Farms
  Turlock, CA 800-787-4372
Vessey & Co Inc
  Holtville, CA 760-356-0130

Spanish

SupHerb Farms
  Turlock, CA 800-787-4372

Orange

A. Gagliano Co Inc
  Milwaukee, WI 800-272-1516
Agrexco USA
  Jamaica, NY 718-481-8700
Bissinger's Handcrafted Chocolatier
  St. Louis, MO 314-615-2400
Cal Harvest Marketing Inc
  Hanford, CA 559-582-4494
Corona College Heights
  Riverside, CA 951-351-7880
Di Mare Fresh Inc
  Fort Worth, TX 817-385-3000
DNE World Fruit Sales
  Fort Pierce, FL 800-327-6676
Dundee Groves
  Dundee, FL 800-294-2266
Fillmore Piru Citrus
  Piru, CA 805-521-1781
Gene's Citrus Ranch
  Palmetto, FL 888-723-2006
Haines City Citrus Growers
  Haines City, FL 800-327-6676
Hale Indian River Groves
  Vero Beach, FL 800-562-4502
Heller Brothers Packing Corp
  Winter Garden, FL 855-543-5537
Hunt Brothers Cooperative
  Lake Wales, FL 863-676-1411
Lane Southern Orchards
  Fort Valley, GA 800-277-3224
Leroy Smith Inc
  Vero Beach, FL 772-569-2059
Magnolia Citrus Assn
  Porterville, CA 559-784-4455
Oneonta Starr Ranch Growers
  Wenatchee, WA 509-663-2191
Orange Cove-Sanger Citrus
  Orange Cove, CA 559-626-4453
P R Farms Inc
  Clovis, CA 559-299-0201
Paradise Inc
  Plant City, FL 813-752-1155
Reed Lang Farms
  Rio Hondo, TX 956-748-2354
Seald Sweet
  Vero Beach, FL 559-636-4400
Tony Vitrano Company
  Jessup, MD 800-481-3784
Unique Ingredients LLC
  Gold Canyon, AZ 480-983-2498
Wonderful Citrus
  Mission, TX 956-205-7300
Yokohl Packing Co
  Lindsay, CA 559-562-1327
Z&S Distributing
  Fresno, CA 800-467-0788

Blood

Z&S Distributing
  Fresno, CA 800-467-0788

Mandarin

Agrocan
  Ville St Laurent, QC 877-247-6226
Au Printemps Gourmet
  Saint-Jerome, QC 800-438-6676
DNE World Fruit Sales
  Fort Pierce, FL 800-327-6676
Ntc Marketing
  Williamsville, NY 800-333-1637

Canned

Ntc Marketing
  Williamsville, NY 800-333-1637

Naval

DNE World Fruit Sales
  Fort Pierce, FL 800-327-6676
Johnston Farms
  Bakersfield, CA 661-366-3201
KERN Ridge Growers LLC
  Arvin, CA 661-854-3141
Magnolia Citrus Assn
  Porterville, CA 559-784-4455

Product Categories / Fruits & Vegetables: Oriental Vegetables

Z&S Distributing
  Fresno, CA 800-467-0788

Peels

Fmali Herb
  Santa Cruz, CA. 831-423-7913

Pieces

Citrico
  Northbrook, IL 800-445-2171

Sections

Canned

Emerling International Foods
  Buffalo, NY. 716-833-7381

Valencia

Magnolia Citrus Assn
  Porterville, CA 559-784-4455
Z&S Distributing
  Fresno, CA 800-467-0788

Oriental Vegetables

Canned

Lee's Food Products
  Toronto, ON 416-465-2407
Nikken Foods
  St Louis, MO. 314-881-5818

Papaya

Brooks Tropicals Inc
  Homestead, FL 800-327-4833
Calavo Growers
  Santa Paula, CA 805-525-1245
Natural Foods Inc
  Toledo, OH 419-537-1711
Organic Planet
  San Francisco, CA 415-765-5590
Setton International Foods
  Commack, NY 800-227-4397
Timber Crest Farms
  Healdsburg, CA 888-766-4233
Unique Ingredients LLC
  Gold Canyon, AZ 480-983-2498

Dried

American Importing Co.
  Minneapolis, MN 855-273-0466
Bedemco Inc
  White Plains, NY 914-683-1119
Fine Dried Foods Intl
  Santa Cruz, CA 831-426-1413
Sunridge Farms
  Royal Oaks, CA 831-786-7000

Peach

Ballantine Produce Company
  Reedley, CA 559-875-2583
Ben B. Schwartz & Sons
  Detroit, MI 313-841-8300
Brandt Farms Inc
  Reedley, CA 559-638-6961
Bridenbaugh Orchards
  Martinsburg, PA 814-793-2364
California Fruit
  San Diego, CA 877-378-4811
Capitol Foods
  Memphis, TN 662-781-9021
Central California Raisin Packing Co, Inc.
  Del Rey, CA 559-888-2195
Cherry Hill Orchards
  Lancaster, PA. 717-872-9311
Cherry Lane Frozen Fruits
  Vineland Station, ON 877-243-7796
Clofine Dairy Products Inc
  Linwood, NJ 609-653-1000
Copper Hills Fruit Sales
  Fresno, CA 559-432-5400
Corrin Produce Sales
  Dinuba, CA 559-596-0517
Custom Produce Sales
  Parlier, CA 559-254-5800
Del Mar Food Products Corp
  Watsonville, CA 831-722-3516
Fruit Acres Farm Market and U-Pick
  Coloma, MI. 269-208-3591

Hialeah Products Co
  Hollywood, FL 800-923-3379
HMC Farms
  Kingsburg, CA 559-897-1025
Kings Canyon
  Reedley, CA 559-638-3571
Lane Southern Orchards
  Fort Valley, GA 800-277-3224
Livingston Farmers Assn
  Livingston, CA 209-394-7941
Mason County Fruit Packers Cooperative
  Hart, MI. 231-873-7504
Miss Scarlett's Flowers
  Juneau, AK 800-345-6734
Naraghi Group
  Escalon, CA 209-579-5253
Natural Foods Inc
  Toledo, OH 419-537-1711
North Bay Produce Inc
  Traverse City, MI 231-946-1941
Nut Factory
  Spokane Valley, WA 888-239-5288
Oneonta Starr Ranch Growers
  Wenatchee, WA. 509-663-2191
Organic Planet
  San Francisco, CA 415-765-5590
Overlake Foods
  Olympia, WA 800-683-1078
P R Farms Inc
  Clovis, CA 559-299-0201
Pandol Brothers Inc
  Delano, CA 661-725-3755
Patterson Vegetable Company
  Patterson, CA 209-892-2611
Peterson Farms Inc
  Shelby, MI. 231-861-0119
Prima® Wawona
  Fresno, CA 559-787-8780
Rice Fruit Co
  Gardners, PA 800-627-3359
Shafer Lake Fruit Inc
  Hartford, MI 269-621-3194
Shawnee Canning Co
  Cross Junction, VA 800-713-1414
Sun Valley Packing
  Reedley, CA 559-591-1515
Sunsweet Growers Inc.
  Yuba City, CA 800-417-2253
Symms Fruit Ranch Inc
  Caldwell, ID 208-459-4821
T.S. Smith & Sons
  Bridgeville, DE. 302-337-8271
Talbott Farms
  Palisade, CO 970-464-5656
Taylor Orchards
  Reynolds, GA 478-847-5963
Terri Lynn Inc
  Elgin, IL 800-323-0775
Timber Crest Farms
  Healdsburg, CA 888-766-4233
Titan Farms
  Ridge Spring, SC 803-685-5381
Tom Ringhausen Orchards
  Hardin, IL 800-258-6645
Trinity Fruit Sale Co
  Fresno, CA 559-433-3777
Unique Ingredients LLC
  Gold Canyon, AZ 480-983-2498
Viva Tierra
  Mt Vernon, WA 360-855-0566
Wawona Frozen Foods Inc
  Clovis, CA 559-299-2901
Z&S Distributing
  Fresno, CA 800-467-0788

Canned

Agrocan
  Ville St Laurent, QC 877-247-6226
Emerling International Foods
  Buffalo, NY. 716-833-7381
George Noroian
  Oakland, CA 510-591-7044
Overlake Foods
  Olympia, WA 800-683-1078
Shafer-Haggart
  Vancouver, BC 604-669-5512
Shawnee Canning Co
  Cross Junction, VA 800-713-1414

Dried

Bedemco Inc
  White Plains, NY 914-683-1119

Frozen

Cherry Lane Frozen Fruits
  Vineland Station, ON 877-243-7796
Emerling International Foods
  Buffalo, NY. 716-833-7381
George Noroian
  Oakland, CA 510-591-7044
Overlake Foods
  Olympia, WA 800-683-1078

Klingstone

Canned - Sliced & Diced

Mountain View Fruit Sales
  Reedley, CA 559-637-9933

Sliced

Producer Marketing Overlake
  Olympia, WA 360-352-9096

Pear

A. Gagliano Co Inc
  Milwaukee, WI 800-272-1516
Adobe Creek Packing Co Inc
  Kelseyville, CA. 707-279-4204
Ben B. Schwartz & Sons
  Detroit, MI 313-841-8300
Brothers International Food Corporation
  Rochester, NY 585-343-3007
California Fruit
  San Diego, CA 877-378-4811
Chelan Fresh Marketing
  Chelan, WA 509-682-2591
Chief Wenatchee
  Wenatchee, WA. 509-662-5197
D'Arrigo Brothers Company of California
  Salinas, CA 831-455-4500
Delta Packing
  Lodi, CA 209-334-1023
Diamond Fruit Growers
  Hood River, OR 541-354-5300
Earthbound Farm
  San Jn Bautista, CA 800-690-3200
George W Saulpaugh & Son
  Germantown, NY 518-537-6500
Giumarra Companies
  Los Angeles, CA. 213-627-2900
HH Dobbins Inc
  Lyndonville, NY 877-362-2467
Hialeah Products Co
  Hollywood, FL 800-923-3379
Matson Fruit Co
  Selah, WA 509-697-7100
Miss Scarlett's Flowers
  Juneau, AK 800-345-6734
Mt. Konocti Growers
  Kelseyville, CA. 707-279-4213
New York Apple Sales Inc
  Glenmont, NY. 888-477-6770
Nuchief Sales Inc
  Wenatchee, WA. 888-269-4638
Oneonta Starr Ranch Growers
  Wenatchee, WA. 509-663-2191
Pavero Cold Storage
  Highland, NY 800-435-2994
Reter Fruit
  Medford, OR 541-772-9560
Rice Fruit Co
  Gardners, PA 800-627-3359
Scotian Gold
  Coldbrook, NS 888-726-8426
Stadelman Fruit LLC
  Zillah, WA. 509-829-5145
Stanley Orchards Sales, Inc.
  Modena, NY 845-883-7351
Symms Fruit Ranch Inc
  Caldwell, ID 208-459-4821
Terri Lynn Inc
  Elgin, IL 800-323-0775
Timber Crest Farms
  Healdsburg, CA 888-766-4233
Trinity Fruit Sale Co
  Fresno, CA 559-433-3777
Truitt Bros Inc
  Salem, OR. 800-547-8712

Product Categories / Fruits & Vegetables: Peas

Unique Ingredients LLC
  Gold Canyon, AZ 480-983-2498
Viva Tierra
  Mt Vernon, WA 360-855-0566
Yakima Fresh
  Yakima, WA 509-248-5770

Asian
Ballantine Produce Company
  Reedley, CA 559-875-2583
Fowler Packing Co
  Fresno, CA 559-834-5911
Giumarra Companies
  Los Angeles, CA 213-627-2900
Naumes, Inc.
  Medford, OR 541-772-6268
Price Co
  Yakima, WA 509-966-4110

Bartlett
Adobe Creek Packing Co Inc
  Kelseyville, CA 707-279-4204

Bosc
Adobe Creek Packing Co Inc
  Kelseyville, CA 707-279-4204

Canned
Agrocan
  Ville St Laurent, QC 877-247-6226
Arbre Farms Inc
  Walkerville, MI 231-873-3337
Emerling International Foods
  Buffalo, NY 716-833-7381
Seneca Foods Corp
  Marion, NY 315-926-8100

D'Anjou/Bosc
Associated Fruit Company
  Phoenix, OR 541-535-1787

Dried
Bedemco Inc
  White Plains, NY 914-683-1119

Frozen
Arbre Farms Inc
  Walkerville, MI 231-873-3337
Emerling International Foods
  Buffalo, NY 716-833-7381

Red
Adobe Creek Packing Co Inc
  Kelseyville, CA 707-279-4204

Peas
Boskovich Farms Inc
  Oxnard, CA 805-487-2299
Camellia Beans
  Harahan, LA 504-733-8480
Caribbean Food Delights Inc
  Tappan, NY 845-398-3000
Castella Imports Inc
  Brentwood, NY 631-231-5500
Garden Valley Corp
  Sutherlin, OR 541-459-9565
Hanover Foods Corp
  Hanover, PA 717-632-6000
Inland Empire Foods
  Riverside, CA 888-452-3267
International Home Foods
  Parsippany, NJ 973-359-9920
Knight Seed Company
  Burnsville, MN 800-328-2999
Lakeside Foods Inc.
  Plainview, MN 507-534-3141
Mezza
  Lake Forest, IL 888-206-6054
Mills Brothers Intl
  Seattle, WA 206-575-3000
Miramar Fruit Trading Company
  Doral, FL 305-883-4774
National Frozen Foods Corp
  Seattle, WA 206-322-8900
New Harvest Foods
  Washington, DC 920-822-2578
Norben Co
  Willoughby, OH 888-466-7236

Northwest Pea & Bean Co
  Spokane Valley, WA 509-534-3821
Pictsweet Co
  Bells, TN 731-663-7600
Royal Caribbean Bakery
  Mt Vernon, NY 888-818-0971
Smith Frozen Foods Inc
  Weston, OR 541-566-3515
Snowcrest Packer
  Abbotsford, BC 800-265-3686
Spokane Seed Co
  Spokane Valley, WA 800-359-8478
Strathroy Foods
  Strathroy, ON 519-245-4600
Symons Frozen Foods
  Centralia, WA 360-736-1321
Talley Farms
  Arroyo Grande, CA 805-489-5400
Twin City Foods Inc.
  Stanwood, WA 206-515-2400
Vege-Cool
  Newman, CA 209-862-2360
Veronica Foods Inc
  Oakland, CA 800-370-5554
Wallace Grain & Pea Company
  Pullman, WA 509-878-1561
Z&S Distributing
  Fresno, CA 800-467-0788

Black-eyed
Pictsweet Co
  Bells, TN 731-663-7600

Canned
Emerling International Foods
  Buffalo, NY 716-833-7381

Frozen
Emerling International Foods
  Buffalo, NY 716-833-7381
Pictsweet Co
  Bells, TN 731-663-7600

Canned
Blue Runner Foods Inc
  Gonzales, LA 225-647-3016
Carriere Foods Inc
  Saint-Denis-Sur-Richelie, QC 450-787-3411
Emerling International Foods
  Buffalo, NY 716-833-7381
Hanover Foods Corp
  Hanover, PA 717-632-6000
International Home Foods
  Parsippany, NJ 973-359-9920
Lakeside Foods Inc.
  Plainview, MN 507-534-3141
Lakeside Foods Inc.
  Manitowoc, WI 800-466-3834
Lodi Canning Co
  Lodi, WI 608-592-4236
New Harvest Foods
  Washington, DC 920-822-2578

Dry
Camellia Beans
  Harahan, LA 504-733-8480
Just Tomatoes
  Westley, CA 800-537-1985
Mills Brothers Intl
  Seattle, WA 206-575-3000
Spokane Seed Co
  Spokane Valley, WA 800-359-8478

Frozen
Cavendish Farms
  Dieppe, NB 506-858-7710
Emerling International Foods
  Buffalo, NY 716-833-7381
Hanover Foods Corp
  Hanover, PA 717-632-6000
Lakeside Foods Inc.
  Plainview, MN 507-534-3141
Lakeside Foods Inc.
  Manitowoc, WI 800-466-3834
Lisa's Organics
  Carnelian Bay, CA 877-584-5711
Lodi Canning Co
  Lodi, WI 608-592-4236
National Frozen Foods Corp
  Seattle, WA 206-322-8900

Paris Foods Corporation
  Trappe, MD 410-200-9595
Pictsweet Co
  Bells, TN 731-663-7600
Smith Frozen Foods Inc
  Weston, OR 541-566-3515
Snowcrest Packer
  Abbotsford, BC 800-265-3686
Strathroy Foods
  Strathroy, ON 519-245-4600
Symons Frozen Foods
  Centralia, WA 360-736-1321
Twin City Foods Inc.
  Stanwood, WA 206-515-2400

Green
Knight Seed Company
  Burnsville, MN 800-328-2999
Northwest Pea & Bean Co
  Spokane Valley, WA 509-534-3821
Pictsweet Co
  Bells, TN 731-663-7600
Sno-Pac Foods Inc
  Caledonia, MN 800-533-2215

Green & Yellow Split - Dried
Country Cupboard
  Lewisburg, PA 570-523-3211
Emerling International Foods
  Buffalo, NY 716-833-7381
New Organics
  Kenwood, CA 734-677-5570
Organic Planet
  San Francisco, CA 415-765-5590
Spokane Seed Co
  Spokane Valley, WA 800-359-8478
Unique Ingredients LLC
  Gold Canyon, AZ 480-983-2498
Vege-Cool
  Newman, CA 209-862-2360

Snap
Miss Scarlett's Flowers
  Juneau, AK 800-345-6734
National Frozen Foods Corp
  Seattle, WA 206-322-8900
Pictsweet Co
  Bells, TN 731-663-7600

Snow
North Bay Produce Inc
  Traverse City, MI 231-946-1941

Southern
Trinidad Benham Corporation
  Denver, CO 303-220-1400

Yellow Split
Knight Seed Company
  Burnsville, MN 800-328-2999
Northwest Pea & Bean Co
  Spokane Valley, WA 509-534-3821
Timeless Seeds
  Ulm, MT 406-866-3340
United Pulse Trading Inc
  Bismarck, ND 701-751-1623

Peppers
Abbott & Cobb Inc
  Feasterville, PA 800-345-7333
AgroCepia
  Miami, FL 305-704-3488
B & G Foods Inc.
  Parsippany, NJ 973-401-6500
Baumer Foods Inc
  Metairie, LA 504-482-5761
Bifulco Four Seasons
  Pittsgrove, NJ 856-692-0778
Big B Barbecue
  Evansville, IN 812-425-5235
Blue Marble Brands
  Providence, RI 888-534-0246
Bob Gordon & Associates
  Oak Park, IL 708-524-9611
Border Foods
  New Hope, MN 763-559-7338
Boskovich Farms Inc
  Oxnard, CA 805-487-2299

Product Categories / Fruits & Vegetables: Peppers

Carando Gourmet Frozen Foods
  Agawam, MA 888-227-2636
Cherchies
  Malvern, PA 800-644-1980
Christopher Ranch LLC
  Gilroy, CA 408-847-1100
Chugwater Chili
  Chugwater, WY 800-972-4454
Comanche Tortilla Factory
  Fort Stockton, TX 432-336-3245
Del Mar Food Products Corp
  Watsonville, CA 831-722-3516
Delta Packing
  Lodi, CA 209-334-1023
Dickinson Frozen Foods
  Eagle, ID 800-886-4326
Dolce Nonna
  Whitestone, NY 718-767-3501
Eckert Cold Storage
  Manteca, CA 209-823-3181
EDCO Food Products Inc
  Hobart, WI 800-255-3768
Emerling International Foods
  Buffalo, NY 716-833-7381
F & S Produce Co Inc
  Vineland, NJ 800-886-3316
Fiesta Canning Co
  Phoenix, AZ 602-212-2424
Food City Pickle Company
  Battle Creek, MI 269-781-9135
Fountain Valley Foods
  Colorado Springs, CO 719-573-6012
Frog Ranch Foods
  Glouster, OH 800-742-2488
Ful-Flav-R Foods
  Alamo, CA 925-838-0300
Garon Foods
  Herrin, IL 618-942-4810
George Chiala Farms Inc
  Morgan Hill, CA 408-778-0562
Giuliano's Specialty Foods
  Garden Grove, CA 714-895-9661
Giumarra Companies
  Los Angeles, CA 213-627-2900
Gl Mezzetta Inc
  American Canyon, CA 800-941-7044
GNS Spices
  Walnut, CA 909-594-9505
Great American Appetizers
  Nampa, ID 800-282-4834
GWB Foods Corporation
  Brooklyn, NY 877-977-7610
Haliburton International Inc
  Ontario, CA 877-980-4295
Harris Farms Inc
  Coalinga, CA 800-311-6211
Hermann Pickle Co
  Garrettsville, OH 800-245-2696
JES Foods
  Cleveland, OH 216-883-8987
Johnston Farms
  Bakersfield, CA 661-366-3201
Kaiser Pickles
  Cincinnati, OH 888-291-0608
Kaplan & Zubrin
  Camden, NJ 856-964-1083
Krinos Foods
  Bronx, NY 718-729-9000
Kruger Foods
  Stockton, CA 209-941-8518
L & S Packing Co
  Farmingdale, NY 800-286-6487
Lakeside Packing Company
  Harrow, ON 519-738-2314
Landry's Pepper Co
  St Martinville, LA 337-394-6097
Mama Lil's Peppers
  Portland, OR 503-206-6746
Matador Processors
  Blanchard, OK 800-847-0797
Michigan Freeze Pack
  Hart, MI 231-873-2175
Miguel's Stowe Away
  Stowe, VT 800-448-6517
Monticello Canning Company
  Crossville, TN
Mt Olive Pickle Co
  Mt Olive, NC 800-672-5041
Nature Quality
  San Martin, CA 408-683-2182
Norpaco Inc
  Middletown, CT 800-252-0222

Pacific Choice Brands
  Fresno, CA 559-476-3581
Pastene Co LTD
  Canton, MA 781-298-3397
Pastorelli Food Products
  Chicago, IL 800-767-2829
Pepper Creek Farms
  Lawton, OK 800-526-8132
Peter Rabbit Farms
  Coachella, CA 760-398-0136
Pure Food Ingredients
  Verona, WI 800-355-9601
Ralph Sechler & Son Inc
  St Joe, IN 800-332-5461
Rene Produce Dist
  Rio Rico, AZ 520-281-0806
Ripon Pickle Co Inc
  Ripon, WI 920-748-7110
Ron Son Foods Inc
  Swedesboro, NJ 856-241-7333
Sargent and Greenleaf
  Nicholasville, KY 800-826-7652
Schiff Food Products Co Inc
  Totowa, NJ 973-237-1990
Sedlock Farm
  Lynn Center, IL 309-521-8284
Snowcrest Packer
  Abbotsford, BC 800-265-3686
South Mill
  Kennett Square, PA 610-444-4800
Strub Pickles
  Brantford, ON 519-751-1717
SupHerb Farms
  Turlock, CA 800-787-4372
Topor's Pickle & Food Svc Inc
  Detroit, MI 313-237-0288
Tropical Foods
  Charlotte, NC 800-438-4470
Vega Food Industries Inc
  Cranston, RI 800-973-7737
Vegetable Juices Inc
  Chicago, IL 888-776-9752
Vincent Formusa Company
  Des Plaines, IL 847-813-6040
Violet Packing Holdings LLC
  Williamstown, NJ 856-629-7428
Wholesum Family Farms
  Nogales, AZ 520-281-9233
Z&S Distributing
  Fresno, CA 800-467-0788

Banana

Food City Pickle Company
  Battle Creek, MI 269-781-9135
Gl Mezzetta Inc
  American Canyon, CA 800-941-7044
Kaplan & Zubrin
  Camden, NJ 856-964-1083
Topor's Pickle & Food Svc Inc
  Detroit, MI 313-237-0288
Trappey's Fine Foods Inc
  New Iberia, LA 337-365-8281

Bell

Christopher Ranch LLC
  Gilroy, CA 408-847-1100
Dehydrates Inc
  Hewlett, NY 800-983-4443
Dickinson Frozen Foods
  Eagle, ID 800-886-4326
Earthbound Farm
  San Jn Bautista, CA 800-690-3200
Eckert Cold Storage
  Manteca, CA 209-823-3181
F & S Produce Co Inc
  Vineland, NJ 800-886-3316
Ful-Flav-R Foods
  Alamo, CA 925-838-0300
Gel Spice Co LLC
  Bayonne, NJ 800-922-0230
George Chiala Farms Inc
  Morgan Hill, CA 408-778-0562
Grasso Foods Inc
  Swedesboro, NJ 856-467-2222
KERN Ridge Growers LLC
  Arvin, CA 661-854-3141
Moody Dunbar Inc
  Johnson City, TN 423-952-0100
Nature Quality
  San Martin, CA 408-683-2182

Oxford Frozen Foods
  Oxford, NS 902-447-2100
Rene Produce Dist
  Rio Rico, AZ 520-281-0806
Ripon Pickle Co Inc
  Ripon, WI 920-748-7110
Schiff Food Products Co Inc
  Totowa, NJ 973-237-1990
SupHerb Farms
  Turlock, CA 800-787-4372
Sure-Fresh Produce Inc
  Santa Maria, CA 888-423-5379
Talley Farms
  Arroyo Grande, CA 805-489-5400
Titan Farms
  Ridge Spring, SC 803-685-5381
Tropical Foods
  Charlotte, NC 800-438-4470
Vegetable Juices Inc
  Chicago, IL 888-776-9752
Z&S Distributing
  Fresno, CA 800-467-0788

Canned

Bob Gordon & Associates
  Oak Park, IL 708-524-9611
Colonna Brothers Inc
  North Bergen, NJ 201-864-1115
Emerling International Foods
  Buffalo, NY 716-833-7381
Ful-Flav-R Foods
  Alamo, CA 925-838-0300
L & S Packing Co
  Farmingdale, NY 800-286-6487
Mancini Packing Co
  Zolfo Springs, FL 800-741-1778
Moody Dunbar Inc
  Johnson City, TN 423-952-0100
Ron Son Foods Inc
  Swedesboro, NJ 856-241-7333
Violet Packing Holdings LLC
  Williamstown, NJ 856-629-7428

Capsicums

Advanced Spice & Trading
  Carrollton, TX 800-872-7811
Emerling International Foods
  Buffalo, NY 716-833-7381
Vegetable Juices Inc
  Chicago, IL 888-776-9752

Frozen

SupHerb Farms
  Turlock, CA 800-787-4372

Cayenne

Trappey's Fine Foods Inc
  New Iberia, LA 337-365-8281

Cherry

B & G Foods Inc.
  Parsippany, NJ 973-401-6500
F & S Produce Co Inc
  Vineland, NJ 800-886-3316
Kaplan & Zubrin
  Camden, NJ 856-964-1083
L & S Packing Co
  Farmingdale, NY 800-286-6487
Norpaco Inc
  Middletown, CT 800-252-0222
Trappey's Fine Foods Inc
  New Iberia, LA 337-365-8281

Chile

American Key Food Products Inc
  Closter, NJ 877-263-7539
Border Foods
  New Hope, MN 763-559-7338
Chili Dude
  Dallas, TX 214-354-9906
Chugwater Chili
  Chugwater, WY 800-972-4454
Dave's Gourmet
  San Rafael, CA 800-758-0372
Emerling International Foods
  Buffalo, NY 716-833-7381
Fiesta Canning Co
  Phoenix, AZ 602-212-2424
Ful-Flav-R Foods
  Alamo, CA 925-838-0300

Product Categories / Fruits & Vegetables: Persimmons

George Chiala Farms Inc
 Morgan Hill, CA............408-778-0562
Gl Mezzetta Inc
 American Canyon, CA........800-941-7044
KERN Ridge Growers LLC
 Arvin, CA.................661-854-3141
Magic Seasoning Blends
 New Orleans, LA...........800-457-2857
Mancini Packing Co
 Zolfo Springs, FL.........800-741-1778
New Mexico Green Chile Company
 Artesia, NM...............505-503-0996
Pepperland Farms
 Ponchatoula, LA...........985-956-6703
Pure Food Ingredients
 Verona, WI................800-355-9601
SupHerb Farms
 Turlock, CA...............800-787-4372
Tropical Commodities
 Miami, FL.................305-471-8120
Vega Food Industries Inc
 Cranston, RI..............800-973-7737
Vegetable Juices Inc
 Chicago, IL...............888-776-9752
Walker Foods
 Los Angeles, CA...........800-966-5199
Z&S Distributing
 Fresno, CA................800-467-0788

Dried Pods
American Key Food Products Inc
 Closter, NJ...............877-263-7539
Emerling International Foods
 Buffalo, NY...............716-833-7381
Gel Spice Co LLC
 Bayonne, NJ...............800-922-0230
Magic Seasoning Blends
 New Orleans, LA...........800-457-2857

Chipotle
Emerling International Foods
 Buffalo, NY...............716-833-7381
Magic Seasoning Blends
 New Orleans, LA...........800-457-2857
Ripon Pickle Co Inc
 Ripon, WI.................920-748-7110
Vegetable Juices Inc
 Chicago, IL...............888-776-9752

Frozen
Carando Gourmet Frozen Foods
 Agawam, MA................888-227-2636
Dickinson Frozen Foods
 Eagle, ID.................800-886-4326
Eckert Cold Storage
 Manteca, CA...............209-823-3181
Emerling International Foods
 Buffalo, NY...............716-833-7381
Grasso Foods Inc
 Swedesboro, NJ............856-467-2222
Great American Appetizers
 Nampa, ID.................800-282-4834
Hermann Pickle Co
 Garrettsville, OH.........800-245-2696
Matador Processors
 Blanchard, OK.............800-847-0797
Monticello Canning Company
 Crossville, TN
Paris Foods Corporation
 Trappe, MD................410-200-9595
Rainsweet Inc
 Salem, OR.................800-363-4293
San Antonio Farms
 Platteville, WI...........800-236-1119
Snowcrest Packer
 Abbotsford, BC............800-265-3686
SupHerb Farms
 Turlock, CA...............800-787-4372
Vegetable Juices Inc
 Chicago, IL...............888-776-9752

Habanero
Brooks Tropicals Inc
 Homestead, FL.............800-327-4833
Garon Foods
 Herrin, IL................618-942-4810
George Chiala Farms Inc
 Morgan Hill, CA...........408-778-0562

Jalapeno
Advanced Spice & Trading
 Carrollton, TX............800-872-7811
AgroCepia
 Miami, FL.................305-704-3488
Arbre Farms Inc
 Walkerville, MI...........231-873-3337
Dehydrates Inc
 Hewlett, NY...............800-983-4443
Eckert Cold Storage
 Manteca, CA...............209-823-3181
EDCO Food Products Inc
 Hobart, WI................800-255-3768
Emerling International Foods
 Buffalo, NY...............716-833-7381
F & S Produce Co Inc
 Vineland, NJ..............800-886-3316
Fountain Valley Foods
 Colorado Springs, CO......719-573-6012
Ful-Flav-R Foods
 Alamo, CA.................925-838-0300
Garon Foods
 Herrin, IL................618-942-4810
George Chiala Farms Inc
 Morgan Hill, CA...........408-778-0562
Gl Mezzetta Inc
 American Canyon, CA.......800-941-7044
Great American Appetizers
 Nampa, ID.................800-282-4834
L & S Packing Co
 Farmingdale, NY...........800-286-6487
Leon's Texas Cuisine
 Mckinney, TX..............972-529-5050
Limited Edition
 Midland, TX...............432-686-2008
Matador Processors
 Blanchard, OK.............800-847-0797
Miguel's Stowe Away
 Stowe, VT.................800-448-6517
Nature Quality
 San Martin, CA............408-683-2182
Pepper Creek Farms
 Lawton, OK................800-526-8132
Pure Food Ingredients
 Verona, WI................800-355-9601
San Antonio Farms
 Platteville, WI...........800-236-1119
Strub Pickles
 Brantford, ON.............519-751-1717
SupHerb Farms
 Turlock, CA...............800-787-4372
Trappey's Fine Foods Inc
 New Iberia, LA............337-365-8281
Vegetable Juices Inc
 Chicago, IL...............888-776-9752
Walker Foods
 Los Angeles, CA...........800-966-5199

Jalapeno & Chiles
Grasso Foods Inc
 Swedesboro, NJ............856-467-2222
La Victoria Foods
 Austin, MN................800-725-7212
Matador Processors
 Blanchard, OK.............800-847-0797
Nature Quality
 San Martin, CA............408-683-2182
Pure Food Ingredients
 Verona, WI................800-355-9601
SupHerb Farms
 Turlock, CA...............800-787-4372

Non-Bell
Grasso Foods Inc
 Swedesboro, NJ............856-467-2222

Pepperoncini
Agrocan
 Ville St Laurent, QC......877-247-6226
Baumer Foods Inc
 Metairie, LA..............504-482-5761
Big B Barbecue
 Evansville, IN............812-425-5235
Bob Gordon & Associates
 Oak Park, IL..............708-524-9611
Castella Imports Inc
 Brentwood, NY.............631-231-5500
Emerling International Foods
 Buffalo, NY...............716-833-7381

Food City Pickle Company
 Battle Creek, MI..........269-781-9135
Gl Mezzetta Inc
 American Canyon, CA.......800-941-7044
L & S Packing Co
 Farmingdale, NY...........800-286-6487
Ron Son Foods Inc
 Swedesboro, NJ............856-241-7333
Vegetable Juices Inc
 Chicago, IL...............888-776-9752

Roasted
Agrocan
 Ville St Laurent, QC......877-247-6226
Bedemco Inc
 White Plains, NY..........914-683-1119
Castella Imports Inc
 Brentwood, NY.............631-231-5500
Ful-Flav-R Foods
 Alamo, CA.................925-838-0300
Mancini Packing Co
 Zolfo Springs, FL.........800-741-1778
Moody Dunbar Inc
 Johnson City, TN..........423-952-0100
Ron Son Foods Inc
 Swedesboro, NJ............856-241-7333
Sunny Dell Foods Inc
 Oxford, PA................610-932-5164
SupHerb Farms
 Turlock, CA...............800-787-4372

Serrano
EDCO Food Products Inc
 Hobart, WI................800-255-3768
Emerling International Foods
 Buffalo, NY...............716-833-7381
F & S Produce Co Inc
 Vineland, NJ..............800-886-3316
San Antonio Farms
 Platteville, WI...........800-236-1119
SupHerb Farms
 Turlock, CA...............800-787-4372

Sweet
Carando Gourmet Frozen Foods
 Agawam, MA................888-227-2636
Coutts Specialty Foods Inc
 Boxborough, MA............800-919-2952
Kaplan & Zubrin
 Camden, NJ................856-964-1083
Mancini Packing Co
 Zolfo Springs, FL.........800-741-1778
Ripon Pickle Co Inc
 Ripon, WI.................920-748-7110

Persimmons
Ballantine Produce Company
 Reedley, CA...............559-875-2583
Copper Hills Fruit Sales
 Fresno, CA................559-432-5400
Emerling International Foods
 Buffalo, NY...............716-833-7381
HMC Farms
 Kingsburg, CA.............559-897-1025
Just Tomatoes
 Westley, CA...............800-537-1985
Naumes, Inc.
 Medford, OR...............541-772-6268
Pandol Brothers Inc
 Delano, CA................661-725-3755
Tufts Ranch
 Winters, CA...............530-795-4144
West Pak Avocado Inc
 Murrieta, CA..............800-266-4414

Pimientos
Emerling International Foods
 Buffalo, NY...............716-833-7381
Monticello Canning Company
 Crossville, TN
Moody Dunbar Inc
 Johnson City, TN..........423-952-0100
Paradise Products Corporation
 Boca Raton, FL............800-826-1235
Strub Pickles
 Brantford, ON.............519-751-1717

Product Categories / Fruits & Vegetables: Pineapple

Pineapple

Chiquita Brands LLC.
  Fort Lauderdale, FL 954-924-5700
Del Monte Fresh Produce Inc.
  Coral Gables, FL. 800-950-3683
F & S Produce Co Inc
  Vineland, NJ. 800-886-3316
Hialeah Products Co
  Hollywood, FL 800-923-3379
J H Verbridge & Son Inc
  Williamson, NY 315-589-2366
Maui Gold Pineapple Company
  Pukalani, HI 808-877-3805
Ntc Marketing
  Williamsville, NY 800-333-1637
Nut Factory
  Spokane Valley, WA 888-239-5288
Organic Planet
  San Francisco, CA 415-765-5590
Pacific Coast Fruit Co
  Portland, OR 503-234-6411
Paradise Inc
  Plant City, FL 813-752-1155
Setton International Foods
  Commack, NY 800-227-4397
Sunfood
  El Cajon, CA. 888-729-3663
Terri Lynn Inc
  Elgin, IL 800-323-0775
Timber Crest Farms
  Healdsburg, CA 888-766-4233
Transpacific Foods Inc
  Irvine, CA. 949-975-9900
Unique Ingredients LLC
  Gold Canyon, AZ 480-983-2498

Canned

Agrocan
  Ville St Laurent, QC 877-247-6226
Emerling International Foods
  Buffalo, NY. 716-833-7381
Maui Gold Pineapple Company
  Pukalani, HI 808-877-3805
Ntc Marketing
  Williamsville, NY 800-333-1637
Transpacific Foods Inc
  Irvine, CA. 949-975-9900

Chunks

Transpacific Foods Inc
  Irvine, CA. 949-975-9900

Crushed

Transpacific Foods Inc
  Irvine, CA. 949-975-9900

Dried

American Importing Co.
  Minneapolis, MN 855-273-0466
Bedemco Inc
  White Plains, NY 914-683-1119
Fine Dried Foods Intl
  Santa Cruz, CA 831-426-1413
Golden Valley Natural
  Shelley, ID. 888-270-7147
King Arthur Flour
  Norwich, VT. 800-827-6836
Made In Nature
  Boulder, CO 800-906-7426
Mariani Packing Co.
  Vacaville, CA 707-452-2800
Sunridge Farms
  Royal Oaks, CA 831-786-7000

Frozen

Emerling International Foods
  Buffalo, NY. 716-833-7381
J H Verbridge & Son Inc
  Williamson, NY 315-589-2366
Pacific Coast Fruit Co
  Portland, OR 503-234-6411
Townsend Farms Inc
  Fairview, OR. 503-666-1780

Plums

Ballantine Produce Company
  Reedley, CA 559-875-2583
Brandt Farms Inc
  Reedley, CA 559-638-6961

Burnette Foods
  Elk Rapids, MI 231-264-8116
Copper Hills Fruit Sales
  Fresno, CA 559-432-5400
Corrin Produce Sales
  Dinuba, CA. 559-596-0517
Custom Produce Sales
  Parlier, CA 559-254-5800
Fowler Packing Co
  Fresno, CA 559-834-5911
Henggeler Packing Company
  Fruitland, ID 208-452-4212
J C Watson Co
  Parma, ID 208-722-5141
Mountain View Fruit Sales
  Reedley, CA 559-637-9933
North Bay Produce Inc
  Traverse City, MI 231-946-1941
Oneonta Starr Ranch Growers
  Wenatchee, WA. 509-663-2191
Oregon Fruit Products Co
  Salem, OR. 800-394-9333
Organic Planet
  San Francisco, CA 415-765-5590
P R Farms Inc
  Clovis, CA 559-299-0201
Pandol Brothers Inc
  Delano, CA 661-725-3755
Peterson Farms Inc
  Shelby, MI. 231-861-0119
Prima® Wawona
  Fresno, CA 559-787-8780
Shafer Lake Fruit Inc
  Hartford, MI 269-621-3194
Stadelman Fruit LLC
  Zillah, WA 509-829-5145
Sun Valley Packing
  Reedley, CA 559-591-1515
Symms Fruit Ranch Inc
  Caldwell, ID 208-459-4821
Terri Lynn Inc
  Elgin, IL 800-323-0775
Timber Crest Farms
  Healdsburg, CA 888-766-4233
Trinity Fruit Sale Co
  Fresno, CA 559-433-3777
Unique Ingredients LLC
  Gold Canyon, AZ 480-983-2498
Viva Tierra
  Mt Vernon, WA. 360-855-0566
Z&S Distributing
  Fresno, CA 800-467-0788

Canned

Burnette Foods
  Elk Rapids, MI 231-264-8116
Emerling International Foods
  Buffalo, NY. 716-833-7381
Honee Bear Canning
  Lawton, MI. 800-626-2327
Oregon Fruit Products Co
  Salem, OR. 800-394-9333
Truitt Bros Inc
  Salem, OR. 800-547-8712

Dried

American Importing Co.
  Minneapolis, MN 855-273-0466
Bedemco Inc
  White Plains, NY 914-683-1119
Made In Nature
  Boulder, CO 800-906-7426
Mariani Packing Co.
  Vacaville, CA 707-452-2800
Setton International Foods
  Commack, NY 800-227-4397

Frozen

Coloma Frozen Foods Inc
  Coloma, MI. 800-642-2723
Emerling International Foods
  Buffalo, NY. 716-833-7381
Fruithill Inc
  Yamhill, OR 503-662-3926
Oregon Fruit Products Co
  Salem, OR. 800-394-9333

Pomegranate

Ballantine Produce Company
  Reedley, CA 559-875-2583

Copper Hills Fruit Sales
  Fresno, CA 559-432-5400
Emerling International Foods
  Buffalo, NY. 716-833-7381
Fowler Packing Co
  Fresno, CA 559-834-5911
HMC Farms
  Kingsburg, CA 559-897-1025
Naumes, Inc.
  Medford, OR. 541-772-6268
North Bay Produce Inc
  Traverse City, MI 231-946-1941
POM Wonderful LLC
  Los Angeles, CA. 866-976-6999

Potatoes

Au Gratin

Captain Ken's Foods Inc
  St Paul, MN. 800-510-3811
Idahoan Foods LLC
  Idaho Falls, ID 800-746-7999

Frozen

Captain Ken's Foods Inc
  St Paul, MN. 800-510-3811

Baked & Stuffed

Sun Glo Of Idaho
  Sugar City, ID 208-356-7346

Frozen

Penobscot Mccrum LLC
  Belfast, ME 800-435-4456
Sun Glo Of Idaho
  Sugar City, ID 208-356-7346

Canned

Burnette Foods
  Elk Rapids, MI 231-264-8116
Emerling International Foods
  Buffalo, NY. 716-833-7381
Nation Wide Canning Ltd.
  Cottam, ON 519-839-4831
New Harvest Foods
  Washington, DC 920-822-2578
Nickabood's Inc
  Los Angeles, CA. 213-746-1541
Ore-Ida Foods
  Pittsburgh, PA 800-255-5750
Weil's Food Processing
  Wheatley, ON 519-825-4572

Dehydrated

Idahoan Foods LLC
  Idaho Falls, ID 800-746-7999
Specialty Ingredients
  Buffalo Grove, IL 847-419-9595

Frozen

Agri-Dairy Products
  Purchase, NY 914-697-9580
Emerling International Foods
  Buffalo, NY. 716-833-7381
Oregon Potato Co
  Boardman, OR 800-336-6311
Unique Ingredients LLC
  Gold Canyon, AZ 480-983-2498

Fresh

AgriNorthwest
  Kennewick, WA. 509-734-1195
Beamon Brothers
  Goldsboro, NC 919-734-4931
Circle Valley Produce LLC
  Idaho Falls, ID 208-524-2628
Earthbound Farm
  San Jn Bautista, CA 800-690-3200
Hanover Potato Products Inc
  Hanover, PA 717-632-0700
Oneonta Starr Ranch Growers
  Wenatchee, WA. 509-663-2191
Oregon Potato Co
  Boardman, OR 800-336-6311
Oregon Potato Co
  Pasco, WA 800-987-2726
Pacific Collier Fresh Company
  Immokalee, FL 800-226-7274

247

Product Categories / Fruits & Vegetables: Powdered Vegetables

R.D. Offutt Farms
  Park Rapids, MN 218-732-1461
Seald Sweet
  Vero Beach, FL 559-636-4400
Symms Fruit Ranch Inc
  Caldwell, ID 208-459-4821

Russet

Baker Produce
  Kennewick, WA 800-624-7553
Bottom Line Foods
  Pembroke Pines, FL 954-843-0562
Les Aliments Livabec Foods
  Sherrington, QC 450-454-7971
McCain Produce Inc.
  Florenceville-Bristol, NB 506-392-3036

White

McCain Produce Inc.
  Florenceville-Bristol, NB 506-392-3036

Frozen

Cavendish Farms
  Dieppe, NB 506-858-7710
Emerling International Foods
  Buffalo, NY 716-833-7381
Endico Potatoes Inc
  Mt Vernon, NY 914-664-1151
McCain Foods USA Inc.
  Oakbrook Terace, IL 800-938-7799
Michael Foods, Inc.
  Minnetonka, MN 952-258-4000
Mr Dell Foods
  Kearney, MO 816-628-4644
Nickabood's Inc
  Los Angeles, CA 213-746-1541
Ore-Ida Foods
  Pittsburgh, PA 800-255-5750
Oregon Potato Co
  Boardman, OR 800-336-6311
Paris Foods Corporation
  Trappe, MD 410-200-9595
Small Planet Foods
  Minneapolis, MN 800-624-4123
Sun Glo Of Idaho
  Sugar City, ID 208-356-7346
Twin City Foods Inc.
  Stanwood, WA 206-515-2400
Washington Potato Company
  Pasco, WA 800-897-2726

Rounds

Penobscot Mccrum LLC
  Belfast, ME 800-435-4456

Wedges

Ore-Ida Foods
  Pittsburgh, PA 800-255-5750
Penobscot Mccrum LLC
  Belfast, ME 800-435-4456

Instant

Gilster-Mary Lee Corp
  Chester, IL 618-826-2361
Idahoan Foods LLC
  Idaho Falls, ID 800-746-7999

Oven Type

Frozen

Sun Glo Of Idaho
  Sugar City, ID 208-356-7346

Potatoes

Aaland Potato Company
  Hoople, ND 701-894-6144
Alsum Farms & Produce
  Cambria, WI 800-236-5127
Baker Produce
  Kennewick, WA 800-624-7553
Ben B. Schwartz & Sons
  Detroit, MI 313-841-8300
Burnette Foods
  Elk Rapids, MI 231-264-8116
Byrnes Packing Shed
  Hastings, FL 904-692-1643
Canon Potato Company
  Center, CO 719-754-3445

Crystal Potato Seed Co
  Crystal, ND 701-657-2143
Dr. Oetker Canada Ltd.
  Mississauga, ON 800-387-6939
Edmonton Potato Growers
  Edmonton, AB 780-447-1860
Grower Shipper Potato Company
  Monte Vista, CO 719-852-3569
Hanover Potato Products Inc
  Hanover, PA 717-632-0700
Idaho Supreme Potatoes Inc
  Firth, ID 208-346-4100
Idahoan Foods LLC
  Idaho Falls, ID 800-746-7999
Isadore A. Rapasadi & Son
  Canastota, NY 800-828-7277
J C Watson Co
  Parma, ID 208-722-5141
J. R. Simplot Co.
  Boise, ID 208-336-2110
Johnston Farms
  Bakersfield, CA 661-366-3201
Kingston Fresh
  Idaho Falls, ID 208-522-2365
Kiska Farms
  Burbank, WA 509-547-7746
Larsen Farms
  Hamer, ID 208-374-5592
Lehr Brothers
  Edison, CA 661-366-3244
Livingston Farmers Assn
  Livingston, CA 209-394-7941
Lone Wolf Farms
  Minto, ND 701-248-3482
Maple Leaf Foods International
  North York, ON 800-268-3708
Martens Fresh
  Port Byron, NY 315-776-8821
McCain Foods USA Inc.
  Oakbrook Terace, IL 800-938-7799
McCain Produce Inc.
  Florenceville-Bristol, NB 506-392-3036
Michael Foods, Inc.
  Minnetonka, MN 952-258-4000
Mr Dell Foods
  Kearney, MO 816-628-4644
Muir Copper Canyon Farms
  Salt Lake City, UT 800-564-0949
Nation Wide Canning Ltd.
  Cottam, ON 519-839-4831
National Harvest
  Kansas City, MO 816-842-9600
New Harvest Foods
  Washington, DC 920-822-2578
Nonpareil Farms
  Blackfoot, ID 800-522-2223
Nu-Way Potato Products
  North York, ON 416-241-9151
O C Schulz & Sons
  Crystal, ND 701-657-2152
Oregon Potato Co
  Boardman, OR 800-336-6311
Penobscot Mccrum LLC
  Belfast, ME 800-435-4456
Sun Glo Of Idaho
  Sugar City, ID 208-356-7346
Twin City Foods Inc.
  Stanwood, WA 206-515-2400
Vauxhall Foods
  Vauxhall, AB 403-654-2771
Vessey & Co Inc
  Holtville, CA 760-356-0130
Washington Potato Company
  Pasco, WA 800-897-2726
Weil's Food Processing
  Wheatley, ON 519-825-4572
Wildcat Produce
  McGrew, NE 308-783-2438

Red

Baker Produce
  Kennewick, WA 800-624-7553
Kiska Farms
  Burbank, WA 509-547-7746
McCain Produce Inc.
  Florenceville-Bristol, NB 506-392-3036
Vessey & Co Inc
  Holtville, CA 760-356-0130

Powdered Vegetables

Emerling International Foods
  Buffalo, NY 716-833-7381
Green Foods Corp.
  Oxnard, CA 800-777-4430
Green Source Organics
  Boynton Beach, FL 561-740-8595
LYNQ
  Montreal, QC
Marshall Ingredients
  Wolcott, NY 800-796-9353
Niagara Foods
  Middleport, NY 716-735-7722
Spreda Group
  Louisville, KY 502-426-9411
Vegetable Juices Inc
  Chicago, IL 888-776-9752
Weinberg Foods
  Kirkland, WA 800-866-3447

Produce

Aaland Potato Company
  Hoople, ND 701-894-6144
Adobe Creek Packing Co Inc
  Kelseyville, CA 707-279-4204
AgriNorthwest
  Kennewick, WA 509-734-1195
Alsum Farms & Produce
  Cambria, WI 800-236-5127
Annapolis Produce & Restaurant
  Annapolis, MD 410-266-5211
Anton Caratan & Son
  Bakersfield, CA 661-725-2575
Apple Acres
  La Fayette, NY 603-893-8596
Appleton Produce Company
  Weiser, ID 208-414-3352
Applewood Orchards Inc
  Deerfield, MI 800-447-3854
Argee Corp
  Santee, CA 800-449-3030
Associated Fruit Company
  Phoenix, OR 541-535-1787
Atlantic Blueberry
  Hammonton, NJ 609-561-8600
Babe Farms Inc
  Santa Maria, CA 800-648-6772
Baker Produce
  Kennewick, WA 800-624-7553
Ballantine Produce Company
  Reedley, CA 559-875-2583
Banana Distributing Company
  San Antonio, TX 210-227-8285
Bay Cities Produce Co Inc
  San Leandro, CA 510-346-4943
Ben B. Schwartz & Sons
  Detroit, MI 313-841-8300
Ben-Bud Growers Inc.
  Boca Raton, FL 561-347-3120
Bifulco Four Seasons
  Pittsgrove, NJ 856-692-0778
Bodek Kosher Produce Inc
  Brooklyn, NY 718-377-4163
Boggiatto Produce Inc
  Salinas, CA 831-424-8952
Boskovich Farms Inc
  Oxnard, CA 805-487-2299
Brandt Farms Inc
  Reedley, CA 559-638-6961
Bridenbaugh Orchards
  Martinsburg, PA 814-793-2364
Brooks Tropicals Inc
  Homestead, FL 800-327-4833
Byrnes Packing Shed
  Hastings, FL 904-692-1643
Cal Harvest Marketing Inc
  Hanford, CA 559-582-4494
Calco of Calgary
  Calgary, AB 403-295-3578
Calif Watercress Inc
  Fillmore, CA 805-524-4808
Capital Produce II Inc
  Jessup, MD 443-755-1733
Caro Foods
  Houma, LA 800-395-2276
Carolina Blueberry Co-Op Assn
  Garland, NC 910-588-4220
Carson City Pickle Company
  Carson City, MI 989-584-3148
Castellini Group
  Newport, KY 800-233-8560

Product Categories / Fruits & Vegetables: Produce

Cates Addis Company
Parkton, NC 800-423-1883
Chazy Orchards
Chazy, NY 518-846-7171
Chief Wenatchee
Wenatchee, WA 509-662-5197
Chris' Farm Stand
Peabody, MA 978-994-4315
Christopher Ranch LLC
Gilroy, CA 408-847-1100
Circle Valley Produce LLC
Idaho Falls, ID 208-524-2628
Concannon Vineyard
Livermore, CA 800-258-9866
Congdon Orchards Inc.
Yakima, WA 509-966-4440
Corona College Heights
Riverside, CA 951-351-7880
Corrin Produce Sales
Dinuba, CA 559-596-0517
Coulter Giufre & Co Inc
Chittenango, NY 315-687-6510
Country Fresh Mushroom Co
Toughkenamon, PA 610-268-3033
Couture Farms
Kettleman City, CA 559-386-9865
Crane & Crane Inc
Brewster, WA 509-689-3447
Crown Packing Company
Salinas, CA 831-424-2067
Crystal Potato Seed Co
Crystal, ND 701-657-2143
D'Arrigo Brothers Company of California
Salinas, CA 831-455-4500
Delta Packing
Lodi, CA 209-334-1023
Di Mare Fresh Inc
Fort Worth, TX 817-385-3000
Diamond Blueberry Inc
Hammonton, NJ 609-561-3661
Diamond Fruit Growers
Hood River, OR 541-354-5300
Dimond Tager Company Products
Tampa, FL 813-238-3111
DNE World Fruit Sales
Fort Pierce, FL 800-327-6676
DNO Inc
Columbus, OH 614-231-3601
Dundee Citrus Growers Assn
Dundee, FL 800-447-1574
E.W. Bowker Company
Pemberton, NJ 609-894-9508
Exeter Produce
Exeter, ON 519-235-0141
F & S Produce Co Inc
Vineland, NJ 800-886-3316
Farm Pak Products Inc
Spring Hope, N.C. 800-367-2799
Federation-Southern Cprtvs
Atlanta, GA 404-765-0991
Ferris Organic Farms
Eaton Rapids, MI 800-628-8736
Fiesta Farms
Toronto, ON 416-537-1235
Fig Garden Packing Inc
Fresno, CA 559-271-9000
Fillmore Piru Citrus
Piru, CA 805-521-1781
Finer Foods Inc
Chicago, IL 773-579-3870
Flippin-Seaman Inc
Tyro, VA 434-277-5828
Florida Citrus
Bartow, FL 863-537-3999
Fresh Express, Inc.
Salinas, CA 800-242-5472
Fruit Ranch Inc
Milwaukee, WI 800-433-3289
Ful-Flav-R Foods
Alamo, CA 925-838-0300
G Cefalu & Brother Inc
Jessup, MD 410-799-2910
Garber Farms
Iota, LA 800-824-2284
Gentile Brothers Company
Cincinnati, OH 800-877-7954
George Chiala Farms Inc
Morgan Hill, CA 408-778-0562
George W Saulpaugh & Son
Germantown, NY 518-537-6500
Glacier Foods
Houston, TX 832-375-6300

Godwin Produce Co
Dunn, NC 910-892-4171
Golden River Fruit Company
Vero Beach, FL 772-562-8610
Golden Town Apple Products
Rougemont, QC 866-552-7643
Great Eastern Sun Trading Co
Asheville, NC 800-334-5809
Grimmway Farms
Bakersfield, CA 800-301-3101
Grower Shipper Potato Company
Monte Vista, CO 719-852-3569
Haines City Citrus Growers
Haines City, FL 800-327-6676
Half Moon Fruit & Produce Company
Yolo, CA 530-662-1727
Harlin Fruit Co
Monett, MO 417-235-7370
Harner Farms
State College, PA 814-237-7919
Harris Farms Inc
Coalinga, CA 800-311-6211
Heller Brothers Packing Corp
Winter Garden, FL 855-543-5537
Henggeler Packing Company
Fruitland, ID 208-452-4212
Herold's Salads
Cleveland, OH 800-427-2523
HH Dobbins Inc
Lyndonville, NY 877-362-2467
Horton Fruit Co Inc
Louisville, KY 800-626-2245
Hunt Brothers Cooperative
Lake Wales, FL 863-676-1411
Indian Bay Frozen Foods
Centreville, NL 709-678-2844
Indian Hollow Farms
Richland Center, WI 800-236-3944
International Specialty Supply
Cookeville, TN 931-526-1106
Isadore A. Rapasadi & Son
Canastota, NY 800-828-7277
J C Watson Co
Parma, ID 208-722-5141
J J Produce
Loxahatchee, FL 561-791-1796
Jack Brown Produce
Sparta, MI 800-348-0834
Jasmine Vineyards, Inc.
Delano, CA 661-792-2141
JES Foods
Cleveland, OH 216-883-8987
Jonathan's Sprouts
Rochester, MA 508-763-2577
Joseph J. White
Browns Mills, NJ 609-893-2332
Kaiser Pickles
Cincinnati, OH 888-291-0608
Kingston Fresh
Idaho Falls, ID 208-522-2365
Kitchen Pride Mushrooms Farm
Gonzales, TX 830-540-4528
Knight Seed Company
Burnsville, MN 800-328-2999
Knight's Appleden Fruit LTD
Colborne, ON 905-349-2521
L F Lambert Spawn Co
Coatesville, PA 610-384-5031
Lagorio Enterprises
Manteca, CA 209-982-5691
Lane Southern Orchards
Fort Valley, GA 800-277-3224
Lehr Brothers
Edison, CA 661-366-3244
Lennox Farm
Shelburne, ON 519-925-6444
Livingston Farmers Assn
Livingston, CA 209-394-7941
Lone Wolf Farms
Minto, ND 701-248-3482
Long Island Cauliflower Assn
Riverhead, NY 631-727-2212
Lou Pizzo Produce
Parkland, FL 954-941-8830
Lucich Santos Farms
Patterson, CA 209-892-6500
M & S Tomato Repacking Co Inc
Springfield, MA 413-737-1308
Magnolia Citrus Assn
Porterville, CA 559-784-4455
Mancuso Cheese Co
Joliet, IL 815-722-2475

Mann Packing Co
Salinas, CA 800-285-1002
Manzana Products Co.
Sebastopol, CA 707-823-5313
Maple Leaf Foods International
North York, ON 800-268-3708
Marley Orchards Corporation
Yakima, WA 509-248-5231
Martens Fresh
Port Byron, NY 315-776-8821
Matson Fruit Co
Selah, WA 509-697-7100
Maui Gold Pineapple Company
Pukalani, HI 808-877-3805
McDaniel Fruit
Fallbrook, CA 760-728-8438
Mcfarling Foods Inc
Indianapolis, IN 317-635-2633
Merrill's Blueberry Farms
Ellsworth, ME. 800-711-6551
Michigan Celery Cooperative
Hudsonville, MI 616-669-1250
Mike & Jean's Berry Farm
Mt Vernon, WA 360-424-7220
Mister Spear
Stockton, CA 800-677-7327
Mixon Fruit Farms Inc
Bradenton, FL 800-608-2525
Montreal Chop Suey Company
Montreal, QC 514-522-3134
Naraghi Group
Escalon, CA 209-579-5253
National Raisin Co.
Fowler, CA 559-834-5981
New York Apple Sales Inc
Glenmont, NY 888-477-6770
Nonpareil Farms
Blackfoot, ID 800-522-2223
Nor-Cliff Farms
Port Colborne, ON 905-835-0808
North Bay Produce Inc
Traverse City, MI 231-946-1941
Northern Feed & Bean Company
Lucerne, CO 800-316-2326
Northwest Pea & Bean Co
Spokane Valley, WA 509-534-3821
NSG Transport Inc
Gothenburg, NE 308-537-7191
Nuchief Sales Inc
Wenatchee, WA 888-269-4638
Nunes Co Inc
Salinas, CA 831-751-7500
Nut Factory
Spokane Valley, WA 888-239-5288
O C Schulz & Sons
Crystal, ND 701-657-2152
Ocean Mist Farms
Castroville, CA 831-633-2144
Ocean Spray International
Lakeville-Middleboro, MA 800-662-3263
Ontario Produce Company
Ontario, OR 541-889-6485
Orange Cove-Sanger Citrus
Orange Cove, CA 559-626-4453
Oregon Potato Co
Boardman, OR 800-336-6311
Oxford Frozen Foods
Oxford, NS 902-447-2100
P R Farms Inc
Clovis, CA 559-299-0201
Pandol Brothers Inc
Delano, CA 661-725-3755
Pavero Cold Storage
Highland, NY 800-435-2994
Peter Rabbit Farms
Coachella, CA 760-398-0136
Pioneer Growers
Belle Glade, FL 229-243-9306
Pleasant Grove Farms
Pleasant Grove, CA 916-655-3391
Post Familie Vineyards
Altus, AR 800-275-8423
Pots de Creme
Lexington, KY 859-299-2254
Prairie Mushrooms
Ardrossan, AB 780-467-3555
Price Co
Yakima, WA 509-966-4110
Prime Produce
Orange, CA 714-771-0718
Produce Buyers Company
Detroit, MI 313-843-0132

Product Categories / Fruits & Vegetables: Prunes

Producers Cooperative
　Bryan, TX 979-778-6000
Quillin Produce Co
　Huntsville, AL 256-883-7374
R & S Mexican Food
　Glendale, AZ. 602-272-2727
R.C. McEntire & Company
　Columbia, SC 803-799-3388
Red Hat Cooperative
　Redcliff, AB 403-548-6208
Reed Lang Farms
　Rio Hondo, TX 956-748-2354
Reinhart Foods
　Toronto, ON 416-645-4910
Rene Produce Dist
　Rio Rico, AZ. 520-281-0806
Reter Fruit
　Medford, OR. 541-772-9560
Rice Fruit Co
　Gardners, PA 800-627-3359
Russo Farms
　Vineland, NJ 856-692-5942
S & E Organic Farms Inc
　Bakersfield, CA 661-325-2644
S & L Produce Inc
　Walnut Hill, IL 618-532-8344
Sales USA
　Salado, TX 800-766-7344
Santanna Banana Company
　Harrisburg, PA 717-238-8321
Schmidt Bros Inc
　Swanton, OH. 800-200-7318
Scotian Gold
　Coldbrook, NS 888-726-8426
Seald Sweet
　Vero Beach, FL 559-636-4400
Sedlock Farm
　Lynn Center, IL. 309-521-8284
Segall Nathan Co Inc
　Montgomery, AL. 334-279-3174
Shields Date Garden
　Indio, CA. 800-414-2555
Snokist Growers
　Yakima, WA 800-377-2857
Solana Gold Organics
　Sebastopol, CA 800-459-1121
South Mill
　Kennett Square, PA. 610-444-4800
Spring Ledge Farm Stand
　New London, NH 603-526-6253
Stadelman Fruit LLC
　Zillah, WA. 509-829-5145
Star Route Farms
　Bolinas, CA. 415-868-1658
Strube Celery & Vegetable Co
　Chicago, IL 773-446-4000
Sun Pacific
　Pasadena, CA 213-612-9957
Superior Mushroom Farms
　Ardrossan, AB 866-687-2242
Sure-Fresh Produce Inc
　Santa Maria, CA 888-423-5379
Surface Banana Company
　Parkersburg, WV 304-485-2400
Talley Farms
　Arroyo Grande, CA. 805-489-5400
Tanimura Antle Inc
　Salinas, CA 800-772-4542
Taylor Farms
　Salinas, CA 831-754-0471
Taylor Farms Pacific
　Tracy, CA 209-830-1086
Taylor Orchards
　Reynolds, GA 478-847-5963
Teixeira Farms, Inc.
　Santa Maria, CA 805-928-3801
Tejon Ranch Co
　Lebec, CA 661-248-3000
Tiger Mushroom Farm
　Nanton, AB 403-646-2578
Tony Vitrano Company
　Jessup, MD 800-481-3784
Topaz Farm
　Portland, OR. 503-708-0008
Trefethen Family Vineyards
　Napa, CA. 707-255-7700
Tru-Blu Cooperative Associates
　New Lisbon, NJ 609-894-8717
True Blue Farms
　Grand Junction, MI. 877-654-2400
Tufts Ranch
　Winters, CA 530-795-4144
Turlock Fruit Co
　Turlock, CA 209-634-7207
Ultimate Foods
　Linden, NJ. 908-486-0800
United Apple Sales
　New Paltz, NY 585-765-2460
United Marketing Exchange
　Delta, CO 970-874-3332
United Pickles
　Bronx, NY. 718-933-6060
Van de Kamps
　Peoria, IL. 800-798-3318
Vaughn Rue Produce
　Wilson, NC 800-388-8138
Venture Vineyards
　Lodi, NY 888-635-6277
Veronica Foods Inc
　Oakland, CA 800-370-5554
Vidalia Sweets Brand
　Lyons, GA 912-565-8881
Vincent B Zaninovich & Sons
　Richgrove, CA 661-725-2497
Walter P Rawl & Sons Inc
　Pelion, SC 803-894-1900
Washington Fruit & Produce Company
　Yakima, WA 509-457-6177
Waugh Foods Inc
　East Peoria, IL. 309-427-8000
Weiser River Packing
　Weiser, ID 208-549-0200
West Pak Avocado Inc
　Murrieta, CA 800-266-4414
Wetherby Cranberry Company
　Warrens, WI 608-378-4813
Whitney & Sons Seafood
　Hudson, FL 727-869-3728
Wileman Brothers & Elliott Inc
　Cutler, CA 559-528-4772
Worldwide Specialties In
　Los Angeles, CA. 800-437-2702
Yakima Fresh
　Yakima, WA 509-248-5770
Yokohl Packing Co
　Lindsay, CA 559-562-1327
Zentis Sweet Ovations
　Philadelphia, PA 800-223-7073
Zuccaro Produce
　Columbia Heights, MN. 612-333-1122

Prunes

Central California Raisin Packing Co, Inc.
　Del Rey, CA 559-888-2195
George W Saulpaugh & Son
　Germantown, NY 518-537-6500
Henggeler Packing Company
　Fruitland, ID 208-452-4212
HH Dobbins Inc
　Lyndonville, NY 877-362-2467
Hialeah Products Co
　Hollywood, FL 800-923-3379
Kalustyan
　New York, NY 800-352-3451
Organic Planet
　San Francisco, CA 415-765-5590
Ramos Orchards
　Winters, CA 530-795-4748
Service Packing Company
　Vancouver, BC 604-681-0264
Sowden Brothers Farm
　Live Oak, CA 530-695-3750
Stadelman Fruit LLC
　Zillah, WA. 509-829-5145
Sunsweet Growers Inc.
　Yuba City, CA. 800-417-2253
Sutter Foods LLC
　Yuba City, CA. 530-682-7776
Terri Lynn Inc
　Elgin, IL 800-323-0775
Timber Crest Farms
　Healdsburg, CA 888-766-4233
Tufts Ranch
　Winters, CA 530-795-4144
Unique Ingredients LLC
　Gold Canyon, AZ 480-983-2498
Valley View Packing Co
　Yuba City, CA. 530-673-7356
Wilbur Packing Company
　Yuba City, CA. 530-671-4911

Canned

Emerling International Foods
　Buffalo, NY. 716-833-7381
Valley View Packing Co
　Yuba City, CA. 530-673-7356

Dried

Bedemco Inc
　White Plains, NY 914-683-1119
Setton International Foods
　Commack, NY 800-227-4397

Frozen

Emerling International Foods
　Buffalo, NY. 716-833-7381
Honee Bear Canning
　Lawton, MI 800-626-2327

Pulps & Purees

Amafruits
　Mokena, IL 877-818-1262
Buddy Fruits
　Rye, NY. 914-514-2098
Homemade Harvey
　Los Angeles, CA. 310-472-4410
Nimeks Organics
　Bethlehem, PA 610-997-0500
Pastorelli Food Products
　Chicago, IL 800-767-2829
Perfect Puree of Napa Valley
　Napa, CA. 707-261-5100
Rainsweet Inc
　Salem, OR. 800-363-4293
Rv Industries
　Buford, GA 770-729-8983
Sunrise Growers
　Placentia, CA 714-630-6292
SupHerb Farms
　Turlock, CA 800-787-4372
Tulkoff's Food Products Inc
　Baltimore, MD 800-638-7343

Fruit & Vegetable

California Custom Fruits
　Baldwin Park, CA 877-558-0056
Emerling International Foods
　Buffalo, NY. 716-833-7381
Golden Town Apple Products
　Rougemont, QC 866-552-7643
Greenwood Associates
　Niles, IL 847-579-5500
Hirzel Canning Co & Farms
　Luckey, OH 419-419-7525
Louis Dreyfus Company Citrus Inc
　Winter Garden, FL 407-656-1000
Pastorelli Food Products
　Chicago, IL 800-767-2829
Peace River Citrus Products
　Vero Beach, FL 772-492-4050
Prima Foods International
　Silver Springs, FL 800-774-8751
Red Gold Inc.
　Elwood, IN 866-729-7187
S & E Organic Farms Inc
　Bakersfield, CA 661-325-2644
Seneca Foods Corp
　Marion, NY. 315-926-8100
True Blue Farms
　Grand Junction, MI. 877-654-2400
Vegetable Juices Inc
　Chicago, IL 888-776-9752
Vita-Pakt Citrus Products Co
　Covina, CA 888-684-8272

Pulp

Dried Beet

Emerling International Foods
　Buffalo, NY. 716-833-7381

Fruit

3V Company
　Brooklyn, NY 718-858-7333
Avo-King Internatl
　Orange, CA 800-286-5464
Calavo Growers
　Santa Paula, CA 805-525-1245
Miramar Fruit Trading Company
　Doral, FL. 305-883-4774

Product Categories / Fruits & Vegetables: Pumpkin

Sunny Avocado
  Jamul, CA 800-999-2862
Tantos Foods International
  Markham, ON 905-943-9993

Vegetable

Pastorelli Food Products
  Chicago, IL 800-767-2829

Puree

Fruit

Beta Pure Foods
  Santa Cruz, CA 831-685-6565
Calavo Growers
  Santa Paula, CA 805-525-1245
Fruithill Inc
  Yamhill, OR 503-662-3926
Gerber Products Co
  Arlington, VA 800-284-9488
Golden Town Apple Products
  Rougemont, QC 866-552-7643
Granny's Best Strawberry Products
  Victoria, ON 519-426-0705
Greenwood Associates
  Niles, IL 847-579-5500
Hartog Rahal Foods
  Norwood, NJ 201-750-0500
Johnson Foods, Inc.
  Sunnyside, WA 509-837-4214
Milne Fruit Products Inc
  Prosser, WA 509-786-2611
Munk Pack
  Greenwich, CT
National Frozen Foods Corp
  Seattle, WA 206-322-8900
Pacific Coast Fruit Co
  Portland, OR 503-234-6411
Rainsweet Inc
  Salem, OR 800-363-4293
RFi Ingredients
  Blauvelt, NY 800-962-7663
Rv Industries
  Buford, GA 770-729-8983
Seneca Foods Corp
  Princeville, IL 309-385-4301
Summerland Sweets
  Summerland, BC 800-577-1277
Sunrise Growers
  Placentia, CA 714-630-6292

Fruit & Vegetable

Ful-Flav-R Foods
  Alamo, CA 925-838-0300
National Frozen Foods Corp
  Seattle, WA 206-322-8900
Pastorelli Food Products
  Chicago, IL 800-767-2829

Orange

KMC Citrus Enterprises Inc
  Weirsdale, FL 863-298-8270

Tomato

Emerling International Foods
  Buffalo, NY 716-833-7381
Hirzel Canning Co & Farms
  Luckey, OH 419-419-7525
Pastorelli Food Products
  Chicago, IL 800-767-2829

Vegetable

Beta Pure Foods
  Santa Cruz, CA 831-685-6565
National Frozen Foods Corp
  Seattle, WA 206-322-8900
Otsuka America Foods Inc
  San Francisco, CA 415-986-5300
Pastorelli Food Products
  Chicago, IL 800-767-2829

Tomato

Canned

Nation Wide Canning Ltd.
  Cottam, ON 519-839-4831
Pastorelli Food Products
  Chicago, IL 800-767-2829

Red Gold Inc.
  Elwood, IN 866-729-7187
Seneca Foods Corp
  Marion, NY 315-926-8100
Tip Top Canning Co
  Tipp City, OH 800-352-2635
Vegetable Juices Inc
  Chicago, IL 888-776-9752
Violet Packing Holdings LLC
  Williamstown, NJ 856-629-7428

Pumpkin

Abbott & Cobb Inc
  Feasterville, PA 800-345-7333
Bay Baby Produce
  Burlington, WA 360-755-2299
Bennett's Apples & Cider
  Ancaster, ON 905-648-6878
Heartland Strawberry Farm
  Waterloo, IA 888-747-7423
Organic Planet
  San Francisco, CA 415-765-5590
Schmidt Bros Inc
  Swanton, OH 800-200-7318
Tom Ringhausen Orchards
  Hardin, IL 800-258-6645
Topaz Farm
  Portland, OR 503-708-0008
Unique Ingredients LLC
  Gold Canyon, AZ 480-983-2498
Wildcat Produce
  McGrew, NE 308-783-2438

Canned

Agrocan
  Ville St Laurent, QC 877-247-6226
Emerling International Foods
  Buffalo, NY 716-833-7381
Harvest-Pac Products
  Chatham, ON 519-436-0446
Lakeside Foods Inc.
  Manitowoc, WI 800-466-3834

Frozen

Emerling International Foods
  Buffalo, NY 716-833-7381
Lakeside Foods Inc.
  Manitowoc, WI 800-466-3834

Radish

Boskovich Farms Inc
  Oxnard, CA 805-487-2299
F & S Produce Co Inc
  Vineland, NJ 800-886-3316
Gouw Quality Onions
  Taber, AB 403-223-1440
Pioneer Growers
  Belle Glade, FL 229-243-9306
Vegetable Juices Inc
  Chicago, IL 888-776-9752

Raisins

Amazing Fruit Products
  Fort Payne, AL 256-273-5363
American Key Food Products Inc
  Closter, NJ 877-263-7539
Bedemco Inc
  White Plains, NY 914-683-1119
Boghosian Raisin Packing Co
  Fowler, CA 559-834-5348
Central California Raisin Packing Co, Inc.
  Del Rey, CA 559-888-2195
Chooljian Bros Packing Co
  Sanger, CA 559-875-5501
Del Rey Packing
  Del Rey, CA 559-888-2031
Dipasa USA Inc
  Brownsville, TX 956-831-4072
Emerling International Foods
  Buffalo, NY 716-833-7381
Fig Garden Packing Inc
  Fresno, CA 559-271-9000
Foley's Chocolates & Candies
  Richmond, BC 888-236-5397
Green Earth Orchards
  Salt Lake City, UT 801-888-7161
Jason & Son Specialty Foods
  Rancho Cordova, CA 800-810-9093
Jewel Date Co
  Thermal, CA 760-399-4474

Just Tomatoes
  Westley, CA 800-537-1985
Kalustyan
  New York, NY 800-352-3451
Lion Raisins Inc
  Selma, CA 559-834-6677
Made In Nature
  Boulder, CO 800-906-7426
Mariani Packing Co.
  Vacaville, CA 707-452-2800
National Raisin Co.
  Fowler, CA 559-834-5981
New Organics
  Kenwood, CA 734-677-5570
Nut Factory
  Spokane Valley, WA 888-239-5288
Organic Planet
  San Francisco, CA 415-765-5590
Reinhart Foods
  Toronto, ON 416-645-4910
Setton International Foods
  Commack, NY 800-227-4397
Sun Valley Raisins Inc
  Fresno, CA 559-233-8070
Sun-Maid Growers of California
  Kingsburg, CA 559-896-8000
Sunfood
  El Cajon, CA 888-729-3663
Sunridge Farms
  Royal Oaks, CA 831-786-7000
Terri Lynn Inc
  Elgin, IL 800-323-0775
Timber Crest Farms
  Healdsburg, CA 888-766-4233
Unique Ingredients LLC
  Gold Canyon, AZ 480-983-2498
Victor Packing
  Madera, CA 559-673-5908
Waymouth Farms Inc
  Minneapolis, MN 800-527-0094

Chocolate Coated

Sun-Maid Growers of California
  Kingsburg, CA 559-896-8000

Dried

Boghosian Raisin Packing Co
  Fowler, CA 559-834-5348
Fig Garden Packing Inc
  Fresno, CA 559-271-9000
Jason & Son Specialty Foods
  Rancho Cordova, CA 800-810-9093
Kalustyan
  New York, NY 800-352-3451
National Raisin Co.
  Fowler, CA 559-834-5981
Nut Factory
  Spokane Valley, WA 888-239-5288

Yogurt Coated

Foley's Chocolates & Candies
  Richmond, BC 888-236-5397
GKI Foods
  Brighton, MI 248-486-0055
Mariani Packing Co.
  Vacaville, CA 707-452-2800
Setton International Foods
  Commack, NY 800-227-4397
Sun-Maid Growers of California
  Kingsburg, CA 559-896-8000
Terri Lynn Inc
  Elgin, IL 800-323-0775

Rhubarb

Bryant Preserving Company
  Alma, AR 800-634-2413
Cajun Brands
  New Iberia, LA 504-408-2252
Coloma Frozen Foods Inc
  Coloma, MI 800-642-2723
Lennox Farm
  Shelburne, ON 519-925-6444
Snowcrest Packer
  Abbotsford, BC 800-265-3686
Washington Rhubarb Grower Assn
  Sumner, WA 800-435-9911
Webster Farms
  Cambridge, NS 800-507-8844

Product Categories / Fruits & Vegetables: Roasted Vegetables

Canned
Emerling International Foods
　Buffalo, NY 716-833-7381

Frozen
Coloma Frozen Foods Inc
　Coloma, MI 800-642-2723
Emerling International Foods
　Buffalo, NY 716-833-7381
Lennox Farm
　Shelburne, ON 519-925-6444
Snowcrest Packer
　Abbotsford, BC 800-265-3686
Washington Rhubarb Grower Assn
　Sumner, WA 800-435-9911
Webster Farms
　Cambridge, NS 800-507-8844

Roasted Vegetables
SupHerb Farms
　Turlock, CA 800-787-4372

Roots & Tubers
American Botanicals
　Eolia, MO 800-684-6070
Emerling International Foods
　Buffalo, NY 716-833-7381
Penn Herb Co
　Philadelphia, PA 800-523-9971

Rutabaga
Arbre Farms Inc
　Walkerville, MI 231-873-3337
Exeter Produce
　Exeter, ON 519-235-0141

Canned
Arbre Farms Inc
　Walkerville, MI 231-873-3337
Emerling International Foods
　Buffalo, NY 716-833-7381

Frozen
Arbre Farms Inc
　Walkerville, MI 231-873-3337
Emerling International Foods
　Buffalo, NY 716-833-7381
Paris Foods Corporation
　Trappe, MD 410-200-9595

Salad Greens
AeroFarms
　Newark, NJ 973-242-2495
Atlanta Bread Co.
　Smyrna, GA 800-398-3728
Boskovich Farms Inc
　Oxnard, CA 805-487-2299
Earthbound Farm
　San Jn Bautista, CA 800-690-3200
Risvold's Inc.
　Gardena, CA 323-770-2674
Taylor Farms Pacific
　Tracy, CA 209-830-1086

Mustard Tips
AeroFarms
　Newark, NJ 973-242-2495

Sauces

Apple
Andros Foods North America
　Mount Jackson, VA 844-426-3767
Blue Jay Orchards
　Bethel, CT 203-748-0119
Cold Hollow Cider Mill
　Waterbury Center, VT 800-327-7537
Commodities Marketing Inc
　Clarksburg, NJ 732-516-0700
Coutts Specialty Foods Inc
　Boxborough, MA 800-919-2952
Del Mar Food Products Corp
　Watsonville, CA 831-722-3516
Emerling International Foods
　Buffalo, NY 716-833-7381
Graves Mountain Lodge Inc.
　Syria, VA 540-923-4231

Knouse Foods Co-Op Inc.
　Peach Glen, PA 717-677-8181
Leahy Orchards
　Franklin Centre, QC 800-667-7380
Leroux Creek
　Hotchkiss, CO 877-970-5670
Love Creek Orchards
　Medina, TX 800-449-0882
Mott's LLP
　Plano, TX 800-426-4891
Nana Mae's Organics
　Sebastopol, CA 707-829-7359
New Era Canning Company
　New Era, MI 231-861-2151
Solana Gold Organics
　Sebastopol, CA 800-459-1121
Tree Top Inc
　Selah, WA 509-697-7251
Unique Ingredients LLC
　Gold Canyon, AZ 480-983-2498
White House Foods
　Winchester, VA 540-662-3401

Canned
Leahy Orchards
　Franklin Centre, QC 800-667-7380
New Era Canning Company
　New Era, MI 231-861-2151

with Other Fruit or Spices
Leahy Orchards
　Franklin Centre, QC 800-667-7380

Cranberry
Coastal Classics
　Duxbury, MA 508-746-6058
Delectable Gourmet LLC
　Deer Park, NY 800-696-1350
Fireside Kitchen
　Halifax, NS 902-454-7387
Johnston's Home Style Products
　Charlottetown, PE 902-629-1300
Ocean Spray International
　Lakeville-Middleboro, MA 800-662-3263
Skjodt-Barrett Foods
　Brampton, ON 877-600-1200
Steel's Gourmet Foods, Ltd.
　Bridgeport, PA 800-678-3357

Jellied
Ocean Spray International
　Lakeville-Middleboro, MA 800-662-3263

Scallions
Emerling International Foods
　Buffalo, NY 716-833-7381
Ferris Organic Farms
　Eaton Rapids, MI 800-628-8736
S & E Organic Farms Inc
　Bakersfield, CA 661-325-2644
SupHerb Farms
　Turlock, CA 800-787-4372
Tanimura Antle Inc
　Salinas, CA 800-772-4542

Seaweeds & Sea Vegetables
Acadian Seaplants
　Dartmouth, NS 800-575-9100
Gimme Health Foods
　San Rafael, CA
Great Eastern Sun Trading Co
　Asheville, NC 800-334-5809
Maine Coast Sea Vegetables
　Franklin, ME 207-565-2907
Maine Seaweed Company
　Steuben, ME 207-546-2875
Ocean's Halo
　Burlingame, CA 650-642-5907
Sea Veggies
　Commerce, CA 323-728-4762

Shallot
California Garlic Co
　San Diego, CA 951-506-8883
Christopher Ranch LLC
　Gilroy, CA 408-847-1100
Haliburton International Inc
　Ontario, CA 877-980-4295

SupHerb Farms
　Turlock, CA 800-787-4372
Vegetable Juices Inc
　Chicago, IL 888-776-9752

Soy
Agri-Dairy Products
　Purchase, NY 914-697-9580
Ajinomoto Heartland Inc
　Chicago, IL 773-380-7000
Avatar Corp
　University Park, IL 800-255-3181
Basic Food Flavors
　North Las Vegas, NV 702-643-0043
Bluechip Group
　Salt Lake City, UT 800-878-0099
California Natural Products
　Lathrop, CA 209-858-2525
Cedar Lake Foods
　Cedar Lake, MI 800-246-5039
Clofine Dairy Products Inc
　Linwood, NJ 609-653-1000
Cricklewood Soyfoods
　Mertztown, PA 610-682-4109
Ener-G Foods
　Seattle, WA 800-331-5222
Flavor House, Inc.
　Adelanto, CA 760-246-9131
Genisoy
　Downsview, OH 866-972-6879
Glennys
　Brooklyn, NY 888-864-1243
Healthy Food Ingredients
　Fargo, ND 844-275-3443
Hialeah Products Co
　Hollywood, FL 800-923-3379
House Foods America Corp
　Garden Grove, CA 877-333-7077
International Service Group
　Alpharetta, GA 770-518-0988
Island Spring Inc
　Vashon, WA 206-463-9848
Lee's Food Products
　Toronto, ON 416-465-2407
Lightlife
　Turners Falls, MA 800-769-3279
Lisanatti Foods
　Oregon City, OR 866-864-3922
Mandarin Soy Sauce Inc
　Middletown, NY 845-343-1505
Mei Shun Tofu Products Company
　Chicago, IL 312-842-7000
MicroSoy Corporation
　Jefferson, IA 515-386-2100
Miyako Oriental Foods Inc
　Baldwin Park, CA 877-788-6476
Modesto WholeSoy
　Ceres, CA 209-523-5119
N D Labs
　Lynbrook, NY 888-263-5227
Nature Soy Inc
　Philadelphia, PA 215-765-3289
Northern Soy Inc
　Rochester, NY 585-235-8970
Pokonobe Industries
　Santa Monica, CA 310-392-1259
Pulmuone Foods USA Inc.
　Fullerton, CA 800-588-7782
Red River Commodities Inc
　Fargo, ND 800-437-5539
San-Ei Gen FFI
　New York, NY 212-315-7850
Schillinger Genetics Inc
　West Des Moines, IA 866-769-7200
Solnuts
　Hudson, IA 800-648-3503
Soyfoods of America
　Washington, DC 202-659-3520
SoyLife Division
　Edina, MN 952-920-7700
Specialty Ingredients
　Buffalo Grove, IL 847-419-9595
Spectrum Foods Inc
　Springfield, IL 217-528-5301
Sunrich LLC
　Hope, MN 800-297-5997
Turtle Island Foods
　Hood River, OR 800-508-8100
Vitasoy USA
　Woburn, MA 800-848-2769

Product Categories / Fruits & Vegetables: Spinach

Fresh

Smoke & Fire Natural Food
 Great Barrington, MA 413-528-8008
Vitasoy USA
 Woburn, MA 800-848-2769

Protein

Texturized

Seneca Foods Corp
 Princeville, IL 309-385-4301
Spectrum Foods Inc
 Springfield, IL 217-528-5301

Soy Bean

Aak USA Inc
 Newark, NJ 973-344-1300
AG Processing Inc
 Omaha, NE 800-247-1345
American Culinary Garden
 Springfield, MO 888-831-2433
DuPont Nutrition & Biosciences
 New Century, KS 913-764-8100
DuPont Pioneer
 Johnston, IA 515-535-5954
Durey-Libby Edible Nuts
 Carlstadt, NJ 800-332-6887
Fizzle Flat Farm, L.L.C.
 Yale, IL 618-793-2060
IMAC
 Oklahoma City, OK 888-878-7827
Ingredient Innovations
 Kansas City, MO 816-587-1426
Knight Seed Company
 Burnsville, MN 800-328-2999
Lone Pine Enterprise Inc
 Carlisle, AR 870-552-3217
Louis Dreyfus Corporation
 Rotterdam,
Myron's Fine Foods, Inc.
 Millers Falls, MA 800-730-2820
Producers Rice Mill Inc.
 Stuttgart, AR 870-673-4444
R&J Farms
 West Salem, OH 419-846-3179
Red River Commodities Inc
 Fargo, ND 800-437-5539
Roberts Seed
 Axtell, NE 308-743-2565
Schillinger Genetics Inc
 West Des Moines, IA 866-769-7200
Seed Enterprises Inc
 West Point, NE 888-440-7333
Shepherd Farms Inc
 Hillsboro, MO 800-383-2676
Sno-Pac Foods Inc
 Caledonia, MN 800-533-2215
Sonne
 Wahpeton, ND. 800-727-6663
T.S. Smith & Sons
 Bridgeville, DE 302-337-8271
Tofu Shop Specialty Foods Inc
 Arcata, CA 707-822-7401

Roasted Whole

Greenwave Foods
 Berkeley, CA 510-898-1973

Soy Milk

Agri-Dairy Products
 Purchase, NY 914-697-9580
Chunco Foods Inc
 Kansas City, MO 816-283-0716
Clofine Dairy Products Inc
 Linwood, NJ 609-653-1000
Commodities Marketing Inc
 Clarksburg, NJ 732-516-0700
Devansoy Farms
 Carroll, IA. 800-747-8605
Eden Foods Inc
 Clinton, MI 888-424-3336
Ener-G Foods
 Seattle, WA 800-331-5222
FarmSoy Company
 Summertown, TN 931-964-2411
Mighty Soy Inc
 Los Angeles, CA 323-266-6969
Nutrisoya Foods
 Saint-Hyacinthe, QC. 877-769-2645

San Diego Soy Dairy
 El Cajon, CA. 619-447-8638
Soyfoods of America
 Washington, DC 202-659-3520
Sunrise Markets
 Vancouver, BC 800-661-2326
Tofu Shop Specialty Foods Inc
 Arcata, CA 707-822-7401
Twin Oaks Community
 Louisa, VA 540-894-5141
Vance's Foods
 San Francisco, CA 415-621-1171
WhiteWave Foods
 Denver, CO 800-488-9283

Soy Protein

DuPont Nutrition & Biosciences
 New Century, KS 913-764-8100
Farbest-Tallman Foods Corp
 Montvale, NJ 201-573-4900
N D Labs
 Lynbrook, NY 888-263-5227
SoyTex
 West Orange, NJ 888-769-8391

Concentrate

DuPont Nutrition & Biosciences
 New Century, KS 913-764-8100
Spectrum Foods Inc
 Springfield, IL 217-528-5301

Grits

Spectrum Foods Inc
 Springfield, IL 217-528-5301

Spinach

Avon Heights Mushrooms
 Avondale, PA 610-268-2092
Boskovich Farms Inc
 Oxnard, CA. 805-487-2299
Earthbound Farm
 San Jn Bautista, CA 800-690-3200
F & S Produce Co Inc
 Vineland, NJ 800-886-3316
Patterson Frozen Foods
 Patterson, CA 209-892-2611
Patterson Vegetable Company
 Patterson, CA 209-892-2611
Pictsweet Co
 Bells, TN. 731-663-7600
Seabrook Brothers & Sons
 Seabrook, NJ 856-455-8080
Snowcrest Packer
 Abbotsford, BC. 800-265-3686
State Garden Inc.
 Chelsea, MA
Unique Ingredients LLC
 Gold Canyon, AZ 480-983-2498
Vegetable Juices Inc
 Chicago, IL 888-776-9752

Canned

Emerling International Foods
 Buffalo, NY. 716-833-7381

Frozen

Emerling International Foods
 Buffalo, NY. 716-833-7381
Paris Foods Corporation
 Trappe, MD. 410-200-9595
Vegetable Juices Inc
 Chicago, IL 888-776-9752

Sponge Gourd

Acme Steak & Seafood
 Youngstown, OH. 800-686-2263
Bifulco Four Seasons
 Pittsgrove, NJ 856-692-0778
Cajun Brands
 New Iberia, LA 504-408-2252

Sprouts

Amigos Canning Company
 San Antonio, TX. 210-798-5360
Boskovich Farms Inc
 Oxnard, CA. 805-487-2299
Calco of Calgary
 Calgary, AB. 403-295-3578

Chunco Foods Inc
 Kansas City, MO. 816-283-0716
Houston Calco, Inc
 Houston, TX 713-236-8668
International Specialty Supply
 Cookeville, TN 931-526-1106
Jonathan's Sprouts
 Rochester, MA 508-763-2577
Montreal Chop Suey Company
 Montreal, QC 514-522-3134
Mung Dynasty
 Pittsburgh, PA 412-381-1350
Snowcrest Packer
 Abbotsford, BC. 800-265-3686

Alfalfa

Chunco Foods Inc
 Kansas City, MO. 816-283-0716
International Specialty Supply
 Cookeville, TN 931-526-1106
Jonathan's Sprouts
 Rochester, MA 508-763-2577
Marjon Specialty Foods Inc
 Plant City, FL 813-752-3482

Bean

Emerling International Foods
 Buffalo, NY. 716-833-7381
International Specialty Supply
 Cookeville, TN 931-526-1106
Marjon Specialty Foods Inc
 Plant City, FL 813-752-3482

Mung Bean

Chunco Foods Inc
 Kansas City, MO. 816-283-0716
NOW Foods
 Bloomingdale, IL 888-669-3663

Squash

Abbott & Cobb Inc
 Feasterville, PA. 800-345-7333
Bay Baby Produce
 Burlington, WA. 360-755-2299
Boskovich Farms Inc
 Oxnard, CA. 805-487-2299
Earthbound Farm
 San Jn Bautista, CA 800-690-3200
F & S Produce Co Inc
 Vineland, NJ 800-886-3316
Giumarra Companies
 Los Angeles, CA. 213-627-2900
Haliburton International Inc
 Ontario, CA. 877-980-4295
Michigan Freeze Pack
 Hart, MI 231-873-2175
National Frozen Foods Corp
 Seattle, WA 206-322-8900
Organically Grown Co
 Eugene, OR 800-937-9677
Pacific Collier Fresh Company
 Immokalee, FL 800-226-7274
Pictsweet Co
 Bells, TN. 731-663-7600
Rene Produce Dist
 Rio Rico, AZ 520-281-0806
Snowcrest Packer
 Abbotsford, BC. 800-265-3686
Tom Ringhausen Orchards
 Hardin, IL 800-258-6645
Vegetable Juices Inc
 Chicago, IL 888-776-9752
Walter P Rawl & Sons Inc
 Pelion, SC 803-894-1900
Wholesum Family Farms
 Nogales, AZ 520-281-9233

Acorn

Bay Baby Produce
 Burlington, WA. 360-755-2299

Canned

Emerling International Foods
 Buffalo, NY. 716-833-7381
Sure-Fresh Produce Inc
 Santa Maria, CA 888-423-5379

Product Categories / Fruits & Vegetables: Star Fruit

Frozen
Emerling International Foods
  Buffalo, NY 716-833-7381
Paris Foods Corporation
  Trappe, MD 410-200-9595
Sure-Fresh Produce Inc
  Santa Maria, CA 888-423-5379
Vegetable Juices Inc
  Chicago, IL 888-776-9752

Golden Scallopino
Zuccaro Produce
  Columbia Heights, MN 612-333-1122

Star Fruit
Brooks Tropicals Inc
  Homestead, FL 800-327-4833

Succotash
Emerling International Foods
  Buffalo, NY 716-833-7381
Pictsweet Co
  Bells, TN 731-663-7600
Symons Frozen Foods
  Centralia, WA 360-736-1321
Twin City Foods Inc.
  Stanwood, WA 206-515-2400

Canned
Emerling International Foods
  Buffalo, NY 716-833-7381
Patterson Frozen Foods
  Patterson, CA 209-892-2611

Frozen
Emerling International Foods
  Buffalo, NY 716-833-7381
Paris Foods Corporation
  Trappe, MD 410-200-9595
Patterson Frozen Foods
  Patterson, CA 209-892-2611
Pictsweet Co
  Bells, TN 731-663-7600
Symons Frozen Foods
  Centralia, WA 360-736-1321

Sun Dried Fruit
Chooljian Bros Packing Co
  Sanger, CA 559-875-5501
Del Rey Packing
  Del Rey, CA 559-888-2031

Sweet Potatoes
B & B Produce
  Cana, VA 800-633-4902
Best Ever Bakery
  Massapequa, NY 516-795-5590
Bissett Produce Company
  Spring Hope, NC 800-849-5073
Bright Harvest Sweet Potato Co
  Clarksville, AR 800-793-7440
Burch Farms
  Hilton, NY 800-466-9668
Carolina Pride Products
  Enfield, NC 252-445-3154
Earthbound Farm
  San Jn Bautista, CA 800-690-3200
Godwin Produce Co
  Dunn, NC 910-892-4171
Johnson Brothers Produce Company
  Whitakers, NC 252-437-2111
Joseph D Teachey Jr Produce Co
  Wallace, NC 910-285-4502
Livingston Farmers Assn
  Livingston, CA 209-394-7941
Moody Dunbar Inc
  Johnson City, TN 423-952-0100
Nash Produce
  Nashville, NC 800-334-3032
Royce C. Bone Farms
  Nashville, NC 252-443-3773
Scott Farms Inc
  Lucama, NC 877-284-4030
Spring Acres Sales Company
  Spring Hope, NC 800-849-5436
Tull Hill Farms Inc
  Kinston, NC 252-523-8052

Wayne E Bailey Produce Co Inc
  Chadbourn, NC 800-845-6149

Frozen
Bright Harvest Sweet Potato Co
  Clarksville, AR 800-793-7440
Emerling International Foods
  Buffalo, NY 716-833-7381

Mashed
Bright Harvest Sweet Potato Co
  Clarksville, AR 800-793-7440

Frozen
Bright Harvest Sweet Potato Co
  Clarksville, AR 800-793-7440

Swiss Chard
Earthbound Farm
  San Jn Bautista, CA 800-690-3200

Tamarind
Cinnabar Specialty Foods Inc
  Prescott, AZ 866-293-6433

Tangelos
Heller Brothers Packing Corp
  Winter Garden, FL 855-543-5537

Tangerines
DNE World Fruit Sales
  Fort Pierce, FL 800-327-6676
Haines City Citrus Growers
  Haines City, FL 800-327-6676
Hale Indian River Groves
  Vero Beach, FL 800-562-4502
Heller Brothers Packing Corp
  Winter Garden, FL 855-543-5537
Hunt Brothers Cooperative
  Lake Wales, FL 863-676-1411
Seald Sweet
  Vero Beach, FL 559-636-4400

Taro
Sweety Novelty
  Monterey Park, CA 626-282-4482

Tartufo
Gelato Fresco
  Toronto, ON 416-785-5415
Vigneri Chocolate Inc.
  Rochester, NY 877-844-6374

Textured Vegetable Protein
Advanced Spice & Trading
  Carrollton, TX 800-872-7811
Clofine Dairy Products Inc
  Linwood, NJ 609-653-1000
DuPont Nutrition & Biosciences
  New Century, KS 913-764-8100
First Spice Mixing Co
  Long Island City, NY 800-221-1105
New Organics
  Kenwood, CA 734-677-5570
Westin Foods
  Omaha, NE 800-228-6098

Tomatillos
Emerling International Foods
  Buffalo, NY 716-833-7381
George Chiala Farms Inc
  Morgan Hill, CA 408-778-0562
Haliburton International Inc
  Ontario, CA 877-980-4295

Tomato
AgroCepia
  Miami, FL 305-704-3488
Agrusa
  Leonia, NJ 201-592-5950
Ballantine Produce Company
  Reedley, CA 559-875-2583
BGS Jourdan & Sons
  Darlington, MD 410-457-4904
Castellini Group
  Newport, KY 800-233-8560

Char-Wil Canning Company
  Trappe, MD 410-476-3167
Del Monte Fresh Produce Inc.
  Coral Gables, FL 800-950-3683
Di Mare Fresh Inc
  Fort Worth, TX 817-385-3000
Earthbound Farm
  San Jn Bautista, CA 800-690-3200
Eden Foods Inc
  Clinton, MI 888-424-3336
Escalon Premier Brand
  Escalon, CA 209-838-7341
F & S Produce Co Inc
  Vineland, NJ 800-886-3316
Fresh Express, Inc.
  Salinas, CA 800-242-5472
George Chiala Farms Inc
  Morgan Hill, CA 408-778-0562
Giumarra Companies
  Los Angeles, CA 213-627-2900
Haliburton International Inc
  Ontario, CA 877-980-4295
Harris Farms Inc
  Coalinga, CA 800-311-6211
Henry Broch & Co
  Gurnee, IL 847-816-6225
Hermann Pickle Co
  Garrettsville, OH 800-245-2696
John N Wright Jr Inc
  Federalsburg, MD 410-754-9044
Kaplan & Zubrin
  Camden, NJ 856-964-1083
Lagorio Enterprises
  Manteca, CA 209-982-5691
Local Roots Farms
  Burt, NY 716-946-3198
M & S Tomato Repacking Co Inc
  Springfield, MA 413-737-1308
Mangia Inc.
  Mission Viejo, CA 866-462-6442
Miramar Pickles & Food Products
  Fort Lauderdale, FL 954-463-0222
Nation Wide Canning Ltd.
  Cottam, ON 519-839-4831
Neil Jones Food Company
  Vancouver, WA 800-291-3862
Northwest Packing Co
  Vancouver, WA 800-543-4356
Pacific Collier Fresh Company
  Immokalee, FL 800-226-7274
Pastorelli Food Products
  Chicago, IL 800-767-2829
Patterson Vegetable Company
  Patterson, CA 209-892-2611
Pure Food Ingredients
  Verona, WI 800-355-9601
Rene Produce Dist
  Rio Rico, AZ 520-281-0806
Royce C. Bone Farms
  Nashville, NC 252-443-3773
Sofo Foods
  Toledo, OH 800-447-4211
Spreda Group
  Louisville, KY 502-426-9411
Stanislaus Food Prod
  Modesto, CA 800-327-7201
Sun Pacific
  Pasadena, CA 213-612-9957
Sun-Brite Canning
  Kingsville, ON 519-326-9033
Surface Banana Company
  Parkersburg, WV 304-485-2400
Talley Farms
  Arroyo Grande, CA 805-489-5400
Thomas Canning/Maidstone
  Maidstone, ON 519-737-1531
Timber Crest Farms
  Healdsburg, CA 888-766-4233
Tip Top Canning Co
  Tipp City, OH 800-352-2635
Topor's Pickle & Food Svc Inc
  Detroit, MI 313-237-0288
Unilever Food Solutions
  Englewood Cliffs, NJ
Vegetable Juices Inc
  Chicago, IL 888-776-9752
Veronica Foods Inc
  Oakland, CA 800-370-5554
Vincent Formusa Company
  Des Plaines, IL 847-813-6040
Violet Packing Holdings LLC
  Williamstown, NJ 856-629-7428

Product Categories / Fruits & Vegetables: Tomato

Waterfield Farms
 Amherst, MA 413-549-3558
Weil's Food Processing
 Wheatley, ON 519-825-4572
Wholesum Family Farms
 Nogales, AZ 520-281-9233
Z&S Distributing
 Fresno, CA 800-467-0788

Canned

Agrocan
 Ville St Laurent, QC 877-247-6226
Agusa
 Lemoore, CA 559-924-4785
B & G Foods Inc
 Parsippany, NJ 973-401-6500
Char-Wil Canning Company
 Trappe, MD 410-476-3167
Dei Fratelli
 Toledo, OH 800-837-1631
Eden Foods Inc
 Clinton, MI 888-424-3336
Escalon Premier Brand
 Escalon, CA 209-838-7341
Hirzel Canning Co.
 Ottawa, OH 800-837-1631
John N Wright Jr Inc
 Federalsburg, MD 410-754-9044
Milroy Canning Company
 Milroy, IN 765-629-2221
Morningstar Foods
 Los Banos, CA 209-826-8000
Nation Wide Canning Ltd.
 Cottam, ON 519-839-4831
Natural Value
 Sacramento, CA 916-836-3561
Neil Jones Food Company
 Vancouver, WA 800-291-3862
Northwest Packing Co
 Vancouver, WA 800-543-4356
Pastene Co LTD
 Canton, MA 781-298-3397
Pastorelli Food Products
 Chicago, IL 800-767-2829
Pure Food Ingredients
 Verona, WI 800-355-9601
Red Gold Inc.
 Elwood, IN 866-729-7187
Rio Valley Canning Co
 Donna, TX 956-464-7843
Shafer-Haggart
 Vancouver, BC 604-669-5512
Small Planet Foods
 Minneapolis, MN 800-624-4123
Stanislaus Food Prod
 Modesto, CA 800-327-7201
Sun-Brite Canning
 Kingsville, ON 519-326-9033
Thomas Canning/Maidstone
 Maidstone, ON 519-737-1531
Tip Top Canning Co
 Tipp City, OH 800-352-2635
Violet Packing Holdings LLC
 Williamstown, NJ 856-629-7428
Weil's Food Processing
 Wheatley, ON 519-825-4572

Crushed

Agrocan
 Ville St Laurent, QC 877-247-6226
Colonna Brothers Inc
 North Bergen, NJ 201-864-1115
Furmano's Foods
 Northumberland, PA 800-952-1111
Hirzel Canning Co & Farms
 Luckey, OH 419-419-7525
Small Planet Foods
 Minneapolis, MN 800-624-4123
Violet Packing Holdings LLC
 Williamstown, NJ 856-629-7428

Cherry

80 Acres Farms
 Hamilton, OH 888-574-1569
Exeter Produce
 Exeter, ON 519-235-0141
Talley Farms
 Arroyo Grande, CA 805-489-5400

Cocktail

Miss Scarlett's Flowers
 Juneau, AK 800-345-6734
Seneca Foods Corp
 Princeville, IL 309-385-4301

Diced

Furmano's Foods
 Northumberland, PA 800-952-1111
Hirzel Canning Co & Farms
 Luckey, OH 419-419-7525
Ingomar Packing Co
 Los Banos, CA 209-826-9494
Small Planet Foods
 Minneapolis, MN 800-624-4123
Tip Top Canning Co
 Tipp City, OH 800-352-2635

Dried

Agusa
 Lemoore, CA 559-924-4785
Emerling International Foods
 Buffalo, NY 716-833-7381
Fine Dried Foods Intl
 Santa Cruz, CA 831-426-1413
Grapevine Trading Company
 Santa Rosa, CA 800-469-6478
Just Tomatoes
 Westley, CA 800-537-1985
Rising Sun Farms
 Phoenix, OR 800-888-0795
Setton International Foods
 Commack, NY 800-227-4397
Terri Lynn Inc
 Elgin, IL 800-323-0775
Timber Crest Farms
 Healdsburg, CA 888-766-4233
Unique Ingredients LLC
 Gold Canyon, AZ 480-983-2498
Valley Sun Products Inc
 Newman, CA 800-426-5444

Fresh

F & S Produce Co Inc
 Vineland, NJ 800-886-3316
Fresh Express, Inc.
 Salinas, CA 800-242-5472
G Cefalu & Brother Inc
 Jessup, MD 410-799-2910
Harris Farms Inc
 Coalinga, CA 800-311-6211
Lagorio Enterprises
 Manteca, CA 209-982-5691
Mixon Fruit Farms Inc
 Bradenton, FL 800-608-2525
Rene Produce Dist
 Rio Rico, AZ 520-281-0806
Talley Farms
 Arroyo Grande, CA 805-489-5400

Frozen

Milroy Canning Company
 Milroy, IN 765-629-2221
Ocean Mist Farms
 Castroville, CA 831-633-2144
Red Gold Inc.
 Elwood, IN 866-729-7187
SupHerb Farms
 Turlock, CA 800-787-4372
Vegetable Juices Inc
 Chicago, IL 888-776-9752

Marinated

American Importing Co.
 Minneapolis, MN 855-273-0466

Plum

Kaplan & Zubrin
 Camden, NJ 856-964-1083

Processed

Agusa
 Lemoore, CA 559-924-4785
Escalon Premier Brand
 Escalon, CA 209-838-7341
Pastorelli Food Products
 Chicago, IL 800-767-2829

Weil's Food Processing
 Wheatley, ON 519-825-4572

Products

Agusa
 Lemoore, CA 559-924-4785
American Chalkis Intl. Food Corp.
 Walnut, CA 562-232-4105
Emerling International Foods
 Buffalo, NY 716-833-7381
Escalon Premier Brand
 Escalon, CA 209-838-7341
F & S Produce Co Inc
 Vineland, NJ 800-886-3316
Fresh Express, Inc.
 Salinas, CA 800-242-5472
George Chiala Farms Inc
 Morgan Hill, CA 408-778-0562
Henry Broch & Co
 Gurnee, IL 847-816-6225
Hermann Pickle Co
 Garrettsville, OH 800-245-2696
International Home Foods
 Parsippany, NJ 973-359-9920
Lagorio Enterprises
 Manteca, CA 209-982-5691
Lake Packing Co Inc
 Lottsburg, VA 800-324-2759
Los Gatos Tomato Products
 Huron, CA 559-945-2700
Milroy Canning Company
 Milroy, IN 765-629-2221
Morningstar Foods
 Los Banos, CA 209-826-8000
Nation Wide Canning Ltd.
 Cottam, ON 519-839-4831
Northwest Packing Co
 Vancouver, WA 800-543-4356
Paradise Tomato Kitchens
 Louisville, KY 502-637-1700
Pasta Factory
 Melrose Park, IL 800-615-6951
Pastorelli Food Products
 Chicago, IL 800-767-2829
Progresso Quality Foods
 Vineland, NJ 856-691-1565
Pure Food Ingredients
 Verona, WI 800-355-9601
Red Gold Inc.
 Elwood, IN 866-729-7187
Small Planet Foods
 Minneapolis, MN 800-624-4123
Spreda Group
 Louisville, KY 502-426-9411
Talley Farms
 Arroyo Grande, CA 805-489-5400
Thomas Canning/Maidstone
 Maidstone, ON 519-737-1531
Timber Crest Farms
 Healdsburg, CA 888-766-4233
Tip Top Canning Co
 Tipp City, OH 800-352-2635
Unilever Food Solutions
 Englewood Cliffs, NJ
Unique Ingredients LLC
 Gold Canyon, AZ 480-983-2498
VCPB Transportation
 Secaucus, NJ 201-770-0070
Vegetable Juices Inc
 Chicago, IL 888-776-9752
Veronica Foods Inc
 Oakland, CA 800-370-5554
Walker Foods
 Los Angeles, CA 800-966-5199
Weil's Food Processing
 Wheatley, ON 519-825-4572
Welch Foods Inc.
 Concord, MA 800-340-6870

Roma (Egg)

Lagorio Enterprises
 Manteca, CA 209-982-5691

Stewed

Furmano's Foods
 Northumberland, PA 800-952-1111
Nation Wide Canning Ltd.
 Cottam, ON 519-839-4831
Northwest Packing Co
 Vancouver, WA 800-543-4356

Product Categories / Fruits & Vegetables: Tropical & Exotic Fruit

Tip Top Canning Co
  Tipp City, OH 800-352-2635

Sun-Dried

Agrocan
  Ville St Laurent, QC 877-247-6226
American Importing Co.
  Minneapolis, MN 855-273-0466
Bedemco Inc
  White Plains, NY 914-683-1119
Bella Sun Luci
  Chico, CA 530-899-2661
Castella Imports Inc
  Brentwood, NY 631-231-5500
Martin Farms
  Brockport, NY 877-838-7369
Mezza
  Lake Forest, IL 888-206-6054
Pacific Choice Brands
  Fresno, CA 559-476-3581
Veronica Foods Inc
  Oakland, CA 800-370-5554

Yellow Cherry

Beckman & Gast Co
  St Henry, OH. 419-678-4195
California Fruit and Tomato Kitchens
  Modesto, CA. 209-574-9407
Supreme Dairy Farms Co
  Warwick, RI 401-739-8180

for Processing

Agusa
  Lemoore, CA. 559-924-4785

Tropical & Exotic Fruit

Ntc Marketing
  Williamsville, NY 800-333-1637
Sambazon
  San Clemente, CA. 877-726-2296
Varet Street Market
  Brooklyn, NY 718-302-0560

Turnip

Boskovich Farms Inc
  Oxnard, CA. 805-487-2299
Pictsweet Co
  Bells, TN 731-663-7600
Snowcrest Packer
  Abbotsford, BC. 800-265-3686
Tom Ringhausen Orchards
  Hardin, IL 800-258-6645
Walter P Rawl & Sons Inc
  Pelion, SC 803-894-1900

Canned

Emerling International Foods
  Buffalo, NY. 716-833-7381

Frozen

Emerling International Foods
  Buffalo, NY. 716-833-7381
Paris Foods Corporation
  Trappe, MD. 410-200-9595

Vegetables

A. Lassonde Inc.
  Rougemont, QC 866-552-7643
Aaland Potato Company
  Hoople, ND. 701-894-6144
Acme Steak & Seafood
  Youngstown, OH. 800-686-2263
Affiliated Rice Milling
  Alvin, TX. 281-331-6176
Agro Foods, Inc.
  Miami, FL. 786-552-9006
Al Pete Meats
  Muncie, IN 765-288-8817
ALDI
  Cincinnati, OH 513-421-1671
Alimentaire Whyte's Inc
  Laval, QC 866-420-9520
Associated Potato Growers
  Grand Forks, ND. 800-437-4685
B & G Foods Inc.
  Parsippany, NJ. 973-401-6500
B.M. Lawrence & Company
  San Francisco, CA 415-981-2926

Baker Produce
  Kennewick, WA 800-624-7553
Baumer Foods Inc
  Metairie, LA 504-482-5761
Bay Cities Produce Co Inc
  San Leandro, CA. 510-346-4943
BCFoods
  Santa Rosa, CA. 707-547-1776
Bean Buddies
  New Hyde Park, NY 516-775-3706
Ben B. Schwartz & Sons
  Detroit, MI 313-841-8300
Big B Barbecue
  Evansville, IN 812-425-5235
Birdseye Food
  Mountain Lakes, NJ 585-383-1850
Bob Gordon & Associates
  Oak Park, IL 708-524-9611
Border Foods
  New Hope, MN. 763-559-7338
Bornt & Sons Inc
  Holtville, CA. 760-356-1066
Bottom Line Foods
  Pembroke Pines, FL 954-843-0562
Bright Harvest Sweet Potato Co
  Clarksville, AR 800-793-7440
Bryant Preserving Company
  Alma, AR 800-634-2413
Bubbles of San Francisco
  Stockton, CA 209-951-6071
Burnette Foods
  Elk Rapids, MI 231-264-8116
Burnham & Morrill Co
  Portland, ME. 800-813-2165
Byrnes Packing Shed
  Hastings, FL 904-692-1643
C.C. Graber Company
  Ontario, CA. 800-996-5483
Cajun Brands
  New Iberia, LA 504-408-2252
California Fruit and Tomato Kitchens
  Modesto, CA. 209-574-9407
Caltex Foods
  Canoga Park, CA 800-522-5839
Carando Gourmet Frozen Foods
  Agawam, MA 888-227-2636
Caribbean Food Delights Inc
  Tappan, NY 845-398-3000
Cascadian Farm Inc
  Sedro Woolley, WA 360-855-0542
Castellini Group
  Newport, KY 800-233-8560
Cates Addis Company
  Parkton, NC 800-423-1883
Cebro Frozen Food
  Newman, CA. 209-862-0150
Christopher Ranch LLC
  Gilroy, CA. 408-847-1100
Chugwater Chili
  Chugwater, WY 800-972-4454
Club Chef LLC
  Covington, KY 859-578-3100
Coloma Frozen Foods Inc
  Coloma, MI. 800-642-2723
Coulter Giufre & Co Inc
  Chittenango, NY 315-687-6510
Country Fresh Inc
  Spring, TX. 281-453-3300
Coutts Specialty Foods Inc
  Boxborough, MA 800-919-2952
Crystal Potato Seed Co
  Crystal, ND. 701-657-2143
D'Arrigo Brothers Company of California
  Salinas, CA. 831-455-4500
Dairy King Milk Farms/Foodservice
  Whitter, CA. 800-900-6455
Dairy Management Inc
  Rosemont, IL. 800-853-2479
Deep Foods Inc
  Union, NJ 908-810-7500
Del Mar Food Products Corp
  Watsonville, CA 831-722-3516
Del Monte Fresh Produce Inc.
  Coral Gables, FL. 800-950-3683
Delicious Valley Frozen Foods
  McAllen, TX 956-631-7177
Delta Packing
  Lodi, CA. 209-334-1023
Dickinson Frozen Foods
  Eagle, ID 800-886-4326
DMH Ingredients Inc
  Libertyville, IL 847-362-9977

DNO Inc
  Columbus, OH 614-231-3601
Dong Kee Company
  Chicago, IL 312-225-6340
East Coast Fresh Cuts Inc
  Laurel, MD
Eckert Cold Storage
  Manteca, CA. 209-823-3181
Eden Foods Inc
  Clinton, MI 888-424-3336
Erba Food Products
  Brooklyn, NY 718-272-7700
Escalon Premier Brand
  Escalon, CA 209-838-7341
F & S Produce Co Inc
  Vineland, NJ 800-886-3316
Faribault Foods, Inc.
  Fairbault, MN 507-331-1400
Federation-Southern Cprtvs
  Atlanta, GA. 404-765-0991
Fiesta Canning Co
  Phoenix, AZ 602-212-2424
Florida Citrus
  Bartow, FL 863-537-3999
Fort Boise Produce Company
  Nyssa, OR 541-372-5174
Foster Family Farm
  South Windsor, CT 860-648-9366
Fountain Valley Foods
  Colorado Springs, CO. 719-573-6012
Fresh Frozen Foods
  Jefferson, GA 800-277-9851
Frieda's Inc
  Los Alamitos, CA 714-826-6100
Ful-Flav-R Foods
  Alamo, CA 925-838-0300
Garber Farms
  Iota, LA 800-824-2284
Garden Valley Corp
  Sutherlin, OR 541-459-9565
Garon Foods
  Herrin, IL 618-942-4810
GC Farms
  Morgan Hill, CA 408-778-0562
Gene Belk Briners
  Bloomington, CA 909-877-1819
George Chiala Farms Inc
  Morgan Hill, CA 408-778-0562
Gl Mezzetta Inc
  American Canyon, CA 800-941-7044
Glacier Foods
  Houston, TX 832-375-6300
GLK Foods, LLC
  Shortsville, NY 855-572-8800
Glory Foods
  Columbus, OH 800-414-5679
Godwin Produce Co
  Dunn, NC 910-892-4171
Gotliebs Guacamole
  Sharon, CT 860-365-0842
Great American Appetizers
  Nampa, ID. 800-282-4834
GS Dunn & Company
  Hamilton, ON 905-522-0833
GWB Foods Corporation
  Brooklyn, NY 877-977-7610
H.K. Canning
  Ventura, CA. 805-652-1392
Haliburton International Inc
  Ontario, CA. 877-980-4295
Hard-E Foods
  St Louis, MO. 314-533-2211
Harner Farms
  State College, PA 814-237-7919
Harris Farms Inc
  Coalinga, CA. 800-311-6211
Harvest-Pac Products
  Chatham, ON 519-436-0446
Heirloom Organic Gardens
  Hollister, CA. 831-637-8497
Henderson's Gardens
  Berwyn, AB 780-338-2128
Henry Broch & Co
  Gurnee, IL. 847-816-6225
Herold's Salads
  Cleveland, OH 800-427-2523
HH Dobbins Inc
  Lyndonville, NY 877-362-2467
HMC Farms
  Kingsburg, CA 559-897-1025
Houston Calco, Inc
  Houston, TX 713-236-8668

Product Categories / Fruits & Vegetables: Vegetables

Inland Empire Foods
   Riverside, CA 888-452-3267
International Home Foods
   Parsippany, NJ 973-359-9920
International Specialty Supply
   Cookeville, TN 931-526-1106
J C Watson Co
   Parma, ID 208-722-5141
J. R. Simplot Co.
   Boise, ID 208-336-2110
JES Foods
   Cleveland, OH 216-883-8987
John N Wright Jr Inc
   Federalsburg, MD 410-754-9044
Jyoti Cuisine India
   Berwyn, PA 610-296-4620
Kaplan & Zubrin
   Camden, NJ 856-964-1083
Kings Processing
   Middleton, NS 902-825-2188
Knight Seed Company
   Burnsville, MN 800-328-2999
L & S Packing Co
   Farmingdale, NY 800-286-6487
L H Hayward & Co
   New Orleans, LA 504-733-8480
Lagorio Enterprises
   Manteca, CA 209-982-5691
Lakeside Foods Inc.
   Plainview, MN 507-534-3141
Lakeside Packing Company
   Harrow, ON 519-738-2314
Lennox Farm
   Shelburne, ON 519-925-6444
Les Trois Petits Cochons
   Brooklyn, NY 800-537-7283
Limited Edition
   Midland, TX 432-686-2008
Livingston Farmers Assn
   Livingston, CA 209-394-7941
Lodi Canning Co
   Lodi, WI 608-592-4236
Lone Wolf Farms
   Minto, ND 701-248-3482
Long Island Cauliflower Assn
   Riverhead, NY 631-727-2212
Made In Nature
   Boulder, CO 800-906-7426
Mancini Packing Co
   Zolfo Springs, FL 800-741-1778
Maple Leaf Foods International
   North York, ON 800-268-3708
Martens Fresh
   Port Byron, NY 315-776-8821
Martha's Garden
   Toronto, ON 866-773-2887
Matador Processors
   Blanchard, OK 800-847-0797
Mccartney Produce Co
   Paris, TN 731-642-2362
Mercer Processing
   Modesto, CA 209-529-0150
Meridian Foods New Inc
   Eaton, IN 765-396-3344
Miami Purveyors Inc
   Miami, FL 800-966-6328
Michael Foods, Inc.
   Minnetonka, MN 952-258-4000
Michigan Celery Cooperative
   Hudsonville, MI 616-669-1250
Miguel's Stowe Away
   Stowe, VT 800-448-6517
Millie's Pierogi
   Chicopee Falls, MA 800-743-7641
Mills Brothers Intl
   Seattle, WA 206-575-3000
Milos
   New York, NY 212-245-7400
Minnesota Dehydrated Veg Inc
   Fosston, MN 218-435-1997
Miramar Fruit Trading Company
   Doral, FL 305-883-4774
Mister Spear
   Stockton, CA 800-677-7327
Mixon Fruit Farms Inc
   Bradenton, FL 800-608-2525
Mother Teresa's
   Clute, TX 888-265-7429
Mrs Mazzula Food Products Inc
   Edison, NJ 732-248-0555
Mt Olive Pickle Co
   Mt Olive, NC 800-672-5041

Nation Wide Canning Ltd.
   Cottam, ON 519-839-4831
National Frozen Foods Corp
   Seattle, WA 206-322-8900
Natural Choice Distribution
   Oakland, CA 510-653-8212
Nature Quality
   San Martin, CA 408-683-2182
New Era Canning Company
   New Era, MI 231-861-2151
New Harvest Foods
   Washington, DC 920-822-2578
Nicola International
   Los Angeles, CA 818-545-1515
Nonpareil Farms
   Blackfoot, ID 800-522-2223
NORPAC Foods Inc
   Salem, OR
Northwest Packing Co
   Vancouver, WA 800-543-4356
Nunes Co Inc
   Salinas, CA 831-751-7500
O C Schulz & Sons
   Crystal, ND 701-657-2152
Ocean Mist Farms
   Castroville, CA 831-633-2144
Ohio Mushroom Company
   Lima, OH 419-221-1721
Olive Growers Council
   Visalia, CA 559-734-1710
Ontario Produce Company
   Ontario, OR 541-889-6485
Oregon Potato Co
   Boardman, OR 800-336-6311
Organically Grown Co
   Eugene, OR 800-937-9677
Osowski Farms
   Minto, ND 701-248-3341
Pacific Choice Brands
   Fresno, CA 559-476-3581
Pacific Collier Fresh Company
   Immokalee, FL 800-226-7274
Pacific Valley Foods Inc
   Bellevue, WA 425-643-1805
Paradise Products Corporation
   Boca Raton, FL 800-826-1235
Paris Foods Corporation
   Trappe, MD 410-200-9595
Pastorelli Food Products
   Chicago, IL 800-767-2829
Pictsweet Co
   Bells, TN 731-663-7600
Pride Enterprises Glades
   Belle Glade, FL 561-996-1091
Proacec USA
   Santa Monica, CA 310-996-7770
Produits Ronald
   St. Damase, QC 800-465-0118
Pure Food Ingredients
   Verona, WI 800-355-9601
Queensway Foods Company
   Burlingame, CA 650-871-7770
R & S Mexican Food
   Glendale, AZ 602-272-2727
R.C. McEntire & Company
   Columbia, SC 803-799-3388
Rainsweet Inc
   Salem, OR 800-363-4293
Ralph Sechler & Son Inc
   St Joe, IN 800-332-5461
Raymond-Hadley Corporation
   Spencer, NY 800-252-5220
Ready Pac Foods Inc
   Irwindale, CA 800-800-4088
Red River Commodities Inc
   Fargo, ND 800-437-5539
Rene Produce Dist
   Rio Rico, AZ 520-281-0806
Ripon Pickle Co Inc
   Ripon, WI 920-748-7110
Ron Son Foods Inc
   Swedesboro, NJ 856-241-7333
Salad Depot
   Moonachie, NJ 201-507-1980
Santa Barbara Olive Company
   Santa Barbara, CA 800-624-4896
Sargent and Greenleaf
   Nicholasville, KY 800-826-7652
Schiff Food Products Co Inc
   Totowa, NJ 973-237-1990
Schmidt Bros Inc
   Swanton, OH 800-200-7318

Seabrook Brothers & Sons
   Seabrook, NJ 856-455-8080
Sedlock Farm
   Lynn Center, IL 309-521-8284
Seneca Foods Corp
   Princeville, IL 309-385-4301
Seneca Foods Corp
   Marion, NY 315-926-8100
Serv-Agen Corporation
   Cherry Hill, NJ 856-663-6966
Seville Olive Company
   Los Angeles, CA 323-261-2218
Shafer Lake Fruit Inc
   Hartford, MI 269-621-3194
Silva Farms
   Gonzales, CA 831-675-2428
Small Planet Foods
   Minneapolis, MN 800-624-4123
Smeltzer Orchard Co
   Frankfort, MI 231-882-4421
Smith Frozen Foods Inc
   Weston, OR 541-566-3515
Snowcrest Packer
   Abbotsford, BC 800-265-3686
Sonne
   Wahpeton, ND 800-727-6663
SOPAKCO Foods
   Mullins, SC 800-276-9678
South Mill
   Kennett Square, PA 610-444-4800
Specialty Food Association
   New York, NY 646-878-0301
Spokane Seed Co
   Spokane Valley, WA 800-359-8478
Spreda Group
   Louisville, KY 502-426-9411
Strathroy Foods
   Strathroy, ON 519-245-4600
Strub Pickles
   Brantford, ON 519-751-1717
Sun Glo Of Idaho
   Sugar City, ID 208-356-7346
Sun-Brite Canning
   Kingsville, ON 519-326-9033
Sunnyside Vegetable Packing
   Millville, NJ 856-451-5077
Superior Bean & Spice Company
   Brush Prairie, WA 360-694-0819
SupHerb Farms
   Turlock, CA 800-787-4372
Surface Banana Company
   Parkersburg, WV 304-485-2400
T.S. Smith & Sons
   Bridgeville, DE 302-337-8271
Talk O'Texas Brands Inc
   San Angelo, TX 800-749-6572
Taylor Farms
   Salinas, CA 831-754-0471
Taylor Farms Pacific
   Tracy, CA 209-830-1086
Teixeira Farms, Inc.
   Santa Maria, CA 805-928-3801
Thomas Canning/Maidstone
   Maidstone, ON 519-737-1531
Timber Crest Farms
   Healdsburg, CA 888-766-4233
Tom Ringhausen Orchards
   Hardin, IL 800-258-6645
Topor's Pickle & Food Svc Inc
   Detroit, MI 313-237-0288
Trans Pecos Foods
   San Antonio, TX 210-228-0896
Tropic Fish Hawaii LLC
   Honolulu, HI 808-591-2936
Tropical Foods
   Charlotte, NC 800-438-4470
Tuscarora Organic Growers Cooperative
   Hustontown, PA 814-448-2173
Twin City Foods Inc.
   Stanwood, WA 206-515-2400
Unilever Food Solutions
   Englewood Cliffs, NJ
United Marketing Exchange
   Delta, CO 970-874-3332
Vegetable Juices Inc
   Chicago, IL 888-776-9752
Veronica Foods Inc
   Oakland, CA 800-370-5554
Violet Packing Holdings LLC
   Williamstown, NJ 856-629-7428
Visalia Produce Sales
   Kingsburg, CA 559-897-6652

Product Categories / Fruits & Vegetables: Vegetables Mixed

Wagshal's Imports
   Washington, DC 202-363-5698
Wallace Grain & Pea Company
   Pullman, WA 509-878-1561
Washington Potato Company
   Pasco, WA 800-897-2726
Washington Rhubarb Grower Assn
   Sumner, WA 800-435-9911
Webster Farms
   Cambridge, NS 800-507-8844
Weil's Food Processing
   Wheatley, ON 519-825-4572
Westin Foods
   Omaha, NE 800-228-6098
Wildcat Produce
   McGrew, NE 308-783-2438
Zuccaro Produce
   Columbia Heights, MN 612-333-1122

IQF (Individual Quick Frozen)

Eckert Cold Storage
   Manteca, CA 209-823-3181
Rainsweet Inc
   Salem, OR 800-363-4293
SupHerb Farms
   Turlock, CA 800-787-4372
Washington Rhubarb Grower Assn
   Sumner, WA 800-435-9911

Vegetables Mixed

Agrocan
   Ville St Laurent, QC 877-247-6226
Birdseye Food
   Mountain Lakes, NJ 585-383-1850
Deep Foods Inc
   Union, NJ 908-810-7500
Di Mare Fresh Inc
   Fort Worth, TX 817-385-3000
Just Tomatoes
   Westley, CA 800-537-1985
New Harvest Foods
   Washington, DC 920-822-2578
Patterson Frozen Foods
   Patterson, CA 209-892-2611
Risvold's Inc.
   Gardena, CA 323-770-2674
Strathroy Foods
   Strathroy, ON 519-245-4600

Broccoli, Peas & Carrots

Faribault Foods, Inc.
   Fairbault, MN 507-331-1400

California Blend

Paris Foods Corporation
   Trappe, MD 410-200-9595

Canned

Bryant Preserving Company
   Alma, AR 800-634-2413
Carriere Foods Inc
   Saint-Denis-Sur-Richelie, QC 450-787-3411

Cates Addis Company
   Parkton, NC 800-423-1883
Deep Foods Inc
   Union, NJ 908-810-7500
Emerling International Foods
   Buffalo, NY 716-833-7381
Faribault Foods, Inc.
   Fairbault, MN 507-331-1400
Moody Dunbar Inc
   Johnson City, TN 423-952-0100
New Harvest Foods
   Washington, DC 920-822-2578

Frozen

Birdseye Food
   Mountain Lakes, NJ 585-383-1850
Deep Foods Inc
   Union, NJ 908-810-7500
Paris Foods Corporation
   Trappe, MD 410-200-9595
Strathroy Foods
   Strathroy, ON 519-245-4600
Symons Frozen Foods
   Centralia, WA 360-736-1321

Peas & Carrots

Cates Addis Company
   Parkton, NC 800-423-1883
Strathroy Foods
   Strathroy, ON 519-245-4600
Symons Frozen Foods
   Centralia, WA 360-736-1321
Twin City Foods Inc.
   Stanwood, WA 206-515-2400

Frozen

Cates Addis Company
   Parkton, NC 800-423-1883
Strathroy Foods
   Strathroy, ON 519-245-4600
Symons Frozen Foods
   Centralia, WA 360-736-1321
Twin City Foods Inc.
   Stanwood, WA 206-515-2400

Water Chestnuts

Dong Kee Company
   Chicago, IL 312-225-6340
Emerling International Foods
   Buffalo, NY 716-833-7381
Lee's Food Products
   Toronto, ON 416-465-2407
SupHerb Farms
   Turlock, CA 800-787-4372

Watercress

AeroFarms
   Newark, NJ 973-242-2495
Calif Watercress Inc
   Fillmore, CA 805-524-4808

Yams

AgriNorthwest
   Kennewick, WA 509-734-1195
Arbre Farms Inc
   Walkerville, MI 231-873-3337
Bright Harvest Sweet Potato Co
   Clarksville, AR 800-793-7440
F & S Produce Co Inc
   Vineland, NJ 800-886-3316
Garber Farms
   Iota, LA 800-824-2284
Godwin Produce Co
   Dunn, NC 910-892-4171
Ocean Mist Farms
   Castroville, CA 831-633-2144
Seneca Foods Corp
   Marion, NY 315-926-8100
Vaughn Rue Produce
   Wilson, NC 800-388-8138
Zuccaro Produce
   Columbia Heights, MN 612-333-1122

Frozen

Bright Harvest Sweet Potato Co
   Clarksville, AR 800-793-7440

Zucchini

Arbre Farms Inc
   Walkerville, MI 231-873-3337
Bifulco Four Seasons
   Pittsgrove, NJ 856-692-0778
Earthbound Farm
   San Jn Bautista, CA 800-690-3200
Emerling International Foods
   Buffalo, NY 716-833-7381
F & S Produce Co Inc
   Vineland, NJ 800-886-3316
Great American Appetizers
   Nampa, ID 800-282-4834
Haliburton International Inc
   Ontario, CA 877-980-4295
Miss Scarlett's Flowers
   Juneau, AK 800-345-6734
Paris Foods Corporation
   Trappe, MD 410-200-9595
Pictsweet Co
   Bells, TN 731-663-7600
Sure-Fresh Produce Inc
   Santa Maria, CA 888-423-5379
Talley Farms
   Arroyo Grande, CA 805-489-5400
Vegetable Juices Inc
   Chicago, IL 888-776-9752

General Grocery

General

731 North Beach LLC
  La Habra, CA 562-697-8888
99 Ranch Market
  Hacienda Heights, CA 626-839-2899
A Gift Basket by Carmela
  Longmeadow, MA 413-746-1400
A.T. Gift Company
  Harpers Ferry, WV 304-876-6680
Aliments Fontaine Sant, Inc
  Ville Saint-Laurent, QC 888-627-2683
Allied Food Products
  Brooklyn, NY 718-230-4227
AmeriQual Foods
  Evansville, IN 812-867-1444
Arctic Glacier
  Winnipeg, MB 888-573-9237
Ashley Food Co Inc
  Sudbury, MA 800-617-2823
Baldwin Richardson Foods
  Oakbrook Terrace, IL 866-644-2732
Binding Brauerei USA
  Norwalk, CT 203-229-0111
Boyajian LLC
  Canton, MA 800-965-0665
Brazilian Home Collection
  Passaic, NJ 973-365-5800
Brookshire Grocery Company
  Tyler, TX 888-937-3776
Capalbo's Fruit Baskets
  Clifton, NJ 800-252-6262
Chicken Of The Sea
  El Segundo, CA 844-267-8862
Chong Mei Trading
  East Point, GA 404-768-3838
Choyce Produce
  Honolulu, HI 808-839-1502
Christmas Point Wild Rice Co
  Baxter, MN 218-828-0603
Classic Foods
  San Francisco, CA 800-574-8122
Colony Foods
  Lawrence, MA 978-682-9677
Cosgrove Distributors Inc
  Spring Valley, IL 800-347-3071
Creative Food Ingredients
  Perry, NY 585-237-2213
Culinary Farms Inc
  Woodland, CA 888-383-2767
DeLallo Foods
  Mount Pleasant, PA 877-355-2556
Dogswell LLC
  Los Angeles, CA 888-559-8833
Eat It Corporation
  Brooklyn, NY 718-768-7950
Ellsworth Foods
  Tifton, GA 229-386-8448
Fabrique Delices
  Hayward, CA 510-441-9500
Farallon Fisheries Co
  S San Francisco, CA 650-583-3474
Fast Fixing Foods
  Boaz, AL 800-317-4232
Festive Foods
  Virginia Beach, VA 757-490-9186
Figueroa Brothers
  Irving, TX 800-886-6354
Formost Friedman Company
  Merrick, NY 516-378-4919
Fountain Shakes/MS Foods
  Minnetonka, MN 952-988-6940
French & Brawn Marketplace
  Camden, ME 207-236-3361
Galland's Institutional Food
  Bakersfield, CA 661-631-5505
Giulia Speciality Food
  Lodi, NJ 973-478-3111
Gold Mine Natural Food Company
  Poway, CA 800-475-3663
Great River Organic Milling
  Arcadia, WI 608-687-9580
Gulf Marine & Industrial Supplies Inc
  Houston, TX 800-886-6252
H & W Foods
  Kapolei, HI 808-682-8300
H-E-B Grocery Co. LP
  San Antonio, TX 800-432-3113
Haile Resources
  Dallas, TX 800-357-1471
Hain Celestial Group Inc
  Lake Success, NY 800-434-4246
Hanmi Inc
  Chicago, IL 773-271-0730
Hatch Chile Company
  Albuquerque, NM 912-267-9909
Healthy Food Ingredients
  Fargo, ND 844-275-3443
Hickey Foods
  Sun Valley, ID 800-215-0646
Holly's Oatmeal Inc
  Torrington, CT 860-618-0090
Ingles Markets
  Black Mountain, NC 828-669-2941
Inland Products
  Carthage, MO 417-358-4048
International Delicacies Inc
  San Pablo, CA 844-974-1030
Ira Higdon Grocery Company
  Cairo, GA 229-377-1272
Island Treasures Gourmet
  Manassas, VA 703-801-4671
Itella Foods
  San Pedro, CA 310-732-5875
Johnston County Hams
  Smithfield, NC 800-543-4267
Julian's Recipe
  Brooklyn, NY 888-640-8880
Kaladi Brothers
  Anchorage, AK 907-644-7400
Karlin Foods
  Northfield, IL 847-441-8330
Kaurina's, LLC
  Dallas, TX 972-888-9990
Kusha Inc.
  Cypress, CA 800-550-7423
La Superior Food Products
  Shawnee Mission, KS 913-432-4933
Lahaha Tea Co
  Arcadia, CA 626-215-6960
Lance Private Brands
  Charlotte, NC 888-722-1163
Lemke Wholesale
  Rogers, AR 479-751-4671
Lopez Foods
  Oklahoma City, OK 405-603-7500
Lotus Manufacturing Company
  San Antonio, TX 210-223-1421
M & M Label Co
  Malden, MA 800-637-6628
M&L Ventures
  Tucson, AZ 520-884-8232
Maher Marketing Services
  Irving, TX 972-751-7700
Marukan Vinegar USA Inc.
  Paramount, CA 562-630-6060
Mathews Packing
  Marysville, CA 530-743-9000
Mcfarling Foods Inc
  Indianapolis, IN 317-635-2633
Meijer Inc
  Grand Rapids, MI 616-453-6711
Milton A. Klein Company
  New York, NY 800-221-0248
Minh Food Corporation
  Pasadena, TX 800-344-7655
Miss Jenny's Pickles
  Kernersville, NC 336-978-0041
Mission Valley Foods
  Fremont, CA 408-254-9387
Mj Kellner Co
  Springfield, IL 217-483-1700
MKE Enterprises LTD
  New York, NY 212-447-0051
Moledina Commodities
  Flower Mound, TX 817-490-1101
Monte Cristo Trading
  Scarsdale, NY 914-725-8025
National Food Co LTD
  Honolulu, HI 808-839-1118
National Importers
  Richmond, BC 888-894-6464
O'Brines Pickling
  Spokane, WA 509-534-7255
Olde Estate
  Boca Raton, FL 561-400-7444
Particle Control
  Albertville, MN 763-497-3075
Penn Dutch Meat & Seafood Market
  Hollywood, FL 954-921-7144
Pon Food Corp
  Ponchatoula, LA 985-386-6941
Publix Super Market
  Lakeland, FL 800-242-1227
Pure Inventions LLC
  Little Silver, NJ 732-842-5777
Quality Food Products Inc
  Chicago, IL 312-666-4559
Ramsen Inc
  Lakeville, MN 952-431-0400
Richards Natural Foods
  Eagle, MI 517-627-7965
Schnuck Markets, Inc.
  St. Louis, MO 800-264-4400
Select Origins
  Mansfield, OH 419-924-5447
Severance Foods Inc
  Hartford, CT 860-724-7063
Solo Worldwide Enterprises
  Falls Church, VA 703-845-7072
Sprouts Farmers Market Inc.
  Phoenix, AZ
Stassen North America
  Louisville, CO 303-563-1016
Sun Garden Sprouts
  Cookeville, TN 931-400-2710
Sun World Intl LLC
  Palm Desert, CA 760-398-9450
Sun-Rise
  Alexandria, MN 320-846-5720
Sunny Delight Beverage Company
  Cincinnati, OH
Tase-Rite Co
  Wakefield, RI 401-783-7300
The Procter & Gamble Company
  Cincinnati, OH 800-692-0132
Thermice Company
  Old Greenwich, CT 203-637-4500
Topco Associates LLC
  Elk Grove Village, IL 847-676-3030
Trade Marcs Group
  Brooklyn, NY 718-387-9696
Tradeshare Corporation
  Brooklyn, NY 718-237-2295
Transnational Foods
  Miami, FL 305-415-9970
Ultimate Foods
  Linden, NJ 908-486-0800
Valley Sun Products Inc
  Newman, CA 800-426-5444
VIP Food Svc
  Kahului, HI 808-877-5055
Wallace Edwards & Sons
  Surry, VA 800-200-4267
WEIS Markets Inc.
  Sunbury, PA 866-999-9347
Winn-Dixie Stores
  Jacksonville, FL 800-967-9105
Wonder Natural Foods Corp
  Water Mill, NY 631-726-4433
Yamamotoyama of America
  Pomona, CA 909-594-7356
Zuccaro Produce
  Columbia Heights, MN 612-333-1122

Product Categories / Ingredients, Flavors & Additives: General

Ingredients, Flavors & Additives

Freeze Dried Ingredients

Freeze-Dry Ingredients
  Elmhurst, IL 630-530-1880
Oregon Freeze Dry, Inc.
  Albany, OR 541-926-6001
SupHerb Farms
  Turlock, CA 800-787-4372
Y Not Foods
  Cape Coral, FL 608-222-2860

General

A Hill of Beans Coffee Roasters
  Omaha, NE 402-333-6048
Accurate Ingredients Inc
  Farmingdale, NY 516-496-2500
AEP Colloids
  Hadley, NY 800-848-0658
Ajinomoto Frozen Foods USA, Inc.
  Ontario, CA. 866-536-8008
Aloecorp, Inc.
  Seattle, WA 800-458-2563
AMCO Proteins
  Burlington, NJ. 609-387-3130
AME Nutrition
  Dublin, OH 614-766-3638
American Ingredients Co
  Lenexa, KS 800-669-4092
American Specialty Foods
  Lancaster, PA 800-335-6663
Ames Company, Inc
  New Ringgold, PA 610-750-1032
AMF Pharma
  Ontario, CA. 888-666-1016
Analyticon Discovery LLC
  Rockville, MD 240-406-1256
Asiamerica Ingredients
  Westwood, NJ 201-497-5531
AuNutra Industries Inc
  Chino, CA 909-628-2600
Axiom Foods, Inc.
  Los Angeles, CA. 800-711-3587
Bakto Flavors
  North Brunswick, NJ 732-354-4492
Batory Foods
  Des Plaines, IL 847-299-1999
Beverage Flavors Intl
  Chicago, IL 773-248-3860
Biothera
  St Paul, MN. 651-675-0300
Blanver USA
  Boca Raton, FL. 561-416-5513
Blue Marble Biomaterials
  Missoula, MT 800-738-0849
Bonnie & Don Flavours Inc.
  Mississauga, ON. 905-625-1813
Budenheim USA, Inc.
  Columbus, OH 614-345-2400
Caldic USA Inc
  Elgin, IL 847-468-0001
Caremoli USA
  Ames, IA 515-233-1255
Carolina Innovative Food Ingredients, Inc.
  Nashville, NC 252-462-1551
Catherych
  Warren, NJ 732-566-6625
Centerchem, Inc.
  Norwalk, CT 203-822-9800
Chaucer Foods, Inc. USA
  Forest Grove, OR
CJ America
  Los Angeles, CA. 213-427-5566
Clara Foods
  San Francisco, CA
Clariant
  Charlottte, NC. 704-331-7000
Corbion
  S San Francisco, CA
Corbion
  Blair, NE. 402-426-0377
Corbion
  Tucker, GA 470-545-7100
Corbion
  Dolton, IL 708-849-8590
Corbion
  Mississauga, ON 800-324-8802

Corbion
  Totowa, NJ 800-526-5261
Corbion
  Lenexa, KS 800-669-4092
Corbion
  Grandview, MO. 816-763-8377
Creative Flavors & Specialties LLP
  Linden, NJ. 908-862-4678
D F Ingredients Inc
  Washington, MO 888-583-0802
D2 Ingredients, LP.
  De Pere, WI. 920-425-8870
Darling Ingredients Inc.
  Irving, TX 800-800-4841
Deko International Company
  Earth City, MO 314-298-0910
Denomega Pure Health
  Brighton, CO. 479-181-2845
Dohler-Milne Aseptics LLC
  Prosser, WA. 509-786-2240
Draco Natural Products Inc
  San Jose, CA. 408-287-7871
Dulcette Technologies
  Lindenhurst, NY 631-752-8700
DuPont Tate & Lyle BioProducts Company, LLC.
  Loudon, TN. 866-404-7933
DyStar Hilton Davis/DyStar Foam Control
  Cuyahoga Falls, OH 330-916-6726
Edlong Corporation
  Elk Grove Village, IL 847-631-6700
Embria Health Sciences
  Ankeny, IA 877-362-7421
EMD Performance Materials
  Philadelphia, PA 888-367-3275
Emerald Hilton Davis LLC
  Cincinnati, OH 513-841-0057
Emerald Performance Materials
  Cuyahoga Falls, OH 330-916-6700
Epogee
  Indianapolis, IN
Escalade Limited
  Huntington, NY 631-659-3373
Ethical Naturals
  San Anselmo, CA 866-459-4454
Expro Manufacturing
  Vernon, CA 323-415-8544
Fallwood Corp
  White Plains, NY 914-304-4065
Fenchem Inc
  Chino, CA 909-597-1113
Fiberstar
  River Falls, WI 715-425-7550
First Choice Ingredients
  Germantown, WI. 262-251-4322
FlavorHealth
  North Brunswick, NJ 732-875-4799
Flavors and Color
  Walnut, CA 909-598-4441
Fontana Flavors Inc
  Janesville, WI 608-754-9668
Fontana Flavors Inc
  Janesville, WI 608-754-9668
Foreign Domestic Chemicals
  Oakland, NJ 201-651-9700
Freeze-Dry Foods Inc
  Albion, NY 585-589-6399
FrieslandCampina Ingredients North America, Inc.
  Paramus, NJ 551-497-7300
Fuji Health Science/Inc
  Burlington, NJ. 609-386-3030
GAF Seelig Inc
  Flushing, NY. 718-899-5000
Garuda International
  Exeter, CA. 559-594-4380
Gelnex Gelatins
  Chicago, IL 312-577-4275
Glanbia Nutritionals
  Twin Falls, ID 208-733-7555
GLG Life Tech Corporation
  Richmond, BC 855-454-7587
Global Preservatives
  Lake Charles, LA 866-491-0816
Golden 100
  Deland, FL 386-734-0113
Graham Chemical Corporation
  Barrington, IL 847-304-4400

Great Earth Chemical
  Portland, OR 503-620-7130
GTC Nutrition
  Westchester, IL 800-443-2746
Hangzhou Sanhe USA Inc.
  Walnut, CA 909-869-6016
Hard Eight Nutrition LLC
  Henderson, NV 702-425-7638
Hawkins Inc
  Roseville, MN. 800-328-5460
Heartland Flax
  Valley City, ND. 866-599-3529
Helm New York Chemical Corp
  Piscataway, NJ 732-981-0528
High Quality Organics
  Reno, NV 775-971-8550
Hilmar Ingredients
  Hilmar, CA 888-300-4465
Horner International
  Raleigh, NC. 919-787-3112
I P Callison & Sons
  Lacey, WA 360-412-3340
ICL Performance Products
  St. Louis, MO 800-244-6169
IFC Solutions
  Linden, NJ. 800-875-9393
Imperial Sensus
  Sugar Land, TX. 281-490-9522
Ingredia Inc
  Wapakoneta, OH 419-738-4060
Ingredient Specialties
  Exeter, CA. 559-594-4380
Innopros Holdings Inc.
  Cranbury, NJ. 609-495-2495
Innova Flavors
  Lombard, IL 630-928-4800
Interfood Ingredients
  Miami, FL. 786-953-8320
J & K Ingredients
  Paterson, NJ 973-340-8700
J Rettenmaier USA LP
  Schoolcraft, MI. 877-895-4099
Javo Beverage Co., Inc.
  Vista, CA. 760-330-1141
Jel Sert
  West Chicago, IL 800-323-2592
Jost Chemical
  St Louis, MO. 314-428-4300
Kenko International
  Los Angeles, CA. 323-721-8300
Latitude, LTD
  Huntington, NY 631-659-3374
Lekithos
  Palm Beach Gardens, FL
Lionel Hitchen Essitional Oils
  Sarasota, FL 941-379-1400
Lipid Nutrition
  Channahan, IL. 815-730-5208
Log 5 Corporation
  Phoenix, MD. 410-329-9580
Log House Foods
  Plymouth, MN. 763-546-8395
Magrabar Chemical Corp
  Morton Grove, IL 847-965-7550
MAK Wood Inc
  Grafton, WI. 262-387-1200
Marroquin Organic Intl.
  Santa Cruz, CA 831-423-3442
Marukan Vinegar USA Inc.
  Paramount, CA 562-630-6060
MGP Ingredients Inc
  Atchison, KS. 800-255-0302
Moore Organics
  Hamilton, OH 513-881-7144
Muntons Ingredients
  Bellevue, WA 425-372-3082
Nantong Acetic Acid Chemical Co., Ltd.
  Hilliard, OH 614-947-0249
Nature's Products Inc
  Sunrise, FL 800-752-7873
New Hope Natural Media
  Boulder, CO 303-939-8440
Newport Ingredients
  Los Angeles, CA. 323-284-5959
North Taste Flavourings
  Anse-Bleue, NB 506-732-0010

Product Categories / Ingredients, Flavors & Additives: Acids

Nutraceutical International
  Park City, UT 800-669-8877
Nutralliance
  Yorba Linda, CA.................. 844-410-1400
NutriFusion
  Naples, FL 239-300-9702
Old Cavendish Products
  Cavendish, VT 800-536-7899
Peter Cremer North America
  Cincinnati, OH 877-901-7262
Phamous Phloyd's Barbecue
  Denver, CO 800-497-3281
Piveg, Inc.
  San Diego, CA 858-688-3070
Procell Polymers
  Baton Rouge, LA 225-978-8069
Reheis Co
  Berkeley Heights, NJ 908-464-1500
San Joaquin Vly Concentrates
  Fresno, CA 800-557-0220
Shanghai Freemen
  Edison, NJ 732-981-1288
SoluBlend Technologies LLC
  Frankfort, IL 815-534-5778
Specialty Minerals Inc
  Bethlehem, PA 800-801-1031
Sunshine International Foods
  Methuen, MA 978-837-3209
Suzhou-Chem Inc
  Wellesley, MA 781-433-8618
Svzusa Inc
  Othello, WA 509-488-6563
Vanilla Corp Of America LLC
  Hatfield, PA 215-996-1978
Ventura Foods LLC
  Brea, CA 800-421-6257
Vida Blend
  Amsterdam, NY 518-620-6216
Wiberg Corporation
  Oakville, ON 905-825-9900
Wildly Organic
  Silver Bay, MN 800-945-3801
Z-Trim Holdings, Inc
  Mundelein, IL 847-549-6002

Acids

Amerol Chemical Corporation
  Farmingdale, NY 631-694-4700
Bartek Ingredients, Inc.
  Stoney Creek, ON 800-263-4165
BASF Corp.
  Florham Park, NJ 800-526-1072
Cargill Inc.
  Minneapolis, MN 800-227-4455
J M Swank Co
  North Liberty, IA 800-593-6375
Jarchem Industries
  Newark, NJ 973-578-4560
Jungbunzlauer Inc
  Newton, MA 617-969-0900
Particle Dynamics
  Saint Louis, MO 800-452-4682
Pfanstiehl Inc
  Waukegan, IL 847-623-0370
PMP Fermentation Products
  Peoria, IL 800-558-1031
Profood International
  Naperville, IL 888-288-0081
Protein Research
  Livermore, CA 800-948-1991
Roquette America Inc.
  Geneva, IL 630-463-9430
Shanghai Freemen
  Edison, NJ 732-981-1288
Silver Fern Chemical Inc
  Seattle, WA 866-282-3384
Symrise Inc.
  Teterboro, NJ 201-288-3200
Trumark
  Linden, NJ 800-752-7877
Wilke International Inc
  Lenexa, KS 800-779-5545

Adipic

Shanghai Freemen
  Edison, NJ 732-981-1288
Silver Fern Chemical Inc
  Seattle, WA 866-282-3384
Universal Preservachem Inc
  Somerset, NJ 732-568-1266

Aminoacetic

ADH Health Products Inc
  Congers, NY 845-268-0027
Ajinomoto Heartland Inc
  Chicago, IL 773-380-7000
AMT Labs Inc
  North Salt Lake, UT 801-294-3126
Anabol Naturals
  Santa Cruz, CA 800-426-2265
Asiamerica Ingredients
  Westwood, NJ 201-497-5531
Belmont Chemicals
  Clifton, NJ 800-722-5070
Catherych
  Warren, NJ 732-566-6625
DMH Ingredients Inc
  Libertyville, IL 847-362-9977
Eckhart Corporation
  Novato, CA 800-200-4201
Jo Mar Laboratories
  Campbell, CA 800-538-4545
Kyowa Hakko
  New York, NY 800-596-9252
NOW Foods
  Bloomingdale, IL 888-669-3663
Nu Naturals Inc
  Eugene, OR 800-753-4372
Stauber Performance Ingrdients
  Fullerton, CA 888-441-4233
Universal Preservachem Inc
  Somerset, NJ 732-568-1266

Benzoic

Emerald Kalama Chemical, LLC
  Kalama, WA 800-223-0035
Luyties Pharmacal Company
  Saint Louis, MO 800-325-8080
Universal Preservachem Inc
  Somerset, NJ 732-568-1266

Boric/Boracic

Universal Preservachem Inc
  Somerset, NJ 732-568-1266

Gluconic (Gluconolactone)

Glucona America
  Janesville, WI 608-752-0449
Jungbunzlauer Inc
  Newton, MA 617-969-0900
PMP Fermentation Products
  Peoria, IL 800-558-1031
Roquette America Inc.
  Geneva, IL 630-463-9430
Universal Preservachem Inc
  Somerset, NJ 732-568-1266

Glutamic

Shanghai Freemen
  Edison, NJ 732-981-1288
Universal Preservachem Inc
  Somerset, NJ 732-568-1266

Succinic

BioAmber
  Plymouth, MN 763-253-4480
Shanghai Freemen
  Edison, NJ 732-981-1288

Tannic

Silvateam USA
  Ontario, CA 909-635-2870

Acidulants

Asiamerica Ingredients
  Westwood, NJ 201-497-5531
Marukan Vinegar USA Inc.
  Paramount, CA 562-630-6060
Newport Ingredients
  Los Angeles, CA 323-284-5959
Tate & Lyle PLC
  Hoffman Estates, IL 847-396-7500
Wenda America Inc
  Naperville, IL 844-999-3632

Acetic

Asiamerica Ingredients
  Westwood, NJ 201-497-5531
Jarchem Industries
  Newark, NJ 973-578-4560
Universal Preservachem Inc
  Somerset, NJ 732-568-1266

Citric

American Key Food Products Inc
  Closter, NJ 877-263-7539
Asiamerica Ingredients
  Westwood, NJ 201-497-5531
Cargill Inc.
  Minneapolis, MN 800-227-4455
Embassy Flavours Ltd.
  Brampton, ON 800-334-3371
FBC Industries
  Schaumburg, IL 888-322-4637
Hosemen & Roche Vitamins & Fine Chemicals
  Nutley, NJ 800-526-6367
International Chemical Corp
  Melbourne, FL 800-914-2436
Jungbunzlauer Inc
  Newton, MA 617-969-0900
Luyties Pharmacal Company
  Saint Louis, MO 800-325-8080
Nichem Co
  Newark, NJ 973-399-9810
Shekou Chemicals
  Waltham, MA 781-893-6878
Universal Preservachem Inc
  Somerset, NJ 732-568-1266

Fumaric

Asiamerica Ingredients
  Westwood, NJ 201-497-5531
Bartek Ingredients, Inc.
  Stoney Creek, ON 800-263-4165
Jungbunzlauer Inc
  Newton, MA 617-969-0900
Silver Fern Chemical Inc
  Seattle, WA 866-282-3384
Universal Preservachem Inc
  Somerset, NJ 732-568-1266

Lactic

Asiamerica Ingredients
  Westwood, NJ 201-497-5531
Fleurchem Inc
  Middletown, NY 845-341-2100
Jungbunzlauer Inc
  Newton, MA 617-969-0900
Pfanstiehl Inc
  Waukegan, IL 847-623-0370
Trumark
  Linden, NJ 800-752-7877
Universal Preservachem Inc
  Somerset, NJ 732-568-1266
Varied Industries Corp
  Mason City, IA 800-654-5617
Wilke International Inc
  Lenexa, KS 800-779-5545

Malic

Asiamerica Ingredients
  Westwood, NJ 201-497-5531
Bartek Ingredients, Inc.
  Stoney Creek, ON 800-263-4165
Jungbunzlauer Inc
  Newton, MA 617-969-0900
Universal Preservachem Inc
  Somerset, NJ 732-568-1266

Phosphoric

Asiamerica Ingredients
  Westwood, NJ 201-497-5531
ICL Performance Products
  St. Louis, MO 800-244-6169
Universal Preservachem Inc
  Somerset, NJ 732-568-1266

Sorbic

Asiamerica Ingredients
  Westwood, NJ 201-497-5531
International Chemical Corp
  Melbourne, FL 800-914-2436
Jungbunzlauer Inc
  Newton, MA 617-969-0900
Silver Fern Chemical Inc
  Seattle, WA 866-282-3384

Product Categories / Ingredients, Flavors & Additives: Additives

Universal Preservachem Inc
  Somerset, NJ..................732-568-1266

Tartaric

American Tartaric Products
  Larchmont, NY..................914-834-1881
Asiamerica Ingredients
  Westwood, NJ..................201-497-5531
Bartek Ingredients, Inc.
  Stoney Creek, ON..................800-263-4165
Frontier Co-op
  Norway, IA..................844-550-6200
H. Interdonati
  Cold Spring Harbour, NY..................800-367-6617
International Chemical Corp
  Melbourne, FL..................800-914-2436
Jungbunzlauer Inc
  Newton, MA..................617-969-0900
Universal Preservachem Inc
  Somerset, NJ..................732-568-1266

Additives

Foreign Domestic Chemicals
  Oakland, NJ..................201-651-9700
Great Earth Chemical
  Portland, OR..................503-620-7130
ICL Performance Products
  St. Louis, MO..................800-244-6169
Jost Chemical
  St Louis, MO..................314-428-4300
Latitude, LTD
  Huntington, NY..................631-659-3374
Magrabar Chemical Corp
  Morton Grove, IL..................847-965-7550

Anticaking

Allied Blending & Ingredients
  Keokuk, IA..................800-758-4080
Asiamerica Ingredients
  Westwood, NJ..................201-497-5531
Atlantic Chemicals Trading
  Glendale, CA..................818-246-0077

Enrichment & Nutrient

Single & Blended

Asiamerica Ingredients
  Westwood, NJ..................201-497-5531

Enzymes

D F Ingredients Inc
  Washington, MO..................888-583-0802
Deerland Probiotics & Enzymes
  Forsyth, MO..................800-825-8545
DSM
  Heerlen,

Free Flow

Amerol Chemical Corporation
  Farmingdale, NY..................631-694-4700
Asiamerica Ingredients
  Westwood, NJ..................201-497-5531
Crompton Corporation
  Greenwich, CT..................800-295-2392
Garuda International
  Exeter, CA..................559-594-4380
Prolume
  Lakeside, AZ..................928-367-1200

Nutrient

Provitas LLC
  Plano, TX..................972-767-8867
Shanghai Freemen
  Edison, NJ..................732-981-1288

Adjuncts

Torkelson Cheese Co
  Lena, IL..................815-369-4265

Brewing

Acadian Seaplants
  Dartmouth, NS..................800-575-9100
Boyd's Coffee Co
  Portland, OR..................800-735-2878
Shanghai Freemen
  Edison, NJ..................732-981-1288
Thymly Products Inc
  Colora, MD..................877-710-2340

Agents

Asiamerica Ingredients
  Westwood, NJ..................201-497-5531
Crest Foods Inc
  Ashton, IL..................877-273-7893
IFC Solutions
  Linden, NJ..................800-875-9393
International Foodcraft Corp
  Linden, NJ..................800-875-9393
MAFCO Worldwide
  Camden, NJ..................856-986-4050
Magrabar Chemical Corp
  Morton Grove, IL..................847-965-7550

Buffering

Thymly Products Inc
  Colora, MD..................877-710-2340

Clarifying

American Laboratories
  Omaha, NE..................402-339-2494

Release, Grease

Edible

International Foodcraft Corp
  Linden, NJ..................800-875-9393

Thickening

PLT Health Solutions Inc
  Morristown, NJ..................973-984-0900
Sno Shack Inc
  Rexburg, ID..................888-766-7425

Arrowroot

Advanced Spice & Trading
  Carrollton, TX..................800-872-7811
Frontier Co-op
  Norway, IA..................844-550-6200
Schiff Food Products Co Inc
  Totowa, NJ..................973-237-1990

Whipping

Kolatin Real Kosher Gelatin
  Lakewood, NJ..................732-364-8700

Alkalis

Caustic

Sodium & Potassium Hydroxides

Xena International
  Polo, IL..................815-946-2626

Ammonium Carbonate

King Arthur Flour
  Norwich, VT..................800-827-6836
Luyties Pharmacal Company
  Saint Louis, MO..................800-325-8080
Universal Preservachem Inc
  Somerset, NJ..................732-568-1266

Analogs

Meat

Caribbean Food Delights Inc
  Tappan, NY..................845-398-3000
Cedar Lake Foods
  Cedar Lake, MI..................800-246-5039
Ivy Foods
  Phoenix, AZ..................877-223-5459
Oogolow Enterprises
  Chico, CA..................800-816-6873
Vitasoy USA
  Woburn, MA..................800-848-2769
Westin Foods
  Omaha, NE..................800-228-6098
Winmix/Natural Care Products
  Englewood, FL..................941-475-7432

Antioxidants

Amerol Chemical Corporation
  Farmingdale, NY..................631-694-4700
Asiamerica Ingredients
  Westwood, NJ..................201-497-5531
Avatar Corp
  University Park, IL..................800-255-3181
Body Breakthrough Inc
  Deer Park, NY..................800-924-3343
Dulcette Technologies
  Lindenhurst, NY..................631-752-8700
Escalade Limited
  Huntington, NY..................631-659-3373
Ethical Naturals
  San Anselmo, CA..................866-459-4454
Fuji Health Science/Inc
  Burlington, NJ..................609-386-3030
Herbal Products & Development
  Aptos, CA..................831-688-8706
International Vitamin Corporation
  Freehold, NJ..................800-666-8482
J M Swank Co
  North Liberty, IA..................800-593-6375
Kenko International
  Los Angeles, CA..................323-721-8300
Latitude, LTD
  Huntington, NY..................631-659-3374
Newport Ingredients
  Los Angeles, CA..................323-284-5959
NOW Foods
  Bloomingdale, IL..................888-669-3663
Nutraceutical International
  Park City, UT..................800-669-8877
PLT Health Solutions Inc
  Morristown, NJ..................973-984-0900
Premier Organics
  Oakland, CA..................866-237-8688
QBI
  South Plainfield, NJ..................908-668-0088
RFi Ingredients
  Blauvelt, NY..................800-962-7663
RPM Total Vitality
  Yorba Linda, CA..................800-234-3092
Shanghai Freemen
  Edison, NJ..................732-981-1288
Uas Laboratories
  Eden Prairie, MN..................800-422-3371
Wenda America Inc
  Naperville, IL..................844-999-3632

Ascorbic Acid

Asiamerica Ingredients
  Westwood, NJ..................201-497-5531
China Pharmaceutical Enterprises
  Baton Rouge, LA..................800-345-1658
International Chemical Corp
  Melbourne, FL..................800-914-2436
King Arthur Flour
  Norwich, VT..................800-827-6836
Shekou Chemicals
  Waltham, MA..................781-893-6878
Universal Preservachem Inc
  Somerset, NJ..................732-568-1266

Aroma Chemicals

Asiamerica Ingredients
  Westwood, NJ..................201-497-5531
Astral Extracts
  Syosset, NY..................516-496-2505
Firmenich Inc.
  Plainsboro, NJ..................800-257-9591
Powder Pure
  The Dalles, OR..................541-298-4800
Terra Flavors & Fragrances
  New York, NY..................212-244-1181

Aroma Chemicals & Materials

Chemicals

Asiamerica Ingredients
  Westwood, NJ..................201-497-5531
Native Scents
  Taos, NM..................800-645-3471

Methyl Salicylate

Asiamerica Ingredients
  Westwood, NJ..................201-497-5531

Fragrances

AFF International
  Marietta, GA..................800-241-7764
AM Todd Co
  Kalamazoo, MI..................269-343-2603
Aroma Vera
  Los Angeles, CA..................800-669-9514

Product Categories / Ingredients, Flavors & Additives: Bases

Aromachem
   Brooklyn, NY 718-497-4664
Asiamerica Ingredients
   Westwood, NJ 201-497-5531
Avoca
   Merry Hill, NC 252-482-2133
Avri Co Inc
   Richmond, CA 800-883-9574
Centflor Manufacturing Co
   New York, NY 212-246-8307
Classic Flavors & Fragrances
   New York, NY 212-777-0004
DreamTime, Inc
   Santa Cruz, CA 877-464-6702
Elan Vanilla Co
   Newark, NJ 973-344-8014
Essential Products of America
   Tampa, FL 800-822-9698
Firmenich Inc.
   Plainsboro, NJ 800-257-9591
Flavor & Fragrance Specialties
   Mahwah, NJ 800-998-4337
Flavormatic Industries
   Wappingers Falls, NY 845-297-9100
Fleurchem Inc
   Middletown, NY 845-341-2100
Flower Essence Svc
   Nevada City, CA 800-548-0075
Green Spot Packaging
   Claremont, CA 800-456-3210
International Flavors & Fragrances Inc.
   New York, NY 212-765-5500
Jogue Inc
   Northville, MI 800-531-3888
Newport Flavours & Fragrances
   Orange, CA 714-744-3700
PMC Specialties Group Inc
   Cincinnati, OH 800-543-2466
SKW Nature Products
   Langhorne, PA 215-702-1000
Symrise Inc.
   Teterboro, NJ 201-288-3200
T Hasegawa USA Inc
   Cerritos, CA 714-522-1900
Technology Flavors & Fragrances
   Amityville, NY 631-789-8228
Treatt USA Inc
   Lakeland, FL 863-668-9500
Ungerer & Co
   Lincoln Park, NJ 973-706-7381

Bases

Al-Rite Fruits & Syrups Co
   Miami, FL 305-652-2540
Ariake USA Inc
   Harrisonburg, VA 540-432-6550
BakeMark Canada
   Laval, QC 800-361-4998
BakeMark Ingredients Canada
   Richmond, BC 800-665-9441
Bartush Schnitzius Foods Co
   Lewisville, TX 972-219-1270
Blount Fine Foods
   Fall River, MA 774-888-1300
California Dairies Inc.
   Visalia, CA 559-625-2200
Chef Hans' Gourmet Foods
   Monroe, LA 800-890-4267
Citrosuco North America Inc
   Lake Wales, FL 800-356-4592
Classic Tea
   Libertyville, IL 630-680-9934
Clofine Dairy Products Inc
   Linwood, NJ 609-653-1000
Concord Foods, LLC
   Brockton, MA 508-580-1700
Consolidated Mills Inc
   Houston, TX 713-896-4196
Crest Foods Inc
   Ashton, IL 877-273-7893
CTL Foods
   Colfax, WI. 800-962-5227
Custom Culinary Inc.
   Schaumberg, IL. 800-621-8827
Dorothy Dawson Food Products
   Jackson, MI. 517-788-9830
Eatem Foods Co
   Vineland, NJ 800-683-2836
Erba Food Products
   Brooklyn, NY 718-272-7700
Finlays
   Lincoln, RI 800-288-6272
Flavor House, Inc.
   Adelanto, CA 760-246-9131
Folklore Foods
   Selby, SD. 605-649-1144
Fuji Foods Corp
   Browns Summit, NC 336-375-3111
Global Food Industries
   Townville, SC 800-225-4152
GS-AFI
   South Plainfield, NJ 800-345-4342
Gum Technology Corporation
   Tucson, AZ 800-369-4867
Hormel Foods Corp.
   Austin, MN 507-437-5611
Illes Seasonings & Flavors
   Carrollton, TX 800-683-4553
Integrative Flavors
   Michigan City, IN 800-837-7687
JMH International
   Park City, UT 888-741-4564
Johnson's Food Products
   Dorchester, MA 617-265-3400
Manildra Milling Corporation
   Fairway, KS. 800-323-8435
Meat-O-Mat Corp
   Brooklyn, NY 718-965-7250
Merci Spring Water
   Maryland Heights, MO 314-872-9323
MicroSoy Corporation
   Jefferson, IA 515-386-2100
Midas Foods Intl
   Oak Park, MI. 877-728-2379
Olympia Oyster Co
   Shelton, WA 877-427-3193
Pacific Harvest Products
   Bellevue, WA 425-401-7990
Particle Dynamics
   Saint Louis, MO 800-452-4682
Produits Ronald
   St. Damase, QC 800-465-0118
Roos Foods
   Kenton, DE 800-343-3642
Serv-Agen Corporation
   Cherry Hill, NJ 856-663-6966
Skjodt-Barrett Foods
   Brampton, ON 877-600-1200
Spice Hunter Inc
   Richmond, VA 800-444-3061
Spicetec Flavors & Seasonings
   Omaha, NE 800-921-7502
Stevens Tropical Plantation
   West Palm Beach, FL 561-683-4701
Sweet Sue Kitchens
   Athens, AL 256-216-0500
Swiss Food Products
   Chicago, IL 312-829-0100
Texas Spice Co
   Round Rock, TX 800-880-8007
Tone Products Inc
   Melrose Park, IL 800-536-8663
United Citrus
   Norwood, MA. 800-229-7300
V & E Kohnstamm Inc
   Brooklyn, NY 800-847-4500
Vita-Pakt Citrus Products Co
   Covina, CA 888-684-8272
Welch Foods Inc.
   Concord, MA 800-340-6870
Western Syrup Company
   Santa Fe Springs, CA 562-921-4485
White Coffee Corporation
   Long Island City, NY 800-221-0140

Beef

Castella Imports Inc
   Brentwood, NY 631-231-5500
Golden Specialty Foods Inc
   Norwalk, CA. 562-802-2537

Broth Cubes

Gel Spice Co LLC
   Bayonne, NJ. 800-922-0230

Beverage

Allen Flavors Inc
   Edison, NJ. 908-561-5995
Astral Extracts
   Syosset, NY. 516-496-2505
Baldwin Richardson Foods
   Oakbrook Terrace, IL 866-644-2732
Bartush Schnitzius Foods Co
   Lewisville, TX 972-219-1270
California Custom Fruits
   Baldwin Park, CA. 877-558-0056
Carmi Flavor & Fragrance Company
   Commerce, CA 800-421-9647
Century Foods Intl LLC
   Sparta, WI 800-269-1901
Classic Tea
   Libertyville, IL 630-680-9934
Consolidated Mills Inc
   Houston, TX 713-896-4196
CTL Foods
   Colfax, WI. 800-962-5227
Delano Growers Grape Products
   Delano, CA 661-725-3255
Essential Flavors & Fragrances
   Corona, CA 888-333-9935
Finlays
   Lincoln, RI 800-288-6272
Folklore Foods
   Selby, SD. 605-649-1144
Franco's Cocktail Mixes
   Pompano Beach, FL 800-782-4508
Fruitcrown Products Corp
   Farmingdale, NY 800-441-3210
Global Food Industries
   Townville, SC 800-225-4152
I Rice & Co Inc
   Philadelphia, PA 800-232-6022
Milne Fruit Products Inc
   Prosser, WA 509-786-2611
Nedlog Company
   Wheeling, IL 800-323-6201
New Organics
   Kenwood, CA 734-677-5570
Plaidberry Company
   Vista, CA 760-727-5403
Quality Naturally Foods
   City Of Industry, CA. 888-498-6986
Rio Syrup Co
   St Louis, MO. 800-325-7666
Roos Foods
   Kenton, DE 800-343-3642
Schlotterbeck & Foss Company
   Portland, ME. 800-777-4666
Singer Extract Laboratory
   Livonia, MI 313-345-5880
Skjodt-Barrett Foods
   Brampton, ON 877-600-1200
Stevens Tropical Plantation
   West Palm Beach, FL 561-683-4701
Tampico Beverages Inc
   Chicago, IL 877-826-7426
Thirs-Tea Corp
   Boca Raton, FL. 561-948-5600
Tova Industries LLC
   Louisville, KY 888-532-8682
Vance's Foods
   San Francisco, CA 415-621-1171
Vegetable Juices Inc
   Chicago, IL 888-776-9752
Wechsler Coffee Corporation
   Teterboro, NJ. 800-800-2633
Welch Foods Inc.
   Concord, MA 800-340-6870
Western Syrup Company
   Santa Fe Springs, CA 562-921-4485
Wild Aseptics, LLC
   Erlanger, KY. 877-787-7221
Winmix/Natural Care Products
   Englewood, FL 941-475-7432

Bouillon

Gel Spice Co LLC
   Bayonne, NJ. 800-922-0230
Hormel Foods Corp.
   Austin, MN 507-437-5611
Massel USA
   Carol Stream, IL 704-573-2299
Organic Gourmet
   Sherman Oaks, CA 800-400-7772

Beef

Hormel Foods Corp.
   Austin, MN 507-437-5611
Supreme Dairy Farms Co
   Warwick, RI 401-739-8180

Product Categories / Ingredients, Flavors & Additives: Bases

Candy
Kolatin Real Kosher Gelatin
   Lakewood, NJ 732-364-8700

Chicken
Castella Imports Inc
   Brentwood, NY 631-231-5500
Golden Specialty Foods Inc
   Norwalk, CA 562-802-2537
Swiss Food Products
   Chicago, IL 312-829-0100

Chocolate
Forbes Chocolate BP
   Broadview Hts, OH 440-838-4400
US Chocolate Corp
   Brooklyn, NY 718-788-8555

Dairy
Johnson's Food Products
   Dorchester, MA 617-265-3400
WILD Flavors (Canada)
   Mississauga, ON 800-263-5286

Non-Dairy & Imitation
Al-Rite Fruits & Syrups Co
   Miami, FL 305-652-2540
BakeMark Ingredients Canada
   Richmond, BC 800-665-9441
California Custom Fruits
   Baldwin Park, CA 877-558-0056
Century Foods Intl LLC
   Sparta, WI 800-269-1901
Clofine Dairy Products Inc
   Linwood, NJ 609-653-1000
Forbes Chocolate BP
   Broadview Hts, OH 440-838-4400
Freeman Industries
   Tuckahoe, NY 800-666-6454
Galloway Co
   Neenah, WI 800-722-8903
Global Food Industries
   Townville, SC 800-225-4152
I Rice & Co Inc
   Philadelphia, PA 800-232-6022
Johnson's Food Products
   Dorchester, MA 617-265-3400
Land O'Lakes Inc
   Arden Hills, MN 800-328-9680
Limpert Bros Inc
   Vineland, NJ 800-691-1353
New Organics
   Kenwood, CA 734-677-5570
Nog Incorporated
   Dunkirk, NY 800-332-2664
Plaidberry Company
   Vista, CA 760-727-5403
Quality Naturally Foods
   City Of Industry, CA 888-498-6986
Tova Industries LLC
   Louisville, KY 888-532-8682
Welsh Farms
   Wallington, NJ 800-221-0663
Westin Foods
   Omaha, NE 800-228-6098

Flavor
Creative Flavors & Specialties LLP
   Linden, NJ 908-862-4678
Essentia Protein Solutions
   Ankeny, IA 515-289-5100
Forbes Chocolate BP
   Broadview Hts, OH 440-838-4400
GS-AFI
   South Plainfield, NJ 800-345-4342
JMH International
   Park City, UT 888-741-4564
Pecan Deluxe Candy Co
   Dallas, TX 800-733-3589

Food
Abimco USA, Inc.
   Mendham, NJ 973-543-7393
Clofine Dairy Products Inc
   Linwood, NJ 609-653-1000
GS-AFI
   South Plainfield, NJ 800-345-4342
I Rice & Co Inc
   Philadelphia, PA 800-232-6022

Summit Hill Flavors
   Somerset, NJ 732-805-0335
Tova Industries LLC
   Louisville, KY 888-532-8682
Vita-Pakt Citrus Products Co
   Covina, CA 888-684-8272
Wild Aseptics, LLC
   Erlanger, KY 877-787-7221

Fruit
Agrana Fruit US Inc
   Cleveland, OH 800-477-3788
California Custom Fruits
   Baldwin Park, CA 877-558-0056
Fee Brothers
   Rochester, NY 800-961-3337
Tova Industries LLC
   Louisville, KY 888-532-8682
Wild Aseptics, LLC
   Erlanger, KY 877-787-7221

Gravy
Bernard Food Industries Inc
   Evanston, IL 800-323-3663
Con Yeager Spice Co
   Zelienople, PA 800-222-2460
Cordon Bleu International
   Anjou, QC 800-363-1182
Custom Culinary Inc.
   Schaumberg, IL 800-621-8827
Dorothy Dawson Food Products
   Jackson, MI 517-788-9830
Eatem Foods Co
   Vineland, NJ 800-683-2836
Felbro Food Products
   Los Angeles, CA 323-936-5266
Fuji Foods Corp
   Browns Summit, NC 336-375-3111
Gel Spice Co LLC
   Bayonne, NJ 800-922-0230
Griffith Foods Inc.
   Alsip, IL 708-371-0900
Hormel Foods Corp.
   Austin, MN 507-437-5611
Integrative Flavors
   Michigan City, IN 800-837-7687
Karlsburger Foods Inc
   Monticello, MN 800-383-6549
Lasco Foods Inc
   St Louis, MO 314-832-1906
Lawry's Foods
   Hunt Valley, MD 800-952-9797
Magic Seasoning Blends
   New Orleans, LA 800-457-2857
Meat-O-Mat Corp
   Brooklyn, NY 718-965-7250
More Than Gourmet
   Akron, OH 800-860-9385
Pacific Foods
   Kent, WA 800-347-9444
Produits Ronald
   St. Damase, QC 800-465-0118
Serv-Agen Corporation
   Cherry Hill, NJ 856-663-6966
Shenandoah Mills
   Lebanon, TN 615-444-0841
Sweet Sue Kitchens
   Athens, AL 256-216-0500
Swiss Food Products
   Chicago, IL 312-829-0100
Tova Industries LLC
   Louisville, KY 888-532-8682
Vogue Cuisine Foods
   Sunnyvale, CA 888-236-4144
World Flavors Inc
   Warminster, PA 215-672-4400

Juice
Citrosuco North America Inc
   Lake Wales, FL 800-356-4592
Delano Growers Grape Products
   Delano, CA 661-725-3255
Merci Spring Water
   Maryland Heights, MO 314-872-9323
Welch's Global Ingredients Group
   Concord, MA 978-371-3692

Sauce
Eatem Foods Co
   Vineland, NJ 800-683-2836

Illes Seasonings & Flavors
   Carrollton, TX 800-683-4553
JMH International
   Park City, UT 888-741-4564
Produits Ronald
   St. Damase, QC 800-465-0118
Summit Hill Flavors
   Somerset, NJ 732-805-0335
UFL Foods
   Mississauga, ON 905-670-7776

Seafood
Blount Fine Foods
   Fall River, MA 774-888-1300
Swiss Food Products
   Chicago, IL 312-829-0100

Soup
Bernard Food Industries Inc
   Evanston, IL 800-323-3663
Blount Fine Foods
   Fall River, MA 774-888-1300
Bluechip Group
   Salt Lake City, UT 800-878-0099
Chef Hans' Gourmet Foods
   Monroe, LA 800-890-4267
Con Yeager Spice Co
   Zelienople, PA 800-222-2460
Custom Culinary Inc.
   Schaumberg, IL 800-621-8827
Dean Distributors, Inc.
   Burlingame, CA 800-792-0816
Dismat Corporation
   Toledo, OH 419-531-8963
Dorothy Dawson Food Products
   Jackson, MI 517-788-9830
Erba Food Products
   Brooklyn, NY 718-272-7700
Five Star Food Base Company
   St Paul, MN 800-505-7827
Flavor House, Inc.
   Adelanto, CA 760-246-9131
Fuji Foods Corp
   Browns Summit, NC 336-375-3111
Gel Spice Co LLC
   Bayonne, NJ 800-922-0230
Griffith Foods Inc.
   Alsip, IL 708-371-0900
Hormel Foods Corp.
   Austin, MN 507-437-5611
Integrative Flavors
   Michigan City, IN 800-837-7687
JMH International
   Park City, UT 888-741-4564
Kent Precision Foods Group Inc
   Muscatine, IA 800-442-5242
Lake City Foods
   Mississauga, ON 905-625-8244
Lasco Foods Inc
   St Louis, MO 314-832-1906
LonoLife
   Oceanside, CA 855-843-8566
Magic Seasoning Blends
   New Orleans, LA 800-457-2857
Meat-O-Mat Corp
   Brooklyn, NY 718-965-7250
Mermaid Spice Corporation
   Fort Myers, FL 239-693-1986
Olympia Oyster Co
   Shelton, WA 877-427-3193
Oskri Corporation
   Lake Mills, WI 920-648-8300
Pacific Foods
   Kent, WA 800-347-9444
Produits Alimentaire
   Laval, QC 800-361-9326
Produits Ronald
   St. Damase, QC 800-465-0118
R C Fine Foods Inc
   Hillsborough, NJ 800-526-3953
R L Schreiber Inc
   Ft Lauderdale, FL 800-624-8777
Senba USA
   Hayward, CA 888-922-5852
Serv-Agen Corporation
   Cherry Hill, NJ 856-663-6966
Spice Hunter Inc
   Richmond, VA 800-444-3061
St. Ours & Company
   East Weymouth, MA 781-331-8520

Product Categories / Ingredients, Flavors & Additives: Benzoate of Soda

Summit Hill Flavors
  Somerset, NJ 732-805-0335
Superior Quality Foods
  Ontario, CA 800-300-4210
Sweet Sue Kitchens
  Athens, AL 256-216-0500
Swiss Food Products
  Chicago, IL 312-829-0100
Tone Products Inc
  Melrose Park, IL 800-536-8663
Tova Industries LLC
  Louisville, KY 888-532-8682
UBF Food Solutions
  Lisle, IL 630-955-5394
UFL Foods
  Mississauga, ON 905-670-7776
Unilever US
  Englewood Cliffs, NJ 800-298-5018
Vogue Cuisine Foods
  Sunnyvale, CA 888-236-4144
White Coffee Corporation
  Long Island City, NY 800-221-0140
World Flavors Inc
  Warminster, PA 215-672-4400
Young Winfield
  Hamilton, ON 905-893-2536

Seafood
Blount Fine Foods
  Fall River, MA 774-888-1300

Vegetable
California Custom Fruits
  Baldwin Park, CA 877-558-0056
Wild Aseptics, LLC
  Erlanger, KY 877-787-7221

Yogurt
Gum Technology Corporation
  Tucson, AZ 800-369-4867
Johanna Foods Inc.
  Flemington, NJ 800-727-6700
Maple Island
  Saint Paul, MN 800-369-1022
Plaidberry Company
  Vista, CA 760-727-5403

Benzoate of Soda
Xena International
  Polo, IL 815-946-2626

Binders
Cereal
Sentry Seasonings
  Elmhurst, IL 630-530-5370

Sausage
Roland Machinery
  Springfield, IL 800-325-1183
Sentry Seasonings
  Elmhurst, IL 630-530-5370
World Flavors Inc
  Warminster, PA 215-672-4400

for Meat Products
Sentry Seasonings
  Elmhurst, IL 630-530-5370

Bioflavinoids
Asiamerica Ingredients
  Westwood, NJ 201-497-5531
H. Interdonati
  Cold Spring Harbour, NY 800-367-6617
PLT Health Solutions Inc
  Morristown, NJ 973-984-0900
QBI
  South Plainfield, NJ 908-668-0088
Test Laboratories Inc
  Reseda, CA 818-881-4251

Biopolymers
CP Kelco
  Atlanta, GA 800-535-2687

Bits
Baking
Erba Food Products
  Brooklyn, NY 718-272-7700

Ham
Imitation
Gel Spice Co LLC
  Bayonne, NJ 800-922-0230

Blends
Cheese
Classic Tea
  Libertyville, IL 630-680-9934
Leprino Foods Co.
  Denver, CO 800-537-7466
Sentry Seasonings
  Elmhurst, IL 630-530-5370

Custom
Maple Island
  Saint Paul, MN 800-369-1022
Old Dominion Spice Company
  Ashland, VA 804-550-2780
Sentry Seasonings
  Elmhurst, IL 630-530-5370
World Flavors Inc
  Warminster, PA 215-672-4400

Enrichment
Sentry Seasonings
  Elmhurst, IL 630-530-5370

Herbs
All Purpose
Sentry Seasonings
  Elmhurst, IL 630-530-5370
Shaanxi Jiahe Phytochem Co., Ltd.
  Parsippany, NJ 973-439-6869
SupHerb Farms
  Turlock, CA 800-787-4372

Herbs & Spices
Asiamerica Ingredients
  Westwood, NJ 201-497-5531
Cajohn's Fiery Foods Co
  Westerville, OH. 888-703-3473
Colorado Spice Co
  Boulder, CO 800-677-7423
Georgia Spice Company
  Atlanta, GA 800-453-9997
Jodie's Kitchen
  Pinellas Park, FL. 800-728-3704
La Flor Spices
  Hauppaugue, NY 631-885-9601
Marion-Kay Spice Co
  Brownstown, IN 800-627-7423
Marnap Industries
  Buffalo, NY. 716-897-1220
Pendery's
  Dallas, TX. 800-533-1870
Sentry Seasonings
  Elmhurst, IL 630-530-5370
St John's Botanicals
  Bowie, MD 301-262-5302
SupHerb Farms
  Turlock, CA 800-787-4372
Wisconsin Spice Inc
  Berlin, WI 920-361-3555

Pepper
Sentry Seasonings
  Elmhurst, IL 630-530-5370

Caffeine
Asiamerica Ingredients
  Westwood, NJ 201-497-5531
Jungbunzlauer Inc
  Newton, MA 617-969-0900
Natra US
  Chula Vista, CA 800-262-6216

Casein & Caseinates
Agri-Dairy Products
  Purchase, NY 914-697-9580
AME Nutrition
  Dublin, OH 614-766-3638
American Pasien Co
  Burlington, NJ 609-387-3130
Blossom Farm Products
  Ridgewood, NJ 800-729-1818
Crest Foods Inc
  Ashton, IL. 877-273-7893
Erie Foods Intl Inc
  Erie, IL 309-659-2233
Kantner Group
  Wapakoneta, OH 877-738-3448

Casein
Austrade
  Palm Beach Gdns, FL 561-209-2447
Century Foods Intl LLC
  Sparta, WI 800-269-1901
Clofine Dairy Products Inc
  Linwood, NJ 609-653-1000
International Casein Corporation
  Great Neck, NY 516-466-4363
Oxford Frozen Foods
  Oxford, NS 902-447-2100
Pacific Cheese Co
  Hayward, CA 510-784-8800
Prestige Proteins
  Boca Raton, FL. 561-997-8770
Prestige Technology
  Boca Raton, FL. 888-697-4141
Silver Creek Specialty Meats
  Oshkosh, WI 800-729-2849

Cellulose Gel
Aromi d'Italia
  Baltimore, MD 877-435-2869
Asiamerica Ingredients
  Westwood, NJ 201-497-5531
J Rettenmaier USA LP
  Schoolcraft, MI 877-895-4099
PLT Health Solutions Inc
  Morristown, NJ 973-984-0900

Chemicals
Natural
Asiamerica Ingredients
  Westwood, NJ 201-497-5531
BASF Corp.
  Florham Park, NJ 800-526-1072
Chempacific Corp
  Baltimore, MD 410-633-5771
Crompton Corporation
  Greenwich, CT 800-295-2392
Flavorchem Corp
  Downers Grove, IL 800-435-2867
Graham Chemical Corporation
  Barrington, IL 847-304-4400
Symrise Inc.
  Teterboro, NJ. 201-288-3200
Van Waters & Roger
  Summit, IL 708-728-6830
Vanco Trading Inc
  Darien, CT. 203-656-2800

Chlorophyll
Asiamerica Ingredients
  Westwood, NJ 201-497-5531
Christopher's Herb Shop
  Springville, UT 888-372-4372
De Souza's
  Banning, CA 800-373-5171
H. Interdonati
  Cold Spring Harbour, NY. 800-367-6617
Verday
  New York, NY
World Organics Corporation
  Huntington Beach, CA 714-893-0017

Chocolate Products
Byrnes & Kiefer Company
  Callery, PA 724-538-5200
Forbes Chocolate BP
  Broadview Hts, OH. 440-838-4400
Golden 100
  Deland, FL 386-734-0113

Product Categories / Ingredients, Flavors & Additives: Coagulants

Log House Foods
  Plymouth, MN. 763-546-8395

Coagulants

Dairy

Forbes Chocolate BP
  Broadview Hts, OH. 440-838-4400

Coatings

Compound

BASF Corp.
  Florham Park, NJ 800-526-1072

Edible

Golden 100
  Deland, FL 386-734-0113
Mantrose-Haeuser Co Inc
  Westport, CT. 800-344-4229

Cocoa Butter

Aak USA Inc
  Newark, NJ. 973-344-1300
Barry Callebaut USA
  Chicago, IL 866-443-0460
Natra US
  Chula Vista, CA 800-262-6216

Colors

Americolor Corp
  Placentia, CA 800-556-0233
Color Garden
  Anaheim, CA 714-572-0444
ColorKitchen
  Bend, OR. 510-227-6174
ColorMaker, Inc.
  Anaheim, CA 714-572-0444
D D Williamson & Co Inc
  Louisville, KY 502-895-2438
DDW: The Color House
  Louisville, KY 502-895-2438
Emerald Performance Materials
  Cuyahoga Falls, OH 330-916-6700
Erba Food Products
  Brooklyn, NY 718-272-7700
Flavorchem Corp
  Downers Grove, IL 800-435-2867
GNT USA
  Tarrytown, NY 914-524-0600
Golden 100
  Deland, FL 386-734-0113
IFC Solutions
  Linden, NJ. 800-875-9393
International Foodcraft Corp
  Linden, NJ. 800-875-9393
Lubrizol Corp
  Wickliffe, OH 440-943-4200
Newport Ingredients
  Los Angeles, CA. 323-284-5959
Particle Dynamics
  Saint Louis, MO 800-452-4682
Prova
  Danvers, MA. 877-776-8287
Roha USA LTD
  St Louis, MO. 888-533-7642
San Joaquin Vly Concentrates
  Fresno, CA 800-557-0220
Sensient Technologies Corp
  Milwaukee, WI. 414-271-6755
Shank's Extracts Inc
  Lancaster, PA 800-346-3135
Weber Flavors
  Wheeling, IL. 800-558-9078

Annatto

Schiff Food Products Co Inc
  Totowa, NJ 973-237-1990
SJH Enterprises
  Middleton, WI. 888-745-3845

Burnt Sugar

D D Williamson & Co Inc
  Louisville, KY 502-895-2438
Four Percent Company
  Highland Park, MI 313-345-5880
Produits Alimentaire
  St Lambert De Lauzon, QC 800-463-1787

RFi Ingredients
  Blauvelt, NY 800-962-7663
Seydel Co
  Pendergrass, GA 706-693-2266

Caramel

Carmi Flavor & Fragrance Company
  Commerce, CA 800-421-9647
Gel Spice Co LLC
  Bayonne, NJ 800-922-0230

Butter & Cheese

Agri-Dairy Products
  Purchase, NY 914-697-9580
Carmi Flavor & Fragrance Company
  Commerce, CA 800-421-9647
Prime Ingredients Inc
  Saddle Brook, NJ 888-791-6655
SJH Enterprises
  Middleton, WI. 888-745-3845

Caramel

D D Williamson & Co Inc
  Louisville, KY 502-895-2438
Sethness Caramel Color
  Skokie, IL 847-329-2080

Cider & Vinegar

Asiamerica Ingredients
  Westwood, NJ. 201-497-5531
Prime Ingredients Inc
  Saddle Brook, NJ 888-791-6655

Dyes

Certified

Castella Imports Inc
  Brentwood, NY 631-231-5500

Grape Skin Extract Color

Asiamerica Ingredients
  Westwood, NJ. 201-497-5531

Natural

Asiamerica Ingredients
  Westwood, NJ. 201-497-5531
D D Williamson & Co Inc
  Louisville, KY 502-895-2438
LaMonde Wild Flavors
  Mississauga, ON 800-263-5286
PLT Health Solutions Inc
  Morristown, NJ. 973-984-0900

Annatto

SJH Enterprises
  Middleton, WI. 888-745-3845

Anthocyanins Grape Skin

Asiamerica Ingredients
  Westwood, NJ. 201-497-5531
RFi Ingredients
  Blauvelt, NY 800-962-7663

Betaine Beet

RFi Ingredients
  Blauvelt, NY 800-962-7663

Carmine

Asiamerica Ingredients
  Westwood, NJ. 201-497-5531
RFi Ingredients
  Blauvelt, NY 800-962-7663

Carotenoids

Asiamerica Ingredients
  Westwood, NJ. 201-497-5531
RFi Ingredients
  Blauvelt, NY 800-962-7663

Others

Asiamerica Ingredients
  Westwood, NJ. 201-497-5531

Turmeric

Asiamerica Ingredients
  Westwood, NJ. 201-497-5531

RFi Ingredients
  Blauvelt, NY 800-962-7663

Compounds

Cooking

Coast Packing Co
  Vernon, CA. 323-277-7700
Prime Ingredients Inc
  Saddle Brook, NJ 888-791-6655

Tenderizing

Chicago Pastry
  Bloomingdale, IL 630-529-6391
Custom Culinary Inc.
  Schaumberg, IL. 800-621-8827
Tova Industries LLC
  Louisville, KY 888-532-8682
World Flavors Inc
  Warminster, PA 215-672-4400

Concentrates

Fruit

3V Company
  Brooklyn, NY 718-858-7333
Apple & Eve LLC
  Port Washington, NY 800-969-8018
Beta Pure Foods
  Santa Cruz, CA. 831-685-6565
Citrosuco North America Inc
  Lake Wales, FL 800-356-4592
Coloma Frozen Foods Inc
  Coloma, MI 800-642-2723
Greenwood Associates
  Niles, IL 847-579-5500
KERR Concentrates Inc
  Salem, OR. 800-910-5377
Minute Maid Company
  Atlanta, GA. 800-520-2653
Monin Inc.
  Clearwater, FL 855-352-8671
Paragon Fruits
  Maple Grove, MN 763-559-0436
Stiebs
  Madera, CA. 559-661-0031
Svzusa Inc
  Othello, WA 509-488-6563

Fruit Puree

Greenwood Associates
  Niles, IL 847-579-5500
Milne Fruit Products Inc
  Prosser, WA 509-786-2611
RFi Ingredients
  Blauvelt, NY 800-962-7663

Vegetable

Beta Pure Foods
  Santa Cruz, CA. 831-685-6565
Greenwood Associates
  Niles, IL 847-579-5500

Whey Protein Concentrates & Isolates

Calpro Ingredients
  Corona, CA. 909-493-4890
Hilmar Ingredients
  Hilmar, CA 888-300-4465
Ingredia Inc
  Wapakoneta, OH 419-738-4060
Kantner Group
  Wapakoneta, OH 877-738-3448
Main Street Ingredients
  La Crosse, WI. 800-359-2345
Milky Whey Inc
  Missoula, MT 800-379-6455

Confectionery

Bakers' & Confectioners' Supplies

Abel & Schafer Inc
  Ronkonkoma, NY. 800-443-1260
Al-Rite Fruits & Syrups Co
  Miami, FL 305-652-2540
American Almond Products Co
  Brooklyn, NY 800-825-6663
American Key Food Products Inc
  Closter, NJ. 877-263-7539

Product Categories / Ingredients, Flavors & Additives: Cultures & Yeasts

AnaCon Foods Company
  Atchison, KS ... 800-328-0291
Ann's House of Nuts, Inc.
  Columbia, MD ... 410-309-6887
Arcor USA
  Coral Gables, FL ... 800-572-7267
Astor Chocolate Corp
  Lakewood, NJ ... 732-901-1001
Baker Boy Bake Shop Inc
  Dickinson, ND ... 800-437-2008
Bama Foods LTD
  Tulsa, OK ... 800-756-2262
Bartlett Milling Co.
  Statesville, NC ... 800-438-6016
Best Maid Cookie Co
  River Falls, WI ... 888-444-0322
Bette's Oceanview Diner
  Berkeley, CA ... 510-644-3230
Blend Pak Inc
  Bloomfield, KY ... 502-252-8000
Blommer Chocolate Co
  Chicago, IL ... 800-621-1606
Blue Pacific Flavors & Fragrances
  City of Industry, CA ... 626-934-0099
Blue Planet Foods
  Collegedale, TN ... 877-396-3145
Bob's Red Mill Natural Foods
  Milwaukie, OR ... 800-349-2173
Brass Ladle Products
  Concordville, PA ... 800-955-2353
Brown & Haley
  Fife, WA ... 800-426-8400
Byrd Mill Co
  Ashland, VA ... 888-897-3336
Byrnes & Kiefer Company
  Callery, PA ... 724-538-5200
California Independent Almond Growers
  Merced, CA ... 209-667-4855
Cangel
  Toronto, ON ... 800-267-4795
Carol Lee Donuts
  Salina, KS ... 785-827-2402
Century Foods Intl LLC
  Sparta, WI ... 800-269-1901
Cereal Food Processors Inc
  Mcpherson, KS ... 800-835-2067
Charles H Baldwin & Sons
  West Stockbridge, MA ... 413-232-7785
Chase Brothers Dairy
  Oxnard, CA ... 800-438-6455
CHS Inc
  Inver Grove Hts., MN ... 800-328-6539
Commodities Marketing Inc
  Clarksburg, NJ ... 732-516-0700
Cream Of The West
  Harlowton, MT ... 800-477-2383
Dakota Specialty Milling, Inc.
  Fargo, ND ... 844-633-2746
De Iorio's Foods Inc
  Utica, NY ... 800-649-7612
Dessert Innovations Inc
  Atlanta, GA ... 800-359-7351
Devansoy Farms
  Carroll, IA ... 800-747-8605
Dorothy Dawson Food Products
  Jackson, MI ... 517-788-9830
Eden Foods Inc
  Clinton, MI ... 888-424-3336
Eden Processing
  Poplar Grove, IL ... 815-765-2000
EFCO Products Inc
  Poughkeepsie, NY ... 800-284-3326
Fizzle Flat Farm, L.L.C.
  Yale, IL ... 618-793-2060
Food Concentrate Corporation
  Oklahoma City, OK ... 405-840-5633
Frankford Candy & Chocolate Co
  Philadelphia, PA ... 800-523-9090
Franklin Foods
  Enosburg Falls, VT ... 800-933-6114
Galloway Co
  Neenah, WI ... 800-722-8903
Ghirardelli Chocolate Co
  San Leandro, CA ... 800-877-9338
Golden Fluff Popcorn Co
  Lakewood, NJ ... 732-367-5448
Gorant Chocolatier
  Youngstown, OH ... 330-726-8821
Greenfield Mills
  North Howe, IN ... 260-367-2394
Guittard Chocolate Co
  Burlingame, CA ... 800-468-2462

Gurley's Foods
  Willmar, MN ... 800-426-7845
Gust John Foods & Products
  Batavia, IL ... 800-756-5886
H B Taylor Co
  Chicago, IL ... 773-254-4805
Hamersmith, Inc.
  Miami, FL ... 305-685-7451
Harlan Bakeries
  Avon, IN ... 800-435-2738
Healthy Food Ingredients
  Fargo, ND ... 844-275-3443
Heartland Food Products
  Westwood, KS ... 866-571-0222
Heidi's Gourmet Desserts
  Tucker, GA ... 800-241-4166
Holton Food Products
  La Grange, IL ... 708-352-5599
Homestead Mills
  Cook, MN ... 800-652-5233
Honeyville Grain Inc
  Brigham City, UT ... 435-494-4200
I Rice & Co Inc
  Philadelphia, PA ... 800-232-6022
J M Swank Co
  North Liberty, IA ... 800-593-6375
J.R. Short Canadian Mills
  Toronto, ON ... 416-421-3463
Kalsec
  Kalamazoo, MI ... 800-323-9320
Kargher Corp
  Hatfield, PA ... 800-355-1247
Kencraft, Inc.
  Alpine, UT ... 800-377-4368
Kimmie Candy Company
  Reno, NV ... 888-532-1325
King Milling Co Inc
  Lowell, MI ... 616-897-9264
Knappen Milling Co
  Augusta, MI ... 800-562-7736
Knouse Foods Co-Op Inc.
  Peach Glen, PA ... 717-677-8181
L & S Packing Co
  Farmingdale, NY ... 800-286-6487
Lacey Milling Company
  Hanford, CA ... 559-584-6634
Lake States Yeast
  Rhinelander, WI ... 715-369-4949
Lawrence Foods Inc
  Elk Grove Village, IL ... 847-437-2400
Leon's Bakery
  North Haven, CT ... 800-223-6844
Little Crow Foods
  Warsaw, IN ... 800-288-2769
Loghouse Foods
  Minneapolis, MN ... 763-546-8395
Louisiana Gourmet Enterprises
  Houma, LA ... 800-328-5586
Lucas Meyer
  Decatur, IL ... 800-769-3660
Lyoferm & Vivolac Cultures
  Indianapolis, IN ... 317-356-8460
Main Street Ingredients
  La Crosse, WI ... 800-359-2345
Malt Diastase Co
  Saddle Brook, NJ ... 800-526-0180
Marx Brothers Inc
  Birmingham, AL ... 800-633-6376
Merlino Italian Baking Company
  Kent, WA ... 800-800-9490
Mills Brothers Intl
  Seattle, WA ... 206-575-3000
Minn-Dak Yeast Co Inc
  Wahpeton, ND ... 701-642-3300
Moorhead & Company
  Rocklin, CA ... 800-322-6325
Morris J Golombeck Inc
  Brooklyn, NY ... 718-284-3505
Northwestern Foods
  Arden Hills, MN ... 800-236-4937
Orlinda Milling Company
  Orlinda, TN ... 615-654-3633
Pacific Westcoast Foods
  Beaverton, OR ... 800-874-9333
Palmer Candy Co
  Sioux City, IA ... 800-831-0828
Pasta Factory
  Melrose Park, IL ... 800-615-6951
Pelican Bay Ltd.
  Dunedin, FL ... 800-826-8982
Pied-Mont/Dora
  Anne Des Plaines, QC ... 800-363-8003

Plaidberry Company
  Vista, CA ... 760-727-5403
Quali Tech Inc
  Chaska, MN ... 800-328-5870
Quality Naturally Foods
  City Of Industry, CA ... 888-498-6986
R&J Farms
  West Salem, OH ... 419-846-3179
Reinhart Foods
  Toronto, ON ... 416-645-4910
Rene Rey Chocolates Ltd
  North Vancouver, BC ... 888-985-0949
Rhodes International Inc
  Salt Lake City, UT ... 800-876-7333
Richmond Baking Co
  Richmond, IN ... 765-962-8535
Roland Machinery
  Springfield, IL ... 800-325-1183
Rv Industries
  Buford, GA ... 770-729-8983
Schlotterbeck & Foss Company
  Portland, ME ... 800-777-4666
Scott's Auburn Mills
  Russellville, KY ... 270-726-2080
Serv-Agen Corporation
  Cherry Hill, NJ ... 856-663-6966
Service Packing Company
  Vancouver, BC ... 604-681-0264
Shawnee Milling Co
  Shawnee, OK ... 405-273-7000
Signature Brands LLC
  Ocala, FL ... 800-456-9573
Skjodt-Barrett Foods
  Brampton, ON ... 877-600-1200
SOUPerior Bean & Spice Company
  Vancouver, WA ... 800-878-7687
Southeastern Mills Inc
  Rome, GA ... 800-334-4468
Star of the West Milling Co.
  Frankenmuth, MI ... 989-652-9971
Strossner's Bakery & Cafe
  Greenville, SC ... 864-233-2990
Sucesores de Pedro Cortes
  Hato Rey, PR ... 787-754-7040
Swatt Baking Co
  Olean, NY ... 800-370-6656
Tara Foods
  Atlanta, GA ... 404-559-0605
Taste Maker Foods
  Memphis, TN ... 800-467-1407
The Lollipop Tree, Inc
  Auburn, NY ... 800-842-6691
TNT Crust
  Green Bay, WI ... 920-431-7240
Tova Industries LLC
  Louisville, KY ... 888-532-8682
Uhlmann Co
  Kansas City, MO ... 866-866-8627
Valley View Blueberries
  Vancouver, WA ... 360-892-2839
VIP Foods
  Flushing, NY ... 718-821-5330
Watson Inc
  West Haven, CT ... 800-388-3481
Weaver Nut Co. Inc.
  Ephrata, PA ... 800-473-2688
West Pac
  Idaho Falls, ID ... 800-973-7407
Whitaker & Assoc Architects
  Atlanta, GA ... 404-266-1265
White-Stokes Company
  Chicago, IL ... 800-978-6537
Willmark Sales Company
  Brooklyn, NY ... 718-388-7141
Yohay Baking Co
  Lindenhurst, NY ... 631-225-0300
Young Winfield
  Hamilton, ON ... 905-893-2536

Cultures & Yeasts

Bacteria

Sour Dough

Cultures for Health
  Morrisville, NC

Yogurt

Cultures for Health
  Morrisville, NC

Product Categories / Ingredients, Flavors & Additives: Curing Preparations

Bacterial Cultures & Starter Media

Cultures for Health
   Morrisville, NC
Kantner Group
   Wapakoneta, OH 877-738-3448

Cultures

Alfer Laboratories
   Chatsworth, CA 818-709-0737
Alternative Health & Herbs
   Albany, OR 800-345-4152
Berkshire Dairy
   Wyomissing, PA 877-696-6455
Crystal Creamery
   Modesto, CA 866-225-4821
Cultures for Health
   Morrisville, NC
Dairy Connection Inc
   Madison, WI 608-242-9030
GEM Cultures
   Lakewood, WA 253-588-2922
IMAC
   Oklahoma City, OK 888-878-7827
Ingredient Innovations
   Kansas City, MO 816-587-1426
Lallemand
   Montreal, QC 514-522-2133
Lallemand American Yeast
   Addison, IL 630-932-1290
Lyoferm & Vivolac Cultures
   Indianapolis, IN 317-356-8460
Old Home Foods Inc
   New Brighton, MN 651-312-8900
Quality Ingredients
   Burnsville, MN 952-898-4002
Sunshine Dairy Foods Inc
   Portland, OR 503-234-7526
Test Laboratories Inc
   Reseda, CA 818-881-4251
Vivolac Cultures Corporation
   Indianapolis, IN 317-356-8460

Yeast

Bakon Yeast
   Scottsdale, AZ 480-595-9370
Bluechip Group
   Salt Lake City, UT 800-878-0099
California Blending Co
   El Monte, CA 626-448-1918
Cardi Foods
   Fuquay Varina, NC 919-557-3866
DSM
   Heerlen,
Fleischmann's Yeast
   Chesterfield, MO 800-777-4959
Hodgson Mill Inc
   Effingham, IL 800-347-0198
Kyowa Hakko
   New York, NY 800-596-9252
Lake States Yeast
   Rhinelander, WI 715-369-4949
Lallemand American Yeast
   Addison, IL 630-932-1290
Lesaffre Yeast Corporation
   Milwaukee, WI 800-770-2714
Luxor California Exports Corp.
   San Diego, CA 619-465-7777
Minn-Dak Yeast Co Inc
   Wahpeton, ND 701-642-3300
Natural Foods Inc
   Toledo, OH 419-537-1711
Organic Gourmet
   Sherman Oaks, CA 800-400-7772
Pascobel Inc
   Longueuil, QC 450-677-2443
Red Star Yeast
   Milwaukee, WI 800-445-4746
Vinquiry Wine Analysis
   Windsor, CA 707-838-6312
Wausau Paper Corp.
   Mosinee, WI 866-722-8675

Autolysates

Lake States Yeast
   Rhinelander, WI 715-369-4949

Bakers'

Lallemand/American Yeast
   Long Island City, NY 773-267-2223

Minn-Dak Yeast Co Inc
   Wahpeton, ND 701-642-3300

Brewers'

Energen Products Inc
   Norwalk, CA 800-423-8837
NPC Dehydrators
   Payette, ID 208-642-4471
Watson Inc
   West Haven, CT 800-388-3481

Extracts

Organic Gourmet
   Sherman Oaks, CA 800-400-7772

Fresh

Lallemand American Yeast
   Addison, IL 630-932-1290

Primary Dried

Lallemand American Yeast
   Addison, IL 630-932-1290

Torula Dried

Lake States Yeast
   Rhinelander, WI 715-369-4949

Whey

Hilmar Ingredients
   Hilmar, CA 888-300-4465

Wine

Lallemand/American Yeast
   Petaluma, CA 800-423-6625

Yogurt

Lyo-San
   Lachute, QC 800-363-3697

Curing Preparations

Meat

First Spice Mixing Co
   Long Island City, NY 800-221-1105

Decorative Items

Petra International
   Mississauga, ON 800-261-7226
Pfeil & Holding Inc
   Woodside, NY 800-247-7955
Scala-Wisell International Inc.
   Floral Park, NY 516-437-8600
Sugar Flowers Plus
   Glendale, CA 800-972-2935

Digestive Aids

Arise & Shine Herbal Products
   Medford, OR 800-688-2444
Bio-K + International Inc.
   Laval, QC 800-593-2465
Bionutritional Research Group
   Irvine, CA 714-427-6990
Deerland Probiotics & Enzymes
   Kennesaw, GA 800-697-8179
Deerland Probiotics & Enzymes
   Forsyth, MO 800-825-8545
Enzymatic Therapy Inc
   Green Bay, WI 800-783-2286
Enzyme Formulations Inc
   Madison, WI 800-614-4400
Russo Farms
   Vineland, NJ 856-692-5942

Emulsifiers

Aromatech USA
   Orlando, FL 407-277-5727
Asiamerica Ingredients
   Westwood, NJ 201-497-5531
Avatar Corp
   University Park, IL 800-255-3181
Bunge Canada
   Oakville, ON 905-825-7900
Enterprise Foods
   Atlanta, GA 404-351-2251
Kerry, Inc
   Beloit, WI 608-363-1200

Lambent Technologies
   Skokie, IL 800-432-7187
Mitsubishi Intl. Corp.
   New York, NY 800-442-6266
Montello Inc
   Tulsa, OK 800-331-4628
Mother Murphy's
   Greensboro, NC 800-849-1277
Newport Ingredients
   Los Angeles, CA 323-284-5959
PLT Health Solutions Inc
   Morristown, NJ 973-984-0900
Profood International
   Naperville, IL 888-288-0081
Ribus Inc.
   St. Louis, MO 314-727-4287
Taiyo International Inc.
   Minneapolis, MN 763-398-3003
Tate & Lyle PLC
   Hoffman Estates, IL 847-396-7500
Wenda America Inc
   Naperville, IL 844-999-3632

Lecithin

Acatris USA
   Edina, MN 952-920-7700
AG Processing Inc
   Omaha, NE 800-247-1345
American Lecithin Company
   Oxford, CT 800-364-4416
Asiamerica Ingredients
   Westwood, NJ 201-497-5531
Avatar Corp
   University Park, IL 800-255-3181
Blue Chip Baker
   Salt Lake City, UT 800-878-0099
Bluechip Group
   Salt Lake City, UT 800-878-0099
CanAmera Foods
   Edmonton, AL 780-447-6960
DuPont Nutrition & Biosciences
   New Century, KS 913-764-8100
Homefree LLC
   Windham, NH 800-552-7172
International Foodcraft Corp
   Linden, NJ 800-875-9393
King Arthur Flour
   Norwich, VT 800-827-6836
Lucas Meyer
   Decatur, IL 800-769-3660
Mid Atlantic Vegetable Shortening Company
   Kearny, NJ 800-966-1645
Natural Foods Inc
   Toledo, OH 419-537-1711
Westin Foods
   Omaha, NE 800-228-6098

Enhancers

Apple Flavor & Fragrance USA
   Edison, NJ 732-393-0600
Bluechip Group
   Salt Lake City, UT 800-878-0099
Cinnabar Specialty Foods Inc
   Prescott, AZ 866-293-6433
First Spice Mixing Co
   Long Island City, NY 800-221-1105
King Arthur Flour
   Norwich, VT 800-827-6836
Lora Brody Products Inc
   Waltham, MA 781-899-3910
Newport Ingredients
   Los Angeles, CA 323-284-5959
Seattle Seasonings
   Port Orchard, WA 360-871-1511

Enzymes

Ajinomoto Heartland Inc
   Chicago, IL 773-380-7000
Amano Enzyme USA Company, Ltd
   Elgin, IL 800-446-7652
American Laboratories
   Omaha, NE 402-339-2494
American Yeast
   Memphis, TN 866-920-9885
Asiamerica Ingredients
   Westwood, NJ 201-497-5531
Bio-Nutritional Products
   Northvale, NJ 201-784-8200
Catherych
   Warren, NJ 732-566-6625

Product Categories / Ingredients, Flavors & Additives: Extenders

Enzyme Development Corporation
  New York, NY 212-736-1580
Enzyme Innovation
  Chino, CA 909-203-4620
George A Jeffreys & Company
  Salem, VA 540-389-8220
Malabar Formulas
  Nuevo, CA 909-866-3678
Mitsubishi Intl. Corp.
  New York, NY 800-442-6266
Novozymes North America Inc
  Franklinton, NC 800-879-6686
Profood International
  Naperville, IL 888-288-0081
SKW Nature Products
  Dubuque, IA 563-588-6244
Test Laboratories Inc
  Reseda, CA 818-881-4251
Universal Formulas
  Kalamazoo, MI 800-342-6960

Extenders

Arboris LLC
  Savannah, GA 912-238-7537
MAFCO Worldwide
  Camden, NJ 856-986-4050
Thymly Products Inc
  Colora, MD 877-710-2340

Chicken

Valley Grain Products
  Fresno, CA 559-675-3400

Coffee

I Rice & Co Inc
  Philadelphia, PA 800-232-6022

Meat

Flavor House, Inc.
  Adelanto, CA 760-246-9131
Gum Technology Corporation
  Tucson, AZ 800-369-4867
Tova Industries LLC
  Louisville, KY 888-532-8682
World Flavors Inc
  Warminster, PA 215-672-4400

Extracts

Active Organics
  Lewisville, TX 800-541-1478
Advanced Food Systems
  Somerset, NJ 800-787-3067
Al-Rite Fruits & Syrups Co
  Miami, FL 305-652-2540
AM Todd Co
  Kalamazoo, MI 269-343-2603
American Instants Inc
  Flanders, NJ 973-584-8811
American Laboratories
  Omaha, NE 402-339-2494
American Mercantile Corp
  Memphis, TN 901-454-1900
Apotheca Inc
  Woodbine, IA 800-736-3130
Asiamerica Ingredients
  Westwood, NJ 201-497-5531
Bakto Flavors
  North Brunswick, NJ 732-354-4492
Bartek Ingredients, Inc.
  Stoney Creek, ON 800-263-4165
Bear Stewart Corp
  Chicago, IL 800-697-2327
Berghausen E Cheml Co
  Cincinnati, OH 800-648-5887
Beta Pure Foods
  Santa Cruz, CA 831-685-6565
Bickford Flavors
  Euclid, OH 800-283-8322
Blessed Herbs
  Oakham, MA 800-489-4372
Blue California Co
  Rancho Sta Marg, CA 949-459-2729
Blue Mountain Enterprise Inc
  Kinston, NC 800-522-1544
Briess Malt & Ingredients Co.
  Chilton, WI 800-657-0806
Brucia Plant Extracts
  Shingle Springs, CA 530-676-2774
Byrnes & Kiefer Company
  Callery, PA 724-538-5200

Cafe Du Monde Coffee Stand
  New Orleans, LA 800-772-2927
Cajun Brands
  New Iberia, LA 504-408-2252
California Custom Foods
  Fullerton, CA 714-870-0490
Capri Sun
  Granite City, IL
Cargill Inc
  Minneapolis, MN 800-227-4455
Castella Imports Inc
  Brentwood, NY 631-231-5500
Cellucon Inc
  Strathmore, CA 559-568-0190
Century Blends LLC
  Hunt Valley, MD 410-771-6606
Chas Boggini Co.
  Coventry, CT. 860-742-2652
Christopher's Herb Shop
  Springville, UT 888-372-4372
Classic Flavors & Fragrances
  New York, NY 212-777-0004
Clements Foods Co
  Oklahoma City, OK 800-654-8355
Concord Foods, LLC
  Brockton, MA 508-580-1700
Consolidated Mills Inc
  Houston, TX 713-896-4196
Crestmont Enterprises
  Camden, NJ 856-966-0700
Dean Distributors, Inc.
  Burlingame, CA 800-792-0816
Draco Natural Products Inc
  San Jose, CA 408-287-7871
Edgar A Weber & Co
  Wheeling, IL 800-558-9078
Erba Food Products
  Brooklyn, NY 718-272-7700
Ethical Naturals
  San Anselmo, CA 866-459-4454
Everfresh Food Corporation
  Minneapolis, MN 612-331-6393
Fenchem Inc
  Chino, CA 909-597-1113
Finlays
  Lincoln, RI 800-288-6272
Flavor House, Inc.
  Adelanto, CA 760-246-9131
Flavor Sciences Inc
  Lenoir, NC 800-535-2867
Flavorchem Corp
  Downers Grove, IL 800-435-2867
Florida Food Products Inc
  Eustis, FL 800-874-2331
Fona International
  Geneva, IL 630-578-8600
Foodscience Corp
  Essex Junction, VT 800-874-9444
Genarom International
  Cranbury, NJ 609-409-6200
Green Foods Corp.
  Oxnard, CA 800-777-4430
H B Taylor Co
  Chicago, IL 773-254-4805
Herbs Etc
  Santa Fe, NM 888-694-3727
High Quality Organics
  Reno, NV 775-971-8550
Horner International
  Raleigh, NC. 919-787-3112
Inter-American Products
  Cincinnati, OH 800-645-2233
J M Swank Co
  North Liberty, IA 800-593-6375
Jiaherb
  Pine Brook, NJ 888-542-4372
Kalsec
  Kalamazoo, MI 800-323-9320
Kefiplant
  Drummondville, QC 819-477-2345
Kerry Foodservice
  Mansfield, OH 800-533-2722
Kerry, Inc
  Beloit, WI 608-363-1200
Lochhead Mfg. Co.
  Fenton, MO. 800-776-2088
MAFCO Worldwide
  Camden, NJ 856-986-4050
Malt Diastase Co
  Garfield, NJ 800-772-0416
Metarom Corporation
  Newport, VT 888-882-5555

Mother Murphy's
  Greensboro, NC 800-849-1277
Muntons Ingredients
  Bellevue, WA 425-372-3082
Natra US
  Chula Vista, CA 800-262-6216
Naturex Inc
  South Hackensack, NJ 201-440-5000
Newtown Foods USA Inc
  Newtown, PA 215-579-2120
Nutricepts
  Burnsville, MN 800-949-9060
Oregon Flavor Rack
Parker Flavors Inc
  Baltimore, MD 800-336-9113
Particle Control
  Albertville, MN. 763-497-3075
Particle Dynamics
  Saint Louis, MO 800-452-4682
Perlarom Technology
  Columbia, MD 410-997-5114
Phyto-Technologies
  Woodbine, IA 877-809-3404
Phytotherapy Research Laboratory
  Lobelville, TN. 800-274-3727
PLT Health Solutions Inc
  Morristown, NJ 973-984-0900
PMC Specialties Group Inc
  Cincinnati, OH 800-543-2466
Prova
  Danvers, MA 877-776-8287
R C Fine Foods Inc
  Hillsborough, NJ 800-526-3953
RFi Ingredients
  Blauvelt, NY 800-962-7663
Royal Foods & Flavor
  Elk Grove Vlg, IL 847-595-9166
San-Ei Gen FFI
  New York, NY 212-315-7850
SAPNA Foods
  Atlanta, GA 404-589-0977
Senba USA
  Hayward, CA 888-922-5852
Shank's Extracts Inc
  Lancaster, PA 800-346-3135
Simpson Spring Co
  South Easton, MA. 508-238-4472
Singer Extract Laboratory
  Livonia, MI 313-345-5880
Sivetz Coffee
  Corvallis, OR 541-753-9713
SJH Enterprises
  Middleton, WI. 888-745-3845
Sno Shack Inc
  Rexburg, ID. 888-766-7425
Spicely
  Fremont, CA 510-440-1044
Star Kay White Inc
  Congers, NY 800-874-8518
Sterling Extract Co Inc
  Franklin Park, IL 847-451-9728
Stiebs
  Madera, CA. 559-661-0031
Target Flavors Inc
  Brookfield, CT 800-538-3350
Technology Flavors & Fragrances
  Amityville, NY 631-789-8228
Texas Coffee Co
  Beaumont, TX. 800-259-3400
Texas Spice Co
  Round Rock, TX 800-880-8007
Triple K Manufacturing Company, Inc.
  Shenandoah, IA. 712-246-4376
United Canadian Malt
  Peterborough, ON 800-461-6400
V & E Kohnstamm Inc
  Brooklyn, NY 800-847-4500
Virginia Dare Extract Co
  Brooklyn, NY 718-788-1776
Weber Flavors
  Wheeling, IL 800-558-9078
Young Winfield
  Hamilton, ON 905-893-2536

Beef

Blue Mountain Enterprise Inc
  Kinston, NC 800-522-1544
Flavor House, Inc.
  Adelanto, CA 760-246-9131
Gold Coast Ingredients
  Commerce, CA 800-352-8673

Product Categories / Ingredients, Flavors & Additives: Extracts

Prime Ingredients Inc
 Saddle Brook, NJ 888-791-6655
RFi Ingredients
 Blauvelt, NY 800-962-7663
Savoury Systems Inc
 Branchburg, NJ 888-534-6621
Superior Quality Foods
 Ontario, CA 800-300-4210
Tastepoint
 Philadelphia, PA 800-363-5286
Vital Proteins LLC
 Elk Grove Village, IL 224-544-9110

Beverages

Muntons Ingredients
 Bellevue, WA 425-372-3082

Botanical

Abkit Camocare Nature Works
 New York, NY 800-226-6227
Active Organics
 Lewisville, TX 800-541-1478
American Biosciences
 Blauvelt, NY 888-884-7770
Apex Marketing Group
 Las Vegas, NV 888-990-2739
Apotheca Inc
 Woodbine, IA 800-736-3130
Asiamerica Ingredients
 Westwood, NJ 201-497-5531
Avoca
 Merry Hill, NC 252-482-2133
Blue California Co
 Rancho Sta Marg, CA 949-459-2729
Botanical Products
 Springville, CA 559-539-3432
Brucia Plant Extracts
 Shingle Springs, CA 530-676-2774
Christopher's Herb Shop
 Springville, UT 888-372-4372
Danisco-Cultor
 Ardsley, NY 914-674-6300
Dolisos America
 Henderson, NV 800-365-4767
Eclectic Institute
 Sandy, OR 503-668-4120
Emerling International Foods
 Buffalo, NY 716-833-7381
Energique
 Woodbine, IA 800-869-8078
Excellentia Intl.
 Fairfield, NJ 737-749-9840
Frutarom Meer Corporation
 Hertzeliya Pituach,
GCI Nutrients
 Foster City, CA 866-580-6549
Graminex
 Saginaw, MI 877-472-6469
Health from the Sun
 Maynard, MA 800-447-2229
Herb Pharm
 Williams, OR 800-348-4372
Herbalist & Alchemist Inc
 Washington, NJ 908-689-9020
Horner International
 Raleigh, NC 919-787-3112
Nature's Apothecary
 Bloomingdale, IL 888-669-3663
Nature's Products Inc
 Sunrise, FL 800-752-7873
Naturex Inc
 South Hackensack, NJ 201-440-5000
Parker Flavors Inc
 Baltimore, MD 800-336-9113
Pharmachem Laboratories
 Kearny, NJ 800-526-0609
PLT Health Solutions Inc
 Morristown, NJ 973-984-0900
Plus Pharma
 Vista, CA 760-597-0200
RFi Ingredients
 Blauvelt, NY 800-962-7663
Sabinsa Corp
 East Windsor, NJ 732-777-1111
Synthite USA Inc.
 Oak Park, IL 708-446-1716
Terra Botanica Products
 Dahlonega, GA 770-718-9340
Terra Flavors & Fragrances
 New York, NY 212-244-1181
Test Laboratories Inc
 Reseda, CA 818-881-4251
Universal Preservachem Inc
 Somerset, NJ 732-568-1266
Verdure Sciences
 Noblesville, IN 888-656-4364
Whole Herb Co
 Sonoma, CA 707-935-1077

Chicken

Blue Mountain Enterprise Inc
 Kinston, NC 800-522-1544
Flavor House, Inc.
 Adelanto, CA 760-246-9131
Prime Ingredients Inc
 Saddle Brook, NJ 888-791-6655

Coffee

Amelia Bay
 Suwanee, GA 770-772-6360
American Instants Inc
 Flanders, NJ 973-584-8811
California Custom Fruits
 Baldwin Park, CA 877-558-0056
Coffee Enterprises
 Burlington, VT 800-375-3398
Finlays
 Lincoln, RI 800-288-6272
Kerry Foodservice
 Mansfield, OH 800-533-2722
Prime Ingredients Inc
 Saddle Brook, NJ 888-791-6655
S & D Coffee Inc
 Concord, NC 800-933-2210
Synergy Flavors Inc
 Wauconda, IL 847-487-1011
Synthite USA Inc.
 Oak Park, IL 708-446-1716
Teawolf LLC
 Pine Brook, NJ 973-575-4600
Virginia Dare Extract Co
 Brooklyn, NY 718-788-1776

Crab

ADM Wild Flavors & Specialty
 Erlanger, KY 859-342-3600
American Instants Inc
 Flanders, NJ 973-584-8811
Barlean's Fisheries
 Ferndale, WA 360-384-0325
Blue Mountain Enterprise Inc
 Kinston, NC 800-522-1544
Boyajian LLC
 Canton, MA 800-965-0665
Cajun Brands
 New Iberia, LA 504-408-2252
Delmonaco Winery & Vineyards
 Baxter, TN 931-858-1177
Embassy Flavours Ltd.
 Brampton, ON 800-334-3371
Empire Spice Mills
 Winnipeg, NB 204-786-1594
FBC Industries
 Schaumburg, IL 888-322-4637
Felbro Food Products
 Los Angeles, CA 323-936-5266
Flavor Sciences Inc
 Lenoir, NC 800-535-2867
Flavor Systems Intl.
 Cincinnati, OH 800-498-2783
Flavormatic Industries
 Wappingers Falls, NY 845-297-9100
Fleurchem Inc
 Middletown, NY 845-341-2100
Four Percent Company
 Highland Park, MI 313-345-5880
Glucona America
 Janesville, WI 608-752-0449
Gold Coast Ingredients
 Commerce, CA 800-352-8673
GSB & Assoc
 Kennesaw, GA 877-472-2776
Ingredient Innovations
 Kansas City, MO 816-587-1426
John I. Haas
 Washington, DC
Joseph Adams Corp
 Valley City, OH 330-225-9135
Lochhead Mfg. Co.
 Fenton, MO 800-776-2088
Magic Ice Products
 Cincinnati, OH 800-776-7923
Ottens Flavors
 Philadelphia, PA 800-523-0767
Prime Ingredients Inc
 Saddle Brook, NJ 888-791-6655
SKW Nature Products
 Langhorne, PA 215-702-1000
Stirling Foods
 Renton, WA 800-332-1714
Takasago International Corp
 Rockleigh, NJ 201-767-9001
Test Laboratories Inc
 Reseda, CA 818-881-4251
The Stephan Company
 Tampa, FL 954-971-0600
Torre Products Co Inc
 New York, NY 212-925-8989
Triple K Manufacturing Company, Inc.
 Shenandoah, IA 712-246-4376

Flavoring

Amoretti
 Oxnard, CA 800-266-7388
Dohler-Milne Aseptics LLC
 Prosser, WA 509-786-2240
I Rice & Co Inc
 Philadelphia, PA 800-232-6022
Paradigm Foodworks Inc
 Lake Oswego, OR 800-234-0250

Fruit

Agrana Fruit US Inc
 Cleveland, OH 800-477-3788
Byrnes & Kiefer Company
 Callery, PA 724-538-5200
Dohler-Milne Aseptics LLC
 Prosser, WA 509-786-2240
Horner International
 Raleigh, NC 919-787-3112
Parker Flavors Inc
 Baltimore, MD 800-336-9113
Synergy Flavors Inc
 Wauconda, IL 847-487-1011
Test Laboratories Inc
 Reseda, CA 818-881-4251

Root Beer

California Custom Fruits
 Baldwin Park, CA 877-558-0056
Four Percent Company
 Highland Park, MI 313-345-5880
Gold Coast Ingredients
 Commerce, CA 800-352-8673
Prime Ingredients Inc
 Saddle Brook, NJ 888-791-6655
Rio Syrup Co
 St Louis, MO 800-325-7666

Seafood

Ocean Cliff Corp
 New Bedford, MA 508-990-7900

Tea

California Custom Fruits
 Baldwin Park, CA 877-558-0056
Ethical Naturals
 San Anselmo, CA 866-459-4454
Jogue Inc
 Northville, MI 800-531-3888
Kerry Foodservice
 Mansfield, OH 800-533-2722
PLT Health Solutions Inc
 Morristown, NJ 973-984-0900
RFi Ingredients
 Blauvelt, NY 800-962-7663
S & D Coffee Inc
 Concord, NC 800-933-2210
Synergy Flavors Inc
 Wauconda, IL 847-487-1011
Synthite USA Inc.
 Oak Park, IL 708-446-1716
Teawolf LLC
 Pine Brook, NJ 973-575-4600
Virginia Dare Extract Co
 Brooklyn, NY 718-788-1776

Product Categories / Ingredients, Flavors & Additives: Fatty Acids

Vanilla

Astral Extracts
  Syosset, NY.....................516-496-2505
Bakto Flavors
  North Brunswick, NJ 732-354-4492
Bickford Flavors
  Euclid, OH 800-283-8322
California Custom Fruits
  Baldwin Park, CA 877-558-0056
Carmi Flavor & Fragrance Company
  Commerce, CA 800-421-9647
Castella Imports Inc
  Brentwood, NY 631-231-5500
Clements Foods Co
  Oklahoma City, OK 800-654-8355
Consolidated Mills Inc
  Houston, TX 713-896-4196
Elan Vanilla Co
  Newark, NJ 973-344-8014
Embassy Flavours Ltd.
  Brampton, ON. 800-334-3371
Emerling International Foods
  Buffalo, NY. 716-833-7381
Everfresh Food Corporation
  Minneapolis, MN 612-331-6393
Flavorchem Corp
  Downers Grove, IL 800-435-2867
Flavorganics
  Newark, NJ 866-972-6879
Four Percent Company
  Highland Park, MI 313-345-5880
Frontier Co-op
  Norway, IA 844-550-6200
Gel Spice Co LLC
  Bayonne, NJ 800-922-0230
Gold Coast Ingredients
  Commerce, CA 800-352-8673
Grapevine Trading Company
  Santa Rosa, CA 800-469-6478
H B Taylor Co
  Chicago, IL 773-254-4805
Homefree LLC
  Windham, NH 800-552-7172
Horner International
  Raleigh, NC 919-787-3112
I Rice & Co Inc
  Philadelphia, PA 800-232-6022
Jogue Inc
  Northville, MI 800-531-3888
Lafaza Foods
  Oakland, CA 510-282-1138
Lochhead Mfg. Co.
  Fenton, MO. 800-776-2088
Nielsen-Massey Vanillas Inc
  Waukegan, IL 800-525-7873
Parker Flavors Inc
  Baltimore, MD 800-336-9113
Prime Ingredients Inc
  Saddle Brook, NJ 888-791-6655
Rio Syrup Co
  St Louis, MO. 800-325-7666
Rodelle Inc
  Fort Collins, CO 800-898-5457
Shank's Extracts Inc
  Lancaster, PA 800-346-3135
Singing Dog Vanilla
  Eugene, OR. 888-343-0002
Sterling Extract Co Inc
  Franklin Park, IL 847-451-9728
Synergy Flavors Inc
  Wauconda, IL 847-487-1011
Tastepoint
  Philadelphia, PA 800-363-5286
Teawolf LLC
  Pine Brook, NJ 973-575-4600
Triple K Manufacturing Company, Inc.
  Shenandoah, IA. 712-246-4376
V & E Kohnstamm Inc
  Brooklyn, NY 800-847-4500
Van Tone Creative
  Terrell, TX. 800-856-0802
Virginia Dare Extract Co
  Brooklyn, NY 718-788-1776
Weber Flavors
  Wheeling, IL 800-558-9078

Vegetable

Basic American Foods
  Walnut Creek, CA 925-472-4000
Cajun Brands
  New Iberia, LA 504-408-2252
Gold Coast Ingredients
  Commerce, CA 800-352-8673
Kalsec
  Kalamazoo, MI 800-323-9320
Prime Ingredients Inc
  Saddle Brook, NJ 888-791-6655
Silvateam USA
  Ontario, CA 909-635-2870
Ted Shear Assoc Inc
  Larchmont, NY 914-833-0017
Varied Industries Corp
  Mason City, IA 800-654-5617
Vegetable Juices Inc
  Chicago, IL 888-776-9752

Yeast

Royal Foods & Flavor
  Elk Grove Vlg, IL 847-595-9166
Savoury Systems Inc
  Branchburg, NJ 888-534-6621

Fatty Acids

Essential

Childlife
  Culver City, CA 800-993-0332
RFi Ingredients
  Blauvelt, NY 800-962-7663

Fillers

Meal

Agri-Dairy Products
  Purchase, NY 914-697-9580

Flakes

Banana

Agvest
  Cleveland, OH 216-464-3737
Emerling International Foods
  Buffalo, NY. 716-833-7381
Gerber Products Co
  Arlington, VA 800-284-9488
Spreda Group
  Louisville, KY. 502-426-9411
Unique Ingredients LLC
  Gold Canyon, AZ 480-983-2498

Oats

Bob's Red Mill Natural Foods
  Milwaukie, OR 800-349-2173
LaCrosse Milling Company
  Cochrane, WI 800-441-5411

Potato

AgraWest Foods
  Prince Edward Island, NS 877-687-1400
Bob's Red Mill Natural Foods
  Milwaukie, OR 800-349-2173
Emerling International Foods
  Buffalo, NY. 716-833-7381
Idaho Pacific Holdings Inc
  Rigby, ID. 800-238-5503
Idaho Supreme Potatoes Inc
  Firth, ID. 208-346-4100
New Organics
  Kenwood, CA 734-677-5570
Oregon Potato Co
  Boardman, OR 800-336-6311
Tova Industries LLC
  Louisville, KY 888-532-8682
Unique Ingredients LLC
  Gold Canyon, AZ 480-983-2498
VCPB Transportation
  Secaucus, NJ 201-770-0070

Soy

MicroSoy Corporation
  Jefferson, IA 515-386-2100
New Organics
  Kenwood, CA 734-677-5570

Flavor Enhancers

Asiamerica Ingredients
  Westwood, NJ 201-497-5531
Batory Foods
  Des Plaines, IL 847-299-1999
International Flavors & Fragrances Inc.
  New York, NY 212-765-5500
Lifem Spice Ingredients
  Palm Beach, FL 561-844-6334
MAFCO Worldwide
  Camden, NJ. 856-986-4050
Mixerz All Natural Cocktail Mixers
  Beverly, MA 978-922-6497
Nutra Food Ingredients, LLC
  Kentwood, MI. 616-656-9928
QST Ingredients
  Rancho Cucamonga, CA 909-989-4343
Savoury Systems Inc
  Branchburg, NJ 888-534-6621
Summit Hill Flavors
  Somerset, NJ 732-805-0335

Gluconates

Asiamerica Ingredients
  Westwood, NJ 201-497-5531
Lifewise Ingredients
  Brookfield, IL 262-788-9141

Flavors

Advanced Food Systems
  Somerset, NJ 800-787-3067
AFF International
  Marietta, GA 800-241-7764
Ajinomoto Heartland Inc
  Chicago, IL 773-380-7000
Al-Rite Fruits & Syrups Co
  Miami, FL. 305-652-2540
Allen Flavors Inc
  Edison, NJ 908-561-5995
AM Todd Co
  Kalamazoo, MI 269-343-2603
American Fruits & Flavors
  Pacoima, CA 818-899-9574
American Instants Inc
  Flanders, NJ 973-584-8811
American Laboratories
  Omaha, NE 402-339-2494
Aromor Flavors & Fragrances
  Englewood Cliffs, NJ 866-425-1600
Arylessence Inc
  Marietta, GA 800-553-2440
Asiamerica Ingredients
  Westwood, NJ 201-497-5531
Austin Special Foods Company
  Austin, TX. 512-372-8665
Avri Co Inc
  Richmond, CA 800-883-9574
AVRON Resources Inc
  Richmond, CA 800-883-9574
Baker's Coconut
  East Hanover, NJ 855-535-5648
Bakto Flavors
  North Brunswick, NJ 732-354-4492
Bartek Ingredients, Inc.
  Stoney Creek, ON 800-263-4165
Bear Stewart Corp
  Chicago, IL 800-697-2327
Bedoukian Research Inc
  Danbury, CT 800-424-9300
Beta Pure Foods
  Santa Cruz, CA 831-685-6565
Blendex Co
  Louisville, KY 800-626-6325
Blue Pacific Flavors & Fragrances
  City of Industry, CA 626-934-0099
Cajun Brands
  New Iberia, LA 504-408-2252
California Custom Foods
  Fullerton, CA 714-870-0490
Capri Sun
  Granite City, IL
Capriccio
  Chatsworth, CA 818-718-7620
Cargill Inc.
  Minneapolis, MN 800-227-4455
Century Blends LLC
  Hunt Valley, MD 410-771-6606
Chr Hansen Inc
  Milwaukee, WI 414-607-5700
Citrop Inc
  Tampa, FL. 813-249-5955
Citrus and Allied Essences
  New Hyde Park, NY 516-354-1200
Classic Flavors & Fragrances
  New York, NY 212-777-0004

Product Categories / Ingredients, Flavors & Additives: Flavors

Clements Foods Co
  Oklahoma City, OK 800-654-8355
Comax Flavors
  Melville, NY 800-992-0629
Commercial Creamery Co
  Spokane, WA 509-747-4131
Consolidated Mills Inc
  Houston, TX 713-896-4196
Cosco International
  Chicago, IL 800-621-4549
Creative Flavors Inc
  Chagrin Falls, OH 800-848-9043
Crestmont Enterprises
  Camden, NJ 856-966-0700
Danisco-Cultor
  Ardsley, NY 914-674-6300
Dean Distributors, Inc.
  Burlingame, CA 800-792-0816
Dohler-Milne Aseptics LLC
  Prosser, WA 509-786-2240
Ecom Manufacturing Corporation
  Markham, ON 905-477-2441
Edlong Corporation
  Elk Grove Village, IL 847-631-6700
Emerald Performance Materials
  Cuyahoga Falls, OH 330-916-6700
Essential Flavors & Fragrances
  Corona, CA 888-333-9935
Everfresh Food Corporation
  Minneapolis, MN 612-331-6393
Excellentia Intl
  Fairfield, NJ 737-749-9840
Fee Brothers
  Rochester, NY 800-961-3337
Finlays
  Lincoln, RI 800-288-6272
First Choice Ingredients
  Germantown, WI 262-251-4322
Flavor Dynamics Two
  South Plainfield, NJ 888-271-8424
Flavor House, Inc.
  Adelanto, CA 760-246-9131
Flavor Producers
  West Hills, CA 818-835-1850
Flavor Systems Intl.
  Cincinnati, OH 800-498-2783
Flavorchem Corp
  Downers Grove, IL 800-435-2867
Florida Food Products Inc
  Eustis, FL 800-874-2331
Fona International
  Geneva, IL 630-578-8600
Fontana Flavors Inc
  Janesville, WI 608-754-9668
Food Ingredient Solutions
  Teterboro, NJ 917-449-9558
French's Flavor Ingredients
  Springfield, MO 800-841-1256
Fuchs North America
  Hampstead, MD 800-365-3229
Genarom International
  Cranbury, NJ 609-409-6200
Givaudan Fragrances Corp
  East Hanover, NJ 973-386-9800
Golden 100
  Deland, FL 386-734-0113
Great Northern Maple Products
  Saint Honor, De Shenley, QC 418-485-7777
Green Spot Packaging
  Claremont, CA 800-456-3210
Griffith Foods Inc.
  Alsip, IL 708-371-0900
Grow Co
  Ridgefield, NJ 201-941-8777
Gum Technology Corporation
  Tucson, AZ 800-369-4867
H B Taylor Co
  Chicago, IL 773-254-4805
Horner International
  Raleigh, NC 919-787-3112
I Rice & Co Inc
  Philadelphia, PA 800-232-6022
Illes Seasonings & Flavors
  Carrollton, TX 800-683-4553
Innova Flavors
  Lombard, IL 630-928-4800
International Bakers Services, Inc.
  South Bend, IN 574-287-7111
International Flavors & Fragrances Inc.
  New York, NY 212-765-5500
J M Swank Co
  North Liberty, IA 800-593-6375
Jean Niel Inc
  Odessa, FL 727-834-8855
Johnson's Food Products
  Dorchester, MA 617-265-3400
Kalsec
  Kalamazoo, MI 800-323-9320
Kerry Foodservice
  Mansfield, OH 800-533-2722
Kerry, Inc
  Beloit, WI 608-363-1200
Latitude, LTD
  Huntington, NY 631-659-3374
Liberty Natural Products Inc
  Oregon City, OR 800-289-8427
Lionel Hitchen Essitional Oils
  Sarasota, FL 941-379-1400
Lochhead Mfg. Co.
  Fenton, MO 800-776-2088
MAFCO Worldwide
  Camden, NJ 856-986-4050
Mane Inc.
  Lebanon, OH 513-248-9876
Marukome USA Inc.
  Irvine, CA 949-863-0110
Metarom Corporation
  Newport, KY 888-882-5555
Mother Murphy's
  Greensboro, NC 800-849-1277
Natural Flavors
  Newark, NJ 973-589-1230
Nature's Products Inc
  Sunrise, FL 800-752-7873
Naturex Inc
  South Hackensack, NJ 201-440-5000
Northeastern Products Company
  S Plainfield, NJ 908-561-1660
Northwestern Extract
  Germantown, WI 800-466-3034
Nutricepts
  Burnsville, MN 800-949-9060
Ocean Cliff Corp
  New Bedford, MA 508-990-7900
Oregon Flavor Rack
OSF Flavors Inc
  Windsor, CT 800-466-6015
Parker Flavors Inc
  Baltimore, MD 800-336-9113
Parrish's Cake Decorating
  Gardena, CA 800-736-8443
Particle Control
  Albertville, MN 763-497-3075
Particle Dynamics
  Saint Louis, MO 800-452-4682
Perlarom Technology
  Columbia, MD 410-997-5114
PMC Specialties Group Inc
  Cincinnati, OH 800-543-2466
Progressive Flavors
  Madison, WI 800-827-0555
Richard E. Colgin Company
  Dallas, TX 888-226-5446
Rio Syrup Co
  St Louis, MO 800-325-7666
Rosebrand Corp
  Brooklyn, NY 800-854-5356
Royal Foods & Flavor
  Elk Grove Vlg, IL 847-595-9166
San-Ei Gen FFI
  New York, NY 212-315-7850
Savoury Systems Inc
  Branchburg, NJ 888-534-6621
Senomyx Inc
  San Diego, CA 858-646-8300
Sensient Flavors and Fragrances
  Hoffman Estates, IL 847-755-5300
Sensient Technologies Corp
  Milwaukee, WI 414-271-6755
Serv-Agen Corporation
  Cherry Hill, NJ 856-663-6966
Shank's Extracts Inc
  Lancaster, PA 800-346-3135
Silesia Flavors
  Hoffman Estates, IL 847-645-0270
Singer Extract Laboratory
  Livonia, MI 313-345-5880
SJH Enterprises
  Middleton, WI. 888-745-3845
SKW Nature Products
  Dubuque, IA 563-588-6244
Sno Shack Inc
  Rexburg, ID 888-766-7425
Southern Flavoring Co
  Bedford, VA 800-765-8565
Spicetec Flavors & Seasonings
  Omaha, NE 800-921-7502
Star Kay White Inc
  Congers, NY 800-874-8518
Stauber Performance Ingrdients
  Fullerton, CA 888-441-4233
Sterling Extract Co Inc
  Franklin Park, IL 847-451-9728
Symrise Inc.
  Teterboro, NJ 201-288-3200
Synergy Flavors Inc
  Wauconda, IL 847-487-1011
T Hasegawa USA Inc
  Cerritos, CA 714-522-1900
Taiyo International Inc.
  Minneapolis, MN 763-398-3003
Target Flavors Inc
  Brookfield, CT 800-538-3350
Tate & Lyle PLC
  Hoffman Estates, IL 847-396-7500
Technology Flavors & Fragrances
  Amityville, NY 631-789-8228
Terra Flavors & Fragrances
  New York, NY 212-244-1181
Test Laboratories Inc
  Reseda, CA 818-881-4251
Texas Spice Co
  Round Rock, TX 800-880-8007
Triple K Manufacturing Company, Inc.
  Shenandoah, IA 712-246-4376
Ungerer & Co
  Lincoln Park, NJ 973-706-7381
US Chocolate Corp
  Brooklyn, NY 718-788-8555
US Ingredients
  Naperville, IL 630-820-1711
V & E Kohnstamm Inc
  Brooklyn, NY 800-847-4500
Valley Grain Products
  Fresno, CA 559-675-3400
Vanlab Corporation
  Rochester, NY 585-232-6647
Virginia Dare Extract Co
  Brooklyn, NY 718-788-1776
Webbpak Inc
  Trussville, AL 800-655-3500
Weber Flavors
  Wheeling, IL 800-558-9078
Western Syrup Company
  Santa Fe Springs, CA 562-921-4485
WILD Flavors (Canada)
  Mississauga, ON 800-263-5286
World Flavors Inc
  Warminster, PA 215-672-4400

Almond

Castella Imports Inc
  Brentwood, NY 631-231-5500
Flavorganics
  Newark, NJ 866-972-6879
Gold Coast Ingredients
  Commerce, CA 800-352-8673
Nielsen-Massey Vanillas Inc
  Waukegan, IL 800-525-7873

Amaretto

Allen Flavors Inc
  Edison, NJ 908-561-5995
Flavorganics
  Newark, NJ 866-972-6879
Gold Coast Ingredients
  Commerce, CA 800-352-8673

Anise (See also Spices/Anise Seed)

Castella Imports Inc
  Brentwood, NY 631-231-5500
Gold Coast Ingredients
  Commerce, CA 800-352-8673

Apple

Allen Flavors Inc
  Edison, NJ 908-561-5995
Gold Coast Ingredients
  Commerce, CA 800-352-8673

Apricot

Gold Coast Ingredients
  Commerce, CA 800-352-8673

Product Categories / Ingredients, Flavors & Additives: Flavors

Artificial
Citrus and Allied Essences
  New Hyde Park, NY 516-354-1200
Clarendon Flavor Engineering
  Louisville, KY 502-634-9215

Banana
Allen Flavors Inc
  Edison, NJ 908-561-5995
Castella Imports Inc
  Brentwood, NY 631-231-5500
Flavorganics
  Newark, NJ 866-972-6879
Gold Coast Ingredients
  Commerce, CA 800-352-8673

Beer
Gold Coast Ingredients
  Commerce, CA 800-352-8673

Berry
Gold Coast Ingredients
  Commerce, CA 800-352-8673

Beverage
Allen Flavors Inc
  Edison, NJ 908-561-5995
Clarendon Flavor Engineering
  Louisville, KY 502-634-9215
Flavor & Fragrance Specialties
  Mahwah, NJ 800-998-4337
Flavors from Florida
  Bartow, FL 800-888-0409
Synergy Flavors Inc
  Wauconda, IL 847-487-1011

Blackberry
Allen Flavors Inc
  Edison, NJ 908-561-5995
Gold Coast Ingredients
  Commerce, CA 800-352-8673

Blueberry
Allen Flavors Inc
  Edison, NJ 908-561-5995
Gold Coast Ingredients
  Commerce, CA 800-352-8673

Brown Sugar
Gold Coast Ingredients
  Commerce, CA 800-352-8673

Butter
DairyChem Inc.
  Fishers, IN 317-849-8400
Edlong Corporation
  Elk Grove Village, IL 847-631-6700
First Choice Ingredients
  Germantown, WI 262-251-4322
Gold Coast Ingredients
  Commerce, CA 800-352-8673

Pecan
Edlong Corporation
  Elk Grove Village, IL 847-631-6700
Gold Coast Ingredients
  Commerce, CA 800-352-8673

Vanilla
Edlong Corporation
  Elk Grove Village, IL 847-631-6700
Gold Coast Ingredients
  Commerce, CA 800-352-8673

Buttermilk
DairyChem Inc.
  Fishers, IN 317-849-8400
Edlong Corporation
  Elk Grove Village, IL 847-631-6700
Gold Coast Ingredients
  Commerce, CA 800-352-8673

Butterscotch
Edlong Corporation
  Elk Grove Village, IL 847-631-6700

Gold Coast Ingredients
  Commerce, CA 800-352-8673

Cajeta
Edlong Corporation
  Elk Grove Village, IL 847-631-6700

Caramel
Edlong Corporation
  Elk Grove Village, IL 847-631-6700
Gold Coast Ingredients
  Commerce, CA 800-352-8673
Mont Blanc Gourmet
  Denver, CO 800-877-3811

Cheese
Dean Distributors, Inc.
  Burlingame, CA 800-792-0816
Edlong Corporation
  Elk Grove Village, IL 847-631-6700
Flavor Dynamics Two
  South Plainfield, NJ 888-271-8424
Gold Coast Ingredients
  Commerce, CA 800-352-8673
H B Taylor Co
  Chicago, IL 773-254-4805
Ingretec
  Lebanon, PA 717-273-0711
Thiel Cheese & Ingredients
  Hilbert, WI 920-989-1440

Cheesecake
Edlong Corporation
  Elk Grove Village, IL 847-631-6700
Gold Coast Ingredients
  Commerce, CA 800-352-8673

Cherry
Allen Flavors Inc
  Edison, NJ 908-561-5995
AM Todd Co
  Kalamazoo, MI 269-343-2603

Chocolate
Allen Flavors Inc
  Edison, NJ 908-561-5995
Gold Coast Ingredients
  Commerce, CA 800-352-8673
H B Taylor Co
  Chicago, IL 773-254-4805
Mont Blanc Gourmet
  Denver, CO 800-877-3811
US Chocolate Corp
  Brooklyn, NY 718-788-8555

Cinnamon
Gold Coast Ingredients
  Commerce, CA 800-352-8673

Citrus
Allen Flavors Inc
  Edison, NJ 908-561-5995
Asiamerica Ingredients
  Westwood, NJ 201-497-5531
Citrus and Allied Essences
  New Hyde Park, NY 516-354-1200
Flavorganics
  Newark, NJ 866-972-6879
Gold Coast Ingredients
  Commerce, CA 800-352-8673
H B Taylor Co
  Chicago, IL 773-254-4805

Cocoa
Batory Foods
  Des Plaines, IL 847-299-1999
Flavor Dynamics Two
  South Plainfield, NJ 888-271-8424
Gold Coast Ingredients
  Commerce, CA 800-352-8673
Horner International
  Raleigh, NC 919-787-3112
Prova
  Danvers, MA 877-776-8287

Coconut
Castella Imports Inc
  Brentwood, NY 631-231-5500

Gold Coast Ingredients
  Commerce, CA 800-352-8673

Coffee
A Hill of Beans Coffee Roasters
  Omaha, NE 402-333-6048
Acqua Blox LLC
  Santa Fe Springs, CA 562-693-9599
American Instants Inc
  Flanders, NJ 973-584-8811
Beck Flavors
  Loveland, OH 314-878-7522
Coffee Grounds
  Falcon Heights, MN 651-644-9959
Finlays
  Lincoln, RI 800-288-6272
Flavor & Fragrance Specialties
  Mahwah, NJ 800-998-4337
Flavor Dynamics Two
  South Plainfield, NJ 888-271-8424
Gold Coast Ingredients
  Commerce, CA 800-352-8673
Prova
  Danvers, MA 877-776-8287
U Roast Em Inc
  Hayward, WI 715-634-6255

Cultured
DairyChem Inc.
  Fishers, IN 317-849-8400
Edlong Corporation
  Elk Grove Village, IL 847-631-6700

Dairy
Beck Flavors
  Loveland, OH 314-878-7522
Blossom Farm Products
  Ridgewood, NJ 800-729-1818
Dairy Farmers Of America
  Kansas City, KS 888-332-6455
DairyChem Inc.
  Fishers, IN 317-849-8400
Edlong Corporation
  Elk Grove Village, IL 847-631-6700
First Choice Ingredients
  Germantown, WI 262-251-4322
Gold Coast Ingredients
  Commerce, CA 800-352-8673
H B Taylor Co
  Chicago, IL 773-254-4805
Hilmar Ingredients
  Hilmar, CA 888-300-4465
Ingretec
  Lebanon, PA 717-273-0711
Nature's Products Inc
  Sunrise, FL 800-752-7873
Saputo Inc.
  Montreal, QC 800-672-8866

Egg
Gold Coast Ingredients
  Commerce, CA 800-352-8673

Extract
Asiamerica Ingredients
  Westwood, NJ 201-497-5531
Bell Flavors & Fragrances
  Northbrook, IL 847-291-8300
Bickford Flavors
  Euclid, OH 800-283-8322
California Custom Fruits
  Baldwin Park, CA 877-558-0056
Carmi Flavor & Fragrance Company
  Commerce, CA 800-421-9647
Charles H Baldwin & Sons
  West Stockbridge, MA 413-232-7785
Citrus and Allied Essences
  New Hyde Park, NY 516-354-1200
Crest Foods Inc
  Ashton, IL 877-273-7893
Crestmont Enterprises
  Camden, NJ 856-966-0700
Edlong Corporation
  Elk Grove Village, IL 847-631-6700
Essentia Protein Solutions
  Ankeny, IA 515-289-5100
Fona International
  Geneva, IL 630-578-8600
Freeman Industries
  Tuckahoe, NY 800-666-6454

Product Categories / Ingredients, Flavors & Additives: Flavors

Frutarom Meer Corporation
   Hertzeliya Pituach,
Fuji Foods Corp
   Browns Summit, NC 336-375-3111
GLCC Co
   Paw Paw, MI 269-657-3167
H R Nicholson Co
   Baltimore, MD 800-638-3514
Hosemen & Roche Vitamins & Fine Chemicals
   Nutley, NJ 800-526-6367
Jogue Inc
   Northville, MI 800-531-3888
Kloss Manufacturing Co Inc
   Allentown, PA 800-445-7100
Marnap Industries
   Buffalo, NY 716-897-1220
Master Mix
   Placentia, CA 714-524-1698
National Flavors
   Kalamazoo, MI 800-525-2431
Newport Flavours & Fragrances
   Orange, CA 714-744-3700
Nielsen-Massey Vanillas Inc
   Waukegan, IL 800-525-7873
Pecan Deluxe Candy Co
   Dallas, TX 800-733-3589
Red Arrow Products Co LLC
   Manitowoc, WI 920-769-1100
Robertet Flavors
   Piscataway, NJ 732-981-8300
Senomyx Inc
   San Diego, CA 858-646-8300
Simpson Spring Co
   South Easton, MA 508-238-4472
Sno Wizard Inc
   New Orleans, LA 800-366-9766
Southern Flavoring Co
   Bedford, VA 800-765-8565
Southern Snow
   Belle Chasse, LA 504-393-8967
Tara Foods
   Atlanta, GA 404-559-0605
Tastepoint
   Philadelphia, PA 800-363-5286
Van Tone Creative
   Terrell, TX 800-856-0802
Vegetable Juices Inc
   Chicago, IL 888-776-9752

Fat
Choco Finesse, LLC
   Indianapolis, IN 317-476-6034
Edlong Corporation
   Elk Grove Village, IL 847-631-6700
Gold Coast Ingredients
   Commerce, CA 800-352-8673

Fish
Fontana Flavors Inc
   Janesville, WI 608-754-9668
Gold Coast Ingredients
   Commerce, CA 800-352-8673
North Taste Flavourings
   Anse-Bleue, NB 506-732-0010

Flavors

Dressing
Edlong Corporation
   Elk Grove Village, IL 847-631-6700

Enhancers
Edlong Corporation
   Elk Grove Village, IL 847-631-6700
Essentia Protein Solutions
   Ankeny, IA 515-289-5100
Flavor & Fragrance Specialties
   Mahwah, NJ 800-998-4337
H&A Health Products, Inc
   Richmond Hill, ON 514-979-3589
Serious Foodie
   Bradenton, FL 844-736-6343
W.T.I.
   Jefferson, GA 800-827-1727

Fruit
Agrana Fruit US Inc
   Cleveland, OH 800-477-3788
Dohler-Milne Aseptics LLC
   Prosser, WA 509-786-2240

Gold Coast Ingredients
   Commerce, CA 800-352-8673
H B Taylor Co
   Chicago, IL 773-254-4805
Silesia Flavors
   Hoffman Estates, IL 847-645-0270

Grain
GKI Foods
   Brighton, MI 248-486-0055

Half & Half
Edlong Corporation
   Elk Grove Village, IL 847-631-6700

Hazelnut
Allen Flavors Inc
   Edison, NJ 908-561-5995
Flavorganics
   Newark, NJ 866-972-6879
Gold Coast Ingredients
   Commerce, CA 800-352-8673

Heat Stable
Edlong Corporation
   Elk Grove Village, IL 847-631-6700

Hickory Smoke Oil
Gold Coast Ingredients
   Commerce, CA 800-352-8673
Talk O' Texas Brands Inc
   San Angelo, TX 800-749-6572

Irish Creme
Edlong Corporation
   Elk Grove Village, IL 847-631-6700
Gold Coast Ingredients
   Commerce, CA 800-352-8673

Lemon
Allen Flavors Inc
   Edison, NJ 908-561-5995
Castella Imports Inc
   Brentwood, NY 631-231-5500
Charles H Baldwin & Sons
   West Stockbridge, MA 413-232-7785
Citromax Flavors Inc
   Carlstadt, NJ 201-933-8405
Frontier Co-op
   Norway, IA 844-550-6200
Gold Coast Ingredients
   Commerce, CA 800-352-8673
Nielsen-Massey Vanillas Inc
   Waukegan, IL 800-525-7873
Serv-Agen Corporation
   Cherry Hill, NJ 856-663-6966
Test Laboratories Inc
   Reseda, CA 818-881-4251
Ungerer & Co
   Lincoln Park, NJ 973-706-7381

Licorice
AM Todd Co
   Kalamazoo, MI 269-343-2603
Asiamerica Ingredients
   Westwood, NJ 201-497-5531
Gold Coast Ingredients
   Commerce, CA 800-352-8673
Horner International
   Raleigh, NC 919-787-3112

Lime
Allen Flavors Inc
   Edison, NJ 908-561-5995
Gold Coast Ingredients
   Commerce, CA 800-352-8673
Ungerer & Co
   Lincoln Park, NJ 973-706-7381

Liqueur
Edgar A Weber & Co
   Wheeling, IL 800-558-9078

Macadamia
Allen Flavors Inc
   Edison, NJ 908-561-5995

Buonitalia
   New York, NY 212-633-9090
Gold Coast Ingredients
   Commerce, CA 800-352-8673

Maple
Allen Flavors Inc
   Edison, NJ 908-561-5995
Castella Imports Inc
   Brentwood, NY 631-231-5500
Gold Coast Ingredients
   Commerce, CA 800-352-8673

Butter
Edlong Corporation
   Elk Grove Village, IL 847-631-6700

Masking
Edlong Corporation
   Elk Grove Village, IL 847-631-6700
Gold Coast Ingredients
   Commerce, CA 800-352-8673
Silesia Flavors
   Hoffman Estates, IL 847-645-0270
Virginia Dare Extract Co
   Brooklyn, NY 718-788-1776
Watson Inc
   West Haven, CT 800-388-3481

Meat
First Choice Ingredients
   Germantown, WI 262-251-4322
Flavor & Fragrance Specialties
   Mahwah, NJ 800-998-4337
Flavor House, Inc.
   Adelanto, CA 760-246-9131
Fontana Flavors Inc
   Janesville, WI 608-754-9668
Genarom International
   Cranbury, NJ 609-409-6200
Innova Flavors
   Lombard, IL 630-928-4800

Microwave
Edlong Corporation
   Elk Grove Village, IL 847-631-6700

Milk
DairyChem Inc.
   Fishers, IN 317-849-8400
Edlong Corporation
   Elk Grove Village, IL 847-631-6700
Fonterra Co-operative Group Limited
   Chicago, IL 888-869-6455
Gold Coast Ingredients
   Commerce, CA 800-352-8673
Ingredia Inc
   Wapakoneta, OH 419-738-4060

Butter
Edlong Corporation
   Elk Grove Village, IL 847-631-6700
Fonterra Co-operative Group Limited
   Chicago, IL 888-869-6455

Nut
Gold Coast Ingredients
   Commerce, CA 800-352-8673
H B Taylor Co
   Chicago, IL 773-254-4805

Orange
Allen Flavors Inc
   Edison, NJ 908-561-5995
Castella Imports Inc
   Brentwood, NY 631-231-5500
Charles H Baldwin & Sons
   West Stockbridge, MA 413-232-7785
Frontier Co-op
   Norway, IA 844-550-6200
Gold Coast Ingredients
   Commerce, CA 800-352-8673
Nielsen-Massey Vanillas Inc
   Waukegan, IL 800-525-7873
Ungerer & Co
   Lincoln Park, NJ 973-706-7381

Product Categories / Ingredients, Flavors & Additives: Glandulars

Passion Fruit
Allen Flavors Inc
  Edison, NJ.................908-561-5995
Gold Coast Ingredients
  Commerce, CA..............800-352-8673

Peach
Allen Flavors Inc
  Edison, NJ.................908-561-5995
Gold Coast Ingredients
  Commerce, CA..............800-352-8673

Peanut
Gold Coast Ingredients
  Commerce, CA..............800-352-8673

Pear
Allen Flavors Inc
  Edison, NJ.................908-561-5995
Gold Coast Ingredients
  Commerce, CA..............800-352-8673

Peppermint
Castella Imports Inc
  Brentwood, NY.............631-231-1500
Frontier Co-op
  Norway, IA................844-550-6200
Gold Coast Ingredients
  Commerce, CA..............800-352-8673
Ungerer & Co
  Lincoln Park, NJ..........973-706-7381

Pickle
Gold Coast Ingredients
  Commerce, CA..............800-352-8673

Pineapple
Allen Flavors Inc
  Edison, NJ.................908-561-5995
Castella Imports Inc
  Brentwood, NY.............631-231-1500
Gold Coast Ingredients
  Commerce, CA..............800-352-8673

Pistachio
Gold Coast Ingredients
  Commerce, CA..............800-352-8673

Potato
Gold Coast Ingredients
  Commerce, CA..............800-352-8673

Poultry
Flavor House, Inc.
  Adelanto, CA..............760-246-9131

Raspberry
Allen Flavors Inc
  Edison, NJ.................908-561-5995
Gold Coast Ingredients
  Commerce, CA..............800-352-8673

Root Beer
Allen Flavors Inc
  Edison, NJ.................908-561-5995
Gold Coast Ingredients
  Commerce, CA..............800-352-8673

Rum
Butter Toffee
Edlong Corporation
  Elk Grove Village, IL.....847-631-6700

Seafood
Flavor House, Inc.
  Adelanto, CA..............760-246-9131

Smoke
Dean Distributors, Inc.
  Burlingame, CA............800-792-0816
Gold Coast Ingredients
  Commerce, CA..............800-352-8673
Red Arrow Products Co LLC
  Manitowoc, WI.............920-769-1100

Sour
Senomyx Inc
  San Diego, CA.............858-646-8300

Cream
DairyChem Inc.
  Fishers, IN...............317-849-8400
Edlong Corporation
  Elk Grove Village, IL.....847-631-6700
Gold Coast Ingredients
  Commerce, CA..............800-352-8673

Sour Dough
Gold Coast Ingredients
  Commerce, CA..............800-352-8673

Spearmint
Gold Coast Ingredients
  Commerce, CA..............800-352-8673
I P Callison & Sons
  Lacey, WA.................360-412-3340
Ungerer & Co
  Lincoln Park, NJ..........973-706-7381

Strawberry
Allen Flavors Inc
  Edison, NJ.................908-561-5995
Castella Imports Inc
  Brentwood, NY.............631-231-1500
Gold Coast Ingredients
  Commerce, CA..............800-352-8673

Sweet Cream
Gold Coast Ingredients
  Commerce, CA..............800-352-8673

Tea
Acqua Blox LLC
  Santa Fe Springs, CA......562-693-9599
Allen Flavors Inc
  Edison, NJ.................908-561-5995
Beck Flavors
  Loveland, OH..............314-878-7522
Flavor & Fragrance Specialties
  Mahwah, NJ................800-998-4337
Flavor Dynamics Two
  South Plainfield, NJ......888-271-8424
Gold Coast Ingredients
  Commerce, CA..............800-352-8673

Vanilla
Agri-Dairy Products
  Purchase, NY..............914-697-9580
Allen Flavors Inc
  Edison, NJ.................908-561-5995
Bakto Flavors
  North Brunswick, NJ.......732-354-4492
Carmi Flavor & Fragrance Company
  Commerce, CA..............800-421-9647
Charles H Baldwin & Sons
  West Stockbridge, MA......413-232-7785
Clements Foods Co
  Oklahoma City, OK.........800-654-8355
Everfresh Food Corporation
  Minneapolis, MN...........612-331-6393
Gold Coast Ingredients
  Commerce, CA..............800-352-8673
Helm New York Chemical Corp
  Piscataway, NJ............732-981-0528
Jogue Inc
  Northville, MI............800-531-3888
Lafaza Foods
  Oakland, CA...............510-282-1138
Lemur International
  Richmond, CA..............510-620-9708
New Organics
  Kenwood, CA...............734-677-5570
Prova
  Danvers, MA...............877-776-8287
Serv-Agen Corporation
  Cherry Hill, NJ...........856-663-6966
Singing Dog Vanilla
  Eugene, OR................888-343-0002
Sno Wizard Inc
  New Orleans, LA...........800-366-9766
Sterling Extract Co Inc
  Franklin Park, IL.........847-451-9728

Triple K Manufacturing Company, Inc.
  Shenandoah, IA............712-246-4376
Webbpak Inc
  Trussville, AL............800-655-3500

Vanillin
Agri-Dairy Products
  Purchase, NY..............914-697-9580
AM Todd Co
  Kalamazoo, MI.............269-343-2603
Asiamerica Ingredients
  Westwood, NJ..............201-497-5531
Astral Extracts
  Syosset, NY...............516-496-2505
California Custom Fruits
  Baldwin Park, CA..........877-558-0056
Gold Coast Ingredients
  Commerce, CA..............800-352-8673
International Chemical Corp
  Melbourne, FL.............800-914-2436
Nichem Co
  Newark, NJ................973-399-9810
Universal Preservachem Inc
  Somerset, NJ..............732-568-1266
Zink & Triest Company
  Montgomeryville, PA.......800-537-5070

Variegates
Triple K Manufacturing Company, Inc.
  Shenandoah, IA............712-246-4376

Vegetable
Gold Coast Ingredients
  Commerce, CA..............800-352-8673
Kalsec
  Kalamazoo, MI.............800-323-9320
Summit Hill Flavors
  Somerset, NJ..............732-805-0335

Watermelon
Gold Coast Ingredients
  Commerce, CA..............800-352-8673

Wine
Edgar A Weber & Co
  Wheeling, IL..............800-558-9078
Gold Coast Ingredients
  Commerce, CA..............800-352-8673

Wintergreen
Gold Coast Ingredients
  Commerce, CA..............800-352-8673

Yogurt
DairyChem Inc.
  Fishers, IN...............317-849-8400
Edlong Corporation
  Elk Grove Village, IL.....847-631-6700
Gold Coast Ingredients
  Commerce, CA..............800-352-8673
Gum Technology Corporation
  Tucson, AZ................800-369-4867
Johanna Foods Inc.
  Flemington, NJ............800-727-6700
Plaidberry Company
  Vista, CA.................760-727-5403

Glandulars
Ultra Enterprises
  Whittier, CA..............800-543-0627

Grain-Based
Beaumont Rice Mills
  Beaumont, TX..............409-832-2521

Gums
AM Todd Co
  Kalamazoo, MI.............269-343-2603
Asiamerica Ingredients
  Westwood, NJ..............201-497-5531
Au'some Candies
  Monmouth Junction, NJ.....877-287-6649
Batory Foods
  Des Plaines, IL...........847-299-1999
Beehive Botanicals
  Hayward, WI...............800-233-4483

Product Categories / Ingredients, Flavors & Additives: Humectants

Cap Candy
  Napa, CA.........................707-251-9321
DMH Ingredients Inc
  Libertyville, IL...................847-362-9977
El Brands
  Ozark, AL........................334-445-2828
Food Ingredient Solutions
  Teterboro, NJ....................917-449-9558
Fun Factory
  Milwaukee, WI...................877-894-6767
Gum Technology Corporation
  Tucson, AZ.......................800-369-4867
Gurley's Foods
  Willmar, MN.....................800-426-7845
H&A Health Products, Inc
  Richmond Hill, ON................514-979-3589
Jungbunzlauer Inc
  Newton, MA.....................617-969-0900
Kolatin Real Kosher Gelatin
  Lakewood, NJ....................732-364-8700
Lotte USA Inc
  Battle Creek, MI..................269-963-6664
Magic Gumball Intl
  Chatsworth, CA..................800-576-2020
Main Street Ingredients
  La Crosse, WI....................800-359-2345
Montello Inc
  Tulsa, OK........................800-331-4628
Oak Leaf Confections
 877-261-7887
PLT Health Solutions Inc
  Morristown, NJ...................973-984-0900
Polypro International Inc
  Edina, MN.......................800-765-9776
Profood International
  Naperville, IL....................888-288-0081
Richardson Brands Co
  Canajoharie, NY..................518-673-3553
Sahagian & Associates
  Oak Park, IL.....................800-327-9273
Scripture Candy
  Birmingham, AL..................888-317-7333
Snackerz
  Commerce, CA...................888-576-2253
SP Enterprises, Inc.
  Las Vegas, NV...................800-746-4774
SWELL Philadelphia Chewing Gum Corporation
  Havertown, PA...................610-449-1700
Thymly Products Inc
  Colora, MD......................877-710-2340
TIC Gums
  Belcamp, MD....................800-899-3953
Triple-C
  Hamilton, ON...................800-263-9105
Whetstone Chocolates
  St Augustine, FL.................877-261-7887
World Confections Inc
  South Orange, NJ................718-768-8100

Acacia Gum
Alfred L. Wolff, Inc.
  Park Ridge, IL...................847-759-8888
Gum Technology Corporation
  Tucson, AZ.......................800-369-4867
Gumix International Inc
  Fort Lee, NJ.....................800-248-6492
Main Street Ingredients
  La Crosse, WI....................800-359-2345
Nexira
  Somerville, NJ...................800-872-1850
PLT Health Solutions Inc
  Morristown, NJ...................973-984-0900

Agar-Agar
AM Todd Co
  Kalamazoo, MI..................269-343-2603
Gum Technology Corporation
  Tucson, AZ.......................800-369-4867
PLT Health Solutions Inc
  Morristown, NJ...................973-984-0900
Universal Preservachem Inc
  Somerset, NJ.....................732-568-1266

Algin & Alginates
PLT Health Solutions Inc
  Morristown, NJ...................973-984-0900

Arabic
PLT Health Solutions Inc
  Morristown, NJ...................973-984-0900

Carboxymethylcellulose
PLT Health Solutions Inc
  Morristown, NJ...................973-984-0900

Carrageenan
CP Kelco
  Atlanta, GA......................800-535-2687
GPI USA LLC.
  Mokena, IL......................800-929-4248
PLT Health Solutions Inc
  Morristown, NJ...................973-984-0900

Gellan
CP Kelco
  Atlanta, GA......................800-535-2687
PLT Health Solutions Inc
  Morristown, NJ...................973-984-0900

Ghatti
PLT Health Solutions Inc
  Morristown, NJ...................973-984-0900

Guar Gum
Agri-Dairy Products
  Purchase, NY....................914-697-9580
Asiamerica Ingredients
  Westwood, NJ....................201-497-5531
Commodities Marketing Inc
  Clarksburg, NJ...................732-516-0700
Gum Technology Corporation
  Tucson, AZ.......................800-369-4867
H Fox & Co Inc
  Brooklyn, NY....................718-385-4600
PLT Health Solutions Inc
  Morristown, NJ...................973-984-0900
Polypro International Inc
  Edina, MN.......................800-765-9776
Universal Preservachem Inc
  Somerset, NJ.....................732-568-1266

Hydroxypropyl Methylcellulose
Asiamerica Ingredients
  Westwood, NJ....................201-497-5531

Karaya Gum
Gum Technology Corporation
  Tucson, AZ.......................800-369-4867
Universal Preservachem Inc
  Somerset, NJ.....................732-568-1266

Locust Bean Gum
CP Kelco
  Atlanta, GA......................800-535-2687
Gum Technology Corporation
  Tucson, AZ.......................800-369-4867
PLT Health Solutions Inc
  Morristown, NJ...................973-984-0900

Methylcellulose
PLT Health Solutions Inc
  Morristown, NJ...................973-984-0900

Natural
PLT Health Solutions Inc
  Morristown, NJ...................973-984-0900

Pectin
Asiamerica Ingredients
  Westwood, NJ....................201-497-5531
CP Kelco
  Atlanta, GA......................800-535-2687
Silvateam USA
  Ontario, CA......................909-635-2870

Tara
PLT Health Solutions Inc
  Morristown, NJ...................973-984-0900
Silvateam USA
  Ontario, CA......................909-635-2870

Tragacanth
Gum Technology Corporation
  Tucson, AZ.......................800-369-4867
Universal Preservachem Inc
  Somerset, NJ.....................732-568-1266

Vegetable Gum
Functional Foods
  Englishtown, NJ..................800-442-9524
Gum Technology Corporation
  Tucson, AZ.......................800-369-4867
Gumix International Inc
  Fort Lee, NJ.....................800-248-6492

Xanthan Gum
AM Todd Co
  Kalamazoo, MI..................269-343-2603
Asiamerica Ingredients
  Westwood, NJ....................201-497-5531
CP Kelco
  Atlanta, GA......................800-535-2687
Deosen USA
  Piscataway, NJ...................908-292-1165
Gum Technology Corporation
  Tucson, AZ.......................800-369-4867
Hodgson Mill Inc
  Effingham, IL....................800-347-0198
Homefree LLC
  Windham, NH...................800-552-7172

Humectants
Nutricepts
  Burnsville, MN...................800-949-9060

Hydrocolloids
PLT Health Solutions Inc
  Morristown, NJ...................973-984-0900
Silvateam USA
  Ontario, CA......................909-635-2870
TIC Gums
  Belcamp, MD....................800-899-3953

Hydrolyzed Products

Milk Proteins
First Spice Mixing Co
  Long Island City, NY..............800-221-1105
Kantner Group
  Wapakoneta, OH.................877-738-3448
Milk Specialties Global
  Eden Prairie, MN.................952-942-7310

Vegetable Proteins
Flavor House, Inc.
  Adelanto, CA....................760-246-9131
Savoury Systems Inc
  Branchburg, NJ..................888-534-6621
Valley Meats
  Coal Valley, IL...................309-517-6639

Inclusions
Paradise Fruits NA
  Norwood, MA...................781-769-4900

Ingredients
Avafina Organics
  Coquitlam, BC...................604-292-0022
Blue California Co
  Rancho Sta Marg, CA.............949-459-2729
Carolina Ingredients Inc
  Rock Hill, SC....................803-323-6550
Century Foods Intl LLC
  Sparta, WI.......................800-269-1901
Diana Naturals
  Saddle Brook, NJ.................845-729-0942
DSM Food Specialties
  Parsippany, NJ
Espro Manufacturing
  Vernon, CA......................323-415-8544
Excellentia Intl.
  Fairfield, NJ.....................737-749-9840
Fallwood Corp
  White Plains, NY.................914-304-4065
Ful-Flav-R Foods
  Alamo, CA......................925-838-0300
Global Organics
  Cambridge, MA..................781-648-8844
Hayashibara International Inc.
  New York, NY...................212-703-1340
Heartland Ingredients LLC
  Troy, MO........................800-557-2621
Helm New York Chemical Corp
  Piscataway, NJ...................732-981-0528

Product Categories / Ingredients, Flavors & Additives: Leaveners

International Food Products
  Fenton, MO....................800-227-8427
Marukan Vinegar USA Inc.
  Paramount, CA..................562-630-6060
Newtown Foods USA Inc
  Newtown, PA...................215-579-2120
PGP International
  Woodland, CA..................800-233-0110
PLT Health Solutions Inc
  Morristown, NJ.................973-984-0900
Quali Tech Inc
  Chaska, MN....................800-328-5870
SAPNA Foods
  Atlanta, GA...................404-589-0977
Sentry Seasonings
  Elmhurst, IL..................630-530-5370
Sun Ray International
  Davis, CA.....................530-297-1688
Universal Impex Corporation
  Toronto, ON...................416-743-7778
Van Hees Gmbh
  Cary, NC......................919-654-6862

Bakery

American Pasien Co
  Burlington, NJ................609-387-3130
Amoretti
  Oxnard, CA....................800-266-7388
Caremoli USA
  Ames, IA......................515-233-1255
Chaucer Foods, Inc. USA
  Forest Grove, OR
International Food Products
  Fenton, MO....................800-227-8427
New Horizon Foods
  Union City, CA................510-489-8600
P&H Milling Group
  Cambridge, ON.................519-650-6400
White Stokes International
  Chicago, IL...................800-978-6537

Dairy

Century Foods Intl LLC
  Sparta, WI....................800-269-1901
Interfood Ingredients
  Miami, FL.....................786-953-8320
Kantner Group
  Wapakoneta, OH................877-738-3448
Trega Foods
  Weyauwega, WI.................920-867-2137

Food

AmTech Ingredients
  Hudson, WI....................715-381-5746
Anchor Ingredients
  Fargo, ND.....................701-499-1480
Capriccio
  Chatsworth, CA................818-718-7620
Catherych
  Warren, NJ....................732-566-6625
Century Foods Intl LLC
  Sparta, WI....................800-269-1901
Interfood Ingredients
  Miami, FL.....................786-953-8320
International Food Products
  Fenton, MO....................800-227-8427
Land O'Frost Inc.
  Lansing, IL...................800-323-3308
Mantrose-Haeuser Co Inc
  Westport, CT..................800-344-4229
PLT Health Solutions Inc
  Morristown, NJ................973-984-0900
Summit Hill Flavors
  Somerset, NJ..................732-805-0335
White Stokes International
  Chicago, IL...................800-978-6537

Leaveners

Baking Soda

Agri-Dairy Products
  Purchase, NY..................914-697-9580
Bunny Bread
  Evansville, IN
Church & Dwight Co., Inc.
  Ewing, NJ.....................800-833-9532
Clabber Girl Corporation
  Terre Haute, IN...............812-232-9446
Frontier Co-op
  Norway, IA....................844-550-6200

GloryBee
  Eugene, OR....................800-456-7923
Natrium Products Inc
  Cortland, NY..................800-962-4203

Maltodextrin

Agri-Dairy Products
  Purchase, NY..................914-697-9580
California Natural Products
  Lathrop, CA...................209-858-2525
Clofine Dairy Products Inc
  Linwood, NJ...................609-653-1000
Grain Processing Corp
  Muscatine, IA.................800-448-4472
Ingredion Inc.
  Westchester, IL...............800-713-0208
Malt Diastase Co
  Saddle Brook, NJ..............800-526-0180
New Organics
  Kenwood, CA...................734-677-5570
Roquette America Inc.
  Geneva, IL....................630-463-9430

Milk Calcium

Ingredia Inc
  Wapakoneta, OH................419-738-4060
Kantner Group
  Wapakoneta, OH................877-738-3448

Pastes

Almond

Emerling International Foods
  Buffalo, NY...................716-833-7381

Fig

Emerling International Foods
  Buffalo, NY...................716-833-7381
Fig Garden Packing Inc
  Fresno, CA....................559-271-9000
Unique Ingredients LLC
  Gold Canyon, AZ...............480-983-2498

Fruit

Cinnabar Specialty Foods Inc
  Prescott, AZ..................866-293-6433
Citadelle Maple Syrup Producers' Cooperative
  Plessisville, QC..............819-362-3241
Emerling International Foods
  Buffalo, NY...................716-833-7381
Fig Garden Packing Inc
  Fresno, CA....................559-271-9000
Kapaa Poi Factory
  Kapaa, HI.....................808-822-5426
Lion Raisins Inc
  Selma, CA.....................559-834-6677
Unique Ingredients LLC
  Gold Canyon, AZ...............480-983-2498
Vacaville Fruit Co
  Vacaville, CA.................707-447-1085

Tomato

Emerling International Foods
  Buffalo, NY...................716-833-7381
Ingomar Packing Co
  Los Banos, CA.................209-826-9494
International Home Foods
  Parsippany, NJ................973-359-9920
Northwest Packing Co
  Vancouver, WA.................800-543-4356
Pastene Co LTD
  Canton, MA....................781-298-3397
Spreda Group
  Louisville, KY................502-426-9411
Stanislaus Food Prod
  Modesto, CA...................800-327-7201
Unilever Food Solutions
  Englewood Cliffs, NJ

Canned & Frozen

International Home Foods
  Parsippany, NJ................973-359-9920
Unilever Food Solutions
  Englewood Cliffs, NJ

Pectins

Apple

Asiamerica Ingredients
  Westwood, NJ..................201-497-5531
Century Blends LLC
  Hunt Valley, MD...............410-771-6606
Gum Technology Corporation
  Tucson, AZ....................800-369-4867
Spreda Group
  Louisville, KY................502-426-9411
Universal Preservachem Inc
  Somerset, NJ..................732-568-1266

Citrus

Asiamerica Ingredients
  Westwood, NJ..................201-497-5531
Century Blends LLC
  Hunt Valley, MD...............410-771-6606
Citrico
  Northbrook, IL................800-445-2171
Gum Technology Corporation
  Tucson, AZ....................800-369-4867
Universal Preservachem Inc
  Somerset, NJ..................732-568-1266

Fruit

Century Blends LLC
  Hunt Valley, MD...............410-771-6606
Kent Precision Foods Group Inc
  Muscatine, IA.................800-442-5242
Spreda Group
  Louisville, KY................502-426-9411

Phosphates

Asiamerica Ingredients
  Westwood, NJ..................201-497-5531
BK Giulini Corporation
  Ladenburg,
Escalade Limited
  Huntington, NY................631-659-3373
Fiberstar
  River Falls, WI...............715-425-7550
First Spice Mixing Co
  Long Island City, NY..........800-221-1105
Hawkins Inc
  Roseville, MN.................800-328-5460
ICL Performance Products
  St. Louis, MO.................800-244-6169
Innophos Holdings Inc.
  Cranbury, NJ..................609-495-2495
International Food Products
  Fenton, MO....................800-227-8427
Prayon Inc.
  Augusta, GA...................206-213-5572
Wiberg Corporation
  Oakville, ON..................905-825-9900

Ammonium Phosphates

Luyties Pharmacal Company
  Saint Louis, MO...............800-325-8080
Universal Preservachem Inc
  Somerset, NJ..................732-568-1266

Calcium Phosphate

Asiamerica Ingredients
  Westwood, NJ..................201-497-5531
Luyties Pharmacal Company
  Saint Louis, MO...............800-325-8080
Natural Enrichment Industries
  Herrin, IL....................618-942-2112

Potassium Bicarbonate

Innophos Holdings Inc.
  Cranbury, NJ..................609-495-2495

Sodium Phosphate

Agri-Dairy Products
  Purchase, NY..................914-697-9580
Asiamerica Ingredients
  Westwood, NJ..................201-497-5531
Luyties Pharmacal Company
  Saint Louis, MO...............800-325-8080
Universal Preservachem Inc
  Somerset, NJ..................732-568-1266

Product Categories / Ingredients, Flavors & Additives: Potassium Bitartrate (Cream of Tartar)

Potassium Bitartrate (Cream of Tartar)
Advanced Spice & Trading
 Carrollton, TX 800-872-7811
American Tartaric Products
 Larchmont, NY 914-834-1881
Jungbunzlauer Inc
 Newton, MA 617-969-0900

Potassium Bromate
Morre-Tec Ind Inc
 Union, NJ 908-686-0307

Potassium Citrate
Agri-Dairy Products
 Purchase, NY 914-697-9580
Asiamerica Ingredients
 Westwood, NJ 201-497-5531
Cargill Inc.
 Minneapolis, MN 800-227-4455
Jungbunzlauer Inc
 Newton, MA 617-969-0900
Shekou Chemicals
 Waltham, MA 781-893-6878
Universal Preservachem Inc
 Somerset, NJ 732-568-1266

Potassium Lactate
Hawkins Inc
 Roseville, MN 800-328-5460
Trumark
 Linden, NJ 800-752-7877

Potassium Sorbate
Agri-Dairy Products
 Purchase, NY 914-697-9580
Asiamerica Ingredients
 Westwood, NJ 201-497-5531
Jungbunzlauer Inc
 Newton, MA 617-969-0900
Shekou Chemicals
 Waltham, MA 781-893-6878
Silver Fern Chemical Inc
 Seattle, WA 866-282-3384
Universal Preservachem Inc
 Somerset, NJ 732-568-1266

Powders
Expro Manufacturing
 Vernon, CA 323-415-8544
First Choice Ingredients
 Germantown, WI. 262-251-4322
Hayashibara International Inc.
 New York, NY 212-703-1340
Marroquin Organic Intl.
 Santa Cruz, CA 831-423-3442

Adobo
American Key Food Products Inc
 Closter, NJ 877-263-7539
Gel Spice Co LLC
 Bayonne, NJ 800-922-0230
Magic Seasoning Blends
 New Orleans, LA 800-457-2857

Arrowroot
GloryBee
 Eugene, OR 800-456-7923

Baking
Agri-Dairy Products
 Purchase, NY 914-697-9580
American Tartaric Products
 Larchmont, NY 914-834-1881
Erba Food Products
 Brooklyn, NY 718-272-7700
Frontier Co-op
 Norway, IA 844-550-6200
King Arthur Flour
 Norwich, VT 800-827-6836
Lallemand American Yeast
 Addison, IL 630-932-1290
Lynch Foods
 North York, ON. 416-449-5464
Roland Machinery
 Springfield, IL 800-325-1183

Tasty Mix Quality Foods
 Brooklyn, NY 718-855-7680
Young Winfield
 Hamilton, ON 905-893-2536

Beverage
Aromatech USA
 Orlando, FL. 407-277-5727
Baldwin Richardson Foods
 Oakbrook Terrace, IL 866-644-2732
Best Foods
 Englewood Cliffs, NJ 201-894-4000
Cappuccine
 Corona, CA 800-511-3127
First Choice Ingredients
 Germantown, WI. 262-251-4322
Instant Products of America
 Columbus, IN 812-372-9100
J. Crow Company
 New Ipswich, NH 800-878-1965
Lynch Foods
 North York, ON. 416-449-5464
Mele-Koi Farms
 Newport Beach, CA 949-660-9000
Natural Formulas
 Hayward, CA 510-372-1800
Northwestern Foods
 Arden Hills, MN 800-236-4937
Wechsler Coffee Corporation
 Teterboro, NJ. 800-800-2633

Broth
Ancient Nutrition
 North Palm Beach, FL 888-823-4468
Essentia Protein Solutions
 Ankeny, IA 515-289-5100
International Dehydrated Foods
 Springfield, MO 800-641-6509

Buttermilk
Diehl Food Ingredients
 Defiance, OH 800-251-3033
Kantner Group
 Wapakoneta, OH 877-738-3448

Carob
Earth Circle Organics
 Auburn, CA. 877-922-3663
NOW Foods
 Bloomingdale, IL 888-669-3663
Universal Preservachem Inc
 Somerset, NJ 732-568-1266

Carob & Cocoa
Dairy House
 Fenton, MO. 636-343-5444
Earth Circle Organics
 Auburn, CA. 877-922-3663
GloryBee
 Eugene, OR 800-456-7923
Jedwards International Inc
 Braintree, MA. 781-848-1473
Kana Organics
 Westlake Village, CA 213-603-0448

Celery
Advanced Spice & Trading
 Carrollton, TX 800-872-7811
American Key Food Products Inc
 Closter, NJ 877-263-7539
Con Yeager Spice Co
 Zelienople, PA. 800-222-2460
Emerling International Foods
 Buffalo, NY. 716-833-7381
Gel Spice Co LLC
 Bayonne, NJ 800-922-0230
Unique Ingredients LLC
 Gold Canyon, AZ 480-983-2498

Cheese
Anderson Custom Processing
 New Ulm, MN. 877-588-4950
Commercial Creamery Co
 Spokane, WA. 509-747-4131
DMH Ingredients Inc
 Libertyville, IL 847-362-9977
First Choice Ingredients
 Germantown, WI. 262-251-4322

Kantner Group
 Wapakoneta, OH 877-738-3448
Kerry, Inc
 Beloit, WI 608-363-1200
King Arthur Flour
 Norwich, VT 800-827-6836

American
Kantner Group
 Wapakoneta, OH 877-738-3448

Bakers
Kantner Group
 Wapakoneta, OH 877-738-3448

Cheddar
Commercial Creamery Co
 Spokane, WA. 509-747-4131
Kantner Group
 Wapakoneta, OH 877-738-3448

Cream
Kantner Group
 Wapakoneta, OH 877-738-3448

Chicken Stock
Summit Hill Flavors
 Somerset, NJ 732-805-0335

Chili
Advanced Spice & Trading
 Carrollton, TX 800-872-7811
American Key Food Products Inc
 Closter, NJ 877-263-7539
Bruce Foods Corporation
 Lafayette, LA 800-299-9082
Bueno Foods
 Albuquerque, NM 800-888-7336
Commercial Creamery Co
 Spokane, WA. 509-747-4131
Dave's Gourmet
 San Rafael, CA 800-758-0372
Fernandez Chili Co
 Alamosa, CO. 719-589-6043
Gel Spice Co LLC
 Bayonne, NJ 800-922-0230
Monterrey Products
 San Antonio, TX. 210-435-2872
Morris J Golombeck Inc
 Brooklyn, NY 718-284-3505
Santa Cruz Chili & Spice
 Tumacacori, AZ 520-398-2591
Swagger Foods Corp
 Vernon Hills, IL 847-913-1200
Texas Coffee Co
 Beaumont, TX. 800-259-3400
Whole Herb Co
 Sonoma, CA 707-935-1077

Cocoa
Batory Foods
 Des Plaines, IL 847-299-1999
Forbes Chocolate BP
 Broadview Hts, OH. 440-838-4400
Frontier Co-op
 Norway, IA 844-550-6200
Gilster-Mary Lee Corp
 Chester, IL. 618-826-2361
Mont Blanc Gourmet
 Denver, CO 800-877-3811
Natra US
 Chula Vista, CA 800-262-6216
Northwestern Foods
 Arden Hills, MN 800-236-4937
NOW Foods
 Bloomingdale, IL 888-669-3663
Sucesores de Pedro Cortes
 Hato Rey, PR. 787-754-7040
Vivoo
 Verona,
Wildly Organic
 Silver Bay, MN 800-945-3801

Curry
American Key Food Products Inc
 Closter, NJ 877-263-7539
Commissariat Imports
 Los Angeles, CA. 310-475-5628

Product Categories / Ingredients, Flavors & Additives: Powders

Gel Spice Co LLC
  Bayonne, NJ 800-922-0230

Hot
Commissariat Imports
  Los Angeles, CA 310-475-5628

Echinacea Purpurea
Asiamerica Ingredients
  Westwood, NJ 201-497-5531
RFi Ingredients
  Blauvelt, NY 800-962-7663

Egg
Batory Foods
  Des Plaines, IL 847-299-1999

Feverfew
Asiamerica Ingredients
  Westwood, NJ 201-497-5531
RFi Ingredients
  Blauvelt, NY 800-962-7663

Fruit
Agvest
  Cleveland, OH 216-464-3737
Blue California Co
  Rancho Sta Marg, CA 949-459-2729
Carmi Flavor & Fragrance Company
  Commerce, CA 800-421-9647
Emerling International Foods
  Buffalo, NY 716-833-7381
Jiaherb
  Pine Brook, NJ 888-542-4372
Mayfield Farms and Nursery
  Athens, TN 423-746-9859
Niagara Foods
  Middleport, NY 716-735-7722
Paragon Fruits
  Maple Grove, MN 763-559-0436
Powder Pure
  The Dalles, OR 541-298-4800
Prime Ingredients Inc
  Saddle Brook, NJ 888-791-6655
QBI
  South Plainfield, NJ 908-668-0088
RFi Ingredients
  Blauvelt, NY 800-962-7663
Spreda Group
  Louisville, KY 502-426-9411
Unique Ingredients LLC
  Gold Canyon, AZ 480-983-2498
United Citrus
  Norwood, MA 800-229-7300
Valley Fig Growers
  Fresno, CA 559-237-3893

Garlic (See also Spices/Garlic Powder)
Advanced Spice & Trading
  Carrollton, TX 800-872-7811
Alfred L. Wolff, Inc.
  Park Ridge, IL 847-759-8888
American Key Food Products Inc
  Closter, NJ 877-263-7539
Asiamerica Ingredients
  Westwood, NJ 201-497-5531
Emerling International Foods
  Buffalo, NY 716-833-7381
Gel Spice Co LLC
  Bayonne, NJ 800-922-0230
Great Garlic Foods
  Bradley Beach, NJ 732-775-3311
Italian Rose Garlic Products
  Riviera Beach, FL 800-338-8899
RFi Ingredients
  Blauvelt, NY 800-962-7663
Texas Coffee Co
  Beaumont, TX 800-259-3400
Vegetable Juices Inc
  Chicago, IL 888-776-9752

Gingko
Asiamerica Ingredients
  Westwood, NJ 201-497-5531
RFi Ingredients
  Blauvelt, NY 800-962-7663

Ginseng
Asiamerica Ingredients
  Westwood, NJ 201-497-5531
RFi Ingredients
  Blauvelt, NY 800-962-7663

Gotu Kola
Asiamerica Ingredients
  Westwood, NJ 201-497-5531
RFi Ingredients
  Blauvelt, NY 800-962-7663

Ice Cream
Agri-Dairy Products
  Purchase, NY 914-697-9580
America's Classic Foods
  Cambria, CA 805-927-0745
Clofine Dairy Products Inc
  Linwood, NJ 609-653-1000
Quality Naturally Foods
  City Of Industry, CA 888-498-6986

Jelly
Lake City Foods
  Mississauga, ON 905-625-8244

Meat
American Key Food Products Inc
  Closter, NJ 877-263-7539
Flavor House, Inc.
  Adelanto, CA 760-246-9131
QST Ingredients
  Rancho Cucamonga, CA 909-989-4343
Summit Hill Flavors
  Somerset, NJ 732-805-0335

Mesquite Smoke
Earth Circle Organics
  Auburn, CA 877-922-3663

Milk
Abunda Life
  Asbury Park, NJ 732-775-9338
Agri-Dairy Products
  Purchase, NY 914-697-9580
All American Foods Inc
  Mankato, MN 800-833-2661
Berkshire Dairy
  Wyomissing, PA 877-696-6455
Blossom Farm Products
  Ridgewood, NJ 800-729-1818
California Dairies Inc.
  Visalia, CA 559-625-2200
Century Foods Intl LLC
  Sparta, WI 800-269-1901
Challenge Dairy Products, Inc.
  Dublin, CA 800-733-2479
Clofine Dairy Products Inc
  Linwood, NJ 609-653-1000
Commercial Creamery Co
  Spokane, WA 509-747-4131
Con Yeager Spice Co
  Zelienople, PA 800-222-2460
Country Fresh Farms
  Salt Lake City, UT 800-878-0099
CTL Foods
  Colfax, WI 800-962-5227
Devansoy Farms
  Carroll, IA 800-747-8605
F C C
  Mcminnville, OR 503-472-2157
First District Association
  Litchfield, MN 320-693-3236
First Spice Mixing Co
  Long Island City, NY 800-221-1105
Fonterra Co-operative Group Limited
  Chicago, IL 888-869-6455
Graf Creamery Co
  Bonduel, WI 715-758-2137
Humboldt Creamery
  Modesto, CA 888-316-6064
IMAC
  Oklahoma City, OK 888-878-7827
Kantner Group
  Wapakoneta, OH 877-738-3448
Kelly Flour Company
  Addison, IL 630-678-5300
Lake Country Foods Inc
  Oconomowoc, WI 262-567-5521
Land O'Lakes Inc
  Arden Hills, MN 800-328-9680
Main Street Ingredients
  La Crosse, WI 800-359-2345
Maple Island
  Saint Paul, MN 800-369-1022
Meyenberg Goat Milk
  Turlock, CA 800-891-4628
Plainview Milk Products
  Plainview, MN 800-356-5606
Protient
  St Paul, MN 800-328-9680
Ramsen Inc
  Lakeville, MN 952-431-0400
Rv Industries
  Buford, GA 770-729-8983
Saint Albans Cooperative Creamery
  Saint Albans, VT 802-524-6581
Thymly Products Inc
  Colora, MD 877-710-2340
United Dairymen of Arizona
  Tempe, AZ 480-966-7211
Vance's Foods
  San Francisco, CA 415-621-1171
Weinberg Foods
  Kirkland, WA 800-866-3447
Welsh Farms
  Wallington, NJ 800-221-0663
Westin Foods
  Omaha, NE 800-228-6098

Molasses
Rogers Sugar Inc.
  Montreal, QC 514-527-8686
Smolich Bros. Home Made Sausage
  Crest Hill, IL 815-727-2144

Mustard
Kathy's Gourmet Specialties
  Mendocino, CA 707-937-1383

Onion (See also Spices/Onion Powder)
Advanced Spice & Trading
  Carrollton, TX 800-872-7811
American Key Food Products Inc
  Closter, NJ 877-263-7539
Con Yeager Spice Co
  Zelienople, PA 800-222-2460
Emerling International Foods
  Buffalo, NY 716-833-7381
Erba Food Products
  Brooklyn, NY 718-272-7700
Gel Spice Co LLC
  Bayonne, NJ 800-922-0230
Texas Coffee Co
  Beaumont, TX 800-259-3400
Vegetable Juices Inc
  Chicago, IL 888-776-9752

Pau D'Arco Bark
Asiamerica Ingredients
  Westwood, NJ 201-497-5531
RFi Ingredients
  Blauvelt, NY 800-962-7663

Peanut Butter
Crazy Richard's
  Dublin, OH 614-889-4824

Prepared for Further Processing
Akay USA LLC
  Sayreville, NJ 732-254-7177

Protein
Clif Bar & Co
  Emeryville, CA 802-254-3227
Fonterra Co-operative Group Limited
  Chicago, IL 888-869-6455
Kiss My Keto
  Los Angeles, CA 310-765-1553
Lekithos
  Palm Beach Gardens, FL
LonoLife
  Oceanside, CA 855-843-8566
Onnit Labs
  Austin, TX 855-666-4899
Terra Origin, Inc.
  Hauppauge, NY 631-300-2306

Product Categories / Ingredients, Flavors & Additives: Preservatives

Universal Nutrition
   New Brunswick, NJ 800-872-0101
Wisconsin Specialty Protein
   Madison, WI
Zego Foods
   San Francisco, CA 415-706-8094

Saw Palmetto Berry

Asiamerica Ingredients
   Westwood, NJ 201-497-5531
RFi Ingredients
   Blauvelt, NY 800-962-7663

Seafood

American Key Food Products Inc
   Closter, NJ 877-263-7539
Flavor House, Inc.
   Adelanto, CA .760-246-9131

Seasoning

Advanced Food Services
   Lenexa, KS 913-888-8088
American Key Food Products Inc
   Closter, NJ 877-263-7539
Gel Spice Co LLC
   Bayonne, NJ .800-922-0230
Magic Seasoning Blends
   New Orleans, LA 800-457-2857
Summit Hill Flavors
   Somerset, NJ .732-805-0335
Vegetable Juices Inc
   Chicago, IL 888-776-9752

Soy Milk

Cedar Lake Foods
   Cedar Lake, MI 800-246-5039

St. John's Wort

RFi Ingredients
   Blauvelt, NY 800-962-7663

Tofu

Aloha Tofu Factory Inc
   Honolulu, HI 808-845-2669
Clofine Dairy Products Inc
   Linwood, NJ 609-653-1000
Dixie USA
   Tomball, TX 800-233-3668

Tomato

Henry Broch & Co
   Gurnee, IL 847-816-6225

Valerian Root

Asiamerica Ingredients
   Westwood, NJ 201-497-5531
RFi Ingredients
   Blauvelt, NY 800-962-7663

Vanilla

Agri-Dairy Products
   Purchase, NY 914-697-9580
Carmi Flavor & Fragrance Company
   Commerce, CA 800-421-9647
Emerling International Foods
   Buffalo, NY 716-833-7381
H B Taylor Co
   Chicago, IL 773-254-4805
Helm New York Chemical Corp
   Piscataway, NJ 732-981-0528
Prime Ingredients Inc
   Saddle Brook, NJ 888-791-6655
Sterling Extract Co Inc
   Franklin Park, IL 847-451-9728
Sunfood
   El Cajon, CA .888-729-3663
Whole Herb Co
   Sonoma, CA .707-935-1077

Yogurt

Commercial Creamery Co
   Spokane, WA .509-747-4131
Kantner Group
   Wapakoneta, OH 877-738-3448
Maple Island
   Saint Paul, MN 800-369-1022
Master Mix
   Placentia, CA .714-524-1698

Quality Ingredients
   Burnsville, MN 952-898-4002

Preservatives

Atlantic Chemicals Trading
   Glendale, CA .818-246-0077
Emerald Performance Materials
   Cuyahoga Falls, OH 330-916-6700
Escalade Limited
   Huntington, NY 631-659-3373
Grace & I
   Los Angeles, CA 800-584-1736
Great Earth Chemical
   Portland, OR .503-620-7130
Kenko International
   Los Angeles, CA 323-721-8300
Profood International
   Naperville, IL .888-288-0081
Simply Panache
   Hampton, VA .800-313-5613

Food

Brenntag North America
   Reading, PA .610-926-6100
Cargill Inc.
   Minneapolis, MN 800-227-4455
Emerald Kalama Chemical, LLC
   Kalama, WA .800-223-0035
FBC Industries
   Schaumburg, IL 888-322-4637
Hosemen & Roche Vitamins & Fine Chemicals
   Nutley, NJ 800-526-6367
Hurd Orchards
   Holley, NY 585-638-8838
Jarchem Industries
   Newark, NJ 973-578-4560
Jungbunzlauer Inc
   Newton, MA .617-969-0900
Kent Precision Foods Group Inc
   Muscatine, IA 800-442-5242
Macco Organiques
   Valleyfield, QC 450-371-1066
Nutricepts
   Burnsville, MN 800-949-9060
Parish Chemical Company
   Orem, UT 801-226-2018
PMC Specialties Group Inc
   Cincinnati, OH 800-543-2466
Shekou Chemicals
   Waltham, MA .781-893-6878
Silver Fern Chemical Inc
   Seattle, WA 866-282-3384
Tasty Mix Quality Foods
   Brooklyn, NY .718-855-7680
Universal Preservachem Inc
   Somerset, NJ .732-568-1266
Wisconsin Wilderness Food Products
   Lake Bluff, IL .800-359-3039

Proteins

AME Nutrition
   Dublin, OH 614-766-3638
American Pasien Co
   Burlington, NJ 609-387-3130
BioExx Specialty Proteins
   Toronto, ON 416-588-4442
Clara Foods
   San Francisco, CA
Clofine Dairy Products Inc
   Linwood, NJ 609-653-1000
Essentia Protein Solutions
   Ankeny, IA 515-289-5100
Fonterra Co-operative Group Limited
   Chicago, IL 888-869-6455
Ingredia Inc
   Wapakoneta, OH 419-738-4060
International Food Products
   Fenton, MO 800-227-8427
Kantner Group
   Wapakoneta, OH 877-738-3448
Milk Specialties Global
   Eden Prairie, MN 952-942-7310

Releases

Food

Barlean's Fisheries
   Ferndale, WA .360-384-0325
Capri Bagel & Pizza Corporation
   Brooklyn, NY .718-497-4431

Cloud Nine
   Claremont, CA 909-624-3147
Corn Popper
   Tulsa, OK 918-250-9317
Desert King International
   San Diego, CA 800-982-2235
EcoNatural Solutions
   Boulder, CO 303-357-5682
Ferris Organic Farms
   Eaton Rapids, MI 800-628-8736
Flavorganics
   Newark, NJ 866-972-6879
Ingredient Innovations
   Kansas City, MO 816-587-1426
Jewel Date Co
   Thermal, CA .760-399-4474
Leech Lake Wild Rice
   Cass Lake, MN 218-335-8200
Lone Pine Enterprise Inc
   Carlisle, AR 870-552-3217
Lowell Farms
   El Campo, TX 888-484-9213
Marantha Natural Foods
   San Francisco, CA 866-972-6879
Martha Olson's Great Foo
   Sutter Creek, CA 800-973-3966
Montana Specialty Mills LLC
   Great Falls, MT 800-332-2024
Nicola Valley Apiaries
   Merritt, BC 250-378-5208
S & E Organic Farms Inc
   Bakersfield, CA 661-325-2644
Southern Brown Rice
   Weiner, AR 800-421-7423
Stengel Seed & Grain Co
   Milbank, SD 605-432-6030
Sunnyland Mills
   Fresno, CA 800-501-8017
Top Hat Co Inc
   Wilmette, IL 847-256-6565
US Mills
   Bala Cynwyd, PA 800-422-1125

Replacers

Savoury Systems Inc
   Branchburg, NJ 888-534-6621

Egg

Clara Foods
   San Francisco, CA

Fat

Edlong Corporation
   Elk Grove Village, IL 847-631-6700
Epogee
   Indianapolis, IN

Raisin Juice

Dry

Cajun Brands
   New Iberia, LA 504-408-2252

Sodium

Asiamerica Ingredients
   Westwood, NJ 201-497-5531
Erie Foods Intl Inc
   Erie, IL 309-659-2233
Gum Technology Corporation
   Tucson, AZ 800-369-4867
International Food Products
   Fenton, MO 800-227-8427
Jungbunzlauer Inc
   Newton, MA .617-969-0900
Nu-Tek Food Science
   Minnetouka, MN 952-683-7580
Nutricepts
   Burnsville, MN 800-949-9060
PMP Fermentation Products
   Peoria, IL 800-558-1031
Trumark
   Linden, NJ 800-752-7877

Sodium Alginates

Asiamerica Ingredients
   Westwood, NJ 201-497-5531
Gum Technology Corporation
   Tucson, AZ 800-369-4867

Product Categories / Ingredients, Flavors & Additives: Sodium Benzoate

PLT Health Solutions Inc
   Morristown, NJ 973-984-0900
TIC Gums
   Belcamp, MD 800-899-3953

Sodium Benzoate

Agri-Dairy Products
   Purchase, NY 914-697-9580
Asiamerica Ingredients
   Westwood, NJ 201-497-5531
Cargill Inc.
   Minneapolis, MN 800-227-4455
Emerald Kalama Chemical, LLC
   Kalama, WA 800-223-0035
Jarchem Industries
   Newark, NJ 973-578-4560
Jungbunzlauer Inc
   Newton, MA 617-969-0900
Luyties Pharmacal Company
   Saint Louis, MO 800-325-8080
Shekou Chemicals
   Waltham, MA 781-893-6878
Silver Fern Chemical Inc
   Seattle, WA 866-282-3384
Universal Preservachem Inc
   Somerset, NJ 732-568-1266

Sodium Citrate

Asiamerica Ingredients
   Westwood, NJ 201-497-5531
Cargill Inc.
   Minneapolis, MN 800-227-4455
International Chemical Corp
   Melbourne, FL 800-914-2436
Jungbunzlauer Inc
   Newton, MA 617-969-0900
Shekou Chemicals
   Waltham, MA 781-893-6878
Universal Preservachem Inc
   Somerset, NJ 732-568-1266

Sodium Lactate

Hawkins Inc
   Roseville, MN 800-328-5460

Spirulina

Alternative Health & Herbs
   Albany, OR 800-345-4152
Asiamerica Ingredients
   Westwood, NJ 201-497-5531
Christopher's Herb Shop
   Springville, UT 888-372-4372
Cyanotech Corp
   Kailua Kona, HI 800-395-1353
Earth Circle Organics
   Auburn, CA 877-922-3663

Stabilizers

King Arthur Flour
   Norwich, VT 800-827-6836
Marukan Vinegar USA Inc.
   Paramount, CA 562-630-6060
PLT Health Solutions Inc
   Morristown, NJ 973-984-0900
Silvateam USA
   Ontario, CA 909-635-2870
Taiyo International Inc.
   Minneapolis, MN 763-398-3003
Tate & Lyle PLC
   Hoffman Estates, IL 847-396-7500
TIC Gums
   Belcamp, MD 800-899-3953
Watson Inc
   West Haven, CT 800-388-3481
Wenda America Inc
   Naperville, IL 844-999-3632

Lecithinated

Agri-Dairy Products
   Purchase, NY 914-697-9580
Arnhem Group
   Cranford, NJ 800-851-1052
New Organics
   Kenwood, CA 734-677-5570
Universal Preservachem Inc
   Somerset, NJ 732-568-1266

Yogurt

Johanna Foods Inc.
   Flemington, NJ 800-727-6700
Maple Island
   Saint Paul, MN 800-369-1022

Starches

Anderson Custom Processing
   New Ulm, MN. 877-588-4950
Cargill Inc.
   Minneapolis, MN 800-227-4455
Evergreen Sweeteners, Inc
   Hollywood, FL 954-381-7776
Marroquin Organic Intl.
   Santa Cruz, CA 831-423-3442
Marsan Foods
   Toronto, ON 416-755-9262
National Starch Food Innovation
   Bridgewater, NJ 800-743-6343
Norben Co
   Willoughby, OH 888-466-7236
Raymond-Hadley Corporation
   Spencer, NY 800-252-5220
Roquette America Inc.
   Geneva, IL. 630-463-9430
Seydel Co
   Pendergrass, GA 706-693-2266
St. Lawrence Starch
   Mississauga, ON 905-271-8396
Tate & Lyle PLC
   Hoffman Estates, IL 847-396-7500
Westin Foods
   Omaha, NE 800-228-6098

Arrowroot

American Key Food Products Inc
   Closter, NJ. 877-263-7539

Corn

American Key Food Products Inc
   Closter, NJ. 877-263-7539
Evergreen Sweeteners, Inc
   Hollywood, FL 954-381-7776
GloryBee
   Eugene, OR 800-456-7923
Grain Processing Corp
   Muscatine, IA 800-448-4472
Hodgson Mill Inc
   Effingham, IL. 800-347-0198
Ingredion Inc.
   Westchester, IL 800-713-0208
International Food Products
   Fenton, MO. 800-227-8427
Meelunie America
   Farmington Hills, MI 248-473-2100
Mills Brothers Intl
   Seattle, WA 206-575-3000
Nacan Products
   Brampton, ON. 905-454-4466
New Organics
   Kenwood, CA 734-677-5570
Westin Foods
   Omaha, NE 800-228-6098

Dextrin

Seydel Co
   Pendergrass, GA 706-693-2266

Potato

Homefree LLC
   Windham, NH. 800-552-7172
International Food Products
   Fenton, MO. 800-227-8427
King Arthur Flour
   Norwich, VT 800-827-6836
VCPB Transportation
   Secaucus, NJ 201-770-0070

Rice

American Key Food Products Inc
   Closter, NJ. 877-263-7539
Avebe America Inc.
   Cranbury, NJ 609-865-8981
International Food Products
   Fenton, MO. 800-227-8427

Tapioca

Homefree LLC
   Windham, NH. 800-552-7172
King Arthur Flour
   Norwich, VT 800-827-6836

Wheat

Caremoli USA
   Ames, IA 515-233-1255
International Food Products
   Fenton, MO. 800-227-8427

Surfactants & Solubilizers

Stepan Co.
   Northfield, IL 847-446-7500

Solubilizers

PLT Health Solutions Inc
   Morristown, NJ 973-984-0900

Sweeteners

Agri-Dairy Products
   Purchase, NY 914-697-9580
Atlantic Chemicals Trading
   Glendale, CA 818-246-0077
Catherych
   Warren, NJ 732-566-6625
Dulcette Technologies
   Lindenhurst, NY 631-752-8700
Escalade Limited
   Huntington, NY 631-659-3373
Evergreen Sweeteners, Inc
   Hollywood, FL 954-381-7776
GLG Life Tech Corporation
   Vancouver, BC 604-669-2602
GLG Life Tech Corporation
   Richmond, BC 855-454-7587
H&A Health Products, Inc
   Richmond Hill, ON 514-979-3589
Helm New York Chemical Corp
   Piscataway, NJ 732-981-0528
Ingredient Specialties
   Exeter, CA 559-594-4380
International Food Products
   Fenton, MO. 800-227-8427
J M Swank Co
   North Liberty, IA 800-593-6375
Kenko International
   Los Angeles, CA. 323-721-8300
Log House Foods
   Plymouth, MN 763-546-8395
Louisiana Sugar Cane Cooperative
   St Martinville, LA 337-394-3785
Marroquin Organic Intl.
   Santa Cruz, CA 831-423-3442
Natur Sweeteners, Inc.
   Los Angeles, CA 310-445-0020
NOW Foods
   Bloomingdale, IL 888-669-3663
Rare Hawaiian Honey Company
   Kamuela, HI 888-663-6639
Rio Naturals
   El Dorado Hills, CA 916-719-4514
Stauber Performance Ingrdients
   Fullerton, CA 888-441-4233
Sweet'N Low
   Brooklyn, NY
Sweetleaf Co
   Gilbert, AZ 480-921-2160
Techno Food Ingredients Co., Ltd
   San Gabriel, CA 626-288-8478
Wenda America Inc
   Naperville, IL 844-999-3632
Wildly Organic
   Silver Bay, MN 800-945-3801

Dextrose

Agri-Dairy Products
   Purchase, NY 914-697-9580
Cargill Inc.
   Minneapolis, MN 800-227-4455
Evergreen Sweeteners, Inc
   Hollywood, FL 954-381-7776
Ingredion Inc.
   Westchester, IL 800-713-0208
Malt Diastase Co
   Saddle Brook, NJ 800-526-0180
Roquette America Inc.
   Geneva, IL. 630-463-9430

Product Categories / Ingredients, Flavors & Additives: Tenderizers

Westin Foods
  Omaha, NE 800-228-6098

Lactose

Agri-Dairy Products
  Purchase, NY 914-697-9580
Asiamerica Ingredients
  Westwood, NJ 201-497-5531
Blossom Farm Products
  Ridgewood, NJ 800-729-1818
Century Foods Intl LLC
  Sparta, WI 800-269-1901
Clofine Dairy Products Inc
  Linwood, NJ 609-653-1000
First District Association
  Litchfield, MN 320-693-3236
Grande Custom Ingredients Group
  Fond du Lac, WI 800-772-3210
Hilmar Ingredients
  Hilmar, CA 888-300-4465
Leprino Foods Co.
  Denver, CO 800-537-7466
Main Street Ingredients
  La Crosse, WI 800-359-2345
Universal Preservachem Inc
  Somerset, NJ 732-568-1266

Sorbitol

Agri-Dairy Products
  Purchase, NY 914-697-9580
Asiamerica Ingredients
  Westwood, NJ 201-497-5531
Roquette America Inc.
  Geneva, IL 630-463-9430
Universal Preservachem Inc
  Somerset, NJ 732-568-1266

Tenderizers

3V Company
  Brooklyn, NY 718-858-7333
AM Todd Co
  Kalamazoo, MI 269-343-2603
Dean Distributors, Inc.
  Burlingame, CA 800-792-0816
Phamous Phloyd's Barbecue
  Denver, CO 800-497-3281
Sentry Seasonings
  Elmhurst, IL 630-530-5370
W.T.I.
  Jefferson, GA 800-827-1727

Meat

3V Company
  Brooklyn, NY 718-858-7333
Alltech Inc
  Nicholasville, KY 859-885-9613
AM Todd Co
  Kalamazoo, MI 269-343-2603
American Key Food Products Inc
  Closter, NJ. 877-263-7539
Custom Culinary Inc.
  Schaumberg, IL. 800-621-8827
Enzyme Development Corporation
  New York, NY 212-736-1580
Oregon Flavor Rack
Sentry Seasonings
  Elmhurst, IL 630-530-5370
Texas Coffee Co
  Beaumont, TX 800-259-3400
World Flavors Inc
  Warminster, PA 215-672-4400

Thickeners

Gelnex Gelatins
  Chicago, IL 312-577-4275

Gelatin

Asiamerica Ingredients
  Westwood, NJ 201-497-5531
Cangel
  Toronto, ON 800-267-4795
Con Yeager Spice Co
  Zelienople, PA 800-222-2460
Erba Food Products
  Brooklyn, NY 718-272-7700
First Food Co
  Dallas, TX 800-527-1866
Gelita North America
  Sergeant Bluff, IA 800-223-9244

Gelnex Gelatins
  Chicago, IL 312-577-4275
Golden Fluff Popcorn Co
  Lakewood, NJ 732-367-5448
Inter-American Products
  Cincinnati, OH 800-645-2233
Marquez Brothers International
  Hanford, CA 800-858-1119
Milligan & Higgins
  Johnstown, NY 518-762-4638
Nature's Products Inc
  Sunrise, FL 800-752-7873
Nitta Gelatin NA
  Morrisville, NC 800-278-7680
PB Leiner USA
  Plainview, NY 516-822-4040
Protica Inc
  Whitehall, PA 800-776-8422
Qualicaps Inc
  Whitsett, NC 800-227-7853
Rousselot Inc
  Mukwonago, WI 888-455-3556
SKW Nature Products
  Langhorne, PA 215-702-1000
Spring Glen Fresh Foods
  Ephrata, PA 800-641-2853
Tessenderlo Kerley Inc
  Phoenix, AZ 800-669-0559
Tova Industries LLC
  Louisville, KY 888-532-8682
Vital Proteins LLC
  Elk Grove Village, IL 224-544-9110
Vyse Gelatin Co
  Schiller Park, IL 800-533-2152
White Coffee Corporation
  Long Island City, NY 800-221-0140

Toppings

Al-Rite Fruits & Syrups Co
  Miami, FL 305-652-2540
Bake N Joy Foods
  North Andover, MA 800-666-4937
Baldwin Richardson Foods
  Oakbrook Terrace, IL 866-644-2732
Consolidated Mills Inc
  Houston, TX 713-896-4196
Dark Tickle Company
  St Lunaire-Griquet, NL. 709-623-2354
Golden State Foods Corp
  Irvine, CA 949-247-8000
Gumpert's Canada
  Mississauga, ON 800-387-9324
Instant Products of America
  Columbus, IN 812-372-9100
Kerry Foodservice
  Mansfield, OH 800-533-2722
Paulaur Corp
  Cranbury, NJ 609-395-8844
Phillips Syrup Corp
  Cleveland, OH 800-350-8443
Presto Avoset Group
  Claremont, CA 909-399-0062
Scala-Wisell International Inc.
  Floral Park, NY 516-437-8600
Shine Companies
  Spring, TX. 281-353-8392

Cakes & Donuts

Signature Brands LLC
  Ocala, FL 800-456-9573

Confectionery

Paulaur Corp
  Cranbury, NJ 609-395-8844
Ribble Production
  Warminster, PA 215-674-1706

Crunch

American Almond Products Co
  Brooklyn, NY 800-825-6663
Paulaur Corp
  Cranbury, NJ 609-395-8844

Dessert

3V Company
  Brooklyn, NY 718-858-7333
Al-Rite Fruits & Syrups Co
  Miami, FL 305-652-2540
American Almond Products Co
  Brooklyn, NY 800-825-6663

American Classic Ice Cream Company
  Bay Shore, NY 800-736-4100
Aunt Aggie De's Pralines
  Sinton, TX. 800-333-9354
Baldwin Richardson Foods
  Oakbrook Terrace, IL 866-644-2732
Brighams
  Arlington, MA 800-242-2423
Calhoun Bend Mill
  Libuse, LA 800-519-6455
California Balsamic Inc
  Ukiah, CA 888-644-5127
California Custom Foods
  Fullerton, CA 714-870-0490
California Custom Fruits
  Baldwin Park, CA 877-558-0056
Carole's Cheesecake Company
  Toronto, ON 416-256-0000
Chocolaterie Bernard Callebaut
  Calgary, AB. 800-661-8367
Conagra Brands Inc
  Chicago, IL 877-266-2472
Conagra Foodservice
  Chicago, IL 877-266-2472
Consolidated Mills Inc
  Houston, TX 713-896-4196
Country Fresh Food & Confections, Inc.
  Oliver Springs, TN 800-545-8782
Creme Unlimited
  Matteson, IL 800-227-3637
Durkee-Mower
  Lynn, MA 781-593-8007
Felbro Food Products
  Los Angeles, CA 323-936-5266
Gold Coast Ingredients
  Commerce, CA 800-352-8673
Golden West Fruit Company
  Commerce, CA 323-726-9419
H Fox & Co Inc
  Brooklyn, NY 718-385-4600
Hanan Products Co
  Hicksville, NY 516-938-1000
Homemade By Dorothy Boise
  Boise, ID 800-657-7449
I Rice & Co Inc
  Philadelphia, PA 800-232-6022
Instant Products of America
  Columbus, IN 812-372-9100
Instantwhip Foods Inc
  Columbus, OH 800-544-9447
J.M. Smucker Co.
  Orrville, OH 888-550-9555
JER Creative Food Concepts, Inc.
  Commerce, CA 800-350-2462
Jogue Inc
  Northville, MI 800-531-3888
Johnson's Food Products
  Dorchester, MA. 617-265-3400
Kraus & Co
  Irvine, CA 800-662-5871
Lyons Magnus
  Fresno, CA 800-344-7130
Masterson Co Inc
  Milwaukee, WI 414-647-1132
Michigan Desserts
  Oak Park, MI. 800-328-8632
Newport Flavours & Fragrances
  Orange, CA. 714-744-3700
Oak State Products Inc
  Wenona, IL 815-853-4348
Oregon Hill Farms
  St Helens, OR 800-243-4541
Parker Products
  Fort Worth, TX 817-336-7441
Paulaur Corp
  Cranbury, NJ 609-395-8844
Pearson's Berry Farm
  Bowden, AB 403-224-3011
Pecan Deluxe Candy Co
  Dallas, TX. 800-733-3589
Phillips Syrup Corp
  Cleveland, OH 800-350-8443
Rich Products Corp
  Buffalo, NY 800-828-2021
Rosebrand Corp
  Brooklyn, NY 800-854-5356
Rowena
  Norfolk, VA. 800-627-8699
Sea Breeze Fruit Flavors
  Towaco, NJ 800-732-2733
Somebody's Mother's Chocolate
  Houston, TX 713-627-3055

Product Categories / Ingredients, Flavors & Additives: Vitamins & Supplements

Sonoma Syrup Co. Inc.
  Sonoma, CA 707-996-4070
Spruce Mountain Blueberries
  West Rockport, ME. 207-236-3538
Steel's Gourmet Foods, Ltd.
  Bridgeport, PA 800-678-3357
Swatt Baking Co
  Olean, NY .800-370-6656
The Great San Saba River Pecan Company
  San Saba, TX 800-621-8121
Tiller Foods Company
  Dayton, OH. 937-435-4601
Tom & Sally's Handmade Chocolates
  Brattleboro, VT. 800-827-0800
Tone Products Inc
  Melrose Park, IL 800-536-8663
Top Hat Co Inc
  Wilmette, IL 847-256-6565
Tropical Foods
  Lithia Springs, GA 800-544-3762
Valley Grain Products
  Fresno, CA 559-675-3400
Wax Orchards
  Seattle, WA 800-634-6132
Western Syrup Company
  Santa Fe Springs, CA 562-921-4485
White-Stokes Company
  Chicago, IL. 800-978-6537
Williamsburg Chocolatier
  Williamsburg, VA 757-253-1474

Fruit
E.D. Smith Foods Ltd
  Hamilton, ON 905-573-1207

Meringue
Zuccaro Produce
  Columbia Heights, MN. 612-333-1122

Sprinkles
Erba Food Products
  Brooklyn, NY 718-272-7700
King Arthur Flour
  Norwich, VT. 800-827-6836
Weaver Nut Co. Inc.
  Ephrata, PA. 800-473-2688

Whipped
Bunge Canada
  Oakville, ON. 905-825-7900
CanAmera Foods
  Edmonton, AL. 780-447-6960
Fieldbrook Foods Corp.
  Dunkirk, NY. 800-333-0805
Johnson's Food Products
  Dorchester, MA. 617-265-3400
Now & Zen
  Louisville, CO. 800-779-6383
Rich Products Corp
  Buffalo, NY. 800-828-2021
Schneider's Dairy Inc
  Pittsburgh, PA. 412-881-3525
Tiller Foods Company
  Dayton, OH. 937-435-4601

Dairy
Brighams
  Arlington, MA 800-242-2423
Elgin Dairy Foods
  Chicago, IL. 800-786-9900
Instantwhip Foods Inc
  Columbus, OH 800-544-9447
Johnson's Food Products
  Dorchester, MA. 617-265-3400

Non-Dairy
Elgin Dairy Foods
  Chicago, IL. 800-786-9900
Instantwhip Foods Inc
  Columbus, OH 800-544-9447
Johnson's Food Products
  Dorchester, MA. 617-265-3400

Vitamins & Supplements
Aloecorp, Inc.
  Seattle, WA 800-458-2563
Embria Health Sciences
  Ankeny, IA 877-362-7421
Fallwood Corp
  White Plains, NY 914-304-4065
Fenchem Inc
  Chino, CA. 909-597-1113
Great Earth Chemical
  Portland, OR 503-620-7130
Latitude, LTD
  Huntington, NY 631-659-3374

A
Asiamerica Ingredients
  Westwood, NJ 201-497-5531
Banner Pharmacaps
  High Point, NC 800-526-6993
Dong Us I
  Irvine, CA 888-580-0088
Ganeden, Inc
  Mayfield Hts, OH 440-229-5200
New Hope Natural Media
  Boulder, CO 303-939-8440
Synergy Plus
  Freehold, NJ 732-308-3000

B1 - Thiamine
Prinova
  Carol Stream, IL 630-868-0300

B12
Prinova
  Carol Stream, IL 630-868-0300

B2 - Riboflavin
Prinova
  Carol Stream, IL 630-868-0300

B5
Prinova
  Carol Stream, IL 630-868-0300

B6 - Pyridoxine
Prinova
  Carol Stream, IL 630-868-0300

Beta Carotene
Asiamerica Ingredients
  Westwood, NJ 201-497-5531

Biotin
Asiamerica Ingredients
  Westwood, NJ 201-497-5531

C
Asiamerica Ingredients
  Westwood, NJ 201-497-5531
Childlife
  Culver City, CA 800-993-0332
Marlyn Nutraceuticals
  Phoenix, AZ 800-899-4499
Prinova
  Carol Stream, IL 630-868-0300

Ascorbic Acid
World Ginseng Ctr Inc
  San Francisco, CA 800-747-8808

Calcium
Allied Custom Gypsum Company
  Norman, OK. 800-624-5963
American Micronutrients
  Independence, MO 816-252-1060
Asiamerica Ingredients
  Westwood, NJ 201-497-5531
Specialty Minerals Inc
  Bethlehem, PA 800-801-1031

E - Tocopherol
Asiamerica Ingredients
  Westwood, NJ 201-497-5531
World Ginseng Ctr Inc
  San Francisco, CA 800-747-8808

Inositol
Asiamerica Ingredients
  Westwood, NJ 201-497-5531
Tabco Enterprises
  Pomona, CA 909-623-4565

Medical Nutritionals
Alternative Health & Herbs
  Albany, OR. 800-345-4152
Apotheca Inc
  Woodbine, IA 800-736-3130
Asiamerica Ingredients
  Westwood, NJ 201-497-5531
Atrium Biotech
  Quebec, QC. 418-652-1116
Brenntag North America
  Reading, PA 610-926-6100
Champion Nutrition Inc
  Sunrise, FL 800-225-4831
Chattem Chemicals Inc
  Chattanooga, TN. 423-822-5000
Eatem Foods Co
  Vineland, NJ 800-683-2836
Green Turtle Bay Vitamin Company
  Summit, NJ 800-887-8535
Penta Manufacturing Company
  Livingston, NJ 973-740-2300
Tova Industries LLC
  Louisville, KY 888-532-8682
Westar Nutrition Corporation
  Costa Mesa, CA 800-645-1868

Mineral Blends
Asiamerica Ingredients
  Westwood, NJ 201-497-5531
Coral LLC
  Carson City, NV 800-882-9577
M-CAP Technologies
  Wilmington, DE 302-695-5329
World Nutrition, Inc.
  Scottsdale, AZ. 800-548-2710

Minerals
Acta Health Products
  Sunnyvale, CA 408-732-6830
ADH Health Products Inc
  Congers, NY 845-268-0027
Alacer Corp
  Carlisle, PA 888-425-2362
Alta Health Products
  Idaho City, ID 800-423-4155
Ameri-Kal Inc
  Wichita Falls, TX 940-322-5400
Anabol Naturals
  Santa Cruz, CA 800-426-2265
Asiamerica Ingredients
  Westwood, NJ 201-497-5531
Beverly International
  Cold Spring, KY 800-781-3475
Bio-Tech Pharmacal Inc
  Fayetteville, AR 800-345-1199
Brenntag North America
  Reading, PA 610-926-6100
Champion Nutrition Inc
  Sunrise, FL 800-225-4831
Childlife
  Culver City, CA 800-993-0332
Coral LLC
  Carson City, NV 800-882-9577
Designed Nutritional Products
  Orem, UT 801-224-4518
DSM Fortitech Premixes
  Schenectady, NY
Eidon
  Poway, CA. 800-700-1169
Grow Co
  Ridgefield, NJ 201-941-8777
Healthy N Fit International
  Croton On Hudson, NY 800-338-5200
Herbal Products & Development
  Aptos, CA. 831-688-8706
J R Carlson Laboratories Inc
  Arlington Heights, IL 888-234-5656
Jamieson Laboratories
  Windsor, ON. 800-265-5088
Jungbunzlauer Inc
  Newton, MA 617-969-0900
Marlyn Nutraceuticals
  Phoenix, AZ 800-899-4499
Michael's Naturopathic Prgms
  San Antonio, TX. 800-845-2730
Milwhite Inc
  Brownsville, TX 800-442-0082
Naturalife Laboratories
  Torrance, CA 800-231-3670
Nature Most Laboratories
  Middletown, CT 800-234-2112

Product Categories / Ingredients, Flavors & Additives: Vitamins & Supplements

Nature's Bounty Co.
  Ronkonkoma, NY 877-774-3361
Nature's Sunshine Products Company
  Lehi, UT 800-223-8225
NOW Foods
  Bloomingdale, IL 888-669-3663
Nutricepts
  Burnsville, MN 800-949-9060
Nutritech Corporation
  Santa Barbara, CA 800-235-5727
Nutrition 21 Inc
  Purchase, NY 914-701-4500
Particle Dynamics
  Saint Louis, MO 800-452-4682
Performance Labs
  Calabasas, CA 800-848-2537
PLT Health Solutions Inc
  Morristown, NJ 973-984-0900
PMP Fermentation Products
  Peoria, IL 800-558-1031
Pro Pac Labs
  Ogden, UT 888-277-6722
Protein Research
  Livermore, CA 800-948-1991
Randal Optimal Nutrients
  Santa Rosa, CA 800-221-1697
San Francisco Salt
  Hayward, CA 800-480-4540
Seppic Inc
  Fairfield, NJ 877-737-7421
Universal Formulas
  Kalamazoo, MI 800-342-6960
US Foods & Pharmaceuticals Inc
  Madison, WI 800-362-8294
USA Laboratories Inc
  Burns, TN 800-489-4872

Niacin

Asiamerica Ingredients
  Westwood, NJ 201-497-5531
Nu Naturals Inc
  Eugene, OR 800-753-4372

Nutraceuticals

Amcan Industries
  Elmsford, NY 914-347-4838
AquaTec Development
  Sugar Land, TX 281-491-0808
Asiamerica Ingredients
  Westwood, NJ 201-497-5531
BASF Corp.
  Florham Park, NJ 800-526-1072
Bio-Foods
  Pine Brook, NJ 973-808-5856
Bio-Tech Pharmacal Inc
  Fayetteville, AR 800-345-1199
BioTech Corporation
  Glastonbury, CT 800-886-9052
Brenntag North America
  Reading, PA 610-926-6100
Century Foods Intl LLC
  Sparta, WI 800-269-1901
Cyanotech Corp
  Kailua Kona, HI 800-395-1353
Dulcette Technologies
  Lindenhurst, NY 631-752-8700
Embria Health Sciences
  Ankeny, IA 877-362-7421
Fallwood Corp
  White Plains, NY 914-304-4065
Farbest-Tallman Foods Corp
  Montvale, NJ 201-573-4900
GloryBee
  Eugene, OR 800-456-7923
Jarrow Industries Inc
  Santa Fe Springs, CA 562-906-1919
Lallemand Inc
  Montreal, QC 800-452-4364
Natra US
  Chula Vista, CA 800-262-6216
Naturex Inc
  South Hackensack, NJ 201-440-5000
Nutraceutics Corp
  St Louis, MO 877-664-6684
Nutranique Labs
  Santa Rosa, CA 707-545-9017
PLT Health Solutions Inc
  Morristown, NJ 973-984-0900
QBI
  South Plainfield, NJ 908-668-0088

Soluble Products Company
  Lakewood, NJ 732-364-8855
SoyLife Division
  Edina, MN 952-920-7700
Trans-Packers Svc Corp
  Brooklyn, NY 877-787-8837
Unique Ingredients LLC
  Gold Canyon, AZ 480-983-2498
Vitakem Neutraceutical Inc
  Smithtown, NY 855-837-0430
Vitarich Laboratories
  Naples, FL 800-817-9999
Vivolac Cultures Corporation
  Indianapolis, IN 317-356-8460
Westar Nutrition Corporation
  Costa Mesa, CA 800-645-1868

Nutritional Supplements

ADH Health Products Inc
  Congers, NY 845-268-0027
Alfer Laboratories
  Chatsworth, CA 818-709-0737
Ameri-Kal Inc
  Wichita Falls, TX 940-322-5400
American Health
  Ronkonkoma, NY 800-445-7137
Anabol Naturals
  Santa Cruz, CA 800-426-2265
Arizona Natural Products
  Phoenix, AZ 800-255-2823
Arizona Nutritional Supplements
  Chandler, AZ 888-742-7675
Asiamerica Ingredients
  Westwood, NJ 201-497-5531
Atrium Biotech
  Quebec, QC 418-652-1116
Belmont Chemicals
  Clifton, NJ 800-722-5070
Bio-Foods
  Pine Brook, NJ 973-808-5856
BioSynergy
  Boise, ID 800-554-7145
Brickerlabs.Com
  Chandler, AZ 800-274-2537
Bristol-Myers Squibb Co.
  New York, NY 800-332-2056
Century Foods Intl LLC
  Sparta, WI 800-269-1901
Champion Nutrition Inc
  Sunrise, FL 800-225-4831
Cognis
  Cincinnati, OH 800-526-1072
Cyanotech Corp
  Kailua Kona, HI 800-395-1353
Dean Distributors, Inc.
  Burlingame, CA 800-792-0816
Dr. Christopher's Herbal Supplements
  Spanish Fork, UT 800-453-1406
Embria Health Sciences
  Ankeny, IA 877-362-7421
Esteem Products
  Bellevue, WA 800-255-7631
Fallwood Corp
  White Plains, NY 914-304-4065
Food Sciences Corp
  Mt Laurel, NJ 800-346-4422
Foodscience Corp
  Essex Junction, VT 800-874-9444
Genisoy
  San Francisco, CA 866-972-6879
Herbal Products & Development
  Aptos, CA 831-688-8706
I-Health Inc
  Cromwell, CT 800-990-3476
Klaire Laboratories
  Reno, NV 888-488-2488
Lewis Laboratories International Ltd.
  Southport, CT 800-243-6020
Lifestar Millennium
  Sedona, AZ 877-422-4739
Lifestyle Health Guide
  Cheyenne, WY 800-822-3712
Matrix Health Products
  Santee, CA 888-736-5609
Mega Pro Intl
  St George, UT 800-541-9469
Metagenics, Inc.
  Aliso Viejo, CA 800-692-9400
Mushroom Wisdom, Inc
  East Rutherford, NJ 800-747-7418
N D Labs
  Lynbrook, NY 888-263-5227

Natural Balance
  Englewood, CO 800-624-4260
Naturalife Laboratories
  Torrance, CA 800-231-3670
Naturally Scientific
  Leonia, NJ 888-428-0700
Nature's Best Inc
  Hauppauge, NY 800-345-2378
Nature's Nutrition
  Marysville, OH 800-242-1115
New Horizon Foods
  Union City, CA 510-489-8600
Nurture
  Devon, PA 888-395-3300
Nutrition Center Inc
  Douglas, WY 800-443-3333
Nutrition Supply Corp
  Liberty, TX 888-541-3997
Nutritional Labs Intl
  Missoula, MT 406-273-5493
Nutritional Specialties
  Orange, CA 800-333-6168
O'Donnell Formulas Inc
  San Marcos, CA 800-736-1991
Orange Peel Enterprises
  Vero Beach, FL 800-643-1210
P-Bee Products
  Oak Harbor, WA 800-322-5572
Pacific Nutritional
  Vancouver, WA 360-896-2297
Pacific Standard Distributors
  Sandy, OR 760-479-1460
Performance Labs
  Calabasas, CA 800-848-2537
Phoenician Herbals
  Scottsdale, AZ 800-966-8144
Phyto-Technologies
  Woodbine, IA 877-809-3404
Pioneer Nutritional Formula
  Shelburne Falls, MA 800-458-8483
Premier Protein
  Emeryville, CA 888-836-8977
Pro-Source Performance Prods
  Manasquan, NJ 732-528-3260
Protein Research
  Livermore, CA 800-948-1991
Randal Optimal Nutrients
  Santa Rosa, CA 800-221-1697
Royal Products
  Scottsdale, AZ 480-948-2509
Schiff Nutrition International
  Parsippany, NJ 800-526-6251
Shaklee Corp
  Pleasanton, CA 800-742-5533
Soft Cell Technology
  Commerce, CA 800-360-7484
Solgar Vitamin & Herbal
  Leonia, NJ 877-765-4274
St John's Botanicals
  Bowie, MD 301-262-5302
Stimo-O-Stam, Ltd.
  Covington, LA 800-562-7514
Tabco Enterprises
  Pomona, CA 909-623-4565
Twinlab Corporation
  Boca Raton, FL 800-645-5626
Uas Laboratories
  Eden Prairie, MN 800-422-3371
USA Laboratories Inc
  Burns, TN 800-489-4872
Vita-Pure Inc
  Roselle, NJ 908-245-1212
Vitatech Nutritional Sciences
  Tustin, CA 714-832-9700
Wakunaga Of America Co LTD
  Mission Viejo, CA 800-421-2998
WCC Honey Marketing
  City Of Industry, CA 626-855-3086
Wellesse
  Ferndale, WA 800-232-4005
Wilke International Inc
  Lenexa, KS 800-779-5545
World Ginseng Ctr Inc
  San Francisco, CA 800-747-8808
Zone Perfect Nutrition Company
  Columbus, OH 800-390-6690

Pantothenic Acid

Asiamerica Ingredients
  Westwood, NJ 201-497-5531

Product Categories / Ingredients, Flavors & Additives: Vitamins & Supplements

Protein Supplements

Alkinco
  New York, NY 800-424-7118
Asiamerica Ingredients
  Westwood, NJ 201-497-5531
Belmont Chemicals
  Clifton, NJ 800-722-5070
Bio-Foods
  Pine Brook, NJ 973-808-5856
Croda Inc
  Edison, NJ 732-417-0800
Designer Protein
  Carlsbad, CA 800-337-4463
Energenetics International
  Keokuk, IA 319-535-0760
Hilmar Ingredients
  Hilmar, CA 888-300-4465
Mariner Neptune Fish & Seafood Company
  Winnipeg, NB 800-668-8862
World Ginseng Ctr Inc
  San Francisco, CA 800-747-8808

Supplements

Acta Health Products
  Sunnyvale, CA 408-732-6830
ADH Health Products Inc
  Congers, NY 845-268-0027
Agger Fish Corp
  Brooklyn, NY 718-855-1717
Alfer Laboratories
  Chatsworth, CA 818-709-0737
Alkinco
  New York, NY 800-424-7118
Aloe Farms Inc
  Harlingen, TX 800-262-6771
AMT Labs Inc
  North Salt Lake, UT 801-294-3126
Anabol Naturals
  Santa Cruz, CA 800-426-2265
Archon Vitamin Corp
  Edison, NJ 800-848-0089
Arizona Natural Products
  Phoenix, AZ 800-255-2823
Asiamerica Ingredients
  Westwood, NJ 201-497-5531
Atrium Biotech
  Quebec, QC 418-652-1116
Beehive Botanicals
  Hayward, WI 800-233-4483
Belmont Chemicals
  Clifton, NJ 800-722-5070
Bestco Inc
  Mooresville, NC 704-664-4300
Brassica Protection Products
  Baltimore, MD 866-747-0001
CactuLife, LLC
  Corona Del Mar, CA 800-500-1713
Century Foods Intl LLC
  Sparta, WI 800-269-1901
Champion Nutrition Inc
  Sunrise, FL 800-225-4831
Christopher's Herb Shop
  Springville, UT 888-372-4372
Clear Products Inc.
  San Diego, CA 888-257-2532
Dean Distributors, Inc.
  Burlingame, CA 800-792-0816
Deerland Probiotics & Enzymes
  Kennesaw, GA 800-697-8179
Doctor's Best Inc
  San Clemente, CA 800-333-6977
Eckhart Corporation
  Novato, CA 800-200-4201
En Garde Health Products, Inc.
  Van Nuys, CA 800-955-4633
GCI Nutrients
  Foster City, CA 866-580-6549
Global Health Laboratories
  Amityville, NY 631-777-2134
Good For You America
  Concordia, MO 866-329-5969
Herbal Products & Development
  Aptos, CA 831-688-8706
Heritage Books & Gifts
  Virginia Beach, VA 800-862-2923
Hillestad Pharmaceuticals
  Woodruff, WI 800-535-7742
International Vitamin Corporation
  Freehold, NJ 800-666-8482
J R Carlson Laboratories Inc
  Arlington Heights, IL 888-234-5656
Jo Mar Laboratories
  Campbell, CA 800-538-4545
Kiss My Keto
  Los Angeles, CA 310-765-1553
Lang Pharma Nutrition Inc
  Middletown, RI 401-848-7700
LonoLife
  Oceanside, CA 855-843-8566
Maju Superfoods
  San Diego, CA 619-736-0622
Mantrose-Haeuser Co Inc
  Westport, CT 800-344-4229
MegaFood
  Manchester, NH 800-848-2542
Natural Balance
  Englewood, CO 800-624-4260
Nature's Bounty Co.
  Ronkonkoma, NY 877-774-3361
Nature's Herbs
  Merritt, BC 800-437-2257
Nature's Plus
  Melville, NY 800-645-9500
Nature's Provision Company
  Olivebridge, NY 845-657-6020
Nature's Way
  Green Bay, WI 800-962-8873
Navitas Naturals
  Novato, CA 888-645-4282
New Chapter
  Brattleboro, VT 800-543-7279
Nutraceutical International
  Park City, UT 800-669-8877
Nutricepts
  Burnsville, MN 800-949-9060
Nutritional Counselors of America
  Spencer, TN 931-946-3600
Nutriwest
  Douglas, WY 800-443-3333
O'Donnell Formulas Inc
  San Marcos, CA 800-736-1991
Old Fashioned Natural Products
  Santa Ana, CA 800-552-9045
Onnit Labs
  Austin, TX 855-666-4899
Pharmavite LLC
  Northridge, CA 800-276-2878
Pro Form Labs
  Orinda, CA 707-752-9010
Protein Research
  Livermore, CA 800-948-1991
Randal Optimal Nutrients
  Santa Rosa, CA 800-221-1697
Rejuvila
  Boulder, CO 877-480-4402
Source Naturals
  Scotts Valley, CA 800-815-2333
Tova Industries LLC
  Louisville, KY 888-532-8682
TruBrain
  Santa Monica, CA 650-241-8372
Twinlab Corporation
  Boca Raton, FL 800-645-5626
Universal Nutrition
  New Brunswick, NJ 800-872-0101
Vit-Best Nutrition
  Tustin, CA 714-832-9700
Vita-Pure Inc
  Roselle, NJ 908-245-1212
Vitakem Neutraceutical Inc
  Smithtown, NY 855-837-0430
Vital Choice
  Bellingham, WA 800-608-4825
Vitamer Laboratories
  Irvine, CA 800-432-8355
Vitaminerals
  Glendale, CA 800-432-1856
Wakunaga Of America Co LTD
  Mission Viejo, CA 800-421-2998
Wilke International Inc
  Lenexa, KS 800-779-5545
World Organics Corporation
  Huntington Beach, CA 714-893-0017

Minerals

AMT Labs Inc
  North Salt Lake, UT 801-294-3126
Asiamerica Ingredients
  Westwood, NJ 201-497-5531
Bestco Inc
  Mooresville, NC 704-664-4300
BetterBody Foods & Nutrition LLC
  Lindon, UT 866-404-6582
Jamieson Laboratories
  Windsor, ON 800-265-5088
Matrix Health Products
  Santee, CA 888-736-5609
Nutraceutical International
  Park City, UT 800-669-8877
Nutricepts
  Burnsville, MN 800-949-9060
Protein Research
  Livermore, CA 800-948-1991
Randal Optimal Nutrients
  Santa Rosa, CA 800-221-1697
Watson Inc
  West Haven, CT 800-388-3481

Vitamins

AHD International, LLC
  Atlanta, GA 404-233-4022
Asiamerica Ingredients
  Westwood, NJ 201-497-5531
Foodscience Corp
  Essex Junction, VT 800-874-9444
Freeda Vitamins Inc
  Long Island City, NY 800-777-3737
Garcoa Laboratories Inc
  Calabasas, CA 800-831-4247
Healthy N Fit International
  Croton On Hudson, NY 800-338-5200
International Vitamin Corporation
  Freehold, NJ 800-666-8482
Jamieson Laboratories
  Windsor, ON 800-265-5088
MegaFood
  Manchester, NH 800-848-2542
Nature's Way
  Green Bay, WI 800-962-8873
Nhs Labs Inc
  Star, ID 888-546-8694
Nutribiotic
  Lakeport, CA 800-225-4345
Nutrilabs
  San Francisco, CA 877-468-8745
Nutrisciences Labs
  Farmingdale, NY 855-492-7388
Optimum Nutrition
  Aurora, IL 800-763-3444
Protein Research
  Livermore, CA 800-948-1991
Randal Optimal Nutrients
  Santa Rosa, CA 800-221-1697
Sandco International
  Northport, AL 800-382-2075
Scandinavian Formulas Inc
  Sellersville, PA 800-288-2844
Solgar Vitamin & Herbal
  Leonia, NJ 877-765-4274
Twinlab Corporation
  Boca Raton, FL 800-645-5626
Vitatech Nutritional Sciences
  Tustin, CA 714-832-9700
Watson Inc
  West Haven, CT 800-388-3481
Wilke International Inc
  Lenexa, KS 800-779-5545

Vitamins

21st Century Products, Inc.
  Fort Worth, TX 817-284-8299
A. Vogel USA
  Ghent, NY 800-641-7555
Abunda Life
  Asbury Park, NJ 732-775-9338
Acta Health Products
  Sunnyvale, CA 408-732-6830
Action Labs
  Anaheim, CA 800-400-5696
ADH Health Products Inc
  Congers, NY 845-268-0027
Agumm
  Coral Springs, FL 954-344-0607
AHD International, LLC
  Atlanta, GA 404-233-4022
Alacer Corp
  Carlisle, PA 888-425-2362
Alfer Laboratories
  Chatsworth, CA 818-709-0737
Alternative Health & Herbs
  Albany, OR 800-345-4152
Ameri-Kal Inc
  Wichita Falls, TX 940-322-5400

Product Categories / Ingredients, Flavors & Additives: Vitamins & Supplements

American Biosciences
   Blauvelt, NY 888-884-7770
Anabol Naturals
   Santa Cruz, CA 800-426-2265
Animal Pak
   New Brunswick, NJ 800-872-0101
Anmar Nutrition
   Bridgeport, CT 203-336-8330
Apotheca Inc
   Woodbine, IA 800-736-3130
Apple Valley Market
   Berrien Springs, MI 800-237-7436
Archon Vitamin Corp
   Edison, NJ 800-848-0089
Argee Corp
   Santee, CA 800-449-3030
Asiamerica Ingredients
   Westwood, NJ 201-497-5531
At Last Naturals Inc
   Valhalla, NY 800-527-8123
Atkins Nutritionals Inc.
   Denver, CO 800-628-5467
Banner Pharmacaps
   High Point, NC 800-526-6993
BASF Corp.
   Florham Park, NJ 800-526-1072
Belmont Chemicals
   Clifton, NJ 800-722-5070
Beverly International
   Cold Spring, KY 800-781-3475
Bio-Tech Pharmacal Inc
   Fayetteville, AR 800-345-1199
Botanical Products
   Springville, CA 559-539-3432
Brenntag North America
   Reading, PA 610-926-6100
Capsule Works
   Ronkonkoma, NY 877-435-2277
Carob Tree
   Arcadia, CA 626-445-0215
Champion Nutrition Inc
   Sunrise, FL 800-225-4831
Childlife
   Culver City, CA 800-993-0332
China Pharmaceutical Enterprises
   Baton Rouge, LA 800-345-1658
Country Life
   Hauppauge, NY 800-645-5768
CVC4Health
   Vernon, CA 800-421-6175
Cyanotech Corp
   Kailua Kona, HI 800-395-1353
De Souza's
   Banning, CA 800-373-5171
Deerland Probiotics & Enzymes
   Kennesaw, GA 800-697-8179
DMH Ingredients Inc
   Libertyville, IL 847-362-9977
DSM Fortitech Premixes
   Schenectady, NY
Dynapro International
   Kaysville, UT 800-877-1413
Earth Science
   Corona, CA 951-371-7565
Eckhart Corporation
   Novato, CA 800-200-4201
Eclectic Institute
   Sandy, OR 503-668-4120
Edom Labs Inc
   Deer Park, NY 800-723-3366
Energen Products Inc
   Norwalk, CA 800-423-8837
Enzymatic Therapy Inc
   Green Bay, WI. 800-783-2286
ERBL
   Vista, CA 800-275-3725
Esteem Products
   Bellevue, WA 800-255-7631
Europa Sports Products
   Charlotte, NC 800-447-4795
Farbest-Tallman Foods Corp
   Montvale, NJ 201-573-4900
Figuerola Laboratories
   Santa Ynez, CA 800-219-1147
Fortress Systems LLC
   Omaha, NE 888-331-6601
Freeda Vitamins Inc
   Long Island City, NY 800-777-3737
Freeman Industries
   Tuckahoe, NY 800-666-6454
Functional Products LLC
   Atlantic Beach, FL 904-249-8074

Futurebiotics LLC
   Hauppauge, NY 800-645-1721
G M P Laboratories Of Amer Inc
   Anaheim, CA 714-630-2467
Garcoa Laboratories Inc
   Calabasas, CA 800-831-4247
GCI Nutrients
   Foster City, CA 866-580-6549
Goen Technologies Inc
   Wilkes Barre, PA 800-467-3041
Graminex
   Saginaw, MI 877-472-6469
Green Foods Corp.
   Oxnard, CA 800-777-4430
Green Turtle Bay Vitamin Company
   Summit, NJ 800-887-8535
Grow Co
   Ridgefield, NJ 201-941-8777
H. Reisman Corporation
   Orange, NJ 973-882-1670
Health Products Corp
   Yonkers, NY 914-423-2900
Healthy N Fit International
   Croton On Hudson, NY 800-338-5200
Helmuth Country Bakery Inc
   Hutchinson, KS 800-567-6360
Herbal Products & Development
   Aptos, CA 831-688-8706
Heritage Books & Gifts
   Virginia Beach, VA 800-862-2923
Heterochemical Corp
   Valley Stream, NY 516-561-8225
Highland Laboratories
   Mount Angel, OR 888-717-4917
Hillestad Pharmaceuticals
   Woodruff, WI 800-535-7742
Hosemen & Roche Vitamins & Fine Chemicals
   Nutley, NJ 800-526-6367
I-Health Inc
   Cromwell, CT 800-990-3476
Indiana Botanic Gardens Inc
   Hobart, IN 877-909-1502
International Vitamin Corporation
   Freehold, NJ 800-666-8482
J R Carlson Laboratories Inc
   Arlington Heights, IL 888-234-5656
Jamieson Laboratories
   Windsor, ON 800-265-5088
Jarrow Industries Inc
   Santa Fe Springs, CA 562-906-1919
Kemin Industries Inc
   Des Moines, IA 800-777-8307
Lang Pharma Nutrition Inc
   Middletown, RI 401-848-7700
Leiner Health Products
   Carson, CA 310-835-8400
Liberty Natural Products Inc
   Oregon City, OR 800-289-8427
Luyties Pharmacal Company
   Saint Louis, MO 800-325-8080
Madys Inc
   San Francisco, CA 415-822-2227
Marlyn Nutraceuticals
   Phoenix, AZ 800-899-4499
Mega Pro Intl
   St George, UT 800-541-9469
MegaFood
   Manchester, NH 800-848-2542
Metabolic Nutrition
   Tamarac, FL 800-626-1022
Metagenics, Inc.
   Aliso Viejo, CA 800-692-9400
Michael's Naturopathic Prgms
   San Antonio, TX 800-845-2730
Mission Pharmacal Company
   San Antonio, TX 210-696-8400
Motherland International Inc
   Rancho Cucamonga, CA 800-590-5407
Natural Food Supplements Inc
   Canoga Park, CA 818-341-3375
Naturalife Laboratories
   Torrance, CA 800-231-3670
Nature Most Laboratories
   Middletown, CT 800-234-2112
Nature's Bounty Co.
   Ronkonkoma, NY 877-774-3361
Nature's Sunshine Products Company
   Lehi, UT 800-223-8225
New Chapter
   Brattleboro, VT 800-543-7279
Northridge Laboratories
   Chatsworth, CA 818-882-5622

NOW Foods
   Bloomingdale, IL 888-669-3663
Noyes, P J
   Lancaster, NH 800-522-2469
Nu Naturals Inc
   Eugene, OR 800-753-4372
Nutraceutical International
   Corpus Christi, TX 800-338-4788
Nutraceutical International
   Park City, UT 800-669-8877
Nutraceutics Corp
   St Louis, MO 877-664-6684
Nutri-Cell
   Naples, FL 866-953-2355
Nutribiotic
   Lakeport, CA 800-225-4345
Nutrilabs
   San Francisco, CA 877-468-8745
Nutritech Corporation
   Santa Barbara, CA 800-235-5727
Nutritional Counselors of America
   Spencer, TN 931-946-3600
Nutritional Research Associates
   South Whitley, IN 800-456-4931
Nutro Laboratories
   South Plainfield, NJ 800-446-8876
O'Donnell Formulas Inc
   San Marcos, CA 800-736-1991
Oc Lugo Co Inc
   New City, NY 845-480-5121
Old Fashioned Natural Products
   Santa Ana, CA 800-552-9045
Optimal Nutrients
   Foster City, CA 707-528-1800
Ortho-Molecular Products Inc
   Stevens Point, WI 800-332-2351
Pacific Nutritional
   Vancouver, WA 360-896-2297
Parish Chemical Company
   Orem, UT 801-226-2018
Particle Dynamics
   Saint Louis, MO 800-452-4682
Pharmachem Laboratories
   Kearny, NJ 800-526-0609
Phoenix Laboratories
   Farmingdale, NY 800-236-6583
Pro Pac Labs
   Ogden, UT 888-277-6722
Proper-Chem
   Dix Hills, NY 631-420-8000
Protein Research
   Livermore, CA 800-948-1991
Pure Source LLC
   Doral, FL 800-324-6273
Randal Optimal Nutrients
   Santa Rosa, CA 800-221-1697
SADKHIN Complex
   Brooklyn, NY 800-723-5446
Sandco International
   Northport, AL 800-382-2075
Scandinavian Formulas Inc
   Sellersville, PA 800-288-2844
Select Supplements Inc
   Carlsbad, CA 760-431-7509
Solgar Vitamin & Herbal
   Leonia, NJ 877-765-4274
Source Naturals
   Scotts Valley, CA 800-815-2333
Sportabs International
   Los Angeles, CA 888-814-7767
Super Nutrition Life Extension
   Fort Lauderdale, FL 800-678-8989
Tabco Enterprises
   Pomona, CA 909-623-4565
Terra Botanica Products
   Dahlonega, GA 770-718-9340
Texas Coffee Co
   Beaumont, TX 800-259-3400
Thor Inc
   Ogden, UT 888-846-7462
Twinlab Corporation
   Boca Raton, FL 800-645-5626
Unique Vitality Products
   Agoura Hills, CA 818-889-7739
USA Laboratories Inc
   Burns, TN 800-489-4872
Vita-Pure Inc
   Roselle, NJ 908-245-1212
Vitamer Laboratories
   Irvine, CA 800-432-8355
Vitaminerals
   Glendale, CA 800-432-1856

Product Categories / Ingredients, Flavors & Additives: Waxes

Vitamins
   Chicago, IL 312-861-0700
Vitarich Laboratories
   Naples, FL. 800-817-9999
Wakunaga Of America Co LTD
   Mission Viejo, CA 800-421-2998
Westar Nutrition Corporation
   Costa Mesa, CA 800-645-1868
Whole Life Nutritional Supplements
   North Hollywood, CA 800-748-5841
Wilke International Inc
   Lenexa, KS 800-779-5545
World Ginseng Ctr Inc
   San Francisco, CA 800-747-8808

World Nutrition, Inc.
   Scottsdale, AZ. 800-548-2710
World Organics Corporation
   Huntington Beach, CA 714-893-0017
Wright Enrichment Inc
   Crowley, LA 800-201-3096
Wysong Corp
   Midland, MI 800-748-0188

Waxes

Lanaetex Products Incorporated
   Elizabeth, NJ. .908-351-9700

Paraffin

International Food Products
   Fenton, MO. 800-227-8427
Stevenson-Cooper Inc
   Philadelphia, PA 215-223-2600

Rice

International Food Products
   Fenton, MO. 800-227-8427

Jams, Jellies & Spreads

Jams

A Taste of the Kingdom
  Kingdom City, MO............888-592-5080
Alaska Herb & Tea Co
  Anchorage, AK................800-654-2764
Algood Food Co
  Louisville, KY................502-637-3631
Amberland Foods
  Harvey, ND....................800-950-4558
Andros Foods North America
  Mount Jackson, VA.............844-426-3767
Au Printemps Gourmet
  Saint-Jerome, QC..............800-438-6676
B & R Classics LLC
  Huntington, NY................631-427-5675
BakeMark Ingredients Canada
  Richmond, BC..................800-665-9441
Bear Meadow Farm
  Ashfield, MA..................413-628-3970
Bear Stewart Corp
  Chicago, IL...................800-697-2327
Bella Vista Farm
  Lawton, OK....................866-237-8526
Benbow's Coffee Roasters
  Bar Harbor, ME................207-288-2552
Blake Hill Preserves
  Grafton, VT...................802-289-1636
Blue Marble Brands
  Providence, RI................888-534-0246
Bonnie's Jams
  Cambridge, MA.................617-714-5380
Brad's Organic
  Haverstraw, NY................845-429-9080
Bread & Chocolate Inc
  Wells River, VT...............800-524-6715
BRINS
  Brooklyn, NY
Buckhead Gourmet
  Atlanta, GA...................800-673-6338
Buonitalia
  New York, NY..................212-633-9090
Calamondin Cafe
  Fort Myers, FL................239-288-5535
California Custom Fruits
  Baldwin Park, CA..............877-558-0056
Carol Hall's Hot Pepper Jelly
  Fort Bragg, CA................866-737-7379
Carr Valley Cheese Company
  La Valle, WI..................800-462-7258
Chelsea Flower Market
  New York, NY..................888-727-7887
Choice of Vermont
  Destin, FL....................800-444-6261
Clements Foods Co
  Oklahoma City, OK.............800-654-8355
Coco Lopez Inc
  Miramar, FL...................800-341-2242
Colorado Mountain Jams & Jellies
  Palisade, CO..................970-464-0745
Cornabys
  Spanish Fork, UT..............801-830-4530
Cotswold Cottage Foods
  Arvada, CO....................800-208-1977
Crop Pharms, LLC
  Staatsburg, NY................845-266-8999
Daregal
  Princeton, NJ.................609-375-2312
Dark Tickle Company
  St Lunaire-Griquet, NL........709-623-2354
Deborah's Kitchen Inc.
  Littleton, MA.................617-216-9908
Delicae Gourmet
  Tarpon Springs, FL............800-942-2502
Diane's Sweet Heat
  McKinleyville, CA
Doral International
  Bayside, NY...................718-224-7413
Doves and Figs LLC
  Arlington, MA.................781-646-2272
E.D. Smith Foods Ltd
  Hamilton, ON..................905-573-1207
Eat This
  Erwinna, PA...................215-391-5807
EFCO Products Inc
  Poughkeepsie, NY..............800-284-3326
Eleanor's Best LLC
  Garrison, NY..................646-296-6870
Erba Food Products
  Brooklyn, NY..................718-272-7700
Family Food Company
  Paramount, CA.................310-715-2698
Fruit Fillings Inc
  Fresno, CA....................800-995-4514
Fruit of the Land Products
  Thornhill, ON.................877-311-5267
GEM Berry Products
  Orofino, ID...................888-231-1699
Heinz Portion Control
  Jacksonville, FL..............904-695-1300
Herb Bee's Products
  Colchester, VT................802-864-7387
House of Webster
  Rogers, AR....................800-369-4641
Jim's Cheese Pantry
  Waterloo, WI..................800-345-3571
Just Jan's Inc.
  Calabasas, CA.................818-282-6236
Kozlowski Farms
  Forestville, CA...............800-473-2767
Lowcountry Produce
  Raleigh, NC...................800-935-2792
Mad River Farm Kitchen
  Arcata, CA....................707-822-0248
Manassero Farms
  Irvine, CA....................949-554-5103
Mardale Specialty Foods
  Waukegan, IL..................845-299-0285
Middlefield Cheese House
  Middlefield, OH...............800-327-9477
Mixon Fruit Farms Inc
  Bradenton, FL.................800-608-2525
National Grape Co-Op
  Westfield, NY.................800-340-6870
Nature's Hollow
  Charleston, UT
New Canaan Farms
  Dripping Springs, TX..........800-727-5267
Oasis Food Co
  Hillside, NJ..................800-275-0477
Old Country Cheese
  Cashton, WI...................888-320-9469
Pacific Westcoast Foods
  Beaverton, OR.................800-874-9333
Peanut Butter & Co.
  New York, NY..................866-456-8372
Pemberton's Foods Inc
  Gray, ME......................800-255-8401
Potlicker Kitchen
  Stowe, VT.....................802-760-6111
Reid Foods
  Gurnee, IL....................888-295-8478
Rowena
  Norfolk, VA...................800-627-8699
Sapore della Vita
  Sarasota, FL..................941-914-4256
Sargent's Bear Necessities
  North Troy, VT................802-988-2903
Scott Hams
  Greenville, KY................800-318-1353
Shawnee Canning Co
  Cross Junction, VA............800-713-1414
Side Hill Farm
  Brattleboro, VT...............802-254-2018
Sidehill Farm
  Brattleboro, VT...............802-254-2018
Something Special Deli-Foods
  Sherwood Park, AB.............800-461-5892
Spruce Mountain Blueberries
  West Rockport, ME.............207-236-3538
Stanchfield Farms
  Milo, ME......................207-732-5173
Steel's Gourmet Foods, Ltd.
  Bridgeport, PA................800-678-3357
Stonewall Kitchen
  York, ME......................800-826-1752
Summer In Vermont Jams
  Hinesburg, VT.................802-453-3793
Sunfresh Foods
  Seattle, WA...................800-669-9625
Sutter Buttes Olive Oil
  Sutter, CA....................530-763-7921
T.J. Blackburn Syrup Works
  Jefferson, TX.................800-657-5073
T.W. Garner Food Company
  Winston Salem, NC.............800-476-7383
TBJ Gourmet
  West Chester, PA..............856-222-2000
The Jam Stand
  Brooklyn, NY..................718-218-5194
Universal Impex Corporation
  Toronto, ON...................416-743-7778
Valley View Blueberries
  Vancouver, WA.................360-892-2839
Vermont Harvest Spec Food LLC
  Stowe, VT.....................800-338-5354
Vista D'Oro Farms
  Langley, BC...................855-514-3539
Welch Foods Inc.
  Concord, MA...................800-340-6870
Willamette Valley Pie Co
  Salem, OR.....................503-362-8857

Apricot

Allied Old English Inc
  Port Reading, NJ..............732-602-8955
Erba Food Products
  Brooklyn, NY..................718-272-7700

Grape

Allied Old English Inc
  Port Reading, NJ..............732-602-8955
T.W. Garner Food Company
  Winston Salem, NC.............800-476-7383

Strawberry

Allied Old English Inc
  Port Reading, NJ..............732-602-8955
Bear Stewart Corp
  Chicago, IL...................800-697-2327
Erba Food Products
  Brooklyn, NY..................718-272-7700
Knott's Berry Farms
  Orrville, OH..................866-828-5502
New Canaan Farms
  Dripping Springs, TX..........800-727-5267
T.W. Garner Food Company
  Winston Salem, NC.............800-476-7383

Jellies

Alaska Herb & Tea Co
  Anchorage, AK.................800-654-2764
Aloha From Oregon
  Eugene, OR....................800-241-0300
B & B Pecan Processors
  Turkey, NC....................866-328-7322
Bear Meadow Farm
  Ashfield, MA..................413-628-3970
Beetroot Delights
  Foothill, ON..................888-842-3387
Carr Valley Cheese Company
  La Valle, WI..................800-462-7258
Coco Lopez Inc
  Miramar, FL...................800-341-2242
Colorado Mountain Jams & Jellies
  Palisade, CO..................970-464-0745
Deborah's Kitchen Inc.
  Littleton, MA.................617-216-9908
Dundee Groves
  Dundee, FL....................800-294-2266
Just Jan's Inc.
  Calabasas, CA.................818-282-6236
Kettle Master
  Hillsville, VA................276-728-7571
Low Country Produce
  Lobeco, SC....................800-935-2792
Lowcountry Produce
  Raleigh, NC...................800-935-2792
McIlhenny Company
  Avery Island, LA..............800-634-9599
Northeast Kingdom Mustard Company
  Derby, VT.....................866-478-7388
Palmetto Canning
  Palmetto, FL..................941-722-1100
Pennacook Peppers
  Virginia Beach, VA............757-663-8798

Product Categories / Jams, Jellies & Spreads: Marmalades & Preserves

Potlicker Kitchen
   Stowe, VT 802-760-6111
Shenk's Foods
   Lancaster, PA 717-393-4240
Something Special Deli-Foods
   Sherwood Park, AB 800-461-5892

Beets

Beetroot Delights
   Foothill, ON 888-842-3387

Royal

Algood Food Co
   Louisville, KY 502-637-3631
Bear Stewart Corp
   Chicago, IL 800-697-2327
C C Pollen
   Phoenix, AZ 800-875-0096
Campagna Distinct Flavor
   Lebanon, OR. 800-959-4372
Dawes Hill Honey Company
   Nunda, NY 888-800-8075
Delicae Gourmet
   Tarpon Springs, FL 800-942-2502
Fiesta Gourmet of Tejas
   Canyon Lake, TX 800-585-8250
Herb Bee's Products
   Colchester, VT 802-864-7387
Royal Resources
   New Orleans, LA 800-888-9932
Sargent's Bear Necessities
   North Troy, VT 802-988-2903
Stanchfield Farms
   Milo, ME. 207-732-5173
Summer In Vermont Jams
   Hinesburg, VT. 802-453-3793
Vermont Harvest Spec Food LLC
   Stowe, VT. 800-338-5354
WCC Honey Marketing
   City Of Industry, CA. 626-855-3086
Z Specialty Food, LLC
   Woodland, CA. 800-678-1226

Marmalades & Preserves

A Perfect Pear
   Napa, CA. 800-553-5753
A Southern Season
   Hillsborough, NC 800-253-3663
Alaska Jacks
   Anchorage, AK 888-660-2257
Algood Food Co
   Louisville, KY 502-637-3631
Allied Old English Inc
   Port Reading, NJ 732-602-8955
Amberland Foods
   Harvey, ND 800-950-4558
Amcan Industries
   Elmsford, NY 914-347-4838
American Spoon Foods Inc
   Petoskey, MI 888-735-6700
Ana's Salsa
   Austin, TX. 888-849-7054
Arbor Hill Grapery & Winery
   Naples, NY 800-554-7553
Arizona Cowboy
   Phoenix, AZ 800-529-8627
Arome Fleurs & Fruits
   Saint-Jean-Baptiste Day, QC 877-349-3282
Au Printemps Gourmet
   Saint-Jerome, QC 800-438-6676
Bainbridge Festive Foods
   Farmington, TN 800-545-9205
Bartons Fine Foods
   Denniston, KY 888-810-3750
Baumer Foods Inc
   Metairie, LA 504-482-5761
Bear Meadow Farm
   Ashfield, MA 413-628-3970
Bear Stewart Corp
   Chicago, IL 800-697-2327
Blackberry Patch
   Thomasville, GA. 800-853-5598
Blake Hill Preserves
   Grafton, VT. 802-289-1636
Blue Marble Brands
   Providence, RI 888-534-0246
Blueberry Store
   Grand Junction, MI. 877-654-2400
Bono USA
   Fairfield, NJ 862-485-8729

Booneway Farms
   Berea, KY 859-986-2636
BRINS
   Brooklyn, NY
C W Resources Inc
   New Britain, CT 860-229-7700
California Custom Fruits
   Baldwin Park, CA 877-558-0056
Castella Imports Inc
   Brentwood, NY 631-231-5500
Casually Gourmet
   New Haven, VT 800-639-7604
Catamount Specialties of Vermont
   Plainfield, VT 800-639-2406
Cherchies
   Malvern, PA 800-644-1980
Cheri's Desert Harvest
   Tucson, AZ 800-743-1141
Cherith Valley Gardens
   Fort Worth, TX 800-610-9813
Cherry Hut
   Traverse City, MI 888-882-4431
Chris' Farm Stand
   Peabody, MA. 978-994-4315
Chugwater Chili
   Chugwater, WY 800-972-4454
Chukar Cherries
   Prosser, WA. 800-624-9544
Cincinnati Preserving Co
   Cincinnati, OH 800-222-9966
Clements Foods Co
   Oklahoma City, OK 800-654-8355
Coco Lopez Inc
   Miramar, FL 800-341-2242
Cold Hollow Cider Mill
   Waterbury Center, VT. 800-327-7537
Country Cupboard
   Lewisburg, PA 570-523-3211
Coutts Specialty Foods Inc
   Boxborough, MA 800-919-2952
Dillman Farm Inc
   Bloomington, IN 800-359-1362
Dundee Groves
   Dundee, FL. 800-294-2266
E Waldo Ward & Son Marmalades
   Sierra Madre, CA 800-355-9273
Eat This
   Erwinna, PA 215-391-5807
EFCO Products Inc
   Poughkeepsie, NY 800-284-3326
Eleanor's Best LLC
   Garrison, NY. 646-296-6870
Erba Food Products
   Brooklyn, NY 718-272-7700
Esper Products DeLuxe
   Kissimmee, FL 800-268-0892
Eva Gates Homemade Preserves
   Bigfork, MT 800-682-4283
Eweberry Farms
   Brownsville, OR 541-466-3470
Fiesta Gourmet of Tejas
   Canyon Lake, TX 800-585-8250
Fireside Kitchen
   Halifax, NS 902-454-7387
Fischer & Wieser Spec Foods
   Fredericksburg, TX. 877-861-0260
Food For Thought Inc
   Honor, MI 231-326-5444
Forge Mountain Foods
   Hendersonville, NC 800-823-6743
Freed, Teller & Freed
   South San Francisco, CA 800-370-7371
From Oregon
   Springfield, OR. 541-747-4222
Frostproof Sunkist Groves
   Frostproof, FL. 863-635-4873
Gem Berry Products
   Sandpoint, ID 800-231-1699
Graves Mountain Lodge Inc.
   Syria, VA. 540-923-4231
Graysmarsh Berry Farm
   Sequim, WA 800-683-4367
Great Northern Maple Products
   Saint Honor, De Shenley, QC 418-485-7777
Greaves Jams & Marmalades
   Niagara-on-the-Lake, ON 800-515-9939
Green Grown Products Inc
   Marina Del Ray, CA 310-828-1686
Grouse Hunt Farm Inc
   Tamaqua, PA 570-467-2850
H Cantin
   Beauport, QC 800-463-5268

Heinz Portion Control
   Jacksonville, FL 904-695-1300
Hillcrest Orchard
   Lake Placid, FL. 865-397-5273
Hollman Foods
   Des Moines, IA. 888-926-2879
Homemade By Dorothy Boise
   Boise, ID 800-657-7449
Honey Bear Fruit Basket
   Denver, CO 888-330-2327
Huckleberry Patch
   Hungry Horse, MT 800-527-7340
Hurd Orchards
   Holley, NY 585-638-8838
Indian Bay Frozen Foods
   Centreville, NL. 709-678-2844
Inter-American Products
   Cincinnati, OH 800-645-2233
J.M. Smucker Co.
   Orrville, OH 888-550-9555
Jim's Cheese Pantry
   Waterloo, WI. 800-345-3571
JMS Specialty Foods
   Ripon, WI 800-535-5437
Kamish Food Products
   Chicago, IL 773-725-6959
Kent Precision Foods Group Inc
   Muscatine, IA 800-442-5242
Kerr Jellies
   Dana, NC 877-685-8381
Knott's Berry Farms
   Orrville, OH 866-828-5502
Knouse Foods Co-Op Inc
   Peach Glen, PA 717-677-8181
Koloa Rum Corp
   Kalaheo, HI. 808-332-9333
Kozlowski Farms
   Forestville, CA 800-473-2767
La Caboose Specialties
   Sunset, LA 337-662-5401
Lancaster Packing Company
   Myerstown, PA 717-397-9727
Lawrence Foods Inc
   Elk Grove Village, IL 847-437-2400
Lehi Mills
   Lehi, UT 877-311-3566
Leona's Restaurante
   Chimayo, NM 888-561-5569
Lillie's Q
   Chicago, IL 773-772-5500
Love Creek Orchards
   Medina, TX. 800-449-0882
Lowcountry Produce
   Raleigh, NC 800-935-2792
Lynch Foods
   North York, ON. 416-449-5464
Lyons Magnus
   Fresno, CA 800-344-7130
Mad River Farm Kitchen
   Arcata, CA 707-822-0248
Meier's Wine Cellars Inc
   Cincinnati, OH 800-346-2941
Minnestalgia Foods LLC
   Mcgregor, MN 800-328-6731
Mixon Fruit Farms Inc
   Bradenton, FL. 800-608-2525
Mountainbrook of Vermont
   Jeffersonville, VT. 802-644-1988
Mrs Auld's Gourmet Foods Inc
   Reno, NV 800-322-8537
New Canaan Farms
   Dripping Springs, TX. 800-727-5267
New England Cranberry
   Lynn, MA 800-410-2892
Oregon Hill Farms
   St Helens, OR 800-243-4541
Pacific Westcoast Foods
   Beaverton, OR 800-874-9333
Palmetto Canning
   Palmetto, FL. 941-722-1100
Pearson's Berry Farm
   Bowden, AB 403-224-3011
Pepper Creek Farms
   Lawton, OK. 800-526-8132
Pied-Mont/Dora
   Anne Des Plaines, QC 800-363-8003
Plaidberry Company
   Vista, CA. 760-727-5403
Poiret International
   Tamarac, FL 800-237-9151
Post Familie Vineyards
   Altus, AR 800-275-8423

Product Categories / Jams, Jellies & Spreads: Spreads

Purity Factories
 St. John's, NL 800-563-3411
Purity Products
 Plainview, NY 800-256-6102
Quality Naturally Foods
 City Of Industry, CA 888-498-6986
Rapazzini Winery
 Gilroy, CA 800-842-6262
Restaurant Lulu Gourmet Products
 San Francisco, CA 888-693-5800
Robert Rothschild Farm
 Cincinnati, OH 800-222-9966
Rocky Top Farms
 Ellsworth, MI 800-862-9303
Rose City Pepperheads
 Tigard, OR 503-443-3873
Roseland Manufacturing
 Roseland, NJ 973-228-2500
Rowena
 Norfolk, VA 800-627-8699
Sambets Cajun Deli
 Austin, TX 800-472-6238
Sand Hill Berries
 Mt Pleasant, PA 724-547-4760
SBK Preserves
 Bronx, NY 800-773-7378
Sedlock Farm
 Lynn Center, IL 309-521-8284
Seven Keys Co Of Florida
 Pompano Beach, FL 954-946-5010
Shawnee Canning Co
 Cross Junction, VA 800-713-1414
Shenk's Foods
 Lancaster, PA 717-393-4240
Shooting Star Farms
 Bartlesville, OK 888-850-8540
Silver Palate Kitchens
 Cresskill, NJ 201-568-0110
Skjodt-Barrett Foods
 Brampton, ON 877-600-1200
Stickney & Poor Company
 Peterborough, NH 603-924-2259
Sugarman of Vermont
 Hardwick, VT 800-932-7700
Summerland Sweets
 Summerland, BC 800-577-1277
T.J. Blackburn Syrup Works
 Jefferson, TX 800-657-5073
T.W. Garner Food Company
 Winston Salem, NC 800-476-7383
Tait Farm Foods
 Centre Hall, PA 800-787-2716
Tex-Mex Gourmet
 Brenham, TX 888-345-8467
The Great San Saba River Pecan Company
 San Saba, TX 800-621-8121
The Lollipop Tree, Inc
 Auburn, NH 800-842-6691
Trailblazer Foods
 Portland, OR 800-777-7179
Trappist Preserves
 Cleveland, OH 800-472-0425
Tropical Preserving Co Inc
 Los Angeles, CA 213-748-5108
Uncle Fred's Fine Foods
 Rockport, TX 361-729-8320
Valley View Blueberries
 Vancouver, WA 360-892-2839
Vista D'Oro Farms
 Langley, BC 855-514-3539
Wagner Gourmet Foods
 Lenexa, KS 913-469-5411
Wax Orchards
 Seattle, WA 800-634-6132
WCC Honey Marketing
 City Of Industry, CA 626-855-3086
Welch Foods Inc
 Concord, MA 800-340-6870
Welch Foods Inc.
 Concord, MA 800-340-6870
Westport Rivers Vineyard
 Westport, MA 800-993-9695
Wild Thyme Cottage Products
 Pointe Claire, QC 514-695-3602
Z Specialty Food, LLC
 Woodland, CA 800-678-1226

Spreads

A Southern Season
 Hillsborough, NC 800-253-3663
Aak USA Inc
 Newark, NJ 973-344-1300
Alaska Smokehouse
 Woodinville, WA 800-422-0852
Alexian Pâtés
 Neptune, NJ 800-927-9473
Algood Food Co
 Louisville, KY 502-637-3631
Allfresh Food Products
 Evanston, IL 847-869-3100
Allied Old English Inc
 Port Reading, NJ 732-602-8955
Amcan Industries
 Elmsford, NY 914-347-4838
American Almond Products Co
 Brooklyn, NY 800-825-6663
American Spoon Foods Inc
 Petoskey, MI 888-735-6700
Arbor Hill Grapery & Winery
 Naples, NY 800-554-7553
B & G Foods Inc.
 Parsippany, NJ 973-401-6500
Bainbridge Festive Foods
 Farmington, TN 800-545-9205
BakeMark Ingredients Canada
 Richmond, BC 800-665-9441
Bauer's Mustard
 Flushing, NY 718-821-3570
Baumer Foods Inc
 Metairie, LA 504-482-5761
Bear Meadow Farm
 Ashfield, MA 413-628-3970
Beekman 1802
 Sharon Springs, NY 888-801-1802
Bel Brands USA
 Chicago, IL 312-462-1500
Betty Lou's
 McMinnville, OR 800-242-5205
Black Bear Fruits
 New Lisbon, WI 608-547-6133
Blake Hill Preserves
 Grafton, VT 802-289-1636
Blue Jay Orchards
 Bethel, CT 203-748-0119
Boulder Brands, Inc.
 Paramus, NJ 201-421-3970
BP Gourmet
 Hauppauge, NY 631-234-8200
Bread Dip Company
 Maple Valley, WA 425-358-7386
Butterball Farms
 Grand Rapids, MI 888-828-8837
Butternut Mountain Farm
 Morrisville, VT 800-828-2376
Carolina Food Company
 Tulsa, OK 918-519-9338
Castella Imports Inc
 Brentwood, NY 631-231-5500
Chelsea Flower Market
 New York, NY 888-727-7887
Cheri's Desert Harvest
 Tucson, AZ 800-743-1141
Cherry Hut
 Traverse City, MI 888-882-4431
Chocolaterie Bernard Callebaut
 Calgary, AB 800-661-8367
Chris' Farm Stand
 Peabody, MA 978-994-4315
Chugwater Chili
 Chugwater, WY 800-972-4454
Cinnabar Specialty Foods Inc
 Prescott, AZ 866-293-6433
Citadelle Maple Syrup Producers' Cooperative
 Plessisville, QC 819-362-3241
Clements Foods Co
 Oklahoma City, OK 800-654-8355
Cleveland Kraut
 Cleveland, OH 216-264-6895
Cold Hollow Cider Mill
 Waterbury Center, VT 800-327-7537
Consumer Guild Foods Inc
 Toledo, OH 419-726-3406
Cook's Pantry
 Ventura, CA 805-947-4622
Cowboy Caviar
 Berkeley, CA 877-509-1796
Crofter's Food
 Parry Sound, ON 705-746-6301
Cugino's Gourmet Foods
 Crystal Lake, IL 888-592-8446
Dawes Hill Honey Company
 Nunda, NY 888-800-8075
Dutch Gold Honey Inc
 Lancaster, PA 800-338-0587
E Waldo Ward & Son Marmalades
 Sierra Madre, CA 800-355-9273
Earth Balance
 Boulder, CO 866-234-6429
East Wind Inc
 Tecumseh, MO 417-679-4682
Erba Food Products
 Brooklyn, NY 718-272-7700
Esper Products DeLuxe
 Kissimmee, FL 800-268-0892
Eva Gates Homemade Preserves
 Bigfork, MT 800-682-4283
Fireside Kitchen
 Halifax, NS 902-454-7387
Flaum Appetizing
 Brooklyn, NY 718-821-1970
Follow Your Heart
 Chatsworth, CA 818-725-2820
Forge Mountain Foods
 Hendersonville, NC 800-823-6743
Fox Hollow
 Crestwood, KY 502-241-8621
From Oregon
 Springfield, OR 541-747-4222
Gardners Candies Inc
 Tyrone, PA 800-242-2639
GEM Berry Products
 Orofino, ID 888-231-1699
Gem Berry Products
 Sandpoint, ID 888-231-1699
GFA Brands Inc
 Paramus, NJ 201-568-9300
Giovanni's Appetizing Food Co
 Richmond, MI 586-727-9355
Graham Cheese Corporation
 Elnora, IN 800-472-9178
Graves Mountain Lodge Inc.
 Syria, VA 540-923-4231
Graysmarsh Berry Farm
 Sequim, WA 800-683-4367
Great Garlic Foods
 Bradley Beach, NJ 732-775-3311
Greaves Jams & Marmalades
 Niagara-on-the-Lake, ON 800-515-9939
Groeb Farms
 Onsted, MI 800-530-9969
Grouse Hunt Farm Inc
 Tamaqua, PA 570-467-2850
H & B Packing Co
 Waco, TX 254-752-2506
Harold Food Company
 Charlotte, NC 704-588-8061
Heinz Portion Control
 Jacksonville, FL 904-695-1300
Herb Bee's Products
 Colchester, VT 802-864-7387
Hillcrest Orchard
 Lake Placid, FL 865-397-5273
Hillside Lane Farm
 Randolph, VT 802-728-0070
Hollman Foods
 Des Moines, IA 888-926-2879
Homemade By Dorothy Boise
 Boise, ID 800-657-7449
Honey Bear Fruit Basket
 Denver, CO 888-330-2327
Honey Butter Products Co
 Manheim, PA 717-665-9323
Hope Foods
 Boulder, CO 303-248-7019
Huckleberry Patch
 Hungry Horse, MT 800-527-7340
Indian Bay Frozen Foods
 Centreville, NL 709-678-2844
J.M. Smucker Co.
 Orrville, OH 888-550-9555
JMS Specialty Foods
 Ripon, WI 800-535-5437
Just Jan's Inc.
 Calabasas, CA 818-282-6236
Kapow Now!
 North Vancouver, BC 604-726-6391
Kent Precision Foods Group Inc
 Muscatine, IA 800-442-5242
Kerr Jellies
 Dana, NC 877-685-8381
Kevala
 Dallas, TX 877-379-1179
Kind Snacks
 New York, NY 855-884-5463
Knott's Berry Farms
 Orrville, OH 866-828-5502

Product Categories / Jams, Jellies & Spreads: Spreads

Knotts Fine Foods
 Paris, TN 731-642-1961
Knouse Foods Co-Op Inc.
 Peach Glen, PA 717-677-8181
Koloa Rum Corp
 Kalaheo, HI 808-332-9333
Kozlowski Farms
 Forestville, CA 800-473-2767
Krema Nut Co
 Columbus, OH 800-222-4132
Kween Foods
 San Diego, CA 401-343-0805
La Caboose Specialties
 Sunset, LA. 337-662-5401
Lancaster Packing Company
 Myerstown, PA 717-397-9727
Land O'Lakes Inc
 Arden Hills, MN 800-328-9680
Landis Peanut Butter
 Souderton, PA 215-723-9366
Lasco Foods Inc
 St Louis, MO 314-832-1906
Lawry's Foods
 Hunt Valley, MD 800-952-9797
Leavitt Corp., The
 Everett, MA 617-389-2600
Leroux Creek
 Hotchkiss, CO 877-970-5670
Lost Trail Root Beer
 Louisburg, KS 800-748-7765
Love Creek Orchards
 Medina, TX 800-449-0882
Lynch Foods
 North York, ON 416-449-5464
Mad River Farm Kitchen
 Arcata, CA 707-822-0248
Madison Foods
 Saint Paul, MN 651-265-8212
Manassero Farms
 Irvine, CA 949-554-5103
Marantha Natural Foods
 San Francisco, CA 866-972-6879
Marin Food Specialties
 Byron, CA 925-634-6126
Mccutcheon Apple Products
 Frederick, MD 800-888-7537
Meier's Wine Cellars Inc
 Cincinnati, OH 800-346-2941
Minnestalgia Foods LLC
 Mcgregor, MN 800-328-6731
Miss Scarlett's Flowers
 Juneau, AK 800-345-6734
Mixon Fruit Farms Inc
 Bradenton, FL 800-608-2525
Montana Mountain Smoked Fish
 Montana City, MT. 800-649-2959
Mountainbrook of Vermont
 Jeffersonville, VT 802-644-1988
Mrs Annie's Peanut Patch
 Floresville, TX 830-393-7845
National Grape Co-Op
 Westfield, NY 800-340-6870
New Canaan Farms
 Dripping Springs, TX 800-727-5267
Nikki's Coconut Butter
 Hudson, WI
Nutiva
 Richmond, CA 800-993-4367
Once Again Nut Butter
 Nunda, NY 888-800-8075
Oregon Hill Farms
 St Helens, OR 800-243-4541
Organic Gourmet
 Sherman Oaks, CA 800-400-7772
Original Herkimer Cheese
 Ilion, NY 315-895-7428
Pacific Beach Peanut Butter
 La Mesa, CA 630-329-0792
Palmetto Canning
 Palmetto, FL 941-722-1100
Parkers Farm
 Coon Rapids, MN 800-869-6685
Peaceworks
 New York, NY 212-897-3985
Penotti USA
 Westport, CT 877-720-0896
Pied-Mont/Dora
 Anne Des Plaines, QC 800-363-8003
Pine River Pre-Pack Inc
 Newton, WI 920-726-4216
Plochman Inc
 Manteno, IL 800-843-4566

Private Harvest
 El Dorado Hills, CA 916-933-7080
Producers Peanut Company
 Suffolk, VA 800-847-5491
Protient
 St Paul, MN 800-328-9680
Purity Factories
 St. John's, NL 800-563-3411
Purity Farms
 La Farge, WI 877-211-4819
Purity Products
 Plainview, NY 800-256-6102
Quong Hop & Company
 S San Francisco, CA 650-553-9900
Rachael's Smoked Fish
 Springfield, MA 800-327-3412
Rapazzini Winery
 Gilroy, CA 800-842-6262
Rapunzel Pure Organics
 Bloomfield, NJ 800-225-1449
Regal Food Service
 Houston, TX 281-477-3683
Restaurant Lulu Gourmet Products
 San Francisco, CA 888-693-5800
Rocky Top Farms
 Ellsworth, MI 800-862-9303
Roseland Manufacturing
 Roseland, NJ 973-228-2500
Rowena
 Norfolk, VA 800-627-8699
Sabra Blue & White Food Products
 Dallas, TX 888-957-2272
Salmolux Inc
 Federal Way, WA 253-874-6570
Sassafras Enterprises Inc
 Chicago, IL 800-537-4941
SBK Preserves
 Bronx, NY 800-773-7378
Schlotterbeck & Foss Company
 Portland, ME 800-777-4666
Scott-Bathgate
 Winnipeg, MB 800-216-2990
Sedlock Farm
 Lynn Center, IL 309-521-8284
Shawnee Canning Co
 Cross Junction, VA 800-713-1414
Shenk's Foods
 Lancaster, PA 717-393-4240
Silver Palate Kitchens
 Cresskill, NJ 201-568-0110
Skjodt-Barrett Foods
 Brampton, ON 877-600-1200
Small Planet Foods
 Minneapolis, MN 800-624-4123
Something Special Deli-Foods
 Sherwood Park, AB 800-461-5892
Sommer Maid Creamery Inc
 Pipersville, PA. 215-345-6160
Southern Gold Honey Co
 Vidor, TX 808-899-2494
Southern Peanut Co Inc
 Dublin, NC 800-330-3141
St Laurent Brothers
 Bay City, MI 800-289-7688
Stello Foods Inc
 Punxsutawney, PA 800-849-4599
Sugarman of Vermont
 Hardwick, VT 800-932-7700
Summerland Sweets
 Summerland, BC. 800-577-1277
Suzanne's Specialties
 New Brunswick, NJ 800-762-2135
Sweetstacks LLC
 San Diego, CA 619-997-1097
T.W. Garner Food Company
 Winston Salem, NC. 800-476-7383
Tait Farm Foods
 Centre Hall, PA 800-787-2716
Tara Foods
 Atlanta, GA 404-559-0605
Tarazi Specialty Foods
 Chino, CA 909-628-3601
Terrapin Ridge
 Clearwater, FL 800-999-4052
The Great San Saba River Pecan Company
 San Saba, TX 800-621-8121
The Lollipop Tree, Inc
 Auburn, NY. 800-842-6691
Thistledew Farm
 Proctor, WV 800-854-6639
Timber Crest Farms
 Healdsburg, CA 888-766-4233

Trappist Preserves
 Cleveland, OH 800-472-0425
Treasure Foods
 West Valley, UT. 801-974-0911
Tribe Mediterranean
 Taunton, MA 800-848-6687
Tropical Foods
 Charlotte, NC 800-438-4470
Tropical Preserving Co Inc
 Los Angeles, CA 213-748-5108
Valley View Blueberries
 Vancouver, WA 360-892-2839
Ventura Foods LLC
 Brea, CA 800-421-6257
Virginia & Spanish Peanut Co
 Providence, RI 800-673-3562
Wagner Gourmet Foods
 Lenexa, KS 913-469-5411
WCC Honey Marketing
 City Of Industry, CA 626-855-3086
Welch Foods Inc
 Concord, MA 800-340-6870
Welch Foods Inc.
 Concord, MA 800-340-6870
Westbrae Natural Foods
 Melville, NY 800-434-4246
Wild Thymes Farm Inc
 Greenville, NY 845-266-8387
WillowOak Farms
 Amherst, VA 888-963-2767
Wisconsin Milk Mktng Board Inc
 Madison, WI 800-589-5127
Wisconsin Wilderness Food Products
 Lake Bluff, IL 800-359-3039
World Art Foods
 Temple, TX 254-774-8322
Z Specialty Food, LLC
 Woodland, CA. 800-678-1226
Zesty Z: The Za'atar Company
 Brooklyn, NY 917-740-5241

Apple Butter

A.W. Jantzi & Sons
 Wellesley, ON 519-656-2400
Bear Meadow Farm
 Ashfield, MA 413-628-3970
Betty Lou's
 McMinnville, OR 800-242-5205
Blue Jay Orchards
 Bethel, CT 203-748-0119
Centennial Farms
 Augusta, MO 636-228-4338
Clements Foods Co
 Oklahoma City, OK 800-654-8355
Cold Hollow Cider Mill
 Waterbury Center, VT. 800-327-7537
Coutts Specialty Foods Inc
 Boxborough, MA 800-919-2952
Father's Country Hams
 Bremen, KY 270-525-3554
Graves Mountain Lodge Inc.
 Syria, VA 540-923-4231
Hillcrest Orchard
 Lake Placid, FL. 865-397-5273
Kime's Cider Mill
 Bendersville, PA 717-677-7539
Knouse Foods Co-Op Inc.
 Peach Glen, PA 717-677-8181
Lost Trail Root Beer
 Louisburg, KS 800-748-7765
Love Creek Orchards
 Medina, TX 800-449-0882
Mccutcheon Apple Products
 Frederick, MD. 800-888-7537
Shawnee Canning Co
 Cross Junction, VA 800-713-1414
Shenk's Foods
 Lancaster, PA 717-393-4240
Timber Crest Farms
 Healdsburg, CA 888-766-4233
Tropical Preserving Co Inc
 Los Angeles, CA 213-748-5108

Fruit Butter

American Almond Products Co
 Brooklyn, NY 800-825-6663
Applecreek Speciality Foods
 Lexington, KY 800-747-8871
Betty Lou's
 McMinnville, OR 800-242-5205

Product Categories / Jams, Jellies & Spreads: Spreads

Clements Foods Co
  Oklahoma City, OK 800-654-8355
Cold Hollow Cider Mill
  Waterbury Center, VT 800-327-7537
Dillman Farm Inc
  Bloomington, IN 800-359-1362
Hollman Foods
  Des Moines, IA 888-926-2879
JMS Specialty Foods
  Ripon, WI 800-535-5437
Knouse Foods Co-Op Inc.
  Peach Glen, PA 717-677-8181

Kozlowski Farms
  Forestville, CA 800-473-2767
Lancaster Packing Company
  Myerstown, PA 717-397-9727
Leroux Creek
  Hotchkiss, CO 877-970-5670
Lost Trail Root Beer
  Louisburg, KS 800-748-7765
Mccutcheon Apple Products
  Frederick, MD 800-888-7537
Oregon Hill Farms
  St Helens, OR 800-243-4541

Scott Hams
  Greenville, KY 800-318-1353
Shenk's Foods
  Lancaster, PA 717-393-4240
Timber Crest Farms
  Healdsburg, CA 888-766-4233
Tropical Preserving Co Inc
  Los Angeles, CA 213-748-5108
World of Chia
  The Woodlands, TX 800-251-6973

Meats & Meat Products

Canned

ADJR Inc
  Paulding, OH 419-399-3182
Aunt Kitty's Foods Inc
  Vineland, NJ 856-691-2100
B & G Foods Inc.
  Parsippany, NJ. 973-401-6500
Calihan Pork Processors Inc
  Peoria, IL. 309-674-9175
Campbell Soup Co.
  Camden, NJ. 800-257-8443
Cordon Bleu International
  Anjou, QC. 800-363-1182
Dorina So-Good Inc
  Union, IL. 815-923-2144
Gary's Frozen Foods
  Lubbock, TX. 806-745-1933
Grabill Country Meats
  Grabill, IN. 866-333-6328
Hormel Foods Corp.
  Austin, MN. 507-437-5611
Hsin Tung Yang Foods Inc
  S San Francisco, CA. 650-589-6789
J & B Sausage Co Inc
  Waelder, TX. 830-788-7511
Kelly Foods
  Jackson, TN 731-424-2255
Mertz Sausage Co
  San Antonio, TX. 210-433-3263
Opa's Smoked Meats
  Fredericksburg, TX. 800-543-6750
Triple U Enterprises
  Fort Pierre, SD 605-567-3624

Cooked

Burke Corp
  Nevada, IA 800-654-1152
Golden West Food Group
  Vernon, CA 888-807-3663
Omaha Steaks Inc
  800-960-8400
Specialty Foods Group Inc
  Owensboro, KY 800-238-0020

Dried

Alderfer Inc
  Harleysville, PA 800-341-1121
Arctic Beverages
  Winnipeg, MB. 866-503-1270
Asiago PDO & Speck Alto Adige PGI
  New York, NY 646-624-2885
Breslow Deli Products
  Philadelphia, PA 215-739-4200
Chomps
  Naples, FL
Chops Snacks
  Lebanon, GA. 888-571-4442
Citterio USA
  Freeland, PA 800-435-8888
Country Archer Jerky Co.
  San Bernardino, CA 909-370-0155
Duke's
Henningsen Foods Inc
  Omaha, NE 800-228-2769
Hoopeston Foods Inc
  Burnsville, MN 952-854-0903
Hsin Tung Yang Foods Inc
  S San Francisco, CA. 650-589-6789
Oregon Freeze Dry, Inc.
  Albany, OR. 541-926-6001
Perky Jerky
  Greenwood Vlg, CO 888-343-6113
Prime Smoked Meats Inc
  Oakland, CA. 510-832-7167
Ralph's Packing Co
  Perkins, OK. 800-522-3979
Riverview Foods
  Warsaw, KY 859-567-5211
Serv-Rite Meat Co Inc
  Los Angeles, CA. 323-227-1911
Shelton's Poultry Inc
  Pomona, CA 800-541-1833
Silver Star Meats Inc
  Mc Kees Rocks, PA 800-548-1321

SlantShack Jerky
  Brooklyn, NY 201-632-1035
Tillamook Country Smoker
  Bay City, OR
True Jerky
  San Francisco, CA 858-336-2005
Wolf Canyon Foods
  Carmel, CA. 831-626-1323

Frozen

Acme Steak & Seafood
  Youngstown, OH. 800-686-2263
Al Pete Meats
  Muncie, IN 765-288-8817
American Foods Group LLC
  Green Bay, WI. 800-345-0293
AquaCuisine
  Portland, OR. 208-323-2782
Armbrust Meats
  Medford, WI 715-748-3102
Atlantic Meat Company
  Savannah, GA. 912-964-8511
Atlantic Veal & Lamb Inc
  Brooklyn, NY 800-222-8325
B & D Foods
  Boise, ID. 208-344-1183
Blakely Freezer Locker
  Blakeley, GA. 229-723-3622
Bouma Meats
  Provost, AB. 780-753-2092
Branding Iron
  Sauget, IL. 800-851-4684
Broadleaf Venison USA Inc
  Vernon, CA. 800-336-3844
Brook Locker Plant
  Brook, IN 219-275-2611
Brookside Foods
  Cleveland, OH 216-991-7600
Burke Corp
  Nevada, IA 800-654-1152
Bush Brothers Provision Co
  West Palm Beach, FL 800-327-1345
Butterfield Foods
  Noblesville, IN 317-776-4775
Calihan Pork Processors Inc
  Peoria, IL. 309-674-9175
Carando Gourmet Frozen Foods
  Agawam, MA. 888-227-2636
Cardinal Meat Specialists
  Brampton, ON. 800-363-1439
Caribbean Food Delights Inc
  Tappan, NY. 845-398-3000
Carriage House Foods
  Ames, IA. 515-232-2273
Centennial Food Corporation
  Calgary, AB. 403-214-0044
Chef's Requested Foods
  Oklahoma City, OK 405-239-2610
Cher-Make Sausage Co
  Manitowoc, WI. 800-242-7679
Cheraw Packing Plant
  Cheraw, SC 843-537-7426
Clifty Farm Country Meats
  Paris, TN 800-486-4267
Curly's Foods Inc
  Edina, MN. 612-920-3400
Devault Foods
  Devault, PA. 800-426-2874
Dold Foods
  Wichita, KS. 316-838-9101
Duis Meat Processing
  Concordia, KS. 800-281-4295
Duma Meats Inc
  Mogadore, OH 330-628-3438
El Rey Cooked Meats
  St Louis, MO. 314-521-3113
Florida Veal Processors
  Wimauma, FL. 813-634-5545
Garden Protein International
  Richmond, BC 877-305-6777
Gaucho Foods
  Fayetteville, IL 877-677-2282
Golden West Food Group
  Vernon, CA 888-807-3663
Grecian Delight Foods Inc
  Elk Grove Village, IL 800-621-4387

Hall Brothers Meats
  Olmsted Twp, OH. 440-235-3262
Hamms Custom Meats
  Mckinney, TX. 972-542-3359
Hanover Foods Corp
  Hanover, PA 717-632-6000
Hatfield Quality Meats
  Hatfield, PA. 800-743-1191
Heringer Meats Inc
  Covington, KY 859-291-2000
Homestead Meats
  Delta, CO 970-874-1145
Hormel Foods Corp.
  Austin, MN. 507-437-5611
International Food Packers Corporation
  Miami, FL 305-740-5847
John Garner Meats
  Van Buren, AR 800-543-5473
K & K Gourmet Meats Inc
  Leetsdale, PA 724-266-8400
Kelley Foods
  Elba, AL 334-897-5761
Kenosha Beef International LTD
  Kenosha, WI
King Kold Meats
  Englewood, OH 800-836-2797
Kutztown Bologna Company
  Leola, PA 800-723-8824
Ladoga Frozen Food & Retail
  Ladoga, IN 765-942-2225
Leo G Fraboni Sausage Company
  Hibbing, MN. 218-263-5074
M Buono Beef Co
  Philadelphia, PA 215-463-3600
Macfarlane Pheasants
  Janesville, WI 800-345-8348
Mada'n Kosher Foods
  Dania, FL 954-925-0077
Maid-Rite Steak Company
  Dunmore, PA. 800-233-4259
Maple Leaf Foods International
  North York, ON. 800-268-3708
Morrison Lamothe
  Toronto, ON 877-677-6533
Omaha Steaks Inc
  800-960-8400
On-Cor Frozen Foods Redi-Serve
  Aurora, IL 920-563-6391
P.A. Braunger Institutional Foods
  Sioux City, IA 712-258-4515
Pacific Valley Foods Inc
  Bellevue, WA 425-643-1805
Phoenix Agro-Industrial Corporation
  Westbury, NY 516-334-1194
Pierceton Foods Inc
  Pierceton, IN 574-594-2344
Prime Smoked Meats Inc
  Oakland, CA. 510-832-7167
R Four Meats
  Chatfield, MN. 507-867-4180
Rich Products Corp
  Vineland, NJ 800-818-9261
Rymer Foods
  Chicago, IL 800-247-9637
Shelley's
  Jersey City, NJ 201-433-2900
Smith Packing Regional Meat
  Utica, NY 315-732-5125
Smoked Turkey Inc
  Marshville, NC 704-624-6628
Steak-Umm Company
  Shillington, PA 860-928-5900
Sudlersville Frozen Food Locker
  Sudlersville, MD. 410-438-3106
Thompson Packers
  Slidell, LA. 800-989-6328
Travis Meats Inc
  Powell, TN 800-247-7606
Triple U Enterprises
  Fort Pierre, SD 605-567-3624
Tucker Packing Co
  Orrville, OH. 330-683-3311
United Meat Company
  San Francisco, CA 415-864-2118
United Supermarkets
  Lubbock, TX. 806-745-9667

Product Categories / Meats & Meat Products: Spreads

Valley Meat Company
   Modesto, CA............800-222-6328
Valley Meats
   Coal Valley, IL............309-517-6639
W & G Marketing Company
   Ames, IA............515-233-4774
Zartic Inc
   Rome, GA............800-241-0516

Ingredients

Burke Corp
   Nevada, IA............800-654-1152
GPI USA LLC.
   Mokena, IL............800-929-4248

Minced

Groff's Meats
   Elizabethtown, PA............717-367-1246
Reinhart Foods
   Toronto, ON............416-645-4910

Packers

1000 Islands River Rat Cheese
   Clayton, NY............800-752-1341
A.C. Kissling Company
   Philadelphia, PA............800-445-1943
A.L. Duck Jr Inc
   Zuni, VA............757-562-2387
Abattoir Aliments Asta Inc.
   St Alexandre De Kamouras, QC............800-463-1355
Ajinomoto Foods North America, Inc.
   Ontario, CA............909-477-4700
AJM Meat Packing
   San Juan, PR............787-787-4050
Al Safa Halal
   New York City, NY............800-268-8147
Alaska Sausage & Seafood
   Anchorage, AK............800-798-3636
Alewel's Country Meats
   Warrensburg, MO............800-353-8553
Alexian Pâtés
   Neptune, NJ............800-927-9473
Alle Processing Corp
   Flushing, NY............718-894-2000
Amcan Industries
   Elmsford, NY............914-347-4838
Atlantic Meat Company
   Savannah, GA............912-964-8511
Atlantic Veal & Lamb Inc
   Brooklyn, NY............800-222-8325
Atlantis Pak USA Inc
   Coral Gables, FL............305-403-2603
B & D Foods
   Boise, ID............208-344-1183
B & R Quality Meats Inc
   Waterloo, IA............319-232-6328
Bakalars Sausage Co
   La Crosse, WI............608-784-0384
Ball Park Franks
   Peoria, IL............888-317-5867
Baretta Provision
   East Berlin, CT............860-828-0802
Barone Foods
   Tucson, AZ............520-623-8571
BCFoods
   Santa Rosa, CA............707-547-1776
Bellville Meat Market
   Bellville, TX............800-571-6328
Bierig Brothers Inc
   Vineland, NJ............856-691-9765
Big B Barbecue
   Evansville, IN............812-425-5235
Binkert's Meat Products
   Baltimore, MD............410-687-5959
Birchwood Foods Inc
   Kenosha, WI............800-541-1685
Blakely Freezer Locker
   Blakeley, GA............229-723-3622
Blue Ribbon Meats
   Cleveland, OH............800-262-0395
Bluebonnet Meat Company
   Trenton, TX............903-989-2293
Boesl Packing Co
   Baltimore, MD............800-675-1471
Bowser Meat Processing
   Meriden, KS............785-484-2454
Braham Food Locker Service
   Braham, MN............320-396-2636
Branding Iron
   Sauget, IL............800-851-4684

Branding Iron Meats
   Sauk Rapids, MN............800-851-4684
Breslow Deli Products
   Philadelphia, PA............215-739-4200
Broadaway Ham Co
   Jonesboro, AR............870-932-6688
Broadleaf Venison USA Inc
   Vernon, CA............800-336-3844
Brook Locker Plant
   Brook, IN............219-275-2611
Brook Meadow Meats
   Hagerstown, MD............301-739-3107
Brown Packing Company
   South Holland, IL............800-832-8325
Brucepac
   Woodburn, OR............800-899-3629
Brush Locker
   Fort Morgan, CO............970-842-2660
Bryant's Meat Inc.
   Taylorsville, MS............800-844-0507
Buckhead Beef
   Atlanta, GA............800-888-5578
Burgers' Smokehouse
   California, MO............800-345-5185
Burnett & Son
   Monrovia, CA............877-632-5467
Burton Meat Processing
   Burton, TX............979-289-4022
Busseto Foods
   Fresno, CA............800-628-2633
C & C Packing Co
   Stamps, AR............866-365-3759
C Roy & Sons Processing
   Yale, MI............810-387-3957
C&S Wholesale Meat Company
   Atlanta, GA............404-627-3547
Callaway Packing Inc
   Delta, CO............970-874-9743
Calumet Diversified Meats Company
   Pleasant Prairie, WI............800-752-7427
Cambridge Packing Company
   Boston, MA............800-722-6726
Carando Gourmet Frozen Foods
   Agawam, MA............888-227-2636
Cardinal Meat Specialists
   Brampton, ON............800-363-1439
Caribbean Food Delights Inc
   Tappan, NY............845-398-3000
Carl Venezia Fresh Meats
   Plymouth Meeting, PA............610-239-6750
Carlton Farms
   Carlton, OR............800-932-0946
Carolina Packers Inc
   Smithfield, NC............800-682-7675
Catelli Brothers Inc
   Collingswood, NJ............856-869-9293
Caughman's Meat Plant
   Lexington, SC............803-356-0076
Cavens Meats
   Conover, OH............937-368-3841
Caviness Beef Packers LTD
   Hereford, TX............806-357-2333
Caviness Beef Packers LTD
   Amarillo, TX............806-372-5781
Centennial Food Corporation
   Calgary, AB............403-214-0044
Center Locker Svc
   Center, MO............800-884-0737
Central Meat & Provision
   San Diego, CA............619-239-1391
Central Meat Market
   Providence, RI............401-751-6935
Charlie's Country Sausage
   Minot, ND............701-838-6302
Chef's Requested Foods
   Oklahoma City, OK............405-239-2610
Chicago 58 Food Products
   Woodbridge, ON............416-603-4244
Chino Meat Provision Corporation
   Chino, CA............909-627-1997
Chisesi Brothers Meat Packing
   New Orleans, LA............800-966-3550
Cibao Meat Products Inc
   Bronx, NY............718-993-5072
Cifelli & Sons Inc
   South River, NJ............732-238-0090
Clay Center Locker Plant
   Clay Center, KS............800-466-5543
Clifty Farm Country Meats
   Paris, TN............800-486-4267
Cloud's Meat Processing
   Carthage, MO............417-358-5855

Clyde's Italian & German Sausage
   Denver, CO............303-433-8744
Conagra Brands Inc
   Chicago, IL............877-266-2472
Conagra Foodservice
   Chicago, IL............877-266-2472
Conecuh Sausage Co
   Evergreen, AL............800-726-0507
Corfu Foods Inc
   Bensenville, IL............630-595-2510
Country Butcher Shop
   Carlisle, PA............800-272-9223
Country Smoked Meats
   Bowling Green, OH............800-321-4766
Crater Meat Co Inc
   Medford, OR............541-772-6966
Crofton & Sons Inc
   Tampa, FL............800-878-7675
Crystal Lake Farms
   Decatur, AR............800-382-4425
Cudlin's Meat Market
   Newfield, NY............607-564-3443
Culver Duck Farms Inc
   Middlebury, IN............800-825-9225
Curly's Foods Inc
   Edina, MN............612-920-3400
Custom-Pak Meats
   Knoxville, TN............615-687-0871
Dale T Smith & Sons Inc
   Draper, UT............801-571-3611
David Mosner Meat Products
   Bronx, NY............866-928-6428
Dean Sausage Co Inc
   Attalla, AL............800-228-0704
Debragga & Spitler
   Jersey City, NJ
Dennison Meat Locker
   Dennison, MN............507-645-8734
Diggs Packing Company
   Columbia, MO............573-449-2995
Dinner Bell Meat Product
   Lynchburg, VA............434-847-7766
Dold Foods
   Wichita, KS............316-838-9101
Dolores Canning Co Inc
   Los Angeles, CA............323-263-9155
Duis Meat Processing
   Concordia, KS............800-281-4295
Dunham's Meats
   Urbana, WA............509-924-9821
Dutterer's Home Food Service
   Baltimore, MD............410-298-3663
Dyna Tabs LLC
   Brooklyn, NY............718-376-6084
E&H Packing Company
   Detroit, MI............313-567-8286
E.W. Knauss & Son
   Quakertown, PA............800-648-4220
East Dayton Meat & Poultry
   Dayton, OH............937-253-6185
Edelman Meats Inc
   Antigo, WI............715-623-7686
Ehresman Packaging Co
   Garden City, KS............620-276-3791
El Paso Meat Co
   El Paso, TX............915-838-8600
El Rey Cooked Meats
   St Louis, MO............314-521-3113
Elba Custom Meats
   Elba, AL............334-897-2007
Ellsworth Locker
   Ellsworth, MN............507-967-2544
ELP Inc
   Elizabeth, CO............303-688-2240
Enslin & Son Packing Company
   Hattiesburg, MS............800-898-4687
F&Y Enterprises
   Wauconda, IL............847-526-0620
Fairbury Food Products
   Fairbury, NE............402-729-3379
Far West Meats
   Highland, CA............909-864-1990
Farm Boy Food Svc
   Evansville, IN............800-852-3976
Farmers Produce
   Ashby, MN............218-747-2749
Farmington Foods Inc
   Forest Park, IL............800-609-3276
Finchville Farms Country Ham
   Finchville, KY............800-678-1521
Fineberg Packing Company
   Memphis, TN............901-458-2622

Fiorucci Foods USA Inc
S Chesterfield, VA 800-524-7775
Fischer Meats
Issaquah, WA 425-392-3131
Flanders
Waycross, GA 912-283-5191
Florida Veal Processors
Wimauma, FL 813-634-5545
Foell Packing Company
Naperville, IL 919-776-0592
Fortenberry Mini-Storage
Kodak, TN 865-933-2568
Frank Wardynski & Sons Inc
Buffalo, NY 716-854-6083
Freirich Foods
Salisbury, NC 800-221-1315
Fresh Mark Inc.
Massillon, OH 330-832-7491
Frick's Quality Meats
Washington, MO 800-241-2209
Froehlich Alex Packing Co
Johnstown, PA 814-535-7694
Fulton Provision Co
Portland, OR 800-333-6328
Gaiser's European Style
Union, NJ 908-686-3421
Gem Meat Packing Co
Garden City, ID 208-375-9424
Gibbon Packing
Gibbon, NE 308-468-5771
Glazier Packing Co
Malone, NY 518-483-4990
Glen's Packing Co
Hallettsville, TX 800-368-2333
Glier's Meats Inc
Covington, KY 800-446-3882
Global Food Industries
Townville, SC 800-225-4152
Gouvea's & Purity Foods Inc
Honolulu, HI 808-847-3717
Grabill Country Meats
Grabill, IN 866-333-6328
Grandpa Ittel's Meats Inc
Howard Lake, MN 320-543-2285
Grant Park Packing
Chicago, IL 312-421-4096
Greater Omaha Packing Co Inc.
Omaha, NE 800-747-5400
Grecian Delight Foods Inc
Elk Grove Village, IL 800-621-4387
Grote & Weigel Inc
Bloomfield, CT 860-242-8528
Gulf Packing Company
San Benito, TX 956-399-2631
Gunnoe Farms Sausage & Salad
Charleston, WV 304-343-7686
H&K Packers Company
Winnipeg, NB 204-233-2354
Hansen Packing Co
Jerseyville, IL 618-498-3714
Harvest Direct
Norwell, MA 800-733-2106
Hastings Meat Supply
Hastings, NE 402-463-9857
Hatfield Quality Meats
Hatfield, PA 800-743-1191
Henningsen Foods Inc
Omaha, NE 800-228-2769
Herman Falter Packing Co
Columbus, OH 800-325-6328
Herring Brothers Meats
Guilford, ME 207-876-2631
Hightower's Packing
Minden, LA 318-377-5459
Hilltop Meat Co
Andalusia, AL 800-781-0053
Hofmann Sausage Co Inc
Mattydale, NY 800-724-8410
Holly Hill Locker Company
Holly Hill, SC 803-496-3611
Holton Meat Processing
Holton, KS 785-364-2331
Home Delivery Food Service
Jefferson, GA 706-367-9551
Homestead Meats
Delta, CO 970-874-1145
Hoopeston Foods Inc
Burnsville, MN 952-854-0903
Hoople Country Kitchen Inc
Rockport, IN 877-466-7537
Hormel Foods Corp.
Austin, MN 507-437-5611
Hot Springs Packing Co Inc
Hot Springs, AR 800-535-0449
Hsin Tung Yang Foods Inc
S San Francisco, CA 650-589-6789
Hughes Springs Frozen Food Center
Hughes Springs, TX 903-639-2941
Hughson Meat Company
San Marcos, TX 877-462-6328
Humphrey's Market
Springfield, IL 800-747-6328
Indian Valley Meats
Indian, AK 907-653-7511
International Food Packers Corporation
Miami, FL 305-740-5847
International Meat Co
Chicago, IL 773-622-1400
Isernio Sausage Company
Seattle, WA 888-495-8674
Ito Cariani Sausage Company
Hayward, CA 510-887-0882
J F O'Neill & Packing Co
Omaha, NE 402-733-1200
J W Treuth & Sons
Catonsville, MD 410-747-6281
Jackson Brothers Food Locker
Post, TX 806-495-3245
Jackson Meat
Hutchinson, KS 620-259-6066
Jacob & Sons Wholesale Meats
Martins Ferry, OH 740-633-3091
Jacobsmuhlen's Meats
Cornelius, OR 503-359-0479
JD Sweid Foods
Langley, BC 800-665-4355
Jemm Wholesale Meat Company
Chicago, IL 773-523-8161
Jensen Meat Company
San Diego, CA 619-754-6400
John Garner Meats
Van Buren, AR 800-543-5473
John Volpi & Co
St Louis, MO 800-288-3439
Johnson's Wholesale Meats
Opelousas, LA 337-948-4444
Johnson, Nash & Sons Farms
Warsaw, NC 910-289-6842
Johnsonville Sausage LLC
Watertown, WI 888-556-2728
Jones Dairy Farm
Fort Atkinson, WI 800-563-6637
Jordahl Meats
Manchester, MN 507-826-3418
Joseph Kirschner & Company
Augusta, ME 207-623-3544
Keeter's Meat Company
Tulia, TX 800-456-5019
Kelley Foods
Elba, AL 334-897-5761
Kelly Packing Company
Torrington, WY 307-532-2210
Kenosha Beef International LTD
Kenosha, WI
Kent Quality Foods Inc
Grand Rapids, MI 800-748-0141
Kershenstine Beef Jerky
Eupora, MS 662-258-2049
Ketters Meat Market & Locker Plant
Frazee, MN 218-334-2351
Kingsbury Country Market
La Porte, IN 219-393-3016
Kiolbassa Provision Co
San Antonio, TX 800-456-5465
Koegel Meats Inc
Flint, MI 810-238-3685
Konetzko's Meat Market
Browerville, MN 320-594-2915
Kowalski Sausage Co
Hamtramck, MI 800-482-2400
Kruse & Son
Monrovia, CA 626-358-4536
Kruse Meat Products
Alexander, AR 501-316-2100
Kutztown Bologna Company
Leola, PA 800-723-8824
L & L Packing Co
Chicago, IL 800-628-6328
L & M Lockers
Belt, MT 406-277-3522
Lad's Smokehouse Catering
Needville, TX 979-793-6210
Ladoga Frozen Food & Retail
Ladoga, IN 765-942-2225
Lakeside Foods Inc.
Plainview, MN 507-534-3141
Lampost Meats
Grimes, IA 515-288-6111
Land O'Frost Inc
Searcy, AR 800-643-5654
Lee's Sausage Co
Orangeburg, SC 803-534-5517
Lengerich Meats Inc
Zanesville, IN 260-638-4123
Leo G. Fraboni Sausage Company
Hibbing, MN 218-263-5074
Lindner Bison
Northern, CA 530-254-6337
Lombardi Brothers Meat Packers
Denver, CO 303-458-7441
Lord's Sausage & Country Ham
Dexter, GA 800-342-6002
Lynden Meat Co
Lynden, WA 360-354-2449
M Buono Beef Co
Philadelphia, PA 215-463-3600
Mac's Meats Inc
Las Cruces, NM 575-524-2751
Macfarlane Pheasants
Janesville, WI 800-345-8348
MacGregors Meat & Seafood
Toronto, ON 888-383-3663
Maid-Rite Steak Company
Dunmore, PA 800-233-4259
Manger Packing Corp
Baltimore, MD 800-227-9262
Maple Leaf Foods International
North York, ON 800-268-3708
Maple Leaf Meats
Motreal, QC 800-268-3708
Marcel et Henri Charcuterie Francaise
South San Francisco, CA 800-227-6436
Marks Meat
Holmen, WI 608-526-6058
Mclemores Abattoir Inc
Vidalia, GA 912-537-4476
Meat Center
Edna, TX 361-782-3776
Meating Place
Buffalo, NY 716-885-3623
Medeiros Farms
Kalaheo, HI 808-332-8211
Merkley & Sons Packing Co Inc
Jasper, IN 812-482-7020
Michael's Finer Meats/Seafoods
Columbus, OH 800-282-0518
Miller Brothers Packing Company
Sylvester, GA 229-776-2014
Moonlite Bar-B-Q Inn
Owensboro, KY 800-322-8989
Morreale John R Inc
Chicago, IL 312-421-3664
Morrison Lamothe
Toronto, ON 877-677-6533
Morrison Meat Packers
Miami, FL 800-330-4267
Mountain States Rosen
Bronx, NY 800-872-5262
Moyer Packing Co.
Elroy, PA 800-967-8325
Mucke's Meat Products
Hartford, CT 800-726-5598
Napoleon Locker
Napoleon, IN 812-852-4333
National Foods
Indianapolis, IN 800-683-6565
Natural Food Holdings
Sioux Center, IA 800-735-7765
New City Packing Company
Aurora, IL 630-851-8800
New Generation Foods
Burnaby, BC 604-515-7438
Nicky USA Inc
Portland, OR 800-469-4162
Niemuth's Steak & Chop Shop
Waupaca, WI 715-258-2666
Oklahoma City Meat Co Inc
Oklahoma City, OK 405-235-3308
Olson Locker
Fairmont, MN 507-238-2563
Omaha Meat Processors
Omaha, NE 402-554-1965
On-Cor Frozen Foods Redi-Serve
Aurora, IL 920-563-6391
Original Chili Bowl
Ontario, CA 800-548-6363

Product Categories / Meats & Meat Products: Spreads

Oscar's Wholesale Meats
 Ogden, UT...................801-621-5655
Ossian Smoked Meats
 Ossian, IN....................800-535-8862
Our Best Foods
 Tewksbury, MA................978-858-0077
Palmer Meat Packing Co
 Tremonton, UT................435-257-5329
Paradise Locker Inc.
 Trimble, MO..................816-370-6328
Pasqualichio Brothers Inc
 Scranton, PA..................800-232-6233
Peco Foods Inc.
 Tuscaloosa, AL................205-345-4711
Pekarna Meat Market
 Jordan, MN....................952-492-6101
Pender Packing Co Inc
 Rocky Point, NC...............910-675-3311
Petschl's Quality Meats
 Tukwila, WA..................206-575-4400
Phoenix Agro-Industrial Corporation
 Westbury, NY.................516-334-1194
Pie Piper Products
 Wheeling, IL..................800-621-8183
Pierceton Foods Inc
 Pierceton, IN.................574-594-2344
Piller Sausages & Delicatessens
 Waterloo, ON.................800-265-2628
Piller's Fine Foods
 Waterloo, ON.................800-265-2627
Pinter's Packing Plant
 Dorchester, WI................715-654-5444
Plymouth Beef Co.
 Bronx, NY....................718-589-8600
Prairie Cajun Wholesale
 Eunice, LA....................337-546-6195
Premium Meat Co
 Brigham City, UT..............435-723-5944
Prime Smoked Meats Inc
 Oakland, CA..................510-832-7167
Pruden Packing Company
 Suffolk, VA...................757-539-8773
Puueo Poi Shop
 Hilo, HI......................808-935-8435
Quality Food Company
 Providence, RI................877-233-3462
Quality Meats & Seafood
 West Fargo, ND...............800-342-4250
Quality Sausage Company
 Dallas, TX....................214-634-3400
R Four Meats
 Chatfield, MN.................507-867-4180
R M Felts' Packing Co
 Ivor, VA......................757-859-6131
R.E. Meyer Company
 Lincoln, NE...................888-990-2333
Rabbit Barn
 Turlock, CA..................209-632-1123
Raber Packing Co
 Peoria, IL....................800-331-0543
Ralph's Packing Co
 Perkins, OK..................800-522-3979
Randolph Packing Co
 Asheboro, NC.................336-672-1470
Ray's Sausage Co
 Cleveland, OH................216-921-8782
Real Kosher Sausage Company
 Newark, NJ...................973-690-5394
Red Smith Foods Inc
 Davie, FL....................954-581-1996
Register Meat Co
 Cottondale, FL................850-352-4269
Rich Products Corp
 Vineland, NJ..................800-818-9261
Rinehart Meat Processing
 Branson, MO.................417-869-2041
Riverton Packing
 Riverton, WY................307-856-3838
Robbins Packing Company
 Statesboro, GA...............912-764-7503
Robinson Distributing Co
 London, KY..................800-230-5131
Rocky Mountain Packing Company
 Havre, MT...................406-265-3401
Roman Packing Company
 Norfolk, NE..................800-373-5990
Roman Sausage Company
 Santa Clara, CA...............800-497-7462
Roode Packing Company
 Fairbury, NE..................402-729-2253
Rose Packing Co Inc
 South Barrington, IL...........800-323-7363

Royal Center Locker Plant
 Royal Center, IN..............574-643-3275
Royal Home Bakery
 Newmarket, ON...............905-715-7044
Royal Palate Foods
 Inglewood, CA................310-330-7701
Rudolph's Market & Sausage
 Dallas, TX....................214-741-1874
Rymer Foods
 Chicago, IL...................800-247-9637
S.W. Meat & Provision Company
 Phoenix, AZ..................602-275-2000
Sadler's Smokehouse
 Henderson, TX................903-657-5581
Sahlen's
 Buffalo, NY..................800-466-8165
Sambol Meat Company
 Overland Park, KS.............913-334-8404
San Angelo Packing
 San Angelo, TX...............325-949-9401
San Antonio Packing Co
 San Antonio, TX...............210-224-5441
Sanders Meat Packing Inc
 Custer, MI....................800-968-5035
Sardinha's Sausage
 Somerset, MA................800-678-0178
Saval Foods Corp
 Elkridge, MD.................800-527-2825
Savoie's Sausage and Food Products
 Opelousas, LA................337-942-7241
Schaefers Market
 Sauk Centre, MN.............320-352-6490
Schleswig Specialty Meats
 Schleswig, IA.................712-676-3324
Schumacher Wholesale Meats
 Golden Valley, MN............800-432-7020
Seaboard Foods
 Shawnee Mission, KS..........800-262-7907
Serv-Rite Meat Co Inc
 Los Angeles, CA..............323-227-1911
Shaker Valley Foods
 Cleveland, OH................216-961-8600
Shamrock Slaughter Plant
 Shamrock, TX................806-256-3241
Shelley's
 Jersey City, NJ................201-433-2900
Shelton's Poultry Inc
 Pomona, CA.................800-541-1833
Siena Foods
 Toronto, ON.................800-465-0422
Silver Creek Specialty Meats
 Oshkosh, WI.................800-729-2849
Silver Star Meats Inc
 Mc Kees Rocks, PA...........800-548-1321
Skylark Meats
 Omaha, NE..................800-759-5275
Smith Meat Packing
 Detroit, MI...................313-833-1590
Smith Packing Regional Meat
 Utica, NY....................315-732-5125
Smith Provision Co Inc
 Erie, PA......................800-334-9151
SOPAKCO Foods
 Mullins, SC..................800-276-9678
Souris Valley Processors
 Melita, MB...................204-522-8210
Southern Packing Corp
 Chesapeake, VA..............757-421-2131
Spencer Packing Company
 Washington, NC..............252-946-4161
Spring Hill Meat Market
 Spring Hill, KS...............913-592-3501
Springville Meat & Cold Storage
 Springville, UT...............801-489-6391
Stampede Meat, Inc.
 Bridgeview, IL................800-353-0933
Standard Meat Co LP
 Dallas, TX....................866-859-6313
Statewide Meats & Poultry
 New Haven, CT..............203-777-6669
Steak-Umm Company
 Shillington, PA...............860-928-5900
Stewarts Market
 Yelm, WA...................360-458-2091
Stock Yards Packing Company
 Melrose Park, IL..............877-785-9273
Stone Meat Processor
 Ogden, UT...................801-782-9825
Stonie's Sausage Shop
 Perryville, MO................888-546-2540
Strasburg Provision
 Strasburg, OH................800-207-6009

Streit Carl & Son Co
 Neptune, NJ..................732-775-0803
Stripling's General Store
 Moultrie, GA..................229-985-4226
Sudlersville Frozen Food Locker
 Sudlersville, MD..............410-438-3106
Sunergia Soyfoods
 Charlottesville, VA............800-693-5134
Sunnydale Meats Inc
 Gaffney, SC..................864-489-6091
Superior Meat Co
 Vernal, UT...................435-789-3274
Suzanna's Kitchen
 Peachtree Cor, GA............770-476-9900
Swiss-American Sausage Company
 Lathrop, CA..................209-858-5555
T O Williams Inc
 Portsmouth, VA...............757-397-0771
T.L. Herring & Company
 Wilson, NC..................252-291-1141
Taylor Provisions Company
 Trenton, NJ..................609-392-1113
Temptee Specialty Foods
 Denver, CO..................800-842-1233
Tennessee Valley Packing Co
 Columbia, TN...............931-388-2623
Theriault's Abattoir Inc
 Hamlin, ME.................207-868-3344
Thomas Brothers Country Ham
 Asheboro, NC...............336-672-0337
Thomas Packing Company
 Columbus, GA...............800-729-0976
Thompson Packers
 Slidell, LA...................800-989-6328
Thumann Inc.
 Carlstadt, NJ.................201-935-3636
Tiger Meat & Provisions
 Miami, FL...................305-324-0083
Tillamook Meat Inc
 Tillamook, OR...............503-842-4802
Travis Meats Inc
 Powell, TN..................800-247-7606
Triple U Enterprises
 Fort Pierre, SD...............605-567-3624
Troy Pork Store
 Troy, NY....................518-272-8291
Tyler Packing Co
 Tyler, TX....................903-593-9592
Une-Viandi
 St. Jean Sur Richelieu, NB....800-363-1955
United Meat Company
 San Francisco, CA............415-864-2118
United Provision Meat Company
 Columbus, OH...............614-252-1126
V.W. Joyner & Company
 Smithfield, VA...............757-357-2161
Valley Meat Company
 Modesto, CA................800-222-6328
Victor Ostrowski & Son
 Baltimore, MD...............410-327-8935
Vienna Meat Products
 Scarborough, ON............800-588-1931
Vollwerth & Baroni Companies
 Hancock, MI................800-562-7620
W & G Marketing Company
 Ames, IA...................515-233-4774
WACO Beef & Pork Processors
 Waco, TX...................254-772-4669
Wall Meat Processing
 Wall, SD....................605-279-2348
Wampler's Farm Sausage Company
 Lenoir City, TN..............800-728-7243
Wasatch Meats Inc
 Salt Lake City, UT............800-631-8294
Wayco Ham Co
 Goldsboro, NC..............800-962-2614
Western Buffalo Company
 Rapid City, SD...............800-247-3263
Westport Locker LLC
 Westport, IN................877-265-0551
Whitaker & Assoc Architects
 Atlanta, GA.................404-266-1265
White Packing Company
 Fredericksburg, VA...........540-373-9883
Wichita Packing Co Inc
 Chicago, IL..................312-763-3965
Willcox Meat Packing House
 Willcox, AZ.................520-384-2015
Willie's Smoke House LLC
 Harrisville, PA...............800-742-4184
Windcrest Meat Packers
 Port Perry, ON..............800-750-2542

Product Categories / Meats & Meat Products: General

Woodbine
   Norfolk, VA 757-461-2731
World Casing Corp
   Maspeth, NY 800-221-4887
Y & T Packing Co
   Springfield, IL 217-522-3345
Yoakum Packing Co
   Yoakum, TX 800-999-6997
Zartic Inc
   Rome, GA 800-241-0516
Zerna Packing
   Labadie, MO 636-742-4190
Zummo Meat Co
   Beaumont, TX 409-842-1810
Zweigle's Inc
   Rochester, NY 585-546-1740

Patties

Acme Steak & Seafood
   Youngstown, OH 800-686-2263
Branding Iron
   Sauget, IL 800-851-4684
Brucepac
   Woodburn, OR 800-899-3629
Burger Maker Inc
   Carlstadt, NJ 201-939-0444
Caribbean Food Delights Inc
   Tappan, NY 845-398-3000
Chicago Meat Authority Inc
   Chicago, IL 800-383-3811
Corfu Foods Inc
   Bensenville, IL 630-595-2510
CTI Foods
   Wilder, ID 208-482-7844
Fair Oaks Farms LLC
   Pleasant Prairie, WI 800-528-8615
Gouvea's & Purity Foods Inc
   Honolulu, HI 808-847-3717
Karn Meats
   Columbus, OH 800-221-9585
Kenosha Beef International LTD
   Kenosha, WI
Kutztown Bologna Company
   Leola, PA 800-723-8824
Laurent's Meat Market
   Marrero, LA 504-341-1771
Meating Place
   Buffalo, NY 716-885-3623
Mishler Packing Co
   Lagrange, IN 800-860-4156
On-Cor Frozen Foods Redi-Serve
   Aurora, IL 920-563-6391
Pulmuone Foods USA Inc.
   Fullerton, CA 800-588-7782
Roman Sausage Company
   Santa Clara, CA 800-497-7462
S.W. Meat & Provision Company
   Phoenix, AZ 602-275-2000
Springville Meat & Cold Storage
   Springville, UT 801-489-6391
Travis Meats Inc
   Powell, TN 800-247-7606
Valley Meat Company
   Modesto, CA 800-222-6328
Wisconsin Packaging Corp
   Fort Atkinson, WI 920-563-9363
Zartic Inc
   Rome, GA 800-241-0516

Frozen

Birchwood Foods Inc
   Kenosha, WI 800-541-1685
Branding Iron
   Sauget, IL 800-851-4684
Burke Corp
   Nevada, IA 800-654-1152
Cardinal Meat Specialists
   Brampton, ON 800-363-1439
Caribbean Food Delights Inc
   Tappan, NY 845-398-3000
Chicago Meat Authority Inc
   Chicago, IL 800-383-3811
Corfu Foods Inc
   Bensenville, IL 630-595-2510
Edmond's Chile Co
   St Louis, MO 314-772-1499
Flanders
   Waycross, GA 912-283-5191
Jemm Wholesale Meat Company
   Chicago, IL 773-523-8161
John Garner Meats
   Van Buren, AR 800-543-5473
Kenosha Beef International LTD
   Kenosha, WI
King Kold Meats
   Englewood, OH 800-836-2797
Kutztown Bologna Company
   Leola, PA 800-723-8824
Leo G. Fraboni Sausage Company
   Hibbing, MN 218-263-5074
Maid-Rite Steak Company
   Dunmore, PA 800-233-4259
Mellos North End Mfr
   Fall River, MA 800-673-2320
On-Cor Frozen Foods Redi-Serve
   Aurora, IL 920-563-6391
Plymouth Beef Co.
   Bronx, NY 718-589-8600
Thompson Packers
   Slidell, LA 800-989-6328
Valley Meat Company
   Modesto, CA 800-222-6328
Wisconsin Packaging Corp
   Fort Atkinson, WI 920-563-9363
Zartic Inc
   Rome, GA 800-241-0516

Portion Cuts

A To Z Portion Control Meats
   Bluffton, OH 800-338-6328
Atlantic Veal & Lamb Inc
   Brooklyn, NY 800-222-8325
B & D Foods
   Boise, ID 208-344-1183
Beef Products Inc.
   North Sioux City, SD 605-217-8000
Boar's Head
   Sarasota, FL 800-352-6277
Bouma Meats
   Provost, AB 780-753-2092
Broadleaf Venison USA Inc
   Vernon, CA 800-336-3844
Brucepac
   Woodburn, OR 800-899-3629
Bush Brothers Provision Co
   West Palm Beach, FL 800-327-1345
C&S Wholesale Meat Company
   Atlanta, GA 404-627-3547
Cambridge Packing Company
   Boston, MA 800-722-6726
Canal Fulton Provision
   Canal Fulton, OH 800-321-3502
Caribbean Food Delights Inc
   Tappan, NY 845-398-3000
Carolina Pride Foods
   Greenwood, SC 864-229-5611
Chicago Meat Authority Inc
   Chicago, IL 800-383-3811
Clifty Farm Country Meats
   Paris, TN 800-486-4267
Cloverdale Foods
   Mandan, ND 800-669-9511
Corfu Foods Inc
   Bensenville, IL 630-595-2510
Crescent Duck Farm
   Aquebogue LI, NY 631-722-8000
Dairy Fresh Foods Inc
   Taylor, MI 313-299-0735
Devault Foods
   Devault, PA 800-426-2874
Frank Brunckhorst Company
   Sarasota, FL 804-722-4100
King Kold Meats
   Englewood, OH 800-836-2797
L & L Packing Co
   Chicago, IL 800-628-6328
Land O'Frost Inc
   Searcy, AR 800-643-5654
Marshallville Packing Co
   Marshallville, OH 330-855-2871
National Foods
   Indianapolis, IN 800-683-6565
Ohio Association Of Meat
   Frazeysburg, OH 740-828-9900
Pacific Poultry Company
   Honolulu, HI 808-841-2828
Paulsen Foods
   Atlanta, GA 404-873-1804
Quality Meats & Seafood
   West Fargo, ND 800-342-4250
Robinson Distributing Co
   London, KY 800-230-5131
S.W. Meat & Provision Company
   Phoenix, AZ 602-275-2000
SOPAKCO Foods
   Mullins, SC 800-276-9678
Standard Meat Co LP
   Dallas, TX 866-859-6313
Streit Carl & Son Co
   Neptune, NJ 732-775-0803
The Bruss Company
   Chicago, IL 773-282-2900
Triple U Enterprises
   Fort Pierre, SD 605-567-3624
United Meat Company
   San Francisco, CA 415-864-2118
WACO Beef & Pork Processors
   Waco, TX 254-772-4669
Wisconsin Packaging Corp
   Fort Atkinson, WI 920-563-9363

Prepared

Ajinomoto Foods North America, Inc.
   Ontario, CA 909-477-4700
American Foods Group LLC
   Green Bay, WI 800-345-0293
Burke Corp
   Nevada, IA 800-654-1152
Charlito's Cocina
   Brooklyn, NY 718-482-7890
Fair Oaks Farms LLC
   Pleasant Prairie, WI 800-528-8615
Gutheinz Meats Inc
   Scranton, PA 570-344-1191
Henry J's Meat Specialties
   Chicago, IL 800-242-1314
Meat & Supply Co
   New York, NY 646-864-0967
Piller's Fine Foods
   Waterloo, ON 800-265-2627
Roger Wood Foods Inc
   Savannah, GA 800-849-9272
Sofo Foods
   Toledo, OH 800-447-4211
Specialty Foods Group Inc
   Owensboro, KY 800-238-0020
Wisconsin Cheeseman
   Madison, WI 800-693-0834

Proteins

Abbot's Butcher
   Costa Mesa, CA 949-726-2156
Burke Corp
   Nevada, IA 800-654-1152
Fork & Goode
   Brooklyn, NY
Spice Of Life Co
   Sherman Oaks, CA 818-909-0052

General

Aala Meat Market Inc
   Honolulu, HI 808-832-6650
Ajinomoto Foods North America, Inc.
   Ontario, CA 909-477-4700
Alef Sausage Inc
   Mundelein, IL 847-968-2533
Annapolis Produce & Restaurant
   Annapolis, MD 410-266-5211
Arnold's Meat Food Products
   Brooklyn, NY 800-633-7023
Asiago PDO & Speck Alto Adige PGI
   New York, NY 646-624-2885
Aufschnitt Meats
   Owings Mills, MD 410-356-7745
B & R Quality Meats Inc
   Waterloo, IA 319-232-6328
Ballard Custom Meats
   Manchester, ME 207-622-9764
Belleville Brothers Packing
   North Baltimore, OH 419-257-3529
Bernard & Sons
   Bakersfield, CA 661-327-4431
Blalock Seafood & Specialty
   Orange Beach, AL 251-974-5811
Boar's Head
   Sarasota, FL 800-352-6277
Boyle Meat Company
   Kansas City, MO 800-821-3626
Bradley Technologies Canada Inc.
   Delta, BC 866-508-7514
Broadbent B & B Food Products
   Kuttawa, KY 800-841-2202

Product Categories / Meats & Meat Products: Beef & Beef Products

Brookshire Grocery Company
  Tyler, TX 888-937-3776
Brown Foods
  Dallas, GA 770-445-4358
Burke Corp
  Nevada, IA 800-654-1152
C & J Tender Meat Co
  Anchorage, AK 907-562-2838
Casper Foodservice Company
  Chicago, IL 312-226-2265
Charlito's Cocina
  Brooklyn, NY 718-482-7890
Chicago Premier Meats
  Chicago, IL 800-385-0661
Chipper Snax
  Salt Lake City, UT 801-977-0742
Chong Mei Trading
  East Point, GA 404-768-3838
Cimpl Meats
  Yankton, SD 605-665-1665
Coleman Natural
  Kings Mountain, NC 800-442-8666
Consumers Packing Co
  Melrose Park, IL 800-356-9876
Creminelli Fine Meats
  Salt Lake City, UT 801-428-1820
CTI Foods
  Wilder, ID 208-482-7844
Devro Inc
  Swansea, SC 803-796-9730
DiMario Foods
  Oak Brook, IL 630-581-5250
Double B Distributors
  Lexington, KY 859-255-8822
Dr. Pete's/J.C. Specialty Foods
  Savannah, GA 912-233-3035
E-Fish-Ent Fish Company
  Sooke, BC 250-642-4007
Ellsworth Foods
  Tifton, GA 229-386-8448
Fa Lu Cioli
  Union, NJ 908-258-8651
Fork & Goode
  Brooklyn, NY
Frank Brunckhorst Company
  Sarasota, FL 804-722-4100
Galvinell Meat Co Inc
  Conowingo, MD 410-378-3032
Garden Protein International
  Richmond, BC 877-305-6777
Glenoaks Food Inc
  Sun Valley, CA 818-768-9091
Golden Valley Natural
  Shelley, ID 888-270-7147
Golden West Food Group
  Vernon, CA 888-807-3663
Gopicnic Inc
  Chicago, IL 773-328-2490
Grayson Naturla Farms
  Independence, VA 276-773-3712
Gulf Marine & Industrial Supplies Inc
  Houston, TX 800-886-6252
H-E-B Grocery Co. LP
  San Antonio, TX 800-432-3113
Harbison Wholesale Meats
  Cullman, AL 256-739-5105
Heinkel's Packing Co
  Decatur, IL 800-594-2738
Henry J's Meat Specialties
  Chicago, IL 800-242-1314
Higa Food Service
  Honolulu, HI 808-531-3591
Highland Family Farms
  Mapleton, MN 507-524-3797
Ingles Markets
  Black Mountain, NC 828-669-2941
International Farmers Market
  Chamblee, GA 770-455-1777
Ira Higdon Grocery Company
  Cairo, GA 229-377-1272
J M Swank Co
  North Liberty, IA 800-593-6375
Jacob & Sons Wholesale Meats
  Martins Ferry, OH 740-633-3091
Jordan's Meats & Deli
  Lakeland, MN 651-337-2224
JUST Inc
  San Francisco, CA 844-423-5637
Kern Meat Distributing
  Brooksville, KY 606-756-2255
Lamex Foods Inc.
  Bloomington, MN 952-844-0585

Layman Distributing
  Salem, VA 800-237-1319
Les Trois Petits Cochons
  Brooklyn, NY 800-537-7283
Link Snacks Inc.
  Minong, WI 715-466-2234
Lubbers Family Farm
  Grand Rapids, MI 616-453-4257
Manda Fine Meats Inc
  Baton Rouge, LA 800-343-2642
Marathon Enterprises Inc
  Englewood, NJ 800-722-7388
Mcfarling Foods Inc
  Indianapolis, IN 317-635-2633
Mcredmond Brothers
  Nashville, TN 800-251-5930
Me At Corral
  Gainesville, GA 770-536-9188
Meat & Fish Fellas
  Glendale, AZ 623-931-6190
Meijer Inc
  Grand Rapids, MI 616-453-6711
Memphis Meats
  Berkeley, CA
Miami Beef Co
  Miami Lakes, FL 305-621-3252
My Favorite Jerky
  Boulder, CO 303-444-2846
National Meat & Provision Company
  Reserve, LA 985-479-4200
New Grass Bison
  Shawnee, KS 866-422-5888
New Horizon Farms
  Pipestone, MN 800-906-7447
Newport Meat Co North
  Irvine, CA 949-474-4040
Northern Meats
  Anchorage, AK 907-561-1729
Northwest Meat Company
  Chicago, IL 312-733-1418
Oberto Brands
  Kent, WA 877-453-7591
Oberweis Dairy Inc
  North Aurora, IL 866-623-7934
Ohio Association Of Meat
  Frazeysburg, OH 740-828-9900
Olympic Provisions Northwest
  Portland, OR 503-894-8136
Omaha Steaks Inc
   800-960-8400
Oscar's Wholesale Meats
  Ogden, UT 801-621-5655
Park 100 Foods Inc
  Tipton, IN 800-854-6504
Piggie Park Enterprises
  West Columbia, SC 800-628-7423
Piller's Fine Foods
  Waterloo, ON 800-265-2627
Pilot Meat & Sea Food Company
  Galena, IL 319-556-0760
Pioneer Snacks
  Farmington Hills, MI 248-862-1990
Pluester Quality Meat Co
  Hardin, IL 618-396-2224
Pocino Foods
  City Of Industry, CA 800-345-0150
Pon Food Corp
  Ponchatoula, LA 985-386-6941
Porkie Company of Wisconsin
  Cudahy, WI 800-333-2588
Prime Cut Meat & Seafood Company
  Phoenix, AZ 800-277-1054
Primera Meat Service
  Harlingen, TX 956-423-3721
Primo Foods
  Oceanside, CA 760-439-8711
Protos Inc
  Greensburg, PA 724-836-1802
Publix Super Market
  Lakeland, FL 800-242-1227
Quality Snack Foods Inc
  Alsip, IL 708-377-7120
Quirch Foods
  Coral Gables, FL 800-458-5252
RM Heagy Foods
  Lancaster, PA 717-569-1032
Rocky Mountain Natural Meats
  Henderson, CO 800-327-2706
Rougie Foie Gras
  Marieville, QC 450-460-2107
Safeway Inc.
  Pleasanton, CA 877-723-3929

Schenk Packing Co Inc
  Mt Vernon, WA 360-336-2128
Schisa Brothers
  Syracuse, NY 315-463-0213
Seafood Dimensions Intl
  Yorba Linda, CA 714-692-6464
Service Foods
  Norcross, GA 800-872-3484
Shuff's Meat Market
  Thurmont, MD 301-271-2231
Smoke House
  Sagle, ID 208-263-6312
Smoked Turkey Inc
  Marshville, NC 704-624-6628
Snak King Corp
  City Of Industry, CA 626-336-7711
Sofina Foods Inc
  Markham, ON 855-763-4621
Sommers Organic
  Wheeling, IL 877-377-9797
Specialty Food Association
  New York, NY 646-878-0301
Speco Inc
  Schiller Park, IL 800-541-5415
SRA Foods
  Birmingham, AL 205-323-7447
Strassburger Steaks
  Carlstadt, NJ 201-842-8890
Surlean Foods
  San Antonio, TX 800-999-4370
Sweetwood Cattle Co
  Steamboat Spgs, CO 970-879-7456
Teddy's Tasty Meats
  Anchorage, AK 907-562-2320
Thanasi Foods LLC
  Boulder, CO 866-558-7379
The New Primal
  Johns Island, SC 866-723-1386
The Shed Saucery
  Ocean Springs, MS 228-875-9590
Think Jerky
  Chicago, IL 312-380-0039
Thumann Inc.
  Carlstadt, NJ 201-935-3636
Todd's
  Vernon, CA 800-938-6337
Trail's Best Snacks
  Memphis, TN 800-852-1863
Trenton Processing Ctr
  Trenton, IL 800-871-7675
Troyer Foods Inc
  Goshen, IN 800-876-9377
Turkey Creeks Snacks Inc
  Thomaston, GA 800-329-8875
Tuscan Eat/Perdinci
  Sarasota, FL 941-565-7382
UTZ Quality Foods Inc.
  Hanover, PA 800-367-7629
Vanee Foods Co
  Berkeley, IL 708-449-7300
Vantage Foods
  Calgary, AB 403-215-2820
Vermont Smoke and Cure
  Hinesburg, VT 802-482-4666
Vestergaard Farms
  Ann Arbor, MI 734-929-2875
Vity Meat & Provisions Company
  Phoenix, AZ 602-269-7768
Volpi Foods
  St Louis, MO 800-288-3439
Wegmans Food Markets Inc.
  Rochester, NY 800-934-6267
White Oak Pastures
  Bluffton, GA 229-641-2081
Winn-Dixie Stores
  Jacksonville, FL 800-967-9105
YB Meats of Wichita
  Wichita, KS 316-942-1213
Zabiha Halal Meat Processors
  Addison, IL 630-620-5000
Zoe's Meats
  Santa Rosa, CA 707-545-9637
Zuccaro Produce
  Columbia Heights, MN 612-333-1122

Beef & Beef Products

A To Z Portion Control Meats
  Bluffton, OH 800-338-6328
A&H Products, Inc
  Hillsdale, NJ 908-206-8886
A.C. Kissling Company
  Philadelphia, PA 800-445-1943

Product Categories / Meats & Meat Products: Beef & Beef Products

Abbott's Meat Inc
 Flint, MI 800-678-1907
Abbyland Foods Inc
 Abbotsford, WI 800-732-5483
Acme Steak & Seafood
 Youngstown, OH 800-686-2263
Adolf's Meats & Sausage Kitchen
 Hartford, CT 860-522-1588
Advance Pierre Foods
 Cincinnati, OH 800-969-2747
AFI-FlashGril'd Steak
 Salt Lake City, UT 800-382-2862
AJ's Lena Maid Meats Inc
 Lena, IL 815-369-4522
Al Safa Halal
 New York City, NY 800-268-8147
Albert's Meats
 Claysville, PA 800-522-9970
Alderfer Inc
 Harleysville, PA 800-341-1121
Alpine Butcher
 Lowell, MA 978-256-7771
Alpine Cheese Company
 Winesburg, OH 330-359-6291
Alpine Meats
 Stockton, CA 800-399-6328
American Foods Group LLC
 Green Bay, WI 800-345-0293
Amity Packing Co Inc
 Chicago, IL 800-837-0270
Andrews Dried Beef Company
 Quakertown, PA 610-759-5180
Anmar Foods
 Chicago, IL 312-421-6500
Arena & Sons
 Redwood City, CA 650-366-1750
Arizona Sunland Foods
 Tucson, AZ 520-624-7068
Armbrust Meats
 Medford, WI 715-748-3102
Arrowhead Beef
 Chipley, FL 850-270-8804
Atlantic Meat Company
 Savannah, GA 912-964-8511
Aunt Kitty's Foods Inc
 Vineland, NJ 856-691-2100
Aurora Packing Co Inc
 North Aurora, IL 630-897-0551
Ayoba-Yo
 Oakton, VA 202-796-8554
B & R Quality Meats Inc
 Waterloo, IA 319-232-6328
B.W.J.W. Inc.
 Fort Worth, TX 817-831-0051
Bakalars Sausage Co
 La Crosse, WI 608-784-0384
Ball Park Franks
 Peoria, IL 888-317-5867
Baretta Provision
 East Berlin, CT 860-828-0802
Barney Pork House
 Decatur, AL 256-353-8688
Beef Products Inc.
 North Sioux City, SD 605-217-8000
Bellville Meat Market
 Bellville, TX 800-571-6328
Berks Packing Company, Inc.
 Reading, PA 800-882-3757
Berry Processing
 Walla Walla, IL 509-529-2161
Best Chicago Meat
 Chicago, IL
Best Provision Co Inc
 Union, NJ 800-631-4466
Big B Barbecue
 Evansville, IN 812-425-5235
Birchwood Foods Inc
 Kenosha, WI 800-541-1685
Blakely Freezer Locker
 Blakeley, GA 229-723-3622
Bluebonnet Meat Company
 Trenton, TX 903-989-2293
Boone's Butcher Shop
 Bardstown, KY 888-253-3384
Borders Sporting Goods
 Ashland, KY 606-928-6326
Boulder Sausage Co
 Louisville, CO 866-529-0595
Bouma Meats
 Provost, AB 780-753-2092
Bouvry Exports Calgary
 Calgary, AB 403-253-0717

Boyd's Sausage Co
 Washington, IA 319-653-5715
Bradley 3 Ranch
 Memphis, TX 806-888-1062
Braham Food Locker Service
 Braham, MN 320-396-2636
Branding Iron
 Sauget, IL 800-851-4684
Breslow Deli Products
 Philadelphia, PA 215-739-4200
Brook Locker Plant
 Brook, IN 219-275-2611
Brook Meadow Meats
 Hagerstown, MD 301-739-3107
Brookfield Farm
 Amherst, MA 413-253-7991
Brown Foods
 Dallas, GA 770-445-4358
Brown Packing Company
 South Holland, IL 800-832-8325
Brown Thompson & Sons
 Fancy Farm, KY 270-623-6321
Burgers' Smokehouse
 California, MO 800-345-5185
Burke Corp
 Nevada, IA 800-654-1152
Burnett & Son
 Monrovia, CA 877-632-5467
Burton Meat Processing
 Burton, TX 979-289-4022
Bush Brothers Provision Co
 West Palm Beach, FL 800-327-1345
C & J Tender Meat Co
 Anchorage, AK 907-562-2838
C&S Wholesale Meat Company
 Atlanta, GA 404-627-3547
Caddo Packing Co
 Marshall, TX 903-935-2211
Callaway Packing Inc
 Delta, CO 970-874-9743
Campbell Soup Co.
 Camden, NJ 800-257-8443
Campbell's Quality Cuts
 Sidney, OH 937-492-2194
Camrose Packers
 Camrose, AB 780-672-4887
Canal Fulton Provision
 Canal Fulton, OH 800-321-3502
Candelari's Specialty Sausage
 Houston, TX 800-953-5343
Capital Packers Inc
 Edmonton, AB 800-272-8868
Capolla Food Inc
 North York, ON 416-633-0389
Carando Gourmet Frozen Foods
 Agawam, MA 888-227-2636
Cargill Protein
 Wichita, KS
Caribbean Food Delights Inc
 Tappan, NY 845-398-3000
Caribbean Products
 Baltimore, MD 410-235-7700
Carl Rittberger Sr Inc
 Zanesville, OH 740-452-2767
Caro Foods
 Houma, LA 800-395-2276
Castle Rock Meats
 Denver, CO 303-292-0855
Cattaneo Brothers Inc
 San Luis Obispo, CA 800-243-8537
Centennial Food Corporation
 Calgary, AB 403-214-0044
Center Locker Svc
 Center, MO 800-884-0737
Central Meat & Provision
 San Diego, CA 619-239-1391
Century Agricultural Products LLC
 Greenback, TN 865-980-8522
Chandler Foods Inc
 Greensboro, NC 800-537-6219
Charlito's Cocina
 Brooklyn, NY 718-482-7890
Chef's Requested Foods
 Oklahoma City, OK 405-239-2610
Cher-Make Sausage Co
 Manitowoc, WI 800-242-7679
Cheraw Packing Plant
 Cheraw, SC 843-537-7426
Chicago 58 Food Products
 Woodbridge, ON 416-603-4244
Chicago Meat Authority Inc
 Chicago, IL 800-383-3811

Chicago Steaks
 Chicago, IL 773-847-5400
Chip Steak & Provision Co
 Mankato, MN 507-388-6277
Cimpl Meats
 Yankton, SD 605-665-1665
Circle V Meats
 Spanish Fork, UT 801-798-3081
Clay Center Locker Plant
 Clay Center, KS 800-466-5543
Clovervale Farms
 Amherst, OH 800-433-0146
Columbia Packing Co Inc
 Dallas, TX 214-946-8171
Conagra Brands Inc
 Chicago, IL 877-266-2472
Conagra Foodservice
 Chicago, IL 877-266-2472
Continental Grain Company
 New York, NY 212-207-5100
Continental Sausage
 Denver, CO 866-794-7727
Corfu Foods Inc
 Bensenville, IL 630-595-2510
Couch's Country Style Sausages
 Cleveland, OH 216-823-2332
Country Butcher Shop
 Carlisle, PA 800-272-9223
Country Village Meats Inc
 Sublette, IL 800-700-4545
Crescent Foods
 Chicago, IL 800-939-6268
Creuzebergers Meats
 Duncansville, PA 814-695-3061
Critchfield Meats Inc
 Lexington, KY 800-866-2901
Crofton & Sons Inc
 Tampa, FL 800-878-7675
CTI Foods
 Wilder, ID 208-482-7844
Curley's Custom Meats
 Jackson Center, OH 937-596-6518
Curly's Foods Inc
 Edina, MN 612-920-3400
Curtis Packing Co
 Greensboro, NC 336-275-7684
Cyclone Enterprises Inc
 Houston, TX 281-872-0087
Dale T Smith & Sons Inc
 Draper, UT 801-571-3611
Day-Lee Foods, Inc.
 Santa Fe Springs, CA 800-329-5331
Dearborn Sausage Co Inc
 Dearborn, MI 866-900-4426
Debragga & Spitler
 Jersey City, NJ
Decker Food Company
 Garland, TX 972-278-6192
Deen Meat & Cooked Foods
 Fort Worth, TX 800-333-3953
Devault Foods
 Devault, PA 800-426-2874
Dewig Brothers Packing Company
 Haubstadt, IN 812-768-6208
Diazteca Inc
 Rio Rico, AZ 520-761-4621
Diestel Family Turkey Ranch
 209-532-4950
Diggs Packing Company
 Columbia, MO 573-449-2995
Dino's Sausage & Meat Co Inc
 Utica, NY 315-732-2661
Dole & Bailey Inc
 Woburn, MA 781-935-1234
Dom's Sausage Co Inc
 Malden, MA 781-324-6390
Donald E Hunter Meats
 Hillsboro, OH 937-466-2311
Dorina So-Good Inc
 Union, IL 815-923-2144
Drier's Meats
 Three Oaks, MI 269-756-3101
Dryden Provision Co Inc
 Louisville, KY 502-583-1777
Dugdale Beef Company
 Indianapolis, IN 317-520-9981
Duma Meats Inc
 Mogadore, OH 330-628-3438
Dutch Packing Co., Inc.
 Doral, FL 800-723-9249
Dutterer's Home Food Service
 Baltimore, MD 410-298-3663

Product Categories / Meats & Meat Products: Beef & Beef Products

Dynamic Foods
  Lubbock, TX 806-723-5600
E&H Packing Company
  Detroit, MI 313-567-8286
E.W. Knauss & Son
  Quakertown, PA 800-648-4220
East Dayton Meat & Poultry
  Dayton, OH 937-253-6185
Ed Miniat Inc
  South Holland, IL 708-589-2400
Edelman Meats Inc
  Antigo, WI 715-623-7686
Eickman's Processing Co
  Seward, IL 815-247-8451
Eiserman Meats
  Slave Lake, AB 780-849-5507
El Paso Meat Co
  El Paso, TX 915-838-8600
Ellsworth Locker
  Ellsworth, MN 507-967-2544
ELP Inc
  Elizabeth, CO 303-688-2240
Enjoy Foods International
  Fontana, CA 909-823-2228
Eureka Locker Inc
  Eureka, IL 309-467-2731
Eurocaribe Packing Company
  Vega Baja, PR 787-793-6900
Ezzo Sausage Company
  Columbus, OH 800-558-8841
Fabbri Sausage Mfg Co
  Chicago, IL 312-829-6363
Fair Oaks Farms LLC
  Pleasant Prairie, WI 800-528-8615
Far West Meats
  Highland, CA 909-864-1990
Farm Boy Food Svc
  Evansville, IN 800-852-3976
FDI Inc
  Berkeley, IL 708-544-1880
Feed The Party
  Louisville, KY
First Original Texas Chili Company
  Fort Worth, TX 800-507-0009
Flanders
  Waycross, GA 912-283-5191
Four Star Beef
  Omaha, NE
Fred Usinger Inc
  Milwaukee, WI 800-558-9998
Freirich Foods
  Salisbury, NC 800-221-1315
Fremont Beef Co
  Fremont, NE 800-331-4788
Fulton Provision Co
  Portland, OR 800-333-6328
Gary's Frozen Foods
  Lubbock, TX 806-745-1933
Gaucho Foods
  Fayetteville, IL 877-677-2282
Gelsinger Food Products
  Montrose, CA 818-248-7811
Gem Meat Packing Co
  Garden City, ID 208-375-9424
Georgetown Farm
  Free Union, VA 888-328-5326
Godshall's Quality Meats
  Telford, PA 888-463-7425
Golden West Food Group
  Vernon, CA 888-807-3663
GoodMark Foods
  Edina, MN 952-835-6900
Grandpa Ittel's Meats Inc
  Howard Lake, MN 320-543-2285
Grant Park Packing
  Chicago, IL 312-421-4096
Grass Run Farms
  Greeley, CO 800-727-2333
Great Plains Beef LLC
  Lincoln, NE 402-479-2115
Greater Omaha Packing Co Inc.
  Omaha, NE 800-747-5400
Grimm's Fine Food
  Richmond, BC 866-663-4746
Grimm's Locker Service
  Sherwood, OH 419-899-2655
Groff's Meats
  Elizabethtown, PA 717-367-1246
Gwinn's Foods
  St Louis, MO 314-521-8792
H&K Packers Company
  Winnipeg, NB 204-233-2354

Hall Brothers Meats
  Olmsted Twp, OH 440-235-3262
Ham I Am
  Dallas, TX 800-742-6426
Hamilos Bros Inspected Meat
  Madison, IL 618-876-3710
Hamms Custom Meats
  Mckinney, TX 972-542-3359
Happy Acres Packing Company
  Petal, MS 601-584-8301
Harper's Country Hams
  Clinton, KY 888-427-7377
Harris Ranch Beef Co
  Selma, CA 800-742-1955
Hausman Foods LLC
  Corpus Christi, TX 361-883-5521
Heinke Family Farm
  Paradise, CA 530-877-5264
Heinkel's Packing Co
  Decatur, IL 800-594-2738
Henry J's Meat Specialties
  Chicago, IL 800-242-1314
Heringer Meats Inc
  Covington, KY 859-291-2000
Hickory Baked Ham Co
  Castle Rock, CO 303-688-2633
Hickory Farms
  Maumee, OH 800-753-8558
High Valley Farm
  Castle Rock, CO 303-634-2944
Hillbilly Smokehouse
  Rogers, AR 479-636-1927
Hoff's United Food
  Brownsville, WI 800-852-9658
Holly Hill Locker Company
  Holly Hill, SC 803-496-3611
Holton Meat Processing
  Holton, KS 785-364-2331
Home Market Food Inc
  Norwood, MA 800-367-8325
Honeybaked Ham
  Cincinnati, OH 513-583-8792
Horlacher Meats
  Logan, UT 435-752-1287
Hormel Foods Corp.
  Austin, MN 507-437-5611
Houser Meats
  Rushville, IL 217-322-4994
Hsin Tung Yang Foods Inc
  S San Francisco, CA 650-589-6789
Humeniuk's Meat Cutting
  Ranfurly, AB 780-658-2381
Huse's Country Meats
  Malone, TX 254-533-2205
Independent Meat Co
  Twin Falls, ID 800-284-4626
International Food Packers Corporation
  Miami, FL 305-740-5847
International Meat Co
  Chicago, IL 773-622-1400
Isernio Sausage Company
  Seattle, WA 888-495-8674
Ito Cariani Sausage Company
  Hayward, CA 510-887-0882
J F O'Neill & Packing Co
  Omaha, NE 402-733-1200
J W Treuth & Sons
  Catonsville, MD 410-747-6281
J.M. Schneider
  Saint Anselme, QC 418-885-4474
Jackson Brothers Food Locker
  Post, TX 806-495-3245
Jacob's Meats Inc
  Defiance, OH 419-782-7831
Jacobsmuhlen's Meats
  Cornelius, OR 503-359-0479
Jakes Brothers Country Meats
  Joelton, TN 615-876-2911
Janowski's Hamburgers Inc
  Rockville Centre, NY 516-764-9591
JBS USA LLC
  Greeley, CO 970-506-8000
Jemm Wholesale Meat Company
  Chicago, IL 773-523-8161
Jensen Meat Company
  San Diego, CA 619-754-6400
John Garner Meats
  Van Buren, AR 800-543-5473
Jones Packing Co
  Harvard, IL 815-943-4488
Jordahl Meats
  Manchester, MN 507-826-3418

Joyce Farms
  Winston Salem, NC 800-755-6923
K & K Gourmet Meats Inc
  Leetsdale, PA 724-266-8400
Karl Ehmer
  Flushing, NY 800-487-5275
Kelble Brothers Inc
  Berlin Heights, OH 800-247-2333
Kelly Corned Beef Co
  Chicago, IL 800-624-5617
Kelly Packing Company
  Torrington, WY 307-532-2210
Kelly-Eisenberg Gourmet Deli Products
  Chicago, IL 800-624-5617
Kenosha Beef International LTD
  Kenosha, WI
Kershenstine Beef Jerky
  Eupora, MS 662-258-2049
Ketters Meat Market & Locker Plant
  Frazee, MN 218-334-2351
King Kold Meats
  Englewood, OH 800-836-2797
King's Command Foods Inc
  Green Bay, WA 800-345-0293
Kingsbury Country Market
  La Porte, IN 219-393-3016
Kiolbassa Provision Co
  San Antonio, TX 800-456-5465
Klement Sausage Co Inc
  Milwaukee, WI 800-553-6368
Kulana Foods LTD
  Hilo, HI 808-959-9144
Kutztown Bologna Company
  Leola, PA 800-723-8824
L & L Packing Co
  Chicago, IL 800-628-6328
L & M Lockers
  Belt, MT 406-277-3522
L & M Slaughterhouse
  Georgetown, IL 217-662-6841
L. A. Smoking & Curing Company
  Los Angeles, CA 213-624-2369
Ladoga Frozen Food & Retail
  Ladoga, IN 765-942-2225
Lampost Meats
  Grimes, IA 515-288-6111
Land O'Frost Inc
  Searcy, AR 800-643-5654
Land O'Frost Inc.
  Lansing, IL 800-323-3308
Lay Packing Company
  Knoxville, TN 865-522-1147
Lehmann Farms
  Lakeville, MN 800-446-5276
Lengerich Meats Inc
  Zanesville, IN 260-638-4123
Leo G. Fraboni Sausage Company
  Hibbing, MN 218-263-5074
Link Snacks Inc.
  Minong, WI 715-466-2234
Lisbon Sausage Co Inc
  New Bedford, MA 508-994-0453
Lombardi Brothers Meat Packers
  Denver, CO 303-458-7441
Long Food Industries
  Fripp Island, SC 843-838-3205
Longview Meat & Merchandise Ltd
  Longview, AB 866-355-3759
Mac's Meats Inc
  Las Cruces, NM 575-524-2751
MacGregors Meat & Seafood
  Toronto, ON 888-383-3663
Mada'n Kosher Foods
  Dania, FL 954-925-0077
Magnolia Meats
  Knoxville, TN 865-546-7702
Maid-Rite Steak Company
  Dunmore, PA 800-233-4259
Manger Packing Corp
  Baltimore, MD 800-227-9262
Manley Meats Inc
  Decatur, IN 260-592-7313
Marie F
  Markham, ON 800-365-4464
Marks Meat
  Holmen, WI 608-526-6058
Marshallville Packing Co
  Marshallville, OH 330-855-2871
Marubeni America Corp.
  New York, NY 212-450-0100
Matthiesen's Deer & Custom
  De Witt, IA 563-659-8409

Product Categories / Meats & Meat Products: Beef & Beef Products

Mclemores Abattoir Inc
  Vidalia, GA 912-537-4476
Meadowbrook Meat Company
  Rocky Mount, NC 252-985-7200
Meatco Sales Ltd.
  Mirror, AB 403-788-2292
Meating Place
  Buffalo, NY 716-885-3623
Meatland Packers
  Medicine Hat, AB 403-528-4321
Medeiros Farms
  Kalaheo, HI 808-332-8211
Memphis Meats
  Berkeley, CA
Merkley & Sons Packing Co Inc
  Jasper, IN 812-482-7020
Merrill Meat Co
  Encampment, WY 307-327-5345
Mesquite Organic Beef LLC
  Aurora, CO 888-480-2333
Metafoods LLC
  Brookhaven, GA 404-843-2400
Metropolitan Sausage Manufacturing Company
  Flossmoor, IL 708-331-3232
Michael's Finer Meats/Seafoods
  Columbus, OH 800-282-0518
Miko Meat
  Hilo, HI 808-935-0841
Miller Brothers Packing Company
  Sylvester, GA 229-776-2014
Miller's Country Hams
  Dresden, TN 800-622-0606
Miller's Meat Market
  Red Bud, IL 618-282-3334
Mims Meat Company
  Houston, TX 713-453-0151
Mirasco
  Atlanta, GA 770-956-1945
Montana Ranch Brand
  Billings, MT 406-294-2333
Morreale John R Inc
  Chicago, IL 312-421-3664
Mortimer's Fine Foods
  Burlington, ON 905-336-0000
Moweaqua Packing Plant
  Moweaqua, IL 217-768-4714
Munsee Meats
  Muncie, IN 800-662-8001
Napoleon Locker
  Napoleon, IN 812-852-4333
National Foods
  Indianapolis, IN 800-683-6565
National Steak & Poultry
  Owasso, OK 918-274-8787
Natures Sungrown Foods Inc
  San Rafael, CA 415-491-4944
Nebraska Beef Council
  Kearney, NE 800-421-5326
Nema Food Distribution
  Fairfield, NJ 973-256-4415
Nesbitt Processing
  Aledo, IL 309-582-5183
New Braunfels Smokehouse
  New Braunfels, TX 800-537-6932
Nick's Sticks
  Marshfield, WI 715-257-0636
Nodine's Smokehouse Inc
  Torrington, CT 800-222-2059
Nolechek Meats Inc
  Thorp, WI 800-454-5580
Northern Packing Company
  Brier Hill, NY 315-375-8801
Northwest Meat Company
  Chicago, IL 312-733-1418
Nossack Fine Meats
  Red Deer, AB 403-346-5006
Nueske's Applewood Smoked Meat
  Wittenberg, WI 800-720-1153
Oklahoma City Meat Co Inc
  Oklahoma City, OK 405-235-3308
Old Country Meat & Sausage Company
  San Diego, CA 619-297-4301
Old Kentucky Hams
  Cynthiana, KY 859-234-5015
Old Neighborhood
  Lynn, MA 781-595-1557
Olson Locker
  Fairmont, MN 507-238-2563
Omaha Meat Processors
  Omaha, NE 402-554-1965
Omaha Steaks Inc
  800-960-8400

On-Cor Frozen Foods Redi-Serve
  Aurora, IL 920-563-6391
Onoway Custom Packers
  Onoway, AB 780-967-2727
Ossian Smoked Meats
  Ossian, IN 800-535-8862
P G Molinari & Sons
  San Francisco, CA 415-822-5555
Palmer Meat Packing Co
  Tremonton, UT 435-257-5329
Palmyra Bologna Co Inc
  Palmyra, PA 800-282-6336
Panorama Meats
  Fresno, CA 707-765-6756
Paradise Locker Inc.
  Trimble, MO 816-370-6328
Pasqualichio Brothers Inc
  Scranton, PA 800-232-6233
Pat's Meat Discounter
  Mills, WY 307-237-7549
Patrick Cudahy LLC
  Cudahy, WI 800-486-6900
Paul Schafer Meat Products
  Baltimore, MD 410-528-1250
Payne Packing Co
  Artesia, NM 575-746-2779
Pekarna Meat Market
  Jordan, MN 952-492-6101
Pekarski Sausage
  South Deerfield, MA 413-665-4537
Petschl's Quality Meats
  Tukwila, WA 206-575-4400
Pierceton Foods Inc
  Pierceton, IN 574-594-2344
Piller's Fine Foods
  Waterloo, ON 800-265-2627
Pinter's Packing Plant
  Dorchester, WI 715-654-5444
Piper Meat Processing
  Andover, OH 440-293-7170
Plymouth Beef Co.
  Bronx, NY 718-589-8600
Poche's Smokehouse
  Breaux Bridge, LA 800-376-2437
Polarica USA, Inc.
  Pacheco, CA 800-426-3872
Pork Shop of Vermont
  Charlotte, VT 800-458-3441
Premium Meat Co
  Brigham City, UT 435-723-5944
Prime Pak Foods Inc
  Gainesville, GA 770-536-8708
Provost Packers
  Provost, AB 780-753-2415
Quaker Maid Meats
  Reading, PA 610-376-1500
Quality Food Company
  Providence, RI 877-233-3462
Quality Sausage Company
  Dallas, TX 214-634-3400
Quirch Foods
  Coral Gables, FL 800-458-5252
R Four Meats
  Chatfield, MN 507-867-4180
R I Provision Co
  Johnston, RI 401-831-0815
R.E. Meyer Company
  Lincoln, NE 888-990-2333
Ranch Oak Farm
  Fort Worth, TX 800-888-0327
Randall Foods Inc
  Vernon, CA 800-372-6581
Ray's Sausage Co
  Cleveland, OH 216-921-8782
Real Sausage Co
  Chicago, IL 312-842-5330
Red Deer Lake Meat Processing
  Calgary, AB 403-256-4925
Red Hot Chicago
  Chicago, IL 800-249-5226
Red Steer Meats
  Phoenix, AZ 602-272-6677
Redondo's LLC
  Waipahu, HI 808-671-5444
Rinehart Meat Processing
  Branson, MO 417-869-2041
Robbins Packing Company
  Statesboro, GA 912-764-7503
Robertson's Country Meat Hams
  Finchville, KY 800-678-1521
Rocky Mountain Meats
  Rocky Mountain House, AB 403-845-3434

Rocky Mountain Packing Company
  Havre, MT 406-265-3401
Rolet Food Products Company
  Brooklyn, NY 718-497-0476
Roman Packing Company
  Norfolk, NE 800-373-5990
Romanian Kosher Sausage Co
  Chicago, IL 773-761-4141
Roode Packing Company
  Fairbury, NE 402-729-2253
Rosen's Diversified Inc.
  Fairmont, MN 507-238-6001
Royal Center Locker Plant
  Royal Center, IN 574-643-3275
Royal Palate Foods
  Inglewood, CA 310-330-7701
Rubashkin
  Brooklyn, NY 718-436-5511
Rude Custom Butchering
  Mt Morris, IL 815-946-3795
Ruef's Meat Market
  New Glarus, WI 608-527-2554
Rymer Foods
  Chicago, IL 800-247-9637
S.W. Meat & Provision Company
  Phoenix, AZ 602-275-2000
Sadler's Smokehouse
  Henderson, TX 903-657-5581
Salwa Foods
  Lawrenceville, GA 770-263-8207
Sam KANE Beef Processors Inc
  Corpus Christi, TX 800-242-4142
Sampco
  Chicago, IL 800-767-1689
San Angelo Packing
  San Angelo, TX 325-949-9401
Sanders Meat Packing Inc
  Custer, MI 800-968-5035
Sangudo Custom Meat Packers
  Sangudo, AB 888-785-3353
Santa's Smokehouse
  Fairbanks, AK 800-478-3885
Saval Foods Corp
  Elkridge, MD 800-527-2825
Sculli Brothers
  Yeadon, PA 215-336-1223
Shamrock Foods Co
  Phoenix, AZ 800-289-3663
Shelley's
  Jersey City, NJ 201-433-2900
Shirer Brothers Meats
  Adamsville, OH 740-796-3214
Shreve Meats Processing
  Shreve, OH 330-567-2142
Shrums Sausage & Meats
  Stettler, AB 403-742-1427
Silver Lake Sausage Shop
  Providence, RI 401-944-4081
Sky Haven Farm
  Cincinnati, OH 513-681-2303
Skylark Meats
  Omaha, NE 800-759-5275
Slathars Smokehouse
  Lake City, MN 507-753-2080
Slim Jim
  Chicago, IL 877-266-2472
Smith Packing Regional Meat
  Utica, NY 315-732-5125
Smith Provision Co Inc
  Erie, PA 800-334-9151
Smokey Denmark Sausage Co
  Austin, TX 512-385-0718
Sofina Foods Inc
  Markham, ON 855-763-4621
Sommers Organic
  Wheeling, IL 877-377-9797
Souris Valley Processors
  Melita, MB 204-522-8210
Southern Packing Corp
  Chesapeake, VA 757-421-2131
Specialty Foods Group Inc
  Owensboro, KY 800-238-0020
Spring Grove Foods
  Miamisburg, OH 937-866-4311
Springville Meat & Cold Storage
  Springville, UT 801-489-6391
Square-H Brands Inc
  Vernon, CA 323-267-4600
SRA Foods
  Birmingham, AL 205-323-7447
Stallings Head Cheese Co
  Houston, TX 713-523-1751

Product Categories / Meats & Meat Products: Beef & Beef Products

Standard Meat Co LP
  Dallas, TX 866-859-6313
Steak-Umm Company
  Shillington, PA 860-928-5900
Stehlin & Sons Company
  Cincinnati, OH 800-352-7396
Stock Yards Packing Company
  Melrose Park, IL 877-785-9273
Stone Meat Processor
  Ogden, UT 801-782-9825
Straub's
  Clayton, MO 888-725-2121
Strauss Brands International
  Franklin, WI 414-421-5250
Streit Carl & Son Co
  Neptune, NJ 732-775-0803
Stripling's General Store
  Moultrie, GA 229-985-4226
Sudlersville Frozen Food Locker
  Sudlersville, MD 410-438-3106
Sugardale Foods Inc
  800-860-6333
Sun-Rise
  Alexandria, MN 320-846-5720
SunFed Ranch
  Woodland, CA 530-723-5373
Sunnydale Meats Inc
  Gaffney, SC 864-489-6091
Suzanna's Kitchen
  Peachtree Cor, GA 770-476-9900
Sweetwood Cattle Co
  Steamboat Spgs, CO 970-879-7456
Tank's Meats Inc
  Elmore, OH 419-862-3312
Taylor Meat Co
  Taylor, TX 512-352-6357
Taylor's Sausage Co
  St Louis, MO 314-652-3476
Tayse Meats
  Cleveland, OH 216-664-1799
Temptee Specialty Foods
  Denver, CO 800-842-1233
Terra's
  Perham, MN 218-346-4100
Terrell Meats
  Delta, UT 435-864-2600
Texas Reds Steak House
  Red River, NM 575-754-2922
The Bruss Company
  Chicago, IL 773-282-2900
Thompson Packers
  Slidell, LA 800-989-6328
Thomson Meats
  Melfort, SK 306-752-2802
Three Jerks Jerky
  Pacific Palisades, CA 424-703-5375
Tillamook Meat Inc
  Tillamook, OR 503-842-4802
Tolteca Foodservice
  Norcross, GA 800-541-6835
Travis Meats Inc
  Powell, TN 800-247-7606
Tri State Beef Co
  Cincinnati, OH 513-579-1722
Troy Pork Store
  Troy, NY 518-272-8291
Troyer Foods Inc
  Goshen, IN 800-876-9377
Tucker Packing Co
  Orrville, OH 330-683-3311
Turk Brothers Custom Meats Inc
  Ashland, OH 800-789-1051
Tyler Packing Co
  Tyler, TX 903-593-9592
Tyson Foods Inc.
  Springdale, AR 479-290-4000
Tyson Foods Inc.
  Springdale, AR 800-233-6332
Uncle Charley's Sausage
  Vandergrift, PA 724-845-3302
Une-Viandi
  St. Jean Sur Richelieu, NB 800-363-1955
United Meat Company
  San Francisco, CA 415-864-2118
United Provision Meat Company
  Columbus, OH 614-252-1126
Universal Beef Products
  Houston, TX 713-224-6043
US Wellness Meats
  Canton, MO 877-383-0051
Uvalde Meat Processing
  Uvalde, TX 830-278-6247

Valley Meat Company
  Modesto, CA 800-222-6328
Valley Meats
  Coal Valley, IL 309-517-6639
Verde Farms, LLC
  Woburn, MA 617-221-8922
Vestergaard Farms
  Ann Arbor, MI 734-929-2875
Victoria Fancy Sausage
  Edmonton, AB 780-471-2283
Vienna Beef LTD
  Chicago, IL 800-366-3647
Vienna Meat Products
  Scarborough, ON 800-588-1931
Vital Choice
  Bellingham, WA 800-608-4825
Voget Meats Inc
  Hubbard, OR 503-981-6271
W & G Marketing Company
  Ames, IA 515-233-4774
W.A. Beans & Sons
  Bangor, ME 800-649-1958
W.R. Delozier Sausage Company
  Seymour, TN 865-577-5907
WACO Beef & Pork Processors
  Waco, TX 254-772-4669
Waken Meat Co
  Atlanta, GA 404-627-3537
Walker Meats
  Carrollton, GA 800-741-3601
Wall Meat Processing
  Wall, SD 605-279-2348
Waltham Beef Company
  Boston, MA 617-269-2250
Warren & Son Meat Processing
  Whipple, OH 740-585-2421
Wasatch Meats Inc
  Salt Lake City, UT 800-631-8294
Webster City Custom Meats Inc
  Webster City, IA 515-832-1130
Weiss Brothers Smoke House
  Johnstown, PA 814-539-4085
West Liberty Foods LLC
  West Liberty, IA 888-511-4500
Westbrook Trading Company
  Calgary, AB 800-563-5785
Western Buffalo Company
  Rapid City, SD 800-247-3263
Western Meat Co
  Tumwater, WA 866-357-6601
Westport Locker LLC
  Westport, IN 877-265-0551
White Oak Pastures
  Bluffton, GA 229-641-2081
White's Meat Processing
  Fort Gibson, OK 918-478-2347
Willcox Meat Packing House
  Willcox, AZ 520-384-2015
Windcrest Meat Packers
  Port Perry, ON 800-750-2542
Winona Packing Company
  Winona, MS 662-283-4317
Winter Sausage Manufacturing Company
  Eastpointe, MI 800-321-2987
Wisconsin Packaging Corp
  Fort Atkinson, WI 920-563-9363
Wohrles Foods
  Pittsfield, MA 800-628-6114
Woodbine
  Norfolk, VA 757-461-2731
Woods Smoked Meats Inc
  Bowling Green, MO 800-458-8426
Yoakum Packing Co
  Yoakum, TX 800-999-6997
Zartic Inc
  Rome, GA 800-241-0516

Barbecued

Art's Tamales
  Metamora, IL 309-367-2850
Bear Creek Smokehouse Inc
  Marshall, TX 800-950-2327
Burke Corp
  Nevada, IA 800-654-1152
Curly's Foods Inc
  Edina, MN 612-920-3400
Dorina So-Good Inc
  Union, IL 815-923-2144
Gary's Frozen Foods
  Lubbock, TX 806-745-1933
Gaucho Foods
  Fayetteville, IL 877-677-2282

King Kold Meats
  Englewood, OH 800-836-2797
Moonlite Bar-B-Q Inn
  Owensboro, KY 800-322-8989
Sadler's Smokehouse
  Henderson, TX 903-657-5581
The Shed Saucery
  Ocean Springs, MS 228-875-9590
Travis Meats Inc
  Powell, TN 800-247-7606
W & G Marketing Company
  Ames, IA 515-233-4774

Frozen

Art's Tamales
  Metamora, IL 309-367-2850
Burke Corp
  Nevada, IA 800-654-1152
El Rey Cooked Meats
  St Louis, MO 314-521-3113
Gary's Frozen Foods
  Lubbock, TX 806-745-1933
Gaucho Foods
  Fayetteville, IL 877-677-2282
Hormel Foods Corp.
  Austin, MN 507-437-5611
King Kold Meats
  Englewood, OH 800-836-2797

Brisket

Bear Creek Smokehouse Inc
  Marshall, TX 800-950-2327
Henry J's Meat Specialties
  Chicago, IL 800-242-1314
Nueces Canyon Range
  Brenham, TX 800-925-5058
Saval Foods Corp
  Elkridge, MD 800-527-2825

Canned with Natural Juices

Aunt Kitty's Foods Inc
  Vineland, NJ 856-691-2100
International Food Packers Corporation
  Miami, FL 305-740-5847

Chipped

Alderfer Inc
  Harleysville, PA 800-341-1121

Dinners

Campbell Soup Co.
  Camden, NJ 800-257-8443
Henry J's Meat Specialties
  Chicago, IL 800-242-1314

Filet Mignon

Amana Meat Shop & Smoke House
  Amana, IA 800-373-6328
American Foods Group LLC
  Green Bay, WI 800-345-0293
Chef's Requested Foods
  Oklahoma City, OK 405-239-2610
Chicago Steaks
  Chicago, IL 773-847-5400
Miami Beef Co
  Miami Lakes, FL 305-621-3252

Fresh

Amity Packing Co Inc
  Chicago, IL 800-837-0270
Brook Locker Plant
  Brook, IN 219-275-2611
Brookfield Farm
  Amherst, MA 413-253-7991
Buckhead Beef
  Atlanta, GA 800-888-5578
Cattleman Meat & Produce
  Taylor, MI 734-287-8260
Certified Piedmontese Beef
  Lincoln, NE 800-414-3487
Farm Boy Food Svc
  Evansville, IN 800-852-3976
Farmstead At Long Meadow Ranch
  St Helena, CA 877-627-2645
Great Plains Beef LLC
  Lincoln, NE 402-479-2115
Heinkel's Packing Co
  Decatur, IL 800-594-2738

Product Categories / Meats & Meat Products: Beef & Beef Products

International Meat Co
   Chicago, IL 773-622-1400
Lengerich Meats Inc
   Zanesville, IN 260-638-4123
Munsee Meats
   Muncie, IN 800-662-8001
National Beef Packing Co LLC
   Kansas City, MO 800-449-2333
Plymouth Beef Co.
   Bronx, NY 718-589-8600
R Four Meats
   Chatfield, MN 507-867-4180
Schneider Foods
   Etobicoke, ON 416-252-5790
Shelley's
   Jersey City, NJ 201-433-2900
Smith Packing Regional Meat
   Utica, NY 315-732-5125
Temptee Specialty Foods
   Denver, CO 800-842-1233
Teton Waters Ranch LLC
   Denver, CO 720-340-4590
Thumann Inc.
   Carlstadt, NJ. 201-935-3636
Tomer Kosher Foods
   Skokie, IL 847-779-4870
Troy Pork Store
   Troy, NY 518-272-8291
W.A. Beans & Sons
   Bangor, ME. 800-649-1958
WACO Beef & Pork Processors
   Waco, TX 254-772-4669

Frozen

Amity Packing Co Inc
   Chicago, IL 800-837-0270
Armbrust Meats
   Medford, WI 715-748-3102
Art's Tamales
   Metamora, IL 309-367-2850
Atlantic Meat Company
   Savannah, GA 912-964-8511
Birchwood Foods Inc
   Kenosha, WI 800-541-1685
Birdie Pak Products
   Chicago, IL 773-247-5293
Blakely Freezer Locker
   Blakeley, GA 229-723-3622
Bob's Custom Cuts
   Bonnyville, AB 780-826-2627
Branding Iron
   Sauget, IL 800-851-4684
Brook Locker Plant
   Brook, IN 219-275-2611
Brookfield Farm
   Amherst, MA 413-253-7991
Brookview Farms
   Manakin-Sabot, VA 804-784-3131
Buckhead Beef
   Atlanta, GA. 800-888-5578
Burke Corp
   Nevada, IA 800-654-1152
Bush Brothers Provision Co
   West Palm Beach, FL 800-327-1345
Carando Gourmet Frozen Foods
   Agawam, MA 888-227-2636
Caribbean Food Delights Inc
   Tappan, NY 845-398-3000
Caribbean Products
   Baltimore, MD 410-235-7700
Carl Buddig & Co.
   Homewood, IL 888-633-5684
Cattleman Meat & Produce
   Taylor, MI 734-287-8260
Chip Steak & Provision Co
   Mankato, MN 507-388-6277
City Foods Inc
   Chicago, IL 773-523-1566
Curly's Foods Inc
   Edina, MN. 612-920-3400
Devault Foods
   Devault, PA. 800-426-2874
Duma Meats Inc
   Mogadore, OH 330-628-3438
Dynamic Steaks
   Lubbock, TX. 806-723-5600
Edmond's Chile Co
   St Louis, MO. 314-772-1499
El Rey Cooked Meats
   St Louis, MO. 314-521-3113
Fox Deluxe Inc
   Chicago, IL 312-421-3737

Gary's Frozen Foods
   Lubbock, TX. 806-745-1933
Gaucho Foods
   Fayetteville, IL 877-677-2282
Hall Brothers Meats
   Olmsted Twp, OH 440-235-3262
Hamms Custom Meats
   Mckinney, TX. 972-542-3359
Hausman Foods LLC
   Corpus Christi, TX 361-883-5521
Heringer Meats Inc
   Covington, KY 859-291-2000
Hormel Foods Corp.
   Austin, MN 507-437-5611
International Food Packers Corporation
   Miami, FL 305-740-5847
Jemm Wholesale Meat Company
   Chicago, IL 773-523-8161
JTM Food Group
   Harrison, OH 800-626-2308
K & K Gourmet Meats Inc
   Leetsdale, PA 724-266-8400
King Kold Meats
   Englewood, OH 800-836-2797
Kutztown Bologna Company
   Leola, PA. 800-723-8824
Ladoga Frozen Food & Retail
   Ladoga, IN 765-942-2225
Lengerich Meats Inc
   Zanesville, IN 260-638-4123
Leo G. Fraboni Sausage Company
   Hibbing, MN. 218-263-5074
M Buono Beef Co
   Philadelphia, PA 215-463-3600
Maid-Rite Steak Company
   Dunmore, PA. 800-233-4259
Meat-O-Mat Corp
   Brooklyn, NY 718-965-7250
Northern Packing Company
   Brier Hill, NY 315-375-8801
On-Cor Frozen Foods Redi-Serve
   Aurora, IL 920-563-6391
Phoenix Agro-Industrial Corporation
   Westbury, NY 516-334-1194
Pierceton Foods Inc
   Pierceton, IN 574-594-2344
Plymouth Beef Co.
   Bronx, NY 718-589-8600
R Four Meats
   Chatfield, MN 507-867-4180
Sam KANE Beef Processors Inc
   Corpus Christi, TX 800-242-4142
Schneider Foods
   Etobicoke, ON 416-252-5790
Shelley's
   Jersey City, NJ 201-433-2900
Smith Packing Regional Meat
   Utica, NY 315-732-5125
Steak-Umm Company
   Shillington, PA 860-928-5900
Sudlersville Frozen Food Locker
   Sudlersville, MD. 410-438-3106
Thompson Packers
   Slidell, LA. 800-989-6328
Travis Meats Inc
   Powell, TN 800-247-7606
Tucker Packing Co
   Orrville, OH 330-683-3311
United Meat Company
   San Francisco, CA 415-864-2118
Zartic Inc
   Rome, GA. 800-241-0516

Ground

Acme Steak & Seafood
   Youngstown, OH. 800-686-2263
American Foods Group LLC
   Green Bay, WI. 800-345-0293
Atlantic Meat Company
   Savannah, GA 912-964-8511
Caribbean Food Delights Inc
   Tappan, NY 845-398-3000
Centennial Food Corporation
   Calgary, AB. 403-214-0044
Chicago Steaks
   Chicago, IL 773-847-5400
Chip Steak & Provision Co
   Mankato, MN 507-388-6277
Devault Foods
   Devault, PA. 800-426-2874
Fulton Provision Co
   Portland, OR. 800-333-6328

Grass Run Farms
   Greeley, CO. 800-727-2333
Jensen Meat Company
   San Diego, CA 619-754-6400
John Garner Meats
   Van Buren, AR 800-543-5473
Karn Meats
   Columbus, OH 800-221-9585
Kenosha Beef International LTD
   Kenosha, WI
Miami Beef Co
   Miami Lakes, FL. 305-621-3252
Nurture Ranch
   Frisco, TX. 866-467-2624
Palmer Meat Packing Co
   Tremonton, UT 435-257-5329
Quality Food Company
   Providence, RI 877-233-3462
Rinehart Meat Processing
   Branson, MO. 417-869-2041
S.W. Meat & Provision Company
   Phoenix, AZ 602-275-2000
Sommers Organic
   Wheeling, IL. 877-377-9797
Springville Meat & Cold Storage
   Springville, UT 801-489-6391
Stanley Provision Company
   Manchester, CT. 888-688-6347
Stone Meat Processor
   Ogden, UT. 801-782-9825
Thompson Packers
   Slidell, LA. 800-989-6328
Valley Meat Company
   Modesto, CA 800-222-6328
Valley Meats
   Coal Valley, IL 309-517-6639

Coarse Frozen

Devault Foods
   Devault, PA. 800-426-2874

Frozen

Acme Steak & Seafood
   Youngstown, OH. 800-686-2263
Caribbean Food Delights Inc
   Tappan, NY 845-398-3000
Chip Steak & Provision Co
   Mankato, MN 507-388-6277
Kenosha Beef International LTD
   Kenosha, WI
Thompson Packers
   Slidell, LA. 800-989-6328

Hamburger

Acme Steak & Seafood
   Youngstown, OH. 800-686-2263
Alpine Butcher
   Lowell, MA. 978-256-7771
American Foods Group LLC
   Green Bay, WI. 800-345-0293
Atlantic Meat Company
   Savannah, GA 912-964-8511
Bakalars Sausage Co
   La Crosse, WI. 608-784-0384
Birchwood Foods Inc
   Kenosha, WI 800-541-1685
Brucepac
   Woodburn, OR 800-899-3629
Burger Maker Inc
   Carlstadt, NJ 201-939-0444
Burke Corp
   Nevada, IA 800-654-1152
Chicago Meat Authority Inc
   Chicago, IL 800-383-3811
Chicopee Provision Co Inc
   Chicopee, MA. 800-924-6328
Crocetti's Oakdale Packing Co
   East Bridgewater, MA 508-587-0035
Devault Foods
   Devault, PA. 800-426-2874
Edmond's Chile Co
   St Louis, MO. 314-772-1499
Gouvea's & Purity Foods Inc
   Honolulu, HI 808-847-3717
Hormel Foods Corp.
   Austin, MN 507-437-5611
Marathon Enterprises Inc
   Englewood, NJ 800-722-7388
Miami Beef Co
   Miami Lakes, FL. 305-621-3252

Product Categories / Meats & Meat Products: Beef & Beef Products

Ossian Smoked Meats
  Ossian, IN 800-535-8862
Pierceton Foods Inc
  Pierceton, IN 574-594-2344
Rinehart Meat Processing
  Branson, MO 417-869-2041
Rymer Foods
  Chicago, IL 800-247-9637
Saad Wholesale Meats
  Detroit, MI 313-831-8126
Thompson Packers
  Slidell, LA 800-989-6328
Travis Meats Inc
  Powell, TN 800-247-7606
Valley Meat Company
  Modesto, CA 800-222-6328

Cooked Frozen

Burke Corp
  Nevada, IA 800-654-1152
Maid-Rite Steak Company
  Dunmore, PA 800-233-4259

Uncooked Frozen

Al Safa Halal
  New York City, NY 800-268-8147
Caribbean Food Delights Inc
  Tappan, NY 845-398-3000
Maid-Rite Steak Company
  Dunmore, PA 800-233-4259
Pierceton Foods Inc
  Pierceton, IN 574-594-2344

Italian

Burke Corp
  Nevada, IA 800-654-1152
Henry J's Meat Specialties
  Chicago, IL 800-242-1314

Liver

American Foods Group LLC
  Green Bay, WI 800-345-0293
Caughman's Meat Plant
  Lexington, SC 803-356-0076
Dynamic Foods
  Lubbock, TX 806-723-5600
Fremont Beef Co
  Fremont, NE 800-331-4788
Giovanni's Appetizing Food Co
  Richmond, MI 586-727-9355
Lee's Sausage Co
  Orangeburg, SC 803-534-5517
Skylark Meats
  Omaha, NE 800-759-5275

London Broil

Burnett & Son
  Monrovia, CA 877-632-5467

NY Strip Steak

Amana Meat Shop & Smoke House
  Amana, IA 800-373-6328
Certified Piedmontese Beef
  Lincoln, NE 800-414-3487
Chef's Requested Foods
  Oklahoma City, OK 405-239-2610
Sommers Organic
  Wheeling, IL 877-377-9797

Patties

Alpine Butcher
  Lowell, MA 978-256-7771
Brucepac
  Woodburn, OR 800-899-3629
Burke Corp
  Nevada, IA 800-654-1152
Field Roast
  Seattle, WA 800-311-9497
Fulton Provision Co
  Portland, OR 800-333-6328
Grass Run Farms
  Greeley, CO 800-727-2333
International Meat Co
  Chicago, IL 773-622-1400
Jensen Meat Company
  San Diego, CA 619-754-6400
Miami Beef Co
  Miami Lakes, FL 305-621-3252
On-Cor Frozen Foods

Sommers Organic
  Wheeling, IL 877-377-9797

Frozen

Branding Iron
  Sauget, IL 800-851-4684
Caribbean Food Delights Inc
  Tappan, NY 845-398-3000
Centennial Food Corporation
  Calgary, AB 403-214-0044
Corfu Foods Inc
  Bensenville, IL 630-595-2510
John Garner Meats
  Van Buren, AR 800-543-5473
Kenosha Beef International LTD
  Kenosha, WI
King Kold Meats
  Englewood, OH 800-836-2797
Kutztown Bologna Company
  Leola, PA 800-723-8824
Maid-Rite Steak Company
  Dunmore, PA 800-233-4259
Meat-O-Mat Corp
  Brooklyn, NY 718-965-7250
SunFed Ranch
  Woodland, CA 530-723-5373
Travis Meats Inc
  Powell, TN 800-247-7606
Valley Meat Company
  Modesto, CA 800-222-6328
Wisconsin Packaging Corp
  Fort Atkinson, WI 920-563-9363

Jamacaín

Royal Home Bakery
  Newmarket, ON 905-715-7044

Porterhouse

Arrowhead Beef
  Chipley, FL 850-270-8804
Certified Piedmontese Beef
  Lincoln, NE 800-414-3487
Chef's Requested Foods
  Oklahoma City, OK 405-239-2610
Chicago Steaks
  Chicago, IL 773-847-5400

Pot Roast

Fontanini Italian Meats
  McCook, IL 800-331-6328
Freirich Foods
  Salisbury, NC 800-221-1315

Processed

Al Safa Halal
  New York City, NY 800-268-8147
Alderfer Inc
  Harleysville, PA 800-341-1121
Alewel's Country Meats
  Warrensburg, MO 800-353-8553
Alpine Meats
  Stockton, CA 800-399-6328
American Foods Group LLC
  Green Bay, WI 800-345-0293
Aunt Kitty's Foods Inc
  Vineland, NJ 856-691-2100
Best Chicago Meat
  Chicago, IL
Best Provision Co Inc
  Union, NJ 800-631-4466
Big B Barbecue
  Evansville, IN 812-425-5235
Buckhead Beef
  Atlanta, GA 800-888-5578
Bush Brothers Provision Co
  West Palm Beach, FL 800-327-1345
Caddo Packing Co
  Marshall, TX 903-935-2211
Campbell Soup Co.
  Camden, NJ 800-257-8443
Carando Gourmet Frozen Foods
  Agawam, MA 888-227-2636
Caribbean Food Delights Inc
  Tappan, NY 845-398-3000
Cattaneo Brothers Inc
  San Luis Obispo, CA 800-243-8537
Central Meat & Provision
  San Diego, CA 619-239-1391
Chandler Foods Inc
  Greensboro, NC 800-537-6219

Cher-Make Sausage Co
  Manitowoc, WI 800-242-7679
Cheraw Packing Plant
  Cheraw, SC 843-537-7426
Chip Steak & Provision Co
  Mankato, MN 507-388-6277
Columbia Packing Co Inc
  Dallas, TX 214-946-8171
Corfu Foods Inc
  Bensenville, IL 630-595-2510
Dutterer's Home Food Service
  Baltimore, MD 410-298-3663
E.W. Knauss & Son
  Quakertown, PA 800-648-4220
F&Y Enterprises
  Wauconda, IL 847-526-0620
Hamms Custom Meats
  Mckinney, TX 972-542-3359
Horlacher Meats
  Logan, UT 435-752-1287
Hsin Tung Yang Foods Inc
  S San Francisco, CA 650-589-6789
Jensen Meat Company
  San Diego, CA 619-754-6400
John Garner Meats
  Van Buren, AR 800-543-5473
Kershenstine Beef Jerky
  Eupora, MS 662-258-2049
King's Command Foods Inc
  Green Bay, WA 800-345-0293
Kutztown Bologna Company
  Leola, PA 800-723-8824
Land O'Frost Inc
  Searcy, AR 800-643-5654
Link Snacks Inc.
  Minong, WI 715-466-2234
Longview Meat & Merchandise Ltd
  Longview, AB 866-355-3759
Lower Foods, Inc.
  Richmond, UT 800-295-7898
Moyer Packing Co.
  Elroy, PA 800-967-8325
National Beef Packing Co LLC
  Kansas City, MO 800-449-2333
Nebraska Beef Council
  Kearney, NE 800-421-5326
People's Sausage Co
  Los Angeles, CA 213-627-8633
Pierceton Foods Inc
  Pierceton, IN 574-594-2344
Plumrose USA
  Chicago, IL 800-526-4909
Plymouth Beef Co.
  Bronx, NY 718-589-8600
Rinehart Meat Processing
  Branson, MO 417-869-2041
Saval Foods Corp
  Elkridge, MD 800-527-2825
Smith Provision Co Inc
  Erie, PA 800-334-9151
Sunset Farm Foods Inc
  Valdosta, GA 800-882-1121
Temptee Specialty Foods
  Denver, CO 800-842-1233
Terrell Meats
  Delta, UT 435-864-2600
The Bruss Company
  Chicago, IL 773-282-2900
Thompson Packers
  Slidell, LA 800-989-6328
Tri State Beef Co
  Cincinnati, OH 513-579-1722
Tyson Foods Inc.
  Springdale, AR 800-233-6332
Valley Meat Company
  Modesto, CA 800-222-6328
Weaver Nut Co. Inc.
  Ephrata, PA 800-473-2688
Wisconsin Packaging Corp
  Fort Atkinson, WI 920-563-9363
Woods Smoked Meats Inc
  Bowling Green, MO 800-458-8426

Products

Alderfer Inc
  Harleysville, PA 800-341-1121
Alewel's Country Meats
  Warrensburg, MO 800-353-8553
Bakalars Sausage Co
  La Crosse, WI 608-784-0384
Best Chicago Meat
  Chicago, IL

Product Categories / Meats & Meat Products: Beef & Beef Products

Big B Barbecue
   Evansville, IN 812-425-5235
Birchwood Foods Inc
   Kenosha, WI 800-541-1685
Branding Iron
   Sauget, IL 800-851-4684
Buona Vita Inc
   Bridgeton, NJ 856-453-7972
Bush Brothers Provision Co
   West Palm Beach, FL 800-327-1345
Caddo Packing Co
   Marshall, TX 903-935-2211
Campbell Soup Co.
   Camden, NJ 800-257-8443
Caribbean Food Delights Inc
   Tappan, NY 845-398-3000
Carl Buddig & Co.
   Homewood, IL 888-633-5684
Chicago Meat Authority Inc
   Chicago, IL 800-383-3811
Columbia Packing Co Inc
   Dallas, TX 214-946-8171
Daily Nutrition
   Tucson, AZ 888-612-5037
Dino's Sausage & Meat Co Inc
   Utica, NY 315-732-2661
Dutterer's Home Food Service
   Baltimore, MD 410-298-3663
E.W. Knauss & Son
   Quakertown, PA .800-648-4220
Edmond's Chile Co
   St Louis, MO 314-772-1499
El Rey Cooked Meats
   St Louis, MO 314-521-3113
Elmwood Locker Svc
   Elmwood, IL 309-742-8929
F&Y Enterprises
   Wauconda, IL 847-526-0620
Grandpa Ittel's Meats Inc
   Howard Lake, MN 320-543-2285
Groff's Meats
   Elizabethtown, PA. 717-367-1246
Harris Ranch Beef Co
   Selma, CA 800-742-1955
Hazle Park Quality Meats
   West Hazleton, PA 800-238-4331
Holly Hill Locker Company
   Holly Hill, SC 803-496-3611
Hormel Foods Corp.
   Austin, MN 507-437-5611
Ito Cariani Sausage Company
   Hayward, CA 510-887-0882
John Garner Meats
   Van Buren, AR 800-543-5473
K & K Gourmet Meats Inc
   Leetsdale, PA 724-266-8400
Karn Meats
   Columbus, OH 800-221-9585
Kelly Corned Beef Co
   Chicago, IL 800-624-5617
Kenosha Beef International LTD
   Kenosha, WI
Kershenstine Beef Jerky
   Eupora, MS 662-258-2049
Kutztown Bologna Company
   Leola, PA 800-723-8824
Leo G. Fraboni Sausage Company
   Hibbing, MN. 218-263-5074
Lower Foods, Inc.
   Richmond, UT. 800-295-7898
Maid-Rite Steak Company
   Dunmore, PA 800-233-4259
Meating Place
   Buffalo, NY 716-885-3623
National Foods
   Indianapolis, IN .800-683-6565
On-Cor Frozen Foods Redi-Serve
   Aurora, IL 920-563-6391
Opa's Smoked Meats
   Fredericksburg, TX. 800-543-6750
Peer Foods Group Inc
   Chicago, IL 800-365-5644
People's Sausage Co
   Los Angeles, CA. 213-627-8633
Pinter's Packing Plant
   Dorchester, WI 715-654-5444
Plumrose USA
   Chicago, IL 800-526-4909
Plymouth Beef Co.
   Bronx, NY. 718-589-8600
Rinehart Meat Processing
   Branson, MO. 417-869-2041

Rymer Foods
   Chicago, IL 800-247-9637
S.W. Meat & Provision Company
   Phoenix, AZ 602-275-2000
Sadler's Smokehouse
   Henderson, TX 903-657-5581
Sanders Meat Packing Inc
   Custer, MI 800-968-5035
Saval Foods Corp
   Elkridge, MD 800-527-2825
Sheinman Provision Co
   Philadelphia, PA .215-473-7065
Steak-Umm Company
   Shillington, PA 860-928-5900
Stripling's General Store
   Moultrie, GA. 229-985-4226
Temptee Specialty Foods
   Denver, CO 800-842-1233
Terrell Meats
   Delta, UT. 435-864-2600
The Bruss Company
   Chicago, IL 773-282-2900
Une-Viandi
   St. Jean Sur Richelieu, NB 800-363-1955
Vienna Meat Products
   Scarborough, ON 800-588-1931
Weaver Nut Co. Inc.
   Ephrata, PA 800-473-2688
Wisconsin Packaging Corp
   Fort Atkinson, WI. 920-563-9363
Woods Smoked Meats Inc
   Bowling Green, MO 800-458-8426

Raw

Caribbean Food Delights Inc
   Tappan, NY 845-398-3000
Maid-Rite Steak Company
   Dunmore, PA 800-233-4259

Rib Eye Roast

Certified Piedmontese Beef
   Lincoln, NE. 800-414-3487

Rib Eye Steak

Amana Meat Shop & Smoke House
   Amana, IA. 800-373-6328
Arrowhead Beef
   Chipley, FL 850-270-8804
Chef's Requested Foods
   Oklahoma City, OK 405-239-2610
Chicago Steaks
   Chicago, IL 773-847-5400
Father's Country Hams
   Bremen, KY 270-525-3554
Sommers Organic
   Wheeling, IL. 877-377-9797
Woods Smoked Meats Inc
   Bowling Green, MO 800-458-8426

Rib Steak

Chicago Steaks
   Chicago, IL 773-847-5400

Roast Beef

Alderfer Inc
   Harleysville, PA .800-341-1121
Alpine Butcher
   Lowell, MA. 978-256-7771
Applegate Farms
   Bridgewater, NJ .866-587-5858
Arrowhead Beef
   Chipley, FL 850-270-8804
Berks Packing Company, Inc.
   Reading, PA 800-882-3757
Burnett & Son
   Monrovia, CA. 877-632-5467
Carando Gourmet Frozen Foods
   Agawam, MA 888-227-2636
Chip Steak & Provision Co
   Mankato, MN 507-388-6277
Curly's Foods Inc
   Edina, MN. 612-920-3400
Dom's Sausage Co Inc
   Malden, MA 781-324-6390
Dorina So-Good Inc
   Union, IL. 815-923-2144
Dutterer's Home Food Service
   Baltimore, MD 410-298-3663
El Rey Cooked Meats
   St Louis, MO . . . ./314-521-3113

Hormel Foods Corp.
   Austin, MN 507-437-5611
Ito Cariani Sausage Company
   Hayward, CA 510-887-0882
Lower Foods, Inc.
   Richmond, UT. 800-295-7898
Miami Beef Co
   Miami Lakes, FL .305-621-3252
Saval Foods Corp
   Elkridge, MD 800-527-2825
Sheinman Provision Co
   Philadelphia, PA .215-473-7065
Vienna Meat Products
   Scarborough, ON 800-588-1931

Rolls - Frozen

Columbia Packing Co Inc
   Dallas, TX 214-946-8171
Travis Meats Inc
   Powell, TN 800-247-7606

Sirloin Cubes

Chicago Steaks
   Chicago, IL 773-847-5400

Sliced

E.W. Knauss & Son
   Quakertown, PA .800-648-4220
Henry J's Meat Specialties
   Chicago, IL 800-242-1314
Plymouth Beef Co.
   Bronx, NY. 718-589-8600

Dried

Alderfer Inc
   Harleysville, PA .800-341-1121
E.W. Knauss & Son
   Quakertown, PA .800-648-4220
Palmyra Bologna Co Inc
   Palmyra, PA. 800-282-6336

Frozen

Burke Corp
   Nevada, IA 800-654-1152
Philadelphia Cheese Steak
   Philadelphia, PA .800-342-9771

Special Trim

Buckhead Beef
   Atlanta, GA. 800-888-5578

Steak

Alaskan Gourmet Seafoods
   Anchorage, AK 800-288-3740
Alpine Butcher
   Lowell, MA. 978-256-7771
American Foods Group LLC
   Green Bay, WI. 800-345-0293
Arrowhead Beef
   Chipley, FL 850-270-8804
Bakalars Sausage Co
   La Crosse, WI 608-784-0384
Bear Creek Smokehouse Inc
   Marshall, TX. 800-950-2327
Burnett & Son
   Monrovia, CA. 877-632-5467
Campbell Soup Co.
   Camden, NJ 800-257-8443
Dom's Sausage Co Inc
   Malden, MA 781-324-6390
Grass Run Farms
   Greeley, CO. 800-727-2333
Jemm Wholesale Meat Company
   Chicago, IL 773-523-8161
Joe Fazio's Famous Italian
   Charleston, WV .304-344-3071
Karn Meats
   Columbus, OH 800-221-9585
Kutztown Bologna Company
   Leola, PA 800-723-8824
Mattingly Foods Of Louisville
   Louisville, KY 502-253-2000
Omaha Steaks Inc
  800-960-8400
Pine Point Seafood
   Scarborough, ME 207-883-4701
Pinter's Packing Plant
   Dorchester, WI 715-654-5444

Product Categories / Meats & Meat Products: Frankfurters

Rymer Foods
   Chicago, IL 800-247-9637
Sommers Organic
   Wheeling, IL 877-377-9797
Steak-Umm Company
   Shillington, PA 860-928-5900
Strassburger Steaks
   Carlstadt, NJ 201-842-8890
Woods Smoked Meats Inc
   Bowling Green, MO 800-458-8426

Stew

Burnett & Son
   Monrovia, CA 877-632-5467
Campbell Soup Co.
   Camden, NJ 800-257-8443
Johnston's Home Style Products
   Charlottetown, PE 902-629-1300
Miami Beef Co
   Miami Lakes, FL 305-621-3252
Plymouth Beef Co.
   Bronx, NY .718-589-8600

Frozen

Edmond's Chile Co
   St Louis, MO 314-772-1499

Tongue

Fremont Beef Co
   Fremont, NE 800-331-4788
Saval Foods Corp
   Elkridge, MD 800-527-2825

Veal

A To Z Portion Control Meats
   Bluffton, OH 800-338-6328
A.C. Kissling Company
   Philadelphia, PA 800-445-1943
Adolf's Meats & Sausage Kitchen
   Hartford, CT 860-522-1588
Alpine Butcher
   Lowell, MA 978-256-7771
Arena & Sons
   Redwood City, CA 650-366-1750
Atlantic Veal & Lamb Inc
   Brooklyn, NY 800-222-8325
B & R Quality Meats Inc
   Waterloo, IA 319-232-6328
Baretta Provision
   East Berlin, CT 860-828-0802
Borders Sporting Goods
   Ashland, KY 606-928-6326
Branding Iron
   Sauget, IL .800-851-4684
Brook Locker Plant
   Brook, IN .219-275-2611
Buckhead Beef
   Atlanta, GA 800-888-5578
Bush Brothers Provision Co
   West Palm Beach, FL 800-327-1345
Buzz Food Svc
   Charleston, WV 304-925-4781
Capital Packers Inc
   Edmonton, AB 800-272-8868
Catelli Brothers Inc
   Collingswood, NJ 856-869-9293
Central Meat & Provision
   San Diego, CA 619-239-1391
Country Village Meats Inc
   Sublette, IL 800-700-4545
Cusack Meats
   Oklahoma City, OK 800-241-6328
David Mosner Meat Products
   Bronx, NY .866-928-6428
Debragga & Spitler
   Jersey City, NJ
Dom's Sausage Co Inc
   Malden, MA 781-324-6390
Feed The Party
   Louisville, KY
Florida Veal Processors
   Wimauma, FL 813-634-5545
Fulton Provision Co
   Portland, OR 800-333-6328
Heringer Meats Inc
   Covington, KY 859-291-2000
International Meat Co
   Chicago, IL 773-622-1400
Jordahl Meats
   Manchester, MN 507-826-3418

King Kold Meats
   Englewood, OH 800-836-2797
King's Command Foods Inc
   Green Bay, WA 800-345-0293
L & L Packing Co
   Chicago, IL 800-628-6328
L & M Slaughterhouse
   Georgetown, IL 217-662-6841
Lay Packing Company
   Knoxville, TN 865-522-1147
Lombardi Brothers Meat Packers
   Denver, CO 303-458-7441
Maid-Rite Steak Company
   Dunmore, PA 800-233-4259
Malcolm Meats Co
   Northwood, OH 800-822-6328
Marcho Farms Inc
   Harleysville, PA 215-721-7131
Meat-O-Mat Corp
   Brooklyn, NY 718-965-7250
Miami Beef Co
   Miami Lakes, FL 305-621-3252
Michael's Finer Meats/Seafoods
   Columbus, OH 800-282-0518
Mountain States Rosen
   Bronx, NY .800-872-5262
Northwest Meat Company
   Chicago, IL 312-733-1418
On-Cor Frozen Foods Redi-Serve
   Aurora, IL .920-563-6391
Pasqualichio Brothers Inc
   Scranton, PA 800-232-6233
Petschl's Quality Meats
   Tukwila, WA 206-575-4400
Quaker Maid Meats
   Reading, PA 610-376-1500
Rendulic Meat Packing Corp
   Mckeesport, PA 412-678-9541
Sculli Brothers
   Yeadon, PA 215-336-1223
Shelley's
   Jersey City, NJ 201-433-2900
Smith Packing Regional Meat
   Utica, NY .315-732-5125
Southern Packing Corp
   Chesapeake, VA 757-421-2131
Standard Meat Co LP
   Dallas, TX .866-859-6313
Stock Yards Packing Company
   Melrose Park, IL 877-785-9273
Strassburger Steaks
   Carlstadt, NJ 201-842-8890
Streit Carl & Son Co
   Neptune, NJ 732-775-0803
Superior Farms
   Sacramento, CA 800-228-5262
Suzanna's Kitchen
   Peachtree Cor, GA 770-476-9900
The Bruss Company
   Chicago, IL 773-282-2900
Thompson Packers
   Slidell, LA .800-989-6328
Travis Meats Inc
   Powell, TN 800-247-7606
Tyler Packing Co
   Tyler, TX 903-593-9592
Une-Viandi
   St. Jean Sur Richelieu, NB 800-363-1955
United Meat Company
   San Francisco, CA 415-864-2118
United Provision Meat Company
   Columbus, OH 614-252-1126
Valley Meats
   Coal Valley, IL 309-517-6639
Wasatch Meats Inc
   Salt Lake City, UT 800-631-8294
Windcrest Meat Packers
   Port Perry, ON 800-750-2542

Breaded Frozen

Branding Iron
   Sauget, IL .800-851-4684
King's Command Foods Inc
   Green Bay, WA 800-345-0293
Meat-O-Mat Corp
   Brooklyn, NY 718-965-7250
On-Cor Frozen Foods Redi-Serve
   Aurora, IL .920-563-6391
Valley Meats
   Coal Valley, IL 309-517-6639

Burgers

Meat-O-Mat Corp
   Brooklyn, NY 718-965-7250

Cutlet

On-Cor Frozen Foods Redi-Serve
   Aurora, IL .920-563-6391

Fresh

Florida Veal Processors
   Wimauma, FL 813-634-5545
Provimi Foods
   Seymour, WI 800-833-8325
Shelley's
   Jersey City, NJ 201-433-2900
Smith Packing Regional Meat
   Utica, NY .315-732-5125

Frozen

Atlantic Veal & Lamb Inc
   Brooklyn, NY 800-222-8325
Branding Iron
   Sauget, IL .800-851-4684
Brook Locker Plant
   Brook, IN .219-275-2611
Buckhead Beef
   Atlanta, GA 800-888-5578
Bush Brothers Provision Co
   West Palm Beach, FL 800-327-1345
Florida Veal Processors
   Wimauma, FL 813-634-5545
Heringer Meats Inc
   Covington, KY 859-291-2000
King Kold Meats
   Englewood, OH 800-836-2797
Maid-Rite Steak Company
   Dunmore, PA 800-233-4259
Meat-O-Mat Corp
   Brooklyn, NY 718-965-7250
On-Cor Frozen Foods Redi-Serve
   Aurora, IL .920-563-6391
Provimi Foods
   Seymour, WI 800-833-8325
Shelley's
   Jersey City, NJ 201-433-2900
Smith Packing Regional Meat
   Utica, NY .315-732-5125
Thompson Packers
   Slidell, LA .800-989-6328
Travis Meats Inc
   Powell, TN 800-247-7606
United Meat Company
   San Francisco, CA 415-864-2118

Ground

M Buono Beef Co
   Philadelphia, PA 215-463-3600

Loin Chop

Chicago Steaks
   Chicago, IL 773-847-5400

Rib Chop

Chicago Steaks
   Chicago, IL 773-847-5400

Frankfurters

Al Pete Meats
   Muncie, IN 765-288-8817
Albert's Meats
   Claysville, PA 800-522-9970
Anmar Foods
   Chicago, IL 312-421-6500
Applegate Farms
   Bridgewater, NJ 866-587-5858
AquaCuisine
   Portland, OR 208-323-2782
Ball Park Franks
   Peoria, IL 888-317-5867
Best Provision Co Inc
   Union, NJ .800-631-4466
Big City Reds
   Omaha, NE 800-759-5275
Boesl Packing Co
   Baltimore, MD 800-675-1471
C.W. Brown Foods, Inc.
   Mountt Royal, NJ 856-423-3700
Carolina Packers Inc
   Smithfield, NC 800-682-7675

Product Categories / Meats & Meat Products: Game

Chicago 58 Food Products
   Woodbridge, ON 416-603-4244
Chicopee Provision Co Inc
   Chicopee, MA 800-924-6328
Chisesi Brothers Meat Packing
   New Orleans, LA 800-966-3550
Cloverdale Foods
   Mandan, ND 800-669-9511
Country Village Meats Inc
   Sublette, IL 800-700-4545
Curtis Packing Co
   Greensboro, NC 336-275-7684
Dennison Meat Locker
   Dennison, MN 507-645-8734
Dietz & Watson Inc.
   Philadelphia, PA 215-831-9000
Double B Foods Inc
   Arlington, TX 800-679-0349
Dutterer's Home Food Service
   Baltimore, MD 410-298-3663
Fair Oaks Farms LLC
   Pleasant Prairie, WI 800-528-8615
Far West Meats
   Highland, CA 909-864-1990
Fare Foods Corp
   Du Quoin, IL. 618-542-2155
Field Roast
   Seattle, WA 800-311-9497
Gary's Frozen Foods
   Lubbock, TX. 806-745-1933
Glazier Packing Co
   Malone, NY. 518-483-4990
Gouvea's & Purity Foods Inc
   Honolulu, HI. 808-847-3717
Grote & Weigel Inc
   Bloomfield, CT. 860-242-8528
Hatfield Quality Meats
   Hatfield, PA. 800-743-1191
Hazle Park Quality Meats
   West Hazleton, PA 800-238-4331
Health is Wealth Foods
   Moonachie, NJ 201-933-7474
Hormel Foods Corp.
   Austin, MN 507-437-5611
Hummel Brothers Inc
   New Haven, CT 800-828-8978
Kayem Foods
   Chelsea, MA 800-426-6100
Kelly Corned Beef Co
   Chicago, IL. 800-624-5617
Kent Quality Foods Inc
   Grand Rapids, MI 800-748-0141
Kilgus Meats
   Toledo, OH 419-472-9721
Koegel Meats Inc
   Flint, MI 810-238-3685
Little Rhody Brand Frankfurts
   Johnston, RI 401-831-0815
Marathon Enterprises Inc
   Englewood, NJ 800-722-7388
Martin Rosols
   New Britain, CT 860-223-2707
Matthiesen's Deer & Custom
   De Witt, IA 563-659-8409
Milling Sausage Inc
   Milwaukee, WI 414-645-2677
National Foods
   Indianapolis, IN 800-683-6565
Omaha Steaks Inc
   800-960-8400
P & L Poultry
   Spokane, WA. 509-892-1242
Pie Piper Products
   Wheeling, IL. 800-621-8183
Principe Foods USA
   Long Beach, CA 310-680-5500
Quong Hop & Company
   S San Francisco, CA. 650-553-9900
R.L. Zeigler Company
   Selma, AL. 800-392-6328
Roger Wood Foods Inc
   Savannah, GA. 800-849-9272
Saag's Products LLC
   San Leandro, CA. 855-287-6562
Sahlen's
   Buffalo, NY. 800-466-8165
Saugy Inc
   Cranston, RI 866-467-2849
Schaefers Market
   Sauk Centre, MN 320-352-6490
Schneider Foods
   Kitchener, ON 519-741-5000

Sechrist Brothers
   Dallastown, PA 717-244-2975
Shelton's Poultry Inc
   Pomona, CA 800-541-1833
Smith Packing Regional Meat
   Utica, NY 315-732-5125
Smith Provision Co Inc
   Erie, PA 800-334-9151
Smithfield Foods Inc.
   Smithfield, VA 757-365-3000
Stawnichy Holdings
   Mundare, AB 888-764-7646
Stevens Sausage Co
   Smithfield, NC 800-338-0561
Sunnydale Meats Inc
   Gaffney, SC. 864-489-6091
Tecumseh Poultry, LLC
   Waverly, NE 402-786-1000
Tennessee Valley Packing Co
   Columbia, TN 931-388-2623
Teton Waters Ranch LLC
   Denver, CO 720-340-4590
Thomas Packing Company
   Columbus, GA 800-729-0976
Thumann Inc.
   Carlstadt, NJ 201-935-3636
Troy Foods Inc
   Troy, IL. 618-667-6332
Tyson Foods Inc.
   Springdale, AR 800-233-6332
Vienna Beef LTD
   Chicago, IL. 800-366-3647
Zweigle's Inc
   Rochester, NY. 585-546-1740

Beef

American Foods Group LLC
   Green Bay, WI. 800-345-0293
Berks Packing Company, Inc.
   Reading, PA 800-882-3757
Big City Reds
   Omaha, NE 800-759-5275
Grote & Weigel Inc
   Bloomfield, CT. 860-242-8528
Health is Wealth Foods
   Moonachie, NJ 201-933-7474
Heinkel's Packing Co
   Decatur, IL 800-594-2738
Hormel Foods Corp.
   Austin, MN 507-437-5611
Kelly Corned Beef Co
   Chicago, IL. 800-624-5617
Milling Sausage Inc
   Milwaukee, WI 414-645-2677
National Foods
   Indianapolis, IN 800-683-6565
Pie Piper Products
   Wheeling, IL. 800-621-8183
Red Hot Chicago
   Chicago, IL. 800-249-5226
Teton Waters Ranch LLC
   Denver, CO 720-340-4590
True Story Foods
   San Francisco, CA 888-277-1171

Kosher

American Foods Group LLC
   Green Bay, WI. 800-345-0293

Chicken

Applegate Farms
   Bridgewater, NJ 866-587-5858
P & L Poultry
   Spokane, WA. 509-892-1242
True Story Foods
   San Francisco, CA 888-277-1171

Corn Dogs

Al Pete Meats
   Muncie, IN 765-288-8817
Fare Foods Corp
   Du Quoin, IL. 618-542-2155
Foster Farms Inc.
   Livingston, CA 800-255-7227
Hormel Foods Corp.
   Austin, MN 507-437-5611
Suzanna's Kitchen
   Peachtree Cor, GA 770-476-9900
Tyson Foods Inc.
   Springdale, AR 479-290-4000

Hot Dogs

Grass Run Farms
   Greeley, CO. 800-727-2333
Harvin Choice Meats
   Sumter, SC 800-849-6328
Heinkel's Packing Co
   Decatur, IL 800-594-2738
Saad Wholesale Meats
   Detroit, MI 313-831-8126
Specialty Foods Group Inc
   Owensboro, KY 800-238-0020
SunFed Ranch
   Woodland, CA. 530-723-5373
Vermont Smoke and Cure
   Hinesburg, VT. 802-482-4666

Mini

Grote & Weigel Inc
   Bloomfield, CT. 860-242-8528
Hormel Foods Corp.
   Austin, MN 507-437-5611

Pork

C.W. Brown Foods, Inc.
   Mountt Royal, NJ 856-423-3700
Heinkel's Packing Co
   Decatur, IL 800-594-2738

Soy

Lightlife
   Turners Falls, MA 800-769-3279
Quong Hop & Company
   S San Francisco, CA. 650-553-9900

Turkey

Applegate Farms
   Bridgewater, NJ 866-587-5858
P & L Poultry
   Spokane, WA. 509-892-1242
Sardinha's Sausage
   Somerset, MA 800-678-0178

Game

Alewel's Country Meats
   Warrensburg, MO 800-353-8553
Alpine Butcher
   Lowell, MA 978-256-7771
Bayou Land Seafood
   Breaux Bridge, LA 337-667-6118
Bob's Custom Cuts
   Bonnyville, AB. 780-826-2627
Boyd's Sausage Co
   Washington, IA 319-653-5715
Broadleaf Venison USA Inc
   Vernon, CA 800-336-3844
Brome Lake Ducks Ltd
   Knowlton, QC. 888-956-1977
Bryant Preserving Company
   Alma, AR 800-634-2413
Burgers' Smokehouse
   California, MO 800-345-5185
Camrose Packers
   Camrose, AB. 780-672-4887
Carolina Blueberry Co-Op Assn
   Garland, NC 910-588-4220
Charlito's Cocina
   Brooklyn, NY 718-482-7890
Clay Center Locker Plant
   Clay Center, KS 800-466-5543
Debragga & Spitler
   Jersey City, NJ
Eickman's Processing Co
   Seward, IL. 815-247-8451
Eiserman Meats
   Slave Lake, AB. 780-849-5507
Ellsworth Locker
   Ellsworth, MN 507-967-2544
Farmers Meat Market
   Viking, AB 780-336-3241
Fossil Farms
   Boonton, NJ 973-917-3155
Georgetown Farm
   Free Union, VA 888-328-5326
Goodheart Brand Specialty Food
   San Antonio, TX 888-466-3992
Grandview Farms
   Thornbury, ON 519-599-6368
Hickory Baked Ham Co
   Castle Rock, CO 303-688-2633

Product Categories / Meats & Meat Products: Game

Humeniuk's Meat Cutting
   Ranfurly, AB 780-658-2381
Indian Valley Meats
   Indian, AK 907-653-7511
Jewel Date Co
   Thermal, CA 760-399-4474
Joyce Farms
   Winston Salem, NC 800-755-6923
Ketters Meat Market & Locker Plant
   Frazee, MN .218-334-2351
Macfarlane Pheasants
   Janesville, WI 800-345-8348
Mahantongo Game Farm
   Dalmatia, PA 800-982-9913
Matthiesen's Deer & Custom
   De Witt, IA .563-659-8409
McLane's Meats
   Wetaskiwin, AB 780-352-4321
Meat-O-Mat Corp
   Brooklyn, NY 718-965-7250
Meatco Sales Ltd.
   Mirror, AB 403-788-2292
Michael's Finer Meats/Seafoods
   Columbus, OH 800-282-0518
Miller's Meat Market
   Red Bud, IL .618-282-3334
Musicon Deer Farm
   Goshen, NY 845-294-6378
Nicky USA Inc
   Portland, OR 800-469-4162
Onoway Custom Packers
   Onoway, AB 780-967-2727
Oxford Frozen Foods
   Oxford, NS .902-447-2100
Palmetto Pigeon Plant
   Sumter, SC .803-775-1204
Payne Packing Co
   Artesia, NM .575-746-2779
Pekarna Meat Market
   Jordan, MN .952-492-6101
Pinter's Packing Plant
   Dorchester, WI 715-654-5444
Prairie Cajun Wholesale
   Eunice, LA .337-546-6195
R Four Meats
   Chatfield, MN 507-867-4180
Rabbit Barn
   Turlock, CA 209-632-1123
Rocky Mountain Meats
   Rocky Mountain House, AB 403-845-3434
Specialty Meats & Gourmet
   Hudson, WI 800-310-2360
Springville Meat & Cold Storage
   Springville, UT 801-489-6391
Squab Producers of California
   Modesto, CA 209-537-4744
Stonie's Sausage Shop
   Perryville, MO 888-546-2540
Tofield Packers Ltd
   Tofield, AB .780-662-4842
United Meat Company
   San Francisco, CA 415-864-2118
Uvalde Meat Processing
   Uvalde, TX .830-278-6247
Victoria Fancy Sausage
   Edmonton, AB 780-471-2283
Wall Meat Processing
   Wall, SD 605-279-2348
Western Buffalo Company
   Rapid City, SD 800-247-3263
White Oak Pastures
   Bluffton, GA 229-641-2081

Alligator

Acadian Ostrich Ranch
   Clinton, LA .800-350-0167
Alpine Butcher
   Lowell, MA .978-256-7771
Bayou Land Seafood
   Breaux Bridge, LA 337-667-6118
Nicky USA Inc
   Portland, OR 800-469-4162
Prairie Cajun Wholesale
   Eunice, LA .337-546-6195

Boar

Alpine Butcher
   Lowell, MA .978-256-7771
Broadleaf Venison USA Inc
   Vernon, CA 800-336-3844

Grandview Farms
   Thornbury, ON 519-599-6368
Nicky USA Inc
   Portland, OR 800-469-4162

Buffalo

Alewel's Country Meats
   Warrensburg, MO 800-353-8553
Alpine Butcher
   Lowell, MA .978-256-7771
Broadleaf Venison USA Inc
   Vernon, CA 800-336-3844
Clay Center Locker Plant
   Clay Center, KS 800-466-5543
Golden Valley Natural
   Shelley, ID .888-270-7147
Miller's Meat Market
   Red Bud, IL .618-282-3334
Nicky USA Inc
   Portland, OR 800-469-4162
Pinter's Packing Plant
   Dorchester, WI 715-654-5444
Rocky Mountain Natural Meats
   Henderson, CO 800-327-2706
Springville Meat & Cold Storage
   Springville, UT 801-489-6391
Superior Farms
   Sacramento, CA 800-228-5262
Triple U Enterprises
   Fort Pierre, SD 605-567-3624
Vital Choice
   Bellingham, WA 800-608-4825
Wall Meat Processing
   Wall, SD 605-279-2348
Western Buffalo Company
   Rapid City, SD 800-247-3263
YB Meats of Wichita
   Wichita, KS 316-942-1213

Caribou

Grandview Farms
   Thornbury, ON 519-599-6368

Emu

Dino-Meat Company
   White House, TN 877-557-6493
Grandview Farms
   Thornbury, ON 519-599-6368
YB Meats of Wichita
   Wichita, KS 316-942-1213

Farm-Raised

Clay Center Locker Plant
   Clay Center, KS 800-466-5543
Sunnyside Farms LLC
   Washington, VA 540-675-3669
Triple U Enterprises
   Fort Pierre, SD 605-567-3624
Wall Meat Processing
   Wall, SD 605-279-2348
Western Buffalo Company
   Rapid City, SD 800-247-3263

Meat & Poultry

Becker Foods
   Westminster, CA 714-891-9474
Bon Secour Fisheries Inc
   Bon Secour, AL 251-949-7411
Broadleaf Venison USA Inc
   Vernon, CA 800-336-3844
Clay Center Locker Plant
   Clay Center, KS 800-466-5543
Crescent Duck Farm
   Aquebogue LI, NY 631-722-8000
Czimer's Game & Seafoods
   Homer Glen, IL 888-294-6377
Eickman's Processing Co
   Seward, IL .815-247-8451
Ellsworth Locker
   Ellsworth, MN 507-967-2544
Fox Deluxe Inc
   Chicago, IL 312-421-3737
Grandview Farms
   Thornbury, ON 519-599-6368
Grimaud Farms-California Inc
   Stockton, CA 800-466-9955
Hickory Baked Ham Co
   Castle Rock, CO 303-688-2633
Indian Valley Meats
   Indian, AK 907-653-7511

Ketters Meat Market & Locker Plant
   Frazee, MN .218-334-2351
Lindner Bison
   Northern, CA 530-254-6337
Macfarlane Pheasants
   Janesville, WI 800-345-8348
Metzer Farms
   Gonzales, CA 800-424-7755
Miller Brothers Packing Company
   Sylvester, GA 229-776-2014
Musicon Deer Farm
   Goshen, NY 845-294-6378
Palmetto Pigeon Plant
   Sumter, SC .803-775-1204
Pekarna Meat Market
   Jordan, MN .952-492-6101
Pinter's Packing Plant
   Dorchester, WI 715-654-5444
R Four Meats
   Chatfield, MN 507-867-4180
Schiltz Foods Inc
   Sisseton, SD 877-872-4458
Springville Meat & Cold Storage
   Springville, UT 801-489-6391
Squab Producers of California
   Modesto, CA 209-537-4744
Stonie's Sausage Shop
   Perryville, MO 888-546-2540
Triple U Enterprises
   Fort Pierre, SD 605-567-3624
United Meat Company
   San Francisco, CA 415-864-2118
Uvalde Meat Processing
   Uvalde, TX .830-278-6247
Wall Meat Processing
   Wall, SD 605-279-2348
Wapsie Produce
   Decorah, IA 563-382-4271
Western Buffalo Company
   Rapid City, SD 800-247-3263

Muskox

Grandview Farms
   Thornbury, ON 519-599-6368

Ostrich

Acadian Ostrich Ranch
   Clinton, LA .800-350-0167
Broadleaf Venison USA Inc
   Vernon, CA 800-336-3844
Clay Center Locker Plant
   Clay Center, KS 800-466-5543
Grandview Farms
   Thornbury, ON 519-599-6368
Kingsbury Country Market
   La Porte, IN 219-393-3016
Meat-O-Mat Corp
   Brooklyn, NY 718-965-7250
Nicky USA Inc
   Portland, OR 800-469-4162
Pokanoket Ostrich Farm
   South Dartmouth, MA 508-992-6188
Prime Ostrich International
   Morinville, AB 800-340-2311
Protos Inc
   Greensburg, PA 724-836-1802
YB Meats of Wichita
   Wichita, KS 316-942-1213

Pheasant

Alpine Butcher
   Lowell, MA .978-256-7771
Burgers' Smokehouse
   California, MO 800-345-5185
Hickory Baked Ham Co
   Castle Rock, CO 303-688-2633
Macfarlane Pheasants
   Janesville, WI 800-345-8348
Mahantongo Game Farm
   Dalmatia, PA 800-982-9913
Nicky USA Inc
   Portland, OR 800-469-4162
Squab Producers of California
   Modesto, CA 209-537-4744

Quail (See also Eggs: Quail)

Alpine Butcher
   Lowell, MA .978-256-7771
Burgers' Smokehouse
   California, MO 800-345-5185

Product Categories / Meats & Meat Products: Goat

Manchester Farms
  Columbia, SC 800-845-0421
Nicky USA Inc
  Portland, OR 800-469-4162
Nueces Canyon Range
  Brenham, TX 800-925-5058
Squab Producers of California
  Modesto, CA 209-537-4744
Urgasa
  Coral Gables, FL 786-543-6693

Rabbit

Nicky USA Inc
  Portland, OR 800-469-4162
Rabbit Barn
  Turlock, CA 209-632-1123

Fryer

Mahantongo Game Farm
  Dalmatia, PA 800-982-9913
Squab Producers of California
  Modesto, CA 209-537-4744
Tarazi Specialty Foods
  Chino, CA 909-628-3601

Squab

Palmetto Pigeon Plant
  Sumter, SC 803-775-1204
Squab Producers of California
  Modesto, CA 209-537-4744

Venison

AJ's Lena Maid Meats Inc
  Lena, IL 815-369-4522
Alewel's Country Meats
  Warrensburg, MO 800-353-8553
Alpine Butcher
  Lowell, MA 978-256-7771
Bellville Meat Market
  Bellville, TX 800-571-6328
Blakely Freezer Locker
  Blakeley, GA 229-723-3622
Boyd's Sausage Co
  Washington, IA 319-653-5715
Broadleaf Venison USA Inc
  Vernon, CA 800-336-3844
Brookview Farms
  Manakin-Sabot, VA 804-784-3131
Ellsworth Locker
  Ellsworth, MN 507-967-2544
Grandview Farms
  Thornbury, ON 519-599-6368
Heinkel's Packing Co
  Decatur, IL 800-594-2738
Houser Meats
  Rushville, IL 217-322-4994
Indian Valley Meats
  Indian, AK 907-653-7511
Jackson Brothers Food Locker
  Post, TX 806-495-3245
Ketters Meat Market & Locker Plant
  Frazee, MN 218-334-2351
MacGregors Meat & Seafood
  Toronto, ON 888-383-3663
Matthiesen's Deer & Custom
  De Witt, IA 563-659-8409
Musicon Deer Farm
  Goshen, NY 845-294-6378
Nesbitt Processing
  Aledo, IL 309-582-5183
Nicky USA Inc
  Portland, OR 800-469-4162
R Four Meats
  Chatfield, MN 507-867-4180
Smokey Denmark Sausage Co
  Austin, TX 512-385-0718
Specialty Meats & Gourmet
  Hudson, WI 800-310-2360
Stonie's Sausage Shop
  Perryville, MO 888-546-2540
Superior Farms
  Sacramento, CA 800-228-5262
United Meat Company
  San Francisco, CA 415-864-2118
Uvalde Meat Processing
  Uvalde, TX 830-278-6247
YB Meats of Wichita
  Wichita, KS 316-942-1213

Canned

Indian Valley Meats
  Indian, AK 907-653-7511

Frozen

Broadleaf Venison USA Inc
  Vernon, CA 800-336-3844
Brookview Farms
  Manakin-Sabot, VA 804-784-3131
Indian Valley Meats
  Indian, AK 907-653-7511
R Four Meats
  Chatfield, MN 507-867-4180
United Meat Company
  San Francisco, CA 415-864-2118

Wild

Clay Center Locker Plant
  Clay Center, KS 800-466-5543
Eickman's Processing Co
  Seward, IL 815-247-8451
Triple U Enterprises
  Fort Pierre, SD 605-567-3624
Wall Meat Processing
  Wall, SD 605-279-2348
Western Buffalo Company
  Rapid City, SD 800-247-3263

Goat

Braham Food Locker Service
  Braham, MN 320-396-2636
Caribbean Food Delights Inc
  Tappan, NY 845-398-3000
ELP Inc
  Elizabeth, CO 303-688-2240
Halsted Packing House
  Chicago, IL 312-421-5147
Jones Packing Co
  Harvard, IL 815-943-4488
Madani Halal
  Ozone Park, NY 718-323-9732
Nesbitt Processing
  Aledo, IL 309-582-5183
Red Deer Lake Meat Processing
  Calgary, AB 403-256-4925
White Oak Pastures
  Bluffton, GA 229-641-2081
Windcrest Meat Packers
  Port Perry, ON 800-750-2542

Horse

Bouvry Exports Calgary
  Calgary, AB 403-253-0717
Phoenix Agro-Industrial Corporation
  Westbury, NY 516-334-1194

Lamb

A.C. Kissling Company
  Philadelphia, PA 800-445-1943
Acme Steak & Seafood
  Youngstown, OH 800-686-2263
AJ's Lena Maid Meats Inc
  Lena, IL 815-369-4522
Alpine Butcher
  Lowell, MA 978-256-7771
Alpine Meats
  Stockton, CA 800-399-6328
B & R Quality Meats Inc
  Waterloo, IA 319-232-6328
Blakely Freezer Locker
  Blakeley, GA 229-723-3622
Borders Sporting Goods
  Ashland, KY 606-928-6326
Brookview Farms
  Manakin-Sabot, VA 804-784-3131
Bush Brothers Provision Co
  West Palm Beach, FL 800-327-1345
Callaway Packing Inc
  Delta, CO 970-874-9743
Campbell's Quality Cuts
  Sidney, OH 937-492-2194
Canal Fulton Provision
  Canal Fulton, OH 800-321-3502
Catelli Brothers Inc
  Collingswood, NJ 856-869-9293
Center Locker Svc
  Center, MO 800-884-0737
Chicago Steaks
  Chicago, IL 773-847-5400
Clay Center Locker Plant
  Clay Center, KS 800-466-5543
Country Butcher Shop
  Carlisle, PA 800-272-9223
Country Village Meats Inc
  Sublette, IL 800-700-4545
Cusack Meats
  Oklahoma City, OK 800-241-6328
Dale T Smith & Sons Inc
  Draper, UT 801-571-3611
David Mosner Meat Products
  Bronx, NY 866-928-6428
Debragga & Spitler
  Jersey City, NJ
Dino's Sausage & Meat Co Inc
  Utica, NY 315-732-2661
Dole & Bailey Inc
  Woburn, MA 781-935-1234
Dom's Sausage Co Inc
  Malden, MA 781-324-6390
Duma Meats Inc
  Mogadore, OH 330-628-3438
Eickman's Processing Co
  Seward, IL 815-247-8451
Eiserman Meats
  Slave Lake, AB 780-849-5507
ELP Inc
  Elizabeth, CO 303-688-2240
Eureka Locker Inc
  Eureka, IL 309-467-2731
Feed The Party
  Louisville, KY
Fulton Provision Co
  Portland, OR 800-333-6328
Halsted Packing House
  Chicago, IL 312-421-5147
Heringer Meats Inc
  Covington, KY 859-291-2000
Houser Meats
  Rushville, IL 217-322-4994
International Meat Co
  Chicago, IL 773-622-1400
Isernio Sausage Company
  Seattle, WA 888-495-8674
JBS USA LLC
  Greeley, CO 970-506-8000
Jones Packing Co
  Harvard, IL 815-943-4488
Jordahl Meats
  Manchester, MN 507-826-3418
Kelble Brothers Inc
  Berlin Heights, OH 800-247-2333
Kelly Packing Company
  Torrington, WY 307-532-2210
L & L Packing Co
  Chicago, IL 800-628-6328
L & M Slaughterhouse
  Georgetown, IL 217-662-6841
Lay Packing Company
  Knoxville, TN 865-522-1147
Lombardi Brothers Meat Packers
  Denver, CO 303-458-7441
Madani Halal
  Ozone Park, NY 718-323-9732
Maid-Rite Steak Company
  Dunmore, PA 800-233-4259
Malcolm Meats Co
  Northwood, OH 800-822-6328
Manger Packing Corp
  Baltimore, MD 800-227-9262
Marks Meat
  Holmen, WI 608-526-6058
Matthiesen's Deer & Custom
  De Witt, IA 563-659-8409
Meatland Packers
  Medicine Hat, AB 403-528-4321
Miami Beef Co
  Miami Lakes, FL 305-621-3252
Miller Brothers Packing Company
  Sylvester, GA 229-776-2014
Mountain States Rosen
  Bronx, NY 800-872-5262
Nesbitt Processing
  Aledo, IL 309-582-5183
Northwest Meat Company
  Chicago, IL 312-733-1418
Oklahoma City Meat Co Inc
  Oklahoma City, OK 405-235-3308
Omaha Steaks Inc
  800-960-8400
Onoway Custom Packers
  Onoway, AB 780-967-2727

309

Product Categories / Meats & Meat Products: Meat Meal

Pasqualichio Brothers Inc
  Scranton, PA .800-232-6233
Petschl's Quality Meats
  Tukwila, WA 206-575-4400
Premium Meat Co
  Brigham City, UT 435-723-5944
R Four Meats
  Chatfield, MN 507-867-4180
Ralph's Packing Co
  Perkins, OK 800-522-3979
Red Deer Lake Meat Processing
  Calgary, AB 403-256-4925
Rendulic Meat Packing Corp
  Mckeesport, PA 412-678-9541
Rocky Mountain Meats
  Rocky Mountain House, AB 403-845-3434
Royal Center Locker Plant
  Royal Center, IN 574-643-3275
Shelley's
  Jersey City, NJ 201-433-2900
Smith Packing Regional Meat
  Utica, NY 315-732-5125
Springville Meat & Cold Storage
  Springville, UT 801-489-6391
SRA Foods
  Birmingham, AL 205-323-7447
Standard Meat Co LP
  Dallas, TX 866-859-6313
Stock Yards Packing Company
  Melrose Park, IL 877-785-9273
Strassburger Steaks
  Carlstadt, NJ .201-842-8890
Strauss Brands International
  Franklin, WI .414-421-5250
Streit Carl & Son Co
  Neptune, NJ .732-775-0803
Superior Farms
  Sacramento, CA 800-228-5262
Terrell Meats
  Delta, UT 435-864-2600
Thompson Packers
  Slidell, LA 800-989-6328
Tillamook Meat Inc
  Tillamook, OR 503-842-4802
Tucker Packing Co
  Orrville, OH 330-683-3311
Turk Brothers Custom Meats Inc
  Ashland, OH .800-789-1051
Une-Viandi
  St. Jean Sur Richelieu, NB 800-363-1955
United Meat Company
  San Francisco, CA 415-864-2118
United Provision Meat Company
  Columbus, OH 614-252-1126
Uvalde Meat Processing
  Uvalde, TX 830-278-6247
Vestergaard Farms
  Ann Arbor, MI 734-929-2875
Victoria Fancy Sausage
  Edmonton, AB 780-471-2283
Wall Meat Processing
  Wall, SD 605-279-2348
Warren & Son Meat Processing
  Whipple, OH .740-585-2421
Wasatch Meats Inc
  Salt Lake City, UT 800-631-8294
Westport Locker LLC
  Westport, IN .877-265-0551
White's Meat Processing
  Fort Gibson, OK 918-478-2347
Willcox Meat Packing House
  Willcox, AZ 520-384-2015
Windcrest Meat Packers
  Port Perry, ON 800-750-2542
YB Meats of Wichita
  Wichita, KS 316-942-1213

Fresh

Atlantic Veal & Lamb Inc
  Brooklyn, NY 800-222-8325
R Four Meats
  Chatfield, MN 507-867-4180
Shelley's
  Jersey City, NJ 201-433-2900
Smith Packing Regional Meat
  Utica, NY 315-732-5125

Frozen

Atlantic Veal & Lamb Inc
  Brooklyn, NY 800-222-8325

Maid-Rite Steak Company
  Dunmore, PA 800-233-4259
Phoenix Agro-Industrial Corporation
  Westbury, NY 516-334-1194
R Four Meats
  Chatfield, MN 507-867-4180
Shelley's
  Jersey City, NJ 201-433-2900
Smith Packing Regional Meat
  Utica, NY 315-732-5125
Thompson Packers
  Slidell, LA 800-989-6328
United Meat Company
  San Francisco, CA 415-864-2118

Leg of

Alpine Butcher
  Lowell, MA 978-256-7771
Chicago Steaks
  Chicago, IL 773-847-5400

Loin Chop

Alpine Butcher
  Lowell, MA 978-256-7771
Chicago Steaks
  Chicago, IL 773-847-5400

Loin Roast

Alpine Butcher
  Lowell, MA 978-256-7771

Rib Chop

Chicago Steaks
  Chicago, IL 773-847-5400

Meat Meal

Mcredmond Brothers
  Nashville, TN 800-251-5930

Mutton

Center Locker Svc
  Center, MO .800-884-0737

Packaged

Burke Corp
  Nevada, IA 800-654-1152
Fair Oaks Farms LLC
  Pleasant Prairie, WI 800-528-8615

Pates & Fois Gras

Foie Gras

Hudson Valley Foie Gras
  Ferndale, NY 845-292-2500

Pates

Alexian Pâtés
  Neptune, NJ .800-927-9473
Caughman's Meat Plant
  Lexington, SC 803-356-0076
Cordon Bleu International
  Anjou, QC 800-363-1182
Ducktrap River Of Maine
  Belfast, ME .800-434-8727
Giovanni's Appetizing Food Co
  Richmond, MI 586-727-9355
Hickory Baked Ham Co
  Castle Rock, CO 303-688-2633
International Trading Company
  Houston, TX 713-224-5901
Les Trois Petits Cochons
  Brooklyn, NY 800-537-7283
Marcel et Henri Charcuterie Francaise
  South San Francisco, CA 800-227-6436
Michel's Magnifique
  New York, NY 212-431-1070
Olympic Provisions Northwest
  Portland, OR 503-894-8136
Organic Gourmet
  Sherman Oaks, CA 800-400-7772
Phoenicia Patisserie
  Arlington, TX 817-261-2898
Piller's Fine Foods
  Waterloo, ON 800-265-2627
Salmolux Inc
  Federal Way, WA 253-874-6570
Sunset Farm Foods Inc
  Valdosta, GA 800-882-1121

Taste of Gourmet
  Indianola, MS 800-833-7731

Pork & Pork Products

A To Z Portion Control Meats
  Bluffton, OH .800-338-6328
Abattoir Aliments Asta Inc
  St Alexandre De Kamouras, QC 800-463-1355
Acornseekers Inc
  Flatonia, TX .786-338-8160
Alaska Sausage & Seafood
  Anchorage, AK 800-798-3636
Albert's Meats
  Claysville, PA 800-522-9970
Alderfer Inc
  Harleysville, PA 800-341-1121
Alpine Butcher
  Lowell, MA 978-256-7771
Amana Meat Shop & Smoke House
  Amana, IA 800-373-6328
Arizona Sunland Foods
  Tucson, AZ .520-624-7068
Armbrust Meats
  Medford, WI .715-748-3102
Atlantic Pork & Provisions
  Jamaica, NY 800-245-3536
B & D Foods
  Boise, ID 208-344-1183
B & R Quality Meats Inc
  Waterloo, IA .319-232-6328
Bear Creek Smokehouse Inc
  Marshall, TX 800-950-2327
Best Chicago Meat
  Chicago, IL
Big B Barbecue
  Evansville, IN 812-425-5235
Bluebonnet Meat Company
  Trenton, TX .903-989-2293
Bodin Foods
  New Iberia, LA 337-367-1344
Boone's Butcher Shop
  Bardstown, KY 888-253-3384
Brucepac
  Woodburn, OR 800-899-3629
Burgers' Smokehouse
  California, MO 800-345-5185
Burke Corp
  Nevada, IA 800-654-1152
Burnett & Son
  Monrovia, CA 877-632-5467
Bush Brothers Provision Co
  West Palm Beach, FL 800-327-1345
Buzz Food Svc
  Charleston, WV 304-925-4781
C Roy & Sons Processing
  Yale, MI 810-387-3957
Caddo Packing Co
  Marshall, TX 903-935-2211
Calihan Pork Processors Inc
  Peoria, IL 309-674-9175
Calumet Diversified Meats Company
  Pleasant Prairie, WI 800-752-7427
Cargill Protein
  Wichita, KS
Caribbean Products
  Baltimore, MD 410-235-7700
Carmelita Provisions Company
  Monterey Park, CA 323-262-6751
Carolina Pride Foods
  Greenwood, SC 864-229-5611
Caughman's Meat Plant
  Lexington, SC 803-356-0076
Central Meat & Provision
  San Diego, CA 619-239-1391
Chandler Foods Inc
  Greensboro, NC 800-537-6219
Chef's Requested Foods
  Oklahoma City, OK 405-239-2610
Cheraw Packing Plant
  Cheraw, SC .843-537-7426
Chicago Steaks
  Chicago, IL 773-847-5400
Chip Steak & Provision Co
  Mankato, MN 507-388-6277
Chisesi Brothers Meat Packing
  New Orleans, LA 800-966-3550
Cimpl Meats
  Yankton, SD .605-665-1665
Circle B Ranch
  Seymour, MO 417-683-0271
Circle V Meats
  Spanish Fork, UT 801-798-3081

Product Categories / Meats & Meat Products: Pork & Pork Products

Clem Becker Meats
  Two Rivers, WI 920-793-1391
Clougherty Packing LLC
  Los Angeles, CA 800-846-7635
Cloverdale Foods
  Mandan, ND 800-669-9511
Coleman Natural
  Kings Mountain, NC 800-442-8666
Columbia Packing Co Inc
  Dallas, TX 214-946-8171
Continental Grain Company
  New York, NY 212-207-5100
Cordon Bleu International
  Anjou, QC 800-363-1182
Country Butcher Shop
  Carlisle, PA 800-272-9223
Country Smoked Meats
  Bowling Green, OH 800-321-4766
Country Village Meats Inc
  Sublette, IL 800-700-4545
Crawford Sausage Co Inc
  Chicago, IL 773-277-3095
Crofton & Sons Inc
  Tampa, FL 800-878-7675
Curtis Packing Co
  Greensboro, NC 336-275-7684
Cusack Meats
  Oklahoma City, OK 800-241-6328
Dailys Premium Meats
  Salt Lake City, UT 800-328-7695
Debragga & Spitler
  Jersey City, NJ
Diestel Family Turkey Ranch
  209-532-4950
Dietz & Watson Inc.
  Philadelphia, PA 215-831-9000
Dohar Meats Inc
  Cleveland, OH 216-241-4197
Dolores Canning Co Inc
  Los Angeles, CA 323-263-9155
Dom's Sausage Co Inc
  Malden, MA 781-324-6390
Dreymiller & KRAY Inc
  Hampshire, IL 847-683-2271
Duma Meats Inc
  Mogadore, OH 330-628-3438
East Dayton Meat & Poultry
  Dayton, OH 937-253-6185
Edelmann Provision Company
  Harrison, OH 513-881-5800
Edmond's Chile Co
  St Louis, MO 314-772-1499
Fabbri Sausage Mfg Co
  Chicago, IL 312-829-6363
Fair Oaks Farms LLC
  Pleasant Prairie, WI 800-528-8615
Fanestil Packing Company
  Emporia, KS 800-658-1652
Feed The Party
  Louisville, KY
Fletcher's Fine Foods
  Auburn, WA 253-735-0800
Fork & Goode
  Brooklyn, NY
Fortenberry Mini-Storage
  Kodak, TN 865-933-2568
Freirich Foods
  Salisbury, NC 800-221-1315
Frick's Quality Meats
  Washington, MO 800-241-2209
Fulton Provision Co
  Portland, OR 800-333-6328
Golden West Food Group
  Vernon, CA 888-807-3663
Gouvea's & Purity Foods Inc
  Honolulu, HI 808-847-3717
Grant Park Packing
  Chicago, IL 312-421-4096
Groff's Meats
  Elizabethtown, PA 717-367-1246
Gulf Marine & Industrial Supplies Inc
  Houston, TX 800-886-6252
Hamms Custom Meats
  Mckinney, TX 972-542-3359
Harvin Choice Meats
  Sumter, SC 800-849-6328
Hatfield Quality Meats
  Hatfield, PA 800-743-1191
Hazle Park Quality Meats
  West Hazleton, PA 800-238-4371
Hickory Baked Ham Co
  Castle Rock, CO 303-688-2633

Higa Food Service
  Honolulu, HI 808-531-3591
Hillbilly Smokehouse
  Rogers, AR 479-636-1927
Holly Hill Locker Company
  Holly Hill, SC 803-496-3611
Hoople Country Kitchen Inc
  Rockport, IN 877-466-7537
Hormel Foods Corp.
  Austin, MN 507-437-5611
Humphrey's Market
  Springfield, IL 800-747-6328
JBS USA LLC
  Greeley, CO 970-506-8000
John Hofmeister & Son Inc
  Chicago, IL 800-923-4267
Johnsonville Sausage LLC
  Watertown, WI 888-556-2728
Jones Dairy Farm
  Fort Atkinson, WI 800-563-6637
JTM Food Group
  Harrison, OH 800-626-2308
Karn Meats
  Columbus, OH 800-221-9585
Kelley Foods
  Elba, AL 334-897-5761
Kilgus Meats
  Toledo, OH 419-472-9721
Kowalski Sausage Co
  Hamtramck, MI 800-482-2400
Kubla Khan Food Company
  Portland, OR 503-234-7494
Kutztown Bologna Company
  Leola, PA 800-723-8824
L & L Packing Co
  Chicago, IL 800-628-6328
Land O'Frost Inc
  Searcy, AR 800-643-5654
Lay Packing Company
  Knoxville, TN 865-522-1147
Lee's Sausage Co
  Orangeburg, SC 803-534-5517
Leidy's
  Harleysville, PA 800-222-2319
Leo G. Fraboni Sausage Company
  Hibbing, MN 218-263-5074
Leona Meat Plant
  Troy, PA 570-297-3574
Les Trois Petits Cochons
  Brooklyn, NY 800-537-7283
Levesque
  Montreal, QC 877-539-1702
Locustdale Meat Packing
  Locustdale, PA 570-875-1270
Lord's Sausage & Country Ham
  Dexter, GA 800-342-6002
Lubbers Family Farm
  Grand Rapids, MI 616-453-4257
Malcolm Meats Co
  Northwood, OH 800-822-6328
Maple Leaf Foods
  Winnipeg, NB 800-564-6253
Marshallville Packing Co
  Marshallville, OH 330-855-2871
Marubeni America Corp.
  New York, NY 212-450-0100
Meating Place
  Buffalo, NY 716-885-3623
Mellos North End Mfr
  Fall River, MA 800-673-2320
Metafoods LLC
  Brookhaven, GA 404-843-2400
Miami Beef Co
  Miami Lakes, FL 305-621-3252
Mirasco
  Atlanta, GA 770-956-1945
Mitchell Foods
  Barbourville, KY 888-202-9745
Montana Ranch Brand
  Billings, MT 406-294-2333
Morreale John R Inc
  Chicago, IL 312-421-3664
Morrison Meat Packers
  Miami, FL 800-330-4267
Morse's Sauerkraut
  Waldoboro, ME 866-832-5569
National Steak & Poultry
  Owasso, OK 918-274-8787
New Braunfels Smokehouse
  New Braunfels, TX 800-537-6932
New Horizon Farms
  Pipestone, MN 800-906-7447

Niemuth's Steak & Chop Shop
  Waupaca, WI 715-258-2666
Northwest Meat Company
  Chicago, IL 312-733-1418
Oklahoma City Meat Co Inc
  Oklahoma City, OK 405-235-3308
Olymel
  Saint-Hyacinthe, QC 450-771-0400
Omaha Steaks Inc
  800-960-8400
Ossian Smoked Meats
  Ossian, IN 800-535-8862
Parma Sausage Products
  Pittsburgh, PA 877-294-4207
Pasqualichio Brothers Inc
  Scranton, PA 800-232-6233
Payne Packing Co
  Artesia, NM 575-746-2779
Pederson's Natural Farms
  Hamilton, TX
Peer Foods Group Inc
  Chicago, IL 800-365-5644
Perdue Farms Inc.
  Salisbury, MD 800-473-7383
Pierceton Foods Inc
  Pierceton, IN 574-594-2344
Pioneer Packing Co
  Bowling Green, OH 419-352-5283
Plumrose USA
  Chicago, IL 800-526-4909
Quality Snack Foods Inc
  Alsip, IL 708-377-7120
Quirch Foods
  Coral Gables, FL 800-458-5252
R M Felts' Packing Co
  Ivor, VA 757-859-6131
R.L. Zeigler Company
  Selma, AL 800-392-6328
Randall Foods Inc
  Vernon, CA 800-372-6581
Ray's Sausage Co
  Cleveland, OH 216-921-8782
Red Smith Foods Inc
  Davie, FL 954-581-1996
Register Meat Co
  Cottondale, FL 850-352-4269
Rendulic Meat Packing Corp
  Mckeesport, PA 412-678-9541
Rinehart Meat Processing
  Branson, MO 417-869-2041
Robertson's Country Meat Hams
  Finchville, KY 800-678-1521
Rose Packing Co Inc
  South Barrington, IL 800-323-7363
Sadler's Smokehouse
  Henderson, TX 903-657-5581
Sanders Meat Packing Inc
  Custer, MI 800-968-5035
Saval Foods Corp
  Elkridge, MD 800-527-2825
Savoie's Sausage and Food Products
  Opelousas, LA 337-942-7241
Schaller & Weber Inc
  Astoria, NY 800-847-4115
Sculli Brothers
  Yeadon, PA 215-336-1223
Seaboard Foods
  Shawnee Mission, KS 800-262-7907
Sechrist Brothers
  Dallastown, PA 717-244-2975
Sheinman Provision Co
  Philadelphia, PA 215-473-7065
Smolich Bros. Home Made Sausage
  Crest Hill, IL 815-727-2144
Sofina Foods Inc
  Markham, ON 855-763-4621
Sommers Organic
  Wheeling, IL 877-377-9797
SRA Foods
  Birmingham, AL 205-323-7447
Stevens Sausage Co
  Smithfield, NC 800-338-0561
Stevison Ham Co
  Portland, TN 800-844-4267
Stonie's Sausage Shop
  Perryville, MO 888-546-2540
Strassburger Steaks
  Carlstadt, NJ 201-842-8890
Stripling's General Store
  Moultrie, GA 229-985-4226
Sugar Creek
  Washington Ct Hs, OH 800-848-8205

311

Product Categories / Meats & Meat Products: Pork & Pork Products

Suncrest Farms
   Princeton, KY 973-595-0214
Sunnydale Meats Inc
   Gaffney, SC 864-489-6091
Taylor Meat Co
   Taylor, TX 512-352-6357
Teton Waters Ranch LLC
   Denver, CO 720-340-4590
The Bruss Company
   Chicago, IL 773-282-2900
Thomas Packing Company
   Columbus, GA 800-729-0976
Tolteca Foodservice
   Norcross, GA 800-541-6835
Triumph Foods, LLC
   St. Joseph, MO 800-262-7907
Troy Foods Inc
   Troy, IL 618-667-6332
Tyson Foods Inc.
   Springdale, AR 479-290-4000
Tyson Foods Inc.
   Springdale, AR 800-233-6332
V.W. Joyner & Company
   Smithfield, VA 757-357-2161
Valley Meats
   Coal Valley, IL 309-517-6639
Vestergaard Farms
   Ann Arbor, MI 734-929-2875
Vital Choice
   Bellingham, WA .800-608-4825
Vollwerth & Baroni Companies
   Hancock, MI 800-562-7620
W.A. Beans & Sons
   Bangor, ME 800-649-1958
WACO Beef & Pork Processors
   Waco, TX 254-772-4669
Waken Meat Co
   Atlanta, GA 404-627-3537
Wayco Ham Co
   Goldsboro, NC 800-962-2614
White Oak Pastures
   Bluffton, GA 229-641-2081
Wichita Packing Co Inc
   Chicago, IL 312-763-3965
Williams Pork
   Chadbourn, NC 910-654-0204
Willie's Smoke House LLC
   Harrisville, PA. 800-742-4184
YB Meats of Wichita
   Wichita, KS 316-942-1213

Barbecued

Big B Barbecue
   Evansville, IN 812-425-5235
Chandler Foods Inc
   Greensboro, NC .800-537-6219
Dorina So-Good Inc
   Union, IL 815-923-2144
Moonlite Bar-B-Q Inn
   Owensboro, KY .800-322-8989
Piggie Park Enterprises
   West Columbia, SC 800-628-7423
Sadler's Smokehouse
   Henderson, TX 903-657-5581
Stevison Ham Co
   Portland, TN 800-844-4267
W & G Marketing Company
   Ames, IA 515-233-4774
Woods Smoked Meats Inc
   Bowling Green, MO 800-458-8426

Frozen

Burke Corp
   Nevada, IA 800-654-1152
Clifty Farm Country Meats
   Paris, TN 800-486-4267

Boneless Picnic

Roger Wood Foods Inc
   Savannah, GA 800-849-9272

Breaded

King's Command Foods Inc
   Green Bay, WA 800-345-0293
Valley Meats
   Coal Valley, IL 309-517-6639

Fresh

Abattoir A. Trahan Company
   Yamachiche, QC .819-296-3791

Aliments Jolibec, Inc
   St Jacques De Montcalm, QC. 450-861-6082
Amity Packing Co Inc
   Chicago, IL 800-837-0270
Botsford Fisheries
   Cap Pele, NB. 506-577-4327
Brook Locker Plant
   Brook, IN 219-275-2611
Buckhead Beef
   Atlanta, GA 800-888-5578
Camrose Packers
   Camrose, AB. 780-672-4887
Charcuterie LaTour Eiffel
   Blainville, QC. 800-361-0001
Farm Boy Food Svc
   Evansville, IN 800-852-3976
Independent Meat Co
   Twin Falls, ID 800-284-4626
J & M Wholesale Meat Inc
   Modesto, CA. 855-522-1248
J W Treuth & Sons
   Catonsville, MD .410-747-6281
Les Salaisons Brochu
   St. Henri De Levis, QC. 418-882-2282
Les Viandes or Fil
   Laval, QC 450-687-5664
Maple Leaf Pork
   Montreal, QC 800-268-3708
Ontario Pork
   Guelph, ON. 877-668-7675
Pure Foods Meat
   Toronto, ON 416-236-1163
R Four Meats
   Chatfield, MN 507-867-4180
Schwab Meat Co
   Oklahoma City, OK 800-888-8668
Shelley's
   Jersey City, NJ 201-433-2900
Smith Packing Regional Meat
   Utica, NY 315-732-5125
Sommers Organic
   Wheeling, IL 877-377-9797
Sunterra Meats
   Trochu, AB 403-442-4202
Thomson Meats
   Melfort, SK 306-752-2802
Troy Pork Store
   Troy, NY 518-272-8291
True Story Foods
   San Francisco, CA 888-277-1171

Frozen

Abattoir A. Trahan Company
   Yamachiche, QC .819-296-3791
Aliments Jolibec, Inc
   St Jacques De Montcalm, QC. 450-861-6082
Amity Packing Co Inc
   Chicago, IL 800-837-0270
B & D Foods
   Boise, ID 208-344-1183
Blakely Freezer Locker
   Blakeley, GA. 229-723-3622
Bob's Custom Cuts
   Bonnyville, AB. 780-826-2627
Botsford Fisheries
   Cap Pele, NB. 506-577-4327
Branding Iron
   Sauget, IL 800-851-4684
Brook Locker Plant
   Brook, IN 219-275-2611
Brookfield Farm
   Amherst, MA 413-253-7991
Buckhead Beef
   Atlanta, GA 800-888-5578
Burke Corp
   Nevada, IA 800-654-1152
Charcuterie LaTour Eiffel
   Blainville, QC. 800-361-0001
Clifty Farm Country Meats
   Paris, TN 800-486-4267
Curly's Foods Inc
   Edina, MN. 612-920-3400
Edmond's Chile Co
   St Louis, MO. 314-772-1499
El Rey Cooked Meats
   St Louis, MO. 314-521-3113
Hatfield Quality Meats
   Hatfield, PA. 800-743-1191
J & M Wholesale Meat Inc
   Modesto, CA. 855-522-1248
Kutztown Bologna Company
   Leola, PA. 800-723-8824

Ladoga Frozen Food & Retail
   Ladoga, IN 765-942-2225
Lengerich Meats Inc
   Zanesville, IN 260-638-4123
Les Salaisons Brochu
   St. Henri De Levis, QC. 418-882-2282
Les Viandes du Breton
   Riviere-Du-Lup, QC. 418-863-6711
Les Viandes or Fil
   Laval, QC 450-687-5664
M Buono Beef Co
   Philadelphia, PA .215-463-3600
Maid-Rite Steak Company
   Dunmore, PA. 800-233-4259
Maple Leaf Pork
   Montreal, QC 800-268-3708
Phoenix Agro-Industrial Corporation
   Westbury, NY 516-334-1194
Pierceton Foods Inc
   Pierceton, IN. 574-594-2344
Pure Foods Meat
   Toronto, ON 416-236-1163
R Four Meats
   Chatfield, MN 507-867-4180
Schwab Meat Co
   Oklahoma City, OK 800-888-8668
Shelley's
   Jersey City, NJ 201-433-2900
Smith Packing Regional Meat
   Utica, NY 315-732-5125
Sommers Organic
   Wheeling, IL 877-377-9797
Springhill Farms
   Neepawa, NB 204-476-3393
Steak-Umm Company
   Shillington, PA 860-928-5900
Sudlersville Frozen Food Locker
   Sudlersville, MD .410-438-3106
Thompson Packers
   Slidell, LA. 800-989-6328
Thomson Meats
   Melfort, SK 306-752-2802
Travis Meats Inc
   Powell, TN 800-247-7606

Loin Baby Back Ribs

Wichita Packing Co Inc
   Chicago, IL 312-763-3965

Loin Chop

Amana Meat Shop & Smoke House
   Amana, IA. 800-373-6328
Calumet Diversified Meats Company
   Pleasant Prairie, WI 800-752-7427
Chicago Steaks
   Chicago, IL 773-847-5400

Loins

Bear Creek Smokehouse Inc
   Marshall, TX. 800-950-2327
Black's Barbecue
   Lockhart, TX. 888-632-8225
Calihan Pork Processors Inc
   Peoria, IL. 309-674-9175
Calumet Diversified Meats Company
   Pleasant Prairie, WI 800-752-7427
Chicago Steaks
   Chicago, IL 773-847-5400
Country Smoked Meats
   Bowling Green, OH 800-321-4766
Father's Country Hams
   Bremen, KY 270-525-3554
Pasqualichio Brothers Inc
   Scranton, PA 800-232-6233
Saval Foods Corp
   Elkridge, MD 800-527-2825

Pigs' Feet

Canned

Peer Foods Group Inc
   Chicago, IL 800-365-5644
Red Smith Foods Inc
   Davie, FL 954-581-1996

Prepared

Frozen

Advance Pierre Foods
   Cincinnati, OH 800-969-2747

Product Categories / Meats & Meat Products: Poultry

Branding Iron
  Sauget, IL 800-851-4684
Brookview Farms
  Manakin-Sabot, VA 804-784-3131
Buckhead Beef
  Atlanta, GA 800-888-5578
Burke Corp
  Nevada, IA 800-654-1152
Chicago Meat Authority Inc
  Chicago, IL 800-383-3811
Hall Brothers Meats
  Olmsted Twp, OH 440-235-3262
Hamms Custom Meats
  Mckinney, TX 972-542-3359
King Kold Meats
  Englewood, OH 800-836-2797
Land O'Frost Inc
  Searcy, AR 800-643-5654
Pierceton Foods Inc
  Pierceton, IN 574-594-2344
Puueo Poi Shop
  Hilo, HI 808-935-8435
Roger Wood Foods Inc
  Savannah, GA 800-849-9272
Tucker Packing Co
  Orrville, OH 330-683-3311

Raw

Duma Meats Inc
  Mogadore, OH 330-628-3438
Ralph's Packing Co
  Perkins, OK 800-522-3979

Rib Center Cut

Bear Creek Smokehouse Inc
  Marshall, TX 800-950-2327
Chicago Steaks
  Chicago, IL 773-847-5400
Farm Boy Food Svc
  Evansville, IN 800-852-3976
Stevison Ham Co
  Portland, TN 800-844-4267

Sausage

Alaska Sausage & Seafood
  Anchorage, AK 800-798-3636
Albert's Meats
  Claysville, PA 800-522-9970
Alef Sausage Inc
  Mundelein, IL 847-968-2533
Arnold's Meat Food Products
  Brooklyn, NY 800-633-7023
Battistoni Italian Spec Meats
  Buffalo, NY 800-248-2705
Bear Creek Smokehouse Inc
  Marshall, TX 800-950-2327
Bellville Meat Market
  Bellville, TX 800-571-6328
Big Fork Brands
  Chicago, IL 321-206-9444
Bilinski Sausage Mfg Co
  Cohoes, NY 877-873-9102
Broadbent B & B Food Products
  Kuttawa, KY 800-841-2202
Brooklyn Cured LLC
  New York, NY 907-282-2221
Brucepac
  Woodburn, OR 800-899-3629
Burke Corp
  Nevada, IA 800-654-1152
C.W. Brown Foods, Inc.
  Mountt Royal, NJ 856-423-3700
Carr Valley Cheese Company
  La Valle, WI 800-462-7258
Caughman's Meat Plant
  Lexington, SC 803-356-0076
Chisesi Brothers Meat Packing
  New Orleans, LA 800-966-3550
Cimpl Meats
  Yankton, SD 605-665-1665
Clougherty Packing LLC
  Los Angeles, CA 800-846-7635
Crofton & Sons Inc
  Tampa, FL 800-878-7675
Den's Hot Dogs
  Brooklyn, NY 718-355-9636
Devro
  Swansea, SC 803-796-9730
Dom's Sausage Co Inc
  Malden, MA 781-324-6390

East Dayton Meat & Poultry
  Dayton, OH 937-253-6185
Ebro Foods
  Chicago, IL 773-696-0150
Edelmann Provision Company
  Harrison, OH 513-881-5800
F B Purnell Sausage Co Inc
  Simpsonville, KY 800-626-1512
Field Roast
  Seattle, WA 800-311-9497
Fortenberry Mini-Storage
  Kodak, TN 865-933-2568
Fred Usinger Inc
  Milwaukee, WI 800-558-9998
Gouvea's & Purity Foods Inc
  Honolulu, HI 808-847-3717
Hoople Country Kitchen Inc
  Rockport, IN 877-466-7537
Humphrey's Market
  Springfield, IL 800-747-6328
International Meat Co
  Chicago, IL 773-622-1400
Johnsonville Sausage LLC
  Watertown, WI 888-556-2728
Korte Meat Processors Inc
  Highland, IL 618-654-3813
Kowalski Sausage Co
  Hamtramck, MI 800-482-2400
Kramarczuk's Sausage Co
  Minneapolis, MN 612-379-3018
Kubisch Sausage Mfg Co
  Shelby Twp, MI 800-852-5019
Laxson Co
  San Antonio, TX 210-226-8397
Lee's Sausage Co
  Orangeburg, SC 803-534-5517
Leidy's
  Harleysville, PA 800-222-2319
Leo G. Fraboni Sausage Company
  Hibbing, MN 218-263-5074
Les Trois Petits Cochons
  Brooklyn, NY 800-537-7283
Lord's Sausage & Country Ham
  Dexter, GA 800-342-6002
Magic Seasoning Blends
  New Orleans, LA 800-457-2857
Manns Sausage Company
  Blacksburg, VA 540-605-0867
Meating Place
  Buffalo, NY 716-885-3623
Miami Beef Co
  Miami Lakes, FL 305-621-3252
Morrison Meat Packers
  Miami, FL 800-330-4267
Morse's Sauerkraut
  Waldoboro, ME 866-832-5569
New Braunfels Smokehouse
  New Braunfels, TX 800-537-6932
Niemuth's Steak & Chop Shop
  Waupaca, WI 715-258-2666
Nodine's Smokehouse Inc
  Torrington, CT 800-222-2059
Old Wisconsin Sausage Inc
  Sheboygan, WI 877-451-7988
Olympic Provisions Northwest
  Portland, OR 503-894-8136
R M Felts' Packing Co
  Ivor, VA 757-859-6131
Ray's Sausage Co
  Cleveland, OH 216-921-8782
Red Smith Foods Inc
  Davie, FL 954-581-1996
Register Meat Co
  Cottondale, FL 850-352-4269
Rinehart Meat Processing
  Branson, MO 417-869-2041
Roger Wood Foods Inc
  Savannah, GA 800-849-9272
Rose Packing Co Inc
  South Barrington, IL 800-323-7363
Sausage Kitchen
  Lisbon Falls, ME 888-453-5503
Savoie's Sausage and Food Products
  Opelousas, LA 337-942-7241
Smith Provision Co Inc
  Erie, PA 800-334-9151
Specialty Foods Group Inc
  Owensboro, KY 800-238-0020
Stonie's Sausage Shop
  Perryville, MO 888-546-2540
Stripling's General Store
  Moultrie, GA 229-985-4226

Sunnydale Meats Inc
  Gaffney, SC 864-489-6091
Sunset Farm Foods Inc
  Valdosta, GA 800-882-1121
Teton Waters Ranch LLC
  Denver, CO 720-340-4590
Thomas Packing Company
  Columbus, GA 800-729-0976
Vermont Smoke and Cure
  Hinesburg, VT 802-482-4666
Vollwerth & Baroni Companies
  Hancock, MI 800-562-7620
WACO Beef & Pork Processors
  Waco, TX 254-772-4669
Williams Pork
  Chadbourn, NC 910-654-0204
YB Meats of Wichita
  Wichita, KS 316-942-1213
Zweigle's Inc
  Rochester, NY 585-546-1740

Ardouille

Burke Corp
  Nevada, IA 800-654-1152
Magic Seasoning Blends
  New Orleans, LA 800-457-2857
Sunset Farm Foods Inc
  Valdosta, GA 800-882-1121

Scrapple

Arnold's Meat Food Products
  Brooklyn, NY 800-633-7023
Kirby Holloway Provision Co
  Harrington, DE 800-995-4729

Spareribs

Calihan Pork Processors Inc
  Peoria, IL 309-674-9175
RJ Balson and Sons Inc
  Asheville, NC 321-281-9473

Tenderloin Roast

Amana Meat Shop & Smoke House
  Amana, IA 800-373-6328
Bear Creek Smokehouse Inc
  Marshall, TX 800-950-2327
New Braunfels Smokehouse
  New Braunfels, TX 800-537-6932
Opa's Smoked Meats
  Fredericksburg, TX 800-543-6750

Poultry

50th State Poultry Processors
  Pearl City, HI 808-845-5902
Adolf's Meats & Sausage Kitchen
  Hartford, CT 860-522-1588
AJM Meat Packing
  San Juan, PR 787-787-4050
Al Safa Halal
  New York City, NY 800-268-8147
Alderfer Inc
  Harleysville, PA 800-341-1121
All-States Quality Foods
  Charles City, IA 800-247-4195
Allen Harim Foods LLC
  Seaford, DE 877-397-9191
Alpine Butcher
  Lowell, MA 978-256-7771
American Egg Products Inc
  Blackshear, GA 912-449-5700
Amick Farms LLC
  Batesburg, SC 800-926-4257
Anmar Foods
  Chicago, IL 312-421-6500
Applegate Farms
  Bridgewater, NJ 866-587-5858
Arizona Sunland Foods
  Tucson, AZ 520-624-7068
Armbrust Meats
  Medford, WI 715-748-3102
B & B Poultry Co
  Norma, NJ 800-535-7646
B & D Foods
  Boise, ID 208-344-1183
Barber Foods
  Kings Mountain, NC 877-447-3279
Bear Creek Smokehouse Inc
  Marshall, TX 800-950-2327
Becker Foods
  Westminster, CA 714-891-9474

Product Categories / Meats & Meat Products: Poultry

Bell & Evans
　Fredericksburg, PA 717-865-6626
Bird-In-Hand Farms Inc
　Lancaster, PA 717-291-9904
Birdie Pak Products
　Chicago, IL 773-247-5293
Black's Barbecue
　Lockhart, TX 888-632-8225
Blakely Freezer Locker
　Blakeley, GA 229-723-3622
Blue Ridge Poultry
　Athens, GA 706-546-6767
Boar's Head
　Sarasota, FL 800-352-6277
Bon Ton Products
　Wheeling, IL 847-520-8300
Bowman & Landes Turkeys
　New Carlisle, OH 877-466-9466
Brakebush Brothers
　Westfield, WI 800-933-2121
Brook Locker Plant
　Brook, IN 219-275-2611
Brown Foods
　Dallas, GA 770-445-4358
Bryant's Meat Inc.
　Taylorsville, MS 800-844-0507
Burgers' Smokehouse
　California, MO 800-345-5185
Burke Corp
　Nevada, IA 800-654-1152
Bush Brothers Provision Co
　West Palm Beach, FL 800-327-1345
Butterball LLC
　Garner, NC 919-255-7900
Butterfield Foods
　Noblesville, IN 317-776-4775
Campbell Soup Co.
　Camden, NJ 800-257-8443
Canal Fulton Provision
　Canal Fulton, OH 800-321-3502
Caribbean Food Delights Inc
　Tappan, NY 845-398-3000
Case Farms Ohio Division
　Winesburg, OH 330-359-7141
Chandler Foods Inc
　Greensboro, NC 800-537-6219
Charles Poultry Company
　Lancaster, PA 717-872-7621
Chef Hans' Gourmet Foods
　Monroe, LA 800-890-4267
Chef's Requested Foods
　Oklahoma City, OK 405-239-2610
Chester's International , LLC
　Mountain Brook, AL 800-288-1555
Chestertown Natural Foods
　Chestertown, MD 410-778-1677
Chick-Fil-A Inc.
　Atlanta, GA 866-232-2040
Chisesi Brothers Meat Packing
　New Orleans, LA 800-966-3550
Choctaw Maid Farms
　Jackson, MS 601-683-4000
Clifty Farm Country Meats
　Paris, TN 800-486-4267
Conagra Brands Inc
　Chicago, IL 877-266-2472
Conagra Foodservice
　Chicago, IL 877-266-2472
Continental Grain Company
　New York, NY 212-207-5100
Cordon Bleu International
　Anjou, QC 800-363-1182
Corfu Foods Inc
　Bensenville, IL 630-595-2510
Couch's Country Style Sausages
　Cleveland, OH 216-823-2332
Country Smoked Meats
　Bowling Green, OH 800-321-4766
Crescent Duck Farm
　Aquebogue LI, NY 631-722-8000
Crescent Foods
　Chicago, IL 800-939-6268
Crystal Lake Farms
　Decatur, AR 800-382-4425
Culver Duck Farms Inc
　Middlebury, IN 800-825-9225
Cusack Meats
　Oklahoma City, OK 800-241-6328
Debel Food Products
　Elizabeth, NJ 800-421-3447
Debragga & Spitler
　Jersey City, NJ
Delphos Poultry Products
　Delphos, OH 419-692-5816
Dietz & Watson Inc.
　Philadelphia, PA 215-831-9000
Dole & Bailey Inc
　Woburn, MA 781-935-1234
Double B Foods Inc
　Arlington, TX 800-679-0349
Draper Valley Farms
　Mt Vernon, WA 800-562-2012
Dutterer's Home Food Service
　Baltimore, MD 410-298-3663
E.C. Phillips & Son
　Ketchikan, AK 907-247-7975
East Dayton Meat & Poultry
　Dayton, OH 937-253-6185
East Poultry Co
　Austin, TX 512-476-5367
Eberly Poultry, Inc.
　Stevens, PA 717-336-6440
Edelman Meats Inc
　Antigo, WI 715-623-7686
El Jay Poultry Corporation
　Voorhees, NJ 856-435-0900
Empire Kosher Foods
　Mifflintown, PA 800-367-4734
Exceldor Cooperative
　Levis, QC 418-830-5600
Fair Oaks Farms LLC
　Pleasant Prairie, WI 800-528-8615
Farbest Foods Inc
　Jasper, IN 812-683-4200
Farmers Produce
　Ashby, MN 218-747-2749
Feed The Party
　Louisville, KY
Fieldale Farms
　Baldwin, GA 800-241-5400
Fried Provisions Company
　Evans City, PA 724-538-3160
Gentry's Poultry
　Ward, SC 800-926-2161
George's Inc
　Springdale, AR 800-800-2449
Gerber's Poultry Inc
　Kidron, OH 800-362-7381
Giovanni's Appetizing Food Co
　Richmond, MI 586-727-9355
Golden Platter Foods
　Newark, NJ 973-344-8770
Golden West Food Group
　Vernon, CA 888-807-3663
Grabill Country Meats
　Grabill, IN 866-333-6328
Grant Park Packing
　Chicago, IL 312-421-4096
Gress Enterprises
　Scranton, PA 570-561-0150
Grimaud Farms-California Inc
　Stockton, CA 800-466-9955
Hall Brothers Meats
　Olmsted Twp, OH 440-235-3262
Hamilos Bros Inspected Meat
　Madison, IL 618-876-3710
Health is Wealth Foods
　Moonachie, NJ 201-933-7474
Heinkel's Packing Co
　Decatur, IL 800-594-2738
Hickory Baked Ham Co
　Castle Rock, CO 303-688-2633
Hillbilly Smokehouse
　Rogers, AR 479-636-1927
Hollman Foods
　Des Moines, IA 888-926-2879
Hormel Foods Corp.
　Austin, MN 507-437-5611
House of Raeford Farms Inc.
　Rose Hill, NC 910-289-3191
Indian Valley Meats
　Indian, AK 907-653-7511
International Home Foods
　Parsippany, NJ 973-359-9920
International Meat Co
　Chicago, IL 773-622-1400
J & G Poultry & Seafood
　Gainesville, GA 770-536-5540
J.R. Poultry
　Fults, IL 618-458-7194
Jacob's Meats Inc
　Defiance, OH 419-782-7831
Janes Family Foods
　Mississauga, ON 800-565-2637
JD Sweid Foods
　Langley, BC 800-665-4355
Jennie-O Turkey Store
　Willmar, MN 320-235-6080
Joe Jurgielwicz & Sons
　Hamburg, PA 800-543-8257
John Garner Meats
　Van Buren, AR 800-543-5473
Johnson, Nash & Sons Farms
　Warsaw, NC 910-289-6842
Joyce Farms
　Winston Salem, NC 800-755-6923
K & K Gourmet Meats Inc
　Leetsdale, PA 724-266-8400
Kelly Gourmet Foods Inc
　San Francisco, CA 415-648-9200
King Cole Ducks Limited
　Newmarket, ON 800-363-3825
King's Command Foods Inc
　Green Bay, WA 800-345-0293
L. Craelius & Company
　Chicago, IL 312-666-7100
Lake Charles Poultry
　Lake Charles, LA 337-433-6818
Land O'Frost Inc
　Searcy, AR 800-643-5654
Land O'Frost Inc.
　Lansing, IL 800-323-3308
Lendy's Cafe Raw Bar
　Virginia Beach, VA 757-491-3511
Lilydale Foods
　Markham, ON 800-661-5341
Locustdale Meat Packing
　Locustdale, PA 570-875-1270
Long Food Industries
　Fripp Island, SC 843-838-3205
LSK Smoked Turkey Products
　Bronx, NY 718-792-1300
Macfarlane Pheasants
　Janesville, WI 800-345-8348
MacGregors Meat & Seafood
　Toronto, ON 888-383-3663
Mada'n Kosher Foods
　Dania, FL 954-925-0077
Madani Halal
　Ozone Park, NY 718-323-9732
Mahantongo Game Farm
　Dalmatia, PA 800-982-9913
Maid-Rite Steak Company
　Dunmore, PA 800-233-4259
Malcolm Meats Co
　Northwood, OH 800-822-6328
Manchester Farms
　Columbia, SC 800-845-0421
Manger Packing Corp
　Baltimore, MD 800-227-9262
Manley Meats Inc
　Decatur, IN 260-592-7313
Maple Leaf Farms
　St Leesburg, IN 800-348-2812
Mar-Jac Poultry Inc.
　Gainesville, GA 770-531-5000
Marshall Durbin Companies
　Birmingham, AL 800-768-2456
Marshallville Packing Co
　Marshallville, OH 330-855-2871
McFarland Foods
　Riverton, UT 800-441-9596
Meat-O-Mat Corp
　Brooklyn, NY 718-965-7250
Metafoods LLC
　Brookhaven, GA 404-843-2400
Miami Beef Co
　Miami Lakes, FL 305-621-3252
Miller Brothers Packing Company
　Sylvester, GA 229-776-2014
Mirasco
　Atlanta, GA 770-956-1945
Moretti's Poultry
　Columbus, OH 614-486-2333
Moroni Feed Company
　Moroni, UT 435-436-8202
Mountain Valley Poultry
　Brandon, FL 813-689-2616
Mountaire Corporation
　Millsboro, DE 877-887-1490
Murray's Chickens
　South Fallsburg, NY 800-588-5051
Nema Food Distribution
　Fairfield, NJ 973-256-4415
New Braunfels Smokehouse
　New Braunfels, TX 800-537-6932

Product Categories / Meats & Meat Products: Poultry

New Wave Cuisine
   Mount Holly, NJ 800-486-0276
Nodine's Smokehouse Inc
   Torrington, CT 800-222-2059
Norfolk Hatchery
   Norfolk, NE 800-345-2449
Northwest Meat Company
   Chicago, IL 312-733-1418
Ok Industries
   Fort Smith, AR 800-635-9441
Olson Locker
   Fairmont, MN 507-238-2563
Omaha Steaks Inc
   800-960-8400
On-Cor Frozen Foods Redi-Serve
   Aurora, IL 920-563-6391
P & L Poultry
   Spokane, WA 509-892-1242
Pacific Poultry Company
   Honolulu, HI 808-841-2828
Paisano Food Products
   Elk Grove Village, IL 800-672-4726
Palmetto Pigeon Plant
   Sumter, SC 803-775-1204
Pasqualichio Brothers Inc
   Scranton, PA 800-232-6233
Peco Foods Inc.
   Tuscaloosa, AL 205-345-4711
Pennfield Farms
   Mt Joy, PA 800-732-0009
Petaluma Poultry
   Petaluma, CA 800-556-6789
Petschl's Quality Meats
   Tukwila, WA 206-575-4400
Piller's Fine Foods
   Waterloo, ON 800-265-2627
Pinty's Premium Foods
   Burlington, ON 800-263-7223
Pintys Delicious Foods
   Burlington, ON 800-263-9710
Prime Pak Foods Inc
   Gainesville, GA 770-536-8708
Puueo Poi Shop
   Hilo, HI 808-935-8435
Quirch Foods
   Coral Gables, FL 800-458-5252
Randall Foods Inc
   Vernon, CA 800-372-6581
Ray's Sausage Co
   Cleveland, OH 216-921-8782
Registry Steak & Seafood
   Bridgeview, IL 708-458-3100
Rod Golden Hatchery Inc
   Cullman, AL 256-734-0941
Roman Sausage Company
   Santa Clara, CA 800-497-7462
Rose Acre Farms
   Wolcott, IN 765-258-4015
Rose Hill Distributors
   Branford, CT 203-488-7231
Rus Dun Farms Inc
   Collierville, TN 901-853-0931
Rymer Foods
   Chicago, IL 800-247-9637
Sadler's Smokehouse
   Henderson, TX 903-657-5581
Schaefers Market
   Sauk Centre, MN 320-352-6490
Schaller & Weber Inc
   Astoria, NY 800-847-4115
Schiltz Foods Inc
   Sisseton, SD 877-872-4458
Schneider Foods
   Kitchener, ON 519-741-5000
Schneider Foods
   Saint Marys, ON 800-567-1890
Selwoods Farm Hunting Preserve
   Alpine, AL 800-522-0403
Serenade Foods
   Milford, IN 574-658-4121
Shelley's
   Jersey City, NJ 201-433-2900
Shelton's Poultry Inc
   Pomona, CA 800-541-1833
Simmons Foods Inc
   Siloam Springs, AR 888-831-7007
SJH Enterprises
   Middleton, WI 888-745-3845
Smith Packing Regional Meat
   Utica, NY 315-732-5125
Smoked Turkey Inc
   Marshville, NC 704-624-6628

Sofina Foods Inc
   Markham, ON 855-763-4621
Sommers Organic
   Wheeling, IL 877-377-9797
SOPAKCO Foods
   Mullins, SC 800-276-9678
Springville Meat & Cold Storage
   Springville, UT 801-489-6391
Squab Producers of California
   Modesto, CA 209-537-4744
Standard Meat Co LP
   Dallas, TX 866-859-6313
Starkel Poultry
   Puyallup, WA 253-845-2876
Steak-Umm Company
   Shillington, PA 860-928-5900
Streit Carl & Son Co
   Neptune, NJ 732-775-0803
Sunday House Foods
   Fredericksburg, TX 830-997-2136
Sunnydale Meats Inc
   Gaffney, SC 864-489-6091
Sure-Good Food Distributors
   Syracuse, NY 315-422-1196
Suzanna's Kitchen
   Peachtree Cor, GA 770-476-9900
Sweet Sue Kitchens
   Athens, AL 256-216-0500
Taylor's Poultry Place
   Lexington, SC 803-356-3431
Thomas Packing Company
   Columbus, GA 800-729-0976
Tillamook Meat Inc
   Tillamook, OR 503-842-4802
Tip Top Poultry Inc
   Marietta, GA 800-241-5230
Tolteca Foodservice
   Norcross, GA 800-541-6835
Troyer Foods Inc
   Goshen, IN 800-876-9377
Turkey Store
   Faribault, MN 507-334-5555
Tyson Foods Inc.
   Springdale, AR 479-290-4000
United Provision Meat Company
   Columbus, OH 614-252-1126
Universal Poultry Company
   Athens, GA 706-546-6767
Vestergaard Farms
   Ann Arbor, MI 734-929-2875
Vienna Meat Products
   Scarborough, ON 800-588-1931
Vitale Poultry Company
   Columbus, OH 614-267-1874
W & G Marketing Company
   Ames, IA 515-233-4774
WACO Beef & Pork Processors
   Waco, TX 254-772-4669
Walden Foods
   Winchester, VA 800-648-7688
Walker Meats
   Carrollton, GA 800-741-3601
Waltkoch Limited
   Tucker, GA 404-378-3666
Wapsie Produce
   Decorah, IA 563-382-4271
Wasatch Meats Inc
   Salt Lake City, UT 800-631-8294
Wayco Ham Co
   Goldsboro, NC 800-962-2614
Wayne Farms LLC.
   Oakwood, GA 800-392-0844
Whitaker & Assoc Architects
   Atlanta, GA 404-266-1265
White Fence Farm
   Romeoville, IL 630-739-1720
White Oak Pastures
   Bluffton, GA 229-641-2081
Willie's Smoke House LLC
   Harrisville, PA 800-742-4184
Willow Tree Poultry Farm Inc
   Attleboro, MA 508-222-3621
Woods Smoked Meats Inc
   Bowling Green, MO 800-458-8426
World Flavors Inc
   Warminster, PA 215-672-4400
Wornick Company
   Cincinnati, OH 800-860-4555
Yoakum Packing Co
   Yoakum, TX 800-999-6997
Zabiha Halal Meat Processors
   Addison, IL 630-620-5000

Zacky Farms
   Fresno, CA 800-888-0235
Zartic Inc
   Rome, GA 800-241-0516

Chicken

50th State Poultry Processors
   Pearl City, HI 808-845-5902
Al Safa Halal
   New York City, NY 800-268-8147
All-States Quality Foods
   Charles City, IA 800-247-4195
Alpine Butcher
   Lowell, MA 978-256-7771
Amylu Foods
   Chicago, IL
B & D Foods
   Boise, ID 208-344-1183
Bear Creek Smokehouse Inc
   Marshall, TX 800-950-2327
Black's Barbecue
   Lockhart, TX 888-632-8225
Blakely Freezer Locker
   Blakeley, GA 229-723-3622
Brakebush Brothers
   Westfield, WI 800-933-2121
Brook Locker Plant
   Brook, IN 219-275-2611
Brucepac
   Woodburn, OR 800-899-3629
Bryant's Meat Inc
   Taylorsville, MS 800-844-0507
Burgers' Smokehouse
   California, MO 800-345-5185
Burke Corp
   Nevada, IA 800-654-1152
Buzz Food Svc
   Charleston, WV 304-925-4781
Caribbean Food Delights Inc
   Tappan, NY 845-398-3000
Caribbean Products
   Baltimore, MD 410-235-7700
Case Farms
   Troutman, NC 704-528-4501
CBP Resources
   Gastonia, NC 704-868-4573
Cericola Farms
   Bradford, ON 905-939-2962
Charles Poultry Company
   Lancaster, PA 717-872-7621
Chef Hans' Gourmet Foods
   Monroe, LA 800-890-4267
Chester's International , LLC
   Mountain Brook, AL 800-288-1555
Chick-Fil-A Inc
   Atlanta, GA 866-232-2040
Chisesi Brothers Meat Packing
   New Orleans, LA 800-966-3550
Choctaw Maid Farms
   Jackson, MS 601-683-4000
Coleman Natural
   Kings Mountain, NC 800-442-8666
Cordon Bleu International
   Anjou, QC 800-363-1182
Corfu Foods Inc
   Bensenville, IL 630-595-2510
Crystal Lake Farms
   Decatur, AR 800-382-4425
Culver Duck Farms Inc
   Middlebury, IN 800-825-9225
Delphos Poultry Products
   Delphos, OH 419-692-5816
Dom's Sausage Co Inc
   Malden, MA 781-324-6390
Double B Foods Inc
   Arlington, TX 800-679-0349
East Poultry Co
   Austin, TX 512-476-5367
Eberly Poultry, Inc.
   Stevens, PA 717-336-6440
Exceldor Cooperative
   Levis, QC 418-830-5600
Fair Oaks Farms LLC
   Pleasant Prairie, WI 800-528-8615
Farmers Produce
   Ashby, MN 218-747-2749
Fieldale Farms
   Baldwin, GA 800-241-5400
Foster Farms Inc.
   Livingston, CA 800-255-7227
Golden West Food Group
   Vernon, CA 888-807-3663

Product Categories / Meats & Meat Products: Poultry

Gress Enterprises
  Scranton, PA 570-561-0150
Health is Wealth Foods
  Moonachie, NJ 201-933-7474
Home Delivery Food Service
  Jefferson, GA 706-367-9551
Horizon Poultry
  Toronto, ON 519-364-3200
Hormel Foods Corp.
  Austin, MN 507-437-5611
Hunter Food Inc
  Anaheim, CA 714-666-1888
International Home Foods
  Parsippany, NJ 973-359-9920
Janes Family Foods
  Mississauga, ON 800-565-2637
Javed & Sons
  Houston, TX 713-835-6850
JBS USA LLC
  Greeley, CO 970-506-8000
JD Sweid Foods
  Langley, BC 800-665-4355
Joyce Farms
  Winston Salem, NC 800-755-6923
K & K Gourmet Meats Inc
  Leetsdale, PA 724-266-8400
Karn Meats
  Columbus, OH 800-221-9585
Kelly Gourmet Foods Inc
  San Francisco, CA 415-648-9200
King Food Service
  Rock Island, IL 309-787-4488
King's Command Foods Inc
  Green Bay, WA 800-345-0293
Koch Foods Inc
  Park Ridge, IL 800-837-2778
La Nova Wings
  Buffalo, NY 800-652-6682
Land O'Frost Inc
  Searcy, AR 800-643-5654
Land O'Frost Inc.
  Lansing, IL 800-323-3308
Locustdale Meat Packing
  Locustdale, PA 570-875-1270
Magnolia Meats
  Knoxville, TN 865-546-7702
Manger Packing Corp
  Baltimore, MD 800-227-9262
Maple Leaf Farms
  St Leesburg, IN 800-348-2812
Mar-Jac Poultry Inc.
  Gainesville, GA 770-531-5000
Meat-O-Mat Corp
  Brooklyn, NY 718-965-7250
Memphis Meats
  Berkeley, CA
Mexi-Frost Specialties Company
  Brooklyn, NY 718-625-3324
Michael's Finer Meats/Seafoods
  Columbus, OH 800-282-0518
Mitchell Foods
  Barbourville, KY 888-202-9745
Moretti's Poultry
  Columbus, OH 614-486-2333
Murray's Chickens
  South Fallsburg, NY 800-588-5051
Norfolk Hatchery
  Norfolk, NE 800-345-2449
North Country Smokehouse
  Claremont, NH 800-258-4304
Ok Industries
  Fort Smith, AR 800-635-9441
Oklahoma City Meat Co Inc
  Oklahoma City, OK 405-235-3308
Olymel
  Saint-Hyacinthe, QC 450-771-0400
On-Cor Frozen Foods Redi-Serve
  Aurora, IL 920-563-6391
P & L Poultry
  Spokane, WA 509-892-1242
Paisano Food Products
  Elk Grove Village, IL 800-672-4726
Palmetto Pigeon Plant
  Sumter, SC 803-775-1204
Perdue Farms Inc.
  Salisbury, MD 800-473-7383
Petaluma Poultry
  Petaluma, CA 800-556-6789
Petschl's Quality Meats
  Tukwila, WA 206-575-4400
Pinty's Premium Foods
  Burlington, ON 800-263-7223
Prime Pak Foods Inc
  Gainesville, GA 770-536-8708
Puueo Poi Shop
  Hilo, HI 808-935-8435
Randall Foods Inc
  Vernon, CA 800-372-6581
Roman Sausage Company
  Santa Clara, CA 800-497-7462
Roy Dick Company
  Griffin, GA 770-227-3916
Royal Harvest Foods Inc
  Springfield, MA 413-737-8392
Royal Palate Foods
  Inglewood, CA 310-330-7701
Rymer Foods
  Chicago, IL 800-247-9637
Salwa Foods
  Lawrenceville, GA 770-263-8207
Shamrock Foods Co
  Phoenix, AZ 800-289-3663
Simmons Foods Inc
  Siloam Springs, AR 888-831-7007
SJH Enterprises
  Middleton, WI 888-745-3845
Smith Packing Regional Meat
  Utica, NY 315-732-5125
Sommers Organic
  Wheeling, IL 877-377-9797
SOPAKCO Foods
  Mullins, SC 800-276-9678
SRA Foods
  Birmingham, AL 205-323-7447
Steak-Umm Company
  Shillington, PA 860-928-5900
Sunnydale Meats Inc
  Gaffney, SC 864-489-6091
Suzanna's Kitchen
  Peachtree Cor, GA 770-476-9900
Sweet Sue Kitchens
  Athens, AL 256-216-0500
Tecumseh Poultry, LLC
  Waverly, NE 402-786-1000
Thomson Meats
  Melfort, SK 306-752-2802
Tony Downs Foods
  Mankato, MN 866-731-4561
True Story Foods
  San Francisco, CA 888-277-1171
Vital Choice
  Bellingham, WA 800-608-4825
WACO Beef & Pork Processors
  Waco, TX 254-772-4669
Waken Meat Co
  Atlanta, GA 404-627-3537
Wasatch Meats Inc
  Salt Lake City, UT 800-631-8294
Wayne Farms LLC.
  Oakwood, GA 800-392-0844
West Liberty Foods LLC
  West Liberty, IA 888-511-4500
Wornick Company
  Cincinnati, OH 800-860-4555
Zartic Inc
  Rome, GA 800-241-0516

Barbecued

Black's Barbecue
  Lockhart, TX 888-632-8225
The Shed Saucery
  Ocean Springs, MS 228-875-9590
Woods Smoked Meats Inc
  Bowling Green, MO 800-458-8426

Barbecued Frozen

Burke Corp
  Nevada, IA 800-654-1152

Breaded

Americhicken
  Cape Girardeau, MO 573-651-6485
Barber Foods
  Kings Mountain, NC 877-447-3279
Blendco Inc
  Hattiesburg, MS 888-253-6326
Delphos Poultry Products
  Delphos, OH 419-692-5816
House-Autry Mills Inc
  Four Oaks, NC 800-849-0802
Janes Family Foods
  Mississauga, ON 800-565-2637

Meat-O-Mat Corp
  Brooklyn, NY 718-965-7250

Broilers

Holmes Foods
  Nixon, TX 830-582-1551
Koala Moa
  Honolulu, HI 808-523-6701

Bulk - Leg Quarters - Legs - Thighs

Pennfield Farms
  Mt Joy, PA 800-732-0009

Canned Boned

Criders Poultry
  Stillmore, GA 800-342-3851
International Home Foods
  Parsippany, NJ 973-359-9920

Cooked - Breaded - Frozen

Advance Pierre Foods
  Cincinnati, OH 800-969-2747
Bear Creek Smokehouse Inc
  Marshall, TX 800-950-2327

Cut-Up Frozen

Wayne Farms LLC.
  Oakwood, GA 800-392-0844

Cut-Up IQF (Individually Quick Frozen)

Bell & Evans
  Fredericksburg, PA 717-865-6626

Diced & Cooked

Brucepac
  Woodburn, OR 800-899-3629

Diced Frozen

Burke Corp
  Nevada, IA 800-654-1152

Fajita Strips

Burke Corp
  Nevada, IA 800-654-1152
Chef's Requested Foods
  Oklahoma City, OK 405-239-2610

Fillets

Delphos Poultry Products
  Delphos, OH 419-692-5816
Eberly Poultry, Inc.
  Stevens, PA 717-336-6440

Fresh

Becker Foods
  Westminster, CA 714-891-9474
Bell & Evans
  Fredericksburg, PA 717-865-6626
Brook Locker Plant
  Brook, IN 219-275-2611
Choctaw Maid Farms
  Jackson, MS 601-683-4000
Exceldor Cooperative
  Levis, QC 418-830-5600
Fieldale Farms
  Baldwin, GA 800-241-5400
Holmes Foods
  Nixon, TX 830-582-1551
Just Bare
  Greeley, CO 877-328-2838
Koch Foods Inc
  Park Ridge, IL 800-837-2778
Petaluma Poultry
  Petaluma, CA 800-556-6789
Pilgrim's Pride Corp.
  Greeley, CO 970-506-8000
Sanderson Farms
  Laurel, MS 800-844-4030
Smith Packing Regional Meat
  Utica, NY 315-732-5125
Sommers Organic
  Wheeling, IL 877-377-9797
Wayne Farms LLC.
  Oakwood, GA 800-392-0844

Product Categories / Meats & Meat Products: Poultry

Frozen

Americhicken
  Cape Girardeau, MO 573-651-6485
B & D Foods
  Boise, ID 208-344-1183
Blakely Freezer Locker
  Blakeley, GA 229-723-3622
Brakebush Brothers
  Westfield, WI 800-933-2121
Brook Locker Plant
  Brook, IN 219-275-2611
Burke Corp
  Nevada, IA 800-654-1152
Caribbean Food Delights Inc
  Tappan, NY 845-398-3000
Caribbean Products
  Baltimore, MD 410-235-7700
Choctaw Maid Farms
  Jackson, MS 601-683-4000
Draper Valley Farms
  Mt Vernon, WA 800-562-2012
Exceldor Cooperative
  Levis, QC 418-830-5600
Fieldale Farms
  Baldwin, GA 800-241-5400
Foster Farms Inc.
  Livingston, CA 800-255-7227
Gress Enterprises
  Scranton, PA 570-561-0150
Health is Wealth Foods
  Moonachie, NJ 201-933-7474
Janes Family Foods
  Mississauga, ON 800-565-2637
K & K Gourmet Meats Inc
  Leetsdale, PA 724-266-8400
Koch Foods Inc
  Park Ridge, IL 800-837-2778
Manchester Farms
  Columbia, SC 800-845-0421
Maple Leaf Farms
  St Leesburg, IN 800-348-2812
Mar-Jac Poultry Inc.
  Gainesville, GA 770-531-5000
Mexi-Frost Specialties Company
  Brooklyn, NY 718-625-3324
On-Cor Frozen Foods Redi-Serve
  Aurora, IL 920-563-6391
Paisano Food Products
  Elk Grove Village, IL 800-672-4726
Palmetto Pigeon Plant
  Sumter, SC 803-775-1204
Phoenix Agro-Industrial Corporation
  Westbury, NY 516-334-1194
Pilgrim's Pride Corp.
  Greeley, CO. 970-506-8000
Rymer Foods
  Chicago, IL 800-247-9637
Sanderson Farms
  Laurel, MS 800-844-4030
Simmons Foods Inc
  Siloam Springs, AR 888-831-7007
SJH Enterprises
  Middleton, WI. 888-745-3845
Smith Packing Regional Meat
  Utica, NY 315-732-5125
Sommers Organic
  Wheeling, IL. 877-377-9797
Steak-Umm Company
  Shillington, PA 860-928-5900
Tecumseh Poultry, LLC
  Waverly, NE. 402-786-1000
Tony Downs Foods
  Mankato, MN 866-731-4561
Wayne Farms LLC.
  Oakwood, GA. 800-392-0844
Zartic Inc
  Rome, GA. 800-241-0516

Liver

Holmes Foods
  Nixon, TX. 830-582-1551

Nuggets

Bell & Evans
  Fredericksburg, PA 717-865-6626
Crafty Counter
  Austin, TX. 512-643-2412
Health is Wealth Foods
  Moonachie, NJ. 201-933-7474
JD Sweid Foods
  Langley, BC 800-665-4355

On-Cor Frozen Foods Redi-Serve
  Aurora, IL 920-563-6391
Pinty's Premium Foods
  Burlington, ON 800-263-7223
Saad Wholesale Meats
  Detroit, MI 313-831-8126

Patties

Caribbean Food Delights Inc
  Tappan, NY 845-398-3000
Royal Caribbean Bakery
  Mt Vernon, NY 888-818-0971
Saad Wholesale Meats
  Detroit, MI 313-831-8126
Sommers Organic
  Wheeling, IL. 877-377-9797

Patties Breaded

Americhicken
  Cape Girardeau, MO 573-651-6485
Meat-O-Mat Corp
  Brooklyn, NY 718-965-7250

Prepared

Caribbean Food Delights Inc
  Tappan, NY 845-398-3000
Delphos Poultry Products
  Delphos, OH 419-692-5816
Foster Farms Inc.
  Livingston, CA 800-255-7227
Pasqualichio Brothers Inc
  Scranton, PA 800-232-6233
Sommers Organic
  Wheeling, IL. 877-377-9797

Prepared Frozen

Americhicken
  Cape Girardeau, MO 573-651-6485
Burke Corp
  Nevada, IA 800-654-1152
Caribbean Food Delights Inc
  Tappan, NY 845-398-3000
Chang Food Company
  Garden Grove, CA 714-265-9990
Chef Hans' Gourmet Foods
  Monroe, LA 800-890-4267
Hormel Foods Corp.
  Austin, MN 507-437-5611
Meat-O-Mat Corp
  Brooklyn, NY 718-965-7250
Morrison Lamothe
  Toronto, ON 877-677-6533
Paisano Food Products
  Elk Grove Village, IL 800-672-4726
SJH Enterprises
  Middleton, WI. 888-745-3845

Raw

Caribbean Food Delights Inc
  Tappan, NY 845-398-3000
Eberly Poultry, Inc.
  Stevens, PA 717-336-6440
J W Treuth & Sons
  Catonsville, MD 410-747-6281
Kelly Gourmet Foods Inc
  San Francisco, CA 415-648-9200

Tenders

Americhicken
  Cape Girardeau, MO 573-651-6485

Cornish Game Hens

Eberly Poultry, Inc.
  Stevens, PA 717-336-6440
Norfolk Hatchery
  Norfolk, NE. 800-345-2449
Woods Smoked Meats Inc
  Bowling Green, MO 800-458-8426

Duck

Bear Creek Smokehouse Inc
  Marshall, TX. 800-950-2327
Crescent Duck Farm
  Aquebogue LI, NY 631-722-8000
Culver Duck Farms Inc
  Middlebury, IN 800-825-9225
Hudson Valley Foie Gras
  Ferndale, NY 845-292-2500

Memphis Meats
  Berkeley, CA
North Country Smokehouse
  Claremont, NH 800-258-4304

Goose

Schiltz Foods Inc
  Sisseton, SD 877-872-4458
Wenk Foods Inc
  Madison, SD 605-256-4569

Guineas

Eberly Poultry, Inc.
  Stevens, PA 717-336-6440

Turkey

Alderfer Inc
  Harleysville, PA 800-341-1121
Alpine Butcher
  Lowell, MA. 978-256-7771
Amana Meat Shop & Smoke House
  Amana, IA. 800-373-6328
Applegate Farms
  Bridgewater, NJ 866-587-5858
Bear Creek Smokehouse Inc
  Marshall, TX. 800-950-2327
Becker Foods
  Westminster, CA 714-891-9474
Bowman & Landes Turkeys
  New Carlisle, OH 877-466-9466
Brucepac
  Woodburn, OR 800-899-3629
Burgers' Smokehouse
  California, MO 800-345-5185
Burke Corp
  Nevada, IA 800-654-1152
Campbell Soup Co.
  Camden, NJ. 800-257-8443
Cargill Protein
  Wichita, KS
Carl Buddig & Co.
  Homewood, IL 888-633-5684
Cericola Farms
  Bradford, ON 905-939-2962
Charles Poultry Company
  Lancaster, PA 717-872-7621
Chef's Requested Foods
  Oklahoma City, OK 405-239-2610
Clifty Farm Country Meats
  Paris, TN 800-486-4267
Couch's Country Style Sausages
  Cleveland, OH 216-823-2332
Country Smoked Meats
  Bowling Green, OH 800-321-4766
Diestel Family Turkey Ranch
   209-532-4950
Dietz & Watson Inc.
  Philadelphia, PA 215-831-9000
Eberly Poultry, Inc.
  Stevens, PA 717-336-6440
Far West Meats
  Highland, CA 909-864-1990
Farbest Foods Inc
  Jasper, IN 812-683-4200
Foster Farms Inc.
  Livingston, CA 800-255-7227
Godshall's Quality Meats
  Telford, PA 888-463-7425
Grabill Country Meats
  Grabill, IN. 866-333-6328
Heinkel's Packing Co
  Decatur, IL 800-594-2738
Hickory Baked Ham Co
  Castle Rock, CO 303-688-2633
Hillbilly Smokehouse
  Rogers, AR 479-636-1927
Hollman Foods
  Des Moines, IA 888-926-2879
Hormel Foods Corp.
  Austin, MN 507-437-5611
Jaindl Farms
  Orefield, PA 800-475-6654
Jennie-O Turkey Store
  Willmar, MN 320-235-6080
Land O'Frost Inc
  Searcy, AR 800-643-5654
Lindner Bison
  Northern, CA 530-254-6337
Locustdale Meat Packing
  Locustdale, PA 570-875-1270

Product Categories / Meats & Meat Products: Smoked, Cured & Deli Meats

Mada'n Kosher Foods
   Dania, FL 954-925-0077
Meat-O-Mat Corp
   Brooklyn, NY 718-965-7250
Moretti's Poultry
   Columbus, OH 614-486-2333
Moroni Feed Company
   Moroni, UT 435-436-8202
New Braunfels Smokehouse
   New Braunfels, TX 800-537-6932
Norbest, LLC
   Moroni, UT 800-453-5327
Norfolk Hatchery
   Norfolk, NE 800-345-2449
Olymel
   Saint-Hyacinthé, QC 450-771-0400
P & L Poultry
   Spokane, WA 509-892-1242
Pasqualichio Brothers Inc
   Scranton, PA 800-232-6233
Perdue Farms Inc.
   Salisbury, MD 800-473-7383
Piggie Park Enterprises
   West Columbia, SC 800-628-7423
Plainville Farms
   New Oxford, PA 800-724-0206
Quaker Maid Meats
   Reading, PA 610-376-1500
Ray's Sausage Co
   Cleveland, OH 216-921-8782
Roman Sausage Company
   Santa Clara, CA 800-497-7462
Sahlen's
   Buffalo, NY 800-466-8165
Selwoods Farm Hunting Preserve
   Alpine, AL 800-522-0403
Smith Packing Regional Meat
   Utica, NY 315-732-5125
Smoked Turkey Inc
   Marshville, NC 704-624-6628
Sommers Organic
   Wheeling, IL 877-377-9797
Specialty Foods Group Inc
   Owensboro, KY 800-238-0020
Standard Meat Co LP
   Dallas, TX 866-859-6313
Sunnydale Meats Inc
   Gaffney, SC 864-489-6091
Suzanna's Kitchen
   Peachtree Cor, GA 770-476-9900
Sweet Sue Kitchens
   Athens, AL 256-216-0500
Talisman Foods
   Salt Lake City, UT 801-487-6409
Thomas Packing Company
   Columbus, GA 800-729-0976
Turkey Store
   Faribault, MN 507-334-5555
Vienna Meat Products
   Scarborough, ON 800-588-1931
W & G Marketing Company
   Ames, IA 515-233-4774
Wayco Ham Co
   Goldsboro, NC 800-962-2614
West Liberty Foods LLC
   West Liberty, IA 888-511-4500
Woods Smoked Meats Inc
   Bowling Green, MO 800-458-8426
Zacky Farms
   Fresno, CA 800-888-0235

Breast

Alderfer Inc
   Harleysville, PA 800-341-1121
Amana Meat Shop & Smoke House
   Amana, IA 800-373-6328
Berks Packing Company, Inc.
   Reading, PA 800-882-3757
Dietz & Watson Inc.
   Philadelphia, PA 215-831-9000
Grote & Weigel Inc
   Bloomfield, CT 860-242-8528
Hickory Baked Ham Co
   Castle Rock, CO 303-688-2633
Rose Packing Co Inc
   South Barrington, IL 800-323-7363
Smith Packing Regional Meat
   Utica, NY 315-732-5125
Woods Smoked Meats Inc
   Bowling Green, MO 800-458-8426

Canned

Bowman & Landes Turkeys
   New Carlisle, OH 877-466-9466
Grabill Country Meats
   Grabill, IN 866-333-6328
Sweet Sue Kitchens
   Athens, AL 256-216-0500

Fresh

Becker Foods
   Westminster, CA 714-891-9474
Blue Ridge Poultry
   Athens, GA 706-546-6767
Cooper Farms Cooked Meats
   Van Wert, OH 419-238-4056
Moroni Feed Company
   Moroni, UT 435-436-8202
Smith Packing Regional Meat
   Utica, NY 315-732-5125
Turkey Store
   Faribault, MN 507-334-5555

Frozen

Burke Corp
   Nevada, IA 800-654-1152

Ground

Eberly Poultry, Inc.
   Stevens, PA 717-336-6440
Sommers Organic
   Wheeling, IL 877-377-9797

Leg

Karn Meats
   Columbus, OH 800-221-9585

Patties

Brucepac
   Woodburn, OR 800-899-3629
Sommers Organic
   Wheeling, IL 877-377-9797

Raw

Carl Buddig & Co.
   Homewood, IL 888-633-5684

Sausage

C.W. Brown Foods, Inc.
   Mountt Royal, NJ 856-423-3700
Golden Platter Foods
   Newark, NJ 973-344-8770
Roger Wood Foods Inc
   Savannah, GA 800-849-9272

Whole Frozen

Hickory Baked Ham Co
   Castle Rock, CO 303-688-2633

Smoked, Cured & Deli Meats

814 Americas Inc
   Elizabeth, NJ 908-354-2674
Andalusia Distributing Co Inc
   Andalusia, AL 334-222-3671
Applegate Farms
   Bridgewater, NJ 866-587-5858
Aries Prepared Beef
   Burbank, CA 800-424-2333
Best Chicago Meat
   Chicago, IL
Blue Grass Quality Meat
   Covington, KY 859-331-7100
Boone's Butcher Shop
   Bardstown, KY 888-253-3384
Boyd's Sausage Co
   Washington, IA 319-653-5715
Braham Food Locker Service
   Braham, MN 320-396-2636
Buffalo Bills Premium Snacks
   Lebanon, PA 717-273-7499
Burke Corp
   Nevada, IA 800-654-1152
Caddo Packing Co
   Marshall, TX 903-935-2211
Campbell Soup Co.
   Camden, NJ 800-257-8443
Chef's Cut: Real Jerky
   Naples, FL 586-615-0329

Chicopee Provision Co Inc
   Chicopee, MA 800-924-6328
Chip Steak & Provision Co
   Mankato, MN 507-388-6277
Circle V Meats
   Spanish Fork, UT 801-798-3081
Cloverdale Foods
   Mandan, ND 800-669-9511
Columbia Packing Co Inc
   Dallas, TX 214-946-8171
Crawford Sausage Co Inc
   Chicago, IL 773-277-3095
Curtis Packing Co
   Greensboro, NC 336-275-7684
Cusack Meats
   Oklahoma City, OK 800-241-6328
Daniele Inc
   Pascoag, RI 800-451-2535
Di Bruno Bros
   Philadelphia, PA 215-922-2876
Field Roast
   Seattle, WA 800-311-9497
Foster Farms Inc.
   Livingston, CA 800-255-7227
Freirich Foods
   Salisbury, NC 800-221-1315
Freybe Gourmet Foods Ltd
   Langley, BC 800-879-3739
Frick's Quality Meats
   Washington, MO 800-241-2209
Fusion Jerky
   South San Francisco, CA 650-589-8899
Gary's Frozen Foods
   Lubbock, TX 806-745-1933
H & B Packing Co
   Waco, TX 254-752-2506
Harrington's of Vermont
   Richmond, VT
Heringer Meats Inc
   Covington, KY 859-291-2000
Hummel Brothers Inc
   New Haven, CT 800-828-8978
Independent Meat Co
   Twin Falls, ID 800-284-4626
J & B Sausage Co Inc
   Waelder, TX 830-788-7511
Kayem Foods
   Chelsea, MA 800-426-6100
Koegel Meats Inc
   Flint, MI 810-238-3685
Korte Meat Processors Inc
   Highland, IL 618-654-3813
LA Quercia LLC
   Norwalk, IA 515-981-1625
Lay Packing Company
   Knoxville, TN 865-522-1147
Liguria Foods Inc
   Humboldt, IA 515-332-4121
Little Rhody Brand Frankfurts
   Johnston, RI 401-831-0815
Lord's Sausage & Country Ham
   Dexter, GA 800-342-6002
Mada'n Kosher Foods
   Dania, FL 954-925-0077
Matthiesen's Deer & Custom
   De Witt, IA 563-659-8409
Mckenzie Country Classic's
   Burlington, VT 800-426-6100
Mertz Sausage Co
   San Antonio, TX 210-433-3263
Milano's Of New York City
   New York, NY 800-643-6328
Miller's Meat Market
   Red Bud, IL 618-282-3334
Neese Country Sausage Inc
   Greensboro, NC 800-632-1010
Nema Food Distribution
   Fairfield, NJ 973-256-4415
New Packing Company
   Chicago, IL 312-666-1314
OLLI Salumeria Americana
   Oceanside, CA 877-655-4937
Olympia Provisions
   Portland, OR 503-894-8275
Olympic Provisions Northwest
   Portland, OR 503-894-8136
Opa's Smoked Meats
   Fredericksburg, TX 800-543-6750
Patrick Cudahy LLC
   Cudahy, WI 800-486-6900
Paulsen Foods
   Atlanta, GA 404-873-1804

Product Categories / Meats & Meat Products: Smoked, Cured & Deli Meats

Pederson's Natural Farms
  Hamilton, TX
Peer Foods Group Inc
  Chicago, IL 800-365-5644
Piller's Fine Foods
  Waterloo, ON 800-265-2627
Plumrose USA
  Chicago, IL 800-526-4909
Pocino Foods
  City Of Industry, CA 800-345-0150
Principe Foods USA
  Long Beach, CA 310-680-5500
Quirch Foods
  Coral Gables, FL 800-458-5252
R M Felts' Packing Co
  Ivor, VA 757-859-6131
Shaker Valley Foods
  Cleveland, OH 216-961-8600
SnackMasters, LLC
  Hilmar, CA 800-597-9770
Stevens Sausage Co
  Smithfield, NC 800-338-0561
Stonie's Sausage Shop
  Perryville, MO 888-546-2540
SunFed Ranch
  Woodland, CA 530-723-5373
Terrell Meats
  Delta, UT 435-864-2600
Thomas Packing Company
  Columbus, GA 800-729-0976
Thumann Inc.
  Carlstadt, NJ 201-935-3636
Troy Foods Inc
  Troy, IL 618-667-6332
True Story Foods
  San Francisco, CA 888-277-1171
Tyson Foods Inc.
  Springdale, AR 479-290-4000
Tyson Foods Inc.
  Springdale, AR 800-233-6332
Vermilion Packers Ltd
  Vermilion, AB 780-853-4622
Vermont Smoke and Cure
  Hinesburg, VT 802-482-4666
Vienna Beef LTD
  Vernon, CA 800-733-6063
Wagshal's Imports
  Washington, DC 202-363-5698
Webster City Custom Meats Inc
  Webster City, IA 515-832-1130
Weyauwega Star Dairy
  Weyauwega, WI 888-813-9720
Yoakum Packing Co
  Yoakum, TX 800-999-6997

Bacon

Alderfer Inc
  Harleysville, PA 800-341-1121
Aliments Prince SEC
  Anjou, QC 800-361-3898
Amana Meat Shop & Smoke House
  Amana, IA 800-373-6328
Applegate Farms
  Bridgewater, NJ 866-587-5858
Arnold's Meat Food Products
  Brooklyn, NY 800-633-7023
Bacon America
  Drummondville, QC 819-475-3030
Bear Creek Smokehouse Inc
  Marshall, TX 800-950-2327
Blakely Freezer Locker
  Blakeley, GA 229-723-3622
Broadbent B & B Food Products
  Kuttawa, KY 800-841-2202
Burke Corp
  Nevada, IA 800-654-1152
Chef's Requested Foods
  Oklahoma City, OK 405-239-2610
Chisesi Brothers Meat Packing
  New Orleans, LA 800-966-3550
Circle B Ranch
  Seymour, MO 417-683-0271
Cloverdale Foods
  Mandan, ND 800-669-9511
Di Bruno Bros
  Philadelphia, PA 215-922-2876
Father's Country Hams
  Bremen, KY 270-525-3554
Ferris, Stahl-Meyer
  Fort Lee, NJ 201-242-2500
Hickory Baked Ham Co
  Castle Rock, CO 303-688-2633

Leidy's
  Harleysville, PA 800-222-2319
Manda Fine Meats Inc
  Baton Rouge, LA 800-343-2642
Maple Leaf Consumer Foods
  Fair Oaks, CA 800-999-7603
Naked Bacon
  Ste. Genevieve, MO
Niemuth's Steak & Chop Shop
  Waupaca, WI 715-258-2666
North Country Smokehouse
  Claremont, NH 800-258-4304
Olympic Provisions Northwest
  Portland, OR 503-894-8136
Outstanding Foods
  Venice, CA
Patrick Cudahy LLC
  Cudahy, WI 800-486-6900
Pederson's Natural Farms
  Hamilton, TX
Piller's Fine Foods
  Waterloo, ON 800-265-2627
R.L. Zeigler Company
  Selma, AL 800-392-6328
Rinehart Meat Processing
  Branson, MO 417-869-2041
Rose Packing Co Inc
  South Barrington, IL 800-323-7363
Saad Wholesale Meats
  Detroit, MI 313-831-8126
Scott Hams
  Greenville, KY 800-318-1353
Seaboard Foods
  Shawnee Mission, KS 800-262-7907
Sugar Creek
  Washington Ct Hs, OH 800-848-8205
Sunnydale Meats Inc
  Gaffney, SC 864-489-6091
Sunset Farm Foods Inc
  Valdosta, GA 800-882-1121
Thomas Packing Company
  Columbus, GA 800-729-0976
V.W. Joyner & Company
  Smithfield, VA 757-357-2161
Vermont Smoke and Cure
  Hinesburg, VT 802-482-4666
Woods Smoked Meats Inc
  Bowling Green, MO 800-458-8426

Bits Imitation

American Key Food Products Inc
  Closter, NJ 877-263-7539
Con Yeager Spice Co
  Zelienople, PA 800-222-2460
Fairbury Food Products
  Fairbury, NE 402-729-3379
Schiff Food Products Co Inc
  Totowa, NJ 973-237-1990
Tova Industries LLC
  Louisville, KY 888-532-8682
Westin Foods
  Omaha, NE 800-228-6098

Bits Real

Burke Corp
  Nevada, IA 800-654-1152
Con Yeager Spice Co
  Zelienople, PA 800-222-2460
Sugar Creek
  Washington Ct Hs, OH 800-848-8205
Tova Industries LLC
  Louisville, KY 888-532-8682

Canadian Style

Al & John's Glen Rock Ham
  West Caldwell, NJ 800-969-4990
Burgers' Smokehouse
  California, MO 800-345-5185
Burke Corp
  Nevada, IA 800-654-1152
Calihan Pork Processors Inc
  Peoria, IL 309-674-9175
Country Smoked Meats
  Bowling Green, OH 800-321-4766
Hickory Baked Ham Co
  Castle Rock, CO 303-688-2633
Hormel Foods Corp.
  Austin, MN 507-437-5611
Peer Foods Group Inc
  Chicago, IL 800-365-5644

Pioneer Packing Co
  Bowling Green, OH 419-352-5283
Rose Packing Co Inc
  South Barrington, IL 800-323-7363

Slices

Carolina Pride Foods
  Greenwood, SC 864-229-5611
Country Smoked Meats
  Bowling Green, OH 800-321-4766
Jimmy Dean Foods
  Springdale, AR 800-925-3326
Sugar Creek
  Washington Ct Hs, OH 800-848-8205
Webster City Custom Meats Inc
  Webster City, IA 515-832-1130

Slices Thick

Jimmy Dean Foods
  Springdale, AR 800-925-3326
Westbrae Natural Foods
  Melville, NY 800-434-4246

Beef Jerky

Alderfer Inc
  Harleysville, PA 800-341-1121
Alewel's Country Meats
  Warrensburg, MO 800-353-8553
Amana Meat Shop & Smoke House
  Amana, IA 800-373-6328
Baier's Sausage & Meats
  Red Deer, AB 403-346-1535
Better Made Snack Foods
  Detroit, MI 800-332-2394
Big Chief Meat Snacks Inc
  Calgary, AB 403-264-2641
Boyd's Sausage Co
  Washington, IA 319-653-5715
Brooklyn Biltong
  Brooklyn, NY 407-538-8876
Buffalo Bills Premium Snacks
  Lebanon, PA 717-273-7499
Cattaneo Brothers Inc
  San Luis Obispo, CA 800-243-8537
Chickasaw Trading Company
  Denver City, TX 800-848-3515
Chudabeef Jerky Co.
  Long Beach, CA
Debbie D's Jerky & Sausage
  Tillamook, OR 503-842-2622
E.W. Knauss & Son
  Quakertown, PA 800-648-4220
Eastside Deli Supply
  Lansing, MI 800-349-6694
Eiserman Meats
  Slave Lake, AB 780-849-5507
Enjoy Foods International
  Fontana, CA 909-823-2228
F&Y Enterprises
  Wauconda, IL 847-526-0620
Golden Valley Natural
  Shelley, ID 888-270-7147
Grandpa Ittel's Meats Inc
  Howard Lake, MN 320-543-2285
Hi Country Snack Foods
  Lincoln, MT 406-362-4050
Hsin Tung Yang Foods Inc
  S San Francisco, CA 650-589-6789
J & B Sausage Co Inc
  Waelder, TX 830-788-7511
Kershenstine Beef Jerky
  Eupora, MS 662-258-2049
King B Meat Snacks
  Minong, WI 800-346-6896
Link Snacks Inc.
  Minong, WI 715-466-2234
Longview Meat & Merchandise Ltd
  Longview, AB 866-355-3759
Middlefield Cheese House
  Middlefield, OH 800-327-9477
New Braunfels Smokehouse
  New Braunfels, TX 800-537-6932
Norpaco Inc
  Middletown, CT 800-252-0222
Palmer Meat Packing Co
  Tremonton, UT 435-257-5329
Patagonia Provisions
  Sausalito, CA 888-221-8208
People's Sausage Co
  Los Angeles, CA 213-627-8633

Product Categories / Meats & Meat Products: Smoked, Cured & Deli Meats

Rinehart Meat Processing
 Branson, MO 417-869-2041
Terrell Meats
 Delta, UT 435-864-2600
Tommy's Jerky Outlet
 Mentor, OH 866-448-6942
Trail's Best Snacks
 Memphis, TN 800-852-1863
W.A. Beans & Sons
 Bangor, ME 800-649-1958
Weaver Nut Co. Inc.
 Ephrata, PA 800-473-2688
Western Beef Jerky
 Edmonton, AB 780-469-4817
Wild Bill's Foods
 Martinsville, VA 800-848-3236
Willie's Smoke House LLC
 Harrisville, PA 800-742-4184
Woods Smoked Meats Inc
 Bowling Green, MO 800-458-8426

Frozen

KRAVE Jerky
 Sonoma, CA 707-935-1035

Bologna

Alderfer Inc
 Harleysville, PA 800-341-1121
Atlantic Pork & Provisions
 Jamaica, NY 800-245-3536
Boesl Packing Co
 Baltimore, MD 800-675-1471
Boyd's Sausage Co
 Washington, IA 319-653-5715
C Roy & Sons Processing
 Yale, MI. 810-387-3957
Carolina Packers Inc
 Smithfield, NC 800-682-7675
Carolina Pride Foods
 Greenwood, SC 864-229-5611
Chisesi Brothers Meat Packing
 New Orleans, LA 800-966-3550
Curtis Packing Co
 Greensboro, NC 336-275-7684
Far West Meats
 Highland, CA 909-864-1990
Frank Wardynski & Sons Inc
 Buffalo, NY. 716-854-6083
Gouvea's & Purity Foods Inc
 Honolulu, HI 808-847-3717
Groff's Meats
 Elizabethtown, PA. 717-367-1246
Grote & Weigel Inc
 Bloomfield, CT 860-242-8528
Hazle Park Quality Meats
 West Hazleton, PA 800-238-4331
Ito Cariani Sausage Company
 Hayward, CA 510-887-0882
Kilgus Meats
 Toledo, OH 419-472-9721
Kitt's Meat Processing
 Dedham, IA. 712-683-5622
Locustdale Meat Packing
 Locustdale, PA 570-875-1270
Palmyra Bologna Co Inc
 Palmyra, PA 800-282-6336
Rendulic Meat Packing Corp
 Mckeesport, PA. 412-678-9541
Saad Wholesale Meats
 Detroit, MI 313-831-8126
Schaefers Market
 Sauk Centre, MN 320-352-6490
Sechrist Brothers
 Dallastown, PA. 717-244-2975
Sheinman Provision Co
 Philadelphia, PA. 215-473-7065
Silver Star Meats Inc
 Mc Kees Rocks, PA 800-548-1321
Spring Grove Foods
 Miamisburg, OH 937-866-4311
Stawnichy Holdings
 Mundare, AB 888-764-7646
Sunset Farm Foods Inc
 Valdosta, GA 800-882-1121
Tennessee Valley Packing Co
 Columbia, TN 931-388-2623
Thumann Inc.
 Carlstadt, NJ 201-935-3636
Troy Foods Inc
 Troy, IL 618-667-6332

Zweigle's Inc
 Rochester, NY. 585-546-1740

Bratwurst

Country Smoked Meats
 Bowling Green, OH 800-321-4766
Elmwood Locker Svc
 Elmwood, IL. 309-742-8929
Far West Meats
 Highland, CA 909-864-1990
Fontanini Italian Meats
 McCook, IL. 800-331-6328
Kilgus Meats
 Toledo, OH 419-472-9721
Koegel Meats Inc
 Flint, MI 810-238-3685
S.W. Meat & Provision Company
 Phoenix, AZ 602-275-2000
Saugy Inc.
 Cranston, RI 866-467-2849
Silver Star Meats Inc
 Mc Kees Rocks, PA 800-548-1321
Smolich Bros. Home Made Sausage
 Crest Hill, IL. 815-727-2144
Sunset Farm Foods Inc
 Valdosta, GA 800-882-1121
WACO Beef & Pork Processors
 Waco, TX 254-772-4669
Woods Smoked Meats Inc
 Bowling Green, MO 800-458-8426

Corned Beef

Alderfer Inc
 Harleysville, PA 800-341-1121
Art's Tamales
 Metamora, IL 309-367-2850
Best Provision Co Inc
 Union, NJ 800-631-4466
Burnett & Son
 Monrovia, CA 877-632-5467
Carando Gourmet Frozen Foods
 Agawam, MA 888-227-2636
Chicopee Provision Co Inc
 Chicopee, MA. 800-924-6328
Curly's Foods Inc
 Edina, MN 612-920-3400
Dutterer's Home Food Service
 Baltimore, MD 410-298-3663
Hormel Foods Corp.
 Austin, MN 507-437-5611
International Food Packers Corporation
 Miami, FL 305-740-5847
Kelly Corned Beef Co
 Chicago, IL 800-624-5617
Kelly Foods
 Jackson, TN 731-424-2255
Lower Foods, Inc.
 Richmond, UT. 800-295-7898
Nossack Fine Meats
 Red Deer, AB 403-346-5006
Peer Foods Group Inc
 Chicago, IL 800-365-5644
Plumrose USA
 Chicago, IL 800-526-4909
Saval Foods Corp
 Elkridge, MD 800-527-2825
Sheinman Provision Co
 Philadelphia, PA. 215-473-7065
Stawnichy Holdings
 Mundare, AB 888-764-7646
Thompson Packers
 Slidell, LA. 800-989-6328
Vienna Meat Products
 Scarborough, ON 800-588-1931

Deli Foods

ASK Foods Inc
 Palmyra, PA. 800-879-4275
Bagels By Bell
 Brooklyn, NY 718-272-2780
Billingsgate Fish Company
 Calgary, AB. 403-571-7700
Bloomfield Bakers
 Los Alamitos, CA 800-594-4111
Bottom Line Foods
 Pembroke Pines, FL 954-843-0562
Bouma Meats
 Provost, AB 780-753-2092
Boyd's Sausage Co
 Washington, IA 319-653-5715

Carl Buddig & Co.
 Homewood, IL 888-633-5684
Carolina Packers Inc
 Smithfield, NC 800-682-7675
Chicago 58 Food Products
 Woodbridge, ON 416-603-4244
Cibao Meat Products Inc
 Bronx, NY. 718-993-5072
Corfu Foods Inc
 Bensenville, IL 630-595-2510
Cumberland Gap Provision Company
 Middlesboro, KY 855-411-7675
Curtis Packing Co
 Greensboro, NC 336-275-7684
Czimer's Game & Seafoods
 Homer Glen, IL. 888-294-6377
Dairy Fresh Foods Inc
 Taylor, MI 313-299-0735
Eastside Deli Supply
 Lansing, MI. 800-349-6694
Frank Brunckhorst Company
 Sarasota, FL 804-722-4100
Fratelli Beretta USA
 Mount Olive, NJ 201-438-0723
Global Food Industries
 Townville, SC 800-225-4152
Heinkel's Packing Co
 Decatur, IL 800-594-2738
HFI Foods
 Redmond, WA. 425-883-1320
Home Style Foods Inc
 Hamtramck, MI. 313-874-3250
Hormel Foods Corp.
 Austin, MN 507-437-5611
Hummel Brothers Inc
 New Haven, CT 800-828-8978
Kay Foods Co
 Detroit, MI 313-393-1100
Kelly Corned Beef Co
 Chicago, IL 800-624-5617
Kelly Foods
 Jackson, TN 731-424-2255
Kitt's Meat Processing
 Dedham, IA. 712-683-5622
Klein's Kosher Pickles
 Phoenix, AZ 800-437-4255
Liguria Foods Inc
 Humboldt, IA 515-332-4121
Lower Foods, Inc.
 Richmond, UT. 800-295-7898
Manda Fine Meats Inc
 Baton Rouge, LA 800-343-2642
Marshallville Packing Co
 Marshallville, OH 330-855-2871
Meadows Country Products
 Hollidaysburg, PA 888-499-1001
Norbest, LLC
 Moroni, UT. 800-453-5327
Palmyra Bologna Co Inc
 Palmyra, PA 800-282-6336
Pederson's Natural Farms
 Hamilton, TX
Plumrose USA
 Chicago, IL 800-526-4909
Rachael's Smoked Fish
 Springfield, MA 800-327-3412
Real Kosher Sausage Company
 Newark, NJ 973-690-5394
Schneider Foods
 Kitchener, ON. 519-741-5000
Siena Foods
 Toronto, ON 800-465-0422
Silver Star Meats Inc
 Mc Kees Rocks, PA 800-548-1321
Smith Provision Co Inc
 Erie, PA 800-334-9151
Smithfield Foods Inc.
 Smithfield, VA 757-365-3000
Spring Glen Fresh Foods
 Ephrata, PA. 800-641-2853
Spring Grove Foods
 Miamisburg, OH 937-866-4311
Stevens Sausage Co
 Smithfield, NC 800-338-0561
Temptee Specialty Foods
 Denver, CO 800-842-1233
Tyson Foods Inc.
 Springdale, AR 800-233-6332
Vegi-Deli
 San Rafael, CA 888-473-3667

Product Categories / Meats & Meat Products: Smoked, Cured & Deli Meats

Deli Meats

Alderfer Inc
  Harleysville, PA 800-341-1121
Alpine Butcher
  Lowell, MA 978-256-7771
Atlantic Pork & Provisions
  Jamaica, NY 800-245-3536
Berks Packing Company, Inc.
  Reading, PA 800-882-3757
Binkert's Meat Products
  Baltimore, MD 410-687-5959
Boar's Head
  Sarasota, FL 800-352-6277
Boesl Packing Co
  Baltimore, MD 800-675-1471
Broadaway Ham Co
  Jonesboro, AR 870-932-6688
Burke Corp
  Nevada, IA 800-654-1152
C Roy & Sons Processing
  Yale, MI 810-387-3957
Carl Buddig & Co.
  Homewood, IL 888-633-5684
Carolina Packers Inc
  Smithfield, NC 800-682-7675
Carolina Pride Foods
  Greenwood, SC 864-229-5611
Charlie's Country Sausage
  Minot, ND 701-838-6302
Charlie's Pride
  Vernon, CA 877-866-0992
Citterio USA
  Freeland, PA 800-435-8888
Country Smoked Meats
  Bowling Green, OH 800-321-4766
Curtis Packing Co
  Greensboro, NC 336-275-7684
Dietz & Watson Inc.
  Philadelphia, PA 215-831-9000
Dohar Meats Inc
  Cleveland, OH 216-241-4197
Dutterer's Home Food Service
  Baltimore, MD 410-298-3663
Far West Meats
  Highland, CA 909-864-1990
Frank Brunckhorst Company
  Sarasota, FL 804-722-4100
Frank Wardynski & Sons Inc
  Buffalo, NY 716-854-6083
Fried Provisions Company
  Evans City, PA 724-538-3160
Gaiser's European Style
  Union, NJ 908-686-3421
Gouvea's & Purity Foods Inc
  Honolulu, HI 808-847-3717
Groff's Meats
  Elizabethtown, PA 717-367-1246
Hans Kissle Co
  Haverhill, MA 978-556-4500
Hazle Park Quality Meats
  West Hazleton, PA 800-238-4331
Heinkel's Packing Co
  Decatur, IL 800-594-2738
Hummel Brothers Inc
  New Haven, CT 800-828-8978
Kelly Corned Beef Co
  Chicago, IL 800-624-5617
Kelly Foods
  Jackson, TN 731-424-2255
Kilgus Meats
  Toledo, OH 419-472-9721
Kitt's Meat Processing
  Dedham, IA 712-683-5622
Land O'Frost Inc
  Searcy, AR 800-643-5654
Lengerich Meats Inc
  Zanesville, IN 260-638-4123
Leona Meat Plant
  Troy, PA 570-297-3574
Liguria Foods Inc
  Humboldt, IA 515-332-4121
Locustdale Meat Packing
  Locustdale, PA 570-875-1270
Lower Foods, Inc.
  Richmond, UT 800-295-7898
Manda Fine Meats Inc
  Baton Rouge, LA 800-343-2642
Marathon Enterprises Inc
  Englewood, NJ 800-722-7388
Marshallville Packing Co
  Marshallville, OH 330-855-2871
Martin Rosols
  New Britain, CT 860-223-2707
Parma Sausage Products
  Pittsburgh, PA 877-294-4207
Plumrose USA
  Chicago, IL 800-526-4909
Queen City Sausage & Provision
  Cincinnati, OH 877-544-5588
R.L. Zeigler Company
  Selma, AL 800-392-6328
Rendulic Meat Packing Corp
  Mckeesport, PA 412-678-9541
Robinson Distributing Co
  London, KY 800-230-5131
Roman Packing Company
  Norfolk, NE 800-373-5990
Saag's Products LLC
  San Leandro, CA 855-287-6562
Saval Foods Corp
  Elkridge, MD 800-527-2825
Schaefers Market
  Sauk Centre, MN 320-352-6490
Schaller & Weber Inc
  Astoria, NY 800-847-4115
Sculli Brothers
  Yeadon, PA 215-336-1223
Sechrist Brothers
  Dallastown, PA 717-244-2975
Sheinman Provision Co
  Philadelphia, PA 215-473-7065
Smith Packing Regional Meat
  Utica, NY 315-732-5125
Smith Provision Co Inc
  Erie, PA 800-334-9151
Specialities Importers & Distributers
  Millington, NJ 800-899-6689
Spring Grove Foods
  Miamisburg, OH 937-866-4311
Standard Meat Co LP
  Dallas, TX 866-859-6313
Stawnichy Holdings
  Mundare, AB 888-764-7646
Stevens Sausage Co
  Smithfield, NC 800-338-0561
Stonie's Sausage Shop
  Perryville, MO 888-546-2540
Temptee Specialty Foods
  Denver, CO 800-842-1233
Tennessee Valley Packing Co
  Columbia, TN 931-388-2623
Troy Foods Inc
  Troy, IL 618-667-6332
Tyson Foods Inc.
  Springdale, AR 800-233-6332
United Provision Meat Company
  Columbus, OH 614-252-1126
V.W. Joyner & Company
  Smithfield, VA 757-357-2161
Vienna Beef LTD
  Chicago, IL 800-366-3647
Vienna Meat Products
  Scarborough, ON 800-588-1931
Warren & Son Meat Processing
  Whipple, OH 740-585-2421

Ham

Albert's Meats
  Claysville, PA 800-522-9970
Aliments Prince SEC
  Anjou, QC 800-361-3898
Ashland Sausage Co
  Carol Stream, IL 630-690-2600
Badger Gourmet Ham
  Milwaukee, WI 414-645-1756
Broadbent B & B Food Products
  Kuttawa, KY 800-841-2202
Calihan Pork Processors Inc
  Peoria, IL 309-674-9175
Chicago Steaks
  Chicago, IL 773-847-5400
Chisesi Brothers Meat Packing
  New Orleans, LA 800-966-3550
Cloverdale Foods
  Mandan, ND 800-669-9511
Father's Country Hams
  Bremen, KY 270-525-3554
Frick's Quality Meats
  Washington, MO 800-241-2209
Grote & Weigel Inc
  Bloomfield, CT 860-242-8528
Hickory Baked Ham Co
  Castle Rock, CO 303-688-2633
Holly Hill Locker Company
  Holly Hill, SC 803-496-3611
Humphrey's Market
  Springfield, IL 800-747-6328
Leidy's
  Harleysville, PA 800-222-2319
Maple Leaf Consumer Foods
  Fair Oaks, CA 800-999-7603
Milling Sausage Inc
  Milwaukee, WI 414-645-2677
Niemuth's Steak & Chop Shop
  Waupaca, WI 715-258-2666
Patrick Cudahy LLC
  Cudahy, WI 800-486-6900
Pederson's Natural Farms
  Hamilton, TX
Piller's Fine Foods
  Waterloo, ON 800-265-2627
Redondo Iglesias USA
  Bayonne, NJ 201-455-5266
Rinehart Meat Processing
  Branson, MO 417-869-2041
Rose Packing Co Inc
  South Barrington, IL 800-323-7363
Scott Hams
  Greenville, KY 800-318-1353
Silver Star Meats Inc
  Mc Kees Rocks, PA 800-548-1321
Smoked Turkey Inc
  Marshville, NC 704-624-6628
Specialty Foods Group Inc
  Owensboro, KY 800-238-0020
Stonie's Sausage Shop
  Perryville, MO 888-546-2540
Thomas Packing Company
  Columbus, GA 800-729-0976
Thumann Inc.
  Carlstadt, NJ 201-935-3636
V.W. Joyner & Company
  Smithfield, VA 757-357-2161
Vermont Smoke and Cure
  Hinesburg, VT 802-482-4666
Wayco Ham Co
  Goldsboro, NC 800-962-2614

Canned

Clifty Farm Country Meats
  Paris, TN 800-486-4267
Dold Foods
  Wichita, KS 316-838-9101
Hickory Baked Ham Co
  Castle Rock, CO 303-688-2633
Horlacher Meats
  Logan, UT 435-752-1287
International Trading Company
  Houston, TX 713-224-5901
S. Wallace Edward & Sons
  Surry, VA 800-222-4267
Wayco Ham Co
  Goldsboro, NC 800-962-2614

Cooked - Water-added Chilled

Ferris, Stahl-Meyer
  Fort Lee, NJ 201-242-5500
Madrange
  Millington, NJ 800-899-6689

Fresh

Amana Meat Shop & Smoke House
  Amana, IA 800-373-6328
Smith Provision Co Inc
  Erie, PA 800-334-9151
Smithfield Foods Inc.
  Smithfield, VA 757-365-3000

Frozen

Burke Corp
  Nevada, IA 800-654-1152

Smoked

Alderfer Inc
  Harleysville, PA 800-341-1121
Badger Gourmet Ham
  Milwaukee, WI 414-645-1756
Bear Creek Smokehouse Inc
  Marshall, TX 800-950-2327
Blakely Freezer Locker
  Blakeley, GA 229-723-3622
Carolina Packers Inc
  Smithfield, NC 800-682-7675

Product Categories / Meats & Meat Products: Smoked, Cured & Deli Meats

Cumberland Gap Provision Company
 Middlesboro, KY 855-411-7675
Finchville Farms Country Ham
 Finchville, KY 800-678-1521
Fresh Mark Inc.
 Massillon, OH 330-832-7491
Frick's Quality Meats
 Washington, MO 800-241-2209
Gaiser's European Style
 Union, NJ 908-686-3421
Groff's Meats
 Elizabethtown, PA 717-367-1246
Hillbilly Smokehouse
 Rogers, AR 479-636-1927
Humphrey's Market
 Springfield, IL 800-747-6328
J & B Sausage Co Inc
 Waelder, TX 830-788-7511
John Hofmeister & Son Inc
 Chicago, IL 800-923-4267
Manger Packing Corp
 Baltimore, MD 800-227-9262
North Country Smokehouse
 Claremont, NH 800-258-4304
Nueske's Applewood Smoked Meat
 Wittenberg, WI 800-720-1153
Parma Sausage Products
 Pittsburgh, PA 877-294-4207
Peer Foods Group Inc
 Chicago, IL 800-365-5644
Quality Meats & Seafood
 West Fargo, ND 800-342-4250
R M Felts' Packing Co
 Ivor, VA 757-859-6131
Rinehart Meat Processing
 Branson, MO 417-869-2041
Rose Packing Co Inc
 South Barrington, IL 800-323-7363
S. Wallace Edward & Sons
 Surry, VA 800-222-4267
Sahlen's
 Buffalo, NY 800-466-8165
Sechrist Brothers
 Dallastown, PA 717-244-2975
Selwoods Farm Hunting Preserve
 Alpine, AL 800-522-0403
Serv-Rite Meat Co Inc
 Los Angeles, CA 323-227-1911
Smith Provision Co Inc
 Erie, PA 800-334-9151
Swiss-American Sausage Company
 Lathrop, CA 209-858-5555
Thomas Packing Company
 Columbus, GA 800-729-0976
Troy Foods Inc
 Troy, IL 618-667-6332
Tyson Foods Inc.
 Springdale, AR 800-233-6332
V.W. Joyner & Company
 Smithfield, VA 757-357-2161
Webster City Custom Meats Inc
 Webster City, IA 515-832-1130
Willie's Smoke House LLC
 Harrisville, PA 800-742-4184

Steak

Grote & Weigel Inc
 Bloomfield, CT 860-242-8528

Head Cheese

Ashland Sausage Co
 Carol Stream, IL 630-690-2600
Chicopee Provision Co Inc
 Chicopee, MA 800-924-6328
Savoie's Sausage and Food Products
 Opelousas, LA 337-942-7241
Sweet Traders
 Huntington Beach, CA 714-903-6800

Knockwurst

Boesl Packing Co
 Baltimore, MD 800-675-1471
Chicopee Provision Co Inc
 Chicopee, MA 800-924-6328
Country Smoked Meats
 Bowling Green, OH 800-321-4766
Far West Meats
 Highland, CA 909-864-1990
Ferris, Stahl-Meyer
 Fort Lee, NJ 201-242-5500

Gouvea's & Purity Foods Inc
 Honolulu, HI 808-847-3717
Matthiesen's Deer & Custom
 De Witt, IA 563-659-8409
Sunset Farm Foods Inc
 Valdosta, GA 800-882-1121

Liverwurst

Atlantic Pork & Provisions
 Jamaica, NY 800-245-3536
Chicopee Provision Co Inc
 Chicopee, MA 800-924-6328
Gaiser's European Style
 Union, NJ 908-686-3421
Grote & Weigel Inc
 Bloomfield, CT 860-242-8528
Silver Star Meats Inc
 Mc Kees Rocks, PA 800-548-1321
Sunset Farm Foods Inc
 Valdosta, GA 800-882-1121

Luncheon Meat

Alderfer Inc
 Harleysville, PA 800-341-1121
Atlantic Pork & Provisions
 Jamaica, NY 800-245-3536
Berks Packing Company, Inc.
 Reading, PA 800-882-3757
Binkert's Meat Products
 Baltimore, MD 410-687-5959
Birchwood Foods Inc
 Kenosha, WI 800-541-1685
Boar's Head
 Sarasota, FL 800-352-6277
Boesl Packing Co
 Baltimore, MD 800-675-1471
Boyd's Sausage Co
 Washington, IA 319-653-5715
Broadaway Ham Co
 Jonesboro, AR 870-932-6688
C Roy & Sons Processing
 Yale, MI 810-387-3957
Carl Buddig & Co.
 Homewood, IL 888-633-5684
Carolina Packers Inc
 Smithfield, NC 800-682-7675
Carolina Pride Foods
 Greenwood, SC 864-229-5611
Charlie's Country Sausage
 Minot, ND 701-838-6302
Chicopee Provision Co Inc
 Chicopee, MA 800-924-6328
Chisesi Brothers Meat Packing
 New Orleans, LA 800-966-3550
Cibao Meat Products Inc
 Bronx, NY 718-993-5072
Citterio USA
 Freeland, PA 800-435-8888
Country Smoked Meats
 Bowling Green, OH 800-321-4766
Curtis Packing Co
 Greensboro, NC 336-275-7684
Dietz & Watson Inc.
 Philadelphia, PA 215-831-9000
Dutterer's Home Food Service
 Baltimore, MD 410-298-3663
Far West Meats
 Highland, CA 909-864-1990
Ferris, Stahl-Meyer
 Fort Lee, NJ 201-242-5500
Frank Brunckhorst Company
 Sarasota, FL 804-722-4100
Frank Wardynski & Sons Inc
 Buffalo, NY 716-854-6083
Fried Provisions Company
 Evans City, PA 724-538-3160
Gouvea's & Purity Foods Inc
 Honolulu, HI 808-847-3717
Groff's Meats
 Elizabethtown, PA 717-367-1246
Hazle Park Quality Meats
 West Hazleton, PA 800-238-4331
Hofmann Sausage Co Inc
 Mattydale, NY 800-724-8410
Hormel Foods Corp.
 Austin, MN 507-437-5611
Hummel Brothers Inc
 New Haven, CT 800-828-8978
Ito Cariani Sausage Company
 Hayward, CA 510-887-0882

John Volpi & Co
 St Louis, MO 800-288-3439
Kelly Corned Beef Co
 Chicago, IL 800-624-5617
Kilgus Meats
 Toledo, OH 419-472-9721
Kitt's Meat Processing
 Dedham, IA 712-683-5622
Land O'Frost Inc
 Searcy, AR 800-643-5654
Land O'Frost Inc.
 Lansing, IL 800-323-3308
Lengerich Meats Inc
 Zanesville, IN 260-638-4123
Leona Meat Plant
 Troy, PA 570-297-3574
Liguria Foods Inc
 Humboldt, IA 515-332-4121
Locustdale Meat Packing
 Locustdale, PA 570-875-1270
Lower Foods, Inc.
 Richmond, UT 800-295-7898
Manda Fine Meats Inc
 Baton Rouge, LA 800-343-2642
Marshallville Packing Co
 Marshallville, OH 330-855-2871
Martin Rosols
 New Britain, CT 860-223-2707
Norbest, LLC
 Moroni, UT 800-453-5327
Palmyra Bologna Co Inc
 Palmyra, PA 800-282-6336
Parma Sausage Products
 Pittsburgh, PA 877-294-4207
Patrick Cudahy LLC
 Cudahy, WI 800-486-6900
Plumrose USA
 Chicago, IL 800-526-4909
R.L. Zeigler Company
 Selma, AL 800-392-6328
Rendulic Meat Packing Corp
 Mckeesport, PA 412-678-9541
Robinson Distributing Co
 London, KY 800-230-5131
Roman Packing Company
 Norfolk, NE 800-373-5990
Saad Wholesale Meats
 Detroit, MI 313-831-8126
Saag's Products LLC
 San Leandro, CA 855-287-6562
Saval Foods Corp
 Elkridge, MD 800-527-2825
Schaefers Market
 Sauk Centre, MN 320-352-6490
Schaller & Weber Inc
 Astoria, NY 800-847-4115
Sculli Brothers
 Yeadon, PA 215-336-1223
Sechrist Brothers
 Dallastown, PA 717-244-2975
Sheinman Provision Co
 Philadelphia, PA 215-473-7065
Siena Foods
 Toronto, ON 800-465-0422
Smith Packing Regional Meat
 Utica, NY 315-732-5125
Smith Provision Co Inc
 Erie, PA 800-334-9151
Spring Grove Foods
 Miamisburg, OH 937-866-4311
Standard Meat Co LP
 Dallas, TX 866-859-6313
Stevens Sausage Co
 Smithfield, NC 800-338-0561
Stonie's Sausage Shop
 Perryville, MO 888-546-2540
Sunset Farm Foods Inc
 Valdosta, GA 800-882-1121
Tennessee Valley Packing Co
 Columbia, TN 931-388-2623
Thumann Inc.
 Carlstadt, NJ 201-935-3636
Troy Foods Inc
 Troy, IL 618-667-6332
United Provision Meat Company
 Columbus, OH 614-252-1126
V.W. Joyner & Company
 Smithfield, VA 757-357-2161
Vienna Meat Products
 Scarborough, ON 800-588-1931
Warren & Son Meat Processing
 Whipple, OH 740-585-2421

Product Categories / Meats & Meat Products: Smoked, Cured & Deli Meats

Canned
Alpine Butcher
  Lowell, MA................978-256-7771
Tyson Foods Inc.
  Springdale, AR............800-233-6332

Olive Loaf
Bryant Preserving Company
  Alma, AR..................800-634-2413
Cajun Brands
  New Iberia, LA............504-408-2252

Pastrami
Alderfer Inc
  Harleysville, PA..........800-341-1121
Best Provision Co Inc
  Union, NJ.................800-631-4466
Bottom Line Foods
  Pembroke Pines, FL........954-843-0562
Carando Gourmet Frozen Foods
  Agawam, MA................888-227-2636
Carl Buddig & Co.
  Homewood, IL..............888-633-5684
Chicago 58 Food Products
  Woodbridge, ON............416-603-4244
Curly's Foods Inc
  Edina, MN.................612-920-3400
Dutterer's Home Food Service
  Baltimore, MD.............410-298-3663
Ferris, Stahl-Meyer
  Fort Lee, NJ..............201-242-5500
Kelly Corned Beef Co
  Chicago, IL...............800-624-5617
Lower Foods, Inc.
  Richmond, UT..............800-295-7898
Marathon Enterprises Inc
  Englewood, NJ.............800-722-7388
Nossack Fine Meats
  Red Deer, AB..............403-346-5006
Saval Foods Corp
  Elkridge, MD..............800-527-2825
Vienna Meat Products
  Scarborough, ON...........800-588-1931
Volpi Foods
  St Louis, MO..............800-288-3439

Pepperoni
Battistoni Italian Spec Meats
  Buffalo, NY...............800-248-2705
Big Chief Meat Snacks Inc
  Calgary, AB...............403-264-2641
Burke Corp
  Nevada, IA................800-654-1152
Busseto Foods
  Fresno, CA................800-628-2633
Cattaneo Brothers Inc
  San Luis Obispo, CA.......800-243-8537
Country Smoked Meats
  Bowling Green, OH.........800-321-4766
Fiorucci Foods USA Inc
  S Chesterfield, VA........800-524-7775
Hormel Foods Corp.
  Austin, MN................507-437-5611
Ito Cariani Sausage Company
  Hayward, CA...............510-887-0882
Liguria Foods Inc
  Humboldt, IA..............515-332-4121
Quality Sausage Company
  Dallas, TX................214-634-3400
Sangudo Custom Meat Packers
  Sangudo, AB...............888-785-3353
Spring Grove Foods
  Miamisburg, OH............937-866-4311
Stawnichy Holdings
  Mundare, AB...............888-764-7646
Swiss-American Sausage Company
  Lathrop, CA...............209-858-5555
Viau Foods
  Laval, QC.................800-663-5492
Volpi Foods
  St Louis, MO..............800-288-3439

Prosciutto
Fiorucci Foods USA Inc
  S Chesterfield, VA........800-524-7775
Hormel Foods Corp.
  Austin, MN................507-437-5611
Olympic Provisions Northwest
  Portland, OR..............503-894-8136

Parma Sausage Products
  Pittsburgh, PA............877-294-4207
Santa Maria Foods
  Branpton, ON..............905-790-1991
Siena Foods
  Toronto, ON...............800-465-0422
Volpi Foods
  St Louis, MO..............800-288-3439

Salami
Alef Sausage Inc
  Mundelein, IL.............847-968-2533
Applegate Farms
  Bridgewater, NJ...........866-587-5858
Baier's Sausage & Meats
  Red Deer, AB..............403-346-1535
Battistoni Italian Spec Meats
  Buffalo, NY...............800-248-2705
Boesl Packing Co
  Baltimore, MD.............800-675-1471
Burke Corp
  Nevada, IA................800-654-1152
Busseto Foods
  Fresno, CA................800-628-2633
Charlie's Country Sausage
  Minot, ND.................701-838-6302
Chicago 58 Food Products
  Woodbridge, ON............416-603-4244
Chicopee Provision Co Inc
  Chicopee, MA..............800-924-6328
Chisesi Brothers Meat Packing
  New Orleans, LA...........800-966-3550
Cibao Meat Products Inc
  Bronx, NY.................718-993-5072
Far West Meats
  Highland, CA..............909-864-1990
Fiorucci Foods USA Inc
  S Chesterfield, VA........800-524-7775
Hormel Foods Corp.
  Austin, MN................507-437-5611
Ito Cariani Sausage Company
  Hayward, CA...............510-887-0882
John Volpi & Co
  St Louis, MO..............800-288-3439
Liguria Foods Inc
  Humboldt, IA..............515-332-4121
Marathon Enterprises Inc
  Englewood, NJ.............800-722-7388
OLLI Salumeria Americana
  Oceanside, CA.............877-655-4937
Parma Sausage Products
  Pittsburgh, PA............877-294-4207
Patrick Cudahy LLC
  Cudahy, WI................800-486-6900
Plumrose USA
  Chicago, IL...............800-526-4909
Santa Maria Foods
  Branpton, ON..............905-790-1991
Schaller & Weber Inc
  Astoria, NY...............800-847-4115
Sculli Brothers
  Yeadon, PA................215-336-1223
Siena Foods
  Toronto, ON...............800-465-0422
Spring Grove Foods
  Miamisburg, OH............937-866-4311
Stawnichy Holdings
  Mundare, AB...............888-764-7646
Swiss-American Sausage Company
  Lathrop, CA...............209-858-5555
Volpi Foods
  St Louis, MO..............800-288-3439

Sausages
A.L. Duck Jr Inc
  Zuni, VA..................757-562-2387
Abbyland Foods Inc
  Abbotsford, WI............800-732-5483
Adolf's Meats & Sausage Kitchen
  Hartford, CT..............860-522-1588
Aidells Sausage Co
  San Lorenzo, CA...........800-546-5795
Alaska Sausage & Seafood
  Anchorage, AK.............800-798-3636
Alewel's Country Meats
  Warrensburg, MO...........800-353-8553
Aliments Prince SEC
  Anjou, QC.................800-361-3898
Alpine Meats
  Stockton, CA..............800-399-6328

Applegate Farms
  Bridgewater, NJ...........866-587-5858
AquaCuisine
  Portland, OR..............208-323-2782
Aries Prepared Beef
  Burbank, CA...............800-424-2333
Armbrust Meats
  Medford, WI...............715-748-3102
Arnold's Meat Food Products
  Brooklyn, NY..............800-633-7023
Ashland Sausage Co
  Carol Stream, IL..........630-690-2600
Baier's Sausage & Meats
  Red Deer, AB..............403-346-1535
Baja Foods LLC
  Chicago, IL...............773-376-9030
Bakalars Sausage Co
  La Crosse, WI.............608-784-0384
Berks Packing Company, Inc.
  Reading, PA...............800-882-3757
Big City Reds
  Omaha, NE.................800-759-5275
Bilinski Sausage Mfg Co
  Cohoes, NY................877-873-9102
Binkert's Meat Products
  Baltimore, MD.............410-687-5959
Black's Barbecue
  Lockhart, TX..............888-632-8225
Blue Grass Quality Meat
  Covington, KY.............859-331-7100
Bob Evans Farms Inc.
 800-939-2338
Boesl Packing Co
  Baltimore, MD.............800-675-1471
Bouma Meats
  Provost, AB...............780-753-2092
Bowser Meat Processing
  Meriden, KS...............785-484-2454
Boyd's Sausage Co
  Washington, IA............319-653-5715
Braham Food Locker Service
  Braham, MN................320-396-2636
Bridgford Foods Corp
  Anaheim, CA...............800-527-2105
Broadleaf Venison USA Inc
  Vernon, CA................800-336-3844
Brook Meadow Meats
  Hagerstown, MD............301-739-3107
Bryant's Meat Inc.
  Taylorsville, MS..........800-844-0507
Burgers' Smokehouse
  California, MO............800-345-5185
Burke Corp
  Nevada, IA................800-654-1152
Burton Meat Processing
  Burton, TX................979-289-4022
Camellia General Provision Co
  Buffalo, NY...............716-893-5352
Caribbean Food Delights Inc
  Tappan, NY................845-398-3000
Carl Buddig & Co.
  Homewood, IL..............888-633-5684
Carolina Packers Inc
  Smithfield, NC............800-682-7675
Casa di Carfagna
  Columbus, OH..............614-846-6340
Casual Gourmet Foods
  Clearwater, FL............727-298-8307
Cattaneo Brothers Inc
  San Luis Obispo, CA.......800-243-8537
Caughman's Meat Plant
  Lexington, SC.............803-356-0076
Center Locker Svc
  Center, MO................800-884-0737
Central Meat Market
  Providence, RI............401-751-6935
Charlie's Country Sausage
  Minot, ND.................701-838-6302
Cher-Make Sausage Co
  Manitowoc, WI.............800-242-7679
Chicopee Provision Co Inc
  Chicopee, MA..............800-924-6328
Chisesi Brothers Meat Packing
  New Orleans, LA...........800-966-3550
Cibao Meat Products Inc
  Bronx, NY.................718-993-5072
Cifelli & Sons Inc
  South River, NJ...........732-238-0090
Cimpl Meats
  Yankton, SD...............605-665-1665
Cloverdale Foods
  Mandan, ND................800-669-9511

Clyde's Italian & German Sausage
Denver, CO 303-433-8744
Conecuh Sausage Co
Evergreen, AL 800-726-0507
Couch's Country Style Sausages
Cleveland, OH 216-823-2332
Country Smoked Meats
Bowling Green, OH 800-321-4766
Crawford Sausage Co Inc
Chicago, IL 773-277-3095
Crocetti's Oakdale Packing Co
East Bridgewater, MA 508-587-0035
Crofton & Sons Inc
Tampa, FL 800-878-7675
Culver Duck Farms Inc
Middlebury, IN 800-825-9225
Cumberland Gap Provision Company
Middlesboro, KY 855-411-7675
Dean Sausage Co Inc
Attalla, AL 800-228-0704
Debbie D's Jerky & Sausage
Tillamook, OR 503-842-2622
Dennison Meat Locker
Dennison, MN 507-645-8734
Diggs Packing Company
Columbia, MO 573-449-2995
DiGregorio Food Products
St Louis, MO 314-776-1062
Dinner Bell Meat Product
Lynchburg, VA 434-847-7766
Dino's Sausage & Meat Co Inc
Utica, NY 315-732-2661
Dohar Meats Inc
Cleveland, OH 216-241-4197
Dreymiller & KRAY Inc
Hampshire, IL 847-683-2271
Duis Meat Processing
Concordia, KS 800-281-4295
Dutch Packing Co., Inc.
Doral, FL 800-723-9249
E.W. Knauss & Son
Quakertown, PA 800-648-4220
Ellsworth Locker
Ellsworth, MN 507-967-2544
Elmwood Locker Svc
Elmwood, IL 309-742-8929
Elore Enterprises Inc
Miami Gardens, FL 305-477-1650
Enslin & Son Packing Company
Hattiesburg, MS 800-898-4687
European Egg Noodle Manufacturing
Edmonton, AB 780-453-6767
Evergood Fine Foods
San Francisco, CA 800-253-6733
F&Y Enterprises
Wauconda, IL 847-526-0620
Fabbri Sausage Mfg Co
Chicago, IL 312-829-6363
Fanestil Packing Company
Emporia, KS 800-658-1652
Far West Meats
Highland, CA 909-864-1990
Ferris, Stahl-Meyer
Fort Lee, NJ 201-242-5500
Foell Packing Company
Naperville, IL 919-776-0592
Fontanini Italian Meats
McCook, IL 800-331-6328
Fortenberry Mini-Storage
Kodak, TN 865-933-2568
Frank Wardynski & Sons Inc
Buffalo, NY 716-854-6083
Fresh Mark Inc.
Massillon, OH 330-832-7491
Frick's Quality Meats
Washington, MO 800-241-2209
Fried Provisions Company
Evans City, PA 724-538-3160
Gaiser's European Style
Union, NJ 908-686-3421
Gaspar's Linguica Co Inc
North Dartmouth, MA 800-542-2038
Gem Meat Packing Co
Garden City, ID 208-375-9424
Glazier Packing Co
Malone, NY 518-483-4990
Glier's Meats Inc
Covington, KY 800-446-3882
Gouvea's & Purity Foods Inc
Honolulu, HI 808-847-3717
Grandpa Ittel's Meats Inc
Howard Lake, MN 320-543-2285
Grant Park Packing
Chicago, IL 312-421-4096
Grimm's Fine Food
Richmond, BC 866-663-4746
Grote & Weigel Inc
Bloomfield, CT 860-242-8528
Gunnoe Farms Sausage & Salad
Charleston, WV 304-343-7686
H & B Packing Co
Waco, TX 254-752-2506
Hatfield Quality Meats
Hatfield, PA 800-743-1191
Hazle Park Quality Meats
West Hazleton, PA 800-238-4331
Heinkel's Packing Co
Decatur, IL 800-594-2738
Hillbilly Smokehouse
Rogers, AR 479-636-1927
Hofmann Sausage Co Inc
Mattydale, NY 800-724-8410
Homestead Meats
Delta, CO 970-874-1145
Hoople Country Kitchen Inc
Rockport, IN 877-466-7537
Hormel Foods Corp.
Austin, MN 507-437-5611
Hot Springs Packing Co Inc
Hot Springs, AR 800-535-0449
Hummel Brothers Inc
New Haven, CT 800-828-8978
Humphrey's Market
Springfield, IL 800-747-6328
Huse's Country Meats
Malone, TX 254-533-2205
Independent Meat Co
Twin Falls, ID 800-284-4626
Indian Valley Meats
Indian, AK 907-653-7511
Isernio Sausage Company
Seattle, WA 888-495-8674
Ito Cariani Sausage Company
Hayward, CA 510-887-0882
J & B Sausage Co Inc
Waelder, TX 830-788-7511
Jody Maroni's Sausage Kingdom
Burbank, CA 818-760-2004
Johnsonville Sausage LLC
Watertown, WI 888-556-2728
Jones Dairy Farm
Fort Atkinson, WI 800-563-6637
Kayem Foods
Chelsea, MA 800-426-6100
Kelley Foods
Elba, AL 334-897-5761
Kent Quality Foods Inc
Grand Rapids, MI 800-748-0141
Kilgus Meats
Toledo, OH 419-472-9721
Kiolbassa Provision Co
San Antonio, TX 800-456-5465
Kirby Holloway Provision Co
Harrington, DE 800-995-4729
Klement Sausage Co Inc
Milwaukee, WI 800-553-6368
Koegel Meats Inc
Flint, MI 810-238-3685
Konetzko's Meat Market
Browerville, MN 320-594-2915
Kowalski Sausage Co
Hamtramck, MI 800-482-2400
Lad's Smokehouse Catering
Needville, TX 979-793-6210
Larry's Sausage Corporation
Fayetteville, NC 910-483-5148
Laurent's Meat Market
Marrero, LA 504-341-1771
Le Pique-Nique
New York, NY 800-699-9822
Lee's Sausage Co
Orangeburg, SC 803-534-5517
Leona Meat Plant
Troy, PA 570-297-3574
Lewis Sausage Corporation
Burgaw, NC 910-259-2642
Liguria Foods Inc
Humboldt, IA 515-332-4121
Link Snacks Inc.
Minong, WI 715-466-2234
Little Rhody Brand Frankfurts
Johnston, RI 401-831-0815
Locustdale Meat Packing
Locustdale, PA 570-875-1270
Lord's Sausage & Country Ham
Dexter, GA 800-342-6002
Louie's Finer Meats
Cumberland, WI 800-270-4297
Lucy's Foods
Latrobe, PA 724-539-1430
Mac's Farms Sausage Co Inc
Newton Grove, NC 910-594-0095
Manda Fine Meats Inc
Baton Rouge, LA 800-343-2642
Marathon Enterprises Inc
Englewood, NJ 800-722-7388
Marcel et Henri Charcuterie Francaise
South San Francisco, CA 800-227-6436
Marshallville Packing Co
Marshallville, OH 330-855-2871
Mckenzie Country Classic's
Burlington, VT 800-426-6100
McLane's Meats
Wetaskiwin, AB 780-352-4321
Meating Place
Buffalo, NY 716-885-3623
Mellos North End Mfr
Fall River, MA 800-673-2320
Mertz Sausage Co
San Antonio, TX 210-433-3263
Michael's Provision Co
Fall River, MA 508-672-0982
Michel's Magnifique
New York, NY 212-431-1070
Milan Provision Co
Corona, NY 718-899-7678
Miller Brothers Packing Company
Sylvester, GA 229-776-2014
Miller's Meat Market
Red Bud, IL 618-282-3334
Milling Sausage Inc
Milwaukee, WI 414-645-2677
Momence Packing Company
Sheboygan Falls, WI 888-556-2728
Neese Country Sausage Inc
Greensboro, NC 800-632-1010
Neto's Market & Grill
Santa Clara, CA 888-482-6386
New Packing Company
Chicago, IL 312-666-1314
Niemuth's Steak & Chop Shop
Waupaca, WI 715-258-2666
Norpaco Inc
Middletown, CT 800-252-0222
North Country Smokehouse
Claremont, NH 800-258-4304
Nossack Fine Meats
Red Deer, AB 403-346-5006
Nueske's Applewood Smoked Meat
Wittenberg, WI 800-720-1153
Odom's Tennessee Pride Sausage Company
Madison, TN 615-868-1360
Omaha Steaks Inc
. 800-960-8400
Opa's Smoked Meats
Fredericksburg, TX 800-543-6750
Ossian Smoked Meats
Ossian, IN 800-535-8862
Parma Sausage Products
Pittsburgh, PA 877-294-4207
Patrick Cudahy LLC
Cudahy, WI 800-486-6900
Peer Foods Group Inc
Chicago, IL 800-365-5644
Pekarna Meat Market
Jordan, MN 952-492-6101
Piller Sausages & Delicatessens
Waterloo, ON 800-265-2628
Pinter's Packing Plant
Dorchester, WI 715-654-5444
Pioneer Packing Co
Bowling Green, OH 419-352-5283
Pokanoket Ostrich Farm
South Dartmouth, MA 508-992-6188
Polka Home Style Sausage
Chicago, IL 773-221-0395
Quality Meats & Seafood
West Fargo, ND 800-342-4250
Queen City Sausage & Provision
Cincinnati, OH 877-544-5588
R & D Sausage Co
Cleveland, OH 216-692-1832
Ray's Sausage Co
Cleveland, OH 216-921-8782
Real Kosher Sausage Company
Newark, NJ 973-690-5394

Product Categories / Meats & Meat Products: Smoked, Cured & Deli Meats

Red Smith Foods Inc
   Davie, FL 954-581-1996
Register Meat Co
   Cottondale, FL 850-352-4269
Rich Products Corp
   Vineland, NJ 800-818-9261
Rinehart Meat Processing
   Branson, MO. 417-869-2041
Robbins Packing Company
   Statesboro, GA 912-764-7503
Robinson Distributing Co
   London, KY 800-230-5131
Roma Packing Company
   East Providence, RI 401-228-7170
Roman Packing Company
   Norfolk, NE. 800-373-5990
Roman Sausage Company
   Santa Clara, CA 800-497-7462
Roode Packing Company
   Fairbury, NE 402-729-2253
Rudolph's Market & Sausage
   Dallas, TX. 214-741-1874
S. Wallace Edward & Sons
   Surry, VA. 800-222-4267
S.W. Meat & Provision Company
   Phoenix, AZ 602-275-2000
Saag's Products LLC
   San Leandro, CA. 855-287-6562
Sahlen's
   Buffalo, NY. 800-466-8165
Sangudo Custom Meat Packers
   Sangudo, AB. 888-785-3353
Sardinha's Sausage
   Somerset, MA 800-678-0178
Sausages by Amy
   Chicago, IL. 312-829-2250
Savoie's Sausage and Food Products
   Opelousas, LA 337-942-7241
Schaefers Market
   Sauk Centre, MN 320-352-6490
Schaller & Weber Inc
   Astoria, NY 800-847-4115
Scott Hams
   Greenville, KY 800-318-1353
Sculli Brothers
   Yeadon, PA 215-336-1223
Sechrist Brothers
   Dallastown, PA 717-244-2975
Selecto Sausage Co
   Houston, TX. 713-926-1626
Serv-Rite Meat Co Inc
   Los Angeles, CA. 323-227-1911
Sheinman Provision Co
   Philadelphia, PA. 215-473-7065
Siena Foods
   Toronto, ON 800-465-0422
Silver Creek Specialty Meats
   Oshkosh, WI. 800-729-2849
Silver Star Meats Inc
   Mc Kees Rocks, PA 800-548-1321
Smith Packing Regional Meat
   Utica, NY 315-732-5125
Smith Provision Co Inc
   Erie, PA. 800-334-9151
Smokey Denmark Sausage Co
   Austin, TX. 512-385-0718
Smolich Bros. Home Made Sausage
   Crest Hill, IL. 815-727-2144
Spring Grove Foods
   Miamisburg, OH 937-866-4311
Stanley Provision Company
   Manchester, CT. 888-688-6347
Stawnichy Holdings
   Mundare, AB. 888-764-7646
Stevens Sausage Co
   Smithfield, NC 800-338-0561
Stewarts Market
   Yelm, WA 360-458-2091
Stonie's Sausage Shop
   Perryville, MO 888-546-2540
Strasburg Provision
   Strasburg, OH 800-207-6009
Streit Carl & Son Co
   Neptune, NJ 732-775-0803
Stripling's General Store
   Moultrie, GA. 229-985-4226
Sunergia Soyfoods
   Charlottesville, VA. 800-693-5134
Sunnydale Meats Inc
   Gaffney, SC 864-489-6091
Swiss-American Sausage Company
   Lathrop, CA 209-858-5555

T.L. Herring & Company
   Wilson, NC 252-291-1141
Tennessee Valley Packing Co
   Columbia, TN 931-388-2623
Texas Sausage Co
   Austin, TX. 512-472-6707
Thomas Packing Company
   Columbus, GA 800-729-0976
Tofield Packers Ltd
   Tofield, AB 780-662-4842
Troy Foods Inc
   Troy, IL 618-667-6332
Uvalde Meat Processing
   Uvalde, TX 830-278-6247
Vermilion Packers Ltd
   Vermilion, AB. 780-853-4622
Viau Foods
   Laval, QC 800-663-5492
Victor Ostrowski & Son
   Baltimore, MD 410-327-8935
Vienna Beef LTD
   Chicago, IL. 800-366-3647
Vienna Meat Products
   Scarborough, ON 800-588-1931
Vollwerth & Baroni Companies
   Hancock, MI 800-562-7620
Volpi Foods
   St Louis, MO. 800-288-3439
W.A. Beans & Sons
   Bangor, ME. 800-649-1958
WACO Beef & Pork Processors
   Waco, TX. 254-772-4669
Wampler's Farm Sausage Company
   Lenoir City, TN. 800-728-7243
Warren & Son Meat Processing
   Whipple, OH 740-585-2421
Willie's Smoke House LLC
   Harrisville, PA. 800-742-4184
Wolfson Casing Corp
   Mt Vernon, NY 800-221-8042
Woods Smoked Meats Inc
   Bowling Green, MO. 800-458-8426
Zummo Meat Co
   Beaumont, TX. 409-842-1810
Zweigle's Inc
   Rochester, NY. 585-546-1740

Andouille

Applegate Farms
   Bridgewater, NJ 866-587-5858
Burke Corp
   Nevada, IA 800-654-1152
Grote & Weigel Inc
   Bloomfield, CT. 860-242-8528
Laurent's Meat Market
   Marrero, LA 504-341-1771
Parma Sausage Products
   Pittsburgh, PA 877-294-4207
Savoie's Sausage and Food Products
   Opelousas, LA 337-942-7241
Thomas Packing Company
   Columbus, GA 800-729-0976

Blood

Bavarian Meat Products
   Seattle, WA. 206-448-3540
Chicopee Provision Co Inc
   Chicopee, MA. 800-924-6328
Gouvea's & Purity Foods Inc
   Honolulu, HI 808-847-3717

Bockwurst

Chicopee Provision Co Inc
   Chicopee, MA. 800-924-6328
Country Smoked Meats
   Bowling Green, OH 800-321-4766
Koegel Meats Inc
   Flint, MI 810-238-3685

Boudin

Comeaux's
   Lafayette, LA 888-264-5460
Marcel et Henri Charcuterie Francaise
   South San Francisco, CA 800-227-6436
Savoie's Sausage and Food Products
   Opelousas, LA 337-942-7241
Stallings Head Cheese Co
   Houston, TX. 713-523-1751
Sunset Farm Foods Inc
   Valdosta, GA 800-882-1121

Woods Smoked Meats Inc
   Bowling Green, MO. 800-458-8426
Zummo Meat Co
   Beaumont, TX. 409-842-1810

Bratwurst

Chicopee Provision Co Inc
   Chicopee, MA. 800-924-6328
Country Smoked Meats
   Bowling Green, OH 800-321-4766
Elmwood Locker Svc
   Elmwood, IL 309-742-8929
F B Purnell Sausage Co Inc
   Simpsonville, KY 800-626-1512
Far West Meats
   Highland, CA 909-864-1990
Grote & Weigel Inc
   Bloomfield, CT. 860-242-8528
Kayem Foods
   Chelsea, MA 800-426-6100
Kilgus Meats
   Toledo, OH 419-472-9721
Koegel Meats Inc
   Flint, MI 810-238-3685
New Braunfels Smokehouse
   New Braunfels, TX. 800-537-6932
S.W. Meat & Provision Company
   Phoenix, AZ 602-275-2000
Smolich Bros. Home Made Sausage
   Crest Hill, IL. 815-727-2144
WACO Beef & Pork Processors
   Waco, TX. 254-772-4669

Cajun

Fontanini Italian Meats
   McCook, IL. 800-331-6328

Casings: Sausage, Pork, Beef

Austrade
   Palm Beach Gdns, FL. 561-209-2447
Con Yeager Spice Co
   Zelienople, PA. 800-222-2460
Dewied International Inc
   San Antonio, TX. 800-992-5600
International Casings Group
   Chicago, IL. 800-825-5151
Koegel Meats Inc
   Flint, MI 810-238-3685
Marie F
   Markham, ON 800-365-4464
Nitta Casings Inc
   Bridgewater, NJ 800-526-3970
Oversea Casing Co
   Seattle, WA. 206-682-6845
Syracuse Casing Co
   Syracuse, NY 315-475-0309
World Casing Corp
   Maspeth, NY 800-221-4887

Chicken

Bell & Evans
   Fredericksburg, PA 717-865-6626
Kayem Foods
   Chelsea, MA 800-426-6100
Lucy's Foods
   Latrobe, PA 724-539-1430
W.A. Beans & Sons
   Bangor, ME. 800-649-1958

Chorizo

Arnold's Meat Food Products
   Brooklyn, NY 800-633-7023
Burke Corp
   Nevada, IA 800-654-1152
Cacique
   Monrovia, CA 800-521-6987
Carmelita Provisions Company
   Monterey Park, CA. 323-262-6751
Country Smoked Meats
   Bowling Green, OH 800-321-4766
F B Purnell Sausage Co Inc
   Simpsonville, KY 800-626-1512
Lucy's Foods
   Latrobe, PA 724-539-1430
Parma Sausage Products
   Pittsburgh, PA 877-294-4207
Sunset Farm Foods Inc
   Valdosta, GA 800-882-1121
WACO Beef & Pork Processors
   Waco, TX. 254-772-4669

Product Categories / Meats & Meat Products: Smoked, Cured & Deli Meats

Chourico
Gaspar's Linguica Co Inc
 North Dartmouth, MA 800-542-2038
Manuel's Odessa Tortilla
 Odessa, TX 800-753-2445
Mertz Sausage Co
 San Antonio, TX 210-433-3263
Sardinha's Sausage
 Somerset, MA 800-678-0178

Hot
Boesl Packing Co
 Baltimore, MD 800-675-1471
Chicopee Provision Co Inc
 Chicopee, MA 800-924-6328
E.W. Knauss & Son
 Quakertown, PA 800-648-4220
H & B Packing Co
 Waco, TX 254-752-2506
Hormel Foods Corp.
 Austin, MN 507-437-5611
Ray's Sausage Co
 Cleveland, OH 216-921-8782
Sheinman Provision Co
 Philadelphia, PA 215-473-7065
Siena Foods
 Toronto, ON 800-465-0422

Hot Italian
Eagle Rock Food Co
 Albuquerque, NM 505-323-1183
F B Purnell Sausage Co Inc
 Simpsonville, KY 800-626-1512
Grote & Weigel Inc
 Bloomfield, CT 860-242-8528
Siena Foods
 Toronto, ON 800-465-0422

Kielbasa
Berks Packing Company, Inc.
 Reading, PA 800-882-3757
Boesl Packing Co
 Baltimore, MD 800-675-1471
Chicopee Provision Co Inc
 Chicopee, MA 800-924-6328
Country Smoked Meats
 Bowling Green, OH 800-321-4766
Far West Meats
 Highland, CA 909-864-1990
Frank Wardynski & Sons Inc
 Buffalo, NY 716-854-6083
Gaspar's Linguica Co Inc
 North Dartmouth, MA 800-542-2038
Grote & Weigel Inc
 Bloomfield, CT 860-242-8528
Hot Springs Packing Co Inc
 Hot Springs, AR 800-535-0449
Leo G. Fraboni Sausage Company
 Hibbing, MN 218-263-5074
Locustdale Meat Packing
 Locustdale, PA 570-875-1270
Marathon Enterprises Inc
 Englewood, NJ 800-722-7388
Martin Rosols
 New Britain, CT 860-223-2707
Norpaco Inc
 Middletown, CT 800-252-0222
Parma Sausage Products
 Pittsburgh, PA 877-294-4207
Roma Packing Company
 East Providence, RI 401-228-7170
Sardinha's Sausage
 Somerset, MA 800-678-0178
Silver Star Meats Inc
 Mc Kees Rocks, PA 800-548-1321
Smith Packing Regional Meat
 Utica, NY 315-732-5125
Stanley Provision Company
 Manchester, CT 888-688-6347
Victor Ostrowski & Son
 Baltimore, MD 410-327-8935

Knockwurst
Boesl Packing Co
 Baltimore, MD 800-675-1471
Country Smoked Meats
 Bowling Green, OH 800-321-4766
Far West Meats
 Highland, CA 909-864-1990

Gouvea's & Purity Foods Inc
 Honolulu, HI 808-847-3717
Grote & Weigel Inc
 Bloomfield, CT 860-242-8528

Legonica (Thin Italian)
Gaspar's Linguica Co Inc
 North Dartmouth, MA 800-542-2038

Linguica
Burke Corp
 Nevada, IA 800-654-1152
Swiss-American Sausage Company
 Lathrop, CA 209-858-5555

Link
Bakalars Sausage Co
 La Crosse, WI 608-784-0384
Bellville Meat Market
 Bellville, TX 800-571-6328
Burke Corp
 Nevada, IA 800-654-1152
Country Smoked Meats
 Bowling Green, OH 800-321-4766
F B Purnell Sausage Co Inc
 Simpsonville, KY 800-626-1512
Father's Country Hams
 Bremen, KY 270-525-3554
Fontanini Italian Meats
 McCook, IL 800-331-6328
H & B Packing Co
 Waco, TX 254-752-2506
Hormel Foods Corp.
 Austin, MN 507-437-5611
Jimmy Dean Foods
 Springdale, AR 800-925-3326
Mellos North End Mfr
 Fall River, MA 800-673-2320
Opa's Smoked Meats
 Fredericksburg, TX 800-543-6750
Ray's Sausage Co
 Cleveland, OH 216-921-8782

Mortadella
Fiorucci Foods USA Inc
 S Chesterfield, VA 800-524-7775
John Volpi & Co
 St Louis, MO 800-288-3439
Parma Sausage Products
 Pittsburgh, PA 877-294-4207
Siena Foods
 Toronto, ON 800-465-0422

Patti
F B Purnell Sausage Co Inc
 Simpsonville, KY 800-626-1512
Father's Country Hams
 Bremen, KY 270-525-3554
Fontanini Italian Meats
 McCook, IL 800-331-6328
Hormel Foods Corp.
 Austin, MN 507-437-5611
Jimmy Dean Foods
 Springdale, AR 800-925-3326
Mellos North End Mfr
 Fall River, MA 800-673-2320
Ray's Sausage Co
 Cleveland, OH 216-921-8782
Roman Sausage Company
 Santa Clara, CA 800-497-7462

Polish
Crawford Sausage Co Inc
 Chicago, IL 773-277-3095
Fontanini Italian Meats
 McCook, IL 800-331-6328

Pork
Crawford Sausage Co Inc
 Chicago, IL 773-277-3095
Grote & Weigel Inc
 Bloomfield, CT 860-242-8528
Lucy's Foods
 Latrobe, PA 724-539-1430

Salmon
Aquatec Seafoods Ltd.
 Comox, BC 250-339-6412

Sicilian Style (with Cheese)
Volpi Foods
 St Louis, MO 800-288-3439

Sweet
Chicopee Provision Co Inc
 Chicopee, MA 800-924-6328

Sweet Italian
Grote & Weigel Inc
 Bloomfield, CT 860-242-8528

Turkey
Couch's Country Style Sausages
 Cleveland, OH 216-823-2332
Eagle Rock Food Co
 Albuquerque, NM 505-323-1183
Gaspar's Linguica Co Inc
 North Dartmouth, MA 800-542-2038
Lucy's Foods
 Latrobe, PA 724-539-1430

Venison
Broadleaf Venison USA Inc
 Vernon, CA 800-336-3844

Smoked Meat
Alewel's Country Meats
 Warrensburg, MO 800-353-8553
Alpine Meats
 Stockton, CA 800-399-6328
Applegate Farms
 Bridgewater, NJ 866-587-5858
Bellville Meat Market
 Bellville, TX 800-571-6328
Berks Packing Company, Inc.
 Reading, PA 800-882-3757
Boesl Packing Co
 Baltimore, MD 800-675-1471
Braham Food Locker Service
 Braham, MN 320-396-2636
Brook Meadow Meats
 Hagerstown, MD 301-739-3107
Burgers' Smokehouse
 California, MO 800-345-5185
Carolina Pride Foods
 Greenwood, SC 864-229-5611
Chicago 58 Food Products
 Woodbridge, ON 416-603-4244
Cloud's Meat Processing
 Carthage, MO 417-358-5855
Country Smoked Meats
 Bowling Green, OH 800-321-4766
Crofton & Sons Inc
 Tampa, FL 800-878-7675
Duis Meat Processing
 Concordia, KS 800-281-4295
E.W. Knauss & Son
 Quakertown, PA 800-648-4220
F&Y Enterprises
 Wauconda, IL 847-526-0620
Fairbury Food Products
 Fairbury, NE 402-729-3379
Far West Meats
 Highland, CA 909-864-1990
Fiorucci Foods USA Inc
 S Chesterfield, VA 800-524-7775
Fresh Mark Inc.
 Massillon, OH 330-832-7491
Frick's Quality Meats
 Washington, MO 800-241-2209
Gaiser's European Style
 Union, NJ 908-686-3421
Grandpa Ittel's Meats Inc
 Howard Lake, MN 320-543-2285
Hickory Baked Ham Co
 Castle Rock, CO 303-688-2633
Hollman Foods
 Des Moines, IA 888-926-2879
Homestead Meats
 Delta, CO 970-874-1145
Hormel Foods Corp.
 Austin, MN 507-437-5611
Humphrey's Market
 Springfield, IL 800-747-6328
John Hofmeister & Son Inc
 Chicago, IL 800-923-4267
John Volpi & Co
 St Louis, MO 800-288-3439

Product Categories / Meats & Meat Products: Steaks

Koegel Meats Inc
   Flint, MI 810-238-3685
Konetzko's Meat Market
   Browerville, MN 320-594-2915
Laurent's Meat Market
   Marrero, LA 504-341-1771
Leo G. Fraboni Sausage Company
   Hibbing, MN 218-263-5074
Lord's Sausage & Country Ham
   Dexter, GA 800-342-6002
Manger Packing Corp
   Baltimore, MD 800-227-9262
Mckenzie Country Classic's
   Burlington, VT 800-426-6100
Nodine's Smokehouse Inc
   Torrington, CT 800-222-2059
Nueces Canyon Range
   Brenham, TX 800-925-5058
Original Chili Bowl
   Ontario, CA 800-548-6363
People's Sausage Co
   Los Angeles, CA 213-627-8633
Pioneer Packing Co
   Bowling Green, OH 419-352-5283
Quality Meats & Seafood
   West Fargo, ND 800-342-4250
R M Felts' Packing Co
   Ivor, VA 757-859-6131
Rinehart Meat Processing
   Branson, MO 417-869-2041
Robbins Packing Company
   Statesboro, GA 912-764-7503
Rose Packing Co Inc
   South Barrington, IL 800-323-7363
Saag's Products LLC
   San Leandro, CA 855-287-6562
Sahlen's
   Buffalo, NY 800-466-8165
Sardinha's Sausage
   Somerset, MA 800-678-0178
Savoie's Sausage and Food Products
   Opelousas, LA 337-942-7241
Schaller & Weber Inc
   Astoria, NY 800-847-4115
Sechrist Brothers
   Dallastown, PA 717-244-2975
Smith Meat Packing
   Detroit, MI 313-833-1590
Stonie's Sausage Shop
   Perryville, MO 888-546-2540
Stripling's General Store
   Moultrie, GA 229-985-4226
Swiss-American Sausage Company
   Lathrop, CA 209-858-5555
Thomas Packing Company
   Columbus, GA 800-729-0976
Triple U Enterprises
   Fort Pierre, SD 605-567-3624

Troy Pork Store
   Troy, NY 518-272-8291
V.W. Joyner & Company
   Smithfield, VA 757-357-2161
Warren & Son Meat Processing
   Whipple, OH 740-585-2421
Wayco Ham Co
   Goldsboro, NC 800-962-2614
Willie's Smoke House LLC
   Harrisville, PA 800-742-4184
Woods Smoked Meats Inc
   Bowling Green, MO 800-458-8426
Yoakum Packing Co
   Yoakum, TX 800-999-6997
Zerna Packing
   Labadie, MO 636-742-4190

Poultry & Game

Selwoods Farm Hunting Preserve
   Alpine, AL 800-522-0403

Tasso

Comeaux's
   Lafayette, LA 888-264-5460
Savoie's Sausage and Food Products
   Opelousas, LA 337-942-7241

Turkey

Deli Breast - Fresh

Norbest, LLC
   Moroni, UT 800-453-5327

Deli Breast - Frozen

Norbest, LLC
   Moroni, UT 800-453-5327

Deli Breast - Honey

Albert's Meats
   Claysville, PA 800-522-9970

Deli Breast - Smoked

Applegate Farms
   Bridgewater, NJ 866-587-5858

Smoked

Applegate Farms
   Bridgewater, NJ 866-587-5858
Burgers' Smokehouse
   California, MO 800-345-5185
Chickasaw Trading Company
   Denver City, TX 800-848-3515
Crofton & Sons Inc
   Tampa, FL 800-878-7675

Hollman Foods
   Des Moines, IA 888-926-2879
North Country Smokehouse
   Claremont, NH 800-258-4304
Ranch Oak Farm
   Fort Worth, TX 800-888-0327
Selwoods Farm Hunting Preserve
   Alpine, AL 800-522-0403
Thomas Packing Company
   Columbus, GA 800-729-0976
Wayco Ham Co
   Goldsboro, NC 800-962-2614

Steaks

B & D Foods
   Boise, ID 208-344-1183
Bakalars Sausage Co
   La Crosse, WI 608-784-0384
Burnett & Son
   Monrovia, CA 877-632-5467
Cambridge Packing Company
   Boston, MA 800-722-6726
Centennial Food Corporation
   Calgary, AB 403-214-0044
Devault Foods
   Devault, PA 800-426-2874
Dynamic Foods
   Lubbock, TX 806-723-5600
Feed The Party
   Louisville, KY
Kutztown Bologna Company
   Leola, PA 800-723-8824
Ossian Smoked Meats
   Ossian, IN 800-535-8862
Pierceton Foods Inc
   Pierceton, IN 574-594-2344
Pinter's Packing Plant
   Dorchester, WI 715-654-5444
Rymer Foods
   Chicago, IL 800-247-9637
S.W. Meat & Provision Company
   Phoenix, AZ 602-275-2000
Stampede Meat, Inc.
   Bridgeview, IL 800-353-0933
Steak-Umm Company
   Shillington, PA 860-928-5900
Valley Meats
   Coal Valley, IL 309-517-6639

Tripe

Bradshaw's Food Products
   Dighton, MA 508-669-6088

Nuts & Nut Butters

Nut Butters

88 Acres
  Allston, MA 617-208-8651
Abby's Better Nut Butter
American Almond Products Co
  Brooklyn, NY 800-825-6663
Amoretti
  Oxnard, CA 800-266-7388
Andalucia Nuts
  Houston, TX 713-977-9090
Betsy's Best
 888-483-2019
Big Spoon Roasters
  Durham, NC 919-309-9100
Cache Creek Foods LLC
  Woodland, CA 530-662-1764
Crazy Go Nuts
  Fower, CA
Crazy Richard's
  Dublin, OH 614-889-4824
Earth Balance
  Boulder, CO 866-234-6429
East Wind Inc
  Tecumseh, MO 417-679-4682
Eliot's Adult Nut Butters
 503-847-9457
Everland Foods
  Burnaby, BC
Everland Parks
  Burnaby, BC
Farmtrue
  North Stonington, CT 860-495-2231
Feridies
  Courtland, VA 800-544-0896
Food Mill
  Oakland, CA 510-482-3848
Fresh Hemp Foods
  Winnipeg, NB 800-665-4367
Georgia Grinders
  Chamblee, GA
Gopal's Healthfoods
  Sidney, TX 866-646-7257
Healing Home Foods
  Pound Ridge, NY 914-764-1303
Jonny Almond Nut Co
  Flint, MI 810-767-6887
Julie's Real
  Dallas, TX 877-659-4375
Justin's Nut Butter
  Boulder, CO 844-448-0302
Kalot Superfood
  Denver, CO 561-757-6541
Laurel Foods
  Hillsboro, OR 503-692-3663
Legendary Foods
  Pasadena, CA 888-698-1708
Love You Foods
  Flagstaff, AZ 844-693-2662
Maisie Jane's California Sunshine
  Chico, CA 530-899-7909
Marin Food Specialties
  Byron, CA 925-634-6126
Naturally Nutty
  Traverse City, MI 888-224-9988
Nikki's Coconut Butter
  Hudson, WI
Nuttzo
  San Diego, CA 888-325-0553
Once Again Nut Butter
  Nunda, NY 888-800-8075
Pacific Grain & Foods
  Fresno, CA 559-276-2580
Perfect Snacks
  Sorrento Valley, CA 866-628-8548
Premier Organics
  Oakland, CA 866-237-8688
Probar
  Salt Lake City, UT 800-921-2294
Purely Pecans
  Valdosta, GA 800-627-6630
Reginald's Homemade LLC
  Manakin Sabot, VA 804-972-4040
Saratoga Peanut Butter Company
  Saratoga Springs, NY 888-967-3268
Solo Foods
  Countryside, IL 800-328-7656
Soynut Butter Co
  Glenview, IL 847-635-9960
SunButter
  Fargo, ND 877-873-4501
SuperFat
  Beaverton, OR
Tierra Farm
  Valatie, NY 519-392-8300
To Your Health Sprouted Flour Co., Inc.
  Floyd, VA 540-283-9589
Tribe 9 Foods
  Madison, WI 608-257-7216
Winn-Dixie Stores
  Jacksonville, FL 800-967-9105
Z Specialty Food, LLC
  Woodland, CA 800-678-1226

Almond

Argania Butter
  Rancho Palos Verdes, CA
Barney Butter
  Fresno, CA 559-442-1752
Big Spoon Roasters
  Durham, NC 919-309-9100
Buff Bake
  Santa Ana, CA 949-274-9464
COnut Butter
  New Orleans, LA
Crazy Richard's
  Dublin, OH 614-889-4824
Everland Foods
  Burnaby, BC
Georgia Grinders
  Chamblee, GA
GloryBee
  Eugene, OR 800-456-7923
Julie's Real
  Dallas, TX 877-659-4375
Justin's Nut Butter
  Boulder, CO 844-448-0302
Marin Food Specialties
  Byron, CA 925-634-6126
Naturalmond Almond Butter
  Chamblee, GA 866-327-9301
No Cow
  Denver, CO
Noosh Brands
  Simi Valley, CA 805-522-5744
Nuts 'N More
  Providence, RI 844-413-2344
Once Again Nut Butter
  Nunda, NY 888-800-8075
Premier Organics
  Oakland, CA 866-237-8688
To Your Health Sprouted Flour Co., Inc.
  Floyd, VA 540-283-9589

Hazelnut

Fine & Raw Chocolate
  Brooklyn, NY 718-366-3633
Nuts 'N More
  Providence, RI 844-413-2344

Peanut Butter

Algood Food Co
  Louisville, KY 502-637-3631
American Almond Products Co
  Brooklyn, NY 800-825-6663
Azar Nut Co
  El Paso, TX 800-351-8178
Bell Plantation
  Tifton, GA 229-387-7238
Bella Vista Farm
  Lawton, OK 866-237-8526
Big Spoon Roasters
  Durham, NC 919-309-9100
Bnutty
  Merrillville, IN 844-426-8889
Buff Bake
  Santa Ana, CA 949-274-9464
CB's Nuts
  Kingston, WA 360-297-1213
Clements Foods Co
  Oklahoma City, OK 800-654-8355
COnut Butter
  New Orleans, LA
Crazy Richard's
  Dublin, OH 614-889-4824
E.F. Lane & Son
  Oakland, CA 510-569-8980
East Wind Inc
  Tecumseh, MO 417-679-4682
Eliot's Adult Nut Butters
 503-847-9457
G.E. Barbour
  Sussex, NB 506-432-2300
Gardners Candies Inc
  Tyrone, PA 800-242-2639
Georgia Grinders
  Chamblee, GA
Good Spread
  Boulder, CO
HomePlate Peanut Butter
  Austin, TX 512-580-9980
J.M. Smucker Co.
  Orrville, OH 888-550-9555
JER Creative Food Concepts, Inc.
  Commerce, CA 800-350-2462
JMS Specialty Foods
  Ripon, WI 800-535-5437
Justin's Nut Butter
  Boulder, CO 844-448-0302
Krema Nut Co
  Columbus, OH 800-222-4132
Landis Peanut Butter
  Souderton, PA 215-723-9366
Leavitt Corp., The
  Everett, MA 617-389-2600
Lynch Foods
  North York, ON 416-449-5464
Marantha Natural Foods
  San Francisco, CA 866-972-6879
Mrs Annie's Peanut Patch
  Floresville, TX 830-393-7845
Nuts 'N More
  Providence, RI 844-413-2344
Once Again Nut Butter
  Nunda, NY 888-800-8075
Pacific Beach Peanut Butter
  La Mesa, CA 630-329-0792
Peanut Butter & Co.
  New York, NY 866-456-8372
Producers Peanut Company
  Suffolk, VA 800-847-5491
Reginald's Homemade LLC
  Manakin Sabot, VA 804-972-4040
Scott-Bathgate
  Winnipeg, MB 800-216-2990
Sessions Co Inc
  Enterprise, AL 334-393-0200
Simple Foods
  Tonawanda, NY 800-234-8850
Southern Peanut Co Inc
  Dublin, NC 800-330-3141
St Laurent Brothers
  Bay City, MI 800-289-7688
Sunland Inc/Peanut Better
  Portales, NM 575-356-6638
Sweet Harvest Foods
  Rosemount, MN 507-263-8599
Tara Foods
  Atlanta, GA 404-559-0605
Virginia & Spanish Peanut Co
  Providence, RI 800-673-3562

Crunchy

Everland Foods
  Burnaby, BC
International Food Products
  Fenton, MO 800-227-8427

Smooth

International Food Products
  Fenton, MO 800-227-8427

Nut Pastes

American Almond Products Co
  Brooklyn, NY 800-825-6663

Product Categories / Nuts & Nut Butters: Nuts

Amoretti
　Oxnard, CA 800-266-7388
Georgia Nut Co
　Skokie, IL 877-674-2993
Solo Foods
　Countryside, IL 800-328-7656

Almond

Bear Stewart Corp
　Chicago, IL 800-697-2327
Georgia Nut Co
　Skokie, IL 877-674-2993
Putney Pasta
　Brattleboro, VT 800-253-3683

Nuts

A La Carte
　Chicago, IL 800-722-2370
Adams & Brooks Inc
　Los Angeles, CA 213-749-3226
Adkin & Son Associated Food Products
　South Haven, MI 269-637-7450
Albanese Confectionery Group
　Merrillville, IN 800-536-0581
All Wrapped Up
　Plantation, FL 800-891-2194
Alldrin Brothers
　Ballico, CA 209-667-1600
American Almond Products Co
　Brooklyn, NY 800-825-6663
American Key Food Products Inc
　Closter, NJ 877-263-7539
American Nut & Chocolate Co
　Boston, MA 800-797-6887
American Yeast
　Memphis, TN 866-920-9885
Ames International Inc
　Fife, WA 888-469-2637
AnaCon Foods Company
　Atchison, KS 800-328-0291
Andalucia Nuts
　Houston, TX 713-977-9090
Ann's House of Nuts, Inc.
　Columbia, MD 410-309-6887
Archer Daniels Midland Company
　Chicago, IL 312-634-8100
Arizona Cowboy
　Phoenix, AZ 800-529-8627
Arizona Pistachio Company
　Tucson, AZ 800-333-8575
Arway Confections Inc
　Chicago, IL 800-695-0612
Aunt Aggie De's Pralines
　Sinton, TX 800-333-9354
Aurora Products
　Orange, CT 800-398-1048
Azar Nut Co
　El Paso, TX 800-351-8178
Baldwin-Minkler Farms
　Orland, CA 530-865-8080
Balsu
　Bay Harbour Islands, FL 305-993-5045
Barcelona Nut Co
　Baltimore, MD 800-296-6887
Bavarian Nut Co
　Buffalo, NY 716-810-6887
Bazzini Holdings LLC
　Allentown, PA 610-366-1606
Bedemco Inc
　White Plains, NY 914-683-1119
Beer Nuts Co Store-Plant
　Bloomington, IL 309-827-8580
Ben Heggy's Candy Co
　Canton, OH 330-455-7703
Berberian Nut Company
　Chico, CA 530-981-4900
Berson Peanuts
　Opp, AL 334-493-0655
Beta Pure Foods
　Santa Cruz, CA 831-685-6565
Birdsong Corp.
　Suffolk, VA 757-539-3456
Bissinger's Handcrafted Chocolatier
　St. Louis, MO 314-615-2400
Blue Diamond Growers
　Sacramento, CA 800-987-2329
Brooks Peanut Co
　Samson, AL 334-898-7194
Buchanan Hollow Nut Co
　Le Grand, CA 800-532-1500

Buddy Squirrel LLC
　St Francis, WI 800-972-2658
Byrd's Pecans
　Butler, MO 866-679-5583
C J Dannemiller Co
　Norton, OH 800-624-8671
Cache Creek Foods LLC
　Woodland, CA 530-662-1764
Cajun Creole Products Inc
　New Iberia, LA 800-946-8688
Cal-Grown Nut Company
　Hughson, CA 209-883-4081
California Almond Packers
　Modesto, CA 209-549-8262
California Fruit & Nut
　Gustine, CA 888-747-8224
California Independent Almond Growers
　Merced, CA 209-667-4855
California Walnut Co
　Los Molinos, CA 530-527-2616
California Wholesale Nut
　Chico, CA 530-895-0512
Camilla Pecan Company
　Camilla, GA 800-526-8770
Capay Canyon Ranch
　Esparto, CA 530-662-2372
Capco Enterprises
　East Hanover, NJ 800-252-1011
Carolina Cracker
　Garner, NC 919-779-6899
Cheese Straws & More
　Monroe, LA 800-997-1921
Chico Nut Company
　Chico, CA 530-891-1493
CHS Inc.
　Inver Grove Hts., MN 800-328-6539
Clic International Inc
　Laval, QC 450-669-2663
Colorado Nut Co
　Denver, CO 800-876-1625
Commodities Marketing Inc
　Clarksburg, NJ 732-516-0700
Crain Ranch
　Los Molinos, CA 530-527-1077
D Steengrafe Co Inc
　Pleasant Valley, NY 845-635-4067
Dakota Gourmet
　Wahpeton, ND 800-727-6663
Del Rio Nut Company
　Livingston, CA 209-394-7945
Derco Foods Intl
　Fresno, CA 559-435-2664
Desert Pepper Trading Co
　El Paso, TX 888-472-5727
Diamond of California
　San Francisco, CA 415-912-3180
Durey-Libby Edible Nuts
　Carlstadt, NJ 800-332-6887
E.F. Lane & Son
　Oakland, CA 510-569-8980
Edison Grainery
　Benicia, CA 510-382-0202
El Brands
　Ozark, AL 334-445-2828
Elegant Edibles
　Houston, TX 800-227-3226
Everland Foods
　Burnaby, BC
Everland Parks
　Burnaby, BC
Fastachi
　Watertown, MA 800-466-3022
Flanigan Farms
　Culver City, CA 800-525-0228
Foley's Chocolates & Candies
　Richmond, BC 888-236-5397
Ford's Gourmet Foods
　Raleigh, NC 800-446-0947
Frazier Nut Farms Inc
　Waterford, CA 209-522-1406
Fresh Roasted Almond Company
　Warren, MI 877-478-6887
Fun Factory
　Milwaukee, WI 877-894-6767
G Scaccianoce & Co
　Bronx, NY 718-991-4462
GAF Seelig Inc
　Flushing, NY 718-899-5000
Georgia Nut Co
　Skokie, IL 877-674-2993
Germack Pistachio Co
　Detroit, MI 800-872-4006

Glennys
　Brooklyn, NY 888-864-1243
GNS Foods
　Arlington, TX 817-795-4671
Golden Kernel Pecan Co
　Cameron, SC 803-823-2311
Goodart Candy Inc
　Lubbock, TX 806-747-2600
Gourmet Nut
　Brooklyn, NY 347-413-5180
Govadinas Fitness Foods
　San Diego, CA 800-900-0108
Grace & I
　Los Angeles, CA 800-584-1736
Great Northern Maple Products
　Saint Honor, De Shenley, QC 418-485-7777
Guerra Nut Shelling Co Inc
　Hollister, CA 831-637-4471
Gulf Pecan Company
　Mobile, AL 251-661-2931
Gurley's Foods
　Willmar, MN 800-426-7845
H&S Edible Products Corporation
　Mount Vernon, NY 800-253-3364
Hammons Products Co
　Stockton, MO 888-429-6887
Hampton Farms
　Severn, NC 800-313-2748
Hancock Peanut Company
　Courtland, VA 757-653-9351
Harris Farms Inc
　Coalinga, CA 800-311-6211
Haven's Candies
　Westbrook, ME 800-639-6309
Hawaiian King Candies
　Honolulu, HI 800-570-1902
Hazelnut Growers Of Oregon
　Cornelius, OR 800-273-4676
HempNut
　Henderson, NV 707-576-7050
Hialeah Products Co
　Hollywood, FL 800-923-3379
Hickory Farms
　Maumee, OH 800-753-8558
Hickory Harvest Foods
　Akron, OH 800-448-6887
HP Schmid
　San Francisco, CA 415-765-5925
Hubbard Peanut Co Inc
　Sedley, VA 800-889-7688
Idaho Candy Co
　Boise, ID 800-898-6986
International Harvest Inc
　Mt Vernon, NY 800-277-4268
International Service Group
　Alpharetta, GA 770-518-0988
Island Snacks
　Buena Park, CA 714-994-1228
Jardine Ranch
　Paso Robles, CA 866-833-5050
Jason & Son Specialty Foods
　Rancho Cordova, CA 800-810-9093
Jerry's Nut House
　Denver, CO 303-861-2262
Jewel Date Co
　Thermal, CA 760-399-4474
JF Braun & Sons Inc.
　Elizabeth, NJ 800-997-7177
Jimbo's Jumbos Inc
　Edenton, NC 800-334-4771
John B. Sanfilippo & Son
　Elgin, IL 847-289-1800
Kalustyan
　New York, NY 800-352-3451
King Nut Co
　Solon, OH 800-860-5464
Koeze Company
　Grand Rapids, MI 800-555-9688
Krema Nut Co
　Columbus, OH 800-222-4132
Krispy Kernels
　Quebec, QC 877-791-9986
L & S Packing Co
　Farmingdale, NY 800-286-6487
LA Wholesale Produce Market
　Los Angeles, CA 888-454-6887
Laurel Foods
　Hillsboro, OR 503-692-3663
Leavitt Corp., The
　Everett, MA 617-389-2600
Lee Seed Co
　Inwood, IA 800-736-6530

329

Product Categories / Nuts & Nut Butters: Nuts

Legendary Foods
  Pasadena, CA 888-698-1708
Livingston Farmers Assn
  Livingston, CA 209-394-7941
Lodi Nut Company
  Lodi, CA 800-234-6887
Lou-Retta's Custom Chocolates
  Buffalo, NY 716-833-7111
Lowery's Home Made Candies
  Muncie, IN 800-541-3340
Mac Farms Of Hawaii Inc
  Captain Cook, HI 808-328-2435
Majestic Foods
  Huntington, NY 631-424-9444
Marantha Natural Foods
  San Francisco, CA 866-972-6879
Mariani Nut Co
  Winters, CA 530-795-1546
Mavuno Harvest
  Philadelphia, PA
McCleskey Mills
  Smithville, GA 229-846-2003
Merritt Pecan Co
  Weston, GA 800-762-9152
Mezza
  Lake Forest, IL 888-206-6054
Midwest Nut Co
  Minneapolis, MN 800-328-5502
Mister Snacks Inc
  Amherst, NY 800-333-6393
Monte Vista Farming Co
  Denair, CA 209-874-1866
Moonlight Mixes LLC
  Little Rock, AR 501-374-2244
Mound City Shelled Nut Inc
  St Louis, MO 888-338-6887
Mount Franklin Foods
  El Paso, TX 800-351-8178
Mrs. Dog's Products
  Grand Rapids, MI 800-267-7364
Mrs. May's Naturals
  Carson, CA 877-677-6297
Naraghi Group
  Escalon, CA 209-579-5253
Natural Foods Inc
  Toledo, OH 419-537-1711
Nature's Candy
  Fredericksburg, TX 800-729-0085
Nature's Select Inc
  Grand Rapids, MI 888-715-4321
Navarro Pecan Co
  Corsicana, TX 800-333-9507
Naylor Candies Inc
  Mt Wolf, PA 717-266-2706
New Century Snacks
  City of Commerce, CA 800-688-6887
New Nissi Corp.
  Paterson, NJ 973-278-4400
New Organics
  Kenwood, CA 734-677-5570
Nichols Farms
  Hanford, CA 559-584-6811
Nimeks Organics
  Bethlehem, PA 610-997-0500
Northwest Chocolate Factory
  Salem, OR 503-362-1340
Northwest Hazelnut Company
  Hubbard, OR 503-982-8030
Nspired Natural Foods
  Boulder, CO 800-434-4246
Nutorious LLC
  Green Bay, WI. 920-288-0483
Nuts + Nuts
  Brooklyn, NY 347-513-9670
Nutty Bavarian
  Sanford, FL 800-382-4788
Olam Spices
  Fresno, CA 559-447-1390
Old Dominion Peanut Corp
  Norfolk, VA. 800-368-6887
Once Again Nut Butter
  Nunda, NY 888-800-8075
Orangeburg Pecan Co
  Orangeburg, SC 803-534-4277
Organic Planet
  San Francisco, CA 415-765-5590
Original Herkimer Cheese
  Ilion, NY 315-895-7428
Osage Pecan Co
  Butler, MO 800-748-8305
Pacific Gold Marketing
  Arlington, TX 817-795-4671

Panoche Creek Packing
  Fresno, CA 559-449-1721
Papes Pecan House
  Seguin, TX 888-688-7273
Patagonia Provisions
  Sausalito, CA 888-221-8208
Patsy's Candy
  Colorado Springs, CO. 866-372-8797
Peanut Patch Gift Shop
  Courtland, VA 800-544-0896
Peanut Roaster
  Henderson, NC 800-445-1404
Pear's Coffee
  Bellevue, NE. 800-828-7688
Pease's Candy
  Springfield, IL. 217-523-3721
Pecan Deluxe Candy Co
  Dallas, TX. 800-733-3589
Picard Peanuts
  Waterdown, ON 888-244-7688
Pippin Snack Pecans
  Albany, GA 800-554-6887
Pleasant Grove Farms
  Pleasant Grove, CA 916-655-3391
Porkie Company of Wisconsin
  Cudahy, WI. 800-333-2588
Priester's Pecans
  Fort Deposit, AL 866-477-4736
Prince of Peace
  Hayward, CA 800-732-2328
Producers Peanut Company
  Suffolk, VA. 800-847-5491
Quality Nut Co
  Modesto, CA. 209-526-3590
Ramos Orchards
  Winters, CA 530-795-4748
Red River Foods Inc
  Richmond, VA. 804-320-1800
Reed Lang Farms
  Rio Hondo, TX 956-748-2354
Regal Health Food
  Chicago, IL 773-252-1044
Restaurant Data
  Irvington, NY 800-346-9390
Richard Green Company
  Indianapolis, IN 317-972-0941
Roberts Ferry Nut Co
  Waterford, CA. 209-874-3247
Ross-Smith Pecan Company
  Thomasville, GA. 800-841-5503
Rpac LLC
  Los Banos, CA 209-826-0272
Sambets Cajun Deli
  Austin, TX. 800-472-6238
Santa Clara Nut Co
  San Jose, CA. 408-298-2425
Sante Specialty Foods
  Santa Clara, CA 408-451-9585
Scala-Wisell International Inc.
  Floral Park, NY 516-437-8600
Schermer Pecan Co
  Glennville, GA 800-841-3403
Service Packing Company
  Vancouver, BC 604-681-0264
Setton Farms
  Terra Bella, CA 559-535-6050
Setton International Foods
  Commack, NY 800-227-4397
Severn Peanut Co
  Severn, NC 252-585-1744
Shields Date Garden
  Indio, CA. 800-414-2555
Shoei Foods USA Inc
  Olivehurst, CA. 530-237-1295
Sivetz Coffee
  Corvallis, OR 541-753-9713
Snackerz
  Commerce, CA. 888-576-2253
Society Hill Snacks
  Philadelphia, PA 800-595-0050
Sole Grano LLC
  Fair Lawn, NJ 201-797-7100
Solnuts
  Hudson, IA 800-648-3503
South Bend Chocolate Co
  South Bend, IN 800-301-4961
South Georgia Pecan Co
  Valdosta, GA 800-627-6630
South Valley Farms
  Wasco, CA 661-391-9000
Southern Peanut Co Inc
  Dublin, NC 800-330-3141

Southern Season
  Chapel Hill, NC 877-929-7133
Southern Style Nuts
  Denison, TX 903-463-3161
Specialty Commodities Inc
  Fargo, ND 701-282-8222
Sprucewood Handmade Cookie Company
  Warkworth, ON 877-632-1300
Squirrel Brand Company
  McKinney, TX 800-624-8242
St Laurent Brothers
  Bay City, MI 800-289-7688
Stahmann Farms
  La Mesa, NM 575-526-2453
Star Snacks
  Jersey City, NJ 888-782-7688
Stone Mountain Pecan Co
  Monroe, GA 800-633-6887
Sugai Kona Coffee
  Holualoa, HI 808-322-7717
Sun Empire Foods
  Kerman, CA 800-252-4786
Sun-Maid Growers of California
  Kingsburg, CA 559-896-8000
Sunny South Pecan Company
  Statesboro, GA 800-764-3687
Sunnyland Farms
  Albany, GA 800-999-2488
Sunray Food Products Corporation
  Bronx, NY 718-548-2255
Sunridge Farms
  Royal Oaks, CA 831-786-7000
Sunridge Farms Inc
  Salinas, CA 831-755-1530
Sunshine Nut Company
  Lewes, DE. 210-732-9460
SunWest Foods, Inc.
  Davis, CA 530-758-8550
Superior Nut & Candy
  Chicago, IL 800-843-2238
Superior Nut Company
  Cambridge, MA 800-251-6060
Superior Pecans
  Eufaula, AL 800-628-2350
Swerseys Chocolate
  Brooklyn, NY 718-497-8800
T M Duche Nut Co
  Orland, CA 530-865-5511
Tejon Ranch Co
  Lebec, CA 661-248-3000
Terri Lynn Inc
  Elgin, IL 800-323-0775
Thanasi Foods LLC
  Boulder, CO 866-558-7379
The Kroger Co.
  Murray, KY 800-632-6900
The Peanut Butter Shop of Williamsburg
  Toano, VA 800-831-1828
Thunderbird Real Food Bar
  Austin, TX. 512-383-8334
Timber Crest Farms
  Healdsburg, CA 888-766-4233
To Your Health Sprouted Flour Co., Inc.
  Floyd, VA 540-283-9589
Todd's
  Vernon, CA 800-938-6337
Torn & Glasser
  Los Angeles, CA. 800-282-6887
Torn Ranch
  Novato, CA. 707-796-7800
Tracy Luckey Pecans
  Harlem, GA 800-476-4796
Treehouse Farms
  Elgin, AZ. 559-757-5020
Trophy Nut Co
  Tipp City, OH 800-219-9004
Tropical Foods
  Charlotte, NC 800-438-4470
Tropical Foods
  Lithia Springs, GA 800-544-3762
Tropical Nut & Fruit Co
  Orlando, FL 800-749-8869
Tucker Pecan Co
  Montgomery, AL 800-239-6540
Twenty First Century Snacks
  Ronkonkoma, NY 800-975-2883
UTZ Quality Foods Inc.
  Hanover, PA 800-367-7629
Vending Nut Co
  Fort Worth, TX 800-429-9260
Virginia & Spanish Peanut Co
  Providence, RI 800-673-3562

Product Categories / Nuts & Nut Butters: Nuts

Virginia Diner Inc
   Wakefield, VA 888-823-4637
Warner Candy
   El Paso, TX 847-928-7200
Warrell Corp
   Camp Hill, PA 800-233-7082
Waymouth Farms Inc
   Minneapolis, MN 800-527-0094
Weaver Nut Co. Inc.
   Ephrata, PA 800-473-2688
Westnut
   Cornelius, OR 800-382-5339
Whaley Pecan Co Inc
   Troy, AL 800-824-6827
Whitley Peanut Factory Inc
   Hayes, VA 800-470-2244
Willamette Valley Walnuts
   McMinnville, OR 503-472-3215
Willmar Cookie & Nut Company
   Willmar, MN 800-426-7845
Wisconsin Cheeseman
   Madison, WI 800-693-0834
Wolfies Roasted Nut Co
   Findlay, OH 419-423-1355
Wonderful Pistachios & Almonds
   Lost Hills, CA 661-797-6500
Young Pecan
   Las Cruces, NM 575-524-4321
Young Pecan, Inc.
   Florence, SC 800-729-6003
Zenobia Co
   Bronx, NY 866-936-6242
Zuccaro Produce
   Columbia Heights, MN 612-333-1122

Almonds

AgStandard Smoked Almonds
   Los Angeles, CA
Alldrin Brothers
   Ballico, CA 209-667-1600
Almond Brothers
   Pheonix, AZ 602-955-0909
American Almond Products Co
   Brooklyn, NY 800-825-6663
American Key Food Products Inc
   Closter, NJ 877-263-7539
Baldwin-Minkler Farms
   Orland, CA 530-865-8080
Barcelona Nut Co
   Baltimore, MD 800-296-6887
Bavarian Nut Co
   Buffalo, NY 716-810-6887
Bedemco Inc
   White Plains, NY 914-683-1119
Bobalu Nuts
   CA 805-223-0919
Buchanan Hollow Nut Co
   Le Grand, CA 800-532-1500
Cache Creek Foods LLC
   Woodland, CA. 530-662-1764
Cal-Grown Nut Company
   Hughson, CA 209-883-4081
California Almond Packers
   Modesto, CA. 209-549-8262
California Independent Almond Growers
   Merced, CA 209-667-4855
Capay Canyon Ranch
   Esparto, CA. 530-662-2372
Capco Enterprises
   East Hanover, NJ. 800-252-1011
Charles H Baldwin & Sons
   West Stockbridge, MA 413-232-7785
Chico Nut Company
   Chico, CA. 530-891-1493
Chocolate Moon
   Asheville, NC 800-723-1236
Commodities Marketing Inc
   Clarksburg, NJ 732-516-0700
Creative Snacks Co LLC
   Greensboro, NC 336-668-4151
Del Rio Nut Company
   Livingston, CA 209-394-7945
Durey-Libby Edible Nuts
   Carlstadt, NJ 800-332-6887
Equal Exchange Inc
   West Bridgewater, MA 774-776-7400
Erba Food Products
   Brooklyn, NY 718-272-7700
Fastachi
   Watertown, MA. 800-466-3022
Foley's Chocolates & Candies
   Richmond, BC 888-236-5397

Frazier Nut Farms Inc
   Waterford, CA. 209-522-1406
Fresh Roasted Almond Company
   Warren, MI 877-478-6887
G Scaccianoce & Co
   Bronx, NY. 718-991-4462
Gourmet Nut
   Brooklyn, NY 347-413-5180
Harris Farms Inc
   Coalinga, CA 800-311-6211
Healing Home Foods
   Pound Ridge, NY 914-764-1303
Hialeah Products Co
   Hollywood, FL 800-923-3379
Hughson Nut Inc
   Hughson, CA. 209-883-0403
Jardine Ranch
   Paso Robles, CA 866-833-5050
Jasmine Vineyards, Inc.
   Delano, CA 661-792-2141
Jerry's Nut House
   Denver, CO 303-861-2262
John B. Sanfilippo & Son
   Elgin, IL 847-289-1800
Krema Nut Co
   Columbus, OH 800-222-4132
Legendary Foods
   Pasadena, CA 888-698-1708
Livingston Farmers Assn
   Livingston, CA 209-394-7941
Lodi Nut Company
   Lodi, CA 800-234-6887
Lou-Retta's Custom Chocolates
   Buffalo, NY 716-833-7111
Maisie Jane's California Sunshine
   Chico, CA 530-899-7909
Mariani Nut Co
   Winters, CA 530-795-1546
Monte Vista Farming Co
   Denair, CA 209-874-1866
Naraghi Group
   Escalon, CA 209-579-5253
Navitas Naturals
   Novato, CA 888-645-4282
Nichols Farms
   Hanford, CA 559-584-6811
NOW Foods
   Bloomingdale, IL 888-669-3663
Nunes Farms Marketing
   Gustine, CA 209-862-3033
Nut Factory
   Spokane Valley, WA 888-239-5288
Nuts About You
   Los Angeles, CA
Nutty Bavarian
   Sanford, FL 800-382-4788
Olomomo Nut Company
   Boulder, CO 877-923-6888
Omega Nutrition
   Bellingham, WA 800-661-3529
Once Again Nut Butter
   Nunda, NY 888-800-8075
Organic Planet
   San Francisco, CA 415-765-5590
Osage Pecan Co
   Butler, MO 800-748-8305
P R Farms Inc
   Clovis, CA 559-299-0201
Pacific Gold Marketing
   Arlington, TX 817-795-4671
Panoche Creek Packing
   Fresno, CA 559-449-1721
Patterson Vegetable Company
   Patterson, CA 209-892-2611
Pearl Crop
   Stockton, CA 209-808-7575
Pleasant Grove Farms
   Pleasant Grove, CA 916-655-3391
Primex International Trading
   Los Angeles, CA 310-410-7100
Q's Nuts
   Somerville, MA 617-764-3741
Ramos Orchards
   Winters, CA 530-795-4748
Red River Foods Inc
   Richmond, VA 804-320-1800
Roberts Ferry Nut Co
   Waterford, CA 209-874-3247
Rotteveel Orchards
   Dixon, CA 707-678-1495
Rpac LLC
   Los Banos, CA 209-826-0272

Select Harvest USA
   Turlock, CA 209-668-2471
Service Packing Company
   Vancouver, BC 604-681-0264
Setton International Foods
   Commack, NY 800-227-4397
Simple Foods
   Tonawanda, NY 800-234-8850
South Valley Farms
   Wasco, CA 661-391-9000
Southern Style Nuts
   Denison, TX 903-463-3161
Sunridge Farms
   Royal Oaks, CA 831-786-7000
SunWest Foods, Inc.
   Davis, CA 530-758-8550
T M Duche Nut Co
   Orland, CA 530-865-5511
Tejon Ranch Co
   Lebec, CA 661-248-3000
Terri Lynn Inc
   Elgin, IL 800-323-0775
The Mapled Nut Co.
   Morrisville, VT 800-726-4661
Timber Crest Farms
   Healdsburg, CA 888-766-4233
To Your Health Sprouted Flour Co., Inc.
   Floyd, VA 540-283-9589
Treehouse Farms
   Elgin, AZ 559-757-5020
Unique Ingredients LLC
   Gold Canyon, AZ 480-983-2498
Weaver Nut Co. Inc.
   Ephrata, PA 800-473-2688
Whitley Peanut Factory Inc
   Hayes, VA 800-470-2244
Wild Things Snacks
   Seattle, WA 720-231-9196
Wolfies Roasted Nut Co
   Findlay, OH 419-423-1355
Wonderful Pistachios & Almonds
   Lost Hills, CA 661-797-6500

Salted

Cache Creek Foods LLC
   Woodland, CA. 530-662-1764
Hialeah Products Co
   Hollywood, FL 800-923-3379
NOW Foods
   Bloomingdale, IL 888-669-3663
Setton International Foods
   Commack, NY 800-227-4397
Terri Lynn Inc
   Elgin, IL 800-323-0775

Brazil

American Almond Products Co
   Brooklyn, NY 800-825-6663
Bedemco Inc
   White Plains, NY 914-683-1119
Cache Creek Foods LLC
   Woodland, CA. 530-662-1764
Durey-Libby Edible Nuts
   Carlstadt, NJ 800-332-6887
Hialeah Products Co
   Hollywood, FL 800-923-3379
LA Wholesale Produce Market
   Los Angeles, CA 888-454-6887
NOW Foods
   Bloomingdale, IL 888-669-3663
Setton International Foods
   Commack, NY 800-227-4397
Terri Lynn Inc
   Elgin, IL 800-323-0775
Weaver Nut Co. Inc.
   Ephrata, PA 800-473-2688

Cashews

American Almond Products Co
   Brooklyn, NY 800-825-6663
American Key Food Products Inc
   Closter, NJ. 877-263-7539
Bavarian Nut Co
   Buffalo, NY. 716-810-6887
Bedemco Inc
   White Plains, NY 914-683-1119
Cache Creek Foods LLC
   Woodland, CA. 530-662-1764
California Fruit & Nut
   Gustine, CA 888-747-8224

Product Categories / Nuts & Nut Butters: Nuts

Commodities Marketing Inc
   Clarksburg, NJ 732-516-0700
Dan-D Foods Ltd
   Richmond, BC 800-633-4788
Durey-Libby Edible Nuts
   Carlstadt, NJ 800-332-6887
Earth Circle Organics
   Auburn, CA 877-922-3663
Equal Exchange Inc
   West Bridgewater, MA 774-776-7400
Fastachi
   Watertown, MA 800-466-3022
Fresh Roasted Almond Company
   Warren, MI 877-478-6887
Germack Pistachio Co
   Detroit, MI 800-872-4006
Gourmet Nut
   Brooklyn, NY 347-413-5180
Healing Home Foods
   Pound Ridge, NY 914-764-1303
Hialeah Products Co
   Hollywood, FL 800-923-3379
Jerry's Nut House
   Denver, CO 303-861-2262
John B. Sanfilippo & Son
   Elgin, IL 847-289-1800
Karma Nuts
   Dublin, CA 925-961-5491
Koeze Company
   Grand Rapids, MI 800-555-9688
Krema Nut Co
   Columbus, OH 800-222-4132
LA Wholesale Produce Market
   Los Angeles, CA 888-454-6887
Landies Candies Co
   Buffalo, NY 800-955-2634
Lou-Retta's Custom Chocolates
   Buffalo, NY 716-833-7111
Marantha Natural Foods
   San Francisco, CA 866-972-6879
Maxwell's Gourmet Food
   Raleigh, NC 800-952-6887
Navitas Naturals
   Novato, CA 888-645-4282
Naylor Candies Inc
   Mt Wolf, PA 717-266-2706
New Organics
   Kenwood, CA 734-677-5570
NOW Foods
   Bloomingdale, IL 888-669-3663
Nut Factory
   Spokane Valley, WA 888-239-5288
Nuts & Stems
   Rosharon, TX 281-464-6887
Nutty Bavarian
   Sanford, FL 800-382-4788
Olomomo Nut Company
   Boulder, CO 877-923-6888
Once Again Nut Butter
   Nunda, NY 888-800-8075
Organic Planet
   San Francisco, CA 415-765-5590
Osage Pecan Co
   Butler, MO 800-748-8305
Pacific Gold Marketing
   Arlington, TX 817-795-4671
Q's Nuts
   Somerville, MA 617-764-3741
Restaurant Data
   Irvington, NY 800-346-9390
Setton International Foods
   Commack, NY 800-227-4397
Southern Style Nuts
   Denison, TX 903-463-3161
Sunfood
   El Cajon, CA 888-729-3663
Sunray Food Products Corporation
   Bronx, NY 718-548-2255
Sunridge Farms
   Royal Oaks, CA 831-786-7000
Terri Lynn Inc
   Elgin, IL 800-323-0775
The Mapled Nut Co.
   Morrisville, VT 800-726-4661
To Your Health Sprouted Flour Co., Inc.
   Floyd, VA 540-283-9589
Tropical Foods
   Lithia Springs, GA 800-544-3762
Weaver Nut Co. Inc.
   Ephrata, PA 800-473-2688
Wolfies Roasted Nut Co
   Findlay, OH 419-423-1355

Chestnuts
Adkin & Son Associated Food Products
   South Haven, MI 269-637-7450

Coated
Golden Kernel Pecan Co
   Cameron, SC 803-823-2311
Wolfies Roasted Nut Co
   Findlay, OH 419-423-1355

Chocolate
Bazzini Holdings LLC
   Allentown, PA 610-366-1606
Bissinger's Handcrafted Chocolatier
   St. Louis, MO 314-615-2400
Jerry's Nut House
   Denver, CO 303-861-2262
Lowery's Home Made Candies
   Muncie, IN 800-541-3340
Osage Pecan Co
   Butler, MO 800-748-8305
Ripple Brand Collective
   Congers, NY 845-353-1251
Schermer Pecan Co
   Glennville, GA 800-841-3403
Weaver Nut Co. Inc.
   Ephrata, PA 800-473-2688

Yogurt
GKI Foods
   Brighton, MI 248-486-0055
Jerry's Nut House
   Denver, CO 303-861-2262
Setton International Foods
   Commack, NY 800-227-4397
Terri Lynn Inc
   Elgin, IL 800-323-0775

Filberts
American Almond Products Co
   Brooklyn, NY 800-825-6663
Cache Creek Foods LLC
   Woodland, CA 530-662-1764
Commodities Marketing Inc
   Clarksburg, NJ 732-516-0700
Durey-Libby Edible Nuts
   Carlstadt, NJ 800-332-6887
Erba Food Products
   Brooklyn, NY 718-272-7700
Germack Pistachio Co
   Detroit, MI 800-872-4006
Hialeah Products Co
   Hollywood, FL 800-923-3379
Jerry's Nut House
   Denver, CO 303-861-2262
Krema Nut Co
   Columbus, OH 800-222-4132
Nut Factory
   Spokane Valley, WA 888-239-5288
Organic Planet
   San Francisco, CA 415-765-5590
Setton International Foods
   Commack, NY 800-227-4397
Terri Lynn Inc
   Elgin, IL 800-323-0775
Weaver Nut Co. Inc.
   Ephrata, PA 800-473-2688

Glazed & Coated
Arway Confections Inc
   Chicago, IL 800-695-0612
Bazzini Holdings LLC
   Allentown, PA 610-366-1606
Betty Lou's
   McMinnville, OR 800-242-5205
Bissinger's Handcrafted Chocolatier
   St. Louis, MO 314-615-2400
Cache Creek Foods LLC
   Woodland, CA 530-662-1764
Cheese Straws & More
   Monroe, LA 800-997-1921
Chocolate Moon
   Asheville, NC 800-723-1236
Crown Candy Corp
   Macon, GA 800-241-3529
Dillon Candy Co
   Boston, GA 800-382-8338
Farr Candy Company
   Idaho Falls, ID 208-522-8215
Foley's Chocolates & Candies
   Richmond, BC 888-236-5397
G Scaccianoce & Co
   Bronx, NY 718-991-4462
GKI Foods
   Brighton, MI 248-486-0055
Golden Kernel Pecan Co
   Cameron, SC 803-823-2311
Goodart Candy Inc
   Lubbock, TX 806-747-2600
Haven's Candies
   Westbrook, ME 800-639-6309
Jason & Son Specialty Foods
   Rancho Cordova, CA 800-810-9093
Jerry's Nut House
   Denver, CO 303-861-2262
Kay Foods Co
   Detroit, MI 313-393-1100
King Nut Co
   Solon, OH 800-860-5464
Knudsen Candy
   Hayward, CA 800-736-6887
Layman Distributing
   Salem, VA 800-237-1319
Lowery's Home Made Candies
   Muncie, IN 800-541-3340
Mac Farms Of Hawaii Inc
   Captain Cook, HI 808-328-2435
Marich Confectionery
   Hollister, CA 800-624-7055
Matangos Candies
   Harrisburg, PA 717-234-0882
Midwest Nut Co
   Minneapolis, MN 800-328-5502
Moore's Candies
   Baltimore, MD 410-836-8840
Mrs Annie's Peanut Patch
   Floresville, TX 830-393-7845
Muth's Candy Store
   Louisville, KY 502-582-2639
Nature's Candy
   Fredericksburg, TX 800-729-0085
Naylor Candies Inc
   Mt Wolf, PA 717-266-2706
Northwest Chocolate Factory
   Salem, OR 503-362-1340
Nuts About You
   Los Angeles, CA
Nutty Bavarian
   Sanford, FL 800-382-4788
Old Dominion Peanut Corp
   Norfolk, VA 800-368-6887
Pippin Snack Pecans
   Albany, GA 800-554-6887
Popcorn Connection
   North Hollywood, CA 800-852-2676
Priester's Pecans
   Fort Deposit, AL 866-477-4736
Prince of Peace
   Hayward, CA 800-732-2328
Setton International Foods
   Commack, NY 800-227-4397
Southern Style Nuts
   Denison, TX 903-463-3161
St Laurent Brothers
   Bay City, MI 800-289-7688
Superior Nut & Candy
   Chicago, IL 800-843-2238
Terri Lynn Inc
   Elgin, IL 800-323-0775
Tom & Sally's Handmade Chocolates
   Brattleboro, VT 800-827-0800
Tonex
   Wallington, NJ 973-773-5135
Tropical Nut Fruit & Bulk Cndy
   Lithia Springs, GA 800-544-3762
Warrell Corp
   Camp Hill, PA 844-234-3217
Waymouth Farms Inc
   Minneapolis, MN 800-527-0094
Weaver Nut Co. Inc.
   Ephrata, PA 800-473-2688
Webb's Candy
   Davenport, FL 800-289-9322
Whitley Peanut Factory Inc
   Hayes, VA 800-470-2244
Wolfies Roasted Nut Co
   Findlay, OH 419-423-1355

Hazelnuts
Balsu
   Bay Harbour Islands, FL 305-993-5045

Product Categories / Nuts & Nut Butters: Nuts

Bedemco Inc
  White Plains, NY 914-683-1119
Cache Creek Foods LLC
  Woodland, CA....................530-662-1764
Commodities Marketing Inc
  Clarksburg, NJ 732-516-0700
Fancy's Candy's
  Rougemont, NC 888-403-2629
Fastachi
  Watertown, MA...................800-466-3022
Hazelnut Growers Of Oregon
  Cornelius, OR....................800-273-4676
Hazy Grove Nuts
  Portland, OR.....................800-574-6887
Hialeah Products Co
  Hollywood, FL....................800-923-3379
Jerry's Nut House
  Denver, CO......................303-861-2262
Krema Nut Co
  Columbus, OH...................800-222-4132
LA Wholesale Produce Market
  Los Angeles, CA..................888-454-6887
Northwest Chocolate Factory
  Salem, OR.......................503-362-1340
Northwest Hazelnut Company
  Hubbard, OR.....................503-982-8030
Omega Nutrition
  Bellingham, WA..................800-661-3529
Organic Planet
  San Francisco, CA................415-765-5590
Setton International Foods
  Commack, NY....................800-227-4397
Terri Lynn Inc
  Elgin, IL.........................800-323-0775
Westnut
  Cornelius, OR....................800-382-5339

Macadamia

American Key Food Products Inc
  Closter, NJ......................877-263-7539
Bedemco Inc
  White Plains, NY 914-683-1119
Cache Creek Foods LLC
  Woodland, CA....................530-662-1764
Durey-Libby Edible Nuts
  Carlstadt, NJ 800-332-6887
Hawaiian Host Inc
  Honolulu, HI.....................888-414-4678
Hawaiian Sun Products
  Honolulu, HI.....................808-845-3211
Hialeah Products Co
  Hollywood, FL....................800-923-3379
Island Princess
  Honolulu, HI.....................866-872-8601
Jerry's Nut House
  Denver, CO......................303-861-2262
Koeze Company
  Grand Rapids, MI.................800-555-9688
Legendary Foods
  Pasadena, CA....................888-698-1708
Lodi Nut Company
  Lodi, CA.........................800-234-6887
Mac Farms Of Hawaii Inc
  Captain Cook, HI.................808-328-2435
Menehune Mac
  Honolulu, HI.....................808-841-3344
NOW Foods
  Bloomingdale, IL..................888-669-3663
Organic Planet
  San Francisco, CA................415-765-5590
Prince of Peace
  Hayward, CA....................800-732-2328
Royal Hawaiian Orchards LP
  Dana Point, CA..................949-661-6304
Setton International Foods
  Commack, NY....................800-227-4397
Sugai Kona Coffee
  Holualoa, HI.....................808-322-7717
Terri Lynn Inc
  Elgin, IL.........................800-323-0775

Mixed Nuts

Bavarian Nut Co
  Buffalo, NY......................716-810-6887
Bazzini Holdings LLC
  Allentown, PA....................610-366-1606
Cibo Vita
  Totowa, NJ......................862-238-8020
Crazy Jerrys Inc Kahuna-Sauces
  Woodstock, GA..................800-347-2823

Gopal's Healthfoods
  Sidney, TX......................866-646-7257
Gourmet Nut
  Brooklyn, NY....................347-413-5180
Jerry's Nut House
  Denver, CO......................303-861-2262
Moonlight Mixes LLC
  Little Rock, AR...................501-374-2244
Nichols Farms
  Hanford, CA.....................559-584-6811
Osage Pecan Co
  Butler, MO......................800-748-8305
Sunridge Farms
  Royal Oaks, CA..................831-786-7000
Swerseys Chocolate
  Brooklyn, NY....................718-497-8800
The Mapled Nut Co.
  Morrisville, VT...................800-726-4661
Wisconsin Cheeseman
  Madison, WI.....................800-693-0834

Nut Meats

American Almond Products Co
  Brooklyn, NY....................800-825-6663
Baldwin-Minkler Farms
  Orland, CA......................530-865-8080
Cache Creek Foods LLC
  Woodland, CA....................530-662-1764
Durey-Libby Edible Nuts
  Carlstadt, NJ 800-332-6887
Hammons Products Co
  Stockton, MO...................888-429-6887
Jerry's Nut House
  Denver, CO......................303-861-2262
King Nut Co
  Solon, OH.......................800-860-5464
Mid Valley Nut Co
  Hughson, CA....................209-883-4491
Mother Earth Enterprises
  New York, NY...................866-436-7688
Service Packing Company
  Vancouver, BC..................604-681-0264
Setton International Foods
  Commack, NY....................800-227-4397
Superior Nut & Candy
  Chicago, IL......................800-843-2238
Superior Pecans
  Eufaula, AL.....................800-628-2350
Terri Lynn Inc
  Elgin, IL.........................800-323-0775
Waymouth Farms Inc
  Minneapolis, MN.................800-527-0094
Whaley Pecan Co Inc
  Troy, AL........................800-824-6827
Willamette Valley Walnuts
  McMinnville, OR.................503-472-3215
Young Pecan, Inc.
  Florence, SC....................800-729-6003

Nut Products

Georgia Nut Co
  Skokie, IL.......................877-674-2993
NutRaw Foods
  Delano, CA
Nuts 'N More
  Providence, RI...................844-413-2344
Royal Hawaiian Orchards LP
  Dana Point, CA..................949-661-6304
Two Moms In The Raw
  Longmont, CO...................720-221-8555
Wisconsin Cheeseman
  Madison, WI.....................800-693-0834

Peanuts

Barcelona Nut Co
  Baltimore, MD...................800-296-6887
Bavarian Nut Co
  Buffalo, NY......................716-810-6887
Belmont Peanuts-Southampton
  Capron, VA.....................434-658-4613
Berson Peanuts
  Opp, AL........................334-493-0655
E.F. Lane & Son
  Oakland, CA....................510-569-8980
Feridies
  Courtland, VA...................866-732-6883
Hampton Farms
  Severn, NC.....................800-313-2748
Hardy Farms
  Hawkinsville, GA.................888-368-6887

Jerry's Nut House
  Denver, CO......................303-861-2262
Kameda USA Inc.
  Torrance, CA....................310-944-9639
Koeze Company
  Grand Rapids, MI.................800-555-9688
Krema Nut Co
  Columbus, OH...................800-222-4132
New Organics
  Kenwood, CA....................734-677-5570
Osage Pecan Co
  Butler, MO......................800-748-8305
Peanut Corporation of America
  Lynchburg, VA...................434-384-7098
Peanut Processors Inc
  Dublin, NC......................800-330-3141
Peanut Shop
  Toano, VA......................800-637-3268
Q's Nuts
  Somerville, MA..................617-764-3741
Queensway Foods Company
  Burlingame, CA..................650-871-7770
Royal Oak Peanuts
  Drewryville, VA..................800-608-4590
Setton International Foods
  Commack, NY....................800-227-4397
Southern Peanut Co Inc
  Dublin, NC......................800-330-3141
Sunfood
  El Cajon, CA....................888-729-3663
Terri Lynn Inc
  Elgin, IL.........................800-323-0775
Virginia Diner Inc
  Wakefield, VA...................888-823-4637
Wolfies Roasted Nut Co
  Findlay, OH.....................419-423-1355

Granulated

American Almond Products Co
  Brooklyn, NY....................800-825-6663
American Key Food Products Inc
  Closter, NJ......................877-263-7539
Cajun Creole Products Inc
  New Iberia, LA...................800-946-8688
Hialeah Products Co
  Hollywood, FL....................800-923-3379
Producers Peanut Company
  Suffolk, VA......................800-847-5491
Terri Lynn Inc
  Elgin, IL.........................800-323-0775

Raw

American Almond Products Co
  Brooklyn, NY....................800-825-6663
Birdsong Corp.
  Suffolk, VA......................757-539-3456
Cajun Creole Products Inc
  New Iberia, LA...................800-946-8688
Hialeah Products Co
  Hollywood, FL....................800-923-3379
Krema Nut Co
  Columbus, OH...................800-222-4132
LA Wholesale Produce Market
  Los Angeles, CA..................888-454-6887
St Laurent Brothers
  Bay City, MI.....................800-289-7688

Raw & Shelled

American Key Food Products Inc
  Closter, NJ......................877-263-7539
Cajun Creole Products Inc
  New Iberia, LA...................800-946-8688
Feridies
  Courtland, VA...................866-732-6883
Hialeah Products Co
  Hollywood, FL....................800-923-3379
King Nut Co
  Solon, OH.......................800-860-5464
McCleskey Mills
  Smithville, GA...................229-846-2003
New Organics
  Kenwood, CA....................734-677-5570
Royal Oak Peanuts
  Drewryville, VA..................800-608-4590
Setton International Foods
  Commack, NY....................800-227-4397
Southern Peanut Co Inc
  Dublin, NC......................800-330-3141
Terri Lynn Inc
  Elgin, IL.........................800-323-0775

Product Categories / Nuts & Nut Butters: Nuts

Roasted

American Almond Products Co
  Brooklyn, NY 800-825-6663
C J Dannemiller Co
  Norton, OH 800-624-8671
Cajun Creole Products Inc
  New Iberia, LA 800-946-8688
E.F. Lane & Son
  Oakland, CA 510-569-8980
King Nut Co
  Solon, OH 800-860-5464
Naylor Candies Inc
  Mt Wolf, PA 717-266-2706
Queensway Foods Company
  Burlingame, CA 650-871-7770
Southern Peanut Co Inc
  Dublin, NC 800-330-3141
St Laurent Brothers
  Bay City, MI 800-289-7688

Salted

Cajun Creole Products Inc
  New Iberia, LA 800-946-8688
Durey-Libby Edible Nuts
  Carlstadt, NJ 800-332-6887
Feridies
  Courtland, VA 866-732-6883
Hialeah Products Co
  Hollywood, FL 800-923-3379
Koeze Company
  Grand Rapids, MI 800-555-9688
LA Wholesale Produce Market
  Los Angeles, CA 888-454-6887
New Organics
  Kenwood, CA 734-677-5570
Setton International Foods
  Commack, NY 800-227-4397
Southern Peanut Co Inc
  Dublin, NC 800-330-3141
St Laurent Brothers
  Bay City, MI 800-289-7688
Terri Lynn Inc
  Elgin, IL 800-323-0775
Virginia & Spanish Peanut Co
  Providence, RI 800-673-3562
Virginia Diner Inc
  Wakefield, VA 888-823-4637

Pecan

American Key Food Products Inc
  Closter, NJ 877-263-7539
Aunt Aggie De's Pralines
  Sinton, TX 800-333-9354
Bavarian Nut Co
  Buffalo, NY 716-810-6887
Bedemco Inc
  White Plains, NY 914-683-1119
Cache Creek Foods LLC
  Woodland, CA 530-662-1764
Carolina Cracker
  Garner, NC 919-779-6899
Carolyn's Gourmet
  Concord, MA 800-656-2940
Cheese Straws & More
  Monroe, LA 800-997-1921
Claxton Bakery Inc
  Claxton, GA 800-841-4211
Country Estate Pecans
  Goldwaite, TX 800-473-2267
Durey-Libby Edible Nuts
  Carlstadt, NJ 800-332-6887
Elegant Edibles
  Houston, TX 800-227-3226
Fancy's Candy's
  Rougemont, NC 888-403-2629
Fresh Roasted Almond Company
  Warren, MI 877-478-6887
George's Candy Shop Inc
  Mobile, AL 800-633-1306
Golden Harvest Pecans
  Cairo, GA 800-597-0968
Golden Kernel Pecan Co
  Cameron, SC 803-823-2311
Green Valley Pecan Company
  Sahuarita, AZ 520-791-2880
Gulf Pecan Company
  Mobile, AL 251-661-2931
Healing Home Foods
  Pound Ridge, NY 914-764-1303
Hialeah Products Co
  Hollywood, FL 800-923-3379
Indianola Pecan House Inc
  Indianola, MS 800-541-6252
Jewel Date Co
  Thermal, CA 760-399-4474
John B. Sanfilippo & Son
  Elgin, IL 847-289-1800
Koeze Company
  Grand Rapids, MI 800-555-9688
Krema Nut Co
  Columbus, OH 800-222-4132
Landies Candies Co
  Buffalo, NY 800-955-2634
Lane Southern Orchards
  Fort Valley, GA 800-277-3224
Lou-Retta's Custom Chocolates
  Buffalo, NY 716-833-7111
Maxwell's Gourmet Food
  Raleigh, NC 800-952-6887
Merritt Pecan Co
  Weston, GA 800-762-9152
Mingo River Pecan Company
  Florence, SC 800-440-6442
Mountain States Pecan
  Roswell, NM 575-623-2216
Navarro Pecan Co
  Corsicana, TX 800-333-9507
New Organics
  Kenwood, CA 734-677-5570
NOW Foods
  Bloomingdale, IL 888-669-3663
Nutty Bavarian
  Sanford, FL 800-382-4788
Orangeburg Pecan Co
  Orangeburg, SC 803-534-4277
Osage Pecan Co
  Butler, MO 800-748-8305
Papes Pecan House
  Seguin, TX 888-688-7273
Pippin Snack Pecans
  Albany, GA 800-554-6887
Priester's Pecans
  Fort Deposit, AL 866-477-4736
Q's Nuts
  Somerville, MA 617-764-3741
Reed Lang Farms
  Rio Hondo, TX 956-748-2354
Ross-Smith Pecan Company
  Thomasville, GA 800-841-5503
Schermer Pecan Co
  Glennville, GA 800-841-3403
Setton International Foods
  Commack, NY 800-227-4397
South Georgia Pecan Co
  Valdosta, GA 800-627-6630
Southern Style Nuts
  Denison, TX 903-463-3161
Stahmann Farms
  La Mesa, NM 575-526-2453
Stone Mountain Pecan Co
  Monroe, GA 800-633-6887
Sunny South Pecan Company
  Statesboro, GA 800-764-3687
Sunnyland Farms
  Albany, GA 800-999-2488
Sunridge Farms
  Royal Oaks, CA 831-786-7000
SunWest Foods, Inc.
  Davis, CA 530-758-8550
Superior Pecans
  Eufaula, AL 800-628-2350
Terri Lynn Inc
  Elgin, IL 800-323-0775
The Mapled Nut Co.
  Morrisville, VT 800-726-4661
Tracy Luckey Pecans
  Harlem, GA 800-476-4796
Tucker Pecan Co
  Montgomery, AL 800-239-6540
Weaver Nut Co. Inc.
  Ephrata, PA 800-473-2688
Whaley Pecan Co Inc
  Troy, AL 800-824-6827
Whitley Peanut Factory Inc
  Hayes, VA 800-470-2244
Wolfies Roasted Nut Co
  Findlay, OH 419-423-1355
Young Pecan
  Las Cruces, NM 575-524-4321
Young Pecan, Inc.
  Florence, SC 800-729-6003

Salted

Golden Kernel Pecan Co
  Cameron, SC 803-823-2311
Schermer Pecan Co
  Glennville, GA 800-841-3403
Stahmann Farms
  La Mesa, NM 575-526-2453

Pignolias

Bedemco Inc
  White Plains, NY 914-683-1119
Castella Imports Inc
  Brentwood, NY 631-231-5500
L & S Packing Co
  Farmingdale, NY 800-286-6487

Pine

American Importing Co.
  Minneapolis, MN 855-273-0466
American Key Food Products Inc
  Closter, NJ 877-263-7539
Durey-Libby Edible Nuts
  Carlstadt, NJ 800-332-6887
Grapevine Trading Company
  Santa Rosa, CA 800-469-6478
Hialeah Products Co
  Hollywood, FL 800-923-3379
NOW Foods
  Bloomingdale, IL 888-669-3663
Setton International Foods
  Commack, NY 800-227-4397
Sunridge Farms
  Royal Oaks, CA 831-786-7000
Terri Lynn Inc
  Elgin, IL 800-323-0775

Pistachio

Arizona Pistachio Company
  Tucson, AZ 800-333-8575
Barcelona Nut Co
  Baltimore, MD 800-296-6887
Bavarian Nut Co
  Buffalo, NY 716-810-6887
Bedemco Inc
  White Plains, NY 914-683-1119
Buchanan Hollow Nut Co
  Le Grand, CA 800-532-1500
Cache Creek Foods LLC
  Woodland, CA 530-662-1764
California Fruit & Nut
  Gustine, CA 888-747-8224
Capco Enterprises
  East Hanover, NJ 800-252-1011
Commodities Marketing Inc
  Clarksburg, NJ 732-516-0700
Durey-Libby Edible Nuts
  Carlstadt, NJ 800-332-6887
Fastachi
  Watertown, MA 800-466-3022
Germack Pistachio Co
  Detroit, MI 800-872-4006
Healing Home Foods
  Pound Ridge, NY 914-764-1303
Hialeah Products Co
  Hollywood, FL 800-923-3379
Jardine Ranch
  Paso Robles, CA 866-833-5050
Kalustyan
  New York, NY 800-352-3451
Keenan Farms
  Kettleman City, CA 559-945-1400
Koeze Company
  Grand Rapids, MI 800-555-9688
Krema Nut Co
  Columbus, OH 800-222-4132
LA Wholesale Produce Market
  Los Angeles, CA 888-454-6887
Leona's Restaurante
  Chimayo, NM 888-561-5569
Maisie Jane's California Sunshine
  Chico, CA 530-899-7909
Mrs. Dog's Products
  Grand Rapids, MI 800-267-7364
Naraghi Group
  Escalon, CA 209-579-5253
Nichols Farms
  Hanford, CA 559-584-6811
NOW Foods
  Bloomingdale, IL 888-669-3663

Product Categories / Nuts & Nut Butters: Nuts

Nunes Farms Marketing
  Gustine, CA 209-862-3033
NutRaw Foods
  Delano, CA
Nuts & Stems
  Rosharon, TX 281-464-6887
Omega Nutrition
  Bellingham, WA 800-661-3529
Organic Planet
  San Francisco, CA 415-765-5590
Pacific Gold Marketing
  Arlington, TX 817-795-4671
Primex International Trading
  Los Angeles, CA 310-410-7100
Santa Barbara Pistachio Co
  Maricopa, CA 800-896-1044
Setton Farms
  Terra Bella, CA 559-535-6050
Setton International Foods
  Commack, NY 800-227-4397
Setton Pistachio
  Terra Bella, CA 559-535-6050
South Valley Farms
  Wasco, CA 661-391-9000
Sunfood
  El Cajon, CA 888-729-3663
Sunray Food Products Corporation
  Bronx, NY 718-548-2255
Sunridge Farms
  Royal Oaks, CA 831-786-7000
SunWest Foods, Inc.
  Davis, CA 530-758-8550
Tejon Ranch Co
  Lebec, CA 661-248-3000
Terri Lynn Inc
  Elgin, IL 800-323-0775
Timber Crest Farms
  Healdsburg, CA 888-766-4233
Weaver Nut Co. Inc.
  Ephrata, PA 800-473-2688
Wonderful Pistachios & Almonds
  Lost Hills, CA 661-797-6500

Pralines (See also Confectionery)

Aunt Aggie De's Pralines
  Sinton, TX 800-333-9354
B & B Pecan Processors
  Turkey, NC 866-328-7322
Blueberry Store
  Grand Junction, MI 877-654-2400
Creole Delicacies Gourmet Shop
  New Orleans, LA 504-525-9508
Landies Candies Co
  Buffalo, NY 800-955-2634
Pecan Deluxe Candy Co
  Dallas, TX 800-733-3589

Roasted

Adkin & Son Associated Food Products
  South Haven, MI 269-637-7450
American Almond Products Co
  Brooklyn, NY 800-825-6663
Baker Candy Company
  Snohomish, WA 425-422-6331
C J Dannemiller Co
  Norton, OH 800-624-8671
Dakota Gourmet
  Wahpeton, ND 800-727-6663
GrandyOats
  Hiram, ME 207-935-7415
Osage Pecan Co
  Butler, MO 800-748-8305
Pacific Grain & Foods
  Fresno, CA 559-276-2580
Q's Nuts
  Somerville, MA 617-764-3741
Solnuts
  Hudson, IA 800-648-3503
Superior Nut & Candy
  Chicago, IL 800-843-2238
Tropical Foods
  Charlotte, NC 800-438-4470

Tropical Nut & Fruit Co
  Orlando, FL 800-749-8869
Willmar Cookie & Nut Company
  Willmar, MN 800-426-7845

Shelled

Alldrin Brothers
  Ballico, CA 209-667-1600
Country Estate Pecans
  Goldwaite, TX 800-473-2267
Crain Walnut Shelling, Inc.
  Los Molinos, CA 530-529-1585
Frazier Nut Farms Inc
  Waterford, CA 209-522-1406
Jerry's Nut House
  Denver, CO 303-861-2262
Pippin Snack Pecans
  Albany, GA 800-554-6887
Ross-Smith Pecan Company
  Thomasville, GA 800-841-5503
Santa Clara Nut Co
  San Jose, CA 408-298-2425
Tracy Luckey Pecans
  Harlem, GA 800-476-4796
Whaley Pecan Co Inc
  Troy, AL 800-824-6827

Soy

Almost Nuts
  Denmark, WI 920-915-0152
American Importing Co.
  Minneapolis, MN 855-273-0466
Amport Foods
  St. Paul, MN 800-236-1119
Don't Go Nuts
  Salida, CO 855-666-8826
Hialeah Products Co
  Hollywood, FL 800-923-3379
Just Tomatoes
  Westley, CA 800-537-1985
Lee Seed Co
  Inwood, IA 800-736-6530
Nature's Select Inc
  Grand Rapids, MI 888-715-4321
New Organics
  Kenwood, CA 734-677-5570
Solnuts
  Hudson, IA 800-648-3503
Sunridge Farms
  Royal Oaks, CA 831-786-7000

Walnuts

American Almond Products Co
  Brooklyn, NY 800-825-6663
Bavarian Nut Co
  Buffalo, NY 716-810-6887
Bedemco Inc
  White Plains, NY 914-683-1119
Berberian Nut Company
  Chico, CA 530-981-4900
Byrd's Pecans
  Butler, MO 866-679-5583
California Walnut Co
  Los Molinos, CA 530-527-2616
Crain Ranch
  Los Molinos, CA 530-527-1077
Crain Walnut Shelling, Inc.
  Los Molinos, CA 530-529-1585
Durey-Libby Edible Nuts
  Carlstadt, NJ 800-332-6887
Erba Food Products
  Brooklyn, NY 718-272-7700
Frazier Nut Farms Inc
  Waterford, CA 209-522-1406
Fresh Roasted Almond Company
  Warren, MI 877-478-6887
Guerra Nut Shelling Co Inc
  Hollister, CA 831-637-4471
Hammons Products Co
  Stockton, MO 888-429-6887
Healing Home Foods
  Pound Ridge, NY 914-764-1303

Hialeah Products Co
  Hollywood, FL 800-923-3379
Jerry's Nut House
  Denver, CO 303-861-2262
John B. Sanfilippo & Son
  Elgin, IL 847-289-1800
Lodi Nut Company
  Lodi, CA 800-234-6887
Mariani Nut Co
  Winters, CA 530-795-1546
Mid Valley Nut Co
  Hughson, CA 209-883-4491
Naraghi Group
  Escalon, CA 209-579-5253
New Organics
  Kenwood, CA 734-677-5570
NOW Foods
  Bloomingdale, IL 888-669-3663
Nut Factory
  Spokane Valley, WA 888-239-5288
Osage Pecan Co
  Butler, MO 800-748-8305
Pearl Crop
  Stockton, CA 209-808-7575
Primex International Trading
  Los Angeles, CA 310-410-7100
Quality Nut Co
  Modesto, CA 209-526-3590
Ramos Orchards
  Winters, CA 530-795-4748
Santa Clara Nut Co
  San Jose, CA 408-298-2425
Service Packing Company
  Vancouver, BC 604-681-0264
Sunridge Farms
  Royal Oaks, CA 831-786-7000
SunWest Foods, Inc.
  Davis, CA 530-758-8550
Tejon Ranch Co
  Lebec, CA 661-248-3000
The Mapled Nut Co.
  Morrisville, VT 800-726-4661
Weaver Nut Co. Inc.
  Ephrata, PA 800-473-2688
Wilbur Packing Company
  Yuba City, CA 530-671-4911
Willamette Valley Walnuts
  McMinnville, OR 503-472-3215

Black

American Key Food Products Inc
  Closter, NJ 877-263-7539
Cache Creek Foods LLC
  Woodland, CA 530-662-1764
Frazier Nut Farms Inc
  Waterford, CA 209-522-1406
Guerra Nut Shelling Co Inc
  Hollister, CA 831-637-4471
Hammons Black Walnuts
  Stockton, MO 888-429-6887
Hammons Products Co
  Stockton, MO 888-429-6887
Hialeah Products Co
  Hollywood, FL 800-923-3379
John B. Sanfilippo & Son
  Elgin, IL 847-289-1800
Lodi Nut Company
  Lodi, CA 800-234-6887
New Organics
  Kenwood, CA 734-677-5570
Organic Planet
  San Francisco, CA 415-765-5590
Setton International Foods
  Commack, NY 800-227-4397
Terri Lynn Inc
  Elgin, IL 800-323-0775
Unique Ingredients LLC
  Gold Canyon, AZ 480-983-2498

Oils, Shortening & Fats

General

Akicorp
  N Miami Beach, FL 786-426-5750
American Hawaiian Soy Company
  Honolulu, HI 800-841-8435
Austrian Trade Commission
  New York, NY 212-421-5250
Capa Di Roma Inc
  East Hartford, CT 860-282-0298
Central Soyfoods
  Lawrence, KS 785-312-8698
CHS Inc.
  Inver Grove Hts., MN. 800-328-6539
Denomega Pure Health
  Brighton, CO. 479-181-2845
DuPont Pioneer
  Johnston, IA 515-535-3200
First Food International
  Linden, NJ. 908-862-5558
Fruit of the Land Products
  Thornhill, ON 877-311-5267
Frutech International Corp
  Pasadena, CA 626-844-0200
G. Banis Company
  Wilmington, DE 617-516-9092
Gourmet Mondiale
  Ste-Catherine, QC. 450-638-6380
Heartland Flax
  Valley City, ND. 866-599-3529
I Heart Olive Oil
  Ft Lauderdale, FL 954-607-1539
International Food Products
  Fenton, MO. 800-227-8427
Maywood International Sales
  Sante Fe, NM 805-500-5500
NAR
  Nashua, NH. 603-888-5420
Nealanders Food Ingredients
  Mississauga, ON. 800-263-1939
Oasis Food Co
  Hillside, NJ. 800-275-0477
Oilseeds International LTD
  San Francisco, CA 415-956-7251
Pacific Soybean & Grain
  San Mateo, CA 650-525-0500
Patrick Cudahy LLC
  Cudahy, WI 800-486-6900
Pondini Imports
  Somerset, NJ. 732-545-1255
Rallis Whole Foods
  Windsor, ON. 519-796-9712
SIGCO Sun Products
  Breckenridge, MN 800-654-4145
Spectrum Foods Inc
  Springfield, IL. 217-528-5301
Sutter Buttes Olive Oil
  Sutter, CA. 530-763-7921
Wegmans Food Markets Inc.
  Rochester, NY. 800-934-6267
Western Pacific Oils, Inc.
  Los Angeles, CA. 213-232-5117

Fats & Lard

Beef

Fatworks
  Niwot, CO

Chicken

All-States Quality Foods
  Charles City, IA 800-247-4195

Dried

Agri-Dairy Products
  Purchase, NY. 914-697-9580

Frozen

Clofine Dairy Products Inc
  Linwood, NJ 609-653-1000

Liquid

Agri-Dairy Products
  Purchase, NY. 914-697-9580

Clofine Dairy Products Inc
  Linwood, NJ 609-653-1000

Powdered

Clofine Dairy Products Inc
  Linwood, NJ 609-653-1000

Hydrogenated

AG Processing Inc
  Omaha, NE. 800-247-1345
Agri-Dairy Products
  Purchase, NY. 914-697-9580
Baker Commodities Inc
  Vernon, CA. 800-427-0696
Blossom Farm Products
  Ridgewood, NJ. 800-729-1818
Bunge Loders Croklaan
  Channahon, IL 800-621-4710
National Starch Food Innovation
  Bridgewater, NJ. 800-743-6343
Theriault's Abattoir Inc
  Hamlin, ME. 207-868-3344
Werling & Sons Slaughterhouse
  Burkettsville, OH 937-338-3281

Lard

CanAmera Foods
  Edmonton, AL. 780-447-6960
Fatworks
  Niwot, CO
OLLI Salumeria Americana
  Oceanside, CA 877-655-4937

Margarine

Allfresh Food Products
  Evanston, IL. 847-869-3100
Bunge Canada
  Oakville, ON. 905-825-7900
Butterball Farms
  Grand Rapids, MI 888-828-8837
CanAmera Foods
  Edmonton, AL. 780-447-6960
CHS Inc.
  Inver Grove Hts., MN. 800-328-6539
GFA Brands Inc
  Paramus, NJ 201-568-9300
Hamersmith, Inc.
  Miami, FL. 305-685-7451
JE Bergeron & Sons
  Bromptonville, QC 800-567-2798
Keller's Creamery
  Kansas City, MO. 800-535-5371
Land O'Lakes Inc
  Arden Hills, MN. 800-328-9680
Madison Foods
  Saint Paul, MN 651-265-8212
Oasis Food Co
  Hillside, NJ. 800-275-0477
Parmalat Canada
  Toronto, ON 800-563-1515
Protient
  St Paul, MN. 800-328-9680
Richardson International
  Winnipeg, MB. 866-217-6211
Schneider's Dairy Inc
  Pittsburgh, PA 412-881-3525
Sommer Maid Creamery Inc
  Pipersville, PA. 215-345-6160
Ventura Foods LLC
  Brea, CA. 800-421-6257
Western Pacific Oils, Inc.
  Los Angeles, CA. 213-232-5117

Oils

AAK
  Louisville, KY 800-622-3055
Abitec Corp
  Columbus, OH 800-555-1255
ACH Food Co Inc
  Oakbrook Terrace, IL 630-586-3740
Agrusa
  Leonia, NJ. 201-592-5950
Akicorp
  N Miami Beach, FL 786-426-5750
Alexander International (USA)
  Brightwaters, NY 866-965-0143
AM Todd Co
  Kalamazoo, MI. 269-343-2603
AME Nutrition
  Dublin, OH 614-766-3638
American Hawaiian Soy Company
  Honolulu, HI 800-841-8435
American Mercantile Corp
  Memphis, TN 901-454-1900
American Yeast
  Memphis, TN 866-920-9885
Archer Daniels Midland Company
  Decatur, IL 217-424-5200
Archer Daniels Midland Company
  Chicago, IL. 312-634-8100
Arista Industries Inc
  Wilton, CT 800-255-6457
Aroma Vera
  Los Angeles, CA. 800-669-9514
Aroma-Life
  Encino, CA 818-905-7761
Arro Corp
  Hodgkins, IL 877-929-2776
Astral Extracts
  Syosset, NY. 516-496-2505
Au Printemps Gourmet
  Saint-Jerome, QC 800-438-6676
Avatar Corp
  University Park, IL. 800-255-3181
Beta Pure Foods
  Santa Cruz, CA 831-685-6565
Bioriginal Food and Science Corp
  Saskatoon, SK. 306-975-1166
Bittersweet Herb Farm
  Shelburne Falls, MA. 800-456-1599
Brand Aromatics Inc
  Lakewood, NJ. 800-363-2080
Bridgewell Resources LLC
  Clackamas, OR 800-481-3557
Buonitalia
  New York, NY 212-633-9090
C W Resources Inc
  New Britain, CT 860-229-7700
C.F. Sauer Co.
  Richmond, VA. 888-723-0052
California Balsamic Inc
  Ukiah, CA. 888-644-5127
California Olive Oil Council
  Berkeley, CA. 888-718-9830
CanAmera Foods
  Edmonton, AL. 780-447-6960
Catania Oils
  Ayer, MA. 978-772-7900
Centflor Manufacturing Co
  New York, NY 212-246-8307
CHS Inc.
  Inver Grove Hts., MN. 800-328-6539
Classic Flavors & Fragrances
  New York, NY 212-777-0004
Clic International Inc
  Laval, QC 450-669-2663
Coast Packing Co
  Vernon, CA 323-277-7700
Coldani Olive Ranch LLC
  Lodi, CA 209-334-0527
Colonna Brothers Inc
  North Bergen, NJ 201-864-1115
Columbus Vegetable Oils
  Des Plaines, IL 847-257-8920
Consumer Guild Foods Inc
  Toledo, OH 419-726-3406
Critelli Olive Oil
  Fairfield, CA. 800-865-4836
Delicae Gourmet
  Tarpon Springs, FL. 800-942-2502
Denomega Pure Health
  Brighton, CO. 479-181-2845
Dow AgroSciences Canada
  Calgary, AB. 403-735-8800
DuPont Nutrition & Biosciences
  New Century, KS 913-764-8100
Erba Food Products
  Brooklyn, NY 718-272-7700
Everland Foods
  Burnaby, BC

Product Categories / Oils, Shortening & Fats: Oils

Everland Parks
  Burnaby, BC
Flavorchem Corp
  Downers Grove, IL 800-435-2867
Follmer Development, Inc
  Newbury Park, CA 805-498-4531
Fratelli Mantova
  Naperville, IL 630-904-0002
Freed, Teller & Freed
  South San Francisco, CA 800-370-7371
Frutech International Corp
  Pasadena, CA 626-844-0200
GFA Brands Inc
  Paramus, NJ 201-568-9300
Golden Eagle Olive Products
  Porterville, CA 559-784-3468
Good Food Inc
  Honey Brook, PA 800-327-4406
Grapevine Trading Company
  Santa Rosa, CA 800-469-6478
Hamersmith, Inc.
  Miami, FL 305-685-7451
Hartsville Oil Mill
  Darlington, SC 843-393-1501
Herbal Products & Development
  Aptos, CA 831-688-8706
Hybco USA
  Los Angeles, CA 323-269-3111
Il Sisters
  Moss Beach, CA 800-282-7058
Ingredion Inc.
  Westchester, IL 800-713-0208
International Food Products
  Fenton, MO 800-227-8427
International Home Foods
  Parsippany, NJ. 973-359-9920
J.M. Smucker Co.
  Orrville, OH 888-550-9555
Kalsec
  Kalamazoo, MI 800-323-9320
Kalustyan
  New York, NY 800-352-3451
Kevala
  Dallas, TX. 877-379-1179
La Tourangelle
  Berkeley, CA. 866-688-6457
Lebermuth Company
  South Bend, IN 800-648-1123
Lesley Elizabeth Inc
  Lapeer, MI. 800-684-3300
Liberty Natural Products Inc
  Oregon City, OR 800-289-8427
Liberty Vegetable Oil Co
  Santa Fe Springs, CA 562-921-3567
Loriva Culinary Oils
  San Francisco, CA 866-972-6879
Love You Foods
  Flagstaff, AZ. 844-693-2662
Lowcountry Produce
  Raleigh, NC 800-935-2792
Lucini Italia Company
  San Francisco, CA 888-558-2464
Marathon Packing Corp
  San Leandro, CA. 510-895-2000
Marnap Industries
  Buffalo, NY. 716-897-1220
Maywood International Sales
  Sante Fe, NM 805-500-5500
Mc Glaughlin Oil Co
  Columbus, OH 614-231-2518
Medallion International Inc
  Pompton Plains, NJ. 973-616-3401
Monini North America
  Shelton, CT. 203-513-2685
Mosby Winery
  Buellton, CA. 800-706-6729
Mott's LLP
  Plano, TX. 800-426-4891
Mountain High Organics
  New Milford, CT 860-210-7805
Mountainbrook of Vermont
  Jeffersonville, VT. 802-644-1988
Napa Valley Kitchens
  Napa, CA. 707-254-3700
National Flavors
  Kalamazoo, MI 800-525-2431
Natural Value
  Sacramento, CA 916-836-3561
Nature Most Laboratories
  Middletown, CT 800-234-2112
Nealanders Food Ingredients
  Mississauga, ON 800-263-1939

Newport Flavours & Fragrances
  Orange, CA 714-744-3700
Nexcel Natural Ingredients
  Springfield, IL 217-391-0091
North American Enterprises
  Tucson, AZ 800-817-8666
Nutiva
  Richmond, CA 800-993-4367
O Olive Oil
  Petaluma, CA 888-827-7148
Odell's
  Reno, NV 800-635-0436
Omega Protein
  Reedville, VA 804-453-6262
Organic Gemini
  Brooklyn, NY 347-662-2900
Pacifica Culinaria
  Vista, CA 800-622-8880
Paradise Products Corporation
  Boca Raton, FL. 800-826-1235
Pastene Co LTD
  Canton, MA 781-298-3397
Pastorelli Food Products
  Chicago, IL. 800-767-2829
Patsy's Italian Restaurant
  New York, NY 212-247-3491
Pompeian Inc
  Baltimore, MD 800-766-7342
Prairie Thyme LTD
  Santa Fe, NM 800-869-0009
Proacec USA
  Santa Monica, CA. 310-996-7770
Pure Indian
  Princeton Jct., NJ 877-588-4433
Purity Products
  Plainview, NY. 800-256-6102
Rising Sun Farms
  Phoenix, OR 800-888-0795
Ron Son Foods Inc
  Swedesboro, NJ 856-241-7333
Rosa Food Products
  Philadelphia, PA 215-467-2214
S S Steiner Inc
  New York, NY 212-838-8901
Salute Sante! Food & Wine
  Napa, CA. 707-251-3900
Santa Barbara Pistachio Co
  Maricopa, CA 800-896-1044
Santini Foods
  San Lorenzo, CA. 800-835-6888
Sieco USA Corporation
  Houston, TX 713-464-1726
Silver Palate Kitchens
  Cresskill, NJ 201-568-0110
Source Food Technology
  Durham, NC 866-277-3849
Sovena USA Inc
  Rome, NY. 315-797-7070
Sparboe Foods Corp
  New Hampton, IA 641-394-3040
Sparrow Lane
  Ceres, CA 866-515-2477
Stauber Performance Ingrdients
  Fullerton, CA 888-441-4233
Sun Grove Foods Inc
  Passaic, NJ. 973-574-1110
Sutter Buttes Olive Oil
  Sutter, CA. 530-763-7921
Tait Farm Foods
  Centre Hall, PA 800-787-2716
Tee Pee Olives, Inc.
  Rye, NY. 800-431-1529
The Coromega Company
  Carlsbad, CA. 877-275-3725
The Dow Chemical Company
  Midland, MI 800-331-6451
Tropical Foods
  Charlotte, NC 800-438-4470
Veronica Foods Inc
  Oakland, CA 800-370-5554
Vitamins
  Chicago, IL. 312-861-0700
Viterra, Inc
  Regina, SK 866-647-4090
Wine Country Kitchens
  Napa, CA. 866-767-9463
Wing Nien Food
  Hayward, CA 510-487-8877

Almond

AG Processing Inc
  Omaha, NE 800-247-1345

Aroma-Life
  Encino, CA 818-905-7761
Astral Extracts
  Syosset, NY. 516-496-2505
Embassy Flavours Ltd.
  Brampton, ON. 800-334-3371
Emerling International Foods
  Buffalo, NY. 716-833-7381
Flora Inc
  Lynden, WA. 800-446-2110
Gold Coast Ingredients
  Commerce, CA 800-352-8673
K L Keller Imports
  Oakland, CA 510-839-7890
Pokonobe Industries
  Santa Monica, CA. 310-392-1259
Tri-State Ingredients
  Mason, OH 800-622-1050
Universal Preservachem Inc
  Somerset, NJ. 732-568-1266

Anise or Aniseed

Astral Extracts
  Syosset, NY. 516-496-2505
Embassy Flavours Ltd.
  Brampton, ON. 800-334-3371
Emerling International Foods
  Buffalo, NY. 716-833-7381
Medallion International Inc
  Pompton Plains, NJ. 973-616-3401
Tri-State Ingredients
  Mason, OH 800-622-1050

Avocado

Arista Industries Inc
  Wilton, CT 800-255-6457
Chosen Foods, Inc.
  San Diego, CA 877-674-2244
Everland Foods
  Burnaby, BC
Primal Kitchen
  Oxnard, CA. 888-774-6259
Primal Nutrition
  Malibu, CA 888-774-6259

Bean

Avatar Corp
  University Park, IL 800-255-3181
Tri-State Ingredients
  Mason, OH 800-622-1050

Black Pepper

Medallion International Inc
  Pompton Plains, NJ. 973-616-3401
Tri-State Ingredients
  Mason, OH 800-622-1050

Borage

Omega Nutrition
  Bellingham, WA 800-661-3529

Canola

ACH Food Co Inc
  Oakbrook Terrace, IL 630-586-3740
AG Processing Inc
  Omaha, NE 800-247-1345
American Vegetable Oils
  Commerce, CA 800-728-8089
Avatar Corp
  University Park, IL 800-255-3181
Bunge Canada
  Oakville, ON. 905-825-7900
California Olive Oil Council
  Berkeley, CA 888-718-9830
DuPont Pioneer
  Johnston, IA 515-535-5954
Emerling International Foods
  Buffalo, NY. 716-833-7381
Flora Inc
  Lynden, WA. 800-446-2110
Gama Products
  Miami, FL 786-235-1515
Good Food Inc
  Honey Brook, PA 800-327-4406
Intermountain Canola Cargill
  Minneapolis, MN 800-822-6652
International Foodcraft Corp
  Linden, NJ. 800-875-9393

Product Categories / Oils, Shortening & Fats: Oils

Loriva Culinary Oils
  San Francisco, CA 866-972-6879
Maywood International Sales
  Sante Fe, NM 805-500-5500
Montana Specialty Mills LLC
  Great Falls, MT. 800-332-2024
Nealanders Food Ingredients
  Mississauga, ON 800-263-1939
New Organics
  Kenwood, CA 734-677-5570
Nexcel Natural Ingredients
  Springfield, IL. 217-391-0091
Odell's
  Reno, NV 800-635-0436
Omega Nutrition
  Bellingham, WA 800-661-3529
Pokonobe Industries
  Santa Monica, CA. 310-392-1259
Riceland Foods Inc.
  Stuttgart, AR 855-742-3929
Richardson International
  Winnipeg, MB. 866-217-6211
Tri-State Ingredients
  Mason, OH 800-622-1050
Universal Preservachem Inc
  Somerset, NJ 732-568-1266

Caraway

Emerling International Foods
  Buffalo, NY 716-833-7381
Medallion International Inc
  Pompton Plains, NJ. 973-616-3401
Tri-State Ingredients
  Mason, OH 800-622-1050

Cardamom

Medallion International Inc
  Pompton Plains, NJ. 973-616-3401
Tri-State Ingredients
  Mason, OH 800-622-1050

Cassia

Embassy Flavours Ltd.
  Brampton, ON. 800-334-3371
Tri-State Ingredients
  Mason, OH 800-622-1050

Castor

Arista Industries Inc
  Wilton, CT 800-255-6457
Avatar Corp
  University Park, IL. 800-255-3181
Heritage Books & Gifts
  Virginia Beach, VA 800-862-2923
Leatex Chemical Co
  Philadelphia, PA 215-739-2000
Salem Oil & Grease Company
  Salem, MA 978-745-0585
Tri-State Ingredients
  Mason, OH 800-622-1050

Celery

Tri-State Ingredients
  Mason, OH 800-622-1050

Cinnamon - Leaf & Bark

Medallion International Inc
  Pompton Plains, NJ. 973-616-3401
Tri-State Ingredients
  Mason, OH 800-622-1050

Citrus

Astral Extracts
  Syosset, NY. 516-496-2505
Boyajian LLC
  Canton, MA 800-965-0665
California Olive Oil Council
  Berkeley, CA. 888-718-9830
Diana's Specialty Foods
  Pingree Grove, IL. 847-683-1200
Embassy Flavours Ltd.
  Brampton, ON. 800-334-3371
Emerling International Foods
  Buffalo, NY 716-833-7381
Frutech International Corp
  Pasadena, CA 626-844-0200
Gold Coast Ingredients
  Commerce, CA 800-352-8673

Louis Dreyfus Company Citrus Inc
  Winter Garden, FL 407-656-1000
Medallion International Inc
  Pompton Plains, NJ. 973-616-3401
Peace River Citrus Products
  Vero Beach, FL 772-492-4050
Prime Ingredients Inc
  Saddle Brook, NJ 888-791-6655
Robertet Flavors
  Piscataway, NJ 732-981-8300
Tri-State Ingredients
  Mason, OH 800-622-1050
Ungerer & Co
  Lincoln Park, NJ 973-706-7381

Clove

Tri-State Ingredients
  Mason, OH 800-622-1050

Coconut

Aak USA Inc
  Newark, NJ 973-344-1300
AG Processing Inc
  Omaha, NE 800-247-1345
Avatar Corp
  University Park, IL. 800-255-3181
Blue Marble Brands
  Providence, RI 888-534-0246
Clofine Dairy Products Inc
  Linwood, NJ 609-653-1000
Emerling International Foods
  Buffalo, NY 716-833-7381
Everland Foods
  Burnaby, BC
First Food International
  Linden, NJ. 908-862-5558
GloryBee
  Eugene, OR 800-456-7923
Gold Coast Ingredients
  Commerce, CA 800-352-8673
Good Food Inc
  Honey Brook, PA 800-327-4406
Kelapo
  Tampa, FL. 800-230-5952
Maywood International Sales
  Sante Fe, NM 805-500-5500
Odell's
  Reno, NV 800-635-0436
Pokonobe Industries
  Santa Monica, CA. 310-392-1259
Pure Life Organic Foods
  Las Vegas, NV 708-990-5817
RE Botanicals
  Boulder, CO 303-214-2118
Sunfood
  El Cajon, CA. 888-729-3663
Tri-State Ingredients
  Mason, OH 800-622-1050
Tropical Link Canada Ltd.
  Burnaby, BC 778-379-3510
Universal Impex Corporation
  Toronto, ON 416-743-7778
Western Pacific Oils, Inc.
  Los Angeles, CA. 213-232-5117

Cod Liver

Jamieson Laboratories
  Windsor, ON 800-265-5088

Cooking

ACH Food Co Inc
  Oakbrook Terrace, IL 630-586-3740
Agrusa
  Leonia, NJ 201-592-5950
Allfresh Food Products
  Evanston, IL 847-869-3100
Arista Industries Inc
  Wilton, CT 800-255-6457
Arro Corp
  Hodgkins, IL 877-929-2776
Avatar Corp
  University Park, IL. 800-255-3181
Butter Buds Food Ingredients
  Racine, WI. 800-426-1119
C&T Refinery
  Minneapolis, MN 800-227-4455
California Oils Corp
  Richmond, CA 800-225-4667
California Olive Oil Council
  Berkeley, CA. 888-718-9830

Capital City Processors
  Winchester, VA 800-473-2731
Coast Packing Co
  Vernon, CA 323-277-7700
Colonna Brothers Inc
  North Bergen, NJ 201-864-1115
Diana's Specialty Foods
  Pingree Grove, IL. 847-683-1200
Dipasa USA Inc
  Brownsville, TX 956-831-4072
Embassy Flavours Ltd.
  Brampton, ON. 800-334-3371
Emerling International Foods
  Buffalo, NY 716-833-7381
Flora Inc
  Lynden, WA. 800-446-2110
Follmer Development, Inc
  Newbury Park, CA 805-498-4531
Gateway Food Products Co
  Dupo, IL 877-220-1963
Good Food Inc
  Honey Brook, PA 800-327-4406
Intermountain Canola Cargill
  Minneapolis, MN 800-822-6652
Liberty Vegetable Oil Co
  Santa Fe Springs, CA 562-921-3567
Loriva Culinary Oils
  San Francisco, CA 866-972-6879
Louis Dreyfus Company Citrus Inc
  Winter Garden, FL 407-656-1000
Marathon Packing Corp
  San Leandro, CA. 510-895-2000
Marina Foods
  Medley, FL 786-888-0129
Morris J Golombeck Inc
  Brooklyn, NY 718-284-3505
Mother Earth Enterprises
  New York, NY 866-436-7688
Mott's LLP
  Plano, TX 800-426-4891
Natural Oils International
  Simi Valley, CA. 805-433-0160
Nick Sciabica & Sons
  Modesto, CA. 800-551-9612
North American Enterprises
  Tucson, AZ 800-817-8666
PAR-Way Tryson Co
  St Clair, MO 636-629-4545
Pastorelli Food Products
  Chicago, IL. 800-767-2829
Pokonobe Industries
  Santa Monica, CA. 310-392-1259
Producers Cooperative Oil Mill
  Oklahoma City, OK 405-232-7555
Progresso Quality Foods
  Vineland, NJ 856-691-1565
Purity Products
  Plainview, NY. 800-256-6102
Ron Son Foods Inc
  Swedesboro, NJ 856-241-7333
Sovena USA Inc
  Rome, NY 315-797-7070
Spectrum Foods Inc
  Springfield, IL. 217-528-5301
Thyme Garden Herb Co
  Alsea, OR 800-482-4372
Tri-State Ingredients
  Mason, OH 800-622-1050

Spray

ACH Food Co Inc
  Oakbrook Terrace, IL 630-586-3740
Butter Buds Food Ingredients
  Racine, WI. 800-426-1119
Follmer Development, Inc
  Newbury Park, CA 805-498-4531
International Home Foods
  Parsippany, NJ. 973-359-9920
PAR-Way Tryson Co
  St Clair, MO 636-629-4545

Coriander Seed

Tri-State Ingredients
  Mason, OH 800-622-1050

Corn

ACH Food Co Inc
  Oakbrook Terrace, IL 630-586-3740
AG Processing Inc
  Omaha, NE 800-247-1345

Product Categories / Oils, Shortening & Fats: Oils

Arro Corp
   Hodgkins, IL 877-929-2776
Avatar Corp
   University Park, IL 800-255-3181
Erba Food Products
   Brooklyn, NY 718-272-7700
Gama Products
   Miami, FL 786-235-1515
Good Food Inc
   Honey Brook, PA 800-327-4406
Ingredion Inc.
   Westchester, IL 800-713-0208
Maywood International Sales
   Sante Fe, NM 805-500-5500
Nealanders Food Ingredients
   Mississauga, ON 800-263-1939
Olde Tyme Food Corporation
   East Longmeadow, MA 800-356-6533
Pacific Soybean & Grain
   San Mateo, CA 650-525-0500
Pastorelli Food Products
   Chicago, IL 800-767-2829
Pokonobe Industries
   Santa Monica, CA 310-392-1259
Purity Products
   Plainview, NY 800-256-6102
Riceland Foods Inc.
   Stuttgart, AR 855-742-3929
Sovena USA Inc
   Rome, NY 315-797-7070
Tri-State Ingredients
   Mason, OH 800-622-1050
Universal Preservachem Inc
   Somerset, NJ 732-568-1266

Cottonseed

AAK
   Louisville, KY 800-622-3055
Aak USA Inc
   Newark, NJ 973-344-1300
Abitec Corp
   Columbus, OH 800-555-1255
AG Processing Inc
   Omaha, NE 800-247-1345
Emerling International Foods
   Buffalo, NY 716-833-7381
Good Food Inc
   Honey Brook, PA 800-327-4406
Hartsville Oil Mill
   Darlington, SC 843-393-1501
Maywood International Sales
   Sante Fe, NM 805-500-5500
Nealanders Food Ingredients
   Mississauga, ON 800-263-1939
Producers Cooperative Oil Mill
   Oklahoma City, OK 405-232-7555
PYCO Industries Inc
   Lubbock, TX 806-747-3434
Riceland Foods Inc.
   Stuttgart, AR 855-742-3929
Southern Cotton Oil Co
   Memphis, TN 901-452-3151
Stevenson-Cooper Inc
   Philadelphia, PA 215-223-2600
Tri-State Ingredients
   Mason, OH 800-622-1050

Dillweed

Tri-State Ingredients
   Mason, OH 800-622-1050

Edible

Aak USA Inc
   Newark, NJ 973-344-1300
Abitec Corp
   Columbus, OH 800-555-1255
ACH Food Co Inc
   Oakbrook Terrace, IL 630-586-3740
AG Processing Inc
   Omaha, NE 800-247-1345
Agri-Dairy Products
   Purchase, NY 914-697-9580
Agrusa
   Leonia, NJ 201-592-5950
Allfresh Food Products
   Evanston, IL 847-869-3100
Arista Industries Inc
   Wilton, CT 800-255-6457
Arro Corp
   Hodgkins, IL 877-929-2776
Avatar Corp
   University Park, IL 800-255-3181
Barlean's Fisheries
   Ferndale, WA 360-384-0325
Boyajian LLC
   Canton, MA 800-965-0665
Bunge Loders Croklaan
   Channahon, IL 800-621-4710
Butter Buds Food Ingredients
   Racine, WI 800-426-1119
C P Vegetable Oil
   Fort Lauderdale, FL 800-398-7154
California Oils Corp
   Richmond, CA 800-225-6457
California Olive Oil Council
   Berkeley, CA 888-718-9830
Capital City Processors
   Winchester, VA 800-473-2731
Capitol Foods
   Memphis, TN 662-781-9021
Colavita USA
   Edison, NJ 888-265-2848
Colonna Brothers Inc
   North Bergen, NJ 201-864-1115
Con Agra Snack Foods
   Hamburg, IA 800-831-5818
Consumer Guild Foods Inc
   Toledo, OH 419-726-3406
Dipasa USA Inc
   Brownsville, TX 956-831-4072
Embassy Flavours Ltd.
   Brampton, ON 800-334-3371
Emerling International Foods
   Buffalo, NY 716-833-7381
Energen Products Inc
   Norwalk, CA 800-423-8837
Erba Food Products
   Brooklyn, NY 718-272-7700
Flora Inc
   Lynden, WA 800-446-2110
Gama Products
   Miami, FL 786-235-1515
Gateway Food Products Co
   Dupo, IL 877-220-1963
Good Food Inc
   Honey Brook, PA 800-327-4406
Grassland Dairy Products Inc
   Greenwood, WI 800-428-8837
Herbal Products & Development
   Aptos, CA 831-688-8706
Intermountain Canola Cargill
   Minneapolis, MN 800-822-6652
John I. Haas
   Washington, DC
Liberty Vegetable Oil Co
   Santa Fe Springs, CA 562-921-3567
Loriva Culinary Oils
   San Francisco, CA 866-972-6879
Louis Dreyfus Company Citrus Inc
   Winter Garden, FL 407-656-1000
Marina Foods
   Medley, FL 786-888-0129
Medallion International Inc
   Pompton Plains, NJ 973-616-3401
Morris J Golombeck Inc
   Brooklyn, NY 718-284-3505
Mother Earth Enterprises
   New York, NY 866-436-7688
Natural Oils International
   Simi Valley, CA 805-433-0160
New Organics
   Kenwood, CA 734-677-5570
Nick Sciabica & Sons
   Modesto, CA 800-551-9612
North American Enterprises
   Tucson, AZ 800-817-8666
Oils Of Aloha
   Waialua, HI 800-367-6010
Ottens Flavors
   Philadelphia, PA 800-523-0767
Paradise Products Corporation
   Boca Raton, FL 800-826-1235
Pastorelli Food Products
   Chicago, IL 800-767-2829
Perdue Farms Inc.
   Salisbury, MD 800-473-7383
Pokonobe Industries
   Santa Monica, CA 310-392-1259
Pompeian Inc
   Baltimore, MD 800-766-7342
Progresso Quality Foods
   Vineland, NJ 856-691-1565
Purity Products
   Plainview, NY 800-256-6102
Ron Son Foods Inc
   Swedesboro, NJ 856-241-7333
Sessions Co Inc
   Enterprise, AL 334-393-0200
Silver Palate Kitchens
   Cresskill, NJ 201-568-0110
Sovena USA Inc
   Rome, NY 315-797-7070
Stuart Hale Co
   Chicago, IL 773-638-1800
Thyme Garden Herb Co
   Alsea, OR 800-482-4372
Tri-State Ingredients
   Mason, OH 800-622-1050
Tropical Foods
   Charlotte, NC 800-438-4470
Universal Preservachem Inc
   Somerset, NJ 732-568-1266
Veronica Foods Inc
   Oakland, CA 800-370-5554

Essential

Allylix Inc
   San Diego, CA 858-909-0595
AM Todd Co
   Kalamazoo, MI 269-343-2603
American Mercantile Corp
   Memphis, TN 901-454-1900
Aroma Vera
   Los Angeles, CA 800-669-9514
Aroma-Life
   Encino, CA 818-905-7761
Aromachem
   Brooklyn, NY 718-497-4664
Avri Co Inc
   Richmond, CA 800-883-9574
Bioriginal Food and Science Corp
   Saskatoon, SK 306-975-1166
Blue California Co
   Rancho Sta Marg, CA 949-459-2729
Centflor Manufacturing Co
   New York, NY 212-246-8307
Classic Flavors & Fragrances
   New York, NY 212-777-0004
Colin Ingram
   Comptche, CA 707-937-1824
Embassy Flavours Ltd.
   Brampton, ON 800-334-3371
Emerling International Foods
   Buffalo, NY 716-833-7381
Essential Products of America
   Tampa, FL 800-822-9698
Excellentia Intl.
   Fairfield, NJ 737-749-9840
Flavor Sciences Inc
   Lenoir, NC 800-535-2867
Flavorchem Corp
   Downers Grove, IL 800-435-2867
Flavormatic Industries
   Wappingers Falls, NY 845-297-9100
Global Botanical
   Barrie, ON 705-733-2117
Green Turtle Bay Vitamin Company
   Summit, NJ 800-887-8535
Greenwood Associates
   Niles, IL 847-579-5500
GuruNanda
   Buena Park, CA 866-421-0309
H B Taylor Co
   Chicago, IL 773-254-4805
Healing Solutions
   Phoenix, AZ 800-819-4098
Heritage Books & Gifts
   Virginia Beach, VA 800-862-2923
Joseph Adams Corp
   Valley City, OH 330-225-9135
Kalsec
   Kalamazoo, MI 800-323-9320
Lebermuth Company
   Mishawaka, IN 800-648-1123
Leeward Resources
   Baltimore, MD 410-837-9003
Lemur International
   Richmond, CA 510-620-9708
Loriva Culinary Oils
   San Francisco, CA 866-972-6879
Maple Ridge Farms
   Mosinee, WI 715-693-4346
Marnap Industries
   Buffalo, NY 716-897-1220

Product Categories / Oils, Shortening & Fats: Oils

Medallion International Inc
  Pompton Plains, NJ 973-616-3401
Mother Earth Enterprises
  New York, NY 866-436-7688
Native Scents
  Taos, NM 800-645-3471
Nature's Fusions
  Provo, UT 801-872-9500
NOW Foods
  Bloomingdale, IL 888-669-3663
Prova
  Danvers, MA 877-776-8287
Robertet Flavors
  Piscataway, NJ 732-981-8300
Starwest Botanicals Inc
  Sacramento, CA 800-800-4372
Synthite USA Inc.
  Oak Park, IL 708-446-1716
Terra Flavors & Fragrances
  New York, NY 212-244-1181
Torre Products Co Inc
  New York, NY 212-925-8989
Treatt USA Inc
  Lakeland, FL 863-668-9500
Tri-State Ingredients
  Mason, OH 800-622-1050
Ungerer & Co
  Lincoln Park, NJ 973-706-7381
Whole Herb Co
  Sonoma, CA 707-935-1077

Natural
Jedwards International Inc
  Braintree, MA 781-848-1473

Fish
Aker BioMarine Antarctic US, LLC.
  Metuchen, NJ 732-917-4000
Daybrook Fisheries
  New Orleans, LA 504-561-6163
Eckhart Corporation
  Novato, CA 800-200-4201
J R Carlson Laboratories Inc
  Arlington Heights, IL 888-234-5656
Jamieson Laboratories
  Windsor, ON 800-265-5088
Omega Pure
  Irvine, CA 562-429-3335
Scandinavian Laboratories
  Belvidere, PA 866-623-2650
Tabco Enterprises
  Pomona, CA 909-623-4565

Fruit
Arista Industries Inc
  Wilton, CT 800-255-6457
Kurtz Orchards Farms
  Niagra-on-the-Lake, ON 905-468-2937

Garlic
Astral Extracts
  Syosset, NY 516-496-2505
California Olive Oil Council
  Berkeley, CA 888-718-9830
Diana's Specialty Foods
  Pingree Grove, IL 847-683-1200
Emerling International Foods
  Buffalo, NY 716-833-7381
Halladay's Harvest Barn
  Bellows Falls, VT 802-463-3471
Lebermuth Company
  Mishawaka, IN 800-648-1123
Loriva Culinary Oils
  San Francisco, CA 866-972-6879
Prime Ingredients Inc
  Saddle Brook, NJ 888-791-6655
Thyme Garden Herb Co
  Alsea, OR 800-482-4372
Tri-State Ingredients
  Mason, OH 800-622-1050
Vegetable Juices Inc
  Chicago, IL 888-776-9752

Ginger
Astral Extracts
  Syosset, NY 516-496-2505
Tri-State Ingredients
  Mason, OH 800-622-1050
Ungerer & Co
  Lincoln Park, NJ 973-706-7381

Grapefruit
Astral Extracts
  Syosset, NY 516-496-2505
Emerling International Foods
  Buffalo, NY 716-833-7381
Gold Coast Ingredients
  Commerce, CA 800-352-8673
Tri-State Ingredients
  Mason, OH 800-622-1050

Grapeseed
AG Processing Inc
  Omaha, NE 800-247-1345
Ameri-Kal Inc
  Wichita Falls, TX 940-322-5400
Arista Industries Inc
  Wilton, CT 800-255-6457
Cuisine Perel
  Richmond, CA 800-887-3735
Diana's Specialty Foods
  Pingree Grove, IL 847-683-1200
Emerling International Foods
  Buffalo, NY 716-833-7381
Food & Vine Inc.
  Napa, CA 707-251-3900
GloryBee
  Eugene, OR 800-456-7923
Lifestar Millennium
  Sedona, AZ 877-422-4739
Pokonobe Industries
  Santa Monica, CA 310-392-1259
Queensway Foods Company
  Burlingame, CA 650-871-7770
Salute Sante! Food & Wine
  Napa, CA 707-251-3900
Tabco Enterprises
  Pomona, CA 909-623-4565
Tri-State Ingredients
  Mason, OH 800-622-1050

Hazelnut
K L Keller Imports
  Oakland, CA 510-839-7890
Loriva Culinary Oils
  San Francisco, CA 866-972-6879
Tri-State Ingredients
  Mason, OH 800-622-1050

Hemp Nut
Ananda Hemp
  Cynthiana, KY
Foods Alive
  Angola, IN 260-488-4497
Herbal Products & Development
  Aptos, CA 831-688-8706
Mother Earth Enterprises
  New York, NY 866-436-7688
Tri-State Ingredients
  Mason, OH 800-622-1050

Lemon
AG Processing Inc
  Omaha, NE 800-247-1345
Astral Extracts
  Syosset, NY 516-496-2505
Boyajian LLC
  Canton, MA 800-965-0665
Citromax Flavors Inc
  Carlstadt, NJ 201-933-8405
Diana's Specialty Foods
  Pingree Grove, IL 847-683-1200
Embassy Flavours Ltd.
  Brampton, ON 800-334-3371
Emerling International Foods
  Buffalo, NY 716-833-7381
Gold Coast Ingredients
  Commerce, CA 800-352-8673
Prime Ingredients Inc
  Saddle Brook, NJ 888-791-6655
Tri-State Ingredients
  Mason, OH 800-622-1050
Ungerer & Co
  Lincoln Park, NJ 973-706-7381

Lemon Grass
Emerling International Foods
  Buffalo, NY 716-833-7381
Tri-State Ingredients
  Mason, OH 800-622-1050

Lime
Astral Extracts
  Syosset, NY 516-496-2505
Boyajian LLC
  Canton, MA 800-965-0665
Emerling International Foods
  Buffalo, NY 716-833-7381
Gold Coast Ingredients
  Commerce, CA 800-352-8673
Tri-State Ingredients
  Mason, OH 800-622-1050
Ungerer & Co
  Lincoln Park, NJ 973-706-7381

Mustard
Emerling International Foods
  Buffalo, NY 716-833-7381
Montana Specialty Mills LLC
  Great Falls, MT 800-332-2024
Tri-State Ingredients
  Mason, OH 800-622-1050

Nutmeg
Emerling International Foods
  Buffalo, NY 716-833-7381
Tri-State Ingredients
  Mason, OH 800-622-1050
Whole Herb Co
  Sonoma, CA 707-935-1077

Olive
Acesur North America
  Purchase, NY 914-925-0450
ACH Food Co Inc
  Oakbrook Terrace, IL 630-586-3740
Advanced Bio Development
  Piermont, NY 845-365-3838
AG Processing Inc
  Omaha, NE 800-247-1345
Agrocan
  Ville St Laurent, QC 877-247-6226
Agrusa
  Leonia, NJ 201-592-5950
Alba Foods, Inc
  Stone Mountain, GA 888-725-4605
Amira Nature Foods Ltd.
  Irvine, CA 949-852-4468
Amphora International
  Lake Forest, CA 888-380-4808
Aralia Olive Oils
  Cambridge, MA 877-585-9510
Arista Industries Inc
  Wilton, CT 800-255-6457
Ariston Specialties
  Bloomfield, CT 860-224-7184
Arnabal International, Inc.
  Tustin, CA 714-665-9477
Athena Oil Inc
  Astoria, NY 718-956-8893
Avatar Corp
  University Park, IL 800-255-3181
B R Cohn Winery & Olive Oil Co
  Glen Ellen, CA 800-330-4064
Bari Olive Oil Co
  Dinuba, CA 877-638-3626
Bella Cucina
  Atlanta, GA 866-350-9040
Bella Vista Farm
  Lawton, OK 866-237-8526
Bozzano Olive Ranch
  Stockton, CA 209-451-3665
Bragg Live Food Products Inc
  Goleta, CA 800-446-1990
California Coast Naturals
  Santa Barbara, CA 805-685-2076
California Olive Growers
  Fresno, CA 888-965-4837
California Olive Oil Council
  Berkeley, CA 888-718-9830
Calio Groves
  Piedmont, CA 800-865-4836
Calivirgin Olive Oils
  Lodi, CA 209-210-3142
Castella Imports Inc
  Brentwood, NY 631-231-5500
Chacewater Winery and Olive Mill
  Kelseyville, CA 707-279-2995
Chaparral Gardens
  Atascadero, CA 805-703-0829

Product Categories / Oils, Shortening & Fats: Oils

Cibaria International
   Riverside, CA 951-823-8490
Colavita USA
   Edison, NJ 888-265-2848
Coldani Olive Ranch LLC
   Lodi, CA 209-334-0527
Colonna Brothers Inc
   North Bergen, NJ 201-864-1115
Corning Olive Oil Company
   Corning, CA 530-824-5447
Creagri Inc
   Hayward, CA 510-732-6478
Critelli Olive Oil
   Fairfield, CA 800-865-4836
Diana's Specialty Foods
   Pingree Grove, IL 847-683-1200
Emerling International Foods
   Buffalo, NY 716-833-7381
Enzo Olive Oil Co.
   Madera, CA 559-299-7278
Erba Food Products
   Brooklyn, NY 718-272-7700
Extravagonzo Gourmet Foods
   Boise, ID 208-639-2926
Fantis Foods Inc
   Carlstadt, NJ 201-933-6200
Farmstead At Long Meadow Ranch
   St Helena, CA 877-627-2645
Filippo Berio Brand
   Lyndhurst, NJ 201-525-2900
Gaea North America LLC
   Hollywood, FL 954-923-7723
GB Ratto International Grocery
   Oakland, CA 800-325-3483
Golden Eagle Olive Products
   Porterville, CA 559-784-3468
Good Food Inc
   Honey Brook, PA 800-327-4406
Grapevine Trading Company
   Santa Rosa, CA 800-469-6478
Holy Smoke LLC
   Johns Island, SC 843-343-5581
Krinos Foods
   Bronx, NY 718-729-9000
La Piccolina
   Decatur, GA 800-626-1624
Laird & Company
   Scobeyville, NJ 877-438-5247
Loriva Culinary Oils
   San Francisco, CA 866-972-6879
Lucero Olive Oil Mfr
   Corning, CA 530-824-2190
Lucero Olive Oil Mfr
   Corning, CA 877-330-2190
Lucini Italia Company
   San Francisco, CA 888-558-2464
M&H Erickson Ranch
   Orland, CA 530-865-9587
Manassero Farms
   Irvine, CA 949-554-5103
Mancini Packing Co
   Zolfo Springs, FL 800-741-1778
Mancuso Cheese Co
   Joliet, IL 815-722-2475
Marconi Italian Specialty Foods
   Chicago, IL 312-421-0485
Marina Foods
   Medley, FL 786-888-0129
Mario Camancho Foods
   Plant City, FL 800-293-9783
McEvoy Ranch
   Petaluma, CA 866-617-6779
Mosti Mondiale/Gourmet Mondiale
   Ste-Catherine, QC 450-638-6380
Mountainbrook of Vermont
   Jeffersonville, VT 802-644-1988
Nick Sciabica & Sons
   Modesto, CA 800-551-9612
North American Enterprises
   Tucson, AZ 800-817-8666
Oliva Verde USA
   Raleigh, NC 919-846-9020
Olive Oil Factor
   Waterbury, CT 475-235-2666
Olive Oil Source
   Santa Ynez, CA 805-688-1014
Olivina. LLC
   Livermore, CA 925-455-8710
Organic Olive Juice
   New York, NY
Organic Planet
   San Francisco, CA 415-765-5590

P R Farms Inc
   Clovis, CA 559-299-0201
Pacific Sun Olive Oil
   Gerber, CA 530-385-1475
Paradise Products Corporation
   Boca Raton, FL 800-826-1235
Pasolivo Willow Creek Olive Ranch
   Paso Robles, CA 805-227-0186
Pastorelli Food Products
   Chicago, IL 800-767-2829
Pokonobe Industries
   Santa Monica, CA 310-392-1259
Pompeian Inc
   Baltimore, MD 800-766-7342
Proacec USA
   Santa Monica, CA 310-996-7770
Purity Products
   Plainview, NY 800-256-6102
Queensway Foods Company
   Burlingame, CA 650-871-7770
Ron Son Foods Inc
   Swedesboro, NJ 856-241-7333
Silverleaf International Corp
   Rosharon, TX 800-442-7542
Southern Season
   Chapel Hill, NC 877-929-7133
Sovena USA Inc
   Rome, NY 315-797-7070
Sun Olive Oil Company
   Jacksonville, FL 904-645-6630
Sutter Buttes Olive Oil
   Sutter, CA 530-763-7921
Sweet Corn Products Co
   Bloomfield, NE 877-628-6115
Tee Pee Olives, Inc.
   Rye, NY 800-431-1529
Terry Foods
   Stoke-on-Trent,
Thyme Garden Herb Co
   Alsea, OR 800-482-4372
Trattore Farms
   Geyserville, CA 707-431-7200
Tri-State Ingredients
   Mason, OH 800-622-1050
Valley Grain Products
   Fresno, CA 559-675-3400
Veronica Foods Inc
   Oakland, CA 800-370-5554
Villa Barone
   Middletown, CA 707-987-8823
Vincent Formusa Company
   Des Plaines, IL 847-813-6040
William Hill Estate Winery
   Napa, CA 707-265-3024

Extra Virgin

Adams Olive Ranch
   Lindsay, CA 888-216-5483
Agrocan
   Ville St Laurent, QC 877-247-6226
Agrusa
   Leonia, NJ 201-592-5950
Arnabal International, Inc.
   Tustin, CA 714-665-9477
Bari Olive Oil Co
   Dinuba, CA 877-638-3626
Bellucci
   Fresno, CA
Bono USA
   Fairfield, NJ 862-485-8729
Bozzano Olive Ranch
   Stockton, CA 209-451-3665
California Olive Ranch
   Chico, CA 530-592-3700
Calio Groves
   Piedmont, CA 800-865-4836
Castella Imports Inc
   Brentwood, CA 631-231-5500
Chacewater Winery and Olive Mill
   Kelseyville, CA 707-279-2995
CHO America
   Baytown, TX 281-712-1549
Colonna Brothers Inc
   North Bergen, NJ 201-864-1115
Corning Olive Oil Company
   Corning, CA 530-824-5447
Critelli Olive Oil
   Fairfield, CA 800-865-4836
Di Alfredo Foods
   Garnet Valley, PA 610-558-2802
Farmstead At Long Meadow Ranch
   St Helena, CA 877-627-2645

Filippo Berio Brand
   Lyndhurst, NJ 201-525-2900
Gemsa Oils
   La Mirada, CA 714-521-1736
GloryBee
   Eugene, OR 800-456-7923
Golden Eagle Olive Products
   Porterville, CA 559-784-3468
Green Gorilla
   Malibu, CA 323-452-5919
K L Keller Imports
   Oakland, CA 510-839-7890
Kana Organics
   Westlake Village, CA 213-603-0448
Lucero Olive Oil Mfr
   Corning, CA 530-824-2190
Lucini Italia Company
   San Francisco, CA 888-558-2464
Natural Earth Products
   Brooklyn, NY 718-552-2727
O Olive Oil
   Petaluma, CA 888-827-7148
Olive Oil Source
   Santa Ynez, CA 805-688-1014
Oliveo LLC
   Rosenberg, TX 888-924-6687
Olivina. LLC
   Livermore, CA 925-455-8710
Pacific Sun Olive Oil
   Gerber, CA 530-385-1475
Paesana Products
   East Farmingdale, NY 631-845-1717
Paradise Products Corporation
   Boca Raton, FL 800-826-1235
Pastorelli Food Products
   Chicago, IL 800-767-2829
Pepper Mill Imports
   Seaside, CA 800-928-1744
Proacec USA
   Santa Monica, CA 310-996-7770
Queensway Foods Company
   Burlingame, CA 650-871-7770
Ron Son Foods Inc
   Swedesboro, NJ 856-241-7333
Sabatino Truffles USA
   West Haven, CT 888-444-9971
Sieco USA Corporation
   Houston, TX 713-464-1726
Specialty Food Association
   New York, NY 646-878-0301
Spruce Foods
   San Clemente, CA 800-326-3612
Stinking Rose, The
   San Francisco, CA 800-995-7674
Sun Grove Foods Inc
   Passaic, NJ 973-574-1110
Sunfood
   El Cajon, CA 888-729-3663
Sutter Buttes Olive Oil
   Sutter, CA 530-763-7921
Terry Foods
   Stoke-on-Trent,
Trattore Farms
   Geyserville, CA 707-431-7200
Veronica Foods Inc
   Oakland, CA 800-370-5554
Villa Barone
   Middletown, CA 707-987-8823

Pomace

Agrocan
   Ville St Laurent, QC 877-247-6226
Olive Oil Source
   Santa Ynez, CA 805-688-1014
Pacific Sun Olive Oil
   Gerber, CA 530-385-1475
Villa Barone
   Middletown, CA 707-987-8823

Onion

Astral Extracts
   Syosset, NY 516-496-2505
Tri-State Ingredients
   Mason, OH 800-622-1050
Vegetable Juices Inc
   Chicago, IL 888-776-9752
Whole Herb Co
   Sonoma, CA 707-935-1077

Product Categories / Oils, Shortening & Fats: Oils

Orange
Astral Extracts
  Syosset, NY 516-496-2505
Boyajian LLC
  Canton, MA 800-965-0665
Diana's Specialty Foods
  Pingree Grove, IL 847-683-1200
Embassy Flavours Ltd.
  Brampton, ON 800-334-3371
Emerling International Foods
  Buffalo, NY 716-833-7381
Gold Coast Ingredients
  Commerce, CA 800-352-8673
Tri-State Ingredients
  Mason, OH 800-622-1050
Ungerer & Co
  Lincoln Park, NJ 973-706-7381
V & E Kohnstamm Inc
  Brooklyn, NY 800-847-4500
Whole Herb Co
  Sonoma, CA 707-935-1077

Palm
Aak USA Inc
  Newark, NJ 973-344-1300
AG Processing Inc
  Omaha, NE 800-247-1345
American Palm Oil
  Washington, DC 202-333-0661
Daabon Organic USA, Inc.
  Miami, FL 305-358-7667
Emerling International Foods
  Buffalo, NY 716-833-7381
Maywood International Sales
  Sante Fe, NM 805-500-5500
Natural Habitats USA
  Boulder, CO 888-958-1967
Nealanders Food Ingredients
  Mississauga, ON 800-263-1939
Pokonobe Industries
  Santa Monica, CA 310-392-1259
Stevenson-Cooper Inc
  Philadelphia, PA 215-223-2600
Tri-State Ingredients
  Mason, OH 800-622-1050
Western Pacific Oils, Inc.
  Los Angeles, CA 213-232-5117

Peanut
AG Processing Inc
  Omaha, NE 800-247-1345
Arro Corp
  Hodgkins, IL 877-929-2776
Avatar Corp
  University Park, IL 800-255-3181
California Olive Oil Council
  Berkeley, CA 888-718-9830
First Food International
  Linden, NJ 908-862-5558
Good Food Inc
  Honey Brook, PA 800-327-4406
K L Keller Imports
  Oakland, CA 510-839-7890
Loriva Culinary Oils
  San Francisco, CA 866-972-6879
Maywood International Sales
  Sante Fe, NM 805-500-5500
Nealanders Food Ingredients
  Mississauga, ON 800-263-1939
Pastorelli Food Products
  Chicago, IL 800-767-2829
Pokonobe Industries
  Santa Monica, CA 310-392-1259
Purity Products
  Plainview, NY 800-256-6102
Riceland Foods Inc.
  Stuttgart, AR 855-742-3929
Sessions Co Inc
  Enterprise, AL 334-393-0200
Sovena USA Inc
  Rome, NY 315-797-7070
Tri-State Ingredients
  Mason, OH 800-622-1050

Pecan
Schermer Pecan Co
  Glennville, GA 800-841-3403

Pepper
Tri-State Ingredients
  Mason, OH 800-622-1050
Whole Herb Co
  Sonoma, CA 707-935-1077

Peppermint
Emerling International Foods
  Buffalo, NY 716-833-7381
Gold Coast Ingredients
  Commerce, CA 800-352-8673
Lebermuth Company
  Mishawaka, IN 800-648-1123
Medallion International Inc
  Pompton Plains, NJ 973-616-3401
Tri-State Ingredients
  Mason, OH 800-622-1050
Ungerer & Co
  Lincoln Park, NJ 973-706-7381

Pimiento
Tri-State Ingredients
  Mason, OH 800-622-1050

Popping Corn
Acatris USA
  Edina, MN 952-920-7700
Avatar Corp
  University Park, IL 800-255-3181
Con Agra Snack Foods
  Hamburg, IA 800-831-5818
Delicious Popcorn
  Waupaca, WI 715-258-7683
Great Western Co LLC
  Hollywood, AL 256-259-3578
Tri-State Ingredients
  Mason, OH 800-622-1050

Poppy Seed
Herbal Products & Development
  Aptos, CA 831-688-8706
Tri-State Ingredients
  Mason, OH 800-622-1050
Whole Herb Co
  Sonoma, CA 707-935-1077

Pumpkin Seed
Arista Industries Inc
  Wilton, CT 800-255-6457

Rice Bran
Arista Industries Inc
  Wilton, CT 800-255-6457
Oilseeds International LTD
  San Francisco, CA 415-956-7251
RiceBran Technologies
  Scottsdale, AZ 602-522-3000
Riceland Foods Inc.
  Stuttgart, AR 855-742-3929

Safflower
AG Processing Inc
  Omaha, NE 800-247-1345
Arista Industries Inc
  Wilton, CT 800-255-6457
California Oils Corp
  Richmond, CA 800-225-6457
Flora Inc
  Lynden, WA 800-446-2110
Loriva Culinary Oils
  San Francisco, CA 866-972-6879
New Organics
  Kenwood, CA 734-677-5570
Pokonobe Industries
  Santa Monica, CA 310-392-1259
Tri-State Ingredients
  Mason, OH 800-622-1050

Sage
Astral Extracts
  Syosset, NY 516-496-2505
Emerling International Foods
  Buffalo, NY 716-833-7381
Tri-State Ingredients
  Mason, OH 800-622-1050
Whole Herb Co
  Sonoma, CA 707-935-1077

Salad
Arista Industries Inc
  Wilton, CT 800-255-6457
Arro Corp
  Hodgkins, IL 877-929-2776
Avatar Corp
  University Park, IL 800-255-3181
Consumer Guild Foods Inc
  Toledo, OH 419-726-3406
Emerling International Foods
  Buffalo, NY 716-833-7381
Sovena USA Inc
  Rome, NY 315-797-7070
Spectrum Foods Inc
  Springfield, IL 217-528-5301
Tri-State Ingredients
  Mason, OH 800-622-1050
Ventura Foods LLC
  Brea, CA 800-421-6257

Sassafras
Astral Extracts
  Syosset, NY 516-496-2505
Tri-State Ingredients
  Mason, OH 800-622-1050
Whole Herb Co
  Sonoma, CA 707-935-1077

Sesame
AG Processing Inc
  Omaha, NE 800-247-1345
Arista Industries Inc
  Wilton, CT 800-255-6457
Avatar Corp
  University Park, IL 800-255-3181
California Olive Oil Council
  Berkeley, CA 888-718-9830
Dipasa USA Inc
  Brownsville, TX 956-831-4072
Emerling International Foods
  Buffalo, NY 716-833-7381
Everland Foods
  Burnaby, BC
Flora Inc
  Lynden, WA 800-446-2110
Loriva Culinary Oils
  San Francisco, CA 866-972-6879
Organic Planet
  San Francisco, CA 415-765-5590
Pokonobe Industries
  Santa Monica, CA 310-392-1259
Tri-State Ingredients
  Mason, OH 800-622-1050
Universal Preservachem Inc
  Somerset, NJ 732-568-1266

Soybean
AAK
  Louisville, KY 800-622-3055
Aak USA Inc
  Newark, NJ 973-344-1300
Abitec Corp
  Columbus, OH 800-555-1255
AG Processing Inc
  Omaha, NE 800-247-1345
Agri-Dairy Products
  Purchase, NY 914-697-9580
American Hawaiian Soy Company
  Honolulu, HI 800-841-8435
Arro Corp
  Hodgkins, IL 877-929-2776
Avatar Corp
  University Park, IL 800-255-3181
California Olive Oil Council
  Berkeley, CA 888-718-9830
Central Soyfoods
  Lawrence, KS 785-312-8698
CHS Inc.
  Inver Grove Hts., MN 800-328-6539
Clofine Dairy Products Inc
  Linwood, NJ 609-653-1000
Dixie USA
  Tomball, TX 800-233-3668
DuPont Pioneer
  Johnston, IA 515-535-3200
Emerling International Foods
  Buffalo, NY 716-833-7381
First Food International
  Linden, NJ 908-862-5558

Product Categories / Oils, Shortening & Fats: Pan Coatings & Sprays

Gama Products
   Miami, FL 786-235-1515
International Foodcraft Corp
   Linden, NJ 800-875-9393
Maywood International Sales
   Sante Fe, NM 805-500-5500
Nealanders Food Ingredients
   Mississauga, ON 800-263-1939
New Organics
   Kenwood, CA 734-677-5570
Nexcel Natural Ingredients
   Springfield, IL 217-391-0091
Organic Planet
   San Francisco, CA 415-765-5590
Owensboro Grain Co
   Owensboro, KY 800-874-0305
Pacific Soybean & Grain
   San Mateo, CA 650-525-0500
Pastorelli Food Products
   Chicago, IL 800-767-2829
Pokonobe Industries
   Santa Monica, CA 310-392-1259
Purity Products
   Plainview, NY 800-256-6102
Riceland Foods Inc.
   Stuttgart, AR 855-742-3929
Sovena USA Inc
   Rome, NY 315-797-7070
Tri-State Ingredients
   Mason, OH 800-622-1050
Universal Preservachem Inc
   Somerset, NJ 732-568-1266

Sunflower

Aak USA Inc
   Newark, NJ 973-344-1300
ACH Food Co Inc
   Oakbrook Terrace, IL 630-586-3740
AG Processing Inc
   Omaha, NE 800-247-1345
Emerling International Foods
   Buffalo, NY 716-833-7381
Everland Foods
   Burnaby, BC
First Food International
   Linden, NJ 908-862-5558
Flora Inc
   Lynden, WA 800-446-2110
GloryBee
   Eugene, OR 800-456-7923
Loriva Culinary Oils
   San Francisco, CA 866-972-6879
Maywood International Sales
   Sante Fe, NM 805-500-5500
New Organics
   Kenwood, CA 734-677-5570
Nexcel Natural Ingredients
   Springfield, IL 217-391-0091
Odell's
   Reno, NV 800-635-0436
Pacific Soybean & Grain
   San Mateo, CA 650-525-0500
Pokonobe Industries
   Santa Monica, CA 310-392-1259
SIGCO Sun Products
   Breckenridge, MN 800-654-4145
Tri-State Ingredients
   Mason, OH 800-622-1050

Tangerine

Astral Extracts
   Syosset, NY 516-496-2505
Emerling International Foods
   Buffalo, NY 716-833-7381
Gold Coast Ingredients
   Commerce, CA 800-352-8673
Tri-State Ingredients
   Mason, OH 800-622-1050

Thyme

Astral Extracts
   Syosset, NY 516-496-2505
Emerling International Foods
   Buffalo, NY 716-833-7381
Tri-State Ingredients
   Mason, OH 800-622-1050
Whole Herb Co
   Sonoma, CA 707-935-1077

Truffle

Alba Foods, Inc
   Stone Mountain, GA 888-725-4605

Vegetable

Aak USA Inc
   Newark, NJ 973-344-1300
Abitec Corp
   Columbus, OH 800-555-1255
ACH Food Co Inc
   Oakbrook Terrace, IL 630-586-3740
Adams Vegetable Oils Inc
   Arbuckle, CA 530-668-2005
AG Processing Inc
   Omaha, NE 800-247-1345
Allfresh Food Products
   Evanston, IL 847-869-3100
Arista Industries Inc
   Wilton, CT 800-255-6457
Arro Corp
   Hodgkins, IL 877-929-2776
Athena Oil Inc
   Astoria, NY 718-956-8893
Avatar Corp
   University Park, IL 800-255-3181
Blue California Co
   Rancho Sta Marg, CA 949-459-2729
Bunge Canada
   Oakville, ON 905-825-7900
C P Vegetable Oil
   Fort Lauderdale, FL 800-398-7154
C&T Refinery
   Minneapolis, MN 800-227-4455
California Oils Corp
   Richmond, CA 800-225-6457
CHS Inc.
   Inver Grove Hts., MN 800-328-6539
Cibaria International
   Riverside, CA 951-823-8490
DuPont Nutrition & Biosciences
   New Century, KS 913-764-8100
Emerling International Foods
   Buffalo, NY 716-833-7381
Follmer Development, Inc
   Newbury Park, CA 805-498-4531
Fuji Vegetable Oil Inc
   White Plains, NY 914-761-7900
Gateway Food Products Co
   Dupo, IL 877-220-1963
Good Food Inc
   Honey Brook, PA 800-327-4406
Hybco USA
   Los Angeles, CA 323-269-3111
International Food Products
   Fenton, MO 800-227-8427
Liberty Vegetable Oil Co
   Santa Fe Springs, CA 562-921-3567
Loriva Culinary Oils
   San Francisco, CA 866-972-6879
Montana Specialty Mills LLC
   Great Falls, MT 800-332-2024
Natural Oils International
   Simi Valley, CA 805-433-0160
Oasis Food Co
   Hillside, NJ 800-275-0477
Ottens Flavors
   Philadelphia, PA 800-523-0767
Pokonobe Industries
   Santa Monica, CA 310-392-1259
Purity Products
   Plainview, NY 800-256-6102
Spruce Foods
   San Clemente, CA 800-326-3612
Starwest Botanicals Inc
   Sacramento, CA 800-800-4372
Tri-State Ingredients
   Mason, OH 800-622-1050
Universal Preservachem Inc
   Somerset, NJ 732-568-1266

Vitamin

Arista Industries Inc
   Wilton, CT 800-255-6457
Green Turtle Bay Vitamin Company
   Summit, NJ 800-887-8535
Jedwards International Inc
   Braintree, MA 781-848-1473
Noyes, P J
   Lancaster, NH 800-522-2469
Tri-State Ingredients
   Mason, OH 800-622-1050
Universal Preservachem Inc
   Somerset, NJ 732-568-1266

Walnut

K L Keller Imports
   Oakland, CA 510-839-7890
Loriva Culinary Oils
   San Francisco, CA 866-972-6879

Wheat Germ

Arista Industries Inc
   Wilton, CT 800-255-6457
Avatar Corp
   University Park, IL 800-255-3181
Energen Products Inc
   Norwalk, CA 800-423-8837
Pokonobe Industries
   Santa Monica, CA 310-392-1259
Tri-State Ingredients
   Mason, OH 800-622-1050
Universal Preservachem Inc
   Somerset, NJ 732-568-1266
Viobin USA
   Monticello, IL 888-473-9645
Vitamins
   Chicago, IL 312-861-0700

Pan Coatings & Sprays

Richardson International
   Winnipeg, MB 866-217-6211

Shortening

AAK
   Louisville, KY 800-622-3055
ACH Food Co Inc
   Oakbrook Terrace, IL 630-586-3740
Allfresh Food Products
   Evanston, IL 847-869-3100
Brand Aromatics Inc
   Lakewood, NJ 800-363-2080
C.F. Sauer Co.
   Richmond, VA 888-723-0052
CanAmera Foods
   Edmonton, AL 780-447-6960
Clofine Dairy Products Inc
   Linwood, NJ 609-653-1000
Coast Packing Co
   Vernon, CA 323-277-7700
DuPont Nutrition & Biosciences
   New Century, KS 913-764-8100
Hamersmith, Inc.
   Miami, FL 305-685-7451
International Food Products
   Fenton, MO 800-227-8427
J.M. Smucker Co.
   Orrville, OH 888-550-9555
JE Bergeron & Sons
   Bromptonville, QC 800-567-2798
Marina Foods
   Medley, FL 786-888-0129
Mid Atlantic Vegetable Shortening Company
   Kearny, NJ 800-966-1645
Pastorelli Food Products
   Chicago, IL 800-767-2829
Richardson International
   Winnipeg, MB 866-217-6211
Source Food Technology
   Durham, NC 866-277-3849
Spectrum Foods Inc
   Springfield, IL 217-528-5301
Ventura Foods LLC
   Brea, CA 800-421-6257
Western Pacific Oils, Inc.
   Los Angeles, CA 213-232-5117

Fluid

DuPont Nutrition & Biosciences
   New Century, KS 913-764-8100
Pastorelli Food Products
   Chicago, IL 800-767-2829

Vegetable

Bunge Canada
   Oakville, ON 905-825-7900
DuPont Nutrition & Biosciences
   New Century, KS 913-764-8100
Gateway Food Products Co
   Dupo, IL 877-220-1963

Product Categories / Oils, Shortening & Fats: Shortening

JE Bergeron & Sons
Bromptonville, QC 800-567-2798
Pastorelli Food Products
Chicago, IL 800-767-2829

Liquid
DuPont Nutrition & Biosciences
New Century, KS 913-764-8100

Pastorelli Food Products
Chicago, IL 800-767-2829

Organic Foods *See also* Organic Foods Major

General

Abunda Life
   Asbury Park, NJ 732-775-9338
Adrienne's Gourmet Foods
   Santa Barbara, CA 800-937-7010
Allegro Coffee Co
   Thornton, CO 800-666-4869
Alliston Creamery
   Alliston, ON 705-435-6751
Alta Dena Certified Dairy LLC
   City Of Industry, CA 800-535-1369
Alvarado Street Bakery
   Petaluma, CA 707-789-6700
American Natural & Organic
   Fremont, CA 510-440-1044
Amy's Kitchen Inc
   Santa Rosa, CA 707-781-6600
Andre-Boudin Bakeries
   San Francisco, CA 415-882-1849
Ankeny Lake Wild Rice
   Salem, OR 800-555-5380
Annie's Naturals
   Berkeley, CA 800-434-1234
Applegate Farms
   Bridgewater, NJ 866-587-5858
Argee Corp
   Santee, CA 800-449-3030
Arico Natural Foods
   Beaverton, OR 503-259-0871
Atwater Foods
   Lyndonville Orleans, NY 585-765-2639
Avalon Organic Coffees
   Albuquerque, NM 800-662-2575
Avenue Gourmet
   Owings Mills, MD 410-902-5701
Barrows Tea Company
   New Bedford, MA 800-832-5024
Beehive Botanicals
   Hayward, WI 800-233-4483
Bel Brands USA
   Chicago, IL 312-462-1500
Belgravia Imports
   Portsmouth, RI 800-848-1127
Bella Vista Farm
   Lawton, OK 866-237-8526
Berardi's Fresh Roast
   Cleveland, OH 800-876-9109
Beta Pure Foods
   Santa Cruz, CA 831-685-6565
Beth's Fine Desserts
   Mill Valley, CA 415-383-3991
Blessed Herbs
   Oakham, MA 800-489-4372
Blue Marble Brands
   Providence, RI 888-534-0246
Boehringer Ingelheim Corp
   Ridgefield, CT 800-243-0127
Brad's Organic
   Haverstraw, NY 845-429-9080
Brass Ladle Products
   Concordville, PA 800-955-2353
Brewster Dairy Inc
   Brewster, OH 800-874-8874
Briess Malt & Ingredients Co.
   Chilton, WI 800-657-0806
Buchanan Hollow Nut Co
   Le Grand, CA 800-532-1500
Bunker Hill Cheese Co Inc
   Millersburg, OH 800-253-6636
Buns & Roses Organic Wholegrain Bakery
   Edmonton, AB 780-438-0098
Buywell Coffee
   Colorado Springs, CO 877-294-6246
Cache Creek Foods LLC
   Woodland, CA 530-662-1764
Cafe Altura
   Santa Paula, CA 800-526-8328
Cafe Society Coffee Company
   Dallas, TX 800-717-6000
California Custom Fruits
   Baldwin Park, CA 877-558-0056
California Independent Almond Growers
   Merced, CA 209-667-4855
California Olive Oil Council
   Berkeley, CA 888-718-9830

Cascadian Farm Inc
   Sedro Woolley, WA 360-855-0542
Cedarlane Foods
   Carson, CA 800-826-3322
Century Foods Intl LLC
   Sparta, WI 800-269-1901
Champlain Valley Milling Corp
   Westport, NY 518-962-4711
Chelten House Products
   Swedesboro, NJ
Cherith Valley Gardens
   Fort Worth, TX 800-610-9813
Chino Valley Ranchers
   Colton, CA 800-354-4503
Chris' Farm Stand
   Peabody, MA 978-994-4315
Christopher Ranch LLC
   Gilroy, CA 408-847-1100
CHS Sunprairie
   Minot, ND 800-556-6807
Chunco Foods Inc
   Kansas City, MO 816-283-0716
Citrus Service
   Winter Garden, FL 407-656-4999
Clear Mountain Coffee Company
   Silver Spring, MD 301-587-2233
Coleman Natural
   Kings Mountain, NC 800-442-8666
Country Choice Organic
   Eden Prairie, MN 952-829-8824
CROPP Cooperative
   La Farge, WI 888-444-6455
Cuizina Food Company
   Woodinville, WA 425-486-7000
Cyanotech Corp
   Kailua Kona, HI 800-395-1353
Daymar Select Fine Coffees
   El Cajon, CA 800-466-7590
Dorothy Dawson Food Products
   Jackson, MI 517-788-9830
Earth Island
   Chatsworth, CA 888-394-3949
East Wind Inc
   Tecumseh, MO 417-679-4682
Eatem Foods Co
   Vineland, NJ 800-683-2836
Eberly Poultry, Inc.
   Stevens, PA 717-336-6440
Eden Foods Inc
   Clinton, MI 888-424-3336
Eden Organic Pasta Company
   Clinton, MI 888-424-3336
Eggology
   Canoga Park, CA 818-610-2222
Emerling International Foods
   Buffalo, NY 716-833-7381
Equal Exchange Inc
   West Bridgewater, MA 774-776-7400
Ethical Naturals
   San Anselmo, CA 866-459-4454
Extracts and Ingredients Ltd
   Union, NJ 908-688-9009
Fairhaven Cooperative Flour Mill
   Bellingham, WA 360-757-9947
FarmGro Organic Foods
   Regina, SK 306-751-2449
Fine Dried Foods Intl
   Santa Cruz, CA 831-426-1413
Fireside Kitchen
   Halifax, NS 902-454-7387
Florence Macaroni Manufacturing
   Chicago, IL 800-647-2782
Florida Crystals Corporation
   West Palm Beach, FL 844-344-9497
Florida Food Products Inc
   Eustis, FL 800-874-2331
French Meadow Bakery & Cafe
   Minneapolis, MN 612-870-7855
Fresh Tofu Inc
   Allentown, PA 610-433-4711
Frontier Co-op
   Norway, IA 844-550-6200
Fungus Among Us
   Snohomish, WA 360-568-3403
Gelato Fresco
   Toronto, ON 416-785-5415

George Chiala Farms Inc
   Morgan Hill, CA 408-778-0562
Ginseng Up Corp
   Worcester, MA 800-446-7364
GKI Foods
   Brighton, MI 248-486-0055
Golden Harvest Pecans
   Cairo, GA 800-597-0968
Golden Town Apple Products
   Rougemont, QC 866-552-7643
Good Groceries
   Brooklyn, NY 347-853-7462
Good Stuff Cacao
   Metamora, MI 248-690-5114
Grandpa Po's Nutra Nuts
   Commerce, CA 323-260-7457
Great Eastern Sun Trading Co
   Asheville, NC 800-334-5809
Great River Organic Milling
   Arcadia, WI 608-687-9580
Green & Black's Organic Chocolate
   Plano, TX 877-299-1254
Grounds for Change
   Poulsbo, WA 800-796-6820
Guayaki
   Sebastopol, CA 888-482-9254
Hain Celestial Group Inc
   Boulder, CO 800-434-4246
Hallcrest Vineyards
   Felton, CA 831-335-4441
Harbar LLC
   Canton, MA 800-881-7040
Hawkhaven Greenhouse International
   Wautoma, WI 800-745-4295
Health Valley Company
   Irwindale, CA 800-334-3204
Healthy Food Ingredients
   Fargo, ND 844-275-3443
HempNut
   Henderson, NV 707-576-7050
Herbal Magic
   Toronto, ON 877-237-7225
Heritage Short Bread
   Hilton Head Isle, SC 843-422-3458
Hialeah Products Co
   Hollywood, FL 800-923-3379
Highland Sugarworks
   Websterville, VT 800-452-4012
Homestead Mills
   Cook, MN 800-652-5233
Horizon Organic Dairy
   Broomfield, CO 888-494-3020
Horner International
   Raleigh, NC 919-787-3112
Hoyt's Honey Farm
   Baytown, TX 281-576-5383
HP Schmid
   San Francisco, CA 415-765-5925
IMAG Organics
   Dallas, TX 855-301-0400
Indigo Coffee Roasters
   Florence, MA 800-447-5450
Ineeka Inc
   Chicago, IL 312-733-8327
Integrative Flavors
   Michigan City, IN 800-837-7687
International Foods
   Bloomfield, NJ 800-225-1449
Island Spring Inc
   Vashon, WA 206-463-9848
Johnson Foods, Inc.
   Sunnyside, WA 509-837-4214
Jonathan's Sprouts
   Rochester, MA 508-763-2577
Kashi Company
   Solana Beach, CA 877-747-2467
KD Canners Inc
   Mississauga, ON 905-602-1825
Kopali Organics
   Miami, FL 305-751-7341
Kozlowski Farms
   Forestville, CA 800-473-2767
Lakeview Bakery
   Calgary, AB 403-246-6127
Larabar
   Denver, CO 800-543-2147

Product Categories / Organic Foods *See also* Organic Foods Major: Baby Foods

Late July Snacks
   Norwalk, CT 888-857-6225
Lifeway
   Morton Grove, IL 877-281-3874
Lily of the Desert
   Denton, TX 800-229-5459
Lowell Farms
   El Campo, TX 888-484-9213
Lundberg Family Farms
   Richvale, CA 530-538-3500
Made In Nature
   Boulder, CO 800-906-7426
Magnum Coffee Roastery
   Nunica, MI 888-937-5282
Mandarin Soy Sauce Inc
   Middletown, NY 845-343-1505
Marroquin Organic Intl.
   Santa Cruz, CA 831-423-3442
Mcfadden Farm
   Potter Valley, CA 800-544-8230
Mediterranean Snack Food Co
   Boonton, NJ 973-402-2644
Mellace Family Brands
   Carlsbad, CA 866-255-6887
Merlino Italian Baking Company
   Kent, WA. 800-800-9490
Mills Brothers Intl
   Seattle, WA 206-575-3000
Minnestalgia Foods LLC
   Mcgregor, MN 800-328-6731
Miyako Oriental Foods Inc
   Baldwin Park, CA. 877-788-6476
Mom's Gourmet, LLC
   Chagrin Falls, OH 440-564-9702
Moore Organics
   Hamilton, OH 513-881-7144
Mountain High Organics
   New Milford, CT 860-210-7805
Mr Espresso
   Oakland, CA 510-287-5200
Mrs. Leeper's Pasta
   Excelsior Springs, MO 800-848-5266
Mrs. Miller's Homemade Noodles
   Fredericksburg, OH 800-227-4487
Mushroom Co
   Cambridge, MD 410-221-8971
Mustard Seed
   Central, SC 877-621-2591
Najla's Specialty Foods Inc
   Louisville, KY 877-962-5527
Native American Natural Foods
   Kyle, SD 800-416-7212
Natural Food Mill
   Corona, CA 800-797-5090
Natural Way Mills Inc
   Middle River, MN. 218-222-3677
Nature's Candy
   Fredericksburg, TX. 800-729-0085
Nature's Legacy Inc.
   Hudson, MI 517-448-2050
Nature's Nutrition
   Marysville, OH 800-242-1115
Naturel
   Rancho Cucamonga, CA 877-242-8344
Natures Sungrown Foods Inc
   San Rafael, CA 415-491-4944
New England Natural Bakers
   Greenfield, MA 800-910-2884
New Organics
   Kenwood, CA 734-677-5570
North Bay Trading Co
   Brule, WI. 800-348-0164
North Country Natural Spring Water
   Port Kent, NY 518-834-9400
NOW Foods
   Bloomingdale, IL 888-669-3663
Nu-World Amaranth Inc
   Naperville, IL 630-369-6851
Nutra Nuts
   Commerce, CA 323-260-7457
Nutrex Hawaii Inc
   Kailua Kona, HI 800-453-1187
O Olive Oil
   Petaluma, CA 888-827-7148
OMG! Superfoods
   Rancho Dominguez, CA 855-664-3663
Once Again Nut Butter
   Nunda, NY 888-800-8075
Organic Germinal
   Los Angeles, CA. 310-846-5901
Organic Girl Produce
   Salinas, CA 831-758-7800

Organic Gourmet
   Sherman Oaks, CA 800-400-7772
Organic Liaison, LLC
   Coral Springs, FL 954-755-4405
Organic Planet
   San Francisco, CA 415-765-5590
Organic Wine Co Inc
   San Francisco, CA 888-326-9463
Oskri Corporation
   Lake Mills, WI 920-648-8300
Pacari Organic Chocolate
   Boca Raton, FL
Palmieri Food Products
   New Haven, CT 800-845-5447
Panos Brands
   Rochelle Park, NJ 201-843-8900
Pappy's Sassafras Tea
   Columbus Grove, OH 877-659-5110
Parthenon Food Products
   Ann Arbor, MI 734-994-1012
Pasta Prima
   Benicia, CA 530-671-7200
Peace Mountain Natural Beverages
   Springfield, MA 413-567-4942
Peace Village Organic Foods
   Berkeley, CA 510-524-4420
Pearl Valley Cheese Inc
   Fresno, OH 740-545-6002
Personal Edge Nutrition
   Ballwin, MO 514-636-4512
Pleasant Grove Farms
   Pleasant Grove, CA 916-655-3391
Prairie Mills Products LLC
   Rochester, IN 574-223-3177
Price Co
   Yakima, WA 509-966-4110
Progenix Corporation
   Wausau, WI 800-233-3356
Purity Farms
   La Farge, WI 877-211-4819
Quality Naturally Foods
   City Of Industry, CA. 888-498-6986
R&J Farms
   West Salem, OH 419-846-3179
R.J. Corr Naturals
   Posen, IL 708-389-4200
RAJB Hog Foods Inc
   Jersey City, NJ 201-395-9400
Rapunzel Pure Organics
   Bloomfield, NJ 800-225-1449
Ravioli Store
   Long Island City, NY 877-727-8269
Red River Commodities Inc
   Fargo, ND 800-437-5539
Regenie's Crunchy Pi
   Haverhill, MA 877-734-3643
RFi Ingredients
   Blauvelt, NY 800-962-7663
Roberts Seed
   Axtell, NE 308-743-2565
Rocky Mountain Honey Company
   Salt Lake City, UT 801-355-2054
Run-A-Ton Group Inc
   Chester, NJ 800-247-6580
Rustic Crust Inc
   Pittsfield, NH 603-435-5119
Seitenbacher America LLC
   Odessa, FL 727-376-3000
Shariann's Organics
   Boulder, CO 800-434-4246
Sierra Madre Coffee
   Denver, CO 303-446-0050
Silver Creek Specialty Meats
   Oshkosh, WI 800-729-2849
SJH Enterprises
   Middleton, WI. 888-745-3845
Sno-Pac Foods Inc
   Caledonia, MN 800-533-2215
Solana Gold Organics
   Sebastopol, CA 800-459-1121
Solnuts
   Hudson, IA 800-648-3503
Sophia's Sauce Works
   Carson City, NV 800-718-7769
Spicely
   Fremont, CA 510-440-1044
Springfield Creamery Inc
   Eugene, OR 541-689-2911
Straus Family Creamery
   Petaluma, CA 800-572-7783
Sunergia Soyfoods
   Charlottesville, VA 800-693-5134

Sunnyside Organics Seedlings
   Washington, VA 510-221-5050
Sunridge Farms
   Royal Oaks, CA 831-786-7000
Sunridge Farms Inc
   Salinas, CA 831-755-1530
Sunshine Farm & Garden
   Renick, WV 304-497-2208
Sure-Fresh Produce Inc
   Santa Maria, CA 888-423-5379
Sustainable Sourcing
   Great Barrington, MA. 413-528-5141
Suzanne's Specialties
   New Brunswick, NJ 800-762-2135
Synergy
   Moab, UT 800-804-3211
Tastybaby
   Malibu, CA 866-588-8278
Tea-n-Crumpets
   San Rafael, CA 415-457-2495
Teeny Tiny Spice Company of Vermont LLC
   Shelburne, VT 802-598-6800
Templar Food Products
   New Providence, NJ 800-883-6752
Thomas Canning/Maidstone
   Maidstone, ON 519-737-1531
Thoughtful Food
   Lafayette, CA 510-910-2581
Three Trees Almondmilk
   San Mateo, CA 855-863-8733
Tomanetti Food Products Inc
   Oakmont, PA 800-875-3040
Tova Industries LLC
   Louisville, KY 888-532-8682
Travel Chocolate
   New York, NY 718-841-7030
Treehouse Farms
   Elgin, AZ. 559-757-5020
Triple Springs Spring Water Co
   Meriden, CT 203-235-8374
Tripper Inc
   Oxnard, CA 805-988-8851
True Organic Product Inc
   Helm, CA 800-487-0379
Tuscarora Organic Growers Cooperative
   Hustontown, PA 814-448-2173
Twin Marquis
   Brooklyn, NY 800-367-6868
Unique Ingredients LLC
   Gold Canyon, AZ 480-983-2498
Vegetable Juices Inc
   Chicago, IL 888-776-9752
Ventre Packing Company
   Syracuse, NY 315-463-2384
Vienna Bakery
   Barrington, RI 401-245-2355
Vogue Cuisine Foods
   Sunnyvale, CA 888-236-4144
WCC Honey Marketing
   City Of Industry, CA. 626-855-3086
Westbrae Natural Foods
   Melville, NY 800-434-4246
Wholesome!
   Sugar Land, TX. 800-680-1896
Wild Aseptics, LLC
   Erlanger, KY 877-787-7221
Wild Rice Exchange
   Woodland, CA. 800-223-7423
Wine Country Chef LLC
   Hidden Valley Lake, CA. 707-322-0406
Wing Nien Food
   Hayward, CA 510-487-8877
Wizards Cauldron, LTD
   Yanceyville, NC 336-694-5665
Wood Sugarbush
   Spring Valley, WI 715-772-4656
Woodstock Farms Manufacturing
   Edison, NJ 800-526-4349
World Casing Corp
   Maspeth, NY 800-221-4887
Xochitl
   Dallas, TX 866-595-8917
Y Z Enterprises Inc
   Maumee, OH 800-736-8779
Your Bar Factory
   LaSalle, QC. 888-366-0258
Zhena's Gypsy Tea
   Commerce, CA 800-448-0803

Baby Foods

Ella's Kitchen
   New Castle, DE. 800-685-7799

Product Categories / Organic Foods *See also* Organic Foods Major: Baked Goods

Gerber Products Co
 Arlington, VA 800-284-9488
Hain Celestial Group Inc
 Lake Success, NY 800-434-4246
Happy Family
 New York, NY 855-644-2779
Little Duck Organics
 New York, NY 877-458-1321
Oh Baby Foods, Inc.
 Fayetteville, AR 800-788-1451
Plum Organics
 Emeryville, CA 877-914-7586
Square One Organics
 River Forest, IL 866-771-7138
Stonyfield Organic
 Londonderry, NH 800-776-2697

Baked Goods

Alvarado Street Bakery
 Petaluma, CA 707-789-6700
Blue Marble Brands
 Providence, RI 888-534-0246
Bread Alone Bakery
 Lake Katrine, NY 800-769-3328
Country Choice Organic
 Eden Prairie, MN 952-829-8824
Fillo Factory, The
 Northvale, NJ 800-653-4556
Foods Alive
 Angola, IN. 260-488-4497
French Meadow Bakery & Cafe
 Minneapolis, MN 612-870-7855
Fullbloom Baking Co
 Newark, NJ 800-201-9909
Good Groceries
 Brooklyn, NY 347-853-7462
Homefree LLC
 Windham, NH 800-552-7172
Inked Organics
 Petaluma, CA
Kashi Company
 Solana Beach, CA 877-747-2467
Kerri Kreations
 Santa Cruz, CA 831-429-5129
Mary's Gone Crackers
 Gridley, CA 888-258-1250
Natural Food Mill
 Corona, CA 800-797-5090
Nature's Path Foods
 Blaine, WA 888-808-9505
Rudi's Organic Bakery
 Boulder, CO 877-293-0876
Rustic Crust Inc
 Pittsfield, NH 603-435-5119
Tram Bar LLC
 Victor, ID 208-354-4790

Beverages

24 Mantra Organic
 Fremont, CA
Allegro Coffee Co
 Thornton, CO 800-666-4869
ALO Drinks
 San Francisco, CA
Bhakti
 Boulder, CO 303-484-8770
Blue Marble Brands
 Providence, RI 888-534-0246
Cafe Kreyol
 Manassas, VA
Caffe Ibis Gallery Deli
 Logan, UT 888-740-4777
California Juice Co.
 Santa Barbara, CA 805-738-8723
Celebrity Tea, LLC
 Tampa, FL 813-600-3317
Cell-Nique
 Norwalk, CT 888-417-9343
Chartreuse Organic Tea
 Trenton, MI 866-315-7832
Choice Organic Teas
 Seattle, WA 866-972-6879
Citromax Flavors Inc
 Carlstadt, NJ 201-933-8405
Dark Dog
 Miami Beach, FL
Davidson's Organics
 Reno, NV 800-882-5888
Evolution Fresh
 Seattle, WA 800-794-9986
Faribault Foods, Inc.
 Fairbault, MN 507-331-1400
Florida Food Products Inc
 Eustis, FL 800-874-2331
Foods Alive
 Angola, IN. 260-488-4497
Frey Vineyards
 Redwood Valley, CA 800-760-3739
Great Eastern Sun Trading Co
 Asheville, NC 800-334-5809
Hain Celestial Group Inc
 Lake Success, NY 800-434-4246
Happy Family
 New York, NY 855-644-2779
Honest Tea Inc
 Atlanta, GA 800-520-2653
J.M. Smucker Co.
 Orrville, OH 888-550-9555
Kombucha Wonder Drink
 Portland, OR 877-224-7331
Lakewood Juice Co.
 Miami, FL 866-324-5900
Mamma Chia
 Carlsbad, CA 855-588-2442
New Barn Organics
 Rohnert Park, CA 888-635-7102
Organic Girl Produce
 Salinas, CA 831-758-7800
Perricone Juices
 Beaumont, CA 951-769-7171
Pyure Brands
 Naples, FL. 305-509-5096
Rooibee Red Tea
 Louisville, KY 502-749-0800
Sambazon
 San Clemente, CA 877-726-2296
Small Planet Foods
 Minneapolis, MN 800-624-4123
Stash Tea Co
 Portland, OR 800-547-1514
Stonyfield Organic
 Londonderry, NH 800-776-2697
Sunfood
 El Cajon, CA 888-729-3663
Tazo Tea
 Kent, WA. 855-829-6832
Templar Food Products
 New Providence, NJ 800-883-6752
The Healthy Beverage Company
 Doylestown, PA 800-295-1388
Third Street Inc
 Louisville, CO. 800-636-3790

Candy & Confectionery

Cocoa Parlor
 Laguna Niguel, CA 949-877-9549
DAGOBA Organic Chocolate
 Ashland, OR 866-972-6879
Dina's Organic Chocolate
 Mt Kisco, NY 888-625-2008
Earth Source Organics
 Vista, CA 760-734-1867
Good Stuff Cacao
 Metamora, MI 248-690-5114
Justin's Nut Butter
 Boulder, CO 844-448-0302
Nelly's Organics
 Chatsworth, CA 310-756-0738
NuGo Nutrition
 Oakmont, PA 888-421-2032
Organic Nectars LLC
 Malden On Hudson, NY 845-246-0506
Pascha Chocolate
 Toronto, Ontario, ... 855-472-7242
Sjaak's Organic Chocolates
 Petaluma, CA 707-775-2434
Sunridge Farms
 Royal Oaks, CA 831-786-7000
Theo Chocolate
 Seattle, WA 206-632-5100
Zazubean
 Vancouver, BC 604-801-5488

Cereals, Grains, Rice & Flour

Back to the Roots
 Oakland, CA 510-922-9758
Bob's Red Mill Natural Foods
 Milwaukie, OR 800-349-2173
Boulder Granola
 Boulder, CO 303-443-1136
Foods Alive
 Angola, IN. 260-488-4497
Great River Organic Milling
 Arcadia, WI. 608-687-9580
Hain Celestial Group Inc
 Lake Success, NY 800-434-4246
Happy Family
 New York, NY 855-644-2779
Heartland Mills Shipping
 Marienthal, KS 800-232-8533
Hodgson Mill Inc
 Effingham, IL 800-347-0198
Homefree LLC
 Windham, NH 800-552-7172
IMAG Organics
 Dallas, TX. 855-301-0400
Kashi Company
 Solana Beach, CA 877-747-2467
King Arthur Flour
 Norwich, VT 800-827-6836
Lundberg Family Farms
 Richvale, CA 530-538-3500
Natural Food Mill
 Corona, CA 800-797-5090
Nature's Legacy Inc.
 Hudson, MI 517-448-2050
Nature's Path Foods
 Blaine, WA 888-808-9505
New England Natural Bakers
 Greenfield, MA 800-910-2884
NOW Foods
 Bloomingdale, IL 888-669-3663
Pacific Grain & Foods
 Fresno, CA 559-276-2580
Santa Barbara Pistachio Co
 Maricopa, CA 800-896-1044
Small Batch Organics
 Manchester Center, VT. 802-367-1054
Small Planet Foods
 Minneapolis, MN 800-624-4123
Smirk's
 Fort Morgan, CO 970-762-0202
Spectrum Foods Inc
 Springfield, IL. 217-528-5301
Teeccino
 Carpinteria, CA 800-498-3434
The Real Co
 Wilmington, DE 347-433-8945
Timeless Seeds
 Ulm, MT 406-866-3340
TresOmega
 New Milford, CT 860-210-7805

Cheese & Cheese Products

Blue Marble Brands
 Providence, RI 888-534-0246
Horizon Organic Dairy
 Broomfield, CO 888-494-3020
Pennsylvania Macaroni Company
 Pittsburgh, PA 800-223-5928

Dairy Products

Ahara Ghee
 Portland, OR 503-997-5050
Alden's Organic
 Camas, WA
Ancient Organics
 Berkeley, CA 510-280-5043
Aurora Organic Dairy
 Boulder, CO 303-284-3313
Boulder Homemade Inc
 Boulder, CO 800-691-5002
Cloud Top
 Pasadena, CA 888-263-1778
Horizon Organic Dairy
 Broomfield, CO 888-494-3020
Oregon Ice Cream Co.
 Vancouver, WA 360-713-6800
Springfield Creamery Inc
 Eugene, OR 541-689-2911
Stonyfield Organic
 Londonderry, NH 800-776-2697
WhiteWave Foods
 Denver, CO 800-488-9283
Windy City Organics
 Northbrook, IL 800-925-0577

Doughs, Mixes & Fillings

Bob's Red Mill Natural Foods
 Milwaukie, OR 800-349-2173

Product Categories / Organic Foods See also Organic Foods Major: Eggs & Egg Products

French Meadow Bakery & Cafe
  Minneapolis, MN 612-870-7855
Hodgson Mill Inc
  Effingham, IL 800-347-0198
Homefree LLC
  Windham, NH 800-552-7172
Nature's Path Foods
  Blaine, WA 888-808-9505

Eggs & Egg Products

Horizon Organic Dairy
  Broomfield, CO 888-494-3020
Pete and Gerry's Organic Eggs
  Monroe, NH 800-210-6657

Ethnic Foods

Bob's Red Mill Natural Foods
  Milwaukie, OR 800-349-2173
French Meadow Bakery & Cafe
  Minneapolis, MN 612-870-7855
Great Eastern Sun Trading Co
  Asheville, NC 800-334-5809
Harbar LLC
  Canton, MA 800-881-7040
San-J International Inc
  Henrico, VA 800-446-5500
SLT Group
  Dayton, NJ 732-837-3096
The Food Collective
  Irvine, CA 866-328-8638

Fruits & Vegetables

Atlantic Laboratories Inc
  Waldoboro, ME 888-662-5357
Bay Baby Produce
  Burlington, WA 360-755-2299
Bedemco Inc
  White Plains, NY 914-683-1119
Blue Marble Brands
  Providence, RI 888-534-0246
Bob's Red Mill Natural Foods
  Milwaukie, OR 800-349-2173
Dole Food Company, Inc.
  Thousand Oaks, CA 800-356-3111
Driscoll Strawberry Assoc Inc
  Watsonville, CA 831-424-0506
Earthbound Farm
  San Jn Bautista, CA 800-690-3200
Faribault Foods, Inc.
  Fairbault, MN 507-331-1400
Farm Fresh to You
  Anaheim, CA 800-796-6009
Fine Dried Foods Intl
  Santa Cruz, CA 831-426-1413
Golden Valley Natural
  Shelley, ID. 888-270-7147
Great Eastern Sun Trading Co
  Asheville, NC 800-334-5809
Happy Family
  New York, NY 855-644-2779
Hodgson Mill Inc
  Effingham, IL 800-347-0198
Lisa's Organics
  Carnelian Bay, CA 877-584-5711
Made In Nature
  Boulder, CO 800-906-7426
Maine Coast Sea Vegetables
  Franklin, ME 207-565-2907
Mushroom Co
  Cambridge, MD 410-221-8971
Mushroom Harvest
  Athens, OH 740-448-7376
Nature's Legacy Inc.
  Hudson, MI 517-448-2050
Organic Girl Produce
  Salinas, CA 831-758-7800
Organics Unlimited
  San Diego, CA 619-710-0658
Ready Pac Foods Inc
  Irwindale, CA 800-800-4088
Sambazon
  San Clemente, CA. 877-726-2296
Season Harvest Foods
  Los Altos, CA 650-968-2273
Small Planet Foods
  Minneapolis, MN 800-624-4123
Spectrum Foods Inc
  Springfield, IL. 217-528-5301
Sunfood
  El Cajon, CA. 888-729-3663

Sunridge Farms
  Royal Oaks, CA 831-786-7000
Sutter Foods LLC
  Yuba City, CA 530-682-7776
Tradin Organics USA
  Scotts Valley, CA 831-685-6565
Viva Tierra
  Mt Vernon, WA 360-855-0566
WhiteWave Foods
  Denver, CO 800-488-9283
Wholesum Family Farms
  Nogales, AZ 520-281-9233

General Grocery

Blue Marble Brands
  Providence, RI 888-534-0246
Faribault Foods, Inc.
  Fairbault, MN 507-331-1400
Happy Family
  New York, NY 855-644-2779
Lisa's Organics
  Carnelian Bay, CA 877-584-5711
Small Planet Foods
  Minneapolis, MN 800-624-4123

Hemp

Colorado Hemp Honey
  Parker, CO 833-233-2256
Curaleaf
  Wakefield, MA 833-760-4367
Earth Circle Organics
  Auburn, CA 877-922-3663
Ella's Flats
  Naples, FL
Hemp Fusion
  Roswell, GA 877-669-4367
Hemp Oil Canada
  Ste. Agathe, MB 800-289-4367
Hemp Production Services
  Saskatoon, SK 844-436-7477
Humming Hemp
  Richland, WA 503-559-6476
Isodiol
  Escondido, CA 855-979-6751
Lumen
  Oakland, CA
Manitoba Harvest Hemp
  Minneapolis, MN 800-665-4367
Minnesota Hemp Farms
  Hastings, MN 877-205-4367
Nature's Love
  Snyder, CO 970-571-7959
Phivida Organics
  San Diego, CA 844-744-6646
RE Botanicals
  Boulder, CO 303-214-2118
San Luis Valley Hemp Co.
  Del Norte, CO. 719-299-5000

Ingredients, Flavors & Additives

Aromatech USA
  Orlando, FL. 407-277-5727
Briess Malt & Ingredients Co.
  Chilton, WI 800-657-0806
California Natural Products
  Lathrop, CA 209-858-2525
Citromax Flavors Inc
  Carlstadt, NJ 201-933-8405
Flavorganics
  Newark, NJ 866-972-6879
Frontier Co-op
  Norway, IA 844-550-6200
Futurebiotics LLC
  Hauppauge, NY 800-645-1721
GloryBee
  Eugene, OR. 800-456-7923
Gold Coast Ingredients
  Commerce, CA 800-352-8673
Homefree LLC
  Windham, NH 800-552-7172
International Foodcraft Corp
  Linden, NJ. 800-875-9393
Lang Pharma Nutrition Inc
  Middletown, RI 401-848-7700
Moore Organics
  Hamilton, OH 513-881-7144
New Chapter
  Brattleboro, VT. 800-543-7279
NOW Foods
  Bloomingdale, IL 888-669-3663

Organic Partners Intl.
  Portland, OR 503-445-1065
Premier Organics
  Oakland, CA 866-237-8688
Primal Essence
  Oxnard, CA. 877-774-6253
Rejuvila
  Boulder, CO 877-480-4402
RFi Ingredients
  Blauvelt, NY 800-962-7663
Sunfood
  El Cajon, CA. 888-729-3663

Jams, Jellies & Spreads

Cook's Pantry
  Ventura, CA 805-947-4622
Food For Thought Inc
  Honor, MI 231-326-5444
Good Spread
  Boulder, CO
Small Planet Foods
  Minneapolis, MN 800-624-4123

Meats & Meat Products

Bilinski Sausage Mfg Co
  Cohoes, NY. 877-873-9102
Coleman Natural
  Kings Mountain, NC 800-442-8666
Eberly Poultry, Inc.
  Stevens, PA 717-336-6440
Golden Valley Natural
  Shelley, ID. 888-270-7147
Mesquite Organic Beef LLC
  Aurora, CO 888-480-2333
Osso Good, LLC
  San Rafael, CA
Panorama Meats
  Fresno, CA 707-765-6756
Petaluma Poultry
  Petaluma, CA 800-556-6789
Sommers Organic
  Wheeling, IL 877-377-9797

Nuts & Nut Butters

Bedemco Inc
  White Plains, NY 914-683-1119
Blue Marble Brands
  Providence, RI 888-534-0246
Divine Organics
  CA 209-532-4950
J.M. Smucker Co.
  Orrville, OH 888-550-9555
Justin's Nut Butter
  Boulder, CO 844-448-0302
NOW Foods
  Bloomingdale, IL 888-669-3663
Nuttzo
  San Diego, CA 888-325-0553
Once Again Nut Butter
  Nunda, NY 888-800-8075
Pacific Grain & Foods
  Fresno, CA 559-276-2580
Premier Organics
  Oakland, CA 866-237-8688
Santa Barbara Pistachio Co
  Maricopa, CA 800-896-1044
Sunco & Frenchie
  Clifton, NJ. 973-478-1011
Sunfood
  El Cajon, CA. 888-729-3663
Sunridge Farms
  Royal Oaks, CA 831-786-7000
Windy City Organics
  Northbrook, IL 800-925-0577

Oils, Shortening & Fats

Blue Marble Brands
  Providence, RI 888-534-0246
CHO America
  Baytown, TX. 281-712-1549
Cibaria International
  Riverside, CA 951-823-8490
Citromax Flavors Inc
  Carlstadt, NJ 201-933-8405
Critelli Olive Oil
  Fairfield, CA 800-865-4836
GloryBee
  Eugene, OR. 800-456-7923
International Foodcraft Corp
  Linden, NJ. 800-875-9393

Product Categories / Organic Foods See also Organic Foods Major: Pasta & Noodles

Santa Barbara Pistachio Co
   Maricopa, CA 800-896-1044
Solazyme Inc
   S San Francisco, CA 650-589-5883
Spectrum Foods Inc
   Springfield, IL. 217-528-5301
Sunfood
   El Cajon, CA 888-729-3663
TresOmega
   New Milford, CT 860-210-7805
Vital Choice
   Bellingham, WA 800-608-4825

Pasta & Noodles

Blue Marble Brands
   Providence, RI 888-534-0246
Caesar's Pasta
   Blackwood, NJ 888-432-2372
Good Citizens
   Simi Valley, CA
Great Eastern Sun Trading Co
   Asheville, NC. 800-334-5809
Hain Celestial Group Inc
   Lake Success, NY. 800-434-4246
Hodgson Mill Inc
   Effingham, IL. 800-347-0198
Lundberg Family Farms
   Richvale, CA. 530-538-3500
Natural Food Mill
   Corona, CA. 800-797-5090
Nature's Legacy Inc.
   Hudson, MI. 517-448-2050

Prepared Foods

24 Mantra Organic
   Fremont, CA
Blue Marble Brands
   Providence, RI 888-534-0246
Boulder Organic Foods
   Niwot, CO. 303-530-0470
Caesar's Pasta
   Blackwood, NJ 888-432-2372
Faribault Foods, Inc.
   Fairbault, MN 507-331-1400
Fig Food Co.
   New York, NY 855-344-3663
Fillo Factory, The
   Northvale, NJ 800-653-4556
Great Eastern Sun Trading Co
   Asheville, NC. 800-334-5809
Hain Celestial Group Inc
   Lake Success, NY. 800-434-4246
Happy Family
   New York, NY 855-644-2779
Kashi Company
   Solana Beach, CA. 877-747-2467
Lightlife
   Turners Falls, MA. 800-769-3279
Lisa's Organics
   Carnelian Bay, CA 877-584-5711
Made In Nature
   Boulder, CO 800-906-7426
Sommers Organic
   Wheeling, IL. 877-377-9797
The Food Collective
   Irvine, CA. 866-328-8638
Vital Choice
   Bellingham, WA 800-608-4825

Relishes & Pickled Products

Food For Thought Inc
   Honor, MI 231-326-5444
Great Eastern Sun Trading Co
   Asheville, NC. 800-334-5809
Small Planet Foods
   Minneapolis, MN 800-624-4123

Sauces, Dips & Dressings

Banzos
   Denver, CO. 303-447-2133
Chelten House Products
   Swedesboro, NJ
Drew's Organics
   Chester, VT. 800-228-2980
Earth Island
   Chatsworth, CA 888-394-3949
Flamous Brands
   Duarte, CA 626-799-7909
Follow Your Heart
   Chatsworth, CA 818-725-2820

Frontier Co-op
   Norway, IA 844-550-6200
Klein Foods, Inc
   Marshall, MN 800-657-0174
Organic Girl Produce
   Salinas, CA 831-758-7800
Salad Girl Inc
   Mahtomedi, MN 651-653-9155
San-J International Inc
   Henrico, VA 800-446-5500
Small Planet Foods
   Minneapolis, MN 800-624-4123

Snack Foods

ALOHA
   New York, NY
Bearded Brothers
   Austin, TX
Bhu Foods
   San Diego, CA 619-855-3258
Blue Marble Brands
   Providence, RI 888-534-0246
Charlton Natural Foods, Inc.
   Huntington Beach, CA 888-611-7753
Dharma Bars
Earthbound Farm
   San Jn Bautista, CA 800-690-3200
Flamous Brands
   Duarte, CA 626-799-7909
Fullbloom Baking Co
   Newark, CA 800-201-9909
Happy Family
   New York, NY 855-644-2779
Late July Snacks
   Norwalk, CT 888-857-6225
Lundberg Family Farms
   Richvale, CA. 530-538-3500
Maine Coast Sea Vegetables
   Franklin, ME. 207-565-2907
Mary's Gone Crackers
   Gridley, CA. 888-258-1250
Mountain Organic Foods
   Moraga, CA. 925-377-0119
Nature's Legacy Inc.
   Hudson, MI. 517-448-2050
Nature's Path Foods
   Blaine, WA. 888-808-9505
New England Natural Bakers
   Greenfield, MA. 800-910-2884
NOW Foods
   Bloomingdale, IL 888-669-3663
NuGo Nutrition
   Oakmont, PA. 888-421-2032
Organic Germinal
   Los Angeles, CA. 310-846-5901
Plum Organics
   Emeryville, CA 877-914-7586
Raw Bite
   Hudson, MA 844-729-2483
Rhythm Superfoods
   Austin, TX. 512-441-5667
Rudi's Organic Bakery
   Boulder, CO 877-293-0876
Sunridge Farms
   Royal Oaks, CA 831-786-7000
Vegan Rob's
   Sea Cliff, NY. 516-671-4411
Vege USA
   Monrovia, CA. 888-772-8343
Watusee Foods
   Washington, DC 202-281-8245
Way Better Snacks
   Minneapolis, MN 612-314-2060
Yogavive
   Tiburon, CA 415-366-6226

Specialty Processed Foods

Cell-Nique
   Norwalk, CT 888-417-9343
Earth Island
   Chatsworth, CA 888-394-3949
Happy Family
   New York, NY 855-644-2779
Heritage Health Food
   Collegedale, TN 888-237-0807
Homefree LLC
   Windham, NH 800-552-7172
Lightlife
   Turners Falls, MA. 800-769-3279
Lundberg Family Farms
   Richvale, CA. 530-538-3500

Natural Food Mill
   Corona, CA. 800-797-5090
NuGo Nutrition
   Oakmont, PA. 888-421-2032
Osso Good, LLC
   San Rafael, CA
Prosperity Organic Foods
   Boise, ID. 888-557-5741
Sunshine Burger & Spec Food Co
   Fort Atkinson, WI 920-568-1100
The Food Collective
   Irvine, CA. 866-328-8638
Wisconsin Specialty Protein
   Madison, WI

Spices, Seasonings & Seeds

24 Mantra Organic
   Fremont, CA
American Natural & Organic
   Fremont, CA. 510-440-1044
Blue Marble Brands
   Providence, RI 888-534-0246
Bob's Red Mill Natural Foods
   Milwaukie, OR 800-349-2173
Davidson's Organics
   Reno, NV 800-882-5888
Foods Alive
   Angola, IN. 260-488-4497
Frontier Co-op
   Norway, IA 844-550-6200
GoAvo
   Montville, NJ 973-534-9951
Great Eastern Sun Trading Co
   Asheville, NC. 800-334-5809
Hodgson Mill Inc
   Effingham, IL. 800-347-0198
Homefree LLC
   Windham, NH 800-552-7172
Maine Coast Sea Vegetables
   Franklin, ME. 207-565-2907
Mountain Rose Herbs
   Pleasant Hill, OR 800-879-3337
Nature's Legacy Inc.
   Hudson, MI. 517-448-2050
NOW Foods
   Bloomingdale, IL 888-669-3663
Pacific Grain & Foods
   Fresno, CA 559-276-2580
Primal Essence
   Oxnard, CA. 877-774-6253
Red Monkey Foods
   Springfield, MO 417-319-7300
Smith & Truslow
   Denver, CO. 303-339-6967
Spicely
   Fremont, CA. 510-440-1044
Sunfood
   El Cajon, CA 888-729-3663
Sunridge Farms
   Royal Oaks, CA 831-786-7000
Sustainable Sourcing
   Great Barrington, MA. 413-528-5141
The Real Co
   Wilmington, DE 347-433-8945
Vital Choice
   Bellingham, WA 800-608-4825

Sugars, Syrups & Sweeteners

Bascom Family Farms Inc
   Brattleboro, VT. 888-266-6271
Bee Seasonal
   Gilbert, AZ
Blue Marble Brands
   Providence, RI 888-534-0246
Divine Organics
   CA 209-532-4950
Finding Home Farms
   Middletown, NY. 845-355-4335
Flavorganics
   Newark, NJ 866-972-6879
Florida Crystals Corporation
   West Palm Beach, FL 844-344-9497
Food For Thought Inc
   Honor, MI 231-326-5444
GloryBee
   Eugene, OR. 800-456-7923
Lundberg Family Farms
   Richvale, CA. 530-538-3500
Madhava Natural Sweeteners
   Boulder, CO 800-530-2900

Product Categories / Organic Foods *See also* Organic Foods Major: Sugars, Syrups & Sweeteners

Maple Valley Cooperative
 Cashton, WI 608-654-7319
NOW Foods
 Bloomingdale, IL 888-669-3663
Once Again Nut Butter
 Nunda, NY 888-800-8075
Organic Nectars LLC
 Malden On Hudson, NY 845-246-0506
Pyure Brands
 Naples, FL 305-509-5096

Runamok Maple
 Fairfax, VT 802-849-7943
SBS Americas
 Valley Cottage, NY 844-727-0827
Skedaddle Maple
 Florenceville-Bristol, NB
Sugar Bob's Smoked Maple Syrup
 Londonderry, VT 802-297-7665
Sunfood
 El Cajon, CA 888-729-3663

Suzanne's Specialties
 New Brunswick, NJ 800-762-2135
Sweet Harvest Foods
 Rosemount, MN 507-263-8599
The Real Co
 Wilmington, DE 347-433-8945
UBC Food Distributors
 Dearborn, MI 877-846-8117
Xooz Gear
 Frisco, TX 214-206-1222

Pasta & Noodles

General

A Zerega's Sons Inc
  Fair Lawn, NJ 201-797-1400
Agrusa
  Leonia, NJ 201-592-5950
Al Dente Pasta Co
  Whitmore Lake, MI 800-536-7278
Alaska Pasta Co
  Anchorage, AK 907-276-2632
Alaska Smokehouse
  Woodinville, WA 800-422-0852
American Italian Pasta Company
  Excelsior Springs, MO 877-328-7278
Armanino Foods of Distinction
  Hayward, CA 800-255-8588
Arrowhead Mills
  Boulder, CO 800-434-4246
Atlanta Bread Co.
  Smyrna, GA 800-398-3728
Belletieri Company
  Allentown, PA 610-433-4334
Bernie's Foods
  Brooklyn, NY 718-417-6677
Better Than Foods USA
  Brookfield, WI 855-691-5900
Bgreen Food
  San Diego, CA 619-825-9330
Biagio's Banquets
  Chicago, IL 800-392-2837
Blue Evolution
  San Mateo, CA 605-741-4074
Blue Marble Brands
  Providence, RI 888-534-0246
Boudreaux's Foods
  New Orleans, LA 504-733-8440
Bruno Specialty Foods
  West Sayville, NY 631-589-1700
Buona Vita Inc
  Bridgeton, NJ 856-453-7972
Buonitalia
  New York, NY 212-633-9090
Caesar's Pasta
  Blackwood, NJ 888-432-2372
Cando Pasta
  Cando, ND 701-968-4401
Canton Noodle Corporation
  New York, NY 212-226-3276
Cappello's
  Denver, CO 844-353-2863
Carando Gourmet Frozen Foods
  Agawam, MA 888-227-2636
Carla's Pasta
  South Windsor, CT 860-436-4042
Castella Imports Inc
  Brentwood, NY 631-231-5500
Cedarlane Foods
  Carson, CA 800-826-3322
Chicago Avenue Pizza
  Chicago, IL 800-244-8935
Chickapea
  Collingwood, ON 888-868-9968
Clic International Inc
  Laval, QC 450-669-2663
Codinos Food Inc
  Scotia, NY 800-246-8908
Colavita USA
  Edison, NJ 888-265-2848
Colony Brands Inc
  Monroe, WI 800-544-9036
Corsetti's Pasta Products
  Woodbury, NJ 800-989-1188
Costas Pasta
  Kennesaw, GA 770-514-8814
Cottage Street Pasta
  Barre, VT 802-476-4024
Country Foods
  Polson, MT 406-883-4384
Cuizina Food Company
  Woodinville, WA 425-486-7000
Dairy Maid Ravioli Mfg Co
  Brooklyn, NY 866-777-3661
Di Fiore Pasta Co
  Hartford, CT 860-296-1077
Drakes Fresh Pasta Co
  High Point, NC 800-737-2783
E.D. Smith Foods Ltd
  Hamilton, ON 905-573-1207
Eden Foods Inc
  Clinton, MI 888-424-3336
Eden Organic Pasta Company
  Clinton, MI 888-424-3336
El Peto Products
  Cambridge, ON 800-387-4064
Elena's
  Auburn Hills, MI 800-723-5362
Ener-G Foods
  Seattle, WA 800-331-5222
Ethnic Gourmet Foods
  Boulder, CO 800-434-4246
European Egg Noodle Manufacturing
  Edmonton, AB 780-453-6767
Explore Cuisine
  Red Bank, NJ
FDI Inc
  Berkeley, IL 708-544-1880
Fiori Bruna Pasta Products
  Miami Lakes, FL 305-705-2534
Florence Macaroni Manufacturing
  Chicago, IL 800-647-2782
Florence Pasta & Cheese
  Marshall, MN 800-533-5290
Florentyna's Fresh Pasta Factory
  Los angeles, CA 800-747-2782
Food City USA
  Arvada, CO 303-321-4447
Fratelli Mantova
  Naperville, IL 630-904-0002
Fresh Market Pasta Company
  Portland, ME 207-773-7146
Fresh Pasta Delights
  Plano, TX 972-422-5907
Fun Foods
  East Rutherford, NJ 800-507-2782
Gaston Dupre
  Excelsior Springs, MO 817-629-6275
Genki USA
  Torrance, CA
Gilster-Mary Lee Corp
  Chester, IL 618-826-2361
Gluten Free Foods Mfg.
  Chino, CA 909-823-8230
Good Old Dad Food Products
  Sault Ste. Marie, ON 800-267-7426
Gourmet's Fresh Pasta
  Pasadena, CA 626-798-0841
Great Eastern Sun Trading Co
  Asheville, NC 800-334-5809
Greenfield Noodle & Spec Co
  Detroit, MI 313-873-2212
Heartline Foods
  Westport, CT 203-222-0381
HFI Foods
  Redmond, WA 425-883-1320
Hodgson Mill Inc
  Effingham, IL 800-347-0198
Hong Tou Noodle Company
  Los Angeles, CA 323-256-3843
Hung's Noodle House
  Calgary, AB 403-250-1663
International Harvest Inc
  Mt Vernon, NY 800-277-4268
International Home Foods
  Parsippany, NJ 973-359-9920
International Noodle Co
  Madison Heights, MI 248-583-2479
Italia Foods
  Schaumburg, IL 800-747-1109
Italian Gourmet Foods Canada
  Calgary, AB 403-283-5350
Itarca
  Los Angeles, CA 800-747-2782
J B & Son LTD
  Yonkers, NY 914-963-5192
Joseph's Gourmet Pasta
  Haverhill, MA 800-863-8998
JSL Foods
  Los Angeles, CA 800-745-3236
Juno Chef's
  Goshen, NY 845-294-5400
Kay Foods Co
  Detroit, MI 313-393-1100
Kemach Food Products
  Brooklyn, NY 718-272-5655
Kozlowski Farms
  Forestville, CA 800-473-2767
La Moderna
  Toluca, MX
LA Pasta Inc
  Silver Spring, MD 301-588-1111
La Piccolina
  Decatur, GA 800-626-1624
La Romagnola
  Orlando, FL 800-843-8359
La Spiga D'Oro Fresh Pasta Co
  Pacifica, CA 800-847-2782
Ladson Homemade Pasta Company
  Charleston, SC 843-588-5088
Landolfi's Food Products
  Trenton, NJ 609-392-1830
Lotsa Pasta
  San Diego, CA 858-581-6777
Louisa Food Products Inc
  St Louis, MO 314-868-3000
Mama Del's Macaroni
  East Haven, CT 203-469-6255
Mama Rosie's Ravioli
  Charlestown, MA 888-246-4300
Mamma Lina Ravioli Company
  San Diego, CA 858-535-0620
Marconi Italian Specialty Foods
  Chicago, IL 312-421-0485
Marsan Foods
  Toronto, ON 416-755-9262
Maruchan Inc
  Irvine, CA 949-789-2300
MI-AL. Corp
  Glen Cove, NY 516-759-0652
Michael Angelo's Inc
  Austin, TX 877-482-5426
Midwest Food
  Chicago, IL 773-927-8870
Modern Macaroni Co LTD
  Honolulu, HI 808-845-6841
Montreal Chop Suey Company
  Montreal, QC 514-522-3134
Morii Foods, Inc.
  Tualatin, OR 503-691-7007
Morrison Lamothe
  Toronto, ON 877-677-6533
Mountain High Organics
  New Milford, CT 860-210-7805
Mrs. Leeper's Pasta
  Excelsior Springs, MO 800-848-5266
Mucci Food Products LTD
  Canton, MI 734-453-4555
MXO Global
  Mount Royal, QC
Nantucket Pasta Company, Inc.
  Nantucket, MA 508-494-5209
Napoli Pasta Manufacturers
  Miami, FL 305-666-1942
Natural Value
  Sacramento, CA 916-836-3561
Nature's Legacy Inc.
  Hudson, MI 517-448-2050
Nissin Foods USA Co Inc
  Gardena, CA 310-327-8478
North American Enterprises
  Tucson, AZ 800-817-8666
Northern Farmhouse Pasta LLC
  Roscoe, NY 607-290-4064
NuPasta
  Markham, ON 855-910-8800
O'Sole Mio
  Boisbriand, QC 844-696-8933
Oakland Noodle Co
  Oakland, IL 217-346-2322
OB Macaroni Company
  844-837-6259
Ocean's Halo
  Burlingame, CA 650-642-5907
Okahara Saimin Factory LTD
  Honolulu, HI 808-949-0588
P & S Ravioli Co
  Philadelphia, PA 215-339-9929
Pappardelle's Inc
  Denver, CO 800-607-2782

Product Categories / Pasta & Noodles: Agnolotti

Pasta Del Mondo
  Carmel, NY 800-392-8887
Pasta Factory
  Melrose Park, IL 800-615-6951
Pasta International
  Mississauga, ON 905-890-5550
Pasta Mami
  Smyrna, GA 770-438-6022
Pasta Mill
  Edmonton, AB 780-454-8665
Pasta Montana
  Great Falls, MT 406-761-1516
Pasta Prima
  Benicia, CA 530-671-7200
Pasta Quistini
  Toronto, ON 416-742-3222
Pasta Shoppe
  Nashville, TN 800-247-0188
Pasta Sonoma
  Rohnert Park, CA 707-584-0800
Pastorelli Food Products
  Chicago, IL 800-767-2829
Peace Village Organic Foods
  Berkeley, CA 510-524-4420
Pede Brothers Italian Food
  Schenectady, NY 518-356-3042
Peking Noodle Co Inc
  Los Angeles, CA 323-223-0897
Pennsylvania Macaroni Company
  Pittsburgh, PA 800-223-5928
Philadelphia Macaroni Co
  Philadelphia, PA 215-923-3141
Pierino Frozen Foods
  Lincoln Park, MI 313-928-0950
Pondini Imports
  Somerset, NJ 732-545-1255
Porinos Gourmet Food
  Central Falls, RI 800-826-3938
Publix Super Market
  Lakeland, FL 800-242-1227
Pure Sales
  Costa Mesa, CA 714-540-5455
Queen Ann Ravioli & Macaroni
  Brooklyn, NY 718-256-1061
Quinoa Corporation
  Gardena, CA 310-217-8125
Ranieri Fine Foods
  Brooklyn, NY 718-599-9520
Ravioli Store
  Long Island City, NY 877-727-8269
Rice Innovations
  Fontana, CA 909-823-8230
Riviera Ravioli Company
  Bronx, NY 718-823-0260
Rocca's Italian Foods Inc
  New Castle, PA 724-654-3344
Ron Son Foods Inc
  Swedesboro, NJ 856-241-7333
Ronzoni
  Largo, FL 800-730-5957
Rosa Food Products
  Philadelphia, PA 215-467-2214
Roses Ravioli
  Oglesby, IL 815-883-8011
Rossi Pasta LTD
  Marietta, OH 800-227-6774
S T Specialty Foods Inc
  Brooklyn Park, MN 763-493-9600
Sabatino Truffles USA
  West Haven, CT 888-444-9971
Salt Lake Macaroni & Noodle Company
  Salt Lake City, UT 801-969-9855
Sam Mills USA
  Boynton Beach, FL 561-572-0510
Savoia Foods
  Chicago Heights, IL 800-867-2782
Sedlock Farm
  Lynn Center, IL 309-521-8284
Sempio Foods
  Cerritos, CA 562-207-9540
Serro Foods LLC
  Catskill, NY 518-943-9255
Severino Pasta Mfg Co Inc
  Westmont, NJ 856-854-3716
Seviroli Foods
  Garden City, NY 516-222-6220
Sfoglia Fine Pastas & Gourmet
  Freeland, WA 360-331-4080
Shanghai Co
  Portland, OR 503-235-2525
Silver Palate Kitchens
  Cresskill, NJ 201-568-0110
Silver State Foods Inc
  Denver, CO 800-423-3351
SOPAKCO Foods
  Mullins, SC 800-276-9678
SOUPerior Bean & Spice Company
  Vancouver, WA 800-878-7687
Spring Glen Fresh Foods
  Ephrata, PA 800-641-2853
Spruce Foods
  San Clemente, CA 800-326-3612
Star Ravioli Mfg Co
  Moonachie, NJ 201-933-6427
Stellar Pasta Company
  Great Barrington, MA 413-528-2150
Sun Noodle
  Honolulu, HI 808-841-5808
Taif Inc
  Folcroft, PA 610-522-0122
Tasty Mix Quality Foods
  Brooklyn, NY 718-855-7680
TexaFrance
  Round Rock, TX 800-776-8937
Tomasso Corporation
  Baie D'Urfe, QC 514-325-3000
Trio's Original Italian Pasta Co.
  Chelsea, MA 800-999-9603
Tropical Foods
  Charlotte, NC 800-438-4470
Turri's Italian Foods
  Roseville, MI 586-773-6010
Twin Marquis
  Brooklyn, NY 800-367-6868
Union
  Irvine, CA 800-854-7292
United Noodle Manufacturing Company
  Salt Lake City, UT 801-485-0951
US Durum Products LTD
  Lancaster, PA 866-268-7268
Varco Brothers
  Chicago, IL 312-642-4740
Vitasoy USA
  Woburn, MA 800-848-2769
Wan Hua Foods
  Seattle, WA 206-622-8417
Wegmans Food Markets Inc.
  Rochester, NY 800-934-6267
Willow Foods
  Beaverton, OR 800-338-3609
Wine Country Pasta
  Sonoma, CA 707-935-1366
Wing's Food Products
  Toronto, ON 416-259-2662
Winn-Dixie Stores
  Jacksonville, FL 800-967-9105
Wisconsin Whey International
  Juda, WI 608-233-5101
Wonton Food
  Brooklyn, NY 800-776-8889
Wornick Company
  Cincinnati, OH 800-860-4555
Young's Noodle Factory Inc
  Honolulu, HI 808-533-6478
Zeroodle
  Richmond Hill, ON 905-889-9880

Agnolotti

Agrusa
  Leonia, NJ 201-592-5950
Caesar's Pasta
  Blackwood, NJ 888-432-2372
Pasta Factory
  Melrose Park, IL 800-615-6951
Putney Pasta
  Brattleboro, VT 800-253-3683
Queen Ann Ravioli & Macaroni
  Brooklyn, NY 718-256-1061
Supreme Dairy Farms Co
  Warwick, RI 401-739-8180
Wisconsin Whey International
  Juda, WI 608-233-5101

Angel Hair

Al Dente Pasta Co
  Whitmore Lake, MI 800-536-7278
Backyard Safari Co
  Covington, GA 770-385-3273
Barilla USA
  Northbrook, IL 800-922-7455
Bgreen Food
  San Diego, CA 619-825-9330
Caesar's Pasta
  Blackwood, NJ 888-432-2372
Cipriani's Spaghetti & Sauce Company
  Chicago Heights, IL 708-755-6212
Costa Macaroni Manufacturing
  Los Angeles, CA 800-433-7785
Food City USA
  Arvada, CO 303-321-4447
Hodgson Mill Inc
  Effingham, IL 800-347-0198
La Romagnola
  Orlando, FL 800-843-8359
Lucy's Foods
  Latrobe, PA 724-539-1430
Mrs. Leeper's Pasta
  Excelsior Springs, MO 800-848-5266
NuPasta
  Markham, ON 855-910-8800
Pasta Factory
  Melrose Park, IL 800-615-6951
Pasta Valente
  Charlottesville, VA 888-575-7670
Putney Pasta
  Brattleboro, VT 800-253-3683

Bows

Hodgson Mill Inc
  Effingham, IL 800-347-0198

Canned

Canton Noodle Corporation
  New York, NY 212-226-3276
Faribault Foods, Inc.
  Fairbault, MN 507-331-1400
International Home Foods
  Parsippany, NJ 973-359-9920
Midwest Food
  Chicago, IL 773-927-8870
Natural Value
  Sacramento, CA 916-836-3561
Seneca Foods Corp
  Marion, NY 315-926-8100
Shanghai Co
  Portland, OR 503-235-2525

Cannelloni

Louisa Food Products Inc
  St Louis, MO 314-868-3000
Marsan Foods
  Toronto, ON 416-755-9262
Pasta Factory
  Melrose Park, IL 800-615-6951
Pasta International
  Mississauga, ON 905-890-5550
Riviera Ravioli Company
  Bronx, NY 718-823-0260
Star Ravioli Mfg Co
  Moonachie, NJ 201-933-6427
Tomasso Corporation
  Baie D'Urfe, QC 514-325-3000
Turri's Italian Foods
  Roseville, MI 586-773-6010

Cavatappi

Costa Macaroni Manufacturing
  Los Angeles, CA 800-433-7785

Cavatelli

Alfredo Aiello Italian Food
  Quincy, MA 617-770-6360
Caesar's Pasta
  Blackwood, NJ 888-432-2372
Fiori Bruna Pasta Products
  Miami Lakes, FL 305-705-2534
J B & Son LTD
  Yonkers, NY 914-963-5192
Landolfi's Food Products
  Trenton, NJ 609-392-1830
Pasta Del Mondo
  Carmel, NY 800-392-8887
Pasta Factory
  Melrose Park, IL 800-615-6951
Queen Ann Ravioli & Macaroni
  Brooklyn, NY 718-256-1061
Riviera Ravioli Company
  Bronx, NY 718-823-0260
Star Ravioli Mfg Co
  Moonachie, NJ 201-933-6427

Product Categories / Pasta & Noodles: Elbow Macaroni

Wisconsin Whey International
  Juda, WI 608-233-5101

Elbow Macaroni

A Zerega's Sons Inc
  Fair Lawn, NJ 201-797-1400
Cando Pasta
  Cando, ND 701-968-4401
Costa Macaroni Manufacturing
  Los Angeles, CA..................... 800-433-7785
Cuizina Food Company
  Woodinville, WA 425-486-7000
Good Citizens
  Simi Valley, CA
Hodgson Mill Inc
  Effingham, IL 800-347-0198
Lundberg Family Farms
  Richvale, CA 530-538-3500
Philadelphia Macaroni Co
  Philadelphia, PA 215-923-3141
Superior Pasta Co
  Philadelphia, PA 215-627-3306

Farfalle

Costa Macaroni Manufacturing
  Los Angeles, CA..................... 800-433-7785
Italia Foods
  Schaumburg, IL 800-747-1109

Fettuccine

Barilla USA
  Northbrook, IL 800-922-7455
Hodgson Mill Inc
  Effingham, IL 800-347-0198
Lucy's Foods
  Latrobe, PA 724-539-1430
NuPasta
  Markham, ON 855-910-8800
Pasta Valente
  Charlottesville, VA 888-575-7670

Gnocchi

Agrusa
  Leonia, NJ 201-592-5950
Capone Foods
  Somerville, MA 617-629-2296
Dixie USA
  Tomball, TX 800-233-3668
Italian Foods Corporation
  Raleigh, NC 888-516-7262
Lucy's Foods
  Latrobe, PA 724-539-1430
Queen Ann Ravioli & Macaroni
  Brooklyn, NY 718-256-1061

Frozen

Lucy's Foods
  Latrobe, PA 724-539-1430
Queen Ann Ravioli & Macaroni
  Brooklyn, NY 718-256-1061
Turri's Italian Foods
  Roseville, MI 586-773-6010

Lasagna

Capone Foods
  Somerville, MA 617-629-2296
Carla's Pasta
  South Windsor, CT 860-436-4042
Hodgson Mill Inc
  Effingham, IL 800-347-0198
Philadelphia Macaroni Co
  Philadelphia, PA 215-923-3141

Frozen

Alfredo Aiello Italian Food
  Quincy, MA 617-770-6360
Bruno Specialty Foods
  West Sayville, NY.................... 631-589-1700
Caesar's Pasta
  Blackwood, NJ 888-432-2372
Cedarlane Foods
  Carson, CA 800-826-3322
Codinos Food Inc
  Scotia, NY........................... 800-246-8908
Italia Foods
  Schaumburg, IL 800-747-1109
Landolfi's Food Products
  Trenton, NJ 609-392-1830

Mamma Lina Ravioli Company
  San Diego, CA 858-535-0620
Marsan Foods
  Toronto, ON 416-755-9262
Molinaro's Fine Italian Foods Ltd.
  Mississauga, ON 905-281-0352
Pasta Factory
  Melrose Park, IL 800-615-6951
Pasta International
  Mississauga, ON 905-890-5550
Riviera Ravioli Company
  Bronx, NY........................... 718-823-0260
Seviroli Foods
  Garden City, NY 516-222-6220
Tomasso Corporation
  Baie D'Urfe, QC 514-325-3000
Wisconsin Whey International
  Juda, WI 608-233-5101

Noodles

A Zerega's Sons Inc
  Fair Lawn, NJ 201-797-1400
Costa Macaroni Manufacturing
  Los Angeles, CA..................... 800-433-7785

Canned

Canton Noodle Corporation
  New York, NY 212-226-3276
Shanghai Co
  Portland, OR 503-235-2525
United Noodle Manufacturing Company
  Salt Lake City, UT 801-485-0951

Chow Mein

Everfresh Food Corporation
  Minneapolis, MN 612-331-6393
Nanka Seimen Company
  Vernon, CA 323-585-9967
Passport Food Group
  Ontario, CA 310-463-0954
Valdez Food Inc
  Philadelphia, PA 215-634-6106
Wan Hua Foods
  Seattle, WA 206-622-8417
Willow Foods
  Beaverton, OR 800-338-3609
Wonton Food
  Brooklyn, NY 800-776-8889

Egg

A Zerega's Sons Inc
  Fair Lawn, NJ 201-797-1400
Costa Macaroni Manufacturing
  Los Angeles, CA..................... 800-433-7785
Eden Organic Pasta Company
  Clinton, MI 888-424-3336
Hodgson Mill Inc
  Effingham, IL 800-347-0198
Manischewitz Co
  Newark, NJ 201-553-1100
Nanka Seimen Company
  Vernon, CA 323-585-9967
Silver State Foods Inc
  Denver, CO 800-423-3351

Mung Bean

Explore Cuisine
  Red Bank, NJ

Oriental

Allied Old English Inc
  Port Reading, NJ.................... 732-602-8955
Annie Chun's
  Los Angeles, CA..................... 415-479-8272
Union
  Irvine, CA 800-854-7292
Vitasoy USA
  Woburn, MA 800-848-2769
Wonton Food
  Brooklyn, NY 800-776-8889

Ramen

Bgreen Food
  San Diego, CA 619-825-9330
Blue Marble Brands
  Providence, RI 888-534-0246
Maruchan Inc
  Irvine, CA 949-789-2300

Pressery
  Denver, CO
Sun Noodle New Jersey
  Carlstadt, NJ 201-530-1100
Union
  Irvine, CA 800-854-7292

Soba

Miracle Noodle
  Los Angeles, CA..................... 800-948-4205
Sun Noodle New Jersey
  Carlstadt, NJ 201-530-1100

Pasta

Alba Foods, Inc
  Stone Mountain, GA 888-725-4605
Banza
Barilla USA
  Northbrook, IL 800-922-7455
Caesar's Pasta
  Blackwood, NJ 888-432-2372
Conte's Pasta Co.
  Vineland, NJ 800-211-6607
Costa Macaroni Manufacturing
  Los Angeles, CA..................... 800-433-7785
Cuizina Food Company
  Woodinville, WA 425-486-7000
Cybele's Free To Eat
  Los Angeles, CA..................... 877-895-3729
Edison Grainery
  Benicia, CA.......................... 510-382-0202
Fantis Foods Inc
  Carlstadt, NJ 201-933-6200
Faribault Foods, Inc.
  Fairbault, MN 507-331-1400
Fiore Di Pasta
  Fresno, CA 559-457-0431
Gabriella's Kitchen
  Mississauga, ON 844-754-6690
Gia Russa
  Boardman, OH 800-527-8772
Intermountain Specialty Food Group
  Salt Lake City, UT 801-977-9077
Jovial Foods
  North Stonington, CT 877-642-0644
Kana Organics
  Westlake Village, CA 213-603-0448
Kashi Company
  Solana Beach, CA................... 877-747-2467
Krinos Foods
  Bronx, NY........................... 718-729-9000
LA Pasta Inc
  Silver Spring, MD 301-588-1111
La Romagnola
  Orlando, FL 800-843-8359
Lucy's Foods
  Latrobe, PA 724-539-1430
Mezza
  Lake Forest, IL 888-206-6054
MI-AL. Corp
  Glen Cove, NY 516-759-0652
Park 100 Foods Inc
  Tipton, IN 800-854-6504
Pasta Prima
  Benicia, CA.......................... 530-671-7200
Queen Ann Ravioli & Macaroni
  Brooklyn, NY 718-256-1061
Ragozzino Foods Inc
  Meriden, CT 800-348-1240
Reid Foods
  Gurnee, IL 888-295-8478
Ronzoni
  Largo, FL 800-730-5957
RP's Pasta Company
  Madison, WI 608-257-7216
Serro Foods LLC
  Catskill, NY.......................... 518-943-9255
Sfoglini Pasta Shop
  Brooklyn, NY 917-338-5955
Simply Shari's Gluten Free
  Thousand Oaks, CA 805-241-5676
Sophia Foods
  Brooklyn, NY 718-272-1110
Superior Pasta Co
  Philadelphia, PA 215-627-3306
Surgital America
  Miramar, FL 954-538-6891
Tribe 9 Foods
  Madison, WI 608-257-7216
Turri's Italian Foods
  Roseville, MI 586-773-6010

Product Categories / Pasta & Noodles: Penne

Vincent Formusa Company
  Des Plaines, IL 847-813-6040
Wisconsin Whey International
  Juda, WI 608-233-5101

Frozen

Fiore Di Pasta
  Fresno, CA 559-457-0431
Homestead Ravioli Company
  South San Francisco, CA 650-615-0750
LA Pasta Inc
  Silver Spring, MD 301-588-1111

Penne

A Zerega's Sons Inc
  Fair Lawn, NJ 201-797-1400
Cando Pasta
  Cando, ND 701-968-4401
Costa Macaroni Manufacturing
  Los Angeles, CA 800-433-7785
Cuizina Food Company
  Woodinville, WA 425-486-7000
Turri's Italian Foods
  Roseville, MI 586-773-6010

Ravioli

Agrusa
  Leonia, NJ 201-592-5950
Alfonso Gourmet Pasta
  Pompano Beach, FL 800-370-7278
Alfredo Aiello Italian Food
  Quincy, MA 617-770-6360
Antoni Ravioli Co
  North Massapequa, NY 800-783-0350
Armanino Foods of Distinction
  Hayward, CA 800-255-8588
Aunt Kitty's Foods Inc
  Vineland, NJ 856-691-2100
Bella Ravioli
  Medford, MA 781-396-0875
Borgattis Ravioli
  Bronx, NY 718-367-3799
Bruno Specialty Foods
  West Sayville, NY 631-589-1700
Caesar's Pasta
  Blackwood, NJ 888-432-2372
Campbell Soup Co.
  Camden, NJ 800-257-8443
Capone Foods
  Somerville, MA 617-629-2296
Chinese Spaghetti Factory
  Boston, MA 617-445-7714
Codinos Food Inc
  Scotia, NY 800-246-8908
Cottage Street Pasta
  Barre, VT 802-476-4024
Cuizina Food Company
  Woodinville, WA 425-486-7000
Dairy Maid Ravioli Mfg Co
  Brooklyn, NY 866-777-3661
Fiori Bruna Pasta Products
  Miami Lakes, FL 305-705-2534
International Home Foods
  Parsippany, NJ 973-359-9920
Italia Foods
  Schaumburg, IL 800-747-1109
J B & Son LTD
  Yonkers, NY 914-963-5192
La Romagnola
  Orlando, FL 800-843-8359
Landolfi's Food Products
  Trenton, NJ 609-392-1830
Louisa Food Products Inc
  St Louis, MO 314-868-3000
Lucy's Foods
  Latrobe, PA 724-539-1430
Mamma Lina Ravioli Company
  San Diego, CA 858-535-0620
Maria & Son
  St Louis, MO 866-481-9009
MI-AL. Corp
  Glen Cove, NY 516-759-0652
New York Ravioli
  New Hyde Park, NY 888-588-7287
Nuovo Pasta Productions LTD
  Stratford, CT 800-803-0033
Pasta Del Mondo
  Carmel, NY 800-392-8887
Pasta Factory
  Melrose Park, IL 800-615-6951
Pasta International
  Mississauga, ON 905-890-5550
Pasta Mill
  Edmonton, AB 780-454-8665
Pasta Prima
  Benicia, CA 530-671-7200
Queen Ann Ravioli & Macaroni
  Brooklyn, NY 718-256-1061
Roses Ravioli
  Oglesby, IL 815-883-8011
Seviroli Foods
  Garden City, NY 516-222-6220
Star Ravioli Mfg Co
  Moonachie, NJ 201-933-6427
Tomasso Corporation
  Baie D'Urfe, QC 514-325-3000
Wisconsin Whey International
  Juda, WI 608-233-5101

Canned

Alfredo Aiello Italian Food
  Quincy, MA 617-770-6360
Campbell Soup Co.
  Camden, NJ 800-257-8443
Cuizina Food Company
  Woodinville, WA 425-486-7000
International Home Foods
  Parsippany, NJ 973-359-9920

Cheese

Alfredo Aiello Italian Food
  Quincy, MA 617-770-6360
Aunt Kitty's Foods Inc
  Vineland, NJ 856-691-2100
Fiori Bruna Pasta Products
  Miami Lakes, FL 305-705-2534
La Romagnola
  Orlando, FL 800-843-8359
Louisa Food Products Inc
  St Louis, MO 314-868-3000
Queen Ann Ravioli & Macaroni
  Brooklyn, NY 718-256-1061

Frozen

Alfredo Aiello Italian Food
  Quincy, MA 617-770-6360
Bruno Specialty Foods
  West Sayville, NY 631-589-1700
Caesar's Pasta
  Blackwood, NJ 888-432-2372
Carla's Pasta
  South Windsor, CT 860-436-4042
Codinos Food Inc
  Scotia, NY 800-246-8908
Cuizina Food Company
  Woodinville, WA 425-486-7000
Fiori Bruna Pasta Products
  Miami Lakes, FL 305-705-2534
Homestead Ravioli Company
  South San Francisco, CA 650-615-0750
Italia Foods
  Schaumburg, IL 800-747-1109
J B & Son LTD
  Yonkers, NY 914-963-5192
Kiki's Gluten-Free
  Park Ridge, IL
Landolfi's Food Products
  Trenton, NJ 609-392-1830
Louisa Food Products Inc
  St Louis, MO 314-868-3000
MI-AL. Corp
  Glen Cove, NY 516-759-0652
Pasta Del Mondo
  Carmel, NY 800-392-8887
Pasta Factory
  Melrose Park, IL 800-615-6951
Pasta International
  Mississauga, ON 905-890-5550
Pasta Prima
  Benicia, CA 530-671-7200
Seviroli Foods
  Garden City, NY 516-222-6220
Star Ravioli Mfg Co
  Moonachie, NJ 201-933-6427
Tomasso Corporation
  Baie D'Urfe, QC 514-325-3000
Turri's Italian Foods
  Roseville, MI 586-773-6010
Wisconsin Whey International
  Juda, WI 608-233-5101

Meat

La Romagnola
  Orlando, FL 800-843-8359
Queen Ann Ravioli & Macaroni
  Brooklyn, NY 718-256-1061

Seafood

La Romagnola
  Orlando, FL 800-843-8359
Queen Ann Ravioli & Macaroni
  Brooklyn, NY 718-256-1061

Vegetable

La Romagnola
  Orlando, FL 800-843-8359
Queen Ann Ravioli & Macaroni
  Brooklyn, NY 718-256-1061

Rigatoni

Al Dente Pasta Co
  Whitmore Lake, MI 800-536-7278
Codinos Food Inc
  Scotia, NY 800-246-8908
Landolfi's Food Products
  Trenton, NJ 609-392-1830
Lucy's Foods
  Latrobe, PA 724-539-1430
Pasta Factory
  Melrose Park, IL 800-615-6951

Rotelle

Cuizina Food Company
  Woodinville, WA 425-486-7000

Rotini

A Zerega's Sons Inc
  Fair Lawn, NJ 201-797-1400
Al Dente Pasta Co
  Whitmore Lake, MI 800-536-7278
Cando Pasta
  Cando, ND 701-968-4401
Hodgson Mill Inc
  Effingham, IL 800-347-0198
Lundberg Family Farms
  Richvale, CA 530-538-3500
Turri's Italian Foods
  Roseville, MI 586-773-6010

Semolina

Florence Macaroni Manufacturing
  Chicago, IL 800-647-2782

Shells

A Zerega's Sons Inc
  Fair Lawn, NJ 201-797-1400
Barilla USA
  Northbrook, IL 800-922-7455
Cando Pasta
  Cando, ND 701-968-4401
Costa Macaroni Manufacturing
  Los Angeles, CA 800-433-7785
Hodgson Mill Inc
  Effingham, IL 800-347-0198

Spaghetti

Barilla USA
  Northbrook, IL 800-922-7455
Caesar's Pasta
  Blackwood, NJ 888-432-2372
Campbell Soup Co.
  Camden, NJ 800-257-8443
Costa Macaroni Manufacturing
  Los Angeles, CA 800-433-7785
Country Cupboard
  Lewisburg, PA 570-523-3211
Hodgson Mill Inc
  Effingham, IL 800-347-0198
International Home Foods
  Parsippany, NJ 973-359-9920
Iwamoto Natto Factory
  Paia, HI 808-579-9935
La Romagnola
  Orlando, FL 800-843-8359
Ladson Homemade Pasta Company
  Charleston, SC 843-588-5088
Landolfi's Food Products
  Trenton, NJ 609-392-1830

Lucy's Foods
 Latrobe, PA 724-539-1430
Lundberg Family Farms
 Richvale, CA 530-538-3500
NuPasta
 Markham, ON 855-910-8800
Pasta Factory
 Melrose Park, IL 800-615-6951
Pasta International
 Mississauga, ON 905-890-5550
Philadelphia Macaroni Co
 Philadelphia, PA 215-923-3141
Superior Pasta Co
 Philadelphia, PA 215-627-3306
Varco Brothers
 Chicago, IL 312-642-4740
Wisconsin Whey International
 Juda, WI 608-233-5101

Canned

International Home Foods
 Parsippany, NJ 973-359-9920
Seneca Foods Corp
 Marion, NY 315-926-8100

Frozen

Caesar's Pasta
 Blackwood, NJ 888-432-2372
Landolfi's Food Products
 Trenton, NJ 609-392-1830
Pasta International
 Mississauga, ON 905-890-5550

Spelt

A Zerega's Sons Inc
 Fair Lawn, NJ 201-797-1400
Costa Macaroni Manufacturing
 Los Angeles, CA 800-433-7785
Nature's Legacy Inc.
 Hudson, MI 517-448-2050

Spinach

Cipriani's Spaghetti & Sauce Company
 Chicago Heights, IL 708-755-6212
La Romagnola
 Orlando, FL 800-843-8359
Marsan Foods
 Toronto, ON 416-755-9262
Wonton Food
 Brooklyn, NY 800-776-8889

Stuffed Shells

Armanino Foods of Distinction
 Hayward, CA 800-255-8588
Lucy's Foods
 Latrobe, PA 724-539-1430
Queen Ann Ravioli & Macaroni
 Brooklyn, NY 718-256-1061
Turri's Italian Foods
 Roseville, MI 586-773-6010

Tagliatelle

Costa Macaroni Manufacturing
 Los Angeles, CA 800-433-7785

Tortellini

Agrusa
 Leonia, NJ 201-592-5950
Alfredo Aiello Italian Food
 Quincy, MA 617-770-6360
Armanino Foods of Distinction
 Hayward, CA 800-255-8588
Bruno Specialty Foods
 West Sayville, NY 631-589-1700
Costa Macaroni Manufacturing
 Los Angeles, CA 800-433-7785
Cuizina Food Company
 Woodinville, WA 425-486-7000
Dairy Maid Ravioli Mfg Co
 Brooklyn, NY 866-777-3661

Fiori Bruna Pasta Products
 Miami Lakes, FL 305-705-2534
Italia Foods
 Schaumburg, IL 800-747-1109
Landolfi's Food Products
 Trenton, NJ 609-392-1830
Lucy's Foods
 Latrobe, PA 724-539-1430
MI-AL. Corp
 Glen Cove, NY 516-759-0652
New York Ravioli
 New Hyde Park, NY 888-588-7287
Pasta Del Mondo
 Carmel, NY 800-392-8887
Pasta Factory
 Melrose Park, IL 800-615-6951
Pasta International
 Mississauga, ON 905-890-5550
Pasta Mill
 Edmonton, AB 780-454-8665
Putney Pasta
 Brattleboro, VT 800-253-3683
Queen Ann Ravioli & Macaroni
 Brooklyn, NY 718-256-1061
Riviera Ravioli Company
 Bronx, NY 718-823-0260
Roses Ravioli
 Oglesby, IL 815-883-8011
Turri's Italian Foods
 Roseville, MI 586-773-6010

Vermicelli

Cipriani's Spaghetti & Sauce Company
 Chicago Heights, IL 708-755-6212
Costa Macaroni Manufacturing
 Los Angeles, CA 800-433-7785
Iwamoto Natto Factory
 Paia, HI 808-579-9935
Superior Pasta Co
 Philadelphia, PA 215-627-3306

Prepared Foods

Battered

BlueWater Seafoods
   Gloucester, MA 888-560-2539
Strong Roots
   Brooklyn, NY 929-466-1639

Refrigerated

Alderfer Inc
   Harleysville, PA 800-341-1121
Alpine Butcher
   Lowell, MA 978-256-7771
AquaCuisine
   Portland, OR 208-323-2782
Atlantic Pork & Provisions
   Jamaica, NY 800-245-3536
Avon Heights Mushrooms
   Avondale, PA 610-268-2092
Binkert's Meat Products
   Baltimore, MD 410-687-5959
Boesl Packing Co
   Baltimore, MD 800-675-1471
Boudreaux's Foods
   New Orleans, LA 504-733-8440
Brookside Foods
   Cleveland, OH 216-991-7600
C Roy & Sons Processing
   Yale, MI 810-387-3957
Charlie's Country Sausage
   Minot, ND 701-838-6302
Chicago 58 Food Products
   Woodbridge, ON 416-603-4244
Chisesi Brothers Meat Packing
   New Orleans, LA 800-966-3550
Citterio USA
   Freeland, PA 800-435-8888
Corfu Foods Inc
   Bensenville, IL 630-595-2510
Country Maid Inc
   Milwaukee, WI 800-628-4354
Dairy Fresh Foods Inc
   Taylor, MI 313-299-0735
Dawn's Foods
   Portage, WI 800-993-2967
Dietz & Watson Inc.
   Philadelphia, PA 215-831-9000
Dohar Meats Inc
   Cleveland, OH 216-241-4197
F & S Produce Co Inc
   Vineland, NJ 800-886-3316
Frank Wardynski & Sons Inc
   Buffalo, NY 716-854-6083
Fried Provisions Company
   Evans City, PA 724-538-3160
Gouvea's & Purity Foods Inc
   Honolulu, HI 808-847-3717
Green Garden Food Products
   Sandpoint, ID 800-669-3169
Groff's Meats
   Elizabethtown, PA 717-367-1246
Hazle Park Quality Meats
   West Hazleton, PA 800-238-4331
Helen's Pure Foods
   Cheltenham, PA 215-379-6433
Herold's Salads
   Cleveland, OH 800-427-2523
HFI Foods
   Redmond, WA 425-883-1320
Hoople Country Kitchen Inc
   Rockport, IN 877-466-7537
House of Thaller Inc
   Knoxville, TN 800-462-3365
Ito Cariani Sausage Company
   Hayward, CA 510-887-0882
John Volpi & Co
   St Louis, MO 800-288-3439
Kelly Corned Beef Co
   Chicago, IL 800-624-5617
Kilgus Meats
   Toledo, OH 419-472-9721
Knotts Fine Foods
   Paris, TN 731-642-1961
Lakeside Foods Inc.
   Manitowoc, WI 800-466-3834
Land O'Frost Inc
   Searcy, AR 800-643-5654

Lengerich Meats Inc
   Zanesville, IN 260-638-4123
Leona Meat Plant
   Troy, PA 570-297-3574
Locustdale Meat Packing
   Locustdale, PA 570-875-1270
Marshallville Packing Co
   Marshallville, OH 330-855-2871
Martin Rosols
   New Britain, CT 860-223-2707
Meadows Country Products
   Hollidaysburg, PA 888-499-1001
Mrs Grissom's Salads Inc
   Nashville, TN 800-255-0571
Parma Sausage Products
   Pittsburgh, PA 877-294-4207
Queen City Sausage & Provision
   Cincinnati, OH 877-544-5588
R.C. McEntire & Company
   Columbia, SC 803-799-3388
Rachael's Smoked Fish
   Springfield, MA 800-327-3412
Real Kosher Sausage Company
   Newark, NJ 973-690-5394
Rendulic Meat Packing Corp
   Mckeesport, PA 412-678-9541
Roman Packing Company
   Norfolk, NE 800-373-5990
Saag's Products LLC
   San Leandro, CA 855-287-6562
Sandridge Food Corp
   Medina, OH 800-627-2523
Saval Foods Corp
   Elkridge, MD 800-527-2825
Schaefers Market
   Sauk Centre, MN 320-352-6490
Schaller & Weber Inc
   Astoria, NY 800-847-4115
Sculli Brothers
   Yeadon, PA 215-336-1223
Sechrist Brothers
   Dallastown, PA 717-244-2975
Sheinman Provision Co
   Philadelphia, PA 215-473-7065
Smith Packing Regional Meat
   Utica, NY 315-732-5125
Spring Glen Fresh Foods
   Ephrata, PA 800-641-2853
Spring Grove Foods
   Miamisburg, OH 937-866-4311
Standard Meat Co LP
   Dallas, TX 866-859-6313
Stawnichy Holdings
   Mundare, AB 888-764-7646
Stonie's Sausage Shop
   Perryville, MO 888-546-2540
Suter Co Inc
   Sycamore, IL 800-435-6942
Tennessee Valley Packing Co
   Columbia, TN 931-388-2623
Teti Bakery
   Etobicoke, ON 800-465-0123
Troy Foods Inc
   Troy, IL 618-667-6332
United Provision Meat Company
   Columbus, OH 614-252-1126
Upstate Niagara Co-Op Inc.
   Buffalo, NJ 716-892-3156
Vienna Meat Products
   Scarborough, ON 800-588-1931
Warren & Son Meat Processing
   Whipple, OH 740-585-2421
Wornick Company
   Cincinnati, OH 800-860-4555

General

A Gift Basket by Carmela
   Longmeadow, MA 413-746-1400
Acme Steak & Seafood
   Youngstown, OH 800-686-2263
Advance Pierre Foods
   Cincinnati, OH 800-969-2747
Agrusa
   Leonia, NJ 201-592-5950
Ajinomoto Foods North America, Inc.
   Ontario, CA 909-477-4700

Al Pete Meats
   Muncie, IN 765-288-8817
Alderfer Inc
   Harleysville, PA 800-341-1121
Alfonso Gourmet Pasta
   Pompano Beach, FL 800-370-7278
Alfonso Gourmet Pasta
   Pompano Beach, FL 800-370-7278
Alfonso Gourmet Pasta
   Pompano Beach, FL 800-370-7278
Alfredo Aiello Italian Food
   Quincy, MA 617-770-6360
Alpine Butcher
   Lowell, MA 978-256-7771
Armanino Foods of Distinction
   Hayward, CA 800-255-8588
Atlantic Pork & Provisions
   Jamaica, NY 800-245-3536
Avalon Gourmet
   Phoenix, AZ 602-253-0343
Avon Heights Mushrooms
   Avondale, PA 610-268-2092
Bake Crafters Food Company
   McDonald, TN 423-396-3392
Barber Foods
   Kings Mountain, NC 877-447-3279
Bay Cities Produce Co Inc
   San Leandro, CA 510-346-4943
Beaver Street Fisheries
   Jacksonville, FL 800-874-6426
Bellisio Foods
   Minneapolis, MN
Bernardi Italian Foods Company
   Bloomsburg, PA 570-389-5500
Biagio's Banquets
   Chicago, IL 800-392-2837
Biagio's Banquets
   Chicago, IL 800-392-2837
Big B Barbecue
   Evansville, IN 812-425-5235
Binkert's Meat Products
   Baltimore, MD 410-687-5959
Blue Marble Brands
   Providence, RI 888-534-0246
BlueWater Seafoods
   Gloucester, MA 888-560-2539
Boesl Packing Co
   Baltimore, MD 800-675-1471
Bouma Meats
   Provost, AB 780-753-2092
Boyd's Sausage Co
   Washington, IA 319-653-5715
Brookside Foods
   Cleveland, OH 216-991-7600
Bruno Specialty Foods
   West Sayville, NY 631-589-1700
Buxton Foods
   Buxton, ND 800-726-8057
C Roy & Sons Processing
   Yale, MI 810-387-3957
Cajun Brands
   New Iberia, LA 504-408-2252
Calendar Islands Maine Lobster LLC
   Portland, ME 207-541-9140
Camino Real Foods Inc
   Vernon, CA 800-421-6201
Campbell Soup Co.
   Camden, NJ 800-257-8443
Campbell Soup Co.
   Camden, NJ 800-257-8443
Canada Bread Co, Ltd
   Etobicoke, ON 800-465-5515
Caribbean Food Delights Inc
   Tappan, NY 845-398-3000
Carl Buddig & Co.
   Homewood, IL 888-633-5684
Carolina Packers Inc
   Smithfield, NC 800-682-7675
Carrington Foods Co Inc
   Saraland, AL 251-675-9700
Cedar Lake Foods
   Cedar Lake, MI 800-246-5039
Cedarlane Foods
   Carson, CA 800-826-3322
Chang Food Company
   Garden Grove, CA 714-265-9990

Product Categories / Prepared Foods: General

Channel Fish Processing
  Gloucester, MA.................800-457-0054
Charlie's Country Sausage
  Minot, ND.....................701-838-6302
Chateau Food Products Inc
  Cicero, IL....................708-863-4207
Chef America
  Chatsworth, CA................818-718-8111
Chef Hans' Gourmet Foods
  Monroe, LA....................800-890-4267
Chicago 58 Food Products
  Woodbridge, ON................416-603-4244
Chicago Meat Authority Inc
  Chicago, IL...................800-383-3811
Chincoteague Seafood Co Inc
  Parsonsburg, MD...............443-260-4800
Chisesi Brothers Meat Packing
  New Orleans, LA...............800-966-3550
Citterio USA
  Freeland, PA..................800-435-8888
Colony Brands Inc
  Monroe, WI....................800-544-9036
Conagra Brands Inc
  Chicago, IL...................877-266-2472
Conagra Foodservice
  Chicago, IL...................877-266-2472
Continental Mills Inc
  Tukwila, WA...................206-816-7000
Corfu Foods Inc
  Bensenville, IL...............630-595-2510
County Gourmet Foods, LLC
  Sewickley, PA.................412-741-8902
Cuisine Solutions Inc
  Sterling, VA..................888-285-4679
Cumberland Gap Provision Company
  Middlesboro, KY...............855-411-7675
Curtis Packing Co
  Greensboro, NC................336-275-7684
Dairy Fresh Foods Inc
  Taylor, MI....................313-299-0735
Deep Foods Inc
  Union, NJ.....................908-810-7500
Devault Foods
  Devault, PA...................800-426-2874
Dietz & Watson Inc.
  Philadelphia, PA..............215-831-9000
Ding Hau Food Co, Ltd
  Richmond, BC..................604-273-1188
Dippy Foods
  Cypress, CA...................800-819-8551
Doerle Food Svc LLC
  Broussard, LA.................800-256-1631
Dohar Meats Inc
  Cleveland, OH.................216-241-4197
Earth Island
  Chatsworth, CA................888-394-3949
Earth Island
  Chatsworth, CA................888-394-3949
Emerling International Foods
  Buffalo, NY...................716-833-7381
Enjoy Foods International
  Fontana, CA...................909-823-2228
Euro Source Gourmet
  Cedar Grove, NJ...............973-857-6000
F & S Produce Co Inc
  Vineland, NJ..................800-886-3316
F & S Produce Co Inc
  Vineland, NJ..................800-886-3316
Fine Choice Foods
  Richmond, BC..................866-760-0888
Fishpeople
  Portland, OR..................503-342-2424
Flavor Right Foods Group
  St Phoenix, AZ................888-464-3734
Frank Wardynski & Sons Inc
  Buffalo, NY...................716-854-6083
Fried Provisions Company
  Evans City, PA................724-538-3160
Garden Protein International
  Richmond, BC..................877-305-6777
GeeFree
  Marina del Ray, CA............310-862-8686
Glendora Quiche Company
  San Dimas, CA.................909-394-1777
Golden Gulf Coast Packing Co
  Biloxi, MS....................228-374-6121
Gonard Foods
  Calgary, AB...................403-277-0991
Gopicnic Inc
  Chicago, IL...................773-328-2490
Gouvea's & Purity Foods Inc
  Honolulu, HI..................808-847-3717

Grecian Delight Foods Inc
  Elk Grove Village, IL.........800-621-4387
Groff's Meats
  Elizabethtown, PA.............717-367-1246
Gutheinz Meats Inc
  Scranton, PA..................570-344-1191
H-E-B Grocery Co. LP
  San Antonio, TX...............800-432-3113
Harold Food Company
  Charlotte, NC.................704-588-8061
Hartselle Frozen Foods
  Hartselle, AL.................256-773-7261
Harvest Time Foods
  Ayden, NC.....................252-746-6675
Hazle Park Quality Meats
  West Hazleton, PA.............800-238-4331
Heinkel's Packing Co
  Decatur, IL...................800-594-2738
Helen's Pure Foods
  Cheltenham, PA................215-379-6433
Herold's Salads
  Cleveland, OH.................800-427-2523
HFI Foods
  Redmond, WA...................425-883-1320
HFI Foods
  Redmond, WA...................425-883-1320
Hip Chick Farms
 707-861-9010
Holland American International Specialties
  Bellflower, CA................562-925-6914
Homestead Fine Foods
  S San Francisco, CA...........650-615-0750
Homestead Fine Foods
  S San Francisco, CA...........650-615-0750
Hoople Country Kitchen Inc
  Rockport, IN..................877-466-7537
House of Thaller Inc
  Knoxville, TN.................800-462-3365
HSR Associates Inc
  Tarzana, CA...................818-757-7152
Hummel Brothers Inc
  New Haven, CT.................800-828-8978
Ian's Natural Food
  Framingham, MA................508-283-1174
Independent Packers Corporation
  Seattle, WA...................206-285-6000
Independent Packers Corporation
  Seattle, WA...................206-285-6000
Ise America Inc
  Galena, MD....................410-755-6300
Ise America Inc
  Galena, MD....................410-755-6300
Ito Cariani Sausage Company
  Hayward, CA...................510-887-0882
John Volpi & Co
  St Louis, MO..................800-288-3439
Karine & Jeff
  Los Angeles, CA
Kay Foods Co
  Detroit, MI...................313-393-1100
Kelly Corned Beef Co
  Chicago, IL...................800-624-5617
Kelly Foods
  Jackson, TN...................731-424-2255
Kerala Curry
  Pittsboro, NC.................919-545-9401
Kilgus Meats
  Toledo, OH....................419-472-9721
King Kold Meats
  Englewood, OH.................800-836-2797
Kitt's Meat Processing
  Dedham, IA....................712-683-5622
Knotts Fine Foods
  Paris, TN.....................731-642-1961
Kubla Khan Food Company
  Portland, OR..................503-234-7494
Lafitte Frozen Foods Corp
  Lafitte, LA...................504-689-2041
Lakeside Foods Inc.
  Manitowoc, WI.................800-466-3834
Land O'Frost Inc
  Searcy, AR....................800-643-5654
Landolfi's Food Products
  Trenton, NJ...................609-392-1830
Lengerich Meats Inc
  Zanesville, IN................260-638-4123
Leona Meat Plant
  Troy, PA......................570-297-3574
Liguria Foods Inc
  Humboldt, IA..................515-332-4121
Lisa Shively's Kitchen Helpers, LLC
  Eden, NC......................336-623-7511

Locustdale Meat Packing
  Locustdale, PA................570-875-1270
Louisiana Packing Company
  Westwego, LA..................800-666-1293
Love Quiches Desserts
  Freeport, NY..................516-623-8800
Lower Foods, Inc.
  Richmond, UT..................800-295-7898
Macabee Foods
  West Nyack, NY................845-623-1300
Made Rite Foods
  Burlington, NC................336-229-5728
Mah Chena Company
  Chicago, IL...................312-226-5100
Manda Fine Meats Inc
  Baton Rouge, LA...............800-343-2642
Maria & Son
  St Louis, MO..................866-481-9009
Marsan Foods
  Toronto, ON...................416-755-9262
Marshallville Packing Co
  Marshallville, OH.............330-855-2871
Martin Rosols
  New Britain, CT...............860-223-2707
Martin Rosols
  New Britain, CT...............860-223-2707
Martin Seafood Company
  Jessup, MD....................410-799-5822
Mcfarling Foods Inc
  Indianapolis, IN..............317-635-2633
Mcgraths Seafood
  Streator, IL..................815-672-2654
Meadows Country Products
  Hollidaysburg, PA.............888-499-1001
Menemsha Fish Market
  Chilmark, MA..................508-645-2282
Metafoods LLC
  Brookhaven, GA................404-843-2400
Mexi-Frost Specialties Company
  Brooklyn, NY..................718-625-3324
Michael Foods, Inc.
  Minnetonka, MN................952-258-4000
Molinaro's Fine Italian Foods Ltd.
  Mississauga, ON...............905-281-0352
Molinaro's Fine Italian Foods Ltd.
  Mississauga, ON...............905-281-0352
Mrs Grissom's Salads Inc
  Nashville, TN.................800-255-0571
Naleway Foods
  Winnipeg, MB..................800-665-7448
Naleway Foods
  Winnipeg, MB..................800-665-7448
Nestle USA
  Mt Sterling, KY...............859-499-1100
Nestle USA Inc
  Glendale, CA..................800-225-2270
Night Hawk Frozen Foods Inc
  Buda, TX......................800-580-4166
Old Fashioned Kitchen Inc
  Lakewood, NJ..................732-364-4100
On-Cor Frozen Foods
On-Cor Frozen Foods Redi-Serve
  Aurora, IL....................920-563-6391
P.A. Braunger Institutional Foods
  Sioux City, IA................712-258-4515
Parma Sausage Products
  Pittsburgh, PA................877-294-4207
Pasta Factory
  Melrose Park, IL..............800-615-6951
Paulsen Foods
  Atlanta, GA...................404-873-1804
Pictsweet Co
  Bells, TN.....................731-663-7600
Plumrose USA
  Chicago, IL...................800-526-4909
Pon Food Corp
  Ponchatoula, LA...............985-386-6941
Preferred Meal Systems Inc
  Moosic, PA....................570-457-8311
Prolimer Foods
  Candiac, QC...................877-535-4631
Queen International Foods
  Monterey Park, CA.............800-423-4414
R.C. McEntire & Company
  Columbia, SC..................803-799-3388
R.L. Zeigler Company
  Selma, AL.....................800-392-6328
Rachael's Smoked Fish
  Springfield, MA...............800-327-3412
Ramona's Mexican Foods
  Gardena, CA...................310-323-1950

357

Product Categories / Prepared Foods: Appetizers

Rancho Sierra
  Salinas, CA 800-398-2929
Real Kosher Sausage Company
  Newark, NJ 973-690-5394
Regal Food Service
  Houston, TX 281-477-3683
Rendulic Meat Packing Corp
  Mckeesport, PA 412-678-9541
Request Foods Inc
  Holland, MI 800-786-0900
Rich Products Corp
  Vineland, NJ 800-818-9261
Roman Packing Company
  Norfolk, NE 800-373-5990
Ruiz Food Products Inc.
  Dinuba, CA 800-477-6474
Saag's Products LLC
  San Leandro, CA 855-287-6562
Sales Associates Of Alaska
  Fairbanks, AK 800-478-2371
Sanderson Farms
  Laurel, MS 800-844-4030
Sandridge Food Corp
  Medina, OH 800-627-2523
Saval Foods Corp
  Elkridge, MD 800-527-2825
Schaefers Market
  Sauk Centre, MN 320-352-6490
Schaller & Weber Inc
  Astoria, NY 800-847-4115
Sculli Brothers
  Yeadon, PA 215-336-1223
Sechrist Brothers
  Dallastown, PA 717-244-2975
Seneca Foods Corp
  Marion, NY 315-926-8100
Seviroli Foods
  Garden City, NY 516-222-6220
Shamrock Foods Co
  Phoenix, AZ 800-289-3663
Sheinman Provision Co
  Philadelphia, PA 215-473-7065
Sims Wholesale
  Batesville, AR 870-793-1109
Smith Packing Regional Meat
  Utica, NY 315-732-5125
SONOCO
  Houma, LA 800-458-7012
Souperb LLC
  Emeryville, CA 415-685-8508
Spring Glen Fresh Foods
  Ephrata, PA 800-641-2853
Spring Grove Foods
  Miamisburg, OH 937-866-4311
Standard Meat Co LP
  Dallas, TX 866-859-6313
Star Ravioli Mfg Co
  Moonachie, NJ 201-933-6427
Starbucks
  Seattle, WA 800-782-7282
Stawnichy Holdings
  Mundare, AB 888-764-7646
Steak-Umm Company
  Shillington, PA 860-928-5900
Stevens Sausage Co
  Smithfield, NC 800-338-0561
Stonie's Sausage Shop
  Perryville, MO 888-546-2540
Strong Roots
  Brooklyn, NY 929-466-1639
Sunburst Foods
  Goldsboro, NC 919-778-2151
Sunset Specialty Foods
  Lake Arrowhead, CA 909-337-7643
Symphony Foods
  Berkeley, CA 510-845-8275
Tampa Maid Foods Inc
  Lakeland, FL 800-237-7637
Tasty Mix Quality Foods
  Brooklyn, NY 718-855-7680
Tennessee Valley Packing Co
  Columbia, TN 931-388-2623
Teti Bakery
  Etobicoke, ON 800-465-0123
Thermo Pac LLC
  Stone Mountain, GA 770-934-3200
Tomanetti Food Products Inc
  Oakmont, PA 800-875-3040
Tomasso Corporation
  Baie D'Urfe, QC 514-325-3000
Troy Foods Inc
  Troy, IL 618-667-6332

Tyson Foods Inc.
  Springdale, AR 800-233-6332
United Provision Meat Company
  Columbus, OH 614-252-1126
Upstate Niagara Co-Op Inc.
  Buffalo, NY 716-892-3156
Vanee Foods Co
  Berkeley, IL 708-449-7300
Vienna Meat Products
  Scarborough, ON 800-588-1931
Viking Seafoods Inc
  Malden, MA 800-225-3020
W.A. Beans & Sons
  Bangor, ME 800-649-1958
Warren & Son Meat Processing
  Whipple, OH 740-585-2421
Wawona Frozen Foods Inc
  Clovis, CA 559-299-2901
Wegmans Food Markets Inc.
  Rochester, NY 800-934-6267
Winn-Dixie Stores
  Jacksonville, FL 800-967-9105
Wornick Company
  Cincinnati, OH 800-860-4555
Wornick Company
  Cincinnati, OH 800-860-4555
Wornick Company
  Cincinnati, OH 800-860-4555
Zartic Inc
  Rome, GA 800-241-0516
Zuccaro Produce
  Columbia Heights, MN 612-333-1122

Appetizers

Ajinomoto Foods North America, Inc.
  Ontario, CA 909-477-4700
Anchor Appetizer Group
  Appleton, WI 920-997-2200
Appetizers And, Inc.
  Wilmington, WA 800-224-7630
B & D Foods
  Boise, ID 208-344-1183
Belle River Enterprises
  Belle River, PE 902-962-2248
Better Baked Foods Inc
  North East, PA 814-725-8778
Biagio's Banquets
  Chicago, IL 800-392-2837
Bylada Foods
  Moonachie, NJ 201-933-7474
Caribbean Food Delights Inc
  Tappan, NY 845-398-3000
Cateraid Inc
  Howell, MI 800-508-8217
Cathay Foods Corporation
  Boston, MA 617-427-1507
Chang Food Company
  Garden Grove, CA 714-265-9990
Chateau Food Products Inc
  Cicero, IL 708-863-4207
Chinese Spaghetti Factory
  Boston, MA 617-445-7714
Conagra Brands Inc
  Chicago, IL 877-266-2472
Conagra Foodservice
  Chicago, IL 877-266-2472
Cordon Bleu International
  Anjou, QC 800-363-1182
Culinaire
  Denver, CO 877-502-9100
Dominex
  St Augustine, FL 904-810-2132
Dufour Pastry Kitchens Inc
  Bronx, NY 800-439-1282
Egg Roll Fantasy
  Auburn, CA 530-887-9197
Fillo Factory, The
  Northvale, NJ 800-653-4556
Fine Choice Foods
  Richmond, BC 866-760-0888
Frozen Specialties Inc
  Perrysburg, OH 419-867-2005
Fry Foods Inc
  Tiffin, OH 800-626-2294
Glendora Quiche Company
  San Dimas, CA 909-394-1777
Great American Appetizers
  Nampa, ID 800-282-4834
Harvest Food Products Co Inc
  Hayward, CA 510-675-0383
Health is Wealth Foods
  Moonachie, NJ 201-933-7474

L & S Packing Co
  Farmingdale, NY 800-286-6487
La Tang Cuisine Manufacturing
  Houston, TX 713-780-4876
Lamb Weston Holdings Inc.
  Eagle, ID 800-766-7783
Lee's Sausage Co
  Orangeburg, SC 803-534-5517
Lemon & Vine
  Napa, CA 707-926-6073
Lucky Foods
  Tualatin, OR 503-612-1300
Mama Amy's Quality Foods
  Mississauga, ON 905-456-0056
Matador Processors
  Blanchard, OK 800-847-0797
McCain Foods USA Inc.
  Oakbrook Terace, IL 800-938-7799
Mt. Olympus Specialty Foods
  Buffalo, NY 716-874-0771
Nancy's Specialty Foods
  Newark, CA 510-494-1100
Paulsen Foods
  Atlanta, GA 404-873-1804
Perfect Bite Co
  Glendale, CA 818-507-1527
Pie Piper Products
  Wheeling, IL 800-621-8183
Piller's Fine Foods
  Waterloo, ON 800-265-2627
Plenus Group Inc
  Lowell, MA 978-970-3832
Produits Belle Baie
  Caraquet, NB 506-727-4414
Sable & Rosenfeld Foods
  Toronto, ON 416-929-4214
Sabra Blue & White Food Products
  Dallas, TX 888-957-2272
Shonna's Gourmet Goodies
  West Bridgewater, MA 888-312-7868
Sinbad Sweets
  Madera, CA 866-746-2232
Sofo Foods
  Toledo, OH 800-447-4211
Steak-Umm Company
  Shillington, PA 860-928-5900
Tampa Maid Foods Inc
  Lakeland, FL 800-237-7637
The Perfect Pita
  Springfield, VA 703-644-0004
Thyme & Truffles Hors d'Oeuvres
  Dollard-Des-Ormeaux, QC 877-785-9759
Tipiak Inc
  Stamford, CT 203-961-9117
Valdez Food Inc
  Philadelphia, PA 215-634-6106
Van-Lang Food Products
  Countryside, IL 708-588-0800
William Poll Inc
  New York, NY 800-993-7655
Willow Foods
  Beaverton, OR 800-338-3609
Wonton Food
  Brooklyn, NY 800-776-8889

Fresh, Canned & Frozen

Belle River Enterprises
  Belle River, PE 902-962-2248
Biagio's Banquets
  Chicago, IL 800-392-2837
Caribbean Food Delights Inc
  Tappan, NY 845-398-3000
Cateraid Inc
  Howell, MI 800-508-8217
Cathay Foods Corporation
  Boston, MA 617-427-1507
Caughman's Meat Plant
  Lexington, SC 803-356-0076
Cedar Key Aquaculture Farms
  Riverview, FL 888-252-6735
Chang Food Company
  Garden Grove, CA 714-265-9990
Chateau Food Products Inc
  Cicero, IL 708-863-4207
Chinese Spaghetti Factory
  Boston, MA 617-445-7714
Cordon Bleu International
  Anjou, QC 800-363-1182
Dufour Pastry Kitchens Inc
  Bronx, NY 800-439-1282
Fine Choice Foods
  Richmond, BC 866-760-0888

Product Categories / Prepared Foods: Baked Beans (see also Pork & Beans)

Frozen Specialties Inc
 Perrysburg, OH 419-867-2005
Glendora Quiche Company
 San Dimas, CA 909-394-1777
Good Wives
 Wilmington, MA 800-521-8160
Gourmet Foods Inc
 Compton, CA 310-632-3300
Great American Appetizers
 Nampa, ID 800-282-4834
La Tang Cuisine Manufacturing
 Houston, TX 713-780-4876
Lancaster Colony Corporation
 Westerville, OH 614-224-7141
Lee's Sausage Co
 Orangeburg, SC 803-534-5517
Matador Processors
 Blanchard, OK 800-847-0797
Nancy's Specialty Foods
 Newark, CA 510-494-1100
Pie Piper Products
 Wheeling, IL 800-621-8183
Piller's Fine Foods
 Waterloo, ON 800-265-2627
Produits Belle Baie
 Caraquet, NB 506-727-4414
Royal Palate Foods
 Inglewood, CA 310-330-7701
Shonna's Gourmet Goodies
 West Bridgewater, MA 888-312-7868
Silverleaf International Corp
 Rosharon, TX 800-442-7542
Steak-Umm Company
 Shillington, PA 860-928-5900
Tampa Maid Foods Inc
 Lakeland, FL 800-237-7637
Thyme & Truffles Hors d'Oeuvres
 Dollard-Des-Ormeaux, QC 877-785-9759
Tipiak Inc
 Stamford, CT 203-961-9117
Van-Lang Food Products
 Countryside, IL 708-588-0800
VLR Food Corporation
 Vaughan, ON 800-387-7437

Frozen

Ajinomoto Foods North America, Inc.
 Ontario, CA 909-477-4700
Appetizers And, Inc.
 Wilmington, WA 800-224-7630
B & D Foods
 Boise, ID 208-344-1183
Bylada Foods
 Moonachie, NJ 201-933-7474
Caribbean Food Delights Inc
 Tappan, NY 845-398-3000
Cathay Foods Corporation
 Boston, MA 617-427-1507
Chang Food Company
 Garden Grove, CA 714-265-9990
Chateau Food Products Inc
 Cicero, IL 708-863-4207
Coastal Seafoods
 Ridgefield, CT 203-431-0453
Cordon Bleu International
 Anjou, QC 800-363-1182
Dufour Pastry Kitchens Inc
 Bronx, NY 800-439-1282
Giorgio Foods
 Temple, PA 800-220-2139
Good Wives
 Wilmington, MA 800-521-8160
Great American Appetizers
 Nampa, ID 800-282-4834
Health is Wealth Foods
 Moonachie, NJ 201-933-7474
Matador Processors
 Blanchard, OK 800-847-0797
McCain Foods Ltd.
 Toronto, ON 416-955-1700
McCain Foods USA Inc.
 Oakbrook Terace, IL 800-938-7799
Neilly's Foods
 York, PA 717-668-3722
Paulsen Foods
 Atlanta, GA 404-873-1804
Stacey's Famous Foods
 Hayden, ID 800-782-2395
Steak-Umm Company
 Shillington, PA 860-928-5900
Strong Roots
 Brooklyn, NY 929-466-1639

Tampa Maid Foods Inc
 Lakeland, FL 800-237-7637
Thyme & Truffles Hors d'Oeuvres
 Dollard-Des-Ormeaux, QC 877-785-9759
Tipiak Inc
 Stamford, CT 203-961-9117
William Poll Inc
 New York, NY 800-993-7655

Refrigerated

Cyclone Enterprises Inc
 Houston, TX 281-872-0087

Baked Beans (see also Pork & Beans)

Canned

Agfinity Inc
 Eaton, CO 800-433-4688
Amigos Canning Company
 San Antonio, TX 210-798-5360
Blue Runner Foods Inc
 Gonzales, LA 225-647-3016
Burnette Foods
 Elk Rapids, MI 231-264-8116
Burnham & Morrill Co
 Portland, ME 800-813-2165
California Fruit and Tomato Kitchens
 Modesto, CA 209-574-9407
Campbell Soup Co.
 Camden, NJ 800-257-8443
Carriere Foods Inc
 Saint-Denis-Sur-Richelie, QC 450-787-3411
Cordon Bleu International
 Anjou, QC 800-363-1182
Eden Foods Inc
 Clinton, MI 888-424-3336
Grandma Browns Beans Inc
 Mexico, NY 315-963-7221
H.K. Canning
 Ventura, CA 805-652-1392
Hanover Foods Corp
 Hanover, PA 717-632-6000
Hoopeston Foods Inc
 Burnsville, MN 952-854-0903
International Home Foods
 Parsippany, NJ 973-359-9920
L & S Packing Co
 Farmingdale, NY 800-286-6487
Lakeside Foods Inc.
 Plainview, MN 507-534-3141
Lakeside Foods Inc.
 Manitowoc, WI 800-466-3834
Mccall Farms
 Effingham, SC 800-277-2012
Meridian Foods New Inc
 Eaton, IN 765-396-3344
Miyako Oriental Foods Inc
 Baldwin Park, CA 877-788-6476
Morgan Foods Inc
 Austin, IN 888-430-1780
Nation Wide Canning Ltd.
 Cottam, ON 519-839-4831
Natural Value
 Sacramento, CA 916-836-3561
New Era Canning Company
 New Era, MI 231-861-2151
New Harvest Foods
 Washington, DC 920-822-2578
NORPAC Foods Inc
 Salem, OR
Red River Commodities Inc
 Fargo, ND 800-437-5539
Rio Valley Canning Co
 Donna, TX 956-464-7843
Seneca Foods Corp
 Princeville, IL 309-385-4301
Truitt Bros Inc
 Salem, OR 800-547-8712
TyRy Inc
 Rocklin, CA 800-322-6325
United Intertrade Corporation
 Houston, TX 800-969-2233
Wornick Company
 Cincinnati, OH 800-860-4555

Breaded Vegetables

Al Pete Meats
 Muncie, IN 765-288-8817
Great American Appetizers
 Nampa, ID 800-282-4834

Lake Erie Frozen Foods Co
 Ashland, OH 800-766-8501
Pictsweet Co
 Bells, TN 731-663-7600
Trans Pecos Foods
 San Antonio, TX 210-228-0896
Westin Foods
 Omaha, NE 800-228-6098

Breakfast Foods: Instant

Bake Crafters Food Company
 McDonald, TN 423-396-3392
Bede Inc
 Haledon, NJ 866-239-6565
Brekki
 Carlsbad, CA 760-487-8895
California Cereal Products
 Oakland, CA 510-452-4500
Campbell Soup Co.
 Camden, NJ 800-257-8443
Continental Mills Inc
 Tukwila, WA 206-816-7000
Country Smoked Meats
 Bowling Green, OH 800-321-4766
Cream Of The West
 Harlowton, MT 800-477-2383
Five Star Home Foods, Inc.
 King of Prussia, PA 800-246-5405
GeeFree
 Marina del Ray, CA 310-862-8686
GFA Brands Inc
 Paramus, NJ 201-568-9300
Hodgson Mill Inc
 Effingham, IL 800-347-0198
Homestead Mills
 Cook, MN 800-652-5233
Ian's Natural Food
 Framingham, MA 508-283-1174
International Home Foods
 Parsippany, NJ 973-359-9920
Jimmy Dean Foods
 Springdale, AR 800-925-3326
Kellogg Co.
 Battle Creek, MI 800-962-1413
Little Crow Foods
 Warsaw, IN 800-288-2769
Maxwell House & Post
 Rye Brook, NY 914-335-2500
Nature's Legacy Inc.
 Hudson, MI 517-448-2050
Quaker Oats Company
 Peterborough, ON 800-267-6287
Real Food Marketing
 Kansas City, MO 816-221-4100
San Francisco Spice Co.
 Woodland, CA 866-972-6879
Sturm Foods Inc
 Manawa, WI 800-347-8876
Tova Industries LLC
 Louisville, KY 888-532-8682
US Mills
 Bala Cynwyd, PA 800-422-1125

Broth

Canned, Frozen, Powdered

Blount Fine Foods
 Fall River, MA 774-888-1300
Bookbinder Specialties LLC
 Media, PA 215-322-1305
Clofine Dairy Products Inc
 Linwood, NJ 609-653-1000
Cordon Bleu International
 Anjou, QC 800-363-1182
Fuji Foods Corp
 Browns Summit, NC 336-375-3111
Hormel Foods Corp.
 Austin, MN 507-437-5611
International Dehydrated Foods
 Springfield, MO 800-641-6509
Organic Gourmet
 Sherman Oaks, CA 800-400-7772
Osso Good, LLC
 San Rafael, CA
Sentry Seasonings
 Elmhurst, IL 630-530-5370
SOUPerior Bean & Spice Company
 Vancouver, WA 800-878-7687
St. Ours & Company
 East Weymouth, MA 781-331-8520

Product Categories / Prepared Foods: Chili

Sweet Sue Kitchens
   Athens, AL 256-216-0500
Tova Industries LLC
   Louisville, KY 888-532-8682

Chicken

All-States Quality Foods
   Charles City, IA 800-247-4195
Bonafide Provisions
   San Diego, CA
Clofine Dairy Products Inc
   Linwood, NJ 609-653-1000
Hain Celestial Group Inc
   Lake Success, NY 800-434-4246
Imagine Foods
   Boulder, CO 800-434-4246
Kettle & Fire
   Austin, TX .415-857-0024
Sentry Seasonings
   Elmhurst, IL 630-530-5370
Sweet Sue Kitchens
   Athens, AL 256-216-0500
The Art of Broth, LLC
   CA 818-715-9320
Vanee Foods Co
   Berkeley, IL 708-449-7300

Chili

Aunt Kitty's Foods Inc
   Vineland, NJ 856-691-2100
Baja Foods LLC
   Chicago, IL 773-376-9030
Big B Barbecue
   Evansville, IN 812-425-5235
Bruce Foods Corporation
   Lafayette, LA 800-299-9082
Burnett & Son
   Monrovia, CA 877-632-5467
Buxton Foods
   Buxton, ND 800-726-8057
Campbell Soup Co.
   Camden, NJ 800-257-8443
Carolina Packers Inc
   Smithfield, NC 800-682-7675
Chandler Foods Inc
   Greensboro, NC 800-537-6219
Cherchies
   Malvern, PA 800-644-1980
Detroit Chili Co
   Southfield, MI 248-440-5933
Edmond's Chile Co
   St Louis, MO 314-772-1499
El Rey Cooked Meats
   St Louis, MO 314-521-3113
Faribault Foods, Inc.
   Fairbault, MN 507-331-1400
Fillo Factory, The
   Northvale, NJ 800-653-4556
Harold Food Company
   Charlotte, NC 704-588-8061
Health Valley Company
   Irwindale, CA 800-334-3204
Hoopeston Foods Inc
   Burnsville, MN 952-854-0903
International Home Foods
   Parsippany, NJ 973-359-9920
Kelly Foods
   Jackson, TN 731-424-2255
Kettle & Fire
   Austin, TX .415-857-0024
Las Cruces Brand Products
   El Paso, TX 915-779-5709
Lee's Sausage Co
   Orangeburg, SC 803-534-5517
Leonard Mountain Inc
   Bixby, OK .800-822-7700
Mi Ranchito Foods
   Phoenix, AZ 602-272-3949
Milnot Company
   Litchfield, IL 800-877-6455
Moonlite Bar-B-Q Inn
   Owensboro, KY 800-322-8989
Mr Jay's Tamales & Chili
   Lynwood, CA 310-537-3932
North of the Border
   Tesuque, NM 800-860-0681
Original Chili Bowl
   Ontario, CA 800-548-6363
Patagonia Provisions
   Sausalito, CA 888-221-8208
Pokanoket Ostrich Farm
   South Dartmouth, MA 508-992-6188
Supreme Frozen Products
   Chicago, IL 773-622-3777
T.L. Herring & Company
   Wilson, NC 252-291-1141
Taylor's Mexican Chili Co Inc
   Carlinville, IL 800-382-4454
Terra Sol Chile Company
   Austin, TX .512-836-3525
Texas Tamale Co
   Houston, TX 713-795-5500
TODDS Enterprises Inc
   Irvine, CA .800-568-6337
Torn & Glasser
   Los Angeles, CA 800-282-6887
Vienna Beef LTD
   Chicago, IL 800-366-3647
Vietti Foods Co Inc
   Nashville, TN 615-244-7864
Wisconsin Packaging Corp
   Fort Atkinson, WI 920-563-9363
Yankee Specialty Foods
   Boston, MA 800-688-9904

Canned

Milnot Company
   Litchfield, IL 800-877-6455
Pure Food Ingredients
   Verona, WI 800-355-9601
Vanee Foods Co
   Berkeley, IL 708-449-7300

Canned & Frozen

Aunt Kitty's Foods Inc
   Vineland, NJ 856-691-2100
Baja Foods LLC
   Chicago, IL 773-376-9030
Big B Barbecue
   Evansville, IN 812-425-5235
Campbell Company of Canada
   Toronto, ON 800-410-7687
Caughman's Meat Plant
   Lexington, SC 803-356-0076
Chandler Foods Inc
   Greensboro, NC 800-537-6219
Edmond's Chile Co
   St Louis, MO 314-772-1499
First Original Texas Chili Company
   Fort Worth, TX 800-507-0009
Kelly Foods
   Jackson, TN 731-424-2255
Marsan Foods
   Toronto, ON 416-755-9262
Mi Ranchito Foods
   Phoenix, AZ 602-272-3949
Milnot Company
   Litchfield, IL 800-877-6455
North of the Border
   Tesuque, NM 800-860-0681
SOPAKCO Foods
   Mullins, SC 800-276-9678
TODDS Enterprises Inc
   Irvine, CA .800-568-6337
Westbrae Natural Foods
   Melville, NY 800-434-4246
Worthmore Food Products Co
   Cincinnati, OH 866-837-7687

Frozen

Bueno Foods
   Albuquerque, NM 800-888-7336
Texas Chili Co
   Fort Worth, TX 800-507-0009

with Cheese

Las Cruces Brand Products
   El Paso, TX 915-779-5709

Chowder

Bay Shore Chowders & Bisques
   Fall River, MA 888-675-6892
Blount Fine Foods
   Fall River, MA 774-888-1300
Campbell Company of Canada
   Toronto, ON 800-410-7687
Campbell Soup Co.
   Camden, NJ 800-257-8443
Cherchies
   Malvern, PA 800-644-1980
Denzer's Food Products
   Baltimore, MD 410-889-1500
Fish Hopper
   Monterey, CA 831-372-3406
LA Monica Fine Foods
   Millville, NJ
Mid-Atlantic Foods Inc
   Easton, MD 800-922-4688
Ronzoni
   Largo, FL .800-730-5957
Triton Seafood Co
   Medley, FL 305-888-0051
Valdez Food Inc
   Philadelphia, PA 215-634-6106
Yankee Specialty Foods
   Boston, MA 800-688-9904

Clam & Fish

Bay Shore Chowders & Bisques
   Fall River, MA 888-675-6892
Blount Fine Foods
   Fall River, MA 774-888-1300
Campbell Company of Canada
   Toronto, ON 800-410-7687
Campbell Soup Co.
   Camden, NJ 800-257-8443
Chincoteague Seafood Co Inc
   Parsonsburg, MD 443-260-4800
Fish Hopper
   Monterey, CA 831-372-3406
Kettle Cuisine
   Lynn, MA .877-302-7687
LA Monica Fine Foods
   Millville, NJ
Mid-Atlantic Foods Inc
   Easton, MD 800-922-4688
Sea Watch Intl
   Easton, MD 410-822-7500

Chutney

A Perfect Pear
   Napa, CA .800-553-5753
Blue Jay Orchards
   Bethel, CT 203-748-0119
Blueberry Store
   Grand Junction, MI 877-654-2400
Chelsea Flower Market
   New York, NY 888-727-7887
Chicama Vineyards
   West Tisbury, MA 888-244-2262
Cinnabar Specialty Foods Inc
   Prescott, AZ 866-293-6433
Coastal Classics
   Duxbury, MA 508-746-6058
Commissariat Imports
   Los Angeles, CA 310-475-5628
Creative Foodworks Inc
   San Antonio, TX 210-212-4761
Cuizina Food Company
   Woodinville, WA 425-486-7000
Curry King Corporation
   Waldwick, NJ 800-287-7987
Delicae Gourmet
   Tarpon Springs, FL 800-942-2502
Graves Mountain Lodge Inc.
   Syria, VA .540-923-4231
Great American Foods Commissary
   Hughes Springs, TX 903-639-1482
J.M. Smucker Co.
   Orrville, OH 888-550-9555
Jay Shah Foods
   Mississauga, ON 905-696-0172
Koloa Rum Corp
   Kalaheo, HI 808-332-9333
Kozlowski Farms
   Forestville, CA 800-473-2767
Outback Kitchens LLC
   Huntington, VT 802-434-5262
Silver Palate Kitchens
   Cresskill, NJ 201-568-0110
Solo Foods
   Countryside, IL 800-328-7656
Spruce Mountain Blueberries
   West Rockport, ME 207-236-3538
Steel's Gourmet Foods, Ltd.
   Bridgeport, PA 800-678-3357
Tait Farm Foods
   Centre Hall, PA 800-787-2716
Vermont Harvest Spec Food LLC
   Stowe, VT .800-338-5354

Product Categories / Prepared Foods: Convenience Food

Wild Thymes Farm Inc
  Greenville, NY 845-266-8387
Wisconsin Wilderness Food Products
  Lake Bluff, IL 800-359-3039

Convenience Food

American Wholesale Grocery
  Mobile, AL 251-433-2528
Andalusia Distributing Co Inc
  Andalusia, AL 334-222-3671
Anmar Foods
  Chicago, IL 312-421-6500
Biagio's Banquets
  Chicago, IL 800-392-2837
Big B Barbecue
  Evansville, IN 812-425-5235
Camino Real Foods Inc
  Vernon, CA 800-421-6201
Crum Creek Mils
  Springfield, PA 888-607-3500
Delicious Frookie
  Des Plaines, IL 847-699-3200
Dorothy Dawson Food Products
  Jackson, MI 517-788-9830
Fantastic World Foods
  Providence, RI
Forkless Gourmet Inc
  Chicago, IL 312-474-5746
Grecian Delight Foods Inc
  Elk Grove Village, IL 800-621-4387
Kelly Foods
  Jackson, TN 731-424-2255
Kraft Heinz Canada
  North York, ON 416-441-5000
Lundberg Family Farms
  Richvale, CA 530-538-3500
McCain Foods Ltd.
  Toronto, ON 416-955-1700
Michael Foods, Inc.
  Minnetonka, MN 952-258-4000
Minsley, Inc.
  Ontario, CA 909-458-1100
Movie Breads Food
  Chateauguay, QC 450-692-7606
Naleway Foods
  Winnipeg, MB 800-665-7448
Nancy's Specialty Foods
  Newark, CA 510-494-1100
Natural Quick Foods
  Seattle, WA 206-365-5757
Sunburst Foods
  Goldsboro, NC 919-778-2151
Super Mom's LLC
  St Paul Park, MN 800-944-7276
Suzanna's Kitchen
  Peachtree Cor, GA 770-476-9900
Troverco
  St. Louis, MO 800-468-3354

Frozen

Advance Pierre Foods
  Cincinnati, OH 800-969-2747
Agrusa
  Leonia, NJ 201-592-5950
Ajinomoto Foods North America, Inc.
  Ontario, CA 909-477-4700
Al Pete Meats
  Muncie, IN 765-288-8817
Applegate Farms
  Bridgewater, NJ 866-587-5858
Barber Foods
  Kings Mountain, NC 877-447-3279
Bernardi Italian Foods Company
  Bloomsburg, PA 570-389-5500
Biagio's Banquets
  Chicago, IL 800-392-2837
Buxton Foods
  Buxton, ND 800-726-8057
Bylada Foods
  Moonachie, NJ 201-933-7474
Camino Real Foods Inc
  Vernon, CA 800-421-6201
Campbell Soup Co.
  Camden, NJ 800-257-8443
Canada Bread Co, Ltd
  Etobicoke, ON 800-465-5515
Catch Up Logistics
  Pittsburgh, PA 412-441-9512
Cedar Lake Foods
  Cedar Lake, MI 800-246-5039

Cedarlane Foods
  Carson, CA 800-826-3322
Endico Potatoes Inc
  Mt Vernon, NY 914-664-1151
English Bay Batter Us Inc
  Columbus, OH 800-253-6844
Fine Choice Foods
  Richmond, BC 866-760-0888
Forte Stromboli Company
  Philadelphia, PA 215-463-6336
Giorgio Foods
  Temple, PA 800-220-2139
Gonard Foods
  Calgary, AB 403-277-0991
Harvest Time Foods
  Ayden, NC 252-746-6675
High Liner Foods Inc.
  Lunenburg, NS 902-634-8811
Hormel Foods Corp.
  Austin, MN 507-437-5611
Juno Chef's
  Goshen, NY 845-294-5400
Landolfi's Food Products
  Trenton, NJ 609-392-1830
Love Quiches Desserts
  Freeport, NY 516-623-8800
Macabee Foods
  West Nyack, NY 845-623-1300
Made Rite Foods
  Burlington, NC 336-229-5728
Maple Leaf Farms
  St Leesburg, IN 800-348-2812
Marsan Foods
  Toronto, ON 416-755-9262
Martin Seafood Company
  Jessup, MD 410-799-5822
Michael Foods, Inc.
  Minnetonka, MN 952-258-4000
Milnot Company
  Litchfield, IL 800-877-6455
Miracapo Pizza
  Elk Grove Village, IL 847-631-3500
Morningstar Farms
  Zanesville, OH 800-535-5644
Morrison Lamothe
  Toronto, ON 877-677-6533
Naleway Foods
  Winnipeg, MB 800-665-7448
Nestle USA Inc
  Glendale, CA 800-225-2270
Nickabood's Inc
  Los Angeles, CA 213-746-1541
Night Hawk Frozen Foods Inc
  Buda, TX 800-580-4166
Old Fashioned Kitchen Inc
  Lakewood, NJ 732-364-4100
On-Cor Frozen Foods Redi-Serve
  Aurora, IL 920-563-6391
Ore-Ida Foods
  Pittsburgh, PA 800-255-5750
Pasta Factory
  Melrose Park, IL 800-615-6951
Queen International Foods
  Monterey Park, CA 800-423-4414
Ragozzino Foods Inc
  Meriden, CT 800-348-1240
Ramona's Mexican Foods
  Gardena, CA 310-323-1950
Request Foods Inc
  Holland, MI 800-786-0900
Ruiz Food Products Inc.
  Dinuba, CA 800-477-6474
Saffron Road
  Stamford, CT 877-425-2587
Steak-Umm Company
  Shillington, PA 860-928-5900
Sunset Specialty Foods
  Lake Arrowhead, CA 909-337-7643
The Food Collective
  Irvine, CA 866-328-8638
Thyme & Truffles Hors d'Oeuvres
  Dollard-Des-Ormeaux, QC 877-785-9759
Tomasso Corporation
  Baie D'Urfe, QC 514-325-3000
Turri's Italian Foods
  Roseville, MI 586-773-6010
United Supermarkets
  Lubbock, TX 806-745-9667
Wawona Frozen Foods Inc
  Clovis, CA 559-299-2901
Zartic Inc
  Rome, GA 800-241-0516

Crepes

Crepini
  Pleasantville, NY 914-533-6645
Echo Lake Foods, Inc.
  Burlington, WI 262-763-9551
Old Fashioned Kitchen Inc
  Lakewood, NJ 732-364-4100
Table De France
  Ontario, CA 909-923-5205

Croquettes

Hanover Foods Corp
  Hanover, PA 717-632-6000

French Fries

Endico Potatoes Inc
  Mt Vernon, NY 914-664-1151
Hanover Potato Products Inc
  Hanover, PA 717-632-0700
Healthy Life Brands LLC
  Wellesley, MA 508-401-7040
Lamb Weston Holdings Inc.
  Eagle, ID 800-766-7783
McCain Foods Ltd.
  Toronto, ON 416-955-1700
McCain Foods USA Inc.
  Oakbrook Terace, IL 800-938-7799
Ore-Ida Foods
  Pittsburgh, PA 800-255-5750
Qualifresh Michel St. Arneault
  St. Hubert, QC 800-565-0550
Strong Roots
  Brooklyn, NY 929-466-1639
Twin City Foods Inc.
  Stanwood, WA 206-515-2400
VCPB Transportation
  Secaucus, NJ 201-770-0070
Yum Yum Potato Chips
  Warwick, QC 800-567-5792

Baked

McCain Foods Ltd.
  Toronto, ON 416-955-1700

Canned

Emerling International Foods
  Buffalo, NY 716-833-7381

Crinkle Cut

Lamb Weston Holdings Inc.
  Eagle, ID 800-766-7783
McCain Foods Ltd.
  Toronto, ON 416-955-1700

Frozen

Emerling International Foods
  Buffalo, NY 716-833-7381
Endico Potatoes Inc
  Mt Vernon, NY 914-664-1151
McCain Foods Ltd.
  Toronto, ON 416-955-1700
Ore-Ida Foods
  Pittsburgh, PA 800-255-5750
Qualifresh Michel St. Arneault
  St. Hubert, QC 800-565-0550
Twin City Foods Inc.
  Stanwood, WA 206-515-2400

Shoestring

Emerling International Foods
  Buffalo, NY 716-833-7381
Ore-Ida Foods
  Pittsburgh, PA 800-255-5750

Sweet

Lamb Weston Holdings Inc.
  Eagle, ID 800-766-7783
McCain Foods Ltd.
  Toronto, ON 416-955-1700

Tater Tots

McCain Foods Ltd.
  Toronto, ON 416-955-1700

Wedges

Lamb Weston Holdings Inc.
  Eagle, ID 800-766-7783

Product Categories / Prepared Foods: French Toast

McCain Foods Ltd.
   Toronto, ON 416-955-1700

French Toast

Continental Mills Inc
   Tukwila, WA 206-816-7000

Frozen

Continental Mills Inc
   Tukwila, WA 206-816-7000

Fresh

Cece's Veggie Co.
   Austin, TX. 512-200-3337
DNO Inc
   Columbus, OH 614-231-3601
G A Food Svc Inc
   St Petersburg, FL. 800-852-2211
Garden Protein International
   Richmond, BC 877-305-6777

Frozen

Ajinomoto Foods North America, Inc.
   Ontario, CA. 909-477-4700
Best Chicago Meat
   Chicago, IL
Better Baked Foods Inc
   North East, PA. 814-725-8778
Blue Marble Brands
   Providence, RI 888-534-0246
Burke Corp
   Nevada, IA 800-654-1152
Caulipower
   Encino, CA 844-422-8544
Charles Rockel & Son
   Cincinnati, OH 513-631-3009
Conagra Brands Inc
   Chicago, IL 877-266-2472
Conagra Foodservice
   Chicago, IL 877-266-2472
Discovery Foods
   Hayward, CA 510-780-9238
Emerling International Foods
   Buffalo, NY. 716-833-7381
Freeze-Dry Foods Inc
   Albion, NY 585-589-6399
Garden Protein International
   Richmond, BC 877-305-6777
Giorgio Foods
   Temple, PA 800-220-2139
Grainful
   Ithaca, NY
Hook Line and Savor
   Gloucester, MA. 833-457-2867
Ian's Natural Food
   Framingham, MA. 508-283-1174
Kraft Heinz Co.
   Chicago, IL. 800-543-5335
Lisa's Organics
   Carnelian Bay, CA 877-584-5711
Luvo Inc.
   Blaine, WA 844-880-5886
Mamie's Pies
   San Francisco, CA 415-870-0390
McCain Foods Ltd.
   Toronto, ON 416-955-1700
On-Cor Frozen Foods
Oscar's Wholesale Meats
   Ogden, UT. 801-621-5655
Paulsen Foods
   Atlanta, GA. 404-873-1804
Popkoff's
   City of Industry, CA 844-767-5633
Red's All Natural
   North Sioux City, SD 605-956-7337
Saffron Road
   Stamford, CT. 877-425-2587
Schwan's Company
   Marshall, MN 800-533-5290
Strong Roots
   Brooklyn, NY 929-466-1639
The Food Collective
   Irvine, CA 866-328-8638
TMI Trading Co
   Brooklyn, NY 718-821-5052

Giardiniera

Castella Imports Inc
   Brentwood, NY. 631-231-5500

Colonna Brothers Inc
   North Bergen, NJ 201-864-1115
Fontanini Italian Meats
   McCook, IL. 800-331-6328
L & S Packing Co
   Farmingdale, NY 800-286-6487
Orleans Packing Co
   Hyde Park, MA 617-361-6611

Hash

Canned & Frozen

Caughman's Meat Plant
   Lexington, SC. 803-356-0076
Hormel Foods Corp.
   Austin, MN 507-437-5611
Kelly Foods
   Jackson, TN 731-424-2255
Lee's Sausage Co
   Orangeburg, SC 803-534-5517
Ninety Six Canning Company
   Ninety Six, SC 864-543-2700
SOPAKCO Foods
   Mullins, SC. 800-276-9678

Hush Puppies

Atkinson Milling Co.
   Selma, NC. 800-948-5707
Delta Pride Catfish
   Indianola, MS 800-228-3474
Fry Krisp Food Products
   Jackson, MI. 877-854-5440
Great American Foods Commissary
   Hughes Springs, TX 903-639-1482
Lakeside Mills
   Rutherfordton, NC 828-286-4866
Lone Star Consolidated Foods Inc.
   Dallas, TX. 800-658-5637
Savannah Food Co
   Savannah, TN 800-795-2550
Shenandoah Mills
   Lebanon, TN. 615-444-0841
Triton Seafood Co
   Medley, FL. 305-888-0051

Frozen & Mixes

Tova Industries LLC
   Louisville, KY 888-532-8682
Triton Seafood Co
   Medley, FL. 305-888-0051
Weisenberger Mills
   Midway, KY 800-643-8678

Individual Packets

Foodservice

Baldwin Richardson Foods
   Oakbrook Terrace, IL 866-644-2732
Heinz Portion Control
   Jacksonville, FL 904-695-1300
Magic Seasoning Blends
   New Orleans, LA 800-457-2857

Individual Quick Frozen Food

Applegate Farms
   Bridgewater, NJ 866-587-5858
Appleton Produce Company
   Weiser, ID 208-414-3352
Bandon Bay Fisheries
   Bandon, OR 541-347-4454
Beef Products Inc.
   North Sioux City, SD 605-217-8000
Boardman Foods Inc
   Boardman, OR 541-481-3000
Burke Corp
   Nevada, IA 800-654-1152
Cherryfield Foods
   Cherryfield, ME 207-546-7573
Christy Wild Blueberry Farms
   Amherst, NS 902-667-3013
Cuizina Food Company
   Woodinville, WA. 425-486-7000
Eckert Cold Storage
   Manteca, CA. 209-823-3181
Emerling International Foods
   Buffalo, NY. 716-833-7381
Fish King
   Glendale, CA 818-244-2161

Gay's Wild Maine Blueberries
   Old Town, ME 207-570-3535
High Liner Foods Inc.
   Lunenburg, NS 902-634-8811
Hillmans Shrimp & Oyster
   Port Lavaca, TX 800-582-4416
Kashi Company
   Solana Beach, CA. 877-747-2467
LA Monica Fine Foods
   Millville, NJ
Leach Farms Inc
   Berlin, WI. 920-361-1880
Lef Bleuges Marinor
   St-Felicien, QC 418-679-4577
Louisiana Packing Company
   Westwego, LA. 800-666-1293
Merrill's Blueberry Farms
   Ellsworth, ME 800-711-6551
Mr Dell Foods
   Kearney, MO. 816-628-4644
Nature Quality
   San Martin, CA. 408-683-2182
On-Cor Frozen Foods
Ore-Cal Corp
   Los Angeles, CA. 800-827-7474
Rainsweet Inc
   Salem, OR 800-363-4293
Sea Snack Foods Inc
   Los Angeles, CA. 213-622-2204
Sun Glo Of Idaho
   Sugar City, ID 208-356-7346
Sun Harvest Foods Inc
   San Diego, CA 619-661-0909
Sure-Fresh Produce Inc
   Santa Maria, CA 888-423-5379
The Food Collective
   Irvine, CA 866-328-8638
Unique Ingredients LLC
   Gold Canyon, AZ 480-983-2498
Washington Rhubarb Grower Assn
   Sumner, WA. 800-435-9911

Knishes

Gabila's Knishes
   Copiague, NY 631-789-2220
Oceanside Knish Factory
   Oceanside, NY 516-766-4445

Meat Balls

Armanino Foods of Distinction
   Hayward, CA 800-255-8588
Buona Vita Inc
   Bridgeton, NJ 856-453-7972
Carando Gourmet Frozen Foods
   Agawam, MA 888-227-2636
Cordon Bleu International
   Anjou, QC. 800-363-1182
DelGrosso Foods
   Tipton, PA 800-521-5880
Devault Foods
   Devault, PA. 800-426-2874
Fontanini Italian Meats
   McCook, IL. 800-331-6328
King's Command Foods Inc
   Green Bay, WA 800-345-0293
Maid-Rite Steak Company
   Dunmore, PA. 800-233-4259
Marcho Farms Inc
   Harleysville, PA 215-721-7131
On-Cor Frozen Foods Redi-Serve
   Aurora, IL 920-563-6391
Quality Sausage Company
   Dallas, TX. 214-634-3400
Rich Products Corp
   Vineland, NJ 800-818-9261

Canned

Acme Steak & Seafood
   Youngstown, OH. 800-686-2263
Campbell Soup Co.
   Camden, NJ. 800-257-8443
Cordon Bleu International
   Anjou, QC. 800-363-1182

Frozen

Burke Corp
   Nevada, IA 800-654-1152
Carando Gourmet Frozen Foods
   Agawam, MA 888-227-2636

Product Categories / Prepared Foods: Meat Loaf

Devault Foods
   Devault, PA 800-426-2874
Maid-Rite Steak Company
   Dunmore, PA 800-233-4259
Mom's Food Company
   Osterville, MA 800-969-6667
On-Cor Frozen Foods
On-Cor Frozen Foods Redi-Serve
   Aurora, IL 920-563-6391
Quaker Maid Meats
   Reading, PA 610-376-1500
Rich Products Corp
   Vineland, NJ 800-818-9261
Turri's Italian Foods
   Roseville, MI 586-773-6010
West Liberty Foods LLC
   West Liberty, IA 888-511-4500

Swedish

Burke Corp
   Nevada, IA 800-654-1152
Rose Packing Co Inc
   South Barrington, IL 800-323-7363

Meat Loaf

Buona Vita Inc
   Bridgeton, NJ 856-453-7972
Burnett & Son
   Monrovia, CA 877-632-5467
Corfu Foods Inc
   Bensenville, IL 630-595-2510
Fontanini Italian Meats
   McCook, IL 800-331-6328
King's Command Foods Inc
   Green Bay, WA 800-345-0293
Marcho Farms Inc
   Harleysville, PA 215-721-7131
Mitchell Foods
   Barbourville, KY 888-202-9745
On-Cor Frozen Foods
Rymer Foods
   Chicago, IL 800-247-9637
Sandridge Food Corp
   Medina, OH 800-627-2523
Sunset Farm Foods Inc
   Valdosta, GA 800-882-1121

Onion Rings

Agri-Pack
   Pasco, WA 509-545-6181
Great American Appetizers
   Nampa, ID 800-282-4834
Matador Processors
   Blanchard, OK 800-847-0797
Oxford Frozen Foods
   Oxford, NS 902-447-2100
Westin Foods
   Omaha, NE 800-228-6098
Yum Yum Potato Chips
   Warwick, QC 800-567-5792

Frozen

Emerling International Foods
   Buffalo, NY 716-833-7381
Fry Foods Inc
   Tiffin, OH 800-626-2294
Great American Appetizers
   Nampa, ID 800-282-4834
Lamb Weston Holdings Inc.
   Eagle, ID 800-766-7783
Matador Processors
   Blanchard, OK 800-847-0797
Oxford Frozen Foods
   Oxford, NS 902-447-2100
Westin Foods
   Omaha, NE 800-228-6098

Pancakes

Continental Mills Inc
   Tukwila, WA 206-816-7000
Cook-In-The-Kitchen
   Hampden, ME 207-848-4900
Old Fashioned Kitchen Inc
   Lakewood, NJ 732-364-4100
Pamela's Products
   Ukiah, CA 707-462-6605
Red Rose Trading Company
   Lancaster, PA 717-293-7833
Ungars Food
   Elmwood Park, NJ 201-773-6846

Frozen

Bake Crafters Food Company
   McDonald, TN 423-396-3392
Continental Mills Inc
   Tukwila, WA 206-816-7000
Old Fashioned Kitchen Inc
   Lakewood, NJ 732-364-4100
Thomas Brothers Country Ham
   Asheboro, NC 336-672-0337

Refrigerated

Echo Lake Foods, Inc.
   Burlington, WI 262-763-9551

with Fruit

Continental Mills Inc
   Tukwila, WA 206-816-7000

Pierogies

Ateeco Inc
   Shenandoah, PA 800-743-7649
Aunt Kathy's Homestyle Products
   Waldheim, SK 306-945-2181
Babci's Specialty Foods
   Chicopee, MA 413-598-8158
Brom Food Group
   St. Laurent, QC 514-744-5152
Giorgio Foods
   Temple, PA 800-220-2139
Heritage Foods USA
   New York, NY 718-389-0985
Millie's Pierogi
   Chicopee Falls, MA 800-743-7641
Mrs. Ts Pierogies
   Shenandoah, PA 800-743-7649
Naleway Foods
   Winnipeg, MB 800-665-7448
Old Fashioned Kitchen Inc
   Lakewood, NJ 732-364-4100
Popkoff's
   City of Industry, CA 844-767-5633
Schwan's Company
   Marshall, MN 800-533-5290

Pizza & Pizza Products

Al Safa Halal
   New York City, NY 800-268-8147
Andre-Boudin Bakeries
   San Francisco, CA 415-882-1849
Avanti Foods Co
   Walnut, IL 800-243-3739
Baja Foods LLC
   Chicago, IL 773-376-9030
BBU Bakeries
   Horsham, PA 800-984-0989
Biagio's Banquets
   Chicago, IL 800-392-2837
Blue Planet Foods
   Collegedale, TN 877-396-3145
Burke Corp
   Nevada, IA 800-654-1152
Bylada Foods
   Moonachie, NJ 201-933-7474
California Blending Co
   El Monte, CA 626-448-1918
Calise & Sons Bakery Inc
   Lincoln, RI 800-225-4737
Canada Bread Co, Ltd
   Etobicoke, ON 800-465-5515
Cappello's
   Denver, CO 844-353-2863
Capri Bagel & Pizza Corporation
   Brooklyn, NY 718-497-4431
Catch Up Logistics
   Pittsburgh, PA 412-441-9512
Chelsea Milling Co.
   Chelsea, MI 800-727-2460
Crestar Crusts
   Washington Court House, OH 740-335-4813
Delgrosso Foods Inc.
   Tipton, PA 800-521-5880
Dorothy Dawson Food Products
   Jackson, MI 517-788-9830
Farm Boy Food Svc
   Evansville, IN 800-852-3976
Fresh Mark Inc.
   Massillon, OH 330-832-7491
Frozen Specialties Inc
   Perrysburg, OH 419-867-2005

GeeFree
   Marina del Ray, CA 310-862-8686
General Mills
   Minneapolis, MN 800-248-7310
Gold Standard Baking Inc
   Chicago, IL 800-648-7904
Home Run Inn Frozen Foods
   Woodridge, IL 800-636-9696
Indian Foods Company, Inc.
   Osseo, MN 866-331-7684
Kamish Food Products
   Chicago, IL 773-725-6959
Kiki's Gluten-Free
   Park Ridge, IL
Kosto Food Products Co
   Wauconda, IL 847-487-2600
KT's Kitchens
   Carson, CA 310-764-0850
L & S Packing Co
   Farmingdale, NY 800-286-6487
Lamonaca Bakery
   Windber, PA 814-467-4909
Leprino Foods Co.
   Denver, CO 800-537-7466
Livermore Falls Baking Company
   Livermore Falls, ME 207-897-3442
Longo's Bakery Inc
   Hazleton, PA 570-454-5825
Magic Seasoning Blends
   New Orleans, LA 800-457-2857
Mama Amy's Quality Foods
   Mississauga, ON 905-456-0056
McCain Foods Ltd.
   Toronto, ON 416-955-1700
Miracapo Pizza
   Elk Grove Village, IL 847-631-3500
Molinaro's Fine Italian Foods Ltd.
   Mississauga, ON 905-281-0352
Nardone Brothers
   Hanover Twp, PA 800-822-5320
Nation Pizza & Foods
   Schaumburg, IL 847-397-3320
Nation Wide Canning Ltd.
   Cottam, ON 519-839-4831
Nestle USA Inc
   Glendale, CA 800-225-2270
Northwestern Foods
   Arden Hills, MN 800-236-4937
O'Neal's Fresh Frozen Pizza Crust
   Springfield, OH 937-323-0050
Palmieri Food Products
   New Haven, CT 800-845-5447
Pecoraro Dairy Products
   Brooklyn, NY 718-388-2379
Pennsylvania Macaroni Company
   Pittsburgh, PA 800-223-5928
Perky's Pizza
   Oldsmar, FL 800-473-7597
Piqua Pizza Supply Co Inc
   Piqua, OH 800-521-4442
Quality Sausage Company
   Dallas, TX 214-634-3400
Rosina Food Holdings Inc
   Buffalo, NY 888-767-4621
Schwan's Company
   Marshall, MN 800-533-5290
Sunset Farm Foods Inc
   Valdosta, GA 800-882-1121
Supreme Dairy Farms Co
   Warwick, RI 401-739-8180
Swiss-American Sausage Company
   Lathrop, CA 209-858-5555
Teeny Foods Inc
   Portland, OR 503-252-3006
Teti Bakery
   Etobicoke, ON 800-465-0123
Tip Top Canning Co
   Tipp City, OH 800-352-2635
TNT Crust
   Green Bay, WI 920-431-7240
Tomanetti Food Products
   Oakmont, PA 800-875-3040
Tomanetti Food Products Inc
   Oakmont, PA 800-875-3040
Tomaro's Bakery
   Clarksburg, WV 304-622-0691
Triple K Manufacturing Company, Inc.
   Shenandoah, IA 712-246-4376
Tyson Foods Inc.
   Springdale, AR 479-290-4000
Valdez Food Inc
   Philadelphia, PA 215-634-6106

Product Categories / Prepared Foods: Pork & Beans (see also Baked Beans)

Violet Packing Holdings LLC
 Williamstown, NJ 856-629-7428
Wanda's Nature Farm
 Lincoln, NE 800-735-6828
Weisenberger Mills
 Midway, KY 800-643-8678
Worthmore Food Products Co
 Cincinnati, OH 866-837-7687

Pizza

Amy's Kitchen Inc
 Santa Rosa, CA 707-781-6600
Andre-Boudin Bakeries
 San Francisco, CA 415-882-1849
Art's Tamales
 Metamora, IL 309-367-2850
Atlanta Bread Co.
 Smyrna, GA 800-398-3728
Aunt Kathy's Homestyle Products
 Waldheim, SK 306-945-2181
Berkshire Mountain Bakery
 Housatonic, MA 866-274-6124
Biagio's Banquets
 Chicago, IL 800-392-2837
BJ's Restaurants Inc.
 Huntington Beach, CA 714-500-2400
Bylada Foods
 Moonachie, NJ 201-933-7474
Cafe Moak
 Rockford, MI 616-866-7625
Catch Up Logistics
 Pittsburgh, PA 412-441-9512
Cedarlane Foods
 Carson, CA 800-826-3322
Chelsea Milling Co.
 Chelsea, MI 800-727-2460
Colors Gourmet Pizza
 Vista, CA 760-597-1400
Dorothy Dawson Food Products
 Jackson, MI 517-788-9830
European Egg Noodle Manufacturing
 Edmonton, AB 780-453-6767
Frozen Specialties Inc
 Perrysburg, OH 419-867-2005
Joe Corbis' Wholesale Pizza
 Darnestown, MD 888-526-7247
Kashi Company
 Solana Beach, CA 877-747-2467
Lucia's Pizza Co
 St Louis, MO 314-843-2553
Macabee Foods
 West Nyack, NY 845-623-1300
McCain Foods Ltd.
 Toronto, ON 416-955-1700
Molinaro's Fine Italian Foods Ltd.
 Mississauga, ON 905-281-0352
Mozzicato De Pasquale Bakery
 Hartford, CT 860-296-0426
Nardone Brothers
 Hanover Twp, PA 800-822-5320
Nestle USA Inc
 Glendale, CA 800-225-2270
New York Pizza
 Daytona Beach, FL 386-257-2050
Newman's Own
 Westport, CT 203-222-0136
Sunset Specialty Foods
 Lake Arrowhead, CA 909-337-7643
Superbrand Dairies
 Montgomery, AL 334-277-6010
Teeny Foods Inc
 Portland, OR 503-252-3006
Teti Bakery
 Etobicoke, ON 800-465-0123
The Perfect Pita
 Springfield, VA 703-644-0004
Troverco
 St. Louis, MO 800-468-3354

Cheese

Avanti Foods Co
 Walnut, IL 800-243-3739
Farm Boy Food Svc
 Evansville, IN 800-852-3976
Leprino Foods Co.
 Denver, CO 800-537-7466
Oh Yes! Foods
 Los Angeles, CA 855-696-4937
Pecoraro Dairy Products
 Brooklyn, NY 718-388-2379
Sun-Re Cheese Co
 Sunbury, PA 570-286-1511
Tomanetti Food Products Inc
 Oakmont, PA 800-875-3040

Crust

Berkshire Mountain Bakery
 Housatonic, MA 866-274-6124
Cali'flour Foods
 Chico, CA 866-422-3568
Calise & Sons Bakery Inc
 Lincoln, RI 800-225-4737
Chelsea Milling Co.
 Chelsea, MI 800-727-2460
Colors Gourmet Pizza
 Vista, CA 760-597-1400
Dorothy Dawson Food Products
 Jackson, MI 517-788-9830
Flamin' Red's Woodfired
 Pawlet, VT 802-325-3641
Giorgio Foods
 Temple, PA 800-220-2139
Livermore Falls Baking Company
 Livermore Falls, ME 207-897-3442
Lone Star Bakery
 Round Rock, TX 512-255-7268
Mama Mary's
 Fairforest, SC 800-813-7574
Mikey's
 480-696-2483
Molinaro's Fine Italian Foods Ltd.
 Mississauga, ON 905-281-0352
Nation Pizza & Foods
 Schaumburg, IL 847-397-3320
Northwestern Foods
 Arden Hills, MN 800-236-4937
Pacific Ocean Produce
 Santa Cruz, CA 831-423-2654
Piqua Pizza Supply Co Inc
 Piqua, OH 800-521-4442
Rustic Crust Inc
 Pittsfield, NH 603-435-5119
Teeny Foods Inc
 Portland, OR 503-252-3006
Teti Bakery
 Etobicoke, ON 800-465-0123
TNT Crust
 Green Bay, WI 920-431-7240
Tomanetti Food Products Inc
 Oakmont, PA 800-875-3040
Tomaro's Bakery
 Clarksburg, WV 304-622-0691
Wrawp
 Pomona, CA 855-972-9748

Frozen

Badger Best Pizzas
 De Pere, WI 920-336-6464
Better Baked Foods Inc
 North East, PA 814-725-8778
Biagio's Banquets
 Chicago, IL 800-392-2837
Bylada Foods
 Moonachie, NJ 201-933-7474
Calise & Sons Bakery Inc
 Lincoln, RI 800-225-4737
Catch Up Logistics
 Pittsburgh, PA 412-441-9512
Caulipower
 Encino, CA 844-422-8544
Cedarlane Foods
 Carson, CA 800-826-3322
Chelsea Milling Co.
 Chelsea, MI 800-727-2460
Chicago Avenue Pizza
 Chicago, IL 800-244-8935
Giorgio Foods
 Temple, PA 800-220-2139
Kashi Company
 Solana Beach, CA 877-747-2467
Lucia's Pizza Co
 St Louis, MO 314-843-2553
Macabee Foods
 West Nyack, NY 845-623-1300
Made In Nature
 Boulder, CO 800-906-7426
Molinaro's Fine Italian Foods Ltd.
 Mississauga, ON 905-281-0352
Nation Pizza & Foods
 Schaumburg, IL 847-397-3320
Nestle USA Inc
 Glendale, CA 800-225-2270
Palermo's Pizza
 Milwaukee, WI 414-643-0919
Randy's Frozen Meats
 Faribault, MN 507-334-7177
Spinato's Fine Foods
 Tempe, AZ 480-275-4319
Sunset Specialty Foods
 Lake Arrowhead, CA 909-337-7643
Superbrand Dairies
 Montgomery, AL 334-277-6010
Tony's Pizza
 Marshall, MN 888-465-8324

Pizza Bagels

Giorgio Foods
 Temple, PA 800-220-2139

Pizza Toppings

Avanti Foods Co
 Walnut, IL 800-243-3739
Baja Foods LLC
 Chicago, IL 773-376-9030
Buona Vita Inc
 Bridgeton, NJ 856-453-7972
Burke Corp
 Nevada, IA 800-654-1152
Farm Boy Food Svc
 Evansville, IN 800-852-3976
Fontanini Italian Meats
 McCook, IL 800-331-6328
Fresh Mark Inc.
 Massillon, OH 330-832-7491
Mama Mary's
 Fairforest, SC 800-813-7574
Patrick Cudahy LLC
 Cudahy, WI 800-486-6900
Pocino Foods
 City Of Industry, CA 800-345-0150
Quality Sausage Company
 Dallas, TX 214-634-3400
Swiss-American Sausage Company
 Lathrop, CA 209-858-5555

Shells

Bowness Bakery
 Calgary, AB 403-250-9760
Lamonaca Bakery
 Windber, PA 814-467-4909
Livermore Falls Baking Company
 Livermore Falls, ME 207-897-3442
Longo's Bakery Inc
 Hazleton, PA 570-454-5825

Frozen

Rosina Food Holdings Inc
 Buffalo, NY 888-767-4621

Pork & Beans (see also Baked Beans)

International Home Foods
 Parsippany, NJ 973-359-9920
Morgan Foods Inc
 Austin, IN 888-430-1780

Canned

Grandma Browns Beans Inc
 Mexico, NY 315-963-7221
International Home Foods
 Parsippany, NJ 973-359-9920

Porkskins

Fried

Cajun

Quality Snack Foods Inc
 Alsip, IL 708-377-7120

Portion Contol & Packaged Foods

A To Z Portion Control Meats
 Bluffton, OH 800-338-6328
Acme Steak & Seafood
 Youngstown, OH 800-686-2263
Advance Pierre Foods
 Cincinnati, OH 800-969-2747
Al Pete Meats
 Muncie, IN 765-288-8817

Product Categories / Prepared Foods: Pot Pies

ASC Seafood Inc
  Largo, FL 800-876-3474
Baldwin Richardson Foods
  Oakbrook Terrace, IL 866-644-2732
Bouma Meats
  Provost, AB 780-753-2092
Branding Iron
  Sauget, IL 800-851-4684
Broadleaf Venison USA Inc
  Vernon, CA 800-336-3844
Bruno Specialty Foods
  West Sayville, NY 631-589-1700
Bush Brothers Provision Co
  West Palm Beach, FL 800-327-1345
C&S Wholesale Meat Company
  Atlanta, GA 404-627-3547
Cal-Tex Citrus Juice LP
  Houston, TX 800-231-0133
Cambridge Packing Company
  Boston, MA 800-722-6726
Canal Fulton Provision
  Canal Fulton, OH 800-321-3502
Cardinal Meat Specialists
  Brampton, ON 800-363-1439
Cloverdale Foods
  Mandan, ND 800-669-9511
Cloverland Dairy
  Saint Clairsville, OH 740-699-0509
Colony Brands Inc
  Monroe, WI 800-544-9036
Cuizina Food Company
  Woodinville, WA 425-486-7000
Devault Foods
  Devault, PA 800-426-2874
Dynamic Foods
  Lubbock, TX 806-723-5600
Elwood International Inc
  Copiague, NY 631-842-6600
Fancy Farms Popcorn
  Bernie, MO 800-833-8154
Good Old Days Foods
  Little Rock, AR 501-565-1257
Gouvea's & Purity Foods Inc
  Honolulu, HI 808-847-3717
Heinz Portion Control
  Jacksonville, FL 904-695-1300
Italia Foods
  Schaumburg, IL 800-747-1109
Jemm Wholesale Meat Company
  Chicago, IL 773-523-8161
John Garner Meats
  Van Buren, AR 800-543-5473
Kenosha Beef International LTD
  Kenosha, WI
King Kold Meats
  Englewood, OH 800-836-2797
King's Command Foods Inc
  Green Bay, WA 800-345-0293
Knouse Foods Co-Op Inc
  Peach Glen, PA 717-677-8181
Kutiks Honey Farm
  Norwich, NY 607-336-4105
Kutztown Bologna Company
  Leola, PA 800-723-8824
L & L Packing Co
  Chicago, IL 800-628-6328
Land O'Frost Inc
  Searcy, AR 800-643-5654
Leahy Orchards
  Franklin Centre, QC 800-667-7380
Love Quiches Desserts
  Freeport, NY 516-623-8800
Lynch Foods
  North York, ON 416-449-5464
M Buono Beef Co
  Philadelphia, PA 215-463-3600
Maid-Rite Steak Company
  Dunmore, PA 800-233-4259
Marcho Farms Inc
  Harleysville, PA 215-721-7131
Mardale Specialty Foods
  Waukegan, IL 845-299-0285
Maxim's Import Corporation
  Miami, FL 800-331-6652
Meat-O-Mat Corp
  Brooklyn, NY 718-965-7250
National Foods
  Indianapolis, IN 800-683-6565
New Generation Foods
  Burnaby, BC 604-515-7438
Ocean Beauty Seafoods Inc
  Seattle, WA 800-365-8950
Okuhara Foods Inc
  Honolulu, HI 808-848-0581
Omaha Steaks Inc
  800-960-8400
On-Cor Frozen Foods Redi-Serve
  Aurora, IL 920-563-6391
Ossian Smoked Meats
  Ossian, IN 800-535-8862
Pacific Poultry Company
  Honolulu, HI 808-841-2828
Peggy Lawton Kitchens
  East Walpole, MA 800-843-7325
Pierceton Foods Inc
  Pierceton, IN 574-594-2344
Plymouth Beef Co.
  Bronx, NY 718-589-8600
Pokanoket Ostrich Farm
  South Dartmouth, MA 508-992-6188
Preferred Meal Systems Inc
  Moosic, PA 570-457-8311
Premier Meat Co
  Vernon, CA 800-555-5539
Prime Ostrich International
  Morinville, AB 800-340-2311
Quality Croutons
  Chicago, IL 800-334-2796
Quality Meats & Seafood
  West Fargo, ND 800-342-4250
Quality Naturally Foods
  City Of Industry, CA 888-498-6986
Schneider's Dairy Inc
  Pittsburgh, PA 412-881-3525
Serv-Rite Meat Co Inc
  Los Angeles, CA 323-227-1911
Skylark Meats
  Omaha, NE 800-759-5275
Smith Packing Regional Meat
  Utica, NY 315-732-5125
Spilke's Baking Company
  Moosic, PA 570-457-2400
Stampede Meat, Inc.
  Bridgeview, IL 800-353-0933
Stickney & Poor Company
  Peterborough, NH 603-924-2259
Streit Carl & Son Co
  Neptune, NJ 732-775-0803
Taku Smokehouse
  Juneau, AK 800-582-5122
Temptee Specialty Foods
  Denver, CO 800-842-1233
The Bruss Company
  Chicago, IL 773-282-2900
Tiller Foods Company
  Dayton, OH 937-435-4601
Travis Meats Inc
  Powell, TN 800-247-7606
Triple U Enterprises
  Fort Pierre, SD 605-567-3624
TyRy Inc
  Rocklin, CA 800-322-6325
Tyson Foods Inc.
  Springdale, AR 479-290-4000
Ultra Seal
  New Paltz, NY 845-255-2490
United Meat Company
  San Francisco, CA 415-864-2118
United Provision Meat Company
  Columbus, OH 614-252-1126
Valley Meat Company
  Modesto, CA 800-222-6328
WACO Beef & Pork Processors
  Waco, TX 254-772-4669
Wawona Frozen Foods Inc
  Clovis, CA 559-299-2901
Wing Nien Food
  Hayward, CA 510-487-8877
Wing's Food Products
  Toronto, ON 416-259-2662

Pot Pies

Cedarlane Foods
  Carson, CA 800-826-3322
Morrison Lamothe
  Toronto, ON 877-677-6533
Real Food Marketing
  Kansas City, MO 816-221-4100
Stacey's Famous Foods
  Hayden, ID 800-782-2395
Twin Hens
  Princeton, NJ 908-925-9040

Pot Stickers

Ajinomoto Foods North America, Inc.
  Ontario, CA 909-477-4700
Chang Food Company
  Garden Grove, CA 714-265-9990
Harvest Food Products Co Inc
  Hayward, CA 510-675-0383
Health is Wealth Foods
  Moonachie, NJ 201-933-7474
Kubla Khan Food Company
  Portland, OR 503-234-7494
Peking Noodle Co Inc
  Los Angeles, CA 323-223-0897
Shine Foods Inc
  Torrance, CA 310-533-6010
Wan Hua Foods
  Seattle, WA 206-622-8417

Potato Products

Alexia Foods
  Long Island City, NY 718-937-0100
Bob Evans Farms Inc.
  800-939-2338
Idahoan Foods LLC
  Idaho Falls, ID 800-746-7999
Maple Leaf Foods International
  North York, ON 800-268-3708
McCain Foods Ltd.
  Toronto, ON 416-955-1700
McCain Produce Inc.
  Florenceville-Bristol, NB 506-392-3036
Pacific Valley Foods Inc
  Bellevue, WA 425-643-1805
Rices Potato Chips
  Biloxi, MS 228-396-5775
Seneca Foods Corp
  Marion, NY 315-926-8100

Hash Browned Potatoes

Emerling International Foods
  Buffalo, NY 716-833-7381
Idahoan Foods LLC
  Idaho Falls, ID 800-746-7999
McCain Foods Ltd.
  Toronto, ON 416-955-1700
Michael Foods, Inc.
  Minnetonka, MN 952-258-4000
Mr Dell Foods
  Kearney, MO 816-628-4644
Sun Glo Of Idaho
  Sugar City, ID 208-356-7346

Prepared Meals

A Dozen Cousins
  Berkeley, CA
Amigos Canning Company
  San Antonio, TX 210-798-5360
Aunt Kitty's Foods Inc
  Vineland, NJ 856-691-2100
Bakkavor USA
  Charlotte, NC 800-842-3025
Barber Foods
  Kings Mountain, NC 877-447-3279
Big Mountain Foods
  Vancouver, BC
BlueWater Seafoods
  Gloucester, MA 888-560-2539
Chandler Foods Inc
  Greensboro, NC 800-537-6219
Cheating Gourmet
  Auburn, ME 800-239-9731
Chef Hans' Gourmet Foods
  Monroe, LA 800-890-4267
Feel Good Foods
  Brooklyn, NY 800-638-8949
Gardein
  Marina del Ray, CA 310-862-8686
Garden Protein International
  Richmond, BC 877-305-6777
Good Food Made Simple
  Wellesley, MA 800-535-3447
Grandcestors
  Golden, CO
Halal Fine Foods
  Toronto, ON 416-679-8000
Hans Kissle Co
  Haverhill, MA 978-556-4500
Henry J's Meat Specialties
  Chicago, IL 800-242-1314

Product Categories / Prepared Foods: Prepared Meals

J B & Son LTD
   Yonkers, NY 914-963-5192
J&M Food Products Co
   Deerfield, IL 847-948-1290
Jackfruit Company, The
   Boulder, CO 877-433-4024
JTM Food Group
   Harrison, OH 800-626-2308
Kashi Company
   Solana Beach, CA 877-747-2467
Melba's Old School Po Boys
   New Orleans, LA 504-267-7765
Modern Table
   Walnut Creek, CA
Molinaro's Fine Italian Foods Ltd.
   Mississauga, ON 905-281-0352
O'Sole Mio
   Boisbriand, QC 844-696-8933
Pacific Foods of Oregon
   Tualatin, OR 503-692-9666
Patty Palace Foods
   Toronto, ON 416-297-0510
Rosina Food Holdings Inc
   Buffalo, NY 888-767-4621
Schwan's Company
   Marshall, MN 800-533-5290
Seneca Foods Corp
   Marion, NY 315-926-8100
Snapdragon Foods
   Oakland, CA 877-881-7627
Soylent
   Los Angeles, CA
Stonewall Kitchen
   York, ME 800-826-1752
Suji's Korean Cuisine
   Seattle, WA 206-985-6640
The Food Collective
   Irvine, CA 866-328-8638
TreeHouse Foods, Inc.
   Oak Brook, IL 708-483-1300
Tyson Foods Inc.
   Springdale, AR 479-290-4000

Beef Dinner

Big B Barbecue
   Evansville, IN 812-425-5235
Henry J's Meat Specialties
   Chicago, IL 800-242-1314
Kelly Foods
   Jackson, TN 731-424-2255
Melba's Old School Po Boys
   New Orleans, LA 504-267-7765
Night Hawk Frozen Foods Inc
   Buda, TX 800-580-4166

Breakfast

Good Food Made Simple
   Wellesley, MA 800-535-3447
Ise America Inc
   Galena, MD 410-755-6300
Jimmy Dean Foods
   Springdale, AR 800-925-3326
Michael Foods, Inc.
   Minnetonka, MN 952-258-4000

Burritos

Chimichangas

Burrito Kitchens
   Longmont, CO 720-652-9000
Camino Real Foods Inc
   Vernon, CA 800-421-6201
Good Food Made Simple
   Wellesley, MA 800-535-3447
Queen International Foods
   Monterey Park, CA 800-423-4414
Red's All Natural
   North Sioux City, SD 605-956-7337
Troverco
   St. Louis, MO 800-468-3354

Canned

Kelly Foods
   Jackson, TN 731-424-2255

Casseroles

Dynamic Foods
   Lubbock, TX 806-723-5600
Good Old Days Foods
   Little Rock, AR 501-565-1257

Marsan Foods
   Toronto, ON 416-755-9262
Savannah Food Co
   Savannah, TN 800-795-2550

Convenience

Chef Hans' Gourmet Foods
   Monroe, LA 800-890-4267
Crafty Counter
   Austin, TX 512-643-2412
Homegrown Naturals
   Napa, CA 800-288-1089
Patty Palace Foods
   Toronto, ON 416-297-0510
Soylent
   Los Angeles, CA

Corn Fritters

Triton Seafood Co
   Medley, FL 305-888-0051

Crab

Stuffed

Boja's Foods Inc
   Bayou La Batre, AL 251-824-4186

Eggplant Parmigiana

Bruno Specialty Foods
   West Sayville, NY 631-589-1700
Pasta Factory
   Melrose Park, IL 800-615-6951

Eggs

Dixie Egg Co
   Jacksonville, FL 800-394-3447
Good Food Made Simple
   Wellesley, MA 800-535-3447
Great Valley Mills
   Barto, PA 800-688-6455
Ise America Inc
   Galena, MD 410-755-6300
Michael Foods, Inc.
   Minnetonka, MN 952-258-4000

Entrees

Ajinomoto Frozen Foods USA, Inc.
   Ontario, CA 866-536-8008
Bellisio Foods
   Minneapolis, MN
Bernardi Italian Foods Company
   Bloomsburg, PA 570-389-5500
Blue Runner Foods Inc
   Gonzales, LA 225-647-3016
Boudreaux's Foods
   New Orleans, LA 504-733-8440
Burnett & Son
   Monrovia, CA 877-632-5467
Carando Gourmet Frozen Foods
   Agawam, MA 888-227-2636
Culinary Revolution
   La Jolla, CA 858-454-4390
Deep Foods Inc
   Union, NJ 908-810-7500
Ethnic Gourmet Foods
   Boulder, CO 800-434-4246
Five Star Home Foods, Inc.
   King of Prussia, PA 800-246-5405
Good Food Made Simple
   Wellesley, MA 800-535-3447
Heinz Quality Chef Foods Inc
   Cedar Rapids, IA 800-356-8307
HFI Foods
   Redmond, WA 425-883-1320
JTM Food Group
   Harrison, OH 800-626-2308
Kent Precision Foods Group Inc
   Muscatine, IA 800-442-5242
King Kold Meats
   Englewood, OH 800-836-2797
Marsan Foods
   Toronto, ON 416-755-9262
Melba's Old School Po Boys
   New Orleans, LA 504-267-7765
Natural Quick Foods
   Seattle, WA 206-365-5757
Paulsen Foods
   Atlanta, GA 404-873-1804

Plenus Group Inc
   Lowell, MA 978-970-3832
Ragozzino Foods Inc
   Meriden, CT 800-348-1240
Ruggiero Seafood
   Newark, NJ 866-225-2627
Spring Glen Fresh Foods
   Ephrata, PA 800-641-2853
Steak-Umm Company
   Shillington, PA 860-928-5900
Stefano Foods
   Charlotte, NC 800-340-4019
Sugar Foods Corp
   Sun Valley, CA 818-768-7900
Tamarind Tree
   Neshanic Station, NJ 800-432-8733
Taste Traditions Inc
   Omaha, NE 800-228-2170
Thyme & Truffles Hors d'Oeuvres
   Dollard-Des-Ormeaux, QC 877-785-9759
Wild Zora Foods
   Loveland, CO 970-541-9672

Frozen

Alfredo Aiello Italian Food
   Quincy, MA 617-770-6360
Amy's Kitchen Inc
   Santa Rosa, CA 707-781-6600
Beetnik Foods, LLC
   Austin, TX 512-548-8228
Bellisio Foods
   Minneapolis, MN
Bernardi Italian Foods Company
   Bloomsburg, PA 570-389-5500
Carando Gourmet Frozen Foods
   Agawam, MA 888-227-2636
CK Living LLC
   River Edge, NJ 201-261-2078
Deep Foods Inc
   Union, NJ 908-810-7500
Dynamic Foods
   Lubbock, TX 806-723-5600
Fairfield Farm Kitchens
   Brockton, MA 508-584-9300
Grainful
   Ithaca, NY
HFI Foods
   Redmond, WA 425-883-1320
Kashi Company
   Solana Beach, CA 877-747-2467
Kelly Gourmet Foods Inc
   San Francisco, CA 415-648-9200
Kent Precision Foods Group Inc
   Muscatine, IA 800-442-5242
King Kold Meats
   Englewood, OH 800-836-2797
Lenchner Bakery
   Concord, ON 905-738-8811
Marsan Foods
   Toronto, ON 416-755-9262
Michael Angelo's Inc
   Austin, TX 877-482-5426
Milmar Food Group
   Goshen, NY 845-294-5400
Night Hawk Frozen Foods Inc
   Buda, TX 800-580-4166
Oven Poppers
   Manchester, NH 603-644-3773
Paulsen Foods
   Atlanta, GA 404-873-1804
Royal Palate Foods
   Inglewood, CA 310-330-7701
Ruggiero Seafood
   Newark, NJ 866-225-2627
Steak-Umm Company
   Shillington, PA 860-928-5900
The Food Collective
   Irvine, CA 866-328-8638
Thyme & Truffles Hors d'Oeuvres
   Dollard-Des-Ormeaux, QC 877-785-9759

Microwavable

Conagra Brands Inc
   Chicago, IL 877-266-2472
Conagra Foodservice
   Chicago, IL 877-266-2472
Vana Life Foods
   Seattle, WA 347-446-6504

Product Categories / Prepared Foods: Prepared Meals

Shelf Stable

Cordon Bleu International
  Anjou, QC 800-363-1182
Dorina So-Good Inc
  Union, IL 815-923-2144
Good For You America
  Concordia, MO 866-329-5969
Hanover Foods Corp
  Hanover, PA 717-632-6000
Health Valley Company
  Irwindale, CA 800-334-3204
Hormel Foods Corp.
  Austin, MN 507-437-5611
Joelle's Choice Specialty Foods LLC
  Fairfield, IA 800-880-2779
Lundberg Family Farms
  Richvale, CA 530-538-3500
Mr Jay's Tamales & Chili
  Lynwood, CA 310-537-3932
My Own Meals Inc
  Deerfield, IL 847-948-1118
Sabra Dipping Company,LL
  Oceanside, CA 800-748-5523
SOPAKCO Foods
  Mullins, SC 800-276-9678
Spring Glen Fresh Foods
  Ephrata, PA 800-641-2853
Sugar Foods Corp
  Sun Valley, CA 818-768-7900
Truitt Bros Inc
  Salem, OR 800-547-8712
Vigo Importing Co
  Tampa, FL 800-282-4130

Etoufee

Chef Hans' Gourmet Foods
  Monroe, LA 800-890-4267

Fish

Carrington Foods Co Inc
  Saraland, AL 251-675-9700
Cuizina Food Company
  Woodinville, WA 425-486-7000
Fishpeople
  Portland, OR 503-342-2424
Janes Family Foods
  Mississauga, ON 800-565-2637
Love The Wild
  Boulder, CO 844-424-9875
Melba's Old School Po Boys
  New Orleans, LA 504-267-7765
Menemsha Fish Market
  Chilmark, MA 508-645-2282
Quinault Pride
  Taholah, WA 360-276-4431
Stacey's Famous Foods
  Hayden, ID 800-782-2395

Stuffed

Anchor Frozen Foods
  Westbury, NY 800-566-3474
Beaver Street Fisheries
  Jacksonville, FL 800-874-6426
King & Prince Seafood Corp
  Brunswick, GA 800-841-0205
Sweet Water Seafood
  Carlstadt, NJ 201-939-6622
Tampa Maid Foods Inc
  Lakeland, FL 800-237-7637

Fish & Chips

Viking Seafoods Inc
  Malden, MA 800-225-3020

Fish Patties

Pacific Salmon Company
  Edmonds, WA 425-774-1315
Viking Seafoods Inc
  Malden, MA 800-225-3020

Fish Sticks

Channel Fish Processing
  Gloucester, MA 800-457-0054
Ungars Food
  Elmwood Park, NJ 201-773-6846
Viking Seafoods Inc
  Malden, MA 800-225-3020

Frozen

Al Safa Halal
  New York City, NY 800-268-8147
BlueWater Seafoods
  Gloucester, MA 888-560-2539
Tichon Sea Food Corp
  New Bedford, MA 508-999-5607
Viking Seafoods Inc
  Malden, MA 800-225-3020

Fried Rice

Willow Foods
  Beaverton, OR 800-338-3609

Frozen

Bake Crafters Food Company
  McDonald, TN 423-396-3392
Biagio's Banquets
  Chicago, IL 800-392-2837
Birdseye Food
  Mountain Lakes, NJ 585-383-1850
Cuizina Food Company
  Woodinville, WA 425-486-7000
G A Food Svc Inc
  St Petersburg, FL 800-852-2211
Grandcestors
  Golden, CO
Heinkel's Packing Co
  Decatur, IL 800-594-2738
High Liner Foods Inc.
  Lunenburg, NS 902-634-8811
Kidfresh
  New York, NY 212-686-4303
McCain Foods Ltd.
  Toronto, ON 416-955-1700
Monsoon Kitchens
  Shrewsbury, MA 508-842-0070
Neilly's Foods
  York, PA 717-668-3722
Path of Life
  Warrenville, IL 844-248-9997
Philadelphia Cheese Steak
  Philadelphia, PA 800-342-9771
Quorn Foods
  Chicago, IL
The Food Collective
  Irvine, CA 866-328-8638

Gyros

Corfu Foods Inc
  Bensenville, IL 630-595-2510
Corfu Foods Inc
  Bensenville, IL 800-874-9767
Kronos
  Glendale Heights, IL 800-621-0099

Lasagna

Alfredo Aiello Italian Food
  Quincy, MA 617-770-6360
Homestead Fine Foods
  S San Francisco, CA 650-615-0750

Macaroni

Campbell Soup Co.
  Camden, NJ 800-257-8443
Gilster-Mary Lee Corp
  Chester, IL 618-826-2361
Molinaro's Fine Italian Foods Ltd.
  Mississauga, ON 905-281-0352

Mozzarella Sticks

Giorgio Foods
  Temple, PA 800-220-2139
Matador Processors
  Blanchard, OK 800-847-0797

Pasta & Noodle Dishes

Agrusa
  Leonia, NJ 201-592-5950
Alfredo Aiello Italian Food
  Quincy, MA 617-770-6360
Antoni Ravioli Co
  North Massapequa, NY 800-783-0350
Barilla USA
  Northbrook, IL 800-922-7455
Bernardi Italian Foods Company
  Bloomsburg, PA 570-389-5500
Bruno Specialty Foods
  West Sayville, NY 631-589-1700
Carando Gourmet Frozen Foods
  Agawam, MA 888-227-2636
Cuizina Food Company
  Woodinville, WA 425-486-7000
Dabruzzi's Italian Foods
  Hudson, WI 715-386-3653
Food City USA
  Arvada, CO 303-321-4447
Landolfi's Food Products
  Trenton, NJ 609-392-1830
On-Cor Frozen Foods
Plentiful Pantry
  Salt Lake City, UT 801-977-9077
Ragozzino Foods Inc
  Meriden, CT 800-348-1240
Rich Products Corp
  Vineland, NJ 800-818-9261
S T Specialty Foods Inc
  Brooklyn Park, MN 763-493-9600
Sandridge Food Corp
  Medina, OH 800-627-2523
Seviroli Foods
  Garden City, NY 516-222-6220
Sidari's Italian Foods
  Cleveland, OH 216-431-3344
Star Ravioli Mfg Co
  Moonachie, NJ 201-933-6427
The Food Collective
  Irvine, CA 866-328-8638

Rice

Amalgamated Produce
  Bridgeport, CT 800-358-3808
Chef Soraya
  Boulder, CO 800-677-7423
Minsley, Inc.
  Ontario, CA 909-458-1100
Penguin Natural Food Inc
  Vernon, CA 323-727-7980
Tony Chachere's Creole Foods
  Opelousas, LA 800-551-9066

Salad

Classic Commissary
  Binghamton, NY 800-929-3486
Club Chef LLC
  Covington, KY 859-578-3100
F & S Produce Co Inc
  Vineland, NJ 800-886-3316
Hans Kissle Co
  Haverhill, MA 978-556-4500
Lakeside Foods Inc.
  Manitowoc, WI 800-466-3834
Paisley Farms Inc
  Willoughby, OH 800-474-5688
R.C. McEntire & Company
  Columbia, SC 803-799-3388
Ready Pac Foods Inc
  Irwindale, CA 800-800-4088
Sandridge Food Corp
  Medina, OH 800-627-2523
Suter Co Inc
  Sycamore, IL 800-435-6942
Troverco
  St. Louis, MO 800-468-3354

Sandwiches

B-S Foods Company
  Oklahoma City, OK 405-949-9797
Bake Crafters Food Company
  McDonald, TN 423-396-3392
Better Baked Foods Inc
  North East, PA 814-725-8778
Black's Barbecue
  Lockhart, TX 888-632-8225
Bridgford Foods Corp
  Anaheim, CA 800-527-2105
Camino Real Foods Inc
  Vernon, CA 800-421-6201
Chef's Pride Gifts LLC
  Taylor, MI 800-878-1800
Chicken Salad Chick
  Auburn, AL 334-275-4578
Classic Delight Inc
  St Marys, OH 800-274-9828
Corfu Foods Inc
  Bensenville, IL 630-595-2510
Country Smoked Meats
  Bowling Green, OH 800-321-4766

Product Categories / Prepared Foods: Prepared Salads

E A Sween Co
  Eden Prairie, MN 800-328-8184
Eastside Deli Supply
  Lansing, MI. 800-349-6694
Food Factory
  Honolulu, HI 808-593-2633
Helen's Pure Foods
  Cheltenham, PA 215-379-6433
Hormel Foods Corp.
  Austin, MN 507-437-5611
JTM Food Group
  Harrison, OH. 800-626-2308
Knotts Fine Foods
  Paris, TN 731-642-1961
Lilydale Foods
  Markham, ON 800-661-5341
Made-Rite Sandwich Co
  Ooltewah, TN 800-343-1327
Maui Bagel
  Kahului, HI 808-270-7561
Meat & Supply Co
  New York, NY 646-864-0967
Piemonte Bakery Co
  Rockford, IL 815-962-4833
Royal Touch Foods
  Etobicoke, ON 416-213-1077
Safeway Inc.
  Pleasanton, CA 877-723-3929
Southern Belle Sandwich Company
  Baton Rouge, LA 800-344-4670
Steak-Umm Company
  Shillington, PA 860-928-5900
Sunburst Foods
  Goldsboro, NC 919-778-2151
Troverco
  St. Louis, MO 800-468-3354
UBF Food Solutions
  Lisle, IL. 630-955-5394
Zartic Inc
  Rome, GA 800-241-0516

Pocket
Applegate Farms
  Bridgewater, NJ 866-587-5858
Nestle USA Inc
  Glendale, CA 800-225-2270
Patty Palace Foods
  Toronto, ON 416-297-0510

Scampi

Shrimp Frozen
Cheating Gourmet
  Auburn, ME 800-239-9731

Seafood
AquaCuisine
  Portland, OR 208-323-2782
Carnival Brands Mfg
  New Orleans, LA 800-925-2774
Carrington Foods Co Inc
  Saraland, AL 251-675-9700
Channel Fish Processing
  Gloucester, MA. 800-457-0054
Chincoteague Seafood Co Inc
  Parsonsburg, MD 443-260-4800
Cuizina Food Company
  Woodinville, WA. 425-486-7000
Fish King
  Glendale, CA 818-244-2161
Gulf City Marine Supply
  Bayou La Batre, AL 251-824-2516
King & Prince Seafood Corp
  Brunswick, GA 800-841-0205
Melba's Old School Po Boys
  New Orleans, LA 504-267-7765
Menemsha Fish Market
  Chilmark, MA. 508-645-2282
Neptune Fisheries
  Newport News, VA 800-545-7474
Oven Poppers
  Manchester, NH 603-644-3773
Ruggiero Seafood
  Newark, NJ 866-225-2627
Sea Pearl Seafood
  Bayou La Batre, AL 800-872-8804
Tex-Mex Cold Storage
  Brownsville, TX 956-831-9433
Triton Seafood Co
  Medley, FL 305-888-0051
Weyand's Fishery
  Wyandotte, MI 800-521-9815

Spaghetti

Canned
Campbell Soup Co.
  Camden, NJ. 800-257-8443
Hormel Foods Corp.
  Austin, MN 507-437-5611
Seneca Foods Corp
  Marion, NY 315-926-8100

with Meatballs
Burnett & Son
  Monrovia, CA. 877-632-5467
JTM Food Group
  Harrison, OH. 800-626-2308

Stuffed Cabbage
Morrison Lamothe
  Toronto, ON 877-677-6533

Stuffed Peppers
L & S Packing Co
  Farmingdale, NY 800-286-6487
Matador Processors
  Blanchard, OK 800-847-0797
Norpaco Inc
  Middletown, CT 800-252-0222
Vega Food Industries Inc
  Cranston, RI 800-973-7737

Stuffed Shells
Antoni Ravioli Co
  North Massapequa, NY 800-783-0350
Bruno Specialty Foods
  West Sayville, NY. 631-589-1700
Caesar's Pasta
  Blackwood, NJ 888-432-2372
Codinos Food Inc
  Scotia, NY. 800-246-8908
J B & Son LTD
  Yonkers, NY 914-963-5192
Landolfi's Food Products
  Trenton, NJ. 609-392-1830
Pasta Del Mondo
  Carmel, NY. 800-392-8887
Pasta Factory
  Melrose Park, IL. 800-615-6951
Seviroli Foods
  Garden City, NY 516-222-6220
Star Ravioli Mfg Co
  Moonachie, NJ 201-933-6427
Wisconsin Whey International
  Juda, WI 608-233-5101

Tamales
Tucson Tamale Company
  Tucson, AZ 520-398-6282

Turkey Dinner
Morrison Lamothe
  Toronto, ON 877-677-6533

Vegetarian
Atlantic Natural Foods
  Nashville, NC 888-491-0524
Dixie USA
  Tomball, TX 800-233-3668
F & S Produce Co Inc
  Vineland, NJ. 800-886-3316
Garden Protein International
  Richmond, BC 877-305-6777
Health Valley Company
  Irwindale, CA 800-334-3204
Kashi Company
  Solana Beach, CA 877-747-2467
Les Palais Des Thes
  New York, NY 917-515-2887
Mortimer's Fine Foods
  Burlington, ON 905-336-0000
Tamarind Tree
  Neshanic Station, NJ. 800-432-8733
The Food Collective
  Irvine, CA 866-328-8638

Prepared Salads
Avon Heights Mushrooms
  Avondale, PA 610-268-2092
Baba Foods
  San Diego, CA 619-426-6946
Bay Cities Produce Co Inc
  San Leandro, CA. 510-346-4943
Black's Barbecue
  Lockhart, TX. 888-632-8225
Brookside Foods
  Cleveland, OH 216-991-7600
Cedar's Mediterranean Foods
  Ward Hill, MA 978-372-8010
Chef's Pride Gifts LLC
  Taylor, MI 800-878-1800
Chiquita Brands LLC.
  Fort Lauderdale, FL 954-924-5700
Conifer Foods
  Medina, WA 800-588-9160
Dole Food Company, Inc.
  Thousand Oaks, CA 800-356-3111
FiveStar Gourmet Foods
  Ontario, CA 909-390-0032
Giovanni's Appetizing Food Co
  Richmond, MI. 586-727-9355
Hanover Foods Corp
  Hanover, PA 717-632-6000
Harold Food Company
  Charlotte, NC 704-588-8061
Helen's Pure Foods
  Cheltenham, PA 215-379-6433
Herold's Salads
  Cleveland, OH 800-427-2523
HFI Foods
  Redmond, WA 425-883-1320
Home Style Foods Inc
  Hamtramck, MI. 313-874-3250
Hoople Country Kitchen Inc
  Rockport, IN 877-466-7537
House of Thaller Inc
  Knoxville, TN 800-462-3365
Kay Foods Co
  Detroit, MI 313-393-1100
Kings Processing
  Middleton, NS. 902-825-2188
L & S Packing Co
  Farmingdale, NY 800-286-6487
Meadows Country Products
  Hollidaysburg, PA. 888-499-1001
Melba's Old School Po Boys
  New Orleans, LA 504-267-7765
Mrs Grissom's Salads Inc
  Nashville, TN 800-255-0571
Mrs Stratton's Salads Inc
  Birmingham, AL 205-940-9640
Sally Sherman
  Mt Vernon, NY 718-822-1100
Sandridge Food Corp
  Medina, OH. 800-627-2523
Sidari's Italian Foods
  Cleveland, OH 216-431-3344
Soupergirl
  Washington, DC 202-609-7177
Spring Glen Fresh Foods
  Ephrata, PA 800-641-2853
Summer Fresh
  Woodbridge, ON 877-472-5237
Vega Food Industries Inc
  Cranston, RI 800-973-7737
Zuccaro Produce
  Columbia Heights, MN. 612-333-1122

Antipasto
Giovanni's Appetizing Food Co
  Richmond, MI. 586-727-9355
L & S Packing Co
  Farmingdale, NY 800-286-6487
Pastene Co LTD
  Canton, MA 781-298-3397

Chicken
Chicken Salad Chick
  Auburn, AL 334-275-4578
Mrs Stratton's Salads Inc
  Birmingham, AL 205-940-9640
Old Dutch Mustard Company
  Great Neck, NY 516-466-0522

Product Categories / Prepared Foods: Quiche

Cole Slaw

Avon Heights Mushrooms
   Avondale, PA 610-268-2092
Black's Barbecue
   Lockhart, TX 888-632-8225
Dawn's Foods
   Portage, WI 800-993-2967
Flaum Appetizing
   Brooklyn, NY 718-821-1970
Kay Foods Co
   Detroit, MI 313-393-1100
Mrs Stratton's Salads Inc
   Birmingham, AL 205-940-9640
Spring Glen Fresh Foods
   Ephrata, PA 800-641-2853

Egg

Dawn's Foods
   Portage, WI 800-993-2967

Iceberg Lettuce Based

Bay Cities Produce Co Inc
   San Leandro, CA 510-346-4943
Zuccaro Produce
   Columbia Heights, MN 612-333-1122

Macaroni

Black's Barbecue
   Lockhart, TX 888-632-8225
Hanover Foods Corp
   Hanover, PA 717-632-6000
Spring Glen Fresh Foods
   Ephrata, PA 800-641-2853

Pasta

Dawn's Foods
   Portage, WI 800-993-2967
Herold's Salads
   Cleveland, OH 800-427-2523
HFI Foods
   Redmond, WA 425-883-1320
Home Style Foods Inc
   Hamtramck, MI 313-874-3250
Kay Foods Co
   Detroit, MI 313-393-1100
Sandridge Food Corp
   Medina, OH 800-627-2523
Spring Glen Fresh Foods
   Ephrata, PA 800-641-2853

Potato

Black's Barbecue
   Lockhart, TX 888-632-8225
Dawn's Foods
   Portage, WI 800-993-2967
Hanover Foods Corp
   Hanover, PA 717-632-6000
Herold's Salads
   Cleveland, OH 800-427-2523
Kay Foods Co
   Detroit, MI 313-393-1100
Mrs Stratton's Salads Inc
   Birmingham, AL 205-940-9640
Sandridge Food Corp
   Medina, OH 800-627-2523
Spring Glen Fresh Foods
   Ephrata, PA 800-641-2853

Salmon

Rachael's Smoked Fish
   Springfield, MA 800-327-3412

Seafood

Rachael's Smoked Fish
   Springfield, MA 800-327-3412

Tuna

Flaum Appetizing
   Brooklyn, NY 718-821-1970
Mrs Stratton's Salads Inc
   Birmingham, AL 205-940-9640

Quiche

Classic Cookings, LLC
   Jamaica, NY 718-439-0200
Glendora Quiche Company
   San Dimas, CA 909-394-1777

Hans Kissle Co
   Haverhill, MA 978-556-4500
Love Quiches Desserts
   Freeport, NY 516-623-8800
Nancy's Specialty Foods
   Newark, CA 510-494-1100
Pie Piper Products
   Wheeling, IL 800-621-8183
Quelle Quiche
   Brentwood, MO 314-961-6554
Stacey's Famous Foods
   Hayden, ID 800-782-2395
Wholesome Bakery
   San Francisco, CA 415-343-5414

Soups & Stews

4C Foods Corp
   Brooklyn, NY 718-272-4242
Alaska Smokehouse
   Woodinville, WA 800-422-0852
All American Foods Inc
   Mankato, MN 800-833-2661
Alvalle
   Denver, CO
Andersen's Pea Soup
   Buellton, CA 805-688-5581
Annie Chun's
   Los Angeles, CA 415-479-8272
Atlanta Bread Co.
   Smyrna, GA 800-398-3728
Aunt Kitty's Foods Inc
   Vineland, NJ 856-691-2100
B&H Foods
   Charlotte, NC 704-332-4106
Back to Nature Foods
   855-346-2225
Bakkavor USA
   Charlotte, NC 800-842-3025
Bay Shore Chowders & Bisques
   Fall River, MA 888-675-6892
Baycliff Co Inc
   Garwood, NJ 866-772-7569
Bear Creek Country Kitchens
   Heber City, UT 800-516-7286
Bellisio Foods
   Minneapolis, MN
Blount Fine Foods
   Fall River, MA 774-888-1300
Blue Crab Bay
   Melfa, VA 800-221-2722
Boston Chowda
   Haverhill, MA 800-992-0054
Bou Brands
   New York, NY 858-401-3356
Boudreaux's Foods
   New Orleans, LA 504-733-8440
Boulder Organic Foods
   Niwot, CO 303-530-0470
Cajun Fry Co Inc
   Pierre Part, LA 888-272-2586
California Natural Products
   Lathrop, CA 209-858-2525
California Wild Rice Growers
   Fall River Mills, CA 800-626-4366
Caltex Foods
   Canoga Park, CA 800-522-5839
Cambridge Food
   Monterey, CA 800-433-2584
Campbell Company of Canada
   Toronto, ON 800-410-7687
Campbell Soup Co.
   Camden, NJ 800-257-8443
Catania Hospitality Group
   Hyannis, MA 888-774-5511
Chef Hans' Gourmet Foods
   Monroe, LA 800-890-4267
Cherchies
   Malvern, PA 800-644-1980
Chimayo To Go / Cibolo Junction
   Albuquerque, NM 800-683-9628
Chincoteague Seafood Co Inc
   Parsonsburg, MD 443-260-4800
Christie's
   Stroughton, MA 781-341-3341
Clarmil Manufacturing Corp
   Hayward, CA 888-252-7645
Classic Cookings, LLC
   Jamaica, NY 718-439-0200
Comfort Foods
   Albuquerque, NM 800-460-5803
Conifer Specialties Inc
   Woodinville, WA 800-588-9160

Cooke Tavern LTD
   Spring Mills, PA 866-422-7687
Country Cupboard
   Lewisburg, PA 570-523-3211
Crush Foods Service
   Westlake Village, CA 818-699-6381
Cugino's Gourmet Foods
   Crystal Lake, IL 888-592-8446
Custom Culinary Inc.
   Schaumberg, IL 800-621-8827
Daily Soup
   New York, NY 888-393-7687
Denzer's Food Products
   Baltimore, MD 410-889-1500
Diversified Foods & Seasonings
   Covington, LA 800-914-2382
Dorothy Dawson Food Products
   Jackson, MI 517-788-9830
Dr. McDougall's Right Foods
   Woodland, CA 866-972-6879
Eatem Foods Co
   Vineland, NJ 800-683-2836
Edmond's Chile Co
   St Louis, MO 314-772-1499
El Peto Products
   Cambridge, ON 800-387-4064
Ellie's Country Delights
   Wainscott, NY 631-478-5200
Erba Food Products
   Brooklyn, NY 718-272-7700
Fair Scones
   Medina, WA 800-588-9160
Fantastic World Foods
   Providence, RI
Fawen
   Brooklyn, NY 888-737-7052
Fig Food Co.
   New York, NY 855-344-3663
Fish Hopper
   Monterey, CA 831-372-3406
Flavor House, Inc.
   Adelanto, CA 760-246-9131
FOND Bone Broth
   San Antonio, TX
George F Brocke & Sons
   Moscow, ID 208-289-4231
GoBio!
   Action, ON 519-853-2958
Grace Foods International
   Astoria, NY 718-433-4789
Grandma Browns Beans Inc
   Mexico, NY 315-963-7221
Grandma Pat's Products
   Albin, WY 307-631-0801
Great Eastern Sun Trading Co
   Asheville, NC 800-334-5809
Griffith Foods Inc.
   Alsip, IL 708-371-0900
H.K. Canning
   Ventura, CA 805-652-1392
Hain Celestial Group Inc
   Lake Success, NY 800-434-4246
Halal Fine Foods
   Toronto, ON 416-679-8000
Hale and Hearty Soups
   New York, NY 212-255-2433
Hanover Foods Corp
   Hanover, PA 717-632-6000
Hans Kissle Co
   Haverhill, MA 978-556-4500
Health Valley Company
   Irwindale, CA 800-334-3204
Heartline Foods
   Westport, CT 203-222-0381
Heinz Quality Chef Foods Inc
   Cedar Rapids, IA 800-356-8307
Hirzel Canning Co & Farms
   Luckey, OH 419-419-7525
Hoopeston Foods Inc
   Burnsville, MN 952-854-0903
Hormel Foods Corp.
   Austin, MN 507-437-5611
Idaho Pacific Holdings Inc
   Rigby, ID 800-238-5503
Imagine Foods
   Boulder, CO 800-434-4246
Integrative Flavors
   Michigan City, IN 800-837-7687
Jager Foods
   Sauk Centre, MN 800-358-7251
JMAC Trading, Inc.
   Torrance, CA 877-566-4569

Product Categories / Prepared Foods: Soups & Stews

Juanita's Foods
   Wilmington, CA 800-303-2965
Just Delicious Gourmet Foods
   Seal Beach, CA 800-871-6085
Jyoti Cuisine India
   Berwyn, PA 610-296-4620
Karine & Jeff
   Los Angeles, CA
Karlsburger Foods Inc
   Monticello, MN 800-383-6549
Kay Foods Co
   Detroit, MI 313-393-1100
KD Canners Inc
   Mississauga, ON 905-602-1825
Kent Precision Foods Group Inc
   Muscatine, IA 800-442-5242
Kettle Cuisine
   Lynn, MA 877-302-7687
Le Grand
   Blainville, QC 450-623-3000
Leonard Mountain Inc
   Bixby, OK 800-822-7700
Les Aliments Ramico Foods
   St. Leonard, QC 514-329-1844
Loffredo Produce
   Rock Island, IL 800-383-3367
LonoLife
   Oceanside, CA 855-843-8566
Manischewitz Co
   Newark, NJ 201-553-1100
Marsan Foods
   Toronto, ON 416-755-9262
McCormick & Company
   Hunt Valley, MD 410-527-6189
Meat-O-Mat Corp
   Brooklyn, NY 718-965-7250
Mercer Processing
   Modesto, CA 209-529-0150
Mid-Atlantic Foods Inc
   Easton, MD 800-922-4688
Moonlite Bar-B-Q Inn
   Owensboro, KY 800-322-8989
Morgan Foods Inc
   Austin, IN 888-430-1780
Near East Food Products
   Leominster, MA 800-822-7423
Nissin Foods USA Co Inc
   Gardena, CA 310-327-8478
Nona Lim
   Oakland, CA 415-513-5328
North Aire Market, Inc.
   Shakopee, MN 800-662-3781
North of the Border
   Tesuque, NM 800-860-0681
Numo Broth
   San Jose, CA
Organic Gourmet
   Sherman Oaks, CA 800-400-7772
Overhill Farms Inc
   Vernon, CA 800-859-6406
Pacific Foods of Oregon
   Tualatin, OR 503-692-9666
Park 100 Foods Inc
   Tipton, IN 800-854-6504
Patagonia Provisions
   Sausalito, CA 888-221-8208
Perez Food Products
   Kansas City, MO 816-931-8761
Pioneer Foods Industries
   Stuttgart, AR 870-673-4444
Plentiful Pantry
   Salt Lake City, UT 801-977-9077
Plenus Group Inc
   Lowell, MA 978-970-3832
Pressery
   Denver, CO
Progresso Quality Foods
   Vineland, NJ 856-691-1565
Ragozzino Foods Inc
   Meriden, CT 800-348-1240
Rapunzel Pure Organics
   Bloomfield, NJ 800-225-1449
Ronzoni
   Largo, FL 800-730-5957
Royal Palate Foods
   Inglewood, CA 310-330-7701
San Francisco Spice Co.
   Woodland, CA 866-972-6879
Sandridge Food Corp
   Medina, OH 800-627-2523
Sea Watch Intl
   Easton, MD 410-822-7500

Shelton's Poultry Inc
   Pomona, CA 800-541-1833
Skinny Souping
   Chicago, IL
Souperb LLC
   Emeryville, CA 415-685-8508
Soupergirl
   Washington, DC 202-609-7177
SOUPerior Bean & Spice Company
   Vancouver, WA 800-878-7687
Spice Hunter Inc
   Richmond, VA 800-444-3061
Sprague Foods
   Belleville, ON 613-966-1200
Spring Glen Fresh Foods
   Ephrata, PA 800-641-2853
St. Ours & Company
   East Weymouth, MA 781-331-8520
Sudbury Soups and Salads
   Sudbury, MA 888-783-7687
Sun Opta Inc.
   Mississauga, ON 952-820-2518
Sweet Earth Foods
   Moss Landing, CA 800-737-3311
Sweet Sue Kitchens
   Athens, AL 256-216-0500
Swiss Food Products
   Chicago, IL 312-829-0100
Tabatchinick Fine Foods
   Somerset, NJ 732-247-6668
Tex-Mex Gourmet
   Brenham, TX 888-345-8467
The Sprout House
   Lake Katrine, NY 800-777-6887
Timber Peaks Gourmet
   Parker, CO 800-982-7687
Tio Gazpacho
   New York, NY 917-946-1160
Turtle Island Foods
   Hood River, OR 800-508-8100
Twin Marquis
   Brooklyn, NY 800-367-6868
Unilever Canada
   Toronto, ON 416-415-3000
Unilever Food Solutions
   Englewood Cliffs, NJ
Vienna Beef LTD
   Chicago, IL 800-366-3647
Vietti Foods Co Inc
   Nashville, TN 615-244-7864
Vince's Seafoods
   Gretna, LA 504-368-1544
VIP Foods
   Flushing, NY 718-821-5330
Westbrae Natural Foods
   Melville, NY 800-434-4246
White Coffee Corporation
   Long Island City, NY 800-221-0140
Wild Zora Foods
   Loveland, CO 970-541-9672
William Poll Inc
   New York, NY 800-993-7655
Wong Wing
   Florenceville-Bristol, NB 866-622-2461
Worthmore Food Products Co
   Cincinnati, OH 866-837-7687
Yankee Specialty Foods
   Boston, MA 800-688-9904

Beef Soup

Country Cupboard
   Lewisburg, PA 570-523-3211
Erba Food Products
   Brooklyn, NY 718-272-7700
Integrative Flavors
   Michigan City, IN 800-837-7687

Beef Stew

Aunt Kitty's Foods Inc
   Vineland, NJ 856-691-2100
Caltex Foods
   Canoga Park, CA 800-522-5839
Campbell Company of Canada
   Toronto, ON 800-410-7687
Chimayo To Go / Cibolo Junction
   Albuquerque, NM 800-683-9628
Hoopeston Foods Inc
   Burnsville, MN 952-854-0903
Kelly Foods
   Jackson, TN 731-424-2255

Marsan Foods
   Toronto, ON 416-755-9262
Midwest Food
   Chicago, IL 773-927-8870
Spring Glen Fresh Foods
   Ephrata, PA 800-641-2853
Sweet Sue Kitchens
   Athens, AL 256-216-0500

Borscht

Gold Pure Food Products Co. Inc.
   Hempstead, NY 800-422-4681

Canned Soup

Amy's Kitchen Inc
   Santa Rosa, CA 707-781-6600
Bookbinder Specialties LLC
   Media, PA 215-322-1305
Caltex Foods
   Canoga Park, CA 800-522-5839
Carriere Foods Inc
   Saint-Denis-Sur-Richelie, QC 450-787-3411
Chef Hans' Gourmet Foods
   Monroe, LA 800-890-4267
Chincoteague Seafood Co Inc
   Parsonsburg, MD 443-260-4800
Colonna Brothers Inc
   North Bergen, NJ 201-864-1115
Dynamic Foods
   Lubbock, TX 806-723-5600
Faribault Foods, Inc.
   Fairbault, MN 507-331-1400
Hoopeston Foods Inc
   Burnsville, MN 952-854-0903
Mid-Atlantic Foods Inc
   Easton, MD 800-922-4688
Overhill Farms Inc
   Vernon, CA 800-859-6406
Progresso Quality Foods
   Vineland, NJ 856-691-1565
Sea Watch Intl
   Easton, MD 410-822-7500
Shelton's Poultry Inc
   Pomona, CA 800-541-1833
Sweet Sue Kitchens
   Athens, AL 256-216-0500
Unilever US
   Englewood Cliffs, NJ 800-298-5018
Vanee Foods Co
   Berkeley, IL 708-449-7300
Worthmore Food Products Co
   Cincinnati, OH 866-837-7687

Canned Stew

Aunt Kitty's Foods Inc
   Vineland, NJ 856-691-2100
Caltex Foods
   Canoga Park, CA 800-522-5839
Campbell Company of Canada
   Toronto, ON 800-410-7687
Campbell Soup Co.
   Camden, NJ 800-257-8443
Cordon Bleu International
   Anjou, QC 800-363-1182
Faribault Foods, Inc.
   Fairbault, MN 507-331-1400
Hoopeston Foods Inc
   Burnsville, MN 952-854-0903
Kelly Foods
   Jackson, TN 731-424-2255
Midwest Food
   Chicago, IL 773-927-8870
Sweet Sue Kitchens
   Athens, AL 256-216-0500

Chicken & Noodles

Aunt Kathy's Homestyle Products
   Waldheim, SK 306-945-2181
Country Cupboard
   Lewisburg, PA 570-523-3211
Hain Celestial Group Inc
   Lake Success, NY 800-434-4246
Imagine Foods
   Boulder, CO 800-434-4246
Shelton's Poultry Inc
   Pomona, CA 800-541-1833
Swagger Foods Corp
   Vernon Hills, IL 847-913-1200

Product Categories / Prepared Foods: Stuffing

Chicken & Rice

Hain Celestial Group Inc
 Lake Success, NY 800-434-4246
Hale and Hearty Soups
 New York, NY 212-255-2433

Chowder

Fish Hopper
 Monterey, CA 831-372-3406
Fishpeople
 Portland, OR 503-342-2424
LA Monica Fine Foods
 Millville, NJ
Mid-Atlantic Foods Inc
 Easton, MD 800-922-4688
Plenus Group Inc
 Lowell, MA 978-970-3832
Ronzoni
 Largo, FL 800-730-5957
Sea Watch Intl
 Easton, MD 410-822-7500
Vanee Foods Co
 Berkeley, IL 708-449-7300
Yankee Specialty Foods
 Boston, MA 800-688-9904

Corn

Hain Celestial Group Inc
 Lake Success, NY 800-434-4246

Manhattan

LA Monica Fine Foods
 Millville, NJ

New England

Campbell Company of Canada
 Toronto, ON 800-410-7687
Custom Culinary Inc.
 Schaumberg, IL 800-621-8827
Hormel Foods Corp.
 Austin, MN 507-437-5611
LA Monica Fine Foods
 Millville, NJ
Vanee Foods Co
 Berkeley, IL 708-449-7300

Cream of Broccoli

Imagine Foods
 Boulder, CO 800-434-4246

Cream of Mushroom

Aunt Kitty's Foods Inc
 Vineland, NJ 856-691-2100
Imagine Foods
 Boulder, CO 800-434-4246
Vanee Foods Co
 Berkeley, IL 708-449-7300

Dehydrated Soup

Chef Merito Inc
 Van Nuys, CA 800-637-4861

Conifer Foods
 Medina, WA 800-588-9160
Dorothy Dawson Food Products
 Jackson, MI 517-788-9830
Flavor House, Inc.
 Adelanto, CA 760-246-9131
Frontier Soups
 Waukegan, IL 800-300-7867
Integrative Flavors
 Michigan City, IN 800-837-7687
Maruchan Inc
 Irvine, CA 949-789-2300
Mayacamas Fine Foods
 Sonoma, CA 800-826-9621
Northwestern Foods
 Arden Hills, MN 800-236-4937
Sentry Seasonings
 Elmhurst, IL 630-530-5370
Serv-Agen Corporation
 Cherry Hill, NJ 856-663-6966
SOUPerior Bean & Spice Company
 Vancouver, WA 800-878-7687
Tropical Nut Fruit & Bulk Cndy
 Lithia Springs, GA 800-544-3762
VIP Foods
 Flushing, NY 718-821-5330
Vogue Cuisine Foods
 Sunnyvale, CA 888-236-4144

Fresh Stew

Midwest Food
 Chicago, IL 773-927-8870

Frozen Soup

Bellisio Foods
 Minneapolis, MN
Chincoteague Seafood Co Inc
 Parsonsburg, MD 443-260-4800
Crystal Noodle
 Torrance, CA 310-781-9734
Dorothy Dawson Food Products
 Jackson, MI 517-788-9830
Edmond's Chile Co
 St Louis, MO 314-772-1499
Fairfield Farm Kitchens
 Brockton, MA 508-584-9300
Marsan Foods
 Toronto, ON 416-755-9262
Progresso Quality Foods
 Vineland, NJ 856-691-1565
Shelton's Poultry Inc
 Pomona, CA 800-541-1833
Taste Traditions Inc
 Omaha, NE 800-228-2170
William Poll Inc
 New York, NY 800-993-7655

Frozen Stew

Campbell Soup Co.
 Camden, NJ 800-257-8443
Edmond's Chile Co
 St Louis, MO 314-772-1499

Marsan Foods
 Toronto, ON 416-755-9262
Midwest Food
 Chicago, IL 773-927-8870

Gumbo

Cajun Crawfish Distributors
 Branch, LA 888-254-8626
Cajun Fry Co Inc
 Pierre Part, LA 888-272-2586
Chef Hans' Gourmet Foods
 Monroe, LA 800-890-4267
Cuizina Food Company
 Woodinville, WA 425-486-7000
Kajun Kettle Foods
 New Orleans, LA 800-331-9612
Louisiana Gourmet Enterprises
 Houma, LA 800-328-5586
Vince's Seafoods
 Gretna, LA 504-368-1544
Yankee Specialty Foods
 Boston, MA 800-688-9904

Lentil Soup

Boulder Organic Foods
 Niwot, CO 303-530-0470
Colonna Brothers Inc
 North Bergen, NJ 201-864-1115
Country Cupboard
 Lewisburg, PA 570-523-3211
Hain Celestial Group Inc
 Lake Success, NY 800-434-4246

Miso

Great Eastern Sun Trading Co
 Asheville, NC 800-334-5809
Kettle & Fire
 Austin, TX 415-857-0024
Ocean's Halo
 Burlingame, CA 650-642-5907
San-J International Inc
 Henrico, VA 800-446-5500

Potato Leek Soup

Boulder Organic Foods
 Niwot, CO 303-530-0470

Wonton Soup

Maruchan Inc
 Irvine, CA 949-789-2300

Stuffing

Meat

Texas Crumb & Food Products
 Farmers Branch, TX 800-522-7862
World Flavors Inc
 Warminster, PA 215-672-4400

Relishes & Pickled Products

Pickled Products

A-1 Eastern-Homemade Pickle Co
  Los Angeles, CA 323-223-1141
Baensch Food Products Co
  Milwaukee, WI 414-562-4643
Big B Barbecue
  Evansville, IN 812-425-5235
Bob Gordon & Associates
  Oak Park, IL 708-524-9611
Bryant Preserving Company
  Alma, AR 800-634-2413
Cajun Brands
  New Iberia, LA 504-408-2252
Campbell Soup Co.
  Camden, NJ 800-257-8443
Carson City Pickle Company
  Carson City, MI 989-584-3148
Commissariat Imports
  Los Angeles, CA 310-475-5628
Cordon Bleu International
  Anjou, QC 800-363-1182
Corsair Pepper Sauce
  Gulfport, MS 228-452-0311
Dolores Canning Co Inc
  Los Angeles, CA 323-263-9155
F & S Produce Co Inc
  Vineland, NJ 800-886-3316
Feature Foods
  Brampton, ON 905-452-7741
Flamm Pickle & Packing
  Eau Claire, MI 800-742-5531
Food City Pickle Company
  Battle Creek, MI 269-781-9135
Food For Thought Inc
  Honor, MI 231-326-5444
Foster Family Farm
  South Windsor, CT 860-648-9366
Freestone Pickle Co
  Bangor, MI 877-874-2553
Gene Belk Briners
  Bloomington, CA 909-877-1819
Giovanni's Appetizing Food Co
  Richmond, MI 586-727-9355
Gl Mezzetta Inc
  American Canyon, CA 800-941-7044
Granny Blossom Specialty Foods
  Wells, VT 802-645-0507
Grillo's Pickles
  Needham Heights, MA
Hell On The Red Inc
  Telephone, TX 903-664-2573
Hermann Pickle Co
  Garrettsville, OH 800-245-2696
JNB Foods, LLC
  Albany, NY 607-267-5874
L & S Packing Co
  Farmingdale, NY 800-286-6487
Lakeside Packing Company
  Harrow, ON 519-738-2314
Lancaster Packing Company
  Myerstown, PA 717-397-9727
Mama O's Premium Kimchi
  Brooklyn, NY 917-326-1557
McClure's Pickles LLC
  Detroit, MI 248-837-9323
Mccutcheon Apple Products
  Frederick, MD 800-888-7537
Money's Mushrooms
  Vancouver, BC 800-669-7992
Paisley Farms Inc
  Willoughby, OH 800-474-5688
Paradise Products Corporation
  Boca Raton, FL 800-826-1235
Peer Foods Group Inc
  Chicago, IL 800-365-5644
Pepperland Farms
  Ponchatoula, LA 985-956-6703
Pernicious Pickling
  Costa Mesa, CA 714-794-9845
Pickled Pink
  Norcross, GA 770-998-1500
Porinos Gourmet Food
  Central Falls, RI 800-826-3938
Rachael's Smoked Fish
  Springfield, MA 800-327-3412
Red Smith Foods Inc
  Davie, FL 954-581-1996
Renfro Foods
  Fort Worth, TX 800-332-2456
Safie Specialty Foods
  Chesterfield, MI 586-598-8282
Sargent and Greenleaf
  Nicholasville, KY 800-826-7652
Seneca Foods Corp
  Marion, NY 315-926-8100
Stanchfield Farms
  Milo, ME 207-732-5173
Stonewall Kitchen
  York, ME 800-826-1752
Talk O'Texas Brands Inc
  San Angelo, TX 800-749-6572
Troy Pork Store
  Troy, NY 518-272-8291
Tucker Cellars
  Sunnyside, WA 509-837-8701
United Pickles
  Bronx, NY 718-933-6060
Yergat Packing Co
  Fresno, CA 559-276-9180

Cauliflower

Gene Belk Briners
  Bloomington, CA 909-877-1819
Paisley Farms Inc
  Willoughby, OH 800-474-5688
Sargent and Greenleaf
  Nicholasville, KY 800-826-7652

Eggs

Cordon Bleu International
  Anjou, QC 800-363-1182
Feature Foods
  Brampton, ON 905-452-7741
Red Smith Foods Inc
  Davie, FL 954-581-1996

Meats

Troy Pork Store
  Troy, NY 518-272-8291

Onions

Screamin' Onionz
  Poughkeepsie, NY

Peppers

Apecka Peppered Pickles
  Rockwall, TX 972-771-7628
F & S Produce Co Inc
  Vineland, NJ 800-886-3316
Gene Belk Briners
  Bloomington, CA 909-877-1819
Gl Mezzetta Inc
  American Canyon, CA 800-941-7044
Paisley Farms Inc
  Willoughby, OH 800-474-5688
Porinos Gourmet Food
  Central Falls, RI 800-826-3938
Sargent and Greenleaf
  Nicholasville, KY 800-826-7652

Pickles

A-1 Eastern-Homemade Pickle Co
  Los Angeles, CA 323-223-1141
Alimentaire Whyte's Inc
  Laval, QC 866-420-9520
Allen's Pickle Works
  Glen Cove, NY 516-676-0640
B & G Foods Inc.
  Parsippany, NJ 973-401-6500
Bainbridge Festive Foods
  Farmington, TN 800-545-9205
Batampte Pickle Prods Inc
  Brooklyn, NY 718-251-2100
Bay Valley Foods
  El Paso, TX 800-236-1119
Bessinger Pickle Co
  Au Gres, MI 989-876-8008
Best Maid Products, Inc.
  Fort Worth, TX 800-447-3581
Blazzin Pickle Company
  McAllen, TX 956-630-0733
Brooklyn Brine Co LLC
  Brooklyn, NY 347-223-4345
Bubbies Fine Foods
  Stockton, CA 805-947-4622
Caltex Foods
  Canoga Park, CA 800-522-5839
Campbell Soup Co.
  Camden, NJ 800-257-8443
Carson City Pickle Company
  Carson City, MI 989-584-3148
Clic International Inc
  Laval, QC 450-669-2663
Commissariat Imports
  Los Angeles, CA 310-475-5628
Conscious Choice Foods
  Lewisville, TX 877-898-6158
Cook's Pantry
  Ventura, CA 805-947-4622
Country Cupboard
  Lewisburg, PA 570-523-3211
Erba Food Products
  Brooklyn, NY 718-272-7700
Flaum Appetizing
  Brooklyn, NY 718-821-1970
Forge Mountain Foods
  Hendersonville, NC 800-823-6743
Gene Belk Briners
  Bloomington, CA 909-877-1819
GFA Brands Inc
  Paramus, NJ 201-568-9300
Gielow Pickles Inc
  Lexington, MI 810-359-7680
GWB Foods Corporation
  Brooklyn, NY 877-977-7610
Hausbeck Pickle Co
  Saginaw, MI 866-754-4721
Hermann Pickle Co
  Garrettsville, OH 800-245-2696
House of Herbs LLC
  Passaic, NJ 973-779-2422
House of Spices
  Flushing, NY 718-507-4600
Howard Foods Inc
  Danvers, MA 978-774-6207
Hurd Orchards
  Holley, NY 585-638-8838
Island Spring Inc
  Vashon, WA 206-463-9848
J G Van Holten & Son Inc
  Waterloo, WI 800-256-0619
Kaiser Pickles
  Cincinnati, OH 888-291-0608
Kaplan & Zubrin
  Camden, NJ 856-964-1083
Klein's Kosher Pickles
  Phoenix, AZ 800-437-4255
Kruger Foods
  Stockton, CA 209-941-8518
L & S Packing Co
  Farmingdale, NY 800-286-6487
Lakeside Packing Company
  Harrow, ON 519-738-2314
Lancaster Packing Company
  Myerstown, PA 717-397-9727
Limited Edition
  Midland, TX 432-686-2008
Lowcountry Produce
  Raleigh, NC 800-935-2792
Miramar Pickles & Food Products
  Fort Lauderdale, FL 954-463-0222
Miss Ginny's Orginal Vermont Pickle Works
  Northfield, VT 802-485-3057
Mister Pickle's Inc
  Auburn, CA 530-885-1000
Mixon Fruit Farms Inc
  Bradenton, FL 800-608-2525
Mt Olive Pickle Co
  Mt Olive, NC 800-672-5041
Olde Tyme Mercantile
  Arroyo Grande, CA 805-489-7991
Olympic Provisions Northwest
  Portland, OR 503-894-8136

Product Categories / Relishes & Pickled Products: Relishes

Original Tony Packo's
  Toledo, OH 866-472-2567
Paisley Farms Inc
  Willoughby, OH 800-474-5688
Paradise Products Corporation
  Boca Raton, FL 800-826-1235
Patriot Pickel Inc
  Wayne, NJ 973-709-9487
Pemberton's Foods Inc
  Gray, ME 800-255-8401
Picklesmith Inc
  Taft, TX 800-499-3401
Porter's Pick-A-Dilly
  Stowe, VT 802-253-6338
Purity Products
  Plainview, NY 800-256-6102
Ralph Sechler & Son Inc
  St Joe, IN 800-332-5461
Regal Crown Foods Inc
  Worcester, MA 508-752-2679
Ripon Pickle Co Inc
  Ripon, WI 920-748-7110
Sambets Cajun Deli
  Austin, TX 800-472-6238
Sargent and Greenleaf
  Nicholasville, KY 800-826-7652
Sargent's Bear Necessities
  North Troy, VT 802-988-2903
Shawnee Canning Co
  Cross Junction, VA 800-713-1414
Stan-Mark Food Products Inc
  Chicago, IL 800-651-0994
Strub Pickles
  Brantford, ON 519-751-1717
SuckerPunch Gourmet
  Bridgeview, IL 708-784-3000
Sunshine Fresh
  North Las Vegas, NV 800-832-8081
Sutter Buttes Olive Oil
  Sutter, CA 530-763-7921
Topor's Pickle & Food Svc Inc
  Detroit, MI 313-237-0288
United Pickles
  Bronx, NY 718-933-6060
Vaughn Rue Produce
  Wilson, NC 800-388-8138
William Harrison Winery LLC
  St Helena, CA 800-913-9463

Dill

Allen's Pickle Works
  Glen Cove, NY 516-676-0640
Batampte Pickle Prods Inc
  Brooklyn, NY 718-251-2100
Bessinger Pickle Co
  Au Gres, MI 989-876-8008
Best Maid Products, Inc.
  Fort Worth, TX 800-447-3581
Bubbies Fine Foods
  Stockton, CA 805-947-4622
Conscious Choice Foods
  Lewisville, TX 877-898-6158
Flamm Pickle & Packing
  Eau Claire, MI 800-742-5531
Food City Pickle Company
  Battle Creek, MI 269-781-9135
Hausbeck Pickle Co
  Saginaw, MI 866-754-4721
Hermann Pickle Co
  Garrettsville, OH 800-245-2696
Kaplan & Zubrin
  Camden, NJ 856-964-1083
Sechler's Fine Pickles
  Saint Joe, IN 800-332-5461
Strub Pickles
  Brantford, ON 519-751-1717
United Pickles
  Bronx, NY 718-933-6060

Gherkins

Conscious Choice Foods
  Lewisville, TX 877-898-6158
Paradise Products Corporation
  Boca Raton, FL 800-826-1235
Sargent and Greenleaf
  Nicholasville, KY 800-826-7652
Sechler's Fine Pickles
  Saint Joe, IN 800-332-5461

Kosher

Best Maid Products, Inc.
  Fort Worth, TX 800-447-3581
Bubbies Fine Foods
  Stockton, CA 805-947-4622
Kaplan & Zubrin
  Camden, NJ 856-964-1083

Sweet

Best Maid Products, Inc.
  Fort Worth, TX 800-447-3581
Flamm Pickle & Packing
  Eau Claire, MI 800-742-5531
Food City Pickle Company
  Battle Creek, MI 269-781-9135
Hausbeck Pickle Co
  Saginaw, MI 866-754-4721
Kaplan & Zubrin
  Camden, NJ 856-964-1083
Sechler's Fine Pickles
  Saint Joe, IN 800-332-5461
United Pickles
  Bronx, NY 718-933-6060

Vegetables

Apecka Peppered Pickles
  Rockwall, TX 972-771-7628
Batampte Pickle Prods Inc
  Brooklyn, NY 718-251-2100
Bob Gordon & Associates
  Oak Park, IL 708-524-9611
Carson City Pickle Company
  Carson City, MI 989-584-3148
Columbia Valley Farms Inc.
  Pasco, WA 855-261-6395
EDCO Food Products Inc
  Hobart, WI 800-255-3768
F & S Produce Co Inc
  Vineland, NJ 800-886-3316
Foster Family Farm
  South Windsor, CT 860-648-9366
Gene Belk Briners
  Bloomington, CA 909-877-1819
Gl Mezzetta Inc
  American Canyon, CA 800-941-7044
Hell On The Red Inc
  Telephone, TX 903-664-2573
Hermann Pickle Co
  Garrettsville, OH 800-245-2696
Johnson Foods, Inc. - Cannery Plant
  Sunnyside, WA 509-837-4188
L & S Packing Co
  Farmingdale, NY 800-286-6487
Lancaster Packing Company
  Myerstown, PA 717-397-9727
Leonard Mountain Inc
  Bixby, OK 800-822-7700
Miramar Pickles & Food Products
  Fort Lauderdale, FL 954-463-0222
Money's Mushrooms
  Vancouver, BC 800-669-7992
Olympic Provisions Northwest
  Portland, OR 503-894-8136
Paisley Farms Inc
  Willoughby, OH 800-474-5688
Paradise Products Corporation
  Boca Raton, FL 800-826-1235
Pepperland Farms
  Ponchatoula, LA 985-956-6703
Pickled Planet
  Ashland, OR 541-201-2689
Talk O'Texas Brands Inc
  San Angelo, TX 800-749-6572
Tucker Cellars
  Sunnyside, WA 509-837-8701
Yergat Packing Co
  Fresno, CA 559-276-9180

Relishes

Alimentaire Whyte's Inc
  Laval, QC 866-420-9520
Aloha From Oregon
  Eugene, OR 800-241-0300
Alto Rey Food Corp
  Studio City, CA 323-969-0178
American Culinary Garden
  Springfield, MO 888-831-2433
American Fine Food Corporation
  Doral, FL 305-392-5000
Amigos Canning Company
  San Antonio, TX 210-798-5360
Arizona Pepper Products
  Mesa, AZ 800-359-3912
Au Printemps Gourmet
  Saint-Jerome, QC 800-438-6676
Baldwin Richardson Foods
  Oakbrook Terrace, IL 866-644-2732
Barhyte Specialty Foods Inc
  Pendleton, OR 800-227-4983
Bauer's Mustard
  Flushing, NY 718-821-3570
Bay Valley Foods
  El Paso, TX 800-236-1119
BBQ Bunch
  Kansas City, MO 816-941-4534
Best Provision Co Inc
  Union, NJ 800-631-4466
Big B Barbecue
  Evansville, IN 812-425-5235
Blue Jay Orchards
  Bethel, CT 203-748-0119
Boetje Foods Inc
  Rock Island, IL 877-726-3853
Bogland
  Pembroke, MA 781-829-9549
Bryant Preserving Company
  Alma, AR 800-634-2413
C & E Canners Inc
  Hammonton, NJ 609-561-1078
C.F. Sauer Co.
  Richmond, VA 888-723-0052
Cajun Brands
  New Iberia, LA 504-408-2252
Campbell Soup Co.
  Camden, NJ 800-257-8443
Carolina Treet
  Wilmington, NC 800-616-6344
Catskill Mountain Specialties
  Saugerties, NY 800-311-3473
Chandler Foods Inc
  Greensboro, NC 800-537-6219
Cherith Valley Gardens
  Fort Worth, TX 800-610-9813
Christie's
  Stroughton, MA 781-341-3341
Cinnabar Specialty Foods Inc
  Prescott, AZ 866-293-6433
Clements Foods Co
  Oklahoma City, OK 800-654-8355
Commissariat Imports
  Los Angeles, CA 310-475-5628
Conroy Foods
  Pittsburgh, PA 412-781-0977
Consumer Guild Foods Inc
  Toledo, OH 419-726-3406
Corfu Foods Inc
  Bensenville, IL 630-595-2510
Cosmopolitan Foods
  Glen Ridge, NJ 973-680-4560
Country Cupboard
  Lewisburg, PA 570-523-3211
Curry King Corporation
  Waldwick, NJ 800-287-7987
Cyclone Enterprises Inc
  Houston, TX 281-872-0087
Daisy Brand
  Dallas, TX 877-292-9830
Davis Food Company
  Plantation, FL 954-791-5868
Delallo's Italian Store
  Jeannette, PA 724-523-5000
Delgrosso Foods Inc.
  Tipton, PA 800-521-5880
Dhidow Enterprises
  Oxford, PA 610-932-7868
Dickson's Pure Honey
  San Angelo, TX 915-655-9233
E Waldo Ward & Son Marmalades
  Sierra Madre, CA 800-355-9273
Elwood International Inc
  Copiague, NY 631-842-6600
Firth Maple Products
  Spartansburg, PA 814-654-2435
Flamm Pickle & Packing
  Eau Claire, MI 800-742-5531
Flavormatic Industries
  Wappingers Falls, NY 845-297-9100
Flavors of the Heartland
  Rocheport, MO 800-269-3210
Fliinko
  South Dartmouth, MA 800-266-9609

Product Categories / Relishes & Pickled Products: Sauerkraut

Food City Pickle Company
  Battle Creek, MI 269-781-9135
Forge Mountain Foods
  Hendersonville, NC 800-823-6743
Fountain Valley Foods
  Colorado Springs, CO. 719-573-6012
Fox Hollow
  Crestwood, KY 502-241-8621
Garden Row Foods
  St Charles, IL 800-505-9999
Garden Row Foods
  Franklin Park, IL 800-555-9798
Gil's Gourmet Gallery
  Seaside, CA 800-438-7480
Golding Farms Foods
  Winston Salem, NC 336-766-6161
Graves Mountain Lodge Inc.
  Syria, VA 540-923-4231
Green Garden Food Products
  Sandpoint, ID 800-669-3169
Grouse Hunt Farm Inc
  Tamaqua, PA 570-467-2850
Half Moon Bay Trading Co
  Atlantic Beach, FL 888-447-2823
Halifax Group
  Washington, DC 202-530-8300
Hanson Thompson Honey Farms
  Redfield, SD 605-472-0474
Hausbeck Pickle Co
  Saginaw, MI 866-754-4721
Heintz & Weber Co
  Buffalo, NY. 716-852-7171
Heluva Good Cheese
  Lynnfield, MA 800-644-5473
Hendon & David
  Millbrook, NY 845-677-9696
Herlocher Foods
  State College, PA 800-437-5625
Howard Foods Inc
  Danvers, MA. 978-774-6207
Hudson Valley Homestead
  Craryville, NY. 518-851-7336
Hume Specialties
  Chester, VT 802-875-3117
Imus Ranch Foods
  Darien, CT. 888-284-4687
J G Van Holten & Son Inc
  Waterloo, WI. 800-256-0619
J.N. Bech
  Elk Rapids, MI 800-232-4583
Jardine Foods
  Buda, TX. 800-544-1880
Jay Shah Foods
  Mississauga, ON 905-696-0172
Joe Hutson Foods
  Jacksonville, FL 904-731-9065
Kaiser Pickles
  Cincinnati, OH 888-291-0608
Khatsa & Company
  Bellevue, WA 888-234-6781
Klein's Kosher Pickles
  Phoenix, AZ 800-437-4255
Kozlowski Farms
  Forestville, CA 800-473-2767
Kruger Foods
  Stockton, CA. 209-941-8518
LA Vencedora Products Inc
  Los Angeles, CA. 800-327-2572
Lakeside Packing Company
  Harrow, ON. 519-738-2314
Lancaster Packing Company
  Myerstown, PA 717-397-9727
Landry's Pepper Co
  St Martinville, LA 337-394-6097
Laredo Tortilleria & Mexican
  Fort Wayne, IN 800-252-7336
Lounsbury Foods
  Toronto, ON. 416-656-6330
M.A. Hatt & Sons
  Lunenburg, NS 902-634-8407
Mardale Specialty Foods
  Waukegan, IL 845-299-0285
Mccutcheon Apple Products
  Frederick, MD. 800-888-7537
Mendocino Mustard
  Fort Bragg, CA 800-964-2270
Mo Hotta Mo Betta
  Savannah, GA. 912-748-2766
Monticello Canning Company
  Crossville, TN
Mrs. Dog's Products
  Grand Rapids, MI 800-267-7364

Mt Olive Pickle Co
  Mt Olive, NC 800-672-5041
Nature Quality
  San Martin, CA. 408-683-2182
Nestelle's, Inc.
  Salem, OR. 503-393-7056
New Canaan Farms
  Dripping Springs, TX 800-727-5267
Newly Weds Foods Inc
  Modesto, CA. 800-487-7423
NPC Dehydrators
  Eden, NC 336-635-5190
NutraSweet Company
  Chicago, IL 800-323-5321
O'Garvey Sauces
  New Braunfels, TX. 830-620-6127
Oasis Food Co
  Hillside, NJ 800-275-0477
Ocean Spray International
  Lakeville-Middleboro, MA 800-662-3263
Ojai Cook
  Los Angeles, CA. 886-571-1551
Old Dutch Mustard Company
  Great Neck, NY 516-466-0522
Olds Products Co
  Pleasant Prairie, WI 262-947-3500
Original Tony Packo's
  Toledo, OH 866-472-2567
Orleans Packing Co
  Hyde Park, MA 617-361-6611
Paisley Farms Inc
  Willoughby, OH 800-474-5688
Palmieri Food Products
  New Haven, CT 800-845-5447
Peaceworks
  New York, NY 212-897-3985
Pepper Creek Farms
  Lawton, OK. 800-526-8132
Peter's Mustards
  Sharon, CT 860-364-0842
Plochman Inc
  Manteno, IL 800-843-4566
Precise Food Ingredients
  Carrollton, TX. 972-323-4951
Quaker Sugar Company
  Brooklyn, NY 718-387-6500
Ragsdale-Overton Food Traditions
  Smithfield, NC 888-424-8863
Raye's Mustard
  Eastport, ME 800-853-1903
Red Pelican Food Products
  Detroit, MI 313-881-4095
RENFRO Foods Inc
  Fort Worth, TX 817-336-3849
Ripon Pickle Co Inc
  Ripon, WI 920-748-7110
Robert & James Brands
  Birmingham, MI 248-646-0578
Rubys Apiaries
  Milnor, ND 701-427-5200
Salad Oils Intl Corp
  Chicago, IL 773-261-0500
San Antonio Farms
  Platteville, WI 800-236-1119
Seminole Foods
  Springfield, OH 800-881-1177
Seneca Foods Corp
  Marion, NY 315-926-8100
Shenk's Foods
  Lancaster, PA 717-393-4240
Silver Spring Foods
  Eau Clair, MI. 800-826-7322
Smiling Fox Pepper Company
  North Aurora, IL 972-754-2820
Snowizard Extracts
  New Orleans, LA 800-366-9766
Sperry Apiaries
  Kindred, ND 701-428-3000
St Mary Sugar Co-Op
  Jeanerette, LA. 337-276-6761
Stan-Mark Food Products Inc
  Chicago, IL 800-651-0994
Stickney & Poor Company
  Peterborough, NH 603-924-2259
Strub Pickles
  Brantford, ON. 519-751-1717
Sun Valley Mustard
  Hailey, ID 800-628-7124
Sunshine Fresh
  North Las Vegas, NV 800-832-8081
Tapatio Hot Sauce
  Vernon, CA 323-587-8933

Target Flavors Inc
  Brookfield, CT 800-538-3350
Terrapin Ridge
  Clearwater, FL 800-999-4052
Thistledew Farm
  Proctor, WV 800-854-6639
Tipp Distributors Inc
  El Paso, TX. 888-668-2639
Ultimate Gourmet
  Hillsborough, NJ 908-359-4050
United Pickles
  Bronx, NY 718-933-6060
Vidalia Sweets Brand
  Lyons, GA 912-565-8881
Wild Thyme Cottage Products
  Pointe Claire, QC 514-695-3602
Wing's Food Products
  Toronto, ON 416-259-2662
Wing-Time
  Lynn, MA 781-592-1069
Wisconsin Wilderness Food Products
  Lake Bluff, IL 800-359-3039
Ye Olde Pepper Co
  Salem, MA. 866-526-2376

Beets

Beetroot Delights
  Foothill, ON 888-842-3387
Bubbies Fine Foods
  Stockton, CA 805-947-4622
Paisley Farms Inc
  Willoughby, OH 800-474-5688

Relishes & Condiments

Baldwin Richardson Foods
  Oakbrook Terrace, IL 866-644-2732
Best Maid Products, Inc.
  Fort Worth, TX. 800-447-3581
Bubbies Fine Foods
  Stockton, CA 805-947-4622
Grandma Hoerner's Inc
  Alma, KS. 785-765-2300
HerbNZest LLC
  Princeton, NJ 917-582-1191
Howard Foods Inc
  Danvers, MA. 978-774-6207
J.M. Smucker Co.
  Orrville, OH 888-550-9555
JaynRoss Creations LLC
  Whitmore Lake, MI 734-657-5852
JNB Foods, LLC
  Albany, NY 607-267-5874
Lowcountry Produce
  Raleigh, NC 800-935-2792
Marathon Enterprises Inc
  Englewood, NJ 800-722-7388
Paisley Farms Inc
  Willoughby, OH 800-474-5688
Reva Foods
  Saint Petersburg, FL 727-692-1292
Shawnee Canning Co
  Cross Junction, VA 800-713-1414
Small Planet Foods
  Minneapolis, MN 800-624-4123
Virginia Chutney Company
  Washington, VA 540-675-1984

Sauerkraut

A.C. Kissling Company
  Philadelphia, PA. 800-445-1943
Alimentaire Whyte's Inc
  Laval, QC 866-420-9520
Batampte Pickle Prods Inc
  Brooklyn, NY 718-251-2100
Bubbies Fine Foods
  Stockton, CA 805-947-4622
Cook's Pantry
  Ventura, CA. 805-947-4622
Dietz & Watson Inc.
  Philadelphia, PA. 215-831-9000
Emerling International Foods
  Buffalo, NY. 716-833-7381
Farmhouse Culture
  Watsonville, CA 831-466-0499
Fermenting Fairy
  Santa Monica, CA
Flaum Appetizing
  Brooklyn, NY 718-821-1970
Fremont Authentic Brands
  Fremont, OH 419-334-8995

Product Categories / Relishes & Pickled Products: Sauerkraut

GLK Foods, LLC
  Shortsville, NY 855-572-8800
Hirzel Canning Co & Farms
  Luckey, OH 419-419-7525
Kaiser Pickles
  Cincinnati, OH 888-291-0608
Kaplan & Zubrin
  Camden, NJ 856-964-1083
Kruger Foods
  Stockton, CA 209-941-8518
Lakeside Packing Company
  Harrow, ON 519-738-2314
Marathon Enterprises Inc
  Englewood, NJ 800-722-7388
Miramar Pickles & Food Products
  Fort Lauderdale, FL 954-463-0222
New Harvest Foods
  Washington, DC 920-822-2578

Pickled Planet
  Ashland, OR 541-201-2689
Red Pelican Food Products
  Detroit, MI 313-881-4095
Ripon Pickle Co Inc
  Ripon, WI 920-748-7110
Strub Pickles
  Brantford, ON 519-751-1717
United Pickles
  Bronx, NY 718-933-6060
Victor Preserving Company
  Ontario, NY 315-524-2711

Juice

Fremont Authentic Brands
  Fremont, OH 419-334-8995

Hirzel Canning Co & Farms
  Luckey, OH 419-419-7525
Kaiser Pickles
  Cincinnati, OH 888-291-0608
Leo G. Fraboni Sausage Company
  Hibbing, MN 218-263-5074
M.A. Hatt & Sons
  Lunenburg, NS 902-634-8407
Smithfield Foods Inc.
  Smithfield, VA 757-365-3000

Sauces, Dips & Dressings

Condiments

3 Gyros Inc
  Tecumseh, ON 519-737-0389
505 Southwestern
  Meridian, ID
A Taste of the Kingdom
  Kingdom City, MO 888-592-5080
A&B American Style, LLC
  New York, NY 917-720-7009
Ajinomoto Foods North America, Inc.
  Ontario, CA. 909-477-4700
Alimentaire Whyte's Inc
  Laval, QC 866-420-9520
Allied Old English Inc
  Port Reading, NJ 732-602-8955
Aloha Shoyu Co LTD
  Pearl City, HI 808-456-5929
American Spoon Foods Inc
  Petoskey, MI 888-735-6700
Amphora International
  Lake Forest, CA 888-380-4808
Appledore Cove LLC
  North Berwick, ME. 207-676-4088
Ashman Manufacturing & Distributing Company
  Virginia Beach, VA 800-641-9924
Au Printemps Gourmet
  Saint-Jerome, QC 800-438-6676
August Kitchen
  Armonk, NY 914-219-5249
Bartush Schnitzius Foods Co
  Lewisville, TX 972-219-1270
Baumer Foods Inc
  Metairie, LA 504-482-5761
Bear Meadow Farm
  Ashfield, MA 413-628-3970
Beetroot Delights
  Foothill, ON 888-842-3387
Bel Brands USA
  Chicago, IL 312-462-1500
Bessinger Pickle Co
  Au Gres, MI 989-876-8008
Bettah Buttah, LLC
  Kansas City, KS 800-568-8468
Betty Lou's
  McMinnville, OR 800-242-5205
Big B Barbecue
  Evansville, IN 812-425-5235
Bob Gordon & Associates
  Oak Park, IL 708-524-9611
Bobby D'S
  Minnetonka, MN. 952-278-7810
Boetje Foods Inc
  Rock Island, IL 877-726-3853
Bone Doctors' BBQ, LLC
  Charlottesville, VA 434-296-7766
Border Foods
  New Hope, MN. 763-559-7338
Brad's Taste of New York
  Floral Park, NY 516-354-9004
Bradley Technologies Canada Inc.
  Delta, BC. 866-508-7514
Brooklyn Delhi
  Brooklyn, NY
Brothers Sauces
  Fort Worth, TX 817-821-3374
Bryant Preserving Company
  Alma, AR 800-634-2413
C & E Canners Inc
  Hammonton, NJ 609-561-1078
Cajohn's Fiery Foods Co
  Westerville, OH. 888-703-3473
Cajun Brands
  New Iberia, LA 504-408-2252
Caltex Foods
  Canoga Park, CA 800-522-5839
Canyon Specialty Foods
  Dallas, TX. 214-352-1771
Capa Di Roma Inc
  East Hartford, CT 860-282-0298
Carol Hall's Hot Pepper Jelly
  Fort Bragg, CA 866-737-7379
Carolina Treet
  Wilmington, NC 800-616-6344
Casa Visco
  Schenectady, NY 888-607-2823

Cedarvale Food Products
  Toronto, ON 416-656-3330
Chandler Foods Inc
  Greensboro, NC 800-537-6219
Chef Silvio's of Wooster Street
  Guilford, CT 203-453-1064
Chef Tim Foods, LLC
  Etters, PA 717-802-0350
Chicago 58 Food Products
  Woodbridge, ON 416-603-4244
Christie's
  Stroughton, MA 781-341-3341
Christopher Ranch LLC
  Gilroy, CA 408-847-1100
Cinnabar Specialty Foods Inc
  Prescott, AZ 866-293-6433
Clements Foods Co
  Oklahoma City, OK 800-654-8355
Clic International Inc
  Laval, QC 450-669-2663
CMS Fine Foods
  Healdsburg, CA 707-473-9561
Cold Hollow Cider Mill
  Waterbury Center, VT. 800-327-7537
Commissariat Imports
  Los Angeles, CA. 310-475-5628
Cook's Pantry
  Ventura, CA. 805-947-4622
Cordoba Foods LLC
  Hialeah, FL 786-202-2988
Corfu Foods Inc
  Bensenville, IL 630-595-2510
Creative Foodworks Inc
  San Antonio, TX 210-212-4761
Creole Fermentation Indu
  Abbeville, LA 337-898-9377
Cuizina Food Company
  Woodinville, WA. 425-486-7000
Del Monte Foods Inc.
  Walnut Creek, CA
Desert Pepper Trading Co
  El Paso, TX 888-472-5727
Diamond Crystal Brands Inc
  Savannah, GA 800-654-5115
Doral International
  Bayside, NY 718-224-7413
Dorina So-Good Inc
  Union, IL. 815-923-2144
Dragunara LLC
  Palos Verdes Estate, CA 310-618-8818
Earth Island
  Chatsworth, CA 888-394-3949
Ed Roller Inc
  Rochester, NY. 585-458-8020
Edward & Sons Trading Co
  Carpinteria, CA. 805-684-8500
El Toro Food Products
  Watsonville, CA 831-728-9266
Elwood International Inc
  Copiague, NY 631-842-6600
Enrico's/Ventre Packing
  Syracuse, NY 888-472-8237
Erba Food Products
  Brooklyn, NY 718-272-7700
Famous Chili Inc
  Fort Smith, AR 479-782-0096
Fernandez Chili Co
  Alamosa, CO. 719-589-6043
Filfil Foods LLC
  Brooklyn, NY 917-971-3493
Fireside Kitchen
  Halifax, NS 902-454-7387
Follow Your Heart
  Chatsworth, CA 818-725-2820
Ford's Gourmet Foods
  Raleigh, NC 800-446-0947
Fountain Valley Foods
  Colorado Springs, CO. 719-573-6012
Fratelli Mantova
  Naperville, IL 630-904-0002
Fremont Authentic Brands
  Fremont, OH 419-334-8995
G.E. Barbour
  Sussex, NB 506-432-2300
Garden Complements Inc
  Kansas City, MO. 800-966-1091

Gedney Foods Co
  Sun Valley, CA 888-244-0653
GFA Brands Inc
  Paramus, NJ 201-568-9300
Gibbons Bee Farm
  Ballwin, MO. 877-736-8607
Gingras Vinegar
  Rougemont, QC 866-469-4954
Girard's Food Service Dressings
  City of Industry, CA 888-327-8442
GoAvo
  Montville, NJ 973-534-9951
Golden Specialty Foods Inc
  Norwalk, CA. 562-802-2537
Good Food For Good
  Markham, ON. 647-449-4922
Goya Foods Inc.
  Jersey City, NJ. 201-348-4900
Graysmarsh Berry Farm
  Sequim, WA 800-683-4367
Greaves Jams & Marmalades
  Niagara-on-the-Lake, ON. 800-515-9939
Green Garden Food Products
  Sandpoint, ID 800-669-3169
GWB Foods Corporation
  Brooklyn, NY 877-977-7610
H-E-B Grocery Co. LP
  San Antonio, TX 800-432-3113
Happy Goat
  Boston, MA. 617-549-2776
Harpo's
  Honolulu, HI 808-735-6456
Heinz Portion Control
  Jacksonville, FL 904-695-1300
Hell On The Red Inc
  Telephone, TX. 903-664-2573
Homegrown Naturals
  Napa, CA. 800-288-1089
Hoople Country Kitchen Inc
  Rockport, IN. 877-466-7537
Hormel Foods Corp.
  Austin, MN 507-437-5611
House of Spices
  Flushing, NY. 718-507-4600
Howjax
  Pembroke Pines, FL 954-441-2491
HSR Associates Inc
  Tarzana, CA. 818-757-7152
Hyde & Hyde Inc
  Corona, CA. 951-279-5239
I Heart Olive Oil
  Ft Lauderdale, FL 954-607-1539
International Food Products
  Fenton, MO. 800-227-8427
International Home Foods
  Parsippany, NJ. 973-359-9920
J.N. Bech
  Elk Rapids, MI 800-232-4583
Jasmine & Bread
  South Royalton, VT 802-763-7115
Jayone Foods Inc
  Paramount, CA 562-633-7400
JMS Specialty Foods
  Ripon, WI 800-535-5437
Joe Bertman Foods
  Cleveland, OH 216-431-4460
John Volpi & Co
  St Louis, MO. 800-288-3439
Junuis Food Products
  Palatine, IL 847-359-4300
Kamish Food Products
  Chicago, IL 773-725-6959
KARI-Out Co
  White Plains, NY 800-433-8799
Kathy's Gourmet Specialties
  Mendocino, CA. 707-937-1383
KC Innovations Inc
  Kansas City, KS 816-506-9023
Ken's Foods Inc
  Marlborough, MA 508-229-1100
Knese Enterprise
  Bellerose, NY 516-354-9004
Koloa Rum Corp
  Kalaheo, HI. 808-332-9333
Kozlowski Farms
  Forestville, CA 800-473-2767

Product Categories / Sauces, Dips & Dressings: Dips

Kraft Heinz Canada
   North York, ON.....................416-441-5000
Kraft Heinz Co.
   Chicago, IL..........................800-543-5335
Krinos Foods
   Bronx, NY...........................718-729-9000
Kruger Foods
   Stockton, CA........................209-941-8518
L & S Packing Co
   Farmingdale, NY....................800-286-6487
La Ferme Martinette
   Coaticook, QC......................888-881-4561
La Morena
   Huamantla,..........................222-211-0515
Lakeside Packing Company
   Harrow, ON..........................519-738-2314
Landry's Pepper Co
   St Martinville, LA..................337-394-6097
Lasco Foods Inc
   St Louis, MO........................314-832-1906
Le Caramel
   La Mesa, CA........................619-562-0713
Lea & Perrins
   Glenview, IL
Lefty Spices
   Waldorf, MD........................301-399-3145
Letterman Enterprises Inc.
   State College, PA..................814-574-4339
Li'l Guy Foods
   Kansas City, MO...................800-886-8226
Lounsbury Foods
   Toronto, ON........................416-656-6330
Mad Will's Food Company
   Auburn, CA.........................888-275-9455
Marathon Enterprises Inc
   Englewood, NJ.....................800-722-7388
Mardale Specialty Foods
   Waukegan, IL......................845-299-0285
Marsa Specialty Products
   Vernon, CA........................800-628-0500
Marukan Vinegar USA Inc.
   Paramount, CA....................562-630-6060
McIlhenny Company
   Avery Island, LA..................800-634-9599
Miguel's Stowe Away
   Stowe, VT.........................800-448-6517
Mizkan Americas Inc
   Kansas City, MO..................800-323-4358
Modern Packaging
   Duluth, GA........................770-622-1500
Montana Mex
   Bozeman, MT
Morgan Foods Inc
   Austin, IN.........................888-430-1780
Morse's Sauerkraut
   Waldoboro, ME....................866-832-5569
Mother Raw
   Toronto, ON.......................855-464-0117
Mother Shucker's Original Cocktail Sauce
   Columbia, SC.....................803-261-3802
Mrs Clark's Foods
   Ankeny, IA........................800-736-5674
Mullins Food Products
   Broadview, IL.....................708-344-3224
Nature Quality
   San Martin, CA...................408-683-2182
New Canaan Farms
   Dripping Springs, TX............800-727-5267
Northwest Packing Co
   Vancouver, WA..................800-543-4356
Oasis Food Co
   Hillside, NJ.......................800-275-0477
Oberweis Dairy Inc
   North Aurora, IL.................866-623-7934
Ojai Cook LLC
   Ojai, CA...........................888-657-1155
Olde Tyme Mercantile
   Arroyo Grande, CA.............805-489-7991
Olympia International
   Belvidere, IL.....................815-547-5972
Pacific Choice Brands
   Fresno, CA......................559-476-3581
Palmieri Food Products
   New Haven, CT.................800-845-5447
Paradise Products Corporation
   Boca Raton, FL.................800-826-1235
Passage Foods LLC
   Collinsville, CT..................800-860-1045
Pastene Co LTD
   Canton, MA.....................781-298-3397
Phamous Phloyd's Barbecue
   Denver, CO.....................800-497-3281

Piknik Products Company
   Montgomery, AL.................334-240-2218
Pilgrim Foods
   Great Neck, NY.................516-466-0522
Pineland Farms
   New Gloucester, ME............207-688-4539
Pondini Imports
   Somerset, NJ....................732-545-1255
Porinos Gourmet Food
   Central Falls, RI.................800-826-3938
Prairie Thyme LTD
   Santa Fe, NM...................800-869-0009
Primal Kitchen
   Oxnard, CA.....................888-774-6259
Primal Nutrition
   Malibu, CA.....................888-774-6259
Productos Del Plata
   Miami, FL......................786-357-8261
Purity Farms
   La Farge, WI..................877-211-4819
Purity Products
   Plainview, NY.................800-256-6102
Ralph Sechler & Son Inc
   St Joe, IN.....................800-332-5461
Rapazzini Winery
   Gilroy, CA....................800-842-6262
Raye's Mustard
   Eastport, ME.................800-853-1903
Ready Foods Inc
   Denver, CO...................800-748-1218
Reckitt Benckiser LLC
   Parsippany, NJ..............973-404-2600
Red Duck Foods
   Portland, OR.................530-219-0150
Renfro Foods
   Fort Worth, TX..............800-332-2456
Restaurant Lulu Gourmet Products
   San Francisco, CA..........888-693-5800
REX Pure Foods
   New Orleans, LA...........800-344-8314
Rowena
   Norfolk, VA..................800-627-8699
Royal Food Products
   Indianapolis, IN.............317-782-2660
Sabra Dipping Company,LL
   Oceanside, CA.............800-748-5523
Sambets Cajun Deli
   Austin, TX.................800-472-6238
Santa Barbara Olive Company
   Santa Barbara, CA........800-624-4896
Sargent and Greenleaf
   Nicholasville, KY.........800-826-7652
Savoie's Sausage and Food Products
   Opelousas, LA...........337-942-7241
Schlotterbeck & Foss Company
   Portland, ME.............800-777-4666
Scott-Bathgate
   Winnipeg, MB...........800-216-2990
Sea Salt Superstore
   Everett, WA.............425-249-2331
Seneca Foods Corp
   Marion, NY..............315-926-8100
Shenk's Foods
   Lancaster, PA..........717-393-4240
Silver Palate Kitchens
   Cresskill, NJ............201-568-0110
Silver Spring Foods
   Eau Clair, MI..........800-826-7322
Sir Kensington's
   New York, NY.........646-450-5735
Sisler's Ice & Ice Cream
   Ohio, IL................888-891-3856
Skillet Street Food
   Seattle, WA...........425-998-9817
Skjodt-Barrett Foods
   Brampton, ON.......877-600-1200
Sky Valley Foods
   Danville, VA
Spanish Gardens Food Manufacturing
   Kansas City, KS....913-831-4242
Sprague Foods
   Belleville, ON.......613-966-1200
Steel's Gourmet Foods, Ltd.
   Bridgeport, CT.....800-678-3357
Stickney & Poor Company
   Peterborough, NH...603-924-2259
Stonewall Kitchen
   York, ME...........800-826-1752
Strub Pickles
   Brantford, ON.....519-751-1717
T. Marzetti Company
   Westerville, OH...800-999-1835

Tamarind Tree
   Neshanic Station, NJ..........800-432-8733
Target Flavors Inc
   Brookfield, CT.................800-538-3350
Taste Teasers
   Dallas, TX.....................800-526-1840
Terrell's Potato Chip Co
   Syracuse, NY.................315-437-2786
Tessemae's All Natural
   Essex, MD....................855-698-3773
Texas Heat
   San Antonio, TX.............800-656-5916
The Lollipop Tree, Inc
   Auburn, NY..................800-842-6691
The Truffleist
   Astoria, NY..................917-325-3374
Thompson's Fine Foods
   Shoreview, MN..............800-807-0025
Thor-Shackel Horseradish Company
   Eau Claire, WI..............800-826-7322
Trappist Preserves
   Cleveland, OH..............800-472-0425
TreeHouse Foods, Inc.
   Oak Brook, IL...............708-483-1300
Tropical Foods
   Charlotte, NC...............800-438-4470
Tulkoff's Food Products Inc
   Baltimore, MD..............800-638-7343
Twang Partners LTD
   San Antonio, TX...........800-950-8095
Two Chefs on a Roll
   Carson, CA.................800-842-3025
Ultra Seal
   New Paltz, NY.............845-255-2490
Unilever Food Solutions
   Englewood Cliffs, NJ
Ventura Foods LLC
   Brea, CA...................800-421-6257
Victoria Fine Foods
   Brooklyn, NY.............718-927-3000
Vienna Beef LTD
   Chicago, IL...............800-366-3647
Wagner Gourmet Foods
   Lenexa, KS..............913-469-5411
Walker Foods
   Los Angeles, CA........800-966-5199
Wei-Chuan USA Inc
   Bell Gardens, CA.......562-372-2020
Welch Foods Inc
   Concord, MA............800-340-6870
Welch Foods Inc.
   Concord, MA............800-340-6870
Westbrae Natural Foods
   Melville, NY............800-434-4246
Westin Foods
   Omaha, NE............800-228-6098
Westport Rivers Vineyard
   Westport, MA.........800-993-9695
Wild Thymes Farm Inc
   Greenville, NY........845-266-8387
Wing Nien Food
   Hayward, CA.........510-487-8877
Wings Foods of Alberta Ltd
   Edmonton, AB........780-433-6406
Winn-Dixie Stores
   Jacksonville, FL......800-967-9105
Wisconsin Spice Inc
   Berlin, WI.............920-361-3555
Woeber Mustard Mfg Co
   Springfield, OH......800-548-2929
Wood Brothers Inc
   West Columbia, SC...803-796-5146
Woodlake Ranch
   Woodlake, CA.......559-564-2161
Woody's Bar-B-Q Sauce Company
   Waldenburg, AR....888-747-9229
World Harbors
   Auburn, ME........800-355-6221
York Mountain Winery
   Templeton, CA.....805-237-7575

Dips

A&B American Style, LLC
   New York, NY.....917-720-7009
Abraham's Natural Foods
   Long Branch, NJ...800-327-9903
Amigos Canning Company
   San Antonio, TX...210-798-5360
Anderson Erickson Dairy
   Des Moines, IA....515-265-2521
Anderson Erickson Dairy
   Kansas City, KS...913-621-4801

Product Categories / Sauces, Dips & Dressings: Dips

Appledore Cove LLC
  North Berwick, ME.................207-676-4088
Arbor Hill Grapery & Winery
  Naples, NY........................800-554-7553
Ashman Manufacturing & Distributing Company
  Virginia Beach, VA................800-641-9924
ASK Foods Inc
  Palmyra, PA.......................800-879-4275
Au Printemps Gourmet
  Saint-Jerome, QC..................800-438-6676
Baba Foods
  San Diego, CA.....................619-426-6946
Banzos
  Denver, CO........................303-447-2133
Baptista's Bakery
  Franklin, WI......................414-409-2000
Baruvi Fresh LLC
  New York, NY......................646-346-1074
Bel Brands USA
  Chicago, IL.......................312-462-1500
Bison Foods
  Buffalo, NY.......................716-892-3156
Bitchin' Sauce
  Carlsbad, CA
Blue Moose of Boulder
  Lafayette, CO.....................303-926-0664
Bread Dip Company
  Maple Valley, WA..................425-358-7386
Byrne Dairy, Inc.
  Syracuse, NY......................800-899-1535
Cass-Clay Creamery
  Fargo, ND.........................701-293-6455
Cedar's Mediterranean Foods
  Ward Hill, MA.....................978-372-8010
Chelten House Products
  Swedesboro, NJ
Country Cupboard
  Lewisburg, PA.....................570-523-3211
Crazy Jerrys Inc Kahuna-Sauces
  Woodstock, GA.....................800-347-2823
Creamland Dairies Inc
  Albuquerque, NM...................505-247-0721
Creative Foodworks Inc
  San Antonio, TX...................210-212-4761
Custom Ingredients Inc
  New Braunfels, TX.................800-457-8935
Delighted By
Dixie Dew Prods Co
  Erlanger, KY......................800-867-8548
Do Anything Foods
  New York, NY
Dorina So-Good Inc
  Union, IL.........................815-923-2144
El Toro Food Products
  Watsonville, CA...................831-728-9266
Elki Coporation
  Everett, WA.......................425-261-1002
Flamous Brands
  Duarte, CA........................626-799-7909
Foods Alive
  Angola, IN........................260-488-4497
Fountain Valley Foods
  Colorado Springs, CO..............719-573-6012
Franklin Foods
  Enosburg Falls, VT................800-933-6114
Fresh Nature Foods
  Spokane, WA.......................509-368-7260
Frontier Co-op
  Norway, IA........................844-550-6200
Garden Complements Inc
  Kansas City, MO...................800-966-1091
Golden Specialty Foods Inc
  Norwalk, CA.......................562-802-2537
Goldwater's Food's Of Arizona
  Fredericksburg, TX................866-779-7241
Gourmet du Village
  Morin-Heights, QC.................800-668-2314
Guiltless Gourmet
  Newark, NJ........................201-553-1100
Haig's Delicacies
  Hayward, CA.......................510-782-6285
Halladay's Harvest Barn
  Bellows Falls, VT.................802-463-3471
Havana's Limited
  Titusville, FL....................321-267-0513
Havoc Maker Products
  Guilford, CT......................800-681-3909
Heidi's Salsa
  Los Angeles, CA...................310-821-0511
Helen's Pure Foods
  Cheltenham, PA....................215-379-6433

Heluva Good Cheese
  Lynnfield, MA.....................800-644-5473
Herb Patch of Vermont
  Bellows Falls, VT.................800-282-4372
Herlocher Foods
  State College, PA.................800-437-5625
Hirzel Canning Co & Farms
  Luckey, OH........................419-419-7525
Hope Foods
  Boulder, CO.......................303-248-7019
Hummustir
  New York, NY
Intercorp Excelle Foods
  North York, ON....................888-473-6337
Kentucky Beer Cheese
  Nicholasville, KY.................859-887-1645
Knese Enterprise
  Bellerose, NY.....................516-354-9004
Lakeview Farms
  Delphos, OH.......................800-755-9925
Lancaster Colony Corporation
  Westerville, OH...................614-224-7141
Lantana Hummus
  Austin, TX........................844-907-7626
Leigh Olivers
  Tyler, TX.........................903-245-9183
Litehouse Foods
  Sandpoint, ID.....................800-669-3169
Lost Trail Root Beer
  Louisburg, KS.....................800-748-7765
Low Country Produce
  Lobeco, SC........................800-935-2792
Lowcountry Produce
  Raleigh, NC.......................800-935-2792
Manassero Farms
  Irvine, CA........................949-554-5103
Mayfield Dairy Farms LLC
  Athens, TN........................800-362-9546
Michelle's RawFoodz
  Chicago, IL.......................312-442-0406
Mixon Fruit Farms Inc
  Bradenton, FL.....................800-608-2525
Mother Raw
  Toronto, ON.......................855-464-0117
New Canaan Farms
  Dripping Springs, TX..............800-727-5267
One Culture Foods
  Duarte, CA........................646-650-2989
Oregon Harvest
  Portland, OR......................503-249-0092
Original Herkimer Cheese
  Ilion, NY.........................315-895-7428
Outta the Park Eats
  Cary, NC..........................919-462-0012
Pied-Mont/Dora
  Anne Des Plaines, QC..............800-363-8003
Prairie Farms Dairy Inc.
  Edwardsville, IL..................618-659-5700
Productos Del Plata
  Miami, FL.........................786-357-8261
Quality Foods
  Qualicum Beach, BC................877-833-7890
Renfro Foods
  Fort Worth, TX....................800-332-2456
RENFRO Foods Inc
  Fort Worth, TX....................817-336-3849
Road's End Organics
  Carpinteria, CA...................877-247-3373
S A L T Sisters
  Goshen, IN........................574-971-8368
Sabra Blue & White Food Products
  Dallas, TX........................888-957-2272
Sabra-Go Mediterranean
  Dallas, TX........................888-957-2272
Salvy Sousa Dealer Locator
  Arkansas City, KS.................620-442-2700
Sambets Cajun Deli
  Austin, TX........................800-472-6238
Schneider-Valley Farms Inc
  Williamsport, PA..................570-326-2021
Sea Gold Seafood Products Inc
  New Bedford, MA...................508-993-3060
Sentry Seasonings
  Elmhurst, IL......................630-530-5370
Sheila's Select Gourmet Recipe
  Heber City, UT....................800-516-7286
Shine Companies
  Spring, TX........................281-353-8392
Shooting Star Farms
  Bartlesville, OK..................888-850-8540
Smith Dairy
  Orrville, OH......................800-776-7076

Sterzing Food Co
  Burlington, IA....................800-754-8467
Taste Weavers
  Urbana, OH........................888-810-8365
Texas Heat
  San Antonio, TX...................800-656-5916
The Honest Stand
  Denver, CO
Thompson's Fine Foods
  Shoreview, MN.....................800-807-0025
Toom Dips
  Saint Paul, MN....................651-447-8666
Tova Industries LLC
  Louisville, KY....................888-532-8682
Tribe Mediterranean
  Taunton, MA.......................800-848-6687
Tropical Link Canada Ltd.
  Burnaby, BC.......................778-379-3510
Two Chefs on a Roll
  Carson, CA........................800-842-3025
United Dairy Inc.
  Martins Ferry, OH.................800-252-1542
US Chocolate Corp
  Brooklyn, NY......................718-788-8555
Vegy Vida
  Cincinnati, OH....................513-659-0781
Ventre Packing Company
  Syracuse, NY......................315-463-2384
Victoria Fine Foods
  Brooklyn, NY......................718-927-3000
White Camel Foods Group
  Carlstadt, NJ.....................201-848-1215
Wild West Spices
  Cody, WY..........................888-587-8887
William Poll Inc
  New York, NY......................800-993-7655

Bean

Collaborative Advantage Marketing
  Detroit, MI.......................248-723-0793
Garden Complements Inc
  Kansas City, MO...................800-966-1091
Hormel Foods Corp.
  Austin, MN........................507-437-5611
La Esquina Food Products
  New York, NY......................646-710-3183
Sentry Seasonings
  Elmhurst, IL......................630-530-5370
Ventre Packing Company
  Syracuse, NY......................315-463-2384

Cheese

Better Made Snack Foods
  Detroit, MI.......................800-332-2394
Hell On The Red Inc
  Telephone, TX.....................903-664-2573
Hormel Foods Corp.
  Austin, MN........................507-437-5611
JTM Food Group
  Harrison, OH......................800-626-2308
Kentucky Beer Cheese
  Nicholasville, KY.................859-887-1645
Leaf Cuisine
  Santa Monica, CA
Litehouse Foods
  Sandpoint, ID.....................800-669-3169
Sentry Seasonings
  Elmhurst, IL......................630-530-5370
Texas Heat
  San Antonio, TX...................800-656-5916
Ventre Packing Company
  Syracuse, NY......................315-463-2384

Chili

Food Processor of New Mexico
  Albuquerque, NM...................877-634-3772
Golden Specialty Foods Inc
  Norwalk, CA.......................562-802-2537
Sentry Seasonings
  Elmhurst, IL......................630-530-5370

Chip

Amigos Canning Company
  San Antonio, TX...................210-798-5360
Dorina So-Good Inc
  Union, IL.........................815-923-2144
Sentry Seasonings
  Elmhurst, IL......................630-530-5370

Product Categories / Sauces, Dips & Dressings: Glazes

Guacamole

Frontera Foods
  Chicago, IL.....................800-509-4441
Sentry Seasonings
  Elmhurst, IL.....................630-530-5370

Salsa

A&B American Style, LLC
  New York, NY....................917-720-7009
Alicita-Salsa
  Great Falls, VA..................703-340-5323
Allied Old English Inc
  Port Reading, NJ................732-602-8955
Arizona Beverage Company
  Cincinnati, OH..................800-832-3775
Bachman Company
  Wyamissing, PA..................800-523-8253
Bel Brands USA
  Chicago, IL.....................312-462-1500
Bettah Buttah, LLC
  Kansas City, KS.................800-568-8468
Bingo Salsa, LLC
  Poulsbo, WA.....................360-779-6746
Border Foods
  New Hope, MN...................763-559-7338
C & G Salsa
  Fishers, IN......................317-569-9099
Canyon Specialty Foods
  Dallas, TX.......................214-352-1771
Casa Visco
  Schenectady, NY................888-607-2823
Choice of Vermont
  Destin, FL.......................800-444-6261
Colorado Salsa Company
  Littleton, CO....................303-932-2617
Desert Pepper Trading Co
  El Paso, TX.....................888-472-5727
Food For Thought Inc
  Honor, MI.......................231-326-5444
Fountain Valley Foods
  Colorado Springs, CO..........719-573-6012
Franklin Foods
  Enosburg Falls, VT..............800-933-6114
Frontera Foods
  Chicago, IL.....................800-509-4441
Golden Specialty Foods Inc
  Norwalk, CA....................562-802-2537
Granny Blossom Specialty Foods
  Wells, VT.......................802-645-0507
Green Mountain Gringo
  Winston-Salem, NC..............888-875-3111
Heidi's Salsa
  Los Angeles, CA................310-821-0211
Herlocher Foods
  State College, PA...............800-437-5625
JNB Foods, LLC
  Albany, NY.....................607-267-5874
Kind Snacks
  New York, NY..................855-884-5463
Li'l Guy Foods
  Kansas City, MO................800-886-8226
Maggie's Salsa
  Charleston, WV.................304-550-5460
Mesa Salsa
  Santa Barbara, CA..............805-448-3836
Mission Foods Corp.
  Irving, TX......................214-583-5113
My Brother Bobby's Salsa
  Poughkeepsie, NY..............845-462-6227
New Canaan Farms
  Dripping Springs, TX...........800-727-5267
North of the Border
  Tesuque, NM...................800-860-0681
Old Home Foods Inc
  New Brighton, MN..............651-312-8900
Oregon Harvest
  Portland, OR...................503-249-0092
Pacific Choice Brands
  Fresno, CA.....................559-476-3581
Pita Pal
  Houston, TX...................713-777-7482
Quality Foods
  Qualicum Beach, BC............877-833-7890
Ready Foods Inc
  Denver, CO....................800-748-1218
Royal Resources
  New Orleans, LA...............800-888-9932
Sentry Seasonings
  Elmhurst, IL....................630-530-5370
Shooting Star Farms
  Bartlesville, OK.................888-850-8540
Small Planet Foods
  Minneapolis, MN................800-624-4123
Stinking Rose, The
  San Francisco, CA..............800-995-7674
T.W. Garner Food Company
  Winston Salem, NC.............800-476-7383
Terrell's Potato Chip Co
  Syracuse, NY...................315-437-2786
Ventre Packing Company
  Syracuse, NY...................315-463-2384

Glazes

A Taste of the Kingdom
  Kingdom City, MO..............888-592-5080
Abel & Schafer Inc
  Ronkonkoma, NY...............800-443-1260
Ashman Manufacturing & Distributing Company
  Virginia Beach, VA..............800-641-9924
BakeMark Ingredients Canada
  Richmond, BC..................800-665-9441
De Nigris
  Totowa, NJ....................973-837-6791
Genarom International
  Cranbury, NJ..................609-409-6200
Gracious Gourmet
  Bridgewater, CT...............860-350-1213
Howard Foods Inc
  Danvers, MA..................978-774-6207
International Food Products
  Fenton, MO...................800-227-8427
Newly Weds Foods Inc
  Chicago, IL....................800-621-7521
Newport Flavours & Fragrances
  Orange, CA....................714-744-3700
Puratos Canada
  Mississauga, ON...............905-362-3668
Sentry Seasonings
  Elmhurst, IL....................630-530-5370
Valley View Blueberries
  Vancouver, WA.................360-892-2839

Gravy

Atlantic Seasonings
  Kinston, NC...................800-433-5261
Aunt Kitty's Foods Inc
  Vineland, NJ..................856-691-2100
Campbell Soup Co.
  Camden, NJ...................800-257-8443
Cordon Bleu International
  Anjou, QC.....................800-363-1182
Custom Culinary Inc.
  Schaumberg, IL................800-621-8827
Diversified Foods & Seasonings
  Covington, LA.................800-914-2382
Edmond's Chile Co
  St Louis, MO..................314-772-1499
Griffith Foods Inc.
  Alsip, IL.......................708-371-0900
Imagine Foods
  Boulder, CO...................800-434-4246
Mayacamas Fine Foods
  Sonoma, CA...................800-826-9621
Mcclancy Seasonings Co
  Fort Mill, SC....................800-843-1968
R L Schreiber Inc
  Ft Lauderdale, FL...............800-624-8777
Sambets Cajun Deli
  Austin, TX.....................800-472-6238
Schlotterbeck & Foss Company
  Portland, ME..................800-777-4666
Select Food Products
  Toronto, ON...................800-699-8016
Sentry Seasonings
  Elmhurst, IL....................630-530-5370
Taste Maker Foods
  Memphis, TN..................800-467-1407
United Supermarkets
  Lubbock, TX...................806-745-9667
Vanee Foods Co
  Berkeley, IL...................708-449-7300

Prepared

Aunt Kitty's Foods Inc
  Vineland, NJ..................856-691-2100
Campbell Soup Co.
  Camden, NJ...................800-257-8443
Cordon Bleu International
  Anjou, QC.....................800-363-1182
Custom Culinary Inc.
  Schaumberg, IL................800-621-8827

Lawry's Foods
  Hunt Valley, MD................800-952-9797
Mayacamas Fine Foods
  Sonoma, CA...................800-826-9621
Sentry Seasonings
  Elmhurst, IL....................630-530-5370
United Supermarkets
  Lubbock, TX...................806-745-9667

Ketchup

A&B American Style, LLC
  New York, NY..................917-720-7009
Alimentaire Whyte's Inc
  Laval, QC......................866-420-9520
Baldwin Richardson Foods
  Oakbrook Terrace, IL...........866-644-2732
C & E Canners Inc
  Hammonton, NJ................609-561-1078
De Nigris
  Totowa, NJ....................973-837-6791
E.D. Smith Foods Ltd
  Hamilton, ON..................905-573-1207
Erba Food Products
  Brooklyn, NY..................718-272-7700
Fine Foods Of America Inc
  Leawood, KS..................913-451-2525
Golden State Foods Corp
  Irvine, CA.....................949-247-8000
Good Food For Good
  Markham, ON.................647-449-4922
Heinz Portion Control
  Jacksonville, FL................904-695-1300
KARI-Out Co
  White Plains, NY...............800-433-8799
Mountain Fire Foods
  Huntington, VT................802-434-2685
Mucky Duck Mustard Company
  Ferndale, MI...................248-544-4610
Nature's Hollow
  Charleston, UT
New Business Corp
  Gary, IN......................219-885-1476
Northwest Packing Co
  Vancouver, WA.................800-543-4356
Portlandia Foods
  Portland, OR..................833-739-3663
Red Duck Foods
  Portland, OR..................530-219-0150
Salvy Sousa Dealer Locator
  Arkansas City, KS..............620-442-2700
Sir Kensington's
  New York, NY.................646-450-5735
Small Planet Foods
  Minneapolis, MN................800-624-4123
Stickney & Poor Company
  Peterborough, NH..............603-924-2259
Ultra Seal
  New Paltz, NY.................845-255-2490
Victoria Amory & Co LLC
  Greenwich, CT................203-220-6454
Westport Rivers Vineyard
  Westport, MA.................800-993-9695
Wing's Food Products
  Toronto, ON..................416-259-2662
World Art Foods
  Temple, TX...................254-774-8322

Marinades

A Perfect Pear
  Napa, CA.....................800-553-5753
A. Lassonde Inc.
  Rougemont, QC...............866-552-7643
Allegro Fine Foods Inc
  Paris, TN......................731-642-6113
Angelo Pietro Honolulu
  Honolulu, HI..................808-941-0555
Annie's Naturals
  Berkeley, CA..................800-434-1234
Applecreek Speciality Foods
  Lexington, KY.................800-747-8871
Appledore Cove LLC
  North Berwick, ME............207-676-4088
Ashman Manufacturing & Distributing Company
  Virginia Beach, VA..............800-641-9924
B & G Foods Inc.
  Parsippany, NJ................973-401-6500
Bavaria Corp International
  Apopka, FL...................407-880-0322
Bea & B Foods
  San Diego, CA................858-490-6205

379

Product Categories / Sauces, Dips & Dressings: Mayonaise

Blendex Co
   Louisville, KY 800-626-6325
Blue Smoke Salsa
   Ansted, WV. 888-725-7298
Bunker Foods Corp.
   New York, NY 646-738-4020
Cajohn's Fiery Foods Co
   Westerville, OH. 888-703-3473
Cajun Original Foods Inc
   New Iberia, LA. 337-367-1344
Chaparral Gardens
   Atascadero, CA. 805-703-0829
CHS Inc.
   Inver Grove Hts., MN. 800-328-6539
Cinnabar Specialty Foods Inc
   Prescott, AZ 866-293-6433
CMS Fine Foods
   Healdsburg, CA. 707-473-9561
Colonna Brothers Inc
   North Bergen, NJ 201-864-1115
Con Yeager Spice Co
   Zelienople, PA. 800-222-2460
Creative Foodworks Inc
   San Antonio, TX. 210-212-4761
Cugino's Gourmet Foods
   Crystal Lake, IL 888-592-8446
Cuizina Food Company
   Woodinville, WA. 425-486-7000
Dixie Trail Farms
   Wilmington, NC 800-665-3968
Dorothy Dawson Food Products
   Jackson, MI. 517-788-9830
Dr Pete's
   Savannah, GA. 888-599-0047
Dr. Pete's
   Savannah, GA. 912-233-3035
Ford's Gourmet Foods
   Raleigh, NC 800-446-0947
Fox Hollow
   Crestwood, KY 502-241-8621
Funnibonz LLC
   Princeton Jct, NJ 877-300-2669
Garden Complements Inc
   Kansas City, MO. 800-966-1091
Genarom International
   Cranbury, NJ. 609-409-6200
Girard's Food Service Dressings
   City of Industry, CA 888-327-8442
Halmoni's Divine Marinade
   Demarest, NJ. 917-913-8961
Havana's Limited
   Titusville, FL. 321-267-0513
Intercorp Excelle Foods
   North York, ON. 888-473-6337
J.T. Pappy's Sauce
   Los Angeles, CA. 323-969-9605
Jake's Grillin
   Hopewell Jct, NY 845-226-4656
Judicial Flavors
   Auburn, CA. 530-885-1298
Kaari Foods
   Brooklyn, NY
Kinder's BBQ
   Walnut Creek, CA. 925-939-7242
L & S Packing Co
   Farmingdale, NY 800-286-6487
Lawry's Foods
   Hunt Valley, MD. 800-952-9797
Louisiana Fish Fry Products
   Baton Rouge, LA 800-356-2905
Love'n Herbs
   Waterbury, CT. 203-756-4932
Mad Will's Food Company
   Auburn, CA. 888-275-9455
Magic Seasoning Blends
   New Orleans, LA 800-457-2857
Manassero Farms
   Irvine, CA. .949-554-5103
Maple Grove Farms Of Vermont
   St Johnsbury, VT. 802-748-5141
Marin Food Specialties
   Byron, CA. 925-634-6126
McIlhenny Company
   Avery Island, LA. 800-634-9599
Mod Squad Martha
   Johns Island, SC 615-476-3696
Molli
   Dallas, TX
Montebello Kitchens
   Gordonsville, VA. 800-743-7687
Mountain Fire Foods
   Huntington, VT. 802-434-2685

Mt. Olympus Specialty Foods
   Buffalo, NY. 716-874-0771
Napa Valley Kitchens
   Napa, CA. .707-254-3700
Nature's Kitchen
   Roswell, GA 678-845-6897
Newly Weds Foods Inc
   Chicago, IL 800-621-7521
Newman's Own
   Westport, CT. 203-222-0136
North Coast Processing
   Carlsbad, CA. 760-931-6809
One Culture Foods
   Duarte, CA 646-650-2989
Parthenon Food Products
   Ann Arbor, MI 734-994-1012
Phamous Phloyd's Barbecue
   Denver, CO. 800-497-3281
Porinos Gourmet Food
   Central Falls, RI 800-826-3938
Primal Kitchen
   Oxnard, CA. 888-774-6259
Primal Nutrition
   Malibu, CA. 888-774-6259
Produits Ronald
   St. Damase, QC. 800-465-0118
Quality Foods
   Qualicum Beach, BC 877-833-7890
Red Creek Marinade Company
   Amarillo, TX. 800-687-9114
Restaurant Lulu Gourmet Products
   San Francisco, CA 888-693-5800
River Town Foods Corp
   St Louis, MO. 800-844-3210
Rosmarino Foods/R.Z. Humbert Company
   Odessa, FL 888-926-9053
Salvy Sousa Dealer Locator
   Arkansas City, KS. 620-442-2700
Sambets Cajun Deli
   Austin, TX. 800-472-6238
Santa Barbara Salsa/California Creative
   Oceanside, CA. 800-748-5523
Sentry Seasonings
   Elmhurst, IL 630-530-5370
Serro Foods LLC
   Catskill, NY 518-943-9255
Soy Vay Enterprises
   Felton, CA. 800-444-6369
Surlean Foods
   San Antonio, TX. 800-999-4370
Swagger Foods Corp
   Vernon Hills, IL 847-913-1200
Sweet Peas Floral Design
   Stockton, CA. 209-472-9284
Sweetwater Spice Company
   Austin, TX. 800-531-6079
Tessemae's All Natural
   Essex, MD. 855-698-3773
Tillie's Gourmet
   Doylestown, PA 215-272-8326
Tone Products Inc
   Melrose Park, IL. 800-536-8663
Tova Industries LLC
   Louisville, KY 888-532-8682
Trailblazer Foods
   Portland, OR 800-777-7179
Ultimate Gourmet
   Hillsborough, NJ. 908-359-4050
Vita Food Products Inc
   Chicago, IL 800-989-8482
Wickers Food Products Inc
   Hornersville, MO 800-847-0032
Wild Thymes Farm Inc
   Greenville, NY 845-266-8387
Wine Country Chef LLC
   Hidden Valley Lake, CA. 707-322-0406

Beef

Lawry's Foods
   Hunt Valley, MD. 800-952-9797
Sentry Seasonings
   Elmhurst, IL 630-530-5370

Chicken

Delphos Poultry Products
   Delphos, OH. 419-692-5816
Sentry Seasonings
   Elmhurst, IL 630-530-5370
Sunchef Farms
   Vernon, CA 323-588-5800

Fajita

Magic Seasoning Blends
   New Orleans, LA 800-457-2857
San Antonio Farms
   Platteville, WI. 800-236-1119
Sentry Seasonings
   Elmhurst, IL 630-530-5370
Tova Industries LLC
   Louisville, KY 888-532-8682

Lamb

Sentry Seasonings
   Elmhurst, IL 630-530-5370

Meat

A. Lassonde Inc.
   Rougemont, QC 866-552-7643
Allegro Fine Foods Inc
   Paris, TN. .731-642-6113
American Culinary Garden
   Springfield, MO 888-831-2433
Booneway Farms
   Berea, KY. 859-986-2636
Bunker Foods Corp.
   New York, NY 646-738-4020
Cajun Original Foods Inc
   New Iberia, LA. 337-367-1344
Centennial Food Corporation
   Calgary, AB. 403-214-0044
Cinnabar Specialty Foods Inc
   Prescott, AZ 866-293-6433
Con Yeager Spice Co
   Zelienople, PA. 800-222-2460
D & D Foods Inc
   West Des Moines, IA 800-772-4098
Favorite Foods
   Burnaby, BC 604-420-5100
Genarom International
   Cranbury, NJ. 609-409-6200
L & S Packing Co
   Farmingdale, NY 800-286-6487
Lawry's Foods
   Hunt Valley, MD. 800-952-9797
Magic Seasoning Blends
   New Orleans, LA 800-457-2857
Mrs. Dog's Products
   Grand Rapids, MI 800-267-7364
Newly Weds Foods Inc
   Chicago, IL 800-621-7521
Parthenon Food Products
   Ann Arbor, MI 734-994-1012
Passetti's Pride
   Hayward, CA 800-521-4659
Produits Ronald
   St. Damase, QC. 800-465-0118
Red Creek Marinade Company
   Amarillo, TX. 800-687-9114
Rob Salamida Co Inc
   Johnson City, NY 800-545-5072
San Antonio Farms
   Platteville, WI. 800-236-1119
Sentry Seasonings
   Elmhurst, IL 630-530-5370
Sparrow Lane
   Ceres, CA .866-515-2477
Stanchfield Farms
   Milo, ME. 207-732-5173
Sweet Peas Floral Design
   Stockton, CA. 209-472-9284
Tova Industries LLC
   Louisville, KY 888-532-8682

Mayonaise

C.F. Sauer Co.
   Richmond, VA. 888-723-0052
Clements Foods Co
   Oklahoma City, OK 800-654-8355
Consumer Guild Foods Inc
   Toledo, OH 419-726-3406
Conway Import Co Inc
   Franklin Park, IL. 800-323-8801
Cuisine Perel
   Richmond, CA 800-887-3735
Empire Mayonaise Company, LLC.
   Brooklyn, NY 718-636-2069
Erba Food Products
   Brooklyn, NY 718-272-7700
GFA Brands Inc
   Paramus, NJ 201-568-9300

Product Categories / Sauces, Dips & Dressings: Mustard

Girard's Food Service Dressings
   City of Industry, CA 888-327-8442
GoAvo
   Montville, NJ 973-534-9951
Green Garden Food Products
   Sandpoint, ID 800-669-3169
Heinz Portion Control
   Jacksonville, FL 904-695-1300
IFM
   New York, NY 212-229-1633
Intercorp Excelle Foods
   North York, ON 888-473-6337
JUST Inc
   San Francisco, CA 844-423-6637
Kruger Foods
   Stockton, CA 209-941-8518
Litehouse Foods
   Sandpoint, ID 800-669-3169
Mardale Specialty Foods
   Waukegan, IL 845-299-0285
Oasis Food Co
   Hillside, NJ 800-275-0477
Olde Tyme Mercantile
   Arroyo Grande, CA 805-489-7991
Piknik Products Company
   Montgomery, AL 334-240-2218
Primal Nutrition
   Malibu, CA 888-774-6259
Purity Products
   Plainview, NY 800-256-6102
Rapazzini Winery
   Gilroy, CA 800-842-6262
Restaurant Lulu Gourmet Products
   San Francisco, CA 888-693-5800
Royal Food Products
   Indianapolis, IN 317-782-2660
San Gennaro Foods Inc
   Kent, WA 800-462-1916
Stickney & Poor Company
   Peterborough, NH 603-924-2259
Stonewall Kitchen
   York, ME 800-826-1752
Unilever US
   Englewood Cliffs, NJ 800-298-5018
Ventura Foods LLC
   Brea, CA 800-421-6257
Victoria Amory & Co LLC
   Greenwich, CT 203-220-6454
Wood Brothers Inc
   West Columbia, SC 803-796-5146

Mustard

G.S. Dunn Limited
   Hamilton, ON 905-522-0833

Brown

G.S. Dunn Limited
   Hamilton, ON 905-522-0833
GoldRush Mustard
   Dallas, TX 214-335-8345
International Food Products
   Fenton, MO 800-227-8427
Mizkan Americas Inc
   Mount Prospect, IL 800-323-4358
Monastary Mustard
   Angel, OR 503-949-6321
Raye's Old Fashioned Gourmet Mustard
   Eastport, ME 800-853-1903
Reckitt Benckiser LLC
   Parsippany, NJ 973-404-2600
Stickney & Poor Company
   Peterborough, NH 603-924-2259
Stonewall Kitchen
   York, ME 800-826-1752

Oriental

G.S. Dunn Limited
   Hamilton, ON 905-522-0833
GS Dunn & Company
   Hamilton, ON 905-522-0833
HerbNZest LLC
   Princeton, NJ 917-582-1191

Yellow

CMS Fine Foods
   Healdsburg, CA 707-473-9561
Country Cupboard
   Lewisburg, PA 570-523-3211
Finding Home Farms
   Middletown, NY 845-355-4335

Flaherty Inc
   Skokie, IL 847-966-1005
G.S. Dunn Limited
   Hamilton, ON 905-522-0833
GS Dunn & Company
   Hamilton, ON 905-522-0833
Honey Acres
   Neosho, WI 920-474-4411
International Food Products
   Fenton, MO 800-227-8427
Marathon Enterprises Inc
   Englewood, NJ 800-722-7388
Miller's Mustard LLC
   Gibsonia, PA 412-894-7172
Portlandia Foods
   Portland, OR 833-739-3663
Raye's Mustard
   Eastport, ME 800-853-1903
Reckitt Benckiser LLC
   Parsippany, NJ 973-404-2600
Silver Spring Foods
   Eau Clair, MI 800-826-7322
Stickney & Poor Company
   Peterborough, NH 603-924-2259
Stonewall Kitchen
   York, ME 800-826-1752
Victoria Amory & Co LLC
   Greenwich, CT 203-220-6454

Salad Dressings

A Perfect Pear
   Napa, CA 800-553-5753
Allied Old English Inc
   Port Reading, NJ 732-602-8955
American Spoon Foods Inc
   Petoskey, MI 888-735-6700
Angelo Pietro Honolulu
   Honolulu, HI 808-941-0555
Annie's Naturals
   Berkeley, CA 800-434-1234
Arbor Hill Grapery & Winery
   Naples, NY 800-554-7553
Arcobasso Foods Inc
   Hazlewood, MO 800-284-0620
Argee Corp
   Santee, CA 800-449-3030
Argo Century, Inc.
   Jacksonville, FL 800-446-7108
Arizona Sunland Foods
   Tucson, AZ 520-624-7068
Ashman Manufacturing & Distributing Company
   Virginia Beach, VA 800-641-9924
Atlantic Seasonings
   Kinston, NC 800-433-5261
B & G Foods Inc.
   Parsippany, NJ 973-401-6500
Bahama Specialty Foods
   Durham, NC 919-471-4051
Baldwin Richardson Foods
   Oakbrook Terrace, IL 866-644-2732
Bartush Schnitzius Foods Co
   Lewisville, TX 972-219-1270
Baycliff Co Inc
   Garwood, NJ 866-772-7569
Bear Meadow Farm
   Ashfield, MA 413-628-3970
Best Foods
   Englewood Cliffs, NJ 201-894-4000
Best Maid Products, Inc.
   Fort Worth, TX 800-447-3581
Betty Lou's
   McMinnville, OR 800-242-5205
Boudreaux's Foods
   New Orleans, LA 504-733-8440
BP Gourmet
   Hauppauge, NY 631-234-8200
Buckhead Gourmet
   Atlanta, GA 800-673-6338
C W Resources Inc
   New Britain, CT 860-229-7700
C.F. Sauer Co.
   Richmond, VA 888-723-0052
California Custom Foods
   Fullerton, CA 714-870-0490
Carole's Cheesecake Company
   Toronto, ON 416-256-0000
Chelten House Products
   Swedesboro, NJ
Chicama Vineyards
   West Tisbury, MA 888-244-2262
Choice Food Distributors LLC
   Nashville, TN 615-350-6070

Christie's
   Stroughton, MA 781-341-3341
CHS Inc.
   Inver Grove Hts., MN 800-328-6539
Clements Foods Co
   Oklahoma City, OK 800-654-8355
CMS Fine Foods
   Healdsburg, CA 707-473-9561
Consumer Guild Foods Inc
   Toledo, OH 419-726-3406
Conway Import Co Inc
   Franklin Park, IL 800-323-8801
Corsair Pepper Sauce
   Gulfport, MS 228-452-0311
Country Fresh Food & Confections, Inc.
   Oliver Springs, TN 800-545-8782
Creative Foodworks Inc
   San Antonio, TX 210-212-4761
Cuisine Perel
   Richmond, CA 800-887-3735
D & D Foods Inc
   West Des Moines, IA 800-772-4098
Delicae Gourmet
   Tarpon Springs, FL 800-942-2502
Diane's Signature Products
   Edmond, OK 405-509-3311
Dorina So-Good Inc
   Union, IL 815-923-2144
Drusilla Seafood
   Baton Rouge, LA 800-364-8844
Dynamic Foods
   Lubbock, TX 806-723-5600
Earth & Vine Provisions Inc
   Lincoln, CA 888-723-8463
Earth Balance
   Boulder, CO 866-234-6429
Earth Island
   Chatsworth, CA 888-394-3949
Farmdale Creamery Inc
   San Bernardino, CA 800-346-7306
Food Source Company
   Mississauga, ON 905-625-8404
Foods Alive
   Angola, IN 260-488-4497
Gedney Foods Co
   Sun Valley, CA 888-244-0653
GFA Brands Inc
   Paramus, NJ 201-568-9300
Girard's Food Service Dressings
   City of Industry, CA 888-327-8442
Gold Pure Food Products Co. Inc.
   Hempstead, NY 800-422-4681
Golden Specialty Foods Inc
   Norwalk, CA 562-802-2537
Golden State Foods Corp
   Irvine, CA 949-247-8000
Green Garden Food Products
   Sandpoint, ID 800-669-3169
Greenjoy
   Okatie, SC
Griffith Foods Inc.
   Alsip, IL 708-371-0900
Grouse Hunt Farm Inc
   Tamaqua, PA 570-467-2850
Hagerty Foods
   Orange, CA 714-628-1230
Hanley's Foods Inc.
   Baton Rouge, LA 225-366-0992
Harpo's
   Honolulu, HI 808-735-6456
Hartville Kitchen
   Hartville, OH 330-877-9353
Haven's Kitchen Sauces
   New York, NY 212-929-7900
Hell On The Red Inc
   Telephone, TX 903-664-2573
House of Herbs LLC
   Passaic, NJ 973-779-2422
IFM
   New York, NY 212-229-1633
Intercorp Excelle Foods
   North York, ON 888-473-6337
Jed's Maple Products
   Derby, VT 802-766-2700
JUST Inc
   San Francisco, CA 844-423-6637
Kaari Foods
   Brooklyn, NY
Kauai Organic Farms
   Kilauea, HI 808-651-8843
Ken's Foods Inc
   Marlborough, MA 508-229-1100

Product Categories / Sauces, Dips & Dressings: Salad Dressings

Kerry Foodservice
  Mansfield, OH 800-533-2722
Kosto Food Products Co
  Wauconda, IL 847-487-2600
Kozlowski Farms
  Forestville, CA 800-473-2767
Kraft Heinz Canada
  North York, ON 416-441-5000
KT's Kitchens
  Carson, CA 310-764-0850
L & S Packing Co
  Farmingdale, NY 800-286-6487
Lasco Foods Inc
  St Louis, MO 314-832-1906
Litehouse Foods
  Sandpoint, ID 800-669-3169
Live A Little Gourmet Foods
  Oakland, CA 888-744-2300
Love'n Herbs
  Waterbury, CT 203-756-4932
Lynch Foods
  North York, ON 416-449-5464
Mad Will's Food Company
  Auburn, CA 888-275-9455
Maple Grove Farms Of Vermont
  St Johnsbury, VT 802-748-5141
Mardale Specialty Foods
  Waukegan, IL 845-299-0285
Marie's Quality Foods
  Brea, CA 800-339-1051
Marina Foods
  Medley, FL 786-888-0129
Marjon Specialty Foods Inc
  Plant City, FL 813-752-3482
Marukan Vinegar USA Inc.
  Paramount, CA 562-630-6060
Marzetti
  Columbus, OH 614-846-2232
Mayacamas Fine Foods
  Sonoma, CA 800-826-9621
Mccutcheon Apple Products
  Frederick, MD 800-888-7537
Mermaid Spice Corporation
  Fort Myers, FL 239-693-1986
Michelle's RawFoodz
  Chicago, IL 312-442-0406
Milani
  Muscatine, IA 800-442-5242
Milos Whole World Gourmet
  Athens, OH 866-589-6456
Mixon Fruit Farms Inc
  Bradenton, FL 800-608-2525
Mod Squad Martha
  Johns Island, SC 615-476-3696
Mother Raw
  Toronto, ON 855-464-0117
Mother Teresa's
  Clute, TX 888-265-7429
Mucky Duck Mustard Company
  Ferndale, MI 248-544-4610
Mullens Dressing
  Palestine, IL 618-586-2727
Mullins Food Products
  Broadview, IL 708-344-3224
Napa Valley Kitchens
  Napa, CA 707-254-3700
Nonna Pia's Gourmet Sauces
  Whistler, BC 888-372-1534
North American Enterprises
  Tucson, AZ 800-817-8666
North Coast Farms
  Santa Cruz, CA 831-426-3733
North Coast Processing
  Carlsbad, CA 760-931-6809
O'Brian Brothers Food
  Cincinnati, OH 513-791-9909
Oasis Food Co
  Hillside, NJ 800-275-0477
Ocean Spray International
  Lakeville-Middleboro, MA . . . 800-662-3263
Olde Tyme Mercantile
  Arroyo Grande, CA 805-489-7991
Ott Food Products Co
  Carthage, MO 800-866-2585
Pacific Harvest Products
  Bellevue, WA 425-401-7990
Pacific Westcoast Foods
  Beaverton, OR 800-874-9533
Parthenon Food Products
  Ann Arbor, MI 734-994-1012
Piknik Products Company
  Montgomery, AL 334-240-2218
Porinos Gourmet Food
  Central Falls, RI 800-826-3938
Primal Kitchen
  Oxnard, CA 888-774-6259
Primal Nutrition
  Malibu, CA 888-774-6259
Purity Products
  Plainview, NY 800-256-6102
Quality Foods
  Qualicum Beach, BC 877-833-7890
Quong Hop & Company
  S San Francisco, CA 650-553-9900
Risvold's Inc.
  Gardena, CA 323-770-2674
River Town Foods Corp
  St Louis, MO 800-844-3210
Rosmarino Foods/R.Z. Humbert Company
  Odessa, FL 888-926-9053
Royal Food Products
  Indianapolis, IN 317-782-2660
Royal Resources
  New Orleans, LA 800-888-9932
Salad Girl Inc
  Mahtomedi, MN 651-653-9155
San Diego Soy Dairy
  El Cajon, CA 619-447-8638
San Gennaro Foods Inc
  Kent, WA 800-462-1916
San-J International Inc
  Henrico, VA 800-446-5500
Saratoga Salad Dressing
  Canton, MA 781-821-1010
Schlotterbeck & Foss Company
  Portland, ME 800-777-4666
Select Food Products
  Toronto, ON 800-699-8016
Sentry Seasonings
  Elmhurst, IL 630-530-5370
Shawnee Canning Co
  Cross Junction, VA 800-713-1414
Silver Palate Kitchens
  Cresskill, NJ 201-568-0110
Sky Valley Foods
  Danville, VA
Southern Art Company, LLC
  Atlanta, GA 800-257-6606
Sprague Foods
  Belleville, ON 613-966-1200
Stickney & Poor Company
  Peterborough, NH 603-924-2259
Swagger Foods Corp
  Vernon Hills, IL 847-913-1200
Sweet Earth Foods
  Moss Landing, CA 800-737-3311
T'Lish Dressings and Marinades
  Opelika, AL 205-503-8603
T. Marzetti Company
  Westerville, OH 800-999-1835
Tasty Toppings Inc
  Columbus, NE 800-228-4148
Tessemae's All Natural
  Essex, MD 855-698-3773
Tex-Mex Gourmet
  Brenham, TX 888-345-8467
TexaFrance
  Round Rock, TX 800-776-8937
The Lollipop Tree, Inc
  Auburn, NY 800-842-6691
Thistledew Farm
  Proctor, WV 800-854-6639
Tillie's Gourmet
  Doylestown, PA 215-272-8326
Trader Vic's Food Products
  Emeryville, CA 877-762-4824
Triple H Food Processors Inc
  Riverside, CA 951-352-5700
Tulocay Cemetery
  Napa, CA 888-627-2859
Unilever US
  Englewood Cliffs, NJ 800-298-5018
Valley Grain Products
  Fresno, CA 559-675-3400
Ventura Foods LLC
  Brea, CA 800-421-6257
Vincent Formusa Company
  Des Plaines, IL 847-813-6040
Virginia Honey Company
  Inwood, WV 304-267-8500
Vita Food Products Inc
  Chicago, IL 800-989-8482
Vitasoy USA
  Woburn, MA 800-848-2769
Walden Farms
  Linden, NJ 800-229-1706
Westin Foods
  Omaha, NE 800-228-6098
White Oak Farm and Table
  Westport, CT 203-716-1577
Wild Thymes Farm Inc
  Greenville, NY 845-266-8387
WillowOak Farms
  Amherst, VA 888-963-2767
Wine Country Kitchens
  Napa, CA 866-767-9463
Wizards Cauldron, LTD
  Yanceyville, NC 336-694-5665
Wood Brothers Inc
  West Columbia, SC 803-796-5146
World Flavors Inc
  Warminster, PA 215-672-4400
Yo Mama's Foods
  Gainesville, FL
York Mountain Winery
  Templeton, CA 805-237-7575

Balsamic Vinegar

Adams Olive Ranch
  Lindsay, CA 888-216-5483
Buckhead Gourmet
  Atlanta, GA 800-673-6338
Colonna Brothers Inc
  North Bergen, NJ 201-864-1115
Conway Import Co Inc
  Franklin Park, IL 800-323-8801
De Nigris
  Totowa, NJ 973-837-6791
Manassero Farms
  Irvine, CA 949-554-5103
Milani
  Muscatine, IA 800-442-5242
Newman's Own
  Westport, CT 203-222-0136

Blue Cheese

Conway Import Co Inc
  Franklin Park, IL 800-323-8801
Litehouse Foods
  Sandpoint, ID 800-669-3169
Wood Brothers Inc
  West Columbia, SC 803-796-5146

Ceasar

Conway Import Co Inc
  Franklin Park, IL 800-323-8801
HV Food Products Co
  Oakland, CA 877-853-7262
Litehouse Foods
  Sandpoint, ID 800-669-3169
Newman's Own
  Westport, CT 203-222-0136

Creamy Dijon

Conway Import Co Inc
  Franklin Park, IL 800-323-8801
Mullens Dressing
  Palestine, IL 618-586-2727
Stinking Rose, The
  San Francisco, CA 800-995-7674

French

Litehouse Foods
  Sandpoint, ID 800-669-3169
Milani
  Muscatine, IA 800-442-5242
O'Brian Brothers Food
  Cincinnati, OH 513-791-9909
Ott Food Products Co
  Carthage, MO 800-866-2585
Wood Brothers Inc
  West Columbia, SC 803-796-5146

Gourmet

Betty Lou's
  McMinnville, OR 800-242-5205
Olde Tyme Mercantile
  Arroyo Grande, CA 805-489-7991
Salad Girl Inc
  Mahtomedi, MN 651-653-9155

Product Categories / Sauces, Dips & Dressings: Salsa

Italian Style

Conway Import Co Inc
 Franklin Park, IL 800-323-8801
Hartville Kitchen
 Hartville, OH 330-877-9353
HV Food Products Co
 Oakland, CA 877-853-7262
Litehouse Foods
 Sandpoint, ID 800-669-3169
Mullens Dressing
 Palestine, IL 618-586-2727
Newman's Own
 Westport, CT 203-222-0136
O'Brian Brothers Food
 Cincinnati, OH 513-791-9909
Olde Tyme Mercantile
 Arroyo Grande, CA 805-489-7991
Ott Food Products Co
 Carthage, MO 800-866-2585
Wood Brothers Inc
 West Columbia, SC 803-796-5146

Mixes

CHS Inc.
 Inver Grove Hts., MN 800-328-6539
Frontier Co-op
 Norway, IA 844-550-6200
Gourmet du Village
 Morin-Heights, QC 800-668-2314
House of Thaller Inc
 Knoxville, TN 800-462-3365
Kokopelli's Kitchen
 Phoenix, AZ 888-943-9802
R C Fine Foods Inc
 Hillsborough, NJ 800-526-3953

Oil & Vinegar

Marukan Vinegar USA Inc.
 Paramount, CA 562-630-6060

Ranch

Ott Food Products Co
 Carthage, MO 800-866-2585

Non-Fat

Betty Lou's
 McMinnville, OR 800-242-5205
Marukan Vinegar USA Inc.
 Paramount, CA 562-630-6060
Walden Farms
 Linden, NJ 800-229-1706

Oil & Vinegar

Au Printemps Gourmet
 Saint-Jerome, QC 800-438-6676
Conway Import Co Inc
 Franklin Park, IL 800-323-8801
Gourm, Mist
 Sunny Isles Beach, FL 866-502-8472
Litehouse Foods
 Sandpoint, ID 800-669-3169
Marukan Vinegar USA Inc.
 Paramount, CA 562-630-6060
Newman's Own
 Westport, CT 203-222-0136

Ranch

Conway Import Co Inc
 Franklin Park, IL 800-323-8801
Hartville Kitchen
 Hartville, OH 330-877-9353
HV Food Products Co
 Oakland, CA 877-853-7262
Litehouse Foods
 Sandpoint, ID 800-669-3169
Newman's Own
 Westport, CT 203-222-0136
O'Brian Brothers Food
 Cincinnati, OH 513-791-9909

Raspberry Vinegrette

Litehouse Foods
 Sandpoint, ID 800-669-3169
Rising Sun Farms
 Phoenix, OR 800-888-0795

Thousand Island

Conway Import Co Inc
 Franklin Park, IL 800-323-8801
Wood Brothers Inc
 West Columbia, SC 803-796-5146

Salsa

505 Southwestern
 Meridian, ID
Alimentaire Whyte's Inc
 Laval, QC 866-420-9520
Allied Old English Inc
 Port Reading, NJ 732-602-8955
American Spoon Foods Inc
 Petoskey, MI 888-735-6700
Amigos Canning Company
 San Antonio, TX 210-798-5360
Ana's Salsa
 Austin, TX. 888-849-7054
Appledore Cove LLC
 North Berwick, ME 207-676-4088
Arizona Cowboy
 Phoenix, AZ 800-529-8627
Ashman Manufacturing & Distributing Company
 Virginia Beach, VA 800-641-9924
B & G Foods Inc.
 Parsippany, NJ 973-401-6500
Bartush Schnitzius Foods Co
 Lewisville, TX 972-219-1270
BBQ Bunch
 Kansas City, MO 816-941-4534
Beaverton Foods Inc
 Hillsboro, OR 800-223-8076
Bel Brands USA
 Chicago, IL 312-462-1500
Better Made Snack Foods
 Detroit, MI 800-332-2394
Bien Padre Foods Inc
 Eureka, CA 707-442-4585
Big B Barbecue
 Evansville, IN 812-425-5235
Blueberry Store
 Grand Junction, MI 877-654-2400
Border Foods
 New Hope, MN 763-559-7338
C W Resources Inc
 New Britain, CT 860-229-7700
Cajohn's Fiery Foods Co
 Westerville, OH 888-703-3473
California-Antilles Trading
 San Diego, CA 800-330-6450
Casa Visco
 Schenectady, NY 888-607-2823
Catamount Specialties of Vermont
 Plainfield, VT 800-639-2406
Cedar's Mediterranean Foods
 Ward Hill, MA 978-372-8010
Cervantes Food Products Inc
 Albuquerque, NM 877-982-4453
Charlie Beigg's Sauce Company
 Windham, ME 888-502-8595
Chelten House Products
 Swedesboro, NJ
Chimayo To Go / Cibolo Junction
 Albuquerque, NM 800-683-9628
Choice of Vermont
 Destin, FL 800-444-6261
Cinnabar Specialty Foods Inc
 Prescott, AZ 866-293-6433
Circle R Ranch
 Flower Mound, TX 800-247-3077
Ciro Foods
 Pittsburgh, PA 412-771-9018
Colorado Salsa Company
 Littleton, CO 303-932-2617
Country Cupboard
 Lewisburg, PA 570-523-3211
Cowgirl Chocolates
 Moscow, ID 888-882-4098
Creative Foodworks Inc
 San Antonio, TX 210-212-4761
Cuizina Food Company
 Woodinville, WA 425-486-7000
Custom Food Solutions LLC
 Louisville, KY 800-767-2993
Dave's Gourmet
 San Rafael, CA 800-758-0372
Dei Fratelli
 Toledo, OH 800-837-1631
DelGrosso Foods
 Tipton, PA 800-521-5880

Delgrosso Foods Inc.
 Tipton, PA 800-521-5880
Desert Pepper Trading Co
 El Paso, TX 888-472-5727
Dockside Market
 Key Largo, FL 800-813-2253
Dorina So-Good Inc
 Union, IL 815-923-2144
E.D. Smith Foods Ltd
 Hamilton, ON 905-573-1207
Edward Johnson's Salsa
 Flemington, NJ
El Toro Food Products
 Watsonville, CA 831-728-9266
Famous Chili Inc
 Fort Smith, AR 479-782-0096
Fiesta Gourmet of Tejas
 Canyon Lake, TX 800-585-8250
Fischer & Wieser Spec Foods
 Fredericksburg, TX 877-861-0260
Food Processor of New Mexico
 Albuquerque, NM 877-634-3772
Ford's Gourmet Foods
 Raleigh, NC 800-446-0947
Forge Mountain Foods
 Hendersonville, NC 800-823-6743
Fountain Valley Foods
 Colorado Springs, CO 719-573-6012
Fremont Authentic Brands
 Fremont, OH 419-334-8995
Frog Ranch Foods
 Glouster, OH 800-742-2488
Galena Canning Co
 Galena, IL 815-777-9495
Garden Complements Inc
 Kansas City, MO 800-966-1091
Garden Fresh Gourmet
 Ferndale, MI 866-725-7239
Gedney Foods Co
 Sun Valley, CA 888-244-0653
Gingro Corp
 Manchester Center, VT 802-362-0836
Giovanni Food Co Inc
 Syracuse, NY 315-457-2373
Gold Pure Food Products Co. Inc.
 Hempstead, NY 800-422-4681
Golden Specialty Foods Inc
 Norwalk, CA 562-802-2537
Green Mountain Gringo
 Winston-Salem, NC 888-875-3111
Gringo Jack's
 Manchester Ctr, VT 802-362-0836
Guiltless Gourmet
 Newark, NJ 201-553-1100
Gumpert's Canada
 Mississauga, ON 800-387-9324
Hagerty Foods
 Orange, CA 714-628-1230
Havana's Limited
 Titusville, FL 321-267-0513
Heidi's Salsa
 Los Angeles, CA 310-821-0211
Hirzel Canning Co & Farms
 Luckey, OH 419-419-7525
Hol, Mol,
 Long Beach, CA 877-310-8453
Hormel Foods Corp.
 Austin, MN 507-437-5611
Hot Licks
 Spring Valley, CA 888-766-6468
Hot Mama's Foods
 Springfield, MA 413-737-6572
Hot Wachula's
 Lakeland, FL 877-883-8700
Hume Specialties
 Chester, VT 802-875-3117
Imus Ranch Foods
 Darien, CT 888-284-4687
Indel Food Products Inc
 El Paso, TX 800-472-0159
JC's Midnite Salsa
 Tucson, AZ 800-817-2572
Jillipepper
 Albuquerque, NM 505-609-8409
JNB Foods, LLC
 Albany, NY 607-267-5874
Joe Hutson Foods
 Jacksonville, FL 904-731-9065
Kettle Master
 Hillsville, VA 276-728-7571
Kind Snacks
 New York, NY 855-884-5463

Product Categories / Sauces, Dips & Dressings: Sauces

Kozlowski Farms
   Forestville, CA 800-473-2767
LA Canasta Mexican Foods
   Phoenix, AZ 855-269-7721
La Esquina Food Products
   New York, NY 646-710-3183
LA Vencedora Products Inc
   Los Angeles, CA 800-327-2572
La Victoria Foods
   Austin, MN 800-725-7212
Laredo Tortilleria & Mexican
   Fort Wayne, IN 800-252-7336
Las Cruces Brand Products
   El Paso, TX 915-779-5709
Leigh Olivers
   Tyler, TX. 903-245-9183
Leona's Restaurante
   Chimayo, NM 888-561-5569
Li'l Guy Foods
   Kansas City, MO. 800-886-8226
Litehouse Foods
   Sandpoint, ID 800-669-3169
Los Chileros
   Albuquerque, NM 505-768-1100
Lowcountry Produce
   Raleigh, NC 800-935-2792
Mad Will's Food Company
   Auburn, CA. 888-275-9455
Miguel's Stowe Away
   Stowe, VT 800-448-6517
Mixon Fruit Farms Inc
   Bradenton, FL. 800-608-2525
My Brother's Salsa
   Bentonville, AR 479-271-9404
Naked Infusions LLC
   Calabasas, CA 818-239-9058
Native Kjalii Foods
   San Francisco, CA 415-522-5580
O'Garvey Sauces
   New Braunfels, TX. 830-620-6127
Ocean Spray International
   Lakeville-Middleboro, MA 800-662-3263
Paisley Farms Inc
   Willoughby, OH 800-474-5688
Palmieri Food Products
   New Haven, CT 800-845-5447
Paradise Products Corporation
   Boca Raton, FL 800-826-1235
Patricia Quintana
   Los Angeles, CA
Pepper Creek Farms
   Lawton, OK. 800-526-8132
Plocky's Fine Snacks
   Hinsdale, IL 630-323-8888
Quality Foods
   Qualicum Beach, BC 877-833-7890
Rapazzini Winery
   Gilroy, CA. 800-842-6262
Ready Foods Inc
   Denver, CO 800-748-1218
Red Gold Inc.
   Elwood, IN 866-729-7187
Renfro Foods
   Fort Worth, TX 800-332-2456
Reva Foods
   Saint Petersburg, FL 727-692-1292
Riba Foods
   Houston, TX. 800-327-7422
Royal Resources
   New Orleans, LA 800-888-9932
Ruffner's
   Wayne, PA. 610-687-9800
Sabor Mexicano
   Berkeley, CA
Sabra Dipping Company,LL
   Oceanside, CA 800-748-5523
Sabra-Go Mediterranean
   Dallas, TX. 888-957-2272
Salsa God
   New York, NY 646-359-0573
Sambets Cajun Deli
   Austin, TX. 800-472-6238
San Antonio Farms
   Platteville, WI 800-236-1119
Santa Barbara Olive Company
   Santa Barbara, CA 800-624-4896
Santa Barbara Salsa/California Creative
   Oceanside, CA 800-748-5523
Sechler's Fine Pickles
   Saint Joe, IN 800-332-5461
Select Food Products
   Toronto, ON 800-699-8016

Shawnee Canning Co
   Cross Junction, VA 800-713-1414
Sky Valley Foods
   Danville, VA
Slawsa
   Cramerton, NC
Smiling Fox Pepper Company
   North Aurora, IL 972-754-2820
Southern Bar-B-Que
   Jennings, LA 866-612-2586
Southwest Spirit
   Socorro, NM 800-838-0773
Soylent Brand
   Irving, TX. 972-255-4747
Spruce Foods
   San Clemente, CA 800-326-3612
Steel's Gourmet Foods, Ltd.
   Bridgeport, PA 800-678-3357
Stello Foods Inc
   Punxsutawney, PA. 800-849-4599
Steve Mendez
   Woodland, CA. 530-662-0512
Stinking Rose, The
   San Francisco, CA 800-995-7674
SuckerPunch Gourmet
   Bridgeview, IL 708-784-3000
Sun Harvest Foods Inc
   San Diego, CA 619-661-0909
Sunny Dell Foods Inc
   Oxford, PA 610-932-5164
T.W. Garner Food Company
   Winston Salem, NC. 800-476-7383
Taste Weavers
   Urbana, OH 888-810-8365
Tenayo
   New York, NY 917-677-7607
Terrell's Potato Chip Co
   Syracuse, NY 315-437-2786
Texas Heat
   San Antonio, TX. 800-656-5916
Texas Tamale Co
   Houston, TX. 713-795-5500
The Brooklyn Salsa Co LLC
   Ridgewood, NY 347-470-5493
The Vine
   Manhasset, NY 516-365-8463
Timber Peaks Gourmet
   Parker, CO. 800-982-7687
Todd's Salsa
   Bangor, ME. 844-328-7257
Ultimate Salsa
   Charlotte, NC 888-827-2572
Uncle Fred's Fine Foods
   Rockport, TX 361-729-8320
Vegetable Juices Inc
   Chicago, IL. 888-776-9752
Vita Food Products Inc
   Chicago, IL. 800-989-8482
Walker Foods
   Los Angeles, CA 800-966-5199
Wing Nien Food
   Hayward, CA 510-487-8877
Ximena's Latin Flavors
   Spicewood, TX 817-821-3246
Xochitl
   Dallas, TX. 866-595-8917
Zuni Foods
   San Antonio, TX. 800-906-3876

Canned

Kozlowski Farms
   Forestville, CA 800-473-2767
Palmieri Food Products
   New Haven, CT 800-845-5447
T.W. Garner Food Company
   Winston Salem, NC. 800-476-7383

Chunky

Newman's Own
   Westport, CT. 203-222-0136
T.W. Garner Food Company
   Winston Salem, NC. 800-476-7383

Mild

Garden Fresh Gourmet
   Ferndale, MI 866-725-7239
Hot Wachula's
   Lakeland, FL. 877-883-8700
JC's Midnite Salsa
   Tucson, AZ 800-817-2572

Sabra Dipping Company,LL
   Oceanside, CA 800-748-5523
T.W. Garner Food Company
   Winston Salem, NC. 800-476-7383
Ultimate Salsa
   Charlotte, NC 888-827-2572

Picante

Bartush Schnitzius Foods Co
   Lewisville, TX 972-219-1270
Garden Fresh Gourmet
   Ferndale, MI 866-725-7239
Hormel Foods Corp.
   Austin, MN 507-437-5611
Hot Wachula's
   Lakeland, FL. 877-883-8700
JC's Midnite Salsa
   Tucson, AZ 800-817-2572
T.W. Garner Food Company
   Winston Salem, NC. 800-476-7383
Texas Heat
   San Antonio, TX. 800-656-5916
Ultimate Salsa
   Charlotte, NC 888-827-2572

with Cheese

Amigos Canning Company
   San Antonio, TX. 210-798-5360
Delgrosso Foods Inc.
   Tipton, PA. 800-521-5880

Sauces

505 Southwestern
   Meridian, ID
A Southern Season
   Hillsborough, NC 800-253-3663
Ajinomoto Foods North America, Inc.
   Ontario, CA 909-477-4700
Ajinomoto Heartland Inc
   Chicago, IL. 773-380-7000
Al Dente Pasta Co
   Whitmore Lake, MI 800-536-7278
Alimentaire Whyte's Inc
   Laval, QC 866-420-9520
Allegro Fine Foods Inc
   Paris, TN 731-642-6113
Allied Old English Inc
   Port Reading, NJ 732-602-8955
American Culinary Garden
   Springfield, MO 888-831-2433
American Spoon Foods Inc
   Petoskey, MI 888-735-6700
Amigos Canning Company
   San Antonio, TX. 210-798-5360
Amy's Kitchen Inc
   Santa Rosa, CA 707-781-6600
Angelo Pietro Honolulu
   Honolulu, HI 808-941-0555
Ankle Deep Foods
   Norfolk, NE. 402-371-6707
Annie Chun's
   Los Angeles, CA 415-479-8272
Annie's Naturals
   Berkeley, CA. 800-434-1234
Apecka Peppered Pickles
   Rockwall, TX 972-771-7628
Archie Moore's
   Milford, CT. 203-876-5088
Argo Century, Inc.
   Jacksonville, FL 800-446-7108
Arizona Sunland Foods
   Tucson, AZ 520-624-7068
Arlen S Gould & Assoc
   Arlington Hts, IL 847-577-2122
Armanino Foods of Distinction
   Hayward, CA 800-255-8588
Ashman Manufacturing & Distributing Company
   Virginia Beach, VA. 800-641-9924
ASK Foods Inc
   Palmyra, PA. 800-879-4275
Atlanta Burning Bush
   Newnan, GA. 800-665-5611
Atlantic Seasonings
   Kinston, NC 800-433-5261
Au Printemps Gourmet
   Saint-Jerome, QC 800-438-6676
Aunt Aggie De's Pralines
   Sinton, TX 800-333-9354
Aunt Jenny's Sauces/Melba Foods
   Brooklyn, NY 718-383-3192

Product Categories / Sauces, Dips & Dressings: Sauces

Austin Slow Burn
 Austin, TX....................877-513-3192
B & B Pecan Processors
 Turkey, NC....................866-328-7322
B & G Foods Inc.
 Parsippany, NJ................973-401-6500
Bainbridge Festive Foods
 Farmington, TN................800-545-9205
Bakkavor USA
 Charlotte, NC.................800-842-3025
Baldwin Richardson Foods
 Oakbrook Terrace, IL..........866-644-2732
Barefoot Contessa Pantry
 York, ME......................800-826-1752
Barhyte Specialty Foods Inc
 Pendleton, OR.................800-227-4983
Bartush Schnitzius Foods Co
 Lewisville, TX................972-219-1270
Basic Food Flavors
 North Las Vegas, NV...........702-643-0043
Baumer Foods Inc
 Metairie, LA..................504-482-5761
Bay Valley Foods
 El Paso, TX...................800-236-1119
Baycliff Co Inc
 Garwood, NJ...................866-772-7569
BBQ Bunch
 Kansas City, MO...............816-941-4534
BBQ Shack
 Paola, KS.....................913-294-5908
BBQ'n Fools Catering, LLC
 Greenfield, NJ................800-671-8652
Beaverton Foods Inc
 Hillsboro, OR.................800-223-8076
Beetnik Foods, LLC
 Austin, TX....................512-548-8228
Bel Brands USA
 Chicago, IL...................312-462-1500
Bellisio Foods
 Minneapolis, MN
Berner Food & Beverage LLC
 Dakota, IL....................800-819-8199
Bettah Buttah, LLC
 Kansas City, KS...............800-568-8468
Bien Padre Foods Inc
 Eureka, CA....................707-442-4585
Big B Barbecue
 Evansville, IN................812-425-5235
Big Poppa Smokers
 Coachella, CA.................877-828-0727
Bittersweet Herb Farm
 Shelburne Falls, MA...........800-456-1599
Blackberry Patch
 Thomasville, GA...............800-853-5598
Blair's Sauces & Snacks
 Highlands, NJ.................800-982-5247
Blue Jay Orchards
 Bethel, CT....................203-748-0119
Blue Smoke Salsa
 Ansted, WV....................888-725-7298
Bodin Foods
 New Iberia, LA................337-367-1344
Bongiovi Brand Pasta Sauces
 Valley Village, CA............434-296-7766
Border Foods
 New Hope, MN..................763-559-7338
Bove's of Vermont
 Burlington, VT................802-862-6651
Brateka Enterprises
 Ocala, FL.....................877-549-3227
Brooklyn Delhi
 Brooklyn, NY
Brother Bru Bru's
 Venice, CA....................310-396-9033
Bruno Specialty Foods
 West Sayville, NY.............631-589-1700
Buckhead Gourmet
 Atlanta, GA...................800-673-6338
Buffalo Wild Wings
 Minneapolis, MN...............763-546-1891
Bunker Foods Corp.
 New York, NY..................646-738-4020
C & E Canners Inc
 Hammonton, NJ.................609-561-1078
C.F. Sauer Co.
 Richmond, VA..................888-723-0052
Cafe Chilku
 Colchester, VT................802-878-4645
Cafe Tequila
 San Francisco, CA.............415-264-0106
Cajohn's Fiery Foods Co
 Westerville, OH...............888-703-3473

Cajun Brands
 New Iberia, LA................504-408-2252
California Balsamic Inc
 Ukiah, CA.....................888-644-5127
California Custom Foods
 Fullerton, CA.................714-870-0490
Campagna Distinct Flavor
 Lebanon, OR...................800-959-4372
Campbell Soup Co.
 Camden, NJ....................800-257-8443
Canada Bread Co, Ltd
 Etobicoke, ON.................800-465-5515
Canyon Specialty Foods
 Dallas, TX....................214-352-1771
Capone Foods
 Somerville, MA................617-629-2296
Captain Bob's Jet Fuel
 Fort Wayne, IN................877-486-6468
Carando Gourmet Frozen Foods
 Agawam, MA....................888-227-2636
Carmela's Gourmet
 Monterey, CA..................831-373-6291
Carol's Country Cuisine
 Glen Ellen, CA................707-996-1124
Carole's Cheesecake Company
 Toronto, ON...................416-256-0000
Carolina Treet
 Wilmington, NC................800-616-6344
Carriere Foods Inc
 Saint-Denis-Sur-Richelie, QC..450-787-3411
Cary Randall's Sauces & Dressings
 Highlands, NJ.................732-872-6353
Casa di Carfagna
 Columbus, OH..................614-846-6340
Casa Di Lisio Products Inc
 Mt Kisco, NY..................800-247-4199
Casa Visco
 Schenectady, NY...............888-607-2823
Catamount Specialties of Vermont
 Plainfield, VT................800-639-2406
Catskill Mountain Specialties
 Saugerties, NY................800-311-3473
Cattle Boyz Foods
 Okotoks, Alberta,, CA.........888-662-9366
Cedarvale Food Products
 Toronto, ON...................416-656-3330
Cervantes Food Products Inc
 Albuquerque, NM...............877-982-4453
Charlie Palmer Group
 New York, NY..................866-458-7224
Chef Merito Inc
 Van Nuys, CA..................800-637-4861
Chef Philippe LLC
 Arlington, TX.................817-461-9049
Chef Shells Catering & Roadside Cafe
 Downtown Port Huron, MI.......810-966-8371
Chef-A-Roni Fancy Foods
 East Greenwich, RI............401-884-8798
Chelten House Products
 Swedesboro, NJ
Cherchies
 Malvern, PA...................800-644-1980
Cherry Hut
 Traverse City, MI.............888-882-4431
Chincoteague Seafood Co Inc
 Parsonsburg, MD...............443-260-4800
Choclatique
 Los Angeles, CA...............310-479-3849
Chocolaterie Bernard Callebaut
 Calgary, AB...................800-661-8367
Christie's
 Stroughton, MA................781-341-3341
Christopher Ranch LLC
 Gilroy, CA....................408-847-1100
Chukar Cherries
 Prosser, WA...................800-624-9544
Cinnabar Specialty Foods Inc
 Prescott, AZ..................866-293-6433
Cipriani's Spaghetti & Sauce Company
 Chicago Heights, IL...........708-755-6212
Circle B Ranch
 Seymour, MO...................417-683-0271
Ciro Foods
 Pittsburgh, PA................412-771-9018
City Saucery
 Staten Island, NY.............718-753-4006
Clarmil Manufacturing Corp
 Hayward, CA...................888-252-7645
Classy Delites
 Austin, TX....................800-440-2648
Clements Foods Co
 Oklahoma City, OK.............800-654-8355

Clofine Dairy Products Inc
 Linwood, NJ...................609-653-1000
CMS Fine Foods
 Healdsburg, CA................707-473-9561
Coach Sposato's Bar-B-Que
 Lincoln, AR...................800-264-7535
Cold Hollow Cider Mill
 Waterbury Center, VT..........800-327-7537
Colgin Co
 Dallas, TX....................888-226-5446
Colonna Brothers Inc
 North Bergen, NJ..............201-864-1115
Colorado Salsa Company
 Littleton, CO.................303-932-2617
Conifer Foods
 Medina, WA....................800-588-9160
Continental Seasoning
 Teaneck, NJ...................800-631-1564
Cook's Pantry
 Ventura, CA...................805-947-4622
Cookies Food Products
 Wall Lake, IA.................800-331-4995
Cordon Bleu International
 Anjou, QC.....................800-363-1182
Corfu Foods Inc
 Bensenville, IL...............630-595-2510
Corine's Cuisine
 Sparks, MD
Corsair Pepper Sauce
 Gulfport, MS..................228-452-0311
Costa Deano's Gourmet Foods
 Canton, OH....................800-337-2823
Country Bob's Inc
 Centralia, IL.................800-373-2140
Country Fresh Food & Confections, Inc.
 Oliver Springs, TN............800-545-8782
Country Village Meats Inc
 Sublette, IL..................800-700-4545
Cowboy Food & Drink
 Chagrin Falls, OH.............800-759-5489
Crave Natural Foods
 Los Angeles, CA...............877-425-2599
Crazy Jerrys Inc Kahuna-Sauces
 Woodstock, GA.................800-347-2823
Creative Foodworks Inc
 San Antonio, TX...............210-212-4761
Crustacean Foods
 Los Angeles, CA...............866-263-2625
Cucina Antica Foods Corp
 Mt Kisco, NY..................877-728-2462
Cugino's Gourmet Foods
 Crystal Lake, IL..............888-592-8446
Cuizina Food Company
 Woodinville, WA...............425-486-7000
Curry King Corporation
 Waldwick, NJ..................800-287-7987
Custom Culinary Inc.
 Schaumberg, IL................800-621-8827
Custom Food Solutions LLC
 Louisville, KY................800-767-2993
Custom Ingredients Inc
 New Braunfels, TX.............800-457-8935
Cyclone Enterprises Inc
 Houston, TX...................281-872-0087
D & D Foods Inc
 West Des Moines, IA...........800-772-4098
D'Oni Enterprises
 San Juan Capistrano, CA.......800-809-8298
Dabruzzi's Italian Foods
 Hudson, WI....................715-386-3653
Daregal
 Princeton, NJ.................609-375-2312
Dean Distributors, Inc.
 Burlingame, CA................800-792-0816
Del Mar Food Products Corp
 Watsonville, CA...............831-722-3516
Delgrosso Foods Inc.
 Tipton, PA....................800-521-5880
Dell'Amore Enterprises
 Colchester, VT................800-962-6673
Desert Pepper Trading Co
 El Paso, TX...................888-472-5727
Dhidow Enterprises
 Oxford, PA....................610-932-7868
DiGregorio Food Products
 St Louis, MO..................314-776-1062
Dillard's Bar-B-Q Sauce
 Durham, NC....................919-286-1080
Dipasa USA Inc
 Brownsville, TX...............956-831-4072
Diversified Foods & Seasonings
 Covington, LA.................800-914-2382

Product Categories / Sauces, Dips & Dressings: Sauces

Divine Foods
   Elizabethtown, NC 910-862-2576
Dixie Trail Farms
   Wilmington, NC 800-665-3968
Do Anything Foods
   New York, NY
Dorina So-Good Inc
   Union, IL 815-923-2144
Dorothy Dawson Food Products
   Jackson, MI. 517-788-9830
Dr Pete's
   Savannah, GA 888-599-0047
Drew's Organics
   Chester, VT 800-228-2980
E Waldo Ward & Son Marmalades
   Sierra Madre, CA 800-355-9273
E.D. Smith Foods Ltd
   Hamilton, ON 905-573-1207
Earth & Vine Provisions Inc
   Lincoln, CA 888-723-8463
East Wind Inc
   Tecumseh, MO 417-679-4682
Eastern Food Industries Inc
   East Greenwich, RI 401-884-8798
Eatem Foods Co
   Vineland, NJ 800-683-2836
Eden Foods Inc
   Clinton, MI 888-424-3336
Edmond's Chile Co
   St Louis, MO. 314-772-1499
El Charro Mexican Food Ind
   Roswell, NM. 575-622-8590
El Rancho Tortilla
   San Antonio, TX 210-922-8411
El Rey Cooked Meats
   St Louis, MO. 314-521-3113
El Toro Food Products
   Watsonville, CA 831-728-9266
EMD Sales Inc
   Baltimore, MD 410-385-3023
Escalon Premier Brand
   Escalon, CA 209-838-7341
Essen Nutrition Corp
   Romeoville, IL 800-582-6064
Ethnic Gourmet Foods
   Boulder, CO 800-434-4246
Excalibur Seasoning
   Pekin, IL 800-444-2169
Famous Chili Inc
   Fort Smith, AR 479-782-0096
Father's Country Hams
   Bremen, KY 270-525-3554
Favorite Foods
   Burnaby, BC 604-420-5100
Felbro Food Products
   Los Angeles, CA. 323-936-5266
Fernandez Chili Co
   Alamosa, CO. 719-589-6043
Festive Foods
   Virginia Beach, VA. 757-490-9186
Fiesta Canning Co
   Phoenix, AZ 602-212-2424
Figaro Company
   Mesquite, TX 972-288-3587
Fireside Kitchen
   Halifax, NS 902-454-7387
Fischer & Wieser Spec Foods
   Fredericksburg, TX 877-861-0260
Flavor House, Inc.
   Adelanto, CA 760-246-9131
Follow Your Heart
   Chatsworth, CA 818-725-2820
Food Concentrate Corporation
   Oklahoma City, OK 405-840-5633
Food Masters
   Griffin, GA 888-715-4394
Food Source Company
   Mississauga, ON 905-625-8404
Fool Proof Gourmet Products
   Grapevine, TX 817-329-1839
Ford's Gourmet Foods
   Raleigh, NC 800-446-0947
Formosa Enterprises Inc
   San Jose, CA. 408-297-3300
Fountain Valley Foods
   Colorado Springs, CO. 719-573-6012
Fox Hollow
   Crestwood, KY 502-241-8621
Fremont Authentic Brands
   Fremont, OH. 419-334-8995
Fresh Pasta Delights
   Plano, TX 972-422-5907

Frontera Foods
   Chicago, IL 800-509-4441
Frontier Co-op
   Norway, IA 844-550-6200
Fusion Gourmet
   Gardena, CA 310-532-8938
Fuzzy's Wholesale Bar-B-Q
   Madison, NC 336-548-2283
Galassi Foods
   Coralville, IA 319-339-7409
Galena Canning Co
   Galena, IL. 815-777-9495
Garden Complements Inc
   Kansas City, MO. 800-966-1091
Garden Row Foods
   Franklin Park, IL. 800-555-9798
Garlic Festival Foods
   Hollister, CA. 888-427-5423
Gator Hammock Corp
   Felda, FL. 800-664-2867
Gayle's Sweet N' Sassy Foods
   Beverly Hills, CA. 310-246-1792
Gedney Products Co
   Sun Valley, CA 888-244-0653
Gehl Foods, Inc.
   Germantown, WI. 800-521-2873
Genarom International
   Cranbury, NJ. 609-409-6200
Gia Russa
   Boardman, OH 800-527-8772
Gingro Corp
   Manchester Center, VT. 802-362-0836
Giovanni Food Co Inc
   Syracuse, NY 315-457-2373
Girard's Food Service Dressings
   City of Industry, CA 888-327-8442
GMB Specialty Foods
   San Juan Capistrano, CA 800-809-8298
GoBio!
   Action, ON 519-853-2958
Gold Dollar Products
   Memphis, TN 800-971-8964
Gold Pure Food Products Co. Inc.
   Hempstead, NY. 800-422-4681
Golden Specialty Foods Inc
   Norwalk, CA. 562-802-2537
Golden State Foods Corp
   Irvine, CA 949-247-8000
Golden West Specialty Foods
   Brisbane, CA. 800-584-4481
Goldwater's Food's Of Arizona
   Fredericksburg, TX 866-779-7241
Good Food For Good
   Markham, ON 647-449-4922
Gourmet Conveniences Ltd
   Litchfield, CT. 866-793-3801
Gourmet's Secret
   North Highlands, CA 916-334-6161
Grain Processing Corp
   Muscatine, IA 800-448-4472
Gravymaster, Inc.
   Canajoharie, NY. 800-839-8938
Great American Barbecue Company
   White Plains, NY 914-686-2277
Green Garden Food Products
   Sandpoint, ID 800-669-3169
Griffith Foods Inc.
   Alsip, IL 708-371-0900
Gringo Jack's
   Manchester Ctr, VT 802-362-0836
Grouse Hunt Farm Inc
   Tamaqua, PA 570-467-2850
Guido's International Foods
   Pasadena, CA 877-994-8436
Gumpert's Canada
   Mississauga, ON 800-387-9324
Gunther's Gourmet
   Richmond, VA. 804-240-1796
Habby Habanero's Food Products
   Jacksonville, FL 904-333-9758
Hagerty Foods
   Orange, CA. 714-628-1230
Haig's Delicacies
   Hayward, CA 510-782-6285
Halal Fine Foods
   Toronto, ON 416-679-8000
Halifax Group
   Washington, DC 202-530-8300
Hampton Chutney Company
   Amagansett, NY 631-267-3131
Hanan Products Co
   Hicksville, NY 516-938-1000

Hanover Foods Corp
   Hanover, PA 717-632-6000
Harry's Cafe
   Mount Holly, VT. 802-259-2996
Hartville Kitchen
   Hartville, OH 330-877-9353
Hartville Locker Service
   Hartville, OH 330-877-9547
Harvest-Pac Products
   Chatham, ON 519-436-0446
Havana's Limited
   Titusville, FL. 321-267-0513
Havoc Maker Products
   Guilford, CT 800-681-3909
Heartbreaking Dawns Artisan Foods
   Glendale, AZ. 646-957-3484
Heartline Foods
   Westport, CT. 203-222-0381
Heffy's BBQ Co.
   Kansas City, MO. 816-200-2271
Heidi's Salsa
   Los Angeles, CA. 310-821-0211
Heintz & Weber Co
   Buffalo, NY. 716-852-7171
Heinz Portion Control
   Jacksonville, FL 904-695-1300
Heinz Quality Chef Foods Inc
   Cedar Rapids, IA. 800-356-8307
Heluva Good Cheese
   Lynnfield, MA 800-644-5473
Heritage Family Specialty Foods Inc
   Grand Prairie, TX 800-648-2837
Hillside Lane Farm
   Randolph, VT 802-728-0070
Hirzel Canning Co & Farms
   Luckey, OH. 419-419-7525
Hollman Foods
   Des Moines, IA. 888-926-2879
Homestead Fine Foods
   S San Francisco, CA 650-615-0750
Honey Bear Fruit Basket
   Denver, CO 888-330-2327
Honeydrop Beverages
   Houston, TX
HongryHawg of Louisiana
   Prairieville, LA 888-772-4294
Hoopeston Foods Inc
   Burnsville, MN 952-854-0903
Hopkins Inn Of Lake Waramaug
   Warren, CT 860-868-7295
Hormel Foods Corp.
   Austin, MN 507-437-5611
Horseshoe Brand
   Milan, NY 845-240-2390
House of Herbs LLC
   Passaic, NJ 973-779-2422
Howjax
   Pembroke Pines, FL 954-441-2491
Hume Specialties
   Chester, VT 802-875-3117
HV Food Products Co
   Oakland, CA 877-853-7262
Illes Seasonings & Flavors
   Carrollton, TX 800-683-4553
Imus Ranch Foods
   Darien, CT 888-284-4687
Integrative Flavors
   Michigan City, IN. 800-837-7687
Intercorp Excelle Foods
   North York, ON. 888-473-6337
International Home Foods
   Parsippany, NJ. 973-359-9920
Island Spice
   Doral, FL. 786-473-3465
Italia Foods
   Schaumburg, IL. 800-747-1109
Iya Foods LLC
   North Aurora, IL. 630-854-7107
J.A.M.B. Low Carb Distributor
   Pompano Beach, FL 800-708-6738
J.N. Bech
   Elk Rapids, MI 800-232-4583
J.T. Pappy's Sauce
   Los Angeles, CA. 323-969-9605
Jack Miller's Food Products
   Ville Platte, LA 800-646-1541
Jake's Grillin
   Hopewell Jct, NY 845-226-4656
Jesben
   Pittsburgh, PA
Jets Le Frois Corp
   Brockport, NY 585-637-5003

Product Categories / Sauces, Dips & Dressings: Sauces

Jillipepper
  Albuquerque, NM 505-609-8409
Jimtown Store
  Healdsburg, CA 707-433-1212
JMS Specialty Foods
  Ripon, WI 800-535-5437
Joe Hutson Foods
  Jacksonville, FL 904-731-9065
Johnny Harris Famous Barbecue Sauce
  Savannah, GA 888-547-2823
Juanita's Foods
  Wilmington, CA 800-303-2965
Kaari Foods
  Brooklyn, NY
Kagome USA Inc
  Los Banos, CA 209-826-8850
Kajun Kettle Foods
  New Orleans, LA 800-331-9612
KARI-Out Co
  White Plains, NY 800-433-8799
Kathy's Gourmet Specialties
  Mendocino, CA 707-937-1383
Kelchner's Horseradish
  Allentown, PA 800-424-1952
Kemach Food Products
  Brooklyn, NY 718-272-5655
Ken's Foods Inc
  Marlborough, MA 508-229-1100
Kent Precision Foods Group Inc
  Muscatine, IA 800-442-5242
Kentucky Bourbon
  Louisville, KY 866-472-7797
Kerala Curry
  Pittsboro, NC 919-545-9401
Kettle Master
  Hillsville, VA 276-728-7571
Kill Sauce
  Pasadena, CA
Kilwons Foods
  Santa Cruz, CA 831-426-9670
Kind Snacks
  New York, NY 855-884-5463
Kinder's BBQ
  Walnut Creek, CA 925-939-7242
King Cupboard
  Red Lodge, MT 800-962-6555
Knouse Foods Co-Op Inc.
  Peach Glen, PA 717-677-8181
Koloa Rum Corp
  Kalaheo, HI 808-332-9333
Kozlowski Farms
  Forestville, CA 800-473-2767
Kraft Heinz Co.
  Chicago, IL 800-543-5335
Kraus & Co
  Irvine, CA 800-662-5871
L & S Packing Co
  Farmingdale, NY 800-286-6487
L & S Packing Co
  Farmingdale, NY 877-879-6453
La Piccolina
  Decatur, GA 800-626-1624
LA Vencedora Products Inc
  Los Angeles, CA 800-327-2572
Lancaster Fine Foods
  Lancaster, PA 717-397-9578
Laredo Tortilleria & Mexican
  Fort Wayne, IN 800-252-7336
Las Cruces Brand Products
  El Paso, TX 915-779-5709
Lasco Foods Inc
  St Louis, MO 314-832-1906
Lassonde Pappas & Company, Inc.
  Carneys Point, NJ 800-257-7019
Le Frois Foods Corporation
  Brockport, NY 585-637-5003
Le Grand
  Blainville, QC 450-623-3000
Lea & Perrins
  Glenview, IL
Leams
  Hutchinson, KS 316-662-4287
Lee Kum Kee USA Inc
  City Of Industry, CA 800-654-5082
Lee's Sausage Co
  Orangeburg, SC 803-534-5517
Lemmes Company
  Coventry, RI 401-821-2575
Lendy's Cafe Raw Bar
  Virginia Beach, VA 757-491-3511
Leroux Creek
  Hotchkiss, CO 877-970-5670

Les Aliments Livabec Foods
  Sherrington, QC 450-454-7971
Li'l Guy Foods
  Kansas City, MO 800-886-8226
LiDestri Food & Drink
  Fairport, NY 585-377-7700
Lillie's Q
  Chicago, IL 773-772-5500
Longmeadow Building Dept
  Longmeadow, MA 413-565-4153
Louis Maull Co
  St Louis, MO 314-241-8410
Louisa Food Products Inc
  St Louis, MO 314-868-3000
Louisiana Fish Fry Products
  Baton Rouge, LA 800-356-2905
Louisiana Gourmet Enterprises
  Houma, LA 800-328-5586
Lounsbury Foods
  Toronto, ON 416-656-6330
Lowcountry Produce
  Raleigh, NC 800-935-2792
Lucky Foods
  Tualatin, OR 503-612-1300
LWC Brands Inc.
  Dallas, TX 800-552-8006
Lynch Foods
  North York, ON 416-449-5464
Lyons Magnus
  Fresno, CA 800-344-7130
Mad Chef Enterprise
  Mentor, OH 800-951-2433
Mad Will's Food Company
  Auburn, CA 888-275-9455
Madison Foods
  Saint Paul, MN 651-265-8212
Magic Seasoning Blends
  New Orleans, LA 800-457-2857
Mandarin Soy Sauce Inc
  Middletown, NY 845-343-1505
Mansmith's Barbeque
  San Jn Bautista, CA 800-626-7648
Maple Grove Farms Of Vermont
  St Johnsbury, VT 802-748-5141
Marina Foods
  Medley, FL 786-888-0129
Marsan Foods
  Toronto, ON 416-755-9262
Martha Olson's Great Foo
  Sutter Creek, CA 800-973-3966
Matouk International USA Inc
  Sunrise, FL 954-742-2204
Mayacamas Fine Foods
  Sonoma, CA 800-826-9621
Mcclancy Seasonings Co
  Fort Mill, SC 800-843-1968
McCormick & Company
  Hunt Valley, MD 410-527-6189
Mccutcheon Apple Products
  Frederick, MD 800-888-7537
Meditalia
  New York, NY 212-616-3006
Mid-Atlantic Foods Inc
  Easton, MD 800-922-4688
Midas Foods Intl
  Oak Park, MI 877-728-2379
Miguel's Stowe Away
  Stowe, VT 800-448-6517
Millflow Spice Corp.
  Hauppauge, NY 866-227-8355
Minnestalgia Foods LLC
  Mcgregor, MN 800-328-6731
Mix-A-Lota Stuff LLC
  Fort Pierce, FL 727-365-7328
Miyako Oriental Foods Inc
  Baldwin Park, CA 877-788-6476
Mizkan Americas Inc
  Kansas City, MO 800-323-4358
Mo Hotta Mo Betta
  Savannah, GA 912-748-2766
Mod Squad Martha
  Johns Island, SC 615-476-3696
Molinaro's Fine Italian Foods Ltd.
  Mississauga, ON 905-281-0352
Molli
  Dallas, TX
Monin Inc.
  Clearwater, FL 855-352-8671
Montebello Kitchens
  Gordonsville, VA 800-743-7687
Monterrey Products
  San Antonio, TX 210-435-2872

Monterrey Products
  San Antonio, TX 800-872-1652
Moonlite Bar-B-Q Inn
  Owensboro, KY 800-322-8989
More Than Gourmet
  Akron, OH 800-860-9385
Morgan Foods Inc
  Austin, IN 888-430-1780
Morningstar Foods
  Los Banos, CA 209-826-8000
Mother Teresa's
  Clute, TX 888-265-7429
Mott's
  Plano, TX 800-426-4891
Mott's LLP
  Plano, TX 800-426-4891
Mrs. Dog's Products
  Grand Rapids, MI 800-267-7364
Mullens Dressing
  Palestine, IL 618-586-2727
Mullins Food Products
  Broadview, IL 708-344-3224
Myron's Fine Foods, Inc.
  Millers Falls, MA 800-730-2820
Nana Mae's Organics
  Sebastopol, CA 707-829-7359
Nation Wide Canning Ltd.
  Cottam, ON 519-839-4831
Native Kjalii Foods
  San Francisco, CA 415-522-5580
New Business Corp
  Gary, IN 219-885-1476
New Canaan Farms
  Dripping Springs, TX 800-727-5267
New Era Canning Company
  New Era, MI 231-861-2151
Nog Incorporated
  Dunkirk, NY 800-332-2664
Nonna Pia's Gourmet Sauces
  Whistler, BC 888-372-1534
North American Enterprises
  Tucson, AZ 800-817-8666
North Coast Processing
  Carlsbad, CA 760-931-6809
Northwest Packing Co
  Vancouver, WA 800-543-4356
Nuovo Pasta Productions LTD
  Stratford, CT 800-803-0033
O'Brian Brothers Food
  Cincinnati, OH 513-791-9909
O'Garvey Sauces
  New Braunfels, TX 830-620-6127
O'Sole Mio
  Boisbriand, QC 844-696-8933
Ocean Spray International
  Lakeville-Middleboro, MA 800-662-3263
Ocean's Halo
  Burlingame, CA 650-642-5907
Ojai Cook
  Los Angeles, CA 886-571-1551
Old World Spices Inc
  Overland Park, KS 800-241-0070
On The Verandah
  Highlands, NC 828-526-2338
One Culture Foods
  Duarte, CA 646-650-2989
Otafuku Foods
  Santa Fe Springs, CA 562-404-4700
Ott Food Products Co
  Carthage, MO 800-866-2585
Overhill Farms Inc
  Vernon, CA 800-859-6406
Pacific Choice Brands
  Fresno, CA 559-476-3581
Pacific Foods of Oregon
  Tualatin, OR 503-692-9666
Pacific Harvest Products
  Bellevue, WA 425-401-7990
Pacific Poultry Company
  Honolulu, HI 808-841-2828
Palmieri Food Products
  New Haven, CT 800-845-5447
Papa Leone Food Enterprises
  Beverly Hills, CA 310-552-1660
Paradise Products Corporation
  Boca Raton, FL 800-826-1235
Park 100 Foods Inc
  Tipton, IN 800-854-6504
Parthenon Food Products
  Ann Arbor, MI 734-994-1012
Passetti's Pride
  Hayward, CA 800-521-4659

Pasta Factory
Melrose Park, IL 800-615-6951
Pastor Chuck Orchards
Portland, ME 207-773-1314
Pastorelli Food Products
Chicago, IL 800-767-2829
Peaceworks
New York, NY 212-897-3985
Pearson's Homestyle
Bowden, AB 877-224-3339
Pecan Deluxe Candy Co
Dallas, TX 800-733-3589
Pemberton's Foods Inc
Gray, ME 800-255-8401
Pepper Creek Farms
Lawton, OK 800-526-8132
Peppers
Lewes, DE 800-998-3473
Perky's Pizza
Oldsmar, FL 800-473-7597
Pett Spice Products Inc
Atlanta, GA 404-691-5235
Pierino Frozen Foods
Lincoln Park, MI 313-928-0950
Piggie Park Enterprises
West Columbia, SC 800-628-7423
Pino's Pasta Veloce
Staten Island, NY 718-273-6660
Plenus Group Inc
Lowell, MA 978-970-3832
Poison Pepper Company
Floral City, FL 888-539-5540
Pomodoro Fresca Foods
Millburn, NJ 973-467-6609
Ponti USA
New York, NY
Porinos Gourmet Food
Central Falls, RI 800-826-3938
Porky's Gourmet Foods
Gallatin, TN 800-767-5911
Prairie Thyme LTD
Santa Fe, NM 800-869-0009
Private Harvest
El Dorado Hills, CA 916-933-7080
Private Label Foods
Rochester, NY 585-254-9205
Produits Ronald
St. Damase, QC 800-465-0118
Progresso Quality Foods
Vineland, NJ 856-691-1565
PS Seasoning & Spices
Iron Ridge, WI 920-387-2204
Purity Products
Plainview, NY 800-256-6102
Quality Foods
Qualicum Beach, BC 877-833-7890
R L Schreiber Inc
Ft Lauderdale, FL 800-624-8777
R&R Homestead Kitchen
Saumico, WI 888-779-8245
Ragozzino Foods Inc
Meriden, CT 800-348-1240
Ragsdale-Overton Food Traditions
Smithfield, NC 888-424-8863
Rancho's
Memphis, TN 901-276-8820
Randazzo's Honest To Goodness Sauces
Glen Rock, NJ 201-543-1195
Rao's Specialty Foods Inc
New York, NY 212-269-0151
Ray's Sausage Co
Cleveland, OH 216-921-8782
Raye's Mustard
Eastport, ME 800-853-1903
Raye's Old Fashioned Gourmet Mustard
Eastport, ME 800-853-1903
Reckitt Benckiser LLC
Parsippany, NJ 973-404-2600
Red Lion Spicy Foods Company
Red Lion, PA 717-309-8303
Reily Foods Company
New Orleans, LA 800-535-1961
Renfro Foods
Fort Worth, TX 800-332-2456
RENFRO Foods Inc
Fort Worth, TX 817-336-3849
Restaurant Lulu Gourmet Products
San Francisco, CA 888-693-5800
Reva Foods
Saint Petersburg, FL 727-692-1292
REX Pure Foods
New Orleans, LA 800-344-8314
Reynolds Sugar Bush
Aniwa, WI 715-449-2057
Riba Foods
Houston, TX 800-327-7422
Richelieu Foods Inc
Braintree, MA 781-786-6800
Rio Valley Canning Co
Donna, TX 956-464-7843
River Town Foods Corp
St Louis, MO 800-844-3210
Robert Rothschild Farm
Cincinnati, OH 800-222-9966
Robinson's No 1 Ribs
Oak Park, IL 800-836-6750
Ronzoni
Largo, FL 800-730-5957
Rosa Mexicano
New York, NY 212-757-5447
Roses Ravioli
Oglesby, IL 815-883-8011
Rosmarino Foods/R.Z. Humbert Company
Odessa, FL 888-926-9053
Rossi Pasta LTD
Marietta, OH 800-227-6774
Routin America
Delray Beach, FL
Rowena
Norfolk, VA 800-627-8699
Royal Baltic LTD
Brooklyn, NY 718-385-8300
Royal Food Products
Indianapolis, IN 317-782-2660
Rufus Teague
Shawnee, KS 913-706-3814
Ruskin Redneck Trading Company
Ruskin, FL 813-645-7710
S.D. Mushrooms
Avondale, PA 610-268-8082
Sabatino Truffles USA
West Haven, CT 888-444-9971
Sable & Rosenfeld Foods
Toronto, ON 416-929-4214
Sabra Dipping Company,LL
Oceanside, CA 800-748-5523
Sadler's Smokehouse
Henderson, TX 903-657-5581
Saffron Road
Stamford, CT 877-425-2587
Salvy Sousa Dealer Locator
Arkansas City, KS 620-442-2700
Sambets Cajun Deli
Austin, TX 800-472-6238
Santa Barbara Olive Company
Santa Barbara, CA 800-624-4896
Santa Barbara Salsa/California Creative
Oceanside, CA 800-748-5523
Santa Cruz Chili & Spice
Tumacacori, AZ 520-398-2591
Saratoga Salad Dressing
Canton, MA 781-821-1010
Sau-Sea Foods
Tarrytown, NY 914-631-1717
Sauces N' Love
Lynn, MA 781-595-7771
Savoie's Sausage and Food Products
Opelousas, LA 337-942-7241
Schiavone's Casa Mia
Middletown, OH 513-422-8650
Schlotterbeck & Foss Company
Portland, ME 800-777-4666
Scott's Sauce Co Inc
Goldsboro, NC 800-734-7282
Select Food Products
Toronto, ON 800-699-8016
Seminole Foods
Springfield, OH 800-881-1177
Senba USA
Hayward, CA 888-922-5852
Seneca Foods Corp
Marion, NY 315-926-8100
Sentry Seasonings
Elmhurst, IL 630-530-5370
Serious Foodie
Bradenton, FL 844-736-6343
Serro Foods LLC
Catskill, NY 518-943-9255
Shirley J Ventures, LLC
Lindon, UT 801-225-5073
Sidari's Italian Foods
Cleveland, OH 216-431-3344
Sieco USA Corporation
Houston, TX 713-464-1726
Silver Palate Kitchens
Cresskill, NJ 201-568-0110
Silver Spring Foods
Eau Clair, MI 800-826-7322
Silver State Foods Inc
Denver, CO 800-423-3351
Simply Delicious
Cedar Grove, NC 919-732-5294
Skjodt-Barrett Foods
Brampton, ON 877-600-1200
Slather Brand Foods LLC
Charleston, SC 843-513-1750
Solana Gold Organics
Sebastopol, CA 800-459-1121
Solo Foods
Countryside, IL 800-328-7656
SOPAKCO Foods
Mullins, SC 800-276-9678
Sopakco Foods
Mullins, SC 843-464-7851
Sopako Foods
Mullins, SC 843-464-7851
Sophia Foods
Brooklyn, NY 718-272-1110
Sophia's Sauce Works
Carson City, NV 800-718-7769
South Ceasar Dressing Company
Novato, CA 415-897-0605
Southern Art Company, LLC
Atlanta, GA 800-257-6606
Southern Delight Gourmet Foods
Bowling Green, KY 866-782-9943
Southern Okie
Edmond, OK 405-657-7765
Southwest Specialty Food
Goodyear, AZ 800-536-3131
Soy Vay Enterprises
Felton, CA 800-444-6369
Spanish Gardens Food Manufacturing
Kansas City, KS 913-831-4242
Stanislaus Food Prod
Modesto, CA 800-327-7201
Starport Foods
San Francisco, CA 866-206-9343
Stello Foods Inc
Punxsutawney, PA 800-849-4599
Stickney & Poor Company
Peterborough, NH 603-924-2259
Stonewall Kitchen
York, ME 800-826-1752
Stubb's Legendary BBQ
Austin, TX 800-227-2283
Sun Harvest Foods Inc
San Diego, CA 619-661-0909
Sunny Dell Foods Inc
Oxford, PA 610-932-5164
Super Smokers Bar-B-Que
Eureka, MO 636-938-9742
Surlean Foods
San Antonio, TX 800-999-4370
Sutter Buttes Olive Oil
Sutter, CA 530-763-7921
Swatt Baking Co
Olean, NY 800-370-6656
Sweet & Saucy Inc
Centennial, CO 303-807-5132
Sweet Baby Ray's
Chicago, IL 877-729-2229
Sweet Peas Floral Design
Stockton, CA 209-472-9284
Sweetwater Spice Company
Austin, TX 800-531-6079
Swiss Food Products
Chicago, IL 312-829-0100
T. Marzetti Company
Westerville, OH 800-999-1835
T.W. Garner Food Company
Winston Salem, NC 800-476-7383
Tait Farm Foods
Centre Hall, PA 800-787-2716
Tantos Foods International
Markham, ON 905-943-9993
Tapatio Hot Sauce
Vernon, CA 323-587-8933
Taste Weavers
Urbana, OH 888-810-8365
Tasty Tomato
San Antonio, TX 210-822-2443
Teasdale Quality Foods Inc
Atwater, CA 209-358-5616
Terlato Kitchen
Bannockburn, IL 855-805-7221

Product Categories / Sauces, Dips & Dressings: Sauces

Tex-Mex Gourmet
  Brenham, TX 888-345-8467
Texas Heat
  San Antonio, TX 800-656-5916
Texas Tamale Co
  Houston, TX 713-795-5500
The Saucey Sauce Company Inc.
  Brooklyn, NY 646-648-0159
Thistledew Farm
  Proctor, WV 800-854-6639
Thomas Gourmet Foods
  Greensboro, NC 800-867-2823
Thompson's Fine Foods
  Shoreview, MN 800-807-0025
Thor-Shackel Horseradish Company
  Eau Claire, WI 800-826-7322
Thornton Foods Company
  Eden Prairie, MN 952-944-1735
Timber Crest Farms
  Healdsburg, CA 888-766-4233
Tip Top Canning Co
  Tipp City, OH 800-352-2635
TMI Trading Co
  Brooklyn, NY 718-821-5052
Todd's
  Des Moines, IA 800-247-5363
Tomasso Corporation
  Baie D'Urfe, QC 514-325-3000
Tone Products Inc
  Melrose Park, IL 800-536-8663
Top Hat Co Inc
  Wilmette, IL 847-256-6565
Trader Vic's Food Products
  Emeryville, CA 877-762-4824
Trappey's Fine Foods Inc
  New Iberia, LA 337-365-8281
Trio's Original Italian Pasta Co.
  Chelsea, MA 800-999-9603
Triple H Food Processors Inc
  Riverside, CA 951-352-5700
Triple K Manufacturing Company, Inc.
  Shenandoah, IA 712-246-4376
Tulkoff's Food Products Inc
  Baltimore, MD 800-638-7343
Twin Marquis
  Brooklyn, NY 800-367-6868
Two Chefs on a Roll
  Carson, CA 800-842-3025
UBF Food Solutions
  Lisle, IL 630-955-5394
Ultimate Gourmet
  Hillsborough, NJ 908-359-4050
United Foods USA
  Hayward, CA 510-264-5850
Valley Grain Products
  Fresno, CA 559-675-3400
Vegetable Juices Inc
  Chicago, IL 888-776-9752
Ventre Packing Company
  Syracuse, NY 315-463-2384
Vermont Signature Sauces
  Saxtons River, VT 802-869-5000
Vidalia Brands Inc
  Reidsville, GA 800-752-0206
Vidalia Sweets Brand
  Lyons, GA 912-565-8881
Viki's Montana Classics
  Bigfork, MT 800-248-1222
Vincent's Food Corporation
  Carle Place, NY 516-481-3544
Violet Packing Holdings LLC
  Williamstown, NJ 856-629-7428
Vivienne Dressings
  St Louis, MO 800-827-0778
Wagner Gourmet Foods
  Lenexa, KS 913-469-5411
Wagshal's Imports
  Washington, DC 202-363-5698
Walden Farms
  Linden, NJ 800-229-1706
Walker Foods
  Los Angeles, CA 800-966-5199
Webbpak Inc
  Trussville, AL 800-655-3500
Wei-Chuan USA Inc
  Bell Gardens, CA 562-372-2020
Well Dressed Food Company
  Tupper Lake, NY 518-359-5280
West Pac
  Idaho Falls, ID 800-973-7407
Westbrae Natural Foods
  Melville, NY 800-434-4246

Westin Foods
  Omaha, NE 800-228-6098
Whole in the Wall
  Binghamton, NY 607-722-5138
Wickers Food Products Inc
  Hornersville, MO 800-847-0032
Widow's Mite Vinegar Company
  Washington, DC 877-678-5854
WILD Flavors (Canada)
  Mississauga, ON 800-263-5286
Wild Thymes Farm Inc
  Greenville, NY 845-266-8387
William Poll Inc
  New York, NY 800-993-7655
Williamsburg Chocolatier
  Williamsburg, VA 757-253-1474
WillowOak Farms
  Amherst, VA 888-963-2767
Wing It Inc
  Falmouth, MA 508-540-9860
Wing Nien Food
  Hayward, CA 510-487-8877
Wing-Time
  Lynn, MA 781-592-1069
Wizards Cauldron, LTD
  Yanceyville, NC 336-694-5665
Woeber Mustard Mfg Co
  Springfield, OH 800-548-2929
Wood Brothers Inc
  West Columbia, SC 803-796-5146
World Art Foods
  Temple, TX 254-774-8322
World Famous Buffalo Wing Sauce
  Buffalo, NY 716-912-9068
World Flavors Inc
  Warminster, PA 215-672-4400
World Harbors
  Auburn, ME 800-355-6221
World Herbs Gourmet
  Old Saybrook, CT 860-388-3781
Worthmore Food Products Co
  Cincinnati, OH 866-837-7687
Yai's Thai
  Denver, CO
Yamasa Corp USA
  Salem, OR 503-363-8550
Ying's Kitchen
  Lake Villa, IL 847-403-7078
Yo Mama's Foods
  Gainesville, FL
Yoshida Food Products Co
  Portland, OR 800-653-1114
Zarda Bar-B-Q & Catering Company
  Blue Springs, MO 800-776-7427

Alfredo

Al Dente Pasta Co
  Whitmore Lake, MI 800-536-7278
Amanida USA Corp
  Coral Gables, FL
Barilla USA
  Northbrook, IL 800-922-7455
Casa Di Lisio Products Inc
  Mt Kisco, NY 800-247-4199
Classy Delites
  Austin, TX 800-440-2648
Cuizina Food Company
  Woodinville, WA 425-486-7000
Genarom International
  Cranbury, NJ 609-409-6200
LiDestri Food & Drink
  Fairport, NY 585-377-7700
Marsan Foods
  Toronto, ON 416-755-9262
Newman's Own
  Westport, CT 203-222-0136
Pasta Factory
  Melrose Park, IL 800-615-6951
Sargento Foods Inc
  Plymouth, WI 800-243-3737
Tomasso Corporation
  Baie D'Urfe, QC 514-325-3000
Victoria Fine Foods
  Brooklyn, NY 718-927-3000

Barbecue

A Southern Season
  Hillsborough, NC 800-253-3663
A. Lassonde Inc.
  Rougemont, QC 866-552-7643

Allied Old English Inc
  Port Reading, NJ 732-602-8955
Annie's Naturals
  Berkeley, CA 800-434-1234
Arbor Hill Grapery & Winery
  Naples, NY 800-554-7553
Ashman Manufacturing & Distributing Company
  Virginia Beach, VA 800-641-9924
Baker's Ribs No 2
  Dallas, TX 214-748-5433
Baldwin Richardson Foods
  Oakbrook Terrace, IL 866-644-2732
Bartush Schnitzius Foods Co
  Lewisville, TX 972-219-1270
Baumer Foods Inc
  Metairie, LA 504-482-5761
BBQ Bunch
  Kansas City, MO 816-941-4534
BBQ'n Fools Catering, LLC
  Greenfield, IN 800-671-8652
BBS Bodacious BBQ Company
  Coral Springs, FL 800-537-5928
Bettah Buttah, LLC
  Kansas City, KS 800-568-8468
Big B Barbecue
  Evansville, IN 812-425-5235
Blair's Sauces & Snacks
  Highlands, NJ 800-982-5247
Blueberry Store
  Grand Junction, MI 877-654-2400
Bone Suckin' Sauce
  Raleigh, NC 919-833-7647
Buffalo Wild Wings
  Minneapolis, MN 763-546-1891
Bunker Foods Corp.
  New York, NY 646-738-4020
Cafe Chilku
  Colchester, VT 802-878-4645
Cafe Tequila
  San Francisco, CA 415-264-0106
Cajohn's Fiery Foods Co
  Westerville, OH 888-703-3473
California-Antilles Trading
  San Diego, CA 800-330-6450
Captain Bob's Jet Fuel
  Fort Wayne, IN 877-486-6468
Carolina Treet
  Wilmington, NC 800-616-6344
Casa Visco
  Schenectady, NY 888-607-2823
Casually Gourmet
  New Haven, VT 800-639-7604
Catamount Specialties of Vermont
  Plainfield, VT 800-639-2406
Catskill Mountain Specialties
  Saugerties, NY 800-311-3473
Charlie Beigg's Sauce Company
  Windham, ME 888-502-8595
CHS Inc.
  Inver Grove Hts., MN 800-328-6539
Cinnabar Specialty Foods Inc
  Prescott, AZ 866-293-6433
Clements Foods Co
  Oklahoma City, OK 800-654-8355
Coach Sposato's Bar-B-Que
  Lincoln, AR 800-264-7535
Colgin Co
  Dallas, TX 888-226-5446
Conway Import Co Inc
  Franklin Park, IL 800-323-8801
Cookies Food Products
  Wall Lake, IA 800-331-4995
Cookshack
  Ponca City, OK 800-423-0698
Country Bob's Inc
  Centralia, IL 800-373-2140
Country Cupboard
  Lewisburg, PA 570-523-3211
Crazy Mary's
  New York, NY 212-889-8124
Creative Foodworks Inc
  San Antonio, TX 210-212-4761
Cugino's Gourmet Foods
  Crystal Lake, IL 888-592-8446
Cuisine Perel
  Richmond, CA 800-887-3735
Cuizina Food Company
  Woodinville, WA 425-486-7000
Culver Duck Farms Inc
  Middlebury, IN 800-825-9225
D & D Foods Inc
  West Des Moines, IA 800-772-4098

389

Product Categories / Sauces, Dips & Dressings: Sauces

Desert Pepper Trading Co
  El Paso, TX 888-472-5727
Dillard's Bar-B-Q Sauce
  Durham, NC 919-286-1080
Dorina So-Good Inc
  Union, IL 815-923-2144
Douglas Cross Enterprises
  Seattle, WA 206-448-1193
Dynamic Foods
  Lubbock, TX 806-723-5600
E.D. Smith Foods Ltd
  Hamilton, ON 905-573-1207
El Rey Cooked Meats
  St Louis, MO 314-521-3113
Favorite Foods
  Burnaby, BC 604-420-5100
Felbro Food Products
  Los Angeles, CA 323-936-5266
Fiesta Gourmet of Tejas
  Canyon Lake, TX 800-585-8250
Figaro Company
  Mesquite, TX 972-288-3587
Food Concentrate Corporation
  Oklahoma City, OK 405-840-5633
Food Ingredient Solutions
  Teterboro, NJ 917-449-9558
Food Processor of New Mexico
  Albuquerque, NM 877-634-3772
Fremont Authentic Brands
  Fremont, OH 419-334-8995
Funnibonz LLC
  Princeton Jct, NJ 877-300-2669
Garden Complements Inc
  Kansas City, MO 800-966-1091
Gayle's Sweet N' Sassy Foods
  Beverly Hills, CA 310-246-1792
Gedney Foods Co
  Sun Valley, CA 888-244-0653
Golden Specialty Foods Inc
  Norwalk, CA 562-802-2537
Golding Farms Foods
  Winston Salem, NC 336-766-6161
Good Food For Good
  Markham, ON 647-449-4922
Gumpert's Canada
  Mississauga, ON 800-387-9324
Hak's
  Los Angeles, CA 424-235-0516
Havana's Limited
  Titusville, FL 321-267-0513
Head Country
  Ponca City, OK 888-762-1227
Heinz Portion Control
  Jacksonville, FL 904-695-1300
Hollman Foods
  Des Moines, IA 888-926-2879
Hormel Foods Corp.
  Austin, MN 507-437-5611
Horseshoe Brand
  Milan, NY 845-240-2390
Hot Licks
  Spring Valley, CA 888-766-6468
Hot Wachula's
  Lakeland, FL 877-883-8700
J.N. Bech
  Elk Rapids, MI 800-232-4583
JMS Specialty Foods
  Ripon, WI 800-535-5437
Johnny Harris Famous Barbecue Sauce
  Savannah, GA 888-547-2823
Judicial Flavors
  Auburn, CA 530-885-1298
Kinder's BBQ
  Walnut Creek, CA 925-939-7242
King's Hawaiian Holding Co Inc.
  Torrance, CA 877-695-4227
Kozlowski Farms
  Forestville, CA 800-473-2767
L & S Packing Co
  Farmingdale, NY 800-286-6487
Lea & Perrins
  Glenview, IL
Lee's Sausage Co
  Orangeburg, SC 803-534-5517
Lendy's Cafe Raw Bar
  Virginia Beach, VA 757-491-3511
Litehouse Foods
  Sandpoint, ID 800-669-3169
Lounsbury Foods
  Toronto, ON 416-656-6330
Mad Will's Food Company
  Auburn, CA 888-275-9455

Mansmith's Barbeque
  San Jn Bautista, CA 800-626-7648
Mccutcheon Apple Products
  Frederick, MD 800-888-7537
Millflow Spice Corp.
  Hauppauge, NY 866-227-8355
Mucky Duck Mustard Company
  Ferndale, MI 248-544-4610
Nature's Hollow
  Charleston, UT
New Business Corp
  Gary, IN 219-885-1476
North of the Border
  Tesuque, NM 800-860-0681
O'Brian Brothers Food
  Cincinnati, OH 513-791-9909
Ott Food Products Co
  Carthage, MO 800-866-2585
Pacific Choice Brands
  Fresno, CA 559-476-3581
Pacific Poultry Company
  Honolulu, HI 808-841-2828
Palmetto Canning
  Palmetto, FL 941-722-1100
Palmieri Food Products
  New Haven, CT 800-845-5447
Paradise Products Corporation
  Boca Raton, FL 800-826-1235
Passetti's Pride
  Hayward, CA 800-521-4659
Piggie Park Enterprises
  West Columbia, SC 800-628-7423
Porinos Gourmet Food
  Central Falls, RI 800-826-3938
Produies Ronald
  St. Damase, QC 800-465-0118
Reckitt Benckiser LLC
  Parsippany, NJ 973-404-2600
Rib Rack
  Birmingham, MI
River Town Foods Corp
  St Louis, MO 800-844-3210
Rob Salamida Co Inc
  Johnson City, NY 800-545-5072
Robbie's Natural Products
  Vancouver, WA 360-433-2325
Robinson's No 1 Ribs
  Oak Park, IL 800-836-6750
Rosmarino Foods/R.Z. Humbert Company
  Odessa, FL 888-926-9053
Sadler's Smokehouse
  Henderson, TX 903-657-5581
Sambets Cajun Deli
  Austin, TX 800-472-6238
San Gennaro Foods Inc
  Kent, WA 800-462-1916
Savoie's Sausage and Food Products
  Opelousas, LA 337-942-7241
Schlotterbeck & Foss Company
  Portland, ME 800-777-4666
Scott's Sauce Co Inc
  Goldsboro, NC 800-734-7282
Sky Valley Foods
  Danville, VA
Southern Bar-B-Que
  Jennings, LA 866-612-2586
Southern Delight Gourmet Foods
  Bowling Green, KY 866-782-9943
Stanchfield Farms
  Milo, ME 207-732-5173
Steel's Gourmet Foods, Ltd.
  Bridgeport, PA 800-678-3357
Stinking Rose, The
  San Francisco, CA 800-995-7674
Stuart & CO
  Brooklyn, NY 347-292-7456
Subco Foods Inc
  Sheboygan, WI 800-473-0757
Sweet Baby Ray's
  Chicago, IL 877-729-2229
Sweet Peas Floral Design
  Stockton, CA 209-472-9284
T. Marzetti Company
  Westerville, OH 800-999-1835
T.W. Garner Food Company
  Winston Salem, NC 800-476-7383
Taste Weavers
  Urbana, OH 888-810-8365
The Shed Saucery
  Ocean Springs, MS 228-875-9590
Thompson's Fine Foods
  Shoreview, MN 800-807-0025

Todd's
  Des Moines, IA 800-247-5363
Triple H Food Processors Inc
  Riverside, CA 951-352-5700
Tulkoff's Food Products Inc
  Baltimore, MD 800-638-7343
Ubons Sauce LLC
  Yazoo City, MS 662-716-7100
Valley Grain Products
  Fresno, CA 559-675-3400
Ventre Packing Company
  Syracuse, NY 315-463-2384
Vermont Made Richard's Sauces
  St Albans, VT 802-524-3196
Vidalia Sweets Brand
  Lyons, GA 912-565-8881
We Rub You
  Brooklyn, NY 718-387-9797
Webbpak Inc
  Trussville, AL 800-655-3500
Wei-Chuan USA Inc
  Bell Gardens, CA 562-372-2020
West Pac
  Idaho Falls, ID 800-973-7407
Westin Foods
  Omaha, NE 800-228-6098
Wine Country Chef LLC
  Hidden Valley Lake, CA 707-322-0406
Wing Nien Food
  Hayward, CA 510-487-8877
Wing-Time
  Lynn, MA 781-592-1069
Wizards Cauldron, LTD
  Yanceyville, NC 336-694-5665
Wood Brothers Inc
  West Columbia, SC 803-796-5146
World Famous Buffalo Wing Sauce
  Buffalo, NY 716-912-9068
World Flavors Inc
  Warminster, PA 215-672-4400
Zarda Bar-B-Q & Catering Company
  Blue Springs, MO 800-776-7427

Black Bean

Favorite Foods
  Burnaby, BC 604-420-5100
Lee Kum Kee USA Inc
  City Of Industry, CA 800-654-5082

Cheese

Berner Food & Beverage LLC
  Dakota, IL 800-819-8199
Clofine Dairy Products Inc
  Linwood, NJ 609-653-1000
Cuizina Food Company
  Woodinville, WA 425-486-7000
Fountain Valley Foods
  Colorado Springs, CO 719-573-6012
Galassi Foods
  Coralville, IA 319-339-7409
Genarom International
  Cranbury, NJ 609-409-6200
Kent Precision Foods Group Inc
  Muscatine, IA 800-442-5242
Knouse Foods Co-Op Inc.
  Peach Glen, PA 717-677-8181
Marsan Foods
  Toronto, ON 416-755-9262
Sargento Foods Inc
  Plymouth, WI 800-243-3737
Thornton Foods Company
  Eden Prairie, MN 952-944-1735

Nacho

Bel Brands USA
  Chicago, IL 312-462-1500
Knouse Foods Co-Op Inc.
  Peach Glen, PA 717-677-8181
Olde Tyme Food Corporation
  East Longmeadow, MA 800-356-6533
Vanee Foods Co
  Berkeley, IL 708-449-7300

Chili

Baldwin Richardson Foods
  Oakbrook Terrace, IL 866-644-2732
Big B Barbecue
  Evansville, IN 812-425-5235
Cervantes Food Products Inc
  Albuquerque, NM 877-982-4453

Product Categories / Sauces, Dips & Dressings: Sauces

Commodities Marketing Inc
  Clarksburg, NJ 732-516-0700
El Charro Mexican Food Ind
  Roswell, NM 575-622-8590
Fernandez Chili Co
  Alamosa, CO 719-589-6043
Fiesta Canning Co
  Phoenix, AZ 602-212-2424
First Original Texas Chili Company
  Fort Worth, TX 800-507-0009
Hurd Orchards
  Holley, NY 585-638-8838
Ingleby Farms
  Dublin, PA 877-728-7277
Las Cruces Brand Products
  El Paso, TX 915-779-5709
Le Grand
  Blainville, QC 450-623-3000
Lee Kum Kee USA Inc
  City Of Industry, CA 800-654-5082
Miguel's Stowe Away
  Stowe, VT 800-448-6517
Mrs Auld's Gourmet Foods Inc
  Reno, NV 800-322-8537
North of the Border
  Tesuque, NM 800-860-0681
Red Gold Inc.
  Elwood, IN 866-729-7187
Santa Cruz Chili & Spice
  Tumacacori, AZ 520-398-2591
Sky Valley Foods
  Danville, VA
Stokes Canning Company
  Aurora, CO 800-978-6537
T.W. Garner Food Company
  Winston Salem, NC 800-476-7383

Clam

Casa Di Lisio Products Inc
  Mt Kisco, NY 800-247-4199
Chincoteague Seafood Co Inc
  Parsonsburg, MD 443-260-4800
Colonna Brothers Inc
  North Bergen, NJ 201-864-1115
Cuizina Food Company
  Woodinville, WA 425-486-7000
Mid-Atlantic Foods Inc
  Easton, MD 800-922-4688
Pasta Factory
  Melrose Park, IL 800-615-6951
Victoria Fine Foods
  Brooklyn, NY 718-927-3000

Cocktail

Baldwin Richardson Foods
  Oakbrook Terrace, IL 866-644-2732
Cedarvale Food Products
  Toronto, ON 416-656-3330
Clements Foods Co
  Oklahoma City, OK 800-654-8355
Cuizina Food Company
  Woodinville, WA 425-486-7000
E Waldo Ward & Son Marmalades
  Sierra Madre, CA 800-355-9273
Ed Roller Inc
  Rochester, NY 585-458-8020
Golding Farms Foods
  Winston Salem, NC 336-766-6161
Joe Hutson Foods
  Jacksonville, FL 904-731-9065
Kelchner's Horseradish
  Allentown, PA 800-424-1952
Lounsbury Foods
  Toronto, ON 416-656-6330
Palmieri Food Products
  New Haven, CT 800-845-5447
Paradise Products Corporation
  Boca Raton, FL 800-826-1235
Sau-Sea Foods
  Tarrytown, NY 914-631-1717
T.W. Garner Food Company
  Winston Salem, NC 800-476-7383
Thor-Shackel Horseradish Company
  Eau Claire, WI 800-826-7322
Tulkoff's Food Products Inc
  Baltimore, MD 800-638-7343
Vegetable Juices Inc
  Chicago, IL 888-776-9752

Curry

Baldwin Richardson Foods
  Oakbrook Terrace, IL 866-644-2732
Curry King Corporation
  Waldwick, NJ 800-287-7987
HerbNZest LLC
  Princeton, NJ 917-582-1191

Dessert

Amoretti
  Oxnard, CA 800-266-7388
Applecreek Speciality Foods
  Lexington, KY 800-747-8871
Graeter's Mfg. Co.
  Cincinnati, OH 800-721-3323
Sutter Buttes Olive Oil
  Sutter, CA 530-763-7921

Duck

Allied Old English Inc
  Port Reading, NJ 732-602-8955
KARI-Out Co
  White Plains, NY 800-433-8799
L & S Packing Co
  Farmingdale, NY 800-286-6487

Fish

24Vegan
  Arcadia, CA
Stacey's Famous Foods
  Hayden, ID 800-782-2395

Fra Diavolo

Cuizina Food Company
  Woodinville, WA 425-486-7000
L & S Packing Co
  Farmingdale, NY 800-286-6487
Palmieri Food Products
  New Haven, CT 800-845-5447
Papa Leone Food Enterprises
  Beverly Hills, CA 310-552-1660
Victoria Fine Foods
  Brooklyn, NY 718-927-3000

Frozen

Bellisio Foods
  Minneapolis, MN
Carando Gourmet Frozen Foods
  Agawam, MA 888-227-2636
Casa Di Lisio Products Inc
  Mt Kisco, NY 800-247-4199
Cuizina Food Company
  Woodinville, WA 425-486-7000
Dynamic Foods
  Lubbock, TX 806-723-5600
Louisa Food Products Inc
  St Louis, MO 314-868-3000
Marsan Foods
  Toronto, ON 416-755-9262
Overhill Farms Inc
  Vernon, CA 800-859-6406
Pierino Frozen Foods
  Lincoln Park, MI 313-928-0950
Tomasso Corporation
  Baie D'Urfe, QC 514-325-3000
Trio's Original Italian Pasta Co.
  Chelsea, MA 800-999-9603
Two Chefs on a Roll
  Carson, CA 800-842-3025
Vegetable Juices Inc
  Chicago, IL 888-776-9752

Fudge

Paradigm Foodworks Inc
  Lake Oswego, OR 800-234-0250

Garlic

Baldwin Richardson Foods
  Oakbrook Terrace, IL 866-644-2732
Bunker Foods Corp.
  New York, NY 646-738-4020
Captain Bob's Jet Fuel
  Fort Wayne, IN 877-486-6468
CHS Inc.
  Inver Grove Hts., MN 800-328-6539
Cuizina Food Company
  Woodinville, WA 425-486-7000

L & S Packing Co
  Farmingdale, NY 800-286-6487
Lee Kum Kee USA Inc
  City Of Industry, CA 800-654-5082
Marsan Foods
  Toronto, ON 416-755-9262
Pasta Factory
  Melrose Park, IL 800-615-6951
Robbie's Natural Products
  Vancouver, WA 360-433-2325
Soy Vay Enterprises
  Felton, CA 800-444-6369
Vegetable Juices Inc
  Chicago, IL 888-776-9752

Ginger

Baldwin Richardson Foods
  Oakbrook Terrace, IL 866-644-2732
Bunker Foods Corp.
  New York, NY 646-738-4020
Cuizina Food Company
  Woodinville, WA 425-486-7000
Vegetable Juices Inc
  Chicago, IL 888-776-9752

Gourmet

Beaverton Foods Inc
  Hillsboro, OR 800-223-8076
Hot Mama's Foods
  Springfield, MA 413-737-6572
Kagome USA Inc
  Los Banos, CA 209-826-8850
Vita Food Products Inc
  Chicago, IL 800-989-8482
Wildly Delicious
  Toronto, ON 888-545-9995

Habanero

Baldwin Richardson Foods
  Oakbrook Terrace, IL 866-644-2732
Captain Bob's Jet Fuel
  Fort Wayne, IN 877-486-6468
Catskill Mountain Specialties
  Saugerties, NY 800-311-3473
Chili Dude
  Dallas, TX 214-354-9906
Havana's Limited
  Titusville, FL 321-267-0513
Horseshoe Brand
  Milan, NY 845-240-2390
Kill Sauce
  Pasadena, CA
Lendy's Cafe Raw Bar
  Virginia Beach, VA 757-491-3511
Mo Hotta Mo Betta
  Savannah, GA 912-748-2766
Mrs. Dog's Products
  Grand Rapids, MI 800-267-7364
New Canaan Farms
  Dripping Springs, TX 800-727-5267
Porky's Gourmet Foods
  Gallatin, TN 800-767-5911
Tex-Mex Gourmet
  Brenham, TX 888-345-8467
Vegetable Juices Inc
  Chicago, IL 888-776-9752
Wing-Time
  Lynn, MA 781-592-1069

Hoisin

Baldwin Richardson Foods
  Oakbrook Terrace, IL 866-644-2732
Cuizina Food Company
  Woodinville, WA 425-486-7000
Hormel Foods Corp.
  Austin, MN 507-437-5611
Lee Kum Kee USA Inc
  City Of Industry, CA 800-654-5082
Miyako Oriental Foods Inc
  Baldwin Park, CA 877-788-6476
Soy Vay Enterprises
  Felton, CA 800-444-6369
Wei-Chuan USA Inc
  Bell Gardens, CA 562-372-2020

Hollandaise

Century Blends LLC
  Hunt Valley, MD 410-771-6606
Cuizina Food Company
  Woodinville, WA 425-486-7000

Product Categories / Sauces, Dips & Dressings: Sauces

Teasdale Quality Foods Inc
  Atwater, CA 209-358-5616

Horseradish

Bartush Schnitzius Foods Co
  Lewisville, TX 972-219-1270
Beaverton Foods Inc
  Hillsboro, OR 800-223-8076
Cedarvale Food Products
  Toronto, ON 416-656-3330
Ed Roller Inc
  Rochester, NY 585-458-8020
Grouse Hunt Farm Inc
  Tamaqua, PA 570-467-2850
Hoople Country Kitchen Inc
  Rockport, IN 877-466-7537
Kelchner's Horseradish
  Allentown, PA. 800-424-1952
Lounsbury Foods
  Toronto, ON 416-656-6330
Mother's Mountain Pantry
  Falmouth, ME 800-440-9891
Sau-Sea Foods
  Tarrytown, NY 914-631-1717
Seminole Foods
  Springfield, OH 800-881-1177
Silver Spring Foods
  Eau Clair, MI. 800-826-7322
Southwest Specialty Food
  Goodyear, AZ 800-536-3131
Strub Pickles
  Brantford, ON 519-751-1717
Thor-Shackel Horseradish Company
  Eau Claire, WI 800-826-7322
Tulkoff's Food Products Inc
  Baltimore, MD 800-638-7343
Westin Foods
  Omaha, NE 800-228-6098
Woeber Mustard Mfg Co
  Springfield, OH 800-548-2929

Hot

Archie Moore's
  Milford, CT. 203-876-5088
Arizona Cowboy
  Phoenix, AZ 800-529-8627
Ashman Manufacturing & Distributing Company
  Virginia Beach, VA. 800-641-9924
B & G Foods Inc.
  Parsippany, NJ. 973-401-6500
Baldwin Richardson Foods
  Oakbrook Terrace, IL 866-644-2732
Baumer Foods Inc
  Metairie, LA 504-482-5761
BBQ'n Fools Catering, LLC
  Greenfield, IN 800-671-8652
Blair's Sauces & Snacks
  Highlands, NJ 800-982-5247
Boston Spice & Tea Company
  Boston, VA 800-966-4372
Brother Bru Bru's
  Venice, CA 310-396-9033
Bruce Foods Corporation
  Lafayette, LA 800-299-9082
Buds Kitchen
  New Castle, PA 724-654-9216
Buffalo Wild Wings
  Minneapolis, MN 763-546-1891
Cafe Tequila
  San Francisco, CA 415-264-0106
Cajohn's Fiery Foods Co
  Westerville, OH. 888-703-3473
Cajun Brands
  New Iberia, LA 504-408-2252
California-Antilles Trading
  San Diego, CA 800-330-6450
Cannon's Sweets Hots
  Las Cruces, NM 800-214-6639
Canyon Specialty Foods
  Dallas, TX. 214-352-1771
Captain Bob's Jet Fuel
  Fort Wayne, IN 877-486-6468
Carriere Foods Inc
  Saint-Denis-Sur-Richelie, QC 450-787-3411
Colorado Salsa Company
  Littleton, CO. 303-932-2617
Country Bob's Inc
  Centralia, IL 800-373-2140
Cyclone Enterprises Inc
  Houston, TX 281-872-0087
Dave's Gourmet
  San Rafael, CA 800-758-0372
Dhidow Enterprises
  Oxford, PA 610-932-7868
Dockside Market
  Key Largo, FL 800-813-2253
E. H. Gourmet
  Virginia Beach, VA 757-431-1996
Favorite Foods
  Burnaby, BC 604-420-5100
Festive Foods
  Virginia Beach, VA 757-490-9186
Fire Fruits International
  Orlando, FL. 407-480-6580
Ford's Gourmet Foods
  Raleigh, NC 800-446-0947
Forge Mountain Foods
  Hendersonville, NC 800-823-6743
Garden Complements Inc
  Kansas City, MO. 800-966-1091
Garden Row Foods
  Franklin Park, IL. 800-555-9798
Havana's Limited
  Titusville, FL. 321-267-0513
Heartbreaking Dawns Artisan Foods
  Glendale, AZ. 646-957-3484
Heintz & Weber Co
  Buffalo, NY. 716-852-7171
Hormel Foods Corp.
  Austin, MN 507-437-5611
Horseshoe Brand
  Milan, NY 845-240-2390
Hot Licks
  Spring Valley, CA 888-766-6468
Hot Wachula's
  Lakeland, FL. 877-883-8700
Ingleby Farms
  Dublin, PA. 877-728-7277
Joe Hutson Foods
  Jacksonville, FL 904-731-9065
Juanita's Foods
  Wilmington, CA 800-303-2965
Judicial Flavors
  Auburn, CA. 530-885-1298
K-Mama Sauce
  Minneapolis, MN 612-460-5156
KARI-Out Co
  White Plains, NY 800-433-8799
L & S Packing Co
  Farmingdale, NY 800-286-6487
LA Canasta Mexican Foods
  Phoenix, AZ 855-269-7721
Las Cruces Brand Products
  El Paso, TX. 915-779-5709
Lendy's Cafe Raw Bar
  Virginia Beach, VA 757-491-3511
Leonard Mountain Inc
  Bixby, OK. 800-822-7700
Lounsbury Foods
  Toronto, ON 416-656-6330
Mad Will's Food Company
  Auburn, CA. 888-275-9455
Magic Seasoning Blends
  New Orleans, LA 800-457-2857
MAK Enterprises
  Palmdale, CA 661-272-1867
Maple Grove Farms Of Vermont
  St Johnsbury, VT. 802-748-5141
Millflow Spice Corp.
  Hauppauge, NY 866-227-8355
Mizkan Americas Inc
  Kansas City, MO. 800-323-4358
Mo Hotta Mo Betta
  Savannah, GA. 912-748-2766
Mrs. Dog's Products
  Grand Rapids, MI 800-267-7364
Native Kjalii Foods
  San Francisco, CA 415-522-5580
Natural Value
  Sacramento, CA 916-836-3561
North of the Border
  Tesuque, NM. 800-860-0681
O'Garvey Sauces
  New Braunfels, TX. 830-620-6127
Original Juan
  Kansas City, KS 800-568-8468
Paradise Products Corporation
  Boca Raton, FL. 800-826-1235
Pepper Creek Farms
  Lawton, OK. 800-526-8132
Pepper Island Beach
  Lawrence, PA 724-746-2401
Peppered Palette
  Bellingham, WA 866-829-9151
Peppers
  Lewes, DE. 800-998-3473
Picaflor
  Boulder, CO 720-442-3816
Porky's Gourmet Foods
  Gallatin, TN 800-767-5911
Quality Foods
  Qualicum Beach, BC 877-833-7890
Ray's Sausage Co
  Cleveland, OH 216-921-8782
Reckitt Benckiser LLC
  Parsippany, NJ. 973-404-2600
Red Hot Foods
  Santa Paula, CA 805-258-3650
Robinson's No 1 Ribs
  Oak Park, IL 800-836-6750
Royal Resources
  New Orleans, LA 800-888-9932
Sabra Dipping Company,LL
  Oceanside, CA 800-748-5523
Sam's Leon Mexican Food
  Omaha, NE 402-733-3809
Sambets Cajun Deli
  Austin, TX. 800-472-6238
San Antonio Farms
  Platteville, WI 800-236-1119
Simmons Hot Gourmet Products Corp.
  Lethbridge, AB 403-327-9087
Sinai Gourmet
  Montreal, QC 844-887-4624
Southwest Specialty Food
  Goodyear, AZ 800-536-3131
Spice House International Specialties
  Hicksville, NY 516-942-7248
Sweet Baby Ray's
  Chicago, IL. 877-729-2229
T.W. Garner Food Company
  Winston Salem, NC. 800-476-7383
Tantos Foods International
  Markham, ON 905-943-9993
Tapatio Hot Sauce
  Vernon, CA 323-587-8933
Texas Tamale Co
  Houston, TX 713-795-5500
Thistledew Farm
  Proctor, WV 800-854-6639
Thompson's Fine Foods
  Shoreview, MN 800-807-0025
Tomorrow Enterprise
  New Iberia, LA 337-783-2666
Trappey's Fine Foods Inc
  New Iberia, LA 337-365-8281
Tucson Tamale Company
  Tucson, AZ 520-398-6282
Uncle Dougie's
  Chicago, IL
Vegetable Juices Inc
  Chicago, IL 888-776-9752
Whitfield Foods Inc
  Montgomery, AL. 800-633-8790
Wing It Inc
  Falmouth, MA. 508-540-9860
Wing-Time
  Lynn, MA 781-592-1069
Wizards Cauldron, LTD
  Yanceyville, NC 336-694-5665
World Famous Buffalo Wing Sauce
  Buffalo, NY. 716-912-9068

Jerk

Baldwin Richardson Foods
  Oakbrook Terrace, IL 866-644-2732
Buffalo Wild Wings
  Minneapolis, MN 763-546-1891
Catskill Mountain Specialties
  Saugerties, NY 800-311-3473
Cinnabar Specialty Foods Inc
  Prescott, AZ 866-293-6433
Cuizina Food Company
  Woodinville, WA. 425-486-7000
Doctor Dread's Jerk
  Glen Echo, MD. 301-908-9450
Mix-A-Lota Stuff LLC
  Fort Pierce, FL 727-365-7328
Nature's Kitchen
  Roswell, GA 678-845-6897

Product Categories / Sauces, Dips & Dressings: Sauces

Lemon
Baldwin Richardson Foods
  Oakbrook Terrace, IL 866-644-2732
Genarom International
  Cranbury, NJ 609-409-6200
Wei-Chuan USA Inc
  Bell Gardens, CA 562-372-2020

Marinara
Baldwin Richardson Foods
  Oakbrook Terrace, IL 866-644-2732
Campbell Soup Co.
  Camden, NJ. 800-257-8443
Casa Di Lisio Products Inc
  Mt Kisco, NY 800-247-4199
CHS Inc.
  Inver Grove Hts., MN 800-328-6539
Colonna Brothers Inc
  North Bergen, NJ 201-864-1115
Cowboy Caviar
  Berkeley, CA. 877-509-1796
Cuizina Food Company
  Woodinville, WA. 425-486-7000
Dell'Amore Enterprises
  Colchester, VT 800-962-6673
Hot Wachula's
  Lakeland, FL. 877-883-8700
Kozlowski Farms
  Forestville, CA 800-473-2767
L & S Packing Co
  Farmingdale, NY 800-286-6487
LiDestri Food & Drink
  Fairport, NY 585-377-7700
Mad Will's Food Company
  Auburn, CA. 888-275-9455
Mamma Lombardi's All Natural Sauces
  Holbrook, NY. 631-471-6609
Marsan Foods
  Toronto, ON 416-755-9262
Molinaro's Fine Italian Foods Ltd.
  Mississauga, ON 905-281-0352
Nello's Sauce
  Raleigh, NC 919-428-4338
Newman's Own
  Westport, CT. 203-222-0136
Palmieri Food Products
  New Haven, CT 800-845-5447
Pasta Factory
  Melrose Park, IL 800-615-6951
Pasta Valente
  Charlottesville, VA. 888-575-7670
Pastorelli Food Products
  Chicago, IL 800-767-2829
Red Gold Inc.
  Elwood, IN 866-729-7187
Sargento Foods Inc
  Plymouth, WI 800-243-3737
Stanislaus Food Prod
  Modesto, CA. 800-327-7201
Vanee Foods Co
  Berkeley, IL. 708-449-7300
Ventre Packing Company
  Syracuse, NY 315-463-2384
Victoria Fine Foods
  Brooklyn, NY 718-927-3000
Violet Packing Holdings LLC
  Williamstown, NJ 856-629-7428
Webbpak Inc
  Trussville, AL 800-655-3500

Meat
J.M. Smucker Co.
  Orrville, OH 888-550-9555
Victoria Fine Foods
  Brooklyn, NY 718-927-3000
Woods Smoked Meats Inc
  Bowling Green, MO 800-458-8426

Mediterranean
Baldwin Richardson Foods
  Oakbrook Terrace, IL 866-644-2732
Cookies Food Products
  Wall Lake, IA 800-331-4995
Cuizina Food Company
  Woodinville, WA. 425-486-7000
L & S Packing Co
  Farmingdale, NY 800-286-6487
Papa Leone Food Enterprises
  Beverly Hills, CA 310-552-1660

Parthenon Food Products
  Ann Arbor, MI 734-994-1012

Mexican Food
Art's Mexican Products
  Kansas City, KS 913-371-2163
B & G Foods Inc.
  Parsippany, NJ. 973-401-6500
Big B Barbecue
  Evansville, IN 812-425-5235
Border Foods
  New Hope, MN 763-559-7338
Casa Visco
  Schenectady, NY. 888-607-2823
Fernandez Chili Co
  Alamosa, CO. 719-589-6043
Garden Complements Inc
  Kansas City, MO. 800-966-1091
Golden Specialty Foods Inc
  Norwalk, CA. 562-802-2537
Golding Farms Foods
  Winston Salem, NC. 336-766-6161
Heluva Good Cheese
  Lynnfield, MA. 800-644-5473
New Canaan Farms
  Dripping Springs, TX 800-727-5267
Palmieri Food Products
  New Haven, CT 800-845-5447
Pepper Creek Farms
  Lawton, OK. 800-526-8132
Subco Foods Inc
  Sheboygan, WI 800-473-0757
Walker Foods
  Los Angeles, CA. 800-966-5199

Mint
Baldwin Richardson Foods
  Oakbrook Terrace, IL 866-644-2732
Cedarvale Food Products
  Toronto, ON 416-656-3330
Lounsbury Foods
  Toronto, ON 416-656-6330
Top Hat Co Inc
  Wilmette, IL 847-256-6565

Mixes
Century Blends LLC
  Hunt Valley, MD. 410-771-6606
CHS Inc.
  Inver Grove Hts., MN 800-328-6539
Clorox Company
  Oakland, CA. 510-271-7000
Lawry's Foods
  Hunt Valley, MD. 800-952-9797
Produits Alimentaire
  Laval, QC 800-361-9326
R C Fine Foods Inc
  Hillsborough, NJ. 800-526-3953
Serv-Agen Corporation
  Cherry Hill, NJ 856-663-6966
Superior Quality Foods
  Ontario, CA. 800-300-4210
UFL Foods
  Mississauga, ON 905-670-7776

Mole
Juanita's Foods
  Wilmington, CA 800-303-2965

Mushroom
Cipriani's Spaghetti & Sauce Company
  Chicago Heights, IL 708-755-6212
Cuizina Food Company
  Woodinville, WA. 425-486-7000
Galassi Foods
  Coralville, IA 319-339-7409
The Truffleist
  Astoria, NY. 917-325-3374
Vanee Foods Co
  Berkeley, IL. 708-449-7300
Vegetable Juices Inc
  Chicago, IL 888-776-9752
Worthmore Food Products Co
  Cincinnati, OH 866-837-7687

Orange
Bunker Foods Corp.
  New York, NY 646-738-4020

Papa Leone Food Enterprises
  Beverly Hills, CA 310-552-1660
San-J International Inc
  Henrico, VA 800-446-5500

Organic
Fiore Di Pasta
  Fresno, CA 559-457-0431
Imagine Foods
  Boulder, CO 800-434-4246
Lassonde Pappas & Company, Inc.
  Carneys Point, NJ 800-257-7019
Vegy Vida
  Cincinnati, OH 513-659-0781

Oyster
Favorite Foods
  Burnaby, BC 604-420-5100
Lee Kum Kee USA Inc
  City Of Industry, CA. 800-654-5082
Wei-Chuan USA Inc
  Bell Gardens, CA 562-372-2020

Pasta
Amanida USA Corp
  Coral Gables, FL
Barilla USA
  Northbrook, IL 800-922-7455
Colavita USA
  Edison, NJ. 888-265-2848
Coupla Guys Foods
  Chicago, IL 312-829-2332
Dei Fratelli
  Toledo, OH 800-837-1631
Del Monte Foods Inc.
  Walnut Creek, CA
Fiore Di Pasta
  Fresno, CA 559-457-0431
Milos Whole World Gourmet
  Athens, OH 866-589-6456
Mondiv/Division of Lassonde Inc
  Boisbriand, QC 450-979-0717
Newman's Own
  Westport, CT. 203-222-0136
Nona Vegan Foods
  Toronto, ON 416-836-9387
Pacific Choice Brands
  Fresno, CA 559-476-3581
Paesana Products
  East Farmingdale, NY. 631-845-1717
Pastene Co LTD
  Canton, MA 781-298-3397
Patsy's Brands
  New York, NY 212-247-3491
Serro Foods LLC
  Catskill, NY 518-943-9255
Summer Garden Food Manufacturing
  Boardman, OH 330-965-8455
The Sunshine Tomato Company
  New Cumberland, PA 717-909-0844
Victoria Fine Foods
  Brooklyn, NY 718-927-3000
White Oak Farm and Table
  Westport, CT. 203-716-1577

Peanut
Rowena
  Norfolk, VA. 800-627-8699

Pepper
Brother Bru Bru's
  Venice, CA 310-396-9033
Colibri Pepper Company
  Elmer, LA 316-730-6528
Genarom International
  Cranbury, NJ 609-409-6200
Judicial Flavors
  Auburn, CA. 530-885-1298
Landry's Pepper Co
  St Martinville, LA. 337-394-6097
Pepper Source Inc
  Metairie, LA 504-885-3223
Pepper Source LTD
  Rogers, AR 479-246-1030
Pepper Source, Rogers
  Van Buren, AR 479-474-5178
Porky's Gourmet Foods
  Gallatin, TN 800-767-5911
Small Axe Peppers
  Long Island City, NY

Product Categories / Sauces, Dips & Dressings: Sauces

T.W. Garner Food Company
  Winston Salem, NC 800-476-7383

Hot

Brother Bru Bru's
  Venice, CA 310-396-9033
Horseshoe Brand
  Milan, NY 845-240-2390
Kill Sauce
  Pasadena, CA
Mother's Mountain Pantry
  Falmouth, ME 800-440-9891
Porky's Gourmet Foods
  Gallatin, TN 800-767-5911

Pesto

Al Dente Pasta Co
  Whitmore Lake, MI 800-536-7278
Armanino Foods of Distinction
  Hayward, CA 800-255-8588
Barilla USA
  Northbrook, IL 800-922-7455
Bella Cucina
  Atlanta, GA 866-350-9040
Casa Di Lisio Products Inc
  Mt Kisco, NY 800-247-4199
Christopher Ranch LLC
  Gilroy, CA 408-847-1100
Cuizina Food Company
  Woodinville, WA 425-486-7000
Delectable Gourmet LLC
  Deer Park, NY 800-696-1350
Golden Specialty Foods Inc
  Norwalk, CA 562-802-2537
Gracious Gourmet
  Bridgewater, CT 860-350-1213
Great Garlic Foods
  Bradley Beach, NJ 732-775-3311
HerbNZest LLC
  Princeton, NJ 917-582-1191
Kind Snacks
  New York, NY 855-884-5463
La Maison Le Grand
  St-Joseph-du-Lac, QC 450-623-3000
Le Grand
  Blainville, QC 450-623-3000
Les Aliments Livabec Foods
  Sherrington, QC 450-454-7971
Millflow Spice Corp.
  Hauppauge, NY 866-227-8355
Mondiv/Division of Lassonde Inc
  Boisbriand, QC 450-979-0717
North American Enterprises
  Tucson, AZ 800-817-8666
Pasta Factory
  Melrose Park, IL 800-615-6951
Peaceworks
  New York, NY 212-897-3985
Pestos with Panache
  Brooklyn, NY 917-656-3082
Randazzo's Honest To Goodness Sauces
  Glen Rock, NJ 201-543-1195
Red Gold Inc.
  Elwood, IN 866-729-7187
Rising Sun Farms
  Phoenix, OR 800-888-0795
TexaFrance
  Round Rock, TX 800-776-8937
Tulkoff's Food Products Inc
  Baltimore, MD 800-638-7343
Victoria Fine Foods
  Brooklyn, NY 718-927-3000
Waterfield Farms
  Amherst, MA 413-549-3558

Pizza

Alimentaire Whyte's Inc
  Laval, QC 866-420-9520
Baldwin Richardson Foods
  Oakbrook Terrace, IL 866-644-2732
Big B Barbecue
  Evansville, IN 812-425-5235
Canada Bread Co, Ltd
  Etobicoke, ON 800-465-5515
Cuizina Food Company
  Woodinville, WA 425-486-7000
DelGrosso Foods
  Tipton, PA 800-521-5880
Delgrosso Foods Inc.
  Tipton, PA 800-521-5880
Dorothy Dawson Food Products
  Jackson, MI 517-788-9830
Furmano's Foods
  Northumberland, PA 800-952-1111
Giovanni Food Co Inc
  Syracuse, NY 315-457-2373
Hirzel Canning Co & Farms
  Luckey, OH 419-419-7525
Leonardo's of Vermont, LLC
  South Burlington, VT 902-863-8404
Mama Mary's
  Fairforest, SC 800-813-7574
Nation Wide Canning Ltd.
  Cottam, ON 519-839-4831
Palmieri Food Products
  New Haven, CT 800-845-5447
Paradise Tomato Kitchens
  Louisville, KY 502-637-1700
Pastorelli Food Products
  Chicago, IL 800-767-2829
Perky's Pizza
  Oldsmar, FL 800-473-7597
Rustic Crust Inc
  Pittsfield, NH 603-435-5119
Sargento Foods Inc
  Plymouth, WI 800-243-3737
Sassafras Enterprises Inc
  Chicago, IL 800-537-4941
Sky Valley Foods
  Danville, VA
Spinato's Fine Foods
  Tempe, AZ 480-275-4319
Stanislaus Food Prod
  Modesto, CA 800-327-7201
Tip Top Canning Co
  Tipp City, OH 800-352-2635
Triple K Manufacturing Company, Inc.
  Shenandoah, IA 712-246-4376
Violet Packing Holdings LLC
  Williamstown, NJ 856-629-7428
Worthmore Food Products Co
  Cincinnati, OH 866-837-7687

Plum

Baldwin Richardson Foods
  Oakbrook Terrace, IL 866-644-2732
Cuizina Food Company
  Woodinville, WA 425-486-7000
Favorite Foods
  Burnaby, BC 604-420-5100
Lee Kum Kee USA Inc
  City Of Industry, CA 800-654-5082
Wei-Chuan USA Inc
  Bell Gardens, CA 562-372-2020
Wing's Food Products
  Toronto, ON 416-259-2662

Primavera

Cuizina Food Company
  Woodinville, WA 425-486-7000
L & S Packing Co
  Farmingdale, NY 800-286-6487

Puttanesca

Baldwin Richardson Foods
  Oakbrook Terrace, IL 866-644-2732
Casa Di Lisio Products Inc
  Mt Kisco, NY 800-247-4199
Cuizina Food Company
  Woodinville, WA 425-486-7000
L & S Packing Co
  Farmingdale, NY 800-286-6487
Papa Leone Food Enterprises
  Beverly Hills, CA 310-552-1660

Seafood

Beaverton Foods Inc
  Hillsboro, OR 800-223-8076
Blue Crab Bay
  Melfa, VA 800-221-2722
Chincoteague Seafood Co Inc
  Parsonsburg, MD 443-260-4800
Clements Foods Co
  Oklahoma City, OK 800-654-8355
Cuizina Food Company
  Woodinville, WA 425-486-7000
E Waldo Ward & Son Marmalades
  Sierra Madre, CA 800-355-9273
Heinz Portion Control
  Jacksonville, FL 904-695-1300
J.M. Smucker Co.
  Orrville, OH 888-550-9555
Lounsbury Foods
  Toronto, ON 416-656-6330
Mid-Atlantic Foods Inc
  Easton, MD 800-922-4688
Myron's Fine Foods, Inc.
  Millers Falls, MA 800-730-2820
New Business Corp
  Gary, IN 219-885-1476
New Canaan Farms
  Dripping Springs, TX 800-727-5267
Palmieri Food Products
  New Haven, CT 800-845-5447
Paradise Products Corporation
  Boca Raton, FL 800-826-1235
Rosmarino Foods/R.Z. Humbert Company
  Odessa, FL 888-926-9053
Silver Spring Foods
  Eau Clair, MI 800-826-7322
T.W. Garner Food Company
  Winston Salem, NC 800-476-7383
Woeber Mustard Mfg Co
  Springfield, OH 800-548-2929

Soy

Ajinomoto Heartland Inc
  Chicago, IL 773-380-7000
Alimentaire Whyte's Inc
  Laval, QC 866-420-9520
American Culinary Garden
  Springfield, MO 888-831-2433
Baldwin Richardson Foods
  Oakbrook Terrace, IL 866-644-2732
Bartush Schnitzius Foods Co
  Lewisville, TX 972-219-1270
Basic Food Flavors
  North Las Vegas, NV 702-643-0043
Baumer Foods Inc
  Metairie, LA 504-482-5761
Baycliff Co Inc
  Garwood, NJ 866-772-7569
Castella Imports Inc
  Brentwood, NY 631-231-5500
Clements Foods Co
  Oklahoma City, OK 800-654-8355
Commodities Marketing Inc
  Clarksburg, NJ 732-516-0700
Dixie USA
  Tomball, TX 800-233-3668
Edward & Sons Trading Co
  Carpinteria, CA 805-684-8500
Favorite Foods
  Burnaby, BC 604-420-5100
Felbro Food Products
  Los Angeles, CA 323-936-5266
Flavor House, Inc.
  Adelanto, CA 760-246-9131
Hormel Foods Corp.
  Austin, MN 507-437-5611
Inter-American Products
  Cincinnati, OH 800-645-2233
KARI-Out Co
  White Plains, NY 800-433-8799
Lee Kum Kee USA Inc
  City Of Industry, CA 800-654-5082
Lee's Food Products
  Toronto, ON 416-465-2407
Mandarin Soy Sauce Inc
  Middletown, NY 845-343-1505
McIlhenny Company
  Avery Island, LA 800-634-9599
Millflow Spice Corp.
  Hauppauge, NY 866-227-8355
Myron's Fine Foods, Inc.
  Millers Falls, MA 800-730-2820
Nikken Foods
  St Louis, MO 314-881-5818
San-J International Inc
  Henrico, VA 800-446-5500
Sempio Foods
  Cerritos, CA 562-207-9540
Serv-Agen Corporation
  Cherry Hill, NJ 856-663-6966
Sobaya
  Cowansville, QC 800-319-8808
Tomasso Corporation
  Baie D'Urfe, QC 514-325-3000
Wei-Chuan USA Inc
  Bell Gardens, CA 562-372-2020
Wing Nien Food
  Hayward, CA 510-487-8877

Product Categories / Sauces, Dips & Dressings: Sauces

Wing's Food Products
  Toronto, ON 416-259-2662
Wizards Cauldron, LTD
  Yanceyville, NC 336-694-5665
Yamasa Corp USA
  Salem, OR 503-363-8550

Spaghetti

Alimentaire Whyte's Inc
  Laval, QC 866-420-9520
Baldwin Richardson Foods
  Oakbrook Terrace, IL 866-644-2732
Campbell Soup Co.
  Camden, NJ 800-257-8443
Casa Visco
  Schenectady, NY 888-607-2823
Chef-A-Roni Fancy Foods
  East Greenwich, RI 401-884-8798
Cipriani's Spaghetti & Sauce Company
  Chicago Heights, IL 708-755-6212
Cuizina Food Company
  Woodinville, WA 425-486-7000
DelGrosso Foods
  Tipton, PA 800-521-5880
Delgrosso Foods Inc.
  Tipton, PA 800-521-5880
Eden Foods Inc
  Clinton, MI 888-424-3336
Furmano's Foods
  Northumberland, PA 800-952-1111
Giovanni Food Co Inc
  Syracuse, NY 315-457-2373
Gumpert's Canada
  Mississauga, ON 800-387-9324
Hagerty Foods
  Orange, CA 714-628-1230
Hanover Foods Corp
  Hanover, PA 717-632-6000
Hirzel Canning Co & Farms
  Luckey, OH 419-419-7525
L & S Packing Co
  Farmingdale, NY 800-286-6487
Marsan Foods
  Toronto, ON 416-755-9262
Molinaro's Fine Italian Foods Ltd.
  Mississauga, ON 905-281-0352
Mom's Food Company
  Osterville, MA 800-969-6667
Nation Wide Canning Ltd.
  Cottam, ON 519-839-4831
Nicola Pizza
  Rehoboth Beach, DE 302-226-2654
Palmieri Food Products
  New Haven, CT 800-845-5447
Peaceworks
  New York, NY 212-897-3985
Pino's Pasta Veloce
  Staten Island, NY 718-273-6660
Porinos Gourmet Food
  Central Falls, RI 800-826-3938
Progresso Quality Foods
  Vineland, NJ 856-691-1565
Ragozzino Foods Inc
  Meriden, CT 800-348-1240
Red Gold Inc.
  Elwood, IN 866-729-7187
Seneca Foods Corp
  Marion, NY 315-926-8100
Silver State Foods Inc
  Denver, CO 800-423-3351
Todd's
  Des Moines, IA 800-247-5363
Triple H Food Processors Inc
  Riverside, CA 951-352-5700
Violet Packing Holdings LLC
  Williamstown, NJ 856-629-7428
Westin Foods
  Omaha, NE 800-228-6098
Worthmore Food Products Co
  Cincinnati, OH 866-837-7687

Meat

Campbell Soup Co.
  Camden, NJ 800-257-8443
Chef-A-Roni Fancy Foods
  East Greenwich, RI 401-884-8798
Cipriani's Spaghetti & Sauce Company
  Chicago Heights, IL 708-755-6212
DelGrosso Foods
  Tipton, PA 800-521-5880

Gaucho Foods
  Fayetteville, IL 877-677-2282
Vanee Foods Co
  Berkeley, IL 708-449-7300

Meatless

Campbell Soup Co.
  Camden, NJ 800-257-8443
Chef-A-Roni Fancy Foods
  East Greenwich, RI 401-884-8798
DelGrosso Foods
  Tipton, PA 800-521-5880
Molinaro's Fine Italian Foods Ltd.
  Mississauga, ON 905-281-0352

Steak

Ashman Manufacturing & Distributing Company
  Virginia Beach, VA 800-641-9924
Baumer Foods Inc
  Metairie, LA 504-482-5761
Creative Foodworks Inc
  San Antonio, TX 210-212-4761
Golding Farms Foods
  Winston Salem, NC 336-766-6161
Joe Hutson Foods
  Jacksonville, FL 904-731-9065
Kozlowski Farms
  Forestville, CA 800-473-2767
L & S Packing Co
  Farmingdale, NY 800-286-6487
Lea & Perrins
  Glenview, IL
Magic Seasoning Blends
  New Orleans, LA 800-457-2857
Myron's Fine Foods, Inc.
  Millers Falls, MA 800-730-2820
Newman's Own
  Westport, CT 203-222-0136
Paradise Products Corporation
  Boca Raton, FL 800-826-1235
Quality Foods
  Qualicum Beach, BC 877-833-7890
Webbpak Inc
  Trussville, AL 800-655-3500
Wine Country Chef LLC
  Hidden Valley Lake, CA 707-322-0406
Wizards Cauldron, LTD
  Yanceyville, NC 336-694-5665

Stir-Fry

Baldwin Richardson Foods
  Oakbrook Terrace, IL 866-644-2732
Cuizina Food Company
  Woodinville, WA 425-486-7000
Flavor House, Inc.
  Adelanto, CA 760-246-9131
Hormel Foods Corp.
  Austin, MN 507-437-5611
L & S Packing Co
  Farmingdale, NY 800-286-6487
Marjon Specialty Foods Inc
  Plant City, FL 813-752-3482
Myron's Fine Foods, Inc.
  Millers Falls, MA 800-730-2820
Wei-Chuan USA Inc
  Bell Gardens, CA 562-372-2020
Wing Nien Food
  Hayward, CA 510-487-8877
Wizards Cauldron, LTD
  Yanceyville, NC 336-694-5665

Sweet & Sour

Baldwin Richardson Foods
  Oakbrook Terrace, IL 866-644-2732
Big B Barbecue
  Evansville, IN 812-425-5235
Cuizina Food Company
  Woodinville, WA 425-486-7000
Garden Complements Inc
  Kansas City, MO 800-966-1091
Gumpert's Canada
  Mississauga, ON 800-387-9324
KARI-Out Co
  White Plains, NY 800-433-8799
L & S Packing Co
  Farmingdale, NY 800-286-6487
Lee Kum Kee USA Inc
  City Of Industry, CA 800-654-5082
Robbie's Natural Products
  Vancouver, WA 360-433-2325

Vanee Foods Co
  Berkeley, IL 708-449-7300
Wei-Chuan USA Inc
  Bell Gardens, CA 562-372-2020
Wing Nien Food
  Hayward, CA 510-487-8877

Szechuan

Baldwin Richardson Foods
  Oakbrook Terrace, IL 866-644-2732
Favorite Foods
  Burnaby, BC 604-420-5100
Myron's Fine Foods, Inc.
  Millers Falls, MA 800-730-2820
San-J International Inc
  Henrico, VA 800-446-5500

Taco

Amigos Canning Company
  San Antonio, TX 210-798-5360
Baldwin Richardson Foods
  Oakbrook Terrace, IL 866-644-2732
Bartush Schnitzius Foods Co
  Lewisville, TX 972-219-1270
Bien Padre Foods Inc
  Eureka, CA 707-442-4585
Big B Barbecue
  Evansville, IN 812-425-5235
Cookies Food Products
  Wall Lake, IA 800-331-4995
El Rancho Tortilla
  San Antonio, TX 210-922-8411
Famous Chili Inc
  Fort Smith, AR 479-782-0096
Fernandez Chili Co
  Alamosa, CO 719-589-6043
Golden Specialty Foods Inc
  Norwalk, CA 562-802-2537
Golding Farms Foods
  Winston Salem, NC 336-766-6161
Hagerty Foods
  Orange, CA 714-628-1230
Heluva Good Cheese
  Lynnfield, MA 800-644-5473
Hirzel Canning Co & Farms
  Luckey, OH 419-419-7525
Hormel Foods Corp.
  Austin, MN 507-437-5611
Hume Specialties
  Chester, VT 802-875-3117
Imus Ranch Foods
  Darien, CT 888-284-4687
Judicial Flavors
  Auburn, CA 530-885-1298
LA Vencedora Products Inc
  Los Angeles, CA 800-327-2572
La Victoria Foods
  Austin, MN 800-725-7212
Laredo Tortilleria & Mexican
  Fort Wayne, IN 800-252-7336
Li'l Guy Foods
  Kansas City, MO 800-886-8226
New Canaan Farms
  Dripping Springs, TX 800-727-5267
Palmieri Food Products
  New Haven, CT 800-845-5447
Pepper Creek Farms
  Lawton, OK 800-526-8132
Red Duck Foods
  Portland, OR 530-219-0150
Red Gold Inc.
  Elwood, IN 866-729-7187
Spanish Gardens Food Manufacturing
  Kansas City, KS 913-831-4242

Tahini

Dipasa USA Inc
  Brownsville, TX 956-831-4072
East Wind Inc
  Tecumseh, MO 417-679-4682
Once Again Nut Butter
  Nunda, NY 888-800-8075
Premier Organics
  Oakland, CA 866-237-8688

Tartar

Baldwin Richardson Foods
  Oakbrook Terrace, IL 866-644-2732
Cedarvale Food Products
  Toronto, ON 416-656-3330

Product Categories / Sauces, Dips & Dressings: Vinegar

Cuizina Food Company
  Woodinville, WA 425-486-7000
Golding Farms Foods
  Winston Salem, NC 336-766-6161
Heinz Portion Control
  Jacksonville, FL 904-695-1300
Kelchner's Horseradish
  Allentown, PA 800-424-1952
Lounsbury Foods
  Toronto, ON 416-656-6330
Sau-Sea Foods
  Tarrytown, NY 914-631-1717
Schlotterbeck & Foss Company
  Portland, ME 800-777-4666
Silver Spring Foods
  Eau Clair, MI. 800-826-7322
Westin Foods
  Omaha, NE 800-228-6098
Wood Brothers Inc
  West Columbia, SC 803-796-5146

Teriyaki

Argo Century, Inc.
  Jacksonville, FL 800-446-7108
Baldwin Richardson Foods
  Oakbrook Terrace, IL 866-644-2732
Baycliff Co Inc
  Garwood, NJ 866-772-7569
BBQ'n Fools Catering, LLC
  Greenfield, IN 800-671-8652
Buffalo Wild Wings
  Minneapolis, MN 763-546-1891
California Custom Foods
  Fullerton, CA 714-870-0490
Conway Import Co Inc
  Franklin Park, IL. 800-323-8801
Cuizina Food Company
  Woodinville, WA 425-486-7000
Dynamic Foods
  Lubbock, TX 806-723-5600
Favorite Foods
  Burnaby, BC 604-420-5100
Golden Specialty Foods Inc
  Norwalk, CA 562-802-2537
Hormel Foods Corp.
  Austin, MN 507-437-5611
L & S Packing Co
  Farmingdale, NY 800-286-6487
Miyako Oriental Foods Inc
  Baldwin Park, CA 877-788-6476
Myron's Fine Foods, Inc.
  Millers Falls, MA 800-730-2820
Passetti's Pride
  Hayward, CA 800-521-4659
Red Duck Foods
  Portland, OR 530-219-0150
Sagawa's Savory Sauces
  Tualatin, OR 503-692-4334
San-J International Inc
  Henrico, VA 800-446-5500
Sky Valley Foods
  Danville, VA
T. Marzetti Company
  Westerville, OH. 800-999-1835
Triple H Food Processors Inc
  Riverside, CA 951-352-5700
Valley Grain Products
  Fresno, CA 559-675-3400
World Flavors Inc
  Warminster, PA 215-672-4400
Yamasa Corp USA
  Salem, OR. 503-363-8550

Tomato

Barilla USA
  Northbrook, IL 800-922-7455
City Saucery
  Staten Island, NY 718-753-4006
Furmano's Foods
  Northumberland, PA 800-952-1111
Galassi Foods
  Coralville, IA 319-339-7409
Mamma Lombardi's All Natural Sauces
  Holbrook, NY 631-471-6609
Rosa Food Products
  Philadelphia, PA 215-467-2214
Small Planet Foods
  Minneapolis, MN 800-624-4123
The Jersey Tomato Company
  Hillsdale, NJ

Canned

Bartush Schnitzius Foods Co
  Lewisville, TX 972-219-1270
Bruno Specialty Foods
  West Sayville, NY. 631-589-1700
Cajun Brands
  New Iberia, LA 504-408-2252
Casa Di Lisio Products Inc
  Mt Kisco, NY 800-247-4199
Casa Visco
  Schenectady, NY. 888-607-2823
City Saucery
  Staten Island, NY 718-753-4006
Colonna Brothers Inc
  North Bergen, NJ 201-864-1115
Costa Deano's Gourmet Foods
  Canton, OH. 800-337-2823
Cucina Antica Foods Corp
  Mt Kisco, NY 877-728-2462
Cuizina Food Company
  Woodinville, WA 425-486-7000
Escalon Premier Brand
  Escalon, CA 209-838-7341
Gumpert's Canada
  Mississauga, ON 800-387-9324
Hanover Foods Corp
  Hanover, PA 717-632-6000
Hirzel Canning Co & Farms
  Luckey, OH 419-419-7525
International Home Foods
  Parsippany, NJ. 973-359-9920
Kozlowski Farms
  Forestville, CA 800-473-2767
L & S Packing Co
  Farmingdale, NY 800-286-6487
Molinaro's Fine Italian Foods Ltd.
  Mississauga, ON. 905-281-0352
Nation Wide Canning Ltd.
  Cottam, ON 519-839-4831
Northwest Packing Co
  Vancouver, WA 800-543-4356
Palmieri Food Products
  New Haven, CT 800-845-5447
Papa Leone Food Enterprises
  Beverly Hills, CA 310-552-1660
Pasta Factory
  Melrose Park, IL. 800-615-6951
Pastorelli Food Products
  Chicago, IL. 800-767-2829
Progresso Quality Foods
  Vineland, NJ 856-691-1565
Seneca Foods Corp
  Marion, NY. 315-926-8100
Small Planet Foods
  Minneapolis, MN 800-624-4123
Tip Top Canning Co
  Tipp City, OH 800-352-2635
Tomasso Corporation
  Baie D'Urfe, QC 514-325-3000
Walker Foods
  Los Angeles, CA. 800-966-5199

Diced

Small Planet Foods
  Minneapolis, MN 800-624-4123

Frozen

Cajun Brands
  New Iberia, LA 504-408-2252
Casa Di Lisio Products Inc
  Mt Kisco, NY 800-247-4199
Cuizina Food Company
  Woodinville, WA 425-486-7000
Hanover Foods Corp
  Hanover, PA 717-632-6000
Marsan Foods
  Toronto, ON 416-755-9262
Molinaro's Fine Italian Foods Ltd.
  Mississauga, ON. 905-281-0352
Progresso Quality Foods
  Vineland, NJ 856-691-1565
Seneca Foods Corp
  Marion, NY. 315-926-8100

with Spices

Palmieri Food Products
  New Haven, CT 800-845-5447
Patsy's Italian Restaurant
  New York, NY 212-247-3491

Small Planet Foods
  Minneapolis, MN 800-624-4123

Worcestershire

A. Lassonde Inc.
  Rougemont, QC 866-552-7643
Annie's Naturals
  Berkeley, CA. 800-434-1234
Baldwin Richardson Foods
  Oakbrook Terrace, IL 866-644-2732
Baumer Foods Inc
  Metairie, LA 504-482-5761
Big B Barbecue
  Evansville, IN 812-425-5235
Cajun Brands
  New Iberia, LA 504-408-2252
Clements Foods Co
  Oklahoma City, OK 800-654-8355
Colgin Co
  Dallas, TX. 888-226-5446
Felbro Food Products
  Los Angeles, CA. 323-936-5266
Gold Coast Ingredients
  Commerce, CA 800-352-8673
Illes Seasonings & Flavors
  Carrollton, TX. 800-683-4553
Inter-American Products
  Cincinnati, OH 800-645-2233
Lea & Perrins
  Glenview, IL
McIlhenny Company
  Avery Island, LA. 800-634-9599
Millflow Spice Corp.
  Hauppauge, NY 866-227-8355
New Business Corp
  Gary, IN. 219-885-1476
Portlandia Foods
  Portland, OR 833-739-3663
Reckitt Benckiser LLC
  Parsippany, NJ. 973-404-2600
Robbie's Natural Products
  Vancouver, WA 360-433-2325
Serv-Agen Corporation
  Cherry Hill, NJ 856-663-6966
T.W. Garner Food Company
  Winston Salem, NC 800-476-7383
Vegetable Juices Inc
  Chicago, IL. 888-776-9752

Vinegar

A Perfect Pear
  Napa, CA. 800-553-5753
Agrusa
  Leonia, NJ. 201-592-5950
American Culinary Garden
  Springfield, MO 888-831-2433
Arbor Hill Grapery & Winery
  Naples, NY 800-554-7553
Arnabal International, Inc.
  Tustin, CA. 714-665-9477
Au Printemps Gourmet
  Saint-Jerome, QC 800-438-6676
B R Cohn Winery & Olive Oil Co
  Glen Ellen, CA 800-330-4064
Baycliff Co Inc
  Garwood, NJ 866-772-7569
Belton Foods Inc
  Dayton, OH 800-443-2266
Big B Barbecue
  Evansville, IN 812-425-5235
Bittersweet Herb Farm
  Shelburne Falls, MA. 800-456-1599
Blueberry Store
  Grand Junction, MI 877-654-2400
Boston Spice & Tea Company
  Boston, VA. 800-966-4372
Boyajian LLC
  Canton, MA 800-965-0665
Buonitalia
  New York, NY 212-633-9090
C W Resources Inc
  New Britain, CT 860-229-7700
California Balsamic Inc
  Ukiah, CA. 888-644-5127
California Olive Oil Council
  Berkeley, CA. 888-718-9830
Castella Imports Inc
  Brentwood, NY. 631-231-5500
Chicama Vineyards
  West Tisbury, MA 888-244-2262

Product Categories / Sauces, Dips & Dressings: Vinegar

Clements Foods Co
  Oklahoma City, OK 800-654-8355
Colonna Brothers Inc
  North Bergen, NJ 201-864-1115
Consumers Vinegar & Spice Co
  Chicago, IL 773-376-4100
Creole Fermentation Indu
  Abbeville, LA 337-898-9377
Dark Tickle Company
  St Lunaire-Griquet, NL. 709-623-2354
De Nigris
  Totowa, NJ 973-837-6791
Delicae Gourmet
  Tarpon Springs, FL 800-942-2502
Eden Foods Inc
  Clinton, MI 888-424-3336
Emerling International Foods
  Buffalo, NY. 716-833-7381
Fleischmann's Vinegar Co Inc
  Cerritos, CA 800-443-1067
Fleischmann's Yeast
  Chesterfield, MO 800-777-4959
Four Chimneys Farm Winery Trust
  Himrod, NY 607-243-7502
Fredericksburg Herb Farm
  Fredericksburg, TX. 800-259-4372
Gedney Foods Co
  Sun Valley, CA 888-244-0653
Gold Pure Food Products Co. Inc.
  Hempstead, NY. 800-422-4681
Grapevine Trading Company
  Santa Rosa, CA. 800-469-6478
Halladay's Harvest Barn
  Bellows Falls, VT 802-463-3471
Herb Bee's Products
  Colchester, VT 802-864-7387
Hinzerling Winery
  Prosser, WA. 800-727-6702
Hudson Valley Fruit Juice
  Highland, NY 845-691-8061
Hurd Orchards
  Holley, NY 585-638-8838
II Sisters
  Moss Beach, CA 800-282-7058
K L Keller Imports
  Oakland, CA. 510-839-7890
KARI-Out Co
  White Plains, NY 800-433-8799
Kedem
  Bayonne, NJ 718-369-4600
Ken's Foods Inc
  Marlborough, MA 508-229-1100
Knouse Foods Co-Op Inc.
  Peach Glen, PA 717-677-8181
Kozlowski Farms
  Forestville, CA 800-473-2767
Lesley Elizabeth Inc
  Lapeer, MI. 800-684-3300
Lounsbury Foods
  Toronto, ON 416-656-6330
Mandarin Soy Sauce Inc
  Middletown, NY 845-343-1505
Mange
  Somerville, MA 917-880-2104
Marina Foods
  Medley, FL 786-888-0129
Marukan Vinegar USA Inc.
  Paramount, CA 562-630-6060
Mizkan Americas Inc
  Kansas City, MO. 800-323-4358
Modena Fine Foods Inc
  Clifton, NJ. 973-470-8499
Morehouse Foods Inc
  City Of Industry, CA. 888-297-9800
Myron's Fine Foods, Inc.
  Millers Falls, MA 800-730-2820
Nakano Foods
  Mt Prospect, IL 800-323-4358
National Fruit Product Co Inc
  Winchester, VA 540-723-9614
National Vinegar Co
  St Louis, MO. 314-962-4111
Nonna Pia's Gourmet Sauces
  Whistler, BC 888-372-1534
North American Enterprises
  Tucson, AZ 800-817-8666
O Olive Oil
  Petaluma, CA 888-827-7148
Oasis Food Co
  Hillside, NJ 800-275-0477
Old Dutch Mustard Company
  Great Neck, NY 516-466-0522
Olds Products Co
  Pleasant Prairie, WI 262-947-3500
Pastorelli Food Products
  Chicago, IL. 800-767-2829
Patsy's Italian Restaurant
  New York, NY 212-247-3491
Pilgrim Foods
  Great Neck, NY 516-466-0522
Pompeian Inc
  Baltimore, MD 800-766-7342
Ponti USA
  New York, NY
Prairie Thyme LTD
  Santa Fe, NM 800-869-0009
Proacec USA
  Santa Monica, CA. 310-996-7770
Purity Products
  Plainview, NY 800-256-6102
Red Pelican Food Products
  Detroit, MI 313-881-4095
Reinhart Foods
  Toronto, ON 416-645-4910
Restaurant Lulu Gourmet Products
  San Francisco, CA 888-693-5800
REX Pure Foods
  New Orleans, LA 800-344-8314
Roanoke Apple Products
  Salem, VA 540-375-3782
Robert Rothschild Farm
  Cincinnati, OH 800-222-9966
Rosa Food Products
  Philadelphia, PA 215-467-2214
Santa Barbara Olive Company
  Santa Barbara, CA 800-624-4896
Sargent and Greenleaf
  Nicholasville, KY 800-826-7652
Satiety Winery & Cafe
  Davis, CA 530-757-2699
Sedlock Farm
  Lynn Center, IL 309-521-8284
Sempio Foods
  Cerritos, CA 562-207-9540
Sherrill Orchards
  Arvin, CA 661-858-2035
Sieco USA Corporation
  Houston, TX 713-464-1726
Silver Palate Kitchens
  Cresskill, NJ 201-568-0110
Slide Ridge LLC
  Mendon, UT 435-752-4956
Solana Gold Organics
  Sebastopol, CA 800-459-1121
Southern Season
  Chapel Hill, NC 877-929-7133
Sparrow Lane
  Ceres, CA 866-515-2477
Spruce Mountain Blueberries
  West Rockport, ME. 207-236-3538
Stickney & Poor Company
  Peterborough, NH 603-924-2259
Thistledew Farm
  Proctor, WV 800-854-6639
Thyme Garden Herb Co
  Alsea, OR 800-482-4372
Todhunter Foods
  Lake Alfred, FL 863-956-1116
Tropical Foods
  Charlotte, NC 800-438-4470
Vincent Formusa Company
  Des Plaines, IL 847-813-6040
Walker Foods
  Los Angeles, CA. 800-966-5199
Webbpak Inc
  Trussville, AL 800-655-3500
White House Foods
  Winchester, VA 540-662-3401
Widow's Mite Vinegar Company
  Washington, DC 877-678-5854
Wild Thymes Farm Inc
  Greenville, NY 845-266-8387
Wing's Food Products
  Toronto, ON 416-259-2662
Woeber Mustard Mfg Co
  Springfield, OH. 800-548-2929

Apple Cider

Bragg Live Food Products Inc
  Goleta, CA 800-446-1990
Comvita USA
  Santa Barbara, CA 855-449-2201
De Nigris
  Totowa, NJ 973-837-6791
Eden Foods Inc
  Clinton, MI 888-424-3336
Emerling International Foods
  Buffalo, NY. 716-833-7381
Ethan's
  Boulder, CO 720-432-8384
GloryBee
  Eugene, OR. 800-456-7923
Kevala
  Dallas, TX. 877-379-1179
Knouse Foods Co-Op Inc.
  Peach Glen, PA 717-677-8181
Mizkan Americas Inc
  Kansas City, MO 800-323-4358
Nana Mae's Organics
  Sebastopol, CA 707-829-7359
National Vinegar Co
  St Louis, MO 314-962-4111
Pastorelli Food Products
  Chicago, IL 800-767-2829
Ponti USA
  New York, NY
Reinhart Foods
  Toronto, ON 416-645-4910
Roanoke Apple Products
  Salem, VA. 540-375-3782
Sieco USA Corporation
  Houston, TX 713-464-1726
Solana Gold Organics
  Sebastopol, CA 800-459-1121
Vermont Village
  Barre, VT
Walker Foods
  Los Angeles, CA. 800-966-5199
Webbpak Inc
  Trussville, AL 800-655-3500
White House Foods
  Winchester, VA 540-662-3401
Widow's Mite Vinegar Company
  Washington, DC 877-678-5854

Balsamic

Acetifico Marcello Denigris
  Westwood, NJ 973-837-6791
Agrusa
  Leonia, NJ. 201-592-5950
California Olive Oil Council
  Berkeley, CA. 888-718-9830
Chaparral Gardens
  Atascadero, CA. 805-703-0829
Coldani Olive Ranch LLC
  Lodi, CA 209-334-0527
Consumers Vinegar & Spice Co
  Chicago, IL. 773-376-4100
Emerling International Foods
  Buffalo, NY. 716-833-7381
Enzo Olive Oil Co.
  Madera, CA. 559-299-7278
Modena Fine Foods Inc
  Clifton, NJ. 973-470-8499
Mosby Winery
  Buellton, CA. 800-706-6729
Mosti Mondiale/Gourmet Mondiale
  Ste-Catherine, QC. 450-638-6380
North American Enterprises
  Tucson, AZ 800-817-8666
Olive Oil Factor
  Waterbury, CT. 475-235-2666
Organic Planet
  San Francisco, CA 415-765-5590
Pastorelli Food Products
  Chicago, IL. 800-767-2829
Ponti USA
  New York, NY
Proacec USA
  Santa Monica, CA. 310-996-7770
Putney House Trading LLC
  New London, NH 603-526-2336
Reinhart Foods
  Toronto, ON 416-645-4910
Restaurant Lulu Gourmet Products
  San Francisco, CA 888-693-5800
S A L T Sisters
  Goshen, IN 574-971-8368
Sieco USA Corporation
  Houston, TX 713-464-1726
Sutter Buttes Olive Oil
  Sutter, CA 530-763-7921
Valley Grain Products
  Fresno, CA 559-675-3400
Wild Thymes Farm Inc
  Greenville, NY 845-266-8387

Product Categories / Sauces, Dips & Dressings: Vinegar

Liquid

Clements Foods Co
  Oklahoma City, OK 800-654-8355
Colonna Brothers Inc
  North Bergen, NJ 201-864-1115

Malt

Consumers Vinegar & Spice Co
  Chicago, IL 773-376-4100
Eden Foods Inc
  Clinton, MI 888-424-3336
Reinhart Foods
  Toronto, ON 416-645-4910

Raspberry

Reinhart Foods
  Toronto, ON 416-645-4910
Thistledew Farm
  Proctor, WV 800-854-6639

Sherry

National Vinegar Co
  St Louis, MO 314-962-4111

White Distilled

Big B Barbecue
  Evansville, IN 812-425-5235
Consumers Vinegar & Spice Co
  Chicago, IL 773-376-4100
Creole Fermentation Indu
  Abbeville, LA 337-898-9377
Emerling International Foods
  Buffalo, NY 716-833-7381
Knouse Foods Co-Op Inc.
  Peach Glen, PA 717-677-8181
Mizkan Americas Inc
  Kansas City, MO 800-323-4358
National Vinegar Co
  St Louis, MO 314-962-4111
Pastorelli Food Products
  Chicago, IL 800-767-2829
Reinhart Foods
  Toronto, ON 416-645-4910
Roanoke Apple Products
  Salem, VA 540-375-3782
Walker Foods
  Los Angeles, CA 800-966-5199
Webbpak Inc
  Trussville, AL 800-655-3500
White House Foods
  Winchester, VA 540-662-3401

Wine

B & G Foods Inc.
  Parsippany, NJ 973-401-6500
California Balsamic Inc
  Ukiah, CA 888-644-5127
Consumers Vinegar & Spice Co
  Chicago, IL 773-376-4100
De Nigris
  Totowa, NJ 973-837-6791
Eden Foods Inc
  Clinton, MI 888-424-3336
Knouse Foods Co-Op Inc.
  Peach Glen, PA 717-677-8181
Modena Fine Foods Inc
  Clifton, NJ 973-470-8499
Nakano Foods
  Mt Prospect, IL 800-323-4358
National Vinegar Co
  St Louis, MO 314-962-4111
Pastorelli Food Products
  Chicago, IL 800-767-2829
Pompeian Inc
  Baltimore, MD 800-766-7342
Ponti USA
  New York, NY
Reinhart Foods
  Toronto, ON 416-645-4910
Roanoke Apple Products
  Salem, VA 540-375-3782
Satiety Winery & Cafe
  Davis, CA 530-757-2699
Sieco USA Corporation
  Houston, TX 713-464-1726
Wine Country Kitchens
  Napa, CA 866-767-9463

Snack Foods

General

34-Degrees
  Denver, CO 303-861-4818
3PM Bites
  New York, NY
88 Acres
  Allston, MA 617-208-8651
Ajinomoto Frozen Foods USA, Inc.
  Ontario, CA. 866-536-8008
America's Classic Foods
  Cambria, CA 805-927-0745
American Importing Co.
  Minneapolis, MN 855-273-0466
Amplify Snack Brands
  Austin, TX 512-600-9893
Arico Natural Foods
  Beaverton, OR 503-259-0871
B.O.S.S. Food Co.
 800-344-8584
Bake City
  Atlanta, GA. 855-336-4777
Balance Bar Company
  Bohemia, NY .800-346-2194
Barbara's Bakery
  Lakeville, MN. 800-343-0590
Barkthins Snacking Chocolate
  Congers, NY .845-770-5802
Barrel O' Fun Snack Foods
  Perham, MN .800-346-4910
Bazaar Inc
  River Grove, IL 800-736-1888
Beanitos
  Austin, TX. 512-609-8017
Bearded Brothers
  Austin, TX
Bearitos
  Boulder, CO .310-886-8200
Because Cookie Dough
Betsy's Cheese Straws
  Millbrook, AZ 877-902-3141
Biena Foods
  Allston, MA 617-202-5210
Big Spoon Roasters
  Durham, NC .919-309-9100
Big Steer
  Houston, TX .800-421-4951
Blue Crab Bay
  Melfa, VA 800-221-2722
Bountiful Larder LLC
  Crested Butte, CO. 800-676-5057
Brothers All Natural
  Rochester, NY. 877-842-7477
Buffalo Bills Premium Snacks
  Lebanon, PA .717-273-7499
Calif Snack Foods
  South El Monte, CA 626-454-4099
CarbRite Diet
  New Brunswick, NJ 800-872-0101
Caveman Foods
  Lafayette, CA 925-979-9515
Chasquis Natural Foods
  St. Catharines, ON
Chic Naturals
  Lahaina, HI. 808-463-7878
Conn's Potato Chips
  Zanesville, OH 740-452-4615
Cornfields Inc
  Waukegan, IL 847-263-7000
Countertop Productions
  Alexandria, VA
Crazy Richard's
  Dublin, OH 614-889-4424
Creative Snacks Co LLC
  Greensboro, NC 336-668-4151
Crunch-A-Mame
  Mulberry, AR
Crunchsters
 303-545-9000
Crunchy Rollers
  Dallas, TX
Del Monte Foods Inc.
  Walnut Creek, CA
Dieffenbach's Potato Chips
  Womelsdorf, PA 610-589-2385
Divvies
  South Salem, NY 914-533-2804

DNX Foods
  Tucson, AZ 888-612-5037
Don Bugito
  San Francisco, CA
Double B Distributors
  Lexington, KY 859-255-8822
Eagle Family Foods
  Richfield, OH 888-656-3245
East Kentucky Foods
  Winchester, KY. 859-744-2218
Eat Your Coffee
  Boston, MA
EatKeenwa, Inc.
  Jersey City, NJ 855-453-3692
Elemental Superfood
  Torrance, CA
Ello Raw
Empact Bars
  Boulder, CO .877-836-7228
Enjoy Life Foods
  Chicago, IL 888-503-6569
Farmwise LLC
  Wellesley, MA. 508-401-7040
Flamous Brands
  Duarte, CA 626-799-7909
From the Ground Up
  Fairfield, NJ
General Mills
  Minneapolis, MN 800-248-7310
GKI Foods
  Brighton, MI .248-486-0055
Gluck Brands
  Sugar Land, TX. 281-903-7082
Golden Flake Snack Foods
  Birmingham, AL. 800-367-7629
Golden Island Jerky Co.
  Rancho Cucamonga, CA 844-362-3222
Goldilocks USA
  Hayward, CA 510-476-0700
Good Lovin' Foods
 877-760-6833
Good! Snacks
  Walnut, CA 415-762-0600
GoodBites Snacks
  Venice, CA
Goodness Knows
Gopal's Healthfoods
  Sidney, TX 866-646-7257
Gourmet Basics
  Brooklyn, NY 718-509-9366
Gourmet Kitchen, Inc.
  Neptune, NJ .800-492-3663
Govadinas Fitness Foods
  San Diego, CA 800-900-0108
Grandma Emily
  Montreal, QC 877-943-3661
Growing Roots Foods
  Englewood Cliffs, NJ
H-E-B Grocery Co. LP
  San Antonio, TX. 800-432-3113
Hale and Hearty Soups
  New York, NY 212-255-2433
Happy Family
  New York, NY 855-644-2779
Happy Herberts Food Co Inc
  Jersey City, NJ 800-764-2779
Hearthside Food Solutions
  Downers Grove, IL. 630-967-3600
Hippeas
  Plainview, NY
Hippie Snacks
  Burnaby, BC .877-769-6887
Humbly Hemp
  Los Angeles, CA. 424-259-3521
Humming Hemp
  Richland, WA 503-559-6476
Hungry Sultan
  Lake Forest, CA 949-215-0000
Husman Snack Food Company
  Peoria, IL. 859-282-7490
I'm Different Snacks
  Los Angeles, CA
Ideal Snacks Corp
  Liberty, NY 845-292-7000
Jonny Almond Nut Co
  Flint, MI 810-767-6887

Kateri Foods
  Hopkins, MN 800-330-8351
KAYS Processing LLC
  Clara City, MN 320-847-3220
Kellogg Co.
  Battle Creek, MI 800-962-1413
Kind Snacks
  New York, NY 855-884-5463
King Henry's Inc
  Valencia, CA .661-295-5566
Kraft Heinz Co.
  Chicago, IL 800-543-5335
Krema Nut Co
  Columbus, OH 800-222-4132
Late July Snacks
  Norwalk, CT .888-857-6225
Laurel Hill Foods
  Attleboro, MA. 877-759-8141
Leaf Jerky
  Battle Creek, MI 800-962-1413
Lesserevil Brand Snack Co
  Danbury, CT .203-529-3555
Levant Mediterranean Snack Foods LLC
  Haverhill, MA. 978-241-9986
Lillie's Q
  Chicago, IL 773-772-5500
LivBar
  Salem, OR. 971-239-1209
Lost Trail Root Beer
  Louisburg, KS. 800-748-7765
Love Good Fats
  Toronto, ON
Love You Foods
  Flagstaff, AZ. 844-693-2662
Lundberg Family Farms
  Richvale, CA. 530-538-3500
LWC Brands Inc.
  Dallas, TX. 800-552-8006
Maine Coast Sea Vegetables
  Franklin, ME. 207-565-2907
Manischewitz Co
  Newark, NJ .201-553-1100
Maplegrove Foods
  Ontario, CA. .909-545-6075
McIlhenny Company
  Avery Island, LA. 800-634-9599
Mediterranean Snack Food Co
  Boonton, NJ .973-402-2644
MetaBall
  Chester, NJ 800-247-6580
Mezza
  Lake Forest, IL 888-206-6054
Mister Bee Potato Chips Co
  Parkersburg, WV. 304-428-6133
Modern Pod Co.
  Providence, RI
Mondelez International
  East Hanover, NJ 855-535-5648
Mountain Organic Foods
  Moraga, CA. 925-377-0119
Nebraska Bean
  Clearwater, NE 800-253-6502
New Nissi Corp.
  Paterson, NJ .973-278-4400
Nomi Snacks
  Minneapolis, MN
Nora Snacks
  Santa Fe Springs, CA 562-404-9888
NOW Foods
  Bloomingdale, IL 888-669-3663
Nu-World Amaranth Inc
  Naperville, IL 630-369-6851
Nush Foods
  Salt Lake City, UT 801-953-1370
Nutty Goodness
  Charleston, SC
OHi Food
  Costa Mesa, CA 808-281-7815
ONE Brands
  Charlotte, NC 888-231-2684
Organic Amazon
  Key Biscayne, FL
Organic Gemini
  Brooklyn, NY 347-662-2900
Organic RealBar
  Diamond Bar, CA 888-622-8828

Product Categories / Snack Foods: Cheese Curls

Orto Foods
   Congers, NY 516-725-5422
Pacific Gold Snacks
   Kent, WA. 253-854-7056
Paleo Ranch
   Lakeway, TX
Papa Dean's Popcorn
   San Antonio, TX 877-855-7272
Patagonia Provisions
   Sausalito, CA 888-221-8208
Peaceful Fruits
   330-356-8515
Peeled Snacks
   Cumberland, RI. 401-437-4386
Perfect Snacks
   Sorrento Valley, CA 866-628-8548
Phyter Foods
   West Chicago, IL 630-206-3701
Pippin Snack Pecans
   Albany, GA 800-554-6887
Power Crunch
   Irvine, CA
Prana
   Ville St Laurent, QC 844-447-7262
Probar
   Salt Lake City, UT 800-921-2294
Ramsey Popcorn Co Inc
   Ramsey, IN 800-624-2060
Raw Rev
   Hawthorne, NY. 914-326-4095
Real Coconut Co. Inc., The
   CA
Rhythm Superfoods
   Austin, TX. 512-441-5667
Ripple Brand Collective
   Congers, NY 845-353-1251
Rise Bar
   Irvine, CA. 800-440-6476
Royal Hawaiian Orchards LP
   Dana Point, CA. 949-661-6304
Rudolph Foods Co
   Lima, OH. 419-648-3611
Safely Delicious
   Overland Park, KS 913-963-5140
Sargento Foods Inc
   Plymouth, WI 800-243-3737
Schwan's Company
   Marshall, MN 800-533-5290
Seapoint Farms
   Huntington Beach, CA 714-374-9831
Sensible Foods LLC
   Santa Rosa, CA. 888-222-0170
Setton International Foods
   Commack, NY 800-227-4397
Sheffa Foods
   New York, NY 800-494-1956
Simply 7 Snacks
   Houston, TX. 877-682-2359
Small Planet Foods
   Minneapolis, MN 800-624-4123
Snack Works/Metrovox Snacks
   Orange, CA 800-783-9870
Snikiddy, LLC
   Boulder, CO 303-444-4405
Snyder's-Lance Inc.
   Charlotte, NC 800-438-1880
Sophia Foods
   Brooklyn, NY 718-272-1110
Squire Boone Village
   New Albany, IN 888-934-1804
Sugar Foods Corp
   New York, NY
Sun Opta Inc.
   Mississauga, ON. 952-820-2518
Sun-Maid Growers of California
   Kingsburg, CA 559-896-8000
Sun-Rype Products
   Kelowna, BC. 888-786-7973
Sunridge Farms Inc
   Salinas, CA 831-755-1530
SuperEats
   New York, NY 802-760-7075
Superseedz
   North Haven, CT. 203-407-0546
Sweetwood Cattle Co
   Steamboat Spgs, CO 970-879-7456
Terrell's Potato Chip Co
   Syracuse, NY 315-437-2786
Terri Lynn Inc
   Elgin, IL 800-323-0775
Thanasi Foods LLC
   Boulder, CO 866-558-7379

Thatcher's Gourmet Specialties
   San Francisco, CA 800-926-2676
The Humphrey Co
   Lockport, NY 716-597-1974
The Konery
   Brooklyn, NY 917-750-4147
The Matzo Project
   Brooklyn, NY 929-276-2896
The Naked Edge, LLC
   Boulder, CO 888-297-9426
The Safe + Fair Food Company
   Chicago, IL
TMI Trading Co
   Brooklyn, NY 718-821-5052
Touche Bakery
   London, ON 518-455-0044
TreeHouse Foods, Inc.
   Oak Brook, IL. 708-483-1300
Tri-Sum Potato Chip Company
   Leominster, MA 978-697-2447
Tropical Valley Foods
   Plattsburgh, NY 877-756-6831
Watusee Foods
   Washington, DC 202-281-8245
Wegmans Food Markets Inc.
   Rochester, NY. 800-934-6267
WholeMe
   Minneapolis, MN 612-247-9728
Wicked Crisps
   Greensboro, NC
Wicked Mix
   Little Rock, AR. 501-374-2244
Wild Zora Foods
   Loveland, CO 970-541-9672
Wilde Brands
   Boulder, CO 720-328-0843
Windy City Organics
   Northbrook, IL. 800-925-0577
Winn-Dixie Stores
   Jacksonville, FL 800-967-9105
Wise Foods Inc
   Berwick, PA 888-438-9473
Wyandot Inc
   Marion, OH. 800-992-6368
Yogavive
   Tiburon, CA 415-366-6226
Your Bar Factory
   LaSalle, QC. 888-366-0258

Cheese Curls

Cheeze Kurls
   Grand Rapids, MI 616-784-6095
Elmers Fine Foods Inc
   New Orleans, LA 888-570-0764
Golden Flake Snack Foods
   Birmingham, AL. 800-367-7629
Happy's Potato Chip Co
   Minneapolis, MN 612-781-3121
Hartley's Potato Chip Co
   Lewistown, PA 717-248-0526
Tri-Sum Potato Chip Company
   Leominster, MA 978-697-2447
Wyandot Inc
   Marion, OH. 800-992-6368

Cheese Twists

Aileen Quirk & Sons Inc
   Kansas City, MO. 816-471-4580
American Blanching Company
   Fitzgerald, GA 229-423-4098
American Nut & Chocolate Co
   Boston, MA. 800-797-6887
American Skin LLC
   Burgaw, NC. 800-248-7463
Amsnack
   Stockton, CA. 209-982-5545
Archie Moore's
   Milford, CT. 203-876-5088
Arizona Pistachio Company
   Tucson, AZ 800-333-8575
Austinuts
   Austin, TX. 877-329-6887
B. Lloyd's Pecans
   Barwick, GA. 800-322-6887
Bachman Company
   Wyomissing, PA 800-523-8253
Ballreich's Potato Chips
   Tiffin, OH 800-323-2447
Barrel O' Fun Snack Foods
   Perham, MN 800-346-4910

Berberian Nut Company
   Chico, CA 530-981-4900
Bickel's Snack Foods Inc
   York, PA 800-233-1933
Black Jewell Popcorn
   Columbus, IN. 800-948-2302
Boyd's Sausage Co
   Washington, IA 319-653-5715
Brandmeyer Popcorn Co
   Ankeny, IA 800-568-8276
Bremner Biscuit Company
   Denver, CO 866-972-6879
Brennan Snacks Manufacturing
   Bogalusa, LA 800-290-7486
Browns' Ice Cream Company
   Minneapolis, MN 612-378-1075
C.J. Distributing
   Surf City, NC 800-990-2366
Cafe Fanny
   Berkeley, CA. 800-441-5413
Calbee America Inc
   Fairfield, CA. 707-427-2500
California Fruit & Nut
   Gustine, CA 888-747-8224
Capri Bagel & Pizza Corporation
   Brooklyn, NY 718-497-4431
Carolina Fine Snacks
   Greensboro, NC 336-605-0773
Cattaneo Brothers Inc
   San Luis Obispo, CA 800-243-8537
Central Snacks
   Carthage, MS 601-267-3112
Chappaqua Crunch
   Marblehead, MA 781-631-8118
Cheese Straws & More
   Monroe, LA. 800-997-1921
Chelsea Milling Co.
   Chelsea, MI. 800-727-2460
City Farm/Rocky Peanut Company
   Detroit, MI 800-437-6825
Cloud Nine
   Claremont, CA 909-624-3147
Colorado Popcorn Co
   Sterling, CO 866-491-2676
Columbia Empire Farms Inc
   Sherwood, OR. 503-538-2156
Community Orchards
   Fort Dodge, IA 888-573-8212
Con Agra Snack Foods
   Hamburg, IA 800-831-5818
Corbin Foods-Edibowls
   Santa Ana, CA 800-695-5655
Corn Popper
   Tulsa, OK 918-250-9317
Dellaco Classic Confections
   Burlington, WI 866-537-2656
Dieffenbach's Potato Chips
   Womelsdorf, PA 610-589-2385
Door County Potato Chips
   Milwaukee, WI 414-964-1428
Durey-Libby Edible Nuts
   Carlstadt, NJ 800-332-6887
Durham Ellis Pecan Co
   Comanche, TX 800-732-2629
Eddy's Bakery
   Boise, ID 208-377-8100
El Grano De Oro
   Pacifica, CA 650-355-8417
Elegant Edibles
   Houston, TX. 800-227-3226
Exquisita Tortillas Inc
   Edinburg, TX 956-383-6712
Fairchester Snacks Corp
   White Plains, NY 914-761-2824
Fairmont Snacks Group
   Independence, OH 216-642-3336
Fastachi
   Watertown, MA. 800-466-3022
Fisher's Popcorn
   Ocean City, MD 888-395-0335
Foley's Chocolates & Candies
   Richmond, BC 888-236-5397
Fontazzi/Metrovox Snacks
   Orange, CA 800-428-0522
Food Products Corporation
   Phoenix, AZ 602-273-7139
Fortella Fortune Cookies
   Chicago, IL 312-567-9000
Fresh Roasted Almond Company
   Warren, MI 877-478-6887
Fun City Popcorn
   Las Vegas, NV 800-423-1710

Product Categories / Snack Foods: Chips

Furukawa Potato Chip Factory
  Captain Cook, HI 808-323-3785
Garrett Popcorn Shops
  Chicago, IL 888-476-7267
Germack Pistachio Co
  Detroit, MI 800-872-4006
GH Bent Company
  Milton, MA 617-322-9287
Gilda Industries Inc
  Hialeah, FL 305-887-8286
Glacial Ridge Foods
  Starbuck, MN 320-239-2215
Golden Peanut and Tree Nuts
  Alpharetta, GA 770-752-8160
Govatos Chocolates
  Wilmington, DE 888-799-5252
Great Western Co LLC
  Hollywood, AL 256-259-3578
Guy's Food
  Overland Park, KS 800-821-2405
Haby's Alsatian Bakery
  Castroville, TX 830-538-2118
Hammond's Candies
  Denver, CO 888-226-3999
Happy Herberts Food Co Inc
  Jersey City, NJ 800-764-2779
Harvest Manor Farms
  Princeton, KY 877-984-6639
Hazelnut Growers Of Oregon
  Cornelius, OR 800-273-4676
Hillson Nut Co
  Cleveland, OH 800-333-2818
Hume Specialties
  Chester, VT 802-875-3117
Humphrey Co
  Cleveland, OH 800-486-3739
Imus Ranch Foods
  Darien, CT 888-284-4687
J.W. Haywood & Sons Dairy
  Louisville, KY 502-774-2311
Jay Shah Foods
  Mississauga, ON 905-696-0172
Jenny's Old Fashioned
  North Ridgeville, OH 800-452-3235
Jerrell Packaging
  Birmingham, AL 205-426-8930
JMS Specialty Foods
  Ripon, WI 800-535-5437
Joel Harvey Distributing
  Brooklyn, NY 718-629-2690
John W Macy's Cheesesticks Inc
  Elmwood Park, NJ 800-643-0573
Judy's Cream Caramels
  Sherwood, OR 503-625-7161
Kendrick Gourmet Products
  Columbus, GA 800-356-1858
Kevton Gourmet Tea
  Streetman, TX 888-538-8668
Kids Kookie Company
  San Clemente, CA 800-350-7577
LA Vencedora Products Inc
  Los Angeles, CA 800-327-2572
Laredo Tortilleria & Mexican
  Fort Wayne, IN 800-252-7336
Larosa Bakery Inc
  Shrewsbury, NJ 800-527-6722
Las Cruces Brand Products
  El Paso, TX 915-779-5709
Lima Grain Cereal Seeds LLC
  Fort Collins, CO 970-498-2200
Longleaf Plantation
  Purvis, MS 800-421-7370
Longview Meat & Merchandise Ltd
  Longview, AB 866-355-3759
Los Angeles Nut House Brands
  Los Angeles, CA 213-481-0134
Louise's
  Shelbyville, KY 502-633-9700
Ludwick's Frozen Donuts
  Grand Rapids, MI 800-366-8816
Madhouse Munchies
  South Burlington, VT 888-323-4687
Mama Amy's Quality Foods
  Mississauga, ON 905-456-0056
Manuel's Odessa Tortilla
  Odessa, TX 800-753-2445
Marantha Natural Foods
  San Francisco, CA 866-972-6879
Maxin Marketing Corporation
  Aliso Viejo, CA 949-362-1177
Mexican Accent
  New Berlin, WI 262-784-4422

Mission Foods Corp.
  Irving, TX 972-232-5200
Mitchum Potato Chips
  Charlotte, NC 704-372-6744
Molinaro's Fine Italian Foods Ltd.
  Mississauga, ON 905-281-0352
Mrs. Dog's Products
  Grand Rapids, MI 800-267-7364
Natchez Pecan Shelling Company
  Taylorsville, MS 601-785-4333
National Foods
  Bronx, NY 800-683-6565
Nips Potato Chips
  Honolulu, HI 808-593-8549
Noble Popcorn
  Sac City, IA 800-537-9554
Northwoods Candy Emporium
  Branson, MO 417-332-1010
Nustef Foods
  Mississauga, ON 877-306-7562
Nutty Bavarian
  Sanford, FL 800-382-4788
Oasis Mediterranean Cuisine
  Toledo, OH 419-269-1516
Old Dutch Foods LTD
  Roseville, MN
Old Sacramento Popcorn Company
  Sacramento, CA 916-446-1980
Packaged Products Division
  Largo, FL 888-833-2247
Paddack Enterprises
  Escalon, CA 209-838-1536
Papes Pecan House
  Seguin, TX 888-688-7273
Pepe's Mexican Restaurant
  Anaheim, CA 714-952-9410
Perfections by Allan
  Owings Mills, MD 800-581-8670
Picard Peanuts
  Waterdown, ON 888-244-7688
Pickle Cottage
  Bucklin, KS 316-826-3502
Pizza Products
  Farmington Hills, MI 800-600-7482
Plantation Pecan & Gift Company
  Waterproof, LA 800-477-3226
Plehn's Bakery Inc
  Louisville, KY 502-896-4438
Pond Brothers Peanut Company
  Suffolk, VA 757-539-2356
Poore Brothers
  Phoenix, AZ 623-932-6200
Popcorn Popper
  Monon, IN 800-270-2705
Popcorner
  Swansea, IL 618-277-2676
Poppin Popcorn
  Naples, FL 941-262-1691
Premiere Packing Company
  Greenacres, WA 888-239-5288
REED'S Inc
  Los Angeles, CA 800-997-3337
Reiter Dairy
  Newport, KY 800-544-6455
Rices Potato Chips
  Biloxi, MS 228-396-5775
Ricos Candy Snack & Bakery
  Hialeah, FL 305-885-7392
Ripensa A/S
  Lehigh Acres, FL 941-561-5882
Rolet Food Products Company
  Brooklyn, NY 718-497-0476
Route 11 Potato Chips
  Mount Jackson, VA 800-294-7783
Rural Route 1 Popcorn Co
  Livingston, WI 800-828-8115
Rygmyr Foods
  South Saint Paul, MN 800-545-3903
Sanarak Paper & Popcorn Supplies
  Buffalo, NY 716-874-5662
Savory Foods
  Grand Rapids, MI 800-878-2583
Sesaco Corp
  Austin, TX 800-737-2260
Severance Foods Inc
  Hartford, CT 860-724-7063
Shallowford Farms Popcorn, Inc.
  Yadkinville, NC 800-892-9539
Shearer's Foods Inc
  Massillon, OH 330-767-4030
Snack Factory
  Princeton, NJ 888-683-5400

Snappy Popcorn
  Breda, IA 800-742-0228
Snelgrove Ice Cream Company
  Salt Lake City, UT 800-569-0005
Snikiddy, LLC
  Boulder, CO 303-444-4405
Sommer's Food Products
  Salisbury, MO 660-388-5511
Southern Popcorn Company
  Memphis, TN 901-362-5238
Southern Roasted Nuts
  Fitzgerald, GA 912-423-5616
Spilke's Baking Company
  Moosic, PA 570-457-2400
St. Amour Inc/French Cookies
  Costa Mesa, CA 714-754-1900
Story's Popcorn Company
  Charleston, MO 573-649-2727
Sunnyside Farms
  Neligh, NE 402-791-2210
Tabard Farm Potato Chips
  Middletown, VA 540-869-0104
Texas Tito's
  Austin, TX . . . . 877-99 -OTEX
The Great Western Tortilla Co.
  Denver, CO 303-298-0705
Thyme Garden Herb Co
  Alsea, OR 800-482-4372
Tim's Cascade Snacks
  Auburn, WA 800-533-8467
Tom Sturgis Pretzels Inc
  Reading, PA 800-817-3834
Trinidad Benham Corporation
  Denver, CO 303-220-1400
Trotter Soft Pretzels
  Hatfield, PA 215-855-2197
Tuscan Bakery
  Portland, OR 800-887-2261
Twin Valley Developmental Services
  Greenleaf, KS 800-748-7416
Uncle Ralph's Cookies
  Frederick, MD 800-422-0626
Uncle Ray's Potato Chips
  Detroit, MI 800-800-3286
Van-Lang Food Products
  Countryside, IL 708-588-0800
Vande Walle's Candies Inc
  Appleton, WI 800-738-1020
Vic's Corn Popper
  Omaha, NE 402-932-0426
Wachusset Potato Chip Co Inc
  Fitchburg, MA 800-551-5539
Warden Peanut Company
  Portales, NM 575-356-6691
Weaver Popcorn Co Inc
  Van Buren, IN
Wynnewood Pecan Company
  Wynnewood, OK 800-892-4985
Yick Lung Company
  Honolulu, HI 808-841-3611
Young Pecan
  Las Cruces, NM 575-524-4321

Chips

Bagel Chips

Basic Grain Products
  Coldwater, OH 866-411-6677
Greater Knead, The
  Bensalem, PA 267-522-8523
Harlan Bakeries
  Avon, IN 800-435-2738
Hometown Bagel Inc
  Alsip, IL 708-385-0002
Old London Foods
  Yadkinville, NC
Soloman Baking Company
  Denver, CO 303-371-2777
Weaver Nut Co. Inc.
  Ephrata, PA 800-473-2688

Baked

Abuelita Mexican Foods
  Manassas Park, VA 703-369-0232
Azteca Foods Inc
  Chicago, IL 708-563-6600
C J Vitner Co
  Chicago, IL 773-523-7900
Dang Foods
  Berkeley, CA 510-338-3345

Product Categories / Snack Foods: Chips

Fuller Foods
   Portland, OR 503-308-3814
Golden Fluff Popcorn Co
   Lakewood, NJ 732-367-5448
Harlan Bakeries
   Avon, IN 800-435-2738
Imus Ranch Foods
   Darien, CT 888-284-4687
LA Canasta Mexican Foods
   Phoenix, AZ 855-269-7721
LA Mexicana Tortilleria
   Chicago, IL 773-247-5443
Laredo Tortilleria & Mexican
   Fort Wayne, IN 800-252-7336
Li'l Guy Foods
   Kansas City, MO 800-886-8226
Luna's Tortillas
   Dallas, TX 214-747-2661
Mexican Accent
   New Berlin, WI 262-784-4422
Natural Intentions, Inc.
   Folsom, CA
Olde Tyme Food Corporation
   East Longmeadow, MA 800-356-6533
Ozuna Food Products Corporation
   Sunnyvale, CA 408-400-0495
Pepe's Mexican Restaurant
   Anaheim, CA 714-952-9410
Puebla Foods Inc
   Passaic, NJ 973-473-0201
R&J Farms
   West Salem, OH 419-846-3179
Rudy's Tortillas
   Carrollton, TX 800-878-2401
Severance Foods Inc
   Hartford, CT 860-724-7063
Shallowford Farms Popcorn, Inc.
   Yadkinville, NC 800-892-9539
Spanish Gardens Food Manufacturing
   Kansas City, KS 913-831-4242
TH Foods, Inc.
   Loves Park, IL 815-636-9500
The Safe + Fair Food Company
   Chicago, IL
Tom's Snacks Company
   Charlotte, NC 800-995-2623
Vintage Italia
   Windermere, FL 407-217-5910
Westbrae Natural Foods
   Melville, NY 800-434-4246

Banana

American Importing Co.
   Minneapolis, MN 855-273-0466
Bubba's Fine Foods
   Loveland, CO

Cassava

Arico Natural Foods
   Beaverton, OR 503-259-0871
Tantos Foods International
   Markham, ON 905-943-9993
Wai Lana Snacks
   Sacramento, CA 888-924-5252

Chocolate

Sheryl's Chocolate Creations
   Hicksville, NY 888-882-2462
The Good Bean
   Berkeley, CA 561-243-7773

Corn

Abuelita Mexican Foods
   Manassas Park, VA 703-369-0232
Art's Mexican Products
   Kansas City, KS 913-371-2163
Barrel O' Fun Snack Foods
   Perham, MN 800-346-4910
C J Vitner Co
   Chicago, IL 773-523-7900
Delicious Popcorn
   Waupaca, WI 715-258-7683
Frito-Lay Inc.
   Plano, TX 800-352-4477
G.E.F. Gourmet Foods Inc
   Mountain Lake, MN 800-692-6762
Golden Flake Snack Foods
   Birmingham, AL 800-367-7629
Inka Crops
   Citrus Heights, CA .916-723-1450

LA Mexicana Tortilleria
   Chicago, IL 773-247-5443
Old Dutch Foods LTD
   Roseville, MN
Pippin Snack Pecans
   Albany, GA 800-554-6887
Tom's Snacks Company
   Charlotte, NC 800-995-2623
Xochitl
   Dallas, TX 866-595-8917

Fried

Abuelita Mexican Foods
   Manassas Park, VA 703-369-0232
Archie Moore's
   Milford, CT 203-876-5088
Bickel's Potato Chip Company
   York, PA 800-233-1933
C J Vitner Co
   Chicago, IL 773-523-7900
Calbee America Inc
   Fairfield, CA 707-427-2500
Delicious Popcorn
   Waupaca, WI 715-258-7683
El Milagro
   Chicago, IL 773-579-6120
Elmers Fine Foods Inc
   New Orleans, LA 888-570-0764
Evans Food Group LTD
   Chicago, IL 866-254-7400
Happy's Potato Chip Co
   Minneapolis, MN 612-781-3121
Hartley's Potato Chip Co
   Lewistown, PA 717-248-0526
Jones Potato Chip Co
   Mansfield, OH 800-466-9424
Kitchen Cooked Inc
   Farmington, IL 800-752-1535
LA Mexicana Tortilleria
   Chicago, IL 773-247-5443
LA Vencedora Products Inc
   Los Angeles, CA 800-327-2572
Laredo Tortilleria & Mexican
   Fort Wayne, IN 800-252-7336
Manhattan Food Brands, LLC
   Metuchen, NJ 732-906-2168
Maui Potato Chip Factory
   Kahului, HI 808-877-3652
Mexican Accent
   New Berlin, WI 262-784-4422
Middleswarth Potato Chips
   Kingston, PA 570-288-2447
Miguel's Stowe Away
   Stowe, VT 800-448-6517
Mrs Fisher's Potato Chips
   Rockford, IL 815-964-9114
Olde Tyme Food Corporation
   East Longmeadow, MA 800-356-6533
Ozuna Food Products Corporation
   Sunnyvale, CA 408-400-0495
Pepe's Mexican Restaurant
   Anaheim, CA 714-952-9410
Puebla Foods Inc
   Passaic, NJ 973-473-0201
Revonah Pretzel LLC
   Hanover, PA 717-630-2883
Route 11 Potato Chips
   Mount Jackson, VA 800-294-7783
Severance Foods Inc
   Hartford, CT 860-724-7063
Shearer's Foods Inc
   Massillon, OH 330-767-4030
Spanish Gardens Food Manufacturing
   Kansas City, KS 913-831-4242
Sun Pac Foods
   Brampton, ON 905-792-2700
Terrell's Potato Chip Co
   Syracuse, NY 315-437-2786
Tim's Cascade Snacks
   Auburn, WA 800-533-8467
Tom's Foods
   Charlotte, NC 877-309-6361
Tom's Snacks Company
   Charlotte, NC 800-995-2623
Westbrae Natural Foods
   Melville, NY 800-434-4246
Yum Yum Potato Chips
   Warwick, QC 800-567-5792

Nacho

Arizona Beverage Company
   Cincinnati, OH 800-832-3775
Luna's Tortillas
   Dallas, TX 214-747-2661
Old Dutch Foods LTD
   Roseville, MN
Olde Tyme Food Corporation
   East Longmeadow, MA 800-356-6533
Ozuna Food Products Corporation
   Sunnyvale, CA 408-400-0495

Peanut Butter

Perfect Life Nutrition
   West Orange, NJ .973-980-2298

Pita

Argo Fine Foods
   Saint James, NY 631-703-0443
Baba Foods
   San Diego, CA 619-426-6946
Basic Grain Products
   Coldwater, OH 866-411-6677
Bearitos
   Boulder, CO 310-886-8200
Cedar's Mediterranean Foods
   Ward Hill, MA 978-372-8010
Regco
   Haverhill, MA 978-521-4370
Regenie's Crunchy Pi
   Haverhill, MA 877-734-3643
Sensible Portions
   Boulder, CO 800-913-6637
Soloman Baking Company
   Denver, CO 303-371-2777

Plantain

ARA Food Corp
   Miami, FL 800-533-8831
Inka Crops
   Citrus Heights, CA .916-723-1450
Lam's Food Inc
   Queens Village, NY 718-217-0476

Potato

All American Snacks
   Midland, TX 800-840-2455
Arctic Beverages
   Winnipeg, MB 866-503-1270
Bachman Company
   Wyamissing, PA 800-523-8253
Backer's Potato Chip Company
   Fulton, MO 573-642-2833
Barrel O' Fun Snack Foods
   Perham, MN 800-346-4910
Better Made Snack Foods
   Detroit, MI 800-332-2394
Bickel's Potato Chip Company
   York, PA 800-233-1933
Bickel's Snack Foods Inc
   York, PA 800-233-1933
Bountiful Larder LLC
   Crested Butte, CO 800-676-5057
Brad's Taste of New York
   Floral Park, NY 516-354-9004
Coney Island Classics
   Valley Stream, NY .516-823-3001
Conn's Potato Chips
   Zanesville, OH 740-452-4615
Covered Bridge Potato Chip Company
   Waterville, NB 506-375-2447
Deep River Snacks
   Deep River, CT 860-434-7347
Delicious Popcorn
   Waupaca, WI 715-258-7683
Dieffenbach's Potato Chips
   Womelsdorf, PA 610-589-2385
Doctor Dread's Jerk
   Glen Echo, MD 301-908-9450
Eli's Bread Inc
   New York, NY 866-354-3547
Elmers Fine Foods Inc
   New Orleans, LA 888-570-0764
Frito-Lay Inc.
   Plano, TX 800-352-4477
Golden Flake Snack Foods
   Birmingham, AL 800-367-7629
Gringo Jack's
   Manchester Ctr, VT 802-362-0836

Product Categories / Snack Foods: Chips

Grippo Foods
   Cincinnati, OH 800-626-1824
Hanover Foods Corp
   Hanover, PA 717-632-6000
Happy's Potato Chip Co
   Minneapolis, MN 612-781-3121
Hartley's Potato Chip Co
   Lewistown, PA 717-248-0526
Herr Foods Inc.
   Nottingham, PA. 800-523-5030
Husman Snack Food Company
   Peoria, IL. 859-282-7490
Inka Crops
   Citrus Heights, CA 916-723-1450
Jackson's Honest
   Crested Butte, CO
Joe Tea and Joe Chips
   Upper Montclair, NJ 973-744-7502
Jones Potato Chip Co
   Mansfield, OH 800-466-9424
Kay's Naturals, Inc.
   Clara City, MN 866-873-5499
Kettle Brand
   Charlotte, NC 800-438-1880
Kitchen Cooked Inc
   Farmington, IL 800-752-1535
Knese Enterprise
   Bellerose, NY 516-354-9004
Luke's Organic
   Santa Cruz, CA
Martin's Potato Chips
   Thomasville, PA 800-272-4477
Maui Potato Chip Factory
   Kahului, HI 808-877-3652
Mediterranean Snack Food Co
   Boonton, NJ 973-402-2644
Middleswarth Potato Chips
   Kingston, PA. 570-288-2447
Mikesell's Potato Chip Company
   Dayton, OH. 937-228-9400
Mister Bee Potato Chips Co
   Parkersburg, WV. 304-428-6133
Mrs Fisher's Potato Chips
   Rockford, IL. 815-964-9114
Naturally Homegrown
   Surrey, BC. 604-465-7751
Old Dutch Foods LTD
   Roseville, MN
Ole Salty's Potato Chips
   Loves Park, IL. 815-637-2447
One Potato Two Potato
   Womelsdorf, PA 610-589-6500
Osem USA Inc
   Englewood Cliffs, NJ 800-200-6736
PepsiCo.
   Purchase, NY 914-253-2000
Pippin Snack Pecans
   Albany, GA 800-554-6887
Pop Gourmet LLC
   Tukwila, WA. 206-397-3896
Popchips
   San Francisco, CA 866-217-9327
Revonah Pretzel LLC
   Hanover, PA. 717-630-2883
Rick's Chips
   San Anselmo, CA 415-420-8151
Rock-N-Roll Gourmet
   Marina Del Ray, CA 800-518-3891
Snak King Corp
   City Of Industry, CA. 626-336-7711
Snyder's-Lance Inc.
   Charlotte, NC 800-438-1880
Sterzing Food Co
   Burlington, IA 800-754-8467
Stuart & CO
   Brooklyn, NY 347-292-7456
Terrell's Potato Chip Co
   Syracuse, NY 315-437-2786
That's How We Roll, LLC
   Fairfield, NJ 973-602-3011
The Good Crisp Company
Tim's Cascade Snacks
   Auburn, WA. 800-533-8467
Tom's Foods
   Charlotte, NC 877-309-6361
Tom's Snacks Company
   Charlotte, NC 800-995-2623
Tri-Sum Potato Chip Company
   Leominster, MA 978-697-2447
UTZ Quality Foods Inc.
   Hanover, PA. 800-367-7629

Wachusset Potato Chip Co Inc
   Fitchburg, MA 800-551-5539
Westbrae Natural Foods
   Melville, NY 800-434-4246
Wysong Corp
   Midland, MI 800-748-0188
Yum Yum Potato Chips
   Warwick, QC. 800-567-5792

Alternative

AvoLov
   Bend, OR. 541-419-4078
Bare Snacks
   800-940-0019
Beanfields
   855-328-2326
Daily Crave, The
   Folsom, CA
Ka-POP!
   Erie, CO
Kiwa
   Ontario, CA
Mediterranean Snack Food Co
   Boonton, NJ 973-402-2644
Naturally Homegrown
   Surrey, BC. 604-465-7751
Pop Gourmet LLC
   Tukwila, WA. 206-397-3896
ProFormance Foods
   Brooklyn, NY 703-869-3413
Snikiddy, LLC
   Boulder, CO 303-444-4405
The Good Crisp Company

Baked

Bickel's Snack Foods Inc
   York, PA 800-233-1933
That's How We Roll, LLC
   Fairfield, NJ 973-602-3011
Wyandot Inc
   Marion, OH. 800-992-6368

Barbecue

Backer's Potato Chip Company
   Fulton, MO 573-642-2833
Barrel O' Fun Snack Foods
   Perham, MN 800-346-4910
Martin's Potato Chips
   Thomasville, PA 800-272-4477
Mister Bee Potato Chips Co
   Parkersburg, WV. 304-428-6133
Tim's Cascade Snacks
   Auburn, WA. 800-533-8467
Wachusset Potato Chip Co Inc
   Fitchburg, MA 800-551-5539

Gourmet

Boulder Canyon Natural Foods
   Boulder, CO 303-546-9939

No Salt

Wachusset Potato Chip Co Inc
   Fitchburg, MA 800-551-5539

Ridges

Arctic Beverages
   Winnipeg, MB. 866-503-1270
Backer's Potato Chip Company
   Fulton, MO 573-642-2833
Barrel O' Fun Snack Foods
   Perham, MN 800-346-4910
Wachusset Potato Chip Co Inc
   Fitchburg, MA 800-551-5539

Salt & Vinegar

Small Planet Foods
   Minneapolis, MN 800-624-4123
Tim's Cascade Snacks
   Auburn, WA. 800-533-8467
Wachusset Potato Chip Co Inc
   Fitchburg, MA 800-551-5539

Salted

Barrel O' Fun Snack Foods
   Perham, MN 800-346-4910
International Trading Company
   Houston, TX 713-224-5901
Mediterranean Snack Food Co
   Boonton, NJ 973-402-2644

Sour Cream & Onion

Backer's Potato Chip Company
   Fulton, MO 573-642-2833
Barrel O' Fun Snack Foods
   Perham, MN 800-346-4910
Martin's Potato Chips
   Thomasville, PA 800-272-4477
Mister Bee Potato Chips Co
   Parkersburg, WV. 304-428-6133
Tim's Cascade Snacks
   Auburn, WA. 800-533-8467
Wachusset Potato Chip Co Inc
   Fitchburg, MA 800-551-5539

Sweet Potatoes

ARA Food Corp
   Miami, FL 800-533-8831
Rhythm Superfoods
   Austin, TX. 512-441-5667
Small Planet Foods
   Minneapolis, MN 800-624-4123
The Good Bean
   Berkeley, CA. 561-243-7773

Taco

Li'l Guy Foods
   Kansas City, MO 800-886-8226

Tortilla

Abuelita Mexican Foods
   Manassas Park, VA 703-369-0232
Arizona Cowboy
   Phoenix, AZ 800-529-8627
Art's Mexican Products
   Kansas City, KS 913-371-2163
Azteca Foods Inc
   Chicago, IL 708-563-6600
Bachman Company
   Wyamissing, PA 800-523-8253
Bake Crafters Food Company
   McDonald, TN 423-396-3392
Barrel O' Fun Snack Foods
   Perham, MN 800-346-4910
Bearitos
   Boulder, CO 310-886-8200
Better Made Snack Foods
   Detroit, MI 800-332-2394
Bickel's Snack Foods Inc
   York, PA 800-233-1933
Bountiful Larder LLC
   Crested Butte, CO. 800-676-5057
C J Vitner Co
   Chicago, IL 773-523-7900
Copak Solutions
   Conover, NC. 828-261-0255
Deep River Snacks
   Deep River, CT. 860-434-7347
El Matador Foods
   Baytown, TX. 800-470-2447
El Milagro
   Chicago, IL 773-579-6120
Food Should Taste Good
   Denver, CO 877-588-3784
Frog Ranch Foods
   Glouster, OH. 800-742-2488
Golden Flake Snack Foods
   Birmingham, AL. 800-367-7629
Golden Fluff Popcorn Co
   Lakewood, NJ 732-367-5448
Herr Foods Inc.
   Nottingham, PA. 800-523-5030
Husman Snack Food Company
   Peoria, IL. 859-282-7490
LA Canasta Mexican Foods
   Phoenix, AZ 855-269-7721
LA Mexicana Tortilleria
   Chicago, IL 773-247-5443
LA Tapatia Tortilleria Inc
   Fresno, CA 559-441-1030
Los Amigo Tortilla Mfg Co
   Atlanta, GA. 800-969-8226
Luke's Organic
   Santa Cruz, CA
Miguel's Stowe Away
   Stowe, VT. 800-448-6517
Mikesell's Potato Chip Company
   Dayton, OH. 937-228-9400
Mission Foodservice
   Oldsmar, FL 800-443-7994

Product Categories / Snack Foods: Corn Nuts

Ozuna Food Products Corporation
  Sunnyvale, CA 408-400-0495
Pan De Oro Tortilla Chip Co
  Hartford, CT 860-724-7063
PepsiCo.
  Purchase, NY 914-253-2000
Plocky's Fine Snacks
  Hinsdale, IL 630-323-8888
Puebla Foods Inc
  Passaic, NJ 973-473-0201
R.W. Garcia
  Scotts Valley, CA 408-287-4616
Rudy's Tortillas
  Carrollton, TX 800-878-2401
RW Garcia
  San Jose, CA 408-287-4616
Small Planet Foods
  Minneapolis, MN 800-624-4123
Snak King Corp
  City Of Industry, CA 626-336-7711
Snyder's-Lance Inc.
  Charlotte, NC 800-438-1880
Spanish Gardens Food Manufacturing
  Kansas City, KS 913-831-4242
Sun Pac Foods
  Brampton, ON 905-792-2700
T.W. Garner Food Company
  Winston Salem, NC 800-476-7383
Tom's Snacks Company
  Charlotte, NC 800-995-2623
UTZ Quality Foods Inc.
  Hanover, PA 800-367-7629
Way Better Snacks
  Minneapolis, MN 612-314-2060
Westbrae Natural Foods
  Melville, NY 800-434-4246
Wyandot Inc
  Marion, OH 800-992-6368

Corn Nuts

California Nuggets Inc
  Ripon, CA 209-599-7131
Dakota Gourmet
  Wahpeton, ND 800-727-6663
Hialeah Products Co
  Hollywood, FL 800-923-3379
Setton International Foods
  Commack, NY 800-227-4397
Waymouth Farms Inc
  Minneapolis, MN 800-527-0094

Popcorn

479 Degrees
  San Francisco, CA 815-552-6039
A La Carte
  Chicago, IL 800-722-2370
American Pop Corn Co
  Sioux City, IA 712-239-1232
Angelic Gourmet Inc
  Naples, NY 800-294-0947
Angie's Artisan Treats LLC
  North Mankato, MN 888-982-4984
Bachman Company
  Wyamissing, PA 800-523-8253
Better Made Snack Foods
  Detroit, MI 800-332-2394
Black Jewell Popcorn
  Columbus, IN 800-948-2302
Black Shield
  Albuquerque, NM 800-653-9357
Brandmeyer Popcorn Co
  Ankeny, IA 800-568-8276
Brimhall Popcorn
  Bartlett, TN 800-628-6559
Buddy Squirrel LLC
  St Francis, WI 800-972-2658
C & F Foods Inc
  City Of Industry, CA 626-723-1000
C J Dannemiller Co
  Norton, OH 800-624-8671
C J Vitner Co
  Chicago, IL 773-523-7900
Calif Snack Foods
  South El Monte, CA 626-454-4099
Cape Cod Potato Chips
  Hyannis, MA 800-438-1880
Carmadhy's Foods
  Waterloo, ON 519-746-0551
Cheeze Kurls
  Grand Rapids, MI 616-784-6095

Chester Inc Information
  Valparaiso, IN 800-778-1131
Cloud Nine
  Claremont, CA 909-624-3147
Clutter Farms
  Gambier, OH 740-427-3515
Colorado Popcorn Co
  Sterling, CO 866-491-2676
Con Agra Snack Foods
  Hamburg, IA 800-831-5818
Coney Island Classics
  Valley Stream, NY 516-823-3001
Corn Popper
  Tulsa, OK 918-250-9317
Crickle Company
  Thomasville, GA 800-237-8689
De Met's Candy Co
  Stamford, CT 800-872-7622
Deep River Snacks
  Deep River, CT 860-434-7347
Delicious Popcorn
  Waupaca, WI 715-258-7683
Double Good
  Burr Ridge, IL 630-568-5544
Eagle Family Foods
  Richfield, OH 888-656-3245
Elmers Fine Foods Inc
  New Orleans, LA 888-570-0764
Fancy Farms Popcorn
  Bernie, MO 800-833-8154
Fernando C Pujals & Bros
  Guaynabo, PR 787-792-3080
Fizzle Flat Farm, L.L.C.
  Yale, IL 618-793-2060
Frankford Candy & Chocolate Co
  Philadelphia, PA 800-523-9090
Fresh Ideas
  Las Vegas, NV 702-701-4272
Frito-Lay Inc.
  Plano, TX 800-352-4477
Front Range Snacks Inc
  Centennial, CO 303-744-8850
Fun City Popcorn
  Las Vegas, NV 800-423-1710
Funkychunky Inc.
  Edina, MN 888-473-8659
Gaslamp Co Popcorn
  Riverside, CA 877-237-8276
Gilster-Mary Lee Corp
  Chester, IL 618-826-2361
Gluck Brands
  Sugar Land, TX 281-903-7082
Golden Flake Snack Foods
  Birmingham, AL 800-367-7629
Golden Fluff Popcorn Co
  Lakewood, NJ 732-367-5448
Grandpa Po's Nutra Nuts
  Commerce, CA 323-260-7457
Great American Popcorn Works of Pennsylvania
  Telford, PA 855-542-2676
Great Western Co LLC
  Hollywood, AL 256-259-3578
Hain Celestial Group Inc
  Lake Success, NY 800-434-4246
Halfpops Inc
  Scottsdale, AZ 480-494-5117
Happy Herberts Food Co Inc
  Jersey City, NJ 800-764-2779
Happy's Potato Chip Co
  Minneapolis, MN 612-781-3121
Herr Foods Inc.
  Nottingham, PA 800-523-5030
International Home Foods
  Parsippany, NJ 973-359-9920
International Service Group
  Alpharetta, GA 770-518-0988
Jerry's Nut House
  Denver, CO 303-861-2262
Jess Jones Vineyard
  Dixon, CA 707-678-3839
Jody's Gourmet Popcorn
  Virginia Beach, VA 757-422-8646
Kernel Fabyan's Gourmet Popcorn
  St Charles, IL 847-483-1377
Kernel Seasons LLC
  Elk Grove Vlg, IL 866-328-7672
Kloss Manufacturing Co Inc
  Allentown, PA 800-445-7100
Koeze Company
  Grand Rapids, MI 800-555-9688
Kornfections
  Chantilly, VA 800-469-8886

Krispy Kernels
  Quebec, QC 877-791-9986
Lima Grain Cereal Seeds LLC
  Fort Collins, CO 970-498-2200
Martin's Potato Chips
  Thomasville, PA 800-272-4477
Metzger Popcorn Co
  Delphos, OH 800-819-6072
Michele's Chocolate Truffles
  Clackamas, OR 800-656-7112
Midwest Nut Co
  Minneapolis, MN 800-328-5502
Mikesell's Potato Chip Company
  Dayton, OH 937-228-9400
Mills Brothers Intl
  Seattle, WA 206-575-3000
Morrison Farms
  Clearwater, NE 402-887-5335
Nebraska Bean
  Clearwater, NE 800-253-6502
Newman's Own
  Westport, CT 203-222-0136
Noble Popcorn
  Sac City, IA 800-537-9554
Nutra Nuts
  Commerce, CA 323-260-7457
Old Dutch Foods LTD
  Roseville, MN
Old Sacramento Popcorn Company
  Sacramento, CA 916-446-1980
Olson Livestock & Seed
  Haigler, NE 308-297-3283
Oogie's Snack LLC
  Denver, CO 303-455-2107
Organic Planet
  San Francisco, CA 415-765-5590
Papa Dean's Popcorn
  San Antonio, TX 877-855-7272
Patsy's Candy
  Colorado Springs, CO 866-372-8797
Pleasant Grove Farms
  Pleasant Grove, CA 916-655-3391
Pop Art Snacks
  Salt Lake City, UT 801-983-7470
Pop Gourmet LLC
  Tukwila, WA 206-397-3896
Popcorn Connection
  North Hollywood, CA 800-852-2676
Popcorn Popper
  Monon, IN 800-270-2705
Popcorn World
  Sedalia, MO 800-443-8226
Popcorner
  Swansea, IL 618-277-2676
Popcornopolis LLC
  Vernon, CA 800-767-2489
Poppers Supply Company
  Allentown, PA 800-457-9810
Popsalot
  Beverly Hills, CA 213-761-0156
Preferred Popcorn
  Chapman, NE 308-986-2526
Preston Farms Popcorn
  Louisville, KY 866-767-7464
Primrose Candy Co
  Chicago, IL 800-268-9522
Quinn Snacks
  Boulder, CO 303-927-6655
R&J Farms
  West Salem, OH 419-846-3179
Ramsey Popcorn Co Inc
  Ramsey, IN 800-624-2060
Reist Popcorn Co
  Mt Joy, PA 717-653-8078
Richard Green Company
  Indianapolis, IN 317-972-0941
Rivard Popcorn Products
  Lancaster, PA 717-898-7131
Roberts Ferry Nut Co
  Waterford, CA 209-874-3247
Rock-N-Roll Gourmet
  Marina Del Ray, CA 800-518-3891
Rygmyr Foods
  South Saint Paul, MN 800-545-3903
Sahagian & Associates
  Oak Park, IL 800-327-9273
Sexy Pop LLC
  Sea Cliff, NY 877-476-2755
Shallowford Farms Popcorn, Inc.
  Yadkinville, NC 800-892-9539
Shepherd Farms Inc
  Hillsboro, IL 800-383-2676

Product Categories / Snack Foods: Pork Rinds

Sheryl's Chocolate Creations
   Hicksville, NY 888-882-2462
Snack Works/Metrovox Snacks
   Orange, CA 800-783-9870
Snak King Corp
   City Of Industry, CA 626-336-7711
Snappy Popcorn
   Breda, IA 800-742-0228
Snikiddy, LLC
   Boulder, CO 303-444-4405
Snyder's-Lance Inc.
   Charlotte, NC 800-438-1880
Stock Popcorn Ind Inc
   Lake View, IA 712-657-2811
Sugar Plum
   Kingston, PA 800-447-8427
Teelee Popcorn
   Shannon, IL. 800-578-2363
The Hampton Popcorn Company
   Bethpage, NY 888-947-6726
The Little Kernel
   Manalapan, NJ 732-607-3880
Tiny But Mighty Popcorn
   Shellsburg, IA 800-330-4692
Todd's
   Vernon, CA 800-938-6337
Treier Popcorn Farms
   Bloomdale, OH 419-454-2811
Tri-Sum Potato Chip Company
   Leominster, MA 978-697-2447
Trinidad Benham Corporation
   Denver, CO 303-220-1400
UTZ Quality Foods Inc.
   Hanover, PA 800-367-7629
Vande Walle's Candies Inc
   Appleton, WI 800-738-1020
Vegan Rob's
   Sea Cliff, NY. 516-671-4411
Velvet Creme Popcorn Co
   Westwood, KS. 888-553-6708
Vogel Popcorn
   Lakeville, MN. 952-469-7482
Wabash Valley Farms
   Monon, IN. 877-888-7077
Wachusset Potato Chip Co Inc
   Fitchburg, MA 800-551-5539
Weaver Popcorn Co Inc
   Van Buren, IN
Westbrae Natural Foods
   Melville, NY. 800-434-4246
Wildly Organic
   Silver Bay, MN 800-945-3801
Yaya's
   Corona Del Mar, CA. 949-675-7708

Coated

Black Shield
   Albuquerque, NM. 800-653-9357
Calif Snack Foods
   South El Monte, CA 626-454-4099
Double Good
   Burr Ridge, IL. 630-568-5544
Golden Fluff Popcorn Co
   Lakewood, NJ. 732-367-5448
Jody's Gourmet Popcorn
   Virginia Beach, VA. 757-422-8646
Kernel Seasons LLC
   Elk Grove Vlg, IL. 866-328-7672
Lou-Retta's Custom Chocolates
   Buffalo, NY. 716-833-7111
The Safe + Fair Food Company
   Chicago, IL

Flavored

479 Degrees
   San Francisco, CA 815-552-6039
Black Shield
   Albuquerque, NM. 800-653-9357
Calif Snack Foods
   South El Monte, CA 626-454-4099
Dale & Thomas Popcorn
   Englewood, NJ. 800-767-4444
DGZ Chocolate
   Houston, TX. 877-949-9444
Double Good
   Burr Ridge, IL. 630-568-5544
Eda's Sugar Free
   Philadelphia, PA 215-324-3412
G.H. Cretors
   Richfield, OH

Golden Fluff Popcorn Co
   Lakewood, NJ. 732-367-5448
Halfpops Inc
   Scottsdale, AZ. 480-494-5117
Happy's Potato Chip Co
   Minneapolis, MN 612-781-3121
Jody's Gourmet Popcorn
   Virginia Beach, VA. 757-422-8646
Kernel Seasons LLC
   Elk Grove Vlg, IL. 866-328-7672
Live Love Pop
   Addison, TX 214-697-6370
Maddy & Maize
   Saint Paul, MN 612-405-9155
Maria's Premium
Middlefield Cheese House
   Middlefield, OH 800-327-9477
Midwest Nut Co
   Minneapolis, MN 800-328-5502
Mini Pops Inc
   Stoughton, MA 781-436-5864
Noble Popcorn
   Sac City, IA. 800-537-9554
Nouveau Foods
   Mountain View, CA
Oogie's Snack LLC
   Denver, CO 303-455-2107
Pipsnacks
   New York, NY 973-723-4246
Pop Gourmet LLC
   Tukwila, WA 206-397-3896
Pop Zero
   Salt Lake City, UT 801-456-5757
Popcorn World
   Sedalia, MO 800-443-8226
Popcornopolis LLC
   Vernon, CA. 800-767-2489
Poppy Hand-Crafted Popcorn
   Asheville, NC 828-552-3149
POPTime
   Clifton, NJ. 862-225-9549
Quality Snacks
   New York, NY
Quinn Snacks
   Boulder, CO 303-927-6655
Rivard Popcorn Products
   Lancaster, PA 717-898-7131
Tastebuds Popcorn
   Belmont, NC 704-461-8755
The Little Kernel
   Manalapan, NJ 732-607-3880
Tim's Cascade Snacks
   Auburn, WA 800-533-8467
Tri-Sum Potato Chip Company
   Leominster, MA 978-697-2447
Velvet Creme Popcorn Co
   Westwood, KS. 888-553-6708
Victoria's Catered Traditions
   Manteca, CA. 877-272-5208
Wabash Valley Farms
   Monon, IN. 877-888-7077
Yaya's
   Corona Del Mar, CA. 949-675-7708

Pork Rinds

ARA Food Corp
   Miami, FL. 800-533-8831
Bacon's Heir
   706-688-9534
Better Made Snack Foods
   Detroit, MI 800-332-2394
Evans Food Group LTD
   Chicago, IL. 866-254-7400
Golden Flake Snack Foods
   Birmingham, AL. 800-367-7629
Mac's Snacks
   Arlington, TX 817-640-5626
Manda Fine Meats Inc
   Baton Rouge, LA 800-343-2642
Rudolph Foods Co
   Lima, OH. 419-648-3611
Sau-Sea Foods
   Tarrytown, NY 914-631-1717
Tom's Snacks Company
   Charlotte, NC 800-995-2623

Bacon

Evans Food Group LTD
   Chicago, IL. 866-254-7400
Rudolph Foods Co
   Lima, OH. 419-648-3611

Potato Sticks

Golden Fluff Popcorn Co
   Lakewood, NJ. 732-367-5448
Wachusset Potato Chip Co Inc
   Fitchburg, MA 800-551-5539

Pretzels

All American Snacks
   Midland, TX 800-840-2455
All Wrapped Up
   Plantation, FL 800-891-2194
Amoroso's Baking Co
   Bellmawr, PA. 215-471-4740
Angelic Gourmet Inc
   Naples, NY 800-294-0947
Bachman Company
   Wyamissing, PA 800-523-8253
Bake Crafters Food Company
   McDonald, TN 423-396-3392
Barrel O' Fun Snack Foods
   Perham, MN 800-346-4910
Benzel's Pretzel Bakery
   Altoona, PA. 800-344-4438
Better Made Snack Foods
   Detroit, MI 800-332-2394
Bickel's Snack Foods Inc
   York, PA 800-233-1933
Bissinger's Handcrafted Chocolatier
   St. Louis, MO 314-615-2400
Brad's Taste of New York
   Floral Park, NY. 516-354-9004
Brimhall Foods
   Bartlett, TN 800-628-6559
Buckeye Pretzel Company
   Williamsport, PA. 800-257-6029
Buddy Squirrel LLC
   St Francis, WI. 800-972-2658
Candy Cottage Company
   Huntingdon Valley, PA 215-953-8288
Cape Cod Potato Chips
   Hyannis, MA. 800-438-1880
Clara Foods
   Clara City, MN 888-844-8518
Dave's Gourmet
   San Rafael, CA 800-758-0372
Dieffenbach's Potato Chips
   Womelsdorf, PA. 610-589-2385
Dream Confectioners LTD
   Teaneck, NJ. 201-836-9000
Fatty Sundays
   Brooklyn, NY 646-762-2555
Frito-Lay Inc.
   Plano, TX 800-352-4477
From the Ground Up
   Fairfield, NJ
GKI Foods
   Brighton, MI 248-486-0055
Gratify Gluten Free
   Englewood Cliffs, NJ 800-200-6736
GWB Foods Corporation
   Brooklyn, NY 877-977-7610
Happy Herberts Food Co Inc
   Jersey City, NJ 800-764-2779
Hartley's Potato Chip Co
   Lewistown, PA 717-248-0526
Herr Foods Inc.
   Nottingham, PA. 800-523-5030
Hialeah Products Co
   Hollywood, FL 800-923-3379
J & J Snack Foods Corp
   Pennsauken, NJ 800-486-9533
Julius Sturgis Pretzel Bakery
   Lititz, PA 717-626-4354
Kay's Naturals, Inc.
   Clara City, MN 866-873-5499
Key III Candies
   Fort Wayne, IN 800-752-2382
Keystone Pretzel Bakery
   Lititz, PA. 888-572-4500
Kim & Scott's Gourmet Pretzels
   Chicago, IL. 800-578-9478
Knese Enterprise
   Bellerose, NY 516-354-9004
Krispy Kernels
   Quebec, QC. 877-791-9986
Martin's Potato Chips
   Thomasville, PA 800-272-4477
Mary's Gone Crackers
   Gridley, CA 888-258-1250
Mikesell's Potato Chip Company
   Dayton, OH. 937-228-9400

Product Categories / Snack Foods: Rice Cakes

Mister Snacks Inc
  Amherst, NY..................800-333-6393
Nature's Legacy Inc.
  Hudson, MI....................517-448-2050
Old Dutch Foods LTD
  Roseville, MN
Palmer Candy Co
  Sioux City, IA.................800-831-0828
PepsiCo.
  Purchase, NY..................914-253-2000
Porkie Company of Wisconsin
  Cudahy, WI....................800-333-2588
Port City Pretzels
  Portsmouth, NH................603-502-7946
Pretzel Perfection
  Vancouver, WA.................360-635-3886
Pretzel Pete
  Montgomeryville, PA...........877-857-1727
Pretzels Inc
  Bluffton, IN...................800-456-4838
Quinn Snacks
  Boulder, CO...................303-927-6655
R&J Farms
  West Salem, OH................419-846-3179
S B Global Foods Inc
  Lansdale, PA..................877-857-1727
Savor Street
  Reading, PA...................800-523-8253
Sheryl's Chocolate Creations
  Hicksville, NY.................888-882-2462
Snack Works/Metrovox Snacks
  Orange, CA....................800-783-9870
Snak King Corp
  City Of Industry, CA...........626-336-7711
Snyder's of Hanover
  Charlotte, NC..................800-233-7125
Sole Grano LLC
  Fair Lawn, NJ..................201-797-7100
Sporting Colors LLC
  St. Louis, MO..................888-394-2292
Sweet City Supply
  Virginia Beach, VA.............888-793-3824
Tell City Pretzel Company
  Tell City, IN...................812-548-4499
Todd's
  Vernon, CA....................800-938-6337
Triple-C
  Hamilton, ON..................800-263-9105
Tru Chocolate
  Medford, MA..................855-878-2462
Unique Pretzel Bakery, Inc.
  Reading, PA...................610-929-3172
UTZ Quality Foods Inc.
  Hanover, PA...................800-367-7629
Vermont Pretzel & Cookie Co.
  Bellows Falls, VT...............888-671-4774
Weaver Nut Co. Inc.
  Ephrata, PA...................800-473-2688
Wege Pretzel Company
  Hanover, PA...................800-888-4646
Westbrae Natural Foods
  Melville, NY...................800-434-4246

Flavored
Creative Snacks Co LLC
  Greensboro, NC...............336-668-4151
Dream Pretzels
  New York, NY.................877-966-8434
Grippo Foods
  Cincinnati, OH.................800-626-1824
Kim & Scott's Gourmet Pretzels
  Chicago, IL...................800-578-9478
Unique Pretzel Bakery, Inc.
  Reading, PA...................610-929-3172

Nubs
Kim & Scott's Gourmet Pretzels
  Chicago, IL...................800-578-9478
Pretzel Pete
  Montgomeryville, PA...........877-857-1727

Soft
Bakers Best Snack Food Corp.
  Pennsauken, NJ...............215-822-3511

Hammond Pretzel Bakery Inc
  Lancaster, PA.................717-392-7532
Kim & Scott's Gourmet Pretzels
  Chicago, IL...................800-578-9478
New York Pretzel
  Brooklyn, NY..................718-366-9800
Rudi's Organic Bakery
  Boulder, CO...................877-293-0876
Vermont Pretzel & Cookie Co.
  Bellows Falls, VT..............888-671-4774

Sticks or Rods
Barrel O' Fun Snack Foods
  Perham, MN..................800-346-4910
Confectionately Yours LTD
  Buffalo Grove, IL..............800-875-6978
Handy Pax
  Randolph, MA................781-963-8300
Kim & Scott's Gourmet Pretzels
  Chicago, IL...................800-578-9478
Quinn Snacks
  Boulder, CO..................303-927-6655
Sheryl's Chocolate Creations
  Hicksville, NY.................888-882-2462

Twists
Jerry's Nut House
  Denver, CO...................303-861-2262
Kim & Scott's Gourmet Pretzels
  Chicago, IL...................800-578-9478
Pretzel Pete
  Montgomeryville, PA..........877-857-1727
Sheryl's Chocolate Creations
  Hicksville, NY.................888-882-2462

Rice Cakes
Basic Grain Products
  Coldwater, OH................866-411-6677
Blue Marble Brands
  Providence, RI................888-534-0246
Element Snacks
  New York, NY.................212-966-7696
GWB Foods Corporation
  Brooklyn, NY.................877-977-7610
Happy Family
  New York, NY.................855-644-2779
Hawaii Candy Inc
  Honolulu, HI..................800-303-2507
Lundberg Family Farms
  Richvale, CA..................530-538-3500
Ohta Wafer Factory
  Honolulu, HI..................808-949-2775
Westbrae Natural Foods
  Melville, NY...................800-434-4246

Snack Pellets
Preformed
Fashion Snackz
  Pomona, CA..................909-598-0880
Rudolph Foods Co
  Lima, OH.....................419-648-3611
Urban Foods LLC
  Sacramento, CA...............916-372-3663

Trail Mix
American Importing Co.
  Minneapolis, MN..............855-273-0466
Bavarian Nut Co
  Buffalo, NY...................716-810-6887
Bhuja Snacks
  Kennesaw, GA
Big Steer
  Houston, TX..................800-421-4951
Bite Fuel
  Oregon City, OR
Bubba's Fine Foods
  Loveland, CO
C J Vitner Co
  Chicago, IL...................773-523-7900
Cibo Vita
  Totowa, NJ...................862-238-8020

Creative Snacks Co LLC
  Greensboro, NC...............336-668-4151
Desert Pepper Trading Co
  El Paso, TX...................888-472-5727
East Kentucky Foods
  Winchester, KY...............859-744-2218
Essential Living Foods
  Torrance, CA.................310-319-1555
Grandma Emily
  Montreal, QC.................877-943-3661
GrandyOats
  Hiram, ME....................207-935-7415
Greenjoy
  Okatie, SC
Healing Home Foods
  Pound Ridge, NY..............914-764-1303
Hickory Harvest Foods
  Akron, OH....................800-448-6887
Inn Maid Food
  Lenox, MA...................413-637-2732
Jerry's Nut House
  Denver, CO..................303-861-2262
Kohler Original Recipe Chocolates
  Kohler, WI...................920-208-4930
Lehi Valley Trading Company
  Mesa, AZ....................480-684-1402
Marin Food Specialties
  Byron, CA....................925-634-6126
Midwest Nut Co
  Minneapolis, MN.............800-328-5502
Mister Snacks Inc
  Amherst, NY.................800-333-6393
Nature Kist Snacks
  Commerce, CA................323-278-9578
Navitas Naturals
  Novato, CA..................888-645-4282
New England Natural Bakers
  Greenfield, MA...............800-910-2884
Nspired Natural Foods
  Boulder, CO..................800-434-4246
Nut Factory
  Spokane Valley, WA..........888-239-5288
Old Dutch Foods LTD
  Roseville, MN
Patience Fruit & Co.
  Villeroy, QC
Prana
  Ville St Laurent, QC..........844-447-7262
Setton Farms
  Terra Bella, CA...............559-535-6050
Setton International Foods
  Commack, NY...............800-227-4397
Sole Grano LLC
  Fair Lawn, NJ.................201-797-7100
Sonne
  Wahpeton, ND...............800-727-6663
Sun-Rype Products
  Kelowna, BC.................888-786-7973
Sunridge Farms
  Royal Oaks, CA..............831-786-7000
Sunridge Farms Inc
  Salinas, CA...................831-755-1530
Superior Nut & Candy
  Chicago, IL...................800-843-2238
Terri Lynn Inc
  Elgin, IL......................800-323-0775
Thoughtful Food
  Lafayette, CA.................510-910-2581
Tierra Farm
  Valatie, NY...................519-392-8300
Timber Peaks Gourmet
  Parker, CO...................800-982-7687
Tropical Foods
  Charlotte, NC................800-438-4470
Valley View Blueberries
  Vancouver, WA..............360-892-2839
Waymouth Farms Inc
  Minneapolis, MN.............800-527-0094
Weaver Nut Co. Inc.
  Ephrata, PA..................800-473-2688
Wysong Corp
  Midland, MI..................800-748-0188

/ProductCategories/Specialty&OrganicFoods:General

Specialty & Organic Foods

General

Arico Natural Foods
  Beaverton, OR 503-259-0871
Fallwood Corp
  White Plains, NY 914-304-4065

Aquaculture

Bayou Land Seafood
  Breaux Bridge, LA 337-667-6118
Bourbon Barrel Foods
  Louisville, KY 502-333-6103
Chef Silvio's of Wooster Street
  Guilford, CT 203-453-1064
GS Gelato & Desserts Inc
  Fort Walton Bch, FL 888-435-2767
Idaho Trout Company
  Buhl, ID 866-878-7688
Marion's Smart Delights
  Arlington, VA 703-593-3450
Nora Snacks
  Santa Fe Springs, CA 562-404-9888
Ocean's Balance
  Cape Elizabeth, ME
Silver Streak Bass Co
  El Campo, TX 979-543-6343
Southern Pride Catfish Company
  Seattle, WA 800-343-8046
T. Marzetti Company
  Westerville, OH 800-999-1835
Treats Island Fisheries
  Scaly Mountain, NC 207-733-4580

CBD

Curaleaf
  Wakefield, MA 833-760-4367
GoodBites Snacks
  Venice, CA
Green Gorilla
  Malibu, CA 323-452-5919
Green Roads CBD
  Deerfield Beach, FL 833-462-8922
Irwin Naturals
  Los Angeles, CA 888-223-1548
Medterra CBD
  Irvine, CA 800-971-1288
Nature's Fusions
  Provo, UT 801-872-9500
NuLeaf Naturals
  Denver, CO 720-372-4842
Plus CBD Oil
  San Diego, CA 855-758-7223
PureForm CBD
  Los Angeles, CA
Sagely Naturals
  Santa Monica, CA 424-262-6614

Dietary Products

Alfred L. Wolff, Inc.
  Park Ridge, IL 847-759-8888
Avenue Gourmet
  Owings Mills, MD 410-902-5701
Cave Shake
  Los Angeles, CA
Cell-Nique
  Norwalk, CT 888-417-9343
Clara Foods
  San Francisco, CA
Grandcestors
  Golden, CO
Health Warrior
  Richmond, VA 804-381-5305
Kalifornia Keto
  Villa Park, CA
Personal Edge Nutrition
  Ballwin, MO 514-636-4512
Prosperity Organic Foods
  Boise, ID 888-557-5741
Steve's PaleoGoods
  Pennsauken, NJ 856-356-2258
Synergy
  Moab, UT 800-804-3211

Diet & Weight Loss Aids

Alkinco
  New York, NY 800-424-7118
Almased USA
  St. Petersburg, FL 727-867-4444
Body Breakthrough Inc
  Deer Park, NY 800-924-3343
CarbRite Diet
  New Brunswick, NJ 800-872-0101
Eckhart Corporation
  Novato, CA 800-200-4201
Himalayan Heritage
  Fredonia, WI 888-414-9500
Inbalance Health
  Wayland, MI 269-792-1977
LonoLife
  Oceanside, CA 855-843-8566
Natural Balance
  Englewood, CO 800-624-4260
Nature's Plus
  Melville, NY 800-645-9500
Nellson Candies Inc
  Irwindale, CA 626-334-4508
Nestle USA Inc
  Glendale, CA 800-225-2270
Nutraceutical International
  Park City, UT 800-669-8877
Organic Liaison, LLC
  Coral Springs, FL 954-755-4405
Pro Form Labs
  Orinda, CA 707-752-9010
Russo Farms
  Vineland, NJ 856-692-5942
Soluble Products Company
  Lakewood, NJ 732-364-8855
The Sola Company
  Houston, TX 800-277-1486
Tova Industries LLC
  Louisville, KY 888-532-8682
USA Laboratories Inc
  Burns, TN 800-489-4872
VitaThinQ Inc.
  Davie, FL
Zevia
  Culver City, CA 855-469-3842

Dietary Supplements

Acta Health Products
  Sunnyvale, CA 408-732-6830
Alacer Corp
  Carlisle, PA 888-425-2362
Archon Vitamin Corp
  Edison, NJ 800-848-0089
Balanced Health Products
  New York, NY 212-794-9878
BetaStatin Nutritional Rsearch
  Greenwich, CT 800-660-9570
Century Foods Intl LLC
  Sparta, WI 800-269-1901
CHiKPRO
  417-708-0988
Edom Labs Inc
  Deer Park, NY 800-723-3366
Green Roads CBD
  Deerfield Beach, FL 833-462-8922
Hero Nutritionals
  Santa Ana, CA 800-500-4376
Immu Dyne Inc
  Florence, KY 888-246-6839
Life Extension Foundation
  Fort Lauderdale, FL 888-895-4771
Maat Nutritionals
  Los Angeles, CA 888-818-6228
Montana Naturals
  Park City, UT 800-650-9597
Naturalife Laboratories
  Torrance, CA 800-231-3670
Nature's Herbs
  Merritt, BC 800-437-2257
Nellson Nutraceutical LLC
  Anaheim, CA 844-635-5766
North West Pharmanaturals Inc
  Brea, CA 714-529-0980
NOW Foods
  Bloomingdale, IL 888-669-3663
Power Crunch
  Irvine, CA
QBI
  South Plainfield, NJ 908-668-0088
Rainbow Light Nutritional Systems
  Santa Cruz, CA 800-635-1233
SimplyFUEL, LLC
  Leawood, KS 913-269-1889
Source Naturals
  Scotts Valley, CA 800-815-2333
Trace Minerals Research
  West Haven, UT 800-624-7145
Valentine Enterprises Inc
  Lawrenceville, GA 770-995-0661
Vita-Pure Inc
  Roselle, NJ 908-245-1212
Vitamer Laboratories
  Irvine, CA 800-432-8355
Wilke International Inc
  Lenexa, KS 800-779-5545

Health Products

Abunda Life
  Asbury Park, NJ 732-775-9338
Acta Health Products
  Sunnyvale, CA 408-732-6830
Action Labs
  Anaheim, CA 800-400-5696
ADH Health Products Inc
  Congers, NY 845-268-0027
Agger Fish Corp
  Brooklyn, NY 718-855-1717
Alacer Corp
  Carlisle, PA 888-425-2362
Alfer Laboratories
  Chatsworth, CA 818-709-0737
Alkinco
  New York, NY 800-424-7118
Alli & Rose
  Lincolnton, NC 828-446-8420
Aloe Farms Inc
  Harlingen, TX 800-262-6771
Aloe Laboratories
  Harlingen, TX 800-258-5380
Alternative Health & Herbs
  Albany, OR 800-345-4152
Amcan Industries
  Elmsford, NY 914-347-4838
American Almond Products Co
  Brooklyn, NY 800-825-6663
American Spoon Foods Inc
  Petoskey, MI 888-735-6700
Anabol Naturals
  Santa Cruz, CA 800-426-2265
Annie's Naturals
  Berkeley, CA 800-434-1234
Apotheca Inc
  Woodbine, IA 800-736-3130
Archon Vitamin Corp
  Edison, NJ 800-848-0089
Arizona Natural Products
  Phoenix, AZ 800-255-2823
Arro Corp
  Hodgkins, IL 877-929-2776
Aspire
  Chicago, OH
Atkins Nutritionals Inc.
  Denver, CO 800-628-5467
Atrium Biotech
  Quebec, QC 418-652-1116
Bake N Joy Foods
  North Andover, MA 800-666-4937
BBS Bodacious BBQ Company
  Coral Springs, FL 800-537-5928
Bede Inc
  Haledon, NJ 866-239-6565
Beehive Botanicals
  Hayward, WI 800-233-4483
Bel Brands USA
  Chicago, IL 312-462-1500
Betty Lou's
  McMinnville, OR 800-242-5205
Bevco Sales International Inc.
  Surrey, BC 800-663-0090
Beverly International
  Cold Spring, KY 800-781-3475

Product Categories / Specialty & Organic Foods: Dietary Products

Bio-Foods
   Pine Brook, NJ 973-808-5856
Black Ranch Organic Grains
   Etna, CA 916-467-3387
Blessed Herbs
   Oakham, MA. 800-489-4372
Blue Chip Baker
   Salt Lake City, UT 800-878-0099
Blue Planet Foods
   Collegedale, TN 877-396-3145
Botanical Products
   Springville, CA. 559-539-3432
Brucia Plant Extracts
   Shingle Springs, CA 530-676-2774
Buckhead Gourmet
   Atlanta, GA. 800-673-6338
Bunker Hill Cheese Co Inc
   Millersburg, OH 800-253-6636
Butter Buds Food Ingredients
   Racine, WI. 800-426-1119
CactuLife, LLC
   Corona Del Mar, CA. 800-500-1713
California Fruit
   San Diego, CA 877-378-4811
California Natural Products
   Lathrop, CA 209-858-2525
California Olive Oil Council
   Berkeley, CA. 888-718-9830
Caltex Foods
   Canoga Park, CA 800-522-5839
Carole's Cheesecake Company
   Toronto, ON 416-256-0000
Cascade Fresh
   Seattle, WA 800-511-0057
Caveman Foods
   Lafayette, CA 925-979-9515
Cedar Crest Specialties
   Cedarburg, WI. 800-877-8341
Cedar Lake Foods
   Cedar Lake, MI. 800-246-5039
Cedarlane Foods
   Carson, CA 800-826-3322
Champlain Valley Milling Corp
   Westport, NY. 518-962-4711
Chase Brothers Dairy
   Oxnard, CA. 800-438-6455
China Mist Brands
   Scottsdale, AZ. 800-242-8807
Christopher Ranch LLC
   Gilroy, CA. 408-847-1100
Christopher's Herb Shop
   Springville, UT 888-372-4372
Clif Bar & Co
   Emeryville, CA. 802-254-3227
Coca-Cola Beverages Northeast
   Bedford, NH 844-619-3388
Cookie Tree Bakeries
   Salt Lake City, UT 801-268-2253
Countertop Productions
   Alexandria, VA
Cyanotech Corp
   Kailua Kona, HI 800-395-1353
Dairy Maid Dairy LLC
   Frederick, MD. 301-663-5114
Dean Distributors, Inc.
   Burlingame, CA 800-792-0816
Deerland Probiotics & Enzymes
   Kennesaw, GA 800-697-8179
Devansoy Farms
   Carroll, IA. 800-747-8605
Diamond Crystal Brands Inc
   Savannah, GA 800-654-5115
Dolphin Natural Chocolates
   Cambria, CA. 800-236-5744
Dorothy Dawson Food Products
   Jackson, MI. 517-788-9830
Dr. In The Kitchen
   Minneapolis, MN 952-746-3007
DSM Fortitech Premixes
   Schenectady, NY
Dulce de Leche Delcampo Products
   Miami, FL. 877-472-9408
Earth Island
   Chatsworth, CA 888-394-3949
Eda's Sugar Free
   Philadelphia, PA 215-324-3412
Edner Corporation
   Hayward, CA 510-441-8504
Elwood International Inc
   Copiague, NY 631-842-6600
Emkay Trading Corporation
   Elmsford, NY. 914-592-9000

Ener-G Foods
   Seattle, WA 800-331-5222
Energen Products Inc
   Norwalk, CA. 800-423-8837
Essential Nutrients Inc
   Emery, UT. 435-286-2460
Evo Hemp
   Boulder, CO
Evolve
   Walnut Creek, CA. 888-298-6629
Faber Foods and Aeronautics
   Evergreen, CO. 800-237-3255
Falcone's Cookie Land LTD
   Brooklyn, NY 718-236-4200
Fat Snax
   Brooklyn, NY. 347-496-5834
Fieldbrook Foods Corp.
   Dunkirk, NY 800-333-0805
First District Association
   Litchfield, MN 320-693-3236
FitPro USA
   Fairfield, CA. 877-645-5776
FODY Food Co.
   Westmount, QC. 818-835-1850
Food First
   Walhalla, ND. 800-241-0799
Freeda Vitamins Inc
   Long Island City, NY 800-777-3737
Frontier Co-op
   Norway, IA 844-550-6200
Garuda International
   Exeter, CA 559-594-4380
Germack Pistachio Co
   Detroit, MI 800-872-4006
Gertrude & Bronner's Magic Alpsnack
   Vista, CA .877-786-3649
Gifford's Ice Cream
   Skowhegan, ME 800-950-2604
Ginger Shots
   Huntington Beach, CA 888-413-1487
Ginseng Up Corp
   Worcester, MA 800-446-7364
Global Health Laboratories
   Amityville, NY 631-777-2134
Glover's Ice Cream Inc
   Frankfort, IN 800-686-5163
Goldthread
   Santa Monica, CA. 413-325-8987
GoMacro
   Viola, WI. .800-788-9540
GoodBelly Probiotics
   Boulder, CO 303-443-3631
Govadinas Fitness Foods
   San Diego, CA 800-900-0108
Great Circles
   Bellows Falls, VT 877-877-2120
Green Foods Corp.
   Oxnard, CA 800-777-4430
Green Options
   San Rafael, CA 888-473-3667
Grow Co
   Ridgefield, NJ. 201-941-8777
Gust John Foods & Products
   Batavia, IL. 800-756-5886
GWB Foods Corporation
   Brooklyn, NY 877-977-7610
H Fox & Co Inc
   Brooklyn, NY 718-385-4600
H. Reisman Corporation
   Orange, NJ 973-882-1670
H2rOse, LLC
   Los Angeles, CA
Harvest Valley Bakery Inc
   La Salle, IL 815-224-9030
Haydenergy Health
   Valley Stream, NY 800-255-1660
Health Valley Company
   Irwindale, CA 800-334-3204
Healthy Grain Foods LLC
   Northbrook, IL 847-272-5576
Healthy Skoop
   Boulder, CO 720-545-1753
Healthy Times Baby Food
   San Diego, CA 858-513-1550
Heart to Heart Foods
   Hyde Park, UT 435-753-9602
Heavenly Hemp Foods
   Nederland, CO 888-328-4367
Hello Water
  888-474-3556
Hemp Fusion
   Roswell, GA 877-669-4367

Hemp2o
   San Leandro, CA. 510-382-1231
Herbal Products & Development
   Aptos, CA. 831-688-8706
Herbs America
   Murphy, OR 541-846-6222
Heritage Books & Gifts
   Virginia Beach, VA. 800-862-2923
Heritage Farms Dairy
   Murfreesboro, TN. 615-895-2790
Heterochemical Corp
   Valley Stream, NY 516-561-8225
HFI Foods
   Redmond, WA 425-883-1320
Hillestad Pharmaceuticals
   Woodruff, WI 800-535-7742
Hillside Candy Co
   Hillside, NJ. 800-524-1304
Hinckley Springs Bottled Water
  800-201-6218
Holistic Products Corporation
   Englewood, NJ 800-221-0308
Homestead Mills
   Cook, MN 800-652-5233
Hormel Foods Corp.
   Austin, MN 507-437-5611
Host Defense Mushrooms
  800-780-9126
House Foods America Corp
   Garden Grove, CA 877-333-7077
Howard Foods Inc
   Danvers, MA. 978-774-6207
Hsu's Ginseng Enterprises Inc
   Wausau, WI. 800-826-1577
Humbly Hemp
   Los Angeles, CA 424-259-3521
Humco Holding Group Inc
   Texarkana, TX. 903-831-7808
I-Health Inc
   Cromwell, CT 800-990-3476
ICONIC Protein
   San Clemente, CA
Imlak'esh Organics
   Goleta, CA 805-689-2269
Integrative Flavors
   Michigan City, IN 800-837-7687
Inter Health Nutraceuticals
   Benicia, CA. 800-783-4636
Interbake Foods
   Richmond, VA. 800-221-1002
International Casings Group
   Chicago, IL 800-825-5151
International Vitamin Corporation
   Freehold, NJ 800-666-8482
Island Spring Inc
   Vashon, WA. 206-463-9848
J R Carlson Laboratories Inc
   Arlington Heights, IL 888-234-5656
J.N. Bech
   Elk Rapids, MI 800-232-4583
Jamieson Laboratories
   Windsor, ON 800-265-5088
Jason & Son Specialty Foods
   Rancho Cordova, CA 800-810-9093
Jason Pharmaceuticals
   Owings Mills, MD 800-638-7867
Jaxon's Ice Cream Parlor
   Dania Beach, FL 954-923-4445
JiMMY! Bars
   Chicago, IL. 888-676-7971
JMS Specialty Foods
   Ripon, WI. 800-535-5437
Jonathan's Sprouts
   Rochester, MA 508-763-2577
Julian Bakery
   Oceanside, CA 760-721-5200
Kapaa Poi Factory
   Kapaa, HI 808-822-5426
Kemach Food Products
   Brooklyn, NY 718-272-5655
Keto Foods
   Neptune, NJ 732-922-0009
KiiTO, Inc.
   Los Angeles, CA
Klinke Brothers Ice Cream Co
   Memphis, TN 901-322-6640
Knouse Foods Co-Op Inc.
   Peach Glen, PA 717-677-8181
Koia
   Los Angeles, CA
Kolb-Lena Bresse Bleu Inc
   Lena, IL. 815-369-4577

Product Categories / Specialty & Organic Foods: Dietary Products

Kor Shots
   Malibu, CA
Korea Ginseng Corp.
   Cerritos, CA
Kozlowski Farms
   Forestville, CA 800-473-2767
Kura Nutrition
   Manchester, NH 603-217-2665
Le Bleu Corp
   Advance, NC. 800-854-4471
Life Extension Foundation
   Fort Lauderdale, FL 888-895-4771
Lifeway
   Morton Grove, IL 877-281-3874
Lifewise Ingredients
   Brookfield, IL 262-788-9141
Living Farms
   Tracy, MN 507-629-3517
Longreen Corp.
   San Gabriel, CA 626-287-4700
Lucas Meyer
   Decatur, IL 800-769-3660
Lukas Confections
   York, PA 717-843-0921
Magnetic Springs
   Columbus, OH 800-572-2990
Main Street Gourmet
   Cuyahoga Falls, OH 800-678-6246
Maju Superfoods
   San Diego, CA 619-736-0622
Manhattan Food Brands, LLC
   Metuchen, NJ 732-906-2168
Maple Grove Farms Of Vermont
   St Johnsbury, VT. 802-748-5141
Marsa Specialty Products
   Vernon, CA 800-628-0500
Marsan Foods
   Toronto, ON 416-755-9262
Masala Chai Company
   Santa Cruz, CA 831-475-8881
Master Mix
   Placentia, CA 714-524-1698
Mayway Corp
   Oakland, CA. 800-262-9929
Mccutcheon Apple Products
   Frederick, MD. 800-888-7537
Meadow Brook Dairy Co
   Erie, PA 800-352-4010
MegaFood
   Manchester, NH 800-848-2542
Mei Shun Tofu Products Company
   Chicago, IL 312-842-7000
Merlino Italian Baking Company
   Kent, WA. 800-800-9490
Michigan Dairy LLC
   Livonia, MI. 734-367-5390
Michigan Desserts
   Oak Park, MI. 800-328-8632
MicroSoy Corporation
   Jefferson, IA 515-386-2100
Midwest Nut Co
   Minneapolis, MN 800-328-5502
Mills Brothers Intl
   Seattle, WA. 206-575-3000
Monarch Beverage Company
   Atlanta, GA. 800-241-3732
Morinaga Nutritional Foods, Inc.
   Torrance, CA 310-787-0200
Morningland Dairy Cheese Company
   Mountain View, MO. 417-855-0588
Mountain High Yogurt
   Minneapolis, MN 866-964-4878
Mrs. Leeper's Pasta
   Excelsior Springs, MO 800-848-5266
Mrs. Malibu Foods
   Malibu, CA. 800-677-6254
Mt Sterling Co-Op Creamery
   Highland, WI 866-289-4628
Murray Cider Co Inc
   Roanoke, VA. 540-977-9000
Mustard Seed
   Central, SC 877-621-2591
Natural Balance
   Englewood, CO. 800-624-4260
Natural Company
   Baltimore, MD 410-628-1262
Natural Food Supplements Inc
   Canoga Park, CA 818-341-3475
Natural Food World
   Culver City, CA 310-836-7770
Nature Zen USA
   Essex Junction, VT

Nature's Bounty Co.
   Ronkonkoma, NY 877-774-3361
Nature's Herbs
   Merritt, BC 800-437-2257
Nature's Legacy Inc.
   Hudson, MI. 517-448-2050
Nature's Plus
   Melville, NY 800-645-9500
Naturex Inc
   South Hackensack, NJ 201-440-5000
Nellson Candies Inc
   Irwindale, CA 626-334-4508
Nestle USA Inc
   Glendale, CA 800-225-2270
New Chapter
   Brattleboro, VT. 800-543-7279
New England Country Bakers
   Watertown, CT 800-225-3779
NewGem Products
   Fife, WA 253-896-3089
Nomolas Corp
   Woodmere, NY 516-569-3093
Nootra Life
Norimoor Lic
   Flushing, NY. 718-423-6667
North Country Natural Spring Water
   Port Kent, NY 518-834-9400
North Peace Apiaries
   Fort St. John, BC. 250-785-4808
Now & Zen
   Louisville, CO. 800-779-6383
NOW Foods
   Bloomingdale, IL 888-669-3663
Noyes, P J
   Lancaster, NH 800-522-2469
NuGo Nutrition
   Oakmont, PA 888-421-2032
Nush Foods
   Salt Lake City, UT 801-953-1370
Nut Factory
   Spokane Valley, WA 888-239-5288
Nutraceutical International
   Park City, UT 800-669-8877
Nutrilabs
   San Francisco, CA 877-468-8745
Nutrisport Pharmacal
   Franklin, NJ 833-403-2861
Nutriwest
   Douglas, WY. 800-443-3333
O'Boyle's Ice Cream Company
   Bristol, PA. 215-788-3882
O'Donnell Formulas Inc
   San Marcos, CA 800-736-1991
Ola Loa
   San Francisco, CA 800-800-9550
Old Fashioned Natural Products
   Santa Ana, CA 800-552-9045
Olde Tyme Mercantile
   Arroyo Grande, CA. 805-489-7991
OMG! Superfoods
   Rancho Dominguez, CA. 855-664-3663
Once Again Nut Butter
   Nunda, NY 888-800-8075
Onnit Labs
   Austin, TX. 855-666-4899
Oorganik
   Houston, TX. 281-240-7992
Optimum Nutrition
   Aurora, IL 800-763-3444
Organic Gourmet
   Sherman Oaks, CA 800-400-7772
Osso Good, LLC
   San Rafael, CA
Ota Tofu
   Portland, OR 503-232-8947
OWYN
   Fairfield, NJ 833-533-7061
Pappy's Sassafras Tea
   Columbus Grove, OH 877-659-5110
Particle Dynamics
   Saint Louis, MO 800-452-4682
Pecan Deluxe Candy Co
   Dallas, TX. 800-733-3589
Pecoraro Dairy Products
   Brooklyn, NY 718-388-2379
Peggy Lawton Kitchens
   East Walpole, MA. 800-843-7325
Penta Manufacturing Company
   Livingston, NJ. 973-740-2300
Perfect Foods Inc
   Goshen, NY. 800-933-3288

Perry's Ice Cream Co Inc
   Akron, NY. 800-873-7797
Phillips Syrup Corp
   Cleveland, OH 800-350-8443
Pied-Mont/Dora
   Anne Des Plaines, QC 800-363-8003
Pines International
   Lawrence, KS 800-697-4637
Plainview Milk Products
   Plainview, MN 800-356-5606
Pleasant View Dairy
   Highland, IN 219-838-0155
Pleasoning Gourmet Seasonings
   La Crosse, WI 800-279-1614
Power of 3
   Tenants Harbor, ME 888-211-7911
Premium Water
   Kansas City, MO. 800-332-3332
Pro Form Labs
   Orinda, CA 707-752-9010
Pro Portion Food
   Sayville, NY 631-567-4494
Progenix Corporation
   Wausau, WI. 800-233-3356
Proper-Chem
   Dix Hills, NY 631-420-8000
Protein Research
   Livermore, CA 800-948-1991
Protient
   Woodland, CA. 651-638-2600
Purity Dairies LLC
   Nashville, TN 615-244-1900
Quality Naturally Foods
   City Of Industry, CA. 888-498-6986
Quong Hop & Company
   S San Francisco, CA. 650-553-9900
R.J. Corr Naturals
   Posen, IL 708-389-4200
Ramos Orchards
   Winters, CA 530-795-4748
Ramsen Inc
   Lakeville, MN. 952-431-0400
Randal Optimal Nutrients
   Santa Rosa, CA. 800-221-1697
RawFusion
   Oxnard, CA. 888-852-3350
Regal Health Food
   Chicago, IL 773-252-1044
Rinehart Meat Processing
   Branson, MO. 417-869-2041
Rio Syrup Co
   St Louis, MO. 800-325-7666
Roquette America Inc.
   Geneva, IL. 630-463-9430
Royal Products
   Scottsdale, AZ. 480-948-2509
Russo Farms
   Vineland, NJ 856-692-5942
Sahadi Fine Foods Inc
   Brooklyn, NY 800-724-2341
Sally Lane's Candy Farm
   Paris, TN 731-642-5801
Saratoga Spring Water Co
   Saratoga Springs, NY 888-426-8642
Schneider's Dairy Inc
   Pittsburgh, PA. 412-881-3525
Sells Best
   Mishawaka, IN 800-837-8368
Setton International Foods
   Commack, NY 800-227-4397
Shenk's Foods
   Lancaster, PA 717-393-4240
Siren Snacks
   San Francisco, CA
Sisler's Ice & Ice Cream
   Ohio, IL. 888-891-3856
Sneaky Chef Foods, The
   Boca Raton, FL 561-757-6541
So Delicious Dairy Free
   Springfield, OR. 866-388-7853
Solana Gold Organics
   Sebastopol, CA 800-459-1121
Solnuts
   Hudson, IA 800-648-3503
Source Naturals
   Scotts Valley, CA 800-815-2333
Sovena USA Inc
   Rome, NY. 315-797-7070
Staff Of Life Natural Foods
   Santa Cruz, CA 831-423-8632
Star of the West Milling Co.
   Frankenmuth, MI 989-652-9971

Product Categories / Specialty & Organic Foods: Gluten-Free

Subco Foods Inc
   Sheboygan, WI 800-473-0757
Sunergia Soyfoods
   Charlottesville, VA 800-693-5134
Sunfood
   El Cajon, CA 888-729-3663
Sunray Food Products Corporation
   Bronx, NY 718-548-2255
Sunsweet Growers Inc.
   Yuba City, CA 800-417-2253
Super Stores Industries
   Turlock, CA 209-668-2100
Swagger Foods Corp
   Vernon Hills, IL 847-913-1200
Swiss Premium Dairy Inc
   Lebanon, PA 800-222-2129
Synergy
   Moab, UT 800-804-3211
Terra Origin, Inc.
   Hauppauge, NY 631-300-2306
The Coromega Company
   Carlsbad, CA 877-275-3725
The Valpo Velvet Shoppe
   Valparaiso, IN 219-464-4141
Tigo+
   FL 786-207-4772
Timber Crest Farms
   Healdsburg, CA 888-766-4233
Toft Dairy Inc
   Sandusky, OH 800-521-4606
Tomanetti Food Products Inc
   Oakmont, PA 800-875-3040
Tova Industries LLC
   Louisville, KY 888-532-8682
Tropical Foods
   Charlotte, NC 800-438-4470
Tropical Foods
   Lithia Springs, GA 800-544-3762
Truth Bar LLC
   Waltham, MA 888-886-8959
TruVibe Organics
   Santa Monica, CA
Tu Me Beverage Company
   CA 818-237-5105
Tulkoff's Food Products Inc
   Baltimore, MD 800-638-7343
Turveda
   CA
Twinlab Corporation
   Boca Raton, FL 800-645-5626
TyRy Inc
   Rocklin, CA 800-322-6325
Ultima Health Products Inc.
   Cortland, OH. 888-663-8584
Unique Ingredients LLC
   Gold Canyon, AZ 480-983-2498
Urban Moonshine
   Burlington, VT 802-428-4707
Utzy, Inc.
   Lake Geneva, WI 877-307-6142
Valley View Blueberries
   Vancouver, WA 360-892-2839
Vance's Foods
   San Francisco, CA 415-621-1171
Varni Brothers/7-Up Bottling
   Modesto, CA. 209-521-1777
Vaxa International
   Tampa, FL 877-622-8292
Ventre Packing Company
   Syracuse, NY 315-463-2384
Venus Wafers Inc
   Hingham, MA 800-545-4538
Verday
   New York, NY
VIP Foods
   Flushing, NY 718-821-5350
Vit-Best Nutrition
   Tustin, CA 714-832-9700
Vital Proteins LLC
   Elk Grove Village, IL 224-544-9110
Vitality Works
   Albuquerque, NM 505-268-9950
Vitamer Laboratories
   Irvine, CA 800-432-8355
Vitamins
   Chicago, IL 312-861-0700
Vitasoy USA
   Woburn, MA. 800-848-2769
Vitatech Nutritional Sciences
   Tustin, CA 714-832-9700
Vive Organic
   Venice, CA 877-774-9291

Vogue Cuisine Foods
   Sunnyvale, CA 888-236-4144
Wah Yet Group
   Hayward, CA 800-229-3392
Walden Farms
   Linden, NJ. 800-229-1706
Wax Orchards
   Seattle, WA 800-634-6132
Wellington Foods
   Corona, CA 951-547-7000
Westin Foods
   Omaha, NE 800-228-6098
White Rock Products Corp
   Flushing, NY 800-969-7625
Whitey's Ice Cream Inc
   Moline, IL. 888-594-4839
Whole Herb Co
   Sonoma, CA 707-935-1077
Wilke International Inc
   Lenexa, KS 800-779-5545
Wilson's Fantastic Candy
   Memphis, TN 901-767-1900
Wing Nien Food
   Hayward, CA 510-487-8877
Winmix/Natural Care Products
   Englewood, FL 941-475-7432
Wisconsin Specialty Protein
   Madison, WI
World Flavors Inc
   Warminster, PA 215-672-4400
World Ginseng Ctr Inc
   San Francisco, CA 800-747-8808
World Organics Corporation
   Huntington Beach, CA 714-893-0017
Y Z Enterprises Inc
   Maumee, OH. 800-736-8779
Yoshida Food Products Co
   Portland, OR 800-653-1114

Low-Calorie Desserts

Eden Creamery
   Los Angeles, CA
Wink Frozen Desserts
   Stamford, CT. 516-323-5283

Sugar-Free Foods

American Instants Inc
   Flanders, NJ 973-584-8811
Aunt Gussie Cookies & Crackers
   Garfield, NJ. 800-422-6654
Bissinger's Handcrafted Chocolatier
   St Louis, MO 800-325-8881
California Custom Fruits
   Baldwin Park, CA 877-558-0056
Clemmy's
   Randcho Mirage, CA 877-253-6698
Dresden Stollen Co USA
   Albertson, NY. 516-746-5802
Eda's Sugar Free
   Philadelphia, PA 215-324-3412
GKI Foods
   Brighton, MI 248-486-0055
Gust John Foods & Products
   Batavia, IL 800-756-5886
Howard Foods Inc
   Danvers, MA 978-774-6207
Inn Maid Food
   Lenox, MA 413-637-2732
International Brownie
   East Weymouth, MA. 800-230-1588
Kinnikinnick Foods
   Edmonton, AB 877-503-4466
Kiss My Keto
   Los Angeles, CA. 310-765-1553
Main Street Gourmet
   Cuyahoga Falls, OH 800-678-6246
Maple Grove Farms Of Vermont
   St Johnsbury, VT. 802-748-5141
MATI Energy
   Durham, NC 866-924-8005
Mccutcheon Apple Products
   Frederick, MD. 800-888-7537
Michigan Desserts
   Oak Park, MI. 800-328-8632
Mrs. Leeper's Pasta
   Excelsior Springs, MO 800-848-5266
NuGo Nutrition
   Oakmont, PA. 888-421-2032
Nui Foods
   Anaheim, CA

Olde Tyme Mercantile
   Arroyo Grande, CA. 805-489-7991
Perry's Ice Cream Co Inc
   Akron, NY. 800-873-7797
Sally Lane's Candy Farm
   Paris, TN 731-642-5801
Sells Best
   Mishawaka, IN 800-837-8368
Setton International Foods
   Commack, NY 800-227-4397
Shenk's Foods
   Lancaster, PA 717-393-4240
Silver Tray Cookies
   Fort Lauderdale, FL 305-883-0800
The Sola Company
   Houston, TX 800-277-1486
Tova Industries LLC
   Louisville, KY 888-532-8682
Unique Beverage Company
   Everett, WA 425-267-0959

Gluten-Free

3 Gyros Inc
   Tecumseh, ON. 519-737-0389
Alicita-Salsa
   Great Falls, VA 703-340-5323
American Natural & Organic
   Fremont, CA 510-440-1044
American Specialty Foods
   Lancaster, PA 800-335-6663
Amrita Snacks
   Hartsdale, NY 888-728-7779
Andean Naturals LLC
   Foster City, CA. 650-303-1780
Antoni Ravioli Co
   North Massapequa, NY 800-783-0350
Ariel Natural Foods
   Bellevue, WA 425-637-3345
Aunt Aggie De's Pralines
   Sinton, TX. 800-333-9354
Aunt Gussie Cookies & Crackers
   Garfield, NJ. 800-422-6654
Avena Foods Ltd.
   Regina, SK 306-757-3663
Beanitos
   Austin, TX. 512-609-8017
Beetnik Foods, LLC
   Austin, TX. 512-548-8228
Boulder Granola
   Boulder, CO 303-443-1136
Brothers Sauces
   Fort Worth, TX 817-821-3374
Buns & Roses Organic Wholegrain Bakery
   Edmonton, AB 780-438-0098
Chef Tim Foods, LLC
   Etters, PA 717-802-0350
Cherrybrook Kitchen
   Burlington, MA. 866-458-8225
Clemmy's
   Randcho Mirage, CA 877-253-6698
Cup 4 Cup LLC
   Napa, CA. 707-754-4263
D I Mfg LLC
   Omaha, NE 402-330-5650
Delicious Without Gluten
   Dollard Des Ormeaux, QC 514-542-3943
Dharma Bars
Dowd & Rogers
   San Clemente, CA. 800-232-8619
Dream Foods Intl
   Santa Monica, CA. 310-315-5739
Earth Source Organics
   Vista, CA. 760-734-1867
Eat Real Snacks USA
   Marietta, GA. 404-432-0842
Emmy's Organics
   Ithaca, NY. 855-463-6697
Ener-G Foods
   Seattle, WA 800-331-5222
Enjoy Life Foods
   Chicago, IL 888-503-6569
FAGE USA Dairy Ind Inc
   Johnstown, NY 866-962-5912
Falafel Republic
   Needham Heights, MA. 781-878-6027
Feridies
   Courtland, VA 800-544-0896
Figamajigs
   San Mateo, CA. 650-227-3830
Firebird Artisan Mills
   Harvey, ND 701-324-4330

Product Categories / Specialty & Organic Foods: Gourmet & Specialty Foods

Foods Alive
   Angola, IN......................260-488-4497
French Meadow Bakery & Cafe
   Minneapolis, MN................612-870-7855
Garden Spot Distributors
   New Holland, PA................800-829-5100
Glutino
   Laval, QC......................800-363-3438
Go Max Go Foods
Gold Mine Natural Food Company
   Poway, CA......................800-475-3663
Gopicnic Inc
   Chicago, IL....................773-328-2490
Gracious Gourmet
   Bridgewater, CT................860-350-1213
Grain-Free JK Gourmet, Inc.
   Toronto, ON....................800-608-0465
Greater Knead, The
   Bensalem, PA...................267-522-8523
GS Gelato & Desserts Inc
   Fort Walton Bch, FL............888-435-2767
Healing Home Foods
   Pound Ridge, NY................914-764-1303
Hearthy Foods
   Los Angeles, CA................213-372-5093
Hodgson Mill Inc
   Effingham, IL..................800-347-0198
Honey Mama's
   Portland, OR...................888-506-2627
Integrative Flavors
   Michigan City, IN..............800-837-7687
Jayone Foods Inc
   Paramount, CA..................562-633-7400
Jilz Gluten Free
   Ventura, CA....................805-585-5297
Jovial Foods
   North Stonington, CT...........877-642-0644
Julian Bakery
   Oceanside, CA..................760-721-5200
Kateri Foods
   Hopkins, MN....................800-330-8351
Kay's Naturals, Inc.
   Clara City, MN.................866-873-5499
Kayco
   Bayonne, NJ....................718-369-4600
Kedem
   Bayonne, NJ....................718-369-4600
Kerala Curry
   Pittsboro, NC..................919-545-9401
Kerri Kreations
   Santa Cruz, CA.................831-429-5129
Kind Snacks
   New York, NY...................855-884-5463
King Arthur Flour
   Norwich, VT....................800-827-6836
Kinnikinnick Foods
   Edmonton, AB...................877-503-4466
Koegel Meats Inc
   Flint, MI......................810-238-3685
Lifeway
   Morton Grove, IL...............877-281-3874
Lisa Shively's Kitchen Helpers, LLC
   Eden, NC.......................336-623-7511
Litehouse Foods
   Sandpoint, ID..................800-669-3169
Little Duck Organics
   New York, NY...................877-458-1321
LivBar
   Salem, OR......................971-239-1209
Luna & Larry's Coconut Bliss
   Eugene, OR.....................541-345-0020
Maple Grove Farms Of Vermont
   St Johnsbury, VT...............802-748-5141
MariGold Foods
   Willis, TX.....................936-344-0444
Marion's Smart Delights
   Arlington, VA..................703-593-3450
Marjie's Plantain Foods, Inc.
   New York, NY...................908-627-5627
Mary's Gone Crackers
   Gridley, CA....................888-258-1250
Mediterranean Snack Food Co
   Boonton, NJ....................973-402-2644
Mercer's Dairy
   Boonville, NY..................866-637-2377
Mikey's
  480-696-2483
Mini Pops Inc
   Stoughton, MA..................781-436-5864
Minsa Corp
   Lubbock, TX....................800-852-8291

Modern Day Masala, LLC
   Marietta, GA...................866-611-3757
Mom's Gourmet, LLC
   Chagrin Falls, OH..............440-564-9702
Moo Chocolate/Organic Children's Chocolate LLC
   Cos Cob, CT....................203-561-8864
Mrs. Leeper's Pasta
   Excelsior Springs, MO..........800-848-5266
Mrs. May's Naturals
   Carson, CA.....................877-677-6297
Native American Natural Foods
   Kyle, SD.......................800-416-7212
Nature's Hilights
   Chico, CA......................800-313-6454
Now & Zen
   Louisville, CO.................800-779-6383
NOW Foods
   Bloomingdale, IL...............888-669-3663
Nu-World Amaranth Inc
   Naperville, IL.................630-369-6851
Omega Nutrition
   Bellingham, WA.................800-661-3529
Oregon Bark
   Portland, OR
Outta the Park Eats
   Cary, NC.......................919-462-0012
Pamela's Products
   Ukiah, CA......................707-462-6605
Pineland Farms
   New Gloucester, ME.............207-688-4539
Plocky's Fine Snacks
   Hinsdale, IL...................630-323-8888
Pocino Foods
   City Of Industry, CA...........800-345-0150
Preferred Brands Inc
   Stamford, CT...................800-827-8900
Purely Elizabeth
   Boulder, CO....................720-242-7525
Real Coconut Co. Inc., The
   CA
Red Rose Trading Company
   Lancaster, PA..................717-293-7833
Rhythm Superfoods
   Austin, TX.....................512-441-5667
Rice Innovations
   Fontana, CA....................909-823-8230
Rigoni Di Asiago
   Miami, FL......................305-470-7583
Root Cellar Preserves
   Wellesley, MA..................781-864-7440
San-J International Inc
   Henrico, VA....................800-446-5500
Sensible Foods LLC
   Santa Rosa, CA.................888-222-0170
Soozy's Grain-Free
   New York, NY
Soynut Butter Co
   Glenview, IL...................847-635-9960
Sprecher Brewing Co
   Milwaukee, WI..................888-650-2739
Suzanne's Specialties
   New Brunswick, NJ..............800-762-2135
Swapples
   Washington, DC
Tamarind Tree
   Neshanic Station, NJ...........800-432-8733
The Amazing Chickpea
   St. Louis Park, MN.............612-548-1099
The Art of Broth, LLC
   CA.............................818-715-9320
The Good Crisp Company
The Piping Gourmets
  786-233-8660
The Power of Fruit
   Lebanon, NJ....................908-450-9806
The Safe + Fair Food Company
   Chicago, IL
The Soulfull Project
   Camden, NJ
The Toasted Oat Bakehouse
   Columbus, OH
Thinkthin, LLC
   Los Angeles, CA................866-988-4465
This Bar Saves Lives, LLC
   Culver City, CA................310-730-5060
Thoughtful Food
   Lafayette, CA..................510-910-2581
Thunderbird Real Food Bar
   Austin, TX.....................512-383-8334
Tierra Farm
   Valatie, NY....................519-392-8300

Tribe 9 Foods
   Madison, WI....................608-257-7216
Trumps Food Interest
   Vancouver, BC..................604-732-8473
Twin Hens
   Princeton, NJ..................908-925-9040
Ultimate Biscotti
   Eugene, OR.....................541-344-8220
UnReal Brands
   Boston, MA
Urban Foods LLC
   Sacramento, CA.................916-372-3663
Van's International Foods
   Torrance, CA...................310-320-8611
West Thomas Partners, LLC
   Grand Rapids, MI...............616-755-8432
Wholesome Bakery
   San Francisco, CA..............415-343-5414
Wrawp
   Pomona, CA.....................855-972-9748
Yai's Thai
   Denver, CO
Yogavive
   Tiburon, CA....................415-366-6226

Gourmet & Specialty Foods

Gourmet & Specialty Foods

4th & Heart
   CA.............................213-880-2559
Aketta
Al Safa Halal
   New York City, NY..............800-268-8147
Alexian Pâtés
   Neptune, NJ....................800-927-9473
Alfonso Gourmet Pasta
   Pompano Beach, FL..............800-370-7278
Amaranth Resources
   Albert Lea, MN.................800-842-6689
American Lecithin Company
   Oxford, CT.....................800-364-4416
Ames International Inc
   Fife, WA.......................888-469-2637
Ancora Coffee Roasters
   Madison, WI....................800-260-0217
Andre-Boudin Bakeries
   San Francisco, CA..............415-882-1849
Annie's Homegrown
   Berkeley, CA...................800-288-1089
Applecreek Speciality Foods
   Lexington, KY..................800-747-8871
Arbor Hill Grapery & Winery
   Naples, NY.....................800-554-7553
Arbuckle Coffee Roasters
   Tucson, AZ.....................800-533-8278
Art CoCo Chocolate Company
   Geneva, IL.....................877-232-9901
Ashland Plantation Gourmet
   Bunkie, LA.....................318-346-6600
Ashman Manufacturing & Distributing Company
   Virginia Beach, VA.............800-641-9924
Avary Farms
   Odessa, TX.....................432-332-4139
Babe Farms Inc
   Santa Maria, CA................800-648-6772
Barhyte Specialty Foods Inc
   Pendleton, OR..................800-227-4983
Barrie House Gourmet Coffee
   Elmsford, NY...................800-876-2233
Basketfull
   New York, NY...................800-645-4438
Bay Shore Chowders & Bisques
   Fall River, MA.................888-675-6892
Bella Cucina
   Atlanta, GA....................866-350-9040
Berardi's Fresh Roast
   Cleveland, OH..................800-876-9109
Biagio's Banquets
   Chicago, IL....................800-392-2837
Big Steer
   Houston, TX....................800-421-4951
Biscotti & Co.
   White Plains, NY...............914-682-2165
Blue Crab Bay
   Melfa, VA......................800-221-2722
Boetje Foods Inc
   Rock Island, IL................877-726-3853
Boston's Best Coffee Roasters
   South Easton, MA...............800-898-8393
Boyd's Coffee Co
   Portland, OR...................800-735-2878

Product Categories / Specialty & Organic Foods: Gourmet & Specialty Foods

Brad's Taste of New York
  Floral Park, NY.....................516-354-9004
Brandmeyer Popcorn Co
  Ankeny, IA.........................800-568-8276
Brass Ladle Products
  Concordville, PA...................800-955-2353
Brateka Enterprises
  Ocala, FL..........................877-549-3227
Brazos Legends
  Houston, TX........................800-882-6253
Breaktime Snacks
  Paramount, CA......................800-677-1968
Bremner Biscuit Company
  Denver, CO.........................866-972-6879
British American Tea & Coffee
  Durham, NC.........................919-471-1357
Brutocao Cellars
  Hopland, CA........................800-433-3689
BTS Company/Hail Caesar Dressings
  Nashville, TN......................800-617-8899
Bubbles Baking Co
  Van Nuys, CA.......................800-777-4970
Buckmaster Coffee Co
  Hillsboro, OR......................800-962-9148
Buona Vita Inc
  Bridgeton, NJ......................856-453-7972
Busseto Foods
  Fresno, CA.........................800-628-2633
Buxton Foods
  Buxton, ND.........................800-726-8057
Buzzn Bee Farms
  West Palm Beach, FL................561-881-1551
Byrd Cookie
  Savannah, GA.......................800-291-2973
C W Resources Inc
  New Britain, CT....................860-229-7700
C.C. Graber Company
  Ontario, CA........................800-996-5483
Cafe Sark's Gourmet Coffee
  Yorba Linda, CA....................626-579-6000
Caffe D'Oro
  Chino, CA..........................800-200-5005
California Balsamic Inc
  Ukiah, CA..........................888-644-5127
California Oils Corp
  Richmond, CA.......................800-225-6457
Calistoga Food Company
  New York, NY.......................212-879-4940
Caltex Foods
  Canoga Park, CA....................800-522-5839
Cape Cod Specialty Foods
  Sagamore, MA.......................508-888-7099
Cappuccine
  Corona, CA.........................800-511-3127
Carando Gourmet Frozen Foods
  Agawam, MA.........................888-227-2636
Carl Buddig & Co.
  Homewood, IL.......................888-633-5684
Carolyn's Gourmet
  Concord, MA........................800-656-2940
Cateraid Inc
  Howell, MI.........................800-508-8217
Cedarlane Foods
  Carson, CA.........................800-826-3322
Champignon North America Inc
  Englewood Cliffs, NJ...............201-871-7211
Chatz Roasting Co
  Ceres, CA..........................209-541-1100
Chef Hans' Gourmet Foods
  Monroe, LA.........................800-890-4267
Chef Zachary's Gourmet Blended Spices
  Detroit, MI........................313-226-0000
Chef's Pride Gifts LLC
  Taylor, MI.........................800-878-1800
Cherchies
  Malvern, PA........................800-644-1980
Cheryl's Cookies
  Westerville, OH....................800-443-8124
Chewys Rugulach
  San Diego, CA......................800-241-3456
Chex Finer Foods Inc
  Mansfield, MA......................800-227-8114
Chocolate Street of Hartville
  Hartville, OH......................888-853-5904
Chocolates by Mark
  Houston, TX........................832-736-2626
Choice of Vermont
  Destin, FL.........................800-444-6261
Christie's
  Stroughton, MA.....................781-341-3341
Christopher Ranch LLC
  Gilroy, CA.........................408-847-1100

Citterio USA
  Freeland, PA.......................800-435-8888
Clara Foods
  San Francisco, CA
Clem's Seafood & Specialties
  Buckner, KY........................502-222-7571
Clement's Pastry Shops Inc
  Hyattsville, MD....................301-277-6300
Cloud Nine
  Claremont, CA......................909-624-3147
Coffee Masters
  Spring Grove, IL...................800-334-6485
Cold Fusion Foods
  West Hollywood, CA.................310-287-3244
Colony Brands Inc
  Monroe, WI.........................800-544-9036
Colorado Popcorn Co
  Sterling, CO.......................866-491-2676
Colors Gourmet Pizza
  Vista, CA..........................760-597-1400
Coltsfoot/Golden Eagle Herb
  Grants Pass, OR....................800-736-8749
Conifer Foods
  Medina, WA.........................800-588-9160
Cook's Gourmet Foods
  Riverside, CA......................951-352-5700
Cookie Tree Bakeries
  Salt Lake City, UT.................801-268-2253
Cordon Bleu International
  Anjou, QC..........................800-363-1182
Corfu Foods Inc
  Bensenville, IL....................630-595-2510
Corn Popper
  Tulsa, OK..........................918-250-9317
Cosentino Winery
  Napa, CA...........................800-764-1220
Costa Deano's Gourmet Foods
  Canton, OH.........................800-337-2823
CostaDeano's Enterprises
  Canton, OH.........................330-453-1555
Cottonwood Canyon Vineyard
  Santa Maria, CA....................805-937-8463
Cowboy Caviar
  Berkeley, CA.......................877-509-1796
Creative Cotton
  Northbrook, IL.....................847-291-4128
Creole Delicacies Gourmet Shop
  New Orleans, LA....................504-525-9508
Crown Pacific Fine Foods
  Kent, WA...........................425-251-8750
Crustacean Foods
  Los Angeles, CA....................866-263-2625
CTC Manufacturing
  Calgary, AB........................800-668-7677
Cucina & Amore
  San Pablo, CA......................510-964-4838
Cugino's Gourmet Foods
  Crystal Lake, IL...................888-592-8446
Culinary Masters Corporation
  Alpharetta, GA.....................800-261-5261
Cyclone Enterprises Inc
  Houston, TX........................281-872-0087
Dave's Gourmet
  San Rafael, CA.....................800-758-0372
Davis Bakery & Delicatessen
  Cleveland, OH......................216-292-3060
Dean Distributors, Inc.
  Burlingame, CA.....................800-792-0816
Deep Foods Inc
  Union, NJ..........................908-810-7500
Delftree Corp
  North Adams, MA....................800-243-3742
DeMedici Imports
  Elizabeth, NJ......................908-372-0965
Deneen Foods
  Santa Fe, NM.......................800-866-4695
Desserts by David Glass
  South Windsor, CT..................860-462-7520
Diana's Specialty Foods
  Pingree Grove, IL..................847-683-1200
Dinkel's Bakery Inc
  Chicago, IL........................800-822-8817
Dobake
  Oakland, CA........................800-834-3134
Dole & Bailey Inc
  Woburn, MA.........................781-935-1234
Dolores Canning Co Inc
  Los Angeles, CA....................323-263-9155
Don Alfonso Foods
  Austin, TX.........................800-456-6100
Dorina So-Good Inc
  Union, IL..........................815-923-2144

Dowd & Rogers
  San Clemente, CA...................800-232-8619
Dr. Tima Natural Products
  Los Angeles, CA....................310-472-2181
Dufour Pastry Kitchens Inc
  Bronx, NY..........................800-439-1282
Dumbee Gourmet Foods
  Albany, GA.........................800-569-1657
E Waldo Ward & Son Marmalades
  Sierra Madre, CA...................800-355-9273
Eagle Coffee Co Inc
  Baltimore, MD......................410-685-5893
East Indies Coffee & Tea Co
  Lebanon, PA........................800-220-2326
East Shore Specialty Foods
  Hartland, WI.......................800-236-1069
Egg Roll Fantasy
  Auburn, CA.........................530-887-9197
Eilenberger Bakeries
  Palestine, TX......................800-831-2544
Endangered Species Chocolate
  Indianapolis, IN...................800-293-0160
Enjoy Life Foods
  Chicago, IL........................888-503-6569
Eweberry Farms
  Brownsville, OR....................541-466-3470
Exo Inc.
  Brooklyn, NY.......................818-744-4140
Fairwinds Gourmet Coffee
  Lincoln, CA........................800-829-1300
Fantasy Chocolates
  Boynton Beach, FL..................800-804-4962
Fantis Foods Inc
  Carlstadt, NJ......................201-933-6200
Fillo Factory, The
  Northvale, NJ......................800-653-4556
Finlays
  Lincoln, RI........................800-288-6272
Fiorucci Foods USA Inc
  S Chesterfield, VA.................800-524-7775
First District Association
  Litchfield, MN.....................320-693-3236
Fliinko
  South Dartmouth, MA................800-266-9609
Food For Thought Inc
  Honor, MI..........................231-326-5444
Fox Hollow
  Crestwood, KY......................502-241-8621
Fox Meadow Farm
  Chester Springs, PA................610-827-9731
Fox's Fine Foods
  Laguna Beach, CA...................888-522-3697
France Delices
  Montreal, QC.......................800-663-1365
Fratello Coffee Roasters
  Calgary, AB........................800-465-7227
Frontera Foods
  Chicago, IL........................800-509-4441
Fruit Ranch Inc
  Milwaukee, WI......................800-433-3289
Fun Foods
  East Rutherford, NJ................800-507-2782
Future Bakery & Cafe
  Toronto, ON........................416-231-1491
Gadsden Coffee/Caffe
  Arivaca, AZ........................888-514-5282
Geneva Food Products
  Sanford, FL........................800-240-2326
Gift Basket Supply World
  Jacksonville, FL...................800-786-4438
Gillies Coffee
  Brooklyn, NY.......................800-344-5526
Giovanni's Appetizing Food Co
  Richmond, MI.......................586-727-9355
GKI Foods
  Brighton, MI.......................248-486-0055
Glacial Ridge Foods
  Starbuck, MN.......................320-239-2215
Golden Malted
  South Bend, IN.....................888-596-4040
Golden Moon Tea
  Bristow, VA........................877-327-5473
Golden West Specialty Foods
  Brisbane, CA.......................800-584-4481
Goldstar Brands LLC
  Tucker, GA.........................888-296-7191
Good Fortunes & Edible Art
  Canoga Park, CA....................800-644-9474
Good Health Natural Foods
  Greensboro, NC.....................336-285-0735
Gourmet Market
  Knoxville, TN......................865-330-0123

Product Categories / Specialty & Organic Foods: Gourmet & Specialty Foods

Gourmet Products
   Thomaston, CT 860-283-5147
Goya Foods Inc.
   Jersey City, NJ 201-348-4900
Grace Tea Co
   Acton, MA 978-635-9500
Granowska's
   Toronto, ON 416-533-7755
Great American Popcorn Works of Pennsylvania
   Telford, PA 855-542-2676
Green Mountain Gringo
   Winston-Salem, NC 888-875-3111
Greenwell Farms Inc
   Kealakekua, HI 888-592-5662
Grey Owl Foods
   Grand Rapids, MN 800-527-0172
Grounds For Thought
   Bowling Green, OH 419-354-3266
GWB Foods Corporation
   Brooklyn, NY 877-977-7610
Habby Habanero's Food Products
   Jacksonville, FL 904-333-9758
Hale and Hearty Soups
   New York, NY 212-255-2433
Hancock Gourmet Lobster Co
   Topsham, ME 207-725-1855
Happy & Healthy Products Inc
   Boca Raton, FL 561-367-0739
Harbar LLC
   Canton, MA 800-881-7040
Harrington's of Vermont
   Richmond, VT
Harrison Napa Valley
   Saint Helena, CA 707-963-8762
Hawthorne Valley Farm
   Ghent, NY 518-672-7500
Hearthstone Whole Grain Bakery
   Bozeman, MT 800-757-7919
Hendricks Apiaries
   Englewood, CO 303-789-3209
Heritage Fancy Foods Marketing
   Erlanger, KY 859-282-3782
Hialeah Products Co
   Hollywood, FL 800-923-3379
Hickory Baked Ham Co
   Castle Rock, CO 303-688-2633
Hickory Farms
   Maumee, OH. 800-753-8558
High Liner Foods Inc.
   Lunenburg, NS 902-634-8811
Hollman Foods
   Des Moines, IA. 888-926-2879
Homestead Baking Co
   Rumford, RI 800-556-7216
Honey Acres
   Neosho, WI 920-474-4411
House of Coffee Beans
   Houston, TX 800-422-1799
Humphrey's Market
   Springfield, IL. 800-747-6328
Hungry Sultan
   Lake Forest, CA 949-215-0000
Hunt Country Foods Inc
   Marshall, VA. 540-364-2622
Hye Cuisine
   Del Rey, CA 559-834-3000
Hye Quality Bakery
   Fresno, CA 877-445-1778
Impromtu Gourmet
   Owings Mills, MD 877-632-5766
Improved Nature
   Gardner, NC
Indian Foods Company, Inc.
   Osseo, MN 866-331-7684
Indigo Coffee Roasters
   Florence, MA 800-447-5450
Intermountain Canola Cargill
   Minneapolis, MN 800-822-6652
International Brownie
   East Weymouth, MA. 800-230-1588
International Trading Company
   Houston, TX 713-224-5901
Ivy Foods
   Phoenix, AZ 877-223-5459
J.A.M.B. Low Carb Distributor
   Pompano Beach, FL 800-708-6738
J.B. Peel Coffee Roasters
   Red Hook, NY 800-231-7372
J.N. Bech
   Elk Rapids, MI 800-232-4583
James Frasinetti & Sons
   Sacramento, CA 916-383-2444

Jason & Son Specialty Foods
   Rancho Cordova, CA 800-810-9093
Jay Shah Foods
   Mississauga, ON 905-696-0172
Jeremiah's Pick Coffee Co
   San Francisco, CA 877-537-3642
Jim's Cheese Pantry
   Waterloo, WI 800-345-3571
Jodyana Corporation
   Miami, FL 888-563-5282
Joy's Specialty Foods
   Mancos, CO 800-831-5697
Joyva Corp
   Brooklyn, NY 718-497-0170
Just Desserts
   Fairfield, CA 415-780-6860
Kay Foods Co
   Detroit, MI 313-393-1100
KD Canners Inc
   Mississauga, ON 905-602-1825
Kelly Gourmet Foods Inc
   San Francisco, CA 415-648-9200
Kennedy Gourmet
   Glendale Heights, IL. 800-729-8116
Kerry Foodservice
   Mansfield, OH 800-533-2722
Kevton Gourmet Tea
   Streetman, TX 888-538-8668
Keystone Coffee Co
   San Jose, CA 408-998-2221
Kids Kookie Company
   San Clemente, CA 800-350-7577
Knese Enterprise
   Bellerose, NY 516-354-9004
Knudsen Candy
   Hayward, CA 800-736-6887
Koegel Meats Inc
   Flint, MI 810-238-3685
Kokopelli's Kitchen
   Phoenix, AZ 888-943-9802
Kolb-Lena Bresse Bleu Inc
   Lena, IL. 815-369-4577
Kornfections
   Chantilly, VA. 800-469-8886
Krinos Foods
   Bronx, NY. 718-729-9000
L & S Packing Co
   Farmingdale, NY 800-286-6487
L'Esprit De Campagne
   Berryville, VA. 800-692-8008
L.A. Libations
   El Segundo, CA
La Cookie
   Houston, TX 713-784-2722
La Vigne Enterprises
   Fallbrook, CA. 760-723-9997
Larosa Bakery Inc
   Shrewsbury, NJ 800-527-6722
Laska Stuff
   Rochester, MI 248-652-8473
Leech Lake Wild Rice
   Deer River, MN 877-246-0620
Lesley Elizabeth Inc
   Lapeer, MI. 800-684-3300
Lindsay Farms
   Pike Road, AL. 800-243-4608
Live A Little Gourmet Foods
   Oakland, CA 888-744-2300
Lodi Nut Company
   Lodi, CA 800-234-6887
Lotus Brands
   Twin Lakes, WI 800-824-6396
Louisiana Fish Fry Products
   Baton Rouge, LA 800-356-2905
Louisiana Gourmet Enterprises
   Houma, LA. 800-328-5586
Love Creek Orchards
   Medina, TX. 800-449-0882
Lovebiotics LLC
   Los Osos, CA
M&L Gourmet Ice Cream
   Baltimore, MD 410-276-4880
M. Marion & Company
   Santa Rosa, CA 707-836-0551
Mad Chef Enterprise
   Mentor, OH 800-951-2433
Mad Will's Food Company
   Auburn, CA. 888-275-9455
Madhava Natural Sweeteners
   Boulder, CO 800-530-2900
Madrona Specialty Foods LLC
   Seattle, WA 425-656-2997

Magic Ice Products
   Cincinnati, OH 800-776-7923
Magnum Coffee Roastery
   Nunica, MI 888-937-5282
Main Street Gourmet
   Cuyahoga Falls, OH 800-678-6246
Mama Rose's Gourmet Foods
   Phoenix, AZ 855-809-2848
Mama Vida's Inc
   Randallstown, MD 877-521-0742
Mancini Packing Co
   Zolfo Springs, FL 800-741-1778
Manitok Food & Gifts
   Callaway, MN 800-726-1863
Maple Leaf Foods International
   North York, ON 800-268-3708
Marantha Natural Foods
   San Francisco, CA 866-972-6879
Marcel et Henri Charcuterie Francaise
   South San Francisco, CA 800-227-6436
Mardi Gras
   Verona, NJ 973-857-3777
Marich Confectionery
   Hollister, CA 800-624-7055
Marin Food Specialties
   Byron, CA 925-634-6126
Market Square Food Co.
   Park City, IL 800-232-2299
Marukai Market
   Gardena, CA 310-660-6300
MarySue.com
   Baltimore, MD 800-662-2639
Meat-O-Mat Corp
   Brooklyn, NY 718-965-7250
Mendocino Mustard
   Fort Bragg, CA 800-964-2270
Merlino Italian Baking Company
   Kent, WA 800-800-9490
Mills Brothers Intl
   Seattle, WA 206-575-3000
Minnestalgia Foods LLC
   Mcgregor, MN 800-328-6731
Miracapo Pizza
   Elk Grove Village, IL 847-631-3500
Modern Gourmet Foods
   Irvine, CA 949-250-3129
Morningland Dairy Cheese Company
   Mountain View, MO 417-855-0588
Mother Earth Enterprises
   New York, NY 866-436-7688
Mrs Auld's Gourmet Foods Inc
   Reno, NV 800-322-8537
Mrs. Leeper's Pasta
   Excelsior Springs, MO 800-848-5266
MSRF, Inc.
   Chicago, IL 773-227-1115
Mt. Olympus Specialty Foods
   Westminster, MD 410-848-7080
Mt. Olympus Specialty Foods
   Buffalo, NY. 716-874-0771
Murvest
   Fort Lauderdale, FL 954-772-6440
Mustard Seed
   Central, SC 877-621-2591
Nancy's Specialty Foods
   Newark, CA 510-494-1100
National Foods
   Kansas City, MO. 620-624-1851
National Importers
   Richmond, BC 888-894-6464
Natural Exotic Tropicals
   Pompano Beach, FL 800-756-5267
Natural Intentions, Inc.
   Folsom, CA
Natural Quick Foods
   Seattle, WA 206-365-5757
Nature's Finest Products
   Dallas, TX. 800-237-5205
Nell Baking Company
   Kenedy, TX. 800-215-9190
Neshaminy Valley Natural Foods
   Warminster, PA 215-443-5545
Nest Eggs
   Chicago, IL 773-525-4952
New Canaan Farms
   Dripping Springs, TX 800-727-5267
Newmarket Foods
   Petaluma, CA 707-778-3400
Niche Import Co
   Cedar Knolls, NJ 800-548-6882
Nina's Gourmet Dip
   Mc Lean, VA 703-356-1667

Product Categories / Specialty & Organic Foods: Gourmet & Specialty Foods

North American Enterprises
  Tucson, AZ 800-817-8666
Northern Flair Foods
  Mound, MN 888-530-4453
Northwoods Candy Emporium
  Branson, MO 417-332-1010
Nostalgic Specialty Foods
  Boca Raton, FL 561-391-8600
Nueske's Applewood Smoked Meat
  Wittenberg, WI 800-720-1153
Nutty Bavarian
  Sanford, FL 800-382-4788
OH Chocolate
  Seattle, WA 206-329-8777
Olde Tyme Mercantile
  Arroyo Grande, CA 805-489-7991
Oregon Hill Farms
  St Helens, OR 800-243-4541
Oregon Pride
  The Dalles, OR 888-697-4767
Organic Gourmet
  Sherman Oaks, CA 800-400-7772
Organic Nectars LLC
  Malden On Hudson, NY 845-246-0506
Orleans Packing Co
  Hyde Park, MA 617-361-6611
P & M Staiger Vineyard
  Boulder Creek, CA 831-338-0172
Pacific Westcoast Foods
  Beaverton, OR 800-874-9333
Palmetto Pigeon Plant
  Sumter, SC 803-775-1204
Palmieri Food Products
  New Haven, CT 800-845-5447
Panola Pepper Co
  Lake Providence, LA 800-256-3013
Papa Dean's Popcorn
  San Antonio, TX 877-855-7272
Paradise Products Corporation
  Boca Raton, FL 800-826-1235
Parma Sausage Products
  Pittsburgh, PA 877-294-4207
Parny Gourmet
  Miami, FL 305-798-5177
Pastry Chef
  Pawtucket, RI 800-639-8606
Pati-Petite Cookies Inc
  Bridgeville, PA 800-253-5805
Paulaur Corp
  Cranbury, NJ 609-395-8844
Paulsen Foods
  Atlanta, GA 404-873-1804
Peanut Patch Gift Shop
  Courtland, VA 800-544-0896
Pearl Coffee Co
  Akron, OH 800-822-5282
Peerless Coffee & Tea
  Oakland, CA 800-310-5662
Pelican Bay Ltd.
  Dunedin, FL 800-826-8982
Phipps Desserts
  North York, ON 416-391-5800
Picard Peanuts
  Waterdown, ON 888-244-7688
Pickwick Catfish Farm
  Counce, TN 731-689-3805
PJ's Coffee & Tea
  Covington, LA 800-527-1055
Plaidberry Company
  Vista, CA 760-727-5403
Plaza de Espana Gourmet
  Sunny Isles Beach, FL 305-971-3468
Pontiac Coffee Break
  Waterford, MI 248-332-6333
POP Fishing & Marine
  Honolulu, HI 808-537-2905
Popcorn Connection
  North Hollywood, CA 800-852-2676
Popcorner
  Swansea, IL 618-277-2676
Porinos Gourmet Food
  Central Falls, RI 800-826-3938
Prairie Thyme LTD
  Santa Fe, NM 800-869-0009
Premium Brands
  Bardstown, KY 502-348-0081
Prince of Peace
  Hayward, CA 800-732-2328
Private Harvest
  El Dorado Hills, CA 916-933-7080
Pulmuone Foods USA Inc.
  Fullerton, CA 800-588-7782

Pure Planet
  Rancho Dominguez, CA 800-695-2017
Purely American
  Norfolk, VA 800-359-7873
Purity Farms
  La Farge, WI 877-211-4819
R C Fine Foods Inc
  Hillsborough, NJ 800-526-3953
R L Schreiber Inc
  Ft Lauderdale, FL 800-624-8777
Rabbit Barn
  Turlock, CA 209-632-1123
Rainbow Valley Frozen Yogurt
  White Lake, MI 800-979-8669
Rainforest Company
  Maryland Heights, MO 314-344-1000
Rao's Specialty Foods Inc
  New York, NY 212-269-0151
Raymond-Hadley Corporation
  Spencer, NY 800-252-5220
Reading Coffee Roasters
  Birdsboro, PA 800-331-6713
Real Coconut Co. Inc., The
  CA
Restaurant Lulu Gourmet Products
  San Francisco, CA 888-693-5800
Rich Products Corp
  Buffalo, NY 800-828-2021
Righetti Specialties Inc
  Santa Maria, CA 800-268-1041
Rio Trading Company
  Baltimore, MD 443-384-2500
Robert Rothschild Farm
  Cincinnati, OH 800-222-9966
Ron Son Foods Inc
  Swedesboro, NJ 856-241-7333
Rosmarino Foods/R.Z. Humbert Company
  Odessa, FL 888-926-9053
Rossi Pasta LTD
  Marietta, OH 800-227-6774
Rowena
  Norfolk, VA 800-627-8699
Royal Baltic LTD
  Brooklyn, NY 718-385-8300
Royal Palm Popcorn Company
  Edison, NJ 800-526-8865
Rubschlager Baking Corp
  800-661-7246
Rudolph's Specialty Bakery
  Toronto, ON 800-268-1589
Russ & Daughters
  New York, NY 800-787-7229
Russian Chef
  New York, NY 212-249-1550
Saguaro Food Products
  Tucson, AZ 800-732-2447
Sambets Cajun Deli
  Austin, TX 800-472-6238
San Francisco Popcorn Works
  San Francisco, CA 800-777-2676
San Gennaro Foods Inc
  Kent, WA 800-462-1916
Sandridge Food Corp
  Medina, OH 800-627-2523
Santa Barbara Olive Company
  Santa Barbara, CA 800-624-4896
Santa Barbara Salsa
  Oceanside, CA 800-748-5523
Santa Fe Seasons
  Belen, NM 800-866-4695
Sardinha's Sausage
  Somerset, MA 800-678-0178
Sassafras Enterprises Inc
  Chicago, IL 800-537-4941
Savannah Cinnamon & Cookie Company
  Bradenton, FL 800-288-0854
Schwan's Food Service Inc.
  Marshall, MN 877-302-7426
Scooty's Wholesome Foods
  Boulder, CO 303-440-4025
Selma's Cookies
  Apopka, FL 800-992-6654
Senor Felix's Gourmet Mexican
  Baldwin Park, CA 626-960-2800
Serranos Salsa
  Austin, TX 512-328-9200
Sfoglia Fine Pastas & Gourmet
  Freeland, WA 360-331-4080
Shady Grove Orchards
  Onalaska, WA 360-985-7033
Sheila's Select Gourmet Recipe
  Heber City, UT 800-516-7286

Shine Foods Inc
  Torrance, CA 310-533-6010
Signature Foods
  Pendergrass, DR 706-693-0098
Silver Palate Kitchens
  Cresskill, NJ 201-568-0110
Simply Divine
  New York, NY 212-541-7300
Simpson & Vail
  Brookfield, CT 800-282-8327
Sonoma Gourmet
  Sonoma, CA 707-939-3700
Southern Gold Honey Co
  Vidor, TX 808-899-2494
Southern Heritage Coffee Company
  Indianapolis, IN 800-486-1198
Southern Season
  Chapel Hill, NC 877-929-7133
Southern Style Nuts
  Denison, TX 903-463-3161
Specialty Coffee Roasters
  Delray Beach, FL 800-253-9363
Specialty Foods South LLC
  Charleston, SC 800-538-0003
Spice Galleon
  Belgium, WI 877-668-4800
Spring Creek Natural Foods
  Spencer, WV 518-436-7603
Sprout House
  Ramona, CA 800-777-6887
Star Ravioli Mfg Co
  Moonachie, NJ 201-933-6427
Steel's Gourmet Foods, Ltd.
  Bridgeport, PA 800-678-3357
Stirling Foods
  Renton, WA 800-332-1714
Summerfield Farm Products
  Orange, VA 800-898-3276
Sun West Foods
  Davis, CA 530-758-8550
Sunfood
  El Cajon, CA 888-729-3663
Sunset Specialty Foods
  Lake Arrowhead, CA 909-337-7643
Sweet Shop USA
  Mt Pleasant, TX 888-957-9338
Sweety Novelty
  Monterey Park, CA 626-282-4482
Swiss American Inc
  St Louis, MO 800-325-8150
Swiss Chalet Fine Foods
  Doral, FL 800-347-9477
T.W. Garner Food Company
  Winston Salem, NC 800-476-7383
Table De France
  Ontario, CA 909-923-5205
Taft Street Winery
  Sebastopol, CA 707-823-2049
Tait Farm Foods
  Centre Hall, PA 800-787-2716
Tarazi Specialty Foods
  Chino, CA 909-628-3601
Teeccino
  Carpinteria, CA 800-498-3434
Thackrey & Co
  Bolinas, CA 415-868-9543
The Honest Stand
  Denver, CO
The Real Co
  Wilmington, DE 347-433-8945
The Water Kefir People
  Bend, OR
Thistledew Farm
  Proctor, WV 800-854-6639
Tipiak Inc
  Stamford, CT 203-961-9117
Tokunaga Farms
  Selma, CA 559-896-0949
Tom & Sally's Handmade Chocolates
  Brattleboro, VT 800-827-0800
Tomanetti Food Products Inc
  Oakmont, PA 800-875-3040
Too Good Gourmet
  San Lorenzo, CA 877-850-4663
Topolos at Russian River Vine
  Forestville, CA 707-887-3344
Torn Ranch
  Novato, CA 707-796-7800
Torrefazione Italia
  Seattle, WA 800-827-2333
Tova Industries LLC
  Louisville, KY 888-532-8682

Product Categories / Specialty & Organic Foods: Health & Dietary

Treat Ice Cream Co
  San Jose, CA....................408-292-9321
Trinity Spice
  Midland, TX....................800-460-1149
Tropical Foods
  Charlotte, NC..................800-438-4470
Tropical Foods
  Lithia Springs, GA.............800-544-3762
Tropical Nut & Fruit Co
  Orlando, FL....................800-749-8869
Two Chefs on a Roll
  Carson, CA.....................800-842-3025
Uncle Ralph's Cookies
  Frederick, MD..................800-422-0626
Unibroue/Unibrew
  Chambly, QC....................450-658-7658
Unique Foods
  Raleigh, NC....................919-779-5600
Upton's Naturals
  Chicago, IL
Valley View Blueberries
  Vancouver, WA..................360-892-2839
Van-Lang Food Products
  Countryside, IL................708-588-0800
Vega Food Industries Inc
  Cranston, RI...................800-973-7737
VegGuide.org
  Chicago, IL....................773-363-3939
Venus Wafers Inc
  Hingham, MA....................800-545-4538
Vermont Food Experience
  Shelburne, VT..................802-985-8101
Vermont Natural Co
  Jacksonville, VT...............802-368-2231
Vermont Village
  Barre, VT
Vigneri Chocolate Inc.
  Rochester, NY..................877-844-6374
Vine Village Day
  Napa, CA.......................707-255-4116
Viola's Gourmet Goodies
  Los Angeles, CA................323-731-5277
Vital Proteins LLC
  Elk Grove Village, IL..........224-544-9110
Volcano Island Honey Company
  Honokaa, HI....................888-663-6639
W.S. Wells & Sons
  Wilton, ME.....................207-645-3393
Wagner Gourmet Foods
  Lenexa, KS.....................913-469-5411
Walden Foods
  Winchester, VA.................800-648-7688
Warren & Son Meat Processing
  Whipple, OH....................740-585-2421
Weaver Nut Co. Inc.
  Ephrata, PA....................800-473-2688
Wechsler Coffee Corporation
  Teterboro, NJ..................800-800-2633
Wege of Hanover
  Hanover, PA....................800-888-4646
Wenner Bakery
  Bayport, NY....................800-869-6262
Westbrae Natural Foods
  Melville, NY...................800-434-4246
Wild Rice Exchange
  Woodland, CA...................800-223-7423
Will-Pak Foods
  Ontario, CA....................800-874-0883
Woeber Mustard Mfg Co
  Springfield, OH................800-548-2929
Worldwide Specialties In
  Los Angeles, CA................800-437-2702
Yankee Specialty Foods
  Boston, MA.....................800-688-9904
Yayin Corporation
  Valley Village, CA.............707-829-5686
Yorktown Baking Company
  Yorktown Heights, NY...........800-235-3961
Your Bar Factory
  LaSalle, QC....................888-366-0258
Yvonne's Gourmet Sensations
  Marlton, NJ....................856-985-7677
Z Specialty Food, LLC
  Woodland, CA...................800-678-1226
Zitos Specialty Foods
  Port Charlotte, FL.............941-625-0806

Health & Dietary

Energy Bars

Abbott Laboratories
  Abbott Park, IL................847-938-3887
Amrita Snacks
  Hartsdale, NY..................888-728-7779
Barn Stream Natural Foods
  Alstead, NH....................603-756-4395
Better Than Coffee
  Torrance, CA
Bonk Breaker
  Santa Monica, CA...............310-315-4129
CarbRite Diet
  New Brunswick, NJ..............800-872-0101
Clif Bar & Co
  Emeryville, CA.................802-254-3227
Dharma Bars
DNX Foods
  Tucson, AZ.....................888-612-5037
Epic Provisions
  Austin, TX.....................512-944-8502
Foodie Fuel
  Boulder, CO
Gertrude & Bronner's Magic Alpsnack
  Vista, CA......................877-786-3649
GU Energy Labs
  Berkeley, CA...................800-400-1995
GURU Organic Energy
  San Francisco, CA
Immordl
  San Clemente, CA...............844-466-6735
Joj, Bar
  Encinitas, CA..................877-643-3575
Kalifornia Keto
  Villa Park, CA
Kiss My Keto
  Los Angeles, CA................310-765-1553
KiZE Concepts
  Oklahoma City, OK
LivBar
  Salem, OR......................971-239-1209
MariGold Foods
  Willis, TX.....................936-344-0444
MATI Energy
  Durham, NC.....................866-924-8005
MetaBall
  Chester, NJ....................800-247-6580
MODe Sports Nutrition
  Costa Mesa, CA.................949-274-9948
Navitas Naturals
  Novato, CA.....................888-645-4282
Nutraplex
  Altamonte Springs, FL
Nutri-Nation
  Port Coquitlam, BC.............604-552-5549
ONE Brands
  Charlotte, NC..................888-231-2684
Onnit Labs
  Austin, TX.....................855-666-4899
Optimum Nutrition
  Aurora, IL.....................800-763-3444
Phat Fudge
  Marina del Rey, CA
Probar
  Salt Lake City, UT.............800-921-2294
Quantum Energy Squares
  Santa Monica, CA
Rise Bar
  Irvine, CA.....................800-440-6476
Skratch Labs
  Boulder, CO....................800-735-8904
This Bar Saves Lives, LLC
  Culver City, CA................310-730-5060
Thunderbird Real Food Bar
  Austin, TX.....................512-383-8334
Tram Bar LLC
  Victor, ID.....................208-354-4790
TruBrain
  Santa Monica, CA...............650-241-8372
West Thomas Partners, LLC
  Grand Rapids, MI...............616-755-8432
YoFiit
  Vaughan, ON....................647-997-7846

Organic Foods

Abunda Life
  Asbury Park, NJ................732-775-9338
Adrienne's Gourmet Foods
  Santa Barbara, CA..............800-937-7010
Alliston Creamery
  Alliston, ON...................705-435-6751
Alta Dena Certified Dairy LLC
  City Of Industry, CA...........800-535-1369
American Natural & Organic
  Fremont, CA....................510-440-1044
Amy's Kitchen Inc
  Santa Rosa, CA.................707-781-6600
Andre-Boudin Bakeries
  San Francisco, CA..............415-882-1849
Ankeny Lake Wild Rice
  Salem, OR......................800-555-5380
Annie's Naturals
  Berkeley, CA...................800-434-1234
Applegate Farms
  Bridgewater, NJ................866-587-5858
Atlantic Laboratories Inc
  Waldoboro, ME..................888-662-5357
Aurora Organic Dairy
  Boulder, CO....................303-284-3313
Avalon Organic Coffees
  Albuquerque, NM................800-662-2575
Barrows Tea Company
  New Bedford, MA................800-832-5024
Bedemco Inc
  White Plains, NY...............914-683-1119
Bedrock Farm Certified Organic Medicinal Herbs
  Wakefield, RI..................888-874-7393
Beech-Nut Nutrition Corp
  Amsterdam, NY..................518-595-6600
Beetnik Foods, LLC
  Austin, TX.....................512-548-8228
Bel Brands USA
  Chicago, IL....................312-462-1500
Belgravia Imports
  Portsmouth, RI.................800-848-1127
Bella Vista Farm
  Lawton, OK.....................866-237-8526
Berardi's Fresh Roast
  Cleveland, OH..................800-876-9109
Beta Pure Foods
  Santa Cruz, CA.................831-685-6565
Beth's Fine Desserts
  Mill Valley, CA................415-383-3991
Blessed Herbs
  Oakham, MA.....................800-489-4372
Blue Marble Brands
  Providence, RI.................888-534-0246
Boehringer Ingelheim Corp
  Ridgefield, CT.................800-243-0127
Boulder Granola
  Boulder, CO....................303-443-1136
Brad's Organic
  Haverstraw, NY.................845-429-9080
Brass Ladle Products
  Concordville, PA...............800-955-2353
Brewster Dairy Inc
  Brewster, OH...................800-874-8874
Buchanan Hollow Nut Co
  Le Grand, CA...................800-532-1500
Buchi Kombucha
  Marshall, NC...................828-394-2360
Bunker Hill Cheese Co Inc
  Millersburg, OH................800-253-6636
Buns & Roses Organic Wholegrain Bakery
  Edmonton, AB...................780-438-0098
Butter Buds Food Ingredients
  Racine, WI.....................800-426-1119
Buywell Coffee
  Colorado Springs, CO...........877-294-6246
Cafe Altura
  Santa Paula, CA................800-526-8328
Cafe Society Coffee Company
  Dallas, TX.....................800-717-6000
Caffe Ibis Gallery Deli
  Logan, UT......................888-740-4777
California Custom Fruits
  Baldwin Park, CA...............877-558-0056
California Independent Almond Growers
  Merced, CA.....................209-667-4855
California Olive Oil Council
  Berkeley, CA...................888-718-9830
Carob Tree
  Arcadia, CA....................626-445-0215
Cascadian Farm Inc
  Sedro Woolley, WA..............360-855-0542
Cedarlane Foods
  Carson, CA.....................800-826-3322
Celebrity Tea, LLC
  Tampa, FL......................813-600-3317
Cell-Nique
  Norwalk, CT....................888-417-9343
Century Foods Intl LLC
  Sparta, WI.....................800-269-1901
Champlain Valley Milling Corp
  Westport, NY...................518-962-4711
Chartreuse Organic Tea
  Trenton, MI....................866-315-7832

415

Product Categories / Specialty & Organic Foods: Organic Foods

Chelten House Products
  Swedesboro, NJ
Cherith Valley Gardens
  Fort Worth, TX 800-610-9813
Chino Valley Ranchers
  Colton, CA 800-354-4503
Chris' Farm Stand
  Peabody, MA 978-994-4315
Christopher Ranch LLC
  Gilroy, CA 408-847-1100
CHS Sunprairie
  Minot, ND 800-556-6807
Chunco Foods Inc
  Kansas City, MO 816-283-0716
Citromax Flavors Inc
  Carlstadt, NJ 201-933-8405
Citrus Service
  Winter Garden, FL 407-656-4999
Clear Mountain Coffee Company
  Silver Spring, MD 301-587-2233
Cloud Top
  Pasadena, CA 888-263-1778
Coleman Natural
  Kings Mountain, NC 800-442-8666
Country Choice Organic
  Eden Prairie, MN 952-829-8824
CROPP Cooperative
  La Farge, WI 888-444-6455
Cuizina Food Company
  Woodinville, WA 425-486-7000
Cyanotech Corp
  Kailua Kona, HI 800-395-1353
DAGOBA Organic Chocolate
  Ashland, OR 866-972-6879
Daymar Select Fine Coffees
  El Cajon, CA 800-466-7590
Dharma Bars
Dorothy Dawson Food Products
  Jackson, MI 517-788-9830
East Wind Inc
  Tecumseh, MO 417-679-4682
Eatem Foods Co
  Vineland, NJ 800-683-2836
Eberly Poultry, Inc.
  Stevens, PA 717-336-6440
Eden Foods Inc
  Clinton, MI 888-424-3336
Eden Organic Pasta Company
  Clinton, MI 888-424-3336
Eggology
  Canoga Park, CA 818-610-2222
Extracts and Ingredients Ltd
  Union, NJ 908-688-9009
Fairhaven Cooperative Flour Mill
  Bellingham, WA 360-757-9947
FarmGro Organic Foods
  Regina, SK 306-751-2449
Fig Food Co.
  New York, NY 855-344-3663
Fine Dried Foods Intl
  Santa Cruz, CA 831-426-1413
Firebird Artisan Mills
  Harvey, ND 701-324-4330
Fireside Kitchen
  Halifax, NS 902-454-7387
Flamous Brands
  Duarte, CA 626-799-7909
Florence Macaroni Manufacturing
  Chicago, IL 800-647-2782
Florida Crystals Corporation
  West Palm Beach, FL 844-344-9497
Florida Food Products Inc
  Eustis, FL 800-874-2331
Foods Alive
  Angola, IN 260-488-4497
French Meadow Bakery & Cafe
  Minneapolis, MN 612-870-7855
Fresh Tofu Inc
  Allentown, PA 610-433-4711
Frey Vineyards
  Redwood Valley, CA 800-760-3739
Frontera Foods
  Chicago, IL 800-509-4441
Fruit d'Or
  Villeroy, QC 819-385-1126
Fullbloom Baking Co
  Newark, CA 800-201-9909
Fungus Among Us
  Snohomish, WA 360-568-3403
Gelato Fresco
  Toronto, ON 416-785-5415

George Chiala Farms Inc
  Morgan Hill, CA 408-778-0562
Gerber Products Co
  Arlington, VA 800-284-9488
Ginseng Up Corp
  Worcester, MA 800-446-7364
Golden Harvest Pecans
  Cairo, GA 800-597-0968
Good Groceries
  Brooklyn, NY 347-853-7462
Good Stuff Cacao
  Metamora, MI 248-690-5114
Grandpa Po's Nutra Nuts
  Commerce, CA 323-260-7457
Great Eastern Sun Trading Co
  Asheville, NC 800-334-5809
Great River Organic Milling
  Arcadia, WI 608-687-9580
Green & Black's Organic Chocolate
  Plano, TX 877-299-1254
Guayaki
  Sebastopol, CA 888-482-9254
Hain Celestial Group Inc
  Boulder, CO 800-434-4246
Hallcrest Vineyards
  Felton, CA 831-335-4441
Happy Family
  New York, NY 855-644-2779
Harbar LLC
  Canton, MA 800-881-7040
Hawkhaven Greenhouse International
  Wautoma, WI 800-745-4295
Healing Home Foods
  Pound Ridge, NY 914-764-1303
Health Valley Company
  Irwindale, CA 800-334-3204
Healthy Food Ingredients
  Fargo, ND 844-275-3443
Healthy Times Baby Food
  San Diego, CA 858-513-1550
HempNut
  Henderson, NV 707-576-7050
Herbal Magic
  Toronto, ON 877-237-7225
Heritage Short Bread
  Hilton Head Isle, SC 843-422-3458
Highland Sugarworks
  Websterville, VT 800-452-4012
Hodgson Mill Inc
  Effingham, IL 800-347-0198
Hodo
  Oakland, CA 510-464-2977
Homefree LLC
  Windham, NH 800-552-7172
Homestead Mills
  Cook, MN 800-652-5233
HP Schmid
  San Francisco, CA 415-765-5925
Indigo Coffee Roasters
  Florence, MA 800-447-5450
Ineeka Inc
  Chicago, IL 312-733-8327
International Foods
  Bloomfield, NJ 800-225-1449
Island Spring Inc
  Vashon, WA 206-463-9848
Johnson Foods, Inc.
  Sunnyside, WA 509-837-4214
Kay's Naturals, Inc.
  Clara City, MN 866-873-5499
KD Canners Inc
  Mississauga, ON 905-602-1825
Kombucha Wonder Drink
  Portland, OR 877-224-7331
Kopali Organics
  Miami, FL 305-751-7341
Kozlowski Farms
  Forestville, CA 800-473-2767
Lakeview Bakery
  Calgary, AB 403-246-6127
Lakewood Juice Co.
  Miami, FL 866-324-5900
Late July Snacks
  Norwalk, CT 888-857-6225
Lifeway
  Morton Grove, IL 877-281-3874
Little Duck Organics
  New York, NY 877-458-1321
LivBar
  Salem, OR 971-239-1209
Lowell Farms
  El Campo, TX 888-484-9213

Luna & Larry's Coconut Bliss
  Eugene, OR 541-345-0020
Lundberg Family Farms
  Richvale, CA 530-538-3500
Made In Nature
  Boulder, CO 800-906-7426
Magnum Coffee Roastery
  Nunica, MI 888-937-5282
Maine Coast Sea Vegetables
  Franklin, ME 207-565-2907
Makana Beverages Inc.
  Oxnard, CA
Mamma Chia
  Carlsbad, CA 855-588-2442
Mandarin Soy Sauce Inc
  Middletown, NY 845-343-1505
MariGold Foods
  Willis, TX 936-344-0444
Mary's Gone Crackers
  Gridley, CA 888-258-1250
Mcfadden Farm
  Potter Valley, CA 800-544-8230
Mediterranean Snack Food Co
  Boonton, NJ 973-402-2644
Mellace Family Brands
  Carlsbad, CA 866-255-6887
Merlino Italian Baking Company
  Kent, WA 800-800-9490
Mills Brothers Intl
  Seattle, WA 206-575-3000
Minnestalgia Foods LLC
  Mcgregor, MN 800-328-6731
Miyako Oriental Foods Inc
  Baldwin Park, CA 877-788-6476
Mom's Gourmet, LLC
  Chagrin Falls, OH 440-564-9702
Mountain Organic Foods
  Moraga, CA 925-377-0119
Mr Espresso
  Oakland, CA 510-287-5200
Mrs. Leeper's Pasta
  Excelsior Springs, MO 800-848-5266
Mrs. Miller's Homemade Noodles
  Fredericksburg, OH 800-227-4487
Mushroom Co
  Cambridge, MD 410-221-8971
Mushroom Harvest
  Athens, OH 740-448-7376
Mustard Seed
  Central, SC 877-621-2591
Najla's Specialty Foods Inc
  Louisville, KY 877-962-5527
Native American Natural Foods
  Kyle, SD 800-416-7212
Natural Food Mill
  Corona, CA 800-797-5090
Natural Way Mills Inc
  Middle River, MN 218-222-3677
Nature's Candy
  Fredericksburg, TX 800-729-0085
Nature's Legacy Inc.
  Hudson, MI 517-448-2050
Nature's Nutrition
  Marysville, OH 800-242-1115
Naturel
  Rancho Cucamonga, CA 877-242-8344
Natures Sungrown Foods Inc
  San Rafael, CA 415-491-4944
New England Natural Bakers
  Greenfield, MA 800-910-2884
North Bay Trading Co
  Brule, WI 800-348-0164
North Country Natural Spring Water
  Port Kent, NY 518-834-9400
NOW Foods
  Bloomingdale, IL 888-669-3663
NuGo Nutrition
  Oakmont, PA 888-421-2032
Nutra Nuts
  Commerce, CA 323-260-7457
Nutrex Hawaii Inc
  Kailua Kona, HI 800-453-1187
O Olive Oil
  Petaluma, CA 888-827-7148
Once Again Nut Butter
  Nunda, NY 888-800-8075
Organic Gourmet
  Sherman Oaks, CA 800-400-7772
Organic Nectars LLC
  Malden On Hudson, NY 845-246-0506
Organic Wine Co Inc
  San Francisco, CA 888-326-9463

Product Categories / Specialty & Organic Foods: Organic Foods

Oskri Corporation
  Lake Mills, WI 920-648-8300
Pacari Organic Chocolate
  Boca Raton, FL
Palmieri Food Products
  New Haven, CT 800-845-5447
Panos Brands
  Rochelle Park, NJ 201-843-8900
Pappy's Sassafras Tea
  Columbus Grove, OH 877-659-5110
Parthenon Food Products
  Ann Arbor, MI 734-994-1012
Pasta Prima
  Benicia, CA. 530-671-7200
Peace Mountain Natural Beverages
  Springfield, MA 413-567-4942
Peace Village Organic Foods
  Berkeley, CA. 510-524-4420
Peaceful Fruits
  330-356-8515
Pearl Valley Cheese Inc
  Fresno, OH. 740-545-6002
Perricone Juices
  Beaumont, CA. 951-769-7171
Personal Edge Nutrition
  Ballwin, MO 514-636-4512
Phillips Gourmet Inc
  Kennett Square, PA. 610-925-0520
Pleasant Grove Farms
  Pleasant Grove, CA 916-655-3391
Prairie Mills Products LLC
  Rochester, IN. 574-223-3177
Probar
  Salt Lake City, UT 800-921-2294
Progenix Corporation
  Wausau, WI. 800-233-3356
Purity Farms
  La Farge, WI. 877-211-4819
R&J Farms
  West Salem, OH 419-846-3179
R.J. Corr Naturals
  Posen, IL. 708-389-4200
RAJB Hog Foods Inc
  Jersey City, NJ 201-395-9400
Rapunzel Pure Organics
  Bloomfield, NJ 800-225-1449
Ravioli Store
  Long Island City, NY 877-727-8269
Red River Commodities Inc
  Fargo, ND 800-437-5539
Regenie's Crunchy Pi
  Haverhill, MA. 877-734-3643
Rhythm Superfoods
  Austin, TX. 512-441-5667
Rocky Mountain Honey Company
  Salt Lake City, UT 801-355-2054
Rooibee Red Tea
  Louisville, KY 502-749-0800
Run-A-Ton Group Inc
  Chester, NJ 800-247-6580
Rustic Crust Inc
  Pittsfield, NH 603-435-5119
Santa Barbara Pistachio Co
  Maricopa, CA 800-896-1044
Shariann's Organics
  Boulder, CO 800-434-4246
Sierra Madre Coffee
  Denver, CO. 303-446-0050
Silver Creek Specialty Meats
  Oshkosh, WI. 800-729-2849
Simply Gum
  New York, NY
SJH Enterprises
  Middleton, WI. 888-745-3845
Small Planet Foods
  Minneapolis, MN 800-624-4123
Solana Gold Organics
  Sebastopol, CA 800-459-1121
Solnuts
  Hudson, IA 800-648-3503
Sophia's Sauce Works
  Carson City, NV 800-718-7769
Springfield Creamery Inc
  Eugene, OR. 541-689-2911
Sprouts Farmers Market Inc.
  Phoenix, AZ
Straus Family Creamery
  Petaluma, CA 800-572-7783
Sunergia Soyfoods
  Charlottesville, VA 800-693-5134
Sunfood
  El Cajon, CA. 888-729-3663

Sunridge Farms
  Royal Oaks, CA 831-786-7000
Sunridge Farms Inc
  Salinas, CA 831-755-1530
Sunshine Burger & Spec Food Co
  Fort Atkinson, WI. 920-568-1100
SunWest Foods, Inc.
  Davis, CA. 530-758-8550
Sustainable Sourcing
  Great Barrington, MA. 413-528-5141
Suzanne's Specialties
  New Brunswick, NJ 800-762-2135
Tastybaby
  Malibu, CA 866-588-8278
Tea-n-Crumpets
  San Rafael, CA 415-457-2495
Teeny Tiny Spice Company of Vermont LLC
  Shelburne, VT 802-598-6800
Templar Food Products
  New Providence, NJ 800-883-6752
The Coromega Company
  Carlsbad, CA 877-275-3725
The Naked Edge, LLC
  Boulder, CO 888-297-9426
The Tea Spot, Inc.
  Boulder, CO 303-444-8324
Thomas Canning/Maidstone
  Maidstone, ON 519-737-1531
Tierra Farm
  Valatie, NY 519-392-8300
Tomanetti Food Products Inc
  Oakmont, PA 800-875-3040
Tova Industries LLC
  Louisville, KY 888-532-8682
Travel Chocolate
  New York, NY 718-841-7030
Treehouse Farms
  Elgin, AZ 559-757-5020
Triple Springs Spring Water Co
  Meriden, CT 203-235-8374
Tripper Inc
  Oxnard, CA 805-988-8851
Tropical Açaí LLC
  Pompano Beach, FL 855-550-2224
True Organic Product Inc
  Helm, CA 800-487-0379
TruVibe Organics
  Santa Monica, CA
Twin Marquis
  Brooklyn, NY 800-367-6868
Uncle Matt's Organic
  Clermont, FL 833-729-8625
Unique Beverage Company
  Everett, WA. 425-267-0959
Vegetable Juices Inc
  Chicago, IL 888-776-9752
Ventre Packing Company
  Syracuse, NY 315-463-2384
Verde Farms, LLC
  Woburn, MA 617-221-8922
Vermont Village
  Barre, VT
Vienna Bakery
  Barrington, RI 401-245-2355
Vive Organic
  Venice, CA. 877-774-9291
Vivoo
  Verona,
Vixen Kitchen
  Santa Cruz, CA 707-223-5627
Vogue Cuisine Foods
  Sunnyvale, CA 888-236-4144
WCC Honey Marketing
  City Of Industry, CA. 626-855-3086
Westbrae Natural Foods
  Melville, NY 800-434-4246
Wild Rice Exchange
  Woodland, CA 800-223-7423
Wing Nien Food
  Hayward, CA 510-487-8877
Wizards Cauldron, LTD
  Yanceyville, NC 336-694-5665
World Casing Corp
  Maspeth, NY 800-221-4887
Xochitl
  Dallas, TX. 866-595-8917
Y Z Enterprises Inc
  Maumee, OH. 800-736-8779
Yogavive
  Tiburon, CA 415-366-6226
Your Bar Factory
  LaSalle, QC 888-366-0258

Zhena's Gypsy Tea
  Commerce, CA. 800-448-0803

Certified

Briess Malt & Ingredients Co.
  Chilton, WI 800-657-0806
Caffe Ibis Gallery Deli
  Logan, UT. 888-740-4777
California Custom Fruits
  Baldwin Park, CA. 877-558-0056
Clofine Dairy Products Inc
  Linwood, NJ 609-653-1000
Crosby Molasses Company
  Saint John, NB 800-561-2206
Emerling International Foods
  Buffalo, NY. 716-833-7381
Frontier Co-op
  Norway, IA 844-550-6200
Gold Mine Natural Food Company
  Poway, CA 800-475-3663
Hoyt's Honey Farm
  Baytown, TX. 281-576-5383
Jonathan's Sprouts
  Rochester, MA 508-763-2577
Kozlowski Farms
  Forestville, CA 800-473-2767
Lily of the Desert
  Denton, TX 800-229-5459
Marukan Vinegar USA Inc.
  Paramount, CA 562-630-6060
New Organics
  Kenwood, CA. 734-677-5570
Nu-World Amaranth Inc
  Naperville, IL 630-369-6851
Once Again Nut Butter
  Nunda, NY 888-800-8075
Organic Gourmet
  Sherman Oaks, CA 800-400-7772
Organic Planet
  San Francisco, CA 415-765-5590
Osso Good, LLC
  San Rafael, CA
Raye's Mustard
  Eastport, ME 800-853-1903
Red Monkey Foods
  Springfield, MO 417-319-7300
RFi Ingredients
  Blauvelt, NY. 800-962-7663
Roberts Seed
  Axtell, NE 308-743-2565
Sure-Fresh Produce Inc
  Santa Maria, CA 888-423-5379
The Food Collective
  Irvine, CA 866-328-8638
The Honest Stand
  Denver, CO
The Lancaster Food Company
  Lancaster, PA
True Story Foods
  San Francisco, CA 888-277-1171
Tuscarora Organic Growers Cooperative
  Hustontown, PA 814-448-2173
Wild Aseptics, LLC
  Erlanger, KY. 877-787-7221
Wisconsin Specialty Protein
  Madison, WI
Wood Sugarbush
  Spring Valley, WI 715-772-4656

Beef

Sunnyside Organics Seedlings
  Washington, VA 510-221-5050
Tribali Foods
  San Marino, CA 310-592-5420

Fruit

Kozlowski Farms
  Forestville, CA 800-473-2767

Poultry

Tribali Foods
  San Marino, CA 310-592-5420

Produce

Argee Corp
  Santee, CA 800-449-3030
Price Co
  Yakima, WA 509-966-4110
Tierra Farm
  Valatie, NY 519-392-8300

Product Categories / Specialty & Organic Foods: Sun-Dried Foods

Fruits

Atwater Foods
   Lyndonville Orleans, NY 585-765-2639
California Custom Fruits
   Baldwin Park, CA 877-558-0056
Crunchies Natural Food Company
   Westlake Village, CA 888-997-1866
Emerling International Foods
   Buffalo, NY 716-833-7381
Fine Dried Foods Intl
   Santa Cruz, CA 831-426-1413
Global Organics
   Cambridge, MA 781-648-8844
Golden Town Apple Products
   Rougemont, QC 866-552-7643
Hallcrest Vineyards
   Felton, CA 831-335-4441
Hialeah Products Co
   Hollywood, FL 800-923-3379
Made In Nature
   Boulder, CO 800-906-7426
Organic Planet
   San Francisco, CA 415-765-5590
Price Co
   Yakima, WA 509-966-4110
Setton International Foods
   Commack, NY 800-227-4397
Solana Gold Organics
   Sebastopol, CA 800-459-1121
Sunfood
   El Cajon, CA 888-729-3663
Sunshine Farm & Garden
   Renick, WV 304-497-2208
Tropical Açaí LLC
   Pompano Beach, FL 855-550-2224
Unique Ingredients LLC
   Gold Canyon, AZ 480-983-2498

Ingredients

Global Organics
   Cambridge, MA 781-648-8844
Marroquin Organic Intl.
   Santa Cruz, CA 831-423-3442
Wildly Organic
   Silver Bay, MN 800-945-3801

Natural

Amrita Snacks
   Hartsdale, NY 888-728-7779
Arico Natural Foods
   Beaverton, OR 503-259-0871
Avenue Gourmet
   Owings Mills, MD 410-902-5701
Cache Creek Foods LLC
   Woodland, CA 530-662-1764
California Custom Fruits
   Baldwin Park, CA 877-558-0056
Earthrise Nutritionals
   Irvine, CA 800-949-7473
Ethical Naturals
   San Anselmo, CA 866-459-4454
GKI Foods
   Brighton, MI 248-486-0055
Global Organics
   Cambridge, MA 781-648-8844
Healthy Times Baby Food
   San Diego, CA 858-513-1550
Horner International
   Raleigh, NC 919-787-3112
Hudson River Foods
   Castleton, NY 888-417-9343
Internatural Foods
   Bloomfield, NJ 800-225-1449
Larabar
   Denver, CO 800-543-2147
New Organics
   Kenwood, CA 734-677-5570
Organic Planet
   San Francisco, CA 415-765-5590
Pasta Prima
   Benicia, CA 530-671-7200
Pyure Brands
   Naples, FL 305-509-5096
Quality Naturally Foods
   City Of Industry, CA 888-498-6986
Seitenbacher America LLC
   Odessa, FL 727-376-3000
Sure-Fresh Produce Inc
   Santa Maria, CA 888-423-5379
Unique Ingredients LLC
   Gold Canyon, AZ 480-983-2498

Vegetable Juices Inc
   Chicago, IL 888-776-9752
Wine Country Chef LLC
   Hidden Valley Lake, CA 707-322-0406
Your Bar Factory
   LaSalle, QC 888-366-0258

Antioxidants

Ax Water
   Fargo, ND

Vegetables

CROPP Cooperative
   La Farge, WI 888-444-6455
Emerling International Foods
   Buffalo, NY 716-833-7381
Global Organics
   Cambridge, MA 781-648-8844
Healthy Times Baby Food
   San Diego, CA 858-513-1550
Made In Nature
   Boulder, CO 800-906-7426
Pleasant Grove Farms
   Pleasant Grove, CA 916-655-3391
R&J Farms
   West Salem, OH 419-846-3179
Sno-Pac Foods Inc
   Caledonia, MN 800-533-2215
The Naked Edge, LLC
   Boulder, CO 888-297-9426
Vegetable Juices Inc
   Chicago, IL 888-776-9752

Sun-Dried Foods

Tropical Link Canada Ltd.
   Burnaby, BC 778-379-3510

Survival Foods

Good For You America
   Concordia, MO 866-329-5969
Hialeah Products Co
   Hollywood, FL 800-923-3379
J&M Food Products Co
   Deerfield, IL 847-948-1290
SOPAKCO Packaging
   Mullins, SC 843-464-7851
TyRy Inc
   Rocklin, CA 800-322-6325

Vegetarian Products

Abbot's Butcher
   Costa Mesa, CA 949-726-2156
Adventist Book & Food
   Trenton, NJ 800-765-6955
Big Mountain Foods
   Vancouver, BC
Bixby & Co., LLC
   Rockland, ME 207-691-1778
Boulder Organic Foods
   Niwot, CO 303-530-0470
Butler Foods LLC
   Grand Ronde, OR 503-437-9133
Caribbean Food Delights Inc
   Tappan, NY 845-398-3000
CHS Inc.
   Inver Grove Hts., MN 800-328-6539
Cricklewood Soyfoods
   Mertztown, PA 610-682-4109
Dixie USA
   Tomball, TX 800-233-3668
Earth Island
   Chatsworth, CA 888-394-3949
EatPastry LLC
   San Diego, CA 858-755-7456
Emmy's Organics
   Ithaca, NY 855-463-6697
Flamous Brands
   Duarte, CA 626-799-7909
Fora Foods
   Brooklyn, NY
Forager Project
   San Francisco, CA
Franklin Farms
   Parsippany, NJ
Go Max Go Foods
Gold Mine Natural Food Company
   Poway, CA 800-475-3663
Good PLANeT Foods
   Bellevue, WA 425-449-8134

Gopal's Healthfoods
   Sidney, TX 866-646-7257
Hilary's Eat Well
   Lawrence, KS 785-856-3399
Hudson River Foods
   Castleton, NY 888-417-9343
JUST Inc
   San Francisco, CA 844-423-6637
Jyoti Cuisine India
   Berwyn, PA 610-296-4620
Levant Mediterranean Snack Foods LLC
   Haverhill, MA 978-241-9986
Lightlife
   Turners Falls, MA 800-769-3279
Marjon Specialty Foods Inc
   Plant City, FL 813-752-3482
Modern Table
   Walnut Creek, CA
Morningstar Farms
   Zanesville, OH 800-535-5644
N D Labs
   Lynbrook, NY 888-263-5227
Natural Food Mill
   Corona, CA 800-797-5090
Nature's Path Foods
   Blaine, WA 888-808-9505
Neat Foods
   Lancaster, PA 866-637-6328
New Barn Organics
   Rohnert Park, CA 888-635-7102
No Evil Foods
   Asheville, NC 828-367-1536
Nona Vegan Foods
   Toronto, ON 416-836-9387
Nuts For Cheese
   London, ON 519-601-5070
Oogolow Enterprises
   Chico, CA 800-816-6873
Pita Pal
   Houston, TX 713-777-7482
Probar
   Salt Lake City, UT 800-921-2294
Quorn Foods
   Chicago, IL
Small Planet Foods
   Minneapolis, MN 800-624-4123
Spice Of Life Co
   Sherman Oaks, CA 818-909-0052
Sweet Earth Foods
   Moss Landing, CA 800-737-3311
The Art of Broth, LLC
   CA 818-715-9320
The Piping Gourmets
   786-233-8660
The Soulfull Project
   Camden, NJ
Turtle Island Foods
   Hood River, OR 800-508-8100
Twin Oaks Community
   Louisa, VA 540-894-5141
Unique Ingredients LLC
   Gold Canyon, AZ 480-983-2498
Upton's Naturals
   Chicago, IL
Vana Life Foods
   Seattle, WA 347-446-6504
Vegetable Juices Inc
   Chicago, IL 888-776-9752
Veggie Land
   Parsippany, NJ 888-808-5540
Vegi-Deli
   San Rafael, CA 888-473-3667
Violife
   Thessaloniki,
Vitasoy USA
   Woburn, MA 800-848-2769
Vtopian Artisan Cheeses
   Portland, OR
Wholesome Bakery
   San Francisco, CA 415-343-5414
Wine Country Chef LLC
   Hidden Valley Lake, CA 707-322-0406
Yai's Thai
   Denver, CO
Your Bar Factory
   LaSalle, QC 888-366-0258

Burgers

Beyond Meat
   El Segundo, CA 866-756-4112
Big Mountain Foods
   Vancouver, BC

Product Categories / Specialty & Organic Foods: Vegetarian Products

Boca Foods Company
  Madison, WI 608-285-3311
Dixie USA
  Tomball, TX 800-233-3668
Five Star Foodies
  Cincinnati, OH
Goodseed Burgers
  512-698-7907
Impossible Foods
  Redwood City, CA 855-877-6365
Neat Foods
  Lancaster, PA 866-637-6328
Quaker Maid Meats
  Reading, PA 610-376-1500
Quorn Foods
  Chicago, IL

Sunshine Burger & Spec Food Co
  Fort Atkinson, WI 920-568-1100
Ungars Food
  Elmwood Park, NJ 201-773-6846
Vitasoy USA
  Woburn, MA 800-848-2769

Patties

Big Mountain Foods
  Vancouver, BC
Caribbean Food Delights Inc
  Tappan, NY 845-398-3000
Hilary's Eat Well
  Lawrence, KS 785-856-3399
JD Sweid Foods
  Langley, BC 800-665-4355

Neat Foods
  Lancaster, PA 866-637-6328
Neese Country Sausage Inc
  Greensboro, NC 800-632-1010
Pulmuone Foods USA Inc.
  Fullerton, CA 800-588-7782
Quorn Foods
  Chicago, IL
Vitasoy USA
  Woburn, MA 800-848-2769

Breaded

Neat Foods
  Lancaster, PA 866-637-6328

Specialty Processed Foods

Barbecue Products (See also Specific Foods)

A Southern Season
  Hillsborough, NC 800-253-3663
A. Lassonde Inc.
  Rougemont, QC 866-552-7643
Allied Old English Inc
  Port Reading, NJ 732-602-8955
Arbor Hill Grapery & Winery
  Naples, NY 800-554-7553
Art's Tamales
  Metamora, IL 309-367-2850
Aunt Kitty's Foods Inc
  Vineland, NJ 856-691-2100
Baker's Ribs No 2
  Dallas, TX 214-748-5433
Bartush Schnitzius Foods Co
  Lewisville, TX 972-219-1270
Baumer Foods Inc
  Metairie, LA 504-482-5761
BBQ Bunch
  Kansas City, MO 816-941-4534
Big B Barbecue
  Evansville, IN 812-425-5235
Black's Barbecue
  Lockhart, TX 888-632-8225
Broadaway Ham Co
  Jonesboro, AR 870-932-6688
Bunker Foods Corp.
  New York, NY 646-738-4020
Cafe Tequila
  San Francisco, CA 415-264-0106
California Custom Foods
  Fullerton, CA 714-870-0490
California-Antilles Trading
  San Diego, CA 800-330-6450
Calumet Diversified Meats Company
  Pleasant Prairie, WI 800-752-7427
Captain Bob's Jet Fuel
  Fort Wayne, IN 877-486-6468
Carolina Treet
  Wilmington, NC 800-616-6344
Casa Visco
  Schenectady, NY 888-607-2823
Catskill Mountain Specialties
  Saugerties, NY 800-311-3473
Caughman's Meat Plant
  Lexington, SC 803-356-0076
Chandler Foods Inc
  Greensboro, NC 800-537-6219
Cinnabar Specialty Foods Inc
  Prescott, AZ 866-293-6433
Clements Foods Co
  Oklahoma City, OK 800-654-8355
Clifty Farm Country Meats
  Paris, TN 800-486-4267
Coach Sposato's Bar-B-Que
  Lincoln, AR 800-264-7535
Colgin Co
  Dallas, TX 888-226-5446
Cookies Food Products
  Wall Lake, IA 800-331-4995
Corky's Ribs & BBQ
  Pigeon Forge, TN 865-453-7427
Creative Foodworks Inc
  San Antonio, TX 210-212-4761
Curly's Foods Inc
  Edina, MN 612-920-3400
D & D Foods Inc
  West Des Moines, IA 800-772-4098
Dillard's Bar-B-Q Sauce
  Durham, NC 919-286-1080
Dorina So-Good Inc
  Union, IL 815-923-2144
Dorothy Dawson Food Products
  Jackson, MI 517-788-9830
El Rey Cooked Meats
  St Louis, MO 314-521-3113
Favorite Foods
  Burnaby, BC 604-420-5100
Felbro Food Products
  Los Angeles, CA 323-936-5266
Figaro Company
  Mesquite, TX 972-288-3587
Food Concentrate Corporation
  Oklahoma City, OK 405-840-5633
Fremont Authentic Brands
  Fremont, OH 419-334-8995
Fry Krisp Food Products
  Jackson, MI 877-854-5440
Garden Complements Inc
  Kansas City, MO 800-966-1091
Gary's Frozen Foods
  Lubbock, TX 806-745-1933
Gaucho Foods
  Fayetteville, IL 877-677-2282
Gayle's Sweet N' Sassy Foods
  Beverly Hills, CA 310-246-1792
Gedney Foods Co
  Sun Valley, CA 888-244-0653
Golden Specialty Foods Inc
  Norwalk, CA 562-802-2537
Golding Farms Foods
  Winston Salem, NC 336-766-6161
Gumpert's Canada
  Mississauga, ON 800-387-9324
Harold Food Company
  Charlotte, NC 704-588-8061
Head Country
  Ponca City, OK 888-762-1227
Heinz Portion Control
  Jacksonville, FL 904-695-1300
Hollman Foods
  Des Moines, IA 888-926-2879
Hormel Foods Corp.
  Austin, MN 507-437-5611
J & B Sausage Co Inc
  Waelder, TX 830-788-7511
J.N. Bech
  Elk Rapids, MI 800-232-4583
JD Sweid Foods
  Langley, BC 800-665-4355
JMS Specialty Foods
  Ripon, WI 800-535-5437
Johnny Harris Famous Barbecue Sauce
  Savannah, GA 888-547-2823
King Kold Meats
  Englewood, OH 800-836-2797
Kozlowski Farms
  Forestville, CA 800-473-2767
Kubla Khan Food Company
  Portland, OR 503-234-7494
L & S Packing Co
  Farmingdale, NY 800-286-6487
Lea & Perrins
  Glenview, IL
Lee's Sausage Co
  Orangeburg, SC 803-534-5517
Lendy's Cafe Raw Bar
  Virginia Beach, VA 757-491-3511
Lounsbury Foods
  Toronto, ON 416-656-6330
Mad Will's Food Company
  Auburn, CA 888-275-9455
Magic Seasoning Blends
  New Orleans, LA 800-457-2857
Mansmith's Barbeque
  San Jn Bautista, CA 800-626-7648
Mccutcheon Apple Products
  Frederick, MD 800-888-7537
Mitchell Foods
  Barbourville, KY 888-202-9745
Moonlite Bar-B-Q Inn
  Owensboro, KY 800-322-8989
Mullens Dressing
  Palestine, IL 618-586-2727
New Business Corp
  Gary, IN. 219-885-1476
Ninety Six Canning Company
  Ninety Six, SC 864-543-2700
O'Brian Brothers Food
  Cincinnati, OH 513-791-9909
Original Chili Bowl
  Ontario, CA 800-548-6363
Ott Food Products Co
  Carthage, MO 800-866-2585
Pacific Poultry Company
  Honolulu, HI 808-841-2828
Palmieri Food Products
  New Haven, CT 800-845-5447
Paradise Products Corporation
  Boca Raton, FL 800-826-1235
Piggie Park Enterprises
  West Columbia, SC 800-628-7423
Porinos Gourmet Food
  Central Falls, RI 800-826-3938
Produits Ronald
  St. Damase, QC 800-465-0118
River Town Foods Corp
  St Louis, MO. 800-844-3210
Riverview Foods
  Warsaw, KY 859-567-5211
Robinson's No 1 Ribs
  Oak Park, IL 800-836-6750
Roos Foods
  Kenton, DE 800-343-3642
Rosmarino Foods/R.Z. Humbert Company
  Odessa, FL 888-926-9053
Sadler's Smokehouse
  Henderson, TX 903-657-5581
Savoie's Sausage and Food Products
  Opelousas, LA 337-942-7241
Schiff Food Products Co Inc
  Totowa, NJ 973-237-1990
Schlotterbeck & Foss Company
  Portland, ME 800-777-4666
Scott's Sauce Co Inc
  Goldsboro, NC 800-734-7282
Steel's Gourmet Foods, Ltd.
  Bridgeport, PA 800-678-3357
Suzanna's Kitchen
  Peachtree Cor, GA 770-476-9900
Sweet Baby Ray's
  Chicago, IL 877-729-2229
Sweet Peas Floral Design
  Stockton, CA 209-472-9284
T. Marzetti Company
  Westerville, OH 800-999-1835
T.W. Garner Food Company
  Winston Salem, NC 800-476-7383
Thompson's Fine Foods
  Shoreview, MN 800-807-0025
Todd's
  Des Moines, IA 800-247-5363
Travis Meats Inc
  Powell, TN 800-247-7606
Triple H Food Processors Inc
  Riverside, CA 951-352-5700
Triple K Manufacturing Company, Inc.
  Shenandoah, IA. 712-246-4376
Triple U Enterprises
  Fort Pierre, SD 605-567-3624
Valley Grain Products
  Fresno, CA 559-675-3400
Vidalia Sweets Brand
  Lyons, GA. 912-565-8881
W & G Marketing Company
  Ames, IA. 515-233-4774
Webbpak Inc
  Trussville, AL 800-655-3500
Wei-Chuan USA Inc
  Bell Gardens, CA 562-372-2020
West Pac
  Idaho Falls, ID 800-973-7407
Westin Foods
  Omaha, NE 800-228-6098
Wing Nien Food
  Hayward, CA 510-487-8877
Wood Brothers Inc
  West Columbia, SC 803-796-5146
Woods Smoked Meats Inc
  Bowling Green, MO 800-458-8426
World Famous Buffalo Wing Sauce
  Buffalo, NY. 716-912-9068
Zarda Bar-B-Q & Catering Company
  Blue Springs, MO 800-776-7427

Dehydrated Food (See also Specific Foods)

Agvest
  Cleveland, OH 216-464-3737
Alkinco
  New York, NY. 800-424-7118
American Dehydrated Foods, Inc.
  Springfield, MO 800-456-3447
American Nut & Chocolate Co
  Boston, MA. 800-797-6887

Product Categories / Specialty Processed Foods: Fermented Products (See also Specific Foods)

Amport Foods
   St. Paul, MN 800-236-1119
Anderson Custom Processing
   New Ulm, MN. 877-588-4950
Atrium Biotech
   Quebec, QC. 418-652-1116
Basic American Foods
   Walnut Creek, CA 925-472-4000
Blossom Farm Products
   Ridgewood, NJ 800-729-1818
Boghosian Raisin Packing Co
   Fowler, CA .559-834-5348
California Fruit
   San Diego, CA 877-378-4811
Caltex Foods
   Canoga Park, CA 800-522-5839
Casados Farms
   Ohkay Owingeh, NM 505-852-2433
Century Blends LLC
   Hunt Valley, MD. 410-771-6606
Challenge Dairy Products, Inc.
   Dublin, CA .800-733-2479
Chef Merito Inc
   Van Nuys, CA 800-637-4861
Chooljian Bros Packing Co
   Sanger, CA .559-875-5501
Chukar Cherries
   Prosser, WA. 800-624-9544
Clofine Dairy Products Inc
   Linwood, NJ 609-653-1000
Commercial Creamery Co
   Spokane, WA. 509-747-4131
Consumers Vinegar & Spice Co
   Chicago, IL .773-376-4100
Country Cupboard
   Lewisburg, PA. 570-523-3211
Dairy King Milk Farms/Foodservice
   Whitter, CA. 800-900-6455
Dairy-Mix Inc
   St Petersburg, FL 800-955-6101
Del Rey Packing
   Del Rey, CA 559-888-2031
Desert Valley Date
   Coachella, CA. 760-398-0999
Devansoy Farms
   Carroll, IA. .800-747-8605
Dismat Corporation
   Toledo, OH .419-531-8963
Emerling International Foods
   Buffalo, NY. 716-833-7381
Fig Garden Packing Inc
   Fresno, CA .559-271-9000
Fine Dried Foods Intl
   Santa Cruz, CA 831-426-1413
First District Association
   Litchfield, MN 320-693-3236
Freeman Industries
   Tuckahoe, NY 800-666-6454
Fuji Foods Corp
   Browns Summit, NC. 336-375-3111
Garden Valley Corp
   Sutherlin, OR 541-459-9565
Global Food Industries
   Townville, SC 800-225-4152
Golden Town Apple Products
   Rougemont, QC 866-552-7643
Good For You America
   Concordia, MO 866-329-5969
Graf Creamery Co
   Bonduel, WI 715-758-2137
Grandpa Ittel's Meats Inc
   Howard Lake, MN 320-543-2285
Henningsen Foods Inc
   Omaha, NE 800-228-2769
Hialeah Products Co
   Hollywood, FL 800-923-3379
Honeyville Grain Inc
   Brigham City, UT 435-494-4200
Humco Holding Group Inc
   Texarkana, TX. 903-831-7808
Idaho Pacific Holdings Inc
   Rigby, ID. 800-238-5503
Idaho Supreme Potatoes Inc
   Firth, ID. 208-346-4100
Kamish Food Products
   Chicago, IL .773-725-6959
Kozlowski Farms
   Forestville, CA 800-473-2767
Land O'Lakes Inc
   Arden Hills, MN 800-328-9680
Larsen Farms
   Hamer, ID 208-374-5592

Leroux Creek
   Hotchkiss, CO 877-970-5670
Made In Nature
   Boulder, CO 800-906-7426
Main Street Ingredients
   La Crosse, WI 800-359-2345
Maine Wild Blueberry Company
   Cherryfield, ME 800-243-4005
Maruchan Inc
   Irvine, CA . . . . , ...949-789-2300
Master Mix
   Placentia, CA 714-524-1698
Mayacamas Fine Foods
   Sonoma, CA 800-826-9621
Mercer Processing
   Modesto, CA. 209-529-0150
Morris J Golombeck Inc
   Brooklyn, NY 718-284-3505
Niagara Foods
   Middleport, NY. 716-735-7722
North Bay Trading Co
   Brule, WI. 800-348-0164
Northern Feed & Bean Company
   Lucerne, CO 800-316-2326
Oakland Bean Cleaning & Storage
   Knights Landing, CA 530-735-6203
Ontario Foods
   Guelph, ON. 888-466-2372
Oregon Potato Co
   Boardman, OR 800-336-6311
Paisano Food Products
   Elk Grove Village, IL 800-672-4726
Pines International
   Lawrence, KS 800-697-4637
Plainview Milk Products
   Plainview, MN 800-356-5606
Pro Form Labs
   Orinda, CA .707-752-9010
Producers Cooperative
   Bryan, TX 979-778-6000
Produits Alimentaire
   Laval, QC 800-361-9326
Protient
   St Paul, MN. 800-328-9680
Quality Ingredients
   Burnsville, MN 952-898-4002
Ramos Orchards
   Winters, CA 530-795-4748
Ramsen Inc
   Lakeville, MN. 952-431-0400
Reinhart Foods
   Toronto, ON 416-645-4910
Rinehart Meat Processing
   Branson, MO. 417-869-2041
Russell E. Womack, Inc.
   Lubbock, TX. 877-787-3559
Schiff Food Products Co Inc
   Totowa, NJ .973-237-1990
Serv-Agen Corporation
   Cherry Hill, NJ 856-663-6966
Shields Date Garden
   Indio, CA. 800-414-2555
SlantShack Jerky
   Brooklyn, NY 201-632-1035
Smeltzer Orchard Co
   Frankfort, MI 231-882-4421
Smuggler's Kitchen
   Dundee, FL. 800-604-6793
Solana Gold Organics
   Sebastopol, CA 800-459-1121
SOUPerior Bean & Spice Company
   Vancouver, WA 800-878-7687
South Mill
   Kennett Square, PA. 610-444-4800
Spice Hunter Inc
   Richmond, VA. 800-444-3061
Spreda Group
   Louisville, KY. 502-426-9411
St. Ours & Company
   East Weymouth, MA. 781-331-8520
Sugar Foods Corp
   Sun Valley, CA 818-768-7900
ThreeWorks Snacks
   259 Niagara St., ON
Tova Industries LLC
   Louisville, KY 888-532-8682
Triple U Enterprises
   Fort Pierre, SD 605-567-3624
Tropical Foods
   Charlotte, NC 800-438-4470
Tropical Foods
   Lithia Springs, GA 800-544-3762

Tropical Nut Fruit & Bulk Cndy
   Lithia Springs, GA 800-544-3762
Unique Ingredients LLC
   Gold Canyon, AZ 480-983-2498
United Dairymen of Arizona
   Tempe, AZ. .480-966-7211
Ursula's Island Farms Company
   Seattle, WA .206-762-3113
Valley View Packing Co
   Yuba City, CA 530-673-7356
Verhoff Alfalfa Mill Inc
   Ottawa, OH. 800-834-8563
VIP Foods
   Flushing, NY. 718-821-5330
Vogue Cuisine Foods
   Sunnyvale, CA 888-236-4144
W.A. Beans & Sons
   Bangor, ME. 800-649-1958
Washington Potato Company
   Pasco, WA. .800-897-2726
Welsh Farms
   Wallington, NJ 800-221-0663
Westin Foods
   Omaha, NE 800-228-6098

Fermented Products (See also Specific Foods)

Lovebiotics LLC
   Los Osos, CA
Makana Beverages Inc.
   Oxnard, CA
Roland Machinery
   Springfield, IL. 800-325-1183
The Water Kefir People
   Bend, OR

Freeze Dried Food (See also Specific Foods)

BCFoods
   Santa Rosa, CA. 707-547-1776
Emerling International Foods
   Buffalo, NY. 716-833-7381
Good For You America
   Concordia, MO. 866-329-5969
Hanover Foods Corp
   Hanover, PA 717-632-6000
Tierra Farm
   Valatie, NY .519-392-8300
Tru Fru, LLC
   Salt Lake City, UT 888-437-2497
Unique Ingredients LLC
   Gold Canyon, AZ 480-983-2498
Van Drunen Farms
   Momence, IL. 815-472-3100
Vivolac Cultures Corporation
   Indianapolis, IN 317-356-8460

Frozen Foods (See also Specific Foods)

Abbotsford Growers Ltd.
   Abbotsford, BC 604-864-0022
Acme Steak & Seafood
   Youngstown, OH. 800-686-2263
Agfinity Inc
   Eaton, CO 800-433-4688
Aglamesis Bros Ice Cream
   Cincinnati, OH 513-531-5196
Agripac
   Denver, CO 503-981-0111
Agropur
   Granby, QC 800-363-5686
Agvest
   Cleveland, OH 216-464-3737
Ajinomoto Foods North America, Inc.
   Ontario, CA. 909-477-4700
Al Gelato Bornay
   Franklin Park, IL. 847-455-5355
Al Pete Meats
   Muncie, IN .765-288-8817
Al-Rite Fruits & Syrups Co
   Miami, FL 305-652-2540
Aladdin Bakers
   Brooklyn, NY 718-499-1818
Alaskan Gourmet Seafoods
   Anchorage, AK 800-288-3740
Alati-Caserta Desserts
   Montr,al, QC 877-377-5680
Alexia Foods
   Long Island City, NY 718-937-0100

Product Categories / Specialty Processed Foods: Frozen Foods (See also Specific Foods)

Alfredo Aiello Italian Food
  Quincy, MA................617-770-6360
Aliotti Wholesale Fish Company
  Monterey, CA..............408-722-4597
All Round Foods Bakery Prod
  Westbury, NY..............800-428-8802
Allen Harim Foods LLC
  Seaford, DE...............877-397-9191
Allen's Blueberry Freezer Inc
  Ellsworth, ME.............207-667-5561
Alpenrose Dairy
  Portland, OR..............503-244-1133
Alyeska Seafoods
  Unalaska, AK..............907-581-1211
Amano Fish Cake Factory
  Hilo, HI..................808-935-5555
American Classic Ice Cream Company
  Bay Shore, NY.............800-736-4100
American Seafoods
  Seattle, WA...............206-448-0300
Andrew & Williamson Sales Co
  San Diego, CA.............619-661-6000
Angy's Food Products Inc
  Westfield, MA.............413-572-1010
Annie's Frozen Yogurt
  Minneapolis, MN...........800-969-9648
Appleton Produce Company
  Weiser, ID................208-414-3352
AquaCuisine
  Portland, OR..............208-323-2782
Arista Industries Inc
  Wilton, CT................800-255-6457
Armbrust Meats
  Medford, WI...............715-748-3102
Arrowac Fisheries
  Seattle, WA...............206-282-5655
Art's Tamales
  Metamora, IL..............309-367-2850
Artuso Pastry
  Bronx, NY.................718-367-2515
ASC Seafood Inc
  Largo, FL.................800-876-3474
Athens Foods Inc
  Brookpark, OH.............843-916-2000
Atkinson Milling Co.
  Selma, NC.................800-948-5707
Atlantic Blueberry
  Hammonton, NJ.............609-561-8600
Atlantic Meat Company
  Savannah, GA..............912-964-8511
Atlantic Veal & Lamb Inc
  Brooklyn, NY..............800-222-8325
Aurora Frozen Foods Division
  Saint Louis, MO...........314-801-2800
Austin Special Foods Company
  Austin, TX................512-372-8665
Avanti Foods Co
  Walnut, IL................800-243-3739
Avo-King Internatl
  Orange, CA................800-286-5464
Awrey Bakeries
  Livonia, MI...............800-950-2253
B & D Foods
  Boise, ID.................208-344-1183
B G Smith & Sons Oyster Co
  Sharps, VA................877-483-8279
Badger Best Pizzas
  De Pere, WI...............920-336-6464
Baja Foods LLC
  Chicago, IL...............773-376-9030
Baker Boy Bake Shop Inc
  Dickinson, ND.............800-437-2008
Baker Boys
  Calgary, AB...............877-246-6036
Baker's Point Fisheries
  Oyster Pond Jeddore, NS...902-845-2347
Balboa Dessert Co Inc
  Santa Ana, CA.............800-974-9699
Bama Foods LTD
  Tulsa, OK.................800-756-2262
Bama Frozen Dough
  Tulsa, OK.................800-756-2262
Bandon Bay Fisheries
  Bandon, OR................541-347-4454
Barber Foods
  Kings Mountain, NC........877-447-3279
Barnes Ice Cream Company
  Manchester, ME............207-622-0827
Bavarian Specialty Foods, LLC
  Los Angeles, CA...........626-856-3188
Bay Oceans Sea Foods
  Garibaldi, OR.............503-322-3316

Bayou Land Seafood
  Breaux Bridge, LA.........337-667-6118
BCFoods
  Santa Rosa, CA............707-547-1776
Beaver Street Fisheries
  Jacksonville, FL..........800-874-6426
Beck's Waffles of Oklahoma
  Shawnee, OK...............800-646-6254
Becker Foods
  Westminster, CA...........714-891-9474
Behm Blueberry Farms
  Grand Haven, MI...........616-846-1650
Bellisio Foods
  Minneapolis, MN
Bernardi Italian Foods Company
  Bloomsburg, PA............570-389-5500
Bernie's Foods
  Brooklyn, NY..............718-417-6677
Best Maid Cookie Co
  River Falls, WI...........888-444-0322
Beta Pure Foods
  Santa Cruz, CA............831-685-6565
Biagio's Banquets
  Chicago, IL...............800-392-2837
Biloxi Freezing Processing Inc.
  Biloxi, MS................228-436-0017
Birch Street Seafoods
  Digby, NS.................902-245-6551
Birchwood Foods Inc
  Kenosha, WI...............800-541-1685
Birdie Pak Products
  Chicago, IL...............773-247-5293
Birdsall Ice Cream Company
  Mason City, IA............641-423-5365
Blakely Freezer Locker
  Blakeley, GA..............229-723-3622
Bland Farms INC
  Glennville, GA............800-752-0206
Blend Pak Inc
  Bloomfield, KY............502-252-8000
Blount Fine Foods
  Fall River, MA............774-888-1300
Blue Ridge Poultry
  Athens, GA................706-546-6767
BlueWater Seafoods
  Gloucester, MA............888-560-2539
Bob's Custom Cuts
  Bonnyville, AB............780-826-2627
Boboli Intl. Inc.
  Stockton, CA..............209-473-3507
Bodin Foods
  New Iberia, LA............337-367-1344
Bon Secour Fisheries Inc
  Bon Secour, AL............251-949-7411
Bonnie Doon LLC
  Elkhart, IN...............574-264-3390
Boston Chowda
  Haverhill, MA.............800-992-0054
Brakebush Brothers
  Westfield, WI.............800-933-2121
Branding Iron
  Sauget, IL................800-851-4684
Bridgford Foods Corp
  Anaheim, CA...............800-527-2105
Brighams
  Arlington, MA.............800-242-2423
Bright Harvest Sweet Potato Co
  Clarksville, AR...........800-793-7440
Broadleaf Venison USA Inc
  Vernon, CA................800-336-3844
Brom Food Group
  St. Laurent, QC...........514-744-5152
Brook Locker Plant
  Brook, IN.................219-275-2611
Brooklyn Bagel Company
  Staten Island, NY.........800-349-3055
Brookside Foods
  Cleveland, OH.............216-991-7600
Brookview Farms
  Manakin-Sabot, VA.........804-784-3131
Brown Produce Company
  Farina, IL................618-245-3301
Brown's Ice Cream Co
  Minneapolis, MN...........612-378-1075
Browns' Ice Cream Company
  Minneapolis, MN...........612-378-1075
Bruno Specialty Foods
  West Sayville, NY.........631-589-1700
Bubbies Homemade Ice Cream
  Aiea, HI..................808-487-7218
Buck's Spumoni Company
  Milford, CT...............888-222-8257

Bueno Foods
  Albuquerque, NM...........800-888-7336
Burke Corp
  Nevada, IA................800-654-1152
Bush Brothers Provision Co
  West Palm Beach, FL.......800-327-1345
Butterfield Foods
  Noblesville, IN...........317-776-4775
Buxton Foods
  Buxton, ND................800-726-8057
Bylada Foods
  Moonachie, NJ.............201-933-7474
C F Gollott & Son Seafood
  Diberville, MS............228-392-2747
Caesar's Pasta
  Blackwood, NJ.............888-432-2372
Cahoon Farms
  Wolcott, NY...............315-594-9610
Callis Seafood
  Lancaster, VA.............804-462-7634
Camino Real Foods Inc
  Vernon, CA................800-421-6201
Campbell Soup Co.
  Camden, NJ................800-257-8443
Captain Ken's Foods Inc
  St Paul, MN...............800-510-3811
Carando Gourmet Frozen Foods
  Agawam, MA................888-227-2636
Caribbean Food Delights Inc
  Tappan, NY................845-398-3000
Caribbean Products
  Baltimore, MD.............410-235-7700
Carla's Pasta
  South Windsor, CT.........860-436-4042
Carolina Blueberry Co-Op Assn
  Garland, NC...............910-588-4220
Carolina Foods Inc
  Charlotte, NC.............800-234-0441
Carousel Cakes
  Nanuet, NY................800-659-2253
Carriere Foods Inc
  Saint-Denis-Sur-Richelie, QC..450-787-3411
Carrington Foods Co Inc
  Saraland, AL..............251-675-9700
Casa di Carfagna
  Columbus, OH..............614-846-6340
Casa Di Lisio Products Inc
  Mt Kisco, NY..............800-247-4199
Catch Up Logistics
  Pittsburgh, PA............412-441-9512
Cateraid Inc
  Howell, MI................800-508-8217
Cathay Foods Corporation
  Boston, MA................617-427-1507
CBC Foods
  Little River, KS..........800-276-4770
Cedar Crest Specialties
  Cedarburg, WI.............800-877-8341
Cedar Key Aquaculture Farms
  Riverview, FL.............888-252-6735
Cedar Lake Foods
  Cedar Lake, MI............800-246-5039
Cedarlane Foods
  Carson, CA................800-826-3322
Centreside Dairy
  Renfrew, ON...............800-889-9974
Challenge Dairy Products, Inc.
  Dublin, CA................800-733-2479
Chandler Foods Inc
  Greensboro, NC............800-537-6219
Chang Food Company
  Garden Grove, CA..........714-265-9990
Channel Fish Processing
  Gloucester, MA............800-457-0054
Chases Lobster Pound
  Port Howe, NS.............902-243-2408
Chateau Food Products Inc
  Cicero, IL................708-863-4207
Chef America
  Chatsworth, CA............818-718-8111
Chef Hans' Gourmet Foods
  Monroe, LA................800-890-4267
Chef's Pride Gifts LLC
  Taylor, MI................800-878-1800
Cher-Make Sausage Co
  Manitowoc, WI.............800-242-7679
Cherbogue Fisheries
  Yarmouth, NS..............902-742-9157
Cherry Hill Orchards
  Lancaster, PA.............717-872-9311
Cherry Lane Frozen Fruits
  Vineland Station, ON......877-243-7796

Chester W. Howeth & Brother
Crisfield, MD 410-968-1398
Chewys Rugulach
San Diego, CA 800-241-3456
Chicago Meat Authority Inc
Chicago, IL 800-383-3811
Chill & Moore
Fort Worth, TX 800-676-3055
Chincoteague Seafood Co Inc
Parsonsburg, MD 443-260-4800
Chocolate Shoppe Ice Cream Co
Madison, WI 800-466-8043
Chocolaterie Bernard Callebaut
Calgary, AB 800-661-8367
Choctaw Maid Farms
Jackson, MS 601-683-4000
CHR Foods
Watsonville, CA 831-728-0157
Christie Cookie
Nashville, TN 800-458-2447
Christy Wild Blueberry Farms
Amherst, NS 902-667-3013
Ciao Bella Gelato Company
Irvington, NJ 800-435-2863
Cinderella Cheese Cake Co
Riverside, NJ 800-521-1171
Citrico
Northbrook, IL 800-445-2171
Citrosuco North America Inc
Lake Wales, FL 800-356-4592
Citrus Service
Winter Garden, FL 407-656-4999
Classic Delight Inc
St Marys, OH 800-274-9828
Clear Springs Foods Inc.
Buhl, ID 800-635-8211
Clearwater Fine Foods
Bedford, NS 902-443-0550
Clifty Farm Country Meats
Paris, TN 800-486-4267
Clyde's Delicious Donuts
Addison, IL 630-628-6555
Coastal Seafoods
Ridgefield, CT 203-431-0453
Codinos Food Inc
Scotia, NY 800-246-8908
Cohen's Bakery
Ellenville, NY 845-647-2200
Cole's Quality Foods
Grand Rapids, MI 616-975-0081
Coloma Frozen Foods Inc
Coloma, MI 800-642-2723
Con Agra Foods Inc
Troy, OH 937-335-2115
Conoley Citrus Packers Inc
Winter Garden, FL 407-656-3300
Consolidated Mills Inc
Houston, TX 713-896-4196
Continental Mills Inc
Tukwila, WA 206-816-7000
Cookie Tree Bakeries
Salt Lake City, UT 801-268-2253
Corky's Ribs & BBQ
Pigeon Forge, TN 865-453-7427
Cozy Harbor Seafood Inc
Portland, ME 800-225-2586
Creighton Brothers
Warsaw, IN 574-267-3101
Creme Curls
Hudsonville, MI 800-466-1219
Creme D'Lite
Irving, TX 972-255-7255
Crescent Duck Farm
Aquebogue LI, NY 631-722-8000
Crest International Corporation
San Diego, CA 800-548-1232
Crestar Crusts
Washington Court House, OH 740-335-4813
Crevettes Du Nord
Gaspe, QC 418-368-1414
Crown Valley Food Service
Beaumont, CA 951-769-8786
Crystal Creamery
Modesto, CA 866-225-4821
Cuisine Solutions Inc
Sterling, VA 888-285-4679
Cuizina Food Company
Woodinville, WA 425-486-7000
Culinary Institute Lenotre
Houston, TX 888-536-6873
Culver Duck Farms Inc
Middlebury, IN 800-825-9225

Curly's Foods Inc
Edina, MN 612-920-3400
Cutie Pie Corp
Salt Lake City, UT 800-453-4575
Cyclone Enterprises Inc
Houston, TX 281-872-0087
Dairy Fresh Foods Inc
Taylor, MI 313-299-0735
Dairy King Milk Farms/Foodservice
Whitter, CA 800-900-6455
Dakota Brands Intl
Jamestown, ND 800-844-5073
Dannon Yo Cream
Portland, OR 800-962-7326
De Iorio's Foods Inc
Utica, NY 800-649-7612
Deconna Ice Cream
Reddick, FL 800-824-8254
Deep Creek Custom Packing
Ninilchik, AK 800-764-0078
Deep Foods Inc
Union, NJ 908-810-7500
Del's Lemonade & Refreshments
Cranston, RI 401-463-6190
Del's Seaway Shrimp & Oyster Company
Biloxi, MS 228-432-2604
Delta Pride Catfish
Indianola, MS 800-228-3474
Desserts Of Distinction
Tigard, OR 503-654-8370
Detroit Chili Co
Southfield, MI 248-440-5933
Devault Foods
Devault, PA 800-426-2874
Devine Foods
Elwyn, PA 888-338-4631
Diamond Blueberry Inc
Hammonton, NJ 609-561-3661
Dickinson Frozen Foods
Eagle, ID 800-886-4326
Dillman Farm Inc
Bloomington, IN 800-359-1362
Dimitria Delights Baking Co
North Grafton, MA 800-763-1113
Diversified Avocado Products
Mission Viejo, CA 800-879-2555
Dol Cice' Gelato Company
Yardley, PA 215-499-5661
Dold Foods
Wichita, KS 316-838-9101
Dorothy Dawson Food Products
Jackson, MI 517-788-9830
Dr Praeger's Sensible Foods
Elmwood Park, NJ 877-772-3437
Draper Valley Farms
Mt Vernon, WA 800-562-2012
Dufour Pastry Kitchens Inc
Bronx, NY 800-439-1282
Duma Meats Inc
Mogadore, OH 330-628-3438
Dutch Ann Foods Company
Natchez, MS 601-445-5566
Dwayne Keith Brooks Company
Orangevale, CA 916-988-1030
Dynamic Foods
Lubbock, TX 806-723-5600
E. Gagnon & Fils
St Therese-De-Gaspe, QC 418-385-3011
E.W. Bowker Company
Pemberton, NJ 609-894-9508
Eastern Fish Company
Teaneck, NJ 800-526-9066
Eberhard Creamery
Redmond, OR 541-548-5181
Eckert Cold Storage
Manteca, CA 209-823-3181
Edmond's Chile Co
St Louis, MO 314-772-1499
Edner Corporation
Hayward, CA 510-441-8504
Edwards Baking Company
Marshall, MN 866-739-2328
El Paso Meat Co
El Paso, TX 915-838-8600
El Rey Cooked Meats
St Louis, MO 314-521-3113
Elena's Food Specialties
S San Francisco, CA 800-376-5368
Eli's Cheesecake
Chicago, IL 800-354-2253
Endico Potatoes Inc
Mt Vernon, NY 914-664-1151

Enfield Farms Inc
Lynden, WA 360-354-2919
English Bay Batter Us Inc
Columbus, OH 800-253-6844
Enterprises Pates et Croutes
Boucherville, QC 800-265-7790
Ever Fresh Fruit Co
Boring, OR 800-239-8026
Exceldor Cooperative
Levis, QC 418-830-5600
Fairmont Foods Of Minnesota
Fairmont, MN 507-238-9001
Fairview Dairy Inc
Latrobe, PA 724-537-7111
Fantasia
Sedalia, MO 660-827-1172
Farr Candy Company
Idaho Falls, ID 208-522-8215
Fendall Ice Cream Company
Salt Lake City, UT 801-355-3583
Ferroclad Fishery
Batchawana Bay, ON 705-882-2295
Field's Pies
Pauls Valley, OK 800-286-7501
Fieldale Farms
Baldwin, GA 800-241-5400
Fieldbrook Foods Corp.
Dunkirk, NY 800-333-0805
Fiera Foods
Toronto, ON 800-675-6356
Fine Choice Foods
Richmond, BC 866-760-0888
Fiori Bruna Pasta Products
Miami Lakes, FL 305-705-2534
First Original Texas Chili Company
Fort Worth, TX 800-507-0009
Fish King
Glendale, CA 818-244-2161
Fish Market Inc
Louisville, KY 502-587-7474
Flavors from Florida
Bartow, FL 800-888-0409
Fleischer's Bagels
Macedon, NY 315-986-9999
Florentyna's Fresh Pasta Factory
Los angles, CA 800-747-2782
Florida Veal Processors
Wimauma, FL 813-634-5545
Florida's Natural Growers
Lake Wales, FL 888-657-6600
Food City USA
Arvada, CO 303-321-4447
Forte Stromboli Company
Philadelphia, PA 215-463-6336
Fran's Healthy Helpings
Burlingame, CA 650-652-5772
France Delices
Montreal, QC 800-663-1365
French Gourmet Inc
Sparks, NV 775-525-2525
Fresh Frozen Foods
Jefferson, GA 800-277-9851
Fresh Juice Delivery
Beverly Hills, CA 310-271-7373
Frio Foods
San Antonio, TX 210-278-4525
Frozen Specialties Inc
Perrysburg, OH 419-867-2005
Frozfruit Corporation
Gardena, CA 310-217-1034
Fruit Belt Canning Inc
Lawrence, MI 269-674-3939
Fruithill Inc
Yamhill, OR 503-662-3926
Fry Foods Inc
Tiffin, OH 800-626-2294
G M Allen & Son Inc
Orland, ME 207-469-7060
Gabila's Knishes
Copiague, NY 631-789-2220
Gad Cheese Retail Store
Medford, WI 715-748-4273
Galliker Dairy Co
Johnstown, PA 800-477-6455
Galloway Co
Neenah, WI 800-722-8903
Garber Ice Cream Co Inc
Winchester, VA 800-662-5422
Gardner Pie Co
Akron, OH 330-245-2030
Gary's Frozen Foods
Lubbock, TX 806-745-1933

Product Categories / Specialty Processed Foods: Frozen Foods (See also Specific Foods)

Gaucho Foods
   Fayetteville, IL 877-677-2282
Gelato Fresco
   Toronto, ON 416-785-5415
George Chiala Farms Inc
   Morgan Hill, CA 408-778-0562
George Robberecht Seafood
   Montross, VA 804-472-3556
Gerard & Dominique Seafoods
   Harbor, OR 800-858-0449
Gesco ENR
   Gaspe, QC 418-368-1414
Gifford's Ice Cream
   Skowhegan, ME 800-950-2604
Giorgio Foods
   Temple, PA 800-220-2139
Glacier Foods
   Houston, TX 832-375-6300
Glendora Quiche Company
   San Dimas, CA 909-394-1777
Glover's Ice Cream Inc
   Frankfort, IN 800-686-5163
Gold Standard Baking Inc
   Chicago, IL 800-648-7904
Golden Gulf Coast Packing Co
   Biloxi, MS 228-374-6121
Golden Platter Foods
   Newark, NJ 973-344-8770
Golden Town Apple Products
   Rougemont, QC 866-552-7643
Gonard Foods
   Calgary, AB 403-277-0991
Gonnella Baking Company
   Schamburg, IL 800-322-8829
Good Harbor Fillet Company
   New Bedford, MA 800-343-8046
Good Old Days Foods
   Little Rock, AR 501-565-1257
Good Wives
   Wilmington, MA 800-521-8160
Gorton's Inc.
   Gloucester, MA 800-222-6846
Gourmet Croissant
   Brooklyn, NY 718-499-4911
Goya Foods Inc
   Jersey City, NJ 201-348-4900
Great American Appetizers
   Nampa, ID 800-282-4834
Great Northern Baking Company
   Minneapolis, MN 612-331-1043
Great Northern Products Inc
   Cranston, RI 401-490-4590
Great Valley Mills
   Barto, PA 800-688-6455
Grecian Delight Foods Inc
   Elk Grove Village, IL 800-621-4387
Gregory's Foods, Inc.
   St Paul, MN 800-231-4734
Gress Enterprises
   Scranton, PA 570-561-0150
Grimaud Farms-California Inc
   Stockton, CA 800-466-9955
Grossingers Home Bakery
   New York, NY 800-479-6996
Grow-Pac
   Cornelius, OR 503-357-9691
Gulf Pride Enterprises
   Biloxi, MS 888-689-0560
Guttenplan's Frozen Dough
   Middletown, NJ 888-422-4357
GWB Foods Corporation
   Brooklyn, NY 877-977-7610
H&H Fisheries Limited
   Eastern Passage, NS 866-773-4400
Haines Packing Company
   Haines, AK 907-766-2883
Hall Brothers Meats
   Olmsted Twp, OH 440-235-3262
Hallmark Fisheries
   Charleston, OR 541-888-3253
Hamms Custom Meats
   Mckinney, TX 972-542-3359
Handy International Inc
   Salisbury, MD 800-426-3977
Hanover Foods Corp
   Hanover, PA 717-632-6000
Harker's Distribution
   Le Mars, IA 800-798-7700
Harlan Bakeries
   Avon, IN 800-435-2738
Harold Food Company
   Charlotte, NC 704-588-8061

Harrisburg Dairies Inc
   Harrisburg, PA 800-692-7429
Hartog Rahal Foods
   Norwood, NJ 201-750-0500
Harvest Time Foods
   Ayden, NC 252-746-6675
Hatfield Quality Meats
   Hatfield, PA 800-743-1191
Health is Wealth Foods
   Moonachie, NJ 201-933-7474
Heidi's Gourmet Desserts
   Tucker, GA 800-241-4166
Heinz Quality Chef Foods Inc
   Cedar Rapids, IA 800-356-8307
Herb's Seafood
   Westampton, NJ 800-486-0276
Heringer Meats Inc
   Covington, KY 859-291-2000
Hermann Pickle Co
   Garrettsville, OH 800-245-2696
Hershey Creamery Co
   Harrisburg, PA 888-240-1905
HFI Foods
   Redmond, WA 425-883-1320
Higgins Seafood
   Lafitte, LA 504-689-3577
Hillard Bloom Packing Co Inc
   Port Norris, NJ 856-785-0120
Hillmans Shrimp & Oyster
   Port Lavaca, TX 800-582-4416
Holton Food Products
   La Grange, IL 708-352-5599
Home Delivery Food Service
   Jefferson, GA 706-367-9551
Home Market Foods Inc.
   Norwood, MA 781-948-1500
Home Run Inn Frozen Foods
   Woodridge, IL 800-636-9696
Homer's Ice Cream
   Wilmette, IL 847-251-0477
Homestead Meats
   Delta, CO 970-874-1145
Hormel Foods Corp.
   Austin, MN 507-437-5611
Horst Seafood
   Juneau, AK 877-518-4300
Houdini Inc
   Fullerton, CA 714-525-0325
House of Flavors Inc
   Ludington, MI 800-930-7740
House of Spices
   Flushing, NY 718-507-4600
Hudsonville Ice Cream
   Holland, MI 616-546-4005
Humboldt Creamery
   Modesto, CA 888-316-6064
Hunter Farms - High Point Division
   High Point, NC 800-446-8035
Ice Cream Bowl
   Zanesville, OH 740-452-5267
Ice Cream Club Inc
   Boynton Beach, FL 800-535-7711
Ice Cream Specialties Inc
   St Louis, MO 800-662-7550
Ideal Dairy Farms
   Hudson Falls, NY 518-747-5059
Il Gelato
   Astoria, NY 800-899-9299
Incredible Cheesecake
   San Diego, CA 619-563-9722
Independent Packers Corporation
   Seattle, WA 206-285-6000
Indian Ridge Shrimp Co
   Chauvin, LA 800-594-0920
Indian Valley Meats
   Indian, AK 907-653-7511
Inn Foods Inc
   Watsonville, CA 800-708-7836
Inovata Foods
   Tillsonburg, ON 800-265-5731
Inshore Fisheries
   Middle West Pubnico, NS 902-762-2522
International Food Packers Corporation
   Miami, FL 305-740-5847
International Specialty Supply
   Cookeville, TN 931-526-1106
Island Marine Products
   Clarks Harbour, NS 902-745-2222
Island Oasis Frozen Cocktail
   Beloit, WI 800-777-4752
Island Scallops
   Qualicum Beach, BC 250-757-9811

It's It Ice Cream Co
   Burlingame, CA 800-345-1928
Italia Foods
   Schaumburg, IL 800-747-1109
Itarca
   Los Angeles, CA 800-747-2782
J & J Wall Bakery Co
   Sacramento, CA 916-381-1410
J B & Son LTD
   Yonkers, NY 914-963-5192
J H Verbridge & Son Inc
   Williamson, NY 315-589-2366
J. Matassini & Sons Fish Company
   Tampa, FL 813-229-0829
J.W. Haywood & Sons Dairy
   Louisville, KY 502-774-2311
Jack & Jill Ice Cream
   Moorestown, NJ 856-813-2300
James Skinner Company
   Omaha, NE 800-358-7428
Janes Family Foods
   Mississauga, ON 800-565-2637
Jaxon's Ice Cream Parlor
   Dania Beach, FL 954-923-4445
Jazz Fine Foods
   Montreal, QC 514-255-0110
JBS Packing Inc
   Port Arthur, TX 409-982-3216
Jecky's Best
   Santa Clarita, CA 888-532-5972
Jel Sert
   West Chicago, IL 800-323-2592
Jemm Wholesale Meat Company
   Chicago, IL 773-523-8161
Jessie's Ilwaco Fish Company
   San Francisco, CA 360-642-3773
Joe Jurgielwicz & Sons
   Hamburg, PA 800-543-8257
John Garner Meats
   Van Buren, AR 800-543-5473
Johnson's Real Ice Cream
   Columbus, OH 614-231-0014
Josh & John's Ice Cream
   Colorado Springs, CO 800-530-2855
Jubilee Foods
   Bayou La Batre, AL 251-824-2110
Juno Chef's
   Goshen, NY 845-294-5400
Junuis Food Products
   Palatine, IL 847-359-4300
K & K Gourmet Meats Inc
   Leetsdale, PA 724-266-8400
Kan-Pak
   Arkansas City, KS 800-378-1265
Karn Meats
   Columbus, OH 800-221-9585
Katrina's Tartufo
   Port Jeffrsn Sta, NY 800-480-8836
Kelley Foods
   Elba, AL 334-897-5761
Kenosha Beef International LTD
   Kenosha, WI
Kent Foods Inc
   Gonzales, TX 830-672-7993
Kent Precision Foods Group Inc
   Muscatine, IA 800-442-5242
Key Largo Fisheries
   Key Largo, FL 800-432-4358
Keyser Brothers
   Lottsburg, VA 804-529-6837
King Cole Ducks Limited
   Newmarket, ON 800-363-3825
King Kold Meats
   Englewood, OH 800-836-2797
Kitchens Seafood
   Plant City, FL 800-327-0132
Klinke Brothers Ice Cream Co
   Memphis, TN 901-322-6640
Kodiak Salmon Packers
   Larsen Bay, AK 907-847-2250
Kona Cold Lobsters
   Kailua Kona, HI 808-329-4332
Konto's Foods
   Patterson, NJ 973-278-2800
KT's Kitchens
   Carson, CA 310-764-0850
Kubla Khan Food Company
   Portland, OR 503-234-7494
Kutztown Bologna Company
   Leola, PA 800-723-8824
Kyger Bakery Products
   Lafayette, IN 765-447-1252

Product Categories / Specialty Processed Foods: Frozen Foods (See also Specific Foods)

L&C Fisheries
   Kensington, PE 902-886-2770
La Cookie
   Burbank, CA 818-495-5732
LA Monica Fine Foods
   Millville, NJ
La Nova Wings
   Buffalo, NY 800-652-6682
Ladoga Frozen Food & Retail
   Ladoga, IN 765-942-2225
Lady Gale Seafood
   Baldwin, LA 337-923-2060
Lafitte Frozen Foods Corp
   Lafitte, LA 504-689-2041
Lake Packing Co Inc
   Lottsburg, VA 800-324-2759
Lakeside Foods Inc.
   Plainview, MN 507-534-3141
Land O'Lakes Inc
   Arden Hills, MN 800-328-9680
Landolfi's Food Products
   Trenton, NJ 609-392-1830
Leader Candies
   Brooklyn, NY 718-366-6900
Leelanau Fruit Co
   Peshawbestown, MI 231-271-3514
Leidenheimer Baking Co
   New Orleans, LA 800-259-9099
Lenchner Bakery
   Concord, ON 905-738-8811
Lengerich Meats Inc
   Zanesville, IN 260-638-4123
Lennox Farm
   Shelburne, ON 519-925-6444
Leon's Bakery
   North Haven, CT 800-223-6844
Leonetti's Frozen Food
   Philadelphia, PA 866-551-7168
Les Boulangers Associes Inc
   Seatac, WA 800-522-1185
Lombardi's Seafood
   Winter Park, FL 800-879-8411
Lone Star Bakery
   Round Rock, TX 512-255-7268
Lougheed Fisheries
   Owen Sound, ON 519-376-1586
Louis Dreyfus Company Citrus Inc
   Winter Garden, FL 407-656-1000
Louisa Food Products Inc
   St Louis, MO 314-868-3000
Louisiana Packing Company
   Westwego, LA 800-666-1293
Love Quiches Desserts
   Freeport, NY 516-623-8800
Lucia's Pizza Co
   St Louis, MO 314-843-2553
Ludwick's Frozen Donuts
   Grand Rapids, MI 800-366-8816
Ludwig Fish & Produce Company
   La Porte, IN 800-362-2608
Luxury Crab
   St John's, NL 709-739-6668
M Buono Beef Co
   Philadelphia, PA 215-463-3600
M&L Gourmet Ice Cream
   Baltimore, MD 410-276-4880
M.A. Johnson Frozen Foods
   Marion, IN 317-664-8023
Macabee Foods
   West Nyack, NY 845-623-1300
Macfarlane Pheasants
   Janesville, WI 800-345-8348
Mack's Bill Ice Cream
   Dover, PA 717-292-1931
Mackie International, Inc.
   Riverside, CA 800-733-9762
Mada'n Kosher Foods
   Dania, FL 954-925-0077
Maid-Rite Steak Company
   Dunmore, PA 800-233-4259
Main Street Gourmet
   Cuyahoga Falls, OH 800-678-6246
Maine Wild Blueberry Company
   Cherryfield, ME 800-243-4005
Majestic Foods
   Huntington, NY 631-424-9444
Mama Rosie's Ravioli
   Charlestown, MA 888-246-4300
Mamma Lina Ravioli Company
   San Diego, CA 858-535-0620
Manchester Farms
   Columbia, SC 800-845-0421

Mancuso Cheese Co
   Joliet, IL 815-722-2475
Mannhardt Inc
   Sheboygan Falls, WI 800-423-2327
Maola Milk & Ice Cream Co.
   844-287-1970
Maple Donuts Inc
   Lake City, PA 877-774-3668
Maple Leaf Farms
   St Leesburg, IN 800-348-2812
Maple Leaf Foods International
   North York, ON 800-268-3708
Maplehurst Bakeries LLC
   Brownsburg, IN 800-428-3200
Mar-Jac Poultry Inc.
   Gainesville, GA 770-531-5000
Mar-Key Foods
   Vidalia, GA 912-537-4204
Mardi Gras
   Verona, NJ 973-857-3777
Mario's Gelati
   Vancouver, BC 604-879-9411
Marsan Foods
   Toronto, ON 416-755-9262
Martin Brothers Seafood Co
   Westwego, LA 504-341-2251
Martin Seafood Company
   Jessup, MD 410-799-5822
Marzetti Foodservice
   Westerville, OH 800-247-4194
Mason County Fruit Packers Cooperative
   Hart, MI 231-873-7504
Matador Processors
   Blanchard, OK 800-847-0797
Maxim's Import Corporation
   Miami, FL 800-331-6652
Mayfield Farms and Nursery
   Athens, TN 423-746-9859
McCain Foods Ltd.
   Toronto, ON 416-955-1700
McCain Foods USA Inc.
   Oakbrook Terace, IL 800-938-7799
McConnell's Fine Ice Cream
   Santa Barbara, CA 805-963-8813
Meat-O-Mat Corp
   Brooklyn, NY 718-965-7250
Mehaffies Pies
   Dayton, OH 800-289-7437
Mel-O-Cream Donuts Intl
   Springfield, IL 800-500-5414
Meleddy Cherry Plant
   Sturgeon Bay, WI 920-743-2858
Menemsha Fish Market
   Chilmark, MA 508-645-2282
Merrill's Blueberry Farms
   Ellsworth, ME 800-711-6551
Mexi-Frost Specialties Company
   Brooklyn, NY 718-625-3324
Mi Ranchito Foods
   Phoenix, AZ 602-272-3949
Mia Products
   Scranton, PA 570-207-5328
Michael Foods, Inc.
   Minnetonka, MN 952-258-4000
Michael's Cookies
   Clear Lake, IA 800-822-5384
Michele's Family Bakery
   York, PA 717-741-2027
Michelle Chocolatiers
   Colorado Springs, CO 888-447-3654
Michigan Dairy LLC
   Livonia, MI 734-367-5390
Mid-Atlantic Foods Inc
   Easton, MD 800-922-4688
Mikawaya LLC
   Vernon, CA 323-587-5504
Mike & Jean's Berry Farm
   Mt Vernon, WA 360-424-7220
Mill Cove Lobster Pound
   Trevett, ME 207-633-3340
Milmar Food Group
   Goshen, NY 845-294-5400
Milne Fruit Products Inc
   Prosser, WA 509-786-2611
Minh Food
   Pasadena, TX 713-475-1970
Minh Food Corporation
   Pasadena, TX 800-344-7655
Minor Fisheries
   Port Colborne, ON 905-834-9232
Minterbrook Oyster Co
   Gig Harbor, WA 253-857-5251

Minute Maid Company
   Atlanta, GA 800-520-2653
Miracapo Pizza
   Elk Grove Village, IL 847-631-3500
Mister Cookie Face
   Dunkirk, NY 800-333-0305
Mobile Processing
   Mobile, AL 251-438-6944
Model Dairy LLC
   Reno, NV 800-433-2030
Modern Pod Co.
   Providence, RI
Molinaro's Fine Italian Foods Ltd.
   Mississauga, ON 905-281-0352
Momence Packing Company
   Sheboygan Falls, WI 888-556-2728
Mooresville Ice Cream Co
   Mooresville, NC 800-304-7172
Morey's Seafood Intl LLC
   Motley, MN 800-808-3474
Morgan Foods Inc
   Austin, IN 888-430-1780
Moroni Feed Company
   Moroni, UT 435-436-8202
Morrison Lamothe
   Toronto, ON 877-677-6533
Morrison Meat Pies
   West Valley, UT 801-977-0181
Morrison Milling Co
   Denton, TX 800-531-7912
Mortimer's Fine Foods
   Burlington, ON 905-336-0000
Mozzicato De Pasquale Bakery
   Hartford, CT 860-296-0426
Mushroom Co
   Cambridge, MD 410-221-8971
Mutual Fish Co
   Seattle, WA 206-322-4368
Myers Frozen Food Provisions
   St Paul, IN 765-525-6304
Naleway Foods
   Winnipeg, MB 800-665-7448
Nan Sea Enterprises of Wisconsin
   Waukesha, WI 262-542-8841
Nancy's Specialty Foods
   Newark, CA 510-494-1100
National Fish & Oyster
   Olympia, WA 360-491-5550
National Frozen Foods Corp
   Seattle, WA 206-322-8900
Natural Feast Corporation
   Dover, MA 508-785-3322
Natural Fruit Corp
   Hialeah, FL 305-887-7525
Nature Quality
   San Martin, CA 408-683-2182
Nelson Crab Inc
   Tokeland, WA 800-262-0069
Nelson Ice Cream
   Stillwater, MN 651-430-1103
Neptune Fisheries
   Newport News, VA 800-545-7474
Nestle
   Mt Sterling, KY 859-499-1100
Nestle USA Inc
   Glendale, CA 800-225-2270
New England Muffin Co Inc
   Fall River, MA 508-675-2833
New York Frozen Foods Inc
   Bedford, OH 216-292-5655
Newfound Resources
   St Josephs, NL 709-579-7676
Niagara Foods
   Middleport, NY 716-735-7722
Nickabood's Inc
   Los Angeles, CA 213-746-1541
Night Hawk Frozen Foods Inc
   Buda, TX 800-580-4166
Nor-Cliff Farms
   Port Colborne, ON 905-835-0808
Norbest, LLC
   Moroni, UT 800-453-5327
Nordic Group Inc
   Boston, MA 800-486-4002
Norfood Cherry Growers
   Simcoe, ON 519-426-5784
NORPAC Foods Inc
   Salem, OR
North Pacific Seafoods Inc
   Seattle, WA 206-726-9900
Northern Products Corporation
   Seattle, WA 888-599-6290

Product Categories / Specialty Processed Foods: Frozen Foods (See also Specific Foods)

Northern Wind Inc
 New Bedford, MA 888-525-2525
Notre Dame Seafoods Inc.
 Comfort Cove, NL 709-244-5511
O'Boyle's Ice Cream Company
 Bristol, PA 215-788-3882
O'Hara Corp
 Rockland, ME 207-594-4444
Ocean Beauty Seafoods Inc
 Seattle, WA 800-365-8950
Ocean Food Co. Ltd.
 Toronto, ON 416-285-6487
Ocean Spray International
 Lakeville-Middleboro, MA 800-662-3263
Ocean Springs Seafood
 Ocean Springs, MS 228-875-0104
Okuhara Foods Inc
 Honolulu, HI 808-848-0581
Old Fashioned Kitchen Inc
 Lakewood, NJ 732-364-4100
Omaha Steaks Inc
 800-960-8400
On-Cor Frozen Foods
On-Cor Frozen Foods Redi-Serve
 Aurora, IL 920-563-6391
Orange Bakery
 Irvine, CA 949-863-1377
Ore-Ida Foods
 Pittsburgh, PA 800-255-5750
Oregon Fruit Products Co
 Salem, OR 800-394-9333
Oregon Potato Co
 Boardman, OR 800-336-6311
Otis Spunkmeyer
 Brockport, NY 855-427-9982
Out of a Flower
 Lancaster, TX 800-743-4696
Oven Poppers
 Manchester, NH 603-644-3773
Overhill Farms Inc
 Vernon, CA 800-859-6406
Overlake Foods
 Olympia, WA 800-683-1078
Oxford Frozen Foods
 Oxford, NS 902-447-2100
P. Janes & Sons
 Hant's Harbor, NL 709-586-2252
Pacific American Fish Co Inc
 Vernon, CA 800-625-2525
Pacific Coast Fruit Co
 Portland, OR 503-234-6411
Pacific Ocean Produce
 Santa Cruz, CA 831-423-2654
Pacific Salmon Company
 Edmonds, WA 425-774-1315
Pacific Seafoods International
 Port Hardy, BC 250-949-8781
Pacific Valley Foods Inc
 Bellevue, WA 425-643-1805
Paisano Food Products
 Elk Grove Village, IL 800-672-4726
Palmetto Pigeon Plant
 Sumter, SC 803-775-1204
Pamlico Packing Company
 Grantsboro, NC 800-682-1113
Paradise Island Foods
 Nanaimo, BC 800-889-3370
Pasta Del Mondo
 Carmel, NY 800-392-8887
Pasta Factory
 Melrose Park, IL 800-615-6951
Pasta International
 Mississauga, ON 905-890-5550
Pastry Chef
 Pawtucket, RI 800-639-8606
Patterson Frozen Foods
 Patterson, CA 209-892-2611
Paul Piazza & Son Inc
 New Orleans, LA 800-969-6011
Pede Brothers Italian Food
 Schenectady, NY 518-356-3042
PEI Mussel King
 Morrell, PE 800-673-2767
Pellman Foods Inc
 New Holland, PA 717-354-8070
Penguin Frozen Foods Inc
 Northbrook, IL 800-323-1485
Penobscot Mccrum LLC
 Belfast, ME 800-435-4456
Pepe's Inc
 Chicago, IL 312-733-2500

Pepe's Mexican Restaurant
 Anaheim, CA 714-952-9410
Perfect Addition
 Newport Beach, CA 949-640-0220
Perfect Foods Inc
 Goshen, NY 800-933-3288
Perry's Ice Cream Co Inc
 Akron, NY 800-873-7797
Peter Pan Seafoods Inc.
 Bellevue, WA 206-728-6000
Petersen Ice Cream Company
 Oak Park, IL 708-386-6130
Phillips Foods
 Baltimore, MD 888-234-2722
Phoenix Agro-Industrial Corporation
 Westbury, NY 516-334-1194
Phranil Foods
 Spokane, WA 509-534-7770
Pictsweet Co
 Bells, TN 731-663-7600
Pierceton Foods Inc
 Pierceton, IN 574-594-2344
Pierino Frozen Foods
 Lincoln Park, MI 313-928-0950
Pinocchio Italian Ice Cream Company
 Edmonton, AB 780-455-1905
Piqua Pizza Supply Co Inc
 Piqua, OH 800-521-4442
Platte Valley Creamery
 Scottsbluff, NE 308-632-4225
Plehn's Bakery Inc
 Louisville, KY 502-896-4438
Plymouth Beef Co.
 Bronx, NY 718-589-8600
POG
 Grand Bend, ON 519-238-5704
Portland Shellfish Company
 Portland, ME 207-799-9290
Positively 3rd St Bakery
 Duluth, MN 218-724-8619
Prairie Cajun Wholesale
 Eunice, LA 337-546-6195
Prairie Farms Dairy Inc.
 Edwardsville, IL 618-659-5700
Preferred Meal Systems Inc
 Moosic, PA 570-457-8311
Price's Creameries
 El Paso, TX 915-565-2711
Pride Dairies
 Bottineau, ND 701-228-2216
Prime Smoked Meats Inc
 Oakland, CA 510-832-7167
Puritan/ATZ Ice Cream
 Kendallville, IN 260-347-2700
Purity Dairies LLC
 Nashville, TN 615-244-1900
Purity Ice Cream Co
 Ithaca, NY 607-272-1545
QualiGourmet
 Boisbriand, QC 514-287-3530
Quality Food Products Inc
 Chicago, IL 312-666-4559
Quality Seafood
 Apalachicola, FL 850-653-9696
Queen International Foods
 Monterey Park, CA 800-423-4414
Quelle Quiche
 Brentwood, MO 314-961-6554
R Four Meats
 Chatfield, MN 507-867-4180
Ragozzino Foods Inc
 Meriden, CT 800-348-1240
Rainsweet Inc
 Salem, OR 800-363-4293
Ralph's Famous Italian Ices
 Babylon, NY 631-893-5646
Ramona's Mexican Foods
 Gardena, CA 310-323-1950
Ranaldi Bros. Frozen Food Products
 Warwick, RI 401-737-5130
Ready Foods Inc
 Denver, CO 800-748-1218
Red Baron
 Marshall, MN 800-769-7980
Reinhold Ice Cream Company
 Pittsburgh, PA 412-321-7600
Reiter Dairy
 Newport, KY 800-544-6455
Reiter Dairy LLC
 Springfield, OH 937-323-5777
Request Foods Inc
 Holland, MI 800-786-0900

Resource Trading Company
 Portland, ME 207-772-2299
Restaurant Systems International
 Staten Island, NY 718-494-8888
Rhodes International Inc
 Salt Lake City, UT 800-876-7333
Rich Products Corp
 Vineland, NJ 800-818-9261
Rich Products Corp
 Buffalo, NY 800-828-2021
Rich's Ice Cream Co Inc
 West Palm Beach, FL 561-833-7585
Riviera Ravioli Company
 Bronx, NY 718-823-0260
Rosati Italian Water Ice
 Clifton Heights, PA 855-476-7284
Rose Frozen Shrimp
 Los Angeles, CA 213-626-8251
Roselani Tropics Ice Cream
 Wailuku, HI 808-244-7951
Rowena
 Norfolk, VA 800-627-8699
Royal Harvest Foods Inc
 Springfield, MA 413-737-8392
Royal Madera Vineyards
 Madera, CA 559-486-6666
Royal Seafood Inc
 Brooklyn, NY 718-769-1517
Rubschlager Baking Corp
 800-661-7246
Ruggiero Seafood
 Newark, NJ 866-225-2627
Ruiz Food Products Inc.
 Dinuba, CA 800-477-6474
Rymer Foods
 Chicago, IL 800-247-9637
S & E Organic Farms Inc
 Bakersfield, CA 661-325-2644
S.D. Mushrooms
 Avondale, PA 610-268-8082
Sahadi Fine Foods Inc
 Brooklyn, NY 800-724-2341
Santa Monica Seafood Co.
 Rancho Dominguez, CA 800-969-8862
Saveur Food Group
 New york, NY 212-595-5425
Savino's Italian Ices
 Deerfield Beach, FL 954-426-4119
Saxby Foods
 Edmonton, AB 780-440-4179
Scenic Fruit Co
 Gresham, OR 877-927-3434
Schaefers Market
 Sauk Centre, MN 320-352-6490
Schneider Foods
 Saint Marys, ON 800-567-1890
Schneider's Dairy Inc
 Pittsburgh, PA 412-881-3525
Schneider-Valley Farms Inc
 Williamsport, PA 570-326-2021
Sea Pearl Seafood
 Bayou La Batre, AL 800-872-8804
Sea Safari
 Belhaven, NC 800-688-6174
Sea Snack Foods Inc
 Los Angeles, CA 213-622-2204
Sea Watch Intl
 Easton, MD 410-822-7500
Seaberghs Frozen Foods
 White Plains, NY 914-948-6377
Seabrook Brothers & Sons
 Seabrook, NJ 856-455-8080
Seafood Producers Co-Op
 Bellingham, WA 360-733-0120
Seatech Corporation
 Lynnwood, WA 425-487-3231
Sesinco Foods
 New York, NY 212-243-1306
Seviroli Foods
 Garden City, NY 516-222-6220
Seviroli Foods Inc
 Garden City, NY 516-222-6220
Seymour & Sons Seafoods Inc
 Diberville, MS 228-392-4020
Shaw's Southern Belle Frozen, Inc.
 Jacksonville, FL 888-742-9772
Shawmut Fishing Company
 Anchorage, AK 709-334-2559
Shelley's
 Jersey City, NJ 201-433-2900
Shonna's Gourmet Goodies
 West Bridgewater, MA 888-312-7868

Product Categories / Specialty Processed Foods: Frozen Foods (See also Specific Foods)

Sidari's Italian Foods
 Cleveland, OH 216-431-3344
Sill Farm Market
 Lawrence, MI 269-674-3755
Silver Lining Seafood
 Seattle, WA 800-426-5490
Silver State Foods Inc
 Denver, CO 800-423-3351
Simmons Foods Inc
 Siloam Springs, AR 888-831-7007
Sisler's Ice & Ice Cream
 Ohio, IL 888-891-3856
Smeltzer Orchard Co
 Frankfort, MI 231-882-4421
Smith Dairy
 Orrville, OH 800-776-7076
Smith Frozen Foods Inc
 Weston, OR 541-566-3515
Smith Packing Regional Meat
 Utica, NY 315-732-5125
Smoked Turkey Inc
 Marshville, NC 704-624-6628
Snelgrove Ice Cream Company
 Salt Lake City, UT 800-569-0005
Sno-Co Berry Pak
 Marysville, WA 360-659-3555
Snowbear Frozen Custard
 W Lafayette, IN 765-746-2930
Snowcrest Packer
 Abbotsford, BC 800-265-3686
So Delicious Dairy Free
 Springfield, OR 866-388-7853
Southern Ice Cream Specialties
 Marietta, GA 770-428-0452
Sparboe Foods Corp
 New Hampton, IA 641-394-3040
Specialty Meats & Gourmet
 Hudson, WI 800-310-2360
Spruce Lane Investments
 Stratford, PE 902-892-2600
Squab Producers of California
 Modesto, CA 209-537-4744
St. Ours & Company
 East Weymouth, MA 781-331-8520
Star Ravioli Mfg Co
 Moonachie, NJ 201-933-6427
Starkel Poultry
 Puyallup, WA 253-845-2876
Steak-Umm Company
 Shillington, PA 860-928-5900
Sterling Caviar LLC
 Elverta, CA 800-525-0333
Stewart's Shops Corp
 Ballston Spa, NY 518-581-1200
Stone Crabs Inc
 Miami Beach, FL 800-260-2722
Stone's Home Made Candy Shop
 Oswego, NY 888-223-3928
Strathroy Foods
 Strathroy, ON 519-245-4600
Strebin Farms
 Troutdale, OR 503-665-8328
Sudlersville Frozen Food Locker
 Sudlersville, MD 410-438-3106
SugarCreek
 Cincinnati, OH 800-445-2715
Sun Glo Of Idaho
 Sugar City, ID 208-356-7346
Sunny Avocado
 Jamul, CA 800-999-2862
Sunrise Growers
 Placentia, CA 714-630-6292
Sunset Specialty Foods
 Lake Arrowhead, CA 909-337-7643
Sunshine Dairy Foods Inc
 Portland, OR 503-234-7526
Sunshine Food Sales
 Miami, FL 305-696-2885
Super Snooty Sea Food Corporation
 Boston, MA 617-426-6390
Super Stores Industries
 Turlock, CA 209-668-2100
Superbrand Dairies
 Montgomery, AL 334-277-6010
Supreme Frozen Products
 Chicago, IL 773-622-3777
Sutherland's Foodservice
 Forest Park, GA 404-366-8550
Suzanna's Kitchen
 Peachtree Cor, GA 770-476-9900
Sweet Fortunes of America
 Woodstock, NY 845-679-7327

Sweet Water Seafood
 Carlstadt, NJ 201-939-6622
Sweety Novelty
 Monterey Park, CA 626-282-4482
Switzer's Inc
 Belleville, IL 618-234-2225
Symons Frozen Foods
 Centralia, WA 360-736-1321
Table De France
 Ontario, CA 909-923-5205
Taif Inc
 Folcroft, PA 610-522-0122
Taku Smokehouse
 Juneau, AK 800-582-5122
Tampa Maid Foods Inc
 Lakeland, FL 800-237-7637
Tantos Foods International
 Markham, ON 905-943-9993
Tasty Mix Quality Foods
 Brooklyn, NY 718-855-7680
Tasty Selections
 Concord, ON 905-760-2353
Taylor Shellfish Farms
 Shelton, WA 360-426-6178
Tebay Dairy Company
 Parkersburg, WV 304-863-3705
Tex-Mex Cold Storage
 Brownsville, TX 956-831-9433
The Pillsbury Company
 Chelsea, MA 800-370-7834
The Valpo Velvet Shoppe
 Valparaiso, IN 219-464-4141
Thompson Packers
 Slidell, LA 800-989-6328
Thyme & Truffles Hors d'Oeuvres
 Dollard-Des-Ormeaux, QC 877-785-9759
Tichon Sea Food Corp
 New Bedford, MA 508-999-5607
Tillamook County Creamery Association
 Tillamook, OR 503-842-4481
Tipiak Inc
 Stamford, CT 203-961-9117
TNT Crust
 Green Bay, WI 920-431-7240
Toft Dairy Inc
 Sandusky, OH 800-521-4606
Tolteca Foodservice
 Norcross, GA 800-541-6835
Tomanetti Food Products Inc
 Oakmont, PA 800-875-3040
Tomasso Corporation
 Baie D'Urfe, QC 514-325-3000
Tony's Ice Cream Co
 Gastonia, NC 704-867-7085
Totino's
 Minneapolis, MN 800-248-7310
Trade Winds Pizza
 Green Bay, WI 920-336-7810
Trans Pecos Foods
 San Antonio, TX 210-228-0896
Travis Meats Inc
 Powell, TN 800-247-7606
Trident Seafoods Corp
 Wrangell, AK 907-874-3346
Trio's Original Italian Pasta Co.
 Chelsea, MA 800-999-9603
Triple D Orchards Inc
 Empire, MI 231-326-5174
Triple U Enterprises
 Fort Pierre, SD 605-567-3624
Triton Seafood Co
 Medley, FL 305-888-0051
Tropical Illusions
 Trenton, MO 660-359-5422
Tropical Treets
 North York, ON 888-424-8229
Tropicana Products Inc.
 Chicago, IL 800-237-7799
Tru-Blu Cooperative Associates
 New Lisbon, NJ 609-894-8717
True Blue Farms
 Grand Junction, MI 877-654-2400
Turano Baking
 Berwyn, IL 708-788-9220
Turk Brothers Custom Meats Inc
 Ashland, OH 800-789-1051
Turkey Store
 Faribault, MN 507-334-5555
Turri's Italian Foods
 Roseville, MI 586-773-6010
Two Chefs on a Roll
 Carson, CA 800-842-3025

Umpqua Dairy
 Roseburg, OR 888-672-6455
Uncle Ralph's Cookies
 Frederick, MD 800-422-0626
Unique Ingredients LLC
 Gold Canyon, AZ 480-983-2498
United Meat Company
 San Francisco, CA 415-864-2118
United Supermarkets
 Lubbock, TX 806-745-9667
Valley Meat Company
 Modesto, CA 800-222-6328
Valley Meats
 Coal Valley, IL 309-517-6639
Van Oriental Food Inc
 Dallas, TX 214-630-0111
Van-Lang Food Products
 Countryside, IL 708-588-0800
VegGuide.org
 Chicago, IL 773-363-3939
Velda Farms
 Orlando, FL 800-795-4649
Velvet Ice Cream Co Inc
 Utica, OH 800-589-5000
Viking Seafoods Inc
 Malden, MA 800-225-3020
Vince's Seafoods
 Gretna, LA 504-368-1544
Vincent Piazza Jr & Sons
 Harahan, LA 800-259-5016
Virginia Trout Co
 Monterey, VA 540-468-2280
Vitamilk Dairy
 Bellingham, WA 206-529-4128
Vivolac Cultures Corporation
 Indianapolis, IN 317-356-8460
W & G Marketing Company
 Ames, IA 515-233-4774
W.L. Petrey Wholesale Inc.
 Luverne, AL 334-230-5674
Waltkoch Limited
 Tucker, GA 404-378-3666
Wanchese Fish Co Inc
 Suffolk, VA 757-673-4500
Wapsie Produce
 Decorah, IA 563-382-4271
Warwick Ice Cream
 Warwick, RI 401-821-8403
Washington Potato Company
 Pasco, WA 800-897-2726
Washington Rhubarb Grower Assn
 Sumner, WA 800-435-9911
Waugh Foods Inc
 East Peoria, IL 309-427-8000
Wawona Frozen Foods Inc
 Clovis, CA 559-299-2901
Wayfield Foods
 Atlanta, GA 404-559-3200
Wayne Dairy Products Inc
 Richmond, IN 765-935-7521
Webster Foods
 Cambridge, NS 800-507-8844
Welch Foods Inc
 Concord, MA 800-340-6870
Welch Foods Inc.
 Concord, MA 800-340-6870
Weldon Ice Cream Co
 Millersport, OH 740-467-2400
Welsh Farms
 Wallington, NJ 800-221-0663
Welsh Farms
 Clifton, NJ 973-772-2388
Wenk Foods Inc
 Madison, SD 605-256-4569
Wenner Bakery
 Bayport, NY 800-869-6262
Westco-BakeMark
 Pico Rivera, CA 562-949-1054
Westin Foods
 Omaha, NE 800-228-6098
Weyand's Fishery
 Wyandotte, MI 800-521-9815
White Cap Fish Market
 Islip, NY 631-277-6577
White Toque
 Secaucus, NJ 800-237-6936
Whitey's Ice Cream Inc
 Moline, IL 888-594-4839
Wick's Pies Inc
 Winchester, IN 800-642-5880
Wild Rice Exchange
 Woodland, CA 800-223-7423

Product Categories / Specialty Processed Foods: Frozen Foods (See also Specific Foods)

Williams Institutional Foods
　Douglas, GA 912-384-5270
Winmix/Natural Care Products
　Englewood, FL 941-475-7432
Wolferman's
　Medford, OR 800-798-6241
Wolfgang Puck Food Company
　Santa Monica, CA 310-432-1350

Wornick Company
　Cincinnati, OH 800-860-4555
Wright's Ice Cream Co
　Cayuga, IN 800-686-9561
Ya-Hoo Baking Co
　Sherman, TX 888-869-2466
Yamasa Fish Cake Co
　Los Angeles, CA 213-626-2211

Yorktown Baking Company
　Yorktown Heights, NY 800-235-3961
Zartic Inc
　Rome, GA 800-241-0516
Ziegenfelder Ice Cream Co
　Wheeling, WV 800-322-3642

Spices, Seasonings & Seeds

General

Deko International Company
  Earth City, MO 314-298-0910

Herbs

ACH Food Co Inc
  Oakbrook Terrace, IL 630-586-3740
Agrexco USA
  Jamaica, NY 718-481-8700
AM Todd Co
  Kalamazoo, MI 269-343-2603
American Botanicals
  Eolia, MO 800-684-6070
American Mercantile Corp
  Memphis, TN 901-454-1900
Ana's Salsa
  Austin, TX 888-849-7054
Ashland Sausage Co
  Carol Stream, IL 630-690-2600
August Kitchen
  Armonk, NY 914-219-5249
Backyard Safari Co
  Covington, GA 770-385-3273
Badia Spices Inc.
  Doral, FL 877-629-8000
BDS Natural
  Long Beach, CA 310-747-0444
Belmont Chemicals
  Clifton, NJ 800-722-5070
Beta Pure Foods
  Santa Cruz, CA 831-685-6565
Better Living Products
  Princeton, TX 972-736-6691
Bijol & Spices Inc
  Miami, FL 888-245-6570
Bolner's Fiesta Spices
  San Antonio, TX
Castella Imports Inc
  Brentwood, NY 631-231-5500
Chef Tim Foods, LLC
  Etters, PA 717-802-0350
Choice Food Distributors LLC
  Nashville, TN 615-350-6070
Christopher's Herb Shop
  Springville, UT 888-372-4372
Cinnabar Specialty Foods Inc
  Prescott, AZ 866-293-6433
Colorado Spice Co
  Boulder, CO 800-677-7423
Crush Foods Service
  Westlake Village, CA 818-699-6381
Crystal Star Herbal Nutrition
  Salinas, CA 831-422-7500
Cyclone Enterprises Inc
  Houston, TX 281-872-0087
Daregal
  Princeton, NJ 609-375-2312
Dion Herbs & Spices
  St-Jerome, QC 877-569-8001
Dizzy Pig BBQ Co
  Manassas, VA 571-379-4884
Dragunara LLC
  Palos Verdes Estate, CA 310-618-8818
Dried Ingredients, LLC.
  Miami, FL 786-999-8499
Dynapro International
  Kaysville, UT 800-877-1413
Eckhart Corporation
  Novato, CA 800-200-4201
Fantis Foods Inc
  Carlstadt, NJ 201-933-6200
Freed, Teller & Freed
  South San Francisco, CA 800-370-7371
Georgia Spice Company
  Atlanta, GA 800-453-9997
Golden State Herbs
  Thermal, CA 800-730-3575
Great Spice Company
  Reno, NV 800-730-3575
Guayaki
  Sebastopol, CA 888-482-9254
Hari Om Farms
  Eagleville, TN 615-368-7778
Health Concerns
  Oakland, CA 800-233-9355
Health Products Corp
  Yonkers, NY 914-423-2900
HealthBest
  San Marcos, CA 760-752-5230
Heffy's BBQ Co.
  Kansas City, MO 816-200-2271
Herb Patch of Vermont
  Bellows Falls, VT 800-282-4372
Herbal Science LLC
  Bonita Springs, FL 239-597-8822
Herbs Etc
  Santa Fe, NM 888-694-3727
High Quality Organics
  Reno, NV 775-971-8550
International Spice
  Lakewood, NJ 609-838-1717
Jodie's Kitchen
  Pinellas Park, FL 800-728-3704
Kalustyan
  New York, NY 800-352-3451
Kevala
  Dallas, TX 877-379-1179
La Flor Spices
  Hauppauge, NY 631-885-9601
Lebermuth Company
  South Bend, IN 800-648-1123
Leeward Resources
  Baltimore, MD 410-837-9003
Lefty Spices
  Waldorf, MD 301-399-3145
Maine Coast Sea Vegetables
  Franklin, ME 207-565-2907
McCormick & Company
  Hunt Valley, MD 410-527-6189
Mermaid Spice Corporation
  Fort Myers, FL 239-693-1986
Mezza
  Lake Forest, IL 888-206-6054
Modern Day Masala, LLC
  Marietta, GA 866-611-3757
Mom's Gourmet, LLC
  Chagrin Falls, OH 440-564-9702
Morris J Golombeck Inc
  Brooklyn, NY 718-284-3505
Mother Shucker's Original Cocktail Sauce
  Columbia, SC 803-261-3802
Mountain Rose Herbs
  Pleasant Hill, OR 800-879-3337
Nature's Sunshine Products Company
  Lehi, UT 800-223-8225
Oak Hill Farm
  Glen Ellen, CA 800-878-7808
Pacific Spice Co
  Commerce, CA 323-890-0895
Pereg Gourmet Spices
  Flushing, NY 718-261-6767
Phamous Phloyd's Barbecue
  Denver, CO 800-497-3281
Pots de Creme
  Lexington, KY 859-299-2254
Primal Essence
  Oxnard, CA 877-774-6253
Prince of Peace
  Hayward, CA 800-732-2328
Pure Ground Ingredients
  Minden, NV 775-297-4047
QBI
  South Plainfield, NJ 908-668-0088
Realsalt
  Heber City, UT 800-367-7258
Red Monkey Foods
  Springfield, MO 417-319-7300
Republic of Tea
  Novato, CA 800-298-4832
Rodelle Inc
  Fort Collins, CO 800-898-5457
S A L T Sisters
  Goshen, IN 574-971-8368
Sampac Enterprises
  S San Francisco, CA 650-876-0808
SAPNA Foods
  Atlanta, GA 404-589-0977
See Smell Taste
  San Francisco, CA 415-986-4216
Sentry Seasonings
  Elmhurst, IL 630-530-5370
Shashi Foods
  Toronto, ON 866-748-7441
Silva International
  Momence, IL 815-472-3535
Smith & Truslow
  Denver, CO 303-339-6967
Specialty Food America Inc
  Hopkinsville, KY 888-881-1633
Spice House International Specialties
  Hicksville, NY 516-942-7248
Spicely
  Fremont, CA 510-440-1044
Sunshine Farm & Garden
  Renick, WV 304-497-2208
Sup Herb Farms
  Turlock, CA 800-787-4372
Superior Foods
  Watsonville, CA 831-728-3691
SupHerb Farms
  Turlock, CA 800-787-4372
Test Laboratories Inc
  Reseda, CA 818-881-4251
Tolteca Foodservice
  Norcross, GA 800-541-6835
Universal Formulas
  Kalamazoo, MI 800-342-6960
Van Drunen Farms
  Momence, IL 815-472-3100
Van Eeghen International Inc
  St Laurent, QC 514-332-6455
Wagner Gourmet Foods
  Lenexa, KS 913-469-5411
Whole Herb Co
  Sonoma, CA 707-935-1077
Wisdom Natural Brands-Uani
  Gilbert, AZ 800-899-9908
World Spice
  Roselle, NJ 800-234-1060
Yellow Emperor Inc
  Eugene, OR 877-485-6664
Young Winfield
  Hamilton, ON 905-893-2536
Zuccaro Produce
  Columbia Heights, MN 612-333-1122

Herbal Supplements

Abunda Life
  Asbury Park, NJ 732-775-9338
Acta Health Products
  Sunnyvale, CA 408-732-6830
ADH Health Products Inc
  Congers, NY 845-268-0027
Advanced Spice & Trading
  Carrollton, TX 800-872-7811
Agumm
  Coral Springs, FL 954-344-0607
Alfred L. Wolff, Inc.
  Park Ridge, IL 847-759-8888
Alta Health Products
  Idaho City, ID 800-423-4155
Alternative Health & Herbs
  Albany, OR 800-345-4152
AM Todd Co
  Kalamazoo, MI 269-343-2603
Amazing Herbs Nutraceuticals
  Buford, GA 800-241-9138
Ameri-Kal Inc
  Wichita Falls, TX 940-322-5400
American Biosciences
  Blauvelt, NY 888-884-7770
Arise & Shine Herbal Products
  Medford, OR 800-688-2444
Asiamerica Ingredients
  Westwood, NJ 201-497-5531
Auroma International Inc
  Silver Lake, WI 262-889-8569
Bedrock Farm Certified Organic Medicinal Herbs
  Wakefield, RI 888-874-7393
Bionutritional Research Group
  Irvine, CA 714-427-6990
Blessed Herbs
  Oakham, MA 800-489-4372
Bodyonics Limited
  Farmingdale, NY 516-822-1230
Botanical Products
  Springville, CA 559-539-3432

Product Categories / Spices, Seasonings & Seeds: Salt

Brucia Plant Extracts
   Shingle Springs, CA 530-676-2774
Christopher's Herb Shop
   Springville, UT 888-372-4372
CHS Sunprairie
   Minot, ND 800-556-6807
Cinnabar Specialty Foods Inc
   Prescott, AZ 866-293-6433
Country Life
   Hauppauge, NY 800-645-5768
Cyanotech Corp
   Kailua Kona, HI 800-395-1353
Dr. Christopher's Herbal Supplements
   Spanish Fork, UT 800-453-1406
Eclectic Institute
   Sandy, OR 503-668-4120
Emerling International Foods
   Buffalo, NY 716-833-7381
Empire Spice Mills
   Winnipeg, NB 204-786-1594
En Garde Health Products, Inc.
   Van Nuys, CA 800-955-4633
Essential Flavors & Fragrances
   Corona, CA 888-333-9935
Essiac Canada International
   Ottawa, ON 888-900-2299
Fmali Herb
   Santa Cruz, CA 831-423-7913
Freeman Industries
   Tuckahoe, NY 800-666-6454
Functional Products LLC
   Atlantic Beach, FL 904-249-8074
Fungi Perfecti
   Olympia, WA 800-780-9126
Gaia Herbs Inc
   Brevard, NC 888-917-8269
GCI Nutrients
   Foster City, CA 866-580-6549
Ginco International
   Simi Valley, CA. 800-284-2598
Global Botanical
   Barrie, ON 705-733-2117
Global Health Laboratories
   Amityville, NY 631-777-2134
Graminex
   Saginaw, MI 877-472-6469
Green Gold Group LLC
   Marathon, WI 888-533-7288
Green Grown Products Inc
   Marina Del Ray, CA 310-828-1686
Green Turtle Bay Vitamin Company
   Summit, NJ 800-887-8535
H. Reisman Corporation
   Orange, NJ 973-882-1670
Health & Nutrition Systems International
   Boynton Beach, FL 561-433-0733
Health & Wholeness Store
   Fairfield, IA 800-255-8332
Health Plus
   Chino, CA 800-822-6225
Health Products Corp
   Yonkers, NY 914-423-2900
Heart Foods Company
   Minneapolis, MN 800-229-3663
Herbal Magic
   Toronto, ON 877-237-7225
Herbal Products & Development
   Aptos, CA 831-688-8706
Herbalist & Alchemist Inc
   Washington, NJ 908-689-9020
HerbaSway Laboratories
   Wallingford, CT 800-672-7322
HerbCo International
   Duvall, WA 888-643-7226
Himalayan Heritage
   Fredonia, WI 888-414-9500
Honso USA
   Chandler, AZ 888-461-5808
Humco Holding Group Inc
   Texarkana, TX. 903-831-7808
ILHWA American Corporation
   Belleville, NJ 800-446-7364
Indena USA Inc
   Seattle, WA 206-340-0863
Indiana Botanic Gardens Inc
   Hobart, IN 877-909-1502
International Vitamin Corporation
   Freehold, NJ 800-666-8482
Jaguar Yerba Company
   Ashland, OR 800-839-0775
Jarrow Industries Inc
   Santa Fe Springs, CA 562-906-1919

JR Laboratories
   Honesdale, PA. 570-253-5826
Kalustyan
   New York, NY 800-352-3451
Kingchem
   Allendale, NJ. 800-211-4330
LA Lifestyle Nutritional Products
   Santa Ana, CA 800-387-4786
LifeTime
   Orange, CA. 800-333-6168
Mayway Corp
   Oakland, CA. 800-262-9929
Mcfadden Farm
   Potter Valley, CA 800-544-8230
Meridian Trading Co.
   Boulder, CO 303-442-8683
Michael's Naturopathic Prgms
   San Antonio, TX. 800-845-2730
Mincing Overseas Spice Company
   Dayton, NJ 732-355-9944
Motherland International Inc
   Rancho Cucamonga, CA 800-590-5407
Naturalife Laboratories
   Torrance, CA. 800-231-3670
Nature Most Laboratories
   Middletown, CT 800-234-2112
Nature's Bounty Co.
   Ronkonkoma, NY 877-774-3361
Nature's Herbs
   Merritt, BC 800-437-2257
North West Pharmanaturals Inc
   Brea, CA. 714-529-0980
Northridge Laboratories
   Chatsworth, CA 818-882-5622
Pendery's
   Dallas, TX. 800-533-1870
Phyto-Technologies
   Woodbine, IA 877-809-3404
Prince of Peace
   Hayward, CA. 800-732-2328
Pro Form Labs
   Orinda, CA 707-752-9010
Pro Pac Labs
   Ogden, UT. 888-277-6722
Progenix Corporation
   Wausau, WI. 800-233-3356
Rainbow Light Nutritional Systems
   Santa Cruz, CA 800-635-1233
Restaurant Lulu Gourmet Products
   San Francisco, CA 888-693-5800
SADKHIN Complex
   Brooklyn, NY 800-723-5446
Sandbar Trading Corp
   Louisville, CO. 303-499-7480
Schiff Food Products Co Inc
   Totowa, NJ 973-237-1990
Shaker Museum
   New Gloucester, ME. 888-624-6345
Soft Cell Technology
   Commerce, CA. 800-360-7484
Starwest Botanicals Inc
   Sacramento, CA 800-800-4372
Sundial Herb Garden
   Higganum, CT. 860-345-4290
Swagger Foods Corp
   Vernon Hills, IL 847-913-1200
Test Laboratories Inc
   Reseda, CA 818-881-4251
Tova Industries LLC
   Louisville, KY 888-532-8682
Turtle Island Herbs
   Boulder, CO 800-684-4060
Tusitala
   Grand Bay, AL 251-865-4353
Twin Oaks Community
   Louisa, VA 540-894-5141
Uptime Energy, Inc.
   Canoga Park, CA
Urban Moonshine
   Burlington, VT 802-428-4707
Utzy, Inc.
   Lake Geneva, WI 877-307-6142
Verdure Sciences
   Noblesville, IN 888-656-4364
Virgin Raw Foods LLC
   Los Angeles, CA. 800-830-7047
Vit-Best Nutrition
   Tustin, CA. 714-832-9700
Vitality Works
   Albuquerque, NM 505-268-9950
Vitamer Laboratories
   Irvine, CA 800-432-8355

Vitarich Laboratories
   Naples, FL. 800-817-9999
Whole Herb Co
   Sonoma, CA 707-935-1077
World Ginseng Ctr Inc
   San Francisco, CA 800-747-8808
World Organics Corporation
   Huntington Beach, CA 714-893-0017
Yerba Prima
   Ashland, OR 800-488-4339

for Beef

Sentry Seasonings
   Elmhurst, IL 630-530-5370

for Pork

Sentry Seasonings
   Elmhurst, IL 630-530-5370

for Poultry

Sentry Seasonings
   Elmhurst, IL 630-530-5370

for Seafood

Hsu's Ginseng Enterprises Inc
   Wausau, WI. 800-826-1577
Sentry Seasonings
   Elmhurst, IL 630-530-5370

Salt

Adluh Flour
   Columbia, SC 800-692-3584
Agri-Dairy Products
   Purchase, NY 914-697-9580
Ajinomoto Heartland Inc
   Chicago, IL 773-380-7000
Amphora International
   Lake Forest, CA 888-380-4808
Bespoke Provisions
   Boulder, CO 646-963-1245
Bluechip Group
   Salt Lake City, UT 800-878-0099
Cabo Rojo Enterprises
   Boqueron, PR 787-254-0015
Chef Salt
   Center Valley, PA 215-782-1730
Con Yeager Spice Co
   Zelienople, PA. 800-222-2460
Dr. Paul Lohmann Inc.
   Islandia, NY 631-851-8810
Earth Circle Organics
   Auburn, CA. 877-922-3663
Foods Alive
   Angola, IN. 260-488-4497
Franco's Cocktail Mixes
   Pompano Beach, FL 800-782-4508
Frontier Co-op
   Norway, IA 844-550-6200
Gustus Vitae Condiments LLC
   Pasadena, CA 424-229-2367
Heinz Portion Control
   Jacksonville, FL 904-695-1300
HimalaSalt
   Sheffield, MA 413-528-5141
Himalayan Chef
   Sheffield, MA 413-528-5141
ICL Performance Products
   St. Louis, MO 800-244-6169
Java-Gourmet/Keuka Lake Coffee Roaster
   Penn Yan, NY 888-478-2739
Jungbunzlauer Inc
   Newton, MA 617-969-0900
K+S Windsor Salt Ltd.
   Pointe Claire, QC 514-630-0900
Lawry's Foods
   Hunt Valley, MD 800-952-9797
Morton Salt Inc.
   Chicago, IL 800-725-8847
Nutricepts
   Burnsville, MN 800-949-9060
Peg's Salt
   Greenwood, VA. 434-249-2495
Rapunzel Pure Organics
   Bloomfield, NJ 800-225-1449
S A L T Sisters
   Goshen, IN 574-971-8368
Salty Wahine Gourmet Hawaiian Sea Salt
   Hanapepe, HI 808-378-4089
Seattle Seasonings
   Port Orchard, WA 360-871-1511

Product Categories / Spices, Seasonings & Seeds: Seasonings

Smith & Truslow
  Denver, CO 303-339-6967
Stickney & Poor Company
  Peterborough, NH 603-924-2259
Sunfood
  El Cajon, CA 888-729-3663
Sustainable Sourcing
  Great Barrington, MA 413-528-5141
Sutter Buttes Olive Oil
  Sutter, CA 530-763-7921
Swagger Foods Corp
  Vernon Hills, IL 847-913-1200
The Chili Lab
  Brooklyn, NY
Twang Partners LTD
  San Antonio, TX 800-950-8095
United Salt Corp
  Houston, TX 800-554-8658
WBM International
  Flemington, NJ 866-802-9366

Active
Dr. Paul Lohmann Inc.
  Islandia, NY 631-851-8810
Particle Dynamics
  Saint Louis, MO 800-452-4682

Celery
American Key Food Products Inc
  Closter, NJ 877-263-7539
Gel Spice Co LLC
  Bayonne, NJ 800-922-0230

Garlic
American Key Food Products Inc
  Closter, NJ 877-263-7539
Bolner's Fiesta Spices
  San Antonio, TX
Gel Spice Co LLC
  Bayonne, NJ 800-922-0230

MSG & Salt Mixture
ACH Food Co Inc
  Oakbrook Terrace, IL 630-586-3740
American Food Ingredients Inc
  Oceanside, CA 760-967-6287
Compass Minerals
  Overland Park, KS 913-344-9200
De Souza's
  Banning, CA 800-373-5171
Dr. Paul Lohmann Inc.
  Islandia, NY 631-851-8810

Onion
American Key Food Products Inc
  Closter, NJ 877-263-7539
Gel Spice Co LLC
  Bayonne, NJ 800-922-0230

Rock
Frontier Co-op
  Norway, IA 844-550-6200
Morton Salt Inc.
  Chicago, IL 800-725-8847

Sea
Blue Crab Bay
  Melfa, VA 800-221-2722
Blue Marble Brands
  Providence, RI 888-534-0246
Celtic Sea Salt
  Arden, NC 800-867-7258
Evolution Salt Co.
  Austin, TX 877-868-7979
Jacobsen's Salt Co.
  Portland, OR 503-719-4973
Redmond Minerals Inc
  Heber City, UT 866-312-7258
Riega
  Kansas City, MO 816-744-8260
Sea Salt Superstore
  Lynnwood, WA 866-999-7258
Selina Naturally
  Arden, NC 800-867-7258
Smith & Truslow
  Denver, CO 303-339-6967
Spice Lab
  Pompano Beach, FL 954-275-4478

Sutter Buttes Olive Oil
  Sutter, CA 530-763-7921

Substitutes
Ajinomoto Heartland Inc
  Chicago, IL 773-380-7000
Mermaid Spice Corporation
  Fort Myers, FL 239-693-1986
Morre-Tec Ind Inc
  Union, NJ 908-686-0307
Spice Hunter Inc
  Richmond, VA 800-444-3061

Tablets
Dr. Paul Lohmann Inc.
  Islandia, NY 631-851-8810

Enriched
Dr. Paul Lohmann Inc.
  Islandia, NY 631-851-8810

Seasonings
A.C. Legg
  Calera, AL 800-422-5344
Adluh Flour
  Columbia, SC 800-692-3584
Advanced Food Systems
  Somerset, NJ 800-787-3067
All American Seasonings
  Denver, CO 303-623-2320
All Seasonings Ingredients Inc
  Oneida, NY 800-255-7748
Alpine Touch Spices
  Choteau, MT 877-755-2525
AM Todd Co
  Kalamazoo, MI 269-343-2603
American Food Ingredients Inc
  Oceanside, CA 760-967-6287
American Key Food Products Inc
  Closter, NJ 877-263-7539
Andy's Seasoning
  St Louis, MO 800-305-3004
Arizona Natural Products
  Phoenix, AZ 800-255-2823
Atlantic Seasonings
  Kinston, NC 800-433-5261
Au Printemps Gourmet
  Saint-Jerome, QC 800-438-6676
Autin's Cajun Cookery
  Covington, LA 800-877-7290
Backyard Safari Co
  Covington, GA 770-385-3273
Badia Spices Inc.
  Doral, FL 877-629-8000
Baker's Ribs No 2
  Dallas, TX 214-748-5433
Bakon Yeast
  Scottsdale, AZ 480-595-9370
Barataria Spice Company
  Barataria, LA 800-793-7650
BBQ'n Fools Catering, LLC
  Greenfield, IN 800-671-8652
Bell Flavors & Fragrances
  Northbrook, IL 847-291-8300
Benson's Gourmet Seasonings
  Azusa, CA 800-325-5619
Bettah Buttah, LLC
  Kansas City, KS 800-568-8468
Big Poppa Smokers
  Coachella, CA 877-828-0727
Bittersweet Herb Farm
  Shelburne Falls, MA 800-456-1599
BKW Seasonings
  Knoxville, TN 865-851-8657
Blend Pak Inc
  Bloomfield, KY 502-252-8000
Blendex Co
  Louisville, KY 800-626-6325
Blue Crab Bay
  Melfa, VA 800-221-2722
Bolner's Fiesta Spices
  San Antonio, TX
Boston Spice & Tea Company
  Boston, VA 800-966-4372
C&P Additives
  Boca Raton, FL 877-857-2623
C.F. Sauer Co.
  Richmond, VA 888-723-0052
Cabo Rojo Enterprises
  Boqueron, PR 787-254-0015

Cajun Boy's Louisiana Products
  Church Point, LA 800-880-9575
Cajun Brands
  New Iberia, LA 504-408-2252
Cajun Original Foods Inc
  New Iberia, LA 337-367-1344
California Blending Co
  El Monte, CA 626-448-1918
Caribbean Food Delights Inc
  Tappan, NY 845-398-3000
Catamount Specialties of Vermont
  Plainfield, VT 800-639-2406
Cedar Hill Seasonings
  Edmond, OK 800-342-1986
Char Crust
  Chicago, IL 800-311-9884
Chef Hans' Gourmet Foods
  Monroe, LA 800-890-4267
Chef Merito Inc
  Van Nuys, CA 800-637-4861
Chef Paul Prudhomme's Magic Seasonings Blends
  New Orleans, LA 800-457-2857
Chef Shells Catering & Roadside Cafe
  Downtown Port Huron, MI 810-966-8371
Cherchies
  Malvern, PA 800-644-1980
Chester's International , LLC
  Mountain Brook, AL 800-288-1555
Chimayo To Go / Cibolo Junction
  Albuquerque, NM 800-683-9628
Chr Hansen Inc
  Milwaukee, WI 414-607-5700
Christie's
  Stroughton, MA 781-341-3341
Christopher Ranch LLC
  Gilroy, CA 408-847-1100
Chugwater Chili
  Chugwater, WY 800-972-4454
Colonna Brothers Inc
  North Bergen, NJ 201-864-1115
Colorado Spice Co
  Boulder, CO 800-677-7423
Commercial Creamery Co
  Spokane, WA 509-747-4131
Common Folk Farm
  Naples, ME 207-787-2764
Con Yeager Spice Co
  Zelienople, PA 800-222-2460
Consumers Vinegar & Spice Co
  Chicago, IL 773-376-4100
Continental Seasoning
  Teaneck, NJ 800-631-1564
Creative Seasonings
  Wakefield, MA 617-246-1461
Crest Foods Inc
  Ashton, IL 877-273-7893
Custom Culinary Inc.
  Schaumberg, IL 800-621-8827
Davis & Davis Gourmet Foods
  Allison Park, PA 412-487-7770
Dean Distributors, Inc.
  Burlingame, CA 800-792-0816
Deko International Company
  Earth City, MO 314-298-0910
Demitri's Bloody Mary Seasonings
  Seattle, WA 800-627-9649
Dismat Corporation
  Toledo, OH 419-531-8963
Dona Yiya Foods
  San Sebastian, PR 787-896-4007
Dorothy Dawson Food Products
  Jackson, MI 517-788-9830
Elite Spice Inc
  Jessup, MD 800-232-3531
Enrico's/Ventre Packing
  Syracuse, NY 888-472-8237
Erba Food Products
  Brooklyn, NY 718-272-7700
Everglades Foods
  Sebring, FL 800-689-2221
Everson Spice Co
  Signal Hill, CA 800-421-3753
Excalibur Seasoning
  Pekin, IL 800-444-2169
Fernandez Chili Co
  Alamosa, CO 719-589-6043
First Spice Mixing Co
  Long Island City, NY 800-221-1105
Five Star Food Base Company
  St Paul, MN 800-505-7827
Flavor Dynamics Two
  South Plainfield, NJ 888-271-8424

Product Categories / Spices, Seasonings & Seeds: Seasonings

Flavorbank Company
  Tucson, AZ 800-835-7603
Fmali Herb
  Santa Cruz, CA 831-423-7913
Food Concentrate Corporation
  Oklahoma City, OK 405-840-5633
Food Ingredient Solutions
  Teterboro, NJ 917-449-9558
Foran Spice Inc
  Oak Creek, WI 800-558-6030
Fox Meadow Farm of Vermont
  Rutland, VT 888-754-4204
Fresh Ideas
  Las Vegas, NV 702-701-4272
Fuchs North America
  Hampstead, MD 800-365-3229
Garden of the Gods Gourmet
  Colorado Springs, CO. 877-229-1548
Georgia Spice Company
  Atlanta, GA 800-453-9997
Golden Specialty Foods Inc
  Norwalk, CA 562-802-2537
Good Rub
  Morrisville, NC 919-371-0329
Gravymaster, Inc.
  Canajoharie, NY 800-839-8938
Green Mountain Gringo
  Winston-Salem, NC 888-875-3111
Grouse Hunt Farm Inc
  Tamaqua, PA 570-467-2850
Guapo Spices Company
  Los Angeles, CA. 213-322-8900
Guido's International Foods
  Pasadena, CA 877-994-8436
Gustus Vitae Condiments LLC
  Pasadena, CA 424-229-2367
Halladay's Harvest Barn
  Bellows Falls, VT 802-463-3471
Harris Farms Inc
  Coalinga, CA 800-311-6211
Head Country
  Ponca City, OK 888-762-1227
Health & Wholeness Store
  Fairfield, IA 800-255-8332
Heartline Foods
  Westport, CT 203-222-0381
Heidi's Salsa
  Los Angeles, CA 310-821-0211
Herb Society Of America
  Willoughby, OH 440-256-0514
Himalayan Chef
  Sheffield, MA 413-528-5141
Hollman Foods
  Des Moines, IA 888-926-2879
Homegrown Naturals
  Napa, CA 800-288-1089
Illes Seasonings & Flavors
  Carrollton, TX 800-683-4553
Ingredients Corp Of America
  Memphis, TN 888-242-2669
Integrative Flavors
  Michigan City, IN 800-837-7687
International Spice
  Lakewood, NJ 609-838-1717
Jagulana Herbal Products
  Badger, CA 888-465-3686
JM All Purpose Seasoning
  Lincoln, NE 402-421-8326
K+S Windsor Salt Ltd.
  Pointe Claire, QC 514-630-0900
Kent Precision Foods Group Inc
  Muscatine, IA 800-442-5242
La Flor Spices
  Hauppauge, NY 631-885-9601
Lawry's Foods
  Hunt Valley, MD 800-952-9797
Life Spice & Ingredients LLC
  Chicago, IL 312-274-9992
Louisiana Gourmet Enterprises
  Houma, LA 800-328-5586
Lucile's
  Boulder, CO 800-727-3653
Luhr Jensen & Sons Inc
  Hood River, OR 541-386-3811
Mad Chef Enterprise
  Mentor, OH 800-951-2433
Magic Seasoning Blends
  New Orleans, LA 800-457-2857
Mane Inc.
  Lebanon, OH 513-248-9876
Mansmith's Barbeque
  San Jn Bautista, CA 800-626-7648

Marin Food Specialties
  Byron, CA 925-634-6126
Marion-Kay Spice Co
  Brownstown, IN 800-627-7423
Marnap Industries
  Buffalo, NY 716-897-1220
Massel USA
  Carol Stream, IL 704-573-2299
Mayacamas Fine Foods
  Sonoma, CA 800-826-9621
Mcclancy Seasonings Co
  Fort Mill, SC 800-843-1968
McCormick & Company
  Hunt Valley, MD 410-527-6189
Meat-O-Mat Corp
  Brooklyn, NY 718-965-7250
Mermaid Spice Corporation
  Fort Myers, FL 239-693-1986
Metarom Corporation
  Newport, VT 888-882-5555
Mild Bill's Spices
  Ennis, TX 972-875-2975
Misty's Restaurant & Lounge
  Lincoln, NE 402-466-7222
Modern Products Inc
  Mequon, WI 800-877-8935
Morris J Golombeck Inc
  Brooklyn, NY 718-284-3505
Morton Salt Inc.
  Chicago, IL 800-725-8847
Mrs. McGarrigle's Fine Foods
  Merrickville, ON 877-768-7827
Newly Weds Foods Inc
  Chicago, IL 800-621-7521
Nonna Pia's Gourmet Sauces
  Whistler, BC 888-372-1534
North Coast Farms
  Santa Cruz, CA 831-426-3733
North Coast Processing
  Carlsbad, CA 760-931-6809
Nu Products Co Inc
  South Hackensack, NJ 800-836-7692
Old World Spices Inc
  Overland Park, KS 800-241-0070
One Source
  Concord, MA 800-554-5501
Oregon Flavor Rack
Oregon Spice Co Inc
  Portland, OR 800-565-1599
Organic Gourmet
  Sherman Oaks, CA 800-400-7772
Pacific Foods
  Kent, WA 800-347-9444
Paleo Powder Seasoning
  979-540-9137
Pappy Meat Company
  Fresno, CA 559-291-0218
PAR-Way Tryson Co
  St Clair, MO 636-629-4545
Pearson's Homestyle
  Bowden, AB 877-224-3339
Pelican Bay Ltd.
  Dunedin, FL 800-826-8982
Pemberton's Foods Inc
  Gray, ME 800-255-8401
Pleasoning Gourmet Seasonings
  La Crosse, WI 800-279-1614
Precise Food Ingredients
  Carrollton, TX 972-323-4951
Produits Alimentaire
  Laval, QC 800-361-9326
PS Seasoning & Spices
  Iron Ridge, WI 920-387-2204
R C Fine Foods Inc
  Hillsborough, NJ 800-526-3953
Rector Foods
  Brampton, ON 888-314-7834
Red Lion Spicy Foods Company
  Red Lion, PA 717-309-8303
Restaurant Lulu Gourmet Products
  San Francisco, CA 888-693-5800
Reva Foods
  Saint Petersburg, FL 727-692-1292
REX Pure Foods
  New Orleans, LA 800-344-8314
Rezolex LLC
  Radium Springs, NM 575-527-1730
Riega
  Kansas City, MO 816-744-8260
Robinson's No 1 Ribs
  Oak Park, IL 800-836-6750

Royal Foods & Flavor
  Elk Grove Vlg, IL 847-595-9166
S&B International Corporation
  Torrance, CA 310-257-0177
Salmolux Inc
  Federal Way, WA 253-874-6570
Saratoga Food Specialties
  Bolingbrook, IL 800-451-0407
Schiff Food Products Co Inc
  Totowa, NJ 973-237-1990
Seattle Seasonings
  Port Orchard, WA 360-871-1511
Secret Garden
  Park Rapids, MN 800-950-4409
Sentry Seasonings
  Elmhurst, IL 630-530-5370
Shine Companies
  Spring, TX 281-353-8392
Shirley J Ventures, LLC
  Lindon, UT 801-225-5073
Silver Palate Kitchens
  Cresskill, NJ 201-568-0110
Soteria
  Fairburn, GA 404-768-5161
SOUPerior Bean & Spice Company
  Vancouver, WA 800-878-7687
Southern Culture Foods
  Peachtree Corners, GA
Southern Delight Gourmet Foods
  Bowling Green, KY 866-782-9943
Spice Galleon
  Belgium, WI 877-668-4800
Spice Hunter Inc
  Richmond, VA 800-444-3061
Spice King Corporation
  Beverly Hills, CA 310-836-7770
Spicely
  Fremont, CA 510-440-1044
Spicetec Flavors & Seasonings
  Omaha, NE 800-921-7502
Spike Seasoning Magic
  Mequon, WI 262-242-2400
St Charles Trading Inc
  Batavia, IL 630-377-0608
Superior Quality Foods
  Ontario, CA 800-300-4210
Swagger Foods Corp
  Vernon Hills, IL 847-913-1200
T Hasegawa USA Inc
  Cerritos, CA 714-522-1900
Tampico Spice Co
  Los Angeles, CA 323-235-3154
Taste Maker Foods
  Memphis, TN 800-467-1407
Texas Coffee Co
  Beaumont, TX 800-259-3400
Texas Crumb & Food Products
  Farmers Branch, TX 800-522-7862
Texas Traditions Gourmet
  Georgetown, TX 800-547-7062
Todd's
  Des Moines, IA 800-247-5363
Tommy Tang's Thai Seasonings
  Los Angeles, CA 818-442-0219
Tony Chachere's Creole Foods
  Opelousas, LA 800-551-9066
Trader Vic's Food Products
  Emeryville, CA 877-762-4824
Tropical Foods
  Charlotte, NC 800-438-4470
Tropical Link Canada Ltd.
  Burnaby, BC 778-379-3510
UFL Foods
  Mississauga, ON 905-670-7776
Unilever Food Solutions
  Englewood Cliffs, NJ
United Foods USA
  Hayward, CA 510-264-5850
US Ingredients
  Naperville, IL 630-820-1711
Vanns Spices LTD
  Gwynn Oak, MD 800-583-1693
Victoria Gourmet Inc
  Woburn, MA 800-403-8981
Wagner Gourmet Foods
  Lenexa, KS 913-469-5411
West Pac
  Idaho Falls, ID 800-973-7407
Whole Herb Co
  Sonoma, CA 707-935-1077
WILD Flavors (Canada)
  Mississauga, ON 800-263-5286

Product Categories / Spices, Seasonings & Seeds: Seasonings

Wildly Delicious
   Toronto, ON 888-545-9995
William E. Martin & Sons Company
   Roslyn, NY 516-605-2444
Wixon Inc.
   St. Francis, WI 800-841-5304
Woody's Bar-B-Q Sauce Company
   Waldenburg, AR 888-747-9229
World Flavors Inc
   Warminster, PA 215-672-4400
World Harbors
   Auburn, ME 800-355-6221
Young Winfield
   Hamilton, ON 905-893-2536

Baking
Hodgson Mill Inc
   Effingham, IL 800-347-0198
Sentry Seasonings
   Elmhurst, IL 630-530-5370
World Spice
   Roselle, NJ 800-234-1060

Barbecue
Applecreek Speciality Foods
   Lexington, KY 800-747-8871
Bolner's Fiesta Spices
   San Antonio, TX
Captain Foods, Inc.
   Edgewater, FL 800-749-5047
Frontier Co-op
   Norway, IA 844-550-6200
Mansmith's Barbeque
   San Jn Bautista, CA 800-626-7648
Red Monkey Foods
   Springfield, MO 417-319-7300
Rufus Teague
   Shawnee, KS 913-706-3814
Sentry Seasonings
   Elmhurst, IL 630-530-5370

Blackening
Sentry Seasonings
   Elmhurst, IL 630-530-5370

Cajun Style
A Cajun Life®, LLC
   Damascus, OR
Bolner's Fiesta Spices
   San Antonio, TX
Cajun Creole Products Inc
   New Iberia, LA 800-946-8688
Frontier Co-op
   Norway, IA 844-550-6200
Louisiana Fish Fry Products
   Baton Rouge, LA 800-356-2905
Red Monkey Foods
   Springfield, MO 417-319-7300
Reggie Balls Cajun Foods
   Lake Charles, LA 337-436-0291
Sentry Seasonings
   Elmhurst, IL 630-530-5370
Slap Ya Mama Cajun Seasoning
   Ville Platte, LA 800-485-5217

Cheese
Sentry Seasonings
   Elmhurst, IL 630-530-5370

Chinese Style
Sentry Seasonings
   Elmhurst, IL 630-530-5370
Smith & Truslow
   Denver, CO 303-339-6967

Curd
Sentry Seasonings
   Elmhurst, IL 630-530-5370

Dairy Products
Sentry Seasonings
   Elmhurst, IL 630-530-5370

Fajita
Bolner's Fiesta Spices
   San Antonio, TX
Sentry Seasonings
   Elmhurst, IL 630-530-5370

Fried Rice
Sentry Seasonings
   Elmhurst, IL 630-530-5370

Greek Style
Sentry Seasonings
   Elmhurst, IL 630-530-5370
Smith & Truslow
   Denver, CO 303-339-6967

Italian Herbs
Sentry Seasonings
   Elmhurst, IL 630-530-5370
Smith & Truslow
   Denver, CO 303-339-6967

Italian Style
Schiff Food Products Co Inc
   Totowa, NJ 973-237-1990
Sentry Seasonings
   Elmhurst, IL 630-530-5370

Lemon & Basil
Sentry Seasonings
   Elmhurst, IL 630-530-5370

Lemon & Dill
Sentry Seasonings
   Elmhurst, IL 630-530-5370

Lemon Pepper
Red Monkey Foods
   Springfield, MO 417-319-7300
Sentry Seasonings
   Elmhurst, IL 630-530-5370

Meat Products
A.C. Legg
   Calera, AL 800-422-5344
All American Seasonings
   Denver, CO 303-623-2320
Charissa
   Cutchogue, NY 631-734-8878
JM All Purpose Seasoning
   Lincoln, NE 402-421-8326
Nueces Canyon Range
   Brenham, TX 800-925-5058
Ralph's Packing Co
   Perkins, OK 800-522-3979
Rector Foods
   Brampton, ON 888-314-7834
Robinson's No 1 Ribs
   Oak Park, IL 800-836-6750
Sentry Seasonings
   Elmhurst, IL 630-530-5370
Wixon Inc.
   St. Francis, WI 800-841-5304
World Flavors Inc
   Warminster, PA 215-672-4400

Mexican Style
Bea & B Foods
   San Diego, CA 858-490-6205
Bolner's Fiesta Spices
   San Antonio, TX
Golden Specialty Foods Inc
   Norwalk, CA 562-802-2537
Red Monkey Foods
   Springfield, MO 417-319-7300
Schiff Food Products Co Inc
   Totowa, NJ 973-237-1990
Sentry Seasonings
   Elmhurst, IL 630-530-5370

Pizza
California Blending Co
   El Monte, CA 626-448-1918
Dorothy Dawson Food Products
   Jackson, MI 517-788-9830
Sentry Seasonings
   Elmhurst, IL 630-530-5370

Rib Rub
Bolner's Fiesta Spices
   San Antonio, TX
Reva Foods
   Saint Petersburg, FL 727-692-1292

Rufus Teague
   Shawnee, KS 913-706-3814
Sentry Seasonings
   Elmhurst, IL 630-530-5370
Swagger Foods Corp
   Vernon Hills, IL 847-913-1200
Uncle Dougie's
   Chicago, IL

Sausage
Sentry Seasonings
   Elmhurst, IL 630-530-5370

Andouille
Sentry Seasonings
   Elmhurst, IL 630-530-5370

Hot Italian
Sentry Seasonings
   Elmhurst, IL 630-530-5370

Kielbasa
Sentry Seasonings
   Elmhurst, IL 630-530-5370

Sweet Italian
Sentry Seasonings
   Elmhurst, IL 630-530-5370

Snack

Butter
Sentry Seasonings
   Elmhurst, IL 630-530-5370

Cajun Spice
Sentry Seasonings
   Elmhurst, IL 630-530-5370

Cheddar
Sentry Seasonings
   Elmhurst, IL 630-530-5370

Cinnamon Toast
Bolner's Fiesta Spices
   San Antonio, TX
Sentry Seasonings
   Elmhurst, IL 630-530-5370

Mesquite BBQ
Middleswarth Potato Chips
   Kingston, PA 570-288-2447
Mrs Fisher's Potato Chips
   Rockford, IL 815-964-9114
Sentry Seasonings
   Elmhurst, IL 630-530-5370

Nacho Cheese
Sentry Seasonings
   Elmhurst, IL 630-530-5370

Ranch
Sentry Seasonings
   Elmhurst, IL 630-530-5370

Sour Cream & Onion
Middleswarth Potato Chips
   Kingston, PA 570-288-2447
Mrs Fisher's Potato Chips
   Rockford, IL 815-964-9114
Sentry Seasonings
   Elmhurst, IL 630-530-5370

Southwest
Sentry Seasonings
   Elmhurst, IL 630-530-5370

Tomato Pesto
Sentry Seasonings
   Elmhurst, IL 630-530-5370

for Corned Beef
Sentry Seasonings
   Elmhurst, IL 630-530-5370

Product Categories / Spices, Seasonings & Seeds: Seeds

for Tacos

Badia Spices Inc.
  Doral, FL 877-629-8000
Bolner's Fiesta Spices
  San Antonio, TX
Riega
  Kansas City, MO 816-744-8260
Sentry Seasonings
  Elmhurst, IL 630-530-5370

Seeds

American Mercantile Corp
  Memphis, TN 901-454-1900
Ann's House of Nuts, Inc.
  Columbia, MD 410-309-6887
Brock Seed Company
  Finley, TN 731-286-2430
Buddy Squirrel LLC
  St Francis, WI 800-972-2658
CHS Sunflower
  Grandin, ND 701-484-5313
Cibo Vita
  Totowa, NJ 862-238-8020
Con Yeager Spice Co
  Zelienople, PA 800-222-2460
Corteva Agriscience
  Wilmington, DE 302-485-3000
Dipasa USA Inc
  Brownsville, TX 956-831-4072
DuPont Pioneer
  Johnston, IA 515-535-5954
Eden Foods Inc
  Clinton, MI 888-424-3336
Edison Grainery
  Benicia, CA 510-382-0202
El Brands
  Ozark, AL 334-445-2828
Everspring Farms
  Seaforth, ON 519-527-0990
Farmer Direct Organic
  Regina, SK 306-563-7815
Fernando C Pujals & Bros
  Guaynabo, PR 787-792-3080
Foods Alive
  Angola, IN 260-488-4497
Fresh Hemp Foods
  Winnipeg, NB 800-665-4367
Frito-Lay Inc.
  Plano, TX 800-352-4477
Giusto's Specialty Foods Inc
  S San Francisco, CA 650-873-6566
Go Raw
  San Jose, CA 408-272-4722
GoldFoods
  Miami, FL 305-924-4825
Gourmet Nut
  Brooklyn, NY 347-413-5180
Govadinas Fitness Foods
  San Diego, CA 800-900-0108
Gurley's Foods
  Willmar, MN 800-426-7845
H B Taylor Co
  Chicago, IL 773-254-4805
HempNut
  Henderson, NV 707-576-7050
Hialeah Products Co
  Hollywood, FL 800-923-3379
High Mowing Organic Seeds
  Wolcott, VT 866-735-4454
HP Schmid
  San Francisco, CA 415-765-5925
International Harvest Inc
  Mt Vernon, NY 800-277-4268
Kalustyan
  New York, NY 800-352-3451
King Arthur Flour
  Norwich, VT 800-827-6836
Krispy Kernels
  Quebec, QC 877-791-9986
Mezza
  Lake Forest, IL 888-206-6054
Midwest Nut Co
  Minneapolis, MN 800-328-5502
Mincing Overseas Spice Company
  Dayton, NJ 732-355-9944
Minn-Dak Growers LTD
  Grand Forks, ND 701-746-7453
Monsanto Co
  West Fargo, ND 800-437-4120
Natural Foods Inc
  Toledo, OH 419-537-1711
Nature's Candy
  Fredericksburg, TX 800-729-0085
Nature's Select Inc
  Grand Rapids, MI 888-715-4321
New Century Snacks
  City of Commerce, CA 800-688-6887
New Nissi Corp.
  Paterson, NJ 973-278-4400
Nu-World Amaranth Inc
  Naperville, IL 630-369-6851
Nutiva
  Richmond, CA 800-993-4367
One Degree Organic Foods
  Abbotsford, BC 855-834-2642
Osage Pecan Co
  Butler, MO 800-748-8305
Patsy's Candy
  Colorado Springs, CO 866-372-8797
Plantation Products Inc
  Norton, MA 508-285-5800
R&J Farms
  West Salem, OH 419-846-3179
Red River Commodities Inc
  Fargo, ND 800-437-5539
Schiff Food Products Co Inc
  Totowa, NJ 973-237-1990
Scott-Bathgate
  Winnipeg, MB 800-216-2990
Seeds of Change
  Rancho Dominguez, CA 888-762-7333
Smirk's
  Fort Morgan, CO 970-762-0202
Snackerz
  Commerce, CA 888-576-2253
Sole Grano LLC
  Fair Lawn, NJ 201-797-7100
Sonne
  Wahpeton, ND 800-727-6663
Specialty Commodities Inc
  Fargo, ND 701-282-8222
Spitz USA
  Loveland, CO 970-613-9319
Sunray Food Products Corporation
  Bronx, NY 718-548-2255
Sunridge Farms
  Royal Oaks, CA 831-786-7000
Sunshine Farm & Garden
  Renick, WV 304-497-2208
Tantos Foods International
  Markham, ON 905-943-9993
Tasty Seeds Ltd
  Winkler, NB 888-632-6906
Texas Coffee Co
  Beaumont, TX 800-259-3400
Thanasi Foods LLC
  Boulder, CO 866-558-7379
To Your Health Sprouted Flour Co., Inc.
  Floyd, VA 540-283-9589
Todd's
  Vernon, CA 800-938-6337
Torn & Glasser
  Los Angeles, CA 800-282-6887
Trophy Nut Co
  Tipp City, OH 800-219-9004
Tropical Foods
  Charlotte, NC 800-438-4470
Tropical Foods
  Lithia Springs, GA 800-544-3762
Tropical Nut & Fruit Co
  Orlando, FL 800-749-8869
TruVibe Organics
  Santa Monica, CA
Urban Foods LLC
  Sacramento, CA 916-372-3663
Weaver Nut Co. Inc.
  Ephrata, PA 800-473-2688
Westin Foods
  Omaha, NE 800-228-6098
Whole Herb Co
  Sonoma, CA 707-935-1077
Willmar Cookie & Nut Company
  Willmar, MN 800-426-7845
Zenobia Co
  Bronx, NY 866-936-6242

Alfalfa

Corteva Agriscience
  Wilmington, DE 302-485-3000
DuPont Pioneer
  Johnston, IA 515-535-5954
NOW Foods
  Bloomingdale, IL 888-669-3663

Anise or Aniseed

Chesapeake Spice Company
  Belcamp, MD 410-272-6100
Commodities Marketing Inc
  Clarksburg, NJ 732-516-0700
Morris J Golombeck Inc
  Brooklyn, NY 718-284-3505
Smith & Truslow
  Denver, CO 303-339-6967

Annatto

Gel Spice Co LLC
  Bayonne, NJ 800-922-0230
Morris J Golombeck Inc
  Brooklyn, NY 718-284-3505
Organic Planet
  San Francisco, CA 415-765-5590
Schiff Food Products Co Inc
  Totowa, NJ 973-237-1990

Caraway

Bedemco Inc
  White Plains, NY 914-683-1119
Bob's Red Mill Natural Foods
  Milwaukie, OR 800-349-2173
Chesapeake Spice Company
  Belcamp, MD 410-272-6100
Frontier Co-op
  Norway, IA 844-550-6200
Organic Planet
  San Francisco, CA 415-765-5590
Smith & Truslow
  Denver, CO 303-339-6967

Cardamom

Advanced Spice & Trading
  Carrollton, TX 800-872-7811
American Key Food Products Inc
  Closter, NJ 877-263-7539
Con Yeager Spice Co
  Zelienople, PA 800-222-2460
Consumers Vinegar & Spice Co
  Chicago, IL 773-376-4100
Frontier Co-op
  Norway, IA 844-550-6200
Organic Planet
  San Francisco, CA 415-765-5590
Schiff Food Products Co Inc
  Totowa, NJ 973-237-1990
Smith & Truslow
  Denver, CO 303-339-6967

Celery

Advanced Spice & Trading
  Carrollton, TX 800-872-7811
American Key Food Products Inc
  Closter, NJ 877-263-7539
Con Yeager Spice Co
  Zelienople, PA 800-222-2460
Schiff Food Products Co Inc
  Totowa, NJ 973-237-1990
Smith & Truslow
  Denver, CO 303-339-6967
Unique Ingredients LLC
  Gold Canyon, AZ 480-983-2498
Whole Herb Co
  Sonoma, CA 707-935-1077

Ground

Chesapeake Spice Company
  Belcamp, MD 410-272-6100

Coriander

Smith & Truslow
  Denver, CO 303-339-6967

Whole

Smith & Truslow
  Denver, CO 303-339-6967

Cumin

Con Yeager Spice Co
  Zelienople, PA 800-222-2460
Consumers Vinegar & Spice Co
  Chicago, IL 773-376-4100
Smith & Truslow
  Denver, CO 303-339-6967

Product Categories / Spices, Seasonings & Seeds: Seeds

Ground
Bolner's Fiesta Spices
  San Antonio, TX
Smith & Truslow
  Denver, CO 303-339-6967

Dill
Advanced Spice & Trading
  Carrollton, TX 800-872-7811
Con Yeager Spice Co
  Zelienople, PA 800-222-2460
Organic Planet
  San Francisco, CA 415-765-5590
Schiff Food Products Co Inc
  Totowa, NJ 973-237-1990
Smith & Truslow
  Denver, CO 303-339-6967
Vegetable Juices Inc
  Chicago, IL 888-776-9752

Fennel
Acatris USA
  Edina, MN 952-920-7700
Advanced Spice & Trading
  Carrollton, TX 800-872-7811
American Key Food Products Inc
  Closter, NJ 877-263-7539
Commodities Marketing Inc
  Clarksburg, NJ 732-516-0700
Con Yeager Spice Co
  Zelienople, PA 800-222-2460
Organic Planet
  San Francisco, CA 415-765-5590
Schiff Food Products Co Inc
  Totowa, NJ 973-237-1990
Smith & Truslow
  Denver, CO 303-339-6967

Ground
Smith & Truslow
  Denver, CO 303-339-6967

Fenugreek
Acatris USA
  Edina, MN 952-920-7700
Smith & Truslow
  Denver, CO 303-339-6967

Flax
Bedemco Inc
  White Plains, NY 914-683-1119
Bob's Red Mill Natural Foods
  Milwaukie, OR 800-349-2173
Dixie USA
  Tomball, TX 800-233-3668
Foods Alive
  Angola, IN 260-488-4497
Gel Spice Co LLC
  Bayonne, NJ 800-922-0230
Gourmet Nut
  Brooklyn, NY 347-413-5180
Hialeah Products Co
  Hollywood, FL 800-923-3379
King Arthur Flour
  Norwich, VT 800-827-6836
Minn-Dak Growers LTD
  Grand Forks, ND 701-746-7453
Montana Specialty Mills LLC
  Great Falls, MT 800-332-2024
Natural Way Mills Inc
  Middle River, MN 218-222-3677
New Organics
  Kenwood, CA 734-677-5570
Organic Planet
  San Francisco, CA 415-765-5590
Pizzey's Milling & Baking Company
  Twin Falls, ID 208-733-7555
Premium Gold Flax Products & Processing
  Denhoff, ND 866-570-1234
Red River Commodities Inc
  Fargo, ND 800-437-5539

Mustard
American Key Food Products Inc
  Closter, NJ 877-263-7539
Commodities Marketing Inc
  Clarksburg, NJ 732-516-0700
Con Yeager Spice Co
  Zelienople, PA 800-222-2460

New Organics
  Kenwood, CA 734-677-5570
Phamous Phloyd's Barbecue
  Denver, CO 800-497-3281

Ground Yellow
Smith & Truslow
  Denver, CO 303-339-6967

Whole Brown
Smith & Truslow
  Denver, CO 303-339-6967

Whole Yellow
Smith & Truslow
  Denver, CO 303-339-6967

Peanut
Adkin & Son Associated Food Products
  South Haven, MI 269-637-7450

Poppy
Advanced Spice & Trading
  Carrollton, TX 800-872-7811
American Key Food Products Inc
  Closter, NJ 877-263-7539
Bedemco Inc
  White Plains, NY 914-683-1119
Bob's Red Mill Natural Foods
  Milwaukie, OR 800-349-2173
Con Yeager Spice Co
  Zelienople, PA 800-222-2460
Frontier Co-op
  Norway, IA 844-550-6200
HP Schmid
  San Francisco, CA 415-765-5925
New Organics
  Kenwood, CA 734-677-5570
Organic Planet
  San Francisco, CA 415-765-5590
Patisserie Wawel
  Montreal, QC 614-524-3348
Red Monkey Foods
  Springfield, MO 417-319-7300
Schiff Food Products Co Inc
  Totowa, NJ 973-237-1990
Smith & Truslow
  Denver, CO 303-339-6967
Texas Coffee Co
  Beaumont, TX 800-259-3400

Pumpkin
Advanced Spice & Trading
  Carrollton, TX 800-872-7811
American Key Food Products Inc
  Closter, NJ 877-263-7539
Bedemco Inc
  White Plains, NY 914-683-1119
Bob's Red Mill Natural Foods
  Milwaukie, OR 800-349-2173
Cache Creek Foods LLC
  Woodland, CA 530-662-1764
Durey-Libby Edible Nuts
  Carlstadt, NJ 800-332-6887
Emerling International Foods
  Buffalo, NY 716-833-7381
Hialeah Products Co
  Hollywood, FL 800-923-3379
Kathie's Kitchen
  North Haven, CT 203-407-0546
Midwest Nut Co
  Minneapolis, MN 800-328-5502
New Organics
  Kenwood, CA 734-677-5570
NOW Foods
  Bloomingdale, IL 888-669-3663
Organic Planet
  San Francisco, CA 415-765-5590
Sunfood
  El Cajon, CA 888-729-3663
Sunray Food Products Corporation
  Bronx, NY 718-548-2255
Sunridge Farms
  Royal Oaks, CA 831-786-7000
Superseedz
  North Haven, CT 203-407-0546

Rape
American Key Food Products Inc
  Closter, NJ 877-263-7539
New Organics
  Kenwood, CA 734-677-5570

Rice
Bob's Red Mill Natural Foods
  Milwaukie, OR 800-349-2173

Sesame
American Key Food Products Inc
  Closter, NJ 877-263-7539
Bedemco Inc
  White Plains, NY 914-683-1119
Chesapeake Spice Company
  Belcamp, MD 410-272-6100
New Organics
  Kenwood, CA 734-677-5570
NOW Foods
  Bloomingdale, IL 888-669-3663
Organic Planet
  San Francisco, CA 415-765-5590
Red Monkey Foods
  Springfield, MO 417-319-7300
Setton International Foods
  Commack, NY 800-227-4397
Spice & Spice
  Rolling Hills Estates, CA 866-729-7742

Black
Foods Alive
  Angola, IN 260-488-4497

White
Bob's Red Mill Natural Foods
  Milwaukie, OR 800-349-2173
Spice & Spice
  Rolling Hills Estates, CA 866-729-7742

Spice
Advanced Spice & Trading
  Carrollton, TX 800-872-7811
American Key Food Products Inc
  Closter, NJ 877-263-7539
Fantis Foods Inc
  Carlstadt, NJ 201-933-6200
Stan-Mark Food Products Inc
  Chicago, IL 800-651-0994

Sunflower
Advanced Sunflower
  Huron, SD 605-554-1301
American Importing Co.
  Minneapolis, MN 855-273-0466
American Key Food Products Inc
  Closter, NJ 877-263-7539
Bedemco Inc
  White Plains, NY 914-683-1119
Cache Creek Foods LLC
  Woodland, CA 530-662-1764
CHS Sunflower
  Grandin, ND 701-484-5313
Commodities Marketing Inc
  Clarksburg, NJ 732-516-0700
Corteva Agriscience
  Wilmington, DE 302-485-3000
DuPont Pioneer
  Johnston, IA 515-535-5954
Durey-Libby Edible Nuts
  Carlstadt, NJ 800-332-6887
Eden Foods Inc
  Clinton, MI 888-424-3336
Fastachi
  Watertown, MA 800-466-3022
Heartland Mills Shipping
  Marienthal, KS 800-232-8533
Hialeah Products Co
  Hollywood, FL 800-923-3379
HP Schmid
  San Francisco, CA 415-765-5925
Inn Maid Food
  Lenox, MA 413-637-2732
Marantha Natural Foods
  San Francisco, CA 866-972-6879
Midwest Nut Co
  Minneapolis, MN 800-328-5502
Minn-Dak Growers LTD
  Grand Forks, ND 701-746-7453

Product Categories / Spices, Seasonings & Seeds: Spices

New Organics
  Kenwood, CA 734-677-5570
NOW Foods
  Bloomingdale, IL 888-669-3663
Organic Planet
  San Francisco, CA 415-765-5590
R&J Farms
  West Salem, OH 419-846-3179
Red River Commodities Inc
  Fargo, ND 800-437-5539
Scott-Bathgate
  Winnipeg, MB 800-216-2990
Setton International Foods
  Commack, NY 800-227-4397
Sonne
  Wahpeton, ND 800-727-6663
Sunray Food Products Corporation
  Bronx, NY 718-548-2255
Sunridge Farms
  Royal Oaks, CA 831-786-7000
Westin Foods
  Omaha, NE 800-228-6098

Vegetable

Abbott & Cobb Inc
  Feasterville, PA 800-345-7333
Corteva Agriscience
  Wilmington, DE 302-485-3000
Harris Moran Seed Co
  Modesto, CA 209-579-7333
Plantation Products Inc
  Norton, MA 508-285-5800
Seeds of Change
  Rancho Dominguez, CA 888-762-7333
Seminis Vegetable Seeds Inc
  Oxnard, CA 805-485-7317

Spices

A.C. Legg
  Calera, AL 800-422-5344
Abunda Life
  Asbury Park, NJ 732-775-9338
Adventure Foods
  Whittier, NC 828-497-4113
All American Seasonings
  Denver, CO 303-623-2320
AM Todd Co
  Kalamazoo, MI 269-343-2603
American Food Ingredients Inc
  Oceanside, CA 760-967-6287
American Key Food Products Inc
  Closter, NJ 877-263-7539
American Mercantile Corp
  Memphis, TN 901-454-1900
American Natural & Organic
  Fremont, CA 510-440-1044
Arizona Natural Products
  Phoenix, AZ 800-255-2823
Au Printemps Gourmet
  Saint-Jerome, QC 800-438-6676
Badia Spices Inc.
  Doral, FL 877-629-8000
Barataria Spice Company
  Barataria, LA 800-793-7650
Bell Flavors & Fragrances
  Northbrook, IL 847-291-8300
Bi Nutraceuticals
  Long Beach, CA 310-669-2100
Big B Barbecue
  Evansville, IN 812-425-5235
Bijol & Spices Inc
  Miami, FL 888-245-6570
Boston Spice & Tea Company
  Boston, VA 800-966-4372
Boyd's Coffee Co
  Portland, OR 800-735-2878
Bueno Foods
  Albuquerque, NM 800-888-7336
C.F. Sauer Co.
  Richmond, VA 888-723-0052
California Blending Co
  El Monte, CA 626-448-1918
Castella Imports Inc
  Brentwood, NY 631-231-5500
Century Blends Company
  Hunt Valley, MD 410-771-6606
Chef Hans' Gourmet Foods
  Monroe, LA 800-890-4267
Chef Merito Inc
  Van Nuys, CA 800-637-4861

Chef Paul Prudhomme's Magic Seasonings Blends
  New Orleans, LA 800-457-2857
Chef Zachary's Gourmet Blended Spices
  Detroit, MI 313-226-0000
Chesapeake Spice Company
  Belcamp, MD 410-272-6100
Chic Naturals
  Lahaina, HI 808-463-7878
Chimayo To Go / Cibolo Junction
  Albuquerque, NM 800-683-9628
Choice Food Distributors LLC
  Nashville, TN 615-350-6070
Christopher Ranch LLC
  Gilroy, CA 408-847-1100
Christopher's Herb Shop
  Springville, UT 888-372-4372
Chugwater Chili
  Chugwater, WY 800-972-4454
Colonna Brothers Inc
  North Bergen, NJ 201-864-1115
Colorado Spice Co
  Boulder, CO 800-677-7423
Commodities Marketing Inc
  Clarksburg, NJ 732-516-0700
Con Yeager Spice Co
  Zelienople, PA 800-222-2460
Consolidated Mills Inc
  Houston, TX 713-896-4196
Consumers Vinegar & Spice Co
  Chicago, IL 773-376-4100
Continental Seasoning
  Teaneck, NJ 800-631-1564
Creole Delicacies Gourmet Shop
  New Orleans, LA 504-525-9508
Cyclone Enterprises Inc
  Houston, TX 281-872-0087
D Steengrafe Co Inc
  Pleasant Valley, NY 845-635-4067
Davidson's Organics
  Reno, NV 800-882-5888
Delicae Gourmet
  Tarpon Springs, FL 800-942-2502
Desert Pepper Trading Co
  El Paso, TX 888-472-5727
Dona Yiya Foods
  San Sebastian, PR 787-896-4007
Drusilla Seafood
  Baton Rouge, LA 800-364-8844
Ecom Manufacturing Corporation
  Markham, ON 905-477-2441
Elite Spice Inc
  Jessup, MD 800-232-3531
Emerling International Foods
  Buffalo, NY 716-833-7381
Empire Spice Mills
  Winnipeg, NB 204-786-1594
Enrico's/Ventre Packing
  Syracuse, NY 888-472-8237
Erba Food Products
  Brooklyn, NY 718-272-7700
Excalibur Seasoning
  Pekin, IL 800-444-2169
Excellentia Intl.
  Fairfield, NJ 737-749-9840
Farmtrue
  North Stonington, CT 860-495-2231
Feature Foods
  Brampton, ON 905-452-7741
Fernandez Chili Co
  Alamosa, CO 719-589-6043
Flavorbank Company
  Tucson, AZ 800-835-7603
Fmali Herb
  Santa Cruz, CA 831-423-7913
Food Ingredient Solutions
  Teterboro, NJ 917-449-9558
Fool Proof Gourmet Products
  Grapevine, TX 817-329-1839
Foran Spice Inc
  Oak Creek, WI 800-558-6030
Fox Meadow Farm of Vermont
  Rutland, VT 888-754-4204
Freed, Teller & Freed
  South San Francisco, CA 800-370-7371
Frontier Co-op
  Norway, IA 844-550-6200
Ful-Flav-R Foods
  Alamo, CA 925-838-0300
GB Ratto International Grocery
  Oakland, CA 800-325-3483
George Chiala Farms Inc
  Morgan Hill, CA 408-778-0562

Georgia Spice Company
  Atlanta, GA 800-453-9997
Giusto's Specialty Foods Inc
  S San Francisco, CA 650-873-6566
Global Botanical
  Barrie, ON 705-733-2117
Gourmantra Foods
  Markham, ON 416-225-6711
Great Lakes Tea & Spice
  Glen Arbor, MI 877-645-9363
Great Spice Company
  Reno, NV 800-730-3575
Green Mountain Gringo
  Winston-Salem, NC 888-875-3111
Griffith Foods Inc.
  Alsip, IL 708-371-0900
GS Dunn & Company
  Hamilton, ON 905-522-0833
Guapo Spices Company
  Los Angeles, CA 213-322-8900
Gustus Vitae Condiments LLC
  Pasadena, CA 424-229-2367
Hamersmith, Inc.
  Miami, FL 305-685-7451
Harbor Spice
  Forest Hill, MD 410-893-9500
Harris Farms Inc
  Coalinga, CA 800-311-6211
HealthBest
  San Marcos, CA 760-752-5230
Henry Broch & Co
  Gurnee, IL 847-816-6225
Herb Society Of America
  Willoughby, OH 440-256-0514
Hollman Foods
  Des Moines, IA 888-926-2879
Homegrown Naturals
  Napa, CA 800-288-1089
Ingretec
  Lebanon, PA 717-273-0711
Instant Products of America
  Columbus, IN 812-372-9100
International Spice
  Lakewood, NJ 609-838-1717
Italian Rose Garlic Products
  Riviera Beach, FL 800-338-8899
Iya Foods LLC
  North Aurora, IL 630-854-7107
Jagulana Herbal Products
  Badger, CA 888-465-3686
Jiaherb
  Pine Brook, NJ 888-542-4372
Just Cook Foods
  San Francisco, CA 415-269-2705
K+S Windsor Salt Ltd.
  Pointe Claire, QC 514-630-0900
Kalsec
  Kalamazoo, MI 800-323-9320
Kalustyan
  New York, NY 800-352-3451
Kent Precision Foods Group Inc
  Muscatine, IA 800-442-5242
Kevala
  Dallas, TX 877-379-1179
La Flor Spices
  Hauppaugue, NY 631-885-9601
La Flor Spices Company
  Hauppauge, NY 631-851-9601
Lakeside Mills
  Rutherfordton, NC 828-286-4866
Lawry's Foods
  Hunt Valley, MD 800-952-9797
Lebermuth Company
  Mishawaka, IN 800-648-1123
Leeward Resources
  Baltimore, MD 410-837-9003
Li'l Guy Foods
  Kansas City, MO 800-886-8226
Lillie's Q
  Chicago, IL 773-772-5500
Lost Trail Root Beer
  Louisburg, KS 800-748-7765
Lowcountry Produce
  Raleigh, NC 800-935-2792
Magic Seasoning Blends
  New Orleans, LA 800-457-2857
Mansmith's Barbeque
  San Jn Bautista, CA 800-626-7648
Maple Grove Farms Of Vermont
  St Johnsbury, VT 802-748-5141
Marin Food Specialties
  Byron, CA 925-634-6126

Product Categories / Spices, Seasonings & Seeds: Spices

Marion-Kay Spice Co
  Brownstown, IN 800-627-7423
Marnap Industries
  Buffalo, NY 716-897-1220
Mcclancy Seasonings Co
  Fort Mill, SC 800-843-1968
McCormick & Company
  Hunt Valley, MD 410-527-6189
Mermaid Spice Corporation
  Fort Myers, FL 239-693-1986
Mezza
  Lake Forest, IL 888-206-6054
Mild Bill's Spices
  Ennis, TX 972-875-2975
Milton A. Klein Company
  New York, NY 800-221-0248
Mincing Overseas Spice Company
  Dayton, NJ 732-355-9944
Modern Products Inc
  Mequon, WI 800-877-8935
Monterrey Products
  San Antonio, TX 210-435-2872
Morris J Golombeck Inc
  Brooklyn, NY 718-284-3505
Morton & Bassett Spices
  Rohnert Park, CA 415-883-8530
Morton Salt Inc.
  Chicago, IL 800-725-8847
Mountain High Organics
  New Milford, CT 860-210-7805
Mountain Rose Herbs
  Pleasant Hill, OR 800-879-3337
Natural Foods Inc
  Toledo, OH 419-537-1711
Nature Quality
  San Martin, CA 408-683-2182
Northwestern Coffee Mills
  Mason, WI 800-243-5283
Oak Grove Smoke House Inc
  Prairieville, LA 225-673-6857
Ocean Cliff Corp
  New Bedford, MA 508-990-7900
Olam Spices
  Fresno, CA 559-447-1390
Old Mansion Inc
  Petersburg, VA 800-476-1877
Old World Spices Inc
  Overland Park, KS 800-241-0070
One Source
  Concord, MA 800-554-5501
Oregon Flavor Rack
Oregon Spice Co Inc
  Portland, OR 800-565-1599
Organic Planet
  San Francisco, CA 415-765-5590
Ottens Flavors
  Philadelphia, PA 800-523-0767
Paca Foods Inc
  Tampa, FL 800-388-7419
Pacific Grain & Foods
  Fresno, CA 559-276-2580
Pacific Spice Co
  Commerce, CA 323-890-0895
Palmieri Food Products
  New Haven, CT 800-845-5447
Pappy Meat Company
  Fresno, CA 559-291-0218
Papy's Foods Inc
  Mchenry, IL 815-385-3313
Particle Dynamics
  Saint Louis, MO 800-452-4682
Pearson's Homestyle
  Bowden, AB 877-224-3339
Pecos Valley Spice Company
  Corrales, NM 505-243-2622
Pelican Bay Ltd.
  Dunedin, FL 800-826-8982
Pemberton's Foods Inc
  Gray, ME 800-255-8401
Pendery's
  Dallas, TX 800-533-1870
Pereg Gourmet Spices
  Flushing, NY 718-261-6767
Pett Spice Products Inc
  Atlanta, GA 404-691-5235
Precise Food Ingredients
  Carrollton, TX 972-323-4951
Precision Blends
  Baldwin Park, CA 800-836-9979
Proacec USA
  Santa Monica, CA 310-996-7770

PS Seasoning & Spices
  Iron Ridge, WI 920-387-2204
Pure Indian
  Princeton Jct., NJ 877-588-4433
R & S Mexican Food
  Glendale, AZ 602-272-2727
R C Fine Foods Inc
  Hillsborough, NJ 800-526-3953
R L Schreiber Inc
  Ft Lauderdale, FL 800-624-8777
Rapazzini Winery
  Gilroy, CA 800-842-6262
Raymond-Hadley Corporation
  Spencer, NY 800-252-5220
Red Lion Spicy Foods Company
  Red Lion, PA 717-309-8303
REX Pure Foods
  New Orleans, LA 800-344-8314
Rufus Teague
  Shawnee, KS 913-706-3814
Sambets Cajun Deli
  Austin, TX 800-472-6238
Sandbar Trading Corp
  Louisville, CO 303-499-7480
Santa Cruz Chili & Spice
  Tumacacori, AZ 520-398-2591
Saratoga Food Specialties
  Bolingbrook, IL 800-451-0407
Schiff Food Products Co Inc
  Totowa, NJ 973-237-1990
Sea Salt Superstore
  Lynnwood, WA 866-999-7258
Season Harvest Foods
  Los Altos, CA 650-968-2273
See Smell Taste
  San Francisco, CA 415-986-4216
Selecto Sausage Co
  Houston, TX 713-926-1626
Sentry Seasonings
  Elmhurst, IL 630-530-5370
Serv-Agen Corporation
  Cherry Hill, NJ 856-663-6966
Shank's Extracts Inc
  Lancaster, PA 800-346-3135
SJH Enterprises
  Middleton, WI 888-745-3845
SOUPerior Bean & Spice Company
  Vancouver, WA 800-878-7687
South Texas Spice Co LTD
  San Antonio, TX 210-436-2280
Spanish Gardens Food Manufacturing
  Kansas City, KS 913-831-4242
Specialty Commodities Inc
  Fargo, ND 701-282-8222
Specialty Food America Inc
  Hopkinsville, KY 888-881-1633
Spice & Spice
  Rolling Hills Estates, CA 866-729-7742
Spice Chain
  Avenel, NJ 732-499-9070
Spice Hunter Inc
  Richmond, VA 800-444-3061
Spice O' Life
  Seattle, WA 206-789-4195
Spiceland
  Chicago, IL 800-352-8671
Spicely
  Fremont, CA 510-440-1044
St Charles Trading Inc
  Batavia, IL 630-377-0608
St John's Botanicals
  Bowie, MD 301-262-5302
Stan-Mark Food Products Inc
  Chicago, IL 800-651-0994
Starwest Botanicals Inc
  Sacramento, CA 800-800-4372
Stickney & Poor Company
  Peterborough, NH 603-924-2259
Sundial Herb Garden
  Higganum, CT 860-345-4290
SupHerb Farms
  Turlock, CA 800-787-4372
Sutter Buttes Olive Oil
  Sutter, CA 530-763-7921
Swagger Foods Corp
  Vernon Hills, IL 847-913-1200
Tampico Spice Co
  Los Angeles, CA 323-235-3154
Taste Maker Foods
  Memphis, TN 800-467-1407
Teeny Tiny Spice Company of Vermont LLC
  Shelburne, VT 802-598-6800

Terra Flavors & Fragrances
  New York, NY 212-244-1181
Texas Coffee Co
  Beaumont, TX 800-259-3400
Texas Traditions Gourmet
  Georgetown, TX 800-547-7062
To Market To Market
  Loveland, CO 970-278-1000
Tommy Tang's Thai Seasonings
  Los Angeles, CA 818-442-0219
Trader Vic's Food Products
  Emeryville, CA 877-762-4824
Trinity Spice
  Midland, TX 800-460-1149
Triple H Food Processors Inc
  Riverside, CA 951-352-5700
Tripper Inc
  Oxnard, CA 805-988-8851
Tropical Foods
  Charlotte, NC 800-438-4470
Tropical Nut & Fruit Co
  Orlando, FL 800-749-8869
Two Guys Spice Company
  Jacksonville, FL 800-874-5656
Uncle Fred's Fine Foods
  Rockport, TX 361-729-8320
Urban Accents
  Chicago, IL 877-872-7742
Us Spice Mill Inc
  Chicago, IL 773-378-6800
Van Eeghen International Inc
  St Laurent, QC 514-332-6455
Van Roy Coffee Co
  Cleveland, OH 877-826-7669
Vanns Spices LTD
  Gwynn Oak, MD 800-583-1693
Vegetable Juices Inc
  Chicago, IL 888-776-9752
Vincent Formusa Company
  Des Plaines, IL 847-813-6040
Wabash Heritage Mfg LLC
  Vincennes, IN 812-886-0147
Wagner Gourmet Foods
  Lenexa, KS 913-469-5411
Weaver Nut Co. Inc.
  Ephrata, PA 800-473-2688
West Pac
  Idaho Falls, ID 800-973-7407
Wheeling Coffee & Spice Co
  Wheeling, WV 800-500-0141
Whole Herb Co
  Sonoma, CA 707-935-1077
Wild West Spices
  Cody, WY 888-587-8887
William Bounds
  Torrance, CA 800-473-0504
William E. Martin & Sons Company
  Roslyn, NY 516-605-2444
Wine Country Chef LLC
  Hidden Valley Lake, CA 707-322-0406
Wisconsin Spice Inc
  Berlin, WI 920-361-3555
Wixon Inc.
  St. Francis, WI 800-841-5304
World Flavors Inc
  Warminster, PA 215-672-4400
World Harbors
  Auburn, ME 800-355-6221
World of Spices
  Stirling, NJ 908-647-1218
World Spice
  Roselle, NJ 800-234-1060
Young Winfield
  Hamilton, ON 905-893-2536

Adobo

Frontier Co-op
  Norway, IA 844-550-6200

Allspice

Chesapeake Spice Company
  Belcamp, MD 410-272-6100
Commodities Marketing Inc
  Clarksburg, NJ 732-516-0700
Ecom Manufacturing Corporation
  Markham, ON 905-477-2441
Emerling International Foods
  Buffalo, NY 716-833-7381
Erba Food Products
  Brooklyn, NY 718-272-7700

Product Categories / Spices, Seasonings & Seeds: Spices

Frontier Co-op
  Norway, IA 844-550-6200
Gel Spice Co LLC
  Bayonne, NJ 800-922-0230
Morris J Golombeck Inc
  Brooklyn, NY 718-284-3505
Old Mansion Inc
  Petersburg, VA 800-476-1877
Organic Planet
  San Francisco, CA 415-765-5590
Red Monkey Foods
  Springfield, MO 417-319-7300
Schiff Food Products Co Inc
  Totowa, NJ 973-237-1990
Smith & Truslow
  Denver, CO 303-339-6967
Texas Coffee Co
  Beaumont, TX 800-259-3400
Tova Industries LLC
  Louisville, KY 888-532-8682
Whole Herb Co
  Sonoma, CA 707-935-1077

Ground

Con Yeager Spice Co
  Zelienople, PA 800-222-2460
Consumers Vinegar & Spice Co
  Chicago, IL 773-376-4100
Schiff Food Products Co Inc
  Totowa, NJ 973-237-1990
Smith & Truslow
  Denver, CO 303-339-6967
Wabash Heritage Mfg LLC
  Vincennes, IN 812-886-0147
Whole Herb Co
  Sonoma, CA 707-935-1077

Whole

Con Yeager Spice Co
  Zelienople, PA 800-222-2460
Whole Herb Co
  Sonoma, CA 707-935-1077

Anise - Star

Ground

Chesapeake Spice Company
  Belcamp, MD 410-272-6100
Frontier Co-op
  Norway, IA 844-550-6200
Smith & Truslow
  Denver, CO 303-339-6967

Whole

Smith & Truslow
  Denver, CO 303-339-6967

Apple Pie Spices

Frontier Co-op
  Norway, IA 844-550-6200
Smith & Truslow
  Denver, CO 303-339-6967

Basil

Advanced Spice & Trading
  Carrollton, TX 800-872-7811
American Key Food Products Inc
  Closter, NJ 877-263-7539
Chesapeake Spice Company
  Belcamp, MD 410-272-6100
Con Yeager Spice Co
  Zelienople, PA 800-222-2460
Emerling International Foods
  Buffalo, NY 716-833-7381
Gel Spice Co LLC
  Bayonne, NJ 800-922-0230
Golden State Herbs
  Thermal, CA 800-730-3575
Lebermuth Company
  Mishawaka, IN 800-648-1123
Morris J Golombeck Inc
  Brooklyn, NY 718-284-3505
Red Monkey Foods
  Springfield, MO 417-319-7300
Schiff Food Products Co Inc
  Totowa, NJ 973-237-1990
Smith & Truslow
  Denver, CO 303-339-6967
Specialty Food America Inc
  Hopkinsville, KY 888-881-1633
Spice Chain
  Avenel, NJ 732-499-9070
SupHerb Farms
  Turlock, CA 800-787-4372
Tova Industries LLC
  Louisville, KY 888-532-8682
Vegetable Juices Inc
  Chicago, IL 888-776-9752
Waterfield Farms
  Amherst, MA 413-549-3558
Whole Herb Co
  Sonoma, CA 707-935-1077

Basil Leaf

Frontier Co-op
  Norway, IA 844-550-6200
Morris J Golombeck Inc
  Brooklyn, NY 718-284-3505
Old Mansion Inc
  Petersburg, VA 800-476-1877
Schiff Food Products Co Inc
  Totowa, NJ 973-237-1990

Bay Leaves

Advanced Spice & Trading
  Carrollton, TX 800-872-7811
American Key Food Products Inc
  Closter, NJ 877-263-7539
Bolner's Fiesta Spices
  San Antonio, TX
Chesapeake Spice Company
  Belcamp, MD 410-272-6100
Con Yeager Spice Co
  Zelienople, PA 800-222-2460
Consumers Vinegar & Spice Co
  Chicago, IL 773-376-4100
Frontier Co-op
  Norway, IA 844-550-6200
Gel Spice Co LLC
  Bayonne, NJ 800-922-0230
Pendery's
  Dallas, TX 800-533-1870
Red Monkey Foods
  Springfield, MO 417-319-7300
Smith & Truslow
  Denver, CO 303-339-6967
Spice Chain
  Avenel, NJ 732-499-9070
Tova Industries LLC
  Louisville, KY 888-532-8682
Vegetable Juices Inc
  Chicago, IL 888-776-9752
Wabash Heritage Mfg LLC
  Vincennes, IN 812-886-0147
Whole Herb Co
  Sonoma, CA 707-935-1077

Ground

Emerling International Foods
  Buffalo, NY 716-833-7381

Black Pepper - Ground

Chesapeake Spice Company
  Belcamp, MD 410-272-6100
Spice & Spice
  Rolling Hills Estates, CA 866-729-7742
Swagger Foods Corp
  Vernon Hills, IL 847-913-1200

Capers

Alimentaire Whyte's Inc
  Laval, QC 866-420-9520
Blue Marble Brands
  Providence, RI 888-534-0246
Castella Imports Inc
  Brentwood, NY 631-231-5500
Emerling International Foods
  Buffalo, NY 716-833-7381
Gl Mezzetta Inc
  American Canyon, CA 800-941-7044
J.M. Smucker Co.
  Orrville, OH 888-550-9555
L & S Packing Co
  Farmingdale, NY 800-286-6487
Orleans Packing Co
  Hyde Park, MA 617-361-6611
Paradise Products Corporation
  Boca Raton, FL 800-826-1235
Proacec USA
  Santa Monica, CA 310-996-7770

Ron Son Foods Inc
  Swedesboro, NJ 856-241-7333
Vegetable Juices Inc
  Chicago, IL 888-776-9752

Cardamom

Fiesta Gourmet of Tejas
  Canyon Lake, TX 800-585-8250
Flavouressence Products
  Mississauga, ON 866-209-7778
Min Tong Herbs
  Oakland, CA 800-562-5777
Old Mansion Inc
  Petersburg, VA 800-476-1877
Sill Farm Market
  Lawrence, MI 269-674-3755
Sunja's Oriental Foods
  Waterbury, VT 802-244-7644

Ground

Chesapeake Spice Company
  Belcamp, MD 410-272-6100
Smith & Truslow
  Denver, CO 303-339-6967
Wabash Heritage Mfg LLC
  Vincennes, IN 812-886-0147

Whole

Smith & Truslow
  Denver, CO 303-339-6967

Carob Powder

American Key Food Products Inc
  Closter, NJ 877-263-7539
Gel Spice Co LLC
  Bayonne, NJ 800-922-0230

Cassia (Cinnamon)

American Key Food Products Inc
  Closter, NJ 877-263-7539
Commodities Marketing Inc
  Clarksburg, NJ 732-516-0700
Smith & Truslow
  Denver, CO 303-339-6967

Cayenne

Chesapeake Spice Company
  Belcamp, MD 410-272-6100
Frontier Co-op
  Norway, IA 844-550-6200
Marion-Kay Spice Co
  Brownstown, IN 800-627-7423
Vegetable Juices Inc
  Chicago, IL 888-776-9752

Cayenne Pepper

American Key Food Products Inc
  Closter, NJ 877-263-7539
Christopher's Herb Shop
  Springville, UT 888-372-4372
Morris J Golombeck Inc
  Brooklyn, NY 718-284-3505
Pepper Creek Farms
  Lawton, OK 800-526-8132
Red Monkey Foods
  Springfield, MO 417-319-7300
Tova Industries LLC
  Louisville, KY 888-532-8682
Wabash Heritage Mfg LLC
  Vincennes, IN 812-886-0147

Ground

Smith & Truslow
  Denver, CO 303-339-6967

Whole

Texas Coffee Co
  Beaumont, TX 800-259-3400

Celery Flakes

Frontier Co-op
  Norway, IA 844-550-6200
Swagger Foods Corp
  Vernon Hills, IL 847-913-1200

Product Categories / Spices, Seasonings & Seeds: Spices

Celery Salt
Frontier Co-op
  Norway, IA 844-550-6200
Old Mansion Inc
  Petersburg, VA 800-476-1877
Red Monkey Foods
  Springfield, MO 417-319-7300

Chervil
American Key Food Products Inc
  Closter, NJ 877-263-7539
Frontier Co-op
  Norway, IA 844-550-6200
Muirhead Canning Co
  The Dalles, OR 541-298-1660
SupHerb Farms
  Turlock, CA 800-787-4372

Chile Pepper
Chesapeake Spice Company
  Belcamp, MD 410-272-6100
Chugwater Chili
  Chugwater, WY 800-972-4454
Frontier Co-op
  Norway, IA 844-550-6200
Pendery's
  Dallas, TX 800-533-1870

Chili Crush
Spice & Spice
  Rolling Hills Estates, CA .. 866-729-7742

Chili Pods
Whole & Dried
Spice & Spice
  Rolling Hills Estates, CA .. 866-729-7742

Chili Powder
Frontier Co-op
  Norway, IA 844-550-6200
Leona's Restaurante
  Chimayo, NM 888-561-5569
Mezza
  Lake Forest, IL 888-206-6054
Red Monkey Foods
  Springfield, MO 417-319-7300
Smith & Truslow
  Denver, CO 303-339-6967
Spice & Spice
  Rolling Hills Estates, CA .. 866-729-7742
The Chili Lab
  Brooklyn, NY

Chinese
Red Monkey Foods
  Springfield, MO 417-319-7300
Smith & Truslow
  Denver, CO 303-339-6967

Chipotle Chile Peppers
Dried
Frontier Co-op
  Norway, IA 844-550-6200

Chives
Advanced Spice & Trading
  Carrollton, TX 800-872-7811
American Key Food Products Inc
  Closter, NJ 877-263-7539
Chesapeake Spice Company
  Belcamp, MD 410-272-6100
Frontier Co-op
  Norway, IA 844-550-6200
Gel Spice Co LLC
  Bayonne, NJ 800-922-0230
Red Monkey Foods
  Springfield, MO 417-319-7300
Schiff Food Products Co Inc
  Totowa, NJ 973-237-1990
Smith & Truslow
  Denver, CO 303-339-6967
SupHerb Farms
  Turlock, CA 800-787-4372

Cinnamon
Advanced Spice & Trading
  Carrollton, TX 800-872-7811
American Key Food Products Inc
  Closter, NJ 877-263-7539
Chesapeake Spice Company
  Belcamp, MD 410-272-6100
Con Yeager Spice Co
  Zelienople, PA 800-222-2460
Emerling International Foods
  Buffalo, NY 716-833-7381
Erba Food Products
  Brooklyn, NY 718-272-7700
Frontier Co-op
  Norway, IA 844-550-6200
Lebermuth Company
  Mishawaka, IN 800-648-1123
Morris J Golombeck Inc
  Brooklyn, NY 718-284-3505
Organic Planet
  San Francisco, CA 415-765-5590
Pendery's
  Dallas, TX 800-533-1870
Red Monkey Foods
  Springfield, MO 417-319-7300
Schiff Food Products Co Inc
  Totowa, NJ 973-237-1990
Spice & Spice
  Rolling Hills Estates, CA .. 866-729-7742
Swagger Foods Corp
  Vernon Hills, IL 847-913-1200
Texas Coffee Co
  Beaumont, TX 800-259-3400
Tova Industries LLC
  Louisville, KY 888-532-8682
Tripper Inc
  Oxnard, CA 805-988-8851

Cassia
Advanced Spice & Trading
  Carrollton, TX 800-872-7811
Morris J Golombeck Inc
  Brooklyn, NY 718-284-3505
Schiff Food Products Co Inc
  Totowa, NJ 973-237-1990
Tova Industries LLC
  Louisville, KY 888-532-8682

Ground
Con Yeager Spice Co
  Zelienople, PA 800-222-2460
Homefree LLC
  Windham, NH 800-552-7172
Jedwards International Inc
  Braintree, MA 781-848-1473
Smith & Truslow
  Denver, CO 303-339-6967
Wabash Heritage Mfg LLC
  Vincennes, IN 812-886-0147

Whole
Red Monkey Foods
  Springfield, MO 417-319-7300
Smith & Truslow
  Denver, CO 303-339-6967
Spice & Spice
  Rolling Hills Estates, CA .. 866-729-7742

Citron
Emerling International Foods
  Buffalo, NY 716-833-7381
Seald Sweet
  Vero Beach, FL 559-636-4400

Cloves
Chesapeake Spice Company
  Belcamp, MD 410-272-6100
Con Yeager Spice Co
  Zelienople, PA 800-222-2460
Emerling International Foods
  Buffalo, NY 716-833-7381
Frontier Co-op
  Norway, IA 844-550-6200
Old Mansion Inc
  Petersburg, VA 800-476-1877
Red Monkey Foods
  Springfield, MO 417-319-7300
Schiff Food Products Co Inc
  Totowa, NJ 973-237-1990
Smith & Truslow
  Denver, CO 303-339-6967
Tova Industries LLC
  Louisville, KY 888-532-8682

Ground
Con Yeager Spice Co
  Zelienople, PA 800-222-2460
Schiff Food Products Co Inc
  Totowa, NJ 973-237-1990
Smith & Truslow
  Denver, CO 303-339-6967
Texas Coffee Co
  Beaumont, TX 800-259-3400
Wabash Heritage Mfg LLC
  Vincennes, IN 812-886-0147

Coriander (Cilantro)
Advanced Spice & Trading
  Carrollton, TX 800-872-7811
Chesapeake Spice Company
  Belcamp, MD 410-272-6100
Con Yeager Spice Co
  Zelienople, PA 800-222-2460
Frontier Co-op
  Norway, IA 844-550-6200
Gel Spice Co LLC
  Bayonne, NJ 800-922-0230
Morris J Golombeck Inc
  Brooklyn, NY 718-284-3505
Red Monkey Foods
  Springfield, MO 417-319-7300
Schiff Food Products Co Inc
  Totowa, NJ 973-237-1990
Smith & Truslow
  Denver, CO 303-339-6967
Spice & Spice
  Rolling Hills Estates, CA .. 866-729-7742
Tova Industries LLC
  Louisville, KY 888-532-8682

Cumin
Advanced Spice & Trading
  Carrollton, TX 800-872-7811
American Key Food Products Inc
  Closter, NJ 877-263-7539
Chesapeake Spice Company
  Belcamp, MD 410-272-6100
Commodities Marketing Inc
  Clarksburg, NJ 732-516-0700
Con Yeager Spice Co
  Zelienople, PA 800-222-2460
Emerling International Foods
  Buffalo, NY 716-833-7381
Famarco Limited
  Virginia Beach, VA 757-460-3573
Frontier Co-op
  Norway, IA 844-550-6200
Gel Spice Co LLC
  Bayonne, NJ 800-922-0230
Red Monkey Foods
  Springfield, MO 417-319-7300
Smith & Truslow
  Denver, CO 303-339-6967
Spice & Spice
  Rolling Hills Estates, CA .. 866-729-7742
Tova Industries LLC
  Louisville, KY 888-532-8682
Wabash Heritage Mfg LLC
  Vincennes, IN 812-886-0147

Curry Powder
Frontier Co-op
  Norway, IA 844-550-6200
Red Monkey Foods
  Springfield, MO 417-319-7300
Smith & Truslow
  Denver, CO 303-339-6967
Texas Coffee Co
  Beaumont, TX 800-259-3400

Dill
Chesapeake Spice Company
  Belcamp, MD 410-272-6100
Con Yeager Spice Co
  Zelienople, PA 800-222-2460
Frontier Co-op
  Norway, IA 844-550-6200
Gel Spice Co LLC
  Bayonne, NJ 800-922-0230

Product Categories / Spices, Seasonings & Seeds: Spices

SupHerb Farms
  Turlock, CA 800-787-4372
Tova Industries LLC
  Louisville, KY 888-532-8682

Dill Weed

Con Yeager Spice Co
  Zelienople, PA. 800-222-2460
Golden State Herbs
  Thermal, CA 800-730-3575
Red Monkey Foods
  Springfield, MO 417-319-7300
Smith & Truslow
  Denver, CO 303-339-6967
SupHerb Farms
  Turlock, CA 800-787-4372

Dried

Island Spice
  Doral, FL. 786-473-3465
Van Drunen Farms
  Momence, IL. 815-472-3100

Extracts

Norac Technologies
  Edmonton, AB 780-414-9595
Synthite USA Inc.
  Oak Park, IL 708-446-1716

Fennel

Chesapeake Spice Company
  Belcamp, MD 410-272-6100
Frontier Co-op
  Norway, IA 844-550-6200
Old Mansion Inc
  Petersburg, VA 800-476-1877
Red Monkey Foods
  Springfield, MO 417-319-7300
Smith & Truslow
  Denver, CO 303-339-6967
SupHerb Farms
  Turlock, CA 800-787-4372
Wabash Heritage Mfg LLC
  Vincennes, IN 812-886-0147

Fenugreek

Advanced Spice & Trading
  Carrollton, TX. 800-872-7811
Chesapeake Spice Company
  Belcamp, MD 410-272-6100
Gel Spice Co LLC
  Bayonne, NJ 800-922-0230

Garam Masala

Frontier Co-op
  Norway, IA 844-550-6200

Garlic

Arizona Natural Products
  Phoenix, AZ 800-255-2823
Badia Spices Inc.
  Doral, FL. 877-629-8000
Beaverton Foods Inc
  Hillsboro, OR. 800-223-8076
Bio-Nutritional Products
  Northvale, NJ 201-784-8200
Bolner's Fiesta Spices
  San Antonio, TX
California Garlic Co
  San Diego, CA 951-506-8883
Christopher Ranch LLC
  Gilroy, CA. 408-847-1100
Christopher's Herb Shop
  Springville, UT 888-372-4372
Con Yeager Spice Co
  Zelienople, PA. 800-222-2460
Derlea Foods
  Pickering, ON 888-430-7777
Ecom Manufacturing Corporation
  Markham, ON 905-477-2441
Freeda Vitamins Inc
  Long Island City, NY 800-777-3737
Frontier Co-op
  Norway, IA 844-550-6200
Ful-Flav-R Foods
  Alamo, CA 925-838-0300
Garlic Co
  Bakersfield, CA 661-393-4212

Garlic Valley Farms Inc
  Glendale, CA 800-424-7990
George Chiala Farms Inc
  Morgan Hill, CA. 408-778-0562
Haliburton International Inc
  Ontario, CA. 877-980-4295
Hamersmith, Inc.
  Miami, FL. 305-685-7451
Harris Farms Inc
  Coalinga, CA 800-311-6211
Kimball Enterprise International
  Hacienda Heights, CA 213-276-8898
L & S Packing Co
  Farmingdale, NY 800-286-6487
Lawry's Foods
  Hunt Valley, MD. 800-952-9797
Lebermuth Company
  Mishawaka, IN 800-648-1123
Marin Food Specialties
  Byron, CA. 925-634-6126
Morris J Golombeck Inc
  Brooklyn, NY 718-284-3505
Nature Quality
  San Martin, CA. 408-683-2182
Nu Naturals Inc
  Eugene, OR. 800-753-4372
Old Mansion Inc
  Petersburg, VA 800-476-1877
Pacific Choice Brands
  Fresno, CA 559-476-3581
Pendery's
  Dallas, TX. 800-533-1870
Rapazzini Winery
  Gilroy, CA. 800-842-6262
Schiff Food Products Co Inc
  Totowa, NJ 973-237-1990
Specialty Food America Inc
  Hopkinsville, KY 888-881-1633
Spice Chain
  Avenel, NJ. 732-499-9070
Spice World Inc
  Orlando, FL
SupHerb Farms
  Turlock, CA 800-787-4372
Swagger Foods Corp
  Vernon Hills, IL 847-913-1200
Texas Coffee Co
  Beaumont, TX. 800-259-3400
Three Springs Farm
  Oaks, OK. 918-868-5450
Tova Industries LLC
  Louisville, KY 888-532-8682
Trout Lake Farm
  Trout Lake, WA. 800-655-6988
Tulkoff's Food Products Inc
  Baltimore, MD 800-638-7343
Vessey & Co Inc
  Holtville, CA. 760-356-0130

Chopped

California Garlic Co
  San Diego, CA 951-506-8883
Ful-Flav-R Foods
  Alamo, CA 925-838-0300
L & S Packing Co
  Farmingdale, NY 800-286-6487
Spice World Inc
  Orlando, FL
Tulkoff's Food Products Inc
  Baltimore, MD 800-638-7343

Granulated

Advanced Spice & Trading
  Carrollton, TX. 800-872-7811
Gel Spice Co LLC
  Bayonne, NJ 800-922-0230
Smith & Truslow
  Denver, CO 303-339-6967
Spice & Spice
  Rolling Hills Estates, CA 866-729-7742
Tova Industries LLC
  Louisville, KY 888-532-8682
Wabash Heritage Mfg LLC
  Vincennes, IN 812-886-0147

Minced

Con Yeager Spice Co
  Zelienople, PA. 800-222-2460
Red Monkey Foods
  Springfield, MO 417-319-7300

Smith & Truslow
  Denver, CO 303-339-6967
Spice World Inc
  Orlando, FL
Wabash Heritage Mfg LLC
  Vincennes, IN 812-886-0147

Powdered

Con Yeager Spice Co
  Zelienople, PA. 800-222-2460
Erba Food Products
  Brooklyn, NY 718-272-7700
Red Monkey Foods
  Springfield, MO 417-319-7300
Smith & Truslow
  Denver, CO 303-339-6967
Texas Coffee Co
  Beaumont, TX. 800-259-3400
Whole Herb Co
  Sonoma, CA 707-935-1077

Garlic Salt

Red Monkey Foods
  Springfield, MO 417-319-7300
Smith & Truslow
  Denver, CO 303-339-6967
Texas Coffee Co
  Beaumont, TX. 800-259-3400

Ginger

Advanced Spice & Trading
  Carrollton, TX. 800-872-7811
American Key Food Products Inc
  Closter, NJ. 877-263-7539
California Garlic Co
  San Diego, CA 951-506-8883
Chesapeake Spice Company
  Belcamp, MD 410-272-6100
Christopher Ranch LLC
  Gilroy, CA. 408-847-1100
Christopher's Herb Shop
  Springville, UT 888-372-4372
Con Yeager Spice Co
  Zelienople, PA. 800-222-2460
D Steengrafe Co Inc
  Pleasant Valley, NY 845-635-4067
Erba Food Products
  Brooklyn, NY 718-272-7700
Frontier Co-op
  Norway, IA 844-550-6200
Gel Spice Co LLC
  Bayonne, NJ 800-922-0230
Hialeah Products Co
  Hollywood, FL 800-923-3379
Morris J Golombeck Inc
  Brooklyn, NY 718-284-3505
Old Mansion Inc
  Petersburg, VA 800-476-1877
Pendery's
  Dallas, TX. 800-533-1870
Red Monkey Foods
  Springfield, MO 417-319-7300
Royal Foods Inc
  Marina, CA 800-551-5284
Specialty Food America Inc
  Hopkinsville, KY 888-881-1633
Spice World Inc
  Orlando, FL
SupHerb Farms
  Turlock, CA 800-787-4372
Texas Coffee Co
  Beaumont, TX. 800-259-3400
Tova Industries LLC
  Louisville, KY 888-532-8682
Wabash Heritage Mfg LLC
  Vincennes, IN 812-886-0147

Crystallized

Frontier Co-op
  Norway, IA 844-550-6200
Hialeah Products Co
  Hollywood, FL 800-923-3379

Ground

Con Yeager Spice Co
  Zelienople, PA. 800-222-2460
Smith & Truslow
  Denver, CO 303-339-6967

Product Categories / Spices, Seasonings & Seeds: Spices

Pieces

Ful-Flav-R Foods
   Alamo, CA 925-838-0300
Spice World Inc
   Orlando, FL

Ginseng

Alternative Health & Herbs
   Albany, OR 800-345-4152
Atkins Ginseng Farms
   Waterford, ON 800-265-0239
Fmali Herb
   Santa Cruz, CA 831-423-7913
Ginco International
   Simi Valley, CA 800-284-2598
Heise Wausau Farms
   Wausau, WI 800-764-1010
ILHWA American Corporation
   Belleville, NJ 800-446-7364
Madys Company
   San Francisco, CA 415-822-2227
Master Mix
   Placentia, CA 714-524-1698
Penn Herb Co
   Philadelphia, PA 800-523-9971
Prince of Peace
   Hayward, CA 800-732-2328
Progenix Corporation
   Wausau, WI 800-233-3356
St John's Botanicals
   Bowie, MD 301-262-5302
Sun Chlorella USA
   Torrance, CA 800-829-2828
Triple Leaf Tea Inc
   S San Francisco, CA 800-552-7448
Yellow Emperor Inc
   Eugene, OR 877-485-6664

Gumbo File (Powdered Sassafras)

Frontier Co-op
   Norway, IA 844-550-6200

Herbes de Provence

Frontier Co-op
   Norway, IA 844-550-6200
King Arthur Flour
   Norwich, VT 800-827-6836
Red Monkey Foods
   Springfield, MO 417-319-7300
Smith & Truslow
   Denver, CO 303-339-6967
SupHerb Farms
   Turlock, CA 800-787-4372

Horseradish

Buedel Food Products
   Bridgeview, IL 708-496-3500
Feature Foods
   Brampton, ON 905-452-7741
Frontier Co-op
   Norway, IA 844-550-6200
Gold Pure Food Products Co. Inc.
   Hempstead, NY 800-422-4681
Heintz & Weber Co
   Buffalo, NY 716-852-7171
Junuis Food Products
   Palatine, IL 847-359-4300
Palmieri Food Products
   New Haven, CT 800-845-5447
Red Pelican Food Products
   Detroit, MI 313-881-4095
Strub Pickles
   Brantford, ON 519-751-1717
Thor-Shackel Horseradish Company
   Eau Claire, WI 800-826-7322
United Pickles
   Bronx, NY 718-933-6060

Jerk Chicken

Bolner's Fiesta Spices
   San Antonio, TX
Frontier Co-op
   Norway, IA 844-550-6200

Juniper Berries

Frontier Co-op
   Norway, IA 844-550-6200

Lavender

Smith & Truslow
   Denver, CO 303-339-6967

Lavender Flowers

Wabash Heritage Mfg LLC
   Vincennes, IN 812-886-0147

Lemon Grass

SupHerb Farms
   Turlock, CA 800-787-4372

Lemon Peel

Frontier Co-op
   Norway, IA 844-550-6200
Smith & Truslow
   Denver, CO 303-339-6967

Liquid

Emerling International Foods
   Buffalo, NY 716-833-7381
Jogue Inc
   Northville, MI 800-531-3888
Sentry Seasonings
   Elmhurst, IL 630-530-5370
Spice World Inc
   Orlando, FL
Vegetable Juices Inc
   Chicago, IL 888-776-9752
World Flavors Inc
   Warminster, PA 215-672-4400

Mace (See also Nutmeg)

Advanced Spice & Trading
   Carrollton, TX 800-872-7811
American Key Food Products Inc
   Closter, NJ 877-263-7539
Chesapeake Spice Company
   Belcamp, MD 410-272-6100
Con Yeager Spice Co
   Zelienople, PA 800-222-2460
Emerling International Foods
   Buffalo, NY 716-833-7381
Frontier Co-op
   Norway, IA 844-550-6200
Gel Spice Co LLC
   Bayonne, NJ 800-922-0230
Old Mansion Inc
   Petersburg, VA 800-476-1877
Specialty Food America Inc
   Hopkinsville, KY 888-881-1633
Tova Industries LLC
   Louisville, KY 888-532-8682

Ground

Con Yeager Spice Co
   Zelienople, PA 800-222-2460

Marjoram

American Key Food Products Inc
   Closter, NJ 877-263-7539
Con Yeager Spice Co
   Zelienople, PA 800-222-2460
Emerling International Foods
   Buffalo, NY 716-833-7381
Frontier Co-op
   Norway, IA 844-550-6200
Gel Spice Co LLC
   Bayonne, NJ 800-922-0230
Golden State Herbs
   Thermal, CA 800-730-3575
Old Mansion Inc
   Petersburg, VA 800-476-1877
Red Monkey Foods
   Springfield, MO 417-319-7300
Smith & Truslow
   Denver, CO 303-339-6967
SupHerb Farms
   Turlock, CA 800-787-4372
Tova Industries LLC
   Louisville, KY 888-532-8682
Wabash Heritage Mfg LLC
   Vincennes, IN 812-886-0147

Mint

Whole Herb Co
   Sonoma, CA 707-935-1077

Mint Leaves

Advanced Spice & Trading
   Carrollton, TX 800-872-7811
Charles H Baldwin & Sons
   West Stockbridge, MA 413-232-7785
Emerling International Foods
   Buffalo, NY 716-833-7381

Spearmint

Gel Spice Co LLC
   Bayonne, NJ 800-922-0230
SupHerb Farms
   Turlock, CA 800-787-4372

Mulling

Aspen Mulling Company Inc.
   San Francisco, CA 866-972-6879

Mustard

Dry - Prepared

American Key Food Products Inc
   Closter, NJ 877-263-7539
Au Printemps Gourmet
   Saint-Jerome, QC 800-438-6676
Baldwin Richardson Foods
   Oakbrook Terrace, IL 866-644-2732
Catamount Specialties of Vermont
   Plainfield, VT 800-639-2406
Frontier Co-op
   Norway, IA 844-550-6200
GS Dunn & Company
   Hamilton, ON 905-522-0833
Herlocher Foods
   State College, PA 800-437-5625
J.N. Bech
   Elk Rapids, MI 800-232-4583
Kozlowski Farms
   Forestville, CA 800-473-2767
Minn-Dak Growers LTD
   Grand Forks, ND 701-746-7453
New Canaan Farms
   Dripping Springs, TX 800-727-5267
Old Mansion Inc
   Petersburg, VA 800-476-1877
Pepper Creek Farms
   Lawton, OK 800-526-8132

Prepared

Walker Foods
   Los Angeles, CA 800-966-5199

Mustard Powder

Red Monkey Foods
   Springfield, MO 417-319-7300
Wabash Heritage Mfg LLC
   Vincennes, IN 812-886-0147

Mustards

Chesapeake Spice Company
   Belcamp, MD 410-272-6100
Con Yeager Spice Co
   Zelienople, PA 800-222-2460

Natural Flavorings

Spice King Corporation
   Beverly Hills, CA 310-836-7770

Nutmeg (See also Mace)

Advanced Spice & Trading
   Carrollton, TX 800-872-7811
American Key Food Products Inc
   Closter, NJ 877-263-7539
Commodities Marketing Inc
   Clarksburg, NJ 732-516-0700
Con Yeager Spice Co
   Zelienople, PA 800-222-2460
Emerling International Foods
   Buffalo, NY 716-833-7381
Frontier Co-op
   Norway, IA 844-550-6200
Gel Spice Co LLC
   Bayonne, NJ 800-922-0230
Red Monkey Foods
   Springfield, MO 417-319-7300
Schiff Food Products Co Inc
   Totowa, NJ 973-237-1990

Product Categories / Spices, Seasonings & Seeds: Spices

Smith & Truslow
  Denver, CO 303-339-6967
Spice & Spice
  Rolling Hills Estates, CA 866-729-7742
Texas Coffee Co
  Beaumont, TX 800-259-3400
Tripper Inc
  Oxnard, CA 805-988-8851

Ground
Con Yeager Spice Co
  Zelienople, PA 800-222-2460

Whole
Con Yeager Spice Co
  Zelienople, PA 800-222-2460

Onion
ACH Food Co Inc
  Oakbrook Terrace, IL 630-586-3740
Con Yeager Spice Co
  Zelienople, PA 800-222-2460
Frontier Co-op
  Norway, IA 844-550-6200
Ful-Flav-R Foods
  Alamo, CA 925-838-0300
Gel Spice Co LLC
  Bayonne, NJ 800-922-0230
Marin Food Specialties
  Byron, CA 925-634-6126
Old Mansion Inc
  Petersburg, VA 800-476-1877
Red Monkey Foods
  Springfield, MO 417-319-7300
Texas Coffee Co
  Beaumont, TX 800-259-3400

Chopped
Con Yeager Spice Co
  Zelienople, PA 800-222-2460
Ful-Flav-R Foods
  Alamo, CA 925-838-0300

Granulated
Con Yeager Spice Co
  Zelienople, PA 800-222-2460
Smith & Truslow
  Denver, CO 303-339-6967
Wabash Heritage Mfg LLC
  Vincennes, IN 812-886-0147

Minced
Con Yeager Spice Co
  Zelienople, PA 800-222-2460
Erba Food Products
  Brooklyn, NY 718-272-7700
Red Monkey Foods
  Springfield, MO 417-319-7300
Smith & Truslow
  Denver, CO 303-339-6967

Onion Salt
Red Monkey Foods
  Springfield, MO 417-319-7300

Oregano
Advanced Spice & Trading
  Carrollton, TX 800-872-7811
Bolner's Fiesta Spices
  San Antonio, TX
Castella Imports Inc
  Brentwood, NY 631-231-5500
Chesapeake Spice Company
  Belcamp, MD 410-272-6100
Con Yeager Spice Co
  Zelienople, PA 800-222-2460
Emerling International Foods
  Buffalo, NY 716-833-7381
Frontier Co-op
  Norway, IA 844-550-6200
Morris J Golombeck Inc
  Brooklyn, NY 718-284-3505
Old Mansion Inc
  Petersburg, VA 800-476-1877
Red Monkey Foods
  Springfield, MO 417-319-7300
Schiff Food Products Co Inc
  Totowa, NJ 973-237-1990

Smith & Truslow
  Denver, CO 303-339-6967
Specialty Food America Inc
  Hopkinsville, KY 888-881-1633
Spice Chain
  Avenel, NJ 732-499-9070
SupHerb Farms
  Turlock, CA 800-787-4372
Texas Coffee Co
  Beaumont, TX 800-259-3400
Trout Lake Farm
  Trout Lake, WA 800-655-6988
Vegetable Juices Inc
  Chicago, IL 888-776-9752
Whole Herb Co
  Sonoma, CA 707-935-1077

Greek
Agrocan
  Ville St Laurent, QC 877-247-6226
Golden State Herbs
  Thermal, CA 800-730-3575

Mexican
Wabash Heritage Mfg LLC
  Vincennes, IN 812-886-0147

Paprika
Advanced Spice & Trading
  Carrollton, TX 800-872-7811
American Key Food Products Inc
  Closter, NJ 877-263-7539
Chesapeake Spice Company
  Belcamp, MD 410-272-6100
Con Yeager Spice Co
  Zelienople, PA 800-222-2460
Emerling International Foods
  Buffalo, NY 716-833-7381
Erba Food Products
  Brooklyn, NY 718-272-7700
Frontier Co-op
  Norway, IA 844-550-6200
Gel Spice Co LLC
  Bayonne, NJ 800-922-0230
Heartline Foods
  Westport, CT 203-222-0381
Morris J Golombeck Inc
  Brooklyn, NY 718-284-3505
Old Mansion Inc
  Petersburg, VA 800-476-1877
Pendery's
  Dallas, TX 800-533-1870
Red Monkey Foods
  Springfield, MO 417-319-7300
Schiff Food Products Co Inc
  Totowa, NJ 973-237-1990
SJH Enterprises
  Middleton, WI 888-745-3845
Smith & Truslow
  Denver, CO 303-339-6967
Spice & Spice
  Rolling Hills Estates, CA 866-729-7742
Spice Chain
  Avenel, NJ 732-499-9070
Swagger Foods Corp
  Vernon Hills, IL 847-913-1200
Wabash Heritage Mfg LLC
  Vincennes, IN 812-886-0147

Parsley
Bifulco Four Seasons
  Pittsgrove, NJ 856-692-0778
Chesapeake Spice Company
  Belcamp, MD 410-272-6100
Frontier Co-op
  Norway, IA 844-550-6200
Golden State Herbs
  Thermal, CA 800-730-3575
Red Monkey Foods
  Springfield, MO 417-319-7300
Smith & Truslow
  Denver, CO 303-339-6967
Specialty Food America Inc
  Hopkinsville, KY 888-881-1633
SupHerb Farms
  Turlock, CA 800-787-4372

Dehydrated
Alfred L. Wolff, Inc.
  Park Ridge, IL 847-759-8888

American Key Food Products Inc
  Closter, NJ 877-263-7539
Emerling International Foods
  Buffalo, NY 716-833-7381
Gel Spice Co LLC
  Bayonne, NJ 800-922-0230
Unique Ingredients LLC
  Gold Canyon, AZ 480-983-2498

Pepper
Advanced Spice & Trading
  Carrollton, TX 800-872-7811
American Key Food Products Inc
  Closter, NJ 877-263-7539
Casablanca Foods LLC
  New York, NY 212-317-1111
Con Yeager Spice Co
  Zelienople, PA 800-222-2460
Eatem Foods Co
  Vineland, NJ 800-683-2836
Lawry's Foods
  Hunt Valley, MD 800-952-9797
Morris J Golombeck Inc
  Brooklyn, NY 718-284-3505
Old Mansion Inc
  Petersburg, VA 800-476-1877
Pepper Mill Imports
  Seaside, CA 800-928-1744
Red Monkey Foods
  Springfield, MO 417-319-7300
Schiff Food Products Co Inc
  Totowa, NJ 973-237-1990
Smith & Truslow
  Denver, CO 303-339-6967
Spice & Spice
  Rolling Hills Estates, CA 866-729-7742
Swagger Foods Corp
  Vernon Hills, IL 847-913-1200
Texas Coffee Co
  Beaumont, TX 800-259-3400
Tripper Inc
  Oxnard, CA 805-988-8851
Walker Foods
  Los Angeles, CA 800-966-5199
Wine Country Chef LLC
  Hidden Valley Lake, CA 707-322-0406

Black - White - Red
ACH Food Co Inc
  Oakbrook Terrace, IL 630-586-3740
Frontier Co-op
  Norway, IA 844-550-6200
Marion-Kay Spice Co
  Brownstown, IN 800-627-7423
Spice & Spice
  Rolling Hills Estates, CA 866-729-7742

White Ground
Chesapeake Spice Company
  Belcamp, MD 410-272-6100
Smith & Truslow
  Denver, CO 303-339-6967

White Whole
Frontier Co-op
  Norway, IA 844-550-6200
Smith & Truslow
  Denver, CO 303-339-6967

Pepper Mash
Emerling International Foods
  Buffalo, NY 716-833-7381
Vegetable Juices Inc
  Chicago, IL 888-776-9752

Peppercorns
Amphora International
  Lake Forest, CA 888-380-4808
Frontier Co-op
  Norway, IA 844-550-6200
Smith & Truslow
  Denver, CO 303-339-6967
Wabash Heritage Mfg LLC
  Vincennes, IN 812-886-0147

Whole
Smith & Truslow
  Denver, CO 303-339-6967

Product Categories / Spices, Seasonings & Seeds: Spices

Peppermint
Smith & Truslow
  Denver, CO 303-339-6967
Trout Lake Farm
  Trout Lake, WA. 800-655-6988

Pickling Spices
Frontier Co-op
  Norway, IA 844-550-6200
Texas Coffee Co
  Beaumont, TX. 800-259-3400

Red Pepper

Crushed
Marion-Kay Spice Co
  Brownstown, IN 800-627-7423
Swagger Foods Corp
  Vernon Hills, IL 847-913-1200

Flaked
Smith & Truslow
  Denver, CO 303-339-6967

Rosemary
Advanced Spice & Trading
  Carrollton, TX. 800-872-7811
American Key Food Products Inc
  Closter, NJ. 877-263-7539
Chesapeake Spice Company
  Belcamp, MD 410-272-6100
Con Yeager Spice Co
  Zelienople, PA. 800-222-2460
Emerling International Foods
  Buffalo, NY. 716-833-7381
Frontier Co-op
  Norway, IA 844-550-6200
Gel Spice Co LLC
  Bayonne, NJ 800-922-0230
Morris J Golombeck Inc
  Brooklyn, NY 718-284-3505
Old Mansion Inc
  Petersburg, VA 800-476-1877
Red Monkey Foods
  Springfield, MO 417-319-7300
RFi Ingredients
  Blauvelt, NY 800-962-7663
Schiff Food Products Co Inc
  Totowa, NJ 973-237-1990
Smith & Truslow
  Denver, CO 303-339-6967
SupHerb Farms
  Turlock, CA 800-787-4372
Universal Preservachem Inc
  Somerset, NJ. 732-568-1266
Wabash Heritage Mfg LLC
  Vincennes, IN 812-886-0147

Cut
RFi Ingredients
  Blauvelt, NY 800-962-7663

Ground
Con Yeager Spice Co
  Zelienople, PA. 800-222-2460
RFi Ingredients
  Blauvelt, NY 800-962-7663
Schiff Food Products Co Inc
  Totowa, NJ 973-237-1990

Saffron
Advanced Spice & Trading
  Carrollton, TX. 800-872-7811
American Key Food Products Inc
  Closter, NJ. 877-263-7539
Chesapeake Spice Company
  Belcamp, MD 410-272-6100
Emerling International Foods
  Buffalo, NY. 716-833-7381
Gel Spice Co LLC
  Bayonne, NJ 800-922-0230
Rumi Spice
  Chicago, IL 213-447-6112
Schiff Food Products Co Inc
  Totowa, NJ 973-237-1990
Shank's Extracts Inc
  Lancaster, PA 800-346-3135

Smith & Truslow
  Denver, CO 303-339-6967
Whole Herb Co
  Sonoma, CA 707-935-1077

Sage
Castella Imports Inc
  Brentwood, NY 631-231-5500
Chesapeake Spice Company
  Belcamp, MD 410-272-6100
Con Yeager Spice Co
  Zelienople, PA. 800-222-2460
Consumers Vinegar & Spice Co
  Chicago, IL 773-376-4100
Frontier Co-op
  Norway, IA 844-550-6200
Old Mansion Inc
  Petersburg, VA 800-476-1877
Red Monkey Foods
  Springfield, MO 417-319-7300
Smith & Truslow
  Denver, CO 303-339-6967
SupHerb Farms
  Turlock, CA 800-787-4372

Leaves
Advanced Spice & Trading
  Carrollton, TX. 800-872-7811
Con Yeager Spice Co
  Zelienople, PA. 800-222-2460
Emerling International Foods
  Buffalo, NY. 716-833-7381
Gel Spice Co LLC
  Bayonne, NJ 800-922-0230
SupHerb Farms
  Turlock, CA 800-787-4372

Rubbed
Con Yeager Spice Co
  Zelienople, PA. 800-222-2460

Savory
All American Foods Inc
  Mankato, MN 800-833-2661
American Key Food Products Inc
  Closter, NJ. 877-263-7539
Flavor House, Inc.
  Adelanto, CA 760-246-9131
Golden State Herbs
  Thermal, CA 800-730-3575
Silver Palate Kitchens
  Cresskill, NJ 201-568-0110
Smith & Truslow
  Denver, CO 303-339-6967
Swagger Foods Corp
  Vernon Hills, IL 847-913-1200
Tastepoint
  Philadelphia, PA 800-363-5286

Shallots
Spice World Inc
  Orlando, FL
SupHerb Farms
  Turlock, CA 800-787-4372

Sorrel
SupHerb Farms
  Turlock, CA 800-787-4372

Spearmint
Golden State Herbs
  Thermal, CA 800-730-3575
SupHerb Farms
  Turlock, CA 800-787-4372
Trout Lake Farm
  Trout Lake, WA. 800-655-6988

Star Anise
Chesapeake Spice Company
  Belcamp, MD 410-272-6100
Frontier Co-op
  Norway, IA 844-550-6200
Smith & Truslow
  Denver, CO 303-339-6967

Tandoori
Frontier Co-op
  Norway, IA 844-550-6200

Tarragon
Advanced Spice & Trading
  Carrollton, TX. 800-872-7811
Chesapeake Spice Company
  Belcamp, MD 410-272-6100
Con Yeager Spice Co
  Zelienople, PA. 800-222-2460
Frontier Co-op
  Norway, IA 844-550-6200
Old Mansion Inc
  Petersburg, VA 800-476-1877
Red Monkey Foods
  Springfield, MO 417-319-7300
Schiff Food Products Co Inc
  Totowa, NJ 973-237-1990
Smith & Truslow
  Denver, CO 303-339-6967
Specialty Food America Inc
  Hopkinsville, KY 888-881-1633
SupHerb Farms
  Turlock, CA 800-787-4372
Wabash Heritage Mfg LLC
  Vincennes, IN 812-886-0147

Tartar

Cream
King Arthur Flour
  Norwich, VT 800-827-6836
Universal Preservachem Inc
  Somerset, NJ. 732-568-1266

Teas
Castella Imports Inc
  Brentwood, NY 631-231-5500
O'Neill Coffee Co
  West Middlesex, PA 724-528-2244

Thyme
Advanced Spice & Trading
  Carrollton, TX. 800-872-7811
American Key Food Products Inc
  Closter, NJ. 877-263-7539
Chesapeake Spice Company
  Belcamp, MD 410-272-6100
Con Yeager Spice Co
  Zelienople, PA. 800-222-2460
Emerling International Foods
  Buffalo, NY. 716-833-7381
Frontier Co-op
  Norway, IA 844-550-6200
Golden State Herbs
  Thermal, CA 800-730-3575
Morris J Golombeck Inc
  Brooklyn, NY 718-284-3505
Old Mansion Inc
  Petersburg, VA 800-476-1877
Red Monkey Foods
  Springfield, MO 417-319-7300
Schiff Food Products Co Inc
  Totowa, NJ 973-237-1990
Smith & Truslow
  Denver, CO 303-339-6967
Specialty Food America Inc
  Hopkinsville, KY 888-881-1633
SupHerb Farms
  Turlock, CA 800-787-4372

Ground
Schiff Food Products Co Inc
  Totowa, NJ 973-237-1990
Wabash Heritage Mfg LLC
  Vincennes, IN 812-886-0147

Turmeric
Agri-Dairy Products
  Purchase, NY 914-697-9580
American Key Food Products Inc
  Closter, NJ. 877-263-7539
Con Yeager Spice Co
  Zelienople, PA. 800-222-2460
Emerling International Foods
  Buffalo, NY. 716-833-7381
Frontier Co-op
  Norway, IA 844-550-6200
Red Monkey Foods
  Springfield, MO 417-319-7300
Schiff Food Products Co Inc
  Totowa, NJ 973-237-1990

Product Categories / Spices, Seasonings & Seeds: Spices

SJH Enterprises
  Middleton, WI....................888-745-3845
Tu Me Beverage Company
  CA..............................818-237-5105
Tumericalive Healing Enterprise
  New York, NY....................347-559-6760
Turveda
  CA

Ground

Natural Earth Products
  Brooklyn, NY....................718-552-2727
Schiff Food Products Co Inc
  Totowa, NJ......................973-237-1990
Smith & Truslow
  Denver, CO......................303-339-6967
Wabash Heritage Mfg LLC
  Vincennes, IN...................812-886-0147

Vanilla

Agri-Dairy Products
  Purchase, NY....................914-697-9580
Nielsen-Massey Vanillas Inc
  Waukegan, IL....................800-525-7873
Texas Coffee Co
  Beaumont, TX....................800-259-3400
Tripper Inc
  Oxnard, CA......................805-988-8851
Wabash Heritage Mfg LLC
  Vincennes, IN...................812-886-0147

Vanilla Beans

Emerling International Foods
  Buffalo, NY.....................716-833-7381
Jedwards International Inc
  Braintree, MA...................781-848-1473

Red Monkey Foods
  Springfield, MO.................417-319-7300
Smith & Truslow
  Denver, CO......................303-339-6967
Zink & Triest Company
  Montgomeryville, PA.............800-537-5070

Wasabi

Great Eastern Sun Trading Co
  Asheville, NC...................800-334-5809

White Pepper
Ground

Smith & Truslow
  Denver, CO......................303-339-6967
Spice & Spice
  Rolling Hills Estates, CA.......866-729-7742

Sugars, Syrups & Sweeteners

General

Bear Stewart Corp
  Chicago, IL 800-697-2327
Century Blends LLC
  Hunt Valley, MD 410-771-6606
Colorado Sweet Gold
  Lakewood, CO 303-384-1101
Crop Pharms, LLC
  Staatsburg, NY 845-266-8999
Crosby Molasses Company
  Saint John, NB 800-561-2206
Deborah's Kitchen Inc.
  Littleton, MA 617-216-9908
Deer Creek Honey Farms LTD
  London, OH 740-852-0899
E.F. Lane & Son
  Oakland, CA 510-569-8980
EFCO Products Inc
  Poughkeepsie, NY 800-284-3326
Evergreen Sweeteners, Inc
  Hollywood, FL 954-381-7776
Hoyt's Honey Farm
  Baytown, TX 281-576-5383
In The Raw
  Brooklyn, NY 800-611-7434
Indiana Sugars
  Lemont, IL 630-986-9150
JK Sucralose
  Edison, NJ 732-512-0889
Kerry Foodservice
  Mansfield, OH 800-533-2722
Kevala
  Dallas, TX 877-379-1179
Maple Products
  Sherbrooke, QC 819-569-5161
Monin Inc.
  Clearwater, FL 855-352-8671
NOW Foods
  Bloomingdale, IL 888-669-3663
Particle Control
  Albertville, MN 763-497-3075
Paulaur Corp
  Cranbury, NJ 609-395-8844
PureCircle USA
  Chicago, IL 630-361-0374
Sugarright
  Fairless Hills, PA 215-486-2105
Swerve Sweetener
  New Orleans, LA 888-979-3783
Tate & Lyle PLC
  Hoffman Estates, IL 847-396-7500
TresOmega
  New Milford, CT 860-210-7805
Tropical Link Canada Ltd.
  Burnaby, BC 778-379-3510
Western New York Syrup Corporation
  Lakeville, NY 585-346-2311
Whitfield Foods Inc
  Montgomery, AL 800-633-8790

Artificial

Heartland Sweeteners
  Carmel, IN 317-566-9750
Merisant
  Chicago, IL 312-840-6000
Niutang Chemical, Inc.
  Chino, CA 909-631-2895
Silver Fern Chemical Inc
  Seattle, WA 866-282-3384
Sweet'N Low
  Brooklyn, NY
Techno USA
  San Gabriel, CA 626-288-8478
Universal Preservachem Inc
  Somerset, NJ 732-568-1266
US Sugar Company
  Clewiston, FL 863-983-8121

Fructose

Agri-Dairy Products
  Purchase, NY 914-697-9050
Cargill Inc.
  Minneapolis, MN 800-227-4455
Evergreen Sweeteners, Inc
  Hollywood, FL 954-381-7776
H. Interdonati
  Cold Spring Harbour, NY 800-367-6617
Hunter Farms - High Point Division
  High Point, NC 800-446-8035
Malt Diastase Co
  Saddle Brook, NJ 800-526-0180
Oxford Frozen Foods
  Oxford, NS 902-447-2100
Scenic Fruit Co
  Gresham, OR 877-927-3434
Sensus America Inc
  Lawrence Twp, NJ 646-452-6140
St. Lawrence Starch
  Mississauga, ON 905-271-8396
True Blue Farms
  Grand Junction, MI 877-654-2400

Crystalline

Farbest-Tallman Foods Corp
  Montvale, NJ 201-573-4900

Honey

Adee Honey Farm
  Bruce, SD 605-627-5621
Alaska Herb & Tea Co
  Anchorage, AK 800-654-2764
Apiterra
  Garland, TX 972-485-1005
Babe's Honey Farm
  Victoria, BC 250-658-8319
Barkman Honey
  Hillsboro, KS 800-364-6623
Bee Harmony Honey
  Hillsboro, KS
Bee Raw Honey
  Brooklyn, NY 888-660-0090
Bella Vista Farm
  Lawton, OK 866-237-8526
Bloom Honey
   877-555-9300
Burleson Honey
  Waxahachie, TX 972-937-2809
Castella Imports Inc
  Brentwood, NY 631-231-5500
Cloister Honey LLC
  Charlotte, NC 704-517-6190
Clover Blossom Honey
  La Fontaine, IN 765-981-4443
Colorado Hemp Honey
  Parker, CO 833-233-2256
Comvita USA
  Santa Barbara, CA 855-449-2201
Country Cupboard
  Lewisburg, PA 570-523-3211
Dundee Groves
  Dundee, FL 800-294-2266
Dutch Gold Honey Inc
  Lancaster, PA 800-338-0587
Ed's Honey Co
  Dickinson, ND 701-225-9223
Eleanor's Best LLC
  Garrison, NY 646-296-6870
Emerling International Foods
  Buffalo, NY 716-833-7381
Fischer Honey Company
  North Little Rock, AR 501-758-1123
Fisher Honey Co
  Lewistown, PA 717-242-4373
GloryBee
  Eugene, OR 800-456-7923
Gold Sweet Company
  Lake Wales, FL 863-676-0963
Govadinas Fitness Foods
  San Diego, CA 800-900-0108
Hanna's Honey
  Salem, OR 503-393-2945
Honey Acres
  Neosho, WI 920-474-4411
Honey Bee Company
  Alpharetta, GA 800-572-8838
Honey Blossom
  The Colony, TX 469-582-7508
Honey Stinger
  Steamboat Sprints, CO 866-464-6639
Hoyt's Honey Farm
  Baytown, TX 281-576-5383
Island of the Moon Apiaries
  Esparto, CA 530-787-3993
John Paton Inc
  Doylestown, PA 215-348-7050
Kevala
  Dallas, TX 877-379-1179
Klein Foods, Inc
  Marshall, MN 800-657-0174
Leighton's Honey Inc
  Haines City, FL 863-422-1773
Life Force Specialty Foods
  Moscow, ID 877-657-9471
Madhava Natural Sweeteners
  Boulder, CO 800-530-2900
Malt Diastase Co
  Saddle Brook, NJ 800-526-0180
Meluka Honey
  Santa Clarita, CA
Merrimack Valley Apiaries
  Billerica, MA 978-667-2337
Mike's Hot Honey
  Brooklyn, NY 347-450-4722
Mixon Fruit Farms Inc
  Bradenton, FL 800-608-2525
Monin Inc.
  Clearwater, FL 855-352-8671
Nature's Hollow
  Charleston, UT
Once Again Nut Butter
  Nunda, NY 888-800-8075
Orchard Pond
  Tallahassee, FL 850-894-0154
Queen of America
  Belleview, FL 352-245-3600
R D Laney Family Honey Co
  North Liberty, IN 574-656-8701
Round Rock Honey Co, LLC
  Round Rock, TX 512-828-5416
Savannah Bee Co.
  Savannah, GA 800-955-5080
Scott Hams
  Greenville, KY 800-318-1353
Shawnee Canning Co
  Cross Junction, VA 800-713-1414
Sioux Honey Assn.
  Sioux City, IA 712-258-0638
Slide Ridge LLC
  Mendon, UT 435-752-4956
Strawberry Hill Grand Delights
  Everett, MA 617-319-3557
Sutter Buttes Olive Oil
  Sutter, CA 530-763-7921
Sutton Honey Farms
  Lancaster, KY 859-792-4277
Suzanne's Specialties
  New Brunswick, NJ 800-762-2135
Sweet Harvest Foods
  Rosemount, MN 507-263-8599
Sweetener Supply Corp
  Brookfield, IL 888-784-2799
Tropical Blossom Honey Co
  Edgewater, FL 386-428-9027
Vintage Bee Inc.
  Durham, NC 919-699-6788
Virgin Raw Foods LLC
  Los Angeles, CA 800-830-7047
Virginia Honey Company
  Inwood, WV 304-267-8500
Vita Food Products Inc
  Chicago, IL 800-989-8482

Bee Pollen & Propolis

Alfred L. Wolff, Inc.
  Park Ridge, IL 847-759-8888
Babe's Honey Farm
  Victoria, BC 250-658-8319
C C Pollen
  Phoenix, AZ 800-875-0096
Green Grown Products Inc
  Marina Del Ray, CA 310-828-1686
Hsu's Ginseng Enterprises Inc
  Wausau, WI 800-826-1577
Island of the Moon Apiaries
  Esparto, CA 530-787-3993

Product Categories / Sugars, Syrups & Sweeteners: Molasses

Lenny's Bee Productions
  Bearsville, NY 845-679-4514
Natural Foods Inc
  Toledo, OH 419-537-1711
Nature Cure Northwest
  Poulsbo, WA 800-957-8048
Nicola Valley Apiaries
  Merritt, BC 250-378-5208
North Peace Apiaries
  Fort St. John, BC. 250-785-4808
Paradis Honey
  Girouxville, AB 780-323-4283
Penauta Products
  Stouffville, ON 905-640-1564
QBI
  South Plainfield, NJ 908-668-0088
Rocky Mountain Honey Company
  Salt Lake City, UT 801-355-2054
Southern Gold Honey Co
  Vidor, TX 808-899-2494
Thistledew Farm
  Proctor, WV 800-854-6639
Z Specialty Food, LLC
  Woodland, CA. 800-678-1226

Bees Wax

Adee Honey Farm
  Bruce, SD 605-627-5621
Babe's Honey Farm
  Victoria, BC 250-658-8319
D Steengrafe Co Inc
  Pleasant Valley, NY 845-635-4067
Paradis Honey
  Girouxville, AB 780-323-4283
Pure Food Ingredients
  Verona, WI 800-355-9601
Rocky Mountain Honey Company
  Salt Lake City, UT 801-355-2054
Silverbow Honey Company
  Moses Lake, WA 866-444-6639
Southern Gold Honey Co
  Vidor, TX 808-899-2494
Thistledew Farm
  Proctor, WV 800-854-6639
Wixson Honey Inc
  Dundee, NY 800-363-8209
Z Specialty Food, LLC
  Woodland, CA 800-678-1226

Butter

Dundee Groves
  Dundee, FL 800-294-2266
Honey Acres
  Neosho, WI 920-474-4411
Honey Butter Products Co
  Manheim, PA 717-665-9323
Kevala
  Dallas, TX 877-379-1179
Kurtz Orchards Farms
  Niagra-on-the-Lake, ON 905-468-2937
Limited Edition
  Midland, TX 432-686-2008
Treasure Foods
  West Valley, UT 801-974-0911

Granules

Natural

Groeb Farms
  Onsted, MI 800-530-9969

Liquid

Champlain Valley Apiaries
  Middlebury, VT. 800-841-7334
Deer Creek Honey Farms LTD
  London, OH 740-852-0899
Dutch Gold Honey Inc
  Lancaster, PA 800-338-0587
E.F. Lane & Son
  Oakland, CA 510-569-8980
Fischer Honey Company
  North Little Rock, AR 501-758-1123
GloryBee
  Eugene, OR 800-456-7923
Groeb Farms
  Onsted, MI 800-530-9969
Honey Acres
  Neosho, WI 920-474-4411
Hoyt's Honey Farm
  Baytown, TX 281-576-5383

In The Raw
  Brooklyn, NY 800-611-7434
Jacobsen's Salt Co.
  Portland, OR. 503-719-4973
Leighton's Honey Inc
  Haines City, FL 863-422-1773
Leona's Restaurante
  Chimayo, NM 888-561-5569
Nature Nate's
  McKinney, TX 469-452-4429
Western New York Syrup Corporation
  Lakeville, NY 585-346-2311

Molasses

Alma Plantation
  Lakeland, LA 225-627-6632
Amalgamated Sugar Company
  Boise, ID 208-383-6500
B & G Foods Inc.
  Parsippany, NJ. 973-401-6500
Baldwin Richardson Foods
  Oakbrook Terrace, IL 866-644-2732
C & H Sugar Co Inc
  Crockett, CA 800-773-1803
C S Steen Syrup Mill Inc
  Abbeville, LA 800-725-1654
Cora Texas Mfg Co Inc
  White Castle, LA 225-545-3679
Crosby Molasses Company
  Saint John, NB 800-561-2206
Deer Creek Honey Farms LTD
  London, OH 740-852-0899
Emerling International Foods
  Buffalo, NY. 716-833-7381
GloryBee
  Eugene, OR. 800-456-7923
Golding Farms Foods
  Winston Salem, NC. 336-766-6161
Lafourche Sugar LLC
  Thibodaux, LA 985-447-3210
Louisiana Sugar Cane Co-Op Inc
  St Martinville, LA. 337-394-3785
Malt Diastase Co
  Saddle Brook, NJ 800-526-0180
Malt Diastase Co
  Garfield, NJ. 800-772-0416
Michigan Desserts
  Oak Park, MI 800-328-8632
Mott's LLP
  Plano, TX 800-426-4891
New Organics
  Kenwood, CA 734-677-5570
Osceola Farms Sugar Warehouse
  Pahokee, FL 561-924-7156
Pacific Westcoast Foods
  Beaverton, OR 800-874-9333
Pure Foods
  Sultan, WA 360-793-2241
Pure Life Organic Foods
  Las Vegas, NV 708-990-5817
Pure Sweet Honey Farms Inc
  Verona, WI 800-355-9601
Raceland Raw Sugar Corporation
  Raceland, LA 985-537-3533
Rio Grande Valley Sugar Growers
  Santa Rosa, TX 956-636-1411
Rogers Sugar Inc.
  Montreal, QC 514-527-8686
Savoie Industries
  Belle Rose, LA 225-473-9293
Scott Hams
  Greenville, KY 800-318-1353
Southern Minnesota Beet Sugar Cooperative
  Renville, MN 320-329-8305
St. James Sugar Cooperative
  Saint James, LA 225-265-4056
Sugar Cane Growers Co-Op of Florida
  Belle Glade, FL. 561-996-5556
Suzanne's Specialties
  New Brunswick, NJ 800-762-2135
Sweetener Supply Corp
  Brookfield, IL 888-784-2799
T.J. Blackburn Syrup Works
  Jefferson, TX. 800-657-5073
Tova Industries LLC
  Louisville, KY 888-532-8682
WCC Honey Marketing
  City Of Industry, CA. 626-855-3086
Westway Trading Corporation
  New Orleans, LA 701-282-5010
Whitfield Foods Inc
  Montgomery, AL. 800-633-8790

Wholesome!
  Sugar Land, TX. 800-680-1896

Natural Sweeteners

Abunda Life
  Asbury Park, NJ 732-775-9338
Adee Honey Farm
  Bruce, SD 605-627-5621
Alfred L. Wolff, Inc.
  Park Ridge, IL. 847-759-8888
Alma Plantation
  Lakeland, LA 225-627-6632
Amalgamated Sugar Company
  Boise, ID 208-383-6500
Artesian Honey Producers
  Artesian, SD 605-527-2423
Babe's Honey Farm
  Victoria, BC 250-658-8319
Barkman Honey
  Hillsboro, KS 800-364-6623
BioVittoria USA
  Libertyville, IL 847-226-3467
Briess Malt & Ingredients Co.
  Chilton, WI 800-657-0806
C S Steen Syrup Mill Inc
  Abbeville, LA 800-725-1654
California Natural Products
  Lathrop, CA 209-858-2525
Cargill Inc.
  Minneapolis, MN 800-227-4455
Champlain Valley Apiaries
  Middlebury, VT 800-841-7334
Cleveland Syrup Corporation
  Cleveland, OH 216-883-1845
Clover Blossom Honey
  La Fontaine, IN 765-981-4443
Cora Texas Mfg Co Inc
  White Castle, LA 225-545-3679
Crockett Honey
  Tempe, AZ 800-291-3969
Crop Pharms, LLC
  Staatsburg, NY 845-266-8999
Dawes Hill Honey Company
  Nunda, NY 888-800-8075
Deer Creek Honey Farms LTD
  London, OH 740-852-0899
Dixie USA
  Tomball, TX 800-233-3668
Domino Specialty Ingredients
  West Palm Beach, FL
Doyon
  800-265-2600
Dutch Gold Honey Inc
  Lancaster, PA 800-338-0587
E.F. Lane & Son
  Oakland, CA 510-569-8980
Eden Foods Inc
  Clinton, MI 888-424-3336
Evergreen Sweeteners, Inc
  Hollywood, FL 954-381-7776
Farbest-Tallman Foods Corp
  Montvale, NJ. 201-573-4900
Fischer Honey Company
  North Little Rock, AR 501-758-1123
Florida Crystals Corporation
  West Palm Beach, FL 844-344-9497
Garuda International
  Exeter, CA. 559-594-4380
Gateway Food Products Co
  Dupo, IL 877-220-1963
Golding Farms Foods
  Winston Salem, NC. 336-766-6161
Grain Processing Corp
  Muscatine, IA 800-448-4472
Great Eastern Sun Trading Co
  Asheville, NC 800-334-5809
Greenwood Associates
  Niles, IL 847-579-5500
Groeb Farms
  Onsted, MI 800-530-9969
H. Interdonati
  Cold Spring Harbour, NY 800-367-6617
Hanna's Honey
  Salem, OR. 503-393-2945
Healthy Food Ingredients
  Fargo, ND 844-275-3443
Heinz Portion Control
  Jacksonville, FL 904-695-1300
Hendricks Apiaries
  Englewood, CO. 303-789-3209
Honey World
  Parker, SD 605-297-4188

Product Categories / Sugars, Syrups & Sweeteners: Sucrose

Hoyt's Honey Farm
  Baytown, TX 281-576-5383
Indiana Sugars
  Lemont, IL 630-986-9150
Ingredion Inc.
  Westchester, IL 800-713-0208
Jiaherb
  Pine Brook, NJ 888-542-4372
Jogue Inc
  Northville, MI 800-531-3888
Kerry Foodservice
  Mansfield, OH 800-533-2722
Kutiks Honey Farm
  Norwich, NY 607-336-4105
Lafourche Sugar LLC
  Thibodaux, LA 985-447-3210
Leighton's Honey Inc
  Haines City, FL 863-422-1773
Leprino Foods Co.
  Denver, CO 800-537-7466
Les Industries Bernard et Fils
  Saint Victor, QC 418-588-3590
Louisiana Sugar Cane Co-Op Inc
  St Martinville, LA 337-394-3785
M.A. Patout & Son LTD
  Jeanerette, LA 337-276-4592
Madhava Natural Sweeteners
  Boulder, CO 800-530-2900
Malt Diastase Co
  Saddle Brook, NJ 800-526-0180
Maple Products
  Sherbrooke, QC 819-569-5161
Michele Foods
  South Holland, IL 708-331-7453
Minn-Dak Farmers Co-Op
  Wahpeton, ND 701-642-8411
Minnestalgia Foods LLC
  Mcgregor, MN 800-328-6731
New Organics
  Kenwood, CA 734-677-5570
Nickabood's Inc
  Los Angeles, CA 213-746-1541
Nicola Valley Apiaries
  Merritt, BC 250-378-5208
North Peace Apiaries
  Fort St. John, BC 250-785-4808
NOW Foods
  Bloomingdale, IL 888-669-3663
Once Again Nut Butter
  Nunda, NY 888-800-8075
Organic Nectars LLC
  Malden On Hudson, NY 845-246-0506
Organic Planet
  San Francisco, CA 415-765-5590
Osceola Farms Sugar Warehouse
  Pahokee, FL 561-924-7156
Ouachita Lumber Co
  West Monroe, LA 318-396-1960
Particle Control
  Albertville, MN 763-497-3075
Paulaur Corp
  Cranbury, NJ 609-395-8844
Pied-Mont/Dora
  Anne Des Plaines, QC 800-363-8003
Pure Food Ingredients
  Verona, WI 800-355-9601
Pure Foods
  Sultan, WA 360-793-2241
Pure Sweet Honey Farms Inc
  Verona, WI 800-355-9601
Pyure Brands
  Naples, FL 305-509-5096
R Weaver Apiaries
  Navasota, TX 936-825-2333
Raceland Raw Sugar Corporation
  Raceland, LA 985-537-3533
Rio Grande Valley Sugar Growers
  Santa Rosa, TX 956-636-1411
Rocky Mountain Honey Company
  Salt Lake City, UT 801-355-2054
Roquette America Inc.
  Geneva, IL 630-463-9430
Sandt's Honey Co
  Easton, PA 800-935-3960
Savoie Industries
  Belle Rose, LA 225-473-9293
Shady Maple Farm
  Mississauga, ON 905-206-1455
Silverbow Honey Company
  Moses Lake, WA 866-444-6639
Sno Shack Inc
  Rexburg, ID 888-766-7425

Southern Minnesota Beet Sugar Cooperative
  Renville, MN 320-329-8305
St. James Sugar Cooperative
  Saint James, LA 225-265-4056
Steviva Ingredients
  Portland, OR 800-851-6314
Stickney & Poor Company
  Peterborough, NH 603-924-2259
Sugar Cane Growers Co-Op of Florida
  Belle Glade, FL 561-996-5556
Sunfood
  El Cajon, CA 888-729-3663
Suzanne's Specialties
  New Brunswick, NJ 800-762-2135
Thistledew Farm
  Proctor, WV 800-854-6639
Unique Ingredients LLC
  Gold Canyon, AZ 480-983-2498
United Canadian Malt
  Peterborough, ON 800-461-6400
Universal Preservachem Inc
  Somerset, NJ 732-568-1266
Valentine Chemicals
  Lockport, LA 985-532-2541
Valley View Blueberries
  Vancouver, WA 360-892-2839
VIP Foods
  Flushing, NY 718-821-5330
WCC Honey Marketing
  City Of Industry, CA 626-855-3086
Western New York Syrup Corporation
  Lakeville, NY 585-346-2311
Westway Trading Corporation
  New Orleans, LA 701-282-5010
Whitfield Foods Inc
  Montgomery, AL 800-633-8790
Wholesome!
  Sugar Land, TX 800-680-1896
Wixson Honey Inc
  Dundee, NY 800-363-8209
Woodworth Honey & Bee Co
  Halliday, ND 701-938-4647
Z Specialty Food, LLC
  Woodland, CA 800-678-1226

Sucrose

Evergreen Sweeteners, Inc
  Hollywood, FL 954-381-7776
NOW Foods
  Bloomingdale, IL 888-669-3663
Rogers Sugar Inc.
  Montreal, QC 514-527-8686
Universal Preservachem Inc
  Somerset, NJ 732-568-1266

Sugar

Adirondack Maple Farms
  Fonda, NY 518-853-4022
Agri-Dairy Products
  Purchase, NY 914-697-9580
Alma Plantation
  Lakeland, LA 225-627-6632
Amalgamated Sugar Company
  Boise, ID 208-383-6500
American Crystal Sugar Co.
  Moorhead, MN 218-236-4400
Bateman Products
  Rigby, ID 208-745-9033
Beneo Inc
  Morris Plains, NJ 973-539-6644
Bonumose LLC
  Charlottesville, VA
C & H Sugar Co Inc
  Crockett, CA 800-773-1803
Cleveland Syrup Corporation
  Cleveland, OH 216-883-1845
Cora Texas Mfg Co Inc
  White Castle, LA 225-545-3679
Domino Specialty Ingredients
  West Palm Beach, FL
ECOM Agroindustrial Corporation Ltd
  Pully,
Erba Food Products
  Brooklyn, NY 718-272-7700
Evergreen Sweeteners, Inc
  Hollywood, FL 954-381-7776
Florida Crystals Corporation
  West Palm Beach, FL 844-344-9497
Franco's Cocktail Mixes
  Pompano Beach, FL 800-782-4508

Global Organics
  Cambridge, MA 781-648-8844
Greenwell Farms Inc
  Kealakekua, HI 888-592-5662
Heinz Portion Control
  Jacksonville, FL 904-695-1300
Honey Ridge Farms
  Brush Prairie, WA 360-256-0086
Imperial Sugar Company
  Sugar Land, TX 800-727-8427
Indiana Sugars
  Lemont, IL 630-986-9150
Jakeman's Maple Products
  Beachville, ON 800-382-9795
Kerry Foodservice
  Mansfield, OH 800-533-2722
Lafourche Sugar LLC
  Thibodaux, LA 985-447-3210
Lantic Sugar
  Montreal, QC 514-527-8686
Louisiana Sugar Cane Co-Op Inc
  St Martinville, LA 337-394-3785
M.A. Patout & Son LTD
  Jeanerette, LA 337-276-4592
Madhava Natural Sweeteners
  Boulder, CO 800-530-2900
Maple Products
  Sherbrooke, QC 819-569-5161
Mapleland Farm
  Salem, NY 518-854-7669
Marubeni America Corp.
  New York, NY 212-450-0100
Michigan Sugar Company
  Bay City, MI 989-686-0161
Minn-Dak Farmers Co-Op
  Wahpeton, ND 701-642-8411
Olam Spices
  Fresno, CA 559-447-1390
Organic Planet
  San Francisco, CA 415-765-5590
Osceola Farms Sugar Warehouse
  Pahokee, FL 561-924-7156
Particle Control
  Albertville, MN 763-497-3075
Paulaur Corp
  Cranbury, NJ 609-395-8844
Penta Manufacturing Company
  Livingston, NJ 973-740-2300
Quaker Sugar Company
  Brooklyn, NY 718-387-6500
Raceland Raw Sugar Corporation
  Raceland, LA 985-537-3533
Rapunzel Pure Organics
  Bloomfield, NJ 800-225-1449
Rice Company
  Fair Oaks, CA 916-784-7745
Rio Grande Valley Sugar Growers
  Santa Rosa, TX 956-636-1411
Rogers Sugar Inc.
  Taber, AB 403-223-3535
Rogers Sugar Inc.
  Montreal, QC 514-527-8686
Rogers Sugar Inc.
  Vancouver, BC 604-253-1131
S A L T Sisters
  Goshen, IN 574-971-8368
Savoie Industries
  Belle Rose, LA 225-473-9293
Shady Maple Farm
  Mississauga, ON 905-206-1455
Southern Minnesota Beet Sugar Cooperative
  Renville, MN 320-329-8305
St. James Sugar Cooperative
  Saint James, LA 225-265-4056
Sugar Foods Corp
  Sun Valley, CA 818-768-7900
Sugarright
  Fairless Hills, PA 215-486-2105
Sweeteners Plus Inc
  Lakeville, NY 585-346-3193
US Sugar Company
  Clewiston, FL 863-983-8121
Valentine Chemicals
  Lockport, LA 985-532-2541
Western Sugar Cooperative
  Denver, CO 800-523-7497
Westin Foods
  Omaha, NE 800-228-6098
William Bounds
  Torrance, CA 800-473-0504

Product Categories / Sugars, Syrups & Sweeteners: Sugar Substitutes

Brown
Agri-Dairy Products
  Purchase, NY 914-697-9580
C & H Sugar Co Inc
  Crockett, CA 800-773-1803
Evergreen Sweeteners, Inc
  Hollywood, FL 954-381-7776
Florida Crystals Corporation
  West Palm Beach, FL 844-344-9497
Sweetener Supply Corp
  Brookfield, IL 888-784-2799
US Sugar Company
  Clewiston, FL 863-983-8121
Westin Foods
  Omaha, NE 800-228-6098

Cane
Agri-Dairy Products
  Purchase, NY 914-697-9580
C & H Sugar Co Inc
  Crockett, CA 800-773-1803
Evergreen Sweeteners, Inc
  Hollywood, FL 954-381-7776
Global Organics
  Cambridge, MA 781-648-8844
Homefree LLC
  Windham, NH 800-552-7172
Just Panela
  Boulder, CO 720-600-0522
M.A. Patout & Son LTD
  Jeanerette, LA 337-276-4592
New Organics
  Kenwood, CA 734-677-5570
Organic Planet
  San Francisco, CA 415-765-5590
Rio Grande Valley Sugar Growers
  Santa Rosa, TX 956-636-1411
Sweetener Supply Corp
  Brookfield, IL 888-784-2799
Wholesome!
  Sugar Land, TX 800-680-1896

Granulated
Amalgamated Sugar Company
  Boise, ID 208-383-6500
Diazteca Inc
  Rio Rico, AZ 520-761-4621
Evergreen Sweeteners, Inc
  Hollywood, FL 954-381-7776
Michigan Sugar Company
  Bay City, MI 989-686-0161
Paulaur Corp
  Cranbury, NJ 609-395-8844
Rogers Sugar Inc.
  Montreal, QC 514-527-8686
Sweetener Supply Corp
  Brookfield, IL 888-784-2799
US Sugar Company
  Clewiston, FL 863-983-8121
Westin Foods
  Omaha, NE 800-228-6098

Icing
BakeMark USA
  Schaumburg, IL 847-519-3135
Domino Specialty Ingredients
  West Palm Beach, FL
Lantic Sugar
  Montreal, QC 514-527-8686
Signature Brands LLC
  Ocala, FL 800-456-9573

Invert
Agri-Dairy Products
  Purchase, NY 914-697-9580
Evergreen Sweeteners, Inc
  Hollywood, FL 954-381-7776
Florida Crystals Corporation
  West Palm Beach, FL 844-344-9497
Malt Diastase Co
  Saddle Brook, NJ 800-526-0180
Paulaur Corp
  Cranbury, NJ 609-395-8844

Liquid
Amalgamated Sugar Company
  Boise, ID 208-383-6500
Evergreen Sweeteners, Inc
  Hollywood, FL 954-381-7776
Flavouressence Products
  Mississauga, ON 866-209-7778
Lantic Sugar
  Montreal, QC 514-527-8686
Paulaur Corp
  Cranbury, NJ 609-395-8844
Wholesome!
  Sugar Land, TX 800-680-1896

Liquid & Granulated
Agri-Dairy Products
  Purchase, NY 914-697-9580
Amalgamated Sugar Company
  Boise, ID 208-383-6500
C & H Sugar Co Inc
  Crockett, CA 800-773-1803
Evergreen Sweeteners, Inc
  Hollywood, FL 954-381-7776
Lantic Sugar
  Montreal, QC 514-527-8686

Maple
Brown Family Farm
  Brattleboro, VT 866-254-8718
Butternut Mountain Farm
  Morrisville, VT 800-828-2376
Citadelle Maple Syrup Producers' Cooperative
  Plessisville, QC 819-362-3241
Emerling International Foods
  Buffalo, NY 716-833-7381
Finding Home Farms
  Middletown, NY 845-355-4335
Food For Thought Inc
  Honor, MI 231-326-5444
GloryBee
  Eugene, OR 800-456-7923
J.M. Smucker Co.
  Orrville, OH 888-550-9555
Maple Hollow
  Merrill, WI 715-536-7251
Maple Products
  Sherbrooke, QC 819-569-5161
Maple Valley Cooperative
  Cashton, WI 608-654-7319
Richards Maple Products
  Chardon, OH 800-352-4052
Shady Maple Farm
  Mississauga, ON 905-206-1455
Vermont Country Naturals
  Charlotte, VT 800-528-7021
Whitfield Foods Inc
  Montgomery, AL 800-633-8790

Butter
Butternut Mountain Farm
  Morrisville, VT 800-828-2376
Choice of Vermont
  Destin, FL 800-444-6261
Whitfield Foods Inc
  Montgomery, AL 800-633-8790

Organic
Florida Crystals Corporation
  West Palm Beach, FL 844-344-9497
In The Raw
  Brooklyn, NY 800-611-7434
NOW Foods
  Bloomingdale, IL 888-669-3663
Sunfood
  El Cajon, CA 888-729-3663
Wholesome!
  Sugar Land, TX 800-680-1896

Powdered
Agri-Dairy Products
  Purchase, NY 914-697-9580
C & H Sugar Co Inc
  Crockett, CA 800-773-1803
Cleveland Syrup Corporation
  Cleveland, OH 216-883-1845
Evergreen Sweeteners, Inc
  Hollywood, FL 954-381-7776
Flavouressence Products
  Mississauga, ON 866-209-7778
Michigan Sugar Company
  Bay City, MI 989-686-0161
US Sugar Company
  Clewiston, FL 863-983-8121
Vermont Country Naturals
  Charlotte, VT 800-528-7021

Westin Foods
  Omaha, NE 800-228-6098

Turbinado
In The Raw
  Brooklyn, NY 800-611-7434

Sugar Substitutes
Abunda Life
  Asbury Park, NJ 732-775-9338
Agri-Dairy Products
  Purchase, NY 914-697-9580
Amcan Industries
  Elmsford, NY 914-347-4838
Fasweet Co
  Jonesboro, AR 888-223-6693
Franco's Cocktail Mixes
  Pompano Beach, FL 800-782-4508
GLG Life Tech Corporation
  Richmond, BC 855-454-7587
GloryBee
  Eugene, OR 800-456-7923
Great Eastern Sun Trading Co
  Asheville, NC 800-334-5809
H. Interdonati
  Cold Spring Harbour, NY 800-367-6617
Health Garden USA
  Spring Valley, NY 845-877-7090
Jungbunzlauer Inc
  Newton, MA 617-969-0900
M. Licht & Son
  Knoxville, TN 865-523-5593
Madhava Natural Sweeteners
  Boulder, CO 800-530-2900
Malt Diastase Co
  Saddle Brook, NJ 800-526-0180
McNeil Nutritionals
  Fort Washington, PA 215-273-7000
McNeil Specialty Products Company
  New Brunswick, NJ 732-524-3799
Minnestalgia Foods LLC
  Mcgregor, MN 800-328-6731
Nickabood's Inc
  Los Angeles, CA 213-746-1541
North Peace Apiaries
  Fort St. John, BC 250-785-4808
NOW Foods
  Bloomingdale, IL 888-669-3663
NuNaturals
  Eugene, OR 800-753-4372
Once Again Nut Butter
  Nunda, NY 888-800-8075
Paulaur Corp
  Cranbury, NJ 609-395-8844
PMC Specialties Group Inc
  Cincinnati, OH 800-543-2466
Rocky Mountain Honey Company
  Salt Lake City, UT 801-355-2054
Roquette America Inc.
  Geneva, IL 630-463-9430
St. Lawrence Starch
  Mississauga, ON 905-271-8396
Steviva Ingredients
  Portland, OR 800-851-6314
Stickney & Poor Company
  Peterborough, NH 603-924-2259
Sugar Foods Corp
  Sun Valley, CA 818-768-7900
Suzanne's Specialties
  New Brunswick, NJ 800-762-2135
Sweet'N Low
  Brooklyn, NY
Sweetleaf Co
  Gilbert, AZ 800-899-9908
Universal Preservachem Inc
  Somerset, NJ 732-568-1266
VIP Foods
  Flushing, NY 718-821-5330
WCC Honey Marketing
  City Of Industry, CA 626-855-3086
Westin Foods
  Omaha, NE 800-228-6098
Wholesome!
  Sugar Land, TX 800-680-1896

Aspartame
Ajinomoto Heartland Inc
  Chicago, IL 773-380-7000
McNeil Nutritionals
  Fort Washington, PA 215-273-7000

Product Categories / Sugars, Syrups & Sweeteners: Syrups

Saccharin

Jungbunzlauer Inc
  Newton, MA 617-969-0900
PMC Specialties Group Inc
  Cincinnati, OH 800-543-2466
Roquette America Inc.
  Geneva, IL 630-463-9430
Sweet'N Low
  Brooklyn, NY

Sugar Alternatives

GLG Life Tech Corporation
  Richmond, BC 855-454-7587
McNeil Nutritionals
  Fort Washington, PA 215-273-7000
Stevita Naturals
  Arlington, TX 800-577-8409

Syrups

A.C. Calderoni
  Brisbane, CA 866-468-1897
A.W. Jantzi & Sons
  Wellesley, ON 519-656-2400
Abunda Life
  Asbury Park, NJ 732-775-9338
Advanced Ingredients, Inc.
  Minneapolis, MN 888-238-4647
Al-Rite Fruits & Syrups Co
  Miami, FL 305-652-2540
Alaska Herb & Tea Co
  Anchorage, AK 800-654-2764
Alimentaire Whyte's Inc
  Laval, QC 866-420-9520
Amalgamated Sugar Company
  Boise, ID 208-383-6500
Baldwin Richardson Foods
  Oakbrook Terrace, IL 866-644-2732
Bay Valley Foods
  El Paso, TX 800-236-1119
Belton Foods Inc
  Dayton, OH 800-443-2266
Ben's Sugar Shack
  Temple, NH 603-924-3177
Blueberry Store
  Grand Junction, MI 877-654-2400
Bosco Products Inc
  Towaco, NJ 800-438-2672
Boyd's Coffee Co
  Portland, OR 800-735-2878
Briess Malt & Ingredients Co.
  Chilton, WI 800-657-0806
C S Steen Syrup Mill Inc
  Abbeville, LA 800-725-1654
California Custom Foods
  Fullerton, CA 714-870-0490
California Natural Products
  Lathrop, CA 209-858-2525
Cameron Birch Syrup & Confections
  Wasilla, AK 800-962-4724
Carborator Rental Svc
  Philadelphia, PA 800-220-3556
Cargill Inc.
  Minneapolis, MN 800-227-4455
Carolina Beverage Corp
  Salisbury, NC 704-633-4550
Carolina Treet
  Wilmington, NC 800-616-6344
Castella Imports Inc
  Brentwood, NY 631-231-5500
Cheri's Desert Harvest
  Tucson, AZ 800-743-1141
Citadelle Maple Syrup Producers' Cooperative
  Plessisville, QC 819-362-3241
Classic Tea
  Libertyville, IL 630-680-9934
Clear Mountain Coffee Company
  Silver Spring, MD 301-587-2233
Clements Foods Co
  Oklahoma City, OK 800-654-8355
Cleveland Syrup Corporation
  Cleveland, OH 216-883-1845
Cold Hollow Cider Mill
  Waterbury Center, VT 800-327-7537
Con Yeager Spice Co
  Zelienople, PA 800-222-2460
Consolidated Mills Inc
  Houston, TX 713-896-4196
Cora Italian Specialties
  Countryside, IL 800-696-2672
Cora Texas Mfg Co Inc
  White Castle, LA 225-545-3679
Crosby Molasses Company
  Saint John, NB 800-561-2206
Davinci Gourmet LTD
  Seattle, WA 800-640-6779
Daymar Select Fine Coffees
  El Cajon, CA 800-466-7590
Dean Distributors, Inc.
  Burlingame, CA 800-792-0816
Deer Creek Honey Farms LTD
  London, OH 740-852-0899
Domino Specialty Ingredients
  West Palm Beach, FL
E.D. Smith Foods Ltd
  Hamilton, ON 905-573-1207
Emerling International Foods
  Buffalo, NY 716-833-7381
Entner-Stuart Premium Syrups
  Albany, OR 800-926-6886
Eva Gates Homemade Preserves
  Bigfork, MT 800-682-4283
Evergreen Sweeteners, Inc
  Hollywood, FL 954-381-7776
Eweberry Farms
  Brownsville, OR 541-466-3470
Felbro Food Products
  Los Angeles, CA 323-936-5266
Ferrara Bakery & Cafe
  New York, NY 212-226-6150
Finlays
  Lincoln, RI 800-288-6272
Flavorganics
  Newark, NJ 866-972-6879
Flavors from Florida
  Bartow, FL 800-888-0409
Flavors of Hawaii Inc
  Honolulu, HI 808-597-1727
Flavouressence Products
  Mississauga, ON 866-209-7778
Florida Citrus
  Bartow, FL 863-537-3999
Folklore Foods
  Selby, SD 605-649-1144
Forge Mountain Foods
  Hendersonville, NC 800-823-6743
Foxtail Foods
  Fairfield, OH 800-487-2253
Gateway Food Products Co
  Dupo, IL 877-220-1963
Gedney Foods Co
  Sun Valley, CA 888-244-0653
GEM Berry Products
  Orofino, ID 888-231-1699
Gem Berry Products
  Sandpoint, ID 800-231-1699
Golden Eagle Syrup
  Fayette, AL 205-932-5294
Golden State Foods Corp
  Irvine, CA 949-247-8000
Great Valley Mills
  Barto, PA 800-688-6455
Great Western Co LLC
  Hollywood, AL 256-259-3578
Great Western Juice Co
  Maple Heights, OH 800-321-9180
Groeb Farms
  Onsted, MI 800-530-9969
Gust John Foods & Products
  Batavia, IL 800-756-5886
H & H Products Co
  Orlando, FL 800-678-8448
H Fox & Co Inc
  Brooklyn, NY 718-385-4600
Heinz Portion Control
  Jacksonville, FL 904-695-1300
Highland Sugarworks
  Websterville, VT 800-452-4012
Homemade By Dorothy Boise
  Boise, ID 800-657-7449
Honey Run Winery
  Chico, CA 530-345-6405
Howard Foods Inc
  Danvers, MA 978-774-6207
Huckleberry Patch
  Hungry Horse, MT 800-527-7340
I Rice & Co Inc
  Philadelphia, PA 800-232-6022
Ingredion Inc.
  Westchester, IL 800-713-0208
Instant Products of America
  Columbus, IN 812-372-9100
International Food Products
  Fenton, MO 800-227-8427
J.M. Smucker Co.
  Orrville, OH 888-550-9555
Jakeman's Maple Products
  Beachville, ON 800-382-9795
JER Creative Food Concepts, Inc.
  Commerce, CA 800-350-2462
JMS Specialty Foods
  Ripon, WI 800-535-5437
Jogue Inc
  Northville, MI 800-531-3888
Josef Aaron Syrup Company
  Redmond, WA 425-820-7221
Jus-Made
  Dallas, TX 800-969-3746
Just Date Syrup
  San Mateo, CA
Kemach Food Products
  Brooklyn, NY 718-272-5655
Kerry Foodservice
  Mansfield, OH 800-533-2722
Kloss Manufacturing Co Inc
  Allentown, PA 800-445-7100
Koloa Rum Corp
  Kalaheo, HI 808-332-9333
Kozlowski Farms
  Forestville, CA 800-473-2767
Kurtz Orchards Farms
  Niagra-on-the-Lake, ON 905-468-2937
Lafourche Sugar LLC
  Thibodaux, LA 985-447-3210
Lancaster Packing Company
  Myerstown, PA 717-397-9727
Les Industries Bernard et Fils
  Saint Victor, QC 418-588-3590
Limpert Bros Inc
  Vineland, NJ 800-691-1353
Lost Trail Root Beer
  Louisburg, KS 800-748-7765
Louisiana Sugar Cane Co-Op Inc
  St Martinville, LA 337-394-3785
Lowery's Premium Roast Gourmet Coffee
  Snohomish, WA 800-767-1783
Lundberg Family Farms
  Richvale, CA 530-538-3500
Lynch Foods
  North York, ON 416-449-5464
Lyons Magnus
  Fresno, CA 800-344-7130
Magic Ice Products
  Cincinnati, OH 800-776-7923
Malt Diastase Co
  Garfield, NJ 800-772-0416
Maple Grove Farms Of Vermont
  St Johnsbury, VT 802-748-5141
Maple Products
  Sherbrooke, QC 819-569-5161
Mapleland Farm
  Salem, NY 518-854-7669
Mardale Specialty Foods
  Waukegan, IL 845-299-0285
Marsa Specialty Products
  Vernon, CA 800-628-0500
Masterson Co Inc
  Milwaukee, WI 414-647-1132
Melchers Flavors of America
  Indianapolis, IN 800-235-2867
Michele Foods
  South Holland, IL 708-331-7453
Michigan Sugar Company
  Bay City, MI 989-686-0161
Minnestalgia Foods LLC
  Mcgregor, MN 800-328-6731
Monin Inc.
  Clearwater, FL 855-352-8671
Morris Kitchen
  Brooklyn, NY 347-457-6994
National Flavors
  Kalamazoo, MI 800-525-2431
National Fruit Flavor Co Inc
  New Orleans, LA 800-966-1123
Naturel
  Rancho Cucamonga, CA 877-242-8344
New Organics
  Kenwood, CA 734-677-5570
Newport Flavours & Fragrances
  Orange, CA 714-744-3700
Nog Incorporated
  Dunkirk, NY 800-332-2664
Northwestern Extract
  Germantown, WI 800-466-3034
Orange Bang Inc
  Sylmar, CA 818-833-1000

Product Categories / Sugars, Syrups & Sweeteners: Syrups

Oregon Hill Farms
  St Helens, OR 800-243-4541
Organic Nectars LLC
  Malden On Hudson, NY 845-246-0506
Osceola Farms Sugar Warehouse
  Pahokee, FL 561-924-7156
Pacific Westcoast Foods
  Beaverton, OR 800-874-9333
Paradigm Foodworks Inc
  Lake Oswego, OR 800-234-0250
Paulaur Corp
  Cranbury, NJ 609-395-8844
Phillips Syrup Corp
  Cleveland, OH 800-350-8443
Pied-Mont/Dora
  Anne Des Plaines, QC 800-363-8003
Poppers Supply Company
  Allentown, PA 800-457-9810
Pride of Dixie Syrup Company
  Bono, AR 800-530-7654
Prima Foods International
  Silver Springs, FL 800-774-8751
Pure Foods
  Sultan, WA 360-793-2241
Purity Factories
  St. John's, NL 800-563-3411
R Torre & Co
  S San Francisco, CA 800-775-1925
Raceland Raw Sugar Corporation
  Raceland, LA 985-537-3533
Richards Maple Products
  Chardon, OH 800-352-4052
Rio Syrup Co
  St Louis, MO 800-325-7666
Rocky Ridge Maple
  Middlebury Center, PA 607-742-9566
Roquette America Inc.
  Geneva, IL 630-463-9430
Routin America
  Delray Beach, FL
Santini Foods
  San Lorenzo, CA 800-835-6888
Savoie Industries
  Belle Rose, LA 225-473-9293
SBK Preserves
  Bronx, NY 800-773-7378
Sea Breeze Fruit Flavors
  Towaco, NJ 800-732-2733
Shady Maple Farm
  Mississauga, ON 905-206-1455
Shank's Extracts Inc
  Lancaster, PA 800-346-3135
Shawnee Canning Co
  Cross Junction, VA 800-713-1414
Singer Extract Laboratory
  Livonia, MI 313-345-5880
Skjodt-Barrett Foods
  Brampton, ON 877-600-1200
Somerset Syrup & Concessions
  Edison, NJ 800-526-8865
Sonoma Syrup Co. Inc.
  Sonoma, CA 707-996-4070
St. James Sugar Cooperative
  Saint James, LA 225-265-4056
Star Kay White Inc
  Congers, NY 800-874-8518
Stasero International
  Kent, WA 888-929-2378
Steel's Gourmet Foods, Ltd.
  Bridgeport, PA 800-678-3357
Stevens Tropical Plantation
  West Palm Beach, FL 561-683-4701
Stirling Foods
  Renton, WA 800-332-1714
Sugar Cane Growers Co-Op of Florida
  Belle Glade, FL 561-996-5556
Sugarman of Vermont
  Hardwick, VT 800-932-7700
Sugarright
  Fairless Hills, PA 215-486-2105
Suzanne's Specialties
  New Brunswick, NJ 800-762-2135
Sweet Additions
  Palm Beach Gardens, NY 561-472-0178
Sweetstacks LLC
  San Diego, CA 619-997-1097
T. Marzetti Company
  Westerville, OH 800-999-1835
T.J. Blackburn Syrup Works
  Jefferson, TX 800-657-5073
Texas Coffee Traders Inc
  Austin, TX 800-343-4875

Toms Moms Foods, LLC
  Centreville, VA 614-716-9436
Tone Products Inc
  Melrose Park, IL 800-536-8663
Tonewood Maple
  Waitsfield, VT 802-496-5512
Torani
  San Francisco, CA 855-972-0508
Tova Industries LLC
  Louisville, KY 888-532-8682
Trader Vic's Food Products
  Emeryville, CA 877-762-4824
Trailblazer Foods
  Portland, OR 800-777-7179
Triple H Food Processors Inc
  Riverside, CA 951-352-5700
Turtle Island Herbs
  Boulder, CO 800-684-4060
United Canadian Malt
  Peterborough, ON 800-461-6400
Valley Grain Products
  Fresno, CA 559-675-3400
Valley View Blueberries
  Vancouver, WA 360-892-2839
Van Tone Creative
  Terrell, TX 800-856-0802
Ventura Foods LLC
  Brea, CA 800-421-6257
Vita Food Products Inc
  Chicago, IL 800-989-8482
Wagner Excello Food Products
  Broadview, IL 708-338-4488
WCC Honey Marketing
  City Of Industry, CA 626-855-3086
Webbpak Inc
  Trussville, AL 800-655-3500
Western Syrup Company
  Santa Fe Springs, CA 562-921-4485
Westin Foods
  Omaha, NE 800-228-6098
Westway Trading Corporation
  New Orleans, LA 701-282-5010
White-Stokes Company
  Chicago, IL 800-978-6537
Whitfield Foods Inc
  Montgomery, AL 800-633-8790
Willamette Valley Pie Co
  Salem, OR 503-362-8857
Wing Nien Food
  Hayward, CA 510-487-8877

Bar

Davinci Gourmet LTD
  Seattle, WA 800-640-6779

Beverages

ARCO Coffee
  Superior, WI 800-283-2726
Davinci Gourmet LTD
  Seattle, WA 800-640-6779
EFCO Products Inc
  Poughkeepsie, NY 800-284-3326
Flavouressence Products
  Mississauga, ON 866-209-7778
Folklore Foods
  Selby, SD 605-649-1144
Great Western Juice Co
  Maple Heights, OH 800-321-9180
Refresco Beverages US Inc.
  Tampa, FL 888-260-3776
Rio Syrup Co
  St Louis, MO 800-325-7666
Skjodt-Barrett Foods
  Brampton, ON 877-600-1200
Van Tone Creative
  Terrell, TX 800-856-0802

Cane

Agri-Dairy Products
  Purchase, NY 914-697-9580
Evergreen Sweeteners, Inc
  Hollywood, FL 954-381-7776
Flavorganics
  Newark, NJ 866-972-6879
Malt Diastase Co
  Saddle Brook, NJ 800-526-0180
New Organics
  Kenwood, CA 734-677-5570
Osceola Farms Sugar Warehouse
  Pahokee, FL 561-924-7156

Ouachita Lumber Co
  West Monroe, LA 318-396-1960
Webbpak Inc
  Trussville, AL 800-655-3500

Corn

Archer Daniels Midland Company
  Decatur, IL 217-424-5200
Archer Daniels Midland Company
  Chicago, IL 312-634-8100
Crosby Molasses Company
  Saint John, NB 800-561-2206
Evergreen Sweeteners, Inc
  Hollywood, FL 954-381-7776
Malt Diastase Co
  Saddle Brook, NJ 800-526-0180
Whitfield Foods Inc
  Montgomery, AL 800-633-8790

Blends

Evergreen Sweeteners, Inc
  Hollywood, FL 954-381-7776

Dextrose

Archer Daniels Midland Company
  Decatur, IL 217-424-5200
Archer Daniels Midland Company
  Chicago, IL 312-634-8100
Evergreen Sweeteners, Inc
  Hollywood, FL 954-381-7776

Glucose - Etc.

Archer Daniels Midland Company
  Decatur, IL 217-424-5200
Archer Daniels Midland Company
  Chicago, IL 312-634-8100
Baldwin Richardson Foods
  Oakbrook Terrace, IL 866-644-2732
Cargill Inc.
  Minneapolis, MN 800-227-4455
Con Yeager Spice Co
  Zelienople, PA 800-222-2460
Evergreen Sweeteners, Inc
  Hollywood, FL 954-381-7776
Gateway Food Products Co
  Dupo, IL 877-220-1963
Ingredion Inc.
  Westchester, IL 800-713-0208
Malt Diastase Co
  Saddle Brook, NJ 800-526-0180
New Organics
  Kenwood, CA 734-677-5570
Paulaur Corp
  Cranbury, NJ 609-395-8844
Roquette America Inc.
  Geneva, IL 630-463-9430
WCC Honey Marketing
  City Of Industry, CA 626-855-3086
Westin Foods
  Omaha, NE 800-228-6098

High Fructose

Evergreen Sweeteners, Inc
  Hollywood, FL 954-381-7776
Ingredion Inc.
  Westchester, IL 800-713-0208
Sweetener Supply Corp
  Brookfield, IL 888-784-2799

Fruit

3V Company
  Brooklyn, NY 718-858-7333
Al-Rite Fruits & Syrups Co
  Miami, FL 305-652-2540
Baldwin Richardson Foods
  Oakbrook Terrace, IL 866-644-2732
Bernard & Sons Maple Products
  St-Victor, QC 418-588-6109
Blackberry Patch
  Thomasville, GA 800-853-5598
California Custom Fruits
  Baldwin Park, CA 877-558-0056
Cold Hollow Cider Mill
  Waterbury Center, VT 800-327-7537
Davinci Gourmet LTD
  Seattle, WA 800-640-6779
Eva Gates Homemade Preserves
  Bigfork, MT 800-682-4283
GEM Berry Products
  Orofino, ID 888-231-1699

Product Categories / Sugars, Syrups & Sweeteners: Syrups

Great Valley Mills
  Barto, PA..................800-688-6455
H & H Products Co
  Orlando, FL.................800-678-8448
H Fox & Co Inc
  Brooklyn, NY................718-385-4600
I Rice & Co Inc
  Philadelphia, PA.............800-232-6022
Inn Maid Food
  Lenox, MA...................413-637-2732
J.M. Smucker Co.
  Orrville, OH................888-550-9555
Jogue Inc
  Northville, MI..............800-531-3888
Koloa Rum Corp
  Kalaheo, HI.................808-332-9333
Maple Grove Farms Of Vermont
  St Johnsbury, VT............802-748-5141
Minnestalgia Foods LLC
  Mcgregor, MN................800-328-6731
Orange Bang Inc
  Sylmar, CA..................818-833-1000
Pacific Westcoast Foods
  Beaverton, OR...............800-874-9333
Phillips Syrup Corp
  Cleveland, OH...............800-350-8443
Purity Factories
  St. John's, NL..............800-563-3411
Sea Breeze Fruit Flavors
  Towaco, NJ..................800-732-2733
Summerland Sweets
  Summerland, BC..............800-577-1277
Valley View Blueberries
  Vancouver, WA...............360-892-2839
Van Tone Creative
  Terrell, TX.................800-856-0802
Vermont Specialty Food Association
  Randolph, VT................802-728-0070
Western Syrup Company
  Santa Fe Springs, CA........562-921-4485

Malt Extract

Briess Malt & Ingredients Co.
  Chilton, WI.................800-657-0806
Grounds For Thought
  Bowling Green, OH...........419-354-3266
Lake Country Foods Inc
  Oconomowoc, WI..............262-567-5521
Malt Diastase Co
  Saddle Brook, NJ............800-526-0180
Premier Malt Products Inc
  Warren, MI..................800-521-1057
Roquette America Inc.
  Geneva, IL..................630-463-9430
United Canadian Malt
  Peterborough, ON............800-461-6400

Maple

A Perfect Pear
  Napa, CA....................800-553-5753
Adirondack Maple Farms
  Fonda, NY...................518-853-4022
Arnold Farm Sugarhouse
  Jackman, ME.................207-668-4110
B & G Foods Inc.
  Parsippany, NJ..............973-401-6500
Baldwin Richardson Foods
  Oakbrook Terrace, IL........866-644-2732
Bascom Family Farms Inc
  Brattleboro, VT.............888-266-6271
Bernard & Sons Maple Products
  St-Victor, QC...............418-588-6109
Brown Family Farm
  Brattleboro, VT.............866-254-8718
Butternut Mountain Farm
  Morrisville, VT.............800-828-2376
Citadelle Maple Syrup Producers' Cooperative
  Plessisville, QC............819-362-3241
Coombs Family Farm
  Brattleboro, VT.............888-266-6271
Couture's Maple Shop/B & B
  Westfield, VT...............800-845-2733
D & D Sugarwoods Farm
  Glover, VT..................800-245-3718
Dole Pond Maple Products
  Jackman, ME.................418-653-5322
Eleanor's Best LLC
  Garrison, NY................646-296-6870
Emerling International Foods
  Buffalo, NY.................716-833-7381
Green River Chocolates
  Hinesburg, VT...............802-482-6727
Hidden Springs Maple
  Putney, VT..................802-387-5200
Highland Sugarworks
  Websterville, VT............800-452-4012
Hillside Lane Farm
  Randolph, VT................802-728-0070
Howard Foods Inc
  Danvers, MA.................978-774-6207
Jed's Maple Products
  Derby, VT...................802-766-2700
JMS Specialty Foods
  Ripon, WI...................800-535-5437
King Arthur Flour
  Norwich, VT.................800-827-6836
L.B. Maple Treat
  Granby, QC..................888-775-1111
Les Industries Bernard et Fils
  Saint Victor, QC............418-588-3590
Maple Acres Inc
  Kewadin, MI.................231-264-9265
Maple Grove Farms Of Vermont
  St Johnsbury, VT............802-748-5141
Maple Hollow
  Merrill, WI.................715-536-7251
Maple Products
  Sherbrooke, QC..............819-569-5161
Maple Valley Cooperative
  Cashton, WI.................608-654-7319
Mc Lure's Honey & Maple Prod
  Littleton, NH...............603-444-6246
Middlefield Cheese House
  Middlefield, OH.............800-327-9477
Minnestalgia Foods LLC
  Mcgregor, MN................800-328-6731
Mount Mansfield Maple Products
  Winooski, VT................802-497-1671
Nature's Hollow
  Charleston, UT
NOW Foods
  Bloomingdale, IL............888-669-3663
Phillips Syrup Corp
  Cleveland, OH...............800-350-8443
Pride of Dixie Syrup Company
  Bono, AR....................800-530-7654
Richards Maple Products
  Chardon, OH.................800-352-4052
Sea Breeze Fruit Flavors
  Towaco, NJ..................800-732-2733
Shady Maple Farm
  Mississauga, ON.............905-206-1455
Subco Foods Inc
  Sheboygan, WI...............800-473-0757
Sugarman of Vermont
  Hardwick, VT................800-932-7700
Swisser Sweet Maple
  Castorland, NY..............315-346-1034
The Maple Guild
  Island Pond, VT.............802-723-6753
Tonewood Maple
  Waitsfield, VT..............802-496-5512
Turkey Hill Sugarbush
  Waterloo, QC................450-539-4822
Vermont Specialty Food Association
  Randolph, VT................802-728-0070
Wagner Excello Food Products
  Broadview, IL...............708-338-4488
Webbpak Inc
  Trussville, AL..............800-655-3500

Pancake

Bernard & Sons Maple Products
  St-Victor, QC...............418-588-6109
California Custom Foods
  Fullerton, CA...............714-870-0490
Finding Home Farms
  Middletown, NY..............845-355-4335
Golden Eagle Syrup
  Fayette, AL.................205-932-5294
Gust John Foods & Products
  Batavia, IL.................800-756-5886
Marina Foods
  Medley, FL..................786-888-0129
Pride of Dixie Syrup Company
  Bono, AR....................800-530-7654
Sea Breeze Fruit Flavors
  Towaco, NJ..................800-732-2733
T. Marzetti Company
  Westerville, OH.............800-999-1835
Tone Products Inc
  Melrose Park, IL............800-536-8663
Vermont Country Naturals
  Charlotte, VT...............800-528-7021
Whitfield Foods Inc
  Montgomery, AL..............800-633-8790

Toppings

Sundae

California Custom Fruits
  Baldwin Park, CA............877-558-0056
I Rice & Co Inc
  Philadelphia, PA............800-232-6022
Tahana Confections LLC
  Portsmouth, NH..............603-498-6246

Waffle

Golden Eagle Syrup
  Fayette, AL.................205-932-5294
Pride of Dixie Syrup Company
  Bono, AR....................800-530-7654
T. Marzetti Company
  Westerville, OH.............800-999-1835

# Food Manufacturers / A-Z

1. 1-2-3 Gluten Free
125 Orange Tree Dr.
Chagrin Falls, OH 44022
216-378-9233
info@123glutenfree.com
www.123glutenfree.com
Gluten free baking mixes.
Owner: Kimberlee Ullner
kim@123glutenfree.com
Square Footage: 80000
Brands:
  1-2-3 Gluten Free

2. 10 Strawberry Street
3837 Monaco Pkwy
Denver, CO 80207
800-428-9397
www.tenstrawberrystreet.com
Serveware, dinnerwear, glassware and flatware
VP, Sales & Marketing: Ruby Hershberger
Year Founded: 1983

3. 1000 Islands River Rat Cheese
242 James St
Clayton, NY 13624-1010
315-686-2480
Fax: 315-686-4701 800-752-1341
support@riverratcheese.net
www.riverratcheese.net
Distributor: NYS Cheese, Adirondack Sausage
President: Mary Scudera
1000islandsriverratcheese@gmail.com
Estimated Sales: $2,500,000
Number Employees: 10-19
Type of Packaging: Consumer, Food Service, Private Label, Bulk
Brands:
  Adirondack Cheese
  Gold Cup
  River Rat Cheese

4. 1642
2025 rue Parthenais
Suite 318
Montreal, QC H2K 3T2
Canada
800-774-4907
info@1642.ca www.1642.ca
Soft drinks

5. 18 Rabbits Inc.
995 Market Street
2nd Floor
San Francisco, CA 94103
415-922-6006
blackjack@18rabbits.com
www.18rabbits.com
Organic, non-GMO and kosher granola bars
Founder and CEO: Alison Vercruysse
COO: Kent Spalding
Brands:
  18 RABBITS

6. 21st Century Products, Inc.
2692 Gravel Dr
Bldg 5
Fort Worth, TX 76118-6976
817-284-8299
Fax: 817-284-4844
Processor and exporter of vitamins; also, mineral and weight loss drinks
President: Greg Harris
Vice President: Dixon Ray
National Sales Director: Richard Fabose
Estimated Sales: $100,000
Number Employees: 2
Type of Packaging: Consumer, Food Service, Private Label, Bulk

7. 21st Century Snack Foods
921 S 2nd St
Ronkonkoma, NY 11779
631-588-8000
www.21snackshop.com
Chocolate, nuts, seeds, trail mixes, dried fruit, candy, gummies, marzipan and gifts.
President: Royce Keller
Estimated Sales: $2.5-5 Million
Number Employees: 20-49
Type of Packaging: Bulk

8. 24 Mantra Organic
Fremont, CA 94538
www.24mantra.com
Organic processed foods and drinks

9. 24Vegan
Arcadia, CA 91077-1743
www.24vegan.com
Fish sauce

10. 3 Gyros Inc
5270 Brendan Lane
Tecumseh, ON N0R 1L0
Canada
519-737-0389
Fax: 888-678-8584 info@3gyros.com
Gluten-free, sugar-free, other condiments, salad dressing, other sauces, seasonings and cooking enhancers.
President/Founder: Thanos Zikantas
National Account Manager: Tim Fittler
Customer Service: Angelo Zikantas
Product Development: Jason Verbeen

11. 3 Springs Water Co
1800 Pine Run Rd
Laurel Run, PA 18706-9419
570-823-7019
Fax: 570-822-6177 800-332-7873
info@3springs.com www.3springs.com
Processor and bottler of low-mineral and sodium-free spring water
President: Jim Tosh
info@3springs.com
Estimated Sales: $3-5 Million
Number Employees: 20-49
Square Footage: 80000
Type of Packaging: Consumer, Food Service, Private Label
Brands:
  3 Springs

12. 3 Water
Huntington, NY 11743
877-371-8704
info@drink3water.com www.drink3water.com
Caffeinated water
Parent Co: EuroVita Corp.
Type of Packaging: Consumer

13. 34-Degrees
2825 Larimer St
Denver, CO 80216
303-861-4818
Fax: 303-484-4664 info@34-degrees.com
www.34-degrees.com
Wafer crackers made with all natural ingredients. Natural, sesame, cracked pepper, rosemary, and whole grain varieties.
Founder/President: Craig Lierberman
EVP: Jennifer Margoles
Marketing Manager: Jen Swift
VP of Operations: Wes Brasher
Number Employees: 5-9
Type of Packaging: Consumer
Brands:
  34 Degrees

14. 350 Cheese Straws
1003 Lennoxville Rd.
Beaufort, NC 28516
252-838-9080
www.350cheesestraw.com
Cheese straws.
Founder and President: Ashley Sellars
Square Footage: 330230

15. 360 Nutrition
1689 Beverly Blvd
Los Angeles, CA 90026
213-805-3015
inquiry@360nutritionusa.com
360nutritionusa.com
Drink blends
Number of Brands: 5
Number of Products: 20
Type of Packaging: Consumer
Brands:
  360 NUTRITION
  BLENDS WITH BENEFITS
  GO MATCHA
  PRO-SHAKE
  SLIM SHAKE

16. 3PM Bites
New York, NY
3pmbites.com
Superfood snacks
Founder: Tisha Agarwal
Year Founded: 2016
Number Employees: 1-10
Number of Brands: 1
Number of Products: 3
Type of Packaging: Consumer
Brands:
  3PM BITES

17. 3V Company
110 Bridge Street
Brooklyn, NY 11201
718-858-7333
Fax: 718-858-7371 3v.co
Fruit-based beverage products.
CEO: Eren Spring
Contact: Hershy Gombo
hgombo@3v.co
Number of Brands: 3
Type of Packaging: Consumer, Food Service, Private Label, Bulk
Brands:
  3V Classic™
  3V Fresh™
  Smartfruit™

18. 4505 Meats LLC
1246 Howard St
San Francisco, CA 94103
415-255-3094
Pork rinds
General Manager: Adam Bailey
Culinary Operations Manager: Cole Mayfield

19. 479 Degrees
3450 Sacramento Street
San Francisco, CA 94118
815-552-6039
customer_service@479degrees.com
www.479degrees.com
Flavored popcorn.
Founder: Jean Arnold
Contact: Virginia Bryant
virginia@479degrees.com
Brands:
  479 Degrees

20. 4C Foods Corp
580 Fountain Ave
Brooklyn, NY 11208-6002
718-272-4242
Fax: 718-272-2899 inthekitchen@4c.com
www.4c.com
Iced tea, soft drink mix; imported cheese; bread crumbs and soup mix.
Founder and President: John Celauro
sally@4c.com
SVP Operations: Wayne Celauro
Number Employees: 100-249
Square Footage: 420000
Type of Packaging: Food Service, Private Label
Brands:
  4C Foods
  4C Beverages

21. 4Pure
207-831-1030
www.drink4pure.com
Lemonade
Founder & CEO: Will Boyle
Number of Brands: 1
Number of Products: 3
Type of Packaging: Consumer
Brands:
  4PURE

22. 4th & Heart
213-880-2559
wecare@4thandheart.com
fourthandheart.com
Modern food staples
Co-Founder: Raquel Gunsagar
Co-Founder: Lillian Wunsch
Number of Brands: 1
Number of Products: 12
Type of Packaging: Consumer
Brands:
  4TH & HEART

23. 505 Southwestern
Meridian, ID 83642
www.flagshipfoodgroup.com
Salsas, cooking sauces and condiments

453

Food Manufacturers / A-Z

24 50th State Poultry Processors
98-715 Kuahao Place
Pearl City, HI 96782
808-845-5902
Fax: 808-847-7040 derronuezu@yahoo.com
www.50thstatepoultry.biz
Poultry
President: Darryl Uezu
VP: Linda Uezu
Estimated Sales: $10-20 Million
Number Employees: 20-49
Type of Packaging: Consumer, Food Service

25 51 Fifty Enterprises
436 Second St
Livingston, CA 95334
855-513-4389
info@51fiftyenergydrink.com
www.51fiftyenergydrink.com
Energy drinks
Number of Brands: 1
Number of Products: 11
Type of Packaging: Consumer
Brands:
  51FIFTY

26 731 North Beach LLC
731 N. Beach Blvd
La Habra, CA 90631-3657
562-697-8888
Fax: 562-697-8288
Groceries
Owner: Han K Ng
Estimated Sales: $2.5-5 000,000
Number Employees: 5-9

27 80 Acres Farms
345 High St.
7th Fl.
Hamilton, OH 45011
888-574-1569
www.80acresfarms.com
Herbs, leafy greens, and select vegetables.
Co-Founder & President: Tisha Livingston
Co-Founder & CEO: Mike Zelkind
Year Founded: 2015
Type of Packaging: Private Label

28 814 Americas Inc
814 2nd Ave
Elizabeth, NJ 07202-3804
908-354-2674
Fax: 908-354-7170 www.814americas.com
Sausage
Founder: Severino Abuin
CFO: Michael Patratuolla
Manager: Michael Patracuolla
Estimated Sales: $5-10 Million
Number Employees: 20-49
Brands:
  El Mino
  Riojano

29 88 Acres
P.O. Box 79
Allston, MA 02121
617-208-8651
hello@88acres.com
88acres.com
Seed bars, seed granola, and seed butters
Co-Founder: Rob Dalton
Co-Founder: Nicole Ledoux
Marketing Manager: Dayna Scandone
Director of Sales: J.D. Collins
Other Locations:
  Bakery
  Dorchester MA

30 8th Wonder
Denver, CO 80209
303-868-6296
reed@8thwondertea.com
www.8thwondertea.com
Superfood RTD teas
Founder: Parker Rush

31 99 Ranch Market
1625 S Azusa Ave
Hacienda Heights, CA 91745-3832
626-839-2899
Fax: 626-839-2127 www.99ranch.com
Asian American groceries
Founder/CEO: Roger Chen

Year Founded: 1984
Estimated Sales: $500,000
Number Employees: 50-99
Other Locations:
  Manufacturing Facility-Sugarland
  Sugarland TX

32 A B Munroe Dairy Inc
151 N Brow St
East Providence, RI 02914-4415
401-438-4450
Fax: 401-438-0035 info@cowtruck.com
Fluid milk
President: Robert Armstrong
Director, Sales: Bob Munroe
Site Manager: Steve Viall
sviall@monroedairy.com
Plant Manager: John Sherman
Estimated Sales: $7-20 Million
Number Employees: 50-99
Brands:
  Munroe Dairy

33 A Cajun Life®, LLC
Damascus, OR 97089
info@acajunlife.com
www.acajunlife.com
Cajun seasonings
Founder: Chris Fontenot

34 A Couple of Squares, Inc
501-B Nightingale Avenue
London, ON N5W 4C8
Canada
519-672-6979
Fax: 519-672-4487 866-672-6979
info@acoupleofsquares.com
www.acoupleofsquares.com
Cookie manufacturer and wholesaler.
Director of Marketing: Bernadette Erb
Sales Marketing: Carol Dobbin
Square Footage: 9000

35 A Dozen Cousins
Berkeley, CA 94710
support@adozencousins.com
adozencousins.com
Ready-to-heat beans
Founder & CEO: Ibraheem Basir

36 A Gift Basket by Carmela
64 Magnolia Cir
Longmeadow, MA 01106
413-746-1400
Fax: 413-746-1441
Customized gift baskets; importer of plum tomatoes, olive oil, balsamic vinegar, coffee, cookies, cakes, artichokes and gourmet foods from Italy
President: Carmela Denille
Estimated Sales: Less than $500,000
Number Employees: 1-4
Square Footage: 32800
Brands:
  Gift Baskets By Carmela

37 A Hill of Beans Coffee Roasters
14512 West Center Rd
Omaha, NE 68144
402-333-6048
Fax: 402-333-7113 www.ahillofbeans.com
Roasted coffee beans.
Owner: Leo Hill
Estimated Sales: $5-10 000,000 appx.
Number Employees: 2-10

38 A J's Edible Arts
313 S 4th Ave
Pasco, WA 99301-5510
USA
509-547-3440
Fax: 509-380-0142 www.ajsediblearts.com
Mustard, sauces, giftboxes
Presiden: Alice Jones
alice@ajsediblearts.com
Co-Owner: Juli Massingale
Number Employees: 1-4

39 A La Carte
5610 W Bloomingdale Ave
Chicago, IL 60639-4110
773-237-3000
Fax: 773-237-3075 800-722-2370
service@alacarteline.com
Custom promotional products including hard candy and popcorn in decorative tins, jars, boxes, etc.

President: Michael Shulkin
CEO: Adam Robins
Sales Director: James Janowski
Purchasing: Marly Robins
Estimated Sales: $10-20 Million
Number Employees: 50-99
Parent Co: David Scott Industries
Type of Packaging: Food Service, Private Label, Bulk

40 A Perfect Pear
1283 Monticello Rd
Napa, CA 94558
707-251-8532
Fax: 707-257-6830 800-553-5753
All natural pear products to include vinegars, preserves, jellies, chutneys, marinades, salad dressings and maple syrup

41 A Plus Label
3215 W Warner Ave
Santa Ana, CA 92704
714-229-9811
apluslabel.com
Tag and label manufacturer

42 A Southern Season
505 Eno St
Hillsborough, NC 27278-2357
919-929-7133
Fax: 800-646-1118 800-253-3663
www.southernseason.com
Cheesestraws, BBQ sauces, lemon drops, cookies, jams and jellies
Owner: Michael Barefoot
Marketing Director: Deborah Miller
Manager: Tom Baker
tom@southernseason.com
Number Employees: 10-19
Brands:
  Carolina Cupboard

43 A Taste of the Kingdom
3773 County Road 210
Kingdom City, MO 65262-2018
573-592-7373
Fax: 573-642-8680 888-592-5080
Natural, kosher condiments and glazes
Owner: Julie Price
Estimated Sales: $3-5 Million
Number Employees: 5-9

44 A Tavola Together
6262 Crooked Stick Cir
Stockton, CA 95219-1857
USA
209-608-5455
Fax: 209-475-0954
Focaccia, pizza dough, baking mixes, gluten free, recipes
Owner: Rima Barkett
Owner: Claudia Pruett
Estimated Sales: 500,000.00
Number Employees: 4

45 A To Z Portion Control Meats
201 N Main St
Bluffton, OH 45817-1297
419-358-2926
Fax: 419-358-8876 800-338-6328
www.atozmeats.com
Beef and pork products.
President: Lee A Kagy
leek@atozmeats.com
Year Founded: 1945
Estimated Sales: G
Number Employees: 20-49
Type of Packaging: Consumer, Food Service, Private Label, Bulk

46 A Zerega's Sons Inc
20-01 Broadway
P.O. Box 241
Fair Lawn, NJ 07410
201-797-1400
Fax: 201-797-0148 sales@zerega.com
www.zerega.com
Dry pasta.
Director: John Vermylen
jvermylen@zerega.com
Treasurer: Nicholas Pugliese
Vice President: Mark Vermylen
Marketing Project Manager: Judi Pollack
Production Manager: Joseph Anzalone

Food Manufacturers / A-Z

Year Founded: 1848
Estimated Sales: $48.1 Million
Number Employees: 100-249
Square Footage: 125000
Type of Packaging: Consumer, Food Service, Private Label, Bulk
Other Locations:
   Zerega's Pasta Plant
   Lee's Summit MO
   Zerega's Pasta Plant
   Fair Lawn NJ
Brands:
   Antoine's
   Columbia

47 A la Cart
Advanced meal delivery systems
President, Unified Brands: Dave Herring
Parent Co: Unified Brands

48 A to Z Wineworks
30835 N Hwy 99 W
Newburg, OR 97132
   800-739-4455
info@AtoZwineworks.com
www.AtoZwineworks.com
Wine
Founder, CEO: Bill Hatcher
Founder, Chief Marketing & Sales Officer: Deb Hatcher
Founder, Consulting Winemaker: Cheryl Francis
Founder, Director of Winemaking: Sam Tannahill
Year Founded: 2002
Number Employees: 20-49
Brands:
   Rex Hill

49 A&A Marine & Drydock Company
10417 Front Line
PO Box 547
Blenheim, ON N0P 1A0
Canada
   519-676-2030
Fax: 519-676-4343 www.aamarine.ca
Frozen perch and pickerel.
President: George Anderson
Vice President: Sherry Anderson
Estimated Sales: $3.5 Million
Number Employees: 25
Type of Packaging: Consumer, Food Service

50 A&B American Style, LLC
PO Box 949
New York, NY 10013-0861
   917-720-7009
www.abamerican.com
Sauces, seasonings, condiments: mayo, ketchup, salsa, dips.
Co-Founder: Arial Fliman
Co-Founder: Brian Ballan
brianballan@abamerican.com
Number Employees: 2

51 A&C Quinlin Fisheries
1220 Highway 330
Centreville, NS B0W 2G0
Canada
   902-745-2742
Fax: 902-745-1788
Salted fish and seafood.
President: Aaron Quinlin
Estimated Sales: $5-10 Million
Number Employees: 20
Type of Packaging: Consumer, Food Service
Brands:
   A&C
   Chelsea

52 A&H Products, Inc
739 Ramsey Avenue
Hillsdale, NJ 07205
   908-206-8886
Fax: 908-206-8632 sl@aandh.us
www.abeles-heymann.com
Producer of salami, pastrami, corned beef, brisket, hot dogs, beef fry, smoked turkey, and knockwurst.
President: Seth Leavitt
Estimated Sales: $5-10 Million
Number Employees: 5-9

53 A-1 Eastern-Homemade Pickle Co
1832 Johnston St
Los Angeles, CA 90031-3499
   323-223-1141
Fax: 323-227-8951 info@a1pickle.com
www.a1pickle.com
Kosher pickles and assorted pickle products
President: Martin Morhar
Vice President: Murray Berger
Estimated Sales: $3.6 Million
Number Employees: 20-49
Type of Packaging: Food Service
Brands:
   A-1 Pickle

54 A-Treat Bottling Co
2001 Union Blvd
Allentown, PA 18109-1631
   610-434-6139
Fax: 610-434-5511 800-220-1531
www.a-treat.com
Soft drinks
President: Joseph Garvey
j.garvey@a-treat.com
VP: Curt Thomas
Estimated Sales: $9 Million
Number Employees: 50-99
Brands:
   A-Treat
   Big Blue
   Green Spot
   Treat-Up

55 A. Gagliano Co Inc
300 N Jefferson St # 1
PO Box 511382
Milwaukee, WI 53202-5920
   414-272-1515
Fax: 414-272-7215 800-272-1516
info@agagliano.com
Fresh fruits and vegetables
Owner: Anthony Gagliano
tony@agagliano.com
Owner: Nick Gagliano
Owner: Mike Gagliano
Warehouse Manager: Rick Alsum
Estimated Sales: $20 Million
Number Employees: 50-99
Number of Brands: 1
Number of Products: 500
Square Footage: 200000
Type of Packaging: Consumer, Food Service, Private Label, Bulk
Brands:
   A. Gagliano

56 A. Lassonde Inc.
755 Rue Principale
Rougemont, QC J0L 1M0
Canada
   866-552-7643
www.lassonde.com
Fruit juices and drinks.
President/CEO: Jean Gattuso
Chairman/CEO: Pierre-Paul Lassonde
Vice President/CFO: Guy Blanchette
Year Founded: 1918
Estimated Sales: 1.5 Billion
Number Employees: 2,100
Number of Brands: 32
Parent Co: Lassonde Industries, Inc.
Type of Packaging: Food Service
Brands:
   Allen's
   Rougemont
   Fairlee
   Orange Maison
   Everfresh
   Fruite
   Graves
   Oasis
   Sunlike
   Del Monte
   Tropical Grove
   Fruit Drop
   Ruby Kist
   Bombay
   Apple & Eve
   Northland
   Old Orchard
   Madeleine
   Canadian Club
   Antico
   Canton
   The Shrink
   Pomme De Coeur
   Aroma Mi Amore
   Bortilly
   Arte Nova
   Au Quotidien
   Vivre Une Double Vie
   Dublin's Pub
   Vivre Dans La Nuit
   Facies
   The Red Plane

57 A. Nonini Winery
2640 N Dickenson Ave
Fresno, CA 93723-9644
   559-275-1936
Fax: 209-241-7119 noniniwinery@gmail.com
Wine
President & Wine Maker: James Jordan
noniniwinery@gmail.com
Estimated Sales: $1-2.5 Million
Number Employees: 1-4
Type of Packaging: Private Label
Brands:
   A Nonini

58 A. Rafanelli Winery
4685 W Dry Creek Rd
Healdsburg, CA 95448-8124
   707-433-1385
Fax: 707-433-3836 www.arafanelliwinery.com
Wines which include; Zinfandel, Cabernet Sauvignon and Merlot
Owner: Stacy Rafanelli
stacy@arafanelliwinery.com
Estimated Sales: $500,000-$1 Million
Number Employees: 1-4
Number of Brands: 1
Number of Products: 1
Type of Packaging: Private Label
Brands:
   A. Rafanelli

59 A. Smith Bowman Distillery
1 Bowman Dr
Fredericksburg, VA 22408
   540-373-4555
Fax: 540-371-2236 www.asmithbowman.com
Bourbon, scotch, rum, tequila, whiskey, gin and vodka
President/CEO: John Adams Jr
CFO/COO: Kent Broussard
VP Production and Distiller: Joseph Dangler
Estimated Sales: $20-50 Million
Number Employees: 20-49
Number of Brands: 2
Number of Products: 9
Brands:
   Bowman's
   Virginia Gentleman

60 A.C. Calderoni
99 N. Hill Dr
Brisbane, CA 94005-1201
   415-468-2282
Fax: 415-468-5967 866-468-1897
calderoni@value.net www.accalderoni.com
Juices, juice concentrates, and cocktail mixes
President: Bob Baciocco
Purchasing: Scott Hawley
Estimated Sales: $2.5-5 Million
Number Employees: 1-4
Brands:
   A.C. Calderoni

61 A.C. Inc.
125 Black Duck Cove Rd
Beals, ME 04611
   207-497-2261
Fax: 207-497-2731
Seafood wholesaler
President, CEO & Co-Owner: Albert Carver
Vice President & Co-Owner: Patrick Robinson

62 A.C. Kissling Company
161 E Allen St
Philadelphia, PA 19125-4194
   215-423-4700
Fax: 215-425-0525 800-445-1943
Sauerkraut
President: R W Kissling Jr
Contact: R Kissling
kaultejk@yahoo.com

Food Manufacturers / A-Z

Estimated Sales: $2 Million
Number Employees: 10-19
Type of Packaging: Consumer
Brands:
    Kissling

63 A.C. LaRocco Pizza
12412 E. Desmet Ave
Suite D
Spokane Valley, WA 99216-5082
509-924-9113
Fax: 509-922-3085
Vegetarian pizzas
President/CEO: Clarence Scott
Marketing Director: Karen Leffler
k.leffler@aclarocco.com
Estimated Sales: $2 Million
Number Employees: 1-4
Brands:
    A.C. Larocco Vegetarian Pizza

64 A.C. Legg
6330 Highway 31
PO Box 709
Calera, AL 35040-5131
205-324-3451
Fax: 205-324-5971 800-422-5344
sales@aclegg.com www.aclegg.com
Processor of custom-blended seasonings for meat, poultry, seafood and snack foods.
President/CEO: James Purvis
jpurvis@aclegg.com
EVP: Charles Purvis
EVP: Sandra Purvis
Year Founded: 1923
Estimated Sales: $20-50 Million
Number Employees: 100-249
Number of Brands: 1
Square Footage: 131000
Type of Packaging: Food Service, Private Label, Bulk
Brands:
    Legg's Old Plantation

65 A.L. Duck Jr Inc
26231 River Run Trail
Zuni, VA 23898-3215
757-562-2387
Smoked sausage
President: Brenda Redd
Estimated Sales: $1-2.5 Million
Number Employees: 5-9
Type of Packaging: Consumer, Food Service

66 A.T. Gift Company
RR 3
Box 802
Harpers Ferry, WV 25425-9310
304-876-6680
Fax: 304-876-2757
Wine related products
President: Angela Gift
Sales Manager: Frank Gift
Estimated Sales: Less than $500,000
Number Employees: 2

67 A.Vogel USA
6 Grandinetti Drive
Ghent, NY 12075
518-828-9111
Fax: 888-798-7555 800-641-7555
info@BioforceUSA.com www.bioforceusa.com
Natural products, vitamins, etc.
President: Paul Ross
Sales Manager: Rich Manziello
Operations Manager: Roberts Sheets
Estimated Sales: $300,000-500,000
Number Employees: 1-4
Parent Co: Bioforce USA
Brands:
    A. Vogel

68 A.W. Jantzi & Sons
3800 Nafziger Rd
PO Box 27
Wellesley, ON N0B 2T0
Canada
519-656-2400
Fax: 519-656-3370 sales@wellappleproducts.com
www.wellappleproducts.com
Apple cider and apple butter
President: Steve Jantzi
Vice President: Kevin Jantzi

Number Employees: 15
Square Footage: 40000
Type of Packaging: Consumer, Bulk
Brands:
    Wellesley

69 A2 Milk Company
P.O. Box 20651
Boulder, CO 80308
844-422-6455
hello@a2milk.com
www.a2milk.com
Milk
Chief Executive USA: Blake Waltrip
Parent Co: Hain Celestial Group

70 AAK
2520 7th Street Rd
Louisville, KY 40208-1029
502-636-1321
Fax: 502-636-3904 800-622-3055
www.aak.com
Shortenings including flaked, creamy liquid and votated; also, soybean and cottonseed oils; as well as identity preserved oils for GMO-free market.
President/CEO: Timothy Helson
Regional Sales Manager: Jason Glaser
Operations Manager: Sam Marrillia
Estimated Sales: $11.6 Million
Number Employees: 100-249
Square Footage: 200000
Parent Co: AAK USA Inc.
Type of Packaging: Food Service, Bulk
Brands:
    Golden Brands
    Golden Foods

71 AB InBev
One Busch Pl.
St. Louis, MO 63118
314-577-7427
www.ab-inbev.com
Beer, malt liquor, ales, lagers, and non-alcoholic brews.
Zone President, North America: Michel Dukeris
CEO: Carlos Brito
Chief Financial/Solutions Officer: Felipe Dutra
Chief Marketing Officer: Pedro Earp
Chief Sales Officer: Ricardo Tadeu
Year Founded: 2008
Estimated Sales: $56.6 Billion
Number Employees: 182,915
Number of Brands: 500+
Type of Packaging: Consumer, Food Service, Bulk
Other Locations:
    Brewery
    Baldwinsville NY
    Brewery
    Cartersville GA
    Brewery
    Columbus OH
    Brewery
    Fairfield CA
    Brewery
    Fort Collins CO
    Brewery
    Houston TX
    Brewery
    Jacksonville FL
    Brewery
    Los Angeles CA
    Brewery
    Merrimack NH
    Brewery
    St. Louis MO
    Brewery
    Williamsburg VA
    Brewery
    Newark NJ
Brands:
    Budweiser
    Corona
    Stella Artois
    Beck's
    Leffe
    Hoegaarden
    Aguila
    Brahma
    Canvas
    Cass
    Eagle Lager
    Hero
    Jupiler
    Modelo
    Patagonia
    Victoria
    Wals Brut

72 ABC Tea House
14520 Arrow Hwy
Baldwin Park, CA 91706-1732
626-813-1333
Fax: 626-813-1338 888-220-3988
Tea and teabags
Owner: West Huang
west_huang@solteras.com
Estimated Sales: $5-10 Million
Number Employees: 20-49
Parent Co: Cathay International
Brands:
    Abc Tea (A Better Choice)

73 ACH Food Co Inc
One Parkview Plz
5th Floor
Oakbrook Terrace, IL 60181
630-586-3740
Fax: 630-954-6661 www.achfood.com
ACH's spice and seasonings brands, oils and shortenings, canola, vegetable, olive, and mixed blends.
Vice President & General Manager: Robert Soth
Chief Executive Officer: Imad Bazzi
EVP & Chief Financial Officer: Steve Zaruba
Vice President, Human Resources: Sarah Blankenship
sblankenship@achfood.com
Year Founded: 1868
Estimated Sales: $20-50 Million
Number Employees: 1000-4999
Square Footage: 768000
Type of Packaging: Consumer, Food Service, Private Label
Brands:
    Argo Corn Starch
    Decacake
    French's Dry Spice Mixes
    Spice Islands
    Durkee
    French's
    Patak's
    Wber Seasonings

74 ACP, Inc.
225 49th Avenue Dr SW
Cedar Rapids, IA 52404
319-368-8120
Fax: 319-368-8198 800-233-2366
acpsolutions.com
Commercial ovens
President/Owner: Tim Garbett
Parent Co: Ali Group

75 ADH Health Products Inc
215 N Route 303
Congers, NY 10920-1726
845-268-0027
Fax: 845-268-2988 info@adhhealth.com
www.adhhealth.com
All-natural vitamins, minerals, botanicals and high-quality health supplements.
President: Balu Advani
Chairman/CEO: Balram Advani
CFO: Navin Advani
VP/Vice Chairman/Human Resource Director: Maya Advani
COO: Ashwin Advani
VP Production: Arun Deshpande
Estimated Sales: $12.6 Million
Number Employees: 50-99
Square Footage: 100000
Type of Packaging: Private Label
Brands:
    Centra-Vit
    Daily Multiple S/C
    One Daily Essential With Iron
    Prenatal Formula
    Stress Formula With Zinc
    Thera-M Multiple

76 ADJR Inc
7909 Broughton Pike
Paulding, OH 45879
419-399-3182
Fax: 419-399-3189
Canned meat

Food Manufacturers / A-Z

President: Rex Bowersock
Treasurer: Angela Bowersock
Vice President: Dean Bowesock
Manager: Dawn Trentman
Estimated Sales: $2.6 Million
Number Employees: 20
Square Footage: 44100
Type of Packaging: Consumer, Food Service, Private Label

77 ADM Wild Flavors & Specialty
1261 Pacific Ave
Erlanger, KY 41018-1260
859-342-3600
Fax: 859-342-3610 info@wildflavors.com
www.wildflavors.com
Processor and exporter of flavors, colors and other ingredients for food and beverage
President: Kody Gibson
kcgibson@sbts.edu
Marketing Manager: Oliver Hodapp
Estimated Sales: $5-10 Million
Number Employees: 1000-4999
Parent Co: Archer Daniels Midland Company
Type of Packaging: Food Service, Private Label

78 AEP Colloids
6299 Route 9N
Hadley, NY 12835
518-696-9900
Fax: 518-696-9997 800-848-0658
www.aepcolloids.com
Supplier and manufacturer of gums including agar agar, guar, karaya, locust bean, tragacanth, carrageenan and psyllium husk.
Quality Manager: Drew Tomis
Contact: Adam Strouse
a.strouse@aepcolloids.com
Year Founded: 1966
Number Employees: 5-9
Square Footage: 40000
Parent Co: Sarcom Inc
Type of Packaging: Bulk

79 AFF International
1265 Kennestone Circle
Marietta, GA 30066-6037
770-427-8177
Fax: 770-427-0964 800-241-7764
Processor and exporter of aromatic flavors and fragrances
President/Owner: Richard Neill
Estimated Sales: $10-20 Million
Number Employees: 20-49
Type of Packaging: Bulk

80 AFI-FlashGril'd Steak
780 Layton Ave
Salt Lake City, UT 84104-1727
801-972-0055
Fax: 801-972-2050 800-382-2862
afisteak@aol.com
Frozen sandwich steaks
Manager: Goran Cvetkovic
CFO: Eugene Hill
VP, Marketing: Noel Working
Estimated Sales: $5-10 Million
Number Employees: 20-49
Brands:
  Flashgril'd

81 AG Processing Inc
12700 W Dodge Rd
Omaha, NE 68154-2154
402-496-7809
Fax: 402-492-7721 800-247-1345
info@agp.com www.agp.com
Emulsifiers, lecithin, vegetable fats, soybean flours, soy proteins and oils including vegetable, almond, amaranth, avocado, canola, coconut, corn, cottonseed, grape seed, lemon, olive, palm, peanut, and safflower.
Chairman: Brad Davis
CEO: J Keith Spackler
CFO/Group VP: Scott Simmelink
Senior VP: Mark Craigmile
mcraigmile@agp.com
VP: Matt Caswell
SVP, HR: Duke Vair
SVP, Operations: Mark Craigmile
Estimated Sales: Over $1 Billion
Number Employees: 1000-4999
Parent Co: AGP
Other Locations:
  AG Processing Plant
  Eagle Grove IA
  AG Processing Plant
  Emmetsburg IA
  AG Processing Plant
  Manning IA
  AG Processing Plant
  Mason City IA
  AG Processing Plant
  Sergeant Bluff IA
  AG Processing Plant
  Sheldon IA
  AG Processing Plant
  Dawson MN
  AG Processing Plant
  St. Joseph MO
  AG Processing Plant
  Hastings NE
Brands:
  Aep
  Agp Grain Ltd
  Agp Grain Marketing
  Aminoplus
  Masterfeeds
  Soygold

82 AGRO Merchants Grp NA
1150 Sanctuary Pkwy
Suite 125
Alpharetta, GA 30009
888-599-5512
info@agromerchants.com www.agromerchants.com
Fresh and frozen food handling solutions
President, North America: Dave Moore
CEO: Carlos Rodriguez
CFO: Arjan Kaaks
Year Founded: 2013

83 AGT Foods USA
1611 E Century Ave
Suite 102
Bismarck, ND 58503-0780
701-751-1623
Fax: 701-751-1626 info@agtfoods.com
www.agtfoods.com
Supplier of food ingredients. Specialize in red split lentils, football red lentils, whole lentils, chickpeas/garbonzo beans, peas and yellow split peas.
President/CEO: Murad Al-Katib
Parent Co: AGT Food & Ingredients
Type of Packaging: Consumer, Food Service, Private Label, Bulk
Other Locations:
  Williston Facility
  Williston ND
  Minot Factory
  Minot ND

84 AHD International, LLC
3340 Peachtree Rd NE
Suite 1685
Atlanta, GA 30326-1143
404-233-4022
Fax: 404-233-4041 info@ahdintl.com
www.ahdintl.com
Contract manufacturer of vitamins and nutritional products; Importer and exporter of nutritional raw materials and oils
President: John Alkire
Estimated Sales: $10-20 Million
Number Employees: 10-19
Type of Packaging: Bulk

85 AJ's Lena Maid Meats Inc
500 W Main St
Lena, IL 61048-9726
815-369-4522
Fax: 815-369-2075
Beef, pork, lamb and venison
Owner: Marcia Pax
Secretary/Treasurer: Suzanne McGiveron
Estimated Sales: $500000
Number Employees: 10-19
Type of Packaging: Bulk
Brands:
  Lena Maid

86 AJM Meat Packing
PO Box 13922
Park Court
San Juan, PR 00926-3922
787-787-4050
Fax: 787-787-2445
Manufactures approved USDA, FDA, and AMS meat and poultry for the industry which processes products for the school lunch program
VP of Operations: Sabah Yassin

87 ALDI
220 E 4th St
Cincinnati, OH 45202-4102
513-421-1671
Fax: 513-421-1671 www.aldi.us
Manager: Amy Denny
Marketing Director: Bill Still
Estimated Sales: Under $500,000
Number Employees: 20-49

88 ALO Drink
377 Swift Ave
South San Francisco, CA 94080
650-616-7777
Fax: 650-616-4808 info@alodrink.com
www.alodrink.com
Non-carbonated beverage: juice, cider
Executive VP: Henry Chen
Sales&Marketing: Jordan Ferchill
Contact: Brian Choi
brianchoi@alodrink.com
Parent Co: SPI West Port, Inc.

89 ALO Drinks
377 Swift Ave
San Francisco, CA 94080
info@alodrink.com
alodrink.com
Aloe vera drinks
Brands:
  alo

90 ALOHA
New York, NY 10005
aloha.com
Organic protein drinks, bars and powders

91 AM Todd Co
1717 Douglas Ave
Kalamazoo, MI 49007
269-343-2603
Fax: 269-343-3399 www.wildflavors.com
Processor and exporter of natural flavor extracts including alfalfa, black walnut hulls, wild cherry bark, dandelion, spice, oleoresins, xanthan gum, agar agar, fruit aromas (essences), essential oils, papain, coffeeechinacea and ginseng
Director, Business Development: Matt Redd
Estimated Sales: $50-100 Million
Number Employees: 50-99
Square Footage: 95000
Parent Co: Wild Flavours
Type of Packaging: Bulk

92 AMCO Proteins
109 Elbow Lane
Burlington, NJ 08016-4123
609-387-3130
Fax: 609-387-7204 info@amcoproteins.com
www.amcoproteins.com
Manufacturer of functional protein ingredients.
CEO: Adam Cabot
Vice President: Nancy Kraus
Product Development Manager: Jeffrey Brous
Other Locations:
  Quality Distribution Inc.
  Salt Lake City UT

93 AME Nutrition
545 Metro Place S
Suite 100
Dublin, OH 43017
614-766-3638
sales@amenutrition.com
www.amenutrition.com
Plant- and dairy-based ingredients manufacturer
Director of Sales & Marketing: Bill Brickson

94 AMF Pharma
1931 S Lynx Place
Ontario, CA 91761
909-930-9599
Fax: 909-930-9499 888-666-1016
info@amfpharma.com amfpharma.com
Dietary supplements
Number of Brands: 1
Type of Packaging: Private Label

95 AMT Labs Inc
680 N 700 W
North Salt Lake, UT 84054-2733
801-294-3126
Fax: 801-299-0220 customercare@amtlabs.net

Food Manufacturers / A-Z

Processor and exporter of food supplements including mineral supplements, amino acid chelates, ascorbates, citrates, etc.
President: Bing Fang
President: Layne Hadley
Chairman: Dr Sen-Maw Fang PhD
VP/Research & Development: Dr. Oliver Fang MD
VP Manufacturing: Todd Rasmussen
Estimated Sales: $8.2 Million
Number Employees: 50-99
Square Footage: 400000
Type of Packaging: Private Label, Bulk

96 AOI Matcha
16651 Gothard St
Unit M
Huntington Beach, CA 92647
714-841-2716
877-264-0877
info@aoimatcha.com www.aoimatcha.com
Green tea
Type of Packaging: Bulk

97 AOI Tea Company
16651 Gothard Street
Unit M
Huntington Beach, CA 92647
714-841-2716
877-264-0877
consumer@AOItea.com www.aoitea.com
Matcha green tea
Madam President: Ayano Honda
Contact: Andrew Ge
age@aoimatcha.com

98 APC Inc
2425 SE Oak Tree Ct
Ankeny, IA 50021-7199
515-289-7600
Fax: 515-289-4360 800-369-2672
www.functionalproteins.com
Manufacturer of dairy replacer for bakery, confectionery and beverage applications.
CEO: Ryan Black
rblack@proliant.com
Number Employees: 50-99
Parent Co: Lauridsen Group
Other Locations:
   U.S. Office
   Ankeny IA
   Mexico Office
   El Marqu,s, Quer,taro
   Production
   Melrose MN
Brands:
   VersiLac®

99 APS BioGroup
2235 South Central Ave
Phoenix, AZ 85004
602-353-8800
info@apsbiogroup.com
www.apsbiogroup.com
Producer of colostrum, and private label vitamins.
CEO: Bob Davies
Parent Co: Pantheryx, Inc.
Type of Packaging: Consumer, Private Label

100 ARA Food Corp
8001 NW 60th St
Miami, FL 33166-3412
305-468-6659
Fax: 305-592-6035 800-533-8831
info@arafood.com www.tropicalchips.net
Plantain, taro and cassava tropical chips
Vice President: Alberto Abrante
salesdep@arafood.com
Estimated Sales: $10-20 Million
Number Employees: 50-99
Number of Brands: 9
Type of Packaging: Private Label
Brands:
   Bananitas
   Donita
   Rico's
   ARA Real
   Top Banana
   Yu-qui-tas
   Mariquitas Classic
   Natura
   Tropical Chips

101 ARCO Coffee
2206 Winter St
Superior, WI 54880-1400
715-392-4771
Fax: 715-392-4776 800-283-2726
Pete@arcocoffee.com www.arcocoffee.com
Coffee and coffee syrups
Owner: John Andresen
President: B Fleming
Contact: Chris Devaney
chris@arcocoffee.com
Director Manufacturing: Vern Suby
Estimated Sales: Less than $500,000
Number Employees: 1-4
Type of Packaging: Consumer, Food Service
Brands:
   Arco

102 ASC Seafood Inc
6340 118th Ave
Largo, FL 33773-3728
727-541-6896
Fax: 727-545-0582 800-876-3474
fred@ascseafood.com www.ascseafood.com
Quality seafood products
Owner: Steve Annas
steve@ascseafood.com
VP Sales/Marketing: Fred Kunder
Estimated Sales: $4 Million
Number Employees: 5-9
Brands:
   Gulf-Maid

103 ASK Foods Inc
77 N Hetrick Ave
Palmyra, PA 17078-1529
717-838-6356
Fax: 717-838-7458 800-879-4275
tasmith@askfoods.com www.askfoods.com
Desserts, dips, deli salads, sauces, soups, entrees and natural juices.
CEO: Wendy Dimatteo
wdimatteo@askfoods.com
CFO: Rich Rutowski
Director Sales & Marketing: Terry Smith
Estimated Sales: $10-20 Million
Number Employees: 100-249
Square Footage: 400
Type of Packaging: Consumer, Food Service, Private Label, Bulk
Brands:
   Ask Foods
   Homestyle

104 ASV Wines
1998 Road 152
Delano, CA 93215-9437
661-792-3159
Fax: 661-792-3995 sales@asvwines.com
www.asvwines.com
Wines
CEO: Marko Zaninovich
markozaninovich@asvwines.com
Vice President: William Nakata
Plant Manager: John Sleeman
Estimated Sales: $3.2 Million
Number Employees: 20-49
Type of Packaging: Food Service, Private Label, Bulk
Other Locations:
   San Martin Winery
   San Martin CA
Brands:
   Canyon Oaks
   Crow Canyon
   Muirwood
   Steel Creek

105 AVRON Resources Inc
1080 Essex Ave
Richmond, CA 94801-2113
510-233-0633
Fax: 510-233-0636 800-883-9574
avron@avron.com
Flavors
President: Carl Arvold
Estimated Sales: $5-10 Million
Number Employees: 5-9
Type of Packaging: Private Label

106 Aak USA Inc
131 Marsh St
Newark, NJ 07114
973-344-1300
betterwithaak@aak.com
www.aak.com
Processor and importer of cocoa butter substitutes and oils including coconut, cottonseed, palm, soybean, sunflower, vegetable, etc.; exporter of lauric oil products
President, USA & North Latin America: Octavio Diaz de Leon
VP, Operations: Frank Miller
Estimated Sales: $50-100 Million
Number Employees: 50-99
Parent Co: AAK AB
Type of Packaging: Bulk
Other Locations:
   AAK USA Inc-Port Newark Plant
   Port Newark NJ
   AAK USA K1/K2-Lousiville Plant
   Lousiville KY
   AAK Foodservice, USA
   Hillside NJ
   AAK USA Richmond Corp.
   Richmond CA

107 Aala Meat Market Inc
751 Waiakamilo Rd
Honolulu, HI 96817-4312
808-832-6650
Fax: 808-832-6659
Meats
President: Sandra Moribe
gmoribe5@hawaiiantel.net
Estimated Sales: $1-3 Million
Number Employees: 10-19

108 Aaland Potato Company
PO Box 304
101 Railroad Avenue
Hoople, ND 58243
701-894-6144
Fax: 701-894-6423
Potatoes
Manager: Jim Bailey
Estimated Sales: $2.5-5 Million
Number Employees: 10-19
Type of Packaging: Consumer
Brands:
   Aaland

109 Abattoir A. Trahan Company
860 Chemin Des Acadiens
Yamachiche, QC G0X 3L0
Canada
819-296-3791
Fax: 819-296-3364
Fresh and frozen pork
President: Rene Trahan
Marketing Director: Dennis Trahan
Number Employees: 50-99
Type of Packaging: Consumer, Food Service, Private Label, Bulk

110 Abattoir Aliments AstaInc.
511 Av De La Gare
St Alexandre De Kamouras, QC G0L 2G0
Canada
418-495-2728
Fax: 418-495-2879 800-463-1355
www.alimentsasta.com
Pork. Slaughtering services available
CEO: Jacques Poitras
Financial Services Director: Carol Levesque
Supervisor, IT Services And Procurement: Jean Francois Thoral
Quality Services Director: Chanel Fournier
Sales Director: Andre Poitras
Human Resources Director: Edith Laplante
VP, Operations: Stephanie Poitras
Number Employees: 405
Type of Packaging: Bulk

111 Abbot's Butcher
350 Clinton St.
Costa Mesa, CA 92626
949-726-2156
hello@theabbotsbutcher.com
www.abbotsbutcher.com
Plant-based meats including imitation ground beef, chicken, and chorizo
Founder, CEO: Kerry Song

Food Manufacturers / A-Z

112 Abbotsford Growers Ltd.
31825 Marshall Road
Abbotsford, BC V2T 5Z8
Canada
604-864-0022
Fax: 604-864-0020 info@abbotsfordgrowers.com
www.abbotsfordgrowers.com
Raspberry & blueberry packer; frozen purees; and pasteurized and aseptic purees.
General Manager: Colin Hutchinson
Quality Assurance Supervisor: Dan Sigfusson
Sales/Plant/Production: Stephen Evans
Estimated Sales: $10-24 Million
Number Employees: 250
Square Footage: 100000
Type of Packaging: Bulk
Brands:
  Abbotsford Growers Co-Op

113 Abbott & Cobb Inc
4151 E Street Rd
Feasterville, PA 19053-4995
215-245-6666
Fax: 215-245-9043 800-345-7333
acseed@abbottcobb.com www.abbottcobb.com
Breeder, producer and marketer of vegetable seeds, specifically corn, peppers, pumpkins, beans, squash and cucumbers.
Owner: Art Abbott
aandcseeds@aol.com
VP of Sales & Product Management: Luther McLaugglin
Vice President of Public Relations: Harriett Ryan
Senior Vice President of Operations: Bob Rumer
Estimated Sales: $38.7 Million
Number Employees: 20-49
Type of Packaging: Private Label, Bulk
Other Locations:
  Nogales AZ
  West Palm Beach FL
  Caldwell ID
  Los Mochis, Mexico

114 Abbott Laboratories
100 Abbott Park Rd
Abbott Park, IL 60064-3500
847-938-3887
Fax: 847-937-9555 www.abbottvascular.com
Offers a variety of pediatric and adult nutritional products, pharmaceuticals and enteral feeding products. Processor of evaporated and condensed milk.
Chairman/CEO: Miles White
CFO: Thomas Freyman
Senior VP: Gary McCullough
Contact: Roberto Abalos
roberto.abalos@abbott.com
Number Employees: 1-4
Parent Co: Abbott Laboratories
Type of Packaging: Consumer

115 Abbott's Candy Shop
48 E Walnut St
Hagerstown, IN 47346-1542
765-489-4442
Fax: 765-489-5501 877-801-1200
abbottscandy@abbottscandy.com
www.abbottscandy.com
Gourmet chocolates and caramels
President: Suanna Goodnight
Vice President: Gordon Goodnight
Manager: Becky Diercks
abbottscandy@abbottscandy.com
Estimated Sales: $780,000
Number Employees: 20-49
Square Footage: 28
Type of Packaging: Private Label
Brands:
  Abbott's Candy

116 Abbott's Meat Inc
3623 Blackington Ave
Flint, MI 48532-3874
810-232-7128
Fax: 810-232-7960 800-678-1907
www.abbottsmeat.com
Beef and beef products
President: Rebecca Shepler
rshepler@abbottsmeat.com
Estimated Sales: $5-10 Million
Number Employees: 10-19
Brands:
  Abbotts Meat

117 Abby's Better Nut Butter
abbysbetter.com
Nut butters
Founder: Abby Kircher
Number of Brands: 1
Number of Products: 5
Type of Packaging: Consumer
Brands:
  ABBY'S BETTER NUT BUTTER

118 Abbyland Foods Inc
502 E Linden St
P.O. Box 69
Abbotsford, WI 54405
715-223-6386
Fax: 715-223-6388 800-732-5483
abbyland@abbyland.com www.abbyland.com
Meat, sausage and boneless beef.
Chief Insurance & Financial Officer: Paul Hess
Director of Specialty Meats: Brian O'Connor
Specialty Meats Sales: Patty Patterson
Office Manager: Jane Langman
715-223-6386 Ext. 7216
Sausage Production: Sean Wagner
Year Founded: 1977
Estimated Sales: $127 Million
Number of Brands: 1,000
Square Footage: 122000
Type of Packaging: Food Service, Private Label, Bulk
Brands:
  Abbuland
  London Classic Broil
  Tailgate

119 Abdallah Candies & Gifts
3501 County Road 42 W
Burnsville, MN 55306-3805
952-890-0859
Fax: 952-890-3664 service@abdallahcandies.com
www.abdallahcandies.com
Chocolate, caramels and candy mixes.
President: Steve Hegedus
stevenh@abdallahcandies.com
Number Employees: 100-249
Number of Brands: 5
Square Footage: 55000

120 Abe's Vegan Muffins
845-735-5100
www.abesmuffins.com
Muffins and cakes
Number of Brands: 1
Number of Products: 30
Type of Packaging: Consumer
Brands:
  ABE'S

121 Abel & Schafer Inc
20 Alexander Ct
Ronkonkoma, NY 11779-6573
631-737-2220
Fax: 631-737-2335 800-443-1260
info@kompletusa.com us.komplet.com
Mixes including bread, cake, muffin, dough conditioners, glazes and fillings
Vice President: Joanne Oakes
roy.donna@cdphp.com
VP: Frank Triedman
R&D Manager: Diego Grassi
Head of Quality Control: Bert Wiegand
Sales Manager: Joseph Piotte
Director of Operations: Carl Wittig
Production Manager: Christopher Weber
Estimated Sales: $20-25 Million
Number Employees: 50-99
Parent Co: Abel & Schafer Group
Type of Packaging: Private Label

122 Abimar Foods Inc
5425 N 1st St
Abilene, TX 79603-6424
325-691-5425
Fax: 325-691-5471
salesinquiry@abimarfoods.com
Bakery products including cookies and crackers.
Chief Executive Officer: Patricia Canal
pcanal@abimarfoods.com
Director, Business Development: Rafael Henao
Director, Operations: Brandon Heiser
Plant Manager: Luis Felipe Velasquez Lopez
Director, Procurement: Mauricio Perez
Estimated Sales: $29 Million
Number Employees: 100-249
Number of Brands: 4
Parent Co: Grupo Empresarial Nutresa

Type of Packaging: Consumer
Brands:
  Festy
  Lil Dutch Maid
  Nucita
  Tru Blu

123 Abimco USA, Inc.
43 Hampshire Dr
Mendham, NJ 07945
973-543-7393
Fax: 973-543-2948
Fruit juice concentrates; importer and exporter of dried and frozen fruits and vegetables; Importer of juice concentrates, honey and tomato paste; exporter of fresh mushrooms
President: Paulette Krelman
General Manager: Arthur Kupperman
Number Employees: 1-4
Type of Packaging: Bulk

124 Abingdon Vineyard & Winery
20530 Alvarado Rd
Abingdon, VA 24211
276-623-1255
Fax: 276-623-0125 info@abingdonwinery.com
www.abingdonwinery.com
Wines
Owner: Bob Carlson
Co-Owner: Janet Lee Nordin
Vineyard Manager: Kevin Sutherland
Estimated Sales: $.5-1 million
Number Employees: 1-4

125 Abita Brewing Co
166 Barbee Rd
Covington, LA 70433-8651
985-893-3143
Fax: 985-898-3546 800-737-2311
friends@abita.com www.Abita.com
Lager, ale and caffeine-free root beer.
President: Jim Andrews
jimandrews.mail@abitalumber.com
Year Founded: 1986
Estimated Sales: $20-50 Million
Number Employees: 20-49
Square Footage: 14000
Type of Packaging: Consumer, Private Label
Brands:
  Abita
  Golden
  Purple Haze
  Turbodog

126 (HQ)Abitec Corp
501 W 1st Ave
Columbus, OH 43215
614-429-6464
800-555-1255
info@abiteccorp.com www.abiteccorp.com
Producer of specialty chemicals including vegetable oils and powders.
CEO: Jeff Walton
CFO: Brad Orders
Head, R&D: Jim Williams
VP, Operations: John Bielas
Estimated Sales: $50-100 Million
Number Employees: 50-200
Number of Brands: 9
Parent Co: ABF Ingredients
Other Locations:
  Abitec Corporation
  Janesville WI
  Abitec Corporation
  Paris IL
Brands:
  Acconon®
  Accoquat®
  Capmul®
  Caprol®
  Captex®
  Hydro-Kote®
  Nutri Sperse®
  Pureco®
  Sterotex®

127 Abkit Camocare Nature Works
61 Broadway
Room 1310
New York, NY 10006-2722
212-292-1550
Fax: 212-292-1542 800-226-6227
www.abkit.com
Natural products, vitamins, etc

Food Manufacturers / A-Z

President: Claus Ghringer
Director International Sales: Alison Carley
Estimated Sales: $3-5 Million
Number Employees: 10-19
Brands:
- Catuama
- Kwai
- Nature Works

128 Abraham's Natural Foods
9 Long Branch Ave
PO Box 89
Long Branch, NJ 07740-7121
732-229-5799
Fax: 732-571-0890 800-327-9903
abrahamshummos@gmail.com
www.abrahamsnatural.com
Natural gourmet dips, salads and cookies, and kosher and Middle Eastern foods
President: Louis Fellman
taboule@yahoo.com
Estimated Sales: $1 Million
Number Employees: 5-9
Brands:
- Baba Ghannouj
- Hummos

129 Absopure Water Company
8835 General Drive
Plymouth, MI 48170
800-422-7678
www.absopure.com
Bottled water
President: William Young
Contact: Art Amelotte
amelotte@absopure.com
Estimated Sales: $22.9 Million
Number Employees: 100-249
Number of Brands: 1
Type of Packaging: Consumer, Private Label, Bulk
Brands:
- Absopure

130 Abuelita Mexican Foods
9209 Enterprise Ct
Manassas Park, VA 20111-4809
703-369-0232
Fax: 703-369-0875 office@abuelita.com
www.abuelita.com
Corn tortillas and corn tortilla chips.
President: Eugene Suarez
General Manager: Peggy Suarez
Sales Director: Steve Dill
Estimated Sales: $4.7 Million
Number Employees: 1-4
Number of Brands: 3
Number of Products: 45
Square Footage: 106000
Brands:
- Abuelita
- Casa De Carmen
- Nana's Cocina

131 Abunda Life
208 3rd Ave
Asbury Park, NJ 07712-6097
732-775-9338
Fax: 732-502-0899
Natural health products including vitamins, goat milk powder, fiber supplements, herbal spices, herbal teas, rice bran syrups and sweeteners including: banana, grape, pineapple and orange.
Founder: Dr Robert Sorge
Estimated Sales: $300,000-500,000
Number Employees: 10-19
Square Footage: 16800
Type of Packaging: Consumer, Private Label
Brands:
- 24 Super Amino Acids
- Abunda Body
- Blood Building Broth
- Blood Building Powder
- Brain Invigoration Powder
- Cholesterol Solve
- Cram For Students
- Dieters Tea
- Energy Powder
- Essaic Formula
- Fruit Fiber
- Live Plant Juice
- Liver Detox Formula
- Parasite Annihilation Powder
- Royal Pollen Complex
- Super Bowl Cleanse
- Super C Active
- Super Detox
- Super Green
- Super Salad Oil
- Super Tonic

132 Acacia Vineyard
2750 Las Amigas Rd
Napa, CA 94559
707-226-9991
Fax: 707-226-1685 877-226-1700
acacia.info@acaciavineyard.com
www.acaciavineyard.com
Wines
Owner: Matthew Glynn
Contact: Dawn Angelosante
dangelosante@acaciawinery.com
Estimated Sales: $10-20 Million
Number Employees: 20-49
Parent Co: Chalone Wine Group
Brands:
- Acacia

133 Acadian Fine Foods
228 Saint Charles Ave # 1323
New Orleans, LA 70130-2646
504-581-2355
Fax: 504-525-9841
Frozen stuffed chicken, seafood pies, canned blue crabmeat, frozen crabs, crawfish
President: Charles Williams
VP: Russell Raelston
Estimated Sales: $.5-1 million
Number Employees: 5-9

134 Acadian Ostrich Ranch
9010 Highway 961
Clinton, LA 70722
225-683-9988
Fax: 225-683-9988 800-350-0167
Ostrich and alligator meats
President: Marco Dermody

135 Acadian Seaplants
30 Brown Avenue
Dartmouth, NS B3B 1X8
Canada
902-468-2840
Fax: 902-468-3474 800-575-9100
info@acadian.ca www.acadianseaplants.com
Seaweed based products for food, biochemical, agricultural, and agrichemical markets.
Director of Sales: Robert Sperdakes
Account Manager: Linda Linquist
Year Founded: 1981
Estimated Sales: $20 Million
Number Employees: 300
Type of Packaging: Private Label, Bulk
Brands:
- Drewclar
- Hana-Nori
- Nutramer

136 Açaí Roots
5920 Friars Rd
Suite 206
San Diego, CA 92108
Fax: 619-330-2465 866-401-2224
info@açairoots.com www.açairoots.com
Açaí products
Number of Brands: 1
Number of Products: 10
Type of Packaging: Consumer
Brands:
- ACAI ROOTS

137 Acatris USA
3300 Edinborough Way
Suite 712
Edina, MN 55435-5963
952-920-7700
Fax: 952-920-7704 www.acatris.com
Blended dough conditioners, antioxidant solutions, release agents and lubricants; wholesaler/distributor of soy flour, vitamin/mineral blends and oils including soybean and canola.
President: Laurent Leduc
Manager: Joni Johnson
Sales Manager: Cherie Jones
Estimated Sales: $5-10 Million
Number Employees: 20-49
Number of Brands: 15
Square Footage: 64000
Parent Co: Royal Schouten Group
Type of Packaging: Bulk
Brands:
- Alube
- Dadex
- Daedol
- Daejel
- Daelube
- Daminaide
- Daminco
- Daminet
- Extol
- Fenulife
- Lesoy
- Linumlife
- Myvacet
- Myverol
- Soylife

138 AccuTemp
8415 N Clinton Park Dr
Fort Wayne, IN 46825
800-210-5907
www.accutemp.net
Commercial kitchen equipment, including steamers and griddles
President & CEO: Scott Swogger
EVP, Sales & Marketing: John Pennington
COO: Dave Ogram
Year Founded: 1993

139 Accurate Ingredients Inc
125 Schmitt Blvd
Farmingdale, NY 11735-1403
516-496-2500
Fax: 516-496-2516 info@acing.net
Ingredients
President: Dan Saber
Vice President of Sales: Vince Pasquale
Sales, Vice President of Operations: Rich Hamerschlag
Estimated Sales: $15.6 Million
Number Employees: 20-49
Type of Packaging: Consumer, Food Service, Bulk
Other Locations:
- Accurate Ingredients
- Santa Ana CA

140 Accurex
PO Box 410
Schofield, WI 54476
Fax: 715-241-6191 800-333-1400
www.accurex.com
Kitchen ventilation systems
President/Owner: Damon Childers

141 Ace Bakery
1 Hafis Rd
North York, ON M6M 2V6
Canada
416-241-8433
Fax: 905-565-7098 800-443-7929
bread@acebakery.com www.acebakery.com
Fresh and frozen baguettes, loaves, buns, and bagels; chips, toasts, croutons and granola.
President: Lee Andrews
Year Founded: 1993
Number Employees: 500-999
Parent Co: George Weston Ltd.

142 Ace Development
31194 State Highway 51
Bruneau, ID 83604-5076
208-845-2487
Fax: 208-845-2274 copakarobert@hotmail.com
Aquaculture fisheries.
President: Robert Williams
Year Founded: 1984
Estimated Sales: $800,000
Number Employees: 1-4

143 Ace Farm USA Inc
1343 Lafayette Ave
Bronx, NY 10474-4806
718-991-3816
Fax: 718-679-9125 info@acefarmusa.com
Non-alcoholic beverages, soft drinks.
Marketing: Jean Park
Manager: Jina Park
jina@acefarmusa.com
Number Employees: 20-49

Food Manufacturers / A-Z

144 Aceitunas Losada
Ctra. A-398 km 21.3
Carmona, Sevilla, 41410
Spain
export@aceitunaslosada.com
aceitunaslosada.com
Olives

145 Acesur North America
2700 Westchester Ave
Suite 105
Purchase, NY 10577-2554
914-925-0450
Fax: 914-925-0458 info@acesur.com
www.acesur.com
Olive oil and other specialty Spanish products
USA Director: Antonio Rubiales

146 Acetifico Marcello Denigris
P.O. Box 53
Westwood, NJ 07675-0053
973-837-6791
Fax: 973-837-6794 denigris1889.com
Vinegars
Type of Packaging: Consumer, Food Service, Private Label

147 Acharice Specialties
PO Box 690
Greenville, MS 38702-0690
800-432-4901
Fax: 901-381-3287
Rice and grain products
President/CEO: Jack Stratol
Research & Development: Bill Land
Sales/Marketing: Nelson Wurth
Operations/Production: Mike Well
Plant Manager: Pat Roy
Number Employees: 500-999
Type of Packaging: Private Label

148 Achatz Handmade Pie Co
30301 Commerce Blvd
Chesterfield, MI 48051-1243
586-749-2882
www.achatzpies.com
Handmade pies
Manager: Wendy Achatz
vparis@slpr.net
Estimated Sales: Less Than $500,000
Number Employees: 1-4

149 Ackerman Winery
4406 220th Trl
Amana, IA 52203-8035
319-622-3379
Fax: 319-622-6513 info@ackermanwinery.com
www.ackermanwinery.com
Wine
President: Les Ackerman
Manager: Cassie Bott
cassie@firesidewinery.com
Estimated Sales: $1-2.5 Million
Number Employees: 1-4
Type of Packaging: Bulk

150 Acme Bread Co
1601 San Pablo Ave
Berkeley, CA 94702-1317
510-524-1327
www.acmebread.com
Bread
Founder: Steven Sullivan
Contact: Hannah Jukovsky
hannah@acmebread.com
Estimated Sales: Less Than $500,000
Number Employees: 5-9

151 Acme Smoked Fish Corporation
30-56 Gem Street
Brooklyn, NY 11222
718-383-8585
Fax: 718-383-9115 www.acmesmokedfish.com
Processor and importer of smoked fish and herring.
President: Eric Caslow
CFO: Eduardo Carlajasa
EVP: Robert Caslow
Director of Sales: Buzz Billik
VP of Operations: Davis Caslow
Year Founded: 1901
Estimated Sales: $20-50 Million
Number Employees: 100-249
Brands:
  Acme
  Blue Hill Bay

152 Acme Steak & Seafood
31 Bissell Ave
Youngstown, OH 44505-2707
330-270-8000
Fax: 330-270-8006 800-686-2263
support@acmesteak.com www.acmesteak.com
Fresh produce, seafood, sausage, hamburgers and portion controlled meat.
Owner/President: Michael Mike
mike@acmesteak.com
Year Founded: 1947
Estimated Sales: $2.40 Million
Number Employees: 10-19
Square Footage: 68000
Type of Packaging: Consumer, Food Service, Private Label

153 Acornseekers Inc
5294 FM1115
Flatonia, TX 78941
786-338-8160
www.acornseekers.com
Spanish-style pork
Co-Founder & CEO: Sergio Marsal
Co-Founder & Chief Operations Officer: Manuel Murga

154 Acqua Blox LLC
12000 East Slauson Ave
Suite 3
Santa Fe Springs, CA 90670
562-693-9599
Fax: 562-945-3133 info@aquablox.com
www.aquablox.com
Purified and bacteria free water products specifically designed for emergency preparedness, first responders, and disaster victims
Manager: Mike Harris
Estimated Sales: Below $5 Million
Number Employees: 1-4
Type of Packaging: Consumer, Bulk
Brands:
  Aqua Blox®

155 Across Foods, LLC
608 Coach Drive
New Hope, PA 18938
215-693-6274
Fax: 267-895-6311 info@acrossfoods.com
www.acrossfoods.com
Kosher, organic/natiral, cookies, full-line candy, gummies/jellies/pates de fruits, licorice, health, fitness and energy bars, dried fruit.
President: Michael Sas
mjmas@acrossfoods.com

156 Acta Health Products
380 N Pastoria Avenue
Sunnyvale, CA 94085-4108
408-732-6830
Fax: 408-732-0208 www.actaproducts.com
Processor and exporter of vitamins, minerals, herbal extracts and other dietary supplements; importer of raw materials
President: David Chang
david.chang@actaproducts.com
VP: K Y Chang
Director Quality Control: Michael Chang
Director Marketing/Sales: Cal Bewicke
Director Purchasing: Leo Liu
Estimated Sales: $3 Million
Number Employees: 30
Square Footage: 124000
Type of Packaging: Private Label, Bulk

157 Action Labs
PO Box 1090
2915 East Rickerway
Anaheim, CA 92806
714-630-5941
Fax: 714-630-8221 800-400-5696
actionvit@aol.com www.actionlab.com
Specialty diet and energy supplements for men and women.
President: James R Bailey
Marketing: Mandy Ray
Sales: John Russo
Brands:
  Ginseng 4x

158 Active Organics
1097 Yates St
Lewisville, TX 75057-4829
972-221-7500
Fax: 972-221-3324 800-541-1478
info@activeorganics.com
www.activeorganics.com
Botanical extracts
Vice President: Linda Defratus
ldefratus@organics.com
CFO: Glen Guthmann
VP: Bill Hynes
Human Resources Executive: Angi Rene
VP Operations: Bill Heinz
Estimated Sales: $9.9 Million
Number Employees: 100-249
Square Footage: 484000

159 Acushnet Fish Corporation
46 Middle Street
Fairhaven, MA 02719-3086
508-997-7482
Fax: 508-999-6697
Fish
President: Ralph Parsons

160 Adair Vineyards
52 Allhusen Rd
New Paltz, NY 12561-4217
845-255-1377
adairwines@aol.com
www.adairwine.com
Wines
Owner: Mark Stopkie
Estimated Sales: Less Than $500,000
Number Employees: 1-4
Type of Packaging: Private Label

161 Adam Matthews Inc
2104 Plantside Dr
Jeffersontown, KY 40299-1924
502-499-1244
Fax: 502-499-8331
Bakery products including cheesecakes,and Festival Pie.
President: Vicky Meeks
vmeeks@promediagroup.com
Office Operations: Christie Schneider
Bakery Operations: Matt Mead
National Sales Representative: Mary Anne Burch
VP Operations: Cathy Fleig
Estimated Sales: $1-2.5 Million
Number Employees: 20-49
Square Footage: 80000
Brands:
  Adam Matthews

162 Adam Puchta Winery
1947 Frene Creek Rd
Hermann, MO 65041-4103
573-486-5596
Fax: 573-486-2361 info@adampuchtawine.com
www.adampuchtawine.com
Wines
President: Timothy Puchta
tjp_apwinery@centurytel.net
Estimated Sales: $1-2.5 Million
Number Employees: 10-19
Type of Packaging: Private Label

163 Adams & Brooks Inc
1915 S Hoover St
Los Angeles, CA 90007-1322
213-749-3226
Fax: 213-746-7614 info@adams-brooks.com
Bagged candy including: chocolate cups, candy bars, lollypops, novelty, nut, caramel and taffy. Also vending, fund raising and theatre packaging.
President: John Brooks
Cmo: Steve Misinger
steve.misingerbrooks@adams-brooks.com
VP of Marketing & Product Development: Cindy Brooks
Estimated Sales: $10-20 Million
Number Employees: 100-249
Type of Packaging: Consumer, Private Label, Bulk
Brands:
  Adams & Brooks
  Coffee Rio
  Comic Animal
  Cup-O-Gold
  Fairtime
  P-Nuttles
  P-Nuttles Butter Toffee Peanuts

Food Manufacturers / A-Z

Psycho Pops
Psycho Psours
Unicorn Pops

164 Adams County Winery
251 Peach Tree Rd
Orrtanna, PA 17353-9753
717-334-4631
Fax: 717-334-4026 877-601-7936
vintner@adamscountywinery.com
www.adamscountywinery.com
Wines
Owner: Katherine Bigler
vintner@adamscountywinery.com
Estimated Sales: $1-2.5 Million
Number Employees: 10-19

165 Adams Fisheries Ltd
617 Bear Point Rd
Shag Harbour, NS B0T 1W0
Canada
902-723-2435
Fax: 902-723-2325
Salted cod, pollack and haddock and live lobster
President: Donald Adams
Estimated Sales: $3.2 Million
Number Employees: 8
Square Footage: 34000

166 Adams Foods & Milling
146 Industrial Dr
Box 143a
Dothan, AL 36303
334-983-4233
Fax: 334-983-5596
Cakes including pound, sheet and decorated
President: Ted Adams
Manager: Larry Nowkaiski
Manager: Joy Pettis
Estimated Sales: $5-10 Million
Number Employees: 5-9
Parent Co: Adams Milling Company
Type of Packaging: Consumer, Food Service, Private Label, Bulk
Brands:
 Adams
 Avery
 Baker's Best
 Home Style
 Mother's

167 Adams Olive Ranch
1200 S Aster Ave
Lindsay, CA 93247
559-562-2882
Fax: 559-562-2272 888-216-5483
www.adamsoliveranch.com
Olives
Owner: Denis Bonfilio
Estimated Sales: Less than $500,000
Number Employees: 10-19
Square Footage: 24000
Type of Packaging: Consumer, Private Label
Brands:
 Adam's Ranch
 Raw Earth Organics
 Smith Home Cured

168 Adams USA Inc.
610 S. Jefferson Avenue
Cookeville, TN 10017
212-733-2323
Fax: 800-946-4102 800-251-6857
www.adamsusa.com
Health products
CEO: Ian Read
Contact: Dani Boger
dani.boger@adamsusa.com

169 Adams Vegetable Oils Inc
P.O. Box 956
Arbuckle, CA 95912
530-668-2005
Fax: 530-476-2315 info@adamsgrp.com
www.adamsvegetableoils.com
Vegetable oils, grain and seeds.
Sales Manager: David Hoffsten
Estimated Sales: $100+ Million
Number Employees: 50-99
Square Footage: 5889
Type of Packaging: Bulk

170 AddGarlic!
617 Broadway
Unit 1576
Sonoma, CA 95476
707-996-2999
www.addgarlic.com
Pureed Garlic
President: Andy Davis
andy@addgarlic.com
Brands:
 Aglio Di Mirabella(c)

171 Adee Honey Farm
517 Jay St.
Bruce, SD 57220
605-627-5621
Fax: 605-627-5622 www.adeehoneyfarms.com
Processor of honey and beeswax. Pollination services also available
Owner: Richard Adee
Owner: Kelvin Adee
Owner: Bret Adee
Contact: Kirk Adee
kirkadee@adeehoneyfarms.com
Year Founded: 1957
Estimated Sales: $20-50 Million
Number Employees: 50-99
Type of Packaging: Bulk
Other Locations:
 Bakersfield CA
 Cedar Rapids NE
 Roscoe SD
 Woodville MS

172 Adelaida Cellars Inc
5805 Adelaida Rd
Paso Robles, CA 93446-9783
805-239-8980
Fax: 805-239-4671 800-676-1232
wines@adelaida.com www.adelaida.com
Wines
Owner: Elizabeth Vansteenwyk
wines@adelaida.com
General Manager: Jessica Kollhoff
Director of Retail Sales and Marketing: Sunni Mullinax
National Sales: Paul Sowerby
Hospitality Manager: Pati Coelho
Production: Lalo Escalante
Estimated Sales: $1-2.5 Million
Number Employees: 10-19

173 Adelsheim Vineyard
16800 NE Calkins Ln
Newberg, OR 97132-6572
503-538-3652
Fax: 503-538-2248 info@adelsheim.com
www.chehalemmountains.org
Pinot noir wines and cool-climae white wines from Pinot gris; Chardonnay; Pinot blanc and Auxerrois.
President: David Adelsheim
info@adelsheim.com
Owner: Virginia Adelsheim
Marketing & Communications Manager: Catherine Douglas
Manager of Sales Operations: Kim Bellingar
Controller: Kathi Neal
Vineyard Manager: Chad Vargas
Winemaker: Dave Paige
Estimated Sales: $7 Million
Number Employees: 20-49
Square Footage: 160000
Brands:
 Adelsheim Vineyard

174 Adirondack Beverages Inc
701 Corporation Park
Scotia, NY 12302-1065
518-370-3622
Fax: 518-370-3762 800-316-6096
contact@adkbev.com
www.adirondackbeverages.com
Carbonated and noncarbonated beverages including cola, ginger ale, tonic, fruit drink, seltzer and sparkling and still water
President: Douglas Martin
CFO: Ray Demers
rdemers@adkbev.com
Estimated Sales: $500,000-1 Million
Number Employees: 100-249
Square Footage: 3000000
Parent Co: Polar Corporation
Type of Packaging: Consumer, Food Service, Private Label
Brands:
 Adironack
 Clear 'n' Natural
 Waist Watcher

175 Adirondack Maple Farms
490 Persse Rd
Fonda, NY 12068-5716
518-853-4022
Fax: 518-853-3791 bruceroblee@yahoo.com
www.adirondackmaplefarms.com
Pure maple syrup, sugar and candy.
Owner: Bruce Roblee
broblee@adirondackmaplefarms.com
General Manager: Bruce Roblee
Estimated Sales: Less Than $500,000
Number Employees: 1-4
Type of Packaging: Private Label
Brands:
 Adirondack Maple Farms

176 Adkin & Son Associated Food Products
6645 107th Ave
South Haven, MI 49090-9366
269-637-7450
Fax: 269-637-2636
Edible fresh chestnut
President: Roy Adkin
National Accounts: L Adkin
Research & Development: Shelly Newton
Marketing Director: K Johnson
Production/Quality Control: Harold Bennett
Estimated Sales: $15 Million
Number Employees: 5-9
Square Footage: 44000
Type of Packaging: Food Service, Bulk
Brands:
 Adkin's
 Adkin's Royal Blue

177 Adler Fels Winery
980 Airway Ct
Unit B
Santa Rosa, CA 95403-2000
707-539-3123
Fax: 707-569-8301 info@adlerfels.com
Wines
Owner: David Coleman
Estimated Sales: $20 Million
Number Employees: 5-9
Parent Co: Adams Wine Group

178 Adluh Flour
804 Gervais St
PO Box 1437
Columbia, SC 29201-3126
803-779-2460
Fax: 803-252-0014 800-692-3584
info@adluh.com www.adluh.com
Flour and corn meal
President: William Allen
info@adluh.com
Year Founded: 1900
Estimated Sales: $5 Million
Number Employees: 10-19
Type of Packaging: Food Service
Brands:
 Adluh
 Carolina Gem
 Eatmor
 Gold Bond

179 Admiral Beverage Corp
821 Pulliam Ave
Worland, WY 82401-2325
307-347-4201
Fax: 307-347-3571
meumann@admiralbeverage.com
www.admiralbeverage.com
Soft drinks
President: Forrest K Clay
fclay@admiralbeverage.com
Chief Financial Officer: Keith Hartnett
EVP, General Counsel: Bob Callan
Director of Human Resources: AJ Jenness
VP Operations: Kelly Clay
Estimated Sales: $20-50 Million
Number Employees: 100-249
Parent Co: Pepsi Company
Type of Packaging: Consumer, Food Service

Food Manufacturers / A-Z

180 Adobe Creek Packing Co Inc
4825 Loasa Dr
Kelseyville, CA 95451
707-279-4204
Fax: 707-279-0366 shirleyacp@sbcglobal.net
Bartlett pears
President/Grower: Kenneth Barr
Controller: Shirley Campbell
Shipping Manager: Floyd Saderlund
Office Manager: Margot Hoyt
Estimated Sales: $2.7 Million
Number Employees: 250-499
Type of Packaging: Consumer, Food Service, Bulk
Brands:
  Blazing Star

181 Adobe Springs
PO Box 1417
Patterson, CA 95363-1417
408-897-3023
Fax: 408-897-3028 www.mgwater.com
Bulk magnesium rich mineral water
President: Gary Dutey
Vice President: Paul Mason
paulmason@mgwater.com
Brands:
  Hi0spring
  Noah's Spring Water
  Seven-Up

182 (HQ)Adolf's Meats & Sausage Kitchen
35 New Britain Ave
Hartford, CT 06106-3306
860-522-1588
Meats
President: Joseph Gorski
joegorski@live.com
Estimated Sales: Less Than $500,000
Number Employees: 1-4
Type of Packaging: Consumer, Food Service, Bulk
Other Locations:
  Adolf's Meat & Sausage
  Norwalk CT

183 Adrienne's Gourmet Foods
849 Ward Dr
Santa Barbara, CA 93111
805-964-6848
Fax: 805-964-8698 800-937-7010
Organic and kosher cookies, crackers and high protein pastas.
President: John O'Donnell
Vice President: Adrienne O'Donnell
Contact: Sarah Guiginano
sarah@adriennes.com
Estimated Sales: $5-10 Million
Number Employees: 20-49
Type of Packaging: Consumer, Food Service, Private Label, Bulk
Brands:
  Appeteasers
  California Crisps
  Courtney's
  Courtney's Organic Water Crackers
  Darcia's Organic Crostini
  Lavosh Hawaii
  Papadina Pasta
  Papadini Hi-Protein

184 Advance Pierre Foods
9987 Carver Rd.
Suite 500
Cincinnati, OH 45242
800-969-2747
www.advancepierre.com
Packaged sandwiches, fully cooked chicken and beef products, Philly-style steak, breaded beef, pork and poultry, and bakery products.
President/CEO: John Simons
CFO: Michael Sims
Year Founded: 1946
Estimated Sales: $600 Million
Number Employees: 4,000+
Number of Brands: 10
Parent Co: Tyson Foods
Type of Packaging: Consumer, Food Service, Private Label
Other Locations:
  Advance Food Company
  Caryville TN
  Advance Food Company
  Scanton PA
  Advance Food Company-Sales
  Oklahoma City OK
Brands:
  Barber Foods®
  Better Bakery™
  BIG AZ®
  Fast Fixin'®
  Hot 'n' Ready®
  PB Jamwich®
  Landshire®
  Pierre™
  Steak-EZE®
  The Pub®

185 Advanced Aquaculture Systems
4509 Hickory Creek Ln
Brandon, FL 33511-8013
813-653-2823
Fax: 813-684-7773 800-994-7599
info@advancedaquaculture.com
www.advancedaquaculture.com
Hybrid striped bass
President: Gary Miller
Vice President: Barbara Miller
Estimated Sales: $65,000
Number Employees: 5-9

186 Advanced Bio Development
768 Piermont Ave
Piermont, NY 10968
845-365-3838
info@x2performance.com
www.x2performance.com
Natural energy products
CEO: Dr. Ralph Ferrante

187 (HQ)Advanced Food Products LLC
402 S Custer Ave
New Holland, PA 17557
800-732-5373
info@afpllc.com www.afpllc.com
Dairy based products such as puddings, dips, sauces, spreads, nutritional beverages and soups.
President & CEO: Miro Hosek
miroslav.hosek@afpllc.com
CFO: Kris Smith
R&D Manager: Deb Holzhueter
Director, Quality Assurance: Matthew Brown
Director, National Sales & Marketing: Joe Hillen
SVP, Operations: Gregg Kenitz
Year Founded: 1940
Estimated Sales: $100+ Million
Number Employees: 100-249
Type of Packaging: Private Label
Other Locations:
  Manufacturing Facility
  Clear Lake WI
  Manufacturing Facility
  Visalia CA
Brands:
  Andersen's(c) Soup
  Caf, Classics(c)
  Campo Lindo(c)
  Encircle(c)
  Muy Fresco(c)
  Real Fresh(c)

188 Advanced Food Services
9807 Lackman Rd
Lenexa, KS 66219-1209
913-888-8088
Fax: 913-888-8075 info@advancedfood.com
www.advancedfood.com
Seasonings and bakery mixes
President: Raju Shah
rshah@advancedfood.com
Number Employees: 10-19

189 Advanced Food Systems
21 Roosevelt Ave
Somerset, NJ 08873-5030
732-873-6776
Fax: 732-873-4177 800-787-3067
info@afsnj.com www.afsnj.com
Customized ingredient systems for meat and poultry products, frozen foods, sauces and marinades, and more.
President: Yongkeun Joh
arun.abraham@acegroup.com
CFO: Pamela Cooper
EVP: Warren Love
Sales Executive: Chris Kelly
Operations Director: Bob Lijana
Purchasing Director: Mike Walker
Estimated Sales: $6.5 Million
Number Employees: 50-99
Square Footage: 107200

190 Advanced Ingredients, Inc.
401 N 3rd St
Suite 400
Minneapolis, MN 55401
Fax: 763-201-5820 888-238-4647
info@advancedingredients.com
www.advancedingredients.com
Specialty ingredients
President: Fred Greenland
Estimated Sales: $1-3 Million
Number Employees: 5-9
Brands:
  Bakesmart®
  Energysmart®
  Energysource®
  Fruitrim®
  Fruitsavr®
  Fruitsource®
  Moisturlok®
  Plus and Moisturlok®

191 Advanced Spice & Trading
1808 Monetary Ln Ste 100
Carrollton, TX 75006
972-242-8580
Fax: 972-242-6920 800-872-7811
sales@advancedspice.com
www.advancedspice.com
Spices and ingredients
President: Douglas Hank
CEO: Greg Hank
greg@advancedspice.com
Estimated Sales: $2.3 Million
Number Employees: 15
Square Footage: 268800
Type of Packaging: Consumer, Food Service, Private Label, Bulk
Brands:
  Santaka Chili Pods
  Supper Topper

192 Advanced Sunflower
PO Box 902
740 2nd St SW
Huron, SD 57350
605-554-1301
advancedsunflower.com
Sunflower seeds
CEO: Danny Dale
Number of Brands: 1
Type of Packaging: Consumer, Bulk
Brands:
  ADVANCED

193 Adventist Book & Food
2160 Us Highway 1
Trenton, NJ 08648-4447
609-392-8010
Fax: 609-392-4477 800-765-6955
www.adventistbookcenter.com
Vegetarian meat substitutes
CFO: Herb Shiroma
Owner: New Jersey
Estimated Sales: $.5-1 million
Number Employees: 1-4

194 Adventure Foods
481 Banjo Lane
Whittier, NC 28789-7999
828-497-4113
Fax: 828-497-7529
CustomerService@adventurefoods.com
www.adventurefoods.com
Freeze-dried; dehydrated; shelf stable foods and instant food; food storage programs; health food markets; baking mixes, bulk spices and ingredients; specialty foods and special packing for vegetarian, diabetics, gluten intolerance andother food or health restrictions.
President: Jean Spangenberg
jean@adventurefoods.com
CEO: Sam Spangenberg
Number Employees: 5-9
Parent Co: Jean's Garden Greats
Type of Packaging: Consumer, Food Service, Private Label, Bulk
Brands:
  Adventure Foods
  Bake Packers
  Gsi

Food Manufacturers / A-Z

Hearttline
Lumen
Open Country
Well Seasoned Traveler

195 AeroFarms
212 Rome St
Newark, NJ 07105
973-242-2495
info@aerofarms.com
www.aerofarms.com
Baby greens, microgreens, herbs; Aeroponic technology
Chief Executive Officer: David Rosenberg
Chief Financial Officer: Guy Blanchard
Chief Operating Officer: Roger Post
Chief Science Officer: Ed Harwood
Chief Technology Officer: Roger Buelow
Chief Marketing Officer: Marc Oshima
General Counsel: Ariel Lager
Year Founded: 2004
Number Employees: 50-99
Type of Packaging: Food Service
Brands:
  Dream Greens

196 Affiliated Rice Milling
715 N. 2nd St.
Alvin, TX 77511-3674
281-331-6176
Fax: 281-585-0336
Rice and rice flour.
Manager: Johnny Dunham
VP, Operations: Johnny Dunham
Estimated Sales: $20-50 Million
Number Employees: 1-10
Square Footage: 130000
Parent Co: Rice Belt Warehouse
Brands:
  Eminence

197 Afia Foods
P.O. Box 170651
Austin, TX 78717
512-698-8448
sales@afiafoods.com
www.afiafoods.com
Greek, Mediterranean, and Middle Eastern foods
President: Farrah Moussallati Sibai

198 Afieneur
172 Montague St
Brooklyn, NY 11201
617-480-1340
www.afineur.com
Coffee
CEO & Co-Founder: Camille Delebecque, PhD
CTO & Co-Founder: Sophie Deterre, PhD

199 Afineur
172 Montague St
Brooklyn, NY 11201
617-480-1340
Coffee
Ceo & Co-Founder: Camille Delebecque PhD
Cto & Co-Founder: Sophie Deterre PhD

200 Afton Mountain Vineyards Inc
234 Vineyard Ln
Afton, VA 22920-3702
540-456-8667
Fax: 540-456-8002
finewines@aftonmountainvineyards.com
www.aftonmountainvineyards.com
Wines
President: Tom Corpora
Estimated Sales: $1-2.5 Million
Number Employees: 20-49
Type of Packaging: Private Label

201 AgSource Milk Analysis Laboratory
106 North Cecil Street
Bonduel, WI 54107
715-758-2178
Fax: 715-758-2620 bonduel@agsource.com
Farmer-owned and client focused, we are dedicated to providing comprehensive laboratory analysis.
Co-Owner: Don Niles
Co-Owner: John Pagel
VP: Joel Amdall
Vice President Laboratory: Steve Peterson
Personnel Manager: Bruce Cornish
General Manager: C Smith
Estimated Sales: $1-3 Million
Number Employees: 20-49
Brands:
  Ag Co-Op

202 AgStandard Smoked Almonds
Los Angeles, CA
getagstandard.com
Smoked almonds
Number of Brands: 1
Type of Packaging: Consumer

203 Agave Dream
PO Box 1382
La Canada, CA 91012
USA
818-425-7378
Fax: 800-719-0950 310-619-1575
www.agavedream.com
Frozen desserts, ice cream, sorbet
Owner and Co-Founder: Jean Zwarg
Co-Founder: Stacey Ralphs
Estimated Sales: 150,000
Number Employees: 2
Brands:
  Agave Dream

204 Agfinity Inc
260 Factory Rd
Eaton, CO 80615-3481
970-454-4000
Fax: 970-454-2144 800-433-4688
www.agfinityinc.com
Agricultural services, agronomy, fertilizer, fuel/propane, car maintenance, and hardware equipment.
President: Stuart Agfinity
sagfinity@agfinityinc.com
CEO: Jason Brancel
CFO: Rob Lyons
Year Founded: 1905
Estimated Sales: $10-20 Million
Number Employees: 201-500
Type of Packaging: Consumer
Brands:
  Red Bird

205 Agger Fish Corp
63 Flushing Ave # 313
Brooklyn, NY 11205-1081
718-855-1717
Fax: 718-855-4545 marcagger@gmail.com
www.aggerfish.com
Monkfish, fluke, monkfish liver and shark fins, bones and cartilage for food supplements and ingredients.
President: Marc Agger
marcagger@gmail.com
Estimated Sales: $500,000-$1 Million
Number Employees: 500-999
Square Footage: 12000
Type of Packaging: Bulk

206 Aglamesis Bros Ice Cream
3046 Madison Rd
Cincinnati, OH 45209-1797
513-531-5196
Fax: 513-531-5403 www.aglamesis.com
Ice cream and confectionery products
President: James Aglamesis
sales@aglamesis.com
Estimated Sales: $2.5-5 Million
Number Employees: 20-49
Type of Packaging: Consumer, Food Service

207 AgraWest Foods
PO Box 760
Souris
Prince Edward Island, NS C0A 2B0
Canada
902-687-1400
Fax: 902-687-1401 877-687-1400
agrawest@agrawest.com www.agrawest.com
Dehydrated potato granules
President/CEO: Wally Browning
VP Finance: Baden Burt
VP/GM: John Schodde
Quality Assurance Manager: Kendra Deagle
Sales Manager: Mary Croucher
Production Manager: Jamie Trainor
Parent Co: Idaho Pacific Corporation
Type of Packaging: Food Service, Bulk
Brands:
  Chef Master

208 Agrana Fruit US Inc
6850 Southpointe Pkwy
Cleveland, OH 44141-3260
440-546-1199
Fax: 440-546-0038 800-477-3788
www.agrana.us
Sugar; starch; and processed fruits.
President/CEO: Johann Marihart
Board Member: Fritz Gattermeyer
Estimated Sales: $10-20 Million
Number Employees: 50-99
Parent Co: SIAS MPA
Type of Packaging: Food Service, Private Label, Bulk

209 Agrexco USA
15012 132nd Ave
Jamaica, NY 11434
718-481-8700
Fax: 718-481-8710 amoso@agrexco.com
www.agrexco.com
Fruits including dried dates, grapefruits and oranges, vegetables, herbs, and flowers.
President: Yoram Shalev
CFO/VP, Quality Control: Jack Aschkeigi
Produce Sales Manager: Joseph Benjuya
Contact: Abelardo Zeron
abelardoz@agrexco.com
Estimated Sales: $20-50 Million
Number Employees: 20-49
Brands:
  Alesia
  Carmel

210 Agri-Dairy Products
3020 Westchester Ave
Purchase, NY 10577
914-697-9580
Fax: 914-697-9586
customerservice@agridairy.com
www.agridairy.com
Dairy and food ingredients including whey and lactose, milkfat, milk powders, casein, milk proteins, cheese and butter.
President: Steven Bronfield
CEO: Frank Reeves III
CFO: Mary Ellen Storino
Year Founded: 1985
Estimated Sales: $52 Million
Number Employees: 10
Number of Products: 50+
Square Footage: 1600
Type of Packaging: Bulk

211 Agri-Mark Inc
958 Riverdale St
West Springfield, MA 01089-4621
978-552-5500
Fax: 978-552-5587 information@agrimark.net
www.agrimark.net
whey and Dairy products including butter and nonfat, skim and condensed milk; exporter of butter powder.
President/CEO: Richard Stammer
SVP: Robert Wellington
VP/Marketing: John Burke
Communications Director: Douglas DiMento
Plant Manager: Gary Carlow
Year Founded: 1919
Estimated Sales: $20-50 Million
Number Employees: 50-99
Type of Packaging: Private Label, Bulk
Other Locations:
  Agri-Mark Manufacturing Plant
  West Springfield MA
  Agri-Mark Manufacturing Plant
  Middlebury VT
  Agri-Mark Manufacturing Plant
  Cabot VT
  Agri-Mark Manufacturing Plant
  Chateaugay NY
Brands:
  Cabot
  McCadam

212 Agri-Pack
28 Pasco Kahlotus Road
Pasco, WA 99301
509-545-6181
Fax: 509-545-5748 steve@agri-pack.com
Onions including whole, rings, diced and strips
Manager: Tim Sessions
Account Executive: Jon Josephson
Director Sales/Marketing: Steve Shepard
Plant Manager: Todd Daniko

Food Manufacturers / A-Z

Estimated Sales: $2.5-5 Million
Number Employees: 20-49
Square Footage: 600000
Parent Co: Agri Pack
Type of Packaging: Food Service, Bulk

213 (HQ)AgriNorthwest
6716 W Rio Grande
Kennewick, WA 99336
509-734-1195
contactus@agrinw.com
www.agrinorthwest.com
Grower & supplier of corn, wheat and potatoes.
President: Todd Jones
General Manager: Tom Mackay
Farm Unit Manager: Mike Monger
Year Founded: 1968
Estimated Sales: $31.6 Million
Number Employees: 150
Type of Packaging: Food Service, Bulk
Other Locations:
 Plymouth WA
 Prescott WA

214 Agricor Inc
1626 S Joaquin Dr
Marion, IN 46953-9633
765-662-0606
Fax: 765-662-7189 www.grainmillers.com
Whole grain ingredients
President: Steve Wickes
IT: Bill Cramer
bill.cramer@grainmillers.com
Year Founded: 1983
Number Employees: 20-49
Type of Packaging: Bulk
Brands:
 Grain Millers

215 (HQ)Agricore United
1600 Utica Avenue South
Suite 350
St Louis Park, MN 55416
952-460-7450
Fax: 952-460-7404 877-509-5865
Wheat; barley; oats; 3-grain and instant cereals; pancake mix; organic flour and herb food bars and beans.
President/CEO: Mayo Schmidt
CFO: Rex McLennan
COO-Grain: Fran Malecha
Parent Co: Agricore United Int'l.
Type of Packaging: Consumer, Food Service, Bulk
Other Locations:
 Manitoba
 Saskatchewan
 Alberta
 British Columbia

216 Agripac
PO Box 5110
Denver, CO 80217-5110
503-981-0111
Fax: 503-982-3550 consultas@agripac.com.ar
Frozen red raspberries, strawberries, marionberries, rhubarb, snap beans, broccoli, cauliflower, corn, whole onions, peas and carrots, squash, mixed vegetables, prepared vegetables
Director: Pablo Adreani
Senior VP: Patrick Monaghan
Senior VP, Operations: Russ Grubb
Brands:
 Agripac

217 Agro Farma Inc.
669 County Road 25
New Berlin, NY 13411
607-847-6181
Fax: 607-847-8847 877-847-6181
contact@chobani.com www.chobani.com
Greek yogurt
President/CEO: Hamdi Ulukaya
COO: Mikael Pederson
Controller: Besnik Fetoski
Communications Director: Nicki Briggs
VP/Sales: Kyle O'Brien
Contact: Amanda Adams
a.adams@agro-farma.com
Estimated Sales: $35.0 Million
Number Employees: 12000
Other Locations:
 Manufacturing Facility
 Twin Falls ID
Brands:
 Chobani

218 Agro Foods, Inc.
3531 SW 13th St
Miami, FL 33145
786-552-9006
Fax: 305-361-7639 www.agrofoods.com
Spanish olives
Manager: Isa Knight
Estimated Sales: $1-2.5 Million
Number Employees: 5-9
Square Footage: 526000
Parent Co: Agro Aceitunera SA
Type of Packaging: Consumer, Food Service, Private Label, Bulk
Brands:
 Candelita
 Exporsevilla
 Lola

219 AgroCepia
9703 Dixie Highway
Suite 3
Miami, FL 33156
305-704-3488
Fax: 305-666-6930 www.agrocepia.cl
Low moisture colored apple flakes and nuggets, evaporated apple dices, grinds, rings and wedges, low moisture powders, dehydrated tomato, green bell pepper, red bell pepper and jalapeno pepper dices and granules
Sales Director: Mike Zobel
Contact: George Bartels
gbartels@acusallc.com
Estimated Sales: $3-5 Million
Number Employees: 1-4

220 (HQ)Agrocan
176 Benjamin Hudon
Ville St Laurent, QC H4N 1H8
Canada
514-272-2512
Fax: 514-270-6370 877-247-6226
info@agrocanfoods.com www.agrocanfoods.com
Manufacturer and exporter of fruit, olives, oil, vegetables and miscellaneous products
President: John Karellis
Number Employees: 3
Type of Packaging: Private Label
Other Locations:
 Agrocan
 Aeginion, N. Pierias
Brands:
 Sunmed

221 Agropur
2701 Freedom Rd
Appleton, WI 54913-9315
920-687-2489
Fax: 608-441-3031 kevin.thomson@agropur.com
www.agropur.com
Cheese and cheese products.
Director of Sales: Kevin Thomson
Contact: David Hitner
david.hitner@agropur.com
Number Employees: 50-99
Parent Co: Agropur

222 (HQ)Agropur
510 Rue Principale
Granby, QC J2G 7G2
Canada
450-375-1991
Fax: 450-375-7160 800-363-5686
jarollan@agropur.com www.agropur.com
Dairy products
Chairman: Jacques Cartier
CEO: Claude Menard
Secretary: Andre Gauthier
Director, Dairy Ingredient Sales: Kevin Thomson
Number Employees: 650
Parent Co: Agropur MSI, LLC
Type of Packaging: Consumer, Food Service
Other Locations:
 Agropur Coop. Agro-Alimentair
 Markham ON

223 Agrusa
PO Box 267
117 Fort Lee Road
Leonia, NJ 07605-7244
201-592-5950
Fax: 201-585-7244 agrusa@agrusainc.com
www.agritalia.com
Italian foods, including: pasta, olive oil, balsamic vinegar, tomatoes, risotto, rice and frozen pizza.
President: Jill Bush

Number Employees: 5
Square Footage: 8000
Type of Packaging: Consumer, Food Service, Private Label, Bulk
Brands:
 Bella Italia
 Celio
 Don Peppe
 Private Label

224 Agumm
10636 NW 49th Street
Coral Springs, FL 33076-2702
954-344-0607
Fax: 305-341-6667
Baked products, batters, breading, confectionery, dry mixes
President: Matthew Rutter

225 Agusa
1055 S 19th Ave
Lemoore, CA 93245-9747
559-924-4785
Fax: 559-924-0933 jeff.babb@agusa.biz
www.agusa.biz
Tomato based products
President: Pedro Souchard
COO: Inigo Martinez
CFO: Javier Souchard
VP: Craig Shimomura
Sales Manager: Jeff Babb
jeff.babb@agusa.biz
General Manager: Joel Lira
Estimated Sales: $5.9 Million
Number Employees: 20-49
Square Footage: 56000
Type of Packaging: Food Service, Private Label, Bulk

226 Agvest
7589 First Pl Ste 2
Cleveland, OH 44146
216-464-3737
Fax: 440-735-1680 www.agvest.com
Frozen apples, elderberries, bilberries; sugar infused blueberries, cranberries and cherries; and fruit flakes and powders.
President/CEO: Barry Schneider
CFO: Steve Hamilton
Contact: Bob Newman
bob@agvest.com
Estimated Sales: $1-2.5 Million
Number Employees: 5-9
Type of Packaging: Food Service
Brands:
 North Eastern
 Quality

227 Ah Dor Kosher Fish Corporation
25 Maple Terrace
Monsey, NY 10952-3707
845-425-2060
Fish
President: Joseph Neuman
Estimated Sales: Less than $500,000
Number Employees: 1-4
Type of Packaging: Private Label

228 Ahara Ghee
1630 SE 3rd Ave
Portland, OR 97214
503-997-5050
ahararasaghee@gmail.com
www.iloveghee.com
Organic ghee (clarified butter)
Founder/CEO: Andrea Shuman
Co-Founder/COO: Martin Lemke
Year Founded: 2011

229 Ahlgren Vineyard
Bonded Winery 7464
Boulder Creek, CA 95006
831-338-6071
Fax: 831-338-9111 800-338-6071
www.ahlgrenvineyard.com
Wines
Co-Owner: Valerie Ahlgren
Co-Owner/CEO/Winemaker: Dexter Ahlgren
Estimated Sales: $1-2.5 Million
Number Employees: 1-4
Type of Packaging: Food Service, Private Label
Brands:
 Ahlgren Vineyard
 Tre Vini Rossi

Food Manufacturers / A-Z

230 Ahmad Tea
P.O.Box 876
Deer Park, TX 77536
281-478-0957
Fax: 281-479-0521 800-637-7704
info@ahmadteausa.com www.ahmadtea.com
Tea and tea gift producer
Marketing: Karim Afshar
Contact: Ali Afshar
ali@ahmadtea.com

231 Ai Vy Springrolls, Llc
515 East 72nd St
Suite 4j
New York, NY 10021
897-394-3657
info@aivyspringrolls.com
www.aivyspringrolls.com
Spring rolls
Square Footage: 80000

232 Aidells Sausage Co
2411 Baumann Ave
San Lorenzo, CA 94580-1801
510-614-5450
Fax: 510-614-2287 800-546-5795
info@aidells.com www.aidells.com
Sausage and other deli products.
Founder: Chef Bruce Aidells
CEO: Bob Mc Henry
Manager: Rosa Anders
randers@aidells.com
Number Employees: 20-49
Type of Packaging: Consumer, Food Service, Bulk
Brands:
  Aidell's

233 Aileen Quirk & Sons Inc
235 W 12th Ave
Kansas City, MO 64116-4178
816-471-4580
Fax: 816-842-8063 info@aileenquirkandsons.com
www.aileenquirkandsons.com
Dried edible beans for wholesalers and grocery stores.
Owner: Kelly Quirk
quirksons@aol.com
CEO: Larry Quirk
Traffic Manager: Leslie Quirk
Office Manager: Frances Kuhn
Estimated Sales: $3 Million
Number Employees: 10-19
Type of Packaging: Food Service, Private Label, Bulk
Brands:
  PDQ Puncher

234 Aimonetto and Sons
720 N 10th St
Renton, WA 98057
206-767-2777
Fax: 206-762-6792 866-823-2777
Milk, juice, cottage cheese, sour cream and yogurt; wholesaler/distributor of dairy products
Owner: Jim Aimonetto
Estimated Sales: $10-20 Million
Number Employees: 10-19
Type of Packaging: Consumer, Food Service

235 Airlie Winery
15305 Dunn Forest Rd
Monmouth, OR 97361-9570
503-838-6013
Fax: 503-838-6279 airlie@airliewinery.com
www.airliewinery.com
Wines
Owner: Mary Olson
airlie@airliewinery.com
Marketing/Sales VP: Barry Glassman
Marketing and Sales Director: Sue Shay
Winemaker: Elizabeth Ogg
Estimated Sales: $500,000-$1 Million
Number Employees: 1-4
Type of Packaging: Private Label
Brands:
  Airlie

236 Aiya America Inc
2807 Oregon Ct
Unit D-5
Torrance, CA 90503-2635
310-212-1395
Fax: 310-212-1386 info@aiya-america.com
www.aiya-america.com
Wholesaler and distributor of matcha green tea and premium leaf teas used in many types of food and beverage applications.
Sales Assistant/Customer Service: Daniel Coniglio
daniel@aiya-america.com

237 (HQ)Ajinomoto Foods North America, Inc.
4200 Concours St.
Suite 100
Ontario, CA 91764
909-477-4700
Fax: 919-477-4600 www.ajinomotofoods.com
Specializes in frozen ethnic dishes, such as Italian, Mexican and Asian including lasagna, meat balls, ravioli, spaghetti sauce, potstickers, spring rolls, and burritos.
President/CEO: Takaaki Nishii
President, North America: Bernard Kreilmann
Year Founded: 1909
Estimated Sales: $670 Million
Number Employees: 2,500+
Number of Brands: 14
Parent Co: Ajinomoto Co., Inc.
Type of Packaging: Consumer, Food Service
Other Locations:
  Amino Acid Technologies
  Raleigh NC
  Wellness & Sports Nutrition
  Raleigh NC
  Food Ingredients
  Itasca IL
  Ajinomoto Windsor, Inc.
  Ontario, Canada
  Ajinomoto Heartland, Inc.
  Chicago IL
  Ajinomoto Althea, Inc.
  San Diego CA
  Ajinomoto De Mexico
  Col. Juarez, Mexico
Brands:
  Ajinomoto®
  Posada®
  Bernardi®
  Amoy®
  Fred's®
  Whitey's®
  Chili Bowl®
  Golden Tiger®
  Tai Pei®
  Ling Ling®
  Jose Ole®
  VIP®

238 Ajinomoto Frozen Foods USA, Inc.
4200 Concours Street
Suite 100
Ontario, CA 91764
866-536-8008
www.ajifrozenusa.com
Asian ingredients and prepared foods.
Parent Co: Ajinomoto Co., Inc.
Type of Packaging: Consumer, Food Service, Private Label
Other Locations:
  Los Angeles CA
  Portland OR
  Honolulu HI
Brands:
  Tai Pei®
  Ling Ling®
  Jose Ole®
  Ajinomoto®
  VIP®
  Posada®
  Bernardi®
  Amoy®
  Fred's®
  Whitey's®
  Chili Bowl®
  Golden Tiger®

239 Ajinomoto Heartland Inc
8430 W Bryn Mawr Ave
Suite 650
Chicago, IL 60631-3421
773-380-7000
Fax: 773-380-7006 www.lysine.com
Feed-grade amino acids
President: Daniel Bercovici
Number Employees: 10-19
Parent Co: Ajinomoto Co., Inc.
Type of Packaging: Bulk

Brands:
  L-Lysine
  L-Threonine
  AjiLys®
  L-Tryptophan
  AjiPro®-L
  L-Valine

240 Ajiri Tea Company
PO Box 162
Upper Black Eddy, PA 18972
610-982-5075
Fax: 610-982-9346 ajirifoundation@gmail.com
www.ajiritea.com
Tea and coffee.
Owner: Sara Holby

241 Ak Mak Bakeries
89 Academy Ave
Sanger, CA 93657-2104
559-875-5511
Fax: 559-875-2472 www.akmakbakeries.com
Armenian flat bread and cracker bread.
President: Manoog Soojian
manoog@akmakbakeries.com
Controller: Tanya Hodge
Year Founded: 1893
Estimated Sales: $20-50 Million
Number Employees: 20-49
Number of Brands: 2
Type of Packaging: Consumer
Brands:
  Ak Mak
  Country Style

242 Akay USA LLC
500 Hartle St
Suite E
Sayreville, NJ 08872-2770
732-254-7177
akayusallc@gmail.com
www.akay-group.com
Paprika and other spices.
Senior Vice President of Sales USA: Rajive Joseph
Manager: Balu Maliakel
balu.maliakel@akay-group.com
Number Employees: 1-4
Parent Co: Akay Group

243 Aker BioMarine Antarctic US, LLC.
312 Amboy Ave
Metuchen, NJ 08840
732-917-4000
www.superbakrill.com
Krill oil
Brands:
  Superba

244 Aketta
www.aketta.com
Cricket protein powder
CEO: Mohammed Ashour
COO: Gabriel Mott
Number of Brands: 1
Number of Products: 5
Type of Packaging: Consumer
Brands:
  AKETTA

245 Akicorp
20145 NE 21st CT
N Miami Beach, FL 33179
786-426-5750
ysaac@akinin.com
Oilseeds
Manager: Ysaac Akinin
yakinin@akinin.com

246 Al & John's Glen Rock Ham
147 Clinton Rd.
West Caldwell, NJ 07006
973-521-7928
Fax: 973-521-7929 800-969-4990
www.glenrockhams.com
Canadian bacon and fresh ham including cooked, ready-to-eat, fat-free, semi-boneless, smoked boneless, honey, Virginia maple, apple cinnamon, Black Forest.
President/CEO: Alex Oldja
VP: Jennifer Oldja
Director Quality Assurance: Daniel Oldja
Plant Manager: Alex Oldja, Jr.

Food Manufacturers / A-Z

Estimated Sales: $20-50 Million
Number Employees: 100-249
Brands:
   Kohler Deli Meats
   Freda Deli Meats

247 Al Dente Pasta Co
9815 Main St
Whitmore Lake, MI 48189-9338
     734-449-8522
     800-536-7278
info@aldentepasta.com www.aldentepasta.com
Specialty flavored pasta and sauces.
President/Founder: Monique Deschaine
VP: Dennis Deschaine
Contact: Nanette Carson
nanette@aldentepasta.com
Estimated Sales: $5-10 Million
Number Employees: 50-99
Brands:
   Al Dente
   Al Dente Pasta Selecta
   Al Dente Sure Success
   Monique's Pasta Sauces

248 Al Gelato Bornay
9133 Belden Ave
Franklin Park, IL 60131-3505
     847-455-5355
Fax: 847-455-5553 algelatochicago@gmail.com
www.algelatochicago.com
Ice cream, sorbet, spumoni, natural fruit sorbets, and frozen desserts.
President: Paula DiNardo
pdinardo@laibensebornay.com
Estimated Sales: Less Than $500,000
Number Employees: 5-9
Square Footage: 20000
Type of Packaging: Food Service, Private Label, Bulk
Brands:
   Al Gelato

249 (HQ)Al Pete Meats
2100 E Willard St
Muncie, IN 47302-3737
     765-288-8817
Fax: 765-281-2759 www.petespride.net
Frozen portion control foods; including corn dogs, breaded meat and cheese, raw and cooked breaded mushrooms and cauliflower; Exporter of frozen portion controlled breaded meat products.
President: Arlin Mann
CEO: John Hartmeyer
Purchasing Manager: Paul Whitechair
Estimated Sales: $10-20 Million
Number Employees: 20-49
Square Footage: 450000
Type of Packaging: Consumer, Food Service, Private Label
Other Locations:
   Manufacturing Facility
   Muncie IN
   Manufacturing Facility
   Fairbury IL
Brands:
   Al Pete
   Pete's Pride

250 Al Richard's Chocolates
851 Broadway
Bayonne, NJ 07002
     201-436-0915
Fax: 201-436-0485 888-777-6964
www.alrichardschocolates.com
Chocolates
Estimated Sales: $300,000-500,000
Number Employees: 1-4

251 Al Safa Halal
100 Church St
8th Floor
New York City, NY 10007
     800-268-8147
connect@alsafafoods.com www.alsafahalal.com
Processor and exporter of halal processed foods including pizza, beef burgers, chicken nuggets, fish sticks.
President: David Muller
VP: Steve Hahn
Number Employees: 10-19
Number of Brands: 40
Parent Co: Engro Foods Canada Ltd.
Type of Packaging: Consumer, Food Service

Other Locations:
   Al Safa Halal
   Cambridge, Ontario
Brands:
   Al Safa Halal

252 Al's Beverage Company
1-3 Revay Rd
East Windsor, CT 06088
     860-627-7003
Fax: 860-627-8067 888-257-7632
mfeldman@alsbeverage.com
www.alsbeverage.com
Fountain soft drinks
Owner: Marjorie Feldman
Sr. VP Sales: John Martin
VP: William Melcher
Marketing Consultant: Todd Lemieux
Sales Director: Art Gallegos
Contact: Leslie Gengenbach
lgengenbach@alsbeverage.com
Operations Manager: Michael McCarthy
Estimated Sales: $3-5 Million
Number Employees: 50-99
Type of Packaging: Private Label
Brands:
   Al's
   Barrel Head
   Canada Dry
   Rc
   Stewarts
   Sunkist

253 Al-Rite Fruits & SyrupsCo
18524 NE 2nd Ave
Miami, FL 33179-4427
     305-652-2540
Fax: 305-652-4478 www.al-rite.com
Processor and exporter of kosher products including isotonic iced tea, fountain and slush beverage, ice cream and nondairy bases. Also fudge and chocolate syrups, toppings, frozen cocktail/bar mixes and extracts and flavors forbeverages and desserts
Manager: Alfredo Faubel
Vice President: Cliff Spring
cspring@al-rite.com
Estimated Sales: $5-10 Million
Number Employees: 10-19
Type of Packaging: Consumer, Food Service, Private Label, Bulk
Brands:
   Al-Rite
   Iso-Sport
   Tropical

254 Alabama Gulf Seafood
9280 Seafood House Rd
Bayou La Batre, AL 36509
     251-824-4396
Fax: 251-824-7579 eatalabamaseafood.com
Seafood
President: Richard Gazzier
Vice President: Donna Gazzier
Estimated Sales: $5-10 Million
Number Employees: 10-19

255 Alacer Corp
Carlisle, PA 17013
     888-425-2362
www.emergenc.com
Dietary supplements, mineral ascorbates, vitamins and distilled water.
President: Ron Fugate
Vice President: Bruce Sweyd
Year Founded: 1978
Estimated Sales: $20-50 Million
Number Employees: 50-99
Square Footage: 57000
Type of Packaging: Consumer
Brands:
   Emer'gen-C
   Miracle

256 Aladdin Bakers
240 25th St
Brooklyn, NY 11232-1338
     718-499-1818
Fax: 718-788-5174 kasindorf@aladdinbakers.com
www.aladdinbakers.com
Sandwich wraps and gourmet flour tortillas; pita; panini and specialty breads; bagels; bread sticks; toast; croutons; and flatbreads.

President: Joseph Ayoub
ayoub@aladdinbakers.com
CFO/GM: Donald Guzzi
Quality Control Director: Javier Vasquez
VP Sales/Marketing: Paul Kasindorf
Human Resources Director: Barbara Adams
COO/Plant Manager: Arkadi Karachun
Production Manager: Ed Curran
Year Founded: 1972
Estimated Sales: $20-50 Million
Number Employees: 100-249
Square Footage: 9774
Type of Packaging: Consumer, Food Service, Private Label, Bulk
Brands:
   Aladdin

257 Alakef Coffee Roasters Inc
1330 E Superior St
Suite 1
Duluth, MN 55805-3855
     218-724-6849
Fax: 218-724-7727 800-438-9228
info@alakef.com www.alakef.com
Roasted coffee
Co-Owner: Nessim Bohbot
coffee@alakef.com
VP: Deborah Bohbot
Estimated Sales: $1.7 Million
Number Employees: 10-19
Type of Packaging: Private Label

258 Alamance Foods
840 Plantation Dr
Burlington, NC 27215
info@alamancefoods.com
www.alamancefoods.com
Freeze popsicles; whip cream and classic creamer, water.
President: Bill Scott
Regional Sales Manager: Jerry Schumate
Estimated Sales: $10-100 Million
Number Employees: 100-249
Brands:
   Classic Cream
   Fun Pops
   Fun Whip
   Happy Drinks
   Triton Water

259 (HQ)Alamo Tamale Corporation
3713 Jensen Dr
Houston, TX 77026
     713-228-6446
Fax: 713-228-7513 800-252-0586
www.alamotamale.com
Tamales
President: Louis Webster
VP: Shirleen Webster
Estimated Sales: $10-20 Million
Number Employees: 50-99
Square Footage: 75000
Type of Packaging: Consumer, Food Service, Private Label
Brands:
   Alamo

260 Alaska Aquafarms
P.O. Box 7
Moose Pass, AK 99631-0007
     907-288-3667
Fax: 907-288-3667 jjh@seward.net
Shellfish
Owner: James Hetrick
President/CEO: Willard Fehr
Estimated Sales: $300,000-500,000
Number Employees: 1-4

261 Alaska Bounty Seafoods & Smokery
110 Jarvis Street
Sitka, AK 99835-9806
     907-747-3730
Smoked salmon
Partner: Carol Petraborg
Partner: Gerold Brager
Estimated Sales: $1-2.5 Million
Number Employees: 5-9
Type of Packaging: Consumer, Food Service, Bulk

Food Manufacturers / A-Z

262 Alaska General Seafoods
6425 NE 175th St
Kenmore, WA 98028-4808
425-485-7755
Fax: 425-485-5172 info@akgen.com
www.akgen.com
Socially responsible seafood including fresh, frozen, canned, and roe
Vice President: Gordon Lindquist
g.lindquist@alaskageneralseafoods.com
Controller: Brad Wilkins
Estimated Sales: $20-50 Million
Number Employees: 10-19
Parent Co: Jim Pattison Group
Other Locations:
  Kenmore Warehouse
  Kenmore WA
  Naknek Plant
  Naknek AK
  Ketchikan Plant
  Ketchikan AK
  Egegik Office
  Egegik AK
  Ferndale Shop
  Ferndale WA
Brands:
  Gold Seal

263 Alaska Herb & Tea Co
6710 Weimer Dr
Anchorage, AK 99502-2054
907-245-3499
Fax: 907-245-3499 800-654-2764
herbtea@alaska.net www.alaskaherbtea.com
Tea, honey, syrups, jams and jellies, cocoa, vinegars
President: Charles Walsh
herbtea@alaska.net
VP: Sandra Fongemie
Operations Manager: Ann Stewart
Production Manager: Maria Salizar
Estimated Sales: Less than $500,000
Number Employees: 1-4
Type of Packaging: Private Label
Brands:
  Alaska Wild Teas
  Alaskan Boreal Bouquet
  Alaskan Fireweed
  Alaskan Gold
  Cocoalaska

264 Alaska Jacks
6251 Tuttle Pl
Suite 101
Anchorage, AK 99507-2099
907-248-9999
Fax: 907-243-2044 888-660-2257
Smoked salmon, chocolate, taffy, jams and jellies, salmon, gold crunch, chikoot chews, klondike krisp, sourdough starters, and earthquake bars.
President: Starr Horton
Sales Manager: Dave Berry
Estimated Sales: $5-10 Million
Number Employees: 20-49
Brands:
  Alaska Jack's
  Alaska Tea Traders

265 Alaska Ocean Trading
4101 Westland Cir
Anchorage, AK 99517-1430
907-243-4399
Fax: 907-243-4399
Fish and seafood
CFO: Roger Park
Estimated Sales: Under $500,000
Number Employees: 1-4

266 Alaska Pacific Seafoods
627 Shelikof St
Kodiak, AK 99615
907-486-3234
Seafood
Estimated Sales: $50-100 Million
Number Employees: 100-249
Parent Co: North Pacific Seafoods
Brands:
  North Pacific Seafood

267 Alaska Pasta Co
511 W 41st Ave
Suite A
Anchorage, AK 99503-6643
907-276-2632
Fax: 907-276-2632
Pasta

Owner: Hope Nelson
rvnelson@dci.net
Estimated Sales: $1-2.5 Million
Number Employees: 1-4

268 Alaska Sausage & Seafood
2914 Arctic Blvd
Anchorage, AK 99503-3811
907-562-3636
Fax: 907-562-7343 800-798-3636
aks@ak.net www.alaskasausage.com
Sausage, processed meats and smoked fish; exporter of smoked salmon
President: Herbert Eckmann
Secretary/Treasurer: Eva Eckmann
Quality Control Manager: Martin Eckmann
IT: Amanda Ingram
aks@ak.net
Estimated Sales: $10-20 Million
Number Employees: 20-49
Square Footage: 30000
Type of Packaging: Consumer, Food Service, Private Label, Bulk
Brands:
  Alaskan

269 Alaska Seafood Co
5731 Concrete Way
Juneau, AK 99801-9543
907-780-4808
Fax: 907-780-5140 800-451-1400
info@alaskaseafoodcompany.com
www.alaskaseafoodcompany.com
Fish.
President: Richard Hand
Year Founded: 1987
Estimated Sales: $800,000
Number Employees: 10-19

270 Alaska Smokehouse
21616 87th Ave SE
Woodinville, WA 98072-8017
360-668-9404
Fax: 360-668-1005 800-422-0852
service@alaskasmokehouse.com
www.alaskasmokehouse.com
Smoked salmon, spreads, jerky, cookies, fruit purees and coffee.
President/CEO: Jack Praino
customerservice@alaskasmokehouse.com
SVP: Tiffany Andriesen
Estimated Sales: $1.5 Million
Number Employees: 20-49
Square Footage: 60000
Type of Packaging: Consumer, Private Label
Brands:
  Alaska Smokehouse
  Sleepless In Seattle Coffee
  The Famous Pacific Dessert Company

271 Alaskan Brewing Company
5429 Shaune Drive
Juneau, AK 99801-9540
907-780-5866
Fax: 907-780-4514 www.alaskanbeer.com
Beer, amber, pale and stouts.
Co-Founder/President: Geoffrey Larson
Co-Founder: Marcy Larson
CEO: Linda Thomas
Contact: Cindy Burchfield
lostinalaska@gci.net
Plant Manager: Curtis Holmes
Estimated Sales: $20-50 Million
Number Employees: 56
Number of Brands: 10
Type of Packaging: Private Label
Brands:
  Alaskan Amber
  Alaskan Freeride APA
  Alaskan Hopothermia
  Alaskan Icy Bay IPA
  Alaskan Imperial Red
  Alaskan Kicker Session IPA
  Alaskan Stout
  Alaskan Summer Ale
  Alaskan White
  AlaskaN Winter Ale

272 Alaskan Gourmet Seafoods
1020 International Airport Road
Anchorage, AK 99518
Fax: 907-563-2592 800-288-3740
www.akgourmet.com
Frozen and canned smoked halibut and salmon.

President: Paul Schilling
Estimated Sales: $5-10 Million
Number Employees: 18
Square Footage: 40000
Brands:
  Alaskan Gourmet

273 Alaskan Leader Fisheries
8874 Bender Rd
Suite 201
Lynden, WA 98264-8550
360-318-1280
Fax: 866-649-2675 www.alaskanleader.com
Owner: Rob Wurm
rob@alaskanleaderfisheries.com
Partner: Kevin O'Leary
Partner: Richard Thummel
Estimated Sales: $.5-1 million
Number Employees: 1-4
Brands:
  Alaskan Leader Fisheries

274 Alaskan Smoked Salmon & Seafood
8430 Laviento Dr
Anchorage, AK 99515-1914
907-349-8234
Fax: 907-344-7666
Smoked salmon
President: Christopher Rosauer
aksam@alaska.net
Estimated Sales: $200,000
Number Employees: 1-4
Type of Packaging: Consumer, Food Service

275 Alati-Caserta Desserts
277 Rue Dante
Montr,al, QC H2S 1K3
Canada
514-271-3013
Fax: 514-277-5860 877-377-5680
info@alaticaserta.com www.alaticaserta.com
Desserts including almond cakes, cannoli ricotta and chocolate mousse.
President: Vittorio Caldarone
Co-Owner: Marco Caldarone
Estimated Sales: $243,000
Number Employees: 6
Type of Packaging: Food Service
Brands:
  Alati-Casserta

276 Alba Foods, Inc
1355 Rock Mountain Blvd
Stone Mountain, GA 30083
888-725-4605
info@albafoods.us www.albafoods.us
Tart shells and baking ingredients

277 Alba Vineyard & Winery
269 Route 627
Village of Finesville
Milford, NJ 08848-1771
908-995-7800
Fax: 908-995-7155 wine@albavineyard.com
www.albavineyard.com
Wines
President/Owner: Thomas Sharko
Partner: Rudy Marchesi
Estimated Sales: $2.5-5 Million
Number Employees: 5-9
Type of Packaging: Private Label, Bulk
Brands:
  Alba

278 Albanese Confectionery Group
5441 E Lincoln Hwy
Merrillville, IN 46410-5947
219-942-1877
Fax: 219-769-6897 800-536-0581
retail@albaneseconfectionery.com
www.albanesecandy.com
Chocolate covered nuts, candies, and gummies.
President: Scott Albanese
ciaoalbanese@albaneseconfectionary.com
Vice President: Richard Albanese
Purchasing: Alan Levinson
Estimated Sales: $5-10 Million
Number Employees: 5-9
Other Locations:
  Hobart Manufacturing Facility
  Hobart IN

Food Manufacturers / A-Z

279 Albert's Meats
2992 Green Valley Rd
Claysville, PA 15323
800-522-9970
freshflavor@albertsmeats.com albertsmeats.com
Smoked hams, luncheon meats, sausages and kielbasa.
Owner: George Weiss
Sales Manager: Brian Weiss
Number Employees: 50-99
Parent Co: Green Valley Packing
Type of Packaging: Consumer

280 Alberta Cheese Company
8420 26th Street SE
Calgary, AB T2C 1C7
Canada
403-279-4353
Fax: 403-279-4795 info@albertacheese.com
www.albertacheese.com
Cheese: mozzarella, ricotta, cheddar, feta, provolone and monterey jack
President: Frank Talarico
Sales Manager/GM: Michael Talarico
Estimated Sales: $5-10 Million
Number Employees: 20
Type of Packaging: Consumer, Food Service
Brands:
 Franco's
 Sorento

281 Alca Trading Co.
5301 Blue Lagoon Dr
Suite 570
Miami, FL 33126
305-265-8331
www.alcatradingcorp.com
Banana juices and mango purees.
Contact: Andrea Cordova
andrea@alcatradingcorp.com

282 Alcove Chocolate
1929 Hillhurst Ave.
Los Angeles, CA 90027
USA
323-284-2229
Fax: 323-644-0111 www.alcovecafe.com
Chocolate Bars
Founder: Tom Trellis

283 Alden's Organic
Camas, WA 98607
www.aldensicecream.com
Organic ice cream
Brands:
 Alden's Organic

284 Alder Springs Smoked Salmon
PO Box 97
61 River Road
Sequim, WA 98382-0097
360-683-2829
Fax: 360-683-5359
Smoked salmon, salmon jerky, oysters, cod and trout
Owner: Robert Bearden
Estimated Sales: Less than $500,000
Number Employees: 1-4
Type of Packaging: Private Label
Brands:
 Alder Springs

285 Alderfer Inc
382 Main St
PO Box 2
Harleysville, PA 19438-2310
215-256-8818
Fax: 215-256-6120 800-341-1211
www.alderfermeats.com
Pork, beef and turkey products
President/CEO: Jim Van Stone
jvanstone@alderfermeats.com
CFO: Sandy Sloyer
Marketing Manager: Samantha Alderfer
Sales Executive: Chet Dudzinski
Human Resources Manager: Janise Stauffer
Plant Manager: Brent Shoemaker
Purchasing Manager: Ray Ganser
Estimated Sales: $12 Million
Number Employees: 50-99
Number of Brands: 1
Number of Products: 300
Square Footage: 60000
Type of Packaging: Consumer, Food Service, Private Label, Bulk
Brands:
 Alderfer
 Leidy's

286 AleSmith Brewing Company
9368 Cabot Dr
San Diego, CA 92126
858-549-9888
Fax: 858-549-1052 peter@alesmith.com
www.alesmith.com
Ale including seasonal
Owner: Peter Zien
Contact: Peter Cronin
pcronin@alesmith.com
Estimated Sales: $3-5 Million
Number Employees: 1-4
Square Footage: 12800
Type of Packaging: Food Service, Bulk

287 Alef Sausage Inc
1026 Campus Dr
Mundelein, IL 60060-3831
847-968-2533
Fax: 847-968-3095 www.alefsausage.com
Saugage
President: Alec Mikhaylov
alec@alefsausage.com
Estimated Sales: Less Than $500,000
Number Employees: 5-9

288 Aleias Gluten Free Foods
4 Pin Oak Dr
Branford, CT 06405-6506
203-488-5556
connect@aleias.com
www.aleias.com
Gluten-free cookies, bread crumbs, panko, croutons, breads and stuffing mixes.
Contact: Jim Snow
jims@aleias.com
Estimated Sales: Less Than $500,000
Number Employees: 1-4

289 Alessi Bakery
2909 W Cypress St
Tampa, FL 33609-1630
813-879-4544
Fax: 813-872-9103
Tortes, pastry desserts, cakes, cookies
President: Philip Alessi
pjr@alessibakeries.com
CFO: Debrah Herman
Estimated Sales: $5-10 Million
Number Employees: 50-99
Square Footage: 60000
Type of Packaging: Consumer, Food Service
Brands:
 Alessi Bakery

290 Alewel's Country Meats
911 N Simpson Dr
Junction 13 & 50
Warrensburg, MO 64093-9257
660-747-8261
Fax: 660-747-1857 800-353-8553
ralewel@alewels.com www.country-meats.com
Dry, shelf stable, game and summer sausage, and game jerky including deer and buffalo.
Owner: Randy Alewel
alewels@sprintmail.com
Estimated Sales: $2.5-5 Million
Number Employees: 5-9
Square Footage: 20000
Type of Packaging: Consumer, Food Service, Private Label, Bulk
Brands:
 Alewel's Country Meats
 Grandpa A'S

291 Alexander Gourmet Beverages
670 Hardwick Rd
Bolton, ON L7C 5R5
Canada
905-361-2577
Fax: 905-282-0601 800-265-5081
info@alexanderstea.com www.alexanderstea.com
Teas
President: Dave Elliott
Estimated Sales: $3.5 Million
Number Employees: 60+
Number of Brands: 6
Square Footage: 60000
Type of Packaging: Consumer, Food Service, Private Label, Bulk
Brands:
 Alexander's Gourmet Tea
 Cocoa Creations
 Herbal Teazers

292 Alexander International(USA)
132 Concourse East
Brightwaters, NY 11718
805-218-6628
866-965-0143
service@alexander-usa.com
Drink mixes, herbs and spices, olive and other oils.
Owner: F.Matthias Alexander

293 Alexandra & Nicolay Chocolate Company
507 Delaware Avenue
PO Box 14
Portaland, PA 18351
570-897-6223
Fax: 570-897-5954 anchocolatiers@aol.com
www.alexandraandnicolay.com
Chocolates in milk, white and dark
Founder: Alexandra Mazhirov
Founder: Nicolay Mazhirov
Estimated Sales: $300,000-500,000
Number Employees: 5-9

294 Alexia Foods
5102 21st Street
Suite 3B
Long Island City, NY 11101
718-937-0100
Fax: 718-937-0110 info@alexiafoods.com
www.alexiafoods.com
Frozen potato products including artisan breads, oven blends, onion rings, organic products, mashed potatoes, oven fries and oven reds, julienne fries, and appetizers.
President/CEO: Alex Dzieduszycki
Senior Marketing Manager: Michael Smith
Director of Sales: Jack Acree
Contact: Christine Dubois
christine.dubois@alexiafoods.com
Estimated Sales: G
Parent Co: ConAgra Foods
Type of Packaging: Food Service

295 Alexian Pâtés
1200 7th Ave
Neptune, NJ 07753-5176
732-775-3220
Fax: 732-775-3223 800-927-9473
informationrequest@alexianpate.com
www.alexianpate.com
Specialty meats and sausages. All natural preservative free pâtés and mousses; pork, poultry, vegetarian and vegan pâtés
President: Laurie Cummins
Sales Manager: Paul Klempert
Contact: Alexian Terrines
alexian@alexianpate.com
Accountant: John Stevens
Estimated Sales: $10-20 Million
Number Employees: 10-19

296 Alexis Bailly Vineyard
18200 Kirby Ave S
Hastings, MN 55033-9340
651-437-1413
info@abvwines.com
www.abvwines.com
Wines
Founder: David Bailly
Owner/CEO: Nan Bailly
Estimated Sales: $500,000-$1 Million
Number Employees: 1-4
Type of Packaging: Consumer, Private Label
Brands:
 Alexis Bailly

297 Alfer Laboratories
9566 Vassar Ave
Chatsworth, CA 91311-4141
818-709-0737
Fax: 818-709-5360
Nutritional supplements and vitamins including liquid cal-mag, acidophilus cultures and aloe vera gels/juices
President: Ines Gutierrez
alferlabs@aol.com
Purchasing Manager: Ines Gutierrez
Estimated Sales: $2.5-5 Million
Number Employees: 5-9

Food Manufacturers / A-Z

Type of Packaging: Private Label

298 Alfonso Gourmet Pasta
2211 NW 30th Pl
Pompano Beach, FL 33069-1026
954-960-1010
Fax: 954-974-2773 800-370-7278
customerservice@alfonsogourmetpasta.com
Ravioli and prepared foods including fresh, frozen and processed.
President: Joseph Delfavero
jdelfavero@ppg.com
Estimated Sales: $2.5 Million
Number Employees: 5-9
Square Footage: 48000
Type of Packaging: Food Service
Brands:
   Alfonso Gourmet Pasta

299 Alfred & Sam's Italian Bakery
17 Fairview Ave
Lancaster, PA 17603-5594
717-392-6311
Fax: 717-392-6311
Rolls, breads, cannolis and cookies.
President: Tim Mineo
Owner: Sam Borsellino
Estimated Sales: $500,000-$1 Million
Number Employees: 10-19
Type of Packaging: Consumer
Brands:
   Alfred & Sam's

300 Alfred L. Wolff, Inc.
1440 Renaissance Drive
Park Ridge, IL 60068
847-759-8888
Fax: 312-265-9888 www.alwolff.com
Importer of dehydrated vegetables, herbs, honey and other bee products including royal jelly, bee pollen and propolis; also, gum arabic, acidulating agents and nutritional fiber
General Manager: Magnus von Buddenbrock
Estimated Sales: $5 Million
Number Employees: 3
Parent Co: Alfred L. Wolff GmbH
Type of Packaging: Bulk
Brands:
   Big Onion
   Finest Honey Organic
   Finest Honey Selection
   Qslic
   Quick Acid
   Quick Chew
   Quick Coat
   Quick Fibre
   Quick Glanz
   Quick Gum
   Quick Lac
   Quick Oil
   Quick Shine
   Shellac

301 Alfred Louie Inc
4501 Shepard St
Bakersfield, CA 93313-2310
661-831-2520
Fax: 661-833-9197
Fruits and vegetables, pasta, and Chinese canned goods and vegetables.
President: Susan Louie
Manager: Gordon Louie
peakdragon@yahoo.com
Estimated Sales: $5,115,628
Number Employees: 10-19

302 Alfred Nickles Bakery Inc
26 N Main St
Navarre, OH 44662
330-879-5635
customerservice@nicklesbakery.com
www.nicklesbakery.com
Baked goods
President & CEO: David Gardner
SVP, Finance: Mark Sponseller
Plant Manager: John Nixon
Year Founded: 1909
Estimated Sales: $153 Million
Number Employees: 50-99

303 Alfredo Aiello Italian Food
8 Franklin St
Quincy, MA 02169-4944
617-770-6360
Fax: 617-773-3342 info@aapasta.com
www.aapasta.com
Fresh lasagna, ravioli, cavatelli, tortellini, fettuccini
Owner: Alfredo Aiello
alfredo@aapasta.com
Operations Manager: Lino Aiello
Purchasing Manager: John Lucca
Estimated Sales: $5-10 Million
Number Employees: 1-4
Type of Packaging: Consumer, Food Service, Private Label, Bulk
Brands:
   Alfredo

304 Algonquin Tea
RR#5, 106 Augsburg Road
Eganville, ON K0J 1T0
Canada
613-628-6157
800-292-6671
spirit@algonquintea.com algonquintea.com
Herbal tea
Co-Owner & Office Manager: Kim Elkington
Co-Owner: Steven Martyn
Estimated Sales: $1 Million
Number Employees: 10
Brands:
   The Algonquin Tea Co

305 Algood Food Co
7401 Trade Port Dr
Louisville, KY 40258-1896
502-637-3631
Fax: 502-637-1502 bmcdonald@algoodfood.com
www.algoodfood.com
Processor and exporter of peanut butter, jams, jellies and preserves
President: Nicolas Melhuish
CEO: Cecil Barnett
VP & CFO: Kathleen Powell
Vice President: Gillian Barnett
Sales Manager: Ashley Keeney
Operations Executive: Dan Schmidt
Production Manager: Danny Ludwig
Number Employees: 100-249
Square Footage: 400000
Brands:
   Algood Blue Label
   Algood Jelly
   Algood Marmalade
   Algood Old Fashioned
   Algood Preserves
   Algood Red Label
   Cap 'n Kid

306 Alicita-Salsa
737 Walker Road
Suite 2, Po Box 1064
Great Falls, VA 22066
703-340-5323
Fax: 703-406-1276
Dairy-free, gluten-free, sugar-free, vegetarian, salsa/dips, other sauces, seasonings and cooking enhancers, other snacks, other vegetables/fruit.
Marketing: Suzanne Fields

307 Alimentaire Whyte's Inc
1540 Rue Des Patriotes
Laval, QC H7L 2N6
Canada
866-420-9520
customer.service@whytes.ca www.whytes.ca
Sauces, cherries, olives, condiments, relish, cooking oils, and table syrup
Year Founded: 1892
Estimated Sales: $32.35 Million
Number Employees: 325
Square Footage: 250000

308 Alimentos Finisterre
1109 Little Harbor Drive
Deerfield Beach, FL 33441
954-570-5886
Fax: 954-719-2445
Kosher, full-line cold non-carbonated beverages, RTD-ready to drink (coffee, tea, concentrates, powders), full-line condiments, marinades, full-line spreads & syrup, olives, private label.
Marketing: Tony Grivnovics

309 Aliments Fontaine Sant, Inc
450 Rue Deslauriers
Ville Saint-Laurent, QC H4N 1V8
Canada
514-956-7730
Fax: 514-956-7734 888-627-2683
info@fontainesante.com www.fontainesante.com
Health foods.
Marketing: Sami Damnati

310 Aliments Jolibec, Inc
149 Montee Allard
St Jacques De Montcalm, QC J0K 2R0
Canada
450-861-6082
Fresh and frozen pork
President: Roger Ethier
Number Employees: 43
Type of Packaging: Bulk

311 Aliments Prince SEC
11053 Louis H Lafontaine
Anjou, QC H1J 2Z4
Canada
514-383-0556
Fax: 514-383-4332 800-361-3898
Bacon, ham and sausages
President: Marcel Heroux
GM: Alain Heroux
Director Sales: Sylvain Blais
Number Employees: 800
Type of Packaging: Consumer, Food Service, Private Label

312 Aliments Trigone
93 Ch De L'Aqueduc Rr 1
St-Francois-De-La-Rivier, QC G0R 3A0
Canada
418-259-7414
Fax: 418-259-2417 877-259-7491
bio@alimentstrigone.com
www.alimentstrigone.com
Buckwheat and shelled hempseeds.
President: Jacques Cote
Estimated Sales: $1.3 Million
Number Employees: 9
Brands:
   Trigone

313 Aliotti Wholesale Fish Company
2 Wharf II
PO Box 3325
Monterey, CA 93940
408-722-4597
Fax: 408-722-3456
Processor and exporter of frozen squid
President/Purchasing Manager: Joe Aliotii
Estimated Sales: $2.7 Million
Number Employees: 8
Type of Packaging: Food Service
Brands:
   Prima Quality

314 Alive & Well Olives
Ponte Vedra Beach, FL 32004
www.aliveandwellolives.com
Olives
Founding Partner: Greg Leonard
Founding Partner: Martin Roth
Founding Partner: Bruce Kern
Brands:
   Alive & Well

315 Alive and Radiant
PO Box 920096
Needham, MA 02492
800-385-1417
Fax: 617-229-6244
Kale chips
CEO: Blessing Horowytz
Director of Marketing: Melanie Kingsley
Square Footage: 80000
Brands:
   Alive & Radiant

316 Alkinco
PO Box 278
New York, NY 10116-0278
212-719-3070
Fax: 212-764-7804 800-424-7118
info@Alkincohair.com www.alkincohair.com
Beverage mixes including sugared, chocolate and weight control; also, protein supplements

Food Manufacturers / A-Z

President: Julius Klugman
VP: Stewart Hoffman
Estimated Sales: $5-10 Million
Number Employees: 20-49
Square Footage: 200000
Type of Packaging: Consumer, Private Label
Brands:
   Alkinco

317   All American Foods Inc
121 Mohr Dr
Mankato, MN 56001-3000
                                             507-387-6480
                 Fax: 507-387-6111   800-833-2661
          info@aafoods.com www.aafoods.com
Dairy and non-dairy ingredients, including cheese powders and cheese flavorings, dried cultural ingredients, high-fat powders, dried flavoring ingredients, egg replacement powders, and replacers and substitutes for non-fat dry milkpowder, dry buttermilk powder and dry whole milk powder
President: Connie Stokman
Chief Executive Officer: Jeff Thom
Year Founded: 1987
Estimated Sales: $20 Million
Number Employees: 50-99
Number of Brands: 1
Number of Products: 150
Square Footage: 80000
Parent Co: All American Foods
Type of Packaging: Private Label, Bulk
Brands:
   PRO MIX

318   All American Seasonings
10600 E 54th Ave
Suite B
Denver, CO 80239-2132
                                             303-623-2320
                                  Fax: 303-623-1920
                 www.allamericanseasonings.com
Baking mixes for bread, cakes, other pasteries; assorted seasoned snacks including: chips, popcorn, nuts, & pretzels; sauces; variety of hot and cold beverages, energy drinks, and mixers.
Chairman: Andy Rodriguez
Director Of Quality Assurance: Mary Davis
Marketing Director: Joseph Gallagher
Year Founded: 1968
Estimated Sales: $12 Million
Number Employees: 20-49
Square Footage: 70000
Type of Packaging: Consumer, Food Service, Private Label, Bulk
Brands:
   All American

319   All American Snacks
P.O.Box 3
Midland, TX 79702
                                             432-687-6666
                 Fax: 915-699-2305   800-840-2455
                        www.allamericansnacks.com
White chocolate; cereals; pretzels; and pecan halves.
Owner/Public Relations: Lexie Kauffman
Co-Owner/Manager: Sheri Brockett
Sales Director: Kimberlea Bryand
Estimated Sales: $5-10 Million
Number Employees: 20-49
Brands:
   All American Afternoon Delight
   All American Precious Stones
   All American White Trash

320   All Goode Organics
PO Box 61256
Santa Barbara, CA 93160
                                             805-683-3370
                                  Fax: 805-683-7669
Organic foods, herbal teas

321   All Juice Food & Beverage
740 SE Dalbey Drive
Ankeny, IA 50021
                                             515-299-6457
                 Fax: 515-964-0697   800-736-5674
          info@mrsclarks.com www.mrsclarks.com
Beverages, apple juice
President: Ron Kahrer
Plant Manager: John Weber
Number Employees: 20-49

322   All Round Foods Bakery Prod
437 Railroad Ave
Westbury, NY 11590-4314
                                             516-338-1888
                 Fax: 516-338-5151   800-428-8802
                           www.allroundfoods.com
Processor and exporter of frozen doughnuts including plain, glazed, sugar, cinnamon, jelly, etc.
Owner: Glen Wolther
glen@allroundfoods.com
VP, Sales (Central): John Brahm
Executive VP: Robert Glasser
VP, Sales/Marketing (South): Greg Hanson
Purchasing: Steven Finkelstein
Estimated Sales: $3-5 Million
Number Employees: 10-19
Square Footage: 336000
Type of Packaging: Food Service
Brands:
   All Round Foods

323   All Seasonings Ingredients Inc
1043 Freedom Dr
Oneida, NY 13421-7108
                                             315-361-1066
                 Fax: 315-361-1048   800-255-7748
                        bfarnach@allseasonings.com
                              www.allseasonings.com
Custom blended spices and seasonings
President: Cheryl Ano
cano@allseasonings.com
Controller: Steven Tornabene
VP: Brendan Farnach
Manager/Director: Darby Smith
Estimated Sales: Less than $500,000
Number Employees: 1-4
Square Footage: 199504
Type of Packaging: Consumer, Food Service, Private Label, Bulk

324   All Wrapped Up
801 W Tropical Way
Plantation, FL 33317
                                             954-648-3051
                 Fax: 954-587-2144   800-891-2194
                    pam@allwrappedup-gifts.com
                        www.allwrappedup-gifts.com
Candies, cookies, chocolates, nuts, and pretzels, professionally wrapped.
President/CEO: Pam Schwimmer
pam@allwrappedup-gifts.com
VP: Donna Merill
Estimated Sales: Less than $500,000
Number Employees: 5-9
Type of Packaging: Consumer, Private Label

325   All-States Quality Foods
901 N Main Street
Charles City, IA 50616-2109
                                             641-228-5023
                 Fax: 641-228-2624   800-247-4195
Chicken products including broth, rendered fat, diced cooked meat and turkey and chicken quesadillas.
President: Elliot Jones
Marketing Director: Steve Tenney
Operations Manager: Dan Anderegg
dan@allstates.com
Estimated Sales: $17 Million
Number Employees: 150
Number of Products: 10
Type of Packaging: Consumer, Food Service, Private Label, Bulk

326   Allan Bros. Inc.
31 Allan Rd.
Naches, WA 98937
                                             509-653-2625
                         info@allanbrosfruit.com
                              www.allanbrosfruit.com
Apples, apple juice, and cherries.
CEO: Miles Kohl
Year Founded: 1951
Number Employees: 200-500
Type of Packaging: Private Label

327   Allann Brothers Coffee Roasters
1852 Fescue St SE
Albany, OR 97322-7075
                                             541-812-8013
                 Fax: 541-812-8010   800-926-6886
                        sales@allannbroscoffee.com
Coffee and teas

Owner: Allan Stuart
Sales Director: Michael Harris
info@allannbroscoffee.com
Estimated Sales: Less than $500,000
Number Employees: 10-19
Type of Packaging: Consumer, Food Service, Private Label, Bulk

328   Alldrin Brothers
P.O.Box 10
Ballico, CA 95303-0010
                                             209-667-1600
                 Fax: 209-667-0463 www.almondcafe.com
Processor and exporter of almonds.
President: Gary Alldrin
Purchasing Manager: Gary Alldrin
Estimated Sales: $1-2.5 Million
Number Employees: 50-99
Type of Packaging: Bulk
Brands:
   Alldrin

329   Alle Processing Corp
5620 59th St
Flushing, NY 11378-2314
                                             718-894-2000
                 Fax: 718-326-4642 www.alleprocessing.com
Kosher fresh and frozen meat products, entrees and deli meats.
President: Mendel Weinstock
IT: Shlomo Halberstam
halbycpa@alleprocessing.com
Estimated Sales: $10-20 Million
Number Employees: 50-99
Number of Brands: 4
Square Footage: 150000
Parent Co: Alle Processing
Type of Packaging: Consumer, Food Service, Private Label, Bulk
Brands:
   Meal Mart
   Mou Cuisine
   New York Kosher Deli
   Amazing Meals

330   Alleghany's Fish Farm
2755 Route 281
Saint Philemon, QC G0R 4A0
Canada
                                             418-469-2823
                                  Fax: 418-469-2872
Live trout eggs
GM: Yves Boulanger
Estimated Sales: $1-5 Million
Number Employees: 22
Type of Packaging: Consumer, Food Service
Brands:
   Alleghanys

331   Allegria Italian Bakers
233 E Weddell Dr # I
Sunnyvale, CA 94089-1659
                                             408-734-4300
                 Fax: 408-734-2444   800-467-8648
Baked goods
President: G Giurlani
italbisco@yahoo.com
CFO: Claire Baxter
Marketing Director: R Giurlani
Plant Manager: G Portida
Year Founded: 1984
Estimated Sales: $5-10 Million
Number Employees: 5-9
Type of Packaging: Consumer, Food Service, Private Label, Bulk

332   Allegro Coffee Co
12799 Claude Ct
Suite B
Thornton, CO 80241-3828
                                             303-444-4844
                 Fax: 303-920-5468   800-666-4869
                              www.allegrocoffee.com
Roasted specialty coffees; importer of green coffee beans.
President/General Manager: Jeff Teter
jeff_teter@allegro-coffee.com
CFO: Clarence Peterson
VP: David Kubena
Marketing Director: Tara Cross
Sales Director: Glenda Chamberlain
Human Resources Director: Mimi Fins
Plant Operations Manager: Alejandro Rodolfo
Marketing/Purchasing Manager: Susan Drexel

Food Manufacturers / A-Z

Estimated Sales: $10 Million
Number Employees: 50-99
Square Footage: 50000
Parent Co: Whole Foods Market
Brands:
   Allegro Coffee
   Allegro Tea
   Organic Coffee

333 Allegro Fine Foods Inc
1595 Highway 218 Byp
PO Box 1262
Paris, TN 38242-6632
731-642-6113
Fax: 731-642-6116 info@allegromarinade.com
www.allegromarinade.com
Meat and vegetable marinades
President: John Fuqua
john@allegromarinade.com
VP: Thomas Harrison
Quality Assurance Manager: Marti Jones
Marketing Manager: Tim Phifer
VP Operations: Stan Nelms
Purchasing: Melanie Mathis
Estimated Sales: $3 Million
Number Employees: 50-99
Square Footage: 80000
Type of Packaging: Consumer, Food Service, Private Label, Bulk
Brands:
   Allegro

334 Allegro Winery & Vineyards
3475 Sechrist Rd
Brogue, PA 17309-9415
717-927-9148
Fax: 717-927-1521 info@allegrowines.com
www.cadenzavineyards.com
Wines
Owner: Kris Miller
kris@allegrowines.com
Owner: Carl Helrich
Estimated Sales: $500,000-$1 Million
Number Employees: 1-4
Square Footage: 16000
Brands:
   Allegro

335 (HQ)Allen Flavors Inc
23 Progress St
Edison, NJ 08820-1102
908-561-5995
Fax: 908-561-4164 info@allenflavors.com
www.allenflavors.com
Beverage formulation, flavor and ingredient supply company.
President: Joseph Allen
joeyallen@allenflavors.com
VP: Michel Allen
Chemist: Donald Mull
Vice President of Sales & Marketing: Joe Moran
Assistant Vice President: Dana Allen
Estimated Sales: $38.7 Million
Number Employees: 50-99
Square Footage: 300000
Type of Packaging: Bulk
Other Locations:
   Wet Blending & Distribution Center
   South Plainfield NJ

336 (HQ)Allen Harim Foods LLC
126 N Shipley St
Seaford, DE 19973-3100
302-629-9136
Fax: 302-629-5081 877-397-9191
info@allenharimllc.com www.allenharimllc.com
Poultry products including frozen parts and whole birds; exporter of frozen poultry items
CEO: Steve Evans
Chairman: Warren Allen
CFO: Brian Hildreth
Director of Planning, IT and QA: Allen Harim
Director of Sales and Marketing: Dr.Key Lee
VP Human Resources: Tracy Morris
VP Live Operations: Gary Gladys
Production Coordinator: Karlyn Lemon
Purchasing Director: Gary Lacher
Number Employees: 1000-4999
Type of Packaging: Consumer, Food Service, Private Label, Bulk
Other Locations:
   Allen Family Foods
   Delmar DE
   Allen Family Foods
   Hurlock MD

   Allen Family Foods
   Linkwood MD
Brands:
   Allens

337 Allen's Blueberry Freezer Inc
PO Box 536
Ellsworth, ME 04605
207-667-5561
Fax: 207-667-8315 allensblueberries@gmail.com
Frozen wild blueberries.
President/CEO: Roy Allen
allen@acadia.net
Estimated Sales: $10-20 Million
Number Employees: 10-19
Type of Packaging: Consumer, Food Service
Brands:
   Allen's

338 Allen's Pickle Works
36 Garvies Point Rd
Glen Cove, NY 11542-2821
516-676-0640
Fax: 516-759-5780 bgpickl@aol.com
www.newyorkdelipickle.com
Cold packed sour dill and half sour pickles including whole, spears and chips.
President: Ronald Horman
Estimated Sales: $2.5-5 Million
Number Employees: 10-19
Square Footage: 72000
Type of Packaging: Private Label
Brands:
   Allens
   Alma
   Butterfield
   Clear Sailing

339 Alley Kat Brewing Co, Ltd
9929-60th Avenue
Edmonton, AB T6E 0C7
Canada
780-436-8922
Fax: 780-430-7363 thekats@alleykatbeer.com
www.alleykatbeer.com
Beer, ale, lager and stout
Co-Owner: Neil Herbst
Co-Owner: Lavonne Herbst
Sales Director: Christopher Ducharme
Estimated Sales: $500,000
Number Employees: 8
Square Footage: 15000
Type of Packaging: Consumer, Food Service
Brands:
   Alley Kat Amber
   Aprikat
   Charlie Flint's Original Lager
   Ein Prosit!
   Full Moon Pale Ale
   Olde Deuteronomy
   Razzykat
   Smoked Porter
   St. Paddy's
   Weihnachtskatze

340 Allfresh Food Products
2156 Green Bay Rd
Evanston, IL 60201-3046
847-869-3100
Fax: 847-869-3103 www.allfreshfoodproducts.com
Butter blends, margarine, shortening and vegetable oil
President: Gulshan Wadhwa
allfreshfood@aol.com
VP: Anil Wadhwa
Purchasing Manager: Gulshan Wadhwa
Estimated Sales: $5-10 Million
Number Employees: 5-9
Parent Co: Food Corporation of America
Type of Packaging: Consumer, Food Service
Brands:
   All Fresh
   Big Boy
   Buckson
   Farmer Brothers
   Top Notch

341 Alli & Rose
1422 E Main St
PMB #210
Lincolnton, NC 28092
828-446-8420
Fax: 828-333-5591 customerservice@alli-rose.com
www.alli-rose.com

Chocolate, snacks: pretzels, munchi bites, wafer sticks, veggie straws
Parent Co: C.A.L. Marketing

342 Allied Blending & Ingredients
121 Royal Rd
Keokuk, IA 52632-2028
319-524-1235
Fax: 319-524-9889 800-758-4080
cs@alliedblending.com www.alliedblending.com
Cheese and tortilla products; also baked goods and ingredients.
President: Randy Schmelzel
rschmelzel@alliedblending.com
CFO: Charles Cross
VP Technical Services: John Fannon
Director, Sales & Marketing: Tara Perry
Operations: Matt Stelzer
Plant Manager: Jeff Brunenn
Purchasing: Stephanie Slattery
Number Employees: 50-99
Square Footage: 1200
Brands:
   Free Flow®
   SureFlo™
   SecureFlo™
   Flow Lite®
   Cheese-Mor™
   BatchPak™
   No-Stick™

343 (HQ)Allied Custom Gypsum Company
1550 Double Drive
Norman, OK 73069-8288
Fax: 405-366-9515 800-624-5963
customerservice@alliedcustomgypsum.com
www.alliedcustomgypsum.com
Food
Manager & CFO: Tracy Shirley
Executive VP: Dan Northcutt
VP Operations: Kris Kinder
Estimated Sales: $1-5 Million
Number Employees: 10-19
Number of Products: 1
Square Footage: 200000
Parent Co: Harrison Gypsum
Type of Packaging: Food Service
Brands:
   Acg
   Acg Broadcast Gypsum
   Terra Alba
   Valu-Fil

344 Allied Food Products
251-253 Saint Marks Ave
Brooklyn, NY 11238
718-230-4227
Fax: 718-230-4229 info@alliedfoodproducts.com
www.alliedfoodproducts.com
Kosher soup and gravy bases, gourmet sauces and dressings, dessert mixes and seasoning blends
General Manager: Ernest Stern
Estimated Sales: $1-2,500,000
Number Employees: 5-9
Brands:
   E&S

345 Allied Old English Inc
100 Markley St
Port Reading, NJ 07064-1897
732-602-8955
Fax: 732-636-2538 info@alliedoldenglish.com
www.alliedoldenglish.com
Processor and exporter of Oriental prepared foods including noodles and sauces; also, pancake syrup, molasses, salad dressings, jams, jellies, preserves, salsa and barbecue sauce
President: Brian Dean
COO: Sean Colon
scolon@alliedoldenglish.com
Director of Purchasing: Beverley Gould
Estimated Sales: $8 Million
Number Employees: 50-99
Square Footage: 2000
Type of Packaging: Consumer, Food Service, Private Label, Bulk
Brands:
   Ah-So
   China Pride
   Dai Dairy
   Mee Tu
   Plantation
   Polynesian

Rio Grande
Saucy Susan

346 Allied Wine Corporation
70 Berme Rd
Ellenville, NY 12428
845-796-4160
Fax: 845-796-4161 800-796-4100
l.goldman@alliedwine.com www.alliedwine.com
Kosher wines and spirits
Manager: David Fieldman
VP: Herman Schwartz
Estimated Sales: $500,000-$1 Million
Number Employees: 1-4
Type of Packaging: Food Service, Private Label
Brands:
   Armon

347 Alliston Creamery
26 Dominion Street
Alliston, ON L9R 1L5
Canada
705-435-6751
Fax: 705-435-6797 info@allistoncreamery.com
Butter
President: David Kennedy
Number Employees: 9
Square Footage: 60000
Type of Packaging: Consumer, Food Service, Private Label, Bulk
Brands:
   Golden Dawn

348 Alltech Inc
3031 Catnip Hill Rd
Nicholasville, KY 40356-9765
859-885-9613
Fax: 859-887-3223 info@alltech.com
www.alltech.com
Meat tenderizers, gelating agents, flavor bases and sequestrants
President & CEO: Mark Lyons
COO: Alric Blake
CFO, North America Feed Division: Nathan Hohman
EVP: E Michael Castle II
Chief Marketing Officer: Orla McAleer
VP Business Development: Marc Larousse
VP Operations: Dan Haney
Estimated Sales: $20-50 Million
Number Employees: 500-999

349 Alluserv
4900 W Electric Ave
West Milwaukee, WI 53219
414-902-6400
Fax: 414-902-6446 800-558-8565
info@elakeside.com alluserv.com
Equipment for healthcare food service meal assembly and delivery
President/Owner: Joe Carlson
Principal: Larry Moon
General Manager: Tony Yenzer

350 Allylix Inc
7220 Trade St
Suite 209
San Diego, CA 92121
858-909-0595
Fax: 858-909-0695 info@allylix.com
www.allylix.com
Terpene products and derivatives; food ingredients.
President & CEO: Carolyn Fritz
VP Business Development: Seth Goldblum
VP Research & Development: Richard Burlingame
sgoldblum@allylix.com
VP Sales & Marketing: Leandro Nonino
Contact: Seth Goldblum
sgoldblum@allylix.com
Estimated Sales: $280,000
Number Employees: 5-9

351 Alma Plantation
4612 Alma Plantation Rd
Lakeland, LA 70752
225-627-6632
www.amscl.org
Blackstrap molasses; beet sugar; pure cane sugar; and raw sugars.
CEO: David Stewart
Year Founded: 1859
Estimated Sales: Less than $500,000
Number Employees: 5-9
Type of Packaging: Bulk

352 Almark Foods
2118 Centennial Dr
Gainesville, GA 30504
770-536-4520
Fax: 770-536-4793 800-849-3447
almarkfoods@msn.com www.almarkeggs.com
Egg products
President: Don Stoner
CEO: Mark Papp
Contact: David Cathey
d.cathey@almarkeggs.com
Operations Manager: Paul Heard
Estimated Sales: $5-10 Million
Number Employees: 90
Square Footage: 60000
Type of Packaging: Food Service
Brands:
   Almark

353 Almarla Vineyards & Winery
Highway 510
Shubuta, MS 39360
601-687-5548
Wines
President: Timothy Dunbar
Brands:
   Almarla Black Lightning
   Almarla Soul Train
   Sautene
   Thunder McCloud

354 Almased USA
2861 34th Street South
St. Petersburg, FL 33711
727-867-4444
Fax: 727-866-1438 www.almased.com
Meal replacement powder
Number of Brands: 1
Number of Products: 1
Type of Packaging: Consumer
Brands:
   ALMASED

355 Almond Brothers
4102 Air Lane
Pheonix, AZ 85034
602-955-0909
info@almondbrothers.com
almondbrothers.com
Almonds
Owner: Steve Godber

356 Almost Nuts
PO Box 19
Denmark, WI 54208-0019
920-915-0152
sales@soyalmostnuts.com
www.soyalmostnuts.com
Dry roasted soybeans covered in dark chocolate.
Owner: Darren Kornowske
darren@soyalmostnuts.com
Estimated Sales: $80,000
Number Employees: 2
Square Footage: 3890

357 Aloe Commodities International
2161 Hutton Dr.
Suite 126
Carrollton, TX 75006-8333
972-241-4251
Fax: 972-241-4376 800-701-2563
Aloe vera products, cosmetics and dietary supplement drinks
President/Director: Mark McKnight
CEO: Scott McKnight
CFO: Richard Ellis
VP Sales/Marketing: Jennifer Larson
COO/General Manager: Fred Lauterbach
Estimated Sales: $20-50 Million
Number Employees: 20-49
Number of Brands: 20
Number of Products: 100
Square Footage: 64000
Type of Packaging: Consumer, Private Label
Brands:
   Avera Sport
   Carbmate
   El Toro Loco
   Katahna
   Naturally Aloe

358 Aloe Farms Inc
3102 Wilson Rd
Harlingen, TX 78552-5011
956-425-1289
Fax: 956-425-3390 800-262-6771
info@aloeverafarms.com www.aloeverafarms.com
Aloe vera juice, gel and capsules.
President: Mark Berry
VP: Elvia Berry
Estimated Sales: Less Than $500,000
Number Employees: 1-4
Square Footage: 4224
Type of Packaging: Consumer, Private Label, Bulk
Brands:
   Aloe Farms

359 Aloe Laboratories
5821 E Harrison Ave
Harlingen, TX 78550-1811
956-428-8416
Fax: 956-428-8482 800-258-5380
lrodriguez@aloelabs.com www.aloelabs.com
Organic and conventional aloe vera gel, juice, concentrates and powder.
President: Luis Rodriguez
lrodriguez@aolelabs.com
CEO: Hide Aragaki
Operations and Logistics: Mike Hernandez
Estimated Sales: $3-5 Million
Number Employees: 50-99
Square Footage: 160000
Parent Co: Aloe Farms, Inc.
Brands:
   Aloe Burst
   Aloe Labs

360 Aloe'Ha Drink Products
1908 Augusta Drive
Apt 2
Houston, TX 77057-3717
713-978-6359
Fax: 713-978-6858 www.aloeha.com
Carbonated fruit drinks including rasberry, kiwi-strawberry, peach, lemon-lime, etc.
Operations Manager: Doyle Gaskamp
Number Employees: 5
Type of Packaging: Consumer, Food Service
Brands:
   Aloe'ha

361 Aloecorp, Inc.
3005 1st Ave
Seattle, WA 98121
360-486-7415
800-458-2563
www.aloecorp.com
Aloe vera and other aloe ingredients.
CEO: KS Yoon
Vice President, Chief Scientific Officer: Ken Jones
Quality Unit & Scientific Reg. Affairs: Ramiro Gallegos
Sales Representative: Julia Foo
Customer Service Manager: Norma Garza
Director of Operations: Juan Saldana
Number Employees: 5-9
Other Locations:
   Hainan Aloecorp Co. Ltd
   Shanghai, China

362 Aloha Distillers
5 Sand Island Access Rd
Unit 118
Honolulu, HI 96819-2222
808-841-5787
Fax: 808-847-2903 alohadistillersinc@yahoo.com
Processor and exporter of liqueurs including coffee, chocolate-coconut and chi-chi
President/Purchasing Manager: Dave Fazendin
alohadistillersinc@yahoo.com
Marketing: Ann Fazendin
Estimated Sales: $1-2.5 Million
Number Employees: 1-4
Number of Brands: 1
Number of Products: 1
Type of Packaging: Consumer
Brands:
   Coffee
   Gold
   Kona
   Liqueur

Food Manufacturers / A-Z

363 Aloha From Oregon
1471 Railroad Blvd
Unit 6
Eugene, OR 97402-4187
541-343-5519
Fax: 541-343-5499 800-241-0300
www.alohafromoregon.com
Pepper jellies, chutneys, and other specialty items.
President: Judy Dodson
jd@alohafromoregon.com
Estimated Sales: $5-10 Million
Number Employees: 5-9
Type of Packaging: Consumer, Food Service, Private Label

364 Aloha Poi Factory Inc
800 Lower Main St
Wailuku, HI 96793-1417
808-244-3536
Fax: 808-244-1914
Poi
President: Lester Nakama
Estimated Sales: $2.5-5 Million
Number Employees: 10-19
Type of Packaging: Consumer, Food Service

365 Aloha Shoyu Co LTD
96-1205 Waihona St
Pearl City, HI 96782-1969
808-456-5929
Fax: 808-456-5093 gotshoyu@alohashoyu.com
www.alohashoyu.com
Sauces
President: Brian Tanigawa
btanigawa@alohashoyu.com
Number Employees: 20-49

366 Aloha Tofu Factory Inc
961 Akepo Ln
Honolulu, HI 96817-4503
808-845-2669
Fax: 808-848-4607 www.aloha-tofu.com
Tofu
President: Sharren Sakamaki
VP/Office Manager: Jane Uyehara
Estimated Sales: $2.3 Million
Number Employees: 20-49
Square Footage: 44000

367 Alois J Binder Bakery
940 Frenchmen St
New Orleans, LA 70116-1683
504-947-1111
Fax: 504-947-1122 www.binderbakery.com
Bread and other bakery products
Owner: Alois Binder Jr
Treasurer: Joseph Binder
Estimated Sales: $4 Million
Number Employees: 20-49
Type of Packaging: Consumer, Food Service, Private Label, Bulk

368 Alouette Cheese USA
400 S Custer Ave
New Holland, PA 17557
800-322-2743
customer.service@alouettecheese.com
www.alouettecheese.com
French cheese
President & CEO: Dominique Huth
Director, Research & Development: Steve Schalow
Year Founded: 1974
Estimated Sales: $100 Million
Number Employees: 200-500
Brands:
 alouette(c)

369 Alpen Cellars
2000 E Fork Rd
Trinity Center, CA 96091
530-266-9513
Fax: 530-266-3363 winemaker@alpencellars.com
www.alpencellars.com
Wine
Owner: Mark Groves
winemaker@alpencellars.com
Winemaker: Keith Grooves
Estimated Sales: Less than $500,000
Number Employees: 10-19
Brands:
 Alpen Cellars

370 Alpen Sierra Coffee Company
2222 Park Place
Suite 1A
Minden, NV 89423
775-783-7263
Fax: 775-783-7293 800-531-1405
coffeentea@alpensierra.com www.alpensierra.com
Coffee and tea
President: Christian Waskiewicz
coffeentea@alpensierra.com
Marketing: Megan Waskiewicz
Estimated Sales: $1-2.5 Million
Number Employees: 5-9
Brands:
 Alpen Sierra

371 Alpendough
Cookies and cookie dough
President/Owner: Andrew McKean
Number of Brands: 1
Number of Products: 6
Type of Packaging: Consumer
Brands:
 ALPENDOUGH

372 Alpenglow Beverage Company
3056 Dismel Hollow Road
Linden, VA 22642
540-635-2118
Fax: 304-229-4377
Kosher, organic/natural, juice/cider, non-alcoholic beverages, RTD-ready to drink (coffee, tea, concentrates, powders).
President: Ben Lacy, III
Marketing: Terry Hess

373 Alpenrose Dairy
6149 SW Shattuck Rd
P.O.Box 25030
Portland, OR 97221-1044
503-244-1133
Fax: 503-452-2139 TomBaker@alpenrose.com
www.alpenrose.com
Ice cream; milk; farm eggs; yogurt; orange juice; and butter.
President: Carl Cadanau III
Cmo: Tom Baker
tombaker@alpenrose.com
Operations: Tom Nieradka
Purchasing: Rocky Amick
Estimated Sales: $1.6 Million
Number Employees: 100-249
Type of Packaging: Consumer, Food Service
Brands:
 Alpenrose

374 (HQ)Alpha Baking Company
1910 Lincoln Way West
South Bend, IN 46628
773-261-6000
spowell@alphabaking.com
www.alphabaking.com
Fresh and frozen bread, buns, and bagels sold through wholesale or retail
CEO: Lawrence Marcucci
Vice President of Division: Gary Narcisi
VP of Sales & Marketing: Tim Gill
Estimated Sales: $7 Million
Number Employees: 1000
Square Footage: 600000
Type of Packaging: Consumer, Food Service
Brands:
 S. Rosen's
 Natural Ovens Bakery

375 Alpha Health
104-3686 Bonneville Place
Burnaby, BC V3N 4T6
Canada
888-826-9625
info@assurednatural.com www.alphahealth.ca
Coconut oil, coconut sugar, coconut flour, MCT oil, red palm oil
Number Employees: 10-19
Parent Co: Assured Natural

376 Alpina
5011 AG Park Dr West
Batavia, NY 14020
855-886-1914
alpinaus.com
Smoothies and other dairy products

377 (HQ)Alpine Butcher
963 Chelmsford St
Lowell, MA 01851-5131
978-256-7771
Processor of beef, pork, lamb, chicken, seafood and game meat.
President: Peter Doyle
Treasurer: Dennis Doyle
Owner: Greg Doyle
Owner: Thomas Doyle
Year Founded: 1913
Estimated Sales: $20-50 Million
Number Employees: 10-19
Number of Brands: 1
Square Footage: 3000
Type of Packaging: Consumer, Food Service, Private Label, Bulk
Brands:
 Doyle's

378 Alpine Cheese Company
US Highway 62 E
Winesburg, OH 44690
330-359-6291
Fax: 330-359-0035
Dairy products, natural cheeses and deli
President: Robert Ramseyer
Manager: Joe Nisley
Plant Manager: Brian Barbey
Purchasing Manager: Donald Fudge
Estimated Sales: $35 Million
Number Employees: 45
Type of Packaging: Private Label

379 Alpine Coffee Roasters
894 US Highway 2
Suite J
Leavenworth, WA 98826-1340
509-548-3313
Fax: 509-548-4251 800-246-2761
Coffee
Co-Owner: Dale Harrison
Co-Owner: Veronica Harrison
java@alpinecoffeeroasters.com
Roastmaster: Bill Harrison
Estimated Sales: $2.5-5 Million
Number Employees: 1-4
Brands:
 Alpine Coffee

380 Alpine Meats
7850 Lower Sacramento Rd
Stockton, CA 95210-3912
209-477-2691
Fax: 209-477-1994 800-399-6328
info@alpinemeats.com www.alpinemeats.com
Frankfurters, sausages and hams.
President: Jerry Singer
Quality Control: James Sturgeon
Controller: Cecil McKie
Production: Dennis Saragoza
Purchasing: Robby Jaynes
Estimated Sales: $8 Million
Number Employees: 50-99
Square Footage: 196000
Type of Packaging: Consumer, Food Service, Private Label, Bulk
Brands:
 Alpine

381 Alpine Pure USA
421 Currant Road
Falls River, MA 02720
617-548-8301
Fax: 888-311-6541 888-332-3392
www.alpinepure.net
Teas

382 Alpine Start Foods
1911 11th St
Suite 207
Boulder, CO 80302
info@alpinestartfoods.com
alpinestartfoods.com
Instant coffee
Number of Brands: 1
Number of Products: 1
Type of Packaging: Consumer
Brands:
 ALPINE START

Food Manufacturers / A-Z

383 Alpine Touch Spices
101 3rd St
714 Main Avenue North
Choteau, MT 59422
406-466-2063
Fax: 406-466-2076 877-755-2525
montanaalpinetouch@gmail.com
www.alpinetouch.com
Seasonings
Owner: Mark Southard
Co-Owner: Vicki Southard
Estimated Sales: $500,000-$1 Million
Number Employees: 1-4

384 Alpine Valley Water
16900 Lathrop Ave
Harvey, IL 60426
708-333-3910
Fax: 708-333-3921 sales@AlpineValleyWater.com
www.alpinevalleywater.com
Distilled and bottled water
Owner: Tim Rausch
Estimated Sales: Less than $500,000
Number Employees: 1-4
Square Footage: 40000
Type of Packaging: Food Service
Brands:
 Alpine Valley

385 Alpine Vineyards
25904 Green Peak Rd
Monroe, OR 97456-9773
541-424-5851
Fax: 541-424-5891 www.actionnet.net
Wines
Owner: Dan Jepsen
alpinevineyards@actionnet.net
Estimated Sales: $1-2.5 Million
Number Employees: 5-9

386 Alsum Farms & Produce
N9083 County Road E
Cambria, WI 53923-9668
920-348-5127
Fax: 920-348-5174 800-236-5127
www.alsum.com
Potatoes and onions; fresh fruits and vegetables.
President & CEO: Larry Alsum
CEO: Randy Fischer
randy.fischer@alsum.com
National Sales & Marketing Manager: Heidi Alsum-Randall
Year Founded: 1972
Number Employees: 100-249
Number of Brands: 4
Number of Products: 300
Type of Packaging: Consumer, Food Service, Private Label, Bulk
Brands:
 Alsum Farms & Produce
 Alsum Organics
 Rainbow Organics
 Family Favorite

387 Alta Dena Certified Dairy LLC
17851 E Railroad
City Of Industry, CA 91748
626-923-3182
800-535-1369
www.altadenadairy.com
Dairy products.
Logistics: Carl Reynolds
Year Founded: 1945
Estimated Sales: $48.1 Million
Number Employees: 500-999
Square Footage: 100000
Parent Co: Dean Foods
Brands:
 Alta Dena Classic
 Caribbean Chill
 Crazy Cow
 Dairy Mart
 Decadent Temptations
 Le Younghurt
 Old Tyme

388 Alta Dena Heartland Farms
17851 Railroad St
City Of Industry, CA 91748-1118
626-923-3000
Fax: 626-923-3038 800-395-7004
deanfoods@casupport.com
www.heartlandfarms.com
Dairy products

Manager: Mary Armstrong
mary.armstrong@heartlandfarms.com
Number Employees: 250-499
Square Footage: 500000
Parent Co: Dean Foods
Type of Packaging: Consumer, Private Label
Other Locations:
 Heartland Farms Distribution
 Anaheim CA
 Heartland Farms Distribution
 San Diego CA
 Heartland Farms Distribution
 El Centro CA
 Heartland Farms Distribution
 Ventura CA
 Heartland Farms Distribution
 Santa Barbara CA
 Heartland Farms Distribution
 Desert Hot Springs CA
Brands:
 Knudsen®
 Foremost®
 Arnold Palmer
 Trumoo Chocolate Milk
 Swiss Premium

389 Alta Health Products
300 Main St
Idaho City, ID 83631
208-392-4170
Fax: 208-392-4185 800-423-4155
info@altahealthproducts.com
www.altahealthproducts.com
Herbal supplements, teas and minerals
President: Judy Haswell
Founder: Richard Barmakian
Vice President: Deborah Saw Kims
Product Promotion: Kelli Fischer
Estimated Sales: Less than $500,000
Number Employees: 1-4
Brands:
 Alta

390 Alta Vineyard Cellar
PO Box 980
3081 Lake County Hwy
Calistoga, CA 94515-0980
707-942-6708
Fax: 707-942-5065
Wines
President: Benjamin Falk
Estimated Sales: $500,000-$1 Million
Number Employees: 1-4
Brands:
 Alta

391 Altamura Winery
1700 Wooden Valley Rd
Napa, CA 94558-9617
707-253-2000
Fax: 707-255-3937 altamurawinery@aol.com
www.altamura.com
Wines
President: Frank C Altamura
Estimated Sales: $3-5 Million
Number Employees: 5-9
Number of Brands: 1
Number of Products: 2

392 Alter Eco
2339 3rd St
Suite 70
San Francisco, CA 94107-3100
415-701-1214
Fax: 415-701-1213 sales@alterecofoods.com
www.alterecofoods.com
Fair trade and organic quinoa, rice, sugar, cacao
Co-founder/Co-CEO: Edouard Rollet
Co-founder/Co-CEO: Mathieu Senard
President: Kate Tierney
Quality Assurance: Anissa Bouziane
Director, Marketing: Antoine Ambert
Director, Operations: Jeanne Cloutier
Number Employees: 1-4

393 Alternative Health & Herbs
425 Jackson St SE
Albany, OR 97321
541-791-8400
Fax: 541-791-8401 800-345-4152
healthinfo@healthherbs.com
www.healthherbs.com
Liquid herbal formulations; herbal teas and vitamins.
Owner: Bishop Truman Berst

Estimated Sales: Less than $500,000
Number Employees: 1-4
Square Footage: 12000
Type of Packaging: Consumer, Private Label, Bulk
Brands:
 American Health & Herbs Ministry
 American Naturals
 Truman's

394 Alto Rey Food Corp
11468 Dona Teresa Dr
Studio City, CA 91604-4271
323-969-0178
Fax: 323-969-0197
Condiments, dips, salsas, dressings
President: David Ufberg
davidu@altorey.com
Estimated Sales: $1-2.5 Million
Number Employees: 1-4
Brands:
 Alto Rey

395 Alto Vineyards & Winery
8515 Highway 127
Alto Pass, IL 62905-2033
618-893-4898
Fax: 618-893-4935 www.altovineyards.net
Wines
President / General Manager: Paul Renzaglia
altovin@midwest.net
Estimated Sales: $5-10 Million
Number Employees: 5-9
Type of Packaging: Bulk
Other Locations:
 Alto Vineyards
 Champaign IL

396 Alvalle
Denver, CO 80212
www.alvalle.us
Gazpacho
Brands:
 ALOHA

397 Alvarado Street Bakery
2225 S McDowell Blvd.
Petaluma, CA 94954-5661
707-789-6700
Fax: 707-283-0350
info@alvaradostreetbakery.com
www.alvaradostreetbakery.com
Organic goods including sprouted wheat bread, kosher bagels, tortillas and whole grain and oil-free granola; exporter of frozen organic wheat bread and kosher bagels.
CEO: Bryan Long
Sales Director: Jim Canterbury
Purchasing: Jamie Mitchell
Year Founded: 1979
Estimated Sales: $23 Million
Number Employees: 100-249
Number of Brands: 2
Number of Products: 27
Square Footage: 75000
Type of Packaging: Consumer, Private Label
Brands:
 Alvarado Street Bakery

398 Alvita
8600 Transit Dr
Suite B1
Amherst, NY 14051
833-258-4821
www.alvita.com
Herbal teas and supplement.
Year Founded: 1922
Estimated Sales: $100+ Million
Number Employees: 250-499
Parent Co: Twinlab
Brands:
 Alvita Tea
 Remeteas Detoxitea
 Remeteas Masculinitea
 Remeteas Pms Rescue
 Remeteas Visibilitea

399 Alya Foods
2227 US Hwy 1 #279
North Brunswick, NJ 08902
917-495-0815
info@alyafoods.com
www.alyafoods.com
Dates

Food Manufacturers / A-Z

400 Alyeska Seafoods
551 W Broadway
P.O. Box 530
Unalaska, AK 99685
907-581-1211
Fresh and frozen seafoods
Sales Coordinator: Theresa Koonce
Estimated Sales: $50-100 Million
Number Employees: 20-49
Parent Co: Maruha Nichiro Corporation

401 AmByth Estate
510 Sequoia Ln
Templeton, CA 93465
805-319-6967
gelert@ambythestate.com
www.ambythestate.com
Organic vineyard
Co-Owner: Mary Hart
Co-Owner: Gelert Hart
Estimated Sales: Less than $500,000
Number Employees: 1-4

402 AmTech Ingredients
573 County Route A
Suite 102
Hudson, WI 54016
715-381-5746
www.amtechingredients.com
Producer/distributor of specialty food ingredients, primarily in powder form.
Contact: Andrew Brudevold
abrudevold@amtechingredients.com
Estimated Sales: $330,000
Number Employees: 3
Square Footage: 6734

403 Amador Foothill Winery
12500 Steiner Rd
Plymouth, CA 95669-9510
209-245-6307
Fax: 209-245-3280 800-778-9463
info@amadorfoothill.com
Wines
Owner/President: Ben Zeitman
Owner/Winemaker: Katie Quinn
katie@amadorfoothill.com
Estimated Sales: Less Than $500,000
Number Employees: 1-4
Type of Packaging: Private Label
Brands:
 Amador Foothill

404 Amafruits
8940 W 192nd St
Suite C
Mokena, IL 60448
877-818-1262
custserv@amafruits.com www.amafruits.com
Fruit purees & sorbets
Number of Brands: 1
Number of Products: 11
Type of Packaging: Consumer
Brands:
 AMAFRUITS

405 Amalfitano's Italian Bakery
29 E Commons Blvd
Suite 700
New Castle, DE 19720-1740
302-324-9005
Fax: 302-324-9008
Bakery products
Owner: Ralph Jacobs
Estimated Sales: $2.5-5 Million
Number Employees: 20-49

406 Amalgamated Produce
P.O. Box 5159
1318 Kossuth Street
Bridgeport, CT 06610
203-366-6919
Fax: 203-339-3773 800-358-3808
www.inbusiness.com
Bean soup mixes, dried fruits, stuffings, sprout products and wild rice dishes.
CEO/President: Richard Blackwell
Chief Executive Officer: Richard Westin
Vice President: Adriana Alvarez
Estimated Sales: $10-50 Million
Number Employees: 20-49
Square Footage: 24000
Brands:
 Specialty Farms

407 Amalgamated Sugar Company
1951 S. Saturn Way
Suite 100
Boise, ID 83709
208-383-6500
Fax: 208-383-6688 www.amalgamatedsugar.com
Beet sugar.
President/CEO: John McCreedy
Chairman: Duane Grant
VP of Finance: Craig Hanks
Executive VP/Chief Buisness Dev. Officer: Joe Huff
Vice President, Operations: Kent Quinney
Year Founded: 1897
Estimated Sales: $907 Million
Number Employees: 1,600+
Square Footage: 20000
Parent Co: Snake River Sugar Company
Type of Packaging: Consumer, Food Service, Private Label, Bulk
Brands:
 White Satin®

408 Amalthea Cellars Farm Winery
209 Vineyard Rd
Atco, NJ 08004-2369
856-768-8585
AmaltheaCellars@gmail.com
www.amaltheacellars.com
Wines
Owner: Louis Caracciolo
Manager: Virginia Caracciolo
Estimated Sales: $1-2.5 Million
Number Employees: 5-9

409 Amana Meat Shop & SmokeHouse
4513 F St
Amana, IA 52203-8027
319-622-7586
Fax: 319-622-6245 800-373-6328
info@amanameatshop.com
Hickory-smoked meats including sausage, ham, bacon, pork tenderloin and bratwurst.
Manager: Greg Hergert
Director: Mike Shoup
Estimated Sales: Less than $500,000
Number Employees: 10-19
Parent Co: Amana Society Corporation
Type of Packaging: Consumer, Food Service
Brands:
 Amana Meats

410 Amanda Hills Spring Water
9756 National Road SW
PO Box 301
Etna, OH 43018
740-927-3422
Fax: 740-927-1856 800-375-0885
info@amandahills.com www.amandahills.com
Spring water
Owner: David Betts
Contact: Michael Betts
michael@amandahills.com
Estimated Sales: $300,000-500,000
Number Employees: 1-4
Number of Brands: 1
Square Footage: 40000
Type of Packaging: Private Label
Brands:
 Amanda Hills

411 Amanida USA Corp
2655 Lejeune Rd
Suite 810
Coral Gables, FL 33134
amanida.com/en/
Gourmet Italian and Spanish products
Parent Co: Amanida

412 Amano Artisan Chocolate
496 S 1325 W
Orem, UT 84058-5877
801-655-1996
amano@amanochocolate.com
www.amanochocolate.com
Chocolates
Owner: Art Pollard
Pastry Chef: Rebecca Millican
Number Employees: 20-49
Type of Packaging: Private Label
Brands:
 Amano Ocumare
 Amano Jenbrana

413 Amano Enzyme USA Company, Ltd
1415 Madeline Ln
Elgin, IL 60124
847-649-0101
Fax: 847-649-0205 800-446-7652
sales@amanoenzymeusa.com
Non-animal and non-GMO enzymes for the dietary supplement, nutraceutical, food, diagnostic and pharmaceutical industries.
President: Motoyuki Amano
VP Science/Technology: James Jolly
Contact: Kumiko Paik
kpaik@amanoenzymeusa.com
Estimated Sales: $15 Million
Number Employees: 440
Square Footage: 50000
Parent Co: Amano Enzyme

414 Amano Fish Cake Factory
30 Holomua St
Hilo, HI 96720-5102
808-935-5555
Fax: 808-961-2154
Frozen and canned fish cakes
Owner: Hiroshi Mathubara
Estimated Sales: $1-2.5 Million
Number Employees: 5-9
Type of Packaging: Consumer
Brands:
 Amano

415 Amara Organic Baby Food
584 Page St
San Francisco, CA 94117
267-981-6411
hello@amaraorganicfoods.com
amaraorganicfoods.com
Baby food
Number of Brands: 1
Type of Packaging: Consumer
Brands:
 AMARA

416 Amaranth Resources
139 E William Street
Suite 325
Albert Lea, MN 56007-2535
507-373-0356
Fax: 507-373-4753 800-842-6689
Grains, cereals, spices, seasonings, condiments, allergy free products
CEO: Edward Hubbard
Vice President: R Merrell
Estimated Sales: $2.5-5 Million
Brands:
 Ambake
 Amban
 Amburst
 Amgrain
 Best of Health

417 Amavi Cellars
3796 Peppers Bridge Rd
Walla Walla, WA 99362-7007
509-525-3541
Fax: 509-522-5011 info@amavicellars.com
www.amavicellars.com
Wines
Winemaker/Partner: Jean Francois Pellet
Partner: Eric McKibben
Partner: Travis Goff
Partner: Shane McKibben
Managing Partner: Ray Goff
Tasting Room Manager: Patty Lynch
Number Employees: 5-9

418 Amazing Candy Craft Company
18408 Jamaica Avenue
Hollis, NY 11423-2431
718-264-3031
Fax: 718-264-8437 800-429-9368
Candy
President: Frank Salacuse
VP: Catherine Salacuse
VP Marketing/Sales: Brad Demsky
Brands:
 Candy Activity
 Make Your Own Gummies

Food Manufacturers / A-Z

419 Amazing Fruit Products
501 Airport Rd
Fort Payne, AL 35968
256-273-5363
info@afp-us.com
amazingfruitproducts.com
Flavor-infused raisins
Number of Brands: 1
Number of Products: 7
Type of Packaging: Consumer
Brands:
   AMAZIN' RAISIN

420 Amazing Herbs Nutraceuticals
2709 Faith Industrial Dr
Ste 500
Buford, GA 30518-3564
770-982-4780
Fax: 770-982-0273 800-241-9138
info@amazingherbs.com www.amazingherbs.com
Supplements and natural products
Owner: Tony Goreja
Brands:
   Amazing Herbs
   Theramune Nutritionals

421 Amazon Trading, Ltd.
257 Siri Dhamma Mawatha
Colombo, 10
Sri Lanka
www.amazontea.biz
Loose leaf teas and tea bags.
Owner: Gamini Jayaweera
CEO: Suranga Herath
Square Footage: 80000
Brands:
   Tea of Life
   SUN LEAF

422 Amberg Wine Cellars
2412 Seneca Castle Orleans Road
Clifton Springs, NY 14432
315-462-3455
Fax: 315-462-6512 www.ambergwine.com
Wines
Owner: Ute Amberg
President: Herman Amberg
CFO: Eric Amberg
Marketing Manager: Debbie Amberg
Estimated Sales: $500,000-$1 Million
Number Employees: 1-4
Type of Packaging: Private Label
Brands:
   Amberg Wine Cellars

423 Amberland Foods
1350 Frontage Road
Harvey, ND 58341
701-324-4804
Fax: 701-324-4805 800-950-4558
amberlandfoods@gondtc.com
Dehydrated soup mixes, scone and dip mixes, jams, jellies, seasonings, syrups and toppings
Owner/Manager: Susan K Schwarz
Operations Manager: Elreen Olson
Estimated Sales: $1-2.5 Million
Number Employees: 10-19
Number of Brands: 1
Number of Products: 50
Square Footage: 16000
Type of Packaging: Consumer, Private Label
Brands:
   Dakota Seasonings

424 Ambootia Tea Estate
PO Box 11696
400 N McClurg Ct, Suite 1103
Chicago, IL 60611-0696
312-661-1550
Fax: 312-661-1523 www.teareport.com
Tea
President: Shashank Goel
Estimated Sales: Less than $500,000
Number Employees: 5-9
Brands:
   Ambootia

425 Ambrosi Cheese USA
57-01 49th Place
Maspeth, NY 11378
USA
sales@ambrosifoodusa.com
Cheese
Owner: Ottorino Ambrosi
Sales & Marketing: Giacomo Veraldi

426 Ambrosial Granola
Po Box 090712
Brooklyn, NY 11209
718-491-1335
Fax: 718-425-9932
Granola cereals
President: Hariclia Makoulis

427 Amcan Beverages Inc
1201 Commerce Blvd
American Canyon, CA 94503-9611
707-557-0500
Fax: 707-557-0100 800-972-5962
www.pokka.com.sg
Fruit juices, canned iced coffee, iced tea and yogurt flavored drinks
President: Don Soetaert
CFO: George Lewis
Vice President: Joe Inazuka
Manager: Dave Baldwin
dabaldwin@na.ko.com
Estimated Sales: $18 Million
Number Employees: 100-249
Square Footage: 500000
Parent Co: Pokka Corporation
Type of Packaging: Private Label
Brands:
   Fruit Ole
   Hawaiian Sun
   Premium Tea
   The Coffee

428 Amcan Industries
570 Taxter Road
Elmsford, NY 10523-2356
914-347-4838
Fax: 914-347-4960
Meat, jam, jelly, preserves, health food, nutriceuticals, confectionery, fish, seafood, dairy, beverage and juices, bakery and cereal, natural and artificial sweeteners
President: Bowes Dempsey
VP: Benjamin Dempsey
Contact: Guylaine Boucher
guylaine@dempseycorporation.com
Estimated Sales: $5-10 Million
Number Employees: 7

429 Amelia Bay
3851 Lakefield Dr
Suite 120
Suwanee, GA 30024-1242
770-772-6360
Fax: 770-772-4766 www.ameliabay.com
Liquid concentrates for coffees, teas, cappucinos, chais.
President: John Crandall
john@ameliabay.com
Sales Manager: Ralph Lane
Estimated Sales: $5-10 Million
Number Employees: 5-9
Type of Packaging: Food Service

430 Amella
214 Main Street
Suite 376
El Segundo, CA 90245
USA
Fax: 310-388-3105 800-205-0080
Carmel candy
Owner: Elena Kiamileva
Contact: Emir Kiamilev
ekiamilev@amellacaramels.com

431 Ameri Candy
3618 Saint Germaine Ct
Louisville, KY 40207-3722
502-583-1776
Fax: 502-583-1776 omar@americandybar.com
www.americandybar.com
Chocolates
Owner: Omar Patum
omar@americandybar.com
Estimated Sales: Less than $500,000
Number Employees: 1-4
Type of Packaging: Consumer, Private Label, Bulk
Brands:
   Americandy
   Asher
   Jim Candy
   Rooster Run

432 Ameri-Kal Inc
5405 Centime Drive
Suite 400
Wichita Falls, TX 76305-5271
940-322-5400
Nutritional supplements, vitamins, minerals, herbal formulations, sports nutrition products, herb flavored grapeseed oil, capsules, tablets, bulk powder, liquids, soft gel, etc.
Director: Djoko Soejoto
CEO: Tom Soejoto
Director/Of Marketing: Ron Soejoto
Contact: Keith Mccray
keith@ameri-kal.com
Number Employees: 18
Square Footage: 142000
Type of Packaging: Private Label, Bulk

433 Ameri-Suisse Group
157 Helen Street
South Plainfield, NJ 07080
908-222-1001
Fax: 732-222-1929
Novelty candies
Owner: Lew Demeter

434 AmeriGift
P.O. Box 5767
2300 Celcius Avenue
Oxnard, CA 93030
805-988-0350
Fax: 805-988-4668 800-421-9039
Candy gift items
Owner: Lionel Meff
Estimated Sales: $2.5-5 Million
Number Employees: 50-99
Brands:
   Amerigift Sweet Tooth Originals
   Ghirardelli

435 AmeriQual Foods
18200 Highway 41 North
Evansville, IN 47725
812-867-1444
Fax: 812-867-0278 www.ameriqual.com
Supplier of pre-made food items and manufacturer of heat-sealed microwavable bowls, trays and flexible pouches
CEO: Steve Chancellor
CFO: Sandra Rasche
Finance: Dave Barnes
Contact: Casey Elliott
casey.elliott@thementornetwork.com
Number Employees: 650
Other Locations:
   AmeriQual Packaging
   Evansville IN

436 America's Catch
PO Box 584
Itta Bena, MS 38941
662-254-7207
Fax: 662-254-9776 800-242-0041
solons@catfish.com www.catfish.com
Fresh and frozen farm-raised catfish
President: Solon Scott
VP Sales: John Nelms
Plant Manager: Bill Martin
Estimated Sales: $20-50 Million
Number Employees: 250-499
Type of Packaging: Consumer, Food Service, Private Label, Bulk
Brands:
   America's Catch

437 America's Classic Foods
1298 Warren Rd
Cambria, CA 93428-4642
805-927-0745
Fax: 805-927-2280 webmail@amcf.com
www.amcf.com
Powdered ice cream mix, ice cream freezers, processor and exporter of mixes including ice cream, baking, doughnut, etc.
President: Monty Rice
mgr@amcf.com
Estimated Sales: $1 Million
Number Employees: 1-4
Square Footage: 120000
Type of Packaging: Food Service, Private Label, Bulk
Brands:
   America's Classic Foods
   American Creamery

Food Manufacturers / A-Z

Empower
Mommy's Choice
Smooth & Creamy

438 American Almond Products Co
103 Walworth St
Brooklyn, NY 11205-2807
718-875-8310
Fax: 718-935-1505   800-825-6663
info@americanalmond.com
Processed nuts, natural nut butters & pastes, specialty pastes, marzipan, lekvar, poppy butter, piping gelee, crunch toppings and coconut macaroon mix.
President: Kevin Burn
kbyrne@americanalmond.com
Customer Service: Priscilla Morales
Estimated Sales: $5-10 Million
Number Employees: 20-49
Square Footage: 160000
Type of Packaging: Consumer, Food Service, Private Label, Bulk
Brands:
   America Almond
   American Almond

439 American Beverage Marketers
New Albany, IN 47151
812-944-3585
abm@abmcocktails.com
abmcocktails.com
Liquid cocktail mixes
Brands:
   Agalima
   Master of Mixes
   Finest Call
   Re...l Cocktail

440 American Biosciences
560 Bradley Parkway
Blauvelt, NY 10913
845-727-0800
888-884-7770
info@americanbiosciences.com
www.americanbiosciences.com
Herbs and supplements.
President: David Wales
Vice President: Rick Jahnke
Estimated Sales: $5-10 Million
Number Employees: 5-9
Type of Packaging: Consumer

441 American Blanching Company
155 Rip Wiley Rd
PO Box 1028
Fitzgerald, GA 31750
229-423-4098
Fax: 229-423-3842 info@AmericanBlanching.com
www.americanblanching.com
Blanched peanuts
President/CEO: Jack Warden
Contact: Michael Davis
mdavis@americanblanching.com

442 American Botanicals
24750 Highway Ff
Eolia, MO 63344
573-485-2300
Fax: 573-485-3801   800-684-6070
info@americanbotanicals.com
www.americanbotanicals.com
American herbs.
President: Allen Lockard
ambotncls@aol.com
Quality Control: Denise Kunzweiler
Operations: Chris Zumwalt
Milling Production: Ron Kunzweiler
Purchasing Agent: Tom Duncan
Purchasing Agent: Gennie Martinez
Estimated Sales: $12 Million
Number Employees: 20-49
Number of Products: 200
Square Footage: 35000
Type of Packaging: Bulk

443 American Bottling & Beverage
1756 Industrial Rd
Walterboro, SC 29488-9368
843-538-7937
Fax: 801-975-7185 www.abbperformance.com
Sport beverages
Owner: Olivia Hall
Manager: Ken Farley
kfarley@glanbia.com
Number Employees: 20-49

444 American Canadian Fisheries
6069 Hannegan Rd
Bellingham, WA 98226
360-398-1117
Fax: 360-398-8801   800-344-7942
Fish and gift boxes
President: Andy Vitaljic
Estimated Sales: $500,000-$1 Million
Number Employees: 1-4
Brands:
   Hannegan Seafoods

445 American Chalkis Intl. Food Corp.
20120 Paseo Del Prado Ste A
Walnut, CA 91789
562-232-4105
Fax: 562-232-4106 info@chalkistomato.us
Tomato products & tomato paste, apricot puree, pomegranate, apple & grape concentrates.

446 American Cheesemen
PO Box 261
2522 South Shore Dr
Clear Lake, IA 50428-0261
641-357-7176
Fax: 641-357-7177
Cheese
President: Paul Austin
Estimated Sales: $5-10 Million
Number Employees: 1-4
Brands:
   American Cheesemen
   Choppin N Block
   E-Z Keep

447 American Classic Ice Cream Company
1565 5th Industrial Ct
Bay Shore, NY 11706
631-666-1000
Fax: 631-666-2934   800-736-4100
www.americanclassicicecream.com
Ice cream and novelties including sandwiches, cups, pies, etc.; also, toppings
Owner: Edgar Williams
Owner/VP: Gregory Kronrad
Contact: Greg Kronrad
gregkronrad@yahoo.com
General Manager: Theresa Bellizzi
Estimated Sales: Under $500,000
Number Employees: 5-9
Type of Packaging: Consumer, Food Service

448 American Copak Corporation
9175 Eton Ave
Chatsworth, CA 91311-5806
818-576-1000
Fax: 818-882-1637 www.americancopak.com
Bakers' and confectioners' supplies, beverages, candy, cereals, snack foods, condiments, dairy products, spreads, kosher foods, mixes, pasta, sauces, soups, sugar, syrups, etc.
President: Steven Brooker
Business Development: Wanda Walk
Estimated Sales: $5-10 Million
Number Employees: 50-99
Square Footage: 400000

449 American Crystal Sugar Co.
101 N. 3rd St.
Moorhead, MN 56560
218-236-4400
feedback@crystalsugar.com
www.crystalsugar.com
Sugarbeet cooperative.
President/CEO: Thomas Astrup
Year Founded: 1899
Estimated Sales: Over $1 Billion
Number Employees: 1000-4999
Type of Packaging: Consumer, Private Label, Bulk
Other Locations:
   Crookston MN
   Drayton ND
   East Grand Forks MN
   Hillsboro ND
   Corporate Headquarters
   Moorhead MN
   Sidney MT

450 American Culinary Garden
3508 E Division St
Springfield, MO 65802-2499
417-799-1410
Fax: 417-831-9933   888-831-2433
Balsamic vinegar and soy sauce and also dessert glazes and burgundy soy marinade.
Manager/Sales Director: Gary Anderson
Vice President: Judy Sipe
Order Desk: Lisa Clifford
Estimated Sales: $2.5-5 Million
Number Employees: 1
Type of Packaging: Consumer, Food Service
Brands:
   American Culinary Gardens
   Teatro

451 American Dehydrated Foods, Inc.
3801 E Sunshine St
PO Box 4087
Springfield, MO 65809-2800
417-881-7755
Fax: 417-881-4963   800-456-3447
info@adf.com www.adf.com
Dehydrated foods.
Chairman: Thomas Slaight
CEO: Kurt Hellweg
President: Mike Gerke
Contact: Dan Beeman
dbeeman@adfinc.com
Plant Manager: Mike Scabarozi
Estimated Sales: $20-50 Million
Number Employees: 20-49
Number of Brands: 1
Brands:
   ADF

452 American Egg Products Inc
375 Pierce Industrial Blvd
Blackshear, GA 31516-2358
912-449-5700
Fax: 912-449-2438 www.calmainefoods.com
Egg products
President: James D Hull
CEO: Ken Looper
CFO: Richard Looper
Office Manager: Michelle Kersey
Estimated Sales: $7 Million
Number Employees: 50-99
Parent Co: Cal-Maine Foods, Inc.

453 American Fine Food Corporation
3600 NW 114th Ave
Doral, FL 33178-1842
305-392-5000
Fax: 305-392-5400
Groceries
President: Sam Amoudi
Marketing/Export Manager: Fadi Ladki
Estimated Sales: $5-10 Million
Number Employees: 5-9

454 American Flatbread
Pittsfield, NH 03263
603-435-5119
info@americanflatbreadproducts.com
americanflatbreadproducts.com
Flatbreads
President: George Schenk
flatbread@americanflatbread.com
VP: Camilla Behn
Marketing Director: Jennifer Moffroid
Manager: Paul Krcmar
Purchasing: Amy Troiano
Estimated Sales: $13.9 Million
Number Employees: 20-49

455 American Food Ingredients Inc
4021 Avenida DE LA Plata
Suite 501
Oceanside, CA 92056-5849
760-967-6287
Fax: 760-967-1952 amerfood@aol.com
www.americanfoodingredients.com
Dehydrated fruits and vegetables, mushrooms, truffles, non GMO ingredients, salt and salt mixtures, seasonings, spices and herbs
President/CEO: Karen Koppenhaver
amerfood@aol.com
Estimated Sales: $5-10 Million
Number Employees: 20-49
Brands:
   American Food

Food Manufacturers / A-Z

456 American Food Products Inc
983 Riverside Dr
Methuen, MA 01844
978-682-1855
www.candybreak.com
Candy
Year Founded: 1950
Estimated Sales: $50-100 Million
Number Employees: 50-99
Type of Packaging: Private Label, Bulk

457 American Foods Group LLC
500 S. Washington St.
Green Bay, WI 54301-4219
800-345-0293
info@AmericanFoodsGroup.com
www.americanfoodsgroup.com
Beef products.
President/COO: Steven Van Lannen
Chairman/CEO: Tom Rosen
CFO: David Jagodzinske
Executive Vice President: Jeff Jones
Year Founded: 2005
Estimated Sales: $225.5 Million
Number Employees: 4,500
Square Footage: 60000
Parent Co: Rosen's Diversified, Inc.
Type of Packaging: Consumer, Food Service
Other Locations:
  Mitchell SD
  Sharonville OH
Brands:
  Halal Meats
  America's Heartland Organic Beef
  Server's Choice
  Meyer Natural Angus Beef
  Sheboygan Sausage Company
  Skylark
  Big City Reds
  Great American Hamburgers
  Rock River Cattle

458 American Fruits & Flavors
10725 Sutter Ave
Pacoima, CA 91331
818-899-9574
SalesTeam@americanfruit.com
www.americanfruits-flavors.com
Custom flavors, fruit juice blends, natural sweeteners, juice concentrates and liquid powder blends. Specializing in fruit, vegetable, sweet and savory flavors, flavor bases, fruit concentrates, coconut products, smoothies, and tropical blends.
President: Bill Haddad
CEO: Rodney Sacks
Corporate Controller: Michael Model
Senior Research & Development Chemist: Martin Goldberg
Quality Control Chemist: Linda Valenzuela
VP of Marketing: Richard Linn
Director of Human Resources: Regina Rodriguez
Year Founded: 2016
Estimated Sales: $168 Million
Number Employees: 100-249
Square Footage: 20000
Parent Co: Monster Beverage Corporation

459 American Halal Company
1177 Summer St
3rd Floor
Stamford, CT 06905
203-961-1954
877-425-2587
info@saffronroadfood.com saffronroadfood.com
Gourmet foods
Cheif Executive Officer: Adnan Durrani

460 American Hawaiian Soy Company
274 Kalihi Street
Honolulu, HI 96819
808-841-8435
800-841-8435
Soybean
President: John Morita

461 American Health
2100 Smithtown Avenue
Ronkonkoma, NY 11779
631-244-2021
Fax: 631-244-1777 800-445-7137
www.americanhealthus.com
Vitamins, minerals, food supplements
President/CEO: Dorie Greenblatt
doriegreenblatt@americanhealthus.com
Vice President: Robert Silverman
Estimated Sales: $3-5 Million
Number Employees: 5-9
Type of Packaging: Consumer

462 American Importing Co.
550 Kasota Ave SE
Minneapolis, MN 55414
855-273-0466
www.amportfoods.com
Snack foods including trail mixes, dried fruits and sunflower seeds.
President: Jeff Vogel
Contact: Kim Ewanika
kim@amportfoods.com
Parent Co: Flagstone Foods
Type of Packaging: Consumer, Private Label, Bulk
Brands:
  Amport Foods
  Dessert Jewell
  Salad Expressions

463 American Ingredients Co
7905 Quivira Rd
Lenexa, KS 66215-2732
913-888-4540
Fax: 913-888-4970 800-669-4092
info@caravaningredients.com
Food ingredients including fortification, emulsifiers, functional blends, bakery mixes and bases, frozen dough, and fillings, icings and glazes
President: Les Stanbery
Chairman: Jaap Vink
VP CFO: Joel Krichiver
Product Manager: Dave Pfefer
Marketing Director: Kerrie Medlicott
VP Sales: Jim Eastan
VP Human Resources: Pam Parker
Engineering Director: Bill Becicka
Director of Operations: Gordon Nolan
Plant Manager: Ian Trod
Number Employees: 350
Type of Packaging: Food Service, Bulk
Other Locations:
  North Kansas City MO
  Mississauga ON
Brands:
  Invisible Goodness
  Nutrivan
  Trancendim
  Pristine
  Bake-Soft
  Alphadim
  Bfp
  Pationic

464 American Instants Inc
117 Bartley Flanders Rd
Flanders, NJ 07836
973-584-8811
sales@americaninstants.com
www.americaninstants.com
Instant coffees and teas, cappuccino, granita, chai, fresh brew tea, hot chocolate, drink mixes and liquid coffee extract
President: Martin Wagner
CEO: Christopher Roche
rshipe@americaninstants.com
Director, R&D: Kristin Truglio
Estimated Sales: $30 Million
Number Employees: 50-99
Square Footage: 72000
Type of Packaging: Food Service, Private Label
Brands:
  Cappuccino Supreme
  Deep Rich
  Hot Chocolate Supreme

465 (HQ)American Italian Pasta Company
1000 Italian Way
Excelsior Springs, MO 64024
877-328-7278
www.makesameal.com
Dry pasta
President, TreeHouse Foods: Dennis Riordan
CEO, TreeHouse Foods: Sam Reed
Parent Co: TreeHouse Private Brands, Inc.
Type of Packaging: Consumer, Food Service, Private Label, Bulk
Other Locations:
  Columbia SC
  Kenosha WI
Brands:
  Ronco
  Anthony's
  Luxury
  Mueller's
  Pennsylvania Dutch
  Golden Grain
  Heartland

466 American Key Food Products Inc
1 Reuten Dr
Closter, NJ 07624-2115
201-767-8022
Fax: 201-767-9124 877-263-7539
contactus@akfponline.com www.akfponline.com
Bulk quantity starches, spices and ingredients.
Manager: Luis Mansueto
VP: Ivan Sarda
Sales: Mel Festejo
Manager: Foss Carter
cfoss@akfponline.com
Operations: Edwin Pacia
Purchasing: Connie Ponce de Leon
Number Employees: 1-4
Type of Packaging: Bulk
Brands:
  Emsland
  King Lion

467 American Laboratories
4410 South 102nd Street
Omaha, NE 68127
402-339-2494
Fax: 402-339-0801
sales@americanlaboratories.com
www.americanlaboratories.com
Pancreatin and pepsin enzymes
President: Kenny Soejoto
Chairman/CEO: Jeff Jackson
Senior Vice President: Rod Schake
Vice President of Administration: Janet Giwoyna
Vice President of Quality Assurance: Thomas Langdon
Vice President of Sales: Bret Wyant
Contact: Dan Aase
d.aase@americanlaboratories.com
Vice President of Production: Mark Schufeldt
Purchasing Manager: Tom Hall
Number Employees: 50-99
Number of Products: 960
Type of Packaging: Bulk

468 American Lecithin Company
115 Hurley Road
Unit 2B
Oxford, CT 06478
203-262-7100
Fax: 203-262-7101 800-364-4416
www.americanlecithin.com
Lecithin products and specialty phospholipids; importer of lecithin
President: Randall Zigmont
Contact: Dianne Bukowski
customerService@americanLecithin.Com
Year Founded: 1928
Estimated Sales: $.5-1 million
Number Employees: 6
Square Footage: 28000
Parent Co: The Lipod Group
Type of Packaging: Consumer, Bulk
Brands:
  Alcolec

469 (HQ)American Licorice
1914 Happiness Way
La Porte, IL 46350
219-324-1400
Fax: 219-324-1490 866-442-2783
insidesales@amerlic.com
www.americanlicorice.com
Licorice twists, pieces, and ropes in various flavors. Also sour hard candies and drinking straws.
President & CEO: John Kretchmer
Director of Business Strategy: Aaron Johnson
Director of Innovation: Tim Walsh
Quality Assurance Manager: Ed Silva
Corporate Logistic Manager: Ernie Dacanay
Corporate Supply Chain Manager: Dennie Carff
Year Founded: 1914
Estimated Sales: $39.9 Million
Number Employees: 201-500
Square Footage: 126521

Food Manufacturers / A-Z

Type of Packaging: Consumer, Food Service, Private Label, Bulk
Other Locations:
  Consumer Service
  La Porte IN
Brands:
  Natural Vines
  Black Licorice Vines
  Licorice Ropes
  Red Ropes
  Red Vines
  Snaps
  Sour Punch
  Sugar Free Vines
  Super Ropes
  Twisty Punch
  Sip-N-Chew
  Extinguisher

470 American Mercantile Corp
1270 Warford St
Memphis, TN 38108-3421
901-454-1900
Fax: 901-454-0207 amc@memphi.net
www.americanmercantile.com
Spices, seeds, herbs, botanicals, extracts, essential oils and related natural products
President: Damond Arney
amc@memphi.net
Estimated Sales: Less Than $500,000
Number Employees: 1-4

471 American Micronutrients
PO Box 7129
3120 Weatherford Road
Independence, MO 64055
816-254-6000
Fax: 816-254-6004 816-252-1060
Chelated calcium
President: Mike Davison
Brands:
  American Micronutrients

472 American Mint
1107 Braodway
New York, NY 10010-2731
212-929-1410
Fax: 212-929-1864 800-401-6468
Natural mints
Owner: Sam Hamirani
Estimated Sales: Less than $500,000
Number Employees: 1-4
Type of Packaging: Private Label, Bulk

473 American Natural & Organic
4180 Business Center Dr
Fremont, CA 94538-6354
510-440-1044
info@organicspices.com
www.organicspices.com
Natural and organic spices
CEO & President: John Chansari
Contact: Clara Bonner
clara@organicspices.com
Estimated Sales: $1.2 Million
Number Employees: 5-9
Type of Packaging: Bulk
Brands:
  SPICELY

474 American Nut & Chocolate Co
121 Newmarket Sq
Boston, MA 02118-2603
617-427-1510
Fax: 617-427-1805 800-797-6887
info@amnut.com www.amnut.com
Roasted nuts, chocolates, dried fruits and candies.
President: Robert Novack
Year Founded: 1927
Estimated Sales: $500,000
Number Employees: 1-4
Square Footage: 64000
Type of Packaging: Food Service, Bulk
Brands:
  Harvard

475 American Nuts Inc.
12950 San Fernando Rd
Sylmar, CA 91342
USA
818-364-8855
contact@americannuts.com
www.americannuts.com
Nuts and dried fruits
CEO/Founder: Gary Eshgian

Number Employees: 20-49

476 American Palm Oil
1010 Wisconsin Avenue NW
Suite 307
Washington, DC 20007
202-333-0661
Fax: 202-333-0331 info@americanpalmoil.com
Palm oils
Executive Director: Mohd Salleh Kassim
Contact: Manny Amaya
manuel.amaya@unitedpharmallc.com
Number Employees: 15

477 American Pasien Co
109 Elbow Ln
Burlington, NJ 08016-4123
609-387-3130
Fax: 609-387-7204 info@109elbow.com
www.amcocustomdrying.biz
Functional protein ingredients and protein polymers for edible applications
CEO: Jamil Ahmed
jamilahmed@americancasein.com
CEO: Dennis Bobker
CFO: Jack Pipala
Account Manager: Jane Macey
Sales Manager: Cliff Lang
Human Resources Manager/IT Manager: Ellen Iuliucci
Facilities Manager: Chris Lockard
Estimated Sales: $5.8 Million
Number Employees: 20-49
Square Footage: 120000
Type of Packaging: Bulk

478 American Pop Corn Co
1 Fun Pl
P.O. Box 178
Sioux City, IA 51102
712-239-1232
Fax: 712-239-1268 henry@jollytime-export.com
www.jollytime.com
Various flavours of microwavable and pre-popped popcorn.
President: Jeff Naslund
naslund@americanpopdigital.com
Chairman: Carlton Smith
VP, Production: Greg Hoffman
Year Founded: 1914
Estimated Sales: $30.60 Million
Number Employees: 185
Type of Packaging: Consumer, Bulk
Brands:
  Jolly Time

479 American Quality Foods
353 Banner Farm Rd
Mills River, NC 28759-8707
828-890-8344
www.americanqualityfoods.com
Gluten free and diet dessert mixes
Manager: Debbie Allison
debbie@americanqualityfoods.com
Number Employees: 20-49
Square Footage: 17000

480 American Seafoods
Market Place Tower
2025 First Ave, Suite 900
Seattle, WA 98121
206-448-0300
www.americanseafoods.com
Seafood, including Alaska pollock, Pacific Hake, Yellowfin sole, and Pacific cod.
Chief Executive Officer: Mikel Durham
President: Inge Andreassen
Chief Financial Officer: Kevin McMenimen
EVP, Product & Business Development: Scott McNair
scott.mcnair@americanseafoods.com
Estimated Sales: $430 Million
Number Employees: 1000+
Type of Packaging: Bulk
Other Locations:
  Seattle WA
  Dutch Harbor AK
  New Bedford MA
  Greensboro AL

481 American Skin LLC
140 Industrial Dr
Burgaw, NC 28425
910-259-2232
Fax: 910-259-2535 800-248-7463
Sales@americanskin.net www.pork-rinds.com
Pork rings and pork rinds
Manager: Wes Blake
wes@americanskin.net
Estimated Sales: $300,000-500,000
Number Employees: 20-49

482 American Soy Products Inc
1474 Woodland Dr
Saline, MI 48176-1282
734-429-2310
Fax: 734-429-2112 www.americansoy.com
Aseptic packer of juices, teas and soy products
President: Ron Roller
Estimated Sales: $2.5-5 Million
Number Employees: 50-99
Square Footage: 260000
Type of Packaging: Consumer, Private Label

483 American Specialty Confections
888 County Road D W Ste 100
Saint Paul, MN 55112
651-251-7000
Fax: 651-251-7070 800-776-2085
Candy
President: Jeff Haynes
Marketing Director: Chris Dusk
Sales Manager: Mike Gardener
Number Employees: 100

484 American Specialty Foods
2316 Norman Road
Lancaster, PA 17601
717-397-9578
Fax: 717-397-0951 800-335-6663
www.asfbrands.com
Gluten-free, baking mixes and ingredients, tea, condiments, spices, dessert toppings.
Marketing: Doug Harris
Contact: Michael Fry
mike.fry@asfbrands.com

485 (HQ)American Spoon Foods Inc
1668 Clarion Ave
PO Box 566
Petoskey, MI 49770-9263
231-347-9030
Fax: 231-347-2512 888-735-6700
hello@spoon.com www.spoon.com
Jams, jellies, salsas and condiments.
President: Chris Chickering
chris@spoon.com
VP: Larry Forgione
Human Resources Manager: Dorothy Felton
Plant Manager: Paul Ramey
Purchasing Director: John Kafer
Estimated Sales: $10-20 Million
Number Employees: 50-99
Square Footage: 24000
Type of Packaging: Consumer, Food Service
Other Locations:
  Petosky MI
  Charlevoix MI
  Traverse City MI
  Harbor Springs MI
  Saugatuck MI
  Northville MI
  Ann Arbor MI
Brands:
  American Chef Larry Forgione's
  American Fruit Butters
  American Fruit Toppings
  American Salad Dazzlers
  American Spoon Foods
  American Spoon Fruits
  Salad Dazzlers
  Spoon Fruit
  Spoon Toppers

486 American Tartaric Products
1865 Palmer Ave
Larchmont, NY 10538
914-834-1881
Fax: 914-834-4611 atp@americantartaric.com
www.americantartaric.com
Tartaric acid, cream of tartar and baking powder
President: Emilio Zanin
Vice President: Luca Zanin
Estimated Sales: $5-10 Million
Number Employees: 27

Food Manufacturers / A-Z

Other Locations:
 American Tartaric Products
 Windsor CA

487 American Tuna
4364 Bonita Rd
Unit 331
Bonita, CA 91902
866-817-0497
americantuna.com
Canned tuna
Number of Brands: 1
Number of Products: 9
Type of Packaging: Consumer
Brands:
 AMERICAN TUNA

488 American Vegetable Oils
7244 Condor St
Commerce, CA 90040
800-728-8089
americanvegoil.com
Vegetable oil
Number of Brands: 1
Number of Products: 14
Type of Packaging: Consumer, Bulk
Brands:
 AVO

489 American Vintage Wine Biscuits
4003 27th St
Long Island City, NY 11101-3814
718-361-1003
Fax: 718-361-0204 info@americanvintage.com
www.americanvintage.com
Crackers and snacks made with wine
Owner: Mary Lynn Mondich
Estimated Sales: Less than $500,000
Number Employees: 1-4
Type of Packaging: Consumer

490 American Wholesale Grocery
131 New Jersey Street
Mobile, AL 36603-2111
251-433-2528
Fax: 251-432-7982
Groceries
President: Harold Owens
Secretary/Treasurer: James Statter
Vice President: John Carpenter

491 American Yeast
251 Stiles Dr
Memphis, TN 38127-3500
901-358-4788
Fax: 901-795-6948 866-920-9885
asbe@asbe.org www.lallemand.com
Baking enzymes and baking ingredients
Manager: Bud Spooner
First Vice Chairwoman: Theresa S Cogswell
VP: Christine Merenova
Second Vice-Chairman: Eddie Perrou
Manager: Darrell Philips
Estimated Sales: $5-10 Million
Number Employees: 10-19
Brands:
 Essential
 Fermaid

492 Americana Vineyards & Winery
4367 E Covert Rd
Interlaken, NY 14847-9720
607-387-6801
Fax: 607-387-3852 888-600-8067
gotwine@americanavineyards.com
www.americanavineyards.com
Wines
Owner: Joe Gober
wineinny@aol.com
Estimated Sales: $840,000
Number Employees: 10-19
Brands:
 Americana

493 Americhicken
1330 Copper Dr
Cape Girardeau, MO 63701-1730
573-651-6485
Fax: 573-651-4669 www.americhicken.com
Frozen chicken and entrees
President: Taylor Bass
taylor@americhicken.com
Number Employees: 5-9

494 Americolor Corp
341 S Melrose St
Suite C
Placentia, CA 92870-5974
714-996-1820
Fax: 714-996-7422 800-556-0233
info@americolorcorp.com
www.americolorcorp.com
Food colors for the bakery industry
President: Monika Molina
monika@americolorcorp.com
CFO: Fay Molina
Estimated Sales: $500,000-$1 Million
Number Employees: 1-4
Brands:
 Ameri Color

495 Ameripure Processing Co
803 Willow St
Franklin, LA 70538-6030
337-413-8000
Fax: 337-413-8003 800-328-6729
pfahey@ameripure.com www.ameripure.com
Oysters
President: John Jestvich
john@ameripure.com
Estimated Sales: $5 Million
Number Employees: 50-99
Type of Packaging: Consumer, Food Service, Private Label
Brands:
 Ameripure

496 Amerol Chemical Corporation
71 Carolyn Blvd
Farmingdale, NY 11735
631-694-4700
Fax: 631-694-9177
Synthetic and natural antioxidants and mixed tocopherols.
President: C J Monteleone
CEO: D Sartorio
CFO: A Diaz
R&D: Y Liang
Marketing: S Jean Charles
Operations: F Monteleone
Production: D Ghiglieri
Purchasing Director: D Raleigh
Estimated Sales: $300,000-500,000
Number Employees: 1-4
Square Footage: 46000
Type of Packaging: Private Label, Bulk

497 Ames Company, Inc
PO Box 46
45 Pine Hill Road
New Ringgold, PA 17960
610-750-1032
Fax: 413-604-0541 info@theingredientstore.com
www.theingredientstore.com
Vegetarian meat analogs and dry mixes
Owner: Joseph Ames, Sr.
Number Employees: 5-9

498 Ames International Inc
4401 Industry Dr E
Bldg. A
Fife, WA 98424-1832
253-946-4779
Fax: 253-926-4127 888-469-2637
questions@emilyschocolates.com
www.emilyschocolates.com
Nut products, gourmet chocolates and cookies
President: George Paulose
gpaulose@amesinternational.com
VP: Susan Paulose
Marketing: Amy Paulose
Estimated Sales: $5-10 Million
Number Employees: 50-99
Square Footage: 220000
Type of Packaging: Private Label, Bulk
Brands:
 Amy's
 Ecosnax
 Emily's
 Orchard Hills
 Santa Cruz
 Seven Seas

499 Amest Food
Stony Point, NY 10980
718-360-0886
info@amest.com
www.amest.com
Estonian chocolate, marzipan and dark rye bread

500 Amick Farms LLC
2079 Batesburg Hwy.
Batesburg, SC 29006
803-532-1400
Fax: 803-532-1491 800-926-4257
www.amickfarms.com
Chicken products.
Chief Executive Officer: Ben Harrison
bharrison@amickfarms.com
Vice President, Sales & Marketing: Steve Kernen
Year Founded: 1941
Estimated Sales: $100-499 Million
Number Employees: 1000-4999
Number of Brands: 2
Square Footage: 10992
Parent Co: OSI Industries, LLC
Type of Packaging: Consumer, Food Service, Private Label, Bulk
Other Locations:
 Hurlock MD
Brands:
 Amick Farms Poultry
 Sunrise Farm Fresh

501 Amigos Canning Company
4669 Highway 90 W
San Antonio, TX 78237
210-798-5360
www.amigosfoods.com
Mexican foods, including refried beans, dips, sauces, peppers, and taco shells.
Manager: Clint McNew
Controller: Ivan Kerr
ikerr@amigosfoods.com
Sales Contact: Heather McNew
Plant Manager: Carlos Menchaca
Year Founded: 1925
Estimated Sales: $11.5 Million
Number Employees: 90
Square Footage: 39000
Parent Co: Durrset Amigos
Type of Packaging: Consumer, Private Label
Brands:
 Amigos

502 Amira Nature Foods Ltd.
1 Park Plz Ste 600
Irvine, CA 92614-5987
USA
949-852-4468
Fax: 949-271-3615 amira.net
Grain, cereal, pasta, olive oils, baked goods, dairy products
CEO/Chairman: Karan Chanana
Vice President: Alireza Yazdi

503 Amity Packing Co Inc
4220 S Kildare Ave
Chicago, IL 60632-3930
773-475-9398
Fax: 312-942-0413 800-837-0270
byanz@amitypacking.com www.amitypacking.com
Fresh and frozen pork and beef products.
President: Richard T Samuel
Vice President: Matt Buol
VP Sales/Marketing: Tom Laplant
Contact: Ray Green
rgreen@amitypacking.com
Operations Manager: Jim Stamm
Estimated Sales: $110,000
Number Employees: 10-19
Square Footage: 11224

504 Amity Vineyards
18150 SE Amity Vineyards Rd
Amity, OR 97101-2304
503-835-2362
Fax: 503-835-6451 888-264-8966
amity@amityvineyards.com
www.coelhowinery.com
Wines
President: Myron Redford
myronamity@amityvineyards.com
Sales/Manager: Peter Higbee
Estimated Sales: $830,000
Number Employees: 10-19
Square Footage: 60

Food Manufacturers / A-Z

505 Amizetta Vineyards
1099 Greenfield Rd
St Helena, CA 94574-9625
707-963-1460
Fax: 707-963-1460 cab@amizetta.com
www.amizetta.com
Wines
Owner: Wendy Edelstein
wendy.n.edelstein@nasa.gov
Co-Owner: Amisetta Clark
President: Perry McFadden Clark
Operations/Winemaker: Robert Egelhoff
Estimated Sales: $1-2.5 Million
Number Employees: 1-4

506 Ammerland America
134 South Dixie Hwy
Suite 110
Hallandale Beach, FL 33009
954-350-0325
yunger@molkerei-ammerland.de
www.molkerei-ammerland.de
Dairy Products
President/CEO: Israel Yunger
Parent Co: Molkerei Ammerland eG

507 Amoretti
451 Lombard St
Oxnard, CA 93030-5143
805-983-2903
Fax: 818-718-0204 800-266-7388
www.amoretti.com
Nut flour, paste and butter
Founder, CEO: Jack Barsoumian
info@amoretti.com
Marketing President: Maral Barsoumian
Manufacturing President: Ara Barsoumian
Year Founded: 1989
Estimated Sales: $20+ Million
Number Employees: 20-49
Type of Packaging: Food Service, Bulk
Brands:
 Amoretti
 Baristella
 Capriccio

508 Amoroso's Baking Co
151 Benigno Blvd
Bellmawr, NJ 08031
215-471-4740
info@amorosobaking.com
amorosobaking.com
Rolls, breads, bagels, Jewish bread and pretzels.
President: Lenny Amoroso
lamoroso@amorosobaking.com
Vice President: Jesse Amoroso
CFO: Preston Thomas
Year Founded: 1904
Estimated Sales: $27.7 Million
Number Employees: 400
Square Footage: 80000
Type of Packaging: Consumer, Food Service, Private Label
Brands:
 Merion Park Rye Bread
 Richmond Rye Bread
 Amoroso's Hearth Baked

509 Amphora International
20622 Canada Rd
Lake Forest, CA 92630
949-609-0600
888-380-4808
amphorafoods.com
Olive oil, organic dried fruit, condiments and spices
Number of Brands: 1
Number of Products: 19
Type of Packaging: Consumer
Brands:
 AMPHORA

510 Amplify Snack Brands
500 W 5th St
Suite 1350
Austin, TX 78701
512-600-9893
Fax: 512-640-8757 info@amplifysnacks.com
amplifysnackbrands.com
Healthy snacks

511 Amport Foods
380 St. Peter St.
Suite 1000
St. Paul, MN 55102
612-331-7000
Fax: 612-331-1122 800-236-1119
customers@amportfoods.com
www.amportfoods.com
Dates, dried fruits whole and pressed, soy nuts, and sunflower seeds
President: Andrew Stillman
Vice President: Jeff Vogel
Contact: Aaron Anderson
aaron@amportfoods.com
Production Manager: Mike McIvor
Estimated Sales: $20-50 Million
Number Employees: 20-49
Type of Packaging: Bulk

512 Amrhein's Wine Cellars
9243 Patterson Dr
Bent Mountain, VA 24059-2215
540-929-4632
Fax: 540-929-4632 info@amrheins.com
www.amrheinshop.us
Wines
Owner: Russel Amrhein
vinapple@att.net
Estimated Sales: Less Than $500,000
Number Employees: 1-4

513 Amrita Health Foods
37 Harvard Dr.
Hartsdale, NY 10530
888-728-7779
800-523-8644
www.amritahealthfoods.com
Energy bars
Founder and CEO: Arshad Bahl
Square Footage: 80000

514 Amrita Snacks
Hartsdale, NY 10530
888-728-7779
www.amritahealthfoods.com
Plant-based, vegan, all-natural protein bars, protein snack bites and energy bars in various flavors
Founder/CEO: Arshad Bahl
Number of Brands: 1
Number of Products: 21
Type of Packaging: Consumer, Private Label
Brands:
 Amrita

515 Amsnack
7770 Longe Street
Stockton, CA 95206-3925
209-982-5545
Fax: 209-982-4955
Rice crackers, cookies crackers and chips
President: Satoshi Yamada
Shipping Coordinator: Karen Valterza
Estimated Sales: $5-9.9 Million
Number Employees: 20-49

516 Amstell Holding
209 Theodore Rice Boulevard
New Bedford, MA 02745-1213
508-995-6100
Fax: 508-995-2912
Shelf-stable nonrefrigerated milk, nutritional supplements, juices, teas, and drink beverages.
Director Operations: Cindy Aldrich

517 Amsterdam Brewing Company
21 Bathurst Street
Toronto, ON M5V 2N6
Canada
416-504-1040
Fax: 416-504-1043 416-504-6882
info@amsterdambeer.com
www.amsterdambeer.com
Beer, lager and ale including stout
President: Jeff Carefoote
Number Employees: 12
Type of Packaging: Consumer, Food Service

518 Amwell Valley Vineyard
80 Old York Road
Ringoes, NJ 08551
908-788-5852
Fax: 908-788-1030
Wines
Owner: Jeff Fischer
President: Dr Michael Fisher
Operations Manager: Scott Gares
Estimated Sales: $1-2.5 Million
Number Employees: 1-4
Number of Brands: 1
Number of Products: 20
Type of Packaging: Consumer
Brands:
 Amwell Valley Vineyard

519 Amy & Brian Naturals
6905 Aragon Circle
Buena Park, CA 90620
info@amyandbriannaturals.com
www.amyandbriannaturals.com
Coconut water
Number of Brands: 1
Number of Products: 5
Type of Packaging: Consumer
Brands:
 AMY & BRIAN

520 Amy Food Inc
3324 S Richey St
Houston, TX 77017-6259
713-910-5860
Fax: 713-910-4812 www.amyfood.com
Egg rolls, potstickers, empanadas and party platters, natural and organic foods.
Owner: Phyllis Hsu
amyfood@aol.com
Number Employees: 50-99
Square Footage: 40000
Type of Packaging: Consumer, Food Service, Private Label
Brands:
 Jamy's Three Dragon

521 Amy's Candy Bar
4704 N Damen Ave
Chicago, IL 60625-1512
773-942-6386
amyscandybar@gmail.com
www.amyscandybar.com
Candy and confections
Estimated Sales: Less Than $500,000
Number Employees: 1-4

522 Amy's Kitchen Inc
2330 Northpoint Pkwy
Santa Rosa, CA 95407
707-781-6600
www.amys.com
Frozen organic meals and entrees; also canned soups and bottled pasta sauces.
Co-Owner: Andy Berliner
Co-Owner: Rachel Berliner
EVP: Jack Chipman
Director, Contract Manufacturing: Norma Mery
Estimated Sales: $92.3 Million
Number of Brands: 1
Number of Products: 146
Square Footage: 100000
Type of Packaging: Consumer, Food Service
Brands:
 Amys Kitchen

523 Amylu Foods
1143 West Lake St
Chicago, IL 60607
www.amylufoods.com
Craft meats
CEO: Amylu Kurzawski
Brands:
 Amylu
 Leon's Sausage
 Slotkowski

524 Ana's Salsa
17503 La Cantera Pkwy
Suite 104-473
Austin, TX 78257
512-837-2203
Fax: 512-837-0003 888-849-7054
info@anasfoods.com www.anasfoods.com
Salsas, herbs and jams.
President: Anna Olvera-Ullrich
COO/SVP: Jim Ullrich
Estimated Sales: $500,000
Number Employees: 1-4
Number of Brands: 3
Number of Products: 8
Type of Packaging: Consumer, Food Service, Bulk

Brands:
Ana's

525 AnaCon Foods Company
1145 Main St
PO Box 651
Atchison, KS 66002
913-367-2885
Fax: 913-367-1794 800-328-0291
anacon@journey.com
Processor and exporter of simulated nut and fruit particulates and analogs
Executive Director: Tom Miller
VP Sales/Marketing: Jane Hallas
Director Operations: Marvin Mikkelson
Estimated Sales: $2.5-5 Million
Number Employees: 20-49
Brands:
Bits'n'pops
Bowlby's Bits
Mix-Ups
Nuts'n'pops
Wheat Nuts

526 Anabol Naturals
1550 Mansfield St
Santa Cruz, CA 95062-1720
831-479-1403
Fax: 831-479-1406 800-426-2265
www.anabolnaturals.com
Sports nutrition supplements
President: Roger Prince
anabol@cruzio.com
Estimated Sales: $500,000-$1 Million
Number Employees: 5-9
Square Footage: 20000
Brands:
Anabol Naturals

527 Analyticon Discovery LLC
9700 Great Seneca Hwy
Rockville, MD 20850-3307
240-406-1256
Fax: 240-453-6208 info@ac-discovery.com
www.ac-discovery.com
Natural active ingredients and products.
CEO/Co-Founder: Lutz Muller-Kuhrt
CFO/Co-Founder: Jochen Gatter
VP Research & Development: Karsten Siems
North American/UK Sales Representative: Andrea Christes
Contact: Betsy Manikowski
b.manikowski@ac-discovery.com
VP Operations & Research: Martina Jaensch
Estimated Sales: $4.64 Million
Number Employees: 1-4

528 Ananda Hemp
PO Box 648
Cynthiana, KY 41031
hello@anandahemp.com
www.anandahemp.com
Hemp extract
Number of Brands: 1
Number of Products: 5
Type of Packaging: Consumer
Brands:
ANANDA HEMP

529 Anastasia Confections Inc
1815 Cypress Lake Dr
Orlando, FL 32837-8457
407-816-9944
Fax: 407-816-9901 800-329-7100
customerservice@anastasiaconfections.com
www.anastasiaconfections.com
Specialty candy
President: Mike Constantine
customerservice@anastasiaconfections.com
Estimated Sales: $2 Million
Number Employees: 20-49

530 Anchor Appetizer Group
PO Box 2518
Appleton, WI 54912
920-997-2200
Fax: 920-734-2828
Appetizers
President: Mark Follett
Vice President: Scott Follet
Estimated Sales: $6 Million
Parent Co: McCain Foods USA/H.J. Heinz Company
Type of Packaging: Consumer, Food Service

Brands:
Brew City
Cheese Sensasations
Golden Crisp
Golden Crisp
Moore's
Mozzaluna
Mozzamia
Olivenos
Poppers
Primasamo Cubes
Provago Wheels
Queso Triangulos
Wrappetizers

531 Anchor Brewing Company
1705 Mariposa St
San Francisco, CA 94107
415-863-8350
Fax: 415-552-7094 info@anchorbrewing.com
www.anchorbrewing.com
Beer and ale
Marketing, Communications & Events: Teagan Thompson
VP Sales: Martin Geraghty
VP Logistics: Alfredo Mialma
Year Founded: 1896
Estimated Sales: $20-50 Million
Number Employees: 50-99
Parent Co: Sapporo Holdings
Type of Packaging: Consumer, Private Label
Brands:
Anchor Steam
Liberty Ale
Anchor Porter
Summer Beer
Olf Foghorn
Anchor Small
Christmas Ale

532 Anchor Frozen Foods
32 Urban Ave
PO Box 887
Westbury, NY 11590
516-333-6344
Fax: 516-997-1823 800-566-3474
info@anchorfrozenfoods.com
Seafood including stuffed sole, conch, shrimp, lobster tails, octopus, calamari and king crab legs.
President: Roy Tuccillo
Contact: Stephanie Rusellan
stephanie@anchorfrozenfoods.com
Estimated Sales: $500,000- 1 Million
Number Employees: 5-9
Type of Packaging: Consumer, Food Service, Bulk

533 Anchor Ingredients
5181 38th Street South
Suite B
Fargo, ND 58104
701-499-1480
Fax: 701-499-1481 info@anchoringredients.com
anchoringredients.com
Food ingredients
Co-Founder, Managing Director: Al Yablonski
Co-Founder, Managing Director: Seth Novak
Number of Brands: 1
Type of Packaging: Bulk

534 Ancient Harvest
PO Box 4240
Boulder, CO 80306
310-217-8125
ancientharvest.com
Organic grains
Number of Brands: 1
Number of Products: 10
Brands:
ANCIENT HARVEST
POW! PASTA

535 Ancient Nutrition
1201 US Highway One
Suite 350
North Palm Beach, FL 33408
888-823-4468
info@ancientnutrition.com ancientnutrition.com
Protein supplement
Co-Founder: Jordan Rubin
Number of Brands: 1
Number of Products: 8
Brands:
ANCIENT NUTRITION

536 Ancient Organics
726 Allston Way
Berkeley, CA 94710
510-280-5043
morgyne@ancientorganics.com
www.ancientorganics.com
Organic ghee (clarified butter)
Founder: Peter Malakoff
Owner: Matteo Girard Maxon
CFO: Abinashi Khalsa
VP Sales & Marketing: Greg Glass
National Sales Manager: Tim Transon

537 Ancient Peaks Winery
22720 El Camino Real
Santa Margarita, CA 93453-8668
805-365-7045
Fax: 805-365-7046 info@apwinery.com
www.ancientpeaks.com
Wines
Type of Packaging: Private Label

538 Anco Foods
11421 NW 107 St
Miami, FL 33178
305-651-8489
866-343-1108
www.ancofinecheese.com
Cheese
CEO: Arno Leoni
Estimated Sales: $207 Million
Parent Co: Schratter Foods Inc
Type of Packaging: Bulk

539 Ancora Coffee Roasters
3701 Orin Road
Madison, WI 53704
608-255-2900
Fax: 608-255-2901 800-260-0217
service@ancoracoffee.com www.ancoracoffee.com
Coffees, whole bean and ground; loose leaf teas
President/CEO: George Krug
Quality Control/Production: Rob Jeffries
Marketing: Christy Gibbs
cgibbs@ancoracoffee.com
Estimated Sales: $1-5 Million
Number Employees: 10-19
Square Footage: 60000
Type of Packaging: Consumer, Food Service, Bulk

540 Andalucia Nuts
3505 Bering Dr
Houston, TX 77057
713-977-9090
www.andalucianuts.com
Nuts and nut butters
Type of Packaging: Bulk

541 Andalusia Distributing Co Inc
117 Allen Ave
Andalusia, AL 36420-2501
334-222-3671
www.adc1.com
Deli products
President: Ricky Jones
Vice President: Billy Jones
CFO: Chris Jones
General Manager: Ronnie Taylor
Year Founded: 1956
Estimated Sales: $50-100 Million
Number Employees: 50-99
Brands:
Sara Lee
Bellarico's
Altria
RJReynolds
Hershey's
MARS
Mondelez International
Wrigley
KRAFT
General Mills
Jack Link's
Nestle

542 Andean Naturals LLC
393 Catamaran St
Foster City, CA 94404-2907
650-303-1780
Fax: 707-202-2838 info@andeannaturals.com
www.andeannaturals.com
Quinoa

Food Manufacturers / A-Z

Owner: Sergio Nunez De Arco
sergio_nunez@andeannaturals.com
Finance & Operations Manager: Marcos Guevara
Estimated Sales: $100 Thousand
Number Employees: 1-4
Type of Packaging: Bulk

543 Andersen's Pea Soup
376 Avenue of the Flags
Buellton, CA 93427
805-688-5581
Fax: 805-686-5670 info@peasoupandersens.net
www.peasoupandersens.net
Canned split pea soup
Manager: Tony Picard
Purchasing Director: Brinda Wolf
Estimated Sales: $2.5-5 Million
Number Employees: 50-99

544 Anderson Custom Processing
PO Box 279
New Ulm, MN 56073
507-233-2800
Fax: 507-233-2806 acpi@newulmtel.net
www.andersonprocessing.com
Spray-dried food products including whey, starches, cheese and cream powders
President: Brian Anderson
brian.anderson@andersonprocessing.com
Founder/CEO: Glen Anderson
Production Manager: Jerome Braun
Estimated Sales: $3-5 Million
Number Employees: 1-4
Type of Packaging: Bulk
Other Locations:
  Sleepy Eye MN
  Little Falls WI
  Belleville WI

545 Anderson Dairy Inc
801 Searles Ave
Las Vegas, NV 89101
702-642-7507
Fax: 702-642-3480 comments@andersondairy.com
www.andersondairy.com
Milk and dairy products including milk, cottage cheese, sour cream, cream, buttermilk, half & half, butter, eggs, ice cream and eggnog
President: Dave Coon
Year Founded: 1907
Estimated Sales: $76 Million
Number Employees: 100-249
Number of Brands: 1
Square Footage: 130000
Type of Packaging: Consumer, Bulk
Brands:
  Anderson Dairy

546 Anderson Erickson Dairy
2420 E University Ave
Des Moines, IA 50317
515-265-2521
www.aedairy.com
Milks, orange juice, lemonade, yogurt, cottage cheese, dips, sour cream, eggnog, buttermilk and creams, and ice cream mix.
President: Miriam Erickson Brown
Chief Financial Officer: Warren Erickson
Director of Marketing: Kim Peter
Year Founded: 1930
Estimated Sales: $44.40 Million
Number Employees: 250-499
Square Footage: 190000
Type of Packaging: Food Service
Other Locations:
  Kansas City KS

547 Anderson Erickson Dairy
5431 Speaker Rd
Kansas City, KS 66106
913-621-4801
www.aedairy.com
Milks, orange juice, lemonade, yogurt, cottage cheese, dips, sour cream, eggnog, buttermilk and creams, and ice cream mix.
President: Miriam Erickson Brown
Year Founded: 1930
Estimated Sales: $20-50 Million
Number Employees: 250-499
Type of Packaging: Food Service

548 Anderson Seafood
4780 E Bryson St
Anaheim, CA 92807-1901
714-777-7100
Fax: 714-777-7116
contactus@andersonseafoods.com
www.shopandersonseafoods.com
Fresh and frozen seafood
President: Dennis Anderson
CFO: Alberto Andrade
Vice President: Todd Anderson
VP, Procurement, Sales & Operations: Carl Oliphant
Year Founded: 1979
Number Employees: 20-49
Type of Packaging: Consumer, Food Service

549 Anderson Valley Brewing Co
17700 Highway 253
Boonville, CA 95415
707-895-2337
Fax: 707-895-2353 800-207-2237
info@avbc.com www.avbc.com
Seasonal beer, ale, porter, stout, lager and pilsner
President: Trey White
trewhite@avbc.com
VP Sales: David Gatlin
Estimated Sales: $7 Million
Number Employees: 20-49
Square Footage: 80000
Type of Packaging: Consumer
Brands:
  Barney Flats Oatmeal Stout
  Beik's Esb
  Boont Amber
  High Rollers Wheat
  Hop Ottin' Ipa
  Poleeko Gold
  Winter Solstice

550 Anderson's Conn Valley Vineyards
680 Rossi Rd
St Helena, CA 94574-9646
707-963-8600
Fax: 707-963-7818 800-946-3497
info@connvalleyvineyards.com
www.connvalleyvineyards.com
Wines
President: Todd Anderson
todd@connvalleyvineyards.com
Operations: Mac Sawyer
Estimated Sales: $2.5-5 Million
Number Employees: 5-9

551 Andre Prost Inc
680 Middlesex Tpke
Old Saybrook, CT 06475-1303
860-388-0838
Fax: 860-388-0830 800-243-0897
www.andreprost.com
Candy, confectionery, seasonings and spices.
Owner: Lori Montano
Vice President: Peter Cumings
VP Finance: Charles Landrey
lorimontano@andreprost.com
Estimated Sales: $2 Million
Number Employees: 10-19
Brands:
  A Taste of China
  A Taste of India
  A Taste of Thai
  Ginger Snaps
  Honees
  Notta Pasta
  Odense
  Zotz

552 Andre's Confiserie Suisse
5018 Main St
Kansas City, MO 64112-2755
816-561-3440
Fax: 816-561-2922 800-892-1234
customer_service@andreschocolates.com
www.andreschocolates.com
Swiss style chocolate candies
President: Marcel Bollier
customerservice@andreschocolates.com
CEO: Rene Bollier
CFO: Connie Bollier
Estimated Sales: $2.5-5 Million
Number Employees: 50-99
Type of Packaging: Consumer
Other Locations:
  Andre's Confiserie Suisse
  Overland Park KS
  Andre's Confiserie Suisse
  Denver CO

553 Andre-Boudin Bakeries
221 Main St Ste 1230
San Francisco, CA 94105
415-882-1849
Fax: 415-913-1818 boudin@boudinbakery.com
www.boudinbakery.com
Sourdough bread, specialty breads, and sweet goods
Owner: Sharon Duvall
VP Sales/Marketing: Terry Wight
Contact: Kayla Alexis
kalexis@boudinbakery.com
Plant Manager: Rick Rodrick
Estimated Sales: $300,000-500,000
Number Employees: 1,000-4,999
Type of Packaging: Private Label, Bulk
Brands:
  Boudin

554 Andrew & Williamson Sales Co
9940 Marconi Dr
San Diego, CA 92154-7270
619-661-6000
Fax: 619-661-6007
accounting@andrew-williamson.com
www.bajaclassic.com
Frozen strawberries
President: Fred Williamson
fredwilliamson@andrew-williamson.com
Estimated Sales: $2.5-5 Million
Number Employees: 20-49
Brands:
  A&W

555 Andrew Peller Limited
697 S. Service Rd.
Grimsby, ON L3M 4E8
Canada
905-643-4131
Fax: 905-643-4944 info@andrewpeller.com
www.andrewpeller.com
Wines.
President: Randy Powell
Chairman/CEO: John Peller
Executive VP, IT/CFO: Steve Attridge
Executive VP, Marketing: Shawn MacLeod
Executive VP, National Sales: Erin Rooney
Executive VP, Human Resources: Sara Presutto
Executive VP, Operations: Brendan Wall
Year Founded: 1927
Estimated Sales: $363.8 Million
Number Employees: 1,198
Number of Brands: 10
Square Footage: 89782
Type of Packaging: Consumer, Food Service, Bulk
Brands:
  Peller Estates
  Sandhill
  Wayne Gretzky Estates
  Trius Winery
  Red Rooster
  Calona Vineyards
  Thirty Bench
  Roundpetal
  Vineco
  Winexpert

556 Andrews Brewing Co
565 Aquone Rd
Andrews, NC 28901-7004
828-321-2006
www.andrewsbrewing.com
Beer
Owner: Andrew Hazen
Estimated Sales: $500,000-$1 Million
Number Employees: 1-4
Brands:
  Brown Ale
  English Pale Ale
  St. Nicks Poter
  Summer Golden Ale

557 Andrews Caramel Apples
5001 W Belmont Ave
Chicago, IL 60642
773-286-2224
Fax: 773-286-2258 800-305-3004
Info@AndysSeasoning.com
Caramel apples
President: Daniel De Marco
Treasurer: Sylvia Schuman
Purchasing: Rick Walker

Food Manufacturers / A-Z

Estimated Sales: $2.5-5 Million
Number Employees: 10-19
Type of Packaging: Consumer
Brands:
  Andrews
  Ms. Kays

558 Andrews Dried Beef Company
625 E Broad Street
Quakertown, PA 18951-1713
610-759-5180
Fax: 610-759-1529

Dried beef
President: E William Knauss
Estimated Sales: $10-24.9 Million
Number Employees: 50-99
Parent Co: E.W. Knauss & Sons

559 Andros Foods North America
10119 Old Valley Pike
Mount Jackson, VA 22842
540-217-4100
844-426-3767
sales@androsna.com www.androsna.com
Fruit based food and beverages, confectionary, preserves, frozen desserts
CEO/COO: Terry Stoehr
Estimated Sales: $52.3 Million
Number Employees: 500-999
Parent Co: Andros Group

560 Andy's Seasoning
2829 Chouteau Ave
St Louis, MO 63103-3016
314-664-2149
Fax: 314-664-2149 800-305-3004
www.andysseasoning.com
Seasoning salt and breadings for fish and chicken.
President/CEO: Larry Lee
Manager: Michael Lee
michael@andysseasoning.com
Year Founded: 1981
Estimated Sales: $20-50 Million
Number Employees: 20-49
Number of Brands: 9
Number of Products: 12
Square Footage: 27000
Type of Packaging: Consumer, Food Service, Private Label, Bulk
Brands:
  Andy's Cajun Fish Breading
  Andy's Golden Fish Batter
  Andy's Hot 'N' Spicy Breading
  Andy's Mild Chicken Breading
  Andy's Red Fish Breading
  Andy's Seasoned Salt
  Andy's Shrimp Tempura Batter
  Andy's Vegetable Breading
  Andy's Yellow Fish Breading

561 Anette's Chocolate & Ice Cream
1321 1st St
Napa, CA 94559-2927
707-252-4228
Fax: 707-252-8074 mary@anettes.com
Truffles, creams, brittles, chews, chocolate sauces, caramel sauces, traditional and unique seasonal specialties.
President: Helen Krasovic
helen.krasovic@lajollasportsclub.com
VP: Brent Madsen
Marketing: Mary Stornetta
Number Employees: 10-19

562 Angel's Bakeries
29 Norman Avenue
Brooklyn, NY 11222
718-389-1400
Fax: 718-389-3928 joe@angelsbakery.com
www.angelsbakery.com
Cookies, muffin tops, muffins, florentines, cakes and cake slices.
President: Joseph Angel
Vice President: Adi Angel
Marketing Director: Bill McNamee
Production Manager: Eloy Rojas
Estimated Sales: $4.1 Million
Number Employees: 45

563 Angelic Bakehouse
3275 East Layton Ave
Cudahy, WI 53110
www.angelicbakehouse.com

Crusts, wraps, bread, buns, rolls, baguettes and bread crisps
Co-Founder: Jenny Marino
Co-Founder: James Marino
Year Founded: 2009
Number of Brands: 1
Number of Products: 20
Brands:
  ANGELIC BAKEHOUSE
  FLATZZA
  SPROUTED

564 Angelic Gourmet Inc
P.O.Box 127
8629 State Route 21 South
Naples, NY 14512
800-294-0947
Fax: 800-947-5371
Chocolate dipped pretzels and chocolate drizzled popcorn.
President: Donna Scott
Estimated Sales: $1.8 Million
Number Employees: 20

565 Angelo & Franco U.S.A.
3441 Jack Northrop Ave.
Building 14
Hawthorne, CA 90250
USA
310-263-0506
www.angeloandfranco.com
A variety of cheeses.
Co-Owner: Angelo Tartaglia
Co-Owner: Franco Russo
Brands:
  angelo & franco

566 Angelo Pietro Honolulu
1108 12th Ave # C
Honolulu, HI 96816-3767
USA
808-941-0555
Fax: 808-440-0385 www.angelopietro.com
Sauces, seasonings, cooking enhancers, marinades, salad dressing
President: Kunihiko Murata
Manager: Tomohiko Shiomi
Number Employees: 20-49

567 Angie's Artisan Treats LLC
1918 Lookout Dr
North Mankato, MN 56003-1705
507-387-3886
888-982-4984
www.boomchickapop.com
Kettle corn.
Co-Owner: Dan Bastian
Co-Owner: Angie Bastian
Manager: Joe Atkinson
jatkinson@angiespopcorn.com
Number Employees: 100-249
Square Footage: 80000
Brands:
  BOOMCHICKAPOP

568 Anglo American Trading
P.O.Box 97
Harvey, LA 70059-0097
504-341-5631
Fax: 504-341-5635
Manager: Dennis Skrmetta
CEO: Eric Skrmetta

569 Angry Orchard Cider Company, LLC
2241 Albany Post Rd.
Walden, NY 12586
888-845-3311
www.angryorchard.com
Apple, pear and ros, hard ciders
Head Producer: Ryan Burk
Number of Brands: 1
Number of Products: 6
Type of Packaging: Consumer, Private Label
Brands:
  Angry Orchard

570 Angy's Food Products Inc
77 Servistar Industrial Way
Westfield, MA 01085-5601
413-572-1010
Fax: 413-572-4785 www.angyslandolfi.com
Frozen tortellini, gnocchi, cavatelli, stuffed shells, manicotti and ravioli

Owner: Edward Debartolo
edd@angyslandofi.com
CFO: Liz Campanini
VP: Steve Campanini
Number Employees: 20-49
Square Footage: 92000
Type of Packaging: Consumer, Food Service, Private Label, Bulk
Brands:
  Angy's
  Big Y
  Finast
  Introvigne's
  Shaw's

571 Anheuser-Busch
One Busch Place
St. Louis, MO 63118
800-342-5283
www.anheuser-busch.com
Beers
President & CEO, North America: Michel Doukeris
VP, Finance & Solutions: Nelson Jamel
VP, People: Agostino De Gasperis
VP, Procurement & Sustainability: Ingrid De Ryck
VP, Business & Wholesaler Development: Bob Tallett
VP, Marketing: Marcel Marcondes
VP, Sales: Brendan Whitworth
VP, Legal & Corporate Affairs: Cesar Vargas
Year Founded: 1852
Estimated Sales: $15.5 Billion
Number Employees: 19,000+
Number of Brands: 100+
Type of Packaging: Consumer, Food Service, Private Label
Brands:
  Budweiser
  Bud Light
  Michelob Ultra
  Stella Artois
  Patagonia Cerveza
  Estrella Jalisco
  Busch
  Natural Light
  Landshark Lager
  Presedente
  Hoegaarden
  Shock Top
  10 Barrel Brewing Co.
  Breckenridge Brewery
  Blue Point Brewing Company
  Devils Backbone Brewing Company
  Elysian Brewing
  Golden Road Brewing
  Four Peaks Brewing Co.
  Goose Isalnd
  Karbach Brewing Company
  Platform Beer Co.
  Wicked Weed Brewing
  Veza Sur Brewing Co.
  Virture Cider
  Maha Organic Hard Cider
  LQD
  Ritas
  Bon & Viv Spiked Seltzer
  Babe
  Cutwater Spirits
  Hi Ball Energy
  Kombrewcha

572 Animal Pak
3 Terminal Rd
New Brunswick, NJ 08901-3615
732-545-3130
Fax: 732-509-0458 800-872-0101
info@animalpak.com www.animalpak.com
Vitamins, supplements, and powdered proteins
President: Clyde Rockoff
VP Marketing: Michael Rockoff
VP Sales: Tim Tantum
VP Operations: Bob Glucken
Plant Manager: Dave Mitchell
Estimated Sales: $35.1 Million
Number Employees: 100-249
Square Footage: 100000
Parent Co: Universal Nutrition
Brands:
  Animal Pak
  Forza
  Hardfast
  Natural Sterols
  Yohimbe Bar

Food Manufacturers / A-Z

573 **Anita's Mexican Foods Corporation**
1390 West 4th Street
San Bernardino, CA 92408
909-884-8706
Mexican foods including tortilla chips and taco and tostada shells, plus organic snacks, chips and popcorn
President: Jose Gomez
Contact: Mark Schneeberger
mark.schneeberger@anitasmexicanfood.com
Plant Manager: Frank Coser
Estimated Sales: $20-50 Million
Number Employees: 100-249
Square Footage: 30000
Parent Co: La Reina
Type of Packaging: Consumer, Food Service, Private Label, Bulk
Brands:
    Anita's
    Go-Mex
    La Reina
    Old Pueblo Ranch

574 **Anita's Yogurt**
Brooklyn, NY 11211
anitas.com
Coconut yogurt
Founder: Anita Shepherd

575 **Ankeny Lake Wild Rice**
9594 Sidney Rd S
PO Box 3667
Salem, OR 97306-9448
503-363-3241
Fax: 503-371-9080   800-555-5380
ankenylakes_st.maries@yahoo.com
www.wildriceonline.com
Certified organic wild rice and nonorganic and wild rice blends
Owner: Larry Payne
paynels@netzero.com
Co-Owner: Sharon Jenkins-Payne
Estimated Sales: $500,000
Number Employees: 1-4
Square Footage: 12000
Type of Packaging: Consumer, Food Service, Private Label, Bulk
Brands:
    Canadian Jumbo Lake
    Idaho Lake Wild Rice
    Oregon
    Wild & Ricey

576 **Ankle Deep Foods**
912 W Omaha Avenue
Norfolk, NE 68701-5842
402-371-6707
wings@buffalomaid.com
www.buffalomaid.com
Hot suaces and marinades
Brands:
    Buffalo Maid

577 **Anmar Foods**
2150 W Carroll Ave
Chicago, IL 60612-1604
312-421-6500
Fax: 312-421-4765   www.anmarfoods.com
Beef, burgers, chicken, turkey, pork, and lamb
Owner: Bob Martinelli
President: Michael Casper
Estimated Sales: $20-50 Million
Number Employees: 20-49

578 **Anmar Nutrition**
P.O.Box 2343
540 Barnum Avenue
Bridgeport, CT 06608-0343
203-336-8330
Fax: 203-336-5508   www.anmarinternational.com
Vitamins, nutritional products, excipients, non-prescription pharmaceutical products, herbs, and amino acids.
President: John Blanco
VP: Hongbing Deng
Sales Director: Allan Pollard
Production Manager: John Blanco
Estimated Sales: $10-20 Million
Number Employees: 10-19
Number of Products: 100+
Square Footage: 15000
Type of Packaging: Bulk

579 **Ann Hemyng Candy Inc**
118 N Main St
Trumbauersville, PA 18970
215-536-7004
Fax: 215-536-6848   800-779-7004
ahcchocolate@verizon.net
www.chocolateshop.com
Molded chocolate including lollypops, novelties in chocolates, custom corporate logos
President/Owner: Louise Spindler
Estimated Sales: $.5-1 million
Number Employees: 5-9

580 **Ann's House of Nuts, Inc.**
9212 Berger Road
Suite 300
Columbia, MD 21046
410-309-6887
Fax: 410-312-9144
Nuts, dried fruits and mixes
President: Edward Zinke
Estimated Sales: $2.5-5 Million
Number Employees: 50-99
Square Footage: 800000
Type of Packaging: Consumer, Food Service, Private Label

581 **Anna's Oatcakes**
988 Route 100
Weston, VT 05161-5414
802-824-3535
Oatcakes and other baked goods

582 **Annabella**
Longmont, CO 80504
www.annabella.com
Water buffalo milk yogurt

583 **Annabelle Candy Co Inc**
27211 Industrial Blvd
Hayward, CA 94545-3392
510-783-2900
Fax: 510-785-7675   info@annabellecandy.com
www.annabellecandy.info
Processor of confectionery products including chocolate truffles, candy bars, nougats and taffy
CEO: Susan G Karl
susan@annabelle-candy.com
Year Founded: 1950
Estimated Sales: $15 Million
Number Employees: 50-99
Square Footage: 60000
Type of Packaging: Consumer, Bulk
Brands:
    ABBA-ZABBA(c)
    BIG HUNK(c)
    LOOK!(c)
    Rocky Road(c)
    U-NO(c)

584 **Annabelle Lee**
70 Rear Mills Road
Kennebunkport, ME 04046
207-967-4611
Fax: 207-832-7795
Seafood
President: Frank Minio
Number Employees: 30

585 **Annapolis Produce & Restaurant**
15 Lee St
Annapolis, MD 21401-3980
410-266-5211
Fax: 410-266-0568
Groceries, fish, meats and dairy products.
President: Charles Bassford
Chief Financial Officer: Bobby Goldbeck
Vice President: Elaine Bassford
Estimated Sales: $10-19.9 Million
Number Employees: 5-9

586 **Annapolis Winery**
26055 Soda Springs Rd
Annapolis, CA 95412-9728
707-886-5460
Fax: 707-886-5460   annapoliswinery@gmail.com
www.annapoliswinery.com
Wines
President: Basil Scalabrini
Co-Owner: Barbara Scalabrini
Estimated Sales: $2.5-5 Million
Number Employees: 5-9

587 **Annette Island Packing Company**
PO Box 8
Metlakatla, AK 99926
907-886-4441
Fax: 907-886-4471   info@metlakatla.com
www.metlakatla.com
Salmon and cured seafood
Manager: Freeman McGilton

588 **Annette's Donuts Ltd.**
1965 Lawrence Ave W
Toronto, ON M9N 1H5
Canada
416-656-3444
Fax: 416-656-5400   888-839-7857
Bread, pastries and other bakery products
President: Nicolas Yannopoulos
Board Member: Ariadni Yannopoulos
Estimated Sales: $5.9 Million
Number Employees: 85
Square Footage: 124000
Type of Packaging: Consumer, Food Service, Bulk

589 **Annie Chun's**
PO Box 911170
Los Angeles, CA 90091
415-479-8272
Fax: 415-479-8274   info@anniechun.com
www.anniechun.com
Soup bowls, noodle bowls, noodle express, rice express and organic noodles and sauce kits.
Owner: Annie Chun
President: Mike Keeland
CFO: Han Kim
Estimated Sales: Less than $500,000
Number Employees: 5-9

590 **Annie's Frozen Yogurt**
5200 W 74th St # A
Minneapolis, MN 55439-2223
952-835-2110
Fax: 952-835-2378   800-969-9648
www.anniesyogurt.com
Frozen yogurt
President: Lawrence Cerf
ldcerf@aol.com
Estimated Sales: $500,000-$1 Million
Number Employees: 10-19

591 **Annie's Homegrown**
1610 5th St
Berkeley, CA 94710-1715
510-558-7500
800-288-1089
bernie@annies.com   www.annies.com
Vegan and organic foods
President: Mark Mortimer
CEO: John Foraker
CFO: Zahir Ibrahim
Chief Innovation Officer: Bob Kaake
VP Marketing: Sarah Bird
Strategic Planning: ED Aaron
IT: Kristin Gibson-Lynn
kgibsonlynn@annies.com
Estimated Sales: Less Than $500,000
Number Employees: 5-9
Type of Packaging: Private Label
Brands:
    Annie's Macaroni & Cheese
    Tamarind Tree
    Annie's Organic Foods

592 **Annie's Naturals**
1610 5th St
Berkeley, CA 94710-1715
510-558-7500
Fax: 802-456-8865   800-434-1234
www.annies.com
Dressings and vinaigrettes, BBQ sauces, marinades and Worcestershire sauce.
Owner/Production Development: Annie Christopher
Owner/Sales/Marketing: Peter Backman
Number Employees: 10-19
Type of Packaging: Consumer, Food Service, Private Label
Brands:
    Annie's Naturals
    Annie's Naturals Magic Sauces
    Annie's Naturals Salad Dressings

Food Manufacturers / A-Z

593 Antelope Valley Winery
42041 20th St W
Lancaster, CA 93534-6912
661-722-0145
Fax: 661-722-6035 800-282-8332
wines@avwinery.com www.avwinery.com
Wines
Owner: Cyndee Donato
Winemaker: Cecil McLester
Estimated Sales: $2.5-5 Million
Number Employees: 5-9
Type of Packaging: Private Label
Brands:
  Antelope Valley

594 Anthony & Sons Italian Bakery
1275 Bloomfield Ave
Fairfield, NJ 07004-2708
973-575-5865
Fax: 973-244-1298 anthonyandsons@aol.com
Bread
Owner: Anthony Pio Costa
Plant Manager: Robert Tobia
Estimated Sales: Less than $500,000
Number Employees: 5-9

595 Anthony Road Wine Co
1020 Anthony Rd
Penn Yan, NY 14527-9632
315-536-2182
Fax: 315-536-5851 800-559-2182
info@anthonyroadwine.com
www.anthonyroadwine.com
Wines
Estimated Sales: $2.5-5 Million
Number Employees: 10-19

596 Anthony Thomas Candy Co
1777 Arlingate Ln
Columbus, OH 43228-4114
614-272-1870
877-226-3921
www.anthony-thomas.com
Gourmet-style chocolate including truffles, real butter creams, cordial cherries, creams, peanut butter cups, pecans and English Toffee.
President: Joe Zanetos
EVP Administration/Finance: Greg Zanetos
Marketing/Sales Manager: Clara Davis
EVP Production: Tim Zanetos
Plant Manager: Paul Reeder
Estimated Sales: Less Than $500,000
Number Employees: 1-4
Square Footage: 456000
Type of Packaging: Consumer
Brands:
  Anthony-Thomas Chocolates

597 Anton Caratan & Son
PO Box 2797
1625 Road 160
Bakersfield, CA 93303-2797
661-725-2575
Fax: 661-725-5829
Table grapes
President: Anton Caratan
Sales Manager: George Ann Caratan
Estimated Sales: $10-20 Million
Number Employees: 250-499
Type of Packaging: Consumer
Brands:
  Good Times
  Prosperity

598 Antoni Ravioli Co
879 N Broadway
North Massapequa, NY 11758-2353
516-799-0350
Fax: 516-799-0357 800-783-0350
www.antoniravioli.com
Ravioli, stuffed shells and manicotti, tortellini, cavatelli and gnocchi, fresh pasta, also gluten free products.
President: Gene Saucci
philrino@msn.com
Estimated Sales: $1.5 Million
Number Employees: 10-19
Square Footage: 12000
Type of Packaging: Food Service, Private Label, Bulk
Brands:
  Antoni Ravioli

599 Antonio Mozzarella Factory
71 Springfield Ave
Springfield, NJ 07081-1303
973-379-0033
Fax: 973-379-0099 antoniomozz@verizon.net
www.antoniomozzarella.com
Fresh mozarella
President: Tom Pagpugliese
thomas@antoniomozzarella.com
Estimated Sales: $7.1 Million
Number Employees: 1-4

600 Apac Chemical Corporation
150 N Santa Anita Ave
Suite 850
Arcadia, CA 91006
626-203-0066
Fax: 626-203-0067 866-849-2722
sales@apacchemical.com www.apacchemical.com
Potassium sorbate and sorbic acid
President: Sun Chang
Vice President: Tom Kusaka
Account Executive: Sergio Scarcella
Account Executive: Dave Plowman
Estimated Sales: $4 Million
Number Employees: 7

601 Apani Southwest
5401 N 1st St
Abilene, TX 79603-6424
325-690-1550
Fax: 325-690-1412 drinkapak@sbcglobal.net
www.apanisw.com
Premium drinking water
Owner: Glenda Pickens
Estimated Sales: $2 Million
Number Employees: 10-19
Type of Packaging: Private Label

602 Apecka Peppered Pickles
371 Stevens Road
Rockwall, TX 75032-6754
972-771-7628
Fax: 973-772-2655
Peppered pickles, pickled okra and garlic, green chile sauce
President: Sharon Eisenbraun
Estimated Sales: Less than $500,000
Number Employees: 1-4

603 Apex Marketing Group
7835 S Rainbow Blvd
Suite 17-300
Las Vegas, NV 89139
866-610-6165
Fax: 805-499-4204 888-990-2739
apexmktg@earthlink.net www.hairnomore.com
Personal care products
President/CEO: Mel Landyn
Vice President: Carole Landyn
Marketing Director: Mark Landyn
Operations Manager: Armen Grigorian
Product Manager: Mel Landyn
Estimated Sales: $5 Million
Number Employees: 25
Number of Brands: 2
Number of Products: 6
Square Footage: 32000
Type of Packaging: Consumer, Private Label, Bulk
Other Locations:
  Apex Marketing Group
  Newbury Park CA

604 Aphrodite Divine Confections
2677 Forest Lane
Garland, TX 75042
972-485-1005
Fax: 972-485-8866 baker@aphroditedesserts.com
www.aphroditedesserts.com
Frozen cookie dough and desserts
Founder: Dean d'Ambrosia

605 Apiterra
2677 Forest Lane
Garland, TX 75042
972-485-1005
Fax: 972-485-8866 baker@aphroditedesserts.com
www.aphroditedesserts.com
Flavor-infused honey
Co-Founder & CEO: Dzmitry Hryharovich
Co-Founder & CTO: Aleh Svirchou
Co-Founder: Daria Zarubina
Brands:
  APITERRA

606 Apotheca Inc
201 Apple Boulevard
Woodbine, IA 51579
712-647-3133
Fax: 888-898-0401 800-736-3130
info@apothecacompany.com
www.apothecacompany.com
Homeopathics, botanical extracts, capsules, tablets and sports nutritionals
President: Kathryn Simon
Contact: Mike Evans
mike@apothecacompany.com
Estimated Sales: $10-20 Million
Number Employees: 100
Square Footage: 140000

607 Appetizers And, Inc.
330 Ballardvale Street
Wilmington, WA 01887
773-227-0400
Fax: 773-227-0448 800-224-7630
Frozen hors d'oeuvres
President/CEO/Co-Owner: George King
EVP/Co-Owner: Patricia Domanik
CFO: Scott Forester
SVP Operations/COO: Kristine Holtz
VP Manufacturing: John Trellicoso
Number Employees: 250-499
Type of Packaging: Consumer, Food Service

608 Apple & Eve LLC
2 Seaview Blvd # 100
3rd Floor
Port Washington, NY 11050-4634
516-621-1122
Fax: 516-621-2164 800-969-8018
info@appleandeve.com www.appleandeve.com
Natural juices and juice blends; importer of fruit concentrates
Founder/CEO: Gordon Crane
gordon@appleandeve.com
CFO: Paul Bevilacqua
VP: Joan Segal
VP Innovation & Development: Ken Gootkind
Director of Marketing/Advertising: Jeff Damiano
VP Sales/Marketing: Cary Crane
Operations Executive: Tyron Charles
Plant Manager: John Donlon
Purchasing Manager: Mary Ellen Brothers
Estimated Sales: $15.1 Million
Number Employees: 50-99
Number of Products: 100+
Square Footage: 42000
Type of Packaging: Consumer
Brands:
  Apple & Eve
  Made In the Shade
  Sesame Street
  Tribal

609 Apple Acres
4633 Cherry Valley Turnpike
La Fayette, NY 13084
603-893-8596
Fax: 315-677-5143 sam@appleacres.com
www.appleacres.com
Apples
CEO: Walter Blackler
Co-Owner: Bob Rigdon
Estimated Sales: $10 Million
Number Employees: 20-49
Square Footage: 128000
Type of Packaging: Consumer

610 Apple Flavor & Fragrance USA
55 Carter Dr
Edison, NJ 08817-2066
732-393-0600
Fax: 732-393-1933 www.cnaff.com
Flavor ingredients and enhancers.
President: Maggie Wu
maggieapff@cnaffusa.com
Number Employees: 5-9

611 Apple Valley Market
9067 US Highway 31 # A
Berrien Springs, MI 49103-1806
269-471-3282
Fax: 269-471-6035 800-237-7436
avnf@avnf.com www.avnf.com
Vitamins and vegetarian groceries
Manager: George Schmidt
george@avnf.com
CEO: Frank Williams

Food Manufacturers / A-Z

Estimated Sales: $5-10 Million
Number Employees: 100-249
Square Footage: 200000

612 Applecreek Speciality Foods
PO Box 910089
Lexington, KY 40591
859-881-8010
Fax: 877-869-9184 800-747-8871
bhall@mis.net
Preserves, fruit butters, marinade, salsa, relish, caramel and chocolate fidge dessert sauces, dressings, BBQ seasonings and homemade candies.
Owner: Buddy Hall
Operations Manager: Lynn Abshear
Estimated Sales: $1-3 Million
Number Employees: 1-4
Brands:
  Applecreek Orchards

613 Appledore Cove LLC
19 Buffum Rd Unit 6
North Berwick, ME 03906
207-676-4088
Fax: 207-636-8100
Salsas, condiments & dips, sauces & marinades, preserves & dessert sauces
President: Jeff Garstka

614 Applegate Farms
Rt 202 South
Suite 300
Bridgewater, NJ 08807-5530
908-725-2768
Fax: 908-725-3383 866-587-5858
Organic meat including beef, chicken, turkey and pork. Also cheese, sausage and hotdogs.
Owner: Seven McDonald
Co-Founder: Chris Ely
Number Employees: 50-99
Square Footage: 28000
Type of Packaging: Consumer, Food Service, Private Label, Bulk
Brands:
  Applegate Farms
  Great Organic Hotdog
  Joy Stick

615 Appleton Produce Company
1408 Weiser River Road
PO Box 110
Weiser, ID 83672
208-414-3352
Fax: 208-414-1862 onions@appletonproduce.com
Onions
President: C. Robert Woods
President/Owner: Steve Woods
Marketing/Sales Manager: Steve Walker
Purchasing Manager: Dave Price
Estimated Sales: $12 Million
Number Employees: 50
Type of Packaging: Consumer, Food Service, Private Label, Bulk
Brands:
  Apco
  Appleton
  Gold Nugget

616 Applewood Orchards Inc
2998 Rodesiler Hwy
Deerfield, MI 49238-9789
517-447-3002
Fax: 517-447-3006 800-447-3854
jim@applewoodapples.com
www.applewoodapples.com
Apples
Owner: James Swindeman
james@applewoodapples.com
Vice President: Steve Swindeman
VP: Scott Swindeman
Estimated Sales: $5-10 Million
Number Employees: 20-49
Type of Packaging: Consumer

617 Applewood Seed & Garden Group
5380 Vivian Street
Arvada, CO 80002-1959
303-431-7333
Fax: 303-467-7886 800-232-0666
sales@applewoodseed.com
www.applewoodseed.com
Wildflower and garden seed producers

President: Gene Milstein
General Manager: Norm Poppe
Contact: Kendall Holdrem
kholdren@applewoodseed.com
Estimated Sales: $5-10 Million
Parent Co: Applewood Seed & Garden Group

618 Applewood Winery
82 Four Corners Rd.
Warwick, NY 10990
845-988-9292
info@applewoodwinery.com
www.applewoodwinery.com
Merlot, Cabernet, Riesling, Chardonnay, Red wine blends, fruit-flavoured wine, hard cider
Owner: Jonathan Hull
Year Founded: 1993
Number of Brands: 2
Number of Products: 21
Type of Packaging: Consumer, Private Label
Brands:
  Applewood Winery
  Naked Flock

619 April Hill Inc
190 28th St SE
Grand Rapids, MI 49548
616-245-0595
Fax: 616-245-2368 www.aprilhill.com
Breads, rolls
Plant Manager: William MacKenzie
Estimated Sales: $2.5-5 Million
Number Employees: 10-19

620 Aqua Clara Bottling & Distribution
1315 Cleveland Street
Clearwater, FL 33755-5102
727-446-2999
Fax: 727-446-3999
Oxygen-enriched premium drinking water
Chairman: E Douglas Cifers
President & CEO: Jack Plunkett
Number Employees: 5-9
Brands:
  Aqua Clara

621 Aqua Vie Beverage Corporation
PO Box 6759
333 South Main Street
Ketchum, ID 83340-6759
208-622-7792
Fax: 208-622-8829 800-744-7500
www.aquavie.com
Natural falvored water without carbonation, low-calorie and exotic flavors
President: Thomas Gillespie
Estimated Sales: $1-2.5 Million
Number Employees: 20-49
Type of Packaging: Bulk
Brands:
  Avalanche

622 AquaCuisine
11560 SW 67th Avenue
Suite 200W
Portland, OR 97223
208-323-2782
Fax: 208-323-4730 mgoforth@aquacuisine.com
www.aquacuisine.com
Seafood products as well as fresh and frozen burgers, franks and refrigerated seafood entrees.
President: Mark Goforth
Estimated Sales: $5 Million
Number Employees: 1-4
Number of Products: 7
Square Footage: 20000
Type of Packaging: Consumer
Brands:
  Aquacuisine

623 AquaTec Development
1543 Locke Ln
Sugar Land, TX 77478
281-491-0808
Fax: 281-242-7771
Bulk production of algae and nutraceutical extracts and concentrates. Algae food supplements and food fortificial bulk only
President: Howard Stern
hstern@aquatec.com
Number Employees: 1-4
Type of Packaging: Bulk

624 Aquatec Seafoods Ltd.
820 Shamrock Place
Comox, BC V9M 3P6
Canada
250-339-6412
Fax: 250-339-4951
Fresh and frozen salmon and oysters
President: Malena Tutte
Estimated Sales: $2.7 Million
Number Employees: 20
Square Footage: 28000
Type of Packaging: Consumer, Food Service, Private Label, Bulk

625 Aquatech
6221 Petersburg St
Anchorage, AK 99507-2006
907-563-1387
Fax: 907-563-1852 877-938-2722
www.crabfactory.com
Live, fresh and frozen Alaskan king crab.
Partner: Miki Ballard
Partner: Lamar Ballard
aquatech@ak.net
General Manager: Sarah Ballard
Estimated Sales: $3-5 Million
Number Employees: 5-9

626 Aralia Olive Oils
1105 Massachusetts Avenue
Suite 2E
Cambridge, MA 02138
617-354-8556
Fax: 617-249-1855 877-585-9510
www.araliaoliveoils.com
Olive Oils
President: Emmanuel Daskalakis
Number Employees: 2

627 Arbor Crest Wine Cellars
4705 N Fruit Hill Rd
Spokane, WA 99217-9562
509-927-9463
Fax: 509-927-0574 www.arborcrest.com
Wine
Head Winemaker: Kristina Mielke-van L"ben Sels
Estimated Sales: $1.25 Million
Number Employees: 20-49
Type of Packaging: Private Label
Brands:
  Arbor Crest

628 Arbor Hill Grapery & Winery
6461 State Route 64
Naples, NY 14512-9726
585-374-2870
Fax: 585-374-9198 800-554-7553
www.thegrapery.com
Wines, grape- and fruit-based products, fruit preservatives, wine jellies, dressings, vinegars, barbeque sauces, mustard, spreadable sauces and dips, pretzel dips, wine sauces and tea concentrates.
President: John Brahm
john@thegrapery.com
VP: Katharine Brahm
Public Relations: Sherry Brahm-Orlando
Estimated Sales: Less than $5 Million
Number Employees: 5-9
Type of Packaging: Consumer, Private Label
Brands:
  Arbor Hill Wine
  Brahm's Wine Country
  Mrs. Brahms

629 Arbor Mist Winery
116 Buffalo St
Canandaigua, NY 14424
866-396-7394
www.arbormist.com
Fruit-flavored wines

630 Arbor Springs Water Co
950 Orchard St
Ferndale, MI 48220-1439
248-543-7151
Fax: 248-543-0488 sales@arborspringswater.com
Bottled spring and purified water.
Owner: John Niel
j.niel@arborspringswater.com
Estimated Sales: $5-10 Million
Number Employees: 10-19
Other Locations:
  Arbor Springs Water Company
  Ann Arbor MI

488

Food Manufacturers / A-Z

631 Arboris LLC
1101 W Lathrop Ave
PO Box 2008
Savannah, GA 31415-1021
912-238-7537
Fax: 912-238-7454 info@arboris-us.com
www.arboris-us.com
Sterols used in yogurt, milks, juices and breads.
Vice President/General Manager: Peter Acton
Contact: Elliot Abemayor
elliot.abemayor@arboris-us.com
Purchasing: Jeanne Anderson
Number Employees: 10-19

632 Arbre Farms Inc
6362 N 192nd Ave
Walkerville, MI 49459-8601
231-873-3337
Fax: 231-873-5699 www.arbrefarms.com
Provides food service and frozen food manufacturing industries with the finest quality frozen fruits and vegetables.
President: C O Johnson
cjohnson@arbrefarms.com
Quality Control: Robert Anderson
Marketing: Tripper Showell
Sales: Jean Hovey
Plant Manager: Vince Miskosky
Number Employees: 250-499
Type of Packaging: Food Service, Bulk
Other Locations:
  Willow Cold Storage
  Walkerville MI

633 Arbuckle Coffee Roasters
3550 E Corporate Dr
Tucson, AZ 85706-1821
520-790-5282
Fax: 520-748-7910 800-533-8278
www.arbucklecoffee.com
Coffee and tea.
President: Denney Willis
VP: Josh Willis
Estimated Sales: $500,000-$1 Million
Number Employees: 10-19
Brands:
  Arbuckle

634 Arcadia Biosciences
202 Cousteau Pl.
Ste. 105
Davis, CA 95618
530-756-7077
Fax: 530-756-7027 info@arcadiabio.com
arcadiabio.com
Non-GMO specialty wheat ingredients.
President & CEO: Matthew Plavan
Chief Commercial Officer: Sarah Reiter
CFO: Pam Haley
CTO: Randall Shultz
Year Founded: 2002
Number of Brands: 1
Type of Packaging: Food Service
Brands:
  GoodWheat™

635 Arcadia Dairy Farms Inc
1869 Brevard Rd
34 Arcadia Farms Road
Arden, NC 28704
828-684-3556
Fax: 828-684-7988 info@arcadiafarms.com
www.arcadiadairyfarms.com
Juices including orange, apple, strawberry and grape; also, water
President: James Ward
arcdfinc@aol.com
Vice President: Carolyn Arthur
Estimated Sales: $1 Million
Number Employees: 20-49
Type of Packaging: Consumer
Brands:
  Arcadia
  Sunrise

636 Arcadian Estate Winery
4184 State Route 14
Rock Stream, NY 14878
607-535-2068
Fax: 607-535-4692 800-298-1346
info@arcadianwine.com www.arcadianwine.com
Wines.
Owner: John Dalonzo
Number Employees: 10-19

Type of Packaging: Consumer

637 Archer Daniels Midland Company
4666 Faries Parkway
Decatur, IL 62526
217-424-5200
www.adm.com
Food and feed ingredients, industrial chemicals and biofuels.
Type of Packaging: Food Service, Bulk

638 (HQ)Archer Daniels Midland Company
77 West Wacker Dr.
Suite 4600
Chicago, IL 60601
312-634-8100
www.adm.com
Food and feed ingredients, industrial chemicals and biofuels.
Chairman/CEO: Juan Luciano
Executive VP/CFO: Ray Young
Senior VP/General Counsel: D. Cameron Findlay
Year Founded: 1902
Estimated Sales: $64.3 Billion
Number Employees: 32,000

639 Archibald Frozen Desserts
990 Progress Blvd
New Albany, IN 47150-2259
812-941-8267
Fax: 812-941-5374
Soft serve ice cream and frozen yogurt
CEO: Ed Meyer
Executive VP: Greg Gilbert
greg.gilbert@archibaldfrozendesserts.com
Sales & Marketing Coordinator: Lindsay Usher
National Sales Manager: Alex Mohler
Warehouse/Service Manager: Tim Coy
Estimated Sales: Less Than $500,000
Number Employees: 1-4

640 Archie Moore's
15 Factory Ln
Milford, CT 06460-3306
203-876-5088
Fax: 203-876-0525
Manufacturer and exporter of buffalo wing sauce and flavored potato chips
President: Todd Ressler
tressler@archiemoores.com
Estimated Sales: $.5-1 million
Number Employees: 20-49
Square Footage: 10000
Parent Co: Archie Moore's Bar & Restaurant
Type of Packaging: Consumer, Food Service, Private Label, Bulk
Brands:
  Archie Moore's

641 Archon Vitamin Corp
3775 Park Ave
Suite 1
Edison, NJ 08820-2566
973-371-1700
Fax: 973-371-1277 800-848-0089
purchasing@archonvitamin.com
www.archonvitamin.com
Vitamins, minerals, herbs, and other nutritionals.
President: Tom Pugsley
tpugsley@archonvitamin.com
VP Products Division: Paul Stevens
Quality Assurance Manager: Susan Jackson
Sales Manager: Rick McNall
Operations Executive: Jose Camaano
Purchasing Director: Tracy Daniiel
Estimated Sales: $5-10 Million
Number Employees: 50-99
Number of Brands: 1
Square Footage: 200000
Type of Packaging: Consumer, Private Label, Bulk
Brands:
  Bionutrient

642 Arcobasso Foods Inc
8850 Pershall Road
Hazlewood, MO 63042
314-381-8083
Fax: 314-381-4522 800-284-0620
pat@arcobasso.com www.arcobasso.com
Salad dressings, sauces and marinades.
President: Pat Newsham
Contact: Phyllis Alberici
phyllis@arcobasso.com

643 Arcor USA
550 Biltmore Way-PH11A
Coral Gables, FL 33134
305-592-1080
Fax: 305-592-1081 800-572-7267
info@arcor.com www.arcor.com.ar
Candies
President: Luis Alejandro Pagani
National Sales Manager: Michael Figueras
Product Manager: Damian Cordova
Estimated Sales: $10-20 Million
Number Employees: 20-49
Type of Packaging: Private Label
Brands:
  Arcor Premium Hard Filled Candies
  Arcor Value Line Hard Candies
  Rocklets
  Whisper Chocolate Bon Bons

644 (HQ)Arctic Beverages
107 Mountainview Road
Unit 2
Winnipeg, MB R3C 2E6
Can
204-633-8686
866-503-1270
winnipeg@arcticbev.com www.arcticbev.com
Soft drinks, juices, snack foods, bread, frozen food, chocolate.
Year Founded: 1991
Estimated Sales: $6 Million
Number Employees: 44
Number of Products: 68
Square Footage: 68000
Parent Co: Tribal Councils Investment Group of Manitoba Ltd.
Other Locations:
  Arctic Beverages Ltd.
  The Pas MB
  Arctic Beverages Ltd.
  Thompson MB
  Arctic Beverages Ltd.
  Winnipeg MB

645 Arctic Glacier
625 Henry Avenue
Winnipeg, MB R3A 0V1
Canada
204-772-2473
Fax: 204-783-9857 888-573-9237
info@arcticglacierinc.com
www.arcticglacierinc.com
Ice
President/CEO: Keith McMahon
EVP Operations: Mike Wohlgemuth
Chief Financial Officer: Douglas Bailey
VP Accounting/Financial Reporting: Rosemary Brisson
VP Sales/Marketing: Michael Busch
Estimated Sales: $10-20 Million
Number Employees: 20-49
Parent Co: Arctic Glacier
Other Locations:
  Happy Ice Manufacturing Plant
  Buffalo NY
  Happy Ice Manufacturing Plant
  Utica NY
  Happy Ice Manufacturing Plant
  Corning NY
  Happy Ice Manufacturing Plant
  Albany NY

646 Arctic Ice Cream Co
22 Arctic Pkwy
Ewing, NJ 08638-3093
609-393-4264
Fax: 609-392-3663 800-858-8966
arcticicecream@hotmail.com
www.arcticicecreamco.com
Ice cream
President: Thomas Green
CEO: John Connors
Vice President: Christine Green
Estimated Sales: $1 Million
Number Employees: 10-19

647 Arctic Zero
4241 Jutland Drive
Suite 305
San Diego, CA 92117
888-272-1715
www.arcticzero.com
Low glycemic, lactose free, gluten free and GMO free frozen desserts

Food Manufacturers / A-Z

Founder: Greg Holtman
Contact: Megan Abordo
megan@myarcticzero.com

648 Ardent Mills Corp
1875 Lawrence St
Suite 200
Denver, CO 80202-1847
510-999-2877
800-851-9618
www.ardentmills.com
Flours, mixes, blends, and specialty products.
CEO: Dan Dye
Chief Financial Officer: John Barton
Director of Marketing: Don Trouba
Vice President, Sales: Dean Grossmann
Contact: Andy Alan
andy.allen@ardentmills.com
Senior Director Operations: Troy Anderson
Number Employees: 10-19
Type of Packaging: Food Service, Bulk
Brands:
   American Beauty
   Buccaneer
   Denrado
   Full Power
   Hummer
   Kyrol
   Magnifico Special
   Minnesota Girl
   Pikes Peak
   Producer
   Ramsey Medium Rye
   Urban Special
   and many more

649 Ardith Mae Farmstead Goat Cheese
1094 State Route 9J
Stuyvesant, NY 12173
917-744-4314
www.ardithmae.com
Goat cheese

650 Ardmore Cheese Company
26366 Main Street
Ardmore, TN 38449
931-427-2191
Fax: 931-427-4116
Cheddar cheese
Manager: Abby Woods
VP: Joe Madeo
Plant Manager: Brad Jackson
Estimated Sales: $500-1 Million appx.
Number Employees: 1-4
Square Footage: 40000
Type of Packaging: Consumer, Private Label
Brands:
   Ardmore
   Avalon

651 Ardy Fisher
201-244-3436
877-699-5066
info@ardyfisher.com brislingsardines.com
Sardines
Number of Brands: 1
Number of Products: 5
Brands:
   BRISLING SARDINES

652 Arel Group Wine & Spirits Inc
2870 Pharr Court South NW
Suite 2009
Atlanta, GA 30305-2174
404-869-4387
Fax: 404-506-9242 info@arelgroupws.com
www.tenutapolvaro.com
Wines and spirits
President & Co-Founder: Elviana Candoni
Co-Founder: Armando De Zan
admin@candoniwines.com
Estimated Sales: $1.3 Million
Number Employees: 10-19
Number of Brands: 2
Brands:
   Candoni de Zan
   Tenuta Polvaro

653 Arena & Sons
746 Maple St
Redwood City, CA 94063-2025
650-366-1750
Fax: 650-366-4679
Veal and beef
Owner: Jim Arena
President: Joanne Arena
Estimated Sales: $2.5-5 Million
Number Employees: 5-9
Type of Packaging: Bulk

654 Argania Butter
Rancho Palos Verdes, CA 90275
info@araganiabutter.com
araganiabutter.com
Almond butter
Founder: Nadia Gara

655 Argee Corp
9550 Pathway St
Santee, CA 92071-4169
619-449-5050
Fax: 619-449-8392 800-449-3030
argeecorp@sbcglobal.net www.argeecorp.com
President: Robert Goldman
rgoldman@argeecorp.com
VP Sales/Marketing: Ruth Goldman
Estimated Sales: $10-20 Million
Number Employees: 50-99

656 Argo Century, Inc.
840 Edgewood Ave
Suite 202
Jacksonville, FL 32205
704-525-6180
Fax: 704-525-6280 800-446-7108
info@tontonsauce.com www.tontonsauce.com
Ginger dressing, teriyaki sauce and vinaigrettes.
President: Yoshi Shioda
Estimated Sales: $1-3 Million
Number Employees: 1-4
Type of Packaging: Consumer

657 Argo Fine Foods
PO Box 2077
Saint James, NY 11780
631-703-0443
Tzatziki (yogurt sauce), pita snacks
President/Owner: Christel DeBlasio-Pavlidis

658 Argo Tea
16 W Randolph St
Chicago, IL 60601
612-553-1550
info@argotea.com
www.argotea.com
Tea

659 Argyle Winery
691 Highway 99 W
PO Box 280
Dundee, OR 97115-0280
503-538-8520
Fax: 503-538-2055 888-427-4953
customerservice@argylewinery.com
www.argylewinery.com
Wines.
Director, Sales & Marketing: Chris Cullina
Head, Vineyard Operations: Allen Holstein
Year Founded: 1987
Estimated Sales: $20-50 Million
Number Employees: 50-99
Number of Brands: 3
Parent Co: Distinguished Vineyards & Wine Partners
Type of Packaging: Private Label
Brands:
   Argyle Brut
   Nuthouse
   Spirithouse

660 Ariake USA Inc
1711 N Liberty St
Harrisonburg, VA 22802-4518
540-432-6550
Fax: 540-432-6549 www.ariakeusa.com
Meat stocks, broths, bases, and seasonings.
Technical Manager: Kyle Wellsford
kylewellsford@va.ariake.com
Manager: Joseph Brisby
Purchasing Specialist: Aaron Robinson
Estimated Sales: $18 Million
Number Employees: 50-99
Square Footage: 58000
Parent Co: Ariake Japan Co., Ltd.

661 Arico Natural Foods
3720 Sw 141st Ave
Suite 210
Beaverton, OR 97005
503-259-0871
www.crisproot.com
Casava root chips
President/CEO: Angela Ichwan
CFO/VP: Hermanto Hidajat
Vice President of Sales and Marketing: Duke Field
Estimated Sales: $500,000-1 Million
Number Employees: 5-9

662 Ariel Natural Foods
13400 N 20th St
Suite 32
Bellevue, WA 98005
425-637-3345
Fax: 425-637-8655 www.arielfoods.com
Sugar-free, dairy-free and gluten-free premium dried snacks.

663 Ariel Vineyards
860 Napa Valley Corporate Way
Suite C
Napa, CA 94558-6281
707-258-8050
Fax: 707-258-8052 800-456-9472
info@arielvineyards.com www.arielvineyards.com
Nonalcoholic wine
Manager: Craig Rosser
info@jlohr.com
VP Operations: Jeff Meier
Estimated Sales: $5-10 Million
Number Employees: 1-4
Square Footage: 256000
Parent Co: J. Lohr Vineyards & Wines
Brands:
   Ariel
   Ariel Blanc
   Ariel Brut Cuve
   Ariel Cabernet
   Ariel Chardonnay
   Ariel Merlot
   Ariel Rouge
   Ariel White Zinfandel

664 Aries Prepared Beef
17 W Magnolia Blvd
Burbank, CA 91502-1719
818-526-4855
Fax: 818-845-3041 800-424-2333
aileen@ariesbeef.com www.ariesbeef.com
Meats and sausage including; roast beef, pastrami, corned beef, hot dogs, sausages, and pickled and fresh meats
Owner: Ragip Unal
Director of Quality Control: Rob Unal
VP Sales: Fred Weiss
ragipunal@gmail.com
Director of Production: Luis Rolon
General Manager: Ken McLaughlin
Estimated Sales: $19 Million
Number Employees: 50-99
Type of Packaging: Consumer, Food Service

665 Arise & Shine Herbal Products
P.O.Box 400
Medford, OR 97501
541-282-0891
Fax: 541-773-8866 800-688-2444
www.ariseandshine.com
Digestive aids and herbal supplements.
Founder: Dr. Richard Anderson
CEO: Avona L'Carttier
Contact: Denise Shannon
dshannon@ariseandshine.com
Brands:
   Chomper
   Flora Grow
   Herbal Nutrition
   Super Antioxidant Blend
   Ultimate Food Complex

666 Arista Industries Inc
557 Danbury Rd
Wilton, CT 06897-2218
203-761-1009
Fax: 203-761-4980 800-255-6457
info@aristaindustries.com
www.aristaindustries.com
Oils, frozen shrimp, lobster tails and octopus. Importer of octopus, shrimp, squid, lobster tails, oils and surimi products.

Food Manufacturers / A-Z

President: Alan Weitzer
CEO: Charles Hillyer
Chairman: Stephen Weitzer
steve@aristaindustries.com
Estimated Sales: $2.5-5 Million
Number Employees: 20-49
Type of Packaging: Consumer, Food Service
Brands:
  Arista
  Pacific Treasures
  Sea Devils

667 Ariston Specialties
PO Box 306
Bloomfield, CT 06002
860-224-7184
Fax: 860-726-1263
aristonspecialties@hotmail.com
Olive Oils
Owner: Thomas Doukas
tom.doukas@aristonspecialties.com

668 Ariza Cheese Co
7602 Jackson St
Paramount, CA 90723-4912
562-630-4144
Fax: 562-630-4174   800-762-4736
Mexican cheese
President: Fatima Ariza
Estimated Sales: $5.5 Million
Number Employees: 20-49
Type of Packaging: Consumer, Food Service

669 Arizmendi Bakery
1331 9th Ave
San Francisco, CA 94122-2308
415-566-3117
info@arizmendibakery.com
www.arizmendibakery.com
Pastries, artisan breads, gourmet pizza
Owner: Isaac Hee
isaachee@yahoo.com
Number Employees: 10-19

670 Arizona Beverage Company
644 Linn Street
Suite 318
Cincinnati, OH 45203
Fax: 516-326-4988   800-832-3775
info@drinkarizona.com   www.drinkarizona.com
Teas, juices and iced coffees.
President: John Ferolito
Chairman: Don Vultaggio
CFO/CEO: Rick Adonailo
VP National Sales: Paul O'Donnell
Contact: Taiwo Adekoya
tadekoya@drinkarizona.com
Year Founded: 1992
Estimated Sales: $5-10 Million
Number Employees: 500-999
Brands:
  Arizona
  Ferolito, Vultaggio & Sons
  Rx Extreme Energy Shot

671 Arizona Cowboy
3010 N 24th St
Phoenix, AZ 85016-7816
602-278-1421
Fax: 602-484-9482   800-529-8627
www.ameliocenterprises.com
Salsa, jellies, hot sauces, tortilla chips, honey, candy and nuts.
Owner/President: Amelio Casciato
Estimated Sales: $500,000-1 Million
Number Employees: 5-9
Square Footage: 6600
Type of Packaging: Consumer, Food Service, Private Label

672 Arizona Natural Products
12815 N Cave Creek Rd
Phoenix, AZ 85022-5834
602-997-6098
Fax: 602-288-8331   800-255-2823
info@arizonanatural.com   www.arizonanatural.com
Herbal and vitamin supplements.
President/CEO: Michael Hanna
Contact: Ranna Hanna
rhanna@arizonanatural.com
Estimated Sales: Less Than $500,000
Number Employees: 5-9
Square Footage: 40000

Brands:
  Allirich

673 Arizona Nutritional Supplements
210 S Beck Ave
Chandler, AZ 85226-3311
480-753-3510
Fax: 480-966-9640   888-742-7675
www.aznutritional.com
Nutritional and dietary supplements
Owner: Jonathan Pinkus
jonpinkus@aznutritional.com
Co-Owner: Aaron Blunck
Estimated Sales: $10-20 Million
Number Employees: 100-249
Square Footage: 50000

674 Arizona Pepper Products
710 E Broadway Rd
Mesa, AZ 85204-2081
480-833-1908
Fax: 480-833-0309   800-359-3912
info@azgunslinger.com   www.azgunslinger.com
Hot sauces, olives, spices and pistachios
President: Bill Marko
Year Founded: 1987
Estimated Sales: $2.5-5 Million
Number Employees: 10-19

675 Arizona Pistachio Company
3865 N Businesss Ctr Drive
Suite 115
Tucson, AZ 85705
520-746-0880
Fax: 520-741-9797   800-333-8575
salesapc@azpistachio.com
Pistachios
President: Henry Mollner
Year Founded: 1969
Estimated Sales: $2.5-5 Million
Number Employees: 5-9
Type of Packaging: Consumer, Food Service, Bulk

676 Arizona Sunland Foods
3752 S Broadmont Drive
Tucson, AZ 85713
520-624-7068
www.azsunlandfoods.com
Breaded proteins, sauces and dressings
President: Arnie Jacobsen
arnie@azsunlandfoods.com
Director of Sales & Marketing: Josh Jacobsen
Director of Product Dev. & Operations: Joel Jacobsen
Year Founded: 1983
Type of Packaging: Food Service, Private Label
Brands:
  Sunland

677 Arizona Vineyards
1830 E Patagonia Hwy
Nogales, AZ 85621
520-287-7972
Fax: 520-287-7597
Wines
Owner/President: Arthur Ocheltree
Owner/CEO: Tino Ocheltree
Estimated Sales: Less than $150,000
Number Employees: 1-4
Brands:
  Arizona Vineyards

678 Arla Foods Inc
675 Rivermede Road
Concord, ON L4K 2G9
Canada
905-669-9393
Fax: 905-669-5614   www.arlafoods.com
Cheese
President: Andrew Simpson
Estimated Sales: $19 Million
Number Employees: 120
Square Footage: 200000
Type of Packaging: Consumer, Food Service, Private Label, Bulk
Brands:
  Tre Stelle

679 Arlen S Gould & Assoc
2821 N Vista Rd
Arlington Hts, IL 60004-2108
847-577-2122
Fax: 708-577-4244
Sauces, dips and dressings

Owner: Arlen Gould
Number Employees: 1-4
Brands:
  Dolefam

680 Armanino Foods of Distinction
30588 San Antonio St
Hayward, CA 94544-7102
510-441-9300
Fax: 510-441-0101   800-255-8588
customerservice@armanino.biz
Exporter of Italian foods including sauces, pasta, meatballs and bread. Importer of Italian cheeses.
CEO: Edmond Pera
Estimated Sales: F
Number Employees: 20-49
Square Footage: 24000
Type of Packaging: Consumer, Food Service
Brands:
  Armanino

681 Armbrust Meats
224 S Main St
Medford, WI 54451
715-748-3102
Fax: 715-748-6399
Fresh and frozen sausage, beef, pork and poultry
President: Thomas Armbrust
Estimated Sales: $500,000-$1 Million
Square Footage: 132000
Type of Packaging: Consumer, Bulk

682 Armenia Coffee Corporation
2975 Westchester Avenue
Purchase, NY 10577
914-694-6100
Fax: 914-694-5622   j.apuzzo@armeniacoffee.com
armeniacoffee.net
Coffee
President: Joe Apuzzo
Owner: John Randall
CFO: Alan Macek
VP: Robert Tapia
Estimated Sales: $1.4 Million
Number Employees: 9

683 Armeno Coffee Roasters LTD
75 Otis St
Northborough, MA 01532-2412
508-393-2821
Fax: 508-393-2818   beans@armeno.com
www.armeno.com
Coffee roaster
Owner: Chuck Koffman
beans@armeno.com
Co-Owner: John Parks
Estimated Sales: Under $1 Million
Number Employees: 1-4
Square Footage: 20000
Type of Packaging: Consumer, Private Label
Brands:
  Armeno

684 Armistead Citrus Company
1057 N Greenfield Rd
Mesa, AZ 85205
480-830-2491
Citrus products
Owner: Ken Armistead
Estimated Sales: Under $500,000
Number Employees: 1-4
Brands:
  Armistead Citrus Products

685 Arnabal International, Inc.
13459 Savanna
Tustin, CA 92782
714-665-9477
Fax: 714-665-9477   armen@arnabal.com
www.arnabal.com
Oils and vinegars
Owner: Nairy Balian
Co-Owner: Jeff Stratton
Estimated Sales: $.5-1 million
Number Employees: 1-4

686 Arnel's Originals, Inc
381 Sonoma Ct
Ventura, CA 93004-1169
USA
805-322-6900
www.arnelsoriginals.com
Baking mixes

Food Manufacturers / A-Z

President: Arnel McAtee
Contact: Gabriela Eisenberg
eisenbergg@svusd.org
Estimated Sales: 52,000
Number Employees: 1

687 Arnhem Group
25 Commerce Drive
Suite 130
Cranford, NJ 07016-3605
908-709-4045
Fax: 908-709-9221 800-851-1052
info@arnhemgroup.com www.arnhemgroup.com
Binders and extenders, fat replacers, flavor enhancers, milk products and stabilizers.
President, Chairman, CEO: Michael Bonner
Account Manager: Karyn Rosenberg
National Accounts Manager: Sandra Lyna
Contact: Milagros Fernandez
mfernandez@arnhemgroup.com
Estimated Sales: $1-2.5 Million
Number Employees: 1-4

688 Arnold Farm Sugarhouse
P.O. Box 63
Jackman, ME 04945
207-668-4110
www.arnoldfarm.com
Maple syrup

689 Arnold Foods Company
PO Box 976
Horsham, PA 19044
203-531-2043
Fax: 203-531-2170 800-984-0989
www.gwbakeries.com
Baked goods
Vice President: Rod Cuha
Manager: Vinnie Greco
Number Employees: 1-4
Brands:
  Beck's
  Beck's Dark
  Beck's For Oktoberfest
  Haake Beck Non-Alcoholic

690 Arnold's Meat Food Products
274 Heyward Street
Brooklyn, NY 11209
718-963-1400
Fax: 718-963-2303 800-633-7023
www.arnolds-sausage.com
Smoked sausage, scrapple, chorizos, kielbasa and bacon.
President: Sheldon Dosik
michelle_shao@colpal.com
VP: Jason Judd
Year Founded: 1967
Estimated Sales: $3.6 Million
Number Employees: 25
Square Footage: 33940
Type of Packaging: Consumer, Food Service, Private Label, Bulk
Brands:
  Arnold's Meats
  Caroline's Sausage
  El Cerdito

691 Arns Winery
601 Mund Rd
St Helena, CA 94574-9738
707-963-3429
Fax: 707-963-5780 info@arnswinery.com
www.arnswinery.com
Wines
Owner: John Arns
Co-Owner: Sandi Belcher
sandi@arnswinery.com
Marketing: Sandi Belcher
Sales: Kathi Belcher-Tyler
Purchasing: John Arns
Estimated Sales: $100,000
Number Employees: 1-4
Number of Brands: 1
Number of Products: 1
Square Footage: 4800
Type of Packaging: Consumer
Brands:
  Arns

692 Aroma Coffee Company
7650 Industrial Dr
Forest Park, IL 60130
708-488-8340
Fax: 708-488-8366
Roasted whole bean coffee
President: Gust Papanicholas
Estimated Sales: $5-10 Million
Number Employees: 6
Type of Packaging: Consumer, Food Service, Private Label, Bulk
Brands:
  Aroma Cuisiner's Choice
  Aroma Southern Maison
  Aroma Turkish
  Cuisiniers Choice

693 Aroma Coffee Roasters Inc
1601 Madison St
Hoboken, NJ 07030-2313
201-792-1730
Fax: 201-659-1883 www.aromacoffee.com
Coffee wholesaler
Manager: Ruth Santuccio
Estimated Sales: $1-2.5 Million
Number Employees: 20-49

694 Aroma Ridge
1831 W Oak Pkwy
Suite C
Marietta, GA 30062-2246
770-421-9600
Fax: 770-421-9116 800-528-2123
contact@aromaridge.com www.aromaridge.com
Coffee
Owner: Nawal Shadeed
Number Employees: 5-9

695 Aroma Vera
5310 Beethoven St
Los Angeles, CA 90066-7015
310-204-3392
Fax: 310-306-5873 800-669-9514
cservice@aromavera.com
Processor, importer and exporter of essential oils
President: Marcel Lavabre
CEO: Klee Irwin
Estimated Sales: $59,000
Number Employees: 1
Square Footage: 200000
Brands:
  Aroma Vera

696 Aroma-Life
16161 Ventura Boulevard
Encino, CA 91436-2522
818-905-7761
Fax: 818-905-0292 mzwan@aol.com
Almond and macadamia oils
President: Moshe Zwang
CEO: Diana Zwang
Estimated Sales: $300,000-500,000
Number Employees: 1-4
Number of Brands: 18
Number of Products: 16
Square Footage: 110000
Type of Packaging: Private Label, Bulk
Brands:
  Aroma-Life

697 Aromachem
599 Johnson Ave
Brooklyn, NY 11237
718-497-4664
Fax: 718-821-2193
Flavors, essential oils and fragrances
President: M Edwards
CEO: Leona Levine
Estimated Sales: $3 Million
Number Employees: 30
Square Footage: 100000
Type of Packaging: Bulk

698 Aromatech USA
5770 Hoffner Avenue
Suite 103
Orlando, FL 32822
407-277-5727
Fax: 407-277-5725 americas@aromatech.fr
www.aromatech.fr/en/f.usa.htm
Flavorings for beverages, candies, baking, snacks and pastries.

699 Arome Fleurs & Fruits
6600, chemin des Sept
Saint-Jean-Baptiste Day, QC J0L 2B0
Canada
450-281-0911
Fax: 450-281-0917 877-349-3282
Floral products incorporated into spreads, jellies and syrups.

700 Aromi d'Italia
5 N Calhoun St
Baltimore, MD 21223-1814
443-703-4001
Fax: 443-703-2194 877-435-2869
ashworth@ashworth.com
Gelato
Owner: Boris Ghazarian
Contact: Hannah Follis
hfollis@aromibeauty.com
Estimated Sales: $200,000
Number Employees: 5-9
Brands:
  Aromi D'Italia

701 Aromor Flavors & Fragrances
560 Sylvan Ave # 2030
Englewood Cliffs, NJ 07632-3165
201-503-1662
Fax: 201-503-1663 866-425-1600
Flavors and fragrances
Manager: Carol Feldman
cfeldman@aromor-usa.com
General Manager: Gary Romans
Number Employees: 1-4

702 Arro Corp
7440 Santa Fe Dr # A
Hodgkins, IL 60525-5076
708-639-9063
Fax: 708-352-5293 877-929-2776
Sales@arro.com www.arro.com
Corn, peanut, salad, soybean and vegetable oils.
Owner: Pat Gaughn
arrosales@aol.com
Sales Exec: Timothy Mcnicholas
Estimated Sales: $500,000-1 Million
Number Employees: 50-99
Type of Packaging: Food Service, Private Label, Bulk
Other Locations:
  Chicago IL
  Hodgkins IL

703 Arrowac Fisheries
Fisherman's Commerce Building
4039 21st Ave W, Suite 200
Seattle, WA 98199-1252
206-282-5655
Fax: 206-282-9329 info@arrowac-merco.com
www.arrowac-merco.com
Fresh and frozen seafood.
President: Frank Mercker
Vice President: Waltraut Yanagisawa
Estimated Sales: $25 Million
Number of Brands: 3
Number of Products: 15
Square Footage: 2000
Type of Packaging: Consumer, Food Service, Private Label, Bulk
Brands:
  Arrow
  Merco
  Ocean Dawn

704 Arrowhead Beef
982 Hutchins Ln.
Chipley, FL 32428
850-270-8804
info@arrowheadbeef.com
arrowheadbeef.com
Grass-fed and Waygu beef.
Co-Owner: George Fisher
Co-Owner: Tony DeBlauw
Year Founded: 2010
Type of Packaging: Private Label

705 Arrowhead Mills
4600 Sleepytime Dr.
Boulder, CO 80301
866-595-8917
Fax: 806-364-8242 800-434-4246
www.arrowheadmills.com
Pasta

Food Manufacturers / A-Z

President/CEO: Irwin Simon
Operations: Gary Schultz
Purchasing: Dale Hollingswoth
Number Employees: 50-99
Parent Co: Hain Food Group

706 Arrowood Winery
14347 Hwy 12
PO Box 1240
Glen Ellen, CA 95442-9445
707-935-2600
Fax: 707-938-5947 800-938-5170
www.arrowoodvineyards.com
Wines.
Founder: Richard Arrowood
Founder: Alis Arrowood
Winemaker: Kristina Werner
Manager: Lisa Evich
lisa.evich@arrowoodwinery.com
Estimated Sales: $10-20 Million
Number Employees: 20-49
Number of Brands: 2
Type of Packaging: Private Label
Brands:
  Arrowood
  Grand Archer

707 Art CoCo Chocolate Company
2248 Gary Lane
Geneva, IL 60134
630-232-2500
Fax: 630-232-2528 877-232-9901
info@artcoco.com www.artcoco.com
Chocolates
President: Kenneth Wolf
VP: Gail Zucker
National Retail Sales Director: Michelle Bonnick
Production Manager: Charles Martinez
Estimated Sales: $5-9.9 Million
Number Employees: 5-9
Parent Co: Silvestri Sweets, Inc.
Type of Packaging: Private Label
Brands:
  Art Coco
  Art Fidos Cookies
  Art Topo

708 Art's Mexican Products
615 Kansas Ave
Kansas City, KS 66105-1311
913-371-2163
Fax: 913-371-2052
www.artsmexicanfoodproducts.com
Mexican food specialties including corn chips, tortilla chips and sauces.
Owner: Angela Gutierrez
Owner: Rachael Gutierrez
Manager: Rachael Kelly
Estimated Sales: $10-20 Million
Number Employees: 10-19
Number of Brands: 1
Brands:
  Art's Mexican Products

709 Art's Tamales
574-576 Hickory Point Rd
Metamora, IL 61548
309-367-2850
Beef tamales and BBQ
President: David Chinuge
CEO: Zack Fosdyck
Public Relations: Robin Fosdyck
Production Manager: Bill Sanders
Estimated Sales: $300,000-500,000
Number Employees: 5
Square Footage: 20000
Type of Packaging: Consumer, Food Service, Private Label
Brands:
  Art's Tamales
  Party Time

710 Arteasans Beverages LLC
801 New 167th St
Suite 312
North Miami Beach, FL 33162-3729
305-363-5410
www.arteasan.com
Cold tea

711 Artek USA
3915 Freshwind Circle
Westlake Village, CA 91361
818-874-0885
Fax: 818-874-0802 866-278-3501
sales@artekusa.com www.artekusa.com
President: Larry Jones
Estimated Sales: $.5-1 million
Number Employees: 5

712 Artesa Vineyards & Winery
1345 Henry Rd
Napa, CA 94559-9705
707-224-1668
Fax: 707-224-1672 Info@artesawinery.com
www.artesawinery.com
Wines
President: Mark Beringer
djohnson@nspit.nashville.ihs.gov
CFO: Tim O'Leary
Winemaker: Ana Diogo-Draper
VP Production: Dave Dobson
Estimated Sales: $20-50 Million
Number Employees: 50-99
Type of Packaging: Private Label

713 Artesian Honey Producers
PO Box 6
100 West 1st. Ave
Artesian, SD 57314
605-527-2423
Honey, candy, and confectionary
Owner: John Zen
Estimated Sales: $1-2.5 Million
Number Employees: 5-9
Type of Packaging: Bulk

714 Artisan Confections
100 Crystal A Dr
Hershey, PA 17033-9524
717-534-4200
Fax: 415-626-7991 866-237-0152
Chocolate truffles and chocolate novelties
President: Charles Huggins
CEO: Joseph Scmidt
CFO: Jeff Smith
VP Marketing: Ellen Meuse
Production Manager: Richard Chaeniot
Estimated Sales: $5-10 Million
Number Employees: 50-99
Brands:
  Chocolate Slicks

715 Artisan Kettle
833-605-6929
info@artisankettle.com artisankettle.com
Chocolate chips and bars
Number of Brands: 1
Number of Products: 2
Brands:
  ARTISAN KETTLE

716 Artist Coffee
51 Harvey Road
Unit D
Londonderry, NH 03053-7414
603-434-9385
Fax: 603-216-8029 866-440-4511
Producer of gourmet coffee, tea and candy for promotional trade. Specializing in Custom Labeling with very special products.
President: Tom Rushton
Marketing Director: Dan Sewell
Estimated Sales: $3-5 Million
Number Employees: 1-4
Type of Packaging: Consumer, Private Label
Other Locations:
  Lambent Technologies
  Gurnee IL
Brands:
  Cirashine
  Erucical
  Hodag
  Lamchem
  Lumisolve
  Lumisorb
  Lumulse
  Oleocal
  Polycal

717 Arturo's Spinella's Bakery
750 North Main Street
Waterbury, CT 06705
203-754-3056
Cookies

President: Fred Napolitano
Estimated Sales: $1-2.5 Million appx.
Number Employees: 5-9

718 Artuso Pastry
670 E 187th St
Bronx, NY 10458
718-367-2515
Fax: 718-367-2553 sales@artusopastry.com
artusopastry.com
Italian pastry ingredients, fresh and frozen
CEO: Anthony Artuso
Sales Exec: Natalie Corridori
Estimated Sales: $3 Million
Number Employees: 20-49
Brands:
  Artuso

719 Arway Confections Inc
3425 N Kimball Ave
Chicago, IL 60618-5505
773-267-5770
Fax: 773-267-0610 800-695-0612
craigleva@arwayconfections.com
www.arwayconfections.com
Candy including brittles, butter toffee, panned and enrobed products, sponge candy and glazed nuts
President: James Resnick
jamesresnick@arwayconfections.com
President/Marketing Manager: Craig Leva
General Manager/Purchasing: Rick Johnson
Estimated Sales: $5-10 Million
Number Employees: 20-49
Square Footage: 320000
Type of Packaging: Bulk

720 Arylessence Inc
1091 Lake Dr
Marietta, GA 30066-1073
770-924-3775
Fax: 770-928-5671 800-553-2440
geoffG@arylessence.com www.arylessence.com
Fragrance and flavors
President & CEO: Steve Tanner
ctanner@arylessence.com
Executive Vice President: Cynthia Reichard
Estimated Sales: $23 Million
Number Employees: 50-99
Type of Packaging: Private Label

721 Aryzta
6080 Center Dr
Suite 900
Los Angeles, CA 90045
855-427-9982
www.aryztaamericas.com
Baked and unbaked desserts and breakfast pastries.
Chairman: Gary McGann
CEO: Kevin Toland
Year Founded: 1897
Estimated Sales: $300 Million
Number Employees: 10,000+
Type of Packaging: Consumer, Food Service, Private Label
Other Locations:
  Gourmet Baker
  Burnaby BC
  Gourmet Baker
  Winnipeg MT
Brands:
  Fantasia
  Gourmet Baker

722 Asael Farr & Sons Co
2575 S 300 W
Salt Lake City, UT 84115-2908
801-484-8724
Fax: 801-484-8768 877-553-2777
info@farrsicecream.com www.farrsicecream.com
Ice creams, yogurts, sorbets, ice cream and yogurt mixes, specialty foods, etc
President: Dexter Farr
CEO: Michael Farr
Contact: Blair Boelter
blair.boelter@farrsicecream.com
Estimated Sales: $.5-1 million
Number Employees: 5-9
Brands:
  Farr
  Russell's

Food Manufacturers / A-Z

723 Asarasi
23 Turner Rd #61
Danbury, CT 06810
info@asarasiwater.com
asarasi.com
Bottled water extracted from maple trees
CEO: Adam Lazar

724 Aseltine Cider Company
533 Lamoreaux Dr NW
Comstock Park, MI 49321
616-784-6615
Fax: 616-784-7676
Bottled apple products, manufacturing food preparations
Owner: John Klamt
Secretary: Ronald Klamt
General Manager: John Klamt
Estimated Sales: $2.5-5 Million
Number Employees: 10-19

725 Asher's Chocolates
1555 Gehman Road
Kulpsville, PA 19443
215-721-3276
Fax: 215-721-3265 855-827-4377
customers@ashers.com www.ashers.com
Chocolate and confections, including chocolate-covered pretzels potato chips, and graham crackers. The company also produces boxed assortments (including truffles, chews, nuts, cordials, and creams) and gift baskets, fudgepecan-caramel patties, almond bark, and sugar-free and low-carb assortments.
President/CEO: David Asher
CFO: Charles Clark
VP Sales/Marketing: Jeff Asher
Contact: Lisa Wylie
lwylie@ashers.com
VP Operations: Steve Marcanello
Estimated Sales: A
Number Employees: 120

726 Ashland Milling
PO Box 1775
14471 Washington Highway
Ashland, VA 23005
804-798-8329
Fax: 804-798-9357 888-897-3336
sales@byrdmill.com www.byrdmill.com
Flour, cornmeal and mixes
President: Todd Attkisson
General Manager: Lynwood Atkinson
attkisson@byrdmill.com
Estimated Sales: $10-20 Million
Number Employees: 20-49
Brands:
  Blue Barn
  Diamond
  Eukanuba
  Hyland
  Kalmbach
  Purina

727 Ashland Plantation Gourmet
133 Highway 1177
Bunkie, LA 71322-9773
318-346-6600
Fax: 318-346-4666
Food Producers
President: Kim White
Estimated Sales: Less than $500,000
Number Employees: 1-4

728 Ashland Sausage Co
280 S Westgate Dr
Carol Stream, IL 60188-2243
630-690-2600
Fax: 630-690-2612 contact@ashlandsausage.com
www.ashlandsausage.com
Sausage
President: Stanley Podgorski
ashlandsausage@yahoo.com
Purchasing: Stanley Podgorski
Estimated Sales: $1-2.5 Million
Number Employees: 10-19
Type of Packaging: Consumer, Food Service
Brands:
  Ashland

729 Ashland Vineyards & Winery
2775 E Main St
Ashland, OR 97520-9781
541-488-0088
Fax: 541-488-5857 www.winenet.com
Wines
Owner: Phil Kodak
wines@winenet.com
Owner/CEO: Kathleen Kodak
Estimated Sales: Less Than $500,000
Number Employees: 1-4
Brands:
  Ashland

730 Ashley Food Co Inc
443 North Rd
Sudbury, MA 01776-1017
978-579-8988
Fax: 978-579-8989 800-617-2823
maddog@ashleyfood.com www.ashleyfoodco.com
Sauces
President: David Ashley
maddog@ashleyfood.com
Estimated Sales: $1-2.5 Million
Number Employees: 1-4
Brands:
  Joe Perry's
  Mad Cat
  Mad Dog Hot Sauce
  Weir's

731 Ashman Manufacturing & Distributing Company
P.O.Box 1068
1120 Jensen Drive
Virginia Beach, VA 23451-0068
757-428-6734
Fax: 757-437-0398 800-641-9924
admin@ashmanco.com www.ashmanco.com
A wide variety of gourmet sauces, salsas, hot sauces, dry blends, marinades, dessert sauces and drink mixes
President, Co-Founder: Tim Ashman
Co-Founder: Katharine Ashman
Sales Manager: Joel Lutchin
Estimated Sales: $5-10 million
Number Employees: 10-19
Type of Packaging: Consumer, Private Label

732 Asiago PDO & Speck AltoAdige PGI
26 West 23rd Street
6th Floor
New York, NY 10010
646-624-2885
Fax: 646-624-2893
Cheese, cured meats i.e. prosciutto/bacon.
Marketing: Flavio Innocenzi

733 Asiamerica Ingredients
245 Old Hood Rd #3
Westwood, NJ 07675-3174
201-497-5993
Fax: 201-497-5994 201-497-5531
info@asiamericaingredients.com
www.asiamericaingredients.com
Processor, importer, exporter and distributor of bulk vitamins, amino acids, nutraceuticals, aromatic chemicals, food additives, herbs, mineral nutrients and pharmaceuticals.
President/Owner: Mark Zhang
CFO: Lillian Yang
Quality Control: Michelle Naomi
Sales: Cari Pandero
Contact: Elizabeth Gysbers
egysbers@asiamericaingredients.com
Purchasing: Michelle N. Riley
Estimated Sales: $5-10 Million
Number Employees: 10
Type of Packaging: Bulk

734 Asian Foods Inc
1300 L'Orient St
St Paul, MN 55117
651-558-2400
www.asianfoods.com
Ethnic food products
CEO: Kevin Hourican
Vice President, Sales: Jim Hamel
Estimated Sales: $100+ Million
Number Employees: 100-249
Number of Brands: 3
Square Footage: 68000
Parent Co: SYSCO
Type of Packaging: Food Service, Private Label
Other Locations:
  Kansas City MO
  Hampshire IL

Brands:
  Ji Hao
  Shang Pin

735 Askinosie Chocolate
514 E Commercial St
Springfield, MO 65803-2946
417-862-9900
Fax: 417-862-9904 lawren@askinosie.com
www.askinosie.com
Chocolate/cocoa products
Owner: Shawn Askinosie
mshawn@askinosie.com
Operations Manager: Jill Tilman
Number Employees: 10-19

736 Aspen Mulling Company Inc.
C/O World Pantry Company
1192 Illinois Street
San Francisco, CA 94107
800-622-7736
Fax: 970-925-5408 866-972-6879
aspenspices@worldpantry.com
www.aspenspices.com
Manufacturer and exporter of mulling spices
Manager: Leo Varade
Marketing: David Kallen
Estimated Sales: Under $5 Million
Number Employees: 5-9
Type of Packaging: Consumer, Food Service

737 Aspire
500 N Michigan Ave.
Suite 600
Chicago, OH 60611
customerservice@aspiredrinks.com
aspiredrinks.com
Energy drinks with zero sugar and zero calories.
CEO: Chris Wadlington
Co-Founder & Int'l. Sales Director: Neil Blewitt
Co-Founder & COO: Darren Linnell
Year Founded: 2010
Number Employees: 11-50
Type of Packaging: Private Label

738 Assets Grille & Southwest Brewing Company
6910 Montgomery Boulevard NE
Albuquerque, NM 87109-1406
505-889-6400
Fax: 505-889-0264
Brewer of beer, ale and stout
Owner: Mark Devesti
Estimated Sales: $2.5-5 Million
Number Employees: 50-99
Parent Co: Assets Brewing Company
Type of Packaging: Consumer, Food Service, Bulk

739 Associated Fruit Company
3721 Colver Rd
Phoenix, OR 97535-9705
541-535-1787
Fax: 541-535-6936
Manufacturer and exporter of fresh fruit including plums and pears
President: David Lowry
Purchasing: Scott Martinez
delrae.erickson@exchangebank.com
Estimated Sales: $1-2.5 Million
Number Employees: 6
Type of Packaging: Bulk

740 Associated Milk Producers Inc.
315 N. Broadway St.
PO Box 455
New Ulm, MN 56073
507-354-8295
800-533-3580
www.ampi.com
Cheese, butter and powdered milk products.
Co-President/Co-CEO: Donn DeVelder
Co-President/Co-CEO: Sheryl Meshke
Chairman: Steve Schlangen
schlangens@ampi.com
Estimated Sales: $1.7 Billion
Number Employees: 1000-4999
Type of Packaging: Consumer, Food Service, Private Label

Food Manufacturers / A-Z

741 (HQ)Associated Potato Growers
2001 N 6th St
Grand Forks, ND 58203-1584
701-775-4614
Fax: 701-746-5767 800-437-4685
www.apgspud.com
Potatoes and potato products
CEO: Bryan Miller
Director Sales: Greg Holtman
Estimated Sales: $26 Million
Number Employees: 100-249
Other Locations:
  Associated Potato Growers
  Grafton ND
  Associated Potato Growers
  Drayton ND
Brands:
  Apg
  Dole
  Holsom
  Natives Pride
  Nodark
  Potato Mity Red

742 Asti Holdings Ltd
320 Stewardson Way
Unit 2-3
New Westminster, BC V3M 6C3
Canada
604-523-6866
Fax: 604-523-6880 info@goldenbonbon.com
www.goldenbonbon.com
Nougat candy and caramels
President: Ricardo Mazzucco
Estimated Sales: $1.7 Million
Number Employees: 100-500

743 Astor Chocolate Corp
651 New Hampshire Ave
Lakewood, NJ 08701-5452
732-901-1001
Fax: 732-901-1003 info@astorchocolate.com
www.astorchocolate.com
Manufacturer, importer and exporter of chocolate including fund raising, foiled novelties, bars, truffles, mints, shells and boxed.
President: Teri Aboud
teri.aboud@gmail.com
President: David Grunhut
CFO: Nat Vernaci
Sales Director: Howard Cubberly
Human Resource Executive: Arie Lax
Purchasing Manager: Karen Garrison
Estimated Sales: $25,000
Number Employees: 50-99
Square Footage: 66162
Type of Packaging: Consumer, Food Service, Private Label, Bulk
Brands:
  After Dark
  Le Belge Chocolatier
  Party Favors By Astor
  Pastry Essentials
  Square One

744 Astral Extracts
50 Eileen Way
Unit 6
Syosset, NY 11791-5313
516-496-2505
Fax: 516-496-4248 info@astralextracts.com
www.astralextracts.com
Processor, wholesaler, distributor, importer and exporter of fruit juice concentrates, essential oils and citrus products
President: Cynthia Astrack
info@astralextracts.com
General Manager: Joan Pace
Estimated Sales: $5-10 Million
Number Employees: 5-9
Square Footage: 30000
Type of Packaging: Food Service, Private Label, Bulk

745 Astro Dairy Products
405 The West Mall
10th Floor
Toronto, ON M9C 5S1
Canada
416-622-2511
Fax: 416-622-4180 www.astro.ca
Dairy products including yogurt, cottage cheese, sour cream and cream cheese
President: James Biltekoff
Number Employees: 200
Parent Co: Parmalat Canada
Type of Packaging: Consumer, Food Service, Private Label, Bulk
Brands:
  Astro
  Biobest

746 At Last Naturals Inc
401 Columbus Ave # 2
Valhalla, NY 10595-1375
914-747-3599
Fax: 914-747-3791 800-527-8123
www.alast.com
Manufacturer and exporter of laxative tea and natural herbal health products.
Vice President: Fred Rosen
fred@alast.com
Estimated Sales: $1-3 Million
Number Employees: 1-4
Square Footage: 148000
Type of Packaging: Consumer
Brands:
  Dhea
  Innerclean
  Sul-Ray
  Valerian

747 Ateeco Inc
600 E Centre St
PO Box 606
Shenandoah, PA 17976-1825
570-462-2745
Fax: 570-462-3299 800-743-7649
consumercontact@pierogies.com
www.pierogies.com
Frozen pierogies.
President: Thomas Twardzik
tcoyle@pierogies.com
Director, Public Relations: Wayne Holben
Director, Operations: Ray Stasulli
Estimated Sales: $20-50 Million
Number Employees: 100-249
Number of Brands: 1
Square Footage: 350
Type of Packaging: Private Label
Brands:
  Mrs. T's Pierogies

748 Athena Oil Inc
3082 36th St
Astoria, NY 11103-4705
718-956-8893
Fax: 718-956-5813 info@athenaoil.com
www.athenaoil.com
Wholesale oils vegetable and olive
President/Owner: Moschos Scoullis
mscoullis@gmail.com
Estimated Sales: $1.2 Million
Number Employees: 10-19

749 Athens Baking Company
4589 W Jacquelyn Ave
Fresno, CA 93722-6442
559-485-3024
Fax: 559-485-0671 800-775-2867
sales@athensbaking.com www.athensbaking.com
Baked beans, rolls, and buns
Owner: Dave Smart
Estimated Sales: $5-10 Million
Type of Packaging: Consumer, Food Service, Private Label
Brands:
  Athens

750 Athens Foods Inc
13600 Snow Rd
Brookpark, OH 44142-2546
216-676-8500
Fax: 216-676-0609 843-916-2000
www.athensfoods.com
Fillo dough, fillo shells and other fillo products.
CEO: Scott Sumser
CFO: Bob Tansing
R&D Manager: Jean Myers
VP of Sales/Marketing: Bill Buckingham
VP of Operations: Jeff Swint
Estimated Sales: $29.5 Million
Number Employees: 100-249
Number of Brands: 2
Number of Products: 200
Square Footage: 120000
Type of Packaging: Consumer, Food Service, Private Label, Bulk
Brands:
  Apollo®
  Athens®

751 Athletic Brewing Co.
350 Long Beach Rd
Stratford, CT 06615
203-273-0422
info@athleticbrewing.com
www.athleticbrewing.com
Non-alcoholic craft beer
Founder: Bill Shufelt
Year Founded: 2017

752 Atka Pride Seafoods Inc
302 Gold St
Suite 202
Juneau, AK 99801-1127
907-586-0161
Fax: 907-586-0165 888-927-4232
info@apicda.com www.apicda.com
Supplier of seafood
Chief Executive Officer: Larry Cotter
Chief Financial Officer: Robert Smith
Chief Operating Officer: John Sevier
Number Employees: 1-4
Parent Co: Aleutian Pribilof Island Community Development Association

753 Atkins Elegant Desserts
11852 Allisonville Rd
Fishers, IN 46038-2312
317-570-1850
Fax: 317-773-3766 800-887-8808
Frozen cheesecakes, pies, cakes and pastries.
Manager: Debbie Llewellyn
CEO: Tom Atkins Jr
CFO: Tom Atkins
R&D: Darrell Bell
Quality Control: John Parent
Canadian National Manager: Wayne Barefoot
VP Sales & Marketing: Bob Barry
National Accounts Manager: Lisa Atkins Miller
Operations: Bill Beglin
Production: Jeff Fascko
Plant Manager: Terry Graves
Purchasing: Denise Miller
Estimated Sales: $12-13 Million
Number Employees: 50-99
Square Footage: 70000
Type of Packaging: Consumer, Food Service, Private Label
Brands:
  Atkins

754 Atkins Ginseng Farms
RR 1
PO Box 1125
Waterford, ON N0E 1Y0
Canada
519-443-7236
Fax: 519-443-4565 800-265-0239
Manufacturer, importer and exporter of ginseng products including capsules, also grower of american ginseng
Owner/President: Micheal Atkins
Estimated Sales: $20-50 Million
Number Employees: 5-9
Square Footage: 6000
Type of Packaging: Consumer, Private Label, Bulk
Brands:
  Atkins
  Gin Ultimate
  Golden Dreams
  Golden Grower
  Northern Serenitea
  Northern Spirit

755 Atkins Nutritionals Inc.
1050 17th St
Suite 1000
Denver, CO 80265-2078
303-633-2840
800-628-5467
www.atkins.com
Atkins diet food, candy and nutritional bars.
President & CEO: Joseph Scalzo
Estimated Sales: $5-10 Million
Number Employees: 1-4
Type of Packaging: Consumer, Food Service

Food Manufacturers / A-Z

756 Atkinson Candy Co
1608 W Frank Ave
Lufkin, TX 75904-3109
936-639-2333
Fax: 936-639-2337 contact@atkinsoncandy.com
Manufacturer of candies.
President: Eric Atkinson
eatkinson@atkinsoncandy.com
COO: Doug Hanks
Estimated Sales: $21.8 Million
Number Employees: 100-249
Square Footage: 100000
Type of Packaging: Consumer, Food Service
Brands:
    Mint Twists
    Peanut Butter Bars
    Chick-O-Stick
    Long Boys
    Gemstone Gourmet Candies
    Sophie Mae
    Slo Poke
    Black Cow

757 Atkinson Milling Co.
95 Atkinson Mill Rd.
Intersection Hwy. 42 & 39
Selma, NC 27576
919-965-3547
Fax: 919-202-0523 800-948-5707
information@atkinsonmilling.com
www.atkinsonmilling.com
Flour and other grain mill products including corn meal, hushpuppy mixes, breaders, biscuit mixes, cornbread sticks, and chicken dumplings.
President: Glen Wheeler
Year Founded: 1757
Estimated Sales: $8.3 Million
Number Employees: 50-99
Type of Packaging: Consumer, Food Service, Private Label, Bulk
Brands:
    Atkinson's
    Boddie
    Cattail
    Ellis Davis

758 Atlanta Bread Co.
1200 Wilson Way SE
Suite 100
Smyrna, GA 30082-7212
770-432-0933
Fax: 770-444-1991 800-398-3728
www.atlantabread.com
Bread, pastries, bagels, rolls, muffins, sandwiches, salads and desserts. Also featuring expanded coffee selection
President & CEO: Jerry Couvaras
COO: Basil Couvaras
Estimated Sales: $1-2.5 Million
Number Employees: 100-249
Type of Packaging: Consumer, Food Service
Brands:
    Atlanta Bread

759 Atlanta Burning Bush
3781 Happy Valley Cir
Newnan, GA 30263
770-253-4443
Fax: 770-253-9941 800-665-5511
Hot sauces, BBQ sauce. Supplier of food related products
Owner: Marilyn Witt
Estimated Sales: $500,000-$1,000,000
Number Employees: 1-4
Type of Packaging: Consumer, Bulk
Brands:
    Atlanta Burning

760 Atlanta Coffee & Tea Co
770-981-6774
Fax: 770-981-6697 800-426-4781
sales@atlantacoffeeandtea.com
shop.atlantacoffeeandtea.com/contact-us
Processor and importer of coffee and tea; coffee roaster and tea packer, private label packaging available
VP: Harris Carver
Estimated Sales: Less Than $500,000
Number Employees: 1-4
Number of Products: 16
Type of Packaging: Food Service, Private Label

761 Atlanta Coffee Roasters
2205 Lavista Rd NE
Atlanta, GA 30329-3917
404-636-1038
Fax: 404-255-1189 800-252-8211
info@atlantacoffeeroasters.com
www.atlantacoffeeroasters.com
Coffee
Owner: William Letbetter
bill@atlantacoffeeroasters.com
CFO: Stephen Burress
Estimated Sales: $910,000
Number Employees: 5-9
Brands:
    Brazil Celebes
    Celebes
    Columbian
    Costa Rica
    Jamaica Bluemountain
    Laminita

762 Atlanta Fish Market
265 Pharr Rd NE
Atlanta, GA 30305-2243
404-262-3165
Fax: 404-240-6665 www.buckheadrestaurants.com
Seafood
Manager: Jason Zaleski
bcompton@buckheadrestaurants.com
Site Manager: Brandon Compton
bcompton@buckheadrestaurants.com
Estimated Sales: $5-10 Million
Number Employees: 100-249

763 Atlantic Aqua Farms
918 Brush Wharf Rd
Orwell Cove, PE C0A 2E0
Canada
902-651-2563
Fax: 902-651-2513 terry@canadiancove.pe.ca
www.canadiancove.com
Manufacturer and exporter of fresh mussels, oysters and clams-hardshell
GM: Brian Fortune
Number Employees: 50
Type of Packaging: Consumer, Food Service, Private Label, Bulk

764 Atlantic Blueberry
7201 Weymouth Rd # A
Hammonton, NJ 08037-3414
609-561-8600
Fax: 609-561-5033 staff@atlanticblueberry.com
www.atlanticblueberry.com
Processor and exporter of fresh and frozen blueberries
President/CEO: Arthur Galletta
Harvest Crew Supervisor: Paul Galletta
Food Safety, Security, and Defense, QC: John Galletta
Sales: Art Galletta
General Inquiries, Press Inquiries: Denny Doyle
Operations: Robert Galletta
Year Founded: 1935
Estimated Sales: $5-10 Million
Number Employees: 10-19
Number of Brands: 1
Number of Products: 1
Square Footage: 320000
Type of Packaging: Private Label
Brands:
    Atlantic Blueberry

765 (HQ)Atlantic Capes Fisheries
985 Ocean Dr
Cape May, NJ 08204-1855
609-884-3000
Fax: 609-884-3261 info@atlanticcapes.com
www.atlanticcapes.com
Fresh and frozen scallops, fish, clams, mackerel, squid and monkfish; importer of scallops; exporter of fresh and frozen scallops, squid, butterfish and mackerel
President: Daniel Cohen
dcohen@atlanticcapesfisheries.com
VP, Sales/Marketing: Jeff Bolton
VP, Operations: David Shaw
Estimated Sales: $15 Million
Number Employees: 20-49
Square Footage: 40000
Other Locations:
    ACF Production Facility
    Point Pleasant Beach NJ
    ACF Sales/Marketing Office
    New Bedford MA
Brands:
    Atlantic Capes
    Cape May Salt

766 Atlantic Chemicals Trading
116 N Maryland Ave # 210
Glendale, CA 91206-4270
818-246-0077
Fax: 617-292-0073 usa@act.de
www.act.de
Manufacturer and distributor of flavors such as peppermint & menthol, sweeteners, acidifiers and preservatives. Food additives and preservatives
General Manager: Jaklin Minasian
Number Employees: 5-9

767 Atlantic Fish Specialties
17 Walker Drive
Charlottetown, PE C1A 8S5
Canada
902-894-7005
Fax: 902-566-3546 macneill@cookeaqua.com
www.cookeaqua.com
Manufacturer and exporter of smoked salmon, mackerel and trout
President: Glenn Cooke
General Manager: Doug Galen
Number Employees: 40
Type of Packaging: Consumer, Food Service, Private Label, Bulk

768 Atlantic Foods
2560 US Highway 22
Scotch Plains, NJ 07076
908-889-8182
Fax: 909-322-9993
Seafood
President: Derek Ivey
Estimated Sales: $50-100 Million
Number Employees: 100-200
Type of Packaging: Consumer, Food Service, Private Label, Bulk

769 Atlantic Laboratories Inc
41 Cross St
Waldoboro, ME 04572-5634
207-832-5376
Fax: 207-832-6905 888-662-5357
nak@noamkelp.com www.noamkelp.com
Harvests and processes kelp.
President: Robert Morse, Jr.
Contact: Edward Ernste
eernste@noamkelp.com
Number Employees: 5-9
Type of Packaging: Consumer, Bulk

770 Atlantic Meat Company
2600 Louisville Rd
Savannah, GA 31415
912-964-8511
Fax: 912-964-6831
Fresh and frozen ground beef, including hamburger patties
President/CEO: Lee Javetz
Purchasing Agent: Marc Javetz
Estimated Sales: $20-50 Million
Number Employees: 50
Square Footage: 30000
Type of Packaging: Consumer, Food Service, Private Label, Bulk
Brands:
    Atlantic Meat
    Circle a Brands Beef Patties
    Circlea Beef Patties

771 Atlantic Mussel Growers Corporation
PO Box 70
Pointe Pleasant Road
Murray Harbour, PE C0A 1R0
Canada
902-962-3089
Fax: 902-962-3741 800-838-3106
Manufacturer and exporter of fresh mussels
Executive Manager: John Sullivan
Business Manager: Rollie McInnis
Operations Manager: Marjorie Henderson
Number Employees: 25
Type of Packaging: Consumer, Private Label, Bulk

Food Manufacturers / A-Z

772 Atlantic Natural Foods
110 Industry Ct
Nashville, NC 27856
888-491-0524
www.atlanticnaturalfoods.com
Vegetarian foods and beverages
Number of Brands: 3
Square Footage: 53000
Brands:
   LOMA LINDA
   KAFFREE ROMA
   NEAT

773 Atlantic Pork & Provisions
14707 94th Ave
Jamaica, NY 11435-4513
718-272-9550
Fax: 718-272-9630 800-245-3536
Fresh hams; also, bologna and liverwurst loaves
President/Ceo: Jack Antinori
Number Employees: 50
Type of Packaging: Consumer
Brands:
   Atlantic
   Eidelweiss
   Laurel Hill
   Lifeline

774 Atlantic Salmon of Maine
57 Little River Dr
Belfast, ME 4915
207-338-9028
Fax: 207-338-6288 800-508-7861
www.cookeaqua.com
Fresh salmon
GM: David Peterson
CFO: John Thibodeau
Sales Manager: Mary Warner
Contact: Peter Christensen
pchristensen@majesticsalmon.com
Receptionist: Becky Darres
Number Employees: 200
Type of Packaging: Food Service
Other Locations:
   Atlantic Salmon of Maine
   Swan Island ME

775 Atlantic Sea Pride
16 Fish Pier
Boston, MA 02210-2054
617-269-7700
Fax: 617-269-7766
Processor and wholesaler/distributor of fresh fish and fillets; serving the food service market
President: Anthony Correnti
VP: Frank Mazza
Estimated Sales: $4.30 Million
Number Employees: 20
Type of Packaging: Consumer, Food Service, Bulk

776 Atlantic Seacove Inc
20 Newmarket Sq
Boston, MA 02118-2601
617-442-6206
Fax: 617-482-7733
Wholesale dealers in fresh and frozen fish
President/CEO: John Wojitasinski
Owner: Andrew Bunten
Treasurer: Mitchell Wojitasinski
Estimated Sales: $3.3 Million
Number Employees: 10-19

777 Atlantic Seafood Direct
12 A Portland Fish Pier
PO Box 682
Portland, ME 04104
800-774-6025
Seafood fresh and frozen
President: Jerry Knecht
VP/General Manager: Mike Norton

778 Atlantic Seasonings
417 E Vernon Ave
Kinston, NC 28501-4456
252-522-1515
Fax: 252-522-2485 800-433-5261
Salad dressing and drink mixes, gravies, seasoning and flour blends and sauces; custom blending available
President: Jay Neuhoff
VP Marketing: Ken Neuhoff
Estimated Sales: $2.5-5 Million
Number Employees: 10-19
Square Footage: 72000
Type of Packaging: Food Service, Private Label, Bulk
Brands:
   Atlantic Seasonings

779 Atlantic Veal & Lamb Inc
275 Morgan Ave
Brooklyn, NY 11211
800-222-8325
info@atlanticveal.com www.atlanticveal.com
Processor and exporter of individually vacuumed frozen veal including portion controlled, hand sliced, leg cutlets, roasts and cubed.
Chief Executive Officer: Phillip Peerless
ppeerless@atlanticveal.com
Chairman: Marty Weiner
CFO: Joe Saccardi
VP: Martin Weiner
Lamb Sales Director: Dan Salmon
National Sales Director: John Ricci
Customer Service Manager: Mario Vigorito
Chief Operating Officer: Shawn Peerless
Estimated Sales: $20-50 Million
Number Employees: 100-249
Type of Packaging: Consumer, Food Service
Brands:
   Farm Fed Veal
   Plume De Veau
   The Epicurean

780 Atlantis Pak USA Inc
75 Valencia Ave # 701
Coral Gables, FL 33134-6132
305-403-2603
Fax: 786-249-0454
customerservice@atlantis-pak.com
www.atlantis-pak.com
Meat Packing, manufacturer of acid free packing paper, and recycled paper for meat.
Principle: Vladimir Zhamgotsev
zhamgotsev@atlantis-pak.com
Number Employees: 1-4
Parent Co: Atlantis Pak

781 Atlas Peak Vineyards
3700 Sada Canyon Road
Napa, CA 94558
866-522-9463
Fax: 707-226-2306 707-252-7971
wineclub@atlaspeak.com www.vineyards.com
Red and white wines
Owner: Marchese Piero-Antinori
CFO: Chris Stenzel
Contact: Carlos Ladeland
carlos.ladeland@atlaspeakvineyards.com
VP Operations: Darren Procsal
VP Production: Tony Fernandez
Estimated Sales: $5-10 Million
Number Employees: 20-49
Type of Packaging: Consumer, Food Service
Brands:
   Atlas Peak
   Consenso

782 Atoka Cranberries, Inc.
3025 Route 218
Manseau, Quebec, QC G0X 1V0
Canada
819-356-2001
Fax: 819-356-2111 infoatoka@atoka.qc.ca
Grower and processor of fresh and dried cranberries, and cranberry juice concentrate for industrial applications. Founded in 1984.
President: Mark Bieler

783 (HQ)Atrium Biotech
1405 Boul
Quebec, QC G1P 4P5
Canada
418-652-1116
Fax: 866-628-6661
Processor, importer and exporter of shark cartilage, nutritional supplements and powders. Developers and marketing of value added ingredients
President: Richard Bordeleau
CEO: Luc Dupont
Vice President/CFO: Jocelyn Harvey
Development: Serge Yelle
Sales: Johan Aerts
Purchasing: Rene Augstburger
Estimated Sales: $1.5 Million
Number Employees: 20
Number of Brands: 3
Number of Products: 20
Square Footage: 400000
Brands:
   2-Mix
   Biomega
   Cartcelt
   Cartilade
   Dermanex
   Genista
   Natcelt
   Pepogest
   Phyto-Est
   Prostacare
   Prostavite

784 Attala Development Corporation
101 North Natchez Street
Kosciusko, MS 39090
662-289-2981
Fax: 662-289-3288 info@kadcorp.org
www.kosciusko.ms/development
Corn flour meal and blended wheat flour
President/CEO: Steve Zea
VP Economic Development: Greg Cooper
VP Community Development: Tonya Threet
Purchasing: Joe Cain
Estimated Sales: $345
Number Employees: 4
Type of Packaging: Consumer, Private Label
Brands:
   Magnolia

785 Atwater Block Brewing Company
237 Joseph Campau St
Detroit, MI 48207
313-877-9205
Fax: 313-877-9241 atwater@atwaterbeer.com
www.atwaterbeer.com
German-style lager, ale and beer; importer of malt and hops
President: Mark Rieth
Contact: Chelsea Iadipaolo
chelsea@atwaterbeer.com
Estimated Sales: $.5-1 million
Number Employees: 10-19
Square Footage: 80000
Type of Packaging: Consumer, Food Service, Private Label
Brands:
   Atwater
   Stoney

786 Atwater Foods
10182 Roosevelt Hwy
Route 18
Lyndonville Orleans, NY 14098-9785
585-765-2639
Fax: 585-765-9443 www.shorelinefruit.com
Manufacturer, exporter and wholesaler of many kinds of dried fruit, including apples, cherries, cranberries, blueberries and strawberries. Star-K Kosher. Our customer service support is responsive to timelines and responsible for keeping everything on track
Manager: Randy Atwater
Quality Control: Chris Fraser
Sales/Marketing: Jim Palmer
Contact: Fred Freeman
fred@atwaterfoods.com
Plant Manager: Steve Mohr
Purchasing Manager: Pat Glidden
Estimated Sales: 15-20 Million
Number Employees: 50-99
Number of Products: 50+
Square Footage: 180000
Type of Packaging: Private Label, Bulk
Brands:
   Atwater
   Atwater Dried Fruits
   Shoreline Fruit

787 Atwood Cheese Company
Rural Route 1
7412 Highway 235
Atwood, ON N0G 1B0
Canada
519-356-2271
Fax: 519-356-2170
Largest manufacturer of cheeses including mozzarella, feta, fontina, emmental and parmesan
Manager: Samuel Cadeddo
Number Employees: 19
Square Footage: 120000
Type of Packaging: Bulk

Food Manufacturers / A-Z

Brands:
    Tre Stelle

788 Au Bon Climat Winery
PO Box 113
Los Olivos, CA 93441
805-937-9801
Fax: 805-937-2539 info@aubonclimat.com
www.aubonclimat.com
Wines
Owner: Robert Lindquist
Contact: Michael Main
michael@aubonclimat.com
Winemaker: Jim Clendenen
Estimated Sales: $.5-1 million
Number Employees: 1-4
Type of Packaging: Private Label

789 Au Printemps Gourmet
101-765 Nobel Street
Saint-Jerome, QC J7Z 7A3
Canada
450-438-6676
Fax: 450-438-0080 800-438-6676
services@beaulieuinstant.com
www.beaulieuinstantane.com/en/home-apgourmet
Vinegars, jams, jelly seasonings and gift sets, gourmet foods.
Owner: Chantal Desjardins
Finance Director: Tim Dick
Vice President, Sales/Marketing: Marilyn O'Connell
Operations: Dolores Wilson
Year Founded: 1978
Estimated Sales: $5-9 Million
Number Employees: 20
Number of Brands: 1
Brands:
    Au Printemps Gourmet

790 (HQ)Au'some Candies
2031 Route 130
Suite E, Bldg A
Monmouth Junction, NJ 08852-3014
732-951-8818
Fax: 732-951-8828 877-287-6649
Candy
President: Carlos Yeung
CEO: David Tsu
Sales Manager: Marcos Perales
VP Operations: Rose Downey
Year Founded: 1998
Estimated Sales: $5-10 Million
Number Employees: 10-19
Other Locations:
    Au'some Candies
    Mission Viejo CA
    Au'some Candies
    Coppell TX
    Au'Some Candies
    Mississauga, Ontario
    Au'Some Candies Europe S.L.
    Sitges, Spain
    Au'Some Candy Asia
    Kowloon, Hong Kong
Brands:
    Candy Yo-Yo
    Gummi Alien Invaders
    Pop Magic
    Super Sucker

791 AuNutra Industries Inc
5625 Daniels Street
Chino, CA 91710
909-628-2600
Fax: 909-628-8110 info@aunutra.com
www.aunutra.com
Manufacturer and supplier of botanicals and nutritional ingredients
VP Sales/Marketing: Ken Guest
Regional Sales Manager: Tara Trainor
Contact: Jing Ang
jang@aunutra.com

792 Auburn Dairy Products Inc
702 W Main St
Auburn, WA 98001-5299
253-833-3400
Fax: 253-833-3751 800-950-9264
info@yamiyogurt.com www.instantwhip.com
Sour cream, half and half and yogurt including plain, orange, cherry, strawberry, blueberry and lemon. Lactose free and 100 percent dairy.
Manager: Jerry Dinsmore
Executive Director: Martin Lavine
Purchasing & Plant Manager: Marv Query

Estimated Sales: $10-20 Million
Number Employees: 20-49
Parent Co: Instantwhip Foods
Type of Packaging: Consumer, Food Service
Brands:
    Yami(c) Yogurt
    Zoi Greek Yogurt

793 Aufschnitt Meats
7 Gwynns Mill
Owings Mills, MD 21117
410-356-7745
www.aufschnittmeats.com
Meat products

794 August Foods LTD
4820 Avenue Q
Lubbock, TX 79412-2210
806-744-1918
Fax: 806-744-4934
Fried pies
Owner: Brian Seely
Estimated Sales: $750
Number Employees: 10-19
Square Footage: 14400
Brands:
    August's Fried

795 August Kitchen
PO Box 54
Armonk, NY 10504-0054
914-219-5249
info@augustkitchen.com
Marinades, other sauces, seasonings and cooking enhancers.
Contact: Zina Ovchinnikoff-Santos
zina@augustkitchen.com
Number Employees: 1-4
Brands:
    J-Burger Seasoning

796 August Schell Brewing Co
1860 Schells Rd
New Ulm, MN 56073
507-354-5528
Fax: 507-359-9119 800-770-5020
schells@schellsbrewery.com schellsbrewery.com
Manufacturer of beer, ale and lager.
Year Founded: 1828
Estimated Sales: $21 Million
Number Employees: 50-99
Type of Packaging: Consumer, Private Label
Brands:
    Grain Belt
    Schell's

797 Augusta Winery
5601 High St
Augusta, MO 63332-1703
636-228-4301
Fax: 636-228-4683 888-667-9463
info@augustawinery.com
www.augustawinery.com
Manufacturer of handcrafted wines
President: Tony Kooyumjian
augustawinery@aol.com
Year Founded: 1988
Estimated Sales: $2.5-5 Million
Number Employees: 5-9
Type of Packaging: Bulk

798 Augustin's Waffles
51 Glen Ridge Drive
Long Valley, NJ 07853
908-684-0830
Fax: 908-684-4878
Presweetened belgian waffles, with pearl sugars, dough, cooked waffles, sales of equipment and waffle tools.
President: Al Poe
Vice President: Henry Picquet

799 Aunt Aggie De's Pralines
311 W Sinton St
Sinton, TX 78387-2556
361-364-2711
Fax: 361-692-2971 800-333-9354
sales@auntaggiede.com www.auntaggiede.com
Processor of original, all natural chocolate, chewy, and coconut pralines.

Founder & CEO: Eleanor Harren
aggiede@aol.com
General Counsel & Marketing: Amy Harren de Villarreal
Chief Operating Officer: Michael Pocrass
Year Founded: 1987
Estimated Sales: $5-10 Million
Number Employees: 20-49
Square Footage: 2200
Brands:
    Aunt Aggie De's Pralines

800 Aunt Fannie's Bakery
1039 Grant Street SE
Atlanta, GA 30315-2014
404-622-8146
Baked goods
Manager: Earl Stallworth
Estimated Sales: $20-50 Million
Number Employees: 100-249
Parent Co: Flowers Industries

801 Aunt Gussie Cookies & Crackers
141 Lanza Ave
Bldg 8
Garfield, NJ 07026-3538
973-340-4480
Fax: 973-340-3501 800-422-6654
info@auntgussies.com www.auntgussies.com
Processor of cookies and crackers including sugar-free and gluten-free
President: David Caine
Contact: Joyce Parker
joyce@auntgussies.com
Year Founded: 1980
Estimated Sales: $2.5-5 Million
Number Employees: 5-9
Number of Brands: 1
Number of Products: 45
Square Footage: 60000
Type of Packaging: Consumer, Private Label, Bulk
Brands:
    Aunt Gussie's Cookies & Crackers

802 Aunt Heddy's Bakery
234 N 9th Street
Brooklyn, NY 11211-2012
718-782-0582
Food wholsaler and maufacturer of breads and babka
Owner: Rich Zablocki
Estimated Sales: $63 Thousand
Number Employees: 2

803 Aunt Jenny's Sauces/Melba Foods
186 Huron St
Brooklyn, NY 11222-1706
718-383-3192
Fax: 718-383-3191 www.melbafoods.com
Sauces, melba foods, groceries
President: Marie Cuoco
Year Founded: 1962
Estimated Sales: $2.5-5 Million
Number Employees: 10-20
Type of Packaging: Private Label

804 Aunt Kathy's Homestyle Products
PO Box 279
Waldheim, SK S0K 4R0
Canada
306-945-2181
Fax: 306-945-2043
Manufacturer and distributor of cabbage rolls, filled perogies, pizza, Mennonite farmer sausage and smokies, chicken strips, dry ribs, pies, and crumbles.
Owner: Deah Scott
Owner: Derek Scott
Production Manager: Willie Curtis
Year Founded: 1986
Estimated Sales: A
Number Employees: 5-9
Type of Packaging: Consumer, Bulk

805 Aunt Kitty's Foods Inc
270 N Mill Road
Vineland, NJ 08360
856-691-2100
Fax: 856-696-1295 www.auntkittys.com
Manufacturer, retail private label, and packaging of chili, stew, beef hash, hot dog chili, gravy, condensed soups, broth, beef cubes, and pasta.
Vice President: Craig Adams
Plant Manager: J Keith Griffis

Year Founded: 1924
Estimated Sales: $1-3 Million
Number Employees: 100-249
Number of Brands: 6
Square Footage: 480000
Parent Co: Hanover Foods Corp
Type of Packaging: Consumer, Food Service, Private Label
Brands:
   Aunt Kitty's
   Austex Products
   Bryan Products
   Bunker Hill
   Castleberry Products
   Venice Maid Products

806 Aunt Lizzie's Inc
1531 Overton Park Ave
Memphis, TN 38112-5138
901-274-2966
Fax: 901-274-2902 800-993-7788
www.auntlizzie.com
Gourmet southern cheese straws and other products
President: Ginna Kelley
Founder: Elizabeth Harwell
Year Founded: 1983
Estimated Sales: Under $500,000
Number Employees: 5-9
Type of Packaging: Private Label
Brands:
   Aunt Lizzie's
   Lemon Shortbread
   Libby's Pecan Cookies
   Sharp Cheddar Cheese
   Sun-Dried Tomato Str
   Wind & Willow Key Lime Cheeseball

807 (HQ)Aunt Millie's Bakeries
350 Pearl St
Fort Wayne, IN 46802-1508
260-424-8245
Fax: 260-424-5047 855-755-2253
customerservice@auntmillies.com
www.auntmillies.com
Breads, buns, English muffins, rolls, as well as bread and muffin mixes
President: John Popp
VP Finance: Jay Miller
Estimated Sales: $10-15 Million
Number Employees: 1000-4999
Type of Packaging: Consumer, Food Service
Other Locations:
   Perfection Bakeries Plant
   Michigan
   Perfection Bakeries Plant
   Illinois
   Perfection Bakeries Plant
   Ohio
   Perfection Bakeries Plant
   Kentucky
Brands:
   Aunt Millie's
   Sumbeam

808 Aunt Sally's Praline Shops
750 Saint Charles Ave
New Orleans, LA 70130-3714
504-522-2126
Fax: 504-944-5925 800-642-7257
service@auntsallys.com www.auntsallys.com
New Orleans style creamy praline candies in four flavors, and other specialty food items.
Manager: Bethany Gex
CEO: Frank Simoncioni
Sales: Becky Hebert
Sales: Cherie Cunningham
Director Of Operations: Karl Schmidt
Estimated Sales: $5 Million+
Number Employees: 20-49
Square Footage: 20000
Type of Packaging: Consumer, Food Service, Private Label, Bulk
Brands:
   Aunt Sally's Creamy Pralines
   Aunt Sally's Gourmet

809 Auroma International Inc
1100 E Lotus Dr
Silver Lake, WI 53170-1668
262-889-8569
Fax: 262-889-2461 auroma@lotuspress.com
www.auromaintl.com
Dietary supplements, herbs and herbal formulas.
CEO: Santosh Krinsky
Number Employees: 50-99

810 Aurora Alaska Premium Smoked Salmon & Seafood
PO Box 211376
Anchorage, AK 99521-1376
907-338-2229
Fax: 907-338-2228 800-653-3474
Seafood products
Owner: Bill Dornberger
Owner: Gloria Dornberger

811 Aurora Frozen Foods Division
2067 Westport Center Drive
Saint Louis, MO 63146-2800
314-801-2800
Fax: 314-801-2550
Frozen sea food, pizza and breakfast products, including waffles, french toast
Chairman: Ian Wilson
COO: Eric D Brenk
CFO: William R McManaman
Number Employees: 1017
Brands:
   Aunt Jemima
   Celeste
   Duncan Hines
   Lender's
   Log Cabin
   Mrs Butterworth's
   Mrs Paul's
   Van De Kamp's

812 Aurora Organic Dairy
1919 14th St
Suite 300
Boulder, CO 80302-5321
303-284-3313
Fax: 720-564-0409 info@auroraorganic.com
www.auroraorganic.com
Producer of private-brand organic milk and butter for U.S. retailers.
President and CEO: Marcus Peperzak
President: Scott McGinty
CFO: Cammie Muller
Vice President: Clark Driftmier
Director of Quality: Peggy Colfelt
Marketing Manager: Sonia Tuatelli
Contact: Kristin Anderson
kristin.anderson@auroraorganic.com
Senior VP Farm Operations: Juan Velez
Plant Manager: John Beutler
Estimated Sales: 23.9 Million
Number Employees: 5-9
Square Footage: 2835
Type of Packaging: Private Label, Bulk

813 Aurora Packing Co Inc
125 S Grant St
North Aurora, IL 60542-1603
630-897-0551
Fax: 630-897-0647 www.aurorabeef.com
Processor and exporter of beef. Meat packing plant founded in 1939.
CFO: Don Tanis
dtanis@aurorapacking.com
VP: Marvin Doty
Estimated Sales: $41 Million
Number Employees: 100-249
Number of Brands: 1
Type of Packaging: Consumer, Food Service, Private Label
Brands:
   Aurora Angus Beef

814 Aurora Products
205 Edison Road
Orange, CT 06477
203-375-9956
Fax: 203-375-9734 800-398-1048
ANatural@auroraproduct.com
www.auroraproduct.com
Trail mixes, nuts, dried fruits and candy
Owner/President: Stephanie Blackwell
VP Operations: Scott Magner
Year Founded: 1998
Estimated Sales: $30-40 Million
Number Employees: 100+

815 Aussie Crunch
1877 Air Lane Drive
Suite 4
Nashville, TN 37210-3814
615-983-8280
Fax: 615-261-9055 800-401-6534
Makers of gourmet popcorn, and popcorn supplies

President: Andy Moore
Year Founded: 2004
Number Employees: 7

816 Austin Chase Coffee
4001 21st Ave W
Seattle, WA 98199-1201
206-282-7045
Fax: 206-282-5218 888-502-2333
Coffee
President: Phil Sancken
jane@caffeappassionato.com
Sales Exec: Jane Galloway
Year Founded: 1989
Estimated Sales: $5-10 Million
Number Employees: 20-49
Type of Packaging: Private Label
Brands:
   Nescafe
   Green Mountain
   Peets

817 Austin Slow Burn
PO Box 150042
Austin, TX 78715-0042
512-282-7140
Fax: 512-282-7140 877-513-3192
www.austinslowburn.com
Gourmet fiery foods. Marinades, jams, jellies, hot pepper sauce, red sauce, green sauce and special variety sauces.
President: Jill Lewis
jilllewis@austin.rr.com
VP: Kevin Lewis
Estimated Sales: $300,000-500,000
Number Employees: 1-4

818 Austin Special Foods Company
10000 Inshore Drive
Austin, TX 78730
512-372-8665
Fax: 512-652-2699
Wholesaler of all natural and kosher dairy biscotti, cookies and frozen cookie dough. Many biscotti flavors
Owner: Laura Logan
CEO: Gene Austin
Year Founded: 1994
Estimated Sales: $10-20 Million
Number Employees: 3
Brands:
   Dog Bakery Products
   M&M Cookies
   Granny Cookies

819 Austinuts
2900 W Anderson Ln # 19b
Austin, TX 78757-1364
512-323-6887
Fax: 512-323-6889 877-329-6887
info@austinuts.com www.austinuts.com
Dry Roasted Gourmet Nuts and Seeds, Dried Fruits, Chocolates, Candy, Trail Mixes, Gourmet Food, Go Texan Products, Gift Baskets & Corporate Gifts.
Founder: Doron Ilai
Estimated Sales: $650,000
Number Employees: 5-9
Square Footage: 8
Type of Packaging: Private Label
Brands:
   Austinuts

820 Austrade
3309 Northlake Blvd # 201
Suite 201
Palm Beach Gdns, FL 33403-1705
561-209-2447
Fax: 561-585-7164 info@austradeinc.com
The leader in importing fine chemicals and food products.
President: Gary Bartl
VP: Stephen Barti
Marketing: Joseph Schantl
Sales: Sandra Barti
Year Founded: 1997
Estimated Sales: Less than $500,000
Number Employees: 1-4

Food Manufacturers / A-Z

821 Austrian Trade Commission
120 W 45th St # 900
7th Avenue
New York, NY 10036-4062
212-421-5250
Fax: 212-751-4675
newyork@advantageaustria.org
Specialty foods. Non-alcoholic beverages, water, beer, salad dressing, full-line vinegar, full-line chcoolate, cheese, agency/trade organization.
Contact: Christian Kesberg
Contact: Maichaela Lausegger
Manager: Salomeh Saidi
tehran@advantageaustria.org
Number Employees: 5-9

822 Authentic Marotti Biscotti
749 Red Wing Dr
Lewisville, TX 75067
972-221-7295
Fax: 972-436-4547
Wholesome bakers of gourmet biscotti, brownies and bar cookies.
Owner: Joann Marotti
VP: Glenn Mancini
Estimated Sales: $2.5-5 Million
Number Employees: 1-4
Type of Packaging: Consumer, Private Label, Bulk
Brands:
 Marotti Biscotti

823 Autin's Cajun Cookery
804 W 8th Ave
Covington, LA 70433-2306
985-871-1199
Fax: 985-871-7290 800-877-7290
autinskjun@aol.com www.autinscajuncookery.com
Manufacturer of Cajun dinner mixes and seasonings including jambalaya, etouffee, dirty rice, chili, gumbo, etc
President: Gibson Autin
autinskjun@aol.com
Year Founded: 1910
Estimated Sales: $500,000-$1 Million
Number Employees: 1-4
Type of Packaging: Consumer, Food Service, Private Label, Bulk
Brands:
 Autin's

824 Automatic Rolls Of New Jersey
1 Gourmet Ln
Edison, NJ 08837
877-222-2867
www.nefoods.com
Soft hamburger rolls; serving McDonalds chains
Plant Manager: Charlies Colli
Estimated Sales: $50-100 Million
Number Employees: 100-249
Parent Co: Northeast Foods
Type of Packaging: Food Service

825 Autumn Hill Vineyards/Blue Ridge Wine
301 River Drive
Stanardsville, VA 22973
434-985-6100
autumnhillwine@gmail.com
www.autumnhillwine.com
Wine
Owner: Avra Schwab
Owner: Ed Schwab
Estimated Sales: $1-3 Million
Number Employees: 1-4

826 Autumn Wind Vineyard
15225 NE North Valley Rd
Newberg, OR 97132
503-538-6931
Fax: 503-538-6931
Manufacturer of fine wines
Owner: Patricia Green
Co-Owner: Jim Anderson
Estimated Sales: $500,000-$1 Million
Number Employees: 1-4
Square Footage: 12
Type of Packaging: Private Label
Brands:
 Patricia Green Cellars

827 Avafina Organics
100-1580 Brigantine Dr
Coquitlam, BC V3K 7C1
Canada
604-292-0022
Fax: 604-292-0024 hello@avafina.com
www.avafina.com
Organic ingredients

828 Avalon Gourmet
1051 E Broadway Rd
Phoenix, AZ 85040-2301
602-253-0343
Fax: 480-253-0432
Manufacturer of gourmet foods
President: Richard Du Pree
richdupree@fsiaz.com
Owner: Alan Parker
VP: Dolores DuPree
Year Founded: 1994
Estimated Sales: $5-10 Million
Number Employees: 5-9

829 Avalon International Breads
422 W Willis St
Detroit, MI 48201-1702
313-832-0008
Fax: 313-832-0018 www.avalonbreads.net
Organic breads and baked goods
CEO: Vanessa Blanchard
vanessablanchard@avalonbreads.net
Number Employees: 50-99

830 Avalon Organic Coffees
8308 Corona Loop NE
Albuquerque, NM 87113-1665
505-856-5582
Fax: 505-856-5588 800-662-2575
e-mail@avalonorganic.com
Organic coffee
Contact: Tanya Archuleta

831 Avanti Foods Co
109 Depot Street
Walnut, IL 61376
815-379-2155
800-243-3739
www.avantifoods.com
Frozen pizzas and walnut cheeses
Year Founded: 1964
Estimated Sales: $6 Million
Number Employees: 20-49
Number of Brands: 3
Type of Packaging: Consumer, Food Service, Private Label, Bulk
Brands:
 Gino's
 Swiss Party

832 Avary Farms
2513 North Jackson
Odessa, TX 79761
432-332-4139
Fax: 915-332-4130
Owner: Bob Avary
Sales/Marketing Manager: Angela Avery
Estimated Sales: $300,000-500,000
Number Employees: 1-4

833 Avatar Corp
500 Central Ave
University Park, IL 60484-3147
708-534-5511
Fax: 708-534-0123 800-255-3181
inquiries@avatarcorp.com www.avatarcorp.com
Manufacture, refine and supply raw materials and ingrdients for the food, drug and personal care industries.
Owner: Kari Boykin
k.boykin@avatarholdings.com
President: Michael Shamie
VP Marketing: David Darwin
Chief Operating Officer: Phil Ternes
Plant Manager: Kent Taylor
Purchasing: Kristina Gutyan
Year Founded: 1982
Estimated Sales: $9 Million
Number Employees: 10-19
Square Footage: 80000
Type of Packaging: Private Label, Bulk
Brands:
 Arol
 Arox
 Avox
 Avagel
 Avapol
 Avatar
 Avatech
 Brown 'n' Serve
 Citation
 Dpo
 Lsc
 Protrolley
 Paneze
 Pankote
 Pinnacle
 Probio
 Prochill
 Procon
 Prokote
 Prophos
 Prosyn
 Protech
 Snow White
 Soft White
 Trokote
 Wintrex

834 Avebe America Inc.
101 Interchange Plaza
Suite 101
Cranbury, NJ 08512
609-865-8981
www.avebe.com
Starch specialties for texture, protein enrichment, stability and appearance.
Estimated Sales: $20-50 Million
Number Employees: 20-49
Parent Co: AVEBE Group

835 Aveka Inc
2045 Wooddale Dr
St Paul, MN 55125-2904
651-730-1729
Fax: 651-730-1826 888-317-3700
aveka@aveka.com www.aveka.com
Contract manufacturer and research and development company that focuses on particle technology including spray drying, particle coating or microcapsule technologies.
Owner: John Anderson
aveka@avekamfg.com
CEO/Ownder: William Hendrickson
Environmental Manager: Shain Kroenecke
Process Engineer: Matthew Timmers
Number Employees: 50-99
Other Locations:
 Aveka Manufacturing
 Fredericksberg IA
 Cresco Food Technologies
 Cresco IA
 Aveka Nutra Processing
 Waukon IA
 Aveka CCE Technologies
 Cottage Grove MN

836 Avena Foods Ltd.
316 1st Ave. E
Regina, SK S4N 5H2
Canada
306-757-3663
Fax: 306-757-1218 drichardson@avenafoods.com
www.avenafoods.com
Processor and supplier of gluten-free/wheat free oat products for private label/ingredients market. Allergen free plant with GFCO and OU Kosher Certification. Products include rolled oats, quick flakes, flour, steel cuts oats andbran.
Director: Kevin Meadows
Director: Maryellen Carlson
Quality Control: Nicole Gudmundsson
Sales: Dale Richardson
Operations: Rod Lechner
Plant Manager: Nathalie Paquin
Purchasing: Carryl Litzenberger
Estimated Sales: $746.93 Thousand
Number Employees: 26
Type of Packaging: Private Label, Bulk

837 Avenue Gourmet
11445 Cronridge Drive
Suite Q
Owings Mills, MD 21117
410-902-5701
Fax: 410-902-0600 www.avenuegourmet.com
Manufacturer of specialty and natural foods distribution

Food Manufacturers / A-Z

President: Patricia Lobel
patricia.lobel@avenuegourmet.com
Sales Manager: Sandra Hoffman
Year Founded: 1998
Number Employees: 10-19

838 Avery Brewing Company
5763 Arapahoe Ave. Unit E
Boulder, CO 80303
303-440-4324
Fax: 303-786-8790 877-844-5679
info@averybrewing.com www.averybrewing.com
Producer of various beers
President: Adam Avery
CEO/CFO: Larry Avery
Vice President: Thomas Boogaard
Quality Control Manager: Matt Thrall
Contact: Bernardo Alatorre
bernardo@averybrewing.com
Operations Manager: Steve Breezley
Chief Technology Officer: Shaun Nanavati
Year Founded: 1993
Estimated Sales: $5-10 Million
Number Employees: 9
Brands:
   14'er Esb
   Avery
   Ellie's Brown
   Hog Heaven
   Out of Bounds
   Redpoint
   Salvation
   The Reverend
   White Rascal

839 Avery Dennison Corporation
207 N Goode Avenue
Suite 500
Glendale, CA 91203-1301
626-304-2000
www.averydennison.com
Manufacturer and exporter of pressure sensitive labels.
Chairman/President/CEO: Mitch Butier
SVP/Chief Financial Officer: Greg Lovins
SVP/Chief Human Resources Officer: Anne Hill
SVP/General Counsel/Secretary: Susan Miller
VP/General Manager, Retail Branding: Deon Stander
VP/Global Operations/Supply Chain: Kamran Kian
Year Founded: 1935
Estimated Sales: $7.5 Billion
Number Employees: 30,000
Other Locations:
   Avery Research Center (AEM)
   Irwindale CA
   Business Media
   Buffalo NY
   Corporate
   Framingham MA
   Corporate Int'l Manufacturing
   Covina CA
   Corporate Office at Brea
   Brea CA
   Corporate Office at Framingham
   Framingham MA
   Corporate Shared EHS at Milford
   Milford MA
   Engineered Films Division
   Greenfield IN
   Engineered Films Division
   Painesville OH

840 Avitae
PO Box 93686
Cleveland, OH 44101
888-228-4823
goavitae.com
Caffeinated water
Number of Brands: 3
Number of Products: 15
Brands:
   AVITAE
   SPARKLING AVITAE
   AVITAE XR

841 Avo-King Internatl
2050 W Chapman Ave
Suite 210
Orange, CA 92868-2649
714-937-1551
Fax: 714-937-1974 800-286-5464
info@avo-king.com www.avo-king.com
Processor and importer of frozen guacamole and avocado pulp
Owner: Guido Doddoli
Controller: Francisco Philibert
commets@avo-king.com
Vice President: Pablo Doddoli
Estimated Sales: $2.5 Million
Number Employees: 1-4
Parent Co: Doddoli Hermanos Group
Brands:
   Avo-King

842 AvoLov
20724 Carmen Loop
Suite 120
Bend, OR 97702
541-419-4078
www.avocadochips.com
Avocado chips
Number of Brands: 1
Number of Products: 3
Brands:
   AVOLOV

843 Avoca
PO Box 129
841 Avoca Road
Merry Hill, NC 27957
252-482-2133
Fax: 252-482-8622 www.avocainc.com
Manufacturer and exporter of flavors and fragrances
President: David Peele
Director/ Business Development: Richard Maier
COO: Danny White
Research & Development: Richard Teague
Marketing Director: Shannon Sloan
Plant Manager: Danny White
Number Employees: 50-99

844 Avon Heights Mushrooms
50 Old Baltimore Pike
Avondale, PA 19311
610-268-2092
Fax: 610-268-8706
Manufacturer of coleslaw and salad mixes; also, packer of spinach, broker of vegetables
Owner: Philip Pusey Jr
Year Founded: 1972
Estimated Sales: $2 Millio
Number Employees: 20
Square Footage: 32000

845 Avri Co Inc
1080 Essex Ave
Richmond, CA 94801-2113
510-233-0633
Fax: 510-233-0636 800-883-9574
avrico@avrico.com
Flavoring supplies, flavors, fragrances, essential oils
President: Carl Arvold
av@avrico.com
Estimated Sales: Less than $1 Million
Number Employees: 5-9
Brands:
   Avri Companies

846 Award Baking Intl
206 State Ave S
New Germany, MN 55367-9521
952-353-2533
Fax: 952-353-8066 800-333-3523
awardbaking@oblaten.com www.oblaten.com
Biscottis and all natural specialty baked goods.
Owner: Tim Kraft
tkraft@oblaten.com
Co-Owner: Ken Barron
Marketing: Rhonda Kossack
Year Founded: 1948
Estimated Sales: $1-2.5 Million
Number Employees: 20-49
Square Footage: 40000
Parent Co: Kenny B's Cookie
Brands:
   Auer
   Award Auer/Blaschke
   Award Crunchy Dunkers
   Biscotti Di Roma
   Carlsbad Oblaten

847 Awrey Bakeries
12301 Farmington Rd
Livonia, MI 48150
734-522-1100
Fax: 734-522-1585 800-950-2253
personnel@awrey.com
Frozen baked goods including cakes, bagels, muffins, doughnuts, danish, croissants, biscuits, rolls, english muffins, and marquise desserts.
VP, Contract Sales: Diane Lynch
Contact: Betty Awrey
b.j.awrey@netscape.com
Plant Manager and Director of Operations: Kurt Eddy
Estimated Sales: $34.6 Million
Number Employees: 380
Number of Brands: 4
Number of Products: 200
Square Footage: 60000
Type of Packaging: Consumer, Food Service, Private Label
Brands:
   Awrey's Maestro
   Grande
   Marquise
   Atkins Elegant Desserts

848 Ax Water
Fargo, ND 58104
info@drinkaxwater.com
drinkaxwater.com
Antioxidant water
CEO and Co-Founder: Blake Johnson
President and Co-Founder: Wade Gronwold
Year Founded: 2017

849 Axelsson & Johnson Fish Company
PO Box 180
933 Ocean Drive
Cape May, NJ 08204-0180
609-884-8426
Fax: 609-898-0221 ajfish@bellatlantic.net
www.jerseyseafood.nj.gov
Exporter and importer of fresh seafood
Manager: Andrew Axelsson
Estimated Sales: $5-10 Million
Number Employees: 10-19
Brands:
   A&J Brand

850 Axiom Foods, Inc.
12100 Wilshire Blvd
Suite 800
Los Angeles, CA 90025
310-264-2606
800-711-3587
info@axiomfoods.com www.axiomfoods.com
Organic WGBR protein concentrates and isolates, sugars, sugar solids, honey, milks, flours and starches. (brown rice products)
President & CEO: David Janow
Sales Director: Jason Lee
Estimated Sales: $.5-1 Million

851 Axium Foods
239 Oak Grove Ave
PO Box 187
South Beloit, IL 61080-1936
815-389-3053
800-523-8644
www.axiumfoods.com
Corn-based snack foods
President: Jerry Stokely
jstokely@axiumfoods.com
Number Employees: 100-249
Type of Packaging: Consumer, Food Service, Private Label

852 Ayara Products
6245 W. 87th St.
Los Angeles, CA 90045
310-410-8848
www.ayaraproducts.com
Ethnic sauces.
Founder: Vanda Asapahu
vanda@ayarathaicuisine.com
Square Footage: 80000

853 Ayoba-Yo
P.O. Box 3666
Oakton, VA 22124
202-796-8554
www.ayoba-yo.com
Dried meat snacks

501

Food Manufacturers / A-Z

854 Azar Nut Co
1800 Northwestern Dr
El Paso, TX 79912-1125
915-877-4079
Fax: 915-877-1198 800-351-8178
www.mountfranklinfoods.com
Peanuts, almonds, pecans, walnuts, pine and mixed nuts, dried fruit, candy and snack mixes
CEO: Richard Condie
condie@azarnutco.com
New Business Development Manager: Jay Roehner
VP, Sales & Marketing: Barbara Powell
Operations Manager: James Jamison
Warehouse Manager: Art Romero
Number Employees: 100-249
Other Locations:
  Sunlight Plant
  Juarez, Mexico

855 Azteca Foods Inc
5005 S Nagle Ave
Chicago, IL 60638-1318
708-563-6600
Fax: 708-563-0331 info@aztecafoods.com
www.baja-tortillas.com
Mexican food products including salad shells, tortilla chips and tortillas
President: Renee Togher
renee.togher@aztecafoods.com
Chairman: Arthur Velasquez
Vice Presdient, Finance: Joseh Klomes
Vice President Operations: Julio Martinez
Estimated Sales: $34 Million
Number Employees: 100-249
Number of Brands: 3
Square Footage: 120000
Type of Packaging: Consumer, Food Service
Brands:
  Azteca®
  Buena Vida®
  Ultragrain® Tortillas

856 Azteca Milling
5601 Executive Dr.
Suite 650
Irving, TX 75038-6118
972-232-5300
Fax: 972-232-5370 800-364-0040
info@aztecamilling.com www.aztecamilling.com
Corn tortilla flours; snack flours; retail flours, and speciality flours.
President: Ignacio Hernandez
Vice President: Don Schleppegrell
Corporate Sales Manager: Rick Norton
Snack Manager Sales: Alan Davis
Contact: Hernan Guevara
hernan_guevara@aztecamilling.com
Estimated Sales: $40 Million
Number Employees: 100-249
Parent Co: Gruma Corporation
Type of Packaging: Bulk
Brands:
  Masa Mixta ®
  Maseca ®
  Selecta ®

857 (HQ)Azuma Foods Intl Inc USA
20201 Mack St
Hayward, CA 94545-1224
510-782-1112
Fax: 510-782-1188 www.azumafoods.com
Processor, exporter and importer of frozen seafood, caviar and ready-made sushi
President/CEO: Takahiro Tamura
Chairman: Toshinobu Azuma
Estimated Sales: $5-10 Million
Number Employees: 50-99
Other Locations:
  New York Branch
  East Rutherford NJ
  Hawaii Sales Office
  Honolulu HI
  West Coast American Division Sales
  Novato CA
  East Coast American Division Sales
  Boston MA
Brands:
  Ichiban Delight®
  My-Dol®
  Sea Salad
  Takohachi
  Taste of Island Legends
  Tobikko®

858 B & B Food DistributorsInc
724 S 13th St
Terre Haute, IN 47807-4997
812-238-1438
Fax: 812-232-0670 800-264-1438
www.bandbfoods.net
Manufacturer of general merchandise and foodservice equipment
President: Scott Isles
scott@bandbfoods.net
Year Founded: 1952
Estimated Sales: $10-20 Million
Number Employees: 50-99

859 B & B Pecan Processors
106 Thomson Ave
Turkey, NC 28393-9132
910-533-2229
Fax: 919-553-4610 866-328-7322
bandbpecans@intrstar.net
www.elizabethspecans.com
Pecan praline, brittle, chocolate covered pecans, butter-roasted pecans and BBQ sauce
Owner: Alan Bundy
bandbpecans@intrstar.net
Estimated Sales: $.5-1 million
Number Employees: 5-9
Brands:
  Elizabeth's

860 B & B Poultry Co
110 Almond Rd
Norma, NJ 08347
856-692-8893
Fax: 856-455-7681 800-535-7646
information@bandbpoultry.com
www.bandbpoultry.com
Refrigerated chickens, whole and parts
President: Josh Fisher
CEO: Mark Fisher
Treasurer: Dorothy Fisher
Vice President: Mark Fisher
Contact: Benjamin Fisher
Year Founded: 1945
Estimated Sales: $25 Million
Number Employees: 100-249

861 B & B Produce
12902 Fancy Gap Hwy.
Cana, VA 24317
276-755-4441
Fax: 919-894-2127 800-633-4902
www.bandbproducecana.com
Fruits, vegetables, plants, hanging baskets, candy, jams, jelly, honey, molasses
Founder & Owner: Burlie Bowman
Owner: Eddie Bowman
Owner: Gary Bowman
Estimated Sales: $20-50 Million
Number Employees: 20-49
Brands:
  Sun Beauty

862 B & C Riverside
2155 Highway 18
Vacherie, LA 70090-5405
225-265-8356
Fax: 225-265-9960 www.bncrestaurant.com
Vacuum packed, fresh and frozen alligator and seafood
Owner: Tommy Breaux
Estimated Sales: Under $1 Million
Number Employees: 5-9
Type of Packaging: Consumer, Food Service

863 B & D Foods
3494 S Tk Ave
Boise, ID 83705-5278
208-344-1183
Fax: 208-344-6825 sales@banddfoods.net
www.banddfoods.com
Processor of frozen finger steaks, pork and chicken strips and battered mozzarella cheese sticks
Contact: Tim Anderson
Contact: Don Emlet
Contact: John Tolman
Contact: Carma Christensen
cchristensen@banddfoods.net
Year Founded: 1972
Estimated Sales: $10-20 Million
Number Employees: 10-19
Square Footage: 24000
Type of Packaging: Food Service, Private Label

864 B & G Foods Inc.
4 Gatehall Dr.
Parsippany, NJ 07054
973-401-6500
Fax: 973-630-6522 customercare@mybrands.com
www.bgfoods.com
Frozen and shelf-stable products including hot cereals, jams, jellies, fruit spreads, canned meats, beans and vegetables, taco shells, vinegars and cooking wines, sweeteners, seasonings, pickles, peppers, salsas and various saucessyrups and condiments.
Chairman: Stephen Sherrill
President/CEO/Director: Kenneth Romanzi
EVP, Finance/Chief Financial Officer: Bruce Wacha
EVP/Chief Compliance Officer: Scott Lerner
EVP, Human Resources: Eric Hart
Executive VP/Chief Customer Officer: Ellen Schum
Chief Supply Chain Officer: Erich Fritz
Year Founded: 1889
Estimated Sales: $1.7 Billion
Number Employees: 2,500+
Number of Brands: 50+
Square Footage: 200000
Type of Packaging: Consumer, Food Service
Brands:
  Back to Nature
  Bear Creek®
  Cream of Wheat®
  Green Giant™
  B&M®
  Mrs Dash®
  Ortega
  Victoria®
  Ac'cent®
  Ac'cent Sa-son®
  B&G®
  Baker's Joys®
  Brer Rabbit®
  Buena Vida™
  Canoleo®
  Carey's®
  Crock Pot®
  Dec A Cake®
  Devonsheer®
  Don Pepino®
  Durkee®
  Emeril's®
  Grandma's Molasses®
  Henri's®
  Joan of Arc®
  Las Palmas®
  Le Sueur®
  MacDonald's™
  Mama Mary's™
  Maple Grove Farms of Vermont®
  McCann's®
  Molly McButter
  New York Flatbreads™
  New York Style™
  Old London®
  Polaner®
  Regina®
  Scalfani®
  Skinnygirl™
  SnackWell's®d
  Spice Islands®
  Spring Tree®
  Static Guard®
  Sugar Twin®
  Tone's®
  Trappey's®
  True North®
  Underwood®
  Vermont Maid®
  Weber®
  Wright's®

865 B & J Seafood
1101 US Highway 70 E
New Bern, NC 28560-6617
252-637-0483
Fax: 252-633-0775
Wholesaler of fish and seafood. Canned, frozen and refrigerated blue crabmeat, frozen and refrigerated flounder fillets.
President: Brent Fulcher
bjseafood@earthlink.net
Year Founded: 2006
Estimated Sales: $14 Million
Number Employees: 100-249
Type of Packaging: Private Label
Brands:
  Upper Bay

Food Manufacturers / A-Z

866 B & R Classics LLC
56 Old Field Rd
Huntington, NY 11743
631-427-5675
Fax: 631-421-7471 ctr@brclassics.com
www.brclassics.com
Gluten-free, cakes/pastries, cookies, chocolate bars, chocolate truffles, gummies/jellies/pates de fruits, chips, gift packs.
Marketing: Chris Riley
Contact: Chris Johnson
chris@johnsco-investments.com

867 B & R Quality Meats Inc
200 Park Rd
Waterloo, IA 50703
319-232-6328
Fax: 319-232-8623
customerservice@b-rqualitymeats.com
www.b-rqualitymeats.com
Processor and wholesaler/distributor of meat including beef, pork, veal and poultry; serving the foodservice market
Estimated Sales: $5-10 Million
Number Employees: 10-19
Square Footage: 24000
Type of Packaging: Consumer, Food Service, Bulk

868 B G Smith & Sons Oyster Co
787 Oakley Ln
Sharps, VA 22548
804-394-2721
Fax: 804-394-2741 877-483-8279
Manufacturer and exporter of fresh and frozen oysters; processor and packager of ice
President/CEO: B Smith
Estimated Sales: $2.5-5 Million
Number Employees: 10-19
Number of Brands: 3
Number of Products: 1
Square Footage: 400000
Type of Packaging: Consumer, Food Service, Private Label
Brands:
  Chesapeake Bay Ice
  Chesapeake Pride
  Ocean Spray
  Perch Creek

869 B R Cohn Winery & Olive Oil Co
15000 Hwy 12
Glen Ellen, CA 95442-9454
707-938-4064
Fax: 707-938-4585 800-330-4064
info@brcohn.com www.brcohnwinery.com
Wine, olive oils, vinegars
President: Daniel Cohn
Owner: Bruce Cohn
Accounts Manager: Kelly Johnson
Marketing and Design Manager: Trevor Swallow
National Sales Manager: Lezette Yearby
Public Relations: Micheal Coats
Winemaker: Tom Montgomery
Purchasing: Bruce Cohn
Estimated Sales: $2.5-5 Million
Number Employees: 20-49
Type of Packaging: Private Label
Brands:
  Balsamic and Herb Dipping Oil
  Balsamic Vinegar of Modena
  Cabernet Vinegar
  Carneros Chardonnay
  Champagne Vinegar
  Chardonnay Vinegar
  Mendocino Cty. Sauvignon Blanc
  Olive Hill Cabernet Sauvignon
  Olive Hill Cabernet Sauvignon
  Olive Hill Pinot Noir
  Organic Extra Virgin Olive Oil
  Raspberry Champagne Vinegar
  Reserve Carneros Chardonnay
  Silver Label Cabernet Sauvignon
  Sonoma Extra Virgin Olive Oil
  Sonoma Valley Merlot
  Sonoma Valley Zinfandel

870 B S & B Safety Systems LLC
7455 E 46th St
Tulsa, OK 74145-6263
918-622-5950
Fax: 918-492-1559 800-272-3475
sales@bsbsystems.com www.bsbsystems.com
Manufactures overpressure protection safety products, pressure relief, both positive and vacuum with pressure relieving products including rupture disks.
VP: Dave Garrison
Number Employees: 5-9

871 B&A Bakery
1820 Ellesmere Road
Toronto, ON M1H 2V5
Canada
416-289-9600
Fax: 416-289-2445 800-263-2878
freshness@breadsource.com
www.breadsource.com
Processor of homestyle sandwich bread and rolls including hamburger, submarine, hot dog, dinner and kaiser
Proprietor: Arif Sunderji
Year Founded: 1985
Estimated Sales: $1.4 Million
Number Employees: 40
Square Footage: 48000
Type of Packaging: Food Service

872 B&D Food Corporation
575 Madison Ave
Suite 1006
New York, NY 10022-8511
212-937-8456
Fax: 212-412-9034
Roasted, ground coffee; chocolate beverages and cappaccinos; and spray dried agglomerated soluble coffee and powdered tea.
Chief Executive Officer/Board Directors: Yaron Arbell
Chief Financial Officer/Board Directors: Yossi Haras
Number Employees: 1-4
Type of Packaging: Food Service

873 B&H Foods
P.O.Box 668568
Charlotte, NC 28266-8568
704-332-4106
Fax: 704-332-5980
Shellfish Shippers
President: Stan Bracey
Plant Manager: Dennis Frost
Estimated Sales: $20-50 Million
Number Employees: 50-99
Parent Co: B&H Foods

874 B&K Coffee
PO Box 1238
Oneonta, NY 13820-5238
607-432-1499
Fax: 607-432-1592 800-432-1499
www.bkcoffee.com
Manufacturer of coffee and tea.
Owner: Paul Karabinis
Owner: Gene Bettiol
Year Founded: 1991
Estimated Sales: $10-24.9 Million
Number Employees: 20-49
Number of Brands: 1
Type of Packaging: Private Label
Brands:
  B&K Coffee

875 B&M Enterprises
4818 S 76th St
Suite 130
Greenfield, WI 53220
414-399-7402
Fax: 414-461-2009 www.bmenterprisez.com
Manufacturer of dairy products
Owner: Marson Berry
Account Manager: Billy Anderson
Year Founded: 1982
Estimated Sales: Under $500,000
Number Employees: 1-4

876 B&M Fisheries
15 Pingree Farm Road
Georgetown, MA 01833
978-352-6663
Fax: 978-352-7565
Manufacturer of seafood
Manager: Matt Lofton
Manager: Brad Zimmerman
Contact: Allan Robicheau
allan@houmardacadie.com

877 B-S Foods Company
1000 Cornell Pkwy
Suite 600
Oklahoma City, OK 73108-1800
405-949-9797
Fax: 405-949-9802
Pre-packaged luncheon meats and sandwiches
Owner: Sandra Henager
Sales Manager: Dave Heinecke
Estimated Sales: $2.5-5 Million
Number Employees: 5-9
Parent Co: B-S Foods Company
Type of Packaging: Consumer

878 B-Tea Beverage, LLC
One International Blvd
Suite 720
Mahwah, NJ 07495
201-512-8400
Fax: 201-791-5800 btkombucha.com
Organic kombucha, organic tea
Operations Manager: Katie Scully
Year Founded: 2016
Number Employees: 1-10

879 B. Lloyd's Pecans
PO Box 354
1073 Clifford Street
Barwick, GA 31720
404-759-2441
800-322-6887
Supplier of Pecans and pecan confections
Owner: Heeth Varnedoe
Estimated Sales: $500-1 Million appx.
Number Employees: 30-99
Type of Packaging: Food Service

880 B. Nutty
655 12th St Apt 305
Oakland, CA 94607-3667
USA
510-374-4658
nutty@nuttyness.com
Chocolate bars, candy, gift packs
CEO: Kristian Salvesen
Chief Marketing: Anis Salvesen
Number Employees: 2

881 B.B. Bean, Coffee
583 County Line Rd
Monument, CO 80132
719-481-1170
bbcoffee@aol.com
Coffee
CEO: Elizabeth Kawczynski
Marketing Director: Elizabeth Kawczynski
Roastmaster: Bob Polito
Brands:
  Bean Coffee

882 B.C. Fisheries
P.O.Box 334
Hanckock Point Road
Hancock, ME 04640-0334
207-422-8205
Fax: 207-422-8206
Seafood
Manager: Pete Daley

883 B.M. Lawrence & Company
601 Montgomery St
Suite 1115
San Francisco, CA 94111-2614
415-981-2926
Fax: 415-981-2926 info@bmlawrence.com
Wholesaler/Processor and distributor of soft drinks, nonalcoholic beer, canned fruits, vegetables, juices and fish
President: B Lawrence
Purchasing Agent: Hugh Ditzler
info@bmlawrence.com
Estimated Sales: $5-10 Million
Number Employees: 5-9
Square Footage: 8000
Brands:
  California Farms
  Grapefruit
  Lemon-Lime
  Us Cola
  Us Select

884 B.O.S.S. Food Co.
800-344-8584
info@bossfoodco.com bossfoodco.com

Food Manufacturers / A-Z

Superfood snack bars
Number of Brands: 1
Number of Products: 5

885 B.W.J.W. Inc.
3517 Conway St
Fort Worth, TX 76111
817-831-0051
Fax: 817-834-6766
Meat
President: John Wehba
Contact: Bill Louis
b.louis@barwmeat.com
Estimated Sales: $10 Million
Number Employees: 65

886 BASF Corp.
100 Park Ave.
Florham Park, NJ 07932
973-245-6000
800-526-1072
www.basf.com
Vitamins and feed additives for human and livestock nutrition and fungicides, insecticides and herbicides for crop protection.
Chairman/CEO, BASF North America: Wayne Smith
Executive VP/CFO, BASF Corporation: Tobias Dratt
Senior VP/General Counsel: Stefan John
Year Founded: 1865
Estimated Sales: $63.8 Billion
Number Employees: 117,628
Parent Co: BASF SE
Other Locations:
  Geismar LA
  Shreveport LA
  Livonia MI
  Wyandotte MI
  Sparks GA
  Aberdeen MI
  Palmyra MO
  Belvidere NJ
  Jamesburg NJ
  Washington NJ
  Enka NC
  Morganton NC
  Wilmington NC

887 BBQ Bunch
13100 Woodland Avenue
Kansas City, MO 64146-1801
816-941-4534
Fax: 816-941-0263 lewieb@aol.com
BBQ and mustard sauce; wholesaler/distrinutor of BBQ products; marketing consultant to the BBQ industry.
Owner: Lewis Bunch
Estimated Sales: $500,000-$1 Million
Number Employees: 1-4
Type of Packaging: Food Service, Private Label, Bulk
Brands:
  Jazzy Barbecue Sauce

888 BBQ Shack
1613 E Peoria St
Paola, KS 66071-1893
913-294-5908
pitmaster@thebbqshack.com
Barbacue meats
Owner: Rick Schoenberger
Director Marketing/Sales: Debbie McCrackin
Estimated Sales: Less Than $500,000
Number Employees: 5-9
Brands:
  Bbq Shack

889 BBQ'n Fools Catering, LLC
20 W. South Street
Greenfield, IN 46140
317-448-5873
Fax: 800-671-8652 800-671-8652
www.bbqnfools.com
BBQ sauces and seasonings.
Owner: Tom Brohamer
Co-Owner: Kurt Weidmann
Contact: Grant Ford
grant@bbqnfools.com
Estimated Sales: $40,000
Number Employees: 3
Brands:
  Bbq'n Fools
  Papa Dan's World Famous Jerky

890 BBS Bodacious BBQ Company
8411 Forest Hills Dr
Suite 103
Coral Springs, FL 33065
954-752-0909
Fax: 954-345-3482 800-537-5928
bbsbbq@aol.com www.800jerky2u.com
Natural and fat-free barbecue sauces, spicy jellies and steak, turkey jerky
President/CEO: Susan Sheldon
Estimated Sales: $500,000-$1 Million
Number Employees: 10-19
Brands:
  Aunt Jayne's
  Bbs Bodacious
  Sammye's Sumptuous

891 BBS Lobster Co
141 Smalls Point Rd
Machiasport, ME 04655-3231
207-255-8888
Fax: 207-255-3987 info@lobstertrap.com
www.lobstertrap.com
Wholesaler of lobsters
Owner: Susan West
General Manager: Blair West
CFO: Greg Menzel
Assistant General Manager: Rosie Barrett
Domestic/International Sales: David Madden
Lobster Purchasing/Operations: Tom Platt
Estimated Sales: $1,600,000
Number Employees: 5-9
Parent Co: Lobster Trap Wholesale Seafood Dealers

892 BBU Bakeries
255 Business Ctr Drive
PO Box 976
Horsham, PA 19044
213-672-8010
Fax: 610-320-9286 800-984-0989
Manufacturer of cakes, pies, muffins, doughnuts, breads, pizza dough and bagels
President: Gary Prince
Plant Manager: Ron Schulthies
Year Founded: 1983
Estimated Sales: $300,000-500,000
Number Employees: 10000-25000
Type of Packaging: Consumer
Brands:
  Mrs Bairds
  Orowheat
  Entemanns
  Thomas
  Arnold
  Boboli
  Freihoffer

893 BCFoods
1330 N Dutton Ave
Suite 100
Santa Rosa, CA 95401
707-547-1776
Fax: 707-545-5270 www.bcfoods.com
Industrial ingredients, dehydrated and freeze dried vegetables, freeze dried fruit, dairy and meat products.
President North America: Adam Lee
Director of Sales & Marketing: Mike Bray
Global Operations Manager: Daniel Mabee
Estimated Sales: $20-50 Million
Number Employees: 20-49

894 BCGA Concept Corporation
39 Canal Street
New York, NY 10002
212-488-0661
Fax: 212-488-0700 info@freshgingerale.com
Soft Drinks, Non Alcoholic.
Founder/CEO: Bruce Cost
Marketing: Jenny Chen

895 BDS Natural
2779 E El Presidio St
Long Beach, CA 90810-1118
310-747-0444
Fax: 310-518-2577 info@bdsnatural.com
www.bdsnatural.com
Manufacturer and distributor of spices and seasoning blends, botanical powders, and herbal teas.

Co-Founder: Steve Brennis
Co-Founder: David Soloman
General Manager: Donna Cook
R&D Manager/Technical Foods Sales: Daniel Alexander
Technnical Director: Pauline Lu
Customer Service Manager: Marlene Sellers
Human Resources Manager: Alexis Torres
Director of Operations: Kevin Witt
Operations Manager: John Kapski
Purchasing: Brandy Guedea
Number Employees: 5-9
Other Locations:
  Operations
  Carson, CA

896 BGS Jourdan & Sons
1415 Stafford Rd
Darlington, MD 21034-1801
410-457-4904
Canned whole tomatoes and various other fruits and vegetables.
Owner: Scott Reezes
Estimated Sales: Less than $120,000
Number Employees: 1-4
Type of Packaging: Consumer, Private Label
Brands:
  Point Pleasant

897 BJ's Restaurants Inc.
7755 Center Ave
Suite 300
Huntington Beach, CA 92647-3084
714-500-2400
Fax: 714-848-8287 dianne@bjsbrewhouse.com
www.bjsrestaurants.com
Beer, ale and lager; also, pizza
President/CEO: Gerald Deitchle
Cfo/Evp: Gregory Levin
Executive VP: Lon F Ledwith
lon@bjsbrewhouse.com
Estimated Sales: 513,000
Number Employees: 10000+
Parent Co: BJ's Restaurants Inc
Brands:
  Bj Beer

898 BK Giulini Corporation
Dr.-Albert-Reimann-Str. 2
Ladenburg, 68526
Germany
Phosphate-based food ingredients for further processed meat, poultry, dairy and seafood.
Chief Scientific Officer: Wolfgang Schneider
Estimated Sales: $24 Million
Number Employees: 15
Square Footage: 4129
Parent Co: ICL
Brands:
  Bekaplus®
  Brifisol®
  Johr®
  Turrisin®

899 BK Specialty Foods
200 Eagle Court
Swedesboro, NJ 08085-1799
856-294-600
Fax: 856-241-8942 800-354-9445
bkfoods.com
Gourmet foods including dairy, baked goods, desserts, beans & rice, fruit and ethnic foods.
CFO: Scott Carey
Vice President of Sales and Marketing: Karen Kratchman-Gold
Number Employees: 51-200

900 BKW Seasonings
3110 Henson Rd
Suite 7
Knoxville, TN 37921-5392
865-851-8657
Fax: 865-966-6963 matt@bkwseasonings.com
www.bkwseasonings.com
Various types of seasonings
Owner: Matt Boeler
Contact: Karen Webb
kwebb@bkwseasonings.com
Year Founded: 2007
Number Employees: 5-9

Food Manufacturers / A-Z

901 BN Soda
PO Box 11
Brookline, MA 02446
617-782-7888
Fax: 240-536-3079
Soda made of natural flavors and cane sugar, also caffeine-free
Founder: Tom Bleier
tombleier@aol.com

902 BOLD Organics
2090 7th Avenue
Suite 201A
New York, NY 10027
consumerinfo@bold-organics.com
Organic foods
President/CEO: Aaron Greenwald
CFO/COO: Justin Kniepman
National Sales Manager: Sasha Sherman

903 BP Gourmet
135 Ricefield Ln
Hauppauge, NY 11788-2046
631-234-8200
Fax: 631-234-8200
Fat-free and organic cookies, sugar free cookies, fruit spreads and salad dressing. Also produces bread sticks and croutons
President: Florence Boris
Estimated Sales: $2.5-5 Million
Number Employees: 20-49
Brands:
 Bp Gourmet
 Freida's Kitchen
 Monte Carlo Bake Shop
 Sweet Nothings

904 BRAMI Snacks
154 Grand St
New York, NY 10013-3141
917-291-1945
info@bramisnacks.com
www.bramisnacks.com
Beans and wholegrain snacks
CEO: Dillon Dandurand
Brands:
 BRAMI Beans

905 BRINS
Brooklyn, NY
orders@staggjam.com
www.brinsjam.com
Jams and marmalades
Founder: Candice Ross
Year Founded: 2015

906 BTS Company/Hail CaesarDressings
PO Box 218015
5157 Traceway Drive
Nashville, TN 37221-8015
615-646-3125
Fax: 615-226-6867 800-617-8899
Gourmet dressings, pasta sauces, marinades. Available in Original, Low-Fat and Fat Free, Wide variety of flavors & sizes.
Owner: Bunny Sundock
Estimated Sales: $1-3 Million
Number Employees: 1-4

907 Baba Foods
San Diego, CA
619-426-6946
Fax: 619-810-0755 inforequest@babafoods.com
www.babafoods.com
Hummus, pita chips, dips and salads
Number of Brands: 1
Number of Products: 33
Brands:
 BABA FOODS

908 Babci's Specialty Foods
193 Fairview Avenue
Chicopee, MA 01013
413-598-8158
Pierogies, kapusta, chrust
President: Eugene Kirejczyk
Year Founded: 1986
Type of Packaging: Food Service, Private Label

909 Babcock Winery & Vineyards
5175 E Highway 246
Lompoc, CA 93436-9613
805-736-1455
Fax: 805-736-3886 info@babcockwinery.com
www.babcockwinery.com
Red and white wines
Owner: Bryan Babcock
info@babcockwinery.com
Year Founded: 1984
Estimated Sales: $5-10 Million
Number Employees: 20-49
Type of Packaging: Private Label

910 Babe Farms Inc
1485 N Blosser Rd
Santa Maria, CA 93458-2043
805-925-4144
Fax: 805-922-3950 800-648-6772
customerservice@babefarms.com
www.babefarms.com
Specialty and baby produce items, including peeled carrots and root vegetables
Founder: Will Souza
CEO: Judy Lundberg
judy@babefarms.com
Finance Manager: Carrie Jordan
Operations: Jeff Lundberg
Year Founded: 1986
Estimated Sales: $7 Million
Number Employees: 100-249
Type of Packaging: Food Service, Private Label
Brands:
 Babe Farms

911 Babe's Honey Farm
4150 Blenkinsop Road
Victoria, BC V8X 2C4
Canada
250-658-8319
Fax: 250-658-8149 www.babes-honey-farm.com
Fireweed and wild flower honey, beeswax
Owner: Brandon Schwartz
Year Founded: 1945
Estimated Sales: $585,000
Number Employees: 60
Square Footage: 48000
Type of Packaging: Food Service
Brands:
 Babe's

912 Baby's Coffee
U.S. 1 Mile Marker 15
Key West, FL 33040
337-442-6359
Fax: 305-744-9843 800-523-2326
info@babyscoffee.com www.babyscoffee.com
Coffee
Manager: Mary Browman
Co-Owner: Olga Teplitsky
Marketing Manager: Alfonse Manosalvas
Estimated Sales: Less than $500,000
Number Employees: 1-4
Type of Packaging: Private Label
Brands:
 Baby's Breakfast Roast
 Baby's Private Buzz
 Baby's Wrelker's Roa
 Hemingway's Hair Of
 Killer Joe
 Old Town Roast
 Sexpresso

913 Bacardi Canada, Inc.
3250 Bloor St. W
East Tower, Suite 1050
Toronto, ON M8X 2X9
Canada
905-451-6100
Fax: 905-451-6753 www.bacardi.com
Rum, vodka, scotch, gin, vermouth, carbonated low proof beverages, liqueurs
General Manager: Blair MacNeil
Estimated Sales: 250-499
Number Employees: 100
Parent Co: Bacardi Limited
Type of Packaging: Consumer, Food Service
Brands:
 Bacardi
 Grey Goose
 Martini & Rossi
 Russian Prince
 Bombay

914 Bacardi USA Inc
2701 S Le Jeune Rd
Suite 400
Coral Gables, FL 33134-5809
305-573-8511
Fax: 305-573-0756 800-222-2734
hrbmusa@bacardi.com
www.bacardilimited.com/us/en
Tropical drink flavored coolers, rum, vodka, prepared mixed drinks
President: Pete Carr
CEO: Mahesh Madhavan
Estimated Sales: $650 Million
Number Employees: 250-499
Parent Co: Bacardi International
Type of Packaging: Consumer, Food Service
Brands:
 Anejo
 B&B/Benedictine
 Bacardi Breezers
 Bacardi Limon
 Bacardi Rum
 Bacardi Spice
 Bombay
 Castillo Rums
 Dewar's Scotch
 Hatuey Beers
 Martini & Rossi Asti
 Martini & Rossi Vermouth
 Pommeroy

915 Bacci Chocolate Design
17 Columbia St # 4
Swampscott, MA 01907-1788
781-595-1511
Fax: 781-595-1544 888-725-2877
sales@baccichocolatedesign.com
Chocolate bars, other chocolate, toffee.
Owner: Carlo Bacci
carlobacci@hotmail.com
Sr VP Marketing/Sales: Erin Calvo-Bacci
Estimated Sales: Less Than $500,000
Number Employees: 1-4

916 Bachman Company
801 Hill Avenue
Wyomissing, PA 19610
610-320-7800
Fax: 610-320-7897 800-523-8253
www.bachmanco.com
Pretzels, jax, tortilla chips, popcorn, potato chips, party mix and onion rings.
President: Scott Carpenter
CEO: Joanne Millisock
Director: Marcia Welch
Sales: Andy Kapusta
Director of Human Resources: Deanna Williams
VP Manufacturing/Operations: Mark Miller
VP Manufacturing: Daniel Meyers
Purchasing Director: Lisa George
Estimated Sales: $10-20 Million
Number Employees: 350
Square Footage: 40000
Type of Packaging: Consumer, Food Service
Brands:
 Bachman
 Kidzels
 Treat
 Valley Maid

917 Back Bay Trading
11800 Wills Rd
Suite 120
Alpharetta, GA 30024
770-772-6360
Fax: 770-772-4766 800-650-8327
info@ameliabay.com www.ameliabay.com
Liquid tea and Coffee Bag-N-box
President/CEO: John Crandall
CFO: Sherry Harder
Vice President: Jason Crandall
Sales Director: Marshall Cartmill
Public Relations: Jackie Hewitt
Operations Manager: Dudley Blizzard
Estimated Sales: $5-10 Million
Number Employees: 5-9
Type of Packaging: Private Label
Brands:
 Amelia Bay
 Private Label

Food Manufacturers / A-Z

918 Back to Basics
PO Box 2780
West Bend, WI 53095-0278
801-523-6500
800-688-1989
www.backtobasicsproducts.com
Confections, candy, equipment
Estimated Sales: $5-10 Million
Number Employees: 50-99
Brands:
  Back To Basics
  Hawaiice
  Nutri Source
  Peel Away

919 Back to Nature Foods
855-346-2225
www.backtonaturefoods.com
Cereal, cookies, crackers, granola, nuts, trail mix, soup and juice
Brands:
  BACK TO NATURE

920 Back to the Roots
424 2nd St
Oakland, CA 94607
510-922-9758
www.backtotheroots.com
Organic cereal and windowsill gardens
Co-Founder: Nikhil Arora
Co-Founder: Alejandro Velez
Year Founded: 2009

921 Backer's Potato Chip Company
1 West Industrial Road
PO Box 128
Fulton, MO 65251
573-642-2833
Fax: 573-642-7617 john@backerchips.com
www.backerchips.com
Potato chips
President: Vicki McDaniel
Contact: Eric Milius
eric@backerchips.com
Estimated Sales: $10-20 Million
Number Employees: 50-99
Number of Brands: 1
Type of Packaging: Consumer, Private Label
Brands:
  Backer's

922 Backyard Safari Co
303 Campbell Rd
Covington, GA 30014-6110
770-385-3273
Fax: 888-821-2241
support@backyardsafarico.com
www.backyardsafarico.com
Spices, herbs, and pastas
Owner: Sherri Hutchison
Contact: Clyde Hutchison
clyde_hutchison@att.net
Estimated Sales: Less Than $500,000
Number Employees: 1-4
Square Footage: 80000
Brands:
  Clyde's Soon to be Famous
  GROW Gardens

923 Bacon America
255 Rue Rocheleau
Drummondville, QC J2C 7G2
Canada
819-475-3030
Fax: 819-475-4164
Bacon
President: Marcel Heroux
Estimated Sales: $5-10 Million
Number Employees: 500-999
Parent Co: J.M. Schneider
Type of Packaging: Consumer, Food Service, Private Label

924 Bacon's Heir
706-688-9534
info@baconsheir.com
baconsheir.com
Pork rinds and pork panko
Number of Brands: 2
Number of Products: 10
Brands:
  PORK PANKO
  PORK CLOUDS

925 Bad Frog Brewery Co
1093 A1a Beach Blvd
Suite 346
St Augustine, FL 32080-6733
904-687-5939
Fax: 734-629-1777 888-223-3764
badfrog@badfrog.com www.badfrog.com
Beer
President: Jim Wauldron
Contact: William Ostrander
williamostrander@badfrog.com
Estimated Sales: $2.5-5 Million
Number Employees: 10-19
Type of Packaging: Private Label
Brands:
  Bad Frog Amber Lager
  Bad Frog Bad Light
  Bad Frog Micro Malt

926 Bad Seed Cider Company, LLC
43 Baileys Gap Rd.
Highland, NY 12528
845-236-0956
info@badseedhardcider.com
www.badseedhardcider.com
Hard dry ciders
Co-Owner/Partner: Albert Wilklow
Co-Owner/Partner: Devin Britton
Co-Owner/Partner: Bram Kincheloe
Year Founded: 2011
Number of Brands: 1
Number of Products: 4
Type of Packaging: Consumer, Private Label
Brands:
  Bad Seed

927 Badger Best Pizzas
1548 Deckner Avenue
De Pere, WI 54185
920-336-6464
Frozen pizza
President: Herm Fredericks
Plant Manager: Peggy Seefeldt
Estimated Sales: $2.5-5 Million
Number Employees: 5-9

928 Badger Gourmet Ham
3521 W Lincoln Avenue
Milwaukee, WI 53215-2394
414-645-1756
Fax: 414-645-5189 www.badgergourmetham.com
Ham
President: Mark Schwellinger
Estimated Sales: $10-20 Million
Number Employees: 20-49
Number of Brands: 1
Type of Packaging: Consumer
Brands:
  Badger

929 Badger Island Shell-Fish & Lobster
2 Badgers Is W
Kittery, ME 03904-1601
207-703-0431
Fax: 207-703-0432 joe@herbertbrothers.com
www.herbertbrothers.com
Seafood, shellfish, lobster
Owner: Joe Herbert
Co-Owner: Dave Herbert
Estimated Sales: $.5-1 million
Number Employees: 1-4
Parent Co: Herbert Brothers Entertainment Inc

930 Badia Spices Inc.
PO Box 226497
Doral, FL 33322-4697
305-629-8000
877-629-8000
info@badiaspices.com www.badiaspices.com
Herbs, spices and seasonings including garlic, buboric, jalapeno, lindo and taco flavoring.
President: Joseph Badia
info@badia-spices.com
Year Founded: 1967
Estimated Sales: $100 Million
Number Employees: 100-249
Number of Brands: 1
Square Footage: 100000
Type of Packaging: Consumer, Food Service, Private Label, Bulk
Brands:
  Badia Spices
  Badia Canned Vegetables
  Badia Hot Sauces
  Badia Nuts & Seeds
  Badia Seasoning Blends
  Badia Teas

931 Baensch Food Products Co
1025 E Locust St
Milwaukee, WI 53212
414-562-4643
Fax: 414-562-5525 www.mabaensch.com
Pickled & creamed herring
Owner/President: Kim Wall
kim@mabaensch.com
GM: David Jackson
Year Founded: 1932
Number Employees: 10-19
Square Footage: 120000
Parent Co: Wild Foods
Type of Packaging: Consumer, Food Service, Private Label, Bulk
Brands:
  Ma Baensch
  Ma Baensch Herring

932 Bagai Tea Company
PO Box 1046
San Marcos, CA 92079-1046
760-591-3084
Fax: 760-510-1904
Tea
President: Arun Bagai
CFO: Sanjay Bagai
VP: Vik Bagai
Production Manager: Maria Bagai
Purchasing Manager: Arun Bagai
Estimated Sales: $1-5 Million
Number Employees: 5-9
Type of Packaging: Private Label
Brands:
  Chaya
  Emerald Green
  Golden Amber

933 Bagel Factory
2320 S Robertson Blvd # 202
Boulevard
Los Angeles, CA 90034-2053
310-836-9865
www.bagelfactoryinc.com
Bagels
Owner: Sanford Brody
sanford@thebagelfactory.com
CEO/President: Jay Epstein
Estimated Sales: Less Than $500,000
Number Employees: 1-4
Square Footage: 10000

934 Bagel Guys
102 Willoughby Street
Brooklyn, NY 11201-5318
718-222-4361
Fax: 718-222-4362 bagelguyscorp@AOL.com
Bagels
President: Jeffrey Gargiulo
Estimated Sales: $120,000
Number Employees: 3

935 Bagel Lites
240 51st Ave
Apt. 1F
Long Island City, NY 11101
844-678-5544
sales@bagellites.com
www.bagellites.com
Bite-size bagels
Owner: Raquel Salas
Estimated Sales: $100,000
Number Employees: 1-4
Type of Packaging: Private Label

936 Bagels By Bell
10013 Foster Avenue
Brooklyn, NY 11236
718-272-2780
Fax: 718-272-2789 info@bialy.com
www.bialy.com
Bagels and bialy
President: Warren Bell
Estimated Sales: $1 Million
Number Employees: 10-19
Type of Packaging: Private Label
Brands:
  Bell Bialy

Bell Mini Bagel
Bagel By Bell

937 Bagelworks
1229 1st Ave # 2
New York, NY 10065-6314
212-744-6444
Fax: 718-358-3076 www.bagelworks-nyc.com
Muffins and bagels including oat bran, sesame, poppy, cinnamon raisin, sundried tomato, chocolate, sourdough, spinach, herb, wholewheat, cheese, broccoli, rye, peanut butter, etc. including fat free
Owner: Mona Hinnawi
munayah@aol.com
CEO: Aliyeh Hinnawi
CFO: Joseph Hinnawi
VP: Ramsey Hinnawi
Estimated Sales: Less Than $500,000
Number Employees: 5-9
Square Footage: 3400
Other Locations:
Bagelworks
New York NY

938 Bagley's
9782 Rt. 414
Hector, NY 14841
607-582-6421
Fax: 607-582-6421
www.Brittany@BagleysPRV.com
Wines
President: Dave Bagley
Estimated Sales: Less than $200,000
Number Employees: 1-4
Type of Packaging: Private Label
Brands:
Poplar Ridge Vineyards

939 Bahama Specialty Foods
614 Shepherd Street
Durham, NC 27701-3133
919-471-4051
Fax: 919-479-4916
Pepper sauces and salad dressings
President: Robert Maehr
CEO: Jeffrey Ensminger
Estimated Sales: $250,000-500,000
Number Employees: 1-4
Number of Brands: 2
Number of Products: 5
Square Footage: 26000
Type of Packaging: Consumer

940 Baier's Sausage & Meats
6022 67a Street
Red Deer, AB T4P 3E8
Canada
403-346-1535
Fax: 403-346-1773
Ham, sausage, beef jerky, bacon and salami
CEO: Keith Baires
Marketing: Keith Baires
Estimated Sales: $5-10 Million
Type of Packaging: Consumer, Food Service, Bulk
Brands:
Baier's

941 Bailey's Basin Seafood
1683 Front Street
Morgan City, LA 70380-3034
985-384-4926
Fax: 985-384-4926
Fish and seafood
President: Nolton Bailey
Estimated Sales: $2.6 Million
Number Employees: 30
Type of Packaging: Consumer, Food Service

942 Baileyana Winery
4915 Orcutt Rd
San Luis Obispo, CA 93401-8335
805-544-9080
Fax: 805-781-3635 www.baileyana.com
Wine
Manager: Michael Blaney
michael@paragonvineyard.com
CFO: John R Nevin
Estimated Sales: Below $5 Million
Number Employees: 20-49
Brands:
Ecclestone
Vintage Port

943 Baily Tea USA Inc
2275 research blvd
Suite 720
Rockville, MD 20850
301-704-1739
sales@bailytea.com
www.bailytea.com
Tea
CEO: Sudath Munasinghe
s.munasinghe@bailytea.com

944 Baily Vineyard & Winery
33440 LA Serena Way
Temecula, CA 92591-5104
951-676-9463
Fax: 951-676-1276 contact@bailywinery.com
www.bailywinery.com
Wine
Owner: Phil Baily
phil@bailywinery.com
Owner: Carol Baily
Year Founded: 1986
Estimated Sales: $2,800,000
Number Employees: 5-9
Brands:
Baily

945 Bainbridge Festive Foods
2630 Nashville Highway
Farmington, TN 37091
931-359-8000
Fax: 662-363-9895 800-545-9205
www.bainbridgefestivefoods.com
Jellies, pickles, preserves, spice tea mix, and parsley mustard sauce
President: Anthony Altavilla
Owner: Kathleen Pegram
Year Founded: 1981
Estimated Sales: $150,000
Number Employees: 1-4
Number of Products: 12
Square Footage: 14000
Type of Packaging: Private Label

946 Baird Dairy LLC
110 N Randolph Ave
Clarksville, IN 47129-2761
812-283-3345
Fax: 812-283-8701
Ice cream
Owner: Randall Baird
Estimated Sales: Less Than $500,000
Number Employees: 1-4
Type of Packaging: Consumer

947 Baja Foods LLC
636 W Root St
Chicago, IL 60609-2630
773-376-9030
Fax: 773-376-9245 lisa@bajafoodsllc.com
Frozen tamales, quesadillas, chimichangas, burritos, enchiladas, taco meat and chili
Owner: Art Velasquez
donraezler@aol.com
Sales/Marketing: Jeff Rothschild
General Manager: Timothy Poisson
Purchasing Manager: Cheryl Canning
Year Founded: 2001
Estimated Sales: $10-20 Million
Number Employees: 20-49
Square Footage: 30000
Type of Packaging: Consumer, Food Service, Private Label, Bulk
Brands:
Amigo
Cafe Amigo
La Marca
Tango

948 Bakalars Sausage Co
2760 Hemstock St
La Crosse, WI 54603-2345
608-784-0384
Fax: 608-784-8361 info@bakalarssausage.com
www.bakalarssausage.com
Sausage, beef, fish, pork, hamburger meat, steak, etc
President: Mike Bakalars
bakalars@centurytel.net
Purchasing Manager: Mike Bakalars
Estimated Sales: $15 Million
Number Employees: 20-49
Type of Packaging: Consumer, Food Service, Private Label, Bulk
Brands:
Bakalars

949 Bake City
1235 Hightower Trail
Suite 300
Atlanta, GA 30350
855-336-4777
info@bakecityusa.com www.bakecityusa.com
Vegan, organic baked snacks

950 Bake Crafters Food Company
10673 S Lee Highway
McDonald, TN 37353
423-396-3392
Fax: 423-396-9604 support@bakecrafters.com
bakecrafters.com
Baked goods manufacturer specializing in school foodservice nationwide.
General Manager: Michael Byrd
Contact: Lonny Byrd
lonny@bakecrafters.com
Type of Packaging: Consumer, Food Service, Private Label, Bulk
Brands:
Bake Crafters

951 Bake N Joy Foods
351 Willow St
North Andover, MA 01845-5973
978-521-5946
Fax: 978-683-1713 800-666-4937
productinfo@bakenjoy.com www.bakenjoy.com
Low-fat, fat-free and frozen batters, bakery mixes, fillings, toppings, icings and ready-to-bake items
President/CEO: Robert Ogan
rogan@bakenjoy.com
CFO: Alice Shephard
VP Sales: Mark Ake
VP Marketing/Business Development: George Fregone
Marketing Manager: Tara Oleary O Donovan
Estimated Sales: $20-50 Million
Number Employees: 100-249
Type of Packaging: Food Service, Bulk
Other Locations:
Bake'n Joy Foods
Chuluota FL
Brands:
Freshbakes
Strawberry Colada Frozen Batter
Triple Berry Blast Frozen Batter

952 Bake Rite Rolls Inc
2945 Samuel Dr
Bensalem, PA 19020
215-638-2400
800-949-5623
www.nefoods.com
Soft sandwich rolls, english muffins, hamburger and hot dog rolls.
Plant Manager: Jackie Eddis
Estimated Sales: $20-50 Million
Number Employees: 100-249
Parent Co: Northeast Foods
Type of Packaging: Private Label

953 BakeMark Canada
2345 Francis-Hughes Avenue
Laval, QC H7S 1N5
Canada
450-667-8888
Fax: 450-667-3342 800-361-4998
www.bakemarkcanada.com
Processor and exporter of bakers' and confectioners' supplies including fondants, cocoa chips and pieces, apricot and strawberry glazes, rainbow and chocolate sprinkles and fruit pie fillings
President: Larry Sullivan
Contact: Stephanie Corrente
Year Founded: 1915
Number Employees: 10-19
Square Footage: 280000
Parent Co: CSM Bakery Supplies North America
Type of Packaging: Food Service, Private Label
Brands:
Golden
Lafave

Food Manufacturers / A-Z

954 BakeMark Ingredients Canada
2480 Viking Way
Richmond, BC V6V 1N2
Canada
604-303-1700
Fax: 604-270-8002 800-665-9441
www.yourbakemark.com
Baked goods, breads, baking mixes, cookies, pie filling, icing, frozen fruit
President: Larry Sullivan
Vice President: Michael Armstrong
Marketing: David Lopez
Sales Manager: Jeff Bligh
General Manager: Rick Barnes
Manufacturing: Ellen Tsang
Estimated Sales: $23 Million
Number Employees: 160
Number of Brands: 12
Number of Products: 2000
Type of Packaging: Private Label, Bulk
Brands:
 Bakemark
 Bib Ulmer Spatz
 Brill
 Caravan
 Degoede
 Diamalt
 Dreidoppel
 Marquerite
 Meistermarken

955 BakeMark USA
1933 N Meacham Road
Suite 530
Schaumburg, IL 60173-4342
847-519-3135
Fax: 847-925-2101 www.bakemarkusa.com
Bakery products
President/CEO: Robert Wallace
CFO: Herman Brons
VP: Tom Gumkowski
Branch Manager: Karen Werner
Estimated Sales: $4 Million
Type of Packaging: Private Label
Other Locations:
 Phoenix AZ
 Burlington NJ
 Pico Rivera CA
 North Las Vegas NV
 Rancho Cordova CA
 Reno NV
 Union City CA
 Buffalo NY
 Denver CO
 Saratoga Springs NY
 Altanta GA
 Fairfield OH
 Carol Stream IL
Brands:
 Bakeqwik
 Bakesense
 Flour Brands
 Produits Marguerite
 Trigal Dorado
 Westco

956 (HQ)BakeMark USA
7351 Crider Ave
Pico Rivera, CA 90660-3705
562-949-1054
Fax: 562-948-5506 866-232-8575
information@bakemark.com
www.yourbakemark.com
Baking mixes, fillings, icings, glazes, and bakery supplies
President & CEO: Gary Schmidt
CFO: Refugio Reynoso
VP Sales & Marketing: Rick Bennett
Estimated Sales: $20-50 Million
Number Employees: 20-49

957 Baked & Wired
1052 Thomas Jefferson St NW
Washington, DC 20007-3813
703-663-8727
info@bakedandwired.com
www.bakedandwired.com
Baked goods, espresso and bread
Owner: Tony Velazquez
email: info@bakedandwired.com
Number Employees: 5-9

958 Bakeology
Torrance, CA

bakeology.co
Cookies, snack bites and bars
Co-Founder: Dawn Martel
Co-Founder: Sasha Crescentini
Number of Brands: 1
Number of Products: 5
Brands:
 BAKEOLOGY

959 Baker Boy Bake Shop Inc
170 Gta Dr
Dickinson, ND 58601-7200
701-225-4444
Fax: 701-225-7981 800-437-2008
Processor of frozen dough products; wholesaler/distributor of bakery supplies including flour, sugar, etc.; serving the foodservice market.
CEO: Guy Moos
guym@bakerboy.com
Year Founded: 1955
Number Employees: 250-499
Square Footage: 135000
Type of Packaging: Consumer, Food Service, Private Label
Brands:
 Baker Boy

960 Baker Boys
2140 Pegasus Road NE
Calgary, AB T2E 8G8
Canada
403-255-4556
Fax: 403-259-5124 877-246-6036
info@bakerboys.net www.bakerboys.net
Processor of cinnamon rolls including thaw and serve, pre-proofed and frozen
President: Barry Walton
Year Founded: 1987
Number Employees: 20-49
Type of Packaging: Consumer, Food Service
Brands:
 Baker Boys Baked Goods

961 Baker Candy Company
12345 139th St Se
Snohomish, WA 98290
425-422-6331
Fax: 206-361-7009 www.bakerscandies.com
Manufacturer of roasted nuts, chocolates and hard candy
Owner: Randy Spoo
VP: Ronald Prevele
Treasurer: Ronald Prevele
VP: Lee Prevele
Year Founded: 2009
Estimated Sales: $5-10 Million
Number Employees: 2
Square Footage: 60000
Type of Packaging: Consumer, Bulk
Brands:
 Pop Candy
 Mars
 Pez
 Skull
 Dylan's

962 Baker Cheese Factory Inc
N5279 County Road G
St Cloud, WI 53079-1644
920-477-7871
Fax: 920-477-2404 info@bakercheese.com
www.bakercheese.com
Manufacturer of various cheese specializing in string cheese.
President: Brian Baker
CFO: Kevin Baker
Cheese Operations Manager: Jeff LeBleu
Year Founded: 1916
Estimated Sales: $25-50 Million
Number Employees: 100-249
Type of Packaging: Consumer, Private Label
Brands:
 Baker

963 Baker Commodities Inc
4020 Bandini Blvd
Vernon, CA 90058-4274
323-268-2883
Fax: 323-268-5166 800-427-0696
info@bakercommodities.com
Protein meal and feeding fats. Rendering company that recycles fats and oils.
Owner: James M Andreoli
jan@bakercommodities.com
CFO: Jim Reynolds
Executive VP: Dennis Luckey
VP Operations: Bill Sikes
Estimated Sales: $10-20 Million
Number Employees: 500-999
Type of Packaging: Bulk
Other Locations:
 Seattle WA
 Spokane WA
 Kerman CA
 Phoenix AZ
 Rochester NY
 North Billerica MA

964 Baker Maid Products, Inc.
2419 Java Street
New Orleans, LA 70119
504-827-5500
Fax: 504-827-5400 800-664-7882
info@bakermaid.com www.bakermaid.com
Brandied fruit cake and cookies
President & CEO: Darryl Sorrensen
Marketing Director: Adrian Smith
Operations Director: Colin Manikin
Plant Manager: Greg Marigny
Year Founded: 1953
Estimated Sales: $1-2.5 Million
Number Employees: 20-49

965 Baker Produce
212 W Railroad Avenue
PO Box 6757
Kennewick, WA 99336
509-586-6174
Fax: 509-582-3694 800-624-7553
pquinn@bakerproduce.com
www.bakerproduce.com
Apples, onions, potatoes
Sales Manager: Pam Quinn
Sales Representative: Savannah Dean
Shipping Clerk: Kiley Dean
Number Employees: 250-499
Type of Packaging: Consumer, Food Service, Bulk
Brands:
 Baker Supreme
 Bakers Beauties
 Golden Beauties
 Goose Hill
 Western Beauty

966 Baker's Candies Factory Store
831 S Baker St
PO Box 88
Greenwood, NE 68366-1000
402-789-2700
Fax: 402-789-2013 800-804-7330
info@bakerscandies.com www.bakerscandies.com
Fine chocolates, including our chocolate meltaways in seven flavors
Owner: Todd Baker
todd@bakerscandies.com
VP: Patty Baker
Estimated Sales: $3-5 Million
Number Employees: 5-9
Type of Packaging: Consumer

967 Baker's Coconut
100 Deforest Ave
East Hanover, NJ 07936
901-381-6636
Fax: 901-381-6524 855-535-5648
www.mondelezinternational.com
Coconut concentrate
Contact: Mary Taylor
Number Employees: 100-249
Parent Co: Kraft Foods
Type of Packaging: Bulk

968 Baker's Dozen & Cafe
225 E State St
Herkimer, NY 13350
315-866-6770
Baked goods including bread, rolls and doughnuts
Owner: Tom Watkins
Manager: Tony Durso
Estimated Sales: Less Than $500,000
Number Employees: 10-19

Food Manufacturers / A-Z

969 Baker's Point Fisheries
33 Bakers Point Rd East
Oyster Pond Jeddore, NS B0J 1W0
Canada
902-845-2347
Fax: 902-845-2770 janette@bakerspoint.ca
Fresh and frozen haddock, cod, pollack, hake and cusk
Co-Owner: Janette Faulkner
Co-Owner: Wyman Baker
Number Employees: 50-99
Type of Packaging: Bulk

970 Baker's Ribs No 2
3033 Main St
Dallas, TX 75226-1506
214-748-5433
Fax: 214-748-8544 www.bakersribs.com
BBQ sauces and seasonings
General Manager: Robert Austin
Owners: Joe and Suzanne Duncan
Estimated Sales: Less Than $500,000
Number Employees: 1-4
Type of Packaging: Consumer, Food Service
Brands:
  Baker's Rib Inc

971 Bakerhaus Veit Limited
70 Whitmore Road
Woodbridge, ON L4L 7Z4
Canada
905-850-9229
Fax: 905-850-9292 800-387-8860
info@backerhausveit.com
www.backerhausveit.com
Artisan breads
President/CEO: Sabine C Veit
Sales/Marketing/Development: Doug Fleck
Brands:
  Bakerhaus Veit

972 Bakers Best Snack Food Corp.
6000 Central Highway
Pennsauken, NJ 08109
215-822-3511
Fax: 215-997-2049
Soft pretzels
Manager: Wayne Childs
President: Jerry Driver
Sales Exec: John Lewandoski
Marketing Manager: Michael Karaban
G.M.: Wayne Childs
Year Founded: 1989
Number Employees: 50-99
Parent Co: J&J Snack Foods Company
Type of Packaging: Consumer
Brands:
  Rold Gold
  Mustard Pretzels
  Peanut Butter Pretzels
  Unique Pretzels

973 Bakers Breakfast Cookie
427 Ohio St.
Bellingham, WA 98225
360-714-9585
Fax: 360-715-8011 877-889-1090
www.bbcookies.com
All natural cookies
Owner: Erin Baker
Contact: G Bryan
bryang@bbcookies.com
Estimated Sales: $5-10 Million
Number Employees: 20-49
Square Footage: 8000

974 Bakers of Paris
99 Park Ln
Brisbane, CA 94005-1309
415-468-9100
Fax: 415-468-4320
customer-service@bakersofparis.com
www.bakersofparis.com
French bread and French pastries
Owner: Lionel Robbe-Jeadu
lionel@bakersofparis.com
VP: Gilles Wicker
Sales Executive: Caroline Hughes
Estimated Sales: $5-10 Million
Number Employees: 20-49

975 Bakery Barn Inc
111 Terence Dr
Pittsburgh, PA 15236-4133
412-655-1113
Fax: 412-655-8566 888-322-BARN
sales@bakery-barn.com
High-protein cookies
President/Owner: Sean Perich
frontoffice@bakery-barn.com
Number Employees: 100-249
Type of Packaging: Private Label

976 Bakery Essentials Inc
2007 Inverness Dr
Vernon Hills, IL 60061-4530
847-573-0844
Fax: 847-573-0945
Flour, wheat and grain
Owner: Michael Kaufman
Estimated Sales: $500,000-$1 Million
Number Employees: 1-4

977 Bakery on Main
127 Park Ave
Suite 100
East Hartford, CT 6108
860-895-6622
Fax: 860-895-6624 info@bakeryonmain.com
bakeryonmain.com
Gluten free baked goods
President/Founder: Michael Smulders
Quality Assurance Manager: Jennifer Salisbury
Senior Marketing Associate: Curtis Dalbon
VP, Sales: Paul Connolly
Operations Manager: Melissa Carducci-Brooks
Production Manager: Frank Guiliano

978 BakeryCorp
15625 NW 15th Ave
Miami, FL 33169-5601
305-623-3838
Fax: 305-626-9189 info@bakerycorp.com
www.bakerycorp.com
Breads, cakes and pastries
Vice President: Juan Carlos Lacal
Operations General Manager: Luis Lacal
Estimated Sales: $10-20 Million
Number Employees: 20-49
Number of Brands: 1
Type of Packaging: Food Service, Bulk
Brands:
  BakeryCorp

979 Baking Leidenheimer
1501 Simon Bolivar Ave
New Orleans, LA 70113-2329
504-525-1596
Fax: 504-525-1596 800-259-9099
info@leidenheimer.com www.leidenheimer.com
Breads
President: Sandy Whann
Estimated Sales: $10-20,000,000
Number Employees: 10-19

980 Bakkavor USA
2700 Westinghouse Blvd
Charlotte, NC 28273
800-842-3025
sales@bakkavor.us www.bakkavor.com
Fresh soups, breads, sauces, hummus, burritos, dips, and ready meals
President & CEO: Ben Waldron
CFO: Mary Barnett
Quality Assurance Manager: Julie Morrison
Director of Marketing: Therese Griffin
VP Strategic Business Development: Stephen Young
Number Employees: 500-999
Parent Co: Bakkavor Group

981 Bakon Yeast
33415 N 64th Place
Scottsdale, AZ 85266-7363
480-595-9370
Fax: 480-595-9371 bakonyeast@aol.com
bakonyeast.samsbiz.com
Vegetable derived bacon flavored seasonings and hickory smoked torula yeast
President: Phyll Ray
VP: Larry Ray
Plant Manager: Rebecca Schaefer
Year Founded: 1933
Estimated Sales: $600,000
Number Employees: 2-4
Square Footage: 40000
Parent Co: Bakon Yeast
Type of Packaging: Consumer, Food Service, Bulk
Brands:
  Bakon Seasonings
  Bakon Yeast

982 Bakto Flavors
59 Dudley Rd.
North Brunswick, NJ
732-354-4492
Fax: 732-626-5677 info@baktoflavors.com
www.baktoflavors.com
Vanilla products, flavors, spices & herbs, and vinegars
Founder: Daphna Havkin-Frenkel
Square Footage: 80000
Brands:
  Visionary Vinegars

983 Balagna Winery Company
223 Rio Bravo Dr
Los Alamos, NM 87544
505-672-3678
Fax: 505-672-1482
Wines
Proprietor: John Balagna
Estimated Sales: $.5-1 million
Number Employees: 1-4
Brands:
  Balagna Winery

984 Balance Bar Company
110 Orville Drive
Bohemia, NY 11716
800-346-2194
info@balance.com www.balance.com
Meal replacement dieting aids, energy bars
President/CEO: Peter Wilson
Chief Executive Officer: Jeff Nagel
Vice President, Finance: Kristina Eriksen
Chief Operating Officer: Michele ABO
Estimated Sales: $8 Million
Number Employees: 29
Parent Co: The Carlyle Group, L P
Type of Packaging: Private Label
Brands:
  Balance

985 Balanced Health Products
215 E 68th St Ste 33a
New York, NY 10065
212-794-9878
Fax: 212-794-5108
Dietetic candy and food health supplements
President: Nikki Haskell
Estimated Sales: $790,000
Number Employees: 1-4
Square Footage: 4000
Brands:
  Nikki Bars
  Star Blend
  Star Caps
  Star Sucker Sour
  Star Suckers

986 Balboa Dessert Co Inc
1760 E Wilshire Ave
Santa Ana, CA 92705-4615
714-972-4972
Fax: 714-972-0605 800-974-9699
customerservice@balboadessert.com
Processor and exporter of desserts including frozen cakes, cheesecakes and tortes, gourmet baked goods, wholesale and retail
Owner: Anna Ochoa
aochoa@balboadessert.com
Owner: Brett Pollack
Vice President: Dan Hamilton
Year Founded: 1987
Estimated Sales: $4 Million
Number Employees: 5-9
Square Footage: 72000
Type of Packaging: Food Service

987 Baldinger Baking Co
1256 Phalen Blvd
St Paul, MN 55106-2156
651-224-5761
Fax: 651-224-9047 www.baldingerbakery.com
Breads, breadsticks, buns, rolls, bagels and more.

509

Food Manufacturers / A-Z

Partner: Bob Baldinger
President: Steve Baldinger
Contact: Dawn Almen
dawnalmen@gmail.com
Year Founded: 1888
Estimated Sales: $22 Million
Number Employees: 50-99
Square Footage: 145000
Type of Packaging: Consumer, Food Service, Private Label
Brands:
 Baldinger

988 Baldwin Richardson Foods
#2390, One Tower Lane
Oakbrook Terrace, IL 60181
866-644-2732
www.brfoods.com
Liquid ingredient manufacturer specializing in signature sauces, dessert toppings, beverage and pancake syrups, specialty fruit fillings and condiments. The company also offers processing options such as hot-fill, cold-fillhomogenization, and emulsion.
President & CEO: Eric Johnson
Chief Financial Officer: Evelyn White
Sr. Director of Sales: Cara Hughes
Year Founded: 1916
Estimated Sales: $5-10,000,000
Number Employees: 200-500
Square Footage: 900000
Type of Packaging: Consumer, Food Service, Private Label, Bulk
Other Locations:
 Macedon Manufacturing Facility
 Macedon NY
 Williamson Manufacturing
 East Williamson NY
Brands:
 Mrs. Richardson Toppings
 Nance's Mustards

989 Baldwin Vineyards
176 Hardenburgh Rd
Pine Bush, NY 12566-5720
845-744-2226
Fax: 845-744-6321 Info@BaldwinVineyards.com
www.baldwinvineyards.com
Wines
Owner: Pat Baldwin
bv2@frontiernet.net
Owner/President: Jack Baldwin
VP: John Baldwin
Estimated Sales: $500,000-$1 Million
Number Employees: 1-4
Brands:
 Baldwin

990 Baldwin-Minkler Farms
320 E South St
Orland, CA 95963-9111
530-865-8080
Fax: 530-865-8085 djsoetaert@aol.com
Almonds
Owner: Bill Minkler
Estimated Sales: $20-50 Million
Number Employees: 50-99
Type of Packaging: Bulk

991 Balic Winery
6623 Harding Hwy
Mays Landing, NJ 08330-1022
609-625-2166
Fax: 609-625-1904 www.balicwinery.com
Wine
Owner: Bojan Boskodich
b.boskodich@balicwinery.com
Year Founded: 1933
Estimated Sales: Less than $200,000
Number Employees: 1-4

992 Ball Park Franks
PO Box 3901
Peoria, IL 61612
888-317-5867
www.ballparkbrand.com
Hot dogs, packaged meat products, kosher meats, jerky, beef and chicken patties.
President/CEO: Donnie Smith
Number of Brands: 1
Parent Co: Tyson Foods
Brands:
 Ball Park

993 Ballantine Produce Company
P.O.Box 756
10550 S Button Willeen Ave
Reedley, CA 93654-4400
559-875-2583
Fax: 559-637-2159
Manufacturer and processor of over 200 varieties of plums, peaches, nectarines, pluots, white flesh, apricots, grapes, Asian pears, quince, pomegranates, persimmons and apples.
President: Virgil Rasmussen
Partner: Herbert Kaprielian
CFO: Richard Graham
Manufacturing Executive: Ron Fraughenheim
Year Founded: 1919
Estimated Sales: $10-20 Million
Number Employees: 1-4
Type of Packaging: Consumer, Food Service
Other Locations:
 Reedley Sales Office
 Reedley CA
Brands:
 Ballantine

994 Ballard Custom Meats
55 Myrtle St
Manchester, ME 04351-3251
207-622-9764
Fax: 207-621-0242
Meats and seafood
President: Kenneth Ballard
Year Founded: 1969
Estimated Sales: $2,000,000
Number Employees: 10-19

995 Ballas Egg Products Corp
40 N 2nd St
Zanesville, OH 43701-3446
740-453-0386
Fax: 740-453-0491 www.ballasegg.com
Frozen, dried and liquid egg products.
President: Craig Ballas
Estimated Sales: $10 Million
Number Employees: 50-99
Type of Packaging: Consumer, Bulk
Brands:
 Ballas

996 Ballreich's Potato Chips
186 Ohio Ave
Tiffin, OH 44883-1746
419-447-1814
Fax: 419-447-5635 800-323-2447
chips@ballreich.com www.ballreich.com
Snacks including potato chips; flavors include BBQ, sour cream and onion, southwestern BBQ, salt and vinegar, no salt added, and marcelled
Owner: Brian Reis
brian@ballreich.com
VP: Linda Reis
Year Founded: 1920
Estimated Sales: $4 Million
Number Employees: 20-49
Number of Brands: 1
Number of Products: 52
Square Footage: 200000
Type of Packaging: Private Label

997 Balsu
1160 Kane Concourse
Suite 100A
Bay Harbour Islands, FL 33154
305-993-5045
Fax: 305-993-5047 balsu@balsusa.com
www.balsusa.com
Hazelnuts
President/CHR: H. Zapsu
Director/Sales And Marketing: Sezen Donmezer
Sales Director: Karim Azzaoui
kazzaoui@aol.com
Year Founded: 1980
Estimated Sales: A
Number Employees: 1-4
Type of Packaging: Bulk

998 Balticshop.Com LLC
2842 Main Street
Suite 333
Glastonbury, CT 06033-1036
Fax: 201-300-0146 800-506-2312
margita@balticshop.com www.balticshop.com
Bread, candy & cookies.

999 Baltimore Brewing Company
104 Albemarle St
Baltimore, MD 21202
410-837-5000
Fax: 410-837-5024 theo@degroens.com
www.degroens.com
Beers
President: Theo De Groen
groen@degroens.com
Secretary: Imtraud De Groen
Estimated Sales: Under $500,000
Number Employees: 1-4
Brands:
 De Groen's

1000 Baltimore Coffee & Tea Co Inc
9 W Aylesbury Rd # T
Lutherville, MD 21093-4121
410-561-1080
Fax: 410-561-4816 800-823-1408
orders@baltcoffee.com www.baltcoffee.com
Coffee and tea
Owner: Paul Jakubowski
pjakubowski@easternshoretea.com
VP: Norman Loverde
Estimated Sales: $2.5-5 Million
Number Employees: 50-99
Type of Packaging: Private Label
Brands:
 Easten Shore Tea
 Peets
 Costa Rica
 Lavazza Coffee

1001 Bama Fish Atlanta
3113 Main Street
East Point, GA 30344-4802
404-765-9896
Fax: 404-765-9874
Fresh and frozen fish

1002 Bama Foods LTD
5377 E 66th St N
Tulsa, OK 74117-1813
918-592-0778
Fax: 918-732-2902 800-756-2262
www.bama.com
Frozen baked goods including cookies, pies and biscuits; dough, pastry and crumb crust pie shells
CEO: Matt Alley
alley@bama.com
Chief Executive Officer: Paula A. Marshall
Chief Financial Officer-US Operations: Rocky Moore
Executive Vice President: William L. Chew
Vice President of Research and Developme: Joe McDilda
QC Manager: Maurice Lawry
Director Brand Sales: Gary Wilson
Vice President of Operations: Kevin C. Wilson
Number Employees: 100-249
Type of Packaging: Consumer, Food Service

1003 Bama Frozen Dough
2745 East 11th Street
PO Box 4829
Tulsa, OK 74104
918-732-2600
Fax: 918-592-7499 800-756-2262
dwilson@bama.com www.bama.com
Frozen pizza, yeast, pastry sheet dough
CEO: Paula Marshall
Chief Financial Officer: Rocky Moore
VP R&D/Quality Assurance: Mike Martin
VP Sales/Marketing: Alvaro Gomez
Contact: Adam Ailey
aailey@bama.com
VP Operations: Kevin Wilson
Estimated Sales: $20-50 Million
Number Employees: 100-249
Parent Co: Bama Companies
Other Locations:
 Bama Companies
 Tulsa OK
 Bama Foods Ltd.
 Tulsa OK
 Beijing Bama Food Processing Co.
 Daxing County, Beijing

1004 Banana Distributing Company
1500 S Zarzamora Street
Unit 405
San Antonio, TX 78207
210-227-8285
Fax: 210-227-8285 www.banana-distributing.com

Food Manufacturers / A-Z

Bananas, plantains, hass avocados, oranges, apples, sugar cane
Owner/Manager: Jim Scarsdale
Year Founded: 2007
Estimated Sales: $5-10 Million
Number Employees: 10-19
Parent Co: Barshop Enterprises
Type of Packaging: Consumer, Food Service, Bulk

1005 Bandon Bay Fisheries
PO Box 485
250 1st Street SW
Bandon, OR 97411-0485
541-347-4454
Fax: 541-347-4313
Seafood, shrimp meat and crab meat
Manager: Graydon Stinnett
Number Employees: 50-99
Square Footage: 40000
Parent Co: S&S Seafood
Type of Packaging: Private Label

1006 Banfi Vintners
1111 Cedar Swamp Rd
Old Brookville, NY 11545-2109
516-626-9200
Fax: 516-626-9218 800-645-6511
banfiwines@gmail.com www.banfiwines.com
Wine
Principal: James Mariani
President & CEO: Cristina Mariani-May
Marketing Director: Gary Clayton
VP Public Relations: Lars Leicht
Estimated Sales: $34 Million
Number Employees: 50-99
Brands:
 Almaviva
 Bell' Agio
 Borgogno
 Cecchi
 Concha Y Toro
 Cono Sur
 Costello Banfi
 Entree
 Florio
 Old Brookville
 Placido
 Riunite
 Sartori
 Sincerity
 Stone Haven
 Stone Haven
 Stone's
 Sunrise
 Vigne Regali
 Walnut Crest
 Wisdom & Warter

1007 Bang & Soderlund Inc
9240 Bonita Beach Rd SE # 1118
Bonita Springs, FL 34135-4250
239-498-0600
Fax: 239-498-0606 soderlund@aol.com
Dairy products
Manager: Michael Cunningham
Estimated Sales: $2.5-5,000,000
Number Employees: 1-4
Type of Packaging: Private Label

1008 Banner Candy Manufacturing Company
700 Liberty Avenue
Brooklyn, NY 11208-2115
718-647-4747
Candy and confectionary
President: Peter Stone
Partner: Laura Stone
Contact: Rose Grunther
bannercandy700@yahoo.com
Estimated Sales: $10-20 Million
Number Employees: 29-49
Type of Packaging: Bulk

1009 Banner Pharmacaps
4100 Mendenhall Oaks Pkwy
Suite 301
High Point, NC 27265
336-812-7003
Fax: 336-812-7030 800-526-6993
www.patheon.com
Vitamins
President/CEO: Roger Gordon
CFO: Damien Reynolds
Global VP/R&D/Operations: Aqeel Fatmi
kevin.cogdell@wellsfargo.com
Contact: Kevin Cogdell
kevin.cogdell@wellsfargo.com
Global VP/Commercial Operations: Timothy Doran
Parent Co: Sobel-Holland
Other Locations:
 Banner Pharmacaps
 Chatsworth CA
 Banner Pharmacaps
 Alberta, Canada
 Gelcaps Exportadora De Mexico
 Naucalpan, Edo. de Mexico
 Banner Pharmacaps Europe BV
 Tilburg, The Netherlands
 Banner Pharmacaps India Pvt. Ltd.
 Bangalore, India
Brands:
 Sofgels®
 Entericare®
 Solvatrol™
 Soflet® Gelcaps
 Liquisoft™
 Chewels®
 Versatrol™
 Ecocaps®

1010 Banquet Schusters Bakery
115 E Abriendo Ave
Pueblo, CO 81004-4201
719-544-1062
Baked goods
President: Janet Monack
Year Founded: 1946
Estimated Sales: Less Than $500,000
Number Employees: 10-19
Type of Packaging: Consumer

1011 Bantam Bagels
283 Bleecker St
New York, NY 10014
646-852-6320
contact@bantambagels.com
www.bantambagels.com
Gourmet bagels
Co-Owner: Nick Oleksak
Co-Owner: Elyse Olesak
Year Founded: 2015
Estimated Sales: $500,000
Number Employees: 1-4
Type of Packaging: Consumer, Food Service
Brands:
 MarieBelle(c)

1012 Banza
info@eatbanza.com
www.eatbanza.com
Chickpea pasta
Number of Brands: 1
Type of Packaging: Consumer
Brands:
 BANZA

1013 Banzos
5500 East Pacific Place
Denver, CO 80222
303-447-2133
info@eatbanzos.com
Garbonzo bean dips and snacks
Parent Co: Wild Thyme Naturals
Type of Packaging: Consumer

1014 Baptista's Bakery
4625 W Oakwood Park Dr
Franklin, WI 53132-8872
414-409-2000
Fax: 414-423-4375 info@baptistas.com
www.baptistas.com
Snack products
President: Thomas Howe
thowe@baptistas.com
Research & Development: Kelli Lara
Product Development & Culinary Science: Mike Huber
Business Development & Customer Service: Ed Creamean
Materials/Distribution Manager: Neil Stockman
Plant Technical Manager: Brent Butterfield
Supply Chain Process Specialist: John Susko
Number Employees: 100-249
Square Footage: 135000
Parent Co: Snyder's-Lance Inc.
Type of Packaging: Food Service, Private Label

1015 Bar Harbor Brewing Company
8 Mount Desert Street
Bar Harbor, ME 04609
207-288-4592
www.barharborbrewing.com
Brewering company
President: Andre Lozano
Operations: Tod Foster
Year Founded: 1990
Estimated Sales: $1-2.5 Million
Number Employees: 1-4
Brands:
 Bar Harbor Ginger Ale
 Bar Harbor Peach Ale
 Cadillac Mountain Stout
 Harbor Lighthouse Ale
 Thunder Hole Ale
 True Blue

1016 Bar Harbor Foods
1112 Cutler Rd
Whiting, ME 04691-3436
207-259-3341
Fax: 207-259-3343 info@barharborfoods.com
www.barharborfoods.com
Seafood
Contact: Mike Sansing
msansing@barharborfoods.com

1017 Bar-S Foods Co
5090 N 40th St # 300
Phoenix, AZ 85018-2185
602-264-7272
Fax: 602-285-5252 800-699-4115
www.bar-s.com
Meat products
CEO: Delilah Aguilar
delilah.aguilar@bar-sfoods.com
Number Employees: 50-99

1018 Baraboo Candy Co LLC
E10891 Coop Ln
Baraboo, WI 53913
608-356-7425
Fax: 608-356-1815 800-967-1690
sales@baraboocandy.com www.baraboocandy.com
Chocolate candy sugar free, dark, milk and white chocolate
President: Michael Ford
CEO: Walter Smith
Chief Executive: Dennis Roney
Year Founded: 1981
Estimated Sales: $1 Million
Number Employees: 5-9
Type of Packaging: Private Label, Bulk
Brands:
 Chewy Gooey Pretzel Sticks
 Cow Lick
 Cow Pie
 Green Bay Puddles
 Lick-A-Pig
 Moo Chew
 Upper Fingers
 Wally Walleye

1019 Barataria Spice Company
PO Box 239
Barataria, LA 70036
504-689-7650
800-793-7650
www.seasoningspice.com
Spices
Co-Owner/President: Mike Hymel
Co-Owner/CEO: Cynthia Hymel
Estimated Sales: Less than $500,000
Number Employees: 2
Type of Packaging: Consumer, Food Service
Brands:
 Captain Mike's

1020 Barbara's Bakery
20802 Kensington Blvd
Lakeville, MN 55044
800-343-0590
www.barbaras.com
Organic and natural cereals, crackers, cookies, bars, puffs and chips.
President: Barabara Jaffe
Research & Development Manager: Deborah Flindall
Vice President, Marketing: Kent Spalding
Year Founded: 1971
Estimated Sales: $20-50 Million

Food Manufacturers / A-Z

Number Employees: 175
Square Footage: 102500
Type of Packaging: Consumer, Private Label
Other Locations:
   Barbara's Bakery
   Sacramento CA
Brands:
   Barbara's Bakery
   Nature's Choice
   Weetabix

1021 Barber Dairies
36 Barber Ct
Birmingham, AL 35209-6435
205-942-2351
Fax: 205-943-0296 www.barbersdairy.com
Dairy products, fruit juices and teas.
Controller: Martin Walden
General Manager/VP: P Flagg
Chief Marketing Officer: Johnny Collins
Sales: Terri Smith
Human Resource Executive: Sharon Williams
Manager: Lew Mccravy
Plant Manager: Valerie Meyers
Estimated Sales: $5-10 Million
Number Employees: 250-499
Parent Co: Dean Foods
Type of Packaging: Consumer, Food Service, Private Label, Bulk

1022 Barber Foods
PO Box 219
Kings Mountain, NC 28086
877-447-3279
www.barberfoods.com
Frozen chicken: stuffed breasts
Year Founded: 1955
Estimated Sales: $3-5 Million
Square Footage: 600000
Parent Co: Advance Pierre Foods
Type of Packaging: Consumer, Food Service
Other Locations:
   Barber Foods Production Plant
   Portland ME
Brands:
   Barber Foods

1023 Barber's Farm Distillery LLC
3609 NY-30
Middleburgh, NY 12122
www.1857spirits.com
Gluten-free, farm-to-bottle vodka
President/General Manager: Dorcas Roehrs
Head Distiller: Elias Barber
Marketing/Sales Director: Larry Friedberg
Number of Brands: 1
Number of Products: 1
Type of Packaging: Consumer, Private Label
Brands:
   1857 Spirits

1024 Barbero Bakery, Inc.
61 Conrad St
Trenton, NJ 08611
609-394-5122
Fax: 609-394-5567 www.barberobakery.com
Specialty cakes, pastries, italian cookies, deserts, deli breads and rolls
President: Robert McVicker
Contact: Lou Commiso
lcommiso@barberobakery.com
Year Founded: 1925
Estimated Sales: $2.5-5 Million
Number Employees: 20-49

1025 Barboursville Vineyards
17655 Winery Rd
P.O. Box 136
Barboursville, VA 22923-8321
540-832-3824
Fax: 540-832-7572 bvvy@barboursvillewine.com
Wines
Manager: Luca Paschina
CMO: Carter Nicholas
nicholas.carter@barboursvillewine.com
Number Employees: 20-49

1026 Barca Wine Cellars
PO Box 1150
Roseville, CA 95678
916-786-0770
Fax: 916-740-2220
barcaintlwines@barcawines.net
barcawines.net
Wines

General Manager/CEO: Gino Barca
Year Founded: 1881
Estimated Sales: $3-5 Million
Number Employees: 5-9
Brands:
   Barbousville Vineyards

1027 Barcelona Nut Co
502 S Mount St
Baltimore, MD 21223-3495
410-233-5252
Fax: 410-233-6555 800-296-6887
sales@barcelonanut.com www.barcelonanut.com
Trail mixes, snack mixes, popcorn and cotton candy
President: Tony Tsonis
ttsonis@barcelonanut.com
EVP: Mike Adams
Estimated Sales: $20-50 Million
Number Employees: 100-249
Number of Brands: 5
Square Footage: 55000
Type of Packaging: Consumer, Food Service, Private Label, Bulk
Brands:
   Barcelona
   Candyman Lane
   Healthnut
   Snacknut
   Stonehedge

1028 Bard Valley Medjool Date Growers
2575 E 23rd Lane
Yuma, AZ 85365
928-726-0901
Fax: 928-726-9413 edwardo@datepac.com
www.datepac.com
Medjool dates
President: Edward O'Malley
President of Sales Operations: Dave Nelson
Production Manager: Camen Wilson
General Manager: Glen Vandervoort
Year Founded: 2004
Number Employees: 50-99

1029 Bare Snacks
800-940-0019
baresnacks.com
Fruit and vegetable chips
Number of Brands: 1
Type of Packaging: Consumer
Brands:
   BARE

1030 Barefoot Contessa Pantry
2 Stonewall Lane
York, ME 03909
207-351-2712
Fax: 207-351-2715 800-826-1752
kbouchie@stonewallkitchen.com
www.stonewallkitchen.com
French citrus, dessert baking mixes, breakfast baking mixes, dessert toppings, sauces and marinades, pancakes and syrups, preserves and lemon curd, coffee and hot chocolate
Co-Founder/President/CEO: Jonathan King
Co-Founder/VP: James Stott
Year Founded: 1991

1031 Barely Bread
www.barelybread.com
Grain-free bread and bagels
Founder: Amanda Orso
Chief Marketing Officer: Elyssa Sanders
Number of Brands: 1
Type of Packaging: Consumer
Brands:
   BARELY BREAD

1032 Baretta Provision
172 Commerce St
East Berlin, CT 06023-1105
860-828-0802
Fax: 860-828-8699 www.barettaprovision.com
Meats including beef, pork and veal
Owner: William Baretta
President: Daniel Baretta
Contact: Lori Wright
lori.wright@barettaprovision.com
Year Founded: 1967
Estimated Sales: $3-5 Million
Number Employees: 10-19
Type of Packaging: Food Service

Brands:
   Lenora

1033 Bargetto Winery
3535 N Main St
Soquel, CA 95073-2530
831-475-2258
Fax: 831-475-2664 800-422-7438
customerservice@bargetto.com www.bargetto.com
Wines
President: Martin Bargetto
Operations: Michael Sones
Year Founded: 1918
Estimated Sales: $5-9.9 Million
Number Employees: 20-49
Type of Packaging: Private Label
Brands:
   Bargetto
   Chaucers
   Lavita

1034 Barhyte Specialty Foods Inc
912 Airport Rd
Pendleton, OR 97801-4589
541-276-0259
Fax: 503-691-8918 800-227-4983
chris@mustardpeople.com www.barhyte.com
Mustards
Owner: Brad Hill
Secretary/Treasurer: Irene Barhyte
Director Sales Marketing: Chris Barhyte
chris@barhyte.com
Public Relation President: Kelly M. Mooney
Year Founded: 1982
Estimated Sales: $2.5-5,000,000
Number Employees: 5-9
Brands:
   Aviator Ale Micro Brew Mustards
   Food and Wine
   Food and Wine Mustards
   Haus Barhyte Mustard
   Williamette Valley Mustard

1035 Bari & Gail
761 Main Street
Walpole, MA 02081
508-668-2634
Fax: 508-850-9555 800-828-9318
Chocolates
President: Joseph Sesnovich
Owner: Barrie Steinberg
Vice President: Lisa Gail Sesnovich
Year Founded: 1932
Estimated Sales: $500,000
Number Employees: 1-4
Type of Packaging: Bulk

1036 Bari Olive Oil Co
40063 Road 56
Dinuba, CA 93618-9708
559-595-9260
877-638-3626
orders@bariliveoil.com www.bariliveoil.com
Olive oils
President: Robert Sawatzky
Contact: Breann Borges
borgesbreann@bariliveoil.com
Number Employees: 1-4

1037 Barilla USA
885 Sunset Ridge Road
Northbrook, IL 60062
847-405-7500
Fax: 847-405-7505 800-922-7455
www.barilla.com
Pastas and pasta sauces.
President: Jean-Pierre Comte
VP Marketing: Melissa Tendick
Contact: Carroll Alba
alba.carroll@barilla.com
Logistics Customer Manager: Pasquale DeChiara
Number Employees: 100-249
Number of Brands: 3
Type of Packaging: Food Service
Brands:
   Barilla Pasta
   Barilla Pronto™
   Barilla ProteinPLUS™

Food Manufacturers / A-Z

1038 Barkeater Chocolates
3235 State Route 28
PO Box 286
North Creek, NY 12853
518-251-4438
www.barkeaterchocolates.com
Chocolates
Co-Founder: Jim Morris
Co-Founder: Deb Morris
Contact: Louisa Giaquinto
lgiaquinto@allstatecorporateservices.com
Square Footage: 80000
Brands:
 Barkeater Chocolates

1039 Barker System Bakery
209 S Oak St
Mt Carmel, PA 17851-2147
570-339-3380
Baked goods
President: Cathy Saukatis
Owner: Paul Saukatis
Estimated Sales: Less than $500,000
Number Employees: 1-4

1040 Barkman Honey
120 Santa Fe St
Hillsboro, KS 67063-9688
620-947-3173
Fax: 620-947-3640 800-364-6623
www.barkmanhoney.com
Honey
CEO: Dwight Stoller
dstoller@ghfllc.com
Director of Operations: Tom Harmon
Year Founded: 1920
Number Employees: 50-99
Type of Packaging: Consumer, Food Service
Other Locations:
 Latty OH
Brands:
 Naked Wild Honey
 Busy Bee
 Pure Harmony Dakota Clover
 Pure 'N Simple
 Thrifty Bee

1041 Barkthins Snacking Chocolate
225 N Route 303 Ste 101
Congers, NY 10920-3001
USA
845-770-5802
Fax: 845-353-5276 www.barkTHINS.com
Chocolate
Executive Vice President: Tom Riggio
Chief Marketing Officer: Deborah Holt
Contact: Dominic Alvarado
dalvarack@barkthins.com

1042 Barlean's Fisheries
3660 Slater Rd
Ferndale, WA 98248-9518
360-384-0325
Fax: 360-384-1746 bfmain@barleansfishery.com
www.barleansfishery.com
Organic flaxseed oil, fish oil
Owner/President: Cindy Smith
Vice President: Ronan Smith
Marketing Director: Andreas Koch
Manager: Yehya Ahmed
yahmed@barleans.com
Year Founded: 1972
Number Employees: 10-19

1043 Barn Stream Natural Foods
PO Box 896
52 McClean Road
Alstead, NH 03602-3326
603-756-4395
Health foods
Owner: Nicholas Raynor
Year Founded: 1992
Estimated Sales: $1 Million
Number Employees: 2

1044 Barnana
1746 Berkeley St
Unit B
Santa Monica, CA 90404
858-480-1543
info@barnana.com
barnana.com
Dried banana snacks

Co-Founder/CEO: Caue Suplicy
CMO: Nik Ingersoll
COO: Matt Clifford
Year Founded: 2012
Type of Packaging: Private Label

1045 Barnes & Watson Fine Teas
270 S Hanford St # 211
Seattle, WA 98134-1941
206-625-9435
Fax: 206-625-0345 800-447-8832
tea@barnesandwatson.com www.bwt.com
Tea
Owner: Ken Rudee
Estimated Sales: $1-2,500,000
Number Employees: 1-4
Number of Products: 50+
Type of Packaging: Consumer, Food Service, Bulk
Brands:
 Barnes
 Watson Fine Teas

1046 Barnes Ice Cream Company
475 Pond Rd
Manchester, ME 04351-3612
207-622-0827
Ice cream and frozen desserts
Owner: Richard Barnes
Owner: Carl Barnes
Estimated Sales: $500,000-$1 Million
Number Employees: 1-4
Type of Packaging: Consumer

1047 Barney Butter
2925 S Elm Ave
Suite 101
Fresno, CA 93706-5465
USA
559-442-1752
info@barneybutter.com
www.barneybutter.com
Almond based butters
Chief Financial Officer: Dawn Kelley
Estimated Sales: Less Than $500,000
Number Employees: 1-4

1048 Barney Pork House
New Mourten Road
Decatur, AL 35601-1471
256-353-8688
Sausage
Partner: Billy C Burney II
Estimated Sales: $.5-1 million
Number Employees: 49

1049 Barnie's Coffee and Tea
1030 N Orange Ave
Suite 220
Orlando, FL 32801
800-284-1416
customerservice@barniescoffee.com
www.barniescoffee.com
Coffee and tea
CFO: Tricia Relvini
VP, Sales & Marketing: Scott Uguccioni
Estimated Sales: $94 Million
Number Employees: 50-99

1050 Baron Vineyards
PO Box 624
1516 Fairway Drive
Paso Robles, CA 93446
805-239-3313
Fax: 805-239-2789
Wines
Owner: Tom Baron
Co-Owner: Sharon Baron
Number Employees: 20-49
Brands:
 Baron

1051 Barone Foods
345 S Kino Pkwy
Tucson, AZ 85719
520-623-8571
Fax: 520-622-1599
Cooked and processed meats including sausage
Chief Operating Officer: Tim Barone
Estimated Sales: $5-10 Million
Number Employees: 10-19
Parent Co: City Meat
Type of Packaging: Consumer, Food Service, Private Label, Bulk

1052 Barrel O' Fun Snack Foods
400 Lakeside Dr
PO Box 230
Perham, MN 56573-2202
330-346-7000
Fax: 218-346-7003 800-346-4910
www.barrelofunsnacks.com
Snacks
President/CEO: Ken Nelson
VP: Charlie Nelson
VP Sales & Marketing: Randy Johnson
Contact: Terry Enerson
tenerson@klnfamilybrands.com
General Manager: Kevin Keil
Estimated Sales: $20-50 Million
Number Employees: 5-9
Number of Brands: 1
Parent Co: Shearer's Foods
Type of Packaging: Private Label
Brands:
 Barrel O'Fun

1053 Barrie House Gourmet Coffee
4 Warehouse Lane
Elmsford, NY 10523
914-233-1561
800-876-2233
www.barriehouse.com
Coffees, teas, accessories and equipment
President: Paul Goldstein
CEO: Craig M James
CFO/COO: George Ercolino
Quality/R&D Director: Zurab Jacobi
VP Sales & Customer Service: Kathleen Collins
Contact: Edward Goldstein
egoldstein@barriehouse.com
Year Founded: 1934
Estimated Sales: $20-50 Million
Number Employees: 20-49
Number of Products: 200
Type of Packaging: Food Service, Private Label, Bulk
Brands:
 Barrie House
 Cafe Bodega
 Cafe Excellence
 Donut Shop

1054 Barrington Coffee Roasting
165 Quarry Hill Rd
Lee, MA 01238-9623
413-243-3008
Fax: 413-528-0614 800-528-0998
coffee@barringtoncoffee.com
www.barringtoncoffee.com
Coffee
Owner: Barth Anderson
barth@barringtoncoffee.com
Owner: Gregg Charbonneau
General Manager: Christina Stanton
Production Director: Karli Cassavant
Year Founded: 1993
Estimated Sales: $2.5-5 Million
Number Employees: 5-9
Type of Packaging: Private Label
Brands:
 Barrington Estate
 Barrington Gold
 Dark Roast
 Limited Edition
 Organic/Fair Trade
 Single Origin

1055 Barrows Tea Company
PO Box 40278
New Bedford, MA 02744-0003
774-488-8684
Fax: 508-990-2760 800-832-5024
www.barrowstea.com
Teas
President: Sam Barrows
Estimated Sales: $1-2.5 Million
Number Employees: 1-4
Number of Brands: 1
Number of Products: 15
Type of Packaging: Consumer, Food Service
Brands:
 Barrows

Food Manufacturers / A-Z

1056 Barry Callebaut USA
600 West Chicago Ave
Suite 860
Chicago, IL 60654
312-496-7300
866-443-0460
www.barry-callebaut.com
Chocolate and cocoa
Chief Executive Officer: Antoine de Saint-Affrique
Chief Financial Officer: Victor Balli
President, Americas: David Johnson
Contact: Mark Adriaenssens
mark.adriaenssens@barry-callebaut.com
Number Employees: 10,000
Number of Brands: 14
Brands:
  Barry Callebaut
  Bensdorp
  Cacao Barry
  Callebaut®
  Caprimo
  Carma®
  Chocolate Masters™
  Chocovic
  IBC
  Le Royal
  Mona Lisa
  Sicao
  Van Houten Drinks
  Van Houten Professional
  VanLeer
  La Morella Nuts

1057 Barry Group
415 Griffin Dr
Corner Brook, NL A2H 3E9
Canada
709-785-7387
bgi@barrygroupinc.com
www.barrygroupinc.com
Frozen fish and seafood; grenadier fillets; fish oil.
Founder & CEO: Bill Barry
VP, Sales: Kevin Baldwin
Year Founded: 1854
Estimated Sales: $283.03 Million
Number Employees: 3,000
Parent Co: Westfish International
Type of Packaging: Consumer, Food Service, Private Label, Bulk
Brands:
  Ocean Leader
  Seafreez
  Pacific
  Icelandic

1058 Barsotti Family Juice Co.
2239 Hidden Valley Lane
Camino, CA 95709-9722
530-622-4629
Fax: 530-642-9703 info@barsottijuice.com
www.barsottijuice.com
Fruit and vegetable juices
Co-Founder: Gael Barsotti
Co-Founder: Joan Barsotti
Number of Brands: 1
Number of Products: 11
Type of Packaging: Consumer

1059 Bartek Ingredients, Inc.
421 Seaman Street
Stoney Creek, ON L8E 3J4
Canada
905-662-1127
Fax: 905-662-8849 800-263-4165
sales@bartek.ca www.bartek.ca
Acidulants
Chief Executive Officer: Raffaele Brancato
Vice President: David Tapajna
Vice President: Jason Perry
Year Founded: 1978
Estimated Sales: $40 Million
Number Employees: 80
Square Footage: 40000

1060 Bartlett Dairy & Food Service
90-04 161 St
Suite 609
Jamaica, NY 11285
718-658-2299
www.bartlettny.com
Dairy and general grocery products
President: Thomas Malave, Jr.
Senior Logistics Analyst: Gary Kwan
gkwan@bartlettny.com
Year Founded: 1990
Estimated Sales: $123.3 Million
Number Employees: 171
Number of Brands: 1
Brands:
  Bartlett Dairy

1061 Bartlett Milling Co.
701 S Center St
Box 831
Statesville, NC 28677
704-872-9581
Fax: 704-873-8956 800-438-6016
www.bartlettmillingfeed.com
Grain merchandising, flour and feed milling
Vice President: Trey Sebus
Year Founded: 1907
Estimated Sales: $50-100 Million
Number Employees: 100-249
Parent Co: Bartlett & Company
Type of Packaging: Consumer, Food Service, Private Label, Bulk
Brands:
  Diamond Cake
  Fine Spun
  Palace Pastry
  White Rock
  Wigwam

1062 Bartolini Ice Cream
967 E 167th St
Bronx, NY 10459-1951
718-589-5151
Fax: 718-893-3171
Ice cream, ices, cheese, eggs, and dairy products
Owner: Michael Bartolini
Year Founded: 1971
Estimated Sales: $3 Million
Number Employees: 10-19

1063 Bartons Fine Foods
Highway 460
Denniston, KY 40316
606-768-3750
Fax: 606-768-3737 888-810-3750
Jellies, jams, mustards, barbecue sauces, molasses and relishes
President: Bryan Allphin
Operations Director: Phil Madrio
Estimated Sales: $2.5-5 Million
Number Employees: 5-9
Square Footage: 24000
Type of Packaging: Consumer, Food Service, Private Label

1064 Bartush Schnitzius Foods Co
425 E Jones St
1137 North Kealy
Lewisville, TX 75057-2613
972-219-1270
Fax: 972-436-5719 sales@bartushfoods.com
www.bartushfoods.com
Bar mixes, salad dressing and sauces including horseradish, salsa, barbecue, taco, picante and tomato
President/CEO: John Rubi
jrubi@bartushfoods.com
Sales Executive: Joe Bartush
Year Founded: 1968
Estimated Sales: $12 Million
Number Employees: 50-99
Number of Products: 200+
Square Footage: 100000
Type of Packaging: Consumer, Food Service, Private Label
Brands:
  Bar-Snitz
  Fairway
  Melcer
  Schnitzius
  Texas

1065 Baruvi Fresh LLC
535 Fifth Ave
27th Flr
New York, NY 10017
646-346-1074
info@baruvi.com
www.hummustir.com
Hummus
CEO/Co-Founder: Rakesh Barmecha
COO/Co-Founder: Alon Kruvi
Vice President of Sales: Brian Stuckleman
Operations Manager: Johnny Makkar
Year Founded: 2015
Number Employees: 1-10
Type of Packaging: Food Service, Private Label

1066 Basciani Foods Inc
944 Penn Green Rd.
Avondale, PA 19311-9749
610-268-3610
Fax: 610-268-2186 john@bascianifoods.com
www.bascianifoods.com
Mushrooms including crimini, portabella, oyster, shiitake, white, and other exotic mushrooms; Blackberries
President: Mario Basciani Sr
COO: Michael Basciani Sr
Food Safety & Sanitation Specialist: Fred Recchiuti
Head of Sales/Logistics: John Basciani Sr
Head of Sales/Logistics: Richard Basciani Jr
Estimated Sales: $20-50 Million
Number Employees: 100-249

1067 Bascom Family Farms Inc
74 Cotton Mill Hl # A106
Brattleboro, VT 05301-8603
802-254-5529
Fax: 802-257-8111 888-266-6271
sales@bascomfamilyfarms.com
www.maplesource.com
Pure maple syrup and sugar; organic and kosher varieties available
President: Bruce Bascom
Director of Sales and Marketing: Arnold Coombs
Estimated Sales: $.5-1 million
Number Employees: 10-19
Number of Brands: 3
Type of Packaging: Consumer, Food Service, Private Label, Bulk
Brands:
  Coombs Family Farms

1068 Base Culture
5160 140th Ave N
Clearwater, FL 33760
baseculture.com
Paleo baked goods
Founder & CEO: Jordan Windschauer
Number of Brands: 1
Type of Packaging: Consumer

1069 Basic American Foods
2185 N California Blvd
Suite 215
Walnut Creek, CA 94596-3566
925-472-4000
Fax: 925-472-4360 www.baf.com
Mashed potatoes, hashbrowns & cut potatoes, potato casseroles, and beans & chili
President & CEO: Loren Kimura
lkimura@baf.com
CFO: John Argent
Brand Manager: Hans Kohte
Development Manager: Gary Eversoll
Production Supervisor: Leon Mortensen
Marketing Manager: Jane Foreman
Director, Ingredient Sales: Daniela Boyd
Senior Manager Media Relations: Pat Burke
VP Supply Chain Operations: Mark Klompien
Project Manager: Jerome Bullock
Purchasing: Chris Gentry
Number Employees: 100-249
Square Footage: 13814
Type of Packaging: Consumer, Food Service, Private Label, Bulk
Brands:
  Hungry Jack
  Nana's Own
  Basic American Foods
  Nature's Own Potato Pearls
  Potato Pearls Excel
  Potato Pearls
  Golden Grill
  Redi-Shred
  Quick-Start Home Style Chili
  Santiago Beans
  Classic Casserole
  Redi-Shred Potato Cheese Bake

1070 Basic Food Flavors
3950 E Craig Rd
North Las Vegas, NV 89030-7504
702-643-0043
Fax: 702-643-6149 info@basicfoodflavors.com
www.basicfoodflavors.com

Industrial ingredients, including hydrolyzed vegetable proteins, processed flavors, soy sauce and soy bases
President & CFO: Cathy Staley
cstaley@staleyinc.com
Vice President: Bill Robertson
Lab Manager; R&D: Randy Pierce
Quality Assurance Manager: Geetika Duggal
Customer Service: Cathy Hooper
Director of Sales & Marketing: Dave Wood
Operations Director: Phil Price
Estimated Sales: $10 Million
Number Employees: 50-99
Square Footage: 60000
Type of Packaging: Food Service, Bulk

1071 Basic Grain Products
300-310 East Vine Street
Coldwater, OH 45828-1399
614-408-3091
Fax: 419-678-4647 866-411-6677
info@tastemorr.com www.tastemorr.com
Whole grain rice cakes, multigrain crisps, pita chips, and potato crisps.
President: Carol Knapke
Estimated Sales: $20-50 Million
Number Employees: 100-249
Number of Brands: 1
Type of Packaging: Consumer, Private Label
Brands:
   Tastemorr Snacks

1072 Basignani Winery
15722 Falls Rd
Sparks Glencoe, MD 21152-9582
410-472-0703
Fax: 410-472-2536
Wines
Owner: Lynne Basignani
lynne@basignani.com
Year Founded: 1986
Estimated Sales: Less Than $500,000
Number Employees: 1-4

1073 Basin Crawfish Processors
P.O.Box 25
522 Parkway Drive
Breaux Bridge, LA 70517-4306
337-332-6655
Fax: 337-332-5917 www.bbcrawfest.com
Crawfish, frozen fish and seafood
President: Brayon Blanchard
Estimated Sales: $300,000-500,000
Number Employees: 1-4

1074 Basketfull
276 5th Ave Rm 201
New York, NY 10001
212-686-2175
Fax: 212-255-9019 800-645-4438
Gourmet food and fruit and gift baskets
President: Nancy Forest
Estimated Sales: Less than $500,000
Number Employees: 5-9

1075 Baskin-Robbins LLC
130 Royall St
Canton, MA 02021
800-859-5339
www.baskinrobbins.com
Ice cream, specialty frozen desserts, bases for dairy beverages, nondairy flavors
President: David Hoffmann
CEO: Nigel Travis
Chief Information & Strategy Officer: Jack Clare
COO: Scott Murphy
Year Founded: 1945
Estimated Sales: Over $1 Billion
Number Employees: 1,000-4,999
Number of Brands: 2
Parent Co: Dunkin' Brands, Inc.
Type of Packaging: Consumer, Food Service
Brands:
   Baskin Robbins
   Dunkin' Donuts

1076 Basque French Bakery
2625 Inyo St
Fresno, CA 93721-2787
559-268-7088
Fax: 559-268-0510 www.pyreneesbakery.com
Baked goods, breads and rolls
President/Owner: Al Lewis
al.lewis@pyreneesbakery.com
Vice President: Rita Ingmire
Production Manager: Ed Kwiecien
Year Founded: 1994
Estimated Sales: $2.5-5 Million
Number Employees: 20-49

1077 Bass Lake Cheese Factory
598 Valley View Trl
Somerset, WI 54025-6800
715-247-5586
Fax: 715-549-6617 800-368-2437
blcheese@blcheese.com www.blcheese.com
Cheese
Owner: Scott Erickson
Co-Owner: Julie Erickson
Year Founded: 1918
Estimated Sales: 500,000
Number Employees: 5-9
Type of Packaging: Consumer
Brands:
   Master's Mark

1078 (HQ)Bassett's
1211 Chestnut St
Suite 410
Philadelphia, PA 19107-4114
215-864-2771
Fax: 215-864-2766 888-999-6314
www.bassettsicecream.com
Ice cream, yogurt, sorbet
President: Michael Strange
CEO: Ann Bassett
Estimated Sales: $5-10 Million
Number Employees: 5-9
Other Locations:
   Bassetts Ice Cream
   Philadelphia PA
Brands:
   Bassett's

1079 Batampte Pickle Prods Inc
77 Brooklyn Terminal Market
Brooklyn, NY 11236-1511
718-251-2100
Fax: 718-531-9212
Pickles and pickled products.
President/CEO: Barry Silberstein
Vice President: Scott Silberstein
Estimated Sales: $20-50 Million
Number Employees: 50-99
Number of Brands: 1
Type of Packaging: Consumer
Brands:
   Ba-Tampte

1080 Batavia Wine Cellars
235 N Bloomfield Road
Canandaigua, NY 14424-1059
585-396-7600
Fax: 585-396-7833
Wines
President: Ned Cooper
Ceo/Vice President: Tim Richenberg
Contact: Marty Bognanno
marty.bognanno@cwine.com
Number Employees: 100-249
Parent Co: Canandaigua Wine Company
Type of Packaging: Consumer, Food Service, Private Label, Bulk
Brands:
   Capri
   Henri Merchant
   Vinter's Choice

1081 Batdorf & Bronson
200 Market St NE
Olympia, WA 98501-6965
360-753-7531
Fax: 360-754-5283 800-955-5282
coffee@batdorf.com www.batdorfcoffee.com
Coffee
President: Larry Challain
larryc@batdorf.com
CFO: Dave Wasson
Vice President: Scott Merle
Quality Control: Michael Elvin
Public Relations: Lois Maffeo
Operations Manager: Heather Ringwood
Production Manager: Brian Meyers
Plant Manager: Shelia Smith
Estimated Sales: $5-10 Million
Number Employees: 20-49
Type of Packaging: Consumer, Food Service, Private Label, Bulk

1082 Bateman Products
251 W Main Street
Rigby, ID 83442-1351
208-745-9033
Fax: 208-357-5317 www.mrsbateman.com
Fat products, sugar and egg replacements
Owner: Mrs Bateman
Estimated Sales: $.5-1 million
Number Employees: 5-9

1083 Batory Foods
1700 E Higgins Rd
Suite 300
Des Plaines, IL 60018-3800
847-299-1999
Fax: 847-299-2750 info@batoryfoods.com
www.batoryfoods.com
Distributor of cocoa products, dairy products, cereals, candies and corn syrup solids, commodity syrups, condiments, sauces, egg powders, dough conditioners, emulsifiers and fibers.
President: Ron Friedman
CFO: Alan Kessler
Number Employees: 50-99

1084 Battistoni Italian SpecMeats
81 Dingens St
Buffalo, NY 14206-2307
716-826-2700
Fax: 716-826-0603 800-248-2705
Italian meat products including salami, pepperoni, capacollo and chorizo.
President: Eric Naber
Manager: Anne Ashley
aashley@battistonibrand.com
Year Founded: 1931
Estimated Sales: $10-24.9 Million
Number Employees: 20-49
Number of Brands: 1
Parent Co: Providential Foods Corporation
Type of Packaging: Private Label
Brands:
   Battistoni

1085 Bauducco Foods Inc.
1705 NW 133 Ave
Suite 101
Miami, FL 33182
305-477-9270
Fax: 305-477-4703 sales@bauduccofoods.com
www.bauducco.com
Panettone, wafers, cookies, crackers and bars
President/General Manager: Stefano Mozzi
Manager: Fred Rodrigues
Contact: Alfredo Rivera
alfredor@bauduccofoods.com
Year Founded: 2004
Estimated Sales: $5 Million
Number Employees: 1-4
Brands:
   Bauducco

1086 Bauer's Mustard
5340 Metropolitan Ave
Flushing, NY 11385-1218
718-821-3570
Fax: 718-366-3055 bart@abauersmustard.com
www.abauersmustard.com
Mustard
Owner: Bart Druery
bart@abauersmustard.com
Number Employees: 1-4
Type of Packaging: Consumer, Food Service
Brands:
   A. Bauer's

1087 Baumer Foods Inc
2424 Edenborn Ave
Suite 510
Metairie, LA 70001
504-482-5761
www.baumerfoods.com
Sauces, including hot sauce, steak sauce, worcestershire, oriental and wing sauce.
Regional Sales Manager: Kevin Eber
Vice President, Exports: Marwan Kabbani
Year Founded: 1923
Estimated Sales: $39.9 Million
Number Employees: 100-249
Number of Brands: 1

Food Manufacturers / A-Z

Number of Products: 11
Square Footage: 120000
Type of Packaging: Consumer, Food Service, Private Label
Brands:
　Chef's Recipe
　Figaro
　Ditka
　Crystal

1088　Bautista Family OrganicDate
93800 Hammond Rd
Mecca, CA 92254-6706
　　　　760-396-2337
www.7hotdates.com
Dehydrated fruits and vegetables
Owner: Enrique Bautista
Year Founded: 1975
Estimated Sales: Less Than $500,000
Number Employees: 1-4

1089　Bavaria Corp International
515 Cooper Commerce Dr
Suite 100
Apopka, FL 32703-6222
　　　　407-880-0322
Fax: 407-880-1932　bavaria@bavariacorp.com
www.bavariacorp.com
Specialty blends, marinades, and dips
Owner: Dennis Koo
Sales Director, North America: Steven Fore
bavaria@fdn.com
Estimated Sales: $5-$10 Million
Number Employees: 5-9
Type of Packaging: Food Service, Bulk
Brands:
　Bafos

1090　Bavarian Meat Products
2934 Western Ave
Seattle, WA 98121-1021
　　　　206-448-3540
Fax: 206-956-0526
Sausage
Owner: Lila Ridgeway
lila@bavarianmeats.com
Co-Owner: Robert Hofstatter
Vice President: Lynn Stewart
Estimated Sales: $2.5-5 Million
Number Employees: 10-19
Type of Packaging: Consumer, Food Service

1091　Bavarian Nut Co
822 Elmwood Ave
Buffalo, NY 14222-1408
　　　　716-810-6887
sales@bavariannut.com
www.bavariannut.com
Nuts, including almonds, pecans, cashews, pistachios, salted peanuts, walnuts and trail mixes
Owner: Dan Desrosiers
Year Founded: 1994
Estimated Sales: $20-50 Million
Number Employees: 50-99

1092　Bavarian Specialty Foods, LLC
22417 S Vermont St
Los Angeles, CA 90502-2449
　　　　626-856-3188
Bakery products
Number Employees: 100-249
Type of Packaging: Food Service, Private Label, Bulk

1093　Baxters Vineyards & Winery
2010 Parley St
Nauvoo, IL 62354-1355
　　　　217-453-2528
Fax: 217-453-6600　800-854-1396
www.nauvoowinery.com
Wines
Co-owner: Kelly Logan
Co-owner: Brenda Logan
baxters@nauvoo.net
Year Founded: 1857
Estimated Sales: $500,000-$1 Million
Number Employees: 5-9
Brands:
　Baxters Old Nauvoo

1094　Bay Baby Produce
424 Greenleaf Ave
Burlington, WA 98233-1800
　　　　360-755-2299
Fax: 360-755-8010　info@baybabyproduce.com
www.baybabyproduce.com
Organic pie pumpkins, spaghetti squash, butternut squash, acorn squash, carnival squash, delicata squash, kabocha squash, and red kuri squash
Founder/President: Michele Youngquist
Sales: Tyann Schlimmer

1095　Bay Cities Produce Co Inc
2109 Williams St
San Leandro, CA 94577
　　　　510-346-4943
Fax: 510-352-4704　www.baycitiesproduce.com
Frozen and prepared fruits and vegetables.
President: Steve Del Masso
Vice President: Vince Del Masso
Secretary/Treasurer/VP: Diana Del Masso
diana@baycitiesproduce.com
Office Manager/Accounts Payable: JoLynn Eala
Quality Control: Luis Vaca
General Manager: Jason Shipps
Sales Manager: Tony D'Amato
Frozen Foods Supervisor: Jeff Christensen
Senior Buyer: Mike Short
Year Founded: 1947
Estimated Sales: $20-50 Million
Number Employees: 20-49
Square Footage: 55000
Type of Packaging: Food Service

1096　Bay Haven Lobster Pound
280 Chases Pond Rd
York, ME 3909
　　　　207-363-5265
Fax: 907-486-6417
Lobster, fish, and seafood
Owner: Randy Small
President: Tim Small
Year Founded: 1998
Estimated Sales: $1-3 Million
Number Employees: 5-9

1097　Bay Hawk Ales
2000 Main St
Irvine, CA 92614-7202
　　　　949-442-7565
Fax: 949-442-7566　info@bayhawkales.com
Beers
Manager: Carl Zappa
President: David Voorhies
Sales: Robert Fischer
General Manager: Karl Zappa
Year Founded: 1994
Estimated Sales: $2.5-5 Million
Number Employees: 5
Type of Packaging: Consumer, Food Service, Private Label
Brands:
　Amber Ale
　Bayhawk Ipa
　Bayhawk Stout
　Beach Blonde
　California Pale Ale (Cpa)
　Chocolate Porter
　Hefe Weizen
　Honey Blonde
　O.C. Lager

1098　Bay Hundred Seafood Inc
23713 Saint Michaels Rd
St Michaels, MD 21663-2431
　　　　410-745-9329
Fax: 410-745-9176
www.chesapeakelandingrestaurant.com
Oysters and crabs
President: Joseph Spurry
Estimated Sales: $10-20 Million
Number Employees: 10-19
Type of Packaging: Consumer
Brands:
　Miles River

1099　Bay Oceans Sea Foods
PO Box 348
Garibaldi, OR 97118-0348
　　　　503-322-3316
Fax: 503-322-0049　www.localocean.net
Products include gourmet albacore tuna, chinook salmon, dungeness crab and shrimp, as well as canned tuna and salmon.

Owner: Jeff Princehouse
Estimated Sales: $10-20 Million
Number Employees: 20-49
Type of Packaging: Consumer, Food Service

1100　Bay Pac Beverages
1150 Civic Drive
Suite 300
Walnut Creek, CA 94596-8221
　　　　925-279-0800
Fax: 925-279-0804　baypac@pacbell.net
Sports beverages
President: Jackson Bays
Manager of Export Sales: Alan Wirsig
Estimated Sales: $2.5-5 Million
Number Employees: 5-9
Type of Packaging: Bulk

1101　Bay Shore Chowders & Bisques
360 Currant Road
Fall River, MA 02720
　　　　888-675-6892
info@bayshorechowders.com
www.bayshorechowders.com
Gourmet lobster bisque, New England and Manhattan clam chowders, New England fish chowder, lobster, mussels, shrimp and roasted corn chowder, crab bisque
Estimated Sales: $780,000
Number Employees: 4
Type of Packaging: Consumer, Food Service, Bulk
Brands:
　Bay Shore

1102　Bay State Milling Co.
100 Congress St.
Quincy, MA 02169
　　　　800-553-5687
infobsm@bsm.com　www.baystatemilling.com
Flour and grain products.
President/CEO: Peter Levangie
Head of Business Development: Brian Rothwell
CFO: Peter Banat
Senior Director Marketing & Product Dev.: Colleen Zammar
VP, Sales & Customer Development: Douglas Dewitt
Vice President of Operations: Kevin Kavanaugh
Year Founded: 1899
Estimated Sales: $61.2 Million
Type of Packaging: Consumer, Food Service, Private Label, Bulk
Other Locations:
　Tolleson AZ
　Platteville CO
　Minneapolis MN
　Winona MN
　Indiantown FL
　Mooresville NC
　Clifton NJ
　Wichita KS

1103　Bay Valley Foods
1390 Pullman Dr.
El Paso, TX 79936
　　　　800-236-1119
www.bayvalleyfoods.com
Pickles, powder, syrups & sauces, aseptic, liquid creamer, refrigerated dressing & egg substitutes, soup, broth & gravy, infant foods, salsa, salad dressings, marinades & barbecue sauces, fruit spreads & sauces, salad dressingsmarinades and mayonnaise.
President/CEO: Steve Oakland
CFO: Matthew Foulston
Executive VP/General Counsel: Thomas O'Neill
Year Founded: 1862
Estimated Sales: $116.3 Million
Number Employees: 1,000
Square Footage: 50000
Parent Co: TreeHouse Foods, Inc.
Type of Packaging: Consumer, Food Service, Private Label, Bulk
Brands:
　Hoffman House®
　Bennetts®
　Mocha Mix®
　Borden®
　Cremora®
　Flavor Charm
　Bay Valley™
　E.D. Smith
　Second Nature®
　Steinfeld's®
　Nalley®
　Farman's®

Food Manufacturers / A-Z

Heifetz®
Roddenbery's®
Northwoods®

1104 Bay View Farm
PO Box 680
Honaunau, HI 96726
808-328-9658
Fax: 808-328-8693 800-662-5880
www.bayviewfarmcoffees.com
Coffee
President: Andrew Roy
VP: Roslyn Roy
Estimated Sales: $5-10 Million
Number Employees: 10-19

1105 Baycliff Co Inc
608 South Ave.
Garwood, NJ 07027
212-772-6078
Fax: 212-472-8980 866-772-7569
www.sushichef.com
Rice vinegar, soy sauce, soy salad dressing, teriyaki sauce, rice, rice cracker mix, green tea, and soups
President: Helen Tandler
ht@sushichef.com
VP: Alan Johnson
Estimated Sales: $20-50 Million
Number Employees: 20-49
Type of Packaging: Consumer, Food Service
Brands:
 Sushi Chef

1106 Baycliff Company
242 E 72nd St
New York, NY 10021
212-772-6078
Fax: 212-472-8980 www.sushichef.com
Japansese food and ingredients; vinegar; sauces; vegetables; spices.
President: Helen Tandler
Year Founded: 1982
Brands:
 The Sushi Chef

1107 Bayley's Lobster Pound
9 Avenue Six
Pine Point
Scarborough, ME 04074-8838
207-883-4571
Fax: 207-510-7317 800-932-6456
bayleys@bayleys.com www.bayleys.com
Fresh and frozen shrimp, clams and lobster
Owner: William Bayley
bill@bayleys.com
Year Founded: 1915
Number Employees: 5-9

1108 Bayou Crab
10380 Foots Rd
Grand Bay, AL 36541-6491
251-824-2076
Fax: 251-824-1484
Cajum foods
Owner: Dan Viravong
Estimated Sales: $3-5 Million
Number Employees: 10-19

1109 Bayou Food Distributors
949 Industry Rd
Kenner, LA 70062-6848
504-469-1745
Fax: 504-469-1852 800-516-8283
bayoufoods@hughes.com
Fillet fish, crabs, shrimp; frozen foods, such as beef, pork, poultry and seafood
CEO: Arthur Mitchell
bayoufoods@hughes.net
Estimated Sales: $5-10 Million
Number Employees: 5-9
Square Footage: 54400
Type of Packaging: Food Service

1110 Bayou Land Seafood
1108 Vincent Berard Rd
Breaux Bridge, LA 70517
337-667-6118
Fax: 337-667-6059 bayoulandseafood@aol.com
Seafood, including fresh and frozen crawfish, fish, crabs and shrimp; also, alligator and turtle
Owner: Adam Johnson
bayoulandseafood@aol.com
VP: Sharon Difatta
Plant Manager: Jeff Guidry
Year Founded: 2000
Estimated Sales: $2 Million
Number Employees: 50-99
Number of Products: 100
Square Footage: 38400
Type of Packaging: Consumer, Food Service, Bulk
Brands:
 Bayou Land Seafood

1111 Bays English Muffin Corporation
PO Box 1455
1026 Jackson Blvd
Chicago, IL 60607-2914
312-346-5757
Fax: 316-226-3435 800-367-2297
www.bays.com
Breads, rolls, buns
President: James Bay
Year Founded: 1933
Estimated Sales: $1-2.5 Million
Number Employees: 35

1112 Baywood Cellars
5573 W Woodbridge Rd
Lodi, CA 95242
209-334-0445
Fax: 209-334-0132 800-214-0445
Wines
Founder: Joe Cotta Jr
President: John Cotta
Co-Owner: James Cotta
Estimated Sales: Under $500,000
Number Employees: 1-4
Brands:
 Baywood Cellars

1113 Bazaar Inc
1900 5th Ave
River Grove, IL 60171-1931
708-583-1800
Fax: 708-583-9782 800-736-1888
www.thebazaarinc.com
Candy, snacks and spices
President: Rob Nardick
rnardick@thebazaarinc.com
Finance Executive: Tony Ligenza
VP: Arlene Nardick
Sales Executive: Arnie Fishbain
VP Purchasing: Gene Wisniewski
Year Founded: 1960
Estimated Sales: $15 Million
Number Employees: 100-249
Square Footage: 590000

1114 Bazzini Holdings LLC
1035 Mill Rd
Allentown, PA 18106-3101
610-366-1606
Fax: 610-366-1606 www.bazzininuts.com
Nuts, mixes, bars and pistachios
Owner/President: Rocco Damato
COO: Richard Toltzis
VP of Marketing: Carrie Madigan
Manager: Jen Bowman
jbowman@cherrydalefarms.com
Number Employees: 1-4
Square Footage: 200000
Other Locations:
 Allentown PA
Brands:
 Bazzini
 Candy Club
 House of Bazzini
 Natures Club
 Nut Club

1115 Be-Bop Biscotti
601 NE 1st St
Bend, OR 97701
Fax: 541-389-6185 888-545-7487
info@be-bop.net www.be-bop.net
Biscotti
President/Owner: Robert Golden
Contact: Glenna Gibson
ggibson@be-bop.net
Number Employees: 99

1116 Bea & B Foods
PO Box 178837
San Diego, CA 92117
858-490-6205
pilarcitas@aol.com
www.pilarcitas.com
Mexican seasonings and marinades
President: Bea Knapp
Estimated Sales: $3-5 Million
Number Employees: 1-4
Brands:
 Pilarcitas

1117 Beachaven Vineyards & Winery
1100 Dunlop Ln
Clarksville, TN 37040-9319
931-645-8867
Fax: 931-645-3522
thefolks@beachavenwinery.com
www.westgateinnclarksville.com
Wines
President/Owner: Louisa Cooke
bbwinery@aol.com
VP: Edward Cooke
Estimated Sales: $2.5-5 Million
Number Employees: 10-19

1118 Beacon Drive Inn
255 John B White Sr Blvd
Spartanburg, SC 29360-6047
864-585-9387
Fax: 864-585-2888
Iced tea
General Manager: Kenny Church
CEO: Steve McManus
CEO: Sam Maw
Year Founded: 1946
Estimated Sales: $3-5 Million
Number Employees: 50-99
Square Footage: 20000
Type of Packaging: Food Service, Private Label
Brands:
 Beacon Drive-In Iced Tea

1119 Beal's Lobster Pier
186 Clark Point Rd
SW Harbor, ME 04679
207-244-3202
Fax: 207-244-9479 800-244-7178
orders@bealslobster.com www.bealslobster.com
Lobster
President/Owner: Sam Beal
Year Founded: 1930
Estimated Sales: $1-3 Million
Number Employees: 10-19

1120 Beam Suntory
222 W. Merchandise Mart Plaza
Suite 1600
Chicago, IL 60654
312-964-6999
www.beamsuntory.com
Alcohol, including cognac, bourbon and bourbon mixes, whisky, rum, and tequila.
President/CEO: Albert Baladi
President, Brands: Jessica Spence
Senior VP/CFO: Marc Andre Tousignant
Senior VP/General Counsel: Todd Bloomquist
Senior VP/Chief Human Resources Officer: Paula Erickson
EVP/Chief Supply Chain Officer: David Hunter
Year Founded: 2014
Estimated Sales: $3.1 Billion
Number Employees: 4,800
Number of Brands: 50+
Square Footage: 50000
Parent Co: Suntory Holdings
Type of Packaging: Consumer, Food Service
Other Locations:
 Jim Beam Brands Co.
 Geyserville CA
Brands:
 Baker's®
 Basil Hayden's®
 Booker's®
 Bourbon deLuxe®
 Jim Beam®
 Knob Creek®
 Maker's Mark®
 Old Crow®
 Old Grand-Dad®
 Red Stag
 Ardmore®
 Auchentoshan
 Bowmore
 Glen Garioch
 Laphroaig®
 McClelland's
 Teacher's®
 Sumiwataru Umeshu
 Suntory Umeshu
 Yamazaki Aged Umeshu
 Dai Juhyo

Food Manufacturers / A-Z

Kuromaru
Muginoka
Nanko
Super Juhyo
Wanko
Suntory Whisky
2 GINGERS®
Connemara®
Kilbeggan®
Tyrconnell®
Alberta Premium®
Canadian Club®
Tangle Ridge®
Old Overholt®
DYC Whisky
100 ANOS®
El Tesoro de Don Felipe®
Hornitos®
Sauza®
Tres Generaciones®
Calico Jack®
Cruzan®
Ronrico®
AO Vodka
EFFEN®
Kamchatka®
Pinnacle®
VOX®
Courvoisier®
Salignac®
After Shock®
DeKuyper®
Hermes
Japone
JDK & Sons™
Kamora®
Lejay Lagoute
Leroux®
Midori Melon
Sourz®
Square
The Blue
Gilbey's®
Larios®
Sipsmith®
SkinnygirL®
Larios®
Sipsmith®
SkinnygirL®
-196 C
Kaori Horoyoi
Kokushibori

1121 Beamon Brothers
3392 Us Highway 117 N
Goldsboro, NC 27530-8175
919-734-4931
Fax: 919-736-1849
Potatoes, sweet potatoes
President: Robert Rackley
Estimated Sales: Under $500,000
Number Employees: 3
Brands:
Mount Herman
Stoney Hill

1122 Bean Buddies
1804 Plaza Avenue
New Hyde Park, NY 11040-4937
516-775-3706
Fax: 516-775-3706
Chocolate, coffee candy, candy and confectionary retail
President: Nina Cole
Estimated Sales: $2.5-5 Million
Number Employees: 5-9

1123 Bean Forge
93753 Coos Sumner Lane
PO Box 1073
Coos Bay, OR 97420-1614
541-267-5191
Fax: 888-354-0491 888-292-1632
sales@thebeanforge.com www.thebeanforge.com
Coffees
Manager: Adam Hinkle
Owner: David Herold
Estimated Sales: $500,000-$1 Million
Number Employees: 5-9
Brands:
Bean Forge
Guido & Sals Old Chicago
Kenya Aa
Lighthouse
Menehune Magic
Tanzanian Peaberry
Whiskey Run

1124 Beanfields
855-328-2326
info@beanfields.com www.beanfields.com
Bean chips
CEO: Mark Rampolla
Number of Brands: 1
Number of Products: 7
Type of Packaging: Consumer
Brands:
BEANFIELDS

1125 Beanitos
3601 South Congress
Suite B-500
Austin, TX 78704
512-609-8017
Fax: 512-609-8094 www.beanitos.com
Vegetarian chips and snacks
Marketing: Dave Forman
Contact: Mike Larocca
mike@beanitos.com
Type of Packaging: Private Label

1126 Bear Creek Country Kitchens
325 W 600 S
Heber City, UT 84032-2230
516-333-9326
Fax: 435-654-5449 800-516-7286
www.bearcreekcountrykitchens.com
Soup and pasta mixes
Owner: Donald White
President/CEO: Kevin Ruda
CFO: Al Van Leeuwen
Director R&D: Brian Brinkerhoff
VP Sales/Marketing: Stephen White
VP Operations: Kevin Kowalski
Purchasing Manager: Mark Hartman
Estimated Sales: $40 Million
Number Employees: 100-249
Square Footage: 180000
Parent Co: American Capital Strategies
Type of Packaging: Consumer, Food Service
Brands:
Bear Creek Country Kitchens
Sheila's Select Gourmet Recipes

1127 Bear Creek Smokehouse Inc
10857 State Highway 154
Marshall, TX 75670-8105
903-935-5217
Fax: 903-935-2871 800-950-2327
info@bearcreeksmokehouse.com
www.bearcreeksmokehouse.com
Smoked chicken, turkey and turkey products, smoked and cured ham, salted pork, soup mixes, smoked bacon, sausages, pork ribs and desserts.
President: Charles Shoults
VP: Robbie Shoults
Secretary/Treasurer: Brenda Shoults
Year Founded: 1943
Estimated Sales: $10-20 Million
Number Employees: 20-49
Square Footage: 60000
Type of Packaging: Consumer
Brands:
Bear Creek Brand

1128 Bear Creek Winery
4210 Holland Loop Road
PO Box 609
Cave Junction, OR 97523
541-592-3977
Fax: 541-592-2127 877-273-4843
bvw@bridgeviewwine.com
www.bridgeviewwine.com
Wines
CEO: Rene Eichmann
Marketing: Lorie Eichmann
Year Founded: 1997
Estimated Sales: Less than $500,000
Number Employees: 1-4
Brands:
Dijon Clone
Rogue Valley

1129 Bear Meadow Farm
926 Watson-Spruce Corner Rd
Ashfield, MA 01330
413-628-3970
Apples, jellies, preserves, jams, salad dressings
Owner: Matt Shearer
Year Founded: 2002
Estimated Sales: $1-2.5 Million
Number Employees: 1-4
Square Footage: 12000
Type of Packaging: Consumer, Food Service, Private Label
Brands:
Bear Meadow Farm
Rt 66 Foods

1130 Bear Naked, Inc.
PO Box 649
Solana Beach, CA 92075
866-374-4442
www.bearnaked.com
Granola, energy bars, snack bars and trail mix.
Parent Co: Kellogg Company

1131 Bear Stewart Corp
1025 N Damen Avenue
Chicago, IL 60622
773-276-0400
Fax: 773-276-3512 800-697-2327
info@bearstewart.com www.bearstewart.com
Fillings, jams, jellies, and premade mixes for bakers and confectioners.
VP of Sales: Michael Hoffman
COO: Jason Brooks
Year Founded: 1966
Estimated Sales: $5-10 Million
Number Employees: 1-4
Square Footage: 200000
Type of Packaging: Food Service, Bulk

1132 Bearded Brothers
Austin, TX 78736
www.beardedbros.com
Vegan, organic snack bars
Co-Founder: Caleb Simpson
Co-Founder: Chris Simpson

1133 Bearitos
4600 Sleepytime Drive
Boulder, CO 80301
310-886-8200
Fax: 310-886-8219 www.bearitos.com
Puffed snacks and tortilla chips.
President/CEO: Irwin Simon
Estimated Sales: $10-20 Million
Number Employees: 20-49
Brands:
Bearitos

1134 Beatrice Bakery Co
201 S 5th St
Beatrice, NE 68310-4408
402-223-2358
Fax: 402-223-4465 800-228-4030
www.beatricebakery.com
Dessert cakes, fruit cakes, and liqueur-filled cakes
President: Greg Leech
greg@beatricebakery.com
Quality Control/Production Manager: Robin Dickinson
Sales Manager: Connie Warnsing
Public Relations: Brooklyn Soft
Estimated Sales: $5-10 Million
Number Employees: 20-49
Number of Brands: 10
Number of Products: 125
Square Footage: 200000
Type of Packaging: Private Label
Brands:
Grandma's Bake Shoppe
Grandma's Fruit Cake
Innkeeper's Own
Ye Olde English

1135 Beaucanon Estate Wines
1006 Monticello Rd
Napa, CA 94558-2032
707-254-1460
Fax: 707-254-1462 800-660-3520
www.beaucanonestate.com
Wines
President: Louis De Coninck
louis@beaucanonestate.com
Estimated Sales: $2.5-5,000,000
Number Employees: 10-19

Food Manufacturers / A-Z

1136 Beaujolais Panforte
3200 Dutton Ave
Suite 320
Santa Rosa, CA 95407-5735
707-357-1566
Fax: 707-937-3656 800-776-1778
www.beaujoilaisgranola.com
Granola products
CEO: David LaMonica
Partner: Andrea Sarnataro
Type of Packaging: Private Label
Brands:
 McConnell's(c)

1137 Beaulieu Vineyard
1960 St. Helena Hwy
Rutherford, CA 94573
707-257-5749
cs_bv@bvwines.com
www.bvwines.com
Wines
Marketing Manager: Graham Jones
Estimated Sales: $25-49 Million
Number Employees: 80
Parent Co: Diageo Chateau & Estate Wines Co.
Type of Packaging: Bulk

1138 Beaumont Rice Mills
1800 Pecos Street
Beaumont, TX 77701
409-832-2521
lbroussard@gtbizclass.com
www.bmtricemills.com
Rice
President: Louis Broussard
lbroussard@gtbizclass.com
Vice President: Ben Broussard
Secretary: Sheryl Graham
Assistant Secretary/Treasurer: Brenda Cook
Estimated Sales: $17.5 Million
Number Employees: 50-99
Type of Packaging: Consumer

1139 Beaver Street Brewery
11 S Beaver St # 1
Flagstaff, AZ 86001-5500
928-779-0079
Fax: 928-779-0029 info@beaverstreetbrewery.com
www.beaverstreetbrewery.com
Beers
President/Owner: Evan Hanseth
we2k@aol.com
VP: Winnie Hanseth
Estimated Sales: $248 Million
Number Employees: 100-249
Type of Packaging: Consumer, Food Service
Brands:
 Bramble Berry Brew
 Hefe Weizen
 India Pale Ale
 Marzen Lager
 Pilsener
 R&R Oatmeal Stout
 Rail Head Red Ale
 Vienna Lager

1140 Beaver Street Fisheries
1741 W. Beaver St.
Jacksonville, FL 32209
800-252-5661
800-874-6426
www.beaverstreetfisheries.com
Lobster tail, clams, oysters, shrimp, crab, mussels, swai fillets, tilapia fillets, breaded fish, imitation crab, smoked salmon, frog legs, crawfish, conch, squid & calamari and octopus & scallops. Also manufactures beef, porkpoultryand lamb.
President: Alfred Frisch
CFO: Jeff Edwards
Executive Vice President: Mark Frisch
Director, Marketing: Bluzette Carline
Year Founded: 1950
Estimated Sales: $442.8 Million
Number Employees: 250-499
Number of Brands: 5
Square Footage: 300000
Type of Packaging: Consumer, Food Service, Private Label, Bulk
Brands:
 Sea Best®
 Tropic Seafood®
 Island Queen®
 Island Prince®
 HF's Outstanding

1141 Beaverton Foods Inc
7100 NE Century Boulevard
Hillsboro, OR 97124
503-646-8138
800-223-8076
www.beavertonfoods.com
Horseradish, mustard, garlic and sauces.
Founder: Rose Biggi
CEO: Domonic Biggi
Business/Customer Service Manager: Roger Klingsporn
Estimated Sales: $10-20 Million
Number Employees: 50-99
Number of Brands: 6
Number of Products: 150
Square Footage: 65000
Type of Packaging: Consumer, Food Service, Private Label, Bulk
Brands:
 Beaver
 Charlie's Salsa
 Inglehoffer
 Napa Valley
 Pacific Farms
 Tulelake

1142 Because Cookie Dough
hello@becausecookiedough.com
www.becausecookiedough.com
Cookie dough
Founder: Alexis Chan
Number of Brands: 1
Type of Packaging: Consumer
Brands:
 BECAUSE COOKIE DOUGH

1143 Beck Flavors
1301 Mattec Drive
Loveland, OH 45140
314-878-7522
Fax: 513-889-1268 beckflavors.net
Bakery, beverage, coffee, tea, and dairy flavors.
General Manager: Joe Willoughby
Contact: Darienne Bils
dbils@beckflavors.net
Type of Packaging: Bulk
Other Locations:
 Ardsley NY
 Bakersfield CA
 Lakeland FL
 New Century KS
Brands:
 Beck Cafe
 Beck Flavors

1144 Beck's Ice Cream
3610 Lewisberry Rd
York, PA 17404-8382
717-764-4585
Fax: 717-846-5121
Ice cream
Owner: Jerry Beck
CEO: Lynne Beck
CFO: Kerry Beck
Year Founded: 1979
Estimated Sales: $250,000
Number Employees: 1-4
Brands:
 Becks Ice Cream

1145 Beck's Waffles of Oklahoma
101 S Kickapoo Ave
Shawnee, OK 74801-7686
405-878-0615
Fax: 405-878-8546 800-646-6254
wafflman@swbell.net
Frozen Belgian waffles
President: Betty Beck
Sales: Doyle Beck
Year Founded: 1998
Estimated Sales: $1-3 Million
Number Employees: 10
Square Footage: 80000
Type of Packaging: Consumer, Food Service

1146 Becker Foods
15136 Goldenwest Cir
Westminster, CA 92683-5235
714-891-9474
www.beckerfoods.com
Custom processor and packager of; fresh and frozen poultry, beef, pork, lamb, veal, cheese products, and more
President: Stan Becker
stan@beckerfoods.com
Vice President: Dian Vendel
Number Employees: 5-9
Type of Packaging: Food Service, Private Label

1147 Beckman & Gast Co
282 W Kremer-Hoying Road
PO Box 307
St Henry, OH 45883
419-678-4195
Fax: 419-678-3005 www.beckmangast.com
Canned goods including tomato juice, tomatoes, and cut green beans.
President: William Gast
william.gast@beckmangast.com
Secretary/Treasurer: Paul Moorman
Customer Service Manager: Terri Gast
Operations Manager: Paul Moorman
VP of Manufacturing: Karl Gast
Estimated Sales: $5-9.9 Million
Number Employees: 10-19
Type of Packaging: Consumer, Private Label
Brands:
 Beckman's

1148 Beckmann's Old World Bakery
104 Bronson St # 6
Santa Cruz, CA 95062-3487
831-423-9242
Fax: 831-426-3548
customerhelp@beckmannsbakery.com
www.beckmannsbakery.com
Breads and other baked goods.
President: Peter Beckmann
pbeckmann@beckmannsbakery.com
CEO: Beth Holland
Estimated Sales: $24.2 Million
Number Employees: 100-249
Number of Brands: 1
Square Footage: 17000
Brands:
 Beckmann's

1149 Beckmen Vineyards
2670 Ontiveros Rd
Los Olivos, CA 93441
805-688-8664
Fax: 805-688-9983 info@beckmenvineyards.com
www.beckmenvineyards.com
Wines
President: Tom Beckmen
info@beckmenvineyards.com
Operations Manager: Steve Beckmen
Estimated Sales: $500-1 Million appx.
Number Employees: 5-9

1150 Becky's Blissful Bakery
PO Box 252
Pewaukee, WI 53072
262-327-4111
www.beckysblissfulbakery.com
Manufacturer of desserts made from all natural ingredients. Specializes in caramel.
Owner: Rebecca Scarberry
Square Footage: 80000

1151 Bede Inc
PO Box 8263
Haledon, NJ 07538-0263
973-956-2900
Fax: 973-956-0600 866-239-6565
bedeinc@aol.com
Processor and exporter of instant hot cereals including peanut porridge, banana, plantain, etc.; also, peanut-based health beverage mixes
President: Jasseth Cummings
CFO: Gloria Johnson
Buyer: Sam Cummings
Quality Control: King H
Estimated Sales: $2.5-5,000,000
Number Employees: 1-4
Brands:
 Cream of Peanut
 Crema De Many
 Malted Peanut
 Quick Peanut Porridge
 Vigorteen

Food Manufacturers / A-Z

1152 Bedell Northfork LLC
36225 Main Rd
RT 25
Cutchogue, NY 11935-1346
631-734-7537
Fax: 631-734-5788 wine@bedellcellars.com
www.bedellcellars.com
Wines
Owner: Michael Lynne
CEO: Trent Preszler
Senior Vice President, Events: Amy Finno
EVP- Sales & Marketing: Jonathan Lynne
Contact: Suzanne Baird
sue@bedellcellars.com
COO: Trent Preszler
Plant Manager: Dave Thompson
Estimated Sales: $1-2.5 Million
Number Employees: 5-9
Other Locations:
  Corey Creek Vineyards(Tasting Room)
  Southold NY
Brands:
  Bedell Cellars
  Corey Creek

1153 Bedemco Inc
3 Barker Ave Ste 325
White Plains, NY 10601
914-683-1119
Fax: 914-683-1482 info@bedemco.com
www.bedemco.com
Organic dried fruit, dried vegetables, nuts and seeds.
President: Elazar Demeshulam
Vice President: Roy Demeshulam
Quality Control Manager: Natalie Levy
Marketing Director: Emily Cantor
Sales: Murray Feinblatt
Contact: Roni Detoledo
roni@bedemco.com
Production Manager: Robert Haas
Estimated Sales: $3-5 Million
Number Employees: 1-4
Type of Packaging: Food Service, Private Label, Bulk
Brands:
  HUDSON VALLEY FARMS

1154 Bedoukian Research Inc
21 Finance Dr
Danbury, CT 06810-4133
203-830-4000
Fax: 203-830-4010 800-424-9300
customerservice@bedoukian.com
www.bedoukian.com
Flavors and aromas.
President: Robert Bedoukian
robert@bedoukian.com
Regulatory and Technical Services: Joseph Bania
Year Founded: 1972
Estimated Sales: $10-24 Million
Number Employees: 50-99

1155 Bedre Fine Chocolate
37 N Colbert Rd
Davis, OK 73030-9338
580-369-4200
800-367-5390
bedre.chocolates@chickasaw.net
www.bedrechocolates.com
Chocolate
Contact: Brenda Cloud
brenda.cloud@chickasaw.net
Number Employees: 10-19
Type of Packaging: Consumer, Private Label

1156 Bedrock Farm Certified Organic Medicinal Herbs
106 Woodland Trail
Wakefield, RI 55105
401-789-9943
Fax: 651-227-1387 888-874-7393
Organic medicinal herbs. Founded in 1992.
President: Angie Geary

1157 Bee Harmony Honey
Hillsboro, KS 67063
www.beesponsible.com
Raw honey

1158 Bee International
2311 Boswell Rd
Suite 1
Chula Vista, CA 91914-3512
619-710-1800
Fax: 619-710-1822 800-421-6465
info@beeinc.com www.beeinc.com
Manufacturer and importer of Easter, Valentine, Halloween, Christmas and novelty candy items
Owner/CEO: Louis Block
louisblock@beeinc.com
Quality Assurance Manager: Martin Quezada
VP Operations: Charles Block
Estimated Sales: $18 Million
Number Employees: 20-49
Square Footage: 165000
Type of Packaging: Consumer
Brands:
  Chicle Chips
  Micro Bmx Bike
  Micro Scooter

1159 Bee Raw Honey
Brooklyn, NY 11231
888-660-0090
www.beeraw.com
Honey
Founder: Zeke Freeman
Square Footage: 80000
Brands:
  Bee Raw

1160 Bee Seasonal
Gilbert, AZ 85234
beeseasonal.com
Organic raw honey
Founder: Thomas Hobbe

1161 Beech-Nut Nutrition Corp
1 Nutritious Pl
Amsterdam, NY 12010-8105
518-595-6600
Fax: 518-595-6601 www.beechnut.com
Organic baby foods
CEO: Jeff Boutelle
Chief Financial Officer: Alain Souligny
Vice President of Human Resources: Erin Clemens
Controlled: Marc Ruf
Estimated Sales: $10-20 Million
Number Employees: 20-49
Number of Brands: 2
Parent Co: Hero Group
Type of Packaging: Consumer
Brands:
  Beech-Nut
  Beech-Nut Organic

1162 Beecher's Handmade Cheese
1600 Pike Place
Seattle, WA 98101
206-956-1964
sales@beecherscheese.com
www.beechershandmadecheese.com
Cheese
Owner: Kurt Beecher Dammeier
Year Founded: 2003
Number Employees: 20-40

1163 (HQ)Beef Products Inc.
891 Two Rivers Dr
North Sioux City, SD 57049-5391
605-217-8000
Fax: 605-217-8001 www.beefproducts.com
Lean beef processed from fresh beef trimmings
President/Owner: Richard Jochum
CEO: Eldon Roth
Director: Regina Roth
Contact: David Berghult
dberghult@beefproducts.com
Facilities: Brian Goeden
Purchasing: Dave Rose
Number Employees: 1400
Square Footage: 144000
Type of Packaging: Consumer, Food Service
Other Locations:
  BPI Plant
  South Sioux City NE
  BPI Plant
  Amarillo TX
  BPI Plant
  Garden City KS
  BPI Plant
  Waterloo IA
  BPI Plant
  Finney County KS
Brands:
  Bpi®

1164 Beehive Botanicals
16297 W Nursery Rd
Hayward, WI 54843-7138
715-634-4274
Fax: 715-634-3523 800-233-4483
www.beehivebotanicals.com
Processor and exporter of health supplements derived from honey, propolis, pollen and royal jelly; also, sugar-free propolis chewing gum.
President/CEO: Linda Graham
linda.graham@beehivebotanicals.com
Quality Control Manager: Denise Gregory
Purchasing Manager: Lisa Johnson
Year Founded: 1972
Estimated Sales: $6.5 Million
Number Employees: 20-49
Square Footage: 24000
Brands:
  Beehive Botanicals
  Honey Silk
  Royal Jelly
  Bee Pollen

1165 Beehive Cheese
2440 East 6600 South
Suite 8
Uintah, UT 84405
801-476-0900
Fax: 801-476-3308 www.beehivecheese.com
Cheese
Owner: Tim Welsh
Owner: Pat Ford
Estimated Sales: B
Number Employees: 10-19

1166 Beekman 1802
187 Main St
Sharon Springs, NY 13459
888-801-1802
shop.beekman1802.com
Organic jams, honey, concentrates, coffee beans, and cookbooks.
Co-Founder: Josh Kilmer-Purcell
Co-Founder: Brent Ridge
Year Founded: 2008

1167 Beer Bakers Inc.
5515 Edmondson Pike
Suite 121
Nashville, TN 37211
615-775-3329
soberdough.com
Baked goods made with beer.
Co-Owner: Jordan Mychal
Co-Owner: Veronic Mychal
Type of Packaging: Consumer, Private Label
Brands:
  Soberdough

1168 Beer Nuts Co Store-Plant
103 N Robinson St
Bloomington, IL 61701-5424
309-827-8580
Fax: 309-827-0914 info@beernuts.com
Nuts
President: James Shirk
ashirk@beernuts.com
Marketing Manager: Cindy Shirk
Public Relations: Tom Foster
Media Relations: Georgia Dawson
Year Founded: 1937
Estimated Sales: G
Number Employees: 50-99
Square Footage: 100000
Type of Packaging: Food Service
Brands:
  Beer Nuts(c)

1169 Beetnik Foods, LLC
2600 E. Cesar Chavez
Austin, TX 78702
512-548-8228
customersupport@beetnikfoods.com
www.beetnikfoods.com
Organic sauces and frozen, ready-to-eat meals.
Founder: David Perkins
Contact: Rustin Dodd
rdodd@beetnikfoods.com
Square Footage: 330230
Brands:
  beetnik

Food Manufacturers / A-Z

1170 Beetroot Delights
72 Spruceside Crescent
Foothill, ON L0S 1E1
Canada
888-842-3387
Fax: 905-892-1080
Manufacturer and exporter of beetroot condiments including cherry beet pepper and ginger beet jelly, spiced beet ketchup and beet relish. Founded in 1985.
President: Grace Lallemand
Number Employees: 3
Square Footage: 3200
Type of Packaging: Consumer, Food Service
Brands:
  Beetroot Delights

1171 Behm Blueberry Farms
14904 Canary Drive
Grand Haven, MI 49417
616-846-1650
http://www.behmblueberryfarms.com/
Fresh blueberries. Founded in 1953.
President: Howard Behm
VP: Sharon Behm
Estimated Sales: $3-5 Million
Number Employees: 5
Brands:
  Blueberry King

1172 Bel Brands USA
30 S. Wacker Dr.
Suite 3000
Chicago, IL 60606-7413
312-462-1500
Fax: 847-879-1999 www.belbrandsusa.com
Nacho sauce, salsa and cheeses.
CEO: Bill Graham
Vice President, Human Resources: Kerri Gollias
Vice President, Marketing: Shannon Maher
Year Founded: 1865
Estimated Sales: $103 Million
Number Employees: 250-499
Number of Brands: 7
Square Footage: 130000
Type of Packaging: Consumer, Food Service, Bulk
Other Locations:
  Bel Brands USA
  Little Chute WI
  Bel Brands USA
  Leitchfield KY
  Bel Brands USA
  Brookings SD
Brands:
  Boursin
  Kaukauna
  Laughing Cow
  Merkts
  Mini Babybel
  Owl's Nest
  Price*s

1173 Bel Cheese USA
602 W Main St
Leitchfield, KY 42754-1347
270-259-4071
Fax: 270-259-4560
Manufacturer of spreadable cheese and individual serving-sized cheese wheels.
Plant Manager: Francine Moudry
fmoudry@belbrandsusa.com
Estimated Sales: $20-50 Million
Number Employees: 250-499
Number of Brands: 2
Square Footage: 57500
Parent Co: Bel Brands USA
Type of Packaging: Consumer, Food Service, Bulk
Brands:
  Laughing Cow
  Mini Babybel

1174 BelGioioso Cheese Inc.
4200 Main St
Green Bay, WI 54311
920-863-2123
Fax: 920-863-8791 info@belgioioso.com
www.belgioioso.com
Italian cheeses including provolone, parmesan, romano, asiago, fontina, kasseri, mascarpone, gorgonzola, fresh mozzarella, pepato, peperoncino, parveggiano.
Sales Manager: Mimmo Bruno
Quality Assurance Manager: Helen Schmude
Vice President of Marketing: Francis Wall
Vice President Foodservice Sales: Bob Ekstrom
Human Resources Manager: Barb Altschwager
Year Founded: 1979
Estimated Sales: $31.5 Million
Number Employees: 100-249
Square Footage: 30000
Type of Packaging: Consumer, Food Service, Bulk
Brands:
  Belgioioso
  American Grana
  Auribella
  Unwrap & Roll
  Italico
  Peperoncino
  Ricotta Con Latte

1175 Belcolade
Industriezone Zuid III-B-9320
Pennsauken, NJ 08110
856-661-9123
Fax: 856-665-0005 www.belcolade.com
Couverture chocolate, wholesaler of chocolate and cocoa.
Principak: Taygun Basaran
Estimated Sales: $5-10 Million
Number Employees: 5-9
Parent Co: Belcolade NV/SA
Brands:
  Belcolade
  Belcolade
  Carat

1176 Belgian Boys
140 Carolyn Blvd
Farmingdale, NY 11735
info@belgianboys.com
belgianboys.com
Peanut butter; chips; cookies; pancake and waffle mixes.
Co-Founder: Gregory Galel
Number Employees: 11-50

1177 Belgravia Imports
275 Highpoint Ave
Portsmouth, RI 02871
401-683-3323
Fax: 401-683-2717 800-848-1127
belgravia@belgraviaimports.com
www.belgraviaimports.com
Organic and natural gourmet foods.
President: Ronald Dick
Contact: Vinny Constanza
vin-warehouse@belgraviaimports.com
Year Founded: 1937
Estimated Sales: $1-2.5 Million
Number Employees: 5-9

1178 Bell & Evans
154 W Main St
Fredericksburg, PA 17026
717-865-6626
info@bellandevans.com
www.bellandevans.com
Processor and exporter of fresh chicken, chicken nuggets, sausages, burgers, and diced IQF chicken breast
President: Scott Sechler
CFO: Dan Chirico
Year Founded: 1894
Estimated Sales: Over $1 Billion
Number Employees: 500-999
Number of Brands: 2
Square Footage: 180000
Brands:
  Bell & Evans the Excellent Chicken
  Farmers Pride Natural

1179 Bell Flavors & Fragrances
500 Academy Dr
Northbrook, IL 60062-2497
847-291-8300
Fax: 847-291-1217 info@bellff.com
www.bellff.com
Manufacturer and exporter of natural and artificial flavoring extracts for food and beverages; also, spice compounds.
President: Jim Heinz
jheinz@bellff.com
Director of Marketing: Kelli Heinz
Year Founded: 1912
Estimated Sales: $39 Million
Number Employees: 50-99
Square Footage: 100000
Type of Packaging: Consumer, Food Service
Brands:
  Yuccafoam

1180 Bell Foods International
3213 Waconda Rd.
Gervais, OR 97026
503-390-1425
Fax: 503-390-9526 info@bellfoodsintl.com
www.bellfoodsintl.com
Maraschino cherry manufacturers
Contact: Monica Guzman
monicag@bellfoodsintl.com
Type of Packaging: Consumer, Private Label

1181 Bell Marketing Inc
10135 S Roberts Rd # 208
Palos Hills, IL 60465-1500
708-598-8873
Fax: 708-598-8968 800-426-6113
www.bellmarketing.com
Fruit ingredients, juice concentrates, purees, dried fruit-essences-botanicals
Owner: Mary Bell
Sales Director: Karen McNichols
mbell@bellmktg.com
Operations Manager: Jim Kusmierek
Estimated Sales: $5 Million
Number Employees: 1-4
Type of Packaging: Bulk

1182 Bell Mountain Vineyards
463 Bell Mountain Rd
Willow City, TX 78675-8501
830-685-3297
Fax: 830-685-3657
evelyn@bellmountainwine.com
www.bellmountainwine.com
Wines.
Owner: Robert P Oberhelman
bellmountainwine@ctesc.net
VP: Ames Morrison
Year Founded: 1968
Estimated Sales: $2.5-5 Million
Number Employees: 5-9

1183 Bell Plantation
P.O. Box 943
Tifton, GA 31793
229-387-7238
customerservice@bellplantation.com
bellplantation.com
Organic peanut butter, peanut cooking oil, chocolate and spreads.
Owner: Jill St John
Year Founded: 2007

1184 Bell's Brewery Inc
355 E Kalamazoo Ave
Kalamazoo, MI 49053
269-382-2338
Fax: 269-382-3820 www.bellsbeer.com
Ale and stout
President: Larry Bell
VP: Angie Bell
Estimated Sales: $5-10 Million
Number Employees: 50-99
Type of Packaging: Consumer, Food Service

1185 Bell-Carter Foods Inc
590 Ygnacio Valley Rd.
Suite 300
Walnut Creek, CA 94596
925-284-5933
Fax: 925-284-1289 800-252-3557
contactus@bellcarter.com www.bellcarter.com
Black ripe, spanish, sicilian, kalamata, and other specialty olive products
CEO: Tim Carter
CFO: Paul Adcock
EVP: Doug Reifsteck
Quality Assurance & R/D: Julie Tinsley
VP Strategy & Marketing: Colleen Sparda
VP Sales: Tom Rickard
Director of Operations: Ron Kerr
Estimated Sales: $20-50 Million
Number Employees: 20-49
Type of Packaging: Consumer, Food Service, Private Label, Bulk
Brands:
  Lindsay Olives

Food Manufacturers / A-Z

1186 Bella Chi-Cha Products
216-B Fern Street
Santa Cruz, CA 95060
831-423-1851
Fax: 831-423-0212 ccrusso@pacbell.net
www.bellachicha.com
Pesto and layered tortas
President/Owner: Chi-Cha Russo

1187 Bella Coola Fisheries
3133 188 St
Surrey, BC V3S 9V5
Canada
604-541-0339
Fax: 604-541-0370
Processor and exporter of fresh and frozen herring roe and salmon
General Manager: Frank Taylor
Number Employees: 10-19
Type of Packaging: Consumer, Food Service, Private Label, Bulk

1188 Bella Cucina
1870 Murphy Ave SW
Atlanta, GA 30310-4837
404-755-0404
Fax: 678-539-8401 866-350-9040
customerservice@bellacucina.com
www.bellacucina.com
Olive oils and pestos
Owner: Louise Fili
customerservice@bellacucina.com
Manager: Reginald Weeks
Estimated Sales: $2.5-5 Million
Number Employees: 5-9
Type of Packaging: Private Label

1189 Bella Ravioli
369 Main St
Medford, MA 02155-6149
781-396-0875
Fax: 781-396-0876
Pasta. Founded in 1981.
Owner: Robert DE Pasquale
Co-Owner: Robert De Pasquale
Estimated Sales: Less Than $500,000
Number Employees: 1-4
Brands:
  Bella Ravioli

1190 Bella Sun Luci
1220 Fortress St
Chico, CA 95973-9029
530-899-2661
Fax: 530-899-7746 mooneyfarm@aol.com
www.bellasunluci.com
Sun dried tomatoes, pesto, risotto, olive oil, BBQ marinade and tomato sauces.
Owner: Maryellen Mooney
Partner/Production: Stephen Mooney
Quality Assurance Manager: Jett Uribe
Sales/Marketing: Lisa Mooney
Business Management: Tammy Goss
Estimated Sales: $30 Million
Number Employees: 20-49
Square Footage: 100000
Type of Packaging: Consumer, Food Service, Private Label, Bulk
Brands:
  Bella Sun Luci
  Summer's Choice

1191 Bella Vista Farm
1002 SW Ard St
Lawton, OK 73505-9660
580-536-1300
Fax: 580-536-4886 866-237-8526
craig@peppercreekfarms.com
www.peppercreekfarms.com
Organic jams, honey, peanut butter, popcorn, all nautral pasta sauces, organic pasta and organic olive oil.
Owner: Craig Weissman
Year Founded: 1984
Estimated Sales: Less than $500,000
Number Employees: 5-9
Brands:
  Bella Vista

1192 Bella Viva Orchards
7030 Hughson Ave
Hughson, CA 95326-8014
209-883-9015
Fax: 209-883-0215 800-552-8218
CustomerCare@BellaViva.com
Kosher dried fruit and chocolate fruits packaged for gifts.
Owner: Victor Martino
Year Founded: 1994
Estimated Sales: Less Than $500,000
Number Employees: 1-4

1193 Bella-Napoli Italian Bakery
721 River St
Troy, NY 12180-1233
518-274-8277
Fax: 518-274-2625 888-800-0103
www.bellanapolibakery.com
Italian specialties
President: Dominic Mainella
Sales Executive: Victoria Signore
Estimated Sales: $2.5-5 Million
Number Employees: 50-99
Other Locations:
  Bella Napoli Italian Bakery
  Latham NY

1194 Belle Plaine Cheese Factory
N3473 Wisconsin Ave
Shawano, WI 54166
715-526-2789
866-245-5924
Retailer of cheese including colby, cheddar, monterey jack, rainbow and pepper jack. Founded in 1972.
President: Donald Brandl
Estimated Sales: Less Than $500,000
Number Employees: 1-4
Type of Packaging: Consumer

1195 Belle River Enterprises
12 Waterview Lane
Belle River, PE C0A 1B0
Canada
902-962-2248
Fax: 902-962-4276
Processor and exporter of rock crab combo and minced crab, cocktail claws and salad meat and lobsters. Founded in 1982.
General Manager: Howard Hancock
Vice President: Dean Hancock
Estimated Sales: $1-5 Million
Number Employees: 75
Square Footage: 32000
Brands:
  Belle River

1196 Belleharvest Sales Inc
11900 Fisk Road
Belding, MI 48809-9413
800-452-7753
sales@belleharvest.com www.belleharvest.com
Manufacturer, wholesaler/distributor, exporter, and packer of fresh apples.
President/CEO: Mike Rothwell
bellehar@iserv.net
Controller: Tony Kramer
Director of Marketing: Chris Sandwick
Director of Field Operations: Tony Blattner
Plant Manager: Brad Pitsch
Number Employees: 50-99
Parent Co: Belding Fruit Storage
Type of Packaging: Private Label, Bulk
Brands:
  Evercrisp®
  Smitten®
  SweeTango® Apples
  Topaz

1197 Bellerose Vineyard
435 W Dry Creek Rd
Healdsburg, CA 95448
707-433-1637
Fax: 707-433-7024
Wines (Winery)
Founder/Owner: Charles Richard
Estimated Sales: $500,000 appx.
Number Employees: 5-9
Brands:
  Bellerose

1198 (HQ)Belletieri Company
1207 W Chew St
Allentown, PA 18102-3751
610-433-4334
Italian specialty foods, condiments and sauces. Founded in 1994.
President: Loui Belletieri
Treasurer: Peter Belletieri
Estimated Sales: Under $500,000
Number Employees: 4-6

1199 Belleville Brothers Packing
2545 Insley Rd
North Baltimore, OH 45872
419-257-3529
Fax: 419-257-3529 www.bellevillebrothers.com
Meat products. Founded in 1999.
President: James Belleville
Owner: Ivan Bellevue
Estimated Sales: $500,000
Number Employees: 1-4
Type of Packaging: Consumer, Bulk

1200 (HQ)Bellisio Foods
1201 Harman Pl
Ste 302
Minneapolis, MN 55403
info@bellisiofoods.com
www.bellisiofoods.com
Frozen entrees, sauces and soups.
CEO: Tom Smith
SVP & CFO: Doug Kooren
SVP & Chief People Officer: Margot McManus
SVP, Marketing & Sales: John Plaso
Year Founded: 1912
Estimated Sales: $140.9 Million
Number Employees: 1000+
Square Footage: 40280
Parent Co: Charoen Pokphand Foods
Type of Packaging: Consumer, Food Service
Brands:
  Authentico®
  Budget Gourmet®
  Michelina's Grande
  Michelina's Lean Gourmet®
  Michelina's Pizza Snack Rolls
  Michelina's Signature®
  Zap'ems®

1201 Bellocq
104 West St
Brooklyn, NY 11222
347-463-9231
inquiries@bellocq.com
www.bellocq.com
Manufacturer of a variety of teas and tea sets.
Co-Founder: Michael Shannon
Co-Founder: Heidi Stewart
Co-Founder: Scott Stewart
Square Footage: 80000
Brands:
  Bellocq

1202 Bells Foods International
3213 Waconda Rd NE
Gervais, OR 97026
503-390-1425
Fax: 503-390-9526 info@bellfoodsintl.com
www.bellfoodsintl.com
A food processor, manufacturer specialized in co-packing
President: Craig Bell
CFO: Paul Leipzig
Marketing Director: Cody Bell
VP Sales: Doug Zibell
Plant Manager: Monica Guzman
Estimated Sales: $65,000
Number Employees: 20-49
Parent Co: Bell Farms
Type of Packaging: Consumer, Food Service, Private Label, Bulk
Brands:
  Eola

1203 Bellucci
2904 S Angus Avenue
Fresno, CA 93727
info@belluccipremium.com
belluccipremium.com
Organic extra virgin olive oil

Food Manufacturers / A-Z

1204 Bellville Meat Market
36 S Front St
Bellville, TX 77418-2406
979-865-5782
Fax: 979-865-0550 800-571-6328
www.bellvillemeatmarket.com
Regular and flavored beef and pork smoked sausage links including garlic, jalapeno, cayenne pepper, etc.; also, fresh pork links, dry, all beef summer and pan sausages and venison products available
Owner: Jerrod Poffenberger
jerrod@bellvillemeatmarket.com
Office Manager: Sara Barnet
Plant Manager: Jerrod Daniel Poffenberger
Plant Operator: Marcus J. Poffenberger
Estimated Sales: $2.5-5 Million
Number Employees: 10-19
Square Footage: 6000
Type of Packaging: Consumer, Food Service, Private Label, Bulk
Brands:
Poffenberger's Bellville

1205 Bellwether Farms
PO Box 299
Valley Ford, CA 94972
707-478-8067
Fax: 707-763-2443 info@bellwethercheese.com
Fresh and aged cheese
Owner: Cynthia Callahan
Founder: Cindy Callahan
Vice President: Liam Callahan
liam@bellwetherfarms.com
Sales/Marketing: Lenny Rice Moonsammy
Estimated Sales: Under $500,000
Number Employees: 5-9
Type of Packaging: Private Label
Brands:
Bellwether

1206 Belly Treats, Inc.
210-200 Wellington St W
Toronto, ON M5V 3C7
Canada
416-418-3285
Fax: 905-479-4135 www.bellytreats.com
Candies and nuts
Owner/Sales & Marketing: George Tsioros
Estimated Sales: $1 Million
Number of Products: 500+
Type of Packaging: Bulk

1207 Belmar Spring Water
410 Grove Street
Glen Rock, NJ 07452
201-444-1010
Fax: 201-444-2801 www.belmarspringwater.com
Processor and bottler of spring water.
Estimated Sales: $1-2.5 Million
Number Employees: 10-19
Type of Packaging: Consumer, Private Label

1208 Belmont Brewing Co
25 39th Pl # 25
Long Beach, CA 90803-2806
562-433-3891
Fax: 562-434-0604 www.belmontbrewing.com
Beer and micro brews. Founded in 1990.
Owner: David Hansen
davidhansen@belmontbrewing.com
General Manager: Ben Patterson
VP: Tom Avila
Estimated Sales: $2.5-5 Million
Number Employees: 50-99
Brands:
Bitburger
Black & Tan
Franziskaner Hefe-Weisse
Growler
Long Beach Crude
Marathon
Penny Fogger
Shandy
Strawberry Blonde
Top Sail Amber
Woodchuck Pear Cider

1209 Belmont Chemicals
50 Mount Prospect Ave
Clifton, NJ 07013-1900
973-777-2225
Fax: 973-777-6384 800-722-5070
Processor and exporter of vitamins, nutritional and protein supplements, herbs and amino acids

Owner/President: Paul Egyes
Sales Manager: Paul Egyes
Public Relations: Mary Apuzzo
Estimated Sales: $4.5 Million
Number Employees: 4
Number of Products: 50
Square Footage: 4000
Type of Packaging: Bulk

1210 Belmont Peanuts-Southampton
23195 Popes Station Rd
Capron, VA 23829-2501
434-658-4613
info@belmontpeanuts.com
www.belmontpeanuts.com
Peanut and peanut products. Founded in 1993.
President/Owner: Patsy Marks
pastymarks@belmontpeanuts.com
VP: Robert Marks
Number Employees: 1-4

1211 Belton Foods Inc
2701 Thunderhawk Ct
Dayton, OH 45414-3445
937-890-7768
Fax: 937-890-7780 800-443-2266
dsipos@beltonfoods.com www.beltonfoods.com
Beverages, concentrates, pancake and table syrups, vinegars, drink mixes, enhancing syrups and slush base. Founded in 1971.
President: David Sipos
dsipos@beltonfoods.com
Vice President: Cynthia Gillespie
Sales Executive: Ted Doron
Sales Director: Don Fox
Production Manager: Joe Reece
Manager: Tony Dudon
Estimated Sales: $3.4 Million
Number Employees: 20-49
Number of Brands: 20
Number of Products: 120
Square Footage: 96
Type of Packaging: Consumer, Food Service, Private Label, Bulk

1212 (HQ)Ben & Jerry's Homemade Inc
30 Community Dr # 1
South Burlington, VT 05403-6828
802-846-1500
Fax: 802-846-1555 866-258-6877
info@benjerry.com www.benjerry.com
Processor of ice cream, frozen yogurt, sorbet and smoothies
President/CEO: Perry Odak
CEO: Jostein Solheim
CFO: Michael Graning
Marketing Director: David Stever
Public Relations Manager: Sean Greenwood
Senior Director Operations: Bruce Bowman
Plant Manager: Janette Cole
Purchasing: Daniel Scheidt
Year Founded: 1978
Number Employees: 500-999
Square Footage: 276000
Type of Packaging: Consumer
Other Locations:
Ben & Jerry's
Waterbury VT
Brands:
Ben & Jerry's
Ben & Jerry's Frozen Smoothies
Ben & Jerry's Ice Cream

1213 Ben B. Schwartz & Sons
7201 W. Fort Street
Suite #27
Detroit, MI 48209
313-841-8300
Fax: 313-841-1253 www.benbdetroit.com
Grower of fruits and vegetables including apples, peaches, pears, cucumbers, lettuce and potatoes. Founded in 1906.
Owner/President/CEO: Chris Billmeyer
Contact: Zeena Toma
ztoma@wescommtech.com
COO: Nathan Stone
Estimated Sales: $10-20 Million
Number Employees: 20-49
Type of Packaging: Consumer

1214 Ben Heggy's Candy Co
743 Cleveland Ave NW
Canton, OH 44702-1884
330-455-7703
Fax: 330-455-9865 info@heggys.com
www.heggys.com
Old fashioned candies and handcrafted chocolates.
President/Owner: Richard Wollenberg
info@heggys.com
Estimated Sales: $10-20 Million
Number Employees: 20-49
Type of Packaging: Private Label

1215 Ben's Sugar Shack
83 Webster Hwy
Temple, NH 03084-4124
603-924-3177
benssugarshack@gmail.com
www.bensmaplesyrup.com
Manufacturer of syrup.
Owner: Ben Fisk

1216 Ben-Bud Growers Inc.
9210 Glades Rd
Boca Raton, FL 33434
561-347-3120
Fax: 561-347-3101 www.ben-bud.com
Processor and importer of vegetables.
President: Ben Litowich
Quality Control Manager: Robert Graham
Sales Manager: Andrew Wilson
Year Founded: 1910
Estimated Sales: $20-50 Million
Number Employees: 10-19
Type of Packaging: Consumer, Bulk

1217 Benbow's Coffee Roasters
8 Access Alley
Bar Harbor, ME 04609
207-288-2552
Fax: 207-288-8227 www.benbows.com
Coffee roasters and jams
President/Owner: Ron Greenberg
CEO: Jaren Greenberg
Estimated Sales: Less than $500,000
Number Employees: 1-4
Type of Packaging: Private Label
Brands:
Benbow's

1218 Beneficial Blends
6304 Benjamin Road
Suite 507
Tampa, FL 33634-5128
Fax: 813-902-7261 800-230-5952
erin@beneficialblends.com www.kelapo.com
Other baking mixes and ingredients, other condiments, other oils, other spreads & syrup.
Marketing: Erin Meagher
erin@beneficialblends.com

1219 Beneo Inc
201 Littleton Rd # 100
1st Floor
Morris Plains, NJ 07950-2939
973-539-6644
Fax: 973-867-2141 contact@beneo.com
www.beneo.com
Manufacturer of ingredients derived from chicory roots, beer sugar, rice and wheat.
President: Jon Peters
Executive VP: Joe O'Neill
joe.oneill@beneo.com
Estimated Sales: $170,000
Number Employees: 10-19
Parent Co: Beneo GmbH
Brands:
Isomalt

1220 Benmarl Wine Co
156 Highland Ave
Marlboro, NY 12542-6304
845-236-4265
Fax: 845-236-7271 benmarlwinery@gmail.com
www.benmarl.com
Wines including white, blended red, rose and Chardonnay. Founded in 1971.
Owner: Victor Spaccerelli
President: Mark Miller
General Manager: Matthew Spaccarelli
Estimated Sales: $2.5-5 Million
Number Employees: 5-9
Type of Packaging: Consumer, Food Service

Food Manufacturers / A-Z

Brands:
  Marlboro Village

1221 Bennett's Apples & Cider
944 Garner Road East
Ancaster, ON L9G 3K9
Canada
905-648-6878
Fax: 905-648-3647 www.bennettsapples.com
Sweet and mulled apple and apple cranberry cider, apples, pumpkins and sweet corn; contract packaging available. Founded in 1978.
CEO/President: Todd Bennett
Vice President: Richard Bennett
Estimated Sales: $3 Million
Number Employees: 27
Square Footage: 40000
Type of Packaging: Consumer, Food Service, Private Label, Bulk
Brands:
  Bennett's

1222 Benson's Gourmet Seasonings
P.O. Box 638
Azusa, CA 91702-0638
626-969-4443
Fax: 626-969-2912 800-325-5619
bensons4u@aol.com www.bensonsseasonings.com
Kosher, salt-free and sugar-free seasoning blends including herb/pepper, natural salty flavor, Southwestern, Jamaican, lemon and garlic/herb, big game, game bird and chili. Founded in 1989.
President: Debbie Benson
Estimated Sales: Less than $500,000
Number Employees: 1-4
Square Footage: 4000
Type of Packaging: Consumer, Food Service, Bulk

1223 Benton's Seafood Ctr
711 Central Ave S
Tifton, GA 31794-5212
229-382-4976
Fax: 229-382-0779
Seafood. Founded in 1987.
Owner: Tim Benton
Estimated Sales: $1-3 Million
Number Employees: 1-4

1224 Benzel's Pretzel Bakery
5200 6th Ave
Altoona, PA 16602-1435
814-942-5062
Fax: 814-942-4133 800-344-4438
pretzels@benzels.com www.benzels.com
Pretzels. Founded in 1911.
President: Ann Benzel
pretzels@benzels.com
Owner: William Benzel
Sales Director: Shaun Benzel
Production Manager: Erkin McCaulley
Estimated Sales: $10-20 Million
Number Employees: 98
Number of Products: 36
Square Footage: 180000
Type of Packaging: Consumer, Food Service, Private Label, Bulk
Brands:
  Benzel's Brand
  Pennysticks Brand

1225 Benziger Family Winery
1883 London Ranch Rd
Glen Ellen, CA 95442-9728
707-935-3000
Fax: 707-935-3016 888-490-2739
greatwine@benziger.com www.benziger.com
Fine wines
President: Tim Wallace
erinnbz@benziger.com
VP Winegrowing: Mark Burningham
Marketing: Jennifer Seekon
Sales: Erinn Benziger
General Manager: Mike Benziger
Estimated Sales: $20-50 Million
Number Employees: 5-9

1226 Bequet Confections
8235 Huffine Ln
Bozeman, MT 59718-5986
406-586-2191
Fax: 406-586-7003 877-423-7838
sales@bequetconfections.com
www.bequetconfections.com
Caramels and flavored caramels. Founded in 2001.

President: Joe Sharber
Owner: Robin Bequet
robin@bequetconfections.com
Number Employees: 20-49

1227 Berardi's Fresh Roast
12029 Abbey Rd
Cleveland, OH 44133-2637
440-582-4303
Fax: 440-582-4359 800-876-9109
sales@berardiscoffee.com
www.berardiscoffee.com
Specialty coffees, estates, organic, signature blends, espresso and espresso pods. Green, black, organic and herbal teas. Founded in 1987.
Owner: Sean Leneghan
sleneghan@berardiscoffee.com
CEO: Patrick Leneghan
Estimated Sales: $2.5-5 Million
Number Employees: 20-49
Type of Packaging: Private Label

1228 Berberian Nut Company
6100 Wilson Landing Rd.
Chico, CA 95973-8902
530-981-4900
Fax: 209-465-6008 www.berberiannut.com
Chandler, Howard, Tulare, and Hartley walnuts
Principal: Pete Turner
Quality Assurance Supervisor: Yesica Salcido
Marketing Manager: Ken Wagner
General Manager: Terry Turner
Plant Manager: Ren Fairbanks
Estimated Sales: $20-50 Million
Number Employees: 50-99
Type of Packaging: Consumer, Food Service, Private Label, Bulk

1229 Bergen Marzipan & Chocolate
205 S Washington Ave
Bergenfield, NJ 07621-2918
201-385-8343
Fax: 201-385-0042 bergenmarzipan@optonline.net
www.bergenmarzipan.net
Confections, marzipan and chocolate. Founded in 1987.
Owner: Eddie Sarpon
bergenmarzipan@yahoo.com
Principal: Gunter Schott
Estimated Sales: Under $500,000
Number Employees: 5-9

1230 Berghausen E Cheml Co
4524 Este Ave
Cincinnati, OH 45232-1763
513-541-5631
Fax: 530-683-4011 800-648-5887
www.berghausen.com
Processor and finisher of quillaja and yucca extracts (powder and liquid forms) and food colors. Founded in 1863.
President: Beth Baker
bbaker@berghausen.com
Quality Control Manager: Tom Davlin
Estimated Sales: $1-5 Million
Number Employees: 10-19

1231 Berghoff Brewery
1730 W Superior St # 3w
Chicago, IL 60622-5639
608-358-4992
Fax: 608-325-3198 www.berghoffbeer.com
Beer and malt liquor in kegs, bottles and cans
President/Plant Manager: Gary Olson
CEO: Harry Cumberbatch
Director of Brewing/Quality Control: Kris Kalav
Production Manager: Dick Tschanz
Estimated Sales: $10 Million
Number Employees: 20-49
Brands:
  Berghoff Family
  Blumer's Root Beer
  Braumeister
  Braumeister Light
  Huber
  Huber Bock
  Wisi Club

1232 Bering Sea Fisheries
4413 83rd Avenue SE
Snohomish, WA 98290-5204
425-334-1498
Processor and exporter of frozen salmon. Founded in 1961.

President: H William Bodey
Vice President: Russell Bodey
Estimated Sales: $780,000
Number Employees: 10
Type of Packaging: Private Label

1233 Berke-Blake Fancy Foods, Inc.
150 National Pl # 140
Longwood, FL 32750-6431
407-831-7288
Fax: 407-831-7065 888-386-2253
www.anniepiesbakery.com
Cakes including cheesecakes, and pies. Founded in 1991.
CEO: Anne Resnick
Sales Executive: Marnie Blake Zahn
General Manager: Mark Hanft
Production Manager: Daniele Sansone
Estimated Sales: $5-10 Million
Number Employees: 5-9
Number of Brands: 1
Number of Products: 100
Square Footage: 36000
Type of Packaging: Food Service
Brands:
  Annie Pie's

1234 Berkeley Farms
25500 Clawiter Rd
Hayward, CA 94545
510-265-8600
Fax: 510-265-8748 800-395-7004
sharon_cornelius@deanfoods.com
www.berkeleyfarms.com
Dairy products
Manager: Nick Kelble
Quality Control: Besty Raasch
VP Sales/Marketing: Mike Lasky
General Sales Manager: Dan Atkins
Distribution Manager: Richard Hunter
General Manager: Derek Allbee
Plant Manager: Randy Vick
Number Employees: 500-999
Parent Co: Dean Foods Company

1235 Berks Packing Company, Inc.
307-323 Bingaman St
PO Box 5919
Reading, PA 19610-5919
610-376-7291
Fax: 610-378-1210 800-882-3757
hr@berksfoods.com www.berksfoods.com
Beef frankfurters, smoked sausage and kielbasa, roast beef, turkey breast, regular and reduced-sodium ham, deli meats, etc
President: Mike Boylan
CEO: Charles Boylan
Purchasing Director: David Boylan
Brands:
  Berks

1236 Berkshire Bark Inc
18 Elm Ct
Sheffield, MA 1257
413-229-8120
info@berkshirebark.com
www.berkshirebark.com
Manufacturer of top quality Belgian chocolate.
President: Jerome Bertuglia
Number Employees: 1-4
Brands:
  berkshire bark

1237 Berkshire Brewing Co Inc
12 Railroad St
South Deerfield, MA 01373-1034
413-665-6600
Fax: 413-665-7837 877-222-7468
www.berkshire-brewing.com
Ale and seasonal beer. Founded in 1992.
Owner: Dan Bisson
dbisson@berkshirebrewingcompany.com
CEO: Christopher Lalli
Director: Julia Dvorko
Estimated Sales: $1.2 Million
Number Employees: 20-49
Type of Packaging: Consumer, Food Service
Brands:
  Berkshire Ale
  Cabin Fever Ale
  Coffeehouse Porter
  Drayman's Porter
  Gold Spike Ale
  Hefeweizen

Food Manufacturers / A-Z

Holidale Barley Wine
Imperial Stout
Lost Sailor India Pale Ale
Mailbock Lager
Oktoberfest Lager
Raspberry Barley Wine
River Ale
Shabadoo Black and Tan Ale
Steel Rail Extra Pale Ale

1238 Berkshire Dairy
1258 Penn Ave
Wyomissing, PA 19610-2147
610-378-9999
Fax: 610-378-4975   877-696-6455
info@berkshiredairy.com www.berkshiredairy.com
Manufacturer, importer and exporter of analog extenders, dehydrated dairy products, powders, cheese, creamers, lactose, milk and whey, whole milk powder, Anhydreos milkfat butter, nonfat dry milk, permeate
President & CEO: Dale Mills
dmills@berkshiredairy.com
Sales Director: Steve Cinesi
Estimated Sales: $2.7 Million
Number Employees: 10-19
Parent Co: Dairy Farmers of America, Inc.
Type of Packaging: Private Label, Bulk
Brands:
  Berk-Cap

1239 Berkshire Mountain Bakery
367 Park St
Housatonic, MA 1236
413-274-3412
Fax: 413-274-6124   866-274-6124
info@berkshiremountainbakery.com
www.berkshiremountainbakery.com
Baked goods such as; sourdough bread, ciabatta bread, bread w/chocolate, oat pecan cookies, pizza crusts and pizza's
President: Richard Bourdon
bourdon592@yahoo.com
Number Employees: 10-19

1240 Berlin Natural Bakery
5126 County Rd 120
Berlin, OH 44610
330-893-2734
Fax: 330-893-2157   800-686-5334
www.berlinnaturalbakery.com
Bakery products made with spelt. Founded in 1997.
President: Joy Schrock
cindy@berlinnaturalbakery.com
Managing Executive: Karl Widder
Estimated Sales: $1.3 Million
Number Employees: 20-49
Type of Packaging: Private Label

1241 Bernadette Baking Company
85 Commercial St
Medford, MA 02155
781-393-8700
Fax: 781-393-0414
Crunchy biscotti dipped in brews, coffeees, teas, or wines. Founded in 1998.
President: Bernadette De Vergilio
Vice President: Marie Cooke
Plant Manager: Mario Ruiz
Estimated Sales: Under $500,000
Number Employees: 5-9
Type of Packaging: Private Label
Brands:
  Bernadette's Biscotti
  Bernadette's Biscotti Soave
  Bernadette's Cookies

1242 Bernard & Sons
4011 Jewett Ave
Bakersfield, CA 93303
661-327-4431
Fax: 661-327-7461 www.bernardandsons.com
Meat Products. Founded in 1965.
Owner: Dennis Bernard
General Manager: Hal Ulmer
Estimated Sales: $11,100,000
Number Employees: 20-49

1243 Bernard & Sons Maple Products
104, rue Industrielle du Bois,
St-Victor, QC G0M 2B0
Canada
418-588-6109
Fax: 418-588-6836 info@bernards.ca
www.bernards.ca
Pure maple and fruit syrups

1244 Bernard Food Industries Inc
P.O. Box 1497
Evanston, IL 60204
Fax: 847-869-5315   800-323-3663
www.bernardfoods.com
Dessert toppings, soup bases, drinks and baking ingredients.
President & CEO: Steve Bernard
VP, Sales & Operations: Lou Haan
Year Founded: 1947
Estimated Sales: $20-50 Million
Number Employees: 50-99
Square Footage: 60000
Type of Packaging: Consumer, Food Service, Private Label, Bulk
Brands:
  Bernard
  Beta-Care
  Calorie Control
  Hola
  Kwik-Dish
  Lite-95
  Longhorn Grill
  Sans Sucre
  Tex-Pro
  Thixx

1245 Bernardi Italian Foods Company
595 W 11th St
Bloomsburg, PA 17815
570-389-5500
Fax: 570-784-0293 www.bernardifoodservice.com
Frozen and prepared Italian dinners and cheese foods
Plant Manager: Howard Teufel
Q/A Manager: Julie Simcox
Purchasing: Sharon Lawrence
Year Founded: 1969
Estimated Sales: $20-50 Million
Number Employees: 100-249
Square Footage: 70000
Parent Co: Ajinomoto Foods
Type of Packaging: Consumer, Food Service, Private Label, Bulk

1246 Bernardo Winery
13330 Paseo Del Verano Norte
San Diego, CA 92128-1899
858-487-1866
Fax: 858-673-5376 jim@bernardowinery.com
www.bernardowinery.com
Wine and brandy. Founded in 1932.
President: Ross Rizzo
ross@bernardowinery.com
Marketing & Advertising Manager: Samantha Pewitt
General Manager: Selena Roberts
Estimated Sales: $500,000-$1 Million
Number Employees: 20-49
Type of Packaging: Private Label
Brands:
  Bernardo

1247 Bernardus Winery Tasting Rm
5 W Carmel Valley Rd
21810 Parrot Ranch Road
Carmel Valley, CA 93924
831-298-8021
Fax: 831-659-1676   800-223-2533
www.bernardus.com
Wines
Owner: Ben Pon
bpon@bernardus.com
Operations Manager: Dean DeKorth
Plant Manager: Matthew Shea
Estimated Sales: $5-10 Million
Number Employees: 5-9
Type of Packaging: Private Label
Brands:
  Bernardus

1248 Bernatello's Foods
5625 W 78th St
Suite B
Edina, MN 55439-3153
952-831-6622
800-878-5001
www.bernatellos.com
Frozen pizza manufacturer in the Midwest.
Number Employees: 100-249
Brands:
  Brew Pub
  Bellatoria
  Orv's
  Roma
  Pizza Corner

1249 Berner Food & Beverage LLC
2034 E Factory Rd
Dakota, IL 61018
800-819-8199
berner.sales@bernerfoods.com
bernerfoodandbeverage.com
Shelf stable RTD coffee beverages, dips, and aerosol cheese.
CEO: Kurt Seagrist
CFO: Scott Edgcomb
VP, Manufacturing: Alan Davis
Chief Commercial Officer: Kirby Harris
Year Founded: 1943
Estimated Sales: $250 Million
Number Employees: 600-800
Square Footage: 200000
Type of Packaging: Consumer, Private Label, Bulk
Other Locations:
  Berner Cheese Corp.
  Rock City IL

1250 Bernheim Distilling Company
1416 S 3rd Street
Louisville, KY 40208-2117
502-638-1387
Fax: 502-585-9110   800-303-0053
Bookings@bernheimmansion.com
www.bernheimmansion.com
Spirits, wheat whiskey and bourbon
Owner: Bernard Bernheim
Estimated Sales: $300,000-500,000
Number Employees: 5-9

1251 Bernie's Foods
158 Cook Street
Brooklyn, NY 11206
718-417-6677
Fax: 201-445-2003 www.ratners.com
Canner and food processors of frozen kosher foods.
President: Abraham Ostreicher
Number Employees: 20-49
Number of Brands: 3
Number of Products: 50
Square Footage: 40000
Type of Packaging: Consumer, Food Service, Private Label
Brands:
  Frankel's Homestyle
  Tovli

1252 Berres Brothers Coffee
202 Air Park Dr
PO Box 578
Watertown, WI 53094-7411
920-261-6158
Fax: 920-261-9390   800-233-5443
info@bbcoffee.com www.berresbrothers.com
Coffee
Owner: Pete Berres
info@bbcoffee.com
Number Employees: 50-99

1253 Berri Pro
3159 Donald Douglas Loop S
Santa Monica, CA 90405
berripro.com
Fitness beverage
Founder: Jerome Tse
Number of Brands: 1
Type of Packaging: Consumer
Brands:
  BERRI PRO

1254 Berry Processing
150 Avery Street
Walla Walla, IL 99362
509-529-2161
Fax: 509-527-1331
Beef and pork. Founded in 1955.

Food Manufacturers / A-Z

Owner: Kathreen Berry
Co-Owner: Lowell Berry
Estimated Sales: $500,000-$1 Million
Number Employees: 1-4
Type of Packaging: Consumer, Food Service, Private Label, Bulk

1255 Berryessa Gap Tasting Room
15 Main St
Winters, CA 95694-1722
530-795-3201
Fax: 916-795-1119 orrin@berryessagap.com
www.berryessagap.com
Processors of fine wines
CFO & Owner: Dan Martinez
Owner, Marketing & Sales Director: Corinne Martinez
Owner & Winemaker: Mike Anderson
Owner & Vineyard Operations Manager: Santiago Moreno
Hospitality & Marketing Manager: Megan Foley
Sales Manager: Clint Crow
clintcrow@berryessagap.com
Estimated Sales: $220,000
Number Employees: 1-4

1256 Berson Peanuts
113 Highway 52 E
Opp, AL 36467-3767
334-493-0655
Fax: 334-493-7767
Peanuts
Division Manager: Dennis Finch
Contact: John Reed
john@alafarm.com
Estimated Sales: Less Than $500,000
Number Employees: 5-9
Type of Packaging: Bulk

1257 Bertie County Peanuts
217 U.S. 13 North
Windsor, NC 27983
252-794-2138
Fax: 252-794-9267 800-457-0005
jon@pnuts.net www.pnuts.net
Sugar-free, other chocolate, other candy, health, fitness and energy bars, nuts, gift packs, private label.
Marketing: Jon Powell

1258 Besco Grain Ltd
PO Box 166
30 Railway Avenue
Brunkild, MB R0G 0E0
Canada
204-736-3570
Fax: 204-736-3575 www.bescograin.ca
Grains
President: Renee Caners
Quality Control: Carol Schulz
International Sales: Anthony Krijger
Sales Manager: Fred Nicholson
Office Manager: Sheri Hiebert
Plant Manager: Jamie Stelmachowich

1259 Bespoke Provisions
PO Box 225
Boulder, CO 80306
646-963-1245
hello@bespoke-provisions.com
www.bespoke-provisions.com
Manufacturer of crackers, salt, and candles.
Founder: Rachelle Miller
Square Footage: 80000

1260 Bess Eaton
127 High St
Westerly, RI 02891-1821
401-596-5533
www.besseaton.com
Coffee and baked goods
Management: David Liguori
Estimated Sales: Less Than $500,000
Number Employees: 5-9

1261 Bessinger Pickle Co
537 N Court Street
Au Gres, MI 48703-9204
989-876-8008
Dill pickles, pickled fruits and vegetables.
Year Founded: 1974
Estimated Sales: $1 Million
Number Employees: 50-99
Square Footage: 104000
Type of Packaging: Consumer

1262 Best Chicago Meat
4649 W Armitage Ave
Chicago, IL 60639
www.bestchicagomeat.com
Meat products including frozen hamburger patties, sausages, spare ribs, chitterlings, bacon, ham, breakfast links, chicken nuggets, rib tips and kosher hot dogs
CFO: Paul Dwyer
Regional Sales Manager: Edward Allaway
Estimated Sales: $20-50 Million
Number Employees: 20-49
Number of Brands: 4
Square Footage: 20000
Parent Co: Beavers Holdings
Type of Packaging: Consumer, Food Service
Brands:
   David's Kosher
   Glenmark
   JEMMBURGER
   Moo & Oink

1263 Best Chocolate In Town
880 Massachusetts Avenue
Indianapolis, IN 46204
317-636-2800
Fax: 317-636-2822 888-294-2378
info@bestchocolateintown.com
www.bestchocolateintown.com
Hand-made chocolates
Owner: Elizabeth Garber
Estimated Sales: $100,000
Number Employees: 5-9

1264 Best Cooking Pulses, Inc.
110 10th St NE
Portage la Prairie, MB R1N 1B5
Canada
204-857-4451
margaret@bestcookingpulses.com
www.bestcookingpulses.com
Peas, chickpea, lentil and bean flours and pea fiber. Certified Kosher, Halal, Conventional or Certified-Organic, free of all major allergens, and gluten free.
President: Trudy Heal
Director, Sales & Marketing: Jennifer Evancio
General Manager: Mike Gallais
Estimated Sales: $11.25 Million
Number Employees: 23
Type of Packaging: Bulk

1265 Best Ever Bakery
17 Broadway
Massapequa, NY 11758-5003
516-795-5590
Fax: 516-804-1144 besteverbakery@gmail.com
www.besteverbakeshop.com
Sweet potato and pecan pie, cakes, cookies, and dessert designs.
Owner: Ashley D Elia
President: Vincent D Elia
Estimated Sales: A
Number Employees: 5-9
Type of Packaging: Consumer

1266 Best Express Foods Inc
1458 E Grand River Rd
Williamston, MI 48895-9336
517-655-2288
Fax: 517-655-8568
Frozen pizza and pizza related items
Contact: Dave Spencer
dspencer@bestexpressfoods.com
Number Employees: 20-49
Type of Packaging: Consumer

1267 Best Foods
700 Sylvan Ave
Englewood Cliffs, NJ 07632
201-894-4000
Fax: 201-894-2186 www.bestfoods.com
Best Foods manufactures the best-selling mayonnaise in the United States. East of the Rockies, Best Foods is known as Hellman's.
President, Unilever Foods: Amanda Sourry
Contact: Cordell Price
cordell.price@unilever.com
Number Employees: 44,000
Number of Products: 13
Parent Co: Unilever
Type of Packaging: Consumer, Food Service
Brands:
   Best Foods
   Hellmann's

1268 Best Harvest Bakeries
530 S 65th St
Kansas City, KS 66111-2324
913-287-6300
Fax: 913-287-5408 800-811-5715
info@bestharvest.com www.bestharvest.com
Buns and rolls and breads. Founded in 1999.
President/COO: Ed Honesty
Chairman/CEO: Robert Beavers
VP: Brandon Beavers
Quality Assurance Supervisor: Jason McConico
Manufacturing Executive: Brad Wolf
Purchasing: Rich Lingo
Estimated Sales: $3.4 Million
Number Employees: 20-49
Square Footage: 128000
Type of Packaging: Consumer, Food Service

1269 Best Maid Cookie Co
1147 Benson St
River Falls, WI 54022-1594
715-426-2090
Fax: 715-426-1950 888-444-0322
customerservice@bestmaid.com
www.bestmaid.com
Pre-formed frozen cookie dough and baked cookies; also specialty products available. Founded in 1943.
Owner: Byron Grickson
Vice President: Ron Thielen
Human Resource Manager: Deb Dartsch
Number Employees: 100-249
Square Footage: 80000
Type of Packaging: Food Service, Private Label

1270 Best Maid Products, Inc.
1401 S Riverside Drive
PO Box 1809
Fort Worth, TX 76101-1809
817-335-5494
Fax: 817-534-7117 800-447-3581
www.bestmaidproducts.com
Pickles, sauces, dressings and condiments.
President: Brian Dalton
Technical Director: Mike Wuller
Marketing Director: Roger Fort
Contact: Diaz Alfonso
diaza@aldeasa.com
Estimated Sales: $44.1 Million
Number Employees: 250
Number of Brands: 1
Square Footage: 200000
Type of Packaging: Consumer
Brands:
   Best Maid

1271 Best Provision Co Inc
2401 Morris Ave.
Union, NJ 07083
973-242-5000
Fax: 973-648-0041 800-631-4466
info@bestprovision.com www.bestprovision.com
Corned beef, roast beef, frankfurters, pastrami and bacon
President: Floyd Jason
fjayson@bestprovision.com
Co-Owner: Kevin Karp
Co-Owner: Richard Dolinko
Human Resource Director: Clara Mendez
Year Founded: 1938
Estimated Sales: $35 Million
Number Employees: 100-249
Square Footage: 65000
Type of Packaging: Consumer, Food Service

1272 Bestco Inc
288 Mazeppa Rd
Mooresville, NC 28115-7928
704-664-4300
Fax: 704-664-7493 www.bestco.com
Nutritional supplements, cough drops, lozenges and antacids.
President: Tim Condron
CEO: Richard Zulman
rzulman@bestco.com
CFO: Scott Wattenberg
EVP: Mark Knight
EVP: Steve Berkowitz
EVP: Jonathan Zulman

Food Manufacturers / A-Z

Estimated Sales: $1-9.99 Million
Number Employees: 250-499
Parent Co: Tamanda Holdings USA Inc.
Type of Packaging: Private Label

1273 Beta Pure Foods
2100 Deleware Avenue
Santa Cruz, CA 95060
831-685-6565
Fax: 831-685-6569 www.betapure.com
Organic frozen fruits and vegetables, concentrates and purees, sweeteners. Founded in 1994.
President: Loren Morr
Number Employees: 5-9
Parent Co: SunOpta
Type of Packaging: Food Service, Private Label, Bulk

1274 BetaStatin Nutritional Rsearch
299 Riversville Rd
Greenwich, CT 06831
203-869-7778
Fax: 203-869-7778 800-660-9570
www.betastatin.com
Nutritional and weight loss supplements.
Managing Director: Dr Stephen L Newman

1275 Beth's Fine Desserts
34 Miller Aveue
Mill Valley, CA 94941
415-383-3991
Fax: 707-792-0399
Bite-sized cookies and savory cheese wafers, gourmet gift items, gingerbreads. Produces and markets desserts.
President: Beth Setrakian
Brands:
   Beth's
   Beth's Baking Basics
   Heavenly Little Cookies

1276 Bethel Heights Vineyard
6060 Bethel Heights Rd NW
Salem, OR 97304-9733
503-399-9588
Fax: 503-581-0943 info@bethelheights.com
www.bethelheights.com
Wines
President: Pat Dudley
pat@bethelheights.com
Winemaker: Terry Casteel
Vice President: Ted Casteel
Marketing Director: Pat Dudley
Estimated Sales: $2 Million
Number Employees: 20-49
Type of Packaging: Private Label

1277 Betsy's Best
888-483-2019
info@betsysbest.com betsysbest.com
Nut and seed butters
Founder: Betsy Opyt
Number of Brands: 1
Number of Products: 4
Type of Packaging: Consumer
Brands:
   BETSY'S BEST

1278 Betsy's Cheese Straws
3761 Grandview Road
Millbrook, AZ 36054-3203
334-285-1354
Fax: 800-625-9700 877-902-3141
info@belmontpeanuts.com
Cheese straws. Founded in 1998.
President/Owner: Betsy Parker
Contact: Elizabeth Campbell
elizabethc@betsyscheesestraws.com
Number Employees: 6

1279 Bettah Buttah, LLC
111 Southwest Blvd
Kansas City, KS 66103
913-432-5228
Fax: 913-432-5880 800-568-8468
www.bettahbuttah.com
Specialty foods, snacks, hot sauces, condiments, seasonings, salsas, barbeque sauces. Flavored butters. Founded in 1996.
President: Joe Polo
Branch Manager: Jana Kirke
Contact: Kit Maxfield
Contact: Bryan Richards

Estimated Sales: Less than $500,000
Number Employees: 20-49
Brands:
   Cajun Bayou
   Calido Chile Traders
   Fiesta
   Jose Goldstein
   Original Juan
   Panisgood
   Texas Longhorn
   Wild and Mild

1280 Bette's Oceanview Diner
1807 4th St
Berkeley, CA 94710-1910
510-644-3230
Fax: 510-644-3209 bettesdiner@worldpantry.com
www.bettesdiner.com
Manufacturer and exporter of pancake mixes including buttermilk, oatmeal and buckwheat; also, scone mixes including raisin, cranberry and lemon currant
Owner: Bette Kroening
Number Employees: 20-49
Type of Packaging: Consumer, Food Service
Brands:
   Bette's Oceanview Diner

1281 Better Bagel Bakery
4854 S Tamiami Trl
Sarasota, FL 34231-4352
941-924-0393
Fax: 941-924-0358
Baked goods such as; breads, rolls, bagels, etc
Owner: Jun Park
Estimated Sales: Less than $100,000
Number Employees: 1-4

1282 Better Baked Foods Inc
56 Smedley St
North East, PA 16428-1632
814-725-8778
Fax: 814-725-5021 www.betterbaked.com
French bread pizza, panini sandwiches, appetizers, garlic breads, breakfast items, and desserts.
President/COO: Joseph Pacinelli
CEO: Chris Miller
Director of Manufacturing Operations: Jerry Pacinelli
IT Manager: Brad Harrison
davide@betterbaked.com
Plant Manager: Scott Carpenter
Estimated Sales: $20-50 Million
Number Employees: 100-249
Number of Brands: 3
Square Footage: 200000
Type of Packaging: Food Service, Private Label
Brands:
   Daybreak Classics
   Papa Presto
   Two Sicily's

1283 Better Beverages Inc
10624 Midway Ave
Cerritos, CA 90703-1581
562-924-8321
Fax: 562-924-6204 800-344-5219
customercare@betbev.com www.betbev.com
Soft drinks, juices, energy drinks, coffee, punch syrups, bar mixes, beverage dispensers, and glass washer and sanitizer.
Owner: Harold Harris
haroldh@betbev.com
CEO: G Harris
Estimated Sales: $20-50 Million
Number Employees: 20-49
Type of Packaging: Consumer, Food Service
Brands:
   Rc Cola

1284 Better Bites Bakery
Austin, TX 78737
rachel@betterbitesbakery.com
www.betterbitesbakery.com
Bites, cupcakes and brownies
Founder & CEO: Leah Lopez

1285 Better Living Products
208 Harvard Drive
Princeton, TX 75407
972-736-6691
Fax: 903-298-0014 zetawize@yahoo.com
www.betterlivingusa.com
Processor, importer of kava kava powder, aloe vera juice and herbs. Founded in 1996.

Founder: Don Ansley
COO: Ed Carter
Estimated Sales: Less than $500,000
Number Employees: 1-4
Parent Co: Zeta Wize LLC Company
Brands:
   Kava Kava
   Noni Nonu

1286 Better Made Snack Foods
10148 Gratiot Ave
Detroit, MI 48213
313-925-4774
Fax: 313-925-6028 800-332-2394
info@bettermadesnackfoods.com
www.bettermadesnackfoods.com
Potato chips, popcorn, crunchy chips, pretzels, pork rinds, tortilla chips, beef jerky, chocolate covered potato chips and pretzels, salsas and cheese dips.
President: David Jones
Year Founded: 1930
Estimated Sales: $62 Million
Number Employees: 100-249
Type of Packaging: Consumer, Food Service
Brands:
   Better Made

1287 Better Than Coffee
Torrance, CA 90503
contact@betterthancoffee.com
www.betterthancoffee.com
High energy bars
Founder & Managing Partner: Valerie Milovic

1288 Better Than Foods USA
17000 W Capitol Dr
Brookfield, WI 53005
855-691-5900
www.betterthanfoodsusa.com
Organic noodles, pasta and rice
Number of Brands: 1
Number of Products: 3
Type of Packaging: Consumer
Brands:
   BETTER THAN

1289 BetterBody Foods & Nutrition LLC
1762 W 20 S Ste 500
Lindon, UT 84042-1762
Fax: 801-456-2601 866-404-6582
info@xagave.com www.xagave.com
Supplements
President/Owner: Stephen Richards
Contact: Joshua Faber
jfaber@betterbodyfoods.com

1290 Betty Jane Homemade Candy
3049 Asbury Rd
Dubuque, IA 52001-8459
563-582-4668
Fax: 563-582-2150 800-642-1254
www.bettyjanecandies.com
Candy
President/CEO: Drew Siegert
bjcgremlin@aol.com
Vice President: George Hagge
Sales Exec: Linnae Heinz
Plant Mgr./Head of Production: John Heinz
Estimated Sales: $2 Million
Number Employees: 20-49
Type of Packaging: Consumer
Brands:
   Gremlins

1291 Betty Lou's
750 SE Booth Bend Rd
PO Box 537
McMinnville, OR 97128
503-434-5205
Fax: 503-472-8643 800-242-5205
www.bettylousinc.com
Processor and exporter of oil and, low-fat oven baked apple butter, low-fat and wheat-free fruit bars and fat-free cookies, snack foods and candies, protein bars. Founded in 1978.
Owner: Betty Carrier
VP Sales: John Sizemore
Estimated Sales: $2.5-5 Million
Number Employees: 20-49
Square Footage: 36000
Type of Packaging: Consumer, Private Label
Brands:
   Betty Lou's

Food Manufacturers / A-Z

1292 Bevco Sales International Inc.
9354-194th Street
Surrey, BC V4N 4E9
Canada
604-888-1455
Fax: 604-888-2887 800-663-0090
info@bevco.net www.bevco.net
Processor and co-packer of fruit juices, citrus drinks and bottled water
President/Board Member: Brian Fortier
Board Member: Donna Fortier
Estimated Sales: $5-10 Million
Number Employees: 10-19
Type of Packaging: Consumer, Private Label
Brands:
  Juicetyme Delites
  O-Jay
  Watertyme
  Wild Springs

1293 Beverage America
545 E 32nd St
Holland, MI 49423-5495
616-396-1281
Fax: 616-396-8121
Bottled water, fruit beverages, Snapple, and Dr. Pepper
Plant Manufacturing: Dale Stein
Estimated Sales: $5-10 Million
Number Employees: 5-9

1294 Beverage Capital Corporation
2209 Sulphur Spring Rd
Baltimore, MD 21227-2933
410-242-7404
Fax: 410-247-2977
bevcapsales@beveragecapital.com
Bottled and canned soft and juice drinks and juice; also, seltzer water; contract packaging available
Chairman: Harold Honickman
Controller: John Schmitj
Treasurer: Walter Wilkinson
Vice President: Rick Smith
Contact: Florence Stewart
fstewart@capitol-beverage.com
Purchasing Agent: Kim Quinn
Estimated Sales: $28 Million
Number Employees: 350
Square Footage: 365000
Type of Packaging: Consumer, Private Label
Other Locations:
  Whitehead Court Manufacturing
  Baltimore MD
  30th Street Manufacturing
  Baltimore MD
Brands:
  Bevnet
  Cadbury Schweppes
  Canada Dry
  Energy Brand
  Mistic
  Snapple

1295 Beverage Flavors Intl
3150 N Campbell Ave
Chicago, IL 60618-7921
773-248-3860
Fax: 773-248-3862 info@beverageflavorsintl.com
www.beverageflavorsinternational.com
Beverage flavor emulsions and concentrates to bottlers. Flavor selection includes citrus punch, tropical fruit punch, pineapple-banana, mango peach, apple, strawberry-kiwi, aloha punch and pineapple-guava.
Manager: Daniel Manoogian
Contact: Gregg Goga
ggoga@beverageflavorsintl.com
Office Manager: Barbara Martinez
Estimated Sales: Less Than $500,000
Number Employees: 1-4
Type of Packaging: Bulk

1296 Beverage House Inc
400 High Point Rd SE # 100
Cartersville, GA 30120-6610
770-387-0451
Fax: 770-387-1809 888-367-8327
www.beveragehouse.com
Coffee, tea and beverage concentrates. Founded in 1984.
Manager: Jimmy Garren
CEO: Jim Gollhoffer
Marketing Manager: Robbin McCool
Manager: Monte Ammons
monte@beveragehouse.com
Number Employees: 20-49

Type of Packaging: Private Label
Brands:
  New Southern Tradition Teas
  Reedy Brew Teas

1297 Beverly International
1768 Industrial Rd
Cold Spring, KY 41076-8610
859-781-3474
Fax: 859-781-7590 800-781-3475
www.beverlyinternational.net
Manufacturer and exporter of multiple vitamin and mineral packs; also, protein powders. Founded in 1967.
Owner: Roger Riedinger
Owner: Sandy Riedinger
sandyr@beverlyinternational.net
Estimated Sales: Less Than $500,000
Number Employees: 5-9
Type of Packaging: Consumer, Food Service, Private Label
Brands:
  Beverly International

1298 Bevsource
219 Little Canada Road East
St. Paul, MN 55117
651-797-0113
Fax: 651-482-1337 866-956-4608
sales@bevsource.com www.bevsource.com
Ingredients and packaging for the beverage industry, specifically sweeteners, vitamin blends, juice concentrates, and alcohol.

1299 Beyond Meat
1325 E El Segundo Blvd
El Segundo, CA 90245
866-756-4112
beyondmeat.com
Plant-based burgers and sausages
CEO: Ethan Brown
Number of Brands: 1
Number of Products: 11
Type of Packaging: Consumer
Brands:
  BEYOND MEAT

1300 Bgreen Food
6977 Navajo Rd
Suite 116
San Diego, CA 92119
619-825-9330
hello@bgreenfood.com
www.bgreenfood.com
Organic rice and noodles

1301 Bhakti
939 Pearl St
Suite 200
Boulder, CO 80302-5067
303-484-8770
www.drinkbhakti.com
Chai made with fresh pressed organic ginger and fiery spices.
Founder & CEO: Brook Eddy
brook@bhaktichai.com
Quality Assurance Supervisor: Matthew Sessa
Marketing & Events Manager: Allison Salvati
Food Service Sales Manager: Austin Doll
Director Of Plant Operations: Beau Hagberry
Head Brewer: Jared Mandeville
Shipping Manager: Kyle Hameister
Number Employees: 1-4
Type of Packaging: Consumer, Food Service

1302 Bhu Foods
San Diego, CA 92110
619-855-3258
www.bhufoods.com
Vegan protein bars
Contact: Laura Katleman
Number of Brands: 1
Number of Products: 12
Type of Packaging: Consumer
Brands:
  BHU FIT

1303 Bhuja Snacks
Kennesaw, GA 30152
majans.com
Snack mixes
Parent Co: Majans

1304 Bi Nutraceuticals
2550 El Presidio St
Long Beach, CA 90810-1193
310-669-2100
Fax: 310-637-3644 contact@botanicals.com
www.binutraceuticals.com
Manufacturer and distributor of water soluable extracts, pre-mixes, herb powders and teas.
President: George Pontiakos
Director of Fulfillment Services: Corey Leon
CFO: Christoph Kirchner
VP Technical Services: Emilio Gutierrez
VP Global Quality & Compliance: Rupa Das
Director of Marketing: Randy Kreienbrink
Sales Manager-Pacific Territory: Nicole Robertson
Contact: Patrisha Abergas
patrishaabergas@tmmc.com
Director, Extract Operations: Dr. William Meer

1305 Biagio's Banquets
4242 N Central Ave
Chicago, IL 60634-1810
773-736-9009
Fax: 773-587-3011 800-392-2837
rperrye@aol.com www.suparossa.com
Processor and exporter of pasta, breaded appetizers and pizza including deep dish, thin crust, pan and self-rising. Founded in 1977.
President: Samuel Cirrincione
Sales Director: Michelle Rubino
Contact: Peter Lesniak
peter@suparossa.com
General Manager: Tom Cirrincione
Estimated Sales: $10-20 Million
Number Employees: 50-99
Square Footage: 60000
Brands:
  Suparossa

1306 Bianchi Winery
3380 Branch Rd
Paso Robles, CA 93446-8314
805-226-9922
Fax: 805-226-8230 info@bianchiwine.com
www.bianchiwine.com
Manufacturer and exporter of red and white wines. Founded in 2001.
Owner: Glenn A Bianchi
gl@bianchiwine.com
Principal: Al Smart
CFO: Mike Gardnier
Vice President: Albert Paul
Operations: Edward Ortease
Manager/Winemaster: Tom Lane
Estimated Sales: $5 Million
Number Employees: 5-9
Number of Brands: 3
Number of Products: 20
Type of Packaging: Consumer, Food Service, Bulk
Brands:
  Bianchi Vineyards
  Chateau Cellars
  Domaine Noel
  Vista Verde

1307 Bias Vineyards & Winery
3166 Highway B
Berger, MO 63014-1418
573-834-5475
Fax: 573-834-2046 800-905-2427
info@biaswinery.com www.biaswinery.com
Wines
President: Carol Grass
biaswinery@fenit.com
VP: Kirk Grass
Purchasing Director: Carol Grass
Estimated Sales: Less Than $500,000
Number Employees: 1-4
Type of Packaging: Private Label

1308 Biazzo Dairy Products Inc
1145 Edgewater Ave
Ridgefield, NJ 07657-2102
201-941-6800
Fax: 201-941-4151 info@biazzo.com
www.biazzo.com
Fresh, chunk and shredded mozzarella, ricotta and string cheese.
President: Sergio Espinoza
sergio.espinoza@schreiberfoods.com
Vice President: John Iapichino, Jr.
Food Safety & Quality Assurance Manager: Sanya Bici
Director of Sales: Steven Cilento

Food Manufacturers / A-Z

Estimated Sales: $20-50 Million
Number Employees: 50-99
Square Footage: 58000
Type of Packaging: Consumer, Food Service, Private Label, Bulk
Brands:
 Biazzo Brand

1309 Bickel's Potato Chip Company
51 N Main St
PO Box 2427
York, PA 17405
717-665-2002
Fax: 717-665-5449 800-233-1933
www.bickelssnacks.com
Warehouse location for Bickel's potato chips. Founded in 1954.
President: John Wareheine
Controller: Gary Knisely
Director Sales: Ed Dobkel
Plant Manager: Jay Epstein
Purchasing Director: Nellie Redding
Estimated Sales: $10-24.9 Million
Number Employees: 5-9
Type of Packaging: Consumer
Brands:
 Bickel's

1310 Bickel's Snack Foods Inc
1120 Zinns Quarry Rd
P.O. Box 2427
York, PA 17404-3533
717-843-0738
Fax: 717-843-5192 800-233-1933
www.bickelssnacks.com
Snack food products including barrels, tortilla chips, corn chips, wedge pretzels, kettle cooked chips, cheese products, and potato chips.
General Manager: Dale Warfel
Year Founded: 1954
Estimated Sales: $20-50 Million
Number Employees: 1000-4999
Parent Co: Hanover Foods Corporation
Type of Packaging: Private Label
Brands:
 Bickle Snacks
 Bon Ton
 Cabana
 Golden Gourmet
 Wege

1311 Bickford Daniel LobsterCompany
Lanes Is
Vinalhaven, ME 04863
207-863-4688
Fax: 207-863-4525
Lobster
Estimated Sales: $1-3 Million
Number Employees: 5-9

1312 Bickford Flavors
19007 Saint Clair Ave
Euclid, OH 44117-1001
216-531-6006
Fax: 216-531-2006 800-283-8322
orders@bickfordflavors.com
www.bickfordflavors.com
Extracts including vanilla and assorted flavoring and syrups.
President: Barbara Sofer
orders@bickfordflavors.com
Vice President: Scott Sofer
Operations: Heather Noel
Estimated Sales: $2.5-5 Million
Number Employees: 5-9
Number of Brands: 1
Number of Products: 150
Square Footage: 60000
Type of Packaging: Private Label
Brands:
 Bickford

1313 Bidwell Candies
1610 Broadway Ave
Mattoon, IL 61938-5751
217-234-3858
Fax: 217-234-3856
Manufactures chocolates and candies
Owner: Greg Kuhl
Co-Owner: Lori Kuhl
Plant Manager: Judy Brown
Estimated Sales: Less than $500,000
Number Employees: 5-9

1314 Bidwell Vineyard
18910 Middle Rd
Vineyard 48
Cutchogue, NY 11935-1069
631-734-5200
Fax: 631-734-6763
Fine wines. Founded in 1982.
Owner: Rose Pipia
General Manager: Joseph Pipia
Purchasing Director: James Bidwell
Estimated Sales: $1-2.5 Million appx.
Number Employees: 1-4
Brands:
 Carbernet Sauvignon
 Chardonnay
 Country Gardens Blush Banquet
 Merlot
 Sauvignon Blanc
 White Riesling

1315 Bien Cuit
120 Smith St.
Brooklyn, NY 11201
718-852-0200
info@biencuit.com
www.biencuit.com
Various types of bread.
Chef & Owner: Zachary Golper
Owner: Kate Wheatcroft
Head Baker: Sarah Wilkens
Director, Sales & Marketing: Shelby Jones
Director, Operations: Zachary Greenspon
Type of Packaging: Consumer

1316 Bien Padre Foods Inc
1459 Railroad St
Eureka, CA 95501-2147
707-442-4585
Fax: 707-269-2140 www.bienpadre.com
Manufacturer and exporter of tortilla chips, corn and flour tortillas and salsas. Founded in 1974.
President/Owner: Benito Lim
stevebpf@gmail.com
Sales Exec: Steve Frenz
Estimated Sales: $1-2.5 Million
Number Employees: 20-49
Square Footage: 56000
Type of Packaging: Consumer, Food Service, Private Label, Bulk

1317 Biena Foods
119 Braintree St
Suite 409
Allston, MA 02134-1642
617-202-5210
hello@bienafoods.com
Manufacturer of flavoured chickpea snacks.
Founder and CEO: Poorvi Patodia
poorvi@bienafoods.com
Number Employees: 1-4
Square Footage: 80000
Brands:
 Biena Chickpea Snacks

1318 Bieri's Jackson Cheese
3271 Hwy. P
Jackson, WI 53037
262-677-3227
Fax: 262-677-3480 800-321-6077
annette@bierischeese.com www.bierischeese.com
Retailers of the finest Wisconsin cheeses
Owner: Annette Du Bois
Co-Owner/CEO: Wayne Dubois
Estimated Sales: $300,000-500,000
Number Employees: 5-9
Type of Packaging: Bulk

1319 Bierig Brothers Inc
3539 Reilly Ct
Vineland, NJ 08360-1500
856-691-9765
Fax: 856-692-7869 www.bierigbrothers.com
Veal and lamb products.
Vice President: David Bierig
biebros@aol.com
Operations Manager: Danny Bierig
General Manager: Alan Bierig
Vice President: David Bierig
biebros@aol.com
Estimated Sales: $25 Million
Number Employees: 20-49

1320 Biery Cheese Co
6544 Paris Ave
Louisville, OH 44641-9544
330-875-3381
Fax: 330-875-5896 www.bierycheese.com
Family-owned award-winning cheese manufacturer.
President: Jeff Fairless
CEO: Ben Biery
Number Employees: 100-249
Type of Packaging: Consumer, Food Service, Private Label, Bulk
Brands:
 Biery

1321 Bifulco Four Seasons
590 Almond Rd
Pittsgrove, NJ 08318-4070
856-692-0778
Fax: 856-691-1529 www.bifulcos.com/
Parsley, peppers, tomatoes, zucchini, and melons. Founded in 1971.
President/Owner: Bert Bifullo
Contact: Umberto Bifulco
umbertobifulco@bifulcos.com
Secretary/Sales: Kathleen Bifulco
Estimated Sales: $2.5-5 Million
Number Employees: 10-19
Type of Packaging: Consumer, Bulk
Brands:
 Tall-Boy

1322 Big Al's Seafood
7701 Quacker Neck Rd
PO Box 293
Bozman, MD 21612
410-745-2637
Fax: 410-745-9046
Wholesaler/distributor of crabs, clams, fish and oysters. Founded in 1979.
President: Alan Poore
Estimated Sales: Less than $500,000
Number Employees: 5
Square Footage: 24000
Type of Packaging: Consumer

1323 Big Apple Bagels
500 Lake Cook Rd # 475
Suite 475
Deerfield, IL 60015-5240
847-948-7520
800-251-6101
www.bigapplebagels.com
Bagels and baked goods
Contact: Richard Chou
richard@bodypoint.com
Number Employees: 10-19

1324 Big B Barbecue
2727 N Kentucky Ave
Evansville, IN 47711-6203
812-425-5235
Fax: 812-428-8432 www.bigbbarbecue.com
Sauces, pepperoncinis, chili, pork barbecue, sloppy joes, vinegar, salsa and pickled products. Founded in 1962.
President & CEO: Richard Bonenberger
Estimated Sales: Less Than $500,000
Number Employees: 10-19
Type of Packaging: Consumer, Food Service, Private Label, Bulk
Brands:
 Big B
 Frontier Gold

1325 Big Boss Baking Co
629 Mcway Dr
High Point, NC 27263-2059
336-861-1212
www.bigbossbaking.com
Manufacturer of granola and granola bites.
President and Owner: Lavinia Hensley
lavinia@bigbossbaking.com
Estimated Sales: Less Than $500,000
Number Employees: 5-9
Square Footage: 80000

1326 Big Bucks Brewery & Steakhouse
550 S Wisconsin Street
Gaylord, MI 49735
989-731-0401
Fax: 989-731-2788 info@bigbuck.com
Beer, ale, lager and stout. Founded in 1994.

Food Manufacturers / A-Z

Manager: Tracy Dalman
Contact: Anthony Dombrowski
anthonydombrowski@mathworks.com
Estimated Sales: $2.5-5 Million
Number Employees: 376
Type of Packaging: Consumer, Food Service

1327 Big Chief Meat Snacks Inc
3900 52 Ave NE
Calgary, AB T3J 3X4
Canada
403-264-2641
Fax: 403-262-9053 biteme@bigchief.ca
www.bigchiefbeefjerky.com
Snack meats including pepperoni and teriyaki sticks, beef jerky and kippered beef. Founded in 1971.
Founder: William Klein
Contact: Mary Bendzik
Estimated Sales: C
Number Employees: 20
Type of Packaging: Consumer
Brands:
 Big Chief
 Old Dutch

1328 Big City Reds
4430 S 110th Street
Omaha, NE 68137-1217
847-714-1640
Fax: 847-714-1647 800-759-5275
www.americanfoodsgroup.com
All beef hotdogs, frankfurters and sausage including Polish and cocktail. FOunded in 1996.
President: Michael Sternberg
VP Marketing: Rebecca Sternberg
National Sales Manager: Robin Warren
Estimated Sales: $500,000
Number Employees: 5-10
Type of Packaging: Consumer, Food Service, Private Label
Brands:
 Big City Reds

1329 Big Dipper Dough Co.
2819 Cass Rd E4
Traverse City, MI 49684
231-883-6035
bigdipperdough.com
Cookie dough
Co-Owner/Co-Founder: Dan Fuller
Co-Owner/Co-Founder: Austin Groesser
Type of Packaging: Consumer
Brands:
 BIG DIPPER

1330 Big Easy Foods
3935 Ryan St
Lake Charles, LA 70605-2817
337-477-5499
Fax: 985-563-4202 855-477-9296
info@bigeasyfoods.com www.bigeasyfoods.com
Turduckens, stuffed chickens, shrimp, sausage, boudin, jalapeno poppers, cornbread casserole
Managing Partner: Larry Avery
lavery@bigeasyfoods.com
Managing Partner: Mark Abraham
COO: Scott Arrant
Estimated Sales: $20-50 Million
Number Employees: 50-99

1331 Big Fatty's Flaming Foods
639 County Road 240
Valley View, TX 76272-5912
940-726-3741
Fax: 940-726-6257 888-248-6332
Spicy foods; biscotti, spice rubs and cornbread. Founded in 1996.
President/Owner: Gail Patterson
gforcewind@aol.com
VP: Ricky Patterson
Estimated Sales: Less Than $500,000
Number Employees: 1-4

1332 Big Fork Brands
4241 N Ravenswood Ave
Chicago, IL 60613
321-206-9444
contact@bigforkbrands.com
bigforkbrands.com
Bacon and sausage
Co-Founder/Chef: Lance Avery
Co-Founder: Ann Avery
Year Founded: 2011

1333 Big Island Candies Inc
585 Hinano St
Hilo, HI 96720-4428
808-946-9213
Fax: 808-961-6941 800-935-5510
contactus@bigislandcandies.com
www.bigislandcandies.com
Manufacturer of shortbread cookies, chocolates and baked goods.
President/CEO: Allan Ikawa
allan@bigislandcandies.com
Chief Financial Officer: Bonnie Honda
Estimated Sales: $7 Million
Number Employees: 50-99
Number of Brands: 1
Type of Packaging: Consumer
Brands:
 Big Island Candies

1334 Big Island Seafood, LLC
1201 University Drive NE
Atlanta, GA 30306-2504
404-366-8943
Fax: 404-366-9129
Tuna, swordfish, snapper, grouper, sea bass, mahi-mahi, tilapia, seafood

1335 Big J Milling Co
733 W Forest St
Brigham City, UT 84302-2052
435-723-3459
Fax: 435-723-3450 www.brigham.net
Grain and flour. Founded in 1909.
President: Brent Baugh
bgbaugh@brigham.net
Owner: Mike Chadwick
Owner: Ken Sutton
Vice President: Ray Reese
Sales Executive: Scott Reese
Estimated Sales: $2.6 Million
Number Employees: 10-19
Type of Packaging: Consumer, Food Service, Private Label

1336 Big Mountain Foods
Vancouver, BC V5X 3E8
Canada
bigmountainfoods.com
Vegan prepared meals
Year Founded: 1987

1337 Big Picture Farm LLC
1600 Peaked Mountain Road
PO Box 344
Townshend, VT 05353
802-221-0547
bigpicturefarm@gmail.com
www.bigpicturefarm.com
Candy, caramels, and cheese.
Founder: Iouisa Conrad
Co-Founder: Luke Farrell
Square Footage: 80000

1338 Big Poppa Smokers
53973 Polk St.
Coachella, CA 92236
877-828-0727
customerservice@bigpoppasmokers.com
www.bigpoppasmokers.com
Manufacturer of grills & smokers, rubs, meat sauces and cutlery.
President and CEO: Sterling Ball
Square Footage: 80000

1339 Big Red Bottling
6500 River Place Boulevard
Building 1, Suite 450
Austin, TX 78730
254-772-7791
Fax: 254-772-2441 www.bigred.com
Carbonated soft drinks
Chairman & CEO: Gary Smith
Year Founded: 1937
Estimated Sales: $20-50 Million
Number Employees: 20-49
Parent Co: Dr Pepper Snapple Group
Brands:
 Diet Big Red ®
 Big Blue ®
 Big Red Vanilla Float ®
 Big Peach ®
 Big Pineapple ®
 Nugrape ®
 Nesbitts ®

1340 Big Rock Brewery
5555 76th Avenue SE
Calgary, AB T2C 4L8
Canada
403-720-3239
Fax: 403-236-7523 800-242-3107
beer@bigrockbeer.com www.bigrockbeer.com
Beer, ale, stout and lager
President & CEO: Wayne Arsenault
Chief Financial Officer: Don Sewell
Head Brewmaster: Paul Gautreau
Director of Marketing: Susanne Fox
VP Sales: Paul Howden
Business Development Manager: Dennis Carr
Estimated Sales: G
Number Employees: 100-249
Type of Packaging: Consumer, Food Service

1341 Big Russ Beer Cheese
237 South Main St.
Beaver Dam, KY 42320
270-485-6544
www.bigrussbeercheese.com
Manufacturer of beer cheese.
Square Footage: 80000

1342 Big Shoulders Coffee
1105 W Chicago Ave
Chicago, IL 60642
312-846-1883
information@bigshoulderscoffee.com
www.bigshoulderscoffee.com
Coffee
Founder: Tim Coonan
General Manager: Abigail Helmus
VP Operations: Gregg Piazzi
Director of Sales: Dave Marsalek
Year Founded: 2012
Number Employees: 20-49

1343 (HQ)Big Sky Brands
3289 Lenworth Dr
Unit A
Mississauga, ON L4X 2H1
Canada
416-599-5415
www.bigskybrands.com
Candy, mints and soda.
Co-Founder: Ron Cheng
Co-Founder: Steve Yacht
Type of Packaging: Private Label
Other Locations:
 Big Sky Brands
 Chicago IL
 Big Sky Brands
 Buffalo NY
 Big Sky Brands
 Los Angeles CA
Brands:
 Co2 Hard Candy
 Diablo Ignited Sours
 Drive Activated
 Green-T Energy Mints
 Jones Soda Carbonated Candy
 Jones Soda Carbonated Sours
 Jones Soda Energy Boosters
 Jones Sours
 Love Mints
 Make Out Mints
 Playboy Mints
 Warp Energy Mints
 Warp Micro Hyper Charged Mints
 Sunkist Citrus

1344 Big Sky Brewing Co
5417 Trumpeter Way
P.O.Box 17170
Missoula, MT 59808-8680
406-549-2777
Fax: 406-549-1919 800-559-2774
info@bigskybrew.com www.bigskybrew.com
Ale and stout. Founded in 1995.
President: Neal Leathers
neal@bigskybrew.com
Sales Executive: Bjorn Nabozney
VP Production: Kris Nabozney
Estimated Sales: $3 Million
Number Employees: 20-49
Square Footage: 96000
Type of Packaging: Consumer, Food Service, Bulk
Brands:
 Big Sky Ipa
 Moose Drool Brown Ale
 Powder Hound Winter Ale
 Scape Goat Pale Ale

Food Manufacturers / A-Z

Summer Honey Seasonal Ale
Trout Slayer Ale

1345 Big Spoon Roasters
4517 Hillsborough Rd
#101-B
Durham, NC 27705
919-309-9100
info@bigspoonroasters.com
www.bigspoonroasters.com
Nut butters and nut butter snack bars
Founder: Mark Overbay
Marketing & Communications Manager: Mackenzie Props
Regional Sales Representative: Andrew Anderson
Director of Operations: Michael Silver
Year Founded: 2011
Number Employees: 10-19

1346 Big Steer
9101 Lipan Rd # 108
Houston, TX 77063-5559
713-782-2444
Fax: 713-785-0730 800-421-4951
bigsteer@live.com www.bigsteer.biz
Manufacturer microwave fudge and gourmet snack mixes. Founded in 1989.
President: Grant Nichols
Estimated Sales: $1-5 Million
Number Employees: 5-9
Type of Packaging: Private Label

1347 Big Train Inc
25392 Commercentre Dr
Lake Forest, CA 92630
949-340-8800
Fax: 949-707-1000 800-244-8724
www.bigtrain.com
Ice blended coffees, flavored syrups, and specialty beverage mixes. Founded in 1991.
CEO: Mike Dunn
CFO: Kevin Smith
VP, Supply Chain: Steve Schartg
International Sales: Rachel Pena
Customer Service Supervisor: Shannon Haskill
Estimated Sales: $10-12 Million
Number Employees: 1-4
Square Footage: 72000
Type of Packaging: Bulk

1348 Big Tree Farms
2305 Ashland St
Suite C506
Ashland, OR 97520
541-488-5605
info@bigtreefarms.com
bigtreefarms.com
Coconut products including oil and sugar.
Co-Founder: Ben Ripple
Number Employees: 11-50
Brands:
    Los Cantores

1349 Big Watt Coffee
Minneapolis, MN 55408
info@bigwattcoffee.com
bigwattcoffee.com
Cold press coffee
Co-Founder: Lee Carter
Co-Founder: Jason Westplate
Co-Founder: Caleb Garn

1350 Bigelow Tea
201 Black Rock Tpke
Fairfield, CT 06825
888-244-3569
info@bigelowtea.com www.bigelowtea.com
Tea bags and tea including organic, loose, hot and iced
President: David Bigelow
Executive Vice President: Donald Janezic
Assistant Marketing Manager: Cindy Manning
Warehouse Coordinator: Steve Koch
Year Founded: 1945
Estimated Sales: $94 Million
Number Employees: 250-499
Number of Brands: 1
Brands:
    Bigelow

1351 Bijol & Spices Inc
2154 NW 22nd Ct
Miami, FL 33142-7346
305-634-9030
Fax: 305-634-7454 888-245-6570
info@bijol.com www.bijol.com
Contract packager and exporter of spices and herbs. Founded in 1991.
President: Ida Borges
Vice President: Diego Borges
Estimated Sales: $2.5-5 Million
Number Employees: 5-9
Type of Packaging: Consumer

1352 Bilgore's Groves
807 Court Street
Clearwater, FL 34616-1525
727-442-2171
Fax: 727-446-3998
Fruits
Manager: Evelyn Tumber
Estimated Sales: $500-1 Million appx.
Number Employees: 1-4

1353 Bilinski Sausage Mfg Co
41 Lark St
Cohoes, NY 12047-4618
518-237-0171
Fax: 518-237-0205 877-873-9102
info@bilinski.com www.bilinski.com
Many flavors of all natural and organic chicken sausages. 100% all natural, antibiotic-free, and fully cooked.
Owner: Steve Schonwetter
info@bilinski.com
Number Employees: 20-49
Type of Packaging: Consumer

1354 Bill's Seafood
9016 Belair Rd
Baltimore, MD 21236-2120
410-256-9520
Fax: 410-256-3491
www.billsseafoodandcatering.net
Seafood
Owner: Bill Paulshock
bscrabs@aol.com
Estimated Sales: $5-10 Million
Number Employees: 20-49

1355 (HQ)Billingsgate Fish Company
1941 Uxbridge Drive NW
Calgary, AB T2N 2V2
Canada
403-571-7700
Fax: 403-571-7717 www.billingsgate.com
Processor and packager of fish, meat and deli products; wholesaler/distributor of meats and seafood; serving the food service market. Founded in 1966.
President/Board Member: Bryan Fallwell
Sales Representative: Brenda Shreindorfer
Operations Manager: Mark Puffer
Estimated Sales: $2.8 Million
Number Employees: 20
Square Footage: 140000
Type of Packaging: Consumer, Food Service
Other Locations:
    Billingsgate Fish Company
    Edmonton, Alberta
    Billingsgate Fish Company
    St. Albert, Alberta
Brands:
    Billingsgate
    King of Fish
    Plough Boy

1356 Billy's Seafood Inc
16780 River Rd
Bon Secour, AL 36511-3428
251-949-6288
Fax: 251-949-6505 888-424-5597
billys@gulftel.com www.billys-seafood.com
Seafood
Owner: Billy Parks
billys@gulftel.com
Estimated Sales: $2,000,000
Number Employees: 1-4

1357 Biloxi Freezing Processing Inc.
PO Box 730
Biloxi, MS 39533
228-436-0017
Fax: 228-436-0019 biloxifreezing.com
Frozen shrimp
President: Mark Mavar
Number Employees: 20-49
Type of Packaging: Consumer, Food Service, Private Label
Brands:
    Captain Joey
    M&M
    Suarez

1358 Biltmore Estate Wine Company
1 Lodge St
Asheville, NC 28803
800-411-3812
www.biltmore.com
Wines
President & CEO: Bill Cecil
SVP & CFO: Steve Watson
Director of Marketing: Heather Jordan
hjordan@biltmore.com
Estimated Sales: $138.8 Million
Number Employees: 1,800
Number of Brands: 2
Brands:
    Biltmore
    Antler Hill

1359 Bimbo Bakeries USA Inc.
255 Business Center Dr.
PO Box 976
Horsham, PA 19044
Fax: 610-320-9286 800-984-0989
www.bimbobakeriesusa.com
Bread and sweet baked goods.
President: Fred Penny
Year Founded: 1998
Estimated Sales: Over $1 Billion
Number Employees: 20,000
Number of Brands: 20
Parent Co: Grupo Bimbo
Brands:
    Thomas'®
    Sara Lee®
    Nature's Harvest®
    Arnold®
    Brownberry®
    Oroweat®
    Entenmann's®
    Ball Park®
    Marinela®
    Bimbo®
    Maier's®
    eureka!®
    Beefsteak®
    Boboli®
    Mrs Baird's®
    Freihofer's®
    Heiner's
    Grandma Sycamore's®
    Tia Rosa®
    Stroehmann®
    Beefsteak(c)
    D'Italiano(c)

1360 Bindi North America
630 Belleville Tpke
Kearny, NJ 07032-4407
973-812-8118
Fax: 973-812-5020 info@bindiusa.com
www.bindiusa.com
Manufacturer of cakes, gelato, croissants, dessert sauces and other delicacies.
President: Attilio Bindi
Vice President: Stefano Del Verme
sdelverme@bindiusa.com
Number Employees: 100-249
Square Footage: 80000
Brands:
    bindi

1361 Binding Brauerei USA
194 Main St # 1
Norwalk, CT 06851-3502
203-229-0111
Fax: 203-229-0105 www.bindingusa-beers.com
Beer and ale.
President: Hans Schliebs
CEO: Dilip Mehta
VP Sales: Dave Deuser
Estimated Sales: $5-10 Million
Number Employees: 10-19
Parent Co: Radeberger Gruppe GmbH
Brands:
    Clausthaler
    Dab
    Krusovice

Food Manufacturers / A-Z

Radeberger
Tucher

1362 Bingo Salsa, LLC
2001 Nw Swanlund Street
Poulsbo, WA 98370-9528
360-779-6746
Fax: 360-930-8377 bingosalsa67@yahoo.com
www.bingosalsas.com
Makers of canned fruits and specialties. Founded in 2004.
Principal: Lisa Hudson
mamabread@yahoo.com

1363 Binkert's Meat Products
8805 Philadelphia Rd
Baltimore, MD 21237-4310
410-687-5959
Fax: 410-687-5023 binkertsmeat@comcast.net
www.binkerts.com
Manufacturer and distributor of German style lunch meats and sausages. FOunded in 1964.
President: Sonya Weber
Managing Partner: Luthar Weber
Estimated Sales: $300,000-500,000
Number Employees: 5
Square Footage: 11200

1364 Binns Vineyards & Winery
525 Roadrunner Lane
Las Cruces, NM 8800550348
575-526-6738
Fax: 575-522-1112
Wines
Owner: Eddie Binns
Vice President: Glenn Binns
Estimated Sales: $1-4.9 Million
Number Employees: 5-9
Type of Packaging: Private Label

1365 Bio-Botanica Inc
75 Commerce Dr
Hauppauge, NY 11788-3943
631-231-5522
Fax: 631-231-7332 800-645-5720
www.bio-botanica.com
Botanical extracts and flavors
Owner/CEO: Frank D'Amelio
President: Josephine Perricone
CFO: William O'Reilly
VP R&D: Dr. Youssef Mirhom
Quality Control: William Wilson
Marketing Director: Dorie Greenblatt
VP Sales: Mark Sysler
Estimated Sales: $5-10 Million
Number Employees: 100-249
Number of Products: 300
Square Footage: 560000
Type of Packaging: Food Service, Private Label, Bulk

1366 Bio-Foods
104 Bloomfield Avenue
Pine Brook, NJ 07058
973-808-5856
Fax: 973-396-2999 bobkoetzner@aol.com
www.biofoodsltd.com
Manufacturer and exporter of nutrients and spices.
President: Bharat Patel
Vice President: Robert Koetzner
Number Employees: 5-9
Square Footage: 36000
Type of Packaging: Bulk
Brands:
  Bio-Foods

1367 Bio-Hydration Research Lab
2091 Rutherford Road
Carlsbad, CA 92008
760-438-6686
Fax: 760-268-0808 800-531-5088
sales@pentawater.com www.pentawater.com
Bio-Hydration; a molecular restructured water that hydrates faster and provides enhanced performance and healthy living. Founded in 1999.
CEO: Bill Holloway
Chief Financial Officer: Ernest Ho
CEO: Dennis O'Bryan
Public Relations Manager: Jeffrey Pizzino
Estimated Sales: $5-10 Million
Number Employees: 50-99
Number of Brands: 1
Number of Products: 2
Square Footage: 220000

Type of Packaging: Consumer
Brands:
  Penta

1368 Bio-K + International Inc.
Parc Scientifique
495 boul. Armand-Frappier
Laval, QC H7V 4B3
Canada
450-978-2465
Fax: 450-978-9729 800-593-2465
info@biokplus.com www.biokplus.com
President: Pavel Hamet
Marketing Director: Michael Sirdemt
CFO: Michael Rheault
Year Founded: 1996
Brands:
  Bio K

1369 Bio-Nutritional Products
119 Rockland Ave
Northvale, NJ 07647-2144
201-784-8200
Fax: 201-784-8201
President: Stephen Difolco
Brands:
  Eugalan
  Lacto

1370 Bio-Tech Pharmacal Inc
3481 N Hwy 112
Fayetteville, AR 72704-7437
479-443-9148
Fax: 479-443-5643 800-345-1199
customerservice@bio-tech-pharm.com
www.biotechpharmacal.com
Hypo-allergenic nutraceuticals, vitamins, minerals, herbals, anti-oxidants, amino acids, etc. Founded in 1984.
Chairman: Dale Benedict
service@bio-tech-pharm.com
Director, Sales/Marketing: Lora Daniel
Facility Manager: Mark Leason
Number Employees: 10-19
Number of Brands: 1
Type of Packaging: Consumer, Private Label, Bulk
Brands:
  Bio-Tech Pharmacal

1371 BioAmber
3850 Annapolis Ln N
Suite 180
Plymouth, MN 55447
763-253-4480
kristine.weigal@bio-amber.com
Succinic acid, BDO, plasticizers, polymers and C6 chemicals
President & CEO: Jean-Francois HUC
CTO: Jim Millis
CFO: Andrew Ashworth
Executive VP: Mike Hartmann
Chief Commercial Officer: Babette Pettersen
Contact: Marie Beaumont
marie.beaumont@bio-amber.com
Chief Operations Officer: Fabrice Orecchioni
Estimated Sales: $560 Thousand
Number Employees: 74

1372 BioExx Specialty Proteins
33 Fraser Ave
Suite G11
Toronto, ON M6K 3J9
Canada
416-588-4442
Fax: 416-588-1999 www.bioexx.com
Oil and high-value proteins from Canola.
CEO & Director: Chris Schnarr
CFO: Greg Furyk
EVP: Samah Garringer
VP Operations: Clinton Smith

1373 BioSynergy
PO Box 16833
Boise, ID 83706-6414
208-342-6660
Fax: 208-342-0880 800-554-7145
email@biosynergy.com www.biosynergy.com
Health related products and nutritional supplements. FOunded in 1994.
President/Owner: Ted Kremer
tdoty@cves.org
CEO: Hidemi Ogino
Marketing Director: Hidemi Kremer

Estimated Sales: $200,000
Number Employees: 1-4
Brands:
  Nojo

1374 (HQ)BioTech Corporation
107 Oakwood Dr Ste E
Glastonbury, CT 06033
860-633-8111
Fax: 860-682-6863 800-886-9052
info@dermasilkbrands.com
Nutraceuticals and nutritional supplements. Founded in 1994.
President: Gregory Kelly
Contact: Lisa Livingston
llivingston@biotechcorp.com
Estimated Sales: $5-10 Million
Number Employees: 10-19

1375 BioVittoria USA
357 N Milwaukee Rd
Libertyville, IL 60048
847-226-3467
Processor and supplier of monk fruit, a natural calorie-free sweetener that is a new alternative to sugar and artificial sweeteners.
President: Lan Fusheng
CEO: David Thorrold
CFO: Danny Wai Yen
VP: Garth Smith
VP Sales & Marketing: Paul Paslaski
Estimated Sales: $500 Thousand
Type of Packaging: Food Service, Private Label, Bulk

1376 Bioenergy Life Science
13840 Johnson St NE
Andover, MN 55304-6922
763-757-0032
Fax: 763-757-0588 877-474-2673
info@bioenergyls.com www.theribosecompany.biz
Our focus is on the bulk ribose sale business for food and beverage and dietary supplements. Supplement
President: Tom VonderBrink
Chairman/Chief Executive Officer: Leo Zhang
Regional Director: Marianne McDonagh
EVP/Chief Technology Officer: Alex Xue
Technical Sales Manager: Michael Crabtree
Executive Director, Supply Chain Mgmt.: Adia Edwards
Director of Marketing: Penny Portner
Office Administrator: Greta Kaster
Director, Business Administration: Michelle Wald
Research Scientist: Pat Starks
Warehouse Manager: Nick Jacobson
Shipping & Receiving Manager: Lori Huntley
Number Employees: 10-19

1377 Bionutritional ResearchGroup
15375 Barranca Pkwy
Suite C104
Irvine, CA 92618-2206
714-427-6990
Fax: 714-427-6998
Nutritional products, protein powder and bars, supplements. Founded in 1991.
Owner: Kevin Lawrence
President/CEO: Kevin Stensby
Sales Executive: Ken Braunstein
VP Operations: Tom Williams
Estimated Sales: $15 Million
Number Employees: 5-9
Brands:
  Alpha Glutamine
  Cell Charge®
  Power Crunch®
  Proto Whey®

1378 Bioriginal Food and Science Corp
102 Melville Street
Saskatoon, SK S7J 0R1
Canada
306-975-1166
Fax: 306-242-3829 business@bioriginal.com
www.bioriginal.com
Essential fatty acids, omega 3, omega 6, and omega 9.
President/CEO: Joe Vidal
EVP Global Marketing/Sales: Johan Kamphuis
VP Operations: Cameron Kupper

Food Manufacturers / A-Z

1379 Biospringer
7475 West Main St
Milwaukee, WI 53214
414-615-4100
Fax: 414-615-4005 866-424-1158
customer.service@biospringer-na.com
www.biospringer-na.com
Natural yeast
Marketing Manager: Marilyn Stieve
Contact: Chris Kaltenbach
chris.kaltenbach@lsaf.com

1380 Biotec A Z Laboratories
20809 N 19th Avenue
Suite 1
Phoenix, AZ 85027-3519
800-218-6979
Fax: 623-576-2285
Supplements and vitamins.
President: Tyler Rosales

1381 Biothera
3388 Mike Collins Dr # A
Suite A
St Paul, MN 55121-2409
651-675-0300
Fax: 651-657-0400 info@biothera.com
www.biothera.com
Food-grade immune-enhancing ingredients for the nutritional supplement, functional food, cosmetic and animal feed nutrition markets.
Founder/Chairman: Daniel Conners
Chief Executive Officer: Richard G Mueller
rmueller@biotherapharma.com
Chief Financial Officer: William Gacki
Senior Vice President: James Horstmann
SVP, Research & Development: Donald Cox, Ph.D.
SVP, Marketing & Communications: David Walsh
SVP, Business Development: Steve Smith
COO, Research & Technology: Steven Karel
Estimated Sales: $3-5 Million
Number Employees: 50-99
Type of Packaging: Bulk

1382 Birch Benders
3316 Tejon St
Unit 107
Denver, CO 80211
855-572-6225
Fax: 303-502-1112 info@birchbenders.com
birchbenders.com
Toaster waffles and pancake and waffle mixes
Co-Founder: Matt Lacasse
Co-Founder: Lizzi Ackerman

1383 Birch Street Seafoods
31 Birch St
Digby, NS B0V 1A0
Canada
902-245-6551
Fax: 902-245-6554
Processor and exporter of fresh and frozen salted groundfish
Vice President: William Cottreau
Contact: Janice Oliver
Plant Manager: Alan Frankland
Estimated Sales: $500,000-1 Million
Number Employees: 25
Type of Packaging: Consumer, Food Service, Private Label, Bulk

1384 Birchwood Foods Inc
3111 152nd Ave
PO Box 639
Kenosha, WI 53144-7630
262-859-2272
Fax: 262-859-2078 800-541-1685
bwinfo@bwfoods.com www.bwfoods.com
Manufactuer and exporter of cryogenically frozen and vacuum-packed fresh ground beef in bulk and patties; importer of boneless beef
President, CEO & Director: Dennis Vignieri
CEO: Cindy Anderson
canderson@bwfoods.com
CFO & Director: Jerry King
VP HR & Safety: Phyllis Murray
Quality Assurance Supervisor: Cathy Miller
VP Sales & Marketing: Wayne Wehking
EVP Operations & Procurement: John Ruffolo
Product Manager: Doug Ladd
Manager of Purchasing: Alex Savaglio
Estimated Sales: $2.76 Million
Number Employees: 500-999
Square Footage: 240000
Type of Packaging: Consumer, Food Service, Private Label, Bulk
Other Locations:
Frankfort Manufacturing Facility
Frankfort IN
Columbus Manufacturing Facility
Columbus OH
Atlanta Manufacturing Facility
Atlanta GA

1385 (HQ)Bird-In-Hand Farms Inc
1708 Columbia Ave # 1
Lancaster, PA 17603-4550
717-291-9904
Fax: 717-291-1990 www.bihfarms.com
Poultry. Founded in 1949.
Owner: Frederick Bloom
VP Sales: Ted Bloom
fred.bloom@bihfarms.com
Estimated Sales: $5-10 Million
Number Employees: 5-9
Type of Packaging: Private Label
Other Locations:
Bird-In-Hand Farms
Chapin SC
Bird-In-Hand Farms
Jackson MI
Bird-In-Hand Farms
Huntington IN
Bird-In-Hand Farms
Nacogdoches TX
Bird-In-Hand Farms
Monett MO
Bird-In-Hand Farms
Topsail Beach NC
Bird-In-Hand Farms
Russellville AR
Bird-In-Hand Farms
Southern Pines NC
Brands:
Bird-In-Hand
Truly Dutch

1386 Birdie Pak Products
3925 W 31st St
Chicago, IL 60623-4934
773-247-5293
Fax: 773-247-4280 www.birdiepak.com
Processor and distributor of frozen beef, poultry and fish
President: Thomas Krueger
VP: Kevin Krueger
Estimated Sales: $2.5-5 Million
Number Employees: 10-19
Type of Packaging: Consumer, Food Service, Private Label
Brands:
Birdie Pak

1387 Birdsall Ice Cream Company
518 N Federal Ave
Mason City, IA 50401-3216
641-423-5365
Ice cream. Founded in 1968.
Owner: Vaughn Escher
Owner: Dave Escher
Estimated Sales: $1 Million
Number Employees: 22
Type of Packaging: Consumer, Food Service

1388 Birdseye Dairy-Morning Glory
2325 Memorial Dr
Green Bay, WI 54303-6399
920-494-5388
Fax: 920-494-4388 www.birdseyejuice.com
Apple and orange juice; wholesaler/distributor of dairy products including milk, ice cream, butter and sour cream; serving the food service market. Founded in 1925.
President: Steven Williams
steve.williamss@birdseye.com
Estimated Sales: $10-20 Million
Number Employees: 10-19
Type of Packaging: Consumer, Food Service, Private Label, Bulk
Brands:
Birdseye
Morning Glory

1389 Birdseye Food
1 Old Bloomfield Rd.
Mountain Lakes, NJ 07046
585-383-1850
Fax: 585-385-1281 www.birdseye.com
Frozen vegetables, frozen complete bagged meals, canned pie fillings, chili and bottled salad dressings.
President/CEO, Conagra Brands: Sean Connolly
Year Founded: 1923
Estimated Sales: $399 Million
Number Employees: 100-249
Square Footage: 15333
Parent Co: Conagra Brands, Inc.
Type of Packaging: Consumer, Food Service, Bulk
Other Locations:
Fennville MI
Waseca MN
Fulton NY
Berlin PA
Algona WA
Tacoma WA
Darien WI
Green Bay WI
Brands:
Birds Eye®

1390 Birdsong Corp.
612 Madison Ave.
PO Box 1400
Suffolk, VA 23434-1400
757-539-3456
Fax: 757-539-7360 www.birdsongpeanuts.com
Raw peanuts.
President: Jeff Johnson
CEO: George Birdsong
gbirdsong@birdsong-peanuts.com
CFO: Stephen Huber
Year Founded: 1914
Estimated Sales: $50.50 Million
Number Employees: 500-999
Square Footage: 10000
Type of Packaging: Food Service
Other Locations:
Birdsong Corp.
Gorman TX

1391 Birkett Mills
PO Box 440
Penn Yan, NY 14527
315-536-3311
Fax: 315-536-6740 contact@thebirkettmills.com
www.thebirkettmills.com
Flour
President & COO: Jeff Gifford
CEO: Wayne Wagner
Sales Executive: Cliff Orr
Contact: Don Habberfield
dhabberfield@thebirkettmills.com
Estimated Sales: $1-2.5 Million
Number Employees: 40
Type of Packaging: Consumer, Private Label, Bulk
Brands:
Bessie
Pocono
Puritan
Wolffs

1392 Birkholm's Solvang Bakery
460 Alisal Rd
Solvang, CA 93463-2726
805-688-8188
Fax: 805-686-4407 800-377-4253
www.birkholmsbakery.com
Processor and exporter of bread, cake and Danish tarts
President: Susan Halme
susan@solvangbakery.com
General manager: Melissa Redell
Estimated Sales: Less Than $500,000
Number Employees: 5-9
Type of Packaging: Consumer, Food Service

1393 Birnn Chocolates of Vermont
102 Kimball Ave
Suite 4
South Burlington, VT 05403
Fax: 802-860-1256 800-338-3141
www.birnn.com
Premium wholesale truffles
President: H Birnn
bh@birnn.com
Co-Owner: Bill Birnn
VP: Bill Birnn
Estimated Sales: $2 Million
Number Employees: 20-49
Type of Packaging: Private Label

Food Manufacturers / A-Z

1394 **(HQ)Biscomerica Corporation**
565 West Slover Avenue
PO Box 1070
Rialto, CA 92377-1070
909-877-5997
Fax: 909-877-3593 info@biscomerica.com
www.biscomerica.com
Manufacturer of cookies, chocolates and candies.
President/CEO: Nadi Soltan
Contact: Dina Fangary
dfangar@biscomerica.com
Year Founded: 1980
Estimated Sales: $30 Million
Number Employees: 250-499
Number of Brands: 4
Square Footage: 250000
Type of Packaging: Consumer, Food Service, Private Label, Bulk
Brands:
  Checkers Cookies
  Granny's Oven
  Knott's Berry Farms
  Sun Maid

1395 **(HQ)Biscoti Di Suzy**
1070 40th St
Oakland, CA 94608-3617
510-923-0446
Fax: 510-923-0344 800-211-5903
info@crunchyfoods.com www.crunchyfoods.com
Cookies, other baked goods.
Owner/CEO: Karen Jackson
Marketing: Will Tassi
Estimated Sales: $5-9.9 Million
Number Employees: 10-19
Type of Packaging: Consumer, Food Service, Private Label, Bulk
Brands:
  Biscotti Di Suzy™

1396 **Biscottea**
23216 SE 135th Ct
Issaquah, WA 98027
425-313-1993
Fax: 425-427-0709 info@biscottea.net
www.biscottea.net
Organic, all natural flavored shortbread
President/Owner: Laurance Milner
Number Employees: 2

1397 **Biscotti & Co.**
145-157 St John Street
White Plains, NY EC1V 4PW
914-682-2165
Fax: 914-328-4276
Bulk and wrapped shelf stable biscotti and gourmet cookies
President: Gary Spirer
Marketing Director: Jerry O'Donnell
Sales Director: Debbie Rittberg
General Manager: Jerry O'Donnell
Number Employees: 10-19
Square Footage: 36000
Type of Packaging: Consumer, Bulk
Brands:
  Alex & Dani's Biscotti
  Karen's Fabulous Biscotti

1398 **Biscotti Goddess**
3910 Amberleigh Blvd
Richmond, VA 23236
804-745-9490
www.biscotti-goddess.com
Manufacturer of biscotti. Founded in 2007.
Owner: Jan Defalco
Number Employees: 1-4

1399 **Bishop Brothers**
113 W 5th Ave
Bristow, OK 74010-2824
918-367-2270
Fax: 918-367-2270 800-859-8304
info@bishoptaboli.com www.bishoptaboli.com
Wholesaler/distributor of bulgur wheat including tabbouleh; custom packaging services available. Founded in 1962.
Owner: Eddie Bishop
ebishop07@aol.com
Estimated Sales: $2.5-5 Million
Number Employees: 1-4
Type of Packaging: Consumer, Food Service, Bulk

1400 **Bishop Farms Winery**
500 S Meriden Rd
Cheshire, CT 06410-2968
203-272-8243
Fax: 203-272-7344
Manufacturer of wines
President: John Romanik
Owner: Mary Romanik
Marketing Director: Mary Romanik
Contact: Kevin Clark
crystal6156@yahoo.com
Estimated Sales: $500,000-$1 Million
Number Employees: 1-4

1401 **Bison Brewing Company**
PO Box 4821
Berkeley, CA 94704-4821
510-697-1537
Fax: 510-217-4332 info@bisonbrew.com
www.bisonbrew.com
Organic Beer. Founded in 1989.
Owner: Dan DelGarande
Sales Representative: Rich Schwanbeck
Estimated Sales: $5-10 Million
Number Employees: 10-19
Brands:
  Barley Wine Ale
  Belgian Ale
  Chocolate Stout
  Farmhouse Saison
  Gingerbread Ale
  Honey Basil Ale
  India Pale Ale
  Red Ale
  Winter Warmer

1402 **Bison Foods**
25 Anderson Rd
Buffalo, NY 14225
716-892-3156
www.bisonfoods.com
Dips and sour cream.
Chief Executive Officer: Larry Webster
Chief Operating Officer: Joe Duscher
Year Founded: 1931
Parent Co: Upstate Niagara Cooperative Inc.
Type of Packaging: Consumer

1403 **Bissett Produce Company**
P.O.Box 279
1436 North NC Hwy 581
Spring Hope, NC 27882-0279
252-478-4158
Fax: 252-478-7798 800-849-5073
Bissettproducecompanyinc@msn.com
Grower, packer and exporter of sweet potatoes, pickling cucumbers and banana and specialty peppers and seedless watermelons. Founded in 2001.
Manager: Don Sparks
Finance Executive: Dan Bissett
Vice President: Lee Bissett
Sales Director: Don Sparks
Contact: Dan Bissett
bissettproducecompanyinc@msn.com
Estimated Sales: $2.5-5 Million
Number Employees: 20
Square Footage: 240000
Type of Packaging: Consumer, Food Service, Private Label, Bulk
Brands:
  Bissett's
  Rue's Choice

1404 **(HQ)Bissinger's Handcrafted Chocolatier**
3983 Gratiot Street
St Louis, MO 63110
314-534-2401
Fax: 314-534-2419 800-325-8881
sales@bissingers.com www.bissingers.com
Boxed chocolates, sugar free chocolate and classic gourmet candies. Founded in 1995.
President: Ken Kellerhals
Contact: Charles Anton
canton@bissingers.com
Number Employees: 40

1405 **Bissinger's HandcraftedChocolatier**
1600 North Broadway
St. Louis, MO 63102
314-615-2400
www.bissingers.com
Fine chocolates and caramels.

CEO: Tim Fogerty
Estimated Sales: $6000000
Number Employees: 5-9
Type of Packaging: Consumer, Bulk

1406 **Bitchin' Sauce**
Carlsbad, CA 92010
www.bitchinsauce.com
Almond dip
Number of Brands: 1
Number of Products: 6
Type of Packaging: Consumer
Brands:
  BITCHIN' SAUCE

1407 **Bite Fuel**
Oregon City, OR 97045
info@bitefuel.com
www.bitefuel.com
Cookies and trail mix
CEO: Eric Shen
Production Manager: Isabel Ayala
Number of Brands: 1
Number of Products: 8
Type of Packaging: Consumer
Brands:
  BITE FUEL

1408 **Bite Size Bakery**
504 Frontage Rd NE
Rio Rancho, NM 87124
505-994-3093
www.bitesizebakery.com
Manufacturer of bite-sized cookies in a variety of flavours, including bizcochitos, pinon nut chocolate chip, lemon verde pistachio. ginger snap, and raisin oatmeal.
Owner: Lucia Deichmann
Parent Co: KDK Enterprises
Brands:
  Bite-Size Bakery

1409 **Bitsy's Brainfood**
1 Little West 12th Street
New York, NY 10014
212-461-1572
www.bitsysbrainfood.com
Cookies and crackers
Co-Founder: Maggie Patton
Co-Founder: Alex Voris
Number of Brands: 1
Number of Products: 8
Type of Packaging: Consumer
Brands:
  SMART CRACKERS
  SMART COOKIES

1410 **Bitter Love**
Portland, ME 04101
www.bitterlove.com
Sparkling drinking bitters

1411 **Bittermilk LLC**
P.O. Box 13371
Charleston, SC 29422
843-641-0455
drink@bittermilk.com
bittermilk.com
Alcoholic cocktail mixers with natural ingredients
Co-Founder: Joe Raya
Co-Founder: MariElena Raya
Brands:
  Michel de France(c)

1412 **Bittersweet Herb Farm**
635 Mohawk Trl
Shelburne Falls, MA 01370-9775
413-625-6523
Fax: 413-625-0166 800-456-1599
dave@bittersweetherbfarm.com
www.bittersweetherbfarm.com
Wasabi ginger sauce, lemon garlic sauce, strawberry jam and all natural seasonings. Also flavored oils and balsamic vinegars. Founded in 1983.
Owner: Dave Lemon
dave@bittersweetherbfarm.com
Estimated Sales: $1-2.5 Million
Number Employees: 10-19

1413 **Bittersweet Pastries**
385 Chestnut St
Norwood, NJ 07648-2001
201-768-7005
Fax: 973-882-6998 800-217-2938

Food Manufacturers / A-Z

Desserts including tarts, layer cakes, and flourless chocolate truffle cakes. Also sold frozen and dessert bars. Founded in 1984.
President: Bob Trier
Vice President: Louis Florencia
info@bittersweetpastries.com
Estimated Sales: $1-5 Million
Number Employees: 20-49
Square Footage: 18000
Parent Co: Fairfield Gourmet Foods Corporation
Type of Packaging: Food Service

1414 Bixby & Co., LLC
One Sea Street Place
Rockland, ME 04841
207-691-1778
info@bixbyco.com
www.bixbyco.com
Manufacturer of vegan chocolates.
Founder: Kate McAleer
kate@bixbyco.com
Brands:
   Bixby Bar

1415 Black Bear Farm Winery
248 County Road 1
Chenango Forks, NY 13746-2208
607-656-9863
mamabear@blackbearwinery.com
www.blackbearwinery.com
Wines
President: Mark Stacey
Co-Owner: Sandy Stacey
Chief of Cider Production: Joe Stacey
Number Employees: 1-4

1416 Black Bear Fruits
N7832 County Rd M
New Lisbon, WI 53950
608-547-6133
www.blackbearfruits.com
Fruits and vegetables. Founded in 2010.
Contact: Ron Krizan
greenrugger@yahoo.com

1417 Black Forest Organic
Oakbrook Terrace Tower
1 Tower Lane, Suite 2700
Oakbrook Terrace, IL 60181
800-323-1768
www.ferrarausa.com
Non-chocolate confection
CEO: Todd Siwak
CFO: Tom Polke
Chief Operating Officer: Michael Murray
Year Founded: 1908
Number of Brands: 1
Number of Products: 16
Parent Co: Ferrara Candy Company
Type of Packaging: Consumer
Brands:
   BLACK FOREST ORGANIC
   TROLLI
   NOW AND LATER
   BRACH'S
   BOB'S
   RED HOTS
   LEMONHEAD
   SATHERS
   JUJYFRUITS
   BOSTON BAKED BEANS
   ATOMIC FIREBALL
   JAW BUSTERS
   CHUCKLES
   RAIN BLO
   SUPER BUBBLE
   FRUIT STRIPE

1418 Black Garlic
2499 American Ave
Hayward, CA 94545-1809
510-264-0227
888-811-9065
info@blackgarlic.com www.blackgarlic.com
Garlic. Founded in 2008.
CEO: Scott Kim
Contact: Sohee Lee
slee@myblackgarlic.com
Number Employees: 5-9

1419 Black Hound New York
226 India Street
Brooklyn, NY 11222
212-97-505
Fax: 718-782-0621 800-344-4417
customerservice@blackhoundny.com
www.blackhoundny.com
Hard, soft and chocolate candies, cakes and delectibles. Founded in 2003.
President: Debbie Miller
Estimated Sales: $500,000-$1 Million
Number Employees: 10-19

1420 Black Jewell Popcorn
417 Washington St
Columbus, IN 47201
618-948-2303
Fax: 618-948-2505 800-948-2302
www.blackjewell.com
Black and red popcorn
President: Carole Klein
Owner: Charles Klein
Estimated Sales: $2.5-5 Million
Number Employees: 10-19
Type of Packaging: Private Label
Brands:
   Black Jewell®
   Crimson Jewell®

1421 Black Market Gelato
13158 Saticoy St
North Hollywood, CA 91605
818-983-6040
blackmarketgelato.com
Gelato and sorbet
Owner: Spin Mllynarik
Estimated Sales: Less than $500,000
Number Employees: 1-4
Type of Packaging: Consumer, Private Label

1422 Black Mesa Winery
1502 Highway 68
Velarde, NM 87582
505-852-2820
Fax: 505-852-2820 800-852-6372
jer@blackmesawinery.com
www.blackmesawinery.com
Wine
Co-Owner: Jerry Burd
Co-Owner: Lynda Burd
Event Coordinator: Karen Fielding
Estimated Sales: $500,000-$1 Million
Number Employees: 1-4
Type of Packaging: Private Label
Brands:
   Black Mesa
   Coyote Wine

1423 Black Prince Distillery Inc
691 Clifton Ave
PO Box 1999
Clifton, NJ 07011-4203
973-365-2050
Fax: 973-365-0746 rickn@blackprincedist.com
www.blackprincedistillery.com
Liquor, liqueurs and cordials
President: Robert Guttag
VP, Operations: Rick Noone
rnoone@blackprincedistillery.com
Estimated Sales: $3.2 Million
Number Employees: 20-49
Square Footage: 120000
Brands:
   Black Prince
   Devils Spring
   Dorado
   Llord's
   Tj Toad

1424 Black Ranch Organic Grains
5800 Eastside Road
Etna, CA 96027-9753
916-467-3387
Seven grain cereals including wheat and barley
Owner: Dave Black
Co-Owner: Dawn Black
Estimated Sales: Under $500,000
Number Employees: 1-4
Type of Packaging: Consumer, Food Service
Brands:
   Black Ranch Gourmet Grains

1425 Black River Caviar
0075 Sunset Dr
Breckenridge, CO 80424-7218
970-547-1542
Fax: 970-547-9707 888-315-0575
graham@blackrivercaviar.com
www.blackrivercaviar.com
Caviar
President: Graham Gaspard
Estimated Sales: $500 Thousand
Number Employees: 5
Type of Packaging: Consumer, Food Service

1426 Black Sheep Vintners
221 Main Street
PO Box 1851
Murphys, CA 95247
209-728-2157
Fax: 209-728-2157 info@blacksheepwinery.com
www.blacksheepwinery.com
Fine wines. Founded in 1983.
Owner: Steve Millier
CEO: David Olson
Marketing Director: Janis Olson
Estimated Sales: Less than $500,000
Number Employees: 1-4
Type of Packaging: Private Label

1427 Black Shield
5620 Venice Avenue NE
Albuquerque, NM 87113-2306
562- Ve-ice
Fax: 505-884-5643 800-653-9357
Specialty gourmet popcorn
President: Marc Moore
Estimated Sales: Less than $500,000
Number Employees: 1-4

1428 Black's Barbecue
215 N Main St
Lockhart, TX 78644-2121
512-398-2712
Fax: 512-398-6000 888-632-8225
info@blacksbbq.com www.blacksbbq.com
Barbequed sausage; wholesaler/distributor of meats including brisket, ribs, chicken, pork and loin. Established in 2009.
Manager: Steve Cloud
CEO: Terry Black
Owner: Norma Black
Co-Owner: Edgar Black
Manager: Barrett Black
barrett@blacksbbq.com
Estimated Sales: $300,000-500,000
Number Employees: 5-9
Type of Packaging: Bulk

1429 Blackbear Coffee Company
318 N Main St
Hendersonville, NC 28792-0407
828-692-6333
Fax: 828-692-6333
www.mountainshops.com/bear.html
Coffee
Manager: Bo Rodriquez
Estimated Sales: Less than $500,000
Number Employees: 5-9

1430 Blackberry Patch
PO Box 1639
Thomasville, GA 31799
229-558-9996
Fax: 229-558-9998 800-853-5598
fruittreats@blackberrypatch.com
www.blackberrypatch.com
Natural fruit syrups, jams, jellies, chocolate sauces and pancake mixes. Founded in 1999.
President: Randy Harvey
Owner: Harry Jones
Contact: Sabrina Cannon
sabrinac@blackberrypatch.com
Estimated Sales: $870,000
Number Employees: 11
Number of Brands: 2
Number of Products: 48
Type of Packaging: Consumer, Private Label

1431 Blair's Sauces & Snacks
188 Bay Ave
PO Box 363
Highlands, NJ 07732-1624
732-872-0755
Fax: 732-872-2035 800-982-5247
www.extremefood.com

535

Food Manufacturers / A-Z

Manufacturer of hot sauces, BBQ rubs and snacks.
Owner: Blair Lazar
Number of Brands: 1
Type of Packaging: Consumer
Brands:
   Blair's

1432 Blake Hill Preserves
PO Box 118
Grafton, VT 05146-0118
802-289-1636
vicky@blakehillpreserves.com
www.blakehillpreserves.com
Manufacturer of chutneys, conserves, preserves and marmalades made from organic ingredients.
Co-Founder: Vicky Allard
vicky@blakehillpreserves.com
Co-Founder: Joe Hanglin
Number Employees: 1-4
Square Footage: 80000

1433 Blake's All Natural Foods
178 Silk Farm Rd
Concord, NH 03301-8411
603-225-3532
Fax: 603-225-3390 info@blakesallnatural.com
www.blakesallnatural.com
Frozen natural, organic and family-sized meals
CEO: Sean M Connolly
sean@blakesallnature.com
Number Employees: 20-49

1434 Blakely Freezer Locker
12850 Magnolia Street
Blakeley, GA 31758-7055
229-723-3622
Fax: 229-723-9156
Frozen beef, pork and chicken, also hardwood smoked sausages and hams.
Owner: Douglas Huey Johnson
Owner: Deeann Benton Johnson
Estimated Sales: $2.5-5 Million
Number Employees: 5-9
Type of Packaging: Consumer
Other Locations:
   Blakely GA

1435 Blalock Seafood & Specialty
24822 Canal Rd
Orange Beach, AL 36561-3894
251-974-5811
Fax: 251-974-5812
Manufacturer and wholesaler of seafood. Founded in 1992.
Owner: Pete Blalock
pblalock419@gmail.com
Estimated Sales: $4,000,000
Number Employees: 5-9
Type of Packaging: Consumer

1436 Bland Farms INC
1126 Raymond D Bland Rd
Glennville, GA 30427-7020
912-654-3048
Fax: 912-654-1330 800-752-0206
info@blandfarms.com www.blandfarms.com
Frozen foods and sweet onions. Founded in 2000.
Owner: Delbert Bland
delbert@blandfarms.com
Manager: Elbert Bland
Number Employees: 100-249

1437 Blansh International
2340 West Monte Vista Avenue
Turlock, CA 95380
209-250-1237
Fax: 408-279-8444
Ethnic foods. Founded in 1991.
President: Atoor Eliasnia
Estimated Sales: $250,000
Number Employees: 2

1438 Blanton's
229 West Main Street
Suite 202
Frankfort, KY 40601
502-223-9874
Fax: 423-337-3487 www.blantonsbourbon.com
Hard stick candy, molded and regular chocolate; also, seasonal products available. Founded in 1967.
Owner: Harld Blanton
Vice President: Betty Blanton
Estimated Sales: $500,000
Number Employees: 5-9
Type of Packaging: Consumer
Brands:
   Blanton's

1439 Blanver USA
1515 S Federal Hwy
Suite 204
Boca Raton, FL 33432-7404
561-416-5513
Fax: 561-416-5563 tesau@blanver.com
www.blanver.com.br
Purified cellulose excipients, gums and gels used to increase fiber content, improve texture, stabilize and thicken food products.
President: Sergio Frangioni
Founder: Valdemir Passos
Contact: Scott Geary
scott.geary@blanver.com
Operations Manager: Rehanna Birbal
Estimated Sales: $1.3 Million
Parent Co: Blanver
Type of Packaging: Bulk

1440 Blaser's USA, Inc.
1858 US Highway 63
Comstock, WI 54826
715-822-2437
Fax: 715-822-8459 866-570-2439
Cheeses. Founded in 1947.
CEO: Paul Bauer
National VP Sales/Marketing: Jim Grande
Operations Manager: John Freyholtz
Plant Superintendent: Joe Hines
Estimated Sales: $500,000-$1 Million
Number Employees: 50-99
Parent Co: The Ellsworth Cooperative Creamery
Type of Packaging: Private Label
Brands:
   Blaser's

1441 Blau Oyster Co Inc
11321 Blue Heron Rd
Bow, WA 98232-9326
360-766-6171
Fax: 360-766-6115 www.blauoyster.com
Processor and exporter of oysters. Founded in 1933.
President: Paul E Blau
blauoysterco@gmail.com
Marketing Manager: Pete Nordlund
Director of Operations: Paul Blau
Estimated Sales: $2.5-5 Million
Number Employees: 10-19
Type of Packaging: Consumer, Food Service, Private Label, Bulk

1442 Blazzin Pickle Company
6105 N 32nd Street
McAllen, TX 78505-5006
956-630-0733
Pickles including chips and spears
President: Craig Johnson
VP: Kathy Johnson
Number Employees: 1-4
Square Footage: 8000
Type of Packaging: Consumer, Food Service
Brands:
   Blazzin

1443 Blend Pak Inc
10039 High Grove Rd
PO Box 458
Bloomfield, KY 40008-7178
502-252-8000
Fax: 502-252-8001 salesinfo@blendpak.com
www.blendpak.com
Manufactures batter, breaders, marinades, seasoning blends, specialty mixes, and custom blended dry formulas. Founded in 1990.
CEO/Human Resources Director: Dan Sutherland
dan@blendpak.com
EVP: Sue Sutherland
R&D: Linda Mikels
Quality Control: Rob Elkin
Operations: Dave Montgomery
Plant Manager: Matt Elder
Estimated Sales: $10 Million
Number Employees: 20-49
Square Footage: 44000
Type of Packaging: Food Service, Private Label, Bulk
Brands:
   Blend Pak
   Bloomfield Farms
   Pier Fresh

1444 Blendco Inc
8 J M Tatum Industrial Dr
Hattiesburg, MS 39401-8341
601-544-9800
Fax: 601-544-5634 888-253-6326
csr@blendcoinc.com www.blendcoinc.com
Dry food manufacturer. Provide custom blending and packaging, as well as private labeling and contract packaging services.
President: Charles McCaffrey
Chief Financial Officer: Ken Hrdlica
Estimated Sales: $8 Million
Number Employees: 20-49
Number of Brands: 2
Type of Packaging: Food Service, Private Label, Bulk
Brands:
   Ezy Time
   Chicken-To-Go

1445 Blendex Co
11208 Electron Dr
Louisville, KY 40299-3875
502-267-1003
Fax: 502-267-1024 800-626-6325
www.blendex.com
Dry ingredients blending company specializing in batters, breadings, seasonings, seasonings and marinades. 12 distribution warehouses located across the US.
President: Jacquelyn Bailey
CEO: Ronald Pottinger
rpottinger@blendex.com
Director: Olin Cook
Executive Vice President: Tony Jessee
Vice President Research/Development: Jordan Stivers
Vice President of Sales: Ron Carr
Estimated Sales: $28.5 Million
Number Employees: 50-99
Type of Packaging: Food Service, Private Label, Bulk

1446 Blendtopia
Nashville, TN 37217
www.blendtopiafoods.com
Superfood smoothie kits
Founder: Tiffany Taylor

1447 Blenheim Bottling Company
P0 Box 452
Hamer, SC 29547
843-774-0322
Fax: 843-774-4018 800-270-9344
info@blenheimgingerale.com
www.blenheimgingerale.com
Jamaican ginger ale manufacturer. Founded in 1993.
President: Patty Schafer
CEO: Mackie Hayes
Manager: Ryan Schafer
Sales Director: Sheila McDowell
Estimated Sales: $2.5-5 Million
Number Employees: 5-9
Brands:
   Blenheim

1448 Blessed Herbs
109 Barre Plains Rd
Oakham, MA 01068
508-882-3839
Fax: 508-882-3755 800-489-4372
info@blessedherbs.com www.blessedherbs.com
Manufacturer, importer and exporter of organic and wildcrafted dried herbs, extracts, formulas and tablets; also, echinacea angustifolia root; exporter and importer of dried herbs and colon cleansers.
Co-Founder: Michael Volchok
Co-Founder: Martha Volchok
CEO: Scott Leonard
Marketing Director: Shalom Volchok
Contact: Alicia Rocco
alicia@blessedherbs.com
Estimated Sales: $500,000-$1 Million
Number Employees: 14
Square Footage: 24000
Type of Packaging: Consumer, Bulk

1449 Bletsoe's Cheese Inc
8281 3rd Ln
Marathon, WI 54448-9522
715-443-2526
Fax: 715-443-6407 bletsoecheese@frontier.com

Food Manufacturers / A-Z

This company was founded in 1983 and is a producer of cheeses. Bletsoe's products include up to 27 types of cheese. Varieties include cheese curds, 22 lb. cheddar daises, 40 pound cheddar, pepper jack and colby.
President: David Bletsoe
Marketing Director: Bonnie Bletsoe
Estimated Sales: $5-10 Million
Number Employees: 10-19
Type of Packaging: Consumer
Brands:
  Bletsoe's Cheese

1450 Bleuet Nordic
103 rue Boulianne
Dolbeau-Mistassini, QC G8L 6B1
Canada
418-239-1001
Fax: 418-239-0565 info@bleuetnordic.com
bleuetnordic.com
Frozen wild blueberries
Sales: Tim Dohan

1451 Bliss Brothers Dairy, Inc.
PO Box 2288
711 Park Street
Attleboro, MA 02703
508-222-2884
Fax: 508-226-6320 800-622-8789
www.blissdairy.com
Manufacturers of ice cream, frozen yogurt, sherbert, sorbet, and ice cream mixes
President: Dave Bliss
Chief Financial Officer: Kent Bliss
Contact: Thomas Bliss
tbliss@bristolfarms.com
Estimated Sales: $1-2.5 Million
Number Employees: 50-99

1452 Bliss Gourmet Foods
St. Paul, MN
blissgourmetfoods.com
Granola and muesli
Founder and Chef: Lesley Powers
Year Founded: 1908
Number of Brands: 1
Number of Products: 16
Type of Packaging: Consumer

1453 Blissfully Better
Chester, NJ 07930
www.blissfullybetter.com
Toffee sweetened with coconut nectar
CEO: Bonnie Boroian
Number of Brands: 1
Number of Products: 4
Type of Packaging: Consumer
Brands:
  BLISSFULLY BETTER

1454 Blk Enterprises
214 W 39th Street
Room 202
New York, NY 10018-8323
212-764-3331
Fax: 212-764-3338 c.laurita@blkbeverages.com
Beverages. Founded in 2011
Contact: Chris Laurita
Number Employees: 1

1455 (HQ)Blommer Chocolate Co
600 W Kinzie St
Chicago, IL 60654-5585
312-226-7700
Fax: 312-226-4141 800-621-1606
www.blommer.com
Processor and exporter of chocolate ingredients for the bakery, dairy and confectionery industries including milk and dark chocolate, confectioner and pastel coatings, cookie drops, chocolate liquor, cocoa butter, cocoa powder, icecream ingredients, etc. Founded in 1939.
President: Peter Blommer
Founder, Chairman & CEO: Henry Blommer
CFO: Jack S Larsen
jack@blommer.com
Vice President: Rich Blommer
Manager of Quality Assurance: Radka Kacena
Marketing & Purchasing Manager: Leanna Hicks
Sales Support: Chief Marketing Officer Kidd
VP of Operations: Rich Blommer
Plant Mnaager: Joe Chwala
Purchasing Manager: Faye Garcia
Estimated Sales: $38.4 Million
Number Employees: 1-4
Square Footage: 340000
Type of Packaging: Bulk
Other Locations:
  Union City CA
  East Greenville PA
  Campbellford ON

1456 Blommer Chocolate Co
1101 Blommer Dr
East Greenville, PA 18041-2140
215-679-4472
Fax: 215-679-4196 800-825-8181
klhicks@uc.blommer.com www.blommer.com
Chocolate
President: Peter Blommer
pblommer@uc.blommer.com
Estimated Sales: Less than $500,000
Number Employees: 100-249
Type of Packaging: Bulk
Other Locations:
  Chicago IL
  Union City CA

1457 Bloom Honey
805-379-0040
877-555-9300
www.bloomhoney.com
Raw honey
President/Owner: David Jefferson
Number of Brands: 1
Number of Products: 8
Type of Packaging: Consumer
Brands:
  BLOOM

1458 Bloomfield Bakers
10711 Bloomfield St
Los Alamitos, CA 90720-2503
562-594-4411
Fax: 562-742-0408 800-594-4111
Cookies, cereals, crackers, bars and mixes. Founded in 1981.
President: Sam Calderon
Owner/CEO: William Ross
Research & Development Manager: Christina Lates
Quality Control Manager: Steve Huber
National Sales Manager: Russ Case
Contact: Raiza Bastidas
braiza@phonewareinc.com
COO: Gary Marx
Plant/Production Manager: Ricardo Gonzalez
Estimated Sales: $5-10 Million
Number Employees: 850
Square Footage: 300000
Type of Packaging: Private Label

1459 Bloomfield Farms
575 Spencer Mattingly Ln
Bardstown, KY 40004-9103
502-348-0012
Fax: 502-348-7711 www.thebloomfieldfarms.com
Gluten free mixes including brownies, pancakes, pizza dough and cake mixes
Manager: Davis Chesser
davisc@blendpak.com
Number Employees: 10-19

1460 Bloomington Brewing Co
1795 E 10th St
Bloomington, IN 47408-3975
812-323-2112
Fax: 812-333-3200 www.bloomingtonbrew.com
Ale and stout
Owner: Jessica May
jessica@bloomington.com
General Manager: Micheal Fox
Business Manager: Mark Cady
Marketing Director: Sera Shikh
Number Employees: 1-4
Parent Co: One World Enterprises
Type of Packaging: Consumer, Food Service, Bulk
Brands:
  Bloomington Brewing
  Quarrymen Pale

1461 Bloomsberry LLC
92 Jackson St
Salem, MA 01970-3068
978-745-9100
Fax: 978-745-9150 800-745-5154
sales@bloomsberry.com www.praimgroup.com
Chocolates. Founded in 2005.
Owner: Vanessa Kettelwell
vanessa@bloomsberry.com
VP: Kerry Francis
Estimated Sales: Less Than $500,000
Number Employees: 1-4

1462 Blossom Farm Products
545 State Rt 17
Suite 2003
Ridgewood, NJ 07450
201-493-2626
Fax: 201-493-2666 800-729-1818
Processor, importer and exporter of dairy products including milk powders, dry blends, whey, caseinates, lactose, butter fats, etc.
President: Paul Podell
Manager: Kathy Oviedo
VP: Marcia Podell
Operations Manager: Kathy Oviedo
Number Employees: 5-9
Type of Packaging: Consumer, Food Service, Bulk

1463 Blossom Water, LLC
PO Box 393
Westwood, MA 02090
855-325-5777
info@drinkblossomwater.com
www.drinkblossomwater.com
Flavoured water.
Founder & President: Steve Fortuna
Director of Sales: Mike Penta
Square Footage: 80000
Brands:
  blossom water

1464 Blount Fine Foods
630 Currant Rd
Fall River, MA 02720
774-888-1300
www.blountfinefoods.com
Frozen seafood products including chopped clams, lobster bisque, clam chowder, variety of meats, hearty soups and an array of dips.
President: Todd Blount
Chief Innovation Officer: William Bigelow
bsewall@blountseafood.com
VP, Sales & Marketing: Bob Sewall
Director, Purchasing: Ed Sheehan
Estimated Sales: $46.60 Million
Number Employees: 50-99
Square Footage: 65000
Type of Packaging: Consumer, Food Service, Private Label, Bulk
Brands:
  Blount
  Gourmet Stuffed Clams
  Point Judith
  Sams Clams
  White Cap

1465 Blue Bell Creameries LP
1101 S Blue Bell Rd
Brenham, TX 77833-4413
979-836-7977
Fax: 979-830-7398 800-327-8135
www.bluebell.com
Ice milk mix, ices, ice cream and frozen yogurt. FOunded in 1907.
CEO: Paul W Kruse
paul.kruse@bluebell.com
President/CEO: Paul Kruse
Chief Managing Officer: Melvin Zeigenbein
Number Employees: 1000-4999
Type of Packaging: Consumer, Food Service
Other Locations:
  Sylacauga AL
  Broken Arrow OK
  Brenham TX
Brands:
  Blue Bell Ice Cream
  Blue Bell Dairy

1466 (HQ)Blue California Co
30111 Tomas
Rancho Sta Marg, CA 92688-2125
949-459-2729
Fax: 949-635-1986 info@bluecal-ingredients.com
www.bluecal-ingredients.com
Developer and manufacturer of food ingredients.
President: Steven Chen
steven.chen@gmail.com
Executive Vice President: Cecilia McCollum
Quality Control Manager: Carl Lai
Estimated Sales: $10-20 Million
Number Employees: 10-19

Food Manufacturers / A-Z

Other Locations:
Rockaway NJ

1467 Blue Chip Baker
1911 S 3850 W
Salt Lake City, UT 84104-4914
801-269-0997
Fax: 801-269-9666 800-878-0099
info@bluechipgroup.net www.augasonfarms.com
Lecithins, health foods, wild Mexican yam cream, colloidal silver
President: Mark Augason
CEO: Gary Bringhurst
HR Vice President: Jeff Augason
VP of Information Technology: Fabio Demelo
Estimated Sales: $500,000-$1 Million
Number Employees: 100-249
Square Footage: 40
Type of Packaging: Consumer, Food Service, Private Label, Bulk
Brands:
  Trophic

1468 Blue Chip Cookies
5991 Meijer Dr
Suite 24
Milford, OH 45150-1531
513-697-6610
Fax: 513-297-9494 800-888-9866
www.bluechipcookiesdirect.com
Manufacturer and wholesaler of fresh baked cookies
President/Chief Cookie Officer: Donna Drury
Estimated Sales: Less Than $500,000
Number Employees: 1-4

1469 Blue Circle Foods
4600 Argyle Terrace NW
Washington, DC 20011
202-232-5282
www.bluecirclefoods.com
Fresh and frozen fish
Year Founded: 2005

1470 Blue Crab Bay
29368 Atlantic Dr.
Melfa, VA 23410
757-787-3602
Fax: 757-787-3430 800-221-2722
sales@bluecrabbay.com www.bluecrabbay.com
Wholesaler & retailer of bloody mary mixers, seafood soups, seasonings, snacks, crab meat; also salt, mustard, and marinade, stoneware. Founded in 1985.
President: Pamela Barefoot
pam@baybeyond.net
VP Finance: Dawn Brasure
Marketing Director: Kelly Drummond
Sales Manager: Victoria DiLeo
Chief Operating Officer: Paul Driscoll
Purchasing: Linda Nyborg
Estimated Sales: $1-3 Million
Number Employees: 22
Square Footage: 86000
Parent Co: Bay Beyond, Inc.
Type of Packaging: Consumer
Brands:
  Barnacles Snack Mix
  Blue Crab Bay
  Crab House Nuts
  Salmonberry
  Sting Ray Bloody Mary Mixer
  Watts Island Trading

1471 Blue Diamond Growers
1802 C St.
Sacramento, CA 95811
800-987-2329
www.bluediamond.com
Processor, grower and exporter of almonds, macadamias, pistachios and hazelnuts. Two thousand almond products in many cuts, styles, sizes and shapes for use in confectionary, bakery, dairy and processed foods. In house R/D for customproducts.
President/Chief Executive Officer: Mark Jansen
Chairman of The Board: Clinton Shick
CFO: Dean LaVallee
Vice Chairman: Dale Van Groningen
Quality Assurance Lab Manager: Steven Phillips
Director, Marketing: Al Greenlee
Manager, Communications: Cassandra Keyse
Manager, Operations: Bruce Lisch
Manager, Product Development: Mike Stoddard
Senior Vice President, Procurement: David Hills
Year Founded: 1910
Estimated Sales: $709 Million
Number Employees: 1,100

Type of Packaging: Consumer, Food Service, Private Label, Bulk
Brands:
  Almond Breeze
  Almond Toppers
  Blue Diamond
  Blue Diamond Almonds
  Blue Diamond Hazelnut
  Blue Diamond Macadamias
  Nut Thins
  Smokehouse
  California Nuts

1472 Blue Dog Bakery
3302 Fuhrman Ave E # 301
Suite 301
Seattle, WA 98102-7115
206-323-6958
Fax: 206-666-3835 888-749-7229
BlueDog@bluedogbakery.com
www.bluedogbakery.com
Company produces a variety of premium, natural, low fat dog biscuits and treats. Founded in 1998.
President/Owner: Margot Kenly
CEO: Kyle Polanski
bluedog@bluedogbakery.com
Estimated Sales: $1-3 Million
Number Employees: 1-4
Type of Packaging: Private Label
Brands:
  Mariner Biscuits
  Original Sesame Low Fat Crackers
  Parmesan Low Fat Crackers
  Sweet Onion Low Fat Crackers
  Sweet Pepper Low Fat Crackers

1473 Blue Evolution
1528 El Camino Real
Suite 304
San Mateo, CA 94402
605-741-4074
info@blueevolution.com
www.blueevolution.com
Seaweed-infused pasta
CEO: Beau Perry
Sales Manager: Chris Elders
VP, Operations: Luke Knowles
Number of Brands: 1
Number of Products: 5
Type of Packaging: Consumer
Brands:
  BLUE EVOLUTION

1474 Blue Gold Mussels
38 Blackmer St
P.O.Box 1803
New Bedford, MA 02744
508-993-2635
Fax: 508-994-9508 seagold01@msn.com
www.seagolddips.com
Fresh and frozen mussel products and calamari salad. Founded in 1996.
Owner: Bill Silkes
Director Marketing: Joe Jeffrey
Type of Packaging: Consumer, Food Service, Private Label
Brands:
  Blue Gold

1475 Blue Grass Quality Meat
PO Box 17658
2648 Crescent Springs Pike
Covington, KY 41017-0658
859-331-7100
Fax: 859-331-4273
www.bluegrassqualitymeats.com
Smoked meats and sausage. Founded in 1992.
President/CEO: Paul Rice
Contact: Joan Brewer
jbrewer@bluegrassqualitymeats.com
Estimated Sales: $10-24.9 Million
Number Employees: 50-99
Type of Packaging: Consumer, Food Service, Private Label, Bulk

1476 Blue Green Organics
1923 Record Crossing Rd
Dallas, TX 75235
817-703-2321
bluegreenagave.com
Agave nectar and chia seeds
Number of Brands: 1
Number of Products: 3
Type of Packaging: Consumer, Food Service

Brands:
  BLUE GREEN ORGANICS

1477 Blue Harbour Cheese
P.O. Box 46011 Novalea
Halifax, NS B3K 5V8
Canada
902-240-0305
info@blueharbourcheese.com
www.blueharbourcheese.com
Cheese
Cheese Maker: Lyndell Findlay

1478 Blue Harvest Foods
86 Macarthur Dr
New Bedford, MA 02740-7214
508-993-5700
Fax: 508-991-5133 www.blueharvestfisheries.com
Fresh and frozen scallops including bay and sea and fillets including flounder, cod, yellow tail and haddock; importer of cod fish and scallops; exporter of scallops
President: Albert J Santos
al@scallops-fillets.com
CEO: Linda Wisniewski
Treasurer/Vice President: Carmine Romano
Sales Manager: Patrick Moriarty
Manager: Albert Santos
al@scallops-fillets.com
Estimated Sales: $10-20 Million
Number Employees: 20-49
Square Footage: 60000
Type of Packaging: Consumer, Food Service, Private Label, Bulk
Brands:
  Ding Gua Gua
  Hygrade
  Old Cape Harbor
  Teddy's

1479 Blue Hill Yogurt
630 Bedford Rd.
Pocantico Hills, NY 10591
914-366-9600
www.bluehillyogurt.com
Manufacturer of yogurt.
Co-Founder, Owner: David Barber
david@bluehillfarm.com
Co-Owner: Laureen Barber
Executive Chief and Co-Owner: Dan Barber
Brands:
  Blue Hill

1480 Blue Hills Spring Water Company
441 Quincy Avenue
Quincy, MA 02169
614-715-3900
Fax: 617-770-2720 www.bluehillswater.com
Bottled water manufacturer. Founded in 1984.
President/CEO: Mike Verrochi
COO: Mark Okum
Estimated Sales: $2.5-5 Million
Number Employees: 50-99
Brands:
  Monadnock Mountain Spring Water

1481 Blue Jay Orchards
125 Plumtrees Rd
Bethel, CT 06801-3102
203-748-0119
Fax: 203-748-4814
Apple butter, sauce and chutney; also, pear butter. Founded in 1985.
President: Paul Patterson
pspatterson@qualityseals.com
VP: Mary Patterson
Estimated Sales: $500,000
Number Employees: 5-9
Square Footage: 40000
Type of Packaging: Consumer, Private Label
Brands:
  Blue Jay Orchards

1482 Blue Lakes Trout Farm
133 Warm Creek Rd
Jerome, ID 83338
208-734-7151
Fax: 208-733-0325
Rainbow trout
Manager: Harold Johnson
Estimated Sales: $2.5-5 Million
Number Employees: 5-9
Type of Packaging: Consumer, Food Service

Food Manufacturers / A-Z

Brands:
  Greene's

1483 Blue Marble Biomaterials
5653 Alloy S
Missoula, MT 59808
406-552-0748
Fax: 206-452-5898 800-738-0849
info@bluemarblebio.com www.bluemarblebio.com
Natural, bio-derived flavor and fragrance products including natural esters, thioesters, acids and extracts.
President/Chief Science Officer: James Stephens
Quality Research Scientist: Michalea Finnegan
Director Marketing/Communications: Melanie Calahan
Chief Business Officer: Colby Underwood
Contact: Nathan Snyder
nathan.snyder@bluemarblebio.com
Operations Manager: Wayne Smith
Electrical Systems/Production: Nate Snyder

1484 Blue Marble Brands
313 Iron Horse Way
Providence, RI 02908
888-534-0246
Fax: 866-402-7371
Organic, natural, specialty, ethnic and functional foods.
President: Chris Jensen
Year Founded: 2006
Estimated Sales: $16.2 Million
Number of Brands: 19
Type of Packaging: Food Service
Brands:
  Woodstock®
  Tumaro's®
  Rising Moon Organics®
  Mt. Vikos™
  Mediterranean Organic™
  Harvest Bay®
  Natural Sea™
  Field Day®
  Koyo™
  Mini Me's®
  Fantastic World Foods®
  Old Wessex™
  AH!LASKA®
  Asian Gourmet®
  Bella Famiglia®
  Haddon House®
  Medford Farms®
  Musette®
  Tropical Pepper®

1485 Blue Monkey
Long Beach, CA 90831
info@bluemonkeydrinks.com
www.bluemonkeydrinks.com
Tropical fruit juices and snacks
Co-Owner: Simon Ginsberg
Co-Owner: Mary-Jane Ginsberg
Year Founded: 2010

1486 Blue Moon Foods
568 N Main Street
White River Junction, VT 05001-7026
802-295-1165
Fax: 802-295-2553
Ice cream and frozen desserts. Founded in 1995.
President: John Donaldson
Estimated Sales: $440,000
Number Employees: 7
Brands:
  Blue Moon Tea

1487 Blue Moose of Boulder
1733 Majestic Dr
Unit 103
Lafayette, CO 80026
303-926-0664
customercare@bluemooseofboulder.com
bluemooseofboulder.com
Hummus, dips and spreads, pesto, salsa, and preprepared snacks.
General Manager: Bert Sartori
Year Founded: 1997
Number Employees: 11-50
Type of Packaging: Private Label

1488 Blue Mountain Enterprise Inc
4000 Commerce Dr
Kinston, NC 28504-7906
252-522-1544
Fax: 252-522-2599 800-522-1544
Savory flavors for the food industry, also contract manufacturing and packaging
President: William Baugher
labs@bluemoutainsflavors.com
Manager of Scientific Affairs: Jonathan Baugher
Corporate Secretay/Treasurer: Teresa Baugher
Research/Development: William Recktenwald
Quality Control: Margaret Jones
Customer Service: Maureen Suggs
Operations Manager: Laura Key
Production: Perry Price, Jr
Estimated Sales: $4 Million
Number Employees: 10-19
Number of Products: 150
Square Footage: 67775
Parent Co: Blue Mountain Enterprises
Type of Packaging: Bulk

1489 Blue Mountain Vineyards
7627 Grape Vine Drive
New Tripoli, PA 18066
610-298-3068
Fax: 610-298-8616 info@bluemountainwine.com
www.bluemountainwine.com
Wines
President/Owner: Joseph Greff
VP: Vickie Greff
Estimated Sales: $2.5-5 Million
Number Employees: 10-19

1490 (HQ)Blue Pacific Flavors & Fragrances
1354 Marion Ct
City of Industry, CA 91745
626-934-0099
www.bluepacificflavors.com
Basic manufacturer of natural flavors, extracts, essences and functional ingredients to the beverage, dairy, confectionery, baking and pharmaceutical industries. Founded in 1992.
President: Donald Wilkes
Contact: Kelly Anderson
kelly.anderson@cgtech.com
Estimated Sales: $5-9 Million
Number Employees: 20-49
Number of Brands: 5
Square Footage: 40000
Type of Packaging: Food Service, Private Label, Bulk
Other Locations:
  Blue Pacific Asia
  Malaysia
  Blue Pacific China
  Beijing, China
  Blue Pacific Korea
  Seoul, Korea
Brands:
  Cafe Extract
  Instacafe
  Naturessence
  Sun-Ripened
  Synature

1491 Blue Planet Foods
9104 Apison Pike
PO Box 2178
Collegedale, TN 37315
423-396-3145
Fax: 423-396-3402 877-396-3145
sales@blueplanetfoods.net
Grain based products, granola, nutrition and granola bar components, bread bases and nutritional fillers; exporter of granola products
President: Russell McKee
Human Resources Director: Wayne White
Director of Operations: Deris Bagli
Production Manager: Cliff Myers
Plant Manager: Frank Park
Parent Co: McKee Foods Corporation
Type of Packaging: Consumer, Food Service, Private Label, Bulk
Brands:
  Heartland®
  Hearty Life®

1492 Blue Point Brewing Co
161 River Ave
Patchogue, NY 11772-3304
631-475-6944
Fax: 631-475-5252 pete@bluepointbrewing.com
www.bluepointbrewing.com
The Blue Point Brewing Company is Long Island's first currently-operating microbrewery.
Owner & President: Peter Cotter
Owner & Brewmaster: Mark Burford
getdpoint@aol.com
Chief Financial Officer: Gary Peck
Quality Control Manager: Alan Brady
Director of Branding & Communications: Curt Potter
National Sales Manager: Rob Johnson
Operations: Nick Burford
Number Employees: 20-49
Type of Packaging: Consumer

1493 Blue Ribbon Farm Dairy Fresh
827 Exeter Ave
Exeter, PA 18643-1728
570-655-5579
Fax: 570-655-5637 www.blueribbondairy.com
Ice cream manufacturer. Founded in 1961.
President: Ken Sorick
Estimated Sales: $5-10 Million
Number Employees: 5-9

1494 Blue Ribbon Meats
3316 W 67th Pl
Cleveland, OH 44102
216-631-8850
Fax: 216-631-8934 800-262-0395
www.blueribbonmeats.com
Meat and seafood.
President: Al Radis
Year Founded: 1948
Estimated Sales: $20-50 Million
Number Employees: 100-249

1495 Blue Ridge Poultry
396 Foundry Street
Athens, GA 30601
706-546-6767
Fresh and frozen poultry including turkey; wholesaler/distributor of poultry and eggs
President: Robert Harris
Estimated Sales: $1-3 Million
Number Employees: 5-9
Square Footage: 18000
Type of Packaging: Consumer

1496 Blue Ridge Tea & Herb Co
26 Woodhull St
2nd Floor Suite
Brooklyn, NY 11231-2643
718-625-3100
Fax: 718-935-1874 www.blueridgetea.com
Custom herbal and teabag formulations for private label. Also sales agent for teabags with ten vitamins; flavored. Founded in 1979.
President: Roger Rigolli
rrbrth1@aim.com
Vice President: Troy Rigolli
Estimated Sales: $4.5 Million est.
Number Employees: 10-19
Type of Packaging: Private Label
Brands:
  Blue Ridge Teas

1497 Blue Runner Foods Inc
726 S Burnside Ave
Gonzales, LA 70737-3452
225-647-3016
Fax: 225-647-4017
customerservice@bluerunnerfoods.com
www.bluerunnerfoods.com
Processor and canner of Cajun and Creole creamed beans, peas and heat and serve entrees. Founded in 1993.
President: Richard Thomas
Vice President: Katie Thomas
kthomas@bluerunnerfoods.com
Estimated Sales: $5-10 Million
Number Employees: 20-49
Type of Packaging: Consumer, Food Service
Brands:
  Blue Runner

Food Manufacturers / A–Z

1498 Blue Sky Beverage Company
550 Monica Circle
Suite 201
Corona, CA 92880
505-995-9761
Fax: 505-982-4004 800-426-7367
info@drinkbluesky.com www.drinkbluesky.com
Manufacturer and exporter of natural and energy sodas; also sparkling and artesian drinking water
Chairman/CEO: Rodney Sacks
President/COO/CFO: Hilton Schlosberg
Estimated Sales: $48,000

1499 Blue Smoke Salsa
119 East Main Street
PO Box 244
Ansted, WV 25812
304-658-3800
Fax: 304-658-5400 888-725-7298
bluesmokesalsa@hotmail.com
Jams and jellys, barbecue sauces, sparkling cider, honey, gourmet mustards, specialty butters, pickles, marinades and sauces, salsa, hot and spicy foods, seasonings, and dry mixes. Founded in 1992.
President: Robin Hildebrand
Estimated Sales: $300,000
Number Employees: 7

1500 Blue Star Food Products
3000 NW 109th Ave
Doral, FL 33172
305-836-6858
info@bluestarfoods.com
www.bluestarfoods.com
Seafood
Executive Chairman & CSO: John Keeler
jkeeler@bluestarfoods.com
Estimated Sales: $50-100 Million
Number Employees: 20-49
Number of Brands: 4
Brands:
  Blue Star
  Oceanica
  Pacifika
  Seassentials

1501 Blue Willow Tea Co
1200 10th St
Berkeley, CA 94710-1509
510-524-1933
Fax: 510-420-0260 800-328-0353
info@bluewillowtea.com www.bluewillowtea.com
Teas. Founded in 1994.
Owner: Ali Roth
jacqueline.rodarte@lacdc.org
Estimated Sales: Less Than $500,000
Number Employees: 1-4
Brands:
  Blue Willow
  Wu Wei

1502 BlueWater Seafoods
128 Rogers Street
Gloucester, MA 01930
978-283-3000
888-560-2539
www.bluewater.ca
Haddock and sole, shrimp temptations, five star tilapia, grill fillets, grill salmon and haddock, natural cut fillets, popcorn shrimp, classic family favorites, seasoned fillets and shrimp bowls
Number Employees: 225
Parent Co: Gortons USA
Type of Packaging: Consumer, Food Service

1503 Blueberry Store
PO Box 195
Grand Junction, MI 49056
269-437-6322
Fax: 269-434-6997 877-654-2400
sales@theblueberrystore.com
www.theblueberrystore.com
All natural blueberry preserve, blueberry salsa, blueberry BBQ sauce, blueberry juice, chocolate covered blueberries, blueberry syrup, blueberry mustard, blueberry vinegar and chutney
CEO: Jennifer Montgomery
CFO: Jeff Van Natter
Estimated Sales: $300,000-500,000
Number Employees: 1-4
Number of Products: 20
Parent Co: Michigan Blueberry Growers Association

1504 Bluebird Restaurant
19 N Main St
Logan, UT 84321-4583
435-752-3155
www.thebluebirdrestaurant.com
Candy and confectionery. Founded in 1914.
Owner: Sue Bette
sbette@bluebird-farm.com
Estimated Sales: $1-2.5 Million
Number Employees: 20-49

1505 Bluebonnet Meat Company
719 S. Pearl Street
Trenton, TX 75490-3111
903-989-2293
info@jackswholesalemeat.com
Beef and pork
President: Ben Buses
Vice President: Hannah Buses
Estimated Sales: $3-5 Million
Number Employees: 5-9
Type of Packaging: Consumer

1506 Bluechip Group
432 W 3440 S
Salt Lake City, UT 84115-4228
801-269-0997
Fax: 801-269-9666 800-878-0099
customerservice@bluechipgroup.net
Milk drinks including tofu, rice and soy
President: Mark Augason
CFO: Phil Auguson
Estimated Sales: $5 Million
Number Employees: 10-19
Number of Brands: 16
Number of Products: 160
Square Footage: 70000
Type of Packaging: Consumer, Food Service, Private Label, Bulk
Brands:
  Blue Chip Baker
  Blue Chip Group
  Morning Moo's
  Swiss Whey D'Lite

1507 Bluegrass Brewing Company
3929 Shelbyville Rd
Louisville, KY 40207
502-899-7070
Fax: 502-899-7051 pathagan@bbcbrew.com
www.bbcbrew.com
Brewer of ale, stout and lager. Founded in 1993.
Owner/President: Patrick Hagan
Contact: Jonathan Haeseley
haeseley@aye.net
Estimated Sales: $10-20 Million
Type of Packaging: Consumer, Food Service, Bulk
Brands:
  Altbier
  American Pale Ale
  Bluebird Restaurant
  Dark Star Porter
  Nut Brown Ale

1508 Bluegrass Dairy & Food
1117 Cleveland Ave
Glasgow, KY 42141
Fax: 270-651-8844 800-794-4840
www.bluegrassdairy.com
Powdered ingredients for the food industry.
Plant Manager: Rick Johnson
Purchasing: Trent Walker
Other Locations:
  Sprinfield Facility
  Springfield KY

1509 Bluepoint Bakery
1721 E 58th Ave
Denver, CO 80216-1505
303-298-1100
Fax: 303-298-9797 sales@bluepointbakery.com
www.bluepointbakery.com
Manufacturer of baked goods such as croissants, cinnamon rolls, breads, muffins, scones, danishes, cakes, tarts and pies.
President: Fred Bramhall
CFO: Robb Letterman
robb@bluepointbakery.com
Vice President: Mary Clark
Estimated Sales: $20-50 Million
Number Employees: 50-99
Type of Packaging: Food Service

1510 Blume Honey Water
1382 Old Freeport Rd
Suite 3B
Pittsburgh, PA 15238
412-406-7391
info@blumehoneywater.com
www.blumehoneywater.com
Honey-infused water
Co-Founder: Michele Burchfield
Co-Founder: Carla Frank
Number of Brands: 1
Number of Products: 3
Type of Packaging: Consumer
Brands:
  BLUME HONEY WATER

1511 Blumenhof Vineyards-Winery
13699 South Hwy 94
Dutzow, MO 63342
636-433-2245
Fax: 636-433-5224 800-419-2245
info@blumenhof.com www.blumenhof.com
Wine manufacturer. Founded in 1987.
President: Mark Blumenberg
Estimated Sales: $1-2.5 Million
Number Employees: 10-19

1512 Blundell Seafoods
11351 River Road
Richmond, BC V6X 1Z6
Canada
604-270-3300
Fax: 604-270-6513 info@blundellseafoods.com
www.blundellseafoods.com
Fresh and frozen seafood including clams, oysters, exotic fish, fin fish, freshwater fish, crustaceans, caviar
President: Ian Tak Yen Law
Vice President: Jeremy Kwun Hon Law
VP Sales: Rick Ogilvie
Manager: Bill Leung
Estimated Sales: $30 Million
Number Employees: 75
Type of Packaging: Consumer, Food Service, Private Label, Bulk

1513 Bnutty
Merrillville, IN 46410
844-426-8889
bnutty.com
Gourmet peanut butter
Number Employees: 1-4
Number of Products: 12
Type of Packaging: Consumer, Private Label
Brands:
  Bnutty

1514 Boar's Head
1819 Main St
Suite 800
Sarasota, FL 34236
800-352-6277
boarshead.com
Meat products include bacon, beef, chicken, ham, pre-sliced meats, and turkey. Other products include cheese, condiments, dips, hummus, and spreads.
Year Founded: 1905
Estimated Sales: $100+ Million
Number Employees: 500-999

1515 Boardman Foods Inc
71320 E Columbia Ln
P.O. Box 786
Boardman, OR 97818
541-481-3000
Fax: 801-881-8999 www.boardmanfoodsinc.com
Onions including IQF and peeled
President: Brian Maag
Purchasing: Chris Bacon
Quality Control: Deanna Goodeve
VP Sales: Thomas Flaherty
VP Operations: Debbie Radie
Estimated Sales: $20-50 Million
Number Employees: 100-249
Type of Packaging: Bulk

1516 Bob Evans Farms Inc.
800-939-2338
BEConsumerRelations@bobevansfoods.com
www.bobevansgrocery.com
Sausage, bacon, frozen handheld breakfast items, refrigerated dinner sides, and other convenience foods.
Chairman: Mike Townsley

Food Manufacturers / A-Z

Year Founded: 1953
Estimated Sales: Over $1 Billion
Number Employees: 10000+
Parent Co: Post Holdings, Inc.
Type of Packaging: Consumer, Food Service
Other Locations:
    Corporate Headquarters
    New Albany OH
    Bob Evans Farm
    Rio Grande OH
    Food Production
    Hillsdale MI
    Food Production
    Xenia OH
    Food Production & Distribution
    Springfield OH
    Food Production
    Sulphur Springs TX
Brands:
    Bob Evans®

1517 Bob Gordon & Associates
940 Linden Avenue
Oak Park, IL 60302-1349
708-524-9611
Processor and importer of green and black olives, maraschino cherries, pickled onions, pickled mushrooms and Greek pepperoncini. Founded in 1976.
President: Roberta Seefeldt
Vice President: Aaron Seefeldt
VP of Sales: Marcel Seefeldt
Controller: James Gosling
Estimated Sales: $1.2 Million
Number Employees: 10
Type of Packaging: Food Service, Private Label, Bulk
Brands:
    Marquis
    Splinter

1518 Bob's Custom Cuts
PO Box 6189
Bonnyville, AB T9N 2G8
Canada
780-826-2627
Fax: 780-826-2138
Fresh and frozen beef, pork, lamb, elk, jerky, deer, buffalo, wild boar, ostrich and game sausage
President & Board Member: Robert Belanger
Plant Manager: Ken Wychopen
Estimated Sales: A
Number Employees: 1-4
Square Footage: 19000
Parent Co: Dargis Land & Cattle
Type of Packaging: Consumer, Food Service, Private Label, Bulk

1519 Bob's Red Mill Natural Foods
13521 SE Pheasant Ct
Milwaukie, OR 97222-1248
503-654-3215
Fax: 503-653-1339 800-349-2173
www.bobsredmill.com
Milled whole grain flours, cereals and corn meal; also, mixes, bean flour and fat replacers
President: Bob Moore
CEO: Dennis Gilliam
CFO: John Wagner
Marketing Director: Cassidy Stockton
Head of Customer Service: Elizabeth Nawrocki
Estimated Sales: $25-50 Million
Number Employees: 250-499
Square Footage: 320000
Type of Packaging: Consumer, Food Service, Bulk
Brands:
    Bob's Red Mill

1520 Bobalu Nuts
805-223-0919
bobalunuts.com
Flavored almonds
Owner: Scott Cummings
Number of Brands: 1
Number of Products: 6
Type of Packaging: Consumer
Brands:
    BOBALU NUTS

1521 Bobby D'S
4737 County Road 101
Suite 222
Minnetonka, MN 55345-2634
952-278-7810
Sauces.
Owner: Robert Dechellis

1522 Bobbysue's Nuts LLC
65 North Bedford Rd.
Chappaqua, NY 10514
877-554-6887
getnuts@bobbysuesnuts.com
www.bobbysuesnuts.com
Combining almonds, cashews, pecans, and other nuts.
President: Barb Kobren
Contact: Adam Kobren
adam@bobbysuesnuts.com
Square Footage: 86000

1523 Bobo's Oat Bars
6325 Gunpark Dr
Suite B
Boulder, CO 80301
303-938-1977
info@eatbobos.com
eatbobos.com
Snack bars
Owner: Beryl Stafford
Number of Brands: 1
Number of Products: 18
Type of Packaging: Consumer
Brands:
    BOBO'S

1524 Boboli Intl. Inc.
3439 Brookside Road
Suite 104
Stockton, CA 95219-1754
209-473-3507
Fax: 209-473-0492
Frozen bakery products including cream puffs, eclairs, pastries and breads. Founded in 1986.
CEO: Greg Helland
President/COO: Josh Helland
Estimated Sales: $12.3 Million
Number Employees: 75
Number of Brands: 6
Type of Packaging: Food Service
Brands:
    Ambretta
    Breadeli
    Dutch Choux
    Patissa™
    Tulip Street Bakery
    Van Dierman

1525 Boca Bagelworks
8177 Glades Rd # 1
Boca Raton, FL 33434-4063
561-852-8992
Fax: 561-852-5798 info@bagelworks.com
www.bagelworks.com
Owned and operated by H&L Restaurants. Processor and exporter of bagels
Owner: Paul Herman
VP: Steven Goldstein
Estimated Sales: $500,000 appx.
Number Employees: 20-49

1526 Boca Bons East
5190 Lake Worth Road
Greenacres, FL 33463
954-346-0494
Fax: 954-346-0497 800-314-2835
Manufacturer and exporter of a certified kosher chocolate that is a combination of a truffle, fudge, and a brownie.
President: Susan Kanter
Sales Executive: Robin Kula
Estimated Sales: $1-3 Million
Number Employees: 10-19
Square Footage: 10000
Type of Packaging: Consumer, Food Service, Private Label, Bulk
Brands:
    Boca Bons

1527 Boca Foods Company
910 Mayer Ave
Madison, WI 53704
608-285-3311
Fax: 608-285-6741 bocaburger@kraftheinz.com
www.bocaburger.com
Meatless burgers
President: Kevin Scott
Director: Heather Fries
Brand Manager: Gary Berger
Estimated Sales: $20-50 Million
Number Employees: 35
Parent Co: Kraft Foods
Brands:
    Boca®

1528 Bodacious Foods
339 Gennett Dr
Jasper, GA 30143-1140
706-253-1153
Fax: 706-253-1156 800-391-1979
info@bodaciousfoods.com
www.bodaciousfoods.com
Cheese straws and shortbread, gingerbread, key lime, chocolate and sugar-free brownie bites
CEO: Cathy Cunningham
cathy@bodaciousfoods.com
Shipping Manager: Anthony Russell
Purchasing Manager: Dave Hays
Estimated Sales: $1,4,000,000
Number Employees: 20-49
Square Footage: 16000
Type of Packaging: Consumer
Brands:
    Geraldine's Bodacious

1529 Bodega Chocolates
17290 Newhope St Ste A A
Fountain Valley, CA 92708
714-432-0708
Fax: 714-432-1537 888-326-3342
Fudge truffle bars and confections
Principal: Gary Khazanovich
Owner: Martucci Angiano
Estimated Sales: Under $500,000
Number Employees: 8
Type of Packaging: Consumer, Food Service
Brands:
    Fudgescotti

1530 Bodek Kosher Produce Inc
1294 E 8th St
Brooklyn, NY 11230-5106
718-377-4163
Fax: 718-377-0782 info@bodek.com
www.bodek.com
Grade A, California grown produce, strictly supervised from seedling to harvest to production under the Central Rabbinical Congress, OU, and Rabbi Gissinger.
Owner: Solomon Fried
sfried@bodek.com
Secretary: Zvi Gartenhouse
Vice President: Ike Rosenbluth
Estimated Sales: $1-$2,500,000
Number Employees: 5-9

1531 Bodin Foods
704 Avenue D
New Iberia, LA 70560-0527
337-367-1344
Fax: 337-364-4968 www.cajun-recipes.com
Frozen Cajun foods, browning/seasoning sauce, pork boudin, shrimp boudin, crawfish boudin, dressing mix, crawfish pies, meat pies, shrimp and crabmeat pies, and crawfish and crabmeat pies
Owner: Dennis Higginebotham
CEO: Madine Pacetti
Estimated Sales: $500,000
Number Employees: 5-9
Number of Brands: 2
Number of Products: 11
Square Footage: 25635
Type of Packaging: Consumer, Food Service, Private Label
Brands:
    Bodin's
    Brown Kwik
    Cajun Bites

1532 Body Breakthrough Inc
561 Acorn St # I
St Unit I
Deer Park, NY 11729-3600
631-243-2443
Fax: 631-243-2464 800-924-3343
www.bodybreakthrough.com
Processor and exporter of teas including herbal, dietary and antioxidant; also, weight loss aids
President: Cori Lichter
Executive Director: Glenn Lichter
Estimated Sales: Under $800,000
Number Employees: 5-9
Square Footage: 10000
Type of Packaging: Consumer, Private Label
Brands:
    Anti Oxidant Edge

Food Manufacturers / A-Z

Trim Maxx
Yohimbe

1533 Bodyonics Limited
200 Adams Blvd
Farmingdale, NY 11735-6615
516-822-1230
Fax: 516-822-1252
Sports nutrition, vitamins, herbs and supplements.
President: Mel Rich
Sales/Marketing: Andy Fishman
Number Employees: 50-99

1534 Boeger Winery
1709 Carson Rd
Placerville, CA 95667-5195
530-622-8094
Fax: 530-622-8112 800-655-2634
sue@boegerwinery.com www.boegerwinery.com
Wines
Owner/Secretary & Treasurer: Susan Boeger
sue@boegerwinery.com
Manager; President: Justin Boeger
Manager: Brian Bumgarner
Marketing & Public Relations: Tara De Le Rosa
Sales Executive; Sales Mangager: Carl Keinert
Winemaker: Justin Boeger
Estimated Sales: $2-5,000,000
Number Employees: 20-49
Type of Packaging: Private Label

1535 Boehringer Ingelheim Corp
900 Ridgebury Rd
PO Box 368
Ridgefield, CT 06877-1058
203-798-9988
Fax: 203-431-6556 800-243-0127
webmaster@rdg.boehringer-ingelheim.com
www.us.boehringer-ingelheim.com
Organic mineral salts
President: Paul Fonteyne
Number Employees: 5000-9999

1536 Boesl Packing Co
2322 Belair Rd
Baltimore, MD 21213-1283
410-675-1071
Fax: 410-327-4131 800-675-1471
info@k9kraving.com www.k-9kraving.com
Manufacturer and packer of meat products including smoked frankfurters, knockwurst, bologna, salami and bacon; pig tails, neck bones and chitterlings; sausage: hot, smoked and Polish
Owner: Jeffery Burton
jburton@mr.baltimore.com
Senior Executive: J Boesl
Vice President: Robert Barrett
Estimated Sales: $3.2 Million
Number Employees: 1-4
Type of Packaging: Consumer

1537 Boetje Foods Inc
2736 12th Street
Rock Island, IL 61201
309-788-4352
Fax: 309-788-4365 877-726-3853
www.boetjefoodsinc.com
Gourmet mustard
President: Will Kropp
tavery@coynecollege.edu
Production Manager: Harrison Kropp
Estimated Sales: $2.5-5 Million
Number Employees: 5-9
Square Footage: 24000
Type of Packaging: Consumer, Food Service, Private Label, Bulk
Brands:
Dutch Boy

1538 Boggiatto Produce Inc
850 Work St # 201
Salinas, CA 93901-4378
831-424-8952
Fax: 831-424-1974 produce@boggiatto.com
Artichokes, broccoli, Brussels sprouts, cabbage, celery, cilantro, squash, lettuce, romaine lettuce hearts, kale, onions, leeks, peas, parsley, beets, green beans, rapini, spinach, etc

Owner: Kraig Kuska
Controller: Joann Glennon
Vice President: Jeffry Hitchcock
Consulting Chef: Beat Giger
Food Safety Coordinator: Jose Garcia-Canedo
Sales Manager: Kraig Kuska
kraig@boggiatto.com
Sales: Don Day
Growers & Directors: Ron & Ed Panziera
Estimated Sales: $2.5-5,000,000
Number Employees: 10-19
Type of Packaging: Consumer, Food Service
Brands:
Boggiatto
Garden Hearts

1539 Boghosian Raisin Packing Co
726 S 8th St
PO Box 338
Fowler, CA 93625-2506
559-834-5348
Fax: 559-834-1419
Raisins
Owner: Pete Boghosian
pboghosian@boghosianraisin.com
Owner: Paul Boghosian
Human Resource Executive: Roger Stiles
Manufacturing Supervisor: Richard Lokey
Plant Manager: Richard Lokey
Estimated Sales: $7 Million
Number Employees: 50-99
Square Footage: 33000
Type of Packaging: Consumer, Bulk

1540 Bogland
300 Oak Street
Pembroke, MA 02359-1984
781-829-9549
Fax: 781-829-9567
Cranberry chutney, cranberry mustard, cranberry grill sauce, cranberry cabernet vinaigrette, cranberry orange marmalade, cranberry blueberry preserves, Szechuan peanut sauce, margarita madness mustard, port mustard, seafood mustard
President: Jan Baird
Estimated Sales: $2.5-5,000,000
Number Employees: 1-4
Brands:
Bogland
Bogland By the Sea
Boglandish

1541 Bogle Vineyards Inc
37783 County Road 144
Clarksburg, CA 95612-5009
916-744-1030
Fax: 916-744-1187 info@boglewinery.com
www.boglewinery.com
Wine
President: Warren Bogle
Intl. Sales: Jody Bogle
VP: Ryan Bogle
Manager: Eric Aafedt
Vice President of Sales: Christopher Catterton
Human Resources Executive: Cassie Bandelyufter
Office Manager: Sue Upsite
Director of Winemaking: Christopher Smith
Estimated Sales: $2-5,000,000
Number Employees: 1-4
Type of Packaging: Private Label

1542 Bohemian Brewery
94 E 7200
Midvale, UT 84047
801-566-5474
Fax: 801-566-5321 info@bohemianbrewery.com
www.bohemianbrewery.com
Ale and lager
President: Joe Petras
Vice President: Helen Petras
Estimated Sales: Under $500,000
Number Employees: 10
Type of Packaging: Consumer, Food Service
Brands:
Bohemian

1543 Boisset Family Estates
849 Zinfandel Ln
St Helena, CA 94574-1645
707-963-6900
800-878-1123
info@boisset.com www.boissetfamilyestates.com
Wine

President: Jean-Charles Boisset
Controller: Phillip Marquand
VP: Alain Leonnet
Marketing Manager: Lisa Heisinger
Director of Consumer Marketing: Michelle Sitton
Estimated Sales: $7.8 Million
Number Employees: 5-9
Parent Co: LaFamille des Grands Vins
Brands:
Amberhill
Buena Vista Winery
California Rabbit
Deloach
Fog Mountain
Frenchie Winery
Jcb By Jean-Charles Boisset
Lockwood Vineyard
Lyeth Estate
Raymond Vineyards
Sonoma Cuvee
Bouchard Aine & Fils
Domaine De La Vougeraie
French Rabbit
J.Moreau & Fils
La Captive
Louis Bernard
Ropiteau Freres
Louis Bouillot
Beni Di Batasiolo
Neige
Idol Vodka

1544 Boissons Miami Pomor
704 Boulevard Guimond
Longueuil, QC J4G 1T5
Canada
450-677-3744
Fax: 450-677-7826 877-977-3744
www.boissonsmiami.com
Juices, concentrates and crystals
President: Lise Huneault
Vice President: Andre Brisebois
Vice President: Yves Brisebois
Estimated Sales: $1.4 Million
Number Employees: 9
Square Footage: 13500

1545 Boja's Foods Inc
13120 N Wintzell Ave
Bayou La Batre, AL 36509-2138
251-824-4186
Fax: 251-824-7339 www.bojasfoods.com
Crab meat stuffing
CFO: Nancy West
Vice President: Greg Malone
bojacrab@aol.com
Secretary: John Kramer
Manager: Donald Crammond
Estimated Sales: $1.5-2,000,000
Number Employees: 10-19
Brands:
Boja's
Boja's Chef's Delight
Paulines

1546 Bold Coast Smokehouse
224 County Rd
Lubec, ME 04652
207-733-8912
Fax: 207-733-8986 888-733-0807
www.boldcoastsmokehouse.com
Hot and cold smoked Atlantic salmon, smoked salmon, smoked salmon pate and lox, smoked trout pate, finnan haddie, smoked mackeral, smoked salmon kabobs, graulax, smoked lobster products, smoked mussels and smoke scallops.
President/Owner: Vinny Gartmayer
Estimated Sales: $250,000
Number Employees: 3
Type of Packaging: Consumer, Private Label

1547 Bolner's Fiesta Spices
426 Menchaca St
San Antonio, TX 78207
info@fiestaspices.com
www.fiestaspices.com
Processor and importer of dehydrated vegetables, liquid extracts and spices, herbs and seasonings, including: bay leaves, cinnamon, cloves, cumin, sage, nutmeg, oregano, paprika, onion salt, anise, caraway, garlic, celery and mustardseeds, black pepper.
Founder: Clifton Bolner
Plant Manager: James Morris

Food Manufacturers / A-Z

Estimated Sales: Under $1 Million
Number Employees: 100-249
Type of Packaging: Consumer, Food Service, Private Label, Bulk
Brands:
   Fiesta
   Lynwood Farms
   Papa Joe's
   River Road
   Spice Choice
   Spice Ranch
   Spice Star

1548 Bolt House Farms-Shipping Dept
7200 E Brundage Ln
Bakersfield, CA 93307-3099
661-366-7207
Fax: 661-366-0326 800-467-4683
raust@bolthouse.com www.bolthouse.com
Vegetable and melon farming
Chairman: Andre Hdant
CEO: Jeff Dunn
Vice President: Joe Pryor
Engineering and R&D Manager: Robert Misuraca
Director, Quality Compliance: Bela Chandra
VP Marketing: Bryan Reese
VP Sales: Tim McCorkle
Contact: Anthony Abbate
aabbate@bolthouse.com
Production Manager: Aaron Corbett
Purchasing Manager: Jason Higbee
Estimated Sales: $118 Million
Number Employees: 20-49
Parent Co: Campbell Soup Co
Brands:
   Earth Unt Farm
   Green Gaint

1549 Bon Courage Gourmet
2726 Croasdaile Dr
Suite 103-C
Durham, NC 27705
919-973-0920
888-865-5841
info@boncouragegourmet.com
boncouragegourmet.com
European chocolate and confections
President: Michael Barefoot
michael@boncouragegourmet.Com
Vice President: Tim Manale
General Manager: Angela Joines
Year Founded: 2013
Brands:
   Miracle Tree(c)

1550 Bon Secour Fisheries Inc
17449 County Road 49 S
Bon Secour, AL 36511
251-949-7411
Fax: 251-949-6478
bonsec@bonsecourfisheries.com
www.bonsecourfisheries.com
Fresh and frozen flounder, whiting, snapper, shrimp, oysters, scallops, crawfish, snow, soft shell and king crab, lobster, cod, catfish, tuna, grouper, pollock, shark, mahi, talapia, etc.; also, alligator meat.
CFO: Melani Parker
Vice President: Chris Nelson
Director, Sales: Leon Russell
Procurement Manager: Robert Eckerle
Year Founded: 1896
Estimated Sales: $25.10 Million
Number Employees: 100-249
Square Footage: 60000
Type of Packaging: Consumer, Food Service, Bulk
Brands:
   Bon Secour
   Nelson's

1551 Bon Ton Products
275 E Hintz Rd
Wheeling, IL 60090-6002
847-520-8300
Meat buyer, boxed beef and pork cuts.
Owner: George Christie
Marketing Director: Dave Centino
Human Resources Executive: Leslie Baker
Manager: James Cristy
Estimated Sales: $17 Million
Number Employees: 5-9

1552 Bonafide Provisions
San Diego, CA
bonafideprovisions.com
Organic bone broth
Co-Founder & CEO: Sharon Brown
Co-Founder: Alexandra Rains
Co-Founder: Reb Brown
Number of Brands: 1
Number of Products: 5
Type of Packaging: Consumer
Brands:
   BONAFIDE PROVISIONS

1553 Bonduelle North America
540 Chemin Des Patriotes
Saint-denis-sur-richelieu
Quebec, ON J0H 1K0
Canada
450-787-3411
Fax: 450-787-3537 www.familytradition.com
Manufacturer and importer of frozen fruits and vegetables; exporter of canned corn and IQF vegetables
President/CEO: John Omstead
Number Employees: 100-249
Square Footage: 1284000
Type of Packaging: Consumer, Food Service
Other Locations:
   Family Tradition Foods
   Tecumseh, Ontario
Brands:
   Family Traditions
   John O'S

1554 Bone Doctors' BBQ, LLC
718 Eargil Lane
Charlottesville, VA 22902-4302
434-296-7766
Fax: 434-977-6613 sales@bonedoctorsbbq.com
www.bonedoctorsbbq.com
BBQ sauce, grilling sauces, marinades, spices.
Marketing: David Heilbronner

1555 Bone Suckin' Sauce
1109 Agriculture St
Suite 1
Raleigh, NC 27603
919-833-7647
Fax: 919-821-5781 bonesuckin.com
Barbecue, grilling and marinating sauces
Founder: Phil Ford
Number of Brands: 1
Number of Products: 15
Type of Packaging: Consumer
Brands:
   BONE SUCKIN'

1556 Bonert's Pies Inc
2727 S Susan St
Santa Ana, CA 92704-5817
714-540-3535
Fax: 714-540-9615 susanm@bonertspies.com
Fruit, creme, meringue, no sugar added, and no top-ready to finish pies.
President & CEO: Michael Bonert
michaelb@bonertspies.com
CFO: Harry Kaplan
Vice President of R&D: Greg Guerra
Sales Representative: Devin Kuy
Production Manager: Laura Perez
Purchasing Agent: Jeanne Romig
Estimated Sales: $13 Million
Number Employees: 100-249

1557 Bongard's Creameries
250 Lake Dr E
Chanhassen, MN 55317
952-277-5500
info@bongards.com
www.bongards.com
Dairy products including cheese and whey
President/CEO: Keith Grove
CFO: Chris Freeman
Marketing Executive: Sheri Nadeau
VP, Sales & Marketing: Scott Tomes
VP, Operations: Brent Jewett
Number Employees: 50-99
Parent Co: Land O'Lakes
Type of Packaging: Consumer, Private Label

1558 Bongiovi Brand Pasta Sauces
PO Box 3941
Valley Village, CA 91617
434-296-7766
Fax: 434-977-6613 orders@bongiovibrand.com
www.bongiovibrand.com
Manufacturer of pasta sauces.
President: John Bongiovi
Brands:
   Bongiovi Pasta Sauces

1559 Bonk Breaker
1810-H Berkeley St
Santa Monica, CA 90404
310-315-4129
info@bonkbreaker.com
bonkbreaker.com
Protein bars, nutrition bars and
Founder: Phil Ford
Number of Brands: 1
Number of Products: 21
Type of Packaging: Consumer
Brands:
   BONK BREAKER
   PROTEIN BONK BREAKER
   ENERGY CHEWS
   REAL HYDRATION

1560 Bonnie & Don Flavours Inc.
919 Kamato Dr
Mississauga, ON L4W 2R5
Canada
905-625-1813
Fax: 905-626-1824 info@bdflavours.com
www.bdflavours.com
Artifical and organic flavors and extracts
Manager Marketing & Business Development: Ken Halnan

1561 Bonnie Baking Company
800 Boyd Boulevard
La Porte, IN 46350-4419
219-362-4561
Fax: 219-325-0030
Breads and rolls
Manager: John West
Contact: Ben Vales
englap@lewisbakeries.com
Estimated Sales: $20-50 Million
Number Employees: 100-249

1562 Bonnie Doon LLC
2941 Moose Trl
Elkhart, IN 46514-8230
574-264-3390
Fax: 574-264-6208
Ice cream
President: Samuel Dugan
CEO: Sam Dugan
Vice President: Jim Otis
Office Manager: Jan Miller
Estimated Sales: $1-2 Million
Number Employees: 20-49
Type of Packaging: Food Service, Bulk

1563 Bonnie's Ice Cream
21 Leaman Road
Paradise, PA 17562-9660
717-687-9301
Dairy products
President: Lou Termini
Vice President: Dane Cherry
Estimated Sales: $1-2,500,000
Number Employees: 14

1564 Bonnie's Jams
94 Foster St
Cambridge, MA 02138-4729
617-714-5380
info@bonniesjams.com
www.bonniesjams.com
Jams, preserves and corporate gifts.
President: Bonnie Shershow
Contact: Bonnie Jams
bonnie@bonniesjams.com
Number Employees: 5-9

1565 Bonny Doon Vineyard
328 Ingalls Street
Santa Cruz, CA 95060
831-425-3625
888-819-6789
sales@bonnydoonvineyard.com
www.bonnydoonvineyard.com
Wines
President: Randall Grahm
Owner: Lisa Kohrf
Marketing Director: Nicholas Tucker
National Sales Manager: Keith Shulsky
Contact: Nicole Beatie
nicole@bonnydoonvineyard.com
Operations Manager: Ed Moya

Food Manufacturers / A-Z

Estimated Sales: $21,000,000
Number Employees: 43
Type of Packaging: Private Label

1566 Bono USA
19 Gardner Rd
Suite E
Fairfield, NJ 07004
862-485-8729
www.bonousainc.com
Extra virgin olive oil, table olives and marmalades
Year Founded: 1934

1567 Bonterra Vineyard
12625 E Side Road
Hopland, CA 95449
707-744-7575
Fax: 707-744-1844 www.bonterra.com
Wines
Vineyard Director: Dave Koball
Brands:
   Bonterra

1568 Bonumose LLC
1725 Discovery Dr.
Suite 220
Charlottesville, VA 22911
erogers@bonumose.com
bonumose.com
Sugar
Co-Founder & CEO: Ed Rogers
Co-Founder & Chief Scientific Officer: Daniel Wichelecki
Engineering & Operations Manager: Mansoor Pasha
Year Founded: 2016
Type of Packaging: Private Label

1569 Bookbinder Specialties LLC
601 Beatty Rd
Media, PA 19063-1642
215-322-1305
Fax: 267-687-0112
Canned soups and broths.
President: Sean O'Neil
Contact: Colin O'Neil
colin@bookbinderspecialties.com
Brands:
   Bookbinder's

1570 Boone's Butcher Shop
100 Old Bloomfield Pike
Bardstown, KY 40004
502-348-3668
Fax: 502-348-4046 888-253-3384
info@boonesbutchershop.com
www.boonesbutchershop.com
Packer of processed beef and pork products
President: Jerry Boone
boonesbutcher@bardstown.com
Estimated Sales: $6 Million
Number Employees: 20-49

1571 Booneway Farms
167 Glade Rd
Berea, KY 4043
859-986-2636
Fax: 859-986-3583
Mustards, hamburger marinades, jellies, preserves, seasonings and spices
President: Williams Arant, Jr.
Estimated Sales: $2.5-5,000,000
Number Employees: 20-49
Type of Packaging: Private Label

1572 Boordy Vineyards Inc
12820 Long Green Pike
Hydes, MD 21082-9541
410-592-5015
Fax: 410-592-5385 wine-info@boordy.com
www.boordy.com
Wines
President: Robert Deford
wine-info@deboordy.com
Owner: Julie Deford
Owner: Phillip Wagner
Vice President: Anne Deford
Accounting Director: Laurie Kregecz
Marketing Director: Susan Rayner
Public Relations: Rory Calhoun
Production Manager: Tom Burns
Estimated Sales: Under $700,000
Number Employees: 10-19
Type of Packaging: Private Label

Brands:
   Boordy Vineyards

1573 Boothbay Lobster Wharf
97 Atlantic Ave
Boothbay Harbor, ME 04538-2220
207-633-4900
Fax: 207-633-4077
sales@boothbaylobsterwharf.com
Lobster
Owner: Kim Simmons
ksimmons@boothbaylobsterwharf.com
Estimated Sales: Less Than $500,000
Number Employees: 1-4

1574 Boquet's Oyster House
6645 Highway 56
Chauvin, LA 70344-2630
504-594-5574
Fax: 253-761-0504
Fresh, frozen, shucked oysters
President: Lawrenece Bouquet, Jr.

1575 Borden Canada
6890 Notre Dame Street E
Montreal, QC H1N 2E5
Canada
514-256-1601
Fax: 514-256-2537
Dairy
Quality Assurance: Daniel L'Heureux

1576 Borden Dairy
8750 N Central Expy
Suite 400
Dallas, TX 75231
214-459-1100
855-311-1583
www.bordendairy.com
Milk, cream, buttermilk, dips and sour cream, juices, teas and flavored drinks.
CEO: Steve McCormick
IT: Brad Moore
bmills@dairyfreshcorp.com
Number Employees: 100-249
Number of Brands: 1
Type of Packaging: Consumer, Food Service
Brands:
   Borden Dairy

1577 Border Foods
5425 Boone Ave N
New Hope, MN 55428
763-559-7338
comments@borderfoods.com
www.borderfoods.com
Mexican food products including; green chiles, jalapenos and red jalapenos, salsas, enchilada sauces, tomatillos, chipotles, cascabellas, and red chiles.
Chief Executive Officer: Lee Engler
VP, Operations: Carol Williams
General Manager: Jeremy Poole
Year Founded: 1996
Estimated Sales: $24.7 Million
Number Employees: 150
Square Footage: 24488
Type of Packaging: Food Service, Private Label, Bulk
Other Locations:
   Basic American Foods
   Vacaville CA
Brands:
   Classic Casserole
   Golden Grill
   Nature's Own
   Potatoe Pearls
   Quick Start
   Redi Shred
   Regional Recipe
   Santiago

1578 Borders Sporting Goods
5876 US Route 60
Ashland, KY 41102-9508
606-928-6326
Fax: 606-928-1072
www.borderssportinggoods.com
Beef, pork, veal and lamb
Owner: Greg Borders
sales@borderssportinggoods.com
Owner: Reggie Danzhorn
Estimated Sales: $1-2.5 Million
Number Employees: 10-19
Type of Packaging: Consumer

1579 Bordoni Vineyards
Rte 4
Box 885K
Vallejo, CA 94591-9802
707-642-1504
Manufacturer of wines.
President: Jim Bordoni
Estimated Sales: $5-10,000,000
Number Employees: 1-4

1580 Borgattis Ravioli
632 E 187th St
Bronx, NY 10458
718-367-3799
Fax: 718-367-2229 www.borgattis.com/ravioli
Pasta
Owner: Mario Borgatti
Estimated Sales: $1-2,500,000
Number Employees: 1-4

1581 Borinquen Biscuit Corporation
PO Box 1607
Yauco, PR 00698
787-856-3030
Fax: 787-856-5339
oficina@galletasroyalborinquen.com
www.galletasroyalborinquen.com
Manufacturers of quality soda crackers, cookies and biscuits.
President: Antonio Rodriguez Zamora
Treasurer: Nora Rodriguez
Vice President: Antonio Morales
Secretary: Gevoyeva Rodriguez
Human Relations Manager: Hircio Matey
Purchasing Manager: Antonio Rodriguez Morales
Estimated Sales: $15 Million
Number Employees: 130
Square Footage: 174000
Type of Packaging: Consumer, Private Label
Brands:
   Cien En Boca
   Florecitas
   Rica
   Royal Borinquen Export
   Vanilla Imperial

1582 Bornstein Seafoods
PO Box 188
Bellingham, WA 98225
360-734-7990
Fax: 360-734-5732 www.bornstein.com
Live, fresh and frozen seafood.
CEO: Colin Bornstein
bornstein@bornstein.com
Year Founded: 1934
Estimated Sales: $20-50 Million
Number Employees: 50-99
Number of Brands: 1
Type of Packaging: Consumer, Food Service
Brands:
   Bornstein

1583 Bornt & Sons Inc
2307 E US Highway 98
Holtville, CA 92250-9543
760-356-1066
Fax: 760-356-1066
Organic vegetables
Owner: Alan Bornt
borntfamilyfarms@aol.com
CFO: Mary Bornt
Vice President; Office Manager: Sandra Gaskin
VP Marketing/Sales: John Prock
Estimated Sales: $3,4,000,000
Number Employees: 50-99
Brands:
   Bornt Family Farms
   Ocean Organics

1584 Borra Vineyards
1301 E Armstrong Rd
Lodi, CA 95242-9423
209-368-2446
Fax: 209-369-5116 info@borravineyards.com
www.borravineyards.com
Wine
Owner: Steve Borra
sjb@lodiirrigation.com
CEO: Beverly Borra
VP Marketing: Gina Granlees
Estimated Sales: $1-3,000,000
Number Employees: 1-4
Type of Packaging: Private Label

Food Manufacturers / A-Z

Brands:
  Borra

1585 Bos Smoked Fish Inc
1175 Patullo Avenue
Woodstock, ON N4S 7W3
Canada
519-537-5000
Fax: 519-537-5522 info@bossmokedfish.com
www.bossmokedfish.com
Smoked fish
President: Rein Bos
Sales: Chris Bruines
Sales: Kirk VanderSpek
Plant Manager: Pieter Bos
Estimated Sales: $6 Million
Number Employees: 15
Type of Packaging: Consumer, Food Service, Private Label, Bulk

1586 Bosco Products Inc
441 Main Rd
Towaco, NJ 07082-1201
973-334-7534
Fax: 973-334-2617   800-438-2672
Chocolate and flavored syrup and drink products
President: Steven Sanders
steven@seabreezesyrups.com
Number Employees: 50-99
Brands:
  Bosco

1587 Boscoli Foods Inc
2254 Greenwood St
Kenner, LA 70062-7908
504-469-5500
Fax: 504-469-5548 edmontaldo@yahoo.com
www.boscoli.com
Fine Italian gourmet foods.
Owner/President: John Occhipinti
President: Sybil Klopf
Treasurer: Kathleen Occhipinti
Purchasing: Cindy Lopez
Estimated Sales: $900,000
Number Employees: 5-9

1588 Boskovich Farms Inc
711 Diaz Ave
PO Box 1352
Oxnard, CA 93030-7247
805-487-2299
Fax: 805-487-5189
feedback@boskovichfarms.com
www.boskovichfarms.com
Bok choy, artichokes, cilantro, endive, cebollitas, brussels sprouts, onions, lettuce, celery, carrots, cabbages, bell peppers, apples, radishes, spinach, beets, asparagus, kale, leeks, napa, parsley, radish, strawberries and sugarpeas.
President: Philip Boskovich
Co-CEO: Joseph Boskovich
Co-CEO: George Boskovich
lmartinez@boskovichfarms.com
CFO: Lynn Grayson
Sales Manager: Russ Widerburg
Human Resources Manager: Martha Mayorga
Estimated Sales: Over $1 Billion
Number Employees: 1000-4999
Type of Packaging: Consumer, Food Service
Other Locations:
  Transwest Cooling
  Yuma AZ
  Growers Street Cooling
  Salinas CA
  Shipping Distribution
  Oxnard CA

1589 Boskydel Vineyard
7501 E Otto Rd
Lake Leelanau, MI 49653-9419
231-256-7272
jim@boskydel.com
www.boskydel.com
Wines
Owner: Bernard Rink
jim@boskydel.com
Estimated Sales: Less Than $500,000
Number Employees: 1-4
Type of Packaging: Private Label
Brands:
  Boskydel

1590 Bossen
31010 San Antonio St
Hayward, CA 94544
510-324-0168
service@bossenstore.com
www.bossenstore.com
Bubble tea; iced tea; juice mixes; syrup.
Co-Founder: Haber Tu
Co-Founder: Edward Shen
Year Founded: 2012
Parent Co: Leadway International, Inc.

1591 Boston America Corporation
325 New Boston St
Unit 17
Woburn, MA 01801
781-933-3535
Fax: 781-933-3539
customerservice@bostonamerica.com
www.bostonamerica.com
Tinned candies and cookies
President: Matthew Kavet
Contact: Jim Costa
jim.costa@bostonamerica.com
Estimated Sales: $1-3 Million
Number Employees: 20-49
Brands:
  Bubblegum
  Grinch
  My Little Pony
  Powerpuff Girls
  Scooby Doo
  Spider-Man
  Strawberry Shortcake

1592 Boston Beer Co Inc.
1 Design Center Pl.
Suite 850
Boston, MA 02210
617-368-5000
Fax: 617-368-5500   888-661-2337
www.bostonbeer.com
Beer.
President/CEO: David Burwick
Chairman/Founder: C. James Koch
CFO/Treasurer: Frank Smalla
VP, Brewing: David Grinnell
Chief Sales Manager: John Geist
Year Founded: 1984
Estimated Sales: $921 Million
Number Employees: 1000-4999
Number of Brands: 5
Square Footage: 33500
Type of Packaging: Consumer, Food Service
Brands:
  Angry Orchard®
  Samuel Adams®
  Twisted Tea®
  Truly
  A & S Brewing

1593 Boston Chowda
30 River St
Haverhill, MA 01832-5402
978-478-0500
Fax: 978-478-3588   800-992-0054
info@bostonchowda.com   www.bostonchowda.com
Frozen soups and chowders
President: Richard Lamattina
Director: Paul Cassidy
Director: John Leroy
Director: Alan Katz
Manager: Michael Lamattina
Year Founded: 1987
Estimated Sales: Less Than $500,000
Number Employees: 5-9
Square Footage: 13000
Brands:
  Bay State Chowda

1594 Boston Coffee Cake
351 Willow Street South
North Andover, MA 01845
800-434-0500
customerservice@bostoncoffeecake.com
www.bostoncoffeecake.com
Coffee cake
Founder: Mark Forman
customerservice@bostoncoffeecake.com

1595 Boston Direct Lobsters
207 Iris Ave
Jefferson, LA 70121-2807
504-834-6404
Fax: 504-834-6404
Lobsters
President/Owner: Earl Duke
directlobster@aol.com
Estimated Sales: $340,000
Number Employees: 1-4

1596 Boston Fruit Slice & Confectionery Corporation
250 Canal St
Lawrence, MA 01840
978-686-2699
Fax: 978-686-5898 rick@bostonfruitslice.com
www.bostonfruitslice.com
Jellied fruit slices
President: John Morrissey
Executive Director/Hr Manager: Richard Hiera
Purchasing: Gail Laughlin
Estimated Sales: $3.3 Million
Number Employees: 30
Brands:
  Boston Fruit Slices
  Polly Orchard

1597 Boston Seafarms
119 Marlborough Street
Boston, MA 2116
617-784-4777
Fax: 800-692-9907 bostonseafarms@gmail.com
www.bostonseafarm.com
Processor, wholesaler/distributor, importer and exporter of seafood including fish and shellfish
President/CEO: Adam Weinberg
bostonseafarms@gmail.com
Estimated Sales: $12-13,000,000
Number Employees: 5
Square Footage: 36000

1598 Boston Spice & Tea Company
12207 Obannons Mill Rd
Boston, VA 22713
540-547-3907
Fax: 540-547-3656   800-966-4372
Herbal tea, vinegar, seasonings, mustard, sherry-pepper hot sauce, wassil, mulling and corned beef spices and dry bean soup mixes
President/Owner: Joann Neal
Director, Marketing & Sales: Greaner Neal
Estimated Sales: $.5-1 million
Number Employees: 5-9
Type of Packaging: Consumer
Brands:
  Boston Spices
  Logyan's Garden
  Logyn'S Garden Soups
  O'Bannon's
  Stews and Sauces

1599 Boston Stoker
10855 Engle Rd
Vandalia, OH 45377-9439
937-890-6401
Fax: 937-890-6403 www.bostonstoker.com
Coffee
President: Eckley Adams
adamse@bostonstoker.com
Secretary/Treasurer: Sally Dean
Vice President: Henry Dean
Human Resources Director: Annette Sabwani
Director Of Operation: Travis Qualls
Plant Manager: John McWilliams
Purchasing Manager: Mandi Jamison
Estimated Sales: $6,000,000
Number Employees: 10-19
Type of Packaging: Private Label

1600 Boston Tea Company
560 Hudson St
Suite 3
Hackensack, NJ 07601
201-440-3004
Fax: 201-440-3005   800-495-9026
www.bostontea.com
Teas
President: Andy Jacobs
Vice President: Mary Jacobs
Contact: Carleen Failla
cfailla@bostontea.com
Office Manager: Eva Kotsonas
Director of Product Development: Carleen Violante

Food Manufacturers / A-Z

Estimated Sales: $800,000-$1,000,000
Number Employees: 8
Brands:
  Beddy By
  Lemon Dew
  Magic Mountain
  Ming Cha
  Natco
  Pick O' the Bushel
  Razzle Dazzle
  Spice Bouquet

1601 Boston's Best Coffee Roasters
43 Norfolk Ave
South Easton, MA 02375-1190
508-238-8393
Fax: 508-238-6835 800-898-8393
sales@bostonsbestcoffee.com
www.bostonsbestcoffee.com
Coffee, mixers and filters
President: Jacqueline Dovner
CEO: Stephen Fortune
Director of Fundraising Sales: Erin Woodard
Contact: Mary Burke
marymb@bostonsbestcoffee.com
Production Manager: Rocky Raposa
Estimated Sales: Less Than $500,000
Number Employees: 5-9
Square Footage: 5692
Type of Packaging: Consumer, Food Service, Private Label, Bulk
Brands:
  David's Gourmet Coffee
  Gold Star Coffee
  Premier Coffee
  Tropical Coffee

1602 Botanical Bakery, LLC
PO Box 11083
Napa, CA 94581
707-344-8103
Fax: 707-863-8949
Shortbread cookies.
CEO: Sondra Wells

1603 Botanical Products
34725 Bogart Dr
Springville, CA 93265-9602
559-539-3432
Fax: 559-539-2058
Processor and exporter of tablets, capsules, extracts and powders made from yucca and melatonin
President: Gordon Bean
VP: Joyce Bean
Estimated Sales: $1-2.5 Million
Number Employees: 1-4
Square Footage: 4000
Type of Packaging: Consumer
Brands:
  Desert Pride
  Desert Wonder

1604 Botsford Fisheries
Po Box 1093
Cap Pele, NB E4N 3B3
Canada
506-577-4327
Fax: 506-577-2846 info@botsfordfisheries.com
www.botsfordfisheries.com
Processor and exporter of fresh and smoked herring
President: William LeBlanc
Export Sales Manager: Janice Ryan
Plant Manager: Clement LeBlanc
Estimated Sales: $2,500,000
Number Employees: 50-99
Square Footage: 80000
Type of Packaging: Consumer, Food Service, Private Label, Bulk

1605 Bottle Green Drinks Company
2375 Tedlost
Unit 1
Mississauga, ON L5A 3W7
Canada
905-273-6137
Fax: 905-273-3186 info@bottlegreen.co.uk
www.bottlegreendrinks.com
Nonalcoholic and carbonated beverages including limeflower, elderflower, cranberry and lemongrass
President: Andrew James
CFO: Corrie James
Estimated Sales: $2,3000,000
Number Employees: 13
Number of Brands: 2
Number of Products: 9
Type of Packaging: Consumer, Food Service, Private Label
Brands:
  Bottle Green

1606 Bottom Line Foods
15757 Pines Blvd # 302
Suite 302
Pembroke Pines, FL 33027-1207
954-843-0562
Fax: 954-843-0568
Distributor and packer, exporter for frozen foods, meats, cheese, groceries, seafood, spices, etc.
President: Rein Bos
General Manager: Brandon Koppert
Estimated Sales: $1.1 Million
Number Employees: 1-4
Square Footage: 4000
Type of Packaging: Food Service, Private Label, Bulk

1607 Bou Brands
135 Madison Ave
5th Floor
New York, NY 10016
858-401-3356
bouforyou.com
Bouillon cubes
General Manager: Zach Bluemer
Number of Brands: 1
Number of Products: 7
Type of Packaging: Consumer
Brands:
  BOU

1608 Bouchaine Vineyards
1075 Buchli Station Rd
Napa, CA 94559-9716
707-252-9006
Fax: 707-252-0401 800-654-9463
www.bouchaine.com
Wines
Propietor/President: Tattiana Copeland
Proprietor/Chairman: Gerret Copeland
Vice President, Wine Production &Sales: Greg Gauthier
General Manager & Winemaker: Michael Richmond
mrichmond@bouchaine.com
Estimated Sales: $2.5-5,000,000
Number Employees: 10-19

1609 Bouchard Family Farm
3 Strip Rd
Fort Kent, ME 04743-1550
207-834-3237
Fax: 207-834-7422 800-239-3237
bouchard@ployes.com www.ployes.com
Processor and exporter of buckwheat pancake mixes and flour
Owner: Joseph Bouchard
bouchard@ployes.com
Director: Jane Crawford
Treasurer: Aldan Bouchard
Sales/Marketing Executive: Elaine Mininger
Estimated Sales: Under $200,000
Number Employees: 5-9
Square Footage: 110000
Type of Packaging: Consumer, Food Service
Brands:
  Bouchard Family Farm

1610 Boudreaux's Foods
5401 Toler St
New Orleans, LA 70123
504-733-8440
Fax: 504-866-1965
Refrigerated entrees, salad dressings, breads, whole wheat pasta, soups, etc
President: Vince Hayward
Estimated Sales: $1-3,000,000
Number Employees: 1-4
Square Footage: 2000
Type of Packaging: Consumer
Brands:
  Author's Choice
  Boudreaux's

1611 Boulder Beer
2880 Wilderness Pl
Boulder, CO 80301-5401
303-444-8448
Fax: 303-444-4796 webguy@boulderbeer.com
www.boulderbeer.com
Beer and ale
President: Annie Alwin
aalwin@boulderbeer.com
Marketing Director: Dan Weltz
Area Sales Manager: Marvin Simpson
Public Relations Director: Tess McFadden
VP Brewing Operations: David Zuckerman
Estimated Sales: $6 Million
Number Employees: 50-99
Number of Brands: 9
Number of Products: 1
Square Footage: 36000

1612 Boulder Brands, Inc.
115 West Century Road
Suite 260
Paramus, NJ 07652-1432
201-421-3970
Ed.Bryson@fleishman.com
www.smartbalance.com
Buttery spreads
President/COO: Terrence Schulke
Chairman/CEO: Stephen Hughes
Chief Finacial Officer: Christine Sacco
EVP/General Counsel: Norman Matar
Chief Innovation Officer: Peter Dray
Contact: Michael Adamson
madamson@boulderbrands.com
Estimated Sales: $1.5 Million
Number Employees: 56
Brands:
  Smart Balance®
  Heart Right ®

1613 Boulder Canyon Natural Foods
1898 S Flatiron Court
Suite 120
Boulder, CO 80301
303-546-9939
Fax: 303-546-9133 www.bouldercanyonfoods.com
Kettle chips
Co-Founder: Don Poore
Co-Founder: Jay Poore
Year Founded: 1994
Number of Brands: 1
Number of Products: 30
Type of Packaging: Consumer
Brands:
  BOULDER CANYON

1614 Boulder Cookie
Boulder, CO 80516
bouldercookie.com
Paleo cookies
Number of Brands: 1
Number of Products: 6
Type of Packaging: Consumer
Brands:
  BOULDER COOKIE

1615 Boulder Creek Brewing Company
13040 Highway 9
Boulder Creek, CA 95006-9154
831-338-7882
Fax: 831-338-7583
Beer, ale, lager
Owner: Nancy Long
President: Morgan Scarborough
Estimated Sales: &500,000-1,000,000
Number Employees: 18
Brands:
  Boulder Creek
  Redwood Ale

1616 Boulder Granola
PO Box 6114
Boulder, CO 80308-6114
303-443-1136
www.bouldergranola.com
Organic granola. Gluten free and dairy free varieties available.
Contact: Jody Nagel
jody@bouldergranola.com
Type of Packaging: Consumer

Food Manufacturers / A-Z

1617 Boulder Homemade Inc
2935 Baseline Rd # 200
Boulder, CO 80303-2367
303-494-0366
Fax: 303-494-5589 800-691-5002
glennise@bouldericecream.com
www.bouldericecream.com
Natural and organic ice cream, gelato, sorbet, and base mixes.
Contact: Glennise Humphrey
glennise@bouldericecream.com
Number Employees: 5-9
Type of Packaging: Consumer, Bulk
Brands:
  BOULDER ICE CREAM

1618 Boulder Organic Foods
6363 Horizon Lane
Niwot, CO 80503
303-530-0470
hello@boulderorganicfoods.com
boulderorganicfoods.com
Fresh soup made with organic and gluten-free ingredients. Some of their varietites include vegan, vegetarian, and dariy-free options.
Founder & President: Kate Brown
CEO: Greg Powers
Director, Marketing & Sustainability: Jen-ai Stokesbary
Plant Manager: Wyatt Miller
Year Founded: 2008
Estimated Sales: $200 Million
Number Employees: 51-200
Type of Packaging: Consumer, Food Service, Private Label, Bulk

1619 Boulder Sausage Co
513 S Pierce Ave
Louisville, CO 80027-3019
303-665-6302
Fax: 303-665-3109 866-529-0595
www.bouldersausage.com
Meat
Vice President: Tom Griffiths
bouldersausage@webaccess.net
Secretary/Treasurer: James Burton
Vice President: Donald Gullickson
Saleman Manager: Ronda Haire
Office Manager;Operations Manager: Suzanne Richards
Estimated Sales: $2,4,000,000
Number Employees: 20-49
Number of Products: 14
Type of Packaging: Consumer, Food Service, Private Label, Bulk
Brands:
  Boulder Sausage Products
  Private Label Products
  Rocky Mountain Products

1620 Boulder Vegans LLC
4947 S Urban Ct
Morrison, CO 80465-2017
303-667-5628
info@bouldervegans.com
www.beyond-better.com
Vegan cheese and cheese products.
Owner: Kerry Behrens
Brands:
  Beyond Better

1621 Boulevard Brewing
2501 Southwest Blvd
Kansas City, MO 64108-2345
816-474-7095
Fax: 816-474-1722 fineales@blvdbeer.com
www.boulevardia.com
Ale, lager, stout and seasonal beer
President: John McDonald
COO: Steve Mills
CFO: Jeff Krum
Marketing Director: Jeremy Ragonese
VP Sales: Bob Sullivan
Hr Manager: Nicole Thibodeau
Manager: Joe Palausky
Production Manager: Mike Youngquist
Estimated Sales: $27,000,000
Number Employees: 50-99
Type of Packaging: Consumer, Food Service

1622 Bouma Meats
PO Box 925
Provost, AB T0B 3S0
Canada
780-753-2092
Fax: 780-753-4939 bouma_meats@hotmail.com
www.provostnews.ca/boumameats/
Beef and pork including fresh, frozen, portion controlled, sausage and deli cuts; also, bacon and ham
Joint Owner/ Store Operator: Ben Richter
Joint Owner/ Plant Operator: Tim Rachinski
Estimated Sales: $2,000,000
Number Employees: 8
Type of Packaging: Consumer, Food Service, Private Label, Bulk
Brands:
  Bouma

1623 Boundary Fish Company
225 Sigurdson Ave
Blaine, WA 98230-4004
360-332-6715
Fax: 360-332-8785 arnold@boundaryfish.com
www.boundaryfish.com
Dungeness crab, pacific salmon, halibut, black cod, dogfish.
President: Arnold Yuki
Estimated Sales: $20-50 Million
Number Employees: 20-49
Type of Packaging: Consumer, Food Service

1624 Bountiful Larder LLC
218 Butte Ave.
Crested Butte, CO 81224
303-619-8056
800-676-5057
info@jacksonshonest.com
www.jacksonshonest.com
Manufacturer of tortilla and potato chips.
Co-Founder & CEO: Megan Reamer
Social Media and Marketing: Lindsey Schauer
Director of Sales: Jessica Moore
Director of Operations: David McCormick

1625 Bountiful Pantry
PO Box 179
Nantucket, MA 02584
617-487-8019
Fax: 508-374-5850 info@bountifulpantry.com
www.bountifulpantry.com
Soup mixes, side dishes, waffle mixes, bread, roll, scone and biscuit mixes, cookie and dessert mixes and teas and coffees

1626 Bourbon Barrel Foods
1201 Story Ave # 175
Suite 175
Louisville, KY 40206-1768
502-333-6103
Fax: 502-333-6104 info@bourbonbarrelfoods.com
www.bourbonbarrelfoods.com
Gourmet foods.
President: Matt Jamie
info@bourbonbarrelfoods.com
Number Employees: 10-19

1627 Boutique Seafood Brokers
1326 White St SW
Atlanta, GA 30310-1648
404-752-8852
Fax: 404-752-6634 www.buckheadrestaurants.com
Seafood, red snapper, sea bass, lobster meat, crabmeat, grouper
President/CEO: Pano Karatassos
CFO: Christo Makrides
Senior Director of Marketing: Jennifer Parker
Director of Operations: Niko Karatassos
Estimated Sales: $4.5 Million
Number Employees: 1-4

1628 Bouvry Exports Calgary
222 58 Avenue SW
Suite 312
Calgary, AB T2H 2S3
Canada
403-253-0717
Fax: 403-259-3568
Horse meat, bison and beef
President: Claude Bouvry
CEO: John McNaughton
General Manager: Darin Sjonger
Sales: Alain Bouvry
Estimated Sales: $21,6,000,000
Number Employees: 150

Type of Packaging: Consumer, Bulk

1629 Bove's of Vermont
68 Pearl St
Burlington, VT 05403
802-862-7235
Fax: 802-651-9371 802-862-6651
sauceboy@Boves.com www.boves.com
Marinara sauce, roasted garlic sauce, chianti mushroom sauce, romano pomodoro sauce.
President: Mark Bove
sauceboy@boves.com
Vice President/Secretary/Treasurer: Richard Bove
Estimated Sales: $170,000
Number Employees: 3
Brands:
  Bove's of Vermont

1630 Bow Valley Brewing Company
109 Boulder Crescent
Canmore, AB T1W 1L4
Canada
403-678-2739
Fax: 403-678-8813
Lager
President: Hugh Hancock
Treasurer: Jim Lawson
Secretary: Wayne McNeill
Number Employees: 6
Type of Packaging: Consumer, Food Service
Brands:
  Bow Valley

1631 Bowery Farming Inc.
151 W 26th St.
12th Fl.
New York, NY 10001
boweryfarming.com
Leafy greens grown without pesticides and non-GMO seeds.
Co-Founder & CEO: Irving Fain
Co-Founder: Brian Falther
Co-Founder & Strategic Finance: David Golden
Marketing Director: Katie Seawell
Sales Director: Carmela Cugini
Finance & Legal Director: Darren Thompson
Year Founded: 2015
Number Employees: 51-200
Type of Packaging: Private Label

1632 Bowman & Landes Turkeys
6490 Ross Rd
New Carlisle, OH 45344-8801
937-845-9466
Fax: 937-845-9998 877-466-9466
info@bowmanlandes.com
www.bowmanlandes.com
Free range turkeys
President: Anita Bowman
anita@bowmanlandes.com
Estimated Sales: $10-20 Million
Number Employees: 100-249
Type of Packaging: Consumer, Bulk

1633 Bowness Bakery
4280-23rd Street NE
Calgary, AB T2E 6X7
Canada
403-250-9760
Fax: 403-291-9129
Specialty breads, pretzels and pizza shells
CEO: Shams Habib
Estimated Sales: $5,000,000
Number Employees: 40
Type of Packaging: Consumer, Food Service, Bulk
Brands:
  Bowness Baker
  Frisches Brot
  Pretzeland

1634 Bowser Meat Processing
401 S Palmberg St
Meriden, KS 66512
785-484-2454
Meat including sausage
Owner: Gary Koerner
Manager: Kirsti Petesch
Estimated Sales: $140,000
Number Employees: 4
Type of Packaging: Consumer

Food Manufacturers / A-Z

1635 Boyajian LLC
144 Will Dr
Canton, MA 02021-3704
781-828-9966
Fax: 781-828-9922 800-965-0665
customerservice@boyajianinc.com
www.boyajianinc.com
Vinegars, infused oils and natural flavorings.
Owner/President: John Boyajian
jboyajian@boyajianinc.com
Director of Marketing: Amy Alberti
Human Resources Manager: Zovig Kanarian
General Manager: Zanig Kanarian
Estimated Sales: $1 Million
Number Employees: 10-19
Square Footage: 40000
Type of Packaging: Consumer, Food Service, Private Label, Bulk
Brands:
   Boyajian

1636 (HQ)Boyd's Coffee Co
Portland, OR 97230
800-735-2878
customerservicena@farmerbros.com
www.boydscoffeestore.com
Coffees, teas, cocoa, hot and frozen beverages
Senior Sales Manager: Gabriel Dominguez
VP of Manufacturing: Mitch Karstadt
Estimated Sales: $49 Million
Number Employees: 250-499
Number of Brands: 7
Parent Co: Farmer Bros Co
Type of Packaging: Food Service
Other Locations:
   Boyd's Coffee Company
   Coeur D Alene ID
Brands:
   Boyd's Coffee
   Coffee House Roasters
   Island Mist Iced Tea
   Italia D'Oro Coffee
   Techni-Brew
   Today
   Viaggio Coffee

1637 Boyd's Sausage Co
626 Highway 1 S
Washington, IA 52353-9786
319-653-5715
bls11388@gmail.com
Beef jerky, bologna and deer meat products including sausage
Owner: Brandon Statler
Estimated Sales: $270,000
Number Employees: 5-9
Square Footage: 10500
Type of Packaging: Consumer, Bulk

1638 Boyer Candy Co Inc
821 17th St
Altoona, PA 16601-2074
814-944-9401
Fax: 814-944-4923 www.boyercandies.com
Chocolate confectionery products including shell molded chocolates, cup candy and seasonal novelties
CEO: Robert Faith
rfaith@boyercandies.com
Plant Manager: Jim Lidwell
Estimated Sales: $9,000,000
Number Employees: 50-99
Number of Brands: 8
Square Footage: 150000
Type of Packaging: Consumer, Private Label, Bulk
Brands:
   Bartons
   Boxer
   Boyer
   Casanova
   Hill of Westchester
   Kron
   Schrafft's
   Winters

1639 Boyer's Coffee
7295 Washington St
Denver, CO 80229-6707
303-289-3345
Fax: 303-289-2133 800-452-5282
info@boyerscoffee.com www.boyerscoffee.com
Coffee
President: Mark Goodman
mark@boyerscoffee.com
Marketing Director: Bonnie Rine
Plant & Purchasing Manager: L Smith
Estimated Sales: $2.5-5,000,000
Number Employees: 20-49
Type of Packaging: Private Label

1640 Boylan Bottling Company
74 Lee Avenue
Haledon, NJ 07508-1202
973-790-7093
Fax: 973-790-9097 800-289-7978
Bottled soft drinks
President/CEO: Ronald Fiorina
Executive VP: Mark Fiorina
COO: David Fiorina, Jr.
Estimated Sales: $1-2,500,000
Number Employees: 20-49

1641 Boyle Meat Company
1638 Saint Louis Ave
Kansas City, MO 64101-1130
816-221-6283
Fax: 816-221-3888 800-821-3626
theresa@boylescornedbeef.com
Steaks, corn beef, pastrami and pot roast
President: Don Wendl
Special Project Manager: James Crouch
VP: Christy Chester
Estimated Sales: $20-50 Million
Number Employees: 20-49
Square Footage: 10000
Type of Packaging: Food Service, Private Label, Bulk

1642 Boyton Shellfish
RR 2
Box 85a
Ellsworth, ME 04605
207-667-8580
Fax: 619-474-6103
Shellfish
Owner: Dean Smith

1643 Bozzano Olive Ranch
6880 East Navone Road
PO Box 5009
Stockton, CA 95215
209-451-3665
Fax: 209-467-8362 info@bozzanoranch.com
www.bozzanoranch.com
Olive oils
President: Joe Bozzano
Vice President: Jack Bozzano
jack@bozzanoranch.com
Number Employees: 15

1644 Brad's Organic
7 Hoover Ave
Haverstraw, NY 10927
845-429-9080
Fax: 845-429-9089 sales@bradsorganic.com
www.bradsorganic.com
Organic, all-natural salsa, tortilla chips, honey, jams and peanut butter
Administration: Lisa Salia
Estimated Sales: $73,000
Number Employees: 2

1645 Brad's Taste of New York
P.O.Box 20475
Floral Park, NY 11002-0475
516-354-9004
Fax: 516-354-9004 bradstasteofny@aol.com
Gourmet mustard, pretzel dip, honey wheat pretzel, sourdough honey mustard nuggets, and kettle potato chips
Owner: Bradley Knese
Estimated Sales: $1-3 Million
Number Employees: 5-9

1646 Bradford Co
13500 Quincy St
Holland, MI 49424-9460
616-399-6538
Fax: 616-399-8989 info@bradfordco.com
www.bradfordco.com
Manufacturer of packaging products and material handling systems.
President: Hulda Grin
hgrin@championhealthandfitness.com
Estimated Sales: $2.5-5 Million
Number Employees: 100-249

1647 Bradley 3 Ranch
15591 Cr K
Memphis, TX 79245
806-888-1062
Fax: 806-888-1010 mmll@bradley3ranch.com
www.bradley3ranch.com
Fresh beef processing and packing
President: Mary Lou Bradley
General Manager: James Henderson
Purchasing: Kathleen Lewis
Estimated Sales: $20-50 Million
Number Employees: 50-99
Type of Packaging: Consumer, Food Service
Brands:
   B 3 R
   B C Natural

1648 Bradley Creek Seafood
PO Box 30446
Savannah, GA 31410
912-484-3510
Fax: 912-897-7815 www.bradleycreek.com
Crab au gratin pastries; deviled crab; and crab cakes.
President/CEO: Michael Simmons
Type of Packaging: Food Service

1649 Bradley Technologies Canada Inc.
8380 River Road
Delta, BC V4G 1B5
Canada
309-343-1124
Fax: 309-343-1126 866-508-7514
info@bradleysmoker.com
www.bradleysmoker.com
Other meat/game/pate. other sauces, seasonings and cooking enhancers, private label, cooking implements, housewares.
Marketing: Michael Tostowaryk
Estimated Sales: $2.3 Million
Number Employees: 24

1650 Bradshaw's Food Products
1425 Somerset Avenue
Dighton, MA 02715-1215
508-669-6088
Pickled beef tripe
Partner: D Bradshaw
Partner: R Bradshaw
Estimated Sales: $1-2.5 Million
Number Employees: 1-4

1651 Bradye P. Todd & Son
316 Sunburst Highway/US Route 50
Cambridge, MD 21613-1308
410-228-8633
info@toddseafood.com
www.toddseafood.com
Seafood including crabs, seafood delicatessen and restaurant
Owner: Roy Todd
Estimated Sales: $3 Million
Number Employees: 20-49
Square Footage: 12000
Parent Co: T.A. Ocean Odyssey
Type of Packaging: Consumer

1652 Bragg Live Food Products Inc
199 Winchester Canyon Rd
Goleta, CA 93117-1961
805-968-1020
Fax: 805-968-1001 800-446-1990
info@bragg.com www.bragg.com
Liquid aminos and organic apple cider vinegar and extra-virgin olive oil
Manager: Sandi Enriquez
Controller: Sandy Gooch
Estimated Sales: $5-10 Million
Number Employees: 20-49
Brands:
   Bragg

1653 Braham Food Locker Service
124 Central Dr W
Braham, MN 55006
320-396-2636
Meat products including beef, goat and pork; also, smoked and cured sausage
President: Nicholas Grote
CEO: Diane Grote
Estimated Sales: $250,000
Number Employees: 5-9
Type of Packaging: Consumer

Food Manufacturers / A-Z

1654 (HQ)Brakebush Brothers
N4993 6th Dr
Westfield, WI 53964
800-933-2121
www.brakebush.com
Frozen chicken.
Research & Development Director: Jon Brakebush
Quality Assurance Manager: Donna Halbach
Marketing Manager: Steve Ross
Sales & Marketing Director: Scott Sanders
ssanders@brakebush.com
Production Manager: Steve Deery
VP, Purchasing: Chris Brakebush
Year Founded: 1925
Estimated Sales: $33.5 Million
Number Employees: 500-999
Number of Products: 200+
Square Footage: 500000
Type of Packaging: Consumer, Food Service
Brands:
  Smartshapes®
  Kids Klassics®
  Chik'n'zips®
  Global Creations®
  Squawkers®
  Brakebush®
  Honey-Touched®
  Farm Pantry®
  Country Krisp®
  Southern Select™
  Perfect Answers®
  Cayenne Kicker™
  Gold'n'spice®
  Tappers®
  Crispy-Lishus®
  Oven Lovin' Chik'n™
  Wing-Ditties®
  Zippity Doo-Wa Ditties®
  Inferno Wings®
  Chik'n Gone Wild™
  Bluegrass Bourbon™ Sauce
  Fiery Fingers®
  Touchdown Nuggets™
  Chik'n Stars™
  Lil' Chicks™
  Fry Stix™
  Zoo Crew™
  Chik'n Hoops®
  Chik'n Pretzels™
  Dog-Gone Chik'n®
  Chik'n Giggles®
  Bold Italiano™

1655 Brand Aromatics Inc
1600 Oak St
Lakewood, NJ 08701-5924
732-363-8080
Fax: 732-363-8041   800-363-2080
www.brandaromatics.com
Flavors and seasonings
President: Karl Brand
Co-VP: Barbara Brand
Co-VP: Dennis Shea
Sales Executive: Ed Heraty
Warehouse Manager: Mike Sernotti
Plant Manager: Vince Deangelo
Estimated Sales: $4.9 000,000
Number Employees: 20-49

1656 Brandborg Cellars
PO Box 506
Elkton, OR 97436-0506
510-215-9553
Fax: 415-282-6179
Wine
President: Terry Brandborg
Number Employees: 20-49

1657 Brander Vineyard
2401 N Refugio Rd
Santa Ynez, CA 93460
805-688-2455
Fax: 805-688-8010   800-970-9979
info@Brander.com   www.brander.com
Red and white wines
Owner: Fred Brander
fred@brander.com
Sales/Marketing: Julie Hayek
Operations Assistant: Drew Horton
Office Manager: Kathy Forner
Estimated Sales: $380,000
Number Employees: 5-9
Type of Packaging: Consumer, Food Service
Brands:
  Brander

1658 Branding Iron
1682 Sauget Business Blvd.
Sauget, IL 62206-1454
618-337-8400
Fax: 618-337-3292   800-851-4684
www.bih-us.com
Frozen high quality angus beef, pork, and veal patties
President: Mike Holten
Chairman: Jim Holten
Contact: Joe Dietrich
jdietrich@bih-us.com
CEO: Scott Hudspeth
Estimated Sales: $32 Million
Number Employees: 200
Square Footage: 50000
Type of Packaging: Food Service
Brands:
  The Cloud
  Thick N' Juicy
  Restaurant Quality
  Extra Value
  Double Red Provisions

1659 Branding Iron Meats
245 Industrial Blvd
Sauk Rapids, MN 56379-1238
320-259-0659
Fax: 320-240-0654   800-851-4684
Manufacturer and packer of meats and meat snacks
President: James Hanson
Director, Business Dev.: Rich Blay
Director, Quality: Pat Flanigan
Director, Sales: Dave King
Manager: Paul Bravinder
pbravinder@bih-us.com
Estimated Sales: $15.3 Million
Number Employees: 50-99
Parent Co: Branding Iron Holding Company
Type of Packaging: Consumer, Private Label
Brands:
  Besure
  Huisken
  Rg's

1660 Brandmeyer Popcorn Co
3785 NE 70th Ave
Ankeny, IA 50021-9734
515-262-3243
Fax: 866-631-6276   800-568-8276
www.lottapop.com
Processor and exporter of popcorn including gift boxes and specialty items
Owner: Arlie Brandmeyer
arlie@lottapop.com
Estimated Sales: $110,000
Number Employees: 1-4
Brands:
  Iowa State
  Lotta-Pop

1661 Brands Within Reach
141 Halstead Ave
2nd Floor
Mamaroneck, NY 10543
847-720-9090
contact@bwrgroup.com
bwrgroup.com
Bottled water
Brands:
  Belvoir Fruit Farms
  Saint Geron
  Kusmi Tea
  Nestea
  Grand-MŠre
  Lucien Georgelin
  Volvic
  Evian

1662 Brandt Farms Inc
6040 Avenue 430
P.O. Box 852
Reedley, CA 93654-9008
559-638-6961
Fax: 559-638-6964   www.brandtfarms.com
Peaches, nectarines, plums.
President: Wayne Brandt
CEO: Eleanor Brandt
COO: Jack Brandt
Sales Exec: Dave Maddux
Public Relations: Dave Maddox
davemaddux@treeripe.com
Estimated Sales: $20 Million
Number Employees: 100-249
Square Footage: 60000
Brands:
  Brandt
  Crystal Foods
  Crystal R-Best

1663 Brandt Mills
607 Race Street
Mifflinville, PA 18631
570-752-4271
Fax: 570-752-8712
Flour including pastry and whole wheat
President: Richard Brandt Jr
Secretary-Treasurer: Alan Brandt
Secretary: Lisa Dunn
Retail Sales Manager: John Allen
Estimated Sales: $1.3 Million
Number Employees: 12
Square Footage: 24000

1664 Braren Pauli Winery
7051 N State St
Redwood Valley, CA 95470-9629
707-485-0322
Fax: 707-485-6784   800-423-6519
Wines
President: Charlie Barra
Co-Owner/CEO: Bill Pauli
Marketing Director: Larry Braren
Sales Director: Larry Braren
Winemaker: Larry Braren
Estimated Sales: $.5-1,000,000
Number Employees: 20-49
Brands:
  Braren Pauli

1665 Brass Ladle Products
P.O.Box 39
Concordville, PA 19331
610-565-8664
Fax: 610-565-8665   800-955-2353
frontdesk@brassladle.com   www.brassladle.com
All-natural gourmet cake mixes including carrot, mocha mud(chocolate) and lemon poppy seed.
Owner: Skip Achuff
Estimated Sales: $1,000,000
Number Employees: 1-4
Number of Brands: 1
Number of Products: 3
Square Footage: 6000
Type of Packaging: Consumer, Food Service, Private Label, Bulk
Brands:
  Brass Ladle
  Mocha Mud
  Mocha Mud Cake Mix

1666 Brasserie Brasel Brewery
8477 Rue Cordner
Lasalle, QC H8N 2X2
Canada
514-365-5050
Fax: 514-365-2954   800-463-2728
Processor and exporter of lager beers
President: Marcel Jagermann
Managing Director: Stan Jagermann
Number Employees: 10-19
Square Footage: 24000
Type of Packaging: Consumer, Food Service, Private Label
Brands:
  Brasal Bock
  Brasal Legere
  Brasal Special Amber
  Hopps Aux Pommes
  Hopps Brau

1667 Brassica Protection Products
250 President St # 2000
Baltimore, MD 21202-7806
410-732-1200
Fax: 410-732-1980   866-747-0001
mail@brassica.com
Food ingredients, supplements, nutraceuticals, functional foods (cander preventive products)

Food Manufacturers / A-Z

CEO: Antony Talalay
atalalay@mba1978.hbs.edu
National Account Manager: Shane Fantauzzo
VP Business Development: Earl Hauserman
Estimated Sales: $660,000
Number Employees: 1-4
Brands:
    Brassica
    Brassica Teas With Sgs
    Broccosprouts

1668 Braswell's Winery
7556 Bankhead Highway
Dora, AL 35062-2041
    205-648-8335
Fax: 205-648-8335
Wines
President: Wayne Braswell
Owner: Ruth Braswell
Estimated Sales: $1-4,9,000,000
Number Employees: 1-4

1669 Brateka Enterprises
15680 SW 23rd Avenue
Ocala, FL 34473-4278
    352-307-5459
Fax: 352-307-5459 877-549-3227
Gourmet sauces in gift baskets
CEO: Hyacinth Thomas
Number Employees: 10-19
Brands:
    Lize Jamaican Style Gourmet Bbq

1670 Braum's Inc
3000 NE 63rd St
P.O. Box 25429
Oklahoma City, OK 73125
    405-478-1656
    800-327-6455
    www.braums.com
Frozen desserts, dairy and milk.
Owner: Bill Braum
President & CEO: Drew Braum
Marketing Director: Terry Holden
Purchasing Director: Kenny McDonald
Year Founded: 1933
Estimated Sales: $437 Million
Number Employees: 5000-9999
Square Footage: 260000
Type of Packaging: Food Service

1671 Braun Seafood Co
30840 Main Rd
Cutchogue, NY 11935-1336
    631-734-6700
Fax: 631-734-7462 info@braunseafood.com
braunseafood.com
Processor and distributor of oysters
Vice President: Keith Reda
Estimated Sales: $2.5-5,000,000
Number Employees: 20-49

1672 Bravard Vineyards & Winery
15000 Overton Rd
Hopkinsville, KY 42240-9451
    270-269-2583
Fax: 270-269-2583
Wines including dry, semi-dry, semi-sweet and sweet in white, blush, rose and red
Co-Owner: Janeth Bravard
Member: James Bravard
Estimated Sales: $32,000
Number Employees: 1-4
Square Footage: 500
Type of Packaging: Private Label
Brands:
    Bravard
    Countryside Red
    Foch
    Fruit Hill White
    Lady Genevieve
    Pennyroyal

1673 Brazi Bites
1836 NE 7th Ave
Suite 203
Portland, OR 97212
    503-303-2272
    brazibites.com
Brazilian cheese bread
Co-Founder: Junea Rocha
Year Founded: 2009
Number of Brands: 1
Number of Products: 4
Type of Packaging: Consumer
Brands:
    BRAZI BITES

1674 Brazilian Home Collection
249 Monree Street
Passaic, NJ 07055
    973-365-5800
Fax: 973-365-0007 bhcollection.com
Brazil handicraft.

1675 Brazos Legends
9087 Knight Rd
Houston, TX 77054-4305
    713-795-0266
Fax: 713-795-5534 800-882-6253
sbailey@texastamale.com www.texastamale.com
Gourmet food products
President: J Boles
CEO: Shirley Bailey
sbailey@texastamali.com
Sales Director: Shirley Bailey
Operations Manager: Shirley Bailey
Plant Manager: Ana Flores
Estimated Sales: $3-5,000,000
Number Employees: 10-19
Number of Brands: 5
Number of Products: 125
Square Footage: 25000
Type of Packaging: Consumer, Food Service, Private Label, Bulk
Brands:
    Brazos Legends
    Red Eye

1676 Brazos Valley Cheese
7781 Gholson Rd
Waco, TX 76705
    254-230-2535
info@brazosvalleycheese.com
Cheeses
Contact: Marc Kuehl
marc@brazosvalleycheese.com
Type of Packaging: Consumer, Food Service, Bulk

1677 Bread & Chocolate Inc
1538 Industrial Park
Po Box 692
Wells River, VT 05081-9806
    802-429-2920
Fax: 802-429-2990 800-524-6715
info@burnhamandmills.com
Gourmet lemonade, cocoa, pancake mixes, jams, mustards and iced tea mixes
Owner: Fran Rutstein
fran@burnhamandmills.com
Vice President: Fran Rutstein
Estimated Sales: $500,000-900,000
Number Employees: 1-4
Brands:
    Bear River
    Bread & Chocolate
    Moose Mountain
    Snowman
    Storytime

1678 Bread Alone Bakery
2121 Ulster Avenue
Lake Katrine, NY 12449
    845-657-3328
Fax: 845-657-6228 800-769-3328
info@breadalone.com www.breadalone.com
Artisanal bakery.
CEO: Dan Leader
Vice President: Nels Leader
Contact: Sharon Burns-Leader
sharon@breadalone.com
Year Founded: 1985
Number Employees: 100+
Brands:
    Bread Alone

1679 Bread Box Cafe
4711 11th St
Astoria, NY 11101-5404
Canada
    718-389-9703
    breadboxcafelic.com/
Bread and buns
President: Debby Andrews
Co-Owner: Irene Plaisier
Co-Owner: Dianna Careme
Contact: Tal Shuster
talshuster@yahoo.com

Estimated Sales: Less Than $500,000
Number Employees: 1-4
Square Footage: 2000
Type of Packaging: Consumer

1680 Bread Dip Company
PO Box 607
Maple Valley, WA 98038
    425-358-7386
Fax: 425-413-2104 www.breaddipcompany.com
Gourmet spreads and dips
Contact: Jim McCaslin
jim@breaddipcompany.com
Year Founded: 1994
Number Employees: 1-4

1681 Breads from Anna
3007 Sierra Ct
Iowa City, IA 52240
    319-354-3886
Fax: 319-358-9920 877-354-3886
info@breadsfromanna.com www.breadsfromanna.com
Gluten- and allergen-free baking mixes.

1682 Breadworks
923 Preston Ave # A
Charlottesville, VA 22903-4446
    434-296-4663
Fax: 434-971-6740 info@breadworks.org
www.breadworks.org
Breads including American and French sourdough, twelve grain, Jewish rye, challah, semolina, Irish soda and baguettes; also, cookies, muffins, scones, danish, pies, cakes and deli products
Manager: Jim Baber
jsb5930@aol.com
Chairman: Marc Bridenhagen
Vice President: John Satoski
Production/Sales: Priscilla Fox
Estimated Sales: $670,000
Number Employees: 10-19
Parent Co: Worksource Enterprises
Type of Packaging: Consumer, Food Service

1683 Breaktime Snacks
7723 Somerset Blvd
Paramount, CA 90723
    562-633-6200
Fax: 562-633-8789 800-677-1968
info@breaktimesnacks.com
www.breaktimesnacks.com
Gourmet popcorn
President/CEO: Roger Glade
Estimated Sales: $1-2,500,000
Number Employees: 5-9
Brands:
    Corn Appetit

1684 Breakwater Fisheries
14 O'Briens Hill
St John's, NL A1B 4G4
Canada
    709-754-1999
Fax: 709-754-9712
Processor and exporter of frozen snow crab, capelin, turbot, cod, mackerel, herring, squid and shrimp; importer of frozen squid
President/CEO: Randy Barnes
General Manager/Co-Owner: Lemuel White
Vice President: Ken White
Estimated Sales: $10-20 Million
Number Employees: 500
Number of Brands: 1
Square Footage: 75000
Brands:
    Breakwater

1685 Breakwater Seafoods & Chowder
306 S F St
Aberdeen, WA 98520-4144
    360-532-5693
Fax: 360-533-6488
Seafoods
Owner: Sonny Bridges
President: Lloyd Bridges
Treasurer: Jack Thompson
Vice President: Linda Mertz
Estimated Sales: Less Than $500,000
Number Employees: 5-9

Food Manufacturers / A-Z

1686 Breaux Vineyards
36888 Breaux Vineyards Ln
Purcellville, VA 20132-1748
540-668-6299
Fax: 540-668-6283 800-492-9961
jblosser@breauxvineyards.com
www.breauxvineyards.com
Wines
Owner: Paul Breaux
paul@breauxvineyards.com
Co-Owner: Alexis Breaux
Sales Director: Jennifer Breaux Blosser
paul@breauxvineyards.com
General Manager: Chris Blosser
Wine Maker: Dave Collins
Estimated Sales: $480,000
Number Employees: 10-19
Square Footage: 20000
Type of Packaging: Consumer, Private Label, Bulk

1687 Breckenridge Brewery
471 Kalamath St
Denver, CO 80204
303-573-0431
Fax: 303-573-4877 800-328-6723
freshbeer@breckenridgebrewery.com
www.breckenridgebrewery.com
Ale and stout
Founder/President: Edward A Cerkovnik Jr.
Brew master/Director Brewery Operations: J. Todd Usry
Controller: BJ Langton
Director of Marketing: Todd M Thibault
Director of Sales: George O'Neill
Contact: James Bartley
jamesbartley@subway.com
Director of Operations: Kurt Volker
Brew master and Director of Brewery Oper: J Usry
Estimated Sales: $14,000,000
Number Employees: 200
Parent Co: Breckenridge Brewery
Type of Packaging: Consumer, Food Service, Bulk
Brands:
 Autumn Ale
 Avalanche Ale
 Christmas Ale
 Hefe Proper
 Oatmeal Stout
 Pandora's Bock
 Summerbright Ale
 Trademark Pale Ale

1688 Breitenbach Wine Cellars
5934 Old Route 39 NW
Dover, OH 44622-7787
330-343-3603
Fax: 330-343-8290 www.breitenbachwine.com
Wines
President/CEO: Cynthia Bixler
info@breitenbachwine.com
Accountant: Susan Graber
Director of Sales: Jennifer Kohler
Manager: Anita Davis
Director Manufacturing: Dalton Bixler
Estimated Sales: $540,000
Number Employees: 10-19
Brands:
 Breitenbach
 Charming Nancy
 Dardenella
 Dusty Miller
 Festival
 First Crush
 Frost Fire
 Roadhouse Red
 Rosebarb
 Silver Seyual

1689 Brekki
5661 Palmer Way
Suite G
Carlsbad, CA 92010
760-487-8895
info@brekki.com
www.brekki.com
Overnight oatmeal
Co-Founder: Russell Radebaugh
Co-Founder: Greg Peyser
Number of Brands: 1
Number of Products: 5
Type of Packaging: Consumer
Brands:
 BREKKI

1690 Bremner Biscuit Company
4600 Joliet St
Denver, CO 80239-2922
303-371-8180
Fax: 303-371-8185 866-972-6879
bremner@worldpantry.com
www.bremnerbiscuitco.com
Processor and exporter of gourmet, snack and oyster crackers
Manager: Neil Bremner
Contact: Bryan Dare
bdare@darefoods.com
Estimated Sales: $5-10 Million
Number Employees: 20-49
Square Footage: 126000
Parent Co: Dare Foods
Type of Packaging: Consumer, Food Service, Private Label, Bulk
Brands:
 Bremner
 Bremner Wafers
 Brewski Snack

1691 Brennan Snacks Manufacturing
1220 W 7th Street
Bogalusa, LA 70427-3406
800-290-7486
Fax: 985-732-5397
Snacks and cotton candy
Co-Owner: Bernie Brennan, Jr.
Co-Owner: Christi Brennan
Number Employees: 20-49
Type of Packaging: Food Service, Private Label
Brands:
 Oboy's

1692 Brenntag North America
5083 Pottsville Pike
Reading, PA 19605
610-926-6100
Fax: 610-916-3782 contactus@brenntag.com
www.brenntag.com
Ingredients & additives including: amino acids, bentonite, calcium carbonate, carotenoids, caffeine, cellulose gums, calcium oxide, magnesium oxide, enzymes, conjugated linoleic acid, precipitated silica, zinc oxide, guar gum, foamcontrol agents, magnesium carbonate, magnesium hydroxide, natural sweetener, oat ingredients, omega 3 powders, plant sterols, stearates, vegetable oils, vitamins, waxes & butters, colorants, etc.
CEO: Markus Kl,,hn
CFO: Dieter Woehrle
COO: Steven Terwindt
Estimated Sales: $160 Million
Number Employees: 135
Square Footage: 110000
Parent Co: Brenntag AG
Other Locations:
 Sales Office
 Norcross GA
 Sales Office
 Plainfield IL
 Sales Office
 Philadelphia PA
 Sales Office
 Houston TX
 Sales Office
 Orinda CA
Brands:
 Evonik
 Brenntag
 Specialty Minerals
 Basf
 Lucarotin
 Lycovit
 Xangold
 Vicality Albafil
 Calessence
 Vicron
 Scora S.A.
 Scoralite
 Mississippi Lime
 Ashland
 Aqualon
 Aqualon Klucel
 Aqualon Benecel
 Usg
 Tonalin
 Icl Industrial Products
 Novozymes
 Protamex
 Alcalase
 Ban
 Catazyme
 Celluclast
 Dextranase
 Dextrozyme
 Flavourzyme
 Fungamyl
 Gluzyme
 Lactozym Pure
 Lecitase
 Lipopan
 Lipozyme
 Maltogenase
 Neutrase
 Novo Pro D
 Novoshape
 Novozym
 Palatase
 Pentopan
 Sweetzyme
 Termamyl
 Viscozyme L
 Wacker
 Silfoam
 Ppg
 Flo-Gard
 Supercol
 U.S. Zinc Votorantim Metals
 Pyure Brands, Llc
 Biovelop
 Promoat
 Proatein
 Dry N-3
 Vegapure
 Textron
 Covi-Ox
 Covitol
 Koster Keunen

1693 Breslow Deli Products
1209 N Hancock Street
Philadelphia, PA 19122-4505
215-739-4200
Fax: 215-423-4199
Beef including smoked and dried
President: Jon Breslow
Estimated Sales: $890,000
Number Employees: 6
Type of Packaging: Consumer, Food Service

1694 Brew Dr. Kombucha
PO Box 42291
Portland, OR 97242
760-487-8895
info@brekki.com
www.brekki.com
Kombucha
Founder & CEO: Matt Thomas
Number of Brands: 1
Number of Products: 5
Type of Packaging: Consumer
Brands:
 BREW DR.

1695 Brewers Association
736 Pearl Street
Po Box 1679
Boulder, CO 80302
303-447-0816
Fax: 303-447-2825 888-822-6273
bob@brewersassociation.org
www.brewersassociation.com
Beer.
Marketing: Robert Pease
Contact: Katie Brown
katie@brewersassociation.org

1696 Brewers Outlet-Chestnut Hill
7401 Germantown Ave
Philadelphia, PA 19119-1605
215-247-1265
Fax: 215-247-1855 info@mybrewersoutlet.com
www.mybrewersoutlet.com
Craft and specialty beers
Owner: Paul Egonopoulos
Estimated Sales: $2.5-5 Million
Number Employees: 5-9
Square Footage: 15000
Parent Co: Brewers Outlet

1697 Brewery Ommegang
656 County Highway 33
Cooperstown, NY 13326-4737
607-286-4144
Fax: 607-547-8374 800-544-1809
info@ommegang.com www.ommegang.com

Food Manufacturers / A-Z

Owner: Don Feinberg
info@belgianexperts.com
Innovation Manager: Mike McManus
Number Employees: 20-49
Type of Packaging: Consumer

1698 Brewla Inc.
Brooklyn, NY
855-543-7677
www.brewlabars.com
Manufacturer of specialty brewed bars made from herbs, coffee, teas, and botanicals.
Co-Founder: Daniel Dengrove
Co-Founder: Rebecca Dengrove
Square Footage: 80000

1699 (HQ)Brewster Dairy Inc
800 Wabash Ave S
Brewster, OH 44613
330-767-3492
Fax: 330-767-3386 800-874-8874
www.brewstercheese.com
All natural swiss cheese.
Owner & CEO: Fritz Lehman
VP & Chief Financial Officer: Emil Alecusan
VP Sales & Marketing: James Straughn
Manager National Sales: Mike Walpole
flehman@brewstercheese.com
Plant Manager/Production Development: John Scott
Year Founded: 1965
Estimated Sales: $28.4 Million
Number Employees: 100-249
Square Footage: 78914
Type of Packaging: Consumer, Food Service, Private Label, Bulk
Other Locations:
  Stockton Cheese, Inc.
  Stockton IL
  Brewster West LLC
  Rupert ID

1700 Briannas Fine Salad Dressings
P.O. Box 2243
3015 S Blue Bell Rd
Brenham, TX 77834
979-836-5978
Fax: 979-836-6953 www.briannas.com
Gourmet salad dressings
Sales Director: Jeffrey Sadler
Number Employees: 50
Number of Products: 15
Parent Co: Del Sol Food Company Inc.
Type of Packaging: Private Label

1701 Briceland Vineyards
5959 Briceland Thorn Rd
Redway, CA 95560
707-923-2429
Wines and champagnes
Owner/Partner: Margaret Carey
Partner: Joe Collins
Estimated Sales: $150,000
Number Employees: 2

1702 Brick Brewery
400 Bimgemans Centre Drive
Kitchener, ON N2B 3X9
Canada
519-742-2732
Fax: 519-742-9874 800-505-8971
info@waterloobrewing.com
www.waterloobrewing.com
Light and dark lagers, ales, coolers, ciders, craft beers.
Chairman: Peter Schwartz
President/CEO: George Croft
CFO: David J Birch
Director Brewing, Quality and Logistics: Bill Henry
VP Marketing: Norm Pickering
VP Sales: Craig Prentice
Chief Operating Officer: Russell Tabata
Year Founded: 1984
Estimated Sales: $20-50 Million
Number Employees: 20-49
Square Footage: 45000
Type of Packaging: Consumer
Brands:
  Algonquin Honeybrown
  Andechs
  Anniversary Bock
  Brick Premium
  Conners Best Bitter
  Fix
  Formosa Draft
  Henninger Kaiser Pils
  Laker Family of Beers
  Pacific Real Draft
  Red Baron
  Red Cap
  Waterloo Dark

1703 Brickerlabs.Com
3305 N Delaware St
Chandler, AZ 85225-1134
480-889-9450
Fax: 262-334-7651 800-274-2537
sales@brickerlabs.com
www.nutritionalmfgservices.com
Nutritional supplements
Sales/Marketing Manager: Tami Dechairo
Estimated Sales: $1-2,500,000
Number Employees: 5-9
Type of Packaging: Consumer, Food Service, Private Label, Bulk

1704 Bridenbaugh Orchards
316 Orchard Ln
Martinsburg, PA 16662-8145
814-793-2364
Grower and packer of apples, peaches, cherries, strawberries and raspberries; exporter of apples
Owner: Glenn Bridenbaugh
Co-Owner: David Bridenbaugh
Estimated Sales: Less Than $500,000
Number Employees: 1-4
Square Footage: 8000
Type of Packaging: Consumer, Bulk

1705 Bridge Brands Chocolate
286 12th St
San Francisco, CA 94103-3718
415-677-9194
Fax: 415-362-2080 888-732-4626
www.wineloverschocolate.com
Gourmet chocolates
President/Owner: Michael Litton
mike@bridgebrands.com
Number Employees: 10-19

1706 Bridgetown Coffee
2101 NW York St
Portland, OR 97210-2108
503-224-3330
Fax: 503-224-9529 800-726-0320
orders@bridgetowncoffee.com
www.bridgetowncoffee.com
Processor and exporter of coffee; wholesaler/distributor and exporter of tea; serving the food service market
President: Kirk Jensen
kirkj@bridgetowncoffee.com
CEO: Timothy Timmins
Treasurer: Susan Jensen
Estimated Sales: $3,000,000
Number Employees: 20-49
Number of Brands: 6
Number of Products: 21
Square Footage: 80000
Type of Packaging: Consumer, Food Service, Private Label, Bulk
Brands:
  Bridgetown

1707 Bridgeview Vineyards Winery
4210 Holland Loop Rd
Cave Junction, OR 97523-9758
541-592-4688
Fax: 541-592-2127 877-273-4843
bvw@bridgeviewwine.com
www.bridgeviewwine.com
Wine
President: Robert Kerivan
bvw@bridgeviewwine.com
Secretary/Treasurer: Lelo Kerivan
Sales/Marketing Manager: Tim Woodhead
Estimated Sales: $610,000
Number Employees: 20-49

1708 Bridgewell Resources LLC
124020 SE Carpenter Dr
Clackamas, OR 97015
800-481-3557
webinfo@bridgewellres.com
Edible oils, flours, grains and pulses.
President: Pat McCauley
CEO: Pat McCauley
Chief Financial Officer: Jay Wilson
Vice President of Human Resources: Donna Lesch
Food & Agriculture General Manager: Craig Mullen
Parent Co: Bridgewell Resources
Type of Packaging: Consumer, Food Service, Private Label, Bulk

1709 (HQ)Bridgford Foods Corp
1308 N Patt St
Box 3773
Anaheim, CA 92801-2581
714-526-5533
Fax: 714-526-4360 800-527-2105
info@bridgford.com www.bridgford.com
Breads & rolls, ready to eat sandwiches, meat snacks, deli foods & sandwiches, and foodservice doughs and pull apart bread mixes, deli pack biscuits, sandwiches, fully baked bread and rolls, and frozen ready-to-eat meal kits
President: John V Simmons
jsimmons@bridgford.com
President: John Simmons
Executive VP CFO: Raymond Lancy
Assistant to Chief Financial Officer: Debra Morris
Sales & Marketing Executive: Martin Campbell
Director of Sales: Pat Pallarino
Human Resources Manager: L Allan
jsimmons@bridgford.com
Route Operations Manager: Danny Rossman
Plant Manager: Michael Bridgford
Number Employees: 500-999
Type of Packaging: Consumer, Food Service
Other Locations:
  Frozen Rite Division
  Dallas TX
  Superior Foods Division
  Dallas TX
  Bridgford Foods of North Carolina
  Statesville NC
  Bridgford Foods of Illinois
  Chicago IL

1710 (HQ)Briess Malt & Ingredients Co.
625 S Irish Road
P.O. Box 229
Chilton, WI 53014
920-849-7711
Fax: 920-849-4277 800-657-0806
info@briess.com www.briess.com
All-natural food ingredients including malts, natural sweeteners (grain and starch-based), natural colorants, tapioca maltodextrins, reduced cook-time grains, pregelatinized flakes, and toasted grains. Many are whole grain. Non-GMO Kosher Certified, USDA Certified Organics.
President/COO: Gordon Lane
CEO: Monica Briess
CFO: Craig Kennedy
Research & Development: Bob Hansen
VP, Sales & Marketing: Robert O'Connell
Sales Coordinator: Ann Heus
Product Line Manager-Food Division: Shawn Kohlmeier
Purchasing: Michelle Piepenburg
Estimated Sales: $16.2 Million
Number Employees: 110
Type of Packaging: Bulk
Other Locations:
  Briess Ingredients Company
  Chilton WI
  Waterloo WI
Brands:
  Briess
  Cbw
  Insta Grains
  Maltoferm
  Maltorose

1711 Brighams
1328 Massachusetts Avenue
Arlington, MA 2476
781-648-9000
Fax: 781-646-0507 800-242-2423
brighams-mail@brighams.com
www.brighams.com
Ice cream, frozen yogurt, whipped cream and fudge topping
President/Coo: Charles Green
Vice President/Cfo: Greg Welch
Operations: Claudia Kost
Estimated Sales: $2.5-5 Million
Number Employees: 50
Square Footage: 330000
Type of Packaging: Consumer, Private Label, Bulk
Brands:
  Brigham's
  Elan

Food Manufacturers / A-Z

1712 Bright Greens
PO Box 42291
Portland, OR 97242
760-487-8895
info@brekki.com
www.brekki.com
Ready-to-drink fruit and vegetable smoothies
Founder & CEO: Brian Mitchell
Number of Brands: 1
Number of Products: 5
Type of Packaging: Consumer
Brands:
  BRIGHT GREENS

1713 Bright Harvest Sweet Potato Co
509 E Taylor St
PO Box 528
Clarksville, AR 72830
479-754-6313
Fax: 479-754-7794 800-793-7440
sprice@brightharvest.com www.brightharvest.com
Sweet potato products including patties, mashed sweet potatoes, sweet potato sticks, center cut sweet potatoes and casseroles.
President/CEO: Rex King
rking@brightharvest.com
VP Sales: Kandy Jenkins
VP Technical Services: Jeff Hannon
Food Service Sales Manager: John Coniglio
VP Operations: Sam Winterberg
Customer Service/Logistics Manager: Sabrina Price
Estimated Sales: $20-50 Million
Number Employees: 100-249
Number of Brands: 1
Square Footage: 22000
Type of Packaging: Consumer, Food Service
Brands:
  Bright Harvest

1714 BrightFarms
1 Bridge St.
Suite 002-4
Irvington, NY 10533
866-857-8745
www.brightfarms.com
Leafy greens, including various lettuce, kale, arugula, spinach, and basil.
CEO: Steve Platt
Year Founded: 2011
Number Employees: 11-50
Type of Packaging: Private Label

1715 Brimhall Foods
PO Box 34185
Bartlett, TN 38184-0185
901-377-9016
Fax: 901-377-0476 800-628-6559
brimsnacks.com
Snacks
President: Terry Brimhall
Contact: Dan Scoggin
dscoggin@brimsnacks.com
Estimated Sales: $5-10 Million
Number Employees: 100-249
Type of Packaging: Private Label

1716 Brimstone Hill Vineyard
61 Brimstone Hill Rd
Pine Bush, NY 12566-5300
845-744-2231
Fax: 845-744-4782 bhvwine@frontiernet.net
www.brimstonehillwinery.com
Still and sparkling wines
Owner: Richard Eldridge
bhvwine@frontiernet.net
Owner: Valerie Eldridge
Estimated Sales: $500,000-750,000
Number Employees: 1-4
Type of Packaging: Food Service
Brands:
  Brimstone Hill

1717 Briney Sea Delicaseas
715 78th Ave SW # C
Unit 3
Tumwater, WA 98501-5700
360-956-1797
Fax: 360-956-2503 888-772-5666
www.brineysea.net
Seafood including fresh, vacuum-packed smoked salmon
President: Jay Garrison
Estimated Sales: Less than $500,000
Number Employees: 1-4

Type of Packaging: Consumer, Food Service

1718 Brisk Coffee Co
402 N 22nd St
Tampa, FL 33605-6086
813-248-6264
Fax: 813-248-2947 800-899-5282
customer@briskcoffee.com www.briskcoffee.com
Processor and exporter of roasted coffee; also, leasing of coffee equipment available
President/CEO: Richard Perez
VP/COO: Denise Reddick
dreddick@briskcoffee.com
Finance Executive: Julie Beck
Vice President: Mary Perez
VP, Quality Control & Manufacturing: Randy Gongalez
VP Production: Randall Gonzalez
Estimated Sales: $2.9 Million
Number Employees: 20-49
Square Footage: 40000
Type of Packaging: Food Service
Brands:
  Brisk
  Gold Plus
  Innkeepers Choice

1719 Bristle Ridge Vineyards
98 NE 641
Knob Noster, MO 65336-1910
660-422-5646
800-994-9463
Producer of wines. Some of their products include Seyval Blanc, Sauterne, Mont Rose', Diamond, Burgundy, Montserrat Red, deChaunac, Hard Cider and Villard Noir.
President: Edward Smith
Co-Owner: Vickie Smith
General Manager: Todd Smith
Estimated Sales: $5-9,9,000,000
Number Employees: 5-9
Brands:
  Bristle Ridge

1720 Bristol Brewing Co
1604 S Cascade Ave
Colorado Springs, CO 80905-2237
719-368-6120
Fax: 719-633-2145 info@bristolbrewing.com
www.bristolbrewing.com
Ale and stout
Owner: Mike Bristol
mikeb@bristolbrewing.com
Owner: Nicole Schneider
Accounting: Lynne Blesener
Marketing Guru: Amanda Bristol
Sales Guy: Alex Spinnato
mikeb@bristolbrewing.com
General Manager: Tom Zurenko
Maintenance/Problem Solving: Tad Davis
Estimated Sales: $1,400,000
Number Employees: 10-19
Type of Packaging: Consumer, Food Service, Bulk
Brands:
  Beehive
  Edge City Ipa
  Edge City Pilsner
  Laughing Lab
  Mass Transit
  Old No.23
  Red Rocket
  Scottish
  Winter Warlock

1721 Bristol-Myers Squibb Co.
430 E. 29th St.
14th Floor
New York, NY 10016
212-546-4000
800-332-2056
www.bms.com
Pharmaceuticals and related health care products.
Chairman/CEO: Giovanni Caforio
giovanni.caforio@bms.com
Executive VP/CFO: David Elkins
Executive VP/General Counsel: Sandra Leung
Year Founded: 1887
Estimated Sales: $22.56 Billion
Number Employees: 23,300
Number of Brands: 28
Brands:
  BARACLUDE®
  DAKLINZA™
  ELIQUIS®
  EMPLICITI™
  OPDIVO®
  ORENCIA®
  REYATAZ®
  SPRYCEL®
  SUSTIVA®
  YERVOY®
  ATRIPLA®
  AZACTAM®
  COUMADIN®
  DROXIA®
  ETOPOPHOS®
  EVOTAZ®
  GLUCOPHAGE®
  GLUCOVANCE®
  HYDREA®
  KENALOG®
  LYSODREN®
  MEGACE®
  NULOJIX®
  PLAVIX®
  PRAVACHOL®
  VIDEX®
  ZERIT®

1722 British Aisles, LTD.
25A Progress Avenue
Nashua, NH 03062
Fax: 603-881-3480 800-520-8565
sales@britishaisles.com www.britishaisles.com
Organic/natural, tea, non-alcoholic beverages, full-line condiments, full-line candy, ethnic sauces (soy, curry, etc), spices, full-line spreads & syrup.
Marketing: Stephanie Pressinger
Contact: D Pressinger
sales@britishaisles.com

1723 British American Tea & Coffee
1320 Old Oxford Road
Durham, NC 27704-2470
919-471-1357
Fax: 919-471-1357
Tea and coffee.
President: Christopher Hulbert
CFO: Elizabeth Albert
Estimated Sales: Under $500,000
Number Employees: 20-49
Square Footage: 2
Type of Packaging: Private Label

1724 Brittle Kittle
16285 SW 85th Ave # 101
Tigard, OR 97224-5421
503-639-9037
Fax: 615-449-6263 800-447-2128
bkettle@bellsouth.net
Peanut brittle
Owner: Christine Logue
christine@brittlekittle.com
VP: Howard Wilson
Estimated Sales: Less Than $500,000
Number Employees: 1-4
Type of Packaging: Consumer

1725 Brix Chocolates
590 E Western Reserve Road
PO Box 9111
Youngstown, OH 44513
330-657-5864
Fax: 330-726-0749 866-613-2749
sales@brixchocolate.com www.brixchocolate.com
Chocolate
Principal: Nicholas Proia
Partner/Sales and Marketing: Bruce Barber
Estimated Sales: $190,000
Number Employees: 2

1726 Broad Run Vineyards
10601 Broad Run Rd
Louisville, KY 40299-5417
502-231-0372
info@broadrunvineyards.com
www.broadrunvineyards.com
Dry table and dessert wines
Owner: Gerald J Kushner
finewine@iglou.com
Manager of Sales/Marketing: Marilyn Kushner
finewine@iglou.com
Assistant Vintner: Lloyd Hyatt
Estimated Sales: $50,000
Number Employees: 20-49
Square Footage: 4000
Type of Packaging: Food Service

553

Food Manufacturers / A-Z

1727 Broadaway Ham Co
500 N Culberhouse St
Jonesboro, AR 72401-1690
870-932-6688
Fax: 870-932-6683 ham-man@sbcglobal.net
Meat products including deli barbecued ham and snack sticks
Owner: Bruce Broadway
Plant Manager: John Collins
Estimated Sales: $1-3 Million
Number Employees: 1-4
Square Footage: 15000
Type of Packaging: Consumer
Brands:
Crowley Ridge

1728 Broadbent B & B Food Products
257 Mary Blue Rd
Kuttawa, KY 42055-6299
270-388-0609
Fax: 270-388-0613 800-841-2202
order@broadbenthams.com
www.broadbenthams.com
Cured ham, bacon and sausage
Owner: Beth Drennan
beth@broadbenthams.com
Estimated Sales: Less Than $1 Million
Number Employees: 10-19

1729 Broadhead Brewing Co
1680 Vimont Ct.
Unit 106
Orl,ans, ON K4A 3M3
Canada
613-830-3944
broadheadbeer.com
Microbrewed craft beer.
Co-Founder: Josh Larocque
Co-Founder: Jamie White
Head of Sales: John Buist
Head Brewer: Jon Cormier
Year Founded: 2011
Number Employees: 5-10
Type of Packaging: Consumer, Private Label

1730 Broadleaf Venison USA Inc
5600 S Alameda St
Vernon, CA 90058-3428
323-826-9890
Fax: 323-826-9830 800-336-3844
support@broadleafgame.com
www.broadleafgame.com
Specialty and exotic meats; Wagyu Beef, Buffalo, Cervena Venison, kurobuta Pork
Owner: Mark Mitchell
broadleaf@broadleafgame.com
CEO: Pat McGowan
CFO: Ara Temuryan
Vice President: Annie Mitchell
Sales Director: Nathan Cooney
broadleaf@broadleafgame.com
Operations Manager: Pierre La Breton
Production Manager: Randy Eves
Plant Manager: Jose Madera
Purchasing Manager: Edward Townsend
Estimated Sales: $20-30 Million
Number Employees: 50-99
Square Footage: 56000
Type of Packaging: Consumer, Food Service
Brands:
Broadleaf
Broadleaf Cervena

1731 Broadley Vineyards
265 S 5th St
Monroe, OR 97456-9609
541-847-5934
Fax: 541-847-6018 broadley@peak.org
www.broadleyvineyards.com
Wines
President: Craig Broadley
Estimated Sales: $110,000
Number Employees: 1-4

1732 Brock Seed Company
75 Richwood Rd
Finley, TN 38030-3051
731-286-2430
Fax: 760-353-1693
Manufacturer and exporter of asparagus and asparagus seed

Brands:
Broad Run Vineyards

Owner: Clark Brock
Manager: Don Brock
Estimated Sales: $210,000
Number Employees: 3
Type of Packaging: Consumer, Food Service, Private Label
Brands:
Brock

1733 Brockmann's Chocolates
7863 Progress Way
Delta, BC V4G 1A3
Canada
604-946-4111
Fax: 604-946-4114 888-494-2270
info@brockmannchocolate.com
www.brockmannchocolate.com
Chocolates
President: Norbert Brockmann
CEO: Marianne Brockmann
Founder: Willy Brockmann
Estimated Sales: $1.1 Million
Number Employees: 30
Type of Packaging: Private Label
Brands:
Truffini

1734 Broken Bow Brewery
173 Marbledale Rd.
Tuckahoe, NY 10707
914-268-0900
www.brokenbowbrewery.com
Lagers, IPAs, golden ales, porter, fruit-flavored wheat beer
Head Brewer: Michael Lamother
Head, Marketing: Kristen Stone
Head, Sales: Lyle Lamothe
Year Founded: 2013
Number of Brands: 1
Number of Products: 13
Type of Packaging: Consumer, Private Label
Brands:
Broken Bow

1735 Brolite Products Inc
1900 S Park Ave
Streamwood, IL 60107-2944
630-830-0340
Fax: 630-830-0356 888-276-5483
info@bakewithbrolite.com
www.bakewithbrolite.com
Flavors, stabilizers, yeast foods, dough accelerators and conditioners, egg yolk and whole egg substitutes and fudge, English muffin and bread bases; exporter of white and rye sour dough flavors
President: David Delghingaro
d.delghingaro@broliteproducts.com
R&D: Daniel Garcia
Marketing/Sales VP: Tom MacDonald
Plant Manager: Mike Koziol
Estimated Sales: $15 Million
Number Employees: 50-99
Square Footage: 108000
Type of Packaging: Bulk
Brands:
All Soft
B5000
Bro Egcellent
Bro White Sour
Brolite Ia
Brosoft
Egg-O-Lite
Fever Sours
Vita Plus

1736 Brom Food Group
5595 Cote De Liesse
St. Laurent, QC H4M 1V2
Canada
514-744-5152
Fax: 514-744-8195
Processor, importer and exporter of frozen foods and frozen and fresh pierogies including cheese, potato/onion, beef and chicken
Director Marketing: Tom Luczak
Director Operations: Bruce Luczak, M.B.A.
Square Footage: 36000
Type of Packaging: Consumer, Food Service, Private Label, Bulk
Brands:
Granny's
Ogi's

1737 Brome Lake Ducks Ltd
40 Centre Road
PO Box 3430
Knowlton, QC J0E 1V0
Canada
450-242-3825
Fax: 450-243-0497 888-956-1977
info@canardsdulacbrome.com
www.canardsdulacbrome.com
Duck products
President: Claude Trottier
CFO: Genevieve Grenier
Vice President Sales/Marketing: Bruno Giuliani
R&D Director: Jennifer Caron
Quality Control: Jennifer Caron
Marketing Coordinator: Pier-Luc Fiest
Sales Manager: Claude Cadieux
Human Resources Director: Michele Cote
Account Manager: Abraham Chien-Chung Ho
Plant Manager: Guy Ducharme
Estimated Sales: $28 Million
Number Employees: 170

1738 Bronco Wine Co
6342 Bystrum Rd
Ceres, CA 95307
855-874-2394
info@broncowine.com www.broncowine.com
Wine
Chief Executive Officer: Fred Franzia
Co-President/National Sales & Marketing: Joseph Franzia
Co-President: John Franzia, Jr.
Purchasing Manager: Bob Martina
Year Founded: 1973
Estimated Sales: $250 Million
Number Employees: 1,000-4,999
Square Footage: 10000
Type of Packaging: Private Label
Brands:
Charles Shaw
Estrella
Forestville
Foxhollow
Grand Cru
Hacienda
Montpellier
Napa Ridge
Rutherford Vintners
Silver Ridge

1739 Brook Locker Plant
243 W Main St
Brook, IN 47922-8723
219-275-2611
Meat products and fresh and frozen foods including beef, pork, chicken and veal; also, slaughtering available
Owner: Jeff Laffoon
jefflaffoon@hrblock.com
Vice President: Chris Schoonveld
Bookkeeper: Pam Chamberlin
Estimated Sales: $230,000
Number Employees: 5-9
Type of Packaging: Consumer, Bulk

1740 Brook Meadow Meats
716 Security Rd
Hagerstown, MD 21740-4143
301-739-3107
Pork, beef and sausage
Owner: Donald Hoffman
Estimated Sales: $5-10 Million
Number Employees: 1-4
Type of Packaging: Consumer

1741 Brookema Company
500 Fenton Lane
West Chicago, IL 60185-2667
630-562-2290
Fax: 630-562-2291
Dry mixes including cake, soup, cocoa, coffee and coffee creamer.
President: Dan Clery
Estimated Sales: $2.5-5 Million
Number Employees: 20-49
Type of Packaging: Bulk

1742 Brookfield Farm
24 Hulst Rd.
Amherst, MA 01002
413-253-7991
info@brookfieldfarm.org
www.brookfieldfarm.org

Food Manufacturers / A-Z

Fresh and frozen pork and beef
President/Ceo: Frank Swan
President/Ceo: Dennis Gleason
Manager: Abbe Vredenburg
abbe@brookfieldfarm.org
Estimated Sales: Less Than $500,000
Number Employees: 500-999
Type of Packaging: Consumer, Food Service

1743 Brooklyn Bagel Company
PO Box 120027
Staten Island, NY 10312-0027
718-349-3055
Fax: 718-349-1107   800-349-3055
Frozen bagels
Sales Manager: Stanley Silverman
Sales Manager: Arnie Lichtenstein
General Manager: Donald Santman
Estimated Sales: $1-2.5 Million
Number Employees: 20-49
Square Footage: 40000
Type of Packaging: Consumer, Food Service, Bulk

1744 Brooklyn Baking Company
8 John Street
Waterbury, CT 6708
203-574-9198
Baked goods including sourdough, white and rye bread and cookies
Owner: Peter Belez
Estimated Sales: $450,000
Number Employees: 5
Type of Packaging: Consumer, Bulk
Brands:
  Brooklyn Baking Pumpernickel Bread
  Brooklyn Baking Rye Bread

1745 Brooklyn Bean Roastery
7 Hanson Pl.
Brooklyn, NY 11243
908-205-0018
info@brooklynbeans.com
www.brooklynbeans.com
Coffee beans
Co-Founder: Steven Schreiber
Co-Founder: Mayer Koenig
Co-Founder: Eugene Schreiber
Brands:
  Brooklyn Bean Roastery

1746 Brooklyn Biltong
314 Prospect Ave.
Brooklyn, NY 11215
407-538-8876
info@brooklynbiltong.com
www.brooklynbiltong.com
South African style beef jerkey
Principal CEO: Ben van den Heever
Year Founded: 2012

1747 Brooklyn Brew Shop
20 Jay St
Brooklyn, NY 11201
718-874-0119
info@brooklynbrewshop.com
www.brooklynbrewshop.com
Manufacturer of beer making kits.
Co-Founder: Erica Shea
Co-Founder: Stephen Valand
Contact: Sarah Blumenthal
sarahb@brooklynbrewshop.com

1748 Brooklyn Brewery
1 Brewers Row
79 North 11th Street
Brooklyn, NY 11249
718-486-7422
Fax: 718-486-7440 www.brooklynbrewery.com
Ale, stout and lager
Co-Founder/President: Steve Hindy
CEO: Eric Ottaway
Controller: Debbie Bascome
Quality Control Manager: Mary Wiles
Marketing Director: Ben Hudson
VP/Sales: Robin Ottaway
Operations Manager: Karl Knoop
Estimated Sales: $20-50 Million
Number Employees: 22
Type of Packaging: Consumer, Food Service, Bulk
Brands:
  Brooklyn
  Chimay
  Duvel
  Paulaner

Samuel Smith
Sierra Nevada

1749 Brooklyn Brine Co LLC
67 35th Street
Suite 5-1C
Brooklyn, NY 11232
347-223-4345
www.brooklynbrine.com
Manufacturer of non-GMO, Kosher pickles.
Founder: Briner Jones
Brands:
  Brooklyn Brine

1750 Brooklyn Cider House
1100 Flushing Ave.
Brooklyn, NY 11237
347-295-0308
www.brooklynciderhouse.com
Hard dry craft ciders
Founder/Co-Owner: Peter Yi
Founder/Co-Owner: Susan Yi
Year Founded: 2014
Number of Brands: 1
Number of Products: 5
Type of Packaging: Consumer, Private Label
Brands:
  Brooklyn Cider House

1751 Brooklyn Cookie Company
P.O. Box 170143
Brooklyn, NY 11217
347-973-0568
info@brooklyncookiecompany.com
www.brooklyncookiecompany.com
Meringue cookies
President: Cheryl Surana
Estimated Sales: Under $500,000
Number Employees: 1-4
Brands:
  Just Meringues
  "Mushroom" Meringues Cookies

1752 Brooklyn Cured LLC
326 22nd St
New York, NY 11215-6408
907-282-2221
info@brooklyncured.com
www.brooklyncured.com
Sausaged, cured and smoked meats
Founder: Scott Bridi
Year Founded: 2010

1753 Brooklyn Delhi
Brooklyn, NY 11230
hello@brooklyndelhi.com
brooklyndelhi.com
Condiments and sauces
Founder: Chitra Agrawal

1754 Brooklyn Whatever LLC
27 Cobeck Ct
Brooklyn, NY 11223
917-669-5525
brooklynwhatever.com
sugar free pickled vegetables, mixed olives, and mixed nuts.
Owner: Rachel Shamah
rachel@brooklynwhatever.com
Brands:
  Shmolives
  Shnuts.
  Shpickles
  Brooklyn Whatever

1755 Brookmere Wine & Vineyard
5369 SR 655
Belleville, PA 17004-9303
717-935-5380
Fax: 717-935-5349 www.brookmerewine.com
Wines
Owner: Cheryl Glick
Estimated Sales: $2.5-5,000,000
Number Employees: 5-9
Type of Packaging: Bulk

1756 Brooks Peanut Co
402 E Main St
Samson, AL 36477-1224
334-898-7194
Fax: 334-898-7196 www.brookspeanut.com
Peanuts

Owner: Barrett Brooks
barrettbrooks@msn.com
CEO: Fleming G. Brooks
Secretary/Treasurer: Sherry Brooks
Office Manager: Lucy Adams
Estimated Sales: $8.3 Million
Number Employees: 5-9
Type of Packaging: Bulk

1757 Brooks Tropicals Inc
18400 SW 256th St
Homestead, FL 33031-1892
305-247-3544
Fax: 305-242-7393   800-327-4833
maryo@brookstropicals.com
Grower, packer and shipper of papayas, avocados, starfruit, limes, passion fruit, mangos, guavas, uglyfruit and other tropical produce.
President: Pal Brooks
CEO: Greg Smith
Year Founded: 1928
Number Employees: 100-249
Type of Packaging: Bulk
Brands:
  SlimCado® avocado
  Caribbean Red® papaya

1758 Brookshire Grocery Company
PO Box 1411
Tyler, TX 75710-1411
903-534-3000
888-937-3776
www.brookshires.com
Regional supermarket chain in Texas, Louisiana and Arkansas.
Chairman/CEO: Bradley Brookshire
Year Founded: 1928
Estimated Sales: $2.5 Billion
Number Employees: 14,000+
Brands:
  Brookshire's®
  Full Circle®
  Goldenbrook Farms®
  PAWS Premium™
  Tasty Bakery
  Top Care®
  Valu Time®
  World Classics™

1759 Brookside Foods
17212 Miles Ave
Cleveland, OH 44128
216-991-7600
Fax: 216-991-7739
Fresh and frozen prepared salads and meats
President/Owner: Bernie Polen
CEO: Jack Lain
Sales Executive: Alisa Capriottschrei
Contact: Denis Mcguire
dmcguire@brooksidefoods.com
Office Manager: Jacke Lane
Estimated Sales: $1.3 Million
Number Employees: 12
Type of Packaging: Consumer, Food Service, Private Label
Brands:
  Bosell
  Brookside
  Homestead

1760 Brookside Foods
3899 Mt. Lehman Road
Abbotsford, BC V4X 2N1
Canada
604-607-6650
Fax: 604-607-7046   800-468-1714
info@brooksidefoods.com
www.brooksidefoods.com
Base concentrates, fruit fillings, custom ice cream inclusions, confectionery coatings, and paned and deposited chocolate confections, etc. Importer of cocoa butter, cocoal powder, chocolate liquer, etc. Exporter of real fruit chipschocolate, panned and deposited chocolate confections, etc. Custom dry blending and private labeling.
President: Kenneth Shaver
Director Sales: Alan Whitteker
Estimated Sales: $26.5 Million
Number Employees: 150
Parent Co: Brookside Foods
Type of Packaging: Consumer, Private Label, Bulk

Food Manufacturers / A-Z

1761 Brookview Farms
854 Dover Road
P.O. Box 126
Manakin-Sabot, VA 23103
804-784-3131
Fax: 804-784-2697
themarket@brookviewfarm.com
www.brookviewfarm.com
Fresh and frozen meat including beef, pork, lamb and venison
President: Jack Lugbill
Estimated Sales: $5-10 Million
Number Employees: 10-19
Square Footage: 21000
Type of Packaging: Consumer, Food Service, Bulk

1762 Brother Bru Bru's
PO Box 2964
Venice, CA 90294-2964
310-396-9033
info@brobrubru.com
Producer of natural salt-free sauces, including Original African Hot PepperSauce, Organic Chipotle and Organic Chili Pepper Sauce.
Owner: Cynthia Riddle
Estimated Sales: $5-10,000,000
Number Employees: 50-99
Brands:
   Brother Bru Bru's

1763 Brother's Trading LLC
P.O. Box 2234
San Gabriel, CA 91778-2234
626-378-9323
info@gemgemsweet.com
gemgemsweet.com
Ginger and citrus fruit based candy.
General Manager: Andrew Ma
Purchasing: Marlen Abolafia
Type of Packaging: Private Label
Brands:
   Gem Gem

1764 Brotherhood Winery
100 Brotherhood Plaza Dr
P.O.Box 190
Washingtonville, NY 10992-2279
845-496-3661
Fax: 845-496-8720
contact@brotherhoodwinery.net
www.brotherhood-winery.com
wines.
President: Hernan Donoso
Co-Owner: Cesar Baeza
Vice President: Philip Dunsmore
Commercial Assistant, Marketing & Sales: Ren,e Schweizer
Production Manager: Mark Daigle
Plant Manager: Carol Tepper
Estimated Sales: $10 Million
Number Employees: 50
Type of Packaging: Consumer, Food Service, Private Label, Bulk
Brands:
   Brotherhood

1765 Brothers All Natural
1175 Lexington Ave
Rochester, NY 14606
585-343-3007
Fax: 585-343-4218 877-842-7477
www.brothersallnatural.com
Freeze-dried fruit crisps
President & Co-CEO: Matt Betters
Co-CEO: Travis Betters
Estimated Sales: $4.1 Million
Number Employees: 22

1766 Brothers Desserts
2727 S Susan Street
Santa Ana, CA 92704
949-655-0080
info@brothersdesserts.com
brothersdesserts.com
Ice creams, sorbets, fruit bars and frozen desserts
President/Owner: Gary Winkler
Year Founded: 1973
Type of Packaging: Bulk
Brands:
   Natural Choice
   Absolute Fruit
   Brothers Ice Cream

1767 Brothers International Desserts
2727 S Susan St
Santa Ana, CA 92704
949-655-0080
www.brothersdesserts.com
Frozen desserts, including ice cream, gelato and sorbet
President/Owner: Gary Winkler
Year Founded: 1973
Estimated Sales: C
Number Employees: 150
Number of Brands: 1
Number of Products: 15
Square Footage: 30000
Type of Packaging: Consumer
Brands:
   NATURAL CHOICE
   CLASSIC BON BONS
   ABSOLUTE FRUIT

1768 Brothers International Food Corporation
1175 Lexington Ave
Rochester, NY 14606
585-343-3007
Fax: 585-343-4218
ingredients@brothersinternational.com
brothersinternational.com
Fruit ingredients
President & Co-CEO: Matt Betters
Co-CEO: Travis Betters
Estimated Sales: $6.2 Million
Number Employees: 33

1769 Brothers Sauces
2617 Museum Way
Fort Worth, TX 76107
817-821-3374
Fax: 877-754-3488
Gluten-free, organic/natural, BBQ sauce, dessert toppings (i.e. fudge sauce, caramel sauce, whipped cream, etc.), foodservice, private label.
Mbr: Darryl King
Manager/Mbr: Barry King
Estimated Sales: $100,000
Number Employees: 2

1770 Broughton Foods LLC
PO Box 961447
El Paso, TX 79996
740-373-4121
Fax: 740-373-2861 800-395-7004
www.dairypure.com
Milks, premium and homestyle ice cream, novelty ice cream, juices and fruit drinks, cottage cheese, sour cream, and chip dip.
Principle: Michael McCullum
General Manager: David Broughton
Executive Vice President: George Broughton
Manager of Sales: Neil Schilling
Plant Manager: Mike Depue
Purchasing Agent: Becci Becker
Estimated Sales: $46.6 Million
Number Employees: 100-249
Square Footage: 8000
Parent Co: Dean Foods
Type of Packaging: Consumer, Food Service, Bulk

1771 Brown & Haley
3500 20th St E
Suite C
Fife, WA 98424
800-426-8400
sweets@brown-haley.com www.brown-haley.com
Manufacturer and exporter of confectionery items including Almond Roca.
President & COO: John Melin
jmelin@brown-haley.com
CFO: Clarence Guimond
Year Founded: 1914
Estimated Sales: $86.9 Million
Number of Brands: 3
Type of Packaging: Consumer, Private Label, Bulk
Brands:
   Mountain Bar
   Roca
   Zingos Mints

1772 Brown & Jenkins TradingCompany
286 Old Rt 15
PO Box 236
Cambridge, VT 05444-0236
802-862-2395
Fax: 802-864-7336 800-456-5282
coffee@brownjenkins.com
www.brownjenkins.com
Coffee
Owner: Sandy Riggens
Marketing Director: Sarah Squirrell
Contact: Rich Williams
rich@brownjenkins.com
Estimated Sales: $1-2,500,000
Number Employees: 1-4
Brands:
   Brown & Jenkins Fresh Roasted

1773 Brown County Winery
4520 State Road 46 E
Nashville, IN 47448-8673
812-988-6144
Fax: 812-988-8285 888-298-2984
info@browncountywinery.com
www.browncountywinery.com
Wines
President/Manager: David Schrodt
Owner/Secretary/Treasurer: Cynthai Schrodt
Marketing Manager: Cynthia Schrodt
Estimated Sales: $525,000
Number Employees: 5-9
Square Footage: 5000
Type of Packaging: Bulk

1774 Brown Cow Farm
10 Burton Drive
Londonderry, NH 03053
888-429-5459
www.browncowfarm.com
Yogurt
Contact: Rosy Rodriguez
rosyr@browncowfarm.com
Estimated Sales: $3,000,000
Number Employees: 12
Number of Brands: 1
Type of Packaging: Consumer
Brands:
   Brown Cow Farm

1775 Brown Dairy Inc
95 Browns Ln
Coalville, UT 84017-9419
435-336-5952
Fax: 435-336-5902 www.brownsdairy.com
Dairy products
Owner: Glen Brown
browndairy@hotmail.com
Number Employees: 5-9

1776 Brown Dog Fancy
50 Noroton Ave
Darien, CT 06820-5214
908-251-1723
info@browndogfancy.com
browndogfancy.com
Mustard and condiments
Owner/Manager: Kyle Rothschild

1777 Brown Family Farm
74 Cotton Mill Hl # A106
Brattleboro, VT 05301-8603
802-254-4554
Fax: 802-254-5022 866-254-8718
info@brownfamilyfarmmaple.com
www.brownfamilyfarmmaple.com
Maple products
Estimated Sales: Under $500,000
Number Employees: 10-19

1778 Brown Foods
3659 Atlanta Highway
PO Box 953
Dallas, GA 30132-5731
770-445-4358
Fax: 770-445-5349
Poultry, pork, seafood, produce, beef
Principal: William Brown
Owner: Graham Kirkman
Estimated Sales: $540,000
Number Employees: 4

Food Manufacturers / A-Z

1779 Brown Packing Company
One Dutch Valley Drive
P.O. Box 703
South Holland, IL 60473-8094
708-849-7990
Fax: 708-849-8094 800-832-8325
Meat products including beef carcasses and primal cuts
President: John Oedzes
Vice President: Brian Oedzes
Contact: Steven Blanton
steven@dv-foods.com
Chief Operating Officer: Bryan Scott
Estimated Sales: $10-24 Million
Number Employees: 60
Square Footage: 50000
Type of Packaging: Consumer, Bulk

1780 Brown Produce Company
Route 37
Farina, IL 62838
618-245-3301
Fax: 618-245-3552
Eggs and egg products including frozen, liquid, whites, whole and yolk
President: Larry Seger
Vice President: Larry Pemberton
Plant Supervisor: Larry Jahraus
Estimated Sales: $10-20 Million
Number Employees: 50-99
Square Footage: 20000000
Type of Packaging: Consumer, Bulk

1781 Brown Thompson & Sons
139 State Route 339 N
Fancy Farm, KY 42039
270-623-6321
Fax: 270-623-6928
Beef, beef products
Owner: Penny Lamb
Estimated Sales: $.5-1,000,000
Number Employees: 1-4

1782 (HQ)Brown's Dairy
1300 Baronne St
New Orleans, LA 70113-1206
504-529-2221
Fax: 504-529-9267 800-680-6455
www.brownsdairy.com
Milk
President: Kennon Davis
Cmo: Laurent Barbe
lbarbe@barbedairy.com
Sales Director: Lauren Barre
Plant Manager: John Brousard
Estimated Sales: $300,000-500,000
Number Employees: 250-499
Parent Co: Suiza Dairy Group
Type of Packaging: Consumer
Brands:
  Brown's Dairy
  Bulgarian Style
  Hershey's Milkshake
  Luzianne Ready-To-Drink
  Nesquik

1783 Brown's Ice Cream Co
3501 Marshall St NE # 150
Suite 150
Minneapolis, MN 55418-0073
612-378-1075
Fax: 612-331-9273 info@brownsicecream.com
www.brownsicecream.com
Ice cream
Owner: Robert Nelson
browns@popp.net
Vice President: Robert Nelson
Estimated Sales: $9 Million
Number Employees: 20-49
Parent Co: Upper Lakes Foods
Type of Packaging: Consumer, Food Service, Bulk

1784 Brown-Forman Corp
850 Dixie Hwy.
Louisville, KY 40210
502-585-1100
Fax: 502-774-6633 brown-forman@b-f.com
www.brown-forman.com
Wine, tequila, champagne, whiskey, vodka, scotch, and liqueurs.
Chairman: Garvin Brown
President/CEO: Lawson Whiting
Executive VP/CFO: Jane Morreau
Executive VP/General Counsel/Secretary: Matthew Hamel
Senior VP/Chief Production Officer: Alejandro Alvarez
Year Founded: 1870
Estimated Sales: $3.8 Billion
Number Employees: 4,600
Number of Brands: 18
Type of Packaging: Consumer
Other Locations:
  Atlanta GA
  Baltimore MD
  Braintree MA
  Coral Gables FL
  Dallas TX
  Hauppauge NY
  Irving TX
  Jackson OH
  Louisville KY
  Lynchburg TN
  Nashville TN
  Newport Beach CA
  Pleasanton CA
Brands:
  Jack Daniels
  Woodford Reserve
  Old Forester
  Early Times
  Collingwood Canadian Whisky
  Canadian Whiskey
  Cooper's Craft
  Slane Irish Whiskey
  The Benriach
  The Glendronach
  Glenglassaugh
  Herradura
  El Jimador
  Pepe Lopez
  Finlandia
  Finlandia Frost
  Chambord
  Korbel
  Sonoma-Cutrer

1785 Brownie Baker Inc
4870 W Jacquelyn Ave
Fresno, CA 93722-5027
559-277-7077
Fax: 559-277-7077 800-598-6501
thebrownieb@gmail.com www.browniebaker.com
Baking products such as; muffins, cakes, brownies, cookies, danish, mexican pastries, poundcake slices and cheesecakes
CEO: Dennis Perkins
CFO: Jodi Cox
Director of Marketing: Ryan Perkins
VP Sales: Glenn Jones
VP Operations: Mike Collins
Director of Baking: Dave Robinson
Estimated Sales: $20-50 Million
Number Employees: 50-99
Square Footage: 45000
Brands:
  Pro Treats
  The Brownie Baker

1786 Brownie Brittle, LLC
2253 Vista Pkwy
Suite 8
West Palm Beach, FL 33411-2722
561-688-1890
Fax: 561-584-5881 info@browniebrittle.com
www.browniebrittle.com
Gourmet brownie mixes, cookies, chocolate, and snack foods.
Owner: Sheila Mains
Marketing Brand Manager: Barbara Riley
Brands:
  Brownie Brittle

1787 Brownie Points Inc
5712 Westbourne Ave
Columbus, OH 43213-1400
614-860-8470
Fax: 614-860-8477 800-427-9643
info@browniepointsinc.com
www.browniepointsinc.com
Manufacturer and retailer of award-winning brownies.
Founder & Co-Owner: Lisa King
info@browniepointsinc.com
Estimated Sales: Less Than $500,000
Number Employees: 1-4

1788 Browniepops LLC
12008 Wenonga
Leawood, KS 66209
816-797-0715
Fax: 913-491-0788 www.berries.com
Brownies with a crisp chocolate exterior on a stick lik lollipops. Available in 11 unique flavors.
President/Owner: Marsha Pener Johnston

1789 Browns Brewing Co
417 River St
Troy, NY 12180-2822
518-273-2337
Fax: 518-273-4834 www.brownsbrewing.com
Beer
President: Garrett Brown
garry@brownsbrewing.com
Estimated Sales: $1-3 Million
Number Employees: 20-49
Brands:
  Ales & Lagers
  Brown's Ware
  Revolution Hall
  Taproom

1790 Browns' Ice Cream Company
3501 Marshall St. NE
Suite 150
Minneapolis, MN 55418
612-378-1075
info@brownsicecream.com
www.brownsicecream.com
Distributor of ice cream
President: Jerry Conder
Treasurer: William Brown
Contact: Bob Nelson
bnelson@brownsicecream.com
Estimated Sales: $8.3 Million
Number Employees: 60
Type of Packaging: Consumer, Food Service, Bulk

1791 Bruce Baking Company
229 Union Avenue
New Rochelle, NY 10801-6048
914-636-0808
Fax: 914-636-0808
Baked goods, macrobiotic food
Owner: Bruce Merbaum
Estimated Sales: Under $500,000
Number Employees: 5-9
Brands:
  Bruce Baking
  Tahini Crunch

1792 Bruce Coffee Svc Plan USA
77 Weston St
PO Box 987
Hartford, CT 06120-1593
860-527-7253
Fax: 860-524-9130 800-227-6638
info@baronetcoffee.com www.baronetcoffee.com
Manufacturer and importer of coffee.
President: Bruce Goldsmith
Estimated Sales: $10-20 Million
Number Employees: 10-19
Number of Brands: 1
Type of Packaging: Consumer, Food Service, Private Label
Brands:
  Baronet Coffees

1793 Bruce Cost Ginger Ale
465 Johnson Ave.
Brooklyn, NY 11237
212-488-0661
info@brucecostgingerale.com
www.brucecostgingerale.com
Manufacturer of flavoured ginger ales.
Founder and Co-Owner: Bruce Cost
Co-Owner: Joseph Tang
Co-Owner: Terry Tang
Estimated Sales: $35.8,000,000
Number Employees: 350
Brands:
  Bruce Cost Ginger Ale

Food Manufacturers / A-Z

1794 Bruce Foods Corporation
221 Southpark Plaza
PO Drawer 1030
Lafayette, LA 70508
Fax: 337-364-3742 800-299-9082
info@brucefoods.com www.brucefoods.com
Cajun and Tex Mex food products.
President/CEO: Joseph Brown
Vice President/Director: Norman Brown

Year Founded: 1928
Estimated Sales: $141.7 Million
Number Employees: 1,600
Square Footage: 295000
Type of Packaging: Consumer, Food Service, Bulk
Other Locations:
  Bruce Foods Plant
  El Paso TX
  Bruce Foods Plant
  Wilson NC
  Bruce Foods Plant
  Lozes LA
  Bruce Foods Plant
  Kerkrade, Netherlands
Brands:
  Cajun Injector®
  Casafiesta®
  Louisiana Hot Sauce
  Bruce's® Mixes
  Bruce's® Yams
  Cajun King®
  Louisiana® Gold
  Mexene® Chili
  Louisiana® Wing Sauce

1795 Bruce Tea
info@bruceleetea.com
www.bruceleetea.com
Energy tea
VP, Sales: Jim Venia
Number of Brands: 1
Number of Products: 3
Type of Packaging: Consumer
Brands:
  BRUCE TEA

1796 Brucepac
380 S Pacific Hwy
Woodburn, OR 97071-5931
503-982-3926
Fax: 503-769-5081 800-899-3629
sales@brucepac.com www.brucepac.com
Cooked and seasoned meats
President & CEO: Glen Golomski
Vice President: Terry Buford
National Business Development: Leo Zachman
VP, Sales & Marketing: Rick Wiser
Manager: Matt Rose
Director of Purchasing: Duane Tipton
Estimated Sales: $35 Million
Number Employees: 500-1000
Type of Packaging: Private Label
Other Locations:
  Durant OK
  Silverton OR
  Woodburn OR
Brands:
  Brucepac
  City Grillers
  Urban Bruce
  World Kitchen's

1797 Brucia Plant Extracts
3855 Dividend Dr
Shingle Springs, CA 95682
530-676-2774
Fax: 530-676-0574 brucia@naturex.com
www.naturex.com
Antioxidants, colors, herbs & spices oleoresins and essential oils, and botanical extracts for the food, flavor and nutraceutical industries
CEO: Thierry Lambert
Group Marketing Director: Antoine Dauby
Sales: David Yuengniaux
Plant Manager: Chris Young
Purchasing Manager: Romain Bayzelon
Estimated Sales: $45 Million
Number Employees: 20-49
Number of Brands: 10
Number of Products: 400
Square Footage: 85000
Parent Co: Naturex
Type of Packaging: Bulk
Brands:
  Theraplant

1798 Bruegger's Bagels
496 Main St
Melrose, MA 02176-3841
781-665-1913
Fax: 781-665-4953 www.brueggers.com
Bagels
Co-Owner: Nord Brue
Co-Owner: Mike Dressel
Number Employees: 10-19

1799 Brum's Dairy
631 Bruham Ave
Pembroke, ON K8A 4Z8
Canada
613-735-2325
Fax: 613-735-2068 www.ic.gc.ca
Process and distribute fresh dairy products as well as fresh juice
President: Stanley W. Brum
Manager: D.A. Fleury
Vice President: Barry D. Brum
Estimated Sales: $12.7 Million
Number Employees: 46
Square Footage: 40000
Type of Packaging: Consumer, Private Label
Brands:
  Nature's Pride

1800 Brunkow Cheese Of Wisconsin
17975 County Road F
Darlington, WI 53530-9310
608-776-3716
Fax: 608-776-3716 www.brunkowcheese.com
Natural, cold pack and raw milk cheeses including cheddar, colby, monterey jack, mild, sharp, garlic, bacon, onion, dill, wine, jalapeno, Italian herb, smoked, etc
Owner: Karl Geissbuhler
brunchee@mhtc.net
Partner: Greg Schulte
Estimated Sales: $580,000
Number Employees: 5-9
Square Footage: 6400
Type of Packaging: Bulk
Brands:
  Brunkow Cheese

1801 Brunnett Dairy Co-Op
11631 State Road 70
Grantsburg, WI 54840-7135
715-689-2468
Fax: 715-689-2135 715-689-2748
info@burnettdairy.com www.burnettdairy.com
Mozzarella, provolone, colby, cheddar and monterey jack
Chairman: Bill Haase
President & CEO: Dan Dowling
Year Founded: 1897
Estimated Sales: Less Than $500,000
Number Employees: 1-4
Type of Packaging: Consumer, Food Service, Private Label, Bulk
Brands:
  Fancy Brand

1802 Bruno Specialty Foods
208 Cherry Ave
West Sayville, NY 11796-1223
631-589-1700
Fax: 631-589-6357 info@brunofoods.com
Frozen kosher and nonkosher Italian food products including tomato sauces, tortellini, regular and vegetable lasagnas, eggplant parmagiana, ravioli, manicotti and stuffed shells
President: Louis D'Agrosa
lrd@brunofoods.com
Quality Control: Judi D'Agrosa
Sales Executive: Amy D'Agrosa
Operations Executive: Manuel Guzman
Production Manager: Jim Harwood
Purchasing: Mike McKasty
Estimated Sales: $4.4 Million
Number Employees: 20-49
Number of Brands: 2
Number of Products: 150
Square Footage: 20000
Type of Packaging: Consumer, Food Service, Private Label, Bulk
Brands:
  Bruno
  Tova's Best

1803 Brush Locker
14505 County Road 14
Fort Morgan, CO 80701-8209
970-842-2660
Fax: 970-842-4831
Processor and packer of meat
Principal: Tyler McDonald
Plant Manager: Iram Khan
Estimated Sales: $5-10 Million
Number Employees: 10-19

1804 Brutocao Cellars
1400 Highway 175
Hopland, CA 95449-9754
707-744-1066
Fax: 707-744-1046 800-433-3689
www.brutocaocellars.com
Wines, gourmet foods
Owner: Leonard Brutocao
Owner/DirectorOf Winemaking: David Brutocao
National Sales Manager: Jeff Miller
brutocaocellars@pacific.net
General Manager: Aaron Niderost
Winemaker: Hoss Milone
Estimated Sales: $1,000,000
Number Employees: 20-49

1805 Bryan Foods
PO Box 3901
Peoria, IL 61612
800-544-3870
www.bryanfoods.com
Bacon, sausage, hot dogs, ham, corn dogs and lunchmeat

1806 Bryant Preserving Company
P.O. Box 367
Alma, AR 72921
800-634-2413
Fax: 479-632-2505 sales@bryantpreserving.com
www.oldsouth.com
Pickled fruits and vegetables including sweet watermelon rinds and cucumber relish, baby carrots, green tomatoes and mild and hot okra.
President: Morgan Bryant
General Manager & COO: Steve Bryant
Sales Manager: Leguetta Yates
Contact: Phillip Bryant
phillip@bryantpreserving.com
Estimated Sales: $1-2.5 Million
Number Employees: 6
Square Footage: 75000
Type of Packaging: Consumer, Food Service, Private Label, Bulk
Brands:
  Old South

1807 Bryant Vineyard
1454 Griffitt Bend Rd
Talladega, AL 35160-7255
256-268-2638
kabryant71614@aol.com
www.bryantwines.com
Wines
Co-Owner: Kelly Bryant
Co-Owner: Dan Bryant
Estimated Sales: Less Than $500,000
Number Employees: 1-4
Brands:
  Bryant Autumn Blush
  Bryant Country White
  Bryant Dixie Blush
  Bryant Festive Red
  Bryant Vineyard

1808 Bryant's Meat Inc.
104 Fellowship Rd
PO Box 321
Taylorsville, MS 39168-5501
601-785-6507
Fax: 601-785-6507 800-844-0507
www.bryantsmeat.com
Meat products including smoked sausage, pork and chicken
President: Robert Hunt
rrhunt@bryantsmeat.com
Secretary/Treasurer: Kay Hunt
Manager: Theresa Driskell
Estimated Sales: $2.5 Million
Number Employees: 20-49
Type of Packaging: Consumer
Brands:
  River Road
  Sunrise

Food Manufacturers / A-Z

1809 Bt. McElrath Chocolatier
2010 E Hennepin Ave
Suite 78
Minneapolis, MN 55413
612-331-8800
Fax: 612-331-2881 info@btmcelrath.com
www.btmcelrath.com
Chocolates
President: Brian T Mc Elrath
Partner/Chief Taster: Christine McElrath
Marketing: Nancy Gross
Estimated Sales: $3-5 Million
Number Employees: 5-9

1810 Bubba's Fine Foods
225 42nd Street SW
Suite C
Loveland, CO 80537
bubbasfoods.com
Gourmet chips
Co-Founder & CEO: Jeff Schmidgall
COO: Jared Menzel
Number of Brands: 1
Number of Products: 9
Type of Packaging: Consumer
Brands:
BUBBA'S FINE FOODS

1811 Bubbies Fine Foods
PO Box 7326
Stockton, CA 95267-0326
805-947-4622
contact@bubbies.com
Kosher dill pickles, dill relish, sauerkraut and horseradish
Co-Owner: John Gray
Co-Owner: Kathy Gray
Type of Packaging: Bulk

1812 Bubbies Homemade Ice Cream
99-1267 Waiua Pl # B
Aiea, HI 96701-5642
808-487-7218
Fax: 808-484-5800
bubbiesicecream@hawaii.rr.com
www.bubbiesicecream.com
Mocha ice cream
President: Keith Robbins
bubbiesicecream@hawaii.rr.com
CFO: Sandra Robbins
VP: Gertrude Robbins
Quality Control: Jayci Robbins
Marketing/Sales Director: Rick Wiser
National Sales Manager: Wayne Shervey
Public Relations: Jo Lacar
Estimated Sales: $2.9,000,000
Number Employees: 5-9
Square Footage: 18000
Type of Packaging: Bulk
Brands:
Bubbies Homemade Ice Cream
Mountain Apple
Tutus

1813 Bubbles Baking Co
15215 Keswick St
Van Nuys, CA 91405-1014
818-786-1700
Fax: 818-786-3617 800-777-4970
Sales@BubblesBakingco.com
Gourmet baked goods
President: Torben Jensen
Manager: Sean Naim
Manager: Armando Berument
armando@bubblesbakingco.com
Estimated Sales: 2.4 Million
Number Employees: 50-99
Number of Brands: 1
Brands:
Bubbles

1814 Bubbles of San Francisco
Box 7326
Stockton, CA 95209-1617
209-951-6071
Fax: 209-957-9413 info@bubbies.com
www.bubbies.com
Kosher pickle products
Co-Owner/CEO: John Gray
Co-Owner/COO: Kathy Gray
Estimated Sales: $500,000-$1,000,000
Number Employees: 1-4
Type of Packaging: Private Label, Bulk

1815 Buccia Vineyard
518 Gore Rd
Conneaut, OH 44030
440-593-5976
bucciwin@suite224.net
www.bucciavineyard.com
Wine
Co-Owner/President: Alfred Bucci
Co-Owner: Joanna Bucci
Estimated Sales: $80,000
Number Employees: 2
Type of Packaging: Bulk

1816 Buchanan Hollow Nut Co
6510 Minturn Rd
Le Grand, CA 95333-9710
209-389-4594
Fax: 209-389-4321 800-532-1500
sharleen@bhnc.com www.bhnc.com
Manufacturer and grower of organic pistachio, almonds, variety of nuts, dried fruit and candies
Owner: Sharleen Robson
sharleen@bhnc.com
Owner: Charleen Robson
Estimated Sales: $800,000
Number Employees: 20-49
Square Footage: 8000
Type of Packaging: Bulk

1817 Buchi Kombucha
242 Derringer Dr
Marshall, NC 28753-8909
828-394-2360
www.drinkbuchi.com
kombucha brews
Sales and Book keeper: Virginia Lancianese
Year Founded: 2009
Number Employees: 11-50

1818 Buck's Spumoni Company
229 Pepes Farm Rd
Milford, CT 06460
888-222-8257
bucksicecream.com
Ice cream specialties including nut roll, spumoni and tortoni
President: Charles A Buck Jr
charles.buck@bucksicecream.com
Secretary: Lois Gosselin
Vice President: Charles Buck SR
Estimated Sales: $1.1 Milion
Number Employees: 15
Type of Packaging: Food Service, Bulk

1819 Buckeye Pretzel Company
1253 Deerfield Drive
Williamsport, PA 17701-9307
570-547-6295
Fax: 570-547-6719 800-257-6029
Pretzels
President/Treasurer: John Best
Vice Pres-sec: Susan Best
Vice President: James Haag
Number Employees: 24
Brands:
Buckeye

1820 Buckhead Beef
4500 Wickersham Dr
Atlanta, GA 30337-5122
404-355-4400
Fax: 404-355-4541 800-888-5578
hf@buckheadbeef.com www.buckheadbeef.com
Fresh and frozen specialty cut meat products including beef, veal, lamb and pork
Founder/CEO: Howard Halpern
President: Chad Stine
CFO: Paul Mooring
frostypauly@yahoo.com
Vice President: Andrew Malcolm
Director of Marketing: Rick Morris
Vice President of Sales: Beverly Ham
Human Resources Executive: Sue Kozbiel
Manager: Chris Aloia
Director of Production: Raymond Morehouse
Director of Purchasing: Jason Lees
Number Employees: 500-999
Type of Packaging: Food Service

1821 Buckhead Gourmet
4060 Peachtree Rd NE # D-272
Atlanta, GA 30319-3020
404-256-1399
Fax: 404-256-1335 800-673-6338
Prepared sauces including fat-free gourmet, barbecue, bordeaux, hunter, peppercorn, maderia, marinades, spice ribs, salad dressings, jams, relishes and salsas
President: Stephan Gosch
CEO: Rupert Crawford
Estimated Sales: $1,000,000
Number Employees: 2
Number of Brands: 1
Number of Products: 35
Type of Packaging: Consumer, Food Service, Private Label, Bulk
Brands:
Buckhead Gourmet

1822 Buckingham Valley Vineyards
1521 Rte 413
Buckingham, PA 18912
215-794-7188
Fax: 215-794-3606 ask@pawine.com
www.pawine.com
Wine
Owner/Partner: Gerald Forest
Partner: Jon Forest
Partner: Kevin Forest
Partner: Kathleen Forest
Estimated Sales: $240,000
Number Employees: 5
Brands:
Buckingham

1823 (HQ)Buckmaster Coffee Co
4893 NW 235th Ave # 101
Hillsboro, OR 97124-5835
503-693-0796
Fax: 503-681-0944 800-962-9148
JoeS@BuckmasterCoffee.com
www.buckmastercoffee.com
Roasted whole bean gourmet coffee
President: Joe Schlichte
joes@buckmastercoffee.com
VP: Joe Schlichte
Sales Manager: Paul Hoffmann
Sales and merchandising manager: Scott Perkins
Estimated Sales: $2 Million
Number Employees: 5-9
Type of Packaging: Consumer

1824 Budd Foods
431 Somerville St
Manchester, NH 03103-5129
603-623-3528
Chicken pot-pies and all-in-one meals
Contact: Jenifer Bechtol
jenifer@mrsbudds.com
Number Employees: 1-4

1825 Buddha Brands
9600 Rue Meilleur
Suite 932
Montreal, QC H2N 2E3
Canada
514-382-3805
hello@buddhabrandscompany.com
www.buddhabrandscompany.com
Coconut water and coconut chips
Number of Brands: 1
Number of Products: 13
Type of Packaging: Consumer
Brands:
THIRSTY BUDDHA
HUNGRY BUDDHA

1826 Buddha Teas
5130 Avenida Encinas
Carlsbad, CA 92008
800-642-3754
service@buddhateas.com www.buddhateas.com
Loose leaf, herbal, green, black and specialty teas
Number of Brands: 1
Type of Packaging: Consumer
Brands:
BUDDHA TEAS

1827 Buddy Fruits
555 Theodore Fremd Ave
Suite C-306
Rye, NY 10580
914-514-2098
hello@buddyfruits.com
www.buddyfruits.com
Fruit purees
Number of Brands: 1
Number of Products: 7

Food Manufacturers / A-Z

Type of Packaging: Consumer
Brands:
 BUDDY FRUITS
 BUDDY FRUITS & VEGGIES
 FRUIT TUBES

1828 Buddy Squirrel LLC
1801 E Bolivar Ave
St Francis, WI 53235-5317
414-483-4500
Fax: 414-483-4137 800-972-2658
www.buddysquirrel.com
Processor, exporter and packer of candy including regular and sugar-free boxed, chocolates, brittles, toffees, holiday, mints, molded novelties, etc.; also, nuts, nut mixes and gourmet popcorn
President: Margaret Gile
margaretg@qcbs.com
Number Employees: 100-249
Number of Brands: 2
Number of Products: 2000
Square Footage: 120000
Parent Co: Quality Candy Shoppes
Type of Packaging: Consumer, Food Service, Private Label, Bulk
Brands:
 Buddy Squirrel
 Fairy Food
 Quality Candy

1829 Budenheim USA, Inc.
2219 Westbrooke Dr
Columbus, OH 43228-9605
614-345-2400
info@budenheim.com
www.budenheim.com/en
Supplier of ingredients for the meat, poultry, seafood, beverage, nutrition, dairy and baking industries. Primarily deals with phosphates.
Marketing: Marti Babcock
Vice President of Sales: Doug Lim
Square Footage: 5016
Parent Co: Chemische Fabrik Budenheim KG

1830 Budi Products LLC
PO Box 1325
Marblehead, MA 01945
781-990-3411
info@budibar.com
www.budibar.com
Manufacturer of bars made from superfood ingredients.
Founder: Michael McCarthy
Square Footage: 80000
Brands:
 BUDIBAR

1831 Buds Kitchen
826 Gardner Center Road
New Castle, PA 16101-6020
724-654-9216
Fax: 724-654-9216 bud301@libcom.com
Hot sauce

1832 (HQ)Buedel Food Products
7661 S 78th Ave # A
Bridgeview, IL 60455-1274
708-496-3500
Fax: 708-496-8369 info@buedelfinemeats.com
Refrigerated horseradish and frozen smoked fish
Owner/President/Sales Exec: Kristyn Benson
kristynb@buedelfoods.com
Secretary/Treasurer: Kathleen Myer
Vice President: Kristin Buedel
Sales Director: Fred Buedel
COO: Darren Benson
Estimated Sales: $25,000,000
Number Employees: 20-49
Type of Packaging: Consumer, Private Label
Brands:
 Prince Gourmet Foods

1833 Buehler Vineyards
820 Greenfield Rd
St Helena, CA 94574-9529
707-963-2155
Fax: 707-963-3747
Wine
President: John Buehler
john@buehlervineyard.com
Winemaker: David Cronin
Manager Sales/Marketing: Misha Chelini
Social Media and Sales: Helen Buehler
Person: Lorri Sax
Office Manager: Karan Zumalt
Vineyard and Production Manager: Raul Gloria
Estimated Sales: $2,000,000
Number Employees: 5-9
Type of Packaging: Private Label

1834 Buena Vista Historic Tstng Rm
18000 Old Winery Rd
PO Box 1842
Sonoma, CA 95476-4840
707-996-4438
Fax: 707-252-0392 800-926-1266
info@buenavistawinery.com
www.buenavistawinery.com
Manufacturer, importer and exporter of wine and also, importer of champagne
President/CEO: Harry Parsley
CFO/VP: Peter Kasper
Human Resources: Dorothy Kines
Site Manager: Starla Perez
Estimated Sales: $5-10 Million
Number Employees: 20-49
Square Footage: 240000
Type of Packaging: Consumer, Private Label
Brands:
 Carneros

1835 Bueno Foods
2001 4th St SW
Albuquerque, NM 87102-4520
505-243-2722
Fax: 505-242-1680 800-888-7336
www.buenofoods.com
Frozen Mexican food including green chile and corn and flour tortillas, chile peppers, spices and dry chile powders
President: Jackie Baca
Number Employees: 100-249
Type of Packaging: Consumer, Food Service, Private Label
Brands:
 Bueno
 Chimayo

1836 Buff Bake
811 S Grand Avenue
Santa Ana, CA 92705
949-274-9464
info@buffbake.com
buffbake.com
Protein cookies and nut butters

1837 Buffalo Bill Brewing Company
1082 B St
Hayward, CA 94541-4108
510-886-9823
Fax: 510-886-8157 info@buffalobillsbrewery.com
www.buffalobillsbrewery.com
Ale, stout, lager and fruit flavored beers
President & CEO: Geoff Harries
Head Brewer: Mike Manty
Year Founded: 1983
Estimated Sales: $20-50 Million
Number Employees: 50-99
Type of Packaging: Consumer, Food Service, Bulk
Brands:
 Alimony Ale
 Billy Bock
 Buffalo Brew
 Pumpkin Ale
 Tasmanian Devil
 White Buffalo

1838 Buffalo Bills Premium Snacks
1547 Joel Dr.
P.O. Box 866
Lebanon, PA 17042
717-273-7499
Fax: 717-273-7699
customerservice@choochoorsnacks.com
www.bbjerky.com
Jerky, meat sticks, meat snacks, pickled sausages, gifts
General Manager: Paul Squires
Sales Manager: Patrick Sherburne

1839 Buffalo Trace Distillery
113 Great Buffalo Trce
Frankfort, KY 40601
502-696-5978
800-654-8471
info@buffalotrace.com
www.buffalotracedistillery.com
Bourbon and rum; importer of wine.
Marketing Services Director: Meredith Moody
Public Relations & Events Manager: Amy Preske
Year Founded: 1771
Estimated Sales: $29.3 Million
Number Employees: 100-249
Type of Packaging: Bulk

1840 Buffalo Wild Wings
600 Highway 169 S
Suite 1919
Minneapolis, MN 55426-1205
763-546-1891
Fax: 952-593-9787 info@buffalowildwings.com
www.buffalowildwings.com
Buffalo wings
Owner: Jim Disbrow
Co-Owner: Scott Lowery
Contact: Dale Gallion
dgallion@buffalowildwings.com
Estimated Sales: $300,000-500,000
Number Employees: 10-19

1841 Bull and Barrel Brewpub
988 Rte. 22
Brewster, NY 10509
845-278-2855
www.bullandbarrelbrewpub.com
IPAs and fruit-flavored Ales
Co-Owner: Rick Cipriani
Co-Owner: Wendy Wulkan
Number of Brands: 1
Number of Products: 6
Type of Packaging: Consumer, Private Label
Brands:
 Bull and Barrel

1842 Bull's Head
C.P. 3151
Richmond, QC J0B 2H0
Canada
819-212-1583
info@bulls-head.com
bulls-head.com
Ginger based soda
Founder: John Bryant
Year Founded: 1986

1843 Bully Hill Vineyards
8843 Greyton H Taylor Mem Dr
Hammondsport, NY 14840
607-868-3610
Fax: 607-868-3205 info@bullyhill.com
www.bullyhillvineyards.com
Wines, champagne and grape juice
President: Lillian Taylor
VP Quality Control/Operations: Gregg Learned
Sales: Adam LaPierre
Estimated Sales: $5-9.9 Million
Number Employees: 5-9
Type of Packaging: Consumer

1844 Bumble Bee
Petco Park
900 C St
San Diego, CA 92101
858-715-4000
Fax: 858-560-6045 info@bumblebee.com
www.bumblebee.com
Canned seafood
CEO: Christopher Lischewski
Estimated Sales: $20-50 Million
Number Employees: 50-99

1845 Bumbleberry Farms LLC
119 Stauffer Rd.
Storystown, PA 15563
814-279-8083
www.bumbleberryfarms.com
Manufacturer of honey and honey products.
Founder: Karen Mosholder
Square Footage: 80000

Food Manufacturers / A-Z

1846 Bunge
1391 Timberlake Manor Pkwy.
Chesterfield, MO 63017
314-292-2000
news@bunge.com
www.bunge.com
Oilseed processing, supply milled wheat, corn and rice products to food processors, bakeries, brewers, foodservice companies and snack food producers. Offers distribution services.
CEO: Gregory Heckman
CFO: John Neppl
Chief Legal Officer: Joseph Podwika
Chief HR & Communications Officer: Deborah Borg
President, Global Operations: Raul Padilla
President, Global Supply Chain: Christos Dimopoulos
Year Founded: 1818
Number Employees: 24,000
Type of Packaging: Food Service

1847 Bunge Canada
2190 S. Service Road West
Oakville, ON L6L 5N1
Canada
905-825-7900
www.bungenorthamerica.com
Oil seeds, protein meals and edible oil products.
Director, Bulk Oil Sales: Steve Caloren
Brands:
    Canaplus

1848 Bunge Loders Croklaan
24708 W Durkee Rd
Channahon, IL 60410-5249
815-730-5200
Fax: 815-730-5202 800-621-4710
blc.na@bunge.com
Fats, oils, flavored flakes, emulsifiers, dietary fiber and encapsulates, shortenings
CEO: Julian Veitch
julian.veitch@croklaan.com
CFO: Vincent Geerts
Vice President: Aaron Buettner
VP Innovation/R&D: Paul Shanahan
Quality Assurance Manager: Linda McLaren
VP Marketing: Vanessa Ballard
Director, Human Resources: Hens van Wingerden
VP of Operations: Eugenia Zorila
Facility Manager: Astrid Ackerman
Purchasing Manager: Sherry Shugart
Estimated Sales: $33.6 Million
Number Employees: 250-499
Number of Brands: 25

1849 Bunge North America Inc.
1391 Timberlake Manor Pkwy.
Chesterfield, MO 63017
314-292-2000
www.bungenorthamerica.com
Grain originator, processor and exporter.
CEO: Gregory Heckman
CFO: Luciano Salvatierra
Year Founded: 1918
Estimated Sales: $3.6 Billion
Parent Co: Bunge Limited
Type of Packaging: Consumer, Food Service, Private Label, Bulk
Brands:
    Calrose
    Kaho Mai
    Maruyu
    Pacific International

1850 Bunker Foods Corp.
79 Madison Ave
2nd Floor
New York, NY 10016
646-738-4020
info@bunkerfoodscorp.com
Importer of sunflower and chia seeds; as well as beans, chickpeas, corn, peanuts and other products.
President: Nicolas Lartitigoyen
Parent Co: Bunker Foods
Type of Packaging: Consumer, Food Service, Private Label
Brands:
    Southern Ray's

1851 Bunker Hill Cheese Co Inc
6005 County Road 77
Millersburg, OH 44654-9045
330-893-2131
Fax: 330-893-2079 800-253-6636
info@heinis.com www.heinis.com
Processor and marketor of Heini's Brand Cheese. Products include yogurt, cultured cheese, raw milk cheeses, other natural cheeses and old fashioned churned butter.
Owner/President: Peter Dauwalder
Cmo: Lisa Troyer
ltroyer@heinis.com
Marketing Director: Bob Walker
Finance/Sales Executive: Lisa Troyer
VP Operations: Bob Troyer
Plant Manager: Eric Sheely
Purchasing Manager: Mark Schlabach
Estimated Sales: $8.6 Million
Number Employees: 50-99
Square Footage: 320000
Type of Packaging: Consumer, Bulk
Brands:
    Amish Valley Farms
    Heini's Brand Cheese

1852 Bunny Bread
Evansville, IN
bunnybread.net
Bread
Principal: Nadine Gallaway
VP: Darryl Trainer
Plant Manager: Daryl Mitchell
Estimated Sales: $90,000
Number Employees: 2
Type of Packaging: Consumer

1853 Buns & Roses Organic Wholegrain Bakery
6519-111th Street NW
Edmonton, AB T6H 4R5
Canada
780-438-0098
Fax: 780-437-8805
Breads and specialty baked products including organic whole grain and gluten-free
Owner: Dhammika Jayawickrama
Estimated Sales: $67,000.00
Number Employees: 1
Square Footage: 4800
Type of Packaging: Consumer, Food Service
Brands:
    Buns & Roses

1854 Buona Vita Inc
1 S Industrial Blvd
Bridgeton, NJ 08302-3401
856-453-7972
Fax: 856-453-7978 sales@buonavitainc.com
www.buonavitainc.com
Italian specialties including meatballs, meatloaf, beef bracioli, eggplant, pasta and pizza toppings
President: Paul Infranco
pauljr@buonavitainc.com
SVP Operations: Blake Christy
Estimated Sales: $20-50 Million
Number Employees: 20-49
Square Footage: 25000
Type of Packaging: Consumer, Food Service, Private Label, Bulk
Brands:
    Buona Vita
    Mama Mia

1855 Buonitalia
75 9th Ave
New York, NY 10011
212-633-9090
Fax: 212-633-9717 info@buonitalia.com
www.buonitalia.com
Gourmet Italian foods including pasta, rice, mushrooms, truffles, flour, jams, oils, cheeses, vinegar, fruit mustard, cookies, biscuits and sweets
Owner: Mimmo Majiulo
Contact: Stacey Bonilla
staceybonilla@buonitalia.com
Manager: Scandt Zyleg
Bookkeeper: Yaribeth Dalmonte
Estimated Sales: $3.8 Million
Number Employees: 20-49
Square Footage: 20000
Parent Co: Misono Food
Type of Packaging: Consumer, Food Service, Private Label, Bulk

1856 Burch Farms
527 North Ave
Hilton, NY 14468-9144
585-392-2411
Fax: 585-392-4111 800-466-9668
info@burchfarms.com www.burchfarms.com
Sweet potatoes
President: Jimmy Burch
Partner: Ted Burch
Marketing Director: Jimmy Burch Jr
Contact: John Burch
john@burchfarms.com
Estimated Sales: $5,000,000
Number Employees: 5-9
Brands:
    Candy Yams
    Georgiana
    Sugar & Spice

1857 Burger Maker Inc
666 16th St
Carlstadt, NJ 07072-1922
201-939-0444
Fax: 201-939-1965 www.schweidandsons.com
Hamburger patties
Owner: David Schweid
davidschweid@burgermaker.com
EVP Operations: Brad Schweid
EVP Sales: Jamie Schweid
Regional Manager: Chip Crenshaw
Regional Manager: Bill Breslin
Regional Manager: John Jernagan
davidschweid@burgermaker.com
Number Employees: 100-249

1858 Burgers' Smokehouse
32819 Highway 87
California, MO 65018-3227
573-796-3134
Fax: 573-796-3137 800-345-5185
service@smokehouse.com www.smokehouse.com
Producer of smoked meats, country cured ham, spare ribs, pork chops, smoked bacon, summer sausage, smoked turkey, smoked chicken, beef roasts, steaks, burgers and desserts.
President: Steven Burger
sburger@smokehouse.com
Vice President: Philip Burger
Marketing Director: Chris Mouse
Operations Manager: Keith Fletcher
Year Founded: 1952
Estimated Sales: $20-50 Million
Number Employees: 250-499
Number of Brands: 1
Square Footage: 200000
Type of Packaging: Consumer, Food Service, Private Label, Bulk
Brands:
    Burgers Smokehouse

1859 Burke Brands
521 NE 189th St
Miami, FL 33179-3909
305-249-5628
Fax: 305-651-6018 877-436-7225
info@cafedonpablo.com www.cafedonpablo.com
Fine specialty coffee and gourmet food products.
President: Darron Burke
Vice President: Eliana Burke
Director of International Sales & Market: Thomas Stout
VP Sales: Carl Fiadini
Contact: Brian Vaughn
bvaughn@burkebrands.com
General Manager: Michele Fera
Production: Gladys Menjura
Estimated Sales: $1.8 Million
Number Employees: 19
Number of Brands: 4
Number of Products: 27
Square Footage: 10000
Type of Packaging: Consumer, Food Service, Private Label, Bulk
Other Locations:
    Burke Brands
    N Miami Beach FL
Brands:
    Cafe Don Pablo

561

Food Manufacturers / A-Z

1860 Burke Candy IngredientsInc
3840 N Fratney St
Milwaukee, WI 53212-1341
414-964-7327
Fax: 414-964-7644 888-287-5350
info@burkecandy.com www.burkecandy.com
Chocolate candies and confectionery. Products are certified kosher
Owner/Chef: Julia Burke
Owner/Chef: Tim Burke
burkecandy@aol.com
Estimated Sales: Less Than $500,000
Number Employees: 1-4

1861 Burke Corp
1516 S D Ave
PO Box 209
Nevada, IA 50201-2708
515-382-3575
Fax: 515-382-2834 800-654-1152
sales_info@burkecorp.com www.burkecorp.com
Sausages and other prepared meats
President: William Burke Jr.
CFO: Marcy Hansen
SVP: David Weber
VP Research and Development: Casey Frye
Process and Quality Control Manager: Jim Chittenden
Marketing Director: Liz Hertz
VP Sales/Marketing: Doug Cooprider
Director: Scott Licht
VP Purchasing: Thomas Burke
Estimated Sales: $28.9 Million
Number Employees: 250-499
Type of Packaging: Food Service, Private Label, Bulk
Brands:
  Burke(c)
  Swiss American Sausage Co.
  NaturaSelect(c)
  Premoro(c)
  Magnifoods(c)
  Tezzata(c)

1862 Burleigh Brothers Seafoods
224 Burleigh Rd
Ellerslie, PE C0B 1J0
Canada
902-831-2349
Fax: 902-831-3072 tom@burleigh.pe.ca
www.burleigh.pe.ca
Fresh shellfish, mollusk, trout and smelt
CEO: Roger Burleigh
President: Proy Burleigh
Marketing Director: Tom Bradstaw
Estimated Sales: $3.2 Million
Number Employees: 16
Type of Packaging: Consumer, Food Service, Private Label, Bulk

1863 Burleson Honey
301 Peters St
Waxahachie, TX 75165-2855
972-937-2809
Fax: 972-937-8711 Jodie.d@burlesons-honey.com
www.burlesons-honey.com
Honey
President: T.E. Burleson Jr
Estimated Sales: $1,6,000,000
Number Employees: 20-49
Square Footage: 45
Type of Packaging: Private Label
Brands:
  Burleson Pure Honey

1864 Burn Brae Farms
940 Matheson Blvd E
Mississauga, ON L4W 2R8
Canada
905-624-3600
Fax: 905-624-3363 gdowd@burnbraefarms.com
www.burnbraefarms.com
Packager of eggs
President: Joe Hudson
Marketing Director: Margaret Hudson
COO: Bob Anderson
Sales Manager: Gord Dowd
General Manager: Earl Powers
Estimated Sales: $25,000,000
Number Employees: 100
Parent Co: Burnbrae Farm
Type of Packaging: Consumer, Food Service
Brands:
  Free Run
  Nature's Best
  Omega Pro
  Organic Shell Eggs

1865 Burnett & Son
1420 S Myrtle Ave
Monrovia, CA 91016-4153
626-357-2165
Fax: 626-357-7115 877-632-5467
info@burnettandson.com www.burnettandson.com
Processor of meat including taco, London broil, shredded beef and pork, corned and roast beef, pot roast, steak, pork loin, etc; also, entrees including beef stew, chile, meat loaf, corned beef and cabbage, spaghetti and meatballsetc
President: Donald Burnett
Principal: David Kruse
Vice President: Derald Burnett
Year Founded: 1978
Estimated Sales: $20-50 Million
Number Employees: 50-99
Type of Packaging: Consumer, Food Service

1866 (HQ)Burnette Foods
701 US-31
Elk Rapids, MI 49629
231-264-8116
Fax: 231-264-9597 info@burnettefoods.com
www.burnettefoods.com
Canned fruits and vegetables including cherries, apples, plumbs, kidney beans, asparagus, green beans and potatoes
Owner/President: Teresa Amato
CEO: John Pelizzari
CFO: Jennifer Sherman
Quality Manager/Sales Executive: Jennifer Boyer
Operations Manager: Dave Schroderus
Production Manager: Eric Rockafellow
Plant Manager: Gary Wilson
Estimated Sales: $40-$50 Million
Number Employees: 50-99
Square Footage: 12066
Type of Packaging: Consumer, Food Service
Other Locations:
  Burnette Foods Plant
  East Jordan MI
  Burnette Foods Plant
  Hartford MI
Brands:
  Burnetti's
  Mothers Maid
  Romeo

1867 Burnham & Morrill Co
1 Beanpot Circle
Portland, ME 04103-5336
800-813-2165
www.bmbeans.com
Canned baked beans and brown bread
President: Kenneth Romanzi
CFO: Bruce Sherrill
Year Founded: 1867
Estimated Sales: $350,000
Number Employees: 100-249
Parent Co: B&G Foods
Type of Packaging: Consumer
Brands:
  B&M Baked Beans

1868 Burnley Vineyards
4500 Winery Ln
Barboursville, VA 22923-1833
540-832-2828
bvwinery@gmx.com
www.burnleywines.com
Producer of wines such as Chardonnay, Cabernet Sauvignon, Cabernet Dora, Riesling, Chambourcin, Vidal and Norton.
General Manager: C.J. Reeder
Sales Manager: Patt Reeder
Tasting & Tours: Dawn Reeder
Winemaker: Lee Reeder
Estimated Sales: $5-9,9,000,000
Number Employees: 5-9
Brands:
  Burnley Vineyards

1869 Burrito Kitchens
505 Weaver Pk Rd
Unit A
Longmont, CO 80501
720-652-9000
www.burritokitchens.com
All-natural burritos
Year Founded: 1999
Number of Products: 12

1870 Burt Lewis Ingredients
875 N Michigan Ave
Suite 2720
Chicago, IL 60611
312-640-8899
Fax: 312-640-8890 www.burtlewisingredients.com
Dairy products and ingredients
President: Vince Curtin
Year Founded: 1976

1871 Burton Meat Processing
1120 Navasota St
Burton, TX 77835-6131
979-289-4022
Fax: 978-989-4001
Beef, pork and sausage
Owner: Jerry Schultz
Estimated Sales: $2.5 Million
Number Employees: 1-4
Type of Packaging: Consumer, Bulk

1872 Bush Brothers & Co
800-590-3797
bushbeans.com
Baked beans
President & CEO: Al Williams
Year Founded: 1908
Estimated Sales: $100-499.9 Million
Number Employees: 1,000-4,999
Brands:
  Bush's Best Baked Beans
  Bush's Grilling Beans
  Bush's Chili
  Bush's Canned Beans

1873 Bush Brothers ProvisionCo
1931 N Dixie Hwy
West Palm Beach, FL 33407-6084
561-832-6666
Fax: 561-832-1460 800-327-1345
orders@bush-brothers.com
www.bush-brothers.com
Processor and exporter of fresh and frozen portion cut beef, veal, lamb, pork and poultry; wholesaler/distributor of dairy products; serving the food service market.
President: Harry Bush
sales@bushb-brothers.com
Vice President: Billy Bush
Sales Manager: Doug Bush
Operations Manager: John Bush
Estimated Sales: $13.3 Million
Number Employees: 20-49
Square Footage: 10000
Type of Packaging: Consumer, Food Service, Private Label, Bulk

1874 Busken Bakery
2675 Madison Rd
Cincinnati, OH 45208-1389
513-871-2114
Fax: 513-871-2662 orders@busken.com
Cookies, cakes, doughnuts, breads, rolls, pies and muffins.
Chief Executive Officer: D. Busken
Vice President: Brian Busken
Estimated Sales: $28,050,000
Number Employees: 100-249

1875 Busseto Foods
1090 W Church Ave
Fresno, CA 93706-3917
559-237-9591
Fax: 559-237-5745 800-628-2633
www.busseto.com
Specialty meats, salami, peperoni, prosciutto, chubs, pancetta and genoa
President & CEO: G Michael Grazier
g@busseto.com
CFO: Chuck Laizure
VP: Luca Zaniboni
Quality Assurance/quality Control Manage: Angela Gunadi
Maintenance Manager: Robert Diaz
Estimated Sales: $6.5 Million
Number Employees: 20-49
Parent Co: IBIS
Type of Packaging: Consumer, Food Service, Private Label, Bulk

Food Manufacturers / A-Z

Brands:
   Busseto
   Busseto Special Reserve

1876 Busy Bee Yerba Mate
www.busybeemate.com
Yerba mate
Co-Founder & CEO: Jayme Starrak
COO: Jared Yeager
Number of Brands: 1
Number of Products: 4
Type of Packaging: Consumer
Brands:
   BUSY BEE

1877 Butler Foods LLC
P.O. Box 40
Grand Ronde, OR 97347
503-437-9133
info@butlerfoods.com
www.butlerfoods.com
Vegan products including soy curls, soy jerky, and taco crumbles
Owner: Dan Butler

1878 Butler Winery
6200 E Robinson Rtd
Bloomington, IN 47408
812-332-6660
vineyard@butlerwinery.com
www.butlerwinery.com
Wine and wine making supplies
President/CEO: James Butler
Secretary/Treasurer: Susan Butler
Manager: Amy Butler
Estimated Sales: $540,000
Number Employees: 5
Brands:
   Butler

1879 Butter Baked Goods
4907 Mackenzie Street
Vancouver, BC V6N 2G5
Canada
604-221-4333
Fax: 604-685-8563 info@butterbakedgoods.com
www.butterbakedgoods.com
Scones, muffins, cinnamon buns, cookies, bars, cupcakes, cakes, pies, tarts and mini tarts, loaves, and marshmallow
Propietor/President: Rosie Daykin
Number Employees: 1

1880 Butter Buds Food Ingredients
2330 Chicory Rd
Racine, WI 53403-4113
262-598-9900
Fax: 262-598-9999 800-426-1119
bbfi@bbuds.com www.bbuds.com
Processor and exporter of cholesterol-free butter flavored oils and sprays; also, natural dairy concentrates including butter, cheese and cream.
CEO: Jonh Buhler
Director of Business Development: Tom Buhler
Director of Administration: Jan Schmaus
General Manager: Bill Buhler
Estimated Sales: $5-10 Million
Number Employees: 50
Square Footage: 10000
Type of Packaging: Consumer, Food Service, Private Label, Bulk
Brands:
   Alfredobuds
   Butter Flo
   Butterbuds
   Buttermist
   Cheesebuds

1881 Butter Krust Baking Company
1919 Flowers Circle
Thomasville, GA 31757
229-226-9110
Fax: 570-286-6975 800-282-8093
www.butterkrust.com
Bread, rolls and donuts
President: James G Apple
CFO: Brenda Swisher
Vice President: Randall Kreisher
Director of Sales: Tom Gresh
Manager: Lisa R. Hay
Plant Manager: Barry Hulfizer
Purchasing Manager: Timothy Apple
Estimated Sales: $300,000-500,000
Number Employees: 5-9

Type of Packaging: Consumer, Private Label, Bulk
Other Locations:
   Northumberland PA
Brands:
   Butter-Krust Country
   Holsum
   Milano

1882 Butterball Farms
1435 Buchanan Ave SW
Grand Rapids, MI 49507-1699
616-243-0105
Fax: 616-243-9169 888-828-8837
www.butterballfarms.com
Butter and margarine
President: David Riemersma
david.r@butterballfarms.com
CFO: Steve Whitteberry
Business Development Management: David Smallwood
Quality Assurance Manager: Lucia Falek
VP of Operations: Mike Craig
Plant Manager: Jim Bovee
Director of Purchasing: Ken Berry
Estimated Sales: $25.5 Million
Number Employees: 100-249
Square Footage: 125000
Type of Packaging: Food Service, Private Label
Brands:
   Butterball
   Figure-Maid
   Pack of the Roses
   Pop-Out
   Sweetcorn

1883 Butterball LLC
1 Butterball Ln
PO Box 2389
Garner, NC 27529-5971
919-255-7900
Fax: 919-255-7973 www.butterballcorp.com
Frozen and refrigerated turkeys
President: Rodney Brenneman
CEO: Brenda Abbott
abbottb@johnstoncc.edu
SVP Research/Development: Jay Jandrain
Marketing Director: Kari Lindell
SVP Retail Sales: Dick Sarvas
Plant Manager: Jerry Lankford
Number Employees: 5000-9999
Parent Co: ConAgra Refrigerated Prepared Foods
Other Locations:
   Frozen Turkey Plant
   Carthage MO
   Prepackaging Plant
   Huntsville AR
   Deli Packaging Plant
   Jonesboro AR
   Frozen Turkey Plant
   Mount Olive NC
   Prepackaging Plant
   Ozark AR
Brands:
   Butterball

1884 Butterfield Foods
635 Westfield Rd
Noblesville, IN 46060-1323
317-776-4775
Fax: 317-776-4784 info@butterfield-foods.com
www.butterfield-foods.com
Prepared foods
President: Frank Violi
Estimated Sales: $30 Million
Number Employees: 150
Parent Co: Violi Foods
Type of Packaging: Consumer, Food Service, Private Label, Bulk

1885 Butterfields
2155 S Old Franklin Rd
Nashville, NC 27856-8952
252-459-7771
Fax: 252-459-7606 800-945-5957
Hard candy.
President: Brooks West
Estimated Sales: $670,000
Number Employees: 15

1886 Butterfly Creek Winery
PO Box 967
Mariposa, CA 95338
209-742-4567
Fax: 209-742-5019 www.yosemite.com
Wines

President: John Gerken
Sales: Tolleman Gorham
General Manager: Bob Gerken
Purchasing Manager: Robert Garcia
Estimated Sales: $210,000
Number Employees: 5
Type of Packaging: Private Label

1887 Butternut Mountain Farm
37 Industrial Park Dr
Morrisville, VT 05661-8533
802-888-5909 800-828-2376
sales@butternutmountainfarm.com
www.butternutmountainfarm.com
Distributor and supplier of pure maple syrup and maple sugar.
Owner/Founder: David Marvin
CEO: John Kingston
Sales Manager: Stuart MacFarland
Director of Operations: Richard Harvey
Purchasing Manager: David Ellis
Square Footage: 50000
Parent Co: The Vermont Maple Syrup Company
Type of Packaging: Consumer, Food Service, Private Label, Bulk
Other Locations:
   Butternut Mountain Farm Store
   Johnson VT

1888 Buttonwood Farm Winery & Vineyard
1500 Alamo Pintado Rd
Solvang, CA 93463-9756
805-688-3032
Fax: 805-688-6168 800-715-1404
info@buttonwoodwinery.com
www.buttonwoodwinery.com
Wines
President: Bret Davenport
bret@buttonwoodwinery.com
CFO: Elizabeth Williams
VP: Seyburn Zorthian
Marketing Manager: Sherill Dugin
Secretary: Barry Zorthian
Estimated Sales: $990,000
Number Employees: 20-49

1889 Buxton Foods
401 Broadway
Buxton, ND 58218-4003
701-847-2110
800-726-8057
Gourmet frozen pinto beans and chili fully cooked and packaged in oven/microwaveable trays and boil-in-bags
President: Paul Siewert
CEO: Eileen Siewert
Estimated Sales: $10-20 Million
Number Employees: 1-4
Square Footage: 9000
Type of Packaging: Consumer, Food Service
Brands:
   Paul's Pintos

1890 Buywell Coffee
4850 North Park Drive
Colorado Springs, CO 80918
719-598-7870
877-294-6246
Organic coffee
President: Segundo Guerrero
Treasurer: Benita Quevedo
Secretary: Pedro Castillo

1891 Buzz Food Svc
4818 Kanawha Blvd E
Charleston, WV 25306-6328
304-925-4781
Fax: 304-925-1502 info@buzzfoodsvc.com
www.buzzbutteredsteaks.com
Distributor of; beef, lamb, veal, chicken, pork, seafood, cheese, dairy, produce, canned goods, flour & baking supplies, frozen entrees and appetizers, ethnic specialties, gourmet items, beverage service, concession supplies andequipment, cleaning products and smallwares
President: Dickinson Gould
dickinson@buzzfoodsvc.com
Sales Manager: Jason Jean
General Manager: John Haddy
Operations Manager: Jeramy Kidd
Purchasing: Dennis Benson

Food Manufacturers / A-Z

Estimated Sales: $10.22 Million
Number Employees: 50-99
Square Footage: 90000
Type of Packaging: Consumer, Food Service
Brands:
    Unipro
    Fry Foods
    Buzz Buttered Steaks
    Code
    General Mills
    Haddys
    Red Gold
    Farmland
    Reflections
    Kraft
    Hormel Foods
    Dutch Quality House
    Teays Valley
    Advance
    Vie De France
    Gold Medal
    Simplot

1892 Buzzards Bay Trading Company
PO Box 600
Fairhaven, MA 02719-0600
    508-996-0242
    Fax: 508-996-2421
Fresh and frozen seafood

1893 Buzzn Bee Farms
4700 N Flagler Dr
West Palm Beach, FL 33407-2907
    561-881-1551
    Fax: 561-881-7023 www.buzznbee.com
Honey
Owner/Beekeeper: David Rukin
Estimated Sales: $2.5-5,000,000
Number Employees: 1-4
Brands:
    Buzzn Bee Farms
    Sweet Squeeze

1894 Byblos Bakery
2479 23rd Street NE
Calgary, AB T2E 8J8
Canada
    403-250-3711
    Fax: 403-291-4095 info@byblosbakery.com
    www.byblosbakery.com
Middle Eastern baked goods including pita bread, bagels, baklava and tortilla wraps
President: Salim Daklala
Secretary: Elias Daklala
VP: George Daklala
Estimated Sales: $5,600,000
Number Employees: 80
Number of Brands: 1
Type of Packaging: Consumer, Food Service, Private Label, Bulk
Brands:
    Byblos

1895 Byington Vineyard & Winery
21850 Bear Creek Rd
Los Gatos, CA 95033-9438
    408-354-1111
    Fax: 408-354-2782 tastingroom@byington.com
    www.byington.com
Wines
Manager: Frank Ashton
Secretary/Treasurer: Rod Bravo
VP: Sheryl Brissenden
Manager: Clyde Byington
c.byington@byingtonsteel.com
Manager: Frank Ashton
Estimated Sales: $510,000
Number Employees: 5-9
Square Footage: 15
Type of Packaging: Private Label
Brands:
    Byington

1896 Bylada Foods
140 W Commercial Ave
Moonachie, NJ 07074-1703
    201-933-7474
    Fax: 201-933-1530 www.chefgustofoods.com
Frozen pizza and pizza bagels including regular and bite-size; exporter of pizza bagels

Vice President: Eric Silverman
eric@byladafoods.com
VP: Eric Silbeerman
Office Manager: Fay Campisi
Production Manager: Dan D'Amico
Estimated Sales: $5-10 Million
Number Employees: 10-19
Square Footage: 38000
Type of Packaging: Consumer, Food Service, Private Label
Brands:
    Bocconcino

1897 Byrd Cookie
6700 Waters Ave
Savannah, GA 31406-2718
    912-355-1716
    Fax: 912-355-4431 800-291-2973
    info@byrdcookiecompany.com
    www.byrdcookiecompany.com
Cookies, cheese biscuits and Southern-style condiments
President: Geoff Repella
geoff@byrdcookiecompany.com
CEO: Stephanie Lindley
Chief Financial Officer: Will Brodmann
Director of Retail Operations: Stacy Jennings
Director of Operations: Jamie Lindley
Estimated Sales: $2.7 Million
Number Employees: 50-99
Number of Brands: 2
Number of Products: 75
Square Footage: 65000
Type of Packaging: Consumer, Private Label
Other Locations:
    Byrd's Famous Cookies @ City Market
    Savannah GA
    Byrd's Famous Cookies on River St.
    Savannah GA
    Byrd's Famous Cookies in Pooler
    Pooler GA
Brands:
    Byrd's Famous Cookies
    Byrd Cookies

1898 Byrd Mill Co
14471 Washington Hwy
Ashland, VA 23005
    804-798-3627
    Fax: 804-798-9357 888-897-3336
    sales@byrdmill.com www.byrdmill.com
Specialty mixes including bread, pound cake, cookie, fruit cobbler, biscuit, pancake, waffle, muffin, spoon bread, shortbread, corn bread, hushpuppy, stoneground grits, etc
President: Todd Attkisson
sales@byrdmill.com
Estimated Sales: $300,000-$500,000
Number Employees: 10-19
Square Footage: 3300
Type of Packaging: Consumer, Food Service, Private Label, Bulk

1899 Byrd's Pecans
3 RR Box 196
Butler, MO 64730-9418
    660-925-3253
    866-679-5583
    byrdspecans.com
Pecans
Owner: Loyle Byrd
Owner: Mary Byrd
Estimated Sales: Less than $500,000
Number Employees: 1-4
Type of Packaging: Private Label
Brands:
    Byrd Missouri Grown
    Byrd's Hoot Owl Pecan Ranch Pecans

1900 Byrd's Seafood
101 Potomac St
Crisfield, MD 21817-1448
    410-968-0990
    Fax: 410-968-1424 www.byrdsseafood.com
Crabmeat
Manager: Patti Marshall
Estimated Sales: $3-5,000,000
Number Employees: 5-9

1901 Byrne & Carlson
PO Box 789
Portsmouth, NH 03802
    603-559-9778
    Fax: 603-559-9778 888-559-9778
    info@byrneandcarlson.com
    www.byrneandcarlson.com
Chocolates and confections
Owner: Christopher Carlson
Estimated Sales: $325,000
Number Employees: 2

1902 Byrne Dairy, Inc.
2394 Route 11
P.O. Box 176
Syracuse, NY 13084
    800-899-1535
    info@byrnedairy.com www.byrnedairy.com
Dairy products including fluid milks, flavored milk drinks, ice cream mixes and custard mixes, creamers, cappuccino and mocha cappuccino drink, egg nog, orange juice, apple juice, grape juice, fruit and orange drink, lemon iced teapink lemon drink, lemonade, and heavy cream and buttermilk, whipped cream, ice cream, cheese, cottage cheese, yogurt, butter, sour cream, eggs, dips, and a recovery drink called After Byrne.
President & CEO: F. Fred Sadeghi
EVP & Treasurer: Mark Byrne
Board President & VP, Marketing: Carl Byrne
Year Founded: 1933
Estimated Sales: $44.5 Million
Number Employees: 480
Square Footage: 32000
Type of Packaging: Consumer, Food Service, Private Label, Bulk
Brands:
    Byrne Dairy
    After Byrne Recovery Drink

1903 Byrnes & Kiefer Co
131 Kline Ave
Callery, PA 16024
    724-538-5200
    Fax: 724-538-9292 contactus@bkcompany.com
    www.bkcompany.com
Baked goods
President: Jay Thier
Chief Executive Officer: Edward Byrnes
Contact: Don Bradley
bradley@bkcompany.com
Estimated Sales: $23,000,000
Number Employees: 50
Type of Packaging: Private Label
Brands:
    B&K Manufacturing
    Charlie's Specialties

1904 Byrnes & Kiefer Company
131 Kline Avenue
Callery, PA 16024
    724-538-5200
    contactus@bkcompany.com
    www.bkcompany.com
Bakery products, including baking supplies, fillings and icings, and read-to-eat baked goods, such as brownies, cookies, and pastries.
Year Founded: 1902
Estimated Sales: $10-20 Million
Number Employees: 20-49
Square Footage: 60000
Type of Packaging: Food Service, Private Label
Brands:
    Chefmaster
    Charlie's Specialties

1905 Byrnes Packing Shed
880 Federal Point Rd
Hastings, FL 32145-3210
    904-692-1643
    Fax: 904-692-2002
Grower and packer of whole potatoes
Owner: Daniel Byrnes
byrnesfarms@aol.com
Estimated Sales: $2.5-5 Million
Number Employees: 10-19
Type of Packaging: Consumer

1906 Byron Vineyard & Winery
5250 Tepusquet Rd.
Santa Maria, CA 93454
    805-938-7365
    Fax: 805-938-1581 info@byronwines.com
    www.byronwines.com

Wines
Manager & Winemaker: Jonathan Nagy
Contact: Lea Brandy
lbrandy@byronwines.com
Estimated Sales: $5-10,000,000
Number Employees: 11-50
Type of Packaging: Private Label

1907 C & C Packing Co
1197 Highway 82
Stamps, AR 71860-9008
870-533-2251
Fax: 870-533-4309 866-365-3759
candcpackinginc@hotmail.com
www.candcpackinginc.com
Meat
Owner: Kenny Camp
kcamp@ccpacking.com
Owner/Operations Manager: Kenny Camp
Estimated Sales: Less Than $500,000
Number Employees: 5-9
Type of Packaging: Consumer

1908 C & E Canners Inc
1249 Mays Landing Rd
PO Box 229
Hammonton, NJ 08037-2816
609-561-1078
Fax: 609-567-2776
Processor, exporter and canner of sauces and ketchup
President: Robert Cappuccio
r.cappuccio@chi-rho.com
Corporate Secretary: Joseph Cappuccio
COO: David Cappuccio
Director Manufacturing: Stephen Cappuccio
Estimated Sales: $1.3 Million
Number Employees: 20-49
Square Footage: 320000
Type of Packaging: Consumer
Brands:
   C & E Sugar
   Cappuccio
   Na Po'okela O Honaunau

1909 (HQ)C & F Foods Inc
15620 E Valley Blvd
City Of Industry, CA 91744-3926
626-723-1000
Fax: 626-723-1212 mmendoza@cnf-foods.com
www.cnf-foods.com
Dried beans, lentils, popcorn, peas and rice
President & CEO: Luis Faura
CFO: Alex Tran
VP Sales & Marketing: Paul Cromidas
Sr. Director of Operations: Mark Mendoza
Year Founded: 1975
Estimated Sales: $32.6 Million
Number Employees: 100-249
Type of Packaging: Consumer, Food Service, Private Label
Other Locations:
   C&F Foods
   Hansen ID
   C&F Foods
   Sikeston MO
   C&F Foods
   Manvel ND
   C&F Food
   Raleigh NC
Brands:
   El Orgullo De Mi Tierra
   Kanga Beans
   Premier Fields

1910 C & G Salsa
PO Box 6085
Fishers, IN 46038-6085
317-569-9099
Fax: 317-569-8666 sales@cgsalsa.com
www.cgsalsa.com
Produces a variety of salsa (mild/medium/hot) and chili sauce (mild/zesty) products.
Owner: Charles Ferguson
sales@cgsalsa.com
Co-Owner: Glenda Ferguson
Number Employees: 1-4
Type of Packaging: Food Service

1911 (HQ)C & H Sugar Co Inc
830 Loring Ave
Crockett, CA 94525
800-773-1803
www.chsugar.com
Raw, organic and granulized sugar; sweeteners and baking sugar.
President & CEO: David Koncelik
Year Founded: 1906
Estimated Sales: $169 Million
Number Employees: 200-500
Parent Co: ASR Group
Type of Packaging: Consumer, Food Service, Private Label, Bulk
Brands:
   C&H

1912 C & J Tender Meat Co
324 E Intl Airport Rd
Anchorage, AK 99518-1215
907-562-2838
Fax: 907-561-5846 www.cjtendermeat.com
Meats
Owner: Steve Jones
Treasurer: Arlita Jones
Estimated Sales: $1.1 Million
Number Employees: 5-9

1913 C C Conway Seafoods
2567 Conway Oysterhouse Road
Wicomico, VA 23184
804-642-2853
Fish and seafood
Owner/President: Christopher Conway III
Estimated Sales: $500,000-$1,000,000
Number Employees: 1-4
Type of Packaging: Food Service, Bulk

1914 C C Pollen
3627 E Indian School Rd # 209
Phoenix, AZ 85018-5134
602-957-0096
Fax: 602-381-3130 800-875-0096
beemail1@ccpollen.com www.beepollen.com
Bee pollen and beehive products
President: Bruce Brown
Estimated Sales: $7 Million
Number Employees: 10-19
Number of Brands: 7
Type of Packaging: Consumer, Food Service, Private Label, Bulk
Brands:
   24-Hour Royal Jelly
   Aller Bee-Gone
   Bee Propolis
   Buzz Bars
   Dynamic Trio
   High Desert
   Pollenergy

1915 C F Burger Creamery Co
8101 Greenfield Rd
Detroit, MI 48228-2296
313-584-4040
Fax: 313-584-9870 info@cfburger.com
www.cfburger.com
Dairy products
President: Dean Angott
CEO: Larry Angott
langott@cfburger.com
Number Employees: 50-99
Type of Packaging: Consumer, Food Service, Private Label, Bulk
Brands:
   C.F. Burger
   Goody Shake
   Natures Fountain

1916 C F Gollott & Son Seafood
9357 Central Ave
PO Box 1191
Diberville, MS 39540-5301
228-392-2747
Fax: 228-392-3701 cfgollot@gmail.com
www.gollottseafood.com
Frozen shrimp
Co-Owner: Brian Gollott
Co-Owner: Armond Gollott
Co-Owner: Dale Gollott
Co-Owner: Nicky Gollott
Plant Operations: Todd Gollott
Estimated Sales: $20-50 Million
Number Employees: 50-99
Square Footage: 7800
Type of Packaging: Consumer, Food Service, Private Label
Brands:
   Treasure Chest Shrimp
   Full Moon Shrimp
   Gollots Brand Shrimp
   Mermaid's Supreme Shrimp

1917 C H Guenther & Son Inc
2201 Broadway St
San Antonio, TX 78215-1135
210-227-1401
www.chg.com
Flour meal and prepared mixes; frozen bakery products.
President & CEO: Dale Tremblay
dtremblay@chguenther.com
SVP & CFO: Justin Grubbs
SVP, Corporate Services: Stephen Phillips
SVP & General Counsel: Thomas McRae
SVP & Chief Commercial Officer: Kelly Crouse
SVP & COO: Eric Stockl
Year Founded: 1851
Estimated Sales: $133.2 Million
Number Employees: 500-999
Square Footage: 22869
Type of Packaging: Consumer, Food Service, Private Label, Bulk
Other Locations:
   Williams Foods
   Lenexa KS
   Pioneer Flour Mills
   San Antonio TX
   Pioneer Frozen Foods
   Duncanville TX
   Pioneer Frozen Foods
   Prosperity SC
   The Guenther House
   San Antonio TX
Brands:
   Pioneer
   Williams
   White Wings
   Morrison's
   Sun-Bird

1918 C Howard Co
1007 Station Rd
Bellport, NY 11713-1552
631-286-7940
Fax: 631-286-7947 apratz@chowardcompany.com
www.chowardsdirect.com
Confectionery products including hard candy, mints and chewing gum
President: Kenneth Pratz
inquire@chowardcompany.com
Treasurer: Gene Pratz
Vice President: Arthur Pratz
Estimated Sales: $510,000
Number Employees: 5-9
Square Footage: 20000
Type of Packaging: Consumer, Private Label
Brands:
   Chowards

1919 C J Dannemiller Co
5300 S Hametown Rd
Norton, OH 44203-6199
330-825-7808
Fax: 330-825-3793 800-624-8671
www.cjdannemiller.com
Roasted nuts and popcorn
President: James A Dannemiller
sales@cjdannemiller.com
Secretary: TW Dannemiller
Estimated Sales: $5-10 Million
Number Employees: 20-49
Square Footage: 88000
Type of Packaging: Bulk

1920 C J Vitner Co
4202 W 45th St
Chicago, IL 60660-4390
773-523-7900
Fax: 773-523-9143 www.snakking.com
Potato chips, pork rinds, cheese puffs, popcorn and pretzels.
Year Founded: 1926
Estimated Sales: $20-50 Million
Number Employees: 250-499
Square Footage: 77000
Parent Co: Snak King
Type of Packaging: Consumer, Food Service, Private Label, Bulk

1921 C Nelson Mfg Co
265 N Lake Winds Pkwy
Oak Harbor, OH 43449-9012
419-898-3305
Fax: 419-898-4098

Food Manufacturers / A-Z

Manufacturer of ice cream cabinets, ice cream carts and related equipment.
Owner: Kelley Smith
nelsonoh@aol.com
Marketing/Sales: George Dunlap
Purchasing: Paul Zylka
Estimated Sales: $10-20 000,000
Number Employees: 20-49

1922 C P Vegetable Oil
601 SW 21st Terrace
Suite 1
Fort Lauderdale, FL 33312-2278
Canada
954-584-0420
Fax: 905-792-9461   800-398-7154
info@cpvusa.com   www.cpvegoil.com
Vegetable oils
Ceo: Christian Pellerin
Manager: Giuseppe Vinci
gvinci@cpvusa.com
Number Employees: 10-19
Type of Packaging: Food Service, Bulk
Brands:
 C.P.

1923 C Roy & Sons Processing
444 Roy Dr
Yale, MI 48097
810-387-1654
Fax: 810-387-3957   croyprocessing@hotmail.com
www.yalebologna.com
Meat products including bologna
CEO: Richard Roy
Manager: Nancy Roy
Estimated Sales: $2 Million
Number Employees: 20
Type of Packaging: Consumer

1924 C S Steen Syrup Mill Inc
119 N Main St
Abbeville, LA 70510-4603
337-893-1654
Fax: 337-893-2478   800-725-1654
steens@steensyrup.com   www.steensyrup.com
Molasses and syrup
Owner: Charlie Steen
steens@steensyrup.com
Marketing Director: Cole Thompson
Estimated Sales: $5-10 Million
Number Employees: 20-49
Type of Packaging: Bulk
Brands:
 Steen's Cane Cured Pheasant

1925 C W Resources Inc
200 Myrtle St
New Britain, CT 06053-4160
860-229-7700
Fax: 860-229-6847   info@cwresources.org
www.cwresources.org
Gourmet products including flavored vinegars and oils, salsas, sauces, jellies, baking mixes, dips/dip mixes, baked goods, rubs and salad dressings
President & CEO: Ronald Buccilli
Director of Finance: Marta Kuczek
VP Sales/Production: Alix Capsalors
Operations Manager: Mark Anderson
Production: Bill Blonski
Estimated Sales: $33 Million
Number Employees: 250-499
Square Footage: 100000
Type of Packaging: Consumer, Food Service, Private Label, Bulk
Brands:
 B&B
 Sumptuous Ions

1926 C&J Trading
1140 Revere Ave
San Francisco, CA 94124-3423
415-822-8910
Fax: 415-822-7526
Oriental food
Owner: C Wo
Estimated Sales: $1-2,500,000
Number Employees: 5-9
Type of Packaging: Private Label

1927 C&P Additives
950 Peninsula Corp Cir
Suite 3018
Boca Raton, FL 33487
561-995-7071
Fax: 561-995-7075   877-857-2623
office@cp-additives.com   www.cp-additives.com
Seasonings and enzymes
Type of Packaging: Private Label, Bulk

1928 C&S Wholesale Meat Company
973 Confederate Ave SE
Atlanta, GA 30312
404-627-3547
Fax: 404-627-3549
Portion cut meat including pork and beef
President: Jay Bernath
CEO: Stanley D. Bernath
Chairman of the Board: Stanley Bernath
Marketing Administrator: Ronnie Berneth
Estimated Sales: $10-20 Million
Number Employees: 20-49
Type of Packaging: Food Service, Bulk
Brands:
 C&S

1929 C&T Refinery
PO Box 9300
Minneapolis, MN 55440
804-287-1340
Fax: 804-285-9168   800-227-4455
www.cargill.com
Processor and exporter of vegetable oil
President: C Sauer
VP: Robert Holden
Parent Co: C.F. Sauer Company
Type of Packaging: Consumer, Food Service, Private Label, Bulk
Brands:
 C&T

1930 C'est Gourmet
2 Watson Place
Framingham, MA 01701
508-877-0000
Fax: 508-877-5600   info@cestgourmet.com
Gourmet baked goods
Co-Owner: Chris Gagnon
Co-Owner: Jacques Cohen
Operations Manager: Andrea Gagnon
Number Employees: 1-4
Type of Packaging: Food Service, Private Label

1931 C. Gould Seafoods
PO Box 14566
Scottsdale, AZ 85267-4566
480-314-9250
Fax: 480-314-9240
Seafood
President: Carla Gould
Owner: Carlos Garcia
Secretary/Treasurer: Helen Sambrano
Vice President: Robert Llewellyn
Estimated Sales: $550,000
Number Employees: 4

1932 C.B.S. Lobster Company
41 Union Wharf
Portland, ME 04101
207-775-2917
Fax: 207-772-0169   www.mainelobsterdirect.com
Lobster
Owner: Lee Kressbach
CEO: Joi Kressbach
Estimated Sales: $5-10 Million
Number Employees: 20-49

1933 C.C. Graber Company
315 E Fourth Street
Ontario, CA 91764
909-983-1761
Fax: 909-984-2180   800-996-5483
info@graberolives.com   www.graberolives.com
Manufacturer of vegetables, gourmet foods and olives.
President: Clifford Graber
Co-Owner: Robert Graber
Contact: Sue Bonetti
suebonetti@graberolives.com
Year Founded: 1894
Estimated Sales: $20-50 Million
Number Employees: 100-249
Number of Brands: 1

Brands:
 Graber Olives

1934 C.E. Fish Company
69 Roque Bluffs Road
Jonesboro, ME 4648
207-434-2631
Fax: 207-434-6940
Soft-shelled and steamer clams
President: Barbara Fish
Treasurer: Marge Fish
Vice President: Ralph Fish
Estimated Sales: $83,000
Number Employees: 5-9
Square Footage: 10500
Type of Packaging: Consumer
Brands:
 Uni

1935 C.F. Sauer Co.
2000 W. Broad St.
Richmond, VA 23220
800-688-5676
888-723-0052
www.cfsauer.com
Spices and mixes including cooking spices, griller seasonings, rubs, grinders, bulk spices and seasonings, baking bag mixes, microwave steamer mixes, gravy mixes, seasoning mixes, grilling marinade mixes, sauce mixes, slow cookermixes, extracts, flavorings and food colorings, mayonnaise and mustard, and BBQ sauces.
President/CEO: Conrad Sauer IV
CFO: W.N. Clemons
Vice President: Bradford Sauer
Executive VP, Sales: Mark Sauer
Year Founded: 1887
Estimated Sales: $223 Million
Number Employees: 1000-4999
Number of Brands: 7
Square Footage: 80000
Type of Packaging: Consumer, Food Service, Private Label
Other Locations:
 C.F. Sauer Company
 San Luis Obispo CA
Brands:
 Bama
 C.F. Sauer Company
 Duke's Mayonaise
 Gold Medal
 Mrs. Filberts
 Sauer's Everyday Spices
 The Spice Hunter

1936 C.J. Distributing
P.O.Box 2344
Surf City, NC 28445
910-329-1681
Fax: 910-329-1286   800-990-2366
Peanuts and snack food items
CEO: E Howell
Number Employees: 1-4
Square Footage: 5000
Type of Packaging: Consumer, Private Label, Bulk

1937 C.L. Deveau & Son
PO Box 1
Salmon River, NS B0W 2Y0
Canada
902-649-2812
Fax: 902-649-2812
Salted fish and frozen herring roe
President: Irvan Paul Deveau
Number Employees: 10-19
Type of Packaging: Consumer, Food Service, Private Label, Bulk

1938 C.W. Brown Foods, Inc.
161 Kings Highway
Mountt Royal, NJ 08061
856-423-3700
customerservice@bottosausage.com
www.bottosausage.com
Fresh sausage, meatballs, and case ready meats
Estimated Sales: $10-20 Million
Number Employees: 50-99
Number of Brands: 1
Number of Products: 5
Type of Packaging: Consumer, Bulk
Brands:
 Botto's Genuine Italian Sausage

Food Manufacturers / A-Z

1939 C2O Pure Coconut Water
4000 Cover Street
Suite 110
Long Beach, CA 90808
877-295-0473
contact@c2o-cocowater.com www.drinkC2O.com
Coconut water
Founder/President: Ronald Greene
Year Founded: 2008
Number Employees: 11-50

1940 CA Fortune & Company
141 Covingtion Dr
Bloomingdale, IL 60108-3107
630-539-3100
Fax: 608-634-2400
Dairy products, specialty foods, pizza toppings, pizza crusts and bread.
President: Ken Rzeszutko
Contact: Stephanie Anderson
stephanie.anderson@cafortune.com
Purchasing: Ralph Johnson
Estimated Sales: $1-2,500,000
Number Employees: 15
Type of Packaging: Private Label
Brands:
 Burlle Meats
 New Holstein Cheese
 Rotella Bread

1941 CB Beverage Corporation
PO Box 49
Hopkins, MN 55343
952-935-9905
Fax: 952-938-2731 www.cocknbull.com
Beverages; ginger beer, sarsaparilla, sparkling juice, root beer, etc.
President: Daniel Meyers
Estimated Sales: Less than $300,000
Number Employees: 1-4

1942 CB's Nuts
6013 NE State Hwy 104
Kingston, WA 98346
360-297-1213
www.cbsnuts.com
Peanut butter
President & Owner: Tami Bowen
VP, Marketing: Chris Bowen
Number of Brands: 1
Number of Products: 2
Type of Packaging: Consumer
Brands:
 CB'S NUTS

1943 CBC Foods
305 Main St
PO Box 396
Little River, KS 67457-9073
620-897-6665
Fax: 620-897-5599 800-276-4770
Manufacture frozen cookie dough
President: Carolyn Wright
carolyn@cookiehouse.com
Estimated Sales: $1,000,000
Number Employees: 5-9
Square Footage: 5000
Type of Packaging: Consumer, Food Service, Private Label, Bulk

1944 CBP Resources
5533 York Highway
Gastonia, NC 28052-8729
704-868-4573
Fax: 704-861-9252
Poultry processing plant.
President: JJ Smith
Principal: Paul Humphries
Estimated Sales: $20-50 Million
Number Employees: 100-249
Parent Co: Carolina By-Products Company

1945 CBS Food Products Corporation
2020 Fieldstone Pkwy
Suite 900-179
Franklin, TN 37069
800-216-9605
Fax: 718-452-2516 info@cbsfoods.com
www.cbsfoods.com
Shrimp burgers
President: Chaim Stein
CEO: Bernard Steinberg
Vice President: Phillip Shapiro
Purchasing Agent: Bob Green
Estimated Sales: $2 Million
Number Employees: 15
Type of Packaging: Consumer, Food Service, Private Label
Brands:
 Cbs

1946 CHO America
204 B W YMCA Dr
Baytown, TX 77521
281-712-1549
www.cho-america.com
Organic and extra virgin olive oils and Deglet Nour dates
CEO: Wajih Rekik

1947 CHR Foods
P.O.Box 608
Watsonville, CA 95077-0608
831-728-0157
Fax: 831-728-0459
Frozen mixed vegetables and strawberries including whole and puree
President/CEO: Ray Rodriguez
CFO: Julis Skelton
Estimated Sales: $5-10,000,000
Number Employees: 5-9
Type of Packaging: Food Service
Brands:
 Chr
 New Harvest Foods

1948 CHS Inc.
5500 Cenex Dr.
Inver Grove Hts., MN 55077
651-355-6000
800-328-6539
www.chsinc.com
Agriculture, energy, transportation and business services company, with food products through subsidiary Ventura Foods.
President/CEO: Jay Debertin
Executive VP/CFO: Olivia Nelligan
Executive VP/General Counsel: Jim Zappa
Estimated Sales: $32.6 Billion
Number Employees: 10000+
Type of Packaging: Consumer, Food Service, Private Label, Bulk

1949 CHS Sunflower
220 Clement Ave
Grandin, ND 58038-4017
701-484-5313
Fax: 701-484-5657 sunflower@chsinc.com
www.chssunflower.com
Sunflower kernels, in-shell sunflower, flax, millet, buckwheat, pumpkin seeds, and soybean.
President/CEO: James Krogh
james.krogh@chsinc.com
Research & Development: Joel Schaefer
Sales Director: Wes Dick
Sales Director: Bruce Fjelde
Plant Superintendent: Arvid Terry
Controller: Chuck Schmidt
Number Employees: 100-249
Parent Co: CHS, Inc.
Type of Packaging: Consumer, Food Service, Private Label, Bulk

1950 CHS Sunprairie
1800 13th St SE
Minot, ND 58701-6061
Canada
701-852-1429
Fax: 701-852-2755 800-556-6807
Organic flour, pancake mixes and hot breakfast cereals; exporter of hot organic breakfast cereals, bars and herbal supplements
Member: Peggy Lesueur-Brymer
Broker Sales Manager: Pat Maloney
Sales Coordinator: Sarah Sanders
Manager: Brad Haugeberg
brad.haugegerg@chsinc.com
Operations Manager: Curt Currie
Estimated Sales: $17,500,000
Number Employees: 20-49
Type of Packaging: Consumer, Food Service
Brands:
 Golden Loaf
 Prairie Sun
 Rosebud
 Sunny Boy

1951 CHiKPRO
417-708-0988
www.chikpro.com
Chicken protein powder
Number of Brands: 1
Number of Products: 26
Type of Packaging: Consumer
Brands:
 REAL CLEAN PROTEIN
 BIN CHXN

1952 CJ America
3530 Wilshire Blvd.,
Suite 1220
Los Angeles, CA 90010
213-427-5566
Fax: 213-427-7878 www.cjamerica.com
Manufacturer of amino acids, flavor enhancers and sweeteners.
President: Joonmo Suh
Vice President: Stephen Chang
Food Ingredients Sales Manager: Cecilia Kim
Product Manager: Chris Lee
Purchasing Agent: Jane Cho
Estimated Sales: $.5-1 million
Number Employees: 10
Square Footage: 31304
Parent Co: Cheiljedang
Type of Packaging: Consumer, Food Service, Private Label, Bulk

1953 CJ Foods
4 Centerpointe Dr
Suite 100
La Palma, CA 90623
714-367-7200
Fax: 714-367-7192 info@cjfoods.com
 www.cjfoods.com
Natural, gourmet Pan-Asian foods and sauces including sauces and pastes, condiments, ingredients, cooked rice, seaweed snacks, potstickers and mini wontons.
President: Sung Shin
CEO & Chairman: Tod Morgan
Contact: Brad Schulz
bradschulz@cj.net
Purchasing Manager: Jason Baik
Estimated Sales: $2.1 Million
Type of Packaging: Consumer, Bulk
Brands:
 bibigo
 Annie Chun's
 Cheiljedang

1954 CJ Omni
4591 Firestone Blvd
South Gate, CA 90280
323-567-8171
Korean foods; specialize in mini wontons and korean sauces
President: James Chae
Estimated Sales: $3.5 Million
Number Employees: 50

1955 CJ's Seafood
125 Dixie Drive
Des Allemands, LA 70030-3320
985-758-1237
Fresh and frozen catfish
President: Curtis Matherne
Number Employees: 1-4
Square Footage: 560
Type of Packaging: Consumer, Food Service

1956 CK Living LLC
606 Kinderkarmack Rd Bsmt
River Edge, NJ 07661-2143
201-261-2078
contactus@crazykoreancooking.com
crazykoreancooking.com
Korean preprepared meals; soups; soy sauce; curry
CEO: Grace Lewis
Type of Packaging: Food Service, Private Label

1957 CMA Global Partners/German Foods LLC
719 6th St
NW Washington, DC 20001
301-365-5043
Fax: 202-467-5440 800-881-6419
info@germanfoods.org
Baking mixes; cake decorations; baking ingredients; hot chocolate powders; confections; curred meats; spreads and jellies.

Food Manufacturers / A-Z

Managing Partner: Arnim von Friedeburg
Year Founded: 2009
Number Employees: 1-10
Type of Packaging: Food Service, Private Label
Brands:
  Brandt
  Dallmayr
  Favorit Swiss Premium
  Grafschafter
  Hela
  Hengstenberg
  Kathi
  Manner
  Meica
  Niederegger Lubeck
  Scho-ko-lade
  Seitenbacher

1958 CMS Fine Foods
4791 Dry Creek Rd
Healdsburg, CA 95448
707-473-9561
Fax: 707-473-9765 www.cmsfinefoods.com
sauces, dressings, mustards, marinades and other condiments; offers co-packing and private label services.
Type of Packaging: Consumer, Food Service, Private Label, Bulk

1959 CNS Confectionery Products
33 Hook Rd
Bayonne, NJ 07002-5006
201-823-1400
Fax: 201-823-2452 888-823-4330
sales@cnscoinc.com www.cnscoinc.com
Importer, processor and national distributor of sweetened, toasted and desiccated coconut as well as other sweet, dry baking ingredients. Certified kosher.
Owner: Eva Deutsch
e.deutsch@cnscoinc.com
CFO: Irene Fishman
VP Sales: Miriam Gross
e.deutsch@cnscoinc.com
Chief, Production/Purchasing: Eva Deutsch
Estimated Sales: $1-2.5 Million
Number Employees: 10-19
Type of Packaging: Private Label
Brands:
  Cns

1960 CO YO
Albuquerque, NM 87107
505-247-0012
info@coyo.us
coyo.com
Coconut yogurt
Founder: Henry Gosling
Brands:
  CO YO

1961 COnut Butter
727 Lyons St
New Orleans, LA 70115
info@COnutButter.com
www.COnutButter.com
Nut butters
Owner: Alexandra Pericak
Year Founded: 2015

1962 CP Kelco
Cumberland Center II
3100 Cumberland Blvd, Suite 600
Atlanta, GA 30339
678-247-7300
800-535-2687
www.cpkelco.com
Texturizing and stabilizing ingredients.
President & CEO: Dieder Viala
Year Founded: 1929
Estimated Sales: $370.5 Million
Number Employees: 2,200
Number of Brands: 10
Number of Products: 24
Parent Co: J.M. Huber Company
Other Locations:
  CP Kelco Production Plant
  Okmulgee OK
  CP Kelco Production Plant
  San Diego CA
Brands:
  Cekol
  Genu
  Genu Plus
  Genugel
  Genulacta
  Genulacta
  Genutine
  Genuvisco
  Kelcogel
  Kelgum
  Keltrol
  Simplesse
  Splendid

1963 CROPP Cooperative
One Organic Way
La Farge, WI 54639
Fax: 608-625-2600 888-444-6455
contact.us@organicvalley.coop www.farmers.coop
Organic products including dried and fresh cheeses, eggs, yogurt, milk and butter; also, organic vegetables and certified organic pork, beef and chicken; importer of certified organic bananas.
CEO: Robert Kirchoff
Project Advisor: Mike Bedessem
Executive VP, Marketing: Lewis Goldstein
Year Founded: 1988
Estimated Sales: $1.157 Billion
Number Employees: 932
Number of Brands: 2
Square Footage: 10000
Type of Packaging: Consumer, Food Service, Private Label, Bulk
Brands:
  Organic Valley
  Organic Prairie
  Mighty Organic

1964 CTC Manufacturing
416 Meridian Road SE
Suite B12
Calgary, AB T2A 1X2
Canada
403-235-2428
Fax: 403-272-9558 800-668-7677
Lollypops
President: G Paul Allen
Sales Manager: David Skultety
Plant Manager: Malcolm Steel
Number Employees: 10-19
Square Footage: 6900
Parent Co: Candy Tree Company
Type of Packaging: Consumer, Food Service, Private Label
Brands:
  The Candy Tree

1965 CTI Foods
22303 Hwy 95
Wilder, ID 83676
208-482-7844
info@ctifoods.com
www.ctifoods.com
Processes meat to beef patties, fajitas, taco meat and others.
CEO: Mike Buccheri
Estimated Sales: $134 Million
Number Employees: 500
Parent Co: CTI Foods Holding Co., LLC
Other Locations:
  Plant
  Azusa CA
  Plant
  Signaw TX
  Plant
  Owingsville KY
  Plant
  King of Prussia PA

1966 CTL Foods
514 Main St
Colfax, WI 54730
715-962-3121
Fax: 715-962-4030 800-962-5227
foods@ctlcolfax.com www.ctlcolfax.com
Malted milk powder, dry-form syrup bases and flavored slush drinks and bases; manufacturer of dry powder dispensers; also, custom blending and packaging services available
President: Michael Bean
Estimated Sales: $1.5 Million
Number Employees: 5-9
Square Footage: 40000
Type of Packaging: Food Service, Private Label
Brands:
  Glacier Ice
  Soda Fountain

1967 CVC4Health
4510 S Boyle Ave
Vernon, CA 90058
323-581-0176
Fax: 323-589-6667 800-421-6175
www.cvc4health.com
Vitamins
President: William Ballard
Treasurer: Lillian Beckenfield
VP: Harvey Monastirsky
VP Sales and Marketing: Greg Faull
Contact: Ronald Beckenfeld
ron@cvc4health.com
Estimated Sales: $12.3 Million
Number Employees: 60
Brands:
  Cvc Specialsties
  Superior Source

1968 CVP Systems Inc
2518 Wisconsin Ave
Downers Grove, IL 60515-4230
630-852-1190
Fax: 630-852-1386 800-422-4720
sales@cvpsystems.com www.cvpsystems.com
Owner/CEO: Wes Bork
COO: Chris Van Wandelen
Estimated Sales: $10-20 Million
Number Employees: 20-49
Brands:
  C.V.P. Systems

1969 Cable Car Beverage Corporation
555 17th Street
Denver, CO 80202-3950
303-298-9038
Fax: 303-298-1150
Beverages
Chairman/President: Samuel Simpson
ssimpson@hollandhart.com
Number Employees: 20-49

1970 Cabo Chips
Cypress, CA 90630
www.cabochips.com
Tortillas and tortilla chips

1971 Cabo Rojo Enterprises
3301 Combate
Boqueron, PR 622
787-254-0015
Fax: 787-254-2048
Processor and importer of salt
President: Jeffrey Padilla Montero
Treasurer: Edwin Almodovar
Secretary: Lourdes Collado
Estimated Sales: $380,000
Number Employees: 5
Type of Packaging: Consumer

1972 Cabot Creamery Co-Op
193 Home Farm Way
Waitsfield, VT 05673-7512
802-496-1200
Fax: 802-371-1200 888-792-2268
info@cabotcheese.com www.cabotcheese.com
Cheese and other dairy products
President/CEO: Rich Stammer
Master Cheddar Maker: Marcel Gravel
CFO: Margaret Bertolino
Senior VP: David Hill
david.hill@cabotcheese.com
Director of Q/C: May Leach
Senior VP of Marketing: Roberta Macdonald
Sales & Marketing Manager: Sara Wing
Public Relations Manager: Bob Schiers
VP of Operations: Dick Gilangworthy
Plant Manager: Chris Pearl
Purchasing Manager: Kathleen McDonnell
Estimated Sales: $300 Million
Number Employees: 50-99
Square Footage: 450000
Parent Co: Agri-Mark
Type of Packaging: Consumer, Food Service, Private Label, Bulk
Brands:
  Cabot
  Cabot Cheeses

1973 Cacao Prieto
218 Conover Street
Brooklyn, NY 11231
347-225-0130
www.cacaoprieto.com

Fine chocolates
President/CEO: Dan Preston
VP & Art Director: Michele Clark
Sales Director: Mike Dirksen
Contact: Michele Clark
michele@cacaoholdings.com
Chief Operating Officer: Dennis Walsh
Number Employees: 20

1974 Cachafaz US
3325 NW 70th Ave
Miami, FL 33122
305-779-6340
cachafaz.us
Vegan and gluten-free chocolate, cookies, and spreads.
Manager: Juan Mandayo
Year Founded: 2001
Number Employees: 10-19

1975 Cache Cellars
RR 2 Box 2780
Davis, CA 95616-9604
530-756-6068
Fax: 530-756-6463
Wines
President: Charles Lowe
Estimated Sales: $1-2,500,000
Number Employees: 5-9
Type of Packaging: Private Label

1976 Cache Creek Foods LLC
411 N Pioneer Ave
Woodland, CA 95776-6122
530-662-1764
Fax: 530-662-2529 www.cachecreekfoods.com
Custom flavoring and wholesale manufacturing of almond, cashew, pistachio, nut products and nut butters
President: Nicholas Celek
ncelek@thelabb.com
CEO: Matthew Morehart
Sales and Marketing Executive: Mike Leonard
Office Manager: Connie Stephens
Production: Ana Contreras
Estimated Sales: $10 Million
Number Employees: 20-49
Number of Products: 75
Square Footage: 60000
Type of Packaging: Consumer, Food Service, Private Label, Bulk
Brands:
  Private Label

1977 (HQ)Cacique
800 Royal Oaks Dr
Suite 200
Monrovia, CA 91017
626-961-3399
Fax: 626-369-8083 800-521-6987
www.caciqueinc
Processor and exporter of mozzarella and fresco cheeses, beef chorizo, pork choriso, soy choriso, mexican cremes, yogurts and beverages.
President: Gilbert Decardenas
Manager: Margarita Hodge
Estimated Sales: $50-100 Million
Number Employees: 325
Number of Brands: 5
Square Footage: 200000
Other Locations:
  Cacique
  Cedar City UT
Brands:
  Black & Gold
  Cacique
  Nochebuena
  Ranchero
  Yonique

1978 Cacoco
hello@drinkcacoco.com
drinkcacoco.com
Drinking chocolate
Co-Founder & CEO: Tony Portugal
Co-Founder & COO: Liam Blackmon
Number of Brands: 1
Number of Products: 5
Type of Packaging: Consumer
Brands:
  CACOCO

1979 CactuLife, LLC
PO Box 349
Corona Del Mar, CA 92625-0349
949-640-8991
Fax: 949-640-8992 800-500-1713
info@cactulife.com www.cactulife.com
Health food supplements
President: Jeff Leibfreid
Estimated Sales: $500,000
Number Employees: 1-4
Brands:
  Cactu Life

1980 Cadbury Adams
5000 Yonge Street
Toronto, ON M2N 7E9
Canada
416-590-5000
Fax: 416-590-5600
consumer.relations@brandspeoplelove.com
www.kraftfoodsgroup.com
A variety of confectionery products.
President/ Canada: Dino Bianco
Chief Executive Officer: Todd Stitzer
Chief Financial Officer: Ken Hanna
Chief Legal Officer: Michael Clark
Chief Science & Technology Officer: David MacNair
President Americas Beverages: Gil Cassagne
President Europe/Middle East/Africa: Matt Shattock
Group Strategy Director: Mark Reckitt
Chief Legal Officer: Hank Udow
Chief Human Resources Officer: Bob Stack
Group Secretary: Hester Blanks
President Americas Confectionery: Jim Chambers
President Global Supply Chain: Steve Drive
Number Employees: 1,000-4,999
Parent Co: Cadbury Schweppes
Type of Packaging: Consumer, Food Service, Bulk
Brands:
  Bubbilicious Bubble Gum
  Certs Breath Mints
  Certs Cool Mint Drops
  Certs Powerful Mints
  Chiclets Gum
  Clorets Breath Freshener
  Dentyne Fire Gum
  Dentyne Ice
  Dentyne Tango

1981 Cadbury Beverages Canada
30 Eglinton Avenue W
Mississauga, ON L5R 3E7
Canada
905-712-4121
Fax: 905-712-8635
consumer.relations@brandspeoplelove.com
www.mondelezinternational.com
Beverage brands include 7 UP, Canada Dry, Clamato, Dr. Pepper, Hawaiian Punch, Mott's, Schweppes and Snapple.
President/CEO: Irene Rosenfeld
Chief Financial Officer: Ken Hanna
Vice President/ CFO: David Brearton
Chief Science & Technology Officer: David MacNair
President Americas Beverages: Gil Cassagne
President Europe/Middle East/Africa: Matt Shattock
Group Strategy Director: Mark Reckitt
Chief Legal Officer: Hank Udow
Chief Human Resources Officer: Bob Stack
Group Secretary: Hester Blanks
President Americas Confectionery: Jim Chambers
President Global Supply Chain: Steve Drive
Number Employees: 1,000-4,999
Parent Co: Cadbury Schweppes
Type of Packaging: Consumer, Food Service, Bulk
Brands:
  Cadbury Chocolate
  Cadbury Dairy Milk
  Cadbury Dark
  Cadbury Favourites
  Cadbury Thins
  Caramilk

1982 (HQ)Cadbury Trebor Allan
850 Industrial Boulevard
Granby, QC J2J 1B8
Canada
450-372-1080
Fax: 450-378-4256 800-387-3267
consumer.relations@brandspeoplelove.com
www.cadburyschweppes.com
Candy including hard, filled hard, toffee, mints, licorice, gums, taffy kisses, penny goods, cough drops, jellies and lollypops, chocolates
Chairman And Ceo: Irene Rosenfeld
Number Employees: 3030
Parent Co: Cadbury Schweppes PLC
Type of Packaging: Consumer, Food Service, Private Label, Bulk
Brands:
  Trebor

1983 Caddo Packing Co
609 S Washington Ave
Marshall, TX 75670-5327
903-935-2211
Processors and butchers of beef and pork.
President: Pat Parrish
Secretary/Treasurer: Judy Parrish
Estimated Sales: $1.5 Million
Number Employees: 10-19
Type of Packaging: Consumer

1984 Cadillac Coffee Co
7221 Innovation Blvd.
Ft. Wayne, IN 46818
248-545-2266
Fax: 248-584-4184 800-438-6900
info@cadillaccoffee.com www.cadillaccoffee.com
Coffee, specialty teas, iced teas, flavored syrups, blended drink mixes, iced cappuccino and more.
President: Guy Gehlert
Chairman: John Gehlert
VP Finance: Timothy Mantyla
Contact: Lisa Adkins
l.adkins@cadillaccoffee.com
VP Operations: Doug Bachman
Purchasing Director: John Hunter
Estimated Sales: Less Than $500,000
Number Employees: 5-9
Square Footage: 6580
Type of Packaging: Consumer, Food Service, Private Label, Bulk
Brands:
  Cadillac Coffee

1985 Cady Cheese Factory
126 Hwy. 128
Wilson, WI 54027
715-772-4218
Fax: 715-772-4224 info@cadycheese.com
www.cadycheese.com
Producer of different varieties and flavors of longhorn cheese. Products are 100% natural and include Colby, Monterey Jack, Gold'n Jack and Veg'y Jack. Cady Cheese company also makes flavored cheeses such as Hot Pepper Jack, SalsaCheddar, Garlic Jack, Roasted Garlic Jack, Bacon and Onion Colby, Jack and Dill, and many more.
Plant Manager, Control: Sandy Lee
Estimated Sales: $5,8,000,000
Number Employees: 45
Type of Packaging: Private Label, Bulk
Brands:
  Cady Creek Farms

1986 Caesar's Pasta
1001 Lower Landing Rd
Suite 302
Blackwood, NJ 08012
888-432-2372
www.caesarskitchen.com
Frozen pre-cooked and raw pasta specialties including ravioli, stuffed shells, manicotti with crepes, gnocchi, cavatelli, spaghetti, fettuccine, linguine, angel hair, agnolotti, ravioletti, tortelloni, cheese lasagna, etc
President/CEO: Michael Lodato
Secretary/Treasurer/VP of Sales: Raymond Lodato
VP: Ronald R. Lodato
Director of Sales: Michelle Hennessy
General Manager: Ronald P. Ladato
Purchasing Manager: Ronald Lodato
raylodato@caesarspasta.com
Estimated Sales: $1-2.5 Million
Number Employees: 20-49
Number of Products: 15
Square Footage: 60000
Type of Packaging: Consumer, Food Service, Private Label, Bulk
Brands:
  Caesar's Kitchen

Food Manufacturers / A-Z

1987 Cafe Altura
760 East Santa Maria Street
Santa Paula, CA 93060
805-933-3027
Fax: 805-933-9367 800-526-8328
www.cafealtura.com
Processor, importer and exporter of organic coffee
President: Chris Shepard
Sales Manager: Elizabeth Blatz
Estimated Sales: $2.5-5 Million
Number Employees: 5-9
Square Footage: 4000
Parent Co: Clean Foods
Brands:
 Cafe Altura

1988 Cafe Bustelo
5605 Nw 82nd Avenue
Miami, FL 33166
786-336-8048
Fax: 305-594-7603 800-990-9039
www.javacabana.com
Roasted coffee
President: Jose Souto
Marketing: Fernando Acosta
Estimated Sales: $2.5-5 000,000
Number Employees: 5-9

1989 Cafe Cartago
3835 Elm St Ste D
Denver, CO 80207
303-297-1212
Fax: 303-316-3325 800-443-8666
Coffee
Owner: Steve Larsen
Partner: Chuck Ask
Purchasing Manager: Steve Larsen
Estimated Sales: $2.5-5,000,000
Number Employees: 5-9
Type of Packaging: Private Label, Bulk

1990 Cafe Chilku
433 Bar Road, Unit 2
Colchester, VT 05446-7916
802-878-4645
Producer of BBQ sauces and dipping sauce
Owner: Chilku Yi

1991 Cafe Del Mundo
229 E 51st Ave
Anchorage, AK 99503
907-562-2326
Fax: 907-562-3278 800-770-2326
www.cafedelmundo.com
Coffee, espresso equipment
Owner: Perry Merkel
Manager: Monique Johnston
Purchasing: Perry Merkel
Estimated Sales: $800,000
Number Employees: 12
Type of Packaging: Private Label, Bulk
Brands:
 Cafe Del Mundo

1992 Cafe Descafeinado de Chiapas
3625 NW 82nd Avenue
Suite 404
Doral, FL 33166-7602
305-499-9775
Fax: 305-499-9776
Coffee importers
President: Daniel Robles
Director: Arandio Muguira
Director: Luis Demetrio
Estimated Sales: $500,000-$1,000,000
Number Employees: 1-4
Type of Packaging: Private Label

1993 Cafe Du Monde Coffee Stand
1039 Decatur St
New Orleans, LA 70116-3309
504-581-2914
Fax: 504-587-0847 800-772-2927
office@cafedumonde.com www.cafedumonde.com
Processor and exporter of beignet doughnut mix, coffee and roasted chicory for coffee flavoring
CFO: J Roman
burt@cafedumonde.com
Manager: Burt Benrud
burt@cafedumonde.com
Manager: Robert Maher
Estimated Sales: $500,000 appx.
Number Employees: 10-19
Square Footage: 30000
Other Locations:
 Cafe Du Monde-French Market
 New Orleans LA
 Cafe Du Monde-Riverwalk Marketplace
 New Orleans LA
 Care Du Monde-New Orleans Centre
 New Orleans LA
 Cafe Du Monde-Oakwood Mall
 Gretna LA
 Cafe Du Monde-Lakeside Mall
 Metairie LA
 Cafe Du Monde-Esplanade Mall
 Kenner LA
 Cafe Du Monde-Veterans Boulevard
 Metairie LA
Brands:
 Cafe Du Monde

1994 Cafe Fanny
1619 5th St
Berkeley, CA 94710-1714
510-526-7664
Fax: 510-526-7486 800-441-5413
shop@cafefanny.com www.cafefanny.com
Organic granola.
Owner: James Maser
Contact: Melody Elliott
melliott@cafefanny.com
Manager: Leslie Wilson
Estimated Sales: $1-2,500,000
Number Employees: 20-49

1995 Cafe Grumpy
199 Diamond St
Brooklyn, NY 11222
718-383-0748
info@cafegrumpy.com
cafegrumpy.com
Coffee roasters
Co-Owner: Chris Timbrell
Co-Owner: Caroline Bell
Head Roaster: Chris Cross
Buyer: Cheryl Kingan
Year Founded: 2005
Type of Packaging: Consumer, Private Label

1996 Cafe Kreyol
Manassas, VA 20109
www.coffeehunterproject.com
Organic specialty coffee

1997 Cafe La Semeuse
55 Nassau Ave
Brooklyn, NY 11222-3143
718-387-9696
Fax: 718-782-2471 800-242-6333
www.cafelasemeuse.com
Coffee
Manager: Andi Billow
Contact: Marc Greenberg
marc@cafelasemeuse.com
Estimated Sales: Under $500,000
Number Employees: 1-4
Brands:
 Cafe La Semeuse
 Classique
 Espresso

1998 Cafe Moak
509 E Division Street
Rockford, MI 49341-1342
616-866-7625
Fax: 616-866-6422
Bread sticks, subs, pizzas and coffee; importer of coffee
Owner: Sal Russo
Administrative Assistant: Becky Fate
Brands:
 Russo's

1999 Cafe Moto
2619 National Ave
San Diego, CA 92113-3617
619-239-6686
Fax: 619-239-9344 800-818-3363
www.cafemoto.com
Imported tea and roasted coffee
President: Torrey Lee
CFO: Kimberly Lee
Manager: Chris Peters
Production Manager: Michael Figgins
Estimated Sales: Under $500,000
Number Employees: 20-49
Type of Packaging: Private Label

2000 Cafe Sark's Gourmet Coffee
22800 Savi Ranch Parkway
Yorba Linda, CA 92887-4623
626-579-6000
Gourmet coffee
President: Jeff Shamburger
Estimated Sales: Under $500,000
Number Employees: 5-9

2001 Cafe Society Coffee Company
2910 N Hall St
Dallas, TX 75204
214-922-8888
Fax: 214-922-0280 800-717-6000
Flavored and organic coffee and tea
President: Lauri Sanderfer
Sales Representative: Byron Laszlo
General Manager: Jessie Nickerson
Estimated Sales: $1-$1,4,000,000
Number Employees: 11
Type of Packaging: Private Label

2002 Cafe Spice
677 Little Britain Rd
New Windsor, NY 12553
845-863-0910
info@cafespice.com
cafespice.com
Preprepared meals including Indian and Thai foods; soups; frozen appetizers; sauces; and rice.
Culinary Director: Hari Nayak
R&D Manager: Deepak Rajamani
Year Founded: 2000
Number Employees: 51-200
Type of Packaging: Food Service, Private Label

2003 Cafe Tequila
967 N Point Street
San Francisco, CA 94109-1111
415-264-0106
Fax: 415-674-1740 www.cafetequila.com
Tequila sauces
President/CEO: John Fielder
Sales/Marketing Executive: Julie Fielder
Number Employees: 1-4
Type of Packaging: Consumer, Food Service
Brands:
 Cafe Tequila

2004 Cafe Yaucono/Jimenez & Fernandez
1103 Avenue Fernandez Juncos
Po Box 13097
San Juan, PR 00908-3097
787-721-3337
Fax: 787-722-5590 info@yaucono.com
www.yaucono.com
Coffee
President: Jose Jimenez
VP/Comp/Treasurer: Julio Torres
Marketing Manager: Joaquin Class
Number Employees: 20
Square Footage: 75000
Type of Packaging: Consumer
Brands:
 Yaucono

2005 Caffe Appassionato Coffee
4001 21st Ave W
Seattle, WA 98199-1201
206-281-8040
Fax: 206-282-5218 888-502-2333
www.caffeappassionato.com
Coffee
President/CEO: Phil Sancken
CFO: Tim Schondelmayer
Sales Exec: Tucker McHugh
tucker@caffeappassionato.com
Roastmaster: Richard Oakes
Production Manager: David Crumb
Estimated Sales: $5-10,000,000
Number Employees: 50-99
Type of Packaging: Private Label
Brands:
 Cafe Appassionato

2006 Caffe D'Amore
3400 Milington Road
Beloit, WI 53511
626-792-9146
Fax: 626-932-0152 800-999-0171
support@caffedamore.com www.caffedamore.com
Instant cappuccino

Food Manufacturers / A-Z

President: Chris Julius
Director Marketing: Cheri Hays
National Sales & Marketing Manager: Adelina Mirzakhanyan
Regional Sales Manager: Jill Zimmerman
Estimated Sales: $1-3,000,000
Number Employees: 20-49
Type of Packaging: Consumer, Food Service

2007 Caffe D'Amore Gourmet Beverages
5400 Butler St
Pittsburgh, PA 15201
626-792-9146
Fax: 626-792-4382 800-999-0171
www.caffedamorepgh.com
Specialty coffee beverages
President: Paul Comi
p.comi@caffedamore.com
Marketing Director: Adelina Mirzakhanyan
Regional Sales Manager: Jill Zimmerman
Estimated Sales: $30-50 Million
Number Employees: 50-99
Parent Co: Kerry

2008 Caffe D'Oro
14020 Central Avenue
Suite 580
Chino, CA 91710-5524
909-591-9493
Fax: 909-522-8844 800-200-5005
Specialty coffee and cappuccino
President: Pamela Abbadessa
V P Marketing: Frank Abbadessa
Number Employees: 5-9
Parent Co: Brad Barry Company
Type of Packaging: Private Label
Brands:
  Caffe D'Oro Cappuccino & Cocoa

2009 Caffe D'Vita
14020 Central Avenue
Suite 580
Chino, CA 91710-5524
909-591-9493
Fax: 909-627-3747 800-200-5005
info@caffedvita.com www.caffedvita.com
Instant cappuccino, smoothies, frappes, iced coffees, cocoas and sugar-free products
President & CEO: Bob Greene
Vice President: Frank Abbadessa
Marketing Director: Frank Greene
Operations Manager: Frank Abbadessa
Estimated Sales: Under $500,000
Number Employees: 20-49
Parent Co: Brad Barry Company
Type of Packaging: Consumer, Food Service, Private Label, Bulk
Brands:
  Caffe D'Vita
  Baristatude

2010 Caffe Darte
33926 9th Ave S
Federal Way, WA 98003-6708
253-252-7050
Fax: 206-763-4665 800-999-5334
sales@caffedarte.com www.caffedarte.com
Processor of coffee beans.
General Manager: Joe Mancuso
jmancuso@caffedarte.com
National Sales Manager: Tim Fleming
Director of Operations: John Virden
Estimated Sales: $5-10,000,000
Number Employees: 20-49
Other Locations:
  Boise Caff,
  Boise ID
  Bonney Lake Caff,
  Tehaleh WA
  Portland Caff,
  Portland OR
  Seattle Caff,-1st & Yesler
  Seattle WA
Brands:
  Campania(c)
  Capri(c)
  Fabriano(c)
  Firenze(c)
  Meaning of Life(c)
  Parioli(c)
  Taormina(c)
  Velletri(c)
  and more

2011 Caffe Ibis Gallery Deli
52 Federal Ave
Logan, UT 84321-4641
435-753-4777
Fax: 435-755-9139 888-740-4777
www.caffeibis.com
Artisan custom coffee roasting house. Focus is on Triple Certified, Organic, Fair Trade, and Smithsonian Shade Grown "Bird-Friendly" coffee from around the world.
Owner: Sally Sears
sally@caffeibis.com
Co-Owner & Roastmaster: Randy Wirth
Number Employees: 20-49
Type of Packaging: Consumer

2012 Caffe Luca Coffee Roaste
1025 Industry Drive
Seattle, WA 98188
206-466-5579
Fax: 206-575-0537 800-728-9116
info@caffeluca.com www.caffeluca.com
Processor, exporter and importer of espresso and blended coffee; also, custom roasting available
Owner: Carol Dema
caroldema@caffeluca.com
Estimated Sales: $380,000
Number Employees: 5
Square Footage: 4000
Type of Packaging: Consumer, Food Service
Brands:
  Antonio
  Casa Luca
  Giovanni
  Gregorio
  Leonardo
  Misto
  Misto Dark

2013 Caffe Trieste
1465 25th St
San Francisco, CA 94107-3403
415-550-1107
Fax: 415-550-1239 CaffeTrieste56@aol.com
Coffee
President: Fabio Giotta
postmaster@caffetrieste.com
Secretary: Sonia Panaleo
Estimated Sales: $2,760,000
Number Employees: 5-9
Type of Packaging: Private Label
Brands:
  Caffe Trieste Coffee Beans

2014 Cahoon Farms
10941 Lummisville Rd
Wolcott, NY 14590-9549
315-594-9610
Fax: 315-594-1678
customerservice@cahoonfarms.com
www.cahoonfarms.com
Frozen apples and cherries
Owner: Duane Cahoon
Controller: Jolene Green
Vice President: William B. Cahoon
Quality Control: Kristy Watson
Sales Manager: Chuck Frederick
customerservice@cahoonfarms.com
Operations Manager: Dave Green
Production Manager: Joe Cahoon
Plant Manager: Robert Cahoon
Estimated Sales: $940,000
Number Employees: 100-249
Type of Packaging: Consumer

2015 Cain Vineyard & Winery
3800 Langtry Rd
St Helena, CA 94574-9772
707-963-1616
Fax: 707-963-7952 winery@cainfive.com
www.cainfive.com
Producer of wines.
Owner: James Meadlock
Owner: Nancy Meadlock
Director of Sales & Marketing: Katie Lazar
Operations Manager: J.J. McCarthy
Production Manager: Francois Bugue
Estimated Sales: $5-10,000,000
Number Employees: 20-49
Number of Brands: 3
Brands:
  Cain Concept
  Cain Cuv,e
  Cain Five

2016 Caito Fisheries Inc
19400 Harbor Ave
PO Box 1370
Fort Bragg, CA 95437-5615
707-964-6368
Fax: 707-964-6439 caitofsh@mcn.org
www.caitofisheries.com
Fresh and frozen fish such as albacore, sole, and flounder, dudungeousness crab, shark, octopus, acallops, prawns, rock shrimp, oysters, clams, swwordfish and salmon.
President: Joe Caito
caito@mcn.org
Estimated Sales: $20-50 Million
Number Employees: 100-249
Type of Packaging: Consumer, Food Service, Private Label, Bulk
Brands:
  Caito

2017 Cajohn's Fiery Foods Co
816 Green Crest Dr
Westerville, OH 43081-2839
614-776-5356
Fax: 614-418-0800 888-703-3473
cajohns@cajohns.com www.cajohns.com
Salsas, hot sauce, barbecue sauce, rubs, spice blends, mixes and mustards.
President/Owner: John Hard
cajohn@cajohns.com
Secretary: Wanza Hard
Director of Operations: Jeremy Priwer
Estimated Sales: $125,000
Number Employees: 5-9
Brands:
  Cajohns
  Nate Dog's

2018 Cajun Boy's Louisiana Products
136 Austin Dr
Church Point, LA 70525
337-207-2391
Fax: 225-357-6888 800-880-9575
datcajunboysco@aol.com
datcajunboysco.com/products
Seasoned beans, blended seasonings and mixes.
Owner/President: Gerald Hicks
Number Employees: 1-4
Type of Packaging: Consumer
Brands:
  Cajun Boy's Louisiana

2019 Cajun Brands
2511 Sugar Mill Rd
New Iberia, LA 70560
504-408-2252
info@cajunbrands.com
www.cajunbrands.com
Peppers including pickled, sport, tobasco, cherry, jalapeno, yellow chile, banana and serrano; also, prepared mustard, pure and imitation pepper and flavoring extracts, pickled okra and tomatoes and sauces including hotworcestershire, etc.
Estimated Sales: $9.2 Million
Number Employees: 90
Type of Packaging: Consumer, Food Service, Private Label, Bulk
Brands:
  Big Chief
  Cajun Chef
  Evangeline
  Andy Roo's
  Bird Brine
  Bon Ca Ca
  Bruce Foods
  Cajun Blast
  Cajun Flip N Fry
  Cajun Land
  Louisiana Mixes
  Mello Joy
  Mossy Bayou
  Panola Pepper Corp
  Papa Scotts
  Pepperdoux
  Poche's
  Savoie's
  Slap Ya Mama
  Southern
  Steens

Food Manufacturers / A-Z

2020 Cajun Crawfish Distributors
379 Industrial Blvd
PO Box 393
Branch, LA 70516
Fax: 337-334-8477 888-254-8626
boudreaux@cajuncrawfish.com
www.cajuncrawfish.com
Live crawfish, cooked crawfish, gumbos, Cajun meats, turducken
Co-Owner: Mark Fruge
Co-Owner: Michael Fruge
Administration: Pam Estes
Marketing Director: Courtney Fruge
Sales Manager: Richard Hotard
Public Relations: Carol Schultz
Operations Manager: Ed Guidry
Year Founded: 1972
Estimated Sales: $30 Million
Number Employees: 4

2021 Cajun Creole Products Inc
5610 Daspit Rd
New Iberia, LA 70563-8961
337-229-8464
Fax: 337-229-4814 800-946-8688
info@cajuncreole.com www.cajuncreole.com
Coffee, peanuts and seasoning
President/Manager: Joel Wallins
Secretary/Treasurer: Sandra Wallins
Estimated Sales: $300,000
Number Employees: 5-9
Type of Packaging: Consumer, Food Service, Bulk
Brands:
 Cajun Creole
 Cajun Creole Coffee
 Cajun Creole Hot Nuts
 Cajun Creole Jalapeanuts
 Jalapeanuts

2022 Cajun Fry Co Inc
107 Mike St
Pierre Part, LA 70339-4415
985-252-6438
Fax: 985-252-8010 888-272-2586
cajunfrycompany@aol.com www.cajunfry.com
Cajun rice mixes, jambalaya, spices
President: Clarence Cavalier Jr
Vice President: Marilyn Cavalier
Estimated Sales: $1-2,500,000
Number Employees: 1-4
Brands:
 Cajun Creole Coffee & Chicory
 Jalapeanuts
 Smokeless Blackened Seasoning

2023 Cajun Original Foods Inc
704 Avenue D
New Iberia, LA 70560-0527
337-367-1344
Fax: 337-364-4968 www.cajunoriginal.com
Processor and exporter of liquid injectable marinades for poultry and red meats, and dry seasonings
President/CEO: Dennis Higginbotham
cajunorignal@bellsouth.net
Estimated Sales: $1-2.5 Million
Number Employees: 10-19
Square Footage: 54400
Type of Packaging: Consumer, Bulk
Brands:
 Cajun Aujus
 Cajun Injector
 Cajun Poultry Marinade
 Cajunshake

2024 Cajun Seafood Enterprises
9650 Highway 52 E
Murrayville, GA 30564-6901
706-864-9688
Fax: 706-864-9688
Seafood

2025 Cakebread Cellars
8300 Saint Helena Hwy
PO Box 216
Rutherford, CA 94573
707-963-5221
Fax: 707-967-8620 800-588-0298
cellars@cakebread.com www.cakebread.com
Manufacturer of fine wines
Founder/Chairman/CEO: Jack Cakebread
President/COO: Bruce Cakebread
SVP, Sales & Marketing: Dennis Cakebread
Contact: Samantha Arnold
arnold@cakebread.com
Director, Vineyard Operations: Toby Halkovich
Estimated Sales: $20-50 Million
Number Employees: 50-99
Number of Brands: 1
Brands:
 Cakebread

2026 Cal Harvest Marketing Inc
8700 Fargo Ave
Hanford, CA 93230-9771
559-582-4494
Fax: 559-582-0683 www.calharvest.com
Fresh fruits and vegetables
President: John Fagundes IV
johnf2006@hughes.net
Purchasing: John Fagundes
Estimated Sales: $2 Million
Number Employees: 5-9
Type of Packaging: Consumer, Private Label, Bulk
Brands:
 Cal-King
 Fresh Harvest
 Golden Harvest

2027 Cal India Foods Inc
13591 Yorba Ave
Chino, CA 91710-5071
909-613-1660
Fax: 909-613-1663
www.systemicenzymetherapy.com
Fruit juices, purees and concentrates
President: Vic Rathi
info@4enzymes.com
Quality Control: Vilas Amin
Purchasing Agent: Priscilla Ferreri
Estimated Sales: $5-7 Million
Number Employees: 20-49
Square Footage: 24000
Parent Co: Specialty Enzymes and Biochemicals Company
Type of Packaging: Bulk
Brands:
 Cal India

2028 Cal Ranch
2628 Concord Blvd
Concord, CA 94519
925-429-2900
Fax: 925-476-2017 info@calranchfood.com
calranchfood.com
Dried fruits and nuts
President/Owner: Juliana Colline
Type of Packaging: Consumer, Food Service

2029 Cal-Grown Nut Company
8616 E. Whitmore
Hughson, CA 95326-0069
209-883-4081
Fax: 209-883-0305 www.californiagrown.com
Processor and exporter of almonds
President: Frank Assali
frankassali@californiagrown.com
Vice President: Marie Assali
Office Manager: Linda Thomas
Estimated Sales: $.5-1 million
Number Employees: 5-9

2030 Cal-Java International Inc
19519 Business Center Dr
Northridge, CA 91324
818-718-2707
Fax: 818-718-2715 800-207-2750
sales@caljavaonline.com caljavaonline.com
Cake decorating supplies
Owner: Daniel Budiman
caljava@aol.com
Vice President: Laurie Budiman
Estimated Sales: $9 Million
Number Employees: 10-19

2031 Cal-Maine Foods Inc.
3320 Woodrow Wilson Dr.
Jackson, MS 39209
601-948-6813
Fax: 601-969-0905 ir@cmfoods.com
www.calmainefoods.com
Shell eggs
CEO/Chairman: Adolphus Baker
abaker@cmfoods.com
Chairman Emeritus: Fred Adams
VP/CFO/Treasurer/Secretary/Director: Max Bowman
Vice President/General Counsel: Rob Holladay
VP Sales: Jeff Hardin
VP, Controller: Mike Castleberry
President/COO/Director: Sherman Miller
Year Founded: 1969
Estimated Sales: $1.037 Billion
Number Employees: 1000-4999
Number of Brands: 3
Type of Packaging: Food Service, Private Label, Bulk
Brands:
 Egg-Land's Best™
 Farmhouse™
 4-Grain™

2032 Cal-Tex Citrus Juice LP
402 Yale St
Houston, TX 77007-2530
713-869-3471
Fax: 713-869-3277 800-231-0133
gary.van.liew@cal-texjuice.com
www.cal-texjuice.com
Fresh and frozen concentrate citrus juices
CEO: Ronald Peterson
Quality Control: Alvaro Falquez
National Sales Manager: Vicki White
Operations: Danny Teague
Purchasing: Kory Mason
Estimated Sales: $40 Million
Number Employees: 100-249
Number of Brands: 3
Number of Products: 63
Parent Co: Country Pure Foods
Type of Packaging: Consumer, Food Service, Private Label
Brands:
 Cal-Tex
 Citrus Pride
 Vita-Fresh
 Vita-Most

2033 Calabro Cheese Corp
580 Coe Ave
East Haven, CT 06512
203-469-1311
Fax: 203-469-6929 www.calabrocheese.com
Ricotta, mozzarella and grated cheese
President & CEO: Frank Angeloni
CFO: Sara Estrom
Vice President: Salvatore Calabro
Estimated Sales: $170,000
Number Employees: 50-99
Type of Packaging: Consumer, Food Service, Private Label, Bulk
Brands:
 Calabro

2034 Calafia Cellars
629 Fulton Ln
St Helena, CA 94574-1014
707-963-0114
Fax: 707-963-0114 randle@calafiacellars.com
www.calafiacellars.com
Wines
Owner: Randall Johnson
marylee53@comcast.net
VP Marketing: Mary Lee Johnson
Estimated Sales: Less Than $500,000
Number Employees: 1-4
Brands:
 Calafia Wines

2035 Calamondin Cafe
4600 Summerlin Rd C-2
Fort Myers, FL 33907
239-288-5535
Fax: 239-288-5534 info@calamondincafe.com
www.calamondincafe.com
Cakes, jams, teacakes and coulis
Founder & CEO: Laurie Gutstein

2036 Calapooia Brewing Co
140 NE Hill St
Albany, OR 97321-3002
541-928-1931
Fax: 541-928-4131 web@calapooiabrewing.com
www.calapooiabrewing.com
Beer

Owner: Mark Martin
Treasurer: Nancy Coleman
Estimated Sales: Below $5 Million
Number Employees: 10-19
Brands:
   Oregon Brewers

2037 Calavo Growers
1141A Cummings Rd
Santa Paula, CA 93060
805-525-1245
Fax: 805-921-3232 www.calavo.com
Growers and processors of pineapples, papayas, and avocados; Manufacturer of; salsa and corn chips
Chairman/President/CEO: Lecil Cole
lecil@calavo.com
CEO: Robin Osterhues
COO/CFO/Corporate Secretary: Arthur Bruno
VP/Fresh Sales & Marketing: Rob Wedin
Quality Assurance Manager: Diane Valine
Vice President, Sales & Marketing: Alan Ahmer
Fresh Operations: Mike Browne
Plant Manager: Brett Viera
Purchasing Agent: Bruce Spurrell
Estimated Sales: $551 Million
Number Employees: 1000-4999
Type of Packaging: Consumer, Food Service, Bulk
Other Locations:
   Temecula Packinghouse
   Temecula CA
   Santa Paula Packinghouse
   Santa Paula CA
   Calavo Processing Plant
   Santa Paula CA
Brands:
   Calavo

2038 Calbee America Inc
2600 Maxwell Way
Fairfield, CA 94534-1915
707-427-2500
Fax: 707-428-2900
Processor and exporter of potato chips
President/Ceo: Masanori Yasunaga
Vice President: Doug Warner
Manager Sales and Marketing: Takashi Katsunoi
VP Human Resources: Yoshi Ishiquro
IT Executive: Masa Suito
msaito@calbeeamerica.com
Estimated Sales: $15 Million
Number Employees: 100-249

2039 Calcium Springs Water Company
2442 Lily Langtree Ct
Park City, UT 84060
435-615-7600
Fax: 435-615-7600
Water
Owner: Lavelle Klobes

2040 Calco of Calgary
Bay C 1007 55th Avenue NE
Calgary, AB T2E 6W1
Canada
403-295-3578
Fax: 403-516-0286 www.calcoofcalgary.com
Processor and packer of bean sprouts, pre-cut vegetables, frozen Chinese dumplings, spring and egg rolls and steamed noodles
President: Wing Tam
General Manager: May Yu
Production: Grace Tam
Number Employees: 10-19
Parent Co: Fung Nin Fine Foods
Type of Packaging: Consumer, Food Service
Brands:
   Calgo
   Mr. Egg Roll
   Noodle Delights

2041 Caldic USA Inc
2425 Alft Ln
Elgin, IL 60124-7864
847-468-0001
customerservice@caldic.us
Sourcing, R&D, processing, warehousing and distribution of ingredients.
Owner: Bob Leonard
bleonard@nealanders.com
Number Employees: 10-19
Parent Co: Caldic

2042 Caleb Haley & Co LLC
800 Food Center Dr # 110
Suite 110
Bronx, NY 10474-1259
718-617-7474
Fax: 718-617-7477 www.calebhaley.com
Wholesale provider in both fresh and frozen seafood.
President: Neil Smith
neil@calebhaley.com
Vice President: Michael Driansky
Office Manager: Robby De Vincenzi
Year Founded: 1859
Estimated Sales: $20-50 Million
Number Employees: 20-49
Brands:
   Angel
   Callaway
   Ocean Harvest

2043 Calendar Islands Maine Lobster LLC
6a Portland Fish Pier
Portland, ME 04101
207-541-9140
Fax: 207-518-9049
Hors d'oeuvres/appetizers, ready meals/pizza/soup, full-line soups, stews, beans, shellfish.
Marketing: Emily Lane

2044 Calera Wine Co
11300 Cienega Rd
Hollister, CA 95023-9619
831-637-9170
Fax: 831-637-9070 info@calerawine.com
Wines
President: Josh Jensen
info@calerawine.com
COO: Diana Vita
Number Employees: 10-19
Brands:
   Calera
   Central Coast
   Doe Mill
   Mills
   Mt. Harlan
   Reed
   Selleck
   Viognier

2045 Calgary Italian Bakery
5310 5th Street SE
Calgary, AB T2H 1L2
Canada
403-255-3515
Fax: 403-255-7016 800-661-6868
contact@cibl.com www.cibl.com
Baked goods including bread, buns, pastries and English muffins
CEO: Luigi Bontorin
Marketing Manager: Ralph Knipsthilb
Office Manager: Louis Bontorin
Plant Manager: Dave Bontorin
Estimated Sales: D
Number Employees: 50-99
Square Footage: 60000
Type of Packaging: Consumer, Food Service
Brands:
   Calgary Italian
   Country Boy
   Golden Rich

2046 Calhoun Bend Mill
PO BOX 520
Libuse, LA 71348
318-640-0060
Fax: 318-339-9099 800-519-6455
sales@calhounbendmill.com
www.calhounbendmill.com
Fruit cobbler mixes, cornmeal and seafood coating.
President/CEO: Patrick Calhoun
Treasurer: Monica Calhoun
Vice President: Nathan Martin
Sales Manager: Emma Cash
Corporate Secretary: Martie Hoover
Estimated Sales: $400,000
Number Employees: 5
Number of Brands: 2
Number of Products: 25
Square Footage: 34000
Type of Packaging: Consumer, Food Service, Private Label, Bulk
Brands:
   Calhoun Bend Mill
   Orchard Mills

2047 Cali'flour Foods
1057 Village Lane
Chico, CA 95926
866-422-3568
www.califlourfoods.com
Cauliflower pizza crusts
Founder/Owner: Amy Lacey

2048 Calico Cottage
210 New Hwy
Amityville, NY 11701-1116
631-841-2100
Fax: 631-841-2401 800-645-5345
www.calicocottage.com
Fudge mixes, flavors and colorings.
President & CEO: Mark Wurzel
m.wurzel@calicocottage.com
Chief Financial Officer: Michael Lobacaro
Vice President: Larry Wurzel
Executive VP, Sales & Marketing: David Sank
Director, Human Resources & Admin: Barbara Stone-Carroll
Sr. VP, Operations & Technology: Thomas Montoya
Estimated Sales: $5 Million
Number Employees: 50-99
Square Footage: 45000
Type of Packaging: Consumer
Brands:
   Calico Cottage Fudge Mix
   Mister Fudge

2049 Calidad Foods
1313 Avenue R
Grand Prairie, TX 75053-5008
214-521-7999
Tortillas and other mexican food products.
CEO/President: Bing Graffunder
CFO: Sam Hillin
V.P Sales/Marketing: Gary Fraizer
Estimated Sales: $25,000,000
Number Employees: 250

2050 Calif Snack Foods
2131 Tyler Ave
South El Monte, CA 91733-2754
626-454-4099
Fax: 626-579-3038
info@californiasnackfoods.com
www.caltreats.com
Manufacturer of snack food such as popcorn, candy coated apples, cotton candy and freezies.
President: Steve Nelson
Secretary: Mary Nelson
Vice President: Paul Mullen
Manager: Alva Dallas
Production Manager: John Ohms
Estimated Sales: $5.3,000,000
Number Employees: 20-49
Brands:
   Karm'l Dapples
   Ice Tickles

2051 Calif Watercress Inc
550 E Telegraph Rd
Fillmore, CA 93015-9667
805-524-4808
Fax: 805-524-5295
Herbal supplements and herbs including cilantro and chives; also, vegetables including mixed, watercress and leeks
President/Treasurer: Alfred Beserra
Accounting: Catherine King
cah2ocress@aol.com
Human Resource Director: Susan Barbera
Secretary: Teresa Beserra
Estimated Sales: $5 Million
Number Employees: 50-99
Type of Packaging: Consumer, Food Service, Bulk
Brands:
   Al's Best

2052 Califia Farms
1095 E Green St
Pasadena, CA 91106
844-237-4779
califiafarms.com
Plant and fruit based creamers and espresso blends.
Founder: Greg Steltenpohl
Year Founded: 2010
Type of Packaging: Private Label

Food Manufacturers / A-Z

2053 California Almond Packers
1150 Ninth Street
Suite 1500
Modesto, CA 95354
209-549-8262
Fax: 209-549-8267
Almonds
Manager: Mathieu Esteve
Finance Executive: Chuck Niehues
Human Resources Executive: Mabel Kindel
Estimated Sales: Less than $500,000
Number Employees: 50-99
Brands:
 California Almond

2054 California Balsamic Inc
966 Mazzoni St
Ukiah, CA 95482-3475
707-463-2646
Fax: 707-463-2299 888-644-5127
www.californiabalsamic.com
Gourmet cooking, sauces, dipping oils, dessert sauces and herbed wine vinegars
Owner: Thomas Allen
balsamics@tresclassique.com
Estimated Sales: Under 500,000
Number Employees: 1-4
Number of Products: 38
Type of Packaging: Food Service, Private Label, Bulk
Brands:
 Lemon Splash
 Splash

2055 California Blending Co
2603 Seaman Ave
El Monte, CA 91733-1929
626-448-1918
Fax: 626-448-1998
Pizza spices, dough mixes, dressing mixes, steak salts, and garlic blends. Also provided; custom blending
President: Bill Morehart
calblending@aol.com
Vice President: Roger Morehart
Estimated Sales: Less Than $500,000
Number Employees: 1-4
Square Footage: 14600
Type of Packaging: Private Label, Bulk

2056 California Cereal Products
1267 14th St
Oakland, CA 94607-2246
510-452-4500
Fax: 510-452-4545 californiacereal.com
Gluten-free cereal ingredients, including rice, cereal and flour products.
President: Mark Graham
Co-Founder/Chairman/CEO: Robert Sterling Savely
Accounting: Richard O'Connor
Estimated Sales: $13.9 Million
Number Employees: 75
Square Footage: 600000
Type of Packaging: Consumer, Private Label, Bulk
Other Locations:
 Manufacturing Facility
 Macon GA

2057 California Citrus Producers
525 E Lindmore St
Lindsay, CA 93247-2559
559-562-5169
Fax: 559-562-5691
Producer of orange juice concentrates.
President: Tommy Elliott
CEO: John Barkley
Estimated Sales: $9,000,000
Number Employees: 20-49
Square Footage: 40000

2058 California Coast Naturals
12477 Calle Real
Santa Barbara, CA 93117
805-685-2076
cacoastnaturals.com
Olives and olive oil
CEO: Craig Makela
Number of Brands: 1
Number of Products: 15
Type of Packaging: Consumer
Brands:
 CALIFORNIA COAST NATURALS

2059 California Custom Foods
2325 Moore Ave
Fullerton, CA 92833-2510
714-870-0490
Fax: 714-870-5609 gilbertj@vanlaw.com
www.vanlaw.com
Processor and exporter of refrigerated and shelf stable salad dressings, pancake syrup, syrup concentrates, flavorings, extracts, colorings, ice cream toppings and barbecue and teriyaki sauces; importer of romano and parmesan cheeseolive oil and balsamic vinegar
Owner: Matthew Jones
jonesm@vanlaw.com
Director of Quality Assurance: Anna Tran
VP Sales/Marketing: John Gilbert
jonesm@vanlaw.com
Estimated Sales: $.5-1 million
Number Employees: 100-249
Square Footage: 520000
Type of Packaging: Consumer, Food Service, Private Label
Brands:
 California Classics
 Sunfruit
 Zito

2060 California Custom Fruits
15800 Tapia St
Baldwin Park, CA 91706-2178
626-736-4130
Fax: 626-736-4145 877-558-0056
info@ccff.com www.ccff.com
Fruit products and flavors
Owner: Monica Ahuero
President: Mike Mulhausen
CFO: Jim Fragnoli
Marketing Manager: Christine Long
Director Operations: Jack Miller
Production Manager: Eric Nielsen
Director of Flavor Development: Phillip Barone
Purchasing Director: Phyllis Ferguson
Estimated Sales: $20-35 Million
Number Employees: 100-249
Square Footage: 33000
Type of Packaging: Bulk
Brands:
 B2b
 Ccff
 Private Label

2061 California Dairies Inc.
2000 N. Plaza Dr.
Visalia, CA 93291
559-625-2200
Fax: 559-625-5433 info@californiadairies.com
www.californiadairies.com
Dairy products.
Chairman: Simon Vander Woude
President/CEO: Brad Anderson
Year Founded: 1999
Estimated Sales: Over $1 Billion
Number Employees: 500-999
Type of Packaging: Consumer, Food Service, Bulk
Other Locations:
 Artesia CA
 Fresno CA
 Los Banos CA
 Tipton CA
 Turlock CA
Brands:
 Challenge Dairy Products
 DairyAmerica

2062 California Fruit
8385 Miramar Mall Road
San Diego, CA 92121
559-266-7117
Fax: 559-266-0988 877-378-4811
admin@californiafruit.com
www.californiafruit.com
Dried apricots, peaches, pears and nectarines
President: Mark Melkonian
Contact: Marshal Dohoney
m.dohoney@caconstructionconcepts.com
Estimated Sales: $2.5-5 Million
Number Employees: 10-19
Type of Packaging: Bulk

2063 California Fruit & Nut
295 South Avenue
Gustine, CA 95322-1235
209-854-1819
Fax: 209-854-1819 888-747-8224
Flavored nuts including pistachios, peanuts and cashews; also, dried fruit and fruit rolls including apricot
President: Zaher Shahbaz
z.shahbaz@fruitnnut.com
Estimated Sales: Less than $500,000
Number Employees: 5-9
Square Footage: 10800
Type of Packaging: Consumer, Food Service
Brands:
 Cal-Fruit

2064 California Fruit Processors
2851 Bozzano Rd
Stockton, CA 95215-9152
209-931-1760
Fax: 209-931-0784 www.cafruitprocessors.com
Brined cherries
President: Alan Corradi
acorradi@cafruitprocessors.com
Office Manager: Cindy Haddad
Estimated Sales: $1,500,000
Number Employees: 50-99

2065 California Fruit and Tomato Kitchens
3800 Leckron Road
Modesto, CA 95357
209-574-9407
Fax: 209-529-1340
Canned goods including tomato products and peaches
President: Barbara Langum
Marketing: Nick Kastle
Product Sales: Greg Wuttke
Product Sales: Kelly Hayward
Plant Manager: Ed Harmon
Estimated Sales: $10-20 Million
Number Employees: 20-49
Type of Packaging: Food Service, Private Label
Brands:
 Dinapoli
 Flotta
 Paradise

2066 California Garden Products
31642 Avenida Los Cerritos
San Juan Capistrano, CA 92675
949-215-0000
Fax: 949-215-0965 felabd@californiagarden.com
www.californiagarden.com
Canned beans
President: Fouad El-Abd
Estimated Sales: $5-9,9,000,000
Number Employees: 11-50

2067 California Garlic Co
2707 Boston Avenue
San Diego, CA 92113
951-506-8883
Fax: 951-699-9155 info@garlicking.net
www.garlicking.net
Garlic, ginger, shallots, green onion, herbs and other
President: John Rosingana
Vice President: Peter Tarantino
Quality Control/Production: Larry George
Marketing: Jeff Crace
Estimated Sales: $1 Million
Number Employees: 35
Number of Brands: 4
Number of Products: 60
Square Footage: 24000
Type of Packaging: Consumer, Food Service, Private Label, Bulk

2068 California Independent Almond Growers
13000 Newport Road
Merced, CA 95303-9704
209-667-4855
Fax: 209-667-4854
Growers, packers, processors and shippers worldwide. California grown whole natural almonds direct from the source. State-of-the-art equipment
President: Karen Barstow
Estimated Sales: $2.5-5 Million
Number Employees: 50-99
Square Footage: 60000
Type of Packaging: Consumer, Food Service, Private Label, Bulk
Brands:
 California Independent Brand

Food Manufacturers / A-Z

2069 California Juice Co.
Santa Barbara, CA 93101
805-738-8723
info@caljuiceco.com
caljuiceco.com
Organic cold-pressed juice shots

2070 California Lavash
101 Leavesley Rd
Gilroy, CA 95020-3604
408-846-7705
info@californialavash.com
www.californialavash.com
Manufacturer of flatbreads.
Marketing Associate: Julia Voyvodich
Sales Director: Lilea Eshoo
leshoo@californialavash.com

2071 California Natural Products
1250 Lathrop Rd
Lathrop, CA 95330-9709
209-858-2525
Fax: 209-858-4076 marci.howe@cnp.com
www.cnp.com
Organic food ingredients, rice and soy beverages, nutritional drinks, soups, broths, teas and wine.
President: Robert Hatch
CEO/Owner: Pat Mitchell
patm@californianatural.com
Vice President of Finance: Gene Guelfo
Vice President: Kevin Haslebacher
Vice President of R&D: Khalid Shammet
Quality Regulatory: Connie Gutierrez
Technical Sales Manager: John Ashby
Director of Human Resources: Skip Lindstrom
Operations Manager: Emil Skaria
Purchasing Manager: Chirs Mifsud
Estimated Sales: $42 Million
Number Employees: 250-499
Type of Packaging: Private Label
Brands:
  Dacopa

2072 California Nuggets Inc
23073 S Frederick Rd
Ripon, CA 95366-9616
209-599-7131
Fax: 209-599-1531 www.californianuggets.com
Roasted nuts and peanut butter manufacturer
Owner: Steve Gikas
steve@californianuggets.com
Secretary/Treasurer: Barbara Bain
Marketing Director: Terry Wells-Brown
Sales Executive: Brenda Orlando
Estimated Sales: $2.6 Million
Number Employees: 50-99
Brands:
  California Nuggets

2073 California Oils Corp
1145 Harbour Way S
Richmond, CA 94804-3618
510-233-7660
Fax: 510-233-1329 800-225-6457
www.caloils.com
Vegetable oils and meal; exporter of corn and safflower oils
CEO: Sihira Ito
Controller: Masako Hirose
Vice President/Sales Executive: Joevic Fabregas
Sales and Marketing Manager: Karol Sop
Number Employees: 20-49
Parent Co: Mitsubishi

2074 California Olive Growers
8427 N Millbrook Avenue
Suite 101
Fresno, CA 93720-2197
559-674-8741
Fax: 559-673-3960 888-965-4837
www.californiaolivegrowers.com
Packer of canned California ripe olives, olive oil, tomatoes and pizza sauce
President: Lewis Johnson
CEO: Tom Lindemann
CEO: Fred Avalli
Quality Control: Larry Newby
Production Manager: Bob Marshall
Estimated Sales: $10 Million
Number Employees: 100-249
Number of Brands: 2
Number of Products: 10
Square Footage: 600000
Type of Packaging: Consumer, Food Service, Private Label, Bulk
Brands:
  Madera
  Oberti

2075 California Olive Oil Council
801 Camelia St # D
Suite D
Berkeley, CA 94710-1459
510-524-4523
Fax: 510-898-1530 888-718-9830
oliveoil@cooc.com www.cooc.com
Processor and exporter of oils including garlic, sesame, peanut, olive, canola, mineral, soybean, citrus, infused, organic, cold pressed and unrefined; also, balsamic vinegar and cooking wines; importer of kosher certified soy sauce
Owner: Claudia Siniawski
Vice President: Robert Mandia
CFO: Dave Lofgren
VP Sales/Marketing: Mark Moffitt
Contact: Alison Altomari
alison@cooc.com
Executive Director: Patricia Darragh
Estimated Sales: $420,980
Number Employees: 5-9
Square Footage: 76000
Parent Co: East Coast Olive Corporation
Type of Packaging: Consumer, Food Service, Private Label, Bulk
Brands:
  California Classics
  Montebello
  Oishii
  Virginia

2076 California Olive Ranch
1367 E Lassen Ave
Suite A1
Chico, CA 95973-7881
530-592-3700
Fax: 530-592-3275 cor@cal-olive.com
Olive oil
CEO: Gregory Kelly
Estimated Sales: 5,300,000
Number Employees: 10-19

2077 California Packing Company
1309 Melody Rd
Olivehurst, CA 95961
530-740-1040
Fax: 530-740-1044 info@calprune.com
www.calprune.com
Prunes in consumer and bulk packs.
Number Employees: 10
Type of Packaging: Private Label

2078 California Shellfish Company
505 Beach St
Suite 200
San Francisco, CA 94133-1131
415-923-7400
Fax: 415-923-1677
Crab, smoked salmon, halibut and snapper
President: Eugene Bugatto
CFO/Secretary/Treasurer: David Zellar
Manager: Richard Amundsen
Estimated Sales: $75.4 Million
Number Employees: 723
Type of Packaging: Consumer, Food Service, Private Label, Bulk

2079 California Smart Foods
2565 3rd St # 341
Suite 342
San Francisco, CA 94107-3159
415-826-0449
Fax: 415-826-0435 calsmartfds@att.net
Baked goods including breads, rolls, cakes, cookies, muffins, scones, danishes, tarts and pastries.
Owner: Helaine Melnitzer
calsmartfds@att.net
Estimated Sales: $20-50 Million
Number Employees: 20-49

2080 California Walnut Co
24490 Joseph Ave
Los Molinos, CA 96055-9663
530-527-2616
Fax: 530-527-7991
www.californiawalnutcompany.com
Walnuts
President: Brendon Flynn
brendon@californiawalnutcompany.com
Vice President: Ginger Gilchrist
Estimated Sales: $5 Million
Number Employees: 20-49

2081 California Wholesale Nut
1925 Manzanita Ave
Chico, CA 95926
530-895-0512
Fax: 530-345-1263
Nuts
Owner: Naomi Mc Dermott
Estimated Sales: $100,000
Number Employees: 1

2082 California Wild Rice Growers
41574 Osprey Rd
Fall River Mills, CA 96028-9750
530-336-5222
Fax: 530-336-5265 800-626-4366
www.frwr.com
Wild Rice
General Manager: Walt Oiler
Manager: Hiram Oilar
PLant Manager: Tony Knight
Estimated Sales: $420,000
Number Employees: 4
Brands:
  Fall River

2083 California-Antilles Trading
3735 Adams Ave
San Diego, CA 92116-2220
619-283-4834
Fax: 619-283-4834 800-330-6450
www.calantilles.com
Hot sauces, salsas, barbecue sauces
President: Richard E Gardner
irina.profosovitskaya@kp.org
Operations: Tevor Dyer
Production: Robert Davis
Estimated Sales: $2.5-5,000,000
Number Employees: 1-4
Number of Brands: 2
Number of Products: 25
Type of Packaging: Consumer, Private Label

2084 Calihan Pork ProcessorsInc
1 South St
Peoria, IL 61602
309-674-9175
Fax: 309-674-3003 www.calihanpork.com
Pork products including pre-rigor, boneless hams, Canadian bacon, spareribs, boneless pork tenderloins, pork riblets, pork hearts and pork tongue
President: Tom Landon
CFO: Al Schmid
General Manager: Jason Jones
Plant Manager: Ben Elbert
Year Founded: 1937
Estimated Sales: $20 Million
Number Employees: 50-99
Type of Packaging: Bulk

2085 Calio Groves
58 Calvert Court
Piedmont, CA 94611
707-402-4700
Fax: 707-402-4747 800-865-4836
Olive oil and extra virgin olive oil; importer of olive oil
President: Brendan Frasier
VP Production & Farming: Bob Singletary
Estimated Sales: $20-50 Million
Number Employees: 20-49
Parent Co: NVK Realty
Type of Packaging: Consumer, Food Service, Private Label, Bulk
Brands:
  Calio Groves
  Evo
  Olio Santo
  Stutz Olive Oil
  Vg Buck California Foods

2086 Calise & Sons Bakery Inc
2 Quality Dr
Lincoln, RI 02865-4266
401-334-3444
Fax: 401-334-0938 800-225-4737
Info@calisebakery.com www.calisebakery.com
Fresh Italian bread, rolls and pizza shells.

Food Manufacturers / A-Z

President: Michael Calise
Treasurer: Joseph Calise
CEO: Peter Petrocelli
VP Sales: Michael J. Pritchard
Production Manager: James Fontaine
Purchasing Manager: Anthony Capuzli
Estimated Sales: $34.8 Million
Number Employees: 100-249
Number of Products: 150
Square Footage: 210000
Type of Packaging: Consumer, Food Service, Private Label
Brands:
   Calise
   Sun Ray

2087 Calistoga Food Company
171 E 74th Street
New York, NY 10021-3221
212-879-4940
Fax: 212-879-5005
President: Martin Kreinik
Estimated Sales: $2.5-5,000,000
Number Employees: 5-9
Brands:
   Calistoga Food

2088 Calivirgin Olive Oils
13950 N Thornton Rd
Lodi, CA 95242
209-210-3142
calivirgin.com
Olive oil
Accounting: Julie Coldani
Year Founded: 2007
Type of Packaging: Food Service, Private Label

2089 Calkins & Burke
#800-1500 Georgia St
Vancouver, BC V6G 2Z6
Canada
604-669-3741
Fax: 604-699-9732 800-669-7992
www.calbur.com
Fresh and frozen halibut, salmon and crab
President: David Calkins
Secretary: Micheal Calkins
VP: Micheal Kolinn
Head of Marketing: Ken Jonn
Estimated Sales: $11.95
Number Employees: 60
Type of Packaging: Consumer, Food Service, Private Label
Brands:
   Astra
   Norden
   Royal Canadian

2090 Callaway Packing Inc
663 W 4th St
Delta, CO 81416-1534
970-874-9743
Fax: 970-874-7842
Fresh meat packer of beef, pork and lamb
President: David Dillie
callaway@kaycee.net
Estimated Sales: $20-50 Million
Number Employees: 10-19
Type of Packaging: Consumer

2091 Callaway Vineyards & Winery
32720 Rancho California Road
Temecula, CA 92591
951-676-4001
Fax: 951-676-5209 800-472-2377
info@callawaywinery.com
www.callawaywinery.com
Red and white wine
President: Mike Jellison
Director: Lori Lyn Narlock
VP/Winemaker: Dwayne Helmuth
Associate Public Relations Manager: Kelly Keagy
Vineyard Manager: Craig Weaver
Cellar Foreman: Joe Vera
Plant Manager: Jose Ceja
Estimated Sales: $20-50 Million
Number Employees: 50-99
Parent Co: Hiram Walker-Allied Domeq.
Type of Packaging: Consumer, Food Service

2092 Callie's Charleston Biscuits
1895 Avenue F
North Charleston, SC 29405-1914
843-577-1198
carrie@calliesbiscuits.com
www.calliesbiscuits.com
Bread/biscuits, cakes/pastries, full line of baked goods and frozen desserts.
Owner: Carrie Bailey-Morey
carrie@calliesbiscuits.com
Estimated Sales: Less Than $500,000
Number Employees: 1-4

2093 Callis Seafood
353 Callis Road
Lancaster, VA 22503-4112
804-462-7634
Fax: 804-435-6808
Oysters, crabs and frozen shrimp
President: Diane Callis-Haydon
CEO/VP: Diane Haydon
Pres-treas: Terry Haydon
Estimated Sales: $200,000
Number Employees: 2
Type of Packaging: Consumer

2094 Calmar Bakery
4906 50 Ave
Calmar, AB T0C 0V0
Canada
780-985-3583
Fax: 780-985-3583
Baked goods including fruit cakes and Danish almond rings and wedding cakes
CEO: Doug Campbell
Secretary/Treasurer: Marlene Campbell
Manager: Tork Kristiansen
Estimated Sales: $99,590
Number Employees: 2
Type of Packaging: Consumer, Food Service
Brands:
   Calmar Bakery

2095 Calpro Ingredients
1787 Pomona Road
Corona, CA 951-735-59
909-493-4890
Fax: 909-493-4845 www.calprofoods.com
Whey protein concentrates
President: Garry Johns
Operations: Carole Northup
Number Employees: 5-9
Square Footage: 6000
Parent Co: Golden Cheese Company of California
Type of Packaging: Bulk
Brands:
   Calpro

2096 Caltex Foods
9045-A Eton Ave
Canoga Park, CA 91304
818-700-8657
Fax: 818-700-0285 800-522-5839
www.aasanfoods.com
Ready made meals, Kosher ready made foods, Halal ready made foods, Mediterrenean foods, Middle Eastern Foods.
President/Secretary: Mehrdad Pakravan
Estimated Sales: $3 Million
Number Employees: 8
Square Footage: 10000
Parent Co: Caltex Trading
Type of Packaging: Consumer, Private Label
Brands:
   Aasan
   Aviva
   Beit Hashita
   Jaffer

2097 Calumet Diversified Meats Company
Ten Thousand 80th Avenue
Pleasant Prairie, WI 53158
262-947-7200
Fax: 262-947-7209 800-752-7427
info@porkchops.com www.porkchops.com
Pork including cutlets, loin, barbecued ribs, tenderloins, chops, etc
CEO & President: Andrew Becker
Chief Financial Officer: Tina Novosel
Vice President: Larry Becker
VP Business Development: Russell Findlay
EVP Sales/Marketing: Joy Huskey
VP Operations: Chidel Taylor
Estimated Sales: $24 Million
Number Employees: 125

2098 Calvert's
PO Box 1761
El Paso, TX 79949
915-544-3434
Fax: 915-533-0026 888-472-5727
www.desertpepper.com
Lemonade mix
Owner: William Parker
Estimated Sales: $10-20 Million
Number Employees: 20-49

2099 Calvisius Caviar
444 Madison Ave
Suite 1206
New York, NY 10022-6957
212-207-8222
Fax: 212-207-8333 www.calvisius.com
Caviar; smoked fish; and gift baskets.
Vice President: John Knierim
john.knierim@calvisius.com
Year Founded: 1977
Number Employees: 1-10
Type of Packaging: Food Service

2100 Camas Prairie Winery
110 S Main St
Moscow, ID 83843-2806
208-882-0214
Fax: 208-882-0214 800-616-0214
www.camasprairiewinery.com
Wine
Co-Owner/President: Stuart Scott
Co-Owner/CFO: Susan Scott
Contact: Jeremy Ritter
tastingroom@camasprairiewinery.com
Estimated Sales: $120,000
Number Employees: 2
Number of Products: 22
Type of Packaging: Private Label
Brands:
   Camas

2101 Cambria Winery
5475 Chardonnay Ln
Santa Maria, CA 93454-9600
805-937-8091
Fax: 805-934-3589 888-339-9463
info@cambriawines.com www.cambriawines.com
Producer of wines such as Chardonnay, Pinot Noir, Pinot Gris, Syrah and Viognier.
President: Barbara Banke
Marketing: Holly Evans
Customer Relations: Karen Readey
General Manager: Keith Moak
Vineyard Manager: Matt Mahoney
Winemaker: Denise Shurtleff
Estimated Sales: $5-10,000,000
Number Employees: 50-99
Brands:
   Cambria

2102 Cambridge Brands Inc
810 Main St
Cambridge, MA 02139-3588
617-491-2500
Fax: 617-547-2381 www.tootsie.com
Candy: bagged, bars, caramels, chocolate, chocolate covered cherries, fudge, holiday, gums and jellies, hard, jelly beans, licorice, lollypops, mints, nougats and coated nuts; also, chocolate and cocoa products for bakersconfectioners, etc.
President: Ellen Gordon
Director of Quality Control: John Zhang
Director of Human Resources: Jon Kopera
Manager: Paul Murphy
Prod Superintedent: Val Ponte
Plant Manager: Gerald Chesser
Number Employees: 100-249
Parent Co: Tootsie Roll Industries
Type of Packaging: Consumer, Food Service
Brands:
   Charleston Chew
   Chuckles
   Junior Mints,
   Pearson
   Pom Poms
   Sugar Babies
   Sugar Daddy
   Sugar Mama

Food Manufacturers / A-Z

2103 Cambridge Food
2801 Salinas Hwy # F
Monterey, CA 93940-6240
831-373-2300
Fax: 866-373-0369 800-433-2584
info@cambridgedietusa.com
www.cambridgedietusa.com
Meal replacement formulas, cereals, soups, nutrition bars
Manager: Janet Bishop
Research & Development: Dr Robert Nesheim
Estimated Sales: $300,000-500,000
Number Employees: 1-4
Brands:
 Cambridge Food

2104 Cambridge Packing Company
41 Foodmart Road
Boston, MA 02118
617-269-6700
Fax: 617-269-0266 800-722-6726
salesinfo@cambridgepacking.com
www.cambridgepacking.com
Fine meats and seafoods including beef, lamb, pork, chicken, fish and shellfish
President/CEO: Bruce Rodman
Co-CEO: Alan Roberts
CFO: Wendy DeMonico
Operations: Paul Dias
Year Founded: 1923
Estimated Sales: $45 Million
Number Employees: 62
Square Footage: 30000

2105 Camellia Beans
5401 Toler Street
Harahan, LA 70183
504-733-8480
Fax: 504-733-8155 info@camelliabeans.com
www.camelliabrand.com
Dried beans, peas and lentils
Partner: Ken Hayward
Partner: Connely Hayward
Estimated Sales: $10-20 Million
Number Employees: 20-49
Type of Packaging: Consumer, Food Service, Bulk
Brands:
 Camellia

2106 Camellia General Provision Co
1333 Genesee St
Buffalo, NY 14211-2227
716-893-5352
Fax: 716-895-7713 contact@camelliafoods.com
www.camelliafoods.com
Meat including smoked, sausage and ham
Owner: Adam Cichocki
adam@camelliafoods.com
Vice President: Patrick Cichocki
Vice President: Eric Cichocki
Office Manager: Joell Gilley
Estimated Sales: $5 Million
Number Employees: 20-49

2107 Cameo Confections
543 Juneway Drive
Bay Village, OH 44140-2606
440-871-5732
Fax: 440-892-8656
Confections
President: Gail Barker

2108 Cameron Birch Syrup & Confections
951 Hermon Road
Suite 6
Wasilla, AK 99654-7379
907-373-6275
Fax: 907-373-6274 800-962-4724
Birch syrup, marinades, salad dressing and candy
President: Marlene Cameron
Number Employees: 1-4
Square Footage: 2500
Type of Packaging: Consumer, Food Service, Private Label, Bulk
Brands:
 Birch Bark
 Birch Logs
 Black Tie
 Cameron
 Cameron's
 Sesame Birch Sticks

2109 Cameron Seafood Processors
PO Box 1228
Cameron, LA 70631-1228
318-775-5510
Fax: 318-755-5529
Seafood
President: Bruce Bang

2110 Camilla Pecan Company
P.O.Box 508
275 Industrial Blvd
Camilla, GA 31730-3911
229-336-7282
Fax: 229-336-1177 800-526-8770
info@harrellnut.com
Pecans
President/CEO: Marty Harrell
CFO: Paula Johnson
General Corporate Management: David Stanfield
Estimated Sales: $43,000,000
Number Employees: 250
Number of Brands: 3
Brands:
 Camilla Pecan
 Harrell Nut
 Ole' Henry's Nuthouse

2111 Camino Real Foods Inc
2638 E Vernon Ave
Vernon, CA 90058-1825
323-585-6599
Fax: 323-585-5420 800-421-6201
www.chicknwraps.com
Frozen burritos and stuffed microwaveable sandwiches
President: Robert Cross
rcross@crfoods.com
CFO: Richard Lunsford
Vice President: Juan Salazar
Marketing: Clark Metcalf
VP Sales: Terry McMartin
Human Resource Compliance & Regulatory: Lulu Saiden
Manager: Jim Gatten
Estimated Sales: $40 Million
Number Employees: 250-499
Parent Co: Nissan Foods
Type of Packaging: Consumer, Food Service
Brands:
 Taxco
 Tina's Las Campanas

2112 Campagana Winery
10950 West Road
Redwood Valley, CA 95470-9741
707-485-1221
Fax: 707-485-1225 www.winesandromance.com
Winery
Chairman: Joseph Campagna
CEO: Tony Coturri
CFO/COO: George Pruden
Marketing Director: Paul White
Sales Director: Paul White
Production Manager: Nic Coturri
Estimated Sales: $3,000,000
Number Employees: 8
Type of Packaging: Private Label
Brands:
 Gabrielli
 Gabrielli Winery

2113 Campagna Distinct Flavor
40759 Mcdowell Creek Drive
Lebanon, OR 97355-0995
541-258-6806
Fax: 541-258-7806 800-959-4372
Cooking sauces, fruit, savory, and mustard flavors; hot pepper and garlic jellies
President: Marlene Peterson
CFO: Joseph Peterson
Estimated Sales: $660,000
Number Employees: 7
Type of Packaging: Private Label

2114 Campari
55 E 59th St
Suite 9
New York, NY 10022-1112
212-891-3600
Fax: 212-891-3661 www.campari.com
Alcoholic beverages
CEO: Bob Kunze-Concewitz
General Manager: Gennaro Miccoli
Estimated Sales: $2.5-5,000,000
Number Employees: 10-19
Parent Co: Campari
Brands:
 Campari
 Cinzano
 Skyy
 Aperoi
 Glen Grant
 Wild Turkey

2115 Campbell Company of Canada
2845 Matheson Blvd E
Toronto, ON L4W 5J8
Canada
800-410-7687
www.campbellsoup.ca
Canned foods including condensed soups, broth, chili and ready to serve soups.
President: Julio Gomez
Year Founded: 1930
Estimated Sales: $224 Million
Number Employees: 700
Type of Packaging: Consumer, Food Service, Private Label
Brands:
 Bisto
 Broths
 Campbells Ready To Enjoy Soups
 Campbells Soup At Hand
 Chunky Ready To Go Bowls
 Chunky Ready To Serve Soups/Chili
 Gardennay
 Godiva
 Habitant
 Healthy Request Ready To Serve Soup
 Pace
 Pepperidge Farm
 Red & White Condensed Soups
 V8
 V8 Splash
 V8 Vgo

2116 Campbell Soup Co.
1 Campbell Pl.
Camden, NJ 08103-1701
856-342-4800
Fax: 856-342-3878 800-257-8443
www.campbellsoupcompany.com
Soups, snacks, beverages and simple meals.
President/CEO: Mark Clouse
Executive VP/CFO: Mick Beekhuizen
Executive VP/General Counsel: Adam Ciongoli
Executive VP, Global R&D: Craig Slavtcheff
Executive VP, Global Supply Chain: Bob Furbee
Year Founded: 1869
Estimated Sales: Over $1 Billion
Number Employees: 18,000
Number of Brands: 21
Type of Packaging: Consumer, Food Service, Bulk
Other Locations:
 Toronto, Canada
 Corporate Headquarters
 Camden NJ
 Pepperidge Farm Headquarters
 Norwalk CT
 Bolthouse Farms Headquarters
 Bakersfield CA
 Norre Snede, Denmark
 Selangor, Malaysia
 Bekasi, Indonesia
 Arnott's Headquarters
 Homebush, Australia
 New Market, New Zealand
Brands:
 Campbells
 Campbells Foodservice
 Campbells Canada
 Campbells Chunky
 Cape Cod
 Goldfish
 Kettle Brand
 Lance
 Late July Snacks
 Milano
 Pace
 Pacific Foods
 Pepperidge Farm
 Plum Organics
 Prego
 Snack Factory Pretzel Crisps
 Snyder's of Hanover
 SpaghettiOs
 Swanson

Food Manufacturers / A-Z

V8 Beverages
Well Yes

2117 Campbell's Quality Cuts
2551 Michigan St
Sidney, OH 45365-9083
937-492-2194
Fax: 937-492-4044
Lamb, beef and pork
Owner: Dennis Campbell
Estimated Sales: $380,000
Number Employees: 5
Type of Packaging: Consumer, Bulk

2118 Camrose Packers
5320 47th Street
Camrose, AB T4V 1K6
Canada
780-672-4887
Fresh beef and pork and wild game including deer, elk and moose
Owner: Andrew Anderson
Manager: Debilyn Witvoet Parent
Treasurer/Secretary: Sharon Miller
Estimated Sales: $1,600,000
Number Employees: 5
Type of Packaging: Consumer
Brands:
  Camrose

2119 Can Am Seafood
972 County Road
Lubec, ME 04652
207-733-2267
Fax: 207-733-0927
Seafood
President: William Jackson
Estimated Sales: $200,000
Number Employees: 1

2120 CanAmera Foods
14711-128th Avenue
Edmonton, AL T5L 3H3
Canada
780-447-6960
Fax: 780-452-0541 canamera.lookchem.com
Shortenings, margarines, oils, lard, whipped toppings, stabilizers and emulsifiers including lecithin
President: Murray Davis

2121 Canada Bread Co, Ltd
10 Four Seasons Place
Etobicoke, ON M9B 6H7
Canada
416-622-2040
800-465-5515
www.canadabread.com
Baked goods, snacks and bread company.
President: Joseph McCarthy
Year Founded: 1911
Estimated Sales: $1.3 Billion
Number Employees: 4,175
Number of Brands: 7
Number of Products: 1K+
Parent Co: Grupo Bimbo
Type of Packaging: Consumer, Food Service, Private Label, Bulk
Brands:
  Villaggio®
  Stonemill®
  POM®
  Dempster's®
  Bon Matin®
  Vachon®
  Ben's®

2122 Canadian Fish Exporters
134 Rumford Ave # 202
Suite 202
Auburndale, MA 02466-1377
617-916-0900
Fax: 617-926-8214 800-225-4215
cfe@cfeboston.com www.cfeboston.com
Saltfish including bacalao, pollock, hake, cusk, haddock, herring, mackerel and cod; importer of Italian cheeses and canned tomatoes
CEO: Robert Metafora
CFO/Treasurer: Janelle Calamari
VP: James Scannell
Estimated Sales: $10-20 Million
Number Employees: 10-19
Type of Packaging: Consumer, Private Label, Bulk
Brands:
  Bacala Rico

Buena Ventura
Cristobal

2123 Canadian Harvest-U.S.A.
7301 Ohms Lane
Suite 600
Edina, MN 55439
952-820-2518
Fax: 952-835-1991 888-689-5800
miker@skypoint.com www.sunopta.com
Fiber ingredients including bleached oat fibers, red and white wheat brans, corn brans, oat blends, wheat germs and customized grain blends
President: David Belaney
Marketing Manager: Mike Rudquist
General Manager: John White
Plant Manager: Paul Empanger
Estimated Sales: $4 Million
Number Employees: 40
Other Locations:
  Canadian Harvest
  St. Thomas ON
Brands:
  Snowite

2124 Canadian Mist Distillers
202 MacDonald Road
Collingwood, ON L9Y 4J2
Canada
705-445-4690
Fax: 705-445-7948 www.canadianmist.com
Processor and exporter of whiskey
Officer: Pat Sullivan
Manager Admin./Commodities: Steve Sly
Manager Production: Don Jaques
Plant Manager: Harold Ferguson
Estimated Sales: $24.4 Million
Number Employees: 35
Square Footage: 1000000
Parent Co: Brown-Forman Corporation
Type of Packaging: Consumer, Food Service
Brands:
  Canadian Mist

2125 Canaf Foods International
405 Queen Street S
Po Box 75047
Bolton, ON L7E 2B0
Canada
905-362-0524
Fax: 905-362-0526 info@canaffoods.com
www.canaffoods.com
Bread/biscuits, cakes/pastries, frozen baked goods, frozen desserts, foodservice, private label.
Marketing: Giovanni Bartolomeo

2126 Canal Fulton Provision
2014 Locust St S
Canal Fulton, OH 44614-9477
330-854-3502
Fax: 330-854-3502 800-321-3502
www.canalfultonpro.com
Portion cut poultry and meats including beef, lamb and pork
President: George Mizarek
jmizarek@aol.com
Estimated Sales: $4.5 Million
Number Employees: 20-49
Square Footage: 81000
Type of Packaging: Consumer, Food Service, Private Label, Bulk
Brands:
  Corn King
  Flavor Pack
  Weaver

2127 Canarino
267 Libbey Parkway
Weymouth, MA 02189
Fax: 781-413-8999 800-510-4202
www.canarino.com
Hot lemon beverage

2128 Candelari's Specialty Sausage
6002 Washington Ave
Houston, TX 77007-5015
832-200-1474
Fax: 281-568-8098 800-953-5343
emaillist@candelaris.com www.candelaris.com
Sausage
President: Michael May
michael@candelaris.com
CFO: Michael Freeman
Estimated Sales: $500,000-$1,000,000
Number Employees: 5-9

Type of Packaging: Private Label
Brands:
  Candelari's

2129 Cando Pasta
1301 5th Ave
PO Box 689
Cando, ND 58324-6603
701-968-4401
www.candopasta.weebly.com
Producer of dry pasta products.
Owner: Jim Gibbens
Owner: Bruce Gibbens
Estimated Sales: Less than $500,000
Number Employees: 20-49
Number of Brands: 1
Square Footage: 80000
Type of Packaging: Consumer, Bulk
Brands:
  Cando Pasta

2130 Candy Basket Inc
1924 NE 181st Ave
Portland, OR 97230
503-666-2000
Fax: 503-666-6400 800-864-1924
candybasket@comcast.net
Milk, dark and white chocolate. Truffles, nuts, chews, turtles, creams, toffee's, barks, corns and brittles.
President/Owner: Dale Fuhr
Contact: Amber Allan
aallan-candybasket@comcast.net
Estimated Sales: $4.5 Million
Number Employees: 35

2131 Candy Bouquet of Elko
3362 Dux Avenue
Elko, NV 89801-4432
775-777-9866
Fax: 775-777-3200 888-855-3391
hopkins@sierra.net
Candy bouquets
Co-Owner: Judy Hopkins
Co-Owner: Diane Noble
Manager: Angie Demars
Number Employees: 1-4

2132 Candy Central
905 Murray Rd
East Hanover, NJ 07936
www.candycentral.com
Candy and confections
Year Founded: 1937
Estimated Sales: Less Than $500,000
Number Employees: 50-249
Number of Brands: 70
Parent Co: Consolidated Service Distributors, Inc
Brands:
  100 Grand(c)
  3 Musketeers(c)
  Adams & Brooks, Inc
  Airheads
  Almond Joy
  Altoids
  American Licorice Co.
  Andre Prost, Inc.
  Atomic Fireball
  Au'some
  Baby Ruth
  Basic Promotions
  Big League Chew
  Bonomo
  Boston America Corp
  Bottle Caps
  BreathSavers
  Bubblicious Bubble Gum
  Butterfinger
  C Howard Co.
  Candyrific
  Charleston Chew
  Charms Co.
  Chuckles
  Cold Stone Creamery
  Colombina
  Cry Baby
  Dentyne
  Dryden & Palmer
  Dubble Bubble
  Dum Dums(c) Pops
  Ferrara Candy Co.
  Fluffy Stuff
  Frankford Candy
  Frooties

Food Manufacturers / A-Z

Gerrit J. Verburg Co.
Gobstopper
Haribo
Heath
Hello Kitty
Hershey's(c)
Hilco Corporation
Hospitality Mints
Hubba Bubba(c)
Ice Breakers
Icee
Impact Confections
Jolly Rancher
Just Born, Inc
Kidsmania Inc
KIT KAT(c)
Koko's Confectionary & Novelty
Laffy Taffy
M & M's
Mars, Inc
Mentos
MILKY WAY(c)
Minions
Mondelez International
My M&Ms
NECCO
Nerds
Nestl,
Novelty Specialties
Nutella(c)
Orbit Gum
Pez Candy
Nutella(c)
Orbit Gum
Pez Candy
Pixy Stix
Pop Rocks
Push Pop Candy

2133 Candy Cottage Company
465 Pike Rd Ste 103
Huntingdon Valley, PA 19006
215-953-8288
Fax: 215-357-3035 thecandycottageco@gmail.com
Chocolate covered pretzels
Co-Owner: Al Palagruto
Co-Owner: Joan Palagruto
Estimated Sales: Under $500,000
Number Employees: 3
Type of Packaging: Consumer, Food Service, Private Label, Bulk
Brands:
 Ultimate Petite Pretzels
 Ultimate Pretzel
 Ultimate Pretzel Rods
 Ultimate Pretzel Sculptures

2134 (HQ)Candy Flowers
9286 Mercantile Drive
Mentor, OH 44060-4525
440-974-1333
Fax: 440-974-1338
Chocolate and candy flowers, chocolate covered pretzels, coffee spoons and cookies and theme wrapped chocolate bars; exporter of candy flowers; importer of chocolates
President: Joanne Henry
Marketing: Anthony Henry
Estimated Sales: $5-10,000,000
Number Employees: 20-49
Square Footage: 42000
Type of Packaging: Food Service
Brands:
 Candy Flower Bouquets
 Spoonful of Flavors
 Sweet Blossoms

2135 Candy Mountain Sweets & Treats
1484 Atlanta Industrial Dr NW
Suite A
Atlanta, GA 30331-1031
404-505-7332
Fax: 404-696-4003 800-621-1954
www.tootarts.com
Sugar free candy
President & CEO: Armand Hammer
VP Purchasing: Bob Davis
VP Sales: Al Silva
Estimated Sales: $20-50 Million
Number Employees: 50-99
Brands:
 Tpp Tarts Kids Kandy

2136 Candyrific
3738 Lexington Rd
Louisville, KY 40207-3010
502-893-3626
Fax: 502-893-3951 sales@candyrific.com
www.candyrific.com
Candy
President: Rob Auerbach
robr@candyrific.com
Vice President: Paul Roberts
Vice President: Mike Roberts
Quality Assurance Manager: Joshua Boone
V.P. of Sales: Larry Lindenbaum
Customer Service: Rebecca Raymond
Estimated Sales: $34.9 Million
Number Employees: 20
Brands:
 Cool Pops
 Crayola
 Etch-A-Sketch
 Marvel
 Peeps
 Slinky Brand Candy

2137 Canelake's Candy
414 Chestnut St
Virginia, MN 55792-2526
218-741-1557
Fax: 218-741-1557 888-928-8889
Processor and exporter of candies and chocolates; importer of nuts
President: James Cina
candy@canelakes.com
Estimated Sales: Less Than $500,000
Number Employees: 5-9
Square Footage: 6000
Type of Packaging: Consumer

2138 Cangel
60 Paton Road
Toronto, ON M6H 1R8
Canada
416-532-5111
Fax: 416-532-6231 800-267-4795
Manufacturer and exporter of food, hydrolyzed and technical gelatins
President: Richard Manka
Number Employees: 2
Square Footage: 160000
Type of Packaging: Bulk

2139 Cannoli Factory
75 Wyandanch Ave
Wyandanch, NY 11798-4441
631-643-2700
Fax: 631-643-2777 sales@cannolifactory.com
www.cannolifactory.com
Processor and exporter of Italian and New York style cheesecake, tiramisu, lobster tail pastries and cannoli products including chocolate covered shells, cream and tarts
Owner: Michael Zucaro
Contact: John Edwards
johne@cannolifactory.com
Estimated Sales: $4 Million
Number Employees: 50-99
Type of Packaging: Food Service

2140 Cannon's Sweets Hots
645.S Almada
Las Cruces, NM 880005
575-523-1447
Fax: 575-523-1447 800-214-6639
sweethot@sweethots.com www.sweethots.com
Hot sauces and chili
Co-Owner/President: John Cannon
Co-Owner/CEO: Diane Cannon
Estimated Sales: Under $500,000
Number Employees: 1-4

2141 Canoe Lagoon Oyster Company
118 Bayview Ave
Coffman Cove, AK 99918
907-329-2253
Fax: 425-643-7266
Oyster
Owner: Sharon Gray
Owner: Don Nicholson
Estimated Sales: $310,000
Number Employees: 2
Type of Packaging: Consumer, Food Service, Bulk

2142 Canoe Ridge Vineyard
1102 W Cherry St
Walla Walla, WA 99362-1746
509-527-0885
Fax: 509-527-0886 www.canoeridgevineyard.com
Wines
Manager: Sue Bridwell
sueb@preceptwine.com
Estimated Sales: $500,000-$1 Million
Number Employees: 10-19
Parent Co: Chalone Wine Group

2143 Canon Potato Company
P.O.Box 880
Center, CO 81125-0880
719-754-3445
Potato packer and shipper
President: David Tonso
d.tonso@canonpotato.com
Estimated Sales: $2,689,000
Number Employees: 40
Parent Co: Woerner Holdings, L.P.
Type of Packaging: Private Label

2144 Canton Noodle Corporation
101 Mott St
New York, NY 10013
212-226-3276
Fax: 212-226-8037
Chinese canned noodles
Principal: James Eng
Estimated Sales: $610,000
Number Employees: 8
Type of Packaging: Consumer

2145 Cantrell's Seafood
Sabino Road
Bath, ME 04530
207-442-7261
Fax: 207-770-1600
Seafood
President: S C Cantrell

2146 Canyon Bakehouse LLC
1510 E 11th St
Loveland, CO 80537-5049
970-461-3844
www.canyonglutenfree.com
Gluten free baked goods
Co-Founder: Christi Skow
Co-Founder: Josh Skow
jskow@canyonbakehouse.com
Co-Founder: Ed Miknevicius
Estimated Sales: Less Than $500,000
Number Employees: 1-4

2147 Canyon Specialty Foods
11035 Switzer Ave
Dallas, TX 75238-1333
214-352-1771
Fax: 214-352-3118 aconnally@canyonfoods.com
www.frankievskitchen.com
Gourmet shelf and frozen food, salsa and sauces
Owner, President: Anne Connally
aconnally@canyonspecialtyfoods.com
Estimated Sales: $1,100,000
Number Employees: 10-19
Parent Co: 321 Capital Partners LLC
Type of Packaging: Private Label

2148 Cap Candy
50 Technology Court
Napa, CA 94558-7519
707-251-9321
Fax: 707-251-9482
Candy
VP of Marketing: Deirdre Gonzalez
General Manager: Tom Pritchard
Number Employees: 250-499
Parent Co: Hasbro

2149 Capa Di Roma Inc
358 Burnside Ave
East Hartford, CT 06108-2426
860-282-0298
Fax: 860-289-6211 email@capadiroma.com
www.capadiroma.com
Olive oil, balsamic vinegar, pasta sauce.
Presidnet: Frank Capaccio
frank@capadiroma.com
VP, Marketing: Emilia Capaccio
Estimated Sales: $150,000
Number Employees: 2

579

Food Manufacturers / A-Z

2150 Capalbo's Fruit Baskets
350 Allwood Rd
Clifton, NJ 07012-1701
973-667-6262
Fax: 973-450-1199 800-252-6262
service@capalbosonline.com
www.capalbosonline.com
Produces gift baskets for the specialty food industry.
President: Frank Capalbo
Vice President: Susan Capalbo
Digital Marketing Manager: Joe Wilson
Estimated Sales: $4.8,000,000
Number Employees: 50-99
Type of Packaging: Food Service
Brands:
  Capalbo's

2151 Caparone Winery LLC
2280 San Marcos Rd
Paso Robles, CA 93446-5322
805-610-5308
info@caparone.com
www.caparone.com
Wines
President: Mark Caparone
Partner: David Caparone
Estimated Sales: $100,000
Number Employees: 1-4

2152 Capay Canyon Ranch
P.O. Box 508
Esparto, CA 95627-0508
530-662-2372
Fax: 530-662-2306 capaycanyonranch.com
Processor and exporter of almonds, walnuts and grapes, and inshell chandler walnuts.
Sales Director: Leslie Barth
Contact: Stan Barth
stan@capaycanyon.com
Plant Operations: Todd Barth
Estimated Sales: $1-2,499 Million
Number Employees: 4
Number of Brands: 2
Number of Products: 8
Square Footage: 10000
Type of Packaging: Bulk
Brands:
  Capay Canyon Ranch
  Stan Barth Farms

2153 Capco Enterprises
34 Deforest Ave # 3
East Hanover, NJ 07936-2832
973-884-0044
Fax: 973-884-8711 800-252-1011
www.capcoenterprisesinc.com
Almonds, licorice, baked beans, sugar-coated pistachios and chick peas
President/CEO: Carole Lapone
clapone@capcoenterprisesinc.com
Operations Executive: James Ventola
Plant Manager: Daniel Rivera
Estimated Sales: $1 Million
Number Employees: 5-9

2154 Cape Ann Seafood
44 Grapevine Road
Gloucester, MA 01930-4341
978-283-0687
Fax: 978-282-1870
President: Nickolas Avelis
Treasurer: Faith Avelis
Vice President: James Douglass
Estimated Sales: $2.0 Million
Number Employees: 2

2155 Cape Cod Coffee Roasters
348 Main St
Mashpee, MA 02649-2045
508-477-2400
Fax: 508-477-2989 www.capecodcoffee.com
Coffee
Owner: Demos Young
demos@capecodroasters.com
Office Manager: Bonnie Cohen
Estimated Sales: $340,000
Number Employees: 5-9

2156 Cape Cod Potato Chips
100 Breeds Hill Rd
Hyannis, MA 02601-1886
508-775-3358
Fax: 508-775-2808 800-438-1880
www.capecodchips.com
Popcorn including white cheddar cheese, natural and butter; also, kettle-cooked potato chips
President: Margaret Wicklund
Chief Executive Officer: Roger Gray
Sr Vice President: Dan Collins
Vice President: Chuck Fisher
Estimated Sales: $20-50 Million
Number Employees: 100-249
Square Footage: 30000
Parent Co: Snyder's Lance
Type of Packaging: Consumer
Brands:
  Cape Cod

2157 Cape Cod Provisions
31 Jonathan Bourne Dr # 1
Unit 1
Pocasset, MA 02559-4919
508-564-5840
Fax: 508-564-5844
customerservice@capecodprovisions.com
Chocolate covered cranberries, chocolate covered fruit, fruit truffles
Owner/President/Quality Control: Susan Faria
Finance Manager: Rick Ottaviano
Director of Sales and Marketing: Kristin McGillicuddy
Sales Representative: Erin Mancinelli
Estimated Sales: $1.2 Million
Number Employees: 10-19

2158 Cape Cod Specialty Foods
11 Cranberry Hwy
P.O. Box 519
Sagamore, MA 2561
508-888-7099
Fax: 508-888-6616 orders@ccsfoods.com
Wholesaler/distributor of gourmet condiments including lemon pepper mustard, cranberry chutney, relish and sauces, schnappy peach preserves, chocolate covered cranberries, bog beans, etc.; also mail order available
Owner: Michael Duryea
bogbeans@verizon.net
Estimated Sales: $160,000
Number Employees: 5-9
Square Footage: 2000
Type of Packaging: Consumer, Food Service

2159 Cape Cod Sweets, LLC
31 Jonathan Bourne Dr
Suite 1
Pocasset, MA 02559-4919
508-564-5840
Fax: 508-564-5844
Chocolate, candy, and fruit confections.
Founder: Sue Faria
Year Founded: 1996
Number Employees: 5-9
Brands:
  Harvest Sweets
  Cape Cod Cranberry Candy
  Sweet Cravings

2160 Capital Brewery & Beer Garden
7734 Terrace Ave
Middleton, WI 53562-3163
608-836-7100
Fax: 608-831-9155 capbrew@capitalbrewery.com
Brewer of lager and ale
President, CEO: Carl Nolen
Brew master: Kirby Nelson
Estimated Sales: $5-10,000,000
Number Employees: 20-49
Type of Packaging: Consumer, Food Service, Bulk
Brands:
  Gartenbrau

2161 Capital City Processors
P.O. Box 3588
Winchester, VA 22604-2586
540-877-2590
Fax: 540-877-3215 800-473-2731
www.valleyproteins.com
Cooking oils
President: Gerald Smith
Owner: Mike Smith
Estimated Sales: $20-50 Million
Number Employees: 10-19
Type of Packaging: Bulk

2162 Capital Packers Inc
12907-57th Street
Edmonton, AB T5A 0E7
Canada
780-476-1391
Fax: 780-478-0083 800-272-8868
info@capitalpackers.ca www.capitalpackers.ca
Cooked and smoked meats including beef, pork and veal
President: Brent Komarnicki
Vice President: Augustine Komarnicki
Sales Manager: Peter Andreassen
Plant Manager: Cor Van Miltenburg
Estimated Sales: $20.6,000,000
Number Employees: 120
Number of Brands: 3
Number of Products: 850
Type of Packaging: Food Service, Private Label, Bulk
Brands:
  Bavarian Brand Sausage
  Cajun Brand Sausage
  Ham Sausage
  Polish Sausage

2163 Capital Produce II Inc
8005 Rappahanock Ave
Jessup, MD 20794-9438
443-755-1733
Fax: 443-755-0282 www.capitalseaboard.com
Seafood
Owner: Tom Alascio
tom@capitalseaboard.com
Vice President: Steve Hanson
Estimated Sales: $3.7 Million
Number Employees: 50-99

2164 Capitol Foods
PO Box 751541
Memphis, TN 38175-1541
662-781-9021
Fax: 662-781-0697
Canned vegetables, diced peaches, mixed fruits and edible oils; exporter of canned vegetables; wholesaler/distributor of bakery, dairy and grocery products, soups and bases, produce, syrups, oils, pasta, meats; serving the food servicemarkets
President: Kenneth Porter
CFO: Phillip Duncan
Number Employees: 134
Square Footage: 20000
Type of Packaging: Consumer, Food Service
Brands:
  Capitol Foods
  Orchard Naturals

2165 Capolla Food Inc
25 Lepage Court
North York, ON M3J 3M3
Canada
416-633-0389
Fax: 416-633-7718 www.cappolafood.com
Packaged luncheon meats including beef and pork
CEO: Rick De Vincenzo
Marketing Director: Francefca Ivas
Sales/Marketing: Dion McGuire
Purchasing Agent: John Capolla
Number Employees: 50-99
Parent Co: J.M. Schneider
Type of Packaging: Consumer
Brands:
  Capolla Foods

2166 Capone Foods
14 Bow St. Union Square
Somerville, MA 02143
617-629-2296
Fax: 617-776-0318 albert@caponefoods.com
www.caponefoods.com
Producer of pasta and sauces. Some of their products include fresh pasta, ravioli, tortellini, gnocchi, pizza, entr,es, meatballs, sausage, empanadas and many more items. Their products can be found in several store locationsthroughout Massachusetts, such as Bedford, Boston, Brighton, Brookline, Cambridge, Concord, and other locations.
Owner: Albert Capone
Manager: Jennifer Capone
Estimated Sales: $320,000
Number Employees: 7
Brands:
  Capone Foods

Food Manufacturers / A-Z

2167 Caporale Winery
910 Enterprise Way
Napa, CA 94558-6209
707-253-9230
Fax: 707-253-9232
Wines
President: Mark Caporale
Estimated Sales: $500,000- 1,000,000
Number Employees: 20-49

2168 Cappello's
PO Box 11757
Denver, CO 80211
844-353-2863
talk@cappellos.com cappellos.com
Gluten-free, grain-free cookie dough, pasta and pizza
Co-Founder: Stacey Marcellus
Co-Founder: Benjamin Frohlichstein
Year Founded: 2011

2169 Cappo Drinks
15011 Badillo St.
Baldwin Park, CA 91706
626-813-1006
sales@cappodrinks.com
www.cappodrinks.com
Manufacturer and exporter of smoothie mixes.
CEO: Scott Berberian
Contact: Ara Berberian
aberberian@cappodrinks.com
Brands:
   Cappo

2170 Cappola Foods
25 Lappage Ct
Toronto, ON M3J 3M3
Canada
416-633-0389
Fax: 416-787-1535 sales@cappolafood.com
www.cappolafood.com
Processor and exporter of Italian flavored ices
Owner: Dom Cappola
Type of Packaging: Consumer, Food Service

2171 Cappuccine
375 Klug Cir
Corona, CA 92880-5408
760-864-7355
Fax: 760-864-7360 800-511-3127
www.cappuccine.net
Manufacturer of gourmet instant powder beverage mixes in chai, vanilla, chocolate, fruit, toffe and coconut flavors. Some of these flavors include Caramel Latte, Double Fudge Mocha, Java Chip, Mocha Glacier, Dark Chocolate Chip, LemonVelvet, Tart Culture Smoothie, Indian Chai Latte and many more.
Founder, Owner & CEO: Michael Rubin
Chief Financial Officer: Lawrence Lathrop
Executive VP: Charles Jennings
chuck@cappuccine.net
Estimated Sales: $5,000,000
Number Employees: 10-19
Number of Brands: 1
Number of Products: 18
Square Footage: 3600
Type of Packaging: Consumer, Food Service, Private Label, Bulk
Brands:
   Cappuccine

2172 Capri Bagel & Pizza Corporation
215 Moore St
Brooklyn, NY 11206-3745
718-497-4431
Fax: 718-497-7567
Manufacturer and exporter of pizza, pizza bagels and mini pizzas
President: Adrian Cooper
Plant Manager: Ikey Tuachi
Estimated Sales: $500,000-$1,000,000
Number Employees: 20-49
Square Footage: 31000
Type of Packaging: Consumer, Food Service, Private Label
Brands:
   Big Time
   Boardwalk

2173 Capri Sun
2901 State St
Granite City, IL 62040
parents.caprisun.com
Flavoring, extracts and beverages
CEO: Roland Weening
Estimated Sales: $100+ Million
Parent Co: Kraft Foods

2174 Capriccio
10021 1/2 Canoga Avenue
Chatsworth, CA 91311-0981
818-718-7620
Fax: 818-718-0204
Manufacturer and exporter of food ingredients
CEO: Jack Barsoumian
Estimated Sales: $500,000-$1,000,000
Number Employees: 1-4
Type of Packaging: Food Service

2175 Capricorn Coffees Inc
353 10th St
San Francisco, CA 94103-3804
415-621-8500
Fax: 415-621-9875 800-541-0758
www.capricorncoffees.com
Coffee, Tea, Accessories
Manager: Annie Ngo
Manager: Rachel Akins
rachel.akins@capricorncoffees.com
Estimated Sales: $1-2.5 Million
Number Employees: 10-19
Type of Packaging: Private Label

2176 Caprine Estates
3669 Centerville Road
Bellbrook, OH 45305-0307
937-848-7406
Fax: 937-848-7437
Goat milk cheese, fudge and bottled milk
President: Dennis Dean
VP: Patti Dean
Sales/Marketing VP: Ron Best
Estimated Sales: $250,000
Number Employees: 5
Square Footage: 15000
Type of Packaging: Consumer, Food Service, Private Label, Bulk

2177 Capriole Inc
10329 New Cut Rd
Greenville, IN 47124-9202
812-923-9408
Fax: 812-923-8901
cheese@capriolegoatcheese.com
www.capriolegoatcheese.com
Cheese
President: Judy Schad
judygoat@aol.com
Estimated Sales: Less Than $500,000
Number Employees: 5-9

2178 Caprock Winery Inc
408 E Woodrow Rd
Lubbock, TX 79423-7809
806-863-2704
Fax: 806-863-2712 800-546-9463
www.caprockwinery.com
Wines
President: Don Roark
CEO: Phillip Anderson
phillip@caprockwinery.com
Manager: Jason Butler
Plant Manager: Kim McPherson
Estimated Sales: $1,000,000
Number Employees: 5-9
Type of Packaging: Private Label

2179 Capsule Works
2100 Smithtown Avenue
Ronkonkoma, NY 11779
Fax: 631-472-2817 877-435-2277
Vitamins
President: Kazuo Kawabata
CFO: Jean-Marc Hu%t
Estimated Sales: $10-20 Million
Number Employees: 20-49
Brands:
   Capsule Works

2180 Capt Collier Seafood
14733 Tom Johnson Ave
Coden, AL 36523-3116
251-824-4925
Fax: 251-824-2374
Seafood
Owner: Phil Brannon
brannonmerle@aol.com
Estimated Sales: $3-5 Million
Number Employees: 5-9

2181 Capt Joe & Sons Inc
95 E Main St
Gloucester, MA 01930-3860
978-283-1454
Fax: 978-283-1466 captijoe06@yahoo.com
Seafood
President: Benjamin Ciaramitaro
Treasurer/Clerk: Charles Ciaramitaro
Vice President: Frank Ciaramitaro
Manager: Joe Ciaramitaro
Estimated Sales: Less Than $500,000
Number Employees: 1-4

2182 Captain Alex Seafoods
8874 N Milwaukee Ave
Niles, IL 60714-1752
847-803-8833
Fax: 847-803-9854 www.fishandseafoodniles.com
Seafood
President/Secretary: Alex Malidis
Vice President: Matthew Mallidis
Office Manager: Ilir Veliu
Estimated Sales: $530,000
Number Employees: 5-9

2183 Captain Bob's Jet Fuel
2216 Ladue Ln
Fort Wayne, IN 46804-2794
260-436-3895
877-486-6468
Hot sauces including habanero-garlic, smoked serrano jalapeno and chile de arbol; also, hot barbecue sauces
President: Robert Kitto
Contact: Bob Kitto
bkitto@captainbobs.net
Estimated Sales: $1-2,500,000
Number Employees: 1-4
Brands:
   Captain Bob's Jet Fuel

2184 Captain Cook Coffee Company
79-7415 Mamalahoa Hwy.
Kealakekua, HI 96750
650-766-9149
Fax: 808-322-2087 info@captaincookkona.com
captaincookkona.stores.yahoo.net
Manufacturer of Kona coffee.
Owner: Steven McLaughlin
Estimated Sales: $5-10,000,000
Number Employees: 10-19
Brands:
   Captain Cook Coffee

2185 Captain Foods, Inc.
2732 Hibiscus Dr
Edgewater, FL 32141-5404
Fax: 386-428-9988 800-749-5047
www.captainfoods.com
BBQ sauces and seasonings; grilling sauces.
Sice President of Sales: Chris Feindt
Type of Packaging: Private Label

2186 Captain Ken's Foods Inc
344 Robert St S
St Paul, MN 55107-2200
651-298-0071
Fax: 651-298-0849 800-510-3811
jtraxler@captainkens.com www.captainkens.com
Frozen foods including chili, oven baked beans and au gratin potatoes, taco meat, meatloaf, macaroni and beef
President: John Traxler
jtraxler@captainkens.com
Chairman, Owner: Mike Traxler
Controller: Linda Traxler
VP Business Development/Sales: Tom Traxler
Operations Manager: Kevin Kosel
Plant Manager: Richard Gavin
Estimated Sales: $1.9 Million
Number Employees: 10-19
Square Footage: 124000
Type of Packaging: Consumer, Food Service
Brands:
   Captain Ken's

2187 Captain Lawrence Brewing Co
444 Saw Mill River Rd # 100
Elmsford, NY 10523-1031
914-741-2337
www.captainlawrencebrewing.com

Food Manufacturers / A-Z

Craft beer.
Owner/Brewer: Scott Vaccaro
scott@captainlawrencebrewing.com
CFO: Vince Vaccaro
Quality Control Manager: Jim Elliot
Sales Manager: Keith Feckete
Number Employees: 1-4
Type of Packaging: Consumer

2188 Captain Little Seafood
413 Central Port Mouton Td.
Queens County, NS B0T1T0
Canada
902-947-2087
Fax: 902-947-2088 www.scotiafish.com
Lobster, Atlantic sea cucumber, red sea cucumber, sea urchin, snow crab, Jonah crab, salmon caviar, halibut, herring, capelin fish, whelk, cold water shrimp, tuna, scallops
Procurement: Steven Shi
Square Footage: 72500

2189 Captain's Choice
29629 11th Pl S
Federal Way, WA 98003-3727
253-941-1184
Fax: 253-946-2852
info@captainschoicesalmon.com
www.captainschoicesalmon.com
Honey brine smoked salmon products and gift packages
President: Donald Buchanan
d.buchanan@captains-choice.com
Treasurer/Secretary: Rosalie Buchanan
Estimated Sales: Less Than $500,000
Number Employees: 1-4
Type of Packaging: Consumer, Food Service, Private Label
Brands:
    Captain's Choice Honey Brine Smoked Salmon
    Smoked Spices

2190 Captiva Limited Inc
45 Us Highway 206 Ste 104
Augusta, NJ 7822
973-579-7883
Fax: 973-579-2509
Processor and exporter of bottled water including stilled, carbonated and flavored; also, sports/health drinks
Owner: Don Destefano
VP: Mary Ann Bell
Estimated Sales: $3-5 Million
Number Employees: 1-4
Square Footage: 6000
Type of Packaging: Consumer, Food Service, Private Label, Bulk
Brands:
    Nature's Mist
    Pro-Life

2191 Caputo Cheese
1931 N 15th Ave
Melrose Park, IL 60160-1402
708-450-0074
Fax: 708-450-1670 sales@caputocheese.com
www.caputocheese.com
Dairy and cheese products, including fresh and greated cheeses.
President: Natale Caputo
Sales Manager: Renzo Berardi
General Manager: Brett Piccioni
Type of Packaging: Consumer, Food Service, Private Label, Bulk

2192 Caracolillo Coffee Mills
4419 N Hesperides St
Tampa, FL 33614-7618
813-876-0302
Fax: 813-875-6407 800-682-0023
info@ccmcoffee.com www.ccmcoffee.com
Coffee
President: Julian Faedo
info@ccmcoffee.com
Estimated Sales: $3-5 Million
Number Employees: 5-9
Type of Packaging: Consumer, Food Service, Private Label
Brands:
    Cafe Quisqueva
    Cafe Caracolillo Decafe
    Cafe Caracolillo Expresso
    Cafe Caracolillo Gourmet
    Cafe Regil
    Cafe Rico Rico
    Cafe Riquisimo

2193 Carando Gourmet Frozen Foods
175 Main St
Agawam, MA 01001-1804
413-737-0183
Fax: 413-789-1653 888-227-2636
www.carandogourmet.com
Frozen food and entrees including roast beef, corned beef, pastrami, sauces, Italian stuffed pastas, gourmet meatballs, cabbage and sweet peppers
President/CEO/Chairman: Peter Carando Jr
CFO: Len Lumber
Director Sales: Brian Kelly
Plant Manager: Miguel Velez
Estimated Sales: $3.9 Million
Number Employees: 100-249
Parent Co: Carando Gourmet
Type of Packaging: Consumer, Food Service, Private Label, Bulk
Brands:
    Carando Gourmet

2194 Caraquet Ice Company
20 Rue Du Quai
Caraquet, NB E1W 1B6
Canada
506-727-7211
Fax: 506-727-6769
Fresh and frozen seafood
President: Richard Albert
Type of Packaging: Bulk
Brands:
    Caraquet

2195 Caravan Company
237 Chandler St
Worcester, MA 01609
508-752-3777
Fax: 508-753-4717
Coffee
President/Treasurer: George Drapos
Vice President: Arthur Drapos
Clerk: Alex Drapos
Estimated Sales: $2.1 Million
Number Employees: 17

2196 CarbRite Diet
3 Terminal Rd
New Brunswick, NJ 08901
732-545-3130
Fax: 732-509-0458 800-872-0101
info@carbritediet.com www.carbritediet.com
Low-carb snack bars and brownies
President: Danny Keller
VP: Robert Gluckin
Year Founded: 2000
Parent Co: Universal Nutrition

2197 Carbon's Golden Malted
4101 William Richardson Dr
South Bend, IN 46628
574-247-2270
Fax: 574-247-2280 800-253-0590
retail@goldenmalted.com www.goldenmalted.com
Manufacturer and market flour mix for pancakes and waffles
President: Rick Mc Keel
Chief Financial Officer: Brian Coyne
VP Sales and Marketing: Robert A. Coquillard
National and International Sales Manager: Tom McVey
Vice President of Operations: Mike McKeel
Number Employees: 1-4

2198 Carborator Rental Svc
6500 Eastwick Ave
PO Box 33327
Philadelphia, PA 19142-3399
215-726-8000
Fax: 215-726-6367 800-220-3556
info@carbonatorrental.com
www.carbonatorrental.com
Soda water syrups and bar mixes; wholesaler/distributor of beverage dispensing equipment
President: Andy Pincus
andy@carbonatorrental.com
Chairman: Herbert Pincus
Corporate Secretary: Susan Pincus
Vice President: Leatrice Pincus
Manager: Thomas Moreno
Production: George Rossi
Estimated Sales: $3.7 Million
Number Employees: 20-49
Square Footage: 80000

2199 Cardi Foods
1003 Sethcreek Drive
Fuquay Varina, NC 27526-5156
919-557-3866
schwcscs@cs.com
Yeast extracts, kosher flavors
Vice President: Charles Schweizer
Estimated Sales: $150,000
Number Employees: 1
Number of Brands: 5
Number of Products: 10
Type of Packaging: Consumer, Food Service
Brands:
    Cardi C

2200 Cardinal Meat Specialists
155 Hedgedale Road
Brampton, ON L6T 5P3
Canada
905-459-4436
Fax: 905-459-8099 800-363-1439
www.cardinalmeats.com
Hamburger patties and steaks
President: Brent Cator
Estimated Sales: $5-10 Million
Number Employees: 35
Type of Packaging: Food Service
Brands:
    Cardinal Kettle
    Roadhouse

2201 Cardinale Winery
7600 St Helena Hwy
Oakville, CA 94562
707-948-2643
Fax: 707-944-2824 800-588-0279
info@cardinale.com www.cardinale.com
Cabernet Sauvignon
Winemaker: Christopher Carpenter
ccarpenter@cardinale.com
Vineyard Manager: Pete Richmond
Estimated Sales: $20-50 Million
Number Employees: 50-99

2202 Care Foods International
4715 33rd St
Long Island, NY 11101-2407
718-392-3355
Fax: 718-392-2072
Coconut water and packaged dried fruit chips.
Vice President: Brian Lee
Type of Packaging: Private Label
Brands:
    CoCo Well

2203 Caremoli USA
23959 580th Ave
Ames, IA 50010-9390
515-233-1255
Fax: 515-233-2933 www.caremoligroup.com
Ingredients of naturally processed grains, flours and fibers
President: Andrea Caremoli
a.caremoli@caremoli-usa.com
Quality Manager: Bethany Christensen
VP Sales/Marketing: Devin Miller
Sales Manager, North & South America: Carolina Calvert
Estimated Sales: $24 Million
Number Employees: 20-49

2204 (HQ)Cargill Inc.
P.O. Box 9300
Minneapolis, MN 55440-9300
800-227-4455
www.cargill.com
Stores, trades, processes and distributes grains, oilseeds, vegetable oils and meals; raises livestock and produces animal feed; produces food ingredients such as starches, glucose syrups, oils and fats.
Chairman/CEO: David MacLennan
CFO: David Dines
Chief Compliance Officer/General Counsel: Anna Richo
Cheif Human Resources Officer: LeighAnne Baker
Business Operations & Supply Chain: Ruth Kimmelshue
Year Founded: 1865
Estimated Sales: $114.6 Billion
Number Employees: 166,000

Food Manufacturers / A-Z

2205 Cargill Kitchen Solutions Inc.
15407 McGinty Rd. W.
Wayzata, MN 55391
833-535-5205
CustomerService_Protein@Cargill.com
www.sunnyfresh.com
Eggs and breakfast products for foodservice operatos, convenience stores, chain restaurants, healthcare foodservice facilities, and schools.
Parent Co: Cargill Inc.
Type of Packaging: Bulk
Brands:
  Sunny Fresh™

2206 Cargill Protein
825 E Douglas
Wichita, KS 67202
consumer_affairs@cargill.com
www.cargill.com/meat-poultry/protein-north-america
Beef, turkey, and swine products.
Chief Risk Officer, Protein & Salt: Brian Sikes
Number Employees: 28,000
Parent Co: Cargill Inc.
Type of Packaging: Food Service, Bulk

2207 Caribbean Coffee Co
495 Pine Ave # A
Goleta, CA 93117-3709
805-692-2200
Fax: 805-962-5074 800-932-5282
info@caribbeancoffee.com
www.caribbeancoffee.com
Over 100 varieties of specialty coffees and teas.
President: John Goerke
john@caribbeancoffee.com
Marketing Manager: Putnam Fairbanks
Estimated Sales: $20-50 Million
Number Employees: 10-19
Type of Packaging: Private Label

2208 Caribbean Cookie Company
515 Central Drive
Suite 103
Virginia Beach, VA 23454-5274
757-631-6767
Fax: 757-631-1725 800-326-5200
Gourmet cookies
President: Charles Phelps
Marketing Director: Leo Palomo
Estimated Sales: $1-2,500,000
Number Employees: 10-19

2209 Caribbean Food DelightsInc
117 Route 303 # B
Suite B
Tappan, NY 10983-2136
845-398-3000
Fax: 845-398-2316
info@caribbeanfooddelights.com
www.caribbeanfooddelights.com
Manufacturer and exporter of Jamaican baked goods including breads, fruit cakes and buns; also, beef, chicken and vegetable patties, jerk chicken, sausage, curried goat, rice, peas, etc
President/CEO: Vincent HoSang
CEO: Vincent Hosang
Estimated Sales: $10-20 Million
Number Employees: 50-99
Square Footage: 120000
Parent Co: Royal Caribbean Bakery
Type of Packaging: Consumer, Food Service, Private Label, Bulk

2210 Caribbean Products
3624 Falls Rd Ste 2
Baltimore, MD 21211
410-235-7700
Fax: 410-235-1513
Manufacturer and also processor and packager of beef and pork products.
President: Brian Hartman
bhartman@caribbeanproductsltd.com
Controller: Alan Wilner
Vice President: Mark Sheubrooks
Sales & Marketing Executive: Brad Ambill
Sales Executive: Jim Vogtman
Plant Manager: Scott Sheubrooks
Estimated Sales: $7.1 Million
Number Employees: 46
Type of Packaging: Consumer, Food Service

2211 Caribou Coffee Co Inc
Minneapolis, MN 55429
888-227-4268
www.cariboucoffee.com
Coffee
President & CEO: John Butcher
CFO: Mike Jensen
Brand Marketing Leader: Michelle Chester
Year Founded: 1992
Estimated Sales: $250,904,568
Number Employees: 5,000-9,999
Number of Brands: 1
Parent Co: JAB Holding Company

2212 Carl Buddig & Co.
950 W. 175th St.
Homewood, IL 60430
708-798-0900
Fax: 708-798-1284 888-633-5684
www.buddig.com
Luncheon meats including chipped beef, ham, turkey, chicken, pastrami and turkey ham; also, specialty sausage and meat snacks.
President: John Buddig
CEO: Robert Buddig
rbuddig@buddig.com
CFO: Peter Maciekewski
Executive VP: Thomas Buddig
Year Founded: 1886
Estimated Sales: $162 Million
Number Employees: 500-999
Number of Brands: 5
Square Footage: 15000
Type of Packaging: Consumer, Food Service, Private Label, Bulk
Brands:
  Buddig Original
  Deli Cuts
  Fix Quix
  Old Wisconsin
  Carl Buddig Meats

2213 Carl Rittberger Sr Inc
1900 Lutz Ln
Zanesville, OH 43701-9260
740-452-2767
Fax: 740-452-6001 info@rittbergermeats.com
www.rittbergers.com
Beef and pork
President: Mark Mccabe
markmccabe@rittbergers.com
VP: George Rittberger
VP Sales: Mark McCabe
Estimated Sales: $4.5 Million
Number Employees: 10-19
Square Footage: 400000
Type of Packaging: Consumer, Bulk

2214 Carl Venezia Fresh Meats
1007 Germantown Pike
Plymouth Meeting, PA 19462-2449
610-239-6750
Fax: 610-239-6751 www.carlveneziameats.com
Processor and packer of meat
President: Carl Venezia
carlveneziameats@gmail.com
Sales Manager: Don Venezia
Estimated Sales: $500,000
Number Employees: 1-4

2215 Carla's Pasta
50 Talbot Ln
South Windsor, CT 06074
860-436-4042
www.carlaspasta.com
Pasta sauces and frozen pastas, including ravioli and lasagna.
Founder & President: Carla Squatrito
sergio@carlaspasta.com
VP, Business Development: Sandro Squatrito
VP, Operations: Sergio Squatrito
Year Founded: 1978
Estimated Sales: $21.20 Million
Number Employees: 50-99
Square Footage: 100000
Type of Packaging: Food Service, Private Label, Bulk

2216 Carlisle Cereal Company
PO Box 2775
Bismarck, ND 58502
701-222-3531
Fax: 701-222-3531 800-809-6018
Cereal

President: Charles Fleming
Estimated Sales: $1 Million
Number Employees: 5-9
Type of Packaging: Private Label
Brands:
  Hometown Stars

2217 Carlson Vineyards Winery
461 35 Rd
Palisade, CO 81526-9518
970-464-5554
Fax: 970-464-5542 888-464-5554
www.carlsonvineyards.com
Wines
Owner: Garrett Portra
info@carlsonvineyards.com
Estimated Sales: $1-2.5 Million
Number Employees: 5-9

2218 Carlton Farms
P.O.Box 580
Carlton, OR 97111
503-852-7166
Fax: 503-852-6263 800-932-0946
rita@carltonfarms.com www.carltonfarms.com
Meats
President/CEO: Rita Duyn
Estimated Sales: $13 Million
Number Employees: 75

2219 Carmadhy's Foods
282 Marsland Drive
Waterloo, ON N2J 3Z1
Canada
519-746-0551
Fax: 519-746-0280
Flavored popcorn including caramel, butter, cheese, white cheddar, pizza, barbecue, ranch, salt and vinegar, sour cream and onion, dill pickle, jalapeno, custom packaging and popcorn seasoning
Proprietor: Dave Charlton
Number Employees: 5-9
Square Footage: 18000
Type of Packaging: Consumer, Private Label, Bulk
Brands:
  Country Style
  Olde Fashioned

2220 Carmela's Gourmet
415 English Ave
Monterey, CA 93940-3810
831-373-6291
Fax: 831-375-5313
Salad dressings
Owner: Carmela Cantisani
Co-Owner: Carmela Cantisani
Estimated Sales: Under $500,000
Number Employees: 1-4
Type of Packaging: Private Label
Brands:
  Carmela's

2221 Carmelita Provisions Company
2901 W Floral Dr
Monterey Park, CA 91754-3626
323-262-6751
Fax: 323-262-3503
Pigs' feet including crackling and pickled; also, chorizo
Owner: Mario Lopez
Estimated Sales: $.5-1 million
Number Employees: 20-49
Type of Packaging: Consumer, Food Service

2222 Carmenet Winery
1680 Moon Mountain Rd
Sonoma, CA 95476-3087
707-996-3526
Fax: 707-996-5302
Wines
President: Tom Selfridge
CFO: Paul Ogarzelec
Public Relations: Lisa Yaple
General Manager: Paula Conwell
Estimated Sales: $5-10 Million
Number Employees: 10-19
Parent Co: Chalone Wine Group

Food Manufacturers / A-Z

2223 (HQ)Carmi Flavor & Fragrance Company
6030 Scott Way
Commerce, CA 90040-3516
323-888-9240
Fax: 323-888-9339 800-421-9647
sales@carmiflavors.com www.carmiflavors.com
High quality natural and artificial flavors in liquid or powder form; supplier of packaging products.
President: Eliot Carmi
CEO: Eliot Carmi
Chief Operating Officer: Dan Carmi
Estimated Sales: $12 Million
Number Employees: 40
Number of Brands: 1
Number of Products: 500
Square Footage: 60000
Type of Packaging: Private Label, Bulk
Other Locations:
 Carmi Flavor & Fragrance
 Port Coquitlam, Canada
 Midwest Office & Manufacturing
 Waverly IA
 Southern Office & Warehouse
 Lawrenceville GA
Brands:
 Carmi Flavors
 Flavor Depot

2224 Carmine's Bakery
2100 Country Club Road
Sanford, FL 32771-4051
407-328-4141
Fax: 407-324-1209 marlafrede@aol.com
Baked goods
Principal: John Schlater
Number Employees: 250 to 500

2225 Carneros Creek Winery
PO Box 8090
Napa, CA 94559
707-253-9464
Fax: 707-253-9465 www.mahoneyvineyards.com
Wines
President: Francis Mahoney
Winemaker: Ken Foster
Vice President: Scot Rich
Sales Director: Hadden Guridie
Plant Manager: Greg Opitz
Estimated Sales: $5-10 Million
Number Employees: 10-19
Type of Packaging: Bulk
Brands:
 Carneros
 Carneros Creek
 Cote De Carneros
 Fleur De Carneros

2226 Carnival Brands Mfg
5900 S Front St
New Orleans, LA 70115-2152
504-897-5454
Fax: 504-734-5886 800-925-2774
gumboking@aol.com www.carnivalbrands.com
French bisques, alligator sauce piquante, dry seasoning, boneless stuffed chicken, sauce mix and seafood entrees including gumbo, crab and shrimp cakes, shrimp Creole and crawfish etouffee.
President: Raymond Rathle Jr
Vice President: Stephen Scott
Marketing: E Alexander Stafford
Public Relations: Simone Rathle
Estimated Sales: $1-2.5 Million
Number Employees: 5-9
Square Footage: 28000
Type of Packaging: Consumer, Food Service
Brands:
 Baby Cakes
 Carnival Cajun Classics
 Chef Creole
 Zipp

2227 Caro Foods
2324 Bayou Blue Rd
Houma, LA 70364
985-872-1483
Fax: 985-876-0825 800-395-2276
Fresh meat and produce, canned and dry goods.
Parent Co: Performance Food Group Company
Brands:
 Heritage Ovens

2228 Carob Tree
1008 N Santa Anita Ave
Arcadia, CA 91006
626-445-0215
Fax: 626-445-0215
Natural groceries and vitamins
Owner: Hyun Chung
Estimated Sales: $160,000
Number Employees: 1-4
Type of Packaging: Consumer, Bulk

2229 Carol Hall's Hot PepperJelly
330 North Main Street
Fort Bragg, CA 95437
707-961-1899
Fax: 707-961-0879 866-737-7379
hall@mcn.org www.hotpepperjelly.com
Jams and condiments
President: Carol Hall
CFO: Albert Hall
Marketing Director: John Temples
Contact: William Hall
edward.getty@na.cokecce.com
Production Manager: Bill Hall
Estimated Sales: $1-2.5 Million
Number Employees: 5-9
Type of Packaging: Private Label

2230 Carol Lee Donuts
104 S 5th St
Salina, KS 67401-2804
785-827-2402
www.carolleedonutssalina.com
Blended mixes for bakery products including yeast raised and cake doughnuts, danish, breads and cookies
Owner: Hong Kim
carolleedonutssalina@gmail.com
VP: Agnes Scott
Estimated Sales: Less Than $500,000
Number Employees: 1-4
Square Footage: 27990
Type of Packaging: Consumer
Brands:
 Carol Lee

2231 Carol's Country Cuisine
2546 Warm Springs Road
Glen Ellen, CA 95442-8712
707-996-1124
Fax: 707-996-1124 carolco@vom.com
Marinades, dressings, sauces
Partner & Production Manager: Carol Frankenfield
carolco@vom.com
Sales Director: Susan Wise
Estimated Sales: $5-10 Million
Number Employees: 5-9
Type of Packaging: Private Label

2232 Carole's Cheesecake Company
1275 Castlefield Ave
Toronto, ON M6B 1G3
Canada
416-256-0000
Fax: 416-256-0001 www.carolescheesecake.com
cheesecakes including praline, lemon, blueberry, raspberry and strawberry; also, pies, low-fat salad dressings, pasta sauces and toppings for cakes and ice cream.
President: Edison Carbajal
CEO: Carole Ogus
Executive VP: Michael Ogus
Estimated Sales: $1-5 Million
Number Employees: 30
Number of Brands: 2
Number of Products: 160
Square Footage: 60000
Type of Packaging: Consumer, Food Service, Private Label
Brands:
 Carole's
 Carole's Tops
 Positively Blueberry
 Positively Pralines
 Positively Strawberry

2233 Carolina Atlantic Seafood Enterprises
PO Box 158
Beaufort, NC 28516-0158
252-504-2663
Fax: 252-726-7097
Frozen seafood
President: Doug Brady
CEO: Walter C Brady
Estimated Sales: $5-10,000,000
Number Employees: 10-19
Type of Packaging: Private Label
Brands:
 Carolina Atlantic Seafood

2234 (HQ)Carolina Beverage Corp
1413 Jake Alexander Blvd S
Salisbury, NC 28146-8359
704-633-4550
Fax: 704-633-7491 custserv@cheerwine.com
www.cheerwine.com
Syrups and beverage concentrates; exporter of soft drinks and concentrates; wholesaler/distributor of soft drinks and water
President: Clift Ritchie
critchie@carolinabottlingcompanyinc.com
CFO: Tommy Page
CIO: Bill Barten
VP Operations: David Swaim
Estimated Sales: $10-20 Million
Number Employees: 20-49
Square Footage: 75000
Parent Co: Cheerwine & Diet Cheerwine
Type of Packaging: Consumer
Other Locations:
 Carolina Beverage Corp.
 Hickory NC
 Carolina Beverage Corp.
 Greenville SC
Brands:
 Cheerwine
 Cheerwine Soft Drink
 Diet Cheerwine
 Savage Energy

2235 Carolina Blueberry Co-Op Assn
11421 US Highway 701 N
P.O. Box 368
Garland, NC 28441-9642
910-588-4220
Fax: 910-588-4297 www.carolinablueberry.com
Fresh and frozen blueberries
General Manager: Rod Bangert
rbangert@carolinablueberry.com
Process Facility Manager: Sonny Parker
Estimated Sales: Less Than $500,000
Number Employees: 1-4
Type of Packaging: Consumer, Food Service, Bulk
Brands:
 Bonnie Blue

2236 Carolina Brewery
460 W Franklin St
Chapel Hill, NC 27516-2313
919-942-1800
Fax: 919-942-1809 www.carolinabrewery.com
Ale, stout and lager
Owner: Robert Poitras
rcpoitras@aol.com
Co-Owner: Chris Rice
Estimated Sales: $2.5-5 Million
Number Employees: 50-99
Square Footage: 32000
Type of Packaging: Consumer, Food Service, Bulk
Brands:
 Copperline Amber
 Franklin Street
 Old North State

2237 Carolina Classics Catfish Inc
7178 NC 11 S
P.O. Box 10
Ayden, NC 28513-8404
252-746-2818
Fax: 252-746-3947 www.cccatfish.com
Fresh and frozen catfish
President: Robert Mayo
rmayo@cccatfish.com
Accounting Manager: Mike Walker
Sales Manager: Doug Doering
Sales Manager: Jeff Betcher
VP Operations: Mike McCready
Controller: Mark Lomis
Estimated Sales: $20-50 Million
Number Employees: 100-249
Type of Packaging: Consumer, Food Service
Brands:
 Carolina Classics

Food Manufacturers / A-Z

2238 Carolina Cookie Co
1010 Arnold St
Greensboro, NC 27405-7102
336-294-2100
Fax: 336-294-9537   800-447-5797
gary@carolinacookie.com
www.carolinacookie.com
Cookies
Owner: Chris Belton
chris@carolinacookie.com
Estimated Sales: $3,000,000
Number Employees: 100-249
Square Footage: 24000

2239 Carolina Cracker
P.O.Box 374
Garner, NC 27529-0374
919-779-9338
Fax: 919-779-6899   www.carolinacracker.net
Nut crackers for soft shell nuts, shelled pecans in bulk
President: Dot Woodruff
CEO: Harold Woodruff
Estimated Sales: $1-2.5 Million
Number Employees: 10-19
Number of Brands: 3
Square Footage: 4
Type of Packaging: Bulk
Brands:
    The Carolina Cracker

2240 Carolina Fine Snacks
209 Citation Ct
Greensboro, NC 27409-9026
336-605-0773
Fax: 336-605-0721
Nutrional snacks
Owner: Echo Frye
echo@carolinafinesnacks.com
Estimated Sales: $2.5-5,000,000
Number Employees: 20-49

2241 Carolina Food Company
3642 South 106th East Place
Tulsa, OK 74146
918-519-9338
toastedyum@hotmail.com
www.toastedwinespreads.com
Manufacturer of wine and fruit flavored spread.
Founder: Corey Carolina
corey.carolina@hotmail.com

2242 Carolina Foods Inc
1807 S Tryon St
Charlotte, NC 28203
704-333-9812
800-234-0441
www.carolinafoodsinc.com
Baked goods including sweet rolls, fresh and frozen fried pies, yeast raised doughnuts and cakes, fruit turnovers and pie dough
President: Paul Scarborough
proach@carolinafoods.com
VP of Operations: Kent Byrom
Estimated Sales: $20-50 Million
Number Employees: 250-499
Number of Brands: 3
Square Footage: 110000
Type of Packaging: Consumer, Food Service, Private Label
Brands:
    Duchess
    O'Boy
    Sunbeam

2243 Carolina Ingredients Inc
1595 Cedar Lane Dr
Rock Hill, SC 29730
803-323-6550
Fax: 803-323-6535   www.carolinaingredients.com
Ingredients
President: Doug Meyer-Cuno
Manager of Sales: Kyle Jones
Contact: Mike Cantore
mcantore@carolinaingredients.com
Production Manager: Richard Dawes
Purchasing Director: Glenn Shishido
Number Employees: 5-9

2244 Carolina Innovative Food Ingredients, Inc.
4626 Coleman Dr
Nashville, NC 27856
252-462-1551
info@cifi1.com
cifingredients.com
Domestic manufacturer of sweet potato juice concentrates and dehydrated sweet potato ingredients.
President: Jim Nagey
CEO: John Kimber

2245 Carolina Packers Inc
2999 S Brightleaf Blvd
Smithfield, NC 27577
800-682-7675
info@carolinapackers.com
www.carolinapackers.com
Hot dogs, bologna, smoked sausage, ham and chili
President: Kent Denning
kdenning@carolinapackers.com
Year Founded: 1940
Estimated Sales: $20-50 Million
Number Employees: 100-249
Number of Brands: 1
Type of Packaging: Consumer, Bulk
Brands:
    Bright Leaf

2246 Carolina Pride Foods
1 Packer Ave.
Greenwood, SC 29646
864-229-5611
Fax: 864-229-0541   www.carolinapride.com
Fresh pork and bacon, smoked meats and processed luncheon meats including deli loaves and bologna; exporter of skinned jowls, pork kidneys, liver and stomachs, flat belly skins, etc.
President: Michael Cox
CFO: Mark Litts
Year Founded: 1920
Estimated Sales: $185 Million
Number Employees: 500-999
Number of Brands: 1
Square Footage: 250000
Type of Packaging: Consumer, Food Service, Private Label, Bulk
Brands:
    Carolina Pride

2247 Carolina Pride Products
24488 Nc Highway 561
Enfield, NC 27823
252-445-3154
Fax: 252-445-1033
Sweet potatoes
President: Jake Taylor
Estimated Sales: $1-2.5 Million
Number Employees: 1-4
Brands:
    Carolina Pride

2248 Carolina Products
5519 W. Idlewild Ave.
Tampa, FL 33634
813-313-1800
Fax: 813-881-1926   info@cott.com
www.cliffstar.com
Bottled apple juice
President, CEO: Steven Kitching
Chief Executive Officer: Jerry Fowden
Chief Financial Officer: Jay Wells
Senior Vice President: Gregory Leiter
Quality Control: Angela Lewis
VP Human Resources: Michael Creamer
VP General Counsel: Marni Morgan Poe
Purchasing: Dennis Jones
Estimated Sales: $10-20 Million
Number Employees: 20-49
Square Footage: 58000
Parent Co: Cliffstar
Type of Packaging: Consumer, Private Label
Brands:
    Carolina Gold

2249 Carolina Summit Mountain Spring Water
6557 Garden Road
Unit 9
Riviera Beach, FL 33404-6307
561-841-8841
Fax: 828-743-5483   water123@bellsouth.net
bottledwater123.com
Bottled water
President: Tom Mitchell
Estimated Sales: $1-2.5 Million
Number Employees: 10-19
Parent Co: Mountain Valley Spring Company

2250 Carolina Treet
Po Box 1017
Wilmington, NC 28402
910-762-1950
Fax: 910-762-1438   800-616-6344
info@carolinatreet.com   www.carolinatreet.com
Processor and importer of barbecue sauce, condiments, syrups, brewed tea, bar mixes and beverage concentrates
President: Joe King
Vice President: Lenwood King
General Manager: Allen Finberg
Estimated Sales: $1.4 Million
Number Employees: 13
Number of Brands: 5
Number of Products: 20
Square Footage: 80000
Type of Packaging: Consumer, Food Service, Private Label, Bulk
Brands:
    Aunt Bertie's
    Carolina Treet

2251 Carolyn's Gourmet
40 Beharrell St Ste 2
Concord, MA 01742
978-369-2940
Fax: 978-371-0639   800-656-2940
Pecans, walnuts, peanuts, English toffee, chocolate bars
President: Hans van Putten
Executive VP: Tracey van Putten
Estimated Sales: $5-10 Million
Number Employees: 5-9
Parent Co: 40ParkLake, LLC
Type of Packaging: Consumer, Private Label, Bulk
Brands:
    Tulip

2252 Carousel Cakes
5 Seeger Dr
Suite 3
Nanuet, NY 10954-2332
845-627-2323
Fax: 845-627-0258   800-659-2253
info@carouselcakes.com   www.carouselcakes.com
Fresh and frozen cakes, mousse, cheesecakes and pies, kosher pdairy and non-dairy products
Owner: David Finkelstein
david@carouselcakes.com
Estimated Sales: $500,000-$1 Million
Number Employees: 10-19
Type of Packaging: Consumer, Food Service
Brands:
    Carousel Cakes

2253 Carousel Candies
2248 Gary Ln
Geneva, IL 60134-2519
630-232-2500
Fax: 708-656-0010   888-656-1552
info@silvestrisweets.com
Candy including caramel, caramel apples, caramel sauce, chocolates, chocolate covered strawberries, gift boxes, gift baskets, assortments, bulk, and special occasion gift bags for holidays and special events.
President: Andy Silvestri
andy@carouselcandy.com
Vice President: Andy Silvestri
Estimated Sales: $2.5-5 Million
Number Employees: 10-19
Type of Packaging: Food Service, Bulk
Brands:
    Carousel

2254 Carr Cheese Factory/GileCheese Company
116 North Main Street
Cuba City, WI 53807
608-744-8455
Fax: 608-744-3457   www.gilecheese.com
Cheese and cheese products
Owner: John Gile
Owner: Diane Gile
Contact: Tim Gile
tim@gilecheese.com
Estimated Sales: $2.5-5 Million
Number Employees: 1-4

Food Manufacturers / A-Z

2255 Carr Valley Cheese
1675 Lincoln Ave
Fennimore, WI 53809-2101
608-822-6416
Fax: 608-822-3505 800-462-7258
www.carrvalleycheese.com
Cheese
National Sales Manager: Beth Wyttenbach
Manager: Sid Cook
sid@carrvalleycheese.com
Manager: Linda Parrish
Estimated Sales: $2.5-5 Million
Number Employees: 10-19
Type of Packaging: Consumer, Private Label, Bulk
Brands:
    Bahl Baby

2256 Carr Valley Cheese Company
S3797 County G
La Valle, WI 53941
608-986-2781
Fax: 608-986-2906 800-462-7258
www.carrvalleycheese.com
Monterey jack, cheddar and colby cheese, butter, jams, jellies and sausage.
President: Sid Cook
National Sales Manager: Beth Wyttenbach
Estimated Sales: $15 Million
Number Employees: 25
Number of Brands: 1
Brands:
    Carr Valley

2257 Carrabassett Coffee Roasters
2 Mountain View Rd
North Main St.
Kingfield, ME 4947
207-265-2326
Fax: 207-265-3527 888-292-2326
carrcoff@tdstelme.net
www.carrabassettcoffee.com
Roaster and wholesaler of coffee
Owner: Tom Hildreth
carrcoff@tds.com
CEO: Steve Skaling
Estimated Sales: Less Than $500,000
Number Employees: 5-9
Number of Brands: 35
Number of Products: 1
Square Footage: 7200
Type of Packaging: Bulk
Brands:
    35

2258 Carriage House Foods
1131 Dayton Ave
Ames, IA 50010
515-232-2273
Fax: 515-232-3003
Frozen meat products
President: Jerry Grauf
Plant Manager: Jim Ringelstetter
Estimated Sales: $7.5 Million
Number Employees: 35
Type of Packaging: Consumer, Food Service, Private Label
Brands:
    Carriage House

2259 Carrie's Chocolates
9216-63 Avenue
Edmonton, AB T6E 0G3
Canada
780-435-7900
877-778-2462
Processor and exporter of handmade novelty and gift chocolates, promotional bars, and wedding candy
Owner: Carrie MacKenzie
Number Employees: 2
Square Footage: 1800
Type of Packaging: Consumer, Food Service, Private Label, Bulk

2260 Carriere Foods Inc
540 Chemin Des Patriotes
Saint-Denis-Sur-Richelie, QC J0H 1K0
Canada
450-787-3411
Fax: 450-787-3537 marketing@carrierefoods.com
www.bonduelle.ca
Manufacturer and exporter of frozen and canned vegetables and fruits including peas, waxed beans, chick peas, green beans, asparagus and corn, dried beans, blueberries, cranberries, rasberries, rhubarb, strawberries, soups and sauces; importer of asparagus, carrots and spinach
President: Marcel Ostiguy
Number Employees: 250-499
Type of Packaging: Consumer, Private Label
Brands:
    Arctica Gardens
    Avon
    Carriere
    Festino
    Graves
    Paula
    Sunny Farm
    Stokely

2261 Carrington Foods Co Inc
200 Jacintoport Blvd
PO Box 509
Saraland, AL 36571-3397
251-675-9700
Fax: 251-679-8721 www.carringtonfoods.com
Frozen seafood including stuffed flounder, crab and shrimp
President: David Carrington Sr
Secretary: Sally Carrington
IT: Joshua Boozer
joshua@carringtonfoods.com
Estimated Sales: $10-20 Million
Number Employees: 100-249
Type of Packaging: Consumer, Food Service
Brands:
    Miss Sally's

2262 Carrington Tea Co.
PO Box 102
Closter, NJ 07624
800-505-9546
support@carringtontea.com
Green, black, herbal and organic teas
Number of Brands: 1
Number of Products: 4
Type of Packaging: Consumer
Brands:
    CARRINGTON TEA

2263 Carrousel Cellars
2825 Day Road
Gilroy, CA 95020-8827
408-847-2060
Fax: 831-424-1077
Wines
Winemaker: John DeSantis
Number Employees: 20-49

2264 Carson City Pickle Company
7451 S Garlock Rd
Carson City, MI 48811
989-584-3148
Fax: 517-879-2146
Produce including cucumbers, pickles and pickled and brined vegetables
Manager: Mike Zwerk
Contact: Wyatt Waldron
police@carsoncitymi.com
Manager: Rudy Montoya
Estimated Sales: $1-2.5 Million
Number Employees: 1-4
Parent Co: Funk Enterprises
Type of Packaging: Consumer, Food Service, Bulk

2265 Carta Blanca
3912 Frutas Ave
El Paso, TX 79905-1316
915-544-6367
Fax: 915-544-0109
Beer
Manager: Carmen Bitar
Contact: Elias Ceballos
elias.ceballos@grupodelavega.com
General Manager: Miriam De La Vega
Estimated Sales: $1-3,000,000
Number Employees: 1-4

2266 Carve Nutrition
114 Washington Blvd
Suite B
Marina Del Rey, CA 90292
310-905-8100
hello@carvenutrition.com
carvenutrition.com
Cookie alternative
CEO: Joey Adler
Number of Brands: 1
Number of Products: 4
Type of Packaging: Consumer
Brands:
    CARVE COOKIE

2267 Cary Randall's Sauces & Dressings
PO Box 363
Highlands, NJ 07732-0363
732-872-6353
Fax: 732-872-2035
Fat-free all natural salad dressing, hot sauce
Contact: Cary Lazon
Estimated Sales: Under $500,000
Number Employees: 1-4

2268 Cary's of Oregon
413 Union Ave
Grants Pass, OR 97527-5541
541-474-0030
Fax: 541-474-5924 888-822-9300
English toffee in 7 different flavors.
Number Employees: 10-19

2269 Casa Di Lisio Products Inc
486 Lexington Ave # 3
Mt Kisco, NY 10549-2779
914-666-5021
Fax: 914-666-7209 800-247-4199
info@casadilisio.com www.casadilisio.com
Frozen Italian sauces including walnut and sun dried tomato pesto, clam, marinara, puttanesca, basil pesto, cilantro pesto provencal, alfredo and roasted red peppers pest
Owner: Linda DiLisio
ldilisio@kitchencooked.net
VP: Lucy DiLisio
Year Founded: 1973
Estimated Sales: $20-50 Million
Number Employees: 50-99
Number of Brands: 1
Number of Products: 25
Square Footage: 4000
Type of Packaging: Consumer, Food Service, Private Label, Bulk
Brands:
    Casa Dilisio

2270 Casa Larga Vineyards
2287 Turk Hill Rd
Fairport, NY 14450-9579
585-223-4210
Fax: 585-223-8899 info@casalarga.com
www.casalarga.com
Wines
President: Andrew Colaruotolo
acolaruotolo@casalarga.com
Wine-Making Director: John Colaruotolo
Director, Accounting/IT: Mary Jo Colaruotolo
Marketing Director: Andrea Colaruotolo
Estimated Sales: $1-9 Million
Number Employees: 20-49
Square Footage: 20
Type of Packaging: Private Label

2271 Casa Nuestra Winery & Vineyard
3451 Silverado Trl N
St Helena, CA 94574-9662
707-963-5783
Fax: 707-963-3174 866-844-9463
info@casanuestra.com
Wine
Owner: Shane Brown
brownshane@commission-tracker.com
Co-owner: Cody Gillette Kirkham
General Manager: Katrina Kirkham
Marketing Manager/Apprentice Winemaker: Stephanie Zacharia
Chief Winemaker: Allen Price
Production Assistant: Hector Ortiz
Estimated Sales: $500,000
Number Employees: 5-9
Brands:
    Casa Nuestra

Food Manufacturers / A-Z

2272 Casa Sanchez Foods
P.O. Box 12582
San Francisco, CA 94112
650-697-7525
Fax: 650-697-1810 877-227-2726
info@casasanchez.com
www.casasanchez.com/index.html
Guacamole and salsas
Contact: Roger Esponilla
roger@casasanchez.com

2273 Casa Valdez Inc
502 E Chicago St
Caldwell, ID 83605-3337
208-459-6461
Fax: 208-459-4154 www.casavaldez.com
Corn and flour tortillas
Owner: Jose Valdez
joejr@casavaldez.com
Sales/Marketting: Joe Romero
Estimated Sales: $2 Million
Number Employees: 20-49

2274 (HQ)Casa Visco
819 Kings Rd
Schenectady, NY 12303-2627
518-377-8814
Fax: 518-377-8269 888-607-2823
www.casavisco.com
Kosher products including spaghetti and barbecue sauces, salsa and mustard; exporter of spaghetti sauce
Owner: Joe Viscusi
info@casavisco.com
VP: Michael Viscusi
Sales & Marketing: Adine Gallo
Production Manager: Michael Viscusi, Jr.
Estimated Sales: $1-2.5 Million
Number Employees: 5-9
Square Footage: 100000
Parent Co: Casa Visco Finer Food
Type of Packaging: Consumer, Food Service, Private Label, Bulk
Brands:
  Casa Visco
  My Country Sweet
  Schabers

2275 Casa di Carfagna
1405 E Dublin Granville Rd
Columbus, OH 43229-3357
614-846-6340
Fax: 614-846-0937 www.carfagnas.com
Italian sausages, frozen Italian meals and sauces
President: Sam Carfagna
Estimated Sales: $5-10 Million
Number Employees: 50-99
Brands:
  Carfagna

2276 Casablanca Foods LLC
P.O. Box 287447
New York, NY 10128-0025
212-317-1111
Fax: 866-530-3110 contact@casablancafoods.com
www.casablancafoods.com
Moroccan inspired spices and sauces.
Founder: Mina Kallamni
Estimated Sales: $100,000
Number Employees: 8
Type of Packaging: Private Label
Brands:
  Mina

2277 Casablanca Market
8430 Central Ave
Suite 3A
Newark, CA 94560-3446
650-964-3000
info@casablancamarket.com
casablancamarket.com
Soy sauce; curry; spreads; marinades; olives; pickles and pickled vegetables
President: Katia Essyad
Type of Packaging: Private Label

2278 Casados Farms
201 State Road 582
Ohkay Owingeh, NM 87566
505-852-2433
Dried and dehydrated fruits
President: Peter Casados
Estimated Sales: $200,000
Number Employees: 10-19

Type of Packaging: Consumer

2279 Casani Candy Company
7905 Browning Rd.
Ste. 208
Pennsauken, NJ 08110
856-488-0045
Fax: 456-488-2645 www.casanicandyco.com
Confectionery ingredients
Chairman: John Lees
President: Joey Traynor
VP: Joseph Lees
Contact: Joe Lees
jlees55@comcast.net
Manager: John Lees
Estimated Sales: $2.5-5 000,000
Number Employees: 10-19

2280 Cascade Cheese Co
302 E Water St
Cascade, WI 53011-1606
920-528-8221
Fax: 920-528-7473 trade.eatwisconsincheese.com
Provolone, mozzarella
Owner: Joel Narges
jnarges@wmmb.com
Treasurer: Elizabeth Babler
Estimated Sales: $2.4 Million
Number Employees: 20-49

2281 Cascade Clear Water
4804 NW Bethany Blvd
I-2, #228
Portland, OR 97229
800-888-3879
Fax: 503-616-7971 www.cascadeh2o.com
Clear water
President, CEO: Douglas Mason
Managing Director International Div: Robert Allen
Estimated Sales: $2.5-5 Million
Number Employees: 20-49
Parent Co: Cleary Canadian Beverage Company

2282 Cascade Coffee
1525 75th St SW # 100
Suite 100
Everett, WA 98203-7007
425-347-3995
Fax: 425-347-5076 800-995-9655
info@cascadecoffee.com www.cascadecoffee.com
Custom coffee roasting and packaging.
President: Kelly Johnson
Chairman/Chief Executive Officer: Phil Johnson
Chief Financial Officer: Nick Jonson
VP, Product Development: Patrick Lyon
Director, Quality Assurance: Nichole Hyde
Director, Engineering & Maintenance: Jerry Klobertanz
Plant Manager: Todd Larson
Estimated Sales: $20-50 Million
Number Employees: 100-249
Type of Packaging: Private Label
Brands:
  Organic Altura
  Organic Mexican Altura
  Organic Sierra Madre Blend

2283 Cascade Fresh
14300 Greenwood Ave N Ste E
Seattle, WA 98133
206-363-0991
Fax: 206-363-8191 800-511-0057
yogurt@cascadefresh.com
Fat free, low fat and whole milk yogurts, as well as Greek and Mediterranean style yogurts, sour cream and açaí, peach, raspberry and strawberry smoothies.
President: Satshakti Khalsa
Estimated Sales: $2,600,000
Number Employees: 10-19
Brands:
  Cascade Fresh

2284 Cascade Mountain Winery
835 Cascade Road
Amenia, NY 12501
845-373-9021
Fax: 845-373-7869 info@cascademt.com
www.cascademt.com
Processor and exporter of dry and semi-dry and nonsweet table wines
Owner: William Wathmore
CEO: Margaret Wetmore
Estimated Sales: $3-5 Million
Number Employees: 5-9

Number of Products: 8
Square Footage: 24000
Type of Packaging: Consumer

2285 Cascade Specialties, Inc.
1 Cascade Way
Boardman, OR 97818
541-481-2522
Fax: 541-481-2640 www.cascadespec.com
Dehydrated onion products.
Owner: Fraser Hawley
CEO: Suvan Sharma
Director of Quality: Tina Kovscek
General Manager: Carl Hearn
Production Manager: Jerry Dyer
Estimated Sales: $5-10 Million
Number Employees: 20-49
Parent Co: JAIN
Other Locations:
  Port Warehouse
  Boardman OR
Brands:
  Cascade Specialties

2286 Cascadian Farm Inc
719 Metcalf St
Sedro Woolley, WA 98284-1456
360-855-0542
Fax: 360-855-0444 www.cascadianfarm.com
Processor, importer, manufacturer and marketer of frozen organic foods including fruits, vegetables and juice concentrates; also pickles and fruit spreads.
President: Maria Morgan
CEO: Steve Sanger
Estimated Sales: $10-20 Million
Number Employees: 50-99
Square Footage: 28930
Parent Co: Small Planet Foods
Type of Packaging: Consumer, Food Service, Bulk
Other Locations:
  Cascadian Farm
  Napa CA
Brands:
  Cascadian Farm
  Fantastic Foods
  Muir Glen
  Small Planet Foods

2287 (HQ)Case Farms
385 Pilch Rd
Troutman, NC 28166
704-528-4501
Fax: 704-528-4277 www.casefarms.com
Fresh, partially-cooked and frozen-for-export poultry products.
Chairman & CEO: Tom Shelton
President & COO: Kevin Phillips
Year Founded: 1986
Estimated Sales: $138.4 Million
Number Employees: 3,200
Other Locations:
  Dudley NC
  Winesburg OH
  Goldsboro NC
  Morganton NC
  Strasburg OH
  Mt. Olive NC
  Shelby NC
  Massillon OH
  Troutman NC

2288 Case Farms Ohio Division
1818 County Road 160
Winesburg, OH 44690
330-359-7141
www.casefarms.com
Fresh, partially-cooked and frozen-for-export poultry products.
Parent Co: Case Farms
Type of Packaging: Private Label
Brands:
  Case Farms Amish Country

2289 Case Side Holdings Company
37 Garden Dr
Kensington, PE C0B 1M0
Canada
902-836-4214
Fax: 902-836-3297
Bread, muffins, biscuits, scones, doughnuts, cookies, pastries, cakes and pies
President: Don Caseley
VP & Manager Director: Trudy Caseley
Secretary: Roy Hogan
Estimated Sales: $752,000
Number Employees: 15

587

Food Manufacturers / A-Z

Type of Packaging: Private Label

2290 Casey Fisheries
PO Box 86
Digby, NS B0V 1A0
Canada
902-245-5801
Fax: 902-245-5552 info@caseyfisheries.com
www.caseyfisheries.com
Processor and exporter of fresh and frozen scallops and salmon
President: Joseph Casey
Plant Manager: Duncan Casey
Estimated Sales: $1.6 Million
Number Employees: 15
Type of Packaging: Consumer, Food Service, Private Label, Bulk

2291 Casey's Seafood Inc
807 Jefferson Ave
Newport News, VA 23607-6117
757-928-1979
Fax: 757-928-0257 www.caseysseafood.com
Canned and frozen blue crab meat; also, heat and serve gourmet crab cakes and deviled crabs and crawfish cakes
Owner: Jim Casey
jim@caseysseafood.com
Marketing Director: Mike Casey
Estimated Sales: $3 Million
Number Employees: 50-99
Square Footage: 40000
Type of Packaging: Consumer, Food Service
Brands:
  Casey's
  Chesapeake Bay's Finest

2292 Casino Bakery
2726 N 36th St
Tampa, FL 33605-3126
813-242-0311
Fax: 813-242-4691
Cuban bread
Owner: Mark N Muhsen
Estimated Sales: $1-2.5 Million
Number Employees: 10-19
Type of Packaging: Consumer, Food Service

2293 Casper Foodservice Company
310 N Green St
Chicago, IL 60607-1300
312-226-2265
Fax: 312-226-2686
President: Thomas Casper
Estimated Sales: $1-3 Million
Number Employees: 10-19

2294 Casper's Ice Cream
11805 N 200 E
Richmond, UT 84333-1408
435-258-2477
Fax: 435-258-5633 800-772-4182
fatboy@fatboyicecream.com
Ice cream novelties including sandwiches and nut sundaes on a stick
President: Kyle Smith
CEO: Paul Merrill
Vice President: Shane Petersen
Vice President: Keith Lawes
Estimated Sales: $35 Million
Number Employees: 175
Square Footage: 184000
Type of Packaging: Consumer, Food Service, Private Label, Bulk
Brands:
  Fat Boy

2295 Cass-Clay Creamery
200 20th St N
PO Box 3126
Fargo, ND 58102-4136
701-293-6455
Fax: 701-241-9154
Liquid milk, ice cream, dips, sour cream, cream & butter, juice, cottage cheese, and yogurt.
Cio/Cto: Kurt Quiggle
kurtquig@msn.com
Marketing: Rachel Kyllo
Sales Manager: Brian Day
Plant Manager: Troy Anderson
Purchasing: Brenda Hartmann
Estimated Sales: $28.9 Million
Number Employees: 320
Number of Brands: 1
Square Footage: 5000
Parent Co: Kemps LLC
Type of Packaging: Consumer, Food Service, Private Label, Bulk
Brands:
  Cass-Clay

2296 Cassandra's Gourmet Classics/Island Treasures Gourmet
10681 Wakeman Ct.
Manassas, VA 20110
703-590-7900
www.cassandrasgourmet.com
Manufacturer of rum cakes.
President: Cassandra Craig
General Manager: Pam Brewster
VP/Sales Manager: Ken Craig
Type of Packaging: Private Label
Brands:
  Island Treasures Gourmet

2297 Castella Imports Inc
120 A Wilshire Blvd
Brentwood, NY 11717
631-231-5500
Cheeses, spices, olives and olive oils
Estimated Sales: $100+ Million
Number Employees: 250-499
Square Footage: 66000

2298 (HQ)Castellini Group
PO Box 721610
Newport, KY 41072-1610
800-233-8560
info@castellinicompany.com
www.castellinicompany.com
Produce; private labeling and custom packaging; also, transportation company offering a 48 state authority of transporting
CEO: Brian Kocher
Number Employees: 250-499
Type of Packaging: Consumer, Food Service, Private Label, Bulk
Brands:
  Castellini
  Club Chef
  Crosset Company
  General Produce
  Grant County Foods
  RWI Logistics

2299 Castello di Borghese Vineyard
17150 Rte 48
Cutchogue, NY 11935
631-734-5111
Fax: 631-734-5485 info@castellodiborghese.com
castellodiborghese.com
Vineyard and winery
Owner: Marco Borghese
Owner: Ann Marie Borghese
Estimated Sales: $500-1 Million appx.
Number Employees: 10-19
Type of Packaging: Private Label
Brands:
  Hargrave Vineyards

2300 Castle Beverages Inc
105 Myrtle Ave
Ansonia, CT 06401-2099
203-734-0883
Carbonated beverages
President & General Manager: David Pantalone
Estimated Sales: $2.5-5,000,000
Number Employees: 5-9
Brands:
  Castle Beverages
  Castle Carbonated Beverages

2301 (HQ)Castle Cheese
2850 Perry Hwy
Slippery Rock, PA 16057
724-368-3022
Fax: 724-368-9456 800-252-4373
Processor and exporter of cheese foods including substitutes, imitation and natural blends
President: George Myrter
Purchasing Manager: Michelle Sabol
Estimated Sales: $370,000
Number Employees: 2
Square Footage: 13112
Type of Packaging: Consumer, Food Service, Private Label, Bulk
Other Locations:
  Castle Cheese
  Vernon BC
Brands:
  Castle Cheese
  Vernon Bc

2302 Castle Hill Lobster
333 Linebrook Rd
Suite R
Ipswich, MA 01938-1146
978-356-3947
Fax: 978-356-9883
Whole seafoods; lobsters
Owner: Robert Marcaurelle
Contact: Dennis Wilke
dennis.wilke@castlehillco.com
Estimated Sales: $2 Million
Number Employees: 1-4
Type of Packaging: Food Service

2303 Castle Rock Meats
707 E 50th Ave
Denver, CO 80216-2006
303-292-0855
Fax: 303-292-0680
Meats
President: Michael Andrade
Plant Manager: Allen Rigby
Estimated Sales: $20-50 Million
Number Employees: 20-49

2304 Castor River Farms
Dexter, MO 63841
castorriverfarms.com
Long grain white and brown rice
Principal: Johnny Hunter
Brands:
  Castor River Farms

2305 Casual Gourmet Foods
4500 140th Avenue N
Suite 113
Clearwater, FL 33762-3827
727-298-8307
Fax: 727-298-0616 info@cgfoods.com
www.cgfoods.com
Fully-cooked, all-natural chicken sausages and chicken burgers. Turkey sausage
Marketing/Sales: David Canarelli
Public Relations: Ben Rizzo
Operations/Production/Plant Manager: Robert Hapanowicz
Number Employees: 5-9

2306 Casually Gourmet
PO Box 143
New Haven, VT 5472
80- 63- 760
Fax: 802-870-3061 800-639-7604
info@casuallygourmet.com www.gormlys.com
Pancake and scone mixes, jellies, preserves, mustards, barbecue sauce and spiced apple cider concentrate
President: Bill Gormly
Estimated Sales: $500,000 appx.
Number Employees: 5-9
Square Footage: 19000
Type of Packaging: Consumer, Food Service, Private Label

2307 Catamount Specialties of Vermont
8053 US Route 2
PO BOX 275
Plainfield, VT 05667
802-253-4525
Fax: 802-253-6933 800-639-2406
debhilld@myfairpoint.net
www.catamountspecialties.com
Produces mustards, salsas, BBQ sauces, pepper jellies, pasta sauces and seasonings
Co-Owner: Don Mugford
Co-Owner: George Gooss
Estimated Sales: $.5-1 million
Number Employees: 1-4

2308 Catania Bakery
1404 N Capitol St NW
Washington, DC 20002-3342
202-332-5135
info@cataniabakery.com
www.cataniabakery.com
Italian bread and biscotti

Food Manufacturers / A-Z

President: Nicole Tramonte
General Manager: Carolyn Craig
Estimated Sales: $630,000
Number Employees: 5-9

2309 Catania Hospitality Group
141 Falmouth Rd
Hyannis, MA 02601-2755
508-771-0040
Fax: 508-771-0883 888-774-5511
info@cataniahospitalitygroup.com
www.cataniahospitalitygroup.com
Fresh and frozen soups and chowders
President: William Catania
william@cataniahospitalitygroup.com
VP: Richard Catonia
Estimated Sales: $500,000-$1,000,000
Number Employees: 500-999
Type of Packaging: Private Label
Brands:
   Cape Cod Clam Chowder
   Cape Cod Lobster Bisque
   Cape Cod Lobster Chowder
   Lobster Chowder
   Minestrone

2310 Catania Oils
3 Nemco Way
Ayer, MA 01432
978-772-7900
Fax: 978-722-7970 cataniaoils.com
Specialty oils
Exec. VP, Sales & Marketing: Stephen Basile
Number of Brands: 1
Type of Packaging: Consumer, Food Service, Private Label, Bulk

2311 Catawissa Bottling Co
450 Fisher Ave
PO Box 27
Catawissa, PA 17820-1022
570-356-2301
Fax: 570-356-2304 800-892-4419
www.catawissabottling.com
Soft drinks.
Owner: Michael Gregorowicz
bigbens1926@peoplepc.com
Plant Manager: Stephen Gregorowicz
Purchasing: Paula Clark
Estimated Sales: $10-20 Million
Number Employees: 20-49
Number of Brands: 2
Brands:
   Big Ben
   Moxie

2312 Catch Up Logistics
5711 Friendship Ave
Pittsburgh, PA 15206-3616
412-441-9512
Fax: 412-441-9517 catchup@bellatlantic.net
www.catchuplogistics.com
Processor and exporter of plain and kosher frozen pizza; also, Italian specialties including pasta
Owner: Ronald Pasekoff
ronald.pasekoff@catchuplogistics.com
COO: Donald Paskoff
Estimated Sales: $2.5-5 Million
Number Employees: 5-9
Type of Packaging: Consumer, Food Service, Private Label, Bulk
Brands:
   Cholov Yisrael
   Tambellini

2313 Catelli Brothers Inc
50 Ferry Ave
Collingswood, NJ 08103-3006
856-869-9293
Fax: 856-869-9488 jresnick@catellibrothers.com
www.catellibrothers.com
Veal and lamb
CEO: Anthony Catelli
acatelli@catellibrothers.com
CFO: Norm Gunn
Quality Control Manager: Cheryl Edwards
Director of Marketing: Doug Buchanan
VP of Sales: Anthony Longino
Human Resources: Vanessa Vogt
Purchasing Manager: Harry Edwards
Estimated Sales: $20.4 Million
Number Employees: 250-499
Other Locations:
   Shrewsbury NJ

Brands:
   American Lamb
   Ami
   Namp

2314 Cateraid Inc
1167 Fendt Dr
Howell, MI 48843-6501
517-546-8217
Fax: 517-546-8674 800-508-8217
cateraid@sbcglobal.net www.cateraidinc.com
Frozen European style tortes, cakes, cheesecakes, miniature pastries and hors d'oeuvres
Owner: Rob Katz
cateraidinc@provide.net
Vice President, Director of Marketing: Rob Katz
Estimated Sales: $2.5-5 Million
Number Employees: 20-49
Number of Brands: 2
Number of Products: 85
Square Footage: 68000
Type of Packaging: Food Service, Private Label
Brands:
   Cateraid
   Catered Gourmet

2315 Cates Addis Company
2640 McIver Road
Parkton, NC 28371
910-858-3439
Fax: 910-858-3074 800-423-1883
Grower of fresh vegetables for pre-prepared salads and food services.
President: Curtiss Cates
Estimated Sales: $3-5 Million
Number Employees: 7
Type of Packaging: Bulk

2316 Catfish Wholesale
P.O.Box 759
Abbeville, LA 70511
337-643-6700
Fax: 337-643-1396 800-334-7292
Processor and distributor of catfish, garfish, crawfish, shrimp, crabs, flounder and trout
President: James Rich
Sales Executive: Shab Calahan
Sales Manager: David Lowery
Estimated Sales: $2.5 Million
Number Employees: 60
Number of Brands: 1
Square Footage: 32000
Type of Packaging: Consumer, Food Service, Private Label, Bulk

2317 Cathay Foods Corporation
960 Massachusetts Ave
Boston, MA 02118-2620
617-427-1507
Fax: 617-427-4083
Frozen spring, cocktail and full sized egg rolls including shrimp, lobster, vegetable, pizza, spinach and cheese; also, egg roll wrappers and crab rangoons
President: Victor Wong
Sales: Nancy Tashjian
Estimated Sales: $5-10 Million
Number Employees: 20-49
Square Footage: 36000
Type of Packaging: Consumer, Food Service, Private Label, Bulk
Brands:
   Cathay Foods

2318 Catherych
141 Mountainview Rd
Warren, NJ 07059
732-566-6625
Fax: 732-566-6392 info@catherych.com
www.catherych.com
Bulk ingredient supplier to the nutraceutical industry
Type of Packaging: Bulk

2319 Catoctin Vineyards
805 Greenbridge Rd
Brookeville, MD 20833
301-774-2310
Fax: 301-774-2310
Wines
President: Bob Lyon
Estimated Sales: Less than $500,000
Number Employees: 1

2320 Catoris Candies Inc
981 5th Ave
New Kensington, PA 15068-6307
724-335-4371
Fax: 724-335-1759 www.catoriscandies.com
Confectionery items
Owner: John Gentile
Estimated Sales: $5-10 Million
Number Employees: 10-19
Type of Packaging: Consumer

2321 Catskill Brewery
672 Old Rte. 17
Livingston Manor, NY 12758
845-439-1232
info@catskillbrewery.com
www.catskillbrewery.com
IPA, Pilsner, Lager, Stout and sour beer
Founder: Ramsay Adams
Number of Brands: 1
Number of Products: 14
Type of Packaging: Consumer, Private Label
Brands:
   Catskill Brewery

2322 Catskill Distilling Company
2037 Rte. 17B
Bethel, NY 12720
845-583-3141
www.catskilldistilling.com
Vodka, gin, grappa, whiskey, bourbon and rye
Owner/Distiller: Monte Sachs
Year Founded: 2008
Number of Brands: 1
Number of Products: 8
Brands:
   Catskill Distilling Company

2323 Catskill Mountain Specialties
1411 Route 212
Saugerties, NY 12477-3040
845-246-0900
Fax: 845-246-5313 800-311-3473
www.newworldhomecooking.com
Condiments including roasted habanero, chipotle, barbecue, Jamaican jerk, etc.; importer of hot peppers, spices, etc.; also, co-packer of acidified foods
Owner: Liz Corrado
VP: Edward Palluth
Number Employees: 1-4
Square Footage: 8000
Type of Packaging: Consumer, Food Service, Private Label, Bulk
Brands:
   Mountainman
   New World Home Cooking Co.

2324 Cattaneo Brothers Inc
797 Caudill Streey
San Luis Obispo, CA 93401
800-243-8537
info@cattaneobros.com www.cattaneobros.com
Jerky, pepperoni sticks and sausage
Owner: Kaitlyn Kaney
Marketing Director: Katelyn Kaney
Estimated Sales: $2.5-5 Million
Number Employees: 20-49
Number of Brands: 1
Number of Products: 50
Square Footage: 34000
Type of Packaging: Consumer, Food Service, Private Label
Brands:
   Cattaneo Brothers

2325 Cattle Boyz Foods
Suite 314, #14
900 Village Lane
Okotoks, Alberta,, CA T1S 1Z6
Canada
403-995-2279
Fax: 403-995-2056 888-662-9366
sales@cattleboyz.com www.CattleBoyZ.com
Manufacturer and exporter of unique latchtop bottle containing versatile gourmet sauces for barbecuing, marinades, glaze for all meats and seafoods. Available in 17 and 35 oz. sizes
Managing Partner/Owner: Karen Hope
Managing Partner: Joe Ternes
Quality Control: Roxanne Quest
Sales: Karen Hope
Number Employees: 1-4
Number of Brands: 1
Number of Products: 4

Food Manufacturers / A-Z

Type of Packaging: Consumer, Food Service, Private Label, Bulk
Brands:
 Cattle Boyz

2326 Cattleman Meat & Produce
11400 Telegraph Rd
Taylor, MI 48180-4078
734-287-8260
Fax: 734-287-8368 www.cattlemansmeats.com
Fresh and frozen beef and meat products.
Owner: Peter Synoweic
Number Employees: 20-49
Type of Packaging: Bulk
Brands:
 Cattleman's

2327 Caughman's Meat Plant
164 Meat Plant Rd
Lexington, SC 29073-8911
803-356-0076
Established in 1955. Manufacturer of sausage, poulty, beef, pork, liver pudding, barbecue hash and beef chili.
President: Marguerite Caughman
VP: Ronald Caughman
Estimated Sales: $20-50 Million
Number Employees: 20-49
Type of Packaging: Consumer
Brands:
 Lexington

2328 Caulipower
Encino, CA 91436
844-422-8544
info@eatcaulipower.com www.eatcaulipower.com
Cauliflower flour-based tortillas, pizzas and baking mixes
Founder & CEO: Gail Becker

2329 Cave Shake
Los Angeles, CA 90065
hi@caveshake.com
eatspaceshake.com
Keto, paleo and vegan meal replacements
CEO: Holly Heath

2330 Caveman Foods
3595 Mt. Diablo Blvd
Suite 200
Lafayette, CA 94549
925-979-9515
www.cavemanfoods.com
Paleo-friendly snack bars and chicken jerky
Number of Brands: 1
Number of Products: 4
Type of Packaging: Consumer

2331 Cavender Castle Winery
142 Mitchell Street SW
Suite 300
Atlanta, GA 30303-3432
706-864-4759
Wines
Vineyard Manager: Gerry Carty
Number Employees: 20-49

2332 Cavendish Farms
100 Midland Dr.
Dieppe, NB E1A 6X4
Canada
506-858-7710
Fax: 506-858-7708 www.cavendishfarms.com
Potato products.
President: Robert Irving
Vice President, Sales: Gerald Toews
Year Founded: 1980
Estimated Sales: $294 Million
Number Employees: 16,000
Parent Co: Cavendish Farms Corporation
Brands:
 FreshCut
 Cavendish Farms®
 Double R®
 FlavourCrisp®
 Clear Coat
 Fine Coat®
 Jersey Shore®

2333 Cavens Meats
US Route 36
Conover, OH 45317-0400
937-368-3841
Fax: 937-368-3849

Processor and wholesaler/distributor of meat products; serving the food service market
President: Victor Caven
VP: Dean Caven
Estimated Sales: $10-20 Million
Number Employees: 10-19
Square Footage: 45000
Type of Packaging: Consumer, Food Service

2334 Caves Of Faribault/SwissValley
222 3rd St NE
Faribault, MN 55021
507-334-5260
Fax: 507-332-9011 jeff.jirik@cavesoffaribault.com
www.faribaultdairy.com
Cheese
President/Owner: Sarah Arhameault
CEO: Jeff Jirik
VP: Michael Gilbertson
Estimated Sales: $3.5 Million
Number Employees: 21

2335 Caviness Beef Packers LTD
3255 W Highway 60
P.O. Box 790
Hereford, TX 79045
806-357-2333
Fax: 806-357-2377 www.cavinessbeefpackers.com
Meat products; slaughtering services available.
President: Trevor Caviness
Year Founded: 1962
Estimated Sales: $28.2 Million
Number Employees: 500-999
Square Footage: 100000
Other Locations:
 Manufacturing Plant
 Amarillo TX

2336 Caviness Beef Packers LTD
4206 Amarillo Blvd E
P.O. Box 31117
Amarillo, TX 79120
806-372-5781
Fax: 806-372-1215 www.cavinessbeefpackers.com
Meat products; slaughtering services available.
President: Trevor Caviness
Year Founded: 1962
Estimated Sales: $20-50 Million
Number Employees: 500-999

2337 Cawston Press
Pittsburgh, PA 15241
info@cawstonpress.com
cawstonpress.com
Sparkling fruit soft drinks
Managing Director: Steve Kearns
Number of Products: 4

2338 Cawy Bottling Co
2440 NW 21st Ter
Miami, FL 33142-7182
305-634-2291
Fax: 305-634-2291 877-917-2299
cawy@cawy.net www.cawy.net
Soft drinks
CEO/VP/Public Relations: Vincent Cossio
Quality Control: Ramon Mesa
Sales Director: Harris Padron
Operations Manager: Mayra Alfonsin
Production Manager: Carlos Garcia
Estimated Sales: $10-20 Million
Number Employees: 20-49
Square Footage: 120000
Type of Packaging: Consumer, Food Service
Brands:
 Cawy Cc
 Cawy Lemon-Lime
 Cawy Watermelon
 Champ's Cola
 Coco Solo
 Jupina
 Malta Cawy
 Malta Rica
 Materva
 Quinabeer
 Rica Malt Tonic
 Trimalta

2339 Caymus Vineyards
8700 Conn Creek Rd
Rutherford, CA 94573
707-967-3010
Fax: 707-963-5958 reception@caymus.com
www.caymus.com
Wines

President: Chuck Wagner
VP: Karen Perry
Public Relations: Phyllis Turner
Estimated Sales: $300,000-500,000
Number Employees: 20-49
Number of Brands: 1
Number of Products: 2
Brands:
 Caymus

2340 Cayuga Pure Organics
18 Banks Rd
Brooktondale, NY 14817-9752
607-273-2621
www.cporganics.com
Grain
Farm Owner/Founder: Erick Smith
erick@cporganics.com
Office Mgr / NYC Operations: Amy Martin
Estimated Sales: Less Than $500,000
Number Employees: 1-4
Type of Packaging: Food Service, Bulk

2341 Cayuga Ridge Estate Winery
6800 State Route 89
Ovid, NY 14521-9599
607-869-5158
Fax: 607-869-3412 800-598-9463
www.cayugaridgewinery.com
Wines
Owner: Tom Challen
crew@flpg.net
Owner: Susie Challen
Estimated Sales: Less Than $500,000
Number Employees: 1-4

2342 Cebro Frozen Food
2100 Orestimba Rd
Newman, CA 95360-9788
209-862-0150
Fax: 209-862-0717 www.cebrofrozenfoods.com
Frozen foods
President: William Cerutti
wcerutti@cebrofrozenfood.com
Estimated Sales: $2.5-5 Million
Number Employees: 10-19

2343 Cecchetti Sebastiani Cellar
389 Fourth Street East
Sonoma, CA 95476-1607
707-933-3230
Fax: 707-996-0424 www.sebastiani.com
Wine
President/CEO: Mary Ann Sebastiani-Cuneo
SVP Sales: Jim O'Connor
SVP/Winemaker: Bob Broman
Number Employees: 1-4
Type of Packaging: Private Label
Brands:
 Brandy
 Cecchetti Sebastiani Napa Valley
 Pepperwood Grove
 Quatro
 Wines

2344 Cece's Veggie Co.
3714 Bluestein Dr
Suite 650
Austin, TX 78721
512-200-3337
info@cecesveggieco.com
www.cecesveggieco.com
Organic vegetable spirals
Founder: Mason Arnold
Number of Brands: 1
Number of Products: 9
Type of Packaging: Consumer
Brands:
 CECE'S VEGGIE NOODLE CO.

2345 Cedar Creek Winery
N70 W6340 Bridge Rd
Cedarburg, WI 53012
262-377-8020
Fax: 262-375-9428 800-827-8020
info@cedarcreekwinery.com
www.cedarcreekwinery.com
Bottler of wine
Manager: Steve Danner
Estimated Sales: $5-9.9 Million
Number Employees: 10-19
Square Footage: 48000
Type of Packaging: Consumer, Food Service, Private Label

Food Manufacturers / A-Z

Brands:
    Cedar Creek

2346 Cedar Crest Specialties
7269 Hwy. 60
P.O. Box 260
Cedarburg, WI 53012
                                   262-377-7252
    Fax: 262-377-5554 800-877-8341
                 info@cedarcresticecream.com
                 www.cedarcresticecream.com
Premium ice cream and no-fat ice cream, frozen yogurt, sherbet and Tom and Jerry mix
President: Ken Kohlwey
CEO: Bill Kohlwey
VP: Robert Kohlwey
Marketing Manager: Charlene Leach
Sales: Robert Kohlwey
Purchasing: Nadine Schmitt
Estimated Sales: $16 Million
Number Employees: 50-99
Number of Brands: 2
Number of Products: 400
Square Footage: 135000
Parent Co: Cedar Crest Specialties
Type of Packaging: Consumer, Food Service, Private Label, Bulk
Brands:
    Cedar Crest
    Gustafson's

2347 Cedar Grove Cheese Inc
E5904 Mill Rd
PO Box 185
Plain, WI 53577-9674
                                   608-546-5284
    Fax: 608-546-2805 800-200-6020
                 info@cedargrovecheese.com
                 www.cedargrovecheese.com
Organic cheese and specialty artisan crafted cheese
Owner: Bob Wills
bob@cedargrovecheese.com
Vice President: Beth Nachreiner
Marketing Director: Robert Wills
General Manager: Peter DeWaard
Estimated Sales: $2.5-5 Million
Number Employees: 20-49
Number of Brands: 3
Number of Products: 50
Type of Packaging: Consumer, Food Service, Private Label, Bulk
Brands:
    Cedar Grove
    Family Farmer
    Squeaks

2348 Cedar Hill Seasonings
P.O.Box 4055
Edmond, OK 73034
                                   405-340-1119
    Fax: 405-340-7673 800-342-1986
                 info@cedarhillseasonings.com
                 www.cedarhillseasonings.com
Seasonings, bottled products and packaged mixes, Cedar Hill Seasonings produces a variety of food items including taco mixes; dip mix with seasonings; cheese ball mixes; marinara and sauce mixes, in addition to offering gift packagesand combo samplers.
Co-Owner: Felicia Schaefer
info@cedarhillseasonings.com
Co-Owner: Helen Schaefer
Type of Packaging: Food Service

2349 Cedar Key Aquaculture Farms
11227 Riverview Dr
Riverview, FL 33578-4471
                                   813-681-5796
    Fax: 352-543-9132 888-252-6735
                 custserv@cedarkeyclams.com
                 www.cedarkeyclams.com
Fresh and frozen clams including hors d'oeuvres
President: Dan Solano
Operations Manager: Mike Smith
Contact: Stephen Jaeb
stephen.j@cedarkeyclams.com
Estimated Sales: Less Than $500,000
Number Employees: 1-4
Type of Packaging: Food Service

2350 Cedar Lake Foods
5333 Quarter Line Rd
Cedar Lake, MI 48812
                                   989-427-5143
    Fax: 989-427-5392 800-246-5039
                 www.cedarlakefoods.com
Processor and exporter of canned and frozen vegetable protein entrees including meat analogs; also, dry soy milk and vegetarian foods
President: Alejo Pizzaro
Contact: Cheri Graves
Production Manager: John Sias
Plant Manager: John Sias
Purchasing Manager: Ann Britten
Estimated Sales: $5-9.9 Million
Number Employees: 20-49
Type of Packaging: Consumer, Food Service, Private Label, Bulk
Brands:
    Cedar Lake
    Mgm

2351 Cedar Mountain Winery
7000 Tesla Rd
Livermore, CA 94550
                                   925-373-6636
    Fax: 925-373-6694 cedarmtn@wt.net
                 www.cedarmountainwinery.com
Wines
Owner: Linda Ault
Owner: Earl Ault
Co-Owner: Earl Ault
Marketing Manager: Sigrid Laing
VP Operations/Production Manager: R Michael Hasbrouck
Estimated Sales: $840,000
Number Employees: 12
Type of Packaging: Private Label
Brands:
    Cedar Grove
    Cedar Mountain

2352 Cedar Valley Cheese Store
W3115 Jay Rd
Belgium, WI 53004-9769
                                   920-994-9500
    Fax: 920-994-2317
                 www.cedarvalleycheesestore.com
Cheese
Owner: Tracy Hiller
tracy@cedarvalleycheese.com
Sec: William Peterson
Estimated Sales: $6.5 Million
Number Employees: 5-9

2353 Cedar Valley Fish Market
218 Division St
Waterloo, IA 50703
                                   319-236-2965
    Fax: 253-761-0504
Seafood
Owner: Marilyn Ruvino
Estimated Sales: $370,000
Number Employees: 5-9

2354 Cedar's Mediterranean Foods
50 Foundation Ave
Ward Hill, MA 01835
                                   978-372-8010
                 www.cedarsfoods.com
Mediterranean foods, including hommus, tzatziki, salads, dips, salsa and pita chips
President & CEO: Charlie Hanna
VP: Bruce Rubin
Number of Brands: 1
Type of Packaging: Consumer
Brands:
    CEDAR'S

2355 Cedarlane Foods
1135 E Artesia Blvd
Carson, CA 90746-1602
                                   310-886-7720
    Fax: 310-886-7733 800-826-3322
                 feedback@cedarlanefoods.com
                 www.cedarlanefoods.com
Natural refrigerated and frozen foods including enchiladas, burritos, pot pies, tortillas, specialty breads, pizza and lasagna; varieties include vegetarian, low-fat and cholesterol and lactose-free
Founder, President: Robert Atallah
terry@franklyfresh.com
Vice President: Terry Mayo
Sales Exec: Terry Mayo
Number Employees: 250-499
Square Footage: 64000
Type of Packaging: Consumer, Food Service, Private Label
Brands:
    Cedarlane
    Soypreme

2356 Cedarlane Natural FoodsToc
1135 E Artesia Blvd
Carson, CA 90746-1602
                                   310-527-7833
                 www.cedarlanefoods.com
Breakfast selections, tamales and vegetarian foods
CEO: Robert Atallah
ktorosyan@franklyfresh.com
Number Employees: 5-9
Type of Packaging: Private Label

2357 Cedarvale Food Products
11 Wiltshire Avenue
Toronto, ON M6N 2V7
Canada
                                   416-656-3330
    Fax: 416-656-6803 lounsbury@lounsbury.ca
Mustard and sauces including horseradish, cocktail, mint and tartar; importer of tomato paste
VP: David Higgins
Manager Export Sales/Marketing: Tim Higgins
General Manager: Gil Marks
Estimated Sales: $487,000
Number Employees: 12
Square Footage: 60000
Parent Co: Lounsbury Foods
Type of Packaging: Consumer, Food Service, Private Label, Bulk
Brands:
    Cedarvale
    Lounsbury
    Wiltshire

2358 Ceilidh Fisherman's Cooperative
158 Main St
Port Hood, NS B0E 2W0
Canada
                                   902-787-2666
    Fax: 902-787-2388 www.ceilidhlobster.ca
Processor and exporter of salted cod, live lobster and crab.
General Manager: Bernie MacDonald
Year Founded: 1985
Estimated Sales: $6 Million
Number Employees: 35
Type of Packaging: Consumer, Food Service, Private Label, Bulk

2359 Celebrity Cheesecake
655 Nova Drive
Suite 304
Davie, FL 33317
                                   877-986-2253
Cheesecakes, pies, cakes
Owner: Anita Phillips
President: Susie Bernstein
Estimated Sales: $500,000-$1 Million
Number Employees: 10-19
Square Footage: 24000
Brands:
    Celebrity Cheesecakes

2360 Celebrity Tea, LLC
7010 East Adamo Drive
Building C Unit 1
Tampa, FL 33619
                                   813-600-3317
Ready-to-drink teas made from natural and USDA-certified organic ingredients.
Type of Packaging: Consumer
Brands:
    CELEBRI TEA

2361 Cell-Nique
65 East Avenue, 3rd Floor
Norwalk, CT 06851
                                   888-417-9343
                 dan@cell-nique.com www.cell-nique.com
Organic Super Green drinks made with foods such as Spirulina, Chlorella and Blue-green algae as well as cereal grass juices and sprouts like barley, wheat, oats and alfalfa. Cell-nique also contains the high anti-oxidant Super Fruitslike Noni, Goji berry, and Açaí.

Food Manufacturers / A-Z

Co-founder, CEO and CFO: Dan Ratner
Co-Founder and CMO: Donna Ratner
Contact: Candi Sterling
candi@healthybrandsco.com
National Operations Manager: Shaun Conners
Warehouse & Distribution: Victor Pinto
Type of Packaging: Consumer

2362 Cellone Bakery Inc
193 Chartiers Ave
Pittsburgh, PA 15205-3321
412-922-5335
Fax: 412-922-6940 800-334-8438
info@Cellones.com www.cellones.com
Bread and rolls
Owner: Brandon Cellone
Owner: Randy Cellone
Management Info Systems Manager: Lori Edward
bcellone@cellonebakery.net
Operations Manager: Gary Cellone
Production Manager: Dean Cellone
Estimated Sales: Less Than $500,000
Number Employees: 5-9
Type of Packaging: Private Label

2363 Cellucon Inc
19994 Meredith Dr
Strathmore, CA 93267
559-568-0190
Fax: 559-568-0271 www.cellucon.com
Natural yucca extract
Owner: John Yale
Manager: Carol Hilty
Administrative Assistant: Kelly Smith
Estimated Sales: $1-3 Million
Number Employees: 10-19
Square Footage: 40000

2364 Celsius
2424 North Federal Hwy
Boca Raton, FL 33431
866-423-5748
www.celsius.com
Fitness drink
Interim President & CEO: John Fieldly
EVP, Marketing & Innovation: Vanessa Walker
SVP, Sales-North America: Jon McKillop
Number of Brands: 1
Number of Products: 23
Type of Packaging: Consumer
Brands:
  CELSIUS LIVE FIT
  CELSIUS HEAT

2365 Celtic Sea Salt
Arden, NC 28704
800-867-7258
www.celticseasalt.com
Sea salt

2366 Centennial Farms
199 Jackson St
Augusta, MO 63332-1721
636-228-4338
centfarmaug@aol.com
www.centennialfarms.biz
Apple butters
Owner: Robert Knoernschild
Estimated Sales: Less Than $500,000
Number Employees: 5-9
Number of Brands: 1
Number of Products: 8
Type of Packaging: Consumer, Private Label

2367 (HQ)Centennial Food Corporation
4412 Manilla Rd
Calgary, AB T2G 4A7
Canada
403-214-0044
Fax: 403-214-1656
www.centennialfoodservice.com
Processor and exporter of fresh and frozen meat products including spiced and formed ground beef, beef patties, battered and breaded steaks and cutlets, vacuum sealed and aged beef cuts, bacon wrapped scallops and marinated short ribs; importer of beef and seafood
Chairman: Ron Kovitz
CEO/President: J Kalef
VP/General Manager: Nashir Vasanji
Number Employees: 250-499
Type of Packaging: Consumer, Food Service, Private Label, Bulk
Other Locations:
  Centennial Food Corp.
  Calgary AB
Brands:
  Canadian Gourmet
  Centennial
  Mastercut

2368 Centennial Mills
601 1st St
Cheney, WA 99004-1653
509-235-6216
Fax: 509-235-2144
Flour
Manager: Luke Burger
Estimated Sales: Under $500,000
Number Employees: 10-19
Parent Co: Archer Daniels Midland Company
Type of Packaging: Consumer, Food Service, Bulk

2369 Center Locker Svc
107 S Public St
Center, MO 63436-1217
573-267-3343
Fax: 573-267-3392 800-884-0737
centerlocker@att.net www.centerlocker.com
Beef, pork, sausage and meat and meat products
Owner: Dennis McMillen
Co-Owner: Debby McMillen
Estimated Sales: $500,000-$1 Million
Number Employees: 1-4
Type of Packaging: Food Service, Bulk

2370 Centerchem, Inc.
20 Glover Ave # 4n
Norwalk, CT 06850-1234
203-822-9800
Fax: 203-822-9820 orders@centerchem.com
www.centerchem.com
Manufacturer & distributor of pectin, bittering agents, essential oils, polishing and glazing agents, waxes, release agents & encapsulated specialty ingredients.
President: Jon Packer
Chief Financial Officer & Treasurer: Mary Fcc
Vice President: John Dondero
Marketing Coordinator: Claude Dougherty
Vice President Sales: Ray Sourial
Tech. Sales Rep.: Jennifer Czerner
Estimated Sales: $6.7 Million
Brands:
  Capol®
  Maxinvert®
  Candurin®
  Rapidase®
  Pearex®
  Hazyme®
  Klerzyme®

2371 Centflor Manufacturing Co
545 W 45th St # L1
New York, NY 10036-3490
212-246-8307
Fax: 212-262-9717 www.mcmahonmed.com
Processor and exporter of essential oils and aromatic chemicals
President: Robert Beller
robjbeller@gmail.com
General Manager: Gloria Rose
Estimated Sales: $1.5 Million
Number Employees: 5-9
Square Footage: 48000

2372 Cento Fine Foods
100 Cento Blvd
West Deptford, NJ 08086-2133
856-853-5445
Fax: 856-853-2843 www.cento.com
Manufacturer of over 1,000 Italian products, including tomato brand products, oils, and vinegars.
President: Rick Ciccotelli
sales4@cento.com
National Sales Manager: Bart Ricci
sales4@cento.com
Number Employees: 100-249

2373 Central Bakery
711 Pleasant St
Fall River, MA 02723
508-675-7620
Fax: 508-677-4523
Bread & other bakery products
Owner: Tibeiro Lopes
Contact: David Lopes
dlopes@centralbakery.com

Estimated Sales: $2.3,000,000
Number Employees: 10-19

2374 Central Bean Co
815 E St SW
Quincy, WA 98848-1073
509-787-1544
Fax: 509-787-4040 info@centralbean.com
www.centralbean.com
Dry bean supplier to canneries and packagers.
President: Tom Grebb
tom@centralbean.com
Estimated Sales: G
Number Employees: 10-19
Type of Packaging: Consumer, Food Service, Private Label, Bulk

2375 Central California Raisin Packing Co, Inc.
5316 S Del Rey Ave
Del Rey, CA 93616
559-888-2195
Dried apricots, mixed fruit, peaches, prunes, raisins
President: Dan Milinovich
Estimated Sales: $1.5 Million
Number Employees: 10
Number of Brands: 1
Brands:
  Del Cara

2376 (HQ)Central Coast Seafood
5495 Traffic Way
Atascadero, CA 93422-4246
805-462-3474
Fax: 805-466-6613 800-273-4741
www.ccseafood.com
Wholesaler/distributor and exporter of fresh seafood; serving the food service market in California
CEO: Giovanni Comin
VP Sales/Marketing: Nancy Osorio
Estimated Sales: $5.9 Million
Number Employees: 5-9
Square Footage: 40000
Other Locations:
  Central Coast Seafoods
  Morro Bay CA

2377 Central Dairies
PO Box 8588
Station A
St Johns, NL A1B 3P2
Canada
709-364-7531
Fax: 709-364-8714 800-563-6455
www.centraldairies.com
Milk, cultured products, frozen desserts, cheese, spreads, juices and drinks
VP: Deve Collins
CEO: Kennetch Peacock
VP/General Manager: David Collins
Manager Sales/Marketing: Ron Croke
Plant Manager: Clarence Chaytor
Parent Co: Farmers Co-op Dairy
Type of Packaging: Consumer
Brands:
  Farmers Ice Cream
  Flavoured Milk

2378 Central Dairy
610 Madison St
Jefferson City, MO 65101-3199
573-635-6148
Fax: 573-634-3028 www.centraldairy.biz
Milk, egg nogs, half and half, sour cream. onion dips, cottage cheese, orange juice, bottled water, and ice cream.
President: Gale Hackman
CEO: Chris Hackman
VP: Steve Raithel
Controller: Mike Fennewald
Estimated Sales: $20-50 Million
Number Employees: 50-99

2379 Central Meat & Provision
1603 National Ave
San Diego, CA 92113-1008
619-239-1391
Fax: 619-239-1634 www.centralmeatco.com
Beef, pork and veal
Owner/President: Robert Kuhlken
rkuhlken@centralmeat-market.com
VP Key Accounts: Kevin Gawle
Sales Manager: John Kuhlken
VP Operations: Bert Risley

Food Manufacturers / A-Z

2380 Central Meat Market
113 Gano St
Providence, RI 02906-3822
401-751-6935
Fax: 401-223-0125 www.centralmeatmarket.com
Portuguese sausages
Owner: Tony Cabaral
cabaraltony@centralmeat-market.com
Estimated Sales: $510,000
Number Employees: 5-9

2381 Central Milling Co
122 E Center St
Logan, UT 84321-4607
435-752-6625
Fax: 435-753-7960 reception@centralmilling.com
www.centralmilling.com
Pancake flour, Golden West All Purpose Flour, Red Rose All Purpose Flour, whole wheat flour, and Germade.
President: H Roscoe Weston
Controller: Shaun Owen
Quality Control: Jeff Daniels
Mill Manager: Manuel Solis
Mill Manager: Nathan Shumway
Mill Manager: Melvin Alberta
Secretary: James Weston
Mill Manager/Electrician: Kurtis Williams
Plant Manager: Fred Weston
Estimated Sales: $10-20 Million
Number Employees: 10-19
Type of Packaging: Consumer, Food Service
Brands:
   Golden West
   Red Rose

2382 Central Snacks
1700 N Pearl St
Carthage, MS 39051-8635
601-267-3112
Fax: 601-267-5249 porkskin@aol.com
www.centralsnacks.com
Pork skins
President: Randy Carson
porkskin@aol.com
Estimated Sales: $2.5-5,000,000
Number Employees: 10-19

2383 Central Soyfoods
710 East 22nd Street
Suite C
Lawrence, KS 66046
785-312-8698
Soybean oil manufacturer
General Partner: Jim Cooley
Plant Manager: Lori Kruger
Estimated Sales: $700,000
Number Employees: 12

2384 Centreside Dairy
61 Lorne Street North
Renfrew, ON K7V 1K8
Canada
613-432-2914
Fax: 613-432-5157 800-889-9974
info@traceysicecream.ca traceysicecream.ca
Ice cream; wholesaler/distributor of dairy products
President: Mark Tracey
General Manager: Melany Tracey
Estimated Sales: $2 Million
Number Employees: 15
Type of Packaging: Consumer, Food Service, Private Label
Brands:
   Economy
   Premium
   Tracey's

2385 Century Agricultural Products LLC
7085 Morganton Rd
Greenback, TN 37742
865-980-8523
Beef; pickles and preserves
Co-Owner: Christopher Burger
Co-Owner: Shona Burger
Admistrator: Dana Couch
Type of Packaging: Food Service, Bulk
Brands:
   Century Harvest Farms

2386 (HQ)Century Blends LLC
11110 Pepper Rd # A
Hunt Valley, MD 21031-1204
410-771-6606
Fax: 410-771-6608 jwaynewheeler@sun-ripe.com
Processor and exporter of bakery and confectionery supplies and mixes including dry bar, salad dressings and sauces
Owner: J Wayne Wheeler
Production Manager: Tim Wheeler
Estimated Sales: $1,000,000
Number Employees: 5-9
Type of Packaging: Food Service, Bulk
Brands:
   Coag-U-Loid
   Condex
   Pie Rite
   Sun-Ripe
   T.H. Angermeier
   Veg-A-Loid

2387 Century Foods Intl LLC
400 Century Ct
Sparta, WI 54656-2468
608-269-1900
Fax: 608-269-1910 800-269-1901
www.centuryfoods.com
Century Foods International is a manufacturer of nutritional powders and ready-to-drink beverages under private label and contract manufacturing agreements for food, sports, health and nutritional supplement industries. Other services provided include agglomeration, blending and instantizing, research and development, analytical testing, and packaging from bulk to consumer size.
President: Tom Miskowski
VP R&D: Julie Wagner
VP Sales/Marketing: Gene Quast
VP Operations: Wade Nolte
Number Employees: 250-499
Square Footage: 1680000
Parent Co: Hormel Foods Corporation
Type of Packaging: Private Label, Bulk
Brands:
   Cenprem
   Lacey Delite
   Pizazz
   Ready Cheese

2388 Cereal Food Processors
425 West 500 South Street
Salt Lake City, UT 84101
801-355-2981
info@cerealfood.com
Wheat flour
President: J. Breck Barton
VP: J. Brent Wall
SVP, Sales: Timothy S. Miller
VP, Operations: John C. Erker
Plant Manager: Rick Thomas
Plant Superintendant: Max Horrocks
Estimated Sales: $10-24.9 Million
Number Employees: 10-19
Parent Co: Cereal Food Processors

2389 Cereal Food Processors Inc
416 N Main St
Mcpherson, KS 67460-3404
620-241-2410
Fax: 620-241-7167 800-835-2067
b.wall@cerealfood.com www.cerealfood.com
Miller of flour including, bakery, bread, all-purpose and self-rising; also, pancake and waffle mix, wheat bran and mill feeds
President: J. Breck Barton
Chairman: Fred Merrill
EVP, Finance & Admin: Steven J. Heeney
Vice President: Greg Edelblute
Plant Superintendent: Kendall Allison
SVP, Sales: Timothy S. Miller
Vice President of Operations: John C. Erker
Vice President: Wayne Ford
Plant Manager: Max Streit
Estimated Sales: $10-20 Million
Number Employees: 20-49
Square Footage: 123810
Type of Packaging: Consumer, Food Service, Private Label, Bulk
Brands:
   America's Best
   Bake-Rite H & R
   Kansas Sun
   Utility
   W-R

2390 (HQ)Cereal Food Processors Inc
2001 Shawnee Mission Pkwy #110
Mission Woods, KS 66205-2097
913-890-6300
Fax: 913-890-6382 info@cerealfood.com
Manufacturer and exporter of flour.
President: J. Breck Barton
Executive VP: Mark L Dobbins
m.dobbins@cerealfoods.com
Year Founded: 1972
Estimated Sales: $20-50 Million
Number Employees: 20-49
Type of Packaging: Consumer
Other Locations:
   Cereal Food Processors Plant
   Los Angeles CA
   Cereal Food Processors Plant
   Kansas City MO
   Cereal Food Processors Plant
   McPherson KS
   Cereal Food Processors Plant
   Billings MT
   Cereal Food Processors Plant
   Great Falls MT
   Cereal Food Processors Plant
   Cleveland OH
   Cereal Food Processors Plant
   Portland OR
   Cereal Food Processors Plant
   Ogden UT
   Cereal Food Processors Plant
   Salt Lake City UT
   Cereal Food Processors Plant
   Montreal QC

2391 Cereal Ingredients, Inc.
4720 S 13th St
Leavenworth, KS 66048-5585
913-727-3434
Fax: 913-727-3681 info@cerealingredients.com
www.cerealingredients.com
specialized ingredients developed from wheat fiber concentrates.
Chairman, CEO: Bob Hatch
Vice President: Bruce Hoffmann
Estimated Sales: $1-2.5 Million
Number Employees: 50-99

2392 Ceres Fruit Juices
6370 Lusk Blvd
8th Floor
San Diego, CA 92121B9
800-778-6498
info@ceresjuices.com www.ceresjuices.com
Fruit juices

2393 Cericola Farms
Bradford, ON L3Z 2A4
Canada
905-939-2962
www.cericola.com
Organic, antibiotic-free chicken producer.
President: Amedeo Cericola
VP: Anthony Cericola
Co-Owner/VP: Mary Cericola
Marketing Director: Amedeo Cericola
Type of Packaging: Consumer, Food Service, Private Label, Bulk
Brands:
   Surefresh Foods

2394 Certi Fresh Foods Inc
842 Flint Ave
Wilmington, CA 90744-3739
310-221-6262
Fax: 310-427-6061 sobel@certi-fresh.com
www.certi-fresh.com
Seafood processing and distribution
Owner: Antonino Palma
CFO/COO: Scott Obel
Quality Control: Michael Jamehdor
VP of Sales & Marketing: Maria White
Director of Sales: Pete Palma
apalma@certi-fresh.com
Operator Specialist: Mario Galaz
Plant Manager: Tom Dukescherer
Purchasing: Revi Ayla
Number Employees: 50-99
Type of Packaging: Consumer, Food Service
Brands:
   Certi-Fresh

Food Manufacturers / A-Z

2395 Certi-Fresh Foods, Inc
842 Flint Ave
Wilmington, CA 90744
910-221-6262
Fax: 310-427-6060 www.certi-fresh.com
Seafood
CEO/Owner: Nino Palma
President/COO/Owner: Pete Palma
US Sales Manager: Mario Galaz
International And Domestic Procurement: Ramiro Ayala

2396 Certified Piedmontese Beef
100 West Harvest Drive
PO Box 82545
Lincoln, NE 68521
402-458-4442
Fax: 402-458-4531 800-414-3487
info@piedmontese.com www.piedmontese.com
Prime cuts of beef
President: Billy Swain

2397 Cervantes Food ProductsInc
1125 Arizona St SE
Albuquerque, NM 87108-4829
505-254-9414
Fax: 505-256-1789 877-982-4453
www.cervantessalsa.com
Chiles: red and green; fresh, dried, canned, frozen
Owner: Richard Gonzales
richard@cervantessalsa.com
Estimated Sales: $1-3 Million
Number Employees: 5-9

2398 Chacewater Winery and Olive Mill
5625 Gabby Lane
Kelseyville, CA 95451
707-279-2995
Fax: 707-279-1972 info@chacewaterwine.com
www.chacewaterwine.com
Fine wines, olive oils, and soaps
Owner/General Manager: Paul Manuel
Mill Master: Emilio De La Cruz
Winemaker: Mark Burch
Number Employees: 10

2399 Chaddsford Winery
632 Baltimore Pike
Chadds Ford, PA 19317-9305
610-388-6221
Fax: 610-388-0360 info@chaddsford.com
www.chaddsford.com
Wines
Owner: Eric Miller
Special Events Planner: Betsie Williamson
Marketing Director: Lee Miller
Sales Director: William Harris
Public Relations: Larry D'Antonio
Operations Manager: James Osborn
Estimated Sales: $1-2.5 Million
Number Employees: 20-49
Type of Packaging: Private Label
Brands:
  Chaddsford

2400 Chai Diaries
23052 H Alicia Pkwy
Suite 603
Mission Viejo, CA 92692
917-460-6828
cs@mychaidiaries.com
www.mychaidiaries.com
Premium organic teas
Principal: Ami Bhansali
Year Founded: 2013

2401 Chalet Cheese Co-Op
N4858 County Road N
Monroe, WI 53566-9355
608-325-4343
Fax: 608-325-4409
Cheese
Manager: Myron Olson
chalet@cppweb.com
Owner: Hans Wampfler
Estimated Sales: $2.5 Million
Number Employees: 20-49
Type of Packaging: Private Label

2402 Chalet Debonne Vineyards
7743 Doty Rd
Madison, OH 44057
440-466-3485
Fax: 440-466-6753 info@debonne.com
www.debonne.com
Wines and vineyard
Owner: Anthony Debevc
Treasurer: Rose Debevc
Vice President: Tony Debevc
Contact: Beth Debevc
bdebevc@debonne.com
Estimated Sales: $2.5-5 Million
Number Employees: 10-19

2403 Chalk Hill Estate Winery
10300 Chalk Hill Rd
Healdsburg, CA 95448-9558
707-657-4839
Fax: 707-838-9687 concierge@chalkhill.com
www.chalkhill.com
Wines
Vice President: Mark Lingenfelder
Head Winemaker: Steve Nelson
Estimated Sales: $10-20 Million
Number Employees: 50-99
Number of Brands: 2
Type of Packaging: Private Label
Brands:
  Chalk Hill Estate Bottled
  Chalk Hill Estate Selection

2404 Challenge Dairy Products, Inc.
6701 Donion Way
Dublin, CA 94568
877-883-2479
Fax: 925-551-7591 800-733-2479
consumerinfo@challengedairy.com
www.challengedairy.com
Processor and exporter of butter and dehydrated milk; wholesaler/distributor of butter and frozen foods.
President, CEO: Irv Holmes
Controller: Geoffrey Uy
SR VP Retail & Foodservice: Tim Anderson
EDI Coordinator: Michael Jenkins
Office Manager: Daisrea Smith
Estimated Sales: $500 Thousand
Number Employees: 175
Number of Brands: 2
Square Footage: 8500
Type of Packaging: Consumer, Food Service, Private Label, Bulk
Brands:
  Challenge
  Challenge Danish

2405 Chalone Vineyard
32020 Stonewall Canyon Rd
Soledad, CA 93960
831-678-1717
Fax: 831-678-2742 www.chalonevineyard.com
Wines
Manager: Robert Cook
robert.cook@biateo.com
Public Relations: Lynn Johnston
General Manager/Winemaker: Dan Karlsen
Estimated Sales: $5-10 Million
Number Employees: 5-9
Parent Co: Chalone Wine Group

2406 Cham Cold Brew Tea
300 Park Ave
New York, NY 10022
646-926-0206
www.drinkcham.com
Cold brewed teas
Co-Founder & CEO: Niko Nikolaou
Number of Brands: 1
Number of Products: 3
Type of Packaging: Consumer
Brands:
  CHAM COLD BREW TEA

2407 Chambord
850 Dixie Highway
Louisville, KY 40210
215-425-9300
Fax: 215-425-9438 800-523-3811
Brown-Forman@b-f.com
www.chambordchannel.com
Raspberry liquor
CEO: Lawson Whiting
CFO: Jane Morreau
External Communications: Elizabeth Conway
Estimated Sales: $26 Million
Number Employees: 120
Square Footage: 188000
Parent Co: Brown-Forman
Type of Packaging: Private Label
Brands:
  Chambord

2408 Chameleon Cold Brew
P.O. Box 4518
Austin, TX 78765-4518
chameleoncoldbrew.com
Cold brewed coffee; organic; instant; and concentrates.
Co-Founder: Chris Campbell
Co-Founder: Steve Williams
Year Founded: 2010
Number Employees: 40
Type of Packaging: Food Service, Private Label

2409 Champignon North America Inc
456 Sylvan Ave
Suite 4
Englewood Cliffs, NJ 07632-2707
201-871-7211
Fax: 201-871-7214 info@champignon-usa.com
www.champignon-international.com
Gourmet cheeses.
President: Birgit Bernhard
VP: Olaf Glaser
Estimated Sales: $8 Million
Number Employees: 1-4
Number of Brands: 2
Brands:
  Brie W/Garlic De Luxe
  Cambozola
  Champignon
  Hofmeister
  Mirabo
  Montagnolo
  Rougette
  Royal Bavarian

2410 Champion Beverages
44 Talmadge Hill Road
Darien, CT 06820-2125
203-655-9026
Fax: 203-655-0676
Beer, dairy drinks
President/CEO: Joseph Tighe
COO: Elaine Tighe
Estimated Sales: Under $500,000
Number Employees: 1-4
Brands:
  Erin's Rock Amber and Stout
  Smoothie Sparkling Choc.Egg Cream
  Stallion X Malt Liquor

2411 Champion Nutrition Inc
1301 Sawgrass Corporate Pkwy
Sunrise, FL 33323-2813
954-233-3300
Fax: 925-689-0821 800-225-4831
www.champion-nutrition.com
Processor and exporter of sports nutrition supplements
Owner: Malcolm Borg
VP Finance: Jannie Motta
Industry Contact: Christy Olson
Estimated Sales: Less Than $500,000
Number Employees: 1-4
Square Footage: 18188
Brands:
  Heavyweight Gainer 900
  Met-Max
  Metabolol
  Muscle Nitro
  Oxi Pro Metabolol
  Revenge

2412 Champlain Valley Apiaries
504 Washington Street Ext
Middlebury, VT 05753-8878
802-388-7724
Fax: 802-388-1653 800-841-7334
cva@together.net
www.champlainvalleyhoney.com
Liquid and natural crystallized honey

Food Manufacturers / A-Z

Owner: Charles Mraz
cva@together.net
Office Manager: Sue Synder
Bee Keeper: James Gabriel
Estimated Sales: $2.5-5 Million
Number Employees: 1-4
Type of Packaging: Consumer

2413 Champlain Valley Milling Corp
6679 Main St
Westport, NY 12993
518-962-4711
Fax: 518-962-8799
info@champlainvalleymilling.com
Organic and kosher whole grain flour including spring wheat, stone ground, soy, rye, white, whole pastry, pancake, etc
President: Sam Sherman
samsherman@champlainvalleymilling.com
Vice President: Paul Barton
Operations Manager: Donald White
Estimated Sales: $5-9.9 Million
Number Employees: 5-9
Type of Packaging: Private Label
Brands:
    Champ

2414 Champoeg Wine Cellars Inc
10375 Champoeg Rd NE
Aurora, OR 97002-8657
503-678-2144
Fax: 503-678-1024
champoeg@champoegwine.com
www.champoegwine.com
Wines
Owner: Lounna Eggert
leggert@champoegwine.com
Estimated Sales: Less Than $500,000
Number Employees: 1-4

2415 Champs Chicken
170 Commerce Dr
PO Box 160
Holts Summit, MO 65043-1098
573-896-2500
Fax: 573-896-9583   888-581-9188
customer.service@PFSbrands.com
www.champschicken.com
Chicken products
CEO: Shawn Burcham
CFO: Trevor Monnig
VP, Human Resources: Carla Dowden
VP, Marketing: Carl Christenson
VP, Operations: Brock Blaise
Number Employees: 50-99

2416 Chandler Foods Inc
Greensboro, NC 27407
336-299-1934
Fax: 336-854-4649   800-537-6219
cfoods@chandlerfoodsinc.com
www.chandlerfoodsinc.com
Barbecue products including pork, chicken and beef; also, chili products including frozen, hot dog and con carne
President: Jeff Chandler
jeffc@chandlerfoodsinc.com
Estimated Sales: $5-9.9 Million
Number Employees: 20-49
Square Footage: 159600
Type of Packaging: Food Service
Brands:
    Carolina Barbecue
    Chandler Foods

2417 Chang Food Company
13941 Nautilus Dr
Garden Grove, CA 92843-4026
714-265-9990
Fax: 714-265-9996   www.changs.com
Process frozen egg rolls, spring rolls, soba noodle, egg noodle bowls (stir fried tofu, vegetable, etc)
President: Van Nguyen
service@changs.com
Manager: Nhuan Nguyen
Estimated Sales: $2.5-$3 Million
Number Employees: 21
Square Footage: 19600
Type of Packaging: Consumer, Food Service, Private Label, Bulk
Brands:
    Chang Food

2418 Channel Fish ProcessingCo Inc
18 Food Mart Rd
Boston, MA 02118-2802
617-464-3366
Fax: 617-464-3377   800-536-3474
t.zaffiro@channelfish.com   www.channelfish.com
Fresh and frozen seafood.
President: John Zaffiro
Owner: Roy Zaffiro
Director, Business Development: Thomas Zaffiro
Estimated Sales: $45 Million
Number Employees: 50-99
Number of Brands: 3
Type of Packaging: Consumer, Food Service, Private Label
Other Locations:
    Gloucester MA
Brands:
    Channel
    Fish Crunchies
    North Atlantic

2419 Channel Fish Processing
88 Commercial St
Gloucester, MA 01930-5096
978-283-4121
Fax: 978-283-5948   800-457-0054
t.zaffiro@channelfish.com
Processor and exporter of frozen catfish, cod, halibut, herring, smelt, squid, shrimp, scallops and whiting; portion-controlled breaded and prepared seafood
President: Frank Cefalo
Sales Manager: Joe Bertolino
Contact: Jim Cross
jcross@channelfish.com
Operations Manager: James Stuart
Estimated Sales: $4.20 Million
Number Employees: 20-49
Square Footage: 160000
Type of Packaging: Consumer, Food Service
Brands:
    Better Buy
    Courageous Captain's
    North Atlantic

2420 Channing Rudd Cellars
PO Box 426
Middletown, CA 95461-0426
707-987-2209
Wines
President: J Rudd
Sales: Reese Grandstaff
Sales: Darrel Burns
Number Employees: 20-49

2421 Chaparral Gardens
16422 Morro Rd
Atascadero, CA 93422-1017
USA
805-703-0829
Fax: 805-461-1099
artisans@chaparralgardens.com
www.cgvinegar.com
Marinades, balsamic vinegar, olive oil
Owners/Founders: Craig & Cari Clark
craig@chaparralgardens.com
Estimated Sales: 230,000
Number Employees: 4

2422 Chappaqua Crunch
65 Tedesco St
Marblehead, MA 01945-1039
781-631-8118
Fax: 781-631-8113
Granola, snack foods
President: Debbie Waugh
Estimated Sales: Under $500,000
Number Employees: 1-4

2423 Chappellet Winery
1581 Sage Canyon Rd
St Helena, CA 94574-9628
707-963-7136
Fax: 707-963-7445   800-494-6379
customerservice@chappellet.com
www.chappellet.com
Wines
Owner: Swetha Anbarasan
Founder: Molly Chappallet
Owner: Jon-Mark Chappellet
Marketing/Sales: Cyril Chappellet
Director National Sales: Steve Tamburelli
sanbarasan@cisco.com
Winery/Vineyard Operations: Jon Mark
Winemaker: Phillip Corallo-Titus
Vineyard Manager: David Pirio
Purchasing Manager: Carissa Chappellet
Estimated Sales: $2.5 Million
Number Employees: 20-49
Type of Packaging: Private Label
Brands:
    Chappallet

2424 Char Crust
3017 North Lincoln Avenue
Chicago, IL 60657-4242
773-528-0600
Fax: 773-472-1101   800-311-9884
customerservice@charcrust.com
Dry-rub seasonings for all meat and fish
Founder/President: Bernard Silver
Director/Marketing: Susan Eriksen
Estimated Sales: $500,000-$1 Million
Number Employees: 5-9
Brands:
    Char Crust

2425 Char-Wil Canning Company
5620 Landing Neck Road
Trappe, MD 21643-3318
410-476-3167
Fax: 410-943-3580
Processor and canner of whole and peeled tomatoes
Owner/Partner: Charles Adams
Number Employees: 6
Type of Packaging: Consumer, Food Service, Private Label, Bulk
Brands:
    Char-Wil

2426 Charcuterie LaTour Eiffel
1020, boul. MichŠle-Bohec
Blainville, QC J7C 5E2
Canada
418-687-2840
Fax: 418-688-9558   800-361-0001
www.toureiffel.ca
Processor and exporter of fresh and frozen pork
Marketing Director: Francois Couture
Parent Co: McCain Foods USA
Type of Packaging: Bulk
Brands:
    Bilopage
    Tour Eiffel

2427 Charissa
8595 Cox Ln
Unit 3
Cutchogue, NY 11935
631-734-8878
charissaspice.com
Morrocan seasonings
Co-Founder: Earl Fultz
Co-Founder: Gloria Fultz
Number Employees: 4
Type of Packaging: Private Label

2428 Charles B. Mitchell Vineyards
8221 Stoney Creek Road Fair Play
Somerset, CA 95684
530-620-3467
Fax: 530-620-1005   800-704-9463
info@charlesbmitchell.com
www.charlesbmitchell.com
Wine
Owner: Michael Conti
Estimated Sales: $2.5-5 Million
Number Employees: 5-9
Type of Packaging: Private Label

2429 Charles Chocolates
535 Florida St
San Francisco, CA 94110
www.charleschocolates.com
Handmade chocolates
Founder: Chuck Siegel

Food Manufacturers / A-Z

2430 Charles H Baldwin & Sons
1 Center St
P.O.Box 372
West Stockbridge, MA 01266-9502
413-232-7785
Fax: 413-232-0114 www.baldwinextracts.com
Flavoring extracts and flavors, maple table syrup and supplier of baking supplies.
Owner: Jackie Moffatt
jackie@baldwinextracts.com
Estimated Sales: $500,000-$1 Million
Number Employees: 1-4
Brands:
  Baldwin

2431 Charles H. Parks & Company
2405 Hoopers Island Rd
Fishing Creek, MD 21634
410-397-3400
Fax: 410-397-3400
Fresh, canned and pasteurized crabmeat; also, fresh crabs
President: Virgil Ruark Jr
Estimated Sales: $3-5 Million
Number Employees: 10-19
Square Footage: 9000
Type of Packaging: Consumer
Brands:
  Captain Charlie

2432 Charles Krug Winery
2800 Main St
St Helena, CA 94574-9502
707-967-2200
Fax: 707-967-2291 www.charleskrug.com
Fine wines
Winemaker, CK Mondavi Vineyards: Marc Mondavi
Winemaker, Charles Krug: Peter Mondavi
Year Founded: 1861
Number Employees: 100-249
Brands:
  Charles Krug
  CK Mondavi

2433 Charles Poultry Company
2943 Charlestown Road
Lancaster, PA 17603-9758
717-872-7621
Fax: 717-872-9570
Free range and all natural chicken and turkey including whole cut up, cutlets, legs, wings, whole breasts, drums, thighs, etc
President: Ken Charles
VP: Richard Charles
Estimated Sales: $20-50 Million
Number Employees: 20-49
Square Footage: 9000
Parent Co: Charles Poultry Live Broker
Type of Packaging: Consumer, Food Service, Private Label, Bulk

2434 Charles Rockel & Son
4303 Smith Rd
Cincinnati, OH 45212-4236
513-631-3009
Fax: 513-631-3083
Food brokers of dairy/deli products, frozen foods, general merchandise, groceries, industrial ingredients, etc
President: Charles Rockel
CFO: Don Rockel
Estimated Sales: $2.5-5 Million
Number Employees: 3

2435 Charles Spinetta Winery
12557 Steiner Rd
PO Box 717
Plymouth, CA 95669-9510
209-245-3384
Fax: 209-245-3386
www.charlesspinettawinery.com
Table wine including wines for bulk market
Owner: Charles Spinetta
Estimated Sales: $1-2.5 Million
Number Employees: 1-4
Brands:
  Charles Spinetta Barbera
  Charles Spinetta Primitivo
  Charles Spinetta Zinfanel

2436 Charles Walker North America
2901 Stanley Ave
Fort Worth, TX 76110
817-922-9834
Fax: 817-922-9854 cissy@charlesalaninc.com
www.charlesalanfurniture.com
Furniture manufacturer
Owner: Margaret Sevadjian
Vice President: Jim Boston
Operations Manager: Steve McDonald
Square Footage: 120
Brands:
  Waiker Conveyor Belt & Equipment

2437 Charleston Tea Plantation
6617 Maybank Hwy
Wadmalaw Island, SC 29487-7006
843-559-0383
Fax: 843-559-3049 800-443-5987
www.charlestonteaplantation.com
Tea
Owner: William Hall
lfasig@rcbigelow.com
Estimated Sales: $2,900,000
Number Employees: 5-9
Brands:
  American Classic Tea

2438 Charlie Beigg's Sauce Company
4 Heritage Lane
Windham, ME 04062-4984
888-502-8595
sales@charliebeiggs.com
BBQ sauce and salsa.
Head of Sales/Marketing: Paula Standley
Parent Co: Equitythink Holdings, LLC

2439 Charlie Palmer Group
420 Lexington Avenue
Suite 850
New York, NY 10170
212-967-6942
Fax: 212-750-8613 866-458-7224
info@charliepalmer.com www.charliepalmer.com
Pan sauces, dessert sauces
Owner: Charlie Lee
VP, HR: Sabrina Orque
Marketing Manager: Christie Sheffield
Corporate Sales Director: Rick Becker
Estimated Sales: $2.5-5 Million
Number Employees: 50-99
Brands:
  Charlie Palmer

2440 Charlie's Country Sausage
4005 Burdick Expy E
Minot, ND 58701-5462
701-838-6302
Meat products including salami, honey ham and sausage
Owner: Rod Lynch
Estimated Sales: $1-2.5 Million
Number Employees: 5-9

2441 Charlie's Pride
2650 Leonis Boulevard
Vernon, CA 90058
Fax: 323-587-7317 877-866-0992
www.charliespride.com
Prepared meats manufacturer founded in 1969.
Co-CEO: Jim Dickman
Co-CEO: Robert Dickman
CFO: Ted Murphy
VP, Sales: Peter Goldsberry
Plant Manager: Krystal Valle
Purchasing Manager: Yahaira Martinez
Number Employees: 140
Square Footage: 60000
Type of Packaging: Consumer, Food Service, Private Label, Bulk

2442 Charlie's Specialties Inc
2500 Freedland Rd
Hermitage, PA 16148-9022
724-346-2350
Fax: 724-346-1110 contactus@bkcompany.com
www.bkcompany.com
Fancy cookies
President: Jay Thier
jthier@charliesusa.com
Owner: E.G. Byrnes, Jr.
Sales: Stacy Rouse
Plant Manager: Frank Keck
Purchasing: Thomas Byrnes
Estimated Sales: $5-10 Million
Number Employees: 100-249
Number of Products: 45
Square Footage: 96000
Parent Co: Byrnes Kitchen Company

2443 Charlito's Cocina
21-09 Borden Avenue
Brooklyn, NY
718-482-7890
info@charlitoscocina.com
www.charlitoscocina.com
Cured meats.
Founder: Charles Wekselbaum

2444 Charlotte's Confections
1395 El Camino Real
Millbrae, CA 94030-1410
650-589-1126
Fax: 650-589-1923 800-798-2427
lisa@charlottesconfections.com
www.charlottesconfections.com
Boxed chocolates, taffy, caramel, brittle, fudge, marshmallow, and holiday specialties.
President: Jeffrey Sosnick
Vice President: Sean Callaway
Marketing Director: Susan Muniak
Contact: Lisa Olswing
lisa@charlottesconfections.com
Production Coordinator: Jim Macintire
Purchasing Manager: Jim Macintire
Estimated Sales: $5 Million
Number Employees: 50-99
Square Footage: 96000
Type of Packaging: Consumer, Food Service, Private Label, Bulk

2445 Charlton Charters
P.O.Box 637
Warrenton, OR 97146-0637
503-338-0569
Fax: 503-861-3229 dscharters@qwestoffice.net
Seafood, including halibut, salmon, sturgeon, tuna, bottomfish
President: Mark Charlton
Estimated Sales: $2.5-5 Million
Number Employees: 1-4

2446 Charlton Natural Foods, Inc.
8277 Kendall Dr
Huntington Beach, CA 92646-6932
888-611-7753
www.charltonfoods.com
Snack chips; pellets and granules; quinoa; chocolate covered dried fruit.
Director: Norman Suh
norman_suh@charltonfoods.com
Type of Packaging: Private Label

2447 Chartreuse Organic Tea
2837 W Jefferson Ave
Trenton, MI 48183
734-671-3006
Fax: 734-671-3953 866-315-7832
Aromatic herbal teas made with all organic herbs. Created using the leaves, stems, roots, berries and flowers from different plants, containing no actual tealeaves. 90% of the herbs used are USA and USDA certified organic with noneof the herbs coming from China, Sri Lanka or India
Owner: Linda Shannon
Type of Packaging: Consumer

2448 Chas Boggini Co.
733 Bread & Milk Street
Coventry, CT 06238
860-742-2652
Fax: 860-742-7903 glen@bogginicola.com
www.bogginicola.com
Manufacturer and exporter of flavoring extracts
President: Glen Boggini
VP: David Boggini
Estimated Sales: $5-10 Million
Number Employees: 5-9
Type of Packaging: Consumer

2449 Chase & Poe Candy Co
1307 S 59th St
PO Box 698
St Joseph, MO 64507-8124
816-279-1625
Fax: 816-279-1997 800-786-1625
info@cherrymash.com www.cherrymash.com

Food Manufacturers / A-Z

Candy including bagged, bar, brittle, chocolate, coconut, fund raising, multi-pack, vending, Christmas, Easter, Halloween and Valentine
President: Barry Yantis
Contact: Chris Adams
cadams@cherrymash.com
Estimated Sales: $10-20 Million
Number Employees: 20-49
Square Footage: 60000
Type of Packaging: Consumer, Bulk
Brands:
    Cherry Mash
    Poe Brands

2450 Chase Brothers Dairy
595 S Wolff Rd
Oxnard, CA 93033-2101
805-487-4981
Fax: 805-487-2529 800-438-6455
Milk and related products including fluid, half and half, chocolate, low-fat, nonfat, buttermilk, eggnog and shakes; also, juices, concentrates and drinks including orange, etc
President: Glywn Chase Jr
Vice President: S Chase
Contact: Danny Lopez
dlopez262006@yahoo.com
Estimated Sales: $5-10 Million
Number Employees: 20-49
Square Footage: 28000
Parent Co: Hailwood
Type of Packaging: Consumer, Food Service
Brands:
    Chase Brothers
    Gold Coast

2451 Chases Lobster Pound
7935 Hwy 6
PO Box 1
Port Howe, NS B0K 1K0
Canada
902-243-2408
Fax: 902-243-3334 www.chaseslobsterltd.ca
Processor and exporter of fresh and frozen lobster
Owner/Manager: Earl Chase
Number Employees: 10-19
Type of Packaging: Consumer, Food Service, Private Label, Bulk

2452 Chasquis Natural Foods
35 Yale Cres
Unit 300G
St. Catharines, ON L2R 2Y6
Canada
info@chasquisnaturalfoods.com
www.chasquisnaturalfoods.com
Quinoa-based snacks
President: Dave Orosz
Brands:
    Quinoa Krunch

2453 Chateau Anne Marie
6580 NE Mineral Springs Road
Carlton, OR 97111
503-864-2991
Fax: 503-864-2203 www.anneamie.com
Wines
Owner: Robert Pamplin Jr
Director, Sales & Marketing: Kim McLeod
Director of Operations: Tim Lamers
Estimated Sales: $5-10 Million
Number Employees: 20-49

2454 Chateau Boswell Winery
3468 Silverado Trl N
St Helena, CA 94574-9662
707-963-5472
josh@chateauboswellwinery.com
www.chateauboswell.com
Wines
Owner: Susan Boswell
susan@chateauboswellwinery.com
COO: Susan Boswell
Operations Manager: Joshua Peeples
Estimated Sales: Less Than $500,000
Number Employees: 1-4
Type of Packaging: Consumer
Brands:
    Chateau Boswell
    Chateau Boswell Estate
    Jacquelynn Cuv'e
    Jacquelynn Syrah

2455 Chateau Chevre Winery
2030 Hoffman Ln
Napa, CA 94558
707-944-2184
Fax: 707-944-2408
Wines
Owner: Jerry Hazen
Estimated Sales: Less than $100,000
Number Employees: 1-4
Type of Packaging: Private Label

2456 Chateau Diana Winery
6195 Dry Creek Rd
Healdsburg, CA 95448-8100
707-433-6992
Fax: 707-433-0743 info@chateaud.com
www.chateaud.com
Wines
President: Jose Arreola
josea@chateaud.com
Co-Owner & President of Sales: Dawn Manning
CFO: Donna Gibson
Quality Control Manager: Andrew Moore
Production Manager: Jos, Arreola
Estimated Sales: $5-10 Million
Number Employees: 20-49
Brands:
    Chateau Diana

2457 Chateau Food Products Inc
6137 W Cermak Rd
Cicero, IL 60804-2024
708-863-4207
Fax: 708-863-5806 www.chateaufoods.com
Frozen potato and bread dumplings
President: Donald Shotola
don.shotola@gmail.com
VP: Anita Shotola
Production: Jon Shotola
Estimated Sales: $1 Million
Number Employees: 5-9
Square Footage: 40000
Type of Packaging: Consumer, Food Service
Brands:
    Chateau
    Mihel

2458 Chateau Grand Traverse Winery
12239 Center Rd
Traverse City, MI 49686-8558
231-938-6120
Fax: 231-223-4105 www.cgtwines.com
Wines
Owner: Ed O' Keefe
Founder/Chairma: Edward O'Keefe, Sr
VP: Sean O'Keefe
Marketing Coordinator: Elizabeth Smith
NSM: Rhonda Riebow
edokeefe@cgtwines.com
Operations Manager/Controller: Terrie McClelland
Bottling Production Manager: Peter Francisco
Purchasing Manager: Mark Groenevelt
Estimated Sales: $2.5-5 Million
Number Employees: 50-99

2459 Chateau Julien Winery
8940 Carmel Valley Road
Carmel, CA 93923
831-624-2600
Fax: 831-624-6138
Wines
Owner: Robert Brower
Assistant Director of Marketing: Shonda Kroll
National Sales Manager: Bobby Brower
Contact: Fina Dominquez
dominquez@chateaujulien.com
VP Production: Bill Anderson
Estimated Sales: $1-2.5 Million
Number Employees: 10-19
Brands:
    Chateau Julien
    Emerald Bay Coastak
    Garland Ranch

2460 Chateau LA Fayette Reneau
5081 State Route 414
Hector, NY 14841
607-546-2062
Fax: 607-546-2069 800-469-9463
info@clrwine.com www.clrwine.com
Wine
Owner/Purchasing Manager: Dick Reno
clrwine@aol.com
VP: Betty Reno
General Manager: Heather Lodge
Estimated Sales: $1.4 Million
Number Employees: 20-49
Type of Packaging: Private Label

2461 Chateau Montelena Winery
1429 Tubbs Ln
Calistoga, CA 94515-9726
707-942-5105
Fax: 707-942-4221
customer-service@montelena.com
www.montelena.com
Wines
General Partner: James Barrett
Partner: Bo Barrett
Vice President, Sales/Marketing: Brian Baker
Estimated Sales: $35 Million
Number Employees: 20-49
Number of Brands: 2
Brands:
    Chateau Montelena
    Silverado Cellars

2462 Chateau Morrisette Winery
287 Winery Rd SW
Floyd, VA 24091-4033
540-593-2865
info@thedogs.com
www.thedogs.com
Wines
President: David Morrisette
Marketing Director: Keith Toler
Estimated Sales: $10-20 Million
Number Employees: 20-49

2463 Chateau Potelle Winery
1200 Dowdell Ln
St Helena, CA 94574-1407
707-255-9440
Fax: 707-963-3031 info@chateaupotelle.com
www.vgschateaupotelle.com
Wines
Owner: Jean-Noel Fourmeaux
jean-noel@chateaupotelle.com
Purchasing Manager: Ulysses Montre
Estimated Sales: $2.5-5 Million
Number Employees: 5-9
Brands:
    Chateau Potelle

2464 Chateau Ra-Ha
301 Commerce Blvd
Jerseyville, IL 62052
618-639-4841
Fax: 618-639-0510 866-639-4832
info@gtec.net www.gtec.com
Wines
Owner: Paul Arnold
Estimated Sales: $500,000-$1 Million
Number Employees: 1-4

2465 Chateau Souverain
26150 Asti Road
PO Box 245
Cloverdale, CA 95425-245
707-302-7722
Fax: 707-433-5174 877-687-9463
shawna.hernandez@tweglobal.com
www.souverain.com
Cabernet sauvignon, merlot, sauvignon blanc, chardonnay and zinfandel
President: Dan Leese
Event Manager: Shawna Hernandez
Purchasing Manager: John Peavey
Estimated Sales: $20-50 Million
Number Employees: 50-99
Parent Co: E&J Gallo
Type of Packaging: Private Label
Brands:
    Chateau Souverain

2466 Chateau St Jean Winery
8555 Sonoma Hwy
P.O.Box 293
Kenwood, CA 95452-9026
707-833-4134
Fax: 707-833-4200 www.chateaustjean.com
Table wine

Food Manufacturers / A-Z

Manager: Margo Van Stafvaren
margo.vanstafvaren@scatecsolar.com
Winemaker/Operation Director: Margo Anstaavern
Public Relations Manager: Nicole Breier
Wine Maker: Steven Reeder
Estimated Sales: $10-24.9 Million
Number Employees: 50-99
Parent Co: Beringer Wine Estates
Type of Packaging: Consumer

2467 Chateau des Charmes Wines
PO Box 280
St. Davids, ON L0S 1P0
Canada
905-262-4219
Fax: 905-262-5548   800-263-2541
www.chateaudescharmes.com
Wines and champagnes, ice wine
President: Paul Bosc
Secretary: Rodger Gordon
Director Marketing: Paul-Andre Bosc
Estimated Sales: $1-2.5 Million
Number Employees: 100-249

2468 Chatila's
254 N Broadway
Salem, NH 03079-2132
603-898-5459
Fax: 603-893-1586
customercare@chatilasbakery.com
www.chatilasbakery.com
All sugar-free items. Chatila's muffins, cookies, pastries, cheesecakes, donuts, bagels, pies, breads, chocolates and ice cream. All items sweetend with Splenda and/or Melltitol, low carb, low cal, low fat, low cholestrol, notrans-fat.
President: Mohamad Chatila
cutomercare@chatilas.com
Sales: Jennifer Marks
Estimated Sales: Less Than $500,000
Number Employees: 1-4
Number of Brands: 1
Number of Products: 100+
Square Footage: 24000
Type of Packaging: Consumer, Food Service, Private Label, Bulk

2469 Chatom Vineyards Inc
7449 Esmeralda Rd
San Andreas, CA 95249-9641
209-736-4604
Fax: 209-736-6507   800-435-8852
www.chatomvineyards.com
Wines
Owner: Gay Callan
info@chatomvineyards.com
Director: Nikki FYFE
Production Manager: Scott Klann
Purchasing Manager: Mari Wells
Estimated Sales: Less Than $500,000
Number Employees: 1-4
Number of Products: 7
Square Footage: 16800
Brands:
   Sangiovese
   Syrah

2470 Chattanooga Bakery Inc
900 Manufacturers Rd # 101
Chattanooga, TN 37405-3763
423-267-3351
Fax: 423-266-2169   800-251-3404
moonpiedirect@moonpie.com
Chattanooga Bakery was founded in 1902. An independent bakery offering snack cake and cookie products, including moon pies, pecan pies, coconut pies and marshmallow treats.
President/CEO: Sam Campbell
CFO: Keith Holt
keith@moonpie.com
VP Marketing: Tory Johnston
VP Sales: John Campbell
VP Operations: Guy Callahan
Estimated Sales: $20-50 Million
Number Employees: 100-249
Number of Brands: 1
Type of Packaging: Consumer
Brands:
   MoonPie

2471 Chattem Chemicals Inc
3708 Saint Elmo Ave
Chattanooga, TN 37409-1235
423-822-5000
Fax: 423-825-0507
eva.edwards@chattemchemicals.com
www.chattemchemicals.com
Glycine and creatine monohydrate
President: Jitendra Doshi
Cmo: Herman Echeverri
herman.echeverri@chattemchemicals.com
CFO: Ed Rusk
VP/General Manager: Jason Allen
Research & Development: Nilesh Patel
Quality Assurance/Quality Control: Frank Seymour
Sales/Marketing Hamposyl Surfactants: Art Pavlidis
Sales/Marketing Rheology Modifiers/APIs: Herman Echeverri
VP Operations/Production/Manufacturing: Ray Smith
Manufacturing Director: Scott Newton
Purchasing/ Traffic: Bill Grant
Estimated Sales: $5-10 Million
Number Employees: 50-99
Square Footage: 51948
Parent Co: Elcat
Type of Packaging: Bulk

2472 Chatz Roasting Co
4221 Brew Master Dr # 13
Suite 13
Ceres, CA 95307-7590
209-541-1100
Fax: 209-541-1131   chatzcoffee@yahoo.com
Gourmet coffee, tea and cocoa.
President: Linda Blaney
Partner: Linda Blaney
Estimated Sales: $10-20 Million
Number Employees: 1-4
Brands:
   Chatz

2473 Chaucer Consumer Solutions
Calabasas, CA 91302
info@crunchiesfood.com
Chocolate-covered freeze-dried fruit snacks
President & CEO: Scott Jacobson

2474 Chaucer Foods, Inc. USA
2238 Yew St
Forest Grove, OR 97116
www.chaucergroup.co.uk
Manufacturers freeze dried ingredients and specialty bread products.
CEO: Andy Ducker
Number Employees: 5-9
Parent Co: Chaucer Foods Ltd

2475 Chauvin Coffee Corporation
4160 Meramec St
Saint Louis, MO 63116
314-772-0700
Fax: 314-772-0722   800-455-5282
info@chauvincoffee.com   www.chauvincoffee.com
Coffee
President: Bonnie Charleville
VP: Mike Charleville
Marketing Manager: Verner Earls
Sales Manager: Sonya Miller
Contact: Lisa Contestabile
l.contestabile@chauvincoffee.com
Estimated Sales: $1-3 Million
Number Employees: 10-19
Type of Packaging: Private Label

2476 Chazy Orchards
9486 State Route 9
Chazy, NY 12921
518-846-7171
Fax: 518-846-8171
customerservice@chazyorchards.com
www.chazy.com
Grower of apples
Operations Manager: Craig Reyell
Estimated Sales: $5-10 Million
Number Employees: 20-49
Parent Co: Giroux's Poultry Farm
Brands:
   SweeTango ™

2477 Cheating Gourmet
PO Box 1537
Auburn, ME 04211
800-239-9731
www.scottandjons.com
Flash frozen shrimp bowls
Founder: Scott Demers
Founder: Jon Demers
Number of Products: 10
Brands:
   Scott & Jon's

2478 Chebe Bread Products
1840 Lundberg Dr W
Spirit Lake, IA 51360-7661
712-336-4211
www.chebe.com
Gluten free dry mixes and frozen bread
Owner: Richard Reed
dreed@chebe.com
Number Employees: 5-9

2479 Cheddar Box Cheese House
264 Alpine Dr
Shawano, WI 54166
715-526-5411
Fax: 715-524-9930
Cheese spreads
President: James O'Betts
Estimated Sales: $400,000
Number Employees: 1-4
Brands:
   Cheddar Box Cheese

2480 Cheese Factory
4856 Lake Ave
Buffalo, NY 14219-1314
716-828-0178
Fax: 716-828-0179
President: Edwin Hildebrand
e.hildebrand@cheesefactory.com
Estimated Sales: Less Than $500,000
Number Employees: 1-4
Parent Co: Cheese Factory

2481 Cheese Merchants of America
248 Tubeway Dr
Carol Stream, IL 60188
630-768-0317
Fax: 630-221-0584   johnp@cheesemerchants.com
www.cheesemerchants.com
Processors of custom blends of Italian cheeses, converters of hard Italian cheeses to grated, shredded, and shaved.
EVP/Managing Partner: Robert Greco
Director Purchasing/Quality Assurance: Paul DelleGrazie
Central Regional Sales Manager: Mark Lewis
EVP Sales: Jim Smart
Contact: Brian Barrett
brianb@cheesemerchants.com
Estimated Sales: $19.3 Million
Number Employees: 90
Square Footage: 105000
Type of Packaging: Consumer, Food Service, Bulk

2482 Cheese Straws & More
5717 Desiard Street
Monroe, LA 71203-4793
318-343-4666
Fax: 318-343-6333   800-997-1921
Straws including Cajun cheese and southern tea; also, pecan pralines, candied pecans and pecan brittle
President: Brenda Schwab
Number Employees: 1-4

2483 CheeseLand
P.O.Box 22230
Seattle, WA 98122-0230
206-709-1220
Fax: 206-709-1818
Cheese
President: Jan Kos
Contact: Mark Roeland
info@cheeselandinc.com
Estimated Sales: $1-2,500,000
Number Employees: 1-4

2484 Cheesecake Etc Desserts
400 Swallow Dr
Miami Springs, FL 33166-4432
305-887-0258
Fax: 305-888-5463

Food Manufacturers / A-Z

Cheesecakes, key lime pies, diner style layer cakes, individual dessert cups; including all varieties of layer cakes, cheesecake, and key lime pie
Owner: Frank Romano
cheesecakeemail@aol.com
VP: MILO IRSULA
Office Manager: Rachelle Romano
Estimated Sales: Under $500,000
Number Employees: 1-4
Number of Brands: 3
Number of Products: 25
Square Footage: 40000
Parent Co: Obem Foods, Inc
Type of Packaging: Food Service
Brands:
    Florida Key Lime Pie

2485 ### Cheesecake Factory Inc.
26901 Malibu Hills Rd.
Calabasas Hills, CA 91301
818-871-3000
Fax: 818-871-3100
www.thecheesecakefactory.com
Restaurant chain and dessert distributor, specializing in cheesecakes.
President: David Gordon
Chairman/CEO: David Overton
doverton@thecheesecakefactory.com
Executive VP/CFO: Matthew Clark
Executive V/General Counsel: Scarlett May
Year Founded: 1972
Estimated Sales: $2.26 Billion
Number Employees: 38,800
Brands:
    Cheesecake Factory®

2486 ### Cheesecake Momma
200 W Henry St
Ukiah, CA 95482
707-462-2253
Fax: 707-468-9056 momma@pacific.net
Processor and wholesaler of cheesecake including all natural and 100% organic
President: Robin Collier
Vice President: Alana Rouse
Estimated Sales: $2.5-5 Million
Number Employees: 20-49

2487 ### Cheeze Kurls
2915 Walkent Drive NW
Grand Rapids, MI 49544-9745
616-784-6095
Fax: 616-784-7445
Snack foods including popcorn and cheese curls
President: Tim DeDinas
VP: Bob Franzak
Vice President, Marketing: Dave Krombeen
Contact: Christopher Dedinas
cdedinas@cksnacks.com
Number Employees: 20-49
Square Footage: 120000
Type of Packaging: Consumer, Food Service, Private Label, Bulk
Brands:
    Ck

2488 ### Chef America
9601 Canoga Ave
Chatsworth, CA 91311
818-718-8111
www.chefamerica.com
Prepared frozen foods including stuffed sandwiches and croissants, pizza snacks and waffles
CEO: Paul Merage
CFO: Glenn Lee
VP: Larry Johnson
Research & Development: Phil Mason
V P Finance: Glenn Lee
Contact: John Mccarthy
john.mccarthy@us.nestle.com
Purchasing Director: George Turner
Purchasing Manager: Russ Shroyer
Plant Manager: Mike Crawford
Number Employees: 500-999
Type of Packaging: Consumer, Food Service

2489 ### Chef Hans' Gourmet Foods
310 Walnut St
Monroe, LA 71201-6712
318-322-2334
Fax: 318-322-2340 800-890-4267
ckorrodi@bayou.com
www.ChefHansgourmetfoods.com
Processor and exporter of soup bases, batter, spices, seafood, breading, seasonings, wild rice pilaf, rice, desserts, bran, jambalaya, gumbo, etouffee, etc.
President: Hans Korrodi
ckorrodi@bayou.com
Estimated Sales: $1-2.5 Million
Number Employees: 1-4
Square Footage: 88000
Brands:
    Chef Hans

2490 ### Chef Merito Inc
7915 Sepulveda Blvd
Van Nuys, CA 91405-1032
818-787-0100
Fax: 818-787-5900 800-637-4861
info@chefmerito.com www.chefmerito.com
Processor, importer and exporter of dried spices, seasonings, seasoned rice, batters, breading mixes, soups and sauces
President/CEO: Plinio Garcia, Jr
Project Manager: Sara Nicholson
Estimated Sales: $10-20 Million
Number Employees: 50-99
Number of Brands: 4
Square Footage: 30000
Type of Packaging: Consumer, Food Service, Bulk
Brands:
    Chef Merito
    Pikos Pikosos
    Ppeppers
    Sabrosito

2491 ### Chef Paul Prudhomme's Magic Seasonings Blends
PO Box 23342
New Orleans, LA 70183-0342
504-731-3590
Fax: 504-731-3576 800-457-2857
info@chefpaul.com www.chefpaul.com
Seasonings and spices.
President/CEO: Shawn McBride
CFO: Tiffanie Roppolo
VP, Sales & Marketing: John McBride
International Sales & Marketing: Anna Zuniga
Contact: Wade Anderson
wanderson@chefpaul.com
Director, Operations: Joey Duplechain
VP, Manufacturing: David Hickey
Plant Manager: Buddy Duplechain
Estimated Sales: $10-20 Million
Number Employees: 50-99
Number of Brands: 1
Square Footage: 30000
Type of Packaging: Private Label
Brands:
    Chef Paul Prudhomme's

2492 ### Chef Philippe LLC
715 Ryan Plaza Drive
Suite Ai
Arlington, TX 76011-1714
817-461-9049
Fax: 817-460-0309
www.ChefPhilipeesKitchen.com
Sauces such as pepper brandy sauce, roasted garlic sauce, rosemary sauce, truffle red wine sauce, seafood white wine cream sauce, lingonberry pepper sauce, and apple cider sauce
Estimated Sales: $.5-1 million
Number Employees: 5-9

2493 ### Chef Salt
6025 Vera Cruz Road
Center Valley, PA 18034
215-782-1730
www.chefsalt.com
Manufacturer of salts.
Co-Founder: David Joachim
Co-Founder: Andrew Schloss
Co-Founder: Mark Bitterman

2494 ### Chef Shamy Gourmet
Salt Lake City, UT 84104
chefshamy.com
Gourmet garlic butter
Founder: David Shamy

2495 ### Chef Shells Catering & Roadside Cafe
324 Superior Mall
Downtown Port Huron, MI 48060
810-966-8371
Fax: 810-966-8372 info@chefshells.com
www.chefshells.com
Wine vinaigrettes, sauces, seasonings and dip mixes; gourmet catering available
Owner: Shell Wrubel
Owner: Mark Wrubel
Estimated Sales: $38,000
Number of Products: 45
Square Footage: 7200
Type of Packaging: Consumer, Food Service, Private Label, Bulk

2496 ### Chef Silvio's of Wooster Street
69 Brookward Road
Guilford, CT 06437-1804
203-453-1064
Fax: 203-453-1064 newmedfoods@aol.com
www.chefsilvios.com
Gourmet foods and sauces.

2497 ### Chef Soraya
6350 Gunpark Dr
Boulder, CO 80301
800-677-7423
info@chefsoraya.com www.chefsoraya.com
Prepared rice bowls
CEO: Soraya Fouladi
Number of Brands: 1
Number of Products: 6
Type of Packaging: Consumer
Brands:
    EAT A BOWL

2498 ### Chef Tim Foods, LLC
65 Sam Snead Circle
Etters, PA 17319-9565
717-802-0350
cheftim@ptd.net
www.cheftimfoods.com
Gluten-free, kosher, organic/natural, salad dressing, marinades, other sauces, seasonings and cooking enhancers.
Contact: Sabrena Jutzi
sabrena@cheftimfoods.com

2499 ### Chef Zachary's Gourmet Blended Spices
PO Box 24115
Detroit, MI 48224
313-226-0000
Fax: 313-226-0000 zach4spice@aol.com
Natural, gourmet spice blends
Owner/President: Chef Zachary Smith
Estimated Sales: $300,000-500,000
Number Employees: 1-4
Type of Packaging: Consumer
Brands:
    Blackening Spice
    Chelsea Spice
    Mediterranean
    Shana Spice

2500 ### Chef's Cut: Real Jerky
PO Box 110871
Naples, FL 34108-0115
USA
586-615-0329
www.chefscutrealjerky.com
Jerky, cured meats: prosciutto, bacon
Owner/Chef: Blair Swiler
CEO: Bart Silvestro
Owner: Dennis Riedel
Contact: Nancy Mancini
nancy@chefscutrealjerky.com
Number Employees: 20-49

2501 ### Chef's Pride Gifts LLC
21740 Trolley Industrial # 1
Taylor, MI 48180-1875
313-295-1800
Fax: 313-295-0448 800-878-1800
www.chefspride.com
Fresh and frozen sandwiches; also, salads, desserts and gourmet cinnamon rolls
President/CEO/Owner: Neil Sloman
Manager: Mike Parks
mike@chefspride.com

Food Manufacturers / A-Z

Estimated Sales: Less Than $500,000
Number Employees: 1-4
Square Footage: 200000
Type of Packaging: Consumer, Private Label
Brands:
   Honeybake Farms

2502 Chef's Requested Foods
2600 Exchange Ave
Oklahoma City, OK 73108-2448
405-239-2610
Fax: 405-239-2616
Processor of fresh and frozen meats, including pork, beef and poultry.
President: John Williams
Manager, IT: Jody Lankford
Director, Marketing: John Brewster
VP of Sales/Marketing: Steven Folenius
VP of Operations: Justin Williams
Estimated Sales: $38 Million
Number Employees: 100-249
Type of Packaging: Food Service

2503 Chef-A-Roni Fancy Foods
2832 S County Trl
East Greenwich, RI 02818-1742
401-884-8798
Fax: 401-884-3552 www.chefaroni.com
Spaghetti sauce
President: Henry Caniglia
h.caniglia@chefaroni.com
Vice President: Lillian Caniglia
Estimated Sales: $500,000-$1 Million
Number Employees: 1-4
Type of Packaging: Consumer, Food Service
Brands:
   Chef-A-Roni

2504 Chefwise
2200 NW 102nd Ave # 2
Unit 2
Doral, FL 33172-2225
786-845-3884
Fax: 786-845-9997 866-254-CHEF
chefwise@hotmail.com www.chefwise.com
Au jus, desserts, sauces, soups and stocks
Owner: Daniel Durand
ddurand@chepafusa.com
Chef: Daniel Durand
Number Employees: 1-4

2505 Chelan Fresh Marketing
PO Box 669
Chelan, WA 98816
509-682-2591
Fax: 509-682-4620 www.chelanfresh.com
Apples, pears and cherries from Washington state.
Domestic Sales Manager: Daniel Gebbers
General Manager: Tom Riggan
Type of Packaging: Consumer, Bulk
Brands:
   Crunch Pak®
   Cascade Crest Organics

2506 Chella's Dutch Delicacies
333 2nd St
Lake Oswego, OR 97034-0000
503-534-9888
Fax: 503-635-1399 800-458-3331
Shortbread pastry and bread
President: Ron Kirk
Purchasing Agent: Jake Raymond
Estimated Sales: $10-20 Million
Number Employees: 10-19

2507 Chelsea Flower Market
75 9th Ave
New York, NY 10011-7006
212-727-1111
Fax: 212-727-1778 888-727-7887
info@chelseamarketbaskets.com
www.chelseamarketbasket.com
Custom made gift baskets for various occasions
Owner: David Porat
Contact: Bhago Ramprashad
andy@chelseamarketbaskets.com
Estimated Sales: $500,000-$1 Million
Number Employees: 1-4
Brands:
   Chelsea Market Baskets
   Cottage Delight
   Shortbread Housf

2508 Chelsea Milling Co.
201 W. North St.
P.O. Box 460
Chelsea, MI 48118-0460
734-475-1361
Fax: 734-475-4630 800-727-2460
www.jiffymix.com
Prepared baking mixes including cake, frosting, muffin, brownie, pizza crust, biscuit, etc.
President/Chief Executive Officer: Howard Holmes
Vice President/Chief Financial Officer: John Powers
Vice President, Sales: William McCreadie
Year Founded: 1901
Estimated Sales: $124 Million
Number Employees: 300
Number of Brands: 1
Number of Products: 7
Type of Packaging: Consumer
Other Locations:
   Chelsea Milling Co.
   Marshall MI
Brands:
   Jiffy Mix

2509 Chelten House Products
607 Heron Dr
Swedesboro, NJ 08085
info@cheltenhouse.com
www.cheltenhouse.com
Organic and all-natural dressings, sauces, marinades, salsa and ketchup. QAI certified and OU approved.
President & COO: Jason Dabrow
Chairman & CEO: Steve Dabrow
CFO: Ken Pawloski
VP, Business Development: David Elchynski
VP, Operations: Jeff Skirvin
Estimated Sales: $40 Million
Number Employees: 50-99
Number of Brands: 3
Square Footage: 150000
Type of Packaging: Consumer, Food Service, Private Label
Brands:
   Chelten House
   Marinade Bay
   Simply Natural

2510 Chempacific Corp
6200 Seaforth St # 6200
Baltimore, MD 21224-6536
410-633-5771
Fax: 410-633-5808 sales@chempacific.com
www.chempacific.com
President: Dr Dean Wei
Vice President Of Operations And Co- Fou: Tony Liang
VP, QA/QC Global and Co-Founder: Rebecca Chiu
Chief Technical Officer: Jian Huang
VP Sales/Marketing: Jim Havlin
Vice President Of Operations And Co- Fou: Tony Liang
Director of Production: Wuyi Wang
Estimated Sales: $3-5 Million
Number Employees: 20-49

2511 Cher-Make Sausage Co
2915 Calumet Avenue
Manitowoc, WI 54220
Fax: 920-683-5990 800-242-7679
www.cher-make.com
Processor and exporter of kippered beef, sausage and meat snacks; importer of frozen meat.
Founder: Art Chermak
Director Finance/Vp Fin: Lawrence Franke
VP of Operations: Chuck Hoefner
Plant Manager: Chuck Hoefner
Purchasing Manager: Jim Coulson
Estimated Sales: $10-20 Million
Number Employees: 100-249
Square Footage: 80000
Type of Packaging: Consumer, Private Label
Brands:
   Cher-Make Sausage
   Home Game
   Smokey Mesquite
   Smoky Valley

2512 Cheraw Packing Plant
578 Highway 1 S
Cheraw, SC 29520-3812
843-537-7426
Beef and pork
Estimated Sales: $5-10 Million
Number Employees: 10-19

Type of Packaging: Consumer, Food Service, Private Label, Bulk

2513 Cherbogue Fisheries
98 Cliff St
Yarmouth, NS B5A 4B3
Canada
902-742-9157
Fax: 902-742-7708
Processor and exporter of fresh and frozen seafood
President/ Founder: Alfred Le Blanc
VP: Alfred LeBlanc
Number Employees: 20-49
Type of Packaging: Bulk

2514 Cherchies
One Bacton Hill Rd. North
Suite 109
Malvern, PA 19355
610-640-9440
Fax: 610-644-7937 800-644-1980
info@cherchies.com www.cherchies.com
Gourmet foods including mustard, peppers, pepper jellies, sauces, soups, chowders, preserves and seasonings; also, chili and freeze-dried soup and chowder mixes
President: Anthony Spallone
VP: Patti Spallone
Marketing: Joe Shrum
Contact: Rose Engleka
rose.engleka@cherchies.com
Operations: Lori Hughes
Purchasing: Gayle Snyder
Estimated Sales: $1-2.5 Million
Number Employees: 10-19
Number of Brands: 1
Number of Products: 60
Square Footage: 5600
Type of Packaging: Consumer, Food Service, Private Label
Brands:
   Cherchies

2515 Cheri's Desert Harvest
1840 E Winsett St
Tucson, AZ 85719-6548
520-623-4141
Fax: 520-623-7741 800-743-1141
www.cherisdesertharvest.com
Jellies, marmalade, bread, candies, syrup
Owner: Cheri Romanoski
cheri@cherisdesertharvest.com
Vice President: Jon Romanaski
Production Manager: Nancy Howes
Purchasing Manager: Cheryl Romanaski
Estimated Sales: $1-2.5 Million
Number Employees: 5-9
Brands:
   Cheri's Desert Harvest

2516 Cheribundi
500 Technology Farm Drive
Geneva, NY 14456
315-781-7308
Fax: 315-282-2317 800-699-0460
www.cheribundi.com
Juice/cider.
President: Brian Ross
Contact: Mary Baggott
maryruth@cheribundi.com

2517 Cherith Valley Gardens
4009 Eloop 820 South
Suite B
Fort Worth, TX 76119
817-466-0600
Fax: 817-446-0602 800-610-9813
terriw@cherithvalley.com
Processor, importer and exporter of gourmet pickles, pickled vegetables, salsas, jellies, fruit toppings, peppers, relishes and hors d'oeuvres
President: Alan Werner
Public Relations: Terri Werner
Operations Manager: Christa Werner
Estimated Sales: $5-10 Million
Number Employees: 10-19
Square Footage: 24000
Type of Packaging: Consumer, Food Service
Brands:
   Cherith Valley Gardens

Food Manufacturers / A-Z

2518 Cherry Central Cooperative, Inc.
1771 N. US Highway 31 S.
Traverse City, MI 49684
231-946-1860
Fax: 231-941-4167 info@cherrycentral.com
www.cherrycentral.com
Red tart cherries, apples and blueberries and also a major supplier of cranberries, strawberries, pomegranate arils and asparagus. Supplier to major manufacturers for dried, frozen, canned and custom products.
President/CEO: Steve Eisler
Director, Food Service: David Barger
Retail National Sales Manager: Vince Higgs
Director, Private/Custom Label: Frank Wolff
Year Founded: 1973
Estimated Sales: $154 Million
Number Employees: 100-249
Square Footage: 15500
Type of Packaging: Consumer, Food Service, Private Label, Bulk
Brands:
  Cherry Central
  Traverse Bay Fruit Co
  Indian Summer

2519 Cherry Hill Orchards
400 Long Lane
Lancaster, PA 17603
717-872-9311
www.cherryhillorchards.com
Processor and packer of fresh cherries, nectarines, peaches, apricots, sweet corn, and pumpkins.
Owner: Tom Haas
cherryhillorchards@verizon.net
Plant Manager: Stephen Haun
Year Founded: 1971
Number Employees: 20-49
Square Footage: 100000
Type of Packaging: Consumer, Food Service
Brands:
  Tree Ripe

2520 Cherry Hut
2345 Munson Ave. (North US-31 North)
Traverse City, MI 49686-3755
231-938-8888
Fax: 231-938-3333 888-882-4431
www.cherrytreeinn.com
Products made from cherries, including sauces, jams, jellies, conserves, preserves
General Manager: Jonathan Pack
Owner: Brenda Case
Production VP: Leonard Case
Estimated Sales: Less Than $500,000
Number Employees: 1-4

2521 Cherry Lane Frozen Fruits
4230 Victoria Avenue
Vineland Station, ON L0R 2E0
Canada
905-562-4337
Fax: 905-562-5577 877-243-7796
www.cherrylane.net
Cherries and peaches
President: John Smith
Number Employees: 100
Type of Packaging: Consumer, Food Service

2522 Cherry Moon Farms
4840 Eastgate Mall
San Diego, CA 92121
858-729-2800
800-580-2913
wecare@customercare.cherrymoonfarms.com
Fruit baskets, gift baskets with chocolates and treats, and spa baskets
President/COO: Abe Wynperle
VP Finance: Rex Bosen
VP/General Counsel: Blake Bilstad

2523 Cherrybrook Kitchen
20 Mall Rd # 410
Suite 410
Burlington, MA 01803-4129
781-272-4460
Fax: 781-272-4460 866-458-8225
info@cherrybrookkitchen.com
www.cherrybrookkitchen.com
Peanut free, dairy free, egg free and nut free cake, cookie and brownie mixes, cookies, frostings, breakfast mixes, and wheat free and gluten free mixes

President/CEO: Chip Rosenberg
Founder: Patsy Rosenberg
VP Marketing: Laura Kuykendall
VP Sales: Sallie Bowling
Finance/HR Manager: Sue Giannetti
Estimated Sales: Less Than $500,000
Number Employees: 5-9

2524 Cherryfield Foods
320 Ridge Rd
Cherryfield, ME 04622-4030
207-546-7573
Fax: 207-546-2713 sales@oxfordfrozenfoods.com
www.oxfordfrozenfoods.com
Blueberries
COO: Jeff Vose
Estimated Sales: $50-100 Million
Number Employees: 100-249
Parent Co: Oxford Frozen Foods

2525 Cherryvale Farms
310-910-1124
info@cherryvalefarms.com
www.cherryvalefarms.com
Cookie, brownie and muffin mixes
CEO: Lindsey Rosenberg
Number of Brands: 1
Number of Products: 9
Type of Packaging: Consumer
Brands:
  EVERYTHING BUT THE...
  INSTANT INDULGENCE

2526 Cheryl's Cookies
646 Mccorkle Blvd
Westerville, OH 43082-8778
614-776-1500
Fax: 614-891-8599 800-443-8124
www.cheryls.com
Cookies and baked goods
President: Cheryl Krueger
CFO/COO: Dennis Hicks
dhicks@cherylandco.com
Quality Assurance Director: Sara Reed
VP Creative Services: Lisa Henry
Estimated Sales: $25.5 Million
Number Employees: 250-499
Square Footage: 23103
Parent Co: 1-800-Flowers
Brands:
  Cheryl & Co.

2527 Chesapeake Bay Crab Cakes & More
10711 Red Run Blvd
Owings Mills, MD 21117
800-282-2722
Fax: 800-858-6547 www.cbcrabcakes.com
Crab cakes and gourmet seafood products.
President: Laura McManus
Estimated Sales: $20-50 Million
Number Employees: 20-49
Square Footage: 35000
Parent Co: Chesapeake Fine Food Group
Type of Packaging: Consumer

2528 Chesapeake Spice Company
4613 Mercedes Dr
Belcamp, MD 21017-1224
410-272-6100
Fax: 410-273-2122 www.chesapeakespice.com
Processor and importers of spices and seasonings, including anise, cumin, sage, sage oil, black pepper, paprika, cinnamon, saffron, thyme and ginger.
President: Larry Lessans
Vice President: David Lessans
Estimated Sales: $5-10 Million
Number Employees: 20-49
Square Footage: 200000
Type of Packaging: Bulk
Other Locations:
  Chesapeake Spice Company-Reno
  Reno NV

2529 Chester Dairy Co
1915 State St
Chester, IL 62233-1115
618-826-2394
Fax: 618-826-2395 www.chesterillinois.com
Dairy
President: Jason Ohlau
Estimated Sales: $10-20 Million
Number Employees: 20-49

2530 Chester Inc Information
555 Eastport Centre Dr
Valparaiso, IN 46383-2911
219-465-7555
Fax: 219-462-2652 800-778-1131
clark@chesterinc.com www.chesterinc.com
Processor and exporter of popcorn
Chairman/CEO: Peter Peuquet
President: Larry Holt
EVP: Leonard Clark
Contact: James Chester
jchester@chestertech.com
Estimated Sales: $5-10 Million
Number Employees: 5-9
Type of Packaging: Consumer, Private Label
Other Locations:
  Francesville IN
  Gary IN
  Troy MI
Brands:
  Chester Farms
  Chester Farms Popping Corn
  Golden

2531 Chester River Clam Co
305 Roe Ingleside Rd
Centreville, MD 21617-2012
410-758-3810
Fax: 410-758-4089
Clams
Owner: Mel Hickman
mhickman@chesterriverhealth.org
Estimated Sales: $2,100,000
Number Employees: 5-9

2532 Chester W. Howeth & Brother
P.O. Box 446
Crisfield, MD 21817-0446
410-968-1398
Fax: 410-968-0670
Fresh and frozen seafood
Manager: Arthur Tawes
Estimated Sales: $5-10 Million
Number Employees: 20-49
Square Footage: 8400
Type of Packaging: Food Service
Brands:
  Chas. W. Howeth & Bro.

2533 Chester's International, LLC
2020 Cahaba Rd
Suite 325
Mountain Brook, AL 35223-1179
205-949-4690
Fax: 205-298-0332 800-288-1555
info@chestersinternational.com
www.chestersinternational.com
Manufacturer and exporter of fried chicken products including breading mixes, seasonings, packaging supplies, deep fryers, fry kettles, marinades, warmers, breading tables, etc
President: Blue Akers
bluea@chestersinternational.com
CFO: Wade King
Director of Operations: Jamees Venable
Estimated Sales: $5.9 Million
Number Employees: 5-9
Brands:
  Chester Fried Chicken
  Chesterfried

2534 (HQ)Chester-Jensen Co., Inc.
345 Tilghman St
Chester, PA 19013-3432
610-876-6276
Fax: 610-876-0485 800-685-3750
htxchng@chester-jensen.com
www.chester-jensen.com
stainless steel food processing equipment, including sanitary chillers, ice builders (thermal storage), batch mixing processors, plate heat exchangers & cook-chill equipment.
President: Richard Miller
CEO: Steven Miller
Sales Director: Robert Skoog
Estimated Sales: $10-20 Million
Square Footage: 76000
Type of Packaging: Consumer, Food Service, Private Label, Bulk
Other Locations:
  Chester-Jensen Company
  Cattaraugus NY

Food Manufacturers / A-Z

2535 Chestertown Natural Foods
303 Cannon St
Chestertown, MD 21620-1327
410-778-1677
Fax: 410-778-6386
www.chestertownnaturalfoods.biz
Poultry
Owner: Trish Young-Gruber
CEO: Louis Rothman
Vice President: William Schroeder
Manager Industrial Sales: Michael Carrow
Plant Manager: Jack Laird
Estimated Sales: $5-10 Million
Number Employees: 5-9
Type of Packaging: Private Label
Brands:
  Chestertown

2536 Chestnut Mountain Winery
1123 Highway 124
Hoschton, GA 30548-3421
770-867-6914
Fax: 770-867-6914
Wines
President: James Laikam
General Manager: Jim O'Dell
Estimated Sales: $1-2,500,000
Number Employees: 1-4

2537 Chevalier Chocolates
39 Eastgate Lane
Enfield, CT 06082-6213
860-741-3330
Belgian chocolates, pralines, truffles, mints, also chocolate, cordial, and brandy covered cherries
President: Linda Chevalier
linda@chevalier.ws
Brands:
  Chevalier Chocolates

2538 Chewys Rugulach
7795 Arjons Dr
San Diego, CA 92126-4366
858-271-1234
Fax: 858-271-1346   800-241-3456
chewyssales@aol.com   www.chewys.com
Filled rugulach including baked, unbaked and frozen
President: Ahmad Paksima
chewys123@aol.com
Vice President: Emily Paksima
Marketing Director: Shahriar Paksima
Estimated Sales: $2.5-5 Million
Number Employees: 20-49
Square Footage: 24960
Parent Co: Ahuramazda
Type of Packaging: Consumer, Food Service, Private Label, Bulk
Brands:
  Chewy's

2539 Chex Finer Foods Inc
71 Hampden Rd # 100
Mansfield, MA 02048-1807
508-226-0660
Fax: 508-226-7060   800-227-8114
info@chexfoods.com   www.chexfoods.com
Processor and importer of gourmet foods including biscuits, confectionery items, specialties, etc
President: David Isenberg
Controller: Donald Robillard
Purchasing: Dan Powers
Estimated Sales: $10-20 Million
Number Employees: 20-49
Type of Packaging: Consumer

2540 Chic Naturals
PO Box 11541
Lahaina, HI 96761
808-463-7878
www.chicnaturals.com
Chickpea snacks, chocolate and spice blends from Hawaii

2541 Chicago 58 Food Products
135 Haist Ave
Woodbridge, ON L4L 5V6
Canada
416-603-4244
Fax: 905-265-0566
chicago58foodproducts@bellnet.ca
Meat products including beef, pastrami, smoked salami, frankfurters; also, herring, condiments and cheese; importer of beef cuts
President and Production Manager: Mosho Ami
Secretary and Sales Director: Ted Bernholtz
VP: Shane Reiken
Estimated Sales: $6.8 Million
Number Employees: 12
Square Footage: 60000
Type of Packaging: Consumer, Food Service, Private Label, Bulk
Brands:
  Chicago 58
  Deli-Dogs
  Lanky Franky

2542 Chicago Avenue Pizza
1376 W Hubbard St # 1378
Chicago, IL 60642-6453
312-421-3000
Fax: 312-421-0774   800-244-8935
www.iltaco.com
Frozen pizza, pizza puffs, pasta with marinara sauce, burritos, tamales and taco puffs
President: Warren Shabaz
warren@iltaco.com
Estimated Sales: $10-20 Million
Number Employees: 50-99
Type of Packaging: Consumer, Food Service, Private Label
Brands:
  Iltaco

2543 Chicago Coffee Roastery
11880 Smith Court
Huntley, IL 60142
847-669-1156
Fax: 847-669-1114   800-762-5402
sales@chicagocoffee.com   www.chicagocoffee.com
Coffee, instant cocoa, instant cappuccino, tea
Owner: Sandra Knight
sknight@coffeemasters.com
Vice President: Brian Gosell
Purchasing Manager: Brian Gosell
Estimated Sales: $2 Million
Number Employees: 5-9
Square Footage: 32000
Type of Packaging: Consumer, Food Service, Private Label, Bulk

2544 Chicago Food Market
2245 S Wentworth Ave
Chicago, IL 60616-2011
312-842-4361
Fax: 312-842-6448
President: Matthew Chan
Estimated Sales: $2,500,000
Number Employees: 10-19

2545 Chicago Gourmet Steaks
PO Box 09094
Chicago, IL 60609
773-254-3384
Fax: 773-254-4355   800-997-8325
sales@cgsteaks.com
Steaks
Contact: Gail Glowacki
gail@cgsteaks.com

2546 Chicago Meat Authority Inc
1120 W 47th Pl
Chicago, IL 60609
773-254-3811
Fax: 773-254-5851   800-383-3811
info@chicagomeat.com   www.chicagomeat.com
Pork and pork products as well as beef and beef products.
Founder/Owner/President: Jordan Dorfman
jdorfman@chicagomeat.com
Quality Control Manager: Charles Clayton
Year Founded: 1990
Estimated Sales: $29.7 Million
Number Employees: 250
Square Footage: 50000
Type of Packaging: Consumer, Food Service, Private Label, Bulk

2547 Chicago Pastry
142 N Bloomingdale Rd
Bloomingdale, IL 60108-1017
630-529-6391
Fax: 630-529-4824   www.chicagopastry.com
Bread including rye, wheat and white; also, pastries, Italian cookies and danish including prune, strawberry and blueberry
President: Renato Turano
Contact: Pete Turano
pturano@chicagopastry.com
Number Employees: 5-9
Type of Packaging: Consumer, Food Service

2548 Chicago Premier Meats
822 W Exchange Ave
Chicago, IL 60609-2507
773-847-3364
Fax: 773-847-3364   800-385-0661
tschicagosteak@aol.com   www.chicagosteaks.com
Meat packing
President/CEO/Treasurer: Tom Summers
CEO/Principal: Thomas Campbell
Vice President: Rick Allison
Estimated Sales: $5.50 Million
Number Employees: 10-19

2549 Chicago Steaks
Chicago, IL
773-847-5400
www.chicagosteaks.com
Meat products, value added products, and gift steaks
Estimated Sales: $9 Million
Number Employees: 20-49
Number of Brands: 5
Square Footage: 6560
Type of Packaging: Food Service, Private Label
Brands:
  Chicago Steak

2550 Chicago Vegan Foods
905 N Ridge Ave
Suite 7
Lombard, IL 60148
630-629-9667
info@chicagoveganfoods.com
chicagoveganfoods.com
Vegan alternatives to marshmallows, cheese and ice cream
Co-Founder: Ryan Howard
Co-Founder: Dan Ziegler
Number of Brands: 3
Number of Products: 3
Type of Packaging: Consumer
Brands:
  DANDIES MARSHMALLOWS
  TEESE VEGAN CHEESE
  TEMPTATION ICE CREAM

2551 Chicama Vineyards
PO Box 430
West Tisbury, MA 02575-0430
508-693-0309
Fax: 508-693-5628   888-244-2262
Wines, vinegar and dressings
President: Catherine Mathiesen
Co-Owner: George Mathiesen
Purchasing Manager: Catherine Mathiesen
Estimated Sales: $5-9.9 Million
Number Employees: 1-4
Brands:
  Chicama

2552 Chick-Fil-A Inc.
5200 Buffington Rd.
Atlanta, GA 30349
866-232-2040
www.chick-fil-a.com
American fast food restaurant chain specializing in chicken.
President/COO: Tim Tassopoulos
Chairman/CEO: Dan Cathy
Senior VP/CFO: Brent Ragsdale
Year Founded: 1946
Estimated Sales: $10.5 Billion
Brands:
  Chick-Fil-A®

2553 Chickapea
Collingwood, ON L9Y 3L6
Canada
888-868-9968
hello@choosechickapea.com   choosechickapea.com
Chickpea and lentil pasta
Founder: Shelby Taylor
Year Founded: 2015
Number of Brands: 1
Number of Products: 6
Type of Packaging: Consumer
Brands:
  CHICKAPEA
  CHICKAPEA PASTA

Food Manufacturers / A-Z

2554 Chickasaw Trading Company
PO Box 1418
Denver City, TX 79323
806-592-3515
Fax: 806-592-3460 800-848-3515
Processor and exporter of lean beef jerky and smoked turkey breast strips
Co-Owner: Linda Kay
Co-Owner: Joe Kay
Number Employees: 1-4
Square Footage: 10000
Type of Packaging: Private Label
Brands:
  Texas Lean

2555 Chicken Of The Sea
2150 E. Grand Ave.
El Segundo, CA 90245
844-267-8862
www.chickenofthesea.com
Tuna, salmon, shrimp, crab, oysters, clams, mackerel and sardines.
CEO, Chicken of the Sea International: Valentin Ramirez
Year Founded: 1917
Estimated Sales: $600 Million
Number Employees: 1000-4999
Parent Co: Thai Union Group
Type of Packaging: Consumer, Food Service, Private Label
Brands:
  Chicken of the Sea
  Chicken of the Sea Singles
  Chicken of the Sea Tuna Salad Kit
  Genova Tonno
  Jack Mackerel

2556 Chicken Salad Chick
724 North Dean Road
Suite 100
Auburn, AL 36830
334-275-4578
Fax: 334-209-0251 www.chickensaladchick.com
Chicken salads, sandwiches, and side dishes
Founder/President/VP, Brand Development: Stacy Brown
Chief Executive Officer: Scott Deviney
Chief Financial Officer: David Ostrander
Founder: Kevin Brown
Controller: Shawn Jones
Director of Marketing: Ali Rauch
Human Resources Manager: Angela Hands
Director of Operations: Paul Grilli
Construction Project Manager: Miles Coggins
Year Founded: 2008
Number Employees: 40

2557 Chico Nut Company
2020 Esplanade
Chico, CA 95926
530-891-1493
Fax: 530-893-5381 almonds@chiconut.com
Processor, exporter and packer of almonds
Owner: Peter D Peterson
Contact: Cheri Azevedo
azevedoc@chiconut.com
Estimated Sales: $3-5 Million
Number Employees: 20-49
Type of Packaging: Bulk

2558 Chico Pops
24 Hanover Lane
Suite B
Chico, CA 95973
530-895-1290
Fax: 530-895-1266 844-467-7677
contactus@chicopops.com www.chicopops.com
A gourmet popcorn and nut manufacturer
COO/Brand Manager: Anna Ashley

2559 Chicopee Provision Co Inc
19 Sitarz Ave
Chicopee, MA 01013
800-924-6328
gary@bluesealkielbasa.com
www.bluesealkielbasa.com
Kielbasa and table ready meats, including polish kielbasa, cheese, hot dogs, cold cuts, and sausage
President: Gary Bernatowicz
Estimated Sales: $4.5 Million
Number Employees: 20-49
Number of Brands: 220
Number of Products: 610
Square Footage: 96000
Type of Packaging: Consumer, Food Service, Private Label, Bulk
Brands:
  Blue Seal
  Chicopee Provision
  F Domin and Sons
  Friendship Diaries
  Hatfield

2560 Chief Wenatchee
1705 N Miller St
Wenatchee, WA 98801-1585
509-662-5197
Fax: 509-662-9415
Grower and exporter of apples, cherries and pears
President: Brian Birsall
Operations Manager: Skip Coonfield
Number Employees: 250 to 499
Type of Packaging: Bulk
Brands:
  Chief Chelan
  Chief Supreme
  Chief Wenatchee
  Wenatchee Gold

2561 Chieftain Wild Rice
PO Box 550
1210 Basswood Ave
Spooner, WI 54801-0550
715-635-6401
Fax: 715-635-6415 800-262-6368
www.chieftainwildrice.com
Wild rice and wild rice blends
President: Donald Richards
General Manager: Joan Gerland
Marketing: Lisa Johnson
Operations Manager: Jim Deutsch
Estimated Sales: $1.6 Million
Number Employees: 25
Number of Brands: 1
Type of Packaging: Private Label
Brands:
  Chieftain(c)

2562 Chihon Biotechnology Co., Ltd.
2220 Glouceston Lane
Naperville, IL 60564
630-670-5701
jeff@chihonbio.com
www.chihonbio.com
A leading manufacturer of natamycin and nisin.
US Contact: Jeffrey Liu

2563 Childlife
8690 Hayden Pl
Culver City, CA 90232-2902
310-853-4300
Fax: 310-305-4680 800-993-0332
mailroom@childlife.net www.childlife.net
Liquid supplements & vitamins for infants to children up to twelve years old
President: Murray Clarke
VP: Helen Mauchi
Estimated Sales: $300,000-500,000
Number Employees: 5-9
Number of Products: 9

2564 Chili-Mex
1450 Lake Robbins Dr
Spring, TX 77380-3258
281-298-5364
Fax: 281-364-8452
Estimated Sales: $1-3 Million
Number Employees: 5-9

2565 Chili Dude
745 Kirkwood Dr
Dallas, TX 75218
214-354-9906
Chili
Director: Corrine Lovato
Brands:
  Chili Dude

2566 Chill & Moore
3221 May Street
Fort Worth, TX 76110-4124
505-769-2649
Fax: 505-762-0571 800-676-3055
Frozen ices
Sales Manager (Food Service): Bob Moore
Sales Manager (Retail): Jay Jackson
Type of Packaging: Consumer, Food Service

2567 Chill Pop
PO Box 19092
Cleveland, OH 44119
info@chillpopshop.com
chillpopshop.com
Frozen fruit pops
Co-Founder: Elizabeth Pryor
Co-Founder: Maggie Pryor

2568 Chimayo To Go / Cibolo Junction
500 Broadway SE
Albuquerque, NM 87102
800-683-9628
info@chimayotogo.com www.chimayotogo.com
Soup, stew and bread mixes, salsas, pretzels, herbs, spices and seasonings.
President: Brian McKinsey
Vice President: Susan McKinsey
Type of Packaging: Private Label

2569 Chimere Winery
1800 Sequoia Dr
Santa Maria, CA 93454-7645
805-928-5611
Fax: 805-922-9143 www.vinarium-usa.com
Wines
Owner: Gary R Mosby
gmosby@ymail.com
Estimated Sales: Less Than $500,000
Number Employees: 1-4

2570 China Mist Brands
7435 E Tierra Buena Ln
Scottsdale, AZ 85260-1608
480-998-8807
Fax: 480-443-8384 800-242-8807
info@chinamist.com www.organichotteas.com
China mist and leaves pure teas
President: Rommie Flammer
rommie@chinamist.com
CEO: John Martinson
President/CEO/Finance Executive: Rommie Flammer
Marketing Coordinator: Kiley Biggins
Director of Retail Sales: Ed Baird
Human Resource Manager: Wade McKesson
rommie@chinamist.com
Plant Manager: Kevin McCullough
Estimated Sales: $3.8 Million
Number Employees: 20-49
Square Footage: 70000
Brands:
  China Mist
  Frenzy Mist
  Green Star

2571 China Pharmaceutical Enterprises
8323 Ohara Court
Baton Rouge, LA 70806-6513
225-924-1423
Fax: 225-924-4154 800-345-1658
Processor and importer of ascorbic acid, caffeine anhydrous and vitamin B-12
Office Manager: Susan Giska
Type of Packaging: Bulk

2572 (HQ)Chincoteague Seafood CoInc
7056 Forest Grove Rd
PO Box 88
Parsonsburg, MD 21849-2096
443-260-4800
Fax: 443-260-4900 gourmetsoups@hotmail.com
www.chincoteagueseafood.com
Processor and distributor of gourmet specialty seafood items: canned and frozen products including fried clams, stuffed clams, New England/Manhattan clam chowders, corn chowder, lobster/clam/shrimp/lobster and cheddar bisques, cream of crab/vegetable crab/crab and cheddar soups, white/red clam sauces, chopped clams, clam juice
Owner: Leonard Rubin
lrubin60@aol.com
CEO: Bernard Rubin
CFO: Toby Rubin
Estimated Sales: $1-2.5 Million
Number Employees: 5-9
Number of Brands: 4
Number of Products: 25
Square Footage: 24000
Type of Packaging: Consumer, Food Service, Private Label, Bulk
Brands:
  Cape Cod
  Capt'n Don's

603

Food Manufacturers / A-Z

2573 Chinese Spaghetti Factory
83 Newmarket Sq
Boston, MA 02118-2619
617-445-7714
Fax: 617-427-5918 www.chinese-spaghetti.com
Peking ravioli, chicken and pork dumplings, scallops with bacon and shrimp spring rolls
Owner: David Sou
dsou@chinese-spaghetti.com
General Manager: Henry Moy
Operations Manager: Ken Moy
Estimated Sales: $1 Million
Number Employees: 20-49
Square Footage: 64000
Type of Packaging: Consumer, Food Service, Private Label, Bulk
Brands:
  Capt'n Eds
  Chinoteaque

2574 Chino Meat Provision Corporation
13564 Central Ave
Chino, CA 91710-5105
909-627-1997
Fax: 909-628-5147
Processor and packer of meat products
Owner: Orestes Blanco
Estimated Sales: $2.5-5 Million
Number Employees: 10-19
Square Footage: 12000
Brands:
  El Paso

2575 Chino Valley Dairy
12000 Eastend Ave
Chino, CA 91710-1565
909-628-8516
Fax: 909-591-4292 800-324-7948
sales@scottbrothers.com www.scottbrothers.com
Dairy products
Heardsman: Stan Scott
Heardsman: Brad Scott
Heardsman: Bruce Scott
General Manager: Rene Peauroi
General Manager: Michael Peauroi
General Manager: Vince Sartain
Manager: Ryan Blair
ryan@sbdfarms.com
Number Employees: 50-99

2576 Chino Valley Ranchers
331 W Citrus Street
Colton, CA 92324
626-652-0890
Fax: 626-652-0893 800-354-4503
info@chinovalleyranchers.com
www.chinovalleyranchers.com
Fresh organic, cage free, free range and fertile white and brown eggs
Marketing Director: David Will
Plant Manager: Mario Gonzalez
Type of Packaging: Consumer, Food Service, Private Label
Brands:
  Chino Valley
  Humane Harvest
  Mothers Free Range
  Nutrifresh
  Veg-A-Fed

2577 Chip Steak & Provision Co
232 Dewey St
Mankato, MN 56001-2393
507-388-6277
Fax: 507-388-6279
Wholesales meat & meat products; wholesales packaged frozen foods
President: Michael Miller
ddi95@yahoo.com
Estimated Sales: $5-9.9 Million
Number Employees: 5-9
Square Footage: 16000
Type of Packaging: Consumer, Food Service, Bulk

2578 Chip'n Dipped Cookie Co
342 New York Ave # 2
Huntington, NY 11743-3567
631-470-2579
questions@chipndipped.com
www.chipndipped.com
Manufacturer of cookies and chocolate.
Foudner and Owner: Peter Goldfarb
peter@chipndipped.com
Estimated Sales: Less Than $500,000
Number Employees: 1-4
Square Footage: 80000

2579 Chipper Snax
1750 S 500 W Ste 700
Salt Lake City, UT 84115
801-977-0742
Fax: 801-977-0743
Beef jerky
Manager: Jeffrey Labrum
Executive Vice President: Jeffrey Labrum
National Sales Manager: Steve Pich
Estimated Sales: $10-20 Million
Number Employees: 20-49
Brands:
  Chipper Beef Jerky

2580 Chiquita Brands LLC.
DCOTA Office Center
1855 Griffin Rd., Suite C-346
Fort Lauderdale, FL 33004-2275
954-924-5700
www.chiquita.com
Fruit and vegetable grower and producer of fresh and prepared food products.
President: Carlos Lopez Flores
VP: Chris Dugan
Year Founded: 1899
Estimated Sales: $3 Billion
Number Employees: 20,000
Number of Brands: 3
Parent Co: Cutrale-Safra
Type of Packaging: Consumer, Food Service, Private Label, Bulk
Brands:
  Chiquita®
  Fresh Express®
  Bites

2581 Chisesi Brothers Meat Packing
5221 Jefferson Hwy
New Orleans, LA 70123-5300
504-822-3550
Fax: 504-822-3916 800-966-3550
www.chisesibros.com
Hams, frankforters, and sausage
President: Donald Bordelon
donald@chisesibros.com
Estimated Sales: $15-20 Million
Number Employees: 100-249
Type of Packaging: Consumer, Food Service

2582 Chisholm Bakery
128 8th Street NW
Chisholm, MN 55719-1656
218-254-4006
Baked goods
Owner: Todd Renke
Estimated Sales: $500,000-$1,000,000
Number Employees: 5-9

2583 Chloe's Fruit
New York, NY 10011
646-442-8000
www.chloesfruit.com
Frozen fruit pops
Founder: Chloe Epstein

2584 Chmura's Bakery
14 Pulaski St
Indian Orchard, MA 01151-2215
413-543-2521
Fax: 413-543-2507 www.aawindowcleaning.com
Rye bread and bakery products
CEO: Joe Albes
Estimated Sales: $1-2,500,000
Number Employees: 10-19

2585 Chobani, Inc.
Norwich, NY
www.chobani.com
Strained yogurt, including Greek, plain, blended, smoothies, snack packs and non-Greek yogurts.
Founder & CEO: Hamdi Ulukaya
Year Founded: 2005
Number Employees: 3,000
Number of Brands: 2
Type of Packaging: Consumer

2586 ChocAlive
16 Mt Ebo Road South
Brewster, NY 10509
845-279-1715
orderchocalive@verizon.net
Gluten free, vegan and raw truffles

2587 Chock Full O'Nuts
888-246-2598
www.chockfullonuts.com
Regular and decaffeinated, ground, instant, and flavoured coffees
Estimated Sales: $67,000
Square Footage: 8984
Parent Co: Massimo Zanetti Beverage
Type of Packaging: Consumer, Food Service, Private Label
Other Locations:
  Chock Full O'Nuts Corp.
  Brooklyn NY
Brands:
  Chock Full O'Nuts
  New York Classics

2588 Choclatique
11030 Santa Monica Blvd #301
Los Angeles, CA 90025-7530
310-479-3849
Fax: 310-479-8448 www.choclatique.com
Chocolates, bars, marshmallows, nuts and novelties, sauces, ganaches and beverages, and baking ingredients
Co-Founder: Ed Engoron
Co-Founder: Joan Vieweger
Marketing: Joan Vieweger

2589 Choco Finesse, LLC
5019 N Meridian St
Indianapolis, IN 46208
317-476-6034
epogee.net
Developer and manufacturer of Epogee Fat Replacement, a low-calorie solid fat replacement.
Founder/CEO: David Rowe
Sr Product & Process Development Advisor: Leo Strecker
Sr Regulatory & Toxicology Advisor: David Bechtel
Head of Manufacturing: Chess Mizell

2590 ChocoME US LLC
25241 Derby Circle
Laguna Hills, CA 92653
949-500-8837
Fax: 949-500-8837 www.chocome.us
Manufacturer of chocolates.
Founder and Owner: Gabor Meszaros
Square Footage: 80000

2591 Chocoholics Divine Desserts
14400 E Highway 26
Linden, CA 95236-9744
209-759-3350 800-760-2462
Fax: info@gourmetchocolate.com
Chocolate dessert toppings, carmel sauces, double fudge cookies, truffles and chocolate novelties
President: Ernie Schenone
VP Sales & Operations: Mary Schenone
Estimated Sales: $5-10 Million
Number Employees: 10-19
Type of Packaging: Private Label

2592 Chocolat
2039 Bellevue Sq
Bellevue, WA 98004-5028
425-452-1141
Fax: 425-452-1142 800-808-2462
Beverages
President: Will Deeg
Director Marketing: Rob Scott
Brands:
  Neuhaus
  Teuscher

2593 Chocolat Belge Heyez
16 Ch De La Rabastaliere E
St-Lazare-De-Bellechasse, QC J3V 2A5
Canada
450-653-5616
Fax: 450-653-1445
Processor and importer of chocolates
Chairman: Bernard Falmagne
VP: Marc Voyer
Treasurer: Dominique Tran
Secretary: Claude Leblanc
Administrator: Sharmila Amin
Estimated Sales: $371,000
Number Employees: 6
Square Footage: 16000
Type of Packaging: Consumer, Private Label

Food Manufacturers / A-Z

2594 Chocolat Jean Talon
4620 Boul Thimens
Montreal, QC H4R 2B2
Canada
514-333-8540
Fax: 514-333-8540 888-333-8540
info@jtalon.ca
Molded hollow chocolates for Easter
President: Robert Poirier
VP/Marketing: Richard Poirier
Sales Manager: Johanne Lavallee
Plant Manager: Lyne Lacharite
Purchasing Manager: Marc Plante
Estimated Sales: $6 Million
Number Employees: 93
Number of Products: 100
Square Footage: 220000
Type of Packaging: Food Service
Brands:
  Chocolat Jean Talon

2595 Chocolat Michel Cluizel
199 Madison Ave
New York, NY 10016-4305
646-415-9126
madison@cluizel.us
www.cluizel.us
Chocolates, calissons, candies and caramels
Contact: Michele Laurent
mlaurent@cluizel.us
Number Employees: 10-19

2596 Chocolat Moderne, LLC.
27 W. 20th St.
Suite 904
New York, NY 10011
212-229-4797
orders@chocolatmoderne.com
www.chocolatmoderne.com
Manufacturer of gourmet chocolate.
Founder and President: Joan Coukos
Contact: Jake Ben-Ami
jake@chocolatmoderne.com
Square Footage: 80000

2597 Chocolate By Design Inc
700 Union Pkwy # 4
Ronkonkoma, NY 11779-7427
631-737-0082
Fax: 631-737-0188 800-536-3618
chocobd@aol.com
Gourmet chocolate novelties and coins; also, custom molding available
President: Ellen Motlin
CEO: Richard Motlin
chocobd@aol.com
Estimated Sales: $500,000
Number Employees: 10-19
Number of Products: 350
Square Footage: 20000
Type of Packaging: Consumer, Private Label

2598 Chocolate By Design Inc
700 Union Pkwy # 4
Ronkonkoma, NY 11779-7427
631-737-0082
Fax: 631-737-0188
Confectionery
Owner: Richard Motlin
chocobd@aol.com
Estimated Sales: $500,000-$1 Million
Number Employees: 10-19
Type of Packaging: Private Label
Brands:
  Chocolate By Design

2599 Chocolate Chix
501 N College Street
Waxahachie, TX 75165-3361
214-744-2442
Fax: 214-744-2449 csurana@chocolatechix.com
www.chocolatechix.com
Meringue cookies
President: Cheryl Surana
Estimated Sales: Less than $500,000
Number Employees: 1-4
Brands:
  Just Meringues
  Mushroom Meringue Cookies

2600 Chocolate Chocolate Chocolate
5025 Pattison Ave
St Louis, MO 63110-2037
314-338-3501
Fax: 314-832-2299 www.chocolatechocolate.com
Manufacturer of handcrafted, premium chocolate.
President: Dan Abel
Number Employees: 10-19
Square Footage: 80000

2601 Chocolate Creations
3465 Brodhead Rd # 4
Monaca, PA 15061-3144
724-774-7675
Fax: 724-774-7675 chocolatecreations@msn.com
Full line of specialty and seasonal chocolate gifts
Owner: Tony Unterberger
tunterberger@duquesnelight.com
Estimated Sales: $5-10 Million
Number Employees: 1-4

2602 Chocolate Delivery Systems Inc
85 River Rock Dr
Suite 202
Buffalo, NY 14207-2170
716-854-6050
Fax: 716-854-7363 www.tomric.com
Manufacturer of chocolates.
President: Tim Thill
CFO: Jim Heron
Quality Manager: Robert Short
t.elsinghorst@tomric.com
Number Employees: 10-19
Square Footage: 80000

2603 Chocolate Fantasies
340 Shore Drive
Burr Ridge, IL 60527
630-572-0045
Fax: 630-572-0039 contactus@espressosecrets.net
All natural dark chocolate confections married to rich espresso coffee.
CEO: Leonard Defranco

2604 Chocolate House
4121 South 35th Street
Milwaukee, WI 53221
414-281-7803
Fax: 414-423-2484 800-236-2022
Manufacturer and exporter of chocolate
Manager: Irene Hyducki
Executive Vice President: Gary Winder
Estimated Sales: $10-20 Million
Number Employees: 50-99
Type of Packaging: Consumer
Brands:
  Absolutely Almond
  Chocolate Mint Meltaways
  Fudgie Bears
  Positively Pecan

2605 Chocolate Maven
Chocolate Maven Bakery & Cafe 821
W. San Mateo Rd
Santa Fe, NM 87505
505-984-1980
www.chocolatemaven.com
Pastries and baked goods

2606 Chocolate Moon
2002 Riverside Drive
42F
Asheville, NC 28804
828-253-6060
Fax: 828-253-1020 800-723-1236
info@bluemoonwater.com
www.bluemoonwater.com
Chocolate covered dried cherries, blueberries and apricots, toffee, cocoa and cappuccino chocolate almonds and pistachios
Owner: Chris Mathis
Operations Manager: Jennifer Donnell
Purchasing Manager: Jennifer Donnell
Estimated Sales: $1-2.5 Million
Number Employees: 10-19
Brands:
  Davinci Gourmet
  Ghiardelli
  Guittard
  Lindt
  Marich
  Oregon Chai

2607 Chocolate Shoppe Ice Cream Co
2221 Daniels St
Madison, WI 53718-6745
608-221-8640
Fax: 608-221-8650 800-466-8043
www.chocolateshoppeicecream.com
Frozen desserts
Owner: Chuck Deadman
dave@chocolateshoppeicecream.com
Vice President: Dave Deadman
Purchasing Manager: Dave Deadman
Estimated Sales: $2.5-5 Million
Number Employees: 20-49

2608 Chocolate Signatures LP
166 Norseman St
Toronto, ON M8Z 2R4
Canada
416-234-8528
Fax: 416-234-0627
www.chocolatesignaturesinc.com
Chocolate bars, truffles, toffee, caramel candy
Sales/Corporate: Dina Gama
Brand Manager: Heather Chu

2609 Chocolate Smith
851 Cerrillos Rd # A
Santa Fe, NM 87505-3005
505-473-2111
Fax: 505-982-6897 www.chocolatesmith.com
Chocolates
Owner: Kari Keenan
contact@chocolatesmith.com
Estimated Sales: Less Than $500,000
Number Employees: 5-9

2610 Chocolate Soup
2300 Mount Werner Circle
Unit C-1
Steamboat Springs, CO 80487
970-870-0224
Fax: 970-870-0378
Organic/natural, cakes/pastries, cookies, crackers, other baked goods, other chocolate, other snacks, private label.
Marketing: Lisa Ciraldo

2611 Chocolate Street of Hartville
114 South Prospect Avenue
Hartville, OH 44632-1010
330-877-1999
Fax: 330-877-1100 888-853-5904
www.discoverhartville.com
Custom chocolate products including 3-D corporate logos, bars and personalized gold foil wrapped coins; also, private label available; exporter of chocolate processing equipment including cooling tunnels, vibration tables, measuringpumps, etc
General Manager: Robert Barton
Estimated Sales: $10-20 Million
Number Employees: 20-49
Square Footage: 26000
Type of Packaging: Consumer, Food Service, Private Label, Bulk
Brands:
  Chocolate Street of Hartville

2612 Chocolate Studio
142 W Germantown Pike
Unit A
Norristown, PA 19401
610-272-3872
Fax: 610-272-3872
Chocolates
Owner: John Giaimo
Estimated Sales: $2.5-5 Million
Number Employees: 5-9
Type of Packaging: Consumer, Bulk

2613 Chocolate Works
114 Church St
Freeport, NY 11520
info@chocolateworks.com
www.chocolateworks.com
Chocolate
Founder: Joe Whaley

2614 Chocolaterie Bernard Callebaut
133 1st Street SE
Calgary, AB T2G 5L1
Canada
403-265-5777
Fax: 403-265-7738 800-661-8367
www.bernardcallebaut.com

Food Manufacturers / A-Z

Processor and exporter of quality chocolates and chocolate products, including spreads, sauces and ice cream bars
President/CEO: Bernard Callebaut
Number Employees: 20-49
Type of Packaging: Consumer, Private Label
Brands:
  Chocolaterie Bernard Callebaut

2615 Chocolaterie Stam
2814 Ingersoll Ave
Des Moines, IA 50312-4013
515-282-9575
Fax: 515-282-9763 877-782-6246
ton@stamchocolate.com www.stamchocolate.com
Quality Dutch chocolates
President: Ton Stam
ton@stamchocolate.com
Estimated Sales: $500,000-$1 Million
Number Employees: 10-19
Brands:
  Stam

2616 Chocolates By Mr Roberts
505 NE 20th St
Boca Raton, FL 33431-8141
561-392-3007
Fax: 561-392-3014
chocbymrroberts@bellsouth.net
www.chocolatesbymrroberts.com
Fine chocolates and truffles, chocolate-covered fruit
Owner: Heinz Robert Goldschneider
CEO: Michelle Zander
Contact: Robert Goldschmider
chocbymrroberts@bellsouth.net
Estimated Sales: Less Than $500,000
Number Employees: 1-4

2617 Chocolates El Rey, Inc
1324 West Clay
Houston, TX 77019
800-357-3999
Info@ChocolatesElRey.com
Premium chocolates. Retail/wholesale, block, discos and chips
President: Randall Turner
Contact: Cody Bollig
bolligcody@chocolate.com.ve
Estimated Sales: $2.5-5 Million
Number Employees: 1-4
Brands:
  Carenero
  El Rey
  Rio Caribe

2618 Chocolates Turin
Granite Parkway
Suite 200
Plano, TX 75024
972-731-6771
Fax: 972-731-6774 www.turin.com.mx
Chocolates
National Sales Manager: Jim Hutchins

2619 Chocolates a La Carte
24836 Avenue Rockefeller
Valencia, CA 91355
661-257-3700
Fax: 661-257-4999 800-818-2462
orders@candymaker.com www.candymaker.com
Processor, importer and exporter of chocolate designs for desserts, amenities and gifts including pianos, swans, sea shells, etc
President: Rena Pocrass
CEO/VP: Richard Pocrass
VP Finance and Administration: Michael Pocrass
Marketing Manager: Diane Rudman
Contact: Tony Aguirre
taguirre@candymaker.com
EVP/Head of Operations: Frank Geukens
Estimated Sales: $26 Million
Number Employees: 165
Square Footage: 110000
Type of Packaging: Food Service
Brands:
  Chocolates a La Carte

2620 Chocolates by Mark
2100 Space Park Drive
Suite 102
Houston, TX 77058
832-736-2626
Fax: 603-925-8000 www.chocolatesbymark.com
Custom chocolate wedding/party favors, gifts

President: Mark Caffey
Number Employees: 1-4
Square Footage: 8800
Type of Packaging: Private Label, Bulk

2621 Chocolati Handmade Chocolates
7708 Aurora Ave N
Seattle, WA 98103-4752
206-784-5212
Fax: 206-525-4574 information@chocolati.com
www.chocolati.com
Candy including mint truffles
Owner: Christian Wong
VP: John Berg
Estimated Sales: $100000
Number Employees: 5-9
Square Footage: 20400
Type of Packaging: Consumer, Private Label, Bulk

2622 Chocolatier
27 Water St
Exeter, NH 03833-2440
603-772-5253
Fax: 603-772-0793 888-246-5528
www.the-chocolatier.com
Molded corporate chocolate candy
Owner: Jason Martone
jmartone@the-chocolatier.com
Estimated Sales: $220,000
Number Employees: 5-9

2623 Chocolove
PO Box 18357
Boulder, CO 80308
303-786-7888
Fax: 303-440-8850 888-246-2656
margaret@chocolove.com www.chocolove.com
Belgian chocolate bars
Founder, Owner: Timothy Moley
Marketing: Kerri Gedert
Estimated Sales: $2.5-5 Million
Number Employees: 5-9
Brands:
  Chocolove

2624 Chocomize
30-10 41st Ave.
4th Floor
Long Island City, NY 11101
800-621-3294
info@chocomize.com
www.chocomize.com
Manufacturer of chocolate bars and pieces.
Co-Founder: Eric Heinbockel
Co-Founder: Fabian Kaempfer
Contact: Jeleisa Forbes-Lowry
jeleisa@chocomize.com
Square Footage: 80000

2625 Chocopologie By Knipschildt
12 S Main St
Norwalk, CT 06854-2978
203-854-4754
Fax: 203-838-3137 info@knipschildt.com
www.chocopologie.com
Chocolates
President/Owner: Fritz Knipschildt
chocopologie@gmail.com
Marketing: Amanda Ciaszki
Number Employees: 10-19

2626 Choctal
1 W Mountain St # 12
Pasadena, CA 91103-3070
USA
626-798-1351
www.choctal.com
Ice cream
CEO: Michael Leb
COO: Robert Michero
Chief Strategy Officer: Nancy Hytone Leb
Contact: Marlene Munoz
marlene.munoz@choctal.com
Operations Manager: Marlene Munoz
Estimated Sales: 250,000
Number Employees: 1-4

2627 Choctaw Maid Farms
Old Highway 15 N
Jackson, MS 39209
601-683-4000
Fax: 601-298-5497
Processor, importer and exporter of fresh and frozen chicken parts

Owner: Tammy Etheridge
Purchasing Agent: Ruthie Harper
Number Employees: 250-499
Type of Packaging: Bulk

2628 Choice Food Distributors LLC
6167 Cockrill Bend Cir
Nashville, TN 37209-1051
615-350-6070
Fax: 615-350-6862 www.thechoicefood.com
Manufacturer and marketer of shelf-stable and prepared foods including muffin and baking mixes, salad dressings, sauces, spices and herbs
Chairman: Michael Shmerling
CEO: Jerry Walker
jwalker@thechoicefood.com
CFO: Mark Johnson
National Accounts Sales Manager: Beth Eaton
Estimated Sales: $4.2 Million
Number Employees: 50-99
Brands:
  Mayberry's Finest
  O'Charley's
  Lamont's

2629 Choice Food Group Inc
618 Church St # 220
Nashville, TN 37219-2453
615-248-9255
www.choicefood.com
Shelf-stable and prepared foods
Number Employees: 1-4
Type of Packaging: Consumer, Private Label

2630 Choice Organic Teas
600 S Brandon St
Seattle, WA 98108-2240
206-525-0051
Fax: 206-523-9750 866-972-6879
choiceorganicteas@worldpantry.com
www.choiceorganicteas.com
Processor and exporter of organic teas including black, green and herbal
Founder: Blake Rankin
Estimated Sales: $1-$2.5 Million
Number Employees: 20-49
Parent Co: Granum Inc
Type of Packaging: Consumer, Food Service, Private Label, Bulk
Brands:
  Choice
  Choice Organic Teas
  Granum
  Kaiseki Select
  Mitoku Macrobiotic
  Sound Sea Vegetables

2631 Choice of Vermont
305 Tequesta Drive
Destin, FL 32541-5715
802-888-6261
Fax: 802-888-6244 800-444-6261
Mustard, hummus, black bean salsa, bruschetta toppings, maple pumpkin butter, pesto sauce and horseradish jam
President: Jim Peterson
Sales Director: Kevin Butler
Operations Manager: Robert Nelson
Estimated Sales: $1 Million
Number Employees: 5-9
Number of Brands: 1
Number of Products: 28
Square Footage: 40000
Type of Packaging: Consumer, Food Service, Private Label
Brands:
  Choice of Vermont

2632 Chomps
465 Bayfront Place
Naples, FL 34102
team@chomps.com
chomps.com
Beef chews
Number of Brands: 1
Number of Products: 4
Type of Packaging: Consumer
Brands:
  CHOMPS

Food Manufacturers / A-Z

2633 Chong Mei Trading
1130 Oakleigh Dr
East Point, GA 30344
404-768-3838
Fax: 404-768-0008
Pork, beef, seafood, chicken, dry goods, dairy, produce, Oriental grocery items
President: Kai Chen Wong
Estimated Sales: $1-3 Million
Number Employees: 10-19

2634 Chooljian Bros Packing Co
3192 S Indianola Avenue
PO Box 395
Sanger, CA 93657
559-875-5501
Fax: 559-875-1582
k.elliott@chooljianbrothers.com
www.chooljianbrothers.com
Processor and exporter of raisins; also, custom packaging services
President: Michael Chooljian
mchooljian@chooljianbrothers.com
Estimated Sales: $500,000
Number Employees: 50-99
Parent Co: Chooljian Brothers Packing Company
Type of Packaging: Consumer, Food Service, Private Label, Bulk
Brands:
  Chooljian
  Prize

2635 Chops Snacks
5101 Old Highway 5
Suite 440
Lebanon, GA 30146
Fax: 718-210-2746 888-571-4442
info@chopssnacks.com topchops.com
Beef jerky
Co-Founder: Luke Sellers
Co-Founder: Dusty Jaquins
Marketing: Carole Gervasi
Number of Brands: 1
Number of Products: 4
Type of Packaging: Consumer
Brands:
  T.O.P. Chops

2636 Chosen Foods, Inc.
453 54th St
Suite 102
San Diego, CA 92114-2220
USA
877-674-2244
Fax: 888-503-6591 www.chosen-foods.com
Grain, cereal, pasta, spreads, syrups, oils
President: George Todd
Chief Executive Officer: Carsten Hagen
Contact: Ardith Alexander
ardith@chosen-foods.com
Estimated Sales: 1,200,000
Number Employees: 12

2637 Chouinard Vineyards & Winery
33853 Palomares Rd
Castro Valley, CA 94552-9616
510-582-9900
Fax: 510-733-6274 chouinard@chouinard.com
www.chouinard.com
Wines
Owner: Damian Chouinard
mamachouinard@gmail.com
Estimated Sales: $1-2.5 Million
Number Employees: 1-4
Brands:
  Alicante Bouschet
  California Champagne
  Central Coast Chardonnay
  Chouinard Red
  Chouinard Rose
  Granny Smith Apple
  Lodi Zinfandel
  Monterey Cabernet Sauvignon
  Monterey Chardonnay
  Monterey Petite Syrah
  Paso Robles Cabernet Sauvignon
  Paso Robles Orange Muscat

2638 Choyce Produce
3140 Ualena St
Suite 206
Honolulu, HI 96819-1965
808-839-1502
President: Edmund Choy
Contact: Annette Forness
aforness@choycehi.com
Estimated Sales: $5-10 Million
Number Employees: 5-9

2639 Chozen Ice Cream
171 W 12th Street
Suite 6C
New York, NY 10011-8210
212-675-4191
Fax: 212-675-4191
Kosher, organic/natural, frozen desserts, ice cream/sorbet.
Marketing: Meredith Fisher

2640 Chr Hansen Inc
9015 W Maple St
Milwaukee, WI 53214
414-607-5700
Fax: 414-607-5959 usinfo@chr-hansen.com
www.chr-hansen.com
Health nutritionals and savory, sweet, dairy, and compound blend flavors.
President & CEO: Mauricio Graber
EVP & CFO: Soren Westh Lonning
EVP & CSO: Thomas Schafer
EVP, Global Operations: Torsten Steenholt
Estimated Sales: $100-499.9 Million
Number Employees: 100-249

2641 Chris Candies Inc
1557 Spring Garden Ave
Pittsburgh, PA 15212-3632
412-322-9400
Fax: 412-322-9402 sales@chriscandies.com
Chocolate bars and novelties; also, custom molds, labels and imprints available. Organic and kosher certified
President: Mark Davis
mark.davis@chriscandies.com
VP/CIO: Dave Byard
Human Resources Manager: Lori Cipkins
mark.davis@chriscandies.com
Operations Executive: Mike Gefert
Estimated Sales: $5-9.9 Million
Number Employees: 50-99
Square Footage: 128000
Type of Packaging: Consumer, Food Service, Private Label

2642 Chris Hansen Seafood
134 Chris Ln
Port Sulphur, LA 70083-2814
504-564-2888
Seafood
Owner: Chris Hansen
Estimated Sales: Less Than $500,000
Number Employees: 1-4

2643 Chris' Farm Stand
Stasinos Farm
11 Lake Street
Peabody, MA 01960
978-994-4315
stasinosma@gmail.com
www.chrisfarmstand.com
Organic produce and jams and jellies
President: Thomas Holopainen
Estimated Sales: Less than $500,000
Number Employees: 5-9
Type of Packaging: Consumer

2644 Chris's Cookies
100 Hollister Rd # 5
Unic C-1
Teterboro, NJ 07608-1139
201-288-8881
Fax: 201-438-8444
customerservice@chriscookies.com
www.chriscookies.com
Manufacturer of cookies, brownies, and pastries.
Co-Founder: Chris Gargiulo
CEO and Co-Founder: Manish Wadia
EVP: Betty Osmanoglu
Quality Assurance Manager: Kapila Devkota
Number Employees: 50-99
Square Footage: 80000

2645 Christensen Ridge Winery
HCR 02,
Box 459
Madison, VA 22727
540-923-4800
Wine
President/Owner: J D Hartman
Estimated Sales: $3-5 Million
Number Employees: 5-9

2646 Christie Cookie
1205 3rd Ave N
Nashville, TN 37208-2703
615-242-3817
Fax: 615-242-5572 800-458-2447
www.christiecookies.com
Gourmet cookies and frozen ready to bake dough.
President: Fleming Wilt
fleming.wilt@christiecookies.com
VP, Sales: Jay McKnight
Director, New Business Development: Charles Tommolino
Marketing Manager: Caroline Sloan
Estimated Sales: $10-20 Million
Number Employees: 20-49
Type of Packaging: Food Service

2647 Christie's
220 Canton Street
Stoughton, MA 02072
781-341-3341
Fax: 781-341-3340 info@avonfood.com
avonfood.com
Processor and contract packager salad dressings and marinades
Estimated Sales: $1-2.5 Million
Number Employees: 20-49
Square Footage: 120000
Parent Co: Avon Food Company
Type of Packaging: Consumer, Food Service, Private Label, Bulk
Brands:
  Christie's Instant-Chef

2648 Christie-Brown
200 Deforest Avenue
East Hanover, NJ 07936-2833
973-503-4000
Fax: 973-503-3660
CEO: Chip Clothier
Estimated Sales: Under $500,000
Number Employees: 5-9

2649 Christine & Rob's Inc
41103 Stayton Scio Rd SE
Stayton, OR 97383-9400
503-769-2993
Fax: 503-769-1291 bartell@wvi.com
www.christineandrobs.com
Old-fashioned oatmeal and preserves
Owner: Christine Bartell
Owner: Rob Bartell
bartell@wvi.com
Estimated Sales: Less Than $500,000
Number Employees: 1-4

2650 Christine Woods Winery
3155 Highway 128
Philo, CA 95466
707-895-2115
Fax: 707-895-2748 www.christinewoods.com
Wines
Owner: Vernon Rose
Owner: Jo Rose
Partner: Edward Rose
Partner: Lisa Rose
Estimated Sales: $500,000-$1 Million
Number Employees: 1-4
Type of Packaging: Private Label

2651 Christmas Point Wild Rice Co
14803 Edgewood Dr
Baxter, MN 56425-8455
218-828-0603
Fax: 218-828-0543 info@christmaspoint.com
www.christmaspoint.com
Wild rice products
Manager: Scott Goehring
info@christmaspoint.com
Estimated Sales: $500,000-$1 Million
Number Employees: 20-49

2652 Christopher Creek Winery
641 Limerick Ln
Healdsburg, CA 95448-9586
707-433-2001
Fax: 707-431-0183 www.christophercreek.com
Wines

Food Manufacturers / A-Z

Owner: Juan Escudero
juan@ea.com
Owner: Fred Wasserman
Estimated Sales: $500,000
Number Employees: 5-9
Square Footage: 12
Type of Packaging: Private Label

2653 Christopher Joseph Brewing Company
6812 E Valley Vista Ln
Paradise Valley, AZ 85253
480-948-7882
Beer
President: Joseph Mocca
Estimated Sales: Under $500,000
Number Employees: 10-19
Brands:
 Bandersnatch Milk Stout
 Big Horn Premium
 Cardinal Pale Ale

2654 Christopher Norman Chocolates
PO Box 1145
Hudson, NY 12534
518-822-0300
Fax: 877-220-5751
Manufacturers of hand made chocolates
Founder/Owner: John Down
Estimated Sales: $300,000-500,000
Number Employees: 1-4
Brands:
 Christopher Norman Chocolates

2655 Christopher Ranch LLC
305 Bloomfield Ave.
Gilroy, CA 95020
408-847-1100
Fax: 408-847-5488 Info@christopherranch.com
www.christopherranch.com
Garlic. Varieties include fresh peeled, fresh roasted, whole fresh, chopped and crushed in oil, chopped and minced in water, pickled garlic, elephant garlic, fresh ginger, fresh shallots, specialty onions, sun dried tomatoes, cherriespeeled specialty onions, horseradish, sweet corn, organic, and dried chiles.
President/CEO: Bill Christopher
Year Founded: 1956
Estimated Sales: $135 Million
Number Employees: 1000-4999
Square Footage: 220000
Type of Packaging: Consumer, Food Service, Bulk

2656 Christopher's Herb Shop
188 S Main St
Springville, UT 84663-1849
801-489-4500
Fax: 801-489-4814 888-372-4372
www.drchristophersherbshop.com
Food supplements manufacturer, private label items, herbs and health foods
President: David Christopher
Vice President: Ruth Christopher Bacalla
Manager: Bobbie Henderson
manager@drchristopherhersbshop.com
Production Manager: James Webster
Purchasing Manager: Josh Bruni
Estimated Sales: Less Than $500,000
Number Employees: 5-9
Square Footage: 15000
Type of Packaging: Private Label

2657 Christy Wild Blueberry Farms
1167 Southhampton Road
Amherst, NS B4H 3Y4
Canada
902-667-3013
Fax: 902-667-0350 chrisgaklis@comcast.net
christywildblueberryfarms.com/
Processor and exporter of IQF wild blueberries
President: Chris Gaklis
Estimated Sales: $1.95 Million
Number Employees: 15
Parent Co: International Food Trade
Brands:
 Blue Boy
 Christy Crops

2658 Chuao Chocolatier
2345 Camino Vida Roble
Carlsbad, CA 92011
760-476-1668
Fax: 760-476-1355 888-635-1444
sales@chuaochocolatier.com
www.chuaochocolatier.com
Chocolates
President: Michael Antonorsi
Ceo: Sergio Alvarez
Chairman: Richard Antonorsi
Marketing: Thomas Pineda
Number Employees: 30

2659 Chuck's Seafoods
91135 Cape Arago Hwy
Charleston, OR 97420
541-888-5525
Fax: 541-888-2121 www.chucksseafood.com
Processor and canner of seafood including salmon, tuna, clams, crabs and shrimp
President: Jack Hampel
Secretary: Diana Hampel
Estimated Sales: $5-10 Million
Number Employees: 5-9
Type of Packaging: Consumer
Brands:
 Vandon Sea-Pack

2660 Chudabeef Jerky Co.
Long Beach, CA 90804
chastian@chudabeef.com
www.chudabeef.com
Beef jerky
Founder: Kevin Casey

2661 Chudleigh's
8501 Chudleigh Way
Milton, ON L9T 0L9
Canada
905-878-8781
Fax: 905-878-6979 800-387-4028
farm@chudleighs.com www.chudleighs.com
Fresh fruit pies and baked fruits
President: Dean Chudleigh
VP: Scott Chudleigh
Estimated Sales: $4.8 Million
Number Employees: 120
Brands:
 Chudleigh's

2662 Chugwater Chili
210 1st St
Chugwater, WY 82210
307-422-3345
Fax: 307-422-3357 800-972-4454
chugchili@direcway.com
www.chugwaterchili.com
Chili products including dip and dressing mixes, chili nuts red pepper jelly and ingredients including spices, seasoning blends and peppers, and also steak rub which is new.
Owner: Marcelyn Brown
chugchili@chugwaterchili.com
CEO: Del Ficanz
VP: Karl Wilkerson
Marketing Director: Raece Wilkerson
Sales Director: Raece Wilkerson
chugchili@chugwaterchili.com
Public Relations: Marcelyn Brown
Estimated Sales: $2.5-5 Million
Number Employees: 10-19
Number of Brands: 1
Number of Products: 5
Square Footage: 10240
Type of Packaging: Consumer, Food Service
Brands:
 Chugwater Chili

2663 Chukar Cherries
320 Wine Country Rd
P.O. Box 510
Prosser, WA 99350-9797
509-786-2055
Fax: 509-786-2591 800-624-9544
sales@chukar.com www.chukar.com
Cherries, dried fruit, trail mixes, chocolates, preserves, sauces, baking mixes, tea and fresh cherries
President: Pam Auld
pam@chukar.com
Chief Financial Officer: JT Montgomery
Head of Production: Kathlene Yound
Estimated Sales: $20-50 Million
Number Employees: 20-49

2664 Chunco Foods Inc
1400 E 2nd St
Kansas City, MO 64106-1301
816-283-0716
Fax: 816-472-7779
Fresh tofu, mung bean sprouts, alfalfa sprouts, radish sprouts, authentic koream kim chee, broccoli sprouts, onion sprouts, crispy sprouts and soy milk
Owner: Peter Chun Jr
Estimated Sales: $660,000
Number Employees: 5-9
Square Footage: 8000
Type of Packaging: Food Service

2665 Chungs Gourmet Foods
3907 Dennis St
Houston, TX 77004-2520
713-741-2118
Fax: 713-741-2330 www.chungsfoods.com
Producer of Asian food products, including egg rolls, sprin rolls, potstickers and ready-to-eat entrees.
President: Vreij "Reg" Kolandjian
CEO: Danny Bell
dbell@chungsfoods.com
Number Employees: 250-499
Parent Co: Yellowstone Brands
Type of Packaging: Consumer, Food Service, Private Label
Brands:
 Chung's

2666 Church & Dwight Co., Inc.
Princeton South Corporate Center
500 Charles Ewing Boulevard
Ewing, NJ 08628
609-806-1200
800-833-9532
www.churchdwight.com
Personal care, household cleaning, fabric care, and health and well-being products for the consumer market. Manufacturer of Arm & Hammer brand sodium bicarbonate (baking soda), and other leavening products for the baking industry.
Chairman/President/CEO: Matthew Farrell
Executive VP/CFO: Rick Dierker
Executive VP/General Counsel/Secretary: Patrick de Maynadier
Executive V, Global R&D: Carlos Linares
Executive VP/CMO: Britta Bomhard
Executive VP, U.S. Sales: Paul Wood
Executive VP, Global Operations: Rick Spann
Year Founded: 1846
Estimated Sales: $4.15 Billion
Number Employees: 4,700
Number of Brands: 34
Type of Packaging: Consumer, Food Service, Bulk
Brands:
 ARM & HAMMER
 Arrid
 Answer
 AIM
 Batiste Dry Shampoo
 Close-Up
 Delicare
 Feline Pine
 First Response
 KABOOM
 Lady's Choice
 Legatin
 L'il Critters
 Nair
 Orajel
 Orange Glo
 OxiClean
 PB 8
 Pepsodent
 Pre-Seed
 RepHresh
 Replens
 Simply Saline
 Spinbrush
 Toppik
 Trojan
 Truly Radient
 vitafusion
 Viviscal
 Waterpik
 Wellgate
 XTRA

Food Manufacturers / A-Z

2667 (HQ)Churny Company
705 W Fulton St
Waupaca, WI 54981
715-258-4040
Fax: 715-258-4046 www.churnyfoodservice.com
Cheese
President/CEO: William Gifford
Sr Vice President: Pascal Fernandez
Vice President, General Manager: Cliff Fleet
Contact: Laura Ruzzo
lruzzo@atwoodcherny.com
Asset Manager: Dave Edel
Operations/Plant Manager: Michael Spence
Estimated Sales: $10-20 Million
Number Employees: 100-249
Square Footage: 126000
Parent Co: Kraft Foods
Type of Packaging: Consumer, Food Service, Private Label
Brands:
 Hoffmans
 Polly-O
 Athenos
 Digiorno

2668 Churny Company
114 Waukegan Rd,
Glenview, IL 60025
847-646-5500
Fax: 847-646-5588 www.athenos.com
Feta cheese
Sales: John Curran
Marketing Director: Roy Lubetkin
Manager: Mary Kay Haben
Estimated Sales: $1-2.5 Million
Number Employees: 50-99
Parent Co: Kraft Foods

2669 (HQ)Ciao Bella Gelato Company
25 Vreeland Rd, #A-104
Irvington, NJ 07040
973-373-1200
Fax: 973-373-1224 800-435-2863
info@ciaobellagelato.com
www.ciaobellagelato.com
Gelato and sorbet
CFO: Stan Fabian
VP, Finance: Ray Bialick
Estimated Sales: $5-10 Million
Number Employees: 50
Square Footage: 40000
Type of Packaging: Consumer, Food Service, Private Label, Bulk
Other Locations:
 Ciao Bella Gelato Co.
 San Francisco CA
 Ciao Bella Gelato Co.
 Los Angeles CA
Brands:
 Ciao Bella
 Gelato
 Gotham Dairy
 Sarabeth's
 Ciao Bella Sorbet

2670 Cibao Meat Products Inc
630 Saint Anns Ave
Bronx, NY 10455-1404
718-993-5072
Fax: 718-993-5638 info@cibaomeat.com
www.cibaomeat.com
Processor and exporter of Spanish sausage and salami.
President: Lutzi Vieluf
CEO: Heinz Vielus
Estimated Sales: $5-10 Million
Number Employees: 50-99
Type of Packaging: Food Service, Bulk
Brands:
 Campesino Jamoneta
 Don Pedro Jamonada
 Induveca
 Longaniza Cibao
 Pavolami
 Salami Campesino
 Salami Del Pueblo
 Salami Sosua
 Salapeno Salami
 Ver-Mex
 Villa Mella

2671 Cibaria International
705 Columbia Ave
Riverside, CA 92507
951-823-8490
Fax: 951-823-8495 www.cibaria-intl.com
Oils, vinegars and accessories
Founder: Kathy Griset
Square Footage: 55000
Type of Packaging: Food Service, Private Label, Bulk

2672 Cibo Vita
12 Vreeland Ave
Totowa, NJ 07512
862-238-8020
info@cibovita.com
www.cibovita.com
Natural and organic snacks and chocolate-covered fruits and nuts
Owner: Ahmet Celik

2673 CideRoad, LLC
P.O. Box 520
Mendham, NJ 07945-0520
973-543-9003
www.cideroad.com
Organic switchel
CEO: Kevin Duffy
Brand Manager: Noelle Shea
Year Founded: 2013
Type of Packaging: Private Label

2674 Cielo Foods
9238 Bally Ct
Rancho Cucamonga, CA 91730-5313
909-945-2323
Fax: 909-945-9090 877-652-4356
www.cielousa.com
Frozen yogurt
Owner: Dan Kim
info@cielousa.com
Number Employees: 5-9

2675 Cienega Valley Winery/DeRose
9970 Cienega Road
Hollister, CA 95023
831-636-9143
Fax: 831-636-1435 info@derosewine.com
www.derosewine.com
Producers of red, white and port wines.
Owner: Pat De Rose
Winemaker: Al DeRose
Assistant Winemaker: Ralph Hurd
Estimated Sales: $500,000- 1 Million
Number Employees: 1-4
Type of Packaging: Private Label
Brands:
 De Rose Vineyards

2676 Cifelli & Sons Inc
38 Obert St
PO Box 538
South River, NJ 08882-1235
732-238-0090
Fax: 732-238-7768
Italian sausage
Owner: Anthony Cifelli
Estimated Sales: $2.5 Million
Number Employees: 10-19
Square Footage: 14000
Type of Packaging: Private Label

2677 Cimarron Cellars
P.O.Box 8
Caney, OK 74533
580-889-5997
Fax: 580-889-6312
Wine
Owner/Winemaker: Dwayne Pool
Owner: Suze Pool
President: Linda Pool
Estimated Sales: $1-2,500,000
Number Employees: 1-4
Brands:
 Cimarron Cellars

2678 Cimpl Meats
1000 Cattle Dr.
Yankton, SD 57078
605-665-1665
Fax: 605-665-8908
Sausage and beef.
President: Gary Becker
Senior Vice President: Charleen Ward
Year Founded: 1940
Estimated Sales: $152.3 Million
Number Employees: 2,000
Square Footage: 25265

2679 Cincinnati Preserving Co
3015 E Kemper Rd
Cincinnati, OH 45241-1514
513-771-2000
Fax: 513-771-8381 800-222-9966
www.clearbrookfarms.com
Fruit preserves ,jams,jellies,canned fruit,pie fillings,fruit pie mixes.
Owner/CFO: Andrew Liscow
VP: Dan Cohen
Contact: Joe Heinrich
joe@clearbrookfarms.com
Estimated Sales: 1.8 Million
Number Employees: 18
Square Footage: 120000
Parent Co: Cincinatti Preserving Company
Type of Packaging: Consumer
Brands:
 Clearbrook Frams
 Spreadable Fruit

2680 Cinderella Cheese Cake Co
208 N Fairview St
PO Box 36
Riverside, NJ 08075-3113
856-461-6302
Fax: 856-461-5813 800-521-1171
Processor/Manufacturer of frozen cheesecake
President/CEO: Joseph Makin
Founder: Alfred Rezende
Estimated Sales: $1 Million
Number Employees: 10-19
Square Footage: 80000
Type of Packaging: Consumer, Food Service
Brands:
 Cinderella

2681 Cinnabar Specialty Foods Inc
1134 Haining St # C
Prescott, AZ 86305-1693
928-778-3687
Fax: 928-778-4289 866-293-6433
info@cinnabarfoods.com www.cinnabarfoods.com
Processor and exporter of sauces including ethnic and barbecue; also, fruit chutneys, dry spice blends, Caribbean salsa, kashmiri marinade, rice mixes, soup enhancers, etc
Owner: Alana Morrison
sales@cinnabarfoods.com
Vice President: Ted Schleicher
Estimated Sales: $1-4.9 Million
Number Employees: 1-4
Square Footage: 4000
Type of Packaging: Consumer, Food Service, Private Label, Bulk
Brands:
 Cinnabar Specialty Foods
 Neera's

2682 Cinnabar Winery
14612 Big Basin Way # A
Saratoga, CA 95070-6085
408-867-1010
Fax: 408-741-5860
Wines
President: Suzanne Frontz
General Manager: Suzan Franz
Estimated Sales: $2.5-5 Million
Number Employees: 10-19

2683 Cinnamon Bakery
121 Hancock Street
Braintree, MA 02184-7040
781-843-2867
Fax: 781-849-0015 800-886-2867
cinbak@aol.com
Cinnamon, raspberry and chocolate sticks, pecan sticky buns and cinnamon rolls
President: Tom Pattavina
Treasurer: Frances Pattavina
Estimated Sales: $2.5-5 Million
Number Employees: 5-9
Brands:
 Boston Bakers Exchange
 Cinnamon Bakery

609

Food Manufacturers / A-Z

2684 Cipriani's Spaghetti & Sauce Company
1025 West End Avenue
Chicago Heights, IL 60411-2742
708-755-6212
Fax: 708-755-6272
Processor and exporter of pasta including angel hair, vermicelli, linguine, fettuccine, lasagna, spinach, etc.; also, pasta sauces
President/Purchasing Manager: Annette Johnson
Executive VP: Arthur Petrarca
Estimated Sales: $5-10 Million
Number Employees: 10-19
Square Footage: 43572
Type of Packaging: Consumer, Food Service, Private Label, Bulk
Brands:
 Cipriani's Classic Italian
 Cipriani's Premium

2685 Circle B Ranch
RR2 Box 2824
Seymour, MO 65746
417-683-0271
www.circlebranchpork.com
Pork products, bacon, meat sticks, sauces, chutneys, and gluten free Bloody Mary mix
Owner: Marina Backes
Owner: John Backes

2686 Circle R Ranch
5901 Cross Timbers Rd
Flower Mound, TX 75022-3142
817-430-1561
Fax: 817-430-8108 800-247-3077
www.circlerranch.org
Sauces including black bean salsa, jalapeno jelly, green chili salsa, cheese and spice blend, corn relish and mesquite barbecue; also, snacks including jalapeno popcorn, habanero popcorn and snack mix
Owner: Jason Roberts
jasonroberts@circlerranch.org
CEO: Alan Powdermaker
Chief Financial Officer: Laura Johnson
Sales manager: Robyn Lacasse
jasonroberts@circlerranch.org
Director of Events: Blair Green
Event Services Manager: Ocean Martinez
Estimated Sales: Less than $500,000
Number Employees: 10-19
Parent Co: Sunset Trails
Type of Packaging: Consumer, Private Label
Brands:
 Circle R Gourmet Foods

2687 Circle V Meats
609 Arrowhead Trl
Spanish Fork, UT 84660-9237
801-798-3081
Fax: 801-798-8671 www.circlevmeat.com
Beef and pork including roasts, ham and bacon
Owner: Cliff Voorhees
admin@circlevmeat.com
Estimated Sales: $3 Million
Number Employees: 10-19

2688 Circle Valley Produce LLC
1370 Burgess St
Idaho Falls, ID 83402-1825
208-524-2628
Fax: 208-524-2630 www.idahopotato.com
Processor and exporter of potatoes
President: Kent Cornelison
Communications: Kirk Hart
Purchasing: Dave Owens
Estimated Sales: $8.8 Million
Number Employees: 50-99
Type of Packaging: Consumer, Bulk
Brands:
 Throughbred
 Valley Gold

2689 Circus Man Ice Cream Corporation
1000 Fulton St
Farmingdale, NY 11735-4245
516-249-4400
Fax: 516-249-4435
Ice cream
Owner: Blaise Graziano
Estimated Sales: $1.8,000,000
Number Employees: 10-19
Brands:
 Circus Man

2690 Ciro Foods
PO Box 44096
Pittsburgh, PA 15205-0296
412-771-9018
Fax: 412-771-9018 cirofoods@usa.net
Roasted red pepper spread, Italian salsa, sauces including pizza, barbecue and cooking and hot honey mustard; wholesaler/distributor of hot pepper sauce; serving the food service market; importer of vinegar; exporter of hot honeymustard
President: Robert Pasquarelli
VP: Josephine Proto
Marketing Executive: Armand Pasquarelli
Number Employees: 20
Type of Packaging: Consumer, Food Service, Private Label

2691 Cisco Brewers
5 Bartlett Farm Rd
Nantucket, MA 02554-4341
508-325-5929
Fax: 508-325-5209 tracy@ciscobrewers.com
www.ciscobrewers.com
Producer of ale and lager beers
Owner: Randy Hudson
randy@ciscobrewers.com
CEO: Jay Harman
Web And Social Media Manager: Kristen V Hull
randy@ciscobrewers.com
Estimated Sales: $600,000
Number Employees: 1-4
Square Footage: 12800
Type of Packaging: Consumer
Brands:
 Baggywrinkle
 Bailey's
 Captain Swain's Extra
 Celebration Libation
 Dubbel Felix Caspian
 Moor
 Nobadeer Ginger
 Summer of Lager
 Whale's Tale

2692 Cisse Trading Co
129 Halstead Ave
Mamaroneck, NY 10543-5608
914-381-5555
info@cissetrading.com
www.cissecocoa.com
Baking mixes, hot cocoa, and super thin brownie thins.
Founder: Diana Lovett
Number Employees: 10-19
Brands:
 Super THINS

2693 (HQ)Citadelle Maple Syrup Producers' Cooperative
2100 St-Laurent, CP 310
Plessisville, QC G6L 2Y8
Canada
819-362-3241
Fax: 819-362-2830 citadelle@citadelle.coop
www.citadelle.coop
Processor and exporter of fruit spreads, honey, pure maple syrup and maple sugar.
CEO: Martin Plante
Director Financial Services & Treasurer: Patrick Fleurent, CPA, CMA
Dir. of Corporate Affairs & Secretary: Jean-Marie Chouinard
Director of Marketing: Sylvie Chapron
Princial Sales Director: Stephane Vachon, M.Sc.
Human Resources Director: Richard Cote
Director Operations & Quality: Remi Fortin, ing. MBA
Number Employees: 150
Square Footage: 360000
Type of Packaging: Consumer, Food Service, Private Label, Bulk
Other Locations:
 La Guadeloupe Facility
 Guadeloupe QC
 Restigouche Brand Inc
 Saint-Quentin NB
 Facility & Distribution Centre
 Plessisville QC
 Tertiary Transformation Facility
 Plessisville QC
 Cranberry Transformation Facility
 Aston-Jonction QC
Brands:
 Camp
 Canada Gold
 Citadelle
 O'Canada

2694 Citrico
155 Revere Dr # 1
Northbrook, IL 60062-1558
847-835-4368
Fax: 847-945-7405 800-445-2171
www.creativeimpactgroup.com
An independent manufacturer of citrus products for the food, beverage, pharmaceutical and nutraceutical industries.
Owner: Joanne Brooks
VP Technical Sales: Robert Vieregg
Sales: Timothy Grano
Contact: Todd Heinz
th@citico.com
Estimated Sales: $4.8 Million
Number Employees: 10-19
Number of Brands: 20
Parent Co: Citrico International
Brands:
 Citrico

2695 Citromax Flavors Inc
444 Washington Ave
Carlstadt, NJ 07072-2806
201-933-8405
Fax: 201-549-1261 www.citromax.com
Grower of lemons and producer of oils, juices and lemon by-products such as essential oils, cloudy and clarified concentrated juices and dehydrated peel. Flavors are used in beverages, confection, dairy and baked goods.
President: Angela Begley
angelabegley@citromaxflavors.com
Quality Control Chemist: Joseph Clark
Directory Of Operations/Plant Manager: Max Van Der Linden
Estimated Sales: $560,000
Number Employees: 1-4
Square Footage: 4599

2696 Citrop Inc
5707 W Sligh Ave
Tampa, FL 33634-4435
813-249-5955
Fax: 813-249-5956
Natural flavoring
President/CEO: Jorge Figueredo
Estimated Sales: $1-2.5 000,000
Number Employees: 1-4

2697 Citrosuco North AmericaInc
5937 State Road 60 E
Lake Wales, FL 33898-9279
863-696-7400
Fax: 863-696-1303 800-356-4592
citrosuco@citrosuco.com.br www.citrosuco.com
Orange juice and concentrates; importer of frozen orange and apple concentrates and not from concentrate orange juice; exporter of frozen orange juice concentrates and not from concentrate orange juice
President: Nick Emanuel
CEO: Kathy Baker
kbaker@citrosuco.com
CFO: Dennis Helms
Sales Manager: Michael DuBrul
Plant Manager: Jim Bolden
Purchasing Manager: Gary Brundage
Estimated Sales: Less Than $500,000
Number Employees: 1-4
Square Footage: 38200
Parent Co: Citrosuco
Type of Packaging: Bulk

2698 Citrus International
210 Salvador Sq
Winter Park, FL 32789-5619
407-629-8037
Fax: 407-629-8195
Citrus juice
President: Brian Albertson
Estimated Sales: Under $500,000
Number Employees: 1-4

2699 Citrus Service
120 S Dillard St
Winter Garden, FL 34787
407-656-4999
Fax: 407-656-4999 beroper@iag.net
Manufacturer and exporter of frozen organic citrus juices and frozen juice concentrates

610

Food Manufacturers / A-Z

President: Bert Roper
CEO: Charles Roper
Estimated Sales: $4 Million
Number Employees: 20-49
Square Footage: 42000
Type of Packaging: Bulk
Brands:
    Grove Sweet

2700 Citrus and Allied Essences
3000 Marcus Ave, Ste 3e11
New Hyde Park, NY 11042
516-354-1200
Fax: 516-354-1502 www.citrusandallied.com
Supplier of essential oils, oleoresins, aromatic chemicals and specialty flavor ingredients.
President/CEO/Owner: Richard Pisano Jr.
Executive Vice President: Stephen Pisano
Sales Manager: Ann Heller
Contact: Jodi Adams
jadams@citrusandallied.com
Director Purchasing: Rob Haedrich
Number Employees: 100+
Type of Packaging: Food Service, Bulk

2701 Citterio USA
2008 State Route 940
Freeland, PA 18224-3256
570-636-3171
Fax: 570-636-1267 800-435-8888
sales@citteriousa.com www.citteriousa.com
Processor and importer of Italian Speciality deli meat products
President/COO: Osvaldo Vanucci
CEO: Michelle Basista
mbasista@citteriousa.com
CEO: Nick Dei Tos
VP Sales: Joseph Petruce
VP Manufacturing: Michael Zieminski
Estimated Sales: $5-10 Million
Number Employees: 100-249
Parent Co: Giuseppe Citterio Spa
Type of Packaging: Consumer, Food Service, Private Label, Bulk
Brands:
    Citterio

2702 City Bakery
3 W 18th St # 1
New York, NY 10011-4610
212-366-1414
Fax: 212-645-0810 info@thecitybakery.com
www.thecitybakery.com
Pretzel croissants and other baked goods.
Owner: Maury Rubin
citybakerysara@mac.com
Number Employees: 20-49

2703 City Bakery Cafe
60 Biltmore Ave # 1
Asheville, NC 28801-3643
828-252-4426
Fax: 212-645-0810 877-328-3687
info@thecitybakery.com www.citybakery.net
Pretzel croissants and other baked goods.
Owner: Maury R Rubin
Marketing: Allison Dees
Manager: Craig Peters
citybakery@bellsouth.net
Estimated Sales: Less Than $500,000
Number Employees: 5-9
Brands:
    Maury's Cookie Dough
    The City Bakery

2704 City Bean
5051 W Jefferson Blvd
Los Angeles, CA 90016-3940
323-734-0828
Fax: 310-208-4554 888-248-9232
info@citybean.com www.citybean.com
Coffee, tea
Owner: Gary Salzer
Estimated Sales: $500,000-$1 Million
Number Employees: 5-9

2705 City Brewing Company
925 S 3rd St
La Crosse, WI 54601
608-785-4200
inquiries@citybrewery.com
www.citybrewery.com
Manufacturer/processor of beer for major and private label brands.

VP & Chief Financial Officer: Gregory Inda
Director, Supply Chain: Jeff Glynn
Year Founded: 1939
Estimated Sales: $38 Million
Number Employees: 400
Type of Packaging: Consumer
Other Locations:
    Latrobe PA
    Memphis TN
Brands:
    City Lager
    City Light
    City Slicker
    Kul
    Lacrosse Lager
    Lacrosse Light

2706 City Cafe & Bakery
215 Glynn St S
Fayetteville, GA 30214-2039
770-461-6800
Fax: 770-461-2161 www.citycafeandbakery.com
Bakery products
Owner: Jorg Schatte
citycafebakery@bellsouth.net
Estimated Sales: $3-5 Million
Number Employees: 20-49

2707 City Farm/Rocky Peanut Company
1545 Clay Street
Detroit, MI 48211-1911
313-871-5100
Fax: 313-871-5106 800-437-6825
rocky-peanut.com/city-farm.com
Holiday snack items
President: Joe Russo
Estimated Sales: $2.5-5 Million
Number Employees: 5-9

2708 City Foods Inc
4230 S Racine Ave
Chicago, IL 60609-2526
773-523-1566
Fax: 773-523-1414 info@beasbest.com
www.beasbest.com
Processor, importer and exporter of frozen beef products including corned beef brisket, short ribs, corned, sliced, roast beef, pastrami, and beef bacon
President: Kenneth Kohn
CEO: John Campbell
john@beasbest.com
Information Technology Manager: Chris Humberg
Sales Manager: Scott Weiss
Director Of Purchasing: John Campbell
Estimated Sales: $48 Million
Number Employees: 50-99
Number of Brands: 3
Square Footage: 43000
Type of Packaging: Consumer, Food Service, Private Label, Bulk
Brands:
    Bea's Best
    Chef's Pride
    Silver Label

2709 City Market
1508 Gloucester St
Brunswick, GA 31520-7143
912-265-4430
Fax: 912-261-2191 www.citymarketseafood.com
Fish and seafood
Owner: Michael Howell
m.howell@citymarket.com
Manager: Frank Owens
Estimated Sales: $3,500,000
Number Employees: 5-9

2710 City Saucery
37 Laconia Ave.
Staten Island, NY 11215
718-753-4006
info@citysaucery.com
www.citysaucery.com
A variety of tomato products including tomato sauce, paste, and preserved tomatoes.
Owner and Co-Founder: Michael Marino
Owner and Co-Founder: Jorge Moret

2711 Clabber Girl Corporation
900 Wabash Ave
Terre Haute, IN 47807-3208
812-232-9446
Fax: 812-232-2397 www.clabbergirl.com

Manufacturer of baking powder, baking soda, dessert mixes and corn starch for retail, food service and industrial customers.
National Sales Manager: Mark Rice
Type of Packaging: Consumer, Food Service, Private Label, Bulk
Brands:
    Clabber Girl®
    Rumford®
    Rex Coffee
    Hearth Club
    Davis®
    Fleischmann's Baking Powder
    Royal®
    InnovaPhase™

2712 Claeys Candy Inc
525 S Taylor St
South Bend, IN 46601-2744
574-287-1818
Fax: 574-287-4184
customerservice@claeyscandy.com
www.claeyscandy.com
Candy, old fashioned hard candies, cream fudge, gourmet peanut brittle, chocolate charlie gift boxes, bulk, private label
President: Gregg Claeys
gclaeys@claeyscandy.com
Plant Manager: Brian Machalleck
Estimated Sales: $10-20 Million
Number Employees: 20-49
Number of Brands: 4
Type of Packaging: Consumer, Private Label, Bulk
Brands:
    Chocolate Charlie
    Claeys Gourmet Cream Fudge
    Claeys Gourmet Peanut Brittle
    Claeys Old Fashion Hards Candies

2713 Claiborne & Churchill Vintners
2649 Carpenter Canyon Rd
San Luis Obispo, CA 93401-8934
805-544-4066
Fax: 805-544-7012 info@claibornechurchill.com
www.claibornechurchill.com
Wines
Owner: Clay Thompson
Owner/CEO: Fredericka Churchill
Marketing Manager: Angela Gloeckler
Estimated Sales: $500,000-$1 Million
Number Employees: 1-4
Brands:
    Claiborne & Churchill

2714 Clara Foods
100 First Avenue SE
Clara City, MN 56222-0457
320-847-3680
Fax: 320-847-3939 888-844-8518
Snack foods, pretzels, cereal, baking ingredients and extruded products
President: Massoud Kazemzadeh
VP Sales/Marketing: Tom Condon
Research & Development: Massoud Kazemzadeh
Purchasing Manager: Joe Jeanotte
Estimated Sales: $1.5 Million
Number Employees: 40

2715 Clara Foods
One Tower Pl.
Ste. 800
San Francisco, CA 94080
info@clarafoods.com
www.clarafoods.com
Egg whites, egg replacers, baking products, food and beverage ingredients, nutritional supplements, animal-free protein.
CEO: Arturo Elizondo
VP, Product: Harshal Kshirsagar
VP, Tech: Joel Kreps
Year Founded: 2014
Number Employees: 11-50
Type of Packaging: Consumer, Food Service

2716 Clarendon Flavor Engineering
2500 Stanley Gault Parkway
Louisville, KY 40223
502-634-9215
Fax: 502-634-1438 www.clarendonflavors.com
Manufactures natural and artificial flavors to food and beverage industry. Specializes in natural soft drinks, juice added and flavored sparkling waters
President: Richard Rigney

Food Manufacturers / A-Z

Estimated Sales: $5-10 Million
Number Employees: 6
Square Footage: 80000
Type of Packaging: Bulk

2717 Clariant
4000 Monroe Rd
Charlottte, NC 28205
704-331-7000
Fax: 704-377-1063 www.clariant.com
Chemical and ingredient manufacturer.
CEO: Hariolf Kottmann

2718 Clark Spring Water Co
319 Clark Street
Pueblo, CO 81003
719-543-1594
ar@clarkspringwater.com
www.clarkspringwater.com
Processor and bottler of water
Founder: Silas Clark
Estimated Sales: Less Than $500,000
Number Employees: 5-9
Type of Packaging: Consumer
Brands:
  Alpine

2719 Clarke J F Corp
173 Franklin Ave
Franklin Square, NY 11010-1341
516-328-8333
Fax: 516-328-8346 800-229-7474
jclarke@jfclarke.com www.jfclarke.com
Frozen shrimp and seafood
President: James Clarke
jclarke@jfclarke.com
Estimated Sales: $5-10 Million
Number Employees: 1-4
Type of Packaging: Food Service
Brands:
  Amazonas
  Avila
  Bee Gee
  Fresh Cargo
  Yutaka

2720 Clarkson Scottish Bakery
1715 Lakeshore Road West
Mississauga, ON L5J 1J4
Canada
905-823-1500
Scottish baked goods including pies, pastries and breads; importer of Scottish and English meats, candies and chocolates
Proprietor: Catherine Whitelaw
Number Employees: 1-4
Square Footage: 1800

2721 Clarmil Manufacturing Corp
30865 San Clemente St
Hayward, CA 94544-7136
510-476-0700
Fax: 510-476-0707 888-252-7645
customerservice@goldilocks-usa.com
Manufacturers a full line of breads, rolls, buns, filled buns and pies, pastries, sweet goods, cookies, crackers and snack items. Cakes-pound cake, sponge, devil, chiffon, snack cakes and other specialty cake items. Processes soupssauces, side dishes, stews, processed meat products, meat and vegetable fillings, hors d'ouvers, specialty snacks and appetizers.
President: Marion Ortiz Luis
myoritz-lus@clarmilmfg.com
Estimated Sales: Less than $500,000
Number Employees: 100-249
Number of Products: 200+
Square Footage: 228000
Type of Packaging: Consumer, Food Service, Private Label, Bulk

2722 Clasen Quality Chocolate
5126 W Terrace Dr # 100
Suite 100
Madison, WI 53718-8346
608-467-1130
Fax: 608-249-4573 877-459-4500
info@clasen.us www.clasen.us
Pure chocolate and confectionery coatings, including milk, dark, white, yogurt, peanut, colored and flavored coatings.
President: Jay Jensen
CFO: Andy Gitter
VP: Dennis Tagarelli
Vice President of Sales and Marketing: Joe Lucas

Estimated Sales: Under $500,000
Number Employees: 5-9
Square Footage: 11228
Type of Packaging: Consumer, Bulk
Brands:
  Clasen

2723 Classic Commissary
126 E Arterial Highway
Binghamton, NY 13901-1656
800-929-3486
Fax: 607-722-1415 classiccommissary@aol.com
Fresh salads and fruits; also, frozen dinners, sandwiches and bagels; for the vending and convenience food industry
Owner: Tara Gianfrate
Contact: Cataldo Gianfrate
cataldo.gianfrate@classiccatering.com
Manager: Cataldo Gianfrate
Number Employees: 50-99
Number of Products: 125
Square Footage: 88000
Type of Packaging: Food Service, Private Label, Bulk
Brands:
  Classic Commissary

2724 Classic Confectionery
PO Box 573
Fort Worth, TX 76101-0573
847-674-4490
Fax: 847-674-4435 800-674-4435
TomDetective@yahoo.com
www.candydetective.com
Candy and confectionery
President: Cory Rogin
Co-Founder: Thomas Allen
President: Gail Robinson
General Manager: Trevor Toppen
Number Employees: 50-99

2725 Classic Cookings, LLC
165-35 145th Drive
Jamaica, NY 11434
718-439-0200
www.classiccooking.com
Manufacturer of souffles, quiches, and hearty soups.
Contact: Elliot Huss
elliot@classiccooking.com
Square Footage: 80000

2726 Classic Delight Inc
310 S Park Dr
P.O.Box 367
St Marys, OH 45885-9688
419-394-7955
Fax: 419-394-3199 800-274-9828
orders@classicdelight.com
www.classicdelight.com
Processor and co-packer of USDA and FDA frozen and refrigerated sandwiches, meat and entrees
Owner: Darl Harkleroad
darl@classicdelight.com
Estimated Sales: $5 Million
Number Employees: 50-99
Number of Brands: 25
Number of Products: 60
Square Footage: 74000
Type of Packaging: Consumer, Food Service, Private Label, Bulk
Brands:
  Classic Delight
  Express Delights
  Sensible Delights

2727 Classic Flavors & Fragrances
878 W End Ave Apt 12b
New York, NY 10025
212-777-0004
Fax: 212-353-0404 cffi125@aol.com
Manufacturer, importer and exporter of flavors, essential oils, aromatics, etc
CEO: George Ivolin
Estimated Sales: $2.5-5 Million
Number Employees: 5-9
Square Footage: 3600
Type of Packaging: Bulk

2728 Classic Foods
1592 Union Street
49
San Francisco, CA 94123-4531
800-574-8122
Fax: 866-235-9993

Family owned manufacturer of top quality branded snack foods distributed throughout the United States and Canada.
President: Florencio Cuetara
VP of Sales-Food Service: Shane Gray
Director of Sales-Vending: Lynn Marie Robles
Contact: Jeff Rynearson
jeffr_ims@yahoo.com
Estimated Sales: $5-10 Million
Number Employees: 100-249
Brands:
  Baked Classics
  Kettle Classics
  Kids Klassics
  Stoned Classics

2729 (HQ)Classic Tea
649 Innsbruck Court
Libertyville, IL 60048-1845
630-680-9934
Processor, importer and exporter of ceylon (black) tea, liquid tea syrup and iced tea concentrates
Managing Director: Thomas Rielly
Director: F Court Bailey
Number Employees: 20-49
Square Footage: 80000
Type of Packaging: Consumer, Food Service, Private Label, Bulk
Other Locations:
  Classic Tea Ltd.
  Chicago IL
Brands:
  Ceylon Classic
  Classic Ceylon
  Pearl

2730 Classy Delites
P.O.Box 340189
Austin, TX 78734-0004
512-266-7157
Fax: 512-266-7198 800-440-2648
All-natural, artichoke marvelous melody, basalmic bean sauce, reduced carbs tweed tortilla chips, jamaican sauce, spinach-avacado sauce and portabella sauce.
Owner: Debbie Westbrook
CEO: Drew Westbrook
drew@classydelites.com
Estimated Sales: $1-2.5 Million
Number Employees: 1-4
Type of Packaging: Consumer
Brands:
  Classy Delites

2731 Claudia B Chocolates
663 W Rhapsody Dr
San Antonio, TX 78216-2608
210-366-4602
Fax: 800-375-4602 800-725-4602
sales@claudiab.com www.claudiab.com
Chocolates
President: Don Bankler
sales@claudiab.com
Estimated Sales: Less Than $500,000
Number Employees: 1-4
Square Footage: 8000
Type of Packaging: Consumer, Private Label, Bulk

2732 Claxton Bakery Inc
203 W Main St
PO Box 367
Claxton, GA 30417-1705
912-739-3097
Fax: 912-739-3097 800-841-4211
service@claxtonfruitcake.com
www.claxtonfruitcake.com
Established in 1910. Manufacturer and exporter of fruit cake, pecans, candies, and dressings.
Vice President: Paul Parker
ppgolf912@bellsouth.net
Estimated Sales: $20-50 Million
Number Employees: 100-249
Type of Packaging: Consumer
Brands:
  Claxton

2733 Clay Center Locker Plant
212 6th St
Clay Center, KS 67432-3312
785-632-5550
Fax: 785-632-5550 800-466-5543
brad@claycenterlocker.com
www.claycenterlocker.com
Beef, pork, lamb, buffalo and ostrich

Food Manufacturers / A-Z

Owner: Brad Dieckmann
claycorod@claycountykansas.org
Estimated Sales: $3-5 Million
Number Employees: 5-9
Type of Packaging: Consumer, Food Service

2734 Clayton Coffee & Tea
502 10th St
Modesto, CA 95354-3504
209-576-1120
Fax: 209-576-1123 sales@claytoncoffee.com
www.claytoncoffee.com
Coffee and tea
Owner: Gretchen Peek
billkuhn@claytoncoffe.com
Estimated Sales: $1-2.5 Million
Number Employees: 1-4
Type of Packaging: Bulk
Brands:
 Clayton Coffee & Tea

2735 Clayton's Crab Co
5775 US Highway 1
Rockledge, FL 32955-5729
321-636-6673
Fax: 321-636-4631
www.claytonscrabcompany.com
Crab meat; wholesaler/distributor of fresh, frozen and canned seafood and meat; serving the food service market
Owner: Janet Walker
claytoncrabjan@cfl.rr.com
Estimated Sales: $1-3 Million
Number Employees: 10-19

2736 Cleanfish Inc
450 Bay St
San Francisco, CA 94133-1820
415-626-3500
Fax: 415-626-2505 annette@cleanfish.com
www.cleanfish.com
Fresh seafood
Owner: Gakhan Perain
gpercin@cadence.com
CEO: Tim o'Shea
Controller: Annette Lee
Bay Area Dealer: Kendrick Wu
Number Employees: 10-19

2737 Clear Creek Distillery
2389 NW Wilson St
Portland, OR 97210-2319
503-248-9470
Fax: 503-248-0490 info@clearcreekdistillery.com
www.clearcreekdistillery.com
Wine and liquor
President: Stephen R Mc Carthy
Vice President: Rachel Showaiter
Estimated Sales: $700,000
Number Employees: 5-9
Type of Packaging: Private Label
Brands:
 Bartlett
 Blue Plumb Brandy
 Clear Creek Grappas
 Flamboise
 Kirschwasser (Cherry Brandy)
 McCarthy's Oregon Single Malt
 Pear Brandy
 Pure Fruite

2738 Clear Mountain Coffee Company
9155 Brookville Rd
Silver Spring, MD 20910
301-587-2233
Fax: 301-587-7158
Fourteen varieties of organic and wood roasted coffees, syrups, Choice Tea, Ghiradelli Chocolate
President: Robert Dasilva
Estimated Sales: $1-2.5 Million
Number Employees: 10-19
Number of Brands: 10
Brands:
 10

2739 Clear Products Inc.
6156 Mission Gorge Rd
Suite C
San Diego, CA 92120
619-521-0327
Fax: 619-283-3913 888-257-2532
mail@clearproductsinc.com
www.clearproductsinc.com
Manufacturing

Owner: Del Neville
Estimated Sales: $300,000-500,000
Number Employees: 1-4

2740 Clear Springs Foods Inc.
1500 E. 4424 N. Clear Lakes Rd.
PO Box 712
Buhl, ID 83316
208-543-4316
800-635-8211
csfsales@clearsprings.com www.clearsprings.com
Fresh and frozen rainbow trout, breaded trout portions, shapes and melts.
CEO: Kurt Meyers
COO: Jeff Jermunson
Year Founded: 1991
Estimated Sales: $130 Million
Number Employees: 250-499
Number of Brands: 4
Square Footage: 7200
Type of Packaging: Consumer, Food Service, Private Label
Brands:
 Clear Springs Kitchen®
 Clear Springs®
 ClearùCuts®
 Splash®

2741 Clear-Vu Industries
200 Homer Avenue
Suite 3
Ashland, MA 01721-1716
508-881-9100
Fax: 508-881-9111 www.clear-vu.com
Bulk Candy System
President: Robert McCann
Estimated Sales: $1-2.5 Million
Number Employees: 10-19

2742 Clearly Canadian Beverage Corporation
220 Viceroy Rd
Units 11/12
Vanghan, ON L4K 3CA
Canada
905-761-0597
Fax: 607-742-5301 866-414-2326
www.clearly.ca
Processor and exporter of water including sparkling fruit, carbonated mineral and artesian
President: David Reingold
CEO: Roy Hessel
CFO: Craig Lennox
Director of Business Intelligence & FP&A: Ibrahim Kamar
Director, Human Resources: Nancy Savard
COO: Nancy Morison
Estimated Sales: $10.62million
Number Employees: 20
Type of Packaging: Consumer, Food Service
Brands:
 Clearly Canadian
 Clearly Canadian O+2
 Orbitz
 Quencher
 Tre' Limone

2743 Clearly Kombucha
San Francisco, CA 94533
www.clearlykombucha.com
Sparkling teas
Co-Founder: Alison Zarrow
Co-Founder: Caleb Cargle
Number of Brands: 1
Number of Products: 6
Type of Packaging: Consumer
Brands:
 CLEARLY KOMBUCHA

2744 Clearwater Coffee Company
711 Rose Rd
Lake Zurich, IL 60047-1542
847-540-7711
Fax: 847-540-7719
Coffee
President: Jim Ludwig

2745 Clearwater Fine Foods
757 Bedford Highway
Bedford, NS B4A 3Z7
Canada
902-443-0550
Fax: 902-443-8367 www.clearwater.ca
Processor and exporter of frozen shrimp, lobster, scallops, crabs and clams
Chairman: Colin MacDonald
CEO: Ian Smith
Number Employees: 100-249
Type of Packaging: Consumer, Food Service

2746 Clem Becker Meats
2720 Lincoln Ave
Two Rivers, WI 54241
920-793-1391
Fax: 920-793-1393 clembeckerinc@lakefield.net
Smoked pork products
President: Peter Becker
VP: Oliver Skrivanie
Business Manager: Jan Eycke
Estimated Sales: $5-10 Million
Number Employees: 25
Type of Packaging: Consumer, Food Service, Private Label

2747 Clem's Seafood & Specialties
4505 Mattingly Ct
Buckner, KY 40010-8830
502-222-7571
Fax: 502-222-7598
Seafood
Owner: Michael McAlister
Estimated Sales: $3-5 Million
Number Employees: 1-4

2748 Clemens Family Corporation
2700 Clemens Rd
Hatfield, PA 19440-0902
800-523-5291
www.clemensfamilycorp.com
Pork products
CEO: Douglas C. Clemens
Contact: Michelle Alldred
malldred@cvff.com

2749 Clement's Pastry Shops Inc
3355 52nd Ave # B
Hyattsville, MD 20781-1033
301-277-6300
Fax: 301-277-2897 office@clementspastry.com
www.clementspastry.com
Custom manufacturing of specialty dessert and pastry items.
President: Richard Barrazotto
Co-Owner: Matthew Barrazotto
VP: John Barrazotto
Estimated Sales: $11 Million
Number Employees: 100-249
Number of Brands: 1
Number of Products: 200
Type of Packaging: Food Service, Private Label
Brands:
 Clements Pastry Shop

2750 (HQ)Clements Foods Co
6601 N Harvey Pl
Oklahoma City, OK 73116
405-842-3308
Fax: 405-843-6894 800-654-8355
clementsfoodscompany.com
Apple butter, preserves, jellies, salad dressings, pie fillings, mayonnaise, mustard, sauces, syrups, vinegar, peanut butter and imitation vanilla; exporter of salad dressings and mustards
President: Edward Clements
Executive Vice President: Robert Clements
Year Founded: 1952
Estimated Sales: $61 Million
Number Employees: 100-249
Number of Brands: 8
Square Footage: 150000
Type of Packaging: Consumer, Food Service, Private Label
Other Locations:
 Clements Foods Company
 Lewisville TX
Brands:
 American
 Delicious
 Dorcheste
 Garden Club
 Little Pig
 Par
 Savory
 Win You

613

Food Manufacturers / A-Z

2751 Clemmy's
PO Box 1746
Randcho Mirage, CA 92270
877-253-6698
www.clemmysicecream.com
Lactose free, 100% sugar free and gluten free ice cream.
Founder/Owner: Jon Gordon
Number Employees: 6
Square Footage: 4374
Type of Packaging: Consumer

2752 Clemson Bros. Brewery
22 Cottage St.
Middletown, NY 10940
845-775-4638
info@clemsonbrewing.com
www.clemsonbrewing.com
Flavored ale, IPA, Belgian-style wheat beer, fruit wheat beers, stout & porter
Co-Owner: Kenan Porter
Number of Brands: 1
Number of Products: 19
Type of Packaging: Consumer, Private Label
Brands:
 Clemson Bros.

2753 Cleveland Kraut
4700 Lakeside Ave
Suite 19-1C
Cleveland, OH 44114
216-264-6895
sales@clevelandkraut.com
clevelandkraut.com
Unpasteurized kraut
Co-Founder: Luke Visnic
Estimated Sales: Less than $500,000
Number Employees: 4
Type of Packaging: Private Label

2754 Cleveland Syrup Corporation
4999 Mead Avenue
Cleveland, OH 44127-1107
216-883-1845
Fax: 216-883-6204
Syrup and powdered sugar
Vice President: James Chaney
General Manager: Jim Chaney
President: Virginia Chaney
Estimated Sales: $1-2.5 Million
Number Employees: 1 to 4
Type of Packaging: Food Service, Bulk

2755 Clic International Inc
2185 Av. Francis Hugues
Laval, QC H7S 1N5
Canada
450-669-2663
Fax: 450-667-6799 agtclic@agtclic.com
www.agtclic.com
Grains, rices, beverages, condiments, pasta, dairy products, dried fruit and nuts, and more.
Estimated Sales: $24.5
Number Employees: 123

2756 Clif Bar & Co
1451 66th St
Emeryville, CA 94608-1004
510-547-1144
Fax: 510-558-7872 802-254-3227
www.clifbar.com
Energy bars, nutrition bars, protein bars, energy chews, energy granolas, energy gel, protein drink mixes, and electrolyte drink mixes
CEO: Kevin Cleary
Founder/Owner & Co-CVO: Gary Erickson
Owner & Co-CVO: Kit Crawford
EVP Food & Innovation: Michelle Ferguson
Marketing Director: Joey Steger
Year Founded: 1992
Estimated Sales: $500 Million-$1 Billion
Number Employees: 1200
Type of Packaging: Consumer, Private Label
Brands:
 CLIF BAR
 CLIF KID
 LUNA
 CLIF SHOT
 CLIF BUILDER'S
 CLIF CRUNCH
 CLIF MOJO

2757 Cliff Lede Vineyards
1473 Yountville Cross Rd
Yountville, CA 94599-9471
707-944-8642
Fax: 707-944-8020 800-428-2259
info@CliffLedeVineyards.com
www.cliffledevineyards.com
Wines and champagne
Owner: Cliff Lede
CEO: John Anderson
Vice President of Operations: Remi Cohen
Marketing Manager: Alfred Andreson
Sales Manager: Peter Vanm
Estimated Sales: $430,000
Number Employees: 20-49
Type of Packaging: Consumer, Food Service

2758 Clifty Farm Country Meats
P.O. Box 1146
Paris, TN 38242
731-642-9740
Fax: 731-642-7129 800-486-4267
www.cliftyfarm.com
Frozen portion cuts of bacon, ham and barbecue pork and turkey
President & CEO: Dan Murphey
Marketing & Sales Manager: Adrian Harrod
Number Employees: 100
Square Footage: 800000
Type of Packaging: Consumer, Food Service
Brands:
 Clifty Farm

2759 Cline Cellars
24737 Arnold Dr
Sonoma, CA 95476-9216
707-940-4030
Fax: 707-931-7118 800-543-2070
www.mizpahhotel.info
Wines
Owner: Laura Feinstein
laurafeinstein@gmail.com
CFO: Nancy Cline
Event Planner: Jennifer Alvarez
Production Manager: Matt Cline
Estimated Sales: Under $500,000
Number Employees: 1-4
Type of Packaging: Private Label
Brands:
 Cline Cellars

2760 Clinton St Baking Co
4 Clinton St
New York, NY 10002-1703
646-602-6263
dede@clintonstreetbaking.com
www.clintonstreetbaking.com
Baked goods
Owner: Neal Kleinberg
graybiscuits@earthlink.net
Estimated Sales: Less Than $500,000
Number Employees: 1-4

2761 Clinton Vineyards Inc
450 Schultzville Rd
Clinton Corners, NY 12514-2402
845-266-5372
Fax: 845-266-3395 clintonwine@aol.com
www.dutchesswinetrail.com
Producer of estate bottled champagnes, white wines & dessert wines.
Owner: Phyllis Feder
info@clintonvineyards.com
Marketing Director: Rita Flood
Public Relations: Debbie Groduindo
General Manager: Chris Stuart
Plant Manager: Bill Wentzel
Estimated Sales: Less Than $500,000
Number Employees: 1-4
Type of Packaging: Consumer
Brands:
 Clinton Victory
 Duet
 Embrace
 Nuit
 Peach Gal
 Romance
 Seyval Blanc
 Seyval Naturel

2762 Clio Snacks
Roselle, NJ 07203
info@cliosnacks.com
www.cliosnacks.com
Chocolate-covered Greek yogurt bars
General Manager: Heather MacNeil Cox
Marketing Director: Rachel Moore
Estimated Sales: $6 Million

2763 Clipper City Brewing
4615 Hollins Ferry Rd
Halethorpe, MD 21227
410-247-7822
Fax: 410-247-7829 www.hsbeer.com
Brewer of beer and ale
Owner: Hugh Sisson
Sales Manager: Joe Gold
Contact: J Hugh
hugh@ccbeer.com
Southern Territory Manager: Kevin Fox
Packaging Manager: John Eugeni
Estimated Sales: $2 Million
Number Employees: 20
Type of Packaging: Consumer, Food Service
Brands:
 Loose Cannon
 Heavy Seas Marzen
 Great Pumpkin
 Aarsh
 Big Dipa
 Hang Ten
 Holy Sheet
 Letter of Marquee 2010
 Letter of Marquee 2011
 Plank 1
 Yule Tide

2764 (HQ)Clofine Dairy Products Inc
1407 New Rd
P.O. Box 335
Linwood, NJ 08221
609-653-1000
Fax: 609-653-0127 info@clofinedairy.com
www.clofinedairy.com
Fluid and dried dairy products; proteins, cheeses, milk replacement blends, tofu and soymilk powders, vital wheat gluten, etc.
Chairman: Larry Clofine
lclofine@clofinedairy.com
President & CEO: Frederick Smith
CFO: Butch Harmon
Warehouse Coordinator: Pamela Gerety
Estimated Sales: $20-50 Million
Number Employees: 10-19
Number of Brands: 2
Number of Products: 100
Type of Packaging: Food Service, Private Label, Bulk
Other Locations:
 Midwest Officer
 Chicago IL
Brands:
 Fine-Mix Dairy
 Food Blends
 Soy Products
 Soyfine
 Soymilk

2765 Cloister Honey LLC
3818 Warrington Dr
Charlotte, NC 28211-3956
704-517-6190
www.cloisterhoney.com
Manufacturer of natural honey.
Owner: Joanne Young
Manager: Randall York
randall@cloisterhoney.com
Number Employees: 1-4

2766 Clorox Company
1221 Broadway
Oakland, CA 94612
510-271-7000
corporate.communications@clorox.com
www.thecloroxcompany.com
Dips, dip mixes, bbq sauces, marinades, and dressings; plastic bags and wrap; disinfectants.
Chairman/CEO: Benno Dorer
EVP/General Counsel: Laura Stein
SVP, Corporate Business Development: Bill Bailey
SVP/Chief Innovation Officer: Denise Garner
SVP/Chief Financial Officer: Kevin Jacobsen
SVP/Chief Customer Officer: Troy Dratcher
SVP/Chief People Officer: Kirsten Marriner
SVP/Chief Product Supply Officer: Andy Lowery
EVP, Household & Lifestyle: Eric Reynolds
Year Founded: 1913
Estimated Sales: $6.2 Billion
Number Employees: 8,800

Brands:
- Brita
- Clorox
- Glad Bags
- Kitchen Bouquet
- Hidden Valley
- Masterpiece
- Burt's Bees
- Chux
- Ever Clean
- 409
- Fresh Step
- Green Works
- Kings Ford
- Liquid PlumR
- Poett
- Renew Life
- Scoop Away
- S.O.S.
- Tilex

2767 Clos Du Bois Winery
19410 Geyserville Ave
Geyserville, CA 95441-9603
707-857-3164
Fax: 707-857-1667 800-222-3189
www.closdubois.com
Wine
President: Jon Moramarco
CFO: Kimberly Hernandez
Vice President: Barbara Adair
barbara.adair@cwine.com
VP Operations: Chase Cambron
Estimated Sales: $7 Million
Number Employees: 100-249

2768 Clos Du Lac Cellars
3151 Highway 88
3151 Hwy 88
Ione, CA 95640
209-274-2238
Fax: 209-274-4147 cdltr@earthlink.net
www.closdulac.com
Wines
Owner: Tim Evans
cdltr@earthlink.net
CFO: Robert Neumann
Vice President: Peter Evans
Winemaker: Francois Cardesse
Cellar Manager: Kelly Evans
Estimated Sales: $2.5-5 Million
Number Employees: 10-19

2769 Clos Du Val Co LTD
5330 Silverado Trl
Napa, CA 94558-9410
707-261-5200
Fax: 707-252-6125 cdv@closduval.com
www.closduval.com
Producer and exporter of wines
President: Steve Tamburelli
COO: Lazaro Cardenas
lazaro.cardenas@dgs.ca.gov
Director of Operations: Jon-Mark Chappellet
Estimated Sales: $5.2 Million
Number Employees: 50-99
Square Footage: 128000
Brands:
- Clos Du Val

2770 Clos Pegase Winery
1060 Dunaweal Ln
Calistoga, CA 94515-9642
707-942-4981
Fax: 707-942-4993 800-866-8583
www.clospegase.com
Wines
President: Jon Shrem
Controller/Business Manager: Abbe Bailon
VP: Theodore Sanford
Sales Director: Shannon Beglin
Manager: Jeremy Anderson
jeremy_anderson@clospegase.com
Winemaker: Steven Rogstad
Purchsing Manager: Theodore Sanford
Estimated Sales: $5-10 Million
Number Employees: 20-49
Brands:
- Hommage Chardonnay
- Hommage Cabernet
- Mitsuko's Vineyard
- Napa Valley
- Dunaweal Vineyard
- Late Harvest

2771 Clos Saint-Denis
1150 chemin des Patriotes
Richelieu, QC J0H 1K0
Canada
450-645-9777
Fax: 450-645-3060
Fine apple ciders
President/Owner: Roland Prud'homme
Estimated Sales: $2.59 Million
Number Employees: 15

2772 Cloud Nine
216 W. Second Street
Claremont, CA 91711
909-624-3147
Fax: 909-624-3951 cloudninepaper@hotmail.com
www.cloudninepaper.com
Processor and exporter of hard candy, organic breath mints, caramel popcorn and natural, gourmet, dairy, nondairy, low-fat and organic chocolate bars
President: Josh Taylor
CFO: Lana Nguyen
Marketing Director: Robert Wagg
Sales Director: Sharon Desser
Director Operations: Andrew Spector
Number Employees: 10-19
Square Footage: 8000
Type of Packaging: Consumer, Private Label
Brands:
- Cloud Nine
- Cloud Nine All-Natural Chocolate Environments
- Sorrento Valley Organics
- Tropical Source
- Tropical Source Dairy-Free Gourmet
- Tropical Source Organic

2773 Cloud Top
556 S. Fair Oaks Ave
#101-1
Pasadena, CA 91105
Fax: 626-628-3340 888-263-1778
kathy@cloudtopyogurt.com
www.cloudtopyogurt.com
Organic frozen yogurt made from scratch. Cloud Top is available coast to coast, including the Hawaiian Islands, through distributors. If you are a distributor, please email distributorsales@cloudtopyogurt.com for more information.
Founder: Kathy Kim
kathy@cloudtopyogurt.com
Type of Packaging: Bulk

2774 Cloud's Meat Processing
2051 S Paradise Ln
Carthage, MO 64836-8452
417-358-5855
Fax: 417-358-7639 www.cloudsmeats.com
Smoked meat; slaughtering services available
Marketing Director: Mike Cloud
mcloud@4state.com
Estimated Sales: $5-10 Million
Number Employees: 20-49

2775 Cloudstone Vineyards
27345 Deer Springs Way
Los Altos Hills, CA 94022-4352
650-948-8621
Wines
President: Peter Wolken
CEO: Judith Wolken
Number Employees: 1-4

2776 Clougherty Packing LLC
3049 E. Vernon Ave.
Los Angeles, CA 90058
800-846-7635
www.farmerjohn.com
Bacon, breakfast sausage, fresh pork, ham, hot dogs, lunch meat, and smoked sausage.
Year Founded: 1931
Estimated Sales: $156.6 Million
Number Employees: 1,300
Square Footage: 1000000
Parent Co: Smithfield Foods
Type of Packaging: Consumer, Bulk
Brands:
- Farmer John
- Farmer John Meats

2777 Clover Blossom Honey
7597 E State Road 218
La Fontaine, IN 46940
765-981-4443
Fax: 765-981-4086
Honey
President/Co-Owner: David Shenefield
VP/Co-Owner: Don Shenefield
Estimated Sales: $5-10 Million
Number Employees: 5-9
Type of Packaging: Consumer, Food Service, Private Label, Bulk

2778 Clover Farms Dairy Co Inc
3300 Pottsville Pike
Reading, PA 19605
610-929-6981
Fax: 610-921-9913 800-323-0123
www.cloverfarms.com
Milk, juice and other dairy products including buttermilk, cottage cheese, half & half, non-dairy creamers, sour cream, heavy cream, and iced tea.
President/CEO: Richard Hartman
Treasurer: John Rothenberger
VP, Sales: Thomas Mullery
VP, Operations: Dennis Dietrich
Estimated Sales: $48.8 Million
Number Employees: 100-249
Number of Brands: 1
Type of Packaging: Private Label
Brands:
- Clover Farms

2779 Clover Hill Vineyards & Winery
9850 Newtown Rd
Breinigsville, PA 18031-1808
610-395-2468
Fax: 610-366-1246 800-256-8374
www.cloverhillwinery.com
Wines
Owner: Kari Skrip
kari@cloverhillwinery.com
Owner: Pat Skrip
Estimated Sales: $2.5-5 Million
Number Employees: 10-19
Brands:
- Clover Hill Rose
- Clover Hill Pinot Noir
- Clover Hill Cuvee

2780 Clover Leaf Cheese
1201 45th Avenue NE
Calgary, AB T2E 2P2
Canada
403-250-3780
Fax: 888-835-0127 888-835-0126
www.cloverleafcheese.ca
Packer and wholesaler/distributor of cheese
President: John Downey
Sales Manager: Chris Cameron
Plant Manager: Brad Lake
Estimated Sales: F
Number Employees: 50-99

2781 Clover Sonoma
Petaluma, CA 94954
800-237-3315
cloversonoma.com
Dairy products
President: Ken Gott

2782 Clover Stornetta Farms Inc
91 Lakeville St
Petaluma, CA 94952-3163
707-778-8448
800-237-3315
askclo@cloverstornetta.com
www.cloverpetaluma.com
Dairy products including milk and cream, yogurt, cheese, cottage cheese, sour cream, butter, cage free eggs and kefir.
President/CEO: Marcus Benedetti
Chief Sourcing Officer: Mkulima Britt
Director, Plant Operations: Michael Benedetti
Estimated Sales: $34.6 Million
Number Employees: 250-499
Number of Brands: 1
Type of Packaging: Consumer
Brands:
- Clover Farms

Food Manufacturers / A-Z

2783 (HQ)Cloverdale Foods
3015 34th St NW
Mandan, ND 58554
800-669-9511
www.cloverdalefoods.com
Manufacturer and wholesaler/distributor of meat products including hickory smoked franks, bacon, ham and sausages, along with other quality pork products.
President & CEO: Scott Russell
Estimated Sales: $49 Million
Number Employees: 250-499
Number of Brands: 2
Square Footage: 61000
Type of Packaging: Consumer, Food Service, Private Label, Bulk
Other Locations:
 Cloverdale Foods Plant
 Minot ND
Brands:
 Cloverdale
 Teardrop

2784 Cloverhill Bakery-Vend Corporation
2035 N Narragansett Ave
Chicago, IL 60639-3842
773-745-9800
Fax: 773-745-1647 www.cloverhill.com
Processor and exporter of sweet goods, doughnuts, cakes, muffins, danishes and cinnamon rolls.
President: William Gee
Executive VP: Edward Gee
Quality Control: Dan Gee
VP Sales: Robert Gee
Production Manager: Joe Perez
Year Founded: 1961
Estimated Sales: $20-50 Million
Number Employees: 100-249
Square Footage: 140000
Parent Co: Hostess
Type of Packaging: Consumer, Food Service
Brands:
 Clover Hill

2785 Cloverland Dairy
PO Box 329
Saint Clairsville, OH 43950-0329
740-699-0509
www.cloverlanddairy.com
Portion controlled butter and buttermilk
President: Robert Hyest
Estimated Sales: $.5-1 million
Number Employees: 300
Type of Packaging: Consumer, Private Label, Bulk

2786 Cloverland/Green Spring Dairy
2701 Loch Raven Rd
Baltimore, MD 21218
410-235-4477
Fax: 410-889-3690 800-876-6455
www.cloverlanddairy.com
Fluid milk and dairy products
President: Michael Marcus
Controller: Greg Stech
SVP Research, Development & Engineering: Edward Kennedy
Contact: Kory Carroll
kcarroll@cloverlanddairy.com
Operations Executive: Robert Glessner
Distribution Supervisor: Norman Maxwell
Estimated Sales: $1.3 Million
Brands:
 Cloverland

2787 Clovervale Farms
1833 Cooper Foster Park Rd
Amherst, OH 44001
440-960-0146
Fax: 440-960-2358 800-433-0146
Individual portioned servings of entrees, vegetables, sandwiches, fruits, cobblers, butter and jelly bars, frozen yogurts, sherbets, italian ices, frozen juice pops and milk
President: Richard Cawrse Jr
CEO: Don Russel
Marketing/Sales Manager: Ray Kautzman
VP Sales: Anne Williams
Purchasing Manager: Angela Viglas
Estimated Sales: $20-50 Million
Number Employees: 100

Brands:
 Chef's Pastry
 Cloverdale

2788 Clown Global Brands
3184 Doolittle Dr
Northbrook, IL 60062-2409
847-498-4696
Fax: 847-564-9076 800-323-5778
info@clown-gysin.com
www.clownglobalbrands.com
Producer and importer of marshmallows, snack foods, breadsticks, toasted onion bits, sesame dots, confectionery, and caramel apple dip items; importer of toasted onion bits and breadsticks
President: Herb Horn
Contact: Martin Haver
mhaver@clownglobalbrands.com
Estimated Sales: $7-10 Million
Number Employees: 5-9
Number of Brands: 2
Square Footage: 8000
Parent Co: Food Network
Type of Packaging: Food Service

2789 Club Chef LLC
3776 Lake Park Dr # 1
Covington, KY 41017-8171
859-578-3100
Fax: 859-578-3374 info@clubchef.com
www.clubchef.com
Wet and dry chopped salad items including lettuce, onions and cabbage
Vice President: Jeff Klare
jtklare@clubchef.com
Estimated Sales: $1-2.5 Million
Number Employees: 100-249
Square Footage: 360000
Parent Co: Castellini Company
Type of Packaging: Consumer, Food Service, Private Label, Bulk
Brands:
 Club Chef
 Farm Fresh
 Readypac

2790 Clutter Farms
7283 Millersburg Rd
Gambier, OH 43022-9775
740-427-3515
www.bulkwholesalepopcorn.com
Popcorn including microwaveable
President: Gordon Clutter
V.P.: Larry Clutter
Number Employees: 5-9
Square Footage: 14000
Type of Packaging: Consumer
Brands:
 Clutters Indian Fields

2791 Clyde's Delicious Donuts
1120 W Fullerton Ave
Addison, IL 60101-4304
630-628-6555
Fax: 630-628-6838 info@clydesdonuts.com
www.clydesdonuts.com
Baked goods including bagels, danishes, coffee cakes, sweet rolls, frozen and fresh yeast and cake doughnuts, and apple, blueberry, maple, and cherry fritters.
President: Kent Bickford
CEO: Kim Bickford
SVP, Sales & Marketing: David Bennett
VP, Business Development: John Cheesman
Marketing Director: Sue Nieves
Purchasing Manager: Dave Kells
Estimated Sales: $16-20 Million
Number Employees: 100-249
Number of Brands: 1
Number of Products: 125
Square Footage: 56000
Type of Packaging: Consumer, Food Service, Private Label, Bulk
Brands:
 Clyde's

2792 Clyde's Italian & German Sausage
3655 Inca St
Denver, CO 80211-3030
303-433-8744
Italian and German sausage
President: Michael Tricarco

Estimated Sales: $10 Milion
Number Employees: 1-4
Type of Packaging: Consumer

2793 Coach Farm Enterprises
105 Mill Hill Rd
Pine Plains, NY 12567
518-398-5325
Fax: 518-398-5329 800-999-4628
info@coachfarm.com www.coachfarm.com
Goat's milk products including soft cheese and yogurt
President: Miles Cahn
m.cahn@coachfarm.com
Marketing: Steve Margarites
General Manager: Phil Peeples
Plant Manager: Rosie Parsons
Estimated Sales: $10-20 Million
Number Employees: 20-49
Type of Packaging: Private Label
Brands:
 Coach Farm
 Yo-Goat

2794 Coach Sposato's Bar-B-Que
P.O. Box 957
Lincoln, AR 72744
479-824-3300
Fax: 870-910-0619 800-264-7535
coachbbq@pgtc.com
Barbecue sauce
Chairman: Beth Couch
General Manager: Sharon Spurlock
Estimated Sales: $.5-1 million
Number Employees: 20-49
Square Footage: 24800
Brands:
 Couch's Original

2795 Coach's Oats
22735 LA Palma Ave
Yorba Linda, CA 92887-4772
714-692-6885
Fax: 714-692-6887 coachsoats@coachsoats.com
www.coachsoats.com
Oats
Owner: Lynn Rogers
coachsoats@coachsoats.com
Estimated Sales: $1-3 Million
Number Employees: 5-9

2796 Coast Packing Co
3275 E Vernon Avenue
Vernon, CA 90058
323-277-7700
www.coastpacking.com
Quality shortening products for the restaurant, baking, and food industries. A supplier of animal fat and vegetable oil shortenings.
President: Ronald Gustafson
ronald.gustafson@coastpacking.com
CEO: Eric Gustafson
HR Manager: Washington Paredes
Director of Operations: Chavis Ferguson
Number Employees: 50-99
Type of Packaging: Consumer, Food Service
Brands:
 Bake Lite All Soy
 Bake Lite Soy/Cotton
 Coast Refined Lard
 Flavor King Blue
 Flavor King Red
 Gold Coast
 Golden Bake
 Supreme
 Viva Lard
 VIVA Manteca Mixta
 Viva Retail Lard

2797 Coast Seafoods Company
14711 NE 29th Pl Ste 111
Bellevue, WA 98007
425-702-8800
Fax: 425-702-0400 800-423-2303
info@coastseafoods.com www.coastseafoods.com
Processor and exporter of fresh oysters and clams
President: John Petrie
CFO: Kay Christopher
Contact: Sharon Adams
sharon@cni.org
Manager: Jim Donaldson
Estimated Sales: $2.5-5 Million
Number Employees: 1-4
Parent Co: Coast Seafoods Company

Food Manufacturers / A-Z

2798 Coastal Classics
380 Church St
Duxbury, MA 02332
508-746-6058
Fax: 508-746-6063
Cranberry chutney, cranberry mustard, cranberry preserves, cranberry hot sauce, cranberry orange marmalade, cranberry blueberry grilling sauce, peanut sauce
President: Jan Baird
Brands:
  Bogland
  Bogland By the Sea
  Coastal Gourmet

2799 Coastal Cocktails
18242 McDurmott Street
Irvine, CA 92614
949-250-8951
Fax: 949-250-9787 bbartels@coastalcocktails.com
Cocktail mixers
Contact: Jeff Dun
dun@coastpacificbuilders.com
Brands:
  Ultimate Bartender
  Martini Party

2800 Coastal Goods
44 Old Jail Ln
Barnstable, MA 02630-1418
508-375-1050
Fax: 508-375-1052
customerservice@coastalgoods.com
www.coastalgoods.com
Salt, peppers, rubs and spices.
Co-Founder: Nigel Dyche
Co-Founder: Sarah Chase
Number Employees: 1-4

2801 Coastal Promotions, Inc.
128 Indian Bayou Dr
Destin, FL 32541
850-460-2328
info@tasteoffl.com
www.tasteoffl.com
Cocktail mixers
Founder & CEO: Doug McWhorter
General Manager: Brian Todd
Number of Brands: 3
Number of Products: 21
Type of Packaging: Consumer, Food Service, Private Label, Bulk
Brands:
  Taste of Florida
  Wild Olive

2802 Coastal Seafood Partners
2939 West Grand Avenue
Chicago, IL 60622
773-235-4000
Fax: 773-989-7799
Seafood
President: Chris Costello
Estimated Sales: $1-3 Million
Number Employees: 20-49

2803 Coastal Seafood Processors
134 Brookhollow Esplanade
Harahan, LA 70123
504-734-9444
Fax: 504-736-9447
Seafood
President: Brian Quartano

2804 Coastal Seafoods
39 Acre Ln
Ridgefield, CT 06877-5501
203-431-0453
Fax: 203-438-7099
Seafood
President: Robert Iseley
CFO/Secretary: Linda Iseley
Operations: Manuel Reyes
Estimated Sales: $2.5-5 Million
Number Employees: 10-19
Square Footage: 5000
Type of Packaging: Food Service, Private Label

2805 Coastlog Industries
46755 Magellan Drive
Novi, MI 48375-3000
248-344-9556
Fax: 248-344-9559
Aseptic shelf stable juice and milk products
President: R K Sridharan
VP Sales: Andy Larkin
Type of Packaging: Food Service
Brands:
  Coastlog

2806 Coastside Lobster Company
PO Box 151
Stonington, ME 04681-0151
207-367-2297
Fax: 207-367-5929
Lobster
President: Peter Collin
Purchsing Director: Karen Rains
Number Employees: 5-9

2807 Cobb Hill Cheese
5 Linden Rd
Hartland, VT 05048-8104
802-436-1612
802-436-4360
info@cobbhillcheese.com
www.cobbhillcheese.com
Cheese
President: Gail Holmes
Contact: Jeannine Kilbride
cobbhillcheese@gmail.com
Estimated Sales: Less Than $500,000
Number Employees: 1-4

2808 Cobraz Brazilian Coffee
450 Park Ave
New York, NY 10022-2644
212-759-7700
Fax: 212-725-1170
Coffee
Managing Director: Francisco Barreto
Estimated Sales: $500,000-$1,000,000
Number Employees: 5-9

2809 Cobscook Bay Seafood
PO Box 252
Perry, ME 04667-0252
207-853-2890
Fax: 208-459-3712
Seafood
President: Joyce Pottle

2810 (HQ)Coby's Cookies
17 Vickers Rd
Toronto, ON M9B 1C1
Canada
416-633-1567
Fax: 416-633-9812
Processor and exporter of frozen cookie dough, muffin and brownie batter; also, retail pack rice crispy squares and brownies
President: Michael Topolinkski
Executive VP: Jay Punwasee
Estimated Sales: $9.3 Million
Number Employees: 150
Square Footage: 60000
Type of Packaging: Consumer, Food Service, Private Label
Other Locations:
  Coby's Cookies
  Downsview ON
Brands:
  Coby's Cookies, Inc.
  Just Great Bakers, Inc.

2811 Coca-Cola Beverages Northeast
1 Executive Park Drive
Suite 330
Bedford, NH 03110
603-627-7871
844-619-3388
www.cokenortheast.com
Sparkling soft drinks, still beverages, and emerging brands such as vitamin water
President: Mark Francoeur
VP, Sales Center Operations: Steve Perrelli
VP, Sales & Marketing: Andrew Marchesseault
VP, Operations: David Dumont
Year Founded: 1977
Number Employees: 3,500
Parent Co: Kirin Brewery Company, Ltd.
Type of Packaging: Consumer, Food Service, Bulk
Brands:
  Barq's
  Canada Dry
  Coca-Cola
  Core Power
  Dasani
  Dr Pepper
  Dunkin Donuts
  Fanta
  Fresca
  Fuze
  Gold Peak
  Honest Tea
  Hubert's Lemonade
  McCaf,
  Mello Yello
  Minute Maid
  Monster Energy
  NOS
  Peace Tea
  Powerade
  Reign
  Smartwater
  Sprite
  Vitamin Water
  Yup!
  Zico

2812 Coca-Cola Bottling Co. Consolidated
PO Box 31487
Charlotte, NC 28231
800-866-2653
www.cokeconsolidated.com
Bottled soft drinks and fountain syrup.
Chairman/CEO: J Frank Harrison, III
Year Founded: 1902
Estimated Sales: $4.3 Billion
Number Employees: 15,500
Number of Brands: 300
Type of Packaging: Consumer, Food Service, Bulk

2813 Coca-Cola Bottling Company UNITED, Inc.
46090 East Lake Boulevard
Birmingham, AB 35217
205-841-2653
800-844-2653
cocacolaunited.com
Bottled soft drinks and fountain syrup.
Chairman: Claude Nielsen
President & CEO: John Sherman, III
Executive VP/CAO/CFO: Hafiz Chandiwala
General Counsel/VP: Lucas Gambino
VP, Supply Chain & Operations: Stanley Ellington
VP/Controller/CIO: Eric Steadman
Year Founded: 1902
Estimated Sales: $2.81 Billion
Number Employees: 10,000
Type of Packaging: Consumer, Food Service, Bulk

2814 Coca-Cola Co.
PO Box 1734
Atlanta, GA 30301
404-676-2121
800-438-2653
consumer.relations@coca-cola.com
www.coca-colacompany.com
Non-alcoholic beverage concentrates and syrups.
Chairman/CEO: James Quincey
jaquincey@coca-cola.com
President/COO: Brian Smith
Executive VP/CFO: John Murphy
Senior VP/Chief Innovation Officer: Robert Long
Senior VP/Chief Communications Officer: Beatriz Perez
Year Founded: 1892
Estimated Sales: $31.8 Billion
Number Employees: 62,600
Number of Brands: 500
Number of Products: 4300
Type of Packaging: Consumer, Food Service
Other Locations:
  Bottling Facility
  Honolulu HI
  Bottling Facility
  Kapolei HI
  Bottling Facility
  Charlotte NC
  Bottling Facility
  Lenexa KS
  Bottling Facility
  El Paso TX
  Bottling Facility
  West Memphis AZ
  Bottling Facility
  Columbus OH
Brands:
  Coca-Cola
  Coca-Cola Zero
  DASANI

Food Manufacturers / A-Z

Diet Coke
Fanta
glac,au vitaminwater
Minute Maid
Odwalla
POWERADE
Sprite
Simply Orange
Sprite
Del Valle
Ciel
Fa!rlife
Georgia
Gold Peak Tea
Honest
Mello Yello
Surge
Costa Coffee
Zico
glac,au smart water

2815 Coca-Cola European Partners
Pemberton House
Bakers Road
Uxbridge, Middx, UB8 1EZ
UK
800-418-4223
comms@ccep.com www.cocacolaep.com
Coca-Cola brands products.
Chairman: Sol Daurella
CEO: Damian Gammell
CFO: Nik Jhangiani
Chief Public Affairs Officer: Lauren Sayeski
Estimated Sales: $10.9 Billion
Number Employees: 23,300
Number of Brands: 44
Type of Packaging: Consumer, Food Service, Bulk
Brands:
  5-Alive
  Abbey Well
  Apollinaris
  Appletiser
  aquaBona
  Aquarius
  Bonaqua
  Burn
  Capri-Sun
  Chaqwa
  Chaidfontaine
  Coca-Cola
  Coca-Cola Light/Diet
  Coca-Cola Zero
  Dr. Pepper
  Fanta Still
  Fanta Zero
  Fanta
  Fernandes
  Finley
  Fruit & Nadia
  Fruitopia
  Glaceau vitamin water
  Glaceau smart water
  Kia Ora
  Kinley
  Krystal
  Kuli
  Lift
  Lilt
  MER
  Mezzo Mix
  Minute Maid
  Monster Energy
  Nalu
  Nestea
  Nordic
  Oasis
  Ocean Spray
  Powerade
  Relentless Energy Drink
  Rosport Blue
  Schuss
  Schwepps
  Seagram's
  Sprite
  TAB X-tra
  Toscal
  Urge
  Vilas del Turbon
  ViO
  ViO BiO LiMO
  Viva

2816 Cocina De Mino
6022 S Western Ave
Oklahoma City, OK 73139-1602
405-632-1036
Fax: 405-632-1394 www.cocinademino.com
Ethnic foods
Owner: Tim Wagner
Marketing Manager: Emeleo Perez
Estimated Sales: $1-3 Million
Number Employees: 10-19
Brands:
  Cocina De Mino

2817 Cocktail Crate
23-23 Borden Ave.
Long Island City, NY 11101
718-316-2033
info@cocktailcrate.com
www.cocktailcrate.com
Manufacturer of cocktail mixes.
Founder: Alex Boyd
alex@cocktailcrate.com

2818 Cocktail Kits 2 Go LLC
205 W 95th St
Apt 5A
New York, NY 10025-6324
917-750-3998
cocktailkits2go.com
Premade cocktail mixes
Owner: Justin Durling
Type of Packaging: Private Label

2819 Coco International
6 Highpoint Dr
Suite 1
Wayne, NJ 07470-7423
973-694-1200
Fax: 973-694-1242 info@cocofoods.com
www.cocofoods.com
Manufacturer of energy bars and other snacks.
Contact: Michael Kim
ykim@cocofoods.com
Number Employees: 5-9

2820 Coco Lopez Inc
3401 SW 160th Ave # 350
Miramar, FL 33027-6306
954-450-3111
Fax: 954-450-3111 800-341-2242
customerservice@cocolopez.com
www.cocolopez.com
Canned fruits and vegetables, preserves, jams and jellie. Also manufacturer of cream of coconut, coconut milk, and coconut juice.
President: Leonardo Vargas
VP: Gisela Sanchez
Manager: Nicole Bennett
nbennett@kaplanuniversity.edu
Estimated Sales: $1,888,884
Number Employees: 10-19
Brands:
  Coco Lopez

2821 Coco Polo
320 Cleveland Ave
Highland Park, NJ 08904-1845
732-249-4847
Fax: 732-545-4494 800-433-2462
so@cocopolo.com www.cocopolo.com
Stevia-sweetened, milk chocolate bars.
President: Diane Yamate

2822 Cocoa Metro
929 W Sunset Blvd
Suite 21
St. George, UT 84770-4867
888-676-1527
www.cocoametro.com
Chocolate milk and drinking chocolate
CEO: Mike Dunford
Number of Brands: 1
Number of Products: 6
Type of Packaging: Consumer
Brands:
  COCOA METRO

2823 Cocoa Parlor
31161 Niguel Rd
Suite A
Laguna Niguel, CA 92672
949-877-9549
info@toniscene.com
cocoaparlor.com
Organic chocolate bars
CEO: Richard Pascall
Type of Packaging: Consumer, Private Label

2824 CocoaPlanet Inc.
1198 Ingram Dr
Sonoma, CA 95476-7680
650-454-0757
Fax: 707-721-1338 info@cocoaplanet.com
cocoaplanet.com
Dark chocolate; hot chocolate powders; and chocolate products.
Founder & CEO: Anne McKibben
anne@cocoaplanet.com
Year Founded: 2012
Estimated Sales: Less than $500,000
Number Employees: 5
Type of Packaging: Consumer, Food Service

2825 Cocolalla Winery
463254 Highway 95 N
Cocolalla, ID 83813
208-263-3774
Fax: 208-263-7605
Wines
President/Owner: Mike Wagoner
VP: Vivian Merkeley
Estimated Sales: $1-4.9,000,000
Number Employees: 1-4
Brands:
  Cocolalla

2826 Cocomels by JJ's Sweets
PO Box 3312
Boulder, CO 80307
303-800-6492
www.cocomels.com
Coconut milk caramels
Founder and Owner: JJ Rademaekers
Vice President of Sales: Rasa Kumar
Square Footage: 80000
Brands:
  Cocomels

2827 Cocomira Confections
321 Evans Avenue
Toronto, ON M8Z 1K2
Canada
416-253-4867
Fax: 416-946-1749 866-413-9049
info@cocomira.com www.cocomira.com
Chocolates, hazelnut crunch, dark chocolate crunch, espresso crunch and maple crunch.
President/Owner: Anna Janes
Director of Sales: Betty Baran

2828 Coconut Beach
PO Box 1949
Bonita, CA 91908-1949
info@coconutbeach.com
www.coconutbeach.com
Coconut oil, water and chips
Number of Brands: 1
Number of Products: 11
Type of Packaging: Consumer
Brands:
  COCONUT BEACH

2829 Coconut Bliss
PO Box 288
Eugene, OR 97440
541-345-0020
844-305-5441
coconutbliss.com
Dairy-free frozen desserts
Co-Founder: Larry Kaplowitz
Number of Brands: 1
Number of Products: 21
Type of Packaging: Consumer
Brands:
  COCONUT BLISS

2830 Coconut Collaborative
coconutcollaborative.com
Coconut milk-based yogurt
Number of Brands: 1
Number of Products: 3
Type of Packaging: Consumer
Brands:
  THE COCONUT COLLABORATIVE

Food Manufacturers / A-Z

2831 Codinos Food Inc
704 Corporation Park # 5
Suite 5
Scotia, NY 12302-1091
518-372-3308
Fax: 518-372-2787 800-246-8908
info@codinos.com www.codinos.com
Frozen pasta including lasagna, manicotti, stuffed shells and rigatoni, ravioli, gnocchi and cavatelli
Owner: Leno Codino
scott@codinos.com
Marketing Director: Scott DeVantier
Sales Exec: Scott Devantier
Estimated Sales: $5-10 Million
Number Employees: 20-49
Type of Packaging: Consumer, Food Service, Private Label, Bulk
Brands:
Poppy's Pierogies

2832 Coffee Associates
178 Old River Rd
Edgewater, NJ 07020
201-945-1060
Fax: 201-945-4887 info@coffeeassociates.com
www.coffeeassociates.com
Coffee
Parent Co: Coffee Associates

2833 Coffee Barrel
2237 Aurelius Rd # 1
Holt, MI 48842-6323
517-694-9000
Fax: 517-694-9001 coffeebarrel@gmail.com
www.thecoffeebarrel.com
Coffee
President: William DeGrow
Manager: Mary Vegrow
CEO: Tim Brenner
Estimated Sales: Less Than $500,000
Number Employees: 5-9
Type of Packaging: Private Label
Brands:
Bis Train
David Rio
Ghiradelli Syrup
Guidparg Chocolates
Stirling Syrup

2834 Coffee Bean
1630 W Evans Ave
Englewood, CO 80110-1098
303-922-1238
Fax: 303-937-6336
Coffee
Owner: Carlo Rondn
Estimated Sales: Under $500,000
Number Employees: 1-4
Brands:
Country Spice Tea
Panache Cocoa and Blender Mix
Panache Gourmet Coffee
Xanadu Exotic Tea

2835 (HQ)Coffee Bean & Tea Leaf
2000 NE Court
Bloomington, MN 55425-5506
952-853-1148
Fax: 952-853-0590 www.coffeebean.com
Coffee and tea
Owner: Jim Cone
coffeeandtealtd@aol.com
Vice President: Jim Cone
Estimated Sales: Less Than $500,000
Number Employees: 5-9
Type of Packaging: Private Label

2836 Coffee Bean Intl
9120 NE Alderwood Rd
Portland, OR 97220-1366
503-227-4490
Fax: 503-225-9604 800-877-0474
info@coffeebeanintl.com www.coffeebeanintl.com
Roasted coffee, tea, cocoa, syrups, and confectionary products; manufacturer of coffee equipment, importer of coffee beans and teas.
President & CEO: Patrick Criteser
pcriteser@coffeebeanintl.com
VP Product Development & Training: Bruce Mullins
Creative Director: Audrey Crespo
Vice President of Marketing: Joe Prewett
Vice President of Sales: Rich Sermone
Manager of Internet Marketing: Vickie Grimes
Operations Executive: Les McDonald
Roastmaster: Paul Thornton
Purchasing Manager: Mark Peldyak
Estimated Sales: $29.3 Million
Number Employees: 100-249
Square Footage: 500000
Parent Co: Farmer Brothers Company
Type of Packaging: Consumer, Food Service, Private Label, Bulk

2837 Coffee Bean of Leesburg
110 S King St # A
Leesburg, VA 20175-3009
703-777-9556
Fax: 703-777-4515 800-232-6872
www.beanusa.com
Coffee
Manager: Juanita Frye
Estimated Sales: $250,000
Number Employees: 5-9

2838 Coffee Beanery LTD
3429 Pierson Pl
Flushing, MI 48433-2498
810-733-1020
Fax: 810-733-1536 800-441-2255
info@beanerysupport.com
www.coffeebeanery.com
Began in 1976. Manufacturer of coffees, teas, syrups, dessert drink mixes and coffee accessories such as mugs, coffee grinders and canisters.
President/CEO: JoAnne Shaw
Chairman: Julius Shaw
COO: Laurie Shaw
VP, Development: Kevin Shaw
VP, Franchise Sales: Kurt Shaw
Marketing Manager: Patti Tushim
Operations Manager: Bob Ashley
Estimated Sales: $20 Million
Number Employees: 100-249
Number of Brands: 1
Square Footage: 45000
Type of Packaging: Private Label
Brands:
Coffee Beanery Franchise

2839 Coffee Brothers Inc
1204 Via Roma
Colton, CA 92324-3909
909-370-1100
Fax: 909-370-1101 888-443-5282
info@coffeebrothers.com www.coffeebrothers.com
Coffee and espresso; importer and wholesaler/distributor of espresso machines
Owner: Cal Amodemo
cal@coffeebrothers.com
General Manager: Max Amodeo
Estimated Sales: $2.5-5 Million
Number Employees: 1-4
Square Footage: 44000
Type of Packaging: Private Label, Bulk
Brands:
Coffee Brothers
Il Caffe
Sigma

2840 Coffee Butler Service
3660 Wheeler Avenue
Alexandria, VA 22304-6403
703-823-0028
Fax: 703-823-6943
Coffee
President: H Steve Swink, Ph.D.
COO: Mike Kelsey

2841 Coffee Culture-A House
1311 O Street
Lincoln, NE 68508-1512
402-438-8456
Fax: 402-474-3535
Coffee
General Manager: Terrance Alan Reis
Operations Manager: Gregory Looney
Estimated Sales: Less than $500,000
Number Employees: 1-4

2842 Coffee Enterprises
32 Lakeside Ave
Burlington, VT 05401-5242
802-865-4480
Fax: 802-865-3364 800-375-3398
www.coffeeenterprises.com
Coffee extracts and chilled coffee-based beverage concentrates; laboratory specializing in the testing and analyzing services for coffee; consultant specializing in the marketing and promotion of coffee
Owner/President: Daniel C Cox
dancox@coffee-ent.com
Administrative Assistant: Christine Hibma
Office Manager: Judy Mammorella
Estimated Sales: $1-3 Million
Number Employees: 10-19
Square Footage: 14000
Type of Packaging: Bulk

2843 Coffee Exchange
207 Wickenden St Uppr
Providence, RI 02903-4348
401-273-1198
Fax: 401-273-4440 877-263-3334
info@thecoffeeexchange.com
www.thecoffeeexchange.com
Processor and importer of regular and decaffeinated whole bean organic coffee; gift baskets available
Owner: Charles Fishbein
charlie@mailordercoffee.com
CEO: Susan Wood
Cafe Manager: Tania Montenegro
Estimated Sales: $1-2.5 Million
Number Employees: 20-49
Brands:
Coffee Exchange
Mel's

2844 Coffee Express RoastingCo
47722 Clipper St
Plymouth, MI 48170-2437
734-459-4900
Fax: 734-459-5511 800-466-9000
info@coffeeexpressco.com
www.coffeeexpressco.com
Wholesaler roaster of specialty coffees; distributors of associated products.
President: Tom Isaia
Office Manager: Joyce Novak
Contact: Genevieve Boss
g.boss@coffeeexpressco.com
Production: Scott Novak
Estimated Sales: Less Than $500,000
Number Employees: 1-4
Number of Brands: 8
Number of Products: 20
Square Footage: 32000
Type of Packaging: Consumer, Food Service, Private Label, Bulk
Brands:
Coffee Express
Mountain Country

2845 Coffee Globe LLC
1118 Pacific Coast Hwy
Suite A-441
Huntington Beach, CA 92648
587-966-1171
Ground, instant, and whole bean coffee
Founder & CEO: Alexandra Mogilevskaya
alex@Coffeeglobe.co
Sales Director: Svetlana Fedoseeva
Number Employees: 11-19
Type of Packaging: Private Label
Brands:
Evo Coffee

2846 Coffee Grounds
1579 Hamline Ave N
Falcon Heights, MN 55108-2107
651-644-9959
Fax: 651-776-1143
undergroundcafecommander@gmail.com
www.thecoffeegrounds.net
Coffee flavorings
Owner: David Lawrence
Estimated Sales: $420,000
Number Employees: 5-9

619

Food Manufacturers / A-Z

2847 Coffee Holding Co Inc
3475 Victory Blvd
Staten Island, NY 10314
718-832-0800
Fax: 718-832-0892 800-458-2233
info@coffeeholding.com www.coffeeholding.com
Roaster, vendor and packer of regular and green coffee; also, packer of instant coffees.
Founder: Sterling Gordon
President & CEO: Andrew Gordon
EVP & COO: David Gordon
EVP of Sales: Erik Hansen
Year Founded: 1971
Estimated Sales: $25 Million
Number Employees: 50-99
Number of Brands: 3
Square Footage: 22000
Type of Packaging: Consumer, Food Service, Private Label, Bulk
Other Locations:
  Harmoney Bay Coffee
  Andover MA
  Organic Products Trading Co.
  Vancouver WA
  Sonofresco
  Burlington WA
Brands:
  5th Avenue
  Cafe Caribe
  Cafe Supremo
  Don Manuel 100% Colombian
  S&W
  Via Roma

2848 Coffee Masters
P.O. Box 460
Spring Grove, IL 60081
815-675-0088
Fax: 815-675-3166 800-334-6485
cmaster@coffeemasters.com
www.coffeemasters.com
Gourmet coffee, tea and cocoa
President: Mike Ebert
Marketing Director: Betsy Summers
Sales Director: Alan Denek
Operations Manager: Tony Nowak
Number Employees: 50-99
Square Footage: 186000
Type of Packaging: Consumer, Food Service, Private Label, Bulk
Brands:
  Ashby's Iced Teas
  Ashby's Teas of London
  Bella Crema
  Brew-A-Cup: Perfect Potfuls
  Cocoa Amore
  Coffee Masters

2849 Coffee Mill Roastery
108 Branchwood Drive
Elon, NC 27244-9384
919-929-1727
Fax: 919-929-5899 800-729-1727
Coffee and tea
Owner: Jan Lawrence
Estimated Sales: $1-2,500,000
Number Employees: 10-19
Type of Packaging: Private Label

2850 Coffee Mill Roasting Company
598 Falconbridge Road
Sudbury, ON P3A 5K6
Canada
705-525-2700
Fax: 705-525-2790
Processor and packer of coffee
President: Geoff Hong
Number Employees: 1-4
Type of Packaging: Food Service
Brands:
  The Coffee Mill

2851 Coffee Millers & Roasters
2924 Del Prado Boulevard S
Suite 5
Cape Coral, FL 33904-7224
941-542-1215
Coffee
President: Edward Miller
Estimated Sales: Less than $500,000
Number Employees: 1-4
Parent Co: Spices of Life Gourmet Coffee

2852 Coffee Millers & Roasting
926 SE 9th Ln # B
Cape Coral, FL 33990-3121
239-573-6800
Fax: 239-573-3693
Domestic and European coffees and blends. Over 150 varieties
President: Marcell Miller
Estimated Sales: $1-2.5 Million
Number Employees: 1-4

2853 Coffee People
4130 SW 117th Ave Ste P
Beaverton, OR 97005
503-643-3053
Fax: 503-672-9013 800-354-5282
customerservice@coffeepeople.com
Specialty coffees and teas
Customer Service: Patti Graves
Estimated Sales: $.5-1 million
Parent Co: Diedrich Coffee

2854 Coffee Process
6005 N Shepherd Dr # G1
Houston, TX 77091-4253
713-695-8483
Fax: 713-695-7530
Coffee
Owner: Carlos DE Aldecoa
CFO: Larissa De Aldeco
Vice President: Maria Carmen De Aldecoa
Estimated Sales: $1-2.5 Million
Number Employees: 10-19
Type of Packaging: Private Label
Brands:
  Uvvw Decaff

2855 Coffee Reserve
2030 W Quail Ave
Phoenix, AZ 85027-2610
623-201-1400
Fax: 623-434-0946 888-755-6789
www.crescendobev.com
Coffee roasting
President & Chief Executive Officer: Rick C. Grayson, Jr.
Account Executive: Debbie Teichmann
VP of Operations & Green Coffee Buyer: John Gozbekian
Director of Business Development: Ted Pearson
Manager: Mick Sampson
mick@coffeereserve.com
COO: John Nugent
Production Manager: Jeff Jackson
Estimated Sales: $5-10 Million
Number Employees: 20-49
Type of Packaging: Bulk

2856 Coffee Roasters Inc
29 Edison Ave # 2a
Oakland, NJ 07436-1311
201-337-8221
Fax: 201-337-0622 800-285-2445
info@coffeeroastersinc.com
www.coffeeroastersinc.com
Coffees
President: Lance Wetzel
Founder, Chief Executive Officer: Gerald Comiskey
Vice President: Leonard Grasser
Estimated Sales: $1,300,000
Number Employees: 5-9

2857 Coffee Roasters Of New Orleans
1001 Industry Rd # A
Kenner, LA 70062-6880
504-712-4966
Fax: 504-827-0818 800-737-5464
www.orleanscoffee.com
Coffees including flavored, regular and decaffeinated; also, grinders, coffee makers and tea
Owner: William Siemers
wholesale@coffeeroastersofneworleans.com
Co Owner: Bob Arceneaux
Owner: Kathleen Siemers
Estimated Sales: Less than $500,000
Number Employees: 20-49
Square Footage: 12000
Type of Packaging: Consumer, Private Label, Bulk

2858 Coffee Roasters of New Orleans
712 Orleans Avenue
New Orleans, LA 70116-3111
504-827-0878
Fax: 800-743-5711 800-737-5464
www.orleanscoffee.com
Coffee
Owner: Bob Arceneaux
Director Sales/Marketing: Kathleen Siemers
General Manager: William Siemers
Production Supervisor: Robert Arceneaux
Estimated Sales: $5-9.9 Million
Number Employees: 5-9

2859 Coffee Up
2201 S Halsted Street
Chicago, IL 60608-4585
847-288-9330
Fax: 847-288-9334
Coffee
President: Chris Chacko
Estimated Sales: Under $500,000
Number Employees: 1-4

2860 Coffee Works
3418 Folsom Blvd
Sacramento, CA 95816-5312
916-452-1086
Fax: 916-452-9134 800-275-3335
info@coffeeworks.com www.coffeeworks.com
Coffee
President: John Shahabian
General Manager: Edwin Alagozian
alagozian@coffeeworks.com
Director: Alexandria Shahabian
Estimated Sales: Less Than $500,000
Number Employees: 5-9
Brands:
  Balthazar's Blend
  Dark Star
  Jump Start
  Sweetfire

2861 Cognis
4900 Este Ave
Cincinnati, OH 45232
973-245-6000
Fax: 513-482-5503 800-526-1072
Suppliers of bulk nutritional raw materials for the food industry
CEO: Antonio Trius
CFO: Klaus Edelmann
Executive Vice President, President of B: Beate Ehle
Managing Director: Paul Allen
Estimated Sales: $1-2.5 Million
Number Employees: 500-999

2862 Cohen's Bakery
89 Center Street
Ellenville, NY 12428
845-647-2200
cohens1920@gmail.com
www.cohensbakery.cafe
Fresh bread, rolls and pastries, cookies, danishes, and muffins; also, frozen raw bread, pizza and roll dough
Owner: Bill Tochterman
info@cohensbakery.com
Number Employees: 1-4
Square Footage: 100000
Brands:
  Al Cohen's

2863 Cohen's Original Tasty Coddie
6639 Chippewa Dr
Baltimore, MD 21209-1542
410-539-0111
Snack foods including potato chips.
President: Esther Cohen
Estimated Sales: Under $500,000
Number Employees: 1-4

2864 Colavita USA
1 Runyons Ln
Edison, NJ 08817-2219
732-404-8300
Fax: 732-287-9401 888-265-2848
usa@colavita.com www.colavita.com
Grains and oils including; extra virgin olive oil, vinegar, pasta, sauces, gnocchi, polenta, rice, marinated vegetables, and gift baskets and foodservice bulk supply

Food Manufacturers / A-Z

President: Sophia Aspromatis
sophiaa@colavita.com
CEO: Giovanni Colavita
VP Quality Control: Anthony Profaci
VP of Sales: Tom Marrone
VP Sales & Marketing: John Profaci
Director of Marketing: Nicole Jeannette
Plant Manager: Les Horowitz
VP Purchasing: Robert Profaci
Estimated Sales: $15 Million
Number Employees: 50-99
Brands:
    Colavita 25-Star Gran Riserva Vin.
    Colavita Balsamic Vinegar
    Colavita Classic Hot Sauce
    Colavita Extra Virgin Olive Oil
    Colavita Fat Free Classic Hot Sauce
    Colavita Fat Free Garden Style Sau.
    Colavita Fat Free Marinara Sauce
    Colavita Fat Free Mushroom Sauce
    Colavita Garden Style Sauce
    Colavita Healthy Sauce
    Colavita Marinara Sauce
    Colavita Marinated Vegetables
    Colavita Mushroom Sauce
    Colavita Pasta
    Colavita Pasta Plus
    Colavita Puttanesca Sauce
    Colavita Red Clam Sauce
    Colavita White Clam Sauce

2865 Colchester Bakery
96 Lebanon Ave
Colchester, CT 06415
860-537-2415
Fax: 860-537-4742
Baked breads
Owner: Ursula Paredes
Estimated Sales: $1-2.5 Million
Number Employees: 20-49
Type of Packaging: Consumer

2866 Colchester Foods
17 Schwartz Rd
Bozrah, CT 6334
860-886-2445
Fax: 860-886-1138 800-243-0469
Processor and exporter of brown and white eggs
VP: Kevin O'Brien
Number Employees: 20-49
Parent Co: Kofkoff Egg Farm
Type of Packaging: Consumer, Food Service, Private Label
Brands:
    New England Farms Eggs

2867 Cold Brew EvyTea
253 Amory St
Boston, MA 02130-2337
617-429-5229
evytea.com
Cold brewed tea
Founder: Evy Chen
Year Founded: 2014
Number Employees: 6

2868 Cold Fusion Foods
8787 Shoreham Drive
Apt 308
West Hollywood, CA 90069-2227
310-287-3244
Fax: 310-287-3242
Protein enriched frozen juice bars
President: Collin Madden

2869 Cold Hollow Cider Mill
3600 Waterbury-Stowe Rd
PO Box 420
Waterbury Center, VT 05677-8020
802-244-8771
Fax: 802-244-7212 800-327-7537
info@coldhollow.com www.coldhollow.com
Apple products including cider, cider jelly, butters, syrup, sauce, preserves and juices; exporter of cider jelly; wholesaler/distributor of health and specialty foods, general merchandise, private label items and produce
Owner: Paul Brown
Vice President: Gayle Brown
Estimated Sales: $5-10 Million
Number Employees: 20-49
Square Footage: 40000
Type of Packaging: Consumer, Food Service, Bulk
Brands:
    Cold Hollow Cider Mill

2870 Cold Spring Bakery Inc
308 Main St
Cold Spring, MN 56320-2597
320-685-8681
Fax: 320-685-3634 csb@coldspringbakery.com
www.coldspringbakery.com
Bakery goods
Owner: Phillip Brown
pbrown@globeuniversity.edu
Vice President: Brian Schurman
Estimated Sales: $2.2 Million
Number Employees: 50-99

2871 Coldani Olive Ranch LLC
13950 North Thornton Road
Lodi, CA 95242
209-334-0527
www.calivirgin.com
Manufacturer of olive oils, balsamic vinegar, and other oils.
Owner: Gina Sans
Square Footage: 80000

2872 Coldwater Fish Farms
PO Box 1
Lisco, NE 69148-0001
308-772-3474
Fax: 308-772-3845 800-658-4450
coldwaterfarms.al@gmail.com
Fish
President: Walter Queen
Sales Director: Molly Vogler
Production Manager: Lloyd Harding
Estimated Sales: $5-10 Million
Number Employees: 20-49
Type of Packaging: Private Label

2873 Cole's Quality Foods
4079 Park East Ct
Grand Rapids, MI 49546
616-975-0081
Fax: 616-975-0267 info@coles.com
www.coles.com
Fresh and frozen garlic bread, baguettes, garlic toast, breadsticks, cheesesticks, and cinnamonsticks.
Brand Manager: Alexis Reininger
Year Founded: 1943
Estimated Sales: $76 Million
Number Employees: 200
Type of Packaging: Consumer, Food Service
Brands:
    Home Style

2874 Colectivo Coffee
Milwaukee, WI
414-273-3747
info@colectivocoffee.com
Independent coffee roaster.
Owner: Paul Lincoln Ward
Square Footage: 24000
Brands:
    Session Roasted coffees
    Letterbox Fine Tea
    Colectivo Keg Company beers
    Troubadour artisan breads

2875 (HQ)Coleman Natural
PO Box 768
Kings Mountain, NC 28086
303-468-2920
Fax: 303-277-9263 800-442-8666
info@colemannatural.com
www.colemannatural.com
Premium natural and organic poultry, pork, and prepared foods. No antibiotics or growth hormones, 100% vegetarian diets and no animal byproducts.
Ceo: Mark McKay
Vice President Of Marketing: Gudjon Olafsson
Vice President Of National Sales: Hans Liebl
Vice President Of Operations: Bart Vittori
Plant Manager: George Lofink
Purchasing Manager: Kevin Rafferty
Estimated Sales: $1 million
Number Employees: 2,300
Square Footage: 50000
Type of Packaging: Food Service
Brands:
    COLEMAN NATURAL
    COLEMAN ORGANIC

2876 Colgin Co
4111 Mint Way
Dallas, TX 75237
Fax: 214-951-8668 888-226-5446
www.colgin.com
Barbecue sauces including mesquite, apple and hickory liquid smoke
Vice President: Mark Gardner
Estimated Sales: $2.5-5 Million
Number Employees: 5-9
Type of Packaging: Consumer, Bulk
Brands:
    Colgin
    Liquid Smoke

2877 Colibri Pepper Company
21 Burrough Cemetery Rd
Elmer, LA 71424
316-730-6528
millereric@bellsouth.net
Pepper sauce
President: Eric Miller
Estimated Sales: $25,000
Number Employees: 2
Number of Brands: 1
Number of Products: 1
Square Footage: 1400
Type of Packaging: Consumer

2878 Colin Ingram
P.O.Box 146
Comptche, CA 95427-0146
707-937-1824
Fax: 707-937-5834
Manufacturer, importer and exporter of essential oils
President: John Weir
bill.lechtner@petco.com
Estimated Sales: $2.5-5 Million
Number Employees: 1-4
Type of Packaging: Consumer, Food Service, Private Label, Bulk

2879 Collaborative Advantage Marketing
2987 Franklin St
Detroit, MI 48207
248-723-0793
info@camtrade.com
camtrade.com
Sea salt; beans; pasta sauce; soups
President: Catherine Hanson
Year Founded: 1999
Estimated Sales: $106,300,00
Number Employees: 15
Brands:
    Jack's Beans
    Falk Salt

2880 College Coffee Roaster
115 N Donerville Rd # I
Mountville, PA 17554-1512
717-285-9561
Fax: 717-872-8554
Coffee
President/Owner: Susan Lithgoe
collegecoffeeroasters@dejazzd.com
VP: George Kerekgyarto
Estimated Sales: Less than $500,000
Number Employees: 1-4

2881 Collin Street Bakery
Corsicana, TX 75110
800-267-4657
www.collinstreet.com
Pecan cakes, coffees, cheesecake, cookies, cakes, pecan pies, breads, muffins and candies
Chief Marketing Officer: Hayden Crawford
Plant Manager: Debbie Watson
Purchasing Manager: Marcia Longo
Year Founded: 1896
Estimated Sales: $20-50 Million
Number Employees: 600
Square Footage: 125000
Type of Packaging: Consumer
Brands:
    Apple Cinnamon Pecan Cake
    Apricot Pecan Cake
    Brittle Duet
    Cheesecake Slicer
    Cinchona Coffee
    Deep Dish Pecan Pike
    DeLuxe Fruitcake®
    Double Deep Fudge Pecan Pie
    Golden Rum Cake

Food Manufacturers / A-Z

Key Lime Cheesecake
Lemon Poppy Seed Cake
New York Style Cheesecake
Orange Paradise Cake
Pecan Coffee Cake
Pecan Duet
Pecan Halves & Pieces
Pineapple Pecan Cake
Praline Pecan Cheesecake
Trio of Cheesecake
Triple Chocolate Cake

2882 Collins Cavier Co
113 York St
Michigan City, IN 46360-3653
219-809-8100
Fax: 219-809-8105 cavco@collinscaviar.com
www.collinscaviar.com
American freshwater caviar, caviar creme spreads and custom compound butters
Owner: Rachel Collins
cavco@collinscavier.com
VP: Rachel Collins
Estimated Sales: $500,000-$1 Million
Number Employees: 1-4
Type of Packaging: Private Label

2883 Coloma Frozen Foods Inc
4145 Coloma Rd
Coloma, MI 49038-8967
269-944-1421
Fax: 269-944-3291 800-642-2723
www.colomafrozen.com
Frozen fruits, vegetables, juices and juice concentrates.
President: Brad Wendzel
CFO: Doug Singleton
Estimated Sales: $25 Million
Number Employees: 50-99
Type of Packaging: Food Service, Bulk
Brands:
Coloma

2884 Colombo Bakery
1329 Fee Dr
Sacramento, CA 95815-3911
916-648-1011
Fax: 916-649-2534
Bread, buns and rolls
Plant Manager: Paul Gonzalez
Estimated Sales: $300,000-500,000
Number Employees: 5-9
Parent Co: Metz Group
Type of Packaging: Consumer, Food Service, Private Label, Bulk

2885 Colonial Coffee Roasters Inc
3250 NW 60th St
Miami, FL 33142-2125
305-638-0885
Fax: 305-634-2538 info@colonialcoffee.com
Coffee roaster
Owner/President: Rafael Acevedo
main@colonialcoffee.com
Vice President: Melvin Weinkle
Operations Manager: Al Reyes
Estimated Sales: $6 Million
Number Employees: 10-19
Number of Brands: 3
Square Footage: 120000
Type of Packaging: Food Service, Private Label, Bulk
Brands:
Cafe Europa
Cafe Latino
Colonial International

2886 Colonial Cookies, Ltd
135 Otonabee Drive
Kitchener, ON N2C 1L7
Canada
519-893-6400
Fax: 519-893-9223 800-265-6508
info@colonialcookies.ca
Cookies
President, Bakery Division: Ray Kingdon
President: John Stephens
Senior VP Finance Bakery Division: Brian Paluch
VP Sales: Richard Bordwell
VP Sales/Marketing: Ted Clarke
Number Employees: 500-999
Parent Co: Parmalat Bakery Group North America
Type of Packaging: Consumer

Brands:
A & M Cookie

2887 Colonna Brothers Inc
4102 Bergen Tpke
North Bergen, NJ 07047-2510
201-864-1115
Fax: 201-864-0144
customerservice@colonnabrothers.com
www.colonnabrothers.com
Bread crumbs, grated cheese, sauces, olive oil & vinegar, soups, stuffing mix, roasted peppers, marinated mushrooms, pepperoncini, chopped garlic, artichoke hearts and bread sticks
President: Peter Colonna
cvifoods@aol.com
Estimated Sales: $5.6 Million
Number Employees: 100-249
Type of Packaging: Consumer, Food Service
Brands:
Colonna

2888 Colony Brands Inc
1112 7th Ave
Monroe, WI 53566-1364
608-328-8400
Fax: 608-328-8457 800-544-9036
www.colonybrands.com
Cakes, tortes & pies; cookies & bars; pastries; petits fours; candy & chocolate; boxed assortments of all kinds; cheeses; sausage, ham and other meats; nuts & pre-mixed snacks; home furniture; home d,cor; electronics; jewelry; fitnessequipment; unisex apparel; small appliances
CEO: John Baumann
Chairman: Pat Kubly
VP/CIO: Steve Cretney
Content Marketing Manager: Matt Stetler
Director of Strategic Planning: Ryan Kubly
Number Employees: 1000-4999
Square Footage: 13236
Parent Co: Colony Brands, Inc.
Brands:
Swiss Colony Foods

2889 Colony Foods
439 Haverhill St
Lawrence, MA 01841
978-682-9677
Fax: 978-687-8448
Frozen, fresh and special order food items.
President: Dereck Barbagallo
Contact: George Abdallah
georgeabdallah@colonyfoods.com
Estimated Sales: $10-20 Million
Number Employees: 20-49

2890 Color Garden
1300 Hancock St
Anaheim, CA 92807
714-572-0444
Fax: 714-572-0999 inquire@colormaker.com
Plant-based food colorings
Type of Packaging: Consumer
Brands:
COLOR GARDEN

2891 ColorKitchen
740 NE 3rd Street
Suite 3-143
Bend, OR 97701
510-227-6174
info@colorkitchenfoods.com
www.colorkitchenfoods.com
Plant-based food colorings
Founder: Ashley Phelps
Type of Packaging: Consumer

2892 ColorMaker, Inc.
1300 N Hancock St # A
Anaheim, CA 92807-1928
714-572-0444
Fax: 714-572-0999 inquire@colormaker.com
www.colorgarden.net
custom natural color blends compatible with product, process and package requirements. Products include free-flowing powders, liquid concentrates, liquid emulsions or viscous pastes.

CEO: Stephen Lauro
stephenl@colormaker.com
Accounting: Shannon Lauro
Research & Development Manager: Dr. Gabriel Lauro
Marketing & Social Media Manager: Dan Wegrzyn
Office Manager: Christine White
Production Manager: Carlos Pena
Number Employees: 5-9
Type of Packaging: Bulk

2893 Colorado Cellars
3553 E Rd
Palisade, CO 81526-9558
970-464-7921
Fax: 970-464-0574 info@coloradocellars.com
www.coloradocellars.com
Wines
President: Richard Turley
rturley@vineland.com
Treasurer: Padte Turley
Estimated Sales: Less Than $500,000
Number Employees: 1-4

2894 Colorado Hemp Honey
Frangiosa Farms
41322 London Dr
Parker, CO 80138
833-233-2256
info@frangiosafarms.com
coloradohemphoney.com
Honey with hemp extract
Founder: Nick French
Business Development: Ali French
Brand and Marketing Manager: Matt Seres
Production Lead: Eric Peter
Facilities and Shipping Manager: James Cole

2895 Colorado Mountain Jams & Jellies
3573 G Rd
Palisade, CO 81526
970-464-0745
www.plumdaisy.com
Fruit jams and wine jellies

2896 Colorado Nut Co
2 Kalamath St
Denver, CO 80223-1550
303-733-7311
800-876-1625
sales@coloradonutco.com
www.coloradonutco.com
Manufactures and Imports candies, chocolates, unique trail mixes, snack mixes, dried fruits and gift baskets for any occasion. Also roast nuts on site. Also offer products with private labeling and customized logos for a variety ofspecialized events.
Owner: Mark Goodman
mgoodman@coloradonutco.com
Owner: Roger Renaud
Estimated Sales: Less Than $500,000
Number Employees: 5-9
Type of Packaging: Consumer, Private Label

2897 Colorado Popcorn Co
320 Oak St
Sterling, CO 80751-3306
970-522-7612
Fax: 970-522-8630 866-491-2676
www.coloradopopcorn.com
Gourmet popcorn
Owner: Kathy Littler
coloradopopcorn@bresnan.net
Estimated Sales: Less Than $500,000
Number Employees: 1-4
Number of Products: 13
Type of Packaging: Consumer, Food Service

2898 Colorado Salsa Company
1228 W Littleton Blvd
Littleton, CO 80120-5800
303-932-2617
Fax: 303-297-7752
info_salsacolorado@yahoo.com
Salsa
Owner: David Karas
CEO: Patricia Parkos
Estimated Sales: $1-2.5 Million
Number Employees: 1-4
Square Footage: 6000
Type of Packaging: Consumer
Brands:
Denver

Food Manufacturers / A-Z

2899 Colorado Spice Co
6350 Gunpark Dr
Boulder, CO 80301-3588
303-581-9586
Fax: 303-581-9288 800-677-7423
tzieglerne@prodigy.net www.coloradospice.com
Custom packed spice and herb blends; also, tea and tea blends
President: Tomas Amo
tomas@coloradospice.com
CEO: Rod Smith
Estimated Sales: $900,000 appx.
Number Employees: 1-4
Square Footage: 20400
Type of Packaging: Food Service, Private Label, Bulk
Brands:
    Cinnamon Ridge
    Shadow Mountain Foods, Inc.
    The Colorado Spice Co.
    The Spice Box
    The Spice Co.

2900 Colorado Sweet Gold
1722 S Golden Road
Lakewood, CO 80401
303-384-1101
Fax: 303-384-1118 www.coloradosweetgold.com
Manufacturers of sweeteners and food ingredients
President: Charlie Gilbert
Executive: Tom Herrmann
Estimated Sales: $500,000-$1 Million
Number Employees: 1-4
Number of Products: 6
Type of Packaging: Private Label

2901 Colors Gourmet Pizza
2349 LA Mirada Dr
Vista, CA 92081-7863
760-597-1400
Fax: 760-431-0914 info@colorspizza.com
www.colorspizza.com
Gourmet pizza, handmade crusts, focaccia and panini bread
Chef, Owner: Martial Bricnet
martialb@colorspizza.com
Director of Sales/Distribution: James Tuckwell
Estimated Sales: $1-3 Million
Number Employees: 20-49
Square Footage: 30000
Brands:
    Colors Gourmet Pizza

2902 Colteryahn Dairy
1601 Brownsville Rd
Pittsburgh, PA 15210-3903
412-881-1408
Fax: 412-881-0460
Milk, cream and juices
Owner: Carl Colteryahn
ccolteryahn@colteryahndairy.com
Director: Frank Dean
Estimated Sales: $1 Million
Number Employees: 50-99

2903 Colts Chocolates
609 Overton St
Nashville, TN 37203-4149
615-251-0100
Fax: 615-251-0120
information@coltschocolates.com
www.coltschocolates.com
Chocolate candy and pies
Owner: Mackenzie Colt
coltsbolts@aol.com
Estimated Sales: $1-2.5 Million
Number Employees: 20-49
Brands:
    Animal Crackers
    Brownies & Roses
    Butter Grahams
    Chocolate Covered Marshmallows
    Colts Bolts
    Gooey Butter Bar, New!
    Happy Trails T-Shirts
    Marie McGhee's
    Roy Rogers Happy Trails
    Truffle Babies

2904 Coltsfoot/Golden Eagle Herb
PO Box 5205
Grants Pass, OR 97528
541-476-8267
Fax: 541-476-0205 800-736-8749
sales@goldeneaglechew.com
www.goldeneaglechew.com
Herbs
Owner: Robert Anderson
Owner: Joni Anderson
Estimated Sales: $3-5 Million
Number Employees: 5-9

2905 (HQ)Columbia Empire Farms Inc
31461 NE Bell Rd
Sherwood, OR 97140-8504
503-538-2156
Fax: 503-538-2156
moreinfo@columbiaempirefarms.com
www.columbiaempirefarms.com
Salted and roasted hazelnuts
President: Floyd Aylor
Owner: Robert Pamplin
Director Information Technology: Janet Pendergrass
Director of Marketing: Linda Strand
Estimated Sales: $4.4 Million
Number Employees: 20-49
Type of Packaging: Private Label
Brands:
    America's Northwest
    Chateau Beniot
    Columbia Empire Farms
    Doodleberry
    Northwest Gourmet
    Nutworld

2906 Columbia Packing Co Inc
Dallas, TX 75203
214-946-8171
www.columbiapacking.com
Meat packers, cattle and hog slaughterers and distributors of boxed beef, boxed pork and sausage items
President: Amber Ondrusek
Vice President: Rusty Ondrusek
Year Founded: 1913
Estimated Sales: $20-50 Million
Number Employees: 50-99

2907 Columbia Phyto Technology
250 Steelhead Way
The Dalles, OR 97058-3570
541-298-4800
Fax: 888-765-1720 sales@powderpure.com
www.columbiaphytotechnology.com
Producer of high quality fruit and vegetable powders. Certified organic, Kosher and all non-GMO.
Contact: Travis Aerni
travis@columbiaphytotechnology.com

2908 Columbia Valley Farms Inc.
P.O. Box 2563
911 Crestloch Ln
Pasco, WA 99302-2563
855-261-6395
www.fostersasparagus.com
Pickled asparagus, green beans, and carrots.
President/CFO: Kevin Filbrun
VP/Sales & Marketing: Bryan Lynch
Customer Relations: Sandy Lehrman
Operations Manager: Ryan Brovont
Year Founded: 1984
Estimated Sales: $611,416,00
Number Employees: 7
Type of Packaging: Private Label
Brands:
    Foster's

2909 Columbia Winery
14030 NE 145th St
Woodinville, WA 98072-6994
425-488-2776
Fax: 425-488-3460 www.columbiawinery.com
Producers of various red, white and blush wines.
CEO: Andrew Browne
Vice President: Glenn Coogan
Year Founded: 1962
Estimated Sales: $270,000
Number Employees: 50-99
Brands:
    Alder Ridge
    Battle Creek
    Sawtooth
    Zefina

2910 Columbine Confections LLC
701 Automation Dr
Windsor, CO 80550-3142
970-377-2293
Fax: 970-225-0910
orders@ferncreekconfections.com
www.ferncreekconfections.com
Manufacturer of gourmet sweets, treats, and chocolates.
Estimated Sales: Less Than $500,000
Number Employees: 1-4
Square Footage: 80000

2911 Columbus Brewing Co
525 Short St
Columbus, OH 43215-5614
614-464-2739
Fax: 614-464-0347 www.dinecbccolumbus.com
Beer
Owner: Mike Campbell
Owner: Doug Griggs
dgriggs@columbusbrewingco.com
Vice President: Ben Pridgeon
Estimated Sales: $500,000-$1 Million
Number Employees: 20-49
Brands:
    1859 Porter
    Apricot Ale
    Columbus Pale Ale
    Nut Brown Ale

2912 Columbus Salame
30977 San Antonio Road
Hayward, CA 94544
www.columbussalame.com
Salame and meat products
Contact: Valeria Fiorito
vfiorito@columco.com

2913 Columbus Vegetable Oils
30 E Oakton St
Des Plaines, IL 60018-1945
847-257-8920
Fax: 773-265-6985 www.cvoils.com
A producer of quality oils, fats, and shortenings. Products range from highly competitive commodity oils to exotic specialty oils.
President: Paulette Gagliardo
Production Manager: Benjamin Caffrey
Estimated Sales: Over $1 Billion
Number Employees: 50-99
Parent Co: CFC Inc.

2914 Comanche Tortilla Factory
107 S Nelson St
Fort Stockton, TX 79735-6707
432-336-3245
www.comanche-tortilla-factory.dinehere.us
Mexican products including peppers, tortillas and tamales
Owner: Joe Ben Gallegos
Number Employees: 1-4
Type of Packaging: Consumer

2915 Comanzo & Company Specialty Bakers
10 Industrial Dr
Smithfield, RI 02917-1500
401-231-2361
Fax: 401-232-9826 888-352-5455
Biscotti, European style shortbread
President: Liz Walker
Estimated Sales: Less than $500,000
Number Employees: 1-4

2916 Comax Flavors
130 Baylis Rd
Melville, NY 11747-3808
631-420-0073
Fax: 631-249-9255 800-992-0629
info@comaxflavors.com www.comaxflavors.com
Supplier of flavors
President: Weisz Agneta
CEO: Peter Calabretta
CFO: Virginia Wyan
Vice President: Paul Calabretta
Sr. Flavor Chemist: Mike Crain
Quality Control: Frank Vollaro
EVP Sales & Marketing: Bill Graham
PR/Communications Manager: Laura Ferrante
VP Operations: Joe Piazza
Production Manager: Jorge Quintanilla
Plant Manager: Marion Cunningham
Purchasing Manager: Michael Keppel

Food Manufacturers / A-Z

Estimated Sales: $15 Million
Number Employees: 250-499

2917 Comeau's Seafoods
60 Saulnierville Rd
Saulnierville, NS B0W 2Z0
Canada
902-769-2101
info@comeausea.com
www.comeauseafoods.com
Fresh, frozen and processed seafoods, herring, smoked salmon.
President & CEO: Noel Despres
Vice President & General Manager: Kim d'Entremont
Estimated Sales: $50-100 Million
Number Employees: 375
Type of Packaging: Consumer, Food Service, Private Label, Bulk

2918 Comeaux's
116 Alley 3
Lafayette, LA 70506
337-332-0720
Fax: 337-507-3343   888-264-5460
Kelly@comeaux.com   www.comeaux.com
Vacuum packed seafood including crawfish boudin, oysters, seafood boudin, shrimp, pork and tasso
Owner: Ray Comeaux
Co-Owner: Sonja Comeaux
Estimated Sales: $570,000
Number Employees: 8
Type of Packaging: Consumer, Food Service
Brands:
  Comeaux's Andouille Sausage
  Comeaux's Crawfish Tails
  Comeaux's Tasso

2919 Comfort Foods
9900 Montgomery Blvd Ne
Suite A
Albuquerque, NM 87111
505-281-7083
Fax: 505-323-8721   800-460-5803
www.comfortfoods.com
Soups and dip mixes
President/CEO: Mark Harden
VP: Dawn Johnson
Handles Marketing/Sales: Matthew Coxler
Plant Manager: Debbie Holm
Estimated Sales: $4 Million
Number Employees: 24
Number of Brands: 2
Number of Products: 80
Square Footage: 140000
Type of Packaging: Private Label
Brands:
  Country Gardens Cuisine
  Desert Gardens Chile and Spice

2920 Commercial Bakeries
45 Torbarrie Rd
Toronto, ON M3L 1G5
Canada
416-247-5478
Fax: 416-242-4129   info@commercialbakeries.com
commercialbakeries.com
Private label cookie manufacturer
President/Owner: Anthony Fusco
CFO: Sam Palermo
Quality Control: Sahar Maftoon
Plant Manager: Steve Brain
Type of Packaging: Private Label

2921 Commercial Creamery Co
159 S Cedar St
Spokane, WA 99201
509-747-4131
sales@cheesepowder.com
www.cheesepowder.com
Dried cheese and yogurt powders; processor and exporter of snack seasoning and spray dried dairy flavors
Owner/VP Sales & Marketing: Megan Boell
mboell@cheesepowder.com
Year Founded: 1908
Estimated Sales: $28 Million
Number Employees: 5-9

2922 Commissariat Imports
PO Box 643025
Los Angeles, CA 90064-0271
310-475-5628
Fax: 310-475-8246   info@bombaybrand.com
Processor, importer and exporter of indian chutneys, pickles, curry powder and pastes including curry, biryani, ginger, garlic and tandoori; certified kosher available
President/CEO: Parvez Commissariat
VP: Aban Commissariat
Estimated Sales: Over $500,000
Number Employees: 2
Type of Packaging: Food Service, Private Label
Brands:
  Bombay

2923 Commodities Marketing Inc
6 Stone Tavern Dr
Clarksburg, NJ 08510
732-516-0700
Fax: 732-516-0600   weldonrice@usa.net
www.weldonfoods.com
Jasmine rice, Basmati rice, Coconut drinks, Coconut milk, Fruits, Beans, Guar gum, Fruit juices and Cashews, Almonds, Saffron (Spain) White Rice/Parboiled Rice.
President: Herbander Sahni
herbandersahni@weldonfoods.com
CEO: Gagandeep Sahni
CFO: Soena Sahni
VP: Avneet Sodhi
R&D: Manoj Hedge
Marketing: Harbinder Singh Sahni & Dee Mirchandai
Sales: Avneet Sodhi
Public Relations: Mr. Dough & Harshida Shaw
Operations: Harshida Shah
Production: Mr Nobpsaul
Plant Manager: Mr Chandej
Estimated Sales: $25 Million
Number Employees: 5-9
Number of Brands: 3
Number of Products: 6
Square Footage: 3000
Type of Packaging: Consumer, Food Service, Private Label, Bulk
Brands:
  Meher
  Weldon

2924 Common Folk Farm
PO Box 141
Naples, ME 04055-0141
207-787-2764
Fax: 207-787-3894
Processor and exporter of herbal teas, seasonings and culinary mixes
Owner: Betz Golon
Owner: Dale Golon
Type of Packaging: Consumer, Private Label, Bulk
Brands:
  Common Folk Farm, Inc.

2925 Community Bakeries
3250 Lacey Rd.
Suite 600
Downers Grove, IL 60515
630-455-5200
Fax: 630-455-5202   800-952-5754
Muffins
President: Charles Huber Jr.
CFO: James Wojciechowski
VP Retail Sales and Marketing: Mark Leopold
Number Employees: 3000
Brands:
  Community Bakeries

2926 Community Coffee Co.
3332 Partridge Ln.
Building A
Baton Rouge, LA 70809
800-884-5282
Fax: 800-643-8199
customerservice@communitycoffee.com
www.communitycoffee.com
Coffee and tea; importer of green coffee; and wholesaler/distributor of coffee creamer.
President/CEO: David Belanger
dbelanger@communitycoffee.com
Chairman: Matthew Saurage
CFO: Annette Vaccaro
Year Founded: 1919
Estimated Sales: $195 Million
Number Employees: 1000-4999
Type of Packaging: Consumer, Food Service, Private Label, Bulk
Brands:
  Community Coffee

2927 Community Mill & Bean
267 State Route 89
Savannah, NY 13146-9711
315-365-2664
Fax: 315-365-2690   800-755-0554
Organic flour milling
CEO: Richard Corichi
Estimated Sales: $1-2.5 Million
Number Employees: 1-4

2928 Community Orchards
2237 160th St
Fort Dodge, IA 50501-8547
515-573-8212
Fax: 515-576-0489   888-573-8212
mail@communityorchards.com
Apple cider, pie and dumplings
President: Greg Baedke
VP: Bev Baedke
Estimated Sales: $678,000
Number Employees: 20-49

2929 Company of a Philadelphia Gentleman
2824 N 2nd St
Philadelphia, PA 19133-3515
215-427-2827
Fax: 215-739-0871   sim4033@aol.com
Teas
Owner: Morton Simkins
Estimated Sales: $500,000-$1 Million
Number Employees: 6
Square Footage: 160000

2930 Compass Minerals
9900 W 109th St
Suite 100
Overland Park, KS 66210
913-344-9200
www.compassminerals.com
Food grade salt products.
President & CEO: Kevin Crutchfield
Chief Financial Officer: Jamie Standen
Chief Legal & Administrative Officer: Mary Frontczak
Chief Commercial Officer: Brad Griffith
Chief Operating Officer: George Schuller
Year Founded: 1844
Estimated Sales: Over $1 Billion
Number Employees: 3,500
Type of Packaging: Consumer, Food Service, Private Label, Bulk

2931 Compton Dairy
25 Walker Street
Shelbyville, IN 46176-1332
317-398-8621
Fax: 317-392-9777
Milk, dairy products-noncheese
President: Dan Compton
Estimated Sales: $2.5-5 Million
Number Employees: 10-19

2932 Comte Cheese Association
152 West 36th Street
Suite 601
New York, NY 10018
646-515-9209
www.comte.com
Cheese, agency/trade organization.

2933 Comvita USA
Santa Barbara, CA 93101
855-449-2201
usacustomerservice@comvita.com
www.comvita.com
Manuka honey and apple cider vinegar
SVP & General Manager: Corey Blick

2934 Con Agra Foods Inc
801 Dye Mill Rd
Troy, OH 45373-4223
937-335-2115
Fax: 937-339-6930   www.conagrafoods.com
Pizza
Plant Manager: Scott Adkins
Estimated Sales: $10-20 Million
Number Employees: 250-499
Parent Co: A.M. Gilardi & Sons

Food Manufacturers / A-Z

2935 Con Agra Snack Foods
2301 Washington St
Hamburg, IA 51640-1835
712-382-2202
Fax: 712-382-1357   800-831-5818
www.vogelpopcorn.com
Processor and exporter of popcorn and popping oils; importer of popcorn and popcorn seeds.
President/CEO: Sean Connolly
Estimated Sales: $20-50 Million
Number Employees: 50-99
Number of Brands: 2
Parent Co: ConAgra Foods
Type of Packaging: Consumer, Food Service, Private Label, Bulk
Brands:
   Act II
   Vogel

2936 Con Yeager Spice Co
144 Magill Rd
Zelienople, PA 16063-3424
724-452-4120
Fax: 724-452-6171   800-222-2460
www.conyeagerspice.com
Seasonings and meat cures and binders; wholesaler/distributor of meat casings and spices
Owner: Bill Kreuer
VP: Rodney Schaffer
Sales Rep.: Rod Schaffer
rschaffer@conyeagermail.com
Production Manager: William Wolford
Estimated Sales: $2.8 Million
Number Employees: 10-19
Square Footage: 54000
Type of Packaging: Consumer, Food Service, Private Label, Bulk
Brands:
   Con Yeager Spices

2937 ConSup North America
170 Beaverbrook Rd
Unit 2
Lincoln Park, NJ 07035-1441
973-628-7330
Fax: 973-628-2919   customerservice@consup.us
www.consupna.com
Importer of German food brands
Owner: Martin Moog
m.moog@consup.us
Marketing: Russ Harlock
Estimated Sales: $5-10 Million
Number Employees: 5-9

2938 Conagra Brands Canada
5055 Satellite Drive
Mississauga, ON L4W 5K7
Canada
416-679-4200
800-461-4556
www.conagrabrands.ca
Consumer brands.
VP/General Manager: Ian Roberts
Number Employees: 500
Square Footage: 20000
Parent Co: Conagra Brands
Type of Packaging: Consumer, Food Service
Other Locations:
   Boisbriand Office
   Boisbriand QC

2939 (HQ)Conagra Brands Inc
222 W. Merchandise Mart Plaza
Chicago, IL 60654
312-549-5000
877-266-2472
www.conagrafoods.com
Consumer brands.
President & CEO: Sean Connolly
Executive VP/CFO: David Marberger
Executive Vice President: Colleen Batcheler
Executive VP/Co-COO: Tom McGough
Estimated Sales: $11 Billion
Number Employees: 18,000
Number of Brands: 70
Type of Packaging: Consumer, Food Service, Bulk
Brands:
   ACT II®
   Alexia®
   Andy Capp's®
   Angie's BOOMCHICKAPOP®
   Armour Star®
   Aunt Jemima®
   Banquet®
   Bernstein's®
   Bertoli®
   BIGS®
   Birds Eye®
   Birds Eye C&W
   Birds Eye Voila
   Blake's®
   Blue Bonnet®
   Brooks®
   Celeste® Pizza for One
   Chef Boyardee®
   Crunch 'n Munch®
   DAVID® Seeds
   Dennison's®
   Duke's®
   Duncan Hines®
   Duncan Hines Comstock®
   Duncan Hies Wilderness®
   Earth Balance®
   Egg Beaters®
   Erin's®
   EVOL®
   Fiddle Faddle®
   Fleischmann's®
   Frontera®
   Gardein®
   Glutino®
   Gulden's®
   H.K. Anderson®
   Hawaiian Snacks®
   Healthy Choice®
   Hebrew National®
   Hungry-Man®
   Hunt's®
   Husman's®
   Jiffy Pop®
   Kangaroo®
   Kid Cuisine®
   La Choy®
   Lender's®
   Libby's®
   Log Cabin®
   Manwich®
   Marie Callender's®
   Mrs.Butterworth's®
   Mrs.Paul's®
   Nalley®
   Odom's Tennessee Pride®
   Open Pit®
   Orville Redencacher'S®
   P.F. Chang's Home Menu®
   PAM®
   Parkay®
   Penrose®
   Peter Pan®
   Poppycock®
   Ranch Style Beans®
   Reddi-wip®
   RO*TEL®
   Rosarita®
   Reddi-wip®
   RO*TEL®
   Rosarita®
   Sandwich Bros. of Wisconsin®
   Slim Jim®
   Smart Balance®

2940 Conagra Foodservice
222 W. Merchandise Mart Plaza
Suite 1300
Chicago, IL 60654
312-549-5000
877-266-2472
www.conagrabrands.com
Supplies restaurants, retailers, commercial customers and other foodservice suppliers.
President/CEO: Sean Connolly
Executive VP/CFO: David Marberger
Executive VP/General Counsel: Colleen Batcheler
Executive VP/Co-COO: Tom McGough
Estimated Sales: K
Number Employees: 10,000+
Number of Brands: 70
Square Footage: 11042
Parent Co: Conagra Brands
Type of Packaging: Consumer, Food Service, Bulk
Other Locations:
   ConAgra Headquarters
   Kennewick WA
   ConAgra Headquarters
   Naperville IL
   Sales Office
   Anaheim CA
   Sales Office
   Mesa AR
   Sales Office
   San Antonio TX
   Sales Office
   Plano TX
   Sales Office
   Tampa FL
   Sales Office
   Baltimore MD
   Sales Office
   Mason OH
   Sales Office
   Troy OH
Brands:
   ACT II®
   Alexia®
   Andy Capp's®
   Angie's BOOMCHICKAPOP®
   Armour Star®
   Aunt Jemima®
   Banquet®
   Bernstein's®
   Bertoli®
   BIGS®
   Birds Eye®
   Birds Eye C&W
   Birds Eye Voila
   Blake's®
   Blue Bonnet®
   Brooks®
   Celeste® Pizza for One
   Chef Boyardee®
   Crunch 'n Munch®
   DAVID® Seeds
   Dennison's®
   Duke's®
   Duncan Hines®
   Duncan Hines Comstock®
   Duncan Hies Wilderness®
   Earth Balance®
   Egg Beaters®
   Erin's®
   EVOL®
   Fiddle Faddle®
   Fleischmann's®
   Frontera®
   Gardein®
   Glutino®
   Gulden's®
   H.K. Anderson®
   Hawaiian Snacks®
   Healthy Choice®
   Hebrew National®
   Hungry-Man®
   Hunt's®
   Husman's®
   Jiffy Pop®
   Kangaroo®
   Kid Cuisine®
   La Choy®
   Lender's®
   Libby's®
   Log Cabin®
   Manwich®
   Marie Callender's®
   Mrs.Butterworth's®
   Mrs.Paul's®
   Nalley®
   Odom's Tennessee Pride®
   Open Pit®
   Orville Redencacher'S®
   P.F. Chang's Home Menu®
   PAM®
   Parkay®
   Penrose®
   Peter Pan®
   Poppycock®
   Ranch Style Beans®
   Reddi-wip®
   RO*TEL®
   Rosarita®
   Reddi-wip®
   RO*TEL®
   Rosarita®
   Sandwich Bros. of Wisconsin®
   Slim Jim®
   Smart Balance®

2941 Concannon Vineyard
4590 Tesla Rd
Livermore, CA 94550-9002
925-456-2505
Fax: 925-583-1160   800-258-9866
info@concannonvineyard.com
www.concannonvineyard.com

Food Manufacturers / A-Z

Processor and exporter of bottled wines; grower of grapes
CFO: Jim Page
Estimated Sales: $1.6 Million
Number Employees: 50-99
Square Footage: 29912
Parent Co: Wine Group
Type of Packaging: Consumer, Private Label
Brands:
   Concannon Vineyard

2942 Concord Farms
2811 Faber St
Union City, CA 94587-1203
510-429-8855
Fax: 510-429-8844 www.concordtapes.com
Grower of fresh shiitake and oyster mushrooms
Owner/President: David Tung
dtung@concordfarms.com
VP: Grace Tung
Estimated Sales: $1.9 Million
Number Employees: 5-9
Type of Packaging: Consumer, Private Label, Bulk
Brands:
   Oringer
   Reddy Glaze

2943 Concord Foods, LLC
10 Minuteman Way
Brockton, MA 02301-7508
508-580-1700
Fax: 508-584-9425 www.concordfoods.com
Supplier of retail food products and custom ingredients. The retail line includes companion items for fresh produce (juices, produce seasoning mixes, smoothie mixes, fresh desserts, dips, etc) and seasoning mixes for ground beef,poultry and seafood. The business ingredients division supplies beverage bases, fountain syrups, toppings, caramels, fruit purees and chocolate products, breadings and batters, and pancake and baking mixes. Recapitalized by Arbor Investments in2015.
President/CEO: Peter Neville
pneville@concordfoods.com
VP: Rich Renna
Marketing Manager: Samantha McCaul
Production Supervisor: Michelle Marvel
Warehouse Team Leader: Gabriel Alves
Estimated Sales: $38 Million
Number Employees: 100-249
Number of Brands: 4
Square Footage: 190000
Parent Co: Arbor Investments
Type of Packaging: Consumer, Food Service, Bulk
Brands:
   Concord Foods
   Tempo
   Oringer
   Red E Made

2944 Conecuh Sausage Co
200 Industrial Park
PO Box 327
Evergreen, AL 36401-1807
251-578-3380
Fax: 251-578-5408 800-726-0507
sales@conecuhsausage.com
www.conecuhsausage.com
Meat products including sausage
President/CEO/Owner: John Sessions
relliott@conecuhsausageco.com
Site Manager: Ronnie Elliott
relliott@conecuhsausageco.com
Estimated Sales: $5.6 Million
Number Employees: 50-99
Type of Packaging: Consumer
Brands:
   Cajun Smoked Sausage
   Hickory Smoked Sausage
   Original Smoked Sausage
   Spicy and Hot Hickory Sausage

2945 Coney Island Classics
65 Roosevelt Ave
Suite 107
Valley Stream, NY 11581
516-823-3001
Fax: 516-823-3003 www.coneyislandclassics.com
Kettle corn, potato chips and cookies

2946 Confection Art Inc
3636 North Williams Avenue
Portland, OR 97227.
503-505-0481
info@chocolatecraftkits.com
www.chocolatecraftkits.com
Molded chocolates
President: Nancy Baggett
Master Pastry Chef: Pierre Herme
Number Employees: 8

2947 Confectionately Yours LTD
160 Lexington Dr
Suite D
Buffalo Grove, IL 60089-6929
847-537-5761
Fax: 847-537-7178 800-875-6978
conyrs@sbcglobal.net
Pretzel rods, English toffee and other homemade style candies
President: Kathy Fish
info@confectionately-yours.com
VP: Tom Fish
Estimated Sales: $600,000
Number Employees: 1-4
Number of Products: 35
Square Footage: 16000
Type of Packaging: Consumer, Food Service, Private Label, Bulk
Brands:
   Big Yummy
   Blasting Powder
   Bola Pop's
   Fizz Wiz
   Fun Stuff
   Joy Stiks
   Lumpy Logs
   Lumpy Lous
   Monster
   Monster Chews
   Nasty Tricks
   Ninja Sticks
   Oogly Eyes
   Rock 'n Roll Chews
   Stickers
   Sweet Stirrings
   Tuesday Toffee

2948 Confoco USA, Inc.
1139 E Jersey St
Suite 415
Elizabeth, NJ 07201
908-659-0566
Fax: 908-659-9339 confocosales@confoco.com
www.confoco.com
Manufacturer and distributor of fruit and vegetable flakes, powder and essences as well as aseptic banana puree. Kosher & Halal Certified products
General Manager: Edwardo Chiriboga
Contact: Francisco Larrea
flarrea@confoco.com
Type of Packaging: Food Service, Bulk

2949 Congdon Orchards Inc.
P.O. Box 2725
Yakima, WA 98907
509-966-4440
Fax: 509-966-4447 www.congdonorchards.com
Apples and pears.
President/CEO: Dick Woodin
CFO: Bob Martin
General Manager: Mark Blore
mblore@congdonorchards.com
Estimated Sales: $1.1 Million
Number Employees: 20-49
Type of Packaging: Consumer, Food Service

2950 Conifer Foods
Medina, WA 98039
425-486-3334
Fax: 425-398-0301 800-588-9160
pgimness@conifer-inc.com conifer-inc.com
Gourmet convenience foods
President/Chief Executive Officer: Mike Maher
Director, Quality: Kurt Larson
Vice President, Marketing: Joanne Ramsay
Vice President, Sales/Marketing: Harry Forsberg
Contact: Bob Benson
rbenson@conifer-inc.com
Plant Manager: Jesse Riojas
Estimated Sales: $40 Million
Number Employees: 32
Number of Brands: 4
Brands:
   Canterbury Naturals
   CrockPot
   Fisher Scones
   Starbucks Hot Cocoa

2951 Conifer Specialties Inc
15500 Woodinville-Redmond Rd
Suite C-400
Woodinville, WA 98072
425-486-3334
Fax: 425-398-0301 800-588-9160
pgimness@conifer-inc.com www.conifer-inc.com
Soups, breads, desserts and Fisher scones
CEO: Mike Maher
Estimated Sales: $2.7 Million
Number Employees: 75

2952 (HQ)Conn's Potato Chips
1805 Kemper Ct
Zanesville, OH 43701-4634
740-452-4615
Fax: 740-452-9272 sales@connschips.com
www.connschips.com
Manufacturer of potato chips and snack foods.
President: Montie Hunter
Founder: Ida Conn
Estimated Sales: $20-50 Million
Number Employees: 20-49
Type of Packaging: Private Label
Brands:
   Conn's Bbq Pork Rinds
   Conn's Bean Dip
   Conn's Caramel Popcorn
   Conn's Cheese Corn Popcorn
   Conn's Cheese Curls
   Conn's Cheese Dip
   Conn's Corn Chips
   Conn's Corn Pops Popcorn
   Conn's Green Onion
   Conn's Honey Bbq Jerky
   Conn's Honey Mustard Dip
   Conn's Jalapeno Dip
   Conn's Nacho Tortilla Chips
   Conn's Oat Bran Pretzels
   Conn's Original
   Conn's Original Beef Jerky
   Conn's Party Mix
   Conn's Picante Dip
   Conn's Pork Rinds
   Conn's Pretzel Rods
   Conn's Pretzel Sticks
   Conn's Pretzel Thins
   Conn's Pretzel Twists
   Conn's Restaurant Tortilla Chips
   Conn's Round Tortilla Chips
   Conn's Salsa Supreme Dip
   Conn's Salt & Vinegar
   Conn's Sour Cream
   Conn's Wavy

2953 Conneaut Cellars Winery LLC
12005 Conneaut Lake Rd
Conneaut Lake, PA 16316
814-382-3999
Fax: 814-382-6151 877-229-9463
www.conneautcellarsdistillery.com
Wines
President: Joel Wolf
Sales/Office Manager: Jackie Elliot
Estimated Sales: $2.5-5 Million
Number Employees: 5-9

2954 Connors Aquaculture
Estes Head
Eastport, ME 04631
207-853-6081
Fax: 207-853-6056
Fish hatchery
President: Ken Hirtle
Treasurer: Charles Crowe
Estimated Sales: $6.9 Million
Number Employees: 150

2955 Conoley Citrus Packers Inc
12488 W Colonial Dr
Winter Garden, FL 34787-4121
407-656-3300
Fax: 407-656-1168 www.conoleyfruit.com
Frozen citrus fruits
President: E. Conoley
CFO: Bill Lewin
bill@conoleyfruit.com
General Manager: Kevin Paffrath

Food Manufacturers / A-Z

Estimated Sales: $11.8 Million
Number Employees: 50-99
Type of Packaging: Private Label

2956 Conrad Rice Mill Inc
P.O. Box 10640
New Iberia, LA 70562-0640
337-364-7242
Fax: 337-365-5806 800-551-3245
sales@conradricemill.com www.conradrice.com
Packed rice including yellow, herb, curry, ranch and wild; also, rice mixes including paella, long grain and wild.
President: Michael Davis
mikedavis@conradricemill.com
Estimated Sales: $20-50 Million
Number Employees: 10-19
Type of Packaging: Consumer, Food Service
Brands:
 Conrad-Davis
 Hol Grain
 Konriko
 R.M.Quiggs

2957 Conrotto A. Winery
1690 Hecker Pass Road
Gilroy, CA 95020-8800
408-847-2233
Wine
President: James Burr
Estimated Sales: $1-2.5 Million
Number Employees: 1-4

2958 Conroy Foods
100 Chapel Harbor Dr # 2
Suite 2
Pittsburgh, PA 15238-4163
412-781-0977
Fax: 412-781-1409 beanos@conroyfoods.com
Deli and seafood condiments
Owner: Jim Conroy
jlc@conroyfoods.com
CEO: William Conroy
Treasurer: Leslee Conroy
Estimated Sales: $1.8 Million
Number Employees: 10-19
Brands:
 Beanos's

2959 Conscious Choice Foods
1620 E. Highway 121
Building C, Suite 700
Lewisville, TX 75056
877-898-6158
Fax: 214-550-2682
consciouschoicefoods@gmail.com
www.consciouschoicefoods.com
Manufacturer of pickles.
CEO: Harold Callaway
Square Footage: 80000

2960 Consolidated Biscuit Company
312 Rader Rd
McComb, OH 45858
info@cbiscuits.com
www.cbiscuits.com
Cookies and crackers.
Estimated Sales: $400 Million
Number Employees: 2,500
Number of Brands: 4
Parent Co: Consolidated Biscuit Co. Ltd.
Brands:
 Healthline
 Devon
 Tal-furnar
 Sunshine Snacks

2961 Consolidated Catfish Co LLC
299 S St
P.O. Box 271
Isola, MS 38754
662-962-3101
Fax: 662-962-0114 sales@countryselect.com
www.countryselect.com
Seafood
President: Dick Stevens
dstevens@countryselect.com
VP of Controller: David Gray
VP: David Allen
VP of Marketing: Jack Perkins
VP of Sales: Joe Forrester
VP of Operations: Lee Parker
Year Founded: 1967
Estimated Sales: $123 Million
Number Employees: 250-499
Number of Brands: 1
Square Footage: 960000
Brands:
 Country Select

2962 Consolidated Mills Inc
7190 Brittmoore Road
Suite 150
Houston, TX 77041
713-896-4196
Fax: 713-896-4199 Info@cmillsinc.com
www.consolidatedmills.com
Specializing in contract packaging and product solutions. Products include frozen drink bases, slush flavors, flavoring extracts, sundae toppings, sno-cone syrups and custom spice blends
President: Scott Vrana
cordner@cmillsinc.com
Executive Vice President: Keith Vrana
Director of Quality Assurances: Cheryl Meche
Customer Service Supervisor: Carol Kirchhoff
Purchasing/Acct. Receivables/Payables: Jo Piercy
Estimated Sales: $3 Million
Number Employees: 20-49
Square Footage: 60000
Parent Co: Consolidated Mills
Type of Packaging: Consumer, Food Service

2963 Consolidated Sea Products
250 N Water St
Suite 112
Mobile, AL 36602-4000
251-433-3240
Fax: 251-433-6721
Seafood
Owner/President: Paul William
Estimated Sales: $740k
Number Employees: 4

2964 Consumer Guild Foods Inc
5035 Enterprise Blvd
Toledo, OH 43612-3839
419-726-3406
Fax: 419-726-8771
Salad dressings and oils, mayonnaise, condiments and relishes
President: Wilbur Ascham
VP: Robert Petrick
Estimated Sales: $2.7 Million
Number Employees: 20-49
Type of Packaging: Consumer, Food Service, Private Label, Bulk
Brands:
 Amhurst Kitchens
 Annie's Supreme
 Cg Supreme

2965 Consumers Packing Co
1301 Carson Dr
Melrose Park, IL 60160-2970
708-345-6780
Fax: 708-345-9052 800-356-9876
www.consumerspacking.com
Meat products
President: William Schutz
Finance Executive: Anthony Barone
VP Sales and Marketing: Mike Gale
Estimated Sales: $17 Million
Number Employees: 100-249

2966 Consumers Vinegar & Spice Co
4723 S Washtenaw Ave
Chicago, IL 60632
773-376-4100
info@cvsco.com
www.cvsco.com
Vinegar, spices and dehydrated garlic and onion
Estimated Sales: $5-10 Million
Number Employees: 10-19
Square Footage: 160000
Type of Packaging: Consumer, Food Service, Private Label, Bulk
Brands:
 Burma
 Consumers

2967 Conte's Pasta Co.
310 Wheat Rd
Vineland, NJ 08360
Fax: 856-697-1757 800-211-6607
customerservice@contespasta.com
contespasta.com
Pasta; sauce; and soup
Founder: Angela Conte
Year Founded: 1970
Number Employees: 11-50
Type of Packaging: Food Service, Private Label

2968 Continental Carbonic Products
2985 East Harrison Avenue
Decatur, IL 62526
217-428-2068
Fax: 217-424-2325 800-379-4232
www.continentalcarbonic.com
Specializes in the manufacture and distribution of dry ice and liquid carbon dioxide, along with sales and rental of dry ice blasting equipment.
President: John Funk
Vice President/Chief Financial Officer: Randy Spitz
General Manager, Manufacturing: Phil Wood
Vice President, Business Development: David Butts
Vice President, Distribution: Jason Taulbee
VP, Manufacturing & Distribution: Mark Hatton

2969 Continental Coffee Products Company
235 N Norwood St
Houston, TX 77011-2311
713-928-6281
Fax: 713-924-9870 800-323-6178
Coffee, tea
President: Peter JW Roorda
Sales Manager: Scott Kolber
Plant Manager: Dan Hickman
Number Employees: 175

2970 Continental Grain Company
787 5th Ave
15th Fl
New York, NY 10153-0015
212-207-5100
information@conti.com
www.continentalgrain.com
Grain, poultry, pork, beef, animal feed, aquaculture, and flour milling.
Directeur General: Charles Fribourg
Chairman & CEO: Paul J. Fribourg
CFO: Frank Baier
General Counsel: Michael Mayberry
Executive Vice President: David Tanner
COO: Robert Golden
Estimated Sales: $2.5 Billion
Number Employees: 11,000
Type of Packaging: Consumer, Bulk
Brands:
 Chiatai Conti Group
 Conti
 ContiParaguay
 Les Moulins D' Haiti
 Moderna Alimentos
 Molinos Champion S.A.
 Santa Elena
 Wayne Farms

2971 Continental Mills Inc
18100 Andover Park W
Tukwila, WA 98188-4703
206-816-7000
Fax: 253-872-7954 www.continentalmills.com
Manufacturer and exporter of baking products including dry flour mixes. Continental Mills has acquired the Pillsbury foodservice small package dry mix business from Best Brands Corporation
President: John Heily
CEO: John M Heily
jheily@continentalmills.com
CFO: Michael Castle
Vice President: Bob Wallach
Research & Development: Dan Donahue
Quality Control: Christy Johnson
Marketing Director: Steve Donley
Sales Director: Steve Giuditta
Public Relations: Clyde Walker
Operations Manager: Mark Harris
Production Manager: Mike Meredith
Year Founded: 1932
Estimated Sales: $43.2 Million
Number Employees: 100-249
Number of Brands: 10
Square Footage: 300000
Parent Co: Pillsbury Food Service
Type of Packaging: Consumer, Food Service, Private Label, Bulk
Brands:
 Albers
 Alpine
 Ghirardelli

Food Manufacturers / A-Z

Kretschmer
Krusteaz
Krusteaz Professional
Old Country Store
Red Lobster
Snowqualmie Falls Lodge
Wild Roots

2972 Continental Sausage
911 E 75th Ave
Denver, CO 80229-6401
303-288-9787
Fax: 303-288-9789 866-794-7727
www.continentalsausage.com
Meats, sausage
Owner: Duane Garrison
dgarrison@llbean.com
Vice President/Treasurer: Ursula Gutknecht
Purchasing Manager: Eric Gutknecht
Estimated Sales: $2.5 Million
Number Employees: 5-9

2973 Continental Seasoning
1700 Palisade Ave
Teaneck, NJ 07666
201-837-6111
Fax: 201-837-9248 800-631-1564
Processor, importer and exporter of sauces, spices, seasonings and food additives
President: Pete Federer
CFO: Jeffrey Bovit
Vice President: Edward Levine
Quality Control: Marty Haas
VP Production: Ann Davis
Plant Manager: Steve Wagner
Estimated Sales: $5 Million
Number Employees: 50
Square Footage: 80000
Type of Packaging: Food Service, Private Label, Bulk

2974 Continental Yogurt
1358 E Colorado Street
Glendale, CA 91205-1474
818-240-7400
Fax: 818-243-3601
Yogurt
Principal: Martha Frazier
Sales Manager: Gary Correll
Purchasing Agent: Juan Garcia
Estimated Sales: $1-3 Million
Number Employees: 10-19
Type of Packaging: Food Service

2975 Conway Import Co Inc
11051 Addison Street
Franklin Park, IL 60131
800-323-8801
info@conwaydressings.com
www.conwaydressings.com
High quality salad dressing and sauce pods for the finest hoels, airlines, cruiselines, and restaurants.
Owner/Vice President, Operations: Gregg Heineman
conwaydressings@mindspring.com
Founder: Albert Heineman
VP Marketing & Sales: Robert Burns
Number Employees: 50-99
Number of Products: 370+
Square Footage: 240000
Type of Packaging: Food Service, Private Label, Bulk

2976 Cook Inlet Processing
909 W 9th Ave
Anchorage, AK 99501-3322
907-243-1166
Fax: 907-243-4231
Manufacturer of fresh seafood, frozen seafood, and canned seafood
Sales Manager: Mike Shupe
VP Operations: Tim Blott
Year Founded: 1977
Estimated Sales: $1-3 Million
Number Employees: 1-4

2977 Cook Natural Products
260 Lafayette Circle
Lafayette, CA 94549
925-283-6897
Fax: 925-283-6086 800-537-7589
www.cooknaturally.com
Organic flour, grains, seeds, beans
President: Brenda McEntee

Estimated Sales: $12 Million
Number Employees: 10-19

2978 Cook's Gourmet Foods
5821 Wilderness Avenue
Riverside, CA 92504
951-352-5700
Fax: 951-352-5710
Co-packers of gourmet foods
President: Tom Harris Jr
General Manager: Tommy Harris
Vice President: Richard Harris
Production Planner: Mike Elsman
Plant Supervisor: Ken Lujan
Estimated Sales: $500,000-$1 Million
Number Employees: 50-99

2979 Cook's Pantry
4125 Market St
Suite 1
Ventura, CA 93003
805-947-4622
cookspantry.com
Spreads, sauces, sauerkrauts and pickles
President/Owner: Matt Hately
Number of Brands: 1
Number of Products: 20
Type of Packaging: Consumer
Brands:
COOK'S PANTRY ORGANIC

2980 Cook-In-The-Kitchen
PO Box 8
Hampden, ME 04444
207-848-4900
Fax: 207-848-4988 www.cookinthekitchen.com
All natural pancake, bakery and soup mixes.
President: Mary Spata
VP/General Manager: Murray Burk
Estimated Sales: $1-2.5 Million
Number Employees: 3
Number of Products: 20
Type of Packaging: Consumer, Private Label

2981 Cooke Aguaculture
874 Main Street
Blacks Harbour, NB E5H-1E6
Canada
506-456-6600
Fax: 506-456-6652 nhalse@cookeaqua.com
www.cookeaqua.com
Distributor of fresh and smoked salmon.
CEO: Glenn Cooke
CFO: Peter Buck
VP Marketing: Jean Lamontagne
VP Sales: Alan Craig
VP Public Relations/Communications: Neil Halse
Purchasing Director: Don Bourque
Number Employees: 20-49
Number of Brands: 3
Number of Products: 60
Square Footage: 10000
Brands:
Appledore
Horton's

2982 Cooke Tavern LTD
4158 Penns Valley Rd
Spring Mills, PA 16875-8306
814-422-7687
Fax: 814-422-8752 866-422-7687
gregw@cooketavernsoups.com
www.cooketavernsoups.com
Soups
President/Owner: Greg Williams
gregw@cooketavernsoups.com
Estimated Sales: Less Than $500,000
Number Employees: 5-9

2983 Cookie Factory
1844 Givan Ave
Bronx, NY 10469-3155
718-379-6223
Fax: 718-379-4417 ggcookies@aol.com
www.thecookiefactory.com
Cookies, cakes and Italian pastries
President: Rose Florio
ggcookies@aol.com
VP: Salvatore Florio Jr
VP Sales: Sal Florio
Finance Executive: Pete Russo
VP Production: Joan Florio
Estimated Sales: $2.5-5 Million
Number Employees: 20-49

Brands:
Mama Rose

2984 Cookie Kingdom
1201 E Walnut St
Oglesby, IL 61348-1344
815-883-3331
Fax: 815-883-3332 ckingdomoffice@gmail.com
www.cookiekingdom.com
Manufacturer of cookies, ice cream wafers and dairy inclusions; co-packer for private label companies; and builder and upgrader of dairy equipment for lease or purchase.
President: Cliff Sheppard
ckingdom@ivnet.com
Director: Patty Smith
Estimated Sales: $13 Million
Number Employees: 100-249
Type of Packaging: Consumer, Private Label, Bulk

2985 Cookie Specialties Inc
482 N Milwaukee Ave
Wheeling, IL 60090-3067
847-537-3888
Fax: 847-537-6709 matt@mattscookies.com
www.mattscookies.info
Cookies
President: Grant Pierce
VP: Matthew Pierce
Contact: Fran Burke
franburke@mattscookies.info
Estimated Sales: $10-20 Million
Number Employees: 10-19
Type of Packaging: Consumer, Food Service, Private Label
Brands:
Matt's Cookies

2986 Cookie Tree Bakeries
4010 W Advantage Circle
Salt Lake City, UT 84104
801-268-2253
www.cookietree.com
Frozen gourmet cookies and cookie dough; also, fat-free available.
Purchasing: Wayne Davis
Year Founded: 1981
Estimated Sales: $20-50 Million
Type of Packaging: Consumer, Food Service, Private Label, Bulk
Brands:
Cookietree Bakeries

2987 Cookies By Design Inc
1865 Summit Ave # 607
Plano, TX 75074-8185
972-398-9536
Fax: 972-398-9542 888-675-1453
customerservice@cookiesbydesign.com
www.cookiesbydesign.com
Cookies and baked goods
Founder: Gwen Wilhite
Contact: Jolene Day
jday@cookiesbydesign.com
Number Employees: 20-49

2988 Cookies Food Products
PO Box 458
Wall Lake, IA 51466
712-664-2437
Fax: 712-664-2675 800-331-4995
www.cookiesbbq.com
Barbecue and taco sauces
President: Speed Herrig
Purchasing Manager: Jeff Herrig
Estimated Sales: $10-20 Million
Number Employees: 10-19
Square Footage: 122000
Type of Packaging: Consumer, Food Service
Brands:
Cookies

2989 Cookies United
141 Freeman Ave
Islip, NY 11751-1428
631-581-4000
Fax: 631-581-4510 info@cookiesunited.com
Manufacturer and national marketer of branded and private label baked goods.
President: Joseph Vitarelli
joseph@silverlakecookie.com
Number Employees: 250-499
Type of Packaging: Consumer, Food Service, Private Label, Bulk

Food Manufacturers / A-Z

2990 Cookiezen, LLC
Po Box 2519
Falls Church, VA 22042-0519
703-389-9274
Fax: 866-496-6034
Cookies
Marketing: Laura Englander
Contact: Emma May
emmamay@cookiezen.com

2991 Cookshack
2304 N Ash St
Ponca City, OK 74601-1109
580-765-3669
Fax: 580-765-2223 800-423-0698
info@cookshack.com www.cookshack.com
Sauces & spices, smoking wood accessories for better barbeque, Cookshack smoked foods cookbooks, electric smoker ovens, pellet fired smokes, charbroilers, pellet grills
President: Brent Matthews
CEO: Sara Birch
j.kenney@varde.com
VP: Edward Aguiar Jr
Marketing Coordinator: Cayley Armstrong
Finance/Marketing/Sales Manager: John Shiflet
General Manager: Stuart Powell
Production Manager: Jim Linnebur
Estimated Sales: $4 Million
Number Employees: 20-49
Number of Brands: 2
Number of Products: 1
Square Footage: 44000
Type of Packaging: Consumer, Food Service, Private Label, Bulk
Brands:
  Fast Eddy's

2992 Cool
801 E Campbell Rd # 348
Richardson, TX 75081-1866
972-437-9352
Fax: 972-644-7231
Sodas and sports drinks
Manager: Dan C Cole
Estimated Sales: $500-1,000,000 appx.
Number Employees: 1-4
Brands:
  Cool Natural Sodas
  Cool Quencher Sports

2993 (HQ)Cool Brands International
4175 Veteran's Memorial Highway
3rd Floor
Ronkonkoma, NY 11779
631-737-9700
Fax: 631-737-9792
Ice cream and ice cream novelties
President/CEO: David Kewer
General Manager: Antonio Brooks
Number Employees: 20-49
Parent Co: CoolBrands International

2994 Cool Mountain BeveragesInc
1065 E Prairie Ave
Des Plaines, IL 60016-3341
847-759-9330
Fax: 847-789-8575 888-838-7632
coolmountn@aol.com www.coolmountain.com
Produces gourmet flavored sodas.
President: Bill Daker
Estimated Sales: $3-5 Million
Number Employees: 5-9
Brands:
  Cool Mountain Gourmet Soda

2995 Coolhaus
8588 Washington Blvd
Culver City, CA 90232
310-853-8995
info@cool.haus
cool.haus
Premium ice cream and ice cream sandwiches
Owner: Natasha Case
Owner: Freya Estreller
Estimated Sales: Less Than $500,000
Number Employees: 5-9

2996 Coombs Family Farm
P.O. Box 117
Brattleboro, VT 05302
888-266-6271
coombsfamilyfarms.com
Maple syrup, sugar, candy, baking mixes, and gift baskets.
Co-Owner: Bruce Bascom
Co-Owner: Arnold Coombs
Estimated Sales: $30 Million
Number Employees: 10-19
Type of Packaging: Private Label

2997 Coon Creek Winery
8711 Silverado Trl S
St Helena, CA 94574-9577
707-963-5133
Fax: 707-963-7840 800-793-7960
info@conncreek.com www.conncreek.com
Wines
Director: Donna Duncanson
COO: David Lawrence
Manager: Paul Asikainen
paul.asikainen@conncreek.com
Number Employees: 10-19

2998 Cooper Farms Cooked Meats
6793 US Route 127
Van Wert, OH 45891-9601
419-238-4056
Fax: 419-238-1587 www.cooperfarms.com
Fresh turkey products
Chief Executive Officer: James Cooper
Treasurer: Anada Cooper
Chief Operating Officer: Gary Cooper
Estimated Sales: $500,000-999,999 Thousand
Number Employees: 100-249

2999 Cooper Lake Farm LLC
203 Cooper Lake Rd
Bearsville, NY 12409
845-679-7822
cooperlakefarm.com
Brittles and cheese
Owner: Gayle Burbank
gayleburbank@gmail.com
Owner: Ken Cohen

3000 Cooper Mountain Vineyards
9480 SW Grabhorn Road
Beaverton, OR 97007
503-649-0027
Fax: 503-649-0702
info@coopermountainwine.com
www.coopermountainwine.com
Wines
Owner: Robert J. Gross
Sales & Marketing Manager: Barbara Gross
Sales Director: Susan Baltus
Winemaker: Rich Cushman
Estimated Sales: $1-2.5 Million
Number Employees: 5-9
Type of Packaging: Private Label

3001 Cooper Street Cookies
320 Martin St
Suite 100
Birmingham, MI 48009
248-283-7700
info@cooperstreetcookies.com
cooperstreetcookies.com
Cookies
President: Max Surnow
Year Founded: 2011
Estimated Sales: $450,000,00
Number Employees: 25
Type of Packaging: Private Label

3002 Cooper Vineyards
13372 Shannon Hill Rd
Louisa, VA 23093-3929
540-894-5474
Fax: 804-285-8773 Info@CooperVineyards.com
www.coopervineyards.com
Wine
Co-Owner: Jaque P. Hogge
Partner: Jacque Hogge
Estimated Sales: Less Than $500,000
Number Employees: 1-4

3003 Cooperative Elevator Co
7211 E Michigan Ave
Pigeon, MI 48755
989-453-3120
Fax: 989-453-3942 800-968-0601
www.coopelev.com
Dried beans
President/CEO: Pat Anderson
panderson@coopelv.com
Chairman: Kurt Ewald
VP Of Finance & Board Treasurer: Mike Wehner
VP of IT & Assistant Board Secretary: Barry Albrecht
Estimated Sales: $500,000-$1 Million
Number Employees: 100-249

3004 Cooperstown Cookie Company
P.O.Box 64
Cooperstown, NY 13326
888-269-7315
Fax: 607-547-2673 888-269-7315
www.cooperstowncookie.com
Baseball cookies
President/Owner: Pati Grady

3005 Copak Solutions
103b Somerset Dr NW
Conover, NC 28613-9217
828-261-0255
Fax: 828-261-0256
Manufacturer of chips.
President: Larry Deal
larry@copaksolutionsinc.net
Number Employees: 20-49
Square Footage: 80000

3006 Copper Hills Fruit Sales
4337 N Golden State Boulevard
Suite 102
Fresno, CA 93722-3801
559-432-5400
Fax: 559-432-5620
Packers of peaches, plums, nectarines, apricots, pomegranates, and persimmons
Managing Member: Wilma J. Deniz

3007 Copper Moon Coffee LLC
1503 Veterans Memorial Parkway East
Lafayette, IN 47905
317-541-9000
Fax: 317-543-0757 www.coppermooncoffee.com
Manufacturer of world coffee blends.
CEO: Brad Gutwein
Square Footage: 80000

3008 Copper Tank Brewing Company
504 Trinity Street
Austin, TX 78701-3714
512-854-9380
Fax: 512-478-1832
Seasonal beer, ale, stout, lager and porter
President: Aaron Scharff
Purchasing: Patrick Bradshaw
Estimated Sales: $2.5-5 Million
Number Employees: 50-99
Type of Packaging: Food Service

3009 Cora Italian Specialties
9630 Joliet Rd
Countryside, IL 60525-4138
708-482-4660
Fax: 708-482-4663 800-696-2672
info@corainc.com www.corainc.com
Monin syrups, Oregon chai, Guitiard and Ghirardelli chocolates, Mocafe, Jet tea etc
President: John Cora
jcora@corainc.com
Sales: Paul Rekstad
Estimated Sales: 1.80 Million
Number Employees: 10-19
Square Footage: 60000
Type of Packaging: Food Service
Brands:
  Danesi
  Dolce
  Ghirardelli
  Guittard
  Jet Tea
  Mocafe
  Monin
  Musetti
  Nikola's Biscotti
  Numi Tea
  Oregon Chai
  Soy Dream
  White Wave

Food Manufacturers / A-Z

3010 Cora Texas Mfg Co Inc
32505 Highway 1
White Castle, LA 70788-3638
225-545-3679
Fax: 225-545-8360 info@coratexas.com
www.coratexas.com
Manufacturer of Louisiana raw sugar and molasses.
President/CEO: Paul Buckley Kessler
Chief Operating Officer/Secretary: Charles Schudmak
Year Founded: 1817
Estimated Sales: $20-50 Million
Number Employees: 100-249
Type of Packaging: Bulk

3011 Coral LLC
5576 Bighorn Dr # B
Carson City, NV 89701-1474
775-883-9853
Fax: 775-883-9858 800-882-9577
sales@coralcalcium.com www.coralcalcium.com
Natural minerals
Sales Director: Alberto Galdamez
Contact: Matt Cuhadar
matt@coralcalcium.com
Number Employees: 5-9

3012 Corazonas Foods, Inc
11900 West Olympic Boulevard
Suite 630
Los Angeles, CA 90064
310-622-9550
Fax: 310-622-9551 800-967-2451
Chips
Contact: Greg Fry
gfry@corazonas.com

3013 Corbin Foods-Edibowls
P.O. Box 28139
Santa Ana, CA 92799-8139
714-966-6695
Fax: 949-640-0279 800-695-5655
www.edibowls.com
Processor and exporter of edible bowls for salads, desserts and tarts; club packs available
Manager: R J Hill
Estimated Sales: $5-10 Million
Number Employees: 5-9
Square Footage: 400000
Type of Packaging: Consumer, Food Service, Bulk
Brands:
 Edibowl

3014 (HQ)Corbion
7905 Quivira Rd
Lenexa, KS 66215-2732
913-890-5500
Fax: 913-888-4970 800-669-4092
foodsus@corbion.com www.corbion.com
Lactic acid, lactic acid derivatives and lactides; functional blends containing enzymes, emulsifiers, minerals, and vitamins; biobased products made from renewable resources and applied in global markets such as bakery, meat, food andbeverages.
CEO: Tjerk de Ruiter
Chief Financial Officer: Eddy van Rhede van der Kloot
Executive VP Biobased Ingredients: Andy Muller
Chief Technology Officer: Marcel Wubbolts
Vice President of Human Resources: Johan van der Hel
Executive Vice President of Operations: Jacqueline van Lemmen
Number Employees: 50-99
Parent Co: Corbion
Other Locations:
 Manufacturing & Product Development
 Totowa NJ
 Manufacturing Facility
 Grandview MO
 Manufacturing Facility
 East Rutherford NJ
 Manufacturing Facility
 Dolton IL
 Manufacturing Facility
 Blair NE
 Manufacturing Facility
 Tucker GA

3015 Corbion
100 Adams Dr
Totowa, NJ 07512
973-256-8886
800-526-5261
www.corbion.com
Lactic acid, lactic acid derivatives and lactides; functional blends containing enzymes, emulsifiers, minerals, and vitamins; biobased products made from renewable resources and applied in global markets such as bakery, meat, food andbeverages.

3016 Corbion
13830 Botts Rd
Grandview, MO 64030
816-763-8377
www.corbion.com
Lactic acid, lactic acid derivatives and lactides; functional blends containing enzymes, emulsifiers, minerals, and vitamins; biobased products made from renewable resources and applied in global markets such as bakery, meat, food andbeverages.

3017 Corbion
96 E Union Ave
East Rutherford, NJ 07073
800-526-5261
www.corbion.com
Lactic acid, lactic acid derivatives and lactides; functional blends containing enzymes, emulsifiers, minerals, and vitamins; biobased products made from renewable resources and applied in global markets such as bakery, meat, food andbeverages.

3018 Corbion
14622 Lakeside Ave
Dolton, IL 60419
708-849-8590
Fax: 708-849-3114 www.corbion.com
Lactic acid, lactic acid derivatives and lactides; functional blends containing enzymes, emulsifiers, minerals, and vitamins; biobased products made from renewable resources and applied in global markets such as bakery, meat, food andbeverages.

3019 Corbion
650 Industrial Park Dr
P.O. Box 38
Blair, NE 68008
402-426-0377
Fax: 402-533-1801 www.corbion.com
Lactic acid, lactic acid derivatives and lactides; functional blends containing enzymes, emulsifiers, minerals, and vitamins; biobased products made from renewable resources and applied in global markets such as bakery, meat, food andbeverages.

3020 Corbion
5150 N Royal Atlanta Dr
Tucker, GA 30084
470-545-7100
Fax: 470-545-7098 www.corbion.com
Lactic acid, lactic acid derivatives and lactides; functional blends containing enzymes, emulsifiers, minerals, and vitamins; biobased products made from renewable resources and applied in global markets such as bakery, meat, food andbeverages.

3021 Corbion
One Tower Place
Suite 6, 6th Floor
S San Francisco, CA 94080
www.corbion.com
Lactic acid, lactic acid derivatives and lactides; functional blends containing enzymes, emulsifiers, minerals, and vitamins; biobased products made from renewable resources and applied in global markets such as bakery, meat, food andbeverages.

3022 Corbion
2500 Meadowpine Blvd
Unit 3
Mississauga, ON L5N 6C4
Canada
905-826-1089
Fax: 905-826-8432 800-324-8802
www.corbion.com
Lactic acid, lactic acid derivatives and lactides; functional blends containing enzymes, emulsifiers, minerals, and vitamins; biobased products made from renewable resources and applied in global markets such as bakery, meat, food andbeverages.

3023 Corbion
Av. Insurgentes Sur 1787 Piso 8
Col. Guadalupe Inn
Ciudad de Mexico, CP., 01020
Mexico
pmx@corbion.com
www.corbion.com
Lactic acid, lactic acid derivatives and lactides; functional blends containing enzymes, emulsifiers, minerals, and vitamins; biobased products made from renewable resources and applied in global markets such as bakery, meat, food andbeverages.

3024 Corby Distilleries
225 King Street West
Suite 1100
Toronto, ON M5V 3M2
Canada
416-479-2400
Fax: 416-369-9809 800-367-9079
corbyweb@adsw.com www.corby.ca
Whiskey, Scotch whiskey, Irish whiskey, bourbon, rum, gin, vodka, tequila, cognac and brandy.
President/CEO: Patrick O'Driscoll
VP/CFO: Thierry Pourchet
VP Marketing: Jeff Agdern
VP Sales: Andy Alexander
VP SP/Customer Service: Chris Chan
VP Production: Jim Stanski
Number Employees: 100-249
Number of Brands: 45
Parent Co: Allied Lyons
Type of Packaging: Consumer, Food Service
Brands:
 Ballantine's Finest
 Barclay's
 Beefeater Dry
 Belvedere
 Canadian Club
 Chopin
 Courvoisier
 D'Eaubonne Vsop Napoleon
 De Kuyper Geneva
 Glendronach
 Hornitos Sauza
 Lamb's Navy
 Lamb's Palm Breeze
 Lamb's White
 Laphroaig
 Lemon Hart
 Maker's Mark
 Malibu Coconut Rum
 Polar Ice Tassel
 Revelstoke
 Royal Reserve
 Sauza Commemorativo
 Sauza Extra Gold
 Sauza Silver
 Sauza Triada
 Scapa Single Malt
 Silk Tassel
 Special Old
 Stolichnaya
 Stolichnaya Razberi
 Stolichnaya Red
 Stolichnaya Vanil
 Teacher's Highland Cream
 Tres Generaciones
 Tullamore Dew
 Wiser's Deluxe
 Wiser's Special Blend
 Wiser's Very Old

3025 Cordoba Foods LLC
15912 NW 48th Avenue
Hialeah, FL 33014-6410
786-202-2988
sales@gauchoranchfoods.com
www.gauchoranchfoods.com
Condiments, BBQ sauce, ethnic sauces (soy, curry, etc.), grilling sauces, marinades, other sauces, seasonings and cooking enhancers, dessert toppings (i.e. fudge sauce, caramel sauce, whipped cream, etc.) other spreads & syrup.

3026 Cordon Bleu International
8383 Rue J Rene Ouimet
Anjou, QC H1J 2P8
Canada
514-352-3000
Fax: 514-352-3226 800-363-1182
info@cordonbleu.ca www.cordonbleu.ca
Processor and exporter of pickled food products, sauces, gravies, chicken broth, meat pates, beef and chicken entrees and red kidney beans in tomato sauce.
Director Advertising/Promotions: Michelle Guibord
Director Sales: Jacques LeGare
Purchasing: Kristen Gerard
Number Employees: 100-249
Parent Co: J-R Ouimet

Food Manufacturers / A-Z

3027 Corea Lobster Cooperative
191 Crowley Island Rd
Corea, ME 04624
207-963-7936
Fax: 207-963-5952
Processors of lobsters
President: Michael Hunt
Treasurer: F.D. Rodgers
VP: Gary Moore
Estimated Sales: $1.5 Million
Number Employees: 4
Type of Packaging: Consumer, Private Label

3028 (HQ)Corfu Foods Inc
755 Thomas Dr
Bensenville, IL 60106-1624
630-595-2510
Fax: 630-595-3884 info@corfufoods.com
www.corfufoods.com
Processor and exporter of pita bread, honey mustard sauce and beef and chicken gyro products including cones, patties, deli kits, sauce and loaves; importer of cheese, olives and stuffed grape leaves.
President: Vasilios Memmos
vmemmos@corfufoods.com
VP: Sophie Maroulis
Purchasing Agent: Ron Fallot
Estimated Sales: $10-20 Million
Number Employees: 50-99
Square Footage: 140000
Other Locations:
  Corfu Foods
  Long Island City NY
Brands:
  Corfu
  Gyros Usa
  Omega
  Tasty

3029 Corfu Foods Inc
755 Thomas Dr
Bensenville, IL 60106-1624
630-595-2510
Fax: 630-595-3884 800-874-9767
www.corfufoods.com
Gyros
President: Vasilios Memmos
vmemmos@corfufoods.com
Estimated Sales: $10-20 Million
Number Employees: 50-99

3030 Corim Industries Inc
1112 Industrial Pkwy
Brick, NJ 08724-2508
732-840-1640
Fax: 732-840-1608 800-942-4201
sales@corimindustries.com
www.corimindustries.com
Manufacturer, wholesaler and exporter of gourmet coffees, custom printed sugar packets, instant cappuccino, chai, and soluble milk for vending machines, custom blending and supplies, and also custom branding for private labelsuppliers.
President: Nathan Teren
nathan.teren@marinemax.com
CEO: Sam Teren
Treasurer/Controller: Nathan Teren
Estimated Sales: $2.1 Million
Number Employees: 20-49
Square Footage: 41672
Type of Packaging: Consumer, Food Service, Private Label, Bulk

3031 Corine's Cuisine
Sparks, MD 21152
www.corinescuisine.com
Gourmet sauces
Owner: Corine Parish
Type of Packaging: Private Label

3032 Corky's Ribs & BBQ
3584 Parkway
Pigeon Forge, TN 37863
865-453-7427
www.corkysbbq.com
Frozen barbecue ribs, pork shoulders and beef brisket
Owner: Barry Pelts
barry@corkysbbq.com
CEO: Andrew Woodman
Principal: Don Pelts
Estimated Sales: $5-10 Million
Number Employees: 100-249
Type of Packaging: Consumer, Food Service

3033 Cormier Rice Milling CoInc
501 W 3rd St
De Witt, AR 72042-2500
870-946-3561
Fax: 870-946-3029 www.cormierrice.com
Processor and exporter of long and medium grain, milled, brown and organic brown rice
Owner: Robert Ellis
robert@cormierrice.com
Vice President: Julie Simpson
VP: J Ferguson
Estimated Sales: $10-20 Million
Number Employees: 10-19
Type of Packaging: Consumer, Food Service, Private Label, Bulk
Brands:
  Lone Pine
  Regal
  Snow Goose

3034 Corn Popper
5584 S Garnett Rd
Tulsa, OK 74146-6814
918-250-9317
Fax: 918-250-7148 www.cornpopper.com
Flavored, organic and plain popcorn.
Owner: Brad Berry
brad@cornpopper.com
CFO: Betty Melton
General Manager: Jose Alves
Estimated Sales: Less Than $500,000
Number Employees: 1-4
Parent Co: Corn Poppers
Brands:
  Popcorn Dippers

3035 Cornabys
421 S 200 E
Spanish Fork, UT 84660-2418
801-830-4530
Fax: 801-423-7838 janetstocks@cornabys.com
www.fruitivia.com
Jams & jellies.
Marketing: Janet Stocks

3036 Cornell Beverages Inc
105 Harrison Pl
Brooklyn, NY 11237-1403
718-381-3000
Fax: 718-381-3001
Carbonated soft drinks
President: Allan Hoffman
allan@cornellbev.com
Treasurer: Donna Hoffman
Purchasing: Jim Dehaan
Estimated Sales: $850,000
Number Employees: 20-49
Brands:
  Cornell Beverages

3037 Cornfields Inc
3898 Sunset Ave
Waukegan, IL 60087-3258
847-263-7000
Fax: 847-263-7090 jbweiler@cornfieldsinc.com
www.cornfieldsinc.com
Chips, nuts, popcorn, pretzels, puffed snacks.
Sales/Marketing: J.B. Weiler
Manager: Henry Cretors
ccretors@cornfieldsinc.com
Number Employees: 1-4

3038 Corning Olive Oil Company
721 Fig Lane
Corning, CA 90621
530-824-5447
Fax: 530-824-5862 sales@corningoliveoil.com
www.corningoliveoil.com
Olive oils
President: John Psyllos
Number Employees: 12

3039 Corona College Heights
8000 Lincoln Ave
Riverside, CA 92504-4343
951-351-7880
Fax: 951-689-5115 www.cchcitrus.org
Processor and exporter of oranges, lemons and grapefruit.
Director: Thomas Chao
Vice President, Field Operations: Ruben Gutierrez
Export Sales Manager: Jessica Chavez
Plant Manager: Brad Tilden
Estimated Sales: $35 Million
Number Employees: 100-249
Square Footage: 180000
Type of Packaging: Consumer, Bulk

3040 Corrin Produce Sales
23667 E Dinuba Ave
Dinuba, CA 93618
559-596-0517
Fax: 559-638-8508
Grower and exporter of fresh fruit including peaches, plums, nectarines and table grapes; also, raisins
President: Harold Seitz
CFO: Robert Greiner
Manager: Lisa Macedo
Estimated Sales: $400,000
Number Employees: 5
Type of Packaging: Bulk

3041 Corsair Pepper Sauce
1110 42nd Avenue
Gulfport, MS 39501-2663
228-452-0311
Fax: 228-452-0152
Pickled fruits and vegetables, vegetable sauces and seasonings and salad dressings.
President: Martha Murphy
Estimated Sales: $120,000
Number Employees: 2

3042 Corsetti's Pasta Products
1001 N Evergreen Ave
Woodbury, NJ 08096-3557
856-853-0999
Fax: 856-853-7438 800-989-1188
Various pasta products such as lasagna and spaghetti.
Owner: Dan Pellegrino
Plant & Purchasing Manager: Michael Corsetti
Estimated Sales: $2.5-5,000,000
Number Employees: 5-9
Type of Packaging: Bulk

3043 Corso's Cookies
314 Lakeside Rd
Syracuse, NY 13209-9729
315-487-2111
Fax: 315-487-4208 800-465-7775
customerservice@corsoscookies.com
www.corsoscookies.com
Cookies and baked goods
CEO: Peter Hess
peter@corsoscookies.com
Number Employees: 20-49

3044 Corteva Agriscience
P.O. Box 80735
Chestnut Run Plaza 735
Wilmington, DE 19805-0735
302-485-3000
www.corteva.com
Agricultural chemicals, seeds and software/digital solutions for farmers.
CEO: James Collins
Executive VP/CFO: Greg Friedman
Senior VP/General Counsel: Cornel Fuerer
Executive VP/Chief Commercial Officer: Tim Glenn
Senior VP, Enterprise Operations: Susan Lewis
Year Founded: 2019
Estimated Sales: $14 Billion
Parent Co: Corteva Agriscience

3045 Cosco International
1826 N Lorel Ave
Chicago, IL 60639-4376
773-889-1400
Fax: 773-889-0854 800-621-4549
Flavors.
President: Patrick Carney
CFO: Joe Hughes
Purchasing Agent: Ken Ciukowski
Estimated Sales: $1-$2.5 Million
Number Employees: 20-49
Brands:
  Apple Sidra
  Cosco Flavors

631

Food Manufacturers / A-Z

3046 Cosentino Winery
7415 Saint Helena Highway
Napa, CA 94558
707-921-2809
Fax: 707-944-2609 800-764-1220
finewines@cosentinowinery.com
www.cosentinowinery.com
Fine red and white wines.
President: Mitch Cosentino
CEO: Larry Soldinger
Marketing Director: Shawn Lutwalla
Public Relations: Julie Weinstock
Estimated Sales: $5-10 Million
Number Employees: 25
Type of Packaging: Private Label

3047 Cosgrove Distributors Inc
120 S Greenwood St
Spring Valley, IL 61362-2014
815-664-4121
Fax: 815-663-1433 800-347-3071
www.cosgrovedistributors.com
Wholesaler/distributor of general line products; serving the food service market.
President: Nora Cosgrove
cosgroves@insightbb.com
Estimated Sales: $2.5-5 Million
Number Employees: 20-49

3048 Cosmo Food Products
200 Callegari Dr
P.O. Box 256
West Haven, CT 06516-6234
203-933-9323
Fax: 203-937-7283 800-942-6766
claudano@cosmosfoods.com
www.cosmosfoods.com
Processor, packer and importer of olives, artichokes, capers, peppers, marinated mushrooms and roasted peppers; also, sun-dried tomatoes, hot cherry peppers, pepperoncini and garlic.
President: Cosmo Laudano
claudano@cosmosfoods.com
VP: Lisa Laudano
Sales Manager: Mario Laudano
Production: Peter Merola
Estimated Sales: $5-10 Million
Number Employees: 20-49
Number of Products: 39
Square Footage: 90000
Type of Packaging: Consumer, Food Service, Private Label, Bulk
Brands:
 Cosmo's

3049 Cosmopolitan Foods
138 Essex Avenue
Glen Ridge, NJ 07028-2409
973-680-4560
Sauces such as BBQ, Worcestershire and Spaghetti
President: Nick Ten Velde
Purchasing Manager: Nick Ten Velde
Number Employees: 5-9

3050 Costa Deano's Gourmet Foods
PO Box 6367
Canton, OH 44706-0367
330-453-1555
Fax: 330-453-9766 800-337-2823
Processor and exporter of gourmet pasta sauces
President: Dean Bacopoulos
VP: Bill Bacopoulos
Number Employees: 5-9
Square Footage: 60000
Parent Co: Costa Deano's Enterprises
Type of Packaging: Consumer, Food Service, Private Label, Bulk
Brands:
 Costa Deano's

3051 Costa Macaroni Manufacturing
PO Box 32308
Los Angeles, CA 90032-0308
Fax: 323-225-1667 800-433-7785
www.costapasta.com
Homemade various shapes and sizes of pastas
West Coast Sales Manager: Stephen Zoccoli
VP Foodservice Sales: Buzz Weisman
Estimated Sales: $5-10 Million
Number Employees: 20-49
Type of Packaging: Food Service, Bulk
Brands:
 Costa

3052 CostaDeano's Enterprises
PO Box 6367
Canton, OH 44706-0367
330-453-1555
Fax: 330-493-9766
Producer of gourmet foods.
President: Dean Bacopoulos
Estimated Sales: $5-10,000,000
Number Employees: 20-49
Square Footage: 10
Type of Packaging: Private Label
Brands:
 Costadeanos Gourmet

3053 Costas Pasta
2045 Attic Pkwy NW
Kennesaw, GA 30152-7610
770-514-8814
Fax: 770-514-9766
Fresh pasta
Owner: Joseph Costa
CFO: Joe Costa
Vice President: Stephen Zoccoli
Sales Director: Stephen Saferite
joe@costapasta.com
Estimated Sales: $2.5-5 Million
Number Employees: 5-9
Brands:
 Costa's Pasta

3054 Cotswold Cottage Foods
9820 W 60th Ave
Arvada, CO 80004
303-423-2987
Fax: 303-423-2987 800-208-1977
cotscotfds@aol.com
Scone mixes, gingerbread mixes, stuffing mixes, lemon curd, jams, and tea
President: Tricia Mackell
Estimated Sales: $300,000-500,000
Number Employees: 5-9
Type of Packaging: Consumer

3055 Cottage Street Pasta
167 S Main Street
Barre, VT 05641-4813
802-476-4024
pastajules@aol.com
Fresh pasta and ravioli.
Purchasing Agent: Karen Gordon
Estimated Sales: $300,000-500,000
Number Employees: 1-4

3056 Cotton Baking Company
3400 S. Macarthur Drive
Alexandria, LA 71302
318-448-6600
Fax: 318-747-0118
Manufacturer of baked products.
Plant Manager: Don Thomas
Sales Manager: Slade Cooper
Estimated Sales: $20-50 Million
Number Employees: 20-49
Type of Packaging: Consumer
Brands:
 Holsum Bread
 Wonder Bread

3057 Cottonwood Canyon Vineyard
3940 Dominion Rd
Santa Maria, CA 93454-9678
805-937-8463
Fax: 805-937-8418 info@cottonwoodcanyon.com
www.cottonwoodcanyon.com
Wine
Owner/Winemaker: Norman Beko
xlntpno@earthlink.net
VP: Stephen Beko
Estimated Sales: $1-2.5 Million
Number Employees: 10-19
Number of Products: 24
Brands:
 Cottonwood Canyon

3058 Couch's Country Style Sausages
4750 Osborn Rd
Cleveland, OH 44128-3138
216-823-2332
Fax: 216-663-3311
Sausage including pork, beef and turkey
President: Ludie Couch
Manager: Stanley Redd

Estimated Sales: $500,000-$1 Million
Number Employees: 1 to 4
Square Footage: 10500
Type of Packaging: Consumer, Bulk

3059 Cougar Mountain Baking Co
4224 24th Ave W
Seattle, WA 98199-1216
206-467-5044
Fax: 206-467-0993 877-328-2622
comments@cougar-mountain.com
www.cookieman.com
Producers of bakery products.
Owner: David Saulnier
david@cougar-mountain.com
Customer Service: Dana Pantley
Estimated Sales: $300,000-500,000
Number Employees: 20-49
Brands:
 Cougar Mountain

3060 Coulter Giufre & Co Inc
8579 Lakeport Rd
Chittenango, NY 13037-9577
315-687-6510
Fax: 315-687-6637
Processor and exporter of produce including onions and turf grass
Owner: Chris Coulter
Estimated Sales: $3-5 Million
Number Employees: 5-9
Brands:
 Bulls Eye

3061 Counter Culture Coffee
812 Mallard Ave
Durham, NC 27701
919-361-5282
888-238-5282
counterculturecoffee.com
Coffee
Coffee Buyer: Chelsea Thoumsin
Year Founded: 1995

3062 Countertop Productions
Alexandria, VA 22304
www.sparkbites.net
Vegan protein bars
Founder: Warren Brown
Number of Products: 5
Brands:
 Spark Bites

3063 Country Archer Jerky Co.
379 E Industrial Rd
San Bernardino, CA 92408
909-370-0155
info@countryarcher.com
www.countryarcher.com
Beef jerky and protein bars
Co-Founder: Eugene Kang
Co-Founder: Susan Kang
Marketing Director: Mathew Thalakotur
VP, Sales: Tim Bateman
COO/CFO: Jeremy White
Year Founded: 1977
Number of Brands: 1
Number of Products: 15
Type of Packaging: Consumer
Brands:
 COUNTRY ARCHER BEEF JERKY

3064 Country Bob's Inc
24000 N US Highway 51
Centralia, IL 62801-8992
618-533-2375
Fax: 618-533-7828 800-373-2140
www.countrybobs.com
Producers of sauces and seasonings.
President: Nate Edison
nate@countrybobs.com
Estimated Sales: $2.5-5 Million
Number Employees: 10-19

3065 Country Butcher Shop
286 Mcallister Church Rd
Carlisle, PA 17015-9504
717-249-4691
Fax: 573-769-4652 800-272-9223
www.countrybutchershopinc.com
Processor and distributor of lamb, beef and pork.
Owner: Mary Finkenbinder
finkenbinder@socket.net

Food Manufacturers / A-Z

Estimated Sales: $10-20 Million
Number Employees: 5-9
Type of Packaging: Private Label

3066 Country Choice Organic
9531 W 78th St # 230
Eden Prairie, MN 55344-8000
952-829-8824
Fax: 952-833-2090
jocelyneg@countrychoiceorganic.com
www.countrychoiceorganic.com
Organic hot cereals, cookies and cocoas.
Chief Cookie Officer: John DePaolis
Director of R&D: Sharon Herzog
Sales Director: Jocelyne Gregg
Contact: Dawn Braam
dawnb@countrychoiceorganic.com
Number of Brands: 1
Number of Products: 35
Type of Packaging: Consumer
Brands:
　Country Choice

3067 Country Club Bakery
1211 Country Club Rd
Fairmont, WV 26554-2318
304-363-5690
Fax: 304-363-6099 www.hollyeats.com
Bread, sandwich rolls, hoagie buns and pepperoni rolls
Owner: Chris Pallotta
Estimated Sales: $5-10 Million
Number Employees: 5-9
Type of Packaging: Consumer, Food Service

3068 Country Clubs Famous Desserts
83 Bustleton Pike
Feasterville Trevose, PA 19053-6465
215-322-0700
Fax: 215-322-1534 800-843-2253
Desserts
Owner: Brian Rothaus
Marketing Executive: Steve Merchant
VP Sales: Bruce Davidsen
Estimated Sales: $20-50 Million
Number Employees: 50-99

3069 Country Cupboard
101 Hafer Rd
Lewisburg, PA 17837-7408
570-523-3211
Fax: 570-524-9299 info@countrycupboardinc.com
www.mattyssporthouse.com
Dehydrated soups, pastas, rices, sauces, relish, jams, beans, sugar-free chocolates, cornbread, honey and salsa, among other products.
Owner: Nicole Edinger
nicicci@dejazzd.com
CEO: Chris Baylor
General Manager: Steve Kulhavy
Events Coordinator: Melissa Swartz
Estimated Sales: $5-10 Million
Number Employees: 250-499

3070 Country Delite Farms LLC
1401 Church St
Nashville, TN 37203-3428
615-320-1440
Fax: 615-329-3017 800-232-4791
www.deanfoods.com
Dairy products
General Manager: Mark Ezell
Marketing Director: Jim Greaving
Public Relations: Royce McClintock
Operations Manager: Charles Hilton
Plant Manager: Eric Steer
Estimated Sales: $25-49.9 Million
Number Employees: 100-249
Brands:
　Country Delight

3071 Country Estate Pecans
1020 West Front Street
Goldwaite, TX 76844
325-648-2200
800-473-2267
retail@pecans.com www.pecans.com
Fresh shelled pecans, inshell pecans, gourmet pecans, and many other unique items
President: Liz Alexander
General Manager: DeWayne McCasland
Year Founded: 1972
Estimated Sales: $20-50 Million

Number Employees: 4
Parent Co: Fermers Investment
Type of Packaging: Private Label

3072 Country Foods
46835 US Highway 93
Polson, MT 59860-7586
406-883-4384
Fax: 406-883-3275 info@countrypasta.com
Manufacturers of pasta.
President: Heather Knutson
knutsonheather@hotmail.com
Vice President: Linda Knutson
Marketing Director: Dan Johnson
Operations Manager: Gary Ivory
Estimated Sales: $2.5-5 Million
Number Employees: 20-49
Type of Packaging: Private Label
Brands:
　Country Pasta

3073 Country Fresh
2555 Buchanan Ave SW
Grand Rapids, MI 49548
616-243-0173
www.enjoycountryfresh.com
Milk, flavored milk, teas & juices, cream, cottage cheese, sour cream & dips, ice cream & frozen novelties.
CEO, Dean Foods Company: Ralph Scozzafava
Year Founded: 1946
Parent Co: Dean Foods Company
Type of Packaging: Consumer, Private Label

3074 (HQ)Country Fresh Farms
432 W 3440 S
Salt Lake City, UT 84115
801-263-6667
Fax: 801-269-9666 800-878-0099
www.bluechipgroup.net
Producers of whey drinks, dairy products and dry mixes.
President: George Moo
CFO: Mike Leonard
Contact: Samuel Howard
howards@domo.com
Estimated Sales: $5 Million
Number Employees: 23
Square Footage: 42400
Type of Packaging: Consumer, Food Service, Private Label, Bulk
Other Locations:
　Country Fresh Farms
　Livonia MI
　Country Fresh Farms
　Grand Rapids MI
Brands:
　Country Fresh Farms
　Swiss Whey D'Lite

3075 Country Fresh Food & Confections, Inc.
405 Main Street
Po Box 604
Oliver Springs, TN 37840
865-435-2655
Fax: 865-435-1930 800-545-8782
info@countryfreshfood.com
www.countryfreshfood.com
Country Fresh Fudge, regular & sugar-free, Pamela Ann Classic Confections, Jim Bean Fudge, Kahula Fudge, Papa Joe's Downhome Gourmet.
President: Edward Stockton
Estimated Sales: $1-2.5 Million
Number Employees: 20-49
Number of Brands: 6
Number of Products: 150
Square Footage: 32000
Type of Packaging: Consumer, Food Service, Private Label, Bulk
Brands:
　Country Fresh
　Country Fresh Fudge
　Papa Joe's Downhome

3076 Country Fresh Inc
3200 Research Forest Dr
Spring, TX 77381
281-453-3300
Fax: 281-453-3304
customerservice@countryfreshinc.com
www.countryfreshinc.com
Fresh-cut fruit, apple slices, vegetable and snacks.
Owner: Bryan Herr

Number Employees: 50
Type of Packaging: Consumer, Private Label

3077 Country Fresh Mushroom Co
289 Chambers Rd
PO Box 490
Toughkenamon, PA 19374
610-268-3033
Fax: 610-268-0479 bbesix@cfmushroom.com
www.cfmushroom.com
Processor of mushrooms including exotic, fresh, processed, whole and sliced.
Chairman/CEO: Edward Leo
President/COO: Laura Matar
SVP, Sales & Marketing: Bob Besix
Director, Warehouse Operations: Dan Tobin
Year Founded: 1925
Estimated Sales: $20-50 Million
Number Employees: 100-249
Number of Brands: 1
Square Footage: 60000
Type of Packaging: Consumer, Food Service, Private Label, Bulk
Brands:
　Country Fresh

3078 Country Home Bakers
720 Metropolitan Pkwy SW
Atlanta, GA 30310
404-215-5540
Fax: 404-527-6690 800-241-6445
Frozen dough including danish, doughnut, roll and cookie; Frozen bread dough including jalapeno/cheese, salsa, spinach/mushroom/cheese, vegetable, focaccia, etc.; also, frozen baked and unbaked pies, frozen cakes, toppings, ice cream and candy
President: Gary Schreiber
Purchasing Executive: Robert Brooks
Regional Sales Manager: Jim Rasmussen
General Manager: Roy Lowery
Plant Manager: Mike Harvison
Year Founded: 2004
Estimated Sales: $20-50 Million
Number Employees: 100-249
Square Footage: 80000
Parent Co: J&J Snack Foods
Type of Packaging: Consumer, Food Service, Private Label, Bulk
Other Locations:
　Country Home Bakers
　Highland Park MI
Brands:
　Chop Block Breads
　Country Home Bakers
　Jessie Lord, Inc.
　Sanders
　Warme Bakker

3079 Country Home Creations Inc
5132 Richfield Rd
Flint, MI 48506-2121
810-244-7348
Fax: 810-244-5348 800-457-3477
chcdips@countryhomecreations.com
Processor and exporter of mixes including cheesecake, cookie, dip and soup.
Owner: Shirley Kautman Jones
chcdips@countryhomecreations.com
Estimated Sales: $-5 Million
Number Employees: 20-49
Square Footage: 40000
Type of Packaging: Consumer, Private Label
Brands:
　Camp Mixes
　Classic Country
　Country Home Creations
　Ginger Kids
　My Mom's Mixes
　Perfect Party Mixes

3080 Country Life
101 Corporate Dr
Hauppauge, NY 11788
631-231-1031
Fax: 631-231-2331 800-645-5768
www.country-life.com
Supplements and health beverages
CEO: Halbert Drexler
Contact: Ramsook Alexis
aramsook-purpura@countrylifevitamins.com
Estimated Sales: $10-20 Million
Number Employees: 100-249
Brands:
　Biochem

Food Manufacturers / A-Z

Country Life
Iron-Tek
Long Life Beverages
Natural Personal Care

3081 Country Maid Inc
1919 S Kinnickinnic Ave
Milwaukee, WI 53204-4000
414-383-3970
Fax: 414-383-9809 800-628-4354
www.countrymaid.com
Refrigerated salads, entrees and desserts
President: Ashley Akridge
ashley@countrymaid.com
CFO: Jordan Plotkin
Office Manager: Pat Plotkin
Estimated Sales: $6.7 Million
Number Employees: 50-99
Square Footage: 160000
Type of Packaging: Consumer, Food Service, Private Label
Brands:
  Country Maid

3082 Country Oven Bakery
2840 Pioneer Dr
Bowling Green, KY 42101-4053
270-782-3203
Fax: 270-782-7170 www.giftagift.com
Pizza dough and pizza shells.
President: Roger Bullion
Cio/Cto: Sam Grado
sam.grado@kroger.com
COO: Jim Bennett
Director Manufacturing: John Madison
Director Engineering: Rick Noall
Plant Manager: Roger Bullion
Purchasing Manager: Wayne Miller
Estimated Sales: $25-49.9 Million
Number Employees: 250-499
Parent Co: Kroger Company

3083 (HQ)Country Pure Foods Inc
222 S Main St
Suite 401
Akron, OH 44308
330-753-2293
Fax: 330-848-4287 877-995-8423
info@juice4u.com www.juice4u.com
Fruit drinks, bottled spring water and juices including apple, orange, grape and pineapple.
Chief Executive Officer: Kenny Sadai
VP, Marketing: Joe Koch
VP, Retail Sales: Jon Hanley
SVP, Operations: Paul Sukalich
Estimated Sales: $44.7 Million
Number Employees: 250-499
Square Footage: 100000
Type of Packaging: Consumer, Food Service, Private Label
Other Locations:
  Ellington CT
  Deland FL
Brands:
  Ardmore Farms®
  Natural Country®
  Glacier Valley®

3084 Country Pure Foods Inc
58 West Rd
Ellington, CT 06029
877-995-8423
info@juice4u.com www.juice4u.com
Fruit drinks, bottled spring water and juices including apple, orange, grape and pineapple.
Number Employees: 100-249
Square Footage: 51266
Type of Packaging: Consumer, Food Service, Private Label
Brands:
  Glacier Valley
  Natural Country
  Sunflo
  Sunny Lea

3085 Country Pure Foods Inc
681 W Waterloo Rd
Akron, OH 44314
877-995-8423
info@juice4u.com www.juice4u.com
Fruit drinks, bottled spring water and juices including apple, orange, grape and pineapple.
Type of Packaging: Consumer, Private Label

3086 Country Pure Foods Inc
1915 N Woodland Blvd
Deland, FL 32724
877-995-8423
info@juice4u.com www.juice4u.com
Fruit drinks, bottled spring water and juices including apple, orange, grape and pineapple.
Type of Packaging: Consumer, Private Label

3087 Country Pure Foods Inc
402 Yale St
Houston, TX 77007
877-995-8423
info@juice4u.com www.juice4u.com
Fruit drinks, bottled spring water and juices including apple, orange, grape and pineapple.
Type of Packaging: Consumer, Private Label

3088 Country Smoked Meats
510 Napolean Road
Bowling Green, OH 43402-0171
419-353-0783
Fax: 419-352-7330 800-321-4766
Processor and exporter of chunked, sliced and deli style Canadian bacon, smoked sausage, pork loins, hocks, turkey parts and ham, pepperoni, bratwurst, kielbasa, chorizos, egg and muffin sandwiches, fresh link sausage and freshboneless pork loins and ten
National Sales Manager: Bruce Schroeder
Estimated Sales: $2.5-5 Million
Number Employees: 20-49
Square Footage: 84000
Type of Packaging: Consumer, Food Service, Private Label, Bulk

3089 Country Village Meats Inc
401 N Pennsylvania St
Sublette, IL 61367-9400
815-849-5532
800-700-4545
www.countryvillagemeats.com
Beef, pork, lamb, veal, sausage, hot dogs, etc.; slaughtering services available
Co-Owner: Edward Morrissey
Estimated Sales: $1-2.5 Million
Number Employees: 1-4
Type of Packaging: Consumer, Bulk

3090 County Gourmet Foods, LLC
751 Chestnut Road
Sewickley, PA 15143-1143
412-741-8902
Fax: 412-741-9176
Gourmet foods
Quality Control: Thomas MacMurray, Ph.D.

3091 Coupla Guys Foods
401 N Racine Ave
Chicago, IL 60642
312-829-2332
Fax: 312-829-8866
Pasta sauces including: sesame; arrabiata; puttanesca; tapenade; buoy base; marinara; and creme de la crimini sauce.
General Manager: Joe Rowley
Sales Manager: Ute Rowley
Contact: Joe Coupla
joe@bbfdirect.com
Type of Packaging: Food Service

3092 Coutts Specialty Foods Inc
1190 Liberty Square Rd
Boxborough, MA 01719-1115
978-263-2952
Fax: 978-263-2953 800-919-2952
csf@couttsspecialtyfoods.com
www.couttsspecialtyfoods.com
Mother's Prize-sweet red pepper, hot sweet red pepper, corn, picclilli relishes, apple butter, and applesauce (with and with no sugar). No preservatives or fillers are added to any of our products. Mother's Pure Preserves-jamsjellies, and marmalades
Owner: Alison Chateauneuf
acouttsspecialty@aol.com
Estimated Sales: $3-5 Million
Number Employees: 1-4
Number of Brands: 2
Number of Products: 38
Type of Packaging: Consumer, Food Service
Brands:
  Mother's Prize
  Mother's Pure Preserves

3093 Couture Farms
30650 Quebec Ave
Kettleman City, CA 93239
559-386-9865
Fax: 559-386-4365
Processor and importer of asparagus, pistachios and mixed melons
Co-Partner: Steve Couture
Co-Partner: Christina Couture
stcou@aol.com
Partner: Chris Couture
stcou@aol.com
Estimated Sales: $2.2 Million
Number Employees: 20-49
Square Footage: 8640
Type of Packaging: Consumer, Food Service, Private Label, Bulk

3094 Couture's Maple Shop/B & B
560 VT Route 100
Westfield, VT 05874-9791
802-744-2733
Fax: 802-744-6275 800-845-2733
www.maplesyrupvermont.com
Maple syrup and candy
Co-Owner: Jacques Couture
Co-Owner: Pauline Couture
jcouture@maplesyrupvt.net
Estimated Sales: Less Than $500,000
Number Employees: 1-4

3095 Couturier Na Inc
2986 US Route 9
Hudson, NY 12534-4407
518-851-2570
Fax: 518-851-2574
Cheese.
President: Alain Foster
afoster@couturierna.com
Marketing: Dominique Penicaud
Number Employees: 5-9

3096 Covered Bridge Potato Chip Company
35 Alwright Ct
Waterville, NB E7P 0A5
Canada
506-375-2447
Fax: 506-375-2448 info@coveredbridgechips.com
www.coveredbridgechips.com
Old fashioned kettle style potato chips
Marketing Manager: Krysten Scott
Production: Mike McCartney
Estimated Sales: $2 Million
Number Employees: 14

3097 Cowart Seafood Corp
755 Lake Landing Dr
Lottsburg, VA 22511-2503
804-529-6101
Fax: 804-529-7374 www.gmail.com
Seafood including fresh, frozen, and breaded oysters, frozen softshell crabs, and canned herring roe
President: S Cowart
cowartsfd@gmail.com
VP: Lake Cowart Jr
Estimated Sales: $10-20 Million
Number Employees: 50-99
Square Footage: 30000
Type of Packaging: Food Service, Private Label
Brands:
  Chesapeake Pride
  Mannings
  Sea Mist

3098 Cowboy Caviar
169 Fairlawn Dr
Berkeley, CA 94708
510-841-0635
Fax: 510-594-8058 877-509-1796
Spreads and chunky marinara sauces
President: Gary Forbes
Estimated Sales: $1-2,500,000
Number Employees: 1-4
Type of Packaging: Private Label

3099 Cowboy Food & Drink
8586 Washington St
Chagrin Falls, OH 44023-5369
440-708-1011
Fax: 406-522-9337 800-759-5489
hucklebuddy@hotmail.com
www.cowboyfoodanddrink.com

Natural barley without hulls; also, barbecue and bean sauces, bean soups, pancake, bread and baking mixes, flours, cereals and whole grains canning fruits and vegies,prepares flour,grain, and mill products.
Co-Owner/President: Jean Clem
Co-Owner: Bud Clem
Estimated Sales: Less Than $500,000
Number Employees: 10-19
Number of Products: 30
Square Footage: 11200
Type of Packaging: Consumer, Food Service, Bulk
Brands:
   Cowboy Foods

3100 **Cowgirl Chocolates**
428 W 3rd St # 3
#3 corner of 3rd and Lilly
Moscow, ID 83843-2284
208-882-4098
Fax: 208-882-0265 888-882-4098
cowgirl@cowgirlchocolates.com
www.cowgirlchocolates.com
Manufacturers of chocolate candies.
Manager: Marilyn Coates
cowgirl@cowgirlchocolates.com
Estimated Sales: Less Than $500,000
Number Employees: 1-4
Brands:
   Cowgirl Chocolates

3101 **Cowgirl Creamery**
80 Fourth St
Point Reyes Station, CA 94956
415-663-9335
Fax: 415-663-5418 www.cowgirlcreamery.com
Artisan organic cheese
Contact: Becky Birkmann
mailorder@cowgirlcreamery.com

3102 **Cowie Wine Cellars & Vineyards**
101 N Carbon City Rd
Paris, AR 72855-4630
479-963-3990
Fax: 479-963-3990 cowie@cswnet.com
www.cowiewinecellars.com
Wines
President: Robert Cowie
cowie@cswnet.com
Sales Room Manager: Katie Cowie
Estimated Sales: Less than $50,000
Number Employees: 1-4
Brands:
   Cowie

3103 **Cozy Harbor Seafood Inc**
75 Saint John St
Portland, ME 04102-3013
207-879-2665
Fax: 207-879-2666 800-225-2586
jnorton@cozyharbor.com www.cozyharbor.com
Buys, processes and distributes premium quality seafood products
Founder and President: John Norton
CEO: John S Norton
jnorton@cozyharbor.com
CFO: Mark Lannon
Co-founder and Technical Manager: Joe Donovan
Domestic and Intl Shrimp Lobster Sales: Tom Keegan
Operations VP: Joseph Donovan Norton
Plant/Production Manager: Roland Jacques
Estimated Sales: $.5-1 million
Number Employees: 100-249
Type of Packaging: Consumer, Food Service, Bulk

3104 **Crab Quarters**
2909 Eastern Ave
Baltimore, MD 21224-3812
410-686-2222
Fax: 410-686-0343
Fresh crab
Owner: Jim Myrick
Estimated Sales: $1-3 Million
Number Employees: 20-49

3105 **Craby's Fish Market**
303 S Black Horse Pike
Blackwood, NJ 08012-2893
856-227-9743
Seafood
Manager: Stephen Palo
Estimated Sales: Less than $500,000
Number Employees: 1-4

3106 **Cracked Candy LLC**
549 10th St
Suite 1
Brooklyn, NY 11215-4401
646-543-1405
hello@crackedcandy.com
www.crackedcandy.com
Sugar-free candy, mints and chips.
Founder: Flora Pringle
Type of Packaging: Private Label

3107 **Craft Brew Alliance**
929 N Russell St
Portland, OR 97227
503-331-7270
contact@craftbrew.com
craftbrew.com
Beer
CEO: Andy Thomas
Number of Brands: 8
Type of Packaging: Private Label
Brands:
   Hefeweizer
   Okio
   Widmer Brothers

3108 **Craft Distillers**
108 W Clay St
Ukiah, CA 95482-5420
707-468-7899
Fax: 707-462-8103 800-782-8145
Distiller and exporter of brandy and specialty spirits
President: Ansley J Coale Jr
VP,CFO: Denise Niderost
Estimated Sales: $1-2,500,000
Number Employees: 5-9
Square Footage: 40000
Type of Packaging: Consumer, Private Label

3109 **Crafty Counter**
PO Box 160361
Austin, TX 78716
512-643-2412
hello@craftycounter.com
www.craftycounter.com
All natural chicken nuggets
Founder: Hema Reddy
CFO: Alejandro Navarro
Marketing: Usha Rao
Operations: Jennifer Martinez
Brands:
   Wundernuggets

3110 **Crain Ranch**
10660 Bryne Ave
Los Molinos, CA 96055-9560
530-527-1077
Fax: 530-529-4143 billcrain@crainranch.com
www.crainranch.com
Processor, grower and exporter of walnuts in the shell.
Owner: Charles R Crain
charles@crainranch.com
Business Office: Kerry Crain
Production: Hal Crain
Estimated Sales: $300,000-500,000
Number Employees: 10-19
Square Footage: 320000
Type of Packaging: Consumer, Private Label, Bulk
Brands:
   Crain Ranch

3111 **Crain Walnut Shelling, Inc.**
10695 Decker Ave
Los Molinos, CA 96055-9628
530-529-1585
Fax: 530-529-1458 crainwalnut@crainwalnut.com
www.crainwalnut.com
Shelled walnuts supplying industrial ingredient needs.
President: Grant Skognes
gskognes@ridefox.com
Owner: Harold Crain
Vice President of Sales & Logistics: Vicki Lapera
Quality Assurance: Devan Wilson
Sales Administrator: Kimberly Gonsalves
Number Employees: 100-249
Type of Packaging: Bulk

3112 **Cramer's Bakery**
14 East Afton Ave.
Yardley, PA 19067
215-493-2760
www.cramerbakery.com
Cakes, pastries, pies, breads and rolls
Founder: John E. Cramer, Jr.

3113 **Cranberry Isles Fisherman's**
1 Water St
Islesford, ME 4646
207-244-5438
Fax: 207-244-9479
Manager: Mark Neighman
Estimated Sales: $.5-1 million
Number Employees: 1-4

3114 **Cranberry Sweets Co**
1005 Newmark Ave
Coos Bay, OR 97420-3102
541-888-9824
Fax: 541-888-2824 800-527-5748
www.cranberrysweets.com
Manufacturers of cranberries, jellies and candies.
Owner: Clayton Shaw
cranberrysweets@frontier.com
Estimated Sales: $1-2.5 Million
Number Employees: 20-49
Brands:
   Cranberry Sweets
   Oregon Berries
   Sweet Basics

3115 **Crane & Crane Inc**
100 Crane Orchard Rd
PO Box 277
Brewster, WA 98812
509-689-3447
Fax: 509-689-2214
Grower and exporter of apples
President: Meg Spellman
meg@craneandcrane.com
Secretary/Treasurer: Margaret Crane
Vice President: Robert Reimmer
Estimated Sales: $930,000
Number Employees: 100-249
Square Footage: 196000
Type of Packaging: Consumer, Food Service, Private Label, Bulk
Brands:
   Crane's Aqua Line
   Crane's Blue Line
   Crane's Gray Line
   Crane's Maroon Line
   Crane's Red Line

3116 **Crane's Pie Pantry Restaurant**
6054 124th Ave
Fennville, MI 49408-9440
269-561-2297
Fax: 269-561-5545 contact@cranespiepantry.com
www.cranespiepantry.com
Pies and wine
Owner: Beckey Crane-Hagger
contact@cranespiepantry.com
Owner: Lue Crane
Winemaker: Rob Crane
Estimated Sales: Less Than $500,000
Number Employees: 10-19

3117 **Crater Meat Co Inc**
2811 Biddle Rd
Medford, OR 97504-4114
541-772-6966
Meat products
Owner: James K Cearley
Estimated Sales: Less Than $500,000
Number Employees: 1-4
Type of Packaging: Consumer
Brands:
   Crater's Meats

3118 **Crave Natural Foods**
2043 Imperial Street
Los Angeles, CA 90021
213-627-8887
877-425-2599
www.cravefoods.com
Nondairy whipped cream, dressings, ice cream and cheese sauce
Owner: Sally A Conway
Contact: Shaheda Sayed
shaheda@cravefoods.com
Number Employees: 1-4
Square Footage: 1600
Type of Packaging: Consumer

Food Manufacturers / A-Z

3119 Craven Crab Company
PO Box 3321
New Bern, NC 28564-3321
252-637-3562
Fax: 252-637-3562
Crab
President: Gaston Fulcher
Brands:
Craven Crab

3120 Craveright
5902 Mount Eagle Dr
Alexandria, VA 22303-2513
703-888-3796
info@craveright.com
www.craveright.com
Gluten free treats.
Owner: Darioush Danaei
ddanaei@craveright.com
Estimated Sales: Less Than $500,000
Number Employees: 1-4

3121 Crawford Sausage Co Inc
2310 S Pulaski Rd
Chicago, IL 60623
773-277-3095
judy@daisybrandsausage.net
www.daisybrandsausage.net
Bratwursts, frankfurters, polish sausage, other linked sausage, sliced lunchmeats, fresh sausages, smoked meats and gift boxes.
Year Founded: 1925
Estimated Sales: $5-10 Million
Number Employees: 20-49
Type of Packaging: Consumer, Food Service, Bulk
Brands:
Daisy Brand Meat Products

3122 Crazy Go Nuts
Fower, CA 93291
www.crazygonutswalnuts.com
Walnut snacks
Founder: Courtney Carini

3123 Crazy Jerrys Inc Kahuna-Sauces
721 Bascomb Commercial Pkwy
Woodstock, GA 30189-2466
770-993-0651
Fax: 770-993-8201 800-347-2823
Sauces, can mixed nuts, garlic mushrooms, maters in spicy vermouth, stuffed olives, can beef stew, soup mix and gumbo mix
President: Jerry Gualtieri
jgualt9817@aol.com
Estimated Sales: $1 Million
Number Employees: 1-4
Type of Packaging: Private Label
Brands:
Crazy Jerry's

3124 Crazy Mary's
300 E. 34th Street
36th Floor
New York, NY 10016
212-889-8124
CrazyMary@CrazyMary.com
www.crazymary.com

3125 Crazy Richard's
P.O. Box 715
Dublin, OH 43017
614-889-4824
info@crazyrichards.com
www.crazyrichards.com
Natural peanut butter, almond butter, cashew butter, peanut powder, and protein snack balls
President & Owner: Kimmi Wernli

3126 Crea Fill Fibers Corp
10200 Worton Rd
Chestertown, MD 21620-3545
410-810-0779
Fax: 410-810-0793 800-832-4462
fiber@creafill.com www.creafill.com
Processor and exporter of powdered cellulose and pure vegetable fibers
President: Paolo Fezzi
pfezzi@creafill.com
Sales Associate: Sara Emgland
Estimated Sales: $5.5 Million
Number Employees: 20-49
Type of Packaging: Bulk

Brands:
Qc Fibers
Sc Fibers

3127 Creagri Inc
25565 Whitesell St
Hayward, CA 94545-3614
510-732-6478
Fax: 510-732-6493 info@creagri.com
www.creagri.com
Extra virgin olive oil
Founder/Chairman: Roberto Crea
rcrea@creagri.com
VP: Paolo Pontoniere
Estimated Sales: $1 Million
Number Employees: 5-9
Type of Packaging: Consumer, Food Service, Bulk
Brands:
Integrale
Supremo

3128 Cream Crock Distributors
50 Worcester Rd
Sterling, MA 01564-1466
978-422-3500
Fax: 978-422-6699 800-423-2736
Ice cream
President: Gary Jonaitis
Estimated Sales: $2.5-5 Million
Number Employees: 5-9

3129 Cream Hill Estates
9633 rue Clement
LaSalle, QC H8R 4B4
Canada
514-363-2066
Fax: 514-363-1614 866-727-3628
info@creamhillestates.com
Producer and distributor of guaranteed pure oats

3130 Cream Of The West
408 Wheatland Ave S
Harlowton, MT 59036-5199
406-632-4804
800-477-2383
cotw@mtintouch.net www.creamofthewest.com
Company products line includes cereals, pancake mixes, jams and jellies, honey, coffee and gift baskets.
Manager: Freida Robertson
Manager: Lian Kent
cotw@itstriangle.com
Production Manager: Bobby Lewis
Estimated Sales: $1-2.5 Million
Number Employees: 5-9
Square Footage: 24000
Type of Packaging: Consumer, Food Service, Bulk
Brands:
Cream of the West

3131 Creamland Dairies Inc
10 Indian School Rd NW
Albuquerque, NM 87105
505-247-0721
Fax: 505-246-9696
Dairy products including ice cream, milk, cultured, cottage cheese, sour cream and dips.
CEO: Howard Miller
CEO: Howard Miller
Public Relations: Connie Holdren
Number Employees: 20-49
Parent Co: Dean Foods Company
Type of Packaging: Consumer
Brands:
Creamland
Dean's

3132 Creation Nation
Calabasas, CA 91301
424-234-5800
hi@foodcreationnation.com
proteinbarmix.com
Protein balls, bars and bites
Founder & CEO: Karen Nation
Year Founded: 2014
Number of Brands: 1
Number of Products: 5
Type of Packaging: Consumer
Brands:
CREATION NATION

3133 Creative Cotton
945 Bermuda Dunes Pl
Northbrook, IL 60062-3125
847-291-4128
alicia@creativeconfections.net
www.creativeconfections.net
Gourmet candy including chocolate and English toffee
President: Alicia Russell
Vice President: Bert Gideon
Estimated Sales: $1-3 Million
Number Employees: 5-9
Type of Packaging: Consumer
Brands:
Creative Confections

3134 Creative Flavors & Specialties LLP
991 E Linden Ave
Linden, NJ 07036
908-862-4678
Fax: 908-862-7458
Flavors for coffee, candy, fruit drinks, bagels, ice cream, ice tea, coffee syrups, snack seasonings, spices and much more. We also customize any flavors, spray drieds and blending
President: Esther Baita
CEO: Mike DiPierro
VP: Danielle Lau
Quality Control: Esther Baita
Production: Fredy Lau
Estimated Sales: $100,000
Number Employees: 5
Number of Products: 5000
Square Footage: 5000
Type of Packaging: Bulk

3135 Creative Flavors Inc
16686 Hilltop Park Pl
Chagrin Falls, OH 44023-4500
440-543-9881
Fax: 440-543-8707 800-848-9043
www.creativeflavorsinc.com
Flavors and ingredients for the dairy industry including cherries, flavors and core powders for novelty bars and sour cream dip bases
President: Michael Ramsey
Public Relations: Cindy Ramsey
Estimated Sales: $2.5-5 Million
Number Employees: 5-9

3136 Creative Food Ingredients
1 Lincoln Ave
Perry, NY 14530
585-237-2213
Fax: 585-237-2735 www.creativefoods.com
Cookies, creme filled cookies, crumble toppings and crushed cookies
President & CEO: Michael O'Flaherty
moflaherty@creativefoods.com
CFO: Jeffrey Arcand
Executive Director, Quality Research: David Humberstone
Executive Director, Operations: Michael Humberstone
Executive Director, Supply Chain: Rodney Smith
Estimated Sales: $100+ Million
Number Employees: 100-249
Brands:
Creative Foods

3137 Creative Foodworks Inc
1011 S Acme Rd
San Antonio, TX 78237-3218
210-212-4761
Fax: 210-212-4919
Private label condiments
President: Dee Dee Garcia
dgarcia@creativefoodworks.com
Quality Control: Michael Billings
Operations Manager: Emilio Herrera
Plant Manager: Norman Diggec
Purchasing Manager: Chris Boynton
Estimated Sales: $5-10 Million
Number Employees: 5-9
Type of Packaging: Consumer, Food Service, Private Label, Bulk

3138 Creative Seasonings
34 Audubon Road
Wakefield, MA 01880-1203
617-246-1461
Fax: 617-246-5381 www.conagrafoods.com
Seasonings

President/CEO: Greg Heckman
CEO: Gary Rodkin

3139 Creative Snacks Co LLC
241 Burgess Rd
Suite B
Greensboro, NC 27409-9333
336-668-4151
Manufacturer of snack foods, ranging from coconut chips to chocolate pretzels and almonds.
Founder and CEO: Marius Andersen
VP of Sales: Scott Feldman
Director of Operations: Zachary Breeden
zacharybreeden@creativesnacks.com
Number Employees: 20-49
Brands:
    CREATIVE SNACKS CO.

3140 Creative Spices
33436 Western Avenue
Union City, CA 94587-3202
510-471-4956
Fax: 510-471-9174
Bread and bakery products
President: Carmella Hagman
Treasurer: Virginia Holmes
VP: Donna Hagman
Contact: Donna Hageman
donna@iconnex.com
Estimated Sales: $10-24.9,000,000
Number Employees: 20-49
Brands:
    Creative Spices

3141 Creemore Springs Brewery
139 Mill St
Creemore, ON L0M 1G0
Canada
705-466-2240
Fax: 705-466-3306 800-267-2240
thefolks@creemoresprings.com
www.creemoresprings.com
Lager beer
President/CEO: Jason Moore
Estimated Sales: $6.9 Million
Number Employees: 90
Type of Packaging: Consumer, Food Service
Brands:
    Creemore Springs Premium Lager
    Creemore Springs Urbock

3142 Creighton Brothers
4217 W Old Road 30
Warsaw, IN 46580-6842
574-267-3101
Fax: 574-267-6446 www.creightonbrothersllc.com
Established in 1925. Processor of fresh, frozen, and hard cooked eggs.
President: Ron Truex
ron@creightonbrothersllc.com
Co-Founder: Russell Creighton
Co-Founder: Hobart Creighton
Estimated Sales: $20,800,000
Number Employees: 100-249
Type of Packaging: Consumer, Food Service, Private Label, Bulk
Brands:
    Good News Eggs
    Grandpa's Choice

3143 Creme Curls
5292 Lawndale Ave
PO Box 276
Hudsonville, MI 49426-1213
616-669-2468
Fax: 616-669-2468 800-466-1219
www.cremecurls.com
Creme horns, eclairs and cream puffs, strudel and turnovers, and pie dough
President: Gary Bierling
gary@cremecurls.com
CFO: Lee Deboer
Vice President: Paul Bierling
VP Sales: Michael Burkett
Estimated Sales: $11.7 Million
Number Employees: 100-249
Square Footage: 66000
Type of Packaging: Consumer, Food Service, Private Label, Bulk
Brands:
    Creme Curls

3144 Creme D'Lite
2366 Hill N Dale Dr
Irving, TX 75038-5619
972-255-7255
A frozen nondairy cream beverage
President: Don Allen
Estimated Sales: $99,000
Number Employees: 2
Square Footage: 10000
Type of Packaging: Consumer, Food Service, Private Label, Bulk
Brands:
    Creme D'Lite
    Tropic D'Lite

3145 Creme Unlimited
600 Holiday Plaza Dr # 520
Matteson, IL 60443-2238
708-748-1336
Fax: 708-748-4985 800-227-3637
Non-dairy whipped toppings and icings
Manager: John Evans
Manager: Cher Vivich
cvicich@cremesunlimited.com
Estimated Sales: $10-20 000,000
Number Employees: 5-9
Brands:
    Cremes

3146 Creminelli Fine Meats
310 N Wright Brothers Dr
Salt Lake City, UT 84116-2881
801-428-1820
Fax: 202-478-0434 www.creminelli.com
Organic/natural, cured meats i.e. prociutto/bacon, other meat/game/pate.
Manager: Samantha Smith
Number Employees: 20-49

3147 Creole Delicacies Gourmet Shop
533 Saint Ann St
New Orleans, LA 70116-3387
504-525-9508
Fax: 504-288-0042 lisette@cookincajun.com
Pralines
President: Lisette Sutton
lisette@cookincajun.com
Estimated Sales: Less Than $500,000
Number Employees: 5-9
Type of Packaging: Consumer
Brands:
    Cookin' Cajun
    Creole Delicacies

3148 Creole Fermentation Indu
7331 Ben Frederick Rd
Abbeville, LA 70510
337-898-9377
Fax: 337-898-9376
Vinegar including white distilled; manufacturer of vinegar production equipment
President: Albert Steen
General Manager: Bill Tribados
Plant Manager: Bill Tribaldos
Estimated Sales: $5-10 Million
Number Employees: 5-9
Type of Packaging: Bulk

3149 Crepini
101 Castleton Street
Pleasantville, NY 10570
914-533-6645
Fax: 914-206-4848
Organic crepes
Production Manager: Mike McCartney
Estimated Sales: A
Number Employees: 1-4

3150 Crepini & The Crepe Team
5600 1st Ave
Brooklyn, NY 11220-2550
USA
718-372-0505
Fax: 914-206-4848 www.crepini.com
Grain, cereal, pasta, cakes, pastries
Executive Officer: Paula Rimer
Contact: Phil Campo
phil@crepini.com

3151 Crescent Duck Farm
10 Edagr Ave
PO Box 500
Aquebogue LI, NY 11931-0500
631-722-8000
www.crescentduck.com
Processor and exporter of fresh and frozen duck. Founded in 1908.
President: Douglas Corwin
Controller: Janet Corwin Wedel
Maintenance Engineer and Manager: Jeffrey Corwin
Plant Manager: Arnold Tilton
Estimated Sales: $7 Million
Number Employees: 50-99
Type of Packaging: Consumer, Food Service
Brands:
    Crescent

3152 Crescent Foods
4343 W 44th Place
Chicago, IL 60632
800-939-6268
communications@crescentfoods.com
www.crescentfoods.com
Halal beef and poultry
President & CEO: Ahmad Adam
VP: Ibrahim Abed
Director of Sales & Marketing: Amna Haq
VP Human Resources: Muneeza Arjmand
Year Founded: 1995
Number Employees: 50-99

3153 Crescent Ridge Dairy
355 Bay Rd
Sharon, MA 02067-1399
781-784-2740
Fax: 781-784-8446 800-660-2740
info@crescentridge.com www.crescentridge.com
Milk
President: Mark Parrish
VP: Jim Carroll
Estimated Sales: $2.5-5 Million
Number Employees: 50-99
Type of Packaging: Private Label
Brands:
    Crescent Ridge Dairy

3154 Crescini Wines
PO Box 216
Soquel, CA 95073-0216
831-462-1466
Wines
President: Richard Crescini
Co-Owner: Paula Crescini
Estimated Sales: $1-2,500,000
Number Employees: 5-9
Square Footage: 3
Type of Packaging: Private Label

3155 Crest Foods Inc
905 Main St.
Ashton, IL 61006
877-273-7893
www.crestfoods.com
Established in 1941. Processor of food ingredients including emulsifying agents, proteins, caseinates, whey, stabilizers and flavors for dips, bases and seasonings; contract packaging available
President: Jeff Meiners
VP of Corporate Sales: Steve Meiners
VP Manufacturing: Mike Meiners
Contact: Rebecca Henson
bhenson@crestfoods.com
Estimated Sales: $20-50 Million
Number Employees: 250-499
Type of Packaging: Consumer, Food Service, Private Label

3156 Crest International Corporation
P.O.Box 83309
San Diego, CA 92138-3309
619-296-4300
Fax: 619-296-3624 800-548-1232
www.crestinternational.com
Fresh or frozen fish and seafoods, fresh and frozen packaged seafood
Owner/President: Stephen Willis
Corporate Secretary: Lourdes Garber
Estimated Sales: $2 Million
Number Employees: 10
Type of Packaging: Food Service, Bulk

Food Manufacturers / A-Z

3157 Crestar Crusts
1104 Clinton Ave.
Washington Court House, OH 43160-1215
740-335-4813
Fax: 781-767-1751 www.richelieufoods.com
Frozen pizza crusts and pizzas
President/CEO: Robbie Jamieson
Director Sales Administration: Steve Deveau
VP Sales: Phillip Scolley
Plant Manager: Jason Yoakum
Estimated Sales: $20-50 Million
Number Employees: 400
Parent Co: Richelieu Foods Inc.

3158 Crestmont Enterprises
1420 Crestmont Ave
Camden, NJ 8103
856-966-0700
Fax: 856-966-6137
Flavors and extracts
President: Amy Baskin
VP: Joseph Shediack, Jr.
VP: Annette Rapaport
Estimated Sales: $5-10 Million
Number Employees: 10-19

3159 Creuzebergers Meats
3001 6th Avenue
Duncansville, PA 16635
814-695-3061
Meat processing
Owner: Sieglinde Creuzberger
Estimated Sales: Less than $500,000
Number Employees: 1-4

3160 Crevettes Du Nord
139 Rue De La Reine
C.P. 6380
Gaspe, QC G4X 2R8
Canada
418-368-1414
Fax: 418-368-1812 gesco@globetrotter.qc.ca
Processor and exporter of fresh and frozen shrimp
President: Amedee La Pierre
Number Employees: 50-99
Type of Packaging: Bulk

3161 Cribari Vineyard Inc
4180 W Alamos Ave # 108
Suite 108
Fresno, CA 93722-3943
559-277-9000
Fax: 559-277-2420 800-277-9095
bulk@cribari.net www.sacramentalwines.com
Processor and exporter of high quality California bulk wine
CEO & CFO: John F. Cribari
Sales: Ben Cribari
Estimated Sales: $730,000
Number Employees: 1-4
Number of Brands: 7
Type of Packaging: Bulk
Brands:
 Cvi Bulk Wines

3162 Crickle Company
90 Genesis Pkwy
Thomasville, GA 31792
229-225-1902
Fax: 229-225-2116 800-237-8689
www.crickle.com
Brittle and popcorn
President/Owner: Harry Jones
VP: Jerry Hunter
Number Employees: 12

3163 Cricklewood Soyfoods
250 Sally Ann Furnace Road
Mertztown, PA 19539-9036
610-682-4109
Fax: 717-484-4789
Kosher vegetarian soy-based foods including burgers and low-fat three bean, organic soy and three grain tempeh, organic and GMO free foods
President: Renate Krummenoehl
Estimated Sales: $380,000
Number Employees: 4
Number of Products: 5
Square Footage: 2400
Type of Packaging: Consumer, Food Service, Bulk
Brands:
 Cricklewood Soyfoods
 Cricklewood Soyfoods

3164 Criders Poultry
1 Plant Avenue
PO Box 398
Stillmore, GA 30464-0398
912-562-4435
Fax: 912-562-4168 800-342-3851
info@criderinc.com www.cridercorp.com
Fresh, frozen, canned and further processed chicken
Owner/CEO: William Crider Jr
CFO: Max Harrell
Research & Development: Phil Hudspeth
Quality Control: Stan Wallen
Operations: Lee Thompkins
Plant Manager: Kenneth Houghton
Purchasing: Ritchie Young
Estimated Sales: $20-50 Million
Number Employees: 400
Type of Packaging: Food Service, Private Label, Bulk
Brands:
 Crider

3165 Crillon Importers LTD
80 E State Rt 4 # 108
Paramus, NJ 07652-2657
201-368-8878
Fax: 201-368-4450 support@crillonimporters.com
www.crillonimporters.com
Wines and liquors
Owner: Michel Roux
roux@crillonimporters.com
Estimated Sales: $10-20 Million
Number Employees: 5-9
Brands:
 Absente
 Agavero
 Aquavits
 Douce Provence
 Elisir Mp Roux
 Hb Pastis
 Magellin Gin
 Rhum Barbancourt
 Rinquinquin
 Talapa Mezcal
 Unicum Zwack

3166 Crispy Green Inc.
144 Fairfield Rd
Fairfield, NJ 07004
973-679-4515
Fax: 973-755-0358 info@crispygreen.com
www.crispygreen.com
Freeze-dried fruits, including all natural and 100-calorie
Chief Executive Officer: Angela Liu
Contact: Kim Driggs
driggs@crispygreen.com
Estimated Sales: $680,000
Number Employees: 7

3167 Cristom Vineyards
6905 Spring Valley Rd NW
Salem, OR 97304-9779
503-375-3068
Fax: 503-391-7057 jeri@cristomwines.com
www.cristomvineyards.com
Wines
Owner: Tom Gerrie
tom@cristomvineyards.com
Co-Owner: Eileen Gerrie
Estimated Sales: $2.5-5 Million
Number Employees: 10-19
Type of Packaging: Private Label

3168 Critchfield Meats Inc
2220 Nicholasville Rd # 166
STE 166
Lexington, KY 40503-2400
859-276-4965
Fax: 859-278-4965 800-866-2901
orders@critchfieldmeats.com
www.critchfieldmeats.com
Meats
President: Mark Critchfield
CEO: Larry McMillan
Secretary/Treasurer: Mike Critchfield
Vice President: Larry Critchfield
ldcritchfield@critchfieldmeats.com
Number Employees: 10-19
Brands:
 Critchfield Meats

3169 Critelli Olive Oil
2445 South Watney Way, Ste D
Fairfield, CA 94533-6721
707-426-3400
Fax: 707-426-3423 800-865-4836
www.critelli.com
Manufacturer of organic olive oil and dipping oil. Importer of culinary oil, Balsamic, Varietal Wine, and flavored vinegars from around the world.
Director Food Service: Mike Brossier
Director Of Operations: Brian Witbracht
Type of Packaging: Food Service, Private Label
Brands:
 Critelli

3170 Criterion Chocolates Inc
125 Lewis St
Eatontown, NJ 07724-3454
732-542-7847
Fax: 732-542-0045 800-804-6060
info@criterionchocolates.com
www.criterionchocolates.com
Chocolates
Owner: George Karagias
criterion@criterionchocolates.com
VP: James Samaras
Marketing Director: Ron Boyadjian
Estimated Sales: $5-10 Million
Number Employees: 20-49
Brands:
 Criterion

3171 Criveller California Corp
185 Grant Ave
Healdsburg, CA 95448-9539
Canada
707-431-2211
Fax: 707-431-2216 888-849-2266
info@criveller.com www.criveller.com
Ale and lager beer
President: Bruce McCubbin
Marketing Director: Matt Johnson
Manager: Barbara Criveller
Number Employees: 5-9
Square Footage: 24000
Type of Packaging: Consumer, Food Service
Brands:
 Eisbock
 Gritstone
 Honey Brown
 Millstone
 Niagara
 Paleao

3172 Crocetti's Oakdale Packing Co
378 Pleasant St
East Bridgewater, MA 02333-1349
508-587-0035
Fax: 508-587-8758 www.crocettis.com
Packer of hamburger meat and sausage
Marketing Director & CFO: Carl Crocetti
Estimated Sales: $5-10 Million
Number Employees: 20-49
Type of Packaging: Consumer, Food Service, Bulk

3173 Crockett Honey
1040 W Alameda Dr
Tempe, AZ 85282-3332
480-731-3936
Fax: 480-731-3938 800-291-3969
bnipper@crocketthoney.com
www.crocketthoney.com
Processor and exporter of honey
Owner: Brian Nipper
Secretary: Linda Nipper
VP: Brian Nipper
Estimated Sales: $5-10 Million
Number Employees: 5-9
Square Footage: 48000
Type of Packaging: Consumer, Food Service, Bulk
Brands:
 Crockett's
 Mrs. Crockett's

3174 Croda Inc
300 Columbus Cir # A
Edison, NJ 08837-3907
732-417-0800
Fax: 732-417-0804 marketing-usa@croda.com
www.crodausa.com
Super refined marine and plant oils, proteins, and peptides for nutraceuticals, functional foods and dietary supplements.

Food Manufacturers / A-Z

President: Sandra Breene
Vice President: Esther Horowitz
ehorowitz@itsadeal.ie
Estimated Sales: $20-50 Million
Number Employees: 100-249
Square Footage: 45000
Parent Co: Croda International P/C

3175 Croft's Crackers
504 14th Avenue
Monroe, WI 53566-1140
608-325-1223
Fax: 608-325-1289 crofts@mail.tds.net
Crackers, granola, cookies
President: John King
Public Relations: John or Kathy King
Estimated Sales: $500,000-$1,000,000
Number Employees: 1-4

3176 Crofter's Food
7 Great North Rd
Parry Sound, ON P2A 2X8
Canada
705-746-6301
www.croftersorganic.com
Organic fruit spreads
Year Founded: 1989
Number of Brands: 1
Number of Products: 26
Type of Packaging: Consumer
Brands:
  CROFTER'S
  CROFTER'S SUPERFRUIT
  CROFTER'S JUST FRUIT

3177 Crofton & Sons Inc
10250 Woodberry Rd
Tampa, FL 33619-8008
813-685-7745
Fax: 813-689-4535 800-878-7675
debbie@unclejohnspride.com
www.unclejohnspride.com
Beef and pork smoked sausage, Italian sausage and smoked turkey links; also, full line of smoked meats
President: Kevin Crofton
kevin@unclejohnspride.com
Co-Owner: Noble Crofton
Estimated Sales: $8 Million
Number Employees: 50-99
Square Footage: 160000
Type of Packaging: Consumer, Food Service, Private Label, Bulk
Brands:
  Bean Brothers
  Smokehouse Favorite
  Uncle John's Pride

3178 Crompton Corporation
One American Lane
Greenwich, CT 06831-2560
203-573-2000
Fax: 203-552-2010 800-295-2392
Chemical ingredients and food additives
Chairman/President/CEO: Craig A. Rogerson
CFO/SVP: Stephen C. Forsyth
VP/Corporate Controller/Principal Acco: Laurence Orton
Global Market Manager: Bob Ruckle
Sales Director: Rick Beitel
Contact: Paul Ellis
paul.ellis@chemtura.com
Number Employees: 20-49

3179 Cronin Vineyards
11 Old La Honda Road
Woodside, CA 94062-2604
650-851-1452
Fax: 650-851-5696
Wines
Proprietor: Duane Cronin
VP: Mora Cronin
Estimated Sales: $300,000
Number Employees: 1-4
Type of Packaging: Consumer
Brands:
  Cizonin Vineyards
  Portola Hills

3180 Crooked River Brewing Company
1101 Center St
Cleveland, OH 44113-2405
216-771-2337
Fax: 216-771-7990
Beer, ale, stout, lager and porter

Owner: Stephen Danckers
Co-Owner: Stuart Sheridan
Estimated Sales: $5-9.9 Million
Number Employees: 10-19
Type of Packaging: Consumer, Food Service, Bulk
Brands:
  Cool Mule
  Crooked River Brewing
  Lighthouse Gold

3181 Crooked Vine/Stony Ridge Wnry
4948 Tesla Rd
Livermore, CA 94550-9530
925-449-0458
Fax: 925-449-0646
bacchus@stonyridgewinery.com
Wines
Owner: Rick Corbett
rick@crookedvine.com
Winemaker: Dale Vaughn-Bowen
Estimated Sales: Below $5 Million
Number Employees: 5-9
Brands:
  Orobianco-California Nv

3182 Crookston Bean
1600 S Main St
Crookston, MN 56716-2445
218-281-2567
Fax: 218-281-2567 www.eteamz.com
Processor and exporter of dried edible beans
President: Paul Biermaier
paul.biermaier@crookston.mn.us
Manager: Dave Seaver
Estimated Sales: $10-20 Million
Number Employees: 5-9
Type of Packaging: Private Label, Bulk

3183 Crop One
2201 Broadway
Oakland, CA 94612
media@cropone.ag
cropone.ag
Leafy greens produced with 95-99% less water than traditional growers and packaged in 100% recycled materials.
CEO: Sonia Lo
Chief Scientific Officer: Dr. Deane Falcone
CFO & SVP of Strategy: Dave Vosburg
Number of Brands: 1
Type of Packaging: Consumer, Private Label
Brands:
  FreshBox Farms

3184 Crop Pharms, LLC
59 Walnut Lane
Staatsburg, NY 12580
845-266-8999
www.currantc.com
Commercial currant farm; developer, marketer and seller of Black Currant products under CurrantC brand. Products include preserves, syrups and frozen currants
Founder/CEO: Greg Quinn
Year Founded: 1999
Number of Brands: 1
Number of Products: 6
Type of Packaging: Private Label
Brands:
  CurrentC

3185 Crosby Molasses Company
327 Rothesay Avenue
Saint John, NB E2J 2C3
Canada
506-634-7515
Fax: 506-634-1724 800-561-2206
feedback@crosbys.com www.crosbys.com
Molasses, corn syrup, and glucose for co-manufactured retail and food service.
President: James Crosby
Senior Vice President: Lorne Goodman
Director of Sales & Marketing: William Crosby
VP of Operations: Jeanette Howley
Estimated Sales: $7.8 Million
Number Employees: 60
Type of Packaging: Consumer, Food Service, Private Label, Bulk
Brands:
  Crosby

3186 Crossings Winery
1289 W Madison Ave
Glenns Ferry, ID 83623-2335
208-366-2539
Fax: 208-366-2458 carmelavineyards@rtci.net
www.carmelavineyards.com
Wines
Winemaker: Neil Glancy
Estimated Sales: $1-2.5 Million
Number Employees: 20-49

3187 Crowley Beverage Corporation
526 Boston Post Road
Wayland, MA 01778-1835
508-358-7177
Fax: 978-358-0057 800-997-3337
Soft drinks
President/CEO: Jill Crowley
Chairman: Edward Crowley
Estimated Sales: $3,000,000
Number Employees: 10-19
Brands:
  Razcal

3188 Crowley Cheese Inc
14 Crowley Ln
Mt Holly, VT 05758-9656
802-259-2340
Fax: 802-259-2347 800-683-2606
sales@crowleycheese.com
www.crowleycheese.com
Cheese including colby, sage, pepper, smoked, dill, garlic and caraway
Manager: Cindy Dawley
rawmilk@vermontel.net
Principal: Jill Jones
President: Galen Jones
Estimated Sales: Less Than $500,000
Number Employees: 5-9
Type of Packaging: Consumer, Food Service, Private Label, Bulk
Brands:
  Crowley

3189 Crown Candy Corp
4145 Mead Rd
Macon, GA 31206
478-781-4911
800-241-3529
info@crowncandy.com www.crowncandy.com
Processor and exporter of confectionery products including brittles, chocolate, coconut, peanut and pecan candies and fudge.
CEO: James Weatherford
jweatherford@crowncandy.com
Estimated Sales: $10-24.9 Million
Number Employees: 100-249
Type of Packaging: Consumer, Private Label, Bulk
Brands:
  Delights
  Royal Recipe

3190 Crown Holdings, Inc.
770 Township Line Rd.
Yardley, PA 19067
215-698-5100
ir@crowncork.com
www.crowncork.com
Bottle caps, can tops, crowns and cans including tin, beer and ale; also, bottling machinery
Chairman: John Conway
President/CEO: Timothy Donahue
Senior VP/CFO: Thomas Kelly
VP/Treasurer: Kevin Clothier
Executive VP/COO: Gerard Gifford
Year Founded: 1892
Estimated Sales: $11.7 Billion
Number Employees: 33,000
Type of Packaging: Consumer, Food Service, Private Label, Bulk
Other Locations:
  Crown Cork & Seal Co.
  Apopka FL

3191 Crown Maple Syrup
47 Mccourt Rd
Dover Plains, NY 12522-5734
USA
845-877-0640
Fax: 845-675-5044 www.crownmaple.com
Maple syrup, baking mixes

Food Manufacturers / A-Z

Owner: Rob Turner
Chief Executive Officer: Compton Chase-Lansdale
Contact: Terriann Albrecht
terriann@crownmaple.com
Estimated Sales: Less Than $500,000
Number Employees: 1-4

3192 Crown Pacific Fine Foods
8809 S 190th St
Kent, WA 98031-1270
425-251-8750
Fax: 425-251-8802 info@cpff.net
www.crownpacificfinefoods.com
Asian foods, baking and pancake mixes, baking goods, chocolates, condiments, and sauces
President/CEO/Founder: Tony Ataee
tony@cpff.net
Year Founded: 1982
Estimated Sales: $20-50 Million
Number Employees: 50-99

3193 (HQ)Crown Packing Company
5 Foster Road
Salinas, CA 93908-9339
831-424-2067
Fax: 831-424-7812
Grower and packer of lettuce, celery and cauliflower; exporter of lettuce and celery
President: Chris Bunn
Sales Manager: Rob Steitz
Sales: Tonya Tempalski
Estimated Sales: $3-5 Million
Number Employees: 2
Type of Packaging: Consumer, Food Service, Private Label, Bulk
Brands:
  Bunny

3194 Crown Prince Inc
18581 Railroad St
City Of Industry, CA 91748-1316
626-912-3700
Fax: 626-854-0350 sales@crownprince.com
www.crownprince.com
Processors and packers of specialty canned seafood.
President: Dustan Hoffman
dhoffman@crownprince.com
Chief Executive Officer: Robert Hoffman
Chief Financial Officer: Chris Bruno
Marketing Manager: Denise Hines
National Sales Manager: Gary Gruettner
Director, Operations: Jeanmarye Stobaugh
Warehouse Manager: John Brassell
Estimated Sales: $20-50 Million
Number Employees: 20-49
Number of Brands: 3
Type of Packaging: Consumer, Private Label
Brands:
  Crown Prince Natural
  Crown Prince Seafood
  Ocean Prince Seafood

3195 Crown Processing Company
10754 Artesia Blvd
Cerritos, CA 90703-2650
562-865-0293
Processor, importer and exporter of citrus rinds including graded, sliced, cooked, canned, made into marmalade. Founded in 1960.
President: John Bowen
Estimated Sales: $5-10 Million
Number Employees: 20-49
Square Footage: 108000
Type of Packaging: Food Service
Brands:
  Crown

3196 Crown Regal Wine Cellars
586 Montgomery St
Brooklyn, NY 11225-3130
718-604-1430
Fax: 718-384-1336 ywine@hotmail.com
Wine and grape juice
Owner: Joseph Baycount
Estimated Sales: $2.5-5,000,000
Number Employees: 5-9

3197 Crown Valley Food Service
550 East First Street
PO Box 2101
Beaumont, CA 92223-1001
951-769-8786
Fax: 951-769-8788
Prepared specialty foods

President: Sheldon Zaritsky
CEO: Mike Cavanaugh
Estimated Sales: $1-3 Million
Number Employees: 10-19

3198 Crum Creek Mils
700 Old Marple Rd
Springfield, PA 19064-1236
610-604-0505
Fax: 413-581-3501 888-607-3500
info@crumcreek.com www.crumcreek.com
Soy-based pastas, breadsticks and soy powders
President: Dr Ara Yeramyan
Contact: Richard Walton
info@crumcreek.com

3199 Crumbs Bake Shop
110 W 40th Street
Suite 2100
New York, NY 10018
877-278-6270
Cupcakes
President: Jason Bauer
Owner/VP: Mia Bauer

3200 Crunch-A-Mame
PO Box 539
Mulberry, AR 72947
hello@crunchamame.com
crunchamame.com
Organic edamame puffs
Number of Brands: 1
Number of Products: 4
Type of Packaging: Consumer
Brands:
  CRUNCH-A-MAME

3201 Crunchies Natural Food Company
733 Lakefield Dr
Suite B
Westlake Village, CA 91361
888-997-1866
crunchiesfood.com
Dried fruit and vegetable snacks
President & CEO: Scott Jacobson
Year Founded: 2004
Number Employees: 11-50
Type of Packaging: Private Label

3202 Crunchsters
303-545-9000
sales@crunchsters.com
www.crunchsters.com
Organic superfood snack
Founder: Frank Lambert
Sales & Marketing: Gina Lambert
Number of Brands: 1
Number of Products: 3
Type of Packaging: Consumer
Brands:
  CRUNCHSTERS

3203 Crunchy Rollers
Dallas, TX 75233
info@crunchyrollers.com
crunchyrollers.com
Organic rice snack bars
Founder: Brian Park

3204 Cruse Vineyards
2883 Lakeshore Dr
Chester, SC 29706
803-377-3944
Wines
Owner: Kenneth Cruse
Owner: susan Cruse
Estimated Sales: $1-4,9,000,000
Number Employees: 1-4
Brands:
  Cruse Vineyards
  Red Vines

3205 Crush Foods Service
Westlake Village, CA 91361
818-699-6381
www.crushfoodservice.com
Portioned herbs, butters and sauces
VP, Business Development: Jon Startz
Type of Packaging: Consumer, Food Service

3206 Crusoe Seafood LLC
9500 El Dorado Avenue
Sun Valley, CA 91352-1339
866-343-7629
Fax: 818-768-2366 jcohen@sugarfoods.com

Seafood.

3207 Crustacean Foods
5369 W Pico Blvd
Los Angeles, CA 90019-4037
323-460-4387
Fax: 323-933-4863 866-263-2625
Gourmet sauces.
Owner: Elizabeth An
Estimated Sales: $300,000-500,000
Number Employees: 5-9

3208 Crusty Bakery Inc
60 Broad St # 35
Suite 3502
New York, NY 10004-2306
917-733-6396
Fax: 646-349-2240
Baked goods.
President: David Banet
Estimated Sales: Less Than $500,000
Number Employees: 5-9

3209 Crystal & Vigor Beverages
174 Sanford Ave
Kearny, NJ 07032-5920
201-991-2342
Fax: 201-991-1882
Alcoholic and non-alcoholic beverages
Owner: Martinho Oliveira
Estimated Sales: $2.5-5,000,000
Number Employees: 10-19
Type of Packaging: Private Label

3210 Crystal Creamery
529 Kansas Ave
Modesto, CA 95351
209-576-3400
866-225-4821
crystalcreamery.com
Milk.
President & CEO: Martin Devine
CFO: Bonnie Chan
VP, Human Resources: Walter Mendez
VP, Manufacturing: Hugo Andrade
Year Founded: 1901
Estimated Sales: $160 Million
Number Employees: 500-999
Type of Packaging: Consumer, Food Service, Private Label, Bulk
Other Locations:
  Crystal Cream & Butter Co.
  Sacramento CA
Brands:
  Crystal

3211 Crystal Farms Dairy Company
Minnetonka, MN
800-672-8260
info@crystalfarms.com www.crystalfarms.com
Cheese and dairy products, including shredded and spreadable cheeses.
VP of Sales: Jason Krzewinski
Supply Chain Leader: John Larson
Number Employees: 30
Square Footage: 92000
Type of Packaging: Consumer
Brands:
  Crystal Farms
  Better'n EGGS

3212 Crystal Geyser Water Co.
Burlingame, CA 94010
800-443-9737
cgwconsumers@crystalgeyser.com
www.crystalgeyser.com
America's first domestic sparkling water
CEO: Yasumasa Iwamoto
VP, Finance: Kevin Moloughney
VP, Sales: Rob Bulot
Operations: Josh Butt
Year Founded: 1977
Number Employees: 50-99

3213 (HQ)Crystal Lake Farms
1200 E Roller Ave
Decatur, AR 72722
479-752-8274
800-382-4425
Processor and exporter of chicken

Food Manufacturers / A-Z

Manager: Daryl Hopkins
Vice President: Lisa Garrett
lisa@crystallakefarms.com
Sr Director, Commodity Sales: Bruce Bayley
VP Human Resources: Janet Wilkerson
Sr VP, Development: Dennis Martin
Estimated Sales: $500,000-$1 Million
Number Employees: 1000-4999
Type of Packaging: Food Service, Private Label, Bulk
Other Locations:
   Crystal Lake
   North Kansas City MO
Brands:
   Crystal Lake

3214 Crystal Lake LLC
6500 W Crystal Lake Rd
Warsaw, IN 46580-8986
   574-858-2514
Fax: 574-858-9886 info@crystallakellc.net
Liquid, frozen and cooked egg products.
President: Ron Truex
Sales Manager: Brian Hayward
Contact: Jeff Johnson
jeff.johnson@crystallakellc.net
Plant Manager: Jason Nichols
Estimated Sales: $10-20 Million
Number Employees: 1-4
Type of Packaging: Food Service, Private Label, Bulk

3215 Crystal Noodle
369 Van Ness Way
Suite 707
Torrance, CA 90501
   310-781-9734
Fax: 310-212-6768 www.crystalnoodle.com
Manufacturer of freeze-dried soups.
President/Owner: Masaki Mizuhashi

3216 Crystal Potato Seed Co
652 6th St
Crystal, ND 58222-4021
   701-657-2143
Fax: 701-657-2366
Seed potatoes
President: Bruce Otto
Partner: Robert Otto
Estimated Sales: $600,000
Number Employees: 1-4
Type of Packaging: Consumer
Brands:
   Dr. Red Norland
   Goldrush
   Norchip
   Red Lasoda
   Shephody
   Snowden

3217 Crystal Rock LLC
1050 Buckingham St
Watertown, CT 06795-6602
   860-945-0661
Fax: 860-274-0397 800-525-0070
www.crystalrock.com
Spring water; also, office coffee service
President: Jack Baker
CEO: Peter Baker
VP of Finance: David Jurasek
VP Sales/Marketing: Peter Guildner
VP of Procurement: Tim Descoteaux
Estimated Sales: $10.7 Million
Number Employees: 100-249
Type of Packaging: Consumer
Brands:
   Crystal Rock Water
   Vermont Pure Water
   Cool Beans Coffee

3218 Crystal Springs
1200 Britannia Road East
Mississauga, ON L4W 4T5
Canada
   905-795-6500
Fax: 905-670-3628 800-822-5889
www.crystalsprings.ca
Bottled water
Marketing Manager: Jeff Smith
Retail Manager: Steve Bondmini
General Manager: Paul Elliot
Production Manager: Eric Chastain
Estimated Sales: $5-10 Million
Number Employees: 100-249
Type of Packaging: Private Label
Brands:
   Crystal Springs
   Value Glacier

3219 Crystal Springs Bottled Water
200 Eagles Landing Blvd
Lakeland, FL 33810
   800-728-5508
www.crystal-springs.com
Bottled water
VP/GM Mid-Atlantic Region: Edward Gemind
Estimated Sales: F
Number Employees: 50-99
Number of Brands: 1
Parent Co: DS Services Of America Inc.

3220 Crystal Springs Water Company
200 Eagles Landing Blvd
Lakeland, FL 33810
   800-728-5508
www.crystal-springs.com
Bottled, spring, purified, distilled and fluoridated drinking water.
President & CEO: Jeff Vinyard
Year Founded: 1921
Estimated Sales: $20-50 Million
Number Employees: 100-249
Number of Brands: 11
Parent Co: DS Services
Brands:
   Alhambra®
   Athena®
   Belmont Springs®
   Crystal Springs®
   Deep Rock®
   Hinckley Springs®
   Kentwood Springs®
   Mount Olympus®
   Nursery®
   Sierra Springs®
   Sparkletts®

3221 Crystal Star Herbal Nutrition
1542 N Sanborn Rd
Salinas, CA 93905-4760
   831-422-7500
Fax: 800-260-4349 www.crystalstar.com
Processor, importer and exporter of herbal extracts, capsules, teas, powdered drink mixes and sports nutrition products
Manager: Julie Lu
Founder: Linda Page PhD
VP Sales: Scott Seabaugh
VP Operations: Glenn Korando
Estimated Sales: Less than $500,000
Number Employees: 1-4
Square Footage: 40000
Parent Co: Jones Products International
Type of Packaging: Consumer, Bulk

3222 Crystal Temptations
67 Porete Ave
North Arlington, NJ 07031
   201-246-7990
Fax: 201-246-7995 info@crystaltemptations.com
crystaltemptations.com
Gourmet popcorn and confections
Manager: Ari Green
VP, Operations: Solomon Green
Year Founded: 1995
Estimated Sales: $170 Million
Number Employees: 50
Type of Packaging: Private Label

3223 Cucina & Amore
2100 Atlas Rd
Unit F01
San Pablo, CA 94806
   510-964-4838
info@cucinaandamore.com
www.cucinaandamore.com
Specialty foods, including gnocchi, oils, vinaigrettes and sauces
Founder & Chairman: Ruth Wilkinson
CEO: Hossein Banejad
Operations: Dean Wilkinson
Year Founded: 2007
Type of Packaging: Consumer
Brands:
   CUCINA & AMORE

3224 Cucina Antica Foods Corp
333 N Bedford Rd # 118
Mt Kisco, NY 10549-1160
   914-244-9700
Fax: 914-244-1794 877-728-2462
info@cucina-antica.com www.montebene.com
Italian sauces
Owner: Niel Fusco
neil@cucina-antica.com
Estimated Sales: $5-10 Million
Number Employees: 1-4

3225 Cudlin's Meat Market
8 Cox Rd
Newfield, NY 14867-9420
   607-564-3443
Meat products; also, slaughtering services available
President: Vince Distefano
Estimated Sales: Less Than $500,000
Number Employees: 1-4
Type of Packaging: Consumer

3226 Cugino's Gourmet Foods
1000 Meyer Dr
Crystal Lake, IL 60014
   815-455-7242
Fax: 815-455-1948 888-592-8446
dhochstatter@cuginos.com www.cuginos.com
Garlic bread spread, gourmet soups, pasta sauce, BBQ sauce and marinades
Owner: Daniel Hochstatter
Estimated Sales: $10-20 Million
Number Employees: 10-19

3227 Cuisine International
1920 Swarthmore Ave
Suite 1
Lakewood, NJ 08701-4589
   732-367-2145
Fax: 732-730-9913 info@cuisinellc.com
www.cuisinellc.com
Frozen hors d'oeuvres
Estimated Sales: Less Than $500,000
Number Employees: 5-9
Type of Packaging: Consumer, Food Service

3228 Cuisine Perel
1001 Canal Blvd Ste A
Richmond, CA 94804
   510-232-0343
Fax: 510-232-0321 800-887-3735
info@cuisineperel.com www.cuisineperel.com
Chocolate, salad dressings, flavored grapeseed oil, mayonnaise, pasta and barbecue sauces, dry pastas and mustard; private label available
Owner: Mark Birchall
mark@cuisineperel.com
Estimated Sales: $2.5-5 Million
Number Employees: 5-9
Square Footage: 24000
Type of Packaging: Private Label

3229 Cuisine Solutions Inc
1501 Moran Rd # 100
Suite 100
Sterling, VA 20166-9338
   703-270-2900
Fax: 703-750-1158 888-285-4679
information@cuisinesolutions.com
www.cuisinesolutions.com
Prepared foods including beef meals, lamb, pork, veal, poultry, rice, pasta, sauces, seafood and vegetarian meals.
Chairman/CEO: Stanislas Vilgrain
President: Felipe Hasselmann
Vice President: Martha Anderson
manderson@jchs.edu
Estimated Sales: $29.2 Million
Number Employees: 250-499
Number of Brands: 2
Square Footage: 58000
Type of Packaging: Food Service
Brands:
   Cuisine Solutions
   Five Leaf

3230 Cuizina Food Company
18565 142nd Ave NE
Woodinville, WA 98072-8523
   425-486-7000
Fax: 425-486-1148

Food Manufacturers / A-Z

Sauces including alfredo, marinara, primavera and spaghetti; also, minestrone and croppino soup and pastas including frozen, filled, extruded and vegetable blends.
President: Ric Ferrera
Contact: Arnold Alvarado
aalvarado@cuizina.com
Estimated Sales: $5 Million
Number Employees: 35
Square Footage: 40000
Type of Packaging: Consumer, Food Service, Private Label, Bulk
Brands:
    Cuizina Italia

3231 Culina
Austin, TX 78701
www.culinayogurt.com
Botanical yogurt alternative
Type of Packaging: Consumer, Food Service

3232 Culinaire
1111 W Exposition Ave
Denver, CO 80223-2335
303-592-9100
Fax: 303-592-7619 877-502-9100
leo@culinairefoods.com www.culinairefoods.com
Hand made gourmet hors d oeuvres and entrees. Custom production available
President: Leo Reiff
Number Employees: 10-19
Number of Brands: 2
Number of Products: 110+
Square Footage: 20000
Type of Packaging: Consumer, Food Service, Private Label
Brands:
    Bistro Faire
    Culinaire

3233 Culinar Canada
58 Av William-Dobell
Baie-Comeau, QC G4Z 1T7
Canada
418-296-4395
Fax: 418-296-4395
Cakes
Head Culinary Chef: Will Franz
Number Employees: 500-999
Parent Co: Culinar Canada
Brands:
    Frenzi

3234 Culinary Farms Inc
1244 E Beamer St
Woodland, CA 95776-6002
916-375-3000
Fax: 916-375-3010 888-383-2767
info@culinaryfarms.com www.culinaryfarms.com
Processors of dried tomatoes, tomato paste and mexican chile peppers.
President: Mohammad Azam
drazam@culinaryfarms.com
CFO: Bal Pattar
National Sales Manager: Deepak Singh
Estimated Sales: $5-10 Million
Number Employees: 10-19
Square Footage: 24000
Type of Packaging: Bulk

3235 Culinary Institute Lenotre
7070 Allensby St
Houston, TX 77022-4322
713-692-0077
Fax: 713-692-7399 888-536-6873
Processor, importer and exporter of frozen strudel, muffins, cakes, cookies, danish, etc
Owner: Alain Lenotre
alenotre@culinaryinstitute.edu
VP: Marie Le Notre
Estimated Sales: $2 Million
Number Employees: 50-99
Square Footage: 120000
Type of Packaging: Private Label

3236 Culinary Masters Corporation
69 Brandywine Trl
Suite 109
Alpharetta, GA 30005
770-667-1688
Fax: 770-667-1682 800-261-5261
www.culinarymasters.com

Wholesaler/distributor and importer of specialty foods, baked goods, equipment and tools; serving the food service market; exporter of spices, blends and specialty equipment
Master Chef/President: Helmut Holzer
Controller: Beth Ann Jackson
Vice President: Sara Jane Holzer
Sales: Michelle Brayley
Estimated Sales: $3-5 Million
Number Employees: 5-9
Square Footage: 16000
Type of Packaging: Food Service, Private Label
Brands:
    Affiorato
    Dreimeister
    Ravifruit
    Stubi
    Symphony Pastries
    Vincotto

3237 Culinary Revolution
1320 Inspiration Drive
La Jolla, CA 92037-6810
858-454-4390
Fax: 323-939-4844 chefakasha@aol.com
Organic and diet food
Owner: Harry Coplan

3238 Culligan International Co
9399 W Higgins Rd # 1100
Suite 1100
Rosemont, IL 60018-4940
847-430-2800
Fax: 732-512-0166 800-231-9283
www.culligan.com
Water Systems, Water
Manager: Bob Prigen
President: Scoot Levy
Chairman: Peter Dixon
Estimated Sales: Under $500,000
Number Employees: 5000-9999
Parent Co: Culligan Water Technologies

3239 Culligan International Company
9399 West Higgins Road
Suite 1100
Rosemont, IL 60018
847-205-6000
Fax: 847-205-6030 www.culligan.com
Water softeners, filtration systems, drinking water systems, commercial and industrial water treatment solutions, whole-house filtration systems and bottled water delivery
Chairman: George Tamke
CEO: Mark Seals
VP Marketing: Eric Rosenthal
VP Sales North America, Comm & Indust: Rod McNelly
Media Contact: Jennifer Griffin
Operations Manager: Jackie McCaleb
Plant Manager: Seth Lewis
Estimated Sales: $26.2 Million
Number Employees: 2000
Brands:
    Culligan

3240 Culture
60 W 8th St
New York, NY 10011
718-499-0207
cultureny.com
Yogurt
Founder: Jenny Ammirati
Type of Packaging: Consumer

3241 Culture Republick
Englewood Cliffs, NJ 07632
800-662-0348
www.culturerepublick.com
Probiotic ice cream
Marketing: Leslie Miller
Number of Products: 7
Type of Packaging: Consumer, Food Service

3242 Culture Systems Inc
3224 N Home St
Mishawaka, IN 46545-4436
574-258-0602
Fax: 574-258-1136 info@culturesystemsinc.com
www.culturesystemsinc.com
Processor, exporter and wholesaler/distributor of dairy ingredients; also, researcher for the food industry

President: David Kim
dhyungkim@aol.com
Estimated Sales: $1-2.5 Million
Number Employees: 10-19
Square Footage: 16000

3243 Cultures for Health
200 Innovation Ave
Suite 150
Morrisville, NC 27560
www.culturesforhealth.com
Starter cultures for cultured and fermented food
Co-Founder: Julie Feickert
Co-Founder: Eric Feickert

3244 Culver Duck Farms Inc
12215 County Road 10
PO Box 910
Middlebury, IN 46540-9694
574-825-9537
Fax: 574-825-2613 800-825-9225
info@culverduck.com www.culverduck.com
Duck, chicken and sausage products.
President: John Metzger
Year Founded: 1858
Estimated Sales: $20-50 Million
Number Employees: 100-249
Square Footage: 30000
Type of Packaging: Food Service
Brands:
    Culver Duck

3245 Culver Fish Farm
1316 W Kansas Ave
Mcpherson, KS 67460-6053
620-241-5200
Fax: 620-241-5202 800-241-5205
Fish
Owner: Brent Culver
culverfish@gmail.com
Estimated Sales: Less Than $500,000
Number Employees: 1-4

3246 Cumberland Creamery
4350 Hurricane Creek Blvd
Antioch, TN 37013-2223
615-641-1027
Fax: 615-641-7038
Dairy
Operations Manager: Jim Monteleone
General Manager: David Moss
Plant Manager: Bill Merrick
Estimated Sales: Under $500,000
Number Employees: 50-99
Parent Co: Suiza Foods

3247 Cumberland Dairy
899 Landis Ave
Rosenhayn, NJ 08352
856-451-1300
Fax: 856-451-1332 800-257-8484
sales@cumberlanddairy.com
www.cumberlanddairy.com
Ice cream mixes, juices, soy products and milk including whole, skim, 1% and 2%; processor of ice cream
President: Carmine Catalana
CFO: Stan Fronczkowski
Director of Research & Development: John Contino
Director of Quality: Richard Grigsby
VP Sales: David A Catalana
VP Operations: Frank Catalana
Year Founded: 1932
Estimated Sales: $20-50 Million
Number Employees: 100-249
Type of Packaging: Consumer, Food Service, Private Label, Bulk
Brands:
    Cumberland Dairy

3248 Cumberland Gap Provision Company
South 23rd Street
PO Box 1797
Middlesboro, KY 40965
606-248-3311
Fax: 606-248-6517 855-411-7675
consumeraffairs@smithfield.com
www.cumberlandgapprovision.com
Fresh smoked sausages and hams

Food Manufacturers / A-Z

President/CEO: Ray Mc Gregor
Vice President: Patrick Flanagan
Quality Control: Kim Treiter
Sales Director: Tim Kreiter
Contact: Michael Bailey
michael.bailey@johnmorrell.com
Purchasing Manager: Gary Evans
Estimated Sales: $20-50 Million
Number Employees: 320
Parent Co: Smithfield Foods
Type of Packaging: Consumer, Food Service, Private Label
Brands:
   Cumberland Gap
   Hickory Hills
   Old Kentucky

3249 **Cummings Studio Chocolates**
679 E 900 S
Salt Lake City, UT 84105-1128
801-328-4858
Fax: 801-328-4801 800-537-3957
candy@CummingsStudioChocolates.com
www.cummingsstudiochocolates.com
Processors of candy including chocolates
President/CEO: Marion Cummings
marion@cummingsstudiochocolates.com
Marketing Manager: Jolend Proter
Estimated Sales: $2.5-5 Million
Number Employees: 50-99
Square Footage: 28000

3250 **Cuneo Cellars**
9360 SE Eola Hills Road
Amity, OR 97101-2416
503-835-2782
Wines
Partner: Gino Cuneo
Estimated Sales: Less than $500,000
Number Employees: 1-4

3251 **Cup 4 Cup LLC**
6540 Washington Street
Yountville, CA 94599
833-287-4287
www.cup4cup.com
Gluten free flour, baking mixes
Owner/Chef: Lena Kwak
Co-Founder: Thomas Keller
National Sales Director: Sarah Robinson
Contact: Magali Delgado
magalidelgado@cup4cup.com

3252 **Cup 4 Cup LLC**
840 Latour Ct
Suite B
Napa, CA 94558-6286
707-754-4263
Fax: 707-927-0130 www.cup4cup.com
Gluten-free baking mixes, flour and other ingredients.
General Manager: Dave Mogridge
Year Founded: 2010
Number Employees: 11-50

3253 **Cupid Candies**
7637 S Western Ave
Chicago, IL 60620-5871
773-925-8191
Fax: 773-925-7736
Candy
President: John Stefanos
cupidcandiesinc@yahoo.com
Estimated Sales: $3 Million
Number Employees: 20-49
Square Footage: 28512
Type of Packaging: Consumer, Private Label

3254 **Cupoladua Oven**
PO Box 266
Wexford, PA 15090
412-592-5378
info@cupoladuaoven.com
www.cupoladuaoven.com
All natural baked goods, sweet treats and savory snacks.

3255 **(HQ)Cupper's Coffee Company**
1502C 3rd Avenu South
Lethbridge, AB T1J 0K8
Canada
403-380-4555
Fax: 403-328-8004 cuppercoffee@gmil.com
Importer and exporter of coffee

President: Al Anctil
Number Employees: 20-49

3256 **Curaleaf**
301 Edgewater Pl
Suite 405
Wakefield, MA 01880
833-760-4367
info@curaleafhemp.com curaleafhemp.com
Hemp-based CBD products including tinctures, topical creams and vape pens
President and CEO: Joe Lusardi

3257 **Curley's Custom Meats**
315 East St
Jackson Center, OH 45334-5078
937-596-6518
Fax: 937-596-6518 www.curlysmeats.com
Meats
President: Larry Edwards
lawrence@curlysjerky.com
Estimated Sales: $2.5-5,000,000
Number Employees: 1-4

3258 **Curly's Foods Inc**
5201 Eden Ave # 181
Suite 370
Edina, MN 55436-2449
612-920-3400
Fax: 612-920-9889 www.curlys.com
Beef including roast, corned, barbecued and cooked and frozen ribs.
President: John Pauley
Vice President: Ken Fineberg
Manager, R&D: Brian Quandt
Estimated Sales: $22 Million
Number Employees: 500-999
Number of Brands: 1
Square Footage: 100000
Parent Co: John Morrell/Smithfield Foods
Type of Packaging: Consumer, Food Service, Private Label, Bulk
Brands:
   Curly's

3259 **Curran's Cheese Plant Inc**
W8850 Davis Rd
Browntown, WI 53522-9741
608-966-3361
Fax: 608-966-3309
Cheese products
Owner: Jim Curran
Estimated Sales: Less Than $500,000
Number Employees: 5-9
Brands:
   Curran Cheese

3260 **Curry King Corporation**
34 West Prospect St
Waldwick, NJ 07463
201-652-6228
Fax: 201-447-3291 800-287-7987
info@curryking.com www.curryking.com
Processor and importer of curry, balti and tandoori sauce; also, mango chutney; exporter of curry sauce
President: Lall Kwatra
lall@addesign.net
Vice President: Pamela Kwatra
Estimated Sales: Under $500,000
Number Employees: 3
Square Footage: 10000
Type of Packaging: Food Service, Private Label, Bulk
Brands:
   Curry King

3261 **Curtice Burns Foods**
11 Clark St
Shortsville, NY 14548-9755
585-289-4414
Fax: 585-289-4280
Canned fruits and vegetables
Chief Financial Officer: Tom Palmer
Manager: Luke Plamondon
Estimated Sales: $1-3 Million
Number Employees: 40
Parent Co: Curtice Burns
Type of Packaging: Consumer, Food Service, Private Label

3262 **Curtis Packing Co**
2416 Randolph Ave
Greensboro, NC 27406-2910
336-275-7684
Fax: 336-275-1901
www.curtispackingcompany.com
Packer of meat products including frankfurters, bologna, bacon, ham, beef and fresh pork
President: Douglas Curtis
douglas.curtis@curtispackingcompany.com
Sales Executive: John Curtis
Estimated Sales: $18 Million
Number Employees: 50-99
Number of Brands: 6
Square Footage: 40000
Type of Packaging: Consumer
Brands:
   Beef Master
   Curtis
   Ibp
   Mbpxl
   Monfort
   Porter House

3263 **Cusa Tea**
1823 Folsom St
Boulder, CO 80302
cusatea.com
Premium instant teas
Founder: Jim Lamancusa
Number of Brands: 1
Number of Products: 6
Type of Packaging: Consumer
Brands:
   CUSA TEA

3264 **Cusack Meats**
301 SW 12th St
Oklahoma City, OK 73109
405-232-2127 800-241-6328
Fax:
cusack@cusackmeats.com www.cusackmeats.com
Beef, pork, lamb, veal and poultry
Owner: Donnie Cusack
General Manager: Al Cusack
Year Founded: 1933
Estimated Sales: $20-50 Million
Number Employees: 20-49
Type of Packaging: Food Service

3265 **Cusano's Baking Company**
2798 SW 32nd Ave
Hallandale, FL 33009
954-458-1010
Fax: 954-458-1052 sales@cusanosbakery.com
www.cusanosbakery.com
Italian bread and bakery products
Owner: Michael Grecco
Co-Owner: Sal Grecco
Director: Mike Hernandez
General Manager: Sal Grego
Estimated Sales: $5-10 Million
Number Employees: 79
Brands:
   Cusano's

3266 **Cushner Seafoods Inc**
4141 Amos Ave
Baltimore, MD 21215-3309
410-358-5564
Fax: 410-358-5558
Fish & Seafood
Owner: Jack Deckelbaum
Estimated Sales: $1,600,000
Number Employees: 5-9

3267 **(HQ)Custom Coffee Plan**
20333 Normandie Ave
Torrance, CA 90502-1215
310-787-5200
Fax: 310-787-5394 800-841-5949
dsdcustomerservice@farmerbros.com
Manufacturer, wholesaler and distributor of coffee, tea, and culinary products.
District Sales Manager: Mike Zankich
Manager: Jon Smith
jsmith@ccpusa.net
Number Employees: 100-249
Type of Packaging: Food Service

3268 **Custom Confections & More**
PO Box 62
Algonquin, IL 60102-0062
832-420-5944
Fax: 208-342-5996

643

Food Manufacturers / A-Z

Hard candy, lollipops
President: Lowell Fugal
Estimated Sales: $5-10 Million
Number Employees: 20-49

3269 Custom Culinary Inc.
1000 E. State Pkwy.
Suite 1
Schaumberg, IL 60173-4569
866-878-3827
800-621-8827
www.customculinary.com
Gravy mixes, soup bases, soup mixes and sauce & gravy concentrates.
Regional Manager: Tom Nemanich
Vice President Operations: David Love
Year Founded: 1945
Estimated Sales: $100 Million
Number Employees: 100-249
Number of Brands: 3
Square Footage: 75000
Parent Co: Griffith Laboratories, Inc.
Type of Packaging: Food Service, Bulk
Brands:
    Gold Label
    Master's Touch
    Panroast

3270 Custom Food Solutions LLC
2505 Data Dr
Louisville, KY 40299-2517
502-671-6966
Fax: 502-671-6906 800-767-2993
www.customfoodsolutions.com
A USDA, FDA and AIB inspected food manufacturing facility specializing in custom batch, fresh ingredient production of soups, sauces, fillings and Sous Vide cooked proteins in flexible sized pouches.
Sales: Karen Reid
Facilities: Chris Smith
Number Employees: 20-49
Number of Products: 50
Square Footage: 130000
Type of Packaging: Food Service

3271 Custom Foods Inc
9101 Commerce Dr
De Soto, KS 66018-8410
913-585-1900
Fax: 913-585-1470 www.customfoodsinc.com
Frozen bakery products
Number Employees: 20-49

3272 Custom House Seafoods
PO Box 7112
Portland, ME 04112
207-773-2778
Fax: 207-761-9458
Fish and seafood.
President: Craig Johnson
Estimated Sales: $820,000
Number Employees: 1-4

3273 Custom Ingredients Inc
1614 N Interstate 35
New Braunfels, TX 78130-2502
830-608-0915
Fax: 830-625-7914 800-457-8935
info@customingredients.com
www.customingredients.com
Ingredients, snacks, dips, bakery, sauces, tortilla
President: James Curry
brcurry@customingredientsinc.com
Marketing: D Ames
Operations: Grey Baker
Production: R Nahn
Estimated Sales: $2.5-5 Million
Number Employees: 10-19
Type of Packaging: Bulk

3274 Custom Produce Sales
13475 E Progress Dr
Parlier, CA 93648-9674
559-254-5800
Fax: 559-646-1003
Peaches, nectarines, blueberries, apricots, plums and grapes
Manager: Bob Melenbacker
Number Employees: 100-249
Brands:
    River Island
    River Valley Farms

3275 Custom-Pak Meats
2013 Dutch Valley Road
Knoxville, TN 37918
615-687-0871
Packer of meat
President: C Hobbs
Executive VP: Christopher Satterfield
Number Employees: 42
Square Footage: 99200
Type of Packaging: Food Service
Brands:
    Nugget
    Pocahontas

3276 Cutie Pie Corp
443 W 400 N
Salt Lake City, UT 84103-1227
801-533-9550
Fax: 801-355-8021 800-453-4575
www.getcutiepie.com
Processor and exporter of frozen fruit snack pies
Principal: Bob Sharp
CFO: Lee Rucker
Director: Lee Wacker
Manager: Williams Arroyo
arroyo@horizonsnackfoods.com
Estimated Sales: Under $500,000
Number Employees: 50-99
Type of Packaging: Consumer, Food Service
Brands:
    Cutie Pies

3277 Cutone Specialty Foods
145 Market Street
Chelsea, MA 02150
617-889-1122
Fax: 617-884-3944
customerservice@cutonespecialtyfoods.com
www.cutonespecialtyfoods.com
Marinated and blanched mushrooms
President/Owner: Mario Cutone

3278 Cutrale Citrus Juices
602 McKean St.
Auburndale, FL 33823-4070
863-965-5000
Fax: 863-965-5311 www.cutrale.com
Grapefruit and orange juices.
President: Hugh Thompson
Year Founded: 1996
Estimated Sales: $173 Million
Number Employees: 400
Square Footage: 16252
Parent Co: Sucocitrico Cutrale Ltda.
Type of Packaging: Consumer, Food Service, Private Label, Bulk

3279 Cutting Edge Beverages
2424 N Federal Hwy
#101
Boca Raton, FL 33431-7796
561-347-5860
Manufacturer of juices, sparkling juices, juice drinks and flavoured waters.
Estimated Sales: $5-10 Million
Number Employees: 5-9
Number of Brands: 4
Parent Co: Whitlock Packaging Corporation
Brands:
    Juice Bowl
    JB'S Extreme
    Fruit Wave H2O
    Juice Bowl Sparkling Juice

3280 Cuvaison Winery
4550 Silverado Trl
Calistoga, CA 94515-9604
707-942-6266
Fax: 707-942-5732 www.cuvaison.com
Red and white wines.
President: Jay Schuppert
jschuppert@cuvaison.com
CFO: Bonnie Schoch
Dir. Of Consumer Sales & Marketing: Mary Pencek
National Sales Manager: Steve Richards
Estimated Sales: $10-20 Million
Number Employees: 20-49
Type of Packaging: Consumer, Food Service
Brands:
    Cuvaison

3281 Cyanotech Corp
73-4460 Queen Kaahumanu
Suite 102
Kailua Kona, HI 96740-2637
808-326-1353
Fax: 808-329-4533 800-395-1353
info@cyanotech.com www.cyanotech.com
Cyanotech Corporation, the world's leader in microalgae technology, produces high-value natural products from microalgae, and is the world's largest commercial producer of natural astaxanthin from microalgae. Products include HawaiiamSpirulina Pacifica, a nutrient-rich dietary supplement; BioAstin, a natural astaxanthin, a powerful antioxidant with expanding applications as a human nutraceutical
CEO: Gerald R Cysewski
gcysewski@cyanotech.com
VP Sales/Marketing: Robert Capelli
Sales Manager: Jeane Vinson
Estimated Sales: F
Number Employees: 100-249
Number of Brands: 3
Number of Products: 2
Square Footage: 1306800
Parent Co: Cyanotech Corporation
Type of Packaging: Consumer, Private Label, Bulk
Brands:
    Bioastin Natural Astaxanthin
    Spirulina Hawaiian Spirulina

3282 Cybele's Free To Eat
Los Angeles, CA 90046
877-895-3729
info@cybelesfreetoeat.com cybelesfreetoeat.com
Vegan cookies and superfood veggie pastas
President & CEO: Cybele Pascal
Number of Brands: 1
Number of Products: 9
Type of Packaging: Consumer
Brands:
    CYBELE'S FREE TO EAT

3283 Cybros
P.O.Box 851
Waukesha, WI 53187-0851
262-547-1821
Fax: 262-547-8946 800-876-2253
Fine breads, rolls, cookies and other products
Owner: Debbie Brooks
General Manager: Paul Geboy
Estimated Sales: $2.5-5 Million
Number Employees: 10-19
Square Footage: 32000

3284 Cyclone Enterprises Inc
146 Knobcrest Dr
Houston, TX 77060-1213
281-872-0087
Fax: 281-872-7645 www.cyclone-ent.com
Processor and importer of Mexican food including hot sauce and peppers. Distributors of dry, canned, processed and frozen grocery items including juices, drinks, dairy products, meats, cheeses, deli products, specialty foods, herbsspices, candy and snac
Owner: Mike Germany
Sales: Jim Petree
mgermany@cyclone-ent.com
Customer Support: Dora Mendoza
General Information: Martha Gibbs
Purchasing: Lam Townsend
Estimated Sales: $2.5-5 Million
Number Employees: 100-249
Type of Packaging: Consumer, Food Service, Private Label

3285 Cygnet Cellars
PO Box 1956
Hollister, CA 95024-1956
831-637-7559
Wine
Partner: Jim Johnson
Estimated Sales: $500,000 appx.
Number Employees: 1-4
Brands:
    Cygnet

3286 Cypress Grove
1330 Q St
Arcata, CA 95521
707-825-1100
Fax: 707-825-1101 info@cypressgrovecheese.com
cypressgrovecheese.com
Goat cheeses

Founder: Mary Keehn
President: Pamela Dressler
Year Founded: 1983
Estimated Sales: $9317243
Number Employees: 51-200
Type of Packaging: Private Label

3287 Cypress Point Creamery
18825 SE 24th Ave
Hawthorne, FL 32640
352-481-2806
www.cypresspointcreamery.com
Cheese

3288 (HQ)Cyrils Bakery
2890 W State Road 84 # 103
Unit 103
Fort Lauderdale, FL 33312-4828
954-797-1832
Fax: 413-473-9708 800-929-7457
sales@cyrils.com www.cyrils.com
Frozen bakery products including breads and pastries.
President: Cyril Cohen
CEO: Adam Weizer
adam@servistree.com
VP: Adam Weizer
Estimated Sales: Less Than $500,000
Number Employees: 1-4
Number of Brands: 1
Number of Products: 75
Type of Packaging: Consumer, Food Service

3289 Czech Stop Grocery & Deli
105 N College Ave
105 N. College St.
West, TX 76691-1455
254-826-4161
Fax: 254-826-5117 Info@CzechStop.net
www.czechstop.net
Baked goods
President: Bill Polk
Number Employees: 50-99

3290 Czepiel Millers Dairy
PO Box 277
Ludlow, MA 01056-0277
413-589-0828
Fax: 413-589-0828
Dairy
President: Stanly Czepiel

3291 Czimer's Game & Seafoods
13136 W 159th St
Homer Glen, IL 60491
708-301-0500
888-294-6377
www.czimers.com
Meat and fish
Owner: Richard Czimer Jr
Estimated Sales: $300,000
Number Employees: 1-4

3292 D & D Foods Inc
5820 Weston Parkway
West Des Moines, IA 50266
515-267-2800
800-772-4098
productinquiry@hy-vee.com www.hy-vee.com
Barbecue sauces, marinades and salad dressings; also, contract packaging available
President: Fred Dodelin
fdodelin@hy-vee.com
CFO: Fred Dodelin
Estimated Sales: $3-5 Million
Number Employees: 5-9
Type of Packaging: Consumer, Food Service, Private Label, Bulk
Brands:
  Foy's B.B.Q. Sauce

3293 D & D Sugarwoods Farm
2287 Glover St
Glover, VT 05839-9356
802-525-3718
Fax: 802-525-4103 800-245-3718
SugarwoodsFarm@comcast.net
Produces Vermont maple syrup, maple candy, maple cream and all natural pancake mixes.
Estimated Sales: Less Than $500,000
Number Employees: 5-9
Type of Packaging: Consumer, Food Service, Private Label

3294 D D Williamson & Co Inc
1901 Payne St
Louisville, KY 40206-1902
502-895-2438
Fax: 502-895-7381
Global manufacturer of natural colour for the food and beverage industries with facilities in Africa, Asia, Europe and North and South America.
Chairman & CEO: Ted Nixon
Type of Packaging: Bulk

3295 D F Ingredients Inc
127 Elm St # 200
Suite 200
Washington, MO 63090-2140
636-583-0802
Fax: 630-583-4877 888-583-0802
michael@dfingredients.com
www.dfingredients.com
Ingredients and dairy products
President: Michael Husmann
Vice President: Larry Rice
Sales Rep: Richard Kuddes
Sales Rep: Kenneth Johnson
Sales Rep: Jim Wesselschmidt
Manager: Megan Bade
megan@dfingredients.com
Number Employees: 1-4

3296 D I Mfg LLC
13335 C St
Omaha, NE 68144-3601
402-330-5650
info@dimanufacturing.com
www.dimanufacturing.com
Specialty food products including gluten free foods, garlic bread, wrapped breads, pizza, cookie dough
Contact: Zack Best
zbest@dimanufacturing.com
Number Employees: 10-19
Type of Packaging: Food Service, Bulk

3297 D Seafood
2723 S Poplar Avenue
Chicago, IL 60608-5915
312-808-1086
Fax: 312-808-0869
Seafood
Owner: De Trinh

3298 D Steengrafe Co Inc
1726 Main St
Pleasant Valley, NY 12569-5611
845-635-4067
Fax: 845-635-4239
Manufacturer and importer of beeswax, botanicals, kola nuts and nut powder, quassia chips, dried ginger and spices
VP: Margot Nordenholt
m_nordenholt@yahoo.com
VP: Carl Schmidt
Estimated Sales: $5 Million
Number Employees: 1-4
Type of Packaging: Bulk

3299 D Waybret & Sons Fisheries
3 Clam Point
Shelburne, NS B0T 1W0
Canada
902-745-3477
Fax: 902-745-2112
Manufacturer and exporter of fresh and salted haddock, cod, halibut and hake; also, fresh lobster
President/Co-Owner: Dewey Waybret
Manager/Co-Owner: Cecil Waybret
Number Employees: 50
Type of Packaging: Bulk

3300 D&M Seafood
135 N King St # 2b
Honolulu, HI 96817-5084
808-531-0687
Fax: 808-531-4947
Seafood
Owner: Hansen Chong

3301 D'Arrigo Brothers Company of California
21777 Harris Rd
Salinas, CA 93908
831-455-4500
Fax: 831-455-4445 bcoleman@darrigo.com
www.andyboy.com
Vegetables: broccoli, fennel, hearts of romaine, broccoli rabe, cauliflower and cactus pear
President & CEO: John D'Arrigo
Chairman: Andy D'Arrigo
VP, Sales & Business Development: Chad Amaral
Director, Business Development: Matt Amaral
Director, Marketing & Culinary: Claudia Villalobos
VP, Sales: Dave Martinez
Director, Sales: John Scherpinski
Estimated Sales: $22 Million
Type of Packaging: Consumer, Bulk
Brands:
  Andy Boy
  Green Head

3302 D'Artagnan
600 Green Ln
Union, NJ 07083-8074
973-344-0565
Fax: 973-465-1870 800-327-8246
www.dartagnan.com
Gourmet foods: beef, duck, lamb
Owner: Lily Hodge
lilyh@unionleague.org
Number Employees: 100-249

3303 D'Oni Enterprises
PO Box 962
San Juan Capistrano, CA 92693-0962
949-240-3053
Fax: 949-240-3086 800-809-8298
www.d-0ni.com
Sauces
President: Greg Bloom
Vice President: David Dallesandro
Vice President: David Bloom
Shipping/Receiving: Linda Trudeau

3304 D-Liteful Baking Company
9012 NW 105 Way
Medley, FL 33178
305-883-6449
Fax: 305-883-8797
Product line includes that of Heavenly Desserts featuring a variety of sugar free products such as cheesecakes and meringues available in vanilla, chocolate, cappuccino, strawberry and lemon flavors. Their Heavenly Harvest line includes sugar free baked products such as sesame and wheat crackers.
Founder: Jorge Guevara
Type of Packaging: Food Service

3305 D2 Ingredients, LP.
1244 Enterprise Dr
De Pere, WI 54115
920-425-8870
Fax: 920-964-0116 info@d2ingredients.com
d2ingredients.com
Functional ingredients and products, including smoke flavorings, alginate products, extrudable yeast-less doughs and savory fillings; spice blends, caramelized sugars and commodities; injection and tumbling products for poulty and meat. Also provide
Vice President of Sales & Marketing: Dan Rose
Type of Packaging: Private Label, Bulk

3306 DAGOBA Organic Chocolate
1105 Benson Way
Ashland, OR 97520-9540
541-482-2001
Fax: 541-482-5661 866-972-6879
dagoba@worldpantry.com
www.dagobachocolate.com
Organic chocolate bars, drinking chocolate, baking products, tasting squares, and professional products.
Estimated Sales: $10-20 Million
Number Employees: 20-49
Type of Packaging: Consumer
Brands:
  Dagoba Organic Chocolate

3307 DB Kenney Fisheries
301 Water Street
PO Box 1210
Westport, NS B0V 1H0
Canada
902-839-2023
Fax: 902-839-2070
dbkenney@dbkenneyfisheries.com
www.dbkenneyfisheries.com
Manufacturer and exporter of scallops, lobster, cod and haddock

Food Manufacturers / A-Z

President: Daniel Kenney Jr
Controller: Steven Lombard
Sales Manager: Dave Titus
Operations manager: Glenn Wadman
Number Employees: 50-99
Type of Packaging: Bulk

3308 DDW: The Color House
1901 Payne Street
Louisville, KY 40206

502-895-2438
Fax: 502-895-7381 www.ddwcolor.com
Natural colors, coloring foods, caramel colors and burnt sugars.
President: Elaine Gravatte
CEO: Ted Nixon
Chief Financial Officer: Ann Joseph
VP Global Human Resources: Ute Purschke-Hamdani
Chief Operating Officer: Elaine Gravatte
Other Locations:
  DDW Global Support Center
  Louisville KY
  D.D. Williamson Colors, LLC
  Port Washington WI

3309 DF Mavens
24-20 49th St
Astoria, NY 11103

347-813-4705
info@falfoodsworldwide.com
dfmavens.com
Fruit based frozen deserts
President: Malcom Stogo
Marketing Manager: Maria Correa
Year Founded: 2013
Estimated Sales: $970000
Number Employees: 20
Type of Packaging: Private Label

3310 DG Yuengling & Son, Inc.
420 Mahantongo St
Pottsville, PA 17901

570-628-4890
marketing@yuengling.com
www.yuengling.com
Beer including ale, porter, lager and light.
President & Owner: Dick Yuengling, Jr.
Chief Operating Officer: David Casinelli
Chief Administrative Officer: Wendy Yuengling
Quality Manager: Joe Frinzi
Sales Administration & Pricing Manager: Debbie Yuengling
Vice President, Operations: Jennifer Yuengling
Order Services: Sheryl Yuengling
Year Founded: 1829
Estimated Sales: $37.7 Million
Number Employees: 185
Square Footage: 36000
Other Locations:
  Yuengling Beer Company
  Pottsville PA
  Yuengling Beer Co of Tampa, Inc
  Tampa FL
Brands:
  Yuengling

3311 DGZ Chocolate
6909 Ashcroft Dr # 315
Suite 315
Houston, TX 77081-5819

713-777-3444
Fax: 713-777-9444 877-949-9444
Chocolates, caramel apples, popcorn covered in chocolate and caramel
Owner: Debbie Zissman
debbie@dgzchocolate.com
Estimated Sales: $5-10 Million
Number Employees: 1-4
Brands:
  Applerazzi
  Poparazzi
  Toffarassi
  Turtlerazzi

3312 DIP Seafood Mudbugs
1870 Dauphin Island Pkwy
Mobile, AL 36605-3000

251-479-0123
Fax: 251-479-9869 info@dipseafoodmudbugs.com
www.dipseafoodmudbugs.com
Seafood
Owner: Phan Nguyen
Estimated Sales: Less Than $500,000
Number Employees: 1-4

3313 DMH Ingredients Inc
1228 American Way
Libertyville, IL 60048-3936

847-362-9977
Fax: 847-362-9977
customerservice@dmhingredients.com
www.dmhingredients.com
Confectionery, gums and stabilizers, cheese and dairy powders, fruit and vegetable products, powdered cellulose, savory flavors, flavor enhancers, sweet flavors, coffee, tea and botanicals, vitamins, amino acids and food chemicalsgrain products, meat aspartame
President: David Damlich
ddamlich@dmhingredients.com
Estimated Sales: $5-10 Million
Number Employees: 10-19

3314 DNE World Fruit Sales
1900 N Old Dixie Hwy
Fort Pierce, FL 34946

Fax: 772-465-1181 800-327-6676
www.dneworld.com
Grower, packer, marketer, and importer of citrus fruit including navel oranges, clementines, lemons and limes; exporter of grapefruit, oranges, tangerines and juice.
Senior Director, Sales: Mark Hanks
Sales: Kevin Carroll
Year Founded: 1914
Estimated Sales: $20-50 Million
Number Employees: 50-99
Parent Co: Wonderful Packing LLC
Type of Packaging: Consumer, Food Service, Private Label, Bulk
Brands:
  Indian River Pride
  Ocean Spray
  Pride

3315 DNO Inc
3650 E 5th Avenue
Columbus, OH 43219

614-231-3601
dno@dnoproduce.com
www.dnoinc.com
Pre-cut prepackaged fresh fruit and vegetables
Founder/Owner: Tony DiNovo
tdinovo@dnoproduce.com
President/COO: Alex DiNovo
Purchasing Manager: Tony DiNovo
Estimated Sales: $10-20 Million
Number Employees: 20-49
Square Footage: 10000
Type of Packaging: Consumer, Food Service, Private Label, Bulk
Brands:
  Fresh Health
  Fresh Health Kids
  OHganics

3316 DNX Foods
120 S Houghton Rd
Suite 138-273
Tucson, AZ 85748

888-612-5037
info@dnxbar.com www.dnxbar.com
Nutrition bars made from meat and superfoods
Founder/CEO: John Rooney
CFO: Josh Nelson
VP Sales: Tim Larsen
Year Founded: 2015

3317 DO, Cookie Dough Confections
550 LaGuardia Pl
New York, NY 10012

646-892-3600
cookiedonyc.com
Cookie dough; baking mixes; frozen desserts
Operations Manager: Nadalyn McNichols
Year Founded: 2014
Number Employees: 1-10

3318 DRY Soda Co.
506 2nd Ave
Suite 1200
Seattle, WA 98104

888-379-7632
drysparkling.com
Sparkling sodas
Founder & CEO: Sharelle Klaus
VP of Marketing: BreeAnna Marchitto
Year Founded: 2005
Number Employees: 11-50
Type of Packaging: Food Service, Private Label

3319 DS Services of America
200 Eagles Landing Blvd.
Lakeland, FL 33810

800-728-5508
www.water.com
Bottled water, water filtration coolers, spring water, purified drinking water, distilled drinking water, and more.
President: Dave Muscato
CEO: Tom Harrington
CFO: Jerry Hoyle
General Manager: Mike Garrity
Year Founded: 1985
Estimated Sales: $787 Million
Number Employees: 5300
Type of Packaging: Consumer, Food Service, Private Label, Bulk
Brands:
  Alhambra®
  Abita Springs®
  Athena®
  Belmont Springs®
  Crystal Springs®
  Deep Rock®
  Hinckley Springs®
  Kentwood Springs®
  Mount Olympus®
  Nursery® Water
  Sierra Springs®
  Sparkletts®
  Standard Coffee®
  My Utapia®

3320 (HQ)DSM
Het Overloon 1
6411 TE
Heerlen,
Netherlands

info@dsm.com
www.dsm.com
Nutrition, health and materials industries, such as food enzymes, cultures and savory ingredients to food and beverage manufacturers.
Co-CEO: Dimitri de Vreeze
Co-CEO: Geraldine Matchett
Chairman, Supervising Board: Rob Routs
Year Founded: 1902
Estimated Sales: $9 Billion
Number Employees: 21,000
Number of Brands: 82
Brands:
  AgiSyn™
  Akulon®
  ALL-Q™
  ALPAFLOR®
  AMPHISOL®
  Arnite®
  Arnitel®
  Bionate®
  BioSpan®
  Brewers Clarex®
  CakeZyme®
  CarboSil®
  CaroCare®
  CAROPHYLL®
  ComfortCoat®
  CRINA®
  CYLACTIN®
  Decovery®
  Delvo®Cheese
  Delvo®Fresh
  Delvotest®
  DeSolite® Supercoatings
  DHAgold™
  Dyneema Purity®
  Dyneema®
  EcoPaXX®
  Elasthane™
  elaVida™
  Epi-Guide®
  Fabuless®
  FloraGLO® LUTEIN
  ForTii®
  Fortitech® Premixes
  Fruitflow®
  geniVida®
  Haloflex™
  Hy-D®
  life's DHA®
  life's™ARA
  life's™GLA
  life's™OMEGA

Maxilact®
Maxiren®
Medeor® Matrix
MEG-3®
Meso BioMatrix®
Multirome®
NeoCryl®
NeoPac™
NeoRad™
NeoRez™
Niaga®
Novamid®
OatWell®
OPTISHARP® Zeaxanthin
OPTRIX®
OsseoFit™
OVN™
Pack-Age®
Panamore®
PARSOL®
PeptoPro®
PurSil®
Quali®-Carotene
Rapidase®
redivivo® Lycopene
resVida®
Rapidase®
redivivo® Lycopene
resVida®
Ronozyme®
Rovimix®
Skins®

3321 DSM Food Specialties
45 Waterview Blvd
Parsippany, NJ 07054
info@dsm.com
www.dsm.com/corporate/about/businesses/dsm-food-specialties.html
DSM Food Specialties is a producer of value-added ingredient solutions for the international food, feed and beverage industries.
President: Patrick Niels
Estimated Sales: K
Number Employees: 10,000+
Parent Co: Koninklijke DSM N.V.

3322 DSM Fortitech Premixes
2105 Technology Dr
Schenectady, NY 12308-1151
info@dsm.com
www.dsm.com
Vitamin and mineral pre mixes, amino acids, nucleotides, nutraceuticals and herbs
VP & CFO: Brian Wilcox
SEVP & Chief Scientific Officer: Ram Chaudhari
Senior QC Specialist: Cindy Grimm
International Project Manager: Dominic Kwiatkowski
Director, Human Resources: Joanne Murphy
Director, Manufacturing: Ed Webster
Purchasing Manager, North America: Thomas Morba
Estimated Sales: K
Number Employees: 10,000+
Square Footage: 68000
Parent Co: DSM
Type of Packaging: Food Service
Other Locations:
 Fortitech
 Europe
 Fortitech
 South America
 Fortitech
 Mexico

3323 DWC Specialities
710 Oak Ln
Horicon, WI 53032
920-485-4550
Fax: 920-485-4035 800-383-8808
www.dwcspecialties.com
Frozen bakery products, organic cookies and bread/specialty distributor of food products and supply goods 80% of WI/Chicago
President: Robert Scott
VP: Kim Gassner
Contact: Brett Anfinson
brett@dwcspecialties.com
Estimated Sales: $500,000-$1 Million
Number Employees: 11
Square Footage: 128000

3324 Daabon Organic USA, Inc.
1110 Brickell Ave
#212
Miami, FL 33131
305-358-7667
Producer of palm oil, and palm oil products including shortenings, hard fats, fry oils, soaps, glycerin and custom oil blends.
President/Owner: Raul Arenas
Vice President: Sergio Espinosa
Sales, North America: Esther Meima
Parent Co: Daabon Organic
Other Locations:
 Daabon Europa GmbH
 Pulheim, Germany
 Daabon Organic Australia Pty Ltd.
 New South Wales
 Daabon Organic Japan Co., Ltd.
 Tokyo

3325 Dabruzzi's Italian Foods
417 2nd St
Hudson, WI 54016-1509
715-386-3653
Fax: 715-549-5202
Ravioli, garlic butter bread and red and white sauces
Owner: Sharon Ellstrom
dabruzzis@earthlink.net
Manager: Nancy Cramer
Estimated Sales: $1-2,500,000
Number Employees: 5-9

3326 Dahlicious
320 Hamilton St
Leominster, MA 01453
www.dahlicious.com
Organic India-styled yogurt drinks
Number of Brands: 1
Number of Products: 5
Type of Packaging: Consumer
Brands:
 DAHLICIOUS

3327 Daily Crave, The
Natural Intentions, Inc.
PO Box 6688
Folsom, CA 95763
thedailycrave.com
Quinoa, lentil and veggie chips and straws
Founder: Hassan Alireza

3328 Daily Greens LLC
PO Box 1437
Austin, TX 78767-1437
512-524-1500
Fax: 512-532-6499 www.drinkdailygreens.com
Juice
Owner/Founder: Shauna Martin
shauna@drinkdailygreens.com
Marketing Manager: Yoshie Yanno-Pennings

3329 Daily Nutrition
120 S Houghton Rd
Suite 138-273
Tucson, AZ 85748
888-612-5037
info@dnxbar.com
Grass-fed meat snack bars
Founder & CEO: John Rooney
CFO: Josh Nelson
Sales: Ali Shouman
Number of Brands: 1
Number of Products: 5
Type of Packaging: Consumer
Brands:
 DNX

3330 Daily Soup
134 E 43rd St # 1
New York, NY 10017-4019
212-949-7687
Fax: 212-687-7839 888-393-7687
Fresh soups
Owner: Young Yoon
Executive Chef: Leslie Kaul
Estimated Sales: Less than $500,000
Number Employees: 10-19
Brands:
 Daily Made

3331 Dailys Premium Meats
3535 S 500 W
Salt Lake City, UT 84115-4205
801-269-1998
Fax: 801-269-1409 800-328-7695
info@dailysmeats.com
A variety of premium meat products, including bacon, hams and breakfast sausages.
President: Samantha Ames
sames@dailysmeats.com
Marketing Manager: John Garlinghouse
VP Sales: Sig Skarland
Production Manager: Dave Caron
Plant Manager: Jeff Lubbers
Number Employees: 250-499
Parent Co: Seaboard Foods
Type of Packaging: Consumer, Food Service
Other Locations:
 Missoula MT
Brands:
 Daily Foods

3332 Dainty Confections
725 Broadway St.
Windsor, ON N9C 0C1
Canada
519-972-8888
Fax: 519-966-3298 800-268-0222
jones@dainty.ca www.daintyrice.com
Candy
President: Catherine Diehl
Marketing: Sherry Jones

3333 Dairiconcepts
3253 E Chestnut Expy
Springfield, MO 65802-2540
417-829-3400
Fax: 417-829-3401 877-596-4374
dcinfo@dairiconcepts.com
www.dairiconcepts.com
Dairy powders and replacement systems, cheese powders and cheese concentrates, block and grated Italian cheeses.
CEO: Jeff Miyake
jeffmiyake@dairiconcepts.com
Number Employees: 1-4

3334 Dairy Connection Inc
501 Tasman St # B
Suite B
Madison, WI 53714-3173
608-242-9030
Fax: 608-242-9036 info@dairyconnection.com
www.dairyconnection.com
Cheese cultures
President: Cathy Potter
getculture@dairyconnection.com
VP/Technical Manager: Dave Potter
Technical Specialist: Sandy S
Customer Service Specialist: Patrick C
Number Employees: 10-19

3335 Dairy Farmers Of America
1405 N. 98th St.
Kansas City, KS 66111
816-801-6455
888-332-6455
webmail@dfamilk.com www.dfamilk.com
Milk, cheese, butter and dairy ingredients.
President/CEO: Rick Smith
rsmith@dfamilk.com
CFO: Greg Wickham
Year Founded: 1998
Estimated Sales: $13.5 Billion
Number Employees: 6,000
Number of Brands: 9
Type of Packaging: Private Label, Bulk
Brands:
 Borden® Cheese
 Cache Valley® Cheese
 Keller's® Creamery Butter
 Plugra® Butter
 Sport Shake
 Kemps®
 Guida's Dairy
 La Vaquita®
 Dairy Maid Dairy®

3336 (HQ)Dairy Fresh Foods Inc
21405 Trolley Industrial Dr
Taylor, MI 48180-1811
313-299-0735
Fax: 313-295-6950

Food Manufacturers / A-Z

Beverages, cheeses, deli foods and frozen foods; importer of cheese and meats including corned beef and ham; exporter of cheese
Co-President: Alan Must
amust@dairyfreshfoods.com
Co-President: Joel Must
Number Employees: 100-249
Square Footage: 800000
Type of Packaging: Consumer, Food Service, Bulk
Brands:
   Brittnia
   Dairy Fresh
   Deli-Fresh
   Gourmet
   Marla
   Oceen Fresh
   Pure Maid

3337 Dairy Group
366 N Broadway # 410
Jericho, NY 11753-2000
      516-433-0080
      Fax: 516-433-7657
Cheese
President: Ned Dorman
ndorman@thedairygroup.com
Estimated Sales: $1-3 Million
Number Employees: 1-4
Brands:
   Dairy Group

3338 Dairy House
150 Larkin Williams Ind Ct
Fenton, MO 63026
      636-343-5444
      Fax: 314-772-4280
Manufacturer and suppliers of cocoa, chocolate dairy powders and beverage flavors.
President: Carl Fitzwater
Vice President: John Hutchinson
Contact: Devine Allen
allen@dairy-house.com
Estimated Sales: 4.6 Million
Number Employees: 30

3339 Dairy King Milk Farms/Foodservice
PO Box 1259
11954 East Washington Blvd
Whitter, CA 90606
      818-243-6455
      Fax: 818-243-2455 800-900-6455
      www.dairyberries.com
Dairy products, frozen vegetables and dry goods; wholesaler/distributor of frozen foods, general merchandise, general line products, produce, meats and seafood; serving the food service market
VP: Joseph Goldstein
Number Employees: 50-99
Square Footage: 280000
Type of Packaging: Consumer

3340 Dairy Maid Dairy LLC
259 E 7th St
Frederick, MD 21701-5227
      301-663-5114
      Fax: 301-695-0431 www.dairymaiddairy.com
Milk, buttermilk, eggnog, whipping cream, creamer, juices and drinks.
Co-President: Jody Vona
Co-President: Jimmy Vona
jvona@dairymaiddairy.com
General Manager: David Staz
Transportation Manager: Bill Fulmer
Plant Manager: Ilir Emini
Estimated Sales: $20-50 Million
Number Employees: 100-249
Number of Brands: 1
Parent Co: Dairy Farmers of America
Type of Packaging: Consumer
Brands:
   Dairy Maid Dairy

3341 Dairy Maid Ravioli Mfg Co
216 Avenue U
Brooklyn, NY 11223-3825
      718-449-2620
      Fax: 718-449-3206 866-777-3661
      dairymaid1@aol.com
Manufacturer and distributor of pasta products including ravioli and tortellini
President/Co-Owner: Louis Ballarino
dairymaid1@aol.com
Co-Owner: Salvatore Ballarino
Vice President: Anthony Ballarino
Estimated Sales: $1-2.5 Million appx.
Number Employees: 5-9
Square Footage: 44000
Type of Packaging: Consumer, Private Label, Bulk
Brands:
   Dairy Maid

3342 Dairy Management Inc
10255 W Higgins Rd # 900
Suite 900
Rosemont, IL 60018-5638
      847-803-2000
      Fax: 847-803-2077 800-853-2479
      www.dairy.org
Bleaching compounds, chocolate, cultures, dairy powders, nonfat dry milk, milk, protiens, vegetable, sweetners
CEO: Thomas Gallagher
thomas.g@rosedmi.com
SVP Nutrition/Product Innovation: Greg Miller, PhD, FACN
VP Nutrition Research: Doug DiRenzom, PhD, FACN
Brand Development Director: Jose Cubillos
Number Employees: 100-249
Parent Co: National Dairy Council

3343 Dairy State Foods Inc
6035 N Baker Rd
Milwaukee, WI 53209-7301
      414-228-1240
      Fax: 414-228-9747 800-435-4499
      sales@dairystatefoods.com
      www.dairystatefoods.com
Manufacturer and exporter of juvenile cookies and animal, oyster crackers, also contract packaging available
President: Larry Rabin
rabin@dairystatefoods.com
Estimated Sales: $1-2.5 Million
Number Employees: 20-49
Square Footage: 120000
Type of Packaging: Consumer, Food Service, Private Label
Brands:
   Alphabet Cookies
   Circus Wagon Animal Crackers
   Toy Bus Animal Crackers
   Wild Jungle Animal Crackers

3344 (HQ)Dairy-Mix Inc
3020 46th Ave N
St Petersburg, FL 33714-3863
      727-525-6101
      Fax: 727-522-0769 800-955-6101
      ecoryn@dairymix.com www.dairymix.com
Manufacturer and exporter of ice cream, ice milk and milk shake mixes, frozen dessert
President: Edward Coryn
ecoryn@dairymix.com
Corporate VP: John Coryn
Sales/Marketing: Mike Costello
Plant Manager: Jerry Maine
Estimated Sales: $8 Million
Number Employees: 10-19
Type of Packaging: Food Service, Bulk

3345 DairyAmerica
4974 E Clinton Way
Suite C-121
Fresno, CA 93727
      559-251-0992
      Fax: 559-251-1078 800-722-3110
      webmaster@dairyamerica.com
      www.dairyamerica.com
Manufacturer and exporter of milk including low heat, medium heat, high heat, whole and dry buttermilk
President/SVP: Keith Gomes
CEO: Hoyt Huffman
Controller: Jean McAbee
CEO: Rich Lewis
Director Sales/Marketing: Dan Block
International Sales: Steve Gulley
Contact: Craig Alexander
acraig@dairyamerica.com
Operations Manager: Frances Zapanta
Estimated Sales: $1-2,500,000
Number Employees: 20-49
Type of Packaging: Bulk
Other Locations:
   Manufacturing Plant
   Los Banos CA
   Manufacturing Facility
   Turlock CA
   Manufacturing Facility
   Visalia CA
   Manufacturing Facility
   Artesia CA
   Manufacturing Facility
   Bactavia NY
Brands:
   Dairyamerica

3346 DairyChem Inc.
9120 Technology Ln
Fishers, IN 46038-2839
      317-849-8400
      Fax: 317-849-8213 cservice@dairychem.com
      www.dairychem.com
Manufacturer and exporter of natural dairy flavors including butter, cream, buttermilk, sour cream, cream cheese, cultured dairy, yogurt, milk, starter distillate and starter flavors.
Owner: Grant Church
VP: Diana Church
Sales Manager: Travis McMahan
gchurch@dairychem.com
Operations Manager/Purchasing: Paul Hampton
Estimated Sales: $1 Million
Number Employees: 10-19
Square Footage: 33400
Type of Packaging: Private Label, Bulk

3347 DairyPure
P.O. Box 961447
El Paso, TX 79996
      800-395-7004
      deanfoods@casupport.com www.dairypure.com
Dairy products; including lowfat milk, lactose free milk, creamers, sour creams, and flavour mixes.
CEO, Dean Foods Company: Ralph Scozzafava
Year Founded: 1931
Number Employees: 1,600
Parent Co: Dean Foods Company
Type of Packaging: Consumer, Private Label

3348 Dairyfood USA Inc
2819 County Highway F
Blue Mounds, WI 53517
      608-437-5598
      Fax: 608-437-8850 800-236-3300
      customerservice@dairyfoodusa.com
      www.dairyfoodusa.com
Cheeses, as well as candies, coffees, sausages and crackers
President/Owner: Daniel Culligan
Human Resources Manager: Teddy White
Purchasing: Vicki Mosure
Estimated Sales: $14.2 Million
Number Employees: 100

3349 Dairytown Products Ltd
49 Milk Board Road
Sussex, NB E4E 5L2
Canada
      506-432-1950
      Fax: 506-432-1940 800-561-5598
      admin@dairytown.com www.dairytown.com
Butter and skim milk, whole milk and buttermilk powders
CEO: Derek Roberts
Quality Assurance: Wendy Palmer
VP Sales/Marketing: George MacPhee
Operations Manager: Lynn McLaughlin
Type of Packaging: Private Label

3350 Daisy Brand
12750 Merit Dr
Suite 600
Dallas, TX 75251
      877-292-9830
      www.daisybrand.com
Sour cream and cottage cheese.
President: David Sokolsky
Director, Human Resources: Julie King
Year Founded: 1917
Estimated Sales: $171 Million
Number Employees: 300
Square Footage: 12000
Type of Packaging: Consumer, Food Service, Private Label, Bulk
Brands:
   Daisy Light Sour Cream
   Daisey Sour Cream

Daisy Cottage Cheese
Daisy Low Fat Cottage Cheese

3351 Daiya Foods
2768 Rupert St
Vancouver, BC V5M 3T7
Canada
877-324-9211
cr@daiyafoods.com daiyafoods.com
Dairy-free cheeze shreds, slices and blocks, dressings and meatless pizza.
Vice President: Michael Lynch

3352 Dakota
4850 Hahns Peak Drive, Ste 240
Loveland, CO 80538
888-586-2209
DBcustomers@dakotaorganic.com
www.grassfedbeef.com
Meat, beef

3353 (HQ)Dakota Brands Intl
2121 13th St NE
Jamestown, ND 58401-3568
701-252-5073
Fax: 701-251-1047 800-844-5073
www.dakotabrands.com
Bagels, rolls and frozen roll dough
President: Rex King
rking@daktel.com
CEO: Donald Kerr
Vice President: Kandy Jenkins
R&D/QA Manager: Colleen Krapp
National Sales Manager: Dick Earle
VP Operations: Darvin Becker
Estimated Sales: $2.5-5 Million
Number Employees: 50-99
Number of Products: 60
Square Footage: 21000
Type of Packaging: Consumer, Food Service, Private Label, Bulk
Brands:
Bagels
Bakeable
Dakota

3354 Dakota Gourmet
896 22nd Ave N
Wahpeton, ND 58075
701-642-3068
Fax: 701-642-9403 800-727-6663
www.dakotagourmet.com
Roasted sunflower nuts, soynuts, and toasted corn
Manager: Lucy Spiekermeier
General Manager: Lucy Spiekermeier
Estimated Sales: $2.5-5,000,000
Number Employees: 20-49
Square Footage: 40000
Parent Co: Sonne
Type of Packaging: Consumer, Food Service, Private Label, Bulk
Brands:
Giants

3355 Dakota Specialty Milling, Inc.
4014 15th Ave N
Fargo, ND 58102-2833
844-633-2746
sales@dakotaspecialtymilling.com
www.dakotaspecialtymilling.com
Producer of grain-based mixes and ingredients.
President: Peter Matthaei
Vice President of Sales & Marketing: Brian Andrews
Senior Director of Sales: Richard Karnemaat
Manager of Customer Logistics: Bernadine King
Director of Milling Operations: Brian Sorenson
bsorenson@dakotaspecialtymilling.com
Director of Technical Services: Bob Meyer
VP of Engineering & Manufacturing: Daryl Bashor
Estimated Sales: $15,000,000
Number Employees: 50-99
Type of Packaging: Consumer, Food Service, Private Label, Bulk

3356 Dakota Style
211 Industrial Dr
Clark, SD 57225-1595
605-532-5278
Fax: 605-532-3599 800-446-2779
www.dakotastyle.com
Kettle cooked potato chips, sunflower seeds
Contact: Riley Dandurand
riley@dakotastyle.com

3357 Dale & Thomas Popcorn
1 Cedar Ln
Englewood, NJ 07631-4802
201-645-4586
Fax: 201-645-4848 800-767-4444
Flavored popcorn
Founder: Richard Demb
Estimated Sales: $40.8 Million
Number Employees: 10-19

3358 (HQ)Dale T Smith & Sons Inc
12450 S Pony Express Rd
Draper, UT 84020-9510
801-571-3611
Fax: 801-571-3685 mail@smithmeats.com
Beef processor.
President: Dale Smith
Vice President: Dennis Smith
Production Manager: Roger McNicol
Number Employees: 50-99
Type of Packaging: Consumer, Food Service

3359 Daley Brothers ltd.
215 Water Street, Suite 301
St John's, NL A1C 6C9
Canada
709-364-8844
Fax: 709-364-7216
Manufacturer and exporter of fresh and frozen seafood
President: Terry Daley
CEO: Steve Hoskins
Sales Manager: Rosemary Buckingham
Number Employees: 20-49
Type of Packaging: Bulk

3360 Dalian Xinfeng International Industry & Trade Co.
1114 Zane Ave N
Golden Valley, MN 55422-4606
612-964-7391
Fax: 612-486-8895
Organic rice, beans, and grains.
Vice President: David Su
Year Founded: 1997
Type of Packaging: Food Service, Private Label

3361 Dalla Valle Vineyards
7776 Silverado Trl
Napa, CA 94558-9739
707-944-2676
Fax: 707-944-8411 info@dallavallevineyards.com
www.dallavallevineyards.com
Wines
President: Naoko Dalla Valle
info@dallavallevineyards.com
Vineyard Manager: Fausto Sanchez
Winemaker: Andy Erikksion
Estimated Sales: $2.5-5,000,000
Number Employees: 10-19
Type of Packaging: Private Label
Brands:
Dalla

3362 Dallis Brothers
11-22 44th Road
Suite 301
Long Island City, NY 11101
718-845-3010
Fax: 718-843-0178 info@dallisbroscoffee.com
www.dallisbroscoffee.com
Manufacturer of coffee.
Director, Sales Technology: Marcelo Crescente
Director, Specialty Coffee: Jon Phillips
Year Founded: 1913
Estimated Sales: $20-50 Million
Number Employees: 20-49
Number of Brands: 1
Parent Co: Lacas Coffee Company
Type of Packaging: Private Label
Other Locations:
Pennsauken NJ
Brands:
Dallis Bros. Coffee

3363 Damascus Bakery
56 Gold St
Brooklyn, NY 11201-1297
USA
718-855-1456
Fax: 718-403-0948
Paninis and pita and lavash breads

President/Owner: Edward Mafoud
edward@damascusbakery.com
Sales Executive: Dave Martz
Number Employees: 100-249

3364 Damiani Wine Cellars LLC
4704 State Route 414
Burdett, NY 14818-9779
607-546-5557
info@damianiwinecellars.com
www.damianiwinecellars.com
Wines
Owner/Winemaker: Lou Damiani
Wine Grower/Maker: Phil Davis
Manager: Michael Cimino
Number Employees: 5-9

3365 Damon Industries
822 Packer Way
Sparks, NV 89431-6445
775-331-3200
Fax: 775-331-3980 800-225-3046
info@fruitful.com www.fruitful.com
Shelf stable juice and beverage concentrates
President: Jeff Baldridge
info@fruitful.com
Quality Control: Richard Johnson
Sales Manager: Larry Grant
Productions: Gary Messerli
Estimated Sales: $5-10,000,000
Number Employees: 20-49
Brands:
Fruitful Juice Products
Juice Direct

3366 Damron Corp
4433 W Ohio St
Chicago, IL 60624-1054
773-826-6001
Fax: 773-826-6004 800-333-1860
info@damrontea.com www.damronplg.com
Tea
President/CEO: Ronald Damper
damrontea@aol.com
General Manager: Gina Gatta
Estimated Sales: $3,000,000
Number Employees: 20-49
Type of Packaging: Bulk
Brands:
Damron
Harvest Delighta

3367 Dan Carter
3018 Helsan Drive
PO Box 282
Richfield, WI 53076-0282
262-677-3407
Fax: 262-677-3806 800-782-0741
www.dcicheeseco.com
Cheese
President: Timothy Omer
Estimated Sales: $500,000-$1,000,000
Number Employees: 20-49
Brands:
Dan Carter

3368 Dan-D Foods Ltd
11760 Machrina Way
Richmond, BC V7A 4V1
Canada
604-274-3263
Fax: 604-274-3268 800-633-4788
www.dan-d-pak.com
Fine food importer, manufacturer and distributor of cashews, dried fruits, rice crackers, snack foods, spices etc. from around the world.
Chairman/President/CEO/Founder: Dan On
Number Employees: 500
Type of Packaging: Food Service, Bulk

3369 Dancing Deer Baking Company
65 Sprague Street
Building-west A
Boston, MA 02136
617-442-7300
Fax: 617-442-8118 888-699-3337
info@dancingdeer.com www.dancingdeer.com
Natural cakes and cookies

Food Manufacturers / A-Z

President/CEO: Patricia Karter
CFO: James Tyson
Marketing: Duane Lefevre
Sales: Dave Lamlein
Contact: Craig Drinkwater
cdrinkwater@dancingdeer.com
Production: Lissa McBurney
Estimated Sales: $59,000
Number Employees: 2
Number of Brands: 1
Number of Products: 25
Square Footage: 14000
Type of Packaging: Consumer, Food Service, Private Label, Bulk

3370 Dandelion Chocolate
740 Valencia St
San Francisco, CA 94110-1735
415-349-0942
800-785-2301
www.dandelionchocolate.com
Chocolates
Owner: Maggi Mcconnell
maggi.m@gmail.com
CEO: Todd Masonis
Number Employees: 5-9

3371 Dang Foods
3254 Adeline St
Suite 210
Berkeley, CA 94703
510-338-3345
Fax: 888-645-6065 hello@dangfoods.com
www.dangfoods.com
Coconut and sticky-rice chips
President/Owner: Vincent Kitirattragarn
vincent.kit@gmail.com
Number Employees: 1-4

3372 Daniel Le Chocolat Belge
88 East 7th Ave
Vancouver, BC V5T 1M2
Canada
604-879-7782
Fax: 604-879-7260 info@danielchocolates.com
www.danielchocolates.com
Fine chocolates and chocolate products including boxed chocolates, chocolate bars, and pastries
Owner: Daniel Poncelet
Secretary/Owner: Monique Poncelet
Estimated Sales: $2.49 Million
Number Employees: 30
Type of Packaging: Consumer, Food Service, Private Label, Bulk

3373 Daniel's Bagel & Baguette Corporation
414 36th Avenue SE
Calgary, AB T2G 1W4
Canada
403-243-3207
www.danielsbagel.foodpages.ca
Baked goods including specialty breads, bagels and pretzels
President: D Oppenheim
Estimated Sales: A
Number Employees: 6
Type of Packaging: Consumer, Food Service

3374 Daniele Inc
105 Davis Dr
Pascoag, RI 02859-3507
401-568-6228
Fax: 401-568-4788 800-451-2535
www.danielefoods.com
Manufacturer of dry-cured delicacies and other gourmet Italian products.
Co-Owner: Stefano Dukcevich
Co-Owner: Davide Dukcevich
Number Employees: 50-99

3375 Danisco-Cultor
430 Saw Mill River Rd
Ardsley, NY 10502-2605
914-674-6300
Fax: 914-674-6538 www.danisco.com
Ingredients for beverage products, including flavor enhancers, and functional botanicals, xylitol, industrial enzymes, sugar
President: Robert Mayer
CEO: Tom Knutzen
VP: Philippe Lavielle
Estimated Sales: $5-10 000,000
Number Employees: 20-49

3376 Danish Maid Butter Co
8512 S Commercial Ave
Chicago, IL 60617-2533
773-731-8787
Fax: 773-731-9812
danishmaidbutter@hotmail.com
www.danishmaid.com
Dairy products including anhydrous milkfat, butter oil and regular and whipped butter; also, packaging services available
President: Susie Wagner
Plant Manager: Matthew Wagner
Estimated Sales: $5 Million
Number Employees: 10-19
Square Footage: 36000
Type of Packaging: Consumer, Food Service, Private Label, Bulk

3377 (HQ)Dannon Company
P.O. Box 90296
Allentown, PA 18109-0296
877-326-6668
Fax: 914-366-2805 877-326-6668
mediainquiries@dannon.com www.dannon.com
Yogurt products
President & CEO: Guastavo Valle
VP Finance, CFO: Antoine Remy
VP Human Resources: Tony Cicio
VP Research & Development North America: Stewart Townsend
VP Quality: Christian Maisonneuve
SVP Marketing: Sergio Fuster
SVP Sales: Lucho Lopez-May
Contact: Jason Moloff
jason.moloff@dannon.com
VP Operations: Fernando Lafuente
Estimated Sales: $198.1 Million
Number Employees: 900
Parent Co: Dannone
Other Locations:
 Dannon Company Plant
 West Jordan UT
 Dannon Company Plant
 Fort Worth TX
 Dannon Company Plant
 Minster OH
Brands:
 Dannon
 Activia
 Danimals
 La Creme
 Light and Fit

3378 Dannon Yo Cream
5858 NE 87th Ave
Portland, OR 97220
800-962-7326
info@yocream.com www.yocream.com
Frozen dessert, snacks and beverages
CFO: W. Douglas Caudell
Estimated Sales: $70 Million
Number Employees: 100-249
Number of Brands: 4
Parent Co: The Dannon Company
Type of Packaging: Consumer, Food Service, Private Label, Bulk
Brands:
 Sorbet By Yo Cream
 The Yogurt Stand
 Yo Cream
 Yo Cream Smoothies

3379 Danone North America
12002 Airport Way
Broomfield, CO 80021
303-635-4000
michael.neuwirth@danone.com
www.danonenorthamerica.com
Organic dairy; fresh dairy; plant-based; coffee creamers & beverages
Year Founded: 2017
Number Employees: 6000
Brands:
 Activia
 DanActive
 Danimals
 Dannon
 Earthbound Farm
 Horizon Organic
 International Delight
 Left Field Farms
 Light & Fit
 Oikos
 Silk
 So Delicious
 Stok
 Vega
 Wallaby Organic
 YoCrunch
 YoCream

3380 Daphne's Creamery
707-762-1760
Fax: 707-542-9601 sales@daphnecreamery.com
daphnecreamery.com
Artisanal cheese and butter
Co-Founder & CEO: George Gavros
Number of Brands: 1
Number of Products: 7
Type of Packaging: Consumer
Brands:
 DAPHNE'S CREAMERY

3381 Daprano & Company
Po Box 49228
Charlotte, NC 28277
704-927-0590
Fax: 704-927-0591 877-365-2337
sales@daprano.com www.daprano.com
Designer chocolates, bonbons, novelties, Italian cookies, biscotti, madeleines, shortbread
President: Angelo Daprano
Brands:
 Amaretti Virginia
 Bonbon Barnier
 Caffarel
 Cantatti
 Flamigni
 Gatsby's/Pierre Koenig
 Jila & Jols
 Reinhardt

3382 Dardimans California
7842 Willis Ave
Panorama City, CA 91402
818-849-5770
dardimans.com
California fruit crisps
CEO: Annie Babayan
Number of Brands: 1
Type of Packaging: Consumer
Brands:
 DARDIMANS

3383 Dare Foods
3750 N. Blackstock Rd
Spartanburg, SC 29303
781-639-1808
Fax: 781-639-2286 800-668-3273
www.darefoods.com
Cookies, candies and crackers; also, ground cookie ingredients
National Sales Manager: Neil S Voutt
Number Employees: 60
Type of Packaging: Bulk

3384 Dare Foods Incorporated
2481 Kingway Drive
PO Box 1058
Kitchener, ON N2C 1A6
Canada
519-893-5500
Fax: 519-893-2644 800-668-3273
www.darefoods.com
Cookies, crackers, fine breads and candy
Number Employees: 1300
Square Footage: 240487
Brands:
 Breaktime
 Dare Creme Cookies
 Pure Chocolate Whippet
 Breton Minis
 Vinta
 Cabaret
 Grainsfirst
 Vivant
 Water Crackers
 Breton
 Bremner Wafers
 Dare Realfruit Candies

3385 Daregal
100 Overlook Ctr
2nd Floor Suite 2014
Princeton, NJ 08540-7814
609-375-2312
Fax: 609-375-2402
Frozen chopped herbs

Food Manufacturers / A-Z

3386 Darifair Foods
4131 Sunbeam Rd
Jacksonville, FL 32257-6027
904-268-9916
Fax: 904-268-8666 sales@darifair.com
www.darifair.com
Cultured dairy ice cream and dessert
President: Andrew Block
CEO: Christiaan Avonda
h.hammond@mpls-synod.org
CFO: William Block
VP Business Development: Jeffrey Block
VP Marketing: Michele Block
VP Operations: Ed Stevens
Executive Chief/VP: John Penland
Estimated Sales: $2.5-5,000,000
Number Employees: 20-49
Type of Packaging: Private Label
Brands:
  Dairfair

3387 Darigold
5601 6th Ave. S.
Suite 300
Seattle, WA 98108
800-333-6455
www.darigold.com
Milk, butter, cottage cheese, cheese, whipping cream, yogurt and sour cream.
President/CEO: Stan Ryan
stan.ryan@darigold.com
Year Founded: 1918
Estimated Sales: Over $1 Billion
Type of Packaging: Consumer, Food Service, Private Label, Bulk
Other Locations:
  Powdered Milk/Butter
  Caldwell ID
  Milk & Cultured
  Boise ID
  Condensed, Powdered Milk
  Jerome ID
  HTST Milk
  Medford OR
  HTST Milk
  Salt Lake UT
  HTST Milk
  Bozeman MT
  UP Milk
  Portland OR
  Powdered Milk
  Chehalis WA
  HTST Milk
  Seattle WA
  HTST Milk
  Spokane WA
  Cheese
  Sunnyside WA
  Cultured/Butter
  Issaquah WA
  Powdered Milk
  Lynden WA
Brands:
  Fred Meyer
  Haggen
  Safeway
  Sysco Products
  Western Family

3388 Dark Dog
3921 Alton Rd
Suite 242
Miami Beach, FL 33140
www.darkdog-organic.com
Organic energy drinks
Year Founded: 1995
Number of Brands: 1
Number of Products: 4
Type of Packaging: Consumer
Brands:
  DARK DOG ORGANIC

3389 Dark Tickle Company
75 Main St.
PO Box 160
St Lunaire-Griquet, NL A0K 2X0
Canada
709-623-2354
Fax: 709-623-2354 www.darktickle.com
Wild berry jams, toppings, beverage concentrate, relish and vinegars
President: Stephen Knudsen
Number Employees: 5-9
Square Footage: 5000
Type of Packaging: Consumer
Brands:
  Dark Tickle

3390 Darling Ingredients Inc.
5601 N MacArthur Blvd.
Irving, TX 75038
927-717-0300
800-800-4841
info@darlingii.com www.darlingii.com
Repurposed beef, poultry and pork by-products into specialty ingredients for use in the pharmaceutical, food, pet food, feed, fuel and fertilizer industries.
CEO: Randall Stuewe
Executive VP/CFO: Brad Phillips
Executive VP/General Counsel: John Sterling
Executive VP/CAO: John Muse
Estimated Sales: $3.4 Billion
Number Employees: 10,000
Number of Brands: 16
Type of Packaging: Private Label, Bulk
Brands:
  Bakery Feeds
  EnviroFlight
  CTH
  Dar Pro Bioenergy
  Dar Pro Ingredients
  Dar Pro Solutions
  Diamond Green Diesel
  Ecoson
  Hepac
  Laru
  NatureSafe
  Peptan
  Rousselot
  Sonac
  Rendac
  Rothsay

3391 Das Foods
2041 W Carroll Avenue
Chicago, IL 60612
312-224-8590
Fax: 800-861-1336 www.dasfoods.com
Gourmet salts, caramels, lollipops and other treats
President: Katie Das
Member: Dhurba Das
Estimated Sales: $500,000-1 Million
Number Employees: 1-4

3392 Date Lady Inc.
900 W Commercial St
Springfield, MO 65803
417-414-2282
info@ilovedatelady.com
ilovedatelady.com
Manufacturer of organic dates, date syrup, and other sauces and syrups sweeteened with dates.
Founder: Colleen Sundlie
Co-Founder: Ryan Sundlie

3393 Dave's Gourmet
4314 Redwood Hwy
Suite 200
San Rafael, CA 94903
Fax: 415-401-9107 800-758-0372
info@davesgourmet.com www.davesgourmet.com
Trail mixes, gourmet hot sauce, salsa, seasoned pretzels, dried chiles and chile powders
Owner: Dave Hirschkop
info@davesgourmet.com
VP: David Lipson
Purchasing Manager: David Lipson
Estimated Sales: $1-2.5 Million
Number Employees: 5-9
Square Footage: 28000
Type of Packaging: Consumer, Food Service
Brands:
  Chile
  Fire Nugget
  Smoked Habanero Pretzels

3394 Dave's Gourmet Albacore
10 Hangar Way
Watsonville, CA 95076
206-999-5517
info.davesalbacore@gmail.com
www.davesalbacore.com
Salmon, albacore tuna, rainbow trout, oysters, dungeness crab, shrimp, pates and mousses
President: Thad Pound
Sales Manager: Lindsay Turner
Contact: Debbie Driessche
davesalbacore@aol.com
Estimated Sales: $1 Million
Number Employees: 1-4
Square Footage: 10000
Type of Packaging: Consumer, Private Label, Bulk
Brands:
  Alder Cove

3395 Dave's Killer Bread
5209 SE International Way
Milwaukie, OR 97222
503-335-8077
www.daveskillerbread.com
Organic sliced bread

3396 David Bradley Chocolatier
92 N Main St # 19
Bldg 19
Windsor, NJ 08561-3209
609-443-4747
Fax: 609-443-8762 877-289-7933
david@dbchocolate.com www.dbchocolate.com
Confectionery
Owner: Robert Hicks
admin@dbchocolate.com
Vice President: Marcy Hicks
Estimated Sales: $1-3 000,000
Number Employees: 10-19
Type of Packaging: Private Label
Brands:
  Gourmet Snack Bags
  Sophisticated Chocol
  Zany Pretzels

3397 David Mosner Meat Products
355 Food Center Dr
Bronx, NY 10474
718-328-5600
866-928-6428
info@davidmosner.com www.davidmosner.com
Packer of veal and lamb.
President: Michael Mosner
VP, Business Development: Benjamin Mosner
Sales: Neil Harris
Year Founded: 1957
Estimated Sales: $20-50 Million
Number Employees: 20-49
Type of Packaging: Consumer, Food Service, Private Label
Brands:
  Mvp

3398 David Rio
PO Box 885462
San Francisco, CA 94188
415-543-2733
Fax: 415-543-2749 800-454-9605
chai@davidrio.com www.davidrio.com
Chai and loose leaf teas
Co-Founder, President and CEO: David Scott Lowe
Co-Founder: Rio H. Miura
Chief Operating Officer: Ai Okuba
Director of Sales: Erin-Kate Whitcomb
Contact: Linda Avilla
lavilla@davidrio.com
Estimated Sales: $2,000,000
Number Employees: 10-19
Number of Brands: 2
Number of Products: 20
Square Footage: 3150
Parent Co: David Rio San Francisco
Type of Packaging: Consumer, Food Service, Private Label, Bulk
Brands:
  David Rio Chai

3399 David's Cookies
11 Cliffside Dr
Cedar Grove, NJ 07009
800-500-2800
custserv@davidscookies.com
www.davidscookies.com
Thaw and serve tarts, layer cakes and single serve desserts, cookies, cookie dough, scones, crumbcake, ruggalach, butter cookies, brownies and mini-muffins
President: Ari Margulies
Vice President: Michael Zuckerman
Year Founded: 1979
Estimated Sales: $90 Million+
Number Employees: 350

Food Manufacturers / A-Z

Number of Brands: 2
Square Footage: 160000
Parent Co: Fairfield Gourmet Foods Corp.
Type of Packaging: Consumer, Food Service
Brands:
Cookie Cupboard
David's Cookies

3400 Davidson's Organics
PO Box 11214
Reno, NV 89510-1214
775-356-1690
Fax: 775-356-3713 800-882-5888
www.davidsonstea.com
Teas, herbs, cocoa, spices, and accessories for the specialty trade and retail use
Estimated Sales: $5-10 Million
Number Employees: 10-19
Square Footage: 50000
Brands:
Davidson's Inc

3401 Davidson's Safest Choice Eggs
2963 Bernice Road
Lansing, IL 60438
708-418-8500
Fax: 708-418-1235 800-410-7519
info@safeeggs.com www.safeeggs.com
Pasteurized eggs
President: Greg West
CFO: Michael Smith

3402 Davinci Gourmet LTD
7224 1st Ave S
Seattle, WA 98108-4103
206-768-7401
Fax: 206-768-1855 800-640-6779
info@davinci-gourmet.com www.kerry.com
Manufacturers flavored syrups, gourmet sauces, and confections
Manager: Gary Sletten
Manager: Greg Desbien
greg@davincigourmet.com
Estimated Sales: $14 Million
Number Employees: 50-99
Number of Products: 120+
Square Footage: 130000
Type of Packaging: Consumer, Food Service, Private Label, Bulk

3403 Davis & Davis Gourmet Foods
3614 William Flynn Hwy
Allison Park, PA 15101-3722
412-487-7770
customerrelations@davisanddavisonline.com
www.davisanddavisonline.com
Manufacturer of gourmet foods including cocktails, seasonings and mixes.
Founder and President: Kenneth Davis
Number Employees: 20-49

3404 Davis Bakery & Delicatessen
28700 Chagrin Blvd # 1
Cleveland, OH 44122-4560
216-292-3060
Fax: 216-292-4588 www.davisbakery.net
Specialty baked goods including cakes, doughnuts and low-sodium
President: Joel Davis
VP Treasurer: Sheldon Davis
Supervisor Sales: Janice Davis
Manager: John Stapleton
jdowling@aspenonnet.com
VP Deli Operations: Sam Perkul
Estimated Sales: $1-2.5 Million
Number Employees: 10-19
Brands:
Kiddie Kakes
Sodex

3405 Davis Bread & Desserts
#O, 720 Olive Dr.
Davis, CA 95616
530-220-4375
tomthebaker@gmail.com
www.davisbreadanddesserts.com
Producer of breads, rolls and desserts. Food items for sale include Cinnamon Rolls, European Danish, Cinnamon Crisps, Raspberry Cheese Pockets, Frosted Brownie, and more. The company sells its products at several farmer's markets throughout the Northern California and Nevada area.
Owner: Tom Kilbourn

Estimated Sales: $320,000
Number Employees: 10
Brands:
Davis Bread

3406 Davis Bynum Winery
8075 Westside Rd.
Healdsburg, CA 95448-3445
866-442-7547
Fax: 707-433-0939 800-826-1073
info@davisbynum.com www.davisbynum.com
Wines
President: Lindley Bynum
GM: Susie Bynum
CFO: Susie Bynum
Contact: Davis Bynum
d.bynum@davisbynum.com
Purchasing: Hampton Bynum
Estimated Sales: $2.5-5,000,000
Number Employees: 10-19
Number of Brands: 2
Type of Packaging: Private Label
Brands:
Davis Bynum
River Bend

3407 Davis Food Company
P.O.Box 16118
Plantation, FL 33318-6118
954-791-5868
Fax: 440-461-2261 www.stadiummustard.com
Mustard
President: Peggy D Davis
Estimated Sales: $1-2,500,000
Number Employees: 1-4
Brands:
Stadium Mustard

3408 Davis Strait Fisheries
71 McQuade Lake Crescent
Halifax, NS B3S 1C4
Canada
902-450-5115
Fax: 902-450-5006 john@davisstrait.com
Seafood products such as northern shrimp, scallops, clams, cod, haddock, and pollack fish
President: Grant Stonehouse
Marketing Director: John Andrews
Operations Manager: Grant Stonehouse
Year Founded: 1991
Estimated Sales: $32 Million
Number Employees: 82
Type of Packaging: Bulk
Brands:
Davis Strait Fisheries Ltd

3409 Davis Street Fish Market
501 Davis Street
Evanston, IL 60201
847-869-3474
Fax: 847-869-6435 davisstreetfish@gmail.com
Seafood
Contact: Ed Huelke
ehuelke@cleanplate.net
Manager: Ed Heulke
Estimated Sales: $3-5 Million
Number Employees: 50-99

3410 Davisco Foods International
11000 W 78th St # 210
Eden Prairie, MN 55344-8012
952-914-0400
Fax: 952-914-0887 800-757-7611
polly@daviscofoods.com www.daviscofoods.com
Whey proteins
Manager: Dana Bellanger
CFO: Jim Ward
VP Finance/Business Administration: John Velgersdyk
Director Quality Assurance: Matt Davis
VP Sales/Marketing/Business Development: Pauline Olson
Contact: Maher Ahmad
maher.ahmad@daviscofoods.com
General Manager: Martin Davis
Estimated Sales: $10-20 000,000
Number Employees: 20-49

3411 Dawes Hill Honey Company
12 S State St
Po Box 429
Nunda, NY 14517
585-468-2535
Fax: 585-468-5995 888-800-8075
info@onceagainnutbutter.com
www.onceagainnutbutter.com
Honey, royal jelly and fruit honey cream spread
Owner: Sandi Alexander
Comptroller: Sandra Alexander
Purchasing Agent: Lloyd Kirwan
Estimated Sales: $10-20 Million
Number Employees: 10-19
Square Footage: 40000
Parent Co: Once Again Nut Butter
Type of Packaging: Consumer, Private Label, Bulk
Brands:
Bee Supreme

3412 Dawn Food Products, Inc
3333 Sargent Rd
Jackson, MI 49201
517-789-4400
800-248-1144
questions@dawnfoods.com www.dawnfoods.com
Doughnut, cake, brownie and other dry mixes, icings and fillings, frozen products.
Chief Executive Officer: Carrie Jones-Barber
Chief Financial Officer: Karl Brown
Chief Legal Officer & Secretary: Scott Thayer
Chief Human Resources Officer: Jason Lioy
Year Founded: 1929
Estimated Sales: Over $1 Billion
Number Employees: 4,000
Square Footage: 95000
Type of Packaging: Consumer, Food Service
Other Locations:
Manufacturing Facilities
Atlanta GA
Baltimore MD
Boston MA
Buffalo NY
Chicago IL
Cleveland OH
Columbus OH
Dallas TX
Denver CO
Las Vegas NV
Little Rock AK
Los Angeles CA
Seattle WA
Brands:
Weight Watchers® Baked Goods
Velvetop™
But-R-Creme™

3413 Dawn's Foods
1530 LaDawn Dr
Portage, WI 53901-8823
608-742-2494
Fax: 608-742-1806 800-993-2967
rrehlinger@dawnsfoods.com
www.dawnsfoodsinc.com
Potato salad, coleslaw, homestyle salads, pasta salads, dips and spreads, quiche, puddings and desserts
President: Greg Drewsen
VP Quality, Food Safety, Training: Dan Waite
VP Sales: Ron Rehlinger
Estimated Sales: $20-50 Million
Number Employees: 20-49
Brands:
Dawn's Foods

3414 Day Foods Company
1901 Durand Ave
Racine, WI 53403
262-634-2164
Fax: 262-634-9929
Frozen pizzas
Manager: Brian Ehmcke
Plant Manager: Ron Harter
Estimated Sales: $10-20 Million
Number Employees: 10-19
Parent Co: Pride of Italy

3415 Day Spring Enterprises
45 Benbro Dr
Cheektowaga, NY 14225-4805
716-685-4340
Fax: 716-685-0810 800-879-7677
www.rainbowpops.com
Hard candy and lollypops; also, seasonal items available

President: Linda Zangerie
Sales Manager: Jeff Baran
Plant Manager: George Sparks
Estimated Sales: $50,000
Number Employees: 1
Square Footage: 32000
Type of Packaging: Consumer, Food Service, Private Label, Bulk
Brands:
   Rainbow Pops

3416 Day-Lee Foods, Inc.
10350 Heritage Park Dr
Suite 111
Santa Fe Springs, CA 90670
                    562-903-3020
       Fax: 562-906-5080 800-329-5331
          info@day-lee.com www.day-lee.com
Meats and poultry
President/CEO: Sumio Somura
Vice President: Kiyoshi Zobe
Marketing: Dan Van Gompel
VP Finance: Misako Ipavec
Contact: Daniel Aigner
daniel.aigner@shopgate.com
General Manager: Yasushi Yokozeki
Director Manufacturing: Toshiyuki Iho
Square Footage: 286240
Parent Co: Nippon Meat Packers
Other Locations:
   Hayward CA
   Santa Fe Springs CA
Brands:
   Day-Lee Foods

3417 Daybreak Coffee Roasters
2377 Main St # C
Glastonbury, CT 06033-4063
                    860-657-4466
       Fax: 860-633-6614 800-882-5282
         freshcoffee@daybreakcoffee.com
              www.daybreakcoffee.com
Coffee
President: Thomas Clarke
Vice President: Linda Kenneman
admin@daybreakcoffee.com
Sales: Cathy Reynolds
Estimated Sales: $500,000-$1,000,000
Number Employees: 10-19
Brands:
   Daybreak

3418 Daybreak Foods Inc
609 6th St NE
Long Prairie, MN 56347-1003
                    320-732-2966
       Fax: 320-732-3690 www.daybreakfoods.com
Egg products
President: Robert Rehm
CEO: Brent Rehm
Finance Manager: Tom Bandevencer
Manager: Tom Vandeventer
tom@daybreakfoods.com
Plant Manager: Steven Masia
Estimated Sales: $10,000,000
Number Employees: 50-99
Type of Packaging: Bulk
Brands:
   Daybreak Foods

3419 Daybrook Fisheries
365 Canal Place
Suite 2300
New Orleans, LA 70130
                    504-561-6163
       Fax: 504-636-4993 www.daybrook.com
Menhaden fishmeal and fish oil.
President: Gregory Holt
CFO: Stephen Morganstern
Executive Vice President: W. Borden Wallace
Senior Vice President, Operations: Lee Alexander
Year Founded: 1898
Estimated Sales: $324.4 Million
Number Employees: 400
Parent Co: Oceana Group
Type of Packaging: Bulk

3420 Daymar Select Fine Coffees
460 Cypress Ln # B
El Cajon, CA 92020-1647
                    619-444-1155
       Fax: 619-444-1985 800-466-7590
       info@daymarcoffee.com www.daymarcoffee.com

Chocolates, syrups, teas and coffees including flavored, organic, roast, ground, whole beans and instant
President: Roy Gallegos
roy@daymarcoffee.com
Secretary: Diana Gallegos
Estimated Sales: $5-10 Million
Number Employees: 10-19
Type of Packaging: Consumer, Food Service, Private Label, Bulk
Brands:
   Cafe El Marino

3421 Dayton Nut Specialties
45 N Pioneer Bld
Springboro, OH 45066
                    937-743-4377
              candyandnutstore.com
Confectionery and nuts
President: Stanley Maschino
Estimated Sales: $2,000,000
Number Employees: 46
Number of Brands: 3
Type of Packaging: Private Label
Brands:
   Dayton Nut Specialties
   Friesinger's Fine Chocolates
   Candy Farm

3422 Dazbog Coffee Co
1090 Yuma St
Denver, CO 80204-3838
                    303-892-9999
       Fax: 303-893-9999 coffee@dazbog.com
                www.dazbog.com
Manufacturer of coffee and tea.
Co-Founder: Anatoly Yuffa
Co-Founder: Leonid Yuffa
coffee@dazbog.com
Number Employees: 10-19

3423 De Boles Nutritional Foods
104 N Common St
Shreveport, LA 71101-2614
                    318-222-6857
              Fax: 318-221-7815
Organic and all natural pastas
President: William Robertson
Vice President: Pete Holcombe
Plant Manager: Monty Phares
Estimated Sales: Under $500,000
Number Employees: 20-49
Parent Co: DeBoles Nutritional Foods

3424 De Bruyn Produce Company
709 NW 12th Ter
Ponpano Beach, FL 33069-2041
                    954-788-6707
       Fax: 954-788-6340 800-733-9177
Onions an carrots
President: Margret DeBruyn
CEO: Mike Diaz
EVP: Ralph Diaz
Sales/Marketing: Betty Aquire
Operations Manager: Kevin Hubbard
Type of Packaging: Consumer, Food Service
Other Locations:
   Cooling And Manufacturing Plant
      Byron Center MI
   Carrot Manufacturing Plant
      Weslaco TX
   Onion Manufacturing Plant
      Farmersville TX
   Vegetable Cooling Plant
      Tifton GA
   Spanish Onion Manufacturing
      Ontario OR
Brands:
   Citation
   Debco
   Gold Rim
   Gulf

3425 De Coty Coffee Co
1920 Austin St
San Angelo, TX 76903-8704
                    325-655-5607
       Fax: 325-655-6837 800-588-8001
       eric@decoty.com www.decoty.com
Importer, Roaster, & Distributor of coffe. Manufacturer of coffee, tea, spices & seasonings.

CEO/President: Michael Agan
agan@decoy.com
Sales/Marketing: Bryan Baker
Operations: Ronnie Wallace
Production Manager: Eric Fischer
Purchasing: Teresa Rocha
Estimated Sales: $12 Million
Number Employees: 50-99
Square Footage: 50000
Type of Packaging: Food Service, Private Label, Bulk

3426 De Fluri's Fine Chocolate
130 N Queen St
Martinsburg, WV 25401-3312
                    304-264-3698
       Fax: 304-264-3698 sales@defluris.com
Truffles, nuts, crunches and chews, creams
President/Owner: Brenda Casabona
sales@defluris.com
Estimated Sales: Less Than $500,000
Number Employees: 1-4

3427 De Iorio's Foods Inc
2200 Bleecker St
Utica, NY 13501-1739
                    315-732-7612
       Fax: 315-732-7621 800-649-7612
              www.deiorios.com
Manufacturer of dough products. Products include dough balls, flats, shells, self rise, breads and sub rolls, breadsticks, and more.
Chairman & CEO: Robert Ragusa
VP, Business Development: Robert Horth
Manager: Fabio Faro
ffaro@deiorios.com
Manager: Donald King
Estimated Sales: $5-10,000,000
Number Employees: 100-249
Number of Brands: 1
Number of Products: 87
Type of Packaging: Consumer, Food Service, Private Label
Other Locations:
   De-Iorio's Frozen Dough
      Utica NY
Brands:
   DeIorio's

3428 De Iorios Frozen Dough Co Inc
2200 Bleecker St
Utica, NY 13501-1739
                    315-724-2401
       Fax: 315-732-7621 800-649-7612
              www.deiorios.com
Frozen dough
President & CEO: Robert J. Ragusa
bhorth@deiorios.com
VP, Business Development: Robert Horth
Sales Exec: Bob Horth
Number Employees: 100-249

3429 De Maria's Seafood
12544 Warwick Blvd
Newport News, VA 23606-2644
                    757-930-3474
              Fax: 757-930-4847
Catfish, cod, flounder, haddock, halibut, mackerel, perch, salmon, shad, tuna, monkfish fillets, blue crabmeat, clams, shrimp
Owner: John DE Maria
oyster1@cox.net
Estimated Sales: $500,000-$1,000,000
Number Employees: 5-9
Brands:
   Demaria Seafood

3430 De Met's Candy Co
30 Buxton Farm Rd
Stamford, CT 06905-1224
                    203-329-4545
       Fax: 203-329-4555 800-872-7622
              www.demetscandy.com
Popcorn snacks
President/CEO: Hendrick Hartong
CEO: David Clarke
CFO: Joanne Prier
CEO: David Clarke
Estimated Sales: $3-5 Million
Number Employees: 5-9
Type of Packaging: Consumer
Brands:
   Fiddle Faddle

Food Manufacturers / A-Z

Golden Gourmet Nuts
Poppycock

3431 De Nigris
31 Vreeland Ave
Totowa, NJ 07512
973-837-6791
Fax: 973-837-6794
Tomato sauce, bruschetta toppings, olive oil, vinegars
CEO Partner: Helena Dane

3432 De Souza's
4092 W Ramsey St
Banning, CA 92220-3518
951-849-5172
Fax: 951-849-1348 800-373-5171
info@desouzas.com www.desouzas.com
Solar-dried sea salt; also, chlorophyll liquid, tablets and capsules
President/CEO: Rosalie DeSouza
VP Operations: K Hill
Estimated Sales: $1-2.5 Million
Number Employees: 1-4
Square Footage: 32000
Type of Packaging: Private Label

3433 DeBeukelaer Cookie Co
228 Industrial Dr N
PO Box 1697
Madison, MS 39110-9481
601-856-7454
Fax: 601-856-1462 www.pirouline.com
Cookies
Founder: Peter DeBeukelaer
Founder: Mireilla DeBeukelaer
SVP Sales: Tim Sullivan
Human Resources Manager: Ana Robinson
Estimated Sales: $22 Million
Number Employees: 100-249
Square Footage: 100000
Brands:
 De Beukelaer

3434 DeBeukelaer Corp
P.O. Box 456
Madison, MS 39130
601-856-7454
swirlmaster@pirouline.com
Cookies
Founder: Peter De Beukelaer
Senior VP of Sales: Tim Sullivan
Year Founded: 1984
Estimated Sales: $23273178
Number Employees: 100
Type of Packaging: Food Service, Private Label

3435 DeLallo Foods
1 DeLallo Way
Mount Pleasant, PA 15666
877-355-2556
www.delallo.com
Organic pasta, sauces and olive oil
VP: Anthony DiPietro
Operations: Jeff Latimer

3436 DeLallo Italian Foods
6390 Route 30
Jeannette, PA 15644-3193
724-523-6577
Fax: 724-853-0141 800-433-9100
www.delallo.com
Olives, antipasti, sauces, pasta, oils & vinegars
Owner: Francis DeLallo
VP Marketing: Robert Lubic
Type of Packaging: Consumer

3437 DeLima Coffee
7546 Morgan Rd
Liverpool, NY 13090
315-457-3725
Fax: 315-457-3730 800-962-8864
info@delimacoffee.com www.delimacoffee.com
Coffee
Principle: Paul Lima
President: Michael Garlick
CFO: Steve Zaremba
Vice President Sales: Donald Hughes
dhughes@delimacoffee.com
VP Human Resources: Peter Sansone
Purchasing Agent: Lisa Priest
Type of Packaging: Consumer, Food Service

3438 DeLuscious Cookies
829 N Highland Ave
Los Angeles, CA 90038
323-460-2370
Fax: 323-460-6301 info@delusciouscookies.com
www.delusciouscookies.com
Gourmet cookies
Owner: Lydia Shayne
Year Founded: 2002
Number of Brands: 1
Number of Products: 11
Type of Packaging: Consumer
Brands:
 DELUSCIOUS

3439 (HQ)DeMedici Imports
One Atalanta Plaza
Elizabeth, NJ 07206
908-372-0965
Fax: 908-372-0960 info@demedici.com
www.demedici.com
Gourmet specialty foods
President: Paul Farber
Contact: Steven Kaufman
sbk@demedici.com
Operations: Marilyn O'Daniels
Estimated Sales: $5-10 Million
Number Employees: 5-9
Type of Packaging: Private Label
Brands:
 Colonna

3440 Dean & De Luca Inc
383 Kalaimoku St
Honolulu, HI 96815
808-729-9720
customercare@deandeluca.com
www.deandeluca.com
Coffee beans
Estimated Sales: $80,000,000
Brands:
 Dean & Deluca

3441 Dean Distributors, Inc.
1350 Bayshore Highway
Suite 400
Burlingame, CA 94010
800-792-0816
corporate@deandistributors.com
www.deandistributors.com
Specialty food products including sauces, kosher and Mexican soups and gravy bases, tenderizers and aid, consomme, smoke and cheese flavors, syrups, extracts and nutritional supplements
President: Ralph Schulz
Controller: Stacey Rusley
VP: Mark Schulz
Director Sales/Marketing: Mark Schulz
Contact: David Mojarro
dmojarro@deandistributors.com
Estimated Sales: $15 Million
Number Employees: 5-9
Square Footage: 140000
Parent Co: Dean Distributors
Type of Packaging: Food Service
Brands:
 Bernard Fine Foods
 Dean
 Flavor-Glow

3442 (HQ)Dean Foods Co.
2711 N. Haskell Ave.
Suite 3400
Dallas, TX 75204
800-395-7004
deanfoods@casupport.com www.deanfoods.com
Milk, ice cream, cultured dairy products, juices, teas and bottled water.
President/CEO: Eric Beringause
Interim CFO/SVP, Finance & Strategy: Gary Rahlfs
SVP/General Counsel: Kristy Waterman
SVP/Chief Commercial Officer: Thomas Murray
Year Founded: 1925
Estimated Sales: $7.7 Billion
Number Employees: 16,000+
Number of Brands: 35
Type of Packaging: Food Service, Private Label
Brands:
 Alta Dena
 Barber's®
 Berkeley Farms
 Broughton®
 Brown's Dairy®
 Country Fresh™
 Creamland
 Dairy Pure®
 Dean's™
 Friendly's®
 Fruit Rush™
 Gandy's
 Garelick Farms®
 Hygeia®
 Jilbert
 Land O Lakes®
 Lehigh Valley®
 Mayfield Creamery™
 Mayfield®
 McArthur Dairy®
 Meadow Brook®
 Meadow Gold®
 Model Dairy
 Oak Farms Dairy
 Orchard Pure™
 PET®
 Price's
 Purity
 Ready Leaf
 Reiter Dairy™
 Swiss Premium®
 T.G. Lee
 TruMoo
 Tuscan™
 Uncle Matt's®

3443 Dean Sausage Co Inc
3750 Pleasant Valley Rd
P.O. Drawer 750
Attalla, AL 35954-5606
256-538-6082
Fax: 256-538-2584 800-228-0704
deansausage@deansausage.com
www.deansausage.com
Sausage
President/Treasurer: Marsue Lancaster
Secretary: Jane Moore
Vice President: Garry Shirley
Marketing Director: Hugh Miller
Estimated Sales: $10-20 Million
Number Employees: 100-249
Square Footage: 75000
Type of Packaging: Consumer, Food Service, Private Label
Brands:
 Dean's Country
 Kentucky Farm

3444 Deanna's Gluten Free Baking Co.
2250 S Escondido Blvd
Suite 110
Escondido, CA 92025
760-432-6100
info@deannasgf.com
deannasglutenfree.com
Gluten free baked goods

3445 Dear North
9301 Glacier Hwy
Suite 200
Juneau, AK 99801-9380
907-789-8500
Fax: 907-789-7896
customercervice@dearnorth.com
dearnorth.com
Smoked seafood; pft,; dried salmon snacks.
Director of Marketing: Ruth Banaszak
Vice President of Sales: Timothy Meskill
Year Founded: 2016
Parent Co: Huna Totem Corperation
Type of Packaging: Private Label

3446 Dearborn Sausage Co Inc
2450 Wyoming St
Dearborn, MI 48120-1518
313-842-2375
Fax: 313-842-2640 866-900-4426
info@dearbornbrand.com
www.dearbornsausage.com
Sausage
Chief Executive Officer: Donald Kosch
Chief Financial Officer: Elizabeth Cooley
Vice President: Michael Kosch
Manager: Mary Kral
mkral45@comcast.net
Estimated Sales: $6,845,000
Number Employees: 50-99
Number of Brands: 1
Brands:
 Dearborn Sausage

Food Manufacturers / A-Z

3447 Deaver Vineyards
12455 Steiner Rd
Plymouth, CA 95669-9504
209-245-4099
Fax: 209-245-4097
deaverwinery@deavervineyard.com
www.deavervineyards.com
Wines
President/Marketing Manager: Ken Deaver
Estimated Sales: $2.5-5,000,000
Number Employees: 5-9
Number of Brands: 19
Number of Products: 1
Type of Packaging: Private Label
Brands:
  19
  Deaver Vineyards Wine

3448 Debbie D's Jerky & Sausage
2210 Main Ave N
Tillamook, OR 97141-7724
503-842-2622
debbie@debbiedssausage.com
www.debbiedssausage.com
Smoked beef jerky and sausage
President: Debbie Downie
debbie.downie@oregoncoast.com
Estimated Sales: Less Than $500,000
Number Employees: 1-4
Type of Packaging: Consumer, Bulk
Brands:
  Debbie D'S

3449 Debel Food Products
2 Papetti Plz
Elizabeth, NJ 07206-1421
908-351-0330
Fax: 908-351-0334   800-421-3447
info@debelfoods.com   www.debelfoods.com
Egg products
President: Elliott Gibber
Manager: John Mckay
jmckay@debelfoods.com
Estimated Sales: $48.3 Million
Number Employees: 50-99
Number of Brands: 2
Square Footage: 75000
Brands:
  Just Whites
  Scramblettes

3450 Deborah's Kitchen Inc.
147 King Street
Suite 406
Littleton, MA 01460
617-216-9908
Fax: 413-552-3259   deborah@deborahskitchen.com
www.deborahskitchen.com
All natural, low-sugar spreadable fruit and relish.
Owner: Deborah Taylore
beborah@deborahskitchen.com
Type of Packaging: Food Service, Private Label

3451 Debragga & Spitler
65-77 Amity St
Jersey City, NJ 07304-3509
info@debragga.com
www.debragga.com
Prime cuts of beef, lamb and pork; wholesaler/distributor of further processed beef, veal, lamb and pork.
President & CEO: Marc John Sarrazin
Year Founded: 1920
Estimated Sales: $20-50 Million
Number Employees: 50-99
Number of Brands: 1
Type of Packaging: Food Service, Bulk
Brands:
  Natural Certified Angus Beef

3452 Debrand Chocolatier
10105 Auburn Park Dr
Fort Wayne, IN 46825-2388
260-969-8333
Fax: 260-969-8334   customerservice@debrand.com
www.debrand.com
Chocolate bars, chocolate truffles, full-line chocolate, other chocolate, toffee.
Owner: Timothy Beere
tbeere@debrand.com
Marketing: Cathy Brand-Beere
Number Employees: 20-49

3453 Deca & Otto Farms
7953 NW 21st Street
Miami, FL 33122
305-629-9335
www.decaotto.com
Buffalo milk yogurts and cheeses
President: Alberto Sasson

3454 Decadence Cheese Cakes
2591 Legacy Way
Grand Junction, CO 81503
970-256-4688
www.decadencecheesecakes.com
Cheese cake
Contact: Lee Mathis
decadencecheesecakes@mindspring.com

3455 Decadent Desserts
831 10th Ave SW
Calgary, AB T2R 0B4
Canada
403-245-5535
Cakes including cheese and wedding; also, pies and cookies
President: Pamela Fortier
Estimated Sales: B
Number Employees: 6
Type of Packaging: Consumer, Food Service

3456 Decas Cranberry Sales Inc
4 Old Forge Way # 1
Carver, MA 02330-1765
508-866-8506
Fax: 508-866-9020   800-649-9811
www.decascranberry.com
All-natural cranberry and fruit products
President/CEO: John Decas
CEO: Charles B Dillon
cdillon@decascranberry.com
VP Sales: Nick Decas
Estimated Sales: $5-10 000,000
Number Employees: 250-499

3457 Decatur Dairy
W1668 Hwy F
Brodhead, WI 53520-9505
608-897-8661
Fax: 608-897-4587   www.decaturdairy.com
Brick, muenster, farmer cheese, pavarti
President: Steven Stettler
Estimated Sales: $500,000-$1,000,000
Number Employees: 10-19
Brands:
  Decatur Dairy

3458 Decker Farms Inc
12475 SW River Rd
Hillsboro, OR 97123-9314
503-628-1532
Fax: 503-628-3696   info@deckerfarm.com
www.deckerfarm.com
Frozen fruits including red and black raspberries and strawberries; also, frozen filberts and hazelnuts
Owner: Priscilla Decker
deckerfarms@frontier.net
Number Employees: 5-9
Type of Packaging: Bulk
Brands:
  Decker Farms Finest

3459 Decker Food Company
3200 W Kingsley Road
Garland, TX 75041-2204
972-278-6192
Fax: 972-278-1983
Meat products
President/CEO: R Belsito
Brand Manager: Mike Rook
Vice President: Dennis Swingle
Sales Director: Denny Swingle
VP Marketing/Sales: Paul Wood
Chief Engineer: Jerry Rhubert
Plant Manager: John Vincent
Estimated Sales: $10-20 Million
Number Employees: 5-9
Parent Co: ConAgra Foods
Type of Packaging: Private Label

3460 Decko Products Inc
2105 Superior St
Sandusky, OH 44870-1891
419-626-5757
Fax: 419-626-3135   800-537-6143
shumphrey@decko.com   www.decko.com
Edible cake and candy decorations and packaged rings, gels
President: F William Niggemyer
Marketing Director: Sara Humphrey
Estimated Sales: $10 Million
Number Employees: 50-99
Square Footage: 105000
Type of Packaging: Private Label
Brands:
  Royal Icing Decoration

3461 Deconna Ice Cream
6300 W Highway 318
Reddick, FL 32686-2334
352-591-1530
Fax: 352-591-4418   800-824-8254
sales@deconna.com   www.deconna.com
Ice cream
President: Vince Deconna
v.conna@deconna.com
Estimated Sales: $36,000,000
Number Employees: 50-99
Number of Brands: 1
Type of Packaging: Bulk
Brands:
  Deconna

3462 DeeBee's Organics
6-798 Fairview Rd
Victoria, BC V9A 5V1
Canada
778-265-8327
Fax: 778-433-8327   855-515-8327
www.deebeesorganics.com
Organic fruit popsicles
Founder: Dr. Dionne Baker

3463 Deen Meat & Cooked Foods
813 E Northside Dr
PO Box 4155
Fort Worth, TX 76102-1017
817-335-2257
Fax: 817-338-9256   800-333-3953
www.deenmeat.com
Meat
President: Danny Deen
danny77@deenmeat.com
VP: Craig Deen
VP: Matthew Deen
Business Development Manager: Steve Dumas
Quality Assurance/ R&D: Marc de Plante
Director of Partner Development: Pat Harrington
VP Operations: Joe Cholopisa
VP, Purchase: Mike Pritchard
Number Employees: 100-249
Brands:
  Deen
  Double L

3464 Deep Creek Custom Packing
Mile 137 Sterling Highway
PO Box 39752
Ninilchik, AK 99639
907-567-3395
Fax: 907-567-3579   800-764-0078
dccp@ptialaska.net
Alaska smoked salmon, halibut, canned giftpacks, custom processing and gourmet seafood
CEO: Jeff Berger
Plant Manager: Chris Baobo
Estimated Sales: $7 Million
Number Employees: 20-49
Square Footage: 24000

3465 Deep Foods Inc
1090 Springfield Rd
Suite 1
Union, NJ 07083-8147
908-810-7500
Fax: 908-810-8482   www.deepfoods.com
Indian foods such as snacks, frozen meals, ice creams and others.
Vice President: Pravin Amin
deepfoods@aol.com
VP Marketing: Archit Amin
Sales Director: Chintam Trivedi
Estimated Sales: $5-10 Million
Number Employees: 50-99
Square Footage: 120000
Type of Packaging: Consumer, Food Service, Bulk
Other Locations:
  Deep Foods
    Mississagua, CANADA ON
Brands:
  Babu's Pocket Sandwiches

Food Manufacturers / A-Z

Bansi
Deep
Deep Dairy
Gujarati
Hot Mix
Hot Wok
Mirch Masala
Reena's
Tandoor Chef
Udupi

3466 Deep River Snacks
PO Box 1127
Deep River, CT 06417
860-434-7347
Fax: 860-434-7512 info@deepriversnacks.com
www.deepriversnacks.com
Chips and popcorn
President: James Goldberg
info@deepriversnacks.com
Estimated Sales: $2 Million
Number Employees: 5-9
Brands:
Deep River Snacks
Honchos

3467 Deep Valley
New York, NY
917-673-5121
Fax: 929-250-2856 www.deepvalleycoffee.com
Organic coffee
Number of Brands: 1
Number of Products: 2
Type of Packaging: Consumer
Brands:
DEEP VALLEY

3468 Deer Creek Honey Farms LTD
551 E High St
London, OH 43140-9521
740-852-0899
Fax: 740-852-4530 www.deercreekhoney.com
Kosher certified honey and molasses
President: Chris Dunham
chris@deercreekhoney.com
Estimated Sales: $650,000
Number Employees: 5-9
Square Footage: 44000
Type of Packaging: Consumer, Food Service, Private Label, Bulk
Brands:
Deer Creek

3469 Deer Park Spring Water Co
925 Cavalier Blvd # D
Chesapeake, VA 23323-1549
757-485-3200
Fax: 757-487-4970 800-832-0271
deerparkwater.com
Bottled spring and distilled water
CFO: Kim Jefferies
General Manager: Michael Difrancesco
Plant Manager: Edgar Gaskins
Estimated Sales: $3-5 Million
Number Employees: 20-49
Square Footage: 146000
Type of Packaging: Consumer, Food Service
Brands:
A&D Water Care
Culligan
Diamond Springs
H2o To Go
Hydrologix
Miller's
The Water Fountain
Water & Health
Water Fountain of Edenton
Yoder Dairies

3470 Deerfield Bakery
201 N Buffalo Grove Rd
Buffalo Grove, IL 60089-1748
847-520-0068
Fax: 847-520-0135 sheila@deerfieldbakery.com
www.deerfieldsbakery.com
Cakes and full service bakery
Owner: Kurt Schmitt
Contact: Paula Schmitt
paula@bodnardesign.com
Estimated Sales: Less than $500,000
Number Employees: 100-249
Type of Packaging: Private Label
Brands:
Deerfield

3471 (HQ)Deerland Probiotics & Enzymes
3800 Cobb International Blvd.
Kennesaw, GA 30152
Fax: 770-919-1194 800-697-8179
www.deerland.com
Manufacturer and exporter of digestive enzymes and nutritional supplements
Chief Executive Officer: Scott Ravech
VP, Science & Technology: John Deaton
Director, Innovation & Education: John Davidson
Director, Quality Assurance & Control: Maggie Leroux
VP, Marketing & Strategy: Sam Michini
Estimated Sales: $20-50 Million
Number Employees: 50-99
Type of Packaging: Private Label, Bulk
Brands:
Eds
Nozimes

3472 Deerland Probiotics & Enzymes
15366 US Highway 160
Forsyth, MO 65653-8107
800-825-8545
www.deerland.com
Manufacturer and exporter of digestive enzymes and nutritional supplements
Type of Packaging: Private Label, Bulk

3473 (HQ)Deerwood Rice & Grain Procng
21926 County Road 10
Deerwood, MN 56444-8486
218-534-3762
Fax: 218-534-3802
Wild rice
President: Dan Mohs
Estimated Sales: $1.20 Million
Number Employees: 20-49
Square Footage: 117000
Type of Packaging: Consumer, Bulk

3474 Dehydrates Inc
1251 Peninsula Blvd
Hewlett, NY 11557-1223
516-295-3700
Fax: 516-295-3777 800-983-4443
dehydrates123@hotmail.com
www.dehydratesinc.com
Dehydrated fruits, vegetables and herbs
President: Steven Reich
Marketing: Gail Whiteford
Public Relations: Lori Zahler
Estimated Sales: $1.5 Million
Number Employees: 1-4
Square Footage: 80000
Type of Packaging: Food Service, Private Label, Bulk
Brands:
Dehydrates

3475 Dei Fratelli
411 Lemoyne Road
Toledo, OH 43619
416-693-0531
Fax: 419-693-0744 800-837-1631
info@hirzel.com www.deifratelli.com
Salsas, tomatoes, tomato juice, pasta sauces
President: Joe Hirzel
Research & Development: Karl Hirzel
Retail Sales: Herb Milem
Human Resources: Sara Monhollen
Square Footage: 250000
Type of Packaging: Consumer

3476 Deko International Company
4283 Shoreline Dr
Earth City, MO 63045-1209
314-298-0910
Fax: 314-298-0081 dekointl@aol.com
www.dekointl.com
Distributor of products and ingredients for the food service industry.
President/CEO: Peter Dekointl
Vice President: Nung Kuo
Sales Coordinator: Jennifer Suen
Customer Service: Johnny Liu
Vice President of Operations: Art Chung
Purchasing Manager: Sarah Zhang
Number Employees: 10-19
Type of Packaging: Food Service
Other Locations:
Rancho Cucamonga CA
Clifton NJ
Norcross GA

3477 Del Mar Food Products Corp
1720 Beach Rd
P.O. Box 891
Watsonville, CA 95077
831-722-3516
Fax: 831-722-7690 www.delmarfoods.com
Apricots, blackberries, peaches, strawberries, brussel sprouts, red bell peppers and spinach
President: P.J. Mecozzi
Vice President, Operations: Lee Haskin
Estimated Sales: $50-99 Million
Number Employees: 500
Number of Brands: 1
Square Footage: 53408
Brands:
Del Mar

3478 Del Monte Foods Inc.
3003 Oak Rd.
Walnut Creek, CA 94598
www.delmonte.com
Canned fruits and vegetables. Not affiliated with Del Monte Fresh Produce.
President & CEO: Gregory Longstreet
CFO: Gene Allen
General Counsel/Chief Compliance Officer: William Sawyers
Chief Marketing Officer: Bibie Wu
Contact: Gerald Abele
gerald.abele@delmontefoods.com
Year Founded: 1886
Estimated Sales: $3.8 Billion
Number Employees: 7,800
Number of Brands: 7
Parent Co: Del Monte Pacific, Ltd.
Type of Packaging: Consumer, Food Service, Private Label
Other Locations:
Del Monte Foods
Cambria WI
Brands:
Del Monte®
Contadina®
College Inn®
S&W®
Fruit & Chia™
Fruit & Oats™
Fruit Refreshers®

3479 (HQ)Del Monte Fresh Produce Inc.
PO Box 149222
Coral Gables, FL 33114-9222
305-520-8400
Fax: 305-567-0320 800-950-3683
contact-us-executive-office@freshdelmonte.com
www.freshdelmonte.com
Fresh and fresh-cut fruit and vegetables.
President/COO: Youssef Zakharia
Chairman/CEO: Mohammad Abu-Ghazaleh
mabughazaleh@freshdelmonte.com
Senior VP/CFO: Eduardo Bezerra
Senior VP/General Counsel/Secretary: Marlene Gordon
Senior VP, North America Operations: Annunciata Cerioli
Year Founded: 1886
Estimated Sales: $3.9 Billion
Number Employees: 45,000
Number of Brands: 11
Type of Packaging: Consumer, Food Service
Other Locations:
Del Monte Fresh Plant
Forest Park GA
Del Monte Fresh Plant
Kankakee IL
Del Monte Fresh Plant
Jessup MD
Del Monte Fresh Plant
Kansas City MO
Del Monte Fresh Plant
Bloomfield NJ
Del Monte Fresh Plant
Mappsville VA
Del Monte Fresh Plant
Canton MA
Del Monte Fresh Plant
Mulberry FL
Del Monte Fresh Plant
Richmond CA
Del Monte Fresh Plant
Eddystone PA
Del Monte Fresh Plant

Food Manufacturers / A-Z

Chicago IL
Del Monte Fresh Plant
Plant City FL
Del Monte Fresh Plant
Columbus OH
Brands:
Del Monte Fresh®
Mann's®
Rosy®
Fruitini
Golden Ripe®
Just Juice
Mission®
MAG® Melon
UTC®
National Poultry Company
De L'Ora®

3480 Del Rey Packing
5287 S Del Rey Ave
P.O. Box 160
Del Rey, CA 93616

559-888-2031
Fax: 559-888-2715
gchooljian@delreypacking.com
www.delreypacking.com

Manufacturer and exporter of raisins.
President: Gerald Chooljian
gchooljian@delreypacking.com
Vice President: Kathy Merlo
Estimated Sales: $20-50 Million
Number Employees: 50-99
Number of Brands: 2
Type of Packaging: Consumer, Food Service, Private Label, Bulk
Brands:
Deluxe
Regent

3481 Del Rio Nut Company
15391 Vinewood Circle
P.O. Box 396
Livingston, CA 95334

209-394-7945
Fax: 209-394-7955 david@delrionut.com
www.delrionut.com

Natural almonds
President/ Marketing Director: David Arakelian
Contact: Barret Arakelian
arakelianbarret@delrionut.com
Operations Manager: Mona Menezes
Estimated Sales: $3-5 Million
Number Employees: 20-49
Square Footage: 36000
Type of Packaging: Consumer, Food Service, Private Label, Bulk
Brands:
Del Rio

3482 Del's Lemonade & Refreshments
1260 Oaklawn Ave
Cranston, RI 02920-2628

401-463-6190
Fax: 401-463-7931 dels@dels.com
www.dels.com

Lemonade
Owner: Bruce DE Lucia
dels@dels.com
VP: Joe Padula
Estimated Sales: $3 Million
Number Employees: 20-49
Brands:
Del's
Del's Italian Ices
Del's Lemonade

3483 Del's Pastry
344 Bering Avenue
Toronto, ON M8Z 3A7
Canada

416-231-4383
Fax: 416-231-3254 800-461-0663
dels@delspastry.com www.delspastry.com

Muffins, turnovers, pies, tea biscuits, cakes and danish
President: Benno Mattes
Vice President: Tom Mattes
Estimated Sales: $9 Million
Number Employees: 170

3484 Del's Seaway Shrimp & Oyster Company
PO Box 648
Biloxi, MS 39533-0648

228-432-2604
Fax: 228-432-8919

Frozen shrimp
President: George Higginbotham
Executive VP: Paul Delcambre
Estimated Sales: $10-20,000,000
Number Employees: 50-99
Type of Packaging: Consumer, Food Service
Brands:
Seaway

3485 DelGrosso Foods
Old Route 220
Tipton, PA 16684

814-684-5880
Fax: 814-684-3943 800-521-5880
info@delgrossos.com www.delgrossos.com

Spaghetti sauce, pizza sauce, salsa, sloppy joe sauce and meatballs.
President: James DelGrosso
VP Global Sales/Marketing: Michael DelGrosso
VP Operations: Joseph DelGrosso
Number Employees: 68
Square Footage: 270000
Type of Packaging: Consumer

3486 DelGrosso Foods
632 Sauce Factory Dr
Tipton, PA 16684

814-684-5880
800-521-5880
info@delgrossosauce.com
www.delgrossofoods.com

Spaghetti sauces, salsas, and Italian-style meatballs
President: James DelGrosso
VP Global Sales & Marketing: Michael DelGrosso
Operations Director: James Mayall
Purchasing Director: Lisa Pier
Estimated Sales: $22 Million
Number Employees: 68
Square Footage: 135000

3487 Delallo's Italian Store
6390 State Route 30
Jeannette, PA 15644-3193

724-523-5000
Fax: 724-523-0981 info@DeLallo.com
www.delallo.com

Olives
Manager: Eric Baker
Manager: Chuck Glona
chuckg@delallo.com
Estimated Sales: $2.5-5 Million
Number Employees: 100-249
Brands:
Delallo

3488 Delancey Dessert Company
573 Grand St
New York, NY 10002-4381

914-393-5209
Fax: 914-574-5270 800-254-5254

Candy and confectionery
Owner: Zvia Levi
Estimated Sales: $1-2.5 Million
Number Employees: 1-4
Brands:
Delancey Dessert

3489 (HQ)Delano Growers Grape Products
32351 Bassett Ave
Delano, CA 93215-9699

661-725-3255
Fax: 661-725-0279

White grape juice concentrate
President: Ray Cox
ray@delanogrowers.com
R&D: Rick Lord
Sales: Ray Cox
Production: Rick Lord
Estimated Sales: $26.30 Million
Number Employees: 50-99
Type of Packaging: Bulk

3490 Delaviuda USA Inc
2100 Salzedo St
Suite 201
Coral Gables, FL 33134

786-599-9814
delaviuda.com

Confections
Marketing development Director: Alvaro Potente
apotente@Delaviuda.com
Year Founded: 1973
Brands:
El Almendro
Delaviuda

3491 Delaware Valley Fish Co
108 W Basin St
Norristown, PA 19401-3859

610-277-4900
Fax: 610-277-4051 www.dvfish.com

Farm raised shellfish, fish, and delicacies
Owner: Barry Kratchman
delvalfish@aol.com
Number Employees: 5-9

3492 Delectable Gourmet LLC
1095 Long Island Ave
Deer Park, NY 11729

631-957-1350
Fax: 631-957-1013 800-696-1350
jeremy@icbakers.com
www.worldsbestcranberries.com

Pesto, cranberry sauce, and gourmet cranberry juice
President: Ted Heim Sr
Estimated Sales: $20-50 Million
Number Employees: 50-99

3493 Delftree Corp
234 Union St
North Adams, MA 01247-3522

413-664-4907
Fax: 413-664-4908 800-243-3742

Gourmet foods and vegetables
Manager: Lori Garvey
selfstorage@delftree.com
VP: Steve Rich
Estimated Sales: $2.5-5,000,000
Number Employees: 10-19
Brands:
Delftree

3494 Delgrosso Foods Inc.
632 Sauce Factory Drive
Tipton, PA 16684

814-684-5880
Fax: 814-684-3943 800-521-5880
michaeld@delgrossofoods.com

Manufacturer and importer of traditional spaghetti sauce, pizza sauce, salsa, sloppy joe sauce, country garden spaghetti sauce and meatballs.
President: James Del Grosso
R&D: Sean Etters
Quality Control: Fredrick Del Grosso
Marketing: Michael Del Grosso
Sales Manager: Robert DelGrosso
Public Relations: Sean Albright
Manager: Joseph Del Grosso
Estimated Sales: $10-20 Million
Number Employees: 50-99
Square Footage: 315000
Type of Packaging: Consumer, Food Service
Brands:
Del Grosso

3495 Delia's Food Co
313 Hilton Pl
Cincinnati, OH 45219-2604

513-221-4322
Fax: 360-248-6677
www.daeliasbiscuitsforcheese.com

Crackers.
Site Manager: Maria Walley
Number Employees: 1-4

3496 Delicae Gourmet
1310 E Lake Dr
Tarpon Springs, FL 34688-8110

727-942-2502
Fax: 727-942-1837 800-942-2502
sales@delicaegourmet.com
www.delicaegourmet.com

Food Manufacturers / A-Z

Bread toppers, slow cooker meals, spice rubs, mustards, relishes, chutneys, jams, jellies, spices, infused oils and vinegars.
Owner/CEO: Barbara Macaluso
sales@delicaegourmet.com
CFO: Linda Parish
VP: Leonard Macaluso
R&D: Eugene Mann
Quality Control: James Parish
Marketing: Janice Strayer
Sales: Janice Strayer
Operations: James Parish
Production: Scott Shepard
Estimated Sales: $1,500,000
Number Employees: 10-19
Number of Brands: 1
Number of Products: 120
Square Footage: 20000
Type of Packaging: Consumer, Food Service, Private Label, Bulk

3497 (HQ)Delicato Family Vineyards
455 Devlin Rd
Suite 201
Napa, CA 94558
707-265-1700
Fax: 707-253-1471 intlmrktg@dfvwines.com
www.delicatofamilyvineyards.com
Wines.
President & CEO: Chris Indelicato
SVP, Operations: Jay Indelicato
VP, Exclusive Brands & Innovation: Jim Ferguson
Regional Accounts Manager: Adam Basala
abasala@dfvwines.com
Year Founded: 1924
Estimated Sales: $29.5 Million
Number Employees: 250-499
Square Footage: 12000
Type of Packaging: Consumer, Food Service, Private Label, Bulk
Brands:
  Delicato

3498 Delicious Desserts
785 5th Ave
Brooklyn, NY 11232-1750
718-680-1156
Fax: 718-369-6665
Italian desserts including spumoni, tartufo, tortoni, tiramisu, cannolis and cakes; importer of fruit sorbet and Italian cakes
President: Joe Fusceo
Contact: D Lisa
lisa@deliciousdesserts.net
Estimated Sales: Less Than $500,000
Number Employees: 1-4
Square Footage: 8000
Type of Packaging: Private Label

3499 Delicious Frookie
2070 Maple Street
Des Plaines, IL 60018-3019
847-699-3200
Fax: 847-699-3201
Cookies.
President: Phil Roos

3500 Delicious Frookie Company
5520 N Northwest Highway
Chicago, IL 60630-1116
773-763-5553
Cookies, crackers
President/CEO: M Kirby
Estimated Sales: $500,000 appx.
Number Employees: 1-4
Parent Co: Delicious Frookie Company

3501 Delicious Popcorn
300 DE Lish US Ave
Waupaca, WI 54981-1260
715-258-7683
Fax: 715-258-1514 www.wisnack.com
Potato chips and popcorn; wholesaler/distributor of pretzels, tostados, tortillas, baked and fried corn curls, party snack mix, corn chips, raw popcorn and popping oil and gourmet popcorn products
President/Co-Owner: James Hollnbacher
CEO/Co-Owner: Jeff Hollnbacher
Marketing/Sales: Jeff Hollnbacher
Production Manager: James Hollnbacher
Purchasing Manager: James Hollnbacher
Estimated Sales: $2-5 Million
Number Employees: 10-19
Type of Packaging: Consumer, Food Service, Private Label, Bulk
Brands:
  De-Lish-Us
  Wisnack

3502 Delicious Valley Frozen Foods
1200 E Ridge Rd # 9
McAllen, TX 78503-1528
956-631-7177
Fax: 956-630-1757
Frozen foods
Manager: Sylvia Villarreal
Estimated Sales: $.5-1,000,000
Number Employees: 1-4

3503 Delicious Without Gluten
90 Brunswick Blvd
Dollard Des Ormeaux, QC H9B 2C5
Canada
514-542-3943
info@deliciouswithout.com
deliciouswithout.com
Baked goods; pizza; cookies
Founder: Miriam Pearl
Number Employees: 5-9

3504 Delighted By
delightedbyhummus.com
Dessert hummus
Founder: Makenzie Marzluff
Number of Brands: 1
Number of Products: 4
Type of Packaging: Consumer
Brands:
  DELIGHTED BY

3505 Delizza
6610 Corporation Pkwy
Battleboro, NC 27809-9804
252-442-0270
info@delizza.us
delizza.us
Frozen pastries
Contact: Ken Martin
kmartin@delizza.us
Estimated Sales: Less Than $500,000
Number Employees: 1-4

3506 Dell'Amore Enterprises
PO BOX 974
Colchester, VT 05446
802-655-6264
Fax: 802-655-6262 800-962-6673
www.dellamore.com
All natural pasta sauces
President: Frank Dell'amore
VP: David Dell'Amore
Estimated Sales: $2.5-5 Million
Number Employees: 5-9
Type of Packaging: Private Label

3507 Dellaco Classic Confections
8002 352nd Ave
Burlington, WI 53105
262-843-1604
Fax: 262-843-1604 866-537-2656
www.pamperedpetscatalog.com
Confections and nuts
Chairman: Cynthia Delligatti
President: Laura Delligatti
Sales/Marketing: Margaret Delligatti
Estimated Sales: $2.5-5 Million
Number Employees: 10-19

3508 (HQ)Delmonaco Winery & Vineyards
600 Lance Dr
Baxter, TN 38544-3530
931-858-1177
barbara@delmonacowinery.com
www.delmonacowinery.com
Wines
President/Winemaker: David Delmonaco
david@delmonacowinery.com
Vice President: Barbara Delmonaco
Estimated Sales: $3 Million
Number Employees: 1-4
Type of Packaging: Bulk

3509 Deloach Vineyards
1791 Olivet Rd
Santa Rosa, CA 95401-3898
707-755-3300
Fax: 707-526-4151
customerservice@deloachvineyards.com
www.deloachvineyards.com
Wines
Vice President: Lisa Heisinger
lisaheisinger@deloachvineyards.com
VP: Christine DeLoach
Winemaker: Cecil DeLoach
Production Manager: Rob Cooper
Estimated Sales: $20-50 Million
Number Employees: 20-49
Brands:
  De Loach

3510 Delorimier Winery
2001 Highway 128
Geyserville, CA 95441-9489
707-857-2000
Fax: 707-857-3262 800-546-7718
www.delorimierwinery.com
Wines
President: Alfred De Lorimier
Marketing: John Woodward
Estimated Sales: $2.5-5,000,000
Number Employees: 10-19
Number of Brands: 1
Number of Products: 10
Type of Packaging: Private Label
Brands:
  De Lorimeir

3511 Delphos Poultry Products
205 S Pierce St
Delphos, OH 45833
419-692-5816
Fax: 419-692-1606
Chicken products including marinated breasts, breaded, breast fillets, hot wings, wingettes and gizzards
President: Thomas J Schimmoller
Estimated Sales: $1-2.5 Million
Number Employees: 10-19
Square Footage: 21000
Type of Packaging: Consumer, Food Service, Private Label, Bulk
Brands:
  Volcano Wings

3512 Delta Catfish Products
602 E Lee St
PO Box 99
Eudora, AR 71640
870-355-4192
Fax: 714-778-0998
Catfish
President/CEO: Thomas Marshall

3513 Delta Food Products
10557 114th Street NW
Edmonton, AB T5H 3J6
Canada
780-424-3636
Fax: 780-424-1536
Frozen Chinese dim sum, fresh noodles, egg and spring rolls, microwaveable Oriental dinners and green onion cakes
President: Gordon Becker
Manager: Mei-ling Chan
Estimated Sales: $1.8 Million
Number Employees: 22
Square Footage: 60000
Type of Packaging: Consumer, Food Service, Private Label
Brands:
  Delta Foods
  Wok Menu

3514 Delta Pacific Seafoods
6001-60 Ave
Delta, BC V4K 4E2
Canada
604-946-5160
www.deltapacific.ca
Fresh and frozen salmon, hake, sardines, halibut
General Manager: Paul Edgett
Estimated Sales: $8 Million
Number Employees: 20
Type of Packaging: Consumer, Food Service

Food Manufacturers / A-Z

3515 Delta Packing
6021 E Kettleman Ln
Lodi, CA 95240-6400
209-334-1023
Fax: 209-334-0811 www.deltapacking.com
Grower, packer and shipper of cherries, wine grapes, grape juice, pears, asparagus and bell peppers.
Manager: Carl Elkins
Manager: Berton Costamagna
Year Founded: 1976
Number Employees: 10-19
Type of Packaging: Consumer, Food Service, Private Label
Brands:
  Delta Fresh

3516 Delta Pride Catfish
1301 Industrial Parkway
Indianola, MS 38751
662-887-5401
Fax: 662-887-5950 800-228-3474
sales@deltapride.com www.deltapride.com
Manufacturer of farm-raised catfish and wholesaler/distributor of fresh and frozen farm raised catfish and hush puppies.
President and CEO: Steve Osso
Owner: Adrian Percy
Contact: Darry Adams
dadams@deltapride.com
Year Founded: 1981
Estimated Sales: $30 Million
Number Employees: 450
Parent Co: Delta Pride Catfish

3517 Deluxe Delight
10700 Santa Monica Blvd
Suite 207
Lost Angeles, CA 90025
424-230-3664
Mediterranean pastries
Owner: Mohamad El Halabi
Year Founded: 1919
Number Employees: 1-10

3518 Demitri's Bloody Mary Seasonings
PO Box 84123
Seattle, WA 98124
206-764-6006
Fax: 206-764-3163 800-627-9649
www.demitris.com
Concentrated Bloody Mary seasonings
President: Demitri Pallis
Contact: Dillon Holmes
dillon@demitris.com
Estimated Sales: Under $300,000
Number Employees: 1-4
Square Footage: 4800
Parent Co: Gourmet Mixes
Type of Packaging: Consumer, Food Service, Bulk
Brands:
  Demitri's Bloody Mary Seasonings

3519 Dempsey's Restaurant & Brewery
50 E Washington St
Petaluma, CA 94952-3115
707-765-9694
Fax: 707-762-1259 www.dempseys.com
Beer
Owner: Peter Burrell
redroosteraile@att.net
CFO: Peter Burrell
Estimated Sales: $1-2.5 Million
Number Employees: 20-49
Square Footage: 24000
Brands:
  Golden Eagle Ale
  Red Rooster Ale
  Sonoma Brewing
  Ugly Dog Stout

3520 Den's Hot Dogs
105 Oceana Dr E
Suite 4E
Brooklyn, NY 11235-6682
718-355-9636
Fax: 718-355-9636 www.denshotdogs.com
Hot dog sandwhiches and condiments
President: Denys Gorbatiuk
Year Founded: 2011
Estimated Sales: $250000
Number Employees: 3
Type of Packaging: Private Label

3521 Denatale Vineyards
11020 Eastside Road
Healdsburg, CA 95448-9487
707-431-8460
Fax: 707-431-8736
Wines
President: Ron DeNatale
Owner: Sandy De Natale
Estimated Sales: $98,000
Number Employees: 2

3522 Deneen Foods
33859 United Avenue
Santa Fe, NM 81001
505-332-2000
Fax: 505-323-7100 800-866-4695
www.santafeseasons.com
Sauces and spice blends
President: Greg Deneen
VP: Edith Deneen
Estimated Sales: $1-2.5 Million
Number Employees: 39009
Number of Brands: 3+
Number of Products: 5+
Square Footage: 68000
Type of Packaging: Consumer, Food Service, Private Label, Bulk
Brands:
  Coyote Cocina
  Santa Fe Seasons
  Go Salsa

3523 Denning's Point Distillery, LLC
10 N. Chestnut St.
Beacon, NY 12508
845-476-8413
info@denningspoint.com
www.denningspointdistillery.com
Brandy, bourbon, whiskey, gin and vodka
Co-Founder: Karl Johnson
Co-Founder: Susan Keramedjian
Year Founded: 2014
Number Employees: 5-9
Number of Brands: 1
Number of Products: 6
Type of Packaging: Private Label

3524 Dennison Meat Locker
109 Farm Rd
Dennison, MN 55018-4108
507-645-8734
dogoods@hotmail.com
www.dennisonmeatlocker.com
Frankfurters and sausage
Owner: Dori Gregory
Estimated Sales: $1-3 Million
Number Employees: 1-4
Type of Packaging: Consumer

3525 Denny's 5th Avenue Bakery
7840 5th Avenue S
Bloomington, MN 55420
952-881-4445
Fax: 952-881-5321 www.dennysbakery.com
Bakery products
Estimated Sales: $1-2.5 Million
Number Employees: 20-49

3526 Denomega Pure Health
992S,4th Ave
Brighton, CO 80601
479-181-2845
Fax: 303-581-9005 jennifer.kibel@denomega.com
www.denomega.com
Edible fats and oils, Omega-3
General Manager: Harold Ranneberg
CEO: Thomas Grys
Marketing Director: Mike OShea
Vice President of Operations: Jarle Wikeby

3527 Denzer's Food Products
PO Box 5632
Baltimore, MD 21210-0632
410-889-1500
Fax: 410-235-7032 jake@denzer.com
Conch chowder, crab soup, lima bean soup, peanut soup. Southeastern and US regional foods
President: Jacob Slagle
Estimated Sales: $1-3,000,000
Number Employees: 1-4
Type of Packaging: Consumer

3528 Deosen USA
1140 Stelton Rd # 205
Suite 205
Piscataway, NJ 08854-5291
908-292-1165
Fax: 908-292-1165 www.deosenusa.com
Ziboxan Xanthan gum.
CEO: Lawrence Herbolsheimer
Director of Sales: John Fritz

3529 Deppeler Cheese Factory
W6805 Deppeler Rd
West 6805 Deppeler Road
Monroe, WI 53566-9709
608-325-6311
Fax: 608-325-6935
Cheese and cheese products
Manager: Silvan Blum
Estimated Sales: Less Than $500,000
Number Employees: 1-4
Type of Packaging: Private Label

3530 Derco Foods Intl
2670 W Shaw Ln # 101
Fresno, CA 93711-2772
559-435-2664
Fax: 559-435-8520 derco@dercofoods.com
www.dercofoods.com
Dried fruits, nuts, specialty foods, pineapple, mushrooms, canned fruit, caned fruit, beans and popcorn
President: Leon Dermenjian
leon@dercofoods.com
Quality Control: Debbie McMillan
VP Sales/Purchasing: Ago Dermanjian
Sales/Marketing: Jeff Margarian
Estimated Sales: $20-50 Million
Number Employees: 10-19
Square Footage: 6000
Brands:
  Derco

3531 Dere Street
5 Shelter Rock Road
Unit 5D
Danbury, CT 06810
203-797-9386
Fax: 203-797-0714 www.derestreet.com
Scones and shortbread
President: David Dere
Vice President: Robin Dere

3532 Derlea Foods
1739 Orangebrook Court
Pickering, ON L1W 3G8
Canada
905-839-7212
Fax: 905-839-7217 888-430-7777
sales@derlea.com www.derlea.com
Fresh garlic
President: Salvatore Geraci
Estimated Sales: $1.2 Million
Number Employees: 30
Type of Packaging: Consumer, Food Service, Private Label, Bulk

3533 Deschutes Brewery
901 SW Simpson Ave
Bend, OR 97702-3118
541-385-8606
Fax: 541-383-4505 www.deschutesbrewery.com
Seasonal beer, ale, stout, lager and porter
President & CEO: Michael LaLonde
Estimated Sales: $44 Million
Number Employees: 100-249
Type of Packaging: Consumer, Food Service
Brands:
  Black Butte
  Cascade Ale
  Mirror Pond Pale Ale
  Obsidian Stout

3534 Deseret Dairy Products
784 W 700 S
Salt Lake City, UT 84104-1415
801-240-7350
Fax: 801-240-7352
Milk and cheese producer; social service and welfare organization.
Manager: Bill Beane
Manager: Pmp Anderson
pranderson@ldschurch.org
Production Supervisor: Curtis Frame
Estimated Sales: $10-25 Million
Number Employees: 20-49

Food Manufacturers / A-Z

Parent Co: The Church of Jesus Christ of Latter-day Saints
Type of Packaging: Food Service

3535 Desert Farms Inc
2708 Wilshire Blvd # 380
Santa Monica, CA 90403-4706
310-430-2096
press@desertfarms.com
www.desertfarms.com
Camel milk
Contact: Walid Abdul-Wahab
walid@desertfarms.com
Number Employees: 5-9

3536 Desert King International
7024 Manya Cir
San Diego, CA 92154-4711
619-429-5222
Fax: 619-429-5001 800-982-2235
info@desertking.com www.desertking.com
Quillaja and yucca extracts for root beer and oil flavors
President: Paul Hiley
philey@desertking.com
VP: Joel Powers
Regional Sales Manager: Raymond Kramer
Estimated Sales: $3-5 Million
Number Employees: 10-19
Square Footage: 60000
Type of Packaging: Private Label, Bulk
Brands:
  Foamation

3537 Desert Pepper Trading Co
PO Box 1761
El Paso, TX 79949
915-533-0008
Fax: 915-533-0026 888-472-5727
www.desertpepper.com
Salsas, condiments, dips and sauces.
Founder: W Park Kerr
Estimated Sales: $3 Million
Number Employees: 37
Type of Packaging: Private Label
Brands:
  Daddy-Q
  Desert Pepper
  Ol' Smokey
  Salsa Del Rio
  Salsa Diablo
  Salsa Divino
  XXX Habanero

3538 Desert Valley Date
86740 Industrial Way
Coachella, CA 92236-2718
760-398-0999
Fax: 760-398-1514 sales@desertvalleydate.com
Dates
President: George Kirkjan
georgekirkjan@desertvalleydate.com
Estimated Sales: $10-20 Million
Number Employees: 50-99

3539 Designed Nutritional Products
1199 South 1480 West
Orem, UT 84058-4907
801-224-4518
Fax: 801-434-8270 info@designednutritional.com
www.designednutritional.com
Dietary supplements including organic germanium, saw palmetto extracts, ascorbigen, melatonin and indole-3-carbinol; exporter of melatonin, gramine, bisindolylmethane and glycogen
President: David Parish
Marketing: Omar Filippelli
Contact: Gus Diaz
customerservice@designednutritional.com
Purchasing Director: Craig Hansen
Estimated Sales: $10-20 Million
Number Employees: 5-9
Square Footage: 10000
Type of Packaging: Bulk

3540 Designer Protein
PO Box 2469
Carlsbad, CA 92018
800-337-4463
info@designerprotein.com designerprotein.com
Whole egg protein powder
CEO: Grace Jeon
Year Founded: 1993
Number of Brands: 1
Number of Products: 10
Type of Packaging: Consumer
Brands:
  DESIGNER WHEY
  ARIA
  SUSTAINED ENERGY
  ESSENTIAL 10
  LITE
  TOTALLY EGG
  SUNSHINE
  ORGANIC PRO 30

3541 Dessert Innovations Inc
25 Enterprise Blvd SW # B
Atlanta, GA 30336-2131
404-691-5000
Fax: 404-691-5001 800-359-7351
sales@dessertinnovations.com
www.classicconfections.com
Industrial dessert manufacturer; barcakes, cupcakes, parfaits, layer cakes, and petit fours
President: Tony Ereiddia
tony@dessertinnovations.com
VP Finance/Operations: Rolf Schittli
General Manager: Tim Guidry
senior sales manager: Bob Lunde
Production Manager: Ralph Ferdinand
Estimated Sales: $10-20 Million
Number Employees: 20-49
Square Footage: 96000
Brands:
  Classic Confections
  Custom Up Cakes
  Singel Serving Sundae

3542 Desserts Of Distinction
14345 SW Pacific Hwy
Tigard, OR 97224-3647
503-654-8370
Fax: 503-654-1322
customerservice@dessertsofdistinction.com
www.dessertsofdistinction.com
Baked goods including frozen cheesecake
Owner: Sue Sanders
ssanders@dessertsofdistinction.com
Estimated Sales: $2.1 Million
Number Employees: 5-9
Type of Packaging: Food Service

3543 Desserts On Us Inc
57 Belle Falor Ct
Arcata, CA 95521-9234
707-822-0160
Fax: 707-822-5908 desonus@aol.com
www.dessertsonus.com
Cookies.
Owner: Emren Essa
desonus@aol.com
Number Employees: 10-19

3544 Desserts by David Glass
400 Chapel Road
Unit 2d Bissell Commons
South Windsor, CT 6074
860-462-7520
Fax: 860-242-4408
Desserts including chocolate truffle cake, cheesecake and chocolate mousse balls
President: David Glass
Estimated Sales: $10-20 Million
Number Employees: 20-49
Square Footage: 20000
Type of Packaging: Consumer, Food Service
Brands:
  Desserts By David Glass

3545 Destileria Serralles Inc
P.O. Box 198
Mercedita, PR 00715-0198
787-840-1000
Fax: 787-840-1155
Rum, vodka, gin, cordials and wine; importer of scotch; exporter of rum; wholesaler/distributor of general merchandise
President & CEO: Felix Serralles, Jr.
Chief Financial Officer: Jorge Vazquez
Product Quality Director: Roberto Pantoja
Chief Marketing Officer: Gabriela Ripepi
State Manager: Vanessa Gehl
Human Resources Director: Daniel Beautista
Estimated Sales: $28.5 Million
Number Employees: 370
Square Footage: 18777
Type of Packaging: Consumer, Private Label, Bulk
Brands:
  Donq Gold
  Donq Cristal
  Donq Limon
  Donq Pasion
  Donq Coco
  Donq Mojito
  Donq Anejo
  Donq Grand Anejo
  Ron Palo Viejo
  Ron Granado
  Ron Llave
  Ron Rico
  Ginebra Calvert
  Vodka Nikolai
  Alcoholado Superior 70
  Alcoholado Baluarte
  Blue Curacao
  Crema De Cacao
  Garandina
  Triple Sec
  Captain Morgan
  Parrot Bay
  Cutty Sark
  Glenrothes
  Glenlivet
  Raynal
  Aguardiente Caldas
  Jim Beam
  El Jimador
  Cinzano
  Skyy Vodka
  Roederer Estate
  Corbett Canyon
  Justin Vineyard
  Sterling Vinyards
  Trave Amaretto
  Kamora
  Trave Amaretto-Decanter
  Anis Paloma
  Sambuca Molinari
  Aqua Best
  Crema De Coco
  Guayabita Best-Pasta De Guayaba
  Sense
  Pares Baltas
  Villaformosa
  Tilenus
  Casa De La Ermita
  Monasterio Sta. Ana Monte
  Condado De Almara
  Priorato-Mas D' En Gil
  Rias Baixas
  Ribera Del Duero
  Rioja
  Montesierra
  Pirineo
  Pirineos
  Senorio De Lazan
  Camparron
  Cano Cosecha
  Bajoz
  Ovacion
  Casa Blanco
  Casa Tinto
  Senorio De Los Llanos
  Pata Negra
  Sandeman Don Fino
  Senorio De Los Llanos
  Pata Negra
  Sandeman Don Fino
  Sandeman Character Oloroso
  Louis Roederer-Remis
  Perrier Jouet-Epernay

3546 Detoxwater
212 7th Street
Brooklyn, NY 11215
888-887-4318
info@detoxwater.com detoxwater.com
Aloe-infused water
Founder: Kenneth Park
Number of Brands: 1
Number of Products: 6
Type of Packaging: Consumer
Brands:
  DETOXWATER

Food Manufacturers / A-Z

3547 Detroit Chili Co
21400 Telegraph Rd
Southfield, MI 48033-4424
248-440-5933
Fax: 248-440-5945 www.dtigroup.biz
Frozen chili
Owner: Tim Keros
Purchasing Agent: Terry Keros
Estimated Sales: $500,000-$1 Million
Number Employees: 5-9
Square Footage: 20000
Type of Packaging: Consumer, Food Service

3548 Devansoy Farms
206 W 7th St
PO Box 885
Carroll, IA 51401-2317
712-792-9665
Fax: 712-792-2712 800-747-8605
info@devansoy.com www.devansoy.com
Powdered and liquid soy milk and soy flours;. Organic and parve available
President: Elmer Schettler
eschettler@devansoy.com
VP/Sales & Mktg: Montgomery Kilburn
VP/Operations: Deb Wycoff
Estimated Sales: $510,000
Number Employees: 1-4
Number of Products: 8
Type of Packaging: Food Service, Private Label, Bulk
Brands:
  Enzact
  Soy Roast

3549 Devault Foods
1 Deveault Lane
Devault, PA 19432
610-644-2536
800-426-2874
info@devaultfoods.com www.devaultfoods.com
Fresh and frozen portion controlled ground beef, hamburgers, pre-cooked meat balls and Philadelphia-style sandwich steaks
President/CEO: Thomas Fillippo
Chief Financial Officer: Carl Sorzano
Vice President, Sales & Marketing: Bill Irwin
COO: Brett Black
Estimated Sales: $41 Million
Number Employees: 120
Number of Brands: 4
Square Footage: 114000
Type of Packaging: Food Service, Private Label, Bulk
Brands:
  Minute Menu
  Mrs Difillippo's
  Steakwich
  Steakwich Lite

3550 Devine Foods
8 S Plum St
Elwyn, PA 19063-3309
610-566-2400
888-338-4631
denise@devinefoods.com
Beverages, frozen confections
President: Denise Devine
Operations: Jerome Renners
Estimated Sales: $5-10 Million
Number Employees: 5-9
Brands:
  Devine Nectar
  Fibrymid
  Fruice
  Simply Devine

3551 Devlin Wine Cellars
PO Box 728
Soquel, CA 95073-0728
831-476-7288
Fax: 831-479-9043 www.webwinery.com/devlin
Wines
President: Cheryl Devlin
Estimated Sales: Less than $500,000
Number Employees: 1-4
Type of Packaging: Private Label

3552 Devro Inc
785 Old Swamp Rd
Sandy Run
Swansea, SC 29160-8387
803-796-9730
Fax: 803-796-1636 www.devro.com
Casings for sausages, hams, salami and other meat products.
VP Product Management: Paul Tutt
Quality Manager: Rocco Del Priore
Business Development Manager: Marco Hobi
Purchasing Agent: Bobbie Fallaw
Estimated Sales: $28.8 Million
Number Employees: 250-499
Number of Brands: 1
Type of Packaging: Consumer
Brands:
  Devro

3553 Dewey's Bakery
100 Vinegar Hill Rd
Winston-Salem, NC 27104-5068
336-765-2095
Fax: 336-748-0501 877-339-3974
mike@deweys.com www.deweys.com
Bakery products
Owner/President: Guy Wilkerson
Estimated Sales: $57,000
Number Employees: 2

3554 (HQ)Dewied International Inc
5010 Interstate 10 E
San Antonio, TX 78219-3352
210-661-6161
Fax: 210-662-6112 800-992-5600
www.dewied.com
Natural and synthetic sausage casings specializing in hog, sheep and beef casings
President: Phil Bohlender
philb@dewiedint.com
VP Sales: George Burt
Estimated Sales: $10-20 Million
Number Employees: 50-99
Brands:
  Dewied

3555 Dewig Brothers Packing Company
100 Maple Street
Haubstadt, IN 47639-0186
812-768-6208
Fax: 812-768-6220 www.dewigmeats.com
Country style meats
President: Thomas Dewig
Finance Executive: Tom Dewig
Estimated Sales: $3,501,748
Number Employees: 35

3556 Dexpa
5503 Kingsley Mnr
Cumming, GA 30041-6119
USA
770-887-7412
Fax: 770-887-8864
Cheese

3557 Dharma Bars
sales@dharmabars.com
www.dharmabars.com
Organic, gluten free, and vegan energy bars
Founder: James Ricciuti

3558 Dhidow Enterprises
PO Box 285
Oxford, PA 19363-0285
610-932-7868
Fax: 509-753-0570
Nonvinegar based hot sauces
President: Dhidow Stephens
CEO: Paulette Colman
Estimated Sales: $300,000
Number Employees: 2
Type of Packaging: Consumer, Food Service, Bulk
Brands:
  Dhidow Enterprise 150x
  Dhidow Enterprise 20x
  Dhidow Enterprise 50x
  Dhidow Enterprise Zero

3559 Di Alfredo Foods
3060 Plaza Dr
Suite 108
Garnet Valley, PA 19060
610-558-2802
dialfredo.com
Pasta; olive oil; vinegar; balsamic glaze; jams and jellies; cookies; crackers; truffles
Director of Sales & Marketing: Thomas Sheridan
tom@dialfredo.com
Type of Packaging: Private Label, Bulk

3560 Di Bruno Bros
930 S 9th St
Philadelphia, PA 19147-3994
215-922-2876
Fax: 215-922-2080 www.dibruno.com
Manufacturer of cured meats, cheeses, and specialty foods such as oils and mixers.
VP of Culinary Pioneering: Emilio Mignucci
Number Employees: 5-9

3561 Di Camillo Baking Co
811 Linwood Ave
Niagara Falls, NY 14305-2517
716-282-2341
Fax: 716-282-2596 800-634-4363
info@dicamillobakery.com
www.dicamillobakery.com
Cakes, biscuits, biscotti, cookies, crispbreads and flatbreads, jams, honey, and confectionary
President: David Di Camillo
dcamillo@dicamillobakery.com
VP: Skip Di Camillo
VP: Tom Di Camillo
VP Marketing: Michael Di Camillo
Year Founded: 1920
Estimated Sales: $20-50 Million
Number Employees: 50-99

3562 Di Cola's Seafood
10754 S Western Ave
Chicago, IL 60643-3199
773-238-7071
Fax: 773-238-8337
www.dicolasseafoodbeverly.com
Seafood
Owner: Robert Di Cola
Estimated Sales: $5-10 Million
Number Employees: 20-49

3563 Di Fiore Pasta Co
556 Franklin Ave
Hartford, CT 06114-3024
860-296-1077
Fax: 860-296-5635
Pasta
Owner: Louise Di Fiore
Manager: Andrea Di Fiore
Estimated Sales: $1-2,500,000
Number Employees: 5-9
Brands:
  Difiore Pasta

3564 Di Lusso & Be Bop Baskote LLC
1950 SW Badger Ave
Suite 105
Redmond, OR 97756
541-388-8164
Fax: 541-389-6185 888-545-7487
orders@be-bop.net www.be-bop.net
Biscotti and specialty roasted coffees
Owner: Bob Golden
bgolden@dilusso.com
Roastmaster: Dona Houtz
Vice President: M Lee
Sales Representative: Abbie Keenan
Estimated Sales: $20-50 Million
Number Employees: 50-99
Square Footage: 6000
Type of Packaging: Consumer, Food Service
Brands:
  Royal Blend

3565 (HQ)Di Mare Fresh Inc
4629 Diplomacy Rd
Fort Worth, TX 76155-2621
817-385-3000
Fax: 817-385-3015 www.dimarefresh.com
Growers, packers and distributors of fresh fruits and vegetables.
President: Paul DiMare
CFO: Cheryl Taylor
cheryl.taylor@dimarefresh.com
Year Founded: 1930
Number Employees: 50-99
Type of Packaging: Consumer, Food Service, Private Label, Bulk
Brands:
  Bermuda Dunes
  Di-Mare Gold Label
  Rancho Palm Springs
  Sea View

Food Manufacturers / A-Z

3566 DiBella Baking Company
3524 Seagate Way
Suite 110
Oceanside, CA 92056
888-857-6151
www.dibellafamiglia.com
Cookies, biscotti and cookie brittle
Number of Brands: 1
Number of Products: 30
Type of Packaging: Consumer
Brands:
  DIBELLA

3567 DiGregorio Food Products
5200 Daggett Ave
St Louis, MO 63110
314-776-1062
Fax: 314-776-3954 www.digregoriofoods.com
Sausage, meat balls and spaghetti sauce
President: Dora Di Gregorio
d.digregorio@digregoriofoods.com
CEO: John DiGregorio
Estimated Sales: $.5-1 million
Number Employees: 20-49
Square Footage: 200000
Type of Packaging: Food Service, Private Label

3568 DiMario Foods
56 Windsor Dr
Oak Brook, IL 60523-2365
630-581-5250
Fax: 630-581-5250 www.dimariofoods.com
Gourmet pork sticks
Co-Owner: Laura DeBartolo
Co-Owner: Nick DeBartolo
Year Founded: 2014
Number Employees: 8
Type of Packaging: Private Label

3569 Diageo Canada Inc.
401 The West Mall
Suite 800
Toronto, ON M9C 5P8
Canada
416-626-2000
Fax: 416-626-2688 www.diageo.com
Processor and exporter of gin and wine
President/Board Member: John Kennedy
Head of Corporate Communications: Rowan Pearman
Parent Co: Grand Metropolitan
Type of Packaging: Consumer, Food Service

3570 (HQ)Diageo North America Inc
801 Main Ave
Norwalk, CT 06851-1163
203-229-2100
Fax: 203-229-8925 www.diageo.com
Distilled liquors, spirits and wines
President: Deirdre Mahlan
deirdre.mahlan@diageo.com
Senior VP: John Adams
Marketing Manager: James Thomson
Number Employees: 1000-4999
Brands:
  Asbach Brandy
  Bell's Scotch
  Black & White
  Canard Duchene
  Cardhu
  Classic Malts
  Dewar's White Label
  Dom Perignon
  George Dickel Whiske
  Glen Ord Scotch
  Gordon's Gin
  Gordon's Vodka
  Gordon's Vodka
  Haig
  Hennessy Cognacs
  Hine Cognac
  I.W. Harper Bourbon
  Johnny Walker Scotch
  Mercier Champagnes
  Safari
  Scoresby Scotch
  Tanqueray Gin
  The Dimple
  Vat 69
  Veuve Cliquot
  Weller Bourbon
  White Horse

3571 (HQ)Diamond Bakery Co LTD
756 Moowaa St
Honolulu, HI 96817-4405
808-847-3551
Fax: 808-847-7482 www.diamondbakery.com
Crackers and cookies, including all natural crackers.
President: Gary Yoshioka
Manager: Katy Leung
kleung@diamondbakery.com
Year Founded: 1921
Estimated Sales: Less Than $500,000
Number Employees: 5-9
Number of Products: 50+
Square Footage: 50500
Type of Packaging: Consumer, Food Service, Private Label, Bulk
Brands:
  Diamond Bakery

3572 Diamond Blueberry Inc
548 Pleasant Mills Rd
Hammonton, NJ 08037-8931
609-561-3661
Fax: 609-567-4423
Fresh and frozen blueberries
Owner: David Berger
Sales: Tim Wetherbee
david@driscolls.com
Manager: Tim Wetherbee
Estimated Sales: $500,000-$1 Million
Number Employees: 20-49
Brands:
  Diamond

3573 Diamond Creek Vineyards
1500 Diamond Mountain Rd
Calistoga, CA 94515-9669
707-942-6926
Fax: 707-942-6936
info@diamondcreekvineyards.com
www.diamondcreekvineyards.com
Wines
President: Al Brounstein
Estimated Sales: $2.5-5 Million
Number Employees: 5-9
Type of Packaging: Private Label

3574 Diamond Crystal Brands Inc
3000 Tremont Rd
Savannah, GA 31405
800-654-5115
www.dcbrands.com
Low-sodium mixes including soup, milk shake, ice cream, sauce, sugar-free dessert and fruit drink; also, instant breakfast beverages, cookies, nutritional chocolate bars and portion packed condiments including jelly, mustard, etc.
President & CEO: Tony Muscato
Director, Information Technology: Arlete Bacon
Year Founded: 1966
Estimated Sales: $45.2 Million
Number Employees: 250-499
Number of Brands: 12
Square Footage: 1200000
Parent Co: Peak Rock Capital of Austin
Type of Packaging: Food Service, Private Label
Other Locations:
  Diamond Crystal Specialty Foo
  Aurora ON
Brands:
  Skippy
  Treemont Farms
  Salt for Life
  True Citrus
  Flavor Fresh
  Chef's Seasoning
  Chef'S Companion
  House Blend
  Single Serv
  Lakeland Dairies
  Caf, Delight Premium Drink Mixes
  Caf, Delight Certified Sweeteners

3575 Diamond Foods
2200 Delaware Avenue
Santa Cruz, CA 95060
831-457-3200
Fax: 831-460-9407 www.emeraldnuts.com
Processor and exporter of gummys, jelly beans, gels, yogurt, chocolate confections and sugar-free and natural candies; also, dried fruit, banana chips and snack and trail mixes
Cfo: Dennis Barrow
Vice President: Dennis Daniels
Estimated Sales: $1-2.5 Million
Number Employees: 100-249
Square Footage: 600000
Type of Packaging: Consumer, Food Service, Private Label, Bulk
Brands:
  Bold Beans
  Harmony Snacks
  Planet Harmony
  Emerald Nuts

3576 Diamond Fruit Growers
3515 Chevron Dr
Hood River, OR 97044
541-354-5300
Fax: 541-354-5394 www.diamondfruit.com
Cooperative grower, packer, shipper and exporter of apples, pears and cherries.
President & CEO: David Garcia
Controller: Linda Gray
Field Representative: Grady Leiblein
Food Safety Coordinator: Corey Yasui
VP, Operations: Bob Wymore
VP, Raw Product: Chad Wimmers
Purchasing Coordinator: Wes Bailey
Year Founded: 1913
Estimated Sales: $20-50 Million
Number Employees: 100-249
Type of Packaging: Bulk

3577 Diamond Seafood
204 N Edgewood Avenue
Wood Dale, IL 60191-1610
630-787-1100
Fax: 630-787-1309
Seafood
President: Thomas Hannagan
Contact: Thomas Hanigan
diamondseafood@yahoo.com
Estimated Sales: $5-10 Million
Number Employees: 10-19

3578 Diamond Water Bottling Fclty
181 Cedar St
Hot Springs, AR 71901
501-623-1251
Fax: 501-623-2648
Bottled spring water
President: Tom Mitchell
Plant Manager: Brian Hinds
Estimated Sales: $5-10 Million
Number Employees: 10-19
Parent Co: Mountain Valley Water
Type of Packaging: Consumer

3579 Diamond of California
600 Montgomery Street
13th Floor
San Francisco, CA 94111
415-912-3180
Fax: 925-251-3820 www.diamondfoods.com
Nuts
President/CEO: Michael Mendes
CFO: Seth Halio
VP: Mario Alioto
Sales: Frank Morgan
Public Relations Manager: Vicki Zeigler

3580 Diana Naturals
250 Pehle Ave Concourse Level
Plaza 1, #207
Saddle Brook, NJ 07663
845-729-0942
www.diana-food.com
Producer of natural ingredients.
President: Yannick Riou
Applications Group Manager: Vinifer Dutia
Sweet & Beverage Category Manager: Teresa Kilgore
Parent Co: Diana Naturals

3581 Diana's Specialty Foods
2305 Aurora Dr
Pingree Grove, IL 60140-6442
847-683-1200
Fax: 847-683-1207
Vinegar, fancy gifts, Italian riviera and provencial bread dippers, grapeseed oils, miniature bread dipping oils, salsa, jams, jelly, mustard, herb mayonnaise, and olive oil
Manager: Mark Pagnoni
Estimated Sales: $12,000
Number Employees: 10-19
Square Footage: 3000

Food Manufacturers / A-Z

3582 Diane's Signature Products
PO Box 2705
Edmond, OK 73083
405-509-3311
sales@dianessignatureproducts.com
www.dianessignatureproducts.com
Manufacturer of signature dressings for salads.
Owner: Brooke Franklin

3583 Diane's Sweet Heat
McKinleyville, CA
dianessweetheat.com
Habanero pepper-infused fruit jams
Owner: Diane Hunt
Year Founded: 2007
Number of Brands: 1
Number of Products: 8
Type of Packaging: Consumer
Brands:
    DIANE'S SWEET HEAT

3584 Diaz Foods
5501 Fulton Industrial Blvd
Atlanta, GA 30336
404-344-5421
Fax: 404-344-3003 www.diazfoods.com
Dry, refrigerated and frozen products

3585 Diazteca Inc
993 E Frontage Rd
Rio Rico, AZ 85648-6234
520-761-4621
Fax: 520-281-1024 www.diazteca.com
Processor and distributor of Mexican fresh mangos, fresh hot peppers, granulated cane sugar, refrigerated and frozen lean beef, frozen shrimp, frozen IQF fruits and vegetables, aseptic fruit purees and other food products.
Owner/President: Ismael Diaz
Vice President: Roderigo Diaz
Estimated Sales: Less Than $500,000
Number Employees: 5-9
Type of Packaging: Consumer, Private Label, Bulk

3586 Dick Garber Company
2295 Parklake Dr NE Ste 165
Atlanta, GA 30345
770-414-0500
Fax: 770-414-9484 m.gokel@inetmail.att.net
Vice President: Mike Goeckel
Estimated Sales: $5-10 Million
Number Employees: 5-9
Parent Co: Dick Garber Company

3587 Dick Garber Company
1202 Tech Blvd
Tampa, FL 33619
813-621-8634
Fax: 813-627-9115 r.i.reynolds@inetmail.att.net
Groceries
President: Dick Garber
Vice President: Bob Reynolds
Contact: Robert Reynolds
r.reynolds@pinnaclefoodsales.com
Estimated Sales: $20-50 Million
Number Employees: 20-49
Parent Co: Dick Garber Company

3588 Dickinson Frozen Foods
1205 Iron Eagle Dr.
Suite B
Eagle, ID 83616
208-452-5200
Fax: 208-452-5365 800-886-4326
customerservice@df-foods.com
www.df-foods.com
Frozen onions, potatoes, and bell peppers
President & CEO: Paul Fox
CFO: Doug Reader
Quality Assurance Manager: George Condie
Director of Sales & Marketing: Aaron Mann
VP Sales: Bruce Robinson
Contact: Lynae Addy
laddy@dickinsonfrozenfoods.com
Director of Operations: Todd Campbell
Plant Manager: Todd Campbell
Purchasing Manager: Tim Burnett
Estimated Sales: $24.1 Million
Number Employees: 462
Square Footage: 100000
Type of Packaging: Consumer, Food Service, Private Label
Brands:
    Dickinson Frozen Foods

3589 Dickson's Pure Honey
4331 Hatchery Road
San Angelo, TX 76903-1513
915-655-9233
Pure honey
President: Andrew Dickson
Estimated Sales: $1-2,500,000 appx.
Number Employees: 1
Brands:
    Dickson's Pure Honey

3590 Didion Milling Inc
520 Hartwig Blvd # C
Johnson Creek, WI 53038-9315
920-348-6816
Fax: 920-699-3628 jdillon@didionmilling.com
www.didionmilling.com
Dry corn miller, corn products
President: Dow Didion
CEO: John Didion
jdidion@didionmilling.com
Vice President: Dow Drachenberg
Vice President of Sales & Marketing: Jeff Dillon
Number Employees: 10-19

3591 Diedrich Coffee
28 Executive Park, Ste 200
Irvine, CA 92614
949-260-1600
Fax: 949-260-1610 800-354-5282
java@diedrich.com
Coffee
President/CFO: Sean McCarthy
Contact: Anthony Barr
barr@gloriajeans.com
Estimated Sales: $18.4 Million
Number Employees: 500
Square Footage: 17620
Parent Co: Green Mountain Coffee
Brands:
    Coffee People
    Diedrich Coffee
    Gloria Jeans

3592 Dieffenbach's Potato Chips
51 Host Rd
Womelsdorf, PA 19567-9421
610-589-2385
Fax: 610-589-2866 www.dieffenbachs.com
Dieffenbach's Old Fashioned Potato Chips; Uglies Kettle-Cooked Chips, which are made from potatoes that do not adhere to USDA cosmetic regulations for produce
President & CEO: Nevin Dieffenbach
VP, Business Development: Dwight Zimmerman
Chief Operating Officer: Michael Marlowe
Estimated Sales: $5-10 Million
Number Employees: 10-19
Number of Brands: 2
Type of Packaging: Consumer, Private Label
Other Locations:
    Factory Outlet Store
    Womelsdorf PA
Brands:
    Dieffenbach's
    Uglies

3593 Diehl Food Ingredients
136 Fox Run Dr
Defiance, OH 43512
419-782-5010
Fax: 419-783-4319 800-251-3033
Lactose free beverages, powdered fat, coffee creamers and whip topping bases.
President: Charles Nicolais
CFO: Darren Lane
CEO: Peter Diehl
Research & Development: Joan Hasselman
Quality Control: Kelly Roach
Marketing Director: Dennis Reid
Sales Director: Jim Holdrieth
Number Employees: 100-249
Parent Co: Diehl
Type of Packaging: Consumer, Food Service, Bulk
Brands:
    Chocomite
    Vitamite

3594 Diestel Family Turkey Ranch
209-532-4950
info@diestelturkey.com
diestelturkey.com
Turkey, ham and beef products
Marketing: Heidi Diestel
Year Founded: 1949
Number of Brands: 1
Type of Packaging: Consumer
Brands:
    DIESTEL TURKEY RANCH

3595 Dietz & Watson Inc.
5701 Tacony St.
Philadelphia, PA 19135
215-831-9000
Fax: 215-831-1044 www.dietzandwatson.com
Meats and cheeses, including kielbasa, scrapple, bacon, ham fillets, franks, grillers, chicken sausages, natural casing sausages, resealable deli meats, sauces and dressings, potato and eggsalad, cole slaw, macaroni salad, greek pastasalad, bruschetta, oriental noodle, pasta parm, pasta primavera, totellini, spinesto, antibasto, black bean, edamame, ambrosia, salami, italian sausage (hot or sweet), pepperoni, etc.
President/CEO: Louis Eni
CFO: Cindy Eni Yingling
COO: Christophe Eni
Year Founded: 1939
Estimated Sales: $245 Million
Number Employees: 500-999
Number of Brands: 1
Square Footage: 180000
Type of Packaging: Consumer, Bulk
Other Locations:
    Black Bear Distribution
    Delanco NJ
    Dietz & Watson
    Baltimore MD
Brands:
    Dietz & Watson

3596 (HQ)Diggs Packing Company
1207 Rogers St
Columbia, MO 65201-4796
573-449-2995
Fax: 573-449-3163
Beef, ham, sausage, meat packing services, distributes fresh meat, provides slaughtering
Owner: Dale Diggs
Public Relations: Dan Reynolds
Estimated Sales: $14.10 Million
Number Employees: 20-49
Type of Packaging: Consumer

3597 Digrazia Vineyards
131 Tower Rd
Brookfield, CT 06804-3654
203-775-1616
Fax: 203-775-3195 800-230-8853
info@digraziavineyards.com
www.digraziavineyards.com
Wine, wholesale & retaile; Altar wine for Church use; winery tours and group events.
Owner: Christopher Kelly
christopherkelly@digrazia.com
Vice President: Mark Longford
Plant Manager: Aaron Cox
Estimated Sales: Less Than $500,000
Number Employees: 1-4
Brands:
    Convetual Franciscan Friars
    Di Grazia Vineyards

3598 Dilettante Chocolates
19016 72nd Avenue South
Kent, WA 98032
425-656-9076
Fax: 425-656-8059 800-800-9490
www.seattlegourmetfoods.com
Candy and confectionery
President: David Taylor
sales@seattlegourmetfoods.com
CEO: Brian Davenport
Director Sales/Marketing: Tom Davis
Sales Manager: Chris Ratliff
Production Manager: Brian Hubbard
Estimated Sales: $1-2.5 Million
Number Employees: 5-9

3599 Dillanos Coffee Roasters
1607 45th St E
Sumner, WA 98390-2202
253-826-1807
Fax: 253-826-1827 800-234-5282
www.dillanos.com
Coffee

Food Manufacturers / A-Z

Owner: Chris Heyer
chrish@dillanos.com
CFO: Rand Hill
Estimated Sales: $3 Million
Number Employees: 50-99
Type of Packaging: Food Service

3600 Dillard's Bar-B-Q Sauce
1058 W Club Boulevard
Ste. 6672
Durham, NC 27701
919-286-1080
Fax: 919-361-3410 sales@carolinasauce.com
Barbecue sauce
Co-Partner: Geneva Dillard
Co-Partner/General Manager: Wilma Dillard
Estimated Sales: Less than $500,000
Number Employees: 10-19
Type of Packaging: Consumer
Brands:
    Dillard's

3601 Dillman Farm Inc
4955 W State Road 45
Bloomington, IN 47403-9362
812-825-8118
Fax: 812-825-4650 800-359-1362
dillman@dillmanfarm.com www.dillmanfarm.com
Fruit butters, preserves, jellies, salsa, mustard, bbq, no preservatives, cane sugar or grape juice to sweeten products
President: Cary Dillman
carydillman@dillmanfarm.com
Treasurer: Amy Dillman
Director of Sales: Jean Brook
Estimated Sales: $820,000
Number Employees: 5-9
Square Footage: 60000
Brands:
    Dillman Farm
    Dillman's All Natural

3602 Dillon Candy Co
19927 US Highway 84 E
Boston, GA 31626-2666
229-498-2051
Fax: 229-498-2201 800-382-8338
Candy including peanut and pecan log rolls, sand brittles, divinity, coated pecans, pralines and pecan puffs
Owner: Tom Cook
Sales: Michele Tull
dcc@dilloncandy.com
Estimated Sales: $10-20 Million
Number Employees: 20-49
Type of Packaging: Consumer

3603 Dimitria Delights Baking Co
81 Creeper Hill Rd
North Grafton, MA 01536-1421
508-839-1638
Fax: 508-839-1685 800-763-1113
sales@dimitriadelights.com
www.dimitriadelights.com
Frozen baked and nonbaked desserts including spinach pies, puff pastries, fruit strudels, regular and filled danish and croissant dough
President/Production Manager: John Colorio
Vice President: Mary Colorio
Estimated Sales: $10-20 Million
Number Employees: 50-99
Square Footage: 70000
Type of Packaging: Consumer, Food Service, Private Label
Brands:
    Mary's
    Pita
    Strudelkins

3604 Dimock Dairy Products
400 S Main St
Dimock, SD 57331
605-928-3833
Fax: 605-928-3390 dimockdairy@santel.net
www.dimockdairy.com
Cheese
GM: Roger Swemby
Manager: Roger Swenby
rogerswenby@dimockdairy.com
Manager: Mike Royston
Estimated Sales: $5-10 Million
Number Employees: 5-9
Square Footage: 18000
Type of Packaging: Consumer

3605 Dimond Tager Company Products
2801 E Hillsborough Ave
Tampa, FL 33610-4410
813-238-3111
Fax: 813-238-3114
Manufacturer and wholesaler/distributor of produce
President: Raymond Charlton
Estimated Sales: $1.7 Million
Number Employees: 10
Square Footage: 16000
Type of Packaging: Consumer, Food Service, Bulk

3606 Dimpflmeier Bakery
26-36 Advance Road
Toronto, ON M8Z 2T4
Canada
416-236-2701
Fax: 416-239-5370 800-268-2421
orders@dimpflmeierbakery.com
www.dimpflmeierbakery.com
German-style breads including rye, pumpernickel, sourdough and monastery; also, rolls and buns
President: Alfonse Dimpflmier
Number Employees: 170
Type of Packaging: Consumer, Food Service
Brands:
    Holzofen
    Klosterbrot
    Muenchner/Stadtbrot

3607 Dina's Organic Chocolate
4 Smith Avenue
Mt Kisco, NY 10549
914-242-0124
Fax: 914-242-5289 888-625-2008
www.dinakhader.com
Line of 74 percent organic dark chocolate products including goji, green tea, omega 3 flax and almond. Also available are 74 percent dark chocolate truffles and rasberry truffles whole line is gluten and dairy free.
President/Owner: Dina Khader
Sales/Marketing/Purchasing: Andre Avdant
Number Employees: 7
Square Footage: 6600

3608 Ding Hau Food Co, Ltd
12760 Bathgate Way
Suite 6
Richmond, BC V6V 1Z4
Canada
604-273-1188
Fax: 604-273-9288
Frozen prepared meals
Owner/President: Yu Lang Chang
Estimated Sales: $3.19 Million
Number Employees: 7
Type of Packaging: Food Service, Private Label, Bulk

3609 Dinkel's Bakery Inc
3329 N Lincoln Ave
Chicago, IL 60657-1107
773-281-7300
Fax: 773-281-6169 800-822-8817
www.dinkels.com
Baked goods including chocolate chip butter cookies, cakes, pecan fudge brownies and snacks; contract baking available
President: N Dinkel
norm@dinkels.com
Controller/Treasurer: Holly Dinkel
General Manager: Luke Karl
Human Resource Manager: J Norman
norm@dinkels.com
Estimated Sales: $870,000
Number Employees: 20-49
Square Footage: 60000
Type of Packaging: Consumer, Food Service, Private Label, Bulk
Brands:
    Dinkel's
    Dinkel's Famous Stollen
    Dinkel's Sip'n
    Dinkel's Southern Double

3610 Dinner Bell Meat Product
1700 17th Street
Lynchburg, VA 24501
434-847-7766
Fax: 434-847-6305
Sausage
President: Butch Anderson
Estimated Sales: $10-20 Million
Number Employees: 10-19
Type of Packaging: Consumer

3611 Dino's Sausage & Meat Co Inc
722 Catherine St
Utica, NY 13501-1304
315-732-2661
Fax: 315-732-3094 www.dinossausage.com
Sausage and beef products; wholesaler/distributor of bacon, ham, pork, lamb, etc
President: Chris Houser
fchousercpa@yahoo.com
Vice President: Anthony Ferrucci
Estimated Sales: $10-20 Million
Number Employees: 10-19
Type of Packaging: Consumer
Brands:
    Dino's

3612 Dino-Meat Company
PO Box 95
White House, TN 37188-0095
615-643-1022
Fax: 615-643-1022 877-557-6493
Emu meat including steaks, ground, breakfast sausage, summer sausage, hot dogs, hot links, meat balls, snack sticks and jerky. Also emu oil and emu oil products
President: Neil Williams
Type of Packaging: Consumer, Food Service
Brands:
    Back Country Emu Products
    Dine-Meat Emu Products

3613 Dion Herbs & Spices
801 Montee St. Nicolas
St-Jerome, QC J7Y 4C7
Canada
450-569-8001
Fax: 450-569-0062 877-569-8001
gaston@alimentsgdion.com
www.alimentsgdion.com
Extracts, herbs, salt, spices, private label.
Marketing: Gaston Dion

3614 Dipaolo Baking Co Inc
598 Plymouth Ave N
Rochester, NY 14608-1629
585-232-3510
Fax: 585-423-5975 sales@dipaolobread.com
Breads, rolls and pastries.
Owner: Jim Acquilano
President/CEO: Dominick Massa
dominick@dipaolobread.com
Estimated Sales: $10-20 Million
Number Employees: 20-49
Type of Packaging: Food Service

3615 Dipasa USA Inc
6600 Ruben Torres Sr Blvd # B
Brownsville, TX 78526-6954
956-831-4072
Fax: 956-831-5893 info@dipasausa.com
www.dipasausa.com
Tahini and sesame seeds, raisins, oil, flour and candy; wholesaler/distributor of onion and cheese breadsticks, baked snacks, halvah and confectionery items, natural colors, oleoresins
Vice President: Garry Lowder
garrylowder@dipasausa.com
Vice President: Garry Lowder
garrylowder@dipasausa.com
Vice President, Marketing: Garry Lowder
Estimated Sales: $8 Million
Number Employees: 10-19
Number of Brands: 2
Number of Products: 10
Square Footage: 80000
Type of Packaging: Consumer, Food Service, Private Label, Bulk
Brands:
    Biladi
    Biladi Tohina
    De Champaque Bakery Snacks
    Dipasa Biladi
    Dipasa De Champagne
    Dipasa Usa
    Sesamin

Food Manufacturers / A-Z

3616 Dippin' Dots LLC
5101 Charter Oak Dr
Paducah, KY 42001-5209
270-443-8994
Fax: 270-443-8997 sales@dippindots.com
www.dippindots.com
Ice cream, yogurt, flavored ices and sherbets
CEO: Scott Fischer
President: Tom Leonard
CFO: Sheri Dikin
Chief Marketing & Sales Officer: Michael Barrette
Public Relations: Terry Reeves
Director Operations: Rick Noble
Estimated Sales: $20-50 Million
Number Employees: 1-4
Brands:
  Dippin' Dots

3617 Dippy Foods
10554 Progress Way Ste K
Cypress, CA 90630
714-816-0150
Fax: 714-816-0153 800-819-8551
Single-serving meals to schools and other institutional food servers
President: Jon Stevenson
VP: Erin Stevenson
Brands:
  Earth's Best
  Hain Kidz
  Health Valley

3618 Discovery Foods
2395 American Ave
Hayward, CA 94545
510-780-9238
Fax: 510-293-1830
Asian inspired frozen foods
President & Founder: Clarence Mou
Founder: Alfred Mou
Contact: John Cotts
jcotts@dfusa.com
Year Founded: 1996
Estimated Sales: $20-50 Million
Number Employees: 100-249

3619 Dismat Corporation
336 N Westwood Ave
Toledo, OH 43607
419-531-8963
Fax: 419-531-8965
Powdered soup mixes and seasonings
President: John Donofrio
mckayssoupmix@bex.net
Operations VP: Sandra Lee Jones
Estimated Sales: $1-$2 Million
Number Employees: 5-9
Number of Brands: 1
Number of Products: 3
Square Footage: 48000
Type of Packaging: Consumer, Bulk
Brands:
  McKay's

3620 Distant Lands Coffee Roaster
801 Houser Way N
Renton, WA 98057
903-592-9771
Fax: 903-593-2699 800-758-4437
info@dlcoffee.com www.dlcoffee.com
Roasters of organic, flavored and fair-trade coffees.
President: Bill McAlpin
Marketing: Kristin Jones
VP Sales: Todd Hughes
Contact: Chris Ashby
ashbyc@dlcoffee.com
Estimated Sales: $5 Million
Number Employees: 50
Type of Packaging: Private Label, Bulk
Brands:
  Country Coffee

3621 Distillata
1608 E 24th Street
Cleveland, OH 44114
800-999-2906
www.distillata.com
Bottler of spring and distilled water, as well as water filtration systems, water coolers, water fountains, and pool filling services.
Owner: Kevin Schroeder
Head of Sales: Adam Schroeder
Operations Manager: Heather Schroeder
Estimated Sales: $10-20 Million
Number Employees: 100-249
Type of Packaging: Consumer, Food Service, Private Label, Bulk
Brands:
  Distillata

3622 Diversified Avocado Products
25950 Acero Street
Suite 360
Mission Viejo, CA 92691-7900
949-837-6464
Fax: 949-837-6464 800-879-2555
Frozen guacamole and fresh avocados
Account Executive: Alberto Castro
Director Sales/Marketing: Ray Flores
Contact: Sam Carson
scarson@dapguacamole.com
Estimated Sales: $500,000- 1 Million
Number Employees: 5-9
Square Footage: 400000
Type of Packaging: Consumer, Food Service

3623 Diversified Foods & Seasonings
1404 Greengate Dr.
Suite 300
Covington, LA 70433
985-809-3600
Fax: 504-834-0395 800-914-2382
sales@diversified-foods.com
www.diversified-foods.com
Frozen specialty foods such as beans, bbq sauces, creole sauces, marinara sauces, side dishes of macaroni and cheese, spinach and artichoke dips, collard greens, soups and chilis, gumbo, rice seasonings, dry marinades, breadings, drygravies, biscuit mixes and custom cheesecakes.
Chairman: Al Copeland Jr.
President & CEO: Peter Smith
CFO: Frank Parent
VP Research & Development: David Smith
Chief Mangement Officer: William Marvin
Estimated Sales: $20-50 Million
Number Employees: 1-4
Parent Co: A.L. Copeland
Type of Packaging: Food Service, Private Label
Brands:
  Chief's Creations

3624 Divine Chocolate
418 7th St SE
Washington, DC 20003
202-332-8913
Fax: 202-332-8916 www.divinechocolateusa.com
Chocolate bars
Ceo: Erin Gorman
Marketing: Niki Lagos
Contact: Amanda White
amanda@divinechocolateusa.com
Estimated Sales: $1 Million
Number Employees: 3

3625 Divine Delights
1250 Holm Rd
Petaluma, CA 94954-1106
707-559-7099
Fax: 707-559-7098 800-443-2836
customerservice@divinedelights.com
www.divinedelights.com
Premium petit fours and petite confections
President: Angelique Fry
Co-owner: Bill Fry
bill@divinedelights.com
Estimated Sales: $5-10 Million
Number Employees: 10-19
Type of Packaging: Private Label, Bulk
Brands:
  Checkerbites
  Divine Delights
  Mice-A-Fours
  Trufflecots

3626 Divine Foods
Po Box 490
Elizabethtown, NC 28337-0490
910-862-2576
Fax: 910-862-2799
Functional (antioxidants), bread/biscuits, juice/cider, wine, salsa/dips, jams, jellies.
Marketing: Miller Taylor

3627 Divine Organics
209-532-4950
www.divineorganics.com
Organic superfoods
Founder: David Kaplan
Number of Brands: 1
Type of Packaging: Consumer
Brands:
  DIVINE ORGANICS

3628 Divvies
700 Oakridge Cmns
South Salem, NY 10590-2440
914-533-2804
www.divvies.com
Dairy free, egg free, peanut free, tree nut free food snacks
Owner: Mark Sandler
mark@divvies.com
Number Employees: 10-19

3629 Dixie Dew Prods Co
1360 Jamike Ave
P.O.Box 18310
Erlanger, KY 41018-3114
859-283-1050
Fax: 859-282-3781 800-867-8548
info@dixiedewproducts.com
Fruit glazes, dips, puddings, toppings, day blends and specialty sauces; contract processing and packaging available
Managing Director: Robert Carl
Quality Controll: Glen Delong
Contact: Margaret Carl
margaretc@dixiedewproducts.com
Estimated Sales: Less Than $500,000
Number Employees: 1-4
Square Footage: 160000
Type of Packaging: Consumer, Food Service, Private Label, Bulk
Brands:
  Classic Traditions
  Harry's Choice
  Heritage Fancy Foods

3630 Dixie Egg Co
5139 Edgewood Ct
Jacksonville, FL 32254-3601
904-783-0950
Fax: 904-786-6227 800-394-3447
kjkeggs@aol.com www.dixieegg.com
Fresh shell eggs
President: Jacques Klempf
CEO: Edward Klempf
sshimoda@dixieegg.com
Controller: Paul Stevenson
IT: Steve Slayter
Feed/Production Manager: Dennis Hughes
Number Employees: 250-499
Parent Co: Foodonics International
Type of Packaging: Consumer, Bulk

3631 Dixie Rice
600 Pasquiere St
Gueydan, LA 70542
337-536-9276
Fax: 337-536-5099
Rice
President: Steven Watson
Chairman: Harold Simmons
Estimated Sales: $460,000
Number Employees: 8
Square Footage: 12000
Brands:
  Dixie

3632 Dixie Trail Farms
PO Box 4082
Wilmington, NC 28406-1082
800-665-3968
Fax: 800-765-7482
Grilling sauces and marinades

3633 Dixie USA
P.O. Box 1969
Tomball, TX 77377
832-616-3366
Fax: 832-201-0765 800-233-3668
info@dixieusa.com www.dixiediner.com
Meat analogs, tofu, soy products and low carb products; exporter of soy
President: Brenda K. Oswalt
Chairman, Founder: Bob Beeley
EVP: Jim Oswalt
Estimated Sales: $5-10 Million
Number Employees: 20-49
Square Footage: 120000

Food Manufacturers / A-Z

Type of Packaging: Consumer, Food Service, Private Label, Bulk
Brands:
  Beef Not
  Chicken Not
  Dutlettes

3634 Dixon's Fisheries
1807 N Main St
East Peoria, IL 61611-2193
    800-373-1457
Fax: 309-694-0539 800-373-1457
internetsales@dixonsseafood.com
www.dixonsseafood.com
Appetizers, caviar, squid, dips, spreads, marinades, sauces, fresh fish & shellfish, frozen fish & shellfish, smoked fish, exotic meats
President: Robert Dixon
Principal: James Dixon
Estimated Sales: $20-50 Million
Number Employees: 5-9

3635 Dizzy Pig BBQ Co
8763 Virginia Meadows Dr
Manassas, VA 20109-7826
    571-379-4884
Fax: 206-984-3736 chris.capell@dizzypigbbq.com
dizzypigbbq.com
Other condiments, rubs, spices, foodservice, gift packs.
Owner: Chris Capell
chris@dizzypigbbq.com
Marketing: Chris Capell
Number Employees: 10-19

3636 Djerdan Burek Corp
9E Wesley St
South Hackensack, NJ 07606
    888-462-8735
info@djerdan.com
djerdan.com
Packed bread rolls; stuffed bread sticks
President/Owner: Selma Medunjanin-Ismajli
Year Founded: 1997
Estimated Sales: Less than $500,000
Number Employees: 8
Type of Packaging: Consumer, Food Service, Private Label

3637 Dl Geary Brewing
38 Evergreen Dr
Portland, ME 04103-1066
    207-878-2337
Fax: 207-878-2388 info@gearybrewing.com
www.gearybrewing.com
Beers
President: David Geary
Marketing: Kelly Lucas
Operations: Kelly Lucas
Estimated Sales: $2 Million
Number Employees: 20-49
Brands:
  Dl Geary Brewing

3638 Do Anything Foods
New York, NY 10007
hello@doanythingfoods.com
www.doanythingfoods.com
Vegetable-based sauces

3639 Dobake
810 81st Avenue
Oakland, CA 94621-2510
    510-834-3134
Fax: 510-834-4408 800-834-3134
dobeinc@aol.com
Gourmet and premium baked sweet goods.
President: Dan Giraudo
Marketing Manager: Lynn Knott
Vice President of Sales: Ron Tallia
Contact: Cecilia Bracamonte
cbracamonte@dobake.com
Number Employees: 100-249
Brands:
  Dobake

3640 Dockside Market
PO Box 1002
Key Largo, FL 33037
    305-283-6678
Fax: 305-397-2389 800-813-2253
donna@docksidemarket.com
www.docksidemarket.com
Cakes, cookies, salsa, sauces, hot sauces, coffee & tea

3641 Doctor Dread's Jerk
PO Box 740
Glen Echo, MD 20812
    301-908-9450
gary@doctordreadsjerk.com
Manufacturer of jerk chicken, fish and salmon burgers.
Owner: Gary Himelfarb
Brands:
  Doctor Dread's

3642 Doctor's Best Inc
197 Avenida LA Pata # A
Suite A
San Clemente, CA 92673-6307
    949-498-3628
Fax: 949-498-3952 800-333-6977
info@drbvitamins.com www.drbvitamins.com
Food supplements
President: Ken Halvorsrude
Cmo: Erin O Gehan
eri@drbvitamins.com
VP Operations: Ranate Halvorsrude
Estimated Sales: $1-2.5 Million
Number Employees: 20-49
Square Footage: 20000

3643 (HQ)Doerle Food Svc LLC
113 Kol Dr
Broussard, LA 70518-3825
    337-252-8551
Fax: 337-252-8558 800-256-1631
www.doerlefoods.com
Fresh and frozen meats and poultry, a wide variety of beverages and chemical supplies, also includes seafood, gourmet foods, fresh produce, dry groceries, dairy products, disposables, small ware and table top items, specialty healthcare products and janitorial supplies
President & CEO: Allen Boudreaux
VP Operations & Transportation: John Romero
VP Sales & Marketing: Charlie Martin
VP Purchasing & Merchandising: Rick Blum
Year Founded: 1950
Estimated Sales: $20-50 Million
Number Employees: 100-249
Other Locations:
  Doerle Food Service
  Shreveport LA

3644 Dogfish Head Craft Brewery
105 Savannah Rd
Lewes, DE 19958
    302-644-8292
    888-834-3474
info@dogfish.com www.dogfish.com
Beer
President & COO: George Pastrana
Vice President: Mariah Calagione
Inventory Coordinator: James Cosby
Year Founded: 1995
Estimated Sales: $226 Million
Number Employees: 150
Number of Brands: 5
Type of Packaging: Consumer, Private Label
Brands:
  Chicory Stout
  Immort Ale
  Indian Brown Ale
  Raison D'Etre
  Shelter Pale Ale

3645 Dogswell LLC
1964 Westwood Boulevard
Suite 350
Los Angeles, CA 90025
    310-651-5200
Fax: 877-327-3145 888-559-8833
info@dogswell.com www.dogswell.com
Functional (antioxidants), other lifestyle, pet food.
Marketing: Marco Giannini

3646 Dogwood Brewing Company
1222 Logan Cir NW
Atlanta, GA 30318
    404-367-0500
Fax: 404-367-0505
Ale and stout beers
President: Crawford Moran
Estimated Sales: $1-2.5 Million
Number Employees: 1-4
Type of Packaging: Consumer, Food Service

Brands:
  Dogwood

3647 Dohar Meats Inc
1979 W 25th St
Cleveland, OH 44113-3455
    216-241-4197
Fax: 216-664-3390
ADempsey@city.cleveland.oh.us
westsidemarket.org/vendor/dohar-lovaszy-meats/?portfolioID=955
Pork including sausage and deli meats
Owner: Angela Dohar
Manager: Mike Szucs
Estimated Sales: Less than $500,000
Number Employees: 1-4
Type of Packaging: Consumer, Bulk

3648 Dohler-Milne Aseptics LLC
804 Bennett Ave
PO Box 111
Prosser, WA 99350-1267
    509-786-2240
Fax: 630-797-2001
Flavoring extracts and syrups
Manager: Dan Villarreal
danv@dmaseptics.com
Controller: Joe Stoops
Estimated Sales: $1.2 Million
Number Employees: 1-4

3649 Dol Cice' Gelato Company
PO Box 343
Yardley, PA 19067
    215-499-5661
Fax: 215-493-6348 Info@DolCice.com
www.dolcice.com
Italian water ices
President: Laurence Dobelle
Type of Packaging: Food Service, Private Label

3650 Dolce Nonna
162-43 12th Avenue
Whitestone, NY 11357
    718-767-3501
Fax: 718-767-3501
Marinated string beans, agri-dolce peppers and marinated eggplant
President/Owner: Gisella Civale

3651 Dolci Gelati
5766 2nd St NE
Washington, DC 20011-2524
    202-257-5323
Fax: 202-526-8064 www.dolcigelati.net
Frozen desserts, ice cream/sorbet, co-packing, private label.
President: Gianluigi Dellaccio
dolcigelati@gmail.com
Number Employees: 1-4

3652 Dold Foods
2929 N Ohio St
Wichita, KS 67219
    316-838-9101
Fax: 316-838-9053 www.hormel.com
Fresh and frozen ham and bacon
Manager: Terry W Hadden
Contact: Brad Blum
brad.blum@hormel.com
Plant Manager: Mark Coffey
Number Employees: 250-499
Square Footage: 400000
Parent Co: Hormel Foods Corporation
Type of Packaging: Consumer

3653 (HQ)Dole & Bailey Inc
16 Conn St
Woburn, MA 01801-5699
    781-935-1234
Fax: 781-935-9085 sales@doleandbailey.com
www.doleandbailey.com
Meats such as lamb, sheep, beef, poultry and pork, as well as maple syrups, cheeses, breads and desserts.
President/CEO: Nancy Matheson-Burns
nancymb@doleandbailey.com
Founder: Cyprus Dole
Co-Founder: Frank Bailey
Vice President: Bill Burns
General Manager/Corporate Chef: Ed Brylczyk
Year Founded: 1868
Estimated Sales: $25 Million
Number Employees: 100-249

Food Manufacturers / A-Z

Brands:
  Chef's Signature
  Northeast Family Farms

3654 Dole Food Company, Inc.
PO Box 5700
Thousand Oaks, CA 91359-5700
800-356-3111
www.dole.com
Fresh fruit, vegetables, prepared foods and salads.
Chairman: David Murdock
President/CEO: Johan Linden
Vice President/CFO: Johan Malmqvist
President, Dole Fresh Vegetables: Michael Solomon
Year Founded: 1851
Estimated Sales: $4.5 Billion
Number Employees: 59,000
Type of Packaging: Consumer, Food Service, Private Label, Bulk
Other Locations:
  Dole Manufacturing Facility
  (9) Arizona
  Dole Manufacturing Facility
  (11) California
  Dole Manufacturing Facility
  (25) Delaware
  Dole Manufacturing Faciltiy
  (27) Florida
  Dole Manufacturing Facility
  (29) Hawaii
  Dole Manufacturing Facility
  (33) Michigan
  Dole Manufacturing Facility
  (35) North Carolina
  Dole Manufacturing Facility
  (37) Ohio
  Dole Manufacturing Facility
  (38) Texas
  Dole Manufacturing Facility
  (39) Ontario, Canada

3655 Dole Pond Maple Products
PO Box 841
Jackman, ME 04945
418-653-5322
Fax: 418-653-5322 jcpare@xplornet.com
www.dolepondmapleproducts.com
Maple syrup
President: Jean-Claude Pare
Number Employees: 1-4

3656 Dolisos America
1710 Whitney Mesa Dr
Henderson, NV 89014-2055
702-871-7153
Fax: 702-871-9670 800-365-4767
Homeopathic medicines.
President/CEO: Luc Clouatre

3657 Dollar Food Manufacturing
1410 Odlum Drive
Vancouver, BC V5L 4X7
Canada
604-253-1422
Fax: 604-253-2226 dollarfood@telus.net
Salted and/or dried salmon, sausage cured, golden pork hock. Founded in 1983.
President: Kelly Chow
Data Provider: Louisa Fung
Number Employees: 35
Type of Packaging: Consumer, Food Service

3658 Dolores Canning Co Inc
1020 N Eastern Ave
Los Angeles, CA 90063-3214
323-263-9155
Fax: 323-269-4876 sales@dolorescanning.com
Pickled pork products, chili bricks and specialty Mexican items
President, Co-Founder: Steve Munoz
Co-Founder: Augustine L. Munoz
Marketing: David Munoz
Sales: Bert Munoz
Estimated Sales: $1 Million
Number Employees: 20-49
Type of Packaging: Consumer, Food Service, Private Label
Brands:
  Dolores

3659 Dolphin Natural Chocolates
1975 Woodview Avenue
Cambria, CA 93428-5168
805-927-7103
Fax: 831-722-0318 800-236-5744
Sugar and dairy-free chocolates; also, chocolate dipped apricots, papaya and pineapple
Owner: Henry McKowen
Estimated Sales: $2.5-5 Million
Number Employees: 5-9
Square Footage: 4000
Type of Packaging: Consumer
Brands:
  Dolphin Natural

3660 Dom's Sausage Co Inc
10 Riverside Park
Malden, MA 02148-6781
781-324-6390
Fax: 781-322-6776 info@domsausage.com
www.domsausage.com
Meats including beef, pork, chicken, lamb and sausages.
President: Angelo Botticelli
CEO: Dominic Botticelli
summerman9@aol.com
Estimated Sales: $15 Million
Number Employees: 20-49
Number of Brands: 1
Type of Packaging: Bulk
Brands:
  Dom's

3661 Domaine Chandon
1 California Dr
Yountville, CA 94599
888-242-6366
clubchandonwine@chandon.com
www.chandon.com
Sparkling and aperitif wines.
Engineer: Mike Morris
Year Founded: 1973
Estimated Sales: $20-50 Million
Number Employees: 250-499
Type of Packaging: Consumer
Brands:
  Blanc De Noirs
  Brut Classic
  Chardonnay
  Mt. Veeder Blanc De Blancs
  Pinot Meunier
  Pinot Noir
  Reserve Brut
  Reserve Brut Rose
  Riche
  Vintage

3662 Domaine St George Winery
1141 Grant Ave
Healdsburg, CA 95448-9570
707-433-5508
Fax: 707-433-5736 dswines@domstgeo.com
www.domainestgeorge.com
Wines
President: Somchai Likitprakong
dswines@domstgeo.com
Chairman: Yu Yee
Estimated Sales: $5-10 Million
Number Employees: 20-49
Type of Packaging: Private Label
Brands:
  Domaine St. George

3663 Domata Living Flour
P.O. Box 24074
Minneapolis, MN 55424
952-303-5484
Fax: 952-303-5955 855-DOM-TA1
domataglutenfree.com
Gluten free flour
Co-Owner: David Madison

3664 Dominex
P.O.Box 5069
St Augustine, FL 32085
904-810-2132
Fax: 904-810-9852 sales@dominexeggplant.com
www.dominexeggplant.com
Eggplant cutlets and appetizers; including peeled, breaded, battered, deep fried and IQF. All natural fully cooked breaded in italian crumbs, eggplant appetizers and cutlets
President: John McGarvey
Director- Sales and Marketing: Miranda Chalke
chalke@dominexeggplant.com
Estimated Sales: 10-19
Number Employees: 50-99
Number of Brands: 10
Number of Products: 145
Type of Packaging: Food Service, Private Label, Bulk
Brands:
  Dominex

3665 Dominion Wine Cellars
PO Box 1057
Culpeper, VA 22701-1057
540-825-8772
Fax: 540-829-0377
Wine
President: Wade D Sampson

3666 Domino Specialty Ingredients
One N Clematis St
West Palm Beach, FL 33401
info@dominospecialtyingredients.com
www.dominospecialtyingredients.com
Organic sugars, tapioca syrup, molasses, malt, honey, rice, rice syrup, rice bran, rice flour, sugar, icing and fondant.
EVP & CFO: Jeff Lawrence
Estimated Sales: $100+ Million
Parent Co: Domino Foods Inc
Brands:
  Florida Crystals
  Domino Sugar
  C&H Sugar
  Redpath Sugar
  Tate+Lyle
  Lyle's Golden Syrup
  Zing
  Sidul

3667 Don Alfonso Foods
7218 McNeil Drive
Austin, TX 78729-7980
512-335-2370
Fax: 512-335-0636 800-456-6100
Mexican food ingredients (prepared moles) dried chiles, spices and sauces
President: Jose Marmolejo
Brands:
  Don Alfonso

3668 Don Bugito
San Francisco, CA 94110
www.donbugito.com
Pre-Columbian Mexican snack foods
Founder: Monica Martinez

3669 Don Hilario Estate Coffee
300 State Street East
Suite 226
Oldsmar, FL 34677
813-814-2888
Fax: 813-814-1788 800-799-1903
info@donhilario.com
Coffee
CEO/Marketing Director: Russell Versaggi
Estimated Sales: $2.5-5 Million
Number Employees: 1-4
Type of Packaging: Private Label
Brands:
  Don Hilario Estate Coffee

3670 Don Jose Foods
8906 N 84th Way
Scottsdale, AZ 85258-2434
480-443-1000
Fax: 480-443-1216 www.donjosefoods.com
Fruit and juice beverages, chocolate drinks and assorted non-dairy items
President: Chuck Kuhlman
Vice President: Robby Kuhlman
Sales Manager: Enrique Ibarra
Number Employees: 1-4
Parent Co: Paradise Valley Foods
Type of Packaging: Private Label
Brands:
  Cereal Match
  Choco D' Lite
  Don Jose Horchata

3671 Don Lee Farms
812 S 5th Ave
Mansfield, TX 76063
817-453-3180
sales@donleefarms.com
www.donleefarms.com
Fully cooked fresh and frozen foods manufacturers.
Type of Packaging: Consumer, Private Label

Food Manufacturers / A-Z

3672 Don Sebastiani & Sons
19150 Highway 12
Sonoma, CA 95476-5412
707-224-0410
Fax: 707-939-7115 hbast@donandsons.com
www.projectpaso.com
Wine
President: Sarah Anderson
sanderson@donandsons.com
VP: Don Staaveren
VP Marketing: Robert Carroll
Account Manager: Mike Wangbickler
President/COO: Mike Holden
Estimated Sales: $9.4 Million
Number Employees: 50-99

3673 Don's Dock Seafood Market
1220 E Northwest Hwy
Des Plaines, IL 60016-3391
847-827-1817
Fax: 847-827-1846 donsdockinc@yahoo.com
Fresh seafood
Owner: Andy Johnson
dkarr4604@yahoo.com
Co-Owner: George Johnson
Co-Owner: Don Johnson
Estimated Sales: $3-5 Million
Number Employees: 10-19

3674 Don's Food Products
4461 Township Line Road
Schwenksville, PA 19473
888-321-3667
www.donssalads.com
Salads, cream cheeses, commodity salads, soups and desserts
President/Owner: Victor Skloff
Contact: Ronnie Carter
rcarter@donssalads.com

3675 Don't Go Nuts
Salida, CO 81201
855-666-8826
dontgonuts.com
Whole grain snack bars and plant-based protein spreads
Co-Founder: Doug Pinto
Co-Founder: Jane Pinto
Number of Brands: 1
Number of Products: 8
Type of Packaging: Consumer
Brands:
DON'T GO NUTS

3676 Dona Yiya Foods
P.O.Box 1623
San Sebastian, PR 00685
787-896-4007
Fax: 787-280-1430 jd@donayiya.com
www.donayiya.com
Manufacturer, exporter and importer of spices and seasonings including garlic in oil or water, soffritto, condiments and tropical candies
President: Javier Quinones
Plant Manager: Luis Denis
Estimated Sales: $3.1 Million
Number Employees: 12
Number of Brands: 2
Number of Products: 23
Square Footage: 40000
Type of Packaging: Consumer, Food Service, Private Label, Bulk

3677 Donald E Hunter Meats
4612 Turkey Rd
Hillsboro, OH 45133-7044
937-466-2311
Beef
Owner: Betty Hunter
Estimated Sales: $1-2.5 Million
Number Employees: 1-4
Type of Packaging: Consumer

3678 Donaldson's Finer Chocolates
600 S State Road 39
Lebanon, IN 46052-9401
765-482-3334
Fax: 765-482-7994 800-975-2336
www.donaldsonschocolates.com
Chocolates and candy
President: George Donaldson
george@donaldsonschocolates.com
Estimated Sales: $5-10 Million
Number Employees: 5-9

Type of Packaging: Consumer

3679 Donatoni Winery
10604 S La Cienega Boulevard
Inglewood, CA 90304-1115
310-645-5445
Fax: 310-645-5445
Wines
President/CEO: Mark Donatoni
Manager Sales: Tina Donatoni
Estimated Sales: Less than $500,000
Number Employees: 1-4
Brands:
Donatoni

3680 Donells Candies
201 E 2nd St # 2
Casper, WY 82601-2576
307-234-6283
Fax: 307-235-9119 877-461-2009
www.donellschocolates.com
Confectionery products including hand-dipped chocolates and fudge
Owner: Mike Stepp
mike@donellschocolates.com
President: Mike Stepp
Estimated Sales: $1-2.5 Million
Number Employees: 5-9
Type of Packaging: Consumer

3681 Dong Kee Company
2252 S Wentworth Ave
Chicago, IL 60616-2042
312-225-6340
Fax: 312-567-9119
Canned Chinese products including egg rolls, water chestnuts, bamboo shoots, mushrooms and fortune and almond cookies
President: Betty Wong
Owner: Herman Wong
Estimated Sales: $500,000-$1 Million
Number Employees: 5-9
Type of Packaging: Consumer, Food Service

3682 Dong Phuong Oriental Bakery
14207 Chef Menteur Hwy
New Orleans, LA 70129
504-254-0214
Fax: 504-254-1744 info@dpbanhmi.com
Baked goods

3683 Dong Us I
2590 Main St
Irvine, CA 92614-6227
949-251-1768
Fax: 949-251-8865 888-580-0088
info@dongyu.us www.dongyu.us
Manufacturer and distributor of L-Carnitine products, amino acids, vitamins, sweeteners, sports nutrition ingredients, food and beverage ingredients
Manager: Weili Zhang
Number Employees: 10-19
Square Footage: 40000

3684 Donna & Company
505 Orange Avenue
Cranford, NJ 07016-2047
908-272-4380
bob@shopdonna.com
www.shopdonna.com
Chocolate bars, chocolate truffles, full-line chocolate, other chocolate, toffee.
Marketing: Robert Koshinskie
Contact: Don Kidd
d.kidd@donna-art.com

3685 Donnelly Fine Chocolates
1509 Mission St
Santa Cruz, CA 95060-4740
831-458-4214
Fax: 831-425-0678 888-685-1871
info@donnellychocolates.com
www.donnellychocolates.com
Chocolate, dessert sauces and mixes; gift boxes available
Owner: Richard Donnelly
donnellyr@donnellychocolates.com
Estimated Sales: Less than $500,000
Number Employees: 1-4
Type of Packaging: Private Label
Brands:
Donnelly Chocolates

3686 Donsuemor Madeleines
2080 N Loop Rd
Alameda, CA 94502-8012
510-865-6406
Fax: 510-865-6947 888-420-4441
remember@donsuemor.com www.donsuemor.com
Gourmet French madeleine cookies
CEO: Susan Davis
susan@donsuemor.com
Number Employees: 50-99

3687 Donut Farm
6037 San Pablo
Oakland, CA 94608
510-338-6319
www.vegandonut.farm
Organic, vegan donuts
Founder: Josh Levine
Year Founded: 2007

3688 Donut Whole
1720 E Douglas Ave
Wichita, KS 67214-4212
316-262-3700
www.thedonutwhole.com
Natural donuts, coffeehouse
Owner: Donni Wempen
donniwempen@hotmail.com
Estimated Sales: Less Than $500,000
Number Employees: 1-4

3689 Doodles Cookies
1748 Rosebud Lane
Aurora, IL 60504
630-701-0847
info@doodlescookies.com
Cookies

3690 Door County Fish Market
2831 Dundee Rd
Northbrook, IL 60062-2501
847-559-9229
Fax: 847-559-9273
Seafood
President: Steven Messner
Secretary/Treasurer: Jeannie Lindwall
Estimated Sales: $1 Million
Number Employees: 6

3691 Door County Potato Chips
3840 N Fratney St
Milwaukee, WI 53212-1341
414-964-1428
Fax: 414-964-1484
Potato chips and pasta and contract packaging
Owner: Jamie Swisher
Number Employees: 1-4
Brands:
Door County Potato Chips
Strendge Pasta

3692 Door Peninsula Winery
5806 State Highway 42
Sturgeon Bay, WI 54235-9767
920-743-7431
Fax: 920-743-5999 800-551-5049
DPW@DCwis.com www.dcwine.com
Wines
Owner: Bob Polman
dpw@dcwis.com
VP/Marketing: Bob Pollman
Estimated Sales: $2.5-5 Million
Number Employees: 10-19
Square Footage: 32
Type of Packaging: Private Label
Brands:
Door-Peninsula

3693 Doral International
215-10 42nd Avenue
Bayside, NY 11361
718-224-7413
Fax: 718-224-7429
Organic/natural, cakes/pastries. cookies, balsamic vinegar, full-line chocolate, gummies/jellies/pates de fruits, pasta (dry), other sauces, seasonings and cooking enhancers.
Marketing: Dora Lara Bonaccolta

3694 (HQ)Dorchester Crab Co
2076 Wingate Bishops Head Rd
Wingate, MD 21675-2015
410-397-8103
Fax: 410-376-3179

Fresh and frozen seafood, shellfish including crabs and crab meat
President: Louis K Woodland
Owner: Zach Seaman
Estimated Sales: $1.70 Million
Number Employees: 5-9
Type of Packaging: Consumer, Bulk

3695 (HQ)Dorina So-Good Inc
17400 Jefferson St
Union, IL 60180-9705
815-923-2144
Fax: 815-923-2151
Manufacturer and exporter of shelf stable barbecue beef and pork; also, mustard, sauces, salsa, salad dressings, chip dips, olive salad and cheesespreads
President: Tim Young
CEO: Darwin Young
Estimated Sales: $.5-1 Million
Number Employees: 20-49
Square Footage: 24000
Type of Packaging: Consumer, Food Service, Private Label, Bulk
Brands:
 Bar-B-Q Fiesta
 Bar-B-Q Treat
 Coney Island
 Duffy
 Farm Country
 Old West Bar-B-Q Delight
 So-Good Bar-B-Q Delight
 So-Good Pork Bar-B-Q
 Super
 Young's Breading

3696 Dorothy Dawson Food Products
251 W Euclid Ave
Jackson, MI 49203-4101
517-788-9830
Fax: 517-788-7852 info@dawsonfoods.com
www.dawsonfoods.com
All-natural, ready-to-use frozen soups, sauces, batters, breadings and mixes including soup, marinade and steak au jus; also, pizza products including sauces, mixes and seasoning blends
President: Laura Bommarito
bbommarito@jacksondawson.com
VP: Brett Crosthwaite
Purchasing: Troy Ghent
Estimated Sales: $10-20 Million
Number Employees: 20-49
Type of Packaging: Food Service, Private Label, Bulk
Brands:
 Emily's Gourmet
 Freshdry
 Kettle Gourmet
 Simon's
 Starters
 Zip

3697 Dorothy Timberlake Candies
2351 Eaton Rd
Madison, NH 03849
603-447-2221
Fax: 603-447-2221 www.timberlakecandies.com
Hard candy and lollipops
President: William Timberlake
Estimated Sales: $1-2.5 Million
Number Employees: 1-4
Brands:
 Dorothy

3698 Dorset Fisheries
215 Water St
Suite 302
St Josephs, NL A1C 6C9
Canada
709-739-7147
Fax: 709-739-0586
Manufacturer and exporter of fresh lobster and cod
President: Derick Philpott
Estimated Sales: $5 Million
Number Employees: 30
Type of Packaging: Bulk

3699 Doscher's Candies Co.
24 W Court St
Cincinnati, OH 45244
513-381-8656
greg@doscherscandies.com
www.doscherscandies.com
Candy including bars, canes and taffy products.
Founded in 1871.

Chairman: Chip Nielson
VP, Operations: Kevin Gilligan
Estimated Sales: $1-2.5 Million
Number Employees: 5-9
Square Footage: 33600
Type of Packaging: Consumer
Brands:
 French Chew
 Gourmet French Chew

3700 Double B Distributors
1031 W New Circle Rd
Lexington, KY 40511-1843
859-255-8822
Fax: 859-233-1241
Meat snack foods
Owner: Bob Heim
bbdis@aol.com
Estimated Sales: $5-10 Million
Number Employees: 10-19

3701 Double B Foods Inc
800 W Arbrook Blvd # 210
Suite 210
Arlington, TX 76015-4393
469-567-6000
Fax: 817-472-8330 800-679-0349
www.doubleb.com
Chicken, eggs, frankfurters and Mexican foods
President: Kevin Macdal
kmacdal@doubleb.com
Chief Executive Officer: Patrick O'Ray
Chief Financial Officer: Don Wall
Year Founded: 1971
Estimated Sales: $25-49.9 Million
Number Employees: 250-499

3702 Double Date Packing
86301 Industrial Way
Coachella, CA 92236
760-398-8900
www.doubledatepacking.com
Medjool dates
CEO: Steven Gilfenbain
General Manager: Rob Carian

3703 Double Good
16W030 83rd St
Burr Ridge, IL 60527
630-568-5544
www.doublegood.com
Popcorn and snacks
Supply Chain & Operations: Justin Barnes
Year Founded: 1998
Estimated Sales: Less Than $500,000
Number Employees: 11-50
Square Footage: 12000

3704 Double Play Foods
500 E 77th Street
Apt 3525
New York, NY 10162-0011
212-682-4611
Fax: 212-570-4488
Peanut butter cups

3705 Double Premium Confections
6630 Kirkley Ave
McLean, VA 22101
202-495-1884
info@dpconfections.com
dpconfections.com
Manufacturer of chocolates, candies, and confections.
Owner: Bailey Kasten

3706 Double Rainbow Gourmet Ice Cream
275 S Van Ness Ave
San Francisco, CA 94103-3733
415-861-5858
Fax: 415-861-5872 800-489-3580
Manufacturers of ice cream and nondairy desserts
President: Steve Fink
CEO: Jeffrey Ross
jeffrey.ross@riverbed.com
Number Employees: 10-19

3707 Double-Cola Company
537 Market Street
Suite 100
Chattanooga, TN 37402
423-267-5691
Fax: 423-267-0793 info@double-cola.com
www.double-cola.com
Soft drinks
President: Alnoor Dhanini
VP Sales/Marketing: Gilford Thomas
Contact: Ramey Arnold
ramey.arnold@double-cola.com
Production: Roy Chisenall
Estimated Sales: $5-10 Million
Number Employees: 5-9
Brands:
 Chaser
 Diet Chaser
 Diet Double-Cola
 Diet Ski
 Double Dry Gingerale
 Double-Cola
 Double-Dry Mixers
 Jumbo Flavors
 Ski

3708 Doug Hardy Company
Mountainville Rd
Deer Isle, ME 04627
207-348-6604
Fax: 207-348-6100
Seafood
Owner: Doug Hardy
Estimated Sales: $3-5 Million
Number Employees: 5-9

3709 Dough-To-Go
3535 DE LA Cruz Blvd
Santa Clara, CA 95054-2112
408-727-4094
Fax: 408-727-4095 betsyl@doughtogo.com
www.dough-to-go.com
Frozen raw dough and cookies, scones and brownies
President: Betsy Lee
Vice President: Rosel Witt
Contact: Lee Betsy
l.betsy@dough-to-go.com
Plant & Purchasing Manager: Tom Natusch
Estimated Sales: $2 Million
Number Employees: 15
Square Footage: 40000
Type of Packaging: Food Service
Brands:
 Dough-To-Go
 Jane Dough

3710 Douglas Cross Enterprises
2030 5th Ave
Seattle, WA 98121-2505
206-448-1193
Fax: 206-448-1979 office@tomdouglas.com
www.tomdouglas.com
BBQ Sauces
Owner: Mauricio Lopez
calimolo209@gmail.com
Estimated Sales: $5-10 Million
Number Employees: 10-19

3711 Douglas Machines Corp
2101 Calumet St
Clearwater, FL 33765-1310
727-461-3477
Fax: 727-449-0029 800-331-6870
info@dougmac.com www.dougmac.com
Douglas Machines Corporation specializes in the design and manufacture of automated industrial and commercial washers and sanitizing equipment for all containers commonly found in the Bakery, Food Processing, Food Service andDistribution industries.
President: Gerri Boyce
boyce@jea.com
Executive Vice President: Kevin Lemen
Vice President Finance & Accounting: Susan Mader
Engineering Manager: Josef Weinberger
Service Manager: Dale Breedlove
Sales & Marketing Coordinator: Rosie Rachel
Operations Manager: Jim Beadling
Technical Support Specialist: John Jurski
Purchasing Manager: Karen McCrae
Number Employees: 50-99

Food Manufacturers / A-Z

3712 Douknie Winery
14727 Mountain Rd
Purcellville, VA 20132-3638
540-668-6464
Fax: 540-668-7679 info@DoukenieWinery.com
Wines
Owner: Hope Bazaco
hbazaco@doukeniewinery.com
Public Relations: Denise Benoi
Number Employees: 10-19

3713 Doumak Inc
2201 Touhy Avenue
Elk Grove Village, IL 60007
800-323-0318
customerservice@doumak.com www.doumak.com
Manufacturer of marshmallows.
CFO: Tim Etzkorn
Director of Operations: Brent Lyons
Estimated Sales: $2.5-5 Million
Number Employees: 50-99
Square Footage: 160000
Type of Packaging: Consumer, Food Service, Private Label
Brands:
 Campfire

3714 Douwe Egberts
771 Dearborn Park Lane
Suite B
Worthington, OH 43085
614-436-6112
Fax: 888-886-1533 800-582-6617
support@enjoybettercoffee.com
www.enjoybettercoffee.com
Coffee
Sales Director: Victor Borsukevich
International Marketing Director: Kerry Owens
Brands:
 Dallmayr
 Jacobs
 Tchibo
 Idee
 Helmut
 Sachers

3715 Doves and Figs LLC
89 Falmouth Rd W
Arlington, MA 02474-1007
781-646-2272
Fax: 866-903-7912 www.dovesandfigs.com
Jams; chutneys; and fruit mustards
Owner: Robin Cohen
Year Founded: 2011
Number Employees: 3
Type of Packaging: Private Label

3716 Dow AgroSciences Canada
450 1st St SW
Suite 2100
Calgary, AB T2P 5H1
Canada
403-735-8800
Fax: 403-735-8841 info@dow.com
www.omega-9oils.com
Omega-9 oils
President/Chief Executive Officer: Jim Wispinski
Estimated Sales: $25.36 Million
Number Employees: 60
Parent Co: DOW Chemical Company
Type of Packaging: Food Service, Bulk

3717 Dow Distribution
524 Ohohia St
Honolulu, HI 96819-1934
808-836-3511
Fax: 808-833-3634
Fish and seafood
President: Craig Mitchell
cmitch@hawaii.rr.com
Estimated Sales: $10-20 Million
Number Employees: 10-19

3718 Dowd & Rogers
1403 N
El Camino Real
San Clemente, CA 92672
916-451-6480
Fax: 800-767-8514 800-232-8619
Premium wheat free and gluten free products
President: Derek Dowd
Number of Brands: 2
Number of Products: 8

Type of Packaging: Consumer, Food Service, Private Label, Bulk
Brands:
 Dowd and Rogers

3719 Down East Specialty Products/Cape Bald Packers
P.O. Box 9739
Suite 1200
Portland, ME 04103
207-878-9170
Fax: 207-878-9104 800-369-6327
www.capebaldpackers.com
Lobster, mussels, rock crab and red crab
Manager: Kathy Nally
Manager: Patrice Landry
Estimated Sales: $1-3 Million
Number Employees: 1-4
Parent Co: Cape Bald Packers
Type of Packaging: Private Label
Brands:
 Downeast

3720 Downeast Candies
P.O.Box 25
Boothbay Harbor, ME 4538
207-633-5178
Fudges and taffy
President: David Carmolli
VP: Elaine Miller
Production Manager: Rick Carmolli
Estimated Sales: $1-2.5 Million
Number Employees: 1-4
Type of Packaging: Consumer, Private Label, Bulk
Brands:
 Downeast Candies

3721 Downeast Cider House
256 Marginal Street
Suite 32
East Boston, MA 02128
857-301-8881
info@downeastcider.com
downeastcider.com
Craft hard cider
Co-Founder: Ross Brockman
Co-Founder: Tyler Mosher
Co-Founder: Ben Manter
Co-Founder: Matt Brockman
Year Founded: 2011
Number Employees: 51-200
Number of Brands: 10
Type of Packaging: Consumer

3722 Downeast Coffee Roasters
259 East Ave
Pawtucket, RI 02860-3801
401-724-6393
Fax: 401-724-0560 800-345-2007
www.downeastcoffee.com
Roasted coffees.
President/CEO: William Kapos
wkapos@excellentcoffee.com
Vice President: Michael Kapos
VP, Retail Sales: Keith McClain
Estimated Sales: $16 Million
Number Employees: 100-249
Number of Brands: 2
Type of Packaging: Private Label
Brands:
 Downeast Coffee
 Ocean Coffee Roasters

3723 Doyon
Canada
800-265-2600
www.mieldoyon.com
Beeswax and honey; exporter of honey; importer of pollen
President: Paul Doyon
CEO: David Sugarman
Number Employees: 15
Square Footage: 60000
Parent Co: McCormick & Co.
Type of Packaging: Consumer, Food Service, Bulk

3724 Dr Konstantin Frank's Vinifera
9749 Middle Rd
Hammondsport, NY 14840-9612
800-320-0735
Fax: 607-868-4888 800-320-0735
info@drfrankwines.com www.drfrankwines.com
Manufacturer and exporter of table wine and champagne

President: Fred Frank
VP & Vineyard Manager: Eric Volz
Consulting Winemaker & Regional Sales Ma:
Barbara Frank
Contact: Peter Bell
pbell@spidergraphics.com
Estimated Sales: $5-10 Million
Number Employees: 5-9
Type of Packaging: Consumer
Brands:
 Chateau Frank Champagne Cellars
 Dr. Konstantin Frank

3725 Dr Pepper Snapple Group
5301 Legacy Dr.
Plano, TX 75024
800-696-5891
www.drpeppersnapplegroup.com
Fruit juices, soft drink, and more.
CEO: Robert Gamgort
CFO: Ozan Dokmecioglu
Chief Legal Officer/General Counsel: Jim Baldwin
Chief Research & Development Officer: David Thomas
Chief Marketing Officer: Andrew Springate
Year Founded: 2008
Estimated Sales: $11 Billion
Number Employees: 21,000
Number of Brands: 34
Parent Co: Keurig Dr Pepper
Type of Packaging: Consumer, Food Service, Bulk
Brands:
 7UP®
 All Sport®
 A&W Root Beer®
 Bai®
 Big Red®
 Canada Dry®
 Clamato®
 Crush®
 Deja Blue®
 Diet Rite®
 Dr Pepper®
 Hawaiian Punch®
 Hires®
 IBC Root Beer®
 Margaritaville®
 Mott's®
 Mr. & Mrs. T®
 Nantucket Nectars®
 Orangina®
 Penafiel®
 RC Cola®
 ReaLemon®
 ReaLime®
 Rose's®
 Schweppes®
 Snapple®
 Squirt®
 Straight Up Tea®
 Stewarts®
 Sun Drop®
 Sunkist®
 Vemon Energy®
 Vernors®
 Yoohoo®

3726 Dr Pete's
P.O. Box 24089
Savannah, GA 31403
912-233-3035
Fax: 912-233-0001 888-599-0047
info@dr-petes.com www.dr-petes.com
Sauces, marinades and dressings
CEO: Joel Coffee
Estimated Sales: $600,000
Number Employees: 5-9
Type of Packaging: Consumer, Food Service
Brands:
 Dr. Pete's

3727 Dr Praeger's Sensible Foods
9 Boumar Pl
Elmwood Park, NJ 07407-2615
201-703-1300
877-772-3437
www.dpsensiblefood.net
Kosher natural frozen products such as veggie burgers, fish sticks and potato pancakes
President: Dr Peter Praeger
CEO: Larry Praeger
larry@drpraegers.com
Director Sales/Marketing: Larry Praeger

Food Manufacturers / A-Z

Estimated Sales: $20-50 Million
Number Employees: 50-99
Type of Packaging: Food Service
Brands:
  Dr Praeger's
  Ungar's

3728 Dr. B's Beverages, LLC
4325 Gerrardstown Rd.
Inwood, WV 25428
304-283-2257
www.docstea.com
Manufacturer of drinks made with tea.
Co-Founder: Ken Banks
Co-Founder: Christopher Banks
Co-Founder: Sarah Banks

3729 Dr. Christopher's Herbal Supplements
155 W 2050 N
Spanish Fork, UT 84660
801-453-1406
Fax: 801-794-6801 800-453-1406
www.drchristopher.com
Supplements and herbal formulas
Sales/Marketing: Troy Fukumitsu
Contact: Robert Scott
rscott@drchristopher.com
Estimated Sales: $20-50 Million
Number Employees: 20-49
Type of Packaging: Consumer, Private Label, Bulk

3730 Dr. Cookie
2112 6th Ave
Seattle, WA 98121-2513
206-389-9321
www.drcookie.com
Cookies, breads, rolls
Manager: Steve Krendall
Estimated Sales: $1-5 Million appx.
Number Employees: 1-4
Brands:
  Dr Cookie

3731 Dr. In The Kitchen
P.O. Box 24868
Minneapolis, MN 55424
952-746-3007
orders@drinthekitchen.com
www.drinthekitchen.com
Snack bars and crackers made with seeds.
Co-Founder: Alison Levitt
Co-Founder: Donna Kelly
Year Founded: 2007
Estimated Sales: $610000
Number Employees: 8
Type of Packaging: Private Label

3732 Dr. Lucy's LLC
930 Denison Ave.
Suite 101-A
Norfolk, VA 23513
757-233-9495
Fax: 757-233-9398 info@drlucys.com
Cookies baked without wheat, gluten, dairy milk, butter, eggs, casein, peanuts or tree nuts.
President/Owner: Lucy Gibney
Contact: Megan Hallman
megan@drlucys.com

3733 Dr. McDougall's Right Foods
Woodland, CA
866-972-6879
www.rightfoods.com
Vegan prepared foods
Founder: Dr. John McDougall
Type of Packaging: Consumer
Brands:
  DR. MCDOUGALL'S

3734 Dr. Oetker Canada Ltd.
2229 Drew Road
Mississauga, ON L5S 1E5
Canada
905-678-1311
Fax: 905-678-9334 800-387-6939
www.oetker.ca
Cake and muffin mixes, mashed potatoes, drink crystals
Chairman: Dr August Oetker
Brands:
  Dr Oetker

3735 Dr. Paul Lohmann Inc.
1757-10 Veterans Memorial Hwy
Islandia, NY 11749
631-851-8810
Fax: 631-851-8815
Specialty mineral salts

3736 Dr. Pete's
2224 Gamble Rd
PO Box 24089
Savannah, GA 31403
912-233-3035
Fax: 912-233-0001 info@dr-petes.com
www.dr-petes.com
Sauces, marinades, dressings, baking mixes
CEO: Joel Coffee
VP: Jan Coffee
Number Employees: 5

3737 Dr. Pete's/J.C. Specialty Foods
P.O. Box 24089
Savannah, GA 31403-4089
912-233-3035
Fax: 912-233-0001 info@dr-petes.com
www.dr-petes.com
Products that complement meats, vegetables and salads, marinades, glazes, salad dressings
Owner: Joel Coffee
Estimated Sales: $2.5-5 Million
Number Employees: 1-4

3738 Dr. Schar USA
1050 Wall Street West
Suite 370
Lyndhurst, NJ 7071
201-355-8470
Fax: 201-355-8624 info.us@drschar.com
www.drschaer.com/en/company/locations/usa/
Gluten free products
Contact: Paul Altieri
paul.altieri@schar.com

3739 Dr. Smoothie Brands
1730 Raymer Avenue
Fullerton, CA 92833
714-449-9787
Fax: 714-449-9474 888-466-9941
info@drsmoothie.com www.drsmoothie.com or www.cafeessentials.com
Dr. Smoothie Brands is a full line beverage company manufacturing shelf-stable, liquid natural fruit smoothies and powdered cocoa, mocha, latte, and chai blends. Manufactures nutritional blends ranging from raw, whole food nutritionbars to a full range of botanicals, including medically endorsed products like The Complete Meal, and Amino line.
Contact: Megan Wood
meganwood@inewsource.org
Number of Brands: 6
Number of Products: 93
Type of Packaging: Consumer, Food Service

3740 Dr. Tima Natural Products
131 Groverton Pl
Los Angeles, CA 90077-3732
310-472-2181
Fax: 310-652-9884
Natural health products and soda
Owner: Potito Depaolis
VP: Mary Caronna
Estimated Sales: $2.5-5,000,000
Number Employees: 5-9
Brands:
  Dr Tima

3741 Draco Natural Products Inc
539 Parrott St
San Jose, CA 95112-4121
408-287-7871
Fax: 408-287-8838 info@dracoherbs.com
www.draconatural.com
Wholesales herbal extracts
CEO: Jerry Wu
Sales: Ed Schack
Estimated Sales: $3 Million
Number Employees: 10-19

3742 Drader Manufacturing Industries
5750-50 Street NW
Edmonton, AB T6B 2Z8
Canada
780-440-2231
Fax: 780-440-2244 800-661-4122
bakery@drader.com www.drader.com

Custom carriers, bread baskets, bakery trays, hand trucks, dollies and bakery shelving
President/General Manager: Gordon McTavish
Account Manager: Chris Gaucher
Operations Manager: Jeff McTavish
Manager: Glenn Eckert
Number Employees: 60
Square Footage: 140000

3743 Dragnet Fisheries
4141 B St
Anchorage, AK 99503-5940
907-276-4551
Fax: 907-274-3617
Fresh and frozen herring, black cod, halibut and salmon
President: Jay Cherrier
Estimated Sales: Less than $500,000
Number Employees: 1-4
Type of Packaging: Consumer, Food Service
Brands:
  Dragnet

3744 Dragunara LLC
Po Box 1111
Palos Verdes Estate, CA 90274
310-618-8818
info@dragunara.com
www.dragunara.com
Other lifestyle, full-line condiments, BBQ sauce, ethnic sauces (soy, curry, etc.), full-line spices, marinades, other sauces, seasonings and cooking enhancers, rubs.

3745 Drake Bakeries
P.O. Box 750
Collegedale, TN 37315
855-403-7253
drakescake.com
Baked goods including snack cakes.
Chief Executive Officer: Mike McKee
Year Founded: 1896
Estimated Sales: $20-50 Million
Number Employees: 50-99
Parent Co: McKee Foods

3746 Drakes Brewing Co
1933 Davis St # 177
Building 177
San Leandro, CA 94577-1256
510-568-2739
Fax: 510-568-9857 drinkdrakes@jbrfoods.com
www.drinkdrakes.com
Beer
Principal: Adolfo Carrera
CFO: Peter Rogers
Manager: John Gittins
john.gittins@drakesbrewing.com
Director Manufacturing: Roger Lind
Estimated Sales: $1-2.5 Million
Number Employees: 1-4
Brands:
  Autumn Fest
  Blood Red
  Chocolate Milk Stout
  Drakes Amber Ale
  Drakes Blond Ale
  Drakes Hefe-Weizen
  Drakes Ipa
  Expedition
  Harvest Ale British Esb
  Imperial Ipa Black Pilsner
  Imperial Ipa Pilsner
  Imperial Stout
  Jolly Rogers
  Sir Francis Stout
  Zatec Pilsner

3747 Drakes Fresh Pasta Co
636 Southwest St
High Point, NC 27260-8107
336-861-5454
Fax: 336-861-4823 800-737-2782
info@drakesfreshpasta.com
Pasta products
President: Richard Drake
rdrake@drakesfreshpasta.com
Vice President: Simone Drake
Sales: Ginger Edward
Estimated Sales: $5 Million
Number Employees: 20-49
Brands:
  Drakes Fresh

671

Food Manufacturers / A-Z

3748 Drangle Foods
300 S Riverside Dr
Gilman, WI 54433
715-447-8241
Fax: 715-447-8242
Flavored processed cheese
President: Tom Hand
Office Manager: Char Hand
Estimated Sales: $1 Million
Number Employees: 80
Square Footage: 80
Type of Packaging: Private Label
Brands:
  Drangle

3749 Draper Valley Farms
1000 Jason Ln
Mt Vernon, WA 98273-2490
360-748-9466
Fax: 360-424-1666 800-562-2012
www.drapervalleyfarms.com
Free range chicken
Vice President: Jeff Power
CFO: Richard Koplowitz
VP & General Manager: Bob Wolfe
Sales & Marketing Manager: Vicki Knutson
Human Resources Manager: Colleen Helgeson
Plant Manager: John Michalak
Head of Purchasing: Jody Dethman
Number Employees: 250-499
Square Footage: 131196
Type of Packaging: Consumer, Food Service

3750 (HQ)Dream Confectioners LTD
540 Cedar Ln
Teaneck, NJ 07666-1742
201-836-9000
Fax: 201-836-9015
Manufacturer and exporter of pretzels
President: Joseph Podolski
Estimated Sales: $2.5-5 Million
Number Employees: 1-4
Type of Packaging: Consumer, Private Label, Bulk
Brands:
  Great

3751 Dream Foods Intl
2116 Wilshire Blvd
Suite 355
Santa Monica, CA 90403-5750
310-315-5739
Fax: 310-388-1322
Dairy-free, functional (antioxidants), gluten-free, kosher, organic/natural, USDA, juice/cider.
Owner: Adriana Kahane
adk@dreamfoods.com
Marketing: Adriana Kahane
Number Employees: 5-9

3752 Dream Pretzels
260 Madison Ave
New York, NY 10016
877-966-8434
www.pressels.com
New York deli-style pretzels
Number of Brands: 1
Number of Products: 4
Type of Packaging: Consumer
Brands:
  DREAM PRETZELS

3753 DreamPak LLC
4717 Eisenhower Avenue
Alexandria, VA 22304
703-751-3511
877-687-4662
info@dreampak.com www.dreampak.com
On-the-go beverages
President/CEO: Dr. Aly Gamay
Executive Vice President: Terry Schneider
Contact: Taufeeque Ali
tali@dreampak.com
Vice President, Operations: Randy Cook
Brands:
  Fruitslim
  Soluflex
  Dogflex
  Trimma
  Enhance To Go
  Joker's Wild Energy
  Chocolate Slim
  Zeniht

3754 DreamTime, Inc
1115 Thompson Ave
#5
Santa Cruz, CA 95062
831-464-6702
Fax: 831-464-6703 877-464-6702
info@dreamtimeinc.com www.dreamtimeinc.com
Natural ingredient health products
Founder/CEO: Judy Day
Contact: Judy Dy
judy.day@dreamtimeinc.com
Estimated Sales: $1-3 Million
Number Employees: 15

3755 Dreaming Cow
www.dreamingcow.com
Grass-based whole milk yogurt and yogurt drinks
Number of Brands: 1
Number of Products: 12
Type of Packaging: Consumer
Brands:
  LUSH
  DREAMING COW

3756 Dresden Stollen Co USA
7 Heathcote Dr
Albertson, NY 11507-2224
516-746-5802
Fax: 516-746-5918 http://www.dresdenstollen.com
Gourmet foods
President/Owner: Joan Greenfield
Estimated Sales: A
Number Employees: 5-9

3757 (HQ)Dressel Collins Fish Company
5131 S Director St
Seattle, WA 98118
206-725-0121
Fax: 206-725-1354
Canned and smoked salmon
President: Mike Bonney
Estimated Sales: $10 Million
Number Employees: 1-4
Type of Packaging: Consumer, Food Service

3758 Drew's Organics
926 VT Route 103 S
Chester, VT 05143-8461
802-875-1184
Fax: 802-875-5126 800-228-2980
info@chefdrew.com www.drewsorganics.com
All-natural salad dressings and salsa. Certified Organic.
President/CEO: Andrew Starkweather
Assistant Controller: Rob Feakes
Manager: John Cummings
johnc@chefdrew.com
Plant Manager: Joe Brent
Estimated Sales: $1.5 Million
Number Employees: 20-49
Type of Packaging: Consumer, Private Label
Brands:
  Drew's All Natural

3759 Dreyer Sonoma
161 Fox Hollow Rd
Woodside, CA 94062-3607
650-851-9448
Fax: 650-851-3268 jdreyer@dreyerwine.com
www.dreyerwine.com
Wines
Co-Owner: Walter Dreyer
Co-Owner: Bettina Dreyer
General Manager: Jonathan Dreyer
Estimated Sales: $2.5-5 Million
Number Employees: 5-9
Brands:
  Dreyer Wine

3760 Dreyer's Grand Ice Cream Inc.
5929 College Ave.
Oakland, CA 94618
877-437-3937
www.dreyers.com
Premium ice creams.
CEO: Kim Peddle Rguem
Year Founded: 1928
Estimated Sales: $1.5 Billion
Number Employees: 10,000
Number of Brands: 28
Parent Co: Nestl, USA
Type of Packaging: Consumer, Food Service
Other Locations:
  Dreyer's Grand Ice Cream
  Fort Wayne IN
Brands:
  Dreyer's
  Edy's

3761 Dreymiller & KRAY Inc
140 S State St
Hampshire, IL 60140-7000
847-683-2271
Fax: 847-683-2272 www.dreymillerandkray.com
Packer/processor of sausage, ham and bacon
President: Ed Reiser
dreymillerandkray@gmail.com
Estimated Sales: $500,000-$1 Million
Number Employees: 5-9
Type of Packaging: Consumer

3762 Dried Ingredients, LLC.
9010 NW 105th Way
Miami, FL 33178
786-999-8499
Fax: 888-893-6595 info@driedingredients.com
www.driedingredients.com
Maufacturer of organic, precooked pulses (beans, lentils, peas); also teas, tea ingredients, herbs, spices, essential oils & dried vegetables. Provide product development & logistics services.
President: Armin Dilles
armin.dilles@driedingredients.com
Sales Manager: Maria Rosello
Parent Co: Dried Ingredients GmbH
Type of Packaging: Food Service, Bulk

3763 Drier's Meats
14 S Elm Street
Three Oaks, MI 49128
269-756-3101
Fax: 269-756-9285 info@driers.com
www.driers.com
Smoked meats
Owner: Carolyn Drier
Estimated Sales: Less than $500,000
Number Employees: 1-4
Brands:
  Drier Meats

3764 Driftwood Dairy
10724 E. Lower Azusa Rd.
El Monte, CA 91731
626-444-9591
www.driftwooddairy.com
Dairy products.
President: Mac Berry
macb@driftwooddairy.com
CEO: James Dolan
Year Founded: 1946
Estimated Sales: $100+ Million
Number Employees: 250-499
Type of Packaging: Consumer, Food Service, Bulk

3765 Driscoll Strawberry Assoc Inc
345 Westridge Dr
Watsonville, CA 95076-4169
831-424-0506
Fax: 831-761-1090 www.driscolls.com
Grower of premium berries.
Chairman & CEO: Miles Reiter
Manager: J M Reiter
jm.reiter@driscolls.com
Number Employees: 50-99
Brands:
  Associates
  Driscoll's
  Dsa
  Islander

3766 Driscoll's
PO Box 50045
Watsonville, CA 95077-5045
800-871-3333
driscolls@allisonpr.com www.driscolls.com
Supplier of fresh berries
Contact: Saumya Lanka
saumya.lanka@driscolls.com

3767 Droga Chocolates
401 East Las Olas Blvd
Suite 800
Fort Lauderdale, FL 33301
800-213-0754
drogachocolates.com
Caramels sweetened with honey

Food Manufacturers / A-Z

President: Michelle Crochet
Partner: Lisa Albani
Contact: Lisa Albani
lisa@drogachocolates.com
Year Founded: 2007
Estimated Sales: B
Number Employees: 5-9
Number of Products: 4
Brands:
  Money on Honey

3768 Droubi's Imports
2721 Hillcroft Street
Houston, TX 77057-5003
713-334-1829
Fax: 713-988-9506
Manufacturer, importer and wholesaler/distributor of tea and coffee
President: A Droubi
VP: Sharon Droubi
Estimated Sales: $1-2.5 Million
Number Employees: 20-49
Square Footage: 48000
Parent Co: Droubi's Bakery & Delicatessen
Brands:
  Gold Star

3769 Drum Rock Specialty Co Inc
44 Fullerton Rd
Warwick, RI 02886-1422
401-737-5165
Fax: 401-737-5060
marketing@drumrockproducts.com
www.drumrockproducts.com
Manufacturer and exporter of fritter breading and batter mixes for vegetables, seafood and poultry; also, custom dry blending and mixing and private labeling services available
President: Stephen Hinger
Sales Manager: Paul Skorupa
Estimated Sales: $1-2.5 Million
Number Employees: 5-9
Type of Packaging: Food Service, Private Label, Bulk
Brands:
  Fis-Chic Wonder Batter

3770 Drusilla Seafood
3482 Drusilla Ln # D
Baton Rouge, LA 70809-1800
225-923-0896
Fax: 225-928-4936 800-364-8844
info@drusillaplace.com www.drusillaplace.com
Manufacturer and packer of seafood, spices, salad dressings and breading mixes
President: James Zito
Cio/Cto: Brad Bito
bradb@drusillaseafood.com
VP: Don Zito
Marketing Manager: Nancy Zito
Estimated Sales: $300,000-$500,000
Number Employees: 100-249
Square Footage: 10000
Parent Co: Seafood Restaurant
Brands:
  Drusilla

3771 Dry Creek Vineyard
3770 Lambert Bridge Rd
Healdsburg, CA 95448-9713
707-433-1000
Fax: 707-433-5329 800-864-9463
dcv@drycreekvineyard.com
www.drycreekvineyard.com
Wines
President: Lynda Abbott
traceyrathjen@cabainc.com
CFO: Dru Cochran
VP: Don Wallace
Consumer Manager: Michael Longerbeam
traceyrathjen@cabainc.com
Estimated Sales: $10-20 Million
Number Employees: 20-49
Type of Packaging: Consumer, Food Service
Brands:
  Dry Creek
  Meritage
  Regatta
  Soleil-Late Harvest Sauvignon

3772 Dryden Provision Co Inc
1016 E Washington St
Louisville, KY 40206-1821
502-583-1777
Fax: 502-583-3006 www.drydenprovidin.com
Meat distributor of pork, poultry, beef, lamb, veal and seafood
President: John Dryden
Co-Owner: Janinne Agee
Manager: Bobby Pound
john@drydenprovidin.com
Estimated Sales: $3 Million
Number Employees: 10-19
Brands:
  Dryden

3773 DuPont Nutrition & Biosciences
4 New Century Pkwy
New Century, KS 66031
913-764-8100
www.food.dupont.com
Ingredients for baking, bars, beverages, confectionery, culinary, diary, frozen desserts, fruit applications, meat alternatives, meat/poultry/seafood, oils and fats, and pet food
President, Nutrition & Biosciences: Matthias Heinzel
Estimated Sales: $4.4 Billion
Number Employees: 10,000
Parent Co: DuPont
Type of Packaging: Consumer, Bulk
Other Locations:
  Central Soya Company-Processing Decatur IN
  Central Soya Company-Processing Gibson City IL
  Central Soya Company-Processing Marion OH
  Central Soya Company-Grain Plant Indianapolis IN
  Central Soya Company-Processing Bellevue OH
  Central Soya Company-Grain Plant Cincinnati OH
  Central Soya Company-Processing Delphos OH
  Central Soya Company-Mfg Remington IN
  Central Soya Company-Processing Morristown IN
  Central Soya Company-Grain Jeffersonville OH
  Central Soya Company-Grain Waterloo IN
  Central Soya Company-Bulk Oil Pawtucket RI
  Central Soya Company-Mfg New Bremen OH
Brands:
  Fibrim
  Solae
  V8 Splash
  Gardenburgers
  Mori-Nu
  Yves Veggie Cuisine
  Medifast

3774 DuPont Pioneer
7100 NW 62nd Ave
P.O. Box 1150
Johnston, IA 50131-941
515-535-5954
www.pioneer.com
Producer of hybrid seeds and other GMO products, focusing on corn, soybeans, alfalfa, sorghum, sunflowers, canola and wheat.
Chairman/CEO: Edward Breen
Chief Financial Officer: Nicholas Fanandakis
Executive Vice President: James Collins Jr.
Senior Marketing Manager: David Tegeder
Sr. VP of Human Resources: Benito Cachinero-Sanchez
Parent Co: DuPont

3775 DuPont Pioneer
P.O. Box 1000
Johnston, IA 50131-0184
515-535-3200
www.pioneer.com
Hybrid and genetically modified seeds.
CEO, Corteva Agriscience: James Collins
Year Founded: 1926
Estimated Sales: $4.3 Billion
Number Employees: 12,300
Number of Brands: 6
Parent Co: Corteva Agriscience
Type of Packaging: Consumer, Food Service, Bulk
Brands:
  Pioneer®
  Plenish™
  Optimum®
  AcreMax®
  AQUAmax™

3776 DuPont Tate & Lyle BioProducts Company, LLC.
198 Blair Bend Dr
Loudon, TN 37774
866-404-7933
www.duponttateandlyle.com
Producer of bio-based 1,30-propanediol.
President: Todd Sutton
Chief Financial Officer: Jennifer Moss
Vice President, Technology: Jim Zahn, Ph.D
Vice President, Marketing & Sales: Stephen Hurff
Vice President, Operations: Sukh Rabeendran
Product Director: Colton Reid

3777 Dubois Seafood
285 Saint Peter St
Houma, LA 70363
985-876-2514
Fax: 985-851-6147
Seafood wholesalers
President: Kerry Dubois
Estimated Sales: $6 Million
Number Employees: 5

3778 Duck Pond Cellars
23145 N Highway 99w
PO Box 429
Dundee, OR 97115-9126
503-538-3199
Fax: 503-538-3190 800-437-3213
dpinfo@duckpondcellars.com
www.duckpondcellars.com
Wines
Owner: Douglas Fries
CFO: Jo Ann Fries
Sales: Scott Jenkins
douglasf@duckpondcellars.com
Wine Club Director: Kathy Wildman
VP Operations: Lisa Jenkins
Estimated Sales: $1-2.5 Million
Number Employees: 10-19
Type of Packaging: Private Label
Brands:
  Duck Pond Cellars

3779 Duckhorn Vineyards
1000 Lodi Ln
St Helena, CA 94574-9410
707-963-7108
Fax: 707-963-7078 888-354-8885
customerservice@duckhorn.com
www.duckhorn.com
Wines
Chairman/Co-Founder: Daniel Duckhorn
President/Chief Executive Officer: Alex Ryan
alex@duckhorn.com
Vice President: Neil Bernardi
Chief Operations Officer: Zach Rasmuson
Estimated Sales: $10-20 Million
Number Employees: 100-249
Number of Brands: 6
Parent Co: GI Manager L.P
Brands:
  Canvasback
  Decoy
  Duckhorn Vineyards
  Goldeneye
  Migration
  Paraduxx

3780 Ducktrap River Of Maine
57 Little River Dr
Belfast, ME 04915-6035
207-338-6280
Fax: 207-338-6288 800-434-8727
ducktrap.sales@marineharvest.com
www.ducktrap.com
Pate and smoked seafood including trout fillets, Atlantic salmon, peppered and herb mackerel, mussels, scallops and shrimp
CEO: Alf-Helge Aarskog
General Manager: Don Cynewski
Estimated Sales: $20-50 Million
Number Employees: 100-249
Square Footage: 25000
Type of Packaging: Consumer, Food Service, Bulk

Food Manufacturers / A-Z

Brands:
Ducktrap
Kendall Brook
Spruce Point
Winter Harbor

3781 Duda Farm Fresh Foods Inc
1200 Duda Trl
Oviedo, FL 32765-4507
407-365-2111
Fax: 407-365-2010 www.dudafresh.com
Fruits and vegetables
Chief Executive Officer: David Duda
Chief Financial Officer: Mark Engwall
Senior Vice President, Corporate Affairs: Rick Hanas
Senior VP, Real Estate/General Counsel: Tracy Duda Chapman
Senior Vice President, Fresh Operations: Dan Duda
Senior Vice President, Duda Ranches: Drew Duda
Sales Exec: Dan Duda
joseph.duda@duda.com
SVP, Mergers & Acquisitions: Tom Duda
Chief Operating Officer: Barton Weeks
Lease Manager: Patrick Schmidt
Number Employees: 20-49
Parent Co: DUDA
Brands:
Dandy(c)

3782 Dufflet Pastries
166 Norseman St
Toronto, ON M8Z ZR4
Canada
416-536-1330
Fax: 416-538-2366 866-238-0899
info@dufflet.com www.dufflet.com
Cakes, tortes, pies, flan, tarts, brownies, cookies, etc.
President: Daniele Bertrand
CEO: Dufflet Rosenberg
Estimated Sales: $11 Million
Number Employees: 65
Number of Products: 100
Square Footage: 40000
Type of Packaging: Consumer, Food Service

3783 Dufour Pastry Kitchens Inc
251 Locust Ave
Bronx, NY 10454-2004
718-402-8800
Fax: 718-402-7002 800-439-1282
forster@convertmedia.com
www.dufourpastrykitchens.com
Manufacturer of frozen puff pastry products including hors d'oeuvres, doughs, snacks, lunch products, tart shells, etc.
Owner: Felicia Forster
forster@convertmedia.com
CEO: Judi Arnold
Year Founded: 1984
Number Employees: 50-99
Type of Packaging: Consumer, Food Service, Bulk
Brands:
Dufour Pastry Kitchens

3784 Dugdale Beef Company
4420 Stout Field North Dr.
Indianapolis, IN 46241
317-520-9981
Fax: 317-298-7608 jeff@dugdalefoods.com
www.dugdalefoods.com
Fine meats, seafood, poultry, cheese, salads, breads, desserts
President: Jean Deering
Founder: Eleanor Dugdale
Contact: Joe Dugdale
joe@dugdalefoods.com
Year Founded: 1975
Estimated Sales: $20-50 Million
Number Employees: 20-49
Type of Packaging: Consumer

3785 Duguay Fish Packers
1062 Bas-Cap-Pele Ch
Cap-Pele, NB E4N 1K9
Canada
506-577-2287
Fax: 506-577-1995
Seafood product preparation and packaging
President: Omer Duguay
Board Member: Alfreda Duguay
Estimated Sales: $3 Million
Number Employees: 20
Type of Packaging: Food Service

3786 (HQ)Duis Meat Processing
1991 E 6th St
Concordia, KS 66901-2621
785-243-7850
800-281-4295
kgduis@aol.com www.duismeatprocessing.com
Quality services for all deer and meat processing needs
Owner: Toby Duis
kgduis@aol.com
CEO: Keith Duis
VP: Toby Duis
Estimated Sales: $1-3 Million
Number Employees: 5-9
Square Footage: 12800
Type of Packaging: Consumer, Food Service, Private Label, Bulk
Other Locations:
Duis Meat Processing
Salina KS

3787 Duke's
dukesmeats.com
Dried sausages and beef brisket strips
Founder: Justin Havlick
Number of Brands: 2
Number of Products: 15
Type of Packaging: Consumer
Brands:
DUKE'S
DUKE'S SMOKED SHORTY

3788 Dulce de Leche DelcampoProducts
15908 NW 48th Ave
Miami, FL 33014
305-620-1444
Fax: 305-624-2728 877-472-9408
Dulce de leche, cholesterol-free white cheese, guava spread and filling
President: Carlos Ruiz DeLuque
Estimated Sales: $37,000
Number Employees: 7
Type of Packaging: Consumer, Food Service, Private Label, Bulk
Brands:
Del Campo

3789 Dulcette Technologies
2 Hicks Street
Lindenhurst, NY 11757
631-752-8700
Fax: 631-752-8117 sales@dulcettetech.com
Sweeteners, nutraceuticals & antioxidants
CEO: M Blum
Quality Control: M Samuels
Marketing: E Saltsberg
Sales: Luke Verdet
Estimated Sales: $500,000-1 Million
Number Employees: 7

3790 Duma Meats Inc
857 Randolph Rd
Mogadore, OH 44260-9343
330-628-3438
Fax: 330-628-2172 d.duma@sbcglobal.net
www.dumameats.com
Supplier of all kinds of cuts of meat and cheeses
President: David Duma Jr
beverley@dumameatsfarmmarket.com
Treasurer: Beverley Duma
Estimated Sales: $840,000
Number Employees: 20-49
Type of Packaging: Consumer, Food Service, Bulk

3791 Dumbee Gourmet Foods
PO Box 70159
Albany, GA 31708-0159
229-435-4800
Fax: 229-420-4108 800-569-1657
Gourmet foods
Owner: Steve Barber
President: Tammy Barber
Estimated Sales: Under $500,000
Number Employees: 1
Brands:
Dummbee Gourmet

3792 Dunbar Foods Corp
1000 S Fayetteville Ave
Dunn, NC 28334-6213
910-892-3175
Fax: 910-892-6311 www.moodydunbar.com
Processor of bell peppers, pimientos and sweet potatoes; products are certified kosher.
President: Jeff Lucas
jeff@moodydunbar.com
Estimated Sales: $10-20 Million
Number Employees: 250-499
Parent Co: Moody Dunbar, Inc.

3793 Duncan Peak Vineyards
PO Box 1473
Lafayette, CA 94549
925-283-3632
www.duncanpeak.com
Wines
President: Hubert Lenczowski
Estimated Sales: Less than $500,000
Number Employees: 2
Type of Packaging: Private Label
Brands:
Duncan

3794 Dundee Brandied Fruit Co
PO Box 445
Dundee, OR 97115-0445
503-537-2500
Fax: 503-538-8599
Brandied fruit
Owner: Richard Sadler
Estimated Sales: Under $500,000
Number Employees: 5-9
Brands:
Dundee Brandied

3795 Dundee Candy Shop
2112 Bardstown Rd
Louisville, KY 40205-1916
502-452-9266
Fax: 502-459-7981 866-877-9266
www.dundeecandy.com
Candy
Owner: Maria Moore
Estimated Sales: $390,000
Number Employees: 5-9
Brands:
Dundee Candy Shop

3796 Dundee Citrus Growers Assn
111 1st St N
Dundee, FL 33838-4002
863-439-1574
Fax: 863-439-1535 800-447-1574
info@dun-d.com www.dun-d.com
Florida citrus fruits including oranges, grapefruit, tangerines and red grapefruit
President & Chairman: W. Lindsay Raley Jr.
Executive VP & CEO: Steve B. Callaham
CFO: Mary Schaal
Quality Control Manager: Mike Mobley
Vice President of Sales: Bobby Finch
VP Human Resource: Missy McGuiness
COO: Greg Dunnahoe
VP Harvesting & Fruit Procurement: Adam Pate
Plant Manager: James Giddens
Purchasing Manager: Nyago Summers
Estimated Sales: $14.9 Million
Number Employees: 500-999
Square Footage: 375000
Type of Packaging: Consumer, Food Service
Brands:
Dun-D

3797 Dundee Groves
28421 US Highway 27
PO Box 829
Dundee, FL 33838
863-439-2284
Fax: 863-439-5049 800-294-2266
info@dundeegroves.com
www.davidsonofdundee.com
Fresh citrus fruit including; oranges, ruby red grapefruits, all natural citrus candies, coconut patties, citrus marmalades, citrus jellies, butters and orange blossom honey. Gift baskets available
President: Glen Davidson
CEO: Susan Davidson
Estimated Sales: $6 Million
Number Employees: 100-249
Number of Brands: 1
Number of Products: 112
Square Footage: 450000
Type of Packaging: Consumer, Private Label

Food Manufacturers / A-Z

3798 Dundee Wine Company
691 Highway 99W
PO Box 280
Dundee, OR 97115-0220
503-538-3922
Fax: 503-538-2055 888-427-4953
wine@argylewinery.com www.argylewinery.com
Wines
Executive Manager: Valeri Cetz
Director of Marketing: Craig Eastman
Estimated Sales: $5 Million
Number Employees: 60
Type of Packaging: Private Label
Brands:
 Dundee

3799 Dunford Bakers
8556 S 2940 W
West Jordan, UT 84088-9660
801-304-0400
Fax: 801-304-0511 800-748-4335
donuts@dunfordbakers.com
www.dunfordbakers.com
Pastries and breads
President: Ron Stevens
Vice President: John R Stevens
VP: Gary E Gottfred
Plant Manager: Dale Hatch
Estimated Sales: $5-10 Million
Number Employees: 100-249
Type of Packaging: Consumer, Private Label, Bulk

3800 Dungeness Development Associates
12969 74th PL. NE
Kirkland, WA 98034
425-823-0770
Fax: 425-823-5049
Producer and importer of Dungeness Crab and Pacific Tiny Shrip
Owner: Joel Van Ornun
Contact: Tena Boggs
tenab@dungenessassoc.com
Plant Manager: Mel Corbitt
Estimated Sales: $5-10 Million
Number Employees: 20-49

3801 Dunham's Lobster Pot
60 Mt Blue Pond Rd
Avon, ME 04966-3301
207-639-2815
Fax: 207-639-2815
Fresh seafood including fish, clams, haddock, scallops, crab meat, mussels, oysters, shrimp, lobster and rib-eye steaks
Owner: Bruce Dunham
Co-Owner: Mary Dunham
Estimated Sales: $220 Thousand
Number Employees: 2
Type of Packaging: Food Service, Bulk

3802 Dunham's Meats
12907 E Wellesley Ave
Spokane Valley
Urbana, WA 99216
509-924-9821
Fax: 937-834-2411 www.dunhammeats.com
Meat products; also, slaughtering services available
Owner/VP: Barry Dunham
Estimated Sales: $1-2.5 Million
Number Employees: 5-9
Type of Packaging: Consumer, Bulk

3803 Dunkin' Brands Inc.
130 Royall St.
Canton, MA 02021
781-737-3000
800-859-5339
www.dunkinbrands.com
Coffee, baked goods and premium ice cream.
President/CEO: David Hoffmann
CFO: Kate Jaspon
Chief Marketing Officer: Tony Weisman
Chief Operating Officer: Scott Murphy
Year Founded: 2004
Estimated Sales: $860 Million
Number Employees: 1,163
Number of Brands: 2
Type of Packaging: Food Service
Brands:
 Baskin-Robbins®
 Dunkin' Donuts®

3804 Dunn Vineyards
805 White Cottage Rd N
Angwin, CA 94508-9616
707-965-3642
Fax: 707-965-3805 dunnvineyards@sbcglobal.net
www.dunnvineyards.com
Wines
Owner: Randy Dunn
dundineyards@sdglobal.net
Director of Marketing: Christina Dunne
Estimated Sales: $390,000
Number Employees: 1-4
Brands:
 Dunn

3805 Duplin Wine Cellars
505 N Sycamore Street
Rose Hill, NC 28458
910-289-3888
Fax: 910-289-3094 800-774-9634
info@duplinwinery.com www.duplinwinery.com
Wines
Owner: David Fussell Jr
Director of Sales: Tabitha Fussell
Contact: Jonathan Fussell
jonathan@duplinwinery.com
Estimated Sales: $5-10 Million
Number Employees: 50
Type of Packaging: Private Label
Brands:
 Duplin

3806 Dupont Cheese
N10140 Hwy 110
Marion, WI 54950
715-754-5424
Fax: 715-754-1313 800-895-2873
info@dupontcheeseinc.com
www.dupontcheeseinc.com
Cheese including colby, mini-horus and longhorn
President: Fred Laack
Estimated Sales: $10-20 Million
Number Employees: 20-49
Type of Packaging: Consumer

3807 Durango Brewing Co
3000 Main Ave
Durango, CO 81301-4245
970-247-3396
scott@durangobrewing.com
www.durangobrewing.com
Beer
Owner: Bob Beardsley
bbeardsley@durangobrewing.com
Estimated Sales: $1-2.5 Million
Number Employees: 5-9
Brands:
 Durango

3808 Durey-Libby Edible Nuts
100 Industrial Rd
Carlstadt, NJ 07072
201-939-2775
Fax: 201-939-0386 800-332-6887
Custom roasted nuts
President: Wendy Dicker
CEO: Billy Dicker
Contact: William Dicker
billythenutman@msn.com
Estimated Sales: $1-2.5 Million
Number Employees: 20-49
Square Footage: 120000
Type of Packaging: Bulk

3809 Durham Ellis Pecan Co
308 S Houston St
Comanche, TX 76442-3237
325-356-5291
Fax: 325-356-3974 800-732-2629
www.durhams.com
Pecans and other nuts
Owner: Hl Dollins
hl.dollins@durhams.com
Estimated Sales: $4 Million
Number Employees: 50-99

3810 Durkee-Mower
2 Empire Street
Lynn, MA 01902
781-593-8007
www.marshmallowfluff.com
Manufacturer and exporter of marshmallow creme
Estimated Sales: $5-10 Million
Number Employees: 24
Square Footage: 140000
Type of Packaging: Consumer, Food Service
Brands:
 Marshmallow Fluff

3811 Dutch Ann Foods Company
28 Col John Pitchford Pkwy
Natchez, MS 39120
601-445-5566
Fax: 601-445-8738
Frozen pie crusts
President: William Jones
Estimated Sales: $1-3 Million
Number Employees: 35
Type of Packaging: Consumer, Food Service, Private Label
Brands:
 Best Way
 Dutch Ann

3812 Dutch Cheese Makers Corp
585 Stewart Ave
Suite 318
Garden City, NY 11530-4701
631-533-9202
Fax: 631-342-8091 www.dutchcheesemakers.com
Dutch cheese
CEO: Steve Margarites
National Sales Director: Tim Sirera
Estimated Sales: $122782
Number Employees: 1-4
Type of Packaging: Private Label

3813 Dutch Farms Inc
700 E 107th St
Chicago, IL 60628-3806
773-660-0900
Fax: 773-660-1044 800-637-3447
support@dutchfarms.com www.dutchfarms.com
Manufacturer/processor of eggs, cheeses, dairy products, deli, bakery and meat items.
Owner: Brian Boomsma
bboomsma@dutchfarms.com
Controller: Kurt Gilbertson
VP: Rachelle Knapper
Marketing Executive: Kevin De Vries
Estimated Sales: $38 Milliom
Number Employees: 100-249
Type of Packaging: Food Service

3814 Dutch Girl Donut Co
19000 Woodward Ave
Detroit, MI 48203-1903
313-368-3020
Doughnuts
Owner: Cecilia Voss
Partner: Gene Timmer
Estimated Sales: $430,000
Number Employees: 10-19

3815 (HQ)Dutch Gold Honey Inc
2220 Dutch Gold Dr
Lancaster, PA 17601
717-393-1716
Fax: 717-393-8687 800-338-0587
info@dutchgoldhoney.com
www.dutchgoldhoney.com
Honey and honey products
VP Finance & Administration: Charles Schatzman
Operations Manager: Jody Gable
Year Founded: 1946
Estimated Sales: $20-50 Million
Number Employees: 20-49
Number of Brands: 4
Square Footage: 100000
Type of Packaging: Consumer, Food Service, Private Label, Bulk
Other Locations:
 Dutch Gold Honey
 Littleton NH
Brands:
 Blossom Hill
 Dutch Gold
 Honey In the Rough
 McLure's Maple

3816 Dutch Henry Winery
4300 Silverado Trl
Calistoga, CA 94515-9603
707-942-5771
Fax: 707-942-5512 888-224-5879
info@dutchhenry.com
Wines

Food Manufacturers / A-Z

Owner: Scott Chafen
info@dutchhenry.com
Customer Service: Less Chafen
Estimated Sales: $2.5-5 Million
Number Employees: 5-9
Type of Packaging: Private Label
Brands:
  Dutch Henry

3817 Dutch Kitchen Bake Shop& Deli
12 John Fitch Hwy
Fitchburg, MA 01420-5902
978-345-1393
Fax: 978-345-6651 peter.raimo@yahoo.com
www.dutchkitchenbakery.com
Breads, rolls, cakes and pastries
Owner: Joe Raimo
VP: Mary Raimo
Sales Manager: Chris Raimo
peter.raimo@yahoo.com
Estimated Sales: $1.50 Million
Number Employees: 20-49
Brands:
  Dutch Kitchen

3818 Dutch Packing Co., Inc.
2800 NW 112th Ave
Doral, FL 33172
305-871-3640
Fax: 305-871-3668 800-723-9249
garciasausagebrand.com
Sausage
President: Raul Rodriguez
Vice President Sales: William Rodriquez
VP Production: Victor Rodriguez
Estimated Sales: $5.2 Million
Number Employees: 36
Type of Packaging: Consumer, Food Service
Brands:
  Garcia Brand

3819 Dutchess Bakery
715 Bigley Ave
Charleston, WV 25302
304-346-4237
Cookies
Owner: Edward S Rada Iii
Estimated Sales: $500,000-$1 Million
Number Employees: 5-9
Type of Packaging: Consumer

3820 Dutchland Frozen Foods
205 Main St
PO Box 148
Lester, IA 51242-7701
712-478-4349
Fax: 712-478-4554 888-497-7243
Pastry puffs and euro classic pastries
Owner: Wayne Van Wyne
CEO: Peter Van Wyhe
pvw@dutchlandfrozenfoods.com
VP: Pete Van Wyne
Number Employees: 20-49

3821 Dutterer's Home Food Service
2700 Lord Baltimore Drive
Baltimore, MD 21244-2648
410-298-3663
Fax: 410-298-1625
Food transporters of meat and refrigerated food
President: Mark Mules
Estimated Sales: $10-20 Million
Number Employees: 6
Type of Packaging: Consumer, Private Label

3822 Duval Bakery Products
1733 Evergreen Ave
Jacksonville, FL 32206-4730
904-354-7878
Fax: 904-354-7828
Stuffing and bread crumbs
Owner: Bob Gorsuch
robertgorsuch@duvalbakeryproducts.com
Plant Manager: Jim Gorsuch
Estimated Sales: $310,000
Number Employees: 5-9
Square Footage: 24000
Type of Packaging: Food Service, Private Label, Bulk

3823 Duverger
Oxnard, CA 93033
www.duvergermacarons.com
Macarons

Founder: Claire Becker

3824 Duxbury Mussel & Seafood Corporation
8 Joseph St # B
Kingston, MA 02364-1122
781-585-5517
Fax: 781-585-2976
Wholesale seafood
President: Robert Marconi

3825 Dwayne Keith Brooks Company
6628 Fiesta Ln
Orangevale, CA 95662-3554
916-988-1030
Fax: 916-988-4442
School and institutional frozen foods
President: Dwayne Brooks
Estimated Sales: $500,000
Number Employees: 2
Square Footage: 7200
Parent Co: SA Products Company
Type of Packaging: Food Service, Bulk

3826 DyStar Hilton Davis/DyStar Foam Control
2020 Front St
Cuyahoga Falls, OH 44221
330-916-6726
Dystar LP manufactures food color & process aids with two divisions focused on the food industry: DyStar Hilton Davis manufactures FD&C Dyes and Lake Color; Dystar Foam Control manufacturers Foam Blast Defoamers.
CEO/Head of Global Sales & Marketing: Eric Hopman
CFO/Vice President of Group Finance: Victor Leendertz
VP, Global Quality & Compliance Mgmt: Kevin Tan
VP, Global Human Resources: Kevin Tan
VP, Global Procurement-North Asia: Vera Huang
VP, Global Manufacturing & Supply Chain: Gerald Talhoff
Parent Co: DyStar Group

3827 Dylan's Candy Bar
1011 Third Ave, 60th St
New York, NY
866-939-5267
customerservice@dylanscandybar.com
www.dylanscandybar.com
Candy, confections

3828 Dyna Tabs LLC
1933 E 12th St
Brooklyn, NY 11229-2703
718-376-6084
sales@dynatabs.com
www.dynatabs.com
Health, wellness, beauty products including oral edible strips, aloe vera drinking gel and passion punch.
Executive Director: Harold Baum
hbaum@dynatabs.com
CFO: Setty Baum
Estimated Sales: $830,000
Number Employees: 10-19
Parent Co: Baum International, Inc
Type of Packaging: Consumer, Private Label

3829 Dynamic Confections
1050 S. 200 West
Salt Lake City, UT 84101-3003
801-355-4422
Fax: 801-355-5546
Quality chocolates
CEO: Taz Murray
President: Keith Elliot
CFO: Jim Loveridge
Executive Assistant: Bonnie Labrum
Estimated Sales: $28 Million
Number Employees: 5

3830 Dynamic Foods
1001 E 33rd St
Lubbock, TX 79404-1816
806-723-5600
Fax: 806-723-5680 jsullivan@dynamicfoods.com
www.dynamicfoods.com
Baked goods, cakes, muffins, cornbread, pies, cobblers, frozen dinner rolls, casseroles, side dishes, soups, sauces, glazes, mexican foods, breaded fish, bread sticks

President: Mike Blasdell
Executive Manager: Gabriel Olivarez
Estimated Sales: $4 Million
Number Employees: 100-249
Number of Brands: 2
Number of Products: 100+
Square Footage: 225000
Type of Packaging: Food Service, Private Label
Brands:
  Dynamic Foods
  Private Label

3831 Dynamic Health Laboratories Inc.
110 Bridge St
Brooklyn, NY 11201
718-472-4009
Fax: 718-392-9301 800-396-2114
info@dynamichealth.com
www.dynamichealth.com
Liquid health products
President: Bruce Burwick
VP: Dan Gombo
Sales Manager: Jane Medress
Contact: Dennis Amaral
dennis@marathonconsulting.com
Estimated Sales: $18 Million
Number Employees: 30

3832 Dynapro International
451 N Main St
Kaysville, UT 84037-1114
801-621-1413
Fax: 801-621-8258 800-877-1413
sales@dynaprointernational.com
www.dynaprointernational.com
Manufacturer and exporter of vitamins and herbal supplements
Owner: Bailey Hall
sales@dynaprointernational.com
Marketing Director: Gary Hoffman
Estimated Sales: Less Than $500,000
Number Employees: 5-9
Square Footage: 15600

3833 (HQ)Dynic USA Corp
4750 NE Dawson Creek Dr
Hillsboro, OR 97124-5799
503-693-1070
Fax: 503-648-1185 800-326-1249
enrique@dynic.com www.dynic.com
Labeling and printing products
President: Gwen Robinson
leej@smccd.edu
CEO/President: Shigeru Tamura
Director of Marketing: Mindy Nybert
Sales Engineer: Cesar Santa
Customer Service Rep: James Brandow
Estimated Sales: $25 Million
Number Employees: 50-99
Parent Co: Dynic Corporation
Other Locations:
  Dynic UK Ltd
  Cardiff, South Wales UK
  Dynic Corporation
  Minatoku, Tokyo, Japan HK
Brands:
  Cabin Air Filters
  Cetus Textile Fabrics
  Oled Desiccant
  Sirius Ttr

3834 (HQ)E & J Gallo Winery
600 Yosemite Blvd.
Modesto, CA 95354-2760
877-687-9463
www.gallo.com
Wines, brandy and sparkling wine.
Chief Marketing Officer: Stephanie Gallo
Year Founded: 1933
Estimated Sales: Over $1 Billion
Number Employees: 5000-9999
Type of Packaging: Consumer, Food Service
Other Locations:
  E&J Gallo Winery
  Mississauga ON
  E&J Gallo Winery
  Fresno CA
  E&J Gallo Winery
  Livingston CA
Brands:
  Argiano®
  Allegrini
  Alamos®
  Andre®
  Apothic®

Barefoot Bubbly®
Barefoot®
Bear Flag®
Ballatore®
Bartles & Jaymes®
Boone's Farm®
Brancaia®
Bridlewood Estate Winery®
Bella Sera®
Carnivor®
Clarendon Hills®
Maso Canali®
Columbia Winery®
Covey Run Winery®
Carlo Rossi®
Canyon Road®
Davinci®
Dancing Bull®
Dark Horse®
Don Miguel Gascon®
Ecco Domani®
Gallo Family Vineyards®
Edna Valley Vineyard®
Copper Ridge Vineyards®
Livingston Cellars®
Ghost Pines®
Jermann®
J Vineyards & Winery®
La Marca®
Las Rocas®
Liberty Creek®
Louis M. Martini®
Laguna®
MacMurray Estate®
Martin Codax®
Dolcea®
Madria Sangria®
Mirassou®
Orin Swift Cellars®
Polka Dot®
Prophecy®
Pieropan®
Peter Vella®
Frei Brothers Reserve®
Renato Ratti®
Red Rock Winery®
Redwood Creek®
Starborough®
Saint Clair Family Estate®
Storypoint®
Fleur de Mer®
Souverain®
Talbott Vineyards®
Tisdale Vineyards®
Turning Leaf®
The Naked Grape®
Tott's®
Tornatore®
Vin Vault®
William Hill Estate®
Whitehaven®
Wild Vines®
William Hill Estate®
Whitehaven®
Wild Vines®
WM. Wycliff Vineyards®
Rancho Zabaco®

3835 E & J Gallo Winery
3387 Dry Creek Rd.
Healdsburg, CA 95448
707-431-1946
www.gallo.com
Wines
Estimated Sales: $1-2.5 Million
Number Employees: 1-4
Parent Co: E & J Gallo Winery

3836 E A Sween Co
16101 W 78th St
Eden Prairie, MN 55344-5798
952-937-9440
Fax: 952-937-0186 800-328-8184
tsween@deliexpress.com www.deliexpress.com
Prepackaged individual sandwiches
President/CEO: Tom Sween
tom.sween@easween.com
CFO: Dick Pearson
Sr. Vice President of Foodservice Sales: Bill Bastian
R&D: Grant Nellis
VP Product Safety: Lavonne Kucera
Marketing: Cheryl Peterson
Vice President of Operations: Tim Engmark
Production: Curt Karger
Plant Manager: Curt Karger
Purchasing: Janet Robling
Estimated Sales: $150,000
Number Employees: 1-4
Parent Co: E.A. Sween Company
Type of Packaging: Consumer
Brands:
  Deli Express
  Sensible Carbs

3837 E L K Run Vineyards
15113 Liberty Rd
Mt Airy, MD 21771-9502
301-363-3156
Fax: 410-875-2009 800-414-2513
elk_run@msn.com www.elkrun.com
Wines
President: Neil Bassford
neil@elkrun.com
Treasurer: Neil Bassford
Marketing Director: Carol Wilson
Estimated Sales: $1-2.5 Million
Number Employees: 1-4
Type of Packaging: Private Label
Brands:
  Elk Run

3838 E Waldo Ward & Son Marmalades
273 E Highland Ave
Sierra Madre, CA 91024-2014
626-355-1218
Fax: 626-355-5292 800-355-9273
service@waldoward.com www.waldoward.com
Manufacturer and importer of gourmet foods including olives, preserves, jellies, marmalades, brandied fruits and sauces including meat, relish and seafood cocktail; exporter of marmalades. Services, private labeling and anufacturing tolarge and small companies. Also offers consulting services
Owner: Richard Ward
richard@waldoward.com
VP: Jeffrey Ward
Estimated Sales: $810,000
Number Employees: 10-19
Number of Brands: 2
Number of Products: 150
Square Footage: 40000
Type of Packaging: Consumer, Private Label
Brands:
  E. Waldo Ward
  Sierra Madre Brand

3839 E&H Packing Company
2453 Riopelle St
Detroit, MI 48207
313-567-8286
Fax: 313-567-8287
Beef
Owner/President: Robert Buzar
Treasurer: Bob Buzar
Estimated Sales: $670,000
Number Employees: 5
Type of Packaging: Consumer, Food Service

3840 E-Fish-Ent Fish Company
1941 Goodridge Road
Sooke, BC V0S 0C6
Canada
250-642-4007
Fax: 250-642-4057 www.e-fish-ent.ca
Manufacturer and exporter of smoked salmon in retort pouch; meat products in pouch, stews, chili, curry.
President: Bryan Mooney
VP: Linda Mooney
Number Employees: 4
Square Footage: 32000
Type of Packaging: Private Label

3841 E. Gagnon & Fils
405 Rte 102
St Therese-De-Gaspe, QC G0C 3B0
Canada
418-385-3011
Fax: 418-385-3021
Manufacturer and exporter of frozen snow crabs, crab
President: Roger Gagnon
Estimated Sales: $2.3 Million
Number Employees: 5
Type of Packaging: Food Service

3842 E. H. Gourmet
575 Lynnhaven Pkwy
Suite 300
Virginia Beach, VA 23452
757-431-1996
info@ehgourmet.com
ehgourmet.com
Hot sauces; sea salt; seasonings; cocktail mixes
Co-Owner: Kerry Takach
Type of Packaging: Private Label

3843 E.C. Phillips & Son
PO Box 7090
Ketchikan, AK 99901-3235
907-247-7975
Fax: 907-225-7250 ecp@ecphillipsalaska.com
www.ecphillipsalaska.com
Buyers and processors of salmon
Owner: Colleen Picillo
CEO: Larry Elliot
VP: Michael Cusack
Estimated Sales: $10-20 Million
Number Employees: 60
Type of Packaging: Consumer

3844 E.D. Smith Foods Ltd
8 Burford Rd
Hamilton, ON L8E 5B1
Canada
905-573-1207
inquiry@edsmith.com
www.edsmith.com
Manufacturer and exporter of jams, ketchup, pie fillings, barbecue and pasta sauces, fruit toppings, salsas and syrups
President/CEO: Michael Burrows
VP Finance: David Smith
VP Operations: Dorothy Pethick
Type of Packaging: Consumer, Food Service, Private Label, Bulk
Brands:
  E.D. Smith
  Habitant
  Lea & Perrins

3845 E.F. Lane & Son
744 Kevin Ct
Oakland, CA 94621
510-569-8980
Fax: 510-569-0240
Manufacturer and exporter of honey and peanut products
Manager: Phyllis Tut
Estimated Sales: $500,000-$1 Million
Number Employees: 1-4
Type of Packaging: Consumer, Food Service, Private Label, Bulk

3846 E.W. Bowker Company
581 New Lasbon
Pemberton, NJ 08068
609-894-9508
Fax: 609-894-2165 ewbowker@yahoo.com
Fresh cranberries and blueberries
President: Ernest Bowker
Estimated Sales: $210,000
Number Employees: 3
Type of Packaging: Consumer, Food Service, Bulk

3847 (HQ)E.W. Knauss & Son
625 East Broad Street
Quakertown, PA 18951-1713
215-536-4220
Fax: 215-536-1129 800-648-4220
www.knaussfoods.com
Sliced dried beef products including beefsticks, beef jerky, hot sausage and pickled meat products.
CEO: Robert Longacre
VP Sales: William Carter
Estimated Sales: $20-50 Million
Number Employees: 50-99

Food Manufacturers / A-Z

Number of Brands: 2
Square Footage: 100000
Type of Packaging: Consumer, Food Service, Private Label, Bulk
Brands:
  Carson's
  Knauss

3848 ECOM Agroindustrial Corporation Ltd
Av Etienne Guillemin 16
PO Box 64
Pully, CH-1009
Switzerland
www.ecomtrading.com
Cotton, cocoa, coffee and sugar.
CFO: Daniel Willett
Year Founded: 1849
Estimated Sales: $5.1 Billion
Number Employees: 6,000
Type of Packaging: Consumer, Food Service, Private Label, Bulk

3849 EDCO Food Products Inc
2815 Packerland Dr # 23
P.O. Box 12511
Hobart, WI 54313-6182
920-499-7651
Fax: 920-499-8023   800-255-3768
sales@edcofood.com   www.edcofood.biz
Processor and importer of peppers including jalapeno, serrano, sport and cascabella; also, cauliflower buttons, chipotle powder and pickled vegetables
President: James Manning
accounting@edcofood.com
VP: Edward Manning
VP: Sylvia Roman
Business Development: David J. Sinkula
Customer Service & Logistics: James Gumtow
Estimated Sales: $3-5 Million
Number Employees: 5-9
Square Footage: 64000
Type of Packaging: Food Service, Private Label, Bulk

3850 EFCO Products Inc
130 Smith St
Poughkeepsie, NY 12601
800-284-3326
info@efcoproducts.com   www.efcoproducts.com
Leading supplier of mixes, fruit and creme style fillings, jellies, glazes and concentrated icing fruits to the baking industry.
CEO: David Miller
Vice President: Andy Herzing
Senior Director of Sales & Marketing: Mark Lowman
Director of Manufacturing Operations: Veronica Miller
Year Founded: 1903
Estimated Sales: $2.5-5 Million
Number Employees: 50-99

3851 EFFi Foods
11620 Wilshire Blvd
Suite 900
Los Angeles, CA 90025
310-582-5938
Fax: 310-388-8798   www.effifoods.com
Chickpea granola
Co-Founder & CEO: Johnny Fayad
Co-Founder & COO: Ali Kothari
Type of Packaging: Consumer
Brands:
  EFFI

3852 EIWA America Inc.
19301 Pacific Gateway Dr
Suite 210
Torrance, CA 90502
310-327-7222
Fax: 310-327-7352   eiwamm.co.jp
Marshmellows and candy
CEO: Hiroya Miyajima
Year Founded: 2010
Estimated Sales: $150000
Number Employees: 3
Type of Packaging: Private Label
Brands:
  Hello Kitty
  Heart
  EIWA
  Suzuki Eikodo
  Ginbis

3853 EJZ Foods
Winston-Salem, NC 27106
tryzen.com
Hazelnut milk chocolate pudding

3854 ELP Inc
366 Grant St
Elizabeth, CO 80107
303-688-2240
Fax: 303-688-2240
Packer of meat including beef, lamb, goat and pork
President: Mike Hundley
VP: Robert Hundley
Estimated Sales: $1-2.5 Million
Number Employees: 10-19
Type of Packaging: Consumer

3855 EMD Performance Materials
One International Plaza
#300
Philadelphia, PA 19113
908-591-7496
Fax: 484-652-5749   888-367-3275
Specialty testing products for the Food and Beverage industry including Microbiology Culture Media featuring granulated media for safety and convenience; the MAS-100 Eco, a lightweight, portable air sampling instrument; the HYLiTE 2system, a portable system for determining the cleanliness of surfaces and work spaces; and Test Strip Kits for rapid testing of Ions and pH measurement. Manufactures a mineral based line of colors for use in foods, dietary supplements and drugs.
President/CEO: Meiken Krebs
Contact: Matthew Girard
mgirard@emdchemicals.com
CFO: Klaus Rueth
Vice President: Octavio Diaz
Research & Development: Jim Morgera
Quality Control: Stephen Bates
Marketing Director: Rebecca Vaiarelli
Key Account Manager: Taina Franke
Public Relations: Rina Spatafore
Operations Manager: Thorsten Hartis
Production Manager: John Alestra
Plant Manager: Bob Jones
Purchasing Manager: Ron Wisda
Estimated Sales: $10-25 Million
Number Employees: 500-999
Parent Co: Merck KgaA Darmstadt

3856 EMD Sales Inc
2010 Washington Blvd
Baltimore, MD 21230-1736
410-385-3023
Fax: 301-322-4504   emdsales@aol.com
www.emdsalesinc.com
International foods distributors of spices, cheeses, groceries, candies, refrigerated and frozen products
Contact: Arly Aguirre
arly.aguirre@emdsalesinc.com
Estimated Sales: $640,000
Number Employees: 50-99

3857 EOS Estate Winery
2300 Airport Rd
Paso Robles, CA 93446-8549
805-591-8050
Fax: 805-239-2317   800-249-9463
customerservice@eosvintage.com
www.eosvintage.com
Wines
Partner: Frank Arciero Jr
Partner: Fern Underwood
CFO: Pati Withers
Marketing: Christopher Vix
Sales: Luis Cota
Public Relations: Denise McLean
Operations: Steve Felten
Production: Leslie Melendez
Plant Manager: Gary Cargill
Purchase Manager: Pat Withers
Estimated Sales: Less Than $500,000
Number Employees: 1-4
Number of Brands: 4
Type of Packaging: Private Label
Brands:
  Aruero
  Cupagranols
  Eos
  Novella

3858 ERBL
2525 Commerce Way
Vista, CA 92081
760-599-6088
Fax: 760-599-6089   800-275-3725
support@coromega.com   www.coromega.com
Omega-3 dietary supplements.
Manager: Suzanne Goodrich
President, Chief Operating Officer: Frank Morley
Estimated Sales: $5-10 Million
Number Employees: 10-19

3859 Eagle Brand
1 Strawberry Lane
Orrville, OH 44667-0280
888-656-3245
www.eaglebrand.com
Sweetened, condensed milk

3860 (HQ)Eagle Coffee Co Inc
1027 Hillen St
Baltimore, MD 21202-4132
410-685-5893
Fax: 410-528-0369   contactus@eaglecoffee.com
www.eaglecoffee.com
Restaurant and gourmet coffees, coffee machines and grinders and coffee beans; serving the food service market
Owner: Nick Constantine
eaglecoffee@aol.com
Controller: Tom Brooks
VP: Jacqueline Parris
Estimated Sales: $1.6 Million
Number Employees: 10-19
Square Footage: 120000
Type of Packaging: Food Service, Private Label
Other Locations:
  Eagle Coffee Co.
  Baltimore MD

3861 Eagle Crest Vineyards LLC
7107 Vineyard Rd
Conesus, NY 14435-9521
585-346-2321
Fax: 585-346-2322   800-977-7117
will@onehda.com   www.eaglecrestvineyards.com
Sacramental and table wine
VP: Bob Quinn
Production Manager: Rose Michaels
Estimated Sales: $2.5-5 Million
Number Employees: 5-9

3862 Eagle Family Foods
4020 Kinross Lakes Pkwy
Richfield, OH 44286
888-656-3245
eaglefoods.com
Snack foods, sweetened condensed milk and evaporated milk products
CEO: Bernard Kreilman
CFO: Joe Sinicropi
Vice President, Finance: Dan Gentile
Vice President, Marketing: Corinne Kelly
Vice President, Sales: Bill Iggins
Vice President, Operations: Rob Miller
Year Founded: 2016
Number Employees: 48
Brands:
  Eagle Brand
  Borden
  PET
  Milnot
  G.H. Cretors
  Skinny Sticks
  Popcorn, Indiana

3863 Eagle Ice Cream Company
90 Broadway Avenue
Cleveland, OH 44146-2059
440-232-0085
Fax: 216-591-2966
Ice Cream
VP: Richard Nye
Estimated Sales: $2.5-5 Million
Number Employees: 20-49
Parent Co: Riser Foods

3864 Eagle Rock Food Co
1225 12th St NW
Albuquerque, NM 87104-2113
505-323-1183
Meat processing
Owner: Mike Perea
Estimated Sales: $1-3 Million
Number Employees: 1-4

Food Manufacturers / A-Z

3865 Eagle Seafood Producers
56 N 3rd Street
Brooklyn, NY 11211-3925
718-963-0939
Fax: 718-963-1306
Fresh and frozen seafood
President: Mark Rudes
VP: Donald Draghi
Estimated Sales: $10-20 Million
Number Employees: 20-49
Type of Packaging: Food Service

3866 Earnest Eats
444 S Cedros Ave
Suite 175
Solana Beach, CA 92075
858-299-4238
Fax: 858-793-3662 earnesteats.com
Superfood cereal, oatmeal and bars
Co-Founder & President: Andrew Aussie
Sales: Andrew Brayton
Year Founded: 2007
Type of Packaging: Consumer
Brands:
EARNEST EATS

3867 Earth & Vine ProvisionsInc
160 Flocchini Cir
Lincoln, CA 95648-1700
916-434-8399
Fax: 916-434-8398 888-723-8463
customerservice@earthnvine.com
www.earthnvine.com
Jams, sauces, beverage elixirs and dressings
Owner: Tressa Cooper
earthnvine@yahoo.com
CEO: Ron Cooper
Number Employees: 10-19

3868 Earth Balance
1600 Pearl St
Suite 300
Boulder, CO 80302
866-234-6429
www.earthbalancenatural.com
Spreads, nut butters, dressings, crackers and snacks
Parent Co: Boulder Brands
Type of Packaging: Consumer
Brands:
EARTH BALANCE

3869 Earth Circle Organics
12745 Earhart Ave
Auburn, CA 95602
877-922-3663
earthcircleorganics.com
Organic ingredients
President & COO: Herb Heller
Founder & CEO: Eric Botner
Vice President, Sales & Marketing: Claire Modjeski
Type of Packaging: Consumer, Bulk

3870 Earth Island
9201 Owensmouth Ave
Chatsworth, CA 91311-5834
818-725-2820
Fax: 818-725-2812 888-394-3949
info@followyourheart.com
www.betterthanmayo.com
Vegan mayonnaise, dips, cheeses, and salad dressings.
Owner: Robert Goldberg
bob@followyourheart.com
Co-Owner: Paul Lewin
Estimated Sales: $1-3 Million
Number Employees: 50-99
Square Footage: 12000
Type of Packaging: Consumer, Food Service, Private Label, Bulk
Brands:
VEGENAISE
VEGAN GOURMET
FOLLOW YOUR HEART

3871 Earth Science
475 N Sheridan St
Corona, CA 92880
951-371-7565
Fax: 909-371-0509
Vitamin C products
President: Kristine Schoenauer
VP: Michael Rutledge
Contract Sales Manager: Diane Smart
Contact: Sergio Aguirre
saguirre@cosmedxscience.com
Number Employees: 100-249
Square Footage: 160000
Type of Packaging: Consumer, Bulk

3872 Earth Song Whole Foods
4880 San Juan Avenue
Suite 216
Fair Oaks, CA 95628-4719
916-332-1355
Fax: 916-332-1355 877-327-8476
Vegan natural food products
Owner: Julie Rogers
Estimated Sales: $300,000-500,000
Number Employees: 1-4
Brands:
Earth Song Whole Food Bars
Grandpa's Secret Omega-3 Muesli

3873 Earth Source Organics
1370 Decision Street
Suite C
Vista, CA 92081
760-734-1867
Fax: 760-734-1576
www.righteouslyrawchocolate.com
Chocolate
Contact: Brittany England
brittany@earthsourceorganics.com

3874 Earth Source Organics
1235 Activity Drive, Suite E
Vista, CA 92081
760-734-1867
Fax: 760-734-1576 info@earthsourceorganics.com
www.righteouslyrawchocolate.com
Gourmet organic raw chocolate bars. Earth Source Organics provides contract food packaging services exclusively for Certified Organic, Vegan, and Kosher raw foods that are Non-GMO, Allergen Free, Nut Free, and Gluten Free.
President: Audrey Darrow
Contact: Dan England
dan@earthsourceorganics.com
Type of Packaging: Consumer
Brands:
RIGHTEOUSLY RAW CHOCOLATE

3875 Earthbound Farm
1721 San Juan Hwy
San Jn Bautista, CA 95045-9780
831-623-7881
800-690-3200
www.earthboundfarm.com
Organic salads, vegetables, frozen fruit, herbs, frozen vegetables, fruit, dried fruit, and snacks.
President: Myra Rubin
myra@ebfarm.com
CEO: Charles Sweat
Chief Financial Officer: Jeff Cook
VP, Product Innovation: Nathalie Fontanilla
Chief Customer & Marketing Officer: Craig Hope
VP, Sales/Customer Service & Product Mgm: Steve Koran
Sr VP, Operations & Organic Integrity: Will Daniels
Chief Production Officer: Otto Kramm
Senior Vice President, Supply Management: Todd Kodet
Number Employees: 1000-4999
Type of Packaging: Consumer

3876 Earthrise Nutritionals
2151 Michelson Dr # 258
Suite 258
Irvine, CA 92612-1382
949-623-0980
Fax: 949-623-0990 800-949-7473
www.earthrise.com
Spirulina based green food nutritional products
President: Hiroyuki Mochizuki
CEO: Sumi Hitoshi
Controller: Adrian Hsu
VP: Rob Kelly
Sales & Marketing Division Manager: Lee Crockett
National Sales: Shiro Nobunaga
COO: Taro Ichimoto
Facility Production Mgr: Antonio Flores
Estimated Sales: Less Than $500,000
Number Employees: 1-4
Type of Packaging: Private Label

3877 Easley Winery
205 N College Ave
Indianapolis, IN 46202-3799
317-636-4516
Fax: 317-974-0128 info@easleywinery.com
www.easleywinery.com
Table wine
President/Winemaker: Mark Easley
measley@500festival.com
Banquet Manager: Meredit Easley
Estimated Sales: $2.6 Million
Number Employees: 10-19
Type of Packaging: Consumer, Food Service, Private Label, Bulk
Brands:
Cape Sandy Vineyards
Easley's

3878 (HQ)East Balt Commissary Inc
1801 W 31st Pl
Chicago, IL 60608-6199
773-376-4444
Fax: 773-376-8137 800-621-8555
www.eastbalt.com
Classic buns, ciabatta breads, and specialty breads
CEO: Mark Bendix
EVP US Region: Lianying "Kelley" Wang
EVP Research & Development: Joe McDilda
VP Global Quality: Mike LaBosky
VP Sales: Daniel Harrison
Estimated Sales: $20-50 Million
Number Employees: 100-249
Type of Packaging: Private Label

3879 East Coast Fresh Cuts Inc
9001 Whiskey Bottom Rd
Laurel, MD 20723
www.eastcoastfresh.com
Fresh cut vegetables including onions, peppers, carrots, celery, etc
CEO: John Corso
CFO: Bob Lahmann
VP, Sales: Jim McWhorter
VP, Customer Care: Tracy Moore
VP, Purchasing: Jason Lambros
Year Founded: 1997
Estimated Sales: $53.35 Million
Number Employees: 300
Square Footage: 330000
Parent Co: Coastal Sun Belt
Type of Packaging: Food Service, Private Label, Bulk

3880 East Dayton Meat & Poultry
1546 Keystone Ave
Dayton, OH 45403
937-253-6185
Fax: 937-253-1040 www.eastdaytonmeat.com
Beef, pork and deer; fresh cut meat, marinades, seasonings, spices, rubs, cheeses, vegetables and salads
Owner: Mike Lakey
Year Founded: 1944
Estimated Sales: $20-50 Million
Number Employees: 5-9
Type of Packaging: Consumer, Food Service

3881 East Indies Coffee & Tea Co
7 Keystone Dr
Lebanon, PA 17042-9791
717-228-2000
Fax: 717-228-2540 800-220-2326
wprog@eastindiescoffeeandtea.com
www.eastindiescoffeeandtea.com
Gourmet and flavored coffees and teas
Owner: Philip Auman
pauman@eastindiescoffeeandtea.com
VP: Mim Enck
Estimated Sales: Less Than $500,000
Number Employees: 1-4

3882 East Kentucky Foods
739 Ecton Road
Winchester, KY 40391
859-744-2218
Fax: 859-744-8511
Packaged frozen goods
President: Greg Ginter
Estimated Sales: $1.4 Million
Number Employees: 7

Food Manufacturers / A-Z

3883 East Point Seafood Company
350 Blake Street
Raymond, WA 98586
360-875-5507
Fax: 360-875-5417   888-317-8459
onlinesales@eastpointseafood.com
www.eastpointseafood.com
Seafood
Owner: Joel Van Ornun
onlinesales@eastpointseafood.com
Estimated Sales: $1-3 Million
Number Employees: 5-9
Type of Packaging: Private Label

3884 East Poultry Co
2615 E 6th St
Austin, TX 78702-3900
512-476-5367
Fax: 512-476-5360   www.eastpoultry.com
Poultry and eggs
President: Ken Aune
eastpoultry@austin.rr.com
Estimated Sales: $4.10 Million
Number Employees: 10-19
Square Footage: 54000
Type of Packaging: Food Service, Bulk

3885 East Shore Specialty Foods
643 Cardinal Ln
Po Box 379
Hartland, WI 53029-2316
262-367-8988
Fax: 262-367-9081   800-236-1069
customerservice@eastshorefoods.com
www.eastshorefoods.com
Gourmet mustards, pretzels, chocolate sauces
Owner: Jeri Mesching
jeri@eastshorefoods.com
CEO: Khristian Graves
Manager: Greg Seales
Marketing: Kristin Graves
Estimated Sales: $760,000
Number Employees: 10-19
Type of Packaging: Private Label

3886 East Side Winery/Oak Ridge Vineyards
6100 E Hwy 12 (Victor Rd)
Lodi, CA 95240
209-369-4758
Fax: 209-369-0202
orderprocessing@oakridgewinery.com
www.oakridgewinery.com
Bottled wines
Owner: Rudy Maggio
Director of Marketing: Marc Lohnes
Director of U.S. Sales and Marketing: Marc M. Lohnes
Estimated Sales: $10-20 Million
Number Employees: 20-49
Type of Packaging: Consumer, Food Service, Private Label, Bulk

3887 East Wind Inc
1361 County Road 547
Tecumseh, MO 65760-7310
417-679-4682
Fax: 417-679-4684   www.eastwind.org
Peanut and organic peanut butters; also, cashew and almond butters and tahini
Manager: Lena Berglund
Sales & Marketing: Shaya Kraut
Sales Director: Sam Lucas
Contact: Virgil Carpenter
virgil.eastwind@gmail.com
Purchasing: Jaime Escobedo
Estimated Sales: $2 Million
Number Employees: 50-99
Square Footage: 28000
Parent Co: East Wind Community
Type of Packaging: Consumer, Food Service, Private Label
Brands:
  East Wind
  East Wind Almond
  East Wind Cashew
  East Wind Organic Peanut Butter
  East Wind Peanut
  East Wind Tahini

3888 Eastern Brewing Corporation
PO Box 497
Hammonton, NJ 08037
609-561-2700
Fax: 609-561-9441
Beer
President: Louis Fatatm
Treasurer: James Penza Jr
Estimated Sales: Less than $500,000
Number Employees: 2

3889 (HQ)Eastern Fish Company
Glennpointe Centre East
300 Frank W Burr Blvd Ste 30
Teaneck, NJ 07666
201-801-0800
Fax: 201-801-0802   800-526-9066
www.easternfish.com
Manufacturer and importer of farm raised shrimp and other seafood, bay and sea scallops, lobster, king crab legs and claws, snow crab clusters, yellow fin tuna
Founder: Bill Bloom
President: Eric Bloom
Secretary: Charna Bloom
Vice President: Lee Bloom
Estimated Sales: $6.7 Million
Number Employees: 30
Square Footage: 18000
Type of Packaging: Private Label
Other Locations:
  Norwestern Sales Office
    Kingston WA
  Western Sales Office
    Anaheim CA
  Northeastern Sales Office
    Gloucester MA
  Southeastern Sales Office
    Coral Springs FL
Brands:
  Sail

3890 Eastern Food IndustriesInc
2832 S County Trl
East Greenwich, RI 02818-1742
401-884-8798
Fax: 401-884-3552   www.chefaroni.com
Pasta sauces
President: Henry Caniglia
h.caniglia@chefaroni.com
VP: Stephen Caniglia
Estimated Sales: $525,000
Number Employees: 5-9

3891 Eastern Sea Products
11 Addison Avenue
Scoudouc, NB E4P 3N3
Canada
506-532-6111
Fax: 506-532-9111   800-565-6364
maurice@easternsea.ca
Manufacturer and exporter of salted and smoked seafood: herring, mackerel, salmon
President: Maurice Allain
Director: Joanne Allain
Estimated Sales: $1.3 Million
Number Employees: 10
Number of Brands: 2
Number of Products: 10
Square Footage: 48000
Type of Packaging: Consumer, Private Label
Brands:
  Cape Royal
  Seapro

3892 Eastern Seafood Co
1020 W Hubbard St
Chicago, IL 60642-6526
312-243-2090
Fax: 312-243-9467
Seafood
President: Mario Falco
easternseafood@att.net
Estimated Sales: $730 Thousand
Number Employees: 5-9

3893 Eastern Shore Tea
9 W Aylesbury Rd # T
Lutherville, MD 21093-4121
410-561-5079
Fax: 410-561-4816   800-823-1408
bct@baltcoffee.com
Tea including whole leaf and bagged
President: Stanley Constantine
sconstantine@easternshoretea.com
CEO: Janice Burns
Estimated Sales: $5-9.9 Million
Number Employees: 5-9
Type of Packaging: Consumer
Brands:
  Baltimore Tea

3894 Eastern Tea Corp
1 Engelhard Dr
Monroe Twp, NJ 08831-3722
609-860-1100
Fax: 609-860-1105   800-221-0865
www.bromleytea.com
Manufacturer, importer and exporter of packaged and loose tea; also, tea bags and tapioca
President: Paul Barbakoff
paul@bromleytea.com
Vice President: Ira Barbakoff
VP of Manufacturing: Glenn Barbakoff
Estimated Sales: $5-10 Million
Number Employees: 50-99
Square Footage: 360000
Type of Packaging: Consumer, Food Service, Private Label

3895 Eastrise Trading Corp.
16025 Arrow Hwy Ste A
Baldwin Park, CA 91706-2063
Fax: 626-330-0205   info@eastriseteas.com
www.eastriseteas.com
Certified organic teas
Owner: Stephen Chau
Treasurer: Lydia Chao
Contact: Stephen Chal
info@foojoyteas.com
Estimated Sales: $1-2.5 Million
Number Employees: 8
Brands:
  Rare Teas

3896 Eastside Deli Supply
2601 W Main St
Lansing, MI 48917
517-485-4630
Fax: 517-485-7904   800-349-6694
products@eastsidedeli.com
Fresh prepared deli sandwiches and beef jerky
President: Jeffrey Jacobs
Route Sales Manager: Kevin Hedley
Contact: Jeff Jacobs
jjacobs@eastsidedeli.com
Estimated Sales: $7.5 Million
Number Employees: 50
Square Footage: 10000
Type of Packaging: Food Service
Brands:
  Eastside Deli
  Fresh From the Deli
  Tillamook Country Smoker

3897 Eastside Seafood
1248 Jeffersonville Rd
Macon, GA 31217-4335
478-743-1888
Fax: 478-272-5800
Seafood
Owner: Riccardo Del Mastro
Estimated Sales: Less Than $500,000
Number Employees: 1-4

3898 Easy Lift Equipment Co Inc
2 Mill Park Ct
Newark, DE 19713-1986
302-737-8784
Fax: 302-737-7333   800-233-1800
sales@easylifteqpt.com   www.easylifteqpt.com
Manufacturers of Drum & Roll handling Equipment
President: Lorea Eastbrun
eastbrun@easylifteqpt.com
Estimated Sales: $5-10 Million
Number Employees: 5-9

3899 Eat Dutch Waffles, LLC
69 W. 500 S.
Orem, UT 84058
801-319-4788
www.eatdutchwaffles.com
Manufacturer of stroopwafels.
Founder: Joost Kling

Food Manufacturers / A-Z

3900 Eat It Corporation
4002 2nd Avenue
Brooklyn, NY 11232
718-768-7950
Fax: 718-832-0406 eatitcorp@aol.com
Soft drinks
President: John Ra
General Manager: Antonio Pichardo

3901 Eat My Waffles
Cardiff By The Sea, CA 92007
www.eatmywaffles.com
Waffle mix

3902 Eat Real Snacks USA
1860 Sandy Plains Rd
Suite 204-125
Marietta, GA 30066
404-432-0842
sales@cofresh.co.uk
eatrealsnacks.com
Organic chips
Director: Priyesh Patel
Type of Packaging: Private Label
Other Locations:
  Headquarters
  Leicester UK

3903 Eat This
75 Headquarters Rd.
Erwinna, PA 18920
215-391-5807
info@eatthisyum.com
www.eatthisyum.com
Manufacturer of sweet jams and marmalades.
Founder: Gino Schrijver

3904 Eat Your Coffee
333 Newbury St
Unit 2B
Boston, MA 02115
info@eatyour.coffee
www.eatyour.coffee
Naturally-caffeinated snacks
Co-Founder & CEO: Johnny Fayad
Co-Founder & COO: Ali Kothari
Type of Packaging: Consumer
Brands:
  EAT YOUR COFFEE

3905 Eat Zi's Market & Bakery
3403 Oak Lawn Ave
Dallas, TX 75219-4215
214-526-1515
Fax: 214-526-1540 feedback@eatzis.com
www.eatzis.com
Market and bakery
Founder: Phil Romano
CEO: Adam Romo
Vice President: Barry Partos
bpartos@eatzis.com
Number Employees: 100-249

3906 EatKeenwa, Inc.
179 Beacon Ave.
Jersey City, NJ 07306
855-453-3692
Manufacturer of quinoa cluster snacks.
Founder: Blake Niemann
Brands:
  Keenwa Krunch

3907 EatPastry LLC
11545 Sorrento Valley Rd
San Diego, CA 92121
858-755-7456
info@eatpastry.com
www.eatpastry.com
vegan cookie dough and baking mixes; gluten free products.
Co-founder: Alfredo Elias
Co-founder: Jessie Williams
Type of Packaging: Consumer

3908 Eatem Foods Co
1829 Gallagher Dr
Vineland, NJ 08360-1548
856-692-1663
Fax: 856-692-0847 800-683-2836
sales@eatemfoods.com www.eatemfoods.com
Food base manufacturing; supplier of savory flavor systems, flavor concentrates, broth concentrates and seasoning bases.
Vice President: Gerrie Bouchard
gerriebouchard@gmail.com
Chief Technical Officer: John Randazzi
Chief Financial Officer: Danine Freeman
Vice President, Treasurer: Mario Riviello
Director, R&D: Bill Cawley
Marketing Manager: Gerrie Bouchard
Vice President, Sales: Don Witherspoon
Director of Operations: Jerry Santo
Estimated Sales: $14 Million
Number Employees: 50-99
Square Footage: 12916
Type of Packaging: Consumer, Food Service, Bulk
Brands:
  Eatem

3909 Eating Evolved
Setauket, NY 11733
631-675-2440
eatingevolved.com
Keto-friendly snack cups and bars
Co-Founder: Rick Gusmano
Co-Founder: Christine Cusano
Brands:
  Keto Cups
  Primal Chocolate

3910 Eau Galle Cheese Factory Shop
N6765 State Highway 25
Durand, WI 54736-4209
715-283-4211
Fax: 715-283-0711 www.eaugallecheese.com
Cheeses.
President: John Buhlman
Estimated Sales: $10-20 Million
Number Employees: 20-49
Number of Brands: 1
Brands:
  Eau Galle Cheese

3911 Eberhard Creamery
235 S.W. Evergreen Ave
P.O. Box 845
Redmond, OR 97756
541-548-5181
Fax: 541-548-7009 ebdairy@eberhardsdairy.com
www.eberhardsdairy.com
Dairy products and frozen foods
President: John Eberhard
Vice President: Ted Eberhard
Manager: Mike Prom
Manager: Ron Jackson
Estimated Sales: $4 Million
Number Employees: 40
Type of Packaging: Consumer, Food Service

3912 Eberle Winery
3810 E Highway 46
Paso Robles, CA 93446-7044
805-238-9607
Fax: 805-237-0344 sales@eberlewinery.com
www.eberlewinery.com
Wine
Owner: Gary Eberle
gary@eberlewinery.com
Estimated Sales: $5-10 Million
Number Employees: 20-49

3913 Eberly Poultry, Inc.
1095 Mount Airy Rd
Stevens, PA 17578
717-336-6440
Fax: 717-336-6905
Organic and specialty poultry.
President: Robert Eberly
Supervisor: Joe Hoover
Manager: Tom Mikus
Contact: Melody Eckenroth
meckenroth@eberlypoultry.com
Estimated Sales: $10-20 Million
Number Employees: 75
Type of Packaging: Consumer

3914 Ebro Foods
1330 W 43rd St
Chicago, IL 60609-3308
773-696-0150
Fax: 773-696-0151 info@ebrofoods.com
www.ebrofoods.com
Manufacturer of Hispanic foods.
VP, Sales & Marketing: Pedro Morales
Manager: Silvio Vega
silvio.vega@ebrofoods.com
Estimated Sales: $14 Million
Number Employees: 10-19
Number of Brands: 1
Type of Packaging: Consumer
Brands:
  Ebro

3915 Echo Farms Puddings
573 Chesterfield Rd
Hinsdale, NH 03451-2210
603-336-7706
Fax: 603-336-5964 866-488-3246
www.echofarmpuddings.com
Desserts, pudding
Owner: Robert Hodge
VP: Shelley Schofield
Contact: Beth Hodge
beth@echofarmpuddings.com
Estimated Sales: $1 Million
Number Employees: 12
Brands:
  Echo Farm Pudding

3916 Echo Lake Foods, Inc.
340 West Grove
Burlington, WI 53105
262-763-9551
Fax: 262-763-4593 info@echolakefoods.com
www.echoforeggs.com
Frozen and liquid egg processing, pancakes, French toast, waffle, omelets, egg pattys, bread rolls, mini pancakes, flavored waffles and pancakes.
Vice President: Jerry Warntjes
VP: Jerry Warntjes
Sales Director: Scott Hall
Retail Sales: Justin Milbradt
Year Founded: 1941
Estimated Sales: $150 Million
Number Employees: 800
Type of Packaging: Consumer, Food Service, Private Label, Bulk

3917 Echo Spring Dairy
706 Oscar St
Eugene, OR 97402
541-342-1291
Fax: 541-342-8379
Dairy products
Manager: Mike Miller
Estimated Sales: $10-20 Million
Number Employees: 20-49
Parent Co: Darigold
Type of Packaging: Consumer, Food Service

3918 Eckert Cold Storage
757 Moffat Blvd
Manteca, CA 95336-5819
209-823-3181
Fax: 209-823-2499
IQF red, green and yellow bell and jalapeno peppers, cabbage leaves, diced cabbage, bok choy, kabocha and mangos
President & CEO: Kevin Mills
CFO: Jack Higgins
HR Executive: Steve West
steve@eckertcoldstorage.com
Researcher: Jason Crichton
Director of Brand Communications: Kevin Kampwerth
Sales & Marketing Manager: Craig West
Purchasing Supervisor: Deborah Haas
Number Employees: 250-499
Square Footage: 77168
Type of Packaging: Bulk

3919 (HQ)Eckhart Corporation
7110 Redwood Blvd Ste A
Novato, CA 94945
415-898-9528
Fax: 415-898-1917 800-200-4201
info@eckhartcorp.com www.eckhartcorp.com
Manufacturer and exporter of vitamins, food supplements and diet aids
President: Deepak Chopra
VP/Latin America: Arnoldo Rosas
Estimated Sales: $500,000-1 Million
Number Employees: 8
Square Footage: 640000
Type of Packaging: Consumer, Food Service, Private Label, Bulk
Brands:
  Nature's Edge
  Stay Well

Food Manufacturers / A-Z

3920 Eckhart Seed Company
531 Eckhart Road
Salinas, CA 93908
831-758-0925
Fax: 831-758-0388 rene@eckhartseed.com
www.eckhartseed.com
Dried beans
President: Richard Eckhart
Secretary: Connie Lord
VP: James Eckhart
Contact: Ed Acrey
beaney12@aol.com
Estimated Sales: $710,000
Number Employees: 12
Type of Packaging: Bulk

3921 Eckroat Seed Company
1106 Martin Luther King Avenue
Oklahoma City, OK 73117
405-427-2484
Fax: 405-427-7174 800-331-7533
www.eckroatseed.com
Manufacturer, importer and exporter of mung beans
President: Robert Eckroat
VP: Don Eckroat
Estimated Sales: $5-10 Million
Number Employees: 10-19
Square Footage: 400000
Type of Packaging: Consumer, Food Service, Private Label, Bulk
Brands:
  Green Dragon

3922 Eclat Chocolate
24 S High St
West Chester, PA 19382-3225
610-692-5206
Fax: 610-692-5207 info@eclatchocolate.com
www.eclatchocolate.com
Chocolate
Owner: Christopher Curtin
info@eclatchoclate.com
Estimated Sales: $510,000
Number Employees: 5-9

3923 Eclectic Institute
36350 Industrial Way
Sandy, OR 97055-7377
503-668-4120
Fax: 503-668-3227
customerservice@eclecticherb.com
www.alstat.com
Organic alcohol extracts, alcohol free glycerins and nutritional supplements.
Owner: Edward Alstat
ealstat@eclecticherb.com
Estimated Sales: $5-10 Million
Number Employees: 50-99

3924 Eco-Planet Cookies
2516 California Ave
Santa Monica, CA 90403
310-829-9050
Fax: 310-829-6745
Croutons, breadcrumbs, breadsticks and cookies including seasonal, butter, natural, wheat-free, fat-free and special dietary baked without refined sugar; also, gingerbread houses and cookies. We also do private label
President: Tom Mosk
Estimated Sales: $2 Million approx.
Number Employees: 1-4
Square Footage: 80000
Type of Packaging: Private Label
Brands:
  Heaven Scent Windmill Cookies
  Heaven Scent
  Heaven Scent Butter Cookies
  Heaven Scent Croutons
  Heaven Scent Fat Free Cookies
  Heaven Scent Natural Foods

3925 EcoNatural Solutions
997 Dixon Rd
Boulder, CO 80302
303-357-5682
Fax: 303-358-4111 sales@stclaires.com
www.stclaires.com
Manufacturer and exporter of organic sweets
CEO: Debra St Claire
d.stclaire@stclaires.com
Estimated Sales: $2.5-5 Million
Number Employees: 5-9
Type of Packaging: Consumer
Brands:
  St. Claire

3926 Ecom Manufacturing Corporation
80 Telson Road
Markham, ON L3R 1E5
Canada
905-477-2441
Fax: 905-477-2551 dsoknacki@ecomcanada.com
www.ecomcanada.com
Natural colors and flavors including garlic, onion, rosemary, allspice, turmeric, jalapeno, cilantro and nutmeg extracts,capsicum,enhancers.
President: David Soknacki
Sales/Marketing: Kan Husband
Estimated Sales: $249,000
Number Employees: 5
Square Footage: 160000
Type of Packaging: Bulk

3927 Ed & Don's Of Hawaii Inc
4462 Malaai St
Honolulu, HI 96818-3134
808-423-8200
Fax: 808-423-0550 sales@edanddons.com
www.edanddons.com
Chocolate candies
President: Vladimir Grave
VP: Earl Kurisu
Marketing: Mark Honda
Estimated Sales: $13 Million
Number Employees: 20-49
Parent Co: Oritz Corporation
Type of Packaging: Private Label
Brands:
  Ed & Don's Chocolate Macadamias
  Ed & Don's Macadamia Brittles
  Ed & Don's Macadamia Chews

3928 (HQ)Ed Miniat Inc
16250 Vincennes Ave
South Holland, IL 60473-1260
708-589-2400
Fax: 708-589-2525 info@miniat.com
www.miniat.com
Frozen prepared meats
President: David Miniat
Chairman: Ronald Miniat
CFO: David Boyle
Executive VP: Michael Miniat
Marketing Manager: Eugene Matern
Sales Manager: Chuck Nalon
Operations Executive: David Jackson
Plant Manager: Darryl Hood
Estimated Sales: $23 Million
Number Employees: 10-19

3929 Ed Miniat Inc
16250 Vincennes Ave
South Holland, IL 60473-1260
708-589-2400
Fax: 708-589-2525 info@miniat.com
www.miniat.com
Prepared frozen meats
President: David Miniat
Director Sales/Marketing: Chuck Nalon
Director Operations: Neil Braderick
Production Manager: Lucio Fragoso
Plant Manager: John Nault
Estimated Sales: $5-10 Million
Number Employees: 10-19
Parent Co: Ed Miniat

3930 Ed Oliveira Winery
155 Center Street
Arcata, CA 95521-6056
707-822-3023
Wines
Owner: Douglas Oliveira
President: Catty Oliveira
Estimated Sales: $62,000
Number Employees: 2

3931 Ed Roller Inc
1115 Ridgeway Ave # 2
Suite 2
Rochester, NY 14615-3755
585-458-8020
Fax: 585-458-8169
Condiments including horseradish and cocktail sauces
Owner: Mike Mendick
edroller@rochester.rr.com
Estimated Sales: $1-2,500,000
Number Employees: 1-4
Number of Products: 2
Square Footage: 10000
Type of Packaging: Consumer, Food Service, Private Label, Bulk
Brands:
  Private Labels
  Rollers

3932 Ed's Honey Co
497 10th Ave SE
Dickinson, ND 58601-7421
701-225-9223
Honey
Owner: Ed Fetch
Estimated Sales: $150,000
Number Employees: 1-4
Type of Packaging: Consumer

3933 Ed's Kasilof Seafoods
26085 Williamson Ln
Kasilof, AK 99610
907-262-7295
Fax: 907-262-1617 800-982-2377
eks@alaska.net www.kasilofseafoods.com
Seafood
President: James Trujillo
eks@alaska.net
Estimated Sales: $960 Thousand
Number Employees: 20-49

3934 Eda's Sugar Free
4900 N 20th St
Philadelphia, PA 19144-2402
215-324-3412
Fax: 888-626-7785 brianberry44@gmail.com
www.edassugarfree.com
Manufacturer, processor and exporter of sugar free hard candies
Owner: Mike Bernert
mbernert@edassugarfree.com
Estimated Sales: Less Than $500,000
Number Employees: 1-4
Number of Brands: 1
Number of Products: 28
Square Footage: 80000
Type of Packaging: Consumer, Food Service, Private Label, Bulk
Brands:
  Eda Sugarfree Hard Candies

3935 Eddy's Bakery
380 N Five Mile Rd
Boise, ID 83713-8959
208-377-8100
Fax: 208-322-7823
Manufacturer of baked goods including bread and cakes
General Manager: Chris Smith
Sales Director: Roy Schmidt
Estimated Sales: $3-5 Million
Number Employees: 1-4
Type of Packaging: Consumer

3936 Edelman Meats Inc
1128 1st Ave
Antigo, WI 54409-1606
715-623-7686
Fax: 715-623-7688
Beef, pork, chicken, fish, etc.
Owner: Joe Edelman
carmin@edelmanmeats.com
President/CEO: Joseph Edelman
Estimated Sales: $20-50 Million
Number Employees: 10-19
Type of Packaging: Food Service

3937 (HQ)Edelmann Provision Company
10000 Martins Way
Harrison, OH 45030
513-881-5800
g.basham@freshsausage.com
www.freshsausage.com
Fresh sausage
President: James Frondorf
jfrondorf@freshsausage.com
Vice President: James Burke
Controller: Casey Flick
Quality Control Manager: Jennifer Stone
Estimated Sales: $17.2 Million
Number Employees: 80

Food Manufacturers / A-Z

3938 Edelweiss Patisserie
19 Blake St
Medford, MA 02155-4921
781-628-0225
Fax: 781-628-0208 sales@edelweisspastry.com
www.edelweisspastry.com
Baked goods including cakes, pastries, muffins, croissants, pullman and tea loaves, rustic breads, cookies, etc
Owner: Elliott Thompson
Owner: Rifat Cebi
Account Manager: Colleen Scribner
Estimated Sales: Less Than $500,000
Number Employees: 5-9
Type of Packaging: Food Service

3939 Eden Creamery
Los Angeles, CA
info@halotop.com
www.halotop.com
Low calorie ice cream
Co-Founder: Justin Woolverton
Co-Founder: Douglas Bouton
Brands:
  Halo Top

3940 Eden Foods Inc
701 Tecumseh Rd
Clinton, MI 49236-9599
517-456-7424
Fax: 517-456-6075 888-424-3336
info@edenfoods.com
Established in 1969. Natural and organic foods including pasta, soymilk, green tea, beans, tomatoes, spaghetti sauce, etc
President/CEO: Michael Potter
CEO: Manuela Della
manueladella@hfhs.org
CFO: Jay Hughes
Vice President: Jim Fox
Quality Control: Jon Solomon
VP Marketing & Sales: Sue Becker
VP Operations: William Swaney
Estimated Sales: $20-50 Million
Number Employees: 100-249
Type of Packaging: Food Service
Brands:
  Eden
  Eden Organic
  Edenbalance
  Edenblend
  Edensoy
  Edensoy Extra

3941 Eden Organic Pasta Company
701 Tecumseh Road
Clinton, MI 49236
517-456-7424
Fax: 517-456-6075 888-424-3336
info@edenfoods.com www.edenfoods.com
Organic and vegetable pastas
President/CEO: Michael Potter
Chief Financial Officer: Jay Hughes
General Manager: Steve Swaney
VP/Marketing: Sue Anne Becker
Manager: Massimo D'Amore
Estimated Sales: $44 Million
Number Employees: 117
Parent Co: Eden Foods
Type of Packaging: Food Service
Other Locations:
  Eden Foods Plant
  Detroit MI
  Eden Foods Plant
  Union City CA
Brands:
  Eden's

3942 Eden Processing
100 East St
Poplar Grove, IL 61065
815-765-2000
Fax: 815-765-2777
Bakers' and confectioners' supplies including maraschino cherries, sweetened coconut, mince meat pie fillings, orange, lemon, melon, grapefruit and citron peels, etc
President, CEO: Louis Tenore, Jr.
Marketing Director: Pam McDowell
Contact: Pam Mcdowell
cherryboss@msn.com
Estimated Sales: $700,000
Number Employees: 14
Square Footage: 220000
Type of Packaging: Bulk

Brands:
  True Blue

3943 Eden Vineyards Winery
19709 Little Ln
Alva, FL 33920
239-728-9463
Fax: 239-728-9463 info@edenwinery.com
www.edenwinery.com
Wines
President: Earl Kiser
VP: Michael Kiser
Estimated Sales: $520,000
Number Employees: 3

3944 Eden's Market
99 Alfred St
Pittsburgh, PA 15228-2309
412-343-1802
Fax: 412-343-1803
edensdownunder@edens-market.com
www.edens-market.com
Gluten free
Owner: Jeff Weiner
edensdownunder@yahoo.com
Estimated Sales: Less Than $500,000
Number Employees: 1-4

3945 Edgar A Weber & Co
549 Palwaukee Dr
Wheeling, IL 60090-6049
847-215-1980
Fax: 847-215-2073 800-558-9078
info@weberflavors.com www.weberflavors.com
Manufacturer and exporter of flavoring extracts for wine, liquor, baked goods and ice cream
Owner: Pam Grossman
pamg@weberflavors.com
CFO: Judith Turyna
Marketing Manager: Roger Passaglia
Plant Manager: Mike Sciore
Purchasing: Carol Myers
Estimated Sales: $3 Million
Number Employees: 50-99
Square Footage: 20000
Brands:
  Hy Van
  Simply Natural
  Simply Natural-Like

3946 Edgewood Estate Winery
607 Airpark Road
Napa, CA 94558-6272
800-755-2374
Fax: 707-254-4920
Wines
CEO: Jeff O'Neill
CFO: John Kelleher
Sales: Steve Lindsay
Purchasing: David Weckerle
Estimated Sales: $1-2.5 Million
Number Employees: 7
Number of Brands: 1
Number of Products: 14
Square Footage: 280000
Parent Co: Golden State Vintners
Type of Packaging: Consumer, Private Label
Brands:
  Edgewood Estate

3947 Edison Grainery
Benicia, CA 94510
510-382-0202
Fax: 510-263-5778 service@edisongrainery.com
edisongrainery.com
Beans, grains, seeds, cereals, super foods, pastas, flours and sweets.
Co-founder: Jeffrey Barnes
Co-founder: Amy Barnes

3948 (HQ)Edlong Corporation
225 Scott St
Elk Grove Village, IL 60007-1299
847-631-6700
info@edlong.com
www.edlong.com
Cheese, butter, milk & cream, cultured, sweet and functional flavors. Concentrated dairy flavors.
President & CEO: Laurette Rondenet
CFO: David Starr
Vice President, Global R&D: Laura Enriquez
Vice President, Operations: Ken Mack
Square Footage: 360000

Type of Packaging: Food Service, Private Label, Bulk
Other Locations:
  Edlong Dairy Flavors
  Suffolk
  Edlong Dairy Flavors
  United Kingdom
  Edlong Dairy Flavors
  Mexico City
Brands:
  Capsulong
  Cheolong
  Ed-Vance
  Vision

3949 Edmond's Chile Co
3236 Oregon Ave
St Louis, MO 63118-3004
314-772-1499
Fax: 314-664-7735
Sliced pork and gravy, sliced beef and gravy, beef au jus, vegetable soup, beef stew, meat sauce, beef chili, chili con carne, beef patties and tamales
President: Mark Adelman
edmondschile@yahoo.com
Estimated Sales: $2.5-5 Million
Number Employees: 10-19
Type of Packaging: Consumer

3950 Edmonton Potato Growers
12220-170 Street
Edmonton, AB T5V 1L7
Canada
780-447-1860
Fax: 780-447-1899 admin@epg.ab.ca
www.epg.ab.ca
Manufacturer and exmporter of potatoes including table, seed and processed, onions
President: Wayne Groot
VP: Ernie Van Boom
Sales: Darcy Olson
General Manager: Bob Jensen
Estimated Sales: $13 Million
Number Employees: 23
Type of Packaging: Consumer, Food Service, Bulk
Brands:
  Canada Goose

3951 Edmunds St. John
1331 Walnut St
Berkeley, CA 94709
510-981-1510
Fax: 510-981-1610 info@edmundsstjohn.com
www.edmundsstjohn.com
Wine
President: Steve Edmunds
s.edmunds@edmundsstjohn.com
Estimated Sales: $1-2.5 Million
Number Employees: 1-4

3952 Edna Valley Vineyard
2585 Biddle Ranch Rd
San Luis Obispo, CA 93401
805-544-5855
Fax: 805-544-0112 866-979-8477
www.ednavalley.com
Table wines including Chardonnay and Pinot Noir
Winemaker: Josh Baker
CEO: Tom Selfridge
Marketing and Customer service: Rebecca Tincher
Sales Manager: Marty Taylor
Contact: Mark Cave
info@ednavalley.com
Plant Manager: Randy Weaver
Estimated Sales: $4 Million
Number Employees: 45
Square Footage: 240000
Parent Co: E&J Gallo Winery
Type of Packaging: Consumer, Food Service, Private Label
Brands:
  Edna Valley
  Videyards

3953 Edner Corporation
1200 Zephyr Ave
Hayward, CA 94544
510-441-8504
Fax: 510-441-9395
Breads (specialty), cakes, cookies, croissants (filled and unfilled), muffins, pastries, & scones (filled and unfilled)
President: Ed Kirschner
VP Technical Sales: Mark Aquilar
Manager: Sandy Caires

Food Manufacturers / A-Z

Estimated Sales: $2 Million
Number Employees: 30
Parent Co: Edner Corporation
Type of Packaging: Consumer, Food Service, Private Label, Bulk
Brands:
    Edna Foods
    Extreme
    Huckleberry
    Jonathan International Foods
    La Patisserie
    Warfarers

3954 (HQ)Edom Labs Inc
100 E Jefryn Blvd
Suite M
Deer Park, NY 11729-5729
    631-586-2266
Fax: 631-586-2385 800-723-3366
info@edomlaboratories.com
www.edomlaboratories.com
Vitamins and dietary supplements
Owner: Eric Pollack
Estimated Sales: Less Than $500,000
Number Employees: 1-4
Type of Packaging: Consumer, Private Label, Bulk

3955 Edoughble
Los Angeles, CA 90034
www.edoughble.com
Edible cookie dough dessert
Founder: Rana Lustyan

3956 Edward & Sons Trading Co
4420 Via Real
Suite C
Carpinteria, CA 93013-1635
    805-684-8500
Fax: 805-684-8220 www.edwardandsons.com
Manufacturer, importer and exporter of natural, organic and specialty foods: condiments, confectionery products, crackers, vegetarian soup mixes, snack foods, canned organic vegetables, vegetarian bouillon cubes, cake decorationsorganic coconut milk
President: Joel Dee
edwardsons@aol.com
Vice President: Alison Cox
Estimated Sales: $1 Million
Number Employees: 10-19
Type of Packaging: Consumer, Food Service, Private Label
Brands:
    Edward&Sons
    Heritage Soups
    Let's Do
    Let's Do Organic
    Native Forest
    Organic Country
    Premier Japan
    Rainforest Organic
    Troy's
    Wizards

3957 Edward Johnson's Salsa
Flemington, NJ 08822
customerservice@ejsalsa.com
ejsalsa.com
Gourmet salsa
Owner: Edward Johnson III
Year Founded: 2014
Number Employees: 1-10
Type of Packaging: Private Label
Brands:
    All-American Squeeze-Salsa

3958 Edward Marc Brands
55 38th St
Pittsburgh, PA 15201
    877-488-1808
edwardmarc.com
Chocolate; confections; and milk shakes
CEO: Mark Edwards
VP of Operations: Steve Brown
Year Founded: 1914
Number Employees: 50-200
Type of Packaging: Food Service, Private Label
Brands:
    MilkShake Factory
    Eward Marc Chocolatier
    Snappers

3959 Edwards Baking Company
115 West College Dr.
Marshall, MN 56258
    404-377-0511
Fax: 404-378-2074 866-739-2328
www.edwardsdesserts.com
Frozen dessert pies
CEO: Dimitrios Smyrnios
Manufacturing Director: Mark Glennon
Estimated Sales: $20-50 Million
Number Employees: 432
Parent Co: Schwan's

3960 Edwards Mill
PO Box 205
Hollister, MO 65673
    417-334-6411
Fax: 417-335-2618 800-222-0525
Josh@StateoftheOzarks.net
www.stateoftheozarks.net
Whole grains that are blended into mixes; pancake, waffle, biscuit, muffin, fruitcakes, jams, jelly, preserves, apple butter
President: Jerry Davis

3961 Edy's Grand Ice Cream
PO Box 2178
Wilkes-Barre, PA 18703
    888-590-3397
Fax: 570-301-4538 www.edys.com
Ice cream

3962 Efco Products Inc
130 Smith St
Poughkeepsie, NY 12601-2109
    845-452-4715
Fax: 845-452-5607 800-284-3326
info@efcoproducts.com www.efcoproducts.com
Bakery mixes and ingredients, fruit and creme-style fillings, jellies, jams, and concentrated icing fruits
Owner: Ira Effron
ieffron@efcoproducts.com
VP/Controller: Kevin Laffin
VP Sales & Marketing: David A. Miller
VP Operations: Andy Herzing
Estimated Sales: $2.5-5 Million
Number Employees: 50-99

3963 Effies Homemade
1 Westinghouse Plz
Hyde Park, MA 02136-2075
    617-364-9300
Fax: 617-364-9333 effie@effieshomemade.com
www.effieshomemade.com
All natural oatcakes and crispy corncakes
Owner: Joan Mac Issac
effie@effieshomemade.com
Partner: Joan MacIsaac
Number Employees: 1-4

3964 Egg Cream America Inc
633 Skokie Blvd
Suite 200
Northbrook, IL 60062-2824
    847-559-2703
Fax: 847-559-2709 getcreamed@aol.com
www.getcreamed.com
Dairy based carbonated beverages
President: Adam Kurlander
CEO: John Beslow
Estimated Sales: Less Than $500,000
Number Employees: 1-4

3965 Egg Innovations
PO Box 1275
Warsaw, IN 46581-1275
Fax: 574-267-7305 800-337-1951
info@egginnovations.com
www.egginnovations.com
Free-range organic eggs
President & CEO: John Brunnquell
VP, Finance: Wes LaRue
VP, Sales & Marketing: Steve Hagopian

3966 Egg Low Farms
35 West State Street
Sherburne, NY 13460
    607-674-4653
Fax: 607-674-9216
Fresh eggs including diced and scrambled. Also salad ready diced eggs and tray ready scrambled eggs; all fresh
President: Helen A. Dunckel
CEO: David Dunckel
VP: David L. Dunckel
Estimated Sales: $850,000
Number Employees: 10
Square Footage: 160000
Type of Packaging: Food Service, Private Label
Brands:
    Egg Low Farms
    The Unbeatable Eatable Egg

3967 Egg Roll Fantasy
PO Box 7895
Auburn, CA 95604-7895
    530-887-9197
Fax: 530-887-9199
Gourmet egg rolls
President: Louie Buendia
VP: Robert DiMiceli
Estimated Sales: $500,000-$1 Million
Number Employees: 10
Number of Brands: 3
Number of Products: 20
Square Footage: 16000
Type of Packaging: Consumer, Food Service, Private Label, Bulk

3968 Eggland's Best Eggs
70 East Sweedsford Road
Suite 150
Malvern, PA 19355
    800-922-3447
www.egglandsbest.com
Dairy, organic eggs.
President/CEO: Charles Lanktree
Director of Quality Assurance: Bart Slaugh
bbarnes@eggland.com
Contact: Barb Barnes
bbarnes@eggland.com
Estimated Sales: $10-20 Million
Number Employees: 10-19
Number of Brands: 1
Type of Packaging: Consumer, Private Label
Brands:
    Eggland's Best

3969 Eggology
6728 Eton Ave
Canoga Park, CA 91303-2813
    818-610-2222
Fax: 818-610-2223 ninag@eggology.com
www.eggology.com
Pure liquid egg whites
President: Brad Halpern
VP: Robyn Mitofsky
Manager: Jose Cardenas
josec@eggology.com
Estimated Sales: $1 Million
Number Employees: 10-19

3970 Egypt Star Bakery Inc
608 N Front St
Allentown, PA 18102-5125
    610-434-8516
Fax: 610-443-1915
Breads, rolls
President: Esther Erdossy
eerdossy@egyptstarbakery.com
VP: Steven Zdrofcoff
Estimated Sales: $3 Million
Number Employees: 20-49

3971 Ehresman Packaging Co
912 E Fulton St
Garden City, KS 67846-6042
    620-276-3791
Fax: 620-276-1916
Meat products; also, custom butchering available
Owner: Mike Plankenhorn
velda.epc@gmail.com
Co-Owner: Velda Plankenhorn
Estimated Sales: $49,000
Number Employees: 10-19
Type of Packaging: Consumer, Private Label

3972 Eickman's Processing Co
3226 S Pecatonica Rd
PO Box 118
Seward, IL 61077
    815-247-8451
Fax: 815-247-8463 www.eickmans.com
Beef, pork, lamb and wild game
President: Michael Eickman
redtail15@aol.com

Estimated Sales: $3 Million
Number Employees: 20-49
Type of Packaging: Consumer, Food Service

3973 Eidon
12330 Stowe Dr
Poway, CA 92064-6802
858-668-0804
Fax: 858-668-3593   800-700-1169
www.eidon.com
Mineral supplements
Manager: Deborah Stewart
CEO: Rick Wagner
info1@eidon.com
VP: Fred Elsner
Production Manager: Cory Wagner
Estimated Sales: $1 Million
Number Employees: 10-19
Number of Brands: 1
Number of Products: 30
Square Footage: 23000
Type of Packaging: Consumer, Private Label, Bulk

3974 Eight O'Clock Coffee Company
5901 West Side Avenue
4th Floor
North Bergen, NJ 07645
800-299-2739
www.eightoclock.com
Roasted coffee.
CFO: Tom Corcoran
SVP, Sales & Marketing: David Allen
Director, Trade Marketing: Robert Hodge
VP, Human Resources: Liesel Bell
Brand Manager: Michael Scalera
Estimated Sales: $44.4 Million
Number Employees: 215
Number of Brands: 1
Parent Co: Tata Coffee Limited
Type of Packaging: Consumer
Other Locations:
   New Providence NJ
Brands:
   Eight O'Clock

3975 Eilenberger Bakeries
512 N John St
Palestine, TX 75801-2725
903-729-0881
Fax: 903-723-2915   800-831-2544
Gourmet cakes and brownies
Owner: Terresa Smith
sales@eilenbergerbakery.com
VP: Stephen Smith
VP/Marketing: Sarah Pryor
Estimated Sales: $720,000
Number Employees: 20-49

3976 Eiserman Meats
401 12 St SE
Slave Lake, AB T0G 2A3
Canada
780-849-5507
Fax: 780-849-6097   info@eisermanmeats.com
www.eisermanmeats.com
Fresh beef, pork, sausage and wild game; also, beef jerky; slaughtering services available
President/Co-Owner: Russell Eiserman
Co-Owner: Annellen Eiserman
Estimated Sales: $527,000
Number Employees: 4
Type of Packaging: Consumer

3977 El Brands
323 Van Heusen Drive
Ozark, AL 36360-1054
334-445-2828
Fax: 334-352-7263
Peanuts
CEO: Ed Lindley
VP Sales/Marketing: Steve Ratliff

3978 El Charro Mexican Food Ind
1711 S Virginia Ave
Roswell, NM 88203-1829
575-622-8590
Fax: 575-622-8590   ectortilla@yahoo.com
Manufacturer and exporter of chili sauce and tortilla chips
Owner: Micheal Trujillo
Owner: Mireya Trujillo
Estimated Sales: $5-10 Million
Number Employees: 10-19
Type of Packaging: Consumer, Food Service, Private Label, Bulk
Brands:
   El Charro
   La Pablanita

3979 El Grano De Oro
1710 Francisco Blvd
Pacifica, CA 94044-2515
650-355-8417
Fax: 650-355-7705   www.hotelgranodeoro.com
Mexican Restaurant
Owner: Mauricio Garcia
Co-Owner: Oscar Garcia
Estimated Sales: $470,000
Number Employees: 10-19

3980 El Jay Poultry Corporation
1010 Haddonfield Berlin # 402
Voorhees, NJ 08043-3514
856-435-0900
Fax: 856-435-3019
Poultry
President: Leo Rubin
Co-Owner: Joseph Milgrim
Estimated Sales: $5-10 Million
Number Employees: 5 to 9
Brands:
   Oak Valley Farms

3981 El Matador Foods
7201 Bayway Dr
Baytown, TX 77520-1303
281-424-0350
Fax: 281-838-1375   800-470-2447
info@elmatadorfoods.com
www.elmatadorfoods.com
Tortilla chips
Owner: Erick Ybarra
elmatador@huston.rr.com
Estimated Sales: $5-10 Million
Number Employees: 20-49
Brands:
   El Matador Tortilla Chip

3982 El Milagro
3050 W 26th St
Chicago, IL 60623-4130
773-579-6120
www.el-milagro.com
Corn and flour tortilla manufacturer in the Midwest.
President: Raphael Lopez
Contact: Phil Crookham
pcrookham@el-milagro.com
Year Founded: 1942
Estimated Sales: Less Than $500,000
Number Employees: 5-9
Type of Packaging: Consumer, Food Service

3983 El Molino Winery
3315 Saint Helena Hwy N
St Helena, CA 94574-9660
707-963-3632
Fax: 707-963-1647   wine@elmolinowinery.com
www.elmolinowinery.com
Wine
Owner: Lily Oliver Berlin
Co-Owner: Jon Berlin
Sales/Marketing: Mimi Buttenheim
Labelling/Foiling Wines: Altagracia Rincon
Estimated Sales: Less Than $500,000
Number Employees: 1-4

3984 El Paso Meat Co
1523 Myrtle Ave
El Paso, TX 79901-1796
915-838-8600
Fax: 915-533-3997
Fresh and frozen beef and pork; slaughtering services available
Owner: Francis Ramos
General Manager: Javier Garcia
Estimated Sales: $3-5 Million
Number Employees: 20-49
Type of Packaging: Consumer, Food Service

3985 El Paso Winery
742 Broadway Route 9 West
Ulster Park, NY 12487
845-331-8642
marylvogel@aol.com
www.elpasowinery.com
Red, white and rose wines
Owner: Maryl Vogel
Operations Manager: Felipe Beltra

Estimated Sales: Less than $500,000
Number Employees: 2
Type of Packaging: Consumer, Food Service

3986 El Perico Charro
204 N 7th St
Garden City, KS 67846-5519
620-275-6454
Manufacturer and retailers of Mexican foods, tortillas
President/CEO: Natividad Hernandez
Estimated Sales: $500,000-$1 Million
Number Employees: 1-4
Number of Products: 2
Type of Packaging: Consumer, Food Service

3987 El Peto Products
65 Saltsman Drive
Cambridge, ON N3H 4R7
Canada
519-650-4614
Fax: 519-650-5692   800-387-4064
info@elpeto.com   www.elpeto.com
Manufacturer and exporter of wheat, gluten and milk-free products including baking mixes, breads, muffins, cakes, buns, pies, cookies, frozen doughs and batters, pastas, soups and specialty flours
President: Elisabeth Riesen
VP: Peter Riesen
Estimated Sales: $3 Million
Number Employees: 18
Number of Brands: 3
Square Footage: 18000
Type of Packaging: Consumer, Food Service, Bulk
Brands:
   El Peto

3988 El Rancho Tortilla
623 New Laredo Hwy
San Antonio, TX 78211
210-922-8411
Fax: 210-922-9159
Corn and flour tortillas, tostadas, taco shells and picante sauce
Owner: Ruben Martinez
Estimated Sales: $2.5-5 Million
Number Employees: 20
Type of Packaging: Consumer

3989 El Rey Cooked Meats
6190 Bermuda Dr
St Louis, MO 63135-3298
314-521-3113
dryan@elreycookedmeats.com
www.elreycookedmeats.com
Manufacturer and exporter of frozen foods including chili, tamales, roast and barbecued beef, taco meat and pork; also, barbecue sauce
Owner: Joseph Frisella
elreyfoods@aol.com
VP, Sales: Don Ryan
Estimated Sales: $10-20 Million
Number Employees: 5-9
Square Footage: 6000
Type of Packaging: Consumer, Food Service
Brands:
   Chef's Helper
   Menu a La Carte

3990 El Toro Brew Pub
17605 Monterey St
Morgan Hill, CA 95037-3620
408-782-2739
Fax: 408-782-0171
Beer
Owner: Geno Acevedo
Estimated Sales: Less Than $500,000
Number Employees: 1-4

3991 El Toro Food Products
504 El Rio Street
Watsonville, CA 95076-3540
831-728-9266
Fax: 831-688-8766
Manufacture of canned salsas varieties including sauces and vegetables
President: Richard Thomas
Estimated Sales: $5-10 Million
Number Employees: 5-9
Number of Brands: 6
Number of Products: 10
Square Footage: 24000
Type of Packaging: Food Service, Private Label, Bulk

Food Manufacturers / A-Z

3992 Elaine's Toffee Co.
PO Box 38
Clayton, CA 94517
925-524-0000
Fax: 925-524-9000 800-883-3050
info@elainestoffee.com www.elainestoffee.com
Kosher, sugar-free, chocolate bars, other chcoolate, toffee, other snacksprivate label.
President: Janet Long
Estimated Sales: $300,000
Number Employees: 7

3993 Elan Vanilla Co
268 Doremus Ave
Newark, NJ 07105-4879
973-344-8014
Fax: 973-344-5880 www.elanvanilla.com
Organic kosher certified vanilla extract, flavoring and synthetic and natural aromatic chemicals
President: Jocelyn Manship
jmanship@elan-chemical.com
Quality Control Manager: Phil Kapp
VP Sales: David Pimentel
Director of Customer Service: Marilyn Santiago
Estimated Sales: $20-50 Million
Number Employees: 50-99
Type of Packaging: Bulk

3994 Elba Custom Meats
405 Alabama Highway 203
Elba, AL 36323-4217
334-897-2007
Meat products
Owner: Billy F Hudson
VP: Douglas Hudson
Estimated Sales: $140,000
Number Employees: 3
Type of Packaging: Consumer

3995 Elco Fine Foods
233 Alden Road
Markham, ON L4B 1G5
Canada
905-731-7337
Fax: 905-731-2391 info@elcofinefoods.com
www.elcofinefoods.com
Distributor of premium confectionery, food and beverage products
CEO: Moe Cussen
Number Employees: 100
Square Footage: 270000

3996 (HQ)Eldorado Artesian Springs Inc
1783 Dogwood St
Louisville, CO 80027-3085
303-499-1316
Fax: 303-499-1339 info@eldoradosprings.com
www.eldoradosprings.com
Bottled water
President/CEO: Douglas Larson
doug@eldoradosprings.com
VP Marketing: Jeremy Martin
VP Operations: Kevin Sipple
Estimated Sales: $5.3 Million
Number Employees: 50-99
Type of Packaging: Private Label
Brands:
 Eldorado Natural Spring Water
 Eldorado Spring Water

3997 Eldorado Coffee Distributors
5675 49th St
Flushing, NY 11378-2012
718-418-4100
Fax: 718-418-4500 800-635-2566
www.eldoradocoffee.com
Established in 1980. Manufacturer and roaster of coffee.
Founder: Segunda Martin
eldoradon1@aol.com
VP: Juan Martin
VP of Sales: Albert Valdes
Estimated Sales: $20-50 Million
Number Employees: 20-49
Type of Packaging: Consumer, Food Service, Private Label
Brands:
 El Dorado Coffee Roasters

3998 Eldorado Seafood Inc
27 Cambridge Street
Burlington, MA 01803
781-270-4290
Fax: 781-270-4242 800-416-5656
Shrimp including breaded, cooked, peeled and deveined
President: Christinne Randazzo
VP: Laura Randazzo
Estimated Sales: $2.5-5 Million
Number Employees: 1-4
Type of Packaging: Consumer, Food Service, Private Label
Brands:
 Eldorado
 Max-Sea

3999 Eleanor's Best LLC
PO Box 9
Garrison, NY 10524
646-296-6870
info@eleanorsbest.com
www.eleanorsbest.com
Handmade, vegan, gluten jams and marmalades, maple syrup, wildflower honey
Founder/Owner: Jennifer Mercurio
Year Founded: 2013
Number Employees: 10
Number of Brands: 1
Number of Products: 16
Type of Packaging: Consumer, Private Label
Brands:
 Eleanor's Best

4000 Elegant Desserts
275 Warren St
Lyndhurst, NJ 07071-2017
201-933-0770
Fax: 201-933-7309 info@elegantdesserts.com
www.elegantdesserts.com
Manufacturer and wholesaler/distributor of pastries including tarts and miniature grand viennas
President: John Mazur
jjmazur@bellatlantic.net
Estimated Sales: $2 Million
Number Employees: 20-49
Type of Packaging: Food Service, Private Label

4001 Elegant Edibles
3311 Mercer St
Houston, TX 77027-6019
713-522-2884
Fax: 713-522-1777 800-227-3226
info@elegantedibles.com www.elegantedibles.com
All natural, gourmet confections, snacks, and recipe ready ingredients
Owner: Diane Dagostino
info@elegantedibles.com
R&D: Francis Jacquinet
Operations: Lori Lake
Production: Amanda Stults
Plant Manager: Ana Olmedo
Estimated Sales: Less than $500,000
Number Employees: 5-9
Number of Brands: 8
Type of Packaging: Consumer, Food Service, Private Label, Bulk
Brands:
 Mrs. Powell's Gourmet

4002 Element Snacks
153 W 27th St
Suite 302
New York, NY 10001-6259
212-966-7696
Fax: 212-994-0392 elementsnacks.com
chocolate covered rice cakes
Founder: Nadia Leonelli
Year Founded: 2012
Estimated Sales: $675000
Number Employees: 1-10
Type of Packaging: Private Label

4003 Elemental Superfood
Torrance, CA 90501
tryzen.com
Organic seedbars and crumble
Founder: Nicole Anderson

4004 Elements Truffles
78 John Miller Way
Kearny, NJ 07032
917-836-2819
we@elementstruffles.com
Chocolate bars and truffles
President: Alak Vasa
Estimated Sales: $74425
Number Employees: 1-4
Type of Packaging: Private Label

4005 Elena's
2650 Paldan
Auburn Hills, MI 48326
248-373-1100
Fax: 248-373-1120 800-723-5362
info@elenas.com www.elenas.com
Manufacturer and exporter of pasta, pasta sauce and pasta salad
President: Elena Houlihan
VP Finance: Caroline Moose
VP Operations: John Houlihan
Estimated Sales: $2.5-5 Million
Number Employees: 20-49
Parent Co: Houlihan's Culinary Traditions
Type of Packaging: Food Service, Private Label, Bulk
Brands:
 Bella Mercato
 Bruschetta

4006 Elena's Food Specialties
405 Allerton Ave
S San Francisco, CA 94080-4818
650-871-8700
Fax: 650-871-0502 800-376-5368
Frozen Mexican foods including enchiladas and burritos
President: Peter Sartorio
VP Product Development: Nathan Steck
R&D Manager: Mark Cooley
Eastern Regional Sales Manager: Alice Pager
Contact: Don Anderson
don@elenasfoods.com
Plant Manager: Manuel Lara
Office Manager: Crystal Snearing
Estimated Sales: $5-10 Million
Number Employees: 50-99
Type of Packaging: Consumer, Food Service

4007 Eleni's Cookies
75 Ninth Avenue
New York, NY 10011-7006
Fax: 800-283-3074 888-435-3647
sales@elenis.com www.elenis.com
Nut-free cookies
Owner: Eleni Giampulos
Contact: Nicholas Colloton
ncolloton@elenis.com
Estimated Sales: $300,000-500,000
Number Employees: 5-9

4008 Elgin Dairy Foods
3707 W Harrison St
Chicago, IL 60624-3622
773-722-7100
Fax: 773-722-3230 800-786-9900
Ice cream, frozen yogurt, dairy and nondairy whipped toppings, sour cream and dairy mixes
President: Edward Gignac
EVP Sales: James Cignac
Marketing Manager: Nathan Langer
Estimated Sales: $12 Million
Number Employees: 95
Square Footage: 58000
Brands:
 Flav'r Top
 Freeze-Thaw

4009 Eli's Bread Inc
403 E 91st St # 1
New York, NY 10128-6800
212-831-4800
Fax: 212-423-9078 866-354-3547
customerservice@elizabar.com www.elizabar.com
Hearth-baked European-style breads, rolls, bagels and crisps based on traditional European recipes
Owner: Eli Zabar
Administrative Executive: Uzziah Phillips
Director Sales: Mark Stewart
Manager: Mark Stewart
mstewart@elizabar.com
Estimated Sales: $5-10 Million
Number Employees: 100-249
Square Footage: 30000

Food Manufacturers / A-Z

4010 Eli's Cheesecake
6701 W Forest Preserve Drive
Chicago, IL 60634
773-308-7000
Fax: 773-736-1169   800-354-2253
info@elicheesecake.com   www.elicheesecake.com
Manufacturer of cheesecakes and desserts sold in Illinois, Indiana, Michigan, Minnesota, Missouri, Ohio and Wisconsin.
President: Marc Schulman
Square Footage: 62000
Type of Packaging: Consumer
Brands:
  Eli's

4011 Eliot's Adult Nut Butters
503-847-9457
info@eliotsadultnutbutters.com
eliotsadultnutbutters.com
Nut butters
Founder: Michael Kanter
Number of Brands: 1
Number of Products: 7
Type of Packaging: Consumer
Brands:
  ELIOT'S ADULT NUT BUTTERS

4012 Elite Spice Inc
7151 Montevideo Rd
Jessup, MD 20794-9308
410-796-1900
Fax: 410-379-6933   800-232-3531
jbrandt@elitespice.com   www.elitespice.com
Spice, seasoning, capsicum, oil & oleoresin, and dehydrated vegetable producer.
President & CEO: Isaac Samuel
CFO/Human Resources Director: Debbie Ingle
R&D Director: Leslie Krause
Quality Control Directory: Dave Anthony
Marketing Executive: Kathy Lyons
VP, Sales: Paul Kurpe
VP/Plant Manager: George Mayer
Purchasing Manager: Margie Schneidman
Year Founded: 1988
Estimated Sales: $20-50 Million
Number Employees: 100-249
Square Footage: 11000
Type of Packaging: Private Label

4013 Elk Cove Vineyards
27751 NW Olson Rd
Gaston, OR 97119-8042
503-985-7760
Fax: 503-985-3525   877-355-2683
info@elkcove.com   www.elkcove.com
Wines
Owner: Adam Campbell
Founder/CEO: Patricia Campbell
Controller: Robert Verant
Sales Manager: Shirley Brooks
adam@elkcove.com
Hospitality Coordinator: Kathy Kennedy
Vineyard Manager: Travis Watson
Estimated Sales: $5-10 Million
Number Employees: 10-19

4014 Elki Coporation
6101 23rd Dr W
Everett, WA 98203
425-261-1002
Fax: 425-261-1006   info@elki.com
elki.com
Bruschettas; jams and preserves; dips; pesto; crostinis; gluten-free snacks; grilled vegetables; tomato sauce
President/Owner: Elizabeth Lie
Year Founded: 1984
Number Employees: 1-4

4015 Ella's Flats
5811 Pelican Bay Blvd
Naples, FL 34106
ellen@ellasflats.com
www.ellasflats.com
Seed crisps
Owner: Ellen Macks

4016 Ella's Kitchen
1209 Orange St
New Castle, DE 19801
800-685-7799
www.ellaskitchen.com
Organic baby food and kids' food
Founder: Paul Lindley
CEO: Mark Cuddigan
Year Founded: 2009
Parent Co: Hain Celestial

4017 Ellenbee-Leggett Co Inc
3765 Port Union Rd
Fairfield, OH 45014-2207
513-874-3200
Fax: 513-874-3323   800-536-1613
service@ellenbee.com   www.ellenbee.com
Distributor of premium foodservice products
President: James Kite
jkite@ellenbee.com
Number Employees: 100-249

4018 Ellenos
5707 Airport Way S
Seattle, WA 98108
206-535-7562
hello@ellenos.com
www.ellenos.com
Greek yogurt
CEO: John Tucker
Vice President, Finance: Adam Karnofski
Vice President, Marketing: Ben Garnero

4019 Ellie's Country Delights
PO Box 1059
Wainscott, NY 11975
631-478-5200
Fax: 631-604-1076
Ratatouille
President: Ellenka Baumrind

4020 Ellio's Pizza
10000 Midlantic Drive
Suite 107W
Mt. Laurel, NJ 8054
866-435-5467
www.ellios.com
Frozen Pizza

4021 Elliott Bay Baking Co.
5601 1st Avenue South
Seattle, WA 98108-3951
206-545-3804
Fax: 206-767-1176
marketing@essentialbaking.com
www.essentialbaking.com
Biscotti bites, java mocha cookies, European tea biscuits
President: Paula Lukoff
Estimated Sales: $2.5-5 Million
Number Employees: 20-49
Brands:
  Ii Biscotto Della Nonna
  My Bubby's

4022 Elliott Seafood Company
53 Stevens Ln
Cushing, ME 04563
207-354-2533
Fax: 207-354-2533
Seafood
President: Stan Elliott

4023 Ellis Coffee Co
2835 Bridge St
Philadelphia, PA 19137-1895
215-537-9500
Fax: 215-534-5311   800-822-3984
www.elliscoffee.com
Coffee
President: Eugene Kestenbaum
Chairman: William Strauss
CFO: Tom McElwee
Executive VP: Frank Parker
VP Sales/Marketing: James O'Ferrell
Estimated Sales: Less Than $500,000
Number Employees: 5-9

4024 Ellison Bakery, Inc.
4108 W Ferguson Rd
Fort Wayne, IN 46899
www.ebakery.com
Cookies, ice-cream sandwich wafers, crunch toppings and inclusion products.
CEO: Stephanie Chattilion
COO: Todd Wallin
todd.wallin@ebakery.com
Production Manager: Matthew Barton
Year Founded: 1945
Estimated Sales: $20-50 Million
Number Employees: 50-99
Number of Brands: 2
Type of Packaging: Consumer, Food Service, Private Label, Bulk
Brands:
  Ella's Oven™
  Ellison

4025 Ellison Milling Company
PO Box 400
Lethbridge, AB T1J 3Z2
Canada
403-328-6622
Fax: 403-327-3772
Durum Semolina, Hard and Soft Wheat Flours
President: Michael Greer
Quality Control: Paolo Santangelo
Marketing Director: Bob Grebinsky
Plant Manager: B McConnell
Number Employees: 65
Parent Co: Parrish & Heimbecker
Type of Packaging: Food Service, Private Label, Bulk
Brands:
  Alebrta
  Baker's Gold
  Dream
  Ellison's
  Royal Pastry
  U-Bake

4026 Elliston Vineyards
463 Kilkare Rd
Sunol, CA 94586-9415
925-862-2377
Fax: 925-862-0316   info@elliston.com
www.elliston.com
Wines
Vice President: Mark Piche
info@elliston.com
VP: Keith Flavetta
Manager: Catherine Neufeld
info@elliston.com
Estimated Sales: $5 Million
Number Employees: 1-4
Type of Packaging: Private Label

4027 Ello Raw
hello@elloraw.com
www.elloraw.com
Superfood snack bites
Founder & CEO: Rebecca Holmes
Number of Brands: 1
Number of Products: 4
Type of Packaging: Consumer
Brands:
  ELLO RAW

4028 Ellsworth Cooperative Creamery
232 N. Wallace St.
PO Box 610
Ellsworth, WI 54011
715-273-4311
Fax: 715-273-5318   www.ellsworthcheese.com
Cheese curds, also available in flavors such as garlic, taco, cajun, natural, premium cheddar and ranch, also breaded and vacuum sealed/freezable.
President/Director: Albert Knegendorf
CEO/Manager: Paul Bauer
paulb@ellsworthcreamery.net
Vice President, Sales/Marketing: Jim Grande
Year Founded: 1910
Estimated Sales: $145 Million
Number Employees: 100-249
Number of Brands: 5
Square Footage: 120000
Type of Packaging: Consumer, Private Label, Bulk
Brands:
  Antonella
  Blaser's
  Ellsworth
  Ellsworth Valley
  Kammerude

4029 Ellsworth Foods
1510 Eastman Dr
Tifton, GA 31793-8228
229-386-8448
Fax: 229-387-9749   www.ellsworthfoods.com
Grocery products
Owner: Ken Ellsworth Jr
kellsworth@ellsworthfoods.com
VP: Rebecca Ellsworth

Food Manufacturers / A-Z

Estimated Sales: $5 Million
Number Employees: 20-49

4030 Ellsworth Locker
317 S Broadway St
Ellsworth, MN 56129-1092
507-967-2544
www.ellsworthamerican.com
Sausage, beef, pork and venison
Owner: Brian Chapa
Co-Owner: Kathy Chapa
Estimated Sales: $1-2.5 Million
Number Employees: 5-9
Type of Packaging: Consumer

4031 Elm City Cheese Co Inc
2240 State St
Hamden, CT 06517-3798
203-865-5768
Fax: 203-865-8303 www.elmcitycheese.com
Grated parmesan cheese
President: Weinstein Margie
wmargie@elmcitycheese.com
Vice President: Marge Weinstein
Estimated Sales: $1.4 Million
Number Employees: 10-19
Type of Packaging: Consumer

4032 Elmer Chocolate®
401 N 5th St
Ponchatoula, LA 70454
985-386-6166
800-843-9537
www.elmerchocolate.com
Only one Elmer Chocolate product can be purchased year-round, which is Gold Brick Topping, also manufactures Christmas, Valentine's and Easter chocolates.
Chairman & CEO: Robert Nelson
Safety Manager: Jeffrey Bell
Year Founded: 1914
Estimated Sales: $26.7 Million
Number Employees: 300
Square Footage: 250000
Type of Packaging: Consumer
Brands:
  Fiddlers
  Gold Brick
  Heavenly Hash
  Just Nuts
  Small Talk Conversation Hearts
  Sweet Occasion

4033 Elmers Fine Foods Inc
2404 Port St
New Orleans, LA 70117-7418
504-949-2716
Fax: 504-948-2537 888-570-0764
sales@elmerscheewees.com
www.elmerscheewees.com
Snack foods including potato chips, popcorn and cheese curls
President: Alan Elmer
alan@elmerscheewees.com
Treasurer: Paul Elmer
VP: Stephen M Elmer
Director of Sales: Gary Langlois
Estimated Sales: $1 Million
Number Employees: 20-49
Type of Packaging: Consumer

4034 Elmhurst Milked
1150 Maple Rd
Elma, NY 14059
888-356-1925
cs@elmhurst1925.com
elmhurst1925.com
Plant-based milks
President: Henry Schwartz
Vice President of Sales: Mike Brown
Year Founded: 1925
Number of Brands: 1
Type of Packaging: Consumer, Food Service
Brands:
  ELMHURST MILKED

4035 Elmwood Locker Svc
214 S Magnolia St
Elmwood, IL 61529-7902
309-742-8929
Fax: 309-742-7071
john@elmwoodmeatlocker.com
Custom butchering and processing. Manufacturer of sausage jerky, beef sticks and bratwurst

Owner: John Powers
Estimated Sales: $500,000-$1 Million
Number Employees: 1-4
Type of Packaging: Consumer, Bulk
Brands:
  J & J

4036 Elmwood Pastry Shop
1136 New Britain Ave
West Hartford, CT 06110-2413
860-233-2029
Fax: 203-865-8303 www.elmwoodpastryshop.com
Hard rolls, bread, doughnuts, cakes and cookies
President: Richard S Winalski Jr
richard.winalski@elmwoodpastryshop.com
Estimated Sales: $500,000-$1 Million
Number Employees: 10-19
Type of Packaging: Consumer

4037 (HQ)Elore Enterprises Inc
1055 NW 159th Dr
Miami Gardens, FL 33169-5805
305-477-1650
Fax: 305-477-2291 www.quijotefoods.com
Spanish sausage
President: Joe Alanso
VP: Juan Alanso
Manager: Sergio Pires
elore@bellsouth.net
Estimated Sales: $1-2.5 Million
Number Employees: 20-49
Type of Packaging: Consumer, Food Service

4038 Elwood International Inc
89 Hudson St
Copiague, NY 11726-1505
631-842-6600
Fax: 631-842-6603 info@elwoodintl.com
Manufacturer and exporter of regular and dietetic portion controlled condiments including dressings, jellies, mayonnaise, mustard, ketchup, peanut butter, table syrups, private label and contract packaging
President: Stuart Roll
Vice President: Richard Roll
IT: Anna Marx
anna@elwoodintl.com
Estimated Sales: $2.90 Million
Number Employees: 10-19
Number of Brands: 3
Number of Products: 40
Square Footage: 92000
Type of Packaging: Consumer, Food Service, Private Label, Bulk
Brands:
  Elwood
  Renaissance
  Winston

4039 Embassy Flavours Ltd.
5 Intermodal Drive
Unit 1
Brampton, ON L6T 5V9
Canada
905-789-3200
Fax: 905-789-3201 800-334-3371
info@embassyflavours.com
www.embassyflavours.com
Manufacturer and exporter of extracts, flavors, colors, essential oils, bases and mixes including cake, pastry and bread. Certifications include BRC, Canadian Celiac Association, Kosher and Halal. Facility is peanut free.
President: Martino Brambilla
R&D: Anne Klingerman
National Sales/Marketing Manager: Mike Taras
Estimated Sales: $1.7 Million
Number Employees: 38
Square Footage: 57600
Type of Packaging: Consumer, Food Service, Private Label, Bulk
Brands:
  Batter-Moist
  Elite
  Embassy
  Prairie Sun

4040 Embria Health Sciences
2105 SE Creekview Dr
Ankeny, IA 50021-8899
515-963-9100
Fax: 515-964-9004 877-362-7421
info@embriahealth.com www.epicorimmune.com

EpiCor® and eXselen®, immune health ingredients for use in all food, beverage and nutritional supplement applications.
President/CEO: Paul Faganel
Research & Development: Larry Robinson
Quality Control Manager: Gayle Kittelson
Marketing Director: Cheryl Sturm
Regional Sales Rep: Naz Kalantari
Regional Sales Rep: Doug Reyes
Director of Operations: Mark Joyner
Estimated Sales: $500,000-1 Million
Number Employees: 10-19

4041 Emerald Hilton Davis LLC
2235 Langdon Farm Rd
Cincinnati, OH 45237-4712
513-841-0057
Fax: 513-841-3771 www.emeraldmaterials.com
Applications for the food and beverage industry.
President/CEO: Jim Donnelly
jimdonnelly@emeraldperformancematerials.com
VP/CFO: Pat McGill
R&D: Joe Uern
Environmental/Safety Manager: Peggy Roundtree
Marketing: Kelly Schaeffer
Sales/Marketing Manager: Bobby Gruber
VP Human Resourced: Thomas Nelson
Plant Manager: Doug Jackson
Purchasing: Jerry McCluskey
Number Employees: 100-249

4042 Emerald Kalama Chemical, LLC
1296 Third Street, N.W.
Kalama, WA 98625
360-673-2550
Fax: 360-673-3564 800-223-0035
kalama@emeraldmaterials.com
www.emeraldmaterials.com/epm/kalama
Manufacturer and exporter of specialty chemicals including benzaldehyde, cinnamic aldehyde, benzyl benzoate, benzyl alcohol, benzylacetate, potassium benzoate, benzoic acid and sodium benzoate
President: Edward T. Gotch
Sr. Vice President, Finance: Daniel Emmett
Vice President Operations and HS&E: Brian A. Denison
Number Employees: 175
Parent Co: Emerald Performance Materials

4043 Emerald Performance Materials
2020 Front St
Cuyahoga Falls, OH 44221-3257
330-916-6700
Fax: 330-916-6734
corporate@emeraldmaterials.com
www.emeraldmaterials.com
Produces and markets technologically advanced speciality chemicals for a broad range of food and industrial applications
President: Carrington Don
carrington.don@winwholesale.com
VP/CFO: Candace Wagner
Number Employees: 500-999

4044 Emerling International Foods
2381 Fillmore Ave
Suite 1
Buffalo, NY 14214-2197
716-833-7381
Fax: 716-833-7386 pemerling@emerfood.com
www.emerlinginternational.com
Bulk ingredients including: Fruits & Vegetables; Juice Concentrates; Herbs & Spices; Oils & Vinegars; Flavors & Colors; Honey & Molasses. Also produces pure maple syrup.
President: J Emerling
jemerling@emerfood.com
Sales: Peter Emerling
Public Relations: Jenn Burke
Year Founded: 1988
Estimated Sales: $10-20 Million
Number Employees: 20-49
Square Footage: 500000

4045 Emery Smith Fisheries Limited
5309 Hwy 3
Shag Harbour, NS B0W 3B0
Canada
902-723-2115
Fax: 902-723-2372
Manufacturer and exporter of salt fish
President: Emery Smith
Estimated Sales: $12 Million
Number Employees: 25

Food Manufacturers / A-Z

4046 Emkay Trading Corporation
250 Clearbrook Road
PO Box 504
Elmsford, NY 10523
914-592-9000
Fax: 914-347-3616 hkpilot@aol.com
Manufacturer and distributor of cheese including cream, bakers, neuchatel, lite, tvorog (Russian style soft cheese) and quark, also, bulk cream, custom fluid diary blends, bulk skim, sour cream, bulk cultured buttermilk and condensedskim milk
Owner: Howard Kravitz
tlindquistturner@limitedbrands.com
Vice President: Ruth Kravitz
Estimated Sales: $2 Million
Number Employees: 30
Square Footage: 800000
Type of Packaging: Consumer, Food Service, Private Label, Bulk
Brands:
  Emkay

4047 Emmi Roth USA
657 2nd St
Monroe, WI 53566-1013
608-845-5796
www.emmiusa.com
Swiss cheese
Brand Manager: Alison Lacey
Managing Director: Tim Omer
Estimated Sales: Less than $500,000
Number Employees: 5-9
Type of Packaging: Food Service, Private Label

4048 Emmy's Candy from Belgium
9816 Emerald Point Drive
Unit 3
Charlotte, NC 28278-6536
205-879-1901
Fax: 205-879-1903 866-879-1901
Candies
President: Emmy Verchecke

4049 Emmy's Organics
629 West Buffalo St
Ithaca, NY 14850
855-463-6697
info@emmysorganics.com
emmysorganics.com
Buckwheat-based cereals
Co-Founder: Ian Gaffney
Co-Founder: Samantha Abrams

4050 Empact Bars
885 Arapahoe Ave
Boulder, CO 80302
877-836-7228
info@empactbars.com empactbars.com
Superfood snack bars
Co-Founder: Melonie Derose
Co-Founder: Zeke Derose
Number of Brands: 1
Number of Products: 3
Type of Packaging: Consumer
Brands:
  EMPACT

4051 Empire Coffee Company
106 Purdy Ave
Port Chester, NY 10573
914-934-1100
Fax: 914-934-1190 800-642-1100
Coffee
Founder & CEO: Robert Richter
VP of Operations: Todd Good
Year Founded: 1984
Square Footage: 40000
Type of Packaging: Private Label

4052 Empire Kosher Foods
247 Empire Dr
Mifflintown, PA 17059
717-436-5921
800-367-4734
www.empirekosher.com
Kosher poultry
President & CEO: Jeff Brown
Director of Quality Assurance: Ahern Tim
VP of Sales: Lisa Nelson
Year Founded: 1938
Estimated Sales: $179.9 Million
Number Employees: 1,000
Square Footage: 240000
Type of Packaging: Private Label
Brands:
  Empire Kosher Poultry Products

4053 Empire Mayonnaise Company, LLC.
564 Vanderbilt Ave.
Brooklyn, NY 11238
718-636-2069
Manufacturer of mayonnaise.
Co-Founder: Sam Mason
Co-Founder: Eilzabeth Valleau

4054 Empire Spice Mills
908 William Avenue
Winnipeg, NB R3E 0Z8
Canada
204-786-1594
Fax: 204-783-2847
Flavoring extracts and whole ground and blended spices, herbs and seeds, seasonings
President: Don Ramage
Estimated Sales: $1 Million
Number Employees: 10
Square Footage: 64000
Type of Packaging: Consumer, Food Service, Private Label, Bulk
Brands:
  Empire's Best

4055 Empire Tea Svc
1965 St James Pl
Columbus, IN 47201-2805
812-375-1937
Fax: 812-376-7382 800-790-0246
sales@empiretea.com www.empiretea.com
Importer of tea in tins, black tea, green tea, herb tea bulk tea, tea bags in wood boxes and various forms of packing
President: Lalith Guy Paranavitana
info@empiretea.com
Plant Manager: Cheryl Paranavitana
Estimated Sales: $250,000
Number Employees: 1-4
Number of Brands: 3
Number of Products: 27
Square Footage: 8000
Type of Packaging: Consumer, Food Service, Private Label, Bulk
Brands:
  Guy's Tea
  Tea Temptations

4056 Empresa La Famosa
PO Box 51968
Toa Baja, PR 00950-1968
787-251-0060
Fax: 787-251-2270
Juice
President: Jose Corripio
VP Operations: Sandy Martin
Purchasing Supervisor: Carmen Menes
Estimated Sales: $5 Million
Number Employees: 61

4057 (HQ)Empresas La Famosa
PO Box 51968
Toa Baja, PR 00950-1968
787-251-0060
Fax: 787-251-2270
Fruit juices, coconut, cream & milk, beans and tomato willow
President: Jose Corripio
Purchasing Supervisor: Carmen Menes
Estimated Sales: $5.6 Million
Number Employees: 61
Square Footage: 960000
Brands:
  Coco Lopez, Usa

4058 Empress Chocolate Company
5518 Avenue N
Brooklyn, NY 11234
718-951-2251
Fax: 718-951-2254 800-793-3809
Manufacturer and exporter of custom and stock molded chocolate novelties, cream filled chocolates, truffles and gift boxes
President: Jack Grunhut
VP: Ernest Grunhut
Sales Director: Jerry Sumner
Estimated Sales: $3 Million
Number Employees: 35
Square Footage: 80000
Parent Co: Ernex Corporation
Type of Packaging: Consumer, Private Label
Brands:
  Empress Chocolates

4059 En Garde Health Products, Inc.
7702 Balboa Blvd
#9
Van Nuys, CA 91406
818-970-9444
Fax: 818-757-0773 800-955-4633
info@engardehealth.com www.engardehealth.com
Health products
President: Hy Null Levy
CEO: Roberta Gabor
Contact: Roberta Chaplanp
roberta@engardehealth.com
Estimated Sales: $410 Thousand
Number Employees: 4

4060 Endangered Species Chocolate
5846 W 73rd St
Indianapolis, IN 46278-1742
317-387-4372
Fax: 317-844-4951 800-293-0160
info@chocolatebar.com www.chocolatebar.com
Gourmet Belgian chocolate, chocolate squares
Co-owner: Wayne Zink
CEO: Curt Meer
Director Finance: Carl Dodds
Operations: Bryan Fuller
Estimated Sales: $9 Million
Number Employees: 50-99
Brands:
  Bug Bites
  Endangered Species Chocolate Bars

4061 Endico Potatoes Inc
160 N Macquesten Pkwy
Mt Vernon, NY 10550-1099
914-664-1151
Fax: 914-664-9267 www.endicopotatoes.com
Frozen potato, vegetable, chicken and appetizer products.
CEO: Mike Edwards
Manager: Mike Acocella
michael.roff@gmail.com
Estimated Sales: $860,000
Number Employees: 20-49
Square Footage: 240000
Type of Packaging: Consumer, Food Service
Brands:
  McCain®
  Sally Sherman Foods
  Tyson®
  Moore's®
  Lambweston®

4062 (HQ)Ener-G Foods
5960 1st Ave S
Seattle, WA 98108-3248
206-767-3928
Fax: 206-764-3398 800-331-5222
samiii@ener-g.com
Manufacturer and exporter of wheat free and gluten free, dairy free, nut free; bread, hamburger buns, cereals, cookies, pasta, mixes, etc.; also allergy-free foods; importer of gluten-free pasta and starches, Medical and diet foodsand low protein foods for PKU.
President: Sam Wylde III
cje@ener-g.com
Marketing/Sales: Jerry Colburn
Sales Exec: Jerry Colburn
Production Manager: Roger Traynor
Purchasing Manager: Sabina Milovic
Estimated Sales: $10 Milion
Number Employees: 20-49
Number of Brands: 2
Number of Products: 200
Square Footage: 40000
Type of Packaging: Consumer, Food Service, Private Label
Brands:
  Ener-G
  Old World

Food Manufacturers / A-Z

4063 (HQ)Energen Products Inc
14631 Best Ave
Norwalk, CA 90650-5258
562-926-5522
Fax: 562-921-0039 800-423-8837
Manufacturer and exporter of vitamins, wheat germ oil and brewers' yeast
President: Joseph Bensler
energen@ix.netcom.com
Estimated Sales: $3 Million
Number Employees: 20-49
Number of Brands: 13
Number of Products: 250
Square Footage: 300000
Type of Packaging: Food Service, Private Label
Brands:
 American Dietary
 Real Life
 The Pierson Company
 Vegetrates

4064 Energenetics International
P.O.Box 845
Keokuk, IA 52632
319-535-0760
Corn-based protein
President: Sammy Pierce
VP: Vincent James
Secretary: Gary Staggs
Number Employees: 5-9

4065 Energique
P.O. Box 121
201 Apple Boulevard
Woodbine, IA 51579
712-647-2499
Fax: 800-503-2588 800-869-8078
inquiry@energiqueherbal.com
Liquefied herbal extracts
President: Scott Beach
CEO/Owner: Jesse Rettig
Sales Manager: Dean Dobmeier
Contact: Joyce Beach
info@energiqueherbal.com
Estimated Sales: $3-5 Million
Number Employees: 10-19
Type of Packaging: Private Label, Bulk
Brands:
 Energique®

4066 Energy Brands/Haute Source
1720 Whitestone Expy
Flushing, NY 11357-3000
718-746-0087
Fax: 718-747-5900 800-746-0087
ebi@energybrands.com
Distilled water
President/CEO: Brent Hastie
SVP Finance: Wadih Khayat
CMO: Rohan Oza
Contact: Charles Alfaro
calfaro@glaceau.com
COO: Glen Ricks
Estimated Sales: Less than $500,000
Number Employees: 1-4
Type of Packaging: Consumer, Food Service
Brands:
 Fruit Water
 Glaceau Vitaminwater
 Go-Go Drinks
 Smart Water
 Soy Water
 Vitamin Water

4067 Energy Foods Intl.
9300 South Dadeland Blvd
Suite 600
Miami, FL 33156
844-772-6622
info@energyfoodsintl.com
www.energyfoodsintl.com
Raw, organic fruit powders
CEO: Laercio Goncalves
Number of Products: 4

4068 Enfield Farms Inc
1064 Birch Bay Lynden Rd
Lynden, WA 98264-9490
360-354-2919
Fax: 360-354-0503 info@enfieldfarms.com
www.nwplant.com
Manufacturer and packer of frozen red raspberries and blueberries
Owner: Marv Enfield
Chairman: Adam Enfield
Secretary/Treasurer: Linda Enfield
Sales Manager: Mike Haveman
menfield@enfieldfarms.com
Human Resources Compliance & Regulatory: Karin Myhre
Estimated Sales: $1.3 Million
Number Employees: 250-499
Square Footage: 17444
Type of Packaging: Food Service, Private Label, Bulk
Brands:
 Enfield Farms

4069 Engel's Bakeries
4709 14 Street NE
Bay 6
Calgary, AB T2E 6S4
Canada
403-250-9560
Fax: 403-250-5381 www.engelsbakeriesltd.ca
Baked and frozen ready-to-bake products including breads, pastries, sausage rolls, cakes, etc
President: Mithoo Gillani
R&D: Brian Hinton
Marketing/Sales: Ron Clappison
Sales Manager: Aaron Goss
Production Manager: Greg Zub
Purchasing: Danoz McKinnon
Estimated Sales: $5 Million
Number Employees: 70
Square Footage: 64000
Type of Packaging: Food Service

4070 English Bay Batter Us Inc
2241 Citygate Dr
Columbus, OH 43219-3564
614-471-9994
Fax: 614-890-9992 800-253-6844
www.englishbaycookies.com
Frozen batter and baked goods
Manager: Dan Rudd
Estimated Sales: $5-10 Million
Number Employees: 20-49
Parent Co: English Bay Batter
Type of Packaging: Consumer, Food Service, Private Label, Bulk
Brands:
 English Batter

4071 Enjoy Foods International
10601 Beech Ave
Fontana, CA 92337
909-823-2228
Fax: 909-355-1573 info@EnjoyBeefJerky.com
www.enjoybeefjerky.com
Manufacturer and exporter of beef and turkey jerky and meat snacks; exporter of steak kabobs
Chairman: Waleed Saab
VP: Mohamad Kabab
Marketing/Sales: Pierre Taylor
Contact: Walter Dorrouh
waleed@enjoybeefjerky.com
Plant Manager: Dennis Quinzon
Estimated Sales: $6.3 Million
Number Employees: 40
Square Footage: 40584
Type of Packaging: Consumer

4072 Enjoy Life Foods
8770 W Bryn Mawr Ave
Suite 1100
Chicago, IL 60631
888-503-6569
enjoylifefoods.com
Gluten-free cookies, snacks, granola and bagels.
President: Federico Meade
Founder/CEO: Scott Mandell
CFO: Bert Cohen
Senior Manager of R&D/Innovation: Lindsey Herman
Quality Assurance Director: Sandy Kasten
Chief Marketing Officer: Joel Warady
Senior Director of Sales: Patricia Marko
Contact: Courtney Benavides
cbenavides@enjoylifefoods.com
Operations Manager: Marvin Rea
Estimated Sales: $6 Million
Number Employees: 50
Square Footage: 60000

4073 Enlightened
101 Lincoln Ave
Suite 100
Bronx, NY 10454-4415
212-888-1120
www.eatenlightened.com
Ice cream and ice cream bars
CEO: Michael Shoretz
Year Founded: 2013
Estimated Sales: Less than $500,000
Number Employees: 1-4
Type of Packaging: Food Service, Private Label

4074 Enray, Inc
6999 Southfront Road
Suite D
Livermore, CA 94551
925-218-2205
Fax: 925-365-0587 800-288-3637
www.truroots.com
Full-line grains, cereal and pasta.
Marketing: Esha Ray
Contact: Steve Fischer
steve@fischer-creative.com

4075 Enrico Biscotti Co
2022 Penn Ave
Pittsburgh, PA 15222-4418
412-281-2602
www.enricobiscotti.com
Italian cookie/biscotti
Owner: Larry Lagattuta
Estimated Sales: Less Than $500,000
Number Employees: 10-19

4076 Enrico's/Ventre Packing
6050 Court Street Rd
Syracuse, NY 13206-1711
315-463-2384
Fax: 315-463-5897 888-472-8237
Sauces and salsas.
President: Marty Ventre
Manager Quality Control: Kurt Alpha
Eastern Regional Sales Manager: Rick Alesia
Estimated Sales: $10-20 Million
Number Employees: 10-19

4077 Ensemble Beverages
600 S Court Street
Suite 460
Montgomery, AL 36104-4106
334-324-7719
Manufacturer, importer and exporter of beverages including carbonated, sports drinks, nutritional shakes, iced tea and powders
President: James Harris
CFO: Cornelius Blanding, Jr
Number Employees: 10-19

4078 Enslin & Son Packing Company
2500 Glendale Ave
Hattiesburg, MS 39401
601-582-9300
Fax: 601-544-2010 800-898-4687
Manufacturer, packer and wholesaler/distributor of sausage
President: August Enslin
Estimated Sales: $4 Million
Number Employees: 30
Square Footage: 32000
Type of Packaging: Consumer, Private Label, Bulk
Brands:
 Bowie River
 Country Morning
 Glendale
 Hickory

4079 Enstrom Candies, Inc.
701 Colorado Ave
Grand Junction, CO 81501
Fax: 970-683-1011 800-367-8766
www.enstrom.com
Manufacturing and sales of confectionery products, including Almond Toffee, Truffles, Chocolates, Brittles, Fudges.

Owner: Doug Simons
Secretary/Treasurer & VP, Marketing: Jamee Simons
Quality Control Manager: Ginny Ansbaugh
National Sales Director: Bob Jackson
Contact Center Manager: Wendy Hanway
wendy@enstrom.com
Chief Technology Officer: Daniel Lively
Manufacturing Director: Doug Tuttle
Buyer: Diana Wilsey
Year Founded: 1929
Estimated Sales: $25 Million
Number Employees: 107
Number of Brands: 1
Square Footage: 19360
Type of Packaging: Consumer
Other Locations:
   Enstrom Candies
   Denver CO
Brands:
   Denver Co
   Enstrom Candies

4080 Entenmann's
930 Riverview Dr
Totowa, NJ 07511
      973-785-7601
Fax: 973-785-0009 www.entenmanns.com
Baked goods
Parent Co: Bimbo Bakeries USA

4081 Enterprise Foods
5315 Tulane Dr SW Ste D
Atlanta, GA 30336
      404-351-2251
Fax: 404-351-3969
Wholesale bakery ingredients and emulsifiers, dough conditioners, bromate replacers
President: Gerald Anderson
Estimated Sales: $1 Million
Number Employees: 10-19
Number of Brands: 1
Number of Products: 10
Square Footage: 300000
Type of Packaging: Bulk
Brands:
   Enterprise
   Sip
   Zeelanco

4082 Enterprises Pates et Croutes
14 Rue De Montgolfier
Boucherville, QC J4B 7Y4
Canada
      450-655-7790
Fax: 450-655-8037 800-265-7790
patesetcroutes.com
Manufacturer and exporter of frozen pie dough and shells; processor of baked muffins, bakery products, pastry products, and food product machinery.
President: Francine Benoit
Estimated Sales: 3.8 Million
Number Employees: 40
Type of Packaging: Consumer, Food Service

4083 Entner-Stuart Premium Syrups
1852 Fescue St SE
Albany, OR 97322-7075
      541-812-8000
Fax: 541-812-8010 800-926-6886
sales@allannbroscoffee.com
www.allannbroscoffee.com
Tea and coffee syrups
President/CEO: Allan Stuart
Estimated Sales: $5-10 Million
Number Employees: 10-19

4084 Enz Vineyards
1781 Limekiln Rd
Hollister, CA 95023-9172
      831-637-6443
Fax: 831-637-9382 www.vinarium-usa.com
Wines
Owner: Robert Enz
Partner: Susan Enz
Estimated Sales: $500,000-$1 Million
Number Employees: 1-4

4085 Enzo Olive Oil Co.
7770 Road 33
Madera, CA 93638
      559-299-7278
Fax: 559-299-7292 info@enzooliveoil.com
enzooliveoil.com
Balsamic vinegars and olive oils
Owner: Pat Ricchiuti
Number of Brands: 3
Number of Products: 13
Type of Packaging: Consumer
Brands:
   ENZO ORGANIC OLIVE OIL
   ENZO ORGANIC BALSAMIC VINEGAR
   ENZO'S TABLE

4086 Enzymatic Therapy Inc
825 Challenger Dr
Green Bay, WI 54311
      920-469-4444 800-783-2286
www.enzymatictherapy.com
Nutritional supplements
President & CEO: Randy Rose
Territory Sales Manager: Ben Bechtolt
pbechtolt@enzy.com
Estimated Sales: $100-499 Million
Number Employees: 250-499
Number of Products: 350
Parent Co: Nature's Way Holding Co.
Type of Packaging: Consumer, Private Label
Brands:
   Acidoplius Pearls
   Remifemin
   Vitaline CoQ10
   Whole Body Cleanse

4087 Enzyme Development Corporation
505 Eighth Avenue
Suite 500
New York, NY 10018
      212-736-1580
Fax: 212-279-0056
info@enzymedevelopment.com
www.enzymedevelopment.com
Manufacturer, importer and exporter of industrial and specialty enzymes.
Technical Sales Representative: Christina Barsa
Contact: Bobby Gau
bobby.gau@scinopharm.com
Type of Packaging: Bulk
Brands:
   Enzeco®

4088 Enzyme Formulations Inc
6421 Enterprise Ln
Madison, WI 53719-1116
      608-273-8100
Fax: 608-273-8111 800-614-4400
www.naturalenzymes.com
Supplements
Owner: Polly Fleming
pfleming@enzymeformulations.com

4089 Enzyme Innovation
13591 Yorba Ave
Chino, CA 91710-5071
      909-203-4620
adm@enzymeinnovation.com
www.enzymeinnovation.com
Enzymes.
Vice President: Dipak Roda
Estimated Sales: Below $1 Million
Number Employees: 1-4

4090 Eola Hills Wine Cellars
501 S Pacific Hwy
Rickreall, OR 97371-9728
      503-623-2405
Fax: 503-623-0350 800-291-6730
www.eolahillswinery.com
Wines
President: Tom Huggins
tom-huggins@eolahillswinery.com
CEO: Eric Rogers
CFO: Cherie Haines
Marketing: Michael Connell
Estimated Sales: $4 Million
Number Employees: 20-49

4091 Epi De France Bakery
1749 Tullie Circle NE
Atlanta, GA 30329
      404-325-1016
Fax: 404-325-0735 800-325-1014
bdoan@epibreads.com www.epibreads.com
Fresh and frozen bread, hoagies, table breads, baguettes, buns and rolls, sliced loaves, and ciabattas.
President: Nic Mulliez
CEO: Hugh Sullins
Sales Manager: B Doan
Estimated Sales: $20-50 Million
Square Footage: 42500
Type of Packaging: Consumer, Food Service, Private Label, Bulk
Brands:
   Epi De France
   Graines De Vie

4092 Epic Provisions
PO Box 684581
Austin, TX 78768
      512-944-8502
Fax: 512-900-7982 eatepic@epicbar.com
epicprovisions.com
Protein bars and snacks; duck fat; cured meats; smoked seafood.
Co-Founder: Taylor Collins
Co-Founder: Katie Forrest
Sales Director: Martha Siskron
marth@epicbar.com
Year Founded: 2012
Estimated Sales: $4 Million
Number Employees: 11-50
Type of Packaging: Private Label

4093 Epic Source Food
PO Box 2244
Frisco, TX 75034
      214-407-7154
epicsourcefoods.com
Goat cheese products and ice cream
CEO & National Sales Manager: Tim Millson
tmillson@epicsourcefoods.com
Sales & Marketing Support: Gayle Franks
Estimated Sales: $2-3 Million
Number Employees: 2-10
Brands:
   Funny Farm
   Laloo's(c)
   Nutritional Noodle
   Planet Harvest

4094 (HQ)Epicurean Butter
9355 Elm Ct
Federal Heights, CO 80260-5211
      303-427-5527
Fax: 303-254-5381 epicureanbutter@msn.com
www.epicureanbutter.com
Compound butters, both sweet and savory.
President: Carlos Garcia
carlos@epicureanbutter.com
VP: Janey Hubschman
Estimated Sales: $6.4 Million
Number Employees: 20-49

4095 Epogee
Indianapolis, IN 46208
www.epogeefoods.com
An alternative ingredient to fat, GMO-free and free of vegetable oils.
CEO: Tom Burrows
Founder & Chief Technology Officer: David Rowe
Chief Commericial Officer: Jayme Caruso
Sr. Director, Marketing: Sarah Malenich
Year Founded: 2011
Number Employees: 10
Type of Packaging: Food Service

4096 (HQ)Equal Exchange Inc
50 United Dr
West Bridgewater, MA 02379-1026
      774-776-7400
Fax: 508-587-0088 orders@equalexchange.coop
www.equalexchange.coop
Organic coffee, tea, chocolate, and nuts
Co-Executive Director: Rink Dickinson
Co-Executive Director: Rob Everts
dabbott@equalexchange.coop
Marketing: Bruce McKinnon
Sales: Mark Sweet
Director Operations: Denise Abbott
Estimated Sales: $20-50 Million
Number Employees: 50-99
Square Footage: 10000
Type of Packaging: Bulk

4097 Equal Exchange Inc
15 Campanelli Circle
Canton, MA 02021
orders@equalexchange.coop
www.equalexchange.coop
Organic coffees
Type of Packaging: Bulk

Food Manufacturers / A-Z

4098 Equal Exchange Inc
3460 NW Industrial St.
Portland, OR 97210
503-847-2000
orders@equalexchange.coop
www.equalexchange.coop
Organic coffees
Type of Packaging: Bulk

4099 Equal Exchange Inc
744 Vandalia St.
St. Paul, MN 55114
651-379-5020
Fax: 651-379-5023 orders@equalexchange.coop
www.equalexchange.coop
Organic coffees
Type of Packaging: Bulk

4100 Equal Exchange Inc
23400 Aurora Rd.
Unit 4
Bedford Heights, OH 44146
440-945-6875
orders@equalexchange.coop
www.equalexchange.coop
Organic coffees
Type of Packaging: Bulk

4101 Equator Coffees & Teas
115 Jordan St
San Rafael, CA 94901-3919
415-485-2213
800-809-7687
orders@equatorcoffees.com
www.equatorcoffees.com
Coffees and teas
Owner: Helen Russell
hrussell@equatorcoffees.com
Number Employees: 20-49

4102 Eragrain
208-867-8416
info@eragrain.com
www.eragrain.com
Ivory and Brown teff.
Brands:
  Eragrain(c)

4103 Erath Vineyards Winery
9409 NE Worden Hill Road
Dundee, OR 97115
503-538-3318
Fax: 503-538-1074 800-539-5463
info@erath.com www.erath.com
Wines
Founder: Dick Erath
Accounting Manager: Doug Moe
Marketing/Sales Manager: Steve Vuylsteke
Contact: Mayo Alba
malba@erath.com
Estimated Sales: $5-10 Million
Number Employees: 20-49
Number of Brands: 1
Number of Products: 1
Type of Packaging: Private Label, Bulk

4104 (HQ)Erba Food Products
2 Metro Tech Ctr. Ste 2000
Brooklyn, NY 11201-3838
718-272-7700
Fax: 718-272-7711
Manufacturer, importer and exporter of kosher foods including vegetables, juices, coffee, spices, seasonings, baked goods, fruits, condiments, fish, nuts, oils, etc
Manager: Heeren Patel
VP of Marketing: Abraham Perkowski
Sales: Jen O'Connor
Number Employees: 10-19
Type of Packaging: Consumer, Food Service
Brands:
  Embassy Wines
  Haddar

4105 Ericas Rugelach & Baking Co
389 4th St
Brooklyn, NY 11215-2901
718-965-3657
Fax: 718-832-6160 ericasrugelach@aol.com
www.ericasrugelach.com
Cookies and rugelach
CEO: Erica Kalick
ekalick@nyc.rr.com
Estimated Sales: Less Than $500,000
Number Employees: 1-4
Brands:
  Erica's Rugelach

4106 Erick Schat's Bakery
763 N Main St
Bishop, CA 93514-2427
760-873-7156
Fax: 760-872-4932 866-323-5854
schatsbakery@mindspring.com
www.schatsbakery.com
Baked goods
Number Employees: 50-99

4107 (HQ)Erie Foods Intl Inc
401 7th Ave
PO Box 648
Erie, IL 61250
309-659-2233
Fax: 309-659-2822 glindsey@eriefoods.com
www.eriefoods.com
Co-dried and concentrated milk proteins; also sodium, calcium, combination and acid-stable caseinates and dairy blends; importer of milk proteins
President/CEO: David Reisenbigler
dreisenbigler@eriefoods.com
CFO: Mark Delaney
COO: Jim Klein
Technical Services Manager: Craig Air
Quality Manager: Rene Perla
Purchasing Manager: Jake VanDeWostine
Process Development Manager: Jim Jacoby
Purchasing Manager: Shawn Larson
Estimated Sales: $1-2.5 Million
Number Employees: 10-19
Square Footage: 120000
Parent Co: Erie Foods International Inc
Type of Packaging: Bulk
Other Locations:
  Erie Foods International
  Beenleigh QLD
Brands:
  Ecco
  Erie

4108 Erivan Dairy
105 Allison Rd
Oreland, PA 19075-1808
215-887-2009
Fax: 215-885-3679 www.erivandairy.com
Yogurt
President: Harry Fereshetian
Plant Manager: Paul Fereshetian
Estimated Sales: $1-2.5 Million
Number Employees: 20-49
Type of Packaging: Consumer

4109 Errol's Cajun Foods
6801 Highway 1001
Belle Rose, LA 70341-5405
225-746-1002
Fax: 225-746-1004 866-746-6003
www.errolscajunfoods.com
Stuffed and frozen jalapeno peppers and value added seafood products including crab and shrimp; also, seafood gumbo and shrimp etouffee and patties
Owner: Errol Perera
bmtheriot@yahoo.com
Estimated Sales: $2.5-5 Million
Number Employees: 10-19
Type of Packaging: Consumer, Food Service

4110 Escalade Limited
37 W Shore Rd # 2
Huntington, NY 11743-7206
631-659-3373
Fax: 631-659-3376 latitudeltd@aol.com
www.latitudeltdusa.com
Ingredients and additives, including anti-oxidants, preservatives, sweeteners and minerals
President: Lourel Mandel
VP: Dedi Avner
Contact: Dedi Avner
escalade@bezeqint.net
Estimated Sales: $500,000- 1 Million
Number Employees: 8

4111 Escalon Premier Brand
1905 McHenry Ave
Escalon, CA 95320
209-838-7341
Fax: 209-838-6206 www.escalon.net
Canned tomatoes and tomato products including sauces
Controller: Steve Kelly
Human Resource Executive: Susan McCready
Product Manager: Dan Milazzo
Plant Manager: John Raggio
Purchasing Agent: Tom Muller
Number Employees: 100-249
Parent Co: Heinz USA
Type of Packaging: Consumer, Food Service
Brands:
  6-In-1
  Bell 'orto
  Bella Rosa
  Christina's Organic
  Heniz
  Mama Linda

4112 Eschete's Seafood
229 New Orleans Blvd
Houma, LA 70364-3345
985-872-4120
Fax: 504-851-6147
Seafood
Owner: John Eschete
Estimated Sales: $300,000-500,000
Number Employees: 1-4

4113 (HQ)Esco Foods Inc
131 Russ St
San Francisco, CA 94103-4009
415-864-2147
info@escofoods.com
www.escofoods.com
Syrups, toppings, salad dressings, marinades, bbq sauce, flavors
President: Marc Bosschart
Contact: Michele Bosschart
info@escofoods.com
Estimated Sales: $2.5-5 Million
Number Employees: 5-9

4114 Eskimo Candy Inc
2665 Wai Wai Pl
Kihei, HI 96753-8178
808-879-5686
Fax: 808-874-0504 www.eskimocandy.com
Seafood and other fine foods.
Owner: Jeff Hansen
eskimo@maui.net
Estimated Sales: $10-20 Million
Number Employees: 20-49

4115 (HQ)Esper Products DeLuxe
2793 N Orange Blossom Trl
Kissimmee, FL 34744-1375
407-847-3726
800-268-0892
colleen1014@webtv.net
Jellies and preserves
President: Andrew McFarland
Estimated Sales: $2.5-5,000,000
Number Employees: 5-9
Brands:
  Esper Deluxe

4116 Espresso Vivace
901 E Denny Way Ste 100
Seattle, WA 98122
206-860-5869
Fax: 206-860-1567 info@espressovivace.com
www.espressovivace.com
Coffee
Founder: David Schomer
Estimated Sales: $1-2.5 Million
Number Employees: 20-49

4117 Espro Manufacturing
2800 Ayers Avenue
Vernon, CA 90058
323-415-8544
Fax: 323-268-4060
Manufacturer and packager of food ingredients, including custom dry powder blends.
Contact: Blas Tiangson
blas.tiangson@kp.org

4118 Essen Nutrition Corp
1414 Sherman Rd
Romeoville, IL 60446-4046
630-739-6700
Fax: 630-739-6464 800-582-6064
sales@essen-nutrition.com
www.essen-nutrition.com

Dietary and health foods
President: Madhavan Anirudhan
manirudhan@essennutritioncorp.com
Vice President: Mike Holland
VP Operations: Tom Grandys
Estimated Sales: $4 Million
Number Employees: 20-49
Type of Packaging: Private Label

4119 Essentia Protein Solutions
2425 SE Oak Tree Court
Ankeny, IA 50021
515-289-5100
Fax: 515-289-5110 essentiaproteins.com
Essentia manufactures functional proteins that improve the taste and texture of commercial food products. It is a global company with operations in the United States, South America, Europe and Asia.
COO: Asger Jacobsen
Executive VP, Global Sales: Moises Contreras
Parent Co: Lauridsen Group
Brands:
 ScanPro™
 APro™
 ExcelPro™
 ExcelPro™ Plus
 Drinde™
 ProBase™
 ProFlavor™

4120 Essentia Water
22833 Bthell Everett Hwy
Street 220
Bothell, WA 98021
425-402-9555
877-293-2239
customerservice@essentiawater.com
www.essentiawater.com
Purifying drinking water
President: Ken Uptain
CFO: Keith Huetson
Estimated Sales: $2 Million
Number Employees: 1-4

4121 Essential Baking Co, The
5601 1st Avenue South
Seattle, WA 98108
206-545-3804
Fax: 206-767-1176
marketing@essentialbaking.com
essentialbaking.com
Artisan breads, pastries and desserts
Chairman: Peter Miller
President & CEO: Tom Campanile
Marketing Manager: Kuanny Yin
HR Generalist: Kanjarin Hiranworawuthikul
Purchasing Manager: Alec Norman
Estimated Sales: $25-50 Million
Number Employees: 200-500
Brands:
 The Essential Baking Company

4122 Essential Flavors & Fragrances
1521 Commerce St
Corona, CA 92880-1730
951-737-3889
Fax: 951-737-4237 888-333-9935
customerservice@essentialflavors.com
www.essentialflavors.com
Drink based concentrates, flavorings, herbal extracts and body building formulas
President: Michael Gulan
mpgro@juno.com
Vice President: Richard Staley
Office Manager: Susan Wakeling
Estimated Sales: $630,000
Number Employees: 5-9
Type of Packaging: Bulk

4123 Essential Living Foods
Torrance, CA 90503
310-319-1555
essentiallivingfoods.com
Trail mixes and smoothie blends

4124 Essential Nutrients Inc
174 E 400 S
Emery, UT 84522
435-286-2460
Fax: 435-286-2471
vickie@essentialnutrientsinc.com
www.essentialnutrientsinc.com
Nutrients

President: Randy Haringa
Vice President: Vicki Heringa
Estimated Sales: $58,000
Number Employees: 1-4
Type of Packaging: Private Label
Brands:
 Super Kmh

4125 Essential Products of America
6710 Benjamin Road
Suite 700
Tampa, FL 33634-4314
813-886-9698
Fax: 813-886-9661 800-822-9698
Manufacturer, importer and exporter of essential oils
President: Michael Alexander
Estimated Sales: $2.5-5 Million
Number Employees: 5
Square Footage: 4800
Type of Packaging: Consumer, Private Label, Bulk
Brands:
 Whole Spectrum

4126 Essiac Canada International
164 Richmond Rd
Ottawa, ON K1Z 6W2
Canada
514-695-2299
888-900-2299
www.essiaccanadainternational.com
Manufacturer and exporter of herbal dietary supplements
President: Terrence Maloney
Estimated Sales: $975,000
Number Employees: 6
Number of Brands: 2
Number of Products: 2
Parent Co: Essiac Canada International
Type of Packaging: Consumer, Food Service
Brands:
 Essiac (Extract)
 Essiac (Powder)

4127 Esteem Products
1800 136th Pl NE
Ste 5
Bellevue, WA 98005
425-562-1281
Fax: 425-562-1284 800-255-7631
customerservice@esteemproducts.com
www.esteemproducts.com
Manufacturer, wholesaler/distributor and exporter of nutritional supplements and specialty vitamins. All combination formulas for consumer simplicity
CEO/President: John Sheaffer
VP: Linda Sheaffer
Marketing: Amy Braisford
Contact: Chana Madsen
chana@esteemproducts.com
Estimated Sales: $500,000-$1 Million
Number Employees: 5-9
Square Footage: 20000
Brands:
 Artho Life
 Cardio Life
 Esteem Plus
 Golden Life
 Immune Life
 Super Life
 Total Man
 Total Woman
 Trim & Firm Am/Pm

4128 Esterlina Vineyard & Winery
435 West Dry Creek Road
Healdsburg, CA 95448
707-895-2920
Fax: 707-895-2972 888-474-7456
Wines
President: Craig Sterling
CEO: Eric Sterling
Marketing Manager: Steve Sterling
Estimated Sales: Under $500,000
Number Employees: 5-9
Brands:
 Esterlina

4129 Esther Price Candies & Gifts
1709 Wayne Ave
Dayton, OH 45410-1711
937-253-2121
Fax: 937-253-6034 855-337-8437
customerservice@epcandies.com
www.estherprice.com

Chocolates
President: James Day
james@epcandies.com
Manager: Barb Dressman
Estimated Sales: Under $500,000
Number Employees: 100-249
Type of Packaging: Consumer, Private Label

4130 Etchandy Farms
Anaheim, CA
Strawberries
President/Owner: Mike Etchandy
Year Founded: 1947
Type of Packaging: Consumer, Private Label

4131 Eternal Water
2950 Buskirk Ave
Suite 312
Walnut Creek, CA 94597
877-854-5494
info@eternalwater.com www.eternalwater.com
Sparkling spring water
Founder & CEO: Karim Mashouf

4132 Ethan's
939 Pearl St
Boulder, CO 80302
720-432-8384
info@ethans.com
www.ethans.com
Apple cider vinegar shots
Founder: Ethan Hirshberg
Number of Brands: 1
Number of Products: 6
Type of Packaging: Consumer
Brands:
 ETHAN'S

4133 Ethel M Chocolates
1 Sunset Way
Henderson, NV 89014
800-438-4356
www.ethelm.com
Chocolate.
Sales Director: Viviana Strahl Dickieson
Estimated Sales: $100-500 Million
Number Employees: 5-9
Parent Co: Mars

4134 Ethel's Baking Co.
22314 Harper Ave
St. Clair Shores, MI 48080
586-552-5110
ethelsbaking.com
Gluten-free dessert bars and cookies
Founder: Jill Bommarito
Year Founded: 2011
Number of Brands: 1
Number of Products: 10
Type of Packaging: Consumer
Brands:
 ETHEL'S BAKING

4135 Ethical Bean Coffee
1315 Kootenay St
Vancouver, BC V5K 4Y3
Canada
604-431-3830
Fax: 604-431-3834 877-431-3830
ethicalbean.com
Roasted coffee beans
Co-Founder: Lloyd Bernhardt
Co-Founder: Kim Schachte
Sales Development & Marketing: Lauren Archibald
Year Founded: 2003
Estimated Sales: $6,000,000
Number Employees: 25
Type of Packaging: Private Label

4136 Ethical Naturals
330 H Sir Francis Drake Blvd
Suite F
San Anselmo, CA 94960
415-459-4454
866-459-4454
info@ethicalnaturals.com
www.ethicalnaturals.com
Natural ingredients and flavors
President: Cal Bewicke
Estimated Sales: Under $500,000
Number Employees: 1

Food Manufacturers / A-Z

4137 Ethnic Edibles
2186 5th Avenue
Apt 17a
New York, NY 10037-2720
718-320-0147
Fax: 718-320-0147 info@ethnicedibles.com
www.ethnicedibles.com
Cookies and cookie cutters with African and Puerto Rico themes
President: Heather McCartney
Contact: Heather Mccartney
heathermccartney@msn.com
Brands:
   Coqui Cookies
   Ethnic Edibles

4138 Ethnic Gourmet Foods
4600 Sleepytime Drive
Boulder, CO 80301
610-692-7575
Fax: 610-719-6399 800-434-4246
www.ethnicgourmet.com
Frozen gourmet foods
Manager: Richard Alexander
Estimated Sales: $20 Million
Number Employees: 50-99
Parent Co: Hain Celestial Group

4139 Etna Brewing Co
131 Callahan St
Etna, CA 96027
530-467-5277
Fax: 530-567-3083 etnabrew@gmail.com
www.etnabrew.com
Beer
Owner: Dave Krell
Brewer: Luke Hurliman
Estimated Sales: $500,000-$1 Million
Number Employees: 10-19
Brands:
   Dark Lager
   Etna Ale
   Etna Bock
   Etna Doppelbock
   Etna Oktoberfest
   Etna Weizen
   Export Lager

4140 (HQ)Ettlinger Corp
175 Olde Half Day Rd # 247
Lincolnshire, IL 60069-3063
847-564-5020
Fax: 847-564-0802
Cereal grains, barley & wheat, reduced lactose whey
President: Peter Ettlinger
peter@ettlingercorp.com
Estimated Sales: $1-2.5 Million
Number Employees: 5-9
Type of Packaging: Food Service, Bulk

4141 Euphoria Chocolate Company
4090 Stewart Rd
Eugene, OR 97402
541-344-4914
Fax: 541-344-5223 www.euphoriachocolate.com
Chocolate truffles, trail mix
President/CEO: Bob Bury
Contact: Lorrie Betty
lorrie@euphoriachocolate.com
Estimated Sales: Less than $500,000
Number Employees: 1-4

4142 Eureka Locker Inc
110 4h Park Rd
Eureka, IL 61530-1706
309-467-2731
Fax: 309-467-2731 www.bittnersmeatco.com
Beef, pork and lamb
President: Scott Bittner
Estimated Sales: $500,000-$1 Million
Number Employees: 1-4
Type of Packaging: Consumer

4143 Eureka Water Co
729 SW 3rd St
Oklahoma City, OK 73109-1100
405-235-8474
Fax: 405-235-6344 800-310-8474
info@ozarkah2o.com
Bottled water
President: Bl Carter
blc@ozarkah2o.com
Plant Manager: Robert DeShazo

Estimated Sales: $5-10 Million
Number Employees: 100-249
Type of Packaging: Consumer, Private Label, Bulk
Brands:
   Mountain Valley
   Ozarka
   Shamrock

4144 Euro Cafe
1150 University Ave # 8
Rochester, NY 14607-1663
585-244-3140
Fax: 585-461-2234 800-298-9410
Biscotti, chocolate, espresso, flavoring. Distributors of cafe and restaurant products
Owner: Barb Campbell
Public Relations: Danny Daniele
Estimated Sales: $1-2.5 000,000
Number Employees: 5-9

4145 Euro Chocolate Fountain
2647 Ariane Dr
San Diego, CA 92117-3422
858-270-9863
Fax: 858-270-6801 800-423-9303
info@eurochocolate.com
Bakery products, chocolate confections and specialty baking
Owner: Urs Huwyler
VP: Don Rein
Estimated Sales: Less Than $500,000
Number Employees: 1-4
Brands:
   Euro Chocolate

4146 Euro Source Gourmet
220 Little Falls Road
Unit 2
Cedar Grove, NJ 07009-1255
973-857-6000
Fax: 973-857-8862 tjvambass@aol.com
Gourmet foods
Owner: Thomas Calvaruso
Sales: Janka Delatte

4147 Euroam Importers Inc
1302 S 293rd Pl
Auburn, WA 98003-3756
253-839-5240
Fax: 253-839-4171 888-839-2702
euroaminc1@aol.com
Coffee
President: Vito Rizzo
euroaminc1@aol.com
VP: Anita Goransson
Estimated Sales: $270,000
Number Employees: 1-4
Number of Brands: 10
Number of Products: 20
Square Footage: 7200
Parent Co: Euro Am Imports

4148 Eurobubblies
58 Union Street
Ashland, MA 01721
508-881-9900
800-273-0750
christian@eurobubblies.com
www.eurobubblies.com
Beverage and food products from Europe
President: Pascal Benichou
Estimated Sales: Under $500,000
Number Employees: 5-9
Type of Packaging: Consumer, Food Service, Private Label, Bulk
Brands:
   Basilic Pistou
   Bel Normande-Spritzers
   Clos Normand
   Dupont D'Isigny-Candies
   Eat Natural
   Efferve
   Eurobubblies
   Eurosupreme
   Harrgate
   Hobgoblin-Beer
   Joker-Fruit Juice
   Lorina-Lemonade
   Pampryl
   Primel
   Seasoning Salt
   Siracuse
   Spoonty
   St Peter's
   Terrafood
   Wychwood

4149 Eurocaribe Packing Company
Vega Baja, PR
787-793-6900
www.matosantos.com/manufacturingsubsidiaries-eurocaribe.htm
Smoked meats
President: Jose Casanova
CFO: John Erickson
Purchasing: Hiram Morales
Estimated Sales: $10-20,000,000
Number Employees: 160
Parent Co: Matosantos Commercial Corp.
Type of Packaging: Private Label, Bulk
Other Locations:
   Zona Industrial
   Carolina PR

4150 Europa Sports Products
11401 Granite St
Charlotte, NC 28273
800-447-4795
sales@europasports.com www.europasports.com
Sports food and nutrition.
CEO: Eric Hillman
erichillman@europasports.com
CFO: Anthony Todaro
COO: Robbie Duncan
Year Founded: 1990
Estimated Sales: $100-499 Million
Number Employees: 250-499
Number of Brands: 280
Brands:
   ABB
   ABN
   Absolute Nutrition
   AccuFitness
   Basic Research
   Best Bar Ever
   Bpi
   Caveman Foods
   Cellucor
   Cytosport
   Designer Protein
   Eat The Bear
   EFX Sports
   Fitmark
   FRS Company
   Clif Bar
   Gatorade
   Hydroxycut
   Jack Links
   Jelly Belly Candy Company
   Kind Snacks
   Mancakes
   Paleo People
   Pure Protein
   Quest Nutrition

4151 European Bakers
5055 S Royal Atlanta Dr
Tucker, GA 30084-3097
770-723-6180
Fax: 770-939-6632 www.europeanbakers.com
Baked goods including breads and buns
President: James Allen
Estimated Sales: $10-20 Million
Number Employees: 100-249
Square Footage: 260000
Parent Co: Flowers Baking Company
Type of Packaging: Consumer

4152 European Coffee
13925 58th Street North
Clearwater, FL 33760
727-535-2111
Fax: 856-428-7262 888-635-4882
ConsumerRelations@melitta.com
www.melitta.com
Coffee
President/CEO: H Radtke
Finance Mananger: Scott Landem
VP: John Masters
Director: Jay Burdette
Operations Manager: Timm Rose
Plant Manager: Vincent Tagliaferro
Estimated Sales: $5-10 Million
Number Employees: 20-49
Brands:
   Frac-Packs

Food Manufacturers / A-Z

4153 European Egg Noodle Manufacturing
14815 Yellowhead Trail Nw
Edmonton, AB T5L 3C4
Canada
780-453-6767
Fax: 780-453-6769
Frozen pastas, sauces, sausages and pizzas
President/Sales: Fausto Chinellato
Operations: Dorothy Chinellato
Estimated Sales: $743,000
Number Employees: 5
Type of Packaging: Consumer
Brands:
  Bella Festa
  Pasta Time

4154 European Roasterie
250 W Bradshaw St
Le Center, MN 56057-1121
507-357-2272
Fax: 507-357-4478 888-588-5282
www.euroroast.com
Coffees and teas
President/CEO: Timothy Tulloch
timothy@euroroast.com
Sales: Cindy Dorzinski
Operations: Thomas Dotray
Estimated Sales: $20-50 Million
Number Employees: 20-49
Type of Packaging: Private Label

4155 European Style Bakery
112 N Hamilton Drive
Unit 107
Beverly Hills, CA 90211-2279
818-368-6876
Blueberry filling, cakes and bakery items
President: Vladimir Landa
vladimir.landa@europeanpastry.com
Estimated Sales: Less than $500,000
Number Employees: 5-9

4156 Eva Gates Homemade Preserves
456 Electric Ave
Bigfork, MT 59911-3641
406-837-4356
Fax: 406-837-4376 800-682-4283
info@evagates.com www.evagates.com
Fruit preserves and fruit syrups
President: Gretchen Gates
Estimated Sales: Less Than $500,000
Number Employees: 1-4
Type of Packaging: Private Label

4157 Evans Creole Candy
848 Decatur St
New Orleans, LA 70116-3375
504-522-7111
Fax: 504-522-7113 800-637-6675
Praline, chocolate candy and syrup
President: Jaye Cuccia
evanscc@bellsouth.net
Estimated Sales: $1-2.5 Million
Number Employees: 5-9
Type of Packaging: Bulk

4158 Evans Food Group LTD
4118 S Halsted St
Chicago, IL 60609-2693
773-254-7400
Fax: 773-254-7791 866-254-7400
www.evansfood.com
Manufacturer and exporter of rendered pork rinds.
Chairman/CEO: Jose Luis Prado
Purchasing: Ed McKenna
Estimated Sales: $20-50 Million
Number Employees: 100-249
Number of Brands: 4
Square Footage: 104000
Type of Packaging: Consumer, Private Label
Brands:
  Bill's
  La Tonita
  Macs
  Porkies

4159 Evans Properties
#301, 660 Beachland Blvd.
Vero Beach, FL 32963
772-234-2410
www.evansprop.com
Agricultural and land-management company. This company has 8 land holdings across Florida, and are responsible for growing citrus.
Chairman of the Board: Jimmy Evans, Jr.
President & CEO: Ronald Edwards
VP, Chief Financial Officer: Jerry Beasman
Vice President: Emmett Evans, III
Estimated Sales: $5-10,000,000
Number Employees: 5-9

4160 Eve Sales Corp
945 Close Ave
Bronx, NY 10473
718-589-6800
Fax: 718-617-6717 executiveoffice@evesales.com
Juice; instant coffee; tea; concentrates and powders; BBQ sauce; marinades; seasonings; and chips
Vice President: Stuart Gale
Year Founded: 1965
Estimated Sales: $299531
Number Employees: 13
Type of Packaging: Private Label

4161 Evensen Vineyards
PO Box 127
Oakville, CA 94562-0127
707-944-2396
Wines
President: Richard Evensen

4162 Ever Fresh Fruit Co
35855 SE Kelso Rd
PO Box 1177
Boring, OR 97009-7064
503-668-8026
Fax: 503-668-5823 800-239-8026
www.everfreshfruit.com
Apples
Owner: Brittany Beem
brittany@everfreshfruit.com
VP: LeAnn Miller
Estimated Sales: $10-20 Million
Number Employees: 50-99
Type of Packaging: Consumer, Food Service, Private Label
Brands:
  Nature's Quest

4163 Everfresh Beverages
6600 E 9 Mile Rd
Warren, MI 48091-2673
586-755-9500
Fax: 586-755-9587 800-323-3416
www.everfreshjuice.com
Manufacturer and exporter of soft drinks and fruit juices including orange and grape
President/CEO: Stan Sheridan
Telecommunications: Ray Laurinaitis
Operations: Dave Piontkowski
Plant Manager: Matt Filipovitch
Purchasing Director: Walter Koziara
Number Employees: 50-99
Square Footage: 500000
Parent Co: National Beverages Corporation
Type of Packaging: Consumer, Private Label
Brands:
  Everfresh
  Lacroix

4164 Everfresh Food Corporation
501 Huron Blvd SE
Minneapolis, MN 55414
612-331-6393
Fax: 612-331-1172 george_edgar@yahoo.com
Chow mein noodles and vanilla including pure and imitation; importer of bamboo shoots and water chestnuts including whole and sliced
VP: Rita Sorsveen
Estimated Sales: $5-10 Million
Number Employees: 10-19
Type of Packaging: Consumer, Food Service, Private Label, Bulk
Brands:
  China Boy

4165 Everglades Foods
441 Webster Turn Drive
Sebring, FL 33870
Fax: 863-655-2214 800-689-2221
sales@evergladesseasoning.com
Seasonings
President: Seth Howard
Owner: Chris Sebring
Marketing Director: Kelli Bronson
Sales: Jenna Buchanan
Estimated Sales: $1-2.5 Million
Number Employees: 5-9
Type of Packaging: Consumer, Food Service
Brands:
  Everglades
  Everglades Heat
  Everglades Original

4166 Evergood Fine Foods
1389 Underwood Ave
San Francisco, CA 94124-3308
415-822-4660
Fax: 415-822-1066 800-253-6733
info@evergoodfoods.com evergoodfoods.com
Sausage manufacturer founded in 1926.
General Manager: Harlan Miller
VP, Sales & Marketing: Don Miller
Estimated Sales: $20-50 Million
Number Employees: 50-99
Type of Packaging: Consumer

4167 Evergreen Juices Inc.
Po Box 1
Don Mills, ON M3C 2R6
Canada
905-886-8090
Fax: 905-886-5633 877-915-8423
info@evergreenjuices.com
www.evergreenjuices.com
Juice
President: Don Mills
Treasurer: Robert MacIntosh

4168 Evergreen Sweeteners, Inc
1936 Hollywood Blvd
Suite 200
Hollywood, FL 33020
954-381-7776
Fax: 954-458-5793 www.esweeteners.com
Bulk liquid sweeteners and bagged sweeteners
President: Arthur Green
Year Founded: 1925
Estimated Sales: $55 Million
Number Employees: 50+
Number of Products: 40
Square Footage: 150000
Type of Packaging: Food Service, Bulk
Other Locations:
  Evergreen Sweeteners, Inc.
  Atlanta GA
  Evergreen Sweeteners, Inc.
  Sanford FL
  Evergreen Sweeteners, Inc.
  Miami FL

4169 Everland Foods
7442 Fraser Park Dr
Burnaby, BC V5J 5B9
Canada
info@everland.ca
everland.ca
Organic, kosher health foods
CEO: Rajinder Bagga
Type of Packaging: Food Service, Private Label

4170 Everland Parks
7442 Fraser Park Dr
Burnaby, BC V5J 5B9
Canada
info@everland.ca
everland.ca
Oils, nuts and nut butters
President & CEO: Kulwant Bagga
Year Founded: 2005
Number of Brands: 1
Number of Products: 400+
Type of Packaging: Consumer
Brands:
  EVERLAND

4171 Everson Spice Co
2667 Gundry Ave
Signal Hill, CA 90755-1808
562-595-4785
Fax: 562-988-0219 800-421-3753
customerservice@eversonspice.com
www.eversonspice.com
Seasonings, dry rubs, stuffing mixes and marinades

695

Food Manufacturers / A-Z

Owner: Tom Everson
tomeverson@eversonspice.com
President: Ken Hopkins
CEO: Kim Everson
Estimated Sales: $2.5-5 Million
Number Employees: 50-99
Type of Packaging: Food Service

4172 Everspring Farms
Seaforth, ON N0K 1W0
Canada
519-527-0990
sales@everspringfarms.ca
www.everspringfarms.ca
Sprouted grains, seeds and beans
Co-Founder: Dale Donaldson
Co-Founder: Marianne Donaldson

4173 Everything Yogurt
1100 Pennsylvania Ave NW
Washington, DC 20004-2501
202-842-2990
Yogurt, salad products
Owner: January Kwak
Estimated Sales: Under $500,000
Number Employees: 20-49

4174 Evo Hemp
Boulder, CO
evohemp.com
Hemp extracts, bars, snacks, seeds and seed oil
Type of Packaging: Consumer
Brands:
  EVO HEMP

4175 Evol Foods
1600 Pearl St # 300
Boulder, CO 80302-5457
303-554-7000
www.evolfoods.com
Frozen foods
Sales: Marcus Seiden
Number Employees: 20-49

4176 Evolution Fresh
Seattle, WA 98134
800-794-9986
info@evolutionfresh.com
www.evolutionfresh.com
Cold-pressed juices and smoothies
Founder: Jimmy Rosenberg
Number of Brands: 1
Number of Products: 24
Type of Packaging: Consumer
Brands:
  EVOLUTION FRESH

4177 Evolution Salt Co.
3310 W Braker Ln
Suite 300-234
Austin, TX 78758-7853
877-868-7979
Fax: 512-828-8789 www.evolutionsalt.com
Himalayan salt products
Owner: Hayden Nasir
VP of Sales: Jordan Holtz
Number Employees: 1-10
Type of Packaging: Food Service, Private Label

4178 Evolve
1340 Treat Blvd
Suite 350
Walnut Creek, CA 94597
888-298-6629
www.drinkevolve.com
Protein bars and shakes

4179 Evy Tea
Boston, MA 02130
www.evytea.com
Ready-to-drink cold brew tea
Founder: Evy Chen

4180 Eweberry Farms
30377 Brownsville Rd
Brownsville, OR 97327-9525
541-466-3470
Gourmet jams and syrups
Owner: John Morrison
Estimated Sales: Less Than $500,000
Number Employees: 1-4

4181 Ex Drinks
1879 Whitney Mesa Dr
Henderson, NV 89014
702-949-6555
Fax: 702-949-6556 866-753-4929
hq@exdrinks.com
Energy drinks and vitamin water
Headquarters Manager: Natasha Platin
Senior Director of Business Development: Clark Wright
Director of Strategic Planning: Kristen Hirtz
Marketing: Travis Arnesen
Contact: Travis Arnesen
tarnesen@exdrinks.com
Estimated Sales: $500,000- 1 Million
Number Employees: 5-9

4182 Excalibur Seasoning
1800 Riverway Dr
Pekin, IL 61554-9307
309-347-1221
Fax: 309-347-9086 800-444-2169
sales@excaliburseasoning.com
www.excaliburseasoning.com
Seasoning
President: Jay Hall
CEO: Blake Taylor
btaylor@lumc.edu
Estimated Sales: $5-10 Million
Number Employees: 50-99

4183 Exceldor Cooperative
5700 Rue J.B.Michaud
Bureau 500
Levis, QC G6V 0B1
Canada
418-830-5600
info@exceldor.com
www.exceldor.ca
Manufacturer and exporter of fresh and frozen chicken.
President & CEO: René Proulx
VP, Operations: Éric Cadoret
VP, Finance: Christian Jacques
VP, Quality Assurance & R&D: Geneviève Arsenault
VP, Communications & Marketing: Isabelle Drouin
VP, Sales: Luc Gagnon
VP, Human Resources: Clémence Drouin
SVP, Chicken Division: Joël Cormier
SVP, Turkey Division: Anthony Tavares
Year Founded: 1945
Estimated Sales: $229 Million
Number Employees: 1400
Square Footage: 7502
Type of Packaging: Consumer, Private Label, Bulk
Brands:
  Exceldor Express

4184 Excellentia Intl.
30 Stewart Place
Fairfield, NJ 07004
737-749-9840
excellentiainternational.com
Ingredient supplier
President/Owner: Tom Buco

4185 Exeter Produce
215 Thames Road West
Exeter, ON N0M 1S3
Canada
519-235-0141
info@exeterproduce.com
exeterproduce.com
Grower, packer and shipper of beans, peppers, lettuce, cabbage and other hydroponic and field produce.
President: Leonard Veri
Director: James Veri
Director: Michael Veri
Year Founded: 1951
Type of Packaging: Bulk
Brands:
  VeriFine

4186 Exo Inc.
94 South 4th Street
Apt. 4
Brooklyn, NY 11249
818-744-4140
exoprotein.com
Protein bars and bites made with cricket flour
Co-Founder: Gabi Lewis
Co-Founder: Greg Sewitz
Year Founded: 2012
Number of Brands: 1
Number of Products: 6
Type of Packaging: Consumer
Brands:
  EXO

4187 Explore Cuisine
308-157 Broad St
Red Bank, NJ 07701
info@explorecuisine.com
www.explorecuisine.com
Bean and pulse pastas
Number of Brands: 1
Number of Products: 15
Type of Packaging: Consumer
Brands:
  EXPLORE CUISINE

4188 Expro Manufacturing
2800 Ayers Avenue
Vernon, CA 90058
323-415-8544
Fax: 323-268-4060
Manufacturer and packager of food ingredients, including custom dry powder blends
President: Peter Ernster
CEO: Douglas Kantner
R&D: Greg Rowland
VP Sales: Michele Mullen
Contact: Daniel Diaz
ddiaz@expromfg.com
Purchasing: James Ernster
Number Employees: 20

4189 Exquisita Tortillas Inc
700 W Chapin St
Edinburg, TX 78541-2416
956-383-6712
Fax: 956-383-1012 info@exquisitatortillas.com
www.exquisitatortillas.com
Corn and flour tortillas, chips, taco & challupa shells, pork skins
Owner: Humberto Rodriguez
hrodriguez@exquisitatortillasinc.com
President & CEO: J Rodriguez
COO: Bill Guerra
Estimated Sales: $26.6 Million
Number Employees: 100-249
Square Footage: 46000
Brands:
  Exquisita

4190 Extracts and Ingredients Ltd
One Gary Road
Union, NJ 07083-5527
908-688-9009
Fax: 908-688-9005 www.morretec.com
Supplier of natural specialty ingredients to the food, nutraceutical and personal care markets. Offer organic specialty oils, Oregano Extract as a natural preservative, Indian spice oleoresins and essential oils, fruit concentrates carrageenans and water-soluble vitamins A, D & E. Manufacture and supply micronized particle powders of TCP, DCP, bran, phytosterols etc. using a patented Vortex milling technology. Also a major distributor of Magnesium, Potassium, and Calciumchlorides.
President: Leonard Glass
Quality Assurance Manager: Anzorena Ramirez
Marketing Coordinator: Melissa Bevilaque
VP Sales/Marketing: David Fondots
Contact: D Fondots
dfondots@morretec.com
VP Administration/Operations: Paul Caskey
Parent Co: Morre-Tec Industries, Inc

4191 Extravagonzo Gourmet Foods
P.O. Box 6346
Boise, ID 83707
208-639-2926
garlic@extravagonzofoods.com
extravagonzofoods.com
Vinegar; olive oil; cooking sauces and seasonings
President: Tom Stevens
Brand Manager: Leah Ryneer
Type of Packaging: Food Service, Private Label

4192 Extreme Creations
4970 Windplay Dr Ste C5
El Dorado Hills, CA 95762
916-941-0444
Fax: 916-941-1777
Jellied lollipops

Food Manufacturers / A-Z

Manager: Kamal Naim
Estimated Sales: $.5-1 million
Number Employees: 1-4

4193 Eyrie Vineyards
935 NE 10th Ave
Mcminnville, OR 97128-4003
503-472-6315
Fax: 503-472-5124 888-440-4970
info@eyrievineyards.com
www.eyrievineyards.com
Wines
Owner: Jason Lett
info@eyrievineyards.com
Vice President: Diana Lett
Estimated Sales: $5-10 Million
Number Employees: 20-49

4194 Ezzo Sausage Company
PO Box 7784
Columbus, OH 43207
614-445-8841
Fax: 614-445-8843 800-558-8841
www.ezzo.com
Sausage, pepperoni
Owner: Bill Ezzo
Contact: Mike Spicer
mspicer@ezzo.com
Plant Manager of Operation: Mike Spicer
Number Employees: 10-19

4195 F & A Dairy Products Inc
212 State Road 35 S
Dresser, WI 54009
715-755-3485
Fax: 715-755-3480 800-657-8582
info@fadairy.com www.fadairy.com
Cheese including mozzarella, provolone, romano and parmesan; importer of pecorino romano
President: Chuck Engdahl
chuck@fadairy.net
Controller: Clyde Loch
CFO: Jay Benusa
QC: Ralph Ramos
Sales: Chris Slavek
Sales: Renzo Sciortino
Human Resources: Carl Gutierrez
VP Wisconsin Operations: Mike Breault
VP New Mexico Operations: Bob Snyder
Estimated Sales: $10-24.9 Million
Number Employees: 50-99
Type of Packaging: Food Service
Other Locations:
  F&A Dairy Products
  Las Cruces NM
Brands:
  F&A

4196 F & S Produce Co Inc
500 W Elmer Rd
Vineland, NJ 08360
800-886-3316
www.freshcutproduce.com
Fresh, whole and pre-cut produce including peppers, onions, lettuce, carrots, spinach, cabbage, tomatoes and cucumbers; brine products including vegetables, cherry and bell peppers, onions and jalapenos; also, salad, vegetable traysand fruit snacks
President: Salvatore Pipitone
CFO: Maddalena Lori
Purchasing Agent: Ted Brode
Estimated Sales: $85 Million
Number Employees: 100-249
Square Footage: 650000
Type of Packaging: Consumer, Food Service, Private Label, Bulk

4197 F B Purnell Sausage Co Inc
6931 Shelbyville Rd
Simpsonville, KY 40067-6511
502-722-5626
Fax: 502-722-5586 800-626-1512
Sausage links, patties and slices.
President: Todd Purnell
tpurnell@itsgood.com
Chairman/CEO: Allen Purnell Jr.
Controller: Dave Fowler
Estimated Sales: $39 Million
Number Employees: 100-249
Number of Brands: 1
Type of Packaging: Consumer, Food Service
Brands:
  Old Folks

4198 (HQ)F B Washburn Candy Corp
137 Perkins Ave
P.O. Box 3277
Brockton, MA 02302-3891
508-588-0820
Fax: 508-588-2205 www.fbwashburncandy.com
Manufactured and distributor of hard candies, specializing in ribbon candies; offer rebagging, private label and wrapping services.
President: James Gilson
jamesgilson@fbwashburncandy.com
Treasurer: Douglas Gilson
Estimated Sales: $10 Million
Number Employees: 20-49
Number of Brands: 2
Square Footage: 150000
Type of Packaging: Consumer, Private Label
Brands:
  Sevigny
  Washburn

4199 F C C
700 NE Highway 99w
Mcminnville, OR 97128-2711
503-472-2157
Fax: 503-472-3821
Milk, butter and powdered milk
President: Dan Bansen
CEO: Michael Anderson
manderson@farmerscoop.org
Estimated Sales: $4.9 Million
Number Employees: 5-9
Square Footage: 224000
Type of Packaging: Consumer, Food Service, Bulk

4200 F W Bryce Inc
8 Pond Rd
Gloucester, MA 01930-1833
978-283-7080
Fax: 978-283-7647 fwbryce@fwbryce.com
www.fwbryce.com
Frozen seafood
President: Kerry Amero
kerryamero@fwbryce.com
CFO: Paul Cantrell
General Counsel: Ian Moores
Logistics Manager: Frank Souza
Quality Assurance Manager: Justin Moores
Director Sales: Glenn Hale
VP Sales: Joe Flammia
Operations Manager: Frank Souza
Warehousing/Logistics: Ralph Pierce
Number Employees: 10-19
Square Footage: 26000

4201 F&Y Enterprises
1205 Karl Ct
Suite 115
Wauconda, IL 60084-1090
847-526-0620
Manufacturer and exporter of hickory smoked meat snacks including sausage sticks and beef jerky
President: Frank Vitek
VP: Bonnie Vitek
Estimated Sales: $2 Million
Number Employees: 40
Parent Co: F&Y Enterprises
Type of Packaging: Consumer, Food Service, Private Label
Brands:
  Texas Brand

4202 F. Gavina & Sons
2700 Fruitland Ave
Vernon, CA 90058
800-428-4627
hello@gavina.com www.gavina.com
Gourmet coffee
CEO: Pedro Gavina
VP, Marketing: Leonor Gavina-Valls
VP, Operations: Carlos Fandino
Brands:
  Gavina
  Don Francisco's
  Caffe La Llave

4203 FAGE USA Dairy Ind Inc
1 Opportunity Dr
Johnstown Industrial Park
Johnstown, NY 12095
518-762-5912
Fax: 518-762-5918 866-962-5912
usa.fage
Greek yogurt and feta cheese

Manager: Antonios Maridakis
Vice President: Ioannis Ravanis
info@fageusa.com
Number Employees: 250-499
Type of Packaging: Consumer

4204 FBC Industries
1933 N Meacham Rd # 550
Suite 550
Schaumburg, IL 60173-4342
847-839-0880
Fax: 847-839-0884 888-322-4637
sales@fbcindustries.com www.fbcindustries.com
Industrial ingredients including dipotassium phosphate, calcium chloride, sodium and potassuim citrates, lactates and benzoates used as buffering agents, emulsifers, firming agents, preservatives, antioxidants, flavorings, etc
President: Robert Bloom
rbloom@fbcindustries.com
VP: John Tramontana
Estimated Sales: $1-3 Million
Number Employees: 10-19
Type of Packaging: Bulk

4205 FDI Inc
5440 Saint Charles Rd
Suite 201
Berkeley, IL 60163-1231
708-544-1880
Fax: 708-544-4117 info@fdiusa.net
www.fdiusa.net
Canned and frozen foods; uses freeze-drying to preserve herbs, fruits, vegetables, spices, meat, pasta and fish
President: Joseph Lucas
National Sales Manager: Barbara Laffey
Manager: Terry Bliudzius
info@fdiusa.net
Estimated Sales: $1.3 Million
Number Employees: 10-19
Parent Co: Groneweg Group
Type of Packaging: Consumer

4206 FIFO Innovations
107-2999 Underhill Ave
Burnaby, BC V5A 3C2
Canada
778-383-6200
800-453-3436
sales@fifobottle.com www.fifobottle.com
Sauce dispensing solutions for restaurants
General Manager: Katie Third

4207 FLAT Tech Inc.
1 North Wacker Dr
Suite 4400
Chicago, IL 60606-2833
855-999-3528
www.flattech.com
Table-stabilising technology
Managing Director: Mike Drake
CFO: Barry Mancell
COO: Ozcan Ozagir
Brands:
  FLAT

4208 FNI Group LLC
188 Lake Street
Sherborn, MA 01770-1606
508-655-4175
Fax: 508-655-8816
All natural cookies that are cholesterol and lactose free
President/Founder: Josephine Ho
Estimated Sales: $200.00 K
Number Employees: 2
Brands:
  Essen Smart Gluten Free
  Essen Smart Single Cookie 2
  Essen Smart Single Cookie 3
  Essen Smart Soy Cookies

4209 FODY Food Co.
376 Victoria Ave
Suite 220
Westmount, QC H3Z 1C3
Canada
818-835-1850
flavorproducers.com
Low FODMAP products for people with irritable bowel syndrome
Founder & CEO: Steven Singer
COO: Sean Surkis

697

Food Manufacturers / A-Z

Year Founded: 2016
Number of Brands: 1
Number of Products: 24
Type of Packaging: Consumer
Brands:
   FODY

4210 FOND Bone Broth
San Antonio, TX 78220
www.fondbonebroth.com
Bone broth tonics
Founder: Alysa Seeland

4211 FW Thurston
2 Steamboat Wharf Road
11 Thurston Rd.
Bernard, ME 04612-0178
207-244-3320
Fax: 207-244-3320
Fresh lobster
President: Michael Radcliffe
Estimated Sales: $3-5 Million
Number Employees: 20-49

4212 Fa Lu Cioli
553 Lehigh Ave
Union, NJ 07083-7976
908-258-8651
Manufacturer of a variety of meats.
Number Employees: 1-4

4213 Fabbri Sausage Mfg Co
166 N Aberdeen St
Chicago, IL 60607-1606
312-829-6363
Fax: 312-829-0396 info@fabbrisausage.com
www.fabbrisausage.com
Italian meats and other pizza supplies including italian sausage, meatballs, italian roast beef, italian style gravy, italian chili.
President: Ray Fabbri
info@fabbrisausage.com
Estimated Sales: $2.5-5 Million
Number Employees: 20-49
Square Footage: 100000
Type of Packaging: Consumer, Food Service, Private Label, Bulk

4214 Faber Foods and Aeronautics
1153 Evergreen Parkway
Suite M105
Evergreen, CO 80439-9501
800-237-3255
Fax: 303-670-0971
Low-fat muesli cereal including strawberry/banana, cranberry/apricot, papaya/peach, blueberry/peach, raspberry/apple, etc.; also, custom blend cereals; exporter of extruded crisp rice, edible seeds, canned oats dried fruit raisins andnuts
President: Maria Faber
Estimated Sales: $300,000-500,000
Number Employees: 10-19
Square Footage: 40000
Type of Packaging: Consumer, Food Service, Private Label, Bulk
Brands:
   Low Fat Body Mueslix

4215 Fabio Imports
6048 De La Rosa Ln
Oceanside, CA 92057-2101
760-726-7040
Fax: 760-726-5731
Italian specialties
Owner/President: Fabio Peraro
Estimated Sales: $1 Million
Number Employees: 35
Square Footage: 12000

4216 Fabrique Delices
1610 Delta Ct
Suite 1
Hayward, CA 94544-7043
510-441-9500
Fax: 510-441-9700 vanessa@fabriquedelices.com
www.fabriquedelices.com
Foie gras, terrine, block and mousse, smoked meats, mousses
President & Co-Owner: Marc Poinsignon
Co-Owner: Antonio Pinheiro
VP, Sales & Marketing: Sebastien Espinasse
Estimated Sales: $2.5-5 Million
Number Employees: 20-49

4217 Faidley Seafood
203 North Paca St
Baltimore, MD 21201
410-727-4898
Fax: 410-837-6495 faidleyseafood@gmail.com
www.faidleyscrabcakes.com
Seafood
President: Nancy Devine
Estimated Sales: $3-5 Million
Number Employees: 10-19

4218 Fair Oaks Farms LLC
7600 95th St
Pleasant Prairie, WI 53158
262-947-0320
Fax: 262-947-0348 800-528-8615
fofcontact@fairoaksfarms.com
www.fairoaksfarms.com
Fresh, ready-to-cook or fully cooked meats including; sausage patties, links & crumbles; bacon strips and bits; hot dogs & smoked sausages; ready-to-cook beef patties, fully-cooked beef patties; pork ribbette and chopette; chickenbreasts, strips and nuggets; salisbury steak; meat loaf
President & CEO: Michael Thompson
Senior Vice President: Joseph Freda
Vice President: Michael Thompson
R&D Manager: Jeannette Falls
Production Supervisor: Sonia Valle
Year Founded: 1985
Estimated Sales: $111.5 Million
Number Employees: 100-249
Square Footage: 55000

4219 Fair Scones
P.O.Box 177
Medina, WA 98039-0177
425-486-3334
Fax: 425-398-0301 800-588-9160
pgimness@conifer-inc.com www.conifer-inc.com
Bean soup and chili mixes, bread, breakfast, dessert and beverage mixes
President: Michael Maher
Contact: John Weber
jweber@conifer-inc.com
Estimated Sales: $10-20 Million
Number Employees: 20-49

4220 Fairbury Food Products
601 2nd St
Fairbury, NE 68352
402-729-3379
Fax: 402-729-2437
Bacon bits
President: Arden Schacht
Number Employees: 20-49
Parent Co: Fairbury Food
Type of Packaging: Food Service, Private Label

4221 Fairchester Snacks Corp
100 Lafayette Ave
White Plains, NY 10603-1612
914-761-2824
www.nysnacks.com
Salty biscuits
Owner: John Barisano
Estimated Sales: $300,000-500,000
Number Employees: 5-9

4222 Fairfield Farm Kitchens
309 Battles Street
Brockton, MA 02301
508-584-9300
Fax: 508-580-9910
Frozen organic soups, entrees, side dishes, sauces, gravies, layer, sheet and pound cakes, etc
Founder/Chairman: Norman Cloutier
Contact: Stephen Korotsky
skorotsky@fairfieldfarmkitchens.com
Year Founded: 2001
Estimated Sales: $20-50 Million
Number Employees: 100-249
Square Footage: 170000
Brands:
   Basic American Frozen Foods
   Fairfield Farm

4223 Fairhaven Cooperative Flour Mill
1115 Railroad Ave
Bellingham, WA 98225-5007
360-757-9947
Fax: 360-734-9947 fairhavenflour@q.com
www.fairhavenflour.com
Manufacturer and exporter of flour including whole grain, wheat, rye, corn, buckwheat, rice, etc
Manager: Bill Distler
Estimated Sales: $1-2.5 Million
Number Employees: 1-4
Type of Packaging: Consumer, Bulk

4224 Fairlife
1001 W Adams St.
Chicago, IL 60607
fairlife.com
Milk and milk products including creamers and protein shakes.
CEO: Tim Doelman
Year Founded: 2012
Parent Co: Coca-Cola Co.
Type of Packaging: Private Label

4225 Fairmont Foods Of Minnesota
905 E 4th St
Fairmont, MN 56031-4014
507-238-9001
Fax: 507-238-9560 www.downsfoodgroup.com
Frozen meals including; entrees, side dishes, soups, sauces and meal kits
President: William Bosshard
william.bosshard@fairmontfoods.com
CEO: Larry McGuire
CFO: William Bosshard
Director Quality Assurance: John Heuer
VP of Operations: Jerald Nasalroad
Production Manager: Pat Meschke
Purchasing: Greg Korth
Estimated Sales: $25.5 Million
Number Employees: 250-499
Square Footage: 152000

4226 Fairmont Snacks Group
6133 Rockside Rd
Suite 208
Independence, OH 44131-2244
216-642-3336
Potato chips, peanuts and snack items
Owner: E. Kelley
Contact: Mark Johnson
mark.johnson@fornuts.com
Estimated Sales: $59,000
Number Employees: 2

4227 Fairview Dairy Inc
1562 Mission Rd
Latrobe, PA 15650-2845
724-537-7111
Fax: 724-537-7249 mblystone@valleydairy.net
www.valleydairy.net
Processor and wholesaler/distributor of ice cream; serving the food service market
President: Melissa Blystone
Vice President: Melissa Blystone
Marketing Director: Virgina Greubel
Contact: Lujean Wasnesky
lwasnesky@valleydairy.net
Director of Operations: Tom Webb
Plant Manager: Ray Sneets
Number Employees: 250-499
Square Footage: 24000
Parent Co: Fairview Dairy
Type of Packaging: Consumer, Food Service
Brands:
   Ice Cream Joe
   Valley Dairy

4228 Fairview Swiss Cheese
1734 Perry Hwy
Fredonia, PA 16124-2720
724-475-4154
Fax: 724-475-4777 www.fairviewsisscheese.com
Cheeses
President: Richard Koller
rkoller54@aol.com
Estimated Sales: $2 Million
Number Employees: 10-19
Square Footage: 80000
Parent Co: John Koller and Son, Inc
Type of Packaging: Consumer, Food Service, Private Label, Bulk

4229 Fairwinds Gourmet Coffee
1731 Aviation Blvd.
Lincoln, CA 95648
916-543-0493
Fax: 603-668-0888 800-829-1300
rogers_service@rogersfamilyco.com
Gourmet Coffee and tea

Food Manufacturers / A-Z

President: Kathy Hybsch
Estimated Sales: $2.5-5 Million
Number Employees: 1-4
Parent Co: JBR Gourmet Foods
Type of Packaging: Bulk
Brands:
   East India Coffee and Tea
   Fairwinds Coffee
   Organic Coffee Co

4230 Fairytale Brownies
4610 E Cotton Center Blvd
Suite #100
Phoenix, AZ 85040-8898
                602-489-5100
   Fax: 602-489-5133 800-324-7982
   juliej@brownies.com www.brownies.com
Brownies, cookies
Co- Founder: Eileen Spitalny
Marketing: Julie Gaffney
Manager: Kim Silva
Number Employees: 20-49

4231 Falafel Republic
800 Hingham St Rockland
Needham Heights, MA 02494
                781-878-6027
   Fax: 781-444-1420 nancy@originalrangoon.com
Dairy-free, gluten-free, vegetarian, helath, fitness and energy bars, other snacks, foodservice.
Marketing: Greg Bukuras

4232 Falcon Rice Mill Inc
600 S Avenue D
PO Box 771
Crowley, LA 70526-5606
                337-783-3825
   Fax: 337-783-1568 800-738-7423
               www.falconrice.com
Long and medium grain rice, jasmine rice, popcorn rice.
President: Mona Trahan
CFO: Robert Trahan
VP, Sales: Charles Trahan
General Manager: Tom Dew
Estimated Sales: $20-50 Million
Number Employees: 20-49
Number of Brands: 6
Type of Packaging: Consumer, Food Service, Private Label, Bulk
Brands:
   Cajun Country
   Falcon
   Home Country
   Jackpot
   Laredo
   Toro

4233 Falcone's Cookie Land LTD
1632 61st St
Brooklyn, NY 11204-2109
                718-236-4200
   Fax: 718-259-6133 www.falconebaking.com
Regular and dietetic cookies; also, crackers, biscuits, breadsticks and flatbread
Owner: Angelo Falcone
falconecookie@aol.com
Vice President: Angelo Falcone
Estimated Sales: $5-9.9 Million
Number Employees: 50-99
Type of Packaging: Consumer, Food Service, Private Label, Bulk
Brands:
   Falcone's
   Falcone's Baked Goods
   Falcone's Cookies
   Falcone's Flatbread

4234 Fall Creek Vineyards
1402 San Antonio St # 200
Austin, TX 78701-1623
                512-476-4477
   Fax: 512-476-6116 www.fcv.com
Wine
Owner: Ed Auler
ed@fcv.com
Co-founder: Susan Auler
Corporate Accountant: Suzette Kramer
VP: Chad Auler
VP Marketting: Chad Auler
VP Sales: Dani Seelig
ed@fcv.com
Operations Manager: Roy Nobles

Estimated Sales: $3-5 Million
Number Employees: 5-9
Type of Packaging: Bulk

4235 Fall River Wild Rice
41577 Osprey Road
Fall River Mills, CA 96028
                530-336-5222
   Fax: 530-336-5265 800-626-4366
               www.frwr.com
Wild rice
General Manager: Walt Oiler
Estimated Sales: $420,000
Number Employees: 4
Square Footage: 56000
Brands:
   Fall River

4236 (HQ)Falla Imports
PO Box 1532
Greenville, ME 04441-1532
                609-476-4106
        Fax: 609-476-0412
Importers of coffee
President: Roderick Falla
Number Employees: 1-4

4237 Fallwood Corp
75 S Broadway
Suite 494
White Plains, NY 10601-4413
                914-304-4065
   Fax: 914-304-4063 ana@fallwoodcorp.com
            www.fallwoodcorp.com
Manufacturer and supplier of all natural nutraceutical ingredients and raw materials. All glanulars-Bovine and Porcine Enzymes
President/CEO: Jorge Millan
Vice President: Graciela Rocchia
Sales: Wayne Battenfield
Manager: Anne-Marie Rodriguez
anna@fallwoodcorp.com
Adminstration: Anne Marie Rodriguez
Estimated Sales: Under $500,000
Number Employees: 1-4
Parent Co: Loboratorio Opoterapico Argentino

4238 Fama Sales Co
450 W 44th St
New York, NY 10036-5205
                212-757-9433
   Fax: 212-765-4193 800-682-0425
Food products
Owner: Ugo R Quazzo
famasales@aol.com
Estimated Sales: $1-2.5 Million
Number Employees: 10-19

4239 Famarco Limited
1381 Air Rail Ave
Virginia Beach, VA 23455-3301
                757-460-3573
        Fax: 757-460-2621
Raw material importer and processor for spice, botanicals and carob
President: Bruce Martin
bruce@famarco.com
VP: Ken Hartfelder
Quality Control: Darrick Bargher
Marketing: Mark Herrick
Plant Manager: James O'Neil
Estimated Sales: $10 Million
Number Employees: 20-49
Square Footage: 80000
Parent Co: B&K International
Type of Packaging: Private Label, Bulk
Brands:
   Martin's Virginia Roast
   Virginia Roast

4240 Family Food Company
6801 De Bie Dr
Paramount, CA 90723-2027
                310-715-2698
        Fax: 562-272-8585
Salads; jams; coffee; sugar; sauces; liquid smoke
Type of Packaging: Private Label

4241 Family Sweets Candy Company
1099 Pratt Boulevard
Elk Grove Village, IL 60007-5120
                336-788-5068
   Fax: 336-784-6708 800-334-1607
Candy

President: LeRoy Mansson

4242 Family Tree Farms
41646 Road 62
Reedley, CA 93654-9124
                559-591-8394
   Fax: 559-595-7795 866-352-8671
           www.familytreefarms.com
Plumcots, white peaches and nectarines, donut peaches and nectarines, yellow peaches and nectarines, apricots, apriums, plums, blueberries, cherries, satsumas
President: David Jackson
djackson@familytreefarms.com
CFO: Dan Clenney
Executive Director of Global Development: Gerome Raco
Director of Research & Development: Eric Wuhl
Quality Control: Mary Ortiz
Director of Marketing: Don Goforth
Estimated Sales: $20-50 Million
Number Employees: 250-499
Brands:
   Eat Smart
   Great Whites
   Flavor Safari
   Farmers Market
   Summerripe
   River Run

4243 Famous Chili Inc
1421 N 7th St
Fort Smith, AR 72901-1320
                479-782-0096
   Fax: 501-782-6825 www.famouschili.com
Chili and salsa
President: David Korkames
famouschili@earthlink.net
Estimated Sales: $5-10 Million
Number Employees: 5-9
Square Footage: 20000
Type of Packaging: Consumer, Food Service, Private Label
Brands:
   Famous
   Four Star
   Heat & Serve
   Star

4244 Famous Specialties Co
55 Saratoga Blvd # B
Island Park, NY 11558-1114
                516-889-9099
   Fax: 516-889-9099 800-894-9218
        famousspecialties@gmail.com
Raw prepared strudel dough
President: Craig Tropp
ctropp@famousspecialties.com
Estimated Sales: $2.5-5 Million
Number Employees: 1-4
Square Footage: 7500
Brands:
   Barney's Town & Country
   Beef International
   Blue Ridge Farms
   Brandt
   Caesar's
   Creative Bakers
   Fancy Foods
   Fancy's Finest
   Fantasia
   Gilda
   Heath & Heather
   High Meadows
   Leaves
   Redi Prep Strudel
   Silver Lake
   Stahl Meyer
   Sweet Street

4245 Fancy Farms Popcorn
2893 County Road 675
Bernie, MO 63822
                573-276-3315
   Fax: 573-276-2287 800-833-8154
        sales@fancyfarmpopcorn.com
        www.fancyfarmpopcorn.com
Portion-packed popcorn
President: Chris Tanner
Sales: J Smith
Estimated Sales: $500,000-$1 Million
Number Employees: 5-9
Parent Co: St. Francis River Farming
Type of Packaging: Food Service, Bulk

Food Manufacturers / A-Z

Brands:
  Fancy Farm

4246 Fancy Lebanese Bakery
2573 Agricola St
Halifax, NS B3K 4C4
Canada
    902-429-0400
Fax: 902-429-0403 fancylebanese@eastlink.ca
    fancylebanesebakery.com
Pita bread and submarine sandwich buns
President: Mary Laba
Manager: Maura Fougere
Estimated Sales: $2.6 Million
Number Employees: 20
Type of Packaging: Consumer, Food Service, Private Label
Brands:
  Fancy Lebanese Bakery
  Flb

4247 Fancy's Candy's
5601 Twin Creeks Trl
Rougemont, NC 27572-8657
    919-644-2573
Fax: 919-732-2070 888-403-2629
    www.sininatin.com
Toffee, milk chocolate, dark chocolate, hazelnuts, white chocolate, and pecans
President: Anne Keller
anne.keller@fancyscandys.com
Estimated Sales: $1-3 Million
Number Employees: 1-4

4248 Fancypants Bakery
160 Elm St # 2
Unit 2
Walpole, MA 02081-1934
    508-660-1140
Manufacturer of cookies.
Principal Owner: Justin Housman
President: Maura Duggan
Number Employees: 20-49

4249 (HQ)Fanestil Packing Company
1542 S Highway 99
Emporia, KS 66801
    620-342-6354
Fax: 620-342-8190 800-658-1652
    www.fanestils.com
Sausage, ham and bacon
President: Scott Sanders
CEO: Dan Smoots
General Manager: Jan Smoots
Estimated Sales: 25,948,000
Number Employees: 52
Type of Packaging: Consumer, Food Service
Brands:
  Fanestil

4250 Fannie May Fine Chocolate
2457 W. North Avenue
Melrose Park, IL 60160
Oakdale, MN 55128
    80- 33- 362
    800-999-3629
customerservice@fanniemay.com
    www.fanniemay.com
Chocolates
President: Terry Mitchell
CEO: David Taiclet
Partner: Michael Givens
Partner: Ulysses Bridgeman
Partner: Rodney Burwell
Number Employees: 5-9
Parent Co: Archibald Candy Corporation
Other Locations:
  Fanny May Fine Chocolates
  Bloomington IN
  Fanny May Fine Chocolates
  Champaign IL
  Fanny May Fine Chocolates
  Peoria IL
  Fanny May Fine Chocolates
  Rockford IL
  Fanny May Fine Chocolates
  Indianapolis IN
  Fanny May Fine Chocolates
  Greenwood IN
  Fanny May Fine Chocolates
  Avon IN
  Fanny May Fine Chocolates
  Terr Haute IN
  Fanny May Fine Chocolates
  Davenport IA
  Fanny May Fine Chocolates
  Springfield IL
  Fanny May Fine Chocolates
  Bourbonnais IL
  Fanny May Fine Chocolates
  Portage MI
  Fanny May Fine Chocolates
  Janesville WI
Brands:
  Fanny May Fine Chocolates
  Harry London
  Fanny Farmer

4251 Fantasia
PO Box 1267
Sedalia, MO 65302-1267
    660-827-1172
Fax: 660-827-3653
Frozen cakes
President: Robert Wright
VP Sales: Thad Bagnato
Plant Manager: Trent Wanamaker
Purchasing Agent: Mike Mallory
Estimated Sales: $10-20,000,000
Number Employees: 150

4252 Fantastic World Foods
313 Iron Horse Way
Providence, RI 02908
    www.fantasticfoods.com
Vegetarian convenience foods including soups and rice; importer of rice.
Estimated Sales: $20-50 Million
Number Employees: 30
Square Footage: 150000
Type of Packaging: Consumer
Brands:
  Fantastic
  Jumping Black Beans
  Nature's Burger Mix
  Tabouli Salad Mix
  Tofu Burger Mix
  Tofu Scrambler Mix

4253 Fantasy Chocolates
2045 High Ridge Rd
Boynton Beach, FL 33426-8713
    561-276-9007
Fax: 561-265-0027 800-804-4962
fantasychocolate@aol.com
    www.williamsandbennett.com
Manufacturer and exporter of chocolate novelties and gourmet pretzels including chocolate, keylime, chocolate pizza, caramel and chocolate apple
President: Becky Gardner
Contact: Bill Gardner
b.gardner@williamsandbennett.com
Products: Bill Gardner
Estimated Sales: $1,2,000,000
Number Employees: 1-4
Type of Packaging: Consumer, Private Label, Bulk
Brands:
  Chocolate Oreos
  Chocolate Pizza
  Forbidden Fruit
  Keylime Graham Crackers
  Logo Chocolates
  Novelty Chocolates
  Party Pretzels
  Peanut Butter Dream

4254 Fantasy Cookie Company
12800 Arroyo Street
Sylmar, CA 91342-5318
    818-361-6901
Fax: 818-365-0040 800-354-4488
    www.fantasycookie.com
Cookies including low fat, fruit juice sweetened and holiday; also, gingerbread houses
President/CEO: Joseph Semder
VP Sales: Richard Semder
Estimated Sales: $2.5-5 Million
Number Employees: 5-9
Type of Packaging: Private Label, Bulk

4255 Fantazzmo Fun Stuff
425 N Martingale Road
Suite 1680
Schaumburg, IL 60173-2214
    847-413-4036
Fax: 847-413-0500
Novelty candy
VP Marketing: Deirdre Gonzalez
Brands:
  Candy Whistler
  Slide Pops
  Sport Totoe 'ems
  Tote 'ems
  Wonka
  Wonka Pixy Stix Mixers
  Xtreme Nerds

4256 Fantini Baking Co Inc
375 Washington St
Haverhill, MA 01832-5377
    978-891-5205
Fax: 978-373-6250 800-343-2110
    www.fantinibakery.com
Breads
President: Robert Fantini
robert@fantinibakery.com
Chief Marketing Officer: Joe Fantini
Estimated Sales: $1-2,500,000
Number Employees: 100-249

4257 Fantis Foods Inc
60 Triangle Blvd
Carlstadt, NJ 07072-2701
    201-933-6200
Fax: 201-933-8797 info@fantisfoods.com
    www.fantisfoods.com
Olive oil, olives, cheese, seafood, gourmet, pasta, mineral water, cookies and baked goods, gyros, frozen pastries, herbs and spices, confectionary, bean and rice, drinks
President: George Makris
fantisfoods@aol.com
VP/CFO: Jerry Makris
VP/Manager: Steve Makris
Sales Executive/Sales Manager: Bill Paelekanos
Estimated Sales: $6 Million
Number Employees: 20-49
Square Footage: 210000
Type of Packaging: Consumer

4258 Far Niente Winery
1350 Acacia Dr
Oakville, CA 94562
    707-944-2861
Fax: 707-944-2312 info@farniente.com
    www.farniente.com
Wines
Partner: Beth Nickel
Partner: Erik Nickel
Contact: Aaron Fishleder
afishleder@farniente.com
Estimated Sales: $10-20,000,000
Number Employees: 100-249
Parent Co: GI Manager L.P.
Brands:
  Bella Union
  Dolce
  Enroute
  Far Niente
  Nickel & Nickel

4259 Far West Meats
7759 Victoria Ave
PO Box 248
Highland, CA 92346-5637
    909-864-1990
Fax: 909-864-0554
Processor and exporter of meat products including smoked sausage, knockwurst, bologna, salami, bratwurst, frankfurters, kielbasa, beef, pork and smoked pork and turkey parts
Owner: Tom Serrato
raemica@pacbell.net
President: Michael Serrato
CFO/Vice President: Wade Snyder
Estimated Sales: $13 Million
Number Employees: 50-99
Square Footage: 50000
Type of Packaging: Consumer, Private Label, Bulk
Brands:
  Far West Meats

4260 Far West Rice Inc
3455 Nelson Road
Nelson, CA 95938
    530-891-1339
Fax: 530-891-0723 sales@farwestrice.com
    www.farwestrice.com
Mill, paakage and market rice for food service and retail demands.
President: C W Johnson
Owner: Greg Johnson
Research & Development: Steve Ross
Marketing Director: Greg Johnson
Operations Manager: Steve Ross

Estimated Sales: $10 Million
Number Employees: 50
Number of Brands: 10
Number of Products: 100
Type of Packaging: Consumer, Food Service, Private Label, Bulk
Brands:
 Calrose Rice
 Fukusuke Rice
 Komachi Premium Rice
 Valley Sun Organic Brown Rice

4261 Farallon Fisheries Co
207 S Maple Ave
S San Francisco, CA 94080-6305
650-583-3474
Fax: 650-583-0137
Seafood
Manager: Juan De Alva
Contact: Aiden Coburn
Manager: Juan De
juande@farallonfisheries.com
Estimated Sales: $500,000-$1,000,000
Number Employees: 5-9
Brands:
 Farallon Foods

4262 Farbest Foods Inc
1155 W 12th Ave
Jasper, IN 47546
812-683-4200
rdownes@farbestfoods.com
www.farbestfoods.com
Turkey and turkey products
Quality Assurance Director: Shawn Archie
Sales & Marketing: Ryan Downes
Plant Manager: Jean Munger
Estimated Sales: $85 Million
Number Employees: 500-999
Number of Brands: 3
Type of Packaging: Consumer, Food Service, Private Label, Bulk
Brands:
 Country Festival
 Farbest Foods
 Heritage Pride

4263 (HQ)Farbest-Tallman Foods Corp
160 Summit Ave # 2
#3101
Montvale, NJ 07645-1721
201-573-4900
Fax: 201-573-0404 www.farbest.com
Manufacturer of dairy and soy proteins, carotenoids, vitamins, sweeteners and nutraceuticals.
President/Chairman: Daniel Meloro
dmeloro@farbest.com
Senior Vice President: Bob Claire
Senior Vice President: Chip Jackson
Vice President: Brent Lambert
Vice President: Paul Guzman
Quality Assurance & Compliance Manager: Shakirul Alom
Sales Director: Michael Sepela
Human Resources Manager: Teresa Lauricella
Director of Operations: Frank Volpe
Dir. Product Management & Supply Chain: Kevin Burke
Estimated Sales: $20-50 Million
Number Employees: 20-49
Number of Brands: 1
Type of Packaging: Consumer, Bulk
Other Locations:
 Kentucky Office
 Louisville KY
 California Office
 Huntington Beach CA
 Farbest Brands Warehousing Center
 Edison NJ
 Farbest Brands Warehousing Center
 Columbus OH
 Farbest Brands Warehousing Center
 Carson CA
Brands:
 Farbest

4264 Fare Foods Corp
208 Cherry Lake Rd
Du Quoin, IL 62832-1248
618-542-2155
Fax: 618-542-2396 www.farefoods.com
Fresh fruits and vegetables
President: Ron Porter
rporter@farefoods.com

Estimated Sales: $10-20 Million
Number Employees: 20-49

4265 Farella-Park Vineyards
2222 N 3rd Ave
Napa, CA 94558-3840
707-254-9489
info@farella.com
www.farella.com
Wines
Owner: Tom Farella
Winemaker/Farm Manager: Tom Farella
Estimated Sales: Less Than $500,000
Number Employees: 1-4

4266 Farfelu Vineyards
13058 Crest Hill Road
Flint Hill, VA 22627-1814
540-364-2930
Fax: 540-364-3930
Wines
Owner: C Raney
Estimated Sales: $500,000-$1,000,000
Number Employees: 1-4

4267 Faribault Foods, Inc.
3401 Park Ave. NW
Fairbault, MN 55021
507-331-1400
ConsumeResponse@faribaultfoods.com
www.faribaultfoods.com
Canned vegetables, sauced beans, refried beans, baked beans, pasta, soup, chili, and organic and Mexican specialties.
President/CEO: Reid MacDonald
CFO: Mike Weber
Executive VP, Sales/Marketing: Frank Lynch
Year Founded: 1888
Estimated Sales: $164 Million
Number Employees: 5
Number of Brands: 8
Parent Co: Arizona Canning Company, LLC
Type of Packaging: Consumer, Private Label, Bulk
Other Locations:
 Faribault Foods Distribution
 Faribault MN
 Faribault Foods Plant
 Cokato MN
Brands:
 Butter Kernel®
 Chilliman®
 Kuner's®
 Luck's®
 Mrs. Grimes®
 SunVista®
 Pride®
 S & W Beans®

4268 Farm & Oven Snacks
Boulder, CO 80304
info@farmandoven.com
farmandoven.com
Vegetable brownies, muffins and cakes
Co-Founder: Kay Allison
Co-Founder: Mike Senackerib
Number of Products: 8

4269 Farm 2 Market
Pier 45 Shed B
San Francisco, CA 94118
Fax: 866-821-9598 800-447-2967
www.farm-2-market.com
Seafood including farm raised shrimp, freshwater prawns, scallops, crawfish and oysters; importer of Australian crawfish and freshwater prawns
President: Marshall Schnider
Estimated Sales: $3-5 Million
Number Employees: 10-19
Type of Packaging: Consumer, Food Service
Brands:
 Sweet-Water

4270 (HQ)Farm Boy Food Svc
2761 N Kentucky Ave
Evansville, IN 47711-6203
812-428-8436
Fax: 812-428-8432 800-852-3976
www.farmboy-foodservice.com
Established in 1952. Manufacturer of beef and pork; wholesaler/distributor of frozen, refrigerated and dry food products, meat, equipment and fixtures. Specializes in pizza toppings and equipment.
President/Co-Owner: Robert Bonenberger
VP/Co-Owner: Richard Bonenberger

Estimated Sales: $38 Million
Number Employees: 50-99
Type of Packaging: Consumer, Food Service, Private Label

4271 Farm Fresh to You
2970 E La Palma Ave Q
Anaheim, CA 92806
800-796-6009
contactus@farmfreshtoyou.com
www.farmfreshtoyou.com
Organic fruits and vegetables

4272 Farm Pak Products Inc
7840 Old Bailey Hwy
Spring Hope, NC 27882
252-459-3101
Fax: 252-459-9020 800-367-2799
sales@farmpak.com www.farmpak.com
Produce including sweet potatoes.
Vice President: Johnny Barnes
International Sales Manager: Jose "Pepe" Calderon
Packing House Supervisor: Frank Salinas
Year Founded: 1969
Estimated Sales: $20-50 Million
Number Employees: 100-249
Type of Packaging: Consumer, Bulk

4273 FarmGro Organic Foods
101-2445 13th Avenue
Regina, SK S4P 0W1
Canada
306-751-2449
Fax: 306-721-3130
Organic food
President: Bruce Johnson
CFO: Dennis Puff
Purchase Manager: Tim Beard

4274 FarmSoy Company
116 Second Road
Summertown, TN 38483
931-964-2411
www.farmsoy.com
Soymilk and tofu
President: Thomas Elliot
VP: Barbara Elliot
Estimated Sales: $50,000
Number Employees: 7
Square Footage: 1200

4275 Farmdale Creamery Inc
1049 W Base Line St
San Bernardino, CA 92411-2310
909-889-3002
Fax: 909-888-2541 800-346-7306
www.farmdale.net
Dairy products including sour cream, sour cream dressing, buttermilk, cheese, whey, cream and butter
Owner: Nick Sibilio
VP & General Manager: Michael Shotts
Customer Service: Wendy Zimmerman
Quality Assurance Manager: Josie Emery
Human Resource Manager: Sam Jimenez
nicksibilio@farmdale.net
VP of Operations: Norman Shotts
nicksibilio@farmdale.net
Production Manager: Shannon Shunk
Planning & Procurement: Norman Crow
Estimated Sales: $8 Million
Number Employees: 50-99
Square Footage: 440000
Type of Packaging: Consumer, Food Service, Private Label, Bulk

4276 Farmer Brothers Company
1912 Farmer Brothers Dr
Northlake, TX 76226
682-549-6600
www.farmerbros.com
Coffee, tea, and culinary products.
President, CEO & Director: Michael Keown
Chairman: Randy Clark
Treasurer & Chief Financial Officer: David Robson
SVP & General Manager, Direct Ship: Scott Siers
General Counsel & Assistant Secretary: Thomas Mattei, Jr.
Secretary: Teri Witteman
Chief Operating Officer: Ellen Iobst
Year Founded: 1912
Estimated Sales: $545.9 Million
Number Employees: 1,800
Type of Packaging: Food Service
Other Locations:
 Farmer Brothers Company

Food Manufacturers / A-Z

Central Point OR
Farmer Brothers Company
Oklahoma City OK
Farmer Brothers Foodservice Plant
Torrance CA
Brands:
 Farmer Brothers
 Spice Products
 Custom Coffee Plan
 Coffee Bean

4277 Farmer Direct Organic
12011 Wascana Heights
Regina, SK S4V 3E2
Canada
306-563-7815
contact@fdorganic.com
www.fdorganic.com
Organic grains, seeds and legumes
Type of Packaging: Consumer

4278 Farmer's Hen House
1956 520th St SW
Kalona, IA 52247-9173
319-683-2206
Fax: 319-683-2256 ryan@farmershenhouse.com
www.farmershenhouse.com
Eggs; commercial, organic and cage free
Owner: Laura Frank
laura@farmershenhouse.com
Estimated Sales: $10-20 Million
Number Employees: 10-19
Brands:
 Farmers Hen House

4279 (HQ)Farmers Cooperative Dairy
4600 Armand-Frappier St
Saint-Hubert, QC
Canada
450-878-2333
800-501-1150
www.farmersdairy.ca
Dairy products including milk, yogurt, ice cream, cheese, sour cream, etc.
President: Roger Massicotte
Estimated Sales: $110.64 Million
Number Employees: 550
Square Footage: 140221
Type of Packaging: Consumer, Food Service, Private Label
Other Locations:
Brands:
 Farmers
 Lacteeze

4280 Farmers Cooperative Grain Co
338 Main St
Kinde, MI 48445-7711
989-874-4200
Fax: 989-874-5793 kindecoop@centurytel.net
www.kindecoop.com
Dried beans
President: Henry Ziel
CEO: Dan Gottschalk
Marketing Director: David Gage
Manager: Adam Farmer
afarmer@kindecoop.com
Estimated Sales: $10-20 Million
Number Employees: 20-49
Type of Packaging: Consumer

4281 Farmers Dairies
7321 N Loop Dr
El Paso, TX 79915
915-772-2736
Fax: 915-772-0907
Dairy products
Partner: Adalberto Navar
Partner: Miguel Navar
Office Manager: Monica Navar
Contact: Ovidio Matamores
ovidiom@mvtvwireless.com
Estimated Sales: $19,000,000
Number Employees: 108

4282 Farmers Meat Market
5213 50 St
Viking, AB T0B 4N0
Canada
780-336-3241
Fax: 780-336-0180
Bologna, cured meats and wild game including deer, elk and moose, famous original viking wieners
President: Eugene Miskew
Sales: Shirley Miskewn
Purchasing Manager: Chris Ferguson
Estimated Sales: $150,000
Number Employees: 3
Type of Packaging: Private Label

4283 Farmers Produce
103 Melby Ave
Ashby, MN 56309-4707
218-747-2749
Chicken
Owner: Gerry Molter
Estimated Sales: $3-5 Million
Number Employees: 10-19
Type of Packaging: Consumer

4284 Farmers Rice Milling Co
3211 Highway 397 S
Lake Charles, LA 70615
337-433-5205
Fax: 337-433-1735 sales@FRMCO.com
www.frmco.com
Processor and grower of rice
General Manager: Philip Bertrand
CEO: Jamie Warshaw
jamiew@frmco.com
By-Product Sales: Jerry Sonnier
Year Founded: 1917
Number Employees: 50-99
Parent Co: The Powell Group
Type of Packaging: Consumer, Food Service

4285 Farmers Seafood Co Wholesale
1192 Hawn Ave
Shreveport, LA 71107-6699
318-222-9504
Fax: 318-424-2029 800-874-0203
farmersseafood@aol.com
www.farmersseafood.com
Wholesaler/distributor of groceries, dairy products and seafood; serving the food service market
Owner: Alex Mijalis
farmersseafood@aol.com
Estimated Sales: $5-10 Million
Number Employees: 50-99

4286 Farmers Way
info@farmerswayus.com
farmerswayus.com
Grains, flours and smoothie blends
Number of Brands: 1
Type of Packaging: Consumer
Brands:
 FARMERS WAY

4287 Farmgate Cheese LLC
3627 1/2 Midvale Ave
Los Angelse, CA 90034-6608
310-733-6853
usa@farmgatecheese.com
www.farmgatecheese.com
Cheese; condiments; jams and preserves.
Owner: Travis Sanders
Year Founded: 2010
Type of Packaging: Private Label
Other Locations:
 Warehouse
 Oakleigh, Australia

4288 Farmhouse Culture
182 Lewis Road
Watsonville, CA 95076
831-466-0499
info@farmhouseculture.com
www.farmhouseculture.com
Manufacturer of organic kraut and kimchi.
CEO: John Tucker
Founder: Kathryn Lukas
COO: Capp Culver
Director of Sales: Heather Dean
Brands:
 Farmhouse Culture

4289 Farmington Foods Inc
7419 West Franklin St
Forest Park, IL 60130-1016
708-771-3600
Fax: 708-771-4140 800-609-3276
info@farmingtonfoods.com
www.farmingtonfoods.com
Pork chops, boneless pork, baby back ribs, St. Louis-style spareribs, pre-packaged kabobs made with beef, chicken and pork, frenched pork racks, and seasoned port tenderloins and roasts
President: Tony Dijohn
tony.dijohn@farmingtonfoods.com
CFO: Albert LaValle
Quality Assurance: Marnie Adamski
Sales Manager: Tony DiJohn
Plant Manager/Director Operations: Dan Bernkopf
Warehouse Manager: Ram McKee
Estimated Sales: $30 Million
Number Employees: 100-249
Square Footage: 55000

4290 Farmland Dairies
520 Main Avenue
Wallington, NJ 07057
973-777-2500
Fax: 973-777-7648 888-727-6252
www.farmlanddairies.com
Milk, ice cream, yogurt, juice and ice tea
President/CEO: Martin Margherio
VP Finance: Anthony Mayzun
Contact: Mayra Olvera
molvera@bordendairy.com
Estimated Sales: $39.4 Million
Number Employees: 490
Square Footage: 150000
Parent Co: Groupo LALA/LALA National Dairy Group
Type of Packaging: Consumer, Food Service
Other Locations:
 Farmland Dairies Facility
 Wallington NJ
 Farmland Dairies Facility
 Newark NJ
 Farmland Dairies Facility
 Grand Rapids MI
Brands:
 Altanta Dairy
 Clinton's
 Farmland Dairies
 Farmland Dairies Special Request
 School Milk!
 Skim Plus
 Sunnydale Farms
 Welsh Farms

4291 Farmland Fresh Dairies
802-814 Bergens St
Newark, NJ 07108
973-961-2500
sales@farmlandmilk.com
farmlandmilk.com
Milk; dairy products
Director of Customer Service: Gabrielle Romeo
Year Founded: 1914
Number Employees: 500-1000
Type of Packaging: Private Label

4292 Farms For City Kids Foundation, Inc.
734 Caper Hill Rd.
Reading, VT 05062
802-484-1236
info@farmsforcitykids.org
www.farmsforcitykids.org
Manufacturer of cheese.
Marketing Manager: Larry Ference
Sales Manager: Cristi Menard
Contact: Curt Allen
curt@farmsforcitychildren.org
Operations Manager: Gary Wojdyla

4293 Farmstead At Long Meadow Ranch
738 Main St
St Helena, CA 94574-2005
707-963-4555
Fax: 707-963-1956 877-627-2645
info@longmeadowranch.com
www.longmeadowranch.com
Olive oils, fine wines, and grass fed beef
President/General Manager: Ted Hall
tedhall@longmeadowranch.com
Director/Chairman: Les Denend
Chief Financial Officer: Devonna Smith
VP/General Manager: Chris Hall
Director of Winemaking: Ashley Heisley
Cellarmaster-Red Wine: Hans Van Dale
Cellarmaster-White Wine: Jeff Restell
Operations Manager: Tony Fernandez
Estimated Sales: $20 Million
Number Employees: 100-249

Food Manufacturers / A-Z

4294 Farmtrue
81 Norwich Westerly Rd
North Stonington, CT 06359
401-474-5073
860-495-2231
info@farmtrue.com www.farmtrue.com
Ghee (clarified butter), ghee-nut butter, tea, spices
Co-Founder: Kim Welch
Co-Founder: Lynn Goodwin

4295 Farmwise LLC
P.O. Box 812428
Wellesley, MA 02482
508-401-7040
Fax: 508-401-7430 eatveggiefries.com
Veggie fries, tots and rings.
Co-Founder & CEO: David Peters
Co-Founder: Christina Peters
Estimated Sales: $1.6 Million
Type of Packaging: Private Label
Brands:
    Veggie Fries
    Veggie Tots
    Veggie Rings

4296 Faroh Candies
7223 Pearl Rd
Middleburg Heights, OH 44130
440-888-9866
Fax: 440-842-4013
Confectionery products including boxed chocolates, chocolate cherries and popcorn specialties.
Owner: George Faroh
Purchasing: Donna Parrot
Estimated Sales: $5-10 Million
Number Employees: 20-49
Type of Packaging: Consumer

4297 Farr Candy Company
345 D Street
Idaho Falls, ID 83402
208-522-8215
Fax: 208-523-3307 www.farrcandy.com
Confectionery products including cherry cordials, peanut clusters and malo nuts; also, ice cream
President/Owner: Kevin W. Call
Estimated Sales: $3-5 Million
Number Employees: 10-19

4298 Farrell Baking Company
26 Stefanak Dr
West Middlesex, PA 16159-3138
724-342-7906
Bread and bakery products
President: Richard Vatavuk
Owner: Richard Vatavuk
Estimated Sales: $1-2,500,000
Number Employees: 10-19
Brands:
    Farrell Baking

4299 Fashion Snackz
3201 W Temple Ave
Suite 275
Pomona, CA 91768
909-598-0880
info.fashionsnackz@gmail.com
www.fashionsnackz.com
Gluten-free fruit and nut clusters
Type of Packaging: Consumer
Brands:
    DEEZ NUTZ

4300 Fast Fixing Foods
1481 US Highway 431
Boaz, AL 35957-1552
256-593-7221
Fax: 256-593-7208 800-317-4232
www.fastfixinfoods.com
Fast foods
Owner: Eugene Davis
eugene.davis@fastfixin.com
Estimated Sales: $10-20 Million
Number Employees: 10-19

4301 Fastachi
598 Mount Auburn St
Watertown, MA 02472-4124
617-924-8787
Fax: 617-924-8844 800-466-3022
Almonds, cashews, pistachios, hazelnuts, peanuts and sunflower seeds; also, gift baskets available
Owner: Souren Etyemezian
sourene@fastachi.com
Estimated Sales: Less Than $500,000
Number Employees: 1-4
Brands:
    Fastachi

4302 (HQ)Fasweet Co
215 N Culberhouse St
Jonesboro, AR 72401-1998
870-932-1562
Fax: 870-932-1114 888-223-6693
www.fasweet.com
Sugar substitutes
President: Jake Morse
Estimated Sales: $5-10 Million
Number Employees: 5-9
Square Footage: 30000
Parent Co: Morse Company
Type of Packaging: Consumer, Food Service
Brands:
    Fasweet

4303 Fat Snax
Brooklyn, NY 11206
347-496-5834
fatsnax.com
Low-carb, keto-friendly cookies and teas
Type of Packaging: Consumer
Brands:
    Fat Snax
    Fat Tea

4304 Fat Toad Farm
787 Kibbee Rd
Brookfield, VT 05036-9615
802-279-0098
info@fattoadfarm.com
www.fattoadfarm.com
Manufacturer of goat's milk.
Co-Owner: Steve Reid
Co-Owner: Judith Irving
Co-Owner: Calley Hastings
Contact: Calley Hastings
calley@fattoadfarm.com
Number Employees: 1-4

4305 FatBoy's Cookie Company
18-01 River Road
Fair Lawn, NJ 07410
201-796-1000
Fax: 201-475-3501 888-328-2690
fatboycookies@aol.com
Cookie dough
President: Joel Ansh

4306 Father Sam's Bakery
105 Msgr Valente Dr
Buffalo, NY 14206-1815
716-853-1071
Fax: 716-853-1062 800-521-6719
www.fathersams.com
Flatbreads, tortilla shells, and flavored wraps.
President: William Sam
Sales: Glenn Povitz
Estimated Sales: $20-50 Million
Number Employees: 50-99
Square Footage: 40000
Type of Packaging: Consumer, Food Service, Private Label
Brands:
    Father Sam's Pocket Breads
    Father Sam's Tortillas
    Father Sam's Wraps

4307 Father's Country Hams
P.O.Box 99 6323 St. Rt 81
Bremen, KY 42325
270-525-3554
Fax: 270-525-3333 info@fatherscountryhams.com
www.fatherscountryhams.com
Ham, bacon, and smoked sausage
President: Charles Gatton Jr
Estimated Sales: $.5-1 million
Number Employees: 5-9

4308 Father's Table Inc
2100 Country Club Rd
P.O. Box 1509
Sanford, FL 32771-4051
407-324-1200
Fax: 407-324-1228 www.thefatherstable.com
Desserts, pizza cheesecake
President: Tim Lambert
tim.lambert@thefatherstable.com
Number Employees: 100-249

4309 Fatty Sundays
630 Flushing Ave
5th Fl
Brooklyn, NY 11206-5026
646-762-2555
Fax: 646-762-2554 info@fattysundays.com
www.fattysundays.com
Gluten-free baked goods; candy; and pretzels.
Co-Founder: Lauren Borowick
Co-Founder: Ali Borowick
Year Founded: 2011
Type of Packaging: Food Service, Private Label

4310 Fatworks
Niwot, CO 80544
fatworksfoods.com
Cooking oils
Number of Brands: 1
Number of Products: 4
Type of Packaging: Consumer
Brands:
    FATWORKS

4311 Favorite Foods
6934 Greenwood Street
Burnaby, BC V5A 1X8
Canada
604-420-5100
Fax: 604-420-9116 www.favoritefoods.com
Manufacturer and exporter of sauces including light and dark soy, oyster, teriyaki, marinade, barbecue, black bean, stir fry, Szechuan spicy hot and plum
President: Chris Barstow
VP of Sales: Chris Langella
Sr. Marketing Manager: Pearl Lyman
Chief Operating Officer: John Libby
Category Managers/Purchasing: Steve Gerasimchik
Estimated Sales: $1-5 million
Number Employees: 24
Square Footage: 70000
Type of Packaging: Consumer, Food Service, Private Label, Bulk
Brands:
    Golden Dragon

4312 Fawen
134 N 4th
2nd Floor
Brooklyn, NY 11249
888-737-7052
drinkfawen.com
Ready-to-drink soups
Number of Brands: 1
Number of Products: 3
Type of Packaging: Consumer
Brands:
    FAWEN

4313 Fayes Bakery Products
216 E McCollum Street
Dexter, MO 63841-1222
573-624-4920
Bakery products
Owner: Dale Parks
Estimated Sales: $.5-1,000,000
Number Employees: 1-4

4314 Faygo Beverages Inc
3579 Gratiot Ave
Detroit, MI 48207
313-925-1600
www.faygo.com
Carbonated soft drinks
President: Alan Chittaro
Controller: Lynn Beauvais
Estimated Sales: $25,000,000-$100,000,000
Number Employees: 500-999
Parent Co: National Beverage Company
Type of Packaging: Consumer, Private Label

4315 Fayter Farms Produce
69400 Jolon Rd
Bradley, CA 93426-9676
831-385-8515
Fax: 831-385-0833
Fresh herbicide pesticide-free Kiss of Burgundy globe artichokes.
President: Thomas Fayter
Estimated Sales: $300,000-500,000
Number Employees: 1-4
Type of Packaging: Private Label, Bulk
Other Locations:
    Fayter Farms Produce
    Bradley CA

Food Manufacturers / A-Z

Brands:
  Globe Artichoke
  Kiss of Burgundy

4316 Fazio's Bakery
1717 Sublette Ave
St Louis, MO 63110-1926
314-645-6239
Fax: 314-645-2410 fazioinfo@faziosbakery.com
Bakery products
President: Charles Fazio
charles@faziosbakery.com
Estimated Sales: Below $5 Million
Number Employees: 100-249
Brands:
  Fazio's

4317 Feature Foods
30 Finley Rd.
Brampton, ON L6T 1A9
Canada
905-452-7741
Fax: 905-452-9210 info@featurefoods.com
www.featurefoods.com
Manufacturer and exporter of pickled eggs and herring; also, herb horseradish
President: Lorne Krongold
Number Employees: 20-49
Type of Packaging: Consumer

4318 Federal Pretzel Baking Company
300 Eagle Court
Bridgeport, NJ 08014
215-467-0505
Fax: 215-467-3153 www.federalpretzel.biz
Pretzels, cookies
President: Florence Sciambi
Plant Manager: Rich Bezila
Estimated Sales: $1-2,500,000
Number Employees: 20-49
Brands:
  Federal Pretzel

4319 Federation-Southern Cprtvs
2769 Church St
Atlanta, GA 30344-3258
404-765-0991
Fax: 404-765-9178 fsc@federation.coop
www.federationsoutherncoop.com
Manufacturer and exporter of fresh vegetables
Chairman: Shirley Williams Blakely
Vice Chair: Daniel Bustamante
Secretary: Satina James
Treasurer: Carrie Fulghum
Estimated Sales: $500,000-$1 Million
Number Employees: 20-49
Type of Packaging: Consumer, Bulk

4320 Fee Brothers
453 Portland Ave
Rochester, NY 14605-1597
585-544-9530
Fax: 585-544-9530 800-961-3337
info@feebrothers.com
Manufacturer and exporter of cocktail mixes including whiskey sour, daiquiri, margarita, pina colada, etc.; also, slush bases, bitters, nonalcoholic cordials, tea and juice concentrates, grenadine, coffee flavoring syrups, maraschinocherries, olives, cocktail
President: John Fee
CEO: Ellen Fee
Treasurer: Joe Fee
Estimated Sales: $1 Million
Number Employees: 10-19
Number of Brands: 1
Number of Products: 90
Square Footage: 96000
Type of Packaging: Food Service, Private Label, Bulk
Brands:
  Fee Brothers

4321 Feed The Party
2055 Nelson Miller Pkwy
Louisville, KY 40223
partyon@feedtheparty.com
feedtheparty.com
Supplier of the finest butcher shop quality meats, including steak, pork, chicken, and lamb.
President & Founder: Matt Kenney
Estimated Sales: $100+ Million
Number Employees: 2-10
Square Footage: 89000
Type of Packaging: Food Service, Bulk

Brands:
  A. Thomas Meats
  Berkwood Farms
  Border Springs Farm Lamb
  Shire Gate
  Shuckman's Fish Co. & Smokery, Inc.
  Joyce Farms
  Big Fork

4322 Feeding the Turkeys, Inc.
745 Atlantic Ave
Suite 327
Boston, MA 02111-2735
207-712-4034
www.eatvicecream.com
Ice cream
Founder: Dan Schorr
Senior Marketing Manager: Molly DeLong
Year Founded: 2016
Number Employees: 1-4
Type of Packaging: Food Service, Private Label

4323 Feel Good Foods
220 36th St
Unit 22
Brooklyn, NY 11232
800-638-8949
tryg@feelgf.com feel-good-foods.com
Gluten-free meals
Contact: Carrie Mcquade
carrie@feelgf.com

4324 Felbro Food Products
5700 W Adams Blvd
Los Angeles, CA 90016
323-936-5266
Fax: 323-936-5946 www.felbro.com
Manufacturer, importer and exporter of fountain syrups, sno cone syrups, dessert toppings, fillings, puddings, sauces, dressings and drink bases for shakes, punches and slushies.
CEO: Mike Feldman
CFO: Brian Seigel
Business Development Manager: Jim DeBiase
COO: Daniel Feldmar
Year Founded: 1946
Estimated Sales: $20-50 Million
Number Employees: 20-49
Number of Brands: 4
Square Footage: 80000
Type of Packaging: Consumer, Food Service, Private Label, Bulk
Brands:
  Coffee Express
  Felbro
  Food Tone
  Marsa

4325 Felix Custom Smoking
17461 147th St SE # 2a
Monroe, WA 98272-1070
425-485-2439
Fax: 425-485-2439 felixcustom@aol.com
Albacore Tuna to Yukon Wild Chum Salmon, smoked seafoods, salmon sausages, dips, ready to eat, etc. Mostly custom work for fisher person.
Owner: Diane Zollinger
felixcustom@aol.com
Plant Manager: Tony Newman
Estimated Sales: More than $500,000
Number Employees: 5-9
Square Footage: 12000
Type of Packaging: Private Label

4326 Felix Roma & Son Inc
2 S Page Ave
Endicott, NY 13760-4693
607-748-3336
Fax: 607-748-3607 www.felixroma.com
Breads, rolls and pizza dough
President: Brian Bertoni
brian@felixroma.com
VP: Barry Roma
VP/Sales Manager: Anthony Roma
Office Manager: Mary Consentio
brian@felixroma.com
Bakery General Manager: James Wasley
VP/Frozen Foods Manager: Michael Roma
Production Manager: Brian Bertoni
Plant Manager: Eugene Roma
brian@felixroma.com
Estimated Sales: $4.3 Million
Number Employees: 50-99
Square Footage: 86000

Type of Packaging: Consumer, Food Service, Private Label, Bulk
Brands:
  Felix Roma

4327 Fenchem Inc
15308 El Prado Rd
Building 8
Chino, CA 91710-7659
909-597-1113
Fax: 909-597-1113 sales@fenchem.com
www.fenchem.com
Manufactures natural ingredients for nutrition supplements and functional foods
President: Yanyan Zhu
Contact: Jason Betts
jasonb@fenchem.com
Estimated Sales: 5-9

4328 Fendall Ice Cream Company
470 South 700 East
Salt Lake City, UT 84102
801-355-3583
Fax: 801-521-0133 sales@fendalls.com
Manufacturer and wholesaler/distributor of ice cream, sherbet, water ices, sorbets and frozen yogurt
Owner: Carol Radinger
Contact: Gunter Radinger
gunter@fendalls.com
Estimated Sales: $1-2.5 Million
Number Employees: 5-9
Type of Packaging: Consumer
Brands:
  Cream of Weber
  Fendall's

4329 Fenestra Winery
83 Vallecitos Rd
Livermore, CA 94550-9603
925-447-5246
Fax: 925-447-4655 800-789-9463
www.fenestrawinery.com
Wines
Owner: Lanny Replogle
l.r@fenestrawinery.com
Estimated Sales: $500,000-$1,000,000
Number Employees: 1-4
Type of Packaging: Private Label
Brands:
  Fenestra Winery

4330 (HQ)Fenn Valley Vineyards
6130 122nd Ave
Fennville, MI 49408-9457
269-561-2396
Fax: 269-561-2973 800-432-6265
winery@fennvalley.com www.fennvalley.com
Wines
President: Vernon Jenewein
vernon@fennvalley.com
Estimated Sales: $500,000-$1,000,000
Number Employees: 10-19

4331 Fenn Valley Vineyards
6130 122nd Ave
Fennville, MI 49408
269-561-2396
www.fennvalley.com
Wines
Asst. Manager, Tasting Room: Chelsea Hundey

4332 Fentimans North America
2286 Holdom Ave
Burnaby, BC V5B 4Y5
Canada
877-326-3248
info@drinkfentimans.com
www.drinkfentimans.com
Botanically brewed beverages-natural sodas
President: Nap Veltri
CEO: Craig James
Marketing: Craig L'Heureux
Sales: Craig James
Public Relations: Samantha James
Year Founded: 1905

4333 Fenton & Lee Chocolatiers
35 E 8th Avenue
Eugene, OR 97401-2906
541-343-7629
Fax: 541-343-6385 800-336-8661
Chocolates and confections
President: Janele Smith

Food Manufacturers / A-Z

Estimated Sales: $2.5-5,000,000
Number Employees: 5-9

4334 Feridies
PO Box 186
28285 Mill Creek Dr
Courtland, VA 23837
800-544-0896
customerservice@feridies.com www.feridies.com
Gluten-free, kosher, organic/natural, other candy, hors d'oeuvres/appetizers, nuts, other snacks, gift packs.
Marketing: Jane Riddick-Fries

4335 Feridies
28285 Mill Creek Dr
Courtland, VA 23837
866-732-6883
www.feridies.com
Virginia peanuts and trail mix
Year Founded: 1973
Type of Packaging: Consumer
Brands:
   FERIDIES

4336 Fermalife
fermalife.com
Fermented soy beverage mix
Type of Packaging: Consumer
Brands:
   FERMALIFE

4337 Ferme Ostreicole Dugas
675 St-Pierre Blvd W
Caraquet, NB E1W 1A2
Canada
506-727-3226
Fax: 506-727-4950
Fresh oysters
President: Gaetan Dugas
Estimated Sales: $520,000
Number Employees: 6
Type of Packaging: Consumer, Food Service

4338 Fermenting Fairy
Santa Monica Blvd
Santa Monica, CA 90403
fatsnax.com
Probiotic foods and beverages
Founder: Lauren Mones

4339 Fernandez Chili Co
8267 County Road 10 S
Alamosa, CO 81101-9176
719-589-6043
Fax: 719-587-0485
Manufacturer and importer of chili and taco sauces, spices and prepared chili mixes; also, Mexican corn products
Vice President: Blair Fernandez
VP: Blair Fernandez
Estimated Sales: $5-10 Million
Number Employees: 5-9
Square Footage: 45000
Type of Packaging: Consumer, Food Service, Bulk

4340 Fernando C Pujals & Bros
B St Cntro De Dist Amlia St
Guaynabo, PR 00968
787-792-3080
Fax: 787-792-8797
Candy
President: Fernando Pujals
Estimated Sales: $24 Million
Number Employees: 80

4341 Ferncreek Confections LLC
2720 Council Tree Ave Ste 224
Fort Collins, CO 80525-6329
970-377-2293
Fax: 970-229-0910
www.ferncreekconfections.com
Confections: toffee
Sales Manager: Dawn Wittstruck

4342 Ferolito Vultaggio & Sons
60 Crossways Park Dr W # 400
Woodbury, NY 11797-2003
516-812-0300
Fax: 516-326-4988   800-832-3775
Beverages, general grocery
President: John Ferolito
CEO: Rick Adonailo
VP Corporate Communications: Francie Patton

Estimated Sales: $10-100,000,000
Number Employees: 500-999
Type of Packaging: Private Label
Brands:
   Arizona Iced Tea
   Ferolito Vultaggio

4343 Ferrante Winery & Ristorante
5585 State Route 307
Geneva, OH 44041
440-466-6046
Fax: 440-466-7370 www.ferrantewinery.com
Wines
Manager: Bob Strickland
Estimated Sales: $2,000,000
Number Employees: 20-49
Brands:
   Ferrante

4344 Ferrara Bakery & Cafe
195 Grand St
b/w Mulberry & Mott St
New York, NY 10013-3717
212-226-6150
Fax: 212-226-0667 information@ferraracafe.com
www.ferraranyc.com
Manufacturer and importer of confectionery products including candies, novelties, Italian and seasonal products; also, syrups, coffee and baked goods
Owner: Ernest Lepore
ernestl@ferraracafe.com
Owner/CEO: Peter Lepore
Estimated Sales: $5-10 Million
Number Employees: 100-249
Type of Packaging: Consumer, Private Label

4345 Ferrara Candy Co Inc
404 W Harrison St
Suite 650
Chicago, IL 60607
800-323-1768
talktous@ferrarausa.com www.ferrarausa.com
Candy including butterscotch, caramels, chocolate, jelly beans, hard, licorice, lollypops, mints, marshmallows, nougats, etc.
CEO: Todd Siwak
CFO: Maurizio Ficarra
VP, Business Development: Willy Pfenning
Chief Customer Officer: Mike Sayles
COO: Michael Murray
Estimated Sales: $50 Million
Number Employees: 500-999
Number of Brands: 18
Square Footage: 365000
Parent Co: Catterton Management Company
Type of Packaging: Food Service, Private Label, Bulk
Other Locations:
   Farley's & Sathers-Distribution
   Chattanooga TN
   Farley's & Sathers-Manufacturing
   Des Plaines IL
   Farley's & Sathers-Manufacturing
   Reynosa MX
Brands:
   Atomic FireBall
   Black Forest Organic
   Bob's
   Boston Baked Beans
   Brach's
   Chuckles
   Fruit Stripe
   Now and Later
   Jaw Busters
   Jujyfruits
   Lemonhead
   Now & Later
   Sweet Stripes
   Rainblo
   Redhots
   Sathers
   Super Bubble
   Trolli

4346 Ferrara Winery
1120 W 15th Ave
Escondido, CA 92025
760-745-7632
Wines
Owner: Gasper D Ferrara
CEO: Vera Ferrara
Estimated Sales: $1-2,500,000
Number Employees: 5-9
Brands:
   Ferrara

4347 Ferrari-Carano
8761 Dry Creek Rd
P.O. Box 1549
Healdsburg, CA 95448-9133
707-433-6700
Fax: 707-431-1742   800-831-0381
info@ferrari-carano.com www.ferrari-carano.com
Wines
President: Don Carano
d.carano@ferrari-carano.com
Co-Owner/Vice President: Rhonda Carano
Director, Vineyard Operations: Steve Domenichelli
Sr. Winemaker: Aaron Piotter
Estimated Sales: $20-50 Million
Number Employees: 100-249
Type of Packaging: Private Label

4348 Ferrero USA Inc
600 Cottontail Ln
Somerset, NJ 08873-1233
732-764-9300
Fax: 732-764-2700   800-337-7376
www.ferrerousa.com
Confectionery items including breath mints, chocolates, chocolate and hazelnut wafers and spread; also, chocolate espresso coffee
Owner: Luigi Cavalotto
CEO: Michael Gilmore
Vice President: F Veglio
VP Of Marketing: Leonardo Limitone
Director of Sales: John Kennington
Estimated Sales: $10-20 Million
Number Employees: 100-249
Parent Co: Ferrero, SPA
Type of Packaging: Consumer
Brands:
   Mon Cheri
   Raffaello
   Rocher
   Silvers
   Tic Tac

4349 Ferrigno Vineyards & Wine
17301 State Route B
St James, MO 65559-8583
573-265-7742
www.ferrignovineyards.com
Wines
CEO: Richard Ferrigno
Estimated Sales: $150,000
Number Employees: 9
Type of Packaging: Private Label
Brands:
   Ferrigno

4350 Ferris Organic Farms
3565 Onondaga Rd
Eaton Rapids, MI 48827-9608
517-628-2506
Fax: 517-628-8257   800-628-8736
ferrisorganicfarm@gmail.com
www.ferrisorganicfarm.com
Manufacturer, grower and exporter of organic beans including black, soy, black turtle and pinto; also, grains including wheat and barley; wholesaler/distributor of organic natural foods
Co-Owner: Richard Ferris
ferrisorganicfarm@excite.com
Estimated Sales: $1-2.5 Million
Number Employees: 1-4
Square Footage: 14000
Type of Packaging: Bulk

4351 (HQ)Ferris, Stahl-Meyer
2071 Lemoine Ave
Suite 202
Fort Lee, NJ 07024
201-242-5500
Fax: 201-242-5516 www.stahlmeyer.com
Cold cuts and frankfurters including; smoked meats, spanish products, beef bacon, cooked hams & deli meats, corned beef & pastrami, and roast beef. Frankfurters include beef, chicken, hot dogs, knockwurst, smoked sausage, andturkey.
President & CEO: Guillermo Gonzalez
Number Employees: 100-249
Number of Brands: 5
Type of Packaging: Consumer, Food Service, Private Label, Bulk
Brands:
   Ferris
   Stahl-Meyer
   Sweet Meadow Farms

Food Manufacturers / A-Z

El Taino
El Conquistador

4352 Ferroclad Fishery
Mamainse Pt
Batchawana Bay, ON P0S 1A0
Canada
705-882-2295
Fax: 705-882-2297
Manufacturer, importer and exporter of herring, trout, whitefish and caviar
Owner: Gary Symons
Number Employees: 20-49
Parent Co: Presteve Foods Limited
Type of Packaging: Consumer, Food Service

4353 Fess Parker Winery
6200 Foxen Canyon Rd
Los Olivos, CA 93441
805-688-1545
Fax: 805-686-1130   800-841-1104
infowinery@fessparker.com   www.fessparker.com
Producer of wines
CEO: Eli Parker
Estimated Sales: $110,000
Number Employees: 11-50
Square Footage: 9
Brands:
   American Tradition Reserve
   Pinot Noir Santa Barbara County
   Santa Barbara County
   Syrah Santa Barbara County
   Viognier Santa Barbara County
   and more

4354 Festive Foods
389 Edwin Dr # 100
Virginia Beach, VA 23462-4548
757-490-9186
Fax: 757-490-9494   www.festivefoods.com
Sauces including spicy and extra spicy
President: Bobby Cannon
bcannon@festivefoods.com
Purchasing: Robert Buchanan
Estimated Sales: $.5-1,000,000
Number Employees: 1-4
Type of Packaging: Consumer
Brands:
   Buffalo Bob's Everything Sauce

4355 Fetzer Vineyards
12901 Old River Rd
Hopland, CA 95449
707-744-1250
www.fetzer.com
Wines
CEO: Giancarlo Bianchetti
CFO: Jorge Lyng Benitez
COO: Cindy DeVries
SVP Sales & Distribution: Barry Marek
Year Founded: 1968
Estimated Sales: $20-50 Million
Number Employees: 100-249

4356 Fiberstar
713 Saint Croix St
River Falls, WI 54022-3600
715-425-7550
Fax: 715-425-7572   sales@fiberstar.net
www.fiberstaringredients.com
Food ingredients and additives
President/CEO: Dale Lindquist
CEO: Greg Aronson
gregaronson@fiberstar.net
VP Technology: Brock Lundberg
Number Employees: 20-49

4357 Fibred
10900 Day Rd SE
Cumberland, MD 21502-8638
301-724-6050
Fax: 301-722-7131   800-598-8894
Customerservice@fibred.com   www.fibred.com
Soy fiber
President: Kim Alkire
kim@fibred.com
Quality Assurance Manager: Rhonda Niland
VP Sales: Karen Ort
Estimated Sales: $10-20 Million
Number Employees: 20-49
Type of Packaging: Bulk
Brands:
   F1-1 Soy Fibre

4358 Ficklin Vineyards Winery
30246 Avenue 7 1/2
Madera, CA 93637-9198
559-674-4598
www.ficklin.com
Wines
President: Peter Ficklin
Assistant Winemaker: Paige Diffenderfer
Marketing: Rick Wilcox
PR/Media, Brand Management and Retail Op: Liz Wilcox
Administrative Manager: Kellie Murpfy
Winemaker: Robeart Simons
Estimated Sales: $500,000-$1,000,000
Number Employees: 5-9

4359 Ficks & Co.
2662 Bush St
San Francisco, CA 94115
ficksdrink.com
Hard seltzers and cocktail mixes
CEO: Ron Alvarado
COO: Mike Williamson
Number of Brands: 1
Number of Products: 8
Type of Packaging: Consumer
Brands:
   FICKS

4360 Ficon
10630 Midwest Industrial Blvd
St Louis, MO 63132-1221
314-427-4099
Fax: 314-427-6646   888-569-4099
www.ficoninc.com
Confectioneries
President: Charlie Hirschi
chirschi@ficoninc.com
Secretary / Treasurer: Gary Sauer
Vice President: Jim Sauer
Estimated Sales: $1-2.5 Million
Number Employees: 1-4

4361 Fidalgo Bay Roasting Co
856 N Hill Blvd
Burlington, WA 98233-4640
360-757-8818
Fax: 360-757-8810   800-310-5540
www.fidalgobaycoffee.com
Coffee
Owner: Gary Swoyer
gary@fidalgobaycoffee.com
CEO: David Evans
VP Sales & Marketing: Darryl Miller
gary@fidalgobaycoffee.com
Purchasing: Gary Sawyer
Estimated Sales: $1-2,500,000
Number Employees: 20-49

4362 Fiddlers Green Farm
16 Mayo St
PO Box 1
North Vassalboro, ME 4962
207-877-7445
Fax: 207-338-3872   800-729-7935
info@fiddlersgreenfarm.com
www.fiddlersgreenfarm.com
Organic and stone ground grains, flour and corn meal
Owner: Marada Cook
Owner: Leah Cook
Vice President: Laine Alexander
Estimated Sales: Under $500,000
Number Employees: 1-4
Square Footage: 600
Type of Packaging: Consumer, Food Service
Brands:
   Belleweather
   Bertha's
   Bread & Biscuits
   Fiddle Cakes
   Fiddlers Green Farms
   Islander's Choice
   Oatbran & Brown Rice
   Penobscot Porridge
   Spice
   Toasted Buckwheat

4363 Field Coffee
6700 Dawson Blvd
Building 3
Norcross, GA 30093
844-343-5326
fieldcoffee.net
Coffee
President: Geoffrey Paul
Controller: Jodi Burkett
Sales Manager: Daniel Lane
Estimated Sales: $10-20 Million
Number Employees: 84
Parent Co: Excelso

4364 Field Roast
3901 7th Ave South
Seattle, WA 98108
800-311-9497
fieldroast.com
Sausages, burgers, deli slices, appetizers and entr,es
Founder: David Lee
Year Founded: 1997
Number of Brands: 1
Number of Products: 20
Type of Packaging: Consumer
Brands:
   FIELD ROAST

4365 Field Stone Winery
10075 Highway 128
Healdsburg, CA 95448-9025
707-433-7266
Fax: 707-433-2231   800-544-7273
Wines
Owner: Roger Hull
soconnor@corvel.com
General and Vineyard Manager: Ben Staten
Owner: Katrina Staten
Tasting Room Manager: Helen Weber
Public Relations: Roger Hull
Estimated Sales: $2.5-5,000,000
Number Employees: 10-19

4366 Field Trip Jerky
630 Flushing Ave
Suite 4
Brooklyn, NY 11206-5026
315-491-8240
Fax: 646-233-0638   www.fieldtripjerky.com
Manufacturer of all natural jerky.
Co-Founder: Matthew Levey
Co-Founder: Tom Donigan
tom@fieldtripjerky.com
Co-Founder: Scott Fiesinger
Estimated Sales: Less Than $500,000
Number Employees: 1-4
Brands:
   FIELD Trip

4367 Field's Pies
100 Fields Row
Pauls Valley, OK 73075-9600
405-238-7381
Fax: 405-238-5075   800-286-7501
fields@fieldspies.com   www.fieldspies.com
Manufacturer of frozen pies including pecan, German chocolate, lemon chess and pumpkin.
President: Chris Field
Vice President: Jenny Wallace
Year Founded: 1975
Estimated Sales: G
Number Employees: 20-49
Square Footage: 12500
Type of Packaging: Consumer, Food Service, Private Label, Bulk
Brands:
   Field's

4368 Fieldale Farms
P.O. Box 558
Baldwin, GA 30511
800-241-5400
www.fieldale.com
Fresh and frozen chicken.
President: Thomas Hensley
General Manager, Further Processing: David Stevens
Year Founded: 1972
Estimated Sales: $473.5 Million
Number Employees: 5,000+
Square Footage: 21000
Type of Packaging: Consumer, Food Service, Private Label, Bulk

Food Manufacturers / A-Z

4369 Fieldbrook Foods Corp.
1 Ice Cream Dr.
P.O. Box 1318
Dunkirk, NY 14048
716-366-5400
Fax: 716-366-3588 800-333-0805
www.fieldbrookfoods.com
Ice cream, frozen yogurt, sherbert and sorbet, sandwiches, ice cream/fudge bars, ice pops, juice and fruit bars, cones, cups, sorbet bars, etc.
President/Chief Executive Officer: Robin Galloway
Chief Financial Officer: Derek Kamholz
Senior VP, Sales & Marketing: James Masood
COO: Mark McLenithan
Vice President, Purchasing: Robert Griewisch
Year Founded: 2001
Estimated Sales: $101 Million
Number Employees: 250-499
Number of Brands: 3
Square Footage: 280000
Type of Packaging: Consumer, Food Service, Private Label, Bulk
Other Locations:
  Fieldbrook Farms
  Columbus GA
Brands:
  Deering
  Howard Johnson
  My Favorite

4370 Fieldbrook Valley Winery
4241 Fieldbrook Rd
Mckinleyville, CA 95519-8130
707-839-4140
Fax: 707-839-2278 www.fieldbrookwinery.com
Wines
Owner: Robert Hodgson
COO: Judith Hodgson
Estimated Sales: Less Than $500,000
Number Employees: 1-4

4371 Fiera Foods
50 Marmora St
Toronto, ON M9M 2X5
Canada
800-675-6356
info@fierafoods.com www.fierafoods.com
French pastries including croissants, danish and turnovers; also, muffin mixes.
President & CEO: Boris Serebryany
COO: Alex Garber
Year Founded: 1987
Estimated Sales: $188.48 Million
Number Employees: 1,200
Square Footage: 200000
Type of Packaging: Food Service

4372 Fiesta Candy Company
25 Old Dover Rd
Suite 1
Rochester, NH 03867
603-335-0003
Fax: 603-994-0333 800-285-9735
Candy
Managing Director: Jose Mayoral
jmayoral@fiestacandy.com
Estimated Sales: $5-10 Million
Number Employees: 5-9

4373 Fiesta Canning Co
1480 E Bethany Home Rd # 110
Suite 110
Phoenix, AZ 85014-2074
602-212-2424
Fax: 602-343-5141
SalesCoordinator@Fiestacan.com
Canned chili pepper paste
President: Gary Johnson
Director: Bob Godfrey
CFO: Bob Myers
bob@fiestacan.com
VP: Stephen Johnson
Marketing: Ernie Jayme
Sales Executive: Iris Marin
Manufacturing Executive: Jesus Ayala
Plant Manager: Bob Godfrey
Number Employees: 5-9
Square Footage: 20000
Brands:
  Cochise Farms
  Fiesta Del Sole
  Macayo Mexican Foods

4374 Fiesta Farms
200 Christie St.
Toronto, ON M6G 3B6
Canada
416-537-1235
Fax: 416-537-1244 www.fiestafarms.ca
Onions including red, yellow and white
President: Garry Bybee
Secretary: Tamara Bybee
VP: Marc Bybee
Estimated Sales: $10-20 Million
Number Employees: 20-49
Type of Packaging: Consumer, Food Service, Private Label, Bulk
Brands:
  Bloombuilder
  Bybee's
  Ff
  Ru-Bee
  Zoombees

4375 Fiesta Gourmet of Tejas
42 Oak Villa Road
Canyon Lake, TX 78133-3102
210-212-5233
Fax: 210-212-5240 800-585-8250
Manufacturer and exporter of Texas-made wines, chiles, salsas, sauces, jellies, oils, coffees and teas; custom-made gift baskets available
Owner: Maricela Smith
Estimated Sales: Less than $500,000
Number Employees: 1-4
Square Footage: 4000
Parent Co: Fiesta Gourmet del Sol
Type of Packaging: Consumer, Food Service, Private Label
Brands:
  Fiesta Del Sol
  Poblanos
  Serranos
  Tejas Sizzle

4376 Fiesta Mexican Foods
979 G St
Brawley, CA 92227-2615
760-344-3580
Fax: 760-344-3580 www.chexfoods.com
Tortillas
President: Raymond Armenta
raymond.armenta@chexfoods.com
Estimated Sales: $3,000,000
Number Employees: 20-49

4377 Fife Vineyards
3620 Road B
Redwood Valley, CA 95470
707-485-0323
Fax: 707-485-0832 info@fifevineyards.com
Wines
President: Dennis Fife
Owner: Karen MacNeil
Estimated Sales: $2.5-5,000,000
Number Employees: 5-9

4378 Fig Food Co.
PO Box 265
New York, NY 10014
855-344-3663
figfood.com
Fig Food offers four ready-to-eat varieties and three condensed varieties of soup. 100% plant-based recipes made with fresh, organic ingredients.
Contact: Joel Henry
joel@figfood.com
Type of Packaging: Consumer
Brands:
  FIG FOOD CO.

4379 Fig Garden Packing Inc
5545 W Dakota Ave
Fresno, CA 93722-9749
559-271-9000
Fax: 559-271-1332
Manufacturer, exporter and packer of dried and diced figs and fig paste including regular and crushed seed
President: Michael Jura
Partner: Lisa Jura
lisa@figgardenpacking.com
Marketing Executive: Bert Zigenman
Estimated Sales: $1.3 Million
Number Employees: 50-99
Square Footage: 9646

4380 Figamajigs
20 North San Mateo Drive
Suite 2
San Mateo, CA 94401
650-227-3830
Fax: 707-581-1753
All natural, gluten free, low fat, kosher fig bars and fig pieces covered in chocolate
Founder: Mel Lefer

4381 Figaro Company
3601 Executive Blvd
Mesquite, TX 75149
972-288-3587
Fax: 972-288-1887
Manufacturer and exporter of hickory liquid smoke, mesquite liquid smoke, fajita marinade, brisket cooking sauce
Owner: J K Mc Kenney
CEO: Dave McCormack
Sales: Dave McCormack
Public Relations: Linda Willett
Operations: Anita Watson
Production: C Platero
Number Employees: 10-19
Number of Products: 6
Square Footage: 42000
Type of Packaging: Consumer, Food Service, Private Label
Brands:
  Figaro

4382 Figueroa Brothers
1740 Hurd Dr
Irving, TX 75038-4324
972-714-0985
Fax: 214-351-9061 800-886-6354
greg@figbros.com www.figbros.com
Habanero pepper sauce
Owner: Greg Figueroa
CEO: Greg P. Figueroa
VP of Sales: Kevin Anderson
greg@figbros.com
Number Employees: 20-49
Brands:
  Melinda's
  Original Habanero Pepper Sauce

4383 Figuerola Laboratories
PO Box 1569
Santa Ynez, CA 93460-1569
805-688-6626
Fax: 805-688-8099 800-219-1147
customerservice@figuerola.net
Dietary supplements
President: Rossana Figuerola
rossana@figuerola.net
Executive Marketing Director: Antonio Figuerola
Number Employees: 5-9
Brands:
  Figuerola

4384 Fiji Water Co LLC
11444 W Olympic Blvd # 210
2nd Floor
Los Angeles, CA 90064-1559
310-312-2850
Fax: 310-312-2828 888-426-3454
info@fijiwater.com www.fijiwater.com
Bottled water
President: James Ahn
james.ahn@mattel.com
CEO: Doug Carlson
SVP: Grace Jeon
SVP Sustainable Growth: Thomas Mooney
Number Employees: 50-99
Parent Co: Roll International Corporation
Brands:
  Fiji

4385 Filfil Foods LLC
457 MacDonough St
Brooklyn, NY 11233-1509
917-971-3493
contact@filfilfoods.com
filfilfoods.com
Vegan spreads, jams, hot sauces, garlic condiments
Co-Founder: Einav Sharon
Co-Founder: Jeff Silva
Year Founded: 2012
Number Employees: 1-4
Type of Packaging: Food Service, Private Label

Food Manufacturers / A-Z

4386 Filippo Berio Brand
9 Polito Ave # 10
Floor 10
Lyndhurst, NJ 07071-3406
201-525-2900
Fax: 201-525-0805 www.filippoberio.com
Olive oil
President: Tom Mueller
Chief Executive Officer: Tonghong Wu
Vice President: Alberto Fontana
Estimated Sales: $10-20,000,000
Number Employees: 10-19
Number of Brands: 11
Parent Co: Societa' Per Azioni Lucchese Olii E Vini
Brands:
  Casale Degli Ulivi
  Centanni
  Filippo Berio Extra Virgin
  Tiger Brand
  Sagri
  Francesconi
  Filippo Berio Green
  Farmhouse
  Fattoria Dell'ulivo
  Filippo Berio
  Filippo Berio Olive

4387 Fillmore Piru Citrus
357 N Main St
P.O. Box 350
Piru, CA 93040
805-521-1781
Fax: 805-521-0990 www.fillmorepirucitrus.com
Oranges, lemons and avocados
President: Brett Kirkpatrick
brett@fpcitrus.com
CFO: Christina Morris
Sales Manager: Lupita Fernandez
VP, Operations: Tim Shugrue
Grower Relations: Samuel Orozco
Plant Supervisor: Antonio Martinez
Year Founded: 1897
Estimated Sales: $20-50 Million
Number Employees: 50-99
Type of Packaging: Consumer, Food Service
Brands:
  Airship
  Belle of Piru
  Cupid
  Cycle
  Desirable
  Glider
  Home of Ramona
  Mansion
  Oriole
  Weaver

4388 Fillo Factory, The
Northvale, NJ 07647
201-439-1036
Fax: 201-385-0012 800-653-4556
ronrex@bellatlantic.net www.fillofactory.com
Gourmet appetizers, baklava, strudel, pastries and fillo dough; importer of dough
President: Ron Rexroth
VP Marketing: Tony Falletta
Contact: Tim Bennett
t.bennett@fillofactory.com
Estimated Sales: $1-3 Million
Number Employees: 60
Square Footage: 12000
Type of Packaging: Consumer, Food Service, Private Label, Bulk
Brands:
  Fillo Factory

4389 Filsinger Vineyards & Winery
39050 De Portola Road
Temecula, CA 92592
951-302-6363
Fax: 877-801-8088 www.filsingerwinery.com
Wines
President: Robert Olson
Contact: William Filsinger
wfilsinger@aol.com
Estimated Sales: $500-1,000,000 appx.
Number Employees: 5-9

4390 Finchville Farms Country Ham
5157 Taylorsville Rd
P.O. Box 56
Finchville, KY 40022-6771
502-834-7952
Fax: 502-834-7095 800-678-1521
www.finchvillefarms.com
Manuafacturer of country ham
Dir: Nathan Arvin
Estimated Sales: $1 Million
Number Employees: 10-19
Type of Packaging: Consumer

4391 Finding Home Farms
140 Eatontown Rd.
Middletown, NY 10940
845-355-4335
www.findinghomefarms.com
Organic maple syrup, waffle and pancake mix, maple mustard and maple candy
Founder/Co-Owner: Laura Putnam
Founder/Co-Owner: Dana Putnam
Year Founded: 2013
Number of Brands: 1
Number of Products: 5
Type of Packaging: Consumer, Private Label
Brands:
  Finding Home Farms

4392 Fine & Raw Chocolate
Brooklyn, NY 11206
718-366-3633
factory@fineandraw.com
www.fineandraw.com
Truffles, chocolate bars, butters and spreads
Owner: Daniel Sklaar

4393 Fine Choice Foods
23111 Fraserwood Way
Richmond, BC V6V 1B3
Canada
604-522-3110
Fax: 866-372-7744 866-760-0888
info@finechoicefoods.com
www.finechoicefoods.com
Dim sum, frozen Chinese entrees and egg rolls
President: Charles Lui
Operations Manager: Christina Lui
Estimated Sales: $5.9 Million
Number Employees: 20-49
Square Footage: 20000
Type of Packaging: Consumer, Food Service, Private Label, Bulk

4394 Fine Dried Foods Intl
2553 Mission St # A
Santa Cruz, CA 95060-5745
831-426-1413
Fax: 831-426-0870 awesomefruit@yahoo.com
www.finedriedfoods.com
Fine Dried Foods International specializes in fresh dried, high quality tropical fruits.
President: Rusty Brown
fdfi@pacbell.net
Estimated Sales: $2.5-5,000,000
Number Employees: 5-9
Type of Packaging: Private Label
Brands:
  True Fruit

4395 Fine Foods Intl
9907 Baptist Church Rd
St Louis, MO 63123-4903
314-842-4473
Fax: 314-843-8846 ffinylp@aol.com
www.dek.de
Tea and coffee industry bags (brick packs), coffee and cappuccino mixes
Manager: Carole Garnett
cagarnett1@aol.com
VP: Keith Sheller
Operations: Carole Garnett
Estimated Sales: Less Than $500,000
Number Employees: 1-4
Type of Packaging: Bulk

4396 Fine Foods Of America Inc
11700 Manor Rd
Leawood, KS 66211-3010
913-451-2525
info@firehook.com
Manufacturer of different types of ketchups.
Owner: Bruce Steinberg
sales@finefoodsofamerica.com
Number Employees: 10-19
Brands:
  Fine Vines

4397 Fine Foods Trading Company
801 New York Ave
Union City, NJ 07087-4115
973-772-2221
Fax: 973-767-2514 info@finecaviar.com
www.finecaviar.com
Caviar
Co-Owner: Irina Walinsky
Year Founded: 1998
Type of Packaging: Consumer, Food Service

4398 Fine Line Seafood
194 Thompson Mill Rd
Newtown, PA 18940-3102
215-598-3359
Fax: 215-598-7235
Producer of fish and seafood.
President: Herbert Young
Estimated Sales: Under $500,000
Number Employees: 1-4

4399 (HQ)Fineberg Packing Company
2875 Starling Place
P.O.Box 80432
Memphis, TN 38108
901-458-2622
Fax: 901-458-7449 katey@finebergpacking.com
www.finebergpacking.com
Meat products: boloney, hot dogs, bacon, smoked hams, packing services available
President: Richard Freudenberg
General Manager: Kay Scott
Estimated Sales: $13.8 Million
Number Employees: 50-99

4400 Finer Foods Inc
3100 W 36th St
Chicago, IL 60632-2304
773-579-3870
Fax: 773-890-1115 finerfoods@aol.com
www.midwestfoods.com
Frozen foods
President: James Fitzgerald
mfitzg3580@aol.com
Estimated Sales: $10-20 Million
Number Employees: 50-99
Square Footage: 100

4401 Finest Call
810 Progress Blvd
New Albany, IN 47150
812-944-3585
finestcallinfo@abmcocktails.com
www.finestcall.com
Alcoholic and nonalcoholic cocktail mixes.
Estimated Sales: $20-50 Million
Number Employees: 50-99
Square Footage: 110000
Type of Packaging: Consumer, Food Service, Private Label
Other Locations:
  American Beverage Marketers
  Overland Park KS
Brands:
  Finest Call
  Master of Mixes

4402 Finestkind Fish Market
855 US Route 1
York, ME 03909-5835
207-363-5000
Fax: 207-363-2664 800-288-8154
Manufacturer and Wholesaler full service seafood company.
Owner: Michael Goslin
Estimated Sales: $2.2 Million
Number Employees: 5

4403 Finger Lakes Coffee Roasters
7330 Route 251
Victor, NY 14564
585-742-6210
Fax: 585-742-6211 800-420-6154
service@fingerlakescoffee.com
www.fingerlakescoffee.com
Fresh roasted coffee
Manager: Kierna McGhan
Co-Owner: Robert Cowdery
Estimated Sales: Less than $500,000
Number Employees: 10-19
Square Footage: 1100

Brands:
    Canandaigua Blend
    Lake Blend
    Seneca Blend

4404 Finkemeier Bakery
3103 Strong Avenue
Kansas City, KS 66106-2113
    913-831-3103
Bakery products
President: Bill Crum
Estimated Sales: $500,000 appx.
Number Employees: 5-9

4405 (HQ)Finlandia Cheese
2001 US Highway 46
Suite 303
Parsippany, NJ 07054-1315
    973-316-6609
Fax: 973-316-6609 www.finlandiacheese.com
Producer and supplier of cheeses and butter. Some of their customers include supermarkets, delis, cheese shops and restaurants. Some of their cheeses include Swiss, Colby Jack, Gouda, Monterey Jack, Harvati, American, Pepper Jack andmany more.
President: Sam Aquino
samaquino@finlandiacheese.com
CEO: Emma Aer
Director, Marketing: Judy Lofgren
Estimated Sales: $5-10,000,000
Number Employees: 10-19
Parent Co: Valio International USA
Brands:
    Finlandia Lappi
    Finlandia Naturals
    Finlandia Swiss
    Heavenly Light
    Muenster
    Sandwich Naturals

4406 Finlay Extracts & Ingredients USA, Inc.
23 Vreeland Road
Suite 201
Florham Park, NJ 07932-1510
    973-539-8030
Fax: 973-539-4816 800-288-6272
infoUSA@finlays.net www.finlayusa.com
Bleding facility for tea and tea products.
Chief Executive Officer: Dushanth Ratwatte
HR Director, Extracts & Ingredients: Tamie Hutchins
Vice President, R&D: Catherine Robinson
NJ Contact: Steve Olyha
Estimated Sales: $10-20 000,000
Number Employees: 5-9
Parent Co: Finlays
Type of Packaging: Bulk
Other Locations:
    Manufacturing Facilty
    Lincoln RI

4407 (HQ)Finlays
10 Blackstone Valley Place
Lincoln, RI 02865
    401-333-3300
    800-288-6272
americas@finlays.net www.finlays.net
Roaster and extractor of gourmet coffee and tea; also, coffee extracts, syrups, concentrates, iced cappuccino, iced coffee, espresso and smoothies available; services include retail, distributor, OCS, food service and foodingredients
Managing Director: Guy Chambers
Finance Director: Julian Rutherford
Technical Director: Wolfgang Tosch
Year Founded: 1895
Number Employees: 100-249
Square Footage: 180000
Parent Co: Swire
Type of Packaging: Consumer, Food Service, Private Label
Brands:
    Autocrat
    Eclipse
    Newport Coffee Traders

4408 Fiore Di Pasta
4776 E Jensen Ave
Fresno, CA 93725-1704
    559-457-0431
Fax: 559-457-0164 info@fioredipasta.com
www.fioredipasta.com
Fresh and frozen organic pastas, sauces, and entrees

Owner: Shanaz Ahmed
ahmed.sarah81@gmail.com
Chief Operating Officer: Benedetta Primavera
Vice President: Anthony Primavera
Purchasing Director: John Day
Number Employees: 20-49
Square Footage: 120000

4409 Fiore Winery
3026 Whiteford Rd
Pylesville, MD 21132-1212
    410-452-0132
Fax: 410-879-4926 contact@fiorewinery.com
www.fiorewinery.com
Wines
Owner: Mike Fiore
mike.fiore@fiorewinery.com
VP: Erich Fiore
Estimated Sales: $1-2,500,000
Number Employees: 5-9

4410 Fiori Bruna Pasta Products
5340 NW 163rd St
Miami Lakes, FL 33014-6228
    305-705-2534
Fax: 305-621-4997 info@fioribruna.com
www.fioribruna.com
Manufacturer and exporter of frozen cheese tortellini, ravioli, cavatelli and potato gnocchi; also, dry egg fettuccine and linguine
President: Romano Fiori
fiori@bellsouth.net
VP Sales/Co-Founder: Cesare Bruna
Estimated Sales: $2.5-5 Million
Number Employees: 10-19
Square Footage: 20000
Type of Packaging: Consumer, Food Service, Private Label, Bulk
Brands:
    Fiori-Bruna

4411 Fiorucci Foods USA Inc
1800 Ruffin Mill Rd
S Chesterfield, VA 23834-5910
    804-520-8392
Fax: 804-520-7180 800-524-7775
marketing@cfg-america.com
www.fioruccifoods.com
Manufacturer and exporter of Italian speciality meats including prosciutto, salami, regional specialty meats, pre-sliced, diced, small salamis, pepperoni, balsamic vinegar
President/CEO: Claudio Colmignoli
CEO: Chris Maze
Finance Executive: Mark Morrison
Quality Assurance Manager: Richard Wilson
Marketing: Keith Amrhein
VP Sales/Marketing: John Jack
Human Resources Manager: Carey Tillett
VP Operations: Oliviero Colmignoli
Plant Manager: Mark Bragalone
Purchasing Manager: Jennifer Erdelyi
Estimated Sales: $10-20 Million
Number Employees: 1-4
Square Footage: 280000
Parent Co: Cesare Fiorucci
Type of Packaging: Consumer, Food Service, Private Label, Bulk
Brands:
    Colosseum
    Fiorucci

4412 Fire Fruits International
5036 Dr Phillips Blvd
Suite 198
Orlando, FL 32819-3310
    407-480-6580
Fax: 321-396-7548 www.firefruits.com
Fruit based hot sauces and condiments.
Founder: Francisco Brignoni
Estimated Sales: $127,346
Number Employees: 2
Type of Packaging: Food Service, Private Label

4413 Firebird Artisan Mills
500 North St W
Harvey, ND 58341-1012
    701-324-4330
Fax: 701-324-4334 www.firebirdmills.com
Manufactuere of gluten free flour and mixes; custom blending available.
President Sales & Procurement: Chris Cairo
Plant Manager: Don Franke

Number Employees: 20-49
Parent Co: Agspring LLC
Type of Packaging: Consumer, Food Service, Private Label, Bulk

4414 Firefly Fandango
3401 Rainier Ave S
Seattle, WA 98144
    206-760-3700
Fax: 206-721-0909
Chocolate and cookies
Estimated Sales: $300,000-500,000
Number Employees: 5-9

4415 Firehook Bakery & Coffeehouse
14701 Flint Lee Rd
Chantilly, VA 20151-1505
    703-263-2253
info@firehook.com
www.firehook.com
Manufacturer of baked goods.
Owner: Bruce Steinberg
Estimated Sales: Less Than $500,000
Number Employees: 1-4

4416 Firelands Winery
917 Bardshar Rd
Sandusky, OH 44870-1507
    419-625-5474
Fax: 419-625-4887 800-548-9463
info@firelandswinery.com
www.firelandswinery.com
Producer of wines. Products include chardonnay, riesling, ice wine, merlot, pinot noir, dolcetto, brut champagne and more.
Owner: Adrian Salvador
asalvador@firelandswinery.com
Sales Manager: David Blankenbeker
Office Manager: Vicky Rogers
Estimated Sales: $5-10,000,000
Number Employees: 10-19
Parent Co: Paramount Distillers

4417 Fireside Kitchen
3430 Prescott Street
Halifax, NS B3K 4Y4
Canada
    902-454-7387
Fax: 902-453-0275 www.prescottgroup.ca
Natural jams, marmalades, cranberry sauce, cookies, muffins and fruit cakes; also, available in gift packs
Executive Director: Susan Slaunwhite
Sales Coordinator: Cindy Kingwell
Production Supervisor: Dorothy O'Reilly
Brands:
    Fireside Kitchen

4418 Firestone Pacific FoodsCo
4211 Fruit Valley Rd
Vancouver, WA 98660-1280
    360-695-9484
Fax: 360-695-0040
sales@firestonepacificfoods.com
www.firestonepacificfoods.com
Wine
Owner: Stan Firestone
stan@firestonepacking.com
Estimated Sales: $2.5-5,000,000
Number Employees: 100-249

4419 Firestone Vineyard
5017 Zaca Station Rd
Los Olivos, CA 93441
    805-688-3940
Fax: 805-686-1256 info@firestonewine.com
www.firestonewine.com
Wines
Owner: William Foley
Estimated Sales: $8,725,246
Number Employees: 20-49
Parent Co: Foley Family Wines, Inc

4420 Firmenich Inc.
250 Plainsboro Rd.
Plainsboro, NJ 08536
    609-452-1000
Fax: 609-520-9780 800-257-9591
www.firmenich.com
Flavors and fragrances.

Food Manufacturers / A-Z

Chairman: Patrick Firmenich
CEO: Gilbert Ghostine
President, Perfumery & Ingredients: Armand de Villoutreys
Chief Research Officer: Genevieve Berger
President, Flavors: Emmanuel Butstraen
COO: Eric Nicolas
Chief Supply Chain Officer: Boet Brinkgreve
Year Founded: 1895
Estimated Sales: $4 Billion
Number Employees: 8,000
Other Locations:
    Firmenich Chemical Plant
    Newark NJ
    Fermenich Citrus Center
    Safety Harbor FL

4421 First Choice Ingredients
N112 W19528 Mequon Rd
Germantown, WI 53022
                                                    262-251-4322
        Fax: 262-251-3881 roddyt@fcingredients.com
                                    www.fcingredients.com
Food flavor and ingredients manufacturers; including cheese powders & pasts, dairy powders, meat flavors, savory flavors, bakery flavors, and beverage liquids & powders
President: Jim Pekar
EVP: Roger Mullins
Sales Manager: Natalie Moore
Contact: Lucas Lieffring
llieffring@fcingredients.com
Estimated Sales: $3 Million
Number Employees: 20

4422 (HQ)First Colony Coffee & Tea Company
204 W 22nd Street
Po Box 11005
Norfolk, VA 23517-2231
                                                    757-622-2224
            Fax: 757-623-2391   800-446-8555
Processor, importer and exporter of teas and coffees including varietal, blends and flavored
President/CEO: Bruce Grembowitz
Marketing Director: Julie Anderson
National Sales Director: Joyce Jordan
Contact: John Bergsten
john.bergsten@orbitalatk.com
Production Manager: Justin Goodman
Estimated Sales: $13 Million
Number Employees: 80
Square Footage: 94000
Type of Packaging: Consumer, Food Service, Private Label, Bulk
Brands:
    Bencheley
    Carolan's
    First Colony
    Frangelico
    Ghirardelli
    Jack Daniel's
    Southern Comfort

4423 First Colony Winery
1650 Harris Creek Rd
Charlottesville, VA 22902-7820
                                                    434-979-7105
            Fax: 434-293-2054   877-979-7105
                        info@firstcolonywinery.com
                        www.firstcolonywinery.com
Wine
Owner: Heather A. Spiess
Owner: Bruce D. Spiess (MD)
Owner: Jeffrey W. Miller
General Manager: Martha Hayman
Estimated Sales: $3-5 Million
Number Employees: 5-9

4424 First District Association
101 S. Swift Ave.
Litchfield, MN 55355
                                                    320-693-3236
                                info@firstdistrict.com
                                www.firstdistrict.com
Dairy products including lactose blends and mixes, specialty cheeses, cream, wheys, whey protein concentrates and milk powders.
President/CEO: Clinton Fall
cfall@firstdistrict.com
Director, Quality Assurance: Dawn Raymond
Director, Sales/Marketing: Glenn Kaping
Director, Operations: Doug Anderson

Year Founded: 1894
Estimated Sales: $476.6 Million
Number Employees: 100-249
Square Footage: 100000
Brands:
    Fieldgate

4425 First Food Co
4561 Leston St
4561 Leston Street
Dallas, TX 75247-5709
                                                    214-637-0214
            Fax: 214-905-0605   800-527-1866
            service@firstfoodco.com www.firstfoodco.com
Gelatins for desserts, salads, etc
Owner: Brooke Hogan
mhogan@fqfood.com
Estimated Sales: $5-10,000,000
Number Employees: 50-99
Type of Packaging: Consumer, Food Service, Private Label, Bulk

4426 First Food International
333 Cantor Ave
Linden, NJ 07036
                                                    908-862-5558
                        Fax: 908-474-1119
Oilseed production (coconut, peanut, soybean and sunflower)
President: Tony Chiang
Estimated Sales: 1-2.5 Million
Number Employees: 7

4427 First Oriental Market
2774 E Ponce DE Leon Ave
Decatur, GA 30030-2715
                                                    404-377-6950
                        Fax: 404-377-7505
Tilapia, flounder, catfish, mackerel, oriental food items
Owner: Diane Bounngaseng
Estimated Sales: $5-10 Million
Number Employees: 5-9

4428 First Original Texas Chili Company
3313 N. Jones
Fort Worth, TX 76164-0281
                                                    817-626-0983
            Fax: 817-626-9105   800-507-0009
                                    www.texaschili.com
Frozen chili con carne, chili sauce and beef taco filling
President: Danny Owens
Estimated Sales: $5-10,000,000
Number Employees: 5-9
Type of Packaging: Consumer, Food Service, Private Label
Brands:
    Our Famous Texas Chili
    Sloppy Joe
    Tex-O-Gold
    Texas One Step

4429 First Roasters of Central Florida
863 N Highway 17/92
Longwood, FL 32750-3167
                                                    407-699-6364
                        Fax: 407-699-6301
Coffee
Manager: Leonardo Lamastus
Estimated Sales: $2.5-5,000,000
Number Employees: 1-4
Brands:
    First Roasters of Central Florida

4430 (HQ)First Spice Mixing Co
3333 Greenpoint Ave
Long Island City, NY 11101-2084
                                                    718-361-2556
            Fax: 718-361-2515   800-221-1105
                                    www.firstspice.com
Seasonings, binders and curing compounds; also, textured vegetable protein, hydrolyzed dairy products, nonfat dry milk, curing ingredients, phosphate compounds, MSG-flavor boosters and spices
President: Peter Epstein
peter@firstspice.com
CEO: Wendy Epstein
Vice President: Vicki Miller
Research & Development: Marcy Epstein
Estimated Sales: $5-10 Million
Number Employees: 10-19

Other Locations:
    First Spice Mixing Company
    San Francisco CA
Brands:
    Albunate
    Flavolin
    Flavor 86
    Savorlok
    Texite
    Tietolin
    Vegolin Hvp
    Vita-Curaid
    Vitaphos

4431 Firth Maple Products
22418 Firth Rd
Spartansburg, PA 16434-3222
                                                    814-654-2435
            Fax: 814-654-7265   877-861-0260
                    www.foundationforsustainableforests.org
Maple syrup
Owner: Troy Firth
firthmaple@aol.com
Estimated Sales: $720,000
Number Employees: 20-49

4432 Fischer & Wieser Spec Foods
411 S Lincoln St
Fredericksburg, TX 78624-4502
                                                    830-997-7194
            Fax: 830-997-0455   877-861-0260
                                    info@jelly.com
Jams, jellies, preserves, marmalades, mustard, sauces, salsa, syrup, honey and snacks
President: Case Fischer
info@jelly.com
President/CEO: Case D Fischer
Director Quality Assurance & Product Dev: Ashley Seelig
Chief Marketing Officer: Deanna Fischer
Sales Director: Mary Llanes Guevera
Director Customer Service: Yvonne Fox
COO: Jenny Wieser Ph.D.
Purchasing: Jenny Wieser
Estimated Sales: $1-3,000,000
Number Employees: 50-99
Type of Packaging: Consumer, Food Service, Private Label
Brands:
    Fischer & Wieser
    Mom's
    Old Chisholm Trail

4433 Fischer Honey Company
2001 N Poplar Street
North Little Rock, AR 72114-2999
                                                    501-758-1123
            Fax: 501-758-8601 fischerhoney@att.net
                                    www.fischerhoney.com
Honey including table, creamed and bakers
Year Founded: 1935
Estimated Sales: $5-10 Million
Number Employees: 5-9
Square Footage: 100000
Type of Packaging: Consumer, Food Service, Private Label, Bulk
Brands:
    Fischer's

4434 Fischer Meats
85 Front St N
Issaquah, WA 98027-3237
                                                    425-392-3131
            Fax: 425-392-0168 www.fischermeatsnw.com
Meat
Owner: Chris Chiechi
fischermeats@gmail.com
Estimated Sales: Less Than $500,000
Number Employees: 5-9
Type of Packaging: Consumer, Food Service

4435 Fish Breeders of Idaho
18374 Hwy 30
Hagerman, ID 83332
                                                    208-837-6114
            Fax: 208-837-6254 fpi@fishbreedersofidaho.com
                                    www.fishbreedersofidaho.com
Breeders of fish. Varieties include trout, sturgeon, catfish, tilapia, and tropical aquarium fish.
Owner: Leo Ray
Vice President: Tod Ray
Sales: Netty Marino
Contact: Judith Ay
judith.ray@alaskasbest.com
Production Manager: Starla Barnes

Food Manufacturers / A-Z

Estimated Sales: $5-10 Million
Number Employees: 2-10
Brands:
  Pride of Idaho

4436 Fish Brothers
203 Taylor Way
PO Box 416
Blue Lake, CA 95525
707-668-9700
Fax: 707-668-9701 800-244-0583
www.fishbrothers.com
Smoked fish including, salmon, nova lox and albacore
Owner: Scott Bradshaw
fishbro@fishbrothers.com
Estimated Sales: $500,000-1 Million
Number Employees: 10-19
Square Footage: 5000
Type of Packaging: Consumer, Food Service, Private Label, Bulk
Brands:
  Fish Brothers

4437 Fish Express
3343 Kuhio Hwy # 10
Suite 10
Lihue, HI 96766
808-245-9918
Fax: 808-246-9188
Seafood
Principal: David Wada
Estimated Sales: $3-5 Million
Number Employees: 10-19

4438 Fish Hopper
700 Cannery Row # K
Monterey, CA 93940-1036
831-372-3406
Fax: 831-372-2026 www.fishhopper.com
Canned clam chowder
CEO: Sabu Shake Jr
Estimated Sales: $2.5-5 Million
Number Employees: 50-99
Type of Packaging: Private Label

4439 Fish King
722 N Glendale Ave
Glendale, CA 91206-2198
818-244-2161
Fax: 818-244-2115 fishkingsfd@aol.com
www.fishkingseafood.com
Seafood including breaded and IQF scallops, shrimp and calamari
President: Tom Furuckawa
Manager: Robert Sperry
fishkingsfd@aol.com
Number Employees: 20-49
Type of Packaging: Consumer, Food Service

4440 Fish King Processors
1 King & Prince Blvd
Brunswick, GA 31520
360-733-9090
Fax: 360-733-9152 800-841-0205
www.kpseafood.com
Smoked salmon
CEO: Terrill Beck
Estimated Sales: $10-20,000,000
Number Employees: 20-49
Parent Co: Unisea Foods
Type of Packaging: Consumer, Food Service
Brands:
  Pride of Alaska
  Salmon Bay

4441 Fish Market Inc
1406 W Chestnut St
Louisville, KY 40203-1776
502-587-7474
Fax: 502-587-7503
Frozen seafood
President: Steven Smith
sseafoods@aol.com
Estimated Sales: $5-10,000,000
Number Employees: 20-49
Square Footage: 14000
Type of Packaging: Consumer, Food Service, Private Label
Brands:
  Fishmarket Seafoods

4442 Fish Market Inc
1406 W Chestnut St
Louisville, KY 40203-1776
502-587-7474
Fax: 502-587-7503
Seafood
President: Steven Smith
sseafoods@aol.com
Estimated Sales: $10 Million
Number Employees: 20-49

4443 Fisher Honey Co
1 Belle Ave # 21
Lewistown, PA 17044-2433
717-242-4373
Fax: 717-242-3978 fisherhoney@fisherhoney.com
www.fisherhoney.com
Manufacturer and exporter of honey, beeswax, beekeepers supplies, containers, glass, metal and plastic
Owner: Scott Fisher
fisherhoney@fisherhoney.com
Plant Supervisor: Scott Fisher
Estimated Sales: $1-2 Million
Number Employees: 1-4
Square Footage: 40000
Type of Packaging: Consumer, Food Service, Private Label, Bulk
Brands:
  Fisher Honey
  Stewarts Honey

4444 Fisher Ridge Wine Co Inc
529 Sheridan Cir
Charleston, WV 25314-1054
304-342-8702
Wines
Owner: Wilson Ward
Estimated Sales: $1-2,500,000
Number Employees: 1-4

4445 Fisher Vineyards
6200 Saint Helena Rd
Santa Rosa, CA 95404-9692
707-539-7511
Fax: 707-539-3601 info@fishervineyards.com
www.fishervineyards.com
Wines
President: Fred Fisher
ffisher@fishervineyards.com
Vice President: Juelle Fisher
Sales/Marketing: Cameron Fisher
General Manager: Robert Fisher
Winemaker: Whitney Fisher
Estimated Sales: $500,000
Number Employees: 10-19
Type of Packaging: Private Label

4446 Fisher's Popcorn
200 S Boardwalk
Ocean City, MD 21842
410-289-5638
Fax: 410-289-1720 888-395-0335
www.fisherspopcorn.com
Caramel-coated popcorn
Owner: Donald Fisher
Marketing: Ben Bauer
Number Employees: 50-99

4447 Fisherman's Market International
607 Bedford Highway
Halifax, NS B3M 2L6
Canada
902-445-3474
Fax: 902-443-5561 retail@fishermansmarket.com
www.fishermansmarket.ca
Live lobster and fresh or frozen seafood
President: Fred Greene
Director International Marketing: Gino Nadalini
Sales: Scott Thompson
General Manager: Monte Snow
Plant Manager: Bill Langdon
Estimated Sales: $20+ Million
Number Employees: 150
Square Footage: 20000
Type of Packaging: Consumer, Food Service, Private Label

4448 Fisherman's Reef Shrimp Company
5192 Fannett Rd
Beaumont, TX 77705
409-842-9520
Fax: 409-842-1212
Frozen domestic shrimp
Owner: Vikki Jones
VP: Trudy Verdine
Contact: Vicki Jones
vsj42@aol.com
Number Employees: 100-249
Parent Co: Farmer Boys Catfish International
Type of Packaging: Food Service, Private Label
Brands:
  Fisherman's Reef

4449 Fishermens Net
849 Forest Ave
Portland, ME 04103-4162
207-772-3565
Fax: 207-828-1726
Seafood
Owner: Benjamin Lindner
Estimated Sales: Less Than $500,000
Number Employees: 1-4

4450 Fishhawk Fisheries
1 4th St
Astoria, OR 97103-4339
503-325-5252
Fax: 503-325-8786
Crab, shrimp, canned fish, salmon, sturgeon, shad, smelt, halibut and black cod
Owner: Steve Fick
fishhawk@ideal-web.com
Director: Carol Fratt
Estimated Sales: $1 Million
Number Employees: 10-19
Square Footage: 12000
Type of Packaging: Bulk
Brands:
  Fishhawk

4451 Fishland Market
117 Ahui Street
Suite C
Honolulu, HI 96813
808-523-6902
Fax: 808-523-6905
Bottomfish, reef fish, Kona crab, white crab, Hawaiian crab
President: Paul Nishimoto

4452 Fishpeople
2540 NE M L King Blvd
Portland, OR 97212
503-342-2424
info@fishpeopleseafood.com
fishpeopleseafood.com
Sustainable seafood
Co-Founder: Duncan Berry
Co-Founder: Kipp Baratoff
Year Founded: 2012
Type of Packaging: Food Service

4453 FitPro USA
2333 Courage Dr
Fairfield, CA 94533
Fax: 707-419-4845 877-645-5776
info@teamfitpro.com www.fitprousa.com
Protein shakes and vitamin supplements
CEO: Gus Malliarodakis
COO: Mike Zumpano
Number of Brands: 1
Number of Products: 8
Type of Packaging: Consumer
Brands:
  FITPRO GO
  EVO

4454 Fitzkee's Candies Inc
2352 S Queen St
York, PA 17402-4939
717-741-1031
Fax: 717-741-5176
Assorted chocolates
President: Robert Fitzkee
Estimated Sales: $2.5-5 Million
Number Employees: 10-19
Type of Packaging: Consumer

4455 Fitzpatrick Winery & Lodge
7740 Fairplay Rd
Somerset, CA 95684-9208
530-620-3248
Fax: 530-620-6838 800-245-9166
Wines

Food Manufacturers / A-Z

Owner: Brian Fitzpatrick
brian@fitzpatrickwinery.com
VP: Diana Fitzpatrick
Estimated Sales: $500,000-$1,000,000
Number Employees: 1-4
Brands:
    Fitzpatrick

4456 Five Acre Farms
44 Court Street
Brooklyn, NY 11201
    718-522-3819
info@fiveacrefarms.com
fiveacrefarms.com

Milk; eggs; and apple cider.
CEO: Daniel Horan
Director of Sales: Jill Bellville
Director of Operations: Patrick Horan
Year Founded: 2011
Estimated Sales: $381,313
Number Employees: 6
Type of Packaging: Food Service, Private Label

4457 Five Ponds Farm
1933 E Mill Rd
Lineville, AL 36266
    256-396-5217
Fax: 256-386-5899

Fruits and vegetables
President: Edward Donlon

4458 Five Star Food Base Company
865 Pierce Butler Rte
St Paul, MN 55104-3073
    651-488-2300
Fax: 651-488-2094   800-505-7827

Soup bases and blended seasonings
Owner: Sid Larson
Estimated Sales: $5-10 000,000
Number Employees: 10-19

4459 Five Star Foodies
3101 Clifton Ave
Cincinnati, OH 45220
info@fivestarfoodies.com
foodiesvegan.com

Vegan burger patties and cold pressed juices
CEO: Valerie Williams
Number of Brands: 1
Number of Products: 8
Type of Packaging: Consumer
Brands:
    FOODIES

4460 Five Star Home Foods, Inc.
234 Mall Boulevard
Suite 140
King of Prussia, PA 19406
    610-337-9004
    800-246-5405
www.fivestarhomefoods.com

Prepared meals, organic vegetables, and juices
President/Owner: Chef Dan
Contact: Gabrielle Delconte
gdelconte@fivestarhomefoods.com
Estimated Sales: $5-10 Million
Number Employees: 9

4461 FiveStar Gourmet Foods
3880 E Ebony Street
Ontario, CA 91761
    909-390-0032
info@fivestargourmetfoods.com
fivestargourmetfoods.com

Sustainable seafood
Co-Founder: Duncan Berry
Co-Founder: Kipp Baratoff
Type of Packaging: Food Service
Brands:
    Simply Fresh

4462 Fizz-O Water Co
809 N Lewis Ave
Tulsa, OK 74110-5365
    918-834-3691
Fax: 918-832-0899   water@fizzowater.com
www.fizzowater.com

Bottler and wholesaler/distributor of spring, drinking and distilled water
President: Harry R Doerner
fizzowater@att.net
Owner: Hency Doerner
Owner: Rick Doerner
Plant Manager: Rick Malkey

Estimated Sales: $1-3 Million
Number Employees: 20-49
Number of Brands: 4
Square Footage: 30000
Type of Packaging: Consumer
Brands:
    Doublepure Distilled
    Mountain Valley
    Ozarka
    Spring House

4463 Fizzle Flat Farm, L.L.C.
18773 E 1600th Avenue
Yale, IL 62448
    618-793-2060
Fax: 618-793-2060   mcmanges@fizzleflatfarm.com
www.fizzleflatfarm.com

Organic popcorn and food grade certified organic grains including white, yellow and blue corn, wheat, soybeans, buckwheat. Grass fed beef raised on certified organic pastures (pasture-raised).
Owner/Manager: Marvin Manges
Owner/Manager: Lori Wells
Estimated Sales: $1-3 Million
Number Employees: 4
Square Footage: 8750
Type of Packaging: Bulk
Brands:
    Fizzle Flat Farm

4464 Fizzy Lizzy
64 Wayne Street
Suite D20
Jersey City, NJ 07302
    212-966-3232
Fax: 888-680-2444   800-203-9336
info@fizzylizzy.com

Whole fruit juice and sparkling water.
CEO: Aaron Morrill
VP: Amy Drown
Estimated Sales: $1.1 Million
Number Employees: 5

4465 Flackers
Minneapolis, MN 55424-0868
hello@flackers.com
flackers.com

Organic flaxseed crackers
Co-Founder: Dr. Alison Levitt
Year Founded: 2008

4466 Flagstaff Brewing Co
16 E Route 66 # 1
Flagstaff, AZ 86001-5792
    928-773-1442
www.flagbrew.com

Beer
President: Jeff Thorsett
jefft@flagbrew.com
Estimated Sales: $8,722,990
Number Employees: 20-49
Brands:
    Agassiz Amber
    Bitterroot Extra Special Bitter
    Blackbird Porter
    Bubbaganouj Ipa
    Great Golden Ale
    Sasquatch Stout
    Three-Pin Pale Ale

4467 Flaherty Inc
9047 Terminal Ave
Skokie, IL 60077-1570
    847-966-1005
Fax: 847-966-1072

Producer of mustard.
Owner: Catherine Flaharty
Finance Manager: Deirdre Flaherty
General Manager: Bridget Flaherty
Estimated Sales: $5-10,000,000
Number Employees: 5-9

4468 Flamin' Red's Woodfired
Robinson Hill Rd
Pawlet, VT 05761
    802-325-3641
Fax: 802-325-3641   woodfire@vermontel.net

Pizza crusts made with organic flour
Owner: Carson Lake
Estimated Sales: $300,000-500,000
Number Employees: 1-4

4469 (HQ)Flamm Pickle & Packing
4502 Hipps Hollow Rd
PO Box 500
Eau Claire, MI 49111
    269-461-6916
Fax: 269-461-6166   800-742-5531
pickles@flammpickle.com   www.flammpickle.com

Sweet pickle relish, dill pickle relish and pickle brine used in salad dressings
President/General Manager: Gina Flamm
Year Founded: 1917
Estimated Sales: $4.20 Million
Number Employees: 10-19
Square Footage: 120000
Type of Packaging: Food Service, Bulk
Brands:
    Flamm's

4470 Flamous Brands
1801 Highland Ave # C
Suite C
Duarte, CA 91010-2833
    626-799-7909
Fax: 626-551-3088   www.flamousbrands.com

Falafel Chips and dip.
Manager: Alejandra Lopez
alejandra@flamousbrands.com
Number Employees: 5-9
Type of Packaging: Consumer

4471 (HQ)Flanders
1104 Gilmore St
Waycross, GA 31501-1307
    912-283-5191
Fax: 912-283-6228   info@flandersburgers.com
www.flandersprovision.com

Manufacturer, distributor and packager of beef patties
President/CEO: Huey Dubberly
CEO: Chris Huff
chuff@flandersprovision.com
CEO/Chief Financial Officer: Chris Huff
Quality Assurance Manager: Michael Denton
Sales: Hollis Yarn
Operations Manager: Rusty Rainey
Year Founded: 1958
Estimated Sales: $36.80 Million
Number Employees: 100-249

4472 Flanigan Farms
9522 Jefferson Blvd
PO Box 347
Culver City, CA 90232
    310-836-8437
Fax: 310-838-0743   800-525-0228
www.flaniganfarms.com

Nut mixes and dried organic persimmons
Owner: Patsy Flanigan
Operations: C Flanigan
Estimated Sales: $3 Million
Number Employees: 10-19
Number of Products: 42
Square Footage: 24000
Type of Packaging: Consumer, Food Service, Private Label
Brands:
    Nuts 'n' Fruit
    Nuts 'n' Things

4473 FlapJacked
960 W 124th Ave
Suite 100
Westminster, CO 80234
    720-476-4758
info@flapjacked.com
www.flapjacked.com

Pancake, muffin and cookie mixes
Co-Founder: Jennifer Bacon
Co-Founder: Dave Bacon
Number of Brands: 1
Number of Products: 18
Type of Packaging: Consumer
Brands:
    FLAPJACKED

4474 Flat Cracker Inc.
143 Washington Ave.
Lawrence, NY 11559-1613
    347-223-2587
Fax: 516-812-9325

Manufacturer of crackers.
Founder: Nicole Dawes

Food Manufacturers / A-Z

4475 (HQ)Flat Tire Bike Shop
6033 E Cave Creek Rd
Cave Creek, AZ 85331-8510
480-488-5261
Fax: 480-577-0177 www.flattirebike.com
Coffee
Owner: David Thompson
Co-Owner/Roastmaster: David Anderson
Estimated Sales: $5-10 Million
Number Employees: 1-4

4476 Flathau's Fine Foods
211 Greenwood Place
Hattiesburg, MS 39402
601-582-9629
Fax: 601-544-2333 888-263-1299
info@flathausfinefoods.com
www.flathausfinefoods.com
Flavored shortbread cookies covered with powdered sugar

4477 Flatout Inc
1422 Woodland Dr
Saline, MI 48176-1633
734-944-5445
Fax: 734-944-5115 866-944-5445
feedback@flatoutbread.com
www.flatoutbread.com
Flatbreads
Owner: Stacey Marsh
Co-Owner: Mike Marsh
Sales/Marketing: Bob Palotta
Number Employees: 100-249

4478 Flaum Appetizing
288 Scholes St
Brooklyn, NY 11206-1728
718-821-1970
Fax: 718-821-9051 info@flaums.com
www.flaumsappetizing.com
Sour pickles, sauerkraut, pickled herring, cole slaw, lox spreads and potato, whitefish, tuna and eggplant salads
Owner: Joel Stern
joel@flaums.com
Production Manager: Salomon Benatar
Estimated Sales: Less than $500,000
Number Employees: 20-49
Square Footage: 50000
Parent Co: M&M Food Products
Type of Packaging: Consumer, Food Service, Private Label, Bulk

4479 (HQ)Flavor & Fragrance Specialties
3 Industrial Ave
Mahwah, NJ 07430-3595
201-825-0352
Fax: 201-825-4785 800-998-4337
customer.care@ffs.com www.ffs.com
Flavor concentrates and fragrance extracts
President: Michael Bloom
m.bloom@ffs.com
Executive Vice President: William Palmer
Director, Sales: Robert C. Frantzen
Estimated Sales: $2.5-5 Million
Number Employees: 20-49
Square Footage: 120000
Type of Packaging: Bulk
Brands:
  Ammonia Guard
  E.O.C.
  High Impact

4480 Flavor Dynamics Two
640 Montrose Ave
South Plainfield, NJ 07080-2602
908-822-8855
Fax: 908-822-8547 888-271-8424
customercare@flavordynamics.com
Food and beverage flavors
President: Dolf DeRovira
R&D Director: Norma Schwarz
Estimated Sales: 20.5 Million
Number Employees: 20-49
Square Footage: 29000
Type of Packaging: Food Service, Private Label, Bulk
Other Locations:
  Flavor Dynamics
  Glenview IL
  Flavor Dynamics
  Corona Del Mar CA
  Flavor Dynamics
  Cape Charles VA

4481 Flavor House, Inc.
9516 Commerce Way
Adelanto, CA 92301-3947
760-246-9131
Fax: 760-246-8431 flavorhouseinc.com
Manufacturer and exporter of flavor concentrates including meat, poultry and seafood; also, hydrolyzed vegetable proteins and liquid and dry soy sauce.
Estimated Sales: $4 Million
Number Employees: 20-49
Square Footage: 84000
Type of Packaging: Bulk

4482 Flavor Producers
8521 Fallbrook Ave
Suite 380
West Hills, CA 91304
818-835-1850
sales@flavorproducers.com
flavorproducers.com
Custom flavors for food and beverage manufacturers
Year Founded: 1981
Type of Packaging: Consumer

4483 Flavor Right Foods Group
2517 E Chambers
St Phoenix, AZ 85040
602-232-2570
Fax: 602-232-2569 888-464-3734
info@flavorright.com
Dessert and pastry toppings and icings, frozen dessert mixes.
President: Doug Smith
Vice President: Rick Warf
Contact: Ivygalliher Galliher
ivygalliher@flavorright.com
Estimated Sales: $5-10 Million
Number Employees: 10-19
Brands:
  Festejos
  Whip N Ice
  Whip N Top

4484 (HQ)Flavor Sciences Inc
652 Nuway Cir
Lenoir, NC 28645-3646
828-758-2525
Fax: 828-758-2424 800-535-2867
information@flavorsciences.com
Natural and artificial flavors and essential oils; exporter of natural and artificial flavors and extracts
President: Roger Kiley
rogerkiley@gmail.com
Vice President: Joyce Kiley
Estimated Sales: $3-5 Million
Number Employees: 5-9

4485 Flavor Systems Intl.
10139 Commerce Park Dr
Cincinnati, OH 45246
513-870-4900
Fax: 513-870-4909 800-498-2783
info@flavorsystems.com
Custom flavorings and specialty food systems
President: William Wasz
Owner: Bob Bahoshy
VP: William Baker
R&D: Angie Lantman
Quality Control: Alan Baker
Contact: Bill Baker
bill.baker@flavorsystems.com
Plant Manager: Rick Messinger
Purchasing: Roger Sage
Estimated Sales: $20 Million
Number Employees: 55
Square Footage: 25000
Type of Packaging: Bulk

4486 FlavorHealth
685 US Hwy 1
North Brunswick, NJ 08902
732-875-4799
Fax: 732-565-1183 info@flavorhealth.com
www.flavorhealth.com
Use natural ingredients to create bitter balancing, sodium reduction and sweet enhancement solutions.
CEO: Christian Kopfli
Senior Director of Finance: Deborah Beckwith
Vice President, Flavor Sciences: Dennis Sawchuk
Vice President, Commerical Development: Shari Joslin

4487 Flavorbank Company
6372 E Broadway Blvd
Tucson, AZ 85710-3538
520-747-5431
Fax: 520-790-9469 800-835-7603
Spices and seasonings
Owner: Jennifer English
Public Relations: Jan Jorden
Operations: Jackie Brooks
Production: James Husser
Plant Manager: Ramona Flores
Estimated Sales: $1-2,500,000
Number Employees: 1-4
Type of Packaging: Private Label
Brands:
  Daniel Orr
  Flavorbank

4488 Flavorchem Corp
1525 Brook Dr
Downers Grove, IL 60515-1024
630-932-8100
Fax: 630-932-4626 800-435-2867
www.flavorchem.com
Manufacturer and exporter of flavorings and food colorings; processor of pure vanilla extract; importer of fine chemicals and essential oils.
President: Ken Malinowski
kmalinowski@flavorchem.com
Year Founded: 1971
Number Employees: 100-249
Square Footage: 215000
Type of Packaging: Consumer, Food Service, Private Label, Bulk
Other Locations:
  Headquarters
  Downers Grove IL
  Flavorchem West
  San Clemente CA
  Flavorchem Europe
  Kerepes, Hungary
Brands:
  Spicery Shoppe Natural

4489 Flavorganics
268 Doremus Ave
Newark, NJ 07105-4875
973-344-8014
Fax: 973-344-1948 866-972-6879
flavorganics@worldpantry.com
www.flavorganics.com
Organic extracts including vanilla, almond, peppermint, lemon and orange
President: Jocelyn Manship
Contact: Jenny Fagundes
jenny@ecsalesco.com
Estimated Sales: $20-50 Million
Number Employees: 50-99
Parent Co: Elan
Type of Packaging: Private Label, Bulk
Brands:
  Flavorganics
  Kogee

4490 (HQ)Flavormatic Industries
230 All Angels Hill Rd
Wappingers Falls, NY 12590
845-297-9100
Fax: 845-297-2881 sales@flavormatic.com
www.flavormatic.com
Manufacturer, importer and exporter of flavors, fragrances and essential oils
President: Judith Back
Executive VP: Ronald Black
Sales: Frank Wells
Operation Manager: Richard Febles
Estimated Sales: $2.5 Million
Number Employees: 20-49
Square Footage: 63000
Type of Packaging: Bulk
Other Locations:

4491 Flavors and Color
20653 Lycoming St
Unit A9
Walnut, CA 91789
909-598-4441
Fax: 909-598-7740 flavorsandcolor.com
Flavorings, colorings and other food ingredients.

4492 Flavors from Florida
203 Bartow Municipal Arprt
Bartow, FL 33830
863-533-0408
Fax: 863-533-9478 800-888-0409

713

Food Manufacturers / A-Z

Ice cream, sherbert, drink base flavoring, flavoring extracts and syrups
President: Robert K Prendes
Contact: Wendy Arsenault
wendy.arsenault@agrana.com
Year Founded: 1971
Estimated Sales: $25-50 Million
Number Employees: 20-49

4493 Flavors of Hawaii Inc
945 Waimanu St
Honolulu, HI 96814-3319
808-597-1727
Fax: 808-597-1728
Coconut syrup, guava syrup, cocopine syrup
President: Alexander Lee
Vice President: Violet Mau
Estimated Sales: $650,000
Number Employees: 5-9
Brands:
  Hawaii

4494 Flavors of the Heartland
201 2nd St
Rocheport, MO 65279
573-698-2063
800-269-3210
Gourmet foods
Manager: Roger Pilkinton
Estimated Sales: Less than $500,000
Number Employees: 1-4
Brands:
  Flavors of the Heartland

4495 Flavouressence Products
1-6750 Davand Drive
Mississauga, ON L5T 2L8
Canada
905-795-0318
Fax: 905-795-0317 866-209-7778
backbaytrading.com
Beverage syrups, juices, bar mixes and slush; exporter of juices, bar mixes and beverage syrups
President/CEO: Mark Weber
CFO: Brain Ferry
Marketing: Bob Graham
Sales: Jolene Davies
Plant Manager: David Milner
Estimated Sales: $5 Million
Number Employees: 5-9
Square Footage: 21000
Type of Packaging: Food Service, Private Label, Bulk

4496 Flax4Life
468 W Horton Rd
Bellingham, WA 98226
360-715-1944
Fax: 360-233-1212 877-352-9487
www.flax4life.net
Flax-based baked goods
General Manager: Kasondra Shippen
Marketing Coordinator: Sarah Bishop
Vice President, Sales: Bob Johnston
Production Manager: Jen Bishop

4497 Fleet Fisheries Inc
20 Blackmer St
New Bedford, MA 02744-2614
508-910-2100
Fax: 508-996-3785 www.fleetfisheries.com
Scallops
President: Lars Vinjerud
lars@oceansfleet.com
Vice President: Rick Miller
Quality Control: Rick Tavis
Operations: Shaun Souza
Accounts Receivable: Dan Pacheco
Plant Manager: Chris Brown
Estimated Sales: $5-10 Million
Number Employees: 10-19

4498 Fleischer's Bagels
1688 N Wayneport Rd
Macedon, NY 14502-8765
315-986-9999
Fax: 315-986-7200 mark@fleischersbagels.com
Fresh, frozen and refrigerated bagels
President: Robert Drago
SVP Operations/CFO: Keith Bleier
Quality Assurance Manager: George Sparks
VP Sales/Marketing: Robert Pim
Contact: Marc Fleischer
mfleischer@fleischersbagels.com
Production Manager: Mike O'Hara
Estimated Sales: $6 Million
Number Employees: 135
Square Footage: 85370
Type of Packaging: Consumer, Food Service, Private Label, Bulk
Brands:
  Fleischer's

4499 Fleischmann's Vinegar Co Inc
12604 Hiddencreek Way
Suite A
Cerritos, CA 90703-2137
Canada
562-483-4600
Fax: 562-483-4644 800-443-1067
sales@fvinegar.com
www.fleischmannsvinegar.com
Vinegar
President/CEO: Ken Simril
CEO: Butch Daugherty
butch.daugherty@fvinegar.com
CFO: Larry McKeown
VP: Sylvain Norton
VP Sales: Roger Arnold
Number Employees: 100-249
Parent Co: Burns Philp Foods
Type of Packaging: Consumer, Food Service, Private Label, Bulk
Brands:
  Allens
  Fleischann's
  Spice Islands

4500 Fleischmann's Yeast
Chesterfield, MO 63017
800-777-4959
info@fleischmannsyeast.com
www.breadworld.com
Active and inactive yeasts, vinegars, leaveners and mold inhibitors; also, technical consulting for bakeries available
Estimated Sales: $50-100 Million
Number Employees: 74
Number of Brands: 1
Parent Co: Garfield Weston Foundation
Type of Packaging: Food Service, Bulk
Brands:
  Fleischmann's Yeast

4501 Fletcher's Fine Foods
502 Boundary Blvd
Auburn, WA 98001-6503
Canada
253-735-0800
www.fletchers.com
Manufacturer and exporter of pork and by-products
President/CEO: Fred Knoedler
President: Michael Lattifi
Manager: Ed Clark
clark@fletchers.com
Number Employees: 100-249
Parent Co: Fletcher's Fine Foods
Type of Packaging: Food Service, Bulk
Brands:
  Fletcher's
  Goodlife

4502 Fleur De Lait Foods Inc
400 S Custer Ave
New Holland, PA 17557-9220
717-355-8580
Fax: 717-355-8561 800-322-2743
alouetteculinary@savenciacheeseusa.com
www.savenciafoodserviceusa.com
Cheese manufacturer
President & CEO: Dominique Huth
National Sales: Larry Rosenberg
Year Founded: 1990
Estimated Sales: $20-50 Million
Number Employees: 250-499

4503 Fleurchem Inc
33 Sprague Ave
Middletown, NY 10940-5128
845-341-2100
Fax: 845-341-2121 info@fleurchem.com
www.fleurchem.com
Natural and synthetic flavoring agents and fragrances including acidulants, anethole, citronellal, eucalyptol, furfural, geraniol, heptanal, methyl acetate, etc
CEO: Charles Barton
cbarton@fleurchem.com
CEO: George Gluck
CFO: Sara Gluck
CEO: Rochele Gluck
Quality Control: Brian Merdler
VP Marketing: Jack Snicolo
Operations Manager: Louis Mercun
Production: Larry Costa
Purchasing Manager: Angie Roman
Estimated Sales: $10-20 Million
Number Employees: 20-49
Square Footage: 400000
Type of Packaging: Private Label, Bulk

4504 Flex Pack USA
6321 Emperor Dr
Orlando, FL 32809-5513
407-857-2883
Fax: 407-857-6970
Packaging/bags
Owner: Mark Dorey
Estimated Sales: $5-10 Million
Number Employees: 50-99

4505 Fliinko
PO Box 80102
South Dartmouth, MA 02748-0102
508-996-9609
Fax: 508-990-1281 800-266-9609
fliinko@ultranet.com
Manufacturer of all natural instant drink mixes.
President: Ingrid Flynn
Treasurer: Thomas Flynn
Estimated Sales: $1-22,500,000
Number Employees: 1-4
Type of Packaging: Private Label
Brands:
  Nectarade

4506 Flippin-Seaman Inc
5529 Crabtree Falls Hwy
Tyro, VA 22976-3103
434-277-5828
Fax: 434-277-9057
Growers, packer and shippers of fine fruit.
Owner: Bill Flippin
Owner: Richard Seaman
info@flippin-seaman.com
Estimated Sales: $10-20 Million
Number Employees: 20-49
Brands:
  Seaman Orchard
  Silver Creek

4507 Flix Candy
6401 W Gross Point Rd
Niles, IL 60714-4507
847-647-1370
Fax: 847-647-0633 info@flixcandy.com
www.flixcandy.com
Candy
President: Sidney Diamond
VP Sales: Jeff Grossman
Contact: Jennifer Baldwin
jenniferb@flixcandy.com
Estimated Sales: Less Than $500,000
Number Employees: 1-4
Brands:
  Disney Princess
  Mickey Mouse
  Rudolph the Red Nosed Reindeer
  Toy Story
  Dippin' Candy

4508 Floating Leaf Fine Foods
28 Christopher St
Winnipeg, MB R2C 2Z2
Canada
204-989-7696
Fax: 204-943-4719 866-989-7696
info@slwr.com eatwildrice.ca
Wild rice
President: Murray Ratuski
murray@slwr.com
Director of Sales: Matthew Ratuski
Coordinator: Sheldon Ratuski
Number Employees: 1-4
Type of Packaging: Food Service, Private Label, Bulk

Food Manufacturers / A-Z

Brands:
- Canadian Wild Rice
- Floating Leaf
- Canoe
- Oh Canada

4509 Flora Inc
805 E Badger Rd
PO Box 73
Lynden, WA 98264-9502
360-354-2110
Fax: 360-354-5355 800-446-2110
info@florahealth.com www.florahealth.com
Digestive enzymes, herbal extracts, herbal teas, herbal tonics, nutritional oils, nutritional supplements, organic chocolates, probiotics and whole foods.
President/Owner: Thomas Greither
Cmo: Gabrial Lightfriend
glightfriend@florahealth.com
Marketing Manager: Gabriel Lightfriend
Estimated Sales: $10-20 Million
Number Employees: 50-99
Type of Packaging: Consumer
Other Locations:
- Flora Manufacturing Facility
- Burnaby BC

Brands:
- Flor-Essence
- Flora

4510 Flora Springs Winery
1978 Zinfandel Ln
St Helena, CA 94574-1611
707-963-5711
Fax: 707-963-7518 info@florasprings.com
www.florasprings.com
Wines
President: John Komes
jkomes@florasprings.com
Finance: Ronette Aiello
Estimated Sales: $1.8,000,000
Number Employees: 10-19

4511 Florence Macaroni Manufacturing
4334 W Chicago Ave
Chicago, IL 60651-3422
773-252-6113
Fax: 773-252-7085 800-647-2782
Macaroni products including regular/orangic semolina and whole wheat
President: Roy Pier Dominici
Sales Executive: Gino Ricciardi
Contact: Tom Behnke
tbenhke@florenceal.org
Manager: Tom Behnke
Plant Manager: Thomas Benhke
Estimated Sales: $3.3 Million
Number Employees: 25
Type of Packaging: Consumer, Food Service, Private Label, Bulk

4512 Florence Pasta & Cheese
115 W College Drive
Marshall, MN 56258-1747
800-533-5290
Fax: 507-537-8159 www.foodpros.com
Frozen pasta and dehydrated cheese
President: Alfred Schwan
Parent Co: Schwann's Sales
Type of Packaging: Consumer, Food Service, Bulk

4513 Florentyna's Fresh Pasta Factory
1864 E 22nd St
Los angles, CA 90058
213-742-9374
Fax: 310-677-2782 800-747-2782
jascha@freshpasta.com www.freshpasta.com
Fresh and fresh frozen pasta products for the food service industry
Manager: Jascha Smuloviez
Contact: Pat Brophy
brophypat@freshpasta.com
Estimated Sales: $1-4,9,000,000
Number Employees: 20-49
Number of Products: 60
Type of Packaging: Food Service, Private Label, Bulk

4514 Florida Brewery
202 Gandy Rd
Auburndale, FL 33823-2726
863-965-1825
Fax: 863-967-6965
Beer
Owner: Ming Tseng
ming@floridabrewery.com
Controller: Julie Williams
Operations: Erich Schalk
Estimated Sales: $3,000,000
Number Employees: 20-49
Square Footage: 62
Type of Packaging: Private Label

4515 Florida Caribbean Distillers
530 Dakota Ave
Lake Alfred, FL 33850
863-956-2002
Fax: 863-956-3979 www.floridadistillers.com
Beverages including wines and spirits
Director Of Bottling Operations: Mike Ryan
Contact: Jacob Call
jacob.call@floridadistillers.com
Estimated Sales: $14.3 Million
Number Employees: 99
Number of Brands: 13
Type of Packaging: Consumer, Bulk
Other Locations:
- Bottling Operations
- Auburndale FL
- Storage/Rum Aging Facility
- Winter Haven FL

Brands:
- Capriccio
- Club Caribe
- Black Roberts
- James Harbour
- Florida Old Reserve
- Minski
- Mad Dragon
- Kentucky's Old Reserve
- Deauville
- Shotball
- Express Load
- Sonavavitch
- Ron Carlos

4516 Florida Citrus
Po Box 9010
Bartow, FL 33831-9010
863-537-3999
Fax: 877-352-2487 www.floridajuice.com
Fruit cocktails, juice and syrup. Product categories are vegetables, canned fruits and fresh fruits
VP: John Roberts
VP: Scott Stallard
Contact: Murat Azik
mazik@citrus.state.fl.us
Estimated Sales: $5-10 Million
Number Employees: 1-4
Type of Packaging: Consumer

4517 Florida Crystals Corporation
1 North Clematis St.
Suite 200
West Palm Beach, FL 33401
561-366-5100
Fax: 561-366-5158 844-344-9497
info@floridacrystals.com www.floridacrystals.com
Sugar, including certified organic, granulated, powdered, and brown sugar, and agave nectar.
Chairman/COO/President: Jose Fanjul
Chairman/CEO: Alfonso Fanjul
Executive VP/CFO: Luis Fernandez
Year Founded: 1960
Estimated Sales: $213.5 Million
Number Employees: 2,000
Number of Brands: 4
Square Footage: 10266
Type of Packaging: Consumer, Bulk
Brands:
- Florida Crystals
- Domino
- C&H
- Redpath

4518 (HQ)Florida Food Products Inc
2231 W County Road 44 # 1
Eustis, FL 32726-2628
352-357-4141
Fax: 352-483-3192 800-874-2331
contact@floridafood.com www.floridafood.com
Vegetable juice concentrates, aloe vera gel, fruit juice powders, vegetable juice powders
President: Jerry Brown
jbrown@floridafood.com
Vice President: Tom Brown
Research & Development: Scott Ruppe
VP Marketing: Thomas Brown
Sales Manager: Mike McIntyre
National Accounts Manager: Randy Blackmar
VP Operations & Manufacturing: Charles Hamrick
Plant Manager: Keith Burt
Purchasing Manager: James Arnett
Estimated Sales: $15-20 Million
Number Employees: 50-99
Square Footage: 300000
Other Locations:
- Florida Food Products
- Sabila

Brands:
- Florida Food Products
- Veg Con Beet
- Veg Con Carrot
- Veg Con Celery

4519 Florida Fruit Juices
7001 W 62nd St
Chicago, IL 60638-3924
773-586-6200
Fax: 773-586-6651 www.puredelitebev.com
Fruit juices including apple, grape, orange, grapefruit, pineapple, etc
President: Donald Franko
clivanos@dupageco.org
VP: Don Franko
VP: Don Franko, Jr.
Estimated Sales: $5-10 Million
Number Employees: 20-49
Type of Packaging: Consumer, Food Service, Private Label

4520 Florida Key West
5470 Division Dr
Fort Myers, FL 33905
239-694-8787
Fax: 239-694-0402 juice@florida-juice.com
Lemon and key lime juices
Owner: Earl Tanner
Director of Sales and Marketing: Sandra Tanner
Estimated Sales: $1-2,500,000
Number Employees: 5-9
Type of Packaging: Consumer, Food Service, Private Label, Bulk
Brands:
- Florida Key West

4521 Florida Natural Flavors
180 Lyman Rd # 120
Casselberry, FL 32707-2805
407-834-5979
Fax: 407-834-6333 800-872-5979
info@floridanaturalflavors.com
www.barcontrolsofflorida.com
Manufacturer, exporter and importer of juice and beverage concentrates including carbonated, noncarbonated and frozen products
Vice President: Garry Erdman
gerdman@floridanaturalflavors.com
COO: Gary Erdman
Manager: Leonard Combs
Estimated Sales: $4,000,000
Number Employees: 20-49
Parent Co: Florida Natural Flavors
Type of Packaging: Private Label
Brands:
- Diet Rite
- Davy's Mix
- Juicemaster
- Mistic Iced Tea
- Nehi Flavors
- Polynesian Pleasure
- R-Own Cola
- Stewart's
- Tropical Pleasure

4522 Florida Veal Processors
6712 State Road 674
Wimauma, FL 33598
813-634-5545
Fax: 813-633-1405
Fresh and frozen veal
President: Richard Nusman
Co-Owner: Max Nusman
Estimated Sales: $5.70 Million
Number Employees: 15
Type of Packaging: Consumer, Food Service

Food Manufacturers / A-Z

4523 Florida's Natural Growers
20205 US Hwy. 27 N.
Lake Wales, FL 33853
863-676-1411
Fax: 863-676-1640   888-657-6600
www.floridasnatural.com
Fresh and frozen fruit juices, concentrates and blends including grapefruit, orange, lemonade, lime, apple and grape.
Owner/President: Frank Hunt
CEO: Bob Behr
CFO: William Hendry
chip.hendry@citrusworld.com
Year Founded: 1933
Estimated Sales: $105 Million
Number Employees: 1,100
Type of Packaging: Consumer, Food Service, Private Label
Brands:
   Florida's Natural

4524 Floron Food Services
2545 96th Street
Edmonton, AB T6N 1E3
Canada
780-438-9300
Fax: 780-438-9200   www.floron.com
Manufacturer of mozzarella and cheddar cheese, manufacturer of private label pasta sauce, full line distribution
President: Ronald Coyle
VP: Stephen Robbins
Year Founded: 1984
Estimated Sales: $20 Million
Number Employees: 40
Square Footage: 20000
Type of Packaging: Consumer, Food Service

4525 Flower Essence Svc
13139 Daisy Blue Mine Rd
Nevada City, CA 95959-9708
530-265-0258
Fax: 530-265-6467   800-548-0075
info@fesflowers.com   www.fesflowers.com
Manufactuer of flower essences
Owner: Richard Katz
rkatz@fesflowers.com
Estimated Sales: $1-3 Million
Number Employees: 10-19

4526 Flowers Baking Co
900 16th St N
Birmingham, AL 35203-1017
205-252-1161
Fax: 205-323-7610   www.flowersfoods.com
Manufacturer and exporter of hamburger buns
President: Carter Wood
carter_wood@flocorp.com
Vice President of Marketing: Janice Anderson
Chief Engineer: Richard Davis
Estimated Sales: $10-20 Million
Number Employees: 250-499
Square Footage: 195000
Parent Co: Flowers Baking Company
Type of Packaging: Consumer

4527 Flowers Baking Co
301 Dallas St
El Paso, TX 79901-1821
915-533-8434
Fax: 915-534-0043   800-328-6111
Baked products including bread, rolls, buns and cake
VP Sales: Jef Dunigan
VP Sales: Tony Ruiz
Number Employees: 20-49
Square Footage: 320000
Parent Co: Flowers Industries
Brands:
   Sunbeam

4528 Flowers Baking Co
546 15th St
Tuscaloosa, AL 35401-4708
205-752-5586
Fax: 205-752-1780
Baked goods including breads, buns and rolls.
President: Keith Singletary
keith_@flocorp.com
CEO: Joe Tashie
Estimated Sales: $.5-1 million
Number Employees: 100-249
Parent Co: Flowers Baking Company
Type of Packaging: Consumer

4529 Flowers Foods Inc.
1919 Flowers Circle
Thomasville, GA 31757
229-226-9110
Fax: 229-225-3823   www.flowersfoods.com
Packaged bakery foods.
President/CEO: A. Ryals McMullian
CFO/Chief Administrative Officer: R. Steve Kinsey
Senior VP/Chief Accounting Officer: Karyl Lauder
Chief Marketing Officer: Debo Mukherjee
Chief Sales Officer: D. Keith Wheeler
COO: Bradley Alexander
Year Founded: 1919
Estimated Sales: Over $1 Billion
Number Employees: 9,800
Number of Brands: 12
Type of Packaging: Consumer, Food Service
Brands:
   Nature's Own
   Tastykake
   Dave's Killer Bread
   Wonder
   Cobblestone Bread Co.
   Canyon Bakehouse
   Mrs. Freshley's
   Alpine Valley Bakery
   Sunbeam Bread
   Merita
   Captain John's Derst's
   Butternut Breads
   Mi Casa
   Bunny Bread
   European Bakers
   Home Pride

4530 Floyd
131 Atlantic Ave
Brooklyn, NY 11201-5504
718-858-5810
info@floydny.com
www.floydny.com
Manufacturer beer cheese and crackers.
Co-Founder: Jim Carden
cardenjim@gmail.com
Co-Founder: Andrew Templar
Co-Founder: Kevin Avanzato
Estimated Sales: Less Than $500,000
Number Employees: 1-4

4531 Flurowater, Inc.
12424 Wilshire Blvd.
Suite 850
Los Angeles, CA 90025
www.wanuwater.com
Manufacturer of flavored water.
Founder & President: Todd O'Gara
CEO: Steve Dollase
CFO: Danelle Larsen
CMO: Jacqueline Gonzalez

4532 Flying Bird Botanicals LLC
905 Squalicum Way Ste 106
Bellingham, WA 98225-2076
USA
360-366-8013
Fax: 360-933-8050   www.flyingbirdbotanicals.com
Tea
Owner/Founder: Scout Urling

4533 Flying Burrito Co
3200 N College Ave
Fayetteville, AR 72703-3565
479-527-0400
Fax: 479-527-0401   arch@flyingburritoco.com
www.flyingburritoco.com
Mexican restaurants serving burritos, tacos, quesadillas, nachos, and salads.
Owner: Mike Rohrbach
mike@flyingburritoco.com
Partner: Archie Schaffer
Estimated Sales: $600,000
Number Employees: 13

4534 Flying Dog Brewery
4607 Wedgewood Blvd
Frederick, MD 21703-7120
301-694-7899
www.flyingdogales.com
Manufacturer and exporter of beer, ale, stout, lager and porter.
President/CFO: Kelly McElroy
CEO: Jim Caruso
jimcaruso@flyingdogales.com
COO: Matt Brophy
CMO: Ben Savage
VP Sales: John Stolins
VP Plant Operations: Mark Matovich
Director, Packaging & Logistics: Christopher Farley
Estimated Sales: $7 Million
Number Employees: 50-99
Square Footage: 114000
Type of Packaging: Consumer, Food Service, Private Label

4535 Flying Embers
Ventura, CA 93003
flyingembers.com
Hard kombucha
Founder & CEO: Bill Moses

4536 Flynn Vineyards Winery
2200 N Pacific Hwy W
Rickreall, OR 97371-9774
503-623-8683
Fax: 503-623-0908   888-427-4953
Producer of wines. Products include Pinot Noir, Chardonnay and Pinot Gris.
President: Howard Rossbach
Estimated Sales: $5-10,000,000
Number Employees: 5-9
Type of Packaging: Private Label

4537 (HQ)Fmali Herb
831 Almar Avenue
Santa Cruz, CA 95060-5899
831-423-7913
Fax: 831-429-5173   sales@fmali.com
Manufacturer and contract packager of ginseng, hibiscus flowers, orange and lemon peels, herbal, green and black teas and chamomile; importer of ginseng, royal jelly and panax extractum; exporter of herbal teas and orange and lemonpeels
President/Co-Founder: Ben Zaricor
Executive VP/Co-Founder: Louise Veninga
Contact: Roberto Avila
ravila@goodearthteas.com
Estimated Sales: $14.0 Million
Number Employees: 50-99
Square Footage: 84000
Type of Packaging: Consumer, Food Service, Private Label, Bulk
Brands:
   Famli
   Good Earth
   Wildcraft

4538 Focus Foodservice
300 Knightsbridge Pkwy
Lincolnshire, IL 60069
Fax: 800-968-4129   800-968-3918
info@focusfoodservice.com
Bakeware, smallwares and storage and transportation solutions
Brands:
   FOCUS FOODSERVICE
   FOCUS FOODSERVICE BAKEWARE
   WEST BEND
   SWING-A-WAY

4539 Foell Packing Company
PO Box 4595
Naperville, IL 60567-4595
919-776-0592
Fax: 919-774-1627   www.foellpacking.com
Manufacturer and exporter of canned meats including tripe, Vienna sausage and pork brains; also, contract packaging available
President: D Johnson
Vice President: T O'Shea
Estimated Sales: $5-10 Million
Number Employees: 20-49
Square Footage: 108000
Type of Packaging: Consumer, Private Label
Brands:
   Beverly
   Rose

4540 Fogo Island Cooperative Society
P.O. Box 70
Seldom Fogo Island, NL A0G 3Z0
Canada
709-627-3452
Fax: 709-627-3495   fogoislandcoop@nf.aibn.com
www.fogoislandcoop.com

Food Manufacturers / A-Z

Manufacturer and exporter of live and frozen crabs
President: Roy Freake
General Manager: Keith Watts
Estimated Sales: $1,4,000,000
Number Employees: 10
Type of Packaging: Consumer, Food Service, Bulk

4541 Foley Estates Vineyard
6121 E Highway 246
Lompoc, CA 93436-9679
805-737-6222
Fax: 805-737-6923 www.foleywines.com
Wines
President: Robert Lidquist
Marketing Manager: Lisa Schaeffer
Sales: Mike Keonig
Manager: Lisa Kekuewa
lkekuewa@foleywines.com
Production Manager: Norm Yost
Estimated Sales: $2.5-5,000,000
Number Employees: 10-19
Type of Packaging: Private Label

4542 Foley's Chocolates & Candies
11520 Horseshoe Way
Richmond, BC V7A 4V5
Canada
604-274-2131
Fax: 604-275-1682 888-236-5397
info@foleyscandies.com
www.foleyschocolates.com
Chocolate and confectionery products including wafers, blocks, chips, almond barks, squares, mints, yogurt covered almonds, raisins, peanuts and coffee beans
Co-Founder: Wade Pugh
Co-Founder: Richard Foley
Number Employees: 20-49
Type of Packaging: Private Label, Bulk

4543 (HQ)Folgers Coffee Co
1 Strawberry Ln
Orrville, OH 44667-0208
800-937-9745
www.folgerscoffee.com
Roasted, ground, regular and decaffeinated coffee. Also, Folgers is the licensed manufacturer and distributor of Dunkin' Donuts retail coffee brand.
Chief Executive Officer: Richard Smucker
SVP/Chief Financial Officer: Mark Belgya
Chief Operating Officer: Vincent Byrd
VP/Controller: John Denman
VP/General Counsel: Jeannette Knudsen
SVP/Corporate Communications: Christopher Resweber
Logistics Leader/Operations Manager: Shane Boddie
Number Employees: 100-249
Parent Co: J.M Smucker Company
Type of Packaging: Consumer
Brands:
   Black Silk
   Classic Complements
   Folger's Filter Pack
   Folger's Flavor
   Folger's Instant
   Folger's Simply Smooth
   Gourmet Selections
   K-Cup Packs
   Mountain Grown

4544 Folie ... Deux Winery
7481 St. Helena Highway
Oakville, CA 94562
707-944-2565
Fax: 707-944-0250 800-535-6400
fadinfo@folieadeux.com www.folieadeux.com
Wines
Manager: Paul Scholfield
CEO: Richard Peterson
CFO: George Schofield
Marketing: Cardace Guridi
Public Relations: David Foster
Operations: Carla Clift
Production: Alejandro Pantoja
Purchasing: Marc Norwood
Number Employees: 10-19
Number of Brands: 3
Type of Packaging: Consumer
Brands:
   Fantaisie
   Folie a Deux
   La Grande Folie
   La Petite Folie

4545 Folklore Foods
2011 Hwy 12 & 83
PO Box 104
Selby, SD 57472
605-649-1144
Fax: 509-865-7363 www.folklorefoods.com
Manufacturer and exporter of espresso syrups and granita concentrate
President/CEO: Daniel Hanson
VP: Chris Hanson
Estimated Sales: $690,000
Number Employees: 5
Square Footage: 22000
Type of Packaging: Consumer, Food Service, Private Label
Brands:
   Folklore
   Folklore Cream Soda
   Folklore Gourmet Syrups
   Folklore Sasaparilla
   Folklore Sparkling Beverages

4546 Follmer Development, Inc
884 Tourmaline Dr
Newbury Park, CA 91320-1205
805-498-4531
Fax: 805-499-4668 fdi@follmerdevelopment.com
www.follmerdevelopment.com
Aerosol cooking, baking and flavoring sprays.
President: Garrett Follmer
Estimated Sales: $9,000,000
Number Employees: 11-50
Type of Packaging: Consumer, Food Service, Private Label

4547 Follow Your Heart
9201 Owensmouth Ave
Chatsworth, CA 91311-5854
818-725-2820
Fax: 818-725-2812 www.followyourheart.com
Organic condiments, sauces, spreads
Owner/Founder: Michael Besancon
Chief Executive Officer: Bob Goldberg
Contact: Pamela Bluestein
pbluestein@followyourheart.com
Purchasing Executive: Lauren Hollenspein
Estimated Sales: F
Number Employees: 50-99

4548 Fona International
1900 Averill Rd
Geneva, IL 60134
630-578-8600
Fax: 630-578-8601 www.fona.com
Flavoring extracts and syrups.
Founder, Chairman & CEO: Joe Slawek
jslawek@fona.com
VP, Accounting & Finance: Chad Hall
EVP: TJ Widuch
EVP: Manon Daoust
COO: Jeremy Thompson
Estimated Sales: $100-500 Million
Number Employees: 100-249

4549 Fontana Flavors Inc
2342 Fulton St
Janesville, WI 53546-1004
608-754-9668
Fax: 608-754-9655
customerservice@fontanaflavors.com
www.fontanaflavors.com
Flavors manufacturer for seafood, meats, prepared foods and vegetarian products
President: Julie Eickstead
jeickstead@fontanaflavors.com
Estimated Sales: $4 Million
Number Employees: 1-4

4550 Fontanini Italian Meats
8751 W 50th St
McCook, IL 60525-3132
708-485-4800
Fax: 708-485-9600 800-331-6328
webinfo@fontanini.com www.fontanini.com
Meatballs, breakfast items, pizza toppings, beef
President: Joanne Fontanini
CEO: Eugene Fontanini
Account Executive: Rita Rufo
Controller Midwest: Eric Divelbiss
Director QC: Anthony Pavel
General Manager: Charles Brown
Regional Manager: Jim Doherty
West Coast Regional Manager: Gene Borgomainero
Director Operations: Mike Catania
Estimated Sales: $46 Million
Number Employees: 5-9
Square Footage: 240000
Parent Co: Hormel Foods Corporation
Type of Packaging: Consumer, Food Service
Brands:
   Mama Ranne

4551 Fontazzi/Metrovox Snacks
612 N. Eckhoff St
Orange, CA 92868
714-634-3478
Fax: 714-634-4424 800-428-0522
questions@giftbasketsupplies.com
www.giftbasketsupplies.com
Popcorn, pretzels, snack mixes, gift packs, gift boxes, sourdough truffles
President: Paul Voxrand
Estimated Sales: $300,000-500,000
Number Employees: 1-4

4552 Fonterra Co-operative Group Limited
8700 W Bryn Mawr Ave
Chicago, IL 60631
888-869-6455
FUSA@fonterra.com www.fonterra.com
Dairy exporter based in New Zealand.
CEO: Miles Hurrell
CFO: Marc Rivers
CEO, Americas: Kelvin Wickham
COO: Fraser Whineray
Year Founded: 2001
Estimated Sales: $19.2 Billion
Number Employees: 21,400
Type of Packaging: Consumer, Food Service
Brands:
   Anchor®
   De Winkel®
   Fresh 'n Fruity®
   Kapiti®
   Mainland®
   Mammoth®
   Perfect Italiano®
   Piako®
   Primo®
   Symbio®
   Tip Top®
   NZMP™

4553 Food & Vine Inc.
68 Coombs St
Suite 2
Napa, CA 94559-3966
707-251-3900
Fax: 707-251-3939 info@grapeseedoil.com
grapeseedoil.com
Grapeseed oil and flour
President/CEO: Valentin Humer
valentin@grapeseedoil.com
Owner: Nanette Humer
Estimated Sales: $620,000
Number Employees: 1-4

4554 Food City Pickle Company
13760 Verona Road
Battle Creek, MI 49014-8920
269-781-9135
Fax: 616-781-3422
Sweet relish, dill relish, whole dill pickles, dill slices, sweet pickles, pepperoncini and peppers including hot and mild banana
President: Ron DeRuiter
Estimated Sales: $2.5-5 Million
Number Employees: 5-9
Square Footage: 44000
Type of Packaging: Consumer, Food Service, Private Label, Bulk
Brands:
   King's Choice

4555 Food City USA
4752 W 60th Ave # A
Suite A
Arvada, CO 80003-6900
303-321-4447
Fax: 303-428-4143 joan@grandmaspasta.com
www.grandmaspasta.com
Fresh and frozen pre-cooked pasta including wide egg noodles, linguini, fettuccine and angel hair
Owner: Moni Piz-Wilson
president@grandmaspasta.com

Food Manufacturers / A-Z

Estimated Sales: $3-5 Million
Number Employees: 5-9
Parent Co: Grandma's Pasta Products
Type of Packaging: Consumer, Food Service
Brands:
   Grandma's

4556 Food Concentrate Corporation
921 NW 72nd St
Oklahoma City, OK 73116
   405-840-5633
   Fax: 405-843-6832
Barbecue sauce concentrate and muffin and seasoning mixes
Owner: Walter Satterman
Estimated Sales: $2.5-5 Million
Number Employees: 6
Square Footage: 8000
Type of Packaging: Consumer, Food Service, Private Label
Brands:
   Food Concentrate Corp.
   Oat-N-Bran
   Uncle Walter's

4557 Food Factory
875 Waimanu St
Suite 535
Honolulu, HI 96813
   808-593-2633
   Fax: 808-591-2943
Frozen foods
President: David Phillips
Estimated Sales: $300,000-500,000
Number Employees: 5-9

4558 Food First
PO Box 499
Walhalla, ND 58282
   701-549-3864
   800-241-0799
info@probiotein.com foodfirstllc.com
Prebiotic fiber and protein blend
Type of Packaging: Consumer

4559 Food For Thought Inc
10704 Oviatt Rd
Honor, MI 49640-9546
   231-326-5444
Fax: 231-326-2649 sales@foodforthought.net
   www.foodforthought.net
Organic and fair trade preserves, salsa, maple syrup, hot sauce, and mustard.
President: Timothy Young
sales@foodforthought.net
Number Employees: 10-19
Type of Packaging: Consumer, Private Label

4560 Food Ingredient Solutions
10 Malcolm Ave
Suite 1
Teterboro, NJ 07608
   917-449-9558
Fax: 201-440-4211 jgreaves@foodcolor.com
   www.foodcolor.com
Manufacturer and distributor of ingredients for barbeque sauces, spices, seasonings, colors, flavors, gums
CEO: Jeff Greaves
jeffgreaves@earthlink.net
VP, Operations: Helen Greaves
Estimated Sales: $6 Million
Number Employees: 10-19
Number of Brands: 2
Number of Products: 80
Type of Packaging: Food Service, Private Label, Bulk
Other Locations:
   Food Ingredients Solutions
   Signal Hill CA
Brands:
   Grill-In-A-Bottle
   Safrante

4561 Food Ingredient Specialties
30003 Bainbridge Road
Solon, OH 44139-2205
   440-248-1820
   Fax: 440-349-3334
Liquid seasonings and food bases
President/CEO: Gary Tortorelli
Parent Co: Nestle USA

4562 Food Masters
PO Box 1565
Griffin, GA 30223-1565
   770-227-0330
Fax: 770-228-4281 888-715-4394
foodmasters@hotmail.com www.foodmasters.com
Mesquite BBQ sauce, Caesar, cucumber dressing and dip, sea sauce, honey mustard, dill delight, vinaigrette, poppy seed
Owner: Pradeep Kumarhia
Estimated Sales: $1-2,500,000
Number Employees: 5-9

4563 Food Matters Again
21 Provost St
Brooklyn, NY 11222
   718-361-3183
   info@foodmattersagain.com
   foodmattersagain.com
Cheese; butter; cured meats; olives and olive oil; honey.
Founder: Brad Dube
Year Founded: 2009
Estimated Sales: $300,000
Number Employees: 6
Type of Packaging: Private Label

4564 Food Mill
3033 Macarthur Blvd
Oakland, CA 94602-3299
   510-482-3848
   Fax: 510-482-0344
Nut butter, cookies and breads
President/Co-Owner: Kirk Watkins
kkcwatkins@yahoo.com
Treasurer/Co-Owner: Arthur Watkins
Sales Exec: Ken Watkins
Estimated Sales: $1-2.5 Million
Number Employees: 10-19
Square Footage: 36000
Type of Packaging: Consumer, Bulk
Brands:
   Food Mill

4565 Food Processor of New Mexico
PO Box 3672
Albuquerque, NM 87190-3672
   505-881-4921
Fax: 505-797-2505 877-634-3772
Bar-b-que sauces, green chile, red chile, habanero
Co-Owner: Phillip Clark
Co-Owner: Wanda Clark

4566 Food Products Corporation
3121 E Washington St
Phoenix, AZ 85034
   602-273-7139
   Fax: 602-275-9429
Mexican foods including flour and corn tortillas, tortilla chips and masa
CEO: David Brennan
Plant Manager: Joaquin Amaro
Estimated Sales: $5-10 Million
Number Employees: 50-99
Square Footage: 120000
Parent Co: Sparta Foods
Type of Packaging: Consumer, Food Service, Private Label, Bulk
Brands:
   Arizona

4567 Food Sciences Corp
821 E Gate Dr
Mt Laurel, NJ 08054-1239
   856-924-5185
Fax: 856-778-4192 800-346-4422
   www.foodsciences.com
Nutritional shakes, puddings; protein snack bars, chips; soups, pastas, hot beverages, other nutritional food supplements
President: Robert Schwartz
Estimated Sales: $10-20 Million
Number Employees: 50-99

4568 Food Should Taste Good
PO Box 9452
Denver, CO 80218
   877-588-3784
   www.foodshouldtastegood.com
Flavored tortilla chips

Founder: Pete Lescoe
VP, Finance: Bob Craig
VP, Marketing: James Borteck
Contact: Amanda Barrasso
amanda@foodshouldtastegood.com
Estimated Sales: $5 Million
Number Employees: 8

4569 Food Source Company
1335 Fewster Drive
Mississauga, ON L4W 1A2
Canada
   905-625-8404
   Fax: 905-238-9160
Manufacturer, exporter and importer of salad dressings, sauces and fat-free mayonnaise
President: Ralph Murray
Estimated Sales: $2,000,000
Number Employees: 18
Square Footage: 40000
Type of Packaging: Consumer, Food Service, Private Label

4570 Food for Life Baking
Corona, CA 92879
   800-797-5090
   www.foodforlife.com
Breads, buns, cereals, pasta, tortillas and waffles
CFO: Scott Kraus
Marketing Manager: Gary Torres
Type of Packaging: Consumer
Brands:
   FOOD FOR LIFE

4571 Food of Our Own Design
1988 Springfield Ave
Maplewood, NJ 7040
   973-762-0985
   Fax: 973-762-7895
Cakes, pastries, brownies and crunch bars
Owner: Timothy Quickel
VP Sales/Operations: Tisha Jackson
Estimated Sales: $10-20 Million
Number Employees: 10-19
Square Footage: 8000

4572 FoodMatch Inc
575 Eight Avenue
Fl 23
New York, NY 10018
   212-244-5050
Fax: 212-334-5042 800-350-3411
info@foodmatch.com www.foodmatch.com
Olives, fig spreads and dolmas
President: Philip Meldrum
President: Phil Meldrum
Contact: Emma Archbold
emma.archbold@foodmatch.com
Estimated Sales: $2.5 Million
Number Employees: 23

4573 Foodie Fuel
Boulder, CO 80303
   foodiefuel.com
Organic, gluten-free energy snacks
CEO: John Herbers
Number of Brands: 1
Number of Products: 4
Type of Packaging: Consumer
Brands:
   FUEL SNACKS

4574 Foods Alive
300 Industrial Dr
Suite C
Angola, IN 46703
   260-488-4497
   foodsalive.com
Flax crackers, artisan cold-pressed oils, super dressings, super foods and hemp foods. Organic, vegan, kosher & gluten-free.
President/Owner: Ellen Moor
info@foodslive.com
CEO: Michael Moor
Operations: Matt Alvord
Number Employees: 5-9
Type of Packaging: Consumer

Food Manufacturers / A-Z

4575 Foodscience Corp
20 New England Dr
PO Box 1
Essex Junction, VT 05452-2896
802-878-5508
Fax: 802-878-0549 800-874-9444
international@foodsciencecorp.com
www.foodsciencecorp.com
Manufacturer and exporter of vitamin supplements, joint and immune support supplements and specialty nutritional formulas
President: Dom Orlandi
CEO: Dale Metz
Financial Executive: Tricia Wunsch
Director of Strategic Planning: Mary Helrich
VP Marketing: Mark Ducharme
Operations: Sarah Oliveira
Estimated Sales: $300,000-500,000
Number Employees: 100-249
Parent Co: FoodScience Corporation
Brands:
 Aangamik Dmg
 Chitolean
 Discovery
 Herb Alchemy

4576 Foodstirs
Santa Monica, CA
844-250-3332
foodstirs.com
Organic baking kits and mixes
CEO: Galit Laibow
Type of Packaging: Consumer
Brands:
 FOODSTIRS

4577 Fool Proof Gourmet Products
1813 Parkwood Dr.
Grapevine, TX 76051
817-329-1839
Fax: 817-329-1819
Manufacturer and exporter of gourmet seasonings, spices, sauces, etc
President: Mark Pierce
VP: Jeff Covington
Estimated Sales: $1-3,000,000
Number Employees: 5-9
Square Footage: 20000
Parent Co: Coulton Associates
Type of Packaging: Consumer, Food Service
Brands:
 Fool Proof Gourmet

4578 (HQ)Foothills Creamery
2825 Bonnybrook Rd. SE
Calgary, AB T2G 4N1
Canada
403-263-7725
Fax: 403-237-5051 800-661-4909
www.foothillscreamery.com
Ice cream, unique cones, various novelties, frozen yogurt, and butter
President: Don Bayrack
Vice President: Barry Northfield
Sales Manager: Randy Wagner
Year Founded: 1969
Estimated Sales: $24 Million
Number Employees: 700
Number of Brands: 3
Number of Products: 24
Type of Packaging: Consumer, Food Service, Private Label, Bulk
Brands:
 Jersey Supreme
 Lone Pine Country
 Rocky Mountain

4579 Foppiano Vineyards
12707 Old Redwood Hwy
PO Box 606
Healdsburg, CA 95448-9241
707-433-7272
Fax: 707-433-0565 info@foppiano.com
www.foppiano.com
Manufacturer and exporter of wines
President: Louis Foppiano
louis@foppiano.com
Winemaker: Bill Regan
Estimated Sales: $10-20 Million
Number Employees: 20-49
Type of Packaging: Consumer
Brands:
 Foppiano

Fox Mountain
Riverside

4580 Fora Foods
Brooklyn, NY 11206
info@forafoods.com
forafoods.com
Dairy-free butter
Co-Founder & CEO: Aidan Altman
Co-Founder & CFO: Andrew McClure

4581 Forager Project
San Francisco, CA 94111
foragerproject.com
Cashew-based yogurt and milk
Founder & CEO: Stephen Williamson
Founder & COO: John-Charles Hanley
Number of Brands: 1
Number of Products: 22
Type of Packaging: Consumer
Brands:
 FORAGER PROJECT

4582 Foran Spice Inc
7616 S 6th St
P.O. Box 109
Oak Creek, WI 53154-2049
414-764-1220
Fax: 414-764-8803 800-558-6030
email@asenzya.com www.asenzya.com
Re-cleaned and sterilized spices, custom engineered seasonings, and value-added food products
President: Patty Goto
patty.goto@foranspice.com
CFO: Andy Gitter
Vice President: Joy Hauser
VP of Business Development & Marketing: Chris Anderson
VP Sales: Paul Duddleston
Engineer: Alan Goto
Estimated Sales: $19 Million
Number Employees: 100-249
Square Footage: 213000
Type of Packaging: Food Service, Private Label, Bulk

4583 Forbes Candies
1300 Taylor Farm Road
Virginia Beach, VA 23453-3141
757-468-6602
Fax: 757-486-0646 800-626-5898
www.forbescandies.com
Confectionery products including salt water taffy, fudge, assorted brittle, and peanuts.
Owner: Jody Crosswhite
CEO: William M. Lawton
Sales Manager: Lynn Watson
Contact: Joanne Friedenson
jo.friedenson@atkinsonrealty.com
Estimated Sales: $5-10 Million
Number Employees: 20-49
Type of Packaging: Consumer

4584 Forbes Chocolate BP
800 Ken Mar Industrial Pkwy
Broadview Hts, OH 44147
440-838-4400
Fax: 440-838-4438 info@forbeschocolate.com
www.forbeschocolate.com
Manufacturer and exporter of cocoa and flavor powders for dairies. Chocolate ,mocha, strawberry, vanilla, orange cream, root beer, banana, mango and others
Owner: Keith Geringer
kgeringer@forbeschocolate.com
VP: Douglas Geringer
Quality Control: Ellon Waters
Director of Marketing: Rick Stunek
Sales: Mike Richter
Estimated Sales: $1.4 Million
Number Employees: 10-19
Square Footage: 17000
Type of Packaging: Bulk

4585 Forbes Co
4855 Kendrick St SE
Grand Rapids, MI 49512-9602
616-940-9900
Fax: 616-940-2028
Magazine publisher
Manager: Bret Foster
Estimated Sales: $3-5 Million
Number Employees: 5-9
Parent Co: Volk Corporation

4586 Ford Gum & Mach Co Inc
18 Newton Ave
Akron, NY 14001-1099
716-542-4561
Fax: 716-542-4610 fordgum@fordgum.com
www.fordgum.com
Manufacturer and distributor of gum balls and gum ball machines.
President: Lindsey Barnick
lbarnick@harrisbeach.com
Sr. Vice President: Steve Greene
Year Founded: 1913
Number Employees: 5-9
Type of Packaging: Consumer, Food Service, Private Label, Bulk
Brands:
 Carousel
 Chunk a Chew
 Yowser!!

4587 Ford's Gourmet Foods
1109 Agriculture St # 1
Raleigh, NC 27603-2371
919-833-7647
Fax: 919-821-5781 800-446-0947
sales@bonesuckin.com www.bonesuckin.com
Producer of sauces, mustards, salsa and nuts. Some of their products include Bone Suckin Sauce, Bone Suckin Mustard, Bone Suckin Hiccuppin Hot, Bone Suckin Seasoning and Bone Suckin Yaki Sauce.
President: Connie Ford
Vice President: Patrick Ford
Estimated Sales: $11.6,000,000
Number Employees: 50-99
Type of Packaging: Private Label
Brands:
 Big Chunks Salsa
 Blessing's Mustard
 Bone Suckin' Sauce
 Ford's Foods
 Hiccuppin' Hot Sauce
 J. Berrie Brown Wine Nuts
 We're Talking Serious Salsa

4588 Ford's Gourmet Foods
1109 Agriculture St # 1
Raleigh, NC 27603-2371
919-833-7647
Fax: 919-821-5781 800-446-0947
Sales@BoneSuckin.com www.bonesuckin.com
Sauces, marinades, mustards, and nuts
Owner: Sandi Ford
sandi@bonesuckin.com
VP: Patrick Ford
Number Employees: 50-99

4589 Foreign Candy Company
1 Foreign Candy Dr
Hull, IA 51239-7499
712-439-1496
Fax: 712-439-3207 800-831-8541
www.foreigncandy.com
Developer and distributor of candy.
CEO, President & Owner: Peter De Yager
VP, Marketing & Sales: Bill Lange
HR Manager: Bethany Bosma
Estimated Sales: $5-10 Million
Number Employees: 11-50
Type of Packaging: Private Label
Brands:
 Mega Warheads
 Rips Toll

4590 Foreign Domestic Chemicals
3 Post Rd
Oakland, NJ 07436-1609
201-651-9700
Fax: 201-651-9703
Manufactures ingredients and additives
President: Heinrich Dieseldorff
Estimated Sales: $500,000-1 Million
Number Employees: 1-4

4591 Foremost Farms USA
E10889 Penny Lane
Baraboo, WI 53913-8115
608-355-8700
800-362-9196
www.foremostfarms.com
Dairy products including cheeses, fresh milk, butter, and whey ingredients.

Food Manufacturers / A-Z

President/CEO: Greg Schlafer
Senior VP/CFO: Bob Bascom
VP, Milk Division & Risk Management: Darin Hanson
Manager: Wally Heil
Year Founded: 1994
Estimated Sales: Over $1 Billion
Number Employees: 1000-4999
Number of Brands: 2
Number of Products: 10
Type of Packaging: Consumer, Food Service, Private Label, Bulk
Brands:
   1950 127 Brand
   Formost Farms USA

4592 Forever Green Food Inc.
5700 E Oplympic Blvd
Commerce, CA 90022-5115
   323-721-9928
Fax: 323-721-1487 info@forevergreenfood.com
forevergreenfood.com
Butter cookies; fruit snacks; crackers; assorted chocolates; pumpkin seeds;
President: John Ren
Director of Sales: Luis Gonzalez
Type of Packaging: Private Label
Brands:
   Bahlsen
   SQUE'EASY
   Hawaiian Host

4593 Forge Mountain Foods
1215 Greenville Hwy
Hendersonville, NC 28792
   828-692-9470
Fax: 828-692-9917 800-823-6743
Specialty foods company with over 250 varieties of old timey food products; jams and jellies, pickles and relishes and more
Owner: Brian Pawling
VP Sales/Marketing: Paul Brim
Estimated Sales: $500,000-$1,000,000
Number Employees: 5-9
Number of Products: 250+
Brands:
   Forge Mountain

4594 Foris Vineyards
654 Kendall Rd
Cave Junction, OR 97523-9721
   541-592-3752
Fax: 541-592-4424 foris@foriswine.com
www.foriswine.com
Wines
Owner: Ted Gerber
Estimated Sales: $2.5-5,000,000
Number Employees: 10-19
Number of Brands: 10
Type of Packaging: Private Label

4595 Fork & Goode
Brooklyn, NY
   hello@forkngoode.com
   www.forkandgoode.com
Pork and other meat products.
CEO: Niyati Gupta
CSO: Gabor Forgacs
Number Employees: 1-4

4596 Forkless Gourmet Inc
10 S Riverside Plz
Chicago, IL 60606-3728
   312-474-5746
Fax: 312-474-6127
Manufacturers forkless bun meals available in several varieties including: chicken sesame teriyaki; thai style chicken; beef & broccoli; pork & vegetables with Five Fortune BBQ Sauce; kung pao shrimp (spicy); vegetarian feast withtofu & edamame; chipotle chicken (spicy); margarita chicken; beef asada; pork & vegetable with Ancho Honey BBQ Sauce, and black bean adobo.
President: Gregory Stahl
CFO: Steven Spiegel
VP: Katie Torres
Type of Packaging: Food Service

4597 Forman Vineyard
1501 Big Rock Rd
St Helena, CA 94574-9613
   707-963-3900
Fax: 707-963-5384 www.formanvineyard.com

Wines, grow produce & bottle cabernet savignon & chardonnay
President/Operations/Prod./Mgr: Ric Forman
forman@sonic.net
Vice President/Operations/Prod./Mgr: Toby Forman
Marketing/Sales/Pub Relations Director: Margaret Hatte
Estimated Sales: $1.8 Million
Number Employees: 5-9
Square Footage: 36000

4598 Formosa Enterprises Inc
111 N Market St
Suite 460
San Jose, CA 95113-1112
   408-297-3300
Fax: 408-297-3311 info@formosasauce.com
www.formosasauce.com
Manufacturer of different sauces.
Owner: Julio Lopez
julio@formosasauce.com
Number Employees: 1-4

4599 Formost Friedman Company
152 Frankel Boulevard
Merrick, NY 11566-4033
   516-378-4919
Fax: 516-379-8301
General grocery
President: William MacMelville
Estimated Sales: $1-2,500,000
Number Employees: 1-4

4600 Fort Boise Produce Company
103 Main St
Nyssa, OR 97913
   541-372-5174
Fax: 541-372-3326
Packed onions
President: Thomas Stephens
Estimated Sales: $1-2,500,000
Number Employees: 50-99

4601 Fort Garry Brewing Company
130 Lowson Crescent
Winnipeg, MB R3P 2H8
Canada
   204-487-3678
Fax: 204-487-0839 info@fortgarry.com
www.fortgarry.com
Beer
President/CEO: Doug Saville
CFO: Denis Chabbert
General Manager: Orest Horechko
Corporate Controller: Maria Nemeth
Sales: Wayne Vanlandeghem
Customer Service: Cathy Di Stefano
Estimated Sales: B
Number Employees: 23
Number of Brands: 13
Number of Products: 1
Square Footage: 50000
Type of Packaging: Private Label, Bulk

4602 Forte Gelato
PO Box 327
Greens Farms, CT 06838
   203-764-1826
Fax: 203-254-3080 info@tasteforte.com
www.tasteforte.com
Manufacturer of low fat, high protein gelato.
Founder: Adrian Pace

4603 Forte Stromboli Company
3129 S 13th Street
Philadelphia, PA 19148-5234
   215-463-6336
Fax: 215-463-8616
Frozen stromboli
President: Ronald Conti
Estimated Sales: $5-10,000,000
Number Employees: 5-9
Type of Packaging: Consumer, Food Service

4604 Fortella Fortune Cookies
214 W 26th St
Chicago, IL 60616-2204
   312-567-9000
Fax: 312-567-9119
Fortune, almond and specialty cookies
Owner: Jatico Francis
bjatico@yahoo.com
Company Manager: Brenda Wong

Estimated Sales: $1-2.5 Million
Number Employees: 10-19
Type of Packaging: Consumer, Food Service

4605 Fortenberry Mini-Storage
3128 Fortenberry Rd
Kodak, TN 37764-2020
   865-933-2568
Fax: 865-933-2568
Ice, cheese and dairy products.
Owner: Regina Underwood
Estimated Sales: Less Than $500,000
Number Employees: 1-4
Type of Packaging: Consumer
Other Locations:
   Fortenberry Ice Company
   Kodak TN

4606 Fortino Winery
4525 Hecker Pass Rd
Gilroy, CA 95020-8807
   408-842-3305
Fax: 408-842-8636 888-617-6606
gino@fortinowinery.com www.fortinowinery.com
Wines
Owner: Gino Fortino
gino@fortinowinery.com
Tasting Room Manager: Jill Fortino
Wine-Club Director & Admin. Assistant: Dawn Jackson
Outside Sales Representative: Bertha Valenzula
Estimated Sales: $900,000
Number Employees: 5-9

4607 Fortitude Brands LLC
6925 Almansa Street
Coral Gables, FL 33146-3809
   305-661-8198
Fax: 305-662-4977
Manufacturer and importer of exotic and natural tropical food products
Principal: Franco Stanzione
CFO: Juan Serna
Marketing: Robert Hunt
Sales: Bob Ottmar
Public Relations: Renee Morales
Estimated Sales: $400,000
Number Employees: 21
Number of Brands: 5
Number of Products: 14
Type of Packaging: Consumer
Brands:
   Casabe Rainforest Crackers
   Isabo Hearts of Palm
   Samai

4608 Forto Coffee
New York, NY 10004
   844-450-7575
fortocoffee.com
Coffee shots
Founder & CEO: Neel Premkumar
Number of Brands: 1
Number of Products: 6
Type of Packaging: Consumer
Brands:
   FORTO

4609 Fortress Systems LLC
2132 S 156th Cir
Omaha, NE 68130-2503
   402-333-3532
Fax: 402-333-3536 888-331-6601
Dietary supplements
CEO: Mike Carnazzo
VP/R&D: Joseph Carnazzo
Consultant: Dr Martha Garcia
Consultant: Dr Brian Sakurada
Number Employees: 1-4
Parent Co: FSI Nutrition

4610 Fortuna Cellars
2124 Fortuna Court
Davis, CA 95616-0603
   530-756-6686
Wines
President: Gerald Bowes

4611 Fortunate Cookie
PO Box 1386
Stowe, VT 05672-1386
   802-888-5706
Fax: 802-888-5563 866-266-5337
portico@stowevt.net www.thefortunatecookie.com

Specialty cookies/gift baskets made from scratch and to order signature offering: fortune cookies in 4 sizes and 19 flavors
Owner/CEO: Portia Arthur
Type of Packaging: Consumer

4612 Fortune Cookie Factory
261 12th St
Oakland, CA 94607-4440
510-832-5552
Fax: 510-832-2565
Personalized fortune cookies
President: Andrew Wong
fcf261@yahoo.com
Estimated Sales: $2.5-5 Million
Number Employees: 5-9

4613 Fortune Seas
42 Rogers Street
Gloucester, MA 01930-5000
978-281-6666
Fax: 978-281-8519
Seafood
President/CEO: Donald Short
VP Sales: Charles Bencal
Brands:
  Fortune's Catch
  Ocean Deli

4614 Fortunes International Teas
11 Tunnel Way
Mc Kees Rocks, PA 15136
412-771-7767
Fax: 412-771-2122 www.fortunescoffee.com
Black, green and herbal teas
Owner: Richard Cefola Sr
r.cefolasr@fortunescoffee.com
VP Marketing: Michael Brunk
Estimated Sales: $500,000-$1,000,000
Number Employees: 1-4
Type of Packaging: Private Label
Brands:
  Commonwealth
  Fortunes
  London Herb & Spice
  Ridgways

4615 Forty Second Street Bagel Cafe
733 W. Westfoot Blvd.
Upland, CA 91786-5603
909-949-7334
Fax: 909-949-0721
Bagels and rolls
Owner: Robert Hall
Estimated Sales: $3-5,000,000
Number Employees: 5-9

4616 Fort, Products
4801 Main St
Suite 205
Kansas City, MO 64112
816-741-3000
www.forteproducts.com
Retail fixtures for the food service industry
CFO: Scott Morris

4617 Fosselman's Ice Cream Co
1824 W Main St
Alhambra, CA 91801-1897
626-282-6533
Fax: 626-282-0246 www.fosselmans.com
Ice cream, sherbet
Owner: Anna Fosselman
acfosselman@charter.net
VP: Christian Fossleman
Estimated Sales: $2.5-5,000,000
Number Employees: 20-49
Type of Packaging: Consumer, Bulk

4618 Fossil Farms
81 Fulton St
Boonton, NJ 07005-1909
973-917-3155
Fax: 973-917-3156 sales@fossilfarms.com
www.fossilfarms.com
Farm raised game and all natural meats
CEO/Co-Owner: Lance Appelbaum
lance@fassilfarms.com
Accounts Payable/Receivable: Denise Polizzotto
Sales Manager: Sturgess Spanos
Customer Service: Kristyn Behnke
COO/Co-Owner: Todd Appelbaum
Warehouse Manager: Jose Rivera
Estimated Sales: $1.1 Million
Number Employees: 20-49

4619 Foster Family Farm
90 Foster St
South Windsor, CT 06074-3873
860-648-9366
www.fosterfarms.com
Manufacturer and exporter of pickled asparagus and beans
Principal: Chris Foster
Co-Owner/Member: Teresa Robertson
Partner: Alexandra Palmer
alexandrapalmer@fosterfarm.com
Estimated Sales: $10-20 Million
Number Employees: 10-19

4620 Foster Fams
P.O. Box 52
Kelso, WA 98626
800-255-7227
www.fosterfarms.com
Chicken and turkey

4621 Foster Farms Inc.
1000 Davis St.
PO Box 306
Livingston, CA 95334
800-255-7227
www.fosterfarms.com
Poultry producer.
CEO: Dan Huber
Estimated Sales: Over $1 Billion
Number Employees: 10000+
Number of Brands: 6
Type of Packaging: Consumer, Food Service, Private Label, Bulk
Brands:
  Foster Farms Fresh & Natural
  Foster Farms Naturally Seasoned
  Foster Farms Simply Raised
  Foster Farms Organic
  Foster Farms Always Natural
  Foster Farms Saut, Ready

4622 Fountain Shakes/MS Foods
13508 Orchard Road
Minnetonka, MN 55305
952-988-6940
Fax: 952-988-6941
Fountain shake in six flavors: chocolate malt, cappuccino, strawberry, vanilla, banana and chocolate
Owner: Alan B Stone
Marketing: Lou Ann Stone
Contact: Alan Stone
astone2454@aol.com
Parent Co: MS Foods
Type of Packaging: Consumer, Bulk
Brands:
  Fountain Shake

4623 (HQ)Fountain Valley Foods
2175 N Academy Circle # 201
PO Box 9882
Colorado Springs, CO 80932
719-573-6012
Fax: 719-573-5192 www.fountainvalleyfoods.com
Salsa, ketchup, bean dip and specialty chili products; Importer/Distributor of cheese sauce, jalapeno peppers, banana peppers, chipotle peppers, green chile.
President: James Loyacono
Contact: Ginger Steineke
ginger@fountainvalleyfoods.com
Estimated Sales: $4.9 Million
Number Employees: 4
Square Footage: 20000
Type of Packaging: Consumer, Food Service, Private Label, Bulk
Other Locations:
  Den-Mar Products
  Trinidad CO
Brands:
  Lone Tree Farm
  Nacho Grande

4624 Four Barrel Coffee
375 Valencia St
San Francisco, CA 94103-3504
415-252-0800
info@fourbarrelcoffee.com
fourbarrelcoffee.com
Coffee
Owner: Jeremy Tooker
jtooker@fourbarrelcoffee.com
Number Employees: 20-49

4625 Four Chimneys Farm Winery Trust
211 Hall Rd
Himrod, NY 14842
607-243-7502
Fax: 607-243-8156
Organically grown grape juice, wine, cooking wine and vinegar
Owner: Scott Smith
ssmith@htva.net
Sales Manager: W Daniel
Estimated Sales: Less than $500,000
Number Employees: 5-9
Type of Packaging: Consumer, Bulk

4626 Four Percent Company
16145 Hamilton Ave
Highland Park, MI 48203-2615
313-345-5880
Fax: 313-345-8686
Flavors
Owner: Harold Samhat
Estimated Sales: $500,000-$1,000,000
Number Employees: 1-4
Type of Packaging: Food Service, Private Label
Brands:
  Seely

4627 Four Seasons Produce Inc
400 Wabash Rd
PO Box 788
Ephrata, PA 17522-9100
717-721-2800
Fax: 717-721-2597 800-422-8384
www.sunrisetransportinc.com
Fruits and vegetables
Owner: David Hollinger
VP Finance: Loretta Radanovic
Quality Manager: Daniel Oloro
National Sales Manager: Stan Paluszewski
davidh@fsproduce.com
VP/General Manager: Rob Kurtz
Number Employees: 500-999
Square Footage: 261000

4628 Four Sigmatic
1629 Abbot Kinney Blvd
Venice, CA 90291
us.foursigmatic.com
Mushroom coffees, elixirs and cacaos
Type of Packaging: Consumer
Brands:
  FOUR SIGMATIC

4629 Four Sisters Winery
783 County Road 519
Belvidere, NJ 07823
908-475-3671
Fax: 908-475-3555 mattyfla@gmail.com
www.foursisterswinery.com
Wines
Owner: Robert Matarazzo
Manager: Valerie Tishuk
Estimated Sales: $1-2,500,000
Number Employees: 5-9
Type of Packaging: Private Label

4630 Four Star Beef
Omaha, NE
www.fourstarbeef.com
Beef
Parent Co: JBS USA, LLC.
Other Locations:
  Tolleson AZ
  Green Bay WI
  Plainwell MI
  Souderton PA

4631 Fournier R & Sons Seafood
14147 Old Highway 67
Biloxi, MS 39532-8803
228-392-4293
Fax: 228-392-7130
Seafood
Owner: Doty Fournier
Secretary: Barbara Fournier
Estimated Sales: $2.5-5 000,000
Number Employees: 20-49

Food Manufacturers / A-Z

4632 Fowler Farms
10273 Lummisville Rd
Wolcott, NY 14590
315-594-8068
Fax: 315-594-8060 800-836-9537
www.fowlerfarms.com
Apples.
Director, Business Development: Mark Sharp
VP, Sales & Marketing: Dave Williams
Sales Assitant: Jennifer Sutton
Year Founded: 1858
Estimated Sales: $100-500 Million
Number Employees: 250-499

4633 Fowler Packing Co
8570 S Cedar Ave
Fresno, CA 93725-8905
559-834-5911
Fax: 559-834-5272 erin@fowlerpacking.com
www.fowlerpacking.com
Table grapes, sorbet grapes, and mandarins
President: Leland Parnagian
CEO: Justin Parnagian
Sales: Chad Nelsen
Year Founded: 1935
Estimated Sales: $20-50 Million
Number Employees: 50-99
Brands:
  Golden State Hops
  SamSonS
  Halos

4634 Fox Deluxe Inc
370 N Morgan St
Chicago, IL 60607
312-421-3737
Fax: 312-421-8067 www.foxdeluxefoods.com
Wholesale frozen meats
Owner: Sam Samano
Estimated Sales: $50-100 Million
Number Employees: 50-99

4635 Fox Hollow
8909 Highway 329
Crestwood, KY 40014-9596
502-241-8621
foxhollow.com
Manufacturer sweet and spicy mustard sauce used as a glaze, marinade and a mustard on meat, fish, chicken and sandwiches
President: Phyllis Fox
Estimated Sales: $500,000-$1 Million
Number Employees: 10-19
Type of Packaging: Consumer
Brands:
  Fox Hollow Farm Mustard
  Fox-More Than a Mustard

4636 Fox Iv Technologies
6011 Enterprise Dr
Export, PA 15632-8969
724-387-3500
Fax: 724-387-3516 877-436-2434
www.foxiv.com
Labels and packing supplies
President/CEO: Rick Fox
Estimated Sales: $10-20 Million
Number Employees: 20-49

4637 Fox Meadow Farm
1439 Clover Mill Road
Chester Springs, PA 19425-1108
610-827-9731
Wines
President: Harry Mandell, Jr.
Estimated Sales: $500,000 appx.
Number Employees: 1-4

4638 Fox Meadow Farm of Vermont
135 N Main St
Suite 5
Rutland, VT 05701-3238
802-259-7805
Fax: 802-773-2242 888-754-4204
www.foxmeadowfarmvt.com
Dry seasoning and herb blends, dry mixes
President: James Harrison
Estimated Sales: $300,000-500,000
Number Employees: 1-4

4639 Fox N Hare Brewing Co.
46 Front St.
Port Jervis, NY 12771
845-672-0100
www.foxnhare-brewing.com
IPAs and American ales; fruit-flavored beers
Co-Owner: Sean Donnelly
Co-Owner: David Krantz
Number of Brands: 1
Number of Products: 9
Type of Packaging: Consumer, Private Label
Brands:
  Fox N Hare

4640 Fox Run Vineyards
670 State Route 14
Penn Yan, NY 14527-9622
315-536-4616
Fax: 315-536-1383 800-636-9786
info@foxrunvineyards.com
www.foxrunvineyards.com
Winery, producing riesling, chardonnay, gewurztraminer, lemberger, cabernet franc and pinot noir.
President/Co-Owner: Scott Osborn
Co-Owner: Albert Zafonte
Co-Owner: Kathy Zafonte
Vice President/Co-Owner: Ruth Osborn
Marketing & Events: Kelli Shaffner
Sales Manager: Dan Mitchell
Vineyard Manager: John Kaiser
Winemaker: Peter Bell
Crush Operations & Inventory: Pete Howe
Estimated Sales: $3.8 Million
Number Employees: 10-19
Number of Brands: 1
Type of Packaging: Consumer
Brands:
  Fox Run

4641 Fox Vineyards & Winery
225 Highway 11 S
Social Circle, GA 30025-5003
770-787-5402
Fax: 770-787-5402 www.foxvinwinery.com
Wines
Owner: John Fuchs
Estimated Sales: $1-2,500,000
Number Employees: 1-4

4642 Fox's Fine Foods
303 Broadway St Ste 106
Laguna Beach, CA 92651
949-497-8910
Fax: 949-497-1763 888-522-3697
Pestos, relishes, condiments, soups
President: Kim Fox
Estimated Sales: Under $500,000
Number Employees: 5-9
Type of Packaging: Private Label

4643 Foxen Foxen 7200
7200 Foxen Canyon Rd
Santa Maria, CA 93454-9581
805-937-4251
Fax: 805-937-0415 www.foxenvineyard.com
Wines
Owner: Richard Dore
Contact: Jesse Cloutier
jesse@foxenvineyard.com
Estimated Sales: $1-2,500,000
Number Employees: 5-9

4644 Foxtail Foods
6880 Fairfield Business Ctr
Fairfield, OH 45014-5476
513-881-7900
Fax: 513-881-7910 800-487-2253
customerservice@foxtailfoods.com
www.foxtailfoods.com
Pies, cookies, muffin batter, mixes and syrups and specialty products
President: Lonnie Howard
VP: Matt Daniel
Director of R&D: Doug Snedden
VP Sales/Marketing: Athos Rostan
Manager: Joe Reinhardt
Purchasing Agent: Rich Frysinger
Estimated Sales: $10-20 Million
Number Employees: 100-249
Square Footage: 179055
Parent Co: Perkins
Type of Packaging: Consumer, Food Service, Private Label, Bulk
Other Locations:
  Foxtail Foods-Corporate
  Memphis
  Foxtail Foods-Corporate
  Tennese
  Foxtail Foods-R&D
  Cincinnati
Brands:
  Foxtail

4645 Fralinger's
1325 Boardwalk # 1
Atlantic City, NJ 08401-7287
609-344-0758
Fax: 609-344-0758 800-938-2339
comments@jamescandy.com
www.jamescandy.com
Taffy and candy
President: Frank Glaser
frank.glaser@jamescandy.com
Controller: Rose Gedicke
VP/Internet Technology: Arthur Gager
EVP Marketing/Sales: Lisa Glaser-Whitney
Sales: Alan Green
VP Operations/Manufacturing: Rob Fisher
Number Employees: 1-4
Type of Packaging: Private Label
Other Locations:
  Fralinger's-Bally's Park
  Atlantic City NJ
  Fralinger's-Tennesee Ave
  Atlantic City NJ
  Fralinger's-Ocean City
  Atlantic City NJ
  Fralinger's-Cape May
  Cape May NJ
Brands:
  Fralinger's
  Bayard's
  James'

4646 Fran's Chocolates
1300 East Pike St
Seattle, WA 98122
206-322-0233
Fax: 203-322-0452 800-422-3726
orders@franschocolates.com
www.franschocolates.com
Chocolates
Owner: Fran Bigelow
Marketing: Adriana Bigelow
Contact: Keita Horn
keitah@franschocolates.com
Estimated Sales: $5 Million
Number Employees: 30

4647 Fran's Healthy Helpings
840 Hinckley Road
Suite 128
Burlingame, CA 94010-1505
650-652-5772
Fax: 650-652-5773
Health foods
President: Fran Lent
VP Operations: Ada Chang
Estimated Sales: $1-2,500,000
Number Employees: 5-9
Brands:
  Fran's Healthy Helpings

4648 France Delices
5065 Rue Ontario E
Montreal, QC H1V 3V2
Canada
514-259-2291
Fax: 514-259-1788 800-663-1365
information@francedelices.com
www.francedelices.com
Manufacturer and exporter of cakes including fresh, frozen and gourmet
President: Colette Durot
VP: Laurent Durot
Estimated Sales: $13million
Number Employees: 3
Square Footage: 100000
Type of Packaging: Consumer, Food Service

4649 Franciscan Estate
1178 Galleron Road at Highway 29
St. Helena, CA 94574
707-967-3830
www.franciscan.com
Winemaker
Director of Winemaking: Janet Myers
Type of Packaging: Consumer

Brands:
- Estancia
- Franciscan Oakville Estate
- Mt Veeder
- Quintessa
- Simi Ravenswood
- Veramonte
- Magnificat
- Cuvee Sauvage
- Napa Valley
- Stylus
- Clos Reserve
- Oakville
- Winemakers Reserve
- Fountain Court
- Rose

4650 Franco's Cocktail Mixes
121 SW 5th Ct
Pompano Beach, FL 33060-7909
954-782-7491
Fax: 954-786-9253 800-782-4508
Francocktl@aol.com
www.francoscocktailmixes.com
Manufacturer and exporter of liquid and dry cocktail mixes; also, colored margarita salt and colored rimming sugars
Owner: Michael A Pitino
Quality Control: Guy Haret
Manager: Laura Schnell
michael@francoscocktailmixes.com
Estimated Sales: $10-24.9 Million
Number Employees: 5-9
Number of Brands: 12
Number of Products: 100+
Square Footage: 50000
Type of Packaging: Food Service, Private Label
Brands:
- Crown's Pride
- Florida Straits Rum Runner
- Florida's Gold Cocktail
- Florida's Pride
- Franco's Margarita Salt Sombrero
- Jose Cuervo Margarita Salt Sombrero
- Pat O'Brien's
- Sauza Margarita Salt With Juicer
- Tout Fini Cocktail Mixes

4651 Frank & Dean's Cocktail Mixes
1395 Coronet Avenue
Pasadena, CA 91107-1639
626-351-4272
Fax: 909-596-4640
Bloody Mary, margarita, pina colada, mai tai, strawberry margarita, lime juice and grenadine
President: Frank Abbadessa
CFO: John Kennick
VP: Dean Carbone
Number Employees: 1-4
Type of Packaging: Private Label
Brands:
- Frank & Dean's Cocktail Mixes

4652 Frank Brunckhorst Company
1819 Main St.
Suite 800
Sarasota, FL 34236
804-722-4100
Fax: 804-863-1409 www.boarshead.com
Boar's Head brands of deli meats and cheeses.
Year Founded: 1905
Estimated Sales: $500+ Million
Number Employees: 250-500
Parent Co: Boar's Head
Brands:
- Boar's Head

4653 Frank Family Vineyards
1091 Larkmead Ln
Calistoga, CA 94515-9675
707-942-0859
Fax: 707-942-2581 880-574-9463
info@frankfamilyvineyards.com
www.frankfamilyvineyards.com
Wines
Owner: Richard Frank
info@frankfamilyvineyards.com
Estimated Sales: $10-20 000,000
Number Employees: 20-49
Type of Packaging: Private Label

4654 Frank Korinek & Co
4828 W 25th St
Cicero, IL 60804-3489
708-652-2870
Fax: 773-242-1917
Pastry fillings, fruit pie filling, donut mixes
President: George Korinek
g.korinek@frankkorinek.com
Estimated Sales: $1-2,500,000
Number Employees: 5-9
Brands:
- Bohemian Maid
- Korinek

4655 Frank Mattes & Sons Reliable Seafood
2327 Edwards Lane
Bel Air, MD 21015-5001
410-879-5444
Fax: 410-734-6061
Seafood

4656 Frank Pagano Company
1513 S State Street
Lockport, IL 60441-3550
815-838-0303
Fax: 815-723-9861
Quality meats
President/CEO: Frank Pagano

4657 Frank Wardynski & Sons Inc
336 Peckham St
PO Box 336
Buffalo, NY 14206-1717
716-854-6083
Fax: 716-854-4887 www.wardynski.com
Smoked polish sausage, italian sausage, natural casing weiners, tender casing weiners, skinless weiners, knockwurst, bologna, cooked salami, liver sausage, kiska, blood tongue, sweet or sour head cheese.
Chairman/President: Raymond Wardynski
rmwardynski@wardynski.com
Estimated Sales: $5-10 Million
Number Employees: 20-49
Square Footage: 105000

4658 Frank-Lin Distributors
2455 Huntington Dr
Fairfield, CA 94533-9734
707-437-1264
Fax: 408-258-9527 800-922-9363
humanresources@frank-lin.com
www.frank-lin.com
Leading producer of wines and distilled spirits
Owner: Frank Lin
bottling@frank-lin.com
President/CEO: Frank Maestri
VP Brand Development: Michael Wasteney
VP Sales/Marketing: Mark Pechusick
Marketing Director: Christina Maestri
VP Sales: David Covello
bottling@frank-lin.com
Estimated Sales: $3-5,000,000
Number Employees: 5-9
Square Footage: 45000
Type of Packaging: Bulk
Brands:
- 8 Seconds Canadian Whiskey
- Beyond Vodka
- Buck
- Bellringer
- Puerto Vallarta

4659 Frankford Candy & Chocolate Co
9300 Ashton Rd
Philadelphia, PA 19114-3532
215-735-5200
Fax: 215-735-0721 800-523-9090
info@frankfordcandy.com
Processor of solid, hollow chocolate molded novelties and nonchocolate candies for Christmas, Easter, Halloween and Valentine's Day.
CEO: Morgan Brehm
mbrehm@inmetco.com
CEO: Stuart Selarnik
Executive VP: Nathan Hoffman
Director, Marketing: Molly Jacobson
Year Founded: 1947
Estimated Sales: $20-50 Million
Number Employees: 250-499
Number of Brands: 7
Square Footage: 65000
Type of Packaging: Bulk

Brands:
- Disney
- Frankford
- Hello Kitty
- Marvel
- Nickelodeon
- SpongeBob SquarePants
- Welchs

4660 Frankfort Cheese
F1705 County Rd N
Edgar, WI 54426-9648
715-352-2345
Fax: 715-352-2346
Cheese
President: Dennis Telschow
Estimated Sales: Less than $500,000
Number Employees: 5-9

4661 Franklin Baker Company
275 Tournament Drive
Southwind Office Center B, Suite 305
Memphis, TN 38125
901-881-6681
Fax: 901-881-6682 www.franklinbaker.com
Baked goods using coconut
President & CEO: Jerry Lorenzo
SVP, Finance: Jim Laurian
SVP, Sales, Marketing & Operations: Ken Gibson
SVP, Operations: Cesar Galvez

4662 Franklin Baking Co.
500 W. Grantham St.
Goldsboro, NC 27530
919-735-0344
Fax: 919-705-2029
Fresh breads and cakes in eastern North Carolina.
President/CEO, Flowers Foods: Allen Shiver
Year Founded: 2000
Estimated Sales: $100-500 Million
Number Employees: 250-499
Parent Co: Flowers Foods
Type of Packaging: Consumer
Brands:
- Sunbeam
- Nature's Own
- Cobblestone Mill
- Bluebird
- Mi Casa

4663 Franklin Baking Company
2004 N Queen Street
Kinston, NC 28501-1621
252-527-1155
Fax: 252-527-9871 800-248-7494
Bakery items
President: Eugene Franklin
Production: Randy Brock
Estimated Sales: $10-24.9,000,000
Number Employees: 100-249

4664 Franklin Farms
222 New Road
Parsippany, NJ 07054
www.franklinfarms.com
Veggie burgers, edamame and veggie breakfast foods
President: Wilhelm Meya
Estimated Sales: $100+ Million
Number Employees: 600
Square Footage: 400000
Brands:
- Veggiballs
- Veggiburger
- Veggidogs
- Vegginuggets

4665 Franklin Foods
68 East St
P.O. Box 486
Enosburg Falls, VT 05450
802-933-4338
Fax: 802-933-4039 800-933-6114
info@franklinfoods.com www.franklinfoods.com
Yogurt and cream cheese
VP of Marketing: Rocco Cardinale
Estimated Sales: $25-49.9 Million
Number Employees: 100-249
Number of Brands: 4
Square Footage: 43000
Type of Packaging: Consumer, Food Service, Private Label, Bulk
Brands:
- All Season's Kitchen

Food Manufacturers / A-Z

Green Mountain Farms
Hahn's
Lombardi's Italian Classics

4666 Franklin Hill Vineyards
7833 Franklin Hill Rd
Bangor, PA 18013-4039
610-588-8708
Fax: 610-588-8158 888-887-2839
franklinhill@enter.net
www.franklinhillvineyards.com
Wines
Owner: Elaine Pivinski
elaine@franklinhillvineyards.com
Estimated Sales: $2.5-5,000,000
Number Employees: 10-19
Type of Packaging: Private Label

4667 Franklin's Cheese
PO Box 8
Los Banos, CA 93635
209-826-6259
Fax: 209-826-8781 franklinsteleme@gmail.com
franklinscheesedotcom.wordpress.com
Rice flour coated Teleme cheese.
President: Franklin Peluso
Year Founded: 1980
Estimated Sales: $20-50 Million
Number Employees: 20-49

4668 Frankly Natural Bakers
7740 Formula Pl
San Diego, CA 92121-2419
858-536-5910
Fax: 858-536-5911 800-727-7229
info@franklynatural.com www.franklynatural.com
Brownies, cookies, energy bars, etc
Owner: Jerry Sarnow
jerry@franklynatural.com
Estimated Sales: $3-5 Million
Number Employees: 10-19
Number of Brands: 3
Number of Products: 26
Square Footage: 20000
Type of Packaging: Consumer, Private Label, Bulk
Brands:
  98% Fat-Free
  Amazingly Tasty
  Beach
  Coast
  Frankly Natural3
  Frankly Organic
  Rice Crunchies
  Vegan Decadence

4669 Franz Bakery Outlet Store
340 NE 11th St
Portland, OR 97293
503-232-2191
www.franzbakery.com
Bakery products.
President & CEO: Bob Albers
CFO: Jerry Boness
VP, Human Resources: Forrest Clayton
Corporate Controller: Keith VanEmmerik
VP, National Sales: Kim Nisbet
Product Wrapper: Sonja Abel
Year Founded: 1906
Estimated Sales: $100-500 Million
Number Employees: 1,000-4,999

4670 Franzia Winery
17000 E State Highway 120
Ripon, CA 95366
209-599-4111
Fax: 209-599-5892 info@franzia.com
www.franzia.com
Wines
CEO: Fred Franzia
CFO: Jim Page
General Manager: Dan Leonard
Sales Executive: Steve Hughs
Head of Operations: Jim Carter
Manufacturing Executive: Lou Dambrosio
Purchasing Executive: Beth Kirkpatrick
Number Employees: 20
Square Footage: 6174
Type of Packaging: Consumer, Food Service, Private Label
Brands:
  Franzia

4671 Fratelli Beretta USA
750 Clark Dr
Mount Olive, NJ 07828
201-438-0723
info@fratelliberettausa.com
www.fratelliberettausa.com
Italian and Spanish meat specialties
President: Lorenzo Beretta
Contact: Simone Bocchina
s.bocchina@fratelliberettausa.com
Estimated Sales: $5-10 Million
Number Employees: 20-49

4672 Fratelli Mantova
2608 Flagstone Circle
Naperville, IL 60564
630-904-0002
Fax: 630-904-0003 info@fineitalianfood.com
www.fineitalianfood.com
Italian foods, including oils, vinegar, pasta, condiments and espresso
Year Founded: 1905

4673 Fratelli Perata
1595 Arbor Rd
Paso Robles, CA 93446-9669
805-238-2809
Fax: 805-238-2809 carol@fratelliperata.com
www.fratelliperata.com
Wines
Owner: Liao Hsinchao
philliao@alum.mit.edu
Estimated Sales: Under $500,000
Number Employees: 1-4

4674 Fratello Coffee Roasters
4021 9th Street SE
Calgary, AB T2G 3C7
Canada
403-265-2112
Fax: 403-263-3255 800-465-7227
info@fratellocoffee.com www.fratellocoffee.com
Gourmet coffee
President: Henry Kutarna
VP: Jason Prefontaine
Marketing Director: David Selley
Number Employees: 20-49
Type of Packaging: Consumer, Food Service
Brands:
  Fratello

4675 Frazier Nut Farms Inc
10830 Yosemite Blvd
Waterford, CA 95386-9637
209-522-1406
Fax: 209-874-9638 fraznut@aol.com
www.fraziernut.com
Manufacturer and exporter of nuts including shelled and in-shell English walnuts and shelled almonds
President: Jim Frazier
jfrazier@fraziernut.com
VP: Steve Slacks
Estimated Sales: $2.5-5 Million
Number Employees: 100-249
Type of Packaging: Bulk
Brands:
  Frazier's Finest

4676 Fred Usinger Inc
1030 N Old World 3rd St
Milwaukee, WI 53203-1300
414-276-9100
Fax: 414-291-5277 800-558-9998
info@usinger.com www.usinger.com
Sausages
President: Fritz Usinger
Vice President: Debra Usinger
VP Marketing/Sales: John Gabe
Estimated Sales: $20-50 Million
Number Employees: 100-249
Brands:
  Sausage a La Carte

4677 Frederick Wildman & Sons LTD
307 E 53rd St # 3
New York, NY 10022-4985
212-355-0700
Fax: 212-355-4719 800-733-9463
info@frederickwildman.com
www.frederickwildman.com
Manufacturer, importer and distributor of fine wines.
President: John Sellar
CEO: Davide Mascalzoni
d.mascalzoni@frederickwildman.com
VP, Finance: James DiCicco
VP/Director, Marketing: Martin Sinkoff
VP/National Sales Manager: Bill Seawright
Assistant VP/Director, Public Relations: Odila Galer-Noel
Year Founded: 1934
Estimated Sales: $20-50 Million
Number Employees: 100-249
Number of Brands: 26
Type of Packaging: Consumer, Food Service
Brands:
  Kanonkop
  Pol Roger
  Chateau Fuisse
  Domaine Armand Rousseau
  Hugo Et Fils
  Marc Roman
  Olivier Leflaive
  Pascal Jolivet
  Potel Aviron
  Egon Muller
  Weingut Wittman
  Grooner
  Astica
  Michel Torino
  Ca Bianca
  Ca Donini
  Castello Monachi
  Lamberti
  Churchills Ports
  Baron De Ley
  El Coto De Rioja
  Maximo
  Museum
  Cartreuse Liqueur
  Edinburgh Gin
  Illegal Mezcal

4678 Fredericksburg Herb Farm
405 Whitney St
Fredericksburg, TX 78624-3785
830-997-8615
Fax: 830-997-5069 800-259-4372
information@fredericksburgherbfarm.com
www.fredericksburgherbfarm.com
Gourmet herbs and vinegars
President: Bill Varney
info@fredericksburgherbfarm.com
Estimated Sales: $1-2.5 Million
Number Employees: 20-49

4679 Free2b Foods
6880 Winchester Circle
Unit E
Boulder, CO 80301
hey@free2bfoods.com
free2bfoods.com
Allergen-free snacks
Type of Packaging: Consumer
Brands:
  free2b

4680 FreeYumm
54 E 69th Ave
Vancouver, BC V5X 4R2
Canada
info@freeyumm.com
www.freeyumm.com
Allergen- and gluten-free snacks
President/Owner: Sarah Clarke
Number of Brands: 1
Number of Products: 8
Type of Packaging: Consumer
Brands:
  FREEYUMM

4681 Freed, Teller & Freed
436 N Canal Street
Suite 2
South San Francisco, CA 94080-4668
650-589-8500
Fax: 650-589-0711 800-370-7371
Tea, coffee, preserves, condiments and sugars
President: A J Techeira Jr
Estimated Sales: $570,000
Number Employees: 7
Number of Brands: 10
Number of Products: 275
Type of Packaging: Consumer, Private Label, Bulk
Brands:
  Dependable

Freed's
Freed, Teller & Fredd

4682 Freeda Vitamins Inc
4725 34th St # 301
Long Island City, NY 11101-2436
718-433-4337
Fax: 212-685-7297   800-777-3737
info@freedavitamins.com
www.freedavitamins.com
Manufacturer and exporter of kosher yeast-free vitamins and supplements including garlic. Our products are also gluten free, dairy free, and free of artificial colors & flavors.
President/CEO: Eliyahu Zimmerman
Estimated Sales: $2.5 Million
Number Employees: 20-49
Number of Brands: 1
Number of Products: 200
Square Footage: 9150
Type of Packaging: Consumer
Brands:
    Freeda

4683 Freedman's Bakery
803 Main St
Belmar, NJ 07719
732-681-2334
Fax: 732-681-1269
Bakery items
President: Herb Freedman
Contact: Herbert Freedman
herb@apex-equip.com
Estimated Sales: $500,000-$1,000,000
Number Employees: 100-249

4684 Freedom Foods LLC
300 Beanville Rd
Randolph, VM 05060
802-728-0070
info@freedom-foods.com
freedom-foods.com
Baked goods; baking mixes and ingredients; soft drinks; snacks; and condiments
President: Eric Woller
Compliance Coordinator: Tara Matthews
Estimated Sales: $2.5-5 Million
Number Employees: 30
Type of Packaging: Private Label

4685 Freekehlicious
P.O. Box 103
Norwood, NJ 07628
201-297-7957
Fax: 201-322-3127   info@freekehlicious.com
freekehlicious.com
Granola; cereal; and pasta
CEO: Barbara Fanelli
Year Founded: 2010
Type of Packaging: Food Service, Private Label

4686 Freeland Bean & Grain Inc
1000 E Washington
PO Box 515
Freeland, MI 48623-8439
989-695-9131
Fax: 989-695-5241   800-447-9131
freeland.i@att.net   www.freelandbeanandgrain.com
Manufacturer and exporter of dried beans and grains
Owner: John Hupfer
freeland.i@att.net
VP: Elenor Hupfer
Estimated Sales: $3.8 Million
Number Employees: 5-9
Type of Packaging: Bulk

4687 Freeman Industries
100 Marbledale Rd
Tuckahoe, NY 10707
914-961-2100
Fax: 914-961-5793   800-666-6454
freeman@lanline.com   www.freemanllc.com
Dairy vitamin concentrates and zein. Importer and exporter of dried fruits and vegetables, pectin, herbal extracts and natural colors. Processor of citrus bioflavonoids and rice bran and rice bran derivates
President/CEO: Joel G Freeman
VP: Paul Freeman
Contact: Joel Freeman
joelfreeman@freemanb2b.com
Estimated Sales: $1-3 Million
Number Employees: 10-19
Square Footage: 10000
Type of Packaging: Bulk

Brands:
    A/D/F
    D' Sol

4688 Freemark Abbey Winery
3022 Saint Helena Hwy N # 5
St Helena, CA 94574-9652
707-963-9698
Fax: 707-963-7633   800-963-9698
info@freemarkabbey.com
www.freemarkabbey.com
Manufacturer and exporter of wines including cabernet sauvignon, chardonnay and johannisberg riesling
Director of Winemaking: Ted Edwards
wineinfo@freemarkabbey.com
Estimated Sales: $5-9.9 Million
Number Employees: 20-49
Type of Packaging: Food Service
Brands:
    Freemark Abbey

4689 Freestone Pickle Co
610 N Center St
Bangor, MI 49013-1434
269-427-7702
Fax: 269-427-5542   877-874-2553
info@freestonepickles.com
www.freestonepickles.com
Pickles, relish and pickled peppers and cauliflower
Owner: Mike Hescott
info@freestonepickles.com
Estimated Sales: $10-20,000,000
Number Employees: 20-49
Type of Packaging: Consumer, Food Service, Private Label, Bulk
Brands:
    Freestone
    Holiday Royal
    Partetime

4690 Freeze-Dry Foods Inc
111 West Ave # 4
Albion, NY 14411-1500
585-589-6399
Fax: 585-589-6402   info@freeze-dry.com
www.freeze-dry.com
Freeze dried ingredients specializing in meat, seafood and protein items
President: Karen Richardson
krichardson@freeze-dry.com
Business Development: Lisa Horvath
Estimated Sales: $4.5 Million
Number Employees: 20-49
Type of Packaging: Consumer

4691 Freeze-Dry Ingredients
188 W Industrial Dr
Suite 200
Elmhurst, IL 60126
630-530-1880
info@fdiusa.net
www.fdiusa.net
Freeze-dried ingredients

4692 Freirich Foods
P.O. Box 1529
Salisbury, NC 28145
800-221-1315
www.freirich.com
Marinated beef and pork, corned beef, roast beef, pastrami, rib roasts, pot roasts, beef sirloin and beef ribs.
President & CEO: Paul Bardinas
CFO & VP of Finance: Doug Sokolowski
VP of Sales & Marketing: Phil Percoco
COO & VP of Operations: Dennis Arrasmith
Estimated Sales: $25 Million
Number Employees: 50-99
Number of Brands: 2
Square Footage: 35000
Type of Packaging: Consumer, Food Service
Brands:
    Freirich Porkette®
    Regal Chef

4693 (HQ)Freixenet USA Inc
967 Broadway
Sonoma, CA 95476-7403
707-996-4981
Fax: 707-996-0720   info@freixenetusa.com
www.gloriaferrer.com
Manufacturer and importer of Spanish champagnes and wines; also, processor of California wines

President: Robert Abel
robert.abel@freixenetusa.com
Number Employees: 50-99
Parent Co: Freixenet SA
Type of Packaging: Consumer
Brands:
    Castellblanch
    Freixenet Spanish Wines
    Freixenet Wines
    Gloria Ferrer
    Henri Abele
    Rene Barbier
    Segura Viudas

4694 Fremont Authentic Brands
802 N Front St
Fremont, OH 43420-1917
419-334-8995
Fax: 419-334-8120   info@fremontcompany.com
www.fremontfoodservice.com
Tomatoes, sauerkraut, salsa and barbecue sauces.
Logistics Manager: Pam Hufford
Year Founded: 1905
Estimated Sales: $28 Million
Number Employees: 250-499
Square Footage: 250000
Type of Packaging: Consumer, Food Service, Private Label
Brands:
    Paisley Farm
    Frank's Kraut

4695 Fremont Beef Co
960 Schneider St
Fremont, NE 68025-6134
402-727-7200
Fax: 402-727-0907   800-331-4788
www.fremontbeef.com
Beef tongue, outside skirts, calf and cow livers
President: Les Leech
Vice President: Jim Pomrenke
Director, Marketing and Sales: Laun Hinkle
Year Founded: 1990
Estimated Sales: $20-50 Million
Number Employees: 100-249

4696 French & Brawn Marketplace
1 Elm St
Camden, ME 04843-1902
207-236-3361
Fax: 207-236-4880   todd@frenchandbrawn.com
www.frenchandbrawn.com
Choice meats, lobsters, soups and sandwiches
Owner: Todd Anderson
todd@frenchandbrawn.com
Estimated Sales: $5-10 Million
Number Employees: 20-49

4697 French Creek Seafood
1097 Lee Road
Parksville, BC V9P 2E1
Canada
250-248-7100
Fax: 250-248-7197   mail@frenchcreek.ca
www.frenchcreek.ca
Manufacturer and exporter of fresh and frozen seafood
President: Brad McLean
President: Brad McLean
Estimated Sales: $6,000,000
Number Employees: 15
Type of Packaging: Bulk

4698 French Feast Inc.
473 S Dean St
Englewood, NJ 07631
201-731-3102
Fax: 201-208-2923
Honey; gingerbread; baking mixes and ingredients; mustard; vinegar; hot chocolate powder; minds; confections; juice; snacks; jams and spreads; olives; salt;
Co-Owner: Phyllis Brooks
Year Founded: 1999
Estimated Sales: $423,431
Number Employees: 5
Number of Products: +700
Type of Packaging: Food Service, Private Label

Food Manufacturers / A-Z

4699 French Gourmet Inc
245 Coney Island Dr
Sparks, NV 89431-6303
775-525-2525
Fax: 775-525-2530 linda@frenchgourmet.com
www.frenchgourmet.com
Frozen dough, croissants, danish, puff pastry, breads, and muffin, cookie batters
Manager: Linda Coffman
lcoffman@frenchgourmet.com
Estimated Sales: $10-49,999,999
Number Employees: 5-9
Number of Brands: 2
Number of Products: 57
Square Footage: 50000
Type of Packaging: Food Service, Private Label, Bulk
Brands:
French Gourmet
Smart Gourmet

4700 French Market Coffee
640 Magazine Street
New Orleans, LA 70130
504-581-7234
Fax: 504-539-5427 800-535-1961
service@reilyproducts.com
www.frenchmarketcoffee.com
Manufacturer and packer of coffee
President: Fraser Bartlett
Year Founded: 1890
Estimated Sales: $2.5-5 Million
Number Employees: 20-49
Parent Co: Reily Foods Company
Type of Packaging: Consumer
Brands:
French Market

4701 French Market Foods
3935 Ryan St
Lake Charles, LA 70605-2817
337-477-9296
www.bigeasyfoods.com
Shrimp, frozen and fresh
President/CEO: Larry Avery
lavery@fmfoods.com
Estimated Sales: $5-9.9 Million
Number Employees: 50-99

4702 French Meadow Bakery & Cafe
2610 Lyndale Ave S
Minneapolis, MN 55408-1321
612-870-7855
Fax: 612-870-1196 www.frenchmeadowcafe.com
Organic and all-natural products including yeast-free, vegan, sprouted grain, gluten-free and Kosher Parve options.
Owner: Steve Shapiro
steve@frenchmeadowcafe.com
Estimated Sales: $5-9.9 Million
Number Employees: 20-49
Number of Brands: 4
Number of Products: 32
Square Footage: 48000
Type of Packaging: Consumer, Food Service, Private Label, Bulk
Other Locations:
French Meadow Bakery
Auburn WA
Brands:
Healthseed
Healthy Hemp
Mens Bread
Womens Bread

4703 French Patisserie
1090 Palmetto Ave
Pacifica, CA 94044
650-738-4990
Fax: 650-738-4995 800-300-2253
gateau@frenchpatisserie.com
www.frenchpatisserie.com
Frozen cakes, tarts, and dessert sauces
President: Marta Spasic
Contact: Frank Spasic
frank@frenchpatisserie.com
Estimated Sales: $5-10 Million
Number Employees: 20-49

4704 French Quarter Seafood
2933 Paris Road
Chalmette, LA 70043-3346
504-277-1679
Fax: 504-277-1679
Seafood
Owner: Philippe Despointes

4705 French's Coffee
1400 Central Rd
Walnut Creek, CA 94596-3794
925-932-5901
Coffee
Owner: Chet Parker
Estimated Sales: Under $500,000
Number Employees: 1-4

4706 French's Flavor Ingredients
4455 E Mustard Way
Springfield, MO 65803
800-841-1256
Provider of flavors to meat and poulty processors in the food manufacturing industry.
Technical Services: Cindy Bernskoetter
Parent Co: Reckitt Benckiser LLC

4707 Fresca Mexican Foods LLC
11193 W Emerald St
Boise, ID 83713-8932
208-376-6922
Fax: 208-375-2330 www.frescamex.com
Flour, corn tortillas and flavored wraps
President: Mike Allen
mallen@frescamex.com
Vice President, Sales/Marketing: Tom Nist
International Sales Manager: Keith Snyder
Estimated Sales: $25,600,000
Number Employees: 100-249
Number of Brands: 1
Number of Products: 60
Type of Packaging: Food Service, Private Label

4708 Fresh Bellies
PO Box 224
White Plains, NY 10605
866-888-0467
info@freshbellies.com freshbellies.com
Organic baby food
President/Owner: Saskia Sorrosa
Number of Brands: 1
Number of Products: 7
Type of Packaging: Consumer
Brands:
FRESH BELLIES

4709 Fresh Express, Inc.
P.O. Box 80599
Salinas, CA 93912
800-242-5472
www.freshexpress.com
Certified organic salads and lettuce, cole slaw & shreds, delicious kits, flavorful spinach, gourmet cafe salads, harvest originals, refreshing mixes, tasty greens mixes, and tender leaf mixes.
President: John Olivo
CEO: Kenneth Diveley
Year Founded: 1926
Estimated Sales: $368.3 Million
Number Employees: 5,000+
Square Footage: 20000
Parent Co: Chiquita Brands International, Inc
Type of Packaging: Bulk
Brands:
Fresh Express

4710 Fresh Frozen Foods
1814 Washington St
PO Box 215
Jefferson, GA 30549-2668
706-367-9851
Fax: 706-367-4646 800-277-9851
wecare@freshfrozenfoods.com
Strawberries, southern peas and beans, carrots, squash, zucchini, green beans, onions, potatoes, turnip roots.
President: Billy Griffin Jr
Year Founded: 1975
Estimated Sales: $40 Million
Number Employees: 50-99
Square Footage: 5600

4711 Fresh Hemp Foods
15.2166 Notre Dame Avenue
Winnipeg, NB R3H 0K1
Canada
800-665-4367
Fax: 204-956-5984
Hemp food products
President/CEO: Mike Fata
Type of Packaging: Bulk

4712 Fresh Ideas
8350 S Durango Dr
Suite 201
Las Vegas, NV 89113-4473
702-701-4272
freshideallc.com
Popcorn, side dishes and seasonings
Number of Brands: 1
Number of Products: 11
Type of Packaging: Consumer
Brands:
FRESH IDEAS

4713 Fresh Island Fish
312 Alamaha St
Unit G
Kahului, HI 96732-2430
808-871-1111
Fax: 808-871-6818 www.freshislandfish.com
Seafood
President: Mike Lee
Owner/Founder/C.E.O: Bruce Johnson
fif@maui.net
Estimated Sales: $10-20 Million
Number Employees: 50-99

4714 Fresh Juice Delivery
269 S Beverly Dr
Suite 1072
Beverly Hills, CA 90212-3851
310-271-7373
Manufacturer and exporter of fresh and fresh-frozen juices including citrus and blended
Estimated Sales: Less Than $500,000
Number Employees: 5-9
Parent Co: Saratoga Beverage
Type of Packaging: Consumer, Food Service
Brands:
Florida Pik't
Fresh Pik't
Just Pik't

4715 Fresh Mark Inc.
1888 Southway St. SW
Massillon, OH 44646
330-832-7491
Fax: 330-830-3174 www.freshmark.com
Bacon, ham, weiners, deli and luncheon meats, dry sausage and other specialty meat items.
CEO: Neil Genshaft
ngenshaft@freshmark.com
Year Founded: 1920
Estimated Sales: $219 Million
Number Employees: 500-999
Square Footage: 80000
Type of Packaging: Consumer, Food Service, Private Label
Brands:
Sugardale
Superior's Brand

4716 Fresh Market Pasta Company
43 Exchange Street
Portland, ME 04101-5009
207-773-7146
Fax: 207-871-7156
Pasta, noodles of all kinds, including ginger and squid's ink
President: Alex Gingrich
Estimated Sales: $500,000-$1,000,000
Number Employees: 10-19

4717 Fresh Nature Foods
8306 N Wall St
Spokane, WA 99208
509-368-7260
Fax: 509-290-6173 info@freshnaturefoods.com
freshnaturefoods.com
Green chickpeas, green hummus and veggie cakes
President/Owner: Ryan Davenport
VP, Food Service Sales: Brad Overberg
Number of Brands: 1
Number of Products: 7
Type of Packaging: Consumer, Food Service
Brands:
FRESH NATURE

4718 Fresh Origins
570 Quarry Rd
San Marcos, CA 92069-9744
760-736-4072
www.freshorigins.com

Food Manufacturers / A-Z

Manufacturer of microgreens.
Co-Founder: David Sasuga
Co-Founder: Kelly Sasuga
Contact: Philip Bosman
philip@freshorigins.com
Number Employees: 1-4
Brands:
  MicroGreens
  Micro Basil Nutmeg
  Micro Cucumber
  Micro Mustard Dijon
  Micro Radish Ruby
  Micro Tangerine Lace
  Micro Wasabi
  Micro Mint Lime
  Petite Green Mixes
  Herb Crystals
  Flower Crystals
  Fruit Crystals
  Mini Herb Crystals
  Mini Flower Crystals

4719 Fresh Pack Seafood
PO Box 1008
Waldoboro, ME 04572-1008
207-832-7720
Fax: 207-832-7795
Fresh seafood
President: Frank Minio
VP/General Manager: Roger Greene

4720 Fresh Pasta Delights
901 W Parker Rd # 135
Plano, TX 75023-7128
972-422-5907
Fax: 972-869-9937
Pasta and sauces
Owner: Jack Rayome
Director Research: Ray Etheridge
Estimated Sales: $5-9.9 000,000
Number Employees: 5-9
Square Footage: 12000
Type of Packaging: Consumer, Food Service, Private Label, Bulk

4721 Fresh Roasted Almond Company
24536 Gibson
Warren, MI 48089
586-619-2400
877-478-6887
warrenproduction@freshroastedalmondco.com
www.freshroastedalmondco.com
Dry roasted, sweetened and flavored kosher nut confections including almonds, pecans, cashews, peanuts and walnuts flavored in cinnamon, honey, maple, vanilla, cherry and spices
Owner: Dan Levy
Contact: Lin Bahni
freshroastedalmondco@freshroastedalmondco.com
Estimated Sales: $1-3 Million
Number Employees: 10-19
Square Footage: 9000
Type of Packaging: Consumer, Private Label, Bulk
Brands:
  Kars
  Ritter

4722 Fresh Samantha
84 Industrial Park Road
Saco, ME 04072-1840
207-284-0011
Fax: 207-284-8331 800-658-4635
Fresh juice
CEO: Doug Levin
Estimated Sales: Less than $500,000
Number Employees: 1-4
Type of Packaging: Consumer
Brands:
  Fresh Samantha

4723 Fresh Seafood Distrib
9910 Milton Jones Rd
Daphne, AL 36526-6143
251-626-1106
Fax: 251-626-1109
Seafood
Co-Owner: Steve Miller
Estimated Sales: $3-5 Million
Number Employees: 5-9

4724 Fresh Start Bakeries
145 S. State College Blvd.
Suite 200
Brea, CA 92821-5806
714-256-8900
Fax: 714-256-8916
Baked goods including hamburger buns and English muffins.
CEO: Russ Doll
info@freshstartbakeries.com
Year Founded: 1962
Estimated Sales: $118 Million
Number Employees: 100-249
Square Footage: 180000
Parent Co: FSB Global Holdings, Inc.
Type of Packaging: Food Service

4725 Fresh Tofu Inc
1101 Harrison St
Allentown, PA 18103-3132
610-433-4711
Fax: 610-433-5611 info@freshtofu.com
www.freshtofu.com
Organic tofu and other soyfood products.
Owner/President: Gary Abramowitz
info@freshtofu.com
Estimated Sales: $2 Million
Number Employees: 20-49
Square Footage: 18000

4726 Freshwater Farms Of Ohio
2624 N US Highway 68
Urbana, OH 43078-9537
937-652-3701
Fax: 937-652-3481 800-634-7434
www.fwfarms.com
Visit our retail store to take home fresh rainbow trout fillets, smoked fillets, marinated fillets, seasoned trout patties, smoked trout spreads and a selection of Ohio foods. We also carry pond supplies and stocking fish, locally-madepottery and garden d,cor. Visit our sturgeon petting zoo, tour Ohio's largest indoor hatchery, & feed our trout by hand. We're open year round!
Owner/President: Dave Smith
drdaveffo@aol.com
Estimated Sales: Less Than $500,000
Number Employees: 5-9

4727 Freshwater Fish Market
1199 Plessis Road
Winnipeg, MB R2C 3L4
Canada
780-413-5370
Fax: 780-495-5384 800-345-3113
edmonton@freshwaterfish.com
www.freshwaterfish.com
Freshwater fish, whitefish and northern pike
President: Tom Dunn
Sales Manager: Doug Clayton
Human Resources: Wendy Matheson
Plant Manager: Dragon Vuksa
Type of Packaging: Consumer, Food Service

4728 Frey Vineyards
14000 Tomki Rd
Redwood Valley, CA 95470-6135
707-485-5177
Fax: 707-485-7875 800-760-3739
info@freywine.com www.freywine.com
Producer of organic wine with no sulfites added. They specialize in Organic Wine, Biodynamic Wine, No Sulfites Added Wine, and GMO Free Wine.
President: Paul Frey
CEO: Katrina Frey
cathie@freywine.com
Vice President, Sales: Jon Frey
Estimated Sales: $5-10,000,000
Number Employees: 10-19
Type of Packaging: Consumer

4729 Freybe Gourmet Foods Ltd
9525-201 St
Suite 203
Langley, BC V1M 4A5
Canada
604-607-7426
Fax: 604-607-7461 800-879-3739
to_freybe@freybe.com www.freybe.com
Manufacturers of sausages including bacon, deli meats, liver sausage & pate, all natural, dry cured, salami, smokies, weiners, and snack foods.
President & CEO: Sven Freybe
Director, Office Services: Karen Hunt
VP, Operations: Angela Doro
Year Founded: 1844
Estimated Sales: $57.52 Million
Number Employees: 350
Square Footage: 110255
Type of Packaging: Consumer, Food Service, Bulk

4730 Frick Winery
23072 Walling Rd
Geyserville, CA 95441-9548
707-857-1980
Fax: 707-857-1980 Frick@frickwinery.com
www.frickwinestore.com
Winery; Alcoholic beverages
Owner: Bill Frick
b.frick@frickwinery.com
Estimated Sales: Less Than $500,000
Number Employees: 1-4

4731 Frick's Quality Meats
360 M E Frick Dr
Washington, MO 63090-1050
636-239-2200
Fax: 636-239-7003 800-241-2209
www.frickmeats.com
Cured and smoked meats including sausage and ham
President: David Frick
Owner: Cindy Frick
cfrick@frickmeats.com
Marketing: Tom Schmiederer
Sales Director: David King
Operations Executive: Rob Rousch
Estimated Sales: $10-20 Million
Number Employees: 100-249

4732 Fried Provisions Company
141 N Washington St Apartment 1
Evans City, PA 16033-2001
724-538-3160
Fax: 724-538-3262
Cheese, luncheon meats, chopped ham, poultry and sausage
President: James Deily
Sales Manager: Tim Deily
Estimated Sales: $1.40 Million
Number Employees: 5
Parent Co: Fort Pitt Brand Meats
Type of Packaging: Consumer, Food Service, Private Label, Bulk
Brands:
  Fort Pitt
  Harmony

4733 Frieda's Inc
4465 Corporate Center Dr
Los Alamitos, CA 90720-2561
714-826-6100
Fax: 714-816-0277 mail@friedas.com
Exotic fruits and vegetables
President: Ann Hawkins
Chief Executive Officer: Karen Caplan
karenc@friedas.com
Vice President: Jackie Caplan
Regional Sales Manager: Dina Boyce
Chief Operating Officer: Jackie Wiggins
Purchasing Manager: Gloria Cardenas
Estimated Sales: $30,000,000
Number Employees: 100-249

4734 Friendship Dairies LLC
6701 County Rd 20
Friendship, NY 14739
585-973-3031
800-854-3243
www.friendshipdairies.com
Dairy products including cottage cheese and whey and whey powders including acid and neutralized; also, calcium lactate powder and sodium lactate
Director of Quality Control: Karen Martin
Director of Marketing: Paige Pistone
Vice President of Sales: Paul Dussault
Year Founded: 1917
Estimated Sales: $60 Million
Number Employees: 100-249
Square Footage: 15000
Parent Co: Saputo Dairy Foods USA, LLC
Type of Packaging: Consumer, Food Service

Food Manufacturers / A-Z

4735 Friendship International
21 Merrill Drive
Rockland, ME 04841-2142
207-594-1111
Fax: 207-236-6103
Manufacturer and exporter of live sea urchins
President: Jim Wadsworth
Contact: Rino Safrizal
safrizal@friends-international.org

4736 FrieslandCampina Ingredients North America, Inc.
61 S Paramus Rd
Suite 535
Paramus, NJ 07652
551-497-7300
www.frieslandcampina.com
Food additives including hydrolized proteins, bioactive peptides and protein fractions.
CEO: Rudy Dieperink
Inside Sales & Marketing: Rae Anne Popjes
Estimated Sales: $17.5 Million
Number Employees: 74
Number of Brands: 11
Parent Co: Royal FrieslandCampina
Other Locations:
   DFE Pharma
   Paramus NJ
   FrieslandCampina Creamy Creation US
   Paramus NJ
   FrieslandCampina Ingredients Plant
   Delhi NY
Brands:
   Aerion
   Esprion
   Glutamine
   Lactoperoxidase
   Lactoval
   Peptide Fm
   Pharmatose
   Primellose
   Primojel
   Respitose
   Textrion

4737 Frio Foods
8600 Wurzbach Road
Suite 500
San Antonio, TX 78240-4331
210-278-4525
Fax: 210-278-1094
Processes frozen foods
President: Ron Trine
Brands:
   Frio

4738 Frisco Baking Co Inc
621 W Avenue 26
Los Angeles, CA 90065-1095
323-225-6111
Fax: 323-225-3554
Sourdough products including par-baked dinner rolls and loaves, full baked rounds and baguettes, double baked loaf, french bread dinner rolls, loaves, party sandwiches, Italian twists and a variety of sandwich rolls from 4-12inches.
Owner: Damon Perata
Owner: Ronald Perata
Sales Manager: Rick Vanzutphen
Estimated Sales: $16.3 Million
Number Employees: 20-49

4739 Frisinger Cellars
2275 Dry Creek Rd
Napa, CA 94558
707-255-3749
Fax: 707-963-7867
Wines
President: Raymond Reyes
Contact: Jim Frisinger
jfrisinger@frisinger.net
Estimated Sales: Under $500,000
Number Employees: 1-4
Parent Co: Consolation Brand

4740 Frisson Normand
2200 Fletcher Avenue
3rd Floor
Fort Lee, NJ 07024
201-585-2179
Fax: 201-585-8575
Fruits
Marketing: Nicolas Lecuqu

4741 Frito-Lay Inc.
7701 Legacy Dr.
Plano, TX 75024-4099
800-352-4477
www.fritolay.com
Corn chips, potato chips, and other snack foods.
CEO, PepsiCo Foods North America: Steven Williams
Senior VP/CFO: Jamie Caulfield
Senior VP/General Counsel: Leanne Oliver
Senior VP/Foods & Global R&D: Denise Lefebvre
Senior VP/Chief Marketing Officer: Rachel Ferdinando
Senior VP, Sales: John Dean
Senior VP/Chief Customer Officer: Mike Del Pozzo
Estimated Sales: $15.79 Billion
Number Employees: 10000+
Number of Brands: 28
Parent Co: PepsiCo
Type of Packaging: Consumer, Food Service
Brands:
   Lay's
   Doritos
   Cheetos
   Tostitos
   Ruffles
   Fritos
   Sun Chips
   Stacy's
   Smartfood
   Rold Gold
   Top N Go
   Simply
   Frito-Lay2GO
   Cracker Jack
   Baken-ets
   Chester's
   Funyun's
   Grandma's
   Matador
   Miss Vickie's
   Munchies
   Munchos
   Sabritones
   Santitas
   Maui Style
   El Isleno

4742 Froehlich Alex Packing Co
77 D Street Ext
Johnstown, PA 15906-2908
814-535-7694
Fax: 814-535-7695
Livestock processor
President: David Froehlich
Estimated Sales: $5-10 Million
Number Employees: 10-19
Type of Packaging: Bulk
Other Locations:
   Alex Froelich Packing Company
   Johnstown PA

4743 Frog City Cheese
PO Box 94
106 Messer Hill Road
Plymouth Notch, VT 5056
802-672-3650
Fax: 802-672-1629
Granular curd (whole milk) cheese
Co-Owner: Jackie McCuin
Co-Owner: Tom Gilbert
Estimated Sales: $3-5 Million
Number Employees: 10-19
Type of Packaging: Consumer

4744 Frog Ranch Foods
5 S High St
Glouster, OH 45732-1051
740-767-3705
Fax: 740-767-3944 800-742-2488
info@froganch.com www.froganch.com
Traditional style salsas, pickles, peppers, tortilla chips
Owner: Craig Cornett
craig@frogranch.com
Estimated Sales: $2.5-5,000,000
Number Employees: 10-19
Type of Packaging: Private Label

4745 Frog's Leap Winery
8815 Conn Creek Rd
Rutherford, CA 94573
707-963-4704
Fax: 707-963-0242 800-959-4704
ribbit@frogsleap.com www.frogsleap.com
Producer of wines such as Cabernet Sauvignon, Sauvignon Blanc, Chardonnay, Zinfandel, Merlot, Petite Sirah, Heritage Blend and Pink.
Owner & Winemaker: John Williams
Chief Financial Officer: Doug Demerritt
Social Media & Marketing Manager: Natalie Barnard
Sales Manager: Michelle Watkins
Hospitality Director: Jami Castro
Vice President, Vineyard Operations: Frank Leeds
General Manager: Jonah Beer
Estimated Sales: $5-10,000,000
Number Employees: 20-49
Brands:
   Cabernet Sauvignon
   Chardonnay
   Merlot
   Sauvignon Blanc
   Zinfandel

4746 From Oregon
2787 Olympic Street
Suite 4
Springfield, OR 97477-7809
541-747-4222
Fax: 541-747-5456
Jams, marmalades and berries
President: Bonnie Koenig
Estimated Sales: $1-4,9,000,000
Number Employees: 1-4

4747 From the Ground Up
Fairfield, NJ 07004
www.fromthegroundupsnacks.com
Cauliflower-based pretzels and crackers

4748 Froma-Dar
378 rue Principale
St. Boniface, QC G0X 2L0
Canada
819-535-3946
Fax: 819-535-7010
Dairy products including cheddar, curd and partly skim cheeses
President: Michel Veillette
Number Employees: 50-99
Square Footage: 40000
Type of Packaging: Consumer, Food Service, Private Label, Bulk
Brands:
   Des Coteaux
   Froma-Dar
   Juneau

4749 (HQ)Front Range Snacks Inc
6547 S Racine Cir # 1800
Centennial, CO 80111-6463
303-744-8850
Fax: 303-389-6859
Processor and exporter of ready-to-eat popcorn
Owner: Tim Bradley
tim@openroadsnacks.com
Estimated Sales: Less Than $500,000
Number Employees: 1-4
Number of Brands: 1
Number of Products: 10
Square Footage: 80000
Type of Packaging: Consumer, Food Service, Private Label, Bulk
Brands:
   Rocky Mountain Popcorn

4750 Frontenac Point Vineyard
9501 State Route 89
Trumansburg, NY 14886-9211
607-387-9619
contactus@frontenacpoint.com
www.frontenacpoint.com
wines. Varieties include Pinot Noir, Chambourcin, Frontenac Red, Chardonnay, Riesling and more.
Co-Owner: Jim Doolittle
Co-Owner: Carol Doolittle
Assistant Manager: Lawrence Doolittle
Estimated Sales: Under $500,000
Number Employees: 1-4
Type of Packaging: Consumer, Food Service, Private Label, Bulk

Food Manufacturers / A-Z

4751 Frontera Foods
449 N Clark St
Chicago, IL 60654
312-595-1624
Fax: 312-595-1625 800-509-4441
info@fronterafoods.com
Producer of Mexican food. Products include tortilla chips, sauces, spices and salsas.
Owner: Manny Valdes
Founder, Owner & Chef: Rick Bayless
Director of Sales: Joseph Valdes
Culinary Director: Jean Marie Brownson
Estimated Sales: $5-10,000,000
Number Employees: 11-50
Type of Packaging: Food Service
Brands:
   Frontera Foods
   Salpica

4752 Frontier Co-op
P.O. Box 299
3021 78th St.
Norway, IA 52318-9520
319-227-7996
Fax: 800-717-4372 844-550-6200
customercare@frontiercoop.com
www.frontiercoop.com
Sustainably sourced and organic herbs, spices, seasonings, teas, sauces, mixes, dips, dressings, dried fruits and vegetables, indgredients, flavors and extracts.
CEO: Tony Bedard
VP Finance: Nicole Erickson
VP Technical Services: Ravin Donald
VP Marketing: Dave Karpick
SVP Business Development: Clint Landis
VP Human Resources: Megan Schulte
EVP Operations: Cole Daily
Year Founded: 1976
Estimated Sales: $100-499.9 Million
Number Employees: 100-249
Type of Packaging: Consumer, Private Label
Brands:
   Frontier
   Aura Cacia
   Simply Organic

4753 Frontier Soups
895 Northpoint Blvd
Waukegan, IL 60085
847-688-1200
Fax: 847-688-1206 800-300-7867
info@frontiersoups.com www.frontiersoups.com
Dried soup and pasta salad mixes
President: Trisha Anderson
Contact: Jane Murphy
jane@frontiersoups.com
Production: Eva Pantoja
Estimated Sales: $2.5-5 Million
Number Employees: 10-19
Square Footage: 16000
Type of Packaging: Consumer
Brands:
   Frontier
   Hearty Originals
   Homemade In Minutes
   I'Ll Bring the Saladd
   Illinois Prairie
   Minnesota Heartland
   New Line Homemade
   Wisconsin Lakeshore

4754 Froozer
1127 Auraria Pkwy
Suite 17
Denver, CO 80204-1896
720-446-0145
hello@froozer.com
www.froozer.com
Frozen whole food fruit snacks
President/Owner: Rich Naha
CEO: Des Hague
Number of Brands: 1
Number of Products: 6
Type of Packaging: Consumer
Brands:
   FROOZER

4755 Frostproof Sunkist Groves
7307 US Highway
27thNorth
Frostproof, FL 33843
863-635-4873
Fax: 863-635-3447 www.frostproofgroves.com
Citrus fruits and juices
Owner: John Stephens
Estimated Sales: $1-3,000,000
Number Employees: 1-4

4756 Frozen Specialties Inc
8600 S Wilkinson Way
Suite G
Perrysburg, OH 43551
419-867-2005
www.frozenspecialties.com
Private label pizza and pizza bites, a multi-line supplier
President & CEO: Rich Alvarez
rich.alvarez@frc.com
Controller: Paul Nungester
Director of Marketing: Lori Hamilton
Vice President, Sales: Dan Burdick
Year Founded: 1969
Estimated Sales: $49.99 Million
Number Employees: 10-19
Number of Brands: 1
Number of Products: 6
Square Footage: 13395
Type of Packaging: Consumer, Private Label, Bulk
Brands:
   Mr. P'S

4757 Frozfruit Corporation
14805 S San Pedro Street
Gardena, CA 90248-2030
310-217-1034
Fax: 310-715-6943
Manufacturer and exporter of frozen ice cream novelties and fruit bars
President: Tom Guinan
Estimated Sales: $500,000-$1 Million
Number Employees: 5-9
Square Footage: 150000
Type of Packaging: Consumer, Food Service, Private Label, Bulk
Brands:
   Frozfruit
   Frozfruit All Natural Fruit Bars
   Summer Naturals

4758 Fru-V
Stouffville, ON
Canada
info@fruvsmoothie.com
www.fruvsmoothie.com
Frozen smoothie blends
Year Founded: 2016
Parent Co: Health Addict Inc

4759 Fruigees
Los Angeles, CA 91423
fruigees.com
Organic fruit snack
CEO: David Czinn
COO: Josh Kahn
Number of Brands: 1
Number of Products: 3
Type of Packaging: Consumer
Brands:
   FRUIGEES

4760 Fruit Acres Farm Marketand U-Pick
3390 Friday Rd
Coloma, MI 49038
269-208-3591
fruitacres@iserv.net
www.fruitacresfarms.com
230 acre fruit farm growing sweet cherries, apples, sweet corn and peaches. Also sells gourmet jams, jellies, honey, sauces, pickles and country gifts.
Co-Owner: Annette Bjorge
Co-Owner: Randy Bjorge
Estimated Sales: $5-10 Million
Number Employees: 10-19

4761 Fruit Belt Canning Inc
54168 60th Ave
P.O. Box 81
Lawrence, MI 49064-9525
269-674-3939
Fax: 269-674-8354 office@fruitbeltfoods.com
www.fruitbeltfoods.com
Manufacturer, wholesaler/distributor of fruits and vegetables such as; asparagus, red tart cherries and strawberries
President: David Frank
davf@fruitbeltfoods.com
Vice President: Warren Frank
Sales Manager: Jim Armstrong
Estimated Sales: $5-9.9 Million
Number Employees: 100-249
Type of Packaging: Food Service, Private Label, Bulk
Brands:
   Fruit Belt
   Solar

4762 Fruit Bliss
1007 Sheffield Ave
Brooklyn, NY 11207
Fax: 718-398-2005 info@fruitbliss.com
Dried fruit infused with water
President/Owner: Susan Leone
Number of Brands: 1
Number of Products: 10
Type of Packaging: Consumer
Brands:
   FRUIT BLISS

4763 Fruit Fillings Inc
2531 E Edgar Ave
Fresno, CA 93706-5410
559-237-4715
Fax: 559-237-0728 800-995-4514
www.fruitfillings.com
Pie and pastry filling, fruit glazes, pectin based jams, fresh California fruit
President: Stephen Norcross
Contact: Bill Barr
bbill@fruitfillings.com
Estimated Sales: $2.5-5 000,000
Number Employees: 20-49

4764 Fruit Growers Supply Company
27770 N Entertainment Drive
Valencia, CA 91355
888-997-4855
news@fruitgrowers.com www.fruitgrowers.com
Cooperative group for agricultural supplies. They manufacture pallets, irrigation systems, and boxes, and they sell other agricultural supplies such as outer wear and pesticides.
President: Bill Dodd
Estimated Sales: $3-5 Million
Number Employees: 1-4
Square Footage: 4800
Type of Packaging: Consumer, Private Label, Bulk

4765 Fruit Ranch Inc
6301 W Bluemound Rd
Milwaukee, WI 53213-4146
414-476-9600
Fax: 414-258-9377 800-433-3289
info@fruitranch.com
Fruit gift baskets. Wholesaler of baskets and supplies
Owner/President: Tanya Gearheart
Estimated Sales: Less Than $500,000
Number Employees: 5-9
Square Footage: 20000
Type of Packaging: Consumer, Private Label, Bulk

4766 Fruit d'Or
306 Route 265
Villeroy, QC G0S 3K0
Canada
819-385-1126
Fax: 819-715-0059 info@fruit-dor.ca
www.fruit-dor.ca
Organic cranberries and blueberries in dried, pureed, concentrated, frozen, and powedered forms; neutraceuticals
Founder/President/CEO: Martin Le Moine
Year Founded: 1999
Estimated Sales: $20-50 Million
Number Employees: 50-99

4767 Fruit of the Boot
5728 NW 27th Pl
Gainesvillve, FL 32606
352-376-3643
Fax: 352-335-9172
Cakes and pastries; cookies; confections; dry pasta; olive oil; balsamic vinegar
Owner/President: Andrea Tosolini
Year Founded: 1999
Estimated Sales: Less than $500,000
Number Employees: 1-4
Type of Packaging: Private Label

Food Manufacturers / A-Z

4768 Fruit of the Land Products
1 Promenade Circle
PO Box 977
Thornhill, ON L4J 8G7
Canada
905-761-9611
Fax: 905-761-9617 877-311-5267
info@fruitoftheland.com www.fruitoftheland.com
Kosher olive oil, honey, jams, jellies, preserves, foodservice, private label.
Marketing: Michael Kurtz

4769 Fruitcrown Products Corp
250 Adams Blvd
Farmingdale, NY 11735-6615
631-694-5800
Fax: 631-694-6467 800-441-3210
info@fruitcrown.com www.fruitcrown.com
Aseptic fruit flavors and bases for beverage, dairy and baking industries
President: Robert Jagenburg
orjagenburg@fruitcrown.com
Number Employees: 50-99
Type of Packaging: Bulk
Brands:
  Asp
  Exquizita
  Fruitcrown
  Huntingcastle

4770 Fruithill Inc
6501 NE Highway 240
Yamhill, OR 97148-8507
503-662-3926
Fax: 503-662-4270 www.fruithillinc.com
Frozen cherries, plums and fruit purees
President: April Ateka
aprila@fruithillinc.com
EVP/Sales: Lee Schrepel
Office Manager: Zach Kanen
Estimated Sales: $10-20,000,000
Number Employees: 50-99
Type of Packaging: Food Service, Private Label

4771 Fruition Northwest LLC
29345 NW W Union Rd
PO Box 130
North Plains, OR 97133
503-880-5193
High-quality infused-dehydrated berry fruits to the wholesale market.
Owner: Alan Krassowski
Estimated Sales: $210 Thousand
Type of Packaging: Bulk

4772 (HQ)FrutStix
1525 State St
Suite 203
Santa Barbara, CA 93101
805-965-1656
Fax: 805-963-8288 info@frutstix.com
www.frutstix.com
Fresh frozen fruit bars, fudge bars
President: William McKinley
Director of Sales/Marketing: Ed Jones
Contact: Lynne Burton
lburton@frutstix.com
Director of Operations: Agustin Munoz
Plant Engineer: Daniel Gavela
Estimated Sales: $5-10 Million
Number Employees: 5-9
Type of Packaging: Food Service, Private Label
Other Locations:
  FrutStix-Manufacturing Plant
  San Diego CA

4773 Frutarom Meer Corporation
Manofim St. Herzeliya
P.O. Box 3088
Hertzeliya Pituach, 46104
Israel
www.iff.com/en/taste/frutarom
Botanicals, extracts, gums, stabilizers, oleoresins, natural colors, enzymes and hydrocolloids
President: Amos Anatot
Year Founded: 1933
Estimated Sales: $20-50 Million
Number Employees: 5600
Number of Products: 70K
Square Footage: 100000
Parent Co: International Flavors-Fragrances
Type of Packaging: Bulk
Brands:
  Merecol
  Meretec
  Merezan
  Stamere

4774 Frutech International Corp
180 S Lake Ave # 335
Suite 335
Pasadena, CA 91101-4735
626-844-0200
Fax: 626-844-0202 info.mx@frutech.com
www.frutech.com
Citrus oil production
Owner: Scott Alexander
scott.a@frutech.com
Treasurer: Gene Adams
VP Finance: Pat Breyer
Estimated Sales: $500,000
Number Employees: 1-4
Parent Co: Frutech International Corporation

4775 Fruvemex
233 Paulin Ave
Calexico, CA 92231
760-203-1896
Fax: 760-203-2389 fcaballero@fruvemex.com
www.fruvemex.com
Refrigerated and frozen fruit and vegetable products
President: Gustavo Caballero
VP Sales/Marketing: Yvonne Brewer
Year Founded: 1986
Number Employees: 85
Square Footage: 180000
Type of Packaging: Bulk

4776 Fry Foods Inc
P.O. Box 837
Tiffin, OH 44883
800-626-2294
orders@fryfoods.com www.fryfoods.com
Frozen, battered and breaded appetizers such as onion rings, cheese sticks, mushrooms, jalapeno poppers, zucchini sticks and breaded cauliflower
President: Norman Fry
Vice President: David Fry
Year Founded: 1961
Estimated Sales: $20-50 Million
Number Employees: 50-99
Number of Brands: 1
Square Footage: 45000
Type of Packaging: Consumer, Food Service
Brands:
  Fry Foods

4777 Fry Krisp Food Products
3360 Spring Arbor Rd
Jackson, MI 49203-3636
517-784-8531
Fax: 517-784-6585 877-854-5440
www.frykrisp.com
Batter mixes for poultry and seafood, funnel cake, corn dogs and onion ring for fairs, and breakfst items such as pancakes, cornbread, biscuit mix and distributor of yellow corn grits.
President: Richard Neuenfeldt
Estimated Sales: $2.5-5 Million
Number Employees: 5-9
Number of Brands: 2
Number of Products: 15
Square Footage: 24000
Type of Packaging: Consumer, Food Service, Private Label, Bulk
Brands:
  Fry Krisp
  Fry Krisp Batter Mixes
  Oven Krisp Coating Mixes

4778 Fuchs North America
3800 Hampstead Mexico Rd
Hampstead, MD 21074
410-363-1700
Fax: 410-363-6619 800-365-3229
Flavors and seasonings
CEO: Daniel Cooper
CFO: Christopher Rodski
Director of Research and Development: Helga Nelson
Director of Marketing: Shannon Cushen
Director of Operations: Derrick Epley
Type of Packaging: Consumer

4779 Fudge Farms
204 N Red Bud Trl
Buchanan, MI 49107-1366
269-695-2008
800-874-0261
Confectionery products including hard and soft, sugar-free, salt-free, caramels, nougats, taffy, fruit chews, coffee, boxed chocolates, candy bars, and sugar-free lollipops
President: Kenneth Harrington
Estimated Sales: $2-2.5 Million
Number Employees: 20-49
Square Footage: 43000
Brands:
  Golden Farm Candies

4780 Fudge Fatale
11950 Ventura Blvd.
Suite 3
Studio City, CA 91604
310-287-0600
Fax: 949-240-3086 800-809-8298
Fudge
President: Alexander Black
Sales: Rich Pariseau
Estimated Sales: $3-5 Million
Number Employees: 5-9

4781 Fuji Foods Corp
6206 Corporate Park Dr
Browns Summit, NC 27214
336-375-3111
Fax: 336-375-3663 information@fujifoodsusa.com
www.fujifoodsusa.com
Chicken, pork and beef broths including concentrated pastes and powders; also, savory flavors, soup bases; and spray dried flavor powders; spray drying services available.
VP Operations & Chief Operating Officer: Michael Russell
Plant Manager: Terry Lawson
Estimated Sales: $20-50 Million
Number Employees: 20-49
Square Footage: 20000
Parent Co: Fuji Foods Corporation
Type of Packaging: Food Service, Bulk

4782 Fuji Health Science/Inc
3 Terri Ln # 12
Unit 12
Burlington, NJ 08016-4903
609-386-3030
Fax: 609-386-3033 contact@fujihealthscience.com
www.fujichemicalusa.com
Markets and manufacturers natural specialty food ingredient, AstaReal astaxanthin, a powerful anti-oxidant
National Sales Manager: Joe Kuncewitch
kuncewitch@fujihealthscience.com
Estimated Sales: Under $500,000
Number Employees: 10-19

4783 Fuji Vegetable Oil Inc
1 Barker Ave # 290
White Plains, NY 10601-1535
914-761-7900
Fax: 914-761-7919 www.fujioilusa.com
Vegetable and other oil
Manager: Andre Cormeau
jcalton@fvo-usa.com
Quality Control: Thomas McBrayer
Sales Exec: Gita Calton
Estimated Sales: $2.5-5 000,000
Number Employees: 5-9

4784 Ful-Flav-R Foods
P.O.Box 82
Alamo, CA 94507
925-838-0300
Fax: 925-838-0310 www.fulflavr.com
Premium Ground Garlic, Minced Garlic (in oil & water), Ground and Minced Ginger, Ground Roasted Garlic, Ground Onion, diced Sweet Bell Peppers, Ground and Diced Jalepeno's, Fire Roasted Anaheim chili's, Ground Chili-Garlic Blends andother unique custom formulated blends. All of our products are pasteurized and pH controlled.
President: Joseph Farrell
Chief Operations Officer: Glen Farrell
Director Sales/Marketing: Steve Linzmeyer
Plant Manager: John Small
Estimated Sales: $1-2.5 Million
Number Employees: 5-9
Type of Packaging: Food Service, Bulk

Brands:
  Ful-Flav-R

4785 Fulcher's Point Pride Seafood
101 South Ave
Oriental, NC 28571-9682
252-249-0123
Fax: 252-249-2337 www.toojays.com
Seafood
Owner: Chris Fulchers
chris.fulcher@toojays.com
Owner: Garland Fulcher
Vice President: Deborah Fulcher
Purchasing: Ralph Bard
Estimated Sales: $4 Million
Number Employees: 50-99
Type of Packaging: Consumer, Food Service, Bulk

4786 Full Sail Brewing Co
506 Columbia St
Hood River, OR 97031-2000
541-386-2247
Fax: 541-386-7316 888-244-2337
www.fullsailbrewing.com
Beers, core brews, seasonal, brews, and special releases.
CEO: Irene Firmat
irenef@fullsailbrewing.com
CFO: Mark Moreland
Executive Brewmaster: Jamie Emmerson
Estimated Sales: $20-50 Million
Number Employees: 20-49
Number of Brands: 2
Brands:
  Full Sail
  Session

4787 Fullbloom Baking Co
6500 Overlake Pl
Newark, CA 94560-1083
510-494-1700
Fax: 510-803-4517 800-201-9909
www.aryzta.com
Fresh, fully-baked and packaged items- your brand or ours. With the latest in mixing, baking and freezing techniques, our goal is to create whatever you need. We manufacture multiple variations of muffins, scones, laminates, bars andbrownies, loaf breads, cookies, and granolas.
CEO and Founder: Karen Trilevsky
CFO: Audrey Heng
Research & Development Manager: Peter Conn
Quality Assurance Manager: Rowena Aquilizan
Sales Director: Laure Chatard
Industrial Engineer: Jagadeesh Dixit
Engineering & Maintenance Manager: Leo Carpio
Number Employees: 100-249
Square Footage: 95000
Type of Packaging: Consumer, Private Label

4788 Fuller Foods
5040 SE Milwaukie Ave
Portland, OR 97202
503-308-3814
fullerfoods.com
Cheesy puffs
President: Jack Kuo
Year Founded: 2012
Estimated Sales: $200,000
Number Employees: 5
Type of Packaging: Private Label

4789 Fulton Fish Market
New York, NY
718-842-8908
customerservice@fultonfishmarket.com
fultonfishmarket.com
Fish, shellfish, and other seafood including caviar, eel, octopus, sea urchin, and squid.
CEO: Mike Spindler
Year Founded: 1822
Type of Packaging: Consumer

4790 Fulton Provision Co
16123 NE Airport Way
Portland, OR 97230-4953
503-254-3000
Fax: 503-254-6328 800-333-6428
Processor of steaks and meats including beef, pork, veal, lamb and poultry.
President: Charlie Benton
SVP Sales: Tom Semke
VP Operations: Mark Vaughan
Business Development Manager: Chad Warneke

Estimated Sales: $20-50 Million
Number Employees: 50-99
Parent Co: Sysco
Type of Packaging: Food Service, Bulk

4791 Fumoir Grizzly
159 Amsterdam
St Augustin, QC G3A 2V5
Canada
418-878-8941
Fax: 418-878-8942 info@grizzly.qc.ca
www.grizzly.qc.ca
Manufacturer and exporter of smoked salmon, trout, halibut
President: Pierre Fontaine
CEO: Laura Boivin
Controller: Sebastian Legault
Director Quality Management: Michele Tessier
Marketing, R&D: Marie-Pier Grondin
Sales Representative-Quebec: Normand Richard
Director Human Resources: Connie Biladeau
Production Manager: Sergiu Parsikov
Estimated Sales: $6,3,000,000
Number Employees: 37
Type of Packaging: Consumer, Food Service, Private Label, Bulk

4792 Fun City Popcorn
3211 Sunrise Ave
Las Vegas, NV 89101
702-367-2676
Fax: 702-876-1099 800-423-1710
www.funcitypopcorn.com
Caramel, cheese and butter popcorn; manufacturer of popcorn processing machinery
President/CEO: Richard Falk
CFO: Maryann Talavera
Estimated Sales: $1-3 Million
Number Employees: 5-9
Square Footage: 40000
Type of Packaging: Consumer, Food Service, Private Label, Bulk

4793 Fun Factory
6223 W Forest Home Ave
Milwaukee, WI 53220
414-543-5887
Fax: 414-543-7850 877-894-6767
Gum, candy
President: Mike Dunlap
mike@funfactoryinc.com
Brands:
  Face Twisters Sour Bubble Gum

4794 Fun Foods
99 Murray Hill Pkwy
Suite D
East Rutherford, NJ 07073-2143
201-896-4949
Fax: 201-896-4911 800-507-2782
funfoodspasta@yahoo.com
Bi- and tri-colored holiday shaped gourmet pasta including Christmas trees, hearts, bunnies, stars and stripes, Jack O'Lanterns, star of David, angels, etc
Manager: Sharon Nicklas
Estimated Sales: $5-10 Million
Number Employees: 5-9
Square Footage: 8000
Type of Packaging: Consumer, Food Service, Private Label, Bulk
Brands:
  All-American Sports Pasta
  Bunny Pasta
  Funfoods Holiday Pasta
  Funfoods Premium
  Harvest Pasta
  Holiday Pasta
  I Love Pasta
  Lucky Pasta
  Pasta Della Festa
  Patriotic Pasta
  Star of David Pasta

4795 Functional Foods
15765 Sturgeon St
Roseville, MI 48066
586-445-0550
Fax: 586-445-1118 877-372-0550
Chocolate
President/CEO: Thomas Morley, Jr
Brands:
  Smartchocolates

4796 Functional Foods
470 US Highway 9
Englishtown, NJ 07726-8239
732-972-2232
Fax: 732-536-9179 800-442-9524
Microcrystalline and hydroxypropyl cellulose, cellulose and psyllium fiber, gum arabic and guar, cellulose and vegetable gums
Marketing Manager: Alpa Nanavati
Manufacturing Manager: Yogi Shah
Estimated Sales: $2.5-5 Million
Number Employees: 20-49

4797 Functional Products LLC
1179 Atlantic Blvd
Atlantic Beach, FL 32233
904-249-8074
Fax: 514-853-6851 info@mueggenburg.com
www.paulmueggenburg.de
Vitamins and food supplements.
Owner: Dirk Mueggenburg
dm4@muepr.com
International Trade: Miguel Chacon
Estimated Sales: $199 Thousand
Number Employees: 2
Parent Co: Muggenburg Pflanzliche Rohstoffe GmbH & Co.
Type of Packaging: Consumer, Bulk

4798 Fungi Perfecti
PO Box 7634
Olympia, WA 98507-7634
360-427-5861
Fax: 360-426-9377 800-780-9126
info@fungi.com
Gourmet and medicinal mushrooms.
Owner: Paul Stamets
stamets1@aol.com
Estimated Sales: $3-5 Million
Number Employees: 20-49

4799 Fungus Among Us
2210 Lake Ave
Po Box 352
Snohomish, WA 98290-1028
360-568-3403
Fax: 360-563-2663 www.fungusamongus.com
Gourmet organic mushrooms
Owner: Lynn Monroe
shrooms@fungusamongus.com
Founder: Lynn Lynn
Estimated Sales: Less Than $500,000
Number Employees: 1-4

4800 Funkychunky Inc.
7452 W 78th St
Edina, MN 55439
952-938-6663
Fax: 952-938-2294 888-473-8659
tore@funkychunkyinc.com
www.funkychunky.com
Chocolate covered pretzels, chocolate popcorn, caramel corn and bars
Marketing: Tore Villberg
Contact: Funkychunky Gracous
funkychunkyincg@funkychunkyinc.com

4801 Funnibonz LLC
3 Lake View Ct
Princeton Jct, NJ 08550-4915
609-915-3685
Fax: 609-845-1806 877-300-2669
info@funnibonz.com www.funnibonz.com
BBQ sauces, rubs and marinades
CEO: Jim Barbour
Co-CEO: Ryan Marrone
Manager: James Barbour
Estimated Sales: Less Than $500,000
Number Employees: 5-9

4802 Furmano's Foods
PO Box 500
Northumberland, PA 17857
570-473-3516
Fax: 570-473-7367 800-952-1111
www.furmanos.com

Food Manufacturers / A-Z

Furmano's heritage of excellence is evident in our stewardship of the land as well as the products we produce. Still guided by the original values that made the Furmano's name synonymous with the quality, the care and dedication withwhich our products are sourced and processed grows with each generation. Furmano's produces healthy, great tasting canned and pouch tomato and bean products for both the retail grocery and foodservice segments of the food industry.
President/CEO: Chad Geise
CEO/Chairman: David Geise
CFO: Ted Hancock
Quality Control: Craig Adams
VP Sales/Marketing: Bob Vanderhook
Contact: Kip Anspach
kip.anspach@furmanos.com
Operations Dir.: Daniel Severn
Purchasing Dir.: David Furman
Year Founded: 1923
Number Employees: 250
Square Footage: 1200000
Type of Packaging: Consumer

4803 Furukawa Potato Chip Factory
P.O.Box 1129
Captain Cook, HI 96704-1129
808-323-3785
Fax: 808- 32-3 37
Potato chips and snack foods
Owner: Jerome Furukawa
Estimated Sales: $1-3,000,000
Number Employees: 1-4

4804 Fusion Gourmet
14824 S Main St
Gardena, CA 90248
310-532-8938
Fax: 310-532-8991 www.fusiongourmet.com
Specializes in authentically prepared, fines quality and all-natural cooking sauces, marinades, and dips from Southeast Asia
President: Annie Chu
Chief Executive Officer: Stephen Liaw
Vice-President: Alexander Shkolnik
Sales: Sandra Liaw
Estimated Sales: $3-5 Million
Number Employees: 1-4
Brands:
  Abc
  Bali's Best
  Fatal Attraction
  Pearl Empress
  Sweet Seduction

4805 Fusion Jerky
405 S Airport Blvd
South San Francisco, CA 94080-6909
USA
650-589-8899
Fax: 650-589-3157
Meat Jerky
Ceo/Founder: Kai Yen Mai
Sales & Marketing Manager: Shruti Dixit
Contact: Kaiyen Mai
kaiyen@fusionjerky.com

4806 Future Bakery & Cafe
483 Bloor Street West
Toronto, ON M8Z 2E2
Canada
416-231-1491
Fax: 416-231-1879 www.zomato.com
Specialty and artisan breads, European pastries and cheesecakes
President/Owner: Borys Wrzesnewskyj
Estimated Sales: $2.5-5 Million
Number Employees: 50-99
Square Footage: 44000
Type of Packaging: Consumer
Brands:
  Future Bakery

4807 Futurebiotics LLC
70 Commerce Dr
Hauppauge, NY 11788-3936
631-273-6300
Fax: 631-273-1165 800-645-1721
customerservice@futurebiotics.com
Manufacturer and distributor of natural health food supplements and vitamins

Owner: Saisul Kibria
skibria@aol.com
Manager: Ed Keenan
Director Operations: Wendy L Kauffman
Estimated Sales: $10-20 Million
Number Employees: 20-49
Type of Packaging: Consumer, Private Label, Bulk
Brands:
  Vital K

4808 Futureceuticals Inc
2692 N State Route 1 17
Momence, IL 60954-3475
815-507-1400
Fax: 815-472-3529 888-452-6853
Sales@futureceuticals.com
Primary processor of nutraceuticals, functional foods and cosmetic ingredients. Processing capabilities include: fermentation, refining, IQF freezing, freeze drying, drum drying, air drying, spray drying, vacuum evaporationextraction, synthesis, milling, grinding and blending.
President: Edward Van Drunen
Director New Business Development Europe: Zheko Kounev
Vice President Business Development: John Hunter
jhunter@futureceuticals.com
Vice President Research & Development: Zbigniew Pietrzkowski
jhunter@futureceuticals.com
Director Quality Control: Boris Nemzer
jhunter@futureceuticals.com
FutureCeuticals Technical Sales: Kit Kats
Number Employees: 5-9
Square Footage: 6000000

4809 Fuzz East Coast
140 Sylvan Avenue
3rd Floor
Englewood Cliffs, NJ 07632
866-438-3893
Fax: 201-461-1091 info@fuzebev.com
www.drinkfuze.com/
Manufacturers a variety of Fuze Health Infusions drinks including green tea and fruit juice flavored beverages.
Co-Founder: Lance Collins
Co-Founder: Joe Rosamilia
Co-Founder: Bruce Lewin
Co-Founder: Paula Grant
Contact: Ashley Nadeau
anadeau@fuzebev.com
Type of Packaging: Food Service

4810 Fuzziwig's Candy Factory
656 Main Ave
Durango, CO 81301-5438
970-247-2770
www.fuzziwigscandyfactory.com
Candy
President: Gordon Allen
gordona@fuzziwigscandyfactory.com
Estimated Sales: Less Than $500,000
Number Employees: 5-9

4811 Fuzzy's Wholesale Bar-B-Q
408 W End Blvd
Madison, NC 27025
336-548-2283
Fax: 336-548-2272
Frozen pork barbecue, brunswick stew, gourmet chicken pot pies, home replacement meals.
President: Fred Nelson
Estimated Sales: Less than $500,000
Number Employees: 1-4

4812 G & J Land & Marine Food Distr
506 Front St
Morgan City, LA 70380-3708
985-385-2251
Fax: 985-385-3614 800-256-9187
order@gjfood.com www.agbr.com
Full service food distributor dedicated to providing an extensive grocery and janitorial product line to the offshore oil and gas, commercial shipping and restaurant industry.
President/Owner: Mike Lind
mike@gjfood.com
Financial Controller: Christine DeHart
Vice President: Erik Lind
Operations: Adam Mayon
Purchasing: Jarrod Leonard
Estimated Sales: $10-20 Million
Number Employees: 100-249

4813 G A Food Svc Inc
12200 32nd Ct N
St Petersburg, FL 33716-1847
727-573-2211
Fax: 727-572-8209 800-852-2211
www.sunmeadow.com
Manufacturer of frozen and shelf stable meals serving senior and child nutrition programs, emergency response and disaster relief services and the military.
President: Glenn Davenport
CEO: Ken Lobianco
Year Founded: 1973
Number Employees: 100-249
Type of Packaging: Consumer, Food Service, Private Label
Brands:
  SunMeadow™

4814 G Cefalu & Brother Inc
8005 Rappahannock Ave
Jessup, MD 20794-9438
410-799-2910
Fax: 410-755-1446 jessup29@aol.com
www.gcefalu.com
Processor/repacker of tomatoes and all types of produce.
Owner: John Cefalu
gessup29@aol.com
Estimated Sales: $10-20 Million
Number Employees: 20-49
Type of Packaging: Consumer, Food Service, Bulk

4815 G Debbas Chocolatier
5877 E Brown Ave
Fresno, CA 93727-1364
559-294-2071
Fax: 559-348-2289 www.ownbrandchocolate.com
Truffles, wine-filled biscotti and chocolate bars with fruits and nut meat
Owner: Maria Gutierrez
maria@gdebbas.com
Estimated Sales: $10-20,000,000
Number Employees: 20-49
Type of Packaging: Consumer
Brands:
  De Bas Vineyard
  Incognito

4816 G M Allen & Son Inc
267 Front Ridge Rd
Orland, ME 4472
207-469-7060
Fax: 207-469-2308
Processing of frozen wild blueberries.
President/CEO: Wayne Allen
HR Executive: Kermit Allen
info@gmallenwildblueberries.com
VP Operations: Kermit Allen
Estimated Sales: $2,000,000
Number Employees: 20-49

4817 G M P Laboratories Of Amer Inc
2931 E LA Jolla St
Anaheim, CA 92806-1306
714-630-2467
Fax: 714-237-1374 info@gmplabs.com
www.gmplabs.com
Leading contract manufacturer of high quality vitamins and nutritional supplements. Our laboratories can assist you in formulating, manufacturing, packaging your products while always maintaining absolute confidentiality.
President/CEO: Suhail Ishaq
sishaq@gmplabs.com
Estimated Sales: $20-50 Million
Number Employees: 50-99

4818 G Scaccianoce & Co
1165 Burnett Pl
Bronx, NY 10474-5716
718-991-4462
Fax: 718-991-0154
Processor and exporter of confectionery including Jordan almonds, French mints and licorice
President: Donald Beck
gscaccianoceinc@hotmail.com
Estimated Sales: $2.5-5 Million
Number Employees: 5-9
Type of Packaging: Consumer, Food Service, Private Label, Bulk

Food Manufacturers / A-Z

4819 G. Banis Company
2711 Centerville Road
Suite 400
Wilmington, DE 19808
617-516-9092
info@banistradition.com
Olive oil, dried fruit, olives, pickles & pickled vegetables, sun-dried tomatoes, foodservice, private label.
Marketing: George Banis

4820 (HQ)G.E. Barbour
165 Stewart Ave
Sussex, NB E4E 3H1
Canada
506-432-2300
Fax: 506-432-2323 www.barbours.ca
Family-owned business since 1867. Manufacturer of tea, nut butters, spices and extracts.
President: Sylvia MacVey
VP: Blair Hystom
Marketing Manager: Gordonna Hache
Director of Sales: Mike Trecartin
Number Employees: 100-249
Type of Packaging: Consumer, Food Service, Private Label
Other Locations:
 G.E. Barbour
 St. John NB
Brands:
 King Cole Tea
 Serious Kick
 Humble Tea
 Nuts About
 Barbours

4821 G.E.F. Gourmet Foods Inc
35584 County Road 8
Mountain Lake, MN 56159-2106
507-427-2631
Fax: 507-427-2631 800-692-6762
greatsnack@frontiernet.net
Manufactures Glad Corn A-maizing Corn Snacks.
Founder/Co-Owner: Stan Friesen
Founder/Co-Owner: Gladys Friesen
greatsnack@frontiernet.net
Type of Packaging: Food Service

4822 G.H. Cretors
Richfield, OH 44286
www.ghcretors.com
Gourmet popcorn
President: Claire Cretors
Brands:
 Vita

4823 G.S. Dunn Limited
80 Park Street N
Hamilton, ON L8R 2M9
Canada
905-522-0833
Fax: 905-522-4423 info@gsdunn.com
www.gsdunn.com
Dry mustard products
President: Don Henry
Estimated Sales: $4.3 Million
Number Employees: 30

4824 GAF Seelig Inc
5905 52nd Ave
Flushing, NY 11377-7480
718-899-5000
Fax: 718-803-1198
Wholesaler and distributor of juice, milk, cheese, yogurt, sour cream, purees, raviolis and pastas, oils and vinegars, chocolate and many more food service items.
President: Rodney Seelig
rseelig@gafseelig.com
Executive Vice President: Gary Lavery Sr.
Director of Sales: John Arena
Estimated Sales: $5-10 Million
Number Employees: 100-249

4825 GB Ratto International Grocery
821 Washington St
Oakland, CA 94607-4029
510-832-6503
Fax: 510-836-2250 800-325-3483
http://rattos.com/
Olives, oils and spices
Owner: Elena Voiron
elena@rattos.com
General Manager: Susan Nelson

Estimated Sales: $2.5-5,000,000
Number Employees: 10-19

4826 GC Farms
15500 Hill Rd
Morgan Hill, CA 95037
408-778-0562
Fax: 408-779-4034 lori.rollins@gcfarms.com
www.gcfarmsinc.com
Frozen vegetables
CFO: Alice Chiala
COO: Tim Chiala
Estimated Sales: $50-100 Million
Number of Brands: 1
Parent Co: George Chiala Farms, Inc.

4827 GCI Nutrients
1163 Chess Dr # H
Foster City, CA 94404-1119
650-376-3534
Fax: 650-697-6300 866-580-6549
mikec@gcinutrients.com www.gcinutrients.com
Processor, importer and exporter of vitamins and supplements including beta carotene, essential fatty acids, herbal products, botanical extracts, food supplements, bulk ingredients, premium raw materials for nutritional and beverage industries with over 42 years of experience
Owner: Richard Merriam
rickm@gcinutrients.com
General Manager: Mike Cronin
Controller: Fransisca Cronin
R&D: William Forgach
Marketing: Michael Sevohon
Production: Derek Cronin
Plant Manager: Mike Cronin
Purchasing Manager: Catherine Sabbah
Estimated Sales: $10 Million
Number Employees: 10-19
Number of Brands: 10
Number of Products: 300
Square Footage: 20000
Brands:
 Abg
 Cm-22
 Eleutherogen
 Gamma-E
 Ge-Oxy 132
 Lipo-Serine
 Olivir
 Oxi-Gamma
 Oxi-Grape

4828 GEM Berry Products
PO Box 709
Orofino, ID 83544
208-263-7503
Fax: 866-357-3505 888-231-1699
gifrep52@gmail.com www.gemberry.com
Processor and exporter of spreads, jams and syrups including raspberry and huckleberry; berry filled chocolates, berry barbecue sauce and many other berry products.
President: Jack O' Brien
CFO: Betty Menser
Marketing: Harry Menser
Contact: Cathy Miller
cathy.miller@gemberryproducts.com
Production: Elizabeth O Brien
Estimated Sales: $50,000-100,000
Number Employees: 1-4
Square Footage: 5000
Type of Packaging: Food Service, Bulk
Brands:
 Gem Berry
 Litehouse
 Taste the Beauty of North Idaho
 Taste the Beauty of the Rockies

4829 GEM Cultures
PO Box 39426
Lakewood, WA 98496
253-588-2922
gemculture@juno.com
www.gemcultures.com
Manufacturer and exporter of shelf stable starters for cultured vegetarian foods including tempeh, miso, shoyu, natto, sourdough, nonyogurt and dairy cultures; importer of koji and natto starters
Owner: Betty Stechmeyer
Public Relations: Gordon McBride
Estimated Sales: $70,000
Number Employees: 1
Square Footage: 2000

Type of Packaging: Private Label
Brands:
 Gem

4830 GF Harvest
1030 E Washington St
Powell, WY 82435
888-941-9922
www.glutenfreeoats.com
Gluten-free oats, oatmeal and oat flour
President/Owner: Seaton Smith
Number of Brands: 1
Number of Products: 18
Type of Packaging: Consumer
Brands:
 CANYON OATS
 GF HARVEST

4831 GFA Brands Inc
115 W Century Rd # 260
Paramus, NJ 07652-1431
201-568-9300
Fax: 201-568-6374 www.smartbalance.com
Cheese, margarine, mayonnaise, cereals, salad dressings, pickles and oils
President: Robert Harris
CEO: Steve Hughes
sh@smartbalance.com
CEO: Steve Hughes
Estimated Sales: $1-3 Million
Number Employees: 10-19
Type of Packaging: Consumer
Brands:
 Gfa
 H-O
 Mrs Fanings
 Spin Blend

4832 GH Bent Company
7 Pleasant St
Milton, MA 02186
617-322-9287
Cookies, brownies and crackers.
Estimated Sales: $500,000-$1 Million
Number Employees: 10-19
Square Footage: 60000
Type of Packaging: Food Service
Brands:
 Bent's

4833 GH Ford Tea Company
PO Box 683
Shokan, NY 12481
845-464-6755
info@ghfordtea.com
www.ghfordtea.com
Processor, importer and exporter of whole leaf teas in tea ball packaging. Offers 30 to 50 blends and flavors utilizing original blending formulas and all natural flavoring.
President: Keith Capolino
ghfordtea@gmail.com
Estimated Sales: $2.5-5 Million
Number Employees: 5-9
Type of Packaging: Consumer, Food Service, Private Label, Bulk
Brands:
 G.H. Ford

4834 GKI Foods
7926 Lochlin Road
Brighton, MI 48116
248-486-0055
Fax: 248-486-9135 www.gkifoods.com
Milk chocolate, sugar free chocolate, yogurt and cards products, panned and enrobed, bulk or packaged. Also produces custom granola (all natural, highly nutritional, low in fat and fat free), trail mixes, etc. Custom formulation. Aidcertified, GMP and HACCP accreditation.
President: Sue Wilts
Contact: Nancy Fletcher
nancy.fletcher@gkifoods.com
General Manager: Jim Frazier
Number Employees: 20-49
Square Footage: 60000
Type of Packaging: Consumer, Private Label, Bulk

Food Manufacturers / A-Z

4835 GLCC Co
39149 W Red Arrow Hwy
PO Box 329
Paw Paw, MI 49079-9389
269-657-3167
Fax: 269-657-4552 glcc@glccflavors.com
www.glccflavors.com
Flavors, juice concentrates and blends; custom re-packaging available
President: Johnathan Davis
Finance Executive: Johnathan Davis
Quality Assurance Manager: Nicole Charron
Sales Exec: Thomas Manion
Human Resources Executive: Lisa Lull
th@glccflavors.com
VP Operations/Plant Manager: Fred Jeffers
Purchasing: Maria Galvan
Estimated Sales: $2.5 Million
Number Employees: 20-49
Square Footage: 70000
Type of Packaging: Bulk

4836 GLG Life Tech Corporation
1050 West Pender Street
Suite 2168
Vancouver, BC V6E 3S7
Canada
604-669-2602
Fax: 604-662-8858 www.glglifetech.com
Supplier of Stevia, which is a natural, zero calorie sweetening additive used in the food and beverage industries.
President/CFO: Brian Meadows
Chairman & CEO: Dr. Luke Zhang
Vice President, Marketing: James Kempland
Vice President, Sales: Jack Tokarczyk

4837 GLG Life Tech Corporation
10271 Shellbridge Way
Suite 100
Richmond, BC V6X 2W8
Canada
604-669-2602
Fax: 604-285-2606 855-454-7587
info@glglifetech.com www.glglifetech.com
Manufactures all-natural sweeteners, stevia extract and monk fruit extract.
Chairman/Chief Executive Officer: Dr. Luke Zhang
Vice Chairman: Brian Palmieri
President/Chief Financial Officer: Brian Meadows
Estimated Sales: $20 Million
Number Employees: 299
Number of Brands: 10
Brands:
  AnySweetPLUS™
  BlendSure™
  MonkGold™
  MonkSweet™
  Organipure™
  P-ProPlus
  PureSTV™
  RebPure™
  RebSweet™
  TasteBoost™

4838 (HQ)GLK Foods, LLC
11 Clark Street
Shortsville, NY 14548
855-572-8800
www.greatlakeskraut.com
Sauerkraut, cabbage products
President: David Flanagan
Contact: David Ford
djford@greatlakeskraut.com
Estimated Sales: $10-20,000,000
Number Employees: 100-249
Type of Packaging: Bulk

4839 GMB Specialty Foods
32422 Alipaz St #G
San Juan Capistrano, CA 92675-4187
949-240-3053
Fax: 949-240-3086 800-809-8298
www.gmbfoods.com
Sauces, toppings, marinades, dressings, rubs and salsas
President: Greg Bloom
Marketing Director: Helen Bloom
Estimated Sales: $1,000,000
Number Employees: 1-4
Type of Packaging: Private Label
Brands:
  Basitan's
  Edelweiss Dressings
  Norman Bishop
  Sallie's
  Scottsdale Mustard Co
  D'Oni Specialty Sauces
  Lean on Me Naturally

4840 GNS Foods
2109 E Division St
Arlington, TX 76011-7817
817-795-4671
Fax: 817-795-4673 sales@gnsfoods.com
www.greatnuts.com
Raw and roasted nuts, packaged pecan candy and dried fruits including raisins, mango, pineapple, apple, banana chips, apricots and mixed; wholesaler/distributor of specialty foods; serving the food service market
President: Kim Peacock
Marketing: Carissa Mark
Contact: Lee Eggleston
sales@gnsfoods.com
Estimated Sales: $5-10 Million
Number Employees: 50-99
Square Footage: 25192
Type of Packaging: Consumer, Food Service, Private Label, Bulk
Brands:
  Grove on the Go
  Grove, Jr
  Pecan Street Sweets
  The Grove

4841 GNS Spices
766 Trotter Ct
Walnut, CA 91789-1277
909-594-9505
Fax: 909-594-5455
Processor and exporter of red savina and orange habanero peppers including pods, flakes and ground
President: Frank Garcia Jr
VP: Mary Garcia
Operations Manager: Frank Garcia Sr
Estimated Sales: $150,000
Number Employees: 2
Type of Packaging: Bulk

4842 GNT USA
660 White Plains Rd
Tarrytown, NY 10591
914-524-0600
info@gntusa.com
exberry.com
Natural colors for the food and beverage industry

4843 GPI USA LLC.
10062 190th Place
Suite 107
Mokena, IL 60448
706-850-7826
Fax: 708-785-0608 800-929-4248
karen.haley@foodgums.com
Specialize in carageenan used for stabilization and as an additive for both dairy products and in the red meat and poultry industries.

4844 GREEN Energy
Kailua, HI 96734
808-396-9454
drinkgreenenergy.com
Organic energy drink

4845 GS Dunn & Company
80 Park Street N
Hamilton, ON L8R 2M9
Canada
905-522-0833
Fax: 905-522-4423 info@gsdunn.com
www.gsdunn.com
Global supplier and manufacturer of dry mustard products
President: Ron Kramer
Director Technical Services: Nancy Post
Estimated Sales: $5 Million
Number Employees: 20-49
Square Footage: 70000
Type of Packaging: Food Service, Private Label, Bulk

4846 GS Gelato & Desserts Inc
1785 Fim Blvd
Fort Walton Bch, FL 32547-1152
850-243-5455
Fax: 850-243-5443 888-435-2767
info@gsgelato.com www.gsgelato.com
Dairy-free, gluten-free, organic frozen desserts
Marketing: Simona Faroni
Manager: Melissa Thompson
melissa@gsgelato.com
Number Employees: 20-49

4847 GS-AFI
238 Saint Nicholas Avenue
South Plainfield, NJ 07080-1810
908-753-9100
Fax: 908-753-9635 800-345-4342
Specialty premixes, spices and seasonings
President: David Hiller
Contact: Dagmar Hiller
Number Employees: 250-499

4848 GSB & Assoc
3115 Cobb International Blvd N
Kennesaw, GA 30152-4354
770-424-1886
Fax: 770-422-1732 877-472-2776
sales@gsbflavorcreators.com
www.gsbflavorcreators.com
Natural and artificial, artificial, water or oil soluble, liquid and spray dried flavors. Flavors are Kosher Certified. We also offer a line of Certified Organic Flavors.
President: Eugene Buday
sales@gsbflavorcreators.com
Estimated Sales: $5-10 Million
Number Employees: 10-19
Type of Packaging: Bulk

4849 GTC Nutrition
5 Westbrook Corporate Ctr #500
Westchester, IL 60154-5795
708-551-2600
Fax: 303-216-2477 800-443-2746
www.ingredion.com
A leading provider of high-quality, science based nutritional ingredients for today's healthy lifestyles. Proudly takes a multi-disciplinary approach to it's business by offering customer support that reaches beyond standard needs. Areas of expertise include scientific and technical counsel, marketing and brand development, applications innovation, logistics and regulatory support and customer service.
CEO: Patrick Smith
Marketing: Trina O'Brien
Estimated Sales: $5-10 000,000
Number Employees: 20-49

4850 GU Energy Labs
1609 4th St
Berkeley, CA 94710
800-400-1995
guenergy.com
Energy gels, chews, capsules and drinks
President & COO: Blair Clark
Type of Packaging: Consumer
Brands:
  GU

4851 GURU Organic Energy
1592 Union St
San Francisco, CA 94123
www.guruenergy.com
Organic energy drinks
Brew Master: Luc Martin-Privat
Type of Packaging: Consumer
Brands:
  GURU

4852 GWB Foods Corporation
PO Box 228
Brooklyn, NY 11204-0228
718-686-6611
Fax: 718-686-6161 877-977-7610
info@gwbfoods.com www.gwbfoods.com
Processor, exporter, importer and wholesaler/distributor of specialty and frozen foods including cookies, candies, crackers, rice cakes, vegetables in jars, bottled water, pickles and pimiento peppers
President: Joshua Weinstein
Export Manager: S Williams
Sales Manager: Jack Yumens
Estimated Sales: $2.5-5 Million
Number Employees: 10-19
Square Footage: 80000
Parent Co: President Baking Company
Type of Packaging: Consumer, Food Service, Private Label, Bulk
Brands:
  Presidor

Food Manufacturers / A-Z

4853 Gabila's Knishes
100 Wartburg Ave
Copiague, NY 11726
631-789-2220
gabilas.com
Processor and exporter of frozen knishes
President: Gloria Gabay
Partner: Sophie Levy
Controller: Linda Ghignone
Estimated Sales: $1-2.5 Million
Number Employees: 20-49
Type of Packaging: Consumer
Brands:
King of Potato Pies

4854 Gabriella's Kitchen
3249 Lenworth Dr
Mississauga, ON L4X 2G6
Canada
844-754-6690
www.gabriellas-kitchen.com
Organic pasta
President: Vincent Micallef
Founder & CEO: Margot Micallef
Chief Marketing Officer: Marc Whitehead
Sr VP of North American Sales: John Shaw
VP of Corporate Development: Christopher Fenn
Type of Packaging: Private Label
Brands:
gaby
TOP-The Oil Plant
Sonoma Pacific
Aunt Zelda's
Gabriella's Kitchen

4855 Gad Cheese Retail Store
2401 County Road C
Medford, WI 54451
715-748-4273
Fax: 715-748-4299
Cheddar cheese, cheese curds, monterey jack, specialty cheese and more than 30 varieties. Retail outlet and an observation window.
President: Bruce Albrecht
VP: Diane Albrecht
Estimated Sales: Less Than $500,000
Number Employees: 1-4
Type of Packaging: Consumer, Food Service, Private Label, Bulk

4856 Gadoua Bakery
150 Bd Industriel
Napierville, QC J0J 1L0
Canada
450-245-7542
Fax: 450-245-7609   800-661-7246
info@gadoua.qc.ca www.gadoua.qc.ca
Bread, buns, bagels, english muffins, and tortillas
President: Pascal Gadoua
Year Founded: 1911
Estimated Sales: $40-60 Million
Number Employees: 550
Square Footage: 150000
Parent Co: George Weston Ltd.
Type of Packaging: Food Service
Brands:
Gadoua

4857 Gadsden Coffee/Caffe
PO Box 460
16850 West Arivaca Rd.
Arivaca, AZ 85601-0460
520-398-3251
Fax: 520-398-2001   888-514-5282
Specialty coffees
Owner: Tom Shook
Estimated Sales: $2.5-5,000,000
Number Employees: 10-19

4858 Gaea North America LLC
1915 Hollywood Blvd
Suite 200
Hollywood, FL 33020
954-923-7723
Fax: 954-923-7732 info@gaeaus.com
gaeaus.com
Greek food, including vinegars and dressings; olive oils.
CEO: David Neuman
Marketing Director: Keli Roberson
Director of Operations: Jimmy Campos
Estimated Sales: $25 Million
Number Employees: 5-9
Type of Packaging: Private Label

4859 Gaia Herbs Inc
101 Gaia Herbs Rd
Brevard, NC 28712-8930
828-884-4242
Fax: 828-883-5960   888-917-8269
info@gaiaherbs.com www.gaiaherbs.com
Organic processor of herbal extracts
Owner: Ric Scalzo
CEO: Ric Scalzo
VP: Daniel Vickers
Quality Control Director: Jim Grant
VP Marketing: Ann Buchman
VP Sales: Angela Guerrant
Human Resources Manager: Cynthia Chandler
kod@gaiaherbs.com
Purchasing: Kate Daigle
Year Founded: 1987
Estimated Sales: $11.5 Million
Number Employees: 100-249
Square Footage: 60000
Brands:
Echinacea
Echinacea/Goldenseal Supreme
Ginseng Extract

4860 Gainey Vineyard
3950 E Highway 246
Santa Ynez, CA 93460
805-688-0558
Fax: 805-688-5864 www.gaineyvineyard.com
Producer of wines, including Pinot Noir, Chardonnay and Syrah.
President: Daniel Gainey
daniel@gaineyvineyard.com
General Manager & Director of Winemaking: John Falcone
Estimated Sales: $5-10 Million
Number Employees: 10-19

4861 Gaiser's European Style
2019 Morris Ave
Union, NJ 07083-6013
908-686-3421
Fax: 908-686-7131
Processor, exporter and wholesaler/distributor of sausage, liverwurst and smoked ham
Owner: Efem Rablov
gaisers@verizon.net
Estimated Sales: $500,000-$1 Million
Number Employees: 10-19
Brands:
Gaiser's

4862 Galante Vineyards
18181 Cachagua Rd
Carmel Valley, CA 93924-9313
831-659-7620
Fax: 831-659-9525   800-425-2683
wine@galantevineyards.com
www.galantevineyards.com
Cabernet Sauvignon
Owner: Jack Galante
jack@gallantv.com
Estimated Sales: Less than $500,000
Number Employees: 5-9
Type of Packaging: Private Label
Brands:
Blackjack Pasture Cabernet
Galante Wines
Rancho Galante Cabernet
Red Rose Hill Cabernet

4863 Galassi Foods
2042 Glen Oaks Drive
Coralville, IA 52241
319-339-7409
lisa@galassifoods.com
www.galassifoods.com
Manufacturer of different pasta sauces.
Founder: Blake Niemann
Contact: Lisa Galassi
lisa@galassifoods.com
Brands:
Galassi

4864 Galasso's Bakery
10820 San Sevaine Way
Mira Loma, CA 91752-1116
951-360-1211
Fax: 951-360-0427 customercare@galassos.com
www.galassos.com
Sourdough, French, specialty and sliced breads, hot dog and hamburger buns, and assorted rolls.
CEO: Jeanette Galasso
CFO: Mark Bailey
mbailey@galassos.com
Sales & Operations Manager: John Galasso
Estimated Sales: $34.9 Million
Number Employees: 250-499
Number of Brands: 1
Square Footage: 110000
Type of Packaging: Consumer, Food Service, Private Label, Bulk
Brands:
Galasso

4865 Galaxy Dairy Products
700 Lake St # E
Ramsey, NJ 07446-1246
201-818-2030
Fax: 201-818-1969 galxdairy@aol.com
Dairy products
President: Thomas Phiebig
VP: Carole Phiebig
Estimated Sales: $30 Million+
Number Employees: 5-9
Type of Packaging: Private Label

4866 Galaxy Desserts
1100 Marina Way
Suite D
Richmond, CA 94804-3727
510-439-3160
Fax: 415-439-3169   800-225-3523
info@galaxydesserts.com
www.galaxydesserts.com
Gourmet desserts
President/CEO/Co-Founder: Paul Levitan
Co-Founder/Master Pastry Chef: John-Yves Charon
Sales/Marketing: Lisa Weaver
Year Founded: 1998
Estimated Sales: $20-50 Million
Number Employees: 250-499
Square Footage: 20000
Type of Packaging: Consumer, Food Service
Brands:
Galaxy Desserts

4867 Galaxy Nutritional Foods Inc
66 Whitecap Dr
Suite 2
North Kingstown, RI 02852-7445
401-667-5000
Fax: 302-655-5049   800-441-9419
www.goveggiefoods.com
Leading producer of healthy dairy products such as soy based dairy, low-fat, and cholestral-free. Category leader in both supermarkets and health food stores.
President, CEO, COO: Brian O'Farrell
CEO: Richard Antonelli
rantonelli@galaxyfoods.com
Executive VP: Jerry Schwartz
Marketing VP: Whitney Velasco-Aznar
VP of Contract Manufacturing: Thomas Perno
Estimated Sales: $25-49.9 Million
Number Employees: 20-49
Number of Brands: 1
Brands:
Go Veggie

4868 Galena Canning Co
107 S Main St
Galena, IL 61036-2224
815-777-9495
Fax: 773-477-5627 info@galenacanning.com
www.galenacanning.com
Specialties in salsas, pasta sauce, BBQ sauces, chili, relishes, pickles, hot sauces, mustard, jams and jellies, fruit butter, syrups, toppings, flavored oils and vinegar.
Owner: Ivo Puidak
Estimated Sales: Less Than $500,000
Number Employees: 5-9

4869 Galena Cellars Winery
515 S Main St
Galena, IL 61036-2352
815-777-3330
Fax: 815-777-3335   800-397-9463
wine@galenacellars.com www.galenacellars.com
Producers, bottles and cellars a variety of wines using grapes, juice and fruit from across the US. Classic dry wines such as Chardonay, Cabernot Sauvignon, White Zinfandel, semi-dry and semi-sweet wines, selection of fruit wines anddessert ports.

Food Manufacturers / A-Z

Owner/President: Scott Lawlor
scott@galenacellars.com
VP: Karen Lawlor
Winemaker: Chris L White
Vineyard Tasting Room Manager: Jan Falson
Estimated Sales: $1,800,000
Number Employees: 20-49
Number of Products: 32
Type of Packaging: Consumer, Bulk
Brands:
  Galena Cellars

4870 Galilean Seafood Inc
16 Broadcommon Rd
Bristol, RI 02809-2722
401-253-3030
Fax: 401-253-9207
Hand shucked clam supplier. Frozen and refrigerated clams, hard shell clams, scallops, conch, and mussels and a full line of hand shucked breaded clam items.
President: Mark Montopoli
Estimated Sales: 1-4,999,999
Number Employees: 50-99
Number of Brands: 3
Brands:
  Galilean
  King Conch
  Pure Brand Products

4871 Galland's Institutional Food
520 Kentucky St
PO Box 3007
Bakersfield, CA 93305-4344
661-631-5505
Fax: 661-631-5513
Distributors of a full service food line, exceptions produce and meat.
President: Joan Galland
Owner: Leonard Galland
CFO: Leonard Galland
Estimated Sales: $3-5 Million
Number Employees: 10-19

4872 Galleano Winery
4231 Wineville Ave
Mira Loma, CA 91752-1412
951-685-5376
Fax: 951-360-9180 info@galleanowinery.com
www.galleanowinery.com
Wines and wine grapes
President/CEO: Donald Galleano
EVP: Charlene Galleano
Human Resources Director: Debbie Kreinbring
Estimated Sales: $810 Million
Number Employees: 10-19
Square Footage: 270000
Type of Packaging: Consumer, Private Label, Bulk
Brands:
  Galleano
  Green Valley

4873 (HQ)Galliker Dairy Co
143 Donald Ln
Johnstown, PA 15907-0159
814-266-8702
800-477-6455
info@gallikers.com www.gallikers.com
Processor and distributor of milk, ice cream, orange juice, iced tea, dips, sour cream, cottage cheese.
President & CEO: Louis Galliker III
Year Founded: 1914
Estimated Sales: $33 Million
Number Employees: 250-499
Square Footage: 94000
Brands:
  Galliker's
  Potomac Farms
  Quality Chekd
  Slim 'n' Trim

4874 Galloway Co
601 S Commercial St
PO Box 609
Neenah, WI 54956-3392
920-722-7741
Fax: 920-722-1927 800-722-8503
www.gallowaycompany.com
Processor of sweetened condensed milk, beverage bases, and dessert mixes.
CEO and Chairman: Timothy Galloway
Sales Exec: Tim Galloway
tgalloway@gallowaycompany.com

Year Founded: 1932
Estimated Sales: $20-50 Million
Number Employees: 20-49
Type of Packaging: Food Service, Private Label, Bulk
Brands:
  Golden Crest

4875 Gallup Sales Company
530 E Historic Highway 66
Gallup, NM 87301
505-863-5241
Fax: 505-863-4219
Distributors of beer and wine.
President: Reed Ferrari
Vice President: Cecil Ferrari
Treasurer: Elsie Bernabe
Estimated Sales: $1-2,500,000
Number Employees: 10-19

4876 Galvinell Meat Co Inc
461 Ragan Rd
Conowingo, MD 21918-1224
410-378-3032
galvinell@zoominternet.net
www.galvinell.com
Custom meat processor, also cooker services and products and private label, custom slaughtering, and party platters, salads, charcoal and ice also available. Beef, pork, goat, and lamb.
President: Dennis Welsh
dennis@galvinell.com
Estimated Sales: $730 Thousand
Number Employees: 5-9
Type of Packaging: Consumer, Food Service, Private Label, Bulk

4877 Gama Products
12200 NW 36th Ave
Miami, FL 33167-2415
786-235-1515
Fax: 786-398-4575 info@gamaproducts.com
www.gamaproducts.com
Processor, importer and exporter of oils including corn, soy, canola, vegetable, rice bran and cottonseed.
President: Jose Abrante
Operations Manager: Rick Samudio
Estimated Sales: $10 Million
Number Employees: 12
Type of Packaging: Consumer, Food Service, Private Label, Bulk
Brands:
  Bekal
  Real

4878 Gamay Flavors
2770 S 171st St
New Berlin, WI 53151-3510
262-785-5104
Fax: 262-789-5149 888-345-4560
caryg@gamayflavors.com
Supplier to the food industry with products such as heat stable cheese flavorings, complete flavor systems and thermostable fillings. Gamay flavors include enzyme modified cheeses, natural cheese flavors, lipolyzed butter oils and creams, natural butter and cream flavors, starter distillate replacers, liquid flavors, sweet flavors, savory flavors, and food colors.
President: Dr. Aly Gamay
Director of Sales and Marketing: Cary Gammons
Contact: Noelle Todd
noellet@gamayflavors.com
Operations: Randy Cook
Estimated Sales: $1-5 000,000
Number Employees: 5-9
Parent Co: R&D Technical Center-Gamay Flavors

4879 (HQ)Gambino's Bakeries Inc
2308 Piedmont St
Kenner, LA 70062-7960
504-712-0809
Fax: 504-466-1507 www.gambinos.com
Distribution of confections, specialty cakes, Italian cookies and pastries, internet specialties, Mardi Gras packages, Doberge cakes and King Cake packaging. Every cake is baked fresh daily and we now ship overnight.
Owner: Sam Scelfo
email@gambinos.com
Estimated Sales: Less Than $500,000
Number Employees: 5-9

4880 Gambino's Bakery
4821 Veterans Memorial Blvd
Metairie, LA 70006-5209
504-885-7500
Fax: 504-887-7442 800-426-2466
kingcakes@gambinosbakery.com
www.gambinos.com
Cakes, cookies, pies and doughnuts
Owner: Sam P Scelfo
samscelfo@gambinos.com
Manager: Theresa Ursin
Estimated Sales: Less Than $500,000
Number Employees: 5-9
Parent Co: Gambino's

4881 (HQ)Gambrinus Co
14800 San Pedro Ave # 310
Third Floor
San Antonio, TX 78232-3735
210-490-9128
Fax: 210-490-9984 www.gambrinus.com
Best known as importer of the Grupo Modelo brand portfolio for the eastern US. Also imports Moosehead Lager from Canada.
President/CEO: Carlos Alvarez
c.alvarez@gambrinusco.com
CFO: James Bolz
Estimated Sales: Under $500,000
Number Employees: 50-99
Other Locations:
  Spoetzel Brewery
  Shiner TX
  Bridgeport Brewery
  Portland OR
  Trumer Brewery
  Berkeley CA
Brands:
  Kosmos Lager
  Lorunita Extra
  Modelo Especial
  Negra Modelo
  Pacifico Clara
  Shiner Bock
  Shiner Premium
  Corona Extra
  Corona Light
  Negro Modelo
  Pacifico Clara
  Modleo Especial

4882 Gandy's Dairies LLC
201 University Ave
Lubbock, TX 79415-3426
806-765-8833
Fax: 806-765-5192 800-338-6841
www.deanfoods.com
Milk, dairy products
Manager: Steve Gerrish
Cio/Cto: Lori Sexton
lori_sexton@deanfoods.com
VP Sales: Bill Murphy
Plant Manager: Larry Hendricks
Year Founded: 1924
Number Employees: 100-249
Parent Co: Dean Foods Company

4883 Ganeden, Inc
5800 Landerbrook Dr
Suite 300
Mayfield Hts, OH 44124
440-229-5200
Fax: 440-229-5240 info@ganedenprobiotics.com
www.ganedenprobiotics.com
Manufacturer and distributor probiotic ingredients.
Chairman of the Board: Andy Lefkowitz
CEO: Michael Bush
Director of Marketing: Erin Marshall

4884 (HQ)Ganong Bros Ltd
One Chocolate Dr
St. Stephen, NB E3L 2X5
Canada
506-465-5600
Fax: 506-465-5610 888-270-8222
feedback@ganong.com www.ganong.com
Confectionery products including bagged candy, boxed chocolate and fruit snacks. Many old fashion varieties such as rich milk caramel, sinful chaocolate truffles, peanut butter cups, delicious double dipped cherries and the one andonly chicken bones.

President & CEO: Bryana Ganong
VP, Innovation & Contract Manufacturing: Nicholas Ganong
CFO: Joe Lacey
Executive Vice Chair: David Ganong
Director, National Sales: John Burgess
Director, Operations: Tim Byrne
Year Founded: 1873
Estimated Sales: $32 Million
Number Employees: 325
Type of Packaging: Consumer, Private Label, Bulk
Brands:
  Between Friends Promotional Candy
  Delecto Chocolates
  Fun Fruits Fruit Snacks-Sunkist
  Ganong Chicken Bones
  Ganong Chocolates
  Ganong Fruitfull
  Ganong Sugar Confections
  Pal-O-Mine Chocolate Bars
  Sunkist Flavour Bursts
  Sunkist Fruit First Fruit Snacks
  Tiffany Bagged Candy
  Wildfruit Fruit Snacks

4885 Ganong Bros Ltd
500 St. George St
Moncton, NB E1C 1Y3
Canada
  506-389-7898
Fax: 506-854-5826 www.ganong.com
Confectionery products including bagged candy, boxed chocolate and fruit snacks. Many old fashion varieties such as rich milk caramel, sinful chocolate truffles, peanut butter cups, delicious double dipped cherries and the one and onlychicken bones.
Estimated Sales: $32 Million
Number Employees: 325
Type of Packaging: Consumer, Private Label, Bulk

4886 Garber Farms
3405 Descannes Hwy
Iota, LA 70543-3118
  337-824-6328
Fax: 337-824-2676 800-824-2284
  www.garberfarm.com
Processor and exporter of long grain white rice and yams
Owner: Wayne Garber
Partner: Wayne Garber
Sales/Marketing Partner: Wayne Garber
layamla@aol.com
Production Manager: Earl Garber
Estimated Sales: $1-2.5 Million
Number Employees: 10-19
Square Footage: 200000
Type of Packaging: Consumer, Food Service, Private Label, Bulk
Brands:
  Creole Classic
  Creole Delights
  Creole Rose
  Louisiana Mini

4887 Garber Ice Cream Co Inc
360 Front Royal Pike
Winchester, VA 22602-7314
  540-662-5422
Fax: 540-722-5088 800-662-5422
  www.garbersicecream.com
Manufacturing of ice cream and frozen desserts and yogurt.
President: Gary Bayliss
garybayliss@garbersicecream.com
Secretary/Treasurer: Arthur Parrish
Marketing Director: Brian Judy
VP, Sales: Brian Judy
Estimated Sales: $5-10 Million
Number Employees: 50-99
Type of Packaging: Consumer, Private Label

4888 (HQ)Garcoa Laboratories Inc
26135 Mureau Rd # 100
Calabasas, CA 91302-3184
  818-225-0113
Fax: 818-225-9251 800-831-4247
  info@garcoa.com www.garcoa.com
Processor and exporter of vitamins and supplements.

President: Richard Soriano
rsoriano@ci.banning.ca.us
CEO: Gregory Rubin
VP/Sales: Terry Williams
R&D: Moh Chizari
Quality Control: Juan Leal
Marketing: Donna Fedecki
Sales: Gregory Rubin
Operations/Purchasing: Jack Clark
Estimated Sales: & 125 Million
Number Employees: 10-19
Square Footage: 8000000
Type of Packaging: Consumer, Private Label
Brands:
  Clean N' Natural
  Nature's Beauty
  Nature's Glory
  Vitamin Classics

4889 Gardein
1046 Princeton Dr
Suite 101
Marina del Ray, CA 90292
  310-862-8686
  www.gardein.com
Meatless prepared foods, including chick'n tenders and meatless meatballs
President/Owner: Yves Potvin
Number of Brands: 1
Number of Products: 25
Type of Packaging: Consumer
Brands:
  GARDEIN

4890 Garden & Valley Isle Seafood
225 N Nimitz Hwy # 3
Honolulu, HI 96817-5349
  808-524-4847
Fax: 808-528-5590 800-689-2733
  info@gvisfd.com www.gvisfd.com
Ahi, sashimi, swordfish and snapper; importer and exporter of fresh seafood; wholesaler/distributor of smoked fish and general merchandise
President: Robert Fram
info@gvisfd.com
CFO: Richard Jenks
Vice President: David Marabella
Operations: Cliff Yamauchi
Estimated Sales: $13,500,000
Number Employees: 20-49
Square Footage: 18000
Type of Packaging: Bulk

4891 (HQ)Garden Complements Inc
920 Cable Rd
Kansas City, MO 64116-4244
  816-421-1090
Fax: 816-421-4220 800-966-1091
  info@gardencomplements.com
  www.gardencomplements.com
Sauces including barbecue, Mexican, Italian and Asian marinades, salsas, salad dressing, gourmet products
President: Don Blackman
Marketing Director: Jim Pirotte
Estimated Sales: $1-2.5 Million
Number Employees: 5-9
Square Footage: 45000
Type of Packaging: Consumer, Food Service, Private Label, Bulk
Brands:
  Amigo
  Aussie
  Aussie Sauce
  Best Choice
  Campfire
  Gaetano's
  Heritage
  Old Southern
  Primo

4892 Garden Fresh Gourmet
1220 E 9 Mile Rd
Ferndale, MI 48220-1972
  248-336-8486
Fax: 248-336-8487 866-725-7239
  info@gardenfreshsalsa.com
  www.gardenfreshgourmet.com
Family owned fresh made salsa company.
Owner/President: Jack Aronson
CFO: Angel Compatna
angel@gardenfreshsalsa.com
Customer Services: Carol Bahri

Estimated Sales: $5-10 Million
Number Employees: 500-999

4893 Garden Protein International
200-12751 Vulcan Way
Richmond, BC V6V 3C8
Canada
  604-278-7300
Fax: 604-278-8238 877-305-6777
  www.gardein.com
Frozen and fresh meals
President: Yves Potvin
Vice President: Ihab Leheta
VP Sales: Richard Bauman
Estimated Sales: $3 Million
Number Employees: 20-49
Type of Packaging: Food Service

4894 Garden Row Foods
411 Stone Drive
St Charles, IL 60174-3301
  630-762-8880
Fax: 630-587-9388 800-505-9999
  eathot.com
Manufacturer and distributor of hot sauces and other products, including Engorphin Rush, Pyromania, Brutal Bajan, and 350 more products.
President: George Kosten
Vice President: John Reeves
Contact: Ed Costen
ek@eathot.com
Number of Products: 15
Square Footage: 2500
Parent Co: Garden Row Foods
Brands:
  Caribbean Marketplace
  Great Grub Rubs
  Tropical Chile Co

4895 Garden Row Foods
9150 Grand Avenue
Franklin Park, IL 60131-3038
  847-455-2200
Fax: 847-455-9100 800-555-9798
Manufacturer and distribuor of hot sauces and other products, including Endorphin Rush, Pyromania, Brutal Bajan and 350 more products.
Owner: Gary Poppins
Principal: George Kosten
Estimated Sales: $2.5-5,000,000
Number Employees: 10-19
Type of Packaging: Consumer, Food Service, Bulk
Brands:
  Brutal Bajan
  Endorphin
  Mongo
  Pyromania

4896 (HQ)Garden Spot Distributors
191 Commerce Dr
New Holland, PA 17557-9114
  717-354-4936
Fax: 717-354-4934 800-829-5100
Natural, organic and specialty foods. Whole grain flours, beans, raw nuts and dried fruits; frozen foods; cereals and granola; breads and baked goods; snack foods; free-range and natural meats and seafood; special-dietary foods andprepared meals including more than 400 gluten free products
President: John Clough
jclough@gardenspotfoods.com
Marketing Coordinator: Amanda Byrd
Sales Director: Jean O'Donnell
General Manager/Operations Director: Brad Crull
Purchasing Manager: Mark Drury
Estimated Sales: $8 Million
Number Employees: 20-49
Number of Brands: 100+
Square Footage: 40000
Type of Packaging: Consumer, Private Label, Bulk
Other Locations:
  Garden Spot Distributors
  Sulphur Springs AR

4897 Garden Valley Corp
850 Garden Valley Cir
Sutherlin, OR 97479-9860
  541-459-9565
Fax: 541-459-1865 gvc@rosenet.net
  www.gvcbeans.com
Dehydrated vegetables: peas, lentils and legumes
Owner: Mark M Sterner
President: Perry Sterner
gvc@rosenet.net

Food Manufacturers / A-Z

Estimated Sales: $2.5-5 000,000
Number Employees: 20-49

4898 Garden of Flavor LLC
7501 Carnegie Ave
Cleveland, OH 44103-4809
216-702-7991
www.gardenofflavor.com
Organic juices; concentrates; powders; coffee and tea.
Owner: Lisa Reed
Number Employees: 1-10
Type of Packaging: Private Label

4899 Garden of the Gods Gourmet
2528 W Cucharras St
Colorado Springs, CO 80904-3029
719-471-2799
Fax: 719-577-4896 877-229-1548
www.godsmarketandcafe.com
A multi-faceted gourmet company. A unique blend of seasonings and spices, plus a variety of fresh and frozen specialty foods.
President: Sandy Vanderstoup
Estimated Sales: Less than $500,000
Number Employees: 20-49

4900 Gardner Pie Co
191 Logan Pkwy
Akron, OH 44319-1188
330-245-2030
Fax: 330-245-2036 www.gardnerpie.com
Frozen pies
Owner: Robert Goff
rgoff@gardnerpie.com
CEO: Tom Gardner
EVP: Kevin Ray
Director, Quality Assurance: Bryan Reynolds
VP, Marketing/Sales: Tom Cavanaugh
Sales Director: Kevin Hickernell
rgoff@gardnerpie.com
Estimated Sales: $3-5 Million
Number Employees: 50-99
Square Footage: 54000
Type of Packaging: Consumer, Food Service, Private Label

4901 Gardner's Gourmet
45450 Industrial Pl # 3
Fremont, CA 94538-6474
510-490-6106
Fax: 510-490-4563 800-676-8558
info@greatdrink.com www.greatdrink.com
Processor and exporter of frosted caffe ghiaccio, granitas, iced cappuccino and smoothie mixes, our original fruit ices, concentrates, frozen cocktails, fruit purees and flavoring syrups.
Owner: Beverly Fritz
Estimated Sales: $3-5,000,000
Number Employees: 1-4
Brands:
  Ghiaccio
  X-Treme Freeze

4902 Gardners Candies Inc
2600 Adams Ave
PO Box E
Tyrone, PA 16686-8850
814-684-3925
Fax: 814-684-3928 800-242-2639
info@gardnerscandies.com
www.gardnerscandies.com
Original Peanut Butter Meltaways®, boxed chocolates, pretzels and popcorn, brittle and roasted nuts, sugar free candy.
President: Sam Phillips
Year Founded: 1897
Estimated Sales: $25-49.9 Million
Number Employees: 100-249
Square Footage: 6708
Type of Packaging: Consumer

4903 Garelick Farms
626 Lynnway
Lynn, MA 01905-3030
781-599-1300
Fax: 781-598-1377 garelickfarms.com
Dairy
Vice President: Phil Littlefield
Vice President: Nicholas Scangas
Marketing Director: C Scangas
Purchasing Manager: D David
Year Founded: 1931
Estimated Sales: $20-50 Million

Number Employees: 500-999
Parent Co: Suiza Foods

4904 (HQ)Garelick Farms
2711 North Haskell Avenue
Suite 3400
Dallas, TX 75204
214-303-3400
Fax: 214-303-2307 800-343-4982
diane_gilley@deanfoods.com
www.garelickfarms.com
Milk, juice, spring water, cider and eggnog
Chairman/CEO: Gregg Engles
Managing Partner: Ton Davis
EVP/CFO: Shaun Mara
SVP/Chief Information Officer: Barbara Carlini
EVP/General Counsel: Steven Kemps
EVP Research/Development: Kelly Duffin-Maxwell
Sales/Marketing: Chris Keyes
Contact: Stephanie Hayward
stephanie_hayward@deanfoods.com
Purchasing: Steve Stewart
Number Employees: 1,000-4,999
Parent Co: Suiza Dairy Group
Type of Packaging: Consumer, Food Service
Other Locations:
  Garelick Farms 508 473-0550
  Mendon MA
  Garelick Farms 800 343-4982
  Franklin MA
  Garelick Farms 800 648-0135
  Burlington NJ
Brands:
  All Natural
  Garelick

4905 Garland Truffles, Inc.
3020 Ode Turner Rd
Hillsborough, NC 27278
919-732-3041
Fax: 919-732-6037 sheila@garlandtruffles.com
www.garlandtruffles.com
Mushrooms including rare truffle mushrooms, also, truffle tree nursery
Estimated Sales: $1.6 Million
Number Employees: 11
Type of Packaging: Food Service

4906 Garlic Co
18602 Zerker Rd
Bakersfield, CA 93263
661-393-4212
Fax: 661-393-9340 www.thegarliccompany.com
Peeled and processed garlic, shallots, onions and ginger
CFO: Gordon Cook
gcook@thegarliccompany.com
Vice President, Sales: John Duffus
Year Founded: 1980
Estimated Sales: $50-100 Million
Number Employees: 100-249

4907 Garlic Festival Foods
PO Box 2309
Hollister, CA 95024
831-638-9556
Fax: 831-638-3505 888-427-5423
custserv@garlicfestival.com
www.garlicfestival.com
Garlic seasoning, sauce, mustard and dressing
President, Founder: Caryl Simpson
CFO: Tracy Taggart
Estimated Sales: $500,000-$1 Million
Number Employees: 5-9
Square Footage: 20600
Parent Co: Randan Corporation
Type of Packaging: Consumer, Bulk
Brands:
  Garli Garni
  Garlic Festival
  Gourmet Gold

4908 Garlic Valley Farms Inc
624 Ruberta Ave
Glendale, CA 91201
818-247-9600
Fax: 818-247-9828 800-424-7990
Info@GarlicValleyFarms.com
www.garlicvalleyfarms.com
Processor, importer and exporter of liquid garlic products including juices and purees

President: William Anderson
CFO: Sonja Anderson
R&D: Bill Brock
Contact: Noli Leoncio
noli@garlicvalleyfarms.com
Estimated Sales: $1.2,000,000
Number Employees: 5-9
Number of Products: 2
Square Footage: 30000
Type of Packaging: Consumer
Brands:
  Garlic Juices

4909 Garman Routing Systems Inc
1612 Barthel Road
PO Box 1126
Taylor, TX 76574
410-561-8085
Fax: 410-561-8086 512-535-0178
www.garmanrouting.com
Route accounting and distribution software for all route distribution applications including that of sales order entry; sales analysis; inventory control; full service vending; truck dispatch. Food industry uses include soft drinkbottlers, bottled water delivery, snack food distributors, dairy delivery, and coffee delivery services.
Sales Manager: Chip Sturm

4910 Garon Foods
900 Camarato Dr
Herrin, IL 62948-6457
618-942-4810
Fax: 618-942-4811 gus@garonfoods.com
www.garonfoods.com
Manufactures peppers including jalapenos, habaneros, and bell, vegetables, herbs and fruits. Value added blending, sauces, and purees
Owner: Gary Griesbach
Sales: Gloryel Griesbach
Estimated Sales: A
Number Employees: 10-19
Number of Brands: 1
Type of Packaging: Bulk
Brands:
  El Gusto

4911 Garrett Popcorn Shops
PO Box 11342
Chicago, IL 60611
312-944-4730
Fax: 312-280-9611 888-476-7267
www.garrettpopcorn.com
Several varieties of popcorn caramel crisp, cheese corn, cashew caramel crisp, macadamia caramel crisp
President: Karen Galaba
Estimated Sales: $300,000-500,000
Number Employees: 1-4
Type of Packaging: Bulk

4912 Garrison Brewing
1149 Marginal Rd
Halifax, NS B3H 4P7
Canada
902-453-5343
Fax: 902-453-4672 beer@garrisonbrewing.com
www.garrisonbrewing.com
Beers
President: Brian Titus
Plant Accountant: Lorna MacPhee
Marketing Coordinator: Katie McDonald
Sales Manager: Todd Johns
Office Administrator: Shelly Simpson
VP Operations: Mark Obermaier
BrewMaster: Daniel Girard
Estimated Sales: $826.6 Thousand
Number Employees: 10

4913 Gartner Studios Inc
220 Myrtle St E
Stillwater, MN 55082-5033
651-351-7700
Fax: 651-351-1408 www.gartnerstudios.com
Cakes, pastries.
Owner: Gregory Gartner
gregory.gartner@gartner.com
Marketing: Steve Griffith
Number Employees: 100-249

Food Manufacturers / A-Z

4914 Garuda International
PO Box 159
Exeter, CA 93221-0159
559-594-4380
Fax: 559-594-4689 www.garudaint.com
Development and marketing of ingredients derived from natural sources
President/CEO: J Roger Matkin
Marketing/Sales: Bassam Faress
Contact: Liang Chen
lchen@garudaint.com
Estimated Sales: $500,000-$1 Million
Number Employees: 5-9
Square Footage: 30000
Type of Packaging: Private Label, Bulk
Brands:
 Cowcium
 Lesstanol
 Milcal
 Milcal-Fg
 Milcal-Tg
 Moo-Calcium
 Octacosanol Gf
 Vege-Coat

4915 Gary Farrell Vineyards-Winery
10701 Westside Rd
Healdsburg, CA 95448-8355
707-473-2909
Fax: 707-433-9060 866-277-9463
concierge@garyfarrellwinery.com
Producer of a 1982 Russian River Valley Pinot Noir. Also produces premium Chardonnay, Merlot, Cabernet Sauvignon and Zinfandel.
President: Gary Farrell
Contact: Tara Albertson
tara@garyfarrellwinery.com
Number Employees: 5-9

4916 Gary's Frozen Foods
2311 109th St
Lubbock, TX 79423-7256
806-745-1933
Fax: 806-745-3141
Barbecue beef, frozen smoked beef brisket, corn dogs and super dogs
President: Buddy Tidwell
Estimated Sales: Under $500,000
Number Employees: 20
Type of Packaging: Consumer, Food Service

4917 Gaslamp Co Popcorn
880 Columbia Ave
Suite 6
Riverside, CA 92507-2159
951-684-6767
Fax: 951-864-6762 877-237-8276
www.rudolphfoods.com
Popcorn and kettle corn
President: John Rudolph
CEO: Leslie Accuar
leslie@gaslamppopcorn.com
Senior VP: Hap Eliott
Estimated Sales: Less Than $500,000
Number Employees: 5-9
Parent Co: Rudolph Foods

4918 Gaspar's Linguica Co Inc
384 Faunce Corner Rd
North Dartmouth, MA 02747-1257
508-998-2012
Fax: 508-998-2015 800-542-2038
gaspars@linguica.com www.linguica.com
Portugese sausage, linguica, chourico, turkey linguica and chourico, andouille, kielbasa, salapicao, chourizos and morcela
President: Charles Gaspar
Sales Director: Randy Gaspar
IT: Annette Scrocca
gaspararap@linguica.com
Plant Manager: Charles Gaspar
Estimated Sales: $6 Million
Number Employees: 20-49
Square Footage: 102000
Type of Packaging: Consumer, Food Service, Private Label

4919 Gaston Dupre
1000 Italian Way
Suite 200
Excelsior Springs, MO 64024-8016
817-629-6275
Fax: 816-502-6722
Wheat products-pasta

President: Terri Webb McMillin
Co-owner: Michelle Muscat
Estimated Sales: $10-20,000,000
Number Employees: 20-49
Brands:
 Eddie's
 Michelle's

4920 Gateway Food Products Co
1728 N Main St
Dupo, IL 62239-1045
618-286-4844
Fax: 618-286-3444 877-220-1963
traines@gatewayfoodproducts.com
www.gatewayfoodproducts.com
Syrups, vegetable oils and shortenings; exporter of corn syrup; wholesaler/distributor of general line items; also shortening flakes, popcorn oils and butter toppings
President: John Crosley
jcrosley@gatewayfoodproducts.com
Vice President: Carroll Crosley
Quality Control: Jeremy Gray
Marketing Director: Teresa Raines
Sales Director: Teresa Raines
Operations Manager: Jeremy Gray
Production Manager: Jim Raines
Plant Manager: Jim Raines
Purchasing Manager: John Crosley
Estimated Sales: $10-20 Million
Number Employees: 10-19
Number of Products: 9
Square Footage: 75000
Type of Packaging: Food Service, Private Label, Bulk
Brands:
 Du Crose
 Du Glaze
 Du Sweet
 Gateway-Du Bake

4921 Gator Hammock Corp
25 S State Route 29
Felda, FL 33930
863-675-0687
Fax: 863-675-4938 800-664-2867
chilegator@msn.com www.gatorhammock.com
Sauces, dressings, mustard, cabbage, pickles, and jam
Owner: Gator Hammock
VP/Quality Control/Production: Larry Stewart
Sales Manager/Public Relations: Jenna Barket
chilegator@msn.com
Estimated Sales: Less Than $500,000
Number Employees: 1-4
Parent Co: Gator Hammock
Type of Packaging: Private Label

4922 Gaucho Foods
2516 Main Avenue
Fayetteville, IL 62258
877-677-2282
Fax: 618-677-2210 info@gauchofoods.com
www.gauchofoods.com
Beef
President: Jack Lachmann
Estimated Sales: $5-9.9 Million
Number Employees: 15
Square Footage: 12000
Type of Packaging: Consumer, Food Service, Private Label, Bulk
Brands:
 Gaucho

4923 Gaudet & Ouellette
Chemin Bas-Cap-Pele
Cap-Pele, NB E4N 1L8
Canada
506-577-4016
Fax: 506-577-4006
Smoked herring
President: Normand Ouellette
Estimated Sales: $5,000,000
Number Employees: 30
Type of Packaging: Bulk

4924 Gay's Wild Maine Blueberries
PO Box 100
Old Town, ME 04468
207-570-3535
Fax: 207-581-3499 wildblueberries@gwi.net
www.wildblueberries.com
Blueberries
President: Paul Gay

4925 Gayle's Sweet N' Sassy Foods
269 S Beverly Dr
Suite 472
Beverly Hills, CA 90212-3851
310-246-1792
Fax: 310-246-1794 info@gaylesbbq.com
www.gaylesbbq.com
Barbecue sauce
Owner: Gayle Gannes
g.gannes@gaylesbbq.com
Estimated Sales: Under $500,000
Number Employees: 20-49

4926 Gaytan Foods Inc
15430 Proctor Ave
City Of Industry, CA 91745-1024
626-330-4553
Fax: 626-330-1224 800-242-9826
ryan@gaytanfoods.com www.gaytanfoods.com
Snacks, pork rinds, cheese puffs
Owner: Rudolph Gaytan
rudolph@gaytanfoods.com
Number Employees: 100-249

4927 Gearharts Fine Chocolates
416 W Main St
Suite C
Charlottesville, VA 22903-5557
434-972-9100
Fax: 434-972-9104 800-625-0595
info@gearhartschocolates.com
www.gearhartschocolates.com
Chocolate
Owner: Tim Gearhart
info@gearhartschocolates.com
Marketing: William Hamilton
Estimated Sales: Less Than $500,000
Number Employees: 1-4

4928 Gedney Foods Co
12243 Branford St
Sun Valley, CA 91352
952-448-2612
888-244-0653
info@gedneypickle.com www.gedneyfoods.com
Condiments, barbecue sauces, vinegars, syrups, pickles, relishes, sauerkraut, salsas, salad dressings, mayonnaise, mustard; cucumbers
CEO: Gary Ethan Kamins
VP, Operations: Rod Prochaska
Estimated Sales: $6-8 Million
Number Employees: 100-249
Parent Co: PMC Global, Inc.
Type of Packaging: Consumer, Food Service, Private Label, Bulk
Brands:
 Devil's Fire
 Gedney
 Geraldo's
 Hiawatha
 Max's
 Minnesaurus Dill Picklodon
 Northland
 Northwoods
 Pep Fest
 State Fair
 Cains
 DelMonte

4929 GeeFree
1046 Princeton Dr
Suite 101
Marina del Ray, CA 90292
310-862-8686
www.gardein.com
Gluten-free puff pastry and prepared foods
President/Owner: Susan Hougui
Number of Brands: 1
Number of Products: 25
Type of Packaging: Consumer
Brands:
 GEEFREE

4930 Gehl Foods, Inc.
N116 W 15970 Main Street
PO Box 1004
Germantown, WI 53022
262-251-8572
Fax: 262-250-6847 800-521-2873
help@gehls.com www.gehls.com
Beverages, savory sauces, wholesome puddings, chips and jalapenos.

Food Manufacturers / A-Z

President: Frank Hughes
CEO: Katherine Gehl
VP: Michael Stewart
VP Marketing: John Slawny
VP Sales: Tracy Propst
Human Resources Manager: Keri Cannestra
VP Operations: John Shaughnessy
Purchasing: Ken St Clair
Number Employees: 220
Square Footage: 633000
Brands:
    Gehl Mainstream Cafe
    Gehl Gourmet

4931 Gel Spice Co LLC
48 Hook Rd
Bayonne, NJ 07002-5007
201-339-0700
Fax: 201-339-0024 800-922-0230
sales@gelspice.com www.gel-spice.com
Spices, seeds and bakery ingredients
President: Harry Blumenfeld
harry@gelspice.com
Vice President: Jacob Engel
Marketing Director: Sherman Engel
Purchasing Manager: Gershon Engel
Number Employees: 50-99
Square Footage: 250000
Type of Packaging: Consumer, Food Service, Private Label, Bulk

4932 Gelateria Naia
736 Alfred Nobel Dr
Hercules, CA 94547-1805
510-724-2479
www.gelaterianaia.com
Gelato and sorbetto
Co-Founder: Trevor Morris
Co-Founder: Chris Tan
Contact: Tiona Beamon
tbeamon@bargelato.com
Estimated Sales: Less Than $500,000
Number Employees: 5-9

4933 Gelati Celesti
612 Meyer Ln # 2
Redondo Beach, CA 90278-5274
310-372-2593
Fax: 310-798-0043 800-550-7550
sales@gelaticelesti.com www.gelaticelesti.com
Gelati, sorbets and gelato truffles
President: Steve Edmonds
sales@gelaticelesti.com
Estimated Sales: $2.5-5,000,000
Number Employees: 10-19
Type of Packaging: Consumer, Food Service, Private Label, Bulk
Brands:
    Gelati Celesti

4934 Gelato Fiasco
74 Maine St
Brunswick, ME 04011-2015
207-607-4262
delicious@gelatofiasco.com
www.gelatofiasco.com
Gelato
Co-Founder and CEO: Joshua Davis
Co-Founder and President: Bruno Tropeano
Marketing Director: Bobby Guerette
Sales Director: Steve Smith
Number Employees: 10-19

4935 Gelato Fresco
60 Tycos Drive
Toronto, ON M6B 1V9
Canada
416-785-5415
Fax: 416-781-3133 info@gelatofresco.com
www.gelatofresco.com
Natural ice cream, sorbet and tartufo
President: Hart Melvin
Estimated Sales: $1.3 Million
Number Employees: 5
Square Footage: 20000
Type of Packaging: Consumer, Food Service
Brands:
    Gelato Fresco

4936 Gelato Giuliana
240 Sargent Dr # 9
110 Terminal Plaza
New Haven, CT 06511-6108
203-772-0607
Fax: 203-772-0612 gelatogiuliana@sbcglobal.net
Gelatos and flavored gelatos
Owner: Deborah Cairo
Vice President: Deborah Cairo
Research & Development: Giuliana Maravalle
Quality Congrol & Marketing Director: Deborah Cairo
Sales & Operations Manager: Mike Desarbo
Public Relations & Production Manager: Jarett Casman
dcairo@gelatogiuliana.com
Plant Manager & Purchasing Director: Giuliana Maravalle
Number Employees: 50-99
Square Footage: 20000

4937 Gelita North America
2445 Port Neal Rd
Sergeant Bluff, IA 51054-7728
712-943-5516
Fax: 712-943-3372 800-223-9244
service.na@gelita.com
Gelatine
President: Jorg Siebert
CFO: Robert Mayberry
robert.mayberry@gelita.com
VP Communications: Michael Teppner
Research & Development: Dr J Michael Dunn
Director Edible Gelatine: Jeremy Kaufmann
National Accounts Manager: Michelle Shapkauski
Senior Sales Manager: Tonja Lipp
Number Employees: 250-499
Brands:
    Gelita

4938 Gelnex Gelatins
30 North Michigan Ave
Suite 1111
Chicago, IL 60601
312-577-4275
Fax: 888-505-1771 www.gelnex.com
Gelatins
President: Alessandro Luize
CEO: Ross Priebbenow
Executive VP: Felipe Chaluppe
fchaluppe@gelnex.com
Estimated Sales: $500,000-1 Million
Number Employees: 4

4939 Gelsinger Food Products
2014 Montrose Avenue
Montrose, CA 91020-1605
818-248-7811
Fax: 818-957-2545
Frozen and refrigerated beef, game meats, lamb, pork, veal, smoked meats, poultry, cured meats, cooked meats
President: Ron Gelsinger
paul@azspinal.org
Sales/Marketing Manager: Kirk Gelsinger
Estimated Sales: $2.5-5,000,000
Number Employees: 20-49

4940 Gem Berry Products
733 Kaniksu Shores Rd
Sandpoint, ID 83864
208-790-2804
Fax: 866-357-3505 800-231-1699
gemberryproducts@gmail.com
www.gemberry.com
Jams, jellies, syrups, gift packs.
President and Owner: Harry Menser
Sales and Marketing: Sandy Dell
Estimated Sales: $500,000-$1,000,000
Type of Packaging: Consumer, Food Service, Bulk

4941 Gem Meat Packing Co
515 E 45th St
Garden City, ID 83714-4896
208-375-9424
Fax: 208-375-1568 gempackonline@live.com
Beef, pork and sausages
President: Tyler Compton
Estimated Sales: $7 Million
Number Employees: 10-19

4942 Gemsa Oils
14370 Gannet St
La Mirada, CA 90638
714-521-1736
www.gemsaoils.com
Olive oil importer
President: Angela Viscomi
Type of Packaging: Consumer, Food Service, Private Label, Bulk
Brands:
    Vita
    Albergo

4943 Genarom International
6 Santa Fe Way
Cranbury, NJ 08512-3288
609-409-6200
Fax: 609-409-6500
Processor and exporter of marinades, sauces and flavors including beef, chicken, turkey, pork, ham, cheese, seafood and creams
CEO: Gary Rodkin
President/Comercial Foods: Paul Maass
Number Employees: 20-49
Square Footage: 60000
Type of Packaging: Food Service, Bulk
Brands:
    Dohlar
    Genarom

4944 Gene & Boots Candies Inc
2939 Pittsburgh Rd
Perryopolis, PA 15473-1005
724-736-2701
800-864-4222
customerservice@geneandboots.com
www.geneandboots.com
Chocolates and old fashion ice cream
Owner: Jan Donati
j.donati@geneandboots.com
Estimated Sales: $5-9.9 Million
Number Employees: 10-19
Square Footage: 8196
Type of Packaging: Consumer

4945 Gene Belk Briners
10380 Alder Ave
Bloomington, CA 92316-2302
909-877-1819
Fax: 909-877-2460 info@genebelkbriners.com
www.genebelkbriners.com
Pickled vegetables
Manager: Curtis Belk
Estimated Sales: $20-50 Million
Number Employees: 20-49
Type of Packaging: Food Service

4946 Gene's Citrus Ranch
4805 Buckeye Road
Palmetto, FL 34221-7400
941-723-0504
Fax: 941-723-3620 888-723-2006
www.citrusranch.com
Oranges and grapefruit
President: Scott Mixon
Vice President: Emory Mixon
Estimated Sales: $10-20,000,000
Number Employees: 10-19
Type of Packaging: Consumer, Food Service

4947 General Mills
1 General Mills Blvd.
Minneapolis, MN 55426
800-248-7310
www.generalmills.com
Branded consumer foods such as snacks, soups, ice cream, baking products, cereals, pasta, spices, and more.
Chairman/CEO: Jeffrey Harmening
CFO: Kofi Bruce
General Counsel/Secretary: Richard Allendorf
Chief Marketing Officer: Ivan Pollard
Year Founded: 1856
Estimated Sales: $15.6 Billion
Number Employees: 38,000
Number of Brands: 42
Type of Packaging: Consumer, Food Service
Other Locations:
    Production Facility
      Albuquerque NM
    Production Facility
      Belvidere IL
    Production Facility
      Buffalo NY
    Production Facility

Food Manufacturers / A-Z

Carlisle IL
Production Facility
Carson CA
Production Facility
Cedar Rapids IA
Production Facility
Covington GA
Production Facility
Golden Valley MN
Production Facility
Great Falls MT
Production Facility
Hannibal MO
Production Facilty
Kansas City MO
Production Facility
Lodi CA
Production Facility
Milwaukee WI
Brands:
  Betty Crocker®
  Bisquick®
  Gold Medal®
  Immaculate Baking®
  Jus-Rol®
  Knack & Back®
  La Saltena®
  Pillsbury®
  Yoki®
  Cascadian Farm®
  Cheerios®
  Chex®
  Cinnamon Toast Crunch®
  Fiber One®
  Kix®
  Lucky Charms®
  Monsters®
  Total®
  Trix®
  Wheaties®
  Haagen-Dazs®
  Annie's®
  Green Giant®
  Hamburger Helper®
  Old El Paso®
  V.Pearl®
  Wanchai Ferry®
  Food Should Taste Good®
  Larabar®
  Liberte®
  Mountain High®
  Muir Glen®
  Latina®
  Blue Buffalo®
  Totino's®
  Bugles®
  Fruit by the Foot®
  Gardetto's®
  Nature Valley®
  Progresso®
  Parampara®
  Yoplait®

4948 Generation Tea
PO Box 907
Monsey, NY 10952-0907
845-352-1216
Fax: 845-352-2973 866-742-5668
info@generationtea.com www.generationtea.com
Chinese tea
Owner: Michael Sanft
msanft@generationtea.com
Co-Owner: Marci Sanft
Estimated Sales: $300,000-500,000
Number Employees: 1-4

4949 Generous Coffee
Denver, CO
info@generousmovement.com
www.generousmovement.com
Roasted coffee beans and ground coffee
President/Co-Founder: Benjamin Higgins
Co-Founder: Riley Fuller
Year Founded: 2017

4950 Genesee Brewing Company
445 Saint Paul Street
Rochester, NY 14605
585-263-9200
Fax: 585-546-8928 www.geneseebeer.com
Beers
President: Johnhen Henderson
CEO: Ramon Sanchez
Marketing Brand Manager: Jennifer McCauley
Vice President, Sales: Donald Cotter
Contact: Michael Baker
mbaker@highfalls.com
Estimated Sales: $2 Million
Number Employees: 460+
Number of Brands: 12
Parent Co: Cerveceria Costa Rica S.A.
Type of Packaging: Consumer, Food Service
Brands:
  Genesee Beer
  Genesee Cream Ale
  Genesee Ice
  Genesee Light
  Genesee N.A.
  Helles Bock
  IPA
  JW Dundee's Honey Brown Lager
  Koch's Golden Anniversary
  Michael Shea's Irish Amber
  Orange Honey Cream Ale
  Scotch Ale

4951 Genesis Today
6800 Burleson Rd # 180
Austin, TX 78744-2325
512-858-1977
800-916-6642
www.genesistoday.com
Superfood supplements
CEO: Lindsey Duncan
lduncan@genesistoday.net
CEO: William Meissner
CFO: Andy Bergad
Vice President: Jeff Brucker
Number Employees: 100-249

4952 Geneva Food Products
2664 Jewett Ln
Sanford, FL 32771-1678
407-323-5518
Fax: 407-323-4394 800-240-2326
Lysanders@genevafoods.com
Dried beans, soups, marinades, dip mixes and seasoning blends
President: Tom Vandermar
tom@genevafoods.com
Senior Partner: Gary Clark
Partner: Angie Fontes
Estimated Sales: $10-20,000,000
Number Employees: 10-19

4953 Genghis Grill Franchise Concepts
18900 Dallas Pkwy # 125
Dallas, TX 75287-6922
214-774-4240
Fax: 214-774-4243 www.genghisgrill.com
Asian prepared foods
CEO: Carrie Waddill
cwaddill@decaturisd.us
Number Employees: 10-19

4954 Genisoy
790 Tennessee Street
San Francisco, CA 94107
866-606-3829
Fax: 415-401-0087 866-972-6879
genisoy@worldpantry.com www.genisoy.com
Powdered beverage mixes, protein bars, sports nutrition products and soy protein bars
President: Tim Bruer
Marketing: Rich Martin
Plant Manager: Jeff Amlin
Estimated Sales: $.5-1 million
Number Employees: 1-4

4955 Genisoy
555 Steeprock Drive
Suite 700
Downsview, OH M3J 2Z6
800-268-7950
Fax: 800-680-8288 866-972-6879
genisoy@worldpantry.com
Soy products
President/CEO: Doug Williamson
CFO: Al Larson
Director Of Marketing: Sharon Jacobson
VP Sales/Marketing: Duke Field
Estimated Sales: $.5-1 million
Number Employees: 350
Parent Co: Genisoy
Brands:
  Genisoy Soy Products
  Mlo Sports Nutrition

4956 Genius Juice
Torrance, CA 90503
800-682-7790
contact@geniusjuice.com geniusjuice.com
Organic coconut smoothie
CEO: Shawn Sugarman

4957 Genki USA
Torrance, CA
www.getskinnynoodles.com
Gluten-free, soy-free noodles and rice
President & COO: Susan Bucher
Year Founded: 2009
Number of Brands: 1
Number of Products: 10
Type of Packaging: Consumer
Brands:
  SMARTCAKE
  SKINNY

4958 Gentile Brothers Company
10310 Julian Dr
Cincinnati, OH 45215
513-531-6000
Fax: 513-771-5569 800-877-7954
Produce
President: Jeff Oaks
CEO: Glen Bryant
CFO, COO: Rick Schimpf
West Virginia Sales Director: Ernie Coe
Director Marketing: Tom Rettig
General Sales: Jim Costello
VP Of Operations & Logistics: Brannon Player
Specialist/Banana/Pineapple: Jim Flehmer
Type of Packaging: Consumer

4959 Gentle Ben's Brewing Co
865 E University Blvd
Tucson, AZ 85719-5046
520-624-4177
Fax: 520-884-9776 www.gentlebens.com
Beers
President: Dennis Arnold
dennis@gentlebens.com
Estimated Sales: $1-2,500,000
Number Employees: 50-99
Type of Packaging: Private Label
Brands:
  Copperhead Pale Ale
  Gentle Ben Winter Brau
  Nolan Porter
  Red Cat Amber
  Taylor Jane's Raspberry Ale
  Tucson Blonde

4960 Gentry's Poultry
262 Speigner Rd
Ward, SC 29166-9438
803-254-8724
Fax: 864-445-2331 800-926-2161
Poultry
President: Wesley Gentry Jr
VP: Wesley Gentry III
Estimated Sales: $5-10 Million
Number Employees: 100-249
Type of Packaging: Consumer, Food Service

4961 George A Dickel & Company
1950 Cascade Hollow Road
P.O. Box 1448
Tullahoma, TN 37388
931-857-4110
888-342-5352
GeorgeDickel@consumer-care.net
www.dickel.com
Whiskey
Master Distiller: John Lunn
Plant Manager: Jennings Backus
Estimated Sales: $10-20 Million
Number Employees: 20-49
Parent Co: Guiness PLC
Type of Packaging: Consumer

4962 George A Jeffreys & Company
504 Roanoke St
Salem, VA 24153-3552
540-389-8220
Fax: 540-387-7418 www.novozymes.com
Enzymes

741

Food Manufacturers / A-Z

Manager: Doug Acksel
dacksel@novozymes.com
Estimated Sales: $5-10 Million
Number Employees: 10-19
Square Footage: 100000

4963 George Chiala Farms Inc
15500 Hill Rd
Morgan Hill, CA 95037-9516
408-778-0562
Fax: 408-779-4034 www.gcfarmsinc.com
Tomatillos, garlic, peppers
President: Alice Chiala
Chief Operating Officer: Tim Chiala
Chief Financial Officer: Christi Becerra
Quality Assurance Manager: Bob See
Sales Director: Joe Trammell
Production Manager: Sam Garcia
Plant Engineer: Rusty McMillan
Estimated Sales: $20-50 Million
Number Employees: 100-249
Number of Products: 300
Square Footage: 40000
Type of Packaging: Food Service, Bulk

4964 George E De Lallo Co Inc
6390 State Route 30
Jeannette, PA 15644-3193
724-523-6577
Fax: 724-523-0981 877-335-2556
info@DeLallo.com www.delallo.com
Pasta, sauces, olives, oils
President: Fran Delallo
fran@delallo.com
Purchasing Agent: J Panichella
Estimated Sales: $500,000-$1 Million
Number Employees: 50-99
Type of Packaging: Consumer

4965 George F Brocke & Sons
223 W 8th Street
Moscow, ID 83843-2326
208-289-4231
Fax: 208-289-4242
Garbanzo beans, rapeseed
President: George Brocke
General Manager: Dean Brocke
Estimated Sales: $10-20,000,000
Number Employees: 20-49

4966 George Noroian
5700 Balboa Drive
Oakland, CA 94611-2315
510-591-7044
Fax: 661-858-2656
Canned and frozen peaches and orange slices
Proprietor: George Noroian
Estimated Sales: $1-2.5 Million
Number Employees: 5-9
Square Footage: 200000

4967 George Robberecht Seafood
440 Mcguires Wharf Road
Montross, VA 22520-3603
804-472-3556
Fax: 804-472-4800
Blue crab, soft-shell crab, oysters, eel, seafood
President/CEO: Maurice Bosse
President: Wilhemina Bosse
Estimated Sales: $2.5-5 Million
Number Employees: 1-4

4968 George W Saulpaugh & Son
1790 Route 9
Germantown, NY 12526-5512
518-537-6500
Fax: 518-537-5555 info@saulpaughapples.com
www.saulpaughapples.com
Apples, pears, grapes and prunes
Vice President: David Jones
Estimated Sales: $10-20 Million
Number Employees: 20-49
Type of Packaging: Consumer, Food Service, Bulk
Brands:
 Clermont

4969 George's Candy Shop Inc
558 S Broad St
Mobile, AL 36603-1124
251-433-1689
Fax: 251-433-3364 800-633-1306
www.3georges.com
Pecans and baked goods

President: Scott Gonzales
scott@3georges.com
VP: Sibhan Gonzales
Estimated Sales: $1500000
Number Employees: 50-99
Square Footage: 120000
Type of Packaging: Consumer
Brands:
 3 George
 Azalea
 Nuthouse

4970 George's Inc
402 W Robinson Ave
Springdale, AR 72764
479-927-7000
800-800-2449
www.georgesinc.com
Frozen chickens.
Chairman: Gary George
Co-CEO & President: Carl George
carl.george@georgesinc.com
Co-CEO & President: Charles George
CFO: Susan White
Chief Strategy & Commercial Officer: Devin Cole
SVP of Foodservice: Brian Coan
Estimated Sales: $410 Million
Number Employees: 1000-4999
Square Footage: 24455
Type of Packaging: Private Label
Brands:
 George's
 Taste O'Spriing

4971 Georgetown Bagelry
5227 River Rd
Bethesda, MD 20816-1415
301-657-4442
Fax: 301-657-5573 www.georgetownbagelry.com
Bagels
Owner: Mary Beall Adler
mary@georgetownbagelry.com
Estimated Sales: Less Than $500,000
Number Employees: 5-9

4972 Georgetown Cupcake
111 Mercer St
New York, NY 10012-5212
212-431-4504
Fax: 212-431-4360
soho@georgetowncupcake.com
www.georgetowncupcake.com
Cupcakes
Contact: Emily Feldstein
efeldstein@citicenter.org
Estimated Sales: Less Than $500,000
Number Employees: 5-9

4973 Georgetown Farm
P.O.Box 106
Free Union, VA 22940
434-973-6761
Fax: 434-973-7715 888-328-5326
www.eatlean.com
Beef and bison meat; sausage and jerky products
Production: Craig Gibson
Plant Manager: Matt Albert
Estimated Sales: $3-5,000,000
Number Employees: 5-9
Brands:
 Georgetown Farm Bison
 Georgetown Farm Piedmontese

4974 Georgia Fruitcake Co
5 S Duval St
Claxton, GA 30417-2027
912-739-2683
Fax: 912-739-3419
www.georgiafruitcakecompany.com
Fruitcakes
Owner: Ira Womble
i.womble@georgiafruitcakecompany.com
Estimated Sales: $5-10 Million
Number Employees: 5-9
Number of Brands: 2
Number of Products: 2
Square Footage: 30000
Type of Packaging: Consumer
Brands:
 Georgia
 Georgia Fruit Cake

4975 Georgia Grinders
301-3400 W Hospital Ave
Chamblee, GA 30341
www.georgiagrinders.com
All-natural nut butters
Founder & CEO: Jaime Foster
Number of Brands: 1
Number of Products: 10
Type of Packaging: Consumer
Brands:
 NATURALMOND
 GEORGIA GRINDERS

4976 Georgia Nut Co
7500 Linder Ave
Skokie, IL 60077-3270
847-324-3600
Fax: 847-674-1173 877-674-2993
web@georgianut.com www.georgianutcorp.com
Confections, snacks, and nuts
President: Rick Drehobl
CEO: Dave Drehobl
CFO: Jack Arends
Director of Sales & Marketing: John Drehobl
Year Founded: 1945
Estimated Sales: $20-50 Million
Number Employees: 100-249
Square Footage: 2000
Type of Packaging: Bulk
Brands:
 Georgia's
 Solo
 Drizzls
 Malt Teenies
 Speckles
 Teenies

4977 Georgia Seafood Wholesale
5634 New Peachtree Rd
Chamblee, GA 30341
770-936-0483
Fax: 770-936-9332
Scallops, frozen seafood, shrimp
President: Liz Wang
Owner: Jack Wong
Estimated Sales: $3-5 Million
Number Employees: 5-9

4978 Georgia Spice Company
3600 Atlanta Industrial Parkway
Atlanta, GA 30331
404-696-6200
Fax: 404-696-4546 800-453-9997
SShapiro@gaspiceco.com gaspiceco.com
Spices and seasonings
Owner/CEO/Plant Manager: Selma Shapiro
R&D Director: Brian Lusty
Human Resources Director: S Lafosse
Manufacturing Director: Bob Kupinsky
Estimated Sales: $5 Million
Number Employees: 19
Square Footage: 78000
Type of Packaging: Food Service, Private Label, Bulk

4979 Georgia Wines Inc
6469 Battlefield Pkwy
Ringgold, GA 30736-5161
706-937-2177
Fax: 706-937-9860 info@georgiawines.com
www.georgiawines.com
Wines
President: Martha Prouty
proutym@georgiawines.com
Estimated Sales: $5-10 Million
Number Employees: 20-49

4980 Georis Winery
4 Pilot Rd
Carmel Valley, CA 93924-9515
831-659-1050
Fax: 831-659-1054 www.georiswine.com
Wines
President: Walter Georis
Purchasing: Sylvia Georis
Estimated Sales: $500,000-$1,000,000
Number Employees: 5-9
Type of Packaging: Private Label
Brands:
 Estate Cabernet Sauvignon
 Estate Merlot

Food Manufacturers / A-Z

4981 Gerard & Dominique Seafoods
16372a Lower Harbor Rd
Harbor, OR 97415
541-469-9494
Fax: 541-469-0757 800-858-0449
www.gdseafoods.com
Canned and frozen seafood
Owner: Julie Tomlinson
Estimated Sales: $190,000
Number Employees: 2
Type of Packaging: Consumer, Food Service
Brands:
Dick & Casey's

4982 Gerber Products Co
1812 N Moore St
Arlington, VA 22209
800-284-9488
www.gerber.com
Infant and toddler food.
President & CEO: Bill Partyka
Year Founded: 1927
Estimated Sales: $477 Million
Number Employees: 5,000-9,999
Parent Co: Nestle
Type of Packaging: Food Service, Bulk
Other Locations:
Production Facility
Fremont MI
Production Facility
Florham Park NJ
Production Facility
Fort Smith NJ
Brands:
Gerber 1st Foods
Gerber 2nd Foods
Gerber 3rd Fodos
Gerber Graduates
Gerber Good Start
Gerber Cereal
Lil'entrees
Pasta Pick Ups
Lil'meals
Nature Select

4983 Gerber's Poultry Inc
5889 Kidron Rd
Kidron, OH 44636
800-362-7381
sales@gerbers.com www.gerbers.com
Poultry.
Owner: Mike Gerber
Year Founded: 1952
Estimated Sales: $20-50 Million
Number Employees: 250-499

4984 Gerhart Coffee Co
224 Wohlsen Way
Lancaster, PA 17603-4043
717-397-8788
Fax: 717-397-3677 800-536-4310
sales@gerhartcoffee.com www.gerhartcoffee.com
Coffee
Owner: Peter Bard
peter_bard@gerhartcoffee.com
Sales: Donald Platt
Estimated Sales: $1-2,500,000
Number Employees: 10-19
Type of Packaging: Private Label

4985 Germack Pistachio Co
2140 Wilkins St
Detroit, MI 48207-2123
313-393-2000
Fax: 313-393-0636 800-872-4006
wholesale@germack.com www.germack.com
Dried fruit, chocolate and nuts
Estimated Sales: $1,000,000-$5,000,000
Number Employees: 20-49
Type of Packaging: Consumer, Food Service

4986 German Bakery at Village Corner
6655 James B Rivers Dr
Stone Mountain, GA 30083
770-498-0329
Fax: 770-498-9863 866-476-6443
germanrestaurant@aol.com
www.germanrestaurant.com
Bakery products
Owner: Hilde Friese
Co-Owner: Clause Friese
Estimated Sales: $1-3,000,000
Number Employees: 10-19
Brands:
Bailey's Irish Cream

4987 Germanton Winery
3530 Hwy 8 & 65
Germanton, NC 27019
336-969-6121
Fax: 336-969-6559 800-322-2894
sales@germantongallery.com
www.germantongallery.com
Wines
President: David Simpson
Treasurer: Judy Simpson
Estimated Sales: Less than $500,000
Number Employees: 1-4

4988 Gertrude & Bronner's Magic Alpsnack
P.O.Box 1958
Vista, CA 92085
844-937-2551
Fax: 760-745-6675 877-786-3649
info@drbronner.com www.drbronner.com
Energy snack bars
President: David Bronner
VP: Ralph Bronner
Estimated Sales: $1-3 Million
Number Employees: 1-4
Type of Packaging: Consumer
Brands:
Dr. Bronner's

4989 Gertrude Hawk Chocolates
901 Keystone Industrial Park Rd
Dunmore, PA 18512
800-822-2032
www.gertrudehawkchocolates.com
Chocolate
President & CEO: Bill Aubrey
baubrey@gertrudehawk.com
Chief Information Officer: Bruce Cottle
Human Resources Director: David Garton
Purchasing Director: Scott Melesky
Year Founded: 1936
Estimated Sales: $100-500 Million
Number Employees: 550

4990 Gesco ENR
139 Rue De La Reine
Gaspe, QC G4X 2R8
Canada
418-368-1414
Fax: 418-368-1812 gesco@globetrotter.qc.ca
Fresh and frozen shrimp
President: Gaetan Denis
Number Employees: 20-49
Type of Packaging: Consumer, Food Service, Private Label, Bulk

4991 Getchell Brothers Inc
1 Union St
P.O. Box 8
Brewer, ME 04412-2040
207-989-7335
Fax: 207-989-7810 800-949-4423
info@getchellbros.com www.getchellbros.com
Wines
President: Doug Farnham
Operations Manager: Bob Morse
Estimated Sales: $2.5-5,000,000
Number Employees: 20-49

4992 Geyser Peak Winery
2306 Magnolia Dr
Healdsburg, CA 95448-9406
707-857-9463
Fax: 707-857-9401 800-255-9463
www.geyserpeakwinery.com
Wines
Winemaker: Ondine Chattan
Manager: Lisa Flohr
lisa.flohr@accoladewinesna.com
Number Employees: 50-99
Brands:
Canyon Road
Geyser Peak
Venezia

4993 Gharana Foods
111 Glendale Ave
Edison, NJ 08817-5280
732-985-9331
Fax: 815-377-3743 orderinfo@gharanafoods.com
www.gharanafoods.com
Indian snacks
Founder: Achyut Patel
Number Employees: 1-4

4994 Ghirardelli Chocolate Co
1111 139th Ave
San Leandro, CA 94578
510-483-6970
800-877-9338
customerservice@ghirardelli.com
www.ghirardelli.com
Chocolates
CEO: Joel Burrows
VP of Professional Products: Chris Eklem
VP of Sales: Rob Budowski
VP of Operations: Samuel Bernegger
Year Founded: 1852
Estimated Sales: $100-500 Million
Number Employees: 250-499
Number of Brands: 1
Type of Packaging: Private Label
Brands:
Ghirardelli

4995 Ghyslain Chocolatier
350 W Deerfield Rd
Union City, IN 47390-1039
765-964-7905
Fax: 765-964-9138 866-449-7524
info@ghyslain.com www.ghyslain.com
Artisan chocolates
President: Ghyslain Maurais
info@ghyslain.com
Estimated Sales: $2.5-5 Million
Number Employees: 20-49

4996 Gia Michaels Confections Inc
318 Meacham Ave
Elmont, NY 11003-3214
516-354-3905
Fax: 516-328-3311 www.giamichaels.com
Cake decorations and confections
Owner: Gia Michaels
g.michaels@giamichaels.com
Marketing: Nicky Juliano
Number Employees: 1-4

4997 Gia Russa
500 McClurg Road
Boardman, OH 44512
330-965-8455
Fax: 330-965-3864 800-527-8772
info@summergardenfood.com
www.summergardenfood.com
Pasta and sauces
Owner/CEO: Thomas R. Zidian
VP Sales/Marketing: Michael Maiello
Plant Operations Manager: Kenny Navoney
Square Footage: 50000
Parent Co: Summer Garden Foods
Other Locations:
Zidian Manufacturing Facility
Youngstown OH

4998 Giambri's Quality Sweets Inc
26 Brand Ave
Clementon, NJ 08021-4211
856-783-1099
Fax: 856-783-6377 866-238-0169
dave@giambris.com www.giambris.com
Hard candies, creamy fudge and chocolates
Owner: David Giambri
dave@giambris.com
Vice President: Josephine Giambri
Number Employees: 10-19

4999 Giant Food
6300 Sherriff Road
Landover, MD 20785
301-341-4100
Fax: 301-618-4967 888-469-4426
www.giantfood.com
Baked products including bread, rolls, cakes, pies, sweetgoods, doughnuts and cookies
Manager: Tarjani Shah
Executive VP/General Manager: Bill Holmes
VP Quality Control: David Richman
Contact: Jennifer Bates
jennifer.bates@usfood.com
Manufacturing Director: Walter Auman
Number Employees: 5,000-9,999
Type of Packaging: Consumer

5000 Gibbon Packing
East Hwy 30
Gibbon, NE 68840
308-468-5771
Fax: 308-468-5262
Boneless beef and offal products

Food Manufacturers / A-Z

Chairman: Rick Elsman
Estimated Sales: $7 Million
Number Employees: 52
Square Footage: 15083
Type of Packaging: Consumer

5001 Gibbons Bee Farm
314 Quinnmoor Dr
Ballwin, MO 63011
636-394-5395
Fax: 636-256-0303 877-736-8607
Honey, salad dressing and honey mustard
Owner: Sharon Gibbons
Sales Manager: John Gibbons
Estimated Sales: $1-3,000,000
Number Employees: 1-4
Type of Packaging: Consumer
Brands:
  Gibbons

5002 Gibbsville Cheese Company
W2663 County Road OO
Sheboygan Falls, WI 53085
920-564-3242
Fax: 920-564-6129 sales@gibbsvillecheese.com
www.gibbsvillecheese.com
Cheeses
Owner: Phillip Van Tatenhove
Estimated Sales: $1-2.5 Million
Number Employees: 10-19
Square Footage: 15000
Type of Packaging: Consumer

5003 Gielow Pickles Inc
5260 Main St
Lexington, MI 48450
810-359-7680
marketing@gielowpickles.com
www.gielowpickles.com
Pickles, sweet relish & peppers
Vice President: Craig Gielow
Year Founded: 1970
Estimated Sales: $40-50 Million
Number Employees: 20-49
Square Footage: 330000
Type of Packaging: Food Service, Private Label
Brands:
  Cool Crisp

5004 Gifford's Ice Cream
25 Hathaway St
Skowhegan, ME 04976
207-474-9821
Fax: 207-474-6120 800-950-2604
info@giffordsicecream.com
www.giffordsicecream.com
Ice cream, non-fat frozen yogurt, sherbet and sorbet
President/Owner: Roger Gifford
CEO: Lindsay Skilling
Treasurer: John Gifford
Contact: Teresa Clement
teresaclement@giffordsicecream.com
Estimated Sales: $10-20 Million
Number Employees: 40+
Type of Packaging: Consumer, Food Service, Private Label, Bulk
Brands:
  Gifford's

5005 Gifford's Ice Cream & Candy Co
8810 Brookville Rd
Silver Spring, MA 02910
800-708-1938
info@giffords.com
Ice cream and candy
President/CEO: Marcelo Ramagem
VP: Neal Lieberman
Number Employees: 5

5006 Gift Basket Supply World
815 Haines Street
Jacksonville, FL 32206-6050
904-353-6278
Fax: 904-633-8764 800-786-4438
Gourmet foods
President: David Paulk
Estimated Sales: $2.5-5,000,000
Number Employees: 5-9

5007 Gil's Gourmet Gallery
577 Ortiz Ave
Seaside, CA 93955-3522
831-394-3305
Fax: 831-394-9144 800-438-7480
gil@gilsgourmet.com www.gilsgourmet.com
Condiments, salsa, pasta sauce, olives
President: Gil Tortolani
gil@gilsgourmet.com
VP: Dylan Tortolani
Marketing Manager: Dave Elgin
Estimated Sales: $1-2,500,000
Number Employees: 10-19
Type of Packaging: Private Label, Bulk

5008 Gilda Industries Inc
2525 W 4th Ave
Hialeah, FL 33010-1339
305-887-8286
Fax: 305-888-4064 www.gildaindustries.com
Crackers
President: Juan Blazquez
gilda@gape.net
Director: Carmen Blazquez
Estimated Sales: $16,000,000
Number Employees: 50-99
Type of Packaging: Private Label

5009 Gile Cheese Store
116 N Main St
Cuba City, WI 53807-1538
608-744-3456
Fax: 608-744-3457 www.gilecheese.com
Cheese, cheese products
Owner: John Gile
Co-Owner: Diane Gile
Marketing: Tim Gile
Estimated Sales: Less Than $500,000
Number Employees: 1-4

5010 Gill's Onions LLC
1051 Pacific Ave
Oxnard, CA 93030-7254
805-240-1931
Fax: 805-271-1932 800-348-2255
sales@gillsonions.com www.gillsonions.com
Onions
President: Steve Gill
Director Sales and Marketing: Nelia Alamo
Estimated Sales: $3.5 Million
Number Employees: 100-249
Square Footage: 160000
Type of Packaging: Food Service, Bulk

5011 Gillians Foods
82 Sanderson Ave # 122
Lynn, MA 01902-1900
781-586-0086
www.gilliansfoodsglutenfree.com
Gluten free foods
Owner: Bob Otolo
chefbob@gilliansfoods.com
Number Employees: 5-9

5012 Gillies Coffee
150 19th St
P.O. Box 320206
Brooklyn, NY 11232-1005
718-499-7766
Fax: 718-499-7771 800-344-5526
info@gilliescoffee.com www.gilliescoffee.com
Coffee
Owner: David Chabbott
davidhchabbott@gmail.com
Estimated Sales: $3.4 Million
Number Employees: 20-49
Square Footage: 28000
Type of Packaging: Food Service, Private Label, Bulk
Brands:
  Brooklyn Java
  Gillies
  Long Island Iced Tea

5013 Gilly's Hot Vanilla
877 East S
PO Box 1991
Lenox, MA 1240
413-637-1515
Fax: 413-637-1515 www.usbizs.com
Hot vanilla drink mixes
Owner: Joanne Deutch
Production: Carl Deutch
Estimated Sales: Under $500,000
Number Employees: 1-4
Type of Packaging: Consumer, Food Service, Bulk
Brands:
  Gilly's Hot Vanilla

5014 Gilmore's Seafoods
129 Court St
Bath, ME 04530-2054
207-443-5231
Fax: 207-386-3271 800-849-9667
gilmore@gilmoreseafood.com gilmoreslobster.com
Seafood
Co-Owner: Kevin Gilmore
Co-Owner: Ben Gilmore
Contact: Danny Gilmore
danny@gilmoreseafood.com
Estimated Sales: $300,000-500,000
Number Employees: 1-4

5015 (HQ)Gilster-Mary Lee Corp
1037 State St
PO Box 227
Chester, IL 62233
618-826-2361
Fax: 618-826-2973
webmaster@gilstermarylee.com
www.gilstermarylee.com
Cake & bread mixes, pancake mixes, drink mixes, cereal, potatoes, frostings, muffin mixes, popcorn, stuffing, chocolate items, brownie mixes, pie shell, baking soda, soups, sauces, and gravies, pastas, cookie mixes, marshmallow itemsmacaroni & cheese, coatings, biscuit mixes, puddings & gelatins, rice, dinners, and organic foods.
VP Sales/Marketing: Tom Welge
Number Employees: 1000-4999
Type of Packaging: Consumer, Food Service, Private Label, Bulk
Other Locations:
  Baking Mix/Shredded Wheat Plants
    Chester IL
  Baking/Mac&Cheese & Pasta Plants
    Steeleville IL
  Cocoa Plant
    Momence IL
  Baking Mix Plant
    Centralia IL
  Popcorn/Cereal Plant Dist, Ctr
    McBride MO
  Corrugated Sheet Plant
    McBride MO
  Baking Mix & Cereal Plants
    Perryville MO
  Popcorn Plant
    Jasper MO
  Cereal Plant
    Joplin MO
  Drink Mix Plant
    Wilson AR
Brands:
  Duff's
  Hospitality
  Py-O-My

5016 Gilt Edge Flour Mills
1090 W 1200 N
Richmond, UT 84333-1413
435-258-2425
Fax: 435-258-2428
customerservice@giltedgeflour.com
www.giltedgeflour.com
Flour
President: Keith Giusto
Vice President: Evan Perry
evan@giltedgeflour.com
Operations Manager: Dave Baker
Estimated Sales: $14 Million
Number Employees: 20-49
Type of Packaging: Consumer, Food Service, Private Label, Bulk
Brands:
  Gilt Edge

5017 Gimbals Fine Candies
250 Hillside Blvd
S San Francisco, CA 94080-1644
650-588-4844
Fax: 650-588-0150 800-344-6225
info@gimbals.net www.gimbalscandy.com
Confectionary
President/CEO: Lance Gimbal
sales@gimbals.net
VP Sales/Marketing: Estle Kominowski
Purchasing: Ward Sims

Food Manufacturers / A-Z

Estimated Sales: $5-10 Million
Number Employees: 20-49
Number of Brands: 1
Number of Products: 100
Square Footage: 90000
Type of Packaging: Consumer, Bulk
Brands:
  Jelly Bean
  Kleergum
  Lowcoom
  Soft Chews
  Taffy Delight
  Taffy Lite
  Ultimate

5018 Gimme Coffee
228 Mott St # 2
New York, NY 10012-5704
212-226-4011
877-446-6325
info@gimmecoffee.com www.gimmecoffee.com
Coffee
Manager: Eva Havle
eva.havle@gimmecoffee.com
Number Employees: 5-9

5019 Gimme Health Foods
San Rafael, CA 94903
gimmesnacks.com
Seaweed products
Co-Founder: Annie Chun
Co-Founder: Steve Broad
Brands:
  gimMe
  gimMe Organic

5020 Ginco International
725 Cochran St
Unit C
Simi Valley, CA 93065-1974
805-520-7500
Fax: 805-520-7509 800-284-2598
sales@ginsengcompany.com
Ginseng
President: Gary Raskin
VP Marketing: Linda Raskin
Sales Exec: Rick Seibert
sales@gincointernational.com
Estimated Sales: Less Than $500,000
Number Employees: 1-4
Square Footage: 30000

5021 Ginger People, The
215 Reindollar Ave
Marina, CA 93933
831-582-2494
Fax: 831-582-2495 800-551-5284
info@gingerpeople.com www.gingerpeople.com
Ginger products
President: Bruce Leeson
VP: Diana Cumberland
Contact: Robert Ballard
rballard@gingerpeople.com
Estimated Sales: $9,000,000
Number Employees: 18
Parent Co: Royal Pacific Foods

5022 Ginger Shots
Huntington Beach, CA 92649
888-413-1487
info@gingershots.com gingershots.com
Organic ginger and fruit juice blends
President & CEO: Zeyad Moussa
Number of Brands: 1
Number of Products: 6
Type of Packaging: Consumer
Brands:
  GINGER SHOTS

5023 Gingerhaus, LLC
7486 North Shore Rd
Norfolk, VA 23505
757-348-4274
Fax: 888-712-4493 lee@gingerhaus.com
www.gingerhaus.com
Baked goods
Contact: Lee Shepherd
lee@indigoart.net

5024 Gingras Vinegar
1132 Grand Caroline
Rougemont, QC J0L 1M0
Canada
514-293-4591
866-469-4954
dgare@pomdial.com www.cidervinegar.com
Vinegars
Founder: Pierre Gingras

5025 Gingro Corp
5103 Main Street
Manchester Center, VT 05255
802-362-0836
Fax: 802-362-0741 candeleros@gmail.com
www.candeleros.net
Ethnic cuisine and all-natural, gourmet sauces, salsas and snacks
Contact: Lindy Bowden
beth@gringojacks.com

5026 Ginny Bakes
3535 NW 60th St
Miami, FL 33142-2026
305-638-5103
Baked goods
Founder: Ginny Simon
Contact: Stephanie Borges
sborges@coach.com
Number Employees: 20-49

5027 Ginseng Up Corp
16 Plum St
Worcester, MA 01604-3600
508-799-6178
Fax: 508-799-0686 800-446-7364
info@ginsengup.com www.ginsengup.com
Natural soft drinks; contract packaging available
President: Sang Han
Manufacturing Executive: Courtney Craite
courtney@ginsengup.com
Estimated Sales: $3-5 Million
Number Employees: 10-19
Parent Co: One Up
Type of Packaging: Consumer
Brands:
  Cold/Hot Pack Tunnel Pasterized
  Flavor
  Ginseng Up

5028 Giorgio Foods
1161 Park Rd
PO Box 96
Temple, PA 19560
610-926-2139
Fax: 610-926-7012 800-220-2139
lbortz@giorgiofoods.com www.giorgiofoods.com
Mushrooms, cheese sticks, pierogies and gravy
President & CFO: Peter Giorgi
Estimated Sales: $5.3 Million
Number Employees: 40
Type of Packaging: Consumer, Food Service, Private Label, Bulk
Brands:
  Brandywine
  Pennsylvania Dutchman
  Giorgio

5029 Giovanni Food Co Inc
6050 Court Street Rd
Syracuse, NY 13206-1711
315-457-2373
sales@giovannifoods.com
www.giovannifoods.com
Sauces
CEO: Louis DeMent
Chief Financial Officer: David Monahan
Vice President of Operations: Tim Budd
Director of Research & Development: Eric Lynch
National Sales Director: Joe Barbara
Production/Purchasing Manager: Katie Weber
Estimated Sales: $20-50 Million
Number Employees: 20-49
Number of Brands: 5
Square Footage: 67000
Type of Packaging: Consumer, Food Service, Private Label
Brands:
  DEMENT'S
  LUIGI GIOVANNI
  TUSCAN TRADITIONS ORGANIC
  TUSCAN TRADITIONS PREMIUM
  JOSE PEDRO

5030 Giovanni's Appetizing Food Co
37775 Division Road
Richmond, MI 48062
586-727-9355
Fax: 586-727-3433 philipjr@gioapp.com
www.gioapp.com
Gourmet foods including antipasto, pickled mushrooms, chopped chicken liver and pates
President: Philip Ricossa
ricossa@gioapp.com
Vice President: Giovanni Ricossa
Estimated Sales: $2.5-5 Million
Number Employees: 10-19
Square Footage: 16000
Type of Packaging: Consumer, Food Service
Brands:
  Champagne Delight
  Giovanni's

5031 Girard Spring Water
1100 Mineral Spring Ave
North Providence, RI 02904-4104
401-725-7298
Fax: 401-725-7913 800-477-9287
Spring water and water coolers
President: John Ponton
Estimated Sales: $500,000-$1 Million
Number Employees: 1 to 4
Square Footage: 7500
Type of Packaging: Consumer, Private Label, Bulk

5032 Girard's Food Service Dressings
145 Willow Avenue
City of Industry, CA 91746
888-327-8442
sales@girardsdressings.com
www.girardsdressings.com
Mayonnaise, salad dressings, sauces and marinades.
Quality Control/R&D Manager: Jeff Stalley
Year Founded: 1935
Estimated Sales: $24 Million
Number Employees: 60
Number of Brands: 3
Number of Products: 175
Square Footage: 25000
Parent Co: HACO
Type of Packaging: Consumer, Food Service, Bulk
Brands:
  Girard's

5033 Girardet Wine Cellar
895 Reston Rd
Roseburg, OR 97471-8611
541-679-7252
Fax: 541-679-9502 wine@girardetwine.com
www.girardetwine.com
Wines
President: Marc Girardet
genuine@gerardetwine.com
CEO: Bonnie Girardet
Winemaker/General Manager: Marc Girardet
Estimated Sales: Under $500,000
Number Employees: 1-4
Type of Packaging: Private Label

5034 Giulia Speciality Food
10 Dell Glen Ave #4
Lodi, NJ 07644-1740
973-478-3111
Fax: 973-478-1133
Mineral water, balsamic vinegar, olive oil, coffee, Easter eggs, rice
Vice President: Carmelo Lamonto
giulia10@optima.net
Estimated Sales: $2.5-5,000,000
Number Employees: 1-4
Brands:
  Basso
  Lasanta Maria
  Mako
  Pasta Maltagliati

5035 Giuliano's Specialty Foods
12132 Knott St
Garden Grove, CA 92841-2801
714-895-9661
Fax: 714-373-6872 www.giulianopeppers.com
Pickled peppers and vegetables
Owner: Errol Guiliano
CEO: Becky Childs
becky@giulianopeppers.com
Estimated Sales: $3.3 Million
Number Employees: 10-19
Square Footage: 40000

Food Manufacturers / A-Z

5036 (HQ)Giumarra Companies
P.O. Box 861200
Los Angeles, CA 90086
213-627-2900
Fax: 213-628-4878 www.giumarra.com
Produce marketing
Senior VP, Strategic Development: Hillary Brick
Director of Quality Control: Jim Heil
Manager: Donald Corsaro

Number Employees: 50-99
Other Locations:
Brands:
  Arra
  Grapeking
  Natuures Partner®
  Agricom
  Arjuan Berry Farm
  Arracado
  Bauza
  Cal Harvest
  Corpora Agricola
  David Del Curto
  Liano Farms
  Luv'ya
  Marthedal Berry Farms
  Payne Family Farms
  Salazar Farms
  Santa Marta
  Subsole
  Vbm
  Yummy Fruit Company
  Zespri

5037 Giusto's Specialty Foods Inc
344 Littlefield Ave
S San Francisco, CA 94080-6103
650-873-6566
Fax: 650-873-2826 getinfo@giustos.com
www.giustos.com
General grocery
President: Craig Moore
craig@giustos.com
Estimated Sales: $24,000,000
Number Employees: 20-49

5038 Givaudan Fragrances Corp
245 Merry Ln.
East Hanover, NJ 07936
973-386-9800
Fax: 973-428-6312 www.givaudan.com
Flavors and fragrances.
CEO: Gilles Andrier
CFO: Tom Hallam
President, Fragrance Division: Maurizio Volpi
President, Flavor Division: Louie D'Amico
Estimated Sales: $4.66 Billion
Other Locations:
  Flavour Production Plant
  Cincinnati OH
  Flavour Creation Plant
  Cincinnati OH
  Flavour Creation Plant
  East Hanover NJ
  Flavour Application Plant
  Elgin IL

5039 Gl Mezzetta Inc
105 Mezzetta Ct
American Canyon, CA 94503-9604
707-648-1050
Fax: 707-648-1060 800-941-7044
www.mezzetta.com
Peppers, olives, pickled vegetables, and other assorted gourmet specialties.
President: Jeff Mezzetta
HR Executive: Maritza Monge
mmonge@mezzetta.com
Director of Product Development: Shea Rosen
Estimated Sales: $20-50 Million
Number Employees: 100-249
Number of Brands: 5
Square Footage: 200000
Type of Packaging: Consumer, Food Service, Private Label
Brands:
  Kona Coast
  Mezzetta
  Napa Valley Homemade
  Deli Sliced
  Gourmet Deli

Type of Packaging: Consumer, Food Service

5040 Glacial Ridge Foods
800 Industrial Dr
Starbuck, MN 56381-9775
320-239-2215
Fax: 313-535-4466
Chips, popcorn and pretzels
President: Mark Shirkey
National Sales Manager: Roger Spagnola
Estimated Sales: $500,000 appx.
Number Employees: 1-4
Brands:
  Country Grown Foods

5041 Glacier Fish Company
2320 West Commodore Way
Suite 200
Seattle, WA 98199
206-298-1200
Fax: 206-298-4750 info@glacierfish.com
www.glacierfish.com
Fish
President: Jim Johnson
CEO: Mike Breivik
CFO: Rob Wood
VP Sales/Marketing: Merle Knapp
Contact: Stephanie Gilbert
stephanie@glacierfish.com
Estimated Sales: $20 Million
Number Employees: 250
Type of Packaging: Food Service, Bulk
Brands:
  Glacier Freeze

5042 Glacier Foods
11303 Antoine Drive
Houston, TX 77066
832-375-6300
Fax: 559-875-3179 www.glazierfoods.com
Frozen and fresh fruit and vegetables
Owner: Jack Mulvaney
Contact: Greg Bohnsack
gregbohnsack@glazierfoods.com
Manager: Alvin Avoy
Plant Manager: Alvin McAvoy
Assistant Plant Manager: Sheila Young
Estimated Sales: $10-20 Million
Number Employees: 50-99
Square Footage: 1496520
Parent Co: JR Wood
Type of Packaging: Consumer, Food Service, Private Label, Bulk

5043 Gladder's Gourmet Cookies
1403 E Mlk Jr Industrial Blvd
Lockhart, TX 78644-3701
512-398-4523
Fax: 512-398-6323 888-398-4523
Raw cookie dough and brownie mixes
Owner: Dusty Baker
dbaker@gladders.com
Marketing Director: Susan Glader
VP Sales/Marketing: Dave Foreman
Director Operations: Kevin Cobb
General Manager: Mark Brown
Estimated Sales: $1-2,500,000
Number Employees: 20-49
Square Footage: 80000
Type of Packaging: Food Service
Brands:
  Gladder's Gourmet Cookie

5044 Gladstone Food Products Company
607 NE 69th St
Kansas City, MO 64188
816-436-1255
Fax: 816-436-1255
Mexican foods
President: Joe Catalano
Vice President: Kim Catalano
Estimated Sales: $1-2,500,000 appx.
Number Employees: 1-4

5045 Glamorgan Bakery
3919 Richmond Rd SW
Building 19
Calgary, AB T3E 4P2
Canada
403-232-2800
glamorganbakery@gmail.com
www.glamorganbakery.com
Freshly baked goods

President/Owner: Douwe Nauta
General Manager: Don Nauta
Sales/Customer Service: Jeremy Nauta
Number Employees: 8

5046 (HQ)Glanbia Nutritionals
121 4th Ave S
Twin Falls, ID 83301-6223
208-733-7555
Fax: 208-733-9222 www.glanbianutritionals.com
Nutritional ingredients
Chief Commercial Officer: Wilf Costello
SVP, Innovation: Eric Bastian
SVP, Product Strategy: Niamh Kelly
SVP, Quality: Barney Krueger
SVP, Procurement & Dairy Economics: Daragh Maccabee
SVP, Global Supply: John Mutchler
Year Founded: 1997
Estimated Sales: $20-50 Million
Number Employees: 50-99
Number of Brands: 1
Parent Co: Glanbia Plc
Brands:
  Glanbia Foods

5047 Glatech Productions LLC
325 2nd St
Lakewood, NJ 08701-3329
732-364-8700
Fax: 732-886-2131 info@kosherGELATIN.com
www.koshergelatin.com
Kolatin kosher gelatin and Elyon confectionery products
CEO: Moshe Eider
glatech@gmail.com
VP: Moshe Eider
Number Employees: 1-4
Type of Packaging: Consumer, Bulk

5048 Glazier Packing Co
3140 State Route 11
Malone, NY 12953-4708
518-483-4990
Fax: 518-483-8300
Sausage and frankfurters; importer of other meat products
President/Owner: John Glazier
jglazier@glazierfoodservice.com
Vice President: Shawn Glazier
General Manager: Lynn Raymond
Estimated Sales: $10-11 Million
Number Employees: 50-99
Square Footage: 90000
Type of Packaging: Consumer, Food Service
Brands:
  Tast-T
  Tast-T Tender

5049 Glean, LLC
Snow Hill, NC 27856
info@liveglean.com
liveglean.com
Vegetable flours
Co-Founder: Annie Chun
Co-Founder: Steve Broad

5050 Glee Gum
305 Dudley St
Providence, RI 02907-1003
401-351-6415
Fax: 401-272-1204 info@gleegum.com
www.gleegum.com
Chewing gum and candy making kits
Contact: Molly Lederer
molly@gleegum.com

5051 Glen Summit Springs Water Company
P.O. Box 129
Mountain Top, PA 18707
570-474-5861
Fax: 570-474-9840 800-621-7596
www.glensummitspringswater.com
Bottled spring water
President: John Tidball
President: Nancy Quin Davis
Estimated Sales: $2.5-5 Million
Number Employees: 20-49

Food Manufacturers / A-Z

5052 Glen's Packing Co
200 E 1st St
Hallettsville, TX 77964
361-798-2601
Fax: 361-798-1201 800-368-2333
www.glenspacking.com
Fresh meats
President: Harold Dolezal
hdolezal@glenspacking.com
VP: Glen Jr Dolezal
Estimated Sales: $5-10 Million
Number Employees: 10-19
Type of Packaging: Consumer

5053 Glendora Quiche Company
210 W Arrow Hwy
San Dimas, CA 91773
909-394-1777
Fax: 909-394-1780
Quiches
Owner: Todd Bilef
President: Brad Kovar
Estimated Sales: $1-3,000,000
Number Employees: 1-4
Square Footage: 3000
Parent Co: Kovar Companies
Type of Packaging: Consumer, Food Service, Private Label, Bulk
Brands:
  Glendora Quiche Co.

5054 Glenn Sales Company
6425 Powers Ferry Rd NW
Suite 120
Atlanta, GA 30339
770-952-9292
Fax: 770-988-9325
Seafood
President: Bruce Pearlman
Estimated Sales: $1,600,000
Number Employees: 5-9

5055 Glennys
1081 East 48th Street
Brooklyn, NY 11234
516-377-1400
Fax: 516-377-9046 888-864-1243
Natural snacks
Manager: Rhonda Talbot
Estimated Sales: $5-10 Million
Number Employees: 20-49
Type of Packaging: Consumer, Food Service
Brands:
  Glenny's

5056 Glenoaks Food Inc
11030 Randall St
Sun Valley, CA 91352-2621
818-768-9091
Fax: 818-767-0742 www.jcrivers.com
Meat snacks
Owner: John Fallon
jjwf3@braincloud.com
Estimated Sales: $1-3,000,000
Number Employees: 20-49
Square Footage: 26000
Type of Packaging: Consumer, Private Label, Bulk
Brands:
  J.C. Rivers Gourmet Jerky

5057 Glenora Wine Cellars
5435 State Route 14
Dundee, NY 14837-8804
607-243-5511
Fax: 607-243-5514 800-243-5513
info@glenora.com www.glenora.com
Wines
President: Gene Pierce
gpierce@glenora.com
Principal: Ed Dalrymple
Principal: Scott Welliver
Director Marketing: Gail Fink
Winemaker: Steve diFrancesco
Estimated Sales: $5-10 Million
Number Employees: 20-49
Square Footage: 35000
Type of Packaging: Consumer, Food Service, Private Label
Brands:
  Finger Lakes
  Glenora
  Peach Orchard Farms
  Trestle Creek

5058 Glier's Meats Inc
533 Goetta Pl
Covington, KY 41011-2203
859-291-1800
Fax: 859-291-1846 800-446-3882
www.goetta.com
German breakfast sausages
Owner: Dan Glier
dan@goetta.com
Director Marketing: Mark Balasa
Plant Manager: Tom Rabe
Estimated Sales: $2.2 Million
Number Employees: 10-19
Square Footage: 24000
Type of Packaging: Food Service, Private Label
Brands:
  Glier's

5059 Global Bakeries Inc
13336 Paxton St
Pacoima, CA 91331-2339
818-896-0525
Fax: 818-896-3237
Baked goods
President: Albert Boyajian
Estimated Sales: $19,762,359
Number Employees: 100-249
Number of Products: 5
Square Footage: 40000
Type of Packaging: Consumer, Food Service, Private Label, Bulk

5060 Global Beverage Company
130 Linden Oaks
Suite C
Rochester, NY 14625-2834
585-381-3560
Fax: 585-381-4025 webmaster@wetplanet.com
Drinks
President: Carl Rapp
COO and CFO: Lowell Patric
Number Employees: 20-49

5061 Global Botanical
545 Welham Road
Barrie, ON L4N 8Z6
Canada
705-733-2117
Fax: 705-733-2391 info@globalbotanical.com
Herbs, spices, oils
President: Sandra Thuna
Office Manager: Therese White
General Manager: Joel Thuna
Number Employees: 12
Square Footage: 40000
Type of Packaging: Private Label, Bulk
Brands:
  Excalibur
  Global Botanical
  Kidz
  Naturalvalves
  Pure-Li Natural

5062 Global Egg Corporation
283 Horner Ave
Toronto, ON M8Z 4Y4
Canada
416-231-2309
Fax: 416-231-8991 info@globalegg.com
www.globalegg.com
Eggs
CEO: Aaron Kwinter
Estimated Sales: $13 Million
Number Employees: 70
Square Footage: 50000
Type of Packaging: Food Service, Bulk
Brands:
  Egg King
  Global

5063 Global Food Industries
307 Circle Dr
Townville, SC 29689
864-287-1212
Fax: 864-287-1335 800-225-4152
info@globalfoodindustries.com
Dairy, dehydrated foods, beverages, and vegetarian foods
President: Neal Pfeiffer
Vice President: Paulette Harary
Office Manager: Sandra Sanoh
Number Employees: 5-9
Number of Brands: 1
Number of Products: 30

Type of Packaging: Food Service, Bulk
Brands:
  Global Food

5064 Global Gardens Group Inc.
10691 Shellbridge Way # 130
Richmond, BC
Canada
855-409-4365
hello@globalgardensgroup.com
Non-dairy, vegetable-based beverage in original, unsweetened and vanilla flavors
President/Chief Executive Officer: Rob Harrison
Chief Financial Officer: Paul Lott
Vice-President, Marketing: Wade Bayne
Number of Brands: 1
Number of Products: 3
Type of Packaging: Consumer, Private Label
Brands:
  Veggemo

5065 Global Health Laboratories
9500 New Horizons Boulevard
Amityville, NY 11701
631-777-2134
Fax: 631-777-3348 www.globalhealthlabs.com
Vitamins and nutritional supplements
Administrator: Susan Mc Guckian
Sales Director: James Gibbons
Contact: Cheryl Manzione
cmanzione@globalhealthlabs.com
Type of Packaging: Consumer, Private Label
Brands:
  Herb Actives
  Nature's Plus
  Source of Life
  Spirutein
  Thermo Tropic

5066 Global Organics
68 Moulton St
Cambridge, MA 02138-1119
781-648-8844
Fax: 781-648-0774 info@global-organics.com
www.global-organics.com
Organic ingredients
President: Dave Alexander
Vice President: Roland Hoch
Account Manager: Dino Scarsella
Sales and Marketing Coordinator: Ravi Arori
Estimated Sales: Under $500,000
Number Employees: 25

5067 Global Preservatives
1401 Hodges Street
Lake Charles, LA 70601
337-491-0816
Fax: 337-433-4291 866-491-0816
Preservatives
President: William Woodward
R&D: Damon Thibodeaux
Operations Director: Tim Vaughan
Plant Manager: Bryan Hymel
Estimated Sales: $2.5 -$5 Million
Number Employees: 1-4
Square Footage: 40000

5068 Globus Coffee LLC
426 Plandome Rd
Manhasset, NY 11030-1943
516-304-5780
Fax: 631-364-4558 www.globuscoffee.com
Coffee
Owner: Kurt Kappeli
public@globuscoffee.com
CFO: Salvatore Errico
Manager: Ronald Levy
Estimated Sales: $820,000
Number Employees: 1-4

5069 Gloria Ferrer Champagne
23555 Highway 121
Sonoma, CA 95476-1427
707-933-1917
Fax: 707-996-0720 info@gloriaferrer.com
www.gloriaferrer.com
White, red, and sparkling wines
President & CEO: Thomas Burnet
Executive Winemaker: Bob Iantosca
VP of Production: Mike Crumly
VP Marketing/Advertising: David Brown
Year Founded: 1986
Estimated Sales: $20-50 Million

Food Manufacturers / A-Z

Number Employees: 50-99
Parent Co: Freixenet America
Brands:
    Freixenet Spanish Wines
    Freixenet Wines

5070 Gloria Jean's Gourmet Coffees
17691 Mitchell N
Irvine, CA 92614-6827
949-589-5040
Fax: 949-589-5041 877-320-5282
www.gloriajeans.com
Coffee
CEO: Neil Gill
VP Marketing: Diane Hays-Hoag
Franchising Manager: Shereen Rai
Contact: James Harris
j.harris@gloriajeans.com
Customer Service: Patti Graves
Estimated Sales: $8 Million
Number Employees: 140
Square Footage: 240000
Parent Co: Diedrich Coffee

5071 Gloria Winery & Vineyard
1648 E 8th St N
Springfield, MO 65802
417-926-6263
Wines
President: Michael Dennis
Estimated Sales: $500,000-$1,000,000
Number Employees: 1-4

5072 Glory Foods
901 Oak St
Columbus, OH 43205
614-252-2042
Fax: 614-252-2043 800-414-5679
www.gloryfoods.com
Fresh and frozen vegetables
President: Jacqueline Neal
Founder: Iris Cooper
Founder/Plant Manager: Dan Charna
Founder: Garth Henley
Controller: Julie Eikenberry
Contact: Dino Allen
dino.allen@gloryfoods.com
Estimated Sales: $3,500,000
Number Employees: 25
Type of Packaging: Food Service, Bulk

5073 GloryBee
PO Box 2744
Eugene, OR 97402
541-689-0913
800-456-7923
sales@glorybee.com glorybee.com
Honey, sweeteners, spices, dried fruits, nuts, oils and ingredients.
President: Richard Turanski
richard.turanski@glorybee.com
Vice President: Alan Turanski
Director of Sales and Marketing: Roger Plant
Purchasing Manager: Randy Djonne
Number Employees: 10-19
Type of Packaging: Consumer, Bulk
Brands:
    GloryBee
    Aunt Patty's
    Honeystix
    Agavestix

5074 Glossop's Syrup
2337 Roscomare Rd
Suite 2173
Los Angeles, CA 90077
424-832-7266
glossops.com
All-natural cocktail syrups
President/Owner: Michael Kaz
Number of Brands: 1
Number of Products: 6
Type of Packaging: Consumer
Brands:
    GLOSSOP'S

5075 Glover's Ice Cream Inc
705 W Clinton St
Frankfort, IN 46041-1824
765-654-6712
Fax: 765-654-7977 800-686-5163
gloversicecream@att.net
www.gloversicecream.com
Ice cream, frozen yogurt and frozen novelties

5076 Glow Gluten Free
New York, NY
800-497-7434
info@glowglutenfree.com
www.glowglutenfree.com
Gluten-free cookies
Cookie Commander in Chief: Jill Brack

5077 Gluck Brands
12320 Cardinal Meadow
Suite 160
Sugar Land, TX 77478
281-903-7082
gluck@glucksnacks.com
www.gluckbrands.com
Veggie sticks, chips, popcorn and protein crisps
Founder: Gabriel Navarro

5078 Glucona America
114 E Conde Street
Janesville, WI 53546-3010
608-752-0449
Fax: 608-752-7643
Gluconates and other supplements
Development Manager: Charles King
Marketing Manager: Scott Wellington
General Manager: Sean Trac
Estimated Sales: $20-50 Million
Number Employees: 20-49
Parent Co: Avebe
Type of Packaging: Food Service
Brands:
    Gluconal

5079 Glunz Family Winery & Cellars
888 E Belvidere Rd # 107
Suite 211
Grayslake, IL 60030-2569
847-548-9463
Fax: 847-548-8038 www.glunzfamilywinery.com
Wines
Owner: Matthew Glunz
VP/Winemaker: Joe Glunz
Cellarmaster: Cipriano Luvieanos
Estimated Sales: Less Than $500,000
Number Employees: 1-4

5080 Gluten Free Foods Mfg.
5010 Eucalyptus Ave
Chino, CA 91710
909-823-8230
glutenfreefoodsmfg.com
Gluten-free pastas
Plant Manager: Bruno Campo
Number of Brands: 1
Number of Products: 8
Type of Packaging: Consumer
Brands:
    PASTARISO

5081 Gluten Free Nation
1014 Wirt Rd # 230
Houston, TX 77055-6857
713-784-7122
Gluten free baked goods
Manager: Randi Markowitz
randi.markowitz@gfhouston.com
Number Employees: 5-9

5082 Gluten Free Sensations
53238 N US Highway 131
Three Rivers, MI 49093-9764
269-273-4090
glutenfreesensations.com
Gluten free foods
Owner: Loretta Hamelink
loretta2@glutenfreesensations.com
Estimated Sales: Less Than $500,000
Number Employees: 1-4

5083 Gluten-Free Heaven
274 S 700 W
Pleasant Grove, UT 84062
801-380-6478
orders@glutenfreeheaven.com
www.glutenfreeheaven.com
Gluten-free baking mixes and flours
Founder & CEO: Andrea Custer
Type of Packaging: Consumer

Brands:
    GLUTEN-FREE HEAVEN

5084 Glutenfreeda Foods Inc
200 E Washington Ave
Burlington, WA 98233-1729
360-755-1300
Karen@glutenfreeda.com
www.glutenfreeda.com
Gluten free foods
CEO: Yvonne Gifford
yvonne@glutenfreeda.com
Chief Marketing Officer: Jessica Hale
Conventional Retail Sales: Kristine Ganes
Number Employees: 20-49

5085 (HQ)Glutino
3750 Ave. Francis Hughes
Laval, QC H7L 5A9
Canada
Fax: 450-629-4781 800-363-3438
www.glutino.com
Gluten free foods
President: Steven Singer
EVP: David Miller

5086 Go Max Go Foods
info@gomaxgofoods.com
www.gomaxgofoods.com
Vegan candy bars free from dairy, eggs, hydrogenated oils, trans fats, artificial ingredients, and cholesterol; 6 gluten-free flavors available
Co-Owner: Scott Ostrander
Co-Owner: Jon Ostrander

5087 Go Raw
1885 Las Plumas Ave
San Jose, CA 95133
408-272-4722
www.goraw.com
Seeds, seed bars, protein bars, crisps, bites and granola
Type of Packaging: Consumer
Brands:
    GO RAW

5088 GoAvo
24 Cheyenne Dr
Montville, NJ 07045-9703
973-534-9951
www.goavospread.com
Avocado-based mayonnaise
Sales: Aaron Glick
Number of Brands: 1
Number of Products: 3
Type of Packaging: Consumer
Brands:
    GOAVO

5089 GoBio!
RR 1
Action, ON L7J 2L7
Canada
519-853-2958
Fax: 519-853-8654 info@gobiofood.com
www.gobiofood.com
Organic foods
President: Anke Kruse
Brands:
    Anke Kruse Organics

5090 GoMacro
415 S Wagoner Ave
Viola, WI 54664
608-627-2310
800-788-9540
www.gomacro.com
Macrobiotic bars
Owner: Jolanta Sonkin
Type of Packaging: Consumer
Brands:
    GOMACRO
    THRIVE

5091 Goat Partners Intl.
1600 Golf Rd
Suite 1200
Rolling Meadows, IL 60008
833-872-4628
askus@greengoatmilk.com greengoatmilk.com
Whole goat milk and goat milk powder

Food Manufacturers / A-Z

5092 Godiva Chocolatier
560 Lexington Ave #A
New York, NY 10022-6828
212-980-9810
Fax: 212-980-9811 800-946-3482
letters@godiva.com www.godiva.com
Chocolate
President, Worldwide: James Goldman
SVP: David Marberger
tommorick@godiva.com
VP Marketing/Merchandising: Michael Simon
Director PR/Promotions: Erica Lapidus
Master Chocolatier: Thierry Muret
Site Manager: Tom Morick
Number Employees: 10-19
Parent Co: Campbell Soup
Type of Packaging: Consumer
Brands:
 Godiva
 Godiva Chocolate
 Godiva Biscuits

5093 Godshall's Quality Meats
675 Mill Rd
Telford, PA 18969-2411
215-256-8867
Fax: 215-256-4965 888-463-7425
Beef, beef products
President: Mark Godshall
Vice President: Floyd Kratz
fkratz@godshalls.com
Number Employees: 50-99
Type of Packaging: Private Label
Brands:
 Godshall's

5094 Godwin Produce Co
1 Yam St
PO Box 163
Dunn, NC 28334
910-892-4171
Fax: 910-892-2232 godwinproduce@aol.com
www.sweettater.com
Sweet potatoes, watermelons and cantaloupes
Owner: Anthony Godwin
Owner: David Godwin
sweettater@aol.com
Office Manager: Susan Moore
Estimated Sales: $5-10 Million
Number Employees: 5-9
Square Footage: 255000
Type of Packaging: Consumer, Food Service, Private Label, Bulk
Brands:
 Dunn's Best
 Godwin
 Godwin Produce
 Godwin's Blue Ribbon
 Sweet Carolina

5095 Goen Technologies Inc
375 Stewart Rd.
Wilkes Barre, PA 18706
973-929-3700
Fax: 973-889-4340 800-467-3041
support@trimspa.com www.trimspa.com
Weight loss supplements
President: Alex Goen
Public Relations Specialist: Chrissy Kulig
Estimated Sales: $20-50 Million
Number Employees: 100-249
Brands:
 Trimspa
 Winsuel

5096 Goetze's Candy Co
3900 E Monument St
Baltimore, MD 21205
410-342-2010
Fax: 410-522-7681 marketing@goetzecandy.com
www.goetzecandy.com
Confectionary, specifically chewy caramel
President: Mitchell Goetze
CEO: Spaulding Goetze
CFO: Dave Long
EVP: Todd Goetze
Year Founded: 1895
Estimated Sales: $20-50 Million
Number Employees: 50-99
Type of Packaging: Consumer, Food Service, Bulk
Brands:
 Caramel Creams®
 Cow Tales®

5097 (HQ)Gold Coast Bakeries
1590 E Saint Gertrude Place
Santa Ana, CA 92705
714-545-2253
Fax: 714-751-2253 orders@goldcoastbakery.com
www.goldcoastbakery.com
Sourdough, buns and rolls, and sliced bread
CEO: Rick Anderson
COO: Paul Cannon
Number Employees: 100-249
Square Footage: 440000
Type of Packaging: Consumer, Food Service, Private Label
Brands:
 Breads of Venice
 Gold Coast Baking Company
 Pioneer French Bakery

5098 Gold Coast Baking Co Inc
1590 E Saint Gertrude Pl
Santa Ana, CA 92705
714-545-2253
Fax: 714-751-2253 orders@goldcoastbakery.com
goldcoastbakery.com
Bakery products and breads
Production Supervisor: Armando Ramirez
Estimated Sales: $76 Million
Number Employees: 100-249
Type of Packaging: Private Label
Other Locations:
 Addison IL
Brands:
 Pioneer French Bakery
 Breads of Venice
 Gold Coast

5099 Gold Coast Ingredients
2429 Yates Ave
Commerce, CA 90040-1917
323-724-8935
Fax: 323-724-9354 800-352-8673
info@goldcoastinc.com goldcoastinc.com
Flavor and color manufacturer
President: Jim Sgro
jim@goldcoastinc.com
CEO: Chuck Brasher
Vice President: Laurie Goddard
Estimated Sales: $12 Million
Number Employees: 20-49
Type of Packaging: Private Label, Bulk

5100 Gold Crust Baking Co Inc
6200 Columbia Park Rd
Landover, MD 20785-3216
301-364-3320
Fax: 301-364-3340 info@goldcrust.com
Bakery goods
Contact: Paul Christou
paul@goldcrust.com
Number Employees: 20-49

5101 Gold Digger Cellars
PO Box 2550
Oroville, WA 98844
509-476-4887
Fax: 509-981-6556
Wines
Preident/Winemaker: Amy Jo Morris
Number Employees: 15

5102 Gold Dollar Products
6073 Mt Moriah Rd Ext Ste 12
Suite 12
Memphis, TN 38115
901-948-8694
Fax: 901-948-0309 800-971-8964
golddoll@bellsouth.net
Vinegar, mustard, hot sauce, lemon juice, bottled water
President/Treasurer: Sondra Abraham
Vice President/Sec: George Abraham
VP, Consultant: Herbert Abraham
VP Marketing: George Abraham
Estimated Sales: $2.5-5,000,000
Number Employees: 1-4
Brands:
 Gold Dollar
 Gold Dollar Lemon
 Gold Dollar/Monedade'oro

5103 Gold Medal Bakery Inc
21 Penn St
Fall River, MA 02724
508-674-5766
www.goldmedalbakery.com
Bread and rolls.
Controller: Claudette Torres
ctorres@goldmedalbakery.com
Year Founded: 1912
Estimated Sales: $50 Million
Number Employees: 250-499
Number of Brands: 2
Square Footage: 410000
Type of Packaging: Private Label
Brands:
 Gold Medal
 Fiber One

5104 Gold Mine Natural Food Company
13200 Danielson St
Suite A-1
Poway, CA 92064
858-537-9830
Fax: 858-695-0811 800-475-3663
customerservice@goldminenaturalfoods.com
www.goldminenaturalfoods.com
Specialty foods
Founder/Owner: Jean Richardson
Contact: David Kirchner
david@goldminenaturalfoods.com

5105 Gold Pure Food ProductsCo. Inc.
1 Brooklyn Rd
Hempstead, NY 11550-6619
516-483-5600
Fax: 516-483-5798 800-422-4681
Kosher salad dressings, sauces, mustards, and vinegar; importer of horseradish roots, dried peaches and dried apricots
President: Steven Gold
Vice President: Herbert Gold
Vice President Sales: Marc Gold
marc@goldshorseradish.com
Estimated Sales: $5-10 Million
Number Employees: 50-99
Square Footage: 300000
Type of Packaging: Consumer, Food Service, Private Label, Bulk
Brands:
 Baker
 Baker's
 Dip N' Joy
 Gold's
 Nathan's
 Old World
 Uncle Dave's

5106 Gold Standard Baking Inc
3700 S Kedzie Ave
Chicago, IL 60632-2768
773-523-2333
Fax: 773-523-7381 800-648-7904
info@gsbaking.com www.gsbaking.com
Bakery products
President: Yianny Caparos
ycaparos@gsbaking.com
VP: Joe Chiodo
Sales Representative: Connie Holston
VP Business Development: Charles Chiodo
Estimated Sales: $2.5-5 Million
Number Employees: 100-249
Square Footage: 100000
Type of Packaging: Consumer, Food Service, Private Label, Bulk
Brands:
 Croissant De Paris
 Gold Standard

5107 Gold Star Seafoods
2300 W 41st St
Chicago, IL 60609-2214
773-376-8080
Fax: 773-376-9879 Vang@goldstarseafood.com
www.goldstarseafood.com
Seafood
President: Van Giragosian
vang@goldstarseafood.com
Estimated Sales: $10-20 Million
Number Employees: 10-19

Food Manufacturers / A-Z

5108 Gold Star Smoked Fish Inc
570 Smith St
Brooklyn, NY 11231-3820
718-522-1545
Fax: 718-260-9194 info@goldstarusa.com
www.goldstarusa.com
Smoked fish and specialty foods
President: Robert Pinkow
Estimated Sales: $10-20 Million
Number Employees: 20-49
Brands:
 Cuetara
 Denmark: Officer
 Germany: Wessergold
 Gerolsteiner
 Gold Star
 Hargita
 Heine's
 Iceland: Armant
 Latvia: Unda
 Poland: Solidarnosc
 Teaports
 Ukraine: Chumak, Nektar

5109 Gold Sweet Company
331 Old Ice House Road
PO Box 247
Lake Wales, FL 33859
863-676-0963
Fax: 863-676-0968 www.goldsweetco.com
Honey
Owner/Manager: Richard Phillips
Estimated Sales: $500,000-$1 Million
Number Employees: 1-4
Square Footage: 9000
Type of Packaging: Consumer, Food Service, Bulk

5110 GoldFoods
10637 N Kendall Dr
Suite 7E
Miami, FL 33176
305-924-4825
info@goldfoodsusa.com
goldfoodsusa.com
Chia and quinoa seeds
Type of Packaging: Consumer

5111 GoldRush Mustard
9540 Garland Rd
Suite 381-298
Dallas, TX 75218
214-335-8345
info@goldrushmustard.com
goldrushmustard.com
Flavored mustards
Empress: Kerry Cole
kerrygoldrush@gmail.com
Type of Packaging: Private Label

5112 Goldcoast Salads
3600 Shaw Blvd.
Naples, FL 34117
239-513-0430
Fax: 239-304-2156
Maine lobster, blue crab and smoked salmon spreads
President: Peter Radno Jr
Co-Owner: Adam Radno
Plant Manager: Ruben Valenzuela

5113 Golden 100
1600 Essex Ave
Deland, FL 32724-2102
386-734-0113
Fax: 386-734-9718
Flavors
President & CEO: Ronald Edmundson
Manager: Jeffrey Ross
jeffreyr@jogue.com
Operations Executive: Mike Bowes
Estimated Sales: $1.7 Million
Number Employees: 10-19
Square Footage: 80000
Parent Co: Jogue Inc.
Type of Packaging: Bulk
Brands:
 Golden 100

5114 Golden Alaska Seafoods LLC
2200 Alaskan Way # 420
Suite 420
Seattle, WA 98121-1684
206-441-1990
Fax: 206-441-8112 www.goldenalaska.com
Frozen seafood
President: Joseph Fleming
Manager: Chris McReynolds
CFO: Markna Franklyn
Sales Manager: Markna Franklyn
Estimated Sales: $1-2,500,000
Number Employees: 5-9

5115 Golden Brown Bakery Inc
421 Phoenix St
South Haven, MI 49090-1309
269-637-3418
Fax: 269-637-7822 www.goldenbrownbakery.com
Bakery products
Owner: David Braschi
dave@goldenbrownbakery.com
Estimated Sales: $1-1,500,000
Number Employees: 20-49
Type of Packaging: Consumer, Food Service, Private Label, Bulk

5116 Golden Cannoli
99 Crescent Ave
Chelsea, MA 02150
617-868-2826
Fax: 617-497-5836 goldencannoli.com
Gourmet cannolis; fillings; cannoli shells; chips
Chairman/CEO: Francesco Bono
Chairman/CEO: Angelo Bresciani
Assistant Vice President: Eric Bresciani
VP of Sales & Marketing: Valerie Bono
Operations Manager: Ed Bresciani
Year Founded: 1970
Estimated Sales: $500,000 To 1 Million
Number Employees: 100-249
Type of Packaging: Private Label

5117 Golden City Brewery
920-12th St
Golden, CO 80401
303-279-8092
Fax: 303-279-8092 info@gcbrewery.com
gcbrewery.com
Beer
President: Jennie Sturdavant
Wholesale Distribution Manager: Josh Norton
Contact: Calvin Cline
ccline@gcbrewery.com
Assistant Brewer & Mad Scientist: Derek Sturdavant
Estimated Sales: $5-9.9 Million
Number Employees: 2-10
Type of Packaging: Private Label

5118 Golden Eagle Olive Products
749 N Plano St
Porterville, CA 93257-6330
559-784-3468
Fax: 559-784-2186
Olive oil
Owner: Jerry Padula
Vice President: Traci Padula
Assistant Manager: Traci Padula
Estimated Sales: $5-10 Million
Number Employees: 1-4
Square Footage: 40000
Type of Packaging: Consumer
Brands:
 Golden Eagle

5119 Golden Eagle Syrup
205 1st Ave SE
Fayette, AL 35555-2719
205-932-5294
Fax: 205-932-5296 info@goldeneaglesyrup.com
www.goldeneaglesyrup.com
Syrups
Co-Owner/President: Trent Mobley
Co-Owner/Plant Manager: Vic Herren
Manager: Jim Herren
Office Manager: Martha Kimbrell
geagle@fayette.net
Estimated Sales: $2.5-5 Million
Number Employees: 5-9
Type of Packaging: Consumer, Food Service, Bulk

5120 Golden Edibles LLC
10396 W State Road 84
Suite 103
Davie, FL 33324
Fax: 973-807-1637 866-779-7781
sales@goldenedibles.com www.goldenedibles.com
Snacks
Co-Owner/President/CEO: Steve Asbaty
Co-Owner: Jenene Carlon
Contact: Ruben Pinchanski
ruben@goldenedibles.com
Type of Packaging: Consumer, Private Label

5121 Golden Eye Seafood
17640 Clarke Rd
Tall Timbers, MD 20690-2055
301-994-2274
Fax: 301-994-9960
Seafood
President: Robert Lumpkins
Estimated Sales: $1.2 Million
Number Employees: 5-9

5122 Golden Flake Snack Foods
1 Golden Flake Dr
Birmingham, AL 35205
800-367-7629
www.goldenflake.com
Snacks
President & CEO: Mark McCutcheon
Estimated Sales: $100-500 Million
Number Employees: 500-999
Number of Brands: 3
Brands:
 Golden Flake
 Maizetos
 Tostados

5123 Golden Fluff Popcorn Co
118 Monmouth Ave
Lakewood, NJ 08701-3347
732-367-5448
Fax: 732-367-5448 goldenfluff@gmail.com
www.goldenfluff.com
Popcorn and other snacks
President: Ephraim Schwinder
goldenfluff@gmail.com
Estimated Sales: Less than $500,000
Number Employees: 10-19
Type of Packaging: Consumer, Bulk
Brands:
 Dontil
 Elyon
 Golden Fluff

5124 Golden Gulf Coast Packing Co
260 Maple St
Biloxi, MS 39530-4501
228-374-6121
Fax: 228-374-0599 wildshrimp@hotmail.com
Shrimp
President/Owner: Richard Gollott
goldengulf123@hotmail.com
Estimated Sales: $10-20 Million
Number Employees: 5-9
Square Footage: 16000

5125 Golden Harvest Pecans
348 Vereen Bell Road
Cairo, GA 39828-4910
229-377-5617
Fax: 229-762-3335 800-597-0968
Pecans and preserves, cookies and jellies
President/CEO: J Van Ponder
Estimated Sales: $250,000
Number Employees: 500-999
Square Footage: 6218
Type of Packaging: Consumer, Food Service, Private Label, Bulk

5126 Golden Island Jerky Co.
Rancho Cucamonga, CA 91730
844-362-3222
www.goldenislandjerky.com
Flavored jerkies
President: Anna Kan
VP, Human Resources: Micki Jack
Number of Brands: 1
Number of Products: 6
Type of Packaging: Consumer
Brands:
 GOLDEN ISLAND

5127 Golden Kernel Pecan Co
5244 Cameron Rd
Cameron, SC 29030-8207
803-823-2311
Fax: 803-823-2080 info@goldenkernel.com
www.goldenkernel.com
Pecans and other snacks

Food Manufacturers / A-Z

Co-Owner: David K Summers
Co-Owner/Sales Executive: Bill Summers
bill@goldenkernel.com
Number Employees: 20-49
Type of Packaging: Consumer, Private Label, Bulk
Brands:
  Golden Kernel

5128 Golden Malted
4101 William Richardson Drive
South Bend, IN 46628
888-596-4040
ncdcs@goldenmalted.com www.goldenmalted.com
Gourmet malted pancake and waffle flour mixes.
President/CEO: Rick McKeel
Sales Manager: Edward Frank
Estimated Sales: $10-20,000,000
Number Employees: 50-100

5129 Golden Moon Tea
PO Box 146
Bristow, VA 20136
425-820-2000
Fax: 425-821-9600 877-327-5473
service@goldenmoontea.com
www.goldenmoontea.com
Tea and chocolates
President: Cynthia Knotts
Owner: Marcus Stout
Number of Products: 30
Type of Packaging: Consumer, Food Service, Private Label, Bulk
Brands:
  Golden Moon Tea

5130 Golden Peanut and Tree Nuts
100 North Point Center East
Suite 400
Alpharetta, GA 30022
770-752-8160
www.goldenpeanut.com
Peanuts and tree nuts.
President: Clint Piper
Year Founded: 2000
Estimated Sales: $500 Million-$1 Billion
Number Employees: 1000+
Parent Co: Archer Daniels Midland
Type of Packaging: Consumer

5131 Golden Platter Foods
37 Tompkins Point Rd
Newark, NJ 07114-2814
973-344-8770
Fax: 973-465-7580 contact@goldenplatter.com
goldenplatter.com
Poultry products
President: Eli Barr
sbarich@goldenplatter.com
Estimated Sales: $6.5 Million
Number Employees: 100-249
Type of Packaging: Consumer, Food Service

5132 Golden River Fruit Company
7150 20th Street #A
Vero Beach, FL 32966-8805
772-562-8610
Fax: 772-567-6008
Grapefruit
CEO: George Lamberth
glambeth@goldenriverfruit.com
VP: David Milwood
General Manager/Purchasing Director: Fred Antwerp
Estimated Sales: $2 Million
Number Employees: 25
Square Footage: 13474
Type of Packaging: Bulk
Brands:
  Bland Farms
  Golden Eagle
  Golden One
  Golden River
  Golden Sun
  National Gold
  National One
  Sundance

5133 Golden Specialty Foods Inc
14605 Best Ave
Norwalk, CA 90650-5258
562-802-2537
Fax: 562-926-4491
wayne@goldenspecialtyfoods.com

Canned dips, salad dressings, sauces, seasonings, chicken and beef bases
CEO: Phil Pisciotto
CFO: Derky Howard
Quality Assurance Director: Javed Atcha
Sales: Andrea Bouras
COO: Jeff Chan
Estimated Sales: $3.5 Million
Number Employees: 50-99
Square Footage: 62000
Type of Packaging: Consumer, Food Service, Private Label, Bulk

5134 Golden State Foods Corp
18301 Von Karman Ave
Suite 1100
Irvine, CA 92612
949-247-8000
www.goldenstatefoods.com
Sauces, dressings, syrups, jams/jellies, meat products, produce, rolls and buns.
CEO & Chairman: Mark Stephen Wetterau
mwetterau@goldenstatefoods.com
SVP & Chief Financial Officer: Joe Heffington
EVP & Chief Administrative Officer: Bill Sanderson
SVP & Chief Legal Officer: John Page
Chief Human Resources Officer: Ed Rodriguez
Year Founded: 1947
Estimated Sales: Over $1 Billion
Number Employees: 1000-4999
Other Locations:
  Phoenix AZ
  Portland OR
  St. Peter MO
  Schertz TX
  Spokane Valley WA
  Suffolk VA
  Tampa FL
  City of Industry CA
  Conyers GA
  Garner NC
  Lemont IL
  Rochester NY
  Whitewater WI

5135 Golden State Herbs
60125 Polk St
P.O. Box 756
Thermal, CA 92274-8944
760-399-1133
Fax: 760-399-1555 800-730-3575
www.goldenstateherbs.com
Herbs
Estimated Sales: $3.4 Million
Number Employees: 5-9
Square Footage: 100000

5136 Golden Town Apple Products
755 Principale St
Rougemont, QC J0L 1M0
Canada
519-599-6300
Fax: 519-599-2103 866-552-7643
pierre.lheureux@lassonde.com www.lassonde.com
Apple processing
Chairman/CEO: Pierre-Paul Lassonde
President/CEO: Jean Gattuso
VP/CFO: Guy Blanchette
Business Manager: Gerry Williams
Technical Director: Doug Johnson
Office Administrator: Darlene Gardner
Maintenance/Engineering Manager: Ron McQuarrie
Juice Production Coordinator: Jennifer Rear
Plant Manager: Bryan Lowe
GM/Purchasing/Sales: Keith Cummings
Number Employees: 20-49
Square Footage: 80000
Parent Co: A. Lassonde, Inc
Type of Packaging: Consumer, Bulk

5137 Golden Valley Dairy Products
1025 E Bardsley Ave
Tulare, CA 93274-5752
559-687-1188
Fax: 559-685-6551 www.saputo.com
Cheese
Manager: Mike Kothbauer
CEO: John Prince
Contact: Eddie Alanis
ealanis@landolakes.com
Estimated Sales: $500,000-$1,000,000
Number Employees: 5-9
Parent Co: DCCA
Type of Packaging: Consumer

Brands:
  Ben & Jerry
  Breyers
  Haagen Dazs
  Klondike

5138 Golden Valley Foods Ltd.
3841 Vanderpol Court
Abbotsford, BC V2T 5W5
Canada
604-857-0704
Fax: 604-607-5504 888-299-8855
www.goldenvalley.com
Eggs and egg products.
Plant & Quality Assurance Manager: Frank Curtis
Regional Sales Manager: Craig Ansell
Year Founded: 1950
Estimated Sales: $24.9 Million
Number Employees: 100
Parent Co: Fresh Start Food Corp.
Type of Packaging: Consumer, Food Service, Private Label
Brands:
  Goldegg
  Canadian Harvest
  Born 3
  Country Golden Yolks
  Freerun
  Freerun Omega 3
  Organic
  Premium Brand
  Golden Valley

5139 Golden Valley Natural
815 E 1400 N
Shelley, ID 83274
888-270-7147
sales@goldenvalleynatural.com
www.goldenvalleynatural.com
Beef, buffalo and turkey jerky; fruit snacks
CEO: Bryce Espline
bryce@goldenvalleynatural.com
Number Employees: 50-99
Type of Packaging: Consumer
Brands:
  Hero Jerky
  Meliora Organic
  Ascend
  Healthy Partner Pet Snacks
  Intermountain Bison

5140 Golden Walnut Specialty Foods
18279 Minnetonka Blvd
Wayzata, MN 55391-3342
95 -76 -079
Fax: 847-731-6433 800-843-3645
sales@goldenwalnut.com
Specialty food products including cookies, cakes, cheesecakes, shortbread and candy
President: Mark Sigel
Estimated Sales: $5-10 Million
Number Employees: 20-49
Parent Co: EMAC International
Type of Packaging: Consumer, Private Label, Bulk
Brands:
  Almond Ingot
  Amelia's Sugar Free Shoppe
  Buckley's
  Golden Walnut
  Ingot
  Monica's
  Razzlenuts
  Sideboard Sweets & Savories
  Thimble

5141 Golden West Food Group
4401 S Downey Rd
Vernon, CA 90058
888-807-3663
Fax: 323-585-8483 info@gwfg.com
www.gwfg.com
Beef, poultry and pork products
CEO: Erik Litmanovich
Chief Sales Officer: Tim White
Contact: Mak Abbasi
it@gwfg.com
Estimated Sales: $100-499 Million
Number Employees: 750
Number of Brands: 14
Type of Packaging: Consumer, Food Service, Private Label
Brands:
  Jack Daniels
  Jack Link's

751

Food Manufacturers / A-Z

Certified Angus Beef
American BBQ Company
Teva Foods
Calle Sabor
Red Moon
Premium Cuts
Royal Poultry
Culver City Meat
Simple Eats
Tabiah Halal

5142 Golden West Fruit Company
2151 Saybrook Ave
Commerce, CA 90040
323-726-9419
Fax: 323-726-9504
Fruits, toppings, syrups, fillings & bottled fruit & beverages
President: Donald Campolo
Estimated Sales: $280,000
Number Employees: 1-4
Square Footage: 20000
Type of Packaging: Private Label, Bulk

5143 Golden West Specialty Foods
300 Industrial Way
Brisbane, CA 94005
415-657-0123
Fax: 415-657-0110 800-584-4481
info@gwsfoods.com www.gwsfoods.com
Sauces, marinades
President: Lawrence Ames
lca@gwsfoods.com
Number Employees: 1-4
Type of Packaging: Private Label
Brands:
  Chinese Chicken Salad Dressing
  Thai Sauce
  Traditional Stir Fry Sauce

5144 Goldenberg's Peanut Chews
1300 Stefko Blvd
Bethlehem, PA 18017
888-645-3453
www.peanutchews.com
Confectionary
President & COO: David Yale
Year Founded: 1917
Estimated Sales: $20-50 Million
Number Employees: 100-249
Square Footage: 100000
Parent Co: Just Born, Inc.
Type of Packaging: Consumer, Food Service, Bulk
Brands:
  Chew-Ets
  Peanut Chews

5145 Goldilocks USA
30865 San Clemente St
Hayward, CA 94544-7136
510-476-0700
Fax: 510-476-0707 www.goldilocks-usa.com
Bakery products
Owner: Rob Yee
Estimated Sales: $5-10,000,000
Number Employees: 20-49

5146 Golding Farms Foods
6061 Gun Club Rd
Winston Salem, NC 27103-9727
336-766-6161
Fax: 336-766-3131
www.mrscampbellschowchow.net
Condiments and sauces
Owner: Ernest Golding
VP/CFO: Violet Golding
EVP: Ron Foster
Technical Director: Daniel Sortwell
Director Sales: Tom Clayton
information@goldingfarmsfoods.com
Operations Manager: Preston Myers
Production Manager: Lawrence Logan
Estimated Sales: 2.5-5 Million
Number Employees: 50-99
Number of Products: 150
Square Footage: 80000
Type of Packaging: Consumer, Food Service, Private Label, Bulk
Brands:
  Golding
  Golding Farms
  Golding Gourmand
  Mrs. Campbells
  Naturally Healthy
  Old Laredo

5147 Goldstar Brands LLC
2121 Tucker Industrial Rd
Tucker, GA 30084-5017
770-938-9884
Fax: 770-938-8964 888-296-7191
info@hongarfarms.com www.hongarfarms.com
Gourmet seasoned oils and vinegars, marinades, bread dippers and specialty items.
President: Joe Oxman
Estimated Sales: $1-2.5 Million
Number Employees: 10-19
Brands:
  Hongar Farms

5148 Goldthread
932 Stanford St
Santa Monica, CA 90403
413-325-8987
info@goldthreadherbs.com
goldthreadherbs.com
Plant-based tonics
Co-Owner: William Siff
Co-Owner: Edith Siff
Number of Brands: 1
Number of Products: 10
Type of Packaging: Consumer
Brands:
  GOLDTHREAD

5149 Goldwater's Food's Of Arizona
Salsa Express
PO Box 9846
Fredericksburg, TX 78624
Fax: 830-990-9481 866-779-7241
www.goldwaters.com
Fruit salsa and bean dips, barbecue sauces and chili
President: Carolyn Ross
Estimated Sales: $1-2,500,000
Number Employees: 1-4
Type of Packaging: Consumer
Brands:
  Goldwater's
  Goldwater's Taste of the Southwest

5150 Goll's Bakery
234 N Washington St
Havre De Grace, MD 21078-2909
410-939-4321
Fax: 410-939-2556
German style bakery products
Owner: Robert Goll
gollsbakery@aol.com
Owner: Susie Goll
Estimated Sales: Less Than $500,000
Number Employees: 5-9

5151 Gonard Foods
3915 Edmonton Trail NE
Unit 7
Calgary, AB T2E 6T1
Canada
403-277-0991
Fax: 403-277-0664
Meat products
President/Owner: Munir Lakha
Estimated Sales: $975,000
Number Employees: 3

5152 Gonnella Baking Company
1117 E Willey Rt
Schamburg, IL 60173
312-733-2020
Fax: 312-733-7056 800-322-8829
www.gonnella.com
Frozen bread and baked goods
President: Nicholas Marcucci
Vice President: Tom Marcucci
Vice President, Food Safety, Compliance: Dan Herzog
General Manager: Kenneth Gonnella

5153 Good Citizens
Simi Valley, CA 93063
hello@goodcitizens.com
goodcitizens.com
Organic macaroni and cheese
Number of Products: 10

5154 Good Culture
1621 Alton Pkwy
Irvine, CA 92606
Fax: 949-545-9965 844-899-8884
www.goodculture.com
Sour cream and cottage cheeses
Co-Founder: Anders Eisner
Co-Founder & CEO: Jesse Merrill

5155 Good Earth Company
890 Mountain Ave
Suite 105
New Providence, NJ 07974
888-625-8227
sales@goodearthteas.com
Teas
President: Ben Zaricor
National Sales Manager: Randy Duarte
Contact: John Ochoa
johno@goodearth.com
Purchasing Agent: Bill Lambert
Estimated Sales: $7.6 Million
Number Employees: 70
Type of Packaging: Private Label
Brands:
  China Collection Teas
  Energy Supplements
  Functional Teas
  Good Earth Teas
  Herbal Teas

5156 Good Food For Good
100 Amber St
Unit 12
Markham, ON L3R 3J8
Canada
647-449-4922
info@goodfoodforgood.ca
goodfoodforgood.ca
Organic condiments
President: Richa Gupta

5157 Good Food Inc
4960 Horseshoe Pike
P.O. Box 160
Honey Brook, PA 19344-1361
610-273-3776
Fax: 610-273-2087 800-327-4406
info@goldenbarrel.com
www.goldenbarrel.com/goodfoodinc
Molasses, syrups, shoofly pie and funnel cake mixes; vegetable, cotton seed, coconut, peanut, corn, olive, canola and blended cooking oils
President: Larry Martin
lmartin@goldenbarrell.com
CEO: Ean Johnson
Year Founded: 1934
Estimated Sales: $20-50 Million
Number Employees: 100-249
Parent Co: Zook Molasses Company
Brands:
  Mrs Schlorers
  Golden Barrel

5158 Good Food Made Simple
180 Linden St
Wellesley, MA 02482
800-535-3447
www.goodfoodmadesimple.com
Prepared foods, including entr,es, burritos, waffles, oatmeal and wraps
VP, Brand Management & Sales: Russ Williams
Type of Packaging: Consumer
Brands:
  GOOD FOOD MADE SIMPLE

5159 (HQ)Good For You America
110 S Bismark St
Concordia, MO 64020-8110
660-463-2158
Fax: 660-463-2459 866-329-5969
www.foodtabs.com
Emergency and survival food tablets and canned freeze-dried foods; importer of bulk ingredients and freeze-dried foods
Manager: Rachel Goring
Manager: Craig Sallin
craig.sallin@frac.org
Wholesale Director: Juanita Haley
Estimated Sales: Less Than $500,000
Number Employees: 1-4
Square Footage: 10000
Type of Packaging: Consumer, Private Label, Bulk

Food Manufacturers / A-Z

Other Locations:
   Food Reserves-Laboratory
   Kansas City MO
   Food Reserves
   Syracuse NY
Brands:
   Food Reserves
   Storehouse Foods

5160 Good Fortunes & Edible Art
6754 Eton Ave
Canoga Park, CA 91303-2813
818-595-1555
Fax: 818-595-1550 800-644-9474
Chocolate-dipped fortune cookies and pretzels
Owner: Karen Staitman
Brands:
   A Dose of Good Fortunes
   Candy Art
   Cookie Art
   Fractured Fortunes
   Good Fortunes
   Pretzel Twisters
   Pretzel Wands
   Sugar Art

5161 Good Groceries
98 4th Street
Brooklyn, NY 11231
347-853-7462
Fax: 718-768-0932 www.goodgroceries.com
Specialty bread products
President/Owner: Martin Sokoloff
VP: Fred Sokoloff
Marketing: Marty Sokoloff
VP Sales/Marketing/Sales Staff: Lu Arcouet
Contact: Steve Cocco
steve@good-groceries.com
Estimated Sales: $1 Million
Number Employees: 6
Type of Packaging: Consumer
Brands:
   SUZIE'S

5162 Good Harbor Fillet Company
40 Herman Melville Blvd
New Bedford, MA 2740
978-281-6360
Fax: 978-281-4166 800-343-8046
Processed seafood products
President: John Cummings
Chief Financial Officer: Robert Fregault
VP: Bill Stride
Southeast Regional Manager: Dave Galloway
Quality Control Manager: Alan Pothier
VP Sales/Marketing: Annette Chalmers
West Coast Sales Manager: Joel Bortz
Chief Operating Officer: Dave Nelson
Purchasing Manager: Alan Gilbert
Number Employees: 50-99
Type of Packaging: Consumer, Food Service

5163 Good Harbor Vineyards & Winery
34 S Manitou Trail
Lake Leelanau, MI 49653-9589
231-256-7165
Fax: 231-256-7378 winery@goodharbor.com
www.goodharbor.com
Wines
Winemaker/Owner: Bruce Simpson
Associate: Richard Flores
Associate: Rocky Flores
Retail Sales/Owner: Debbie Simpson
debbie@goodharbor.com
Operations: William Schaub
Operations: Gary Schaub
Assistant Winemaker: David Hooper
Growing/Management Workforce: Ovidio Chapa
Estimated Sales: Under $500,000
Number Employees: 5-9
Type of Packaging: Private Label

5164 Good Health Natural Foods
3400 West Wendover Avenue
Suite E
Greensboro, NC 27407
336-285-0735
www.goodhealthnaturalfoods.com
Health snacks
CEO: Mark Gillis
Vice President: Terry Meyer
Contact: Don Heon
don.heon@e-goodhealth.com
Estimated Sales: $2.5-5,000,000
Number Employees: 1-4

5165 Good Humor-Breyers Ice Cream
800 Sylvan Ave.
Englewood Cliffs, NJ 07632
800-931-2854
customer.services@unilever.com
www.breyers.com
Ice cream, gelato and frozen dairy desserts.
Estimated Sales: $11 Billion
Number Employees: 1000-4999
Parent Co: Unilever
Type of Packaging: Consumer, Food Service, Private Label, Bulk
Other Locations:
   Breyer's Manufacturing
   Philadelphia PA
   Breyer's Manufacturing
   Long Island NY
   Breyer's Manufacturing
   Brooklyn NY
Brands:
   Breyers®
   Good Humor®
   Carb Smart®
   Fat Free®
   Pure Fruit®
   Breyers Blasts®
   Klondike®
   Popsicle®

5166 Good Karma Foods
2465 Central Ave
Suite 100
Boulder, CO 80301
800-550-6731
goodkarmafoods.com
Flaxmilk and drinkable yogurts
CEO: Doug Radi
CFO: Matt Riegner
Marketing: Brianna Littlepage
VP, Sales: Edward McDonald
COO: Kevin O'Rell
Type of Packaging: Consumer
Brands:
   GOOD KARMA

5167 Good Lovin' Foods
877-760-6833
www.goodlovinfoods.com
Organic, fresh fruit snack bars
CEO: Ryan Smith
VP: Porter Smith
Number of Brands: 1
Number of Products: 4
Type of Packaging: Consumer
Brands:
   GOOD LOVIN' FOODS

5168 Good Old Dad Food Products
185 Industrial Court B
Sault Ste. Marie, ON P6B 5Z9
Canada
705-949-7337
Fax: 705-949-0871 800-267-7426
www.ricos.ca
Frozen and premade pastas
Owner: Richard Palarchio
Number Employees: 10-19
Square Footage: 22000
Type of Packaging: Consumer, Food Service
Brands:
   Rico's

5169 Good Old Days Foods
3300 S Polk St
P.O. Box 191470
Little Rock, AR 72204-7823
501-565-1257
Fax: 501-562-7439 www.goodolddaysfoods.com
Frozen fruit cobblers, corn bread dressing, bread pudding, sweet potato casserole
President: L C Elder
lc@goodolddaysfood.com
CEO: Carroll Elder
CFO: John Zacharison
VP: Robert Cochran
Sales Director: Doyle Rice
Estimated Sales: $10-20 Million
Number Employees: 50-99
Square Footage: 128340
Type of Packaging: Consumer, Food Service, Private Label

5170 Good PLANeT Foods
1813 115th Ave NE
Bellevue, WA 98004
425-449-8134
info@goodplanetfoods.com
goodplanetfoods.com
Plant-based cheeses
CEO: David Israel
VP, Operations: Spencer Oberg
Brands:
   Good PLANeT Foods

5171 Good Rub
PO Box 1088
Morrisville, NC 27560
919-371-0329
distribution@good-rub.com
www.good-rub.com
Natural seasonings
President: Myriam Batista

5172 Good Spread
311 Mapleton Ave
Suite 373
Boulder, CO 80304
www.helpgoodspread.com
Organic peanut butter
Co-Founder: Alex Cox
Co-Founder: Mark Slagle
CEO: Robbie Vitrano
Brand Manager: Lauren Beno
Community Engagement: Daniel Anderson

5173 Good Stuff Cacao
3562 South Lapeer Rd
Metamora, MI 48455
248-690-5114
info@goodstuffcacao.com
www.goodstuffcacao.com
Cacao
Type of Packaging: Consumer

5174 Good Wives
330 Ballardvale St
Wilmington, MA 01887-1012
781-596-0070
Fax: 781-596-1131 800-521-8160
Frozen hors d'oeuvres, pastries, tortilla wraps, and flatbreads
Owner/CEO: Chris Collias
President: Randell Knopf
CFO: Bruce Robertson
Marketing: Sandra Gamble
Manager: Christian Collias
Plant Manager: John Reardon
Estimated Sales: Under $500,000
Number Employees: 100-249
Square Footage: 20000
Type of Packaging: Consumer, Food Service, Private Label

5175 Good Zebra
512-698-7907
info@goodseedburger.com
goodseedburger.com
Honey-sweetened animal crackers
Founder & CEO: Erika Szychowski
Number of Brands: 1
Number of Products: 3
Type of Packaging: Consumer
Brands:
   GOOD ZEBRA

5176 Good! Snacks
340 S Lemon Ave
Unit 8093N
Walnut, CA 91789
415-762-0600
info@goodsnacks.com
goodsnacks.com
Protein bars

5177 Good-O-Beverages Inc
1801 Boone Ave
Bronx, NY 10460-5101
718-328-6400
Fax: 718-328-7002 info@good-o.com
www.good-o.com
Soft drinks, juices, teas and energy drinks
Owner: George Deyarca
slperry8978@yahoo.com
Plant Manager: Irving Mendelson

Food Manufacturers / A-Z

Estimated Sales: $10-20 Million
Number Employees: 50-99
Square Footage: 159000
Type of Packaging: Consumer
Brands:
   Coco Rico
   Kola Champagne
   Red Pop
   West Indian Kola

5178 GoodBelly Probiotics
PO Box 17460
Boulder, CO 80308
303-443-3631
info@goodbelly.com
goodbelly.com
Probiotic fruit juices and bars
Co-Founder: Steve Demos
Co-Founder: Todd Beckman
Type of Packaging: Consumer
Brands:
   GOODBELLY
   GOODBELLY PLUSSHOT
   GOODBELLY STRAIGHTSHOT

5179 GoodBites Snacks
Venice, CA 90291
friends@goodbitesgroup.com
goodbitessnacks.com
Organic superfood snack bites
Founder: Angelica Xavier
Type of Packaging: Consumer
Brands:
   GoodBites
   GoodBites CBD

5180 GoodMark Foods
7700 France Ave S # 200
Edina, MN 55435-5867
952-835-6900
Fax: 952-469-5550 www.slimjim.com
Fries, meat and other snack foods
Manager: David Dart
VP: Paul Brunswick
Marketing Director: Jeff Slater
Sales Director: Michael Ritchey
Merchandise Support Manager: Amy Carroll
Operations Manager: Al Blalock
Number Employees: 50-99
Parent Co: ConAgra Foods
Type of Packaging: Private Label

5181 GoodPop
500 E 4th Street
Suite 603
Austin, TX 78701
888-840-0188
www.goodpops.com
Natural frozen fruit bars
CEO/Founder: Daniel Goetz
Number Employees: 1-4

5182 Goodart Candy Inc
335 E 40th St
Lubbock, TX 79404-2811
806-747-2600
Fax: 806-747-8330
Peanut patties and peanut brittle
Vice President: Ron Harbuck
goodartcandy@yucca.net
Estimated Sales: $500,000-$1 Million
Number Employees: 10-19
Square Footage: 37500
Type of Packaging: Private Label, Bulk
Brands:
   - Goodart's

5183 Goodheart Brand Specialty Food
11122 Nacogdoches Rd
San Antonio, TX 78217-2314
210-637-1963
Fax: 210-637-1391 888-466-3992
amvillarreal@goodheart.com www.goodheart.com
Specialty meats: quail, venison, bison, wild boar, pheasant and Argentinian all-natural beef
Owner: Amalia Palmaz
apalmaz@goodheart.com
Director Sales: Chef Tim Kennedy
Plant Manager: Demetrio Molales
Estimated Sales: $5-10,000,000
Number Employees: 50-99
Square Footage: 30000
Parent Co: Bluebonnet Company
Type of Packaging: Consumer, Food Service
Brands:
   Goodheart

5184 Goodie Girl
Ridgefield, NJ 07657
www.goodiegirlcookies.com
Gluten- and peanut-free cookies
Owner/Founder: Shira Berk
Branding & Packaging: Michelle Suazo
Product Manager: Lauren Growney

5185 Goodness Knows
goodnessknows.com
Fruit and nut snack squares
Number of Brands: 1
Number of Products: 12
Type of Packaging: Consumer
Brands:
   GOODNESS KNOWS

5186 Goodseed Burgers
512-698-7907
info@goodseedburger.com
goodseedburger.com
Hemp seed veggie burgers
Owner: Oliver Ponce
Owner: Erin Shotwell
Number of Brands: 1
Number of Products: 4
Type of Packaging: Consumer
Brands:
   GOODSEED

5187 Goodson Brothers Coffee
138 Sherlake Ln
Knoxville, TN 37922-2307
865-693-3572
Fax: 865-691-8578 800-737-1519
info@goodsonbros.com
Coffee and tea
President: Jeff Goodson
Sales Executive: Kelly Hall
khall@goodsonbros.com
Estimated Sales: $1.2,000,000
Number Employees: 20-49

5188 Goose Island Beer Co
1800 W Fulton St
Chicago, IL 60612-2512
312-226-1119
Fax: 312-733-1692 800-466-7363
info@gooseisland.com
Beers
COO: Tony Bowker
Director of Operations: Mark Kamarauskas
Vice President of Sale: Bob Kenney
Brew master: Greg Hall
General Manager: Tim Lane
Estimated Sales: $2.5-5,000,000
Number Employees: 50-99
Square Footage: 74000
Type of Packaging: Consumer, Food Service
Brands:
   Hey Nut
   Honkers
   Ipa
   Oatmeal

5189 Goosecross Cellars Inc
1119 State Ln
Yountville, CA 94599-9407
707-944-1986
Fax: 707-944-9551 800-276-9210
webmaster@goosecross.com www.goosecross.com
Wines
President/CEO: David Topper
david@goosecross.com
Vice President/Winemaker: Geoff Gorsuch
Hospitality/Public Relations: Colleen Topper
Business Development/Distribution: Pamela Topper
Estimated Sales: $2.5-5,000,000
Number Employees: 10-19
Type of Packaging: Private Label
Brands:
   Aeros
   Bernard Pradel Cabernet
   Goosecross

5190 Gopal's Healthfoods
800 CR 125
Sidney, TX 76474
866-646-7257
customercare@gopalshealthfoods.com
www.gopalshealthfoods.com
Nut and seed mixes, nut and seed butters, vegan parmesan, nori-wrapped energy sticks, fruit and nut bars, brownies, crackers
Founder: Stefan Knueppel

5191 Gopicnic Inc
4011 N Ravenswood Ave # 101
Suite 12
Chicago, IL 60613-4837
773-328-2490
Fax: 773-345-0734 service@gopicnic.com
Gluten-free, organic, vegetarian meals; cured meats and other snacks.
President: Thomas Falduto
tom.falduto@gopicnic.com
Marketing: Carolyn Wiesemann
Number Employees: 5-9

5192 Gorant Chocolatier
8301 Market St
Youngstown, OH 44512-6257
330-726-8821
Fax: 330-726-0325 www.gorant.com
Chocolate-coated candies
Owner: Joseph Miller
jmiller@gorant.com
Director of Operations: Jack Peluse
Number Employees: 100-249
Type of Packaging: Consumer, Private Label
Other Locations:
   PMG Chocolatier
   Niles OH
   Gorant Candies
   Warren Plaza, Warren OH
   Gorant Candies
   Howland Plaza, Warren OH
Brands:
   Gorant & Yum Yum Chocolates

5193 Gordon Biersch Brewery Restaurant
357 E Taylor St
San Jose, CA 95112-3148
408-278-1008
Fax: 408-294-4052 info@gordonbiersch.com
www.gordonbierschbrewing.com
Beer
Co-Founder/President: Dean Biersch
Co-Founder/Director of Operations: Dan Gordon
dgordon@gordonbiersch.com
CFO: Larry Nally
Sales Director: Mark Blecher
Operations Manager: Eddie Sipple
Estimated Sales: $2.5-5,000,000
Number Employees: 20-49
Square Footage: 114000
Brands:
   Gordon Biersch
   Maibock Hefeweizen
   Winter Block
   Braumeister Select IPB

5194 Gorton's Inc.
128 Rogers St.
Gloucester, MA 01930
800-222-6846
www.gortons.com
Seafood.
CEO: Judson Reis
judson.reis@gortons.com
Director Marketing: Mark Lamothe
Year Founded: 1849
Estimated Sales: $280 Million
Number Employees: 1,000-4,999
Parent Co: Nippon Suisan Kaisha
Type of Packaging: Consumer, Food Service
Other Locations:
   Gorton's Seafood
   Cleveland OH
Brands:
   Gorton's Popcorn Shrimp
   Gorton's Fish Sticks
   Gorton's Beer Battered Fillets
   Gorton's Natural Catch
   Gorton's Grilled Tilapia
   Gorton's Shrimp Bowl
   Gorton's Seafood Appetizers
   Gorton's Parmesean Crusted Cod
   Gorton's Pub Style Cod
   Gorton's Simply Bake Salmon

Food Manufacturers / A-Z

5195 Gossner Foods Inc.
1051 N. 1000 West
Logan, UT 84321-6852
435-227-2500
Fax: 435-227-2550 800-944-0454
www.gossner.com
Cheeses.
President/CEO: Dolores Gossner Wheeler
dolores@gossner.com
Vice President: Greg Rowley
Year Founded: 1966
Estimated Sales: $335 Million
Number Employees: 250-499
Number of Brands: 1
Type of Packaging: Consumer, Food Service, Private Label, Bulk
Brands:
  Gossner Foods

5196 Gotliebs Guacamole
PO Box 1036
Sharon, CT 06069-1036
860-365-0842
Guacamole
President: Richard Gotlieb
VP Marketing: Leslie MacKenzie
Production Manager: Laura Mars
Estimated Sales: $500,000-$1,000,000
Number Employees: 5-9
Brands:
  Gotliebs

5197 Gould's Maple Sugarhouse
570 Mohawk Trail
Shelburne Falls, MA 01370
413-625-6170
www.goulds-sugarhouse.com
Maple syrup; pies
Owner/President: Edgar Gould
Owner/President: Helen Gould
Estimated Sales: $1-2,500,000
Number Employees: 5-9

5198 Gouldsboro Enterprises
14 Factory Rd
Gouldsboro, ME 04607-4222
207-963-2203
Fax: 212-925-1913
Lobster
President/Owner: Leonard Bishko
Vice President: Joseph Boyd
Estimated Sales: $300,000-500,000
Number Employees: 1-4

5199 Gourmantra Foods
95 Silver Rose Crescent
Markham, ON L6C 1W6
Canada
416-225-6711
Fax: 416-225-6711
Spices
CEO: Rachna Prasad
VP R&D: Rekha Prasad
COO: Mona Prasad
Number Employees: 5

5200 Gourmedas Inc
2425 Avenue Watt
Dock 4
Quebec, QC G1P 3X2
Canada
418-210-3703
Fax: 418-948-4083
Chocolate
President/CEO: Christoph Klein
Director of Operations: Giordano Perini

5201 Gourmet Basics
67 35th Street
Suite 3
Brooklyn, NY 11232-2200
718-509-9366
Fax: 866-900-7833 info@gourmetbasics.com
www.gourmetbasics.com
Organic chips and snacks
Contact: Jack Benz
jackbenz@gourmetbasics.com

5202 Gourmet Conveniences Ltd
457 Bantam Road
Litchfield, CT 06759
860-567-3529
Fax: 860-631-1012 866-793-3801
sales@sweetsunshine.com
www.sweetsunshine.com
Sauces
Founder/CEO: Paul Sarris
Number Employees: 4

5203 Gourmet Croissant
320 36th St
Brooklyn, NY 11232-2504
718-499-4911
Fax: 718-499-6394
Fresh and frozen baked goods
Co-Owner: Dino Alatsas
Co-Owner: Teddy Alatsas
Principal: Marie Fabrizio
Estimated Sales: Less than $500,000
Number Employees: 10-19
Square Footage: 16000

5204 Gourmet Foods Inc
2910 E Harcourt St
Compton, CA 90221-5502
310-632-3300
Fax: 310-632-0303
Hors d'oeuvres and banquet items
President: Joann Annunziata
jannunziata@gourmetfoodsinc.com
Estimated Sales: $5-10,000,000
Number Employees: 250-499

5205 Gourmet Ghee
Lynbrook, NY 11563
516-744-0770
contact@gourmetghee.com
www.gourmetghee.com
Original and flavored ghee (clarified butter)
Founder & Owner: Nazia Aibani
Year Founded: 2016
Number Employees: 10-19

5206 Gourmet House
PO Box 90340
Allentown, PA 18109-0340
Fax: 888-708-4882 800-226-9522
www.gourmethouserice.com
Rice
Marketing Manager/Sales Executive: Julie Wraa
Operations/Branch Manager: Steve Wraa
Number Employees: 60
Square Footage: 14432
Parent Co: Riviana Foods
Type of Packaging: Consumer, Private Label

5207 Gourmet Kitchen, Inc.
1238 Corlies Avenue
Neptune, NJ 07753
732-775-5222
Fax: 732-775-5225 800-492-3663
kgrossman@gourmetkitcheninc.com
www.gourmetkitcheninc.com
Hors d'oeuvres
Founder: Ray Walsh
Marketing: Kathleen Grossman

5208 Gourmet Market
5107 Kingston Pike
Knoxville, TN 37919-5152
865-330-0123
Fax: 865-584-5661
Gourmet and specialty foods
CEO: Eric Nelson
Estimated Sales: Less Than $500,000
Number Employees: 5-9
Brands:
  Gourmet Foods Market

5209 Gourmet Mondiale
6865 Route 132
Ste-Catherine, QC J5C 1B6
Canada
450-638-6380
Fax: 450-638-7049
nino.piazza@mostimondiale.com
www.gourmetmondiale.com
Cooking wine, olive oil, balsamic vinegar.
Marketing: Nino Piazza

5210 Gourmet Nut
3611 14th Ave
Suite 654
Brooklyn, NY 11218-3787
347-413-5180
info@gourmetnut.com
www.gourmetnut.com
Nuts, dried fruits, seeds, chocolates and salts
President: Morris Elbaz
morris@gourmetnut.com
Estimated Sales: Less Than $500,000
Number Employees: 1-4

5211 Gourmet Products
PO Box 387
Thomaston, CT 06787-0387
860-283-5147
Fax: 860-283-6912
Sauces, mustards, relishes, salsas
Owner: A Yurgelun
Marketing Director: W Yurgelun
VP Operations: David Yurgelun
Production Manager: T Del Gadio
Purchasing Manager: T Curnell
Number Employees: 10-19
Square Footage: 12000
Type of Packaging: Consumer, Private Label, Bulk
Brands:
  Gourmet Products
  New Classics
  New England

5212 Gourmet Sorbet Corporation
159 W 53rd St
New York, NY
646-243-9868
www.sorbabes.com
Manufacturer of sorbet.
Co-Founder: Nicole Cardone
Co-Founder: Deborah Gorman

5213 Gourmet Treats
1860 W 220th St # 445
Torrance, CA 90501-3679
310-212-6975
Fax: 310-212-0709 800-444-9549
info@gourmettreats.com
www.gourmet-treats.myshopify.com
Gourmet regular and fat-free cakes and cookies
President: Shaffin Jinnah
Estimated Sales: Less than $500,000
Number Employees: 1-4
Square Footage: 6000
Type of Packaging: Consumer, Private Label
Brands:
  Gourmet Lite
  Gourmet Treats

5214 Gourmet du Village
539 Village Road
Morin-Heights, QC J0R 1H0
Canada
800-668-2314
www.gourmetduvillage.com
Gourmet dips, seasonings and confectionary
President: Mike Tott
VP Product Development: Rebecca MacDonald
Marketing Assistant: Linda Zechner
Number Employees: 45

5215 Gourmet's Finest
704 Garden Station Rd
PO Box 160
Avondale, PA 19311
610-268-6910
Fax: 610-268-2298 info@gourmetsfinest.com
Mushrooms
Owner: Richard Pia
Type of Packaging: Food Service, Private Label

5216 Gourmet's Fresh Pasta
950 N Fair Oaks Ave
Pasadena, CA 91103-3009
626-798-0841
Fax: 626-798-3591 mayagjian@aol.com
www.gourmetpasta.com
Refrigerated, frozen and precooked pasta
President/CEO: Michael Yagjian
mayagjian@aol.com
Estimated Sales: $2.5-5 Million
Number Employees: 20-49
Square Footage: 60000
Type of Packaging: Consumer, Food Service, Private Label, Bulk

755

Food Manufacturers / A-Z

Brands:
    California Cuisine
    Gourmet Fresh

5217 Gourmet's Secret
5304 Roseville Rd
Suite F
North Highlands, CA 95660-5049
    916-334-6161
Fax: 916-334-6161 gourmetsec@aol.com
Marinades and sauces; vinegars and oils
Partner: Rita Nelson
Estimated Sales: $100,000
Number Employees: 1-4
Brands:
    Bachelor's Brew
    Java Jelly

5218 Gourm, Mist
16850 Collins Ave
Suite 112190
Sunny Isles Beach, FL 33160
    954-608-6858
Fax: 954-252-2247 866-502-8472
Oil and vinegar misters
President/CoFounder: Paige Simona

5219 Gouvea's & Purity Foods Inc
3049 Ualena St # 415
Honolulu, HI 96819-1946
    808-847-3717
Fax: 808-847-6877 www.regospurity.com
Sausages
President: Scott Stevenson
Vice President: Bill Atherton
Manager: Stanley Griffon
stanley@gouveaspurity.com
Estimated Sales: $4000000
Number Employees: 10-19
Type of Packaging: Consumer, Food Service

5220 Gouw Quality Onions
5801-54 Avenue
Taber, AB T1G 1X4
Canada
    403-223-1440
Fax: 403-223-2036
onions@gouwqualityonions.com
www.gouwqualityonions.com
Onions, radishes and red beets
Chairman: Casey Gouw, Sr.
Sales Manager/Controller: Casey Gouw
Warehouse/Plant Operations: Ken Gouw
Farm Manager: Kyle Gouw
Estimated Sales: D
Number Employees: 20-49
Type of Packaging: Consumer

5221 Govadinas Fitness Foods
2651 Ariane Drive
San Diego, CA 92117-3422
    858-270-0691
Fax: 858-270-0696 800-900-0108
Health food bars and natural snacks
CEO: Larry Gatpandan
Accountant: Alberto Hael
VP: Zenaida Gatpandan
Marketing: Michael Pugliese
Sales: Lisa Gatpandan
Production: Jose Marquez
Purchasing: Nila Morrill
Estimated Sales: $3 Million
Number Employees: 20-49
Number of Products: 25
Square Footage: 10000
Type of Packaging: Private Label
Brands:
    Bliss Bar
    Hemp Bar
    Praline Pack
    Raw Power

5222 Govatos Chocolates
4105 Concord Pike
Talleyville Shopping Center
Wilmington, DE 19803-1401
    302-478-5324
Fax: 302-652-3418 888-799-5252
GVTSCANDY@AOL.COM
www.govatoschocolates.com
Chocolates
Owner: Nicholas Govatos
Estimated Sales: Less Than $500,000
Number Employees: 1-4

Type of Packaging: Consumer

5223 Goya Foods Inc.
350 County Rd.
Jersey City, NJ 07307
    201-348-4900
Fax: 201-348-6609 www.goya.com
Latin American food and condiments.
President/CEO: Bob Unanue
Year Founded: 1936
Estimated Sales: $1.5 Billion
Number Employees: 4,000
Number of Products: 2500
Type of Packaging: Consumer, Food Service
Other Locations:
    Goya Foods of South Jersey
    Pedricktown NJ
    Goya Foods of Great Lakes
    Angola NY
    Goya Foods of Long Island
    Bethpage NY
    Goya Foods of Massachusetts
    Webster MA
    Goya Foods of Miami
    Miami FL
    Goya Foods of Orlando
    Orlando FL
    Goya Foods of Virginia
    Prince George VA
    Goya Foods of Illinois
    Bolingbrook IL
    Goya Foods of Texas
    Brookshire TX
    Goya Foods of California
    City of Industry CA
    Goya Foods of Atlanta
    McDonough GA
    Goya Foods of Puerto Rico
    Bayamon PR
    Goya Foods of the Dom. Rep.
    San Cristobal, Dom. Rep.
Brands:
    Goya®

5224 Grabill Country Meats
13211 West St
P.O. Box 190
Grabill, IN 46741-2031
    260-627-3691
Fax: 219-627-2106 866-333-6328
info@grabillmeats.com www.grabillmeats.com
Canned beef, pork, chicken, and turkey products
President: Pat Fonner
Secretary/Treasurer: Dennis Fonner
Estimated Sales: $5-10 Million
Number Employees: 10-19
Type of Packaging: Consumer

5225 Grace & I
Los Angeles, CA
    800-584-1736
delight@graceandi.com
www.graceandi.com
Preserves, fruit and nut presses, granola, and roasted nuts
President: Mina Kolahi

5226 Grace Baking Company
3200 Regatta Blvd
Suite G
Richmond, CA 94804
    510-231-7200
Fax: 510-231-7210 www.gracebaking.com
Baked goods
Founder/Co-Owner: Glenn Mitchell
Co-Owner: Cindy Mitchell
Public Relations and Marketing: Fred Doar
Contact: Tom Deadmore
tdeadmore@goprime.com
Plant Manager: Mike Cassie
Parent Co: Maple Leaf Foods Inc
Type of Packaging: Food Service

5227 Grace Foods International
39-36 32nd Street
Suite 1
Astoria, NY 11106
    718-433-4789
Fax: 718-433-0384 www.gracefoods.com
Beverages, canned meats and fish, chips, coconut products, jams and jellies, ready mixes, rice combos, sauces and condiments, spices and seasoning, teas and veggie meals

5228 Grace Tea Co
14 Craig Rd
Acton, MA 01720-5405
    978-635-9500
Fax: 978-635-9701
customerservice@gracetea.com
www.gracetea.com
Teas
Owner: Hartley Johnson
hejohnson1@gracetea.com
VP: Richard Verdery
Operations Director: Richard Sanders
Estimated Sales: $48,000
Number Employees: 5-9
Number of Brands: 1
Number of Products: 20
Square Footage: 4000
Brands:
    China Yunnan Silver Tip Choice
    Connoisseur Master Blend
    Darjeeling Superb 6000
    Demitasse After Dinner Tea
    Earl Grey Superior Mixture
    Flowery Jasmine-Before the Rain
    Formosa Oolong Champagne of Tea
    Gun Powder Pearl Pinhead Green Tea
    Lapsang Souchong Smoky #1 Blend
    Mountain-Grown Fancy Ceylon
    Owner's Blend Premium Congou
    Pure Assam Irish Breakfast
    Russian Caravan Original China
    Winey Keemun English Breakfast

5229 Graceland Fruit Inc
1123 Main St
Frankfort, MI 49635-9341
    231-352-7181
Fax: 231-352-4881 800-352-7181
info@gracelandfruit.com www.gracelandfruit.com
Infused dried fruits and vegetables
President & CEO: Alan DeVore
CFO: Troy Terwilliger
VP Research Development: Nirmal Sinha PhD
VP Sales/Marketing: Brent Bradley
VP Human Resources: Doug Rath
COO: Dan Engler
Manager/Grower/Processor Relations: Ben Evans
Year Founded: 1976
Estimated Sales: $40 Million
Number Employees: 100-249
Number of Brands: 1
Number of Products: 50
Type of Packaging: Food Service, Private Label, Bulk
Brands:
    Graceland Fruit

5230 Gracious Gourmet
PO Box 218
Bridgewater, CT 06752
    860-350-1213
Fax: 860-350-1214 info@thegraciousgourmet.com
www.thegraciousgourmet.com
Chutneys, glazes, pestos, spreads and tapenades
President: Nancy Wekselbaum
Marketing: Natalie Nablitt
Sales: Deborah Sherman
deborahs@thegraciousgourmet.com
Number Employees: 4

5231 Grady's Cold Brew
819 Garrison Ave
Bronx, NY 10474
    718-860-1600
info@gradyscoldbrew.com
gradyscoldbrew.com
Iced coffee beans, grounds and concentrates
Co-Founder: Kyle Buckley
Co-Founder: Dave Sands
Year Founded: 2011
Number Employees: 8
Square Footage: 15000
Type of Packaging: Food Service, Private Label

5232 Graeter's Mfg. Co.
1175 Regina Graeter Way
Cincinnati, OH 45216
    800-721-3323
www.graeters.com
Ice cream, gelato, sorbet, dessert sauces and confectionary

Food Manufacturers / A-Z

President and CEO: Richard Graeter
Chief of Retail Operations: Chip Graeter
Chief of Quality Assurance: Robert Graeter
VP of Sales and Marketing: George Denman
Contact: Frank Benkalowycz
frank.benkalowycz@key.com

5233 Graf Creamery Co
N4051 Creamery Rd
Bonduel, WI 54107-8441
715-758-2137
Fax: 715-758-8020 www.grafcreamery.com
Butter and condensed and powdered buttermilk
President/CEO: James Bleick
Manager: Jim Bleick
jimb@grafcreamery.com
Plant Manager: Dale Hodmiewicz
Purchasing Director: Jay Winter
Estimated Sales: $10-24.9 Million
Number Employees: 20-49
Square Footage: 168000
Type of Packaging: Private Label, Bulk
Brands:
  Cloverdale
  Gold Medal
  Golden Glow

5234 Graffam Brothers
211 Union St
Rockport, ME 04856-6107
207-236-3396
Fax: 207-236-2569 800-535-5358
sales@lobstertogo.com www.lobstertogo.com
Lobsters and clams
Owner: Janice Graffam
sales@lobstertogo.com
Number Employees: 10-19

5235 Graft Cider
218 Ann St.
Newburgh, NY 12550
410-967-1926
www.graftcidery.com
Hard flavored ciders
Co-Owner: Kyle Sherrer
Co-Owner: Sae Kenney
Number of Brands: 1
Number of Products: 38
Type of Packaging: Consumer, Private Label
Brands:
  Graft Cider

5236 Grafton Village Cheese Co LLC
400 Linden St
Brattleboro, VT 05301-4474
802-246-2221
Fax: 802-843-2210 800-472-3866
info@graftonvillagecheese.com
www.graftonvillagecheese.com
Specialty cheeses
President: Bob Allen
ed@graftonvillagecheese.com
CFO: Bob Donald
Communications/Marketing: Melissa Gullotti
Sales Exec: Ed Reeves
Master Cheesemaker: Dane Huebner
Production Manager: Ellyn Ladd
Facilities Manager: Greg Kathan
Estimated Sales: $10 Million
Number Employees: 50-99
Parent Co: Windham Foundation
Type of Packaging: Consumer, Food Service, Private Label, Bulk
Brands:
  Classic Reserve
  Classic Reserve Ext Sharp Cheddar
  Grafton Gold
  Grafton Gold-Ext Aged Cheddar

5237 Graham & Rollins Inc
19 Rudd Ln
Hampton, VA 23669-4029
757-723-3831
Fax: 757-722-3762 800-272-2728
johnny@grahamandrollins.com
www.grahamandrollins.com
Crab
President: John Graham
VP: Johnny Graham
Manager: Terri Wallace
twallace@grahamandrollins.com
Estimated Sales: $1-2,500,000
Number Employees: 100-249

5238 Graham Cheese Corporation
502 State Road 57 E
Elnora, IN 47529
812-692-5237
Fax: 812-692-5650 800-472-9178
www.grahamcheese.com
Cheese
Plant Manager: Jerry Sims
Estimated Sales: $2,000,000
Number Employees: 20
Type of Packaging: Consumer, Food Service, Private Label, Bulk

5239 Graham Chemical Corporation
1250 S Grove Avenue
Suite 206
Barrington, IL 60010
847-304-4400
Fax: 847-304-8752 www.grahamchemical.com
Specialty chemical intermediates, surfactants, and performance additives.
Owner/Human Resources Executive: Brad Graham
Sales/Marketing Manager: Terri Kent
Estimated Sales: $1 Million
Number Employees: 6
Square Footage: 2000

5240 Graham Fisheries
13890 Shell Belt Rd
Bayou La Batre, AL 36509-2304
251-824-7370
Fax: 251-824-7370 shrimp1951@aol.com
Seafood, shrimp
Owner: Darrell Graham
Estimated Sales: $.5-1 million
Number Employees: 1-4

5241 Grain Belt
1860 Schell Rd
New Ulm, MN 56073-0128
507-354-5528
Fax: 507-359-9119 800-770-5020
schells@schellsbrewery.com grainbelt.com
Craft beer.
Quality Control Manager: Tom Kaehler
Director of Operations: John Stensland
Year Founded: 1890
Estimated Sales: $20-50 Million
Type of Packaging: Consumer, Food Service, Private Label

5242 Grain Craft
201 West Main Street
Suite 203
Chattanooga, TN 37408
423-265-2313
sales@graincraft.com
www.graincraft.com
Flour and grain
President/CEO: Charles Stout
Vice President: Robert Grizzard
Contact: Vicky Heineman
vheineman@graincraft.com
Estimated Sales: $10-19 Million
Number Employees: 20-49

5243 Grain Millers Inc
10400 Viking Dr
Suite 301
Eden Prairie, MN 55344-7268
952-829-8821
Fax: 952-829-8819 800-232-6287
info@grainmillers.com www.grainmillers.com
Specialty grain products
President: Steven Eilertson
steven.eilertson@grainmillers.com
SVP: Rick Schwein
Sales/Marketing Manager: Kris Nelson
Estimated Sales: $20-50 Million
Number Employees: 20-49
Type of Packaging: Food Service, Private Label, Bulk
Brands:
  Grain Millers

5244 Grain Place Foods Inc
1904 N Highway 14
Marquette, NE 68854-2516
402-854-3195
Fax: 402-854-2566 888-714-7246
www.grainplacefoods.com
Grains, cereals
President: David Vetter
dvetter@grainplacefoods.com
Estimated Sales: $1-2,500,000
Number Employees: 20-49
Type of Packaging: Consumer, Private Label, Bulk
Brands:
  Grain Place

5245 Grain Process Enterprises Ltd.
115 Commander Blvd
Scarborough, ON M1S 3M7
Canada
416-291-3226
Fax: 416-291-2159 800-387-5292
gbjr@grainprocess.com
Flours, granola cereals, grain, bread and muffin mixes
President: George Birinyi
Number Employees: 10
Square Footage: 225000
Type of Packaging: Consumer, Private Label, Bulk
Brands:
  Brimley Stone
  Grain-Pro
  Happy Home
  Millbrook

5246 Grain Processing Corp
1600 Oregon St
Muscatine, IA 52761-1404
563-264-4265
Fax: 563-264-4289 800-448-4472
sales@grainprocessing.com
Corn-based products
CEO: Gage Kent
Vice President: David Abbott
d_abbott@grainprocessing.com
R&D: Frank Barresi
Quality Control: Rani Thomas
Marketing/Public Relations: Diane Rieke
Technical Sales: Charles Lambert
Operations: Ron Zitzow
Purchasing: Brian Hasser
Number Employees: 10-19
Square Footage: 300000
Parent Co: Kent Corporation
Brands:
  Incosity
  Instant Pure-Cote
  Maltrin
  Maltrin Qd
  Pure-Bind
  Pure-Cote
  Pure-Dent
  Pure-Gel

5247 Grain-Free JK Gourmet, Inc.
635 Petrolia Rd.
Toronto, ON M3J 2X8
Canada
416-782-0045
Fax: 416-785-0686 800-608-0465
info@jkgourmet.com www.jkgourmet.com
Gluten-free products
President/Owner: Jodi Bager
Vice President: Steven Bager
Number Employees: 5

5248 Grainaissance
1580 62nd St
Emeryville, CA 94608
510-922-8856
Fax: 510-547-0526 800-472-4697
Rice-based products
President: Tony Plotkin
amazake@grainaissance.com
Estimated Sales: $1.4 Million
Number Employees: 11
Type of Packaging: Consumer
Brands:
  Amazake
  Grainaissance
  Mochi

5249 Grainful
950 Danby Rd
Suite 180
Ithaca, NY 14850
info@grainful.com
www.grainful.com
Whole-grain based frozen entrées
President/Owner: Jan Pajerski
Number of Brands: 1
Number of Products: 8
Type of Packaging: Consumer

Food Manufacturers / A-Z

Brands:
  GRAINFUL

5250 Grains of Health LLC
34303 Bodkin Ter
Fremont, CA 94555-2625
510-516-2556
www.laikicrackers.com
Black and red rice crackers
Contact: Pradeep Akkunoor
Number of Brands: 1
Number of Products: 2
Type of Packaging: Consumer

5251 Graminex
95 Midland Rd
Saginaw, MI 48638-5770
989-797-5502
Fax: 989-799-0020 877-472-6469
www.graminex.com
Flower pollen extract and fabales
President: Cynthia May
CEO: Cindy May
graminex@graminex.com
Vice President: Parampal Singh
Estimated Sales: $3-5 Million
Number Employees: 1-4

5252 Grand Central Bakery
4440 NE Fremont
Portland, OR 97213
508-808-9877
Fax: 503-808-9851
gcb.info@grandcentralbakery.com
grandcentralbakery.com
Baked goods

5253 Grand Metropolitan
8710 Central Ave NE # 100
Minneapolis, MN 55434-3305
763-792-3836
Fax: 763-792-3839
Breads
Manager: Deryl R Glaze
VP: Marlene Johnson
Estimated Sales: Less than $500,000
Number Employees: 5-9
Parent Co: Diageo United Distillers and Vinters

5254 Grand River Cellars
5750 S Madison Rd
Madison, OH 44057-9001
440-298-9838
Fax: 440-298-1861 www.grandrivercellars.com
Wines
Manager: Cindy Lindberg
grcinfo@grandrivercellars.com
Vice-President: William Worthy
Estimated Sales: $2.5-5,000,000
Number Employees: 20-49

5255 Grand Teton Brewing Co
430 Old Jackson Hwy
Victor, ID 83455-5500
208-538-0068
Fax: 208-787-4114 888-899-1656
beermail@GrandTetonBrewing.com
www.grandtetonbrewing.com
Beer
President/CEO: Charlie Otto
VP: Ernie Otto
Estimated Sales: $5-10,000,000
Number Employees: 10-19
Type of Packaging: Consumer, Food Service
Brands:
  Grand Teton Brewing
  Teton

5256 Grand View Winery
PO Box 91
East Calais, VT 05667
802-456-7012
Fax: 802-456-7012
Wines
Winemaker/Owner: Phil Tonks
Estimated Sales: $3-5 Million
Number Employees: 5-9

5257 Grandcestors
Golden, CO 80403
grandcestors.com
Frozen paleo diet-friendly prepared meals
Number of Products: 7

5258 Grande Cheese Company
250 Camelot Dr
Fond du Lac, WI 54935
800-678-3122
www.grandecheese.com
Cheese
President: Wayne Matzke
VP Marketing/Sales: Elio Camilotto
filippo.candela@grande.com
Contact: Filippo Candela
filippo.candela@grande.com
Type of Packaging: Consumer, Food Service

5259 Grande Custom Ingredients Group
250 Camelot Dr
Fond du Lac, WI 54935
920-952-7200
Fax: 920-922-2921 800-772-3210
gcig@grande.com www.grandecig.com
Processor and exporter of specialty whey products and lactose.
Group Vice President: Paul Graham
Research & Development: Rory McCarthy
Sales & Marketing: Brad Nielsen
Operations: Lary Turner
Purchasing Director: Chris Richards
Square Footage: 10000
Parent Co: Grande Cheese Company
Type of Packaging: Bulk
Brands:
  Grande Bravo Whey Protein
  Grande Gusto Natural Flavor
  Grande Ultra Nutritional Whey Prot.

5260 Grande River Vineyards
787 Elberta Ave
Palisade, CO 81526-8805
970-464-5867
Fax: 970-464-5427 800-264-7696
info@www.granderiverwines.com
www.granderivervineyards.com
Wines
Founder/Owner/Winemaker: Stephen Smith
bookkeeping@granderiverswines.com
Vineyard Manager: Jim Mayrose
Manager: Javanne Pergola
Estimated Sales: $660,000
Number Employees: 10-19
Type of Packaging: Private Label
Brands:
  Grande River Vineyards
  Grande River Vineyards Everyday
  Grande River Vineyards Meritage

5261 Grande Tortilla Factory
914 N Grande Ave
Tucson, AZ 85745-2404
520-622-8338
Flour and corn tortillas, and tamales
President: Frank Pesqueira Jr
Estimated Sales: $200,000
Number Employees: 5-9
Type of Packaging: Consumer

5262 Grandma Beth's Cookies
1221 Toluca Avenue
Alliance, NE 69301-2447
308-762-8433
Fax: 308-762-6165
Cookies
Owner: Beth Fetcher
Estimated Sales: $500,000-$1,000,000
Number Employees: 1-4
Type of Packaging: Private Label

5263 Grandma Browns Beans Inc
Scenic Ave
Mexico, NY 13114
315-963-7221
Fax: 315-963-4072
grandmabrownsbeans@verizon.net
Beans
President/CFO: Sandra Brown
Estimated Sales: $2.5-3 Million
Number Employees: 10-19
Number of Products: 4
Square Footage: 144000
Type of Packaging: Consumer, Food Service
Brands:
  Grandma Brown's

5264 Grandma Emily
Montreal, QC H4V 2V9
Canada
514-343-3661
877-943-3661
service@grandmaemily.com
www.grandmaemily.com
Granola bars and cereals
President/Owner: Corey Eisenberg
General Manager: Mina Hanna
Controller: Tina D'Onofrio
Sales and Business Development: Awa Diarra
Type of Packaging: Food Service, Bulk

5265 Grandma Hoerner's Inc
31862 Thompson Rd
Alma, KS 66401-9091
785-765-2300
Fax: 785-765-2303 hoerner@kansas.net
www.grandmahoerners.com
Organic reduced sugar preserves, pie fillings, fruit butters, hamburger relish and red pepper jelly
Owner: Duane Mc Coy
dmccoy@grandmahoerners.com
VP: Regina McCoy
Estimated Sales: $7.9 Million
Number Employees: 20-49

5266 Grandma Pat's Products
PO Box 158
Albin, WY 82050-0158
307-631-0801
Fax: 307-673-5765
Soup, chili-bean mixes and popcorn
Co-Owner: Pat Palm
Co-Owner: Chuck Palm

5267 Grandpa Ittel's Meats Inc
704 6th St
Howard Lake, MN 55349-5645
320-543-2285
Fax: 320-543-2285
Beef jerky and summer sausage
Owner: Jim Ittel
Estimated Sales: Less Than $500,000
Number Employees: 1-4
Type of Packaging: Consumer, Food Service, Private Label, Bulk

5268 Grandpa Po's Nutra Nuts
4528 E Washington Blvd
Commerce, CA 90040
323-260-7457
Fax: 888-812-4234 gocorny@nutranuts.com
www.nutranuts.com
Popcorn and soybean snacks
President: Mark Porro
CFO: Michael Porro
Estimated Sales: $200,000
Number Employees: 5
Square Footage: 3300

5269 Grandpops Lollipops
2600 Burlington St # A
Kansas City, MO 64116-3019
816-421-5282
Fax: 816-421-5599 800-255-7873
Lollipops and candy
President: Josh Sitzer
Estimated Sales: Under $500,000
Number Employees: 5-9
Brands:
  Grandpops Lollipops

5270 Grandview Farms
417353 10th Line RR 1
Thornbury, ON N0H 2P0
Canada
519-599-6368
Fax: 519-599-6971 www.grandviewfarms.ca
Meat
President: Desmond Von Teichman
Plant Manager: Bob Hutchinson
Estimated Sales: $100-350,000k
Number Employees: 25
Square Footage: 30000
Type of Packaging: Food Service, Private Label
Brands:
  Grandview Farms

Food Manufacturers / A-Z

5271 GrandyOats
34 Schoolhouse Rd
Hiram, ME 04041
207-935-7415
Fax: 207-935-7416 info@grandyoats.com
www.grandyoats.com
Organic granola, muesli, trail mix, roasted nuts and hot cereals
Co-Owner: Nat Peirce
Co-Owner: Aaron Anker
Year Founded: 1979
Number of Brands: 1
Number of Products: 1
Type of Packaging: Consumer
Brands:
  GRANDYOATS

5272 Granello Bakery
5045 W Mardon Ave
Las Vegas, NV 89139-5521
702-361-0311
Fax: 702-361-0415 orders@granellobakery.com
www.granellobakery.com
Specialty baked goods such as breads, pastry, cake, tarts, cookies and bar cookies.
Owner: Laurie Steed
laurie@granellobakery.com
Year Founded: 1966
Estimated Sales: $20-50 Million
Number Employees: 50-99
Square Footage: 42000

5273 Granite Springs Winery
2860 Omo Ranch Rd
Somerset, CA 95684
530-620-6395
Fax: 530-620-4884 800-638-6041
latcham@directcon.net www.latcham.com
Wines
President: Jon Latcham
Winemaker: Craig Boyd
Estimated Sales: $1-2,500,000
Number Employees: 5-9

5274 Granny Blossom Specialty Foods
Route 30
Wells, VT 05774
802-645-0507
Fax: 802-645-0860
Specialty condiments
Owner: Bob Kopp
Owner: Doris Kopp

5275 Granny Roddy's LLC
4226 Holborn Avenue
Annandale, VA 22003
703-503-3431
Baking mixes
Marketing: Joanne Buto
Type of Packaging: Private Label

5276 Granny's Best Strawberry Products
PO Box 9
Victoria, ON N0E 1W0
Canada
519-426-0705
Fax: 519-426-2573 519-426-0705
Frozen strawberry puree
President: Gary Cooper
Type of Packaging: Private Label

5277 Granowska's
175 Roncesvalles Avenue
Toronto, ON M6R 2L3
Canada
416-533-7755
Fax: 416-533-3261
Baked goods
President: Elizabeth Klodas
Estimated Sales: $813,000
Number Employees: 15
Square Footage: 14000
Brands:
  Granowska's

5278 Grant Park Packing
842 W Lake St
Chicago, IL 60607-1720
312-421-4096
Fax: 312-421-1484 sales@grantparkpacking.com
www.grantparkpacking.com
Pork, beef, poultry, sausage and Italian sausage
Owner: Joseph Maffei
joe@grantparkpacking.com
General Manager/Partner: Vince Maffei
Estimated Sales: $10 Million
Number Employees: 20-49
Square Footage: 35000
Type of Packaging: Consumer

5279 Granville Gates & Sons
60 Fish Plant Rd
Hubbards, NS B0J 1T0
Canada
902-228-2559
Fax: 902-228-2368
Dried and salted seafood
Manager: Garry Harnish
Office Manager: Norma Young
Plant Manager: Ed Grant
Estimated Sales: 5,000,000-9,999,999
Number Employees: 32
Type of Packaging: Bulk

5280 Grapevine Trading Company
738 Wilson St
Santa Rosa, CA 95401
707-576-3950
Fax: 800-469-6808 800-469-6478
Mustards, fruit and balsamic vinegars, olive oils, tapenades, wild mushrooms, chili peppers, pine nuts, dried tomatoes, polenta mixes, vanilla extract
President: Sandra Voorhis
sandra.vanvoorhis@hotmail.com
Estimated Sales: $1,3,000,000
Number Employees: 10
Brands:
  California Harvest
  Gourmet Fare
  Grapevine Trading Co.
  Wine Gift Packaging

5281 Grass Run Farms
Greeley, CO 80634
800-727-2333
grassrunfarms.com
Grass-fed beef

5282 Grassland Dairy Products Inc
N8790 Fairground Ave
Greenwood, WI 54437-7668
715-267-6182
Fax: 715-267-6044 800-428-8837
email@grassland.com www.grassland.com
Butter products
President: Dallas Wuethrich
CFO: Leony Gregorich
Estimated Sales: $38.8 Million
Number Employees: 250-499
Square Footage: 60000
Type of Packaging: Consumer, Food Service, Private Label, Bulk
Brands:
  Grassland
  Wuthrich
  Country Cream
  Fall Creek
  Golden Goodness

5283 Grasso Foods Inc
2111 Kings Hwy
Swedesboro, NJ 08085-3216
856-467-2222
Fax: 856-467-5474 info@grassofoods.com
Peppers
President: Janet Schumann
janet.schumann@grassofoods.com
Number Employees: 5-9
Type of Packaging: Consumer, Food Service, Private Label, Bulk

5284 Gratify Gluten Free
Englewood Cliffs, NJ
Fax: 201-871-8726 800-200-6736
www.gratifyfoods.com
Gluten-free foods
Parent Co: Osem USA, Inc.

5285 Graves Mountain Lodge Inc.
Route 670
Syria, VA 22743-9999
540-923-4231
Fax: 540-923-4312 info@gravesmountain.com
www.gravesmountain.com
Pepper and cucumber relish, fruit preserves, jellies, chutney, apple butter and apple sauce
President: James Graves
Plant Manager: Gail Ford
Estimated Sales: $300,000- $500,000
Number Employees: 6
Number of Brands: 1
Square Footage: 20000
Parent Co: Graves Mountain Lodge
Type of Packaging: Consumer, Private Label
Brands:
  Colonial Williamsburg
  Graves Mountain

5286 Gravity Ciders, Inc.
8 Winkler Rd.
Sydney, NY 13838
www.awestruckciders.com
Homemade hard flavored ciders
Co-Founder: Casey Vitti
Co-Founder: Patti Wilcox
Year Founded: 2014
Number of Brands: 1
Number of Products: 5
Type of Packaging: Private Label
Brands:
  Awestruck Ciders

5287 Gravymaster, Inc.
101 Erie Blvd
Canajoharie, NY 13317
800-526-6872
Fax: 888-673-2451 800-839-8938
info@richardsonbrands.com www.gravy.com
Sauces
President: Stephen Besse
Sales Executive: Cathy Testa
Consultant: John Mills
Sales Coordinator: MaryLou Sweet
Promotional Products Representative: Laurie Bluitt
Supply Chain Manager: Rebecca Woodruff
Estimated Sales: $10-20 Million
Number Employees: 20-49
Parent Co: Richardson Brands
Type of Packaging: Consumer, Food Service
Brands:
  Gravy Master
  Gravymaster

5288 Gray & Company
3325 W Polk Rd
Hart, MI 49420-8149
231-873-5628
Fax: 231-873-0348 800-551-6009
sales@cherryman.com www.grayandcompany.us
Maraschino cherries, glace fruit and chocolate cherry cordials
Director of Finance: Kevin Schulz
Executive Vice President: Joshua Reynolds
Food Scientist: Jillian Clark
Sales: Rich Bertellotti
Director of Cherry Operations: Dirk Williams
Plant Engineer: Benjamin Kirwin
Purchasing Manager: Steve Schauer
Estimated Sales: $28.2 Million
Number Employees: 250-499
Square Footage: 5000
Type of Packaging: Consumer, Food Service, Private Label, Bulk
Other Locations:
  Hart MI
  Dayton OR
Brands:
  Cherryman
  Pennant
  Queen Anne
  Towie
  White Swan

5289 Gray Duck
Minneapolis, MN 55417
www.grayduckchai.com
Organic chai
Co-Founder: Katey Niebur
Co-Founder: Jon Alden

5290 Gray's Brewing Co
2424 W Court St
Janesville, WI 53548-3307
608-752-3552
Fax: 608-752-0821 office@graybrewing.com
www.graybrewing.com
Beer
Owner: Marina Bowser
Sales: Robert Gray
marina@graybrewing.com

Food Manufacturers / A-Z

Estimated Sales: Under $500,000
Number Employees: 10-19
Type of Packaging: Consumer, Food Service

5291 Grays Ice Cream
16 East Rd
Tiverton, RI 02878-3599
401-624-4500
Fax: 401-624-4500 graysicecream@gmail.com
www.graysicecream.com
Homemade ice cream, frozen desserts
President: Marilyn Dennis
mdennis@graysicecream.com
Estimated Sales: $580,000-1,000,000
Number Employees: 20-49

5292 Graysmarsh Berry Farm
6187 Woodcock Rd
Sequim, WA 98382-8144
360-683-5563
Fax: 360-683-6509   800-683-4367
www.graysmarsh.com
Fruit preserves and lavender products; U-pick berries
General Manager: Arturo Flores
Estimated Sales: $20-50 Million
Number Employees: 20-49
Type of Packaging: Consumer, Food Service, Bulk

5293 Grayson Naturla Farms
5630 Wilson Hwy
Independence, VA 24348
276-773-3712
graysonnatural.com
Meat products; health bars and other snacks
Owner: Gary Mitchell
Director of Marketing: Chris Anderson
Manager of Operations: Jenna Heise
Year Founded: 2007
Estimated Sales: $1 Million
Number Employees: 1-10

5294 Great American Appetizers
216 8th St N
Nampa, ID 83687-3029
208-465-5111
Fax: 208-465-5059   800-282-4834
marco@appetizer.com   www.appetizer.com
Appetizers
President: Tammy Mika
tammy.mika@westin.com
Marketing/Sales Coordinator: Debbie Lindley
VP Retail Sales: Frank Benso
COO: Marco Meyer
Purchasing Director: Tammy Mika
Year Founded: 1959
Estimated Sales: $26.6 Million
Number Employees: 250-499
Number of Products: 100
Square Footage: 60000
Parent Co: Westin Foods
Type of Packaging: Consumer, Food Service, Private Label, Bulk
Brands:
 Big Red
 Brew House
 Questias
 Wahoo! Appetizers

5295 Great American Barbecue Company
52 Gedney Way
White Plains, NY 10605
914-686-2277
Fax: 203-661-6162
www.thegreatamericanbbq.com
Frozen and refrigerated beef and chichken
Owner: Dave Mann
Owner: Dan Ferreira
VP Sales: Troy Gall
Contact: Kaye Jackson
kaye@nyhospitalitygroup.com
Brands:
 Great American Barbecue

5296 Great American Cookie Company
1346 Oakbrook Drive
Suite 170
Norcross, GA 30093
877-639-2361
Fax: 404-505-2835
customerservice@gfgmanagement.com
www.greatamericancookies.com
Refrigerated and frozen cookie dough
Manager: Mike Curtis
VP: T Lynch
VP: James Squire
Operations Manager: Danny Breault
Production Manager: Michael Curtis
Number Employees: 1,000-4,999
Parent Co: Mrs. Fields' Original Cookies

5297 (HQ)Great American Dessert Co
5842 Maurice Ave
Flushing, NY 11378-2333
718-894-3494
Fax: 718-894-6105   800-458-6467
info@juniorscheesecake.com
www.juniorscheesecake.com
Gourmet desserts
President: Michael Goodman
michaelgoodman@mycheesecake.com
Public Relations: Theresa Kramer
Purchasing: Grace Pavlak
Estimated Sales: $1-5,000,000
Number Employees: 50-99
Type of Packaging: Private Label
Brands:
 Granny Cheesecakes
 Rode Lee

5298 Great American Foods Commissary
3864 FM 161 North
Hughes Springs, TX 75656
903-639-1482
Fax: 903-968-4376 office@davidbeards.com
www.davidbeards.com
Catfish, tomato relish, hot sauce and hushpuppies
President/CEO: David Beard
Purchasing: Terry Simpler
Estimated Sales: $20-50 Million
Number Employees: 20-49
Brands:
 David Beards
 David Beards Texas Style

5299 Great American Popcorn Works of Pennsylvania
PO Box 214
Telford, PA 18969-0214
215-721-0414
Fax: 215-721-6082   855-542-2676
www.popcornworks.com
Gourmet popcorn
Manager: Alice Barnes
Vice President: Jack Egner
Sales Director: Rob Rosen
Public Relations: Giselle Wetzel
Estimated Sales: Less than $500,000
Number Employees: 1-4
Number of Products: 65
Square Footage: 12000
Type of Packaging: Consumer, Food Service, Private Label, Bulk

5300 Great American Seafood Company
1711 W Kirby Ave
Champaigne, IL 61821-55
217-352-0986
www.greatamericanseafood.com
Seafood
Estimated Sales: $300,000-500,000
Number Employees: 5-9

5301 Great American Smokehouse & Seafood Company
15657 Highway 101 S
Brookings, OR 97415-9556
541-469-6903
Fax: 541-469-9692   800-828-3474
Seafood
Owner: Lee D Myers Sr
Co-Owner: Nancy Myers
Co-Owner: Lee Myers
Estimated Sales: $500,000-$1,000,000
Number Employees: 10-19

5302 Great Atlantic Trading Company
1204 Longstreet Circle
Brentwood, TN 37027-6506
615-661-6678
Fax: 910-575-7978   888-268-8780
www.caviarstar.com
Fresh and frozen seafood, American and imported caviar
President: Dana Leavitt
Estimated Sales: $3.2 Million
Number Employees: 1-4
Square Footage: 5000
Parent Co: Great Atlantic Trading Company

5303 Great Circles
5 Canal Street
PO Box 495
Bellows Falls, VT 05101
802-463-2111
Fax: 802-463-2110   877-877-2120
gcircles@sover.net   http://www.sover.net
Health foods
President: Dwane Kurisu
CEO: Rich Kendall
Estimated Sales: $2.5-5,000,000
Number Employees: 1-4

5304 Great Divide Brewing Co
2201 Arapahoe St
Denver, CO 80205-2512
303-296-9460
Fax: 303-296-9464 info@greatdivide.com
Beer and ale
President/Brew master: Brian Dunn
Vice President: Tara Dunn
Vice President Operations: Mason Thomas
Estimated Sales: $5-10 Million
Number Employees: 1-4
Brands:
 Arapahoe
 Bee Sting
 Denver
 Hibernation
 Saint Brigid's
 Wit
 Whitewater
 Wild Raspberry

5305 Great Earth Chemical
7007 SW Cardinal Ln # 135
Suite 135
Portland, OR 97224-7248
503-620-7130
Fax: 503-670-1737 sales@nawpi.com
www.greatearthchemical.com
Food additives, nutritional supplements, vitamins and preservatives
Owner: Ruth Yein
ruth@greatearthchemical.com
Director of Sales: Daniel Kruszka
Number Employees: 20-49
Parent Co: North American World Trade Group

5306 Great Eastern Sun Trading Co
92 Mcintosh Rd
Asheville, NC 28806-1406
828-665-7790
Fax: 828-667-8051   800-334-5809
weborders@great-eastern-sun.com
Asian organic and natural foods
Owner: Berry Evans
generalmgr@great-eastern-sun.com
Finance: Brett Martin
Sales Manager: Mary Griffin
VP Operations/Purchaser: Jan Paige
Assistant Production Manager: Wendy Young
Warehouse/Shipping: Joe Putnam
Estimated Sales: $5-10 Million
Number Employees: 20-49
Brands:
 MISO MASTER ORGANIC
 EMERALD COVE
 EMPEROR'S KITCHEN
 ORGANIC PLANET
 SUSHI SONIC
 HAIKU
 ONE WORLD
 SWEET CLOUD

5307 Great Expectations Confectionery Gourmet Foods
1911 W Warren Boulevard
Chicago, IL 60612
773-525-4865
Fax: 773-281-5506
Candy and confections
President: John Prescott
Estimated Sales: $110,000
Number Employees: 2
Type of Packaging: Consumer, Private Label
Brands:
 Great Expectations

Food Manufacturers / A-Z

5308 Great Garlic Foods
709 5th Ave
Bradley Beach, NJ 07720-1004
732-775-3311
Fax: 732-774-9386
Garlic products
Owner: Joe DE Santis
ggarlfoods@aol.com
Estimated Sales: $1-3 Million
Number Employees: 5-9
Type of Packaging: Consumer, Food Service, Private Label, Bulk

5309 Great Glacier Salmon
PO Box 1137
Prince Rupert, BC V8J 4H6
Canada
250-627-4955
Fax: 250-627-7945 greatglacier@hotmail.com
Salmon
Accounting: Mary Allen
General Manager: Robert Gould
Estimated Sales: $250,000 To 1,000,000
Number Employees: 20-49
Number of Brands: 2
Square Footage: 6400
Type of Packaging: Private Label, Bulk
Brands:
  Glacier Caviar
  Glacier Salmon

5310 Great Gourmet Inc
5115 Clark Canning House Rd
Federalsburg, MD 21632-2615
410-754-8800
Fax: 410-754-5997 sales@thegreatgourmet.com
Seafood and shellfish
Owner: Kim Scott
kim@thegreatgourmet.com
Number Employees: 20-49

5311 Great Grains Milling Company
105 Four Buttes Railroad Ave W
Scobey, MT 59263
406-783-5581
Red spring wheat flour and bran, cracked wheat cereal, pancake and waffle mixes
President: Alvin Rustebakke
Estimated Sales: $500,000-$1 Million
Number Employees: 1-4
Square Footage: 1600
Type of Packaging: Consumer, Food Service, Private Label

5312 Great Harvest Bread Co
28 S Montana St
Dillon, MT 59725-2434
406-683-6842
Fax: 406-683-5537 800-442-0424
www.greatharvest.com
Bread
President & CEO: Mike Ferretti
mikef@greatharvest.com
Dir.of Bakery Support & Operations: Mark Peterson
Number Employees: 20-49

5313 Great Hill Dairy Inc
160 Delano Rd
Marion, MA 02738-2029
508-748-2208
Fax: 508-748-2282 888-748-2208
www.greathillblue.com
Milk and cheeses
President: Tim Stone
President: Nancy Weaver
Estimated Sales: $500,000-$1,000,000
Number Employees: 1-4
Brands:
  Great Hill Blue

5314 Great Lakes Brewing Co.
2516 Market Ave
Cleveland, OH 44113-3344
216-771-4404
Fax: 216-771-2799
glbcinfo@greatlakesbrewing.com
www.greatlakesbrewing.com
Beers; not to be confused with Canadian "Great Lakes Brewery."
President/CEO: Patrick Conway
Co-Owner: Daniel Conway
Marketing Director: Carey Roberts
Vice President Sales & Marketing: Bridget Barrett
Controller: Kevin Cawneen
Type of Packaging: Consumer, Food Service
Brands:
  Burning River Pale Ale
  Edmund Fitzgerald Porter
  Commodore Perry India Pale Ale
  Conway's Irish Ale
  Dopplerock
  Holy Moses White Ale
  The Wright Pils
  Oktoberfest
  Nosferatu
  Christmas Ale
  Blackout Stout

5315 (HQ)Great Lakes Cheese Company, Inc.
17825 Great Lakes Pkwy
PO Box 1806
Hiram, OH 44234-1806
440-834-2500
Fax: 440-834-1002 glcinfo@greatlakescheese.com
www.greatlakescheese.com
Cheese
Chairman: Hans Epprecht
CEO/President: Gary Vanic
CFO: Russell Mullins
VP Sales: William Andrews
VP Human Resources: Beth Wendell
VP/General Mgr: John W Epprecht
Manufacturing/Operations Director: Steve Scott
Plant Manager: Thomas Eastham
Purchasing Clerk: Shelley Williamson
Estimated Sales: Over $1 Billion
Number Employees: 1000-4999
Square Footage: 400000
Type of Packaging: Private Label
Other Locations:
  Great Lakes Cheese of New York
  Adams NY
  Great Lakes Cheese of Utah
  Fillmore UT
  Great Lakes Cheese Company-HQ
  Hiram OH
  Great Lakes Cheese of La Crosse
  La Crosse WI
  Great Lakes Cheese of Wisconsin
  Plymouth WI

5316 Great Lakes Cheese Company
101 DeVoe Street
Wausau, WI 54403
715-842-3214
Fax: 715-842-4452 www.greatlakescheese.com
Specialty cheese products
COO: Randy Lewis
President of Administration/Treasurer: Daniel E Zagzebski
Estimated Sales: Below $5 Million
Number Employees: 100-249
Parent Co: Great Lakes Cheese Company, Inc.
Brands:
  Great Lakes

5317 Great Lakes Foods
1230 48th Ave
Menominee, MI 49858-1002
906-863-5503
Fax: 906-863-2102 800-800-7492
jvan@greatlakesfoods.com
Canned mushrooms; fruit and vegetable canning, pickling and drying
President: Tom Ireland
Owner: Jerry Vandelaarschot
CFO: Don Kressin
dkressin@greatlakefood.com
Vice President: Johanne Ubbels
Estimated Sales: $1-2.5 Million
Number Employees: 50-99
Parent Co: Ubbelea Farms
Type of Packaging: Consumer, Food Service, Private Label
Brands:
  Chateau
  Riviera

5318 Great Lakes Packing Co
6556 Quarterline Rd
Kewadin, MI 49648-8907
231-264-5561
Fax: 231-264-5594 glpc@greatlakespacking.com
www.greatlakespacking.com
Frozen cherries
President/ Hart Plant Manager: Jon Veliquette
jon@greatlakespacking.com
Vice President: Dean Veliquette
Quality Assurance Manager: Roger Veliquette
Human Resources Manager: Trudy Cullimore
Estimated Sales: $1,7,000,000
Number Employees: 250-499
Type of Packaging: Consumer, Private Label
Brands:
  Great Lakes

5319 Great Lakes Tea & Spice
6610 Western Ave
PO Box 661
Glen Arbor, MI 49636-5103
231-334-6747
Fax: 231-326-2333 877-645-9363
www.teaandspice.com
Loose teas, flowering teas and spices
President/Owner: Chris Sack
CEO: Heather Sack
Estimated Sales: Less Than $500,000
Number Employees: 1-4

5320 Great Lakes Wine & Spirits
373 Victor St
Highland Park, MI 48203-3117
313-453-2200
Fax: 313-867-4039 www.glwas.com
Wines, spirits, and beers.
Co-CEO: Lew Cooper III
Co-CEO: Syd Ross
EVP, Finance: John Queen
EVP, Operations: Lou Grech-Cumbo
EVP, IT: Mike Arkison
VP, National Accounts: Heather Kerr
VP, Wine Sales: Jason Howard
EVP, Sales: Ernier Almeranti
VP, Sales Development: Rick Lopus
VP, Human Resources: Stephanie Lyons
Year Founded: 2008

5321 Great Midwest Seafood Company
5406 Sheridan St
Davenport, IA 52806-2260
563-388-4770
Fax: 563-388-4772
Seafood
Owner: Jeff Melchert
kingfish@gmail.com
Estimated Sales: $10-20 Million
Number Employees: 10-19

5322 Great Northern Baking Company
443 Hoover St NE
Minneapolis, MN 55413
612-331-1043
Fax: 612-331-1052 info@greatnorthernbaking.com
www.greatnorthernbaking.com
Muffins, cakes, cookie bars and pretzels
President: Fred Johnson
Estimated Sales: $5-9.9 000,000
Number Employees: 50-99
Brands:
  Mrs Feldman's Desserts

5323 Great Northern Brewing Co
2 Central Ave
Suite 1
Whitefish, MT 59937-2547
406-863-1000
Fax: 406-863-1001
brewmaster@greatnorthernbrewing.com
www.greatnorthernbrewing.com
Beer and lager
Owner: Dennis Konopatzke
General Manager/ Partner: Marcus Duffey
Controller: Uwe Schaefer
Retail Marketing & Promotion Manager: Jessica Lucey
Head Sales: Orie Roberts
kono@woodtechdoor.com
Tasting Room/Customer Service: Jessica Stanhope
Head Operations: Thomas Sierra
Production Manager: Dan Rasmussen
Estimated Sales: $2.5-5,000,000
Number Employees: 5-9
Parent Co: McKenzie River Partners
Type of Packaging: Consumer, Food Service
Brands:
  Black
  Premium
  Whitefish
  Wild Huckleberry

Food Manufacturers / A-Z

5324 Great Northern Maple Products
331 Rue Principale
Saint Honor, De Shenley, QC G0M 1V0
Canada
418-485-7777
Fax: 418-485-6185 info@greatnorthernmaple.com
www.greatnorthernmaple.com
Organic maple and fruit syrups
Director General: Gary Coppola
International Marketing Manager: Luc Tardiff

5325 Great Northern Products Inc
2700 Plainfield Pike
Cranston, RI 02921-2070
401-490-4590
Fax: 401-633-6051 info@northernproducts.com
www.northernproducts.com
Seafood
President: George Nolan
george@northernproducts.com
Executive Vice President: Peter Bruno
Quality Control/ Compliance: Kyle Wilkens
Domestic Sales: Don Nolan
COO: Jose Pons
Estimated Sales: $10.1 Million
Number Employees: 20-49
Number of Brands: 4
Number of Products: 40
Square Footage: 24000
Brands:
 Commonwealth
 Fruits De Mer
 Langlois
 Sabana
 Sealicious
 Simmonds

5326 Great Pacific Seafoods
PO Box 81165
Seattle, WA 98108
206-764-7180
Fax: 206-764-7187
Fresh and frozen salmon
Manager: Roger Stiles
Estimated Sales: $10-20,000,000
Number Employees: 50-99
Type of Packaging: Consumer, Food Service
Brands:
 Great Pacific

5327 Great Plains Beef LLC
PO Box 82545
Lincoln, NE 68501-2545
402-479-2115
Fax: 402-458-4531 info@piedmontese.com
Beef
President: Billy Swain
Number Employees: 1-4
Brands:
 Lone Creek Cattle Company
 Great Plains
 Certified Piedmontese

5328 Great Recipes
PO Box 647
Beaverton, OR 97075-0647
503-590-1108
Fax: 800-585-2331 800-273-2331
contactus@great-recipes.com
www.great-recipes.com
Bread, cookie, cake, brownie and muffin mixes
President: Mark Bonebrake
markb@great-recipes.com
Estimated Sales: $1-2,500,000
Number Employees: 1-4
Type of Packaging: Private Label
Brands:
 Firenza
 Great Recipes

5329 Great River Organic Milling
W26001 Volds Lane
Arcadia, WI 54612
608-687-9580
Fax: 608-687-3014 contact@greatrivermilling.com
www.greatrivermilling.com
Organic grains, flours and mixes
Owner: Rick Halverson
rhalverson@greatrivermilling.com
Customer Service: Nadine Bayer
Estimated Sales: Less Than $500,000
Number Employees: 1-4
Type of Packaging: Bulk

5330 Great Spice Company
12101 Moya Blvd
Reno, NV 89506-2600
Fax: 760-744-0401 800-730-3575
www.greatspice.com
Dehydrated and fresh herbs
President: Jay Fishman
Inventory Manager: Steve Addison
s.addison@hqorganics.com
Quality Manager: Ja Attaphongse
VP Sales: Jim Slatic
Founder/VP Operations: Jerry Tenenberg
Operations Manager: Dan Sullivan
Shipping Manager: Michael Tenenberg
Global Purchasing Coordinator: Rommina Chavarria
Estimated Sales: $3-5,000,000
Number Employees: 20-49
Type of Packaging: Food Service, Private Label, Bulk

5331 Great Valley Mills
1774 A County Line Rd
Barto, PA 19504-8720
610-754-7800
Fax: 610-754-6490 800-688-6455
Stone ground flour, pancake, muffin, bread and specialty dry food mixes
Owner: Steve Kantoor
Estimated Sales: $690,000
Number Employees: 6
Square Footage: 45000
Type of Packaging: Consumer, Food Service, Private Label
Brands:
 1710
 Covered Bridge Mills
 Flip It
 Great Valley Mills
 Great Valley Mixes

5332 Great Western Brewing Company
519 Second Avenue N
Saskatoon, SK S7K 2C6
Canada
306-653-4653
Fax: 306-653-2166 800-764-4492
info@greatwesternbrewing.com www.gwbc.ca
Beer
President/CEO: Michael Micovcin
Brew master: Garry Johnston
Number Employees: 50-99
Type of Packaging: Consumer, Food Service

5333 Great Western Co LLC
30290 US Highway 72
Hollywood, AL 35752-6134
256-259-3578
Fax: 256-259-7087 www.gwproducts.com
Processor and exporter of popcorn, popping corn oil, cotton candy, sno-cone syrup, candy apple coatings, funnel cakes, waffle cones, corn dog mix, and other concession items
Contact: Tim Ferguson
timf@gwproducts.com
Estimated Sales: Less Than $500,000
Number Employees: 1-4
Number of Brands: 6
Type of Packaging: Consumer, Food Service, Private Label, Bulk
Brands:
 Chillee Snow Cones
 Frostee Snow Cones
 Great Western Products Company
 Peter's Movie Time Products
 Premium America
 Sunglo

5334 Great Western Juice Co
16153 Libby Rd
Maple Heights, OH 44137-1298
216-475-5770
Fax: 216-475-5772 800-321-9180
gwjuice@sbcglobal.net
Beverages
President: Doreen Coons
dcoons@fibreglast.com
VP: Bill Overton
Marketing/Sales: Phil Leroy
Public Relations: Connie Rice
Operations Manager: John Stevens
Plant Manager: John Taziros
Purchasing Manager: Bill Overton
dcoons@fibreglast.com
Estimated Sales: $1.6 Million
Number Employees: 20-49
Square Footage: 60000
Type of Packaging: Food Service, Private Label
Brands:
 Ice & Easy
 Perfection
 Sunny Morning

5335 Great Western Malting Co
1705 NW Harborside Dr
Vancouver, WA 98660
360-693-3661
www.graincorp.com.au
Processed malt
President & CEO: Greg Friberg
Group Chief Financial Officer: Alistair Bell
Chief Information Officer: Andrew Baker
Estimated Sales: $27 Million
Number Employees: 50-99
Square Footage: 13440
Type of Packaging: Bulk
Other Locations:
 Malt Plant
 Vancouver WA
 Malt Plant
 Pocatello ID
 Bagged Malt Country Warehouse
 Vancouver WA
 Bagged Malt Country Warehouse
 Aurora CO
 Bagged Malt Country Warehouse
 Hayward CA
 Bagged Malt Country Warehouse
 Champlain NY
 Bagged Malt Country Warehouse
 Chicago IL
 Bagged Malt Country Warehouse
 Hickory NC
 Bagged Malt Country Warehouse
 British Columbia Canada
 Bagged Malt Country Warehouse
 Alberta Canada

5336 Great Western Tortilla
1761 E 58th Avenue
Denver, CO 80216-1505
303-298-0705
Fax: 303-298-0216
Tortilla chips and other snacks
Director Sales/Marketing: John Amerman
Estimated Sales: $10-20 Million
Number Employees: 50-99

5337 Greater Knead, The
1690 Winchester Rd
Bensalem, PA 19020
267-522-8523
info@thegreaterknead.com
www.thegreaterknead.com
Gluten free bagels and bagel chips
Founder/CEO: Michelle Carfagno
CFO: Christina Cassetti
Product Investigator: Mengyi Hu
Account Manager: Maxie Walsh
Warehouse Manager: Joe Otto
Year Founded: 2012
Number Employees: 20-49

5338 Greater Omaha Packing Co Inc.
3001 L Street
Omaha, NE 68107
402-731-1700
800-747-5400
info@greateromaha.com www.greateromaha.com
Beef.
President/CEO: Henry Davis
Credit/Account Manager: Carol Mesenbrink
Vice President, Sales: Dan Jensen
Year Founded: 1920
Estimated Sales: $1+ Billion
Number Employees: 1,000
Number of Brands: 5
Square Footage: 60000
Type of Packaging: Consumer, Food Service, Private Label, Bulk
Brands:
 Omaha Natural Angus
 Certified Angus Beef
 Greater Omaha
 Hereford Beef
 Omaha Hereford

Food Manufacturers / A-Z

5339 Greaves Jams & Marmalades
PO Box 26
Niagara-on-the-Lake, ON L0S 1J0
Canada
905-468-3608
Fax: 905-468-0071   800-515-9939
greaves@greavesjams.com www.greavesjams.com
Jams, jellies, marmalades and condiments
President: Lloyd Redekopp
Vice President: Angela Redekopp
Production: Rudy Doerwald
Estimated Sales: $1.4 Million
Number Employees: 15
Number of Products: 1
Square Footage: 20000
Type of Packaging: Consumer, Private Label
Brands:
   Greaves

5340 Grebe's Bakery
5132 W Lincoln Ave
Milwaukee, WI 53219-1684
414-543-7001
Fax: 414-543-8863   800-833-3158
info@grebesbakery.com www.grebesbakeries.com
Bakery products
President: Jim Grebe Sr
Year Founded: 1937
Estimated Sales: $10-20 Million
Number Employees: 100-249
Square Footage: 93000
Type of Packaging: Consumer, Bulk
Brands:
   Grebe's

5341 Grecian Delight Foods Inc
1201 Tonne Rd
Elk Grove Village, IL 60007-4925
847-364-2030
Fax: 847-364-1077   800-621-4387
www.gdfsalesportal.com
Frozen Greek baked goods, meat products, pita bread, gyros, entrees and desserts
Owner/Human Resources & Sales Manager: Peter Parthenis
pparthenis@greciandelight.com
VP/CFO: Bill Pierreakeas
Research/Development Manager: John Matchuk
Quality Control Manager: Mary Funteas
Marketing Director: Deme Katsulis
VP Operations: Tom Valnoha
Purchasing Director: George Georganas
Number Employees: 250-499
Type of Packaging: Consumer, Food Service, Private Label
Brands:
   Athenian
   Chicago Style
   Pita Folds

5342 Green & Black's OrganicChocolate
PO Box 259011
Plano, TX 75025
973-909-3900
Fax: 973-909-3930   877-299-1254
greenandblacks@cohnwolfe.com
www.greenandblacks.com/us
Organic choclate
President/Owner: Neil Turpin
CFO: James Reed
Contact: Newell Holt
newell@greenandblacks.com
Number Employees: 8

5343 Green Bay Cheese
1 Overlook Point
Suite 300
Lincolnshire, IL 60069
262-677-3407
Fax: 847-267-3280   800-824-3373
www.saputospecialty.com/en/our-cheeses/green-bay-cheese
Cheeses
Chairman & CEO: Lino Saputo Jr.
CFO: Maxime Therrien
COO, Cheese Division (USA): Terry Brockman
Year Founded: 1975
Estimated Sales: $20-50 Million
Number Employees: 100-249
Parent Co: Saputo Cheese USA

5344 (HQ)Green Bay Packaging Inc.
1700 Webster Ct.
Green Bay, WI 54302
920-433-5111
Fax: 920-433-5471 www.gbp.com
Corrugated shipping containers and labels including coated and stock.
President/CEO: William Kress
bkress@gbp.com
Senior VP/General Counsel: Scott Wochos
Year Founded: 1933
Estimated Sales: $850 Million
Number Employees: 3,200
Type of Packaging: Consumer, Food Service, Private Label, Bulk

5345 Green Beans Coffee Co Inc
4300 Redwood Hwy # 100
San Rafael, CA 94903-2103
415-461-4023
info@greenbeanscoffee.net
www.greenbeanscoffee.com
Coffee
President & Co Founder: Jon Araghi
CEO & Co-Founder: Jason Araghi
Number Employees: 250-499

5346 Green County Foods
PO BOX 2813
Monroe, WI 53566-1364
608-328-8800
Fax: 608-328-8648   800-233-3564
custserv@greencountyfoods.com
www.greencountyfoods.com
Desserts and baked goods
President: Gene Curran
Sales: Wally Wagner
Public Relations: Jim Mason
Operations: Sharee Marzolf
Estimated Sales: $2.5-5,000,000
Number Employees: 10-19
Parent Co: Swiss Colony
Type of Packaging: Consumer, Food Service, Private Label, Bulk
Brands:
   Richly Deserved
   Sweet Treasures

5347 Green Dirt Farm
19915 Mount Bethel Rd
PO Box 74
Weston, MO 64098-9070
816-386-2156
info@greendirtfarm.com
www.greendirtfarm.com
Dairy products
Co-Founder: Jacqueline Smith
Co-Founder: Sarah Hoffman
sarah@greendirtfarm.com
Estimated Sales: Less Than $500,000
Number Employees: 1-4

5348 Green Earth Orchards
1412 Laird Ave
Salt Lake City, UT 84105
801-888-7161
info@greenearthorchards.com
Dried fruits
Number of Brands: 1
Number of Products: 1
Type of Packaging: Consumer, Bulk
Brands:
   GREEN EARTH ORCHARDS

5349 Green Foods Corp.
2220 Camino Del Sol
Oxnard, CA 93030-8905
800-777-4430
info@greenfoods.com greenfoods.com
Powdered protein shakes and juices
President: Takahiko Amano
Chief Administrative Officer: Deborah Pollack
deborah@greenfoods.com
Technical Service Manager: Bob Terry
Estimated Sales: $10-20 Million
Number Employees: 5-9
Square Footage: 19600
Type of Packaging: Consumer
Brands:
   Green Essence

5350 Green Garden Food Products
100 Litehouse Dr.
PO Box 1969
Sandpoint, ID 83864
253-395-4460
Fax: 253-395-0408   800-669-3169
info@ggfoods.com www.ggfoods.com
Condiments
President: Mark Hockman
Director Technical Services: Kyle Anderson
Estimated Sales: $25,000,000
Number Employees: 50-99
Type of Packaging: Consumer, Food Service

5351 Green Gold Group LLC
13905 Stettin Dr
Marathon, WI 54448-9476
715-842-8546
Fax: 715-842-4614   888-533-7288
www.greengoldgroup.com
Ginseng, herbs, whole roots and other health products
Owner: Sam Chen
mail@greengoldgroup.com
CEO: Phouangmala Chen
Estimated Sales: $1-3,000,000
Number Employees: 10-19
Square Footage: 7200
Type of Packaging: Consumer, Bulk

5352 Green Gorilla
22809 Pacific Coast Hwy
Malibu, CA 90265
323-452-5919
ilovegreengorilla.com
CBD-infused extra virgin olive oil
Founder & CEO: Steven Saxton
Senior VP, Sales: Herb Lewis
COO: Steve De Forest

5353 Green Grown Products Inc
13600 Marina Pointe Dr
Suite 315
Marina Del Ray, CA 90292
310-828-1686
Fax: 310-822-6440
Herbs, royal jelly, propolis, bee pollen, chia and sesame seeds, apricot kernels and turbinado sugar
President: Teri Bernardi
CEO: Hal Neiman
Estimated Sales: $2,000,000
Number Employees: 1-4
Square Footage: 16000
Parent Co: Earth Commodities
Type of Packaging: Private Label, Bulk

5354 Green Mountain Chocolate Inc
835 W Central St # 1
Franklin, MA 02038-3189
508-520-7160
Fax: 508-520-7161
info@greenmountainchocolate.com
www.greenmountainchocolate.com
Chocolates
Owner: Betty Duncan
b.duncan@greenmountainchocolate.com
Estimated Sales: Less Than $500,000
Number Employees: 1-4
Brands:
   Green Mountain Chocolate Truffle

5355 Green Mountain Cidery
153 Pond Lane
Middlebury, VT 05753
802-388-0700
Fax: 802-388-0600 www.woodchuck.com
Hard cider
President: Joseph Cerniglia
VP: Dan Rowell
Director Marketing: Alan MacDonald
General Manager: Rob Hyman
Estimated Sales: $2.5-5 Millioin
Number Employees: 20-49
Square Footage: 50
Type of Packaging: Private Label
Brands:
   Woodchuck Draft Cider

5356 Green Mountain Creamery
PO Box 6212
Brattleboro, VT 05302
802-251-2300
855-996-4946
www.greenmountaincreamery.com

Food Manufacturers / A-Z

Greek and Icelandic style yogurts
Type of Packaging: Consumer
Brands:
    GREEN MOUNTAIN CREAMERY
    YOYUMMY

5357 Green Mountain Gringo
4045 Indiana Ave
Winston-Salem, NC 27115
　　　　　　　Fax: 802-875-3140　888-875-3111
　　　　　　　www.greenmountaingringo.com
Salsa
Co-Founder: Christine Hume
Co-Founder: Dave Hume
Parent Co: TW Garner Food Company

5358 Green Options
17 Paul Dr
Suite 104
San Rafael, CA 94903-2043
　　　　　　　　　　　　　415-526-1450
　　　　　　Fax: 415-526-1453　888-473-3667
Health foods
Manager: Michael Madden
Sales Manager: Jill Koperweis
Estimated Sales: $1-3,000,000
Number Employees: 9
Brands:
    Veggie-Deli®
    Veggie-Deli Slices®
    Veggie-Jerky™
    Veggie-Deli®Quick Stick

5359 Green River Chocolates
PO Box 421
Hinesburg, VT 05461
　　　　　　　　　　　　802-482-6727
　　　　　　　　info@adagiochocolates.com
　　　　　　　　　　adagiochocolates.com
Maple syrup, chocolates and chocolate products, butter corn syrup, crepes and pancake mixes, ice cream and pepper sauces
Estimated Sales: $1-3 Million
Number Employees: 5-9

5360 Green Roads CBD
601 Fairway Dr
Deerfield Beach, FL 33441
　　　　　　　　　　　　833-462-8922
　　　　　　　support@greenroadsworld.com
　　　　　　　　www.greenroadsworld.com
CBD-infused dietary supplements
President: Craig Fabel
Co-Founder: Laura Fuentes

5361 Green Source Organics
7290 Kea Lani Dr
Boynton Beach, FL 33437
　　　　　　　　　　　　561-740-8595
　　　　　　　　　　blitz@gsoextracts.com
　　　　　　　　　　　gsoextracts.com
Organic, powdered fruit and vegetable extracts

5362 Green Spot Packaging
100 S Cambridge Ave
Claremont, CA 91711-4842
　　　　　　　　　　　　909-625-8771
　　　　　　Fax: 909-621-4634　800-456-3210
info@greenspotusa.com　www.lagunaliquid.com
Beverages, flavors and fragrances; aseptic packaging services available
CEO: John Tsu
Finance Executive: Don Koury
Sales Executive: Greg Faust
Chief Operating Officer: Dana Staal
Plant Manager: Roy Cooley
Estimated Sales: $6.5 Million
Number Employees: 20-49
Square Footage: 200000
Type of Packaging: Consumer, Food Service, Private Label, Bulk
Brands:
    Action Ade
    Apple Delight
    Apple Royal
    Awesome Orange
    Black Cherry Royal
    Citrus Royal
    Galactic Grape
    Good Buddies
    Green Spot
    Peach Royal
    Superstar Strawberry
    Tropical Royal

5363 Green Turtle Bay Vitamin Company
PO Box 642
Summit, NJ 07902
　　　　　　　　　　　　908-277-2240
　　　　　　Fax: 908-273-9116　800-887-8535
　　　　mail@energywave.com　www.energywave.com
Processor and exporter of vitamin supplement formulas including herbal antioxidants, oils and herbs
President: Karen Horbatt
CEO: Gloria Mckenna
Quality Control: Monica Harris
Marketing: Michele Murphy
Estimated Sales: $600,000
Number Employees: 5
Brands:
    Diabetiks
    Maple Melts
    Powermate
    Powersleep
    Powervites
    Primrose Oile
    Signal 369
    Sunnie

5364 Green Turtle Cannery & Seafood
PO Box 585
81219 Overseas Hwy
Islamorada, FL 33036
　　　　　　　　　　　　305-664-9595
　　　　　　　　　Fax: 305-664-9564
Specialty seafood products
President: Henry Rosenthal Jr.
Estimated Sales: $1-2,500,000
Number Employees: 20-49
Brands:
    Sid and Roxie's

5365 Green Valley Food Corp
1501 Market Center Blvd
Dallas, TX 75207-3913
　　　　　　　　　　　　214-939-3900
　　　　　　Fax: 214-939-3999　800-853-8399
　　　　　　　　www.greenvalleyfood.com
Importer and wholesaler/distributor of cheese, meats, pates, cookies, crackers, breads, jams, jellies, preserves, soups, snack foods, pasta and confections; custom packer of domestic and imported cheeses
Owner: George Chang
Estimated Sales: $2,100,000
Number Employees: 20-49
Square Footage: 120000

5366 Green Valley Foods
1105 Front St NE
Salem, OR 97301
　　　　　　　　　　　　844-588-3535
　　　　　　info@welcometogreenvalley.com
　　　　　　　welcometogreenvalley.com
Organic beans, rice and vegetables
COO: Peri Nathen

5367 Green Valley Pecan Company
1525 W Sahuarita Rd
Sahuarita, AZ 85629-8001
　　　　　　　　　　　　520-791-2880
　　　Fax: 520-629-0119　sales@greenvalleypecan.com
　　　　　　　　www.greenvalleypecan.com
Pecans, nuts
President/CEO: Richard Walden
Controller: Heather Merchant
Chief Marketing Officer: Bruce Caris
bcaris@greenvalleypecan.com
Estimated Sales: $190 Thousand
Number Employees: 250-499
Parent Co: Farmers Investment Company

5368 Green-Go Cactus Water
PO Box 334
Oakville, CA 94562
　　　　　　　　　　　　707-944-2039
　　　　　　　　cactus@drinkgreen-go.com
　　　　　　　　　drinkgreen-go.com
Cactus water
Founder: Sarita Lopez
Type of Packaging: Consumer
Brands:
    GREEN-GO

5369 Greenberg Cheese Co
5743 Smithway St
Suite 308
Commerce, CA 90040-1549
　　　　　　　　　　　　323-727-7735
　　　　　　Fax: 323-727-7941　800-301-4507
　　　　　　www.greenbergcheesecompany.com
Cheese, cheese products
President & COO: Mike Greenberg
mike@greenbergcheesecompany.com
Director of Administration: Richard Holly
CFO: Merilyn Greenberg
Estimated Sales: $30 Million
Number Employees: 20-49
Number of Products: 300
Square Footage: 20000
Parent Co: Dairy Commodities Corporation
Type of Packaging: Food Service, Bulk
Other Locations:
    Commerce CA

5370 Greene Brothers Specialty Coffee Roaster
313 High Street
Hackettstown, NJ 07840-1908
　　　　　　　　　　　　908-979-0022
　　　　　　　　info@greenesbeans.com
　　　　　　　　http://www.greenesbeans.com/
Coffee
Co-President: David Greene
Co-Presidemt: Brian Greene
Estimated Sales: $1-3,000,000
Number Employees: 10-19
Square Footage: 1500

5371 Greenfield Mills
10505 East 750
North Howe, IN 46746
　　　　　　　　　　　　260-367-2394
　　　　　　　　www.newrinkelflour.com
Wheat and buckwheat flour; also, pancake mixes, Certified Organic whole wheat and white soft wheat flour
President: Howard Rinkel
Vice President: Joyce Rinkel
Contact: Dave Rinkel
mazdadoc@yahoo.com
Estimated Sales: $300,000-500,000
Number Employees: 1-4
Square Footage: 24000
Type of Packaging: Consumer, Food Service
Brands:
    New Rinkel

5372 Greenfield Noodle & Spec Co
600 Custer St
Detroit, MI 48202-3128
　　　　　　　　　　　　313-873-2212
　　　　　　　　Fax: 313-873-0515
Noodles
Owner: Kevin Michaels
VP: Mary Michaels
Estimated Sales: $1.3 Million
Number Employees: 10-19
Square Footage: 26000
Type of Packaging: Consumer, Food Service, Private Label, Bulk
Brands:
    Greenfield
    Mrs. Asien

5373 Greenfield Wine Company
205 Jim Oswalt Way Ste B
Vallejo, CA 94503-9695
　　　　　　　　　　　　707-552-5199
　　　　　　　　Fax: 707-963-8537
Wines
Owner: Tony Cartlidge
VP/Partner: Robert Babbe
Vice President: Elijah Selby
Marketing Manager: Dan Waggerman
Contact: Robert Babbe
rgbabbe@aol.com
General Manager: Tony Cartlidge
Estimated Sales: $10-24,9,000,000
Number Employees: 48

5374 Greenhills Irish Bakery
780 Adams St
Dorchester Ctr, MA 02124-5104
　　　　　　　　　　　　617-825-8187
　　　　　　　　info@greenhillsbakery.com
　　　　　　　　www.greenhillsbakery.com
Bakery products

Food Manufacturers / A-Z

5374 (continued)
President: Dermot Quinn
Estimated Sales: $10-20,000,000
Number Employees: 10-19

5375 Greenjoy
Okatie, SC 29909
greenjoylife.com
Superfood dressings and salad mixers

5376 Greenwave Foods
Berkeley, CA
510-898-1973
edazen.com
Edamame snacks
Founder: Rachel Greenberger
Brands:
 eda-zen(c)
 toasta ma-me
 cruncha ma-me(c)

5377 Greenwell Farms Inc
81-6581 Mamalahoa Hwy
Kealakekua, HI 96750
808-323-2862
Fax: 808-323-2584 888-592-5662
sales@greenwellfarms.com
www.greenwellfarms.com
Coffee, specialty confectionary
President: Thomas Greenwell
tom@greenwellfarms.com
CEO: Jennifer Greenwell
Estimated Sales: $1-2.5 Million
Number Employees: 100-249
Type of Packaging: Consumer, Food Service, Private Label, Bulk
Brands:
 Greenwell Farms

5378 Greenwood Associates
6280 W Howard St
Niles, IL 60714-3433
847-579-5500
Fax: 847-579-5501
info@greenwoodassociates.com
www.greenwoodassociates.com
Fruit concentrates and purees
President: Ron Kaplan
Estimated Sales: $5-10 Million
Number Employees: 20-49
Square Footage: 1000
Type of Packaging: Bulk

5379 Greenwood Ice Cream Co
4829 Peachtree Rd
Atlanta, GA 30341-3113
770-455-6166
Fax: 770-455-4152 800-678-6166
orders@greenwoodicecream.com
www.greenwoodicecream.com
Ice cream, frozen desserts
President: Mitchell Williams
mitchell@greenwoodicecream.com
Director: Robert Street
Director: Tony Yen
Estimated Sales: $4,000,000
Number Employees: 20-49
Brands:
 Greenwood

5380 Greenwood Ridge Vineyards
5501 Highway 128
Philo, CA 95466-9477
707-895-2002
Fax: 707-895-2001
everybody@greenwoodridge.com
www.greenwoodridge.com
Wines
Owner: Allan Green
allan@greenwoodridge.com
Estimated Sales: $1-2,500,000
Number Employees: 1-4

5381 Greg's Lobster Company
136 Factory Road
Units 1-3
Harwich Port, MA 02645-1675
508-432-8080
Fax: 508-432-2203
Lobster
President: Leslie Sykes
Estimated Sales: $2.75 Million
Number Employees: 20

5382 Gregory's Foods, Inc.
1301 Trapp Rd
St Paul, MN 55121-1247
651-454-0277
Fax: 651-454-2254 800-231-4734
www.gregorysfoods.com
Frozen baked goods, mixes and bases; bakery ingredients and supplies
President: Greg Helland
cburton@gregorysfoods.com
Quality Control: Tom Hoebbel
Sales/Marketing: Randy Clemons
Estimated Sales: $5.7 Million
Number Employees: 50-99
Square Footage: 44000
Type of Packaging: Food Service, Private Label, Bulk

5383 Gress Enterprises
992 N South Rd
Scranton, PA 18504-1412
570-561-0150
Fax: 570-341-1299 www.gresscold.com
Frozen chicken products
Owner: E Gress
VP/General Manager: Keith Gress
VP Marketing: Glenn Gress
Estimated Sales: $5-10 Million
Number Employees: 10-19
Type of Packaging: Food Service, Bulk

5384 Grey Ghost Bakery
1750 Signal Point Rd.
Suite 2A
Charleston, SC 29412
803-238-1123
www.greyghostbakery.com
Cookies
Founder: Katherine Frankstone

5385 Grey Owl Foods
510 11th St SE
Grand Rapids, MN 55744
218-327-2281
Fax: 218-327-2283 800-527-0172
Rice and rice products
Director Sales/Marketing: Jim McCool
Estimated Sales: $10-20 Million
Number Employees: 10-19
Square Footage: 12000
Parent Co: SIAP Marketing Company
Type of Packaging: Consumer, Food Service, Bulk

5386 Greyston Bakery Inc
21 Park Ave.
Yonkers, NY 10703
914-376-3900
Fax: 914-375-1514 800-289-2253
info@greystonbakery.com www.greyston.org
Baked goods
President/CEO: Mike Brady
Founder: Bernie Glassman
Year Founded: 1982
Estimated Sales: $20-50 Million
Number Employees: 100-249
Type of Packaging: Consumer, Food Service

5387 Griffin's Seafood
24225 Highway 1
Golden Meadow, LA 70357
985-396-2453
Fax: 985-396-2459
Seafood
Owner: Archie Dantin
Estimated Sales: Under $500,000
Number Employees: 1-4

5388 Griffith Foods Inc.
1 Griffith Center
Alsip, IL 60803
708-371-0900
Fax: 708-371-4783 www.griffithfoods.com
Protein, side-dish and snack seasonings; sauces, gravies, and soups mixes; salsa and condiments; and bakery and dough blends.
Chairman: Brian Griffith
CEO: TC Chatterjee
Executive VP/CFO: Matt West
Year Founded: 1919
Estimated Sales: $286.8 Million
Number Employees: 1,000-4,999
Square Footage: 250000
Type of Packaging: Food Service, Private Label, Bulk

5389 Grillo's Pickles
Needham Heights, MA 02494
www.grillospickles.com
Organic pickles
Founder: Travis Grillo
Type of Packaging: Consumer
Brands:
 GRILLO'S PICKLES

5390 Grimaud Farms-California Inc
1320 S Aurora St # A
Stockton, CA 95206-1616
209-466-3200
Fax: 209-466-8910 800-466-9955
Duck and guinea fowl
Owner: Howard Chan
howard@grimaudfarms.com
Vice President: Lauren Bartels
Vice President Sales: Jim Galle
Production/Plant Manager: Diego Davalos
Purchasing Agent: Istvan Deli
Estimated Sales: $6.4 Million
Number Employees: 100-249
Square Footage: 168000
Parent Co: Groupe Grimaud
Type of Packaging: Consumer, Food Service, Private Label, Bulk
Brands:
 Grimaud Farms
 Grimaud Farms Muscovy Ducks
 Sonoma Foie-Gras

5391 Grimm's Fine Food
#100-10991 Shellbridge Way
Richmond, BC V6X 3C6
Canada
780-415-4331
Fax: 780-477-5287 866-663-4746
www.grimmsfinefoods.com
Processed meats and sausages
President: Rick Grimm
Plant Manager: George McCorry
Number Employees: 50-99
Parent Co: Fletcher's Fine Foods
Type of Packaging: Consumer, Food Service, Private Label, Bulk
Brands:
 Deli Flavor
 Fletchers

5392 Grimm's Locker Service
PO Box 4524
Sherwood, OH 43556-0524
419-899-2655
Fax: 419-899-2655
Canned meat and poultry
Owner: Michael Oskey
Estimated Sales: Below $5,000,000
Number Employees: 1-4

5393 (HQ)Grimmway Farms
P.O. Box 81498
Bakersfield, CA 93380
800-301-3101
media@grimmway.com www.grimmway.com
Carrots, potatoes, organic produce and juice
President: Jeff Meger
jmeger@grimmway.com
CFO: Steve Barnes
Vice President: Jeff Huckaby
Quality Assurance: Rory Gonzales
Sales Manager Juice Division: Paul Verderber
Type of Packaging: Consumer, Food Service
Other Locations:
 Grimmway Farms
 Arvin CA
 Cal-Organic Farms
 Lamont CA
Brands:
 Grimmway

5394 Gringo Jack's
5103 Main St
Manchester Ctr, VT 05255-9772
802-362-0836
Fax: 802-362-0741 www.gringojacks.com
Sauces, salsas and dips, chips and soups
Founder and CEO: Jack Gilbert
gringojack@gmail.com
Co-Founder: Michele Kropp
Number Employees: 20-49

Food Manufacturers / A-Z

5395 Grippo Foods
6750 Colerain Ave
Cincinnati, OH 45239-5542
513-923-1900
Fax: 513-923-3645 800-626-1824
info@grippos.com www.grippos.com
Potato chips, pretzels, dips and other snacks
President: Ralph W. Pagel
VP: Nancy Schreiber
Purchasing: Ralph Pagel
Estimated Sales: $7.2 Million
Number Employees: 10-19
Square Footage: 99000
Type of Packaging: Consumer

5396 Groeb Farms
10464 Bryan Hwy
Onsted, MI 49265-0269
517-467-2065
Fax: 517-467-2840 800-530-9969
Honey; UPC labeling, tamper-evident packaging, re-closable cap, easy pour handle and shatterproof containers
President & CEO: Ernest Groeb
VP & CFO: Jack Irvin Jr
VP/COO: Troy Groeb
Director Retail Sales: Jim McCoy
Chief Procurement Officer: Alison Tringale
Type of Packaging: Consumer, Food Service, Private Label, Bulk
Other Locations:
   Belleview FL
   Miller's American Honey
   Colton CA
Brands:
   Gourmet Jose
   Groeb Farms

5397 Groff's Meats
33 N Market St
Elizabethtown, PA 17022-2087
717-367-1246
Fax: 717-367-1952 www.groffsmeats.com
Beef, pork, poultry, deli items and specialty foods
Owner: Nancy Groff
nsgroff@aol.com
VP: Virginia Groff
Estimated Sales: $4 Million
Number Employees: 20-49
Square Footage: 9000
Type of Packaging: Consumer, Food Service, Private Label

5398 Groovy Candies
6770 Brookpark Rd
Cleveland, OH 44129
216-472-0206
Fax: 216-274-9200 888-729-1604
www.groovycandies.com
Candy
President: Ed Kitchen
Chairman: Bert Hiddie
Estimated Sales: $5-9.9 Million
Number Employees: 20-49
Number of Brands: 1
Number of Products: 25
Square Footage: 30000
Type of Packaging: Consumer, Private Label, Bulk
Brands:
   Gladstone Candies

5399 Grossingers Home Bakery
244 W 54th St
New York, NY 10019-5515
212-362-8672
Fax: 212-362-8627 800-479-6996
hrgrsin@aol.com
Ice cream cakes
Owner: Herb Grossinger
Estimated Sales: Less Than $500,000
Number Employees: 5-9
Brands:
   Bombe Glaze

5400 Grote & Weigel Inc
76 Granby St
Bloomfield, CT 06002-3512
860-242-8528
Fax: 860-242-4162
Processed meats and specialty sausages
Owner: Mike Grenier
customerservice@groteandweigel.com
Vice President: John Shieding
Estimated Sales: $5-10 Million
Number Employees: 20-49
Square Footage: 30000
Brands:
   Clearfield
   Grote & Weigel
   Jersey Boardwalk
   Marcello
   Meinel
   Riley's Beef Sausage
   Texan Wiener

5401 Groth Vineyards & Winery
750 Oakville Cross Road
Oakville, CA 94562
707-944-0290
Fax: 707-944-8932 info@grothwines.com
www.grothwines.com
Wines
President: Dennis Groth
CFO: Carl Ebbeson
Vice President: Judith Groth
Marketing Director: Suzanne Groth
Finance Manager: Dawn Selanders
Contact: Mike Ferrante
mferrante@grothwines.com
Winemaker: Michael Weis
Estimated Sales: $1,2,000,000
Number Employees: 20
Type of Packaging: Private Label

5402 Grounds For Thought
174 S Main St
Bowling Green, OH 43402-2909
419-354-3266
Fax: 419-354-7512 www.groundsforthought.com
Coffee
Owner: Kelly Wicks
kelly@groundsforthought.com
Estimated Sales: Under $500,000
Number Employees: 10-19
Square Footage: 3000
Type of Packaging: Consumer, Food Service, Private Label, Bulk
Brands:
   Black Swamp
   Bluegrass
   Grounds For Thought
   John Z'S Big City

5403 Grounds for Change
15773 George Ln NE
Suite 204
Poulsbo, WA 98370
360-779-0402 800-796-6820
info@groundsforchange.com
www.groundsforchange.com
Fair trade organic coffee beans
President/Co-Founder: Kelsey Marshall
Co-Founder: Stacy Marshall
Year Founded: 2003

5404 Groundwork Coffee Co.
5457 Cleon Ave
North Hollywood, CA 91601
818-506-6020
Fax: 818-506-6035 www.groundworkcoffee.com
Organic coffees and teas
Principal: Jeff Chean
Type of Packaging: Consumer
Brands:
   GROUNDWORK

5405 Groupe Paul Masson
110-50, Rue De La Barre
Longueuil, QC J4K 5G2
Canada
514-878-3050
Fax: 450-651-5453 www.bloomberg.com
Alcoholic beverages
President: Jean Denis Cote
VP Marketing Development: Alain Lecours
Number Employees: 100-249
Type of Packaging: Consumer
Brands:
   Aperossimo
   Bau Maniere
   Castelet
   De Lescot
   Dubleuet
   El Condor
   Foret Noire
   L'Ombrelle
   Nobella
   Pica
   Robert De Serbie
   Valentino

5406 Grouse Hunt Farm Inc
458 Fairview St
Tamaqua, PA 18252-4718
570-467-2850
Fax: 570-467-2850 www.woswit.com
Dressings, relishes, mustards, sauces, seasonings, jellies, preserves, butters, fruits, horseradish, etc
Owner: Christopher Thompson
chris@woswit.com
Estimated Sales: Less Than $500,000
Number Employees: 1-4
Number of Brands: 2
Number of Products: 108
Square Footage: 40000
Type of Packaging: Private Label
Brands:
   Grouse Hunt Farms
   Pennsylvania Dutch Foods
   Wos-Wit

5407 Grow Co
55 Railroad Ave
Ridgefield, NJ 07657-2109
201-941-8777
Fax: 201-342-9127 info@growco.us
Vitamins, minerals and flavors
Vice President: Massoud Avanaghi
arvanaghi@growco.us
Estimated Sales: $1-2.5 Million
Number Employees: 10-19
Square Footage: 91200
Brands:
   Re-Natured

5408 Grow-Pac
2220 SW Lafollett Rd
Cornelius, OR 97113
503-357-9691
Fax: 503-357-2155
Frozen blackberries, blueberries, strawberries, marion berries
President: Lloyd Duyck
Co-owner: Geraldine Duyck
Contact: Nick Duyck
nickduyck@valleybluefarms.com
Estimated Sales: Under $500,000
Number Employees: 5
Brands:
   Grow-Pac

5409 Grower Shipper Potato Company
One Fourth Mile Hwy 285
Monte Vista, CO 81144
719-852-3569
Fax: 719-852-5917
Potatoes
Manager: Mark Lounsbury
Vice President: Ron Heersink
Manager: Ken Shepherd
Estimated Sales: $10-20 Million
Number Employees: 20-49
Square Footage: 120000
Type of Packaging: Consumer, Food Service, Bulk
Brands:
   Big Ram
   Colorado Gold
   Diamond
   Jackpot

5410 Growers Cooperative Juice Co
112 N Portage St
Westfield, NY 14787-1054
716-326-3161
Fax: 716-326-6566 www.concordgrapejuice.com
Grape juice and juice concentrate
President: Steve Baran
dmom@concordgrapejuice.com
Quality Assurance Manager: Jim Gillespie
Sales Exec: Dave Momberger
General Manager: David Momberger
Plant Manager: Todd Donato
Estimated Sales: $5-10 Million
Number Employees: 20-49
Type of Packaging: Bulk

5411 Growing Roots Foods
700 Sylvan Ave
Englewood Cliffs, NJ 07632
www.growingrootsfoods.com
Organic corn, coconut and seed bites and clusters

Food Manufacturers / A-Z

Parent Co: Unilever US
Type of Packaging: Consumer
Brands:
    GROWING ROOTS

5412 Grown-up Soda
424 E 57th St
Suite 3C
New York, NY 10022
    212-355-7454
    Fax: 212-208-4444 info@drinkgus.com
    www.drinkgus.com
Sodas
Founder: Steve Hersh
Founder: Jeannette Luoh
Contact: Samantha Garchik
samantha@drinkgus.com
Parent Co: Utmost Brands

5413 Gruet Winery
8400 Pan American Fwy NE
Albuquerque, NM 87113-1832
    505-821-0055
    Fax: 505-857-0066 888-857-9463
    info@gruetwinery.com www.gruetwinery.com
Wines
President/Winemaker: Laurent Gruet
laurent@gruetwinery.com
Vice President: Farid Himeur
Estimated Sales: $1-2,500,000
Number Employees: 20-49
Type of Packaging: Private Label
Brands:
    Domaine St. Vincent
    Gruet Winery

5414 Grumpe's Specialties
140 Market St
Baird, TX 79504-6406
    325-854-1106
    Fax: 325-854-1107 866-854-1106
    artwork@grumpes.com www.grumpes.com
Personalized lollipops
President: Warren Harkins
Number Employees: 10-19

5415 Guapo Spices Company
6200 E Slauson Avenue
Los Angeles, CA 90040-3012
    213-322-8900
    Fax: 213-627-0601
Seasonings, spices
Estimated Sales: $2.5-5,000,000
Number Employees: 20-49
Type of Packaging: Private Label

5416 Guayaki
6782 Sebastopol Ave # 100
Sebastopol, CA 95472-3880
    707-824-6644
    Fax: 707-824-6644 888-482-9254
    info@guayaki.com www.guayaki.com
Organic rainforest herbs
Co-Founder: Alex Pryer
Chief Executive Officer: Chris Mann
info@guayaki.com
Co-Founder: David Karr
VP of Sales: Luke Gernandt
Sales Coordinator: Saskia Baur
Customer Care: Scott Turner
Vice President Operations: Richard Bruehl
Productions: Lucia Diaz
Estimated Sales: $3 Million
Number Employees: 20-49
Number of Brands: 1
Number of Products: 13
Square Footage: 15000
Type of Packaging: Consumer, Food Service, Bulk
Brands:
    Organic Guayaki Yerba Mate

5417 Guenoc & Langtry Estate
21000 Butts Canyon Rd
Middletown, CA 95461-9606
    707-995-7501
    Fax: 707-987-9351 info@langtryestate.com
    www.langtryestate.com
Wines
Owner: Bill Foley
President: Tim Matz
Winemaker: Walter Jorge
Director Marketing: Karen Melander-Magoon
National Sales Manager: Greg Brolin
Media Inquiries: Sarah Johnduff
Year Founded: 1888
Estimated Sales: $20-50 Million
Number Employees: 1
Square Footage: 72000
Brands:
    Domaine Breton
    Guenoc
    Langtry

5418 Guerra Nut Shelling Co Inc
190 Hillcrest Rd
Hollister, CA 95023-4944
    831-637-4471
    Fax: 831-637-1358 walnut@guerranut.com
    www.guerranut.com
Walnuts
President: Frank V Guerra
frank@guerranut.com
CEO: Jeff Guerra
Estimated Sales: $5-10 Million
Number Employees: 50-99
Square Footage: 150000
Type of Packaging: Bulk
Brands:
    Cal Best
    Hillcrest

5419 Guers Dairy
1268 Tumbling Run Rd
Tamaqua, PA 18252-3400
    570-277-6611
    Fax: 570-277-0135 www.guersdairy.com
Milk and milk products
President: Danelle Yaag
dyaag@yahoo.com
Treasurer: William Yaag
VP: Edward Guers
Purchasing Manager: Dwight Manbeck
Estimated Sales: $10-20,000,000
Number Employees: 50-99

5420 Guggisberg Cheese
5060 State Route 557
Millersburg, OH 44654-9266
    330-893-2500
    Fax: 330-893-3240 800-262-2505
    info@babyswiss.com www.babyswiss.com
Cheese
President: Richard Guggisberg
Year Founded: 1950
Estimated Sales: G
Number Employees: 100-249
Square Footage: 10000
Type of Packaging: Consumer, Food Service, Bulk
Brands:
    Amish Farm
    Guggisberg
    Original Baby

5421 Guglielmo Winery
1480 E Main Ave
Morgan Hill, CA 95037-3299
    408-779-2145
    Fax: 408-779-3166 info@guglielmowinery.com
Wines
Winemaker/ President: George E. Guglielmo
george@guglielmowinery.com
CFO: Julie Bradford
Director of Sales: Gene Guglielmo
Dir. Of Retail Operations: Cindy Adams
Estimated Sales: $10-20 Million
Number Employees: 20-49
Type of Packaging: Consumer, Private Label, Bulk
Brands:
    Emile's
    Guflielmo Reserve
    Guglielmo
    Guglielmo Vineyard Selection

5422 Guida's Dairy
433 Park St.
New Britain, CT 06051
    800-832-8929
    www.supercow.com
Dairy products.
President: Michael Young
Estimated Sales: $149 Million
Number Employees: 250-499
Square Footage: 75000
Type of Packaging: Consumer, Food Service, Private Label
Brands:
    Guida's

5423 Guido's International Foods
1669 La Cresta Dr
Pasadena, CA 91103-1260
    626-296-1427
    Fax: 626-296-0306 877-994-8436
Seasonings and sauces
President: Guido Meindl
Estimated Sales: $20,000
Number Employees: 2
Number of Brands: 7
Type of Packaging: Consumer, Food Service, Private Label, Bulk
Brands:
    Guido's Serious

5424 Guidry's Catfish Inc
1093 Henderson Hwy
Breaux Bridge, LA 70517-7728
    337-228-7546
    Fax: 337-228-7544
    www.catfishmarketingassociation.com
Fresh catfish
Owner: Bobby Jules
CAO: Sandra Robertson
sandra@guidryscatfish.com
Operations: Sandra Guidry-Robertson
Administrative Executive: Sandra Robertson
Estimated Sales: $10-20 Million
Number Employees: 100-249

5425 Guilliams Winery
3851 Spring Mountain Rd
St Helena, CA 94574
    707-963-9059
    Fax: 707-963-9059
Wines
President: John Guilliams
Estimated Sales: Less than $500,000
Number Employees: 1-4

5426 Guiltless Gourmet
80 Avenue K
Newark, NJ 7105
    201-553-1100
    deborah.ross@manischewitz.com
    www.guiltlessgourmet.com
Natural, low-fat baked snacks, dips and salsas
President: Michael Shaw
VP Finance: Bart Glaser
VP Sales/Marketing: Robert Greenberg
Number Employees: 20-49
Parent Co: The Manischewitz Company
Type of Packaging: Consumer, Food Service, Private Label, Bulk
Brands:
    Guiltless Gourmet

5427 Guinness Import Co
6 Landmark Sq
Stamford, CT 06901-2704
    203-323-3311
    Fax: 203-359-7209 800-521-1591
    guinness@consumer-care.net www.guiness.com
Beers, stout
President: Tim Kelly
Chief Information Officer: Lynda Gutman
Contact: Charles Ireland
guinness-storehouse@guinness.com
Vice President Operations: Colin Funnell
Number Employees: 5-9
Parent Co: Guiness PLC
Type of Packaging: Consumer
Brands:
    Asahi
    Bass Ale
    Furstenberg
    Guinness Stout
    Harp Lager
    Kaliber
    Guinness®

Food Manufacturers / A-Z

5428 Guittard Chocolate Co
10 Guittard Rd
PO Box 4308
Burlingame, CA 94010-2203
650-697-4427
Fax: 650-692-2761 800-468-2462
sales@guittard.com www.guittard.com
Chocolate and chocolate products
President & CEO: Gary Guittard
gary@guittard.com
Director Sales/Marketing: Mark Spini
Estimated Sales: $20-50 Million
Number Employees: 100-249
Brands:
   Chocolate Products
   Dick Servaes
   Melt-N-Mold
   Smooth-N-Melty

5429 Gulf Atlantic Freezers
PO Box 2493
Gretna, LA 70054-2493
504-392-3590
Fax: 504-392-3443
Frozen seafood
Contact: Al Smith
gafltd@msn.com

5430 Gulf Central Seafood
PO Box 373
Biloxi, MS 39533-0373
228-436-6346
Fax: 228-374-1207
Seafood, fresh, live and frozen
President: Rock Sekul
Estimated Sales: $2.5-5,000,000
Number Employees: 20-49
Brands:
   Gulf Central
   Gulf Star
   Treasure Bay

5431 Gulf City Marine Supply
14650 Shell Belt
Bayou La Batre, AL 36509
251-824-2516
Fax: 251-824-7980
Seafood
President: Charles Graham
Estimated Sales: $500,000-$1 Million
Number Employees: 5-9
Parent Co: Gulf City Seafood

5432 Gulf Crown Seafood Co
306 Jon Floyd Rd
Delcambre, LA 70528-4522
337-685-4722
Fax: 337-685-4241 gulfcrown@gulfcrown.us
www.gulfcrown.us
Shrimp
President: John Floyd
Manager: Bonnie Richard
Sales: Crystal Marcaux
Manager: Stephen Greene
gulfcrown@gulfcrown.us
Estimated Sales: $7 Million
Number Employees: 5-9
Brands:
   Gulf Crown

5433 (HQ)Gulf Food Products Co Inc
509 Commerce Pt
New Orleans, LA 70123-3203
504-733-1516
Fax: 504-733-1517 roberthoy@worldnet.att.net
Seafood
Owner: Albert Lin
gulffoodproducts@aol.com
Estimated Sales: Less than $500,000
Number Employees: 1-4
Square Footage: 16000

5434 Gulf Marine
501 Louisiana St
Westwego, LA 70094-4141
504-436-2682
Fax: 504-436-1585 sales@gulfmarineproducts.com
www.lapack.com
Shrimp, crawfish and other seafood
President: David Lai
Number Employees: 20-49

5435 Gulf Marine & Industrial Supplies Inc
5801 Armour Dr.
Houston, TX 77020
713-514-8010
Fax: 504-525-4761 800-886-6252
service@gulfmarine.net www.gulfmarine.net
Seafood, pork, beef, poultry, canned and frozen foods, fresh vegetables, beer, wine and other general merchandise
President: John Cotsoradis
General Manager: Dimitris Karmoukos
Estimated Sales: $30-50 Million
Number Employees: 50-99
Square Footage: 250000
Type of Packaging: Food Service
Other Locations:
   Houston TX
   New Orleans LA
   Tampa FL
   Long Beach CA

5436 Gulf Packing Company
618 Commerce St
San Benito, TX 78586-4216
956-399-2631
Fax: 956-399-2675
Meat, including heifer calf and packaged meats
CEO: Charlie Booth
VP: Carlos Salinas
Quality Control Manager: Fred Frausto
Manager: Ace Delacerta
Mngr: Frank Esquivel
Estimated Sales: $10-20 Million
Number Employees: 50 to 99
Type of Packaging: Consumer
Brands:
   Quality Minded

5437 Gulf Pecan Company
5456 Highway 90 W
Mobile, AL 36619-4212
251-661-2931
ulfpecanco@yahoo.com
Farm products and raw materials; dried fruits and vegetables
Owner & President: Danny Fritz
Estimated Sales: $5-9.9,000,000
Number Employees: 3

5438 Gulf Pride Enterprises
391 Bayview Ave
Biloxi, MS 39530-2502
228-432-2488
Fax: 228-374-7411 888-689-0560
www.gulfprideenterprises.com
Shrimp
President: Kathy Cruthirds
kathy@gulfprideshrimp.com
Vice President: Wally Gollott
Estimated Sales: $10 Million-$50 Million
Number Employees: 50-99
Type of Packaging: Consumer, Private Label
Brands:
   Captain Pierre
   Gulf Pride
   Magnolia Bay

5439 Gulf Shrimp, Inc.
100 Shrimp Boat Lane
Fort Myers Beach, FL 33931-2925
239-463-8788
Fax: 239-463-3550
Shrimp
Owner: Dennis Henderson
Manager: Dan Schribner
Estimated Sales: $2.5-5,000,000
Number Employees: 20-49

5440 Gulf States Canners Inc
1006 Industrial Park Dr
Clinton, MS 39056
601-924-0511
Canned soft drinks
President & CIO: Albert Clark
Estimated Sales: $75-99 Million
Number Employees: 50-99
Square Footage: 300000
Type of Packaging: Consumer, Food Service

5441 Gulf Stream Crab Company
13871 Shell Belt Rd
Bayou La Batre, AL 36509
251-824-4717
Fax: 251-824-7416
Crabs
President: Bryan Cumbie
Estimated Sales: $.5-1 million
Number Employees: 1-4

5442 Gum Technology Corporation
10860 North Mavinee Drive
Tucson, AZ 85737
520-888-5500
Fax: 520-888-5585 800-369-4867
info@gumtech.com www.gumpert.com
Food gums, hydrocolloids and stabilizing systems
President/CEO: Allen Freed
R&D/Laboratory Director: Aida Prenzno
Marketing Director: Janelle Litel
VP/Sales: Joshua Brooks
Contact: Beth Woodley
beth@milehighingredients.com
Estimated Sales: $5-10 Million
Number Employees: 5-9
Square Footage: 12000
Type of Packaging: Bulk
Brands:
   Coyote
   Coyote Star

5443 Gumix International Inc
2160 N Central Rd # 202
Fort Lee, NJ 07024-7547
201-947-6300
Fax: 201-947-9265 800-248-6492
info@gumix.com
Foods gums
President: Sean Katir
info@gumix.com
Estimated Sales: D
Number Employees: 5-9

5444 Gumpert's Canada
2500 Tedlo Street
Mississauga, ON L5A 4A9
Canada
905-279-2600
Fax: 905-279-2797 800-387-9324
info@gumpert.com www.gumpert.com
Toppings, puddings, flavors & extracts, glazes, icings, cake bases, powder fillings, creme pie fillings, fruit pie fillings, and bavarians
President: George Johnson
R&D/QA Manager: Erica Tulloch
Estimated Sales: $5 Million
Number Employees: 40
Number of Products: 200
Square Footage: 106000
Type of Packaging: Bulk
Brands:
   Gumpert's

5445 Gundlach-Bundschu Winery
2000 Denmark St
Sonoma, CA 95476-9615
707-939-3015
Fax: 707-938-9460 www.gunbun.com
Wines
Owner: Jim Bundschu
jimb@gunbun.com
Winemaker: Keith Emerson
Director of Viticulture: Jim Bundschu
Estimated Sales: $1-2,500,000
Number Employees: 50-99
Number of Brands: 3

5446 Gunnoe Farms Sausage & Salad
2115 Oakridge Dr
Charleston, WV 25311-1499
304-343-7686
Fax: 304-343-4748 gunnoefarm@aol.com
Meat including sausage
President: Nancy Gunnoe
gunnoefarm@aol.com
Vice President: Joy Gunnoe
Sales Executive: Joy Gunnoe
Estimated Sales: $15 Million
Number Employees: 20-49
Type of Packaging: Consumer

Food Manufacturers / A-Z

5447 Gunther's Gourmet
PO Box 18215
Richmond, VA 23226
804-240-1796
Fax: 540-982-2015
chefmike@gunthersgourmet.com
www.gunthersgourmet.com
Salad dressing, salsa/dips, grilling sauces, marinades.
Marketing: Mike Lampros

5448 Gurley's Foods
1118 Highway 12 E
Willmar, MN 56201-3741
320-235-0600
Fax: 320-235-0659   800-426-7845
www.gurleysfoods.com
Nuts, nut mixes, chocolate covered nuts, nut bark
President & General Manager: Tom Taunton
Year Founded: 1979
Estimated Sales: $20-50 Million
Number Employees: 50-99
Brands:
 Gurley's Candy
 Gurley's Golden Recipe Nuts
 Gurley's Natures Harvest
 Rocky Mountain

5449 GuruNanda
6645 Caballero Blvd
Buena Park, CA 90620
866-421-0309
www.gurunanda.com
Essential oils
CFO: David Richards
SVP, Sales & Marketing: Whitney Messens
Type of Packaging: Consumer
Brands:
 GURUNANDA

5450 Gus' Pretzel Shop
1820 Arsenal St # 5
St Louis, MO 63118-2529
314-664-4010
Fax: 314-664-0000 guspretzels.com
Pretzels
Owner: August J Koebbe Jr
Number Employees: 10-19

5451 Gust John Foods & Products
1350 Paramount Pkwy
Batavia, IL 60510-1461
630-879-8700
Fax: 630-879-8708   800-756-5886
www.northern-pines.com
Pancake, waffle and muffin mixes; also, pancake and sugar-free syrups
Owner: Gust Koutselas
gustjohnfoods@aol.com
Estimated Sales: $1 Million
Number Employees: 5-9
Type of Packaging: Consumer, Food Service, Private Label, Bulk
Brands:
 Northern Pines Gourmet

5452 Gustus Vitae Condiments LLC
3016 E Colorado Blvd
Unit 70819
Pasadena, CA 91117
424-229-2367
www.gustusvitae.com
Condiments
Marketing Director: James Evans
Operations Manager: Francis Scanlon

5453 Gutheinz Meats Inc
520 Cedar Ave
Scranton, PA 18505-1191
570-344-1191
Fax: 570-344-1193 www.gutheinz.com
Meat products
President: Allen Leach
Estimated Sales: $2.5-5 Million
Number Employees: 5-9
Type of Packaging: Consumer

5454 Gutsii
12655 W Jefferson Blvd
Level 4
Los Angeles, CA 90066
team@gutsii.com
gutsii.com
Prebiotic chocolate bars

5455 Guttenplan's Frozen Dough
100 Highway 36
Middletown, NJ 07748
Fax: 732-495-2415   888-422-4357
info@guttenplan.com www.guttenplan.com
Frozen rolls, bread, dough and bagels, sweet goods
Owner/President: Jack Guttenplan
Estimated Sales: $10-25 000,000
Number Employees: 50-99
Number of Products: 7
Square Footage: 70000
Type of Packaging: Private Label

5456 Guy's Food
7223 West 95th Street
Suite 230
Overland Park, KS 66212
913-871-3616
Fax: 913-383-8436   800-821-2405
Snacks
President: Ron Hirasawa
CEO: John Morris
CFO: Thomas Price
VP of Sales: Reid Bennett
Operations Manager: Thomas Anderson
Plant Manager: George Flughum
Number Employees: 500-999
Type of Packaging: Private Label
Brands:
 Guy's

5457 Guylian USA Inc.
560 Sylvan Ave
Englewood Cliffs, NJ 07632
201-871-4144
guylian.com
Chocolates and confections
President: Michael Cobb
Director of Sales & Marketing: Nicholas Goh
Year Founded: 1994
Estimated Sales: $1 Million
Number Employees: 1-10
Type of Packaging: Private Label

5458 Gwinn's Foods
6190 Bermuda Dr
St Louis, MO 63135-3264
314-521-8792
Fax: 314-521-8792
Beef, beef products, hot tamales
Owner: Joseph Frisella
Estimated Sales: $1-2,500,000
Number Employees: 5-9

5459 H & B Packing Co
702 Forrest St
Waco, TX 76704-2730
254-752-2506
Fax: 254-752-1451 www.handrfoods.com
Sausages
President: Jake K Bauer
Vice President: David Bauer
Sales Executive: Rick Bauer
IT Executive: Johnny Arispe
jad_jad_007@yahoo.com
Estimated Sales: $20-50 Million
Number Employees: 100-249

5460 H & H Products Co
6600 Magnolia Homes Rd
Orlando, FL 32810-4285
407-299-5410
Fax: 407-298-6966   800-678-8448
info@hartleysbrand.com
www.hhproductscompany.com
Juices, drink bases, liquid teas and syrups
Owner: Morris Hartley
mhartley@hartleysbrand.com
Founder: Len Hartley
Secretary: Betty Hartly
QC Manager: Joy Corbin
Regional Sales Manager: Emily Cooper
Regional Sales Manager: David Lynch
mhartley@hartleysbrand.com
Production Manager: Derrick Abner
Plant Manager: Jason Browning
Purchasing Manager: Mike Bowes
Estimated Sales: $6 Million
Number Employees: 20-49
Square Footage: 120000
Type of Packaging: Food Service, Private Label

Brands:
 Bloody Mary Juice Burst
 Citrus Punch Sugar-Free
 Flavor Burst Liquid Citrus Tea
 Flavor Burst Liquid Sweet Tea
 Flavor Burst Liquid Unsweet Tea
 Flavorburst
 Hartley's
 Juiceburst
 Lemon/Lime Thristaway
 Neutral Slush
 Orange Thirstaway

5461 H & W Foods
2029 Lauwiliwili St
Kapolei, HI 96707-1836
808-682-8300
Fax: 808-841-8687 www.hwfoodservice.com
Refrigerated, frozen and dry meat products
Owner/CEO: Bill Loose
Chief Financial Officer: Jeff Sakamoto
IT Manager: Shelle Andrade
Estimated Sales: $5-10 Million
Number Employees: 5-9
Square Footage: 90000

5462 H B Taylor Co
4830 S Christiana Ave
Chicago, IL 60632-3092
773-254-4805
Fax: 773-254-4563 www.hbtaylor.com
Flavors, colors and food essentials.
President: Leon Juskaitis
Owner/Human Resources Executive: Saul Juskaitis
sjuskaitis@hbtaylor.com
Research & Development Director: Joy Souders
Quality Control Manager: Larry King
Operations Manager: Edward Juskaitis
Purchasing Manager: Mary Power
Estimated Sales: $3 Million
Number Employees: 10-19
Square Footage: 50000
Type of Packaging: Private Label, Bulk
Brands:
 Cocoa Replacers
 Dark Roast
 Golden Roast
 Hyskor
 Lipo Butter
 Liquimul Black
 Mahogany Black
 Sesa-Krunch
 Sesame Seed

5463 H Cantin
1910 Av Du Sanctuaire
Beauport, QC G1E 3L2
Canada
418-663-3523
Fax: 418-663-0717   800-463-5268
cantinh@microtec.ca
Jams, pie fillings, pudding mixes, maple syrup, soup bases, bakery products and candies; importer of frozen fruit; exporter of marshmallow cones and caramels
President/General Manager: Leonce Tremblay
Number Employees: 50-99
Square Footage: 60000
Parent Co: Bon Bons Associates
Type of Packaging: Consumer, Food Service, Private Label, Bulk

5464 H Coturri & Sons Winery
6725 Enterprise Rd
Glen Ellen, CA 95442
707-525-9126
Fax: 707-542-8039   866-268-8774
Wines
Manager: Tony Coturri
Marketing Director: Harry Coturo
Operations Manager: Tony Coturri
Estimated Sales: $500,000-$1,000,000
Number Employees: 1-4

5465 H Fox & Co Inc
416 Thatford Ave
Brooklyn, NY 11212-5895
718-385-4600
Fax: 718-345-4283
Chocolate and fruit flavored syrups, dessert toppings and juice mixes

Food Manufacturers / A-Z

President: David Fox
dfox@foxsyrups.com
Executive VP: Kelly Fox
IT: David Frankum
Estimated Sales: $10-20 Million
Number Employees: 20-49
Square Footage: 36000
Type of Packaging: Food Service
Brands:
   Fox
   Fox's U-Bet
   No-Cal

5466 H Nagel & Son Co
2428 Central Pkwy
Cincinnati, OH 45214-1804
                            513-665-4550
Fax: 513-665-4570 www.brightonmills.com
Flour and flour based mixes
President: Edward Nagel
Estimated Sales: $20-50 Million
Number Employees: 20-49
Number of Brands: 1
Type of Packaging: Food Service, Private Label, Bulk
Brands:
   Brighton Mills

5467 H R Nicholson Co
6320 Oakleaf Ave
Baltimore, MD 21215-2213
                            410-580-0975
Fax: 410-764-9125 800-638-3514
Fruit juices and tea concentrates
President: H Robert Nicholson
Secretary/Treasurer: Su Shaffer
VP Sales/Marketing: Bob Homewood
Number Employees: 20-49
Square Footage: 114000
Type of Packaging: Consumer, Food Service
Brands:
   Bombay Gold 100
   Nicholson's Bestea
   Nicholson's Bottlers
   Nicholson's Chok-Nick

5468 H&A Health Products, Inc
3-180 Brodie Drive
Richmond Hill, ON L4B 3K8
Canada
                            514-979-3589
Fax: 514-694-4543 sales@hacanada.com
                         www.hacanada.com
Flavor enhancers, preservatives, sweeteners, food gums/hydrocolloids, shrink bags and casings.

5469 H&H Fisheries Limited
PO Box 172
Eastern Passage, NS B3G 1M5
Canada
                            902-465-6330
Fax: 902-465-2572 866-773-4400
Fresh and frozen seafood
Contact: Regionald Hartlen
Estimated Sales: $13.8,000,000
Number Employees: 30
Type of Packaging: Consumer, Food Service, Private Label, Bulk

5470 H&K Packers Company
420 Turenne Street
Winnipeg, NB R2J 3W8
Canada
                            204-233-2354
                Fax: 204-235-1258
Pork and beef
President: Albert Kelly
Production: Jake Penner
Plant Manager: Andy Van Patter
Number Employees: 20-49
Square Footage: 20000
Type of Packaging: Bulk
Brands:
   H&K Packers
   Kings Choice

5471 H&S Bakery
620 South Bond Street
Baltimore, MD 21231
                            410-276-7254
      Fax: 410-522-5200 800-959-7655
ematta@hsbakery.com www.hsbakery.com
Bakery products

President: Bill Paterakis
Director of Sales: Charlie Alves
Plant Manager: Matthew Kimmel
Number Employees: 2000+
Square Footage: 336000
Other Locations:
   Community Market
   Baltimore MD
   Crispy Bagel Company
   Baltimore MD
   Baltimore Distribution Center
   Baltimore MD
   Annapolis Junction Dist. Center
   Annapolis Junction MD
   Corporate Office
   Baltimore MD
   Automatic Rolls of Baltimore, Inc.
   Baltimore MD
   Automatic Rolls of North Carolina
   Clayton NC
   Automatic Rolls of New England
   Dayville CT
   Automatic Rolls of New Jersey
   Edison NJ
   Bake Rite Rolls, Inc.
   Bensalem PA
   Mid Atlantic Baking Company
   Baltimore MD
   Schmidt Baking Company
   Baltimore MD

5472 H&S Edible Products Corporation
119 Fulton Lane
Mount Vernon, NY 10550-4697
                            914-664-4041
Fax: 914-664-8304 800-253-3364
Dry bread crumbs, nuts
President: Mari Rowan
Vice President: Peter Rowan
Estimated Sales: $2,000,000
Number Employees: 20-49
Number of Products: 1
Square Footage: 13000
Type of Packaging: Food Service, Private Label, Bulk
Brands:
   H&S Bread Crumbs

5473 H-E-B Grocery Co. LP
PO Box 839999
San Antonio, TX 78283-3999
                            210-938-8357
                            800-432-3113
                            www.heb.com
Processes milk and bread products.
President: Craig Boyan
Chairman/CEO: Charles Butt
butt.charles@heb.com
COO: Martin Otto
Year Founded: 1905
Estimated Sales: $21 Billion
Number Employees: 100,000
Type of Packaging: Consumer
Other Locations:
   Westgate Manufacturing Facility
   Austin TX
   Central Market Manufacturing
   San Antonio TX
   Dairy Manufacturing Facility
   Plano TX
Brands:
   H-E-B
   H-E-Buddy
   H-E-B Select Ingredients
   H-E-B Organics
   H-E-B Kitchen & Table
   Central Market
   Hill Country Products
   Cocinaware
   ChefStyle
   Sear 'n Smoke
   GTC
   Mia's Mirror

5474 H. Interdonati
PO Box 262
Cold Spring Harbour, NY 11724
                            631-367-6611
      Fax: 631-367-6626 800-367-6617
flavorplus@aol.com www.hinterdonati.com
Ingredients and additives
President: Robert Interdonati
Sales Manager: Andrew Interdonati
andrewinterdonati@hinterdonati.com
Estimated Sales: $3 Million
Number Employees: 3
Square Footage: 2000

Brands:
   Alnose

5475 H. Reisman Corporation
377 Crane Street
Orange, NJ 7051
                            973-882-1670
                Fax: 973-882-0323
Vitamins and herbal extracts
Owner/President: Frank Molinaro
Estimated Sales: $5-10 Million
Number Employees: 20-49
Square Footage: 300000
Parent Co: LycoRed Company
Type of Packaging: Bulk
Brands:
   Bionova
   Floraglow
   Lycomato
   Phyto Foods

5476 H.B. Dawe
PO Box 100
Cupids, NL A0A 2B0
Canada
                            709-528-4347
                Fax: 709-528-3463
Groundfish and shellfish
General Manager: Philip Hillyard
Number Employees: 100-249
Type of Packaging: Consumer, Food Service, Private Label, Bulk

5477 H.B. Trading
10 Taft Road
Totowa, NJ 07512-1006
                            973-812-1022
      Fax: 973-812-2191 nico@nideco.com
Cookies and candies
Brands:
   Brent & Sam's
   Cape Cod Cranberry C
   Cow-Town and Rancher's

5478 H.Gass Seafood
38945 Jacqueline Street
Hollywood, MD 20636
                            301-373-6882
                Fax: 301-884-8350
Fresh oysters and crabs
Owner: James Payne
Number Employees: 10-19
Square Footage: 2000

5479 H.K. Canning
130 N Garden St
P.O. BOX 729
Ventura, CA 93002-0729
                            805-652-1392
                       www.whereorg.com
Canned and dry beans, soup and mushrooms
President: Henry Knaust
CFO: Richard Hanson
Vice-President: Carol Knaust
Estimated Sales: $4 Million
Number Employees: 66
Type of Packaging: Consumer, Food Service, Private Label, Bulk
Brands:
   Freshman
   Henry's Kettle
   Knaust Beans
   Meridian Foods
   Norteno
   Sea Valley
   Seaside

5480 H2rOse, LLC
Los Angeles, CA 90046
                        info@drinkh2rose.com
                      www.drinkh2rose.com
Rose water beverage
Co-Founder & President: Kia Illulian
Type of Packaging: Consumer
Brands:
   H2rOse

5481 H3O
PO Box 482
Beckley, WV 25802-0482
                            304-256-0436
     Fax: 304-256-0520 888-436-9287
Bottled water
President: Jamison Humphrey

Food Manufacturers / A-Z

Estimated Sales: Under $500,000
Number Employees: 1-4
Brands:
   H3o

5482 HC Brill Company
1912 Montreal Rd
Tucker, GA 30084
   770-938-3823
Fax: 770-939-2934 800-241-8526
www.hcbrill.com
Ingredients and mixes
President: Cefo Grteor
CEO: Bret Weaver
Estimated Sales: $5-10 000,000
Number Employees: 50-99
Brands:
   Brill's

5483 HFI Foods
17515 Northeast 6th Court
Redmond, WA 98074
   425-883-1320
Fax: 425-861-8341
Surimi products; frozen entrees, mousse desserts and pasta salads
President: Byron Kuroishi
CFO: Yoshinari Kuroishi
Vice President: Christina Gaimaytan
Quality Control: Jenel Lee
Marketing Director: Gwen McLellan
Sales Director: Nori Ishiwari
Public Relations: Cindy Fuller-Stephens
Production Manager: Kazue Yamada
Plant Manager: Kazuo Yamada
Purchasing Manager: Cindy Fuller-Stephens
Estimated Sales: $12 Million
Number Employees: 50-99
Square Footage: 80000
Type of Packaging: Consumer
Brands:
   Fitness First
   Kibun
   King Core
   King Cove
   Seastix

5484 HH Dobbins Inc
99 West Ave
Lyndonville, NY 14098-9744
   585-765-2271
Fax: 585-765-9710 877-362-2467
bbaker@wnyapples.com
www.unitedapplesales.com
Produce, including apples, cabbage, pears and prunes
President: Howard Dobbins
hdobbins@wnyapples.com
Estimated Sales: $3-5 Million
Number Employees: 20-49
Parent Co: United Apple Sales Inc.
Type of Packaging: Consumer, Food Service, Bulk
Brands:
   Old Dobbin

5485 HMC Farms
13138 S Bethel Ave
Kingsburg, CA 93631-9216
   559-897-1025
Fax: 559-897-1610 hmcinfo@hmcmarketing.com
www.hmcfarms.com
Table grapes, peaches, plums, nectarines, and other stone fruit
Owner: Harold McClarty
President: Jon McClarty
CFO: Sarah McClarty
Contact: Joel Booth
joelb@hmcfarms.com
Estimated Sales: $20-50 Million
Number Employees: 20-49

5486 HP Hood LLC
6 Kimball Ln.
Lynnfield, MA 01940
   617-887-3000
   800-343-6592
www.hood.com
Dairy products.
Chairman/CEO: John Kaneb
john.kaneb@hphood.com
President: Gary Kaneb
COO: Jeffrey Kaneb
Senior VP, Milk Procurement: Mike Suever
VP, QS & Regulatory Affairs: Jonathan Fischer
VP, Marketing: Christopher Ross
Executive VP, Sales: James Walsh
Senior VP, Operations: H. Scott Blake
Year Founded: 1846
Estimated Sales: $2 Billion
Number Employees: 3,000
Number of Brands: 4
Type of Packaging: Consumer, Food Service, Private Label, Bulk
Brands:
   Hood®
   Lactaid®
   Hoodsies®
   Simple Smart®

5487 HP Schmid
231 Sansome St
Suite 300
San Francisco, CA 94104-2322
   415-765-5925
Fax: 415-765-5922
Edible seeds; dry peas, beans and lentils; dried fruits, nuts and organic products; dehydrated garlic and onions
President/International Sales: Hans Schmid
hans@hpschmid.com
Sales/Service/Quality Assurance: Brian Kim
Sales/Marketing Manager: Margot Tripier
Materials Manager: Uwe Parl
Year Founded: 1978
Estimated Sales: $20-50 Million
Number Employees: 5-9

5488 HSR Associates Inc
18829 Paseo Nuevo Dr
Tarzana, CA 91356-5136
   818-757-7152
Fax: 818-757-7141
Salad dressings; frozen baked goods, desserts, hors d'oeuvres/appetizers; ready made meals; jams and preserves
President: Steve Goodman
steve@hsrassociates.net
Number Employees: 5-9

5489 HV Food Products Co
1221 Broadway
Oakland, CA 94612
   877-853-7262
www.hiddenvalley.com
Salad dressings, dressing mixes, dips, and salad toppings
Chairman & CEO: Benno Dorer
VP & Chief Marketing Officer: Eric Reynolds
Year Founded: 1954
Estimated Sales: $100-500 Million
Number Employees: 250-499
Number of Brands: 68
Parent Co: Clorox Company
Type of Packaging: Private Label
Brands:
   Farmhouse Originals Ceasar
   Greek Yogurt Lemon Garlic
   Buffalo Ranch(c)
   Greek Yogurt Ranch
   Original Ranch(c) Dips Mix
   Greek Yogurt Salad Dressing Mix
   Homestyle Italian Pasta Salad
   Original Ranch(c) Pasta Salad
   Garlic Parmesan Crouton Bites
   Original Ranch(c) Homestyle
   Three Herb Ranch
   Cheddar & Bacon Flavored Ranch
   Honey BBQ Ranch(c)
   Roasted Garlic Ranch
   Greek Yogurt Spinach & Feta
   Greek Yogurt Creamy Ceasar
   Simply Ranch Cucumber Basil
   Simply Ranch Classic Ranch
   The Original Ranch(c)
   Sriracha Ranch(c)
   Salad Crispins(c)
   Easy Squeeze Bottle
   Light
   and many more

5490 Haagen-Dazs
PO Box 2178
Wilkes-Barre, PA 18703
   800-767-0120
www.haagendazs.us
Dairy, Ice Cream
Owner: Rex Bunzalang
Sr. V.P./Managing Dir., Int'l Div.: John Riccitiello
Senior VP R&D: Ken Snider
Sales Director: Yves Coleon
Estimated Sales: Under $500,000
Number Employees: 1-4
Parent Co: Diageo United Distillers and Vinters

5491 Habby Habanero's Food Products
6475 Ferber Road
Jacksonville, FL 32277-1513
   904-333-9758
http://www.habbys.net/
Barbecue sauces
Contact: Malcolm Quincy
Contact: Jerry Quincy

5492 Habersham Vineyards & Winery
7025 S Main St
Helen, GA 30545-3615
   706-878-9463
Fax: 706-878-8466 info@habershamwinery.com
www.habershamwinery.com
Wines
Owner: Tom Slick
CEO/CFO: Steve Gibson
Wine Maker: Andrew Beaty
Vineyard Manager: Terri Haney
Estimated Sales: $1.5 Million
Number Employees: 10-19
Square Footage: 12000
Type of Packaging: Private Label
Brands:
   Creekstone
   Habersham Estates
   Southern Harvest

5493 Haby's Alsatian Bakery
207 US Highway 90 E
Castroville, TX 78009-5222
   830-538-2118
Fax: 830-931-2194 info@habysbakery.com
www.habysbakery.com
Cookies, pies, cakes, apple fritters, strudels, stollens, bread and coffeecakes.
President: Sammy Tschirhart
VP/Secretary/Treasurer: Yvonne Tschirhart
Estimated Sales: $500,000-$1 Million
Number Employees: 10-19
Square Footage: 16200
Type of Packaging: Consumer

5494 Hadley's Date Gardens
83555 Airport Blvd # 11
Thermal, CA 92274-9127
   760-399-5191
Fax: 760-399-1311 www.hadleys.com
Dates
Owner: Melinda Dougherty
mdougherty@hadleys.com
CEO: John Keck
Vice President: Sean Dougherty
Number Employees: 50-99
Type of Packaging: Consumer, Food Service, Private Label, Bulk
Brands:
   Hadley Date Gardens

5495 Hafner USA
4609 Lewis Rd
Stone Mountain, GA 30083
   678-406-0101
Fax: 678-406-9222 888-725-4605
www.hafner.com
Pastry shells, cream puffs, puff pastries and cake kits
President: Xavier M De Goursac
Marketing: Maria Dziebakowski
Estimated Sales: $5-10 000,000
Number Employees: 5-9

5496 Hafner Vineyard
4280 Pine Flat Rd
Healdsburg, CA 95448
   707-433-4606
Fax: 707-433-1240 info@hafnervineyard.com
www.hafnervineyard.com
Wines

Food Manufacturers / A-Z

Partner/Owner: Richard Hafner
Partner: Julianne Farrell
Partner: Elizabeth Hafner
Managing Partner: Scott Hafner
Winemaker: Sarah Hafner
Estimated Sales: $2,500,000
Number Employees: 10
Type of Packaging: Private Label
Brands:
  Hafner

5497 Hagensborg Chocolates LTD.
3686 Bonneville Place
Unit #103
Burnaby, BC V3N 4T6
Canada
604-215-0234
Fax: 604-215-0235 877-554-7763
sales@hagensborg.com www.hagensborg.com
Canned pate, chocolate and confectionery items, olive oils, sherry vinegar; exporter of smoked salmon fillets
President: Shelley Miller
Marketing: Shelley Wallace
Estimated Sales: $10-20 Million
Number Employees: 10-19
Square Footage: 30000
Type of Packaging: Consumer, Food Service, Private Label
Brands:
  Hagensborg Meltaways Truffles
  Kiss Me Frog Truffles
  Truffles To Go

5498 Hagerty Foods
987 N Enterprise St
Suite J
Orange, CA 92867
714-628-1230
Condiments
President: Francisco Esquivel
Estimated Sales: $220,000
Number Employees: 3
Square Footage: 20000
Type of Packaging: Consumer, Food Service, Private Label
Brands:
  Hagerty Foods
  La Napa
  Winemaker's Choice

5499 Hahn Family Wines
37700 Foothill Rd
Soledad, CA 93960
831-678-4555
Fax: 831-678-0557 info@hahnfamilywines.com
www.hahnwines.com
Wines
President: Bill Leigon
Sr. Director, Marketing: Vince Berry
Regional Sales Manager: Brent Ferro
Director of Winemaking: Paul Clifton
Estimated Sales: $7,500,000
Number Employees: 50-99
Square Footage: 30
Type of Packaging: Private Label
Brands:
  Smith & Hook Winery
  Huntington
  Copa
  Cycles
  Gladiator
  Lucienne
  Bin 36

5500 Hahn's Old Fashioned Cake Co
75 Allen Blvd
Farmingdale, NY 11735-5614
631-249-3456
Fax: 631-249-3492 www.crumbcake.net
Coffee cake
President: Regina Hahn
Chief Operating Officer: Andrew Hahn
Estimated Sales: $2.5-5 Million
Number Employees: 10-19
Type of Packaging: Consumer, Food Service

5501 Haig's Delicacies
25673 Nickel Pl
Hayward, CA 94545-3221
510-782-6285
Fax: 510-782-5428 www.haigsdelicacies.com
Hummus, dips, sauces

Owner/Founder: Haig Takvorian
Marketing: Rita Takvorian
Estimated Sales: Less Than $500,000
Number Employees: 5-9

5502 Haight Brown Vineyard
29 Chestnut Hill Rd
Litchfield, CT 06759-4101
860-567-4045
Fax: 860-818-3770 800-577-9463
haightvineyard@aol.com
www.haightvineyards.com
Wines
Owner: Amy Fenew
Co-Partner: Amy Brown
Manager: Natash Gouey-Guy
Cellar Master: Salvatore Cimino
Estimated Sales: $2.5-5,000,000
Number Employees: 1-4
Brands:
  Haight Vineyard Wines

5503 Hail Merry
9755 Clifford Dr
Unit 150
Dallas, TX 75220
214-905-5005
customerservice@hailmerry.com
www.hailmerry.com
Cups, bites and tarts
Founder: Susan O'Brien
Type of Packaging: Consumer
Brands:
  HAIL MERRY

5504 Haile Resources
2650 Freewood Dr
Dallas, TX 75220-2511
214-357-1471
Fax: 214-357-9381 800-357-1471
www.haileresources.com
Food and beverage ingredients
President: Chris Beninate
chris@haileresources.com
Vice President: Elaine Haile
Estimated Sales: $500,000
Number Employees: 5-9
Type of Packaging: Private Label

5505 (HQ)Hain Celestial Group Inc
1111 Marcus Ave
Suite 100
Lake Success, NY 11042
800-434-4246
www.hain.com
Organic health products.
President/CEO: Mark Schiller
Executive VP/CFO: Javier Idrovo
Senior VP, R&D: Jeff George
Senior VP, Sales: Kevin Lasher
Chief Supply Chain Officer: Jerry Wolfe
Estimated Sales: $2.6 Billion
Number Employees: 6,300
Number of Brands: 29
Brands:
  alba BOTANICA
  Arrowhead Mills
  Avalon Organics
  Bearitos
  BluePrint Organic
  Candle Cafe Vegan
  Casbah
  Celestial Seasonings
  DeBoles
  Dream
  Earth's Best Organic
  Ella's Kitchen
  Empire Kosher
  FreeBird
  Garden of Eatin'
  GG Unique Fiber
  Hain Pure Foods
  Health Valley
  Hollywood
  Imagine
  Jason
  live clean
  MaraNatha
  Nile Spice
  plainville Farms
  Queen Helene
  Rudis
  Sensible Portions
  Spectrum
  SunSpire
  Terra
  The Greek Gods
  Tilda
  Walnut Acres
  Westbrae Natural
  WESTSOY
  Yves Veggie Cuisine

5506 Hain Celestial Group Inc
4600 Sleepytime Dr
Boulder, CO 80301-3284
800-434-4246
www.hainpurefoods.com
Natural and organic foods
Brands:
  Haine Pure Foods
  Celestial Seasonings

5507 Haines City Citrus Growers
8 Railroad Ave
P.O.Box 337
Haines City, FL 33844-4245
863-422-1174
Fax: 863-421-4003 800-327-6676
Citrus fruits
President: Bob Turner
bob@hilltopcitrus.com
Treasurer: Dennis P. Broadaway
Finance Executive: Rod Hamric
Sales Exec: Bob States
Director Field Operations: Charles Counter
Packing House Manager: John Soles
Estimated Sales: $10-20 Million
Number Employees: 100-249
Parent Co: Citrus World

5508 Haines Packing Company
5 Mile Mud Bay Rd.
PO Box 290
Haines, AK 99827
907-766-2883
harry@hainespacking.com
www.hainespacking.com
Salmon, crab, halibut, and shrimp.
President/CEO: William Weisfield
CFO/Controller: Bob Hall
Vice President /Owner: Jan Supler
Year Founded: 1917
Estimated Sales: 100 Million
Number Employees: 40
Square Footage: 5963
Type of Packaging: Consumer, Food Service, Bulk
Other Locations:
  Ward Cove Packing Co.
  Seattle WA
Brands:
  Northern Pride
  Pirate

5509 Hair Of The Dog Brewing
61 SE Yamhill St
Portland, OR 97214-2134
503-232-6585
Fax: 503-235-8743
German style beer
Owner: Denver Bon
denver@hairofthedog.com
Brewer: Pat Savage
Estimated Sales: $500,000-$1,000,000
Number Employees: 1-4

5510 Hak's
1203 S Spaulding Ave
Los Angeles, CA 90019
424-235-0516
support@haksbbq.com
haks.com
Barbecue sauce
Founder: Sharone Hakman

5511 Hakuna Banana
242 N Avenue 25
Los Angeles, CA 90031-1982
323-736-1630
www.hakunabanana.com
Banana-based, non-dairy frozen dessert
Co-Founder: Hannah Hong
Number of Brands: 1
Number of Products: 8
Type of Packaging: Consumer
Brands:
  HAKUNA BANANA

Food Manufacturers / A-Z

5512 Halal Fine Foods
73 Galaxy Blvd
Units 11 & 12
Toronto, ON M9W 5T4
Canada
416-679-8000
info@halalfinefood.com
www.halalfinefood.com
Halal foods including mantu, ashak, sauces, ready meals, cookies, and soups
President: Matin Hakimi
CEO, Director: Mohammad Amin
Account Manager: Rita Raji
Office Manager: Iwona Hakimi
Production Manager: Yusif Zafar

5513 Hale Indian River Groves
1650 90th Ave
Vero Beach, FL 32966
772-581-9915
Fax: 877-329-4253 800-562-4502
customercare@halegroves.com
www.halegroves.com
Fruit juices and fruit gift baskets
VP: Fred Kuester
Internet Marketing Manager: Sean Leis
Sales: Sheila McCue Andrews
Customer Service Lead: Sally Costantini
Estimated Sales: $20-50 Million
Number Employees: 50-99
Type of Packaging: Consumer, Bulk

5514 Hale and Hearty Soups
Chelsea Market
75-9th Ave
New York, NY 10011
212-255-2433
www.haleandhearty.com
Restaurant chain producing homemade soups, sandwiches and salads
CEO: Andy Taylor
Chief Financial Officer: Bob Hernon
Recruitment & Development Manager: David Stafford
Vice President, Sales: Paul Schwartz
Director of Operations: Robert Monti
Estimated Sales: $5-10,000,000
Number Employees: 500-1000

5515 Hale's Brewery
4301 Leary Way NW
Seattle, WA 98107-4538
206-782-0737
Fax: 360-706-1572 info@halesbrewery.com
www.halesbrewery.com
Beers
President/Founder: Michael Hale
Accountant: Brenda Rock
Sales Manager: Bill Preib
Special Events Manager: Dana Hurt
Head Brewer: Chris Sheehan
Year Founded: 1983
Estimated Sales: $20-50 Million
Number Employees: 50-99
Brands:
  Hale's Celebration Porter
  Hale's Pale American Ale
  Hale's Special Bitter
  Moss Bay Extra Ale
  Moss Bay Stout
  Hale's Cream
  Wee Heavy Winter Ale
  Irish Style Nut Brown Ale
  O'Brien Harvest Ale
  Pale American
  Hale's Dublin Style Stout
  German Style Kolsch

5516 Half Moon Bay Trading Co
210 Mayport Rd
Atlantic Beach, FL 32233-3332
904-246-9493
Fax: 904-246-9442 888-447-2823
info@halfmoonbaytrading.com
www.halfmoonbaytrading.com
Condiments, salsas, glaze toppings & mixers
President: Robin Shepherd
CFO: Jeff Hite
VP Sales, Marketing & Product Dev.: Tom Nuijens
Contact: Peggy Cornelius
pcornelius@halfmoonbaytrading.com
Office & Traffic Manager: Ellen Singleton
Year Founded: 1992
Estimated Sales: $1,000,000 +
Number Employees: 1-4
Number of Brands: 5
Number of Products: 21
Square Footage: 10000
Type of Packaging: Consumer, Food Service, Private Label
Brands:
  Beesting
  Caribbean Condiments
  Iguana
  Sweetsting
  Tamarindo Bay

5517 Half Moon Fruit & Produce Company
14275 Cacheville Road
Yolo, CA 95697-3114
530-662-1727
Fax: 530-662-6072
Prunes, plums and melons
President: B E Giovannetti
Operations Manager: Richard Monford
Estimated Sales: $10-20 Million
Number Employees: 7
Brands:
  Buster
  Melo-Glow
  Morning Cheer
  Valley King

5518 Halfpops Inc
16413 N 91st St # 105
Suite 105
Scottsdale, AZ 85260-3052
480-494-5117
info@halfpops.com
www.halfpops.com
Popcorn
CEO: Mike Fitzgerald
Estimated Sales: Less Than $500,000
Number Employees: 1-4

5519 Haliburton International Inc
3855 Jurupa St
Ontario, CA 91761-1404
909-428-8520
Fax: 909-428-8521 877-980-4295
www.haliburton.net
Fire roasted vegetables, including peppers, tomatoes, tomatillos, onions, garlic, shallots, squash, zucchini
Owner: Ian Schenkel
schenkel@haliburton.net
Estimated Sales: $36 Million
Number Employees: 50-99
Type of Packaging: Food Service, Bulk

5520 Halifax Group
1133 Connecticut Avenue, NW
Suite 700
Washington, DC 20036
202-530-8300
Fax: 202-296-7133 jsauter@thehalifaxgroup.com
www.thehalifaxgroup.com
Gourmet sauces, dressings, salsa, condiments and beverages
Principal: Chris Cathcart
Chief Executive Officer: David W. Dupree
Chief Financial Officer: Michael T. Marshall
Vice President: Katherine Trainor
Estimated Sales: $5-10 Million
Number Employees: 10-19
Brands:
  Hill Farms
  Redneck Gourmet
  Scorned Woman
  Southern Sensations
  Wild Man

5521 Hall Brothers Meats
27040 Cook Rd
Olmsted Twp, OH 44138-1111
440-235-3262
Fax: 440-235-6696 www.hallsqualitymeats.com
Fresh and frozen beef, pork, poultry, lamb and seafood
President: Richard Hall
hall@hallbros.com
Estimated Sales: $10-20 Million
Number Employees: 5-9
Type of Packaging: Consumer, Food Service, Bulk

5522 Hall Grain Company
502 E Railroad Avenue
Akron, CO 80720
970-345-2206
Fax: 970-345-6680
Grains
Manager: Tim Mayes
Controller: Kevin Hall
VP: Pat Hall
Estimated Sales: $10-20 Million
Number Employees: 50-99

5523 Halladay's Harvest Barn
6 Webb Ter
Bellows Falls, VT 05101-3157
802-463-3471
Fax: 802-460-1132 halladay@sover.net
www.halladays.com
Seasonings, dips, cheesecake mixes, dry soup mixes, garlic oil and vinegars
Owner: Rick Govotski
holladay@sover.net
Co-Owner: Kathleen Govotski
Estimated Sales: $1-3 Million
Number Employees: 10-19

5524 Hallcrest Vineyards
379 Felton Empire Rd
Felton, CA 95018-9167
831-335-4441
Fax: 831-335-4450 info@hallcrestvineyards.com
www.hallcrestvineyards.com
Wines
President: Yuka Lu
yuka.lu@arbitech.com
Lab Director: Paul Bouswa
Sales Manager: Will Warto
Co-Owner/Public Relations: Lorraine Schumacher
Cellar Master: Giovanni Jovel
Estimated Sales: $2.5-5,000,000
Number Employees: 10-19
Type of Packaging: Private Label
Brands:
  Hallcrest Vineyards
  The Organic Wine Work
  Vinatopia

5525 Hallmark Fisheries
63276 Charleston Ave
P.O. Box 5390
Charleston, OR 97420
541-888-3253
Fax: 541-888-6814 info@hallmarkfisheries.com
www.hallmarkfisheries.com
Fresh, frozen and canned seafood.
Office Manager: Loretta Boyce
Plant Quality Controller: Karen Smith
Estimated Sales: $20-50 Million
Number Employees: 100-249
Parent Co: California Shellfish
Type of Packaging: Consumer, Food Service, Private Label, Bulk
Brands:
  Hallmark
  Peacock
  Point St. George

5526 Halmoni's Divine Marinade
113 Anderson Ave
Demarest, NJ 07627-1318
917-913-8961
www.divinemarinade.com
Marinades; BBQ and grilling sauces; and relish.
Co-Owner: Sandra Rhow-Haik
Co-Owner: Wendy Hegglin
Year Founded: 2013
Type of Packaging: Private Label

5527 Halperns' Purveyors of Steak & Seafood
4685 Welcome All Road
Atlanta, GA 30349
404-767-9229
Fax: 404-767-2611 866-659-6090
info@halperns.com halperns.com
Steak and seafood
President & COO: Ray Hicks
CEO: Kirk Halpern
VP: Jody Hicks

Food Manufacturers / A-Z

5528 Halsted Packing House
445 N Halsted St
Chicago, IL 60642-6518
312-421-5147
Fax: 312-421-4511
Lamb, pork and goat meat
Owner: William Davos
Co-Owner: Ann Davos
Estimated Sales: Less than $500,000
Number Employees: 5-9
Square Footage: 12800
Type of Packaging: Consumer, Food Service

5529 Ham I Am
5505 Longview St
Dallas, TX 75206-5607
972-447-0440
Fax: 972-447-0460   800-742-6426
www.hamiam.com
Pork products, quail, duck, turkey, Texas BBQ, desserts, breakfast ideas, homemade tamales, hors d'oeuvres, and party foods
President: Sharon Meehan
Manager: Meghan Meehan
meghanameehan@gmail.com
Estimated Sales: Under $500,000
Number Employees: 5-9
Type of Packaging: Private Label, Bulk

5530 Hama Hama Oyster® Company
301 N Webb Rd
Lilliwaup, WA 98555
360-877-6938
Fax: 360-877-6942   888-877-5844
Seafood
Owner: David Robins
Sales, Wholesale: Adam James
Estimated Sales: $500,000-$1,000,000
Number Employees: 1-4
Type of Packaging: Private Label, Bulk

5531 Hamersmith, Inc.
3200 NW 125 Street
Miami, FL 33167
305-685-7451
Fax: 305-681-6093 office@hamersmith.com
www.hamersmith.com
Shortenings, margarines, oils, puff paste, pan releases and spices; packagaing services
President: Calvin Theobald
Sales Director: Gerald Delmonico
Estimated Sales: $2.5-5 Million
Number Employees: 10
Number of Brands: 20
Number of Products: 9
Square Footage: 60000
Type of Packaging: Food Service, Private Label, Bulk

5532 Hamilos Bros Inspected Meat
1117 Greenwood St
Madison, IL 62060-1234
618-876-3710
Fax: 618-876-3732
Meat and fresh and frozen fish; wholesaler/distributor of canned goods, paper products and pre-packaged meat
Owner: Mike Skinner
Owner: Jeff Skinner
Estimated Sales: $500,000-$1 Million
Number Employees: 5-9
Type of Packaging: Consumer

5533 Hamilton Marine
20 Park Dr
Rockland, ME 04841-3441
207-594-8181
Fax: 207-594-8161 www.hamiltonmarine.com
Seafood
President: Leni Gronros
COO: Steve Graebert
Manager: Dave Perry
Estimated Sales: $5-10 Million
Number Employees: 5-9

5534 Hammond Pretzel Bakery Inc
716 S West End Ave
Lancaster, PA 17603-5050
717-392-7532
Fax: 717-392-8085 info@hammondpretzels.com
www.hammondpretzels.com
Handmade pretzels and chocolate pretzels
President: Brian Nicklaus
bnicklaus@hammondpretzels.com
General Manager: Brian Nicklaus
Estimated Sales: $10-20 Million
Number Employees: 10-19
Type of Packaging: Consumer
Brands:
    Hammond's

5535 Hammond's Candies
5735 Washington St
Denver, CO 80216-1321
303-333-5588
Fax: 303-333-5622   888-226-3999
www.hammondscandies.com
Chocolates and traditional hard candy and confections
Owner: Bob List
CIO: Ross Chism
Marketing: Andrew Whisler
Contact: Anna Abromovich
anna@hammondscandies.com
Manager: Karlyn Pulst
Master Candymaker: Ralph Nafziger
Estimated Sales: $850,000
Number Employees: 100-249

5536 Hammons Black Walnuts
105 Hammons Dr
PO Box 140
Stockton, MO 65785
Fax: 417-276-5187   888-429-6887
info@black-walnuts.com www.black-walnuts.com
Walnuts
President: Brian Hammons
Year Founded: 1946
Estimated Sales: $1 to 2.5 Million
Number Employees: 80
Type of Packaging: Food Service, Private Label, Bulk

5537 Hammons Products Co
105 Hammons Dr
PO Box 140
Stockton, MO 65785-7608
417-276-5181
Fax: 417-276-5187   888-429-6887
www.hammonsproducts.com
Walnuts
President: Brian Hammons
bhammons@black-walnuts.com
VP Marketing: David Hammons
VP Sales: David Steinmuller
Estimated Sales: $10-20 Million
Number Employees: 100-249
Square Footage: 687000
Type of Packaging: Consumer, Food Service, Bulk
Brands:
    Hammons

5538 Hamms Custom Meats
307 W Louisiana St
Mckinney, TX 75069-4417
972-542-3359
info@hamsdelivered.com
www.hamsdelivered.com
Custom cut meats
Owner: Ken Uselton
Partner: Carrie Galyean
Year Founded: 1954
Estimated Sales: $.5-1 million
Number Employees: 1-4
Type of Packaging: Consumer, Food Service, Bulk

5539 Hampton Associates & Sons
12728 Dogwood Hills Lane
Fairfax, VA 22033-3244
703-968-5847
jamcola@hotmail.com
Soft drinks
CEO/Chairman: Hampton Brown
Estimated Sales: Under $500,000
Number Employees: 1-4
Type of Packaging: Consumer, Food Service
Brands:
    Bahama
    Deep Purple
    Diet Clear Jazz
    Falcon Orange Soda
    Jazz Cola
    Rustler Root Beer

5540 Hampton Chutney Company
6 Main Street
Amagansett, NY 11930
631-267-3131
Fax: 631-267-6169 info@hamptonchutney.com
www.hamptonchutney.com
Fresh chutneys
Owner: Gary MacGurn
Co-Owner: Isabel MacGurn
Chef: Patty Gentry
Estimated Sales: Less than $500,000
Number Employees: 5-9

5541 Hampton Farms
202 Peanut St
Severn, NC 27877
252-585-0916
Fax: 252-585-1242   800-313-2748
www.hamptonfarms.com
Peanuts and peanut products
President & CEO: Dallas Barnes
VP Sales/Marketing: Thomas Nolan
Operations: Dan Hutton
Estimated Sales: $25 Million
Number Employees: 50-99
Parent Co: Meherrin Chemical
Type of Packaging: Private Label, Bulk
Brands:
    Hamptom Farms

5542 Hanan Products Co
196 Miller Pl
Hicksville, NY 11801-1826
516-938-1000
Fax: 516-938-1925 info@hananproducts.com
www.hananproducts.com
Kosher non-dairy products
President: John Bauer
jbauer@hananproducts.com
Estimated Sales: $2.5-5,000,000
Number Employees: 20-49
Type of Packaging: Consumer, Food Service

5543 Hancock Gourmet LobsterCo
46 Park Dr
Topsham, ME 04086-1737
207-725-1855
Fax: 207-725-1856
cal@hancockgourmetlobster.com
www.hancockgourmetlobster.com
Lobster and other specialty seafood products
Founder & President: Cal Hancock
cal@hancockgourmetlobster.com
VP: Jack Rosberg
Executive Chef: Kevin Messier
Wholesale Sales Manager: Laura Meier
Director of Operations & Marketing: Amber Pelletier
Estimated Sales: $1.3 Million
Number Employees: 20-49
Type of Packaging: Consumer, Food Service, Bulk

5544 Hancock Peanut Company
P.O. Box 100
Courtland, VA 23837
757-653-9351
Fax: 757-653-2147
Peanuts
President: J Matthew Pope
VP Sales: Robert Pope
Contact: Melissa Rose
Number Employees: 50-99
Type of Packaging: Consumer, Food Service

5545 Hand Made Lollies
465 S Orlando Avenue
Suite 205
Maitland, FL 32751
877-784-2724
Fax: 877-249-6419 info@handmadelollies.com
www.handmadelollies.com
Handmade and personalized lollipops
President: Timothy Lang

5546 Handley Cellars
3151 Highway 128
Philo, CA 95466
707-895-3876
Fax: 707-895-2603   800-733-3151
info@handleycellars.com www.handleycellars.com
Wines

Food Manufacturers / A-Z

Winemaker & Owner: Milla Handley
milla@handleycellars.com
Director, Sales & Marketing: Travis Scott
National Sales Manager: Lulu McClellan
Hospitality Lead: Chris Richard
Cellar Master: Efrain Garcia
Estate Vineyard Manager: Jos, Jimenez
Estimated Sales: $5-10,000,000
Number Employees: 11-50
Type of Packaging: Private Label

5547 Handy International Inc
700 E Main St # 101
Salisbury, MD 21804-5035
410-912-2000
Fax: 410-968-1592 800-426-3977
www.handycrab.com
Frozen seafood
President: Terry Conway
Senior VP: Rosario D Nero
VP: Todd Conway
Sales Executive: Todd Mcallister
Estimated Sales: $8,000,000
Number Employees: 100-249
Type of Packaging: Consumer, Food Service
Brands:
    Handy

5548 (HQ)Handy Pax
53 York Ave
Randolph, MA 2368
781-963-8300
Snack foods
President: Jay Sussman
Sales Manager: David Sussman
Number Employees: 10-19
Type of Packaging: Consumer, Private Label

5549 Hangzhou Sanhe USA Inc.
20536 Carrey Rd
Walnut, CA 91789
909-869-6016
Fax: 909-869-6015 www.sanheinc.com
Food ingredients and additives.
President: Aili Chen
Contact: Yun Qian
yunqian@sanheinc.com
Estimated Sales: $1 Million
Type of Packaging: Bulk

5550 Hanks Beverage Co
4625 E Street Rd
Feasterville-Trevose, PA 19053-6630
215-396-2809
Fax: 215-396-8077 800-289-4722
info@hanksbeverages.com
www.hanksbeverages.com
Gourmet soda
Manager: Jennifer Brady
Estimated Sales: $5-10 Million
Number Employees: 10-19

5551 Hanley's Foods Inc.
149 Ingram Hall
Baton Rouge, LA 70803
225-366-0992
hanleysfoods.com
Dressings and croutons
CEO: Richard Hanley
COO: Kate Hanley
VP of Manufacturing: Katie Hanley Dunlap
VP of Marketing: Marshall Thompson
VP of Operations: Scott Hallett
Year Founded: 2012
Number Employees: 1-10
Type of Packaging: Private Label

5552 Hanmi Inc
5447 N Wolcott Ave
Chicago, IL 60640-1017
773-271-0730
Fax: 773-271-1756 www.wangfood.com
Korean foods
Owner: Young Kim
chihanmi@yahoo.com
Contact: Sung Sohn
CFO: Michael Winiarski
Vice President: John Kim
Estimated Sales: $10-20 Million
Number Employees: 5-9

5553 Hanna's Honey
4760 Thorman Ave Ne
Salem, OR 97303-4644
503-393-2945
Fax: 503-393-2945 www.hannashoney.com
Package and wholesale gourmet Oregon honey.
President: Jean Hunter
CEO: Claude Hunter
Estimated Sales: $100,000
Number Employees: 2
Type of Packaging: Consumer
Brands:
    Hanna's

5554 Hannah Max Baking
14601 S Main St
Gardena, CA 90248-1916
310-324-9871
Fax: 310-324-9871
Cookies
CEO: Joanne Adirim
joanne@hannahmax.com
Number Employees: 50-99

5555 Hanover Foods Corp
1125 Wilson Ave
P.O. Box 334
Hanover, PA 17331
717-632-6000
Fax: 717-637-2890 www.hanoverfoods.com
Processor and importer of canned, frozen, freeze-dried and fresh vegetables, beans, mushrooms, potato chips, pretzels, juices, sauces, salads, entrees, soups, desserts, etc.; also, spaghetti and meat balls in tomato sauce.
Chief Executive Officer: John Warehime
john.warehime@hanoverfoods.com
Executive Vice President: Gary Knisely
VP, Canning Operations: Dave Still
VP, Sales: Dan Schuchart
Year Founded: 1924
Estimated Sales: $20-50 Million
Number Employees: 250-499
Square Footage: 5161
Type of Packaging: Consumer, Private Label, Bulk
Brands:
    Alcosa
    Aunt Kitty's
    Bickel's
    Casa Maid
    Clayton Farms
    Dawn Glo
    Dutch Farms
    Farmer Girl
    Gibbs
    Hanover
    Hanover Farms
    Lk Burman
    Maryland Chef
    Mitchell's
    Myers
    O & C
    Phillips
    Round the Clock
    Spring Glen
    Spring Glen Fresh Foods
    Sunnyside
    Sunwise
    Super Fine
    Superfine
    Vegetable Cocktail

5556 Hanover Potato Products Inc
60 Black Rock Rd
Hanover, PA 17331-4106
717-632-0700
Fax: 717-632-0756
Potato products
Owner: Kendra Kauffman
office@hanoverchamber.com
Estimated Sales: $250,000
Number Employees: 10-19
Square Footage: 17400
Parent Co: Hanover Foods Corp
Type of Packaging: Food Service

5557 Hans Kissle Co
9 Creek Brook Dr
Haverhill, MA 01832-1548
978-556-4500
Fax: 978-556-4612 www.hanskissle.com
Refrigerated salads, quiches, stuffings, desserts, deli meats and prepared meals
President/CEO: Ken Venti
CFO: Tim Sousa
Sales Exec: Kymberley Feldman
kboyle@hanskissle.com
Plant Manager: Eric Lane
Estimated Sales: $20-50 Million
Number Employees: 50-99
Square Footage: 112000
Type of Packaging: Food Service, Private Label, Bulk

5558 Hansen Caviar Company
881 New York 28
Kingston, NY 12401
845-331-5622
Fax: 845-331-8075 800-735-0441
hcaviar@aol.com
Caviar, foie gras, truffles, smoked fish and other specialty food products
President: Michael Hansen-Sturm
Estimated Sales: $500,000-$1,000,000
Number Employees: 1-4
Type of Packaging: Private Label
Brands:
    Hansen
    Hansen-Norge
    St. Etienne

5559 Hansen Packing Co
807 State Highway 16
Jerseyville, IL 62052-2813
618-498-3714
Fax: 618-498-5507 www.hansenmeatco.com
Meat
Owner: Dave Hansen
Customs Processor/Logistics Operations: Todd Pearse
Customs Processor/Logistics Operations: Jim Woelfel
Marketing/Sales Manager: Ryan Hansen
Retail Manager/Daily Operations: Shon Kennedy
Manager Administrative Operations: Terrie Perry
hansenpacking@gtec.com
Lead Meat Processor: Mike Pearse
Livestock Consultant/Cattle Buyer: Ronnie Hansen
Driver Wholesale Orders: Dan Monroe
Estimated Sales: $3-5 Million
Number Employees: 5-9
Type of Packaging: Bulk
Brands:
    Hansen

5560 Hanson Thompson Honey Farms
P.O.Box 129
Redfield, SD 57469
605-472-0474
Honey
President: Bruce Hanson
Co-Owner: Adrian Thompson
Estimated Sales: Under $500,000
Number Employees: 1-4

5561 Hanzell Vineyards
18596 Lomita Ave
Sonoma, CA 95476-4619
707-996-3860
Fax: 707-996-3862 maildesk@hanzell.com
www.hanzell.com
Wines
President: Jason Jardine
jason@hanzell.com
Director, Vineyard Operations: Jose Ramos Esquivel
Director of Winemaking: Michael McNeill
Estimated Sales: $5-9.9,000,000
Number Employees: 11-50

5562 Happy & Healthy Products Inc
1600 S Dixie Hwy
Suite 200
Boca Raton, FL 33432-7463
561-367-0739
Fax: 561-368-5267 behappy@fruitfull.com
www.happyandhealthy.com
Frozen fruit bars and dessert bars, fruit smoothies, dips and healthy snacks
President: Linda Kamm
president@happyandhealthy.com
Marketing Director: Tabitha Locke
Customer Service Manager: Susan Scotts
Public Relations: Mary Galinat
Operations Manager: Len Murray
General Manager: Rosemary Harris

Food Manufacturers / A-Z

Estimated Sales: $4 Million
Number Employees: 10-19
Number of Brands: 5
Type of Packaging: Consumer, Food Service, Private Label, Bulk
Brands:
    Be Happy 'n Healthy Snacks
    Fruitfull
    Happy Indulgence
    Happy Indulgence Deladent Dips

5563 Happy Acres Packing Company
PO Box 444
Petal, MS 39465-0444
    601-584-8301
Sausage
President: Helen Jernigan
Estimated Sales: $500-1,000,000 appx.
Number Employees: 1-4

5564 Happy Campers
Portland, OR 97223
    www.happycampersgf.com
Gluten-free bread
Co-Founder: Lacy Gillham
Co-Founder: Jan Taborsky

5565 Happy Cow Creamery
332 Mckelvey Rd
Pelzer, SC 29669-9243
    864-243-9699
Fax: 864-869-8687 info@happycowcreamery.com
    www.happycowcreamery.com
Milk, dairy
Owner: Nancy Grubbs
nancy@happycowcreamery.com
Estimated Sales: Less Than $500,000
Number Employees: 1-4

5566 Happy Egg Dealers
3204 E 7th Ave
Tampa, FL 33605-4302
    813-248-2362
    Fax: 813-247-1754
Eggs
Owner: Frank Selph
Estimated Sales: $10-20 Million
Number Employees: 10 to 19
Type of Packaging: Consumer, Bulk
Brands:
    Belle Mead

5567 Happy Family
40 Fulton St
17th Fl.
New York, NY 10038
    212-374-2779
    855-644-2779
    www.happyfamilyorganics.com
Organic foods for babies, toddlers, kids, and adults.
Founder & CEO: Shazi Visram
VP of Marketing: Helen Bernstein
VP Sales: Bob Zimmerman
Contact: Amanda Albers
amanda@happyfamilybrands.com
Founding Partner & COO: Jessica Rolph

5568 Happy Goat
314 Shawmut Ave
Boston, MA 02118
    617-549-2776
    Fax: 415-762-5282
Dessert toppings
Founder/Chief Executive: Michael Winnike
Partner/Director of Marketing/Media & Br: Kyle Pickering
Partner/Director of Operations and Accou: Sharon Winnike
Marketing: Michael Winnike

5569 Happy Herberts Food Co Inc
444 Washington Blvd # 2524
Jersey City, NJ 07310-1916
    201-386-0985
    Fax: 201-386-0984 800-764-2779
    info@HappyHerberts.com
Snacks
Owner: Gary Plutchok
Estimated Sales: Less Than $500,000
Number Employees: 1-4
Brands:
    Happy Herberts

5570 Happy Hive
4476 Tulane St
Dearborn Heights, MI 48125
    313-562-3707
    Fax: 313-562-3707
Candy/confectionery
Owner: Stanley Kozlowicz
Estimated Sales: Less than $100,000
Number Employees: 1-4
Type of Packaging: Consumer, Food Service, Bulk
Brands:
    Happy Hive

5571 Happy Planet Foods
601-4180 Lougheed Hwy
Burnaby, BC V5C 6A7
Canada
    Fax: 604-291-0981 800-811-3213
happy@happyplanet.com happyplanet.com
Juices, smoothies, soups, dairy products and plant milks
Co-Founder: Gregor Robertson
Co-Founder: Randal Ius

5572 Happy's Potato Chip Co
3900 Chandler Dr NE
Minneapolis, MN 55421-4494
    612-781-3121
    Fax: 612-781-3125
Snack foods
President: Steve Aanenson
Finance Executive: Betty Kapsner
Human Resource Executive: Allen Dick
Manager: Finn Henrikssen
Plant Manager: Finn Henrikssen
Estimated Sales: $5 Million
Number Employees: 50-99
Square Footage: 92000
Parent Co: Old Dutch Foods
Type of Packaging: Consumer, Food Service

5573 Harbar LLC
320 Turnpike St
Canton, MA 02021-2703
    781-828-0848
    Fax: 781-828-0849 800-881-7040
Tortillas and specialty flatbreads
Owner: Ezequiel Montemayor
emontemayor@harbar.com
Estimated Sales: $3 Million
Number Employees: 100-249
Square Footage: 80000
Type of Packaging: Consumer, Food Service, Private Label, Bulk
Brands:
    MAYAN FARM
    MARIA AND RICARDO'S
    WRAPPY

5574 Harbison Wholesale Meats
2115 County Road
Suite 401
Cullman, AL 35057
    256-739-5105
    Fax: 256-739-8123
Meat
Proprietor: Gary Harbison

5575 Harbor Fish Market
9 Custom House Wharf
Portland, ME 04101-4708
    207-775-0251
    Fax: 207-879-0611 800-370-1790
    info@harborfish.com www.harborfish.com
Seafood
Owner: Benjamin Alfiero
ben@harborfish.com
Owner: Mike Alfiero
Owner/VP: Michael Alfiero
Estimated Sales: $6.2 Million
Number Employees: 20-49
Square Footage: 16058

5576 Harbor Seafood
969 Lakeville Rd
New Hyde Park, NY 11040-3000
    516-775-2400
    Fax: 516-775-3641 800-645-2211
Seafood

President & CEO: Pete Cardone
peteharbor@aol.com
Director Sales, Marketing & Purchasing: Enrique Oyaga
Sales & Marketing: Trish Albano
VP International Purchasing: Bogdan Swita
Estimated Sales: $6.4 Million
Number Employees: 20-49
Square Footage: 20000

5577 Harbor Spice
100 Industry Ln
Forest Hill, MD 21050-1663
    410-893-9500
    Fax: 410-893-9502 www.harborspice.com
Spices
Manager: Dan Sanchuck
Estimated Sales: $1-2.5 000,000
Number Employees: 10-19

5578 Harbor Sweets
85 Leavitt St
Palmer Cove
Salem, MA 01970-5599
    978-745-7648
    Fax: 978-741-7811 800-243-2115
info@harborsweets.com www.harborsweets.com
Gift chocolates including wedding favors, perennial sweets, classics, dark horse collection, hunt collection, sweet treats, easter and spring gifts, custom chocolates and sugar-free
Owner: Phyllis Le Blanc
phyllis@harborsweets.com
Estimated Sales: $5.6 Million
Number Employees: 100-249
Square Footage: 76000
Brands:
    Dark Horse Chocolates
    Marblehead Mints
    Perennial Sweets
    Sweet Shells
    Sweet Sloops
    Topiary Toffee

5579 Harbor Winery
610 Harbor Blvd
West Sacramento, CA 95691
    916-371-6776
Wines
Owner: Charles Myers
Estimated Sales: Less than $100,000
Number Employees: 1-4
Brands:
    Harbor

5580 Harbour Lobster Ltd
5583 Hwy 3
P.O. Box 69
Shag Harbour, NS B0W 3B0
Canada
    902-723-2500
    Fax: 902-723-2568
Lobster and salted groundfish
President: Wayne Banks
Year Founded: 1972
Number Employees: 5-9
Type of Packaging: Bulk

5581 Hard Eight Nutrition LLC
7511 Eastgate Rd
Henderson, NV 89011
    702-425-7638
    www.bulksupplements.com
Dietary supplements, food ingredients and botanical extracts
CEO: Kevin Baronowsky
Type of Packaging: Consumer, Bulk

5582 Hard-E Foods
3228 N Broadway
St Louis, MO 63147-3515
    314-533-2211
    Fax: 314-533-2656 www.hardefoods.com
Hard cooked and deviled egg products; fresh cut vegetables
President/CEO: Judy Rutz
jrutz@hardefoods.com
Plant Manager: Larry Rutz
Estimated Sales: $2 Million
Number Employees: 20-49
Square Footage: 100000
Type of Packaging: Consumer, Food Service, Private Label

Food Manufacturers / A-Z

Brands:
   Hard-E Foods

5583 Hardscrabble Enterprises
PO Box 1124
Franklin, WV 26807-1124
                                                304-358-2921
Mushrooms
President: Paul Goland
Estimated Sales: Under $500,000
Number Employees: 1-4
Square Footage: 7000
Type of Packaging: Consumer, Food Service, Bulk
Brands:
   American Shiitake
   Hen-Of-The-Woods

5584 Hardy Farms
1659 Eastman Hwy
Hawkinsville, GA 31036-5913
                                                478-783-3044
Fax: 478-783-0606 888-368-6887
info@hardyfarmspeanuts.com
www.hardyfarmspeanuts.com
Fresh green and boiled peanuts
President: Alex Hardy
hardyfarms@cstel.net
Estimated Sales: $1,000,000
Number Employees: 10-19
Number of Brands: 1
Number of Products: 3
Square Footage: 100000
Type of Packaging: Consumer, Food Service, Bulk

5585 Harford Glen Water
PO Box 214
Harford, NY 00001-2838
                                                607-844-8351
Fax: 607-844-8351 866-844-8351
www.harfordglenwater.com
Natural spring water
President/CEO: Edmund McHale
CFO/VP: Lura McHale
Number Employees: 6
Number of Brands: 2
Number of Products: 5
Square Footage: 6000
Type of Packaging: Food Service, Private Label

5586 Hari Om Farms
8416 Shelbyville Hwy
Eagleville, TN 37060-9603
                                                615-368-7778
Fax: 615-368-7650
Herbs and lettuce
Manager: Pedro Lopez
Estimated Sales: $1-2,500,000
Number Employees: 1-4
Square Footage: 120000
Type of Packaging: Consumer, Food Service, Bulk
Brands:
   H2o
   Hari Om Farms

5587 Haribo of America
1825 Woodlawn Dr # 204
Baltimore, MD 21207-4045
                                                847-260-0580
info-us@haribo.com
www.haribo.com
Gummi and licorice candy products.
Vice President, Customer Marketing: Scott Miller
Sales Finance Manager: Lacy Cortez
Human Resources Coordinator: Lourdes Vazquez
Supply Chain Manager: Robert Coffey
Estimated Sales: $5-10,000,000
Number Employees: 51-200
Brands:
   Haribo

5588 Haring Catfish
681 Pete Haring Rd
Wisner, LA 71378
                                                318-724-6133
800-467-3474
info@haringcatfish.com www.haringcatfish.com
Catfish products
President/CEO: Carl Haring
Financial Manager: Josie King
Contact: Andrea Haring
andrea@haringcatfish.com
Purchaser: Hannah Harring Sharp

Estimated Sales: $275-300,000,000
Number Employees: 275-499
Parent Co: Wisener Minnow Hatchery Inc.

5589 Harker's Distribution
801 6th St SW
Le Mars, IA 51031
                                                712-546-8171
Fax: 712-536-3159 800-798-7700
Frozen foods, including meats, poultry and seafood
President: Ron Geiger
CEO: Jim Harker
Sr. VP Sales/Marketing: Stan Dickman
Contact: Dick Blackwell
dblackwell@harkers.com
Purchasing Agent: Kevin Regan
Number Employees: 100-249
Other Locations:
   Harker's Distribution
   Denver CO

5590 Harlan Bakeries
7597 E US Highway 36
Avon, IN 46123
                                                317-272-3600
800-435-2738
www.harlanbakeries.com
Bagels and other bakery products
President & Founder: Hugh Harlan
CFO: John Menne
Executive VP, Sales & Marketing: Joseph Latouf
Year Founded: 1991
Estimated Sales: $92 Million
Number Employees: 1,000-4,999
Number of Brands: 5
Square Footage: 2224
Brands:
   Bagel King
   Bigger Better
   Giant Gourmet
   Harlan Bakeries
   World's Best

5591 Harlin Fruit Co
602 N 17th St
Monett, MO 65708-9178
                                                417-235-7370
Fax: 417-235-7316
Fresh fruits and vegetables
Owner: Jerry Sutton
President: Dennis Hughes
Estimated Sales: $1-2.5 Million
Number Employees: 10-19
Type of Packaging: Consumer, Bulk
Brands:
   Harlin Fruit

5592 Harlon's LA Fish
606 Short St
Kenner, LA 70062-7157
                                                504-467-3809
Fax: 504-466-1503 www.laseafood.com
Seafood
Owner: Harlon Pearce
nolrah@aol.com
Estimated Sales: $10-20 Million
Number Employees: 10-19

5593 Harlow House Company
PO Box 12018
Atlanta, GA 30355
                                                404-325-1270
Fax: 678-560-8355
Confectionery
President: David Swain
Estimated Sales: Less than $500,000
Number Employees: 4
Type of Packaging: Consumer, Bulk

5594 Harmless Harvest
200 Green St
Suite 1
San Francisco, CA 94111
                                             www.harmlessharvest.com
Coconut water and pro-biotics
Type of Packaging: Consumer
Brands:
   HARMLESS HARVEST

5595 Harmon's Original Clam Cakes
PO Box 1113
Kennebunkport, ME 04046-1113
                                                207-967-4100
Fax: 207-967-1008 steve@harmonsclamcakes.com
www.harmonsclamcakes.com

Clam Cakes
Owner: Steven Liautaud

5596 Harmony Bay Coffee
25 Commerce Way # 5
North Andover, MA 01845-1002
                                                978-557-0131
Fax: 978-557-0131 800-514-3663
www.harmonybaycoffee.com
Coffee
President/CEO: Michael Sullivan
VP of Marketing: Stephan Liff
Operations Manager: John Sullivan
Estimated Sales: Less Than $500,000
Number Employees: 5-9
Type of Packaging: Private Label
Brands:
   Benley's Irish Creme
   Harmony Bay

5597 Harmony Cellars
3255 Harmony Valley Rd
Harmony, CA 93435-5000
                                                805-927-1625
Fax: 805-927-0256 800-432-9239
Wines
Co-Owner/Winemaker: Charles Mulligan
info@harmonycellars.com
Co-Owner/Business Manager: Kim Mulligan
Estimated Sales: $500,000-$1,000,000
Number Employees: 10-19
Brands:
   Harmony Cellars

5598 Harner Farms
2191 Whitehall Road
State College, PA 16801
                                                814-237-7919
Produce, including apples, cherries, plums and vegetables
Owner: Daniel Harner
Co-Owner: Pam Harner
Estimated Sales: $220,000
Number Employees: 4
Type of Packaging: Consumer, Food Service

5599 Harney & Sons Tea Co.
5723 Route 22
Millerton, NY 12546-6500
                                                518-789-2100
Fax: 518-789-2100 800-832-8463
ht@harneyteas.com www.harney.com
Teas
President: John Harney
masterteablender@harneyteas.com
Marketing: Lisa Prindle
Sales: Michael Harney
Manager: Paul Harney
Purchasing: Elvira Cardenos
Year Founded: 1983
Estimated Sales: $2.5-5 Million
Number Employees: 200
Square Footage: 90000
Type of Packaging: Consumer, Food Service, Private Label, Bulk
Brands:
   Harney & Sons

5600 Harold Food Company
11949 Steele Creek Road
Charlotte, NC 28273
                                                704-588-8061
Fax: 704-588-4636
Frozen fruit cobblers, salads, spreads, chili and barbecue products; Dry, paper, frozen, fresh and refrigerated products
Marketing Director: Tom Taylor
General Manager: Butch Summey
Estimated Sales: $20-50 Million
Number Employees: 50-99
Square Footage: 46500
Type of Packaging: Food Service, Private Label, Bulk
Brands:
   Harold Food Co.

5601 Harold L King & Co Inc
1420 Stafford St # 2
Redwood City, CA 94063-1077
                                                650-368-2233
Fax: 650-368-3547 888-368-2233
kingcoffee@aol.com www.king-coffee.com
Coffee

Food Manufacturers / A-Z

President & CEO: Robert King
Secretary/Treasurer, CFO: John King
Vice President: Tim Kallok
Traffic Manager: Chris King
Year Founded: 1958
Estimated Sales: $25 Million
Number Employees: 5-9
Type of Packaging: Consumer

5602 Harper's Country Hams
2955 US Highway 51 S
PO Box 122
Clinton, KY 42031-8644
270-653-2081
Fax: 270-653-2409 888-427-7377
Country hams, bacon, and sausage
President: Betty Ellegood
betty@hamtastic.com
Treasurer: Doris Harper
Vice President: Brian Harper
Plant Manager: John Mcauliffe
Purchasing Manager: Brant Dublin
Year Founded: 1952
Estimated Sales: $20-50 Million
Number Employees: 100-249

5603 Harpers Seafood Market
526 W Jackson St
Thomasville, GA 31792-5903
229-226-7525
Fax: 229-228-6446
Oysters
President: Junior Harper
Estimated Sales: $10-20,000,000
Number Employees: 50-99
Type of Packaging: Consumer, Food Service
Brands:
  Harper Seafood

5604 Harpersfield Vineyard
6387 State Route 307 West
Geneva, OH 44041
440-466-4739
info2@harpersfield.com
www.harpersfield.com
Wines
Manager: Adolf Ribic
Co-Owner: Wesley Gerlosky
Contact: Patricia Ribic
zzelda98@aol.com
Estimated Sales: $1-4.9,000,000
Number Employees: 1-4
Type of Packaging: Private Label

5605 Harpo's
477 Kapahulu Avenue
Honolulu, HI 96815
808-735-6456
Fax: 808-735-6456 alohaharpos@hawaii.rr.com
www.harposdressings.com
Gourmet salad dressings, marinades, and pizza
Contact: Mike Trombetta
alohaharpos@hawaii.rr.com
Manager: Ingrid Larsson
Number Employees: 1-4

5606 Harpoon Brewery
306 Northern Ave # 2
Boston, MA 02210-2367
617-574-9551
800-427-7666
www.harpoonbrewery.com
Malt beverages
CEO: David Altrich
altrichanglers@gmail.com
Founder/CEO: Dan Kenary
Estimated Sales: $34 Million
Number Employees: 100-249
Number of Brands: 3
Brands:
  Harpoon
  Pickwick
  U.F.O.

5607 Harrington's of Vermont
210 E Main Rd
PO Box 288
Richmond, VT 05477
Fax: 802-434-3166 info@harringtonham.com
www.harringtonham.com
Smoked meats, cheese, maple syrup, seafood, sweets & snacks, condiments and cakes and pastries.

Owner/Chairman: Peter Klinkenberg
Director: John Balczuk
balczuk@harringtonham.com
CFO: R Klinkenberg
Marketing: Carol Wiseley
Year Founded: 1873
Estimated Sales: $20-50 Million
Number Employees: 10

5608 Harris Crab House
433 Kent Narrow Way N
Grasonville, MD 21638-1307
410-827-9500
Fax: 410-827-9057 www.harrisseafoodco.com
Crabs and oysters
Chairman: William Jerry Harris
Vice President: Art Oertel
Estimated Sales: $5-10 Million
Number Employees: 50-99
Type of Packaging: Consumer
Brands:
  Bay Shore

5609 Harris Farms Inc
27366 W Oakland Ave
Coalinga, CA 93210-9627
559-884-2859
Fax: 559-884-2855 800-311-6211
info@harrisfarms.com www.harrisfarms.com
Tomatoes, onions, melons, almonds, bell peppers and garlic
President & Chairman: John C. Harris
Senior VP: Donald Devine
Office Manager: Janie Davis
Estimated Sales: $5-10 Million
Number Employees: 5-9
Type of Packaging: Consumer, Food Service, Private Label, Bulk
Brands:
  Harris Farms
  Harris Fresh
  Harris Ranch

5610 Harris Moran Seed Co
555 Codoni Ave
Modesto, CA 95357-0507
209-579-7333
Fax: 209-527-5312
Vegetable seeds
President: Matthew Johnston
m.johnston@hmclause.com
CEO: Bruno Carette
VP Research: Jeff McElroy
Marketing Director: Bernie Hamel
US/Canada Sales Director: Dan Bailey
VP Of Production & Operations: Dennis Choate
Purchasing Agent: Maxine Corbett
Estimated Sales: $10-20 Million
Number Employees: 100-249
Parent Co: Groupe Limagrain
Brands:
  Niagra Seed

5611 Harris Ranch Beef Co
16277 S McCall Ave
Selma, CA 93662-9458
559-896-3081
Fax: 559-896-3095 800-742-1955
www.harrisranchbeef.com
Beef products
Chairman: David Wood
Chairman of the Board: John Harris
Chief Financial Officer: Doug Sariss
Estimated Sales: $85 Thousand
Number Employees: 500-999
Number of Brands: 1
Square Footage: 17190
Parent Co: Harris Farms, Inc.
Type of Packaging: Consumer, Food Service, Private Label, Bulk
Brands:
  Harris Ranch

5612 Harris Tea Company
44 New Albany Road
Moorestown, NJ 08057
856-793-0290
info@HarrisTea.com
www.harristea.com
Teas.
President/CEO: Kevin Shah
Estimated Sales: $5-10 Million
Number Employees: 10-19
Parent Co: Harris Freeman Enterprise

Type of Packaging: Food Service, Private Label
Brands:
  BIG TEA
  Dorset Tea
  Newman's Own Organic
  Red Rose
  Salada
  Southern Breeze™
  Tea India ®

5613 Harrisburg Dairies Inc
2001 Herr St
PO Box 2001
Harrisburg, PA 17103-1624
717-233-8701
Fax: 717-231-4584 800-692-7429
sales@harrisburgdairies.com
www.harrisburgdairies.com
Dairy products
President & CEO: Fred Dewey
CMO: Matt Zehring
mzehring@harrisburgdairies.com
VP & CFO: Betsy Albright
VP & COO: Matt Zehring
Quality Control Manager: Rob Madigan
Sales Director: Jim Okum
Plant Manager: Miles Zehring
Number Employees: 100-249
Type of Packaging: Consumer
Brands:
  Harrisburg Dairies

5614 Harrison Napa Valley
1443 Silverado Trail
Saint Helena, CA 94574
707-963-8762
Fax: 707-963-8762 www.whwines.com
Wines
Owner/Winemaker: Lyndsey Harrison
Tasting Room & Wine Club: Shelly Zanoli
Manager: Rob Monaghan
Winemaker: Jim McMahon
Estimated Sales: Less than $500,000
Number Employees: 1-4
Type of Packaging: Private Label
Brands:
  Harrison

5615 Harry & David
2500 S Pacific Hwy
Medford, OR 97501-8724
541-864-2121
Fax: 541-864-2194 877-322-1200
service@harryanddavid.com
Fruit; beef steaks, ham, turkey; frozen truffles, cakes, cheesecakes, cookies and cinnamon rolls
President/CEO: Bill Williams
CAO: Judy Gifford
jgifford@harryanddavid.com
EVP Sales/Marketing: Cathy Fultineer
EVP Operations: Peter Kratz
Number Employees: 500-999
Parent Co: Bear Creek Corporation
Type of Packaging: Consumer, Food Service
Brands:
  Harry & David

5616 Harry London Candies Inc
2457 W. North Avenue
Melrose Park, IL 60160
800-333-3629
customerservice@fanniemay.com
www.fanniemay.com
Chocolate truffles
President: Terry Mitchell
Chief Financial Officer: Matthew Anderson
Contact: Randall Dominowski
randalld@harrylondon.com
Estimated Sales: $20-49.9 Million
Number Employees: 100-249
Parent Co: Fannie May
Brands:
  Harry London Chocolates
  Heartland Chocolates

5617 Harry's Cafe
3621 Route 103
Mount Holly, VT 05758
802-259-2996
www.harryscafe.com
Sauces
Owner/Chef: Trip Pearce
Estimated Sales: $300,000-500,000
Number Employees: 5-9

Food Manufacturers / A-Z

5618 Hart Winery
41300 Avenida Biona
Temecula, CA 92591-5014
951-676-6300
Fax: 951-676-6300 877-638-8788
www.vinhart.com
Wines
Owner/Winemaker: Joe Hart
Owner/CEO: Nancy Hart
Winemaker: Bill Hart
Estimated Sales: $1-2.5 Million
Number Employees: 5-9
Square Footage: 3
Type of Packaging: Private Label
Brands:
   Hart Winery

5619 Hartford Family Winery
8075 Martinelli Rd
Forestville, CA 95436-9255
707-887-8030
Fax: 707-887-7785 www.hartfordwines.com
Wines
General Manager, Winemaker: Jeff Stewart
Consumer Direct Sales Manager: Becky Craig
Hospitality Director: Melissa Cook
Estimated Sales: $5-10,000,000
Number Employees: 5-9
Other Locations:
   Healdsburg Tasting Room & Salon
   Healdsburg CA
Brands:
   Hartford
   Hartford Court

5620 Harting's Bakery
1212 Readings Rd
Bowmansville, PA 17507-0220
717-445-5644
Fax: 717-445-4818
Doughnuts and buns
President/CEO: Jocelyn Heft
COO: Thomas Lester
Plant Manager: William Burkhart
Estimated Sales: $1-2,500,000
Number Employees: 20-49

5621 Hartley's Potato Chip Co
2157 Back Maitland Rd
Lewistown, PA 17044-7311
717-248-0526
Fax: 717-248-3512
hartleyspotatochips@gmail.com
www.hartleyspotatochips.com
Potato chips, pretzels, cheese curls
President: Dan Hartley
dhartley@harkers.com
Estimated Sales: $1 Million
Number Employees: 10-19
Square Footage: 13742
Type of Packaging: Consumer, Food Service

5622 Hartog Rahal Foods
35 Maple Street
Norwood, NJ 07648-2003
201-750-0500
Fax: 212-687-2659
Fruit juice concentrates, fruit purees, frozen fruits and flavoring ingredients
President: Jack Hartog Jr
VP: Randy Loewis
Estimated Sales: $10-20 000,000
Number Employees: 20-49
Parent Co: Hartog Rahal Foods

5623 Hartselle Frozen Foods
411 Main Street West
Hartselle, AL 35640-2421
256-773-7261
Fax: 709-722-1116
Frozen meats
President: Billy Wiley
Secretary/Treasurer: Sam Wiley
Vice President: Danny Wiley

5624 Hartsville Oil Mill
311 Washington St
Darlington, SC 29532-4755
843-393-1501
Fax: 843-395-2690
Cotton oil
President/ Owner: Edgar Lawton
cottonoil@aol.com

Year Founded: 1900
Estimated Sales: $20-50 Million
Number Employees: 50-99

5625 Hartville Kitchen
1015 Edison St NW # 2
Hartville, OH 44632-8510
330-877-9353
Fax: 330-877-2101 info@hartvillekitchen.com
www.hartvillekitchen.com
Salad dressings
President: Vernon Sommers
Vice President: Vernon Sommers Jr.
Marketing & Advertisement Assistant: Sylvia DeMarco
Estimated Sales: $5-10,000,000
Number Employees: 50-200

5626 Hartville Locker Service
119 Sunnyside St SW
Hartville, OH 44632-8933
330-877-9547
www.hartvilleoh.com
Beef processing
Owner: James Young
Estimated Sales: $2.5-5,000,000
Number Employees: 1-4

5627 Harvard Seafood Company
PO Box 208
Grand Bay, AL 36541-0208
251-865-0558
Fax: 251-865-2187
Seafood

5628 Harvest Bakery
101 Windsor Pl # A
Central Islip, NY 11722-3329
631-232-1709
Fax: 631-232-1711 info@harvestbakery.com
www.harvestbakery.com
Bread and pastries
President: Bob Marconti
info@harvestbakery.com
Estimated Sales: $1-2.5 Million appx.
Number Employees: 20-49
Type of Packaging: Consumer
Brands:
   Harvest Bakery

5629 Harvest Direct
61 Accord Park Drive
Norwell, MA 02061
865-539-6305
Fax: 865-523-3372 800-733-2106
info@harvestdirect.com www.harvestdirect.com
Meat and milk alternatives
President: Roger Kilburn
Marketing Director: Monty Kilburn
Contact: Simon George
simon@harvestdirect.com
Manager Wholesale Division: Mary Ellen Kilburn
Estimated Sales: $500,000-$1,000,000
Number Employees: 5-9
Type of Packaging: Private Label
Brands:
   Protflan
   Solait
   Veggie Ribs

5630 Harvest Food Products Co Inc
710 Sandoval Way
Hayward, CA 94544-7111
510-675-0383
Fax: 510-675-0396
sales@harvestfoodproducts.com
Pot stickers, egg rolls, wontons, barbecue pork buns and tempura shrimp
President: Yvonne Cooks
yvonne@womenprisoners.org
Estimated Sales: $10-20 Million
Number Employees: 50-99
Square Footage: 34000
Type of Packaging: Consumer, Food Service, Private Label, Bulk
Brands:
   Harvest Foods

5631 Harvest Innovations
1210 N 14th St
Indianola, IA 50125-1508
515-962-5063
info@harvest-innovations.com
www.harvest-innovations.com

Natural ingredients
President: Jim Boes
jim.boes@harvest-innovations.com
Director Of Research: Dr. Noel Rudie
Product Development & Quality Assurance: Regena Butler
VP Sales/Marketing: Nicole Tomba
Innovation and Sales: Giovanni Santi
Director Food Technology: Dr. Wilmot Wijeratne
Number Employees: 1-4

5632 Harvest Manor Farms
1475 US Hwy 62W
Princeton, KY 42445
319-841-4170
Fax: 319-841-4134 877-984-6639
www.hoodysnuts.com
Nuts and seeds
President & CEO: Joseph Patten
VP Finance & Administration: Kathy Davis
SVP Sales & Commodity Acquisition: John Runck
Industrial Sales Manager: Debbie Parenza
Number of Brands: 1
Parent Co: TreeHouse Foods, Inc.
Brands:
   Hoody's

5633 Harvest Select
730 Energy Center Blvd.
Suite 1402-E
Northport, AL 35473
205-614-6400
Fax: 334-628-2122 800-816-7426
info@harvestselect.com www.harvestselect.com
Alabama catfish
President: Randy Rhodes
VP Operations: Bobby Collins
bobby@harvestselect.com
Quality Assurance Manager: Tammy Spencer
VP Sales: Joe Connor
VP Sales: Shane Gaut
Human Resources Manager: Brenda Cook
Production Manager: Robert Lee
Plant Manager: Chris Hill
Estimated Sales: $20-50 Million
Number Employees: 250-499

5634 Harvest Time Foods
3857 Emma Cannon Rd
Ayden, NC 28513-7413
252-746-6675
Fax: 252-746-3160 www.annesdumplings.com
Frozen dumplings
President: Bryan Grimes
VP: Wendy Grimes
Estimated Sales: $5-9.9 Million
Number Employees: 20-49
Square Footage: 34000
Type of Packaging: Consumer, Food Service
Brands:
   Anne's Chicken Base
   Anne's Dumpling Squares
   Anne's Dumpling Strips
   Anne's Flat Dumplings
   Anne's Old Fashioned
   Anne's Pot Pie Squares
   Mac's Dumplings

5635 Harvest Time Seafood Inc
208 W Elina St
Abbeville, LA 70510-8239
337-893-9029
Fax: 337-898-0614
Fresh and frozen crabmeat
Owner: Kevin E Dartez
kevin@hts.glacoxmail.com
Estimated Sales: $5-10 Million
Number Employees: 20-49

5636 Harvest Valley Bakery Inc
348 Civic Rd
La Salle, IL 61301-9710
815-224-9030
Fax: 815-224-9033 www.harvestvalleybakery.com
Cookies, brownies and bar cookies
President: Nancy Norton
n.norton@harvestvalleybakery.com
Estimated Sales: $10-20,000,000
Number Employees: 20-49
Square Footage: 24000
Type of Packaging: Food Service, Private Label, Bulk

Food Manufacturers / A-Z

5637 Harvest-Pac Products
22131 Bloomfield Rd
Chatham, ON N7M 5J3
Canada
519-436-0446
Fax: 519-436-0319 sales@harvestpac.com
www.harvestpac.com
Canned pumpkin, dark red kidney beans, chick peas and crushed tomatoes
President: Dan O'Neill
Operations Manager: Roger Sterling
Type of Packaging: Food Service, Private Label
Brands:
  Harvest-Pac
  Mom's Choice

5638 Harvin Choice Meats
300 McCrays Mill Road
Sumter, SC 29151-0939
803-775-9367
Fax: 803-775-9369 800-849-6328
harvinmeats@ftc-i.net www.harvinmeats.com
Ham, turkey, sausage, bologna, and hotdogs
Owner: S A Harvin Jr
CEO: W Scott Harvin
Year Founded: 1933
Estimated Sales: $20-50 Million
Number Employees: 50-99

5639 Has Beans Coffee & Tea Co
1078 Humboldt Ave
Chico, CA 95928-5960
530-332-9645
Fax: 530-926-6503 800-427-2326
info@hasbeans.com www.hasbeans.com
Coffee and tea
President: William Vonk
wv@hasbeans.com
Estimated Sales: $1.62 Million
Number Employees: 1-4
Type of Packaging: Private Label

5640 Hastings Co-Op Creamery-Dairy
1701 Vermillion St
PO Box 217
Hastings, MN 55033-3164
651-437-9414
Fax: 651-437-3547 info@hastingscreamery.com
www.hastingscreamery.com
Milk
Manager: David Zwart
david@hastingscreamery.com
General Manager: John Cook
Year Founded: 1922
Estimated Sales: $20-50 Million
Number Employees: 20-49
Type of Packaging: Consumer, Private Label

5641 Hastings Meat Supply
202 W 12th St
PO Box 1167
Hastings, NE 68901-3967
402-463-9857
Fax: 402-463-7181
Meat
Owner: Gary Deal
gary@hastingsfoods.com
Director: Jeff Andreasen
Estimated Sales: $1-3 Million
Number Employees: 1-4
Type of Packaging: Consumer, Food Service, Bulk

5642 Hatch Chile Company
6300 Riverside Plaza Lane NW
Suite 100
Albuquerque, NM 87120
912-267-9909
www.hatchchileco.com
Chiles, chile powder and dip mix
Founder & President: Steve Dawson
Year Founded: 1987

5643 Hatfield Quality Meats
2700 Clemens Rd
P.O. Box 902
Hatfield, PA 19440
215-368-2500
Fax: 215-368-3018 800-743-1191
www.hatfieldqualitymeats.com
Fresh and frozen pork products.
President: Craig Edsill
CEO: Doug Clemens
SVP & CFO: Josh Rennells
Year Founded: 1895
Estimated Sales: $138.3 Million
Number Employees: 1,000-4,999
Square Footage: 850000
Parent Co: Clemens Food Group
Type of Packaging: Consumer, Food Service, Private Label
Other Locations:
  Hatfield Quality Meats
  Chester PA
Brands:
  Beaver Falls
  Butcher Wagon
  Cvf
  Chef Pleaser
  Gold Ribbon
  Hatfield
  Medford
  Olde Philadelphia
  Prima Porta
  Tender Plus

5644 Hathaway Coffee Co Inc
6210 S Archer Rd
Summit Argo, IL 60501-1721
708-458-7666
Fax: 708-458-7668 www.krinos.com
Coffee
President: Michael Corden
Secretary: Joyce Cordon
Number Employees: 1-4

5645 Hausbeck Pickle Co
1626 Hess Ave
Saginaw, MI 48601-3970
989-754-4721
Fax: 989-754-3105 866-754-4721
tim@hausbeck.com www.hausbeck.com
Relish and pickles
CEO: Tim Hausbeck
Treasurer: Richard Hausbeck
Sales Manager: John Schnepf
Estimated Sales: $17,500,000
Number Employees: 20-49
Square Footage: 90000
Type of Packaging: Consumer, Food Service

5646 Hauser Chocolates
59 Tom Harvey Rd
Westerly, RI 02891-3685
401-596-8866
Fax: 401-596-0020 888-599-8231
hauser@hauserchocolates.com
www.hauserchocolates.com
Chocolates
Owner: Ruedi Hauser
hauser@hauserchocolates.com
Estimated Sales: $2.5-5 Million
Number Employees: 10-19
Type of Packaging: Consumer

5647 Hausman Foods LLC
4261 Beacon St
Corpus Christi, TX 78405-3326
361-883-5521
Fax: 361-883-1003 www.hausmanfoods.com
Fresh and frozen beef
President/CEO: Steve R McClure, Sr.
CFO: Amy Seward
aseward@samhausman.com
Vice President/General Manager: Jerry Simpson
Quality Control Manager: Beryl Henry
Vice President/Cold Storage Manager: Amy Seward
Dry Purchasing: Paul des los Santos
Estimated Sales: $46 Million
Number Employees: 100-249
Type of Packaging: Consumer, Food Service, Bulk

5648 Havana's Limited
4420 Coquina Avenue
Titusville, FL 32780-6552
321-267-0513
Fax: 321-267-5340
Hot sauces, dry rubs, seasonings and BBQ sauces
President/CEO: Mark Webber
Vice President: Bruce Webber
Number of Brands: 1
Number of Products: 10
Square Footage: 5000
Type of Packaging: Consumer, Food Service, Private Label, Bulk
Brands:
  Ace Bandito

5649 Haven's Candies
87 County Rd
Westbrook, ME 04092-3807
207-772-1557
Fax: 207-775-0086 800-639-6309
info@havenscandies.com www.havenscandies.com
Chocolates and other confectionary; custom chocolate molding available
Owner: Andy Charles
Marketing Director: Krista Viola
Production Manager: Arthur Dillon
Estimated Sales: $1-2.5 Million
Number Employees: 20-49
Square Footage: 24000
Type of Packaging: Consumer, Private Label, Bulk

5650 Haven's Kitchen Sauces
109 W 17th St
New York, NY 10011
212-929-7900
info@havenskitchen.com www.havenskitchen.com
Sauces and dressings; honey; organic popcorn; granola; peanute butter; pancake mix; baking mixes
Owner: Alison Cayne
Operations Manager: Shell Hatke
Year Founded: 2012
Number Employees: 3
Type of Packaging: Food Service, Private Label

5651 Havi Food Services Worldwide
227 South Blvd
Oak Park, IL 60302-4711
708-445-1700
Fax: 630-351-9479
Breads, rolls, baked goods
CEO: Jeff Somers
Number Employees: 50-99

5652 Havoc Maker Products
121 Old Sachems Head Rd
Guilford, CT 06437-3120
203-453-4943
Fax: 203-453-4943 800-681-3909
Hot sauce, salsa, chili and hot sauce mixes, black bean dip, popcorn and bottled spices
Owner: Ernest Neri
Number Employees: 1-4
Square Footage: 500
Type of Packaging: Food Service, Private Label, Bulk
Other Locations:
  Havoc Maker Products
  Old Lyme CT
Brands:
  Havoc Maker

5653 Hawaii Candy Inc
2928 Ualena St # 4
Honolulu, HI 96819-1937
808-836-8955
Fax: 808-839-4040 800-303-2507
website@hawaiicandy.com www.hawaiicandy.com
Confectionery items and snacks
President: Keith Ohta
info@hawaiicandy.com
Secretary: Richard Ohta
Marketing: Ron Vogel
Estimated Sales: $5-10 Million
Number Employees: 20-49
Square Footage: 33000
Type of Packaging: Consumer, Food Service, Private Label, Bulk
Brands:
  Hawaiian Island Crisp
  Hawaiian Island Crisp Cookies

5654 Hawaii Coffee Company
1555 Kalani St
Honolulu, HI 96817
808-847-3600
Fax: 800-972-0777 800-338-8353
www.hawaiicoffeecompany.com
Coffee
President: Jim Wayman
Chief Marketing Officer: Wenli Lin
National Sales Account Manager: Malia Delapenia
Estimated Sales: $9 000,000
Number Employees: 51-200
Number of Brands: 4
Brands:
  Hawaii Coffee Company
  Lion Coffee

Food Manufacturers / A–Z

Royal Kona Coffee
Tiger Tea

5655 Hawaii International Seafood
371 Aokea Place
PO Box 30486
Kailua, HI 96819-1828
808-839-5010
Fax: 808-833-0712 info@cryofresh.com
www.cryofresh.com
Fish and seafood
President: Bill Kowalski
Estimated Sales: $2,000,000
Number Employees: 5-9

5656 Hawaii Star Bakery
944 Akepo Ln
Suite 3
Honolulu, HI 96817
808-841-3602
Fax: 808-842-7941
Bakery products
Owner: Liane Small
Sales Executive: Kenneth Ticman
Estimated Sales: $10-20 Million
Number Employees: 20-49
Type of Packaging: Consumer, Food Service

5657 Hawaiian Bagel
753 Halekauwila Street
Honolulu, HI 96813-5318
808-596-0638
Fax: 808-593-2434 hibagel@gte.net
Bagels and breads
President: Steve Gelson
Estimated Sales: $5-9,9,000,000
Number Employees: 20-49
Parent Co: Fch Enterprises, Inc.

5658 (HQ)Hawaiian Host Inc
500 Alakawa St
Suite 111
Honolulu, HI 96817-4576
808-848-0500
Fax: 808-845-7466 888-414-4678
info@hawaiianhost.com www.hawaiianhost.com
Chocolates and specialty chocolate products; tea, coffee and cookies
President: Keith Sakamoto
CEO: Dennis Teranishi
Vice President Sales: Tad Teraizumi
Year Founded: 1927
Estimated Sales: $20-50 Million
Number Employees: 100-249

5659 Hawaiian Isles Kona Coffee Co
2839 Mokumoa St
Honolulu, HI 96819-4402
808-833-2244
Fax: 808-839-0277 800-657-7716
mailorder@hawaiianisles.com
www.hawaiianisles.com
Coffee
President: Michael Boulware
Owner: Glenn Boulware
Marketing: Sean Gano
Estimated Sales: $27.1 Million
Number Employees: 100-249
Number of Brands: 2
Brands:
Hawaii Coffee Roasters
Kona

5660 Hawaiian King Candies
550 Paiea St # 501
Honolulu, HI 96819-1837
808-833-0041
Fax: 808-839-7141 800-570-1902
dniiro@lava.net
Macadamia nut snacks
President: David Niiro
Contact: Marvin Sialco
info@hawaiianking.com
Estimated Sales: $10-24,9,000,000
Number Employees: 50-99
Type of Packaging: Consumer, Food Service, Private Label
Brands:
America
Enjoying Las Vegas
Enjoying San Francisco
Favorites of Hawaii
Hawaiian Delight
Hawaiian Joys
Hawaiian King
Hawaiian Majesty
New York Club
Passport
San Francisco Bay Traders
That's Hollywood
Usa

5661 Hawaiian Natural Water Company
98-746 Kuahao Pl Ste F
Pearl City, HI 96782
808-483-0520
Fax: 808-483-0536 hisprings@aol.com
www.hawaiianspring.com
Bottled spring water
President/CEO: Marcus Bender
CFO: Willard D Irwin
CFO: David Leaha
CEO: Tom Van Dixhorn
Executive VP Marketing: Ray Riss
Contact: Joan Teraizumi
k.crumley@unm.edu
Operations Manager: Tony Persson
Number Employees: 5-9
Type of Packaging: Private Label
Brands:
Hawaiian Natural Water

5662 Hawaiian Sun Products
259 Sand Island Access Rd
Honolulu, HI 96819-2227
808-845-3211
Fax: 808-842-0532
customerservice@hawaiiansunproducts.com
www.hawaiiansunproducts.com
Tropical fruit juices; Macadamia nut candy and spreads
President: Burt K Okura
Vice President: Kent Kurihara
Year Founded: 1952
Estimated Sales: $20-50 Million
Number Employees: 50-99
Brands:
Hawaiian Sun
Pokka

5663 (HQ)Hawkhaven Greenhouse International
W9554 Blackhawk Ct.
Wautoma, WI 54982
920-540-3536
Fax: 920-787-4295 800-745-4295
verdegrass@gmail.com www.hawkhaven.com
Wheat grass
President/Owner: Timothy Paegelow
Estimated Sales: Under $300,000
Number Employees: 1-4
Square Footage: 10000
Type of Packaging: Consumer
Brands:
Grower's Pack
Hawkhaven
Verdegrass

5664 Hawkins Farm
20015 116th St
Bristol, WI 53104-9232
262-857-2616
Fax: 506-755-6241
Corn and soybeans
Owner: Steve Hawkins
hawkinss@ih.k12.oh.us
Estimated Sales: Less Than $500,000
Number Employees: 5-9

5665 Hawkins Inc
2381 Rosegate
Roseville, MN 55113
800-328-5460
customer.service@hawkinsinc.com
www.hawkinsinc.com
Ingredients for meat, poultry, seafood, dairy and beverage industries
President & CEO: Patrick Hawkins
patrick.hawkins@hawkinsinc.com
CFO, VP & Treasurer: Jeffrey Oldenkamp
General Counsel, VP & Secretary: Richard Erstad
VP of Operations: Drew Grahek
VP of Purchasing, Logistics, and Sales: Theresa Moran
Year Founded: 1938
Estimated Sales: $345 Million
Number Employees: 500-999
Number of Brands: 3
Type of Packaging: Private Label
Brands:
e(Lm)inate®
Ultralac
Ultra-Pure Bestate

5666 Hawthorne Valley Farm
327 County Route 21C
Ghent, NY 12075-1927
518-672-7500
Fax: 518-672-4887 info@hawthornevalleyfarm.org
Value-added products, including yogurt, cheese, sauerkraut and baked goods.
Executive Director: Martin Ping
Marketing: Karen Press
Farm Tours: Rachel Schneider
Manager: John Kidney
john@hawthornevalleyfarm.org
Estimated Sales: $2.5-5,000,000
Number Employees: 100-249
Type of Packaging: Private Label
Brands:
Hawthorne Valley Farm

5667 Hayashibara International Inc.
546 Fifth Avenue
16th Floor
New York, NY 10036-5000
212-703-1340
Fax: 212-398-0687
Carbohydrate-based ingredients
Director- North America: Tomonari Mozumi
VP: Alan Richards
Sales: Akihiro Hashino
Number Employees: 10
Type of Packaging: Bulk

5668 Haydel's Bakery
4037 Jefferson Hwy
New Orleans, LA 70121-1643
504-837-0190
Fax: 504-837-5512 800-442-1342
www.haydelbakery.com
Specialty cakes
Owner: David Haydel
david.haydel@haydelbakery.com
Estimated Sales: $1-2,500,000
Number Employees: 20-49

5669 Haydenergy Health
9 Riva Court
Valley Stream, NY 11581
212-888-1008
Fax: 212-246-9344 800-255-1660
www.naura.com
Health food products
President: Naura Hayden
Vice President: Nancy Leonard
Estimated Sales: $2.5-5 Million
Number Employees: 1-4
Number of Brands: 1
Number of Products: 3
Square Footage: 8000
Type of Packaging: Consumer
Brands:
Dynamite Energy Shake
Dynamite Vites

5670 Hazel Creek Orchards
227 Smiling Apple Dr
Mt Airy, GA 30563-2714
706-754-4899
Fax: 706-754-1524
Apples, apple juice and fruit ciders
Owner: Horace Yearwood
Estimated Sales: $1-2.5 Million
Number Employees: 1-4
Square Footage: 16800
Type of Packaging: Consumer, Bulk
Brands:
Hazel Creek

5671 Hazelnut Growers Of Oregon
401 N 26th Ave
Cornelius, OR 97113-8510
503-648-4176
Fax: 503-648-9515 800-273-4676
nutsales@hazelnut.com www.hazelnut.com
Hazelnuts

Food Manufacturers / A-Z

President & CEO: Tim Ramsey
Quality Control: Don Marshall
VP Sales & Marketing: Patrick Gabrish
Customer Service & Logistics Coordinator: Claudia Arreola
VP Operations: Dick Vanderschuere
Production Manager: Emilio Briones
Plant Manager: Ken Guinn
Purchasing Manager: Mike Sook
Estimated Sales: $32 Million
Number Employees: 50-99
Type of Packaging: Consumer, Bulk
Brands:
    Oregan Orchard

5672 Hazle Park Quality Meats
260 Washington Ave
West Hazleton, PA 18202
570-455-7571
Fax: 570-455-6030 800-238-4331
www.hazlepark.com
Processed meats
CEO: Gary Kreisel
Type of Packaging: Consumer, Food Service, Private Label, Bulk
Brands:
    Hazle

5673 Hazlitt 1852 Vineyards
5712 Route 414
Hector, NY 14841
607-546-9463
Fax: 607-546-5712 888-750-0494
info@hazlitt1852.com hazlitt1852.com
Wines
CEO & Owner: Doug Hazlitt
Marketing Manager: Stephanie Jarvis
Human Resources Manager: Justin Thomas
Estimated Sales: $5-10,000,000
Number Employees: 50-200
Number of Brands: 2
Other Locations:
    Hazlitt's Red Cat Cellars
    Naples NY
Brands:
    Hazlitt

5674 Hazy Grove Nuts
PO Box 25753
Portland, OR 97298-0753
503-670-8344
Fax: 503-968-2111 800-574-6887
lobbok7@gte.net
Hazelnuts.
President: Karen Lobb
Number Employees: 5—9
Type of Packaging: Private Label

5675 Head Country
2116 N Ash St
Ponca City, OK 74601-1105
580-762-1227
Fax: 580-765-8867 888-762-1227
www.headcountry.com
BBQ sauces, seasonings and marinades.
President: Brian Brassfield
bbrassfield@headcountry.com
Vice President, Co-Owner: Paul Schatte
Quality Control: Alan Slater
Marketing: Paul Schatte
Sales: Paul Schatte
Office Manager, Accounting: Linda Groth
Estimated Sales: Less Than $500,000
Number Employees: 10-19
Number of Brands: 1
Number of Products: 6
Type of Packaging: Consumer, Food Service, Private Label, Bulk
Brands:
    Head Country

5676 Healing Home Foods
73 Westchester Ave
P.O. Box 390
Pound Ridge, NY 10576
914-764-1303
info@healinghomefoods.com
www.healinghomefoods.com
Organic, vegan, gluten-free and GMO-free granolas, crackers, chips, nuts, treats, and other snacks
Founder: Shelley Schulz
Wholesale Inquiries: John Schulz

5677 Healing Solutions
4703 W Brill St
Suite 101
Phoenix, AZ 85043
800-819-4098
support@healingsolutions.com
healingsolutions.com
Essential oils
Exec. VP, Sales & Marketing: Jason Kern
Year Founded: 2014
Number Employees: 51-200

5678 Health & Nutrition Systems International
6615 Boyntn Bch Blvd
Suite 117
Boynton Beach, FL 33437-3526
561-433-0733
Fax: 888-478-8467 info@hnsglobal.com
Diet products
President: Christopher Tisi
Controller: Al Dugan
Marketing Director: Steven Sarafian
Product Development/Sales: Jamie Heithoff
Human Resources/Director Operations: Mona Lalia
Graphic Design: Derek Lopez
Graphic Design: Cathy Card
Shipping/Receiving: Tonya Davis
Number Employees: 10-19

5679 Health & Wholeness Store
104 N Main St
Fairfield, IA 52556-2802
641-472-6274
Fax: 719-260-7400 800-255-8332
www.healthandwholenessllc.com
Herbs and herbal products
President: Prakash Srivastava
Senior VP: Steven Barthe
Marketing Director: Russ Guest
Public Relations: Marsha Bonne
Operations Manager: Kevin Olson
Plant Manager: Kishore Nareundkar
Estimated Sales: Less Than $500,000
Number Employees: 1-4
Number of Brands: 4
Number of Products: 600
Square Footage: 188000
Type of Packaging: Consumer
Brands:
    Ayurveda
    Clarified Butter
    Maharishi
    Yata, Pilta, Kapha Teas

5680 Health Concerns
8001 Capwell Dr
Oakland, CA 94621-2107
510-957-5118
Fax: 510-639-9140 800-233-9355
info@healthconcerns.com
Chinese herbs, medicinal mushrooms and energy tonics
President: Laurie Dearborn
laurie@healthconcerns.com
Estimated Sales: $3-5 Million
Number Employees: 10-19
Square Footage: 12000
Type of Packaging: Consumer
Brands:
    Health Concerns

5681 Health Garden USA
750 Chestnut Ridge Rd
Suite 225
Spring Valley, NY 10977
845-877-7090
Fax: 845-364-6713 info@healthgardenusa.com
www.healthgardenusa.com
Sugar substitutes
Founder: Joel Phillip

5682 Health Plus
13837 Magnolia Ave
Chino, CA 91710-7028
909-627-9393
Fax: 909-591-7659 800-822-6225
order_desk@healthplusinc.com
www.healthplusinc.com
Psyllium and nutritional herbs, tablets and capsules
President: Rita Mediratta
ritam@healthplusinc.com
President: Pat Mediratta

Estimated Sales: $1-2.5 Million
Number Employees: 20-49
Square Footage: 34000
Type of Packaging: Bulk
Brands:
    Adrenal Cleanse
    Astazanthin
    Az-One
    Blood Cleanse
    Brain Vita
    Colon Cleanse
    Ener Jet
    Fireball Fat Burner
    Heart Cleanse
    Joint Cleanse
    Kidney Cleanse
    Liver Cleanse
    Ora-Plus
    Pat's Psyllium Slim
    Prostate Cleanse
    Shelly's Hair Care
    Super Fat Burner

5683 Health Products Corp
1060 Nepperhan Ave
Yonkers, NY 10703-1432
914-423-2900
Fax: 914-963-6001 www.hpc7.com
Psyllium and nutritional herbs, tablets and capsules; contract packager of blending and filling powders
President: Joseph Lewin
zurion2@aol.com
Number Employees: 50-99
Brands:
    Aspi-Cor
    Khg-7
    Lactalins
    Malpotane
    Tick Stop

5684 Health Valley Company
16100 Foothill Boulevard
Irwindale, CA 91706
626-334-3241
Fax: 626-334-0220 800-334-3204
www.healthvalley.com
Natural foods
President: Ben Brecher
CFO/Sr VP: Diane Beardsley
Number Employees: 250-499
Parent Co: Intrepid Food Holdings
Type of Packaging: Consumer, Food Service, Private Label, Bulk
Brands:
    Health Valley

5685 Health Warrior
Richmond, VA 23230
804-381-5305
www.healthwarrior.com
Chia snack bars and protein powders
Co-Founder & CEO: Shane Emmett
Co-Founder: Dan Gluck
Co-Founder: Nick Morris

5686 Health from the Sun
1 Clock Tower
Suite 100
Maynard, MA 01754
781-276-0505
Fax: 781-276-7335 800-447-2229
www.healthfromthesun.com
Fatty acids and phytonutrients
Parent Co: Arkopharma
Brands:
    Lean For Less

5687 Health is Wealth Foods
140 W Commercial Ave
Moonachie, NJ 7024
201-933-7474
Fax: 856-629-0378
Boxed, frozen and all natural foods; vegetarian and vegan items
President: Val Vasilief
Vice President: Jerry Colt
Estimated Sales: $5-10 Million
Number Employees: 5-9
Square Footage: 20000
Type of Packaging: Food Service, Private Label
Brands:
    Health Is Wealth

Food Manufacturers / A-Z

5688 Health-Ade LLC
3347 Motor Ave
Suite 200
Los Angeles, CA 90034-9711
844-337-6368
info@health-ade.com
www.health-ade.com
Kombucha
Co-Founder: Vanessa Dew
Co-Founder and CEO: Daina Trout
Co-Founder and COO: Justin Trout
Year Founded: 2012

5689 HealthBest
133 Mata Way
Suite 101
San Marcos, CA 92069
760-752-5230
Fax: 760-752-1322 www.globalkaizen.com
Natural and organic beans, dried fruits, snack foods, grains, herbs, spices, seasonings, nuts, seeds, bee pollen, pasta, sugar-free candy
President: Jamie Hickerson
President: Laurence Hickerson
Director of Operations: Eric Pena
Production Manager: Armando Ramos
Estimated Sales: $3 Million
Number Employees: 20-49
Number of Brands: 2
Number of Products: 300
Square Footage: 80000
Parent Co: Nature's Best
Type of Packaging: Consumer, Private Label, Bulk
Brands:
  Healthbest

5690 Healthco Canada Enterprises
PO Box 8249
Victoria, BC V8W 3R9
Canada
250-382-8384
Fax: 250-868-2195 877-468-2875
www.therebarstore.com
Organic nutrition bars

5691 Healthee
118 E St. Joseph St
Arcadia, CA 91006
626-574-1719
www.healtheeusa.com
Organic brown rice, fruit juices and turmeric drinks
Type of Packaging: Consumer
Brands:
  healthee

5692 Healthmate Products
1510 Old Deerfield Rd Ste 103
Highland Park, IL 60035
847-579-1051
Fax: 847-579-1059 www.healthmateproducts.com
Papaya concentrates
President: Tim Burke
treedburke@gmail.com
CEO/ Manager of Public Relations: Celeste Burke
Estimated Sales: $1 Million
Number Employees: 1-4
Type of Packaging: Consumer, Food Service

5693 Healthy Beverage LLC
200 S Clinton St
Suite 100
Doylestown, PA 18901
Fax: 866-642-9179 800-295-1388
info@steaz.com steaz.com
Organic green tea
Co-Founder: Steven Kessler
Co-Founder: Eric Schnell
Year Founded: 2002
Estimated Sales: $4.5 Million
Number Employees: 8
Type of Packaging: Private Label
Brands:
  Steaz

5694 Healthy Food Brands LLC
992 Bedford Ave
Brooklyn, NY 11205-4502
212-444-9909
www.hfbcandy.com
Candies and chocolates.
President: Sal Asaro
EVP: Russ Asaro
Estimated Sales: $30.6 Million
Number Employees: 1-4
Number of Brands: 2
Type of Packaging: Private Label
Brands:
  Welch's
  Simply Lite

5695 Healthy Food Ingredients
4666 Amber Valley Pkwy
Fargo, ND 58104
844-275-3443
www.hfifamily.com
Wheat, millet, durum, barley, sorghum, oat, rye, triticale, flax and ancient grains
President & CEO: Brad Hennrich
Estimated Sales: $50-100 Million
Number Employees: 20-49
Square Footage: 15000
Type of Packaging: Bulk

5696 Healthy Grain Foods LLC
4125 Yorkshire Ln
Northbrook, IL 60062-2915
847-272-5576
Fax: 847-272-5576
Cereals; research and development
President: Harold Zukerman
haroldzukerman@gmail.com
Estimated Sales: $1-2,500,000
Number Employees: 5-9

5697 Healthy Life Brands LLC
PO Box 812428
Wellesley, MA 02482
508-401-7040
Fax: 508-401-7430 www.eatveggiefries.com
Specialty fries made with a blend of vegetables, legumes, and potatoes
Co-Founder and CEO: David Peters
Co-Founder: Crista Peters
Brands:
  Veggie Fries

5698 Healthy N Fit International
435 Yorktown Rd
Croton On Hudson, NY 10520-3703
914-271-6040
Fax: 914-271-6042 800-338-5200
Info@behealthynfit.com
www.behealthynfit.com/default.asp
Vitamins, minerals and food supplements; importer of herbs, nutraceuticals, ascorbic acid and nutritional raw materials; exporter of food and dietary supplements
CEO: Robert J Sepe
VP/CFO: Irene Sepe
Public Relations: Denise O'Neill
Estimated Sales: $7 Million appx.
Number Employees: 10-19
Number of Products: 1000
Square Footage: 160000
Type of Packaging: Consumer, Food Service, Private Label, Bulk
Brands:
  Doctor's Nutriceuticals
  Healthy'n Fit Nutritionals

5699 Healthy Skoop
2438 30th Street
Boulder, CO 80301
720-545-1753
healthyskoop.com
Protein powders and cookies
President/Owner: Robert Bennett
Marketing: Lauren Langtim
Sales: Bobby Macauley
Operations: Ned Brown
Type of Packaging: Consumer
Brands:
  HEALTHY SKOOP

5700 Healthy Times Baby Food
San Diego, CA 92101
858-513-1550
Fax: 858-513-1533 hello@healthytimes.com
healthytimes.com
Organic baby food, baby cereal and milk formula.
President: Rondi Prescott
Estimated Sales: $5-10,000,000 appx.
Number Employees: 2-10

5701 Heart Foods Company
2235 E 38th St
Minneapolis, MN 55407-3083
612-724-5266
Fax: 612-724-5516 800-229-3663
Herbal cayenne formulas
Owner: Dick Quinn
Contact: Dixie Davidson
dharley-davidson@heartofdixiehd.com
Estimated Sales: $1-2.5 Million
Number Employees: 1-4
Number of Brands: 1
Number of Products: 13
Square Footage: 5000
Type of Packaging: Consumer

5702 Heart to Heart Foods
142 W 3200 N
Hyde Park, UT 84318
435-753-9602
Fax: 435-753-9605
Ice cream products
Owner: Craig Earl
Contact: Kirk Earl
ekirk@healthyheartmarket.com
Estimated Sales: $2.5-5,000,000
Number Employees: 10-19

5703 Heartbreaking Dawns Artisan Foods
PO Box 10877
Glendale, AZ 85318
646-957-3484
heartbreakingdawns.com
Manufacturer of hot sauce.
Co-Founder: Johnny McLaughlin
Co-Founder: Nicole McLaughlin

5704 Hearthside Food Solutions
3500 Lacey Rd
Suite 300
Downers Grove, IL 60515
630-967-3600
info@hearthsidefoods.com
www.hearthsidefoods.com
Nutrition and energy bars, cookies, crackers, snack foods, cereal and granola, and food packaging.
Chairman/CEO & Co-Founder: Rich Scalise
Senior VP/CFO: Fred Jasser
Senior VP Human Resources: Steve England
Year Founded: 2009
Number Employees: 5000-9999
Type of Packaging: Consumer, Private Label

5705 Hearthstone Whole Grain Bakery
4717 Meadow Lane
Bozeman, MT 59715-9631
406-586-1227
Fax: 406-586-1227 800-757-7919
Bakery
President: Gwen Phillips
Manager: Mavis Mason

5706 Hearthy Foods
2043 Imperial St
Los Angeles, CA 90021
213-372-5093
info@hearthyfoods.com
www.hearthyfoods.com
Gluten free desserts & baking flours
President: Riaz Surti
Year Founded: 2012

5707 Heartland Brewery
1430 Broadway
Suite 1513
New York, NY 10018
212-400-2300
Fax: 212-645-8306 info@heartlandbrewery.com
www.heartlandbrewery.com
Beers
CEO: John Bloostein
Marketing Director: Bonnie Bernier
Estimated Sales: $2.5-5,000,000
Number Employees: 50-99
Type of Packaging: Consumer, Food Service
Brands:
  Heartland

Food Manufacturers / A-Z

5708 Heartland Farms Dairy & Food Products, LLC
3668 South Geyer Road
Suite 205
St. Louis, MO 63127
314-965-1110
Fax: 314-965-1118 888-633-6455
info@heartlandfarmsdairy.com
www.heartlandfarmsdairy.com
Dairy products
President: Tom Jacoby
Marketing Assistant: Pat Hittmeier
Sales of Dry Products: Tim Fann
Contact: Christine Anderson
canderson@heartlandfarmsdairy.com
Weights and Tests: Jenn Jacoby
Type of Packaging: Consumer, Bulk

5709 Heartland Flax
849 14th St SW
P.O. Box 777
Valley City, ND 58072
Fax: 701-845-2276 866-599-3529
info@heartlandflax.com www.heartlandflax.com
Flax ingredients
Director of Sales: Bob Larson
Technical Director: Bruce Livingood

5710 Heartland Food Products
1900 W 47th Place
Suite 302
Westwood, KS 66205
913-831-4446
Fax: 913-831-4004 866-571-0222
www.heartlandfoodproducts.com
Mashed potatoes
President: Bill Steeb
Founder: Mary Steeb
Contact: Tom Gray
tom.gray@heartlandfpg.com
Estimated Sales: Less than $500,000
Number Employees: 10-19
Type of Packaging: Bulk

5711 Heartland Gourmet LLC
52205 19th Street
Lincoln, NE 68512
402-423-1234
Fax: 402-423-4586 800-735-6828
www.heartlandgourmet.com
Organic, all natural and gluten free baking mixes; gluten free and gourmet frozen doughs
Sales & Product Development Manager: Susan Zink
Business Development Manager: Mark Zink
Estimated Sales: $2.3 Million
Number Employees: 20-49
Square Footage: 54000
Type of Packaging: Consumer, Private Label
Brands:
  Wanda's

5712 Heartland Ingredients LLC
802 West College Street
Troy, MO 63379
Fax: 877-841-2067 800-557-2621
contactus@heartlandingredients.net
www.heartlandingredients.net
Ingredients, food and technical grade chemicals and colors, dairy products, meat products, sugar, artifical sweeteners, close dated finished products.

5713 Heartland Mills Shipping
124 N Hwy 167
Marienthal, KS 67863-6368
620-379-4467
Fax: 620-379-4459 800-232-8533
info@heartlandmill.com www.heartlandmill.com
Organic grains, flour, oat products and sunflower seeds
President: Larry Decker
VP: Mark Nightengale
Sales Executive: Carl Rosenlund
Manager: Carl Rosenlund
seanc@ekisticsinc.net
Estimated Sales: Less Than $500,000
Number Employees: 1-4
Square Footage: 28000
Type of Packaging: Food Service, Private Label, Bulk
Brands:
  Heartland Mill

5714 Heartland Strawberry Farm
5111 Osage Rd
Waterloo, IA 50703-9390
319-232-3779
Fax: 888-757-7423 888-747-7423
berrypumpkinfarm@earthlink.net
Fruits and vegetables
Owner: Dave Myers
Number Employees: 1-4

5715 Heartland Sweeteners
14390 Clay Terrace Blvd
Suite 250
Carmel, IN 46032
317-566-9750
www.heartlandfpg.com
Coffee, coffee creamers and low-calorie sweeteners
Type of Packaging: Food Service
Other Locations:
  Distribution Center
  Indianapolis IN
  Manufacturing
  Indianapolis IN

5716 Heartland Vinyards
24945 Detroit Rd # G
Westlake, OH 44145-2554
440-871-0701
jwdover@aol.com
www.heartlandvineyards.com
Wines
Owner: Jerome M Welliver
jwdover@aol.com
Estimated Sales: $500-1,000,000 appx.
Number Employees: 5-9

5717 Heartline Foods
PO Box 454
Westport, CT 06881-0454
203-222-0381
Fax: 203-226-6445
Paprika, beans, noodles, sauces, seasonings, pasta, soups and tapiocas.
President: Henry Ellett
Estimated Sales: $.5-1 million
Number Employees: 1-4
Brands:
  China Bowl
  Dinny Robb
  Sinatra
  Wye River

5718 Hearttea Inc.
195 Montague St
Suite 14F
Brooklyn, NY 11201
917-725-3164
info@heartoftea.com
Iced tea
Founder and President: Messi Gerami
Brands:
  Heart of Tea

5719 Hearty Naturals
P.O.Box 3871
West McLean, VA 22103
513-443-2789
contactus@heartynaturals.com
heartynaturals.com
Coconut oil, ghee, moringa powder and coconut sugar.
Director: Amila Abeyseker
Year Founded: 1980
Estimated Sales: $3 Million
Number Employees: 40-50
Brands:
  Hearty Naturals

5720 Heaven Hill Distilleries Inc.
1311 Gilkey Run Rd.
Bardstown, KY 40004
502-337-1000
Fax: 502-348-0162 www.heavenhill.com
Distilled spirits.
President: Max Shapira
Executive Vice President: Harry Shapira
Vice President, Human Resources: Debbie Morris
COO: Allan Latts
Year Founded: 1935
Estimated Sales: $193 Million
Number Employees: 250-499
Number of Brands: 34
Number of Products: 51
Type of Packaging: Consumer, Private Label, Bulk
Brands:
  Admiral Nelson's Spiced Rum
  Ansac Cognac
  Bernheim Original Wheat Whiskey
  Blackheart Premium Spiced Rum
  Burnett's London Dry Gin
  Burnett's Vodkas
  Carolans Irish Cream Liqueur
  Christian Brothers Brandies
  Cinerator Hot Cinnamon Whiskey
  Copa De Oro Coffee Liqueur
  Coronet VSQ Brandy
  Deep Eddy Vodkas
  Domaine de Canton
  Du Bouchett Liqueurs & Cordials
  Dubonnet Apperitifs
  Elijah Craig Bourbons
  Evan Williams Bourbons
  Fighting Cock Bourbon
  Fulton's Harvest Cream Liqueur
  Georgia Moon Corn Whiskey
  Hnery Mckenna Single Barrel
  HPNOTIQ
  Irish Mist Liqueur
  Larceny Bourbon
  Lunazul Tequilas
  Mellow Corn Whiskey
  O'Mara's Irish Country Cream
  Old Fitzgerald Bourbon
  PAMA Pomegranate Liqueur
  Parker's Heritage Collection
  Pikesville Straight Rye Whiskey
  Rittenhouse Straight Rye Whiskey
  Sacred Bond
  Two Fingers Tequilas

5721 Heavenly Hemp Foods
PO Box 1794
Nederland, CO 80466
303-938-0195
Fax: 303-443-1869 888-328-4367
Health foods
President: David Almquist
Marketing Director: Tom White
Operations Manager: Kathleen Chippi
Number Employees: 1
Brands:
  Heaven Scent
  Heaven Scent Windmill Cakes
  Heaven Scent Butter
  Heaven Scent Croutons

5722 Heavenly Organics, LLC
14300 E 125 Frontage Rd
Longmont, CO 80504
641-636-2095
info@heavenlyorganics.com
heavenlyorganics.com
Honey, whole cane sugar, chocolate honey candies
President: Wj Christopher
heavenlyorganics@yahoo.com
Chief Executive Officer/Founder: Amit Hooda
Operations Director: Jaison Lynch
Estimated Sales: A
Number Employees: 1-4

5723 Heavenscent Edibles
402 E 90th Street
New York, NY 10128-5119
212-369-0310
Fax: 212-369-0310
Brownies and holiday cookies

5724 Hebert Candies
574 Hartford Turnpike
Shrewsbury, MA 01545
508-842-5583
Fax: 508-842-3065 866-609-6533
info@herbertcandies.com www.hebertcandies.com
Kosher chocolate candies and confectionery products
CEO: Tom O'Rourke
Chief Financial Officer: Jeff Goodman
Purchasing Manager: Bob Kerekon
Estimated Sales: $10-20,000,000
Number Employees: 50-99
Square Footage: 100000
Type of Packaging: Consumer

5725 Heck Cellars
15401 Bear Mountain Winery Rd
Arvin, CA 93203-9743
661-854-6120
Fax: 661-854-2876

Wines, brandy; also, juices and bottled water
Owner: Gary Heck
gheck@korbel.com
Plant Manager: Tim Holt
Estimated Sales: $10-20 Million
Number Employees: 20-49
Square Footage: 1200000
Parent Co: F. Korbel & Brothers
Type of Packaging: Private Label, Bulk

5726 Hecker Pass Winery
4605 Hecker Pass Rd
Gilroy, CA 95020-8808
408-842-8755
Fax: 408-842-9799 carlo@heckerpasswinery.com
Wines
Owner/President: Mario Fortino
VP/Operations/Marketing: Carlo Fortino
Owner: Frances Fortino
Estimated Sales: Less Than $500,000
Number Employees: 1-4
Type of Packaging: Private Label
Brands:
   Hecker Pass

5727 Heffy's BBQ Co.
Kansas City Southern Rlwy
Kansas City, MO 66117
816-200-2271
Fax: 816-366-3920 www.heffys.com
Sauces and cooking enhancers
CEO: Mike Farag
CMO: Jason Drumright
COO: Jeff Ratzloff

5728 Hegy's South Hills Vineyard & Winery
PO Box 727
Twin Falls, ID 83303-0727
208-599-0074
Fax: 208-734-6369
Wines
Owner/Vineyard Manager: Frank Hegy
Estimated Sales: Under $500,000
Number Employees: 1-4
Brands:
   South Hills

5729 Heidi's Gourmet Desserts
1651 Montreal Cir
Tucker, GA 30084
770-449-4900
Fax: 770-326-6157 800-241-4166
Frozen speciality desserts
President: Larry Obertfell
Operations Director: Brian Schendider
Estimated Sales: $10-20 Million
Number Employees: 100-249
Square Footage: 134000
Type of Packaging: Consumer, Food Service, Private Label
Other Locations:
   Heidi's Gourmet
   Atlanta GA
   Heidi's Gourmet
   Sun Valley CA
   Heidi's Gourmet
   Salt Lake City UT

5730 Heidi's Salsa
12615 Beatrice St
Los Angeles, CA 90066-7003
USA
310-821-0211
heidi@lukofoods.com
www.lukofoods.com
Salsa, dips, sauces, seasonings, cooking enhancers
Owner: Heidi Luko
Co-Owner: Nikki Dougherty
Contact: Heidi Withers
heidi@lukofoods.com

5731 Heineman Winery
978 Catawba Ave
PO Box 300
Put In Bay, OH 43456-5507
419-285-2811
Fax: 419-285-3412 info@HeinemansWinery.com
www.heinemanswinery.com
Fruit juices and wine.
Owner: Louis Heineman
Vice President: Louis Heineman
Assistant Manager: Michael Bianichi
Estimated Sales: $500,000-$1 Million
Number Employees: 1-4
Parent Co: Heineman Beverage
Other Locations:
   Heineman Distributing
   Port Clinton OH
Brands:
   Catawba Grape Juice
   Heineman's

5732 Heinke Family Farm
5365 Clark Rd
Paradise, CA 95969-6392
530-877-5264
Beef, beef products
Owner: Dave Heinke
Estimated Sales: Less Than $500,000
Number Employees: 1-4

5733 Heinkel's Packing Co
2005 N 22nd St
Decatur, IL 62526
217-428-4401
800-594-2738
sales@heinkelspacking.com
www.heinkelspacking.com
Smoked meats, lunch meats and fresh sausages; boxed beef and pork; venison processing
Owner: Miles Wright
President: Wes Wright
Head of Production: Tom McCarthy
Year Founded: 1912
Estimated Sales: $5-9.9 Million
Number Employees: 20-49
Type of Packaging: Consumer, Food Service, Bulk
Brands:
   Heinkel's

5734 Heintz & Weber Co
150 Reading St
Buffalo, NY 14220-2156
716-852-7171
Fax: 716-852-7173 info@webersmustard.com
www.webersmustard.com
Condiments
President: Steven Desmond
sdesmond@webersmustard.com
Executive VP: Suzanne Desmond
CEO: Steven Desmond
Estimated Sales: $5-10 Million
Number Employees: 5-9
Square Footage: 72000
Type of Packaging: Consumer, Bulk
Brands:
   Weber's Horseradish Mustard
   Weber's Hot Garlic M
   Weber's Hot Piocacic
   Weber's Spicy Dill Pickles
   Weber's Sweet Pickle

5735 Heinz Portion Control
7500 Forshee Dr
Jacksonville, FL 32219
904-695-1300
www.heinzfoodservice.com
Manufacturer and exporter of portion controlled sugar, pepper, salt, ketchup, mustard, sauces, dressings, jams, jellies, syrup, preserves, mayonnaise and artificial sweeteners
Parent Co: The Kraft Heinz Company
Type of Packaging: Food Service, Private Label
Other Locations:
   Portion Pac
   Stone Mountain GA
Brands:
   Chatsworth
   Madeira Farms
   Pitch'r Pak
   Salsa Del Sol
   Squeezers
   Sweet Pleasers Gourmet
   Sweet Pleasers
   Taste Pleasers Gourmet

5736 Heinz Quality Chef Foods Inc
5005 C St SW
Cedar Rapids, IA 52404-7601
319-362-9633
Fax: 319-362-3924 800-356-8307
www.heinz.com
Frozen soups, sauces and entrees
President: Shannon Ashby
Plant Manager: Steve Maddocks
Estimated Sales: $10-20 Million
Number Employees: 100-249
Parent Co: Heinz USA
Type of Packaging: Food Service
Brands:
   Quality Chef Foods, Inc.

5737 Heirloom Organic Gardens
743 Shore Rd
Hollister, CA 95023-9427
831-637-8497
www.heirloom-organic.com
Organic vegetables
President: Grant Brians
Estimated Sales: $.5-1,000,000
Number Employees: 10-19

5738 Heise Wausau Farms
2805 Valley View Rd
Wausau, WI 54403-8799
715-675-3862
Fax: 715-675-3256 800-764-1010
heisewausaufarms@yahoo.com
Ginseng, bee pollen capsules
President/Owner: Lyn Heise
heisewausaufarms@yahoo.com
Sales: Dan Heise
Estimated Sales: Less Than $500,000
Number Employees: 1-4
Square Footage: 16000
Brands:
   Heise's
   Jar-Lu

5739 Heitz Wine Cellars
436 Saint Helena Hwy S
St Helena, CA 94574-2206
707-963-3542
Fax: 707-963-7454 www.heitzcellar.com
Wines
President: Asuncion Tolley
tasuncion@heitzcellar.com
Winemaker: David Heitz
Estimated Sales: $5-10 Million
Number Employees: 5-9
Square Footage: 18726
Type of Packaging: Consumer
Brands:
   Heitz

5740 Hela Spice Company
119 Franklin St
PO Box 1479
Uxbridge, ON L9P 1J5
Canada
905-852-5100
Fax: 905-852-1113 877-435-2649
www.helacanada.com
Custom blends, spice mixtures and seasoning blends for the meat and bakery industry
President: Walter Knecht
Senior Vice President-Sales: Paul Hoogenboom
Information Technology Manager: Gary Leung
Quality Assurance Manager: Crista Dagnall
Director of Technical Applications: Uwe Thode
Customer Service/Administration: Rita Irwin
Vice President-Food Safety: Dr. Thomas Varga
Purchasing Manager: Lisa Gay
Estimated Sales: $7 Million
Number Employees: 40

5741 Helados Mexico
Chino, CA 91708
www.heladosmexico.com
Fruit and ice cream bars

5742 Helen's Pure Foods
301 Ryers Ave
Cheltenham, PA 19012
215-379-6433
Fax: 215-663-5340 info@helenspurefoods.com
helenspurefoods.com
Hummus, dips, dressings, spreads and sandwiches.
Owner: Richard Goldberg
rgoldberg@helenspurefoods.com
Estimated Sales: $5-9.9,000,000
Number Employees: 2-10

5743 Helena View/Johnston Vineyard
3500 Highway 128
Calistoga, CA 94515
707-942-4956
Fax: 707-942-4956
Wines

Food Manufacturers / A-Z

Owner/Winemaker: Charles Johnston
Manager Public Relations: Sarah Marie Johnston
Winery Chief: Tom Gary
VP Administration: Charles Johnston
Brands:
   Helena View
   Moon Mountain

5744 Hell On The Red Inc
13716 E Fm 273
Telephone, TX 75488-5450
   903-664-2573
Fax: 903-664-2301
lisa.hamilton@hellontheredinc.com
www.hellontheredinc.com
Pickled fruits and vegetables, vegetable sauces and seasonings & salad dressings
President: Thomas Baugh
Vice President: Patricia Baugh
Estimated Sales: $575,395
Number Employees: 1-4
Type of Packaging: Consumer, Private Label
Brands:
   Hell on the Red

5745 Hella Cocktail
23-23 Borden Ave
Long Island City, NY 11101
   646-854-8004
hellacocktail.co
Cocktail mixes and bitters
Co-Founder: Jomaree Pinkard
Co-Founder: Tobin Ludwig
Co-Founder: Eddie Simeon

5746 Heller Brothers Packing Corp
306 9th St
Winter Garden, FL 34787-3683
   407-656-4986
Fax: 407-656-1751 855-543-5537
ptanner@hellerbros.com www.hellerbros.com
Citrus fruits
Owner/President: Harvey Heller
Owner/CEO: Harry Falk
hfalk@hellerbros.com
CFO: Jeff McKinney
General Manager: Don Barwick
VP Sales/Marketing: Rob Brath
Human Resources/Finance Executive: Jeff McKinney
General Manager: Billy Howard
Production: Al Jefferson
Estimated Sales: $3 Million
Number Employees: 250-499
Square Footage: 1000000
Type of Packaging: Consumer

5747 Heller Estates
69 West Carmel Valley Road
PO Box 999
Carmel Valley, CA 93924
   831-659-6220
Fax: 831-659-6226 800-625-8466
info@hellerestate.com www.hellerestate.com
Organic wines
President: Robert Freeman
Controller: Pat Verde
Contact: Mary Roos
info@hellerestate.com
General Manager: Rene Schober
Estimated Sales: $1-2.5 Million
Number Employees: 7
Type of Packaging: Consumer

5748 Hello Water
   888-474-3556
sayhello@hellowater.com hellowater.com
Fiber-infused water
Number of Brands: 1
Number of Products: 5
Type of Packaging: Consumer
Brands:
   HELLO WATER

5749 Hells Canyon Winery
18835 Symms Rd
Caldwell, ID 83607-9513
   208-454-3300
800-318-7873
hellwine@yahoo.com
Wines
Owner: Stephen C Robertson
hellwine@yahoo.com
Estimated Sales: Less Than $500,000
Number Employees: 1-4
Brands:
   Hells Canyon

5750 Helm New York Chemical Corp
1110 Centennial Ave # 2
Piscataway, NJ 08854-4146
   732-981-0528
Fax: 732-981-0965 www.helmus.com
Ingredients, additives and flavors
President: Beverly Marsh
bmarsh@helmus.com
CFO: Bill Van Fossen
Senior Vice President: Arun Manalkar
Number Employees: 20-49
Parent Co: Helm AG

5751 Helms Bakery
8758 Venice Blvd.
Ste. 100
Los Angeles, CA 90034
helmsinfo@wnmrealty.com
helmsbakerydistrict.com
Baked goods

5752 Helms Candy Co., Inc
3001 Lee Hwy
P.O.Box 607
Bristol, VA 24202-5939
   276-669-2612
Fax: 276-669-0150 276-669-2533
www.helmscandy.com
Candies
President: George Helms
george@helmscandy.com
CEO: Helen Helms
VP Candy Division: Buzz Helms
VP Pharmaceutical Division: Mark Helms
Accounting Department: Deborah Smith
Production Supervisor: Tony Hatcher
Estimated Sales: $5-10,000,000
Number Employees: 2-10
Square Footage: 65000
Brands:
   Cool-E-Pops
   Happy Day Pops
   Helms
   Hot-C-Pops
   Hot-N-Coldpops
   Mint Lumps
   Mint Puffs
   Thank You Pops
   Virginia Beauty
   Zippy Pop

5753 Helmuth Country Bakery Inc
6706 W Mills Ave
Hutchinson, KS 67501-8890
   620-567-2301
Fax: 620-567-2036 800-567-6360
info@helmuthfoods.com www.helmuthfoods.com
Cookies, candies, noodles and cotton candy
Owner: Jim Rein
jrein@helmuthfoods.com
VP: Katie Helmuth
Estimated Sales: Less Than $500,000
Number Employees: 1-4
Square Footage: 12000
Type of Packaging: Consumer, Food Service
Brands:
   Cortland Manor
   Hatties
   Helmuth

5754 Helshiron Fisheries
7 Norman Road
Grand Manan, NB E5G 2G5
Canada
   506-662-3696
Fax: 506-662-3779 lobfish@nbnet.nb.ca
Seafood
President: Ronald Benson
VP/Marketing Director: Morton Benson
Estimated Sales: $1,500,000
Number Employees: 9
Type of Packaging: Bulk
Brands:
   Helshiron

5755 Helthe Brands
Austin, TX 78746
   888-311-2157
hello@helthebrands.com helthebrands.com
Ayurvedic juices
Co-Founder: Swaroopa Masten
Co-Founder: Mark Masten
Brands:
   Geevani
   Senor Cane

5756 Heltzman Bakery
4749 Dixie Hwy
Louisville, KY 40216-2653
   502-447-3515
www.heitzmanbakery.net
Bakery products, custom cakes and deli trays
President: Paul Osting
Manager: Nancy Kasey
Estimated Sales: Less Than $500,000
Number Employees: 5-9
Type of Packaging: Consumer, Food Service
Brands:
   Springerlies

5757 Heluva Good Cheese
6 Kimball Ln
Suite 400
Lynnfield, MA 01940
   617-660-7400
800-644-5473
www.heluvagood.com
Cheese, dips, cocktail sauce and mustard.
Director, Production & Quality Assurance: Bob Fratangelo
Production Manager: Steve De Mass
Year Founded: 1925
Estimated Sales: $20-50 Million
Number Employees: 100-249
Number of Products: 31
Square Footage: 42000
Type of Packaging: Consumer, Food Service, Private Label, Bulk
Brands:
   Heluva Good Cheese

5758 Hemp Fusion
11660 Alpharetta Hwy
Suite 120
Roswell, GA 30076
   877-669-4367
info@hempfusion.com hempfusion.com
Hemp-based nutritional supplements
Co-Founder & President: Jason Mitchell
Number of Brands: 1
Number of Products: 5
Type of Packaging: Consumer
Brands:
   HEMP FUSION

5759 Hemp Oil Canada
PO Box 300
100 Prairie Rd
Ste. Agathe, MB R0G 1Y0
Canada
   204-882-2480
Fax: 204-882-2529 800-289-4367
info@hempoilcan.com hempoilcanada.com
Hemp food ingredients
Controller: Jodi Schreyer Cloutier
Asst. Mgr., Marketing: Timothy Bonnar
Year Founded: 1998
Number Employees: 51-200
Type of Packaging: Bulk

5760 Hemp Production Services
706 6th Ave N
Saskatoon, SK S7K 2S9
Canada
   844-436-7477
customerservice@hempproductionservices.com
www.hempproductionservices.com
Hempseed oil and powders
President: Garry Meier
VP, Operations: Kevin Friesen
Type of Packaging: Bulk

5761 Hemp2o
1000 Beecher St
San Leandro, CA 94577-1250
   510-382-1231
hemp2o.com
Organic hemp beverages
Contact: Jennifer Kleinfeld
Number of Brands: 1
Number of Products: 9
Type of Packaging: Consumer

Food Manufacturers / A-Z

5762 HempNut
1286 Winter Solstice Avenue
Henderson, NV 89014-8869
707-576-7050
Fax: 707-579-0940 steve@thehempnut.com
www.thehempnut.com
Hempnuts
Founder/President: Richard Rose
Brands:
HEMP2O

5763 Hena Inc
660 Berriman St
Brooklyn, NY 11208-5304
718-272-8237
Fax: 718-272-8391
Iced coffee, iced tea mix and liquid concentrates.
President: Lan Tauber
lanny@henacoffee.com
Estimated Sales: $5-10 000,000
Number Employees: 5-9
Type of Packaging: Food Service, Private Label

5764 Henderson's Gardens
P.O. Box 214
Berwyn, AB T0M 0E0
Canada
780-338-2128
Fax: 780-338-2128
Corn, cucumbers, potatoes, tomatoes, cabbage, peas, beans and peppers
President: Robert Henderson
Number Employees: 3
Type of Packaging: Consumer, Food Service
Brands:
Pride of Peace Vegetables

5765 Hendon & David
PO Box 836
Millbrook, NY 999
845-677-9696
Fax: 845-677-9699 hendonco@aol.com
Macadamia nuts, cranberry grand marnier, exotic meat sauces, honeys, latin specialties, relishes, mustards
Owner: Helen Hendon
Brands:
Bushman's Best Mazavaroo
Clove Valley Farms
Hendon

5766 Hendricks Apiaries
4001 S Elati Street
Englewood, CO 80110-4555
303-789-3209
Specialty honey
President: Paul Hendricks
Co-Owner: Linda Hendricks
Estimated Sales: Under $500,000
Number Employees: 1-4
Square Footage: 6800
Type of Packaging: Consumer, Food Service, Private Label, Bulk
Brands:
Colorado Sunshine Honey

5767 Henggeler Packing Company
6730 Elmore Road
Fruitland, ID 83619
208-452-4212
Fax: 208-452-5416
Apples, plums and prunes
President: Gerald Henggeler
Vice President: Anthony Henggeler
Estimated Sales: $4 Million
Number Employees: 12
Type of Packaging: Consumer, Bulk
Brands:
Fortress
Fruitland

5768 Henning Cheese Factory
20201 Point Creek Rd
Kiel, WI 53042-4299
920-894-3032
Fax: 920-894-3022 kay@henningcheese.com
www.henningcheese.com
Cheese
President: Kerry Henning
Estimated Sales: $10-20 Million
Number Employees: 10-19
Type of Packaging: Consumer, Food Service, Private Label, Bulk
Brands:
Henning's

5769 Henningsen Foods Inc
14334 Industrial Rd
Omaha, NE 68144-3398
402-330-2500
Fax: 402-330-0875 800-228-2769
davids@henningsenfoods.com
www.henningsenfoods.com
Dried meats and eggs; contract dehydration
President: Jerry Walker
CEO: Arnulfo Arevalo
arnulfoa@henningsenfoods.com
R&D: Jason Zhang
Vice President, Sales: Aaron Heironimus
Logistics Manager: Gina Blankenau
Estimated Sales: $10-49.9 Million
Number Employees: 100-249
Square Footage: 12000
Type of Packaging: Food Service, Private Label, Bulk

5770 Henry Broch & Co
3940 Porett Dr
Gurnee, IL 60031-1244
847-816-6225
Fax: 847-816-6238 sales@hbroch.com
www.hbroch.com
Tomatoes and tomato powder, spices and vegetables
Manager: Donald Swanson
Sales Manager: James Kuzma
Estimated Sales: $5-10 Million
Number Employees: 5-9

5771 Henry Davis Company
3405 W 15th Ave
Gary, IN 46404-1964
219-949-8555
Fax: 219-949-9764
Seafood
President: Henry Davis
Estimated Sales: $1-3 Million
Number Employees: 20-49

5772 Henry Estate Winery
687 Hubbard Creek Rd
Umpqua, OR 97486-9611
541-459-5120
Fax: 541-459-5146 800-782-2686
winery@henryestate.com www.henryestate.com
Wines
President: Scott Henry
Vice President, Marketing: Syndi Beavers
Sales & Marketing Specialist: Crystal Loftin
Estimated Sales: $5-10,000,000
Number Employees: 11-50
Brands:
Henry Estate

5773 Henry H. Misner Ltd.
469 Norfolk St. N
Simcoe, ON N3Y 3P8
Canada
519-426-5546
Fax: 519-583-1529
Frozen shellfish and groundfish
President: Donald Misner
CFO: Nancy Misner
General Manager: Donald Misner
Number Employees: 20-49
Type of Packaging: Consumer, Food Service

5774 Henry Hill & Co
459 Walnut St
Napa, CA 94559-3101
707-253-1663
Fax: 707-257-2990
Wines
Owner: Mark Koehn
Estimated Sales: Less Than $500,000
Number Employees: 1-4
Brands:
Broken Rock Cellars

5775 Henry J's Meat Specialties
4460 W Armitage Ave
Chicago, IL 60639-3574
773-227-5400
Fax: 773-227-0414 800-242-1314
www.henryjmeats.com
Prepared meats
CEO: Forrest C. Krisco
fkrisco@henryjmeats.com
Executive Corporate Chief, R&D: Faustino Rivera
Quality Assurance, Plant Operations: Lorenzo Jackson
Customer Service: Alicia Vega
Estimated Sales: $1,000,000-1,490,000
Number Employees: 10-19

5776 Herb Bee's Products
210 Mallard Drive
Colchester, VT 05446-7013
802-864-7387
sierrassong@aol.com
Jam, jelly, relish, quick breads, cheese spreads, and vinegars
Owner: Rhonda Tebeau

5777 Herb Patch of Vermont
30 Island Street
Bellows Falls, VT 05101-3122
802-463-1400
Fax: 802-463-1911 800-282-4372
Cocoas, dessert beverages, dips, teas and herb blends; exporter of cocoa
Owner: John Moisis
Estimated Sales: Less than $500,000
Number Employees: 1-4
Square Footage: 13000
Brands:
Country Cow
Country Cow Cocoa
Cowpuccino Toppers

5778 Herb Pharm
PO Box 116
Williams, OR 97544
541-846-6262
Fax: 800-545-7392 800-348-4372
info@herb-pharm.com www.herb-pharm.com
Health supplements and personal care products
Founder/Co-Owner: Ed Smith
Founder/Co-Owner: Sara Katz
Co-Owner: Sara Katz
Number Employees: 50-99

5779 Herb Society Of America
9019 Kirtland Chardon Rd
Willoughby, OH 44094-5156
440-256-0514
Fax: 440-256-0541 herbs@herbsociety.org
www.herbsociety.org
Seasonings, spices
Executive Director: Katrinka Morgan
director@herbsociety.org
Administrative Support: Olivia Yates
Office Administrator: Michelle Milks
Editor: Robert Walland
Horticulturist: Robin Siktberg
HSA Librarian: Tara Coulter
Estimated Sales: $500,000-$1 000,000
Number Employees: 5-9
Type of Packaging: Private Label
Brands:
Herb Society of America

5780 Herb Tea Company
P.O.Box 1962
Oxnard, CA 93032-1962
805-486-6477
Fax: 805-385-3216
Tea
Sales Coordinator: Robert Lessin
Plant Manager: William Ashwell
Estimated Sales: $2.5-5 000,000
Number Employees: 10-19
Type of Packaging: Consumer, Private Label

5781 Herb's Seafood
112 Schoolhouse Road
Westampton, NJ 08060-3774
609-267-0276
Fax: 609-261-1949 800-486-0276
Prepared fish and poultry
Owner: Nash Cohen
VP Sales: Gary Cannard
Sales Manager: Richard Applebam
Plant Manager: William Byrne
Estimated Sales: $10-20 000,000
Number Employees: 2
Type of Packaging: Private Label
Brands:
Herbs Seafood

Food Manufacturers / A-Z

5782 HerbCo International
16661 W Snoqualmie River Rd NE
Duvall, WA 98019-9202
425-788-7903
Fax: 425-844-9114 888-643-7226
herbco@msn.com www.herbco.net
Culinary herbs and edible flowers
Owner: Ted Andrews
tandrews@herbco.net
Estimated Sales: $5-10 Million
Number Employees: 50-99
Brands:
  Herbco
  Generation Farms
  Michigan Fine Herbs

5783 HerbNZest LLC
135 S Barrow Pl
Princeton, NJ 08540
917-582-1191
info@herbnzest.com
Chutney, relish and a variety of sauces.
Founder and CEO: Deboleena Dutta

5784 HerbaSway Laboratories
101 N. Plains Industrial Rd
PO Box 6098
Wallingford, CT 06492-0089
203-269-6991
Fax: 203-269-9703 800-672-7322
www.herbasway.com
Liquid dietary health supplements
Owner: Dr. Franklin St John
Founder/Owner: Lorraine St. John
Estimated Sales: $10-20 Million
Number Employees: 20-49

5785 Herbal Magic
1867 Yonge Street
Suite 700
Toronto, ON M4S 1Y5
Canada
416-487-7009
Fax: 416-487-4569 877-237-7225
melren@aol.com www.herbalmagic.com
Herbs for alternative uses
Founder/Master Herbalist: Renee Ponder
Estimated Sales: $300,000-500,000
Number Employees: 1-4

5786 Herbal Products & Development
1200 Trout Gulch Rd
Aptos, CA 95003-3038
831-688-8706
herbprodinfo@gmail.com
www.herbprod.com
Food concentrates, digestive enzymes, antioxidants, probiotics, tinctures, oils and liquid vitamins and minerals
President: Paul Gaylon
herbprodinfo@gmail.com
Number Employees: 1-4
Square Footage: 2400
Type of Packaging: Consumer, Private Label
Brands:
  Liquid Life Essential Day & Night
  Liver Restore
  Plant Power
  Power Plus
  Pro Plus
  Supreme 7

5787 Herbal Science LLC
3301 Bonita Beach Rd SW
Suite 308
Bonita Springs, FL 34134
239-597-8822
info@herbalsciencegroup.com
herbalsciencegroup.com
Herbs
President: Robert Gow
Year Founded: 2002
Estimated Sales: $800,000
Number Employees: 5-9

5788 Herbal Water, Inc.
901 N. Walton Ave.
Yuba City, CA 95993
610-668-4000
info@herbalwater.com
www.herbalwater.com
Water infused with herbs
Founder: Ayala Cahana

5789 Herbalist & Alchemist Inc
51 S Wandling Ave
Washington, NJ 07882-2192
908-689-9020
Fax: 908-689-9071 herbalist@nac.net
www.herbalist-alchemist.com
Herbs
President: David Winston
CEO: Beth Lambert
herbworld@aol.com
Estimated Sales: $1-3 Million
Number Employees: 10-19
Brands:
  5lung Re-Leaf

5790 Herbs America
PO Box 446
Murphy, OR 97533
541-846-6222
Fax: 541-846-9488 herbs-america.com
Amazonian herbs, therapeutic teas and herbal extracts
Co-Founder: Mila Lazo
Co-Founder: Jerry Black
COO: Kevin Driskell
Type of Packaging: Consumer, Bulk
Brands:
  HERBS AMERICA
  MACA MAGIC

5791 Herbs Etc
1345 Cerrillos Rd
Santa Fe, NM 87505-3508
505-820-0410
Fax: 505-984-9197 888-694-3727
mailorder@herbsetc.com www.herbsetc.com
Liquid herbal extracts and fast acting softgel herbal medicines
Owner: Daniel Gagnon
Manager: Lynn Childson
lynn.childson@herbsetc.com
Estimated Sales: Less Than $500,000
Number Employees: 5-9
Square Footage: 14000
Type of Packaging: Consumer
Brands:
  Allertonic
  Deep Chi Builder
  Deep Sleep
  Depiezac
  Echinacea Triple Source
  Herbs, Etc.
  Kidalin
  Lung Tonic
  Lymphatonic
  Singers Saving Grace

5792 Heringer Meats Inc
16 W 7th St
Covington, KY 41011-2302
859-291-2000
Fax: 859-291-0444
Fresh and frozen meats
President: Ray Niemeyer
Vice President: Robert Hoeweller
Estimated Sales: $2.3 Million
Number Employees: 5-9
Type of Packaging: Consumer, Food Service
Brands:
  Kahns
  Plue Grass
  Sara Lee

5793 Heritage Books & Gifts
308 Laskin Rd
Virginia Beach, VA 23451-3020
757-428-0400
Fax: 757-428-3632 800-862-2923
www.heritagestore.com
Essential oils, health foods, food supplements, vitamins, herbal teas, herbal tonics and supplements
Owner: Tom Johnson
tom.johnson@heritagestore.com
Chief Financial Officer: Jean Baviera
Marketing Director: David Riblet
Estimated Sales: $9 Million
Number Employees: 50-99
Square Footage: 12000
Type of Packaging: Consumer, Private Label, Bulk

5794 Heritage Coffee Co & Cafe
174 S Franklin St
Juneau, AK 99801-1362
907-586-1087
Fax: 907-586-1892 800-478-5282
coffeeinfo@heritagecoffee.com
www.heritagecoffee.com
Coffee
Manager: Gordon Berry
gordon@heritage-coffee.com
Estimated Sales: Less Than $500,000
Number Employees: 5-9
Brands:
  Black Wolf Blend
  Heritage Coffee

5795 Heritage Family Specialty Foods Inc
901 Santerre St
Grand Prairie, TX 75050-1939
972-660-6511
Fax: 972-660-4567 800-648-2837
info@hfsfoods.com www.heritagefamilyfoods.com
Dressings, salsas, soups, beverage mixes, marinades, spreads, mayos, and bbq sauces
President/CEO: Daniel Brackeen
VP/CFO: Cheryl Brackeen
Vice President: Johnny Lee Stanley
VP Quality Assurance: Amy Brackeen
Year Founded: 1991
Estimated Sales: $20-50 Million
Number Employees: 50-99
Square Footage: 65000
Type of Packaging: Food Service, Private Label
Brands:
  Heritage Chipotle Roasted Salsa
  Heritage Fresh Salsa
  Heritage Garlic Mayo

5796 Heritage Fancy Foods Marketing
1360 Jamike Dr
Erlanger, KY 41018-0310
859-282-3782
Fax: 859-282-3781
Gourmet foods
President: Robert Carl
Brands:
  Heritage Fancy Foods

5797 Heritage Farms Dairy
1100 New Salem Hwy
Murfreesboro, TN 37129-6914
615-895-2790
Fax: 615-895-0570 www.kroger.com
Fresh apple and orange juices, dairy products
Manager: Bill Crabtree
Controller: Mike Hunter
Sales Executive: Charlene Duke
Human Resource Executive: Jeff Philips
General Manager: Robert Allard
Number Employees: 100-249
Parent Co: Kroger Company
Type of Packaging: Consumer, Private Label, Bulk
Brands:
  Kroger

5798 Heritage Foods USA
217 West 18th St
New York, NY 10113
718-389-0985
Fax: 718-389-0547 info@heritagefoodsusa.com
www.heritagefoodsusa.com
Frozen cabbage rolls and pierogies.
Principal: Peter Martins
Contact: Laura Campo
laura@heritagefoodsusa.com
Type of Packaging: Consumer, Food Service, Private Label
Brands:
  Cheemo

5799 Heritage Health Food
PO Box 626
Collegedale, TN 37315
888-237-0807
heritagehealthfood.com
Vegetarian, All-Natural and Organic lines of prepared foods
Founder, President & CEO: Don Otis
Marketing: Jon Fish
Sales: Jay Jones
Number of Brands: 3
Type of Packaging: Consumer

Food Manufacturers / A-Z

Brands:
    WORTHINGTON
    HERITAGE HEALTH FOODS
    KIM'S SIMPLE MEALS

5800 Heritage Salmon
P.O.Box 263
Eastport, ME 04631
207-853-6081
Fax: 207-853-6056 877-407-5577
www.heritagesalmon.com
Salmon
President: Glen Cooke
gcooke@heritagesalmon.com
Marketing: Aian Craig
Number Employees: 100-249
Number of Products: 60
Brands:
    Heritage Salmon

5801 Heritage Salmon Company
100-12051 Horseshoe Way
Richmond, BC V7A 4V4
Canada
604-277-3093
Fax: 604-275-8614
Salmon
President: Ken Hirtle
CFO: Rob Reisen
Type of Packaging: Bulk

5802 Heritage Short Bread
35 Hunter Rd
Suite F
Hilton Head Isle, SC 29926-3715
843-422-3458
Fax: 888-744-6697 info@heritageshortbread.com
www.heritageshortbread.com
Shortbread cookies
Contact: Tom Cole
tom.cole@heritageshortbread.com
Estimated Sales: Less Than $500,000
Number Employees: 1-4

5803 Heritage Wine Cellars
12160 E Main Rd
North East, PA 16428-3644
814-725-8015
Fax: 814-725-8654 800-747-0083
matt@heritagewine.biz www.heritagewine.biz
Wines
President: Cathy Hoitink
cathy@heritagewine.biz
CEO: Robert Bostwick
President: Josh Bostwick
General Manager: Bob Bostwick
Estimated Sales: $2.5-5 000,000
Number Employees: 5-9
Brands:
    Heritage

5804 Heritage's Dairy Stores
376 Jessup Rd
West Deptford, NJ 08086-2130
856-845-2855
Fax: 856-845-8392
mstrockbine@heritagesdairy.com
www.heritages.com
Milk, dairy products
President: Mike St Rockbine
mstrockbine@heritagesdairy.com
Number Employees: 500-999

5805 Herlocher Foods
415 E Calder Way
State College, PA 16801-5663
814-237-0134
Fax: 814-237-1893 800-437-5625
info@herlocherfoods.com
www.herlocherfoods.com
Dipping mustard and salsa
President: Neil Herlocher
CEO: Chuck Herlocher
info@herlocherfoods.com
Estimated Sales: $1-2.5 Million
Number Employees: 5-9
Brands:
    Herlocher's Dipping Mustard

5806 Herman Falter Packing Co
384 Greenlawn Ave
Columbus, OH 43223-2610
614-444-1141
Fax: 614-445-3915 800-325-6328
info@faltersmeats.com www.faltersmeats.com
Meat
President: James Falter
Sales Exec: Lana Smith
lana@faltersmeats.com
Estimated Sales: $10-20 Million
Number Employees: 100-249

5807 Herman's Bakery
130 Main St S
Cambridge, MN 55008-1621
763-689-1515
Fax: 763-689-9642
Bakery products
Owner: Herman Oeistriech
hermansbakery@yahoo.com
Estimated Sales: $1-2.5 000,000
Number Employees: 20-49

5808 Hermann J. Wiemer Vineyard
3962 Rte 14
P.O. Box 38
Dundee, NY 14837
607-243-7971
Fax: 607-348-1498 800-371-7971
wines@wiemer.com wiemer.com
Wines
Owner, Manager & Winemaker: Fred Merwarth
Estimated Sales: $5-10 000,000
Number Employees: 10-19
Brands:
    Hermann J. Wiemer

5809 Hermann Pickle Co
11964 State Route 88
Garrettsville, OH 44231-9115
330-527-2696
Fax: 330-527-2327 800-245-2696
www.hermannpicklecompany.com
Dill and kosher pickles, dill tomatoes and peppers
President/CEO: Larry Hermann
larry_hermannpickle@yahoo.com
Treasurer: Ruth Hermann
Vice President: Don Hermann
Estimated Sales: $10-20 Million
Number Employees: 50-99
Type of Packaging: Consumer, Bulk
Brands:
    Hermann Pickle

5810 Hermannhof Vineyards
330 E 1st St
Hermann, MO 65041
573-486-1452
Fax: 573-486-3415 800-393-0100
hermannhofinfo@hermannhof.com
www.hermannhof.com
Wines
President: James Dierberg
Secretary: Mary Dierberg
Contact: Paul Leroy
sales@hermannhof.com
Estimated Sales: $10-20 Million
Number Employees: 5-9

5811 Hernan
1525 South Main Street
Suite 400
Del Rio, TX 78840
646-263-3598
ihernandez@hernanllc.com
www.hernanllc.com
Hot chocolate, chocolate confectionary
Marketing: Isela Hernandez

5812 Hero Nutritionals
1900 Carnegie Ave
Bldg A
Santa Ana, CA 92705
Fax: 949-379-6041 800-500-4376
heronutritionals.com
Gummy vitamins
CEO: Jennifer Hodges

5813 Herold's Salads
17512 Miles Ave
Cleveland, OH 44128-3404
216-991-9565
Fax: 216-991-9565 800-427-2523
www.heroldssalads.com
Salads, side dish vegetables and desserts
President/Owner: Cathy Herold
heroldsalads@yahoo.com
Quality Control: Stephanie Hunt
Marketing: Greg Johns
Sales Manager: Todd Kaminoski
Plant Manager: Walt Doughty
Estimated Sales: $2 Million
Number Employees: 20-49
Square Footage: 72000
Type of Packaging: Consumer, Food Service, Private Label, Bulk

5814 Heron Hill Winery
9301 County Route 76
Hammondsport, NY 14840-9685
607-868-4241
Fax: 607-868-3435 800-441-4241
info@heronhill.com www.heronhill.com
Wines
Owner: Lisa Cannac
mtabla@onthehouse.com
Estimated Sales: $5-10 Million
Number Employees: 20-49
Type of Packaging: Private Label

5815 Herr Foods Inc.
20 Herr Dr.
PO Box 300
Nottingham, PA 19362
800-523-5030
www.herrfoods.com
Snack foods.
Founder: James Herr
james.herr@herrs.com
Chairman: J.M. Herr
President/CEO: Ed Herr
Year Founded: 1946
Estimated Sales: $100-500 Million
Number Employees: 1000-4999
Type of Packaging: Consumer
Other Locations:
    Herr's
        Seaford DE
    Herr's
        Elkridge MD
    Herr's
        Egg Harbor NJ
    Herr's
        Oakland NJ
    Herr's
        Somerset NJ
    Herr's
        Lakewood NJ
    Herr's
        Hainesport NJ
    Herr's
        Newburgh NY
    Herr's
        Chillicothe OH
    Herr's
        Allentown PA
    Herr's
        Philadelphia PA
    Herr's
        Edinburg PA
    Herr's
        Nottingham PA
Brands:
    Herr's®

5816 Herrell's Ice Cream
8 Old South St
Northampton, MA 01060-3847
413-586-9700
Fax: 413-584-5320 www.herrells.com
Ice cream
CEO: Stephen Herrell
Site Manager: Judy Herrell
Number Employees: 20-49

5817 Herring Brothers Meats
350 Water St
Guilford, ME 4443
207-876-2631
Fax: 207-876-2631 herringbros@hotmail.com
www.herringbrothersmeats.com
Meats

Food Manufacturers / A-Z

Owner: Thomas Gilbert
Owner: Trey Gilbert
Owner: Ellie Patterson
Estimated Sales: $5-10 Million
Number Employees: 20-49
Type of Packaging: Consumer, Private Label

5818 Hershey Co.
19 E Chocolate Dr.
Hershey, PA 17033
800-468-1714
www.thehersheycompany.com
Chocolate, confectionery, snack, refreshment and grocery products.
Chairman/President/CEO: Michele Buck
Senior VP/CFO: Steve Voskuil
Senior VP/General Counsel: Damien Atkins
Year Founded: 1894
Estimated Sales: $7.8 Billion
Number Employees: 15,360
Number of Brands: 31
Type of Packaging: Consumer, Food Service, Private Label
Brands:
  Hershey's
  Reese's
  Hershey's Kisses
  Lancaster
  Hershey's Bliss
  Twizzlers
  Almond Joy
  Mounds
  York
  Kit Kat
  Pieces
  5th Avenue
  Brookside
  Cadbury
  Heath
  Whoppers
  Mr. Goodbar
  Krackel
  Take 5
  Whatchamacallit
  Skor
  Symphony
  Allan
  Good & Plenty
  Jolly Rancher
  breathsavers
  Bubble Yum
  Ice Breakers
  Milk Duds
  Payday
  Rolo
  Zagnut
  Zero

5819 Hershey Creamery Co
301 S Cameron St
Harrisburg, PA 17101
888-240-1905
info@hersheyicecream.com
www.hersheyicecream.com
Ice cream.
Vice President Central Region: Mark Scharlau
mrscharlau@aol.com
Executive Brand Manager: Zach Waite
Year Founded: 1894
Estimated Sales: $45.5 Million
Number Employees: 100-249
Square Footage: 65000
Type of Packaging: Consumer, Food Service, Bulk
Brands:
  Hershey®'s Ice Cream
  Benevita
  Classic Banjo
  Tropi-Kool Smoothies
  Blenjavas
  Twisted Peaks

5820 Hess Collection
4411 Redwood Rd
Napa, CA 94558-9708
707-255-1144
Fax: 707-253-1682 info@hesscollection.com
www.hesscollection.com
Wines
Chief Executive Officer: Timothy Persson
tpersson@hesscollection.com
Director Of Winemaking: Dave Guffy
Estimated Sales: $10-19 Million
Number Employees: 100-249

Number of Brands: 4
Square Footage: 100000
Type of Packaging: Private Label
Brands:
  Artezin
  Hess Collection
  Hess Estate
  Hess Select

5821 Heterochemical Corp
111 E Hawthorne Ave
Valley Stream, NY 11580-6319
516-561-8225
Fax: 516-561-8413
Vitamin K
President: Lynne Galler
VP: Raymond Berruti
Estimated Sales: $990,000
Number Employees: 10-19
Square Footage: 80000

5822 Heyday Beverage Co.
701 East 6th St
Austin, TX 78701
512-443-9876
info@drinkheyday.com
drinkheyday.com
Canned, cold-brew coffee
Founder & CEO: Bart Smith
Number of Brands: 1
Number of Products: 4
Type of Packaging: Consumer
Brands:
  HEYDAY

5823 Heyerly Bakery
107 N Jefferson St
Ossian, IN 46777-1103
260-622-4196
Baked goods
President: Ronald Heyerly
Owner: Stan Heyerly
Estimated Sales: $500,000-$1 Million
Number Employees: 10-19
Type of Packaging: Consumer

5824 Hi Country Snack Foods
PO Box 159
Lincoln, MT 59639-0159
406-362-4050
Fax: 406-362-4275 www.hicountry.com
Beef jerky and sausage
President: James Johnson
COO: Fred Shammel
Contact: Chris Castagne
chris.castagne@hicountry.com
Year Founded: 1976
Number Employees: 50-99
Type of Packaging: Consumer, Food Service

5825 Hi Seas
8345 Shrimpers Row
Dulac, LA 70353-2205
985-563-7155
Fax: 985-563-2536
Shrimp
Owner: Eric Authamant
Estimated Sales: $5-10 Million
Number Employees: 10-19

5826 Hi-Country Foods Corporation
P.O. Box 338
Selah, WA 98942
509-697-7292
Fax: 509-697-3498
Fruit juice concentrates, bottled water, teas and new age beverages
President/Owner: Otis Harlan
CFO: Richard Johnson
CEO: Pat Kelly
Quality Control: Judy Groves
VP/Operations/Marketing: Patrick Kelly
Estimated Sales: $10-20 Million
Number Employees: 50-99
Square Footage: 150000
Type of Packaging: Food Service, Private Label, Bulk
Brands:
  Hi-Country
  Wenatchee Valley

5827 HiBix Corporation
5860 W Las Positas Blvd
Suite 21
Pleasanton, CA 94588
925-225-0800
Fax: 925-225-0700
Hibiscus extract
President/CEO: John-David Enright
SMO: Janet DiGiovanna
VP Sales: James Curley

5828 Hialeah Products Co
2207 Hayes St
Hollywood, FL 33020-3437
954-923-3379
Fax: 954-923-4010 800-923-3379
richnuts@aol.com
Nuts, dried fruits, candy and snacks
Owner: Richard Lesser
richard@newurbanfarms.com
CEO: Kathy Lesser
Research & Development: Noah Lesser
Estimated Sales: $10-25 Million
Number Employees: 10-19
Number of Brands: 2
Number of Products: 200+
Square Footage: 120000
Type of Packaging: Consumer, Food Service, Private Label, Bulk
Brands:
  Oh Nuts

5829 Hiball, Inc.
1862 Union St
San Francisco, CA 94123-4308
415-931-1096
Fax: 415-931-1096 833-442-2553
www.hiball.com
Sparkling energy waters
President: Dan Soffer
dsoffer@epicor.com
Director of Sales: Dan Craytor
Sales Director: Dan Craytor

5830 Hibiscus Aloha Corporation
826 Queen St
Suite 200
Honolulu, HI 96813-5286
808-591-8826
Chocolate macadamia nut candy and cookies
President: Elvira Lo
chocolat_email@yahoo.com
Estimated Sales: $1-3 Million
Number Employees: 5-9

5831 Hickey Foods
PO Box 2312
Sun Valley, ID 83353
208-788-9033
Fax: 208-788-8879 800-215-0646
www.smokedtrout.com
Vacuum-packed smoked trout
President: Thomas M Hickey
Estimated Sales: $1-3 Million
Number Employees: 5-9

5832 Hickory Baked Ham Co
3221 Commerce Ct
Castle Rock, CO 80109-9458
303-688-2633
Fax: 303-688-8431
Smoked and cured poultry and meats.
President: Robert Anderson
Purchasing Manager: Robert Anderson
Estimated Sales: Less Than $500,000
Number Employees: 5-9
Square Footage: 18000
Parent Co: Hickory Baked Food
Type of Packaging: Consumer, Food Service, Private Label, Bulk
Brands:
  Hickory Baked
  High Valley Farm

5833 Hickory Farms
P.O. Box 219
1505 Holland Road
Maumee, OH 43537
419-725-9247
Fax: 419-893-0164 800-753-8558
www.hickoryfarms.com
Gourmet sausage and cheese gift baskets.

Food Manufacturers / A-Z

President/CEO: Diane Pearse
CFO: Joe Herman
Chief Marketing Officer: Judy Ransford
Contact: Bryan Bouley
bouley@hickoryfarms.com
COO: Matt James
Year Founded: 1951
Estimated Sales: $37 Million
Number Employees: 500-999
Type of Packaging: Consumer, Food Service, Bulk
Brands:
    Hickory Farms

5834 Hickory Harvest Foods
90 Logan Pkwy
Akron, OH 44319-1177
    330-644-6266
Fax: 330-644-2501   800-448-6887
www.hickoryharvest.com
Snack foods
President: Joe Swiatkowski
joe@hickoryharvest.com
VP, Sales: Mike Swiatkowski
Plant Manager: Nicholas Hamilton
Number Employees: 20-49
Type of Packaging: Consumer, Food Service, Private Label, Bulk
Brands:
    Hickory Harvest Foods
    I.M. Good Snacks

5835 Hidden Mountain Ranch Winery
2740 Hidden Mountain Rd
Paso Robles, CA 93446-8712
    805-226-9907
Fax: 805-238-4997
Wines
Owner: Richard Gumerman
Estimated Sales: $1-2.5 000,000
Number Employees: 5-9

5836 Hidden Springs Maple
162 Westminster Rd
Putney, VT 05346-8812
    802-387-5200
Fax: 802-387-5200   info@hiddenspringsmaple.com
www.hiddenspringsmaple.com
Maple syrup and candy; baking mixes; jams and preserves; cheese; hot and BBQ sauces.
Owner: Peter Cooper-Ellis
Year Founded: 2009
Estimated Sales: Less than $500,000
Number Employees: 20-49
Type of Packaging: Private Label

5837 Hidden Villa Ranch
310 N Harbor Blvd
Suite 205
Fullerton, CA 92832
    800-326-3220
info@hiddenvilla.com   www.hiddenvilla.com
Cheese and cheese products, liquid eggs.
President: Tim Luberski
tluberski@hiddenvilla.com
EVP: Greg Schneider
EVP: Michael Sencer
LA Division General Manager: Richard Schmidt
Year Founded: 1945
Estimated Sales: $500 Million
Brands:
    Arizona Ranch Fresh
    California Ranch Fresh
    California Sunshine Dairy Pproducts
    Hidden Villa Ranch
    Horizon Orangic
    Gold Circle Farms
    Nestfresh
    Smart Balance

5838 Higa Food Service
225 N. Nimitz Hwy
Honolulu, HI 96817
    808-531-3591
Fax: 808-521-4951   www.higafoodservice.com
Meats
President/CEO: Sheldon Wright
Vice President, Processing: Jerry Higa
VP of Sales & Marketing: Shane Wright
Contact: Clifford Suwa
clifford@higafoodservice.com
Chief Operations Officer: Shaun Wright
Estimated Sales: $10-19.9 Million
Number Employees: 20-49

5839 Higgins Seafood
2798 Jean Lafitte Blvd
Lafitte, LA 70067-5206
    504-689-3577
www.higginscrabhouse.com
Frozen seafood including crabs and oysters
President: Denny Higgins
astrocreepxero@aol.com
Estimated Sales: Less Than $500,000
Number Employees: 1-4
Type of Packaging: Consumer

5840 High Brew Coffee
Austin, TX 78704
    www.highbrewcoffee.com
Canned, cold-brew coffee
Founder & CEO: David Smith
Number of Brands: 1
Number of Products: 3
Type of Packaging: Consumer
Brands:
    HIGH BREW

5841 High Country Elevators Inc
62784 Highway 491
Dove Creek, CO 81324-9616
    970-677-2251
Fax: 970-677-2461   hceinc@gmail.com
Dried beans, wheat and oils
Plant Manager: Bruce Riddel
Estimated Sales: Less Than $500,000
Number Employees: 1-4
Type of Packaging: Consumer, Food Service, Bulk

5842 High Country Gourmet
225 Mountain Way Drive
Orem, UT 84058-5121
    801-426-4383
Fax: 801-426-4385   hictrygrmt@aol.com
Dehydrated soup mixes
President: Rod Meldrum
Type of Packaging: Consumer, Food Service, Private Label, Bulk
Brands:
    High Country Gourmet

5843 High Grade Beverage
891 Georges Rd
Monmouth Jct, NJ 08852-3057
    732-821-7600
Fax: 732-821-2898   887-327-4277
info@hgbev.com   www.highgradebeverage.com
Soft drinks
President: Anthony DeMarco
ademarco@hgbev.com
Chairman: Joseph DeMarco
Corporate Controller: Jeffery Epstein
Corporate Vice President: Guy Battaglia
Corporate Secretary/Treasurer: Elizabeth DeMarco
Sales Manager: John Benvenuto
Operations Manager: John Morra
Number Employees: 100-249

5844 High Liner Foods Inc.
100 Battery Point
PO Box 910
Lunenburg, NS B0J 2C0
Canada
    902-634-8811
Fax: 902-634-6228   info@highlinerfoods.com
www.highlinerfoods.com
Prepared, value-added frozen seafood.
Chairman: Henry Demone
President/CEO: Rod Hepponstall
Executive VP/CFO: Paul Jewer
Executive VP/General Counsel: Tim Rorabeck
VP, Quality Assurance/Food Safety: Meggan Hodgson
Senior VP, Marketing/Innovation: Craig Murray
Senior VP, North American Sales: Chris Mulder
Year Founded: 1926
Estimated Sales: $943 Million
Number Employees: 1,652
Number of Brands: 10
Type of Packaging: Consumer, Food Service, Private Label, Bulk
Other Locations:
    High Liner Foods
    Secaucus NJ
Brands:
    Mirabel®
    Icelandic Seafood®
    FPI ® Brand
    Viking®
    High Liner®
    American Pride®
    High Liner Culinary
    Fisher Boy®
    Sea Cuisine®
    Catch of the Day®
    40 Fathoms®

5845 High Mowing Organic Seeds
76 Quarry Rd
Wolcott, VT 05680
    802-472-6174
Fax: 802-472-3201   866-735-4454
www.highmowingseeds.com
Organic vegetable seeds
President/Owner: Tom Stearns
Type of Packaging: Consumer

5846 High Quality Organics
12101 Moya Blvd.
Reno, NV 89506
    775-971-8550
hqorganics.com
Offers organic ingredients, including spices & herbs, spice extracts, dried vegetables, baking ingredients, and select grains.
Founder & President: Raju Boligala
Founder: Jerry Tenenberg
Founder: Jay Fishman
CFO: Rick May
VP, Quality & Operations: Chad Flores
Director, Sales: Jonathan Raju
Director, Customer Services: Cynthia Acuna
Director, Supply Chain: Gina Pepple
Year Founded: 1977
Number Employees: 51-200
Type of Packaging: Consumer, Food Service, Private Label, Bulk

5847 High Ridge Foods LLC
424 Ridgeway
White Plains, NY 10605-4208
    914-761-2900
Fax: 914-761-2901
Dairy products, sugars and flowers
President: Nestor Alzerez
Sales Manager: Nestor Alzerez, Jr
Estimated Sales: $2.5 000,000
Number Employees: 1-4
Type of Packaging: Private Label, Bulk

5848 High Rise Coffee Roasters
2421 W Cucharras St
Colorado Springs, CO 80904-3048
    719-633-1833
Fax: 719-471-4815
www.highrisecoffeeroasters.com
Coffee
President: Toby Anderson
highrisecoffee@hotmail.com
Estimated Sales: $1-2.5 000,000
Number Employees: 1-4

5849 High Road Craft Ice Cream, Inc.
2241 Perimeter Park Drive
Suite 7
Atlanta, GA 30341-1309
    678-701-7623
sales@highroadcraft.com
www.highroadcraft.com
Frozen desserts, ice cream/sorbet
Marketing: Hunter Thornton

5850 High Tide Seafoods Inc
808 Marine Dr
Port Angeles, WA 98363-2104
    360-452-8488
Fax: 360-452-6710   www.hightideseafoods.com
Fresh and frozen salmon
Owner: Jim Shefler
President: Ernest Vail
ernie@hightideseafoodsinc.com
Estimated Sales: $2.5 Million
Number Employees: 50-99
Type of Packaging: Consumer, Food Service
Brands:
    High Tide Seafoods

5851 High Valley Farm
3221 Commerce Court
Castle Rock, CO 80109-9458
    303-634-2944
Fax: 303-688-8431   www.hickorybakedham.com

Food Manufacturers / A-Z

Sausages and other processed meats, soup mixes, elk meat, bison meat
President: Robert Anderson

5852 Highland Dairies
PO Box 2199
Wichita, KS 67201-2199
316-267-4221
Fax: 316-267-1050 800-336-0765
www.hilanddairy.com
Milk, dairy products
Manager: Jerald Grey
President: Gary Aggus
Marketing Director: Ted Barlows
Number Employees: 100-249
Brands:
  Highland
  Old Chester

5853 Highland Family Farms
57746 Hwy 30
Mapleton, MN 56065
507-524-3797
www.highlandfamilyfarmsmn.com
Grains, vegetables and meat.
Owner/Partner: Kim Duncanson
General Operations: Gabriel Duncanson
Year Founded: 2017

5854 Highland Farm Foods
118 Fairfield Ave
Rock Hill, SC 29732
803-396-1439
highlandfarmfoods.com
Quinoa
CEO: Jack Smith
jack@highlandfarmfoods.com
Type of Packaging: Private Label

5855 Highland Fisheries
1E Fareham Park Road
Glace Bay, NS B1A 6C9
Canada
902-849-6016
Fax: 902-849-7794 fish.n.chips@btinternet.com
Fresh and frozen finfish
President: Josh Wallenham
Plant Manager: Greg Mitchelitis
Number Employees: 100-249
Type of Packaging: Bulk

5856 Highland Laboratories
PO Box 199
Mount Angel, OR 97362
503-845-9223
Fax: 503-845-6364 888-717-4917
www.highlandvitamins.com
Vitamins, minerals and protein powders
Owner/President: Kenneth Scott
CEO: Candy Scott
CFO/Human Resources: Jolyn Rothgery
Quality & Compliance Manager: John Mills
Accounts Manager: Kim Lang
kim@highlandvitamins.com
Sales Manager: Brian Taschereau
COO: Michael Carlson
Manufacturing Supervisor: Vadim Osipovich
Purchasing Manager: Michelle Brumer
Estimated Sales: $5.4 Million
Number Employees: 41
Square Footage: 120000
Type of Packaging: Private Label

5857 Highland Manor Winery
2965 S York Hwy
Jamestown, TN 38556-5334
931-879-9519
Fax: 931-879-2907 www.highlandmanorwinery.net
Wines
Owner: Butch Campbell
Co-Owner: Gertie Campbell
Estimated Sales: $2.5-5 Million
Number Employees: 5-9

5858 Highland Sugarworks
49 Parker Rd
Wilson Industrial Park, P.O. Box 58
Websterville, VT 5678
802-479-1747
Fax: 802-479-1737 800-452-4012
jclose@highlandsugarworks.com
www.highlandsugarworks.com
Pure maple syrup and pancake mixes

President: Jim Mac Isaac
jim@highlandsugarworks.com
Sales/Marketing: Jim Close
Operations: Deb Frimodig
Estimated Sales: $500,000-$1 Million
Number Employees: 10-19
Square Footage: 60000
Type of Packaging: Consumer, Food Service, Private Label, Bulk
Brands:
  Highland Sugarworks

5859 Highlandville Packing
PO Box 190
Highlandville, MO 65669
417-443-3365
Fax: 417-443-3365 www.goatworld.com
Meat products
Owner: Neva Smith
Estimated Sales: $1-2.5 Million
Number Employees: 1-4

5860 Hightower's Packing
1713 Highway 518
Minden, LA 71055-8001
318-377-5459
Fax: 318-377-5408
Meat products
President: Marvin Hightower
marvinhightower@hughes.net
Estimated Sales: $2.5-5 Million
Number Employees: 5-9
Type of Packaging: Consumer, Bulk

5861 Highwood Distillers
PO Box 5693
High River, AB T1V 1M7
Canada
403-652-3202
Fax: 403-652-4227 hrplant@telus.net
Whiskey, vodka, rum, tequila, liquers and pre-mixers
President/Sales: Barry Wilde
Chairman/CEO: W Miller
Number Employees: 20-49
Square Footage: 120000
Type of Packaging: Consumer, Private Label
Brands:
  Buccaneer
  China White
  Colita
  Highwood
  Marushka
  Old Mexico
  Triple Sec
  White Lightning

5862 Hikari Miso Intl.
Torrance, CA 90501
hikarimiso.com
Organic miso pastes
Parent Co: Hikari Miso Co., Ltd.

5863 (HQ)Hiland Dairy Foods Co
1133 E Kearney St
Springfield, MO 65803-3435
417-862-9311
Fax: 417-837-1106 800-492-4022
www.hilanddairy.com
Milk, juice, fruit-flavored drinks, lemonade, water, ice cream, creams/half and half, lactose-free milk, butter, cottage cheese, cheese, shredded cheese, yogurt, sour cream, dips, to-go drinks, egg substitute and egg nog.
President/COO: Gary Aggus
gaggus@hilanddairy.com
Estimated Sales: $20-50 Million
Number Employees: 500-999
Type of Packaging: Consumer, Food Service
Other Locations:
  Omaha NE
  Chandler OK
  Fayetteville AR
  Fort Smith AR
  Norman OK
  Kansas City MO
  Wichita KS
  Little Rock AR
  Norfolk NE
  Des Moines IA
  Dallas TX
  Houstan TX
  Waco TX

5864 Hilary's Eat Well
2205 Haskell Ave
Lawrence, KS 66046
785-856-3399
www.hilaryseatwell.com
Vegetarian burgers, sausages, bites and salad dressings
President & CFO: Lydia Butler
VP, Marketing: Becky Harpstrite
SVP, Sales: Greg Easter
Number of Brands: 1
Number of Products: 27
Type of Packaging: Consumer
Brands:
  HILARY'S

5865 Hill Top Berry Farm & Winery
2800 Berry Hill Rd
Nellysford, VA 22958-2034
434-361-1266
Fax: 434-361-1266 www.hilltopberrywine.com
Wines
Owner: Kimberly Pugh
hilltop1@ntelos.net
Estimated Sales: $3-5 Million
Number Employees: 1-4

5866 Hillandale
US Highway 41 North
Lake City, FL 32055
386-397-1300
Fax: 386-397-1130 www.hillandalefarms.com
Eggs
President: Gary Bethel
Vice President: Steve Vendemia
Estimated Sales: $10-20 Million
Number Employees: 100-249
Type of Packaging: Consumer, Food Service

5867 Hillard Bloom Packing Co Inc
2601 Ogden Ave
Port Norris, NJ 08349-3141
856-785-0120
Fax: 856-785-2341
Fresh and frozen clams and oysters
Vice President: Todd Reeves
VP: Todd Reeves
Human Resource Manager: Barbara Huggins
Estimated Sales: $7600000
Number Employees: 1-4
Square Footage: 20000
Parent Co: Tallmadge Brothers

5868 Hillbilly Smokehouse
1801 S 8th St
Rogers, AR 72756
479-636-1927
Fax: 479-636-4590
Smoked ham, bacon, sausage, turkey, chicken, pork and beef
President: Tom Baumgartner
Vice President: Drew Baumgartner
Estimated Sales: $1 Million
Number Employees: 10
Number of Brands: 1
Number of Products: 20
Square Footage: 20000
Type of Packaging: Consumer

5869 Hillcrest Orchard
101 Autumn Ter
Lake Placid, FL 33852-6275
865-397-5273
Fax: 865-397-5273 ftpresto@tnni.net
Apples and grapes; fruit preserves and grape juice
Co-Owner: Frank Preston
Co-Owner: Twylia Preston
Estimated Sales: Under $100,000
Number Employees: 1-4
Number of Brands: 1
Number of Products: 15
Square Footage: 368000
Type of Packaging: Consumer, Food Service, Bulk
Brands:
  Hillcrest Orchard

5870 Hillcrest Vineyards
240 Vineyard Ln
Roseburg, OR 97471-9097
541-673-3709
dyson@hillcrestvineyard.com
www.hillcrestvineyard.com
Wines

Food Manufacturers / A-Z

Manager: Della Terra
Owner: Richard Sommer
Estimated Sales: Less Than $500,000
Number Employees: 1-4

5871 Hillestad Pharmaceuticals
178 US Highway 51 N
Woodruff, WI 54568-9501
715-358-9773
Fax: 715-358-7812 800-535-7742
info@hillestadlabs.com www.hillestadlabs.com
Nutritional products
Marketing: Dan Hillestad
Estimated Sales: $10-20 Million
Number Employees: 20-49
Type of Packaging: Consumer, Private Label

5872 Hillmans Shrimp & Oyster
915 Broadway St
Port Lavaca, TX 77979-2711
361-552-9415
Fax: 281-339-1509 800-584-4416
www.hillmanoysters.com
Oysters, clams and shirmp
Owner: Cliford Hillman
clifordhillman@hillmanoyster.com
VP Marketing: Chris Hillman
Marketing Director: Tricia Roberts
Sales: Dale Rymer
Public Relations: Wendy Taylor
COO: Steve Taylor
Estimated Sales: $15 Million
Number Employees: 250-499
Number of Brands: 1
Number of Products: 12
Square Footage: 29860
Type of Packaging: Consumer, Food Service, Bulk
Brands:
  Hillman

5873 Hillsboro Coffee Company
3803 Corporex Park Dr
#200
Tampa, FL 33619-1184
813-877-2126
Fax: 813-879-0524
Coffee
President: Neil McTague
VP Sales: John Sakkis
Estimated Sales: $5-10 Million
Number Employees: 8

5874 Hillside Candy Co
35 Hillside Ave
Hillside, NJ 07205-1833
973-926-2300
Fax: 973-926-4440 800-524-1304
info@hillsidecandy.com www.hillsidecandy.com
Sugarfree candy
President: Ted Cohen
ted@hillsidecandy.com
Marketing/Export Sales: Sandy Gencarelli
Estimated Sales: $5-10 Million
Number Employees: 10-19
Type of Packaging: Consumer, Food Service, Private Label, Bulk
Brands:
  Golightly Sugar Free Candy
  Shaken Country Meadows Sweets

5875 Hillside Lane Farm
160 Hillside Ln
Randolph, VT 05060
802-728-0070
Fax: 802-728-0071 info@hillsidelane.com
www.hillsidelane.com
Organic maple pancake & baking mixes, infused vinegars and syrups
President: Cathy Bacon
info@hillsidelane.com
Estimated Sales: $1-3 Million
Number Employees: 1-4
Number of Brands: 4
Number of Products: 17
Type of Packaging: Consumer, Food Service, Private Label, Bulk

5876 Hillson Nut Co
3225 W 71st St
Cleveland, OH 44102-5288
216-961-4477
Fax: 216-961-4480 800-333-2818
nuts@hillsonnut.com
Roasted, raw salted nuts and peanut butter

Owner: Edward Hillson
nuts@hillsonnuts.com
Vice President: Troy Sawvel
Estimated Sales: $500,000-$1 Million
Number Employees: 5-9

5877 Hilltop Meat Co
27630 US Highway 29
Andalusia, AL 36421-9465
334-388-2393
Fax: 334-388-3131 800-781-0053
Meat products
Owner: Billy Green
hilltop@alaweb.com
Estimated Sales: $1-2.5 Million
Number Employees: 5-9
Type of Packaging: Consumer

5878 Hilmar Cheese Company
8901 N Lander Ave
P.O. Box 910
Hilmar, CA 95324
209-667-6076
800-577-5772
info@hilmarcheese.com www.hilmarcheese.com
Cheese.
President & CEO: David Ahlem
Chief Financial Officer: Jason Price
VP, Sales & Marketing: Phil Robnett
Operations Manager: Ted Dykzeul
Year Founded: 1984
Estimated Sales: $100-500 Million
Number Employees: 500-999
Type of Packaging: Consumer, Food Service, Private Label
Brands:
  Gina Marie Cream Cheese

5879 (HQ)Hilmar Ingredients
8901 N Lander Ave
PO Box 910
Hilmar, CA 95324
209-667-6076
Fax: 209-656-2557 888-300-4465
info@hilmaringredients.com
www.hilmaringredients.com
Functional whey proteins, high purity lactose and nutritious milk powders
President: Art De Rooy
CEO: John Jeter
CFO: Jay Hicks
Director, New Business & Applications: Grace Harris
Milk Powders, Sales Manager: Emil Skaria
Contact: Mark Petersen
mpetersen@hilmaringredients.com
Number Employees: 600
Other Locations:
  Manufacturing Site & Visitor Center
  Hilmar CA
  Turlock Manufacturing Site
  Turlock CA
  Texas Manufacturing Site
  Dalhart TX

5880 Hilo Fish Company
55 Holomua St
Hilo, HI 96720-5142
808-961-0877
Fax: 808-935-1603 info@hilofish.com
www.hilofish.com
Fresh billfish, bottomfish, tuna, open ocean fish; Frozen tuna, grouper, hamachi, snapper, and other seafood
CEO: Charlie Umamoto
President & COO: Kerry Umamoto
General Manager: Jamiesen Batangan
Marketing: Helene Rousselle
National Sales Manager: Sabrina Vaughn
Operationas Manager: Keith Hayashi
Estimated Sales: $20-50 Million
Number Employees: 20-49

5881 HimalaSalt
Sheffield, MA 01257
413-528-5141
www.himalasalt.com
Organic Himalayan salt
Founder: Melissa Kushi
Type of Packaging: Consumer
Brands:
  HIMALASALT

5882 Himalayan Chef
Sheffield, MA 01257
413-528-5141
www.himalasalt.com
Organic Himalayan salt and seasonings
CFO: Nafees Anjum
Type of Packaging: Consumer
Brands:
  HIMALAYAN CHEF

5883 Himalayan Heritage
N5821 Fairway Dr
Fredonia, WI 53021-9742
608-274-9640
Fax: 262-692-6387 888-414-9500
web@aliveandhealthy.com
Herbal dietary supplements
Co-Owner: Blair Lewis
Co-Owner: Karen Lewis
Estimated Sales: $1-3 Million
Number Employees: 10-19
Type of Packaging: Consumer, Food Service, Private Label, Bulk
Brands:
  Attnetion Span
  Erjuv-Powder
  Five Forces of Nature
  Immuno Force
  Joyful Mind

5884 Hinckley Springs Bottled Water
800-201-6218
www.hinckleysprings.com
Bottled water
President: Dave Muscato
CEO: Tom Harrington
CFO: Jerry Hoyle
General Manager: Mike Garrity
Estimated Sales: $500,000-$1 Million
Number Employees: 50-99
Square Footage: 6000
Parent Co: DS Services of America
Type of Packaging: Consumer, Food Service, Bulk
Brands:
  FIJI Water ®
  LaCroix Sparkling Water
  Mountain Valley Spring Water ™
  Nursery ®
  Polar Sparkling Water
  Sparkling Ice
  VOSS ® Water

5885 Hingham Shellfish
25 Eldridge Ct
Hingham, MA 02043
781-749-1374
Fax: 405-631-8473
Shellfish
President/Treasure: Myrle Derbyshire
Estimated Sales: $.5-1 million
Number Employees: 1-4

5886 Hint Mint
2432 East 8th Street
Los Angeles, CA 90021
213-622-6468
Fax: 213-622-1780 800-991-6468
www.hintmint.com
Breathmints and peppermint
Owner: Cooper Bates
Marketing: Wendy Campbell
Contact: Sue Chiang
sue@hintmint.com
Estimated Sales: $.5-1 million
Number Employees: 5-9
Brands:
  Hint Mint

5887 Hint Water
2124 Union Street
Suite D
San Francisco, CA 94123
415-513-4050
Fax: 415-276-1786 info@drinkhint.com
www.drinkhint.com
Naturally flavored water
CEO/Founder: Kara Goldin
Contact: Nancy Binder
nancy@drinkhint.com

Food Manufacturers / A-Z

5888 Hinzerling Winery
1520 Sheridan Ave
Prosser, WA 99350-1140
509-786-2163
Fax: 509-786-2163 800-727-6702
info@hinzerling.com www.hinzerling.com
Wine, vinegar
Owner: Mike Wallace
info@hinzerling.com
Cellarmaster: Stan Kelly
Estimated Sales: $1-2.5 Million
Number Employees: 1-4
Type of Packaging: Private Label
Brands:
  Hinzerling
  Wallace

5889 Hip Chick Farms
707-861-9010
hipchicks@hipchickfarms.com
hipchickfarms.com
Organic chicken fingers, chicken meatballs and turkey patties
Co-Founder: Jen Johnson
Co-Founder: Serafina Palandech
Number of Brands: 1
Number of Products: 13
Type of Packaging: Consumer
Brands:
  HIP CHICK FARMS

5890 Hippeas
Plainview, NY 11803
hippeas.com
Organic chickpea puffs
Founder: Livio Bisterzo
CEO: Joe Serventi
Number of Brands: 1
Number of Products: 13
Type of Packaging: Consumer

5891 Hippie Snacks
4612 Dawson St
Burnaby, BC V5C 4C3
Canada
877-769-6887
hello@hippiesnacks.com www.hippiesnacks.com
Coconut clusters, veggie clusters, sesame snacks and granola
President/Owner: Ian Walker
Number of Brands: 1
Number of Products: 11
Type of Packaging: Consumer
Brands:
  HIPPIE SNACKS

5892 (HQ)Hiram Walker & Sons
2072 Riverside Drive E
Windsor, ON N8Y 1A7
Canada
519-254-5171
Fax: 519-971-5732 www.hiramwalker.com
Processor and exporter of blended whiskey, gin, scotch, vodka, rum, liqueurs, etc schnapps flavors include...peah,peppermint,blackberry,pumpkin spice,melon,triple sec blend, there are 43 alltogether.
Chairman/CEO: Paul Duffy
CFO: Thibault Cuny
SVP/Operations: Dan Denisoff
General Counsel: Thomas Lalla
SVP/Spirit Sales: Marty Crane
Marketing Director: Matt Aeppli
Estimated Sales: $199.43million
Number Employees: 500
Parent Co: Pernod Ricard
Type of Packaging: Consumer, Food Service
Other Locations:
  Manufacturing Facility
  Fort Smith AR
Brands:
  Ballantine's
  Beefeater
  Canadian Club
  Courvoisier
  Irish Mist
  Kahlua
  Maker's Mark
  Malibu
  Midori
  Sauza
  Stolichnaya

5893 Hirzel Canning Co & Farms
20790 Bradner Rd
Luckey, OH 43443
419-419-7525
www.hirzelfarms.com
Manufacturer and exporter of canned tomatoes and tomato products, sauerkraut, sauces, salsa, tomato juice, tomato soup and more.
President & CEO: Stephen Hirzel
Office Manager: Lynn Hirzel
Manager: William Hirzel
Director, Manufacturing: Karl Hirzel
Crop Production: Lou Kozma, Jr.
Year Founded: 1923
Estimated Sales: $20-50 Million
Number Employees: 50-99
Number of Brands: 4
Number of Products: 30
Square Footage: 500000
Type of Packaging: Consumer, Food Service, Private Label, Bulk
Brands:
  Dei Fratelli
  Silver Fleece
  Starcross

5894 Hirzel Canning Co.
325 W Williamstown Rd
Ottawa, OH 45875
419-523-3225
Fax: 419-523-6145 800-837-1631
info@hirzel.com www.deifratelli.com
Canned tomato products including whole, sliced, crushed, puree and sauce
President: Karl Hirzel
Plant Manager: Carl Hirzel
Estimated Sales: $2.5-5 Million
Number Employees: 5-9
Parent Co: Hirzel Canning
Type of Packaging: Consumer, Food Service, Private Label
Brands:
  Dei Fratelli
  Silver Fleece
  Star Cross

5895 Hnina Gourmet
Los Angeles, CA 90046
323-876-2609
hninagourmet.com
Raw chocolate bars, cacao spreads, seed crackers and cacao truffles
Founder: Vanessa Morgenstern-Kenan

5896 Hobarama Corporation
400 NW 26th St
Miami, FL 33127-4120
305-531-9708
Fax: 305-531-9709 880-439-2295
www.bawls.com
Beverages
President: Hobart Buppert
Vice President: Lisa Karell
Contact: Eric Pyszka
eric.pyszta@bawls.com
Estimated Sales: $2.5-5 Million
Number Employees: 10-19
Type of Packaging: Bulk

5897 Hobe Laboratories Inc
6479 S Ash Ave
Tempe, AZ 85283-3657
480-413-1950
Fax: 480-413-2005 800-528-4482
hobelabs@aol.com www.hobelabs.com
Processor and exporter of weight loss and herbal teas
President: Bill Robertson
brobertson@hobelabs.com
Marketing Director: Brenda Martin
Operations Manager: Peter Samuell
Estimated Sales: $1.4 Million
Number Employees: 10-19
Square Footage: 27940
Type of Packaging: Consumer, Private Label
Brands:
  Slim
  Thermo Slim
  Ultra Slim

5898 Hodgson Mill Inc
1100 Stevens Ave
Effingham, IL 62401-4265
217-347-0105
Fax: 217-347-0198 800-347-0198
customerservice@hodgsonmill.com
www.hodgsonmill.com
All natural and organic foods-flours, cereals, baking mixes, whole wheat pastas, gluten free pastas, gluten free mixes, baking ingredients-producers and manufacturers of whole grain foods. Co-packing for private label available
Owner: Bob Goldstein
bjgoldstein@hodgsonmill.com
Vice President: Cathy Goldstein
Estimated Sales: $25-30 Million
Number Employees: 100-249
Square Footage: 120000
Type of Packaging: Consumer
Brands:
  Don's Chuck Wagon
  Hodgson Mill
  Kentucky Kernel

5899 Hodo
2923 Adeline St
Oakland, CA 94608
510-464-2977
www.hodofoods.com
Soy products, including soymilk, tofu, yuba and ready-to-eat tofu and yuba meals
Type of Packaging: Consumer, Food Service
Brands:
  HODO

5900 Hoff's Bakery
1 Brainard Ave
Medford, MA 02155-5247
781-396-8384
Fax: 781-396-7918 888-871-5100
www.hoffsbakery.com
Cakes and tortes, cheesecakes, pies and tarts, 1/2 sheet tray, individual desserts, and trifle cups
Owner: Vinny Frattura
vfrattura@hoffsbakery.com
Estimated Sales: $1.5 Million
Number Employees: 20-49

5901 Hoff's United Food
617 Main St
P.O.Box 145
Brownsville, WI 53006
920-269-4798
Fax: 920-583-2194 800-852-9658
www.hoffsqualitymeats.com
Smoked sausage, bacon
Owner: Tim Hoff
Marketing: Tim Hoff
Estimated Sales: $1-2.5 000,000
Number Employees: 10-19
Type of Packaging: Private Label, Bulk

5902 Hofmann Sausage Co Inc
6196 Eastern Ave
Mattydale, NY 13211-2209
315-437-7257
Fax: 315-437-2391 800-724-8410
sales@hofmannsausage.com
www.hofmannbrands.com
German-style sausages, deli meats and mustards
President: Rusty Flook
rusty@hofmannsausage.com
CEO: Walter Flook
Estimated Sales: $5-10Million
Number Employees: 20-49
Type of Packaging: Consumer, Bulk
Brands:
  German
  Snappy's

5903 Hog Haus Brewing Company
430 W Dickson St
Fayetteville, AR 72701-5107
479-521-2739
Fax: 479-442-0077
Beers
Owner/Operator: Julie Sill
Front of House: Marueen Robertson
Estimated Sales: Below $5 Million
Number Employees: 50-99
Type of Packaging: Consumer, Food Service
Brands:
  Hoghaus

Food Manufacturers / A-Z

Ploughman's Pils
Woodstock Wheat

5904 Hogtown Brewing Company
2351 Royal Windsor Drive
Unit 6
Mississauga, ON L5J 4S7
Canada
905-855-9065
Fax: 905-822-0990 www.hogtownbrewers.org
Beers; bottling services
President: Maria Lopez
General Manager: Peter Lazaro
Number Employees: 5-9
Type of Packaging: Consumer, Food Service

5905 Hogtowne B-B-Q Sauce Company
1712 W University Avenue
Gainesville, FL 32603
352-375-6969
Fax: 352-373-6969 www.saltydogsaloon.com
Wholesaler/distributor of hot sauces, BBQ sauces, marinades and other specialty food products
Manager: Keith Singleton
Vice President: Pam Taylor-Kinard
Estimated Sales: $500,000-$1 Million
Number Employees: 20-49
Square Footage: 8000
Parent Co: Original Alan's Cubana
Type of Packaging: Consumer, Food Service, Private Label, Bulk

5906 Holey Moses Cheesecake
115 Francis S Gabreski Airport
Westhampton Beach, NY 11978
631-288-8088
Fax: 631-288-0551 800-225-2253
Cheesecake
President: Christopher Weber
Estimated Sales: Less than $500,000
Number Employees: 1-4

5907 Holistic Products Corporation
10 W Forest Avenue
Englewood, NJ 07631-4020
201-569-1188
Fax: 201-569-3224 800-221-0308
Processor, wholesaler/distributor and importer of health food products including propolis lozenges
President: Arnold Gans
a.gans@mdnu.com
VP Sales: Myra Gans
Number Employees: 38
Square Footage: 16000
Parent Co: MNI Group

5908 Holland American International Specialties
10343 Artesia Blvd
Bellflower, CA 90706
562-925-6914
Fax: 562-925-4507 www.1dutchmall.com
European and domestic specialty gourmet foods.
Manager: Maria Cervantes
Estimated Sales: $.5-1 million
Number Employees: 1-4

5909 Hollandia Bakeries Limited
PO Box 100
Mt Brydges, ON N0L 1W0
Canada
519-264-1020
800-265-3480
www.hollandiacookies.com
Cookies
President: Joop De Voest Jr
Controller: Rick Bannister
Quality Control: Mike Hobley
VP Sales: Doug Smith
Brands:
  Kerleens
  Sugar Free Cookies
  Hard Cookies
  Soft Cookies
  Gourmet Specialty Cookies
  Mini Tubs
  Red Label

5910 Hollman Foods
PO Box 41724
Des Moines, IA 50311
308-468-5635
Fax: 308-468-6141 888-926-2879
hollfamilyenterprises@gmail.com
Barbecue sauce, seasonings, spices, smoked turkey, breading mixes, gourmet jellies and fruit butters; also, gift box items, dip mixes, and honey
Owner: Byron Holl
CEO: Judith Holl
Estimated Sales: $3-5 Million
Number Employees: 5-9
Number of Brands: 2
Number of Products: 30
Square Footage: 12000
Type of Packaging: Consumer, Food Service, Private Label
Brands:
  Eden Farms
  Hollmans

5911 Hollow Road Farms
271 Hollow Rd
Stuyvesant, NY 12173-1910
518-758-1881
Fax: 518-758-1899
Yogurt.
President: Joan Snyder
Estimated Sales: $500,000-$1 000,000
Number Employees: 2-4

5912 Holly Camp Springs Inc
PO Box 69
Hudgins, VA 23076-0069
804-795-2096
Fax: 804-795-1280 info@camphollysprings.com
www.camphollysprings.com
Bottled spring water, bulk spring water
Owner: Dusty Dowdy
CFO: Jeannie Pierce
Vice President and Genreal Manager: Roland Dowdy
Contact: Roland Dowdy
rdowdy@camphollysprings.com
Plant Manager: Brandon Clements
Estimated Sales: $1,1,000,000
Number Employees: 5-9

5913 Holly Hill Locker Company
8728 Old State Road
Holly Hill, SC 29059
803-496-3611
Manufactuer of beef and pork
Owner: L Kenneth Folse Jr
Estimated Sales: Less than $500,000
Number Employees: 1-4
Type of Packaging: Consumer, Bulk

5914 Holly's Oatmeal Inc
241 Northside Dr
19 Calhoun Street
Torrington, CT 06790-3315
860-618-0090
Fax: 860-618-3008 hdimauro@optonline.net
Specialty oatmeals
Owner: Holly Dimauro
Estimated Sales: Less Than $500,000
Number Employees: 1-4

5915 Holmes Cheese Co
9444 State Route 39
Millersburg, OH 44654-9764
330-674-6451
Fax: 330-674-6673 www.holmescheese.com
Cheese and whey
President/CEO: Robert Ramseyer
rramseyer@holmescheeseco.com
VP: Walter Ramseyer
Estimated Sales: $4 Million
Number Employees: 20-49
Square Footage: 168000
Type of Packaging: Consumer, Food Service, Private Label, Bulk

5916 Holmes Foods
101 S Liberty Ave
Nixon, TX 78140-2401
830-582-1551
Fax: 830-582-1090 www.holmesfoods.com
Processor of poultry, whole birds, cut up parts, breast meat, and livers and gizzards
President & CEO: Phillip Morris
Controller: Chris Kutac
Assistant Controller: Becky Morris
SVP/Sales Director: Phil Hartung
Director/Live Operations: Keith Staggs
Year Founded: 1925
Estimated Sales: $20-50 Million
Number Employees: 100-249

5917 Holsum Bakery Inc
2322 W Lincoln St
Phoenix, AZ 85009-5827
602-252-2351
Fax: 602-252-6505 www.holsum.com
Baked goods.
Year Founded: 1900
Estimated Sales: $20-50 Million
Number Employees: 500-999
Other Locations:
  Holsum Manufacturing Plant
  Tempe AZ
  Holsum Manufacturing Plant
  Tolleson AZ
Brands:
  Aunt Hattie's
  Aunt Hattie's Quality Breads
  Bar S
  Holsum
  Lefrancias
  Roman Meal
  Smart Kids

5918 Holt's Bakery Inc
101 Sellers St
Douglas, GA 31533-4607
912-384-2202
Fax: 912-384-7467 www.bullsheet.com
Baked goods, pastries, cookies
Owner: Howard Holt
CEO/Manager: Cecil Holt, Jr
Purchasing Agent: Paul Spivey
Estimated Sales: $1-2.5 000,000
Number Employees: 20-49

5919 Holton Food Products
500 W Burlington Ave
La Grange, IL 60525-2227
708-352-5599
Fax: 708-352-3788 info@holtonfp.com
www.holtonfoodproducts.com
Ingredients for frozen pies, cakes and cookies including egg whites and stabilizers
President: Ross Holton
ross.holton@hfpglobal.com
CEO: Paul Holton
Executive VP: John Holton
Estimated Sales: $2.5-5 Million
Number Employees: 10-19
Type of Packaging: Bulk

5920 Holton Meat Processing
701 Arizona Ave
Holton, KS 66436-1247
785-364-2331
biggsbeef.com/meat-processing.html
Beef
Owner: Lynn Brinkes
holtonmeat@gmail.com
Estimated Sales: $1-3 Million
Number Employees: 5-9
Type of Packaging: Consumer

5921 Holy Kombucha
Dallas, TX 75220
469-828-1572
855-694-6595
hello@holykombucha.com holykombucha.com
Carbonated probiotic kombucha
President/Owner: Leo Bienati
Number of Brands: 1
Number of Products: 13
Type of Packaging: Consumer
Brands:
  HOME KOMBUCHA

5922 Holy Smoke LLC
991 Summerall Rd
Johns Island, SC 39455-8935
843-343-5581
www.holysmokeoliveoil.com
Smoked olive oils
Co-Founder: Kyle Payne
Co-Founder: Max Blackman
holysmokeoliveoil@gmail.com
Year Founded: 2012
Estimated Sales: $200,000
Number Employees: 1-4
Type of Packaging: Private Label

Food Manufacturers / A-Z

5923 Hol, Mol,
421 Obispo Ave
Long Beach, CA 90814-1502
562-439-2555
Fax: 512-671-4766 877-310-8453
info@holymole.com www.holemole.com
Salsa
Owner: Scott Bascon
onebite@holemole.com
Estimated Sales: Less Than $500,000
Number Employees: 5-9

5924 Homarus Inc
12-20 36th Ave
Long Island City, NY 11106
917-832-0333
Fax: 347-808-9948 info@homarus.com
Seafood, primarily lobster
Co-Owner/President: Peter Heineman
CEO: Chris Harvey
VP Sales: Thomas Marshall
Type of Packaging: Consumer, Food Service
Brands:
  Homarus
  Riverbank

5925 Home Bakery
300 S Main St
Rochester, MI 48307-2030
248-651-4830
Fax: 248-651-3458 sweet@thehomebakery.com
www.thehomebakery.com
Baked goods and chocolate
President: Tiffany Bruno
home_bakery@att.net
Estimated Sales: $500,000-$1 Million
Number Employees: 20-49
Type of Packaging: Food Service

5926 Home Delivery Food Service
1814 Washington St.
PO Box 215
Jefferson, GA 30549
706-367-9551
Fax: 706-367-4646
Frozen foods, meats and chicken
President: William Griffin, Sr.

5927 Home Maid Bakery
1005 Lower Main St
Wailuku, HI 96793-2008
808-244-7015
Fax: 808-242-8458 www.homemaidbakery.com
Bakery products
President: Jeremy Kozuki
jeremy@homemaidbakery.com
Sales Director: Leighton Saito
Operations: Wayne Takaki
Estimated Sales: $4-5 Million
Number Employees: 50-99
Number of Brands: 1
Number of Products: 100+
Type of Packaging: Consumer, Private Label

5928 Home Market Food Inc
140 Morgan Dr # 100
Norwood, MA 02062-5076
781-948-1500
Fax: 781-702-6171 800-367-8325
info@homemarketfoods.com
www.burgerdogs.com
Cooked steak, cooked meatballs, sausage, Italian sausage, cooked sausage
President: Wesley Atamian
Manager: Andy Stone
VP: Steve Smith
Director Sales: Dana Geremonte
VP Sales: Mike Wieirmiller
Estimated Sales: $1-3 Million
Number Employees: 5-9
Brands:
  Chef's Choice

5929 Home Market Foods Inc.
140 Morgan Dr.
Norwood, MA 02062
781-948-1500
www.homemarketfoods.com
Frozen foods, meal entrees, appteizers and snacks.
Chairman/CEO/President: Douglas Atamian
Year Founded: 1957
Estimated Sales: 1
Number of Brands: 4

Type of Packaging: Consumer, Food Service, Private Label, Bulk
Brands:
  Cooked Perfect®
  RollerBites®
  Bahama Mama®
  Eisenberg®

5930 Home Roast Coffee
25126 State Road 54
Lutz, FL 33559-6256
813-949-0807
Fax: 813-948-6998
Coffee
Owner/President: Marvis Wood
Owner: Jaime Wood
Estimated Sales: $500,000-$1 000,000
Number Employees: 2-4

5931 Home Run Inn Frozen Foods
1300 Internationale Pkwy
Woodridge, IL 60517-4928
630-783-9696
Fax: 630-783-0069 800-636-9696
gyarka@homeruninn.com
www.homerunnpizza.com
Frozen pizza
President: Joe Perrino
jperrino@homeruninn.com
Marketing Director: Gina Bolger
Operations: Dan Costello
Estimated Sales: $10-24.9 Million
Number Employees: 500-999
Type of Packaging: Consumer, Food Service, Private Label
Brands:
  Home Run Inn

5932 Home Style Bakery Of Grand Junction
924 N 7th St
Grand Junction, CO 81501-3108
970-243-1233
www.homestylebakerygj.com
Baked goods
President: Donald Wilke
jdnwilk@juno.com
Estimated Sales: $1-2.5 Million
Number Employees: 20-49
Square Footage: 6000
Type of Packaging: Consumer, Food Service

5933 Home Style Foods Inc
5163 Edwin St
Hamtramck, MI 48212-3388
313-874-3250
Fax: 313-874-1026
Fresh prepared salads
President: Mike Kadian
Estimated Sales: $10-20 Million
Number Employees: 20-49
Type of Packaging: Private Label, Bulk

5934 HomePlate Peanut Butter
PO Box 40794
Austin, TX 78704
512-580-9980
info@homeplatepb.com
homeplatepb.com
Peanut butter
CEO & Co-Founder: Clint Greenleaf
Founding Partner: Danny Peoples
Founding Partner: Josh Beckett
Year Founded: 2015
Estimated Sales: Less than $500,000
Number Employees: 1-4
Type of Packaging: Private Label

5935 Homefree LLC
PO Box 491
Windham, NH 03087-0491
603-898-0172
800-552-7172
sales@homefreetreats.com
www.homefreetreats.com
Peanut, tree nut, egg and dairy free cookies and cakes
Founder: Jill Robbins
info@homefreetreats.com
Vice President, Sales & Marketing: Gail Schnur
Number Employees: 20-49
Type of Packaging: Consumer

5936 Homegrown Naturals
564 Gateway Dr
Napa, CA 94558
707-254-3700
Fax: 707-259-0219 800-288-1089
erciborgstrom@fantasticfoods.com
Natural foods products
Chief Executive Officer: John Foraker
VP Research/Development: Bob Kaake
Brand Team: Kathryn Keslosky
Web Marketing Manager: Mark Berger
Human Resources Manager: Amy Barberi
Consumer Relations Associate: Corrie Aldous
Consumer Relations Manager: Sherrie Crespin
Number Employees: 20-49
Brands:
  Annie's

5937 Homegrown Organic Farms
PO Box 712
Porterville, CA 93258
559-306-1750
info@hgofarms.com
www.hgofarms.com
Fresh and freeze-dried organic fruit
CEO: Scott Mabs
Type of Packaging: Consumer

5938 Homemade By Dorothy Boise
5150 N Montecito Pl
Boise, ID 83704-2355
208-375-3720
800-657-7449
shop@homemadebydorothy.com
www.homemadebydorothy.com
Jellies, syrups, toppings, pancake and baking mixes, soups, beverages, candy, gift crates and baskets, seasonal and holiday products.
Owner: Anna Baumhoff
dorothy@dorthys.cc
Estimated Sales: $1-2.5 Million
Number Employees: 5-9

5939 Homemade Harvey
PO Box 49346
Los Angeles, CA 90049
310-472-4410
Fax: 310-471-4191 info@homemadeharvey.com
homemadeharvey.com
Organic crushed fruit snack pouches
CEO: Lawrence Jackson
Type of Packaging: Consumer

5940 Homer's Ice Cream
1237 Green Bay Rd
Wilmette, IL 60091-1699
847-251-0477
Fax: 847-251-0495 info@homersicecream.com
www.homersicecream.com
Ice cream and sorbet
Owner: Dean Poulos
icdino@yahoo.com
Marketing Director: Tean Poulos
VP: John Poulos
CEO: Stephen Poulos
Estimated Sales: $10-20 Million
Number Employees: 20-49
Square Footage: 16000
Type of Packaging: Consumer, Food Service, Private Label, Bulk

5941 Homer's Wharf Seafood Company
22 S Water Street
New Bedford, MA 02744-2613
508-997-0766
Fax: 508-999-9666
Seafood
Manager: Bruce Fontes
Estimated Sales: $10-20 Million
Number Employees: 50-99
Type of Packaging: Consumer

5942 Homestead Baking Co
145 N Broadway
Rumford, RI 02916-2801
401-434-0551
Fax: 401-438-0542 800-556-7216
pvican@homesteadbaking.com
www.homesteadbaking.com
Bread products
President: Peter Vican
pvican@homesteadbaking.com
VP: Bill Vican
Sales Manager: Vinny Palmiotti

Food Manufacturers / A-Z

Estimated Sales: $7 Million
Number Employees: 50-99
Square Footage: 160000
Type of Packaging: Food Service, Private Label, Bulk
Brands:
  Matthews All Natural
  Mrs Kavanagh's
  New England Premium

5943 Homestead Dairy
11505 13th Rd
Plymouth, IN 46563-9014
574-936-6126
Fax: 315-769-8975
Dairy products
President: Robert Squires
Number Employees: 20-49

5944 Homestead Fine Foods
315 South Maple Ave
Suite 106
S San Francisco, CA 94080
650-615-0750
Fax: 650-615-0764 info@homesteadpasta.com
www.homesteadpasta.com
Fresh and frozen pastas and sauces
President: Terry Hall
Estimated Sales: $.5-1 million
Number Employees: 10-19
Type of Packaging: Consumer, Food Service, Private Label
Brands:
  Homestead

5945 Homestead Meats
741 W 5th St
Delta, CO 81416-1505
970-874-1145
Fax: 970-856-3517 www.homesteadmeats.com
Frozen sausage; custom cut meat available
Owner: Delwin Bates
General Manager: Randy Sunderland
Estimated Sales: $1-2.5 Million
Number Employees: 20-49
Type of Packaging: Consumer, Food Service, Private Label
Brands:
  Colorado Classic

5946 Homestead Mills
221 N River St
Cook, MN 55723-9503
218-666-5233
Fax: 218-666-5236 800-652-5233
www.homesteadmills.com
Grain, wild rice, cereals, flours and pancake mixes
Owner/President: Keith Aho
aho@homesteadmills.com
Owner/Vice President: Carol Aho
Plant Manager: Anita Reinke
Estimated Sales: $1 Million
Number Employees: 5-9
Number of Brands: 2
Number of Products: 27
Square Footage: 52000
Type of Packaging: Consumer, Food Service, Private Label, Bulk
Brands:
  Country Blend Cereal
  Homestead Mills
  Noprthern Lites Pancakes
  Potato Pancake Mix
  South of the Border Chili
  Specialty Flour
  Uncle Waynes Fish Batter

5947 Homestead Ravioli Company
315 South Maple Avenue
Suite 106
South San Francisco, CA 94080
650-615-0750
Fax: 650-615-0764 Info@HomesteadPasta.com
www.homesteadpasta.com
Italian frozen specialties
President: Terry Hall
Estimated Sales: $5-9.9 Million
Number Employees: 10-19

5948 Homestyle Bread Bakery
3305 E Broadway Rd
Phoenix, AZ 85040-2829
602-268-0676
Fax: 602-276-1468

Bread and bakery products
President: James Boots
Vice President, Sales: Robert Schurman
Estimated Sales: $5-9.9 000,000
Number Employees: 20-49

5949 Hometown Bagel Inc
12401 S Kedvale Ave
Alsip, IL 60803-1818
708-385-0002
info@hometownbagel.com
www.hometownbagel.com
Bagel crisps
Co-Founder: Mike Lally
Co-Founder: Dawn Lally
Vice President: Russ Follis
russ@hometownbagel.com
Number Employees: 10-19

5950 Homewood Winery
23120 Burndale Rd
Sonoma, CA 95476-9722
707-996-6353
Fax: 707-996-6935 www.homewoodwinery.com
Wines
President/Vineyard Manager: David Homewood
davidhomewood@vom.com
Estimated Sales: Under $500,000
Number Employees: 1-4
Type of Packaging: Private Label

5951 Honee Bear Canning
72100 M 40
Lawton, MI 49065-8444
269-624-4611
Fax: 269-624-6009 800-626-2327
hbsales@honeebear.com www.honeebear.com
Berries, cherries, plums, asparagus, blueberries; pie fillings
President: Robert Packer
CEO: Steve Packer
steve@honeebear.com
Sales Manager: Ronald Armstrong
Director: Toby Fields
Estimated Sales: $10-20 Million
Number Employees: 50-99
Square Footage: 450000
Type of Packaging: Consumer, Food Service
Brands:
  Michigan Made

5952 Honest Tea Inc
1 Coca-Cola Plz NW
Atlanta, GA 30313
800-520-2653
honestPR@coca-cola.com www.honesttea.com
Organic tea, lemonade, juice, and soda
Co-Founder & CEO Emeritus: Seth Goldman
seth@honesttea.com
Co-Founder: Barry Nalebuff
Marketing Director: Matt O'Brien
Number Employees: 50-99
Parent Co: The Coca-Cola Company
Type of Packaging: Consumer, Bulk

5953 Honey Acres
N1557 Hwy 67
Neosho, WI 53059
920-474-4411
info@honeyacres.com
www.honeyacres.com
Honey and honey products, including honey chocolates, honey mustards, andhoney straws.
CEO: John Gabielian
Marketing Manager: Debra Champeau
Director of Inside Sales & Marketing: Tiarra Detert
Plant Manager: Eugene Brueggeman
eugene@honeyacres.com
Year Founded: 1852
Estimated Sales: $5-9.9 Million
Number Employees: 30
Number of Products: 50
Square Footage: 144000
Type of Packaging: Consumer, Food Service, Private Label, Bulk
Brands:
  Honey Acres

5954 Honey Bear Fruit Basket
6321 Washington St # N
Denver, CO 80216-1100
303-297-3390
Fax: 303-297-3393 888-330-2327
Fine wine jelly, sauce, scone mix, lemon curd

Owner: Carol Kincler
General Manager: Linda Wenz
Contact: Mary Cucarola
honeybearbaskets@gmail.com
Estimated Sales: $500,000-$1 Million
Number Employees: 1-4
Brands:
  Penelope's

5955 Honey Bee Company
3875 Mansell Road
Alpharetta, GA 30022
800-367-7720
Fax: 800-728-4426 800-572-8838
catalogservice@hbham.com
www.honeybakedonline.com
Flavored honey
Manager: Ray Grant
Estimated Sales: $2.5-5 Million
Number Employees: 1-4
Type of Packaging: Private Label, Bulk

5956 Honey Blossom
The Colony, TX 75056
469-582-7508
info@rawhoneyblossom.com
rawhoneyblossom.com
Raw honey

5957 Honey Butter Products Co
103 S Heintzelman St
Manheim, PA 17545-1723
717-665-9323
Fax: 717-665-4422 www.downeyshoneybutter.com
Honey butter
Owner: Kevin Sadd
Estimated Sales: $1 Million
Number Employees: 5-9
Square Footage: 40000
Type of Packaging: Consumer, Food Service
Brands:
  Downey's

5958 Honey Dew Donuts
2 Taunton St # 3
Plainville, MA 02762-2137
508-699-3900
Fax: 508-699-3949 www.honeydewdonuts.com
Donuts
President: Richard Bowen
richard@honeydewdonuts.com
Number Employees: 10-19

5959 Honey Hut
7304 Chippewa Rd
Brecksville, OH 44141-2304
440-526-0606
Fax: 216-661-1883 HoneyHut@Adelphia.net
www.honeyhut.com
Ice cream, frozen desserts
President/Owner: Frank Page
Estimated Sales: Less Than $500,000
Number Employees: 5-9

5960 Honey Mama's
2030 N Williams Ave
Portland, OR 97227-1930
888-506-2627
honeymamas.com
Gluten and dairy free snack bars and fudge.
Owner: Christy Goldsby
Year Founded: 2014
Estimated Sales: $200,000
Number Employees: 2
Type of Packaging: Private Label

5961 Honey Ridge Farms
12310 NE 245th Ave
Brush Prairie, WA 98606-7740
360-256-0086
Fax: 360-883-2679 info@honeyridgefarms.com
www.honeyridgefarms.com
Honey and gourmet honey products
Owner: Leeanne Goetz
info@honeyridgefarms.com
Estimated Sales: Less Than $500,000
Number Employees: 1-4

5962 Honey Run Winery
2309 Park Ave
Chico, CA 95928-6706
530-345-6405
Fax: 530-894-6639 honeyrun@honeyrun.com
Berry wines

Food Manufacturers / A-Z

President: John Hasle
VP: Amy Hasle
Estimated Sales: $.5-1 million
Number Employees: 1-4

5963 Honey Stinger
PO Box 771162
Steamboat Springs, CO 80477
866-464-6639
www.honeystinger.com
Organic waffles, honey, protein bars, energy chews and gels
Number of Brands: 1
Number of Products: 5
Type of Packaging: Consumer
Brands:
  HONEY STINGER

5964 Honey Wafer Baking Co
13952 Kildare Ave
Crestwood, IL 60445-2357
708-388-9010
Fax: 708-388-9680 800-977-9012
info@honeywater.com www.anisihoneywafer.com
Gourmet honey wafers
Owner/President: Tony Lewandowski
Vice President: Adrienne Lewandowski
Estimated Sales: Under $500,000
Number Employees: 1-4
Type of Packaging: Consumer
Brands:
  Anisi

5965 Honey World
165 N Main Avenue
Parker, SD 57053
605-297-4188
Fax: 605-297-4118 candles@iw.net
Honey
President: Glen Wollman
Estimated Sales: $5-10 Million
Number Employees: 1-4
Type of Packaging: Private Label, Bulk

5966 Honeybaked Ham
12170 Mason Montgomery Rd
Cincinnati, OH 45249-1336
513-583-8792
Fax: 513-583-4190 www.honeybaked.com
Baked hams, turkey, frozen desserts and party trays
President/CEO: Craig Kurz
z8407@hbham.com
Site Manager: Ericka Puckett
Estimated Sales: $5-10 Million
Number Employees: 5-9
Brands:
  Honey Baked Ham

5967 Honeydrop Beverages
Houston, TX 77056
www.honeydrop.com
Organic lemonades sweetened with honey
Contact: Becky Byszewski
bbyszewski@honeydrop.com
Brands:
  Obe Sauce
  Obe Sauce Mix

5968 (HQ)Honeyville Grain Inc
1080 N Main St
Suite 100
Brigham City, UT 84302
435-494-4200
Fax: 435-734-9482 www.honeyville.com
Bakery mixes and ingredients
Founder: Lowell Sherratt
VP Finance: Robert Anderson
Executive VP: Trevor Christensen
Director Marketing/Sales: Don Mann
Sales Manager: Craig Dunford
Assistant Operations Manager: Garth Rollins
Estimated Sales: $10-20 Million
Number Employees: 10-19
Square Footage: 120000
Type of Packaging: Consumer, Food Service, Private Label, Bulk
Other Locations:
  California Distribution
  Rancho Cucamonga CA
  Utah Tempsure & Wholesale
  Salt Lake City UT
  Arizona Wholsale Distribution
  Tempe AZ
  Honeyville Grain Mill
  Honeyville UT

Ohio Distribution Center
West Chester OH

5969 Honeywood Winery
1350 Hines St SE
Salem, OR 97302-2521
503-362-4111
Fax: 503-362-4112 800-726-4101
info@honeywoodwinery.com
www.honeywoodwinery.com
Grape and fruit wines
President: Lesley Gallick
info@honeywoodwinery.com
VP: Marlene K Gallick
Estimated Sales: $1 Million+
Number Employees: 5-9
Number of Brands: 5
Number of Products: 45
Square Footage: 88000
Type of Packaging: Private Label
Brands:
  Honeyman & Wood
  Honeywood Grande
  Honeywood North American Grape
  Honeywood Premium

5970 Hong Kong Noodle Company
2350 S Wentworth Ave
Chicago, IL 60616
312-842-0480
Fax: 312-842-7069
Egg noodles
Manager: Glenn Jung
Vice President/Co-Owner: Harry Chung
Estimated Sales: $2.5-5 Million
Number Employees: 20-49
Type of Packaging: Food Service

5971 Hong Kong Supermarket
5495 Jimmy Carter Blvd # F113
Norcross, GA 30093-1537
770-582-6800
Fax: 404-325-3311 www.hongkongmarketga.com
Oriental food items, ethnic foods, full line seafood
Owner: Ly Tieu
Estimated Sales: $10-20 Million
Number Employees: 1-4

5972 Hong Tou Noodle Company
7059 N Figueroa St
Los Angeles, CA 90042
323-256-3843
Noodles
Owner: Peter Kwong
General Manager: Peter Kong
Estimated Sales: $500,000-$1 000,000
Number Employees: 1-4

5973 Hongar Farms Gourmet Foods
2121 Tucker Industrial Rd
Tucker, GA 30084-5017
770-938-9884
Fax: 770-938-8964 888-296-7191
info@hongarfarms.com www.hongarfarms.com
Oils and vinegars
President: Todd Hurst
todd@hungarfarm.com
Estimated Sales: $.5-1 million
Number Employees: 5-9

5974 HongryHawg of Louisiana
P.O. Box 787
Prairieville, LA 70769
225-622-4011
Fax: 225-622-0546 888-772-4294
answers@cajunsauce.com www.cajunsauce.com
Hot sauce, barbecue sauce, jambalaya mix, cajun seasoning and gift boxes.
Owner: Hiram Davis
Estimated Sales: $5-10 Million
Number Employees: 5-9

5975 Honickman Affiliates
8275 Route 130
Pennsauken, NJ 08110-1435
856-665-6200
Fax: 856-661-4684 800-573-7745
Soft drinks
Chairman: Harold Honickman
CEO: Jeffrey Honickman
Chief Financial Officer: Walt Wilkinson
Business Development Manager: Larry Linder
Production Manager: Phil Forte

Estimated Sales: $10-20 Million
Number Employees: 20-49
Parent Co: PepsiCo North America
Type of Packaging: Consumer, Food Service
Brands:
  Cadbury Schweppes
  Coors
  Pepsi-Cola
  Snapple
  South Beach

5976 Honig Vineyard and Winery
850 Rutherford Road
Rutherford, CA 94573
707-963-5618
Fax: 707-963-5639 800-929-2217
www.honigwine.com
Wines
President: Michael Honig
COO: Tony Benedetti
Marketing Director: Regina Weinstein
Estimated Sales: $5-9.9 Million
Number Employees: 5-9
Type of Packaging: Private Label

5977 Honolulu Fish Company
824 Gulick Avenue
Honolulu, HI 96819-1998
808-833-1123
Fax: 808-836-1045 sales@honolulufish.com
www.honolulufish.com
Sashimi-grade fish
Founder, Chief Executive Officer: Wayne Samiere
Contact: William Grafton
william@honolulufish.com

5978 Honso USA
P.O.Box 6729
Chandler, AZ 85246
602-377-8787
Fax: 480-377-6649 888-461-5808
info@honso.com www.HonsoUSA.com
Chinese herbal products.
President: Dan Wen
Estimated Sales: $300,000-500,000
Number Employees: 1-4

5979 Hood Home Service
187 S Winooski Ave
Burlington, VT 05401-4537
802-864-0941
Ice cream, frozen desserts, milk, juices
Plant Manager: David Roberts
Estimated Sales: $500,000 appx.
Number Employees: 1-4
Parent Co: Hood Foods

5980 Hood River Coffee Co
1310 Tucker Rd
Hood River, OR 97031-8647
541-386-3908
Fax: 541-386-3998 800-336-2954
customerservice@hoodrivercoffeeco.com
Coffee
Owner: Mark Hudon
mark@hoodrivercoffeeco.com
Number Employees: 5-9

5981 Hood River Distillers Inc
660 Riverside Dr
Hood River, OR 97031-1177
541-386-1588
Fax: 541-386-2520 HRDsales@HRDspirits.com
www.findmonarch.com
Spirits, including whisky, rum, gin, vodka, schnapps, Irish cream whiskey, scotch and liqueurs
President: Olivia Barker
oliviab@hrdspirits.com
CFO: Gary Goatcher
VP & General Manager: Lynda Webber
Director of Marketing: Tia Bledsoe
VP Sales: Erik Svenson
Materials/Special Projects Manager: Brad Whiting
Estimated Sales: $4.6 Million
Number Employees: 50-99
Square Footage: 212000
Brands:
  Pendleton Whisky
  Pendleton1910™
  Yazi Ginger Vodka
  Broker's London Dry Gin
  Sinfire™ Cinnamon Whisky
  Ullr Nordic Libation
  Knickers Irish Cream Whiskey

Food Manufacturers / A-Z

Broker's Whiskey
Monarch
Hrd

5982 Hood River Vineyards and Winery
4693 Westwood Drive
Hood River, OR 97031
541-386-3772
Fax: 541-386-5880 hoodriverwines@gmail.com
www.hoodrivervineyardsandwinery.com
Wines
President: Bernie Lerch
VP: Anne Lerch
Contact: Anne Lerch
hoodriverwines@gmail.com
Estimated Sales: $1-2.5 Million
Number Employees: 1-4

5983 Hood Sterile Division
P.O. Box 491
Oneida, NY 13421-0491
315-363-3870
Fax: 315-363-9534 www.hphood.com
Coffeemate, beverages
Plant Manager: Steve Pelkey
Estimated Sales: Under $500,000
Number Employees: 100-249
Parent Co: Hood Foods

5984 Hoodsport Winery
23501 N US Highway 101 # 3
Hoodsport, WA 98548-9605
360-877-9894
Fax: 360-877-9508 800-580-9894
www.hoodsport.com
Wines
President: Peggy Patterson
CEO: Ann Patterson
ann@hoodsport.com
Estimated Sales: $5-10 Million
Number Employees: 10-19
Type of Packaging: Private Label
Brands:
  Hoodsport

5985 Hook Line and Savor
Gloucester, MA 01930
833-457-2867
hooklineandsavor.com
Frozen fish
Founder: Freddie Turner
Marketing: Sean Rogerson

5986 Hooks Cheese Co
320 Commerce St
Mineral Point, WI 53565-1240
608-987-3259
Fax: 608-987-2658 hookscheese@yahoo.com
www.hookscheese.com
Cheese
President: Tony Hook
jahduda@yahoo.com
Owner: Julie Hook
Estimated Sales: $1-2.5 000,000
Number Employees: 5-9

5987 Hoopeston Foods Inc
201 W Travelers Trail
Suite 202
Burnsville, MN 55337-2913
952-854-0903
Fax: 952-854-6874 www.hfinc3.qwestoffice.net
Canned dry beans, chili, stews, soups, sauces, tamales and meats
President: Eric Newman
CEO: Tad Ballentyne
SVP: Corey Hoerning
Sales Manager: Lori Kalahar
Plant Manager: Mel Lollar
Estimated Sales: $5-10 Million
Number Employees: 20-49
Type of Packaging: Food Service, Private Label
Brands:
  Nature's Gold
  Tio Franco

5988 Hoople Country Kitchen Inc
714 N 5th St
Rockport, IN 47635-1103
812-649-2351
Fax: 812-649-2836 877-466-7537
customerservice@hooplecountrykitchens.com
www.hooplecountrykitchens.com
Pork sausage, prepared salads, corn meal mush and horseradish
President: David Caskey
Treasurer: Franklin Caskey
VP: Denise Caskey
Estimated Sales: $5-10 Million
Number Employees: 10-19
Type of Packaging: Consumer

5989 Hop Kiln Winery
6050 Westside Rd
Healdsburg, CA 95448
707-433-6491
Fax: 707-433-6436 info@hkgwines.com
www.hopkilnwinery.com
Wines
CEO: David Di Loreto
Contact: Ellissa Anderson
eanderson@hkgwines.com
Plant Manager: Erich Bradley
Estimated Sales: $5-9.9 Million
Number Employees: 10-19
Brands:
  Chardonnay Barrel Select
  Late Harvest Zinfandel
  Marty Griffin Big Red
  Primivito Zinfandel
  Sonoma County Zinfandel
  Thousand Flowers
  Valdiguie

5990 Hope Creamery
9043 SW 37th Ave
Hope, MN 56046-2003
507-451-2029
www.hopecreamery.com
Butter
President/Owner: Victor Mrotz
tim@hopecreamery.com
Operations: Gene Kruckeberg
Estimated Sales: $300,000-$500,000
Number Employees: 1-4
Square Footage: 12000
Type of Packaging: Consumer, Bulk
Brands:
  Hope

5991 Hope Foods
PO Box 3744
Boulder, CO 80307-3744
USA
303-248-7019
info@hopefoods.com
www.hopefoods.com
Hummus, dips, chocolate
President: Robbie Rech
Marketing Director: Will Burger
VP Of Sales: Alek Ramoska
VP Of Operations: Ian Beert
Estimated Sales: 160,000
Number Employees: 20-49

5992 Hopkins Inn Of Lake Waramaug
22 Hopkins Rd
Warren, CT 06777-1016
860-868-7295
Fax: 860-868-9248 info@thehopkinsinn.com
www.thehopkinsinn.com
Gourmet salad dressings
President: Beth Schober
hopkins@gmail.com
Estimated Sales: $1-2.5 Million
Number Employees: 20-49
Brands:
  Hopkins Inn Caesar Dressing
  Hopkins Inn House Dressing

5993 Hopkins Vineyard
25 Hopkins Rd
Warren, CT 06777-1015
860-868-7954
Fax: 860-868-1768 www.hopkinsvineyard.com
Wines
Owner: Hilary Criollo
hopkinsvineyard@charter.net
Estimated Sales: $1-2.5 Million
Number Employees: 5-9
Type of Packaging: Private Label
Brands:
  Highland Estates
  Hopkins Vineyard
  Hopkins Westwind

5994 Hops Extract Corporation of America
1 West Washington Ave.
Yakima, WA 98903
509-248-1530
Fax: 509-457-4638 800-339-8410
sales@hopsteiner.com www.hopsteiner.com
Hops
Manager: Dave Dunmham
ddunmham@hopsteiner.com
Operations: Paul Signorotti
Year Founded: 1845
Estimated Sales: $20-50 Million
Number Employees: 20-49
Parent Co: S. S. Steiner, Inc.

5995 Horizon Cellars Winery
466 Vineyard Ridge
Siler City, NC 27344
919-742-1404
Fax: 919-742-3885 www.horizoncellars.com
Wines
Owner: Guy Loeffler
Contact: Nicole Loeffler
nicole@horizoncellars.com
Estimated Sales: $100,000
Number Employees: 6

5996 Horizon Organic Dairy
12002 Airport Way
Broomfield, CO 80021-2546
303-635-4000
888-494-3020
info@horizonorganic.com
Organic dairy products
President: Mike Ferry
Communication Manager: Sara Loveday
Contact: Heidy Sowatzke
heidys@horizonorganic.com
VP Operations: Jule Taylor
Estimated Sales: $20-50 Million
Number Employees: 50-99
Type of Packaging: Consumer
Brands:
  Organic Cow

5997 Horizon Poultry
92 Cartwright Avenue
Toronto, ON M6A 1V2
Canada
519-364-3200
Fax: 519-364-4692 cphilipp@schneiderfoods.ca
www.schneiderfoods.ca/
Chickens; eggs
Quality Assurance: Cynthia Philippe
Number Employees: 165
Parent Co: J.M. Schneider
Type of Packaging: Consumer, Food Service, Private Label, Bulk

5998 Horizon Snack Foods
7066 Las Positas Rd # G
Livermore, CA 94551-5134
925-373-7700
Fax: 925-373-8303 800-229-2552
customerservice@horizonfoodgroup.com
Pies
Owner: Bob Sharp
Controller: Brett Howell
Estimated Sales: $2.5-5,000,000
Number Employees: 10-19

5999 Horlacher Meats
30 W 700 N # B
Logan, UT 84321-3214
435-752-1287
Fresh and frozen ham, beef jerky and roast beef
Owner: Betty Horlacher
mombetty8@yahoo.com
Estimated Sales: Less Than $500,000
Number Employees: 1-4
Square Footage: 32000
Type of Packaging: Consumer, Bulk

6000 Hormel Foods Corp.
1 Hormel Pl.
Austin, MN 55912
507-437-5611
www.hormelfoods.com
Meat and grocery products.

Food Manufacturers / A-Z

Chairman/President/CEO: Jim Snee
Executive VP/CFO: Jim Sheehan
Senior VP/General Counsel: Lori Marco
Senior VP, R&D: Kevin Myers
Vice President, Quality Management: Richard Carlson
Year Founded: 1891
Estimated Sales: $9 Billion
Number Employees: 20,000
Number of Brands: 52
Type of Packaging: Consumer, Food Service, Private Label
Other Locations:
  Manufacturing Facility
  Austin MN
  Manufacturing Facility
  Algona IA
  Manufacturing Facility
  Alma KS
  Manufacturing Facility
  Atlanta GA
  Manufacturing Facility
  Aurora IL
  Manufacturing Facility
  Barron WI
  Manufacturing Facility
  Beloit WI
  Manufacturing Facility
  Bondurant IA
  Manufacturing Facility
  Bremin GA
  Manufacturing Facility
  Browerville MN
  Manufacturing Facility
  Dayton OH
  Manufacturing Facility
  Dubuque IA
  Manufacturing Facility
  Eldridge IA
Brands:
  Applegate®
  Hormel®
  Jennie-O Turkey®
  Austin Blues BBQ®
  Bacon 1®
  Real Bacon Toppings
  Black Label Bacon®
  Bufalo®
  Burke®
  Cafe H®
  Chi-Chi's®
  Premium Chicken Breast®
  Hormel Chili®
  Columbus®
  Compleats®
  Cure 81®
  Dan's Prize®
  Del Fuerte®
  Deli Meats
  DiLusso Deli Company®
  Dinty Moore®
  Don Miguel®
  Doña María™
  Embasa®
  Evolve™
  Fire Braised Meats®
  Fontanini®
  Fuse Burger™
  Gatherings®
  Herbox®
  Herdez®
  Hormel Health Labs
  House of Tsang®
  Justin's®
  La Victoria®
  Little Sizzlers®
  Lloyds Barbeque Co®
  Mary Kitchen®
  Muscle Milk®
  Natural Choice®
  Not So Sloppy Joe®
  Old Smokehouse®
  Hormel Pepperoni®
  Refrigerated Entre,s
  Hormel Side Dishes
  Skippy®
  SPAM®
  Stagg Chili®
  Hormel Taco Meats®
  Valley Fresh®
  Vital Cuisine™
  Wholly Guacamole®

6001 Hornell Brewing Company
5 Dakota Dr
New Hyde Park, NY 11042-1109
516-812-0300
Fax: 516-326-4988
Beers
President: John Ferolito
Contact: Ann Marie
agallager@arizonaicedt.com
Estimated Sales: F
Number Employees: 500-999

6002 Horner International
5304 Emerson Drive
Raleigh, NC 27609
919-787-3112
Fax: 919-787-4272 sales@hornerintl.com
www.hornerinternational.com
Natural extracts and flavors
Contact: Ladiner Blaylock
ladiner.blaylock@hornerintl.com
Parent Co: Horner International

6003 Horseshoe Brand
1179 Rte. 199
Milan, NY 12571
845-240-2390
info@horseshoebrand.com
www.horseshoebrand.com
Flavored hot sauces and barbecue sauces
Owner: Ryan Fleischhauer
Year Founded: 2008
Number of Brands: 1
Number of Products: 11
Type of Packaging: Consumer, Private Label
Brands:
  Horseshoe Brand

6004 Horst Seafood
2315 Industrial Blvd
Juneau, AK 99801-8534
907-790-4300
Fax: 907-790-5534 877-518-4300
horsts@gci.net
Fresh and frozen seafood
President: Horst Schramm
horsts@gci.net
Estimated Sales: Less Than $500,000
Number Employees: 1-4
Type of Packaging: Consumer

6005 Horton Fruit Co Inc
4701 Jennings Ln
Louisville, KY 40218-2967
502-969-1375
Fax: 502-964-1515 800-626-2245
Tomatoes, onions, spinach, kale, coleslaw, bananas, avocados, pineapples and caramel apples
Chairman/CEO: Albert Horton
ahorton@hortonfruit.com
President/COO: Jackson Woodward
Treasurer: Steve Edelen
Vice President: Bill Benoit
Sales/Procurement: Tom Smith
Transportation Manager: Bobby Harlow
Number Employees: 100-249
Square Footage: 400000
Type of Packaging: Consumer, Food Service, Private Label
Other Locations:
  Louisville Produce Terminal
  Louisville KY

6006 Horton Vineyards
6399 Spotswood Trl
Gordonsville, VA 22942-7735
540-832-7440
Fax: 540-832-7187 800-829-4633
vawinee@aol.com www.hortonwine.com
Wines
President: Dennis Horton
vawinee@aol.com
Estimated Sales: $5-10 Million
Number Employees: 10-19

6007 Hosemen & Roche Vitamins & Fine Chemicals
340 Kingsland Street
Building 787
Nutley, NJ 07110-1199
973-235-5000
Fax: 973-235-7605 800-526-6367
Bulk vitamins, carotenoids and citric acids for food manufacturing
President: Dr Franz B Humer
Chief Executive Officer: Severin Schwan
Chief Operating Officer: Pascal Soriot
Estimated Sales: Less than $500,000
Number Employees: 1-4
Parent Co: Hoffman-La Roche
Type of Packaging: Bulk
Brands:
  Roche

6008 Hosford & Wood Fresh Seafood Providers
2545 E 7th Street
Tucson, AZ 85716-4701
520-795-1920
Fax: 520-795-1010
Seafood
President: Anita Wood
Secretary: Bruce Hosford

6009 Hosmer Mountain Bottling Co
217 Mountain St
Willimantic, CT 06226-3211
860-423-1555
Fax: 860-423-2207 800-763-2445
www.hosmersoda.com
Soft drinks
President/CEO: Andrew Potvin
VP Marketing Manager: Bill Potvin
Estimated Sales: $2.5-5 Million
Number Employees: 5-9
Type of Packaging: Private Label
Brands:
  Hosmer Mountain Soft Drinks

6010 Hospitality Mints LLC
213 Candy Ln
P.O. Drawer 3140
Boone, NC 28607
Fax: 828-264-6933 800-334-5181
mints@hospitalitymints.com
www.hospitalitymints.com
Mint candies
President/CEO: Patrick Viancourt
CFO/COO: Walter Kaudelka
VP of Marketing: Kathi Guy
Estimated Sales: $500,000-$1 Million
Number Employees: 10-19
Square Footage: 252000
Parent Co: Party Sweets
Type of Packaging: Consumer, Food Service, Private Label, Bulk
Brands:
  Hospitality

6011 Hoss-S
12985 Dunnings Hwy
PO Box 219
Claysburg, PA 16625-8202
814-693-3453
Fax: 814-239-5922 800-438-7439
www.hosswares.com
Prepared foods
Owner: Bill Campbell
VP: Mark Spinazzola
Plant Manager: Rocky Rhodes
Estimated Sales: Less Than $500,000
Number Employees: 5-9

6012 Host Defense Mushrooms
800-780-9126
info@fungi.com hostdefense.com
Mushroom capsules, extracts and sprays
Founder: Paul Stamets
Type of Packaging: Consumer

6013 Hostess Brands
PO Box 419593
Kansas City, MO 64141
816-701-4600
www.hostessbrands.com
Prepackaged sweet baked goods.
President/CEO: Andrew Callahan
Executive VP/CFO: Thomas Peterson
Executive VP/Chief Admin. Officer: Andrew Jacobs
Senior VP, Quality/Food Safety/R&D: Darryl Riley
Year Founded: 2013
Estimated Sales: $776 Million
Type of Packaging: Consumer
Brands:
  Twinkies®
  Hostess CupCakes®
  DingDongs®
  Zingers®

800

Food Manufacturers / A-Z

Donettes®
Ho Hos®

6014 Hot Cakes-Molten Chocolate
5427 Ballard Ave NW
Seattle, WA 98107-4052
206-453-3792
kirsten@kirstengrahampr.com
www.getyourhotcakes.com
Hot cakes and sauces
Founder: Autumn Martin
Estimated Sales: Less Than $500,000
Number Employees: 10-19

6015 Hot Licks
2830 Via Orange Way
Suite A
Spring Valley, CA 91978
Fax: 619-660-7429 888-766-6468
orders@hotlickssauces.com
www.hotlickssauces.com
Hot sauces, salsas, mustards, condiments, snacks, mixes and seasonings, bbq sauces, marinades, and gifts.
Estimated Sales: Less than $500,000
Number Employees: 1-4
Brands:
   Amazon Pepper Products
   California Just Chile!
   Death Valley Habanero
   Hot! Hot! Hot!
   Ottimo
   Pepe's Sauce
   Ring of Fire

6016 Hot Mama's Foods
134 Avocado St
Springfield, MA 01104
413-737-6572
Fax: 413-737-6793
Gourmet foods, including salsa, hummus, pesto, prepared salads, dips and ready-to-cook products; custom packaging and consulting
President: Matt Morse
Finance & Business Development: Herb Heller
Executive Chef: Josh Cooper
Director of Human Resources: Lisa Dufour
Director of Operations: Jim Boyle
Estimated Sales: $14.9 Million
Number Employees: 90
Square Footage: 13500

6017 Hot Springs Packing Co Inc
580 Mid America Blvd
Hot Springs, AR 71913-8412
501-767-2363
Fax: 501-767-9715 800-535-0449
hspc@hotspringspacking.com
www.hotspringspacking.com
Specialty sausages, deli meats and hams
President/CEO: John Stubblefield
hspc@hotspringspacking.com
Estimated Sales: $4.3 Million
Number Employees: 20-49
Type of Packaging: Consumer, Food Service

6018 Hot Wachula's
P.O.Box 2376
Lakeland, FL 33806-2376
863-602-0857
Fax: 863-665-0358 877-883-8700
www.hotwachulas.com
Gourmet dips and sauces, marinades
President: Matt Barber
Estimated Sales: $1 Million
Number Employees: 5-9
Brands:
   Hot Wachula's Gourmet Dips & Sauces

6019 Houdini Inc
4225 N Palm St
Fullerton, CA 92835-1045
714-525-0325
Fax: 714-996-9605
www.winecountrygiftbaskets.com
Gourmet food, wine and gift baskets
Owner: Tim Dean
tdean@houdiniinc.com
Estimated Sales: $500,000-$1 Million
Number Employees: 10-19
Brands:
   California Pantry
   Wine Country

6020 Houlton Farms Dairy
25 Commonwealth Ave
Houlton, ME 04730-2347
207-532-3170
Fax: 207-532-3613
Dairy products
Owner: Alice Lincoln
Estimated Sales: $5-10 000,000
Number Employees: 10-19

6021 House Foods America Corp
7351 Orangewood Ave
Garden Grove, CA 92841-1411
714-901-4350
Fax: 714-901-4235 877-333-7077
www.house-foods.com
Tofu and tofu products; importer of curry, spices, ramen noodles and tea.
President: Shigeru Natake
shigeru@house-foods.com
Marketing Manager: Masahiko Kudo
Sales & Foodservice: Hirofumi Fujimura
Production & Supply Chain Management: Hajime Inoue
Purchasing, Cost Reduction, Admin: Keiji Matsumoto
Estimated Sales: $11.2 Million
Number Employees: 100-249
Square Footage: 60000
Parent Co: House Foods Corporation
Other Locations:
   Somerset NJ
   Garden Grove CA
   NY
Brands:
   Hinoichi
   House Foods

6022 House of Coffee Beans
2348 Bissonnet St
Houston, TX 77005-1512
713-524-0057
Fax: 713-795-5410 800-422-1799
contact@houseofcoffeebeans.com
www.houseofcoffeebeans.com
Coffee
Owner: Roger Farber
Estimated Sales: Less than $500,000
Number Employees: 5-9
Square Footage: 56000
Type of Packaging: Consumer, Food Service, Private Label, Bulk

6023 House of Flavors Inc
110 N William St
Ludington, MI 49431-2092
231-845-7369
Fax: 616-845-7371 800-930-7740
www.houseofflavors.com
Kosher ice cream and frozen novelties
Owner: Pat Calder
hfpat@houseofflavors.com
Number Employees: 1-4
Type of Packaging: Consumer, Food Service

6024 House of Herbs LLC
38 Ann St
Passaic, NJ 07055-5889
973-779-2422
Fax: 973-779-6809
Pickles, sauces and salad dressings
Owner: Paul Fischer
Number Employees: 5-9

6025 House of Raeford Farms Inc.
PO Box 699
Rose Hill, NC 28458
910-289-3191
www.houseofraeford.com
Chickens and turkeys.
Chairman: Marvin Johnson
Chief Executive Officer/President: Robert Johnson
President, Cooked Products Group: Donald Taber
Chief Financial Officer: Ken Qualls
Year Founded: 1925
Estimated Sales: $705 Million
Number Employees: 5,500
Number of Brands: 3
Square Footage: 400000
Type of Packaging: Food Service
Other Locations:
   Further Processing Plant/Distrib.
      Raeford NC
   Chicken Processing Plant
      Arcadia LA
   Columbia Farms Chicken Processing
      Columbia SC
   Breaded Chicken & Turkey Products
      Hemingway SC
   Columbia Farms Chicken Plant
      Greenville SC
Brands:
   House of Raeford®
   Speedy Bird®
   Filet Of Chicken®

6026 House of Spices
12740 Willets Point Blvd
Flushing, NY 11368-1506
718-507-4600
Fax: 718-507-4798
customerservice@hosindia.com
www.hosindia.com
Pickles, condiment pastes, chutney, snack foods, candy, ice cream and frozen foods; importer of Indian-Pakistani basmati rice, lentils, spices, oils and nuts; exporter of pickles, condiments and spices.
President: Candace Kuechler
ckuechler@rich.com
Estimated Sales: $5-10 Millio
Number Employees: 50-99
Number of Brands: 25
Number of Products: 2000
Square Footage: 1200000
Type of Packaging: Consumer, Food Service, Private Label, Bulk
Other Locations:
   Manufacturing Facility
      Stafford TX
   Manufacturing Facility
      Elk Grove IL
   Manufacturing Facility
      Forestville MD
   Manufacturing Facility
      Hayward CA
   Manufacturing Facility
      Orlando FL
   Manufacturing Facility
      Norcross GA
   Manufacturing Facility
      Worcester MA
Brands:
   Laxmi
   Bombay Bites
   Masala Craft
   Maazo
   Garvi Gujarat
   Shamiana
   Amma's Kitchen
   Chai Bites

6027 House of Thaller Inc
1600 Harris Rd
Knoxville, TN 37924-2215
865-689-5893
Fax: 865-689-7132 800-462-3365
sales@houseofthaller.com
www.houseofthaller.com
Sandwich spreads and prepared salads
President: John Thaller
sales@houseofthaller.com
Finance Executive/HR Manager: Stephanie Cooper
R&D Director: Beth Ann Disney
Marketing Manager/Sales Executive: John Thaller
Production Manager: Wes Curnutt
Purchasing Agent: Katherine Reed
Estimated Sales: $8 Million
Number Employees: 20-49
Square Footage: 32000
Type of Packaging: Consumer, Food Service, Private Label, Bulk

6028 House of Tsang
2345 3rd St
San Francisco, CA 94107-3108
415-282-9952
Fax: 415-243-0157 lgmarconi@hormel.com
Asian sauces, marinades, oils, vegetables and sauce combinations.
Owner: David Haase
Estimated Sales: $1 Million
Parent Co: Hormel Foods International Corporation

6029 House of Webster
1013 N 2nd St
P.O. Box 1988
Rogers, AR 72757
479-636-2974
Fax: 479-636-2974 800-369-4641
houseofwebster.com

Food Manufacturers / A-Z

Jams, jellies, preserves, spreads; relish; salsa; mustard; syrup; BBQ sauce; pickled products; cheese products; crackers; cured meats; nuts; baking mixes; soups; spices and seasonings; tea and coffee.
President: John Griffin
Year Founded: 1934
Estimated Sales: $13 Million
Number Employees: 65
Type of Packaging: Food Service, Private Label

6030 House-Autry Mills Inc
7000 US Highway 301 S
Four Oaks, NC 27524-7628
919-963-6458
Fax: 910-594-0739 800-849-0802
info@house-autry.com www.house-autry.com
Baking mixes
CEO: Roger Mortenson
Estimated Sales: $10-20 Million
Number Employees: 100-249
Type of Packaging: Private Label

6031 Houser Meats
RR 2 Box 180B
Rushville, IL 62681
217-322-4994
Fax: 217-322-4994 www.housermeats.com
Beef, pork, lamb and venison
Partner: Douglas Houser
Partner: Terri Houser
Estimated Sales: $500,000-$1 Million
Number Employees: 5-9
Square Footage: 10000
Type of Packaging: Bulk

6032 Houston Calco, Inc
2400 Dallas St
Houston, TX 77003-3604
713-236-8668
Fax: 713-236-1920
Bean sprouts
Owner: Alice Chang
Estimated Sales: $5-10 000,000
Number Employees: 20-49
Type of Packaging: Private Label
Brands:
 Calco

6033 Houston Tea & Beverage
7703 Cannon Street
Houston, TX 77055
832-348-7780
Fax: 832-348-7760 800-585-4549
Teas
President: Linda Williams
Contact: Al Hernandez
al@houstonteaandbeverage.com
Estimated Sales: Less than $500,000
Number Employees: 1-4
Square Footage: 8500
Type of Packaging: Private Label

6034 Howard Foods Inc
5 Ray St
Danvers, MA 01923-3531
978-774-6207
Fax: 978-777-2384 info@howardfoods.com
www.howardfoods.com
Specialty condiments, syrups, seasoning juices and chopped and minced garlic
Estimated Sales: $1-3 Million
Number Employees: 5-9
Brands:
 Howard's

6035 Howard Turner & Son
1659 Route 1 Highway 7
Marie Joseph, NS B0J 2G0
Canada
902-347-2616
Fax: 902-347-2714
Fresh and frozen lobster and groundfish
President: Randy Turner
Type of Packaging: Bulk

6036 Howjax
PO Box 246063
Pembroke Pines, FL 33024-0187
954-441-2491
Fax: 954-962-7258
Gourmet condiments, and Caribean style chutney

6037 Howson Mills
320 Blyth Rd
Blyth, ON N0M 1H0
Canada
519-523-4241
866-422-7522
howson@howsons.ca www.howsons.ca
Durum flour.
Sales Manager: Dan Greyerbighl
Year Founded: 1875
Estimated Sales: $35 Million
Number Employees: 65
Type of Packaging: Bulk

6038 Hoyt's Honey Farm
11711 Interstate 10 E
Baytown, TX 77523
281-576-5383
Fax: 281-576-2191 hoyts@imsday.com
Honey
President: Gordon Brown
Estimated Sales: $5-10 Million
Number Employees: 5-9
Square Footage: 30000
Type of Packaging: Consumer, Food Service, Private Label, Bulk
Brands:
 Hoyt's Pure Honey
 Hoyts

6039 Hsin Tung Yang Foods Inc
405 S Airport Blvd
S San Francisco, CA 94080-6909
650-589-6789
Fax: 650-589-3157 info@htyusa.com
www.htyusa.com
Asian meat products
President: Kailen Mai
Contact: Peter Hamilton
p.hamilton@cymi.com
Director Manufacturing: Pin Chong
Estimated Sales: $10-20 Million
Number Employees: 20-49

6040 Hsu's Ginseng Enterprises Inc
T6819 County Rd W
Wausau, WI 54403-9461
715-675-2325
Fax: 715-675-7832 800-826-1577
info@hsuginseng.com www.hsuginseng.com
Ginseng products, royal jelly, bee pollen, astragalus, dong quai and goldenseal
President: Paul Hsu
info@hsuginseng.com
Vice President: Sharon Hsu
Estimated Sales: $5-10 Million
Number Employees: 50-99
Brands:
 Root To Health

6041 Hu Kitchen
78 Fifth Ave
New York, NY 10011
212-510-8919
hukitchen.com
Organic dark chocolate
CEO: Rita Hudetz
Type of Packaging: Bulk

6042 Hubbard Peanut Co Inc
30275 Sycamore Ave
PO Box 94
Sedley, VA 23878
757-562-4081
Fax: 757-562-2741 800-889-7688
hubs@hubspeanuts.com www.hubspeanuts.com
Cocktail peanuts
President: Lynne Rabil
lynne@hubspeanuts.com
Plant Manager: David Benton
Estimated Sales: $10-24.9 Million
Number Employees: 10-19
Square Footage: 90000
Type of Packaging: Consumer, Food Service, Private Label

6043 Hubble
Manhattan Beach, CA 90266
dave@drinkhubble.com
www.drinkhubble.com
Sparkling cold-pressed juice
Founder & President: Dave Burchianti

6044 Hubers Orchard Winery-Vineyards
19816 Huber Rd
Borden, IN 47106-8309
812-923-9813
Fax: 812-923-3013 800-345-9463
info@huberwinery.com www.huberwinery.com
Wines, fruits, berries and vegetables
President: Ted Huber
dana.huber@huberwinery.com
VP: Greg Huber
Estimated Sales: $5-10 Million
Number Employees: 20-49

6045 Hubert's Lemonade
Tustin, CA 92780
877-265-3286
www.hubertslemonade.com
Flavored lemonades
President/Owner: Daniel Barba

6046 Huck's Seafood
508 Cynwood Dr # D
Easton, MD 21601-3892
410-770-9211
Fax: 410-763-8811
Crabs, oysters and clams; fish
Owner/President: James Ford, Jr
Orders: Amber Ford
Estimated Sales: $.5-1 million
Number Employees: 50
Square Footage: 5000
Type of Packaging: Consumer, Food Service, Bulk
Brands:
 Huck's

6047 Huckleberry Patch
8868 US Hwy 2 East
Hungry Horse, MT 59919
406-387-5000
Fax: 406-387-4444 800-527-7340
info@huckleberrypatch.com
www.huckleberrypatch.com
Wildberry jellies, syrups, jams, preserves
Manager: Laurie Carpy
Estimated Sales: $5-10 Million
Number Employees: 10-19

6048 Hudson Henry Baking Co.
221 Palmer Country Ln
Palmyra, VA 22963-5451
817-733-0709
www.hudsonhenrybakingco.com
Granola products
Founder: Hope Lawrence
hope@hudsonhenrybakingco.com
Year Founded: 2012
Estimated Sales: #350,000
Number Employees: 7
Type of Packaging: Food Service

6049 Hudson River Foods
P.O. Box 11
Castleton, NY 12033
888-417-9343
info@hudsonriverfoods.com
www.hudsonriverfoods.com
All natural foods including baking mixes, cakes, brownies, cookies, icings, puddings, muffins, hempmilk, hemp tofu, chia greek yogurt, drink mixes, and Kombucha
Co-Founder: Dan Ratner
Co-Founder: Donna Ratner
Manager: Winston Edmonds
Warehouse Manager: Rebecca Sagendorf
Year Founded: 2005
Number Employees: 50-99
Number of Brands: 6
Brands:
 Cherrybrook Kitchen
 Tempt Hemp
 European Gourmet Bakery
 The Epic Seed
 High Country Kombucha
 Healthy To Go

6050 Hudson Valley Brewery
7 East Main St.
Beacon, NY 12508
845-218-9156
contact@hvbrewery.com
www.hudsonvalleybrewery.com
Beer, ale, sour IPAs
Founder/President: John-Anthony Gargiulo

Food Manufacturers / A-Z

Year Founded: 2016
Number of Brands: 1
Number of Products: 13
Type of Packaging: Consumer, Private Label, Bulk
Brands:
  Hudson Valley

6051 Hudson Valley Farmhouse Cider
Centre Rd.
Staatsburg, NY 12580
845-266-3979
www.hudsonvalleyfarmhousecider.com
Farm-based cider; barrel-aged cider; pub cider; sparkling cider
Owner: Elizabeth Ryan
Year Founded: 1984
Number of Brands: 1
Number of Products: 6
Type of Packaging: Consumer, Private Label, Bulk
Brands:
  Hudson Valley

6052 Hudson Valley Foie Gras
80 Brooks Rd
Ferndale, NY 12734-5101
845-292-2500
Fax: 845-292-3009
www.hudsonvalleyfoiegras.com
Duck foie gras
Operations Manager: Marcus Henley
Vice President: Izzy Yanay
info@hudsonvalleyfoiegras.com
Estimated Sales: $190 Thousand
Number Employees: 100-249

6053 Hudson Valley Fruit Juice
33 White St
Highland, NY 12528-1621
845-691-8061
Fax: 845-691-9056
Fruit and vegetable juices and vinegar
President: Vincent Nemeth
Manager: Sam Campese
Estimated Sales: $1-2.5 000,000
Number Employees: 2-4

6054 Hudson Valley Homestead
102 Sheldon Ln
Craryville, NY 12521-5324
518-851-7336
Fax: 518-851-7553 john102@hughes.net
Gourmet condiments
President: John King
jbk102@gmail.com
Estimated Sales: Less Than $500,000
Number Employees: 1-4
Type of Packaging: Private Label
Brands:
  BushwhacKer's Mustard
  Blow Hard Mustard
  Hudson Valley Homestead

6055 Hudson Valley Hops
PO Box 292
Beacon, NY 12508
845-202-2398
admin@hvhops.com
www.hvhops.com
Harvester, processor and distributor of hops to brewers in the Hudson Valley
Co-Founder: Justin Riccobono
Co-Founder: Shawn McLearen
Year Founded: 2013
Type of Packaging: Bulk

6056 Hudson Valley Malt
320 Co. Rte. 6
Germantown, NY 12526
845-489-3450
info@hudsonvalleymalt.com
www.hudsonvalleymalt.net
Artisan craft malt
Co-Owner: Dennis Nesel
Co-Owner: Jeanette Nesel
Number of Brands: 1
Type of Packaging: Consumer, Bulk
Brands:
  Hudson Valley Malt

6057 Hudsonville Ice Cream
345 E 48th St # 200
Holland, MI 49423-5381
616-546-4005
Fax: 616-546-4020
hello@hudsonvilleicecream.com
www.hudsonvilleicecream.com
Ice cream, frozen yogurt and sherbet
Owner: Heidi Buttrey
heidibuttrey@hudsonvilleicecream.com
VP Marketing & Sales: Jon Vanderwoude
Estimated Sales: $12 Million
Number Employees: 20-49
Number of Brands: 2
Type of Packaging: Consumer, Bulk
Brands:
  Hudsonville Ice Cream

6058 Hue's Seafood
105 S 14th Street
Baton Rouge, LA 70802-4753
225-383-0809
Fax: 225-383-0809
Seafood
President: Tu Nguyen

6059 Hughes Springs Frozen Food Center
105 Foster St
Hughes Springs, TX 75656
903-639-2941
Meat packer
Owner: Alvin Dannelley
Estimated Sales: $1-2.5 Million
Number Employees: 1 to 4
Type of Packaging: Consumer

6060 Hughson Meat Company
407 S Guadalupe St
San Marcos, TX 78666
512-392-3368
Fax: 512-392-4190 877-462-6328
http://www.hughson-meat.com/retail
Meat products; slaughtering also available
Owner: Marvin Rutkowski
Estimated Sales: $3-5 Million
Number Employees: 5-9
Type of Packaging: Consumer

6061 Hughson Nut Inc
1825 Verduga Rd
Hughson, CA 95326-9675
209-883-0403
Fax: 209-883-2973 info@hughsonnut.com
www.hughsonnut.com
Almonds and almond products
President: Martin Pohl
martin@hughsonnut.com
Estimated Sales: $2.5-5 Million
Number Employees: 250-499
Number of Brands: 1
Square Footage: 300000
Type of Packaging: Consumer, Private Label, Bulk

6062 Hulman & Co
900 Wabash Ave
Terre Haute, IN 47807-3208
812-232-9446
Fax: 812-478-7181 www.clabbergirl.com
Baking powder, tobacco, liquor
President: Tony George
CEO: Mark Miles
Estimated Sales: $20-50 Million
Number Employees: 1000-4999

6063 Humbly Hemp
11749 W Pico Blvd
Los Angeles, CA 90064
424-259-3521
Hemp snack bars
CEO: Daniel Crawford
Number of Brands: 1
Number of Products: 3
Type of Packaging: Consumer
Brands:
  HUMBLY HEMP

6064 Humboldt Bay Coffee Co.
526 Opera Alley
Eureka, CA 95501
707-444-3969
info@humboldtcoffee.com
www.humboldtcoffee.com
Organic coffees

CFO: Luci Ramirez
Year Founded: 1991

6065 Humboldt Brews LLC
856 10th St
Arcata, CA 95521-6232
707-826-2739
Fax: 707-826-2045 robinhewitt@hotmail.com
www.humboldtbrews.com
Beers
President: Mario Celotto
humcitypodcast@gmail.com
Number Employees: 10-19
Type of Packaging: Consumer, Food Service, Bulk
Brands:
  Gold Nectar
  Red Nectar

6066 Humboldt Chocolate
PO Box 1206
Eureka, CA 95502
707-630-5355
Fax: 707-312-8235 info@humboldtchocolate.com
www.humboldtchocolate.com
All-natural chocolate bars

6067 Humboldt Creamery
Modesto, CA 95351
888-316-6064
info@humboldtcreamery.com
www.humboldtcreamery.com
Ice cream and milk products
CFO: Ralph Titus
National Sales & Marketing Manager: Rod Masters
Operations Manager: Mike Callihan
Purchasing Manager: Mark McCurtain
Number Employees: 100-249
Parent Co: Foster Dairy Farms
Type of Packaging: Consumer, Food Service, Bulk

6068 Humco Holding Group Inc
7400 Alumax Rd
Texarkana, TX 75501-0282
903-831-7808
Fax: 903-334-6300 www.nomoreitch.com
Liquid and powder herbal supplements
President/CEO: Greg Pulido
gpulido@humco.com
CFO: Steve Woolf
Vice President: Susan Hickey
VP Quality/Regulatory Affairs: Steve Bryant
VP Sales: Alan Fyke
Estimated Sales: $10-20 Million
Number Employees: 100-249

6069 Hume Specialties
291 Pleasant Street
Chester, VT 05143-9351
802-875-3117
Fax: 802-875-3140
www.greenmountaingringo.com
Salsa and tortilla chips
President: Christine Hume
Executive VP/Production Manager: Dave Hume
Estimated Sales: $2.5-5 Million
Number Employees: 20-49
Square Footage: 28000
Type of Packaging: Consumer
Brands:
  Green Mountain Gringo

6070 Humeniuk's Meat Cutting
PO Box 11
Ranfurly, AB T0B 3T0
Canada
780-658-2381
Fax: 780-658-2389
Fresh and frozen beef, pork and venison
President: Nector Humeniuk
Owner/Manager: Gerald Humeniuk
Secretary: Oksana Humeniuk
Number Employees: 10-19
Square Footage: 320000
Type of Packaging: Consumer, Food Service, Private Label, Bulk
Brands:
  Granny's

6071 Humm Kombucha
1125 NE 2nd Street
Bend, OR 97701
541-306-6329
hummkombucha.com
Kombucha

803

Food Manufacturers / A-Z

Co-Founder & CEO: Jamie Danek
Co-Founder: Michelle Mitchell
Marketing: Ren, Mitchell
Sales: Sally Taylor
Operations: Wade Nolte
Number of Brands: 1
Number of Products: 10
Square Footage: 5000
Type of Packaging: Consumer
Brands:
    HUMM

6072 Hummel Brothers Inc
180 Sargent Dr
New Haven, CT 06511-5958
    203-787-4113
    Fax: 203-498-1755 800-828-8978
    www.hummelbrothers.com
Cold cuts, frankfurters and sausage
President: Michael Czekaj
michael@hummelbros.com
Vice President: Robert Hummel
Estimated Sales: $8 Million
Number Employees: 50-99
Square Footage: 188000
Type of Packaging: Consumer, Private Label
Brands:
    Hummel Meats

6073 Humming Hemp
PO Box 487
723 The Parkway
Richland, WA 99352
    503-559-6476
    thehumminggroup.com
Hemp good snacks
CEO: Hilary Kelsay
VP, Sales & Marketing: Ross Elkin
COO: Max Schneider

6074 Hummingbird Kitchens
P.O.Box 1286
Whitehouse, TX 75791
    903-839-6244
    800-921-9470
Gourmet food mixes
President: Janet Faulkner
CEO: William Faulkner
Estimated Sales: $1-2.5 Million
Number Employees: 5-9
Number of Products: 51
Type of Packaging: Consumer, Private Label, Bulk

6075 Hummustir
535 Fifth Ave
27th Floor
New York, NY 10017
    info@stiritup.com
    www.hummustir.com
Hummus
Managing Director: Alon Kruvi
Number of Brands: 1
Number of Products: 4
Type of Packaging: Consumer
Brands:
    HUMMUSTIR

6076 Humphrey Co
20810 Miles Pkwy
Cleveland, OH 44128-5508
    216-662-6629
    Fax: 216-662-6619 800-486-3739
    www.humphreycompany.com
Premium white popcorn
Vice President: Tom Dickerhoof
tdickerhoof@humphreycompany.com
VP: Betsy Humphrey
Estimated Sales: $500,000-$1 Million
Number Employees: 5-9
Number of Brands: 1
Number of Products: 10
Square Footage: 44000
Type of Packaging: Consumer, Private Label

6077 Humphrey's Market
1821 S 15th St
Springfield, IL 62703-3298
    217-544-7445
    Fax: 217-544-7518 800-747-6328
    www.humphreysmarket.com
Specialty sausage and hams
President: T Humphrey
Sales Exec: Grant Bradley
gbradley@humphreysmarket.com
Chairman: E Humphrey
Estimated Sales: $10-20 Million
Number Employees: 20-49
Square Footage: 29200

6078 Humphry Slocombe
2790A Harrison St
San Francisco, CA 94110
    415-550-6971
    info@humphryslocombe.com
    www.humphryslocombe.com
Ice cream, ice cream cakes and ice cream pies
Co-Founder: Jake Godby
Co-Founder: Sean Vahey

6079 Hung's Noodle House
25-1410 40th Avenue NE
Calgary, AB T2E 6L1
Canada
    403-250-1663
    Fax: 403-291-0632 rickhungkee@hotmail.com
Noodles and rice
President: Ricky Chung
Production: Cindy Chung
Parent Co: Hung Kee Holdings Company
Brands:
    Hung's Noodle House

6080 Hungry Sultan
14 Rancho Circle
Lake Forest, CA 92630
    949-215-0000
    Fax: 949-215-0965 info@hungrysultan.com
Mediterranean gourmet snack foods, including hummus
Founder: Fouad El-Abd
felabd@hungrysultan.com
Communications: Christina Romeo
Estimated Sales: Less than $500,000
Number Employees: 10-19

6081 Hunt Brothers Cooperative
20205 US Highway 27 North
Lake Wales, FL 33853-0631
    863-676-1411
    Fax: 863-676-8362 www.floridasnatural.com
Citrus fruits
President: Frank Hunt
Estimated Sales: $20-50 Million
Number Employees: 250-499
Number of Brands: 2
Type of Packaging: Consumer, Food Service, Bulk
Brands:
    Seald Sweet
    Treasure Pak

6082 Hunt Country Foods Inc
4559 Achilles Ln
Marshall, VA 20115-3014
    540-364-2622
    Fax: 540-364-3112 www.send-best-of-luck.com
Specialty cookies, cakes and chocolates
Owner: Maggi Castelloe
best.of.luck@starpower.net
Estimated Sales: Less than $500,000
Number Employees: 10-19
Brands:
    Best of Luck
    Best of Luck Horseshoe Chocolates
    Horseshoe Cake
    Horseshoes and Nails

6083 Hunt Country Vineyards
4021 Italy Hill Rd
Country Road 32
Branchport, NY 14418-9615
    315-595-2835
    Fax: 315-595-2835 800-946-3289
    info@HuntWines.com www.huntwines.com
Wines, sherry and port
Owner: Joyce Hunt
joycehunt@huntwines.com
CEO, Owner: Arthur Hunt
Owner, Winemaker: Jonathan Hunt
Owner: Caroline Boutard Hunt
Marketing Operations Manager: Andy Marshall
General Manager: Jim Alsina
joycehunt@huntwines.com
Vineyard Manager: Dave Mortensen
Estimated Sales: $500,000-$1 Million
Number Employees: 20-49
Square Footage: 32000
Type of Packaging: Consumer, Private Label
Brands:
    Fingerlakes Wine Cellars
    Foxy Lady
    Hunt Country Vineyards

6084 Hunt-Wesson Foods
222 Merchandise Mart Plaza
Chicago, IL 60654
    209-334-3616
    Fax: 209-333-7428 877-266-2472
    www.hunts.com
Tomato products including diced, whole, stewed, sauce, and ketchup
President & CEO: Sean Connolly
EVP/CFO: David Marberger
EVP/General Counsel: Colleen Batcheler
EVP/Chief Human Resources Officer: Charisse Brock
Estimated Sales: $25-49.9 Million
Number Employees: 100-249
Parent Co: ConAgra Foods
Type of Packaging: Food Service
Brands:
    Hunts
    La Choy
    Rosarita
    Orville Redenbacher
    Swiss Miss
    Wesson
    Peter Pan

6085 Hunter Farms-High Point Division
1900 N Main St
High Point, NC 27262-2132
    336-822-2300
    Fax: 336-882-2341 800-446-8035
    kcavanaugh@harristeeter.com
    www.hunterfarms.com
Dairy products
VP: Dwight Moore
Quality Assurance Manager: Gale Walton
Sales Development: Karin Cavanaugh
Director Sales: Bob Cooke
General Manager: Dwight Moore
Estimated Sales: $10-24.9 Million
Number Employees: 100-249
Parent Co: Harris Teeter
Type of Packaging: Consumer

6086 Hunter Food Inc
3707 La Palma Ave
Anaheim, CA 92806-2122
    714-666-1888
    Fax: 714-666-1222 www.hunterfood.com
Fresh, frozen, marinated, and non-marinated poultry
CEO: Huan Hua Le
Year Founded: 1991
Estimated Sales: $20-50 Million
Number Employees: 20-49

6087 Huppen Bakery
8721 Santa Monica Boulevard
Suite 201
Los Angeles, CA 90069-4507
    323-656-7501
    Fax: 323-656-1090
Swiss chocolates and wafer rolls
President: Urs Brauchli
Type of Packaging: Consumer, Bulk

6088 Hurd Orchards
17260 Ridge Rd
Holley, NY 14470-9353
    585-638-8838
    Fax: 585-638-5175 market@hurdorchards.com
    www.hurdorchards.com
Preserves, vinegars, pickles, chili sauce, jams, marmalades; canned, brandied and dried fruit
Owner: Susan Machamer
market@hurdorchards.com
VP: Amy Machamer
Estimated Sales: $.5-1 million
Number Employees: 20-49

6089 Husch Vineyards & Winery
4400 Highway 128
Philo, CA 95466-9476
    707-895-3216
    Fax: 707-895-2068 800-554-8724
    www.huschvineyards.com

Food Manufacturers / A-Z

Wines
President: Zach Robinson
VP: Amanda Robinson Holstine
Contact: Vicky Giusti
vicky@huschvineyards.com
Operations Manager: Al White
Production Manager: Brad Holstine
Estimated Sales: $2.5-5 Million
Number Employees: 10-19

6090 Huse's Country Meats
3697 State Highway 171
Malone, TX 76660
254-533-2205
Fax: 254-533-2498 husecountrymeats@yahoo.com
www.husescountrymeats.com
Smoked beef and pork sausage
Owner: Randy Huse
Estimated Sales: $5-10 Million
Number Employees: 10-19

6091 Husman Snack Food Company
PO Box 3900
Peoria, IL 61612
859-282-7490
Fax: 513-562-2646
techsupport@pinnaclefoods.com
Potato and tortilla chips
President/CEO: David Ray
Quality Assurance Manager: John Barlage
Plant Manager: Leroy Pennekamp
Number Employees: 100-249
Square Footage: 280000
Parent Co: Birds Eye Foods
Type of Packaging: Consumer, Private Label, Bulk
Brands:
   Husman's

6092 Huy Fong Foods Inc
4800 Azusa Canyon Rd
Irwindale, CA 91706-1938
626-286-8328
Fax: 626-286-8522 customerservice@huyfong.com
www.huyfong.com
Chili pepper sauces and pastes
CEO: David Tran
customerservice@huyfong.com
Number Employees: 20-49

6093 Hybco USA
363 S Mission Rd
Los Angeles, CA 90033-3752
323-269-3111
Fax: 323-269-3130 Customerservice@hybco.com
www.hybco.com
Oils, rice and rice flour
President: David Kashani
Manager: Orly Kashani
orlyk126@yahoo.com
Estimated Sales: $2.5-5 Million
Number Employees: 10-19

6094 Hybread
4712 Admiralty Way
Suite 914
Marina del Ray, CA 90292
310-312-1200
info@hybread.com
hybread.com
Vegetable and whole grain bread
Managing Director: Alon Kruvi
Number of Brands: 1
Number of Products: 3
Type of Packaging: Consumer
Brands:
   HYBREAD

6095 Hyde & Hyde Inc
300 El Sobrante Rd
Corona, CA 92879-5757
951-279-5239
Fax: 951-270-3526 www.hydeandhyde.com
Condiments for the fresh-cut produce industry; custom packaging and co-packaging
President: Tim Hyde
Number Employees: 250-499
Type of Packaging: Consumer, Private Label

6096 Hyde Candy Company
1916 E Mercer Street
Seattle, WA 98112
206-322-5743
Candy
President: Alfred Hyde

6097 Hyde Park Brewing Company
4076 Albany Post Rd.
Hyde Park, NY 12538
845-229-8277
www.hydeparkbrewing.com
Lager, pilsner, ale, stout, porter
Owner: Angelo LoBianco-Barone
Year Founded: 1995
Number of Brands: 1
Number of Products: 7
Type of Packaging: Consumer, Private Label

6098 Hydroblend Limited
1801 N Elder St
Nampa, ID 83687-3079
208-467-7441
Fax: 208-318-1445
Coating for potatoes, appetizers, fish, chicken and vegetbles
President: Mike Guthrie
mguthrie@hbspecialtyfoods.com
CEO: Bill Cyr
VP Sales/Marketing: Randy Hobert
R&D: Henning Melvej
Quality Control: Joshua Bevan
Customer Service: Gay Tisdale
Purchasing Director: Matt Haines
Estimated Sales: $10-20 Million
Number Employees: 20-49
Square Footage: 110000
Type of Packaging: Bulk
Brands:
   Hb Batters
   Hb Breadings

6099 Hye Cuisine
4730 S Highland Ave
Del Rey, CA 93616-9716
559-834-3000
Fax: 559-834-5882 hyecuisine@gmail.com
www.hyecuisineinc.com
Grape leaves and roasted eggplant
President: Raffi Santikian
hyecuisine@gmail.com
Secretary: Hilda Santikian
Estimated Sales: $1 Million
Number Employees: 10-19
Square Footage: 32000
Type of Packaging: Food Service, Private Label

6100 Hye Quality Bakery
2222 Santa Clara St
Fresno, CA 93721-2921
559-445-1511
Fax: 559-445-1540 877-445-1778
info@hyequalitybakery.com
Cracker breads
President: Sammy Ganimian
sg@hyequalitybakery.com
Estimated Sales: $10-20 Million
Number Employees: 10-19
Number of Brands: 2
Type of Packaging: Food Service
Brands:
   Hye DeLites
   Hye Roller

6101 Hygeia Dairy Company
5330 Ayers St
Corpus Christi, TX 78415-2104
361-854-4561
Fax: 361-854-7267 www.deanfoods.com
Milk, chocolate milk and orange juice
Manager: Scott Mc Clarren
VP: Doug Purl
Human Resources Director: Robin Somsngyi
Year Founded: 1927
Estimated Sales: $20-50 Million
Number Employees: 45
Square Footage: 34002
Parent Co: Hygeia Dairy Company
Type of Packaging: Consumer, Food Service, Private Label, Bulk
Brands:
   Hygeia
   Super Good

6102 I Heart Keenwah
PO Box 180032
Chicago, IL 60618
www.iheartkeenwah.com
Quinoa puffs, clusters and cereal
Co-Founder & President: Sarah Chalos
Co-Founder & President: Ravi Jolly
Number of Brands: 1
Number of Products: 8
Type of Packaging: Consumer
Brands:
   I HEART KEENWAH

6103 I Heart Olive Oil
1513 SE 2nd Court
Ft Lauderdale, FL 33301-3937
954-607-1539
Fax: 954-761-1166
Olive oils and balsamic vinegars
Marketing: Beth Haralson

6104 I P Callison & Sons
2400 Callison Rd NE
Lacey, WA 98516-3154
360-412-3340
Fax: 360-412-3344
Flavours, specifically mint
President: Jim Burgett
callisons@callisons.com
Chief Financial Officer: Rick Robinson
Vice President: Jeff Johnson
Vice President, Innovation & Technology: Greg Biza
VP, Director of Global Sales: Philippe Job
Vice President, Operations: Damon Smith
Vice President, Controller: Cena Latshaw
Vice President, Purchasing: Les Toews
Number Employees: 50-99

6105 I Rice & Co Inc
11500 Roosevelt Blvd
Building D
Philadelphia, PA 19116-3080
215-673-7423
Fax: 215-673-2616 800-232-6022
amarino@iriceco.com www.iriceco.com
Syrups, flavorings, sundae toppings, fudge, bakery fillings, bases, tea blends and stabilizers.
President/CEO: Steve Kuhl
skuhl@iriceco.com
Plant Engineer/Maintenance Manager: Ashly Marchese
Estimated Sales: $20-50 Million
Number Employees: 20-49
Number of Brands: 1
Number of Products: 1000
Square Footage: 85000
Type of Packaging: Food Service, Private Label, Bulk
Brands:
   Rice's Products

6106 I'm Different Snacks
920 N Formosa Ave
Los Angeles, CA 90046
hello@imdifferentsnacks.com
imdifferentsnacks.com
Coconut clusters
CEO: Eytan Moldovan
Number of Brands: 1
Number of Products: 3
Type of Packaging: Consumer
Brands:
   I'M DIFFERENT

6107 I-Health Inc
55 Sebethe Dr
Suite 102
Cromwell, CT 06416
800-990-3476
www.i-healthinc.com
Vitamins, supplements and health food. Formerly known as Amerifit Brands.
Estimated Sales: $463 Million
Number Employees: 50-99
Parent Co: DSM
Other Locations:
   Amerifit/Strength Systems USA
   Bloomfield CT
Brands:
   Azo
   Culturelle
   Dhea
   Estroven
   Flex Able
   Sootherbs
   Vitaball
   Brainstrong
   I-Cool
   I Flex
   Ovega-3

Food Manufacturers / A-Z

6108 I. Deveau Fisheries LTD
PO Box 577
Barrington Passage, NS B0W 2J0
Canada
902-745-2877
Fax: 902-645-2211 www.ideveau.com
Live lobster.
President: Berton German
Director, Sales: Joel German
Estimated Sales: $7 Million
Number Employees: 15
Type of Packaging: Bulk

6109 ICL Performance Products
622 Emerson Road
Suite 500
St. Louis, MO 63141
800-244-6169
www.icl-perfproductslp.com
Food-grade phosphoric acid, phosphate salts and food additives
President/CEO: Charles Weidhas
VP Finance: Paul Schlessman
Contact: K Amy
amy.zuzack@icl-pplp.com
VP Operations: Terry Zerr
Number Employees: 500-999
Parent Co: ICL Holdings

6110 ICONIC Protein
San Clemente, CA 92673
www.drinkiconic.com
Protein drinks
Founder & CEO: Billy Bosch

6111 IFC Solutions
1601 E Linden Ave
Linden, NJ 07036
908-862-8810
800-875-9393
ifc-solutions.com
Specialty ingredients manufacturer
President: David Dukes
Year Founded: 1939

6112 IFM
20 West 20th Street
Suite 303
New York, NY 10011
212-229-1633
Fax: 212-898-9024 franck@ifm-usa.com
Gourmet products
Marketing: Frank Foulloy

6113 IFive Brands
P.O.Box 9134
Seattle, WA 98109-0134
206-783-2498
Fax: 206-789-1016 800-882-5615
www.peppermints.com
Fat-free and sugar free mints
Owner: Brett Canfield
Estimated Sales: $3-5 Million
Number Employees: 1-4
Brands:
　Penguin

6114 IGZU
hello@igzulife.com
igzulife.com
Bamboo leaf tea
Co-Founder & CEO: Zachary Anderson
Co-Founder & CFO: Courtney McCoy
Number of Brands: 1
Number of Products: 3
Type of Packaging: Consumer
Brands:
　IGZU

6115 II Sisters
850 Airport St Ste 9
Moss Beach, CA 94038
650-728-5613
Fax: 650-728-5611 800-282-7058
summin_t@yahoo.com
Seasoned oils, herbal vinegars
President/Owner: Sudi Taleghani
CFO: Simmin Taleghani
Estimated Sales: $1-2.5 000,000
Number Employees: 5-9
Brands:
　Ii Sisters
　Ii Sisters
　Sorrell Flavours

6116 ILHWA American Corporation
91 Terry St
Belleville, NJ 07109
973-759-1996
Fax: 973-450-0562 800-446-7364
info@ilhwana.com www.ilhwa-usa.com
Korean ginseng
President: Sang Kil Han
Warehouse Manager: Edner Louis
Estimated Sales: $2.5-5 Million
Number Employees: 1-4
Brands:
　Il Hwa

6117 IMAC
1702 N Sooner Rd
Oklahoma City, OK 73141-1222
405-424-8794
Fax: 405-424-4822 888-878-7827
Dried food, anti-caking agents, flavor extenders, soy milk and cheese cultures
President: Jim Baird
Mananager: Ed Price
Manager: Alvin Thompson
Plant Manager: Bill Armstrong
Estimated Sales: $3-5,000,000
Number Employees: 20-49
Square Footage: 80000
Parent Co: ADFAC
Type of Packaging: Private Label, Bulk

6118 IMAG Organics
1923 Record Crossing Ave
Dallas, TX 75235
817-703-2321
855-301-0400
customerservice@bluegreenagave.com
bluegreenagave.com
Organic agave and chia
Contact: Janis Lee

6119 IMO Foods
P.O.Box 236
Yarmouth, NS B5A 4B2
Canada
902-742-3519
Fax: 902-742-0908 imofoods@ns.sympatico.ca
www.imofoods.com
Canned fish
President: Sidney Hughes
Executive VP/General Manager: Phillip Le Blanc
Director Marketing: David Jollimore
Number Employees: 100-249
Parent Co: IMO Foods
Type of Packaging: Consumer, Food Service, Private Label
Other Locations:
Brands:
　Golden Treasure
　Kersen
　West Island

6120 IOE Atlanta
P.O.Box 267
Galena, MD 21635-0267
410-755-6300
Fax: 410-755-6367
Shellfish, sushi
Chairman: Charles Cully
CFO: Denise For
Number Employees: 10-19

6121 IOM Grain
974 E 100 N
Portland, IN 47371
260-726-6224
Fax: 260-726-6225 877-283-8882
info@iomgrain.com www.iomgrain.com
Non-GMO soybeans
President: Ramon Loucks
Plant Manager: Kyle Laux
Year Founded: 2003
Type of Packaging: Food Service, Private Label, Bulk

6122 IQ Juice
PO Box 1352
Bayville, NY 11709
516-864-0034
iqjuice.com
All-natural juice blends
Number of Brands: 1
Number of Products: 9
Type of Packaging: Consumer
Brands:
　iQ Juice

6123 ISF Trading
Hobson's Wharf
P.O Box 772
Portland, ME 04104
207-879-1575
Fax: 207-761-5877 isfco@aol.com
www.seaurchinmaine.com
Urchin, lobster, crab, whelk, salmon and shrimp products
Founder: Atchan Tamaki
Office Manager: Lan Gao
Estimated Sales: $20-49.9 Million
Number Employees: 120

6124 IZZE Beverage
Boulder, CO
877-476-7380
www.izze.com
Sparkling fruit juices
Co-Founder: Todd Woloson
Co-Founder: Greg Stroh
Number of Brands: 1
Number of Products: 13
Type of Packaging: Consumer
Brands:
　IZZE

6125 Ian's Natural Food
190 Fountain St
Framingham, MA 01702
508-283-1174
customerservice@iansnaturalfoods.com
www.iansnaturalfoods.com
Allergy-friendly frozen foods and snacks
Manager: Terrence Dalton
VP Marketing: Jeff Canner
Contact: Bruce Franklin
bruce.franklin@iansnaturalfoods.com
Estimated Sales: Less Than $500,000
Number Employees: 1-4
Type of Packaging: Consumer

6126 Icco Cheese Co
1 Olympic Dr
Orangeburg, NY 10962-2514
845-680-2436
Fax: 845-398-1669 johna@iccocheese.com
www.iccocheese.com
Processor, importer and exporter of grated parmesan cheese in shaker canisters and glass pet containers; processor and exporter of bread crumbs
President: Joseph V Angiolillo
icco@aol.com
Vice President: John Angiolillo
Estimated Sales: $10-15 Million
Number Employees: 50-99
Type of Packaging: Consumer, Food Service, Private Label, Bulk
Brands:
　America's Choice
　American Beauty
　Berkley & Jensen
　D'Agostino
　Dominick's
　Food Club
　Giant
　Icco Brand
　Luigi Vitelli
　Pastene
　Pathmark
　Price Chopper
　Reggano
　Ronzoni
　San Giorgio
　Shop Rite
　Splendido
　Weis

6127 Ice Chips Candy
818A 79th Ave SE
Olympia, WA 98501
866-202-6623
www.icechips.com
Sugar-free hard candy
Co-Founder: Charlotte Clary
Co-Founder: Bev Vines-Haines
Number of Brands: 1
Number of Products: 18
Type of Packaging: Consumer
Brands:
　ICE CHIPS

Food Manufacturers / A-Z

6128 Ice Cream Bowl
532 Mcintire Ave
Zanesville, OH 43701-3342
740-452-5267
Fax: 740-452-0931 www.tomsicecreambowl.com
Ice cream
Owner: William Sullivan
thebowl532@aol.com
Estimated Sales: $1-3 Million
Number Employees: 20-49
Type of Packaging: Consumer

6129 Ice Cream Club Inc
1580 High Ridge Rd
Boynton Beach, FL 33426-8724
561-731-3331
Fax: 561-731-0311 800-535-7711
info@icecreamclub.com www.icecreamclub.com
Ice cream; soft serve machines
Co-President: Marie Lawson
President, CEO: Rich Draper
SVP: Tom Jackson
Estimated Sales: D
Number Employees: 20-49
Type of Packaging: Consumer, Food Service, Private Label, Bulk

6130 Ice Cream Specialties Inc
8419 Hanley Industrial Ct
St Louis, MO 63144
314-962-2550
800-662-7550
info@northstarfrozentreats.com
www.northstarfrozentreats.com
Ice cream
Estimated Sales: $98 Million
Number Employees: 100-249
Square Footage: 250000
Parent Co: Prairie Farms Dairy
Type of Packaging: Consumer

6131 Icelandic Milk and Skyr Corporation
135 W 26th Street
2nd Floor
New York, NY 10001
212-966-6950
Fax: 646-536-8159 info@siggisdairy.com
www.siggisdairy.com
Icelandic-style yogurt
CEO: Vicky Hilmarsson
Contact: Erik Adamsen
erik.adamsen@siggisdairy.com
Number Employees: 4

6132 Icelandic Provisions
New York, NY 10017
866-991-7597
hello@icelandicprovisions.com
www.icelandicprovisions.com
Icelandic-style yogurt
President & COO: Nico Bevers
Number of Brands: 1
Number of Products: 11
Type of Packaging: Consumer
Brands:
 ICELANDIC PROVISIONS

6133 Icicle Seafoods Inc
4019 21st Ave W
Seattle, WA 98199
206-282-0988
Fax: 206-282-7222
customerservice@icicleseafoods.com
www.icicleseafoods.com
Seafoods
Year Founded: 1965
Estimated Sales: $100+ Million
Number Employees: 500-999

6134 Idaho Candy Co
412 S 8th St
Boise, ID 83702-7105
208-342-5505
Fax: 208-384-5310 800-898-6986
info@idahospud.com www.idahospud.com
Candy
President: Bob Allen
bob@idahospud.com
Quality Control Manager: Bob Riter
Estimated Sales: $1-5 Million
Number Employees: 20-49
Square Footage: 84000
Type of Packaging: Consumer, Food Service, Bulk
Brands:
 Idaho Spud
 Old Faithful
 Owyhee

6135 Idaho Frank Association Inc
391 Taylor Blvd # 180
Pleasant Hill, CA 94523-2282
925-609-8458
Fax: 925-609-9318 info@idahofrank.com
www.idahofrank.com
Dehydrated potato
President: Ednalyn Watts
ewatts@idahofrank.com
Sales Manager: Tom Paratore
Estimated Sales: $5-10 Million
Number Employees: 1-4
Type of Packaging: Food Service, Private Label, Bulk

6136 Idaho Milk Products
2249 S Tiger Dr
Jerome, ID 83338-5080
208-644-2882
Fax: 208-644-2899 www.idahomilkproducts.com
Milk cream derivatives
Number Employees: 10-19

6137 Idaho Pacific Holdings Inc
4723 E 100 N
Rigby, ID 83442-5811
208-538-6971
Fax: 208-538-5082 800-238-5503
ipc@idahopacific.com
Dehydrated potato
President/CEO: Wally Browning
wallybrowning@idahopacific.com
CFO: Baden Burt
Quality Control Manager: Paul Eatinger
VP/Sales & Marketing: Jon Schodde
VP/Operations: Todd Sutton
Plant Manager: Steve McLean
Purchasing: Brian Hart
Year Founded: 1987
Estimated Sales: $40-50 Million
Number Employees: 100-249
Type of Packaging: Food Service, Private Label, Bulk
Brands:
 Idaho-Pacific

6138 Idaho Supreme Potatoes Inc
614 E 800 N
PO Box 246
Firth, ID 83236-1112
208-346-4100
Fax: 208-346-4104 www.idahosupreme.com
Potato products
President/General Manager: Wade Chapman
CFO: Steve Prescott
sprescott@idahosupreme.com
Estimated Sales: $37.60 Million
Number Employees: 100-249
Square Footage: 100000
Type of Packaging: Consumer, Food Service, Private Label
Brands:
 Idaho Supreme

6139 Idaho Trout Company
PO Box 72
Buhl, ID 83316-0072
208-543-6444
Fax: 208-543-8476 866-878-7688
rainbowtrout@idahotrout.com
Trout
Manager: Harold Johnson
Vice President: Gregory Kaslo
Sales/Shipping: Janie Higgins
General Manager: Harold Johnson
Estimated Sales: $10-25 Million
Number Employees: 50-99
Type of Packaging: Food Service, Private Label, Bulk
Brands:
 Cold River
 Idaho's Best
 Rainbow Springs

6140 Idahoan Foods LLC
357 Constitution Way
Idaho Falls, ID 83402
800-746-7999
www.idahoan.com
Dehydrated potato products
President & CEO: Drew Facer
Year Founded: 1960
Estimated Sales: $50-99 Million
Number Employees: 500-999
Type of Packaging: Food Service, Private Label
Brands:
 Idahoan

6141 Ideal Dairy Farms
239 Vaughn Rd.
Hudson Falls, NY 12839
518-747-5059
Fax: 518-747-4869 idealdairy1@yahoo.com
www.idealdairyfarms.com
Dairy products
Owner: Kristie Sorsen
Estimated Sales: $10-20 Million
Number Employees: 20-49
Square Footage: 7500
Type of Packaging: Consumer, Food Service

6142 Ideal Distributing Company
23800 7th Place W
Bothell, WA 98021-8508
425-488-6121
Fax: 425-488-8159
Tea, coffee
Principal: John Erdman
Co-Ownr: Cathy Erdman

6143 Ideal Snacks Corp
89 Mill St
Liberty, NY 12754-2038
845-292-7000
Fax: 845-292-3100 www.idealsnacks.com
Snacks
President: Gunther Brinkman
gunther.brinkman@idealsnacks.com
Director of Operations: LJ Goldstock
Estimated Sales: $3-5 Million
Number Employees: 100-249

6144 Il Gelato
2451 46th Street
Astoria, NY 11103-1007
718-937-3033
Fax: 718-786-5543 800-899-9299
Baked goods, gelato and individual desserts
President: Dimitri Pauli
Estimated Sales: $142,000
Number Employees: 30

6145 Il Giardino Del Dolce Inc
2859 N Harlem Ave
Chicago, IL 60707-1638
773-889-2388
Fax: 773-889-5990 info@IlGiardinoDelDolce.com
www.ilgiardinodeldolce.com
Cannoli shells, mini pasteries, butter cookies and cakes
Owner: Maria Ventrella
ilgiardinodeldolce@gmail.com
Estimated Sales: Less than $500,000
Number Employees: 10-19
Type of Packaging: Consumer
Brands:
 Giardino

6146 Illes Seasonings & Flavors
2200 Luna Rd
Suite 120
Carrollton, TX 75006-6559
214-689-1300
800-683-4553
info@illesfoods.com www.illesfoods.com
Dry and liquid flavor solutions
Owner: Cristin Kahale
cristin@illesseasonings.com
CEO: Rick Illes
Estimated Sales: $28 Million
Number Employees: 50-99
Type of Packaging: Consumer, Food Service, Private Label

6147 Illy Espresso of the Americas
15455 N Greenway Hayden Loop
Scottsdale, AZ 85260-1611
480-951-4074
Fax: 480-483-8631 877-469-4559
info@illyusa.com www.illyusa.com
Espresso pods
Contact: Stefano Ripamonti
sripamonti@illyusa.com

Food Manufacturers / A-Z

Estimated Sales: $20-50 Million
Number Employees: 20-49

6148 Illy caffe
800 Westchester Ave
Suite S440
Rye Brook, NY 10573
914-253-4500
Fax: 914-253-4580 www.illy.com
Coffee
President & CEO: Greg Fea
Year Founded: 1933

6149 Imaex Trading Company
65 Crestridge Drive
Suwanee, GA 30024
678-541-0234
Fax: 678-541-0422 info@imaextrading.com
www.imaexseafoods.com
Frozen seafood products
CEO: Seng Angkawijana
pmulyadi@adfoods.com

6150 Imagine Chocolate
2416 W. Victory Blvd.
Suite 225
Burnank, CA 91506
916-837-5772
www.imaginechocolate.net
Chocolates
Founder and CEO: Mitch Koulouris
VP of Marketing: Randy Gordon
Brands:
  Imagine Chocolate

6151 Imagine Foods
4600 Sleepytime Drive
Boulder, CO 80301
800-434-4246
www.imaginefoods.com
Organic soups, broths, stocks, sauces and gravies.
President/CEO: Irwin Simon
EVP/CFO: Stephen Smith
COO: James Meiers
Estimated Sales: $20-50 Million
Number Employees: 130
Number of Brands: 1
Parent Co: Hain Celestial Group
Type of Packaging: Consumer, Food Service
Brands:
  Imagine Natural Creations

6152 Imani Chimani Chocolate
74 Georgia Ave
Brooklyn, NY 11207-2402
718-484-1011
www.imanichocolatiers.com
Chocolate products and crackers
President and Founder: Ramin Imani
general@imanichocolateer.com
Estimated Sales: Less Than $500,000
Number Employees: 1-4

6153 Imlak'esh Organics
6336 Lindmar Dr
Goleta, CA 93117
805-689-2269
connect@imlakeshorganics.com
imlakeshorganics.com
Cacao nibs, powders, wafers and clusters
Number of Brands: 1
Number of Products: 12
Type of Packaging: Consumer
Brands:
  IMLAK'ESH ORGANICS

6154 Immaculate Baking Company
333 North Avenue
Wakefield, MA 01880
828-696-1655
Fax: 828-696-1663 828-826-6567
info@immaculatebaking.com
www.immaculatebaking.com
Cookies
Owner: Scott Blackwell
blackwell@immaculatebaking.com

6155 Immaculate Consumption
933 Main Street
Columbia, SC 29201
803-799-9053
Fax: 828-696-1663 828-826-6567
Bakes goods, cookies, scones, biscotti, and mojos
President/CEO: Scott Blackwell
Vice President: Caroline Blackwell
VP Sales: Don Porter
Estimated Sales: Under $1 Million
Number Employees: 10-19
Number of Brands: 1
Number of Products: 29
Square Footage: 40000
Type of Packaging: Consumer, Food Service, Private Label
Brands:
  Immaculate Consumption

6156 Immordl
San Clemente, CA 92673
844-466-6735
iam@immordl.com immordl.com
Coffee-based superfood energy drink
Co-Founder: Scott Holmes
Number of Brands: 1
Number of Products: 1
Type of Packaging: Consumer
Brands:
  IMMORDL

6157 Immu Dyne Inc
7453 Empire Dr # 300
Florence, KY 41042-2944
859-746-8772
Fax: 859-746-8772 888-246-6839
info@immudyne.com www.immudyne.com
Natural dietary supplements
President & CEO: Mark McLaughlin
markmcl@immudyne.com
Chairman: Anthony Bruzzese
VP: Alfred Munoz
Estimated Sales: Less Than $500,000
Number Employees: 1-4
Type of Packaging: Consumer, Food Service, Bulk

6158 Impact Confections
4017 Whitney St.
Janesville, WI 53546
608-208-1100
800-535-4401
info@impactconfections.com
www.impactconfections.com
Confectionery products
Founder/President: Brad Baker
CEO: Gary Viljoen
CFO: Rick Weina
Quality Manager: Dave Batchelder
Director Marketing: Jenny Doan
Contact: Andy Telatnik
atelatnik@impactconfections.com
Chief Operating Officer: George Wilson
Year Founded: 1981
Estimated Sales: $25-49.9 Million
Number Employees: 20-49
Number of Products: 40
Type of Packaging: Consumer
Brands:
  Alien Pop
  Alien Poppin' Pops
  Carousel Pop
  Color Blaster
  Glow Pop
  Happy Heart Lollipops
  Hoppin' Pops
  Lilliday Pops
  Lollipop Paint Shop
  Pop-A-Bear
  Soccer Pops

6159 Imperial Flavors Beverage Co
6300 W Douglas Ave
Milwaukee, WI 53218-1551
414-536-7788
Fax: 414-536-7730 info@imperialflavors.com
www.imperialflavors.com
Juice and soda concentrates
President: Jack Pettigrew
Manager: Don Kosak
kosak@imperialflavors.com
Estimated Sales: $10-20 Million
Number Employees: 10-19
Square Footage: 36000
Type of Packaging: Consumer, Food Service, Private Label, Bulk
Brands:
  Captain Jack's
  Fruit N' Juice
  Juice Plus
  Juicy Orange
  Milwaukee Seltzer Company
  Tropics

6160 Imperial Foods, Inc.
5014 39th St
Long Island City, NY 11104
718-784-3400
Fax: 718-361-7993
Dairy products
General Manager: Charles Mikhitarian
Estimated Sales: $2.5-5 Million
Number Employees: 10-19
Square Footage: 16000
Brands:
  Greenfield
  Victor's

6161 Imperial Nougat Co
12035 Slauson Ave # C
Santa Fe Springs, CA 90670-8537
562-693-8423
Fax: 562-945-8852
Candy
President: Al Maghsoudi
imperialnougat@yahoo.com
Estimated Sales: $2.5-5 000,000
Number Employees: 5-9

6162 Imperial Salmon House
1632 Franklin Street
Vancouver, BC V5L 1P4
Canada
604-251-1114
Fax: 604-251-3177
Smoked salmon
President: Robert Blair
Number Employees: 5-9
Type of Packaging: Consumer, Food Service, Bulk

6163 Imperial Sensus
PO Box 9
Sugar Land, TX 77487-0009
281-490-9522
Fax: 281-490-9615 www.imperialsugarland.com
Inulin natural extract
VP Sales/Marketing: Sally Brain
VP of Technical Affairs: Bryan Tungland
Parent Co: Johnson Development Group
Type of Packaging: Food Service, Bulk
Brands:
  Frutafit
  Nutralin

6164 Imperial Sugar Company
3 Sugar Creek Center Blvd.
Suite 500
Sugar Land, TX 77478
800-727-8427
www.imperialsugar.com
Sugar.
President/CEO: John Sheptor
Year Founded: 1843
Estimated Sales: $848 Million
Number Employees: 530
Number of Brands: 5
Parent Co: Louis Dreyfus Holding BV
Brands:
  Dixie Crystals®
  Imperial Sugar®
  Holly Sugar®
  Steviacane®
  Savannah Gold®

6165 Impossible Foods
Redwood City, CA 94063
855-877-6365
hello@impossiblefoods.com impossiblefoods.com
Plant-based meat alternative
Founder & CEO: Patrick Brown
Year Founded: 2011
Type of Packaging: Food Service

6166 Impromtu Gourmet
10711 Red Run Blvd
Ste 113
Owings Mills, MD 21117
212-475-4640
Fax: 800-858-6547 877-632-5766
www.impromptugourmet.com
Fresh gourmet foods
Founder/CEO: Max Polaner
Contact: Laura Mcmanus
info@impromptugourmet.com

Food Manufacturers / A-Z

6167 Improper Goods
16313 NE Cameron Blvd
Portland, OR 97230
503-662-7147
impropergoods.com
Cocktail bitters and syrups
Founder & President: Dan Brazelton
VP: Dylan Myers
Founder & CMO: Genevieve Brazelton
Number of Brands: 2
Number of Products: 18
Type of Packaging: Consumer
Brands:
    THE BITTER HOUSEWIFE
    RAFT

6168 Improved Nature
101 Vandora Springs Rd
Gardner, NC 27529
www.improvednature.com
Plant-based meat substitute
Sales: Larry Yates
Number of Brands: 1
Number of Products: 2
Type of Packaging: Consumer
Brands:
    IMPROVED MEAT
    PRIME PRO TEX

6169 Imuraya USA
2502 Barranca Pkwy
Irvine, CA 92606
949-251-9205
info@imuraya-usa.com
www.imuraya-usa.com
Japanese-style desserts
VP: Shin Imura
Number of Brands: 1
Number of Products: 11
Type of Packaging: Consumer

6170 Imus Ranch Foods
16 West Ave
Darien, CT 06820-4401
505-892-0883
Fax: 631-758-8360 888-284-4687
service@imusranchfoods.com
www.imusranchfoods.com
Tortilla chips, salsa and coffee
President: Don Imus
Chief Financial Officer: John Imus
Number Employees: 2
Type of Packaging: Consumer, Food Service
Brands:
    Fred Imus Southwest
    Fred Imus Turquoise
    Imus Brothers Coffee

6171 In Harvest Inc
1012 Paul Bunyan Dr SE
PO Box 428
Bemidji, MN 56601-3447
218-751-8500
Fax: 218-751-8519 800-346-7032
www.indianharvest.com
Beans, grains, pastas and specialty rice blends
CIO/CTO: Mary Dickey
m.dickey@inharvest.com
CFO: Jeffrey Buelow
Director, Sales: Jeff Lande
Director, Culinary Development: Michael Holleman
Estimated Sales: $20-50 Million
Number Employees: 10-19
Number of Brands: 2
Type of Packaging: Consumer, Food Service, Private Label, Bulk
Brands:
    InHarvest
    KAMUT®

6172 In The Raw
2 Cumberland St
Brooklyn, NY 11205
800-611-7434
www.intheraw.com
Sweeteners
Founder: Marvin Eisenstadt
Year Founded: 1956
Number of Brands: 1
Number of Products: 7
Type of Packaging: Consumer
Brands:
    IN THE RAW

6173 Inbalance Health
739 S Main St
Wayland, MI 49348-1320
269-792-1977
Fax: 269-792-1988
Health bars and supplements
CFO and COO: Lowell Johnson
Marketing and PR Lead: Nichole Allen
nallen@inbalancehealthcorp.com
Number Employees: 5-9

6174 Inca Gold Organics
21 Muir Dr
Scarborough, ON M1M 3B5
Canada
416-264-4622
info@incagoldorganics.com
incagoldorganics.com
Organic quinoa seeds, flakes, flour and snacks; chia seeds; maca products
President/Owner: Juana Garcia
Operations: Henry Falcon

6175 Incredible Cheesecake
3161 Adams Ave
San Diego, CA 92116-1638
619-563-9722
Fax: 619-563-1022
theincrediblecheese@yahoo.com
Frozen cheesecakes
Owner: Heladio Santiego
hsantiego@incrediblecheesecake.net
Estimated Sales: Less Than $500,000
Number Employees: 1-4
Square Footage: 14000

6176 Incredible Foods
75 Sprague St
Boston, MA 02136
857-345-9870
www.perfectlyfree.com
Non-dairy frozen desserts
Founder: David Edwards
Brands:
    perfectly free

6177 Indel Food Products Inc
9515 Plaza Cir
El Paso, TX 79927-2005
915-590-5914
Fax: 915-590-5913 800-472-0159
gustavo@indelfoods.net www.indelfoods.net
Jalapenos and salsa
President: Gustavo Deandar
Estimated Sales: $2.5-5 Million
Number Employees: 5-9
Parent Co: Agroindustrias Deandar
Type of Packaging: Consumer, Food Service, Private Label, Bulk
Brands:
    Del Sol

6178 Indena USA Inc
811 1st Ave
Seattle, WA 98104-1457
206-340-0863
Fax: 206-340-0863 greg@indenausa.com
www.indena.com
Herbal extracts
President: Biagio D. Beffa
Managing Director: Luca Giorgetti
Marketing Director: Christian Artaria
VP Sales: Greg Ris
Contact: Carlo Aloni
carlo.aloni@indena.com
Director of Purchasing: Giulio Simoni
Estimated Sales: $1-2.5 Million
Number Employees: 1-4
Parent Co: Indena S.p.A.
Type of Packaging: Bulk

6179 Independent Bakers Association
1223 Potomac St NW
Washington, DC 20007-3212
202-333-8190
Fax: 202-337-3809
Baked goods
President: Robert Pyle
VP Sales: Nicholas Pyle

6180 Independent Dairy Inc
126 N Telegraph Rd
Monroe, MI 48162-3299
734-241-6016
Fax: 734-241-1251 independentdairy@yahoo.com
Ice cream products
President: Michael Cheney
independentdairy@yahoo.com
Estimated Sales: $5-9.9,000,000
Number Employees: 50-99

6181 Independent Meat Co
2072 Orchard Dr E
Twin Falls, ID 83301-7992
208-734-9702
Fax: 208-734-9702 800-284-4626
info@salmoncreekfarms.com
www.independentmeat.com
Pork, hotdogs, bacon, and other cooked and cured meat products
President: Rob Stephens
CEO: Patrick Florence
patrick@fallsbrand.com
Plant Operations Manager: Chris Schmahl
Purchasing Manager: Phillip Burgoyne
Year Founded: 1904
Estimated Sales: $43 Million
Number Employees: 250-499
Type of Packaging: Consumer

6182 Independent Packers Corporation
2001 W Garfield St
C102
Seattle, WA 98119
206-285-6000
Fax: 206-285-9236
Fresh and frozen seafood including crab, cod, halibut, salmon and tuna
President: Jeffery Buske
Contact: Tammy Findlay
tammy@bbaybrewery.com
Estimated Sales: $3-5 Million
Number Employees: 100-249
Square Footage: 60000
Type of Packaging: Food Service, Private Label

6183 India's Rasoi
25 N Euclid Ave
St Louis, MO 63108-1445
314-361-6911
Fax: 314-727-8331 harinder@rasoi.com
www.rasoi.com
Indian specialties
President: Harinder Singh
harinder@rasoi.com
Estimated Sales: Less Than $500,000
Number Employees: 5-9

6184 Indian Bay Frozen Foods
PO Box 160
Centreville, NL A0G 4P0
Canada
709-678-2844
Fax: 709-678-2447 ackermans@ibffinc.com
www.ibffinc.com
Blueberries, lingonberries, jams and pie fillings; fish
President: Calvin Ackerman
Estimated Sales: 2.5-5 Million
Number Employees: 20-49
Square Footage: 40000
Type of Packaging: Consumer, Private Label, Bulk
Brands:
    Ackerman's Wild

6185 Indian Foods Company, Inc.
204 Central Avenue
Suite 1
Osseo, MN 55369-1257
763-593-3000
866-331-7684
www.indianfoodsco.com
Indian specialties
Owner & President: Kavita Mehta
Estimated Sales: $74,000
Number Employees: 2
Square Footage: 8984
Brands:
    Ashoka

6186 Indian Hollow Farms
15321 Us Hwy 14
Richland Center, WI 53581
608-536-3499
800-236-3944

Food Manufacturers / A-Z

Apples and apple cider
Owner: John Symons
ihfarms@mwt.net
Estimated Sales: $1-2.5 Million
Number Employees: 5-9
Square Footage: 200000
Type of Packaging: Consumer, Food Service, Private Label, Bulk
Brands:
   Country Road
   Iddian Hollow

6187 Indian Ridge Shrimp Co
120 Doctor Hugh St Martin Dr
Chauvin, LA 70344-2723
   985-594-5869
Fax: 985-594-2168 800-594-0920
chris@pearlbrandseafood.com
www.louisianashrimpers.com
Shrimp
Owner: Andrew Blanchard
andrew_blanchard@louisianashrimpers.com
COO: Richard Fakier
Sales Manager: Daniel Babin
Estimated Sales: Less Than $500,000
Number Employees: 1-4
Square Footage: 100000
Type of Packaging: Consumer, Food Service
Brands:
   Pearl

6188 Indian River Select® LLC
7929 SW Jack James Drive
Stuart, FL 34997
   772-595-0070
Fax: 772-287-9828 888-373-7426
www.indianriverjuice.com
Orange and grapefruit juice
President: J Patrick Shirard
CEO: Clifford Burg
Contact: Marty Eskenazi
meskenazi@indianriverselect.com
Estimated Sales: $13,80,000,000
Number Employees: 82
Type of Packaging: Consumer, Food Service, Private Label
Brands:
   Indian River Select

6189 Indian Rock Vineyards
1154 Pennsylvania Gulch Rd
Murphys, CA 95247-9589
   209-728-8514
Fax: 209-728-8338 info@indianrockvineyards.com
www.indianrockvineyards.com
Wines
President: Boyd Thompson
Contact: Ed Bauer
ed@indianrockvineyards.com
Estimated Sales: $3-5 Million
Number Employees: 1-4

6190 Indian Springs Vineyards
PO Box 1450
Penn Vally, CA 95946
   530-432-3782
Fax: 530-478-0903 800-375-9311
Wines
President: David McCord
Production Manager: Julie Holmes
Estimated Sales: Under $500,000
Number Employees: 8
Type of Packaging: Private Label

6191 Indian Valley Meats
HC 52 Box 8809
Indian, AK 99540-9604
   907-653-7511
Fax: 907-653-7694 ivm@alaska.net
www.indianvalleymeats.com
Poultry, venison and fish
President: Douglas Drum
Plant Manager: Renia Drum
Estimated Sales: $2.5-5 Million
Number Employees: 10-19
Square Footage: 68000

6192 Indiana Botanic Gardens Inc
3401 W 37th Ave
Hobart, IN 46342-1751
   219-947-4040
Fax: 219-947-4148 877-909-1501
www.botanicchoice.com
Herbal products and vitamins
President: Tim Cleland
Vice President: Tammy Cleland
VP Marketing: Kelly Fuscoe
Sales Executive: Pauline Cleland
Operations Director: Cathy Bilderback
Purchasing: Greg Villaroman
Year Founded: 1910
Estimated Sales: $25 Million
Number Employees: 100-249
Square Footage: 50000

6193 Indiana Grain Company
1700 Beason St
Baltimore, MD 21230-5347
   410-685-6410
Fax: 410-685-0233
Grain and flour
President: Patrick Turner
CEO: Tom Grisafi
Number Employees: 20-49
Type of Packaging: Bulk

6194 Indiana Sugars
1145 101st St
Lemont, IL 60439-9622
   630-986-9150
Fax: 630-739-1030 john@buysugars.com
Sugar
President/COO: John Yonover
Vice President, Marketing: Scott Sievers
Contact: Tina Arteaga
tina@buysugars.com
Estimated Sales: $5-10 Million
Number Employees: 10-19

6195 Indianola Pecan House Inc
1013 Highway 82 E
Indianola, MS 38751-2327
   662-887-5420
Fax: 662-887-2906 800-541-6252
pecan@pecanhouse.com www.pecanhouse.com
Gourmet pecans, cookies and candies
Owner: Wheeler Timbs
ttimbs@pecanhouse.com
Estimated Sales: $2.5-5 Million
Number Employees: 50-99
Number of Brands: 1
Number of Products: 30
Brands:
   Wheeler's

6196 Indias House
1101 E Broadway
Columbia, MO 65201-4909
   573-817-2009
harinder@rasoi.com
Indian specialties
Owner: Balvir Singh
Estimated Sales: Less Than $500,000
Number Employees: 1-4
Parent Co: India's Rasoa

6197 Indigo Coffee Roasters
660 Riverside Dr # 1
Florence, MA 01062-2763
   413-586-4537
Fax: 413-280-0008 800-447-5450
info@indigocoffee.com www.indigocoffee.com
Coffee
President: Lourdes Tallet
Square Footage: 4000
Type of Packaging: Consumer, Food Service, Private Label, Bulk
Brands:
   Indigo

6198 Indulgent Foods
PO Box 10
Farmington, UT 84025
   801-939-9100
Fax: 801-939-9373
customerservice@indulgentfoods.com
www.indulgentfoods.com
Hot cocoa and cappuccino
Owner: David Cowley
Contact: Brad Brower
bbrower@indulgentfoods.com
Estimated Sales: $3-5 Million
Number Employees: 5-9
Type of Packaging: Consumer, Food Service
Brands:
   Cafe Tiamo

6199 Ineeka Inc
2023 W Carroll Ave Ste C263
Chicago, IL 60612
   312-733-8327
Fax: 312-277-2555
Organic teas
Contact: Sumita Goel
sumita.goel@ineeka.com
Number Employees: 5

6200 InfraReady Products Ltd.
1438 Fletcher Road
Saskatoon, SK S7M 5T2
Canada
   306-242-4950
Fax: 306-242-4213 800-510-1828
info@infrareadyproducts.com
www.infrareadyproducts.com
Cereal grains, oilseeds, pulses, ancient grains, and blends
President: Mark Pickard
Estimated Sales: $4.5 Million
Number Employees: 25
Square Footage: 79052

6201 Ingenuity Beverages
2 Cumberland St
Brooklyn, NY 11205
   800-611-7434
www.intheraw.com
Coffee products, tea products and powdered drinks
CEO: George Hou
Year Founded: 1956
Number of Brands: 1
Number of Products: 7
Type of Packaging: Consumer, Bulk

6202 Ingleby Farms
123 N Main Street
Dublin, PA 18917-2107
   215-249-1118
Fax: 215-249-3722 877-728-7277
www.peppersauces.com
Chilies, hot sauce and specialty foods
President: Carin Froehlich
Vice President: Dietrich Froehlich
Plant Manager: Hans Froehlich
Estimated Sales: $1-2.5 Million
Number Employees: 1-4
Type of Packaging: Private Label

6203 Inglenook
1991 St Helena Hwy
Rutherford, CA 94573
   707-968-1100
www.inglenook.com
Wines
Owner: Francis Ford Coppola
Owner: Eleanor Coppola
General Manager: Philippe Bascaules
Manager: Larry Stone
Estimated Sales: $10-20 Million
Number Employees: 100-249

6204 Ingles Markets
2913 US Highway 70 W
Black Mountain, NC 28711-9103
   828-669-2941
Fax: 828-669-3678
customerservice@ingles-markets.com
www.ingles-markets.com
Cakes, cookies, and deli products
President & CEO: James Lanning
CFO/Director/VP Media Relations: Ronald Freeman
Estimated Sales: $31.7 Million
Number Employees: 16,000
Other Locations:
   Dairy Manufacturing
   Asheville NC
Brands:
   Milko
   Sealtest

6205 Ingleside Vineyards
5872 Leedstown Rd
Colonial Beach, VA 22443-5424
   804-224-8687
Fax: 804-224-8573 www.inglesidevineyards.com
Wines
President: Doug Flemer
info@inglesidevineyards.com
Gift Shop Manager: Nancy Flemer
Executive Winemaker: Bill Swain
Assistant Winemaker: Maria Swain

Food Manufacturers / A-Z

6206 Ingomar Packing Co
9950 S Ingomar Grade Rd
P.O. Box 1448
Los Banos, CA 93635
209-826-9494
Fax: 209-854-6292 ingomar-sales@ingomar.com
www.ingomarpacking.com
Diced tomatoes and tomato paste
President & CEO: Greg Pruett
gregp@ingomar.com
COO: Kent Rounds
VP of Sales: William Cahill
Director of Quality Systems: John Palombi
Director of Sales: Mark Stegeman
Plant Manager: David Waggoner
Estimated Sales: $20-50 Million
Number Employees: 50-99
Square Footage: 10000
Type of Packaging: Bulk

6207 Ingredia Inc
625 Commerce Rd
Wapakoneta, OH 45895-8265
419-738-4060
Fax: 419-738-4426
Dairy ingredients
CEO: Alain Thibault
Contact: Harmony Villemin
s.cedat@idi-ingredients.com
General Manager: Benot Leclercq
Number Employees: 50-99
Parent Co: Coop Laitiere Artois Flandre

6208 Ingredient Innovations
313 NW North Shore Dr
Kansas City, MO 64151-1455
816-587-1426
Fax: 816-587-4167
roxanne@ingredientinnovations.com
www.ingredientinnovations.com
Natural dairy, chemical, fruit and meat flavors and colors; cereal ingredients
President: Roxanne Armstrong
roxanne@ingredientinnovations.com
Estimated Sales: $1-3 Million
Number Employees: 1-4

6209 Ingredient Specialties
180 West Chestnut St
Exeter, CA 93221
559-594-4380
Fax: 559-594-4689 www.ingredientspecialties.com
Distributor of food and industrial ingredients; specializes in artificial sweeteners
Director of Marketing and Sales: Bassam Faress
Estimated Sales: $1-2.5 Million
Number Employees: 9

6210 Ingredients Corp Of America
1270 Warford St
Memphis, TN 38108-3421
901-458-5003
Fax: 901-458-5009 888-242-2669
www.memphi.net
Dried beans and spices
Owner: Derenda Ica
dlandrum@memphi.net
Estimated Sales: $1 Million
Number Employees: 20-49
Square Footage: 22000
Brands:
 Barzi

6211 Ingredion Inc.
5 Westbrook Corporate Ctr.
Westchester, IL 60154
708-551-2600
Fax: 708-551-2700 800-713-0208
www.ingredion.com
Sweeteners, starches, corn syrups, glucose, and oils used in food and beverage products.
CEO: James Zallie
Executive VP/CFO: James Gray
Senior VP/General Counsel/CCO: Janet Bawcom
Senior VP/Chief Innovation Officer: Anthony Delio
COO: Robert Stefansic
Year Founded: 1906
Estimated Sales: $5.8 Billion
Number Employees: 11,000
Type of Packaging: Bulk
Brands:
 Abc Carrier
 Brewer's Crystals
 Buffalo
 Cerelose
 Enzose
 Fiberbond
 Globe
 Globe Plus
 Invertose Hfcs
 Proferm
 Royal
 Royal-T
 Stablebond
 Surebond
 Ultrabond
 Unidex

6212 Ingretec
1500 Lehman St
Lebanon, PA 17046-3337
717-273-0711
Fax: 717-273-1364 www.ingretec.com
Dairy ingredients
President: Philippe Jallon
Vice President: Valerie Crouse
Quality Control: Annabel Ries
Estimated Sales: $5 Million
Number Employees: 11-50
Number of Products: 50
Square Footage: 30000
Type of Packaging: Food Service, Bulk

6213 Initiative Foods
1117 K Street
Sanger, CA 93657
559-875-3354
Fax: 559-875-1879 www.initfoods.com
Organic baby food
President/Marketing Director: John Ypma
National Sales Director: Bill Astin
Contact: Richard Aguirre
richard@initfoods.com
Production Manager of Materials: Marvin Canales
Plant Manager: Richard Aguirre
Estimated Sales: $830,000
Number Employees: 6
Square Footage: 9970
Type of Packaging: Consumer

6214 Inka Crops
7011 Sylvan Rd
Suite B
Citrus Heights, CA 95610
916-723-1450
Fax: 916-723-1098 www.inkacrops.com
Corn, plantain, veggie and potato chips
President/Owner: John Chaloux
Type of Packaging: Consumer
Brands:
 INKA CORN
 INKA CHIPS
 INKA CROPS VEGGIE CHIPS
 INKA CROPS KETTLE CHIPS
 INKA CROPS SEEDS & NUTS

6215 Inked Organics
755 Baywood Dr
2nd Floor
Petaluma, CA 94954
info@inkedorganics.com
inkedorganics.com
Organic breads
CEO: Scott Seymour
Number of Brands: 1
Number of Products: 5
Type of Packaging: Consumer
Brands:
 INKED ORGANICS

6216 Inko's Tea
650 Executive Dr
Willowbrook, IL 60517
inkostea.com
Flavored white iced tea
President/Owner: Andy Schamisso
Number Employees: 10-19

6217 Inland Empire Foods
5425 Wilson St
Riverside, CA 92509
951-682-8222
Fax: 951-682-6275 888-452-3267
janelle@inlandempirefoods.com
www.inlandempirefoods.com
Bean and pea products
President: Mark Sterner
Contact: Sharmila Baba
sharmila@inlandempirefoods.com
Year Founded: 1985
Estimated Sales: $20-50 Million
Number Employees: 20-49

6218 Inland Products
545 N Main St
Carthage, MO 64836
417-358-4048
Fax: 417-358-7196
Animal and marine fats and oils
Vice President: Jack Sweeny
Estimated Sales: $10-20 000,000
Number Employees: 20-49

6219 (HQ)Inland Seafood Inc
1651 Montreal Cir
Atlanta, GA 30084
404-350-5850
Fax: 404-601-5539 800-883-3474
marketing@inlandseafood.com
www.inlandseafood.com
Seafood
President: Chris Rosenberger
Founder, Chief Executive Officer: Joel Knox
Executive Vice President: Robert Novotny
Safety Manager: Patricia Washington
Pomp Agency: Rodney Fund
Vice President of Sales: Stephen Musser
Chief Operating Officer: Bill Demmond
Director of Purchasing: Richard Luff
Estimated Sales: $1-3 Million
Number Employees: 100-249
Other Locations:
 Birmingham AL
 New Orleans LA
 Charlotte NC
 Inland Lobster
 S. Portland ME

6220 Inlet Salmon
PO Box 21426
Fort Lauderdale, FL 33335-1426
954-525-9777
Fish and seafood
Sales Manager: Jim Gonzalez
Parent Co: Inlet Salmon

6221 Inn Foods Inc
310 Walker St
Watsonville, CA 95076-4585
831-724-2026
Fax: 831-728-5708 800-708-7836
www.innfoods.com
Frozen vegetables, fruits, french fries, potatoes, custom blends
President & CEO: Byron Johnson
Estimated Sales: $14.2 Million
Number Employees: 100-249
Square Footage: 20000
Parent Co: VPS Companies, Inc.
Type of Packaging: Consumer, Food Service
Brands:
 Freidel's Finest
 Gold Premium
 The Inn
 Valley Pokt

6222 Inn Maid Food
PO Box 1972
Lenox, MA 01240-4972
413-637-2732
Fax: 413-499-3839
Natural foods, including multi-grain cereal, granola, sunflower seeds, trail mix, multi-grain pancake and waffle mix and sugar-free fruit syrups
President: Jane Peters
Estimated Sales: $1-2.5 Million appx.
Number Employees: 1-4
Square Footage: 8000
Type of Packaging: Consumer, Food Service, Private Label, Bulk
Brands:
 Berrylicious

Food Manufacturers / A-Z

Colonial Jacks
New Granola

6223 Inniskillin Wines
1499 Line 3
Niagra Parway
Niagara-On-The-Lake, ON L0S 1J0
Canada
905-468-2187
Fax: 905-468-5355 888-466-4754
inniskil@inniskillin.com www.inniskillin.com
Wines
President: Donald Ziraldo
VP: Karl Kaiser
Estimated Sales: $650,000
Number Employees: 20
Square Footage: 64000
Type of Packaging: Consumer, Food Service
Brands:
Inniskillin

6224 Innocent Chocolate
4360 Oakes Rd
Davie, FL 33314
800-591-0219
www.innocentchocolate.com
Chocolate
Founder: Ty Cherry
Parent Co: EarthCorp Foundation

6225 Innophos Holdings Inc.
259 Prospect Plains Rd.
Cranbury, NJ 08512
609-495-2495
Fax: 609-860-0138 www.innophos.com
Specialty ingredient solutions for food, health, and industrial markets, including phosphates, minerals, botanicals, protiens and other nutrition ingredients.
Chairman/President/CEO: Kim Ann Mink
Senior VP/CFO: Mark Feuerbach
Senior VP/CMO/CTO: Sherry Duff
Year Founded: 2004
Estimated Sales: $785 Million
Number Employees: 1,400

6226 Innova Flavors
2505 S Finley Rd # 100
Lombard, IL 60148-4867
630-928-4800
Fax: 630-928-4830 www.innovaflavors.com
Meat flavors
General Manager: Enrique Medina
emedina@innovaflavors.com
Senior Food Scientist: Jennifer Ma
Manager: Enrique Medina
emedina@innovaflavors.com
Estimated Sales: $680,000
Number Employees: 50-99
Parent Co: Griffith Laboratories

6227 Innovative Beverage Concepts
9600 Research Dr
Irvine, CA 92618-4666
949-831-8656
Fax: 949-831-2390 web@ibevconcepts.com
www.ibevconcepts.com
Oats, teas and coffees
Founder: Rich Principale
Number Employees: 10-19

6228 Innovative Fishery Products
3569 Hwy 1 Saint-Bernard St
PO Box 125
Belliveau Cove, NS B0W 1J0
Canada
902-837-5163
Fax: 902-837-5165 ifp@eastlink.ca
Fresh, frozen and salted clams, scallops, groundfish and lobster
President: Marc Blinn
CEO: Doug Bertram
VP: Victor (Allan) McGuire
Number Employees: 20-49
Square Footage: 64000
Type of Packaging: Bulk

6229 Inny's Wholesale
1068 Puuwai St
Honolulu, HI 96819-4330
808-841-3172
Fax: 808-841-1410
Seafood
President: Stanley Lum
Treasurer: Jane Lum

Estimated Sales: $3-5 Million
Number Employees: 1-4

6230 Inovata Foods
95 Spruce Street
Tillsonburg, ON N4G 5C4
Canada
519-688-3256
Fax: 519-842-4521 800-265-5731
sales@inovatafoods.com
Frozen entrees
President: Steve Parsons
Chief Financial Officer: Jason Yohemas
Chief Operating Officer: Neil Brooks
Director of Culinary Innovation: Jonathan Smid
VP Business Development: Chad Parsons
Estimated Sales: $31 Million
Number Employees: 300
Type of Packaging: Consumer, Food Service, Private Label
Brands:
Otter Valley

6231 Inshore Fisheries
PO Box 118
Middle West Pubnico, NS B0W 2M0
Canada
902-762-2522
Fax: 902-762-3464 www.inshore.ca
Fresh and frozen fish
President: Claude d'Entremont
Number Employees: 50-99
Type of Packaging: Consumer, Food Service

6232 Instant Products of America
835 S Mapleton Street
Columbus, IN 47201-7359
812-372-9100
Fax: 812-372-9132
Instant beverages, dry mixes, syrups and toppings
President: Rolf Walendy
Vice President: George Moon
Contact: Tom Behrman
tbehrman@instantproductsinc.net
Plant Manager: Mike Brannan
Estimated Sales: $10-24.9 Million
Number Employees: 50
Square Footage: 70000
Parent Co: Kruger Gmbh & Company
Type of Packaging: Consumer, Food Service, Private Label, Bulk
Brands:
Impress
Kruger

6233 (HQ)Instantwhip Foods Inc
2200 Cardigan Ave
Columbus, OH 43215-1092
614-488-2536
Fax: 614-488-0307 800-544-9447
info@instantwhipfoods.com
www.instantwhip.com
Distributor of dairy and nondairy toppings, dairy products, eggs, baked goods and desserts.
General Manager: Jim Ring
Vice President: Tom Michaelides
Square Footage: 41674
Type of Packaging: Consumer, Food Service, Private Label, Bulk
Other Locations:
Instantwhip Akron
Stow OH
Instantwhip Baltimore
Landover MD
Instantwhip Buffalo
Buffalo NY
Instantwhip Chicago
Chicago IL
Instantwhip Columbus
Grove City OH
Instantwhip Connecticut
Wallingford CT
Instantwhip Eastern New York
Binghamton NY
Instantwhip Indianapolis
Indianapolis IN
Instantwhip Minneapolis
Minneapolis MN
Instantwhip Pennsylvania
Blandon PA
Instantwhip Rochester
Rochester NY
Brands:
Instantwhip

6234 Integrative Flavors
3501 W Dunes Hwy
Michigan City, IN 46360-6717
219-879-8236
800-837-7687
www.integrativeflavors.com
Soup bases
President: Georgeann Quealy
VP: Brian Quealy
Director of Research & Development: Peter Hargarten
phargarten@integrativeflavors.com
Director of Regulatory Compliance: John True
Customer Service: Taylor Holm
Estimated Sales: $1,100,000
Number Employees: 10-19
Type of Packaging: Consumer, Food Service, Private Label, Bulk
Brands:
Cooks Delight

6235 Intense Milk
25 Anderson Rd
Buffalo, NY 14225
716-892-3156
www.intensemilk.com
Milk
Chief Executive Officer: Larry Webster
Chief Operating Officer: Joe Duscher
Year Founded: 2009
Parent Co: Upstate Niagara Cooperative Inc.
Type of Packaging: Consumer, Private Label

6236 Inter Health Nutraceuticals
5451 Industrial Way
Benicia, CA 94510-1010
707-751-2800
Fax: 707-751-2801 800-783-4636
info.benicia@lonza.com www.interhealthusa.com
Nutritional and botanical ingredients
President/CEO: Paul Dijkstra
CEO: Connelly Ann
cann@disneyconsumerproducts.com
CFO: Mary Helen Lucero
VP, Information Technologies: Fredrick Zilz
VP, International Sales: Jay Martin
COO: Navpreet Singh
Estimated Sales: $10-20 Million
Number Employees: 20-49
Number of Brands: 16
Parent Co: Lonza Group Ltd.
Type of Packaging: Private Label
Brands:
7-Keto
Aller-7
Cardiaslim
ChromeMate
L-OptiZinc
Lowat
Meratrim
OptiBerry
Protykin
Relora
Seditol
SuperCitrimax
Sytrinol
UCII
ZMA
Zychrome

6237 Inter-American Products
1240 State Ave
Cincinnati, OH 45204
513-762-4900
Fax: 513-244-3668 800-645-2233
edi@inter-americanfoods.com
www.interamericanproducts.com
Gelatins and puddings, nuts, powdered beverages, natural processed cheese, tea, extracts, peanut butter, coffee, soy sauce, steak and Worcestershire sauce, coconut, syrup, salad dressing, mayonnaise, preserves, jellies andbeverages.
Senior Marketing Manager: Jeff Pahl
Contact: Sergio Balegno
sbalegno@interamericanproducts.com
Technical Director: Terry Shamblin
Estimated Sales: Under $500,000
Number Employees: 5-9
Parent Co: Kroger Company

Food Manufacturers / A-Z

6238 Inter-Continental Imports Company
149 Louis Street
Newington, CT 06111
860-665-1101
Fax: 860-665-1085 800-424-4422
www.icaffe.com
Coffee
President/CEO: Vincent Saccuzzo
Office Manager: Lucy Pluchino
Purchasing Manager: Vincent Saccuzzo
Estimated Sales: $5-10 Million
Number Employees: 5-9
Type of Packaging: Private Label
Brands:
- Grande Italia
- Miscela Bar
- Miscela Napoli

6239 Interbake Foods
3951 Westerre Parkway
Suite 200
Richmond, VA 23233
800-221-1002
meoakley@interbake.com
Gourmet crackers and cookies.
President: Peter McLaughlin
Year Founded: 1929
Number Employees: 1000-4999
Parent Co: George Weston Ltd.
Type of Packaging: Consumer, Food Service, Private Label, Bulk
Other Locations:
- Interbake Foods
- Green Bay WI

6240 Intercorp Excelle Foods
90 Sheppard Avenue East
Suite 400
North York, ON M2N 7K5
Canada
416-226-5757
Fax: 416-226-7544 888-473-6337
Refrigerated and shelf stable sauces, marinades, dips and dressings
President: Peter Luik
Treasurer: David Sharpe
Year Founded: 1985
Estimated Sales: Under $500,000
Number Employees: 100
Square Footage: 340000
Parent Co: Heinz Canada
Type of Packaging: Consumer, Food Service
Brands:
- Excelle
- Renee's Gourmet

6241 Interfood Ingredients
777 Brickell Ave
Suite 210
Miami, FL 33131
786-953-8320
info@interfood.com
www.interfood.com
Dairy ingredients and products
Managing Director & VP: Reniers Geoffrey
Year Founded: 1970
Estimated Sales: $235 Million
Number Employees: 200
Parent Co: Interfood Holding

6242 Interfrost
349 W Commercial St
East Rochester, NY 14445-2407
585-381-0320
Fax: 585-381-1052
Frozen fruits and vegetables
VP/General Manager: Thomas Crandall
Estimated Sales: $5-10 Million
Number Employees: 5-9
Parent Co: Cobi Foods

6243 Interior Alaska Fish Processors
2400 Davis Rd
Fairbanks, AK 99701-5700
907-456-3885
Fax: 907-456-3889 800-478-3885
order@santassmokehouse.com
Salmon and salmon products
Owner: Janet McCormick
akhunt@ak.net
CEO/President: Virgil Humphenour
Vice President: Marie Mitchell
Marketing Director: Shelbie Umphenour

Estimated Sales: $2.5-5 Million
Number Employees: 10-19
Type of Packaging: Private Label, Bulk

6244 Intermex Products USA LTD
1375 Avenue S # 300
Grand Prairie, TX 75050-1293
972-660-2071
Fax: 972-660-5941 www.intermexproducts.com
Mexican dishes and sauces
President: Juan Carlos Lorenzo
j.carlos@intermexproducts.com
Treasurer: Sandy Eastep
Vice President: David Hagli
Plant Manager: Gonzalo Branch
Estimated Sales: $10-20 Million
Number Employees: 20-49
Number of Brands: 2
Brands:
- La Torre
- La Mexicanita

6245 Intermountain Canola Cargill
2300 N Yellowstone Hwy
PO Box 9300
Minneapolis, MN 55440-9300
208-522-4113
Fax: 208-522-0794 800-822-6652
www.cargill.com
Specialty canola oils
President: Erwin Kelm
Finance Executive: Joann Wages
General Manager: Ernie Unger
Manager: R Covington
Estimated Sales: $10-20 Million
Number Employees: 10-19
Parent Co: Cargill Foods
Type of Packaging: Consumer, Food Service, Bulk

6246 Intermountain Specialty Food Group
265 Plymouth Ave
Salt Lake City, UT 84115
801-977-9077
Fax: 801-977-8202 www.intermountainfood.com
Pasta, sauces, dessert mixes, dip mixes, baking mixes and soup mixes
President: Debbie Chidester
Co-Owner: Jody Chidester
Contact: Jim Hubbard
jimhubbard@intermountainfood.com
Estimated Sales: $700 Thousand
Number Employees: 13
Number of Brands: 4
Type of Packaging: Consumer, Food Service, Bulk
Other Locations:
- Intermountain Foods
- Meridian ID
Brands:
- Plentiful Pantry
- Pasta Partners
- Chidester Farms
- Zpasta

6247 International Bakers Services, Inc.
1902 N Sheridan Ave
South Bend, IN 46628-1592
574-287-7111
Fax: 574-287-7161 info@internationalbakers.com
Flavors and flavor blends
President & CEO: William Busse

6248 International Brownie
602 Middle St
East Weymouth, MA 02189
781-340-1588
Fax: 781-331-1900 800-230-1588
Gourmet brownies
President: Cindy Rice
Contact: Brownie Reese
rbrownie@internationalbrownie.com
Estimated Sales: Less than $500,000
Number Employees: 1-4
Square Footage: 6000
Brands:
- International Brownie

6249 International Casein Corporation
111 Great Neck Rd
Suite 218
Great Neck, NY 11021-5402
516-466-4363
Fax: 516-466-4365
Casein

President: Marvin Match
Number Employees: 5-9

6250 International Casings Group
4420 S Wolcott Ave
Chicago, IL 60609-3159
773-294-8996
Fax: 773-376-9292 800-825-5151
sales@casings.com www.casings.com
Sausage casings
President: Serge Atohoun
satohoun@casings.com
CFO: Bryan Schultz
VP: Eric Svendsen
Director of Sales: Jim Dunbar
Operations Manager: Jim Wilt
Estimated Sales: $10-20 Million
Number Employees: 100-249
Square Footage: 104000
Type of Packaging: Food Service
Other Locations:
- International Casings Group
- Santa Fe Springs CA
Brands:
- Nature's Best

6251 International Cheese Company
67 Mulock Avenue
Toronto, ON M6N 3C5
Canada
416-769-3547
Fax: 416-769-7153 info@internationalcheese.ca
www.internationalcheese.ca
Italian cheese
President: M Pelosi
Number Employees: 10-19
Square Footage: 39996
Type of Packaging: Consumer, Food Service

6252 International Chemical Corp
7654 Progress Cir
Melbourne, FL 32904-1655
321-952-6466
Fax: 321-952-9883 800-914-2436
95263@msn.com
www.internationalchemicalcorp.com
Processor, importer and exporter of acids including ascorbic, citric, sorbic and tartaric; also, sodium citrate, sodium ascorbate and vanillin
Owner: Bob Catroneo
rcatroneo@floridachem.com
Number Employees: 1-4
Square Footage: 200000
Type of Packaging: Private Label, Bulk
Brands:
- Ici

6253 International Coconut Corp
225 W Grand St
PO Box 3326
Elizabeth, NJ 07202-1205
908-289-1555
Fax: 908-289-1556
sales@internationalcoconut.com
Coconut
Owner: A Kaye
Vice President: Richard Kesselhaut
richard@internationalcoconut.com
Estimated Sales: $2.5-5 Million
Number Employees: 5-9
Square Footage: 46000
Type of Packaging: Consumer, Food Service, Private Label, Bulk
Brands:
- Sno-Top

6254 International Dehydrated Foods
3801 E Sunshine St
Springfield, MO 65809
417-881-7820
800-641-6509
realfood@idf.com www.idf.com
Processed meat and poultry ingredients
Founder: William Darr
CEO: Andrew Herr
Senior Director, Sales: Lou Croce
Credit Manager, Corporate Office: Debbie Thomas
Year Founded: 1982
Estimated Sales: $50 Million
Number Employees: 5-9
Number of Brands: 1
Square Footage: 6973
Type of Packaging: Bulk
Brands:
- IDF

Food Manufacturers / A-Z

6255 International Delicacies Inc
2100 Atlas Rd
Suite F
San Pablo, CA 94806-1100
510-669-2444
Fax: 510-669-2446 844-974-1030
Info@intldelicacies.com www.intldelicacies.com
Olive oils, pasta, bastoncini, cookies, panettone, pickles, balsamic vinegar, honey, infused oils, mustard, dolma, dried figs, fruit preserves, artichokes
Founder/CEO: Hossein Banejad
CFO: Ruth Banejad
VP Sales/Marketing: Maxx Sherman
Manager: Amanda Lee
amandal@intldelicacies.com
COO: Dean Wilkinson
Brands:
   Amir
   Anna's
   Audisio & Lori
   Looza
   Pan Ducale
   Rubino & Vero
   Vicenzi

6256 International Enterprises
PO Box 158
Herring Neck, NL A0G 2R0
Canada
709-628-7406
Fax: 709-628-7875
Mussels
President: Wayne Fudge
Estimated Sales: $975,000
Number Employees: 7
Type of Packaging: Consumer, Food Service, Bulk

6257 International Farmers Market
PO Box 81226
Chamblee, GA 30366-1226
770-455-1777
Fax: 770-451-7474
www.internationalfarmersmarket.com
Dairy, meats, seafood, general grocery items, poultry, blue crab, catfish, clams
Contact: Jacqui Chew
jacqui@ifusionmarketing.com

6258 International Flavors &Fragrances Inc.
521 W. 57th St.
New York, NY 10019
212-765-5500
Fax: 212-708-7132 www.iff.com
Scents and flavors.
Chairman/CEO: Andreas Fibig
Executive VP/Integration Officer: Richard O'Leary
Divisional CEO, Scent: Nicolas Mirzayantz
Divisional CEO, Taste: Matthias Haeni
Executive VP, Operations: Francisco Fortanet
Year Founded: 1889
Estimated Sales: $5.1 Billion
Number Employees: 13,600
Number of Products: 38K
Type of Packaging: Bulk

6259 International Food Packers Corporation
4691 SW 71st Avenue
Miami, FL 33155-4657
305-740-5847
Fax: 305-669-1447
Canned corned beef, frozen cooked beef and beef cuts; importer of canned fish and rice
President: Richard Spradling
Estimated Sales: $2.5-5 Million
Number Employees: 5-9
Square Footage: 12000

6260 International Food Products
150 Larkin Williams Industrial Ct
Fenton, MO 63026
800-227-8427
info@ifpc.com www.ifpc.com
Food ingredients and additives
Chairman: Fred Brown, Sr.
CEO: Clayton Brown
VP, Finance: Kathy Langan
VP, Sales & Marketing: Jamie Moritz
VP, Quality & Regulatory: Mary Ellen Rowland
VP, Manufacturing: Mark Warren
VP, Supply Chain: Jennifer Hoerchler
Year Founded: 1974
Estimated Sales: $150 Million
Number Employees: 50-200
Square Footage: 68000
Type of Packaging: Consumer, Food Service
Other Locations:
   St. Louis MO
   Joplin MO
   Kansas City MO
   Houston TX
   Dallas TX
   Laredo TX
   San Antonio TX
   Indianapolis IN
   Cleveland OH
   Denver CO
   Atlanta GA
   Spokane WA
   Plant City FL
Brands:
   Dairy House Chocolate Dairy Powder(c)
   Dairy House(c) Milk Flavors
   Dairy House(c) Stabalizers
   Dairy House(c) Vitamins
   Ingredion(c)

6261 International Foodcraft Corp
1601 E Linden Ave
Linden, NJ 07036-1508
908-862-8810
Fax: 908-862-8825 800-875-9393
info@intlfoodcraft.com www.ifc-solutions.com
Anti-stick lubricants, release agents and food color concentrates
Owner: David Dukes
ddukes@intlfoodcraft.com
Technical Director: Ted Palumbo
Estimated Sales: $2 Million
Number Employees: 10-19
Type of Packaging: Bulk
Brands:
   Coloreze
   Confecto
   Eez-Out
   Pano

6262 International Foodservice Manufacturers' Association
180 N Stetson Ave
Suite 850
Chicago, IL 60601-6766
312-540-4400
Fax: 312-540-4401 ifma@ifmaworld.com
www.ifmaworld.com
President & CEO: Larry Oberkfell
Chief Financial Officer: Jennifer Tarulis
VP, Member Value: Mike Schwartz
Marketing Director: Cassie Kupfer Norris
VP, Sales & Member Services: Anthony R DePaolo
VP, Communications: Janet Rustigan
Estimated Sales: $20-50 Million
Number Employees: 10-19

6263 International Fruit Marketing
1201 S Orlando Ave # 340
Winter Park, FL 32789-7107
407-628-1121
Fax: 407-628-1829 intlfruit@aol.com
Fruit drinks, pure concentrates and citrus purees
President/CEO: Gene Hays
CFO: Robert Keyes
Vice President: Leland Anderson
Estimated Sales: $13 Million+
Number Employees: 1-4
Parent Co: SECO & Golden 100

6264 International Glace
1616 East Lyons Avenue
Spokane, WA 99217
760-731-3220
Fax: 760-731-3221 800-884-5041
alan@internationalglace.com
Importer of ginger, brewers' yeast spread and glace fruits
Manager: Marilyn Guest
Vice President: Bill Davids
Sales Director: Alan Sipole
Estimated Sales: $1-2.5 Million
Number Employees: 1-4
Type of Packaging: Consumer, Bulk

6265 International Glatt Kosher
5600 1st Ave Ste 19
Brooklyn, NY 11220
718-630-5555
Fax: 718-921-1542
Kosher foods
President: Leib Chaimovitz
Estimated Sales: Less than $500,000
Number Employees: 1-4

6266 International Harvest Inc
606 Franklin Ave
Mt Vernon, NY 10550-4518
914-699-5600
Fax: 914-699-5626 800-277-4268
info@internationalharvest.com
www.internationalharvest.com
Dried fruits, nuts, and seeds
President: Dennis Avalos
dennis.avalos@bnymellon.com
Number Employees: 20-49

6267 International Home Foods
1633 Littleton Rd
Parsippany, NJ 07054
973-359-9920
Fax: 973-254-5473
Canned beans, peas, apples, pasta, chicken, tomato paste, chili, mustard, instant hot cereal, nonstick cooking spray and glazed popcorn
Chairman/CEO: C Dean Metropoulos
SVP/CFO: Craig Steeneck
President/COO: Lawrence Hathaway
Sales/Marketing Executive: Mike Larney
Number Employees: 100
Parent Co: ConAgra Foods
Type of Packaging: Consumer
Brands:
   Bumble Bee
   Campfire
   Campfire Marshmallows
   Captain Jac
   Chef Boyardee
   Chef Boyardee Pastas
   Clover Leaf
   Crunch 'n Munch
   Crunch'n'munch Glazed Popcorn
   Dennison
   Dennison's
   Fireside
   Franklin Crunch 'n' Munch
   Golden Touch
   Gulden's
   Iron Kettle
   Jiffy Pop
   Libby's
   Louis Kemp
   Luck's
   Luck's Beans
   Maypo
   Orleans
   Pam
   Pam Cooking Spray
   Paramount
   Ranch Style
   Ranch Style Brand Beans
   Ro*Tel
   Royal Reef
   Seafest
   Swiftwater
   Tuxedo
   Western Gold
   Wheatena

6268 International Meat Co
7107 W Grand Ave
Chicago, IL 60707
773-622-1400
Fax: 773-622-6829
www.internationalmeatcompany.com
Meat products
Owner: Victor Bomprezzi
Estimated Sales: $5-10 Million
Number Employees: 10-19
Type of Packaging: Consumer, Food Service

6269 International Noodle Co
32811 Groveland St
Madison Heights, MI 48071-1330
248-583-2479
Fax: 248-583-3004
Chinese noodle, egg roll wrapper, pasta, perogi wrapper
President: Robert Ip
Estimated Sales: $1-2.5 000,000
Number Employees: 5-9

Food Manufacturers / A-Z

6270 International Seafoods-Alaska
517 Shelikof St
P.O.Box 2997
Kodiak, AK 99615-6049
907-486-4768
Fax: 907-486-4885 info@isa-ak.com
www.isa-ak.com
Fresh or frozen fish and seafoods
Administrator: Ted Kishimoto
Estimated Sales: $4,200,000
Number Employees: 100-249
Type of Packaging: Consumer, Food Service, Private Label
Brands:
  Internation Seafood of Alaska
  Kodiak Seafood

6271 International Seafoods of Chicago
1133 W Lake St
Chicago, IL 60607-1618
312-243-2330
Fax: 312-243-1923
Seafood
President: Inkie Hong
Estimated Sales: $1,800,000
Number Employees: 5-9

6272 International Service Group
4080 Mcginnis Ferry Rd # 1403
Alpharetta, GA 30005-1774
770-518-0988
Fax: 770-518-0299
Peanuts, popcorn
President: John Kopec
j.kopec@isgnuts.com
Estimated Sales: $3-5 Million
Number Employees: 1-4
Type of Packaging: Consumer, Private Label, Bulk

6273 International SpecialtySupply
1011 Volunteer Dr
Cookeville, TN 38506-5026
931-526-1106
Fax: 931-526-8338 www.sproutnet.com
Alfalfa and bean sprouts
Owner: Robert Rust
Contact: Raymond Jones
r_cjones@me.com
Estimated Sales: Less Than $500,000
Number Employees: 1-4
Parent Co: International Specialty Supply
Type of Packaging: Consumer, Food Service, Private Label, Bulk

6274 International Spice
501 Prospect St.
Suite 111
Lakewood, NJ 08701
609-838-1717
www.zingspices.com
Herbs, rubs and spices
CEO: Noah Gross
ngross@intspice.com
Type of Packaging: Food Service, Private Label

6275 International Tea Importers
8551 Loch Lomond Dr
Pico Rivera, CA 90660
562-801-9600
Fax: 323-722-6368 877-832-5263
iti@teavendor.com www.teavendor.com
Tea
Founder: DeVan Shah
Contact: Desiree Nelson
teaconsultantd@gmail.com
Estimated Sales: $2.5-5 Million
Number Employees: 1-4

6276 International Trade Impact Inc
30 Gordon Ave
Lawrenceville, NJ 08648-1033
609-987-0550
Fax: 609-987-0252 800-223-5484
info@ititropicals.com www.ititropicals.com
Tropical juices
Owner: Gerrit Van Manen
gert@ititropicals.com
Estimated Sales: $2.5-5 Million
Number Employees: 10-19
Brands:
  Ititropicals

6277 International Trading Company
300 Portwall Street
Houston, TX 77029
713-224-5901
Fax: 713-678-1718
Importer of gourmet foods
Sales Manager: Lenny Yassie

6278 International Vitamin Corporation
500 Halls Mill Road
Freehold, NJ 07728
732-308-3000
Fax: 855-482-3291 800-666-8482
www.ivcinc.com/
Vitamin supplements, herbal products and antioxidants
Manager: Barb McCleer
Vice President, General Counsel, Secreta: Ellen Chiniara
Contact: Phillip Abbatiello
phillip.abbatiello@ivcinc.com
Number Employees: 250-499
Type of Packaging: Consumer

6279 Internatural Foods
1455 Broad Street
4th Floor
Bloomfield, NJ 07003
973-338-1499
Fax: 973-338-1485 800-225-1449
www.internaturalfoods.com
Organic and natural products
President: Peter Leiendecker
VP: Linda Palame
Contact: Linda Palame
info@internaturalfoods.com
Estimated Sales: $1-2.5 Million
Number Employees: 1-4
Type of Packaging: Private Label
Brands:
  Bio-Familia
  Bisca
  Blanchard & Blanchard
  Cafix
  Clipper
  Davinci
  Drsoy
  Eddie's
  Helwa
  Kavli
  McCann's
  Monari Federzoni
  Mount Hagen
  Mrs Leeper's
  Pero
  Pritikin
  Ryvita
  Vivani

6280 Intervest Trading Company Inc.
106 Chain Lake Drive
Halifax, NS B3S 1A8
Canada
902-425-2018
Fax: 902-420-0763 info@intervest.ca
Fresh and frozen groundfish and shellfish
President: Jeff Whitman
Year Founded: 1988
Estimated Sales: $5 Million
Number Employees: 1,000-4,999
Type of Packaging: Bulk

6281 Inverness Dairy
1631 Woiderski Rd
Cheboygan, MI 49721
231-627-4655
Fax: 231-627-4655
Milk and butter
President: David Woiderski
Estimated Sales: $5-10 000,000
Number Employees: 20-49

6282 Inviting Foods
Chicago, IL 60661
844-782-5374
makeroats.com
Overnight oatmeal
Number of Products: 3
Brands:
  Maker Overnight Oats

6283 Ipswich Ale Brewery
2 Brewery Pl
Ipswich, MA 01938-1196
978-356-3329
Fax: 450-973-1957 info@mercurybrewing.com
www.ipswichalebrewery.com
Soda and beers
President: Rob Martin
Brand Manager: John Thebeau
Sales & Event Coordinator: Mary Gormley
Brewery Operations Manager: Jim Dorau
Production Manager: Dan Lipke
Inventory Manager: Paul Gentile
Estimated Sales: Below $5 Million
Number Employees: 10-19
Type of Packaging: Consumer, Food Service
Brands:
  Blueberry Ale
  Ipswich Ale
  Stone Cat Ale

6284 Ipswich Maritime Product Company
43 Avery St
Ipswich, MA 01938
978-356-9866
Fax: 978-356-9894 www.ipswichmaritime.com
Seafood
President: Peter Maistrellis
Contact: George Delaney
gdelaney@ipswichmaritime.com
Estimated Sales: $10-20 Million
Number Employees: 10-19

6285 Ipswich Shellfish Co Inc
8 Hayward St
Ipswich, MA 01938-2012
978-356-4371
Fax: 978-356-9235 800-477-9424
www.ipswichshellfish.com
Seafood
Owner, President: Chrissi Pappas
CEO: Alexis Pappas
Controller: Lou Cellineri
VP: Alexander Pappas
Sales Manager: Michael Gagne
Director of Human Resources: Kathy Waymous
Operations Manager: Bob Butcher
General Manager: Michael Trupiano
Purchasing Director: Vito Finazzo
Estimated Sales: $22.2 Million
Number Employees: 250-499
Square Footage: 35000

6286 Ira Higdon Grocery Company
150 IGA Way
Cairo, GA 39828
229-377-1272
jdunn@irahigdongc.com
www.irahigdongc.com
Groceries and meat.
President & CEO: Larry Higdon
Vice President: Katie Higdon
Director of Sales & Marketing: Jim Dunn
Year Founded: 1909
Estimated Sales: $106.3 Million
Number Employees: 100
Square Footage: 170000

6287 Irene's Bakery & Gourmet
1746 Winchester Rd
Bensalem, PA 19020-4542
215-244-6200
www.irenesbakery.com
Baked goods
Owner: Irene Zelikovich
Estimated Sales: Less Than $500,000
Number Employees: 5-9

6288 Iris Brands
St. Louis Park, MN 55426
solero.com
Crushed fruit bars and pops
Co-Founder: Joshua Hochschuler
Brands:
  Solero

6289 Iron Horse Vineyards
9786 Ross Station Rd
Sebastopol, CA 95472-2179
707-887-1507
Fax: 707-887-1337 www.ironhorsevineyards.com
Wines

Food Manufacturers / A-Z

Co-Founder: Barry Sterling
barrys@ironhorsevineyards.com
CEO: Joy Anne Sterling
Co-Founder: Audrey Sterling
Partner/Operations Director: Laurence Sterling
Estimated Sales: $10-20 Million
Number Employees: 50-99
Type of Packaging: Private Label

6290 Ironstone Vineyards
1894 6 Mile Rd
Murphys, CA 95247-9543
209-728-1251
Fax: 209-728-1275 info@ironstonevineyards.com
www.ironstonevineyards.com
Wines
President: Stephen Kautz
skautz@ironstonevineyards.com
CEO: John Kautz
CFO: Michael Porten
Vice President: Francis Millier
Director of Operations: Bruce Rohroer
Estimated Sales: $5 Million
Number Employees: 100-249
Type of Packaging: Private Label
Brands:
 Angels Creek
 Creekside
 Delta Bay

6291 Irresistible Cookie Jar
PO Box 3230
Hayden Lake, ID 83835-3230
208-664-1261
Fax: 208-667-1347
service@irresistiblecookiejar.com
Cookie and muffin mixes, cookie cutters and decorations
President: Wanda Hall
Estimated Sales: $300,000-500,000
Number Employees: 10
Brands:
 Boyds' Kissa Bearhugs
 Mimi's Muffins
 Susan Winget

6292 Irwin Naturals
5310 Beethoven St
Los Angeles, CA 90066
888-223-1548
customersupport@irwinnaturals.com
irwinnaturals.com
CBD-infused nutritional supplements
President/Owner: Rebecca Pearman
CEO: Marc Washington

6293 Isaacson & Stein Fish Company
800 W Fulton Market
Chicago, IL 60607-1375
312-421-2444
Fax: 312-421- 432
Sushi-grade fish
President: Ben Willner
Owner: Sherwin Willner
Estimated Sales: $5-10 Million
Number Employees: 20-49

6294 Isadore A. Rapasadi & Son
PO Box 66
800 North Peterboro Road
Canastota, NY 13032
315-697-2216
Fax: 315-697-3300 800-828-7277
datudman@twcny.com
Potatoes and onions
President/CEO: Izzy Rapasadi
Sales Manager: Bob Rapasadi
Estimated Sales: F
Number Employees: 50-99
Square Footage: 180000
Type of Packaging: Bulk
Brands:
 Raps Blue Ribbon
 Stars & Stripes

6295 Ise America Inc
33335 Galena Sassafras Rd
Galena, MD 21635-1919
410-755-6300
Fax: 410-755-6367 www.iseamerica.com
Fresh eggs
Chairman: Hikonobu Ise
Manager: Larry Beck
larry-beck@iseamerica.com

Estimated Sales: $14.5 Million
Number Employees: 10-19
Square Footage: 12000
Type of Packaging: Consumer, Food Service
Other Locations:
 CMC Food, Inc
 Clark NJ
 ISE Newberry, Inc.
 Newberry SC

6296 Isernio Sausage Company
5600 7th Ave S
Seattle, WA 98108-2644
206-762-5259
Fax: 206-762-6207 888-495-8674
info@isernio.com
Pork, beef and lamb sausages
President: Frank Isernio
Contact: Greg Arend
grega@isernio.com
Estimated Sales: $2.5-5 Million
Number Employees: 20-49
Type of Packaging: Consumer, Food Service

6297 Island Aseptics
100 Hope Ave
Byesville, OH 43723-9460
740-685-2548
Fax: 740-685-6550 www.kerry.com
Beverages, including fruit juices
Controller: Sandy Smith
Human Resources: Missy Miller
Operations: Grace Lippolis
Assistant Plant Manager: John Kasinecz
Estimated Sales: $45.4 Million
Number Employees: 50-99
Square Footage: 15254
Type of Packaging: Private Label, Bulk

6298 Island Delights, Inc.
5104 Greenwich Road
Seville, OH 44273
330-769-2800
Fax: 330-769-3935 866-877-4100
acrall@islanddelights.com
www.islanddelights.com
Coconut candies
Sales: Ann Crall
Sales: Greg Miller
Estimated Sales: $5-10 Million
Number Employees: 15

6299 Island Farms Dairies Cooperative Association
2220 Dowler Place
P.O. Box 38
Victoria, BC V8W 2M1
Canada
250-360-5200
Fax: 250-360-5220 www.islandfarms.com
Dairy products
President: George Aylard
CEO: David McMillan
CFO: Eric Erikson
Quality Control: Sam Arora
Marketing: Jona De Jesus
Sales: Art Paulo
Operations: Greg Martin
Plant Manager: Al Snedden
Purchasing Director: Steve Wainwright
Number Employees: 250-499
Number of Products: 500
Type of Packaging: Consumer, Food Service, Private Label, Bulk

6300 Island Lobster
PO Box 258
Matinicus, ME 04851-0258
207-366-3937
Fax: 207-366-3380
Lobster
Owner: Marc Ames

6301 Island Marine Products
2772 Main Road
P.O. Box 40
Clarks Harbour, NS B0W 1P0
Canada
902-745-2222
Fax: 902-745-3247 islandmarine@ss.eastlink.ca
Processor and exporter of haddock, lobster and lobster meat and tuna
President: Cyril Swim

Estimated Sales: $10-20 Million
Number Employees: 15
Type of Packaging: Food Service, Bulk

6302 Island Oasis Frozen Cocktail
3400 Millington Rd.
Beloit, WI 53511
508-660-1177
Fax: 508-660-1435 800-777-4752
www.kerryfoodservice.com
Non-alcoholic beverage mixes; ice shavers and blenders
President & CEO: Gerry Behan
Marketing Director: Abhishek Trivedi
VP of Global & Strategic Accounts: Michael Walsh
Estimated Sales: $20-50 Million
Number Employees: 100-249
Number of Products: 16
Square Footage: 25000
Parent Co: Kerry Food Services
Brands:
 Sb-3x

6303 Island Princess
2846 Ualena Street
Honolulu, HI 96819
808-839-5222
Fax: 808-836-2019 866-872-8601
info@islandprincesshawaii.com
www.islandprincesshawaii.com
Gourmet snack products
President: Michael Purdy
VP: Owen Purdy
Estimated Sales: $8 Million
Number Employees: 50-99
Number of Brands: 10
Number of Products: 100
Square Footage: 48000
Type of Packaging: Consumer, Food Service, Private Label, Bulk
Brands:
 Hawaiian Princess Smoke
 Island Princess

6304 Island Scallops
5552 Island Highway W
Qualicum Beach, BC V9K 2C8
Canada
250-757-9811
Fax: 250-757-8370 www.islandscallops.com
Fresh and frozen scallops; marine research hatchery
President/CEO: Robert Saunders
R&D: Barb Bunting
Processing Manager: Lorraine Hopps
Estimated Sales: $1 Million
Number Employees: 10
Type of Packaging: Consumer, Food Service

6305 Island Seafood
32 Brook Rd
Eliot, ME 03903-1423
207-439-8508
Fax: 207-439-9945 www.islandseafoodlobster.com
Seafood
Owner: Randy Townsend
randyisf@comcast.net
Estimated Sales: $3-5 Million
Number Employees: 20-49

6306 Island Seafoods
317 Shelikof St
Kodiak, AK 99615
907-486-8575
Fax: 907-486-3007 800-355-8575
www.islandseafoods.com
Seafood
Owner: Frank Tulcich
Contact: Claudine Alokli
calokli@pacseafood.com
Estimated Sales: $5-10 Million
Number Employees: 20-49

6307 Island Snacks
7650 Stage Rd
Buena Park, CA 90621
714-994-1228
info@islandsnacksinc.com
islandsnack.com
Nuts, trail mixes, candies and Hispanic snacks
President/Owner: Alin Barak
Year Founded: 1982
Type of Packaging: Consumer

Food Manufacturers / A-Z

6308 Island Spice
1209 NW 93rd Ct
Doral, FL 33172-2838
786-473-3465
Fax: 305-207-9353 Sales@IslandSpice.com
www.islandspice.com
Dry spices and sauces
President: Lawrence Shadeed
lawrence@islandspice.com
Estimated Sales: Less Than $500,000
Number Employees: 1-4

6309 Island Spring Inc
18846 103rd Ave SW
Vashon, WA 98070
206-463-9848
Fax: 206-463-5670
Organic soy and tofu products
President: W Lukoskie
luke@islandspring.com
R&D: Suni Kim Lukoskie
Estimated Sales: $2.5-5 Million
Number Employees: 10-19
Square Footage: 16000
Type of Packaging: Consumer, Food Service, Private Label, Bulk
Brands:
　Island Spring

6310 Island Sweetwater Beverage Company
825 Lafayette Road
Bryn Mawr, PA 19010-1816
610-525-7444
Fax: 610-525-7502 www.peacemountain.com
Soft drinks, bottled waters, energy drinks; exporter of beer
President: Michael Salaman
Square Footage: 40000
Parent Co: A/S Beverage Marketing
Type of Packaging: Private Label
Brands:
　4th of July Cola
　Absolutenergy
　Activin Energy
　Beverly Hills
　Citrimax
　Citrimax-French Diet Cola
　French Paradox
　Island Sweetwater
　Jazz
　Kiwi Kola
　Nicola
　Rebound
　Sangria Cola
　Santa-Claus
　Slender
　Stampede

6311 Island Treasures Gourmet
9413 Center Point Lane
Manassas, VA 20110
703-801-4671
Fax: 703-590-8796 kcraigcgc@yahoo.com
www.islandtreasuresgourmet.com
Gourmet rum cakes
Owner: Cassandra Craig

6312 Island of the Moon Apiaries
17560 Company Road
85-B
Esparto, CA 95627
530-787-3993
Fax: 530-787-3993
Bee pollen, honey
President: Jerry Kaplan
Estimated Sales: $2.5-5 000,000
Number Employees: 1-4

6313 Isodiol
Escondido, CA 92029
855-979-6751
isodiol.com
Hemp-based beverages

6314 Issimo Food Group
PO Box 1991
La Jolla, CA 92038-1991
619-260-1900
Fax: 619-260-8400 www.issimo-group.com
Specialty chocolate candies and desserts
President/Owner: Willing Howard
Sales Manager: Kathleen Hornbacher
Estimated Sales: $1-2.5 Million
Number Employees: 20-49
Brands:
　Chef Howard's Williecake
　Ecco!
　Issimo Celebrations!
　Issimo's Creme Br-L,
　Lilycake

6315 It's It Ice Cream Co
865 Burlway Rd
Burlingame, CA 94010-1705
650-347-2122
Fax: 650-347-2703 800-345-1928
comments@itsiticecream.com
www.itsiticecream.com
Ice cream novelties
President: Charles Shamieh
comments@itsiticecream.com
Sales Executive: Charles Shamieh
Production Manager: Peter Zaru
Plant Manager: Alex McDow
Estimated Sales: $4 Million
Number Employees: 20-49
Square Footage: 68000
Brands:
　It's It

6316 Italia Foods
2365 Hammond Drive
Schaumburg, IL 60173
847-397-4479
Fax: 847-397-6817 800-747-1109
italiainc@aol.com www.italiafoods.com
Frozen pasta and sauces
President: Filippo Carabetta
fillic@aol.com
Chairman: Arsenio Carabetta
Vice President / Operations: Peter Carabetta
Vice President / Sales: Maria Carabetta
Estimated Sales: $4 Million
Number Employees: 60
Square Footage: 24000
Brands:
　Italia
　Mama Lina

6317 Italian Bakery of Virginia
205 1st St S # 205
Virginia, MN 55792-2699
218-741-3464
Fax: 218-741-2531 www.potica.com
Fresh pies
Owner: Joe Prebonich
Estimated Sales: $1-2.5 Million
Number Employees: 20-49
Type of Packaging: Consumer

6318 Italian Connection
55b W Shore Ave
Dumont, NJ 07628-2332
201-385-2226
Fax: 201-385-9026 www.italian-connection.com
Italian specialty foods
Owner: John Stracquadanio
info@italian-connection.com
Estimated Sales: Less Than $500,000
Number Employees: 1-4

6319 Italian Foods Corporation
7330 Chapel Hill Rd
Suite 102
Raleigh, NC 27607
919-341-0605
Fax: 510-868-4522 888-516-7262
sales@italianfoods.com
Pasta, sauces, spreads & toppings, oil & vinegar, rice, risotto, gnocchi, snacks, grilled vegetables, pasta express
President/Owner: Elena Lapiana
Sales: Francesca Lapiana
francesca.lapiana@italianfoods.com
Operations: Kirk Newcross

6320 Italian Gourmet Foods Canada
101-1240 Kensington Road NW
Calgary, AB T2N 3P7
Canada
403-283-5350
Fax: 403-283-3882 sales@peppinogourmet.com
www.peppinogourmet.com
Fresh pasta
President: Peter Bellusci
Type of Packaging: Consumer, Food Service

Brands:
　The Perfect Pasta

6321 Italian Peoples Bakery Inc
31 Scotch Rd
Ewing, NJ 08628-2512
609-771-1369
Fax: 609-771-1369 www.italianpeoplesbakery.com
Baked goods
Manager: Sandy Elmer
Secretary/Treasurer: Carmen Guagliardo
Manager: Carlos Camey
Estimated Sales: $.5-1 000,000
Number Employees: 10-19
Parent Co: Italian Peoples Bakery

6322 Italian Rose Garlic Products
1380 W 15th St
Suite A
Riviera Beach, FL 33404-5310
561-863-5556
Fax: 561-863-1462 800-338-8899
info@italian-rose.com www.italian-rose.com
Garlic products
President/Founder: Ken Berger
CEO: Angelo Fraggos
Marketing Director: Arthur Conlan
Estimated Sales: $30 Million
Number Employees: 100-249
Type of Packaging: Consumer, Food Service, Private Label
Brands:
　Italian Rose

6323 Itarca
1864 E 22nd St
Los Angeles, CA 90058
310-419-6433
Fax: 310-677-2782 800-747-2782
Fresh and frozen Italian pasta
President: Yvonne Smulovitz
Manager: Jascha Smulovitz
Contact: Pat Brophy
pat.brophy@freshpasta.com
Estimated Sales: $1.60 Million
Number Employees: 17

6324 Itella Foods
1622 South Gaffey St.
Suite 201
San Pedro, CA 90731
310-732-5875
info@ittellafoods.com
www.ittellafoods.com
Comfort foods including burritos, wraps, pizza, pasta, flatbreads, risotto, tartufo, biscotti, panettone, and more. Also organic, gluten free, vegan, and vegetarian options.
Owner: Salveatore Gallatti
COO: Stephanie Dieckmann
Vice President: Frank Brigulio
Estimated Sales: $20-50 Million
Number Employees: 100-249

6325 Ithaca Craft Hummus
Escondido, CA 92029
855-979-6751
info@ithacacoldcrafted.com ithacacoldcrafted.com
Cold-pressed hummus
Founder & President: Chris Kirby
Number of Products: 6
Brands:
　Ithaca Cold-Crafted

6326 Ito Cariani Sausage Company
3190 Corporate Place
Hayward, CA 94545-3916
510-887-0882
Fax: 510-887-8323 us.kompass.com/
Meat products
President: Tony Nakashima
VP Finance: Allen Shiroma
Executive VP/General Manager: Ken Kamata
VP Sales: Al Lera
Estimated Sales: $10-20 Million
Number Employees: 50-99
Square Footage: 170000
Type of Packaging: Consumer, Food Service, Private Label, Bulk
Other Locations:
　Ito Cariani Sausage Co.
　Nishinomiya
Brands:
　Cariani Italian Dry Salami
　Cariani Italian Specialty Loaves

Food Manufacturers / A-Z

6327 Ito En USA Inc
20 Jay St.
Suite 530
Brooklyn, NY 11201
808-847-4477
Fax: 808-841-4384 info@itoen-usa.com
www.itoen-usa.com
Fruit juices, sports drinks, iced tea, coffee and canned teas
President: Nadene Tomiyasu
ntomisawa@itoen.com
CEO: Yosuke Honjo
Marketing Director: Alan Pollock
Year Founded: 1987
Estimated Sales: $20-50 Million
Number Employees: 50-99
Type of Packaging: Consumer, Food Service
Brands:
    Aloha Maid
    Itoen

6328 Ivanhoe Cheese Inc
11301 Hwy 62 RR 5
Madoc, ON K0K 2K0
Canada
613-473-4269
Fax: 613-473-5016 www.ivanhoecheese.com
Cheeses
President: Bruce Kingston
Vice President: Larry Hook
Sales: Paul McKinlay
Plant Manager: Chris Spencer
Estimated Sales: $16.5 Million
Number Employees: 80
Type of Packaging: Consumer, Food Service, Private Label, Bulk
Brands:
    Ivanhoe
    Ivanhoe Classics
    Ivanhoe Fresh

6329 Iveta Gourmet Inc
2125 Delaware Ave
Suite F
Santa Cruz, CA 95060-5758
831-423-5149
Fax: 831-423-5169 iveta@iveta.com
www.iveta.com
Baked goods; jams, curds and clotted cream
Owner: John Bilanko
iveta@iveta.com
Co-Owner: Yvette Bilanko
Estimated Sales: $2.5-5 Million
Number Employees: 5-9
Brands:
    Iveta Gourmet

6330 Ivy Cottage Scone Mixes
530 Fremont Ln
S Pasadena, CA 91030
626-441-2761
Fax: 626-441-9657
Prepared mixes for scones
President: Elaine Osmond

6331 Ivy Foods
3851 E. Thunderhill Place
Phoenix, AZ 85044-6679
480-626-2025
Fax: 480-704-4116 877-223-5459
support@nutribase.com www.nutribase.com
Wheat based meat substitutes
President: Mira Blue Machlis
Estimated Sales: $2.5-5 Million
Number Employees: 1-4
Square Footage: 48000
Brands:
    Meat of Wheat

6332 Iwamoto Natto Factory
143 Hana Hwy # C
Paia, HI 96779
808-579-9935
Fax: 808-579-9933
Natto and noodles
Owner: Daryl Yamashita
Estimated Sales: $110,000
Number Employees: 1-4
Type of Packaging: Consumer, Food Service

6333 Iya Foods LLC
North Aurora, IL 60542
630-854-7107
hello@iyafoods.com
www.iyafoods.com
Sauces, powders, spices, herbs and seasonings
President/Owner: Toyin Kolawole
Type of Packaging: Bulk

6334 J & B Sausage Co Inc
100 Main
PO Box 7
Waelder, TX 78959-5329
830-788-7511
Fax: 830-788-7279 contact@jbfoods.com
Smoked sausage, bacon, ham, jerky and barbecued meat
President: Danny Janecka
CEO: Ty Ahrens
tahrens@jbfoods.com
Year Founded: 1959
Estimated Sales: $42040000
Number Employees: 250-499
Type of Packaging: Consumer, Food Service, Private Label, Bulk
Brands:
    J Bar B
    Singletree Farms
    Texas Smokehouse
    Cajun Hollar
    Chefs-In-A-Bag

6335 J & B Seafood
9301 Faith St
Coden, AL 36523-3057
251-824-4512
Fax: 251-824-1260 jbfood1979@aol.com
www.jandbseafood.com
Seafood
Owner: Raymond T. Barbour
Estimated Sales: $7.7 Million
Number Employees: 100-249

6336 J & G Poultry & Seafood
2360 Monroe Dr
Gainesville, GA 30507-7343
770-536-5540
Fax: 770-531-0829
Poultry
Manager: Bob Gregory
jgpoultry@aol.com
Manager: Bob Gregory
Estimated Sales: $10-20 Million
Number Employees: 10-19

6337 J & J Processing
2757 Lawrence 2225
Pierce City, MO 65723-8391
417-476-5451
Fax: 417-529-8273
Beef, pork and deer processing
Owner: James Etter
Number Employees: 1-4

6338 J & J Snack Foods Corp
6000 Central Hwy
Pennsauken, NJ 08109
856-665-9533
800-486-9533
consumerrelations@jjsnack.com www.jjsnack.com
Nutritional snack foods and beverages.
Chairman/CEO: Gerald Shreiber
gshreiber@jjsnack.com
President: Dan Fachner
CFO: Dennis Moore
COO: Robert Radano
Year Founded: 1971
Estimated Sales: $1.08 Billion
Number Employees: 4,200
Number of Brands: 35
Square Footage: 70000
Type of Packaging: Food Service, Private Label
Brands:
    Superpretzel
    ICEE
    Luigi's
    Tio Pepe's Churros
    The Funnel Cake Factory
    WholeFruit
    Country Home Bakery
    Slush Puppie
    Hill & Valley
    Superpretzel Bavarian
    Dutch Waffle
    Readi-Bake
    California Churros
    Mary B's
    Pretzel Fillers
    Minute Maid
    Labriola
    New Day
    Brauhaus Pretzel
    Arctic Blast
    Auntie Annie's
    PhillySwirl
    Supreme Stuffers
    Daddy Ray's
    Sour Patch Kids
    Dogsters
    Sweet Stuffers
    Federal Pretzel Baking Company
    Parrot-Ice
    Corazonas' Heartbar
    Patio
    Kim & Scott's Gourmet Pretzels
    Barq's
    Oreo Churros
    Shape Ups

6339 J & J Wall Bakery Co
8806 Fruitridge Rd
Sacramento, CA 95826-9708
916-381-1410
Fax: 916-381-6008 www.jjwallbaking.com
Frozen bread and rolls
President: Janet Wall
Year Founded: 1979
Number Employees: 50-99
Type of Packaging: Consumer

6340 J & K Ingredients
160 E 5th St
Paterson, NJ 07524-1603
973-340-8700
Fax: 973-340-4994 sales@jkingredients.net
www.jkingredients.net
Bakery ingredients
President: James Sausville
jkfoods1@aol.com
Vice President of Research & Development: Nigel Weston
Vice President of Sales & Marketing: Al Orr
Director of National Sales: Kurt Miller
Customer Service: Cheryl Tirri
General Manager: Fred Denman
Controller: Andrew Madacsi
Senior Bakery Technician: Jeremy Jones
Estimated Sales: $19.5 Million
Number Employees: 20-49
Number of Brands: 11
Brands:
    Bred-Mate
    Cake-Mate
    Milk-Free
    Vita-Ex
    Restore
    Soft Bake
    Verdi Line
    "10" Potato
    Choc-Dip
    Toptex
    Enak

6341 J & L Grain Processing
12456 Addison Ave
Riceville, IA 50466-7096
641-985-4255
Fax: 641-985-4256 800-244-9211
Grains
President/CEO: Joel Yorgey
jlgrain@omnitelcom.com
Estimated Sales: Below $5 000,000
Number Employees: 5-9

6342 J & L Seafood
13991 Shell Belt Rd
Bayou La Batre, AL 36509-2365
251-824-2371
Fax: 251-824-2371
Seafood
President: Joshua Alderman
Estimated Sales: $3-5 Million
Number Employees: 10-19

Food Manufacturers / A-Z

6343 J & M Foods Inc
9100 Frazier Pike
PO Box 250080
Little Rock, AR 72206-3894
501-663-1991
Fax: 501-663-2822 800-264-2278
info@jm-foods.com www.jm-foods.com
Flavored straws.
President: Jamie Parham
VP: Scott Thibault
Quality Control: David Hill
Director Sales/Marketing: Greg Parham
Plant Manager: David Harkey
Purchasing: Bryan Toland
Estimated Sales: $10-20 Million
Number Employees: 20-49
Type of Packaging: Private Label

6344 J & M Wholesale Meat Inc
2300 Hoover Ave
Modesto, CA 95354-3908
Canada
209-522-1248
Fax: 209-522-8834 855-522-1248
Fresh and frozen pork
President: J McCullough
Administrator Quality Control: Kevin McCullough
Sales Manager: Nannette McCullough
Number Employees: 20-49
Square Footage: 72000
Type of Packaging: Consumer, Food Service, Bulk

6345 J B & Son LTD
564 Mile Square Rd
Yonkers, NY 10701-6333
914-963-5192
Fax: 914-963-5192 www.yonkersny.gov
Specialty cheeses and pastas
President: Steven Brunetto
Sales: Steven Brunetto
Estimated Sales: $5-10 Million
Number Employees: 5-9
Square Footage: 6000
Type of Packaging: Consumer, Food Service, Private Label, Bulk

6346 J Bernard Seafood
1142 Front St
Cottonport, LA 71327
318-876-2716
Fax: 318-876-2925 www.crawfish.org
Seafood
President: James Bernard
Estimated Sales: $3.2 Million
Number Employees: 1-4

6347 J C Watson Co
201 E Main St
Parma, ID 83660
208-722-5141
Fax: 208-722-6646 nancy@soobrand.com
www.soobrand.com
Produce, including onions, apples, potatoes and plums
Owner: Jon Watson
Sales Manager: Nancy Carter
jonw@soobrand.com
Transportation Manager: Melanie Steinhaus
Number Employees: 5-9
Type of Packaging: Consumer, Food Service
Brands:
Soo

6348 J Deluca Fish Co Inc
2204 Signal Pl
San Pedro, CA 90731-7227
310-684-5180
Fax: 310-833-5285 www.jdelucafishco.com
Seafood
President/CEO: John DeLuca
Estimated Sales: $10-20 Million
Number Employees: 5-9
Number of Brands: 0
Type of Packaging: Bulk

6349 J F O'Neill & Packing Co
3120 G St
Omaha, NE 68107-1447
402-733-1200
Fax: 402-733-1724
Beef
President: Ron O'Neill
General Production Manager: Brian O'Neill

Estimated Sales: $12.2 Million
Number Employees: 50-99
Type of Packaging: Consumer, Food Service, Private Label, Bulk

6350 J Filippi Winery
12467 Baseline Rd
Rancho Cucamonga, CA 91739-9522
909-899-5755
Fax: 909-899-9196
www.sacramentalaltarwine.com
Wines
President: Joseph Filippi
josephfilippiwinery@aol.com
Vice President: Jared Filippi
Estimated Sales: $10-20 Million
Number Employees: 20-49
Number of Brands: 1
Brands:
J. Filippi

6351 J G Noble Cheese Company
6021 Etiwanda Ave
Etiwanda, CA 91739
909-899-2603
Cheeses
Partner: Bruce McBride
Partner: Mathilda McBride
Estimated Sales: $2.8 Million
Number Employees: 16

6352 J G Townsend Jr & Co
316 N Race St
P.O.Box 430
Georgetown, DE 19947-1166
302-856-2525
Fax: 302-855-0922
Frozen vegetables, including beans and peas
President: Paul Townsend
VP: John Townsend
Plant Manager: Soloman Henry
Estimated Sales: $2.5-5,000,000
Number Employees: 20-49
Type of Packaging: Consumer, Food Service
Brands:
Country Fair
Townsend

6353 J G Van Holten & Son Inc
703 W Madison St
Waterloo, WI 53594-1365
920-478-2144
Fax: 920-478-2316 800-256-0619
info@vanholtenpickles.com
www.vanholtenpickles.com
Pre-packaged pickles and relish
President: Steve Byrnes
sbyrnes@vanholtenpickles.com
President: Steve Byrnes
VP of Sales: Stef Espiritu
Operations Manager: Bruce Dorn
Estimated Sales: $7000000
Number Employees: 50-99
Type of Packaging: Consumer, Private Label, Bulk
Brands:
Big Papa
Garlic Gus
Hot Mama
Lil' Pepe
Van Holten

6354 J H Verbridge & Son Inc
6700 Lake Ave
Williamson, NY 14589-9569
315-589-2366
Fax: 315-589-7478
Frozen cherries, pineapples and strawberries
President: James Verbridge
jverbridge@jhverbridge.com
Executive VP: Gerald Verbridge
Plant Manager: Lloyd Verbridge
Estimated Sales: $1 Million
Number Employees: 20-49
Type of Packaging: Consumer, Food Service
Brands:
Big V

6355 J J Gandy's Pies Inc
3725 Alt 19 # A
Palm Harbor, FL 34683-1477
727-938-7437
Fax: 727-937-0830 ILovePies@JJGandys.com
www.jjgandys.com
Bakery items

Owner: Jeff Schmidt
ilovepies@jjgandys.com
Estimated Sales: Less Than $500,000
Number Employees: 5-9
Type of Packaging: Food Service

6356 J J Produce
4003 Seminole Pratt Whitney Rd
Loxahatchee, FL 33470-3754
561-791-1796
Fax: 561-422-9778 winston@jjproduce.com
Produce: green bell peppers, cucumbers. eggplant, red bell peppers, zucchini squash, tomatoes, and yellow crooked neck squash.
Owner: John Madden
Chief Financial Officer: Mark Campbell
Vice President: Chris Erneston
VP of Food Safety: Michael Bentel
VP of Business Development & Marketing: Brian Rayfield
VP of Sales: Kohl Brown
VP of Operations: David Beecher
Estimated Sales: $5-10 Million
Number Employees: 1-4

6357 J Lohr Vineyards & Wines
1000 Lenzen Ave
San Jose, CA 95126-2739
408-288-5057
Fax: 408-993-2276 sjwinecenter@jlohr.com
www.jlohr.com
Wines
Founder/Proprietor: Jerry Lohr
CEO: Steve Lohr
stevel@jlohr.com
VP Marketing: Cynthia Lohr
SVP Sales: Ken Lee
VP Production/Plant Manager: David Mezynski
Year Founded: 1974
Estimated Sales: $30-50 Million
Number Employees: 50-99
Type of Packaging: Private Label

6358 J M Clayton Co
108 Commerce St
PO Box 321
Cambridge, MD 21613-1862
410-228-1661
Fax: 410-221-0216 800-652-6931
info@jmclayton.com www.jmclayton.com
Chesapeake Bay blue crabs
President: John C Brooks Jr
CEO: William Brooks
bill@jmclayton.com
Estimated Sales: $3000000
Number Employees: 5-9
Square Footage: 116000
Type of Packaging: Consumer, Food Service, Private Label, Bulk
Brands:
Epicure

6359 J M Swank Co
395 Herky St
North Liberty, IA 52317-8523
319-626-3683
Fax: 319-626-3662 800-593-6375
www.jmswank.com
Food ingredients for the dairy, beverage, meat, bakery, snack, confection, ethnic and prepared foods industries
CEO: Shawn Meaney
Chief Financial Officer: Philip Garton
Senior Vice President: Paul Hillen
Vice President, Sales & Customer Service: Linda Loucks
Vice President, Operations: Reggie Hastings
Estimated Sales: $6 Million
Number Employees: 100-249
Parent Co: Conagra Brands
Other Locations:
Swank Great Lakes
Carol Stream IL
Swank South
Dallas TX
Swank West
Denver CO
Tolleson AZ
Buena Park CA
Modesto CA
Atlanta CA
Cedar Rapids IA
Iowa IA
Kansas KS
Wichita KS

Food Manufacturers / A-Z

Louisville KY
Mansfield MA

6360 J Moniz Co Inc
91 Wordell St
Fall River, MA 02721-4307
508-674-8451
Fax: 508-673-6464 www.jmoniz.com
Seafood
President/Treasurer/Clerk: John Moniz
joaomoniz@hotmail.com
Estimated Sales: $1,000,000
Number Employees: 5-9

6361 J Morgan's Confections
2665 Lincoln Ave
Ogden, UT 84401-3461
USA
801-399-3007
Fax: 801-399-3009
Caramels, truffles, fudge
Owner: Brian Squire
brians@jmorgansconfections.com
Estimated Sales: Less Than $500,000
Number Employees: 1-4

6362 J P Green Milling Co
496 E Depot St
Mocksville, NC 27028-2419
336-751-2126
Fax: 336-751-1349
Grits, feed, flour and corn meal
President: Ralph Naylor
Estimated Sales: $5-10 Million
Number Employees: 10-19

6363 J P's Shellfish Co
414 Harold L Dow Hwy
Eliot, ME 3903
207-439-6018
Fax: 207-439-7794 jpinfo@jpshellfish.com
www.jpshellfish.com
Seafood
President: John Price
jshellfish@aol.com
Sales Exec: John Price
Estimated Sales: $10-20 Million
Number Employees: 20-49

6364 J R Carlson Laboratories Inc
600 W University Dr
Arlington Heights, IL 60004
847-255-1600
888-234-5656
carlson@carlsonlabs.com www.carlsonlabs.com
Norwegian fish oils, vitamins, minerals, amino acids, special formulations and nutritional supplements.
President: Carilyn Carlson Anderson
VP, Marketing & Corporate Relations: Kirsten Carlson Cecchin
Year Founded: 1965
Estimated Sales: $24.3 Million
Number Employees: 100-249
Number of Products: 200
Square Footage: 40000
Type of Packaging: Consumer, Private Label
Brands:
  Aces
  Carlson
  E-Gems
  Key-E
  Niacin-Time
  Super-1-Daily

6365 J Rettenmaier USA LP
16369 US Highway 131 S
Schoolcraft, MI 49087-9150
269-679-2340
Fax: 269-679-2364 877-895-4099
info@jrsusa.com www.jrs.de
Researcher, developer and processor of organic fibers derived from vegetable raw materials that are used as functional additives and pulps.
Director of Administration & Controlling: Gerhard Goss
CEO: Thorsten Willmann
Director of Business Development: Curtis Rath
Director of Sales, Food Division: Dia Panzer-Biddle
Manager: Katie Bush
eyeluvme1991@yahoo.com
Estimated Sales: $12 Million
Number Employees: 50-99
Parent Co: J. Rettenmaier & Sohne GmbH & Co KG

6366 J Turner Seafood
4 Smith St
Gloucester, MA 01930-2710
978-281-8535
Fax: 978-281-1710 www.turners-seafood.com
Seafood
Contact: Peter Stark
pete@turners-seafood.com
Estimated Sales: $2,000,000
Number Employees: 5-9

6367 J W Treuth & Sons
328 Oella Ave
Catonsville, MD 21228-5499
410-747-6281
Fax: 410-465-4867 info@jwtreuth.com
www.jwtreuth.com
Meat products, fresh beef, pork, and poultry.
Co-Owner: Jason Trippet
Co-Owner: Mike Trippet
Estimated Sales: $28.1 Million
Number Employees: 50-99
Type of Packaging: Consumer, Food Service

6368 J&D's Foods
8230 5th Ave South
Suite A-1
Seattle, WA 98108
866-692-3980
www.jdfoods.net
Bacon salt

6369 J&M Food Products Co
P.O. Box 334
Deerfield, IL 60015
847-948-1290
Fax: 847-948-0468 sales@halalcertified.com
www.halalcertified.com
Shelf stable halal meals
VP: Mary Anne Jackson
Year Founded: 1991

6370 J&R Fisheries
PO Box 3302
Seward, AK 99664-3302
907-224-5584
Fax: 907-224-5572 kruzof@ak.net
www.jrfisheries.com
Seafood
Estimated Sales: $300,000-500,000
Number Employees: 1-4

6371 J. Crow Company
PO Box 172
New Ipswich, NH 03071-0172
603-878-1965
Fax: 603-878-1965 800-878-1965
jcrow@jcrow.com www.jcrow.com
Herbs, spices, essential oils and teas
Owner: Jeff Krouk
Contact: Michael Hinson
michael@mcnear.com
Estimated Sales: Less than $500,000
Number Employees: 1-4
Square Footage: 200000
Type of Packaging: Consumer
Brands:
  J. Crow's

6372 J. Fritz Winery
24691 Dutcher Creek Rd
Cloverdale, CA 95425
707-894-3389
Fax: 707-894-4781 800-418-9463
info@fritzwinery.com www.fritzwinery.com
Wines
President: Clayton Fritz
cfritz@fritzwinery.com
Winemaker: Christina Pallmann
Estimated Sales: $2.5-5 Million
Number Employees: 10-19
Brands:
  Fritz

6373 J. Matassini & Sons Fish Company
2008 N Garcia Ave
Tampa, FL 33602
813-229-0829
Fax: 813-229-7327
Fresh and frozen seafood
President: Pasquale Matassini
Estimated Sales: $1-3 Million
Number Employees: 5-9
Type of Packaging: Consumer, Food Service
Brands:
  Matassini Seafoods

6374 (HQ)J. R. Simplot Co.
PO Box 27
Boise, ID 83707-0027
208-336-2110
jrs_info@simplot.com
www.simplot.com
Food manufacturing, seed production, farming, fertilizer manufacturing and frozen-food processing.
Chairman: Scott Simplot
President/CEO: Garrett Lofto
CFO/Treasurer: Brent Moylan
VP, Manufacturing & Supply Chain: Michael Johnston
Estimated Sales: K
Number Employees: 11,000+
Number of Products: 1000
Type of Packaging: Consumer, Food Service, Private Label
Other Locations:
  J.R. Simplot Potato Processing
  Aberdeen ID
  J.R. Simplot Potato Processing
  Caldwell ID
  J.R. Simplot Potato Processing
  Grand Forks ND
  J.R. Simplot Potato Processing
  Moses Lake WA
  J.R. Simplot Potato Processing
  Nampa ID
  J.R. Simplot Potato Processing
  Othello WA
  J.R. Simplot Vegetable Processing
  West Memphis AR
Brands:
  Bent Arm Ale®
  Conquest®
  Simplot Harvest Fresh Avocados™
  RoastWorks®
  Simplot Simple Goodness™
  Simplot Classic®
  Simplot Good Grains™
  Farmhouse Originals®
  Freezefridge®
  Infinity®
  Kitchen Craft™
  Megacrunch®
  NaturalCrisp®
  Old Fashioned Way®
  SeasonedCrisp®
  Select Recipe®
  SIDEWINDERS™
  Simplot Sweets®
  Simplot Thunder Crunch®
  Simply Gold®
  Skincredibles®
  Spudsters®
  Tater Pals®
  Traditional
  True Recipe®
  Simplot Daily Pick™
  Batter Bites®
  JR Buffalos®
  Krunchie Wedges®

6375 J. Stonestreet & Sons Vineyard
7111 Highway 128
Healdsburg, CA 95448
707-473-3307
Fax: 707-433-9469 800-355-8008
info@stonestreetwines.com
www.stonestreetwines.com
Wines
President: Jess Jackson
Sales Manager: Mick Unti
Estimated Sales: $2.5-5 Million
Number Employees: 10
Brands:
  Alexander Valley
  Christopher's
  Legacy Red Wine

6376 J.A.M.B. Low Carb Distributor
4100 N Powerline Road
Suite W3
Pompano Beach, FL 33073-3065
954-917-9881
Fax: 954-917-2590 800-708-6738
Low carb and sugar free foods.
CEO: Alan Beyda

Food Manufacturers / A-Z

6377 J.B. Peel Coffee Roasters
7582 North Broadway
Red Hook, NY 12571
845-758-1792
Fax: 845-758-1814 800-231-7372
jbpeel@twcmetrobiz.com www.jbpeelcoffee.com
Gourmet coffee
President: Gil Klein
VP: Pat Klein
Estimated Sales: Less than $500,000
Number Employees: 4
Number of Products: 200
Type of Packaging: Consumer, Private Label, Bulk

6378 J.G. British Imports
15302 21st Ave E
Bradenton, FL 34212-8121
941-745-1474
Fax: 941-926-1701
www.sarasotamilitaryacademy.com
Tea
President: David Grace
CEO: Grace Sern
Manager: Felisa Choi
Estimated Sales: $100,000
Number Employees: 2
Type of Packaging: Private Label
Brands:
  Rather Jolly Tea

6379 J.M. Schneider
254 Rue Principale
Saint Anselme, QC G0R 2N0
Canada
418-885-4474
Fax: 418-885-9408 www.schneiders.ca
Beef and pork
Plant Manager: Narie Claude Lamontadne
Plant Manager: Cal Petraszko
Number Employees: 100-249
Parent Co: J.M. Schneider
Type of Packaging: Consumer, Food Service
Brands:
  Schneider

6380 J.M. Smucker Co.
1 Strawberry Ln.
Orrville, OH 44667-0280
888-550-9555
www.jmsmucker.com
Fruit spreads, juices, ice cream toppings, syrups, peanut butter and coffee.
Executive Chairman: Richard Smucker
President/CEO: Mark Smucker
mark.smucker@jmsmucker.com
Chief Legal & Compliance Officer: Jeannette Knudson
Chief Marketing & Commercial Officer: Geoff Tanner
Year Founded: 1897
Estimated Sales: $7.3 Billion
Number Employees: 7,140
Number of Brands: 40
Type of Packaging: Consumer, Food Service
Brands:
  Smucker's
  Jif
  Folgers
  Rachel Ray Nutrish
  Dunkin' Donuts
  Adams
  Caf, Bustelo
  Crisco
  Crosse & Blackwell
  Dickinson's
  Meow Mix
  Kava
  Knott's Berry Farm
  Laura Scudder's
  Milk Bone
  Medaglia D'Oro
  Natural Balance Pet Foods
  Kibbles 'n Bits
  9 Lives
  Pilon
  R.W. Knudsen
  Sahale Snacks
  Santa Cruz Organic
  Smucker's Natural
  Smucker's Toppings
  Smucker's Uncrustables
  truRoots
  Pup-Peroni
  Nature's Recipe
  Canine Carry Outs
  Gravy Train
  Milo's Kitchen
  Snausages
  Dad's
  Bick's
  Carnation
  Double Fruit
  Five Roses
  Golden Temple
  Robin Hood

6381 J.N. Bech
214 Dexter St
Elk Rapids, MI 49629
231-264-5080
Fax: 231-264-5107 800-232-4583
Mustards and barbecue glazes
President: John Bech
Office Manager: Lynn Haveman
Estimated Sales: $600000
Number Employees: 7
Type of Packaging: Consumer, Food Service, Private Label
Brands:
  Bech

6382 J.P. Sunrise Bakery
14728 119th Avenue NW
Edmonton, AB T5L 2P2
Canada
780-454-5797
Fax: 780-452-7696 office@sunrise-bakery.com
www.sunrisebakery.com
Baked goods
President: Gary Huising
Director: Tony Bron
Director: Hank Renzenbrink
Number Employees: 80
Square Footage: 120000
Type of Packaging: Consumer, Food Service

6383 J.R. Fish Company
224 Front St
Wrangell, AK 99929
907-874-2399
Fax: 907-874-2398
Seafood
President: Janell Privett
Secretary/Treasurer: William Privett

6384 J.R. Poultry
2924 Maus Road
Fults, IL 62244-1506
618-458-7194
Fax: 706-777-8690
Poultry

6385 J.R. Short Canadian Mills
70 Wickstead Avenue
Toronto, ON M4G 2B5
Canada
416-421-3463
Fax: 416-421-2876
Confectioners corn flakes, corn meal, stablized wheat bran, wheat germ and corn germ
Vice President: Alexa Norris
Parent Co: J.R. Short Milling Company

6386 J.R.'s Seafood
9908 Southwest Highway
Oak Lawn, IL 60453
708-422-4555
Fax: 914-624-0329
Seafood
President: Frank Cestro
Owner: Carlos Grijalva
Estimated Sales: $1-3 Million
Number Employees: 5-9

6387 J.S. McMillan Fisheries
12 Orwell St
North Vancouver, BC V7J 2G1
Canada
604-981-4000
Fax: 604-981-4001
Canned salmon and groundfish
President: Steve Parkhill
VP Sales: Guy Dean
Number Employees: 250-499
Parent Co: J.S. McMillan
Type of Packaging: Consumer, Food Service
Brands:
  Hywave
  J.S. McMillan
  Pinnacle
  Snow Cod

6388 J.T. Pappy's Sauce
1909 1/4 N Las Palmas Avenue
Los Angeles, CA 90068-3270
323-969-9605
Fax: 323-969-9659 saucecentral@aol.com
Sauces and marinades
Number Employees: 8
Number of Brands: 1
Number of Products: 12
Type of Packaging: Consumer, Food Service, Private Label

6389 J.W. Haywood & Sons Dairy
1449 Mccloskey Avenue
Louisville, KY 40210-1740
502-774-2311
Ice cream
Owner: Charles Haywood
Estimated Sales: $300,000-500,000
Number Employees: 9
Type of Packaging: Consumer, Food Service

6390 JBS Packing Inc
101 Houston Ave
PO Box 399
Port Arthur, TX 77640-6413
409-982-3216
Fax: 409-982-3549 jbspacking@aol.com
www.jbspackinginc.com
Fresh and frozen shellfish
CFO: Mark Leckich
National Sales Specialist: Mark Malkemus
Estimated Sales: $20-50 Million
Number Employees: 100-249
Type of Packaging: Consumer, Food Service
Brands:
  Lucky Seas
  Sea Market

6391 JBS USA LLC
1770 Promontory Cir.
Greeley, CO 80634
970-506-8000
www.jbssa.com
Beef, pork and chicken.
CEO: Andre Nogueira
CFO: Denilson Molina
Estimated Sales: $27.8 Billion
Number Employees: 78,000
Number of Brands: 17
Parent Co: JBS S.A.
Type of Packaging: Consumer
Brands:
  5 Star®
  1855®
  Chef's Exclusive®
  Aspen Ridge®
  Cedar River Farms®
  Blue Ribbon®
  Swift®
  La Herencia®
  Clear River Farms®
  Showcase®
  Certified Angus Beef®
  Pilgrim's®
  Grass Run Farms®
  Moyer®
  Four Star Beef®
  Swift Premium®

6392 JC's Midnite Salsa
PO Box 89451
Tucson, AZ 85752-9451
520-574-3993
Fax: 520-572-1151 800-817-2572
Salsa
Estimated Sales: $300,000-500,000
Number Employees: 1-4

6393 JC's Pie Pops
20436 Corisco St.
Chatsworth, CA 91311
818-349-1880
Specialty pie products
CEO: Jennifer Constantine
Brands:
  JC's pie bites
  JC's pie pops

Food Manufacturers / A-Z

6394 JD Sweid Foods
9696-199A Street
Langley, BC V1M 2X7
Canada
604-888-8662
Fax: 604-888-0074 800-665-4355
info@jdsweid.com www.jdsweid.com
Poultry and meat products
President & CEO: Blair Shier
Estimated Sales: $49.1 Million
Number Employees: 600+
Type of Packaging: Consumer, Food Service, Private Label, Bulk
Brands:
  Hampton House
  Sensations

6395 JE Bergeron & Sons
7 Rue St John Baptiste
Bromptonville, QC J0B 1H0
Canada
819-846-2761
Fax: 819-846-6217 800-567-2798
www.nuvel.ca
Shortening and margarine
President: Philippe Bergeron
Secretary: Berengere Bergeron
VP: Danielle Bergeron
Number Employees: 20-49
Square Footage: 120000
Parent Co: Margarine Thibault
Type of Packaging: Consumer, Food Service, Private Label, Bulk
Brands:
  Banquet
  Bergeron
  Canolean
  Chef Gaston
  G Blanchet
  Rexpo
  Silver
  Tradition
  Wonder

6396 JER Creative Food Concepts, Inc.
5743 Smithway St
Suite 305
Commerce, CA 90040-1549
323-721-1882
Fax: 323-721-4526 800-350-2462
Confectionery products
President: Jonathan Freed
Secretary/Treasurer: Ezekiel Freed
VP: Rose Freed
Purchasing Manager: Kit Phillips
Estimated Sales: $3.5 Million
Number Employees: 5
Square Footage: 12000
Type of Packaging: Bulk
Brands:
  Gelite
  Pectose-Standard

6397 JES Foods
4703 Broadway Ave
Cleveland, OH 44127
216-883-8987
Fax: 216-883-8984 www.jesfoods.com
Produce, including carrots, onions, celery, peppers and melons
President: Elaine R Freed
Estimated Sales: $5-10 Million
Number Employees: 10-19

6398 JF Braun & Sons Inc.
P.O.Box 6061
Elizabeth, NJ 07207
908-393-7400
Fax: 908-393-7439 800-997-7177
steve@jfbny.com www.jfbny.com
Imported dried fruits and nuts
President: Stephen O'Mara
Number Employees: 20-49
Brands:
  J.F. Braun

6399 JFG Coffee
400 Poydras Str
10th Floor
New Orleans, LA 70130
Fax: 504-539-5427 800-535-1961
service@reilyproducts.com www.jfgcoffee.com
Coffee
President & COO: Mark Reed
Estimated Sales: $100 Million
Parent Co: Reily Foods Company

6400 JJ Martin Group
Newark, NJ 07114
862-240-1813
Fax: 862-240-1812 saluttiusa.com
Aloe vera drinks
Founder & CEO: John Ra
Brands:
  Aloevine
  Salutti

6401 JJ's Tamales & Barbacoa
1611 Culebra Rd
San Antonio, TX 78201-5914
210-737-1300
Fax: 210-733-8133
Mexican foods
Manager: Gilbert Aparipio
Manager: M Rodriguez
Estimated Sales: Under $500,000
Number Employees: 1-4

6402 JK Sucralose
98-A Mayfield Avenue
Edison, NJ 08837
732-512-0889
jkusa@jksucralose.com
www.jksucralose.com
Sweetners, sucralose
General Manager: Hugh Zhang
Quality Control Director: Jianxin An
EVP of Sales & Marketing: Craig Zezima
Contact: Ye Florey
florey@jksucralose.com
Estimated Sales: $25 Million
Number Employees: 219
Number of Brands: 1
Number of Products: 1
Square Footage: 135000
Brands:
  Jk Sweet

6403 JM All Purpose Seasoning
PO Box 22162
Lincoln, NE 68542-2162
402-421-8326
Seasonings herbs and spices
Owner: James Meeks
Number Employees: 1-4

6404 JMAC Trading, Inc.
369 Van Ness Way
Suite 707
Torrance, CA 90501
310-781-9734
Fax: 310-212-6768 877-566-4569
mizuhashi@crystalnoodle.com
www.crystalnoodle.com
Instant noodle soup
President/CEO: Masaki Mizuhashi
Contact: Anthony Brown
anthonybrown@yrcfreight.com

6405 JMH International
1389 Center Dr
Suite 340
Park City, UT 84098-7660
435-645-9100
Fax: 435-645-9109 888-741-4564
info@jmhpremium.com www.jmhpremium.com
Flavor bases
President: Kirk Mellecker
Vice President: Marc Allen
marc@jmhpremium.com
Sales Director: Michael Norman
Estimated Sales: $500,000-$1 Million
Number Employees: 10-19
Type of Packaging: Consumer, Food Service, Bulk
Brands:
  Jmh Premium

6406 JMS Specialty Foods
126 Jefferson St
Ripon, WI 54971-1383
920-748-1317
Fax: 920-745-6150 800-535-5437
Bottled fruit, peanut butter, barbacue and meat sauces, dessert toppings, maple syrup, jams, jellies, preserves and condiments
Principal: David Brink
Marketing Manager: Carrie Hogan
General Manager: Ken Miller
Plant Manager: Tim Carr
Number Employees: 3
Square Footage: 240000
Parent Co: J.M. Smucker Company
Type of Packaging: Consumer, Food Service, Private Label

6407 JNB Foods, LLC
1971 Western Ave.
Suite 177
Albany, NY 12203
607-267-5874
www.jnbfoods.com
Manufacturer of chutney, relish, salsa, and pickled vegetables.
Owner: Barry Moore

6408 JR Laboratories
Smith Hill Rd
Honesdale, PA 18431
570-253-5826
www.jrlaboratories.com/
Chinese herbal products and fluids
President: Jainie Minogue
Estimated Sales: $300,000-500,000
Number Employees: 1-4

6409 JSL Foods
3550 Pasadena Ave
Los Angeles, CA 90031-1946
323-223-2484
Fax: 323-223-9882 800-745-3236
noodles@jslfoods.com www.jslfoods.com
Pre-made pastas and specialty Chinese products
Owner: Steven Aceves
President: Teiji Kawana
EVP: Koji Kawana
Research Manager: Swee Seet
Marketing Director: Brenda Oshita
VP Sales & Marketing: Wayne Nielsen
saceves@jslfoods.com
VP Operations: Jerry Kobayashi
Plant Manager: Julio Castaneda
Purchasing Manager: Gregory Yee
Estimated Sales: $22.3 Million
Number Employees: 100-249
Square Footage: 60000
Type of Packaging: Food Service, Private Label, Bulk
Brands:
  Amber Farms
  Fortune

6410 JTM Food Group
200 Sales Ave
Harrison, OH 45030
800-626-2308
www.jtmfoodgroup.com
Beef patties, buns, bread sticks, dinner rolls, French bread pizza, spaghetti and meatballs, chili, taco and barbecue sauce.
President & CEO: Tony Maas
tonymaas@jtmfoodgroup.com
Chairman: Jack Maas
CFO: Bill Meier
VP, Business Development: Jerry Maas
VP, Operations: Joseph Maas
Year Founded: 1960
Estimated Sales: $100-500 Million
Number Employees: 250-499
Square Footage: 96000
Type of Packaging: Consumer, Food Service
Brands:
  Chef Vito Pasta Meals
  Cincy Style
  J.T.M. Food Group
  Texas Jack's Tex-Mex
  Vito's Bakery

6411 JUST Inc
2000 Folsom St
San Francisco, CA 94110-1318
415-829-2325
Fax: 415-520-2156 844-423-6637
wecare@justforall.com www.ju.st
Vegan egg substitute, mayonnaise, salad dressing, cookie dough, and lab-grown meat
CEO/Co-Founder: Josh Tetrick
Co-Founder: Josh Balk
COO/CFO: Erez Simha
CTO: Peter Licari

Food Manufacturers / A-Z

Year Founded: 2011
Estimated Sales: $30 Million
Number Employees: 10-19

6412 JVM Sales Corp.
3401 A Tremley Point Rd
Linden, NJ 07036
908-862-4866
Fax: 908-862-4867 anthony@jvmsalescorp.com
jvmsales.com
Italian grated cheeses; custom blends
President & CEO: Mary Beth Tomasino
VP of Sales & Marketing: Anthony Caliendo
Estimated Sales: $2-4 Million
Square Footage: 150000
Type of Packaging: Consumer, Food Service, Private Label, Bulk
Other Locations:
JVM Sales South
Delray Beach FL

6413 Ja-Ca Seafood Products
3 Center Plaza
Boston, MA 02108-2003
978-281-8848
Fax: 978-281-2247
Seafood
President: Kenichi Kawauchi

6414 Jack & Jill Ice Cream
101 Commerce Dr
Moorestown, NJ 08057-4212
856-813-2300
Fax: 856-813-2373 info@jjicc.com
www.jjicc.com
Ice cream and frozen yogurt; cakes and fancy desserts
President: Jay Schwartz
jschwartz@jjicc.com
Founder: Mickey Schwartz
Marketing Director: Shawn Brady
VP Sales: John Corral
General Manager: Ken Schwartz
Number Employees: 500-999
Type of Packaging: Consumer, Food Service

6415 Jack Brown Produce
8035 Fruit Ridge Ave NW
Sparta, MI 49345-9758
616-887-9568
Fax: 616-887-9765 800-348-0834
info@jackbrownproduce.com
www.jackbrownproduce.com
Produce
Owner: Steve Thome
Chairman/VP: Philip Succop
Sales Exec: Mitch Brinks
mitch@jackbrownproduce.com
Operations Manager: Pat Chase
Estimated Sales: $6.5 Million
Number Employees: 20-49
Square Footage: 2000000
Type of Packaging: Consumer, Food Service, Private Label, Bulk
Brands:
Apple Ridge
Peach Ridge

6416 Jack Daniel Distillery
280 Lynchburg Hwy.
Lynchburg, TN 37352
931-759-6357
888-551-5225
www.jackdaniels.com
Whiskey.
CEO, Brown-Forman Corp.: Lawson Whiting
Year Founded: 1866
Estimated Sales: $121,700,000
Number Employees: 500+
Parent Co: Brown-Forman Corporation
Type of Packaging: Consumer
Brands:
Jack Daniel's®
Jack Daniel's Old No. 7
Jack Daniel's Tennessee Rye
Jack Daniel's Single Barrel
Jack Daniel's Gentleman Jack
Jack Daniel's Tennessee Fire
Jack Daniel's Tennessee Honey

6417 Jack Miller's Food Products
646 Jack Miller Road
Ville Platte, LA 70586
337-363-1541
Fax: 337-363-4784 800-646-1541
jackmiller@jackmillers.com www.jackmillers.com
Cajun barbecue and cocktail sauces
President/CEO: Kermit Miller
Estimated Sales: Below $5 Million
Number Employees: 5-9
Square Footage: 28000
Type of Packaging: Food Service, Bulk
Brands:
Jack Miller

6418 Jack's Bean Co LLC
402 N Interocean Ave
Holyoke, CO 80734-1000
970-854-3702
Fax: 970-854-3707
Beans and popcorn
General Manager: Steve Brown
Human Resources Manager: Henry Moore
Manufacturing/Operations Director: Rick Daniel
Estimated Sales: $10.3 Million
Number Employees: 10-19
Square Footage: 110000
Parent Co: ConAgra Foods
Type of Packaging: Consumer, Food Service, Private Label, Bulk

6419 Jack's Paleo Kitchen
Ferndale, WA 98248
Fax: 800-263-1688 www.jackfrancisfoods.com
Allergy-friendly paleo cookies
Co-Owner: Josh Francis
Co-Owner: Karissa Francis
Number of Brands: 1
Number of Products: 13
Type of Packaging: Consumer

6420 Jackfruit Company, The
5723 Arapahoe Ave
Suite 1B
Boulder, CO 80303
877-433-4024
knowjack@thejackfruitcompany.com
thejackfruitcompany.com
Organic jackfruit products
Founder: Annie Ryu
Number of Brands: 1
Number of Products: 13
Type of Packaging: Consumer, Food Service, Bulk
Brands:
THE JACKFRUIT COMPANY

6421 Jackson Brothers Food Locker
121 S Avenue H
Post, TX 79356
806-495-3245
Fax: 806-495-3741
jacksonbrothersmeat@gmail.com
www.jacksonbrothersmeat.com
Beef, pork and deer meat; slaughtering services also available
Owner: Joe Rodriguez
Co-Owner: David Hernandez
Estimated Sales: $3-5 Million
Number Employees: 5-9
Type of Packaging: Consumer

6422 Jackson Meat
13 W 6th Ave
Hutchinson, KS 67501-4650
620-259-6066
Fax: 620-259-6066 jacksonmeat@live.com
www.jacksonmeat.com
Meat products
Owner: A Bryan
Estimated Sales: $10-20 Million
Number Employees: 5-9
Type of Packaging: Consumer, Bulk

6423 Jackson's Honest
Crested Butte, CO
info@jacksonshonest.com
jacksonshonest.com
Coconut oil chips, tortillas and grain puffs
Co-Founder & CEO: Megan Reamer
Co-Founder & CFO: Scott Reamer
Operations: David McCormick
Number of Brands: 1
Number of Products: 20
Type of Packaging: Consumer

Brands:
JACKSON'S HONEST

6424 Jacob & Sons Wholesale Meats
306 Center St
PO Box 217
Martins Ferry, OH 43935-1793
740-633-3091
Fax: 740-633-3106
www.jacobandsonsqualitymeats.com
Meats and sausages
President: Michael Jacob
Estimated Sales: $1.60 Million
Number Employees: 10-19

6425 Jacob Leinenkugel Brewing Co
1 Jefferson Ave
Chippewa Falls, WI 54729-1318
715-723-5557
Fax: 715-723-7158 leinielodge@leinenkugels.com
www.leinie.com
Beers
President: Thomas Jacob Leinenkugel
Estimated Sales: $10-19 Million
Number Employees: 10-19
Parent Co: Molson Coors Brewing Company

6426 Jacob's Meats Inc
8127 N State Route 66
Defiance, OH 43512-6724
419-782-7831
Fax: 419-782-8128 www.jacobsmeats.com
Beef, pork and poultry
President: Mike Stork
jacobsmeats@bright.net
Estimated Sales: $1-3 Million
Number Employees: 5-9
Type of Packaging: Consumer, Food Service, Private Label, Bulk

6427 Jacobsen's Salt Co.
602 SE Salmon St
Portland, OR 97214
503-719-4973
jacobsensalt.com
Cooking ingredients, including sea salt, seasonings and spice blends
VP, Sales: Jody Cook
Year Founded: 2011
Type of Packaging: Consumer

6428 Jacobsmuhlen's Meats
1415 NW Susbauer Rd
Cornelius, OR 97113-6331
503-359-0479
Fax: 503-359-0479
jacobsmuhlensllc@frontier.com
Pork and beef
Owner: Larry Jacobsmuhlen
jacobesmuhlenllc@verizon.net
Estimated Sales: $15 Million
Number Employees: 1-4
Type of Packaging: Consumer

6429 Jacques Pastries
128 Main St
Suncook, NH 03275
603-485-4035
Fax: 603-268-0699 www.jacquespastries.com
Bakery products
Founder: Jacques Despres

6430 Jacquet Bakery
401 Park Ave South
10th Fl.
New York, NY 10016
jacquetbakery.com
Breads, cakes, crepes and waffles
VP, Sales and Operations: James Shankin

6431 Jada Foods LLC
3126 John P. Curci Dr.
Bay 1
Hallandale Beach, FL 33009
855-936-3746
www.krunchymelts.com
Meringues
Owner: Daniel Ginsberg
Contact: Moises Mizrahi
mmizrahi@jadafoods.com

6432 Jade Leaf Matcha
San Francisco, CA 94123
support@jadeleafmatcha.com
www.jadeleafmatcha.

Food Manufacturers / A-Z

Organic Japanese matcha
Type of Packaging: Consumer, Bulk

6433 Jager Foods
613 Birch St S
Sauk Centre, MN 56378
320-491-7249
Fax: 320-732-4047   800-358-7251
Dried soup mixes
President: Pete Jager
Brands:
　Jager
　Shitake Mushroom Soup Mixes (4)

6434 Jagger Cone Co Inc
304 Ellis St
Stryker, OH 43557-9329
419-682-1816
jaggercone@aol.com
Ice cream cones
Owner: Jeff Jaggers
jaggercone@aol.com
Owner: Sherry Jagger
Estimated Sales: Less Than $500,000
Number Employees: 10-19
Type of Packaging: Consumer, Food Service

6435 Jaguar Yerba Company
P.O. Box 1192
Ashland, OR 97520
541-482-7745
Fax: 541-482-6780   800-839-0775
ecoteas@worldpantry.com www.yerbamate.com
Yerba mate teas
Owner: Stefan Schachter
Co-Founder: Brendan Girardi
Partner: Joe Chermesino
Estimated Sales: $3-5 Million
Number Employees: 1-4

6436 Jagulana Herbal Products
PO Box 45
Badger, CA 93603
559-337-2200
Fax: 559-337-2354   888-465-3686
www.immortalityherb.com
Dedicated to researching, developing and marketing jiaogulan and jiaogulan-based herbal products of the highest quality
President: Chris Gleen
Research: Michael Blumert
Estimated Sales: $1-3 Million
Number Employees: 1-4

6437 Jain Americas Inc
1819 Walcutt Rd
Suite I
Columbus, OH 43228-9149
614-850-9400
Fax: 614-850-8600   888-473-7539
info@jainamericas.com www.jainamericas.com
Dehydrated vegetables, fruit purees, puree concentrates and clarified juices
CEO: Narinder Gupta
Executive Vice President: Murali Ramanathan
murali@jainamericas.com
Number Employees: 20-49

6438 Jaindl Farms
3150 Coffeetown Rd
Orefield, PA 18069-2599
610-395-3333
Fax: 610-395-8608   800-475-6654
jaindl.com
Turkey
Owner & President: David Jaindl
jaindl2@aol.com
Year Founded: 1935
Number Employees: 100-249
Type of Packaging: Consumer, Food Service, Private Label, Bulk
Brands:
　Grand Champion

6439 Jake's Grillin
76 Loganberry Ct
Hopewell Jct, NY 12533-5378
845-226-4656
Fax: 845-226-4656 jake@jakesgrillin.com
　　www.jakesgrillin.com
Rubs, sauces and marinades
President: Joe Moran
Brands:
　JAKE'S GRILLIN

6440 Jakeman's Maple Products
454414 Trillium Line
RR #1
Beachville, ON N0J 1A0
Canada
519-539-1366
Fax: 519-421-2469   800-382-9795
info@themaplestore.com www.themaplestore.com
Maple syrup, sugar, candy and yogurt; coffee, tea and cookies
President: Robert Jakeman
CFO: Jane Henderson
Quality Control: Melissa Martin
Sales: Mary Jakeman
Production: Heather Crane
Estimated Sales: $1 Million
Number Employees: 11
Number of Brands: 1
Number of Products: 78
Square Footage: 26480
Parent Co: Auvergne Farms
Type of Packaging: Consumer, Food Service, Private Label, Bulk

6441 Jakes Brothers Country Meats
6089 Clarksville Pike
Joelton, TN 37080-8997
615-876-2911
www.stjacobs.com
Cured meats
Owner: Johnny Jakes
Estimated Sales: Less Than $500,000
Number Employees: 1-4

6442 Jamae Natural Foods
PO Box 481096
Los Angeles, CA 90048
323-937-3670
Fax: 323-937-0849   800-343-0052
order@jamae.com www.jamae.com
Cookies, soy nut crunch bars
President: Crystal You
Estimated Sales: $300,000
Number Employees: 3
Type of Packaging: Private Label
Brands:
　Health Cookie
　Soynut Crunch Bar
　Soynuts

6443 Jamaica John Inc
9140 Belden Ave
Franklin Park, IL 60131-3506
847-451-1730
Fax: 847-451-1590 sales@jamaicajohn.com
　　www.jamaicajohn.com
Sauces
President: John Capozzoli
Quality Control: John Capozzoli Jr
Estimated Sales: $5-10 Million
Number Employees: 10-19

6444 Jamaican Gourmet Coffee Company
250 South 18th Street
Suite 802
Philadelphia, PA 19103
800-261-2859
sales@coffeeforless.com
Coffee, tea
President: Lloyd Parchment
Estimated Sales: Below $5 Million
Number Employees: 20
Square Footage: 55200

6445 James Candy Company
1519 Boardwalk
Atlantic City, NJ 08401-7012
609-344-1519
Fax: 609-344-0246   800-441-1404
Confectionery products
President: Frank Glaser
EVP Sales/Marketing: Lisa Glaser Whitley
Contact: Barbara Aleo
baleo@jamescandy.com
VP Operations: Susan Saraceni
Estimated Sales: $2 Million
Number Employees: 50-99
Type of Packaging: Consumer, Bulk
Brands:
　James Chocolate Seal Taffy
　James Cream Mints
　James Salt Water Taffy
　Mumsey

6446 James Frasinetti & Sons
7395 Frasinetti Rd
Sacramento, CA 95828
916-383-2444
Fax: 916-383-5825
Wines
Partner: Howard Frasinetti
Partner: Gary Frasinetti
gary@frassinetti.com
Estimated Sales: $2.5-5 Million
Number Employees: 36

6447 James L. Mood Fisheries
Woods Harbour
Nova Scotia, NS B0W 2E0
Canada
902-723-2360
Fax: 902-723-2880 info@moodfisheries.com
　　www.moodfisheries.com
Fresh seafood
President: Corey Mood
Vice President: Almond Mood
Estimated Sales: $674,000
Number Employees: 10
Type of Packaging: Consumer, Food Service, Private Label, Bulk

6448 James Skinner Company
4657 G St
Omaha, NE 68117-1410
402-734-1672
Fax: 402-734-0516   800-358-7428
www.skinnerbaking.com
Frozen baked goods
President: James Skinner
Chief Executive Officer: Jim Skinner
VP Marketing: Doug Dinnin
Contact: Scott Barrows
sbarrows@skinnerbaking.com
Director of Operations: Dennis Nolan
Plant Manager: Tom Urzendowski
Estimated Sales: $7.6 Million
Number Employees: 100-249
Square Footage: 300000
Type of Packaging: Consumer, Food Service, Private Label, Bulk
Brands:
　Skinner Bakery

6449 Jamieson Laboratories
4025 Rhodes Drive
Windsor, ON N8W 5B5
Canada
519-974-8482
Fax: 519-974-4742   800-265-5088
　　www.jamiesonvitamins.com
Kefir, yogurt, cod liver oil, vitamins, mineral supplements; water purifying systems and filters.
President/CEO: Mark Hornick
Year Founded: 1922
Estimated Sales: $42 Million
Number Employees: 400
Number of Brands: 22
Square Footage: 40000
Parent Co: CCMP Capital Advisors LLC
Type of Packaging: Consumer
Other Locations:
　Toronto ON
Brands:
　Arthrimin GS™
　Baby-D™
　BodyGUARD™
　Digestive Care™
　Effervescent
　Exxtra-C™
　FluShield™
　Healthy SLEEP™
　Mega Cal™
　NEM®
　Neurosome™
　Nutrisentials™
　Omega Complete™
　Omega-3 Brain™
　Omega-3 Calm™
　Omega-3 Select™
　Prostease™
　ProVitamina™
　Red Dragon™
　Relax & Sleep™
　Slimdown®
　Stressease™

Food Manufacturers / A-Z

6450 Jane Bakes
40 S Main St
Pearl River, NY 10965
845-920-1100
Fax: 845-920-1101 jane@janebakes.com
www.janebakes.com
Cookies
Founder: Jane Carroll

6451 Janes Family Foods
3340 Orlando Drive
Mississauga, ON L4V 1C7
Canada
905-673-7145
Fax: 905-677-0607 800-565-2637
www.janesfamilyfoods.com
Frozen breaded and battered seafood, poultry, vegetable and cheese products
Plant Manager: Pat Palmer
Estimated Sales: $19 Million
Number Employees: 100
Square Footage: 300000
Type of Packaging: Consumer, Food Service, Private Label, Bulk
Brands:
  Crisp & Delicious
  Golden Gate
  J&J Gourmet
  Janes Family Favourites

6452 Janowski's Hamburgers Inc
15 S Long Beach Rd
Rockville Centre, NY 11570-5621
516-764-9591
Fax: 516-764-1908
www.janowskishamburgers.com
Hamburger meats
Owner: William Vogelsberg
Estimated Sales: $2,500-4,999,999 Million
Number Employees: 10-19

6453 Japan Gold USA
13200 Danielson St
Poway, CA 92064
858-486-1707
sales@japangoldusa.com
japangoldusa.com
Japanese snacks, ingredients and condiments
President/Owner: Seigo Okada

6454 Jaquelina's
515 S 32nd St
Camp Hill, PA 17011-5106
717-737-9452
Fax: 717-737-9452
Vinegars and oils
President: Jacqueline Magaro
Estimated Sales: Less than $500,000
Number Employees: 1-4

6455 Jarchem Industries
414 Wilson Ave
Newark, NJ 07105
973-578-4560
Fax: 973-344-5743 info@jarchem.com
www.jarchem.com
Ingredients and additives
CEO: Arnold Stern
Contact: Hein Arthur
hein.arthur@jarchem.com
Mngr.: Howard Honing
Estimated Sales: $.5-1 million
Number Employees: 1-4

6456 Jardine Foods
1 Chisholm Trail
Buda, TX 78610-3350
512-295-4600
Fax: 512-295-3020 800-544-1880
www.jardinefoods.com
Ketchup, chilies, sauces, dips, salsa, BBQ saucees and jellies
Manager: Scott Bolding
CEO: Bobby Mcgee
VP Sales/Mearketing: Garth Gardner
VP of Operations: Scott Jackson
Director: Craig Lieberman
Director: Brad Wallace
Estimated Sales: $5-10 Million
Number Employees: 20-49
Number of Brands: 20
Number of Products: 200
Type of Packaging: Consumer, Food Service, Private Label, Bulk
Brands:
  D.J. Jardine

6457 Jardine Ranch
910 Nacimiento Lake Dr
Paso Robles, CA 93446-8713
805-238-2365
Fax: 805-239-4334 866-833-5050
order@jardineranch.com www.jardineranch.com
Gift baskets of nuts
Owner: Bill Jardine
Owner: Mary Jardine
jardine@jardineranch.com
Manager: Duane Jardine
Estimated Sales: Less Than $500,000
Number Employees: 5-9
Type of Packaging: Consumer, Food Service, Bulk

6458 Jarrow Industries Inc
12246 Hawkins St
Santa Fe Springs, CA 90670-3365
562-906-1919
Fax: 562-906-1979
customerservice@jarrowindustries.com
www.jarrow.com
Vitamins and supplements
President: Mohammed Khalid
Estimated Sales: $20-49 Million
Number Employees: 100-249

6459 Jasmine & Bread
4478 Howe Hill Rd
South Royalton, VT 05068
802-763-7115
Fax: 802-763-7115
Condiments
Owner: Sherrie Maurer
Estimated Sales: $500,000-$1 000,000
Number Employees: 1-4
Type of Packaging: Private Label, Bulk

6460 Jasmine Vineyards, Inc.
33319 Pond Road
Delano, CA 93215
661-792-2141
Fax: 661-792-6365 jvine@jasminevineyards.com
www.jasminevineyards.com
Grapes
Number of Brands: 4
Type of Packaging: Consumer, Food Service, Bulk
Brands:
  Havren
  Jasvine
  M and V
  Vinmar

6461 Jason & Son Specialty Foods
2590 Mercantile Dr Ste A
Rancho Cordova, CA 95742
916-635-9590
Fax: 916-635-9711 800-810-9093
Specialty confectionery items, including trail mixes, nut clusters and raisins
President: William Jason
VP: Margaret Jason
General Manager: Richard Antti
Estimated Sales: $1255895
Number Employees: 15
Type of Packaging: Consumer, Food Service, Private Label, Bulk
Brands:
  Jason & Son

6462 Jason Pharmaceuticals
11445 Cronhill Dr
Owings Mills, MD 21117
410-581-2080
Fax: 410-581-8070 800-638-7867
Dietetic products
President: Margaret MacDonald-Sheetz
CEO: Michael C. MacDonald
CFO: Timothy G. Robinson
CMO: Brian Kagen
Contact: Deborah Carey
deborah@medifast.com
Number Employees: 100-249
Parent Co: Medifast Inc.
Brands:
  Jason Pharmaceuticals

6463 Jasper Products Corp
3877 E 27th St
Joplin, MO 64804
417-206-3877
info@jasperproducts.com
www.jasperproducts.com
Dairy products, fruit beverages and prepared foods
President: Ken Haubein
ken.haubein@jasperproducts.com
Plant Manager: Larry Bearden
Year Founded: 2001
Estimated Sales: $100-499 Million
Number Employees: 750
Square Footage: 2000000
Parent Co: Stremicks Heritage Foods, LLC

6464 Jasper Wyman & Son
22 S Main St
Topsfield, MA 01983-1835
978-887-7472
Fax: 978-887-6881 tom@wymans.com
www.wymans.com
Blueberry juice, frozen treats
Contact: Lisa Francis
lfrancis@wymans.com
Estimated Sales: $10-20 Million
Number Employees: 1-4

6465 Java Beans and Joe Coffee
1331 Commerce St.
Petaluma, CA 94549
707-462-6333
800-624-7031
sales@javabeansandjoe.com
Coffee, flavored coffee, K-Cups
Owner: Lauren Mountanos
Parent Co: Mountanos Family Coffee & Tea Co.

6466 Java Cabana
PO Box 520845
Miami, FL 33152-0845
305-592-7302
Fax: 305-592-9471 www.javacabana.com
Coffee
Owner: Jose Souto
Marketing Director: Beatriz Vescovacci
Estimated Sales: $2.5-5 Million
Number Employees: 20-49
Type of Packaging: Food Service, Private Label

6467 Java Sun Coffee Roasters
35 Atlantic Ave
Marblehead, MA 01945-3139
781-631-7788
Coffee
Owner: Cheryl Burka
javasuncoffee@gmail.com
Estimated Sales: Less Than $500,000
Number Employees: 5-9

6468 Java-Gourmet/Keuka LakeCoffee Roaster
2792 Route 54A
Penn Yan, NY 14527
315-536-7843
888-478-2739
susan@java-gourmet.com www.java-gourmet.com
Coffee, rubs, sauces and marinades, and other gourmet items
President/Owner: Susan Atkisson

6469 Javalution Coffee Company
2400 Boswell Road
Chula Vista, CA 91914
619-934-3980
Fax: 619-934-3205 800-982-3197
customerservice@javalution.com
www.javalution.com/index.php
Coffee
President: Scott Pumper
CEO/Chairman of the Board: Steve Wallach
Vice President of Business Development: Brent Jensen
Chief Science Officer: Jose Antonio
Vice President of Operations: Mike Kolinski
Type of Packaging: Food Service

6470 Javed & Sons
6711 Hornwood Dr
Suite 250
Houston, TX 77074
713-835-6850
javed_sons@hotmail.com
javednsons.webs.c-

Food Manufacturers / A-Z

Halal chicken
Owner: Iqbal Javed
Year Founded: 1999

6471 Javo Beverage Co., Inc.
1311 Specialty Dr
Vista, CA 92081
760-330-1141
www.javobeverage.com
Coffee, tea and botanical extracts
Vice President, Ingredients & Flavours: Joanne Sheean

6472 Jaxon's Ice Cream Parlor
128 S Federal Hwy
Dania Beach, FL 33004-3623
954-923-4445
Fax: 954-922-8293 www.jaxsonsicecream.com
Frozen dairy desserts, low calorie ice cream and frozen yogurt
Owner: Monroe Udell
jaxsons@bellsouth.net
Plant Manager: M Day
Number Employees: 20-49
Parent Co: Dillon Corporation
Type of Packaging: Consumer, Food Service, Private Label
Other Locations:
  Jackson Ice Cream Co.
  Hutchinson KS

6473 Jay Shah Foods
1121 Meyerside Drive
Mississauga, ON L5T 1J6
Canada
905-696-0172
Fax: 905-696-0174
East Indian specialty snack foods and chutneys
President: Jayant Shah
Sales/Marketing Manager: Jay Shah
Purchasing Manager: Shushi Shah
Estimated Sales: $1 Million
Number Employees: 6
Square Footage: 40000

6474 JaynRoss Creations LLC
Whitmore Lake, MI
734-657-5852
Manufacturer of south indian spiced relish.
Co-Founder: Peter Johnston

6475 Jayone Foods Inc
7212 Alondra Blvd
Paramount, CA 90723-3902
562-633-7400
Fax: 562-633-7401 info@jayone.com
www.jayonefoods.com
Gluten-free, vegan, non-GMO, sugar-free specialty items; tea, juices, cider; condiments, yogurt, sauces; and other snacks
President: Seung Lee
info@jayone.com
Marketing Director: Jackie Choi
Estimated Sales: $30 Million
Number Employees: 20-49

6476 Jazz Fine Foods
5065 Ontario E Street
Montreal, QC H1V 3V2
Canada
514-255-0110
Fax: 514-259-1788
General grocery
President: Laurent Durot

6477 Jean Niel Inc
2444 Merchant Ave # 105
Suite 105-106
Odessa, FL 33556-3485
727-834-8855
Fax: 727-834-8832 info@nielaromes.com
www.jeanniel.com/niel_inc_en.php
Flavors and fragrances for beverages, dairy, bakery, savory and confectionary products.
President: Angoine Debutiny
Executive Vice President: Michael Uzan
Contact: Marketa Agbanlog
magbanlog@nielaromes.com
Number Employees: 5-9
Parent Co: Jean Niel

6478 Jecky's Best
26450 Summit Cir
Santa Clarita, CA 91350
661-259-1313
Fax: 661-259-5855 888-532-5972
jeckysbest@yahoo.com www.jabfoods.com
Frozen dough and unbaked goods
President: Jecky Bicer
jeckysbest@yahoo.com
VP: Eitay Bicer
VP: Areila Bicer
Estimated Sales: $5-10 Million
Number Employees: 20-49
Type of Packaging: Private Label
Brands:
  Jecky's Best

6479 Jed's Maple Products
259 Derby Pond Rd
Derby, VT 05829-9605
802-744-2095
Fax: 802-766-2702 802-766-2700
www.jedsmaple.com
Maple syrup, candy, cream, lollipops, salad dressings and sauces
Co-Owner: Stephen Wheeler
Co-Owner: Amy Wheeler
Estimated Sales: Less Than $500,000
Number Employees: 5-9

6480 Jedwards International Inc
141 Campanelli Dr
Braintree, MA 02184-5206
781-848-1473
Fax: 617-472-9359 sales@bulknaturaloils.com
www.bulknaturaloils.com
Organic specialty oils, essential oils, butters, waxes and botanicals
Contact: Jeremy Bamsch
jeremy@bulknaturaloils.com

6481 Jeff's Garden
105 Mezzetta Ct
American Canyon, CA 94503
707-266-7444
consumerinfo@jeffsgardenfoods.com
jeffsgardenfoods.com
All-natural olives, peppers, capers and sun-dried tomatoes
President/Owner: Jeff Mezzetta
Number of Brands: 1
Number of Products: 20
Type of Packaging: Consumer
Brands:
  JEFF'S NATURALS

6482 Jefferson Vineyards
1353 Thomas Jefferson Parkway
Charlottesville, VA 22902
434-977-3042
Fax: 434-977-5459 800-272-3042
office@jeffersonvineyards.com
www.jeffersonvineyards.com
Wines
General Manager: Andy Reagan
Contact: Missy Stevens
tastingroom@jeffersonvineyards.com
Winemaker/Vineyard Manager: Frantz Ventre
Estimated Sales: $5-10 Million
Number Employees: 10-19

6483 Jel Sert
501 Conde St
West Chicago, IL 60185
630-876-4838
800-323-2592
www.jelsert.com
Frozen juice pops, juice beverages and mixes
President: Kenneth Wegner
Research & Development Director: John Dobrozsi
Senior Quality Engineer: Erika Scherer
Director of Human Resources: Juan Chavez
Engineer & Plant Manager: Simon Richards
Square Footage: 1600000
Type of Packaging: Consumer, Food Service, Bulk
Brands:
  Dad's Old Fashioned®
  Dove® Chocolate
  Flavor Aid
  Fla-Vor-Ice®
  Hi-C®
  Hostess®
  Jolly Rancher
  Juicy Juice®
  Kool Pops
  My T Fine®
  Otter Pops®
  Pop-ice®
  PureKick®
  Royal®
  Royal Delights
  Skittles®
  Slush Puppie®
  Sonic™
  Sour Patch Kids
  Starbursts®
  Sunkist
  Sunny D®
  SuperC®
  Warheads®
  Welch's®
  Wyler's®
  Wyler's® Light

6484 Jelks Coffee Roasters
P.O.Box 8667
Shreveport, LA 71148-8667
318-636-6391
Fax: 318-635-1384 800-235-7361
www.jelks-coffee.com
Coffee
President: Harvey Jelks
Estimated Sales: $2.5-5 Million
Number Employees: 5-9
Brands:
  Toddy

6485 (HQ)Jelly Belly Candy Co.
One Jelly Belly Lane
Fairfield, CA 94533-6741
707-428-2800
Fax: 707-428-2863 800-522-3267
www.jellybelly.com
Candy
President: Lisa Brasher
CEO: Herman Rowland
hrowland@jellybelly.com
Vice President, Specialty Sales: John Pola
Chief Sales and Marketing Officer: Ryan Schader
Vice President, Sales: Andrew Joffer
Plant Manager: Anthony Habib
hrowland@jellybelly.com
Purchasing Manager: Reg Nelson
Estimated Sales: $215 Million
Number Employees: 500-999
Number of Brands: 2
Number of Products: 150
Square Footage: 350000
Type of Packaging: Consumer, Private Label
Other Locations:
  Distribution Center
  Pleasant Prairie WI
Brands:
  Goelitz
  Jelly Belly

6486 Jemm Wholesale Meat Company
4649 W Armitage Ave
Chicago, IL 60639-3405
773-523-8161
Fax: 773-523-8890
Frozen portion-controlled steaks and ground beef
President: Daniel Goldman
VP: Thomas Nacht
Plant Manager: Dominic Pinto
Estimated Sales: $14,100,000
Number Employees: 20-49
Type of Packaging: Consumer, Food Service
Brands:
  Seasoned Delux

6487 Jeni's Splendid Ice Creams
401 N Front St
Suite 300
Columbus, OH 43215
614-488-3224
contact@jenis.com
www.jenis.com
Ice cream
Founder & CCO: Jeni Bauer
CEO: John Lowe
Contact: Steve Boutros
steve.boutros@jenis.com

Food Manufacturers / A-Z

6488 Jennie-O Turkey Store
1126 Benson Ave SW
Willmar, MN 56201
320-235-6080
Fax: 320-231-0779 turkeyinfo@j-ots.com
www.jennieo.com
Turkey products
President: Michael Tolbert
CEO: Jerry Jerome
CFO: Dwight York
VP Marketing: Bob Tegt
Sales Director: Jime Splinter
Public Relations: Dave Suheke
Operations Manager: Bob Wood
Purchasing Agent: Larry Hammond
Number Employees: 250-499
Parent Co: Hormel Foods Corporation
Type of Packaging: Consumer, Food Service

6489 Jennies Gluten-Free Bakery
590 Rocky Glen Rd
Moosic, PA 18507
570-457-2400
Fax: 570-457-3626 lainiehamlin@outlook.com
jenniesmacaroons.com
Macaroons and cakes
President: Arnold Badner
Estimated Sales: $4,000,000
Number Employees: 20-49
Square Footage: 120000
Type of Packaging: Food Service
Brands:
  Manhattan Gourmet

6490 Jenny's Country Kitchen
438 Main St S
Dover, MN 55929
507-932-3035
Fax: 507-932-4777   800-357-3497
info@jennyscountrykitchen.com
www.jennyscountrykitchen.com
Cocoa and coffee products
President: Jenny Wood
CEO: Dan Wood
Estimated Sales: Below $5 Million
Number Employees: 10
Brands:
  Jenny's Country Kitchen

6491 Jenny's Old Fashioned
38727 Taylor Pkwy
North Ridgeville, OH 44039
440-327-0775
Fax: 440-327-9349   800-452-3235
popcorn@jennyspopcorn.com
www.jennyspopcorn.com
Popcorn
Owner: Becky Finnegan
becky.finnegan@bendix.com
CEO: Bob Shearer
Plant Manager: Jay McGuire
Estimated Sales: $5-10 Million
Number Employees: 20-49
Type of Packaging: Private Label
Brands:
  Jenny's

6492 Jensen Meat Company
2550 Britannia Blvd
Suite 101
San Diego, CA 92154
619-754-6400
Fax: 619-754-6450 info@jensenmeat.com
www.jensenmeat.com
Ground beef hamburger patties
President: Robert Jensen
CEO: Abel Olivera
CFO: Sam Acuna
VP of Executive Accounts: Patricia Lavigne
VP of Production: Anthony Crivello
Year Founded: 1958
Estimated Sales: $26.9 Million
Number Employees: 1-4
Type of Packaging: Consumer, Food Service, Private Label, Bulk
Brands:
  Jensen Solos™
  Slater's 50/50 Bacon Burger™
  UNCUT™ Before the Butcher®

6493 Jensen's Bread and Bakeries
3420 SE 21st Ave
Portland, OR 97202
503-208-3987
Fax: 503-208-3988 www.jensensbread.com
Bread products

6494 Jensen's Old Fashioned Smokehouse
10520 Greenwood Ave N
Seattle, WA 98133
206-364-5569
Fax: 206-364-0880
retail@jensenssmokehouse.com
www.jensenssmokehouse.com
Smoked seafood
President: Michael Jensen
Estimated Sales: Below $5 Million
Number Employees: 5-9
Type of Packaging: Consumer, Food Service
Brands:
  Wild Keta Salmon
  Wild Keta Salmon
  Wild Red King Salmon
  Wild White King Salmon

6495 Jer's Chocolates
437 S Highway 101
Suite 105
Solana Beach, CA 92075
800-540-7265
info@jers.com
www.jers.com
Chocolates
CEO: Jerry Swain

6496 Jerabek's New Bohemian Coffee House
63 Winifred St W
Saint Paul, MN 55107
651-228-1245
Fax: 651-228-3011 info@jerabeks.com
Baked goods, coffees, collectables
Manager: Russell Sprangler
Estimated Sales: $500,000 appx.
Number Employees: 10-19

6497 Jeremiah's Pick Coffee Co
1495 Evans Ave
San Francisco, CA 94124-1706
415-206-9900
Fax: 415-206-9542   877-537-3642
office@jeremiahspick.com
www.jeremiahspick.com
Coffee
Owner: Jermiah Pick
office@jermiahspick.com
Operations Manager: Jay Meltesen
Estimated Sales: Below $5 Million
Number Employees: 10-19
Square Footage: 56000
Type of Packaging: Consumer, Food Service, Private Label, Bulk
Brands:
  Cafe Pick
  Chocatal
  Jeremiah's Pick

6498 Jerrell Packaging
802 Labarge Drive
Birmingham, AL 35022
205-426-8930
Fax: 205-426-8989 john@jerrellpackaging.com
www.jerrellpackaging.com
Popcorn
President: John Lyon
Contact: Barry Cornell
barry@jerrellpackaging.com
Estimated Sales: Below $5 Million
Number Employees: 10-19

6499 Jerry Brothers Industries Inc
4619 Glasgow St
Richmond, VA 23202
804-271-0689
Fax: 804-271-1258 JBI@MIR-belting.com
www.jerrybrothers.com
Wholesaler/distributor of conveyor belts including smooth, incline, weigh scale and feeder for many parts of the food industry, including bakery, meat processing, salad, tobacco, and boxes for packaging.
Operations Manager: Carras Sayre
Estimated Sales: $2.5-5 Million
Number Employees: 10-19

Type of Packaging: Food Service

6500 Jerry's Nut House
2101 N Humboldt St
Denver, CO 80205
303-861-2262
Fax: 303-861-1214 orders@jerrysnuthouse.com
www.jerrysnuthouse.com
Nuts and snacks
President: Claude Julia
Customer Service Representative: Zuzana Baumhardt
baumhardt@jerrysnuthouse.com
Estimated Sales: $2600000
Number Employees: 10-19
Square Footage: 80000
Type of Packaging: Consumer, Food Service, Private Label, Bulk
Brands:
  Jerry's

6501 Jersey Fruit Co-Op
800 Ellis Mill Rd # B
Glassboro, NJ 08028-3204
856-863-9100
Fax: 856-863-9490 sales@jerseyfruit.com
www.jerseyfruit.com
Bluberries, peaches, nectarines, and cranberries.
Owner: Franscio Allende
Director Of Marketing: Bob Von Rohr
Estimated Sales: $10-20 Million
Number Employees: 10-19
Type of Packaging: Food Service

6502 Jersey Italian Gravy
16 Thornton Rd
Oakland, NJ 07436
201-620-2111
info@jerseyitaliangravy.com
www.jerseyitaliangravy.com
Pasta sauce
President: Carlos Vega

6503 Jerusalem House
2425 W 18th Ave
Eugene, OR 97402
541-485-1012
Fax: 541-687-6853
Middle eastern specialty products
President: Simon Oueis
Estimated Sales: Less than $500,000
Number Employees: 1-4

6504 Jeryl's Jems
43 Eagle Lane
Tappan, NY 10983-1810
201-236-8372
Fax: 845-359-7386 jeryls.jems@yahoo.com
Cake truffles, cookies, brownies
President: Jeryl Kipnis Kronish

6505 Jesben
PO Box 38113
Pittsburgh, PA 15238
info@jesben.com
www.jesben.com
Slow cooker sauces
Founder: Susie Schwartz
Number of Products: 4
Brands:
  Jesben

6506 Jess Jones Vineyard
6496 Jones Ln
Dixon, CA 95620-9601
707-678-3839
Fax: 707-678-3898 www.jessjonesvineyard.com
Wines
President: Jess Jones
CEO: Mary Ellen Jones
Estimated Sales: $700,000
Number Employees: 1-4
Square Footage: 20000
Type of Packaging: Consumer, Bulk
Brands:
  California Golden Pop
  Customer's Bags
  Jess Jones Farms

6507 Jessica's Natural Foods
PO Box 145
Birmingham, MI 48012-0145
248-723-7118
Fax: 248-723-7121 info@jessicasnaturalfoods.com
www.jessicasnaturalfoods.com

Food Manufacturers / A-Z

Gluten free products
Estimated Sales: Less Than $500,000
Number Employees: 1-4

6508 Jessie's Ilwaco Fish Company
45 Shed B
Unit 4
San Francisco, CA 94133
360-642-3773
Fax: 360-642-3362 don@alberseafoods.com
Fish and seafood
Owner: Pierre Marchand
VP: Doug Ross
Marketing: George Alexander
Production: Phil Marchand
Estimated Sales: $20-40 Million
Number Employees: 100-249
Square Footage: 25000
Type of Packaging: Consumer, Food Service, Private Label, Bulk
Brands:
  Custom Lable
  Seaside

6509 Jets Le Frois Corp
56 High St
Brockport, NY 14420-2058
585-637-5003
Fax: 585-637-2855
Barbeque sauces and vinegars
Owner: Duncan Tsay
Estimated Sales: $5-10 000,000
Number Employees: 5-9
Type of Packaging: Private Label

6510 Jewel Bakery
1955 W North Ave
Melrose Park, IL 60160-1131
708-531-6000
Fax: 708-343-9450
Breads
CEO: Stephen Bowater
Number Employees: 100-249

6511 Jewel Date Co
84675 60th Ave
Thermal, CA 92274-8780
760-399-4474
Fax: 760-399-4476
Natural and organic pecans, dates, raisins, nuts and dried fruits
President: Gregory Raumin
CEO: Greg Raumin
greg@jeweldate.com
Sales Manager: John Ortiz
Estimated Sales: $1,300,000
Number Employees: 20-49
Parent Co: Covalda
Type of Packaging: Consumer

6512 JiMMY! Bars
Chicago, IL 60661
888-676-7971
support@jimmybars.com jimmybars.com
Protein bars
Co-Founder: Annette Del Prete
Co-Founder & Co-CEO: Jim Simon
Co-CEO: Jason Wadler

6513 Jiaherb
1 Chapin Rd
Unit 1
Pine Brook, NJ 07058
973-439-6869
Fax: 973-439-6879 888-542-4372
info@jiaherbinc.com www.jiaherbinc.com
Natural ingredients
President: Scott Chen

6514 Jianlibao America
420 5th Avenue
26th Floor
New York, NY 10018-2729
212-354-8898
Fax: 212-354-8838 800-526-1488
Beverages, Asian foodstuffs
President: Qishu Lin
Estimated Sales: $3 Million
Number Employees: 20

6515 Jillipepper
PO Box 7546
Albuquerque, NM 87194
505-609-8409
Fax: 505-344-6633 jilli@jillipepper.com
www.jillipepper.com
Salsas, sauces, dips
Founder, Owner: Jill Levin
jilli@swcp.com
VP: Lowell Levin
Production Manager: Martin Dobyns
Estimated Sales: $1-3 Million
Number Employees: 1-4
Type of Packaging: Private Label

6516 Jilz Gluten Free
2155 Sunset Dr
Ventura, CA 93001
805-585-5297
jilzglutenfree.com
Crackers

6517 Jim Foley Company
1121 Chestnut Hill Cir SW
Marietta, GA 30064-4652
770-427-5102
Fax: 770-427-5102
Seafood
President: Jim Foley

6518 Jim's Cheese Pantry
410 Portland Rd
Waterloo, WI 53594-1200
920-478-3571
Fax: 920-478-2320 800-345-3571
Cheese; jams, jellies and crackers
President: James Peschel
CEO: Jim Peschel
VP: Judy Peschel
Estimated Sales: $9.5 Million
Number Employees: 50-99
Square Footage: 100000
Type of Packaging: Consumer, Food Service

6519 Jimbo's Jumbos Inc
185 Peanut Dr
Edenton, NC 27932-9604
252-482-2193
Fax: 252-482-7857 800-334-4771
Snacks and peanuts; custom formulation
Manager: Hal Burns
Manager: Debbie Miller
dmiller@jimbosjumbos.com
Number Employees: 100-249
Type of Packaging: Private Label

6520 Jimmy Dean Foods
PO Box 2020
Springdale, AR 72765
800-925-3326
www.jimmydean.com
Breakfast sandwiches and sausage.
SVP & General Manager: Jeff Caswell
Parent Co: Tyson Foods, Inc.
Type of Packaging: Consumer, Food Service, Private Label, Bulk
Brands:
  Fresh Taste Fast!
  Jimmy Dean

6521 Jimmys Cookies
125 Entin Rd
Clifton, NJ 07014-1424
973-779-8500
info@jimmyscookies.com
www.jimmyscookies.net
Cookies
President/Owner: Michael Pisani
CEO: Howard Hirsch
CFO: Debbie Kinzley
Estimated Sales: Less Than $500,000
Number Employees: 1-4
Square Footage: 90000
Type of Packaging: Consumer, Food Service, Private Label, Bulk

6522 Jimtown Store
6706 Highway 128
Healdsburg, CA 95448-9630
707-433-1212
Fax: 707-433-1252 jimtown@jimtown.com
www.jimtown.com
Vegetable spreads

Owner: Karrie Brown
karriebrown@jimtown.com
Marketing Director: Haley Callahan
Catering: Susan Schmid
Estimated Sales: Less than $500,000
Number Employees: 10-19
Brands:
  Chickpea Chipotle
  Fig & Olive Tapenade
  Spicy Olive

6523 Jin+Ja
New York, NY
215-690-1470
www.drinkjinja.com
Fresh juices
Founder & CEO: Reuben Canada
Brands:
  JINJA

6524 Jo Mar Laboratories
583 Division St # B
Campbell, CA 95008-6915
408-374-5920
Fax: 408-374-5922 800-538-4545
info@jomarlabs.com www.jomarlabs.com
Health products; contract packaging
President: Joanne Brown
joanne@jomarlabs.com
Estimated Sales: $1-3 Million
Number Employees: 10-19
Square Footage: 14000
Parent Co: Jo Mar Labs
Type of Packaging: Consumer, Private Label

6525 Jo's Candies
2560 W 237th St
Torrance, CA 90505-5217
310-257-0260
Fax: 310-257-0266 800-770-1946
sales@joscandies.com
Gourmet chocolates and confectionary
President: Tom King
Controller: Grant Philders
Plant Manager: Dave Good
Estimated Sales: Below $5 Million
Number Employees: 5-9
Type of Packaging: Private Label, Bulk
Brands:
  Chocolate Covered Graham Crackers
  Dr. Peter's Peppermint Crunch
  Jo's Candies
  Jo's Original

6526 JoJo's Chocolate
Mesa, AZ 85205
805-395-6567
jojoschocolate.com
Chocolate bars
Co-Founder: Sterling Jones

6527 Jodar Vineyard & Winery
3405 Carson Ct
Placerville, CA 95667-5104
530-644-3474
Fax: 530-621-0324 jodarwinery@foothill.net
www.jodarwinery.com
Wines
Owner: Vaughn Jodar
jodarwinery@foothill.net
Partner: Byron Joder
Partner: Sherril Jodar
Estimated Sales: $500,000-$1 Million
Number Employees: 1-4
Brands:
  Jodar

6528 Jodie's Kitchen
6349 82nd Ave N
Pinellas Park, FL 33781
Fax: 727-934-9967 800-728-3704
info@jodieskitchen.com www.jodieskitchen.com
Gourmet herb and spice blends
President: Nobert Moore
VP: Vickey Auge
Estimated Sales: $300,000-500,000
Number Employees: 1-4
Square Footage: 9600
Type of Packaging: Consumer, Private Label, Bulk
Brands:
  Country Classic
  Dip-Idy-Dill
  Galloping Garlic
  Garlic Galore

Food Manufacturers / A-Z

Magically Mexican
Obviously Onion

6529 Jody Maroni's Sausage Kingdom
P.O.Box 1487
Burbank, CA 91507
818-760-2004
Fax: 818-760-8341 info@jodymaroni.com
www.jodymaroni.com
Sausages
Owner: Jordan Monkarsh
VP Marketing: Richard Leivenberg
Contact: Scotty Shadix
scotty@jodymaroni.com
Number Employees: 50-99
Type of Packaging: Consumer, Food Service
Brands:
Jody Maroni

6530 Jody's Gourmet Popcorn
1160 Millers Ln
Virginia Beach, VA 23451-5716
757-422-8646
customerservice@jodyspopcorn.com
www.jodyspopcorn.com
Popcorn and fudge
Founder: Jody Wagner
Number Employees: 20-49
Other Locations:
Retail Store , Laskin Road
Virginia Beach VA
Brands:
Jody's

6531 Jodyana Corporation
18367 NE 4th Ct
Miami, FL 33179-4531
305-651-0110
Fax: 305-651-4535 888-563-5282
Coffee
President: Corey Colaciello
Chairman: Joe Colaciello
Estimated Sales: $620,000
Number Employees: 5
Number of Brands: 115
Square Footage: 12000
Type of Packaging: Food Service, Private Label, Bulk

6532 Joe Bertman Foods
P.O. Box 6562
Cleveland, OH 44101-1562
216-431-4460
Fax: 216-561-2232
www.bertmanballparkmustard.com
Mustard and horseradish sauce
President: Pat Mazoh
Type of Packaging: Consumer, Bulk
Brands:
Bertman Raddish Sauce
Joe Bertman's Ballpark Mustard
Mustard
Original

6533 Joe Clark Fund Raising Candies
621 E 1st Ave
Tarentum, PA 15084-2005
724-226-0866
888-459-9520
www.clarkcandies.com
Chocolates
Owner: Bob Clark
bob@clarkcandies.com
Estimated Sales: $3-5 Million
Number Employees: 5-9
Type of Packaging: Consumer
Brands:
Joe Clark's Candies, Inc.

6534 Joe Corbis' Wholesale Pizza
14100 Darnestown Road
Suite E
Darnestown, MD 20874
888-526-7247
www.joecorbi.com
Pizza
President: Drew McManigle
Estimated Sales: $10-20 Million
Number Employees: 260
Number of Brands: 1
Brands:
Joe Corbi's

6535 Joe Fazio's Famous Italian
1008 Bullitt Street
Charleston, WV 25301
304-344-3071
http://www.fazios.net
Italian foods, seafoods, steaks, sandwiches
Owner: Joe Fazio
Quality Control: Nell Fazio
Marketing Manager: Joe Fazio
Manager: Nell Fazio
Estimated Sales: Below $5 Million
Number Employees: 20-49
Brands:
Fazio's

6536 Joe Hutson Foods
8331 Sanlando Avenue
Jacksonville, FL 32211-5135
904-731-9065
Fax: 904-731-9066 keithhutson@juno.com
Sauces
President: Teresa Foster
CEO: Keith Hutson
Chairman Board: Joe Hutson
Number Employees: 1-4
Square Footage: 1200
Parent Co: Joe Hutson Foods
Brands:
Put Me Hot

6537 Joe Jurgielwicz & Sons
189 Cheese Ln
Hamburg, PA 19526-8057
610-562-3825
Fax: 610-562-0219 800-543-8257
joey@tastyduck.com www.tastyduck.com
Frozen ducklings
Owner: Ian Shollenberger
ian@tastyduck.com
CEO: Joe Jurgielwicz
Partner: Tom Jurgielewicz
Marketing: Joseph Jurgielewicz III
Office Manager: Amy Grimminger
Estimated Sales: $860,000
Number Employees: 20-49
Type of Packaging: Consumer, Food Service
Brands:
South Shore
South Side
Twin Lake

6538 Joe Patti's Seafood Co
524 S B St
Pensacola, FL 32502-5422
850-432-3315
Fax: 850-435-7843 800-500-9929
www.joepattis.com
Seafood and seafood products.
President: Frank Patti
Year Founded: 1933
Estimated Sales: $20-50 Million
Number Employees: 100-249

6539 Joe Tea and Joe Chips
PO Box 43255
Upper Montclair, NJ 07043-0255
973-744-7502
www.joetea.com
Iced teas, juices and chips
CEO and Co-Founder: Joe Prato
Co-Founder: Ann Prato

6540 Joel Harvey Distributing
8800 Ditmas Avenue
Brooklyn, NY 11236
718-629-2690
Fax: 718-629-2172
Chocolate, cookies, crackers, jellies and juices
President: Mark Statfeld
Estimated Sales: $1-2.5 Million
Number Employees: 10-19
Brands:
Ferrara
Guylian
Hero
Hershey
Kedem
Perugina
Venus

6541 Joelle's Choice Specialty Foods LLC
1829 Highway 1
Fairfield, IA 52566
641-472-2414
Fax: 641-472-3774 800-880-2779
http://joelleschoice.com
Shelf-stable soy products
President: Larry Sutton
Type of Packaging: Food Service

6542 Joey's Fine Foods
135 Manchester Place
Newark, NJ 07104
973-482-1400
Fax: 973-482-1597 sales@joeysfinefoods.com
www.joeysfinefoods.com
Mixes and baked goods
President: Aaron Aihini
Vice President Sales: Anthony Romano
Contact: Joe Aihini
Estimated Sales: $5.5 Million
Number Employees: 40
Square Footage: 168000
Type of Packaging: Consumer, Food Service, Private Label, Bulk
Brands:
Cottage Bake
Joey's
New Englander

6543 Joey's Home Bakery-Gluten Free
1532 SW 8th St
Boynton Beach, FL 33426-5827
561-292-4004
joey.palmbeach@gmail.com
www.joeyshomebakeryglutenfree.com
Gluten free bakery
Estimated Sales: Less Than $500,000
Number Employees: 1-4

6544 Jogue Inc
One Vanilla Lane
Northville, MI 48167
248-349-1500
Fax: 248-349-1505 800-531-3888
info@jogue.com www.jogue.com
Flavoring extracts, essential oils, food colors, ice cream toppings, juices and syrups
President/Owner: Dattu Sastry
Technical Sales Manager: Gary Holtquist
Estimated Sales: $10-20 Million
Number Employees: 20-49
Type of Packaging: Food Service, Private Label, Bulk
Other Locations:
Jogue
Detroit MI
Western Syrup Company
Santa Fe Springs CA
High Mountain Manufacturing Company
Salt Lake City UT
Brands:
Gold Label

6545 Johanna Foods Inc.
1 Johanna Farms Rd.
PO Box 272
Flemington, NJ 08822
908-788-2200
800-727-6700
info@johannafoods.com www.johannafoods.com
Fruit juices, beverages and yogurt.
President/CEO: Robert Facchina
robertfacchina@johannafoods.com
Quality Systems Coordinator: Nicole Branstetter
Year Founded: 1995
Estimated Sales: $100 Million
Number Employees: 500-999
Number of Brands: 3
Square Footage: 500000
Type of Packaging: Consumer, Food Service, Private Label, Bulk
Brands:
La Yogurt
Ssips
Tree Ripe

6546 Johlin Century Winery
3935 Corduroy Rd
Oregon, OH 43616-1811
419-693-6288
Fax: 419-693-6429 www.wineweb.com
Wines

Food Manufacturers / A-Z

President/Owner: Bolan and Jay Muchewicz
Estimated Sales: $500,000-$1 000,000
Number Employees: 1-4
Type of Packaging: Private Label

6547 John A Vassilaros & SonInc
2905 120th St
Flushing, NY 11354-2505
                                                718-886-4140
Fax: 718-463-5037 info@vassilaroscoffee.com
                                    www.vassilaroscoffee.com
Coffee and tea
President/CEO: Stefanie Kasselakis Kyles
Estimated Sales: $10-20 Million
Number Employees: 20-49
Number of Brands: 4
Type of Packaging: Private Label
Brands:
    Downtown Sumatra
    Midtown Caff
    Vassi Espresso
    Vassilaros

6548 (HQ)John B. Sanfilippo & Son
1703 N Randall Rd
Elgin, IL 60123-7820
                                                847-289-1800
        Fax: 847-289-1843 info@jbssinc.com
                                                        jbssinc.com
Nuts, dried fruit, salad toppers
Chairman & CEO: Jeffrey Sanfillipo
jsanfillipo@jbssinc.com
Group President/Secretary & CFO: Michael Valentine
Year Founded: 1922
Estimated Sales: $520 Million
Number Employees: 1000-4999
Number of Brands: 2
Type of Packaging: Consumer, Food Service, Private Label, Bulk
Other Locations:
    John B. Filippo & Son
    Bainbridge GA
    John B. Filippo & Son
    Garysburg NC
    John B. Filippo & Son
    Gustine CA
    John B. Filippo & Son
    Walnut CA
Brands:
    Orchard Valley Harvest
    Fisher
    Southern Style
    Squirrel Brand

6549 John B. Wright Fish Company
427 Main St
Gloucester, MA 01930
                                                978-283-4205
                                         Fax: 978-281-5944
Seafood
President: Brian Wright
Contact: David Wright
david@johnbwright.com
Estimated Sales: $5-10 Million
Number Employees: 5-9

6550 John Conti Coffee Co
4406 Ole Brickyard Cir
Louisville, KY 40218-3066
                                                859-253-9770
        Fax: 502-499-2944 800-928-5282
info@johnconti.com www.johnconti.com
Coffee
President: John Conti
CFO: Sherry French
sfrench@johnconti.com
Human Resources: Debbie Redmon
Operations Director: Mark Nethery
Estimated Sales: Under $500,000
Number Employees: 50-99

6551 John Copes Food Products
P.O. Box 334
Hanover, PA 17331
                                                717-632-6000
        Fax: 717-367-7317 800-888-4646
                                               www.johncopes.com
Canned corn and frozen vegetables
President & COO: Thomas Cope
Chairman & CEO: Larry Jones
CFO/Treasurer: Don Long
Controller: Stephen Gaukler
VP Sales & Marketing: Steve Davis
Estimated Sales: $30-50 Million
Number Employees: 130
Parent Co: Hanover Foods
Type of Packaging: Consumer, Private Label
Brands:
    Copes
    Dutch Delight

6552 John Garner Meats
2365 N Rudy Road
Van Buren, AR 72956-8702
                                                479-474-6894
        Fax: 479-474-6897 800-543-5473
Portion controlled pork, poultry and beef
President: Dewayne Garner
President: T D Garner
Marketing Director: Ralph Farrar
Sales Director: Gary Scott
Contact: John Garner
jgarner@peppersource.com
Operations Manager: Rusty Underwood
Production Manager: Rusty Polk
Estimated Sales: $5 Million
Number Employees: 30
Square Footage: 40000
Type of Packaging: Food Service, Private Label, Bulk

6553 John Hofmeister & Son Inc
2386 S Blue Island Ave
Chicago, IL 60608-4292
                                                773-847-0700
        Fax: 773-847-6707 800-923-4267
ehofmeis@hofhaus.com www.hofhaus.com
Smoked and boiled hams and turkeys
President: Ej Hofmeister
Vice President: Robert Bukala
Marketing Manager: Matt Hofmeister
Human Resources Manager: Bob Bukala
Production: Chris Chin
Estimated Sales: $32,000
Number Employees: 50-99
Square Footage: 240000
Type of Packaging: Consumer, Food Service, Private Label
Brands:
    Hofmeister Haus

6554 John I. Haas
5185 Macarthur Blvd NW
Suite 300
Washington, DC 20016
                                      info@johnihaas.com
                                  www.barthhaasgroup.com
Hops and hop aroma extract and oils
CEO: Henry Von Eichel
Estimated Sales: $160 Million
Number Employees: 2,000
Number of Brands: 7
Type of Packaging: Food Service, Private Label, Bulk
Brands:
    Aromahop
    Beta Stab
    Hepahop Gold
    Isahop
    Lacto Stab
    Redihop
    Tetrahop Gold

6555 John J. Nissen Baking Company
34 Abbott St
Brewer, ME 4412
                                                207-989-7654
    Fax: 207-989-7654 contact@twinkies.com
Baked goods
President: Michael D Kafoure
President, Chief Executive Officer: Gregory Rayburn
Executive Vice President, Chief Administ: John Stew
CFO: Ronald B Hutchison
Executive Vice President of Operations: Gary Wandschneider
Estimated Sales: $10-20 Million
Number Employees: 20-49
Brands:
    Hostess
    Wonder Bread

6556 John Kelly Chocolates
1506 N Sierra Bonita Ave
Los Angeles, CA 90046-2812
                                              323-851-3269
        Fax: 323-851-1789 800-609-4243
                     service@johnkellychocolates.com
                          www.johnkellychocolates.com
Chocolates
Owner: John Kelson
john@johnkellychocolates.com
Marketing: John Nelson
Number Employees: 10-19

6557 John Koller & Son Inc
1734 Perry Hwy
Fredonia, PA 16124-2720
                                              724-475-4154
  Fax: 724-475-4777 www.fairviewsswisscheese.com
Cheese
President: Richard Koller
rkoller54@aol.com
Estimated Sales: $10-20 000,000
Number Employees: 10-19
Parent Co: Fairview Swiss Chesse
Brands:
    Fairview Swiss Cheese

6558 John N Wright Jr Inc
402 Railroad Ave
Federalsburg, MD 21632-1413
                                              410-754-9044
                                      Fax: 410-754-9045
Canned tomatoes
President: Mary Harding
jmharding@dmv.com
Estimated Sales: Less Than $500,000
Number Employees: 1-4

6559 John Paton Inc
73 E State St
Doylestown, PA 18901-4359
                                              215-348-7050
                                      Fax: 215-348-8147
            questions@goldenblossomhoney.com
                   www.goldenblossomhoney.com
Honey
President: Jon Paton
jp@goldenblossomhoney.com
Estimated Sales: $860,000
Number Employees: 1-4

6560 John Volpi & Co
5263 Northrup Ave
St Louis, MO 63110-2033
                                              314-772-8550
        Fax: 314-772-0411 800-288-3439
        info@volpifoods.com www.volpifoods.com
Italian meat products
CEO: Lorenza Pasetti
lpassetti@volpifoods.com
Year Founded: 1902
Estimated Sales: $20-50 Million
Number Employees: 100-249
Type of Packaging: Consumer, Food Service, Private Label, Bulk
Brands:
    Volpi Foods

6561 John W Macy's Cheesesticks Inc
80 Kipp Ave
Elmwood Park, NJ 07407-1036
                                              201-791-8036
        Fax: 201-797-5068 800-643-0573
                             timmacy@cheesesticks.com
                               www.johnwmmacys.com
Cheesesticks, cheesecrisps and bread sticks
CEO: John Macy
johnmacy@cheesesticks.com
VP/Sales Manager: Tim Macy
Marketing: Julia D'Arcy
Estimated Sales: $8 Million
Number Employees: 50-99
Square Footage: 180000
Type of Packaging: Consumer, Food Service, Private Label, Bulk
Brands:
    John Wm. Macy's Cheesecrips
    John Wm. Macy's Cheesesticks
    John Wm. Macy's Sweetsticks

Food Manufacturers / A-Z

6562 Johnny Harris Famous Barbecue Sauce
1651 East Victory Drive
Savannah, GA 31404
912-354-7810
Fax: 912-354-6567   888-547-2823
ashley@johnnyharris.com   www.johnnyharris.com
Barbecue sauce
President: Maude Donaldson
Chief Financial Officer: Yvonne Donaldson
Vice President: Norman Heidt
Estimated Sales: $5-10 Million
Number Employees: 5-9
Square Footage: 12000
Type of Packaging: Consumer

6563 Johns Cove Fisheries
RR 3
Yarmouth, NS B5A 4B1
Canada
902-742-8691
Fax: 902-742-3574
Lobster, herring roe and scallops
President: Don Cunningham
Number Employees: 60
Type of Packaging: Consumer, Food Service, Bulk

6564 Johnson Brothers Produce Company
Highway 44 E
Whitakers, NC 27891-0730
252-437-2111
Fax: 252-437-2121
Sweet potatoes
President: Hursel Johnson
VP: Lou Johnson
Estimated Sales: $10-20 Million
Number Employees: 20-49
Type of Packaging: Bulk
Brands:
　Norma Lou

6565 Johnson Estate Winery
8419 West Main Road
Westfield, NY 14787
716-326-2191
Fax: 716-326-2131   800-374-6569
jwinery@cecomet.net   www.johnsonwinery.com
Wines
Owner and Vineyard Manager: Frederick Johnson
Marketing Contact: Bob Dahl
Operations Manager: Mark Lancaster
Estimated Sales: $3-5 Million
Number Employees: 5-9
Square Footage: 60000
Type of Packaging: Consumer

6566 (HQ)Johnson Foods, Inc.
336 E Blaine Ave
P.O. Box 916
Sunnyside, WA 98944
509-837-4214
Fax: 509-837-4855   johnsonfoodsinc.blogspot.ca
Processed cherries, asparagus and pickled vegetables
President: Gary Johnson
gary@johnsonfoods.com
Estimated Sales: $10-20 Million
Number Employees: 250-499
Square Footage: 40000
Type of Packaging: Consumer, Food Service, Private Label, Bulk

6567 Johnson Foods, Inc.-Cannery Plant
300 Warehouse Ave
Sunnyside, WA 98944-1310
509-837-4188
Fax: 509-839-3243
Processed cherries, asparagus and pickled vegetables
Manager: Pete Krause
Estimated Sales: $5-10 Million
Number Employees: 20-49
Parent Co: Johnson Foods, Inc.
Type of Packaging: Consumer, Food Service, Private Label
Brands:
　Princess
　Sunnyside

6568 Johnson Sea Products Inc
251-824-2693
Seafood
Manager: Sean Johnson
Estimated Sales: $100+ Million
Number Employees: 50-99

6569 Johnson's Alexander Valley Wines
8333 Highway 128
Healdsburg, CA 95448-9639
707-433-2319
Fax: 707-433-5302   800-888-5532
Wines
President: Ellen Johnson
Estimated Sales: Less than $500,000
Number Employees: 1-4
Type of Packaging: Private Label
Brands:
　Johnson's Alexander Valley

6570 Johnson's Food Products
1 Mount Vernon St
Dorchester, MA 02125-1604
617-265-3400
Fax: 617-265-1099
Baking mixes, bases, flavorings and whipped toppings
President: John Anton
john.anton@johnsonfoods.com
VP: Peter Anton
Estimated Sales: $5-10 Million
Number Employees: 10-19
Square Footage: 80000
Type of Packaging: Consumer, Food Service, Bulk

6571 Johnson's Real Ice Cream
2728 E Main St
Columbus, OH 43209-2534
614-231-0014
Fax: 614-231-5450
www.johnsonsrealicecream.com
Ice cream and sherbet
President: Jim Wilcoxon
sales@johnsonsrealicecream.com
Estimated Sales: $380000
Number Employees: 10-19
Square Footage: 9600
Type of Packaging: Consumer, Food Service

6572 Johnson's Wholesale Meats
161 N Sixth St
Opelousas, LA 70570-2105
337-948-4444
Fax: 337-948-4495
Meat packer
Manager: David Comoeuax
Sales Manager: Billy Baque
Estimated Sales: $1-3 Million
Number Employees: 1 to 4
Type of Packaging: Consumer, Bulk

6573 Johnson, Nash & Sons Farms
415 John Rich Rd
Warsaw, NC 28398
910-289-6842
Fax: 910-289-6917
Fresh poultry and eggs
President: Don Taber
Estimated Sales: $567.8 Million
Number Employees: 5-9
Type of Packaging: Consumer, Food Service, Bulk
Brands:
　House of Raeford

6574 Johnsonville Sausage LLC
1222 Perry Way
Watertown, WI 53094-6052
920-261-1053
Fax: 920-261-1870   888-556-2728
www.summersausagestory.com
Sausage
President: Alice Stayer
Chief Marketing Officer: Duane Draeger
ddraeger@johnsonville.com
Number Employees: 100-249
Type of Packaging: Consumer
Brands:
　Hot'n Zesty Links
　Johnsonville Bratwur
　Johnsonville Country
　Sage'n Pepper
　Table Two Entree

6575 Johnston County Hams
204 N Brightleaf Blvd
Smithfield, NC 27577-4670
919-934-8054
Fax: 919-934-1091   800-543-4267
service@countrycuredhams.com
www.countrycuredhams.com
Hams, bacon and turkey
Cure Master: Rufus Brown
rufus@countrycuredhams.com
Estimated Sales: Below $5 Million
Number Employees: 10-19

6576 Johnston Farms
13031 Packing House Rd
Bakersfield, CA 93307
661-366-3201
Fax: 661-366-6534   johnstongiftfruit@gmail.com
Navel oranges, peppers and potatoes
Owner: Dennis Johnston
Co-Prtnr.: Gerald Johnston
Commercial Sales Department: Derek Vaughn
dennisj@johnstonfarms.com
Packinghouse Operations: Steve Staker
Plant Manager: Steve Stacker
Number Employees: 100-249

6577 Johnston's Home Style Products
PO Box 1737
Charlottetown, PE C1A 7N4
Canada
902-629-1300
Fax: 902-368-1776
Canned cranberry sauce and stews
President: Harris Johnston
Type of Packaging: Food Service, Private Label

6578 Johnston's Winery Inc
5140 Bliss Rd
Ballston Spa, NY 12020-2044
518-882-6310
Fax: 518-882-5551
Wines
President: Kurt Johnston
Estimated Sales: Less Than $500,000
Number Employees: 1-4
Brands:
　Johnston's Winery

6579 Joia All Natural Soda
3440 Belt Line Blvd.
Suite 206
Minneapolis, MN 55416
612-308-2056
www.joialife.com
Sodas
Founder and CEO: Bob Safford
Contact: Carleton Johnson
carleton.johnson@bwbsoda.com
Brands:
　JOIA ALL NATURAL SODA

6580 Joj, Bar
PO Box 232087
Encinitas, CA 92024
877-643-3575
info@jojebar.com   jojebar.com
Energy bars
Co-Founder: John Abate
Co-Founder: Jess Cerra
Number of Brands: 1
Number of Products: 7
Type of Packaging: Consumer
Brands:
　JOJ

6581 Jolly Llama
11805 N 200 3
Richmond, UT 84333
thejollyllama.com
Whole fruit and non-dairy squeezable sorbet pops
President/Owner: Scott Jacobson
Number of Brands: 1
Number of Products: 9
Type of Packaging: Consumer
Brands:
　JOLLY LLAMA

Food Manufacturers / A-Z

6582 Jomart Chocolates
2917 Avenue R
Brooklyn, NY 11229-2525
718-375-1277
Fax: 718-382-7144
michael@jomartchocolates.com
www.jomartchocolates.com
Manufacturer of different chocolates and confections.
Founder and CEO: Michael Rogak
michael@jomartchocolates.com
Number Employees: 10-19

6583 Jon Donaire Desserts
9511 Ann Street
Santa Fe Springs, CA 90670-2615
562-941-1856
Fax: 562-946-3781   877-366-2473
JDdesserts@rich.com
iloveicecreamcakes.com/cake-brand/jon-donaire
Ice cream cakes
President: Mickey Del Duca
Dessert Specialist: Lisa Tanner
Estimated Sales: $10-50 Million
Number Employees: 100-249
Parent Co: Rich Products Corp.
Brands:
  Jon Donaire

6584 Jonathan Lord Cheesecakes
87 Carlough Rd # A
Bohemia, NY 11716-2921
631-517-1271
Fax: 631-563-8505   800-814-7517
info@jonathanlord.com
www.jonathanlordcheesecake.com
Bakery Products
Owner: Carole Kentrup
Sales Director: William Kentrup
jlcorp@optonline.net
Estimated Sales: Below $5 Million
Number Employees: 10-19
Type of Packaging: Consumer, Food Service, Private Label, Bulk

6585 Jonathan's Sprouts
384 Vaughan Hill Rd
Rochester, MA 02770-2035
508-763-2577
Fax: 508-763-3316   bob@jonathansorganic.com
www.jonathanssprouts.com
Alfalfa sprouts, mung bean sprouts, citrus fruits and vegetables
President: Bob Sanderson
Owner/President: Barbara Sanderson
barbara@jonathansorganic.com
CEO: John Musser
Sales Director: Cathy Rounseville
Estimated Sales: $4 Million
Number Employees: 20-49
Square Footage: 60000
Type of Packaging: Consumer
Brands:
  Jonathan's Organics
  Jonathan's Sprouts

6586 Jones Brewing Company
260 2nd St
Smithton, PA 15479
724-483-2400
Fax: 724-565-5743   info@stoneysbeer.com
www.stoneysbeer.com
Beers, including non-alchoholic beer
Owner: Jon King
Brewmaster: Greg King
Purchasing: Joyce Winkler
Type of Packaging: Consumer, Private Label
Brands:
  Equire
  Eureka
  Stoney's
  Stoney's Black & Tan
  Stoney's Harvest Gold
  Stoney's Light
  Stoney's Non-Alcoholic Brew

6587 Jones Dairy Farm
800 Jones Ave
Fort Atkinson, WI 53538
800-563-6637
www.jonesdairyfarmfoodservice.com
Sausage, bacon, ham, and liverwurst products.
President & CEO: Philip Jones
pjones@jonesdairy.com
Marketing Director: Bridget Molthen
Executive Vice President: Richard Lowry
Manager of Human Resources: Katherine Bruns
SVP, Operations: Roger Borchardt
Manager of Purchasing: Joyce Lemke
Year Founded: 1832
Estimated Sales: $30.7 Million
Number Employees: 250-499
Square Footage: 215000
Type of Packaging: Consumer, Food Service, Bulk
Brands:
  Jones Sausagest
  Ralph & Paula Adams Scrapple

6588 Jones Packing Co
22701 Oak Grove Rd
Harvard, IL 60033-8205
815-943-4488
Beef, lamb, pork and goat
Owner: Ray Jones
rjones@jonespacking.com
Estimated Sales: $4 Million
Number Employees: 10-19
Type of Packaging: Consumer, Food Service, Private Label

6589 Jones Potato Chip Co
823 Bowman St
Mansfield, OH 44903-4107
419-529-9424
Fax: 419-529-6789   800-466-9424
chips@joneschips.com
Potato chips
President: Robert Jones
bobmartin@joneschips.com
Quality Assurance Manager: Susie Drushel
Sales Exec: Bob Martin
Office Manager: Jim Ford
Production Manager: Roy Kehl
Plant Manager: Rick Bartram
Estimated Sales: $6 Million
Number Employees: 50-99
Type of Packaging: Consumer, Food Service, Private Label
Brands:
  Jones
  Thomasson's
  Thomasson's Potato Chips

6590 Jones Soda Company
1000 First Ave South
Suite 100
Seattle, WA 98109
206-624-3357
Fax: 206-624-6857   800-656-6050
info@jonessoda.com   www.jonessoda.com
Sodas
CEO: Jennifer Cue
COO: Eric Chastain
CFO: Max Schroedl
Content Creator: Cassie Smith
EVP US Sales: Steve Gress
Operations Manager: Chris Milberger
Year Founded: 1987
Estimated Sales: $20-50 Million
Number Employees: 50-99
Type of Packaging: Consumer
Brands:
  Berry White
  Betty
  Dave
  Purple Carrot

6591 Jonny Almond Nut Co
G4254 Fenton Rd
Flint, MI 48507-3614
810-767-6887
Fax: 810-767-6889   rich@jonnyalmond.com
Nuts, popcorn and other snacks
General Manager: Bob Bossman
Marketing: Rich Krafsur
Manager: Alicia Handlin
alyssa@jonnyalmond.com
Number Employees: 20-49

6592 JonnyPops
3600 Alabama Ave S
Minneapolis, MN 55416
651-243-0705
info@jonnypops.com
www.jonnypops.com
Popsicles
CEO: Erik Brust
CFO: Connor Wray
Number of Brands: 1
Number of Products: 11
Type of Packaging: Consumer, Food Service
Brands:
  JONNYPOPS

6593 Joray Candy
1258 Prospect Avenue
Brooklyn, NY 11218
718-871-6300
Fax: 718-871-6300   joraycandy@msn.com
www.joraycandy.com
Kosher candy, dried fruit and other snacks
Marketing: Ray Shalhoub

6594 Jordahl Meats
25585 State Highway 13
Manchester, MN 56007-5020
507-826-3418
Meat products
Owner: Brian Jordahl
Estimated Sales: Less Than $500,000
Number Employees: 1-4
Type of Packaging: Consumer, Food Service, Private Label, Bulk

6595 Jordan's Meats & Deli
375 St. Croix Trail S
Lakeland, MN 55043
651-337-2224
jordanmeatsdeli.com
Meat products; serving the retail and food service markets; also, portion cutting services available.
Founder & Owner: Tony Jordan
Estimated Sales: $20-50 Million

6596 Josef Aaron Syrup Company
16541 Redmond Way
Suite 206
Redmond, WA 98052-4492
425-820-7221
Fax: 425-702-9292
Tea and coffee flavors, syrups
President: Judy Toller
Number Employees: 5-9

6597 Joseph Adams Corp
5740 Grafton Rd
Valley City, OH 44280-9327
330-225-9135
Fax: 330-225-9105
Oleoresins, essential oils, natural flavors and colors
President: Patrick Adams
Sales: Kathy Adams
Estimated Sales: $3 Million
Number Employees: 10-19

6598 Joseph Campione Inc
2201 W South Branch Blvd
Oak Creek, WI 53154-4906
414-761-8944
Fax: 414-761-2005   www.josephcampione.com
Italian breads
President: Angelina Campione
acampione@josephcampione.com
Number Employees: 100-249

6599 Joseph D Teachey Jr Produce Co
1307 N Norwood St
Wallace, NC 28466-1331
910-285-4502
Fax: 910-285-5491
Sweet potatoes
Owner: Joseph Teachey
Estimated Sales: $10-20 Million
Number Employees: 1-4
Brands:
  Mary Jo's Blueberries
  Mary Jo's Fancy

6600 Joseph Farms
10561 State Highway 140
PO Box 775
Atwater, CA 95301
209-394-7984
Fax: 209-394-4988   jgfinfo@josephfarms.com
www.josephfarms.com
Cheese
CEO: Michael Gallo
Sales Manager, Latin America: Javier Alvarez
jalvarez@josephfarms.com
Type of Packaging: Consumer, Food Service

Food Manufacturers / A-Z

6601 Joseph J. White
1 Pasadena Rd
Browns Mills, NJ 8015
609-893-2332
Fax: 609-893-2316
Cranberries
President: Joe Darlington
Chairman Board: Thomas Darlington
Estimated Sales: $500,000-$1 Million
Number Employees: 10 to 19
Type of Packaging: Bulk

6602 Joseph Kirschner & Company
193 Riverside Dr
Augusta, ME 04330
207-623-3544
Fax: 207-623-1557
Meats
President: Marco Desalle
Purchasing Manager: Daniel Poulin
Estimated Sales: $200,000
Number Employees: 2

6603 Joseph Phelps Vineyards
200 Taplin Rd
St Helena, CA 94574-9544
707-967-9153
Fax: 707-963-4831 800-707-5789
minglis@josephphelps.com
www.josephphelps.com
Wines
Owner: Bill Phelps
bphelps@jpbwines.com
Founder & Chairman Emeritus: Joe Phelps
VP, CFO: Robert Boyd
VP, Director of Winemaking: Damian Parker
Winemaker: Ashley Hepworth
VP, Director of Sales & Marketing: Mike McEvoy
Director of Vineyard Operations: Philippe Pessereau
Vice President, Director of Winemaking: Damian Parker
Estimated Sales: $5 Million
Number Employees: 50-99
Square Footage: 200000
Type of Packaging: Consumer
Brands:
  Insignia
  Backus Vineyard
  Freestone Vineyards
  Ovation
  Estate Grown Olive Oil
  Fogdog
  Napa Syrah
  Viognier
  Eisrebe
  Innisfree

6604 Joseph Swan Vineyards
2916 Laguna Rd
Forestville, CA 95436-3729
707-573-3747
Fax: 707-575-1605 rod@swanwinery.com
www.swanwinery.com
Wines
Owner: Rod Berglund
rod@swanwineries.com
CEO: Lynn Swan-Berglund
Estimated Sales: Less than $500,000
Number Employees: 1-4
Brands:
  Swan Joseph

6605 Joseph's Gourmet Pasta
262 Primrose St
Haverhill, MA 01830-3930
978-521-1718
Fax: 978-374-7917 800-863-8998
www.josephsgourmetpasta.com
Gourmet pastas
President & CEO: David Zwartendijk
Number Employees: 250-499
Square Footage: 150000

6606 Joseph's Lite Cookies
3700 J Street SE
Deming, NM 88030
575-546-2839
Fax: 575-546-6951 800-373-3726
www.josephslitecookies.com
Sugar free cookies, fat free cookies, brownies, syrups
President: Joseph Semprevivo
Contact: Joe Arriaga
joe@josephslitecookies.com
Estimated Sales: $5-10 Million
Number Employees: 20-49
Square Footage: 208000
Type of Packaging: Consumer

6607 Josephine's Feast
30 5th Ave
Apt 8F
New York, NY 10011-8810
917-622-7428
www.josephinesfeast.com
Preserves and chutney
Founder: Laura O'Brien

6608 Josh & John's Ice Cream
111 E Pikes Peak Ave
Colorado Springs, CO 80903
719-632-0299
Fax: 719-632-2833 800-530-2855
hello@joshandjohns.com www.joshandjohns.com
Ice cream
President/CEO/CFO: John Krakauer
krakauer62@gmail.com
Year Founded: 1986
Estimated Sales: Less Than $500,000
Number Employees: 10-19
Brands:
  Josh & John's Ice Cream

6609 Josh Early Candies
4640 W Tilghman St
Allentown, PA 18104
610-395-4321
Fax: 610-398-8502 www.joshearlycandies.com
Candy and confections
Marketing: Barry Bobil
bub@joshearlycandies.com
Estimated Sales: Below $5 000,000
Number Employees: 10

6610 Jost Chemical
8150 Lackland Rd
St Louis, MO 63114-4524
314-428-4300
Fax: 314-428-4366 www.jostchemical.com
Chemical ingredients
President/Owner: Jerry Jost
jerryj@jostchemical.com
CFO: Jeff Lenger
Vice President: Keith Wunderli
Estimated Sales: $15.5 Million
Number Employees: 100-249

6611 Josuma Coffee Co
PO Box 1115
Menlo Park, CA 94026-1115
650-366-5453
Fax: 650-366-5464 info@josuma.com
www.josuma.com
Coffee
President: Joseph John
josuma@aol.com
Vice President: Urmila John
Estimated Sales: Under $300,000
Number Employees: 1-4
Type of Packaging: Private Label
Brands:
  Espresso Blend
  Green Coffee
  Malabar Gorld Premium
  Monsooned Malabar

6612 Joullian Vineyards
2 Village Dr
Suite A
Carmel Valley, CA 93924-9766
831-659-8100
Fax: 831-659-8102 866-659-8101
info@joullian.com www.joullian.com
Wines
Manager: Raymond E Watson III
Owner: Jeannette Joullian Sias
CFO: Robert Fain
Retail Operations Manager: Hal Ellison
Cellar Master: Elisio Cabrera
Office Manager: Holly Huebner
Winemaker/General Manager: Ridge Watson
Assisstant Winemaker: Katherine Chadwell
Estimated Sales: $2.5-5 000,000
Number Employees: 1-4

Brands:
  Joullian Vineyards

6613 Jovial Foods
41 Norwich-Westerly Rd
North Stonington, CT 06359
877-642-0644
info@jovialfoods.com www.jovialfoods.com
Gluten free foods made with einkorn flour
Founder/President: Carla Bartolucci

6614 Joy Cone Co
3435 Lamor Rd
Hermitage, PA 16148
724-962-5747
joycone@joycone.com
www.joycone.com
Ice cream cones
President: David George
CFO: Scott Kalmanek
Year Founded: 1918
Estimated Sales: $99 Million
Number Employees: 250-499
Number of Brands: 2
Brands:
  Joy
  Scoopy

6615 Joy's Specialty Foods
300 N Willow St
Mancos, CO 81328
970-533-1500
Fax: 970-533-2011 800-831-5697
Specialty condiments
President: Joy Kyzer
Vice President: Dave Kyzer
Estimated Sales: $300,000-500,000
Number Employees: 5
Type of Packaging: Consumer, Bulk
Brands:
  Joy's

6616 Joyce Farms
4787 Kinnamon Rd
Winston Salem, NC 27103-9605
336-766-9900
Fax: 336-766-9009 800-755-6923
www.joyce-farms.com
Poultry, beef and game products
President/CEO: Ron Joyce
ronaldjoyce@joycefoods.com
VP, Finance: Ryan Joyce
Quality Assurance Manager: Jimmy Mitchell
Sales Manager: Nate Morgan
VP, Operations: Stuart Joyce
Year Founded: 1962
Estimated Sales: $20-50 Million
Number Employees: 100-249
Type of Packaging: Private Label

6617 Joyfuls
100 Passaic Ave
Suite 100
Fairfield, NJ 07004
888-989-9050
info@joyfuls.com www.joyfuls.com
Dark chocolate snacks
VP, Sales: Barry Octigan
Number of Products: 3
Brands:
  Joyfuls

6618 Joyva Corp
53 Varick Ave
Brooklyn, NY 11237-1523
718-497-0170
Fax: 718-366-8504 info@joyva.com
www.joyva.com
Confectionery products
President: Milton Radutzky
Director: Richard Radutzky
Vice President: Harry Radutzky
Estimated Sales: $10-20 Million
Number Employees: 50-99
Type of Packaging: Consumer

6619 Juanita's Foods
645 Eubank Ave
P.O. Box 847
Wilmington, CA 90748
310-834-5339
Fax: 310-834-5064 800-303-2965
consumercomments@juanitasfoods.com
www.juanitas.com

Food Manufacturers / A-Z

Mexican foods
President: George De La Torre
CEO: Aaron De La Torre
Director, Quality Assurance: Rasheedi Samira
VP, Sales: John Thompson
Director, Human Resources: Diana Rodriguez
Operations Manager: Mark De La Torre
General Manager: Gina Harpur
Plant Manager: Frank Andrade
Purchasing Manager: Leo Medina
Year Founded: 1946
Estimated Sales: $41500000
Number Employees: 100-249
Type of Packaging: Consumer, Food Service, Private Label, Bulk
Brands:
    Juanita's
    Pico Pica
    Tia Anita

6620 Jubelt Variety Bakeries
303 North Old Route 66
Litchfield, IL 62056
217-324-5314
jubelts@jubelts.com
www.jubelts.com
Cakes, breads, doughnuts and cookies
President: Lance Jubelt
Contact: Becky Brown
becky.brown@jubelts.com
Estimated Sales: $1,200,000
Number Employees: 35
Number of Brands: 2
Square Footage: 16000
Type of Packaging: Food Service, Bulk

6621 Jubilations
950 Highway 45 South
West Point, MS 39773
662-328-9210
Fax: 662-329-1558   800-530-7808
cheesecakes@jubilations.com
www.jubilations.com
Cheesecakes.
President and Founder: Tammy Craddock
Sales and Marketing: George Purnell
Purchasing Manager: Ed Griffith
Estimated Sales: B
Number Employees: 5-9
Square Footage: 24000
Type of Packaging: Consumer, Food Service, Private Label
Brands:
    Jubilations

6622 Jubilee Foods
13050 N Wintzell Ave
Bayou La Batre, AL 36509
251-824-2110
www.jubileeseafood.com
Fresh and frozen shrimp
President: Charles Walton Kraver
shannon@jubileeseafood.com
Vice President: Frank Kawana
Quality Control: Mike Williams
Estimated Sales: Below $5 Million
Number Employees: 15
Brands:
    Buyer Label
    Jubilee
    Southern Supreme

6623 Jubilee Gourmet Creations
PO Box 6305-0318
Manchester, NH 03108
603-625-0654
Fax: 603-625-0654
Brandied cherries, peaches and berries
President: Joyce Davis
Type of Packaging: Consumer, Food Service, Bulk

6624 Judicial Flavors
11400 Atwood Road
Auburn, CA 95603-9017
530-885-1298
Fax: 530-888-0311
Sauces, dressings, oils, marinades, mustard, nuts, spices and coffee
Estimated Sales: $1-3 Million
Number Employees: 5-9

6625 Judy's Cream Caramels
19995 SW Chapman Rd
Sherwood, OR 97140
503-625-7161
Fax: 503-625-1602
Cream caramels
Owner: Debbie Judy
Number Employees: 5-9
Type of Packaging: Consumer

6626 Juice Mart
6758 Julie Ln
West Hills, CA 91307
818-992-4442
Fax: 818-992-4479   877-888-1011
Juice concentrates and nutripaks
President: Linda Renaud
Estimated Sales: $500,000-$1 Million
Number Employees: 1-4

6627 Juice Tyme, Inc.
4401 S Oakley Avenue
Chicago, IL 60609
773-579-1291
Fax: 773-579-1251   800-236-5823
www.juicetyme.com
Juices, teas, energy drinks and beverage concentrates
CEO: Sam Lteif
EVP, Sales & Field Service Operations: Jerry Desmond
Contact: Brian Andrade
brian.andrade@bevolutiongroup.com
Estimated Sales: $30 Million
Number Employees: 50
Square Footage: 30000
Type of Packaging: Food Service

6628 Juicy Whip Inc
1668 Curtiss Ct
La Verne, CA 91750-5848
909-392-7500
Fax: 626-814-8016   www.juicywhip.com
Hispanic beverage concentrates
President/CEO: Gus Stratton
Purchasing: Craig Allen
Estimated Sales: $4 Million
Number Employees: 5-9
Square Footage: 88000
Brands:
    Juicy Whip

6629 Julian Bakery
624 Garrison St
Oceanside, CA 92054
760-721-5200
customerservice@julianbakery.com
julianbakery.com
Manufacturer of gluten-free, low-carb products
VP, Sales: Barry Octigan
Number of Products: 115
Brands:
    D-Max
    ProGranola
    PrimalThin
    PaleoThin

6630 Julian's Recipe
Brooklyn, NY 11222
Fax: 888-645-8030   888-640-8880
info@juliansrecipe.com   www.juliansrecipe.com
Waffles, chips, artisanal breads
Owner: Alex Dzieduszycki
Brands:
    Julian's Recipe

6631 Julie Anne's
10634 San Palatina Street
Las Vegas, NV 89141
702-767-4765
www.julieannes.com
Organic breakfast cereals, granola and other snacks
Marketing: Julie Hession

6632 Julie's Real
100 Crescent Ct
Suite 700
Dallas, TX 75201
877-659-4375
info@juliesreal.com   www.juliesreal.com
Nut butters and grain-free granolas
Founder: Julie Fox
Number of Brands: 1
Number of Products: 11
Type of Packaging: Consumer
Brands:
    JULIE'S REAL

6633 Julius Sturgis Pretzel Bakery
219 E Main St
Lititz, PA 17543-2011
717-626-4354
Fax: 717-627-2682   info@juliussturgis.com
www.juliussturgis.com
Pretzels
Owner: Timothy Snyder
General Manager: Kurt Van Gilder
Estimated Sales: B
Number Employees: 25

6634 Jungbunzlauer Inc
95 Wells Ave
Suite 150
Newton, MA 02459
617-969-0900
Fax: 617-964-2921   office-bos@jungbunzlauer.com
www.jungbunzlauer.com
Ingredients and additives
President: Michael Alexandrow
Chief Executive Officer: Tom Knutzen
Chief Financial Officer: Michael Klaproth
Vice President, Product Management: Achim Hergel
Estimated Sales: $3.3 Million
Number Employees: 20-49
Parent Co: Jungbunzlauer Suisse AG
Type of Packaging: Bulk

6635 Junior's Cheesecake
58-42 Maurice Avenue
PO Box 780-208
Maspeth, NY 11378
718-852-5257
Fax: 718-260-9849   800-458-6467
info@juniorscheesecake.com
www.juniorscheesecake.com
Cheesecakes

6636 Juno Chef's
1 6 1/2 Station Rd
Goshen, NY 10924-6723
845-294-5400
Frozen pre-made meals
President: Julius Spessot
Contact: John Augustinski
johna@milmarfood.com
General Manager: Vilma Falcon
Estimated Sales: $6-10 Million
Number Employees: 50-99
Square Footage: 100000
Type of Packaging: Food Service

6637 Junuis Food Products
800 E Northwest Hwy # 510
Palatine, IL 60074-6511
847-359-4300
Fax: 847-359-4364
Frozen and fresh horseradish
President: John Russell
Estimated Sales: Less than $500,000
Number Employees: 1 to 4
Type of Packaging: Consumer, Food Service

6638 Jus-Made
9761 Clifford Dr Ste 100
Dallas, TX 75220
972-241-5544
Fax: 972-241-3399   800-969-3746
info@jus-made.com
Beverages and beverage mixes; beverage equipment
President: Gene Barfield
VP Sales: Jim Tanner
Contact: Matt Cook
mcook@jus-made.com
Operations Manager: Mike Sayre
Estimated Sales: $1-3 Million
Number Employees: 50-99
Square Footage: 14000
Type of Packaging: Consumer, Food Service, Private Label, Bulk
Other Locations:
    Jus-Made
    Houston TX
Brands:
    Floria Julep
    Orogold

Food Manufacturers / A-Z

6639 Just Bagels
527 Casanova St
Bronx, NY 10474
718-328-9700
Fax: 718-328-9997 www.justbagels.com
Bagels
President: Cliff Nordquist

6640 Just Bare
1770 Promontory Circle
Greeley, CO 80634
877-328-2838
wecare@justbarechicken.com
www.justbarechicken.com
American Humane Certified chicken
President/Owner: Steve Jurek

6641 Just Born Inc
1300 Stefko Blvd
Bethlehem, PA 18017-6672
610-867-7568
Fax: 610-543-4981 800-445-5787
Confectionery products
Co-CEO: Ross Born
Co-CEO: David Shaffer
dshaffer@justborn.com
President/COO: David Yale
Year Founded: 1923
Estimated Sales: $20-50 Million
Number Employees: 500-999
Number of Brands: 6
Type of Packaging: Consumer
Brands:
    Goldenberg's Peanut Chews®
    Hot Tamales®
    Just Born®
    Mike and Ike®
    Peeps®
    Teenee Beanee®

6642 Just Cook Foods
158 22nd Ave
San Francisco, CA 94121-1217
USA
415-269-2705
Fax: 415-684-7806 www.justcookfoods.com
Rubs, spices
Owner: Scott Lucas
scott@justcookfoods.com
Co-Founder: Cathy Storfer
Creative Chef: Daniel Capra

6643 Just Date Syrup
1007 Howard Ave
San Mateo, CA 94401
www.justdatesyrup.com
Alternative sweetener made from organic dates
Founder & CEO: Sylvie Charles
Number of Brands: 1
Number of Products: 1
Type of Packaging: Consumer
Brands:
    JUST DATE SYRUP

6644 Just Delicious Gourmet Foods
PO Box 2747
Seal Beach, CA 90740-1747
949-215-5341
Fax: 714-870-0332 800-871-6085
Dry soup, bread and dip mixes
President: Diana Ferguson
Estimated Sales: $500,000
Number Employees: 5-9
Square Footage: 40000
Type of Packaging: Consumer, Food Service, Bulk
Brands:
    Just Delicious

6645 Just Desserts
5000 Fulton Dr
Fairfield, CA 94534
415-780-6860
Fax: 415-780-6861 info@justdesserts.com
www.justdesserts.com
Specialty cakes, pastries, cookies
CEO: Michael Mendes
VP, Sales: Dean Gold
Contact: Ana Speros
asperos@justdesserts.com
Estimated Sales: $.5-1 million
Number Employees: 100-249
Type of Packaging: Private Label

6646 Just Jan's Inc.
22287 Mulholland Hwy #90
Calabasas, CA 91302-5157
USA
818-282-6236
jan@justjans.com
www.justjansjam.com
Jams, spreads, syrups
Chief Executive Officer/Founder: Jan Hogrewe
Estimated Sales: A
Number Employees: 1-4

6647 Just Off Melrose
1196 Montalvo Way
Palm Springs, CA 92262
760-320-7414
Fax: 760-327-0331
inforequest@justoffmelrose.com
www.justoffmelrose.com
Gourmet snacks
CEO: Brandon Tesmer
Contact: Carol Cross
ccross@justoffmelrose.com
Estimated Sales: $10-20 Million
Number Employees: 50
Brands:
    Just Chips
    Just Crisps
    Just Croutons
    Just Flatbread

6648 Just Panela
6676 Gunpark Dr
Suite D
Boulder, CO 80301
720-600-0522
info@justpanela.com
www.justpanela.com
Organic, artisanal cane sugar
Type of Packaging: Consumer, Bulk
Brands:
    JUST PANELA

6649 Just Tomatoes
2101 W Hamilton Rd Wiley CA
Westley, CA 95387
209-894-5371
Fax: 209-894-3146 800-537-1985
customerservice@justtomatoes.com
www.shopkarensnaturals.com
Dried fruits and vegetables
Co-Owner: Karen Cox
Co-Owner: Bill Cox
karen@justtomatoes.com
Estimated Sales: $1.9 Million
Number Employees: 50-99
Type of Packaging: Consumer, Food Service, Private Label, Bulk
Brands:
    Just

6650 Just Truffles
1363 Grand Ave
St Paul, MN 55105-2204
651-690-0075
Fax: 651-690-2052 877-977-9177
justtruffles@cs.com www.justtruffles.com
Truffles
Co-Founder and Owner: Kathleen O'Hehir-Johnson
Co-Founder and Owner: Roger Johnson
Number Employees: 5-9

6651 Justin Vineyards & Winery LLC
11680 Chimney Rock Rd
Paso Robles, CA 93446-9792
805-227-1160
Fax: 805-237-4152 800-237-4152
info@justinwine.com www.justinwine.com
Wines
President: Justin Baldwin
VP/Director Sales/Marketing: Rich Richardson
Marketing Manager: Tracy Dauterman
Regional Sales Manager: Joseph Spellman
Vice President, Director of Production: Fred Holloway
Estimated Sales: $2.5-5 Million
Number Employees: 20-49
Type of Packaging: Private Label
Brands:
    Justin

6652 Justin's Nut Butter
736 Pearl St
Boulder, CO 80302
844-448-0302
www.justins.com
Nut butters and candy
President: Lance Gentry
CEO/Founder: Justin Gold
CFO: Lonna Borden
Director of Marketing: Lauren Lortie
SVP Sales and Marketing: James Borteck
Contact: Aaron Lord
aaron@justinsnutbutter.com
Type of Packaging: Consumer

6653 Jyoti Cuisine India
816 Newtown Rd
Berwyn, PA 19312-2200
610-296-4620
Fax: 610-889-0492 jyoti@jyotifoods.com
Indian foods
Founder: Jyoti Gupta
VP: Vijai Gupta
Number Employees: 5
Type of Packaging: Consumer, Food Service, Private Label
Brands:
    India House
    Jyoti

6654 K & F Select Fine Coffees
2801 SE 14th Ave
Portland, OR 97202-2203
503-234-7788
Fax: 503-231-9827 800-558-7788
Coffee products, torami syrups and sauces, taza rica cocoas, powdered drink mixes, and liquid fruit smoothie products.
Founder: Don Dominguez
ddominguez@kfcoffee.com
Director Sales/Marketing: Sandy Jumonville
Sales: Steve O Brien
Estimated Sales: $3228000
Number Employees: 10-19
Type of Packaging: Consumer, Food Service, Private Label, Bulk
Brands:
    K&F
    Taza Rica Mexican Spiced Cocoa

6655 K & K Gourmet Meats Inc
300 Washington St
Leetsdale, PA 15056-1004
724-266-8400
Fax: 724-266-8402 www.kkgourmetmeats.com
Frozen chicken, philly, and chicken philly steaks.
Owner: Arthur Katz
kkmeats@verizon.net
Number Employees: 20-49
Type of Packaging: Consumer, Food Service

6656 K & S Cakes
13539 Eagles Rest Dr
Leesburg, VA 20176
910-265-6779
kandscakes@hotmail.com
www.kandscakes.com
Cakes, baked goods, and gift baskets.
Owner: Kim Arico
Year Founded: 1997
Estimated Sales: Less Than $500,000
Number Employees: 1-4
Type of Packaging: Consumer, Bulk
Brands:
    K&S

6657 K Horton Specialty Foods
28 Monument Sq
Portland, ME 04101-6447
207-228-2056
Fax: 207-228-2059
Specialty cheeses, olives, dried cured meats and meat pates, smoked seafood.
President: Kris Horton
Number Employees: 1-4

6658 K L Keller Imports
5332 College Ave
Suite 201
Oakland, CA 94618-2805
510-839-7890
Fax: 510-839-7895 orders@klkeller.com
www.klkeller.com

Food Manufacturers / A-Z

Olive, nut and, truffle oils; vinegar; condiments; herbs; spices; sea salts, and confections.
Owner: Kitty Keller
Sales: Lauren Zaira
Number Employees: 1-4

6659 K&N Fisheries
130 Seal Point Rd 1
Upper Port La Tour, NS B0W 3N0
Canada
902-768-2478
Fax: 902-768-2385
Fresh and salted fish.
Owner/Manager: Kirk Nickerson
Vice President: Gregory Nickerson
Estimated Sales: $2.3 Million
Number Employees: 17
Type of Packaging: Bulk

6660 K'ul Chocolate
2211 E Franklin Ave
Minneapolis, MN 55404
612-344-4300
info@kul-chocolate.com
kul-chocolate.com
Chocolate bars
Founder: Peter Kelsey

6661 K+S Windsor Salt Ltd.
755 boul St. Jean
Pointe Claire, QC H9R 5M9
Canada
514-630-0900
Fax: 514-694-2451 www.windsorsalt.com
Salt including table, food processing, water conditioning and ice melting.
President/CEO: Wes Clark
Marketing Manager: Michel Prevost
Year Founded: 1893
Estimated Sales: $4.89 Million
Number Employees: 861
Parent Co: K+S
Type of Packaging: Consumer, Food Service, Bulk
Other Locations:
 Canadian Salt Company
 Pugwash, Nova Scoti
 Canadian Salt Company
 Mines Seleine, Quebec
 Canadian Salt Company-Warehouse
 Goderich, Ontario
 Canadian Salt Company-Warehouse
 Clarkson, Ontario
 Canadian Salt Company-Warehouse
 Anjou, Quebec
 Canadian Salt Company
 Ojibway, Ontario
 Canadian Salt Company
 Windsor, Ontario
 Canadian Salt Company
 Regina, Saskatchewan
 Canadian Salt Company
 Lindbergh, Alberta
Brands:
 Windsor
 Safe-T-Salt
 Morton
 Tender Quick®
 Windsor® Half Salt™
 Windsor Nature's Seasons®

6662 K-Mama Sauce
4301 Benjamin St NE
Minneapolis, MN 55421
612-460-5156
kmamasauce.com
Korean hot sauce
Founder: K.C. Kye

6663 K.B. Hall Ranch
11999 Ojai Santa Paula Road
Ojai, CA 93023-8323
805-525-5875
Harvests apricots and persimmons.
owner: Thomas Hall

6664 K.S.M. Seafood Corporation
PO Box 3057
Baton Rouge, LA 70821-3057
225-383-1517
Fax: 225-387-6641
Seafood
President: Bo Wallenhom
Estimated Sales: $10-20 Million
Number Employees: 50-99

6665 KARI-Out Co
399 Knollwood Rd
Suite 309
White Plains, NY 10603-1941
914-580-3200
Fax: 914-580-3248 800-433-8799
info@kariout.com www.kariout.com
Sauces; cooking sherrt; vinegar and food colors. Also food containers, specialty bags, cleaning supplies, placemats, napkins, cutlery, and chopsticks & skewers.
President: Epstein Paul
Estimated Sales: $361000
Number Employees: 100-249
Square Footage: 3197
Parent Co: Perk-Up Inc.
Brands:
 China Pack
 Chinese-Lady
 Kari-Out

6666 KAS Spirits
46 Miller Rd.
Mahopac, NY 10541
845-750-6000
info@kasspirits.com
www.kasspirits.com
Krupnikas spiced honey liqueur
Founder/Owner: Kestutis (Kas) Katinas
Year Founded: 2013
Number of Brands: 1
Number of Products: 1
Brands:
 KAS

6667 KAYS Processing LLC
100 1st Ave SE
Clara City, MN 56222-1151
320-847-3220
Fax: 320-847-3110 massoud@kaysprocess.com
www.kaysdiabeticfoods.com
High protein snacks and cereals.
Owner: Massoud Kezemzadeh
sales@kaysnaturals.com
Number Employees: 10-19

6668 KC Innovations Inc
2900 W 43rd Ave
Kansas City, KS 66103-3129
816-506-9023
nina@kc-innovations.com
Sauces, dressing, and dips.
President: Antiona Ward
Marketing: Nina Ward
Number Employees: 1-4
Type of Packaging: Private Label, Bulk

6669 KD Canners Inc
4444 Eastgate Pkwy
Unit 9 & 10
Mississauga, ON L4W 4T6
Canada
905-602-1825
Fax: 905-602-1826 KD@kdcanners.com
www.kdcanners.com
Tropical fruit juices; jams; chutney; sauce; organic soups; and Indian curries.
President: Krishna Tripathi
Vice President: Raju Tripathi
Estimated Sales: $2.5 Million
Number Employees: 16
Type of Packaging: Private Label
Brands:
 Sahara

6670 KERN Ridge Growers LLC
25429 Barbara St
Arvin, CA 93203-9748
661-854-3141
Fax: 661-854-7229 kernridge.com
Grower, packer, and shipper of carrots, bell and chile peppers and Sunkist navel oranges.
General Manager: Bob Giragosian
bob@kernridge.com
Sales Manager: Rob Giragosian
Operations Manager: Pete Smith
Number Employees: 250-499
Type of Packaging: Consumer, Bulk
Brands:
 Kern Ridge
 Morn'n Fresh

6671 (HQ)KERR Concentrates Inc
2340 Hyacinth St NE
Salem, OR 97301-7566
503-378-0493
Fax: 503-378-1123 800-910-5377
info@kerrconcentrates.com
www.kerrconcentrates.com
Frozen fruit and vegetable juice concentrates, purees and puree concentrates.
CFO: David Gatti
R&D Technician: Tim Cohan
QA Manager: Jose Guerrero
Director of Sales: Trevor Albee
Manager: Mike Alley
mike.alley@kerrconcentrates.com
Plant Manager: Bart Hoopman
Purchasing: Jerry Mink
Estimated Sales: $5-10 Million
Number Employees: 20-49
Square Footage: 192000
Parent Co: International Flavors & Fragrances
Type of Packaging: Bulk
Other Locations:
 Kerr Concentrates Div.
 Woodburn OR

6672 KMC Citrus Enterprises Inc
16425 SE Highway 42
Weirsdale, FL 32195-2618
352-821-3666
Fax: 352-821-1400 863-298-8270
info@kmccitrus.com
Fresh and frozen orange puree and dried citrus.
President: Maristela Ferrari
VP: Keith Bowen
Estimated Sales: $1-3,000,000
Number Employees: 10-19
Type of Packaging: Consumer, Bulk
Brands:
 KMC Citrus

6673 KODA Farms Inc
22540 Russell Ave
PO Box 10
South Dos Palos, CA 93665
209-392-2191
Fax: 209-392-6558 inquiry@kodafarms.com
www.kodafarms.com
Rice and rice flour.
General Manager/Pub Relations/VP: Ross Koda
VP: Laura Koda
VP: Robin Koda
VP/Secretary: Tama Koda
Estimated Sales: $10.4 Million
Number Employees: 50-99
Number of Products: 9
Square Footage: 60000
Type of Packaging: Consumer
Brands:
 Blue Star Mockiko
 Diamond K
 Kokuho Rose
 Sho Chiku Bai

6674 KOE Organic Kombucha
Vernon, CA 90058
drinkkoe.com
Organic kombucha
Exec. VP: Armen Soghomonian

6675 KOOL Ice & Seafood Co
110 Washington St
Cambridge, MD 21613-2804
410-228-2300
Fax: 410-228-1027 800-437-2417
info@freshmarylandseafood.com
www.freshmarylandseafood.com
Seafood
Owner: Dave Nickerson
Sales Exec: Tom Collins
tom@freshmarylandseafood.com
Estimated Sales: $5-10 Million
Number Employees: 20-49

6676 KOZY Shack Enterprises Inc
P.O. Box 64050
St Paul, MN 55164-0050
855-716-1555
www.kozyshack.com
Ready-to-eat puddings.
Chairman/President/CEO: Robert Striano
Year Founded: 1967
Estimated Sales: $48.5 Million

Food Manufacturers / A-Z

Number Employees: 249-499
Square Footage: 70000
Type of Packaging: Consumer, Food Service, Bulk
Brands:
  Kozy Shack
  Ready Grains™
  Cowrageous!™
  Smartgels
  Simplywell®

6677 KP USA Trading
500 S Anderson Street
Los Angeles, CA 90033-4222
323-881-9871
Fax: 323-268-3669
Soybean, corn, cottonseed, sesame and other vegetable oils; importer of oriental foods including jasmine, sweet rice, noodles, rice stick and candy
VP: Jerry Wong
Manager: Joe Beatly
Manager: Nancy Wong
Number Employees: 10-19
Square Footage: 100000
Type of Packaging: Consumer, Food Service, Private Label, Bulk
Brands:
  King Products
  Mama

6678 KRAVE Jerky
117 W Napa St
Suite C
Sonoma, CA 95476-6647
USA
707-935-1035
info@kravejerky.com
www.kravejerky.com
Beef jerky
Owner: Jon Sebastiani
CEO: Erica Agrodnia
erica@kravejerky.com
Chief Financial Officer: David Lacy
Partner: Jens Hoj
Director Of Marketing: Chelsea Bialla
Vice President Of Operations: Paul Hettler
Number Employees: 5-9

6679 KT's Kitchens
1065 E Walnut Street
Suite C
Carson, CA 90746-1384
310-764-0850
Fax: 310-764-0855 ktaggares@ktskitchens.com
www.ktskitchens.com
Frozen pizza and refrigerated salad dressings.
President: Kathy Taggares
Contact: Mario Ayon
mario@ktskitchens.com
Estimated Sales: $32 Million
Number Employees: 100-249
Number of Brands: 2
Square Footage: 120000
Type of Packaging: Private Label
Brands:
  Bob's Big Boy
  KT's Kitchens

6680 Ka-POP!
Erie, CO 80516
kapopsnacks.com
Ancient grain snacks
Founder: Dustin Finkel

6681 Kaari Foods
Brooklyn, NY 11201
kaarifoods.com
Plant-based salad dressings, marinades and sauces
Co-Founder: Kellie Shoten
Co-Founder: Amanda Johnston

6682 Kachemak Bay Seafood
4470 Homer Spit Rd
Homer, AK 99603-8003
907-235-2799
Fax: 907-235-2799
Various fishes and other seafoods
Owner: William Sullivan
Estimated Sales: $380,000
Number Employees: 5

6683 Kaffe Magnum Opus
412 S Wade Blvd Ste 2
Millville, NJ 08332-3534
856-327-9975
Fax: 856-794-8900 800-652-5282
support@lcafe.com www.kmocoffee.com
Regular, flavored and decaffeinated coffee
President: Robert Johnson
CEO: Robert Kraeuter
VP: Cathy Johnson
Marketing Director: Heidi McDonough
Sales Representative: Meghan Kurz
Contact: Ciara Stupp
ciara@kmocoffee.com
Operations Manager: Paul Johnsones
Production Manager: Terry Kolonich
Estimated Sales: $500,000-$1 Million
Number Employees: 5-9
Brands:
  Coffee Time
  Kaffe Magnum Opus

6684 Kagome USA Inc
333 Johnson Rd
Los Banos, CA 93635
209-826-8850
www.kagomeusa.com
Tomato based sauces, creamy Sauces, oil based sauces, and specialty sauces.
President & CEO: Luis De Oliveira
Senior Human Resource & Safety Manager: Nida Reams
Product Development: Jennifer Hannon
Senior Operations Manager: Jaime Sandoval
Year Founded: 1988
Estimated Sales: $190.9 Million
Number Employees: 200-499
Other Locations:
  R&D Office
  Foster City CA
  Manufacturing
  Los Banos CA
  Manufacturing
  Osceola AR
Brands:
  Kagome

6685 Kahiki Foods Inc
1100 Morrison Rd
Columbus, OH 43230-6645
614-322-3180
Fax: 614-751-0039 855-524-4540
www.kahiki.com
Frozen Asian entrees and appetizers.
President: Martin Kelly
VP, Manufacturing & Logistics: Mark Novak
Director, Marketing/R&D: Scott Corey
Director, Finance & Accounting: Matthew Szerencsits
Director, Operations: Mike Williams
Estimated Sales: $29.1 Million
Number Employees: 100-249
Number of Brands: 5
Square Footage: 119000
Type of Packaging: Food Service
Brands:
  Bowl & Roll™
  Kahiki
  Steam & Serve™
  StirFresh
  Yum Yum Stix™

6686 Kaiser Pickles
500 York St
Cincinnati, OH 45214
513-621-2053
Fax: 513-455-8284 888-291-0608
customerservice@kaiserpickles.com
www.kaiserpickles.com
Pickle and pepper products
President: Ted G Kaiser
Contact: Liz Gast
liz@kaiserpickles.com
Estimated Sales: $10-20 Million
Number Employees: 16
Square Footage: 24616
Type of Packaging: Consumer, Food Service, Private Label, Bulk

6687 Kajun Kettle Foods
698 Saint George Ave
New Orleans, LA 70121-1117
504-733-8800
Fax: 504-736-0517 800-331-9612
www.kajunkettle.com
Sauces, gumbo and corn shrimp soup.
President: Pierre Hilzim
VP & sales exec: Monica Davidson
mdavidson@kajunkettle.com
Estimated Sales: $4 Million
Number Employees: 20-49
Square Footage: 344000
Type of Packaging: Consumer, Food Service, Private Label, Bulk
Brands:
  Crawfish Monica

6688 Kakookies
PO Box 27585
Minneapolis, MN 55427-0585
www.kakookies.com
Cookies
Founder: Sue Kakuk

6689 Kaladi Brothers
6921 Brayton Dr Ste 201
Anchorage, AK 99507
907-644-7400
Fax: 866-893-4708 sales@kaladi.com
www.kaladi.com
Coffee
President: Tim Gravel
Contact: Brad Bigelow
brad@kaladi.com
Estimated Sales: $2.5-5 Million
Number Employees: 20-49

6690 Kalamazoo Creamery
706 Lake Street
Kalamazoo, MI 49001-2201
616-343-2558
Fax: 616-343-1620
Dairy products
President: William Steers
Brands:
  Kalamazoo

6691 Kalena
Chicago, IL 60614
info@kalenasparkling.com
www.kalenasparkling.com
Sparkling coconut water
Number of Brands: 1
Number of Products: 4
Type of Packaging: Consumer
Brands:
  KALENA

6692 Kalifornia Keto
Villa Park, CA 92861
info@kaliforniaketo.com
kaliforniaketo.com
Keto baking mixes and energy bites
Co-Founder: Kellie Shoten
Co-Founder: Amanda Johnston

6693 Kalin Cellars
61 Galli Dr # F
Novato, CA 94949-5701
415-883-3543
Fax: 415-883-2909 www.kalincellars.com
Wines
President: Terrance Leighton
CFO: Frances Leighton
Estimated Sales: Under $500,000
Number Employees: 1-4
Brands:
  Kalin Cellars

6694 Kalot Superfood
Denver, CO
561-757-6541
www.kalotsuperfood.com
Fruit & nut butters
Founder: Jessica Goldstein

6695 (HQ)Kalsec
3713 W Main St
Kalamazoo, MI 49006
269-349-9711
800-323-9320
www.kalsec.com
Natural flavors, colors, extracts; spice oleoresins and essential oils.
Executive Chairman: George Todd
Research & Development: Don Berdahl
Plant Manager: Harry Todd
Estimated Sales: $3-5 Million
Number Employees: 100-249
Parent Co: Kalamazoo Holdings

Food Manufacturers / A-Z

Type of Packaging: Food Service, Bulk
Brands:
  Kalsec

6696 Kalustyan
123 Lexington Ave # 1
New York, NY 10016-8120
212-685-3451
Fax: 212-683-8458 800-352-3451
www.kalustyans.com
Herbs; spices; rice; nuts; dried fruits; beans; seeds; oils, etc.
Owner: Saedul Alam
alam@kalustyans.com
Estimated Sales: $3 Million
Square Footage: 400000
Type of Packaging: Food Service, Bulk

6697 Kameda USA Inc.
3868 W. Carson St.
Suite 312
Torrance, CA 90503
310-944-9639
Fax: 310-868-2555 info@kamedausa.com
www.kamedausa.com
Various rice snacks
Co-Founder and Owner: Kathleen O'Hehir-Johnson
Co-Founder and Owner: Roger Johnson
Contact: Christopher Mur
christophermur@kamedausa.com

6698 Kamish Food Products
5846 N Kolmar Ave
Chicago, IL 60646-5806
773-725-6959
Fax: 773-267-0400
Baking mixes, chocolate products, jams, jellies and dehydrated fruit nuggets
President: Ted Kamish
VP: Ronald Kamish
Estimated Sales: $5 Million
Number Employees: 20-49
Type of Packaging: Food Service, Private Label, Bulk

6699 Kan-Pak
1016 S Summit St
Arkansas City, KS 67005-3339
620-442-6820
Fax: 800-360-7492 800-378-1265
info@kanpak.us www.kanpak.us
Juices, creamers, dairy, ice creams.
President: Janelle Oxford
Vice President: Steven Soza
Contact: Amy Blackburn
amy.blackburn@kanpak.us
Estimated Sales: $10-20 Million
Number Employees: 500-999

6700 Kana Organics
5716 Corsa Ave
Suite 110
Westlake Village, CA 91362
213-603-0448
info@kanaorganics.com
www.kanaorganics.com
Organic cocoa, olive oil, date syrup and soybean pasta
Founder: Ricardo Favareto
Number of Brands: 1
Number of Products: 7
Type of Packaging: Consumer
Brands:
  KANA ORGANICS

6701 Kangaroo Brands
PO Box 3768
Dept. KAN
Omaha, NE 68103-0768
414-355-9696
Fax: 414-355-4295 877-266-2472
sales@kangaroobrands.com
www.kangaroobrands.com
Various types of bread and tortillas.
President: John Kashou
Treasurer: Bill Podewils
VP: George Kashou
Marketing: Salem Kashou
VP Sales: Phillip Gass
Operations Manager: Kristina A Kashou
Estimated Sales: $5-10 Million
Number Employees: 50-99
Number of Brands: 1
Number of Products: 3

Type of Packaging: Private Label

6702 (HQ)Kantner Group
625 Commerce Drive
Wapakoneta, OH 45895
419-738-4060
Fax: 419-738-4426 877-738-3448
www.kantnergroup.com
Dairy proteins and ingredients; and cheese products.
President: Doug Kantner
General Manager: John Sadowsky
CFO: Mike Koon
Quality Control: Joe Chayka
Sales/Operations: Pam Jeffery
Contact: Douglas Kantner
douglaskantner@kantnergroup.com
Purchasing: Paul Sharp
Purchasing: Mark Howell
Estimated Sales: $3-5 Million
Number Employees: 20-49
Type of Packaging: Food Service, Private Label, Bulk
Other Locations:
  Kantner Ingredients
  Wapakoneta OH
  Blue Valley Foods
  Hebron NE
  Chianti Cheese of New Jersey
  Pemberton NJ
Brands:
  Chianti Cheese
  Kantner
  Blue Valley

6703 Kapaa Bakery
Kinipopo Shopping Village
PO Box 688
Kapaa, HI 96746-0688
808-821-0060
Baked goods
President: Paul Nishijo
Estimated Sales: $500,000 appx.
Number Employees: 5-9

6704 Kapaa Poi Factory
1181 Kainahola Rd
Kapaa, HI 96746-8926
808-822-5426
Poi, tofu and kulolo
President: Kenneth Fujinaga
Estimated Sales: $500,000
Number Employees: 1-4
Type of Packaging: Consumer

6705 Kaplan & Zubrin
134 Kaighn Ave.
Camden, NJ 08101
856-964-1083
Fax: 856-964-0510 www.kzpickles.com
Pickles; condiments; relishes; and peppers.
Estimated Sales: $4773872
Number Employees: 20-49
Square Footage: 222000
Parent Co: Patriot Pickles
Type of Packaging: Food Service

6706 Kapow Now!
108-375 Lynn Ave
North Vancouver, BC V7J 2C5
Canada
604-726-6391
info@kapownow.com
kapownow.com
Spreads and crackers
President/Owner: Tiffany Shen

6707 Kara Chocolates
575 E University Pkwy
Suite B43
Orem, UT 84097-7567
801-224-9515
Fax: 801-224-9588 800-284-5272
Chocolates and candy
Manager: Susan Boren
Manager: Steve Peterson
Estimated Sales: $5-10 Million
Number Employees: 20-49
Brands:
  Kara

6708 Kargher Corp
3131 Sandstone Dr
Hatfield, PA 19440-1939
215-822-1186
Fax: 215-822-9666 800-355-1247

Chocolate products; chocolate nonpareils; and confectionary coated pretzels
CEO: Douglas Kargher
dkargher@kerrygroup.com
Estimated Sales: $5-10 Million
Number Employees: 20-49
Type of Packaging: Consumer, Food Service, Private Label, Bulk
Brands:
  Kargher Chocolate Chips

6709 Karine & Jeff
1800 Century Park East
Suite 600
Los Angeles, CA 90067
www.karinejeff.us
Grains, vegetables, soups and purees
Founder & Co-President: Karine Lepillez
Number of Brands: 1
Number of Products: 14
Type of Packaging: Consumer
Brands:
  KARINE & JEFF

6710 Karl Ehmer
6335 Fresh Pond Rd
Flushing, NY 11385-2623
718-456-8100
Fax: 718-456-2270 800-487-5275
info@karlehmer.com www.karlehmer.com
Sausages; deli and smoked meats.
President: Mark Hanssler
Quality Control: Gary Durante
Production Manager/VP: Allen Hanssler
Marketing Director: Will Osanitsch
Contact: Paul Haglich
Purchasing Manager: Daniel Durante
Estimated Sales: $5-10 Million
Number Employees: 20-49

6711 Karl Strauss Brewing Co
5985 Santa Fe St
San Diego, CA 92109-1623
858-273-2739
jobs@karlstrauss.com
www.karlstrauss.com
Beer; amber lager; and pale ale.
Owner: Karl Strauss
CEO: Ashley Freeborn
afreeborn@yourglobalgroup.com
CFO: Matthew Rattner
Marketing Director: Brian Bolten
Sales: Paul Timm
PR Manager: Melody Daversa
Operations: Grant Gotteshon
Production: Paul Segura
Estimated Sales: $.5-1 million
Number Employees: 50-99
Number of Brands: 25
Number of Products: 2
Square Footage: 88000
Parent Co: Associated Micro Breweries
Brands:
  Downtown After Dark
  Endless Summer Gold
  Karl Strauss
  Red Trolley Ale
  Stargazer
  Windansea Wheat

6712 Karla's Smokehouse
P.O.Box 537
Rockaway Beach, OR 97136-0537
503-355-2362
Smoke fish
Owner: Karla Steinhauser
Estimated Sales: Less than $500,000
Number Employees: 1-4

6713 Karlin Foods
1845 Oak St
Suite 19
Northfield, IL 60093-3022
847-441-8330
Fax: 847-441-8640 info@karlinfoods.com
www.karlinfoods.com
Dehydrated soup mixes and sauces; breadcumbs; seasonings; and stuffing mixes.
President: Mitchell Karlin
mkarlin@karlinfoods.com
Quality Assurance Manager: Vince Klemm
Director, National Sales: Jack Hounsell
Director, Operations: Jacob Drew

Food Manufacturers / A-Z

Estimated Sales: $10-20 Million
Number Employees: 10-19
Type of Packaging: Private Label

6714 Karlsburger Foods Inc
3236 Chelsea Rd W
Monticello, MN 55362-4667
763-295-2273
Fax: 763-323-1745 800-383-6549
www.karlsburger.com
Soup, sauce and gravy bases; and seasonings.
Owner: Mike Maher
mike@karlsburger.com
Number Employees: 20-49
Type of Packaging: Food Service
Brands:
  Karlsburger

6715 Karma Candy
356 Emerald St N
Hamilton, ON L8L 8K6
Canada
905-527-6222
Fax: 905-527-6223
Seasonal chocolate and hard candy
General Manager: Joe Castro
VP, Operations: Samuel Singh

6716 Karma Nuts
11501 Dublin Blvd
Suite 200
Dublin, CA 94568
925-961-5491
info@karmanuts.com
www.karmanuts.com
Wrapped and roasted cashews
Founder: Ganesh Nair
Number of Brands: 1
Number of Products: 6
Type of Packaging: Consumer
Brands:
  KARMA

6717 Karmalize.Me
225 Long Ave
Bldg 15
Hillside, NJ 07205
862-955-3492
admin@karmalize.me
www.karmalize.me
Nuts, seeds and nut butters.
Co-Founder: Shubhra Haryani
Co-Founder: Amit Haryani

6718 Karn Meats
922 Taylor Avenue
Columbus, OH 43219
614-252-3712
Fax: 614-252-8273 800-221-9585
info@karnmeats.com www.karnmeats.com
IQF ground beef patties and cooked ground beef crumbles
Contact: Todd Crawford
tcrawford@karnmeats.com
VP Operations: Michael Furr
Production Supervisor: Tony Furr
Plant Manager: Richard Karn
Estimated Sales: $10 Million
Number Employees: 50
Square Footage: 150000
Type of Packaging: Food Service, Private Label, Bulk

6719 Karoun Dairies Inc
13023 Arroyo St
San Fernando, CA 91340
818-767-7000
Fax: 818-767-7024 888-767-0778
contact@karouncheese.com
www.karouncheese.com
Cheese and cultured dairy products.
President & Chairman: Ara Baghdassarian
CFO: Tsolak Khatcherian
COO: Rostom Baghdassarian
Year Founded: 1990
Estimated Sales: $62.5 Million
Number of Brands: 6
Parent Co: Parmalat Canada
Type of Packaging: Consumer, Food Service
Brands:
  Karoun
  Arz
  Queso Del Valle
  Gopi

Yanni
Central Valley Creamery

6720 Kashi Company
PO Box 649
Solana Beach, CA 92075
877-747-2467
info@kashi.com www.kashi.com
Various multi-grain products
President/Owner: Tony Chow
CEO: David Denholm
Estimated Sales: $5-10 Million
Number Employees: 20-49
Parent Co: Kellogg Company
Type of Packaging: Food Service, Private Label
Brands:
  Go Lean
  Good Friends
  Heart To Heart
  Kashi Cereals
  Kashi Frozen Foods
  Kashi Snacks

6721 Kasilof Fish Company
1930 Merrill Creek Pkwy
Everett, WA 98203-5897
360-658-7552
Fax: 360-653-3560 800-322-7552
smokedsales@tridentseafoods.com
Smoked salmon and smoked seafood
President: Drew Ellison
Finance Manager: Julie Lorig
VP Sales & Marketing: Patti Moore
Estimated Sales: $2.5 Million
Number Employees: 25
Parent Co: Trident Seafoods
Type of Packaging: Consumer, Food Service, Private Label, Bulk
Brands:
  Eagle River Brand
  Kasilof Fish

6722 Kasira
5620 Knott Ave
Buena Park, CA 90621
800-220-6131
www.kasiratea.com
Coffee fruit tea
Number of Brands: 1
Number of Products: 5
Type of Packaging: Consumer
Brands:
  KASIRA

6723 Kasseler Food Products Inc.
1031 Brevik Place
Mississauga, ON L4W 3R7
Canada
905-629-2142
Fax: 905-629-1699 sales@kasselerfoods.com
www.kasselerfoods.com
Bread and biscuits.
President: Erich Lamshoeft

6724 Kastner's Pastry Shop & Grocery
9467 Harding Ave
Surfside, FL 33154-2803
305-866-6993
Pastries
Owner: Philip Cohen
Estimated Sales: Less than $500,000
Number Employees: 5-9

6725 Kate Latter Candy Company
937 Decatur St,
New Orleans, LA 70116
504-525-5359
Fax: 504-828-0045 800-825-5359
New Orleans pralines, Southern candies, Cajun and Creole food products.
CEO: Pam Randazza
Estimated Sales: Less than $5 Million
Number Employees: 12
Brands:
  Chef Hans
  Kate Latters Chocolates

6726 Kate's Vineyard
5211 Big Ranch Rd
Napa, CA 94558-1004
707-255-2644
Fax: 707-966-2813
information@katesvineyard.com
www.katesvineyard.com

Wine
President: William Bryant
VP: Sally Bryant
Marketing VP: Kate Bryant
Contact: Kate Brunnell
Kate@Katesvineyard.Com
Estimated Sales: Less than $5 Million
Number Employees: 1-4
Brands:
  Kate's
  Sedna

6727 Kateri Foods
5415 Opportunity Court
Hopkins, MN 55343
952-933-9732
Fax: 952-933-9942 800-330-8351
Gluten-free; chocolate; candy; nuts; popcorn; and gift baskets.
Marketing: Patrick Knight
Type of Packaging: Consumer, Private Label

6728 Kathie's Kitchen
50 Devine St
North Haven, CT 06473-2244
203-407-0546
www.superseedz.com
Gourmet pumpkin seeds.
Founder: Kathie Pelliccio
Estimated Sales: Less than $500,000
Number Employees: 1-4
Brands:
  SUPERSEEDZ

6729 Kathryn Kennedy Winery
13180 Pierce Rd
Saratoga, CA 95070
408-867-4170
Fax: 408-867-9463
cabernet@kathrynkennedywinery.com
www.kathrynkennedywinery.com
Wine
President/Winegrower: Marty Mathis
Directorr of sales: Eric Fountain
Contact: Alison Von Breitenfeld
qb@kathrynkennedywinery.com
Estimated Sales: Less than $5 Million
Number Employees: 1-4
Brands:
  Kathryn Kennedy

6730 Kathy's Gourmet Specialties
PO Box 1058
Mendocino, CA 95460-1058
707-937-1383
Fax: 707-937-1383 info@kathysgourmet.com
Specialty sauces, mustards and condiments.
Owner: Shelley Pittman
Estimated Sales: $81,000
Number Employees: 2
Number of Products: 8
Type of Packaging: Consumer, Food Service, Private Label, Bulk
Brands:
  Kathy's Gourmet Specialties

6731 Katies Korner Inc
1105 Tibbetts Wick Rd
Girard, OH 44420-1137
330-539-4140
Fax: 330-534-1412 www.katieskorner.com
Homemade ice cream and yogurt
Owner/President: Katherine Martin
Secretary/Treasurer: Keith Martin
Estimated Sales: Less than $500,000
Number Employees: 1-4

6732 Katrina's Tartufo
585 Bicycle Path
Port Jeffrsn Sta, NY 11776-3431
516-476-0863
Fax: 516-331-1269 800-480-8836
Ice cream
Owner: Rob Dineon
Estimated Sales: Less than $500,000
Number Employees: 10-19
Square Footage: 6000

Food Manufacturers / A-Z

6733 Katy's Smokehouse
740 Edwards St
Trinidad, CA 95570
707-677-0151
Fax: 707-677-9328
service@katyssmokehouse.com
www.katyssmokehouse.com
various smoked fish.
Owner: Bob Lake
CEO: Judy Lake
Estimated Sales: Less Than $500,000
Number Employees: 1-4
Type of Packaging: Consumer, Food Service
Brands:
Katy's Smokehouse

6734 Katysweet Confectioners Inc.
4321 W State Highway 71
PO Box 1237
La Grange, TX 78945-5150
979-242-5172
Fax: 800-231-5934 info@katysweet.com
www.katysweet.com
Candy and confections
Founder: Kay Carlton
Estimated Sales: Less than $500,000
Number Employees: 5-9

6735 (HQ)Kauai Coffee Co Inc
1 Numila Rd
Kalaheo, HI 96741-6000
808-335-3237
Fax: 808-335-0036 800-545-8605
retail@kauaicoffee.com
Roasted and specialty coffees.
President: Darla Domingo
Accountant: Candi Akita
Institutional Sales Manager: Faith Soto
Manager: Fred Cowell
Chief Operating Officer: Joan Momohara
Estimated Sales: $28 Million
Number Employees: 20-49
Number of Brands: 1
Type of Packaging: Private Label
Brands:
Kauai Coffee

6736 Kauai Kookie
P.O. Box 503
Eleele, HI 96705
808-335-5003
Fax: 808-335-5186 800-361-1126
info@kauaikookie.com www.kauaikookie.com
Cookies and dressings.
Marketing/Director Of Sales: Ruth Hashisaka
Plant Manager: Ellen Albarado
Estimated Sales: $1 Million
Number Employees: 20-49
Number of Brands: 2
Type of Packaging: Consumer, Food Service
Brands:
Hawaiian Hula Dressing
Kauai Kookie

6737 Kauai Organic Farms
P O Box 86
Kilauea, HI 96754
808-651-8843
Fax: 808-828-0151 phil@kauaiorganicfarms.com
www.kauaiorganicfarms.com
Organic Hawaiian yellow ginger and other ginger based products.
Owner/President: Phil Green
Public Relations: Linda Green
Estimated Sales: $.5-1 million
Number Employees: 5
Number of Products: 4
Square Footage: 8000
Type of Packaging: Bulk

6738 Kauai Producers
4334 Rice St
Suite 101
Lihue, HI 96766
808-245-4044
Fax: 808-245-9061 800-262-1400
kauai@hvcb.org www.gohawaii.com
Wholesaler/distributor of produce and dairy, frozen, dry and refrigerated products
President: Scott Nonaka
Vice President: Pearl Nonaka
Marketing Manager: Merle Nonaka
Estimated Sales: $4.5 Million
Number Employees: 23

6739 Kaurina's, LLC
2750 Northaven Road
Suite 302
Dallas, TX 75229-7072
972-888-9990
Fax: 972-888-9991 info@kaurinas.com
www.kaurinas.com
Organic kulfi and ice cream.
Type of Packaging: Consumer

6740 Kava King
123 N Orchard Street
Suite A4
Ormond Beach, FL 32174
386-673-4247
Fax: 386-671-9500 800-638-0082
Instant kava drink mixes.
VP: William Darby
Marketing Director: Jared White
Sales: Richard Bahmann
Contact: Todd Hotaling
todd@kavakingproducts.com
Estimated Sales: $300,000-500,000
Number Employees: 1-4
Type of Packaging: Consumer
Brands:
Kava King Beverage Mixes
Kava King Chocolates

6741 Kay Foods Co
1352 Division St
Detroit, MI 48207-2604
313-393-1100
Fax: 313-393-1083
Pre-made cold salads; also, gourmet candies.
Owner/VP: Mark Kisel
Estimated Sales: $2 Million
Number Employees: 5-9
Square Footage: 80000
Type of Packaging: Consumer, Food Service, Private Label
Brands:
Kay Foods

6742 Kay's Naturals, Inc.
PO Box 669
100 First Ave SE
Clara City, MN 56222
320-847-3220
866-873-5499
www.kaysnaturals.com
Cereals; protein chips; cookies; and pretzels.
Co-Founder: Ann Kazemzadeh
ann@kaysnaturals.com
Co-Founder: Massoud Kazemzadeh

6743 Kayco
72 New Hook Rd
Bayonne, NJ 07002
718-369-4600
customercare@kayco.com
kayco.com
Kosher, all natural, gluten free, vegan, and fair trade products; also specializes in grape juice.
President: Ilan Ron
CEO: Mordy Herzog
Financial Manager: Dov Levi
Executive Vice President: Harold Weiss
Year Founded: 1948
Estimated Sales: $86 Million
Number Employees: 500-999
Number of Brands: 76
Type of Packaging: Consumer, Food Service, Bulk

6744 Kayem Foods
75 Arlington St.
Chelsea, MA 02150
617-889-1600
800-426-6100
www.kayem.com
Deli products and meats, gourmet chicken, sausage and buns.
President/Chief Executive Officer: Matt Monkiewicz
Year Founded: 1909
Estimated Sales: $129 Million
Number Employees: 500-999
Number of Brands: 8
Square Footage: 160000
Type of Packaging: Consumer, Food Service, Private Label, Bulk

Other Locations:
Genoa Sausage Company
Woburn MA
Brands:
Kayem®

6745 KeVita
Oxnard, CA 93030
888-310-6106
www.kevita.com
Fermented beverages
Co-Founder: Bill Moses
Co-Founder: Chakra Earthsong
Year Founded: 2009

6746 Kedem
72 New Hook Rd
Bayonne, NJ 07002
718-369-4600
customercare@kayco.com
www.kayco.com
Kosher, gluten free and all natural products. Kosher grape juice, non-alcoholic wines, jams and, cooking products and biscuits.
President: Ilan Ron
CEO: Mordy Herzog
Financial Manager: Dov Levi
Executive Vice President: Harold Weiss
Year Founded: 1948
Estimated Sales: $50-90 Million
Number of Brands: 23
Parent Co: Kayco
Type of Packaging: Consumer

6747 Keebler Company
PO Box CAMB
Battlecreek, MI 49016
630-956-9742
800-962-1413
www.keebler.com
Baked goods
President and CEO: David Mackay
Contact: Dana Haller
dana_haller@keebler.com
Year Founded: 1898
Estimated Sales: $622 Million
Number Employees: 400
Square Footage: 325000
Parent Co: Kellogg Company
Type of Packaging: Consumer
Brands:
Keebler
Ready Crust
Hollow Tree

6748 Keegan Ales
20 St. James St.
Kingston, NY 12401
845-331-2739
www.keeganales.com
Craft IPA, American ales and stout
Founder/Owner: Tommy Keegan
Year Founded: 2003
Number of Brands: 1
Number of Products: 6
Type of Packaging: Consumer, Private Label
Brands:
Keegan Ales

6749 Keenan Farms
31510 Plymouth Ave
Kettleman City, CA 93239-9721
559-945-1400
Fax: 559-945-1414 info@keenanpistachio.com
www.keenanpistachio.com
Pistachios
President: Robert Keenan
robert@keenanpistachio.com
VP: Charles Keenan
Estimated Sales: $4 Million
Number Employees: 50-99
Brands:
Keenan Farms

6750 Keep Healthy
1019 Fort Salonga Rd
Northport, NY 11768
631-651-9090
info@keephealthyinc.com
keephealthyinc.com
Date bars
Founder: Ron Sowa

Food Manufacturers / A-Z

6751 Keep Moving Inc.
PO Box 1823
New York, NY 10156
contact@gutzyorganic.com
www.gutzyorganic.com
Organic, prebiotic fruit snacks.
Founder: David Istier
david.istier@energyfruits.com
Brands:
 Energyfruits

6752 Keeter's Meat Company
901 U.S. 87
Tulia, TX 79088
806-995-3413
Fax: 806-995-1087 800-456-5019
www.keetersmeatcompany.com
Meat products
Co-Owner: Jerry Keeter
jkeeter@keetersmeatcompany.com
Co-Owner: Kati Keeter
Estimated Sales: $3 Million
Number Employees: 5-9
Type of Packaging: Consumer

6753 Kefiplant
2120, Joseph-St-Cyr
Drummondville, QC J2C 6V8
Canada
819-477-2345
Fax: 819-477-7595 info@kefiplant.com
www.kefiplant.com
Extracts
President & Sales Director: Chantale Houle
General Director: Alain Lambert

6754 Kegg's Candies
4934 Beechnut St
Houston, TX 77096-1605
713-664-3100
Fax: 713-664-4888
Candy
Number Employees: 10-19

6755 Kehr's candies
3533 W Lisbon Ave
Milwaukee, WI 53208-1954
414-344-4305
Fax: 414-933-2985
Candy
Owner: Paul Martinka
Paul@Kehrs.com
Estimated Sales: Less than $500,000
Number Employees: 5-9
Brands:
 Kehr's Kandy

6756 Kelapo
Tampa, FL 33634
800-230-5952
www.kelapo.com
Virgin coconut oil
Number of Brands: 1
Number of Products: 12
Type of Packaging: Consumer
Brands:
 KELAPO

6757 Kelble Brothers Inc
9111 Reiger Rd
Berlin Heights, OH 44814-9644
419-588-2015
Fax: 419-588-3116 800-247-2333
kelblebrosinc@yahoo.com www.kelbebros.com
Beef and lamb
Owner: Bill Fox
kelblebrothersinc@yahoo.com
VP: William Fox
Purchasing Agent: Rose Austin
Estimated Sales: $4 Million
Number Employees: 10-19
Square Footage: 48000
Type of Packaging: Consumer, Food Service, Bulk

6758 Kelchner's Horseradish
7520 Morris Ct., Ste 115
PO Box 245
Allentown, PA 18106
610-674-4450
Fax: 215-249-1931 800-424-1952
www.kelchnershorseradish.com
Prepared horseradish, tartar sauce, cocktail sauce, horseradish mustard and horseradish with beets
President: John Slaymaker
Chairman of the Board: Walter Slaymaker
Production: Richard Rankin
Estimated Sales: $4,700,000
Number Employees: 10-19
Square Footage: 20000
Type of Packaging: Consumer, Food Service
Brands:
 Kelchner's

6759 Keller's Bakery
1012 Jefferson St
Lafayette, LA 70501-7991
337-235-1568
Fax: 337-235-8817
kellersbakerydowntown@gmail.com
www.kellersdowntown.com
Baked products
Owner/Operator: Kenneth Keller
Year Founded: 1973
Estimated Sales: $1-3 Million
Number Employees: 10-19

6760 Keller's Creamery
10220 N. Ambassador Dr
Kansas City, MO 64153
800-535-5371
www.kellerscreamery.com
Butter, butter oil, powdered milk, cream cheese, cheese products, heavy cream.
Chief Executive Officer: Richard Smith
Year Founded: 1906
Estimated Sales: $48 Million
Number Employees: 210
Square Footage: 6500
Parent Co: Dairy Farmers of America
Type of Packaging: Consumer, Food Service, Private Label, Bulk
Other Locations:
 Keller's Creamery
 Winnsboro TX
Brands:
 Borden
 Breakstones
 Falfurrias
 Hotel Bar
 Keller's
 Plugra

6761 Kelley Bean Co Inc
2407 Circle Dr
Scottsbluff, NE 69361
308-635-6438
Fax: 308-635-7345 info@kelleybean.com
www.kelleybean.com
Dried beans.
President: Kevin Kelley
kkelley@kelleybean.com
Chairman: Robert Kelley, Jr.
EVP & Chief Financial Officer: G. Lee Glenn
Director, Finance: Jim Loveridge
Business Development: Bryce Kelley
Controller: Judy Osborn
Human Resources Manager: Kim Ferguson
Operations/Seed Director: Chris Kelley
Year Founded: 1927
Estimated Sales: $36.1 Million
Number Employees: 20-49
Square Footage: 190000
Brands:
 Browns Best

6762 (HQ)Kelley Foods
1697 Lower Curtis Rd
PO Box 708
Elba, AL 36323-8847
334-897-5761
Fax: 334-897-2712 eddiek@kelleyfoods.com
www.kelleyfoods.com
Various meats
President: Erik Ennis
eennis@drinkarizona.com
CEO: Eddie Kelley
Controller: Alex Mount
Vice President: J Kelley
VP Marketing: C Kelley
VP Operations: Dwight Kelley
Plant Manager: Max Glisson
Estimated Sales: $10-20 Million
Number Employees: 100-249
Type of Packaging: Food Service
Brands:
 Bryan
 Excel
 Hormel
 Kelley's

6763 Kelley's Island Wine Company
418 Woodford Road
Kelleys Island, OH 43438
419-746-2678
kiwineco@aol.com
Wines
President: Kirt Zettler
Owner: Toby Zettler
Estimated Sales: $5-9.9 Million
Number Employees: 5-9
Brands:
 Coyote White
 Inscription White
 Long Sweet Red
 Sunset Pink

6764 Kelley's Katch Caviar
210 Washington St
Savannah, TN 38372-1777
731-925-7360
Fax: 731-925-5631 888-681-8565
www.kelleyskatch.com
Paddlefish and sturgeon caviar.
Owner: Vickie Kelley
Estimated Sales: Less than $500,000
Number Employees: 1-4

6765 Kellogg Canada Inc.
5350 Creekbank Rd.
Mississauga, ON L4W 5S1
Canada
888-876-3750
www.kelloggs.ca
Breakfast foods.
President/CEO: Tony Chow
Estimated Sales: $1 Billion
Number of Brands: 18
Parent Co: Kellogg Company
Type of Packaging: Consumer
Brands:
 All-Bran®
 Corn Pops®
 Eggo®
 Froot Loops®
 Just Right®
 Crispix®
 Kellogg's Corn Flakes®
 Kellogg's Frosted Flakes
 Krave®
 Mini-Wheats®
 Muslix®
 Nutri-Grain®
 Pop-Tarts®
 Raisin Bran®
 Rice Krispies Squares®
 Rice Krispies®
 Special K®
 Vector®

6766 (HQ)Kellogg Co.
1 Kellogg Sq.
PO Box 3599
Battle Creek, MI 49017-3599
269-961-2000
Fax: 269-961-2871 800-962-1413
www.kelloggcompany.com
Breakfast foods manufacturer
Chairman/CEO: Steven Cahillane
President, Kellogg North America: Chris Hood
Senior VP/CFO: Amit Banati
Estimated Sales: $13.5 Billion
Number Employees: 34,000
Number of Brands: 28
Type of Packaging: Consumer
Other Locations:
 R&D
 Battle Creek MI
Brands:
 Kellogg's
 Special K
 Cheez-It
 Pringles
 Keebler
 Austin
 Mother's Cookies
 Morning Star Farms
 Carr's
 Gardenburger
 Murray Sugar Free Cookies
 Famous Amos
 Frosted Mini-Wheats
 Rice Krispies

Food Manufacturers / A-Z

Pop-Tarts
Chips Deluxe
Eggo
All-Bran
Nutri-Grain
Frosted Flakes
Crunchy Nut
Krave
Coco Pops
Froot Loops
Corn Flakes
Corn Pops
Fiber Plus
Town House

6767 Kelly Corned Beef Co
3531 N Elston Ave
Chicago, IL 60618-5687
773-588-2882
Fax: 773-588-0810 800-624-5617
www.kellyeisenberg.com
Corn beef and other deli meat products.
President: Marvin Eisenberg
Year Founded: 1929
Estimated Sales: $510000
Number Employees: 10-19
Parent Co: Eisenberg Sausage Company
Brands:
  Eisenberg
  Kelly

6768 (HQ)Kelly Flour Company
1208 N Swift Rd
Addison, IL 60101-6104
630-678-5300
Fax: 630-678-5311
Dry milk replacers and dry egg extenders
Manager: Dan Hoberg
Executive VP: Donald Kelly, Jr.
Plant Manager: Samuel Vergara
Estimated Sales: $3-5 Million
Number Employees: 20-49
Square Footage: 60
Type of Packaging: Food Service, Private Label
Brands:
  Chickadee Products
  Hi-Bak
  Kel-Yolk
  Thel-Egg

6769 Kelly Foods
513 Airways Blvd
Jackson, TN 38301
731-424-2255
info@kellyfoods.com
www.kellyfoods.com
Canned meat products; importer of corned beef.
President: Ann Koch
Contact: Tony Jordan
tony_jordan@kellysfoods.com
VP Operations: Mark Koch
Plant Manager: Bob James
Purchasing Manager: Mike Rushing
Estimated Sales: $5700000
Number Employees: 50
Square Footage: 260000
Type of Packaging: Consumer
Brands:
  Hypower
  Kelly

6770 Kelly Gourmet Foods Inc
2095 Jerrold Ave
Suite 218
San Francisco, CA 94124-1628
415-648-9200
Fax: 415-648-6164
Cooked, smoked and raw meats.
President: Rina Kelly
VP: Chris Kelly
Sales Director: Ed Kelly
Estimated Sales: Less than $500,000
Number Employees: 1-4
Type of Packaging: Consumer, Food Service, Bulk
Brands:
  Fulton Organic Free Range Chicken
  Fulton Valley Farms
  Sierra Sausage Co.

6771 Kelly Packing Company
P.O. Box 27
Torrington, WY 82240
307-532-2210
Fax: 307-532-8482
Meat products
President: David Kelly
Estimated Sales: $4 Million
Number Employees: 5-9
Type of Packaging: Consumer
Brands:
  Kelly

6772 Kelly's Candies
7 Twin Oaks Place
Pooler, GA 31322
254-289-6154
Fax: 412-573-0044 800-523-3051
Homemade fudge and chocolate candies
Owner: Gina Broderick
Estimated Sales: $.5-1 million
Number Employees: 5-9
Type of Packaging: Consumer, Private Label, Bulk
Brands:
  Kelly's

6773 Kelly-Eisenberg Gourmet Deli Products
3531 N Elston Ave
Chicago, IL 60618
773-588-2882
Fax: 773-588-0810 800-624-5617
sales@kellyeisenberg.com
www.kellyeisenberg.com
Corned beef, hot dogs, roast beef, pastrami, Polish sausage
President: Marvin Eisenberg
VP: Cliff Eisenberg
VP: Howard Eisenberg
Operations Manager: Greg Timm
Estimated Sales: Below $5 Million
Number Employees: 20-49
Type of Packaging: Private Label
Brands:
  Eisenberg Beef Hot Dogs
  Eisenberg Corned Bee
  Eisenberg Pastrami
  Kelly Corned Beef

6774 Kelsen, Inc.
40 Marcus Drive
Suite 101
Melville, NY 11747
631-694-8080
Fax: 631-694-8085 888-253-5736
sales.usa@kelsen.com www.kelsen.com
Danish butter cookies
President: Lars Norgaard
Marketing: Gilbert Quiles
Contact: Nicolaj Andersen
na@kelsen.com
Estimated Sales: $5-10 Million
Number Employees: 5-9
Number of Brands: 4
Brands:
  Bisca
  Karenvolf
  Kjeldsens
  Royal Dansk

6775 Kelson Creek Winery
19919 Shenandoah School Rd
Plymouth, CA 95669
209-245-4700
Fax: 209-245-4707
Wine
Manager: April Ysmael
CEO: Tim Tado
Estimated Sales: $500,000-$1 Million
Number Employees: 1-4
Type of Packaging: Private Label
Brands:
  Kelson Creek

6776 Kemach Food Products
9920 Farragut Rd
Brooklyn, NY 11236-2302
718-272-5655
Fax: 718-272-6226 info@kemach.com
www.kemach.net
Drink mixes; soup mixes; crackers; flour; cereals; pasta; baked goods; candy, chocolates, health food, chocolate syrup, juices, pasta sauces, ices, cones, etc.
President: Samuel Salzman
CFO: Aaron Daum
VP: Nik Salzman
Estimated Sales: $2.5-5 Million
Number Employees: 10-19
Square Footage: 15000
Type of Packaging: Consumer, Food Service, Private Label, Bulk
Brands:
  A'Guania
  Kemach
  Matzo Meal
  Mekach

6777 Kemin Industries Inc
2100 Maury St
Des Moines, IA 50317-1100
515-559-5100
Fax: 515-559-5232 800-777-8307
info@kemin.com www.kemin.com
Vitamin and supplement ingredients, natural preservatives, FloraGLO lutein, natural antioxidant preservatives
Co-Founder: Mary Nelson
VP: Charles Brice
Marketing Director: Andy Martin
Sales Manager: Linda Fullmer
Customer Service: Lori Barker
Number Employees: 100-249
Brands:
  Floraglo
  Myco Curb
  Naturox
  Oro Glo
  Palasurance
  Paradigmox
  Roseen
  Satise
  Zenipro

6778 Kemps LLC
1270 Energy Ln
St Paul, MN 55108
www.kemps.com
Frozen yogurt, ice cream, sherbert, milk, juices, cottage cheese, sour cream and dips, and yogurt.
President & CEO: Greg Kurr
CFO: Daniel Jones
SVP, Growth & Innovation: Rachel Kyllo
VP, Operations: Bob Williams
General Manager: Brad Cuthbert
Year Founded: 1914
Estimated Sales: $116.7 Million
Number Employees: 1,125
Square Footage: 40000
Parent Co: Dairy Farmers of America

6779 Ken's Foods Inc
1 D'Angelo Dr
Marlborough, MA 01752
508-229-1100
www.kensfoods.com
Salad dressings, mayonnaise and sauces.
Year Founded: 1958
Estimated Sales: $106.4 Million
Number Employees: 800
Square Footage: 340000
Other Locations:
  Ken's Plant Facility
  McDonough GA
  Ken's Plant Facility
  Las Vegas NV

6780 Kencraft, Inc.
119 East 200 N.
Alpine, UT 84004-1631
801-756-6916
Fax: 801-756-7791 800-377-4368
sales@kencraftcandy.com
www.kencraftcandy.com
Candy and other confectionery products
President & Chief Executive Officer: David Taiclet
Contact: Gil Bowles
gilb@kencraftcandy.com
Estimated Sales: $34 Million
Number Employees: 200
Number of Brands: 12
Square Footage: 95000
Parent Co: Alpine Confections
Brands:
  Bubblegum Buddies
  Candy Climbers
  Choco Pals
  Chummy Chums
  Circus Sticks
  Kencraft Classics
  Kookie Kakes
  Lil' Lollies

Food Manufacturers / A-Z

Lollipals
Puppet Pals
Twist Pops
Twistix

6781 Kendall Frozen Fruits, Inc.
9777 Wilshire Blvd
Suite 818
Beverly Hills, CA 90212-1908
310-288-9920
Fax: 310-288-9913 susan@kendallfruit.com
www.kendallfruit.com
Frozen fruits including dried, juice concentrates, purees, freeze dried fruit, fruit powders, vegetable products, chocolate covered dried fruit, and yogurt covered dried fruit
President: Susan Kendall
Manager/Berkeley: Deborah Kendall
Manager/Littleton: Larry Kendall
VP Finance: Debra Olk
VP: Mike Daems
VP: Frank Abarca
VP: Kelly Marks
Estimated Sales: $3.6 Million
Number Employees: 14

6782 Kendall-Jackson
5007 Fulton Rd
Fulton, CA 95439
866-287-9818
866-287-9818
kjwines@kj.com www.kj.com
Wines
Manager: Mike Ward
Estimated Sales: Less than $500,000
Number Employees: 1-4
Parent Co: Kendall-Jackson Wine

6783 Kendon Candies Inc
460 Perrymont Avenue
San Jose, CA 95125
408-297-6133
Fax: 408-297-4008 800-332-2639
Lollipops
President: Kate Glass
Contact: Holly Anderson
h.anderson@kendoncandies.com

6784 Kendrick Gourmet Products
302 Brown Ave
Columbus, GA 31903-1253
706-687-0161
Fax: 706-682-1528 800-356-1858
Pecan candies, cakes, and brownies.
President: Bryan Stone
Vice President: Liz Kendrick
Manager: Stacey Chambers
Sales Manager: Robbing Carr
Estimated Sales: $5-9.9 Million
Number Employees: 10-19
Square Footage: 240000
Parent Co: Columbus Gourmet

6785 Kenko International
6984 Bandini Blvd
Los Angeles, CA 90040
323-721-8300
Fax: 323-721-9600 ronu@kenko-intl.com
www.kenkoco.com
Sweeteners, food acidulants, antioxidants, preservatives and other food chemicals.
President: Satomi Tsuchibi
Contact: Juliet Cunningham
jcunningham@alere.com
Estimated Sales: $2.7 Million
Number Employees: 15

6786 Kennebec Fruit Company
2 Main St
Lisbon Falls, ME 04252
207-353-8173
Moxie; yellow gentian based soft drink
Owner: Frank Anicetti
Estimated Sales: Less than $500,000
Number Employees: 1-4

6787 Kennedy Gourmet
115 N. Brandon Drive
Glendale Heights, IL 60139
713-795-5500
Fax: 713-795-5534 800-729-8116
info@imperial-foods.com
www.imperial-foods.com
Gourmet candy and foods

President: J Read Boles
Plant Manager: Sandy Lewis
Purchasing Manager: Sue Williams
Estimated Sales: Below $5 Million
Number Employees: 50
Square Footage: 160
Type of Packaging: Private Label
Brands:
  Brazos Legends
  Choc-Quitos
  Chocolate Covered Pretzels
  Chocolate Flavored Coffee Spoons
  Chocolate Fortune Cookies
  Graham Dunks
  Gram Dunks
  Nostalgic Creations
  Sir George Fudge
  Stirring Sticks
  Tea Sickles
  Which Ends

6788 Kennesaw Fruit & Juice
1300 SW 1st Ct
Pompano Beach, FL 33069-3204
954-532-7938
Fax: 954-784-1222 800-949-0371
www.kennesawjuice.com
Citrus juices including orange, grapefruit, lemonade, etc.; also, cored and chunked pineapple, fresh orange and grapefruit slices and fruit salad available
President: Len Roseburg
V.P./Prtnr.: Ed Zukerman
Estimated Sales: $3-5 Million
Number Employees: 20-49
Square Footage: 152000
Type of Packaging: Consumer, Food Service

6789 Kenny's Candy & Confections
Perham, MN 56573
kennyscandy.com
Fruit snacks, gummies, licorice and popcorn
Founder: Ken Nelson
Year Founded: 1987
Type of Packaging: Private Label

6790 (HQ)Kenosha Beef International LTD
Kenosha, WI
www.bwfoods.com
Meat products including frozen boxed beef patties
President, Chief Executive Officer: Dennis Vignieri
CFO: Jerry King
jking@bwfoods.com
VP HR & Safety: Phyllis Murray
VP Sales & Marketing: Wayne Wehking
EVP Operations & Procurement: John Ruffolo
Number Employees: 500-999
Type of Packaging: Consumer, Food Service
Brands:
  Birchwood Foods
  Bistro 36

6791 Kent Foods Inc
2600 Church St
Gonzales, TX 78629
830-672-7993
Fax: 830-672-7223 www.kentfeeds.com
Frozen and liquid egg products
President: Daw Lu
daw.lu@kentfeeds.com
Sales Executive: Ging Lu
Estimated Sales: $1-3 Million
Number Employees: 20-49
Square Footage: 45000
Type of Packaging: Food Service, Bulk
Brands:
  Kent Foods

6792 Kent Precision Foods Group Inc
2905 US-61
Muscatine, IA 52761
800-442-5242
www.precisionfoods.com
Pickle and tomato mixes, pectins, jams, jellies, fruit preservatives, blended spices and seasonings, dessert mixes; exporter of dry soft serve and dessert mixes.
Manager of Business Development: Kirk Kuiper
Vice President of Sales & Marketing: Connie Huck
Year Founded: 1992
Estimated Sales: $69.4 Million
Number Employees: 20-49
Number of Brands: 8

Square Footage: 200000
Parent Co: Kent Corporation
Type of Packaging: Consumer, Food Service, Private Label, Bulk
Other Locations:
  Manufacturing Location
  Bolingbrook IL
Brands:
  Foothill Farms®
  Frostline® Frozen Treats
  DOLE® Soft Serve
  LAND O'LAKES™
  Mrs. Dash® Foodservice
  Sugar Twin®
  Baker's Joy®
  Sqwincher®

6793 Kent Quality Foods Inc
703 Leonard St NW
Grand Rapids, MI 49504-4236
616-459-4595
Fax: 616-459-5802 800-748-0141
information@kqf.com kqf.com
Manufacturer of franks, sausages and specialty meats. Founded in 1967.
President: Steve Soet
Year Founded: 1967
Estimated Sales: $46 Million
Number Employees: 100-249
Type of Packaging: Consumer, Food Service, Private Label, Bulk

6794 Kent's Wharf
31 Steamboat Hl
Swans Island, ME 4685
207-526-4186
Fax: 207-526-4291
Seafood
Owner: David Niquette
kentswharf@aol.com
Estimated Sales: $300,000-500,000
Number Employees: 1-4

6795 Kentucky Beer Cheese
224 Industry Pkwy
Suite A
Nicholasville, KY 40356-8015
859-887-1645
Fax: 859-277-6075 info@kentuckybeercheese.com
www.kentuckybeercheese.com
Processor and wholesaler/distributor of cheese spread and dip including hot, garlic and beer flavored.
Owner, President: Diane Evans
VP, Owner: Chris Evans
Estimated Sales: Less Than $500,000
Number Employees: 1-4
Square Footage: 4000
Parent Co: Evans Gourmet Foods, LLC
Type of Packaging: Consumer, Food Service
Brands:
  Kentucky Beer Cheese

6796 Kentucky Bourbon
925 S. 7th Street
Louisville, KY 40203
866-472-7797
Fax: 866-574-4269 tracy@bourbonQ.com
www.bourbonQ.com
Gourmet sauces & spices
President: Shane Best
Contact: Jennifer Nolte
jennifer@bourbonq.com
Estimated Sales: $300,000-500,000
Number Employees: 10-19
Brands:
  Bear Claw
  Cultured Red Neck T-Shirts
  Fighting Cock
  Kentucky Bourbonq
  Lady In Red
  Moonshine Madness
  Pappy's Best Premmium Marinade
  Pappy's XXX White Lightnin
  Sauce For Sissies
  Shrimp Butler
  Smoky Mountain Trail Rub

6797 Kentwood Springs
200 Eagles Landing Blvd
Lakeland, FL 33810
800-728-5508
www.kentwoodsprings.com
Spring water
President: Don Woods

843

Food Manufacturers / A-Z

Year Founded: 1963
Estimated Sales: $367.9 Million
Number Employees: 5,350
Number of Brands: 5
Parent Co: Ds Waters Holdings, LLC
Brands:
  Abita Golden
  Abita Purple
  Abita Root Beer
  Abita Seasmals
  Abita Turboday

6798 Kenwood Vineyards
9592 Sonoma Hwy
Kenwood, CA 95452
707-833-5891
Fax: 707-833-1146 info@kenwoodvineyards.com
www.kenwoodvineyards.com
Wines
Manager: Alan Jensen
ajensen@kenwoodvineyards.com
Sales/Marketing: Paul Young
Public Relations: Margie Healy
Winemaker: Mike Lee
Number Employees: 50-99
Square Footage: 200000
Parent Co: Korbel Champagne
Type of Packaging: Consumer
Brands:
  Kenwood Vineyards

6799 Kerala Curry
2277 Otis Johnson Rd
Pittsboro, NC 27312
919-545-9401
Fax: 919-545-9402 rolls@keralacurry.com
www.keralacurry.com
Gluten-free, organic/natural, USDA, chutney/relish, hors d'oeuvres/appetizers, ready meals/pizza/soup, ethnic sauces (soy, curry, etc.), foodservice.
Marketing: Rollo Varkey

6800 Kern Meat Distributing
2711 Wagel Rd
Brooksville, KY 41004
606-756-2255
Fax: 606-756-2114 webberfarms.com
Meat
President: Ed Kern
Estimated Sales: $10-20 Million
Number Employees: 20-49

6801 Kernel Fabyan's Gourmet Popcorn
3722 Illinois Avenue
St Charles, IL 60174-2421
630-485-4680
Fax: 630-513-0396 847-483-1377
Popcorn
Marketing: Eddie Nusinow

6802 Kernel Seasons LLC
2401 E Devon Ave
Elk Grove Vlg, IL 60007-6213
847-350-6041
Fax: 773-326-0869 866-328-7672
www.chicagocustomfoods.com
Popcorn seasonings, machines and accessories.
Founder/Owner/President/CEO: Brian Taylor
Marketing: Jean Doyle
Contact: Andrew Abovitz
aabovitz@kernelseasons.com
Number Employees: 5-9

6803 Kerr Brothers
Toronto, ON M8Z 4P6
Canada
416-252-7341
Fax: 416-252-6054 hr@kerrs.com
www.kerrs.com
Confections, candy, and cough drops.
VP of Sales: Lyndon Brown
Year Founded: 1895
Brands:
  Soda Pops®
  Sour Pops®

6804 Kerr Jellies
PO Box 599
Dana, NC 28724-0599
828-685-8381
Fax: 828-685-8381 877-685-8381
Jellies
President: Kathy Thompson

Estimated Sales: $5-10 Million
Number Employees: 5-9

6805 Kerri Kreations
216 Fern St
Santa Cruz, CA 95060
831-429-5129
kerrikreations@hotmail.com
www.kerrikreations.com
Organic, vegan cookies; gluten-free options available
Founder: Kerri O'Neill
Number Employees: 5-9

6806 Kerry Foodservice
30 Paragon Pkwy
Mansfield, OH 44903-8074
419-522-2722
Fax: 419-522-1152 800-533-2722
slinfo@kerrygroup.com
Processor and exporter of Italian syrups, specialty sugars and powdered toppings for coffees; also, coffee and tea flavors and extracts; private labeling available
Business Director: Peter Dillane
Marketing Director: Corrie Byron
Manager: James Powers
jpowers@stearns-lehman.com
Estimated Sales: $7.9 Million
Number Employees: 20-49
Square Footage: 200000
Type of Packaging: Private Label
Brands:
  Dinatura
  Dolce
  Flavor-Mate
  Gift of Bran
  My Hero
  Paradise Bay
  Select Origins
  Senza
  Stearns & Lehman

6807 Kerry Sweet Ingredients
202 Market Street
Gridley, IL 61744
309-747-3541
Food ingredients
President: Gary Ringger
gringger@kerrygroup.com
Parent Co: Kerry Inc.

6808 Kerry, Inc
Global Technology & Innovation Center
3400 Millington Rd
Beloit, WI 53511
608-363-1200
www.kerry.com
Food ingredients, encapsulation, ingredient sourcing, in-house testing and spray drying services.
CEO/Executive Director: Edmond Scanlon
President/CEO, Kerry Taste & Nutrition: Gerry Behan
CFO: Marguerite Larkin
President/CEO, North America: Michael O'Neill
Global COO: Alan Barrett
Year Founded: 1972
Estimated Sales: Over $1 Billion
Number Employees: 25,255
Parent Co: Kerry Group Plc
Type of Packaging: Food Service

6809 Kershenstine Beef Jerky
550 Industrial Park Rd
Eupora, MS 39744
662-258-2049
Fax: 662-258-2002 www.pappysjerky.com
Processor and exporter of beef jerky
President: Timothy Kershenstine
Estimated Sales: $710,000
Number Employees: 5 to 9
Type of Packaging: Consumer

6810 Kervan USA
52 E Union Blvd
Bethlehem, PA 18018
610-866-2300
kervanusa.com
Gummies, licorice and marshmallow
Number of Products: 200+
Type of Packaging: Consumer, Bulk
Brands:
  Crayola

Bebeto
Yumy Yumy

6811 Keto Foods
56 Park Pl
Suite 2
Neptune, NJ 07753
732-922-0009
Fax: 732-643-6677 email@keto.com
Diet coffee, tea and creamer; low carbohydrate foods and snacks.
President: Arnie Bey
Quality Control: Allan Nargolies
VP Corporation Counsel: Dan Majollo
Sales/Marketing Executive: Arnie Bey
Purchasing Agent: Megan Holman
Estimated Sales: $2.5-5 Million
Number Employees: 30
Square Footage: 120000
Type of Packaging: Consumer, Food Service, Bulk
Brands:
  Slim Diez

6812 Ketters Meat Market & Locker Plant
118 W Main Ave
Frazee, MN 56544
218-334-2351
Beef, pork, turtle and deer
President: Kenneth Ketter
Estimated Sales: $1-3 Million
Number Employees: 5-9
Type of Packaging: Consumer, Food Service

6813 Kettle & Fire
Austin, TX 78701
415-857-0024
www.kettleandfire.com
Bone broths and soups
Co-Founder: Justin Mares
Co-Founder: Nick Mares
Year Founded: 2015
Number of Brands: 1
Number of Products: 6
Type of Packaging: Consumer
Brands:
  KETTLE & FIRE

6814 Kettle Brand
PO Box 32368
Charlotte, NC 28232
800-438-1880
kettlebrand.com
Kettle potato and vegetable chips
President/Owner: Cameron Healy
CFO: Marc Cramer
Year Founded: 1982
Number of Brands: 1
Number of Products: 31
Type of Packaging: Consumer
Brands:
  KETTLE BRAND
  KETTLE UPROOTED
  KETTLE BRAND KRINKLE CUT

6815 Kettle Cuisine
330 Lynnway
Lynn, MA 01901
617-409-1100
Fax: 617-884-1341 877-302-7687
www.kettlecuisine.com
Fresh soups and chowders
President/Founder: Jerry Shafir
Chief Executive Officer: Liam McClennon
Chief Financial Officer: James Reed
EVP Sales, Marketing, R&D: Mike Illum
VP Sales: Bob Benson
EVP Human Resources: Nora McCarthy
Chief Operating Officer: Jeremy Kacuba
Estimated Sales: $20-50 Million
Number Employees: 100-249
Type of Packaging: Consumer, Food Service

6816 Kettle Foods Inc
3125 Kettle Ct SE
Salem, OR 97301-5572
503-364-0399
Fax: 503-371-1447 www.kettlebrand.com
Natural potato chips and healthy snacks
Number Employees: 500-999

Food Manufacturers / A-Z

6817 Kettle Master
497 Farmers Market Rd
Hillsville, VA 24343-5106
276-728-7571
sales@kettlemaster.com
www.kettlemaster.com
Jellies, jams, salsa and sauces
Manager: Rex Horton
Marketing Sales Director: Ben Web
Operations Manager: Fred Jones
Number Employees: 5-9
Type of Packaging: Consumer, Private Label
Other Locations:
  Chesapeake Bay Gourmet
  Baltimore MD

6818 Keurig Dr Pepper
5301 Legacy Dr.
Plano, TX 75024
800-696-5891
www.keurigdrpepper.com
Coffee, hot and cold beverage maker systems, flavored soft drinks, teas, waters, juices, juice drinks, and more.
CEO: Robert Gamgort
CFO: Ozan Dokmecioglu
Chief Legal Officer/General Counsel: Jim Baldwin
Chief Research & Development Officer: David Thomas
Chief Marketing Officer: Andrew Springate
Year Founded: 2018
Estimated Sales: $11 Billion
Number Employees: 25,000
Number of Brands: 81
Number of Products: 530+
Type of Packaging: Consumer, Food Service, Bulk
Other Locations:
  Production
  Castroville CA
  R&D, Professional Services
  Burlington MA
  Production
  Knoxville TN
  Production
  Windsor VA
  Production
  Sumner WA
  Keurig Canada
  Montreal, QC, Canada
Brands:
  Green Mountain Coffee®
  Caribou Coffee®
  Laughing Man®
  Peet's Coffee®
  The Original Donut Shop®
  Van Houtte®
  Revv®
  Tully's Coffe®
  Krispy Kreme®
  Newmann's Own Organics®
  Barista Bros®
  Barista Prima Coffeehouse®
  Br-lerie Mont Royal®
  Br-lerie St. Denis®
  Caf, Escapes®
  Caf, Punta del Cielo®
  Cinnabon®
  Coffee People®
  Diedrich Coffee®
  Donut House Collection®
  Emeril®
  Gloria Jean's Coffees®
  Hollys Coffee®
  Kahl£a®
  Laura Secord®
  Orient Express®
  Timothy's®
  Panera Bread®
  High Brew Coffee®
  Gila Caf,®
  Forto®
  Adagio®
  Dr. Pepper®
  7UP®
  A&W Root Beer®
  Canada Dry®
  Schweppes®
  Sunkist®
  Crush®
  Sun Drop®
  IBC®
  Diet Rite®
  Squirt®
  Vernors®
  Royal Crown Cola®
  Hires®
  Stewart's®
  Big Red®
  Cplus®
  Cactus Cooler®
  Nehi Cola®
  Tahitian Treat®
  Bai®
  Deja Blue®
  Penafiel®
  Snapple®
  Straight Up Tea®
  Evian®
  Neuro®
  Vita Coco®
  Cora®
  Clamato®
  Hawaiian Punch®
  Margritaville®
  Mott's®
  Nantucker Nectars®
  Orangina®
  Mott's®
  Nantucker Nectars®
  Orangina®
  ReaLemon®
  Rose's®
  SunnyD®

6819 Keurig, Inc
55 Walkers Brook Drive
Reading, MA 01867
781-928-0162
866-901-2739
www.keurig.com
Single cup coffee and brewers. Also tea, hot cocoa and iced beverages.
President: Michelle Stacy
Chief Financial Officer: Frances Rathke
VP/General Counsel: Howard Malovany
Director of Research: Karl Winkler
Director of Quality: William Hartman
Contact: Christina Adams
christina.adams@keurig.com
VP Manufacturing/Operations: Dick Sweeney
Number Employees: 185
Type of Packaging: Consumer
Brands:
  Donut Shop
  Green Mountain Coffee
  Newmans Own
  Barista Prima
  Cafe Escapes
  Celestial Seasonings
  Coffee People
  Dunkin Donuts
  Emerils
  Ghiradelli
  Gloria Jeans
  Millstone
  Donut House

6820 Kevala
PO Box 670692
Dallas, TX 75367
877-379-1179
info@kevala.net
kevala.net
Spreads, oil, sweeteners, herbs, and spices.
Operations Manager: Gerardo Rodriguez
gerardo@kevala.net

6821 Kevton Gourmet Tea
385 Fm 416
Streetman, TX 75859-3024
903-389-2905
Fax: 903-389-5607 888-538-8668
Honey, flavored mixes, sour cream, tea, cocoa
CEO: Tanya Miller
Brands:
  Bee My Honey
  Good Stuff Cocoa
  Not Just Jam
  Tea Tyme Cookies
  Countrymixes
  Joy
  Tease

6822 Key Colony Red Parrot Juice
16300 103rd St
Lemont, IL 60439-9666
630-783-8572
Fax: 630-783-8791 844-783-8572
www.redparrotjuice.com
Bag-in-box juices
President: Guy Sisto
SVP: Rob Baker
Regional Sales Coordinator: Tom Ambutas
Manager: Janice Baisden
janice@redparrotjuice.com
Estimated Sales: Less Than $500,000
Number Employees: 1-4
Type of Packaging: Food Service
Brands:
  Red Parrot

6823 Key III Candies
4211 Earth Dr
Fort Wayne, IN 46809
260-747-7514
Fax: 260-747-9898 800-752-2382
Milk chocolate confections, caramels and pretzels.
President: Todd Haines
VP/Co-Owner: Richard Dickmeyer
Manager: Gary Yarger
Estimated Sales: $3-5 Million
Number Employees: 10-19
Square Footage: 20000
Type of Packaging: Consumer, Bulk
Brands:
  Key Iii

6824 Key Largo Fisheries
1313 Ocean Bay Dr
Key Largo, FL 33037-4213
305-451-3782
800-432-4358
www.keylargofisheries.com
Seafood
President & Co-Owner: Tom Hill
tomhill13@aol.com
Co-Owner: Rick Hill
Estimated Sales: $10 Million
Number Employees: 20-49
Square Footage: 6000
Type of Packaging: Consumer, Food Service, Private Label

6825 Key West Key Lime Pie Co
225 Key Deer Blvd
Big Pine Key, FL 33043
305-872-7400
Fax: 305-872-7600 877-882-7437
keywestkeylimepieco.com
Key lime products
President: James Brush
Vice President: Alison Sloat
Estimated Sales: $400,000
Number Employees: 5-9
Number of Brands: 4
Number of Products: 100+
Square Footage: 2400
Type of Packaging: Consumer, Food Service, Private Label
Brands:
  Key Lime Pie Slices Dipped In Choco
  Key Lime Pies Assorted Flavors
  Package Bulk Key Lime Filling

6826 Keynes Brothers Inc
1 W Front St
Logan, OH 43138-1825
740-385-6824
Fax: 740-385-9076 800-282-5627
www.keynesbros.com
Soft and whole wheat flour
Executive: William Keynes
wkeynes@keynesbros.com
Executive: Charles Keynes
Estimated Sales: $20-30 Million
Number Employees: 20-49

6827 Keys Fisheries Market &Marina
3502 Gulfview Ave
Marathon, FL 33050-2362
305-743-4353
Fax: 305-743-3562 866-743-4353
keys.fisheries@comcast.net
www.keysfisheries.com
Processor and wholesaler of seafood products.
Owner: Gary Graves
keysfisheries@comcast.net
Vice President: Gary Graves
Estimated Sales: $1-2.5 Million
Number Employees: 20-49
Type of Packaging: Consumer, Food Service

Food Manufacturers / A-Z

6828 Keyser Brothers
1146 Honest Point Rd
Lottsburg, VA 22511-2521
804-529-6837
Fax: 804-529-5144
Fresh and frozen seafood including crabs and pasteurized crab meat
President/CEO: R Calvin Keyser
Executive VP: Norman Keyser
Estimated Sales: $350,000
Number Employees: 20-25
Number of Brands: 1
Square Footage: 52500
Type of Packaging: Private Label
Brands:
   Potomac River
   Potomac River Brand

6829 Keystone Coffee Co
2230 Will Wool Dr
Suite 100
San Jose, CA 95112-2605
408-998-2221
Fax: 408-998-5021 www.keystonecoffee.com
Processor and exporter of gourmet coffee
President: Tim Wright
CEO: Dan Mckenrick
mdan@keystonecoffee.com
Estimated Sales: $3000000
Number Employees: 10-19
Brands:
   Keystone

6830 Keystone Pretzel Bakery
124 W Airport Rd
Lititz, PA 17543-9294
717-560-1882
Fax: 717-560-2241 888-572-4500
www.keystonepretzels.com
Pretzels
President: George Phillips
mschaller@keystonepretzels.com
Sales Exec: Mike Schaller
Estimated Sales: $12 Million
Number Employees: 50-99
Type of Packaging: Consumer, Food Service, Bulk

6831 Khatsa & Company
PO Box 50754
13805 Main St
Bellevue, WA 98005-3733
206-404-9000
Fax: 425-649-0774 888-234-6781
President: Dachs Kyaping
Vice President: Nanang Nornang
Public Relations: Dachen Kyaping
Estimated Sales: $500,000-$1 Million
Number Employees: 1-4
Brands:
   Khatsa
   Liberate Your Senses
   Urban Nomad Food

6832 KiZE Concepts
Oklahoma City, OK 73106
kizeconcepts.com
Energy bars
Business Development Manager: Sam Wolfe
Chief Marketing Officer: Justin Lane

6833 Kibun Foods
2101 4th Ave
Suite 1170
Seattle, WA 98121-2319
206-467-6287
Fax: 206-467-6612 www.kibunusa.com
Beer
President: Kristine Goodman
kgoodman@starbucks.com
Estimated Sales: $7,500,000
Number Employees: 10-19

6834 Kicking Horse Coffee
491 Arrow Rd
Invermere, BC V0A 1K2
Canada
250-342-4489
Fax: 250-342-4450 888-287-5282
mia@kickinghorsecoffee.com
www.kickinghorsecoffee.com
Ground, whole bean and cold brew coffee
Co-Founder: Elana Rosenfeld
Co-Founder: Leo Johnson

6835 Kidfresh
315 Fifth Ave
Suite 401
New York, NY 10016
212-686-4303
Fax: 212-686-4306 info@kidfresh.com
www.kidfresh.com
Frozen kids' meals
Co-Founder: Matt Cohen
Co-Founder: Gilles Deloux
Number of Brands: 1
Number of Products: 21
Type of Packaging: Consumer
Brands:
   KIDFRESH

6836 Kids Kookie Company
1000 Calle Negocio
San Clemente, CA 92673
949-661-7880
Fax: 949-498-5496 800-350-7577
www.kidscookies.com
Holiday, theme, decorated, specialty shaped and pre-baked cookies
Owner: Dennis Sellers
VP: Gay Sellers
Contact: Marcy Sellers
marcy@kidscookies.com
Estimated Sales: $5-10 Million
Number Employees: 5-9
Type of Packaging: Food Service
Brands:
   Kids Cookie

6837 KidsLuv
San Francisco, CA 94131
855-543-7588
hello@kidsluv.com kidsluv.com
Juice-infused water
Consultant: Jenn Goodrum
Number of Products: 4

6838 Kidsmania
12332 Bell Ranch Dr
Santa Fe Springs, CA 90670
562-946-8822
Fax: 562-946-8802 www.candynovelties.com
Candy toys and novelties
Owner: Foreman Lam
Estimated Sales: $300,000-500,000
Number Employees: 1-4
Number of Products: 100

6839 Kii Naturals Inc
100 Ortona Court
Vaughan, ON L4K 0A5
Canada
905-738-8887
Fax: 905-738-8968 www.kiinaturals.com
Artisan crisps, cereals, grains and superfoods
Chief Executive Officer/Founder: Sujay Shah
Number Employees: 50-99

6840 KiiTO, Inc.
Los Angeles, CA 90017
hi@drinkkiito.com
drinkkiito.com
Plant-based protein drinks

6841 Kiki's Gluten-Free
350 S Northwest Hwy
Suite 300
Park Ridge, IL 60068
hello@kikisglutenfree.com
kikisglutenfree.com
Gluten-free pizzas, cake mixes and pastas
Founder & CEO: Kiki Michalakos

6842 Kilgus Meats
3346 W Laskey Rd
Toledo, OH 43623-4030
419-472-9721
Sausage products and lunch meats
President: William Vallongo
General Manager: Till Ballongo
Estimated Sales: $540,000
Number Employees: 1-4
Square Footage: 4800
Type of Packaging: Consumer, Food Service, Bulk

6843 Kill Cliff
3916-199 Armour Dr NE
Atlanta, GA 30324
855-552-5433
customerservice@killcliff.com www.killcliff.com
Sports drinks
Founder: Todd Ehrlich
Number of Brands: 2
Number of Products: 7
Type of Packaging: Consumer
Brands:
   ENDURE
   KILL CLIFF

6844 Kill Sauce
Pasadena, CA 91105
www.killsauce.com
Hot sauces

6845 Killer Creamery
Boise, ID 83703
info@killercreamery.com
killercreamery.com
Keto-friendly ice cream
Founder: Louis Armstrong
Co-Founder: Liz Armstrong
VP, Marketing: Tate Glasgow

6846 Kilwons Foods
PO Box 3088
Santa Cruz, CA 95060
831-426-9670
Fax: 831-426-2720 kilwon@kilwonsfoods.com
www.kilwonsfoods.com
Sauce, gravy, dressing & dip mixes
Owner: Kilwon Poveromo
Estimated Sales: Less than $500,000
Number Employees: 5-9
Brands:
   Kilwons Foods

6847 Kim & Scott's Gourmet Pretzels
2107 West Carroll Ave
Chicago, IL 60612
312-243-9971
800-578-9478
www.kimandscotts.com
Soft pretzels and other baked goods
President/Owner: Kimberly Oster-Holstein
CEO/Owner: Scott Holstein
CFO: Maura Finn
Contact: Mike Connors
mike@kimandscotts.com
Estimated Sales: $10 Million
Number Employees: 50-99

6848 Kim and Jake's
641 S Broadway
Boulder, CO 80305
303-499-9126
info@kimandjakes.com
kimandjakes.com
Gluten-free breads, buns, rolls and cookies
Co-Founder: Jake Rosenbarger
Co-Founder: Kim Rosenbarger

6849 Kimball Enterprise International
3129 S Hacienda Heights Blvd
Suite 410
Hacienda Heights, CA 91745
213-276-8898
Fax: 213-947-1888 sales@garlicpeeler.com
www.garlicpeeler.com
Processor and exporter of roasted, peeled and chopped garlic, peeled and chopped shallots and garlic juice
President: Jimmy Tani
Estimated Sales: $2 Million
Number Employees: 20
Square Footage: 60000
Type of Packaging: Consumer, Food Service, Private Label, Bulk
Brands:
   Kimball

6850 Kime's Cider Mill
171 Church St
Bendersville, PA 17306
717-677-7539
Fax: 717-677-7151
Apple butter and cider
Owner: Rick Kime
kimescider@netzero.com
Partner: Randy Kimes

Food Manufacturers / A-Z

Estimated Sales: Below $5 Million
Number Employees: 10-19
Type of Packaging: Consumer
Brands:
  Kimes

6851 Kimmie Candy Company
525 Reactor Way
Reno, NV 89502
775-284-9200
Fax: 775-284-9206 888-532-1325
sales@kimmiecandy.com www.kimmiecandy.com
Confections
President/CEO: Joseph Dutra
Accounting: Linda Joo
VP Sales/Marketing: Bernie Leas
Sales Manager: Mark Bedingfield
Contact: Alexis Cissell
alexis@kimmiecandy.com
Operations: John Dutra
Production: OoIn Jung
Estimated Sales: $1-5 Million
Number Employees: 20
Square Footage: 40000
Type of Packaging: Consumer, Food Service, Private Label, Bulk
Brands:
  Baby Dino Eggs
  Choco Rocks
  Kandy Kookies
  Peanut Crunchers
  Raisin Royales
  Sunbursts

6852 Kind Snacks
1372 Broadway
Suite 3
New York, NY 10018-6123
212-819-2480
Fax: 212-616-3005 855-884-5463
customerservice@kindsnacks.com
www.kindsnacks.com
Gluten-free snack bars
Marketing: Mariana Rittenhouse
Year Founded: 2004
Number Employees: 20-49

6853 Kinder's BBQ
245 Ygnacio Valley Rd
Suite 200
Walnut Creek, CA 94596
925-939-7242
www.kindersbbq.com
BBQ sauces, marinades and rubs
President: Dan Avery

6854 King & Prince Seafood
1 King & Prince Blvd.
Brunswick, GA 31520
888-391-5223
marketing@kpseafood.com www.kpseafood.com
Seafood
President/CEO: Michael Alexander
Director of Marketing: Michael Tigani
SVP Sales & Marketing: Mark Sutherland
VP Human Resources: Tom Norton
Procurement Manager: Jay M
Estimated Sales: $20-50 Million
Number Employees: 100-249

6855 King & Prince Seafood Corp
1 King And Prince Blvd
PO Box 899
Brunswick, GA 31520-8668
912-265-5155
Fax: 912-264-4812 800-841-0205
sales@kpseafood.com www.kpseafood.com
Shrimp; lobster tails and stuffed fish; importer of frozen shrimp.
CEO: Volker Kuntzsch
vkuntzsch@kpseafood.com
Estimated Sales: $570,000
Number Employees: 500-999
Parent Co: Nippon Suisan Kaisha, Ltd.
Brands:
  King & Prince
  Mrs. Friday's
  Oceanway Seafood
  Pride of Alaska

6856 King 888 Company
PO BOX 51360
Sparks, NV 89436
775-530-5718
Fax: 800-785-3674 800-785-3674
www.king888.com
Energy drinks
Sales Representative: Gary Larson
Type of Packaging: Food Service

6857 King Arthur Flour
135 US Route 5 S
Norwich, VT 05055-9430
802-649-3361
Fax: 802-649-3365 800-827-6836
www.kingarthurflour.com
Flours, specialty flours and mixes
Co-CEO: Suzanne McDowell
Co-CEO: Karen Colberg
Senior VP: Michael Bittel
mikebittel@kingarthurflowers.com
VP, Sales: Beth Kluge
Year Founded: 1790
Estimated Sales: $45 Million
Number Employees: 300+
Number of Brands: 1
Square Footage: 16600

6858 King B Meat Snacks
P.O. Box 397
Minong, WI 54859-0397
715-466-2234
Fax: 715-466-5151 800-346-6896
info@linksnacks.com
Manufacturer and exporter of jerky and meat snacks
President: Troy Link
CEO: John Link
CFO: John Hermeier
Executive Vice President of Supply Chain: Karl Paepke
Director of Marketing: Jeff LeFever
Estimated Sales: $10-20 Million
Number Employees: 250-499
Type of Packaging: Consumer, Food Service, Private Label, Bulk
Brands:
  B. King
  Taylor Country Farms

6859 King Brewing Company
895 Oakland Ave
Pontiac, MI 48340
248-745-5900
Fax: 248-745-0160 kingbrewco@hotmail.com
www.kingbrewing.info
Wines
Owner: Tom King
Operations Manager: Robert Egelhoff
Estimated Sales: Less than $500,000
Number Employees: 1-4
Square Footage: 18
Type of Packaging: Private Label

6860 King Cole Ducks Limited
15351 Warden Ave.
PO Box 185
Newmarket, ON L3Y 4W1
Canada
905-836-9461
Fax: 905-836-4440 800-363-3825
rgrant@kingcoleducks.com
www.kingcoleducks.com
Processor and exporter of fresh and frozen duck including parts, smoked, boneless breast, peppered, fully cooked, etc
President: James Murby
VP: Robert Murby
Square Footage: 4000
Type of Packaging: Consumer, Food Service, Private Label, Bulk
Brands:
  King Cole

6861 King Cupboard
15 Pepsi Dr
Red Lodge, MT 59068-9104
406-446-3060
Fax: 406-446-3070 800-962-6555
www.kingscupboard.com
All natural dessert sauces and hot chocolate mixes
President: Lila Randolph
li@kingscupboard.com
Estimated Sales: $5-10 Million
Number Employees: 50-99
Type of Packaging: Consumer, Food Service, Private Label, Bulk
Brands:
  Beartooth Kitchens

6862 King Estate Winery
80854 Territorial Hwy
Eugene, OR 97405-9715
541-942-9874
Fax: 541-942-9867 800-884-4441
info@kingestate.com
Wines
CEO: Ed King
edk@kingestate.com
Director of Finance: Artie Weiner
Executive Vice President: Steve Thomson
CFO: Doyal Eubank
VP National sales: Rick Durette
Estimated Sales: Less than $500,000
Number Employees: 100-249
Brands:
  Oregon

6863 King Fish Restaurants
7400 New LA Grange Rd
Suite 405
Louisville, KY 40222-8821
502-339-0565
Fax: 502-339-0230 www.kingfishrestaurants.com
Seafood
Owner: Brown Nolte-Meyer
bnoltemeyer@kingfishrestaurants.com
CEO: Kyle Noltmeyer
Estimated Sales: $10,000,000
Number Employees: 5-9

6864 King Floyd's
102 Hamilton Dr
Unit H
Novato, CA 94949
415-475-7811
Fax: 415-488-1424 admin@kingfloyds.com
kingfloyds.com
Bar provisions, including bitters, syrups and salts
Number of Brands: 1
Number of Products: 11
Type of Packaging: Consumer
Brands:
  KING FLOYD'S

6865 King Food Service
7810 42nd St W
Rock Island, IL 61201-7319
309-787-4488
Fax: 309-787-4501 www.kingfoodservice.com
Seafood, poultry & meat
President: Matthew Cutkomp
CEO/CFO: Mike Cutkomp
Director of Sales & Marketing: Kelly McDonald
VP Operations: Chad Gaul
Estimated Sales: $24 Million
Number Employees: 10-19
Number of Products: 1500

6866 King Henry's Inc
29124 Hancock Pkwy
Valencia, CA 91355-1066
661-295-5566
Fax: 661-295-5099 henry@kinghenrys.com
www.kinghenrys.com
Organic chocolate confections; gummies/jellies of fruits and nuts; pretzels, and dried fruit.
Owner: Henry Davidian
henry@kinghenrys.com
Marketing: Joseph DeFelice
Estimated Sales: Less Than $500,000
Number Employees: 1-4

6867 King Juice Co
851 W Grange Ave
Milwaukee, WI 53221-4425
414-482-0303
Fax: 414-482-0719 www.kingjuice.com
Juices
President: Jon Christophersen
kezman@kingjuice.com
Estimated Sales: $500,000-$1 Million
Number Employees: 20-49
Brands:
  Calypso
  King Juice
  Villa Quenchers

Food Manufacturers / A-Z

6868 King Kold Meats
331-333 North Main Street
Englewood, OH 45322-1388
937-836-2731
Fax: 937-836-5919 800-836-2797
dougsmith@kingkoldinc.com
www.kingkoldinc.com
Fresh and frozen meat products and entrees.
President: Doug Smith
Distributor Sales: Mike DeFrancis
Estimated Sales: $10-20 Million
Number Employees: 20-49
Number of Brands: 3
Number of Products: 125
Square Footage: 30000
Type of Packaging: Consumer, Food Service, Private Label, Bulk
Brands:
    Evelyn Sprague
    Hearth & Kettle
    Kingkold

6869 King Milling Co Inc
115 S Broadway St
PO Box 99
Lowell, MI 49331-1666
616-897-9264
Fax: 616-897-4350 jcantrell@kingflour.com
www.kingflour.com
Wheat and white flour
President: Brian Doyle
bdoyle@kingmilling.com
VP: Steve Doyle
SVP: James Doyle
Estimated Sales: $20-50 Million
Number Employees: 20-49
Number of Brands: 6
Type of Packaging: Food Service, Bulk
Brands:
    Ceres®
    Kimco
    Pathfinder
    Pure Gold
    Sincerity
    Super Kleaned Wheat

6870 King Nut Co
31900 Solon Rd
Solon, OH 44139-3536
440-248-8484
Fax: 440-248-0153 800-860-5464
info@kingnut.com www.kingnut.com
Snack mixes, chocolates, nuts, dried fruit, granola and pretzels; exporter of salted nuts.
Chairman: Michael Kanan
President/CEO: Martin Kanan
SVP/CFO: Joseph Valenza
EVP/CMO: Matthew Kanan
VP Quality Assurance/Product Development: Debra Smith
Manufacturing/Plant Operations: Michael Smith
Estimated Sales: $35 Million
Number Employees: 100-249
Number of Brands: 3
Square Footage: 250000
Parent Co: Kanan Enterprises
Type of Packaging: Consumer, Food Service, Private Label, Bulk
Brands:
    King's Delicious®
    Peterson's
    Summer Harvest®

6871 King Oscar
3838 Camino Del Rio North
Unit 115
San Diego, CA 92108
global.kingoscar.com
Canned seafood
President/Owner: John Engle
Number of Brands: 1
Type of Packaging: Consumer
Brands:
    KING OSCAR

6872 King of Pops Inc
337 Elizabeth St NE
Suite B
Atlanta, GA 30307-1969
678-732-9321
Ice pops
CEO and Co-Founder: Steven Carse
Co-Founder: Nick Carse
Contact: Matt Anderson
andersonm@kingofpops.net

6873 King's Command Foods Inc
500 S Washington St
Green Bay, WA 54301-4219
800-345-0293
info@americanfoodsgroup.com
www.americanfoodsgroup.com
Portion controlled, pre-cooked and ready-to-eat beef, chicken, pork and veal products.
President: Ron Baer
Director of Quality Assurance: Alan Whittington
Year Founded: 1966
Estimated Sales: $50-99 Million
Number Employees: 100-249
Parent Co: American Foods Group
Type of Packaging: Consumer, Food Service

6874 King's Hawaiian Holding Co Inc.
19161 Harborgate Way
Torrance, CA 90501-1316
310-533-3250
Fax: 310-533-8732 877-695-4227
khcares@kingshawaiian.com
www.kingshawaiian.com
Hawaiian sweet bread, rolls, sauces and stuffing.
CEO: Mark Taira
Estimated Sales: $10-20 Million
Number Employees: 250-499
Number of Brands: 1
Square Footage: 150000
Brands:
    King's Hawaiian

6875 Kingchem
5 Pearl Ct
Allendale Park
Allendale, NJ 07401-1656
201-825-9988
Fax: 201-825-9148 800-211-4330
customer-service@kingchem.com
www.kingchem.com
Herbal supplements
Owner: Anne Agler
a.agler@kingchem.com
Chief Executive Officer: Stephen Wang
Vice President, Accounting/Planning: Catherine Penetra
Vice President, Business Development: Keith Drouet
Chief Executive Officer: Lillian Wu
Estimated Sales: $1-9 Million
Number Employees: 20-49
Number of Brands: 1
Square Footage: 2500
Brands:
    Kingchem

6876 Kingly Heirs
PO Box 283
Elkhart, IN 46515
574-596-3763
Fax: 527-296-1188 www.kinglyheirs.com/
Gourmet cake mixes.
President: Kingly Heirs

6877 Kings Canyon
1750 S Buttonwillow Ave
Reedley, CA 93654-4400
559-638-3571
Fax: 559-638-6326
Peaches, apricots and other fruits
President: Steve Kenfield
VP Sales: Fred Berry

6878 Kings Processing
14 Freeman St
PO Box 1251
Middleton, NS B0S 1P0
Canada
902-825-2188
Fax: 902-825-2180
Fresh salads and vegetables
Owner: Bruce Rand
Controller: Krysta Hatt
Quality Control: Cynthia Kenneally
Production Manager: Karen Cole
Plant Manager: Frank Ford
Estimated Sales: $6.9 Million
Number Employees: 50
Type of Packaging: Consumer, Food Service

6879 Kings Seafood Co
3185 Airway Ave
Suite H
Costa Mesa, CA 92626-4601
714-432-0400
Fax: 714-432-0111 800-269-8425
samking@kingsseafood.com
www.kingsseafood.com
Seafood
Owner: Steve Rhee
CEO: Sam King
sking@kingsseafood.com
CFO: Roger Doan
Estimated Sales: $5 Million
Number Employees: 20-49
Square Footage: 60000
Type of Packaging: Food Service

6880 Kingsburg Orchards
10363 E Davis Ave
P.O. Box 38
Kingsburg, CA 93631
559-897-5132
Fax: 559-897-4532 info@kingsburgorchards.com
www.kingsburgorchards.com
A variety of fruits
Owner: George Jackson
Estimated Sales: $100+ Million
Number Employees: 100-249
Brands:
    Season Opener
    Dinosaur Brand
    Sugar Tree
    Flavor Farmer
    Flying Saucer
    Apple Pears

6881 Kingsbury Country Market
5001 S Us 35
La Porte, IN 46345
219-393-3016
Beef, hog, rabbit, ostrich and lamb; custom butchering available
President: Jerry Winter
Treasurer: Sandra Winter
Number Employees: 5-9
Brands:
    Butcher Boy

6882 Kingston Fresh
477 Shoup Ave
Suite 207
Idaho Falls, ID 83402-3658
208-522-2365
Fax: 208-552-7488 www.kingstonfresh.com
Potatoes; onions; broccoli; sweet pineapples; and lettuce.
President: Mike Kingston
CEO: Dave Kingston
Number Employees: 5-9
Type of Packaging: Consumer, Food Service
Brands:
    Awesome
    Russetts

6883 Kingsville Fisherman's Company
PO Box 37
Kingsville Dock
Kingsville, ON N9Y 2E8
Canada
519-733-6534
Fax: 519-733-6959
Processor and exporter of fresh and frozen perch and pickerel
President: Carl Fraser
Sales Manager: John Murray
Number Employees: 50-99
Type of Packaging: Bulk

6884 Kinnikinnick Foods
10940-120 Street NW
Edmonton, AB T5H 3P7
Canada
780-424-2900
Fax: 780-421-0456 877-503-4466
info@kinnikinnick.com www.kinnikinnick.com
Gluten-free bakery products
President & CEO: Jerry Bigam
CFO: Lynne Bigam
VP, Operations: Jay Bigam
Number Employees: 60
Number of Products: 120
Square Footage: 120000
Type of Packaging: Consumer, Food Service

Food Manufacturers / A-Z

Brands:
  Kinnikinnick Foods, Inc.

6885 Kiolbassa Provision Co
1325 S Brazos St
San Antonio, TX 78207-6931
210-226-8127
Fax: 210-226-7464 800-456-5465
info@kiolbassa.com www.kiolbassa.com
Sausage products
President: Michael Kiolbassa
CEO: Robert Kiolbassa
rak@kiolbassa.com
Vice President: Sandra Kiolbassa
Secretary/Treasurer: Barbara Kiolbassa
Year Founded: 1949
Estimated Sales: $21 Million
Number Employees: 100-249
Type of Packaging: Consumer

6886 Kiona Vineyards Winery
44612 N Sunset Rd
Benton City, WA 99320-7500
509-588-6716
Fax: 509-588-3219 info@kionawine.com
www.kionawine.com
Wines and wine grapes
Owner: John Williams
kiona1wine@aol.com
Owner: Ann Williams
National Sales Manager: J J Williams
Manager/Winemaker: Scott Williams
Estimated Sales: Below $5 Million
Number Employees: 5-9
Number of Brands: 1
Number of Products: 16
Type of Packaging: Private Label
Brands:
  Kiona

6887 Kirby Holloway Provision Co
966 Jackson Ditch Rd
Harrington, DE 19952-2417
302-398-3705
Fax: 302-398-4088 800-995-4729
www.kirbyandhollowayinc.com
Sausage and scrapple; wholesaler/distributor of meat and cheese products
Owner: Russell Kirby
rkirby@kirbyandhollowayinc.com
Owner: Rudy Kirby
General Manager: Bill Moore
Estimated Sales: $7 Million
Number Employees: 20-49
Type of Packaging: Consumer, Food Service, Private Label, Bulk

6888 Kirigin Cellars
11550 Watsonville Rd
Gilroy, CA 95020-9434
408-847-8827
Fax: 408-847-3820 folks@kirigincellars.com
www.kirigincellars.com
Wines
Manager: Allen Kreutzer
folks@kirigincellars.com
Estimated Sales: Below $5 Million
Number Employees: 10-19
Brands:
  Kirigin Cellars

6889 Kirin Brewery
5230 Pacific Concourse Dr
Suite 310
Los Angeles, CA 90045
310-381-3040
Fax: 310-320-5955
Beer
President: Satoru Shimura
VP, Marketing: Randy Higa
Estimated Sales: $5-10 Million
Number Employees: 5-9
Parent Co: Mitsubishi International
Brands:
  Kirin Beer
  Kirin Ichiban
  Kirin Lager

6890 Kiska Farms
25056 Ice Harbor Dr
Burbank, WA 99323
509-547-7746
Fax: 509-547-7746 kathy@kiskafarms.com
www.kiskafarms.com
Potatos
Owner: Lonnie Blasdel
lonnie@kiskafarms.com
Co-Owner: Judy Johnston
Estimated Sales: Less Than $500,000
Number Employees: 1-4

6891 Kiss My Keto
8066 Melrose Ave
Suite 4
Los Angeles, CA 90046
310-765-1553
hello@kissmyketo.com
www.kissmyketo.com
Ketogenic snack bars, creamers, protein powder, drink mixes, chocolate bars, supplements, and MCT oil
Co-Founder: Michael Herscu
Co-Founder: Alex Bird
Dietician Expert: Sofia Norton
Digital Marketing Manager: Kate Geller
Customer Service Lead: Lyn Villanueva
Number Employees: 35

6892 Kistler Vineyards
4707 Vine Hill Rd
Sebastopol, CA 95472-2236
707-823-5603
Fax: 707-823-6709 info@kistlervineyards.com
www.kistlervineyards.com
Chardonnay and Pinot Noir
President/CEO: Stephen Kistler
Operations: Jason Kesner
Year Founded: 1978
Estimated Sales: $20-50 Million
Number Employees: 50-99
Brands:
  Durell Vineyard
  Dutton Ranch
  Hyde Vineyard
  McCrea Vineyard
  Sonoma Coast

6893 Kitchen Cooked Inc
632 N Main St
Farmington, IL 61531-1076
309-245-2196
Fax: 540-886-0558 800-752-1535
sklasing@kitchencooked.net
Potato chips
President: George Raymond Curry
orders@kitchencooked.net
Sales Exec: Paul Blackhurst
Estimated Sales: $1100000
Number Employees: 20-49
Type of Packaging: Consumer

6894 Kitchen Pride Mushrooms Farm
1034 County Road 348
Gonzales, TX 78629-2774
830-540-4528
Fax: 830-540-4556 sales@kitchenpride.com
www.kitchenpride.com
Mushrooms
President & CEO: Darrell McLain
dmclain@kitchenpride.com
Estimated Sales: $3 Million
Number Employees: 100-249
Square Footage: 400000
Type of Packaging: Consumer, Food Service, Private Label, Bulk
Brands:
  Kitchen Pride Farms

6895 Kitchen Table
41 Princeton Dr
Syosset, NY 11791-6741
516-931-5113
Fax: 516-932-5467 800-486-4582
info@kitchentablebakers.com
Gourmet, wheat, gluten and sugar free wafer crisps
President/Owner: Barry Novick
Contact: Michelle Beamon
manlemi@nyp.org
Estimated Sales: Less Than $500,000
Number Employees: 1-4

6896 Kitchens Seafood
1001 E Baker St
Suite 202
Plant City, FL 33566
813-750-1888
Fax: 813-750-1889 800-327-0132
sales@kitchensseafood.com
www.kitchensseafood.com
Manufacturer, packer and importer of frozen seafood including lobster, crab, shrimp, shrimp meat and langostinos
President: Dan La Fleur
Type of Packaging: Consumer, Food Service, Private Label, Bulk
Other Locations:
  Kitchens Seafood-Production
  Jacksonville FL

6897 Kitchun Grainfree Food
Austin, TX 78726
thekitchun.com
Grain-free granola and cookie mixes
Co-Founder: Gloriana Koll
Co-Founder: Keesha Waits

6898 Kite Hill
3180 Corporate Pl
Hayward, CA 94545
888-588-0994
info@kite-hill.com www.kite-hill.com
Almond milk foods, including plant-based yogurts, pastas and artisanal cheeses
Co-Founder: Tal Ronnen
Number of Brands: 1
Type of Packaging: Consumer
Brands:
  KITE HILL

6899 Kith Treats
337 Lafayette St
New York, NY 10012
646-648-6285
kith.com
Snackbar, including ice cream and cereal.
Founder: Ronnie Fieg
Year Founded: 2011
Estimated Sales: Less than $500,000
Number Employees: 51-200
Type of Packaging: Consumer, Private Label

6900 Kitt's Meat Processing
506 S 4th Ave
Dedham, IA 51440-2000
712-683-5622
www.kittsmeat.com
Bologna
Owner: David Kitt
Partner: Shawn Kitt
Estimated Sales: Less Than $500,000
Number Employees: 5-9

6901 Kittling Ridge Estate Wines & Spirits
271 Chrislea Road
Vaughan, ON L4L 8N6
Canada
905-945-9225
Fax: 905-738-5551 800-461-9463
www.kittlingridge.com
Wine and spirits
President/CEO: Rossanna Magnotta
Year Founded: 1992
Estimated Sales: $20-50 Million
Number Employees: 100-249
Parent Co: Magnotta Winery Corporation
Brands:
  Canadian
  Kingsgate

6902 Kittridge & Fredrickson LTD
2801 SE 14th Ave
Portland, OR 97202-2203
503-234-7788
800-558-7788
www.kfcoffee.com
Coffee and spiced cocoa.
Founder: Don Dominguez
Founder: Bud Dominguez
Estimated Sales: $10-20 Million
Number Employees: 10-19
Number of Brands: 2
Type of Packaging: Private Label

Food Manufacturers / A-Z

6903 Kiwa
Ontario, CA 91761
info@kiwalife.com
www.kiwalife.com
Vegetable chips
Founder: Martin Acosta
Brands:
 Kiwa
 Kiwa Kids

6904 Kiwi Kiss
150 NW 16th Street
Boca Raton, FL 33432
hello@freshkiwikiss.com
www.freshkiwikiss.com
Strawberry-kiwi fruit treats
Number of Brands: 1
Number of Products: 1
Type of Packaging: Consumer
Brands:
 KIWI KISS

6905 Klaire Laboratories
10439 Double R Blvd
Reno, NV 89521-8905
775-850-8800
Fax: 775-850-8810 888-488-2488
www.klaire.com
Processor and exporter of allergen-free nutritional supplements
President: Cary Fereuson
Number Employees: 20-49
Parent Co: Kek Industries
Brands:
 Vital Life

6906 Klara's Gourmet Cookies
18 Railroad St
Lee, MA 01238-1623
413-243-3370
contact@klarasgourmet.com
www.klarasgourmet.com
Cookies
Founder: Klara Sotonova
contact@klarasgourmetcookies.com
Estimated Sales: Less than $500,000
Number Employees: 5-9
Brands:
 KLARA'S GOURMET

6907 Klein Foods, Inc
1501 E Lyon St
Marshall, MN 56258-3614
Fax: 507-537-1940 800-657-0174
www.kleinfoods.com
Gourmet honey cremes, sauces, syrups, preserves, and more.
Owner & President: Stephen Klein
kleinfoods@yahoo.com
Estimated Sales: $5-9.9 000,000
Number Employees: 5-9
Other Locations:
 Walnut Grove Mercantile
 Marshall MN

6908 Klein's Kosher Pickles
4118 W Whitton Ave
Phoenix, AZ 85019
602-269-2072
Fax: 602-269-2069 800-437-4255
sales@kleinpickles.com
Kosher pickles
President: Byron Arnold
VP: Mark Arnold
Manager Sales & Marketing: Gary Allison
Retail Sales Manager: Don Snider
VP Operations: Jeff Knapp
VP Merchandising: Susan Arnold Demura
Estimated Sales: $1-2.5 Million
Number Employees: 20-49
Square Footage: 1200000
Type of Packaging: Consumer, Food Service
Brands:
 Mrs. Klein's

6909 Kleinpeter Farms Dairy LLC
14444 Airline Hwy
Baton Rouge, LA 70817-6899
225-753-2121
Fax: 225-752-8964 www.kleinpeterdairy.com
Dairy products such as milk, cream and cottage cheese.
President/CEO: Sue Anne Kleinpeter Cox
Year Founded: 1913
Estimated Sales: Less Than $500,000
Number Employees: 1-4
Number of Brands: 1
Type of Packaging: Consumer, Food Service
Brands:
 Kleinpeter

6910 Klement Sausage Co Inc
1036 W Juneau Ave
Suite 400
Milwaukee, WI 53233-1447
414-744-2330
Fax: 414-744-2438 800-553-6368
www.klements.com
Meat products
CEO: Ray Booth
bducharme@klementsausageco.com
Site Manager: Bryan Ducharme
bducharme@klementsausageco.com
Estimated Sales: $42.3 Million
Number Employees: 100-249
Number of Brands: 1
Square Footage: 13000
Parent Co: Tall Tree Foods
Type of Packaging: Food Service, Private Label
Brands:
 Klement's

6911 Klingshirn Winery
33050 Webber Rd
Avon Lake, OH 44012-2330
440-933-6666
Fax: 440-933-7896 contactus@klingshirnwine.com
www.klingshirnwine.com
Wines
President: Lee Klingshirn
info@klingshirnwine.com
Estimated Sales: Below $5 Million
Number Employees: 5-9
Brands:
 Klingshirn Winery

6912 Klinke Brothers Ice Cream Co
2450 Scaper St
Memphis, TN 38114-6546
901-322-6640
Fax: 901-743-8254
Ice cream and frozen yogurt.
President and CEO: John Klinke
john.klinke@klinkebrothers.com
VP of Operations: Russell Klinke
Estimated Sales: $20-50 Million
Number Employees: 50-99
Type of Packaging: Consumer, Food Service, Private Label, Bulk
Brands:
 Angel Food

6913 Klondike Cheese Factory
W7839 State Rd 81
Monroe, WI 53566
608-325-3021
Fax: 608-328-9237 cheese@klondikecheese.com
www.klondikecheese.com
Cheese
President: Ronald Buholzer
Financial Controller: Tammy Fetterolf
Treasurer: David Buholzer
Production Manager: Jon Brunner
Year Founded: 1972
Estimated Sales: $82 Million
Number Employees: 100-249
Square Footage: 90000
Type of Packaging: Consumer, Private Label

6914 Kloss Manufacturing Co Inc
7566 Morris Ct
Suite 310
Allentown, PA 18106-9247
610-391-3820
Fax: 610-391-3830 800-445-7100
Processor and exporter of flavoring extracts for Italian ices and slushes; also, concession equipment and supplies, fountain syrups, popcorn, cotton candy, nachos and waffles
Owner: Stephen Lloss
skloss@klossfunfood.com
Estimated Sales: $3-5 Million
Number Employees: 10-19
Square Footage: 120000
Type of Packaging: Food Service, Private Label, Bulk
Brands:
 Kloss

6915 Klosterman Baking Co.
4760 Paddock Rd
Cincinnati, OH 45229-1047
877-301-1004
info@klostermanbakery.com
www.klostermanbakery.com
Breads, buns, hoagies, flat breads and rolls.
President: Chip Klosterman
CEO: Kim Klosterman
CFO: Ross Anderson
Marketing Manager: Mike Braun
Human Resources Manager: Tim McCoy
IT: Brian Fey
bfey@klostermanbakery.com
Year Founded: 1910
Estimated Sales: $47900000
Number Employees: 20-49
Number of Brands: 1
Type of Packaging: Consumer, Food Service
Brands:
 Klosterman

6916 Knapp Vineyards
2770 Ernsberger Rd
Romulus, NY 14541
607-869-9271
Fax: 607-869-3212 800-869-9271
winery@knappwine.com www.knappwine.com
Wines
Owner: Gene Pierce
Vice President: Susanna Knapp
Contact: John Mcnabb
john@knappwine.com
Estimated Sales: Below $5 Million
Number Employees: 20-49
Type of Packaging: Private Label
Brands:
 Knapp

6917 Knappen Milling Co
110 S Water St
P.O. Box 245
Augusta, MI 49012-9781
269-731-4141
Fax: 269-731-5441 800-562-7736
Knappen@knappen.com
Soft wheat, cereal bran, wheat and flour
President/CEO: Charles B. Knappen III
Treasurer: Darrell Roese
Vice President: John Shouse
jshouse@knappen.com
VP of Sales & Grain Purchasing: Todd C. Wright
Plant Manager: Bob Likens
Number Employees: 20-49
Type of Packaging: Private Label, Bulk
Brands:
 100% Flaked Wheat
 Arbutus Flour
 Heavy Bran
 Satin White Flour
 Sotac

6918 Knese Enterprise
27 Huron Rd
Bellerose, NY 11426
516-354-9004
Fax: 516-354-9004
Spicy gourmet mustard, kettle potato chips, pretzels and pretzel dip
President: Brad Knese
VP: Nancy Knese
Estimated Sales: $400,000
Number Employees: 2
Type of Packaging: Consumer
Brands:
 Brad's Pretzel Dip
 Kettle Chips
 Pretzels

6919 (HQ)Knight Seed Company
12550 W Frontage Road
Suite 203
Burnsville, MN 55337-2402
952-894-8080
Fax: 952-894-8095 800-328-2999
Processor, importer and exporter of soybeans, dried beans, peas and buckwheat; exporter of lentils

President/CEO: Dave Dornacker
Export Manager: Jeff Pricco
VP: Tom Kennelly
Marketing: Tim Kukowski
Sales: Dan Dahlquist
Estimated Sales: $3-5 Million
Number Employees: 16
Square Footage: 12000
Other Locations:
   Knight Seed Co.
   Vanscoy SK
Brands:
   Knight
   Ksc
   Legacy

6920 Knight's Appleden Fruit LTD
11687 County Road 2
Colborne, ON K0K 1S0
Canada
905-349-2521
Fax: 905-349-3129 www.knights-appleden.ca
Processor, importer and exporter of apples
President: Roger Knight
Estimated Sales: 1-2.5 Million
Number Employees: 20-49

6921 Knott's Berry Farms
1 Strawberry Lane
Orrville, OH 44667-0280
866-828-5502
www.knottsberryfarmfoods.com
Jams, jellies and preserves
President/CEO: Mark Smucker
CFO: Mark Belgya
Chief Marketing and Commercial Officer: Geoff Tanner
Number Employees: 100-249
Square Footage: 1000000
Parent Co: J.M. Smucker Company
Type of Packaging: Consumer, Food Service

6922 Knotts Fine Foods
125 N Blakemore St
Paris, TN 38242-4197
731-642-1961
Fax: 731-644-1962 joshknott@knottsfoods.com
www.knottsfoods.com
Refrigerated sandwiches and sandwich spreads; wholesaler/distributor of specialty foods
Owner: Josh Knott
joshknott@knottsfoods.com
VP Sales: BJ Knott
Estimated Sales: $5000000
Number Employees: 20-49
Square Footage: 240000
Brands:
   Knott's
   Knott's Meat Snacks
   Knott's Novelty Candy
   Knott's Salads

6923 Knouse Foods Co-Op Inc.
800 Peach Glen Rd.-Idaville Rd.
Peach Glen, PA 17375
717-677-8181
www.knouse.com
Apples and apple products, vinegar, cherries, tomato juice, pie fillings, and more.
President/Chairman: Kenneth Guise
kguise@knouse.com
CEO: Charles Haberkorn
Vice President, Marketing: Robert Fisher
Vice President, Sales: Richard Esser
Year Founded: 1949
Estimated Sales: $290 Million
Number Employees: 1,500
Number of Brands: 5
Square Footage: 557450
Type of Packaging: Consumer, Food Service, Private Label, Bulk
Brands:
   Apple Time
   Lincoln
   Lucky Leaf
   Mussleman's
   Knouse Food Service

6924 Know Allergies
Charleston, SC
www.knowallergies.com
Granola bars
Founder: Amos Bartlett

6925 Know Brainer
Lafayette, CO 80026
303-475-0456
shari@myknowbrainer.com
www.myknowbrainer.com
Ketogenic coffee creamers, instant coffee, chai tea, matcha tea, and instant hot chocolate
Founder/CEO: Shari Leidich
Year Founded: 2016

6926 Knudsen Candy
25067 Viking St
Hayward, CA 94545-2703
510-293-6887
Fax: 510-293-6890 800-736-6887
Gourmet chocolates including bon bons, creams, regular and caramel nut clusters, truffles, etc.; also, private labeling available
President: Gary Love
Chairman: David Knudsen
Treasurer/Secretary: Kathy Knudsen
Vice President: Tod Knudsen
Marketing Director: Tod Knudsen
Estimated Sales: $2.5-5 Million
Number Employees: 10-19
Square Footage: 72000
Type of Packaging: Consumer, Private Label
Brands:
   Enjoymints
   Tropical Wonders

6927 Koala Moa
755 N Nimitz Hwy
Honolulu, HI 96817-5035
808-523-6701
Fax: 808-671-3527 koalamoa@gmail.com
Broiled chicken
Owner: Christina Shimabukuro
VP: Kristana Speach
Estimated Sales: $1-2.5 Million
Number Employees: 10-19
Square Footage: 28

6928 Kobricks Coffee Company
693 Luis Marin Blvd
Jersey City, NJ 07310-1225
201-656-6313
Fax: 201-656-3665 800-562-7491
info@kobrickcoffee.com www.kobrickcoffee.com
Italian espresso, coffee and tea.
President: Lee Kobrick
Co-Owner: Steve Kobrick
Estimated Sales: $10-24.9 Million
Number Employees: 30-50
Type of Packaging: Private Label
Brands:
   Kobricks
   La San Marco
   Leodoro Espresso
   Numi Teas
   Shearer
   Steven Smith Teamaker Teas
   Tazo Teas
   Torani Syrups

6929 Kobu Beverages, LLC
233 Dean St.
Brooklyn, NY 11217-2202
718-566-2739
www.kombrewcha.com
Alcoholic kombucha
Co-Founder: Barry Nalebuff
Co-Founder: John Hillgen
Co-Founder: Ariel Glazer
Brands:
   Kobu Beverages, LLC

6930 Koch Foods Inc
1300 Higgins Rd
Suite 100
Park Ridge, IL 60068-5766
847-384-5940
Fax: 847-384-5961 800-837-2778
info@kochfoods.com www.kochfoods.com
Fresh and frozen chicken
President & CEO: Joe Grendys
CFO: Lance Buckert
Plant Manager: Jim Dunbar
Foodservice Sales: John Marler
Commodity Sales: Hans Schmidt
Operations Manager: Fred Koch
Year Founded: 1985
Estimated Sales: $20-50 Million
Number Employees: 20-49
Type of Packaging: Consumer, Food Service

6931 Koda Farms
PO Box 10
22540 Russell Ave
South Dos Palos, CA 93665
209-392-2191
inquiry@kodafarms.com
www.kodafarms.com
Organic, heirloom, Japanese-style rice
Co-Principal: Robin Koda
Co-Principal: Ross Koda
Number of Brands: 1
Type of Packaging: Consumer
Brands:
   KOKUHO ROSE

6932 Kodiak Cakes
PO Box 980992
Park City, UT 84098
801-328-4067
Fax: 801-328-4068 flapjacks@kodiakcakes.com
www.kodiakcakes.com
Baking mixes, granola and oatmeal
CEO: Joel Clark
Number of Brands: 1
Type of Packaging: Consumer
Brands:
   KODIAK CAKES

6933 Kodiak Salmon Packers
PO Box 30
Larsen Bay, AK 99624-0038
907-847-2250
Fax: 907-847-2244
Frozen and canned wild Alaskan salmon
President: Alan Beardsley
Executive VP: Van Johnson
Plant Manager: Grant Mirick
Estimated Sales: $750000

6934 Koegel Meats Inc
3400 W Bristol Rd
Flint, MI 48507
810-238-3685
Fax: 810-238-2467 www.koegels.com
Sausage, natural casing and long frankfurters, bratwurst, bockwurst and smoked specialties.
Founder: Albert Koegel
Controller: Jonathon Jury
jjury@koegelmeats.com
Sales Director: Tom Lakies
Operations Manager: Jim Lay
Year Founded: 1916
Number Employees: 50-99
Number of Products: 35
Square Footage: 400000
Type of Packaging: Consumer, Food Service

6935 Koeze Company
PO Box 9470
Grand Rapids, MI 49509-2237
616-724-2620
Fax: 866-817-0147 800-555-9688
bdekker@koeze.com www.koeze.com
Nut candies
President: Scott Koeze
CEO: Jeff Koeze
Marketing: Beth Dekker
Sales Director: Tom Lakos
Contact: Martin Andree
mjandree@koeze.com
Purchasing Manager: John Feenstra
Estimated Sales: $9672287
Number Employees: 20-49
Square Footage: 320000
Type of Packaging: Consumer, Bulk

6936 Koffee Kup Bakery
436 Riverside Ave
Burlington, VT 05401-1452
802-863-2696
Fax: 802-860-0116 koffeekupbakery.com
Bakery products including breads, rolls and doughnuts.
Chief Executive Officer: Andy Matthews
CFO: Eddie Matthews
ematthews@koffeekupbakery.biz
EVP, Sales & Marketing: Brian Carpentier
Controller: Shirley Patrick
Human Resources Manager: Judy Schraven
Plant Manager: Ron Roberge Jr.
Purchasing Manager: Steve Hebert

Food Manufacturers / A-Z

Estimated Sales: $10-20 Million
Number Employees: 50-99
Number of Brands: 1
Type of Packaging: Private Label
Brands:
  Koffee Kup

6937 Koha Food
500 Alakawa St
Suite 104
Honolulu, HI 96817-4576
808-845-4232
Fax: 808-841-5398
Oriental foods
President: Paul Kim
Estimated Sales: $5-10 Million
Number Employees: 20-49

6938 Kohana Coffee
1221 S Mopac Expressway
Suite 100
Austin, TX 78746
512-904-1174
Fax: 512-532-0581 info@kohanacoffee.com
www.kohanacoffee.com
Coffee, decaff and cold brew coffee.
Owner: Victoria Lynden
Sales: Nate Creasey
Contact: Joe Browne
joe@kohanacoffee.com
Operations: Piper Jones
Estimated Sales: Under $500,000
Number Employees: 2

6939 Kohinoor Foods
40 Northfield Avenue
Edison, NJ 08837
732-868-4400
Fax: 732-868-3143 888-440-7423
info@kohinoorfoods.com
www.kohinoorfoods.com
Rice
CEO: Ganesh Skandan
Marketing: Rajan Kapoor
Contact: Amber Munir
amber@kohinoorfoods.com
Estimated Sales: $2.5-5 Million
Number Employees: 10-19
Brands:
  Kohinoor
  Satman Overseas

6940 Kohler Original Recipe Chocolates
725 Woodlake Rd
Suite D
Kohler, WI 53044-1334
920-208-4930
kohlerchocolates@kohler.com
www.kohlerchocolates.com
Chocolate and nuts
CEO and Chairman: Herb Koehler
Manager: Ron Tremaroli
ronald.tremaroli@kohler.com
Number Employees: 10-19

6941 Koia
1920 Hillhurst Ave
Unit V911
Los Angeles, CA 90027
info@drinkkoia.com
drinkkoia.com
Plant protein-based drinks
CEO: Christopher Hunter
Number of Brands: 1
Number of Products: 5
Type of Packaging: Consumer
Brands:
  KOIA

6942 Kokopelli's Kitchen
9116 N Cave Creek Rd
Phoenix, AZ 85020
602-943-8882
Fax: 602-943-8740 888-943-9802
www.kokopelliskitchen.com
Gourmet dry baking mixes; rice; salad dressings; salsas; enchilada sauce; cocoas; beans; and soups.
President: Cheryl Joseph
Estimated Sales: $.5-1 million
Number Employees: 1-4
Number of Products: 45
Square Footage: 12000
Type of Packaging: Consumer, Bulk
Brands:
  Kokopelli's Kitchen

6943 Kola
215 W 64th St
New York, NY 10065-6662
212-688-1895
rincakola@aol.com
Processor and exporter of soft drinks
Principal: Louis Jardines
Estimated Sales: $2.5-5 Million
Number Employees: 5-9
Type of Packaging: Consumer, Food Service, Private Label
Brands:
  Golden Kola
  Inca Kola

6944 Kolatin Real Kosher Gelatin
325 Second Street
Lakewood, NJ 08701
732-364-8700
Fax: 732-370-0877 info@koshergelatin.com
www.koshergelatin.com
Kosher gelatin
Parent Co: Glatech Productions

6945 Kolb-Lena Bresse Bleu Inc
3990 N Sunnyside Rd
Lena, IL 61048-9613
815-369-4577
Fax: 815-369-4914
Cheese including camembert, baby and bay Swiss, brie, feta and soft.
Quality Manager: Leisa Hubb
Manager: Randy Jenny
randy.jenny@bcusa.net
Estimated Sales: $35.7 Million
Number Employees: 100-249
Number of Brands: 1
Parent Co: Alouette Cheese USA
Type of Packaging: Consumer, Food Service
Brands:
  Delico

6946 Kollar Cookies
PO Box 535
Long Branch, NJ 07740
732-343-4217
Fax: 732-750-1960 kollarcookies@aol.com
www.kollarcookies.com
Cookies
Owner: Pam Kimble
Estimated Sales: $1-2.5 Million
Number Employees: 5
Brands:
  Kollar

6947 Koloa Rum Corp
2-2741 Kaumualii Hwy
Suite C
Kalaheo, HI 96741-8346
808-332-9333
Fax: 808-332-7650 www.koloarum.com
Hawaiian rums
Owner: Bob Gunter
info@koloarum.com
Public Relations: Jeanne Toulon
Estimated Sales: $2.5-5 Million
Number Employees: 5-9

6948 Kombucha Wonder Drink
PO Box 4244
Portland, OR 97208-4244
503-224-7331
Fax: 503-224-2295 877-224-7331
www.wonderdrink.com
USDA-certified sparkling fermented tea.
Founder/Owner: Steve Lee
stephenlee@wonderdrink.com
CEO: Craig Decker
Research & Development: Koei Kudo
Sales Director: Todd Hager
Estimated Sales: $650,000
Number Employees: 5-9
Type of Packaging: Consumer
Brands:
  Kombucha Wonder Drink
  Tea Tibet

6949 Kona Brewing
74-5612 Pawai Place
Kailua Kona, HI 96740
808-334-1133
Fax: 808-329-8869 webmail@konabrewingco.com
www.konabrewingco.com
Beer including lager, ale, IPA, and wheat beer.
President & CEO: Mattson Davis
Quality Control: Rich Tucciarone
Marketing Director: Steve Cole
Contact: Keala Aiwohi
keala.aiwohi@konabrewingco.com
Estimated Sales: $30-50 Million
Number Employees: 50-99
Type of Packaging: Private Label
Brands:
  Kona Brewing

6950 Kona Coffee Council
PO Box 2077
Kealakekua, HI 96750
808-323-2911
www.kona-coffee-council.com
Coffee
President: Donna Woolley
Chair of Finance and Budget Committee: Jonathan Sechrist
VP: Gary Strawn
Contact: Roger Dilts
customkona@hotmail.com
Estimated Sales: $.5-1 million
Number Employees: 1-4

6951 Kona Cold Lobsters
73-4460 Queen Kaahumanu
Suite 103
Kailua Kona, HI 96740-2637
808-329-4332
Fax: 808-326-2882 info@konacoldlobsters.com
www.konacoldlobsters.com
Lobsters
President: Joseph Wilson
Manager: Philip Wilson
phil@konacoldlobsters.com
Estimated Sales: Less than $300,000
Number Employees: 10-19

6952 Kona Fish Co Inc
73-4776 Kanalani St
Suite 8
Kailua Kona, HI 96740-2625
808-326-7708
Fax: 808-329-3669 www.hilofish.com
Fresh, frozen seafood
Owner: Kerry Umamoto
Estimated Sales: $5-10 Million
Number Employees: 20-49

6953 Kona Premium Coffee Company
78-1095 Bishop Rd.
Holualoa, HI 96725
808-322-4160
Fax: 808-322-9275 888-322-9550
coffeeorders@KonaPremium.com
www.konapremium.com
Commercial and retail coffee
Owner/President: Robert Millslagle
General Manager: Westley Cornwell
CFO: Jeff Woode
Vice President: Barb Millslagle
Estimated Sales: $20-50 Million
Number Employees: 20-49
Type of Packaging: Private Label
Brands:
  Kona Coffee
  Royal Konaccino

6954 KonaRed Corp.
2042 Corte Del Nogal
Suite C
Carlsbad, CA 92011
949-682-4700
Fax: 949-449-8338 sales@konared.com
www.konared.com
Hawaiian coffee and coffee fruit products
Founder: Shaun Roberts
Number of Brands: 1
Number of Products: 9
Type of Packaging: Consumer
Brands:
  KONARED

Food Manufacturers / A-Z

6955 Konetzko's Meat Market
516 Main St S
Browerville, MN 56438-1200
320-594-2915
Smoked meat and sausage
Owner: Jim Becker
Estimated Sales: Less than $500,000
Number Employees: 5-9
Type of Packaging: Consumer

6956 Konto's Foods
P.O.Box 628
Patterson, NJ 07544
973-278-2800
Fax: 973-278-7943 info@kontos.com
www.kontos.com
Flat bread, dough; meat products; cheese; olives; and Greek specialties.
Founder, Partner: Evripides Kontos
Partner: Steve Kontos
Partner: Michael Vorkas
Number Employees: 150
Square Footage: 300000
Type of Packaging: Food Service
Brands:
  Konto's

6957 Konzelmann Estate Winery
1096 Lakeshore Rd
Niagara on the Lake, ON L0S 1J0
Canada
905-935-2866
Fax: 905-935-2864 wine@konzelmann.ca
www.konzelmann.ca
Wines
Owner: Herbert Konzelmann
Owner: Gudrun Konzelmann
VP: Jim Reschke
VP: Bruno Reis
Media Relations & Marketing: Claudia Konzelmann
VP of Marketing: Jansin Ozkur
Events & Retail: Bev Ferrante
Estimated Sales: $1.79 Million
Number Employees: 7
Type of Packaging: Bulk

6958 Kookaburra
14497 Fryelands Blvd SE
Monroe, WA 98272-2941
360-805-6858
www.kookaburralicorice.com
Licorice
President/Owner: Donald Cook
CEO: Bradley Cook
Manager: Robin Faulds
rfkookaburra@aol.com
Number Employees: 5-9

6959 Kopali Organics
8101 Biscayne Blvd
Suite 609
Miami, FL 33138-4668
305-751-7341
Fax: 305-751-7344
Organic foods
Contact: Fernanda Sanchez
fernanda@kopali.com
COO: Norman Brooks

6960 Kopper's Chocolate
45 Jackson Dr
Cranford, NJ 07016
800-325-0026
info@kopperschocolate.com
kopperschocolate.com
Chocolate beans
Co-Owner: Leslye Alexander
Co-Owner: Jeff Alexander
Year Founded: 1937

6961 (HQ)Koppers Chocolate
45 Jackson Drive
Cranford, NJ 07016
212-243-0220
800-325-0026
info@kopperschocolate.com
www.kopperschocolate.com
Processor, importer and exporter of confectionery items including chocolate covered espresso beans, chocolate covered gummy bears and Danish mint lentils.
President: Jeff Alexander
jeff@kopperschocolate.com
Director of Sales: Ellen Silverman
Estimated Sales: $7800000
Number Employees: 51-200

6962 Koppert Cress USA
23423 Middle Road
Route 48.
Cutchogue, NY 11935
631-734-8500
Fax: 631-734- 849 info.usa@koppertcress.com
www.koppertcress.com
Micro-vegetables
Member: Janny Hendrikse

6963 Kor Shots
Malibu, CA
korshots.com
Cold-pressed juice shots
Founder: Jordan Retamar
Number of Brands: 1
Number of Products: 6
Type of Packaging: Consumer
Brands:
  KOR SHOTS

6964 Korbs Baking Company
540 Pawtucket Avenue
Pawtucket, RI 02860-6098
401-726-4422
Fax: 401-726-4446
Baked goods
President: Edmund Korb
Estimated Sales: $1-2.5 000,000
Number Employees: 50

6965 Korea Ginseng Corp.
12750 Center Court Dr S
Cerritos, CA 90703
contact@kgcus.com
www.kgcus.com
Ginseng products
VP, Sales: Adam Goodman

6966 Kornfections
14516 Lee Rd # C
Chantilly, VA 20151-1638
703-378-0009
Fax: 703-817-9560 800-469-8886
kornfections@verizon.net
Gourmet popcorn and confections.
President: Gerald Lerner
Vice President: Helen Lerner
Marketing/Public Relations: Jerry Lerner
Estimated Sales: $3-5 Million
Number Employees: 6
Number of Brands: 1
Number of Products: 22
Square Footage: 4800
Type of Packaging: Consumer, Food Service, Private Label, Bulk

6967 Korte Meat Processors Inc
810 Deal St
Highland, IL 62249
618-654-3813
Fax: 618-654-8207 www.korte-meats.com
Old Style German sausages, party and deli trays, cheese, and cure meats.
Owner: Dave Korte
Owner: Therese Korte
Year Founded: 1969
Estimated Sales: $3-5 Million
Number Employees: 5-9

6968 Koryo Winery Company
13719 Alma Ave
Gardena, CA 90249
310-532-9616
Fax: 310-532-3240
Wines
President: Sarah Kym
Operations Manager: Roy Kym
Estimated Sales: Less than $500,000
Number Employees: 20-49
Type of Packaging: Private Label
Brands:
  Dong Dong Joo Rice Wine
  Mackoly Rice Wine
  Sochu Distilled Rice

6969 Kosher French Baguettes
683 McDonald Ave
Brooklyn, NY 11218
718-633-4994
Baguettes
Owner: Paul Gima
Estimated Sales: $300,000-500,000
Number Employees: 5-9

6970 Kossar's Bagels & Bialys
367 Grand St
New York, NY 10002-3951
212-473-4810
Fax: 212-253-2146 877-424-2597
www.kossarsbialys.com
Bakery products
Owner: Danny Cohen
mail@kossarsbialys.com
Estimated Sales: Less Than $500,000
Number Employees: 5-9
Brands:
  Bialy
  Kashruth

6971 Kosto Food Products Co
1325 N Old Rand Rd
Wauconda, IL 60084-3302
847-487-2600
Fax: 847-487-2654 www.kostofoods.com
Processor and exporter of salad dressings, food colorings, pudding and ice cream mixes; importer of colorants, stabilizers, ice cream mixes, drink crystals, meat extenders and puddings
President: Donald F Colby
General Manager: Steve Colby
Sales Director: Richard Gray
Estimated Sales: $1300000
Number Employees: 10-19
Type of Packaging: Consumer, Food Service, Private Label, Bulk
Brands:
  Dari Pride
  Food Pak
  Freezerta
  Kosto
  Mack's
  Mrs Slaby's
  Slushade

6972 Koukla Delights
4648 St Laurent Blvd
Montreal, QC H2T 1R3
Canada
646-318-9131
info@koukladelights.com
koukladelights.com
Macaroons and cookies
President: Evelyn Jerassy

6973 Kowalski Sausage Co
2270 Holbrook St
Hamtramck, MI 48212-3487
313-873-8200
Fax: 313-873-4220 800-482-2400
www.kowality.com
Sausage
President: Michael Kowalski
Estimated Sales: $32800000
Number Employees: 100-249
Number of Brands: 2
Number of Products: 75
Type of Packaging: Consumer, Food Service
Brands:
  Hunter's Sausage
  Kowalski

6974 Kozlowski Farms
5566 Hwy 116
Forestville, CA 95436-9697
707-887-1587
Fax: 707-887-9650 800-473-2767
koz@kozlowskifarms.com
www.kozlowskifarms.com
Fruit spreads; jams; mustards; preserves; chutneys; jellys; fruit butters; dessert sauces; steak and BBQ sauces; fruit vinegar; salad dressings and chipotle sauces; apples an Pinot Noir grapes.
Vice President: Carol Every
carol@kozlowskifarms.com
CEO: Perry Kozlowski
CFO: Cindy Kozlowski-Hayworth
Estimated Sales: $1,000,000
Number Employees: 20-49
Number of Brands: 1
Number of Products: 90
Square Footage: 80000
Type of Packaging: Consumer, Private Label
Brands:
  Kozlowski Farms
  Sonoma County Classics

Food Manufacturers / A-Z

6975 Kraemer Wisconsin Cheese LTD
1173 N 4th St
Watertown, WI 53098-3201
920-261-6363
Fax: 920-261-9606 800-236-8033
www.kraemercheese.com
Cheese
Owner: Michael Kraemer
kwcheese@execpc.com
Estimated Sales: Below $5 Million
Number Employees: 5-9

6976 Kraft Heinz Canada
95 Moatfield Dr.
North York, ON M3B 3L6
Canada
416-441-5000
www.kraftcanada.com
Condiments, peanut butter, salad dressings, cheeses, desserts, frozen meals, macaroni and cheese, coffee blends, drink mixes, sweeteners, BBQ sauces, and more.
President, Canada Zone: Bruno Keller
CMO: Dana Somerville
VP of Sales: Peter Hall
Estimated Sales: $3.5 Billion
Number Employees: 2,000
Number of Brands: 6
Parent Co: The Kraft Heinz Company
Type of Packaging: Consumer, Food Service
Brands:
  Baker's
  Jell-O
  Certo
  Cool Whip
  Caramels
  Jet-Puffed
  Magic Baking Powder
  Amooza
  Cheez Whiz
  Cracker Barrel
  Philadelphia
  Kraft 100% Parmesan
  Kraft Singles
  P'tit Qu•bec
  Velveeta
  Nabob
  Maxwell House
  Tassimo
  Gevalia Kaffe
  Kool-Aid
  MiO
  Crystal Light
  Tang
  Country Time
  Kraft Salad Dressings
  Ren,e's
  Classico
  Kraft Dinner
  Shake 'n Bake
  Stove Top
  Kraft Peanut Butter
  Miracle Whip
  Kraft BBQ Sauce
  Kraft Mayo
  Claussen
  Oscar Mayer
  Heinz Ketchup
  MAX Boost Coffee
  Crave
  Bagel Bites
  Catelli
  Bull's Eye
  Diana Sauce
  Lea & Perrins

6977 (HQ)Kraft Heinz Co.
200 E. Randolph St.
Suite 7600
Chicago, IL 60601
800-543-5335
www.kraftheinzcompany.com
Food and beverage company manufacturing pasta, snack foods, sauces, cream cheese, beverages, condiments, etc.
President, US Zone: Carlos Abrams-Rivera
CEO: Miguel Patricio
CFO: Paul Basilio
Chief Growth Officer: Nina Barton
Chief Procurement Officer: Marcos Eloi
Year Founded: 1869
Estimated Sales: $26.27 Billion
Number Employees: 38,000
Number of Brands: 54
Type of Packaging: Consumer, Food Service
Brands:
  Oscar Mayer
  Ore-Ida
  Kraft Macaroni & Cheese
  Classico
  Claussen
  Caprisun
  Heinz ABC
  Wattie's
  Weight Watchers Smart Ones
  Kool-Aid
  Jello
  Philadelphia
  Golden Circle
  Lunchables
  Planters
  Pudliszki
  Maxwell House
  Grey Poupon
  Complan
  Master
  Honig
  Plasmon
  Quero
  Velveeta

6978 Kramarczuk's Sausage Co
215 E Hennepin Ave
Minneapolis, MN 55414-1013
612-379-3018
Fax: 612-379-7693 info@kramarczuk.com
www.kramarczuk.com
Sausages
President: Orest Kramarczuk
andrew@arvisev.com
Estimated Sales: $500,000-$1 Million
Number Employees: 20-49

6979 Kramer Vineyards
26830 NW Olson Rd
Gaston, OR 97119-8039
503-662-4545
Fax: 503-662-4033 800-619-4637
info@kramerwine.com www.kramervineyards.com
Wines
President/CEO/Winemaker: Trudy Kramer
trudy@kramervineyards.com
CEO: Kramer
VP/Secretary/Vineyard Manager: Keith Kramer
Marketing VP: Trudy Kramer
Estimated Sales: Less than $500,000
Number Employees: 5-9
Brands:
  Kramer

6980 Kraus & Co
19700 Fairchild # 270
Suite 270
Irvine, CA 92612-2520
949-250-2955
Fax: 949-250-2960 800-662-5871
krausco@krausco.com www.krausco.com
Flavors, extracts, food colors, fruit preps, variegating sauces, toppings
Owner: Tom Kraus
krausco@krausco.com
Co-Founder/CEO: Eva Kraus
CFO: Saad Alhir
Estimated Sales: Less Than $500,000
Number Employees: 1-4
Type of Packaging: Food Service, Bulk

6981 Krave Pure Food
117 W Napa St
Suite C
Sonoma, CA 95476
877-891-1481
info@kravejerky.com www.kravejerky.com
Beef jerky
General Manager: Shane Chambers
VP, Marketing: Rusti Porter
Director of Operations: Ben Berry

6982 Kreher Family Farms
5411 Davison Rd.
P.O. Box 410
Clarence, NY 14031-0410
716-759-6802
Fax: 716-759-8687 www.krehereggs.com
Eggs, corn, soy, and wheat.
Year Founded: 1924
Type of Packaging: Private Label

6983 Krema Nut Co
1000 Goodale Blvd
Columbus, OH 43212-3889
614-299-4131
Fax: 614-299-1636 800-222-4132
nuts@krema.com www.krema.com
Peanut butter and nuts including cashews
President: Mike Giunta
nuts@krema.com
Estimated Sales: Less than $500,000
Number Employees: 5-9
Type of Packaging: Consumer, Food Service, Private Label
Brands:
  Krema

6984 Krenik's Meat Processing
10740 130th St W
Montgomery, MN 56069-1870
507-364-5154
www.kreniks.com
Meats including steaks, pork chops, ribs, wieners, beef, pork, lamb and poultry products. Also, heat & eat, hot beef, bbq pulled pork, pork & kraut, roast pork, cooked potato dumplings, turkey 'n gravy, smoked pork, sausages, bolognabacon swiss & tomato bratwurst, italian bratwurst, breakfast sausage, beef snack sticks, pork jerky, king crab legs, cod, smoked carp, and custom cuts.
Owner: Jim Krenik
jim@kreniks.com
Estimated Sales: Less Than $500,000
Number Employees: 1-4

6985 Krier Foods
520 Wolf Rd
Random Lake, WI 53075-1280
920-994-2469
Fax: 920-994-9898 www.krierfoods.com
Beverages including juice and soda
Chairman of the Board: B Bruce Krier
Executive VP: Thoma Bretza
Contact: Karen Fahrenkrug
karen@krierfoods.com
Estimated Sales: $740,000
Number Employees: 50-99
Square Footage: 16456
Type of Packaging: Consumer
Brands:
  Fruitland
  Jolly Good

6986 Krinos Foods
1750 Bathgate Ave
Bronx, NY 10457
718-729-9000
Fax: 718-361-9725 info@krinos.com
www.krinos.com
Greek olives, sauces, salsas, and oils.
Owner: Eric Moscahlaidis
Year Founded: 1850
Estimated Sales: $304 Million
Number Employees: 100
Type of Packaging: Consumer, Food Service, Bulk
Other Locations:
  Krinos Manufacturing Facility
  Long Island City NY
  Krinos Manufacturing Facility
  Toronto, Canada
  Krinos Manufacturing Facility
  Montreal, Canada
Brands:
  Apollo
  Athens
  Attiki
  Florina
  Haitoglou
  Hermes
  Horio
  Macedonian
  Melissa
  Mevgal
  Minerva
  Mythos
  Sarantis
  Stella
  Vlaha
  Yiotis
  Zanae

6987 Krispy Kernels
2620 Watt Street
Quebec, QC G1P 3T5
Canada
418-658-1515
Fax: 418-657-5971 877-791-9986
www.krispykernels.com
Peanuts, popcorn, candy and dried fruits and nuts
Owner: Denis Jalbert
CEO: Pierce Rivard
Quality Control: Stephen Jackson
Marketing Director: Renee Maude Jalbert
Sales Director: Stephane Gravel
Plant Manager: Jacques Bieion
Purchasing Manager: Marc Parent
Square Footage: 200000
Brands:
 Krispy Kernels

6988 Krispy Kreme Doughnuts Inc
2116 Hawkins St
Charlotte, NC 28203
www.krispykreme.com
Bakery items and coffee including; doughnuts.
CEO: Michael Tattersfield
Year Founded: 1937
Estimated Sales: $518.7 Million
Number Employees: 4,300
Parent Co: JAB Holding Company

6989 Kristian Regale
14 Birkmose Park Ln
Hudson, WI 54016-2286
715-386-8388
Fax: 715-386-9295 info@kristianregale.com
www.kristianregale.com
Manufacturer and Importer of Swedish nonalcoholic apple and pear sparkling ciders,there are six flavors including the following, apple,peach.pear,poegranate-apple,lingonberry-apple,black currant.
Owner: Nancy Bieraugel
CHR/CEO: Ed Doherty
CFO: Dave Baldwin
Evp: Bob Gillespie
Estimated Sales: $3.4 Million
Number Employees: 7
Type of Packaging: Consumer, Food Service
Brands:
 Kristian Regale

6990 Kristin Hill Winery
3330 SE Amity Dayton Hwy
Amity, OR 97101
503-835-4012
Fax: 503-835-4012
Wine
Owner: Eric Aberag
kristinhill1@msn.com
Co-Owner: Eric Aberg
Estimated Sales: Under $300,000
Number Employees: 1-4
Type of Packaging: Private Label
Brands:
 Kristin Hill

6991 Kroger Bakery
16253 SE 122nd Ave
Clackamas, OR 97015-9136
503-650-2000
Fax: 503-650-2128
Bread and bakery products
Principal: Earl Bliven
ebliven@fredmeyer.com
Estimated Sales: $621,874 Thousand
Number Employees: 100-249

6992 Kronos
1 Kronos Dr.
Glendale Heights, IL 60139
224-353-5353
Fax: 224-353-5400 800-621-0099
requests@kronosfoodscorp.com
www.kronosfoodscorp.com
Mediterranean foods including gyro, pita, flatbread, tzatziki sauce, spanakopita, falafel, and tyropita
Chairman: Michael Austin
CEO: Howard Eirinberg
CFO: Herman Brons
Director of Marketing: Karyn Andrew
SVP Sales: Bob Michaels
Year Founded: 1975
Number Employees: 250-499

6993 Kruger Foods
18362 E Highway 4
Stockton, CA 95215-9433
209-941-8518
www.krugerfoods.com
Processor and exporter of condiments including relish, pickles, peppers and sauerkraut.
Chief Executive Officer: Kara Kruger
Contact: Jessica Altamirano
j.altamirano@krugerfoods.com
Director, Operations: Erik Kruger
Director, Technical Services: Christine Ramsey
Year Founded: 1930
Estimated Sales: $22 Million
Number Employees: 100
Square Footage: 120000
Type of Packaging: Consumer, Food Service, Bulk

6994 Krupka's Blueberries
2647 68th St
Fennville, MI 49408
269-857-4278
Fax: 269-857-4018 www.bluestarblueberries.com
Blueberries
Partner: Harold Krupka
Partner: Carmen Krupka
Sales Manager: Connie Krupka
Estimated Sales: $3,000,000
Number Employees: 50-99
Type of Packaging: Consumer, Bulk

6995 Kruse & Son
235 Kruse Ave
Monrovia, CA 91016-4899
626-358-4536
Fax: 626-303-7349
Meats
Owner: David Kruse
stevek@aol.com
Estimated Sales: $3,200,000
Number Employees: 100-249
Type of Packaging: Consumer, Food Service

6996 Kruse Meat Products
2100 Kruse Loop
Alexander, AR 72002
501-316-2100
Fax: 501-794-0256
Meat products
President: Jeanne Hutchinson
Estimated Sales: $1.8 Million
Number Employees: 15
Type of Packaging: Consumer

6997 Kubisch Sausage Mfg Co
50400 Rizzo Dr
Shelby Twp, MI 48315-3275
586-566-4661
Fax: 586-566-8661 800-852-5019
info@kubischsausage.com
www.kubischsausage.com
Sausage and other prepared meats
Owner: Vasilj Markovich
Estimated Sales: Less than $300,000
Number Employees: 10-19

6998 Kubla Khan Food Company
3369 SE Raymond Street
Portland, OR 97202-4360
503-234-7494
Fax: 503-234-7716
Frozen fruits and vegetables
President: Percy Loy
Estimated Sales: $470,000
Number Employees: 5
Type of Packaging: Food Service, Bulk
Brands:
 Kubla Khan

6999 Kuhlmann's Market Gardens & Greenhouses
1320-167 Avenue NW
Edmonton, AB T5Y 6L6
Canada
780-475-7500
Fax: 780-472-9923 info@kuhlmanns.com
www.kuhlmanns.com
Processor, exporter and packer of cabbage, carrots, broccoli, peas and potatoes
Pres.: Dietrich Kuhlmann
Estimated Sales: C
Number Employees: 20-49
Type of Packaging: Consumer, Food Service

7000 Kuju Coffee
San Francisco, CA
415-634-5858
info@kujucoffee.com
www.kujucoffee.com
Instant coffee
Co-Founder & CEO: Jeff Wiguna
Co-Founder & COO: Justin Wiguna
Number of Brands: 1
Type of Packaging: Consumer
Brands:
 KUJU COFFEE

7001 Kulana Foods LTD
590 W Kawailani St # J
Hilo, HI 96720-3173
808-959-9144
Fax: 808-959-8484
www.tasteofthehawaiianrange.com
Beef and pork slaughtering and processing
President: Brady Yagi
Estimated Sales: Below $5 000,000
Number Employees: 10-19
Type of Packaging: Private Label
Brands:
 Fresh Aland Beef and Pork
 Kulana Foods

7002 Kuli Kuli, Inc.
600 Grand Ave
Suite 410b
Oakland, CA 94610
510-350-8325
info@kulikulifoods.com
www.kulikulifoods.com
Superfood bars, moringa power, mooring tea
Owner/Cmo: Valerie Popelka
Chief Executive Officer/Founder: Lisa Curtis
lisa@kulikulibar.com
Chief Creative & Design: Anne Tsuei
COO/CTO: Jordan Moncharmont
Number Employees: 5-9

7003 Kunde Estate Winery
9825 Sonoma Highway
PO Box 639
Kenwood, CA 95452
707-833-5501
Fax: 707-833-2204 wineinfo@kunde.com
www.kunde.com
Ultra premium, estate grown, and sustainably farmed wines.
Chairman: Jeff Kunde
Vice President: Fred Kunde
Marketing Director: Marcia Kunde Mickelson
Contact: Tim Bell
tbell@kunde.com
Operations Manager: Bill Kunde
Winemaker: Zach Long
Year Founded: 1879
Estimated Sales: $30-50 Million
Number Employees: 50-99
Type of Packaging: Private Label
Brands:
 Estate Cabernet Sauvignon
 Estate Chardonnay
 Estate Merlot
 Estate Syrah
 Estate Viognier
 Estate Zinfandel (Ce

7004 Kupris Home Bakery
23 Williams Road
Bolton, CT 06043-7235
860-649-4746
Breads and pastries
Owner: Juris Kupris
Number Employees: 4

7005 Kura Nutrition
670 N Commercial St
Suite 204
Manchester, NH 03101
603-217-2665
kuranutrition.com
Vegan and dairy protein smoothie mixes
CEO: Kelli Rooney Hanzalik
Number of Brands: 1
Number of Products: 6
Type of Packaging: Consumer
Brands:
 KURA

Food Manufacturers / A-Z

7006 Kurtz Orchards Farms
16006 Niagra River Parkway
PO Box 457
Niagra-on-the-Lake, ON L0S 1J0
Canada
905-468-2937
info@kurtzorchards.com
www.kurtzorchards.com
Jams, jellies, fruit butters, fruit sauces, honey butters, and wine jellies.
Pres.: Wilf Kurtz
CEO: Brad Kurtz
VP: Brad Kurtz
Plant Manager: Darren Hedges
Number Employees: 18
Number of Brands: 3
Brands:
  Bethune
  Black Cat
  Superior

7007 Kusha Inc.
11130 Warland Drive
Cypress, CA 90630
949-930-1400
Fax: 949-250-1520 800-550-7423
Rice, basmati, jasmine, tea, grape seed oil, cheese
Vice President: Jerry Taylor
Contact: Mukesh Agrawal
mukesh@ltfoodsamericas.com
Estimated Sales: Under $500,000
Number Employees: 30
Type of Packaging: Consumer, Food Service, Private Label, Bulk
Brands:
  Nasim
  Pari
  Royal

7008 Kusmi Tea
26 W 23rd Street
6th Floor
New York, NY 10010
646-346-1756
Fax: 646-624-2893 info.us@kusmitea.com
Kosher hot beverages and teas
Marketing: Lauriane Penfornis

7009 Kutiks Honey Farm
285 Lyon Brook Rd
Norwich, NY 13815-3420
607-336-4105
Fax: 607-336-4199
Portion packed honey and honey sticks; also, custom gift packs available
Owner/President: Charles Kutik
Owner: Caryn Kutik
Estimated Sales: Less Than $500,000
Number Employees: 1-4
Square Footage: 18740
Type of Packaging: Consumer, Food Service, Private Label, Bulk
Brands:
  Kutik's Honey

7010 Kutztown Bologna Company
1500 Oregon Rd # 100
Leola, PA 17540-9753
717-556-0901
Fax: 717-560-0680 800-723-8824
info@kutztownbologna.com
www.actionvideoinc.com
Frozen beef and pork products
President: Gordon Harrower
VP: Gary Landuy
Estimated Sales: $670000
Number Employees: 1-4
Type of Packaging: Consumer, Private Label
Brands:
  Kutztown

7011 Kwangdong USA
10 Corporate Park
Suite 130
Irvine, CA 92606
949-501-4610
Vitamin C beverage
Year Founded: 1963

7012 Kween Foods
San Diego, CA 92075
401-343-0805
admin@kween.co
kween.co
Granola butter
Co-Founder: Ali Bonar
Co-Founder: Eric Katz

7013 Kwikpak Fisheries
1016 W 6th Avenue
Suite 301
Anchorage, AK 99501-1963
206-443-1565
Fax: 206-443-1912 800-509-3332
ruthc@ydfda.org www.kwikpakfisheries.com
Smoked seafood.
General Manager: Jack Schultheis
Marketing: Ruth Carter
Contact: Marilyn Charles
marilyn@kwikpakfisheries.com

7014 Kyger Bakery Products
3825 State Road 38 E
Lafayette, IN 47905-5212
765-447-1252
Fax: 765-447-7989 info@harlanbakeries.com
Frozen desserts including cream and meringue pies and angel food and sheet cakes; also, retail and institutional packaging available
President: Joseph Latoufe
Vice President: Doug Harlan
Type of Packaging: Consumer
Brands:
  Kyger

7015 Kyler's Catch Seafood Market
2 Washburn St
New Bedford, MA 02740-7336
508-984-5150
Fax: 508-991-4664 888-859-5377
info@kylerseafood.com www.kylerscatch.com
Fresh and frozen cod and flounder
Owner: Jeff Manfelt
jeff@kylerseafood.com
Controller: Steve Souza
EVP: Billy Arruda
Plant Manager: Paul Poliquin
Estimated Sales: $14 Million
Number Employees: 100-249
Type of Packaging: Private Label

7016 Kyong Hae Kim Company
2330 Kalakaua Ave
Suite 85
Honolulu, HI 96815-5001
808-926-8720
Fax: 808-841-2178
Owner: Kyong Kim

7017 Kyowa Hakko
600 Third Avenue
19th Floor
New York, NY 10017-9023
212-319-5353
Fax: 212-421-1283 800-596-9252
info@kyowa-usa.com www.kyowa-usa.com
Amino, nuclei and organic acids; exporter of food ingredients
President & CEO: Leo Cullen
VP Sales: D Christopher Nolte
Contact: Maurice Kirch
kirch@kyowa-usa.com
Estimated Sales: $20-50 Million
Number Employees: 10-19
Parent Co: Kyowa Hakko Kogyo Company
Brands:
  Cognizin
  Lumistor
  Pantesin
  Setria
  Sustamine

7018 (HQ)L & L Packing Co
527 W 41st St
Chicago, IL 60609-2708
773-285-5400
Fax: 773-285-0366 800-628-6328
www.worldsbeststeak.com
Established in 1955. Supplier of prime and choice aged beef, pork, veal and lamb.
President: Joel Lezak
Sales Manager: Phil Lombardi
Estimated Sales: $24000000
Number Employees: 20-49
Type of Packaging: Consumer, Private Label

7019 L & M Bakery
11 Saint Mihiel Dr
Riverside, NJ 08075-1017
856-461-1660
Fax: 856-461-8524 888-887-1335
sales@lmbakery.com www.lmbakery.com
Fruit squares, nut bread, regular and sour cream coffee cakes and macaroons
Owner: John Kahl
VP: Johanne La Plante
Sales Director: Rick Fermoyle
sales@lmbakery.com
Plant Manager: Andy Stoehrer
Estimated Sales: $10-20 Million
Number Employees: 20-49
Square Footage: 20000
Type of Packaging: Consumer, Food Service
Brands:
  L & M Bakery

7020 L & M Lockers
15 Bridge St
Belt, MT 59412
406-277-3522
Fax: 406-277-3522
Meat and fish
Owner: Steve Serquina
Partner: Jerry Wojtala
Estimated Sales: $200,000+
Number Employees: 1-4
Type of Packaging: Consumer, Food Service

7021 L & M Slaughterhouse
903 Mill Rd
Georgetown, IL 61846-6341
217-662-6841
abitor@aol.com
Beef, veal, lamb and pork; slaughtering sevices available
Owner: Todd Green
Estimated Sales: $1-3 Million
Number Employees: 1-4
Type of Packaging: Consumer

7022 (HQ)L & S Packing Co
101 Central Ave
Farmingdale, NY 11735-6915
631-845-1717
Fax: 631-420-7309 800-286-6487
sales@paesana.com www.paesana.com
Importer of gourmet condiments such as olives, capers, pickles, cocktail onions, mushrooms, etc.; serving food service, industrial and private label markets. Also, high quality authentic pasta sauces and Chinese sauces, see our ad onthe back cover of Vol
President: Louis Scaramelli
lou@paesana.com
Estimated Sales: $3-5 Million
Number Employees: 20-49
Type of Packaging: Consumer, Food Service, Private Label, Bulk
Other Locations:
  L&S Packing Co.
  Flushing NY
Brands:
  Mi-Kee
  Paesana
  Table Joy

7023 L & S Packing Co
101 Central Ave
PO Box 709
Farmingdale, NY 11735-6915
631-845-1717
Fax: 631-420-7309 877-879-6453
info@paesana.com www.paesana.com
Olives
President: Louis Scaramelli
lou@paesana.com
Estimated Sales: $3-5 Million
Number Employees: 20-49

7024 L A Burdick Chocolate
47 Main St
P.O. Box 593
Walpole, NH 03608-3300
603-756-3701
Fax: 603-756-4326 800-229-2419
sales@burdickchocolate.com
www.burdickchocolate.com
Chocolates
CEO: Genna Bromley
gbromley@burdickchocolate.com

Food Manufacturers / A-Z

7025 L C Good Candy Company
1825 E Tremont St
Allentown, PA 18109-1615
610-432-3290
Fax: 610-432-7455 lcgoodcandy@gmail.com
Candy and confections
President: Roland R Mink Jr
Estimated Sales: Below $200,000
Number Employees: 1-4

7026 L F Lambert Spawn Co
1507 Valley Rd
Coatesville, PA 19320
610-384-5031
Fax: 610-384-0390 www.lambertbiologicals.com
Processor and exporter of mushroom spawns
President: Hugh Mcintyre
hugh@lambertspawn.com
Owner: Rick McIntyre
VP of Operations: Joseph Mascrangelo
Estimated Sales: $3300000
Number Employees: 50-99

7027 L H Hayward & Co
5401 Toler St
New Orleans, LA 70123-5222
504-733-8480
Fax: 504-733-8155 info@camelliabeans.com
www.camelliabrand.com
Packaging of beans
Owner: Gordon K Hayward
ken@hhco.com
CO-Owner: Rick Hayward
Estimated Sales: $5-10 Million
Number Employees: 20-49
Type of Packaging: Private Label
Brands:
  Camellia

7028 L K Bowman
12 Old Forge Rd
Nottingham, PA 19362-9747
610-932-2240
Fax: 610-932-4186 800-853-1919
Mushrooms
President: Robert Shelton
Vice President: Jack Shelton
jack.shelton@hanoverfoods.com
Estimated Sales: $10-20 Million
Number Employees: 1-4
Square Footage: 54417
Parent Co: Hanover Foods Corporation
Type of Packaging: Food Service, Private Label, Bulk
Brands:
  Garden Path
  Mother Earth
  Nottingham

7029 L Mawby Vineyards
4519 S Elm Valley Rd
Peshawbestown, MI 49682-9373
231-271-3522
Fax: 231-271-2927 info@lmawby.com
www.lmawby.com
Wines
Owner: Stu Laing
stulaing@gmail.com
Estimated Sales: Less Than $500,000
Number Employees: 1-4
Brands:
  L.Mawby
  M.Lawrence

7030 L&C Fisheries
French River
RR #2
Kensington, PE C0B 1M0
Canada
902-886-2770
Fax: 902-886-3003
calvin@greengablesmussels.com
www.greengablesmussels.com
Fresh mussels, oysters, and fresh and frozen lobsters
Owner: Calvin Jollimore
Number Employees: 10-19
Type of Packaging: Consumer, Food Service

7031 L&M Bakers Supply Company
2501 Steeles Avenue W
Unit # 1
Toronto, ON M3J 2P1
Canada
416-665-3005
Fax: 416-665-8975 800-465-7361
www.lmbakersupply.com
Manufacturer & wholesaler/distributor of cake decorations and baking tools and supplies; serving the food service market
General Manager: Sheba Grinhaus
Number Employees: 20-49
Square Footage: 44000

7032 L&M Evans
PO Box 367
Conyers, GA 30012
770-483-9373
Fax: 847-647-1509
Seafood, clams, fish, fillets
President: L W Bill Evans
Owner: Gene Burkett
Estimated Sales: $300,000-500,000
Number Employees: 1-4

7033 L'Esprit De Campagne
1247 Wrights Mill Rd
Berryville, VA 22611-2243
540-955-1014
Fax: 540-955-1018 800-692-8008
lespritfods@hotmail.com
www.lespritdecampagne.com
Dried tomatoes, apples, cherries, blueberries, cranberries
President: Joy Lokey
jlockey@lespritdecampagne.com
CEO: Carey Lokey
Estimated Sales: Below $5 Million
Number Employees: 50-99
Brands:
  L'Esprit

7034 L. A. Smoking & Curing Company
PO Box 21938
Los Angeles, CA 90021-0938
213-624-2369
Smoked and cured products
President: Bill Terhar
Estimated Sales: $10-24.9 Million
Number Employees: 100-249
Parent Co: Obester Winery

7035 L. Craelius & Company
370 N Morgan St
Chicago, IL 60607-1321
312-666-7100
Fax: 312-666-9747
Fresh poultry
President: Lawrence Craelius
Estimated Sales: $20-50 Million
Number Employees: 20-49

7036 L.A. Libations
715-B N Douglas St
El Segundo, CA 90245
lalibations.com
Specialty beverages
President & Co-Founder: Pat Bolden
CEO & Co-Founder: Danny Stepper
Co-Founder: Dino Sarti
Director, Sales: Glenn Marin
Brands:
  The Living Apothecary
  Aloe Gloe
  KonaRed
  trimino

7037 L.B. Maple Treat
1037 Boul. Industriel
Granby, QC J2J 2B8
Canada
450-777-4464
Fax: 450-777-2867 888-775-1111
www.lbmapletreat.com
Maple syrup and maple syrup products
President/Owner: Daniel Cousineau
Number of Brands: 2
Parent Co: Lantic, Inc.
Type of Packaging: Consumer, Private Label, Bulk
Brands:
  L.B. MAPLE TREAT
  UNCLE LUKE'S

7038 L.H. Rodriguez Wholesale Seafood
3541 S 12th Ave
Tucson, AZ 85713-5914
520-623-1931
Fax: 520-623-0737
Seafood
President: Levi Rodriguez
Treasurer: Albert Rodriguez
Vice President: Joe Rodriguez
Estimated Sales: $3-5 Million
Number Employees: 5-9

7039 LA Bou Bakery & Cafe
1179 Grass Valley Hwy
Auburn, CA 95603-3411
530-823-2303
Fax: 530-823-0400 customerservice@labou.com
www.labou.com
Gourmet coffees, pastries, soups, sandwiches, salads, desserts
Owner: Arlene Be
Number Employees: 10-19

7040 LA Boulangerie
7740 Formula Pl
San Diego, CA 92121-2419
858-578-4040
Fax: 858-536-5911 www.franklynatural.com
Baked goods
Owner: Gerald Sarnoo
Estimated Sales: Below $5 000,000
Number Employees: 10-19
Brands:
  La Boulangerie

7041 LA Buena Vida Vineyards
416 E College St
Grapevine, TX 76051-5468
817-481-9463
Fax: 817-421-3635
Wines
Manager: Adam Artho
Marketing Director: Camille McBee
Manager: John Meyer
jmeyer@labuenavida.com
Estimated Sales: $2.5-5 Million
Number Employees: 10-19
Number of Products: 15
Brands:
  La Buena Vida Vineyards

7042 LA Canasta Mexican Foods
3101 W Jackson St
PO Box 6939
Phoenix, AZ 85009-4833
602-269-7721
Fax: 602-269-7725 855-269-7721
www.la-canasta.com
Mexican food products including tortillas, chips, sauces and salsas.
Founder: Carmen Abril
President: Josie Ippolito
jippolito@la-canasta.com
Controller: Roger Kelling
Plant Manager: Ben Garduno
Estimated Sales: $19.9 Million
Number Employees: 100-249
Number of Brands: 2
Square Footage: 72000
Type of Packaging: Food Service, Private Label
Brands:
  La Canasta
  My Nana's

7043 LA Chapalita Inc
9643 Remer St
South El Monte, CA 91733-3032
626-443-8556
Fax: 626-443-7554 www.lachapalita.com
Tortillas, Mexican food
President: Luis Moya
VP Operation: Luis Moya Jr.
Estimated Sales: Below $5 Million
Number Employees: 5-9

7044 LA Chiripada Winery
Highway 75 Dr # 1119
Dixon, NM 87527
505-579-4437
Fax: 505-579-4437 800-528-7801
chiripa@lachiripada.com www.lachiripada.com
Wine

Number Employees: 50-99

Food Manufacturers / A-Z

VP: Michael Johnson
Tasting Room Manager: Minna Santos
Estimated Sales: Below $5 Million
Number Employees: 1-4
Brands:
  La Chiripada

7045 LA Colonial
1700 Rogers Ave
San Jose, CA 95112-1107
　　　　　　　　　　　　408-436-5551
　　　　　　　　　　Fax: 408-441-0430
Flour tortillas
CEO: George Robles
Marketing Director: George Robles
Estimated Sales: Below $5 Million
Number Employees: 20-49

7046 LA Costa Coffee Roasting Co
6965 El Camino Real # 208
Carlsbad, CA 92009-4102
　　　　　　　　　　　　760-438-8160
　　　　　　　　　　Fax: 760-438-5314
Coffee
President: Doug Novak
roastmaster@lacostacoffeeroasting.com
Estimated Sales: $10-20 000,000
Number Employees: 10-19

7047 LA Grander Hillside Dairy Inc
W11299 Broek Rd
Stanley, WI 54768-8215
　　　　　　　　　　　　715-644-2275
　Fax: 715-644-0720 info@lagranderscheese.com
　　　　　　　www.lagranderscheese.com
Cheese and dairy products
Owner: Randy LA Grander
lagranderscheez@yahoo.com
Estimated Sales: $3,500,000
Number Employees: 20-49
Type of Packaging: Consumer

7048 LA Jota Vineyard Co
1102 Las Posadas Rd
Angwin, CA 94508-9607
　　　　　　　　　　　　707-948-2648
　　Fax: 707-965-0324   877-222-0292
　　　　　　　　info@lajotawines.com
Wines
Manager: Ed Farver
VP: Joan Smith
Sales Manager: John Smith
Estimated Sales: Less Than $500,000
Number Employees: 1-4

7049 LA Lifestyle Nutritional Products
2230 Cape Cod Way
Santa Ana, CA 92703-3582
　　　　　　　　　　　　714-835-6367
　　Fax: 714-835-4948   800-387-4786
Processor and wholesaler/distributor of teas and herbal products
Owner: Patricia J Logsdon
Estimated Sales: $10-20 Million
Type of Packaging: Consumer

7050 LA Mar's Donuts
6950 E Belleview Ave # 200
Suite 200
Greenwood Vlg, CO 80111-1626
　　　　　　　　　　　　303-771-9999
　　　Fax: 303-771-9991 www.lamars.com
Donuts
Number Employees: 5-9

7051 LA Mexicana Tortilla
10020 14th Ave SW
Seattle, WA 98146-3703
　　　　　　　　　　　　206-763-1488
　　Fax: 206-768-1050   info@lamexicana.com
　　　　　　　　　www.lamexicana.com
Mexican foods
Owner: Keith Bloxham
keith@lamexicana.com
General Manager: William Fry
Retail Sales Manager: Jos, Cifuentes
keith@lamexicana.com
Estimated Sales: Below $5 Million
Number Employees: 50-99
Type of Packaging: Private Label
Brands:
  Habero
  La Mexicana
  Souena

7052 LA Mexicana Tortilla Factory
715 Skyline Dr
Duncanville, TX 75116-3923
　　　　　　　　　　　　214-943-7770
　　Fax: 214-943-7778 www.lamexicana.com
Manufacturer of tortillas, tostadas, and tortilla chips
President: Ricardo Garza
Manager: Rafael Perez
Treasurer: Rebecca Garza
Year Founded: 1997
Estimated Sales: $18 Million
Number Employees: 50-99
Square Footage: 20000
Type of Packaging: Consumer

7053 LA Mexicana Tortilleria
2703 S Kedzie Ave
Chicago, IL 60623-4735
　　　　　　　　　　　　773-247-5443
　　　　　　　　　　Fax: 773-247-9004
Tortillas and corn chips
President: Rodolfo Guerrero
Estimated Sales: $4600000
Number Employees: 20-49
Type of Packaging: Consumer

7054 LA Monica Fine Foods
PO Box 309
Millville, NJ 08332
　　　　　　　　info@lamonicafinefoods.com
　　　　　　　　www.lamonicafinefoods.com
Surf clams and ocean clams from US certified waters, serving the fresh, canned and frozen markets.
Founder: Peter LaMonica
Number Employees: 20-49
Square Footage: 360000
Type of Packaging: Consumer, Food Service, Private Label, Bulk
Brands:
  Cape May
  Lamonica

7055 LA Pasta Inc
2727 Pittman Dr
Silver Spring, MD 20910-1807
　　　　　　　　　　　　301-588-1111
　　Fax: 301-588-7243 info@lapastainc.com
Manufacture fresh, frozen, and shelf-life pasta
President: Alexis Konownitzine
alexis@lapastainc.com
Estimated Sales: $5-10 Million
Number Employees: 20-49

7056 LA Patisserie Bakery
19758 Stevens Creek Blvd
Cupertino, CA 95014-2456
　　　　　　　　　　　　408-446-4744
　　Fax: 602-253-7430 www.lapatisserie.net
Bakery products
Owner: Eduardo Teixidor
President: Ed Teixidor
Partner: Mojgan Damaghani
mdamaghani@comcast.net
Estimated Sales: Below $5 000,000
Number Employees: 10-19
Type of Packaging: Private Label
Brands:
  La Patisserie

7057 LA Paz Products Inc
345 Oak Pl
Brea, CA 92821-4122
　　　　　　　　　　　　714-990-0982
　　Fax: 714-990-2246 info@lapazproducts.com
　　　　　　　　　www.lapazproducts.com
Cocktail mixes
President: Tim Casey
tcasey@lapazproducts.com
Marketing & Sales Manager: Greg Diem
Operations, Production, Purchasing: Mike Casey
Plant Manager: Mike Casey
Estimated Sales: $10-20 Million
Number Employees: 10-19
Type of Packaging: Consumer, Food Service

7058 LA Quercia LLC
400 Hakes Dr
Norwalk, IA 50211-9644
USA
　　　　　　　　　　　　515-981-1625
　　Fax: 515-981-1628 prosciutto@laquercia.us
　　　　　　　　　　　www.laquercia.us
Cured meats
Owner: Herbert Eckhouse
prosciutto@laquercia.us
Estimated Sales: F
Number Employees: 20-49

7059 LA Reina Inc
316 N Ford Blvd
Los Angeles, CA 90022-1182
　　　　　　　　　　　　323-268-2791
　　Fax: 323-265-4295   800-367-7522
　　sales@lareinainc.com www.lareinainc.com
Flour tortillas
President: Thomas Gonzalez
tomgon@pacbell.net
CEO: Mauro Robles
VP: Walt Boudreaux
Operations: Francisco Arellano
Purchasing: Luis Farfan
Estimated Sales: $16,000,000
Number Employees: 250-499
Type of Packaging: Consumer, Food Service, Private Label
Brands:
  La Reina

7060 LA Rocca Vineyards & Winery
12360 Doe Mill Rd
Forest Ranch, CA 95942
　　　　　　　　　　　　530-899-9463
　　Fax: 530-894-7268   800-808-9463
　　　　　　　　wine@laroccavineyards.com
　　　　　　　　www.laroccavineyards.com
Wines
Owner: Philip LA Rocca
Marketing Director: Phaedre LaRocco Morril
Estimated Sales: Under $500,000
Number Employees: 5-9
Brands:
  La Rocca Vineyards

7061 LA Segunda Bakery
2512 N 15th St
Tampa, FL 33605-3406
　　　　　　　　　　　　813-248-1531
　　Fax: 813-248-3354 lscbakery@hotmail.com
　　　　　　　　　　www.cubanbread.com
Cuban Bread and baked goods
Owner: Rogger Berrocal
rberrocal@lasegundabakery.com
Number Employees: 20-49

7062 LA Tapatia Tortilleria Inc
104 E Belmont Ave
Fresno, CA 93701-1403
　　　　　　　　　　　　559-441-1030
　　　Fax: 559-441-1712 www.tortillas4u.com
Corn and flour tortillas, chips and tostadas.
Owner/President: Helen Chavez-Hansen
SVP: John Hansen
Controller: Jose Angulo
Export Director: Dan Soleno
Regional Sales Manager: Dennis Walsh
Regional Sales Manager: Vickie Maravel
Sales & Marketing: Linda Ghilarducci
Estimated Sales: $25 Million
Number Employees: 100-249
Number of Brands: 2
Type of Packaging: Private Label
Brands:
  La Tapatia
  Sol De Oro

7063 LA Torilla Factory
3300 Westwind Blvd
Santa Rosa, CA 95403-8273
　　　　　　　　　　　　707-586-4000
　　Fax: 707-586-4017   800-446-1516
　　　　　　　　info@latortillafactory.com
　　　　　　　　www.latortillafactory.com
Corn and flour tortillas and tortilla chips and masa
President: Carlos Tamayo
Owner/President/VP Sales/Marketing: Sam Tamayo
CFO: Stan Mead
R&D Manager: Luz Ana Osbun
Executive Director Sales/Marketing: Jan Remak
Human Resources Manager: Jonna Green
COO/VP/Plant Manager: Sam Tamayo
Estimated Sales: $8000000
Number Employees: 250-499
Square Footage: 18160
Type of Packaging: Consumer, Food Service, Private Label, Bulk
Brands:
  La Tortilla Factory

Food Manufacturers / A-Z

Wrap Arounds
Wrappers

7064 LA Vencedora Products Inc
3322 Fowler St
Los Angeles, CA 90063-2594
323-269-7273
Fax: 323-269-8775 800-327-2572
www.elranchochips.com
Fresh salsa, tortilla chips, nacho chips, and specialty chips
Owner: Victor Gregory
gregv7@msn.com
CEO: Richard Victor
Estimated Sales: $500,000-1 Million
Number Employees: 5-9
Square Footage: 32000
Type of Packaging: Consumer, Food Service, Private Label, Bulk
Brands:
El Rancho
El Rancho Bean Chips
El Rancho Salsa Fresca
El Rancho Tortilla Chips
Pocos

7065 LA Vina Winery
4201 Highway 28
Anthony, NM 88021-8551
575-882-7632
Fax: 575-882-7632 stark@lavinawinery.com
www.lavina.wolfep.com
Wine
Owner: Ken Stark
stark@lavinawinery.com
Co-Owner/CEO: Denise Stark
Estimated Sales: Below $5 Million
Number Employees: 1-4
Brands:
La Vina

7066 LA Wholesale Produce Market
1601 E Olympic Boulevard
Los Angeles, CA 90021
Fax: 213-622-7075 888-454-6887
admin@lanuthouse.com www.lanuthouse.com
Manufacturer, importer and exporter of tree nuts and peanuts; also, processor of peanut butter and manufactured and coated materials
Estimated Sales: $3-5 Million
Number Employees: 5-9
Square Footage: 88000
Parent Co: Morven Partners
Type of Packaging: Consumer, Food Service, Private Label, Bulk

7067 LAVVA
Warwick, NY 10990
lovvelavva.com
Plant-based yogurts
Founder: Liz Fisher

7068 LEF McLean Brothers International
PO Box 128
20 Erie St South
Wheatley, ON N0P 2P0
Canada
519-825-4656
Fax: 519-825-7374
Processor and exporter of fresh and frozen lake fish and seafood
President: Robert Ricci
VP Business Development: Danny Ricci
Type of Packaging: Consumer, Food Service, Private Label, Bulk

7069 LFI Inc
271 US Highway 46 # C101
Fairfield, NJ 07004-2495
973-882-0550
Fax: 973-882-0554 lfiinc@aol.com
www.lfiincorporated.com
Imported foods
Owner: Anthony Lisanti
lfiantonio@aol.com
Marketing Director: Danielle Iannacconi
Public Relations: Carol Lisanti
Estimated Sales: Below $5 000,000
Number Employees: 5-9
Type of Packaging: Private Label
Brands:
Antonia
Casa Primo

7070 LIVE Soda
4020 S Industrial Dr
Suite 133
Austin, TX 78744
info@livesoda.com
livesoda.com
Kombucha, drinking vinegar and probiotic soda
Founder: Trevor Ross
Brands:
LIVE Soda
Raw LIVE Soda
Sparkling LIVE Drinking Vinegars

7071 LLJ's Sea Products
PO Box 296
Round Pond, ME 04564-0296
207-529-4224
Fax: 207-529-4223
Canned and cured fish and seafood.
Owner: Stephen J Brackett
Estimated Sales: $3,000,000
Number Employees: 5-9

7072 LSK Smoked Turkey Products
1575 Bronx River Ave
Bronx, NY 10460
718-792-1300
Fax: 718-792-8883
Smoked turkey products
President: Dan Salmon
CEO: Owen Grossblatt
Contact: Owen Grossblatt
lskdan@aol.com
Plant Manager: John Garvin
Estimated Sales: $9 Million
Number Employees: 10-19
Brands:
Lsk

7073 LWC Brands Inc.
151 Regal Row
Dallas, TX 75247
214-630-9101
Fax: 214-630-7360 800-552-8006
orders@ladywaltons.com ladywaltons.com
Cookies, snacks and sauces
President/Owner: Mary Alizon-Walton
Contact: Ron Kirk
rkirk@ladywaltons.com
Estimated Sales: $2.3 Million
Number Employees: 2
Brands:
Lady Walton's
B.Bob's Foods

7074 LYNQ
Montreal, QC H3P 2R2
Canada
lynqlife.com
Superfood powders

7075 La Abra Farm & Winery
1362 Fortunes Cove Ln
Lovingston, VA 22949
434-263-5392
Fax: 434-263-8540
www.mountaincovevineyards.com
Wines
President: Albert C Weed Ii
Estimated Sales: Less than $200,000
Number Employees: 1-4

7076 La Bonita Ole Inc
5804 E Columbus Dr
Tampa, FL 33619
813-319-2252
Fax: 813-319-2263 800-522-6648
Tortillas
Founder/Owner/President/CEO: Tammy Young
Executive Administrator: Melanie Bodiford
Contact: Patrick Gallagher
patrick@tamxicos.com
VP Operations: Dave Waters
Brands:
Tamxicos
Wrapitz

7077 La Brasserie McAuslan Brewing
5080 St-Ambroise
Montreal, QC H4C 2G1
Canada
514-939-3060
Fax: 514-939-2541 info@mcauslan.com
www.mcauslan.com
Processor and exporter of beer and ale including stout
President: Peter McAuslan
Master Brewer and VP, Production: Ellen Bounsall
Number Employees: 100-249
Type of Packaging: Consumer, Food Service

7078 La Brea Bakery Inc
14490 Catalina St
San Leandro, CA 94577
855-427-9982
www.labreabakery.com
Bread and rolls; also, par-baked and frozen available.
President: John Yamin
jyamin@labreabakery.com
Year Founded: 1989
Estimated Sales: $124.4 Million
Number Employees: 100-249
Parent Co: Aryzta AG
Other Locations:
Direct Store Delivery
Los Angeles CA
Store Baked Delivery Nationwide
Swedesboro NJ

7079 La Buena Mexican Foods Products
234 East 22nd Street
Tucson, AZ 85726-6626
520-624-1796
Fax: 520-624-1846
Mexican food products including corn and flour tortillas, tamales and taco and tostado shells
Owner: Carlos Portillo
Contact: William Garcia
williamgarcia@restaurant.com
Estimated Sales: $5-10 Million
Number Employees: 20-49
Type of Packaging: Consumer

7080 La Caboose Specialties
145 S Budd St
Sunset, LA 70584
337-662-5401
Fax: 337-662-5813
Canned fruits, vegetables, preserves, jams and jellies
Owner: Margaret Brinkhaus
Estimated Sales: Under $100,000
Number Employees: 1-4
Type of Packaging: Consumer
Brands:
La Caboose

7081 La Chiquita Tortilla Manufacturing
3451 Atlanta Industrial Parkway
Atlanta, GA 30331
404-351-9822
Fax: 404-351-4446 800-486-3942
custserv@lctortilla.com
www.lachiquitatortilla.com
Flour and corn tortillas, hand cut chips and wraps and flavored tortillas
Owner/President/CEO: Marcelino Solis
EVP/General Manager: Adam Oliaro
Marketing Manager: Jose Solis
Plant Manager: Henry Sanchez
Estimated Sales: $10.7 Million
Number Employees: 90
Square Footage: 22000
Type of Packaging: Food Service
Brands:
La Chiquita
Provecho

7082 La Choy
Conagra Brands
222 w. merchandise mart plz, suite 1300
Chicago, IL 60654
312-549-5000
Fax: 402-595-4709 www.lachoy.com
Chinese food and soups
Estimated Sales: $20-49.9 Million
Number Employees: 20,900
Parent Co: ConAgra Foods

7083 La Cookie
531-A N. Hollywood Way
Burbank, CA 91505
713-784-2722
Fax: 713-784-3415 818-495-5732
Frozen cookie, muffin and brownie dough
Manager: Brian Fung

Food Manufacturers / A-Z

Estimated Sales: $300,000-500,000
Number Employees: 10-19
Square Footage: 20000
Parent Co: Pilsner Group
Type of Packaging: Food Service
Brands:
   Neal's

7084 La Cookie
5700 Savoy Dr
Houston, TX 77036
   713-784-2722
   Fax: 713-784-3415
Baked goods
Manager: Brian Fung
Vice President: Victor Young
Estimated Sales: $1-2.5 000,000
Number Employees: 1-4

7085 La Crema Coffee Company
9848 Crescent Park Dr
West Chester, OH 45069
   513-779-6278
   Fax: 513-779-1908
melissa@lacremacoffeecompany.com
www.lacremacoffeecompany.com
Coffee and tea
President/Owner: Melissa Flohn
m.flohn@lacremacoffeecompany.com
Operations Manager: Cheryl Windhorst

7086 La Crosse Milling Company
105 Hwy 35
P.O. Box 86
Cochrane, WI 54622
   608-248-2222
   Fax: 608-248-2221 800-441-5411
ghartzell@lacrossemilling.com
Whole grain, organic and Kosher grain ingredients including oats, barley and wheat, products include conventional and organic oat flakes, oat flour, oat bran, oat fiber, pearled barley, barley flakes, barley flour, rolled wheat andother specialty milled grains.
President: Dan Ward
Controller/Assistant Treasurer: Teresa Waters
Safety Manager: Bryan Hoch
Quality Control Manager: Lori Dahl
Food Sales Assistant: Michelle Kosidowski
VP Sales: Glen Hartzell
Maintenance Manager: Dale Peterson
Feed Coordinator: Cara Lee Wiersgalla
Estimated Sales: $48.56 Million
Number Employees: 95
Type of Packaging: Bulk

7087 La Cure Gourmande USA
225 Liberty St
New York, NY 10281-1008
   646-935-9329
www.curegourmande.com
Biscuits; confections; chocolate; caramel
Managing Director: Antoine Vera Medina
Year Founded: 1989
Number Employees: 300
Type of Packaging: Private Label

7088 La Esquina Food Products
114 Kenmare
New York, NY 10012
   646-710-3183
   Fax: 973-278-7943 www.esquinanyc.com
Manufacturer of salsa and black bean dip.
Founder: Derek Sanders
Sales Manager: Sean Marrow

7089 La Ferme Martinette
1728, Martineau's road
Coaticook, QC J1A 2S5
Canada
   819-849-7089
   Fax: 819-849-4042 888-881-4561
lisa@finemapleproducts.com
www.lafermemartinette.com
Maple syrup.
Marketing: Lisa Nadeau

7090 La Flor Spices
25 Hoffman Avenue
Hauppaugue, NY 11788-4717
   631-885-9601
   Fax: 631-851-9606
Manufacturer, importer, exporter and contract packager of spices, herbs, blends, seasonings and ground peppers
President: Ruben La Torre
VP: Dan La Torre
Sales/Distribution Manager: Ruben La Torre
Estimated Sales: $5 Million
Number Employees: 45
Square Footage: 124000
Type of Packaging: Private Label

7091 La Flor Spices Company
25 Hoffman Ave
Hauppauge, NY 11788-4717
   631-851-9601
   Fax: 631-851-9606
Spices
President: Reuben Latorre
Estimated Sales: $7.4 Million
Number Employees: 20-49
Type of Packaging: Consumer, Food Service, Bulk
Brands:
   La Flor

7092 La Have Seafoods
3371 Hwy 331
La Have, NS B0R 1C0
Canada
   902-688-2773
   Fax: 902-688-2766 lahaveseafoods@eastlink.ca
Processor and exporter of fresh and salted fish including pollack, cod, haddock and scallops
President: Dave Himmelman
Estimated Sales: $6.2 Million
Number Employees: 45
Type of Packaging: Bulk

7093 La Maison Le Grand
935 Chemin Principal
St-Joseph-du-Lac, QC J0N 1M0
Canada
   450-623-3000
info@maisonlegrand.com
www.maisonlegrand.com
Pesto, savory tapenades and aromatic sauces
Owner: Bernard Le Grand

7094 La Moderna
Leandro Valle No. 404-200
Toluca, MX 50070
Mexico
   www.lamoderna.com.mx
Cookies, flour, pasta (dry), soups/broths.
Marketing: Robert Flegnann

7095 La Morena
Av. Virgen De La Caridad Lote 20 Al 27
Ciudad Industrial Xicohtencatl 2
Huamantla, 90500
Mexico
   222-211-0515
   Fax: 222-237-2700 www.lamorena.com.mx
Mayo/ketchup, salsa/dips, beans, spices, canned of preserved vegetables/fruit.
Marketing: Roberto Romo Michaud

7096 La Newyorkina
61 Commerce St
Brooklyn, NY 11231
   646-861-0727
info@lanewyorkina.com
lanewyorkina.com
Mexican-style ice pops
Founder: Fany Gerson

7097 La Nova Wings
371 W Ferry St
Buffalo, NY 14213
   716-881-3355
   Fax: 716-881-3366 800-652-6682
www.lanova.com
Frozen chicken wings and tenders
President/CEO: Joseph Todaro
Sales, Eastern: Ben Lamonte
Sales (Midwest): Sam Pantano
Contact: Dave Alessi
dalessi@lanova.com
Estimated Sales: $4.1 Million
Number Employees: 15
Type of Packaging: Consumer, Food Service
Brands:
   La Nova

7098 La Panzanella
18300 Cascade Ave S
Suite 260
Tukwila, WA 98188
   206-903-0500
info@lapanzanella.com
lapanzanella.com
Crackers, cookies and snacks.
Owner: Paul Pigott
Brands:
   Croccantini(c)
   La Panzanella(c)

7099 La Pasta, Inc.
715-B N Douglas St
El Segundo, CA 90245
   lalibations.com
Specialty beverages
President & Co-Founder: Pat Bolden
CEO & Co-Founder: Danny Stepper
Co-Founder: Dino Sarti
Director, Sales: Glenn Marin

7100 La Piccolina
1075 N Hills Drive
Decatur, GA 30033-4220
   406-636-1909
   Fax: 404-296-2008 800-626-1624
Processor and exporter of breadsticks, dips, biscotti, gourmet coffee, cranberry pecan bread, pasta, pasta sauces, olive oil, etc.
President: Olympia Manning
VP: Denise Walsh-Bandini
National Sales Manager: Denise Walsh-Bandini
Estimated Sales: $270,000
Number Employees: 5
Square Footage: 14400

7101 La Preferida, Inc.
3400 W 35th St
Chicago, IL 60632
   773-254-7200
info@lapreferida.com
www.lapreferida.com
Mexican and Latin American foods and ingredients.
Owner: Richard Steinbarth
Marketing Manager: Jaime Munoz
Midwest Sales Manager: Bill Nash
Year Founded: 1949
Estimated Sales: $11 Million
Number Employees: 50-99
Number of Products: 250
Square Footage: 50000
Type of Packaging: Consumer, Private Label
Brands:
   La Preferida

7102 La Regina di San Marzano USA
757 Third Ave
20th Floor
New York, NY 10017
   212-461-3699
info@laregina.com
www.lasanmarzano.com
Pasta sauces and canned tomatoes

7103 (HQ)La Rochelle Winery
5443 Tesla Rd
Livermore, CA 94550
   925-243-6442
   Fax: 408-270-5881 888-647-7768
www.lrwine.com
Vintaged varietal wine
Manager: Janice Fisher
Partner: James Mirassou
Partner: Peter Mirassou
Contact: Jennifer Fazio
jennifer@stevenkent.com
Square Footage: 480000
Other Locations:
   Mirassou Vineyards
   Los Gatos CA
Brands:
   Mirassou

7104 La Romagnola
2215 Tradeport Drive
Orlando, FL 32824-7005
   407-856-4343
   Fax: 407-856-7555 800-843-8359
Fettucine, spaghetti, linguine, angel hair pasta, pasta sheets, tortelloni, ravioli, triangoli and gnocchi; also, noodles including tomato, spinach, black and egg
Ceo: Andreas Rieder

Estimated Sales: $190,000
Number Employees: 3
Square Footage: 136000
Brands:
    La Romagnola
    Le Patron

7105 La Rosa Azzurra
2318 27th St
Astoria, NY 11105
    718-777-7119
    Fax: 718-545-3233 larosaazzurra@msn.com
    www.larosaazzurra.com
Pasta

7106 La Selva Beach Spice
453 McQuaide Dr
La Selva Beach, CA 95076
    831-724-4500
    www.laselvabeachspice.com
Organic sugars, salt and spice blends.
Type of Packaging: Private Label

7107 La Societe
1415 Rue De La Montagne
Montreal, QC H3G 1Z3
Canada
    514-507-9223
    Fax: 514-325-6398 www.lasociete.ca
Processor and exporter of aroma coffee; importer of green coffee beans and cocoa; custom blending available
President: M Claude Parent
Sales/Marketing Executive: Andre Richer
Purchasing Agent: Linda McGail
Number Employees: 12
Square Footage: 24000
Type of Packaging: Consumer, Food Service, Private Label, Bulk
Brands:
    Altima
    Aroma
    Bourbon Excelso

7108 La Spiga D'Oro Fresh Pasta Co
75 Pelican Way
Suite J
Pacifica, CA 94901
    650-359-9526
    Fax: 650-359-0654 800-847-2782
Gourmet fresh and frozen pasta.
President: Robert Clifford
Estimated Sales: Below $5 Million
Number Employees: 10
Brands:
    La Spiga Doro

7109 La Superior Food Products
4307 Merriam Dr
Shawnee Mission, KS 66203
    913-432-4933
    Fax: 913-432-0121
Nacho chips, taco shells, flour tortillas, corn tortillas
President: George Young
CFO: Larry O'Brian
R & D: Gordan Grahm
Estimated Sales: $2.5-5 Million
Number Employees: 20-49
Type of Packaging: Private Label, Bulk
Brands:
    La Superior

7110 La Tang Cuisine Manufacturing
3824 Artdale St
Houston, TX 77063-5246
    713-780-4876
    Fax: 713-780-4296
Asian foods including egg rolls, wonton, crab rangoon, spring roll and burritos.
President: Virginia Limbo
CEO: Joey Limbo
Estimated Sales: $250,000-$1 Million
Number Employees: 20-49
Number of Brands: 2
Number of Products: 5
Square Footage: 20000
Type of Packaging: Food Service, Private Label, Bulk
Brands:
    La Tang
    La Vida

7111 La Tempesta
439 Littlefield Ave
S San Francisco, CA 94080-6106
    650-873-8944
    Fax: 650-873-1190 800-762-8330
    ltwebinfo@latempesta.com www.latempesta.com
Biscotti candy and confectionary products
President: Robert Sharp
CFO: Lee Rucker
Vice President, sales: Sam deLucca
VP of Business Development: Rodney bigs
VP Marketing: Karen Hunt
Vice President of Sales: Bob Yurick
Contact: Sonia Azar
sazar@latempesta.com
Plant Manager: Sonia Azar
Estimated Sales: $9000000
Number Employees: 60
Type of Packaging: Consumer
Brands:
    Amore Bianco
    Biscotti Toscani
    Panforte

7112 La Tortilla Factory
3300 Westwind Blvd
Santa Rosa, CA 95403
    707-586-4017 800-446-1516
    Fax:
    info@latortillafactory.com
    www.latortillafactory.com
Tortillas and wraps
President/CEO: Jeff Ahlers
CFO: David Trogdon
EVP: Willie Tamayo
Marketing Project Manager: Lori Chellies Friend
Sr. Director, National Sales: Tom Moore
Year Founded: 1977

7113 La Tourangelle
125 University Ave
Suite 202
Berkeley, CA 94710
    510-970-9960
    Fax: 510-970-9964 866-688-6457
    contact@latourangelle.com latourangelle.com
Artisanal oils
President & CEO: Matthieu Kohlmeyer
CFO: Gwenn Goffin
VP, QA: Hanh Nguyen
Director of Marketing: Rosanne Kim
Contact: Melinda Bruskrud
mbruskrud@latourangelle.com
Director of Production & Engineering: Nick Heiser
Number Employees: 12
Other Locations:
    Oil Mill
    Woodland CA
    Warehouse
    Woodland CA

7114 La Vans Coffee Company
158 2nd St
Bordentown, NJ 00505
    609-298-0688
Coffees
Manager: Kostas Halkiadakis
Estimated Sales: Less than $500,000
Number Employees: 1-4

7115 La Victoria Foods
1 Hormel Place
Austin, MN 55912
    626-312-2925
    Fax: 626-280-4416 800-725-7212
    www.lavictoria.com
Salsa, taco sauce, enchilada sauce, chiles and peppers
CEO: R Tanklage
VP: Jon Tanklage
Estimated Sales: $5-$10 Million
Number Employees: 5-9
Type of Packaging: Private Label
Brands:
    La Victoria
    La Victoria Salsa Su

7116 La Vigne Enterprises
PO Box 2890
Fallbrook, CA 92088-2890
    760-723-9997
    Fax: 760-728-2710 info@lavignefruits.com
    www.lavignefruits.com
Exotic organically grown fruits, packaged frozen in 2 lb. or 28 lb. pails. Also, dried fruits and gourmet condiments.
President: Helene Beck
Contact: Henry Bolden
hbolden@lavignefruits.com
Number of Products: 10
Type of Packaging: Food Service, Private Label
Brands:
    La Vigns

7117 LaCroix
Ft. Lauderdale, FL 33324
    954-581-0922
    888-241-7360
    www.lacroixwater.com
Sparkling water
Founder: Nick Caporella
Brands:
    LaCroix

7118 LaCrosse Milling Company
105 Highway 35
P.O.Box 86
Cochrane, WI 54622-0086
    608-248-2222
    Fax: 608-248-2221 800-441-5411
    jbackus@lacrossemilling.com
    www.lacrossemilling.com
Oatmeal and rolled oat flakes; exporter of milled oat products
President: Dan Ward
Vice President, Sales: Glenn Hartzell
Plant Manager: Bill Brueger
Estimated Sales: $10-20 Million
Number Employees: 60
Number of Products: 50
Type of Packaging: Food Service, Private Label, Bulk
Brands:
    Diamond

7119 LaMonde Wild Flavors
7315 Pacific Circle
Mississauga, CA L5T-1V1
    905-670-1108
    Fax: 905-670-0076 800-263-5286
    www.wildflavors.com
Natural food and pharmaceutical coloring blends
Chief Operating Officer: Erik Donhowe
Estimated Sales: $1-5 Million
Number Employees: 1-4

7120 Labatt Breweries Alberta
10119-45 Ave NW
Edmonton, AB T6E 0G8
Canada
    780-436-6060
    www.labatt.com
Marketing Manager: Blaine Kulak
Number Employees: 100-249
Parent Co: Labatt Brewing Company
Type of Packaging: Consumer, Food Service

7121 Labatt Breweries Newfoundland
60 Leslie St.
St. John's, NL A1E 2V8
Canada
    709-579-0121
    Fax: 709-579-2018 www.labatt.com
Technical Services & Operations Manager: Rod Penney
Number Employees: 85
Parent Co: Labatt Brewing Company

7122 Labatt Brewery London
150 Simcoe St
London, ON N6A 4M3
Canada
    519-850-8687
    Fax: 519-667-7304 www.labatt.com
Director: Doug Higgin
Number Employees: 400+
Parent Co: Labatt Brewing Company
Type of Packaging: Consumer, Food Service

7123 Labatt Brewing Company
207 Queen's Quay W.
Suite 299
Toronto, ON M5J 1A7
Canada
    416-361-5050
    Fax: 416-361-5200 800-268-2337
    www.labatt.com
Beer.

Food Manufacturers / A-Z

President, Labatt Canada: Kyle Norrington
VP, Legal & Corproate Affairs: Charlie Angelakos
Director, Marketing: Andrew Oosterhuis
Year Founded: 1847
Estimated Sales: $296.58 Million
Number Employees: 3,400
Number of Brands: 60
Number of Products: 60
Square Footage: 88587
Parent Co: AB InBev
Type of Packaging: Consumer, Food Service
Brands:
- Alexander Keith's India Pale Ale
- Labatt Blue
- Budweiser
- Bud Light
- Rolling Rock
- Genuine Lager
- Ice Beer
- Wildcat Strong
- Busch
- Guinness Extra Stout
- Kokanee
- Blue Light
- Lakeport
- Lucky Lager
- Labatt 50
- Brava
- Labatt Crystal
- Oland
- Labatt Lite
- Labatt Ice
- Labatt Genuine Honey
- Labatt Sterling
- Kokanee Gold
- Schooner
- Blue Star
- Stella Artois
- Legere
- Bud Light Lime
- Beck's
- Corona Extra
- Hoegaarden
- Leffe
- Michelo Ultra
- Boddingtons Pub Ale
- Bass
- Lowenbrau
- Modelo

7124 Lacas Coffee Co Inc
7950 National Hwy # A
Pennsauken, NJ 08110-1412
856-910-8662
Fax: 856-910-8671 800-220-1133
info@lacascoffee.com www.lacascoffee.com
Coffee, cocoa and tea.
President: John Vastardis
CEO: Louis Abbato
labbato@lacascoffee.com
Chief Financial Officer: Michael Vlahos
Senior Advisor: Tony Chigounis
Estimated Sales: $10-20 Million
Number Employees: 20-49
Number of Brands: 3
Type of Packaging: Food Service, Private Label
Brands:
- Bigelow
- Lacas
- Newman's Own

7125 Lacey Milling Company
217 West Fifth Street
Hanford, CA 93230
559-584-6634
Fax: 559-584-9165
Flour
Owner: Scott Lindrum
Plant Manager: Steve Verschelden
Estimated Sales: $10-20 Million
Number Employees: 10-19
Type of Packaging: Bulk
Brands:
- California Special
- Lacey

7126 Lactalis American GroupInc
2376 S Park Ave
Buffalo, NY 14280
877-522-8254
www.lactalisamericangroup.com
Processor, exporter and importer of cheeses including Brie, Swiss, Roquefort, feta, edam, Gouda, mozzarella, ricotta, fontina, Asiago, shredded/grated, Parmesan and romano, as well as snack and spreadable cheese.
CEO: Thierry Clement
SVP & Chief Legal Officer: Pierre Lorieau
Marketing Director: Karine Blake
VP of Sales: Yann Connan
Year Founded: 1992
Estimated Sales: $415 Million
Number Employees: 1,600
Number of Brands: 10
Square Footage: 16231
Parent Co: Groupe Lactalis
Type of Packaging: Consumer, Food Service, Private Label
Brands:
- Galbani
- iStara
- Le Chatelain
- Galbani Precious
- President
- Rondele
- Societe
- Galbani Sorrento
- Valbreso Feta
- Don Bernardo

7127 Lactalis Ingredients Inc
2376 S Park Ave
Buffalo, NY 14220
liusa@lactalis.us
www.liusa.com
Produces whey products, milk powders, caseins, industrial butters, nutritional and formulated products.
CEO: Frederick Bouisset
VP, Sales: Yann Connan
Estimated Sales: $50,000-99,000 Million
Number Employees: 1,300
Parent Co: Lactalis American Group, Inc.
Type of Packaging: Consumer, Food Service, Private Label, Bulk

7128 Lactalis USA Inc
218 S Park St
Belmont, WI 53510-9639
608-762-5136
Manufacturer of cheese and cheese products.
CEO: Frederick Bouisset
Plant Manager: Renaudeau Christophe
Estimated Sales: $23 Million
Number Employees: 100-249
Parent Co: Lactalis American Group, Inc.
Type of Packaging: Consumer, Food Service, Private Label

7129 Lad's Smokehouse Catering
3731 School St
Needville, TX 77461
979-793-6210
Fax: 979-793-4220
Sausage
President: Robert Case
Estimated Sales: $1-3 Million
Number Employees: 1-4
Type of Packaging: Consumer
Brands:
- Lad's

7130 Ladoga Frozen Food & Retail
237 S Washington St
Ladoga, IN 47954-7019
765-942-2225
Frozen meat including beef and pork; wholesaler/distributor of fruit and vegetables
President: Harold Lowe
Number Employees: 5-9
Type of Packaging: Consumer, Food Service

7131 Ladson Homemade Pasta Company
700 Daniel Ellis Dr
Charleston, SC 29412
843-588-5088
Fax: 843-556-3950 brian@riobertolinispasta.com
www.riobertolinispasta.com
Pastas and noodles from scratch
Owner: Brian Bertolini

7132 Lady Gale Seafood
101 Charenton Rd
Baldwin, LA 70514-0058
337-923-2060
Fax: 337-923-6909
Fresh and frozen shrimp
Owner: Wayne Stevens
CFO: Jessica Burns
Estimated Sales: Below $5 Million
Number Employees: 4
Type of Packaging: Consumer, Food Service

7133 Laetitia Vineyard & Winery
453 Laetitia Vineyard Dr
Arroyo Grande, CA 93420-9701
805-481-1772
Fax: 805-481-6920 888-809-8463
info@laetitiawine.com www.laetitiawine.com
Wine
President & Head Winemaker: Eric Hickey
HR Executive: Jan Wilkinson
jan@laetitiawine.com
Marketing Coordinator: Jackie Ross
Division Sales Manager: Tabitha Alger
Operations: Dave Hickey
President & Head Winemaker: Eric Hickey
Estimated Sales: Below $5 Million
Number Employees: 50-99
Brands:
- Avila
- Barnwood
- Laetitia

7134 Lafayette Brewing Co
622 Main St
Lafayette, IN 47901-1451
765-742-2591
Fax: 765-742-3443 www.lafbrew.com
Ale
Owner: Greg Emig
greg@lafayettebrewingco.com
Brewer: Chris Johnson
Quality Control: Nancy Emig
Estimated Sales: Below $5 Million
Number Employees: 20-49
Type of Packaging: Consumer, Food Service

7135 Lafaza Foods
Oakland, CA
510-282-1138
www.lafaza.com
Manufacturer of vanilla beans. extracts, and pure ground vanilla.
Co-Founder and CEO: Nathaniel Delafield
Brands:
- LAFAZA

7136 Lafitte Frozen Foods Corp
5165 Caroline St
Lafitte, LA 70067-5423
504-689-2041
Fax: 504-689-3270
Fresh and frozen shrimp processor.
President: Paul Poon
rayz1679@aol.com
Estimated Sales: $8.5 Million
Number Employees: 50-99

7137 Lafleur Dairy Products
617 Hill St
New Orleans, LA 70121-1000
504-729-3330
Fax: 504-461-8655
Milk and yogurt
President: Cedric Lafleur
VP: Tommy Baker
CFO: Monica Sosta
Estimated Sales: Below $5 Million
Number Employees: 40
Parent Co: Borden
Type of Packaging: Consumer, Food Service, Bulk
Brands:
- Borden

7138 Lafollette Vineyard & Winery
180 Morris St
Suite 160
Sebastopol, CA 95472
707-395-3902
Fax: 707-395-3905 info@lafollettewines.com
www.lafollettewines.com
Wines

Food Manufacturers / A-Z

Owner: Miriam Summerskill
Direct Sales & Marketing Manager: Andrew Fegelman
National Sales & Distribution Manager: Vikki Tola
Events Manager: Jana Churich
Estimated Sales: $68,000
Number Employees: 1
Type of Packaging: Private Label
Brands:
  La Follette

7139 Lafourche Sugar LLC
141 Leighton Quarters Rd
Thibodaux, LA 70301-6489
985-447-3210
Fax: 985-447-8731
Sugar and blackstrap molasses
President/CEO: Greg Nolan
gn@lafourchesugars.com
Estimated Sales: $1-3 Million
Number Employees: 50-99
Type of Packaging: Consumer

7140 Lago Tortillas International
1700 E 4th St
Austin, TX 78702-4427
512-476-0945
Fax: 512-476-4931 800-369-9017
Tortillas
President, CEO: Luis Centeno
Estimated Sales: $5-10 Million appx.
Number Employees: 100-249

7141 Lagomarcino's Confectionery
1422 5th Ave # 1422
Moline, IL 61265-1334
309-764-1814
Fax: 309-736-5423 lagos@netexpress.net
www.lagomarcinos.com
Ice cream and confections
Owner: Marybeth Lagomarcino
lago1908@aol.com
Estimated Sales: Less Than $500,000
Number Employees: 10-19
Brands:
  Lagomarcino's

7142 Lagorio Enterprises
2771 E French Camp Rd
Manteca, CA 95336-9689
209-982-5691
Fax: 209-982-0235 mail@lagorio.com
www.lagorio.com
Grower, packer and exporter of fresh tomatoes
President: Ed Beckman
Estimated Sales: $5-10 Million
Number Employees: 100-249
Square Footage: 635772
Brands:
  Ace-Hi

7143 Laguna Beach Brewing Company
237 Ocean Avenue
Laguna Beach, CA 92651
949-497-3381
Fax: 949-497-0659 info@oceanbrewing.com
www.oceanbrewing.com
Ale, stout, lager and porter
President: Ross Bartlett
Number Employees: 30-50
Type of Packaging: Consumer, Food Service, Private Label, Bulk
Brands:
  Diver's Hole Dunkelweizen
  Festival Light Ale
  Greeter's Pale Ale
  Laguna Beach Blinde
  Main Beach Brown
  Renaissance Red
  Salt Kriek Cherry Be
  Thousand Steps Stout
  Victoria E.S.B.
  Wipe Out

7144 Lahaha Tea Co
135 E Santa Clara St # B
Suite B
Arcadia, CA 91006-3288
626-215-6960
lahahatea@yahoo.com
Natural teas imported from China
President: Angie Lin
angielin@lahahatea.com
Number Employees: 5-9

7145 Lahtt Sauce
Monterey Park, CA 91754
323-238-9398
www.lahttsauce.com
Chili oil sauce
CEO: Maxine Lau
Year Founded: 2015

7146 Laird & Company
One Laird Road
Scobeyville, NJ 07724
732-542-0312
Fax: 732-542-2244 877-438-5247
sales@lairdandcompany.com
www.lairdandcompany.com
Established in 1780. Processor of apple brandy, bourbon, vodka, gin, blended whiskey and other spirits; importer of wine and bulk alcoholic beverages; imported olive oils and balsamic vinegars.
President: Larrie Laird
EVP: John Laird III
VP: Lisa Laird Dunn
SVP of Sales/Marketing: Tom Alberico
Operations Manager: Raymond Murdock
General Manager: Lester Clements
Estimated Sales: $20-50 Million
Number Employees: 35
Number of Brands: 7
Type of Packaging: Consumer, Private Label, Bulk
Brands:
  Bankers Club
  Barrister
  Captains
  G & W
  Kasser
  Laird's
  Senators Club

7147 Laird Superfood
PO Box 2270
Sisters, OR 97759
888-670-6796
support@lairdsuperfood.com lairdsuperfood.com
Organic coffee and superfood coffee creamers
Founder: Laird Hamilton
Type of Packaging: Consumer
Brands:
  LAIRD SUPERFOOD

7148 Lake Champlain Chocolates
750 Pine St
Burlington, VT 05401-4923
802-864-1808
Fax: 802-864-1806 800-634-8105
sales@lakechamplainchocolates.com
www.lakechamplainchocolates.com
Specialty chocolate candies
Owner: Jim Lampman
Sales Manager: Allyson Meyers
jim@lakechamplainchocolates.com
Estimated Sales: Less than $500,000
Number Employees: 100-249
Square Footage: 96000
Type of Packaging: Consumer, Food Service, Private Label, Bulk
Brands:
  Five Star Bars
  Original Chocolates of Vermont

7149 Lake Charles Poultry
2808 Fruge St
Lake Charles, LA 70615-3699
337-433-6818
Fax: 318-433-7855
Poultry
President: Danny Bellard
Estimated Sales: $5-10 Million
Number Employees: 5-9

7150 Lake City Foods
5185 General Road
Mississauga, ON L4W 2K4
Canada
905-625-8244
Fax: 905-625-8244 hello@lakecityfoods.com
www.lakecityfoods.com
Processor and exporter of drink mixes, jelly powders, soup bases and mixes, army rations, nondairy coffee creamers and camping and trail foods
Proprietor: Eyal Adda
Number Employees: 10-19
Parent Co: Eden Manufacturing Company
Type of Packaging: Consumer, Food Service, Private Label, Bulk

Brands:
  Anytime
  Camp Rite
  Gibbons
  Quickset

7151 Lake Country Foods Inc
140 S Concord Rd
Oconomowoc, WI 53066-3555
262-567-5521
Fax: 262-567-5714
Malted milk, malt extract, dry blended foods, etc
President: Phil Kemppainen
pkemppainen@lcfoods.com
CFO: John Waltenberry
Vice President: Phillip Vanderhyden
VP Sales: Myron Jones
Estimated Sales: $25 Million
Number Employees: 50-99
Square Footage: 150000

7152 Lake Erie Frozen Foods Co
1830 Orange Rd
Ashland, OH 44805-1335
419-289-9204
Fax: 419-281-7624 800-766-8501
mbuckingham@leffco.net www.leffco.net
Breaded cheese and vegetables
President: Mike Buckingham
mbuckingham@leffco.net
Estimated Sales: $2.4 Million
Number Employees: 20-49
Type of Packaging: Consumer, Food Service, Private Label

7153 Lake Packing Co Inc
755 Lake Landing Dr
Lottsburg, VA 22511-2503
804-529-6101
Fax: 804-529-7374 800-324-2759
info@manningshominy.com
www.manningshominy.com
Frozen oysters and canned tomatoes, tomato juice and hominy
Owner: S L Cowart Jr
Estimated Sales: Under $1,000,000
Number Employees: 20-49
Parent Co: Cowart Seafood
Type of Packaging: Consumer, Food Service, Private Label

7154 Lake Sonoma Winery
777 Madrone Rd
Glen Ellen, CA 95442-9522
707-721-1979
Fax: 707-431-8356 877-586-2796
info@lswinery.com www.lakesonomawinery.com
Wines
CEO: Gary Heck
President: David Ready
Sales: Pat Paulson
Marketing Director: Gary Heck
Estimated Sales: $1-$2.5 Million
Number Employees: 5-9
Brands:
  Lake Sonoma Winery

7155 Lake States Yeast
428 W Davenport St
Rhinelander, WI 54501-3325
715-369-4949
Fax: 715-369-4969 lgary@lallemand.com
www.lallemand.com
Manufacturer and exporter of yeasts including inactive dried, torula, autolyzed, formulated and specialty grades that inlcudes smoked, roasted, and grill flavors.
President/Manager: Antoine Chagnon
Quality Control: Joelle Provix
Customer Service Manager: Linda Gary
Plant Manager: Stuart Bacon
Production Manager: Rick Bishop
Plant Manager: Stuart Bacon
Number Employees: 5-9
Parent Co: Rhinelander Paper Company
Type of Packaging: Private Label, Bulk
Brands:
  Lake States

863

Food Manufacturers / A-Z

7156 Lakefront Brewery Inc
1872 N Commerce St
Milwaukee, WI 53212-3701
414-372-8800
Fax: 414-430-4400 info@lakefrontbrewery.com
www.lakefrontbrewery.com
Beer
Owner: Russ Klich
rushelakefront@brewery.com
Marketing Director: Chris Johnson
Dir. Of Communications: Matt Krajnak
Operations Manager: Chris Ranson
Estimated Sales: Below $5 Million
Number Employees: 100-249
Type of Packaging: Private Label
Brands:
  River West Stein

7157 Lakeport Brewing Corporation
180 Henri Dunant St
Moncton, NB E1E 1E6
Canada
905-523-4200
Fax: 905-523-6564 800-268-2337
Processor and exporter of beer, ale, lager and stout
President: Teresa Cascioli
Sales/Marketing Executive: Ian McDonald
Estimated Sales: F
Number Employees: 200
Type of Packaging: Consumer, Food Service
Brands:
  Brava
  Lakeport Honey Lager
  Lakeport Ice
  Lakeport Light
  Lakeport Pilsener
  Lakeport Strong
  Mongoose
  Steeler Lager
  Wee Willy

7158 Lakeridge Winery & Vineyards
19239 US Highway 27
Clermont, FL 34715-9025
352-394-8627
Fax: 352-394-7490 800-768-9463
www.lakeridgewinery.com
Wines
President: Geary Cox
Finance Executive: Mandi Enix
Vice President: Mandi Enix
menix@lakeridgewinery.com
Sales Executive: Kyle Johnson
Estimated Sales: $30 Million
Number Employees: 20-49
Number of Brands: 1
Brands:
  Lakeridge

7159 Lakeshore Winery
5132 State Route 89
Romulus, NY 14541-9779
315-549-7075
Fax: 315-549-7102 info@lakeshorewinery.com
www.lakeshorewinery.com
Farm winery
Owner: Annie Bachman
annie@lakeshorewinery.com
Estimated Sales: Less Than $500,000
Number Employees: 1-4
Brands:
  Lakeshore

7160 Lakeside Foods Inc.
1055 W. Broadway
Plainview, MN 55964
507-534-3141
www.lakesidefoods.com
Frozen and canned vegetables, frozen appetizers and seafood, canned meats and pet food, canned beans, whipped toppings and sauces.
CEO: Glenn Tellock
Estimated Sales: $103 Million
Number Employees: 500-999
Type of Packaging: Consumer
Other Locations:
  Lakeside Foods-Manufacturing
  Manitowoc WI
  Lakeside Foods-Manufacturing
  Belgium WI
  Lakeside Foods-Manufacturing
  Random Lake WI
  Lakeside Foods-Manufacturing
  Reedsburg WI
  Lakeside Foods-Manufacturing
  Seymour WI
  Lakeside Foods-Manufacturing
  Plainview MN
  Lakeside Foods-Manufacturing
  Brooten MN
  Lakeside Foods-Manufacturing
  Owatoona MN
  Lakeside Foods-Manufacturing
  New Richmond WI
  Lakeside Foods-Manufacturing
  Eden WI
  Lakeside Foods-Distribution
  Manitowoc WI
  Lakeside Foods-Distribution
  Plainview MN
  Lakeside Foods-Distribution
  Belgium WI
Brands:
  Eureka
  Hobby
  Lakeside

7161 (HQ)Lakeside Foods Inc.
PO Box 1327
Manitowoc, WI 54221-1327
920-684-3356
Fax: 920-686-4033 800-466-3834
www.lakesidefoods.com
Food manufacturing company for private label consumers, including canned and frozen vegetables, frozen seafood, canned meats, pet food, canned beans, whipped topping and sauces.
CEO: Glenn Tellock
General Manager: Janet De Pirro
CFO: Denise Kitzerow
Quality Assurance Manager: Alex Kiel
Vice President, Sales: Matt Brown
Vice President, Operations: Bruce Jacobson
Year Founded: 1887
Estimated Sales: $103.5 Million
Number Employees: 1,000-4,999
Square Footage: 28500
Type of Packaging: Consumer, Food Service, Private Label
Other Locations:
  Lakeside Foods Processing Plant
  Manitowoc WI
  Lakeside Foods Processing Plant
  Belgium WI
  Lakeside Foods Processing Plant
  Random Lake WI
  Lakeside Foods Processing Plant
  Reedsburg WI
  Lakeside Foods Processing Plant
  Seymour WI
  Lakeside Foods Processing Plant
  Plainview MN
  Lakeside Foods Processing Plant
  Brooten MN
  Lakeside Foods Processing Plant
  New Richmond WI
  Lakeside Foods Processing Plant
  Eden WI
  Lakeside Foods Processing Plant
  Owatonna MN
  Lakeside Foods Processing Plant
  Mondovi WI
  Lakeside Foods Processing Plant
  Poynette WI
Brands:
  Festal
  Read
  Tendersweet

7162 Lakeside Foods Inc.
705 Main St.
PO Box B
Belgium, WI 53004
262-285-3299
www.lakesidefoods.com
Canned and frozen vegetables, frozen appetizers and seafood, canned meats and pet food, canned beans, whipped toppings and sauces.
CEO: Glenn Tellock
Estimated Sales: $50-100 Million
Number Employees: 250-499
Parent Co: Lakeside Foods

7163 Lakeside Mills
PO Box 230
Rutherfordton, NC 28139-0230
828-286-4866
Fax: 828-287-3361 www.lakesidemills.com
Corn meal, hush puppy mix and breadings; importer of peppers and spices
VP: Aaron King
Contact: Kim King
kimking@lakesidemills.com
Number Employees: 10-19
Parent Co: Lakeside Mills
Type of Packaging: Consumer, Food Service, Private Label, Bulk
Brands:
  Blue Ribbon
  Kings Old Fashion

7164 Lakeside Packing Company
667 County Road #50
Harrow, ON N0R 1G0
Canada
519-738-2314
Fax: 519-738-3684 info@lakesidepacking.com
www.lakesidepacking.com
Pickles, peppers, relish, salsa, tomatoes
President/Board Member: Donald Woodbridge
VP/Board Member: Alan Woodbridge
Estimated Sales: $813,000
Number Employees: 20
Type of Packaging: Consumer, Food Service

7165 Lakeview Bakery
6449 Crowchild Trail SW
Calgary, AB T2E 5R7
Canada
403-246-6127
Fax: 403-246-6609
members.shaw.ca/organicbaking/
Bread, buns and pastries
President: Maureen Hinton
Sales & Distribution Manager: David Hinton
Number Employees: 5-9
Type of Packaging: Consumer, Food Service

7166 Lakeview Banquit Cheese
1755 S Fremont Dr
Salt Lake City, UT 84104-4218
801-364-3607
Fax: 801-364-3600 www.banquetcheese.com
Cheese including cheddar, Monterey jack and mozzarella
President: Val Hardcastle
Chief Executive Officer: Calvin Nelson
CFO: Reagan Wood
Secretary: Jenille Tyler
Vice President of Operations: Kirk Mackert
Plant Manager of Distribution: Andrew Pettersson
Estimated Sales: $14 Million
Number Employees: 10-19
Square Footage: 90000
Type of Packaging: Food Service, Private Label, Bulk
Brands:
  Banquet Better Foods
  Banquet Butter
  Banquet Cheese
  Gold Nugget Butter
  Gold Nugget Cheese
  Grand Teton
  Grand Teton Cheese

7167 Lakeview Cheese
3030 N Lamb Blvd # 114
Las Vegas, NV 89115-3496
702-233-2439
lakeviewcheese.com
Cheese products
Owner: Debbie Gaglio
Estimated Sales: Less Than $500,000
Number Employees: 5-9

7168 Lakeview Farms
229 East Second Street
PO Box 98
Delphos, OH 45833-0098
419-695-9925
Fax: 419-695-9900 800-755-9925
sales_mrkt@lakeviewfarms.com
www.lakeviewfarms.com
Sour cream, mousse, cheesecake, fruit gelatins, sour cream dip, soy oil dips, imitation sour cream and specialty products.
CEO: Tom Davis
Contact: Maria Adamiec
madamiec@lakeviewfarms.com
Estimated Sales: $30-50 Million
Number Employees: 100-249
Number of Brands: 6
Type of Packaging: Food Service, Private Label, Bulk

Food Manufacturers / A-Z

Brands:
- Fresh Creations
- Lakeview Farms
- Luisa's
- Salads of the Sea
- Senor Rico
- Winky Foods

7169 Lakewood Juice Co.
Miami, FL 33127

866-324-5900
info@floridabottling.com
www.lakewoodorganic.com

Organic juices bottled fresh, frozen concentrates, supplement juices, and culinary juices.
Manager: Lee Wilson
Sales Manager: Holly Newberry
Contact: Pamela Ford
pford@floridabottling.com
Estimated Sales: $20-50 Million
Number Employees: 20-49
Parent Co: Florida Bottling
Type of Packaging: Consumer

7170 Lakewood Juice Company
1035 NW 21st Ter
Miami, FL 33127

305-324-5932
Fax: 305-325-9573 866-324-5900
info@floridabottling.com

Manufacturer and exporter of glass-packed fruit juices
President: Vivian Calzadilla
CEO: R Fuhrman
VP, Sales: Joseph Letiz
Contact: Pamela Ford
pford@floridabottling.com
Estimated Sales: $7,000,000
Number Employees: 50
Parent Co: Florida Family Trust
Type of Packaging: Consumer, Food Service, Bulk
Brands:
- Coconut Grove
- Lakewood
- Rainberry
- Summer Song

7171 Lakewood Vineyards Inc
4024 State Route 14
Watkins Glen, NY 14891-9630

607-535-9252
Fax: 607-535-6656 877-535-9252
wines@lakewoodvineyards.com
www.lakewoodvineyards.com

Wines
Owner: Beverly Stamp
lwoodwine@aol.com
Estimated Sales: $2.5-5 Million
Number Employees: 10-19
Brands:
- Lakewood Vineyards
- Mystic Mead

7172 (HQ)Lallemand
1620 Rue Prefontaine
Montreal, QC H1W 2N8
Canada

514-522-2133
Fax: 514-522-2884 www.bio-lallemand.com

Manufacturer and exporter of food and dairy microbial cultures, lactobacilli and bifidobacteria; also, custom formulations available
President: Roland Chagnon
Vice President: Francois Leblanc
Estimated Sales: $10-20 Million
Number Employees: 50-99
Square Footage: 100000
Type of Packaging: Consumer, Private Label, Bulk
Brands:
- Ferlac
- Gastro-Ad
- Polylacton
- Probiotic-2000
- Rosell
- Rosellac
- Standard Formulation
- Vitanat

7173 Lallemand American Yeast
1417 W Jeffrey Dr
Addison, IL 60101-4331

630-932-1290
Fax: 630-932-1291 mlegel@lallemand.com
www.lallemand.com

Baking enzymes, baking ingredients, dough conditioners, such as bromate replacers, chocolate, cocoa, eggs, nuts, oils, oxidizers, raisins, spices, sweeteners, yeast foods, yeast (fresh & dry), starter cultures, baking powder, moldinhibitors
President: Gary Edwards
VP: Merna Legel
Quality Control: Mike Hudson
Sales: Steven Marinella
Estimated Sales: Below $5 Million
Number Employees: 10-19
Parent Co: Lallemand, Inc.
Type of Packaging: Food Service, Bulk
Brands:
- American Yeast
- Eagle
- Essential
- Fermaid
- Lallemand

7174 Lallemand Inc
8480 St Laurent Boulevard
Montreal, QC H2P 2M6
Canada

514-381-5631
Fax: 514-383-4493 800-452-4364
americas-hn@lallemand.com www.lallemand.com

Yeast-cultures are fermented before being high density concentrated and granulated. Yeasts are then fluid bed-dried and bacteria are freeze-dried. Certified yeast for many of the wine countries around the world.
Sales Director: Aldo Fuoco

7175 Lallemand/American Yeast
47-00 Northern Boulevard
Long Island City, NY 11101

773-267-2223
Fax: 773-267-4508 gedwards@lallemand.com
www.lallemand.com

Yeast
President: Joanie Joans
Estimated Sales: $300,000-500,000
Number Employees: 5-9
Parent Co: Lallemand, Inc.

7176 Lallemand/American Yeast
PO Box 5512
Petaluma, CA 94955-5512

707-795-1468
Fax: 661-835-4990 800-423-6625
info@lallemand.com www.lallemand.com

Wine industry yeasts
Director: William Pursley
Parent Co: Lallemand, Inc.
Brands:
- Enoferm
- Fermaid
- Lalvin
- Uvaferm

7177 Lam's Food Inc
9723 218th St
Queens Village, NY 11429-1251

718-217-0476
Fax: 718-217-0655 andrew@lamsnacks.com
www.lamsnacks.com

Plantain and yuca chips in different flavors.
President: Andrew Lam
andrew@lamsnacks.com
VP: Trevor Lam
Sales/Marketing: Melissa Gaviria
Estimated Sales: $520,000
Number Employees: 1-4
Square Footage: 9600

7178 Lamagna Cheese Co
1 Lamagna Dr
Verona, PA 15147-1137

412-828-6112
Fax: 412-828-6782
customer_service@lamagnacheese.com
www.lamagnacheese.com

Manufacturer of ricotta, feta, provolone and mozzarella cheeses.
Owner: Michael Lamagna
CEO: John Sottile
jsottile@lamagnacheese.com
Estimated Sales: $10-20 Million
Number Employees: 20-49
Number of Brands: 1
Type of Packaging: Private Label
Brands:
- Lamagna

7179 Lamb Weston Holdings Inc.
599 S. Rivershore Ln.
Eagle, ID 83616

208-938-1047
800-766-7783
www.lambweston.com

Frozen potato products.
President/CEO: Tom Werner
Senior VP/CFO: Robert McNutt
Senior VP/General Counsel: Eryk Spytek
Year Founded: 1950
Estimated Sales: $3.4 Billion
Number Employees: 7,200
Number of Brands: 8
Type of Packaging: Consumer, Food Service
Other Locations:
- Lamb Weston Manufacturing Plant Weston OR
- Lamb Weston Manufacturing Plant Kennewick WA
- Lamb Weston Manufacturing Plant Prosser WA
- Lamb Weston Manufacturing Plant Boise ID
- Lamb Weston Manufacturing Plant Alberta, Canada

Brands:
- Sweet Things
- Colossal Crisp
- CrispyCoat Fries
- Lamb Weston
- Lamb's Seasoned
- Lamb's Supreme
- LW Private Reserve
- Stealth Fries
- Tavern Traditions

7180 Lambent Technologies
7247 Central Park Ave
Skokie, IL 60076

847-675-3951
Fax: 847-675-3013 800-432-7187
www.lambenttech.com

Manufacturer and exporter of nonionic emulsifiers including polysorbates, sorbitan esters and glycerol esters; also, silicone and nonsilicone antifoams and defoamers
President: Michael Hayes
Marketing Manager: Randy Cobb
Sales Manager: Kevin Hrebenar
Estimated Sales: $9800000
Number Employees: 55
Square Footage: 40000
Parent Co: Petroferm
Brands:
- Lambent

7181 Lambert Bridge Winery
4085 W Dry Creek Rd
Healdsburg, CA 95448-9117

707-431-9600
Fax: 707-433-3215 800-975-0555
wines@lambertbridge.com
www.lambertbridge.com

Wine
President: Dean Agostinelli
dean@lambertbridge.com
Winemaker: Jill Davis
Estimated Sales: $1.1 Million
Number Employees: 5-9
Type of Packaging: Private Label
Brands:
- Lambert Bridge Winery

7182 Lamex Foods Inc.
8500 Normandale Lake Blvd.
Suite 1150
Bloomington, MN 55437

952-844-0585
Fax: 952-844-0083 info@lamexfoods.eu
www.lamexfoods.eu

Many types of foods including; beef, fruit, honey, juice, pork, poultry, seafood, and vegetables.
President: Steve Anderson
CEO: Phillip Wallace
Vice President: Mark Barrett
Year Founded: 1966
Estimated Sales: $1.75 Billion
Number Employees: 48
Square Footage: 6000
Parent Co: Lamex Foods

Food Manufacturers / A-Z

7183 Lamitech West
115 Post Street
Santa Cruz, CA 95060
831-425-6625
Fax: 831-425-6627 TPocock@lamitech.com
www.lamitech.com
Manufacturer of paperboard products for food packaging, printing products, custom laminating and other converting services.
Vice President, General Manager: Adam Reiser
Senior Sales Representative: Tim Pocok
Number Employees: 1-4

7184 Lammes Candies
1000 W 38th St
Austin, TX 78705-1003
512-458-1885
Fax: 512-458-1844 800-252-1885
www.lammes.com
Founded 1885. Candy
Manager: Crystal Bertrand
VP: Bryan Teich
Manager: Richard Butler
rbutler@lammes.com
Estimated Sales: Less Than $500,000
Number Employees: 1-4
Number of Products: 1000
Brands:
    Cashew Critters
    Choc-Adillos
    Longhorns
    Peanut Paws
    Texas Chewie Pecan Praline

7185 Lamonaca Bakery
304 7th St
Windber, PA 15963-1343
814-467-4909
Bread products and pizza shells
President: Mary La Monaca
Estimated Sales: $5-10 Million
Number Employees: 10 to 19
Type of Packaging: Consumer, Food Service

7186 Lamoreaux Landing Wine Cellars
9224 State Route 414
Lodi, NY 14860-9641
607-582-6011
Fax: 607-582-6010 info@lamoreauxwine.com
www.lamoreauxwine.com
Wines
Owner: Mark J Wagner
Retail Sales Manager: Susan Whitaker
markw@lamoreauxwine.com
Estimated Sales: $5-10 Million
Number Employees: 10-19
Type of Packaging: Private Label

7187 Lampost Meats
805 Shawver Drive
Grimes, IA 50111-1118
515-288-6111
Fax: 515-288-5727 sglksl@aol.com
Pork and beef offals
President: Stanley Lammers
Number Employees: 2
Parent Co: Walking S Farms

7188 Lanaetex Products Incorporated
151 3rd St
Elizabeth, NJ 7206
908-351-9700
Fax: 908-351-8753
Processor and exporter of food grade waxes
President: Mike Gutowski
Estimated Sales: $10-20 Million
Number Employees: 10-19

7189 Lancaster Colony Corporation
380 Polaris Parkway
Suite 400
Westerville, OH 43082
614-224-7141
www.lancastercolony.com
Amenities including glassware, ice and food molds, iced tea dispensers, wood grain serving trays, ice buckets, aluminum cookware and commercial coffee urns, candles and matting. Foodservice products include frozen appetizers, dips, and salad dressings.
Executive Chairman: John Gerlach
President & CEO: David Ciesinki
Vice President/CFO: Thomas Pigott
General Counsel/Chief Ethics Officer: Matthew Shurte
Vice President, Investor Relations: Dale Ganobsik
Year Founded: 1969
Estimated Sales: $1.13 Billion
Number Employees: 500-1000
Type of Packaging: Consumer, Food Service, Bulk
Brands:
    Marzetti
    Sister Schubert's
    New York Bakery
    Flatout

7190 Lancaster County WineryLTD
799 Rawlinsville Rd
Willow Street, PA 17584-8700
717-464-3555
www.lancastercountywinery.com
Wines
President: Suzanne Dickel
Manager: Todd Dickel
Estimated Sales: Below $5 Million
Number Employees: 5-9

7191 Lancaster Fine Foods
2320 Norman Rd
Lancaster, PA 17601-5930
717-397-9578
Fax: 717-397-0941 info@lancasterfinefoods.com
www.lancasterfinefoods.com
Sauces, dressings
Owner: Dave Esh
dave@beaniesoflancaster.com
CEO: Michael Thompson
Director of Quality: Christie Oliver
Estimated Sales: $5.8 Million
Number Employees: 20-49

7192 Lancaster Fine Foods
2320 Norman Rd
Lancaster, PA 17601-5930
717-397-9578
Fax: 717-397-0941 info@lancasterfinefoods.com
www.lancasterfinefoods.com
Pickled fruits, sauces, dressings
Owner: Dave Esh
dave@beaniesoflancaster.com
Number Employees: 20-49

7193 Lancaster Packing Company
7615 Lancaster Avenue
PO Box 465
Myerstown, PA 17067
717-397-9727
Fax: 717-397-7744 www.jakeandamos.com
Pennsylvania Dutch-style pickles, preserves, relishes, syrups, pickled vegetables and fruits, chow chow and fruit butters packed in glass canning jars
President: David Doolittle
CEO: Sue Doolittle
Estimated Sales: $5-10 Million
Number Employees: 5-9
Square Footage: 40000
Type of Packaging: Consumer, Private Label
Brands:
    Jake & Amos

7194 Lance Private Brands
8600 South Boulevard
Charlotte, NC 28273
704-557-8313
Fax: 704-556-5781 888-722-1163
Kosher, organic/natural, cookies, private label.
Marketing: Drew Snyder
Contact: Teri Edwards
tedwards@lance.com

7195 Lanco
350 Wireless Blvd Ste 200
Hauppauge, NY 11788
631-231-2300
Fax: 631-231-2731 800-938-4500
sales@lancopromo.com www.lancopromo.com
Chocolate candy including squares, circles and triangles
President: Brian Landow
Number Employees: 175
Type of Packaging: Consumer, Food Service

7196 Land O'Frost Inc
911 Hastings Ave
Searcy, AR 72143-7401
501-268-2473
Fax: 501-268-0357 800-643-5654
www.landofrost.com
Processor and importer of ham, beef, chicken and turkey; also, pre-sliced luncheon meats, pre-portioned julienne meat strips and diced meats
President & CEO: David Van Eekeren
COO: William Marion
wmarion@landofrost.com
Number Employees: 500-999
Square Footage: 1052000
Type of Packaging: Consumer, Food Service, Private Label, Bulk
Brands:
    Perfect-O-Portion
    Salad Toppers
    Sandwich Shop

7197 (HQ)Land O'Frost Inc.
16850 Chicago Ave.
Lansing, IL 60438
708-474-7100
Fax: 708-474-9329 800-323-3308
www.landofrost.com
Lunch and deli meats such as; beef, chicken, turkey, ham and meat ingredients.
President: Charles Niementowski
Chairman/CEO: Donna Van Eekeren
Chief Financial Officer: George Smolar
Director of Quality Control: Dayna Nicholas
Estimated Sales: $103.6 Million
Number Employees: 500-999
Square Footage: 100000
Type of Packaging: Consumer, Food Service, Private Label
Brands:
    Delishaved
    Land O'Frost
    Premium
    Bistro Favorites

7198 Land O'Lakes Inc
4001 Lexington Ave. N.
Arden Hills, MN 55126-2998
651-375-2222
800-328-9680
www.landolakesinc.com
A global crop inputs, dairy foods and animal nutrition co-operative.
President/CEO: Beth Ford
Senior VP/CFO: Bill Pieper
Senior VP/General Counsel: Sheilah Stewart
Senior VP/Chief Marketing Officer: Tim Scott
Executive VP/COO: Jerry Kaminski
Chief Supply Chain Officer: Yone Dewberry
Year Founded: 1921
Estimated Sales: $14 Billion
Number Employees: 10,000
Number of Brands: 5
Type of Packaging: Consumer, Food Service, Private Label, Bulk
Brands:
    Land O'Lakes
    Kozy Shack
    Alpine Lace
    WinField
    Purina

7199 Land-O-Sun Dairies Inc
610 E State St
O Fallon, IL 62269-1538
314-436-6820
Fax: 618-628-3309 www.deanfoods.com
Fruit drinks, milk, cottage cheese, sour cream and dips
Manager: Bill Schaefer
COO: Chuck McQuig
Manager: Jeff Powell
Estimated Sales: $10-20 Million
Number Employees: 10-19
Parent Co: Suiza Foods

7200 Landies Candies Co
2495 Main St # 350
Suite 350
Buffalo, NY 14214-2154
716-834-8212
Fax: 716-833-9113 800-955-2634
larrys@landiescandies.com
www.landiescandies.com

Food Manufacturers / A-Z

Boxed chocolates including pecan, peanut, cashew, no sugar, cherry cordials and nut clusters; also, divinity, toffee, taffy, fondant mints, dipped pretzels, peppermint kisses, caramels, truffles and pecan praline dessert topping.
President, CEO & Founder: Larry Szrama
larrys@landiescandies.com
Comptroller: Bob Szrama
Vice President: Bryan Tiech
Health & Safety Director: Alan Nowak
Marketing & Sales: Dennis Hussak
Operations Director: Dennis Hussak
Prod Suprv: Jimmy Del Gaudio
Plant Manager: John Davis
Estimated Sales: $1670977
Number Employees: 10-19
Type of Packaging: Consumer, Private Label, Bulk
Brands:
    Cashew Critters
    Choc Adillos
    Choc'adillos
    Longhorns
    Texas Chewie

7201 Landis Peanut Butter
641 E Cherry Ln
Souderton, PA 18964-1236
215-723-9366
landispeanutbutter@yahoo.com
www.landispeanutbutter.com
Peanut butter
Owner: Raymond Landis
Estimated Sales: $500-1 Million appx.
Number Employees: 1-4

7202 Landlocked Seafoods
219 E 3rd St
Carroll, IA 51401
712-792-9599
Fax: 712-792-9599
mebner@landlockedseafood.com
Seafood
President: Michael Ebner
Contact: Mike Ebner
mebner@landlockedseafood.com

7203 Landmark Vineyards
101 Adobe Canyon Rd
PO Box 340
Kenwood, CA 95452-9045
707-833-0053
Fax: 707-833-1164 info@landmarkwine.com
www.landmarkwine.com
Wines
Owner/CFO: Michael Colhoun
Winemaker: Eric Stern
Public Relations: Mary Colhoun
Estimated Sales: $5-10 Million
Number Employees: 20-49
Brands:
    Landmark Damaris Chardonnay
    Landmark Grand Detou
    Landmark Kastania Pi
    Landmark Overlook Ch

7204 Landolfi's Food Products
302 Cummings Avenue
Trenton, NJ 08611
609-392-1830
Fax: 609-396-6581 landolfis@gmail.com
Frozen pasta, garlic bread and pizza dough
President: Jack Fu
Sales Director: Lori Landolfi
Director Manufacturing: Paul Melovich
Estimated Sales: $2 Million
Number Employees: 16
Square Footage: 40000
Type of Packaging: Consumer, Food Service, Private Label, Bulk

7205 Landreth Wild Rice
2320 Industrial Blvd
Norman, OK 73069-8518
405-360-2333
Fax: 405-360-6644 800-333-3533
Processor and exporter of wild rice
Principal: George Landreth
Estimated Sales: $110,000
Number Employees: 2
Type of Packaging: Consumer, Food Service, Private Label

7206 Landry's Pepper Co
1606 Cypress Island Hwy
PO Box 127
St Martinville, LA 70582-6013
337-394-6097
Fax: 337-394-7629 landry6097@aol.com
Hot sauces.
President: Lamar Bertrand
VP: Toby Bertrand
Estimated Sales: $500,000
Number Employees: 5-9
Square Footage: 120000
Type of Packaging: Consumer, Food Service, Private Label, Bulk
Brands:
    Cajun Gourmet Magic
    Landry's
    Premium

7207 Lane Southern Orchards
50 Lane Rd
Fort Valley, GA 31030-5212
478-825-3266
Fax: 478-825-7995 800-277-3224
www.lanesouthernorchards.com
Packer of peaches, oranges, grapefruit, and pecans
President: Duke Lane
CEO: Mark Sanchez
mark@lanepacking.com
Marketing Director: Wendy Barton
Wholesale: Duke Lane
Purchasing: Lori Buzze
Estimated Sales: $950,000
Number Employees: 250-499
Square Footage: 43152
Type of Packaging: Bulk
Brands:
    Diamond D

7208 Lane's Dairy
310 N Concepcion St
El Paso, TX 79905-1605
915-772-6700
Fax: 915-772-3097
Manufacturer and exporter of milk and canned and bottled fruit juice
President: John Lane
Owner: Hilda Lane
Production Manager: Chris Lane
Estimated Sales: $2 Million
Number Employees: 20-49
Square Footage: 60000
Type of Packaging: Consumer
Brands:
    Lanes Dairy

7209 Lang Creek Brewery
655 Lang Creek Rd
Marion, MT 59925
406-858-2200
Fax: 406-858-2499
Beer and ale
Owner/Brewmaster: John Campbell
Estimated Sales: $2.5-5 Million
Number Employees: 5-9
Number of Brands: 1
Number of Products: 8
Brands:
    Tri-Motor
    Windsock

7210 Lang Pharma Nutrition Inc
20 Silva Ln
Middletown, RI 02842-5638
401-848-7700
Fax: 401-848-7701 customer.service@langpni.com
Dietary supplements and pharma nutrition products.
Owner: Judy Pattie
jpattie@langpni.com
Vice President: Bruce Lang
Estimated Sales: $10-20 Million
Number Employees: 20-49
Number of Products: 250
Type of Packaging: Consumer, Food Service, Private Label, Bulk
Brands:
    Enerjuice
    Mr. Spice
    Tangy Bang

7211 Lang's Chocolates
350 Pine St.
Williamsport, PA 17701
570-323-6320
info@langschocolates.com
www.langschocolates.com
Gourmet handcrafted chocolates and confections
Master Chocolatier: William Lang

7212 Lange Estate Winery & Vineyard
18380 NE Buena Vista Dr
Dundee, OR 97115-9104
503-538-6476
Fax: 503-538-1938 don@langewinery.com
www.langewinery.com
Wines
Owner: Don Lange
donlange@europa.com
Owner/CEO: Wendy Lange
National Sales Manager: Michael Sanders
donlange@europa.com
Owner, Winemaker: Don Lange
General Manager, Winemaker: Jesse Lange
General Manager, Winemaker: Jesse Lange
Estimated Sales: $680,000
Number Employees: 5-9
Brands:
    Lange Winery

7213 Langer Juice Co Inc
City of Industry, CA
626-336-3100
bruce@langers.com
www.langers.com
Juices.
CEO: Bruce Langer
Quality Assurance Manager: Amandeep Kaur
National Sales Manager: Tom Bottiaux
Year Founded: 1960
Estimated Sales: $160 Million
Number Employees: 100-249
Square Footage: 140000
Type of Packaging: Consumer, Food Service, Private Label
Brands:
    Dole
    Langers Juice
    Packers Pride
    Tropicana

7214 Lantana Hummus
PO Box 40639
Austin, TX 78704
844-907-7626
customerservice@lantanafoods.com
www.lantanafoods.com
Gourmet hummus
CEO: Matt Gase
VP, Marketing: Kristin Garro
Number of Brands: 1
Number of Products: 8
Type of Packaging: Consumer
Brands:
    LANTANA

7215 Lanthier Bakery
PO Box 640
58 Dominion Street
Alexandria, ON K0C 1A0
Canada
613-525-2435
Fax: 613-525-2818 info@lanthierbakery.com
Bread and rolls
President/CEO: Marc Lanthier
Type of Packaging: Consumer, Food Service
Brands:
    Lanthier

7216 Lantic Sugar
4026, Notre-Dame Street East
Montreal, QC H1W 2K3
Canada
514-527-8686
Fax: 514-527-1401 info@lantic.ca
www.lantic.ca
Sugar including liquid, bulk, soft, icing, granulated, coarse, medium, instant, etc
President and CEO: Edward Makin
Chairman, Chief Executive Officer: A. Stuart Belkin
Vice-President, finance and secretary: Manon Lacroix, CPA, auditor CA
Consultant: Daniel Lafrance
Vice President of Sales: Mike Walton
Vice President of Operations: Bob Copeland

Food Manufacturers / A-Z

Number Employees: 400
Type of Packaging: Consumer, Food Service, Bulk
Brands:
  Lantic

7217 Lapierre Maple Farms
99 de l'Escale
St-Ludger de Beauce, QC G0M 1W0
Canada
819-548-5454
www.lapierremaple.com
Organic maple syrup
President: Donald Lapierre

7218 Larabar
Denver, CO 80218
800-543-2147
info@larabar.com www.larabar.com
All-natural fruit, nut and dessert bars
Founder: Lara Merriken
Marketing Director: Ashley Capobianco
Contact: Cynthia Abrahamson
abrahamson@larabar.com

7219 Laredo Tortilleria & Mexican
1616 Woodside Ave
Fort Wayne, IN 46816-3942
260-447-2576
Fax: 219-447-2577 800-252-7336
http://www.laredomexicanfoods.com
Processor and wholesaler/distributor of Mexican food products including salsa, tortillas and tortilla chips; serving the food service market
President: Benito Trevino
General Manager: Raul Trevino
VP: Reynol Trevino
Manager: Frank Trevino
Estimated Sales: Less Than $500,000
Number Employees: 1-4
Parent Co: Tregar
Type of Packaging: Consumer, Food Service, Private Label, Bulk
Brands:
  Don Pedro

7220 Lark Fine Foods
8 Scotts Way
Essex, MA 01929-1120
978-768-0012
Fax: 978-890-7135 mamccormick@gmail.com
www.larkfinefoods.com
Cookies, crackers.
Marketing: Mary Ann McCormick
Estimated Sales: Less Than $500,000
Number Employees: 5-9

7221 Larkin Cold Storage
4755 27th St
Long Island City, NY 11101-4410
718-937-2007
Fax: 718-937-3250
Chocolate bars, butter, cheese, other dairy and eggs, yogurt, honey, pickles & pickled vegetables
Owner: Anne Cheneby
anne@larkin.com
Marketing: Adam Moskowitz
Number Employees: 10-19

7222 Laronga Bakery
599 Somerville Ave
Somerville, MA 02143-3296
617-625-8600
Fax: 617-625-1853
customerservice@larongabakery.com
www.larongabakery.com
Bakery goods
Owner: Michael Ronga
mronga@larongabakery.com
Owner: Louis Ronga
General Manager: Steve Weinstein
Estimated Sales: $20-50 Million
Number Employees: 50-99
Brands:
  La Ronga Bakery

7223 Larosa Bakery Inc
79 Newman Springs Rd E
Shrewsbury, NJ 07702-4038
732-842-2592
Fax: 732-842-8029 800-527-6722
www.ecannoli.com
Cannolis, cannoli cream, gourmet butter, cookies and biscotti

Owner: George Delaney
VP: Peter LaRosa
Sales Manager: George Delaney
gdelaney@kingofcannoli.com
Estimated Sales: $1-3 Million
Number Employees: 20-49
Type of Packaging: Consumer, Food Service, Bulk

7224 Larosa Bakery Inc
79 Newman Springs Rd E
Shrewsbury, NJ 07702-4038
732-842-2592
Fax: 732-842-8029 800-527-6722
www.ecannoli.com
Cannoli, cannoli cream, biscotti, cookies
Owner: George Delaney
gdelaney@kingofcannoli.com
Owner/VP: Peter La Rosa
Estimated Sales: $1.3 Million
Number Employees: 20-49
Brands:
  Larosa's Famous Biscotti
  Larosa's Famous Cannoli
  Larosa's Famous Cookies

7225 Larry J. Williams Company
2686 Savannah Hwy
Jesup, GA 31545-5511
912-427-7729
Fax: 912-427-0611
Shrimp, crab, oysters, scallps, flounder, etc.
President: Larry Williams
l.williams@larryjwilliams.com
General Manager: Joey Williams
Estimated Sales: $1-3 Million
Number Employees: 20-49

7226 Larry's Beans
1509 Gavin St
Raleigh, NC 27608-2613
919-828-1234
Fax: 919-833-4567 www.larryscoffee.com
Wholesale coffee roaster
Owner: Charles Nichols
CFO: Brad Lienhart
VP: Kevin Bobal
Marketing: Kyley Schmidt
Sales: Erik Iverson
charlesnichols@larrysbeans.com
Plant Manager: Neal England
Estimated Sales: $3.0 Million
Number Employees: 10-19

7227 Larry's Sausage Corporation
931 S Eastern Boulevard
Fayetteville, NC 28306-7365
910-483-5148
Fax: 910-483-2526 larryssausage.com
Sausage
Founder/Co-Owner: Larry Godwin
CEO/Co-Owner: Sheila Abe
Estimated Sales: $5-10 Million
Number Employees: 20 to 49
Type of Packaging: Consumer

7228 Larry's Vineyards & Winery
3001 Furbeck Road
Altamont, NY 12009
518-355-7365
v1945p@juno.com
Wine
President/Owner: Larry Brooks
Contact: Donna Pace
v1945p@juno.com
Estimated Sales: Under $500,000
Number Employees: 1-4
Brands:
  Larry's Vineyards

7229 Larsen Farms
2650 N 2375 E
Hamer, ID 83425
208-374-5592
Fax: 208-374-5497 www.larsenfarms.com
Producer of dehydrated and prepared potatoes.
President: Blaine Larsen
Cio/Cto: Kuhn Hay
felipe@kuhnhay.com
VP, Dehydration Operations: Jan Nel
Estimated Sales: $39 Million
Number Employees: 250-499
Number of Brands: 1
Square Footage: 125000
Type of Packaging: Consumer, Private Label

Other Locations:
  Dalhart TX
Brands:
  Larsen Farms

7230 Lartigue Seafood
23043 Perdido Beach Blvd
Orange Beach, AL 36561
251-948-2644
Seafood. Founded in 1979
President: Paul Lartigue Jr
Vice President: Paul Lartigue
Number Employees: 5

7231 Las Cruces Brand Products
6860 El Paso Dr
El Paso, TX 79905-3336
915-779-5709
Fax: 915-779-4559 www.las-cruces.com
Taco shells, tostada chips and flour and corn tortillas; also, salsa including jalapeno, red chile and chile con queso
Owner: Armando Viescas
aviescas@las-cruces.org
General Manager: Enrique Galindo
Office Manager: Elvira Martinez
Estimated Sales: $5-10 Million
Number Employees: 10-19
Square Footage: 18000
Type of Packaging: Consumer, Private Label
Brands:
  Las Cruces

7232 (HQ)Las Cruces Foods
3070 Harrelson Street
Las Cruces, NM 88005
575-526-2352
Fax: 575-523-5271
Mexican products including tortillas and taco shells
President: David Grijalva
CEO: Miguel Grijalva
VP: Miguel Grisalva
Estimated Sales: $461,369
Number Employees: 5 to 9
Other Locations:
  Las Cruces Foods
  Albuquerque NM

7233 Las Olas Confections
401 East Las Olas Blvd
Suite 800
Fort Lauderdale, FL 33301
954-940-4000
www.lasolasbrands.com
Confections and snacks, including chocolate, hard candies and taffy.

7234 Lasco Foods Inc
4553 Gustine Ave
St Louis, MO 63116
314-832-1906
Fax: 314-832-7566
customerservice@lascofoods.com
www.lascofoods.com
Mixes including beverage, sauce, gravy, dressing and dessert; also, sauces, mayonnaise and dressings.
Owner: Tom Ellinwood
tellinwood@lascofoods.com
Estimated Sales: $20-50 Million
Number Employees: 20-49
Square Footage: 100000
Parent Co: Allen Foods
Type of Packaging: Food Service

7235 Laska Stuff
132 Griggs Street
Rochester, MI 48307-1414
248-652-8473
Specialty and organic food.
President: Steve Sparks

7236 Lassonde Pappas & Company, Inc.
1 Collins Dr.
Suite 200
Carneys Point, NJ 08069
800-257-7019
info@lassondepappas.com lassondepappas.com
Juices including apple, blueberry, grape, papaya and cranberry sauce, flavored waters, and juice cocktails, lemonades, organic products, and ready to drink teas.
President, Lassonde Pappas: Seth French

Food Manufacturers / A-Z

Year Founded: 1942
Estimated Sales: $450 Million
Number Employees: 650
Number of Brands: 1
Square Footage: 600000
Parent Co: Lassonde Industries, Inc.
Type of Packaging: Consumer, Private Label, Bulk
Other Locations:
    Clement Pappas Food Plant
    Springdale AR
    Clement Pappas Food Plant
    Seabrook NJ
    Clement Pappas Food Plant
    Mountain Home NC
    Clement Pappas Food Plant
    Ontario CA
Brands:
    Clement Pappas

7237 Latah Creek Wine Cellar
13030 E Indiana Ave
Spokane Valley, WA 99216-1118
509-926-0164
Fax: 509-926-0710 www.latahcreek.com
Wines
President: Mike Conway
info@latahcreek.com
VP: Ellena Conway
Estimated Sales: $340,000
Number Employees: 5-9
Type of Packaging: Private Label

7238 Latcham Vineyards
2860 Omo Ranch Rd
Somerset, CA 95684-9204
530-620-6642
Fax: 530-620-5578 800-750-5591
latcham@directcon.net www.latcham.com
Wines
Owner: Franklin Latcham
jonlatcham@directcon.net
Winemaker: Craig Boyd
Sales Manager: Margaret Latcham
jonlatcham@directcon.net
Estimated Sales: $500,000-$1 Million
Number Employees: 10-19
Brands:
    Barbera
    Port

7239 Late July Snacks
595 Westport Ave
Norwalk, CT 06851
888-857-6225
www.latejuly.com
Organic snacks
Owner: Nicole Dawes
Contact: Aimee Allen
aimee.allen@latejuly.com

7240 Latitude, LTD
37 West Shore Road
Huntington, NY 11743
631-659-3374
Fax: 631-659-3376 latitudeltd@aol.com
Food ingredients manufacturer; including: sweeteners, vitamins, antioxidants and preservatives
Director: Laurel Eastman
Office Manager: Elissa Farrugia

7241 Latonia Bakery
3612 Decoursey Ave
Covington, KY 41015-1438
859-491-8855
Fax: 859-431-4169
Baked goods
President: Bernie Holmer
Estimated Sales: Under $500,000
Number Employees: 5-9

7242 Latta USA
Fair Lawn, NJ
201-512-8400
www.lattausa.com
Manufacturer of kefir and kombucha.
Sales Manager: Katie Scully
Brands:
    Latta

7243 Laura Chenel's Chevre
22085 Carneros Vineyard Way
Sonoma, CA 95476-2826
707-996-1252
Fax: 707-996-1816 www.laurachenel.com
Goat cheese
Founder: Laura Chenel
Manager: Brenda Crow
brenda@laurachenel.com
Estimated Sales: Less Than $500,000
Number Employees: 5-9
Number of Brands: 1
Brands:
    Laura Chenel's

7244 Laura Paige Candy Company
13 Jeanne Drive
Newburgh, NY 12550-1702
845-566-4209
Fax: 845-566-4766 infobe@marshalls.com
www.marshalls.com
Lollipops including hand painted seasonal and regular assortment
President: Elissa Koenig
Chairman: Dr. Louis Korngold
Vice President: Tracey Chalupa
Contact: Ellissa Koenig
ekoenig@marshalls.com
Estimated Sales: Less than $500,000
Number Employees: 30
Square Footage: 32000
Type of Packaging: Consumer, Food Service

7245 Laura's French Baking Co
6721 S Alameda St
Los Angeles, CA 90001-2123
323-585-5144
Fax: 323-585-0591 888-353-5144
Bread, croissants, danish, cakes and pastries
President: Sterling Kim
Manager: Charlie Son
charlieson99@gmail.com
Estimated Sales: Below $5 Million
Number Employees: 20-49
Type of Packaging: Food Service
Brands:
    Laura's

7246 Laurel Foods
31181 Southwest Laurel Rd
Hillsboro, OR 97123
503-692-3663
Fax: 503-692-3664 contact@laurelfoods.com
www.laurelfoods.com
Organic nuts, nut butters and oils
Managing Director: Troy Johnson

7247 Laurel Glen Vineyard
969 Carquinez Ave
Glen Ellen, CA 95442
707-933-9877
Fax: 707-526-9801 info@laurelglenvineyard.com
www.laurelglen.com
Wines
Proprietor: Patrick Campbell
Manager: Randall Watkins
randall@laurelglen.com
Winemaker: Patrick Campbell
Estimated Sales: $4 Million
Number Employees: 5-9
Number of Brands: 5
Type of Packaging: Private Label

7248 Laurel Hill Foods
39 Franklin McKay Road
Attleboro, MA 02703
877-759-8141
Fax: 508-226-7060 sales@laurelhillfoods.com
www.laurelhillfoods.com
Chips and other snacks
Marketing: Jen Huntley-Corbin

7249 Laurent's Meat Market
528 Avenue A
Marrero, LA 70072-2117
504-341-1771
Fax: 504-341-0299
Processor and meat packer of fresh and smoked sausages, hogshead cheese, andouille, hamburger and hot patties
Owner: Layton Laurent Sr
Estimated Sales: $500,000
Number Employees: 1-4
Type of Packaging: Consumer, Food Service, Bulk

7250 Laurie & Sons
1580 Park Avenue
New York, NY 10029
212-866-6600
laurie@laurieandsons.com
www.laurieandsons.com
Manufacturer of toffee.
Founder: Laurie Pauker
lpauker@laurieandsons.com

7251 Lava Cap Winery
2221 Fruitridge Rd
Placerville, CA 95667-3700
530-621-0175
Fax: 530-621-4399 800-475-0175
www.lavacap.com
Wines
President: David Jones
Accountant: Barbara Beacham
General Manager: Jeanne Jones
Sales Director: Tim Hogan
Tour Coordinator: Julia Rosenkrantz
Winemaker: Thomas Jones
Vineyard Manager: Charles Jones
Estimated Sales: Below $5 Million
Number Employees: 10-19
Number of Brands: 1
Number of Products: 1
Square Footage: 96000
Type of Packaging: Private Label

7252 Lavash Corp
2835 Newell St
Los Angeles, CA 90039-3817
323-663-5249
Fax: 323-663-8062
Flatbread
Manager: Edmund Hartounian
lavashcorp@att.net
Director Marketing: Arthur Minassian
National Sales Manager: Adam Cardenas
Cust./Technical Support Manager: Lori Akian
Estimated Sales: Below $5,000,000
Number Employees: 10-19
Brands:
    Wrap'n Roll

7253 Lavazza Premium Coffees
3 Park Ave # 35
New York, NY 10016-5902
212-725-9196
Fax: 212-725-9475 800-466-3287
info@lavazzausa.com www.lavazza.com
Lavazza coffees
General Manager: Ennio Ranaboldo
Founder: Luigi Lavazza
Contact: Bidya Alie
balie@sovrana.com
Estimated Sales: Below $5 Million
Number Employees: 20-49
Brands:
    Lavazza

7254 Lavoi Corporation
1749 Tullie Circle
Atlanta, GA 30329
404-325-1016
bdoan@epibreads.com
www.epibreads.com
Bread and baked goods
CEO Emeritus: Robert Gansel
VP, Business Development: Hugh Sullins
Director, Quality Assurance: Mike Heyburn
Manager, Marketing: Brooke Doan
Year Founded: 1985
Estimated Sales: $89.1 Million
Number Employees: 263
Number of Brands: 1
Square Footage: 61000
Parent Co: R.W. Bakers Co
Type of Packaging: Consumer, Food Service
Brands:
    EPI

7255 Lawler Foods LTD
1219 Carpenter Rd
Humble, TX 77396-1535
281-446-0059
Fax: 281-446-3806 800-541-8285
desserts@lawlers.com www.lawlers.com
Frozen cheesecakes, pies, brownies and sheetcakes
President: Bill Lawler
blawler@lawlers.com
CEO: Carol Lawler

Food Manufacturers / A-Z

Estimated Sales: $10-20 Million
Number Employees: 100-249
Square Footage: 220000
Type of Packaging: Consumer, Food Service, Private Label, Bulk

7256 Lawrence Foods Inc
2200 Lunt Ave
Elk Grove Village, IL 60007
847-437-2400
Fax: 847-437-2567 info@lawrencefoods.com
www.lawrencefoods.com
Bakers' and confectioners' supplies including fruit and cream fillings, icings, glazes, preserves and jellies; available in boxes, cans, pails, drums, totes and flexible pouches.
President: Paul Ferenchick
Chairman: Lester Lawrence
Executive Chairman: Cecil Gregory
CEO & General Counsel: Marc Lawrence
Year Founded: 1890
Estimated Sales: $200 Million
Number Employees: 100-249
Square Footage: 293000
Type of Packaging: Food Service, Private Label, Bulk
Brands:
  Lawrence

7257 Lawry's Foods
24 Schilling Rd.
Hunt Valley, MD 21031
800-952-9797
www.mccormick.com/lawrys
Prepared gravy and sauce mixes, marinades, seasoned salt and pepper, spices and breadings.
President/CEO: Lawrence Kurzius
Year Founded: 1922
Estimated Sales: $500 Million-$1 Billion
Number of Brands: 1
Parent Co: McCormick & Company
Type of Packaging: Consumer
Brands:
  Lawry's

7258 Lax & Mandel Bakery
14439 Cedar Rd
South Euclid, OH 44121
216-382-8877
Fax: 216-382-8875 kosher@laxandmandel.com
Cakes, pastries
Co-Owner: Sheldon Weiser
Co-Owner: Helen Weiser
Co-Owner: Jeffrey Weiser
Estimated Sales: $500,000-$1 Million
Number Employees: 3

7259 Laxson Co
264 W Lachapelle
San Antonio, TX 78204-1853
210-226-8397
Fax: 210-226-0537 laxsonco@laxsonco.com
www.laxsonco.com
Sausages, bacon, ham, cheese, spices
President/Director: Gary Laxson
laxsonco@laxsonco.com
Vice President: Lawrence Laxson
Estimated Sales: $20-50 Million
Number Employees: 20-49

7260 Lay Packing Company
622 E Jackson Avenue
Knoxville, TN 37915-1107
865-522-1147
Fax: 865-922-4321
Beef, pork, lamb and veal
Owner: Ira Lay Jr
General Manager: Jerry Simons
Estimated Sales: $1-3 Million
Number Employees: 10 to 19
Parent Co: Lay Packing Company
Type of Packaging: Consumer, Food Service, Private Label, Bulk

7261 Layman Distributing
1630 W Main St
PO Box 1015
Salem, VA 24153
540-389-2000
Fax: 540-389-2062 800-237-1519
lcc@laymandistributing.com
www.laymandistributing.com
Processor and distributor of candy, including brittles, fudge, chocolate, chews, nut clusters and taffy; meat and dairy; and condiments.
Owner: Justin Keen
justin.keen@laymancandy.com
Vice President of Sales: Scott Thomasson
V.P. Customer Relations: Kenny Keen
Estimated Sales: $5-10 Million
Number Employees: 10-19
Number of Brands: 2028
Number of Products: 122
Square Footage: 172000
Brands:
  Layman's

7262 Lazy Creek Vineyards
4741 Highway 128
Philo, CA 95466
707-895-3623
Fax: 707-895-9226 888-529-9275
chandler@lazycreek.com
www.lazycreekvineyards.com
Estate wines
President: Josh Chandler
VP Marketing: Mary Beth Chandler
Estimated Sales: $5-10 Million
Number Employees: 5-9
Brands:
  Lazy Creek Vineyards

7263 Lazzaroni USA
299 Market St
Suite 160
Saddle Brook, NJ 07663-5312
201-368-1240
Fax: 201-368-1262 www.lazzaroni-ita.com
Manufacturer and distributor of chocolates and cookies
President: Stefano Tombetti
Executive VP: Kathy Ecoffey
Contact: Theresa Strunck
tstrunck@lazzaroniusa.com

7264 Le Bleu Corp
3134 Cornatzer Rd
Advance, NC 27006-7212
336-998-2894
Fax: 336-998-4167 800-854-4471
info@lebleu.com www.lebleu.com
Manufacturer and distributor of bottled water
President/CEO: Jerry Smith
CEO: Brock Agee
b.agee@lebleu.com
Owner/Finance/HR & Sales Executive: Andy Scotchie
Director of Public Relations: Debbie Pullen
Plant Manager: Ed Hauser
Estimated Sales: $17.7 Million
Number Employees: 100-249
Square Footage: 300000
Type of Packaging: Consumer
Brands:
  Le Bleu Bottled Water
  Nascar Bottled Water

7265 Le Caramel
8047 El Capitan Dr
La Mesa, CA 91942-5515
619-562-0713
Fax: 619-562-1604 www.le-caramel.com
Caramels, dessert toppings (i.e. fudge sauce, caramel sauce, whipped cream, etc.).
Marketing: Christine Kugener

7266 Le Chef Bakery
7547 Telegraph Rd
Montebello, CA 90640-6516
USA
323-888-2929
Fax: 323-888-2946 www.lechefbakery.com
Baked goods, bread, biscuits, cakes, pastries, cookies
CEO: Jonathan Lau
jonathanl@lechef.net
Number Employees: 50-99

7267 Le Chic French Bakery
1043 Washington Ave
Miami Beach, FL 33139-5017
305-673-5522
Fax: 305-673-5522
Bakery products including baguettes, buttery croissants, danishes; as well as European style cakes, pies, tarts and pastries
Owner: M Sanchez
Estimated Sales: $2.5-5 000,000
Number Employees: 5-9

7268 Le Donne Brothers Bakery
143 Chestnut St
Roseto, PA 18013-1311
610-588-0423
cbath@epix.net
Breads: anchiove, French, Italian, sweet and Viennese, also; tomato pies
Owner: Robert Bath
Co-Owner: Connie Bath
Estimated Sales: Less Than $500,000
Number Employees: 1-4
Type of Packaging: Consumer

7269 Le Frois Foods Corporation
56 High St
Brockport, NY 14420-2058
585-637-5003
Fax: 585-637-2855
Vinegar
President: Duncan Tsay
Estimated Sales: Under $500,000
Number Employees: 5-9

7270 Le Grand
69 □milien Marcoux
Blainville, QC J7C 0B4
Canada
450-623-3000
Fax: 450-623-2300 info@maisonlegrand.com
www.maisonlegrand.com
Soups, sauces, pestos and chilies
Co-Founder: Bernard Le Grand
Co-Founder: Tatiana Bossy

7271 Le Grand Confectionary
4527 Harlin Drive
Sacramento, CA 95826
888-361-2125
Fax: 916-361-2150
customerservice@legrandtruffles.com
www.legrandtruffles.com
Chocolate truffles, other chocolate and candy, gift packs
Marketing: Jack Shaw

7272 Le Macaron
382 Saint Armands Cir
Sarasota, FL 34236-1313
941-552-8872
lemacaronfranchise@gmail.com
Macaron, french pastries
Owner: Audrey Guillem Saba
guillemlia@aol.com
Estimated Sales: Less Than $500,000
Number Employees: 5-9

7273 Le Pique-Nique
5 Penn Plaza
New York, NY 10001
800-400-6454
Fax: 510-339-7141 800-699-9822
www.thomasnet.com
Sausage including chicken, turkey, chicken/apple, cranberries, orange, maple syrup, etc
President: Dennis Donegan
Estimated Sales: Under $500,000
Number Employees: 1-4
Type of Packaging: Consumer, Food Service
Brands:
  Calypso Caribbean
  Tandoori
  Thai Chicken

7274 Le Roy Ren,
14 NE 1st Ave
Suite 501
Miami, FL 33132
786-558-9968
info@thecalisson.com
us.calisson.com
Calissons, nougats, biscuits, chocolates, creams and jams.
Founder: Olivier Baussan

7275 (HQ)Le Sueur Cheese Co
719 N Main St
Le Sueur, MN 56058-1404
507-665-3353
Fax: 507-665-2820 800-757-7611
info@daviscofoods.com www.daviscofoods.com

Variety of cheese including low-fat, no-fat, enzyme-modified cheeses and other customer specified varieties
President: Mark Davis
Vice President: Jim Ward
Manager: Mitch Davis
mitch.davis@daviscofoods.com
Production Manager: Roger Schroder
Purchasing Manager: Gregory Bush
Estimated Sales: $14.90
Number Employees: 100-249
Square Footage: 12000
Parent Co: Davisco Foods International, Inc.
Other Locations:
  Le Sueur Cheese Plant
  Jerome ID

7276 Le Vigne Winery
5115 Buena Vista Dr
Paso Robles, CA 93446-8558
805-227-4000
Fax: 805-227-6128 800-891-6055
info@levignewinery.com www.levignewinery.com
Wines
Co-Owner: Sylvia Filippini
info@sylvesterwinery.com
Accounting Manager: Scott Keller
Marketing Manager: Zina Miakinkova
Sales Manager: Michael Barreto
Estimated Sales: Below $5 Million
Number Employees: 20-49
Brands:
  Sylvester

7277 Lea & Perrins
801 Waukegan Rd
Glenview, IL 60025
www.leaperrins.com
Sauces and condiments specializing in worcestershire sauces and marinades.
Year Founded: 1839
Estimated Sales: $50-100 Million
Number Employees: 100-249
Number of Brands: 1
Parent Co: H.J. Heinz Company
Type of Packaging: Consumer, Food Service
Brands:
  Lea & Perrins

7278 Leach Farms Inc
W1102 Buttercup Ct
P.O. Box 192
Berlin, WI 54923-8327
920-361-1880
Fax: 920-361-4474
www.leachfoods.com/contact.html
Fresh and frozen spinach and celery
Owner: Tom Leach
General Manager: Jacqueline Oldenburg
Chief Financial Officer: John Zander
Personnel Manager: Sara Block
Quality Assurance Manager: Alecia Vermeen
Sales Manager: Marybeth Yonke
Plant Manager: Loreen Greer
Estimated Sales: $30-50 Million
Number Employees: 10-19
Square Footage: 10000
Type of Packaging: Bulk

7279 Leader Candies
132 Harrison Place
Brooklyn, NY 11237-1522
718-366-6900
Fax: 718-417-1723
Processor and exporter of candies including hard, caramels, jelly beans, novelties, lollypops, filled, fundraising, hard toffee, starch jellies, bagged and nonchocolate, and nonfrozen freeze pops
President: Howard Kastin
Sales: Helen Garfield
VP Manufacturing: Malcom Kastin
Number Employees: 155
Square Footage: 320000
Type of Packaging: Consumer, Food Service, Private Label, Bulk
Brands:
  Beaver Pop
  Freez-A-Pops
  Kastin's
  Leader
  Lolly Lo's

7280 Leaf Cuisine
828 Pico Blvd
Unit 2
Santa Monica, CA 90405
leafcuisine.com
Dairy-free spreads, 'cream cheese' and vegan snack packs
Chef: Rod Rotondi
Year Founded: 2004
Number of Brands: 1
Number of Products: 12
Type of Packaging: Consumer
Brands:
  LEAF CUISINE

7281 Leaf Jerky
PO Box CAMB
Battle Creek, MI 49016
800-962-1413
www.leafjerky.com
Plant-based jerky
Parent Co: Kellogg Company

7282 Leahy Orchards
1772 Route 209
Franklin Centre, QC J0S 1E0
Canada
450-827-2544
Fax: 450-827-2470 800-667-7380
www.applesnax.com
Apple sauce in cans, jars and portion packs; also, pie filling
President/CEO: Michael Leahy
CEO: Beahy
VP Finance/Administration: Guylaine Yelle
VP Sales/Marketing/R&D: Doug Anderson
Director of Purchasing: Philip Seguin
Number Employees: 50-99
Type of Packaging: Consumer
Brands:
  Apple Snax

7283 Leams
906 Texas Court
Hutchinson, KS 67502-5136
316-662-4287
Fax: 620-662-4287
Sweet and savory flavors
President: Alice Grigrest
Number Employees: 1-4

7284 Leaner Creamer
Beverly Hills, CA 90210
866-739-2298
leanercreamer.com
Coconut-based coffee creamer and coffee capsules
CEO: Jonathan Kashani
Director of Marketing: Natasha Kashani

7285 Leatex Chemical Co
2722 N Hancock St
Philadelphia, PA 19133-3597
215-739-2000
Fax: 215-739-5910 www.nielsen.com
Sulphonated castor oils
President: Denniston Brown
dennistonbrown@nielsen.com
VP Marketing: L Kevin McChesney
Estimated Sales: $5,000,000
Number Employees: 10-19

7286 Leavenworth Coffee Roast
894 Highway 2
Leavenworth, WA 98826
509-548-3313
Fax: 509-548-4251 800-246-2761
java@alpinecoffeeroasters.com
www.alpinecoffeeroasters.com
Coffee including 25 blends
President: Dale Harrison
VP: Veronica Harrison
Estimated Sales: $1-2.5 Million
Number Employees: 10-19
Type of Packaging: Consumer, Food Service
Brands:
  Chatter Creek

7287 Leaves Pure Teas
7435 E Tierra Buena Lane
Scottsdale, AZ 85260
480-998-8807
Fax: 650-583-1163 800-242-8807
info@chinamist.com www.chinamist.com
Teas
President & Chief Operations Officer: Rommie Flammer
Co Founder, Co Chairman, Co CEO: Dan Schweiker
Operations Manager: Jeff Morris
Number Employees: 5-9
Type of Packaging: Private Label
Brands:
  Leaves Pure Tea

7288 (HQ)Leavitt Corp., The
100 Santilli Hwy
Everett, MA 02149-1938
617-389-2600
Fax: 617-387-9085 contact@teddie.com
teddie.com
Peanut butter, salted and unsalted cashews and peanuts; raw cashews
President: James T Hintlian
jameshint@teddie.com
Executive VP: Mark Hintlian
Quality Control: Christopher Hayes
Operations Manager: Joseph Saraceno
Production Manager: Jack Skamarakas
Purchasing Manager: Frank Ciampa
Estimated Sales: $10-24.9 Million
Number Employees: 50-99
Type of Packaging: Consumer, Food Service, Private Label, Bulk
Brands:
  Teddie
  River Queen

7289 Lebanon Cheese Co
3 Railroad Ave
PO Box 63
Lebanon, NJ 08833-2156
908-236-2611
Fax: 908-236-6870 www.lebanoncheese.com
Cheese
President: Joe Lotito
Estimated Sales: $3 000,000
Number Employees: 5-9
Brands:
  Lebanon Cheese

7290 Lebermuth Company
4004 Technology Dr
South Bend, IN 46628
574-259-7000
Fax: 574-258-7450 800-648-1123
info@lebermuth.com www.lebermuth.com
Essential oils, fragrances and flavors
President & CEO: Rob Brown
Chief Strategic Officer: Alan Brown
VP, Ingredient Bus. Dev.: Mel Brown
VP, Fragrance Bus. Dev.: Craig Sroda
Chief Financial Officer: Rebecca Brown
Exec. VP, Sales: Craig Lupinacci
Director of Operations: Phil Forte
Year Founded: 1908
Estimated Sales: $10-19 Million
Number Employees: 50-99
Type of Packaging: Bulk

7291 (HQ)Lebermuth Company
14000 McKinley Highway
Mishawaka, IN 46545
574-259-7000
Fax: 574-258-7450 800-648-1123
info@lebermuth.com www.lebermuth.com
Fragrance and flavor company
President: Rob Brown
CEO: Irvin Brown
Vice President: Alan Brown
Contact: Jodi Aker
jaker@lebermuth.com
Production Manager: Mike Ryan
Plant Manager: Robert Hall
Purchasing Manager: Jim Gates
Estimated Sales: $5-10 Million
Number Employees: 50
Square Footage: 180000
Type of Packaging: Bulk

7292 Leblanc Seafood
PO Box 509
Lafitte, LA 70067-0509
504-689-2631
Fax: 504-689-4303
Seafood

Food Manufacturers / A-Z

7293 Lecoq Cuisine Corp
35 Union Ave # 1
Bridgeport, CT 06607-2335
203-334-1010
Fax: 203-334-1800 croissant@lecoqcuisine.com
www.lecoqcuisine.com
Cakes/pastries, frozen desserts, full-line frozen, hors d'oeuvres/appetizers, other frozen, puffed snacks.
Owner: Tami Corby
tami@lecoqcuisine.com
Marketing: Eric Lecoq
Number Employees: 100-249

7294 Lee Andersons
51392 Harrison Street
Coachella, CA 92236-1563
760-398-3441
Dates
Marketing Manager: Ann Jolly
Estimated Sales: Under $500,000
Number Employees: 1-4

7295 Lee Kum Kee
#350, 30-56 Whitestone Expy
Whitestone, NY 11354
718-821-2199
Fax: 718-821-2989 800-346-7562
contact@lkkusa.com www.lkk.com
Processor, importer and exporter of condiments and sauces including chili.
Estimated Sales: $190,000
Number Employees: 3
Square Footage: 80000
Parent Co: Lee Kum Kee Company
Type of Packaging: Consumer, Food Service, Private Label, Bulk
Brands:
  Lee Kum Kee
  Panda

7296 (HQ)Lee Kum Kee USA Inc
14841 Don Julian Rd
City Of Industry, CA 91746-3110
626-709-1888
Fax: 626-709-1899 800-654-5082
contact@lkkusa.com us.lkk.com
Producer of authentic Chinese sauces including oyster flavored sauces, soy sauces, chili sauces and cooking sauces for industrial manufacturers.
Chairman: David Lee
Vice President, Finance: Dickson Chan
Sales Director: Grace Chow
HR, Recruiting: David Lo
General Manager: Rob Berry
Estimated Sales: $9.7 Million
Number Employees: 20-49
Square Footage: 50000
Type of Packaging: Private Label
Brands:
  Choy Sun
  Full House
  Kum Chun Brand
  Lee Kum Kee
  Lee Kum Kee Premium
  Panda Brand

7297 Lee Seed Co
2242 Iowa 182 Ave
Inwood, IA 51240-7592
712-753-4403
Fax: 712-753-4542 800-736-6530
www.soynuts.com
Roasted soynuts in 16 flavors
Co-Owner: Paul Lee
Co-Owner: Joyce Lee
joycelee@soynuts.com
Marketing Director: Scott Lee
Estimated Sales: $3-5 Million
Number Employees: 10-19
Type of Packaging: Consumer, Private Label, Bulk
Brands:
  Super Soynuts

7298 Lee's Food Products
1233 Queen Street E
Toronto, ON M4L 1C2
Canada
416-465-2407
Canned soy sauce and Chinese vegetables including bamboo shoots, water chestnuts and mushrooms; importer of mushrooms, instant noodles and mini corn
President: Marilyn Wong
Secretary/Treasurer: L Wong

Estimated Sales: $5-10 Million
Number Employees: 45
Type of Packaging: Consumer, Food Service

7299 Lee's Ice Cream
7137 E. Stetson Dr.
Scottsdale, AZ 85251
410-581-0234
Fax: 410-581-7044 888-669-5337
Makers of premium gourmet ice cream products available in a variety of flavors.
Founder: Leon Garfield
Co-Founder: Jaques Rubin
Co-Founder: Steven Rubin
CEO: Steve Rubin
Number Employees: 100-249

7300 Lee's Sausage Co
1054 Neeses Hwy
Orangeburg, SC 29115-8606
803-534-5517
Fax: 803-531-2809 leessausage@yahoo.com
Sausage, liver pudding, BBQ meat, BBQ hash, BBQ sauce, chili
President: Freddy Lee
leessausage@yahoo.com
Estimated Sales: $2 Million
Number Employees: 20-49
Type of Packaging: Consumer, Private Label

7301 Leech Lake Wild Rice
115 6th St NE
Cass Lake, MN 56633
218-335-8200
Fax: 218-335-8309
Natural lake and river wild rice
Manager: Cheryl Dunn
Number Employees: 1-4
Brands:
  Leech Lake

7302 (HQ)Leech Lake Wild Rice
51664 County Road 137
Deer River, MN 56636
218-246-2746
Fax: 218-246-2748 877-246-0620
llwrice@paulbunyan.net
Natural lake and river wild rice
Prime Manager: George Donnell
CFO: Mike Ziemer
Quality Control: Christine Cummings
R & D: Steve Mortinson
Public Relations: Don June
Production Manager: George Donnell
Estimated Sales: Below $5 Million
Number Employees: 5
Type of Packaging: Private Label
Brands:
  Leech Lake Wild Rice

7303 Leelanau Cellars
5019 North West Bay Shore Drive (M-22)
Omena, MI 49674
231-386-5201
Fax: 231-386-9797 800-782-8128
info@leelanaucellars.com
www.leelanaucellars.com
Wines
Owner: Michael Jacobson
Owner: Bob Jacobson
Vineyard Manager: Marcel Lenz
General Manager: Tony Lentych
Tasting Room Manager: Carrie Hanson
Sales Manager: Scott Vicary
Estimated Sales: $5-10 Million
Number Employees: 10-19
Brands:
  Leelanau

7304 Leelanau Fruit Co
2900 S West Bay Shore Dr
Peshawbestown, MI 49682-9614
231-271-3514
Fax: 231-271-4367 info@leelanaufruit.com
www.leelanaufruit.com
Processer and exporter of frozen and brined cherries and strawberries
President: Glen Lacross
General Manager: Allen Steimel
Estimated Sales: $1-3 Million
Number Employees: 20-49
Type of Packaging: Consumer, Food Service, Private Label, Bulk

7305 Leeward Resources
401 E Pratt Street
Suite 354
Baltimore, MD 21202-3117
410-837-9003
Fax: 410-837-7527
Spices, herbal extracts, botanitals, essential oils, fruit juices
President: William Brown
Estimated Sales: $3.5 Million
Number Employees: 3

7306 Leeward Winery
2511 Victoria Ave
Oxnard, CA 93035-2931
805-656-5054
Fax: 805-656-5092 www.leewardwinery.com
Processor and exporter of table wines
President: Charles Brigham
Co-Owner: Chuck Gardner
Estimated Sales: $260,000
Number Employees: 4
Square Footage: 34000
Type of Packaging: Consumer, Food Service
Brands:
  Leeward

7307 Lef Bleuges Marinor
1015 Rg Double
St-Felicien, QC G8K 2M1
Canada
418-679-4577
Fax: 418-679-9602
Frozen blueberries
President: Jeanne-Pierre Senneville

7308 Lefse House
5210-51 Ave
Camrose, AB T4V 4N5
Canada
780-672-7555
Fax: 780-608-2377 info@thelefsehouse.ca
www.thelefsehouse.ca
Scandinavian all natural baked goods including potato lefse, flatbread and specialty items
President/CFO: Bernell Odegard
Purchasing Manager: Helen Lien
Estimated Sales: Under $300,000
Number Employees: 5-9
Square Footage: 6400
Type of Packaging: Consumer, Food Service
Brands:
  Lefse House

7309 Left Hand Brewing Co
1265 Boston Ave
Longmont, CO 80501-5809
303-772-0258
Fax: 303-772-9572 brewer@lefthandbrewing.com
www.pourhard.com
Processor and wholesaler/distributor of English style ale, stout and porter; also, German style lager and weiss beer
Owner: John Lindberg
jlindberg@boss-cellular.com
Quality Control: Andy Brown
Marketing/Sales/Public Relations: Chris Lennert
Operations Manager: Joe Schiraldi
Estimated Sales: Below $5 Million
Number Employees: 50-99
Square Footage: 52000
Type of Packaging: Food Service, Bulk
Brands:
  Deep Cover Brown
  Imperial
  Juju Ginger
  Left Hand Black Jack
  Sawtooth
  Tabernash

7310 Left Hand Brewing Co
1265 Boston Ave
Longmont, CO 80501-5809
303-772-0258
Fax: 303-772-9572 www.pourhard.com
Seasonal beer and lager
Owner: John Lindberg
CEO: Eric Wallece
Sales Manager: George Barela
jlindberg@boss-cellular.com
Director Manufacturing: Mark Luca
Estimated Sales: $5-9.9 Million
Number Employees: 50-99
Type of Packaging: Consumer, Food Service

Brands:
    Blackjack Porter
    Brown Ale
    Deep Cover
    Ginger Ale
    Haystack
    Interial Stout
    Jack Man
    Juju
    Milk Stout
    Toleftar Pilfen
    Weat
    Weiss

7311 Lefty Spices
Crain Hwy. Waldorf
Waldorf, MD 20601
    301-399-3145
Fax: 240-607-6721
Flour, full-line baking mixes and ingredients, other meat/game/pate, BBQ sauce, other sauces, seasonings and cooking enhancers, rubs, spices.
Marketing: Walter Nash

7312 Legacy Bakehouse
N8w22100 Johnson Dr
Waukesha, WI 53186-1866
    262-547-2447
Fax: 262-547-2047 800-967-2447
www.legacybakehouse.com
Bread and corn based snack chips
Owner: Chris Pinahs
CEO: Michael Heyer
Director Finance: Bill Bruggink
Quality Assurance: Janet Schultz
Vice President of Sales: Tom Reuteman
COO, Sales: Peter Sardina
Plant Manager: Chris Evans
Purchasing & Logistics: Cathy Huspen
Estimated Sales: $3 Million
Number Employees: 20-49
Square Footage: 236000
Type of Packaging: Consumer, Food Service, Private Label, Bulk
Brands:
    Pinah's

7313 Legacy Juice Works
382 Broadway
Saratoga Springs, NY 12866
    518-583-1108
juice@saratogajuicebar.com
saratogajuicebar.com
Wellness shots, cleanses and cold pressed juices
Co-Owner: Colin MacLean
Type of Packaging: Consumer
Brands:
    LEGACY JUICE WORKS

7314 Legally Addictive Foods
630 Flushing Ave
Brooklyn, NY 11206
legallyaddictivefoods.com
Cookies and crackers
Founder: Laura Shafferman

7315 Legend Brewing Co
321 W 7th St
Richmond, VA 23224-2307
    804-232-8871
Fax: 804-231-3417 info56@legendbrewing.com
www.legendbrewing.com
Beer, ale, stout and lager
President: Thomas E Martin
dave@legendbrewing.com
Sales Exec: David Gott
Brewmaster: Brad Mortensen
Estimated Sales: Below $5 Million
Number Employees: 20-49
Type of Packaging: Consumer, Food Service
Brands:
    Brown Ale
    Legand Brown
    Legand Pilsner
    Porter

7316 Legendary Foods
530 South Lake Ave
Suite 161
Pasadena, CA 91101
    888-698-1708
www.legendaryfoodsonline.com
Nut snacks and butters
Founder: Michael Veni
Number of Brands: 1
Number of Products: 9
Type of Packaging: Consumer
Brands:
    LEGENDARY FOODS

7317 Legumex Walker, Inc.
1345 Kenaston Blvd
Winnipeg, MB R6W 4B3
Canada
    204-808-0448
Grains
Investor & Media Relations: Marin Landis

7318 Lehi Mills
833 E Main St
Lehi, UT 84043-2286
    801-768-4401
Fax: 801-768-4557 877-311-3566
customerservice@lehirollermills.com
lehirollermills.com
Processor of flour, feed and meal; also, pancake mixes, cookie mixes, brownie mixes, bread mixes and preserves.
President: Sherman Robinson
COO: Brock Knight
Sales Exec: Steve DE John
sdejohn@lehirollermills.com
Year Founded: 1906
Estimated Sales: $20-50 Million
Number Employees: 20-49
Number of Brands: 3
Type of Packaging: Food Service, Private Label
Brands:
    Lehi Roller Mills
    Peacock
    Turkey

7319 Lehi Valley Trading Company
4955 E McKellips Rd
Mesa, AZ 85215
    480-684-1402
Fax: 480-461-1804 info@lehivalley.com
www.lehivalley.com
Beans, candy, dried fruit, granola, ice cream mix-ins, nuts and seeds, popcorn and nuggets, snack items and trail mix
President/Owner: Lewis Freeman
Contact: Jason Burrell
jason.burrell@lehivalley.com
Estimated Sales: $7.7 Million
Number Employees: 50

7320 Lehigh Valley Dairy Farms
880 Allentown Rd
Lansdale, PA 19446-5298
    215-855-8205
Fax: 215-855-9834 800-395-7004
www.lehighvalleydairyfarms.com
Dairy
Estimated Sales: $10-19.9 Million
Number Employees: 100-249
Number of Brands: 3
Parent Co: Dean Foods
Brands:
    Dairy Pure
    Trumoo
    Orchardpure

7321 Lehmann Farms
21034 Heron Way
Lakeville, MN 55044-8093
    651-247-3377
Fax: 715-247-2226 800-446-5276
www.lehmannfarms.com
Gourmet foods
President: Doug Oaks
Estimated Sales: Less Than $500,000
Number Employees: 1-4
Parent Co: Lehmann Farms

7322 Lehmann Mills Inc
11000 Youngstown Salem Rd
PO Box 1083
Salem, OH 44460-9654
    330-332-9951
Fax: 330-332-2208 888-919-9494
info@lehmannmills.com www.lehmannmills.com
Three-roll horizontal mills, Three-roll vertical mills, Technical field service Installation start-up and supervision, Operator training and maintenance, Consultation services, In-house CAD engineering, Custom-designed upgrades, Problemsolving capabilities
Owner: David Hrovatic
info@lehmannmills.com
Estimated Sales: $5-10 Million
Number Employees: 20-49

7323 Lehr Brothers
12901 Packing House Road
Edison, CA 93220
    661-366-3244
Fax: 661-366-1449 spudron1@aol.com
Processor and exporter of potatoes
President: Ronald Lehr
VP: Ronald Lehr Jr
Estimated Sales: $17,155,306
Number Employees: 50
Square Footage: 45000
Type of Packaging: Bulk

7324 Leiby's Premium Ice Cream
116 Mountain Rd
Tamaqua, PA 18252
    570-668-2399
Fax: 570-668-6065 877-453-4297
sales.leibys@earthlink.net
www.leibysicecream.com
Ice cream including mixes
President: Keith Zimmerman
VP/Secretary: William Parks
Estimated Sales: $5-10 Million
Number Employees: 10-19
Square Footage: 120000
Type of Packaging: Consumer, Bulk

7325 Leidenfrost Vineyards
5677 Route 414
PO Box 221
Hector, NY 14841
    607-546-2800
Wines
Owner: John Leidenfrost
Estimated Sales: $340,000
Number Employees: 4
Brands:
    Leidenfrost Vineyards

7326 Leidenheimer Baking Co
1501 Simon Bolivar Ave
New Orleans, LA 70113-2329
    504-525-1575
Fax: 504-525-1596 800-259-9099
info@leidenheimer.com www.leidenheimer.com
Manufacturer of fresh and frozen New Orleans style French breads and rolls
President: Robert Whann
Year Founded: 1896
Estimated Sales: $20 Million
Number Employees: 50-99
Square Footage: 40000
Type of Packaging: Consumer, Food Service

7327 Leidy's
382 Main Street
PO Box 2
Harleysville, PA 19438-0002
    215-723-4606
Fax: 215-721-2003 800-222-2319
www.leidys.com
Pork processing.
President/CEO: Jim Van Stone
CFO: Sally Schukraft
General Manager: Todd Wood
Contact: Karen Brown
karen@leidys.com
Estimated Sales: $20-50 Million
Number Employees: 100-249
Number of Brands: 1
Type of Packaging: Consumer, Bulk
Brands:
    Leidy's

7328 Leigh Olivers
PO Box 8346
Tyler, TX 75711
    903-245-9183
Fax: 903-421-1669
customerservice@leigholivers.com
www.leigholivers.com
Dips/salsa and cheeses
CEO: Leigh Vickery
VP: Ron Vickery

Food Manufacturers / A-Z

7329 (HQ)Leighton's Honey Inc
1203 W Commerce Ave
Haines City, FL 33844-3271
863-422-1773
Fax: 863-421-2299 leightonshoney@verizon.net
www.leightonshoney.com
Manufacturer and packer of pure honey.
President: Paul McCord
VP: Janet McCord
Year Founded: 1950
Estimated Sales: $2.5-5 Million
Number Employees: 10-19
Number of Brands: 2
Type of Packaging: Consumer, Food Service, Private Label, Bulk
Brands:
  Leighton's
  Orange Blossom Special

7330 Leinenkugel's
124 E Elm St
Chippewa Falls, WI 54729
888-534-6437
leinielodge@leinenkugels.com www.leinie.com
Alcoholic malt beverages, beer
President: Bill Leinenkugel
CFO: Dave Kahn
VP Marketing: Richard Leininkugel
Point-of-Sale Manager: John Leininkugel
Operations Manager: Pete Dawson
Estimated Sales: $5-10 Million
Number Employees: 50-99
Brands:
  Amber Light
  Berry Weiss
  Honey Weiss
  Leinenkugel Original
  Light
  Northwoods
  Oktoberfest
  Red

7331 Leiner Health Products
901 E 233rd St
Carson, CA 90745
310-835-8400
Fax: 310-952-7760
Vitamins
President: Gale Bansussen
CEO: Bob Kaminski
CEO: Robert R Reynolds
Manager Sales/Marketing: Tom Bovich
Contact: Lucy Bartelson
lbartels@leiner.com
Number Employees: 500-999
Brands:
  Beneflex
  Bumble Bee
  Cardio Discovery
  Liquimax
  Natural Life
  Omega Care
  Pharmacist Formula

7332 Lejeune's Bakery Inc
1510 Main St
Jeanerette, LA 70544-3528
337-276-5690
www.lejeunesbakery.com
Baked goods
Owner: Matthew Juene
Estimated Sales: Less Than $500,000
Number Employees: 1-4

7333 Lekithos
Palm Beach Gardens, FL 33403
lekithos.com
Plant protein powders

7334 Lemate Of New England Inc
11 Perry Dr # C
Unit C
Foxboro, MA 02035-1047
508-543-9035
Fax: 781-784-7369 sales@lematecocktailmix.com
www.lematecocktailmix.com
Sweetened cocktail mixes and flavored syrups.
Founded in 1977.
President: Kevin Christman
kevin@lematecocktailmix.com
Vice President: Marianne Christman
Number Employees: 5-9
Type of Packaging: Consumer, Food Service, Private Label, Bulk

7335 Lemke Wholesale
1225 N 8th St
Rogers, AR 72756
479-751-4671
Fax: 501-751-4671
Variety of food products.
President: Arnold E Lemke
Secretary: Lorene Lemke
Vice-President: Ronald Lemke

7336 Lemmes Company
7 Alice Street
Coventry, RI 02816-7300
401-821-2575
Spaghetti sauce, grated cheese, BBQ sauce, relish, jam, mustard
President: Michael Lemme
Estimated Sales: $2.5-5 000,000
Number Employees: 1

7337 Lemon & Vine
1340 4th Street
Napa, CA 94559
707-926-6073
Fax: 707-927-3514 info@lemonandvine.com
www.lemonandvine.com
Greek appetizers

7338 Lemon Creek Winery
533 E Lemon Creek Rd
Berrien Springs, MI 49103-9714
269-471-1321
Fax: 269-471-1322 lemoncreekwinery@gmail.com
www.lemoncreekwinery.com
Wines
Owner: Jeff Lemon
lemoncreekwinery@gmail.com
Estimated Sales: $1.8 Million
Number Employees: 10-19
Brands:
  Lemon Creek Winery

7339 Lemon-X Corporation
168 Railroad Street
Huntington Station, NY 11746
631-424-2850
Fax: 631-424-2852   800-220-1061
sales@lemon-x.com www.lemon-x.com
Juices and cocktail mixes.
President: James Grassi
Co-Founder: Sonja Grassi
Contact: Greg Aluise
galuise@lemon-x.com
Estimated Sales: $20-50 Million
Number Employees: 100-249
Number of Brands: 5
Type of Packaging: Consumer, Food Service, Private Label, Bulk
Brands:
  CareTree
  Growers Fancy Juice
  Honey Bear Farms
  Lemon-X
  Moon Lake

7340 LemonKind
349 5th Avenue
New York, NY 10016
954-678-1700
info@drinklemonkind.com
drinklemonkind.com
Ready-to-drink teas and juice beverages
Founder: Irene Rojas
Number of Brands: 1
Number of Products: 8
Type of Packaging: Consumer
Brands:
  LEMONKIND

7341 Lemoncocco
66 S Hanford St
Suite 150
Seattle, WA 98134
206-624-3357
info@drinklemoncocco.com
drinklemoncocco.com
Coconut and lemon beverage

7342 Lemur International
3701 Collins Ave
Suite 3N
Richmond, CA 94806
510-620-9708
Fax: 510-620-9965 www.lemurinc.com
Organic vanilla and essential oils

7343 Len Libby Chocolatier-Maine
419 Us Route 1
Scarborough, ME 04070
207-883-4897
Fax: 207-885-5824 lenlibby@lenlibby.com
www.lenlibby.com
Chocolates and candies
Owner: Len Libby
Vice President: Maureen Hemond
Estimated Sales: $500,000-$1 Million
Number Employees: 10-19

7344 Lenchner Bakery
50 Drumlin Circle
Concord, ON L4K 3G1
Canada
905-738-8811
Fax: 905-738-3822 www.lenchners.com
Processor and exporter of kosher frozen entrees and dessert pastries including chocolate, almond, cheese, apple, blueberry, cherry, prune, lemon, spinach feta cheese, potato onion, etc.; also, bagels; private labeling available
President: Zeev Lenchner
Estimated Sales: $1-2.5 Million
Number Employees: 20-49
Square Footage: 40000
Parent Co: Lechner's
Type of Packaging: Consumer, Food Service, Private Label, Bulk
Brands:
  Boueka
  Rrrogala

7345 Lender's Bagels
PO Box 971
Miami, FL 33152
800-768-6287
www.lendersbagels.com
Bagels

7346 Lendy's Cafe Raw Bar
1581 General Booth Blvd # 101
Virginia Beach, VA 23454-5106
757-491-3511
Fax: 757-491-8821
Sauces including buffalo wing, habanero hot and barbecue
Owner: Kent Von Fecht
lendys1@cox.net
Estimated Sales: Less than $500,000
Number Employees: 10-19
Square Footage: 5000
Type of Packaging: Consumer, Food Service, Private Label, Bulk
Brands:
  Buckman's Best
  Buckman's Best Snack

7347 Lengacher's Cheese House
5015 Lincoln Highway
Kinzers, PA 17535-9709
717-355-6490
Cheese
President: Arthur Lengacher
Estimated Sales: $500,000 appx.
Number Employees: 1-4

7348 Lengerich Meats Inc
3095 Van Horn
P.O. Box 411
Zanesville, IN 46799-9027
260-638-4123
lengerich@frontier.com
www.lengerichmeatsinc.us
Beef, pork and lunch meats
Owner: Amy Stephan
Sales Manager: Debbie Woods
lengerichmeats@frontier.com
Estimated Sales: $670,000
Number Employees: 10-19
Type of Packaging: Consumer, Food Service

7349 Lennox Farm
518024 County Rd 124/RR 2
Shelburne, ON L0N 1S6
Canada
519-925-6444
Fax: 519-925-3285
Fresh and frozen rhubarb
President: William French

Food Manufacturers / A-Z

Estimated Sales: $1.4 Million
Number Employees: 12
Type of Packaging: Consumer, Food Service
Brands:
    Lennox

7350 Lenny & Larry's
14300 Arminta St
Panorama City, CA 91402
    www.lennylarry.com
Cookies, muffins and brownies
CEO: Barry Turner
Number of Brands: 3
Type of Packaging: Consumer
Brands:
    THE COMPLETE COOKIE
    THE MUSCLE MUFFIN
    THE MUSCLE BROWNIE

7351 Lenny's Bee Productions
403 Wittenberg Road
Bearsville, NY 12409-5635
    845-679-4514
Smoked trout, bee pollen and honey products
President: Leonardo Busciguo
Vice President: Lynn Duvall
Contact: Lenny Bee
lennysbeeproductions@gmail.com
Type of Packaging: Consumer, Food Service, Private Label
Brands:
    Lenny's Bee Productions

7352 Lenox-Martell Inc
89 Heath St
Boston, MA 02130-1402
    617-442-7777
    Fax: 617-522-9455 877-325-2489
    www.lenoxmartell.com
Processor of colas and juices; wholesaler/distributor of refrigerators and ice and soda machines; serving the food service market; also, installation and maintenance of draft beer systems available
CEO/Sales Executive: Jim Lerner
jlerner@lenoxmartell.com
Controller: David Nitishin
VP Marketing: John Dixon
Sales/Marketing: Jessica Miller
Operations Director: Rick Freitas
Year Founded: 1950
Estimated Sales: $8 Million
Number Employees: 50-99
Square Footage: 120000

7353 Lenson Coffee & Tea Company
PO Box 1103
Pleasantville, NJ 08232-6103
    609-646-3003
    Fax: 609-646-8606
Coffee; wholesaler/distributor of tea; serving the food service market
Owner: Jimmie Anderson
Estimated Sales: $5-10 Million
Number Employees: 20-49
Type of Packaging: Consumer, Food Service, Private Label

7354 Lentia Enterprises Ltd.
17733-66th Ave
Surrey, BC V3S 7X1
Canada
    604-576-8838
    Fax: 604-576-1064 888-768-7368
Naturally fermented, dehydrated sourdoughs from both wheat and rye flours, specialty malted products such as whole malted rye kernels, aroma malts, colouring malts and clean label bread mixes.
President/Board Member: Karl Eibensteiner
Director: Gertrude Eibensteiner
Estimated Sales: $4.08 Million
Number Employees: 23

7355 Leo G. Atkinson Fisheries
89 Daniel Head Road
South Side
Clarks Harbor, NS B0W 1P0
Canada
    902-745-3047
    Fax: 902-745-1245
Processor and exporter of fresh, frozen and salted seafood including haddock, cod, halibut and lobster.
Founded in 1983.
President: Leo Atkinson

Estimated Sales: $9.9 Million
Number Employees: 20
Type of Packaging: Consumer, Food Service, Private Label, Bulk

7356 Leo G. Fraboni Sausage Company
1202 13th Ave E
Hibbing, MN 55746-1218
    218-263-5074
    Fax: 218-263-5074 sales@frabonis.com
    www.frabonis.com
Smoked Polish sausages and frozen beef patties
President: Mark Thune
VP: Wayne Thune
Plant Manager: Don Johnson
Estimated Sales: $.5-1 million
Number Employees: 5-9
Type of Packaging: Consumer, Private Label, Bulk

7357 Leo's Bakery
1179 Ocean St
Marshfield, MA 02050
    781-837-3300
    Fax: 781-837-8949
Bakery products
President: Robert Gagnon
Estimated Sales: $500,000-$1 000,000
Number Employees: 10-19

7358 Leo's Bakery & Deli
101 Despatch Dr
East Rochester, NY 14445-1447
    585-249-1000
    Fax: 585-249-9231 www.leoselite.com
Baked goods
Owner: Patrick Bernunzio
bakery@watermark101.com
Estimated Sales: $630,000
Number Employees: 20-49
Type of Packaging: Consumer, Food Service, Private Label, Bulk
Brands:
    Elite Bakery

7359 Leon's Bakery
1000 Universal Dr N
North Haven, CT 06473-3151
    203-234-0115
    Fax: 203-234-7620 800-223-6844
Frozen dough; exporter of wheat and white rolls
President: Luis Alpizar
CEO: John Ruth
CFO: Eric Olson
Sales Manager: Terry Ginn
Plant Manager: Fred Macey
Estimated Sales: $5-10 Million
Number Employees: 5-9
Square Footage: 300000
Type of Packaging: Food Service, Private Label, Bulk

7360 Leon's Texas Cuisine
2100 Redbud Blvd
Mckinney, TX 75069-8215
    972-529-5050
    Fax: 972-529-2244 scott@texascuisine.com
    www.texascuisine.com
Producer of corny dogs and stuffed jalapenos
Senior VP: John Vroman
john@texascuisine.com
Director of Sales: Nickolas Hancock
Human Resources: Michell Ramos
Sr. Vice President of Operations: John Vroman
Estimated Sales: $500,000-$1 Million
Number Employees: 100-249
Brands:
    Leon's Texas Cuisine

7361 Leona Meat Plant
PO Box 156
Troy, PA 16947
    570-297-3574
    Fax: 570-297-3562 www.leonameatplant.com
Meat including ham, bacon and sausage
President: Charles Debach II
Estimated Sales: $1200000
Number Employees: 5-9
Type of Packaging: Consumer

7362 Leona's Restaurante
4 Medina Ln
Chimayo, NM 87522
    505-351-4569
    888-561-5569

Produces a wide range of unique New Mexican products, including ristras; salsas and sauces; ground and dried items; coffee and tea; and preserves and snacks.
Owner: Leona Tiede
leonas@cybermesa.com
Estimated Sales: Less Than $500,000
Number Employees: 1-4
Number of Brands: 1
Type of Packaging: Consumer
Brands:
    LEONA'S

7363 Leonard Fountain Specialties
4601 Nancy Avenue
Detroit, MI 48212-1213
    313-891-4141
    Fax: 313-892-9200 www.leonardssyrups.com
Syrups, juices and frozen cocktails.
CEO: Leonard Bugajewski
CFO: Sherri Iskra
Product Development & Marketing: Stephen Bugajewski
Plant Manager: John Bamford
Estimated Sales: $5-10 Million
Number Employees: 100-249
Number of Brands: 9
Square Footage: 75
Type of Packaging: Food Service, Private Label
Brands:
    Bar-Pak
    Bulk Co2
    Frosty Pak
    Lemon Twist
    Orange Mist
    Polar Pak
    Quali-Tea
    Thrifty Pak
    Tropical Mist

7364 Leonard Mountain Inc
17402 E 176th St S
Bixby, OK 74008-7527
    918-366-2800
    Fax: 918-366-0335 800-822-7700
    office@leonardmountain.com
    www.leonardmountain.com
Fruit and vegetable dips, pasta salads, bread mixes, rice mixes, olives, soups, chili and pickled vegetables.
President: Debbie Berckefeldt
Estimated Sales: $10-20 Million
Number Employees: 5-9
Number of Brands: 7
Type of Packaging: Private Label
Brands:
    Boot Scootin'
    Leonard Mountain
    Mama Leone's
    Miss Leone's
    Pappy's
    Purely American
    Redneck

7365 Leonardo's of Vermont, LLC
1160 Williston Rd.
South Burlington, VT 05403
    902-863-8404
Manufacturer of pizza sauces.
President and Co-Owner: Sara Byers
Co-Owner: Kelly Byers

7366 Leonetti Cellar
1875 Foothills Ln
Walla Walla, WA 99362-9052
    509-525-1670
    Fax: 509-525-4006 info@leonetticellar.com
    www.leonetticellar.com
Wines
Owner: Nancy Figgins
nancy@leonetticellar.com
VP Operations: Chris Figgins
Marketing: Nancy Figgins
Vineyard Manager: Jason Magnaghi
Estimated Sales: $500,000-$1 Million
Number Employees: 10-19
Parent Co: FIGGINS FAMILY WINE ESTATES
Brands:
    Leonetti Cellar

Food Manufacturers / A-Z

7367 Leonetti's Frozen Food
5935 Woodland Ave
Philadelphia, PA 19143-5919
215-729-4200
Fax: 215-729-7581 866-551-7168
leonettifrozenfo@aol.com www.beststromboli.com
Frozen stromboli and calzones
President: Beth Di Pietro
leonettifrozenfo@aol.com
Plant Manager: Leroy Douglas
Estimated Sales: $1500000
Number Employees: 20-49
Square Footage: 132000
Type of Packaging: Consumer, Food Service, Private Label, Bulk
Brands:
  Leonetti's

7368 Lepage Bakeries
Country Kitchen Plaza
PO Box 1900
Auburn, ME 04211-1900
207-783-9161
lbck@lepagebakeries.com
Bread, rolls, English muffins and donuts
President/CEO: Andrew Barowsky
Chairman: Albert Lepage
VP: Thomas Mato
Contact: Betty Bartos
betty.bartos@lepagebakeries.com
Estimated Sales: $5-10 Million
Number Employees: 525
Type of Packaging: Consumer

7369 Leprino Foods Co.
1830 W. 38th Ave.
Denver, CO 80211
303-480-2600
Fax: 303-480-2605 800-537-7466
www.leprinofoods.com
Mozzarella cheese, cheese blends, and pizza cheese made especially for pizzeria and foodservice operators, frozen food manufacturers and private label cheese packagers.
Chairman/CEO: James Leprino
CFO/SVP, Operations: Lance FitzSimmons
Year Founded: 1950
Estimated Sales: Over $1 Billion
Number Employees: 4,000+
Square Footage: 60000
Type of Packaging: Food Service, Bulk
Other Locations:
  Leprino Foods
    Allendale MI
  Leprino Foods
    Fort Morgan CO
  Leprino Foods
    Ravenna NE
  Leprino Foods
    Remus MI
  Leprino Foods
    Roswell NM
  Leprino Foods
    Waverly NY

7370 Leraysville Cheese Factory
42 Chedder Ln
Le Raysville, PA 18829-7922
570-744-2554
Fax: 570-744-1050 800-595-5196
info@leraysvillecheese.com
www.leraysvillecheese.com
Cheese
President: Milton Repsher Jr.
m.repsher@leraysvillecheese.com
Estimated Sales: Less than $500,000
Number Employees: 5-9
Type of Packaging: Private Label

7371 Leroux Creek
9754 3100 Rd
Hotchkiss, CO 81419-6114
970-872-2256
Fax: 970-872-2250 877-970-5670
www.␣lerouxcreek.com
Organic apple sauce and fruit puree.
President: Edward Tuft
edward@lerouxcreek.com
Quality Control: Wende Michael
Marketing: Sarah Tuft
Operations: Amy Sanders
Plant Manager: Arturo Mendoza
Purchasing: Edward Tuft
Estimated Sales: $1500000
Number Employees: 20-49
Number of Products: 14
Type of Packaging: Consumer, Private Label
Brands:
  Leroux Creek

7372 Leroy Hill Coffee Co Inc
3278 Halls Mill Rd
PO Box 6219
Mobile, AL 36606-2502
251-476-1234
Fax: 251-476-1296 800-866-5282
goodtasteiseverything@leroyhillcoffee.com
www.hillandbrooks.com
Coffee and tea.
President: Deborah Hill
CEO: Roger Burchett
rburchett@hillandbrooks.com
General Sales Manager: Greg King
Estimated Sales: $15-20 Million
Number Employees: 100-249
Number of Brands: 1
Type of Packaging: Private Label
Brands:
  Leroy Hill

7373 (HQ)Leroy Smith Inc
4776 Old Dixie Hwy
Vero Beach, FL 32967-1239
772-569-2059
Fax: 772-567-8428 www.leroysmith.com
Manufacturer and exporter of citrus fruit including grapefruit and oranges.
CEO: Elson Smith
elson.smith@leroysmith.com
Year Founded: 1947
Number Employees: 100-249
Type of Packaging: Consumer
Brands:
  Golden Magic
  Island Fruit
  Magic River
  Mystic River

7374 Lerro Candy Company
P.O. Box 106
Darby, PA 19023
610-461-8886
sales@lerrocandyco.com
www.lerrocandyco.com
Confectionery products including chocolate cherries
Owner/Manager: John Lerro
Estimated Sales: $$2.5-5 Million
Number Employees: 10-19
Type of Packaging: Consumer

7375 Les Aliments Livabec Foods
95 Rang St Louis Rr 2
Sherrington, QC J0L 2N0
Canada
450-454-7971
Fax: 450-454-9100 info@livabec.ca
www.livabec.ca/accueil
Processor and exporter of marinated mixed and roasted vegetables and mushrooms in oil; processor of antipasto calabrese, basil and sun-dried tomato pesto; importer of sun-dried tomatoes
President: Lino Cimagila
VP: Lino Cimaglia, Jr.
Estimated Sales: $2 Million
Number Employees: 3
Square Footage: 50000
Brands:
  Livabec
  Livia

7376 Les Aliments Ramico Foods
8245 Rue Le Creusot
St. Leonard, QC HIP 2A2
Canada
514-329-1844
Fax: 514-329-5096
Beans, soups, sauces, chicken and meat with beans
Director: Rami Matta
VP: Galal Matta
Estimated Sales: G
Number Employees: 10-19
Square Footage: 12000
Type of Packaging: Private Label

7377 Les Boulangers AssociesInc
18842 13th Pl S
Seatac, WA 98148-2399
206-241-9343
Fax: 206-433-2844 800-522-1185
gsimeon@lba-inc.com www.lba-inc.com
Frozen dough, thaw and serve pastries
Owner: Michel Robert
michel@lba-inc.com
Owner: Lynne Andagan
Vice President: Randal Chicoine
Food & Beverage Operations Manager: Philippe Janicka
Estimated Sales: $5-10 Million
Number Employees: 20-49
Type of Packaging: Private Label
Brands:
  French Does
  Lba

7378 Les Bourgeois Vineyards
12847 W Highway Bb
Rocheport, MO 65279-9496
573-698-2300
Fax: 573-698-2170 800-690-1830
info@missouriwine.com www.missouriwine.com
Wines
Owner: Curtis Bourgeois
bistro@missouriwine.com
CEO: Rachel Mills
Marketing Specialist: Tia Stratman
Director of Sales: Tim Weiss
bistro@missouriwine.com
VP Winery Operations: Cory Bomgaars
Estimated Sales: Below $5 Million
Number Employees: 50-99
Type of Packaging: Private Label
Brands:
  Les Bourgeois

7379 Les Brasseurs Du Nord
875 Michele Bohec Boulevard
Blainville, QC J7C 5J6
Canada
450-979-8400
Fax: 450-979-3733 800-378-3733
commentaires@boreale.com www.boreale.com/fr
Processor and distributor of beer, ale and stout
Marketing Manager: Bernard Morin
Vice President: Laura Urtinowski
CEO: Daniel Lampron
Estimated Sales: $5-10 Million
Number Employees: 50-99
Square Footage: 140000
Type of Packaging: Consumer, Food Service
Brands:
  Ber Boreale

7380 Les Brasseurs GMT
5585 De La Rouche
Montreal, QC H2J 3K3
Canada
514-274-4941
Fax: 514-274-6138 888-253-8330
info@brasseursrj.com www.brasseursrj.com
Beer, ale, lager and stout
Manager: Alain Hudon
Partner: Brasserie Le Cheval Blanc
Pioneer: Les Brasseurs GMT
Number Employees: 100-249
Type of Packaging: Consumer, Food Service
Brands:
  Belle Gueule

7381 Les Chocolats Vadeboncoeur Inc.
8350 Parkway D'Anjou
Montreal, QC H1K 4S3
Canada
514-493-8504
Fax: 514-483-3956 800-276-8504
www.chocolatvadeboncoeur.com
Chocolate

7382 Les Industries Bernard et Fils
104 Rue Industrielle Du Boise
Saint Victor, QC G0M 2B0
Canada
418-588-3590
Fax: 418-588-6836 martin@bernards.ca
www.bernards.ca
Processor and exporter of pure maple and fruit syrups
President: Yves Bernard
Marketing Director: Martin Bernard

Food Manufacturers / A-Z

Estimated Sales: $4.4 Million
Number Employees: 35
Type of Packaging: Consumer, Food Service, Private Label, Bulk

7383 Les Mouts De P.O.M.
169 Rang 2
Sain-Francois-Xavier, QC J0B 2V0
Canada
819-845-5555
Fax: 819-845-2555
Tea, juice/cider, non-alcoholic and cold non-carbonated beverages
Marketing: Guy Bergeron

7384 Les Palais Des Thes
1001 Ave Of The Americas
Suite 1117
New York, NY 10018
917-515-2887
Fax: 212-813-2883
wholesale@us.palaisdesthes.com
www.palaisdesthes.com
Functional (antioxidants), vegetarian, tea, soft drinks.
Marketing: Cyrille Bessiere

7385 Les Salaisons Brochu
183 Route Du President-Kennedy
St. Henri De Levis, QC G0R 3E0
Canada
418-882-2282
Fax: 418-882-5212
Fresh and frozen pork
Contact: Laurent Brochu
Number Employees: 250-499
Type of Packaging: Consumer, Food Service, Private Label

7386 Les Trois Petits Cochons
4223 1st Ave
2nd Floor
Brooklyn, NY 11232
212-219-1230
Fax: 212-941-9726 800-537-7283
info@3pigs.com 3pigs.com
Pates, mini terrines, mousses, vegetable and seafood terrines, charouterie and pork free products.
President: Alain Sinturel
CEO: Jean Pierre Pradie
Year Founded: 1975
Estimated Sales: $20-50 Million
Number Employees: 20-49

7387 Les Viandes du Breton
150 Ch Des Raymond
Riviere-Du-Lup, QC G5R 5X8
Canada
418-863-6711
Fax: 416-863-6767 service@dubreton.com
www.dubreton.com
Fresh and frozen pork; exporter of hams, spare ribs, bellies, etc.
President: Vincent Breton
VP, Administration & Finance: Marie Jos,e Landry
Year Founded: 1944
Estimated Sales: $169 Million
Number Employees: 550
Parent Co: Bose Corporation
Type of Packaging: Consumer, Food Service, Private Label, Bulk
Brands:
  Dubreton Natural

7388 Les Viandes or Fil
2080 Rue Monterey
Laval, QC H7L 3S3
Canada
450-687-5664
Fax: 450-687-2733
Processor and exporter of fresh and frozen pork
President: Antonio Filice
Vice President: Bernard Paquette
Estimated Sales: $15 Million
Number Employees: 50
Type of Packaging: Bulk

7389 Lesaffre Yeast Corporation
7475 W Main St.
Milwaukee, WI 53214
414-615-4094
800-770-2714
www.lesaffreyeast.com
Yeast
President & CEO: John Riesch

Parent Co: Lesaffre Group

7390 Lesley Elizabeth Inc
877 Whitney Dr
Lapeer, MI 48446-2565
810-667-0706
Fax: 810-667-7287 800-684-3300
sales@lesleyelizabeth.com
Gourmet sauces, oils, vinegarettes, pestos and crisps
President: Lesley Mc Cowen
CFO: Sally Burrell
sally@lesleyelizabeth.com
Marketing: Gary Bates
Estimated Sales: $1-5 Million
Number Employees: 10-19
Type of Packaging: Private Label
Brands:
  Lesley Elizabeth
  Lesley Elizabeth's Crisps
  Lesley Elizabeth's Dipping Oils
  Lesley Elizabeth's Dips
  Lesley Elizabeth's Pesto
  Lesley Elizabeth's Vinegarettes
  Lesley Marinara

7391 Lesley Stowe Fine Foods
Richmond, BC V6V 1J6
Canada
604-238-2180
www.lesleystowe.com
Crackers and crisps
Founder/Consultant: Lesley Stowe

7392 Leslie Leger & Sons
34 Chemin De La Cote
P.O.Box 1061
Cap-Pele, NB E4N 3B3
Canada
506-577-4730
Fax: 506-577-4960 sales@leslieandsons.com
http://www.leslieandsons.com
Processor and exporter of smoked herring and brined alewife
President: Leslie Leger
Estimated Sales: $4.8 Million
Number Employees: 35
Type of Packaging: Bulk

7393 Lesserevil Brand Snack Co
83 Newtown Rd
2nd Floor
Danbury, CT 06810-4118
203-529-3555
talk2us@lesserevil.com
lesserevil.com
All natural snacks
Contact: Corey Benson
corey@lesserevil.com
Number Employees: 1-4

7394 Lesserevil Brand Snack Co
83 Newtown Rd
Second Floor
Danbury, CT 06810-4118
203-529-3555
talk2us@lesserevil.com
lesserevil.com
Healthier snack foods, using black beans and organic popcorn
Contact: Corey Benson
corey@lesserevil.com
Number Employees: 1-4

7395 Let Them Eat Cake
3805 S West Shore Blvd # B
Tampa, FL 33611-1047
813-837-6888
Fax: 813-831-6741
www.chocolateismycrayon.com
Custom mini pastries
Owner: Michael Baugh
letthemeatcake@tampabay.rr.com
Chef of Icing and Decorating: Lori Maniscalco
Chef of Pastry: Jason Lucas
Marketing Manager: Michael Baugh
Estimated Sales: Less Than $500,000
Number Employees: 1-4

7396 Letterman Enterprises Inc.
109 Fairfield Dr
State College, PA 16801-8248
814-574-4339
Fax: 814-466-6820 david@lettermaninc.com
www.feeltheflavors.com

Ethnic sauces (soy, curry, etc.), grilling sauces, marinades, other sauces, seasonings and cooking enhancers, foodservice.
Marketing: David Letterman
Contact: David Letterman
d_letterman1919@hotmail.com

7397 Levain
167 W 74th St # A
New York, NY 10023-2216
212-874-6080
Fax: 212-874-6413 www.levainbakery.com
Baked goods, breads, cookie mix
Owner: Constance Mc Donald
connie@levainbakery.com
Estimated Sales: Less Than $500,000
Number Employees: 5-9

7398 Levant Mediterranean Snack Foods LLC
113 Neck Road
Unit 5
Haverhill, MA 01835
978-241-9986
Fax: 978-241-9566 www.levantsnacks.com
Manufacturer of falafel chips.
President: Joe Dunne

7399 Levesque
500 Beaumont St
Montreal, QC H3N 1T7
Canada
514-273-1702
Fax: 514-273-2325 877-539-1702
ventes@salaisonlevesque.qc.ca
www.salaisonlevesque.qc.ca
Ham products
President/Owner: M Regis Levesque
VP: Mme Annie Levesque
Estimated Sales: $7.1 Million
Number Employees: 30

7400 Lew-Mark Baking Company
Fl 10
1000 N West St
Wilmington, DE 19801-1059
269-962-6205
Fax: 716-237-2735
Baked goods
President/CEO: M Serventi
Marketing Director: John Wheeler
Number Employees: 20-49
Parent Co: Archway Cookies

7401 Lewes Dairy Inc
660 Pilottown Rd
Lewes, DE 19958-1299
302-645-6281
Fax: 302-645-6290 info@lewesdairy.com
www.lewesdairy.com
Dairy products
Owner: Chip Brittingham
lewesdairy@dmv.com
Vice President: Walter Brittingham
Estimated Sales: $2.3 Million
Number Employees: 20-49
Type of Packaging: Consumer

7402 Lewis Bakeries Inc
500 N Fulton Ave
Evansville, IN 47710-1571
812-425-4642
Fax: 812-425-7609 www.lewisbakeries.net
Large independent bakery in the Midwest.
CFO: Jeffery Sankovitch
jsankovitch@lewisbakeries.com
Number Employees: 1000-4999
Type of Packaging: Consumer, Food Service, Private Label, Bulk
Other Locations:
  Headquarters
  Evansville IN
  Bakery
  Murfreesboro TN
  Bakery
  Ft. Wayne IN
  Bakery
  LaPorte IN
  Bakery
  Vincennes IN
Brands:
  Bunny
  Chief Kahai
  Hartford Farms
  Healthy Life

877

Food Manufacturers / A-Z

Gateway
Indiana Spud
Lewis

7403 Lewis Cellars
4101 Big Ranch Rd
Napa, CA 94558-1406
707-255-3400
Fax: 707-255-3402 info@lewiscellars.com
www.lewiscellars.com
Wines
Owner: Randy Lewis
info@lewiscellars.com
CEO: John Lewis
CFO: Debbie Lewis
Estimated Sales: Less Than $500,000
Number Employees: 1-4

7404 Lewis Laboratories International Ltd.
P.O. Box 373
Southport, CT 06890
203-226-7343
Fax: 203-454-0329 800-243-6020
customerservice@lewis-labs.com
Nutritional supplements
President: Diana Lewis
Vice President: Myron Lewis
Estimated Sales: $500,000-$1 Million
Number Employees: 5-9
Brands:
Brewer's
Fabulous Fiber
Famous Original Formula Staminex
Lewis Labs Rda
Super Fabulous Fiber
Weigh Down

7405 Lewis Sausage Corporation
1050 Old Savannah Road
Burgaw, NC 28425
910-259-2642
Fax: 910-259-9881
Smoked and mild sausage
President: Edgar Hardy
Estimated Sales: $3 Million
Number Employees: 25
Type of Packaging: Consumer

7406 Lexington Coffee & Tea
2571 Regency Rd
Lexington, KY 40503-2920
859-277-1102
Fax: 859-277-6490
contactus@lexingtoncoffeeandtea.com
lexingtoncoffeeandtea.com
roasted coffee and tea. Some of their varieties include African City Roast, Costa Rican Tarrazu, Gourmet Five Star, Mocha Java, Indonesian City Roast, French Roast, Chocolate Hazelnut, Hazelnut French Roast and more.
Owner: Terri Wood
accounts@lexingtoncoffeeandtea.com
Estimated Sales: $5-10 000,000
Number Employees: 2-10
Brands:
Lexington Coffee Tea

7407 Li'l Guy Foods
3631 N Kimball Dr
Kansas City, MO 64161-9474
816-241-2000
Fax: 816-241-2025 800-886-8226
www.lilguyfoods.com
Mexican foods including corn tortillas, flour tortillas, flavored tortilla wraps, taco shells, tortilla chips, spices, taco sauce and salsa picante, cheeses and chorizo and chicharones.
President: David Sloan
VP, Director of Sales: Christina Sloan
VP: Edward Sloan
Director of Sales: Roberto Vidal
Office Manager/Customer Service: Jennifer Hart
Plant Manager: Edward Sloan
Estimated Sales: $2000000
Number Employees: 20-49
Square Footage: 120000
Parent Co: Sloan Acquisition Corporation
Type of Packaging: Consumer, Food Service
Brands:
Li'l Guy
V&V Supremo Cheeses & Meats

7408 LiDestri Food & Drink
815 W Whitney Rd
Fairport, NY 14450
585-377-7700
lidestrifoodanddrink.com
Sauces, dips and beverages for contract manufacturing and private label
Co-President, Sales and Supply Chain: John LiDestri
CEO: Giovanni LiDestri
VP, Finance: Jennifer Shepker
Co-President and CMO: Stefani LiDestri
Contact: David Leifer
dleifer@bridgesinc.info
COO: Phil Viruso
Estimated Sales: $285 Million
Number Employees: 500
Number of Brands: 2
Square Footage: 260000
Type of Packaging: Consumer, Private Label, Bulk
Other Locations:
Rochester NY
Fresno CA
Pennsauken NJ
Lansdale PA
Brands:
Cantisano
Francesco Rinaldi

7409 Liberty Natural Products Inc
20949 S Harris Rd
Oregon City, OR 97045-9428
503-631-4488
Fax: 503-631-2424 800-289-8427
jim@libertynatural.com www.libertynatural.com
Processor and exporter of gourmet breath fresheners, natural flavors and oils; processor of vitamins; importer of essential oils and botanical extracts; wholesaler/distributor of gourmet breath fresheners
Owner: Jim Derking
Sales Manager: Tabor Helton
jim@libertynatural.com
Operations Manager: Shane Reaney
Purchasing Manager: Michelle Falls
Estimated Sales: $1-2.5 Million
Number Employees: 20-49
Square Footage: 68000
Type of Packaging: Consumer, Bulk
Brands:
Max
Natural Gourmet Flavor Oil
Tib

7410 Liberty Orchards Co Inc
117 Mission Ave
P.O. Box C
Cashmere, WA 98815-1007
509-782-2191
Fax: 509-782-1487 800-231-3242
sales@libertyorchards.com
www.libertyorchards.com
Processor and exporter of confectionery products including chocolate, holiday and boxed nonchocolate candy
President: Sue Meiner
sue@libertyorchards.com
VP Marketing & Sales: Michael Rainey Sr
Estimated Sales: $12,377,000
Number Employees: 50-99
Type of Packaging: Consumer, Food Service
Brands:
Aplets
Cotlets
Fruit Chocolates
Fruit Delights
Fruit Festives
Fruit Parfaits
Fruit Softees
Grapelets
Hawaiian Festives

7411 Liberty Vegetable Oil Co
15306 Carmenita Rd
Santa Fe Springs, CA 90670-5606
562-921-3567
Fax: 562-802-3476
liberty@libertyvegetableoil.com
www.libertyvegetableoil.com
Tree nut oils, organic and non-GMO oils.
President: Ronald Field
CEO: Irwin Field
rfield@libertyvegetableoil.com
VP: Edward Field
Quality Assurance: William Kelleghan
Sales & Purchasing: Ronald Field
VP Operations: Lee Hibma
Estimated Sales: $7.1 Million
Number Employees: 20-49
Brands:
Lvo

7412 Life Extension Foundation
3600 West Commercial Blvd
Fort Lauderdale, FL 33309
954-766-8144
Fax: 954-761-9199 888-895-4771
customerservice@lifeextension.com
www.lifeextension.com
Health and nutritional supplements.
President: Bill Faloon
Founder: Saul Kent
Chief Financial Officer: James Murray
Vice President, Sales & Marketing: Rey Searles
Vice President of Purchasing: Connie Richter
Estimated Sales: $25-50 Million
Number Employees: 200+
Type of Packaging: Consumer

7413 Life Force Specialty Foods
1055 Saddle Ridge Road
Moscow, ID 83843-8774
208-882-9158
Fax: 208-882-9158 877-657-9471
www.lifeforce-specialty-foods.com
Honey wine
President: Garrick Kruse
Estimated Sales: $5-9.9 Million
Number Employees: 8
Brands:
Life Force

7414 Life Plus Style Gourmet
65 Roosevelt Ave
Suite 107
Valley Stream, NY 11581
516-823-3001
Fax: 516-823-3003 www.coneyislandclassics.com
Kettle corn
Sales: Andy Appell
andyappell@gmail.com
Brands:
Coney Island Classics

7415 Life Spice & Ingredients LLC
216 W Chicago Ave # 2
Chicago, IL 60654-3100
312-274-9992
Fax: 312-274-2381 www.lifespiceingredients.com
Spices
President: Peter Garvy
pgarvy@lifespiceingredients.com
Vice President of Sales & Marketing: Lisa Stern
Vice President of Operations: Holland Schlutz
Estimated Sales: $25 Million
Number Employees: 5-9

7416 LifeAID
2833 Mission St
Santa Cruz, CA 95060
888-558-1113
www.lifeaidbevco.com
Sports drinks
Co-Founder: Orion Melehan
Co-Founder: Aaron Hinde

7417 LifeIce
129 W 20th St
Apt 4C
New York, NY 10011-3642
917-414-0309
855-543-3423
www.lifeice.com
Frozen snacks
Founder: Paulette Fox

7418 LifeTime
1967 N Glassell St
Orange, CA 92865-4320
714-634-9340
Fax: 714-634-9340 800-333-6168
Vitamins
President: Tom Pinkowski
Vice President of Sales/Marketing: Tom Pinkowski

Food Manufacturers / A-Z

7419 Lifeline Food Company, Inc.
426 Orange Avenue
Seaside, CA 93955
831-899-5040
Fax: 831-899-0285 www.lifetimecheese.com
Dairy and cheese
President: Jone Chappell
CEO: Greg Chappell
greg@lifetimecheese.com
CFO: Greg Chappell
Sales: Andres Borowiak
Estimated Sales: Below $5 Million
Number Employees: 5-9
Number of Brands: 2
Type of Packaging: Private Label
Brands:
  Dairytime
  Energy Bars
  Lifetime
  Lifetime Fat Free Cheese
  Lifetime Lactose/Fat Free Cheese
  Lifetime Low Fat Cheese
  Lifetime Low Fat Rice Cheese
  Soy Cheese

7420 Lifem Spice Ingredients
300 Cherry Lane
Palm Beach, FL 33480
561-844-6334
Fax: 561-844-6335 www.lifespiceingredients.com
Supplier of spice blends and flavor systems.
VP Operations: Howard Schultz
Contact: Bruce Armstrong
barmstrong@lifespiceingredients.com

7421 Lifestar Millennium
PO Box 3837
Sedona, AZ 86340
925-202-4302
Fax: 970-422-4739 877-422-4739
lsmail@lifestar.com
Processor and exporter of natural nutritional supplements; importer of grapeseed oil
President: J Bentley
Estimated Sales: $300,000-500,000
Number Employees: 1-4
Type of Packaging: Consumer, Food Service
Brands:
  Living Food Concentrates
  Multiplex

7422 Lifestyle Health Guide
1603 Capitol Ave
Suite 314
Cheyenne, WY 82001
307-529-1239
Fax: 805-650-0997 800-822-3712
Processor, exporter and importer of health products including nutritional supplements
Owner: Larry Permen
President: Jean Koven
VP: Larry Permen
Estimated Sales: $3-5,000,000
Number Employees: 1-4
Brands:
  Bread, Rice & Pasta Lovers Diet
  Dermagest
  Natragest
  Sound Sleep

7423 Lifeway
6431 W Oakton St
Morton Grove, IL 60053
847-967-1010
Fax: 847-967-6558 877-281-3874
lifewaykefir.com
Kefir, frozen kefir, specialty cheeses and probiotic beverages for kids
President and CEO: Julie Smolyansky
julies@lifeway.net
CFO: Eric Hanson
Sr. EVP, Sales: Amy Feldman
COO: Edward Smolyansky
Estimated Sales: $4 Million
Number Employees: 250-499
Square Footage: 240000
Type of Packaging: Consumer
Brands:
  Basics Plus
  Farmer's Cheese
  Kefir
  Kefir Starter
  La Fruta
  Soy Treat
  Sweet Kiss

7424 Lifewise Ingredients
3540 N 126 St
Suite D
Brookfield, IL 53005
262-788-9141
Fax: 262-788-9143 info@lifewise1.com
Processor and exporter of healthy food ingredients including monosodium glutamate replacements, flavor enhancers, and flavor maskers
Founder: Richard Share
Sales Director: Richard Share
Contact: Dean Antczak
dantczak@lifewise1.com
Lab Manager: Millie Galey
General Manager: Carol Bender
Estimated Sales: Below $5 Million
Number Employees: 5-9
Square Footage: 14000
Brands:
  Bitzels
  Lifewise Ingredients
  Potentiator Plus
  Simply Rich

7425 Light Rock Beverage Company
9 Balmforth Ave
Danbury, CT 06810
203-743-3410
Fax: 203-792-7909
Bottled water, other beverages
President: George Antous
Vice President: Fred Antous
General Manager: Thomas Antous
Estimated Sales: Below $5,000,000
Number Employees: 18
Brands:
  Light Rock

7426 Light Vision Confections
1776 Mentor Ave
Cincinnati, OH 45212-3554
513-351-9444
Fax: 253-981-0758 www.lightvision.com
Holographic confectionery items including lollypops, hard candy and chocolate
President: Eric Begleiter
CEO: Mike Wodke
CFO: Paul Graham
Contact: Wodke Krista
krista.wodke@lightvision.com
Estimated Sales: Below $5 Million
Number Employees: 20-30
Type of Packaging: Food Service, Private Label
Brands:
  Holopop
  Popart

7427 Lightlife
153 Industrial Blvd
Turners Falls, MA 01376
413-774-9000
Fax: 413-774-9080 800-769-3279
info@lightlife.com www.lightlife.com
Processor and exporter of soy-based products like chili, sausages, deli meats, ground meat, tempeh, chicken, burgers and bacon
President: Daniel Abrahamson
dabrahamson@lightlife.com
General Manager: Darcy Zbinovec
R&D: Ron Desautels
Human Resources Director: Bobby Riley
Product Manager: Dean Kuhlka
Year Founded: 1979
Estimated Sales: $20-50 Million
Number Employees: 100-249
Square Footage: 80000
Parent Co: Maple Leaf Foods
Brands:
  Gimme Lean
  Light Burgers
  Organic Flax Tempeh
  Organic Garden Veggie Tempeh
  Organic Smoky Tempeh Strips
  Organic Soy Tempeh
  Organic Three Grain Tempeh
  Organic Wild Rice Tempeh
  Smart Bacon
  Smart Bbq
  Smart Chili
  Smart Cutlets
  Smart Deli
  Smart Dogs
  Smart Ground
  Smart Links
  Smart Sausage
  Smart Tenders
  Smart Wings
  Tofu Pups

7428 Liguria Foods Inc
1515 15th St N
Humboldt, IA 50548-1017
515-332-4121
Fax: 515-332-2629 www.liguriafoods.com
Sausage and salami; exporter of hard and Genoa salami and pepperoni.
Owner: Roger Lawson
Estimated Sales: $25 Million
Number Employees: 50-99
Square Footage: 45000
Parent Co: SMG
Type of Packaging: Consumer, Food Service, Private Label, Bulk
Brands:
  Aquila D'Ora
  Beirmeister
  Buon Giorno
  Gratifica
  Liguria

7429 Lillie's Q
1856 W North Ave
Chicago, IL 60622
773-772-5500
www.lilliesq.com
Sauces, rubs, spices, marmalades, chips
Owner: Charlie McKenna
info@lilliesq.com
Number Employees: 20-49

7430 Lily of the Desert
1887 Geesling Rd
Denton, TX 76208
940-566-9914
Fax: 940-566-9925 800-229-5459
contact@lilyofthedesert.com
www.lilyofthedesert.com
Organic aloe vera beverages, cold brew coffee and tea, and dietary supplements
President: Don Lovelace
dlovelace@lilyofthedesert.com
Year Founded: 1971
Estimated Sales: $1-3 Million
Number Employees: 20-49
Type of Packaging: Consumer, Food Service, Private Label, Bulk
Brands:
  Lily of the Desert

7431 Lily's Sweets
4840 Pearl East Cir
Suite 201E
Boulder, CO 80301
877-587-0557
info@lilyssweets.com lilyssweets.com
Chocolate products sweetened with stevia
Co-Founder: Cynthia Tice
Co-Founder: Chuck Genuardi
Type of Packaging: Consumer
Brands:
  LILY'S

7432 Lilydale Foods
100 Commerce Valley Dr W
Markham, ON L3T 0A1
Canada
800-661-5341
www.lilydale.com
Fresh and frozen meats, poultry, sausages and sandwiches; also, further processed poultry products including fully cooked, par cooked, breaded and unbreaded.
Executive Chairman, Sofina Foods: Michael Latifi
President/CEO: Robert Wilt
Year Founded: 1940
Estimated Sales: Over $1 Billion
Number Employees: 2700
Square Footage: 81978
Parent Co: Sofina Foods Incorporated
Type of Packaging: Consumer, Food Service, Bulk
Brands:
  Lilydale

Food Manufacturers / A-Z

7433 Lima Grain Cereal Seeds LLC
2040 SE Frontage Rd
Fort Collins, CO 80525-9717
970-498-2200
Fax: 970-223-4302 LCS-info@limagrain.com
www.limagrain.com
Processor and distributor of breakfast cereals in boxes and bags
President: Bernie Blach
Secretary: Cindy Blach
CFO: Kelly Mundorf
Executive VP: Cedric Audebert
cedric.audebert@limagrain.com
Marketing/Technical Manager: Zach Gaines
Number Employees: 5-9
Square Footage: 80000
Type of Packaging: Consumer, Food Service, Private Label, Bulk
Brands:
  Colorado's Kernels
  Las Palomas Grandes
  Pop'n Snak

7434 Limehouse Produce Co
4791 Trade St # G
North Charleston, SC 29418-2824
843-556-3400
Fax: 843-556-3950 info@limehouseproduce.com
www.limehouseproduce.com
Fresh fruits and vegetables
Owner: John F Limehouse
Vice President: Andrea Limehouse
Sales: Ken Strange
limehouseproduce@comcast.net
Number Employees: 20-49

7435 Limited Edition
3106 N Big Spring St Ste 101
Midland, TX 79705
432-686-2008
Fax: 432-686-2035
Flavored honey butter, dip mixes, jalapenos, pickles and vegetables
Owner: Beverly Vaughan
Controller: Ann Wimberly
Estimated Sales: $300-500,000
Number Employees: 1-4
Square Footage: 20000
Type of Packaging: Consumer, Food Service, Private Label, Bulk
Brands:
  Limited Edition Presents
  Udderly Delightful

7436 Limitless
1500 W Carroll Ave
Chicago, IL 60607
sales@limitlesscoffee.com
limitlesscoffee.com
Cold brew coffee, coffee beans, green tea and sparkling water
Founder: Matt Matros
Co-Founder: Chris Fanucchi
Co-Founder: Craig Alexander

7437 Limpert Bros Inc
202 N West Blvd
Vineland, NJ 8360
856-691-1353
Fax: 856-794-8968 800-691-1353
www.limpertbrothers.com
Processor, importer and exporter of marshmallow fluff, hot fudge, cherries, butterscotch, carmel, and other toppings, flavors and ingredients.
President: Pearl Giordano
limpertbr@aol.com
R&D: Jim Behringer
Quality Control: Donna Phrampus
Estimated Sales: $1 Million
Number Employees: 10-19
Number of Brands: 1
Number of Products: 400
Square Footage: 280000
Type of Packaging: Food Service, Bulk
Brands:
  Limpert Brothers

7438 Lincourt Vineyards
1711 Alamo Pintado Rd
Solvang, CA 93463-9712
805-688-8554
Fax: 805-688-9327
customerservice@lincourtwines.com
www.lincourtwines.com
Red and white wines
Owner: Bill Foley
Number Employees: 10-19
Square Footage: 16000
Parent Co: Folly Estates
Type of Packaging: Consumer
Brands:
  Lin Court Vineyards

7439 Linda's Gourmet Latkes
PO Box 491413
Los Angeles, CA 90049
818-453-8690
Fax: 818-453-8679 888-452-8537
www.lindasgourmetlatkes.com
Latkes
President/Owner: Linda Hausberg
linda@lindasgourmetlatkes.com

7440 Linda's Lollies Company
1 International Blvd
Ste 208
Mahwan, NJ 07495-002
20- 25- 876
Fax: 201-252-8768 800-347-1545
info@lindaslollies.com www.lindaslollies.com
Processor and exporter of gourmet lollypops and confectionery gifts
President: Linda Harkavy
Sales & Marketing: Tammy Demone
Customer Services: Connie Atticella
Estimated Sales: $1500000
Number Employees: 1-4
Type of Packaging: Consumer, Food Service, Bulk
Brands:
  Linda's Little Lollies
  Linda's Lollies

7441 Linden Cheese Factory
P.O.Box 439
Linden, WI 53553
608-623-2531
Fax: 608-623-2567 800-660-5051
Monterey jack, cheddar, colby, longhorn cheese
President: David Schroeder
Estimated Sales: $5-10 000,000
Number Employees: 15

7442 Linden Cookies Inc
25 Brenner Dr
Congers, NY 10920-1397
845-268-5050
Fax: 845-268-5055 sales@lindencookies.com
www.lindencookies.com
Producer of cookies.
President: Paul Sturz
VP: Suzanne Sturz
Assistant VP: Christian Sturz
Manager: Christian Sturz
csturz@lindencookies.com
Estimated Sales: $10-20 Million
Number Employees: 20-49
Number of Brands: 1
Brands:
  Linden's

7443 Lindner Bison
Newhall
Apt 111
Northern, CA 91355-5139
530-254-6337
Fax: 661-254-0224 klindner@lindnerbison.com
www.lindnerbison.com
Bison/turkey burgers
President: Kathy Lindner
COO: Ken Lindner
Number Employees: 1-4
Brands:
  Bison
  Bisurkey

7444 Lindsay Farms
PO Box 640481
Pike Road, AL 36064
800-243-4608
info@lindsayfarms.com www.lindsayfarms.com
Gourmet and specialty salsas, nuts, and pickled foods
Owner: Jon Winton
Type of Packaging: Private Label
Brands:
  Lindsay Farms

7445 Lindsay's Teas
1331 Commerce St.
Petaluma, CA 94549
707-462-6333
800-624-7031
info@lindsaysteas.com www.lindsaysteas.com
Organic specialty teas
Manager: Melanie Mountanos
Estimated Sales: $20-50 Million
Number Employees: 20-49
Parent Co: Mountanos Family Coffee & Tea Co.
Brands:
  Lindsay's Tea

7446 Lindt & Sprungli USA
One Fine Chocolate Pl
Stratham, NH 03885-2592
603-778-8100
www.lindt-spruengli.com
Manufacturer of fine chocolates
CEO: Daniel Studer
Contact: Lisa Cloutier
lcloutier@lindt.com
Year Founded: 1845
Estimated Sales: $30-50 Million
Number Employees: 650
Brands:
  American Classics
  Lindor Truffles
  Lindt Chocolate

7447 Lindy's Homemade Italian Ice
920-A Black Satchel Drive
Charlotte, NC 28216
704-391-7994
Fax: 704-391-9016 lindysitalianice.com
Italian Ice

7448 Lingle Brothers Coffee
6500 Garfield Ave
Bell Gardens, CA 90201-1897
562-927-3317
Fax: 562-928-1505
Coffee
Owner: James Lingle
Estimated Sales: $10-20 000,000
Number Employees: 20-49

7449 Link Snacks Inc.
1 Snack Food Ln.
PO Box 397
Minong, WI 54859
715-466-2234
Fax: 715-466-5151 www.jacklinks.com
Meat and protein snacks, including jerky, sausages, sticks and strips.
Chairman: Jack Link
President/CEO: Troy Link
Estimated Sales: $1 Billion
Number Employees: 250-499
Number of Brands: 1
Type of Packaging: Consumer
Brands:
  Jack Link's

7450 Lion Brewery Inc
700 N Pennsylvania Ave
Wilkes Barre, PA 18705-2451
570-823-8801
Fax: 570-823-6686 888-295-2337
info@lionbrewery.com www.lionbrewery.com
Fifteenth-largest American-owned brewery.
President & CEO: Cliff Risell
CEO: Jb Brombacher
jbrombacher@lionbrewery.com
Number Employees: 100-249
Type of Packaging: Consumer, Bulk
Brands:
  Lionshead Pilsner
  Lionshead Light

7451 Lion Raisins Inc
9500 S DE Wolf Ave
Selma, CA 93662-9534
559-834-6677
Fax: 559-834-6622 www.lionraisins.com
Grower and processor of California raisins and raisin products.
CEO: Al Lion
alion@lionsraisins.com
Number Employees: 250-499
Square Footage: 130000
Type of Packaging: Consumer, Food Service, Private Label, Bulk

Food Manufacturers / A-Z

Brands:
   California Grown
   Lion
   Sunshine California

7452 Lionel Hitchen Essitional Oils
1867 Porter Lake Drive
Sarasota, FL 34240
941-379-1400
Fax: 941-379-1433 www.lheo.co.uk
Natural flavors and oils
President: Alison Barnes
General Manager: Suzy Nolan
snolan@lhitchenusa.com
Estimated Sales: $700,000
Number Employees: 8

7453 Lioni Latticini Inc
555 Lehigh Ave
Union, NJ 07083-7976
908-624-9450
Fax: 908-686-3449 info@lionimozzarella.com
www.lionimozzarella.com
Fresh whole milk mozzarella products
Owner: Michael Virga
Owner/VP: Salvatore Salzarulo
Marketing: Guiseppe (Sal) Salzarulo
Sales Manager: Michelina Salzarulo
Manager: Lori Church
lori@lionimozzarella.com
Operations Director: Guiseppe (Sal) Salarulo
Production Supervisor: Salvatore Salzarulo
Plant Supervisor: Salvatore Salzarulo
Estimated Sales: $5,700,000
Number Employees: 10-19

7454 Lipid Nutrition
24708 W Durkee Road
Channahan, IL 60410
815-730-5208
Fax: 815-730-5202
Manufacturer natural lipid ingredients
Contact: Ramesh Gaga
ramesh.gaga@unilever.com

7455 Lipsey Mountain Spring Water
P.O.Box 1246
Norcross, GA 30091-1246
770-449-0001
Fax: 770-234-6948 www.lipseywater.com
Bottled water
President: Joseph Lipsey Iii
Estimated Sales: $1-2.5 Million
Number Employees: 20-49

7456 Lisa Shively's Kitchen Helpers, LLC
802 Clarkway Ave
Po Box 2123
Eden, NC 27289
336-623-7511
Fax: 336-623-7511 kitchenhelpers@earthlink.net
Gluten-free, organic/natural, meals, hot chocolate, other soups, stews, beans, rubs, spices, cookbooks.
Marketing: Lisa Shively

7457 Lisa's Organics
PO Box 987
Carnelian Bay, CA 96140
530-584-1958
877-584-5711
www.lisasorganics.com
Organic frozen vegetables and vegetable side dishes
Founder: Lisa Marie Boudreau
Type of Packaging: Consumer

7458 Lisanatti Foods
1815 Red Soils Ct
Oregon City, OR 97045-4139
503-652-1988
Fax: 503-653-1979 866-864-3922
www.lisanattifoods.com
Vegetarian and cheese alternatives including soy satin
President: Philip J Lisac
National Sales & Marketing: Teresa Lisac
Production manager: Andy Ingersoll
Estimated Sales: $5-10 Million
Number Employees: 5-9
Parent Co: P&J Lisac Associates
Type of Packaging: Consumer, Food Service
Brands:
   Lisanatti
   Soy-Sation

7459 Lisbon Sausage Co Inc
PO Box 2028
New Bedford, MA 02741-2028
508-994-0453
Fax: 508-994-0453 joan@amarals.com
www.amarals.com
Portuguese sausage
President: Antonio Rodrigues
Vice President: Joan Sparrow
Contact: Joan Sparrow
joan@amarals.com
Estimated Sales: Below $5 000,000
Number Employees: 10-19

7460 Lisbon Seafood Co
1428 S Main St
Fall River, MA 02724-2604
508-672-3617
Fax: 508-672-4698
Seafood
Owner: Victor Da Silva
vncc@aol.com
Estimated Sales: $1-3 Million
Number Employees: 10-19

7461 Litehouse Foods
1109 N Ella Ave
Sandpoint, ID 83864
800-669-3169
www.litehousefoods.com
Dips & dressings.
Estimated Sales: I
Type of Packaging: Consumer

7462 (HQ)Litehouse Foods
100 Litehouse Dr
Sandpoint, ID 83864
800-669-3169
www.litehousefoods.com
Dressings and dips; portion control and bulk available, including vinaigrette, bleu cheese, ranch, caesar, coleslaw dressing, french, cumin citrus, tartar sauce, burger spread, BBQ sauce, cocktail sauce, deli salsa, mayonaisehorseradish, raspberry, honey mustard, Italian, also low calorie, specialty, and gluten free sauces and dressings.
President & CEO: Kelly Prior
VP, Finance & Accounting: Matt Burrows
SVP, Sales & Marketing: Brent Carr
VP, Operations: Rob Tyrrell
VP, Information Technology: Derek Christensen
Year Founded: 1963
Estimated Sales: $100-500 Million
Number Employees: 250-499
Type of Packaging: Consumer, Food Service, Private Label, Bulk

7463 Little Amana Winery
4400 I St
Amana, IA 52203
319-668-9664
Fax: 319-668-2853
Wine
Owner: Bob Zuber
Brands:
   Ackerman
   Breezy Hills
   Jasper
   Little Swan Lake
   Park Farm
   Sugar Grove
   Summerset
   Village

7464 Little Bird
25 Fairchild Ave
Suite 200
Plainview, NY 11803
646-620-6395
littlebirdkitchen.com
Chocolate bark and simple syrup flavored with jalapenos.
Co-Owner: Sara Meyer
Co-Owner: Corey Meyer

7465 Little Crow Foods
PO Box 1038
Warsaw, IN 46581-1038
574-267-7141
Fax: 574-267-2370 800-288-2769
customerservice@littlecrowfoods.com
www.littlecrowfoods.com

Manufacturer and contract packager of dry blended products including flour, pancake mixes and breakfast cereals; exporter of flour, cereals and seasoned coating mixes
President: Dennis Fuller
EVP: Kimberly Fuller
VP Operations: Ron Shipley
Estimated Sales: $8 Million
Number Employees: 50-99
Square Footage: 360000
Type of Packaging: Consumer, Food Service, Private Label, Bulk
Brands:
   Miracle Maize

7466 Little Duck Organics
New York, NY 10017
877-458-1321
hello@littleduckorganics.com
littleduckorganics.com
No-sugar snacks using natural ingredients. Organic, Kosher, and gluten free.
CEO: Arthur Pergament
Contact: Charlee-Ann Charron
charlee@littleduckorganics.com
Number Employees: 5
Square Footage: 3187
Type of Packaging: Consumer
Brands:
   LITTLE DUCK ORGANICS

7467 Little Hills Winery
710 S Main St
St Charles, MO 63301-3443
636-946-6637
Fax: 636-724-1121 877-584-4557
Wines
Owner: David Campbell
david@little-hills.com
Co-Owner: Tammy Campbell
Estimated Sales: $8.5 Million
Number Employees: 5-9

7468 Little I
815 3rd Street
Blaine, WA 98230
360-332-3258
Fax: 360-332-3279 www.littlei.com
Gourmet mints, cold-pressed enery and vitamin gums and other confections
Owner: Sarah Dalrymple

7469 Little Miss Muffin
4014 N Rockwell St
Chicago, IL 60618
773-463-6328
Fax: 773-463-7101 800-456-9328
Fresh and frozen cakes and pastries
Owner: Staci Minic Mintz
Contact: Kenny Munic
kenny@littlemissmuffin.com
Estimated Sales: $1.8 Million
Number Employees: 40
Type of Packaging: Consumer, Food Service
Brands:
   Little Miss Muffin
   Wide Shoulders Bakin

7470 Little Portion Bakery
350 Co Rd 248
Berryville, AR 72616
479-253-7710
877-504-9865
www.littleportionbakery.org
Granola, snack bars, cookies
Founder: Viola Talbot

7471 Little Red Dot Kitchen
PO Box 2571
Sunnyvale, CA 94087
408-673-8227
reddotkitchen.com
Roasted meat snack
CEO: Ching Lee
VP, Sales: Bonnie Frese

7472 Little Red Kitchen
Brooklyn, NY
littleredkitchenbakeshop.com
Cookies and pies
Founder: Susan Palmer

Food Manufacturers / A-Z

7473 Little Rhody Brand Frankfurts
5 Day St
Johnston, RI 02919-4301
401-831-0815
sales@littlerhodyhotdogs.com
www.littlerhodyhotdogs.com
Sausage, frankfurters, meat products and fast foods
President: Ed Robal
Estimated Sales: $3 Million
Number Employees: 1-4
Square Footage: 40000
Type of Packaging: Consumer, Food Service
Brands:
    Little Rhody Brand

7474 Little River Lobster Company
PO Box 507
East Boothbay, ME 04544-0507
207-633-2648
Fax: 604-276-8371
Whole fish/seafood
President: Mike Dalton
Estimated Sales: $810,000
Number Employees: 1-4

7475 Little River Seafood Inc
440 Rock Town Rd
Reedville, VA 22539-3017
804-453-3670
Fax: 804-453-5421 kelly@littleriverseafood.com
www.littleriverseafood.com
Quality crab products.
President: Steven Minor
steve@littleriverseafood.com
Marketing Executive: Kelly Minor
Estimated Sales: $10,026,306
Number Employees: 50-99
Type of Packaging: Consumer, Food Service, Private Label, Bulk
Brands:
    Little River Seafood

7476 Little's Cuisine
49 Locust Ave
Suite 104
New Canaan, CT 06840
203-228-4440
www.littlescuisine.com
Seasoning mixes and blends
President & Owner: Angela Colabella
angela@littlecuisine.com

7477 Liuzzi Angeloni Cheese
86 Rossotto Drive
Hamden, CT 06514
203-287-8477
Fax: 203-287-9898
Manufacturer of different cheeses including ricotta, mozzarella, and fresh curd.
Founder: Pasquale Liuzzi

7478 LivBar
249 Liberty St. NE
Suite 232
Salem, OR 97301
971-239-1209
hello@livbar.com
www.livbar.com
Energy bars that are organic, gluten free, dairy free, soy free, corn free, and GMO-free
Co-Founder: Gabe Johansen
Co-Founder: Jan Johansen
Year Founded: 2012

7479 Live A Little Gourmet Foods
P.O. Box 10916
Oakland, CA 94610
510-744-3683
Fax: 510-744-3684 888-744-2500
www.livealittle.com
Fresh salads dressings and croutons
Executive Chef, Founder, CEO: Virginia Davis
virginia@livealittle.com
Estimated Sales: $1-3 Million
Number Employees: 1-4
Number of Brands: 2
Brands:
    Live a Little Dressings
    Perfect Croutons

7480 Live Gourmet
Carpinteria, CA
info@livegourmet.com
Greenhouse-grown vegetables.
Number Employees: 70
Brands:
    Live Gourmet(c)
    Grower Pete's Certified Organic(c)

7481 Live Love Pop
4385 Sunbelt Dr
Addison, TX 75001-5134
214-697-6370
Fax: 972-380-4234 info@livelovepop.com
livelovepop.com
Gourmet popcorn
CEO: Lauren Brundage
Operations: Molly Brundage
Number of Brands: 1
Number of Products: 6
Type of Packaging: Consumer
Brands:
    LIVE LOVE POP

7482 Live Oaks Winery
3875 Hecker Pass Road
Gilroy, CA 95020
408-842-2401
Wines
President: Richard Blocher
Estimated Sales: $500-1 Million appx.
Number Employees: 20-49

7483 Livermore Falls Baking Company
49 Gilbert St
Livermore Falls, ME 04254-4238
207-897-3442
Fax: 207-897-6381
Baked goods including rolls and pizza crusts
President: Anthony Maxwell
Estimated Sales: $990,000
Number Employees: 5 to 9

7484 Livermore Valley Cellars
1193 Ava St
Livermore, CA 94550
925-454-9463
Fax: 925-454-9463
Producer of wine
President: Chris Lagiss
CEO: Tim Sauer
Marketing Director: Tim Sauer
Estimated Sales: $1-2.5 Million
Number Employees: 1-4
Brands:
    Lvc

7485 Living Farms
352 3rd Street E
Tracy, MN 56175-1527
507-629-3517
Fax: 507-629-4258
Processors of grains and vegetables
Owner: Ardell Anderson
Vice President/CEO: Janet Anderson
Estimated Sales: Under $500,000
Number Employees: 3

7486 Living Harvest Foods
PO Box 4407
Portland, OR 97208
503-274-0755
888-690-3958
www.livingharvest.com
Non dairy hemp milk, ice cream bars, ice cream, hemp protein powder, hemp oil
President/CEO: Hans Faster
CFO/COO: Catherine Hearn
Marketing Manager: Christina Volgyesi
Estimated Sales: $5 Million
Number Employees: 10
Square Footage: 6400

7487 Living Intentions
250 S Garrard Blvd
Richmond, CA 94801
415-824-5483
www.livingintentions.com
Popcorn, cereal, nut blends, seeds and trail mix.
Founder: Joshua McHugh

7488 Living Raw
2422 Douglass Glen Ln
Franklin, TN 37064-6760
312-933-6543
Fax: 678-669-5801
Chocolate truffles
Co-Owner: T.J. Dunham
Co-Owner: Ginger Dunham

7489 Livingston Farmers Assn
641 6th St
PO Box 456
Livingston, CA 95334-1397
209-394-7941
Fax: 209-394-7952 jim@lfa-ca.com
www.lfa-ca.com
Processor and exporter of sweet potatoes, peaches and almonds
President: Steve Moler
General Manager/CEO: James Snyder
Manager: Jenny Allen
jenny@lfa-ca.com
Estimated Sales: $6 Million
Number Employees: 20-49
Square Footage: 95200
Brands:
    Yamato Colony

7490 Livingston Moffett Winery
1895 Cabernet Ln
Saint Helena, CA 94574
707-965-3694
Fax: 707-965-2058 800-788-0370
www.livingstonwines.com
Winery
President: Diane Livingston
Production Manager: Mark Moffett
Estimated Sales: Below $5 Million
Number Employees: 4
Brands:
    Gemstone Vineyard
    Moffett
    Stanley's
    Starrey's Ion
    Syrah

7491 Livingston's Bulls Bay Seafood
631 Morrison St
Mc Clellanville, SC 29458
843-887-3519
Fax: 843-887-3989
Shrimp and oysters
Owner: Bill Livingston
livbullbay@aol.com
Co-Owner/CEO: Kathy Livingston
Estimated Sales: $1,000,000
Number Employees: 5-9

7492 Liz Lovely Inc
167 Mad River Canoe Rd
Waitsfield, VT 05673-4433
802-496-6390
Fax: 802-329-2043
Gluten free, vegan and non-GMO cookies.
Owner: Liz Holtz
liz@lizlovely.com
CEO: Liz Scott
Operations Manager: Emily Potter
Number Employees: 5-9

7493 Llano Estacado Winery
3426 EAST F.M. 1585
Lubbock, TX 79452
806-745-2258
Fax: 806-748-1674 800-634-3854
info@llanowine.com www.llanowine.com
Wine
President: Mark Hyman
CFO: Mary McGill
Vice President: James Morris
Operations Manager: Greg Bruni
Estimated Sales: Below $5 Million
Number Employees: 20-49
Type of Packaging: Private Label

7494 Lloyd's
740 Springdale Drive
Ste. 206
Exton, PA 19341
610-647-3144
Fax: 610-594-8654 lloydsofpa@aol.com
www.lloydspa.com
Frozen dessert mixes
Technical Director: Barry Jones
President: Andy Jones
Estimated Sales: $5-10 Million
Number Employees: 1-4
Number of Brands: 1
Number of Products: 20
Type of Packaging: Food Service, Private Label, Bulk

Food Manufacturers / A-Z

7495 Loacker USA
90 Broad St
Suite 402A
New York, NY 10004
212-742-8510
Fax: 212-747-8752 www.loackerusa.com
Wafers and chocolate bars
VP, Marketing: Crystal Black Davis
Year Founded: 1925
Estimated Sales: $349 Million
Number Employees: 834

7496 Loafin' Around
555 Eastview Dr
Madison, AL 35758-7824
301-570-4513
Fax: 301-216-1575
Breads
President: Blake Daniel
Estimated Sales: $62 K
Number Employees: 1

7497 Lobster 4 Dinner
106 Wharf Rd
Cape Wolf, PE C0B 1V0
Canada
888-230-0707
www.lobster4dinner.com
Lobster meat

7498 Lobster Gram
4664 N Lowell Ave
Chicago, IL 60630-4263
773-777-8315
Fax: 773-777-5546 800-548-3562
customerservice@lobstergram.com
www.lobstergram.com
Lobster
President: Michael Robinson
michael@livelob.com
Estimated Sales: $1-3 Million
Number Employees: 10-19

7499 Loc Maria Biscuits
Philadelphia, PA 19123
www.locmaria.fr
French biscuits
Number Employees: 350
Brands:
  Gavottes
  Traou Mad

7500 Local Roots Farms
RT 18 W. Lake Rd.
Burt, NY 14028
716-946-3198
localrootsfarmrt18.com
Various produce including, but not limited to tomatoes, beets, carrots, and onions.
Co-Owner: Jerry Winsquist
Co-Owner: Kristi Winquist
Type of Packaging: Consumer

7501 Lochhead Mfg. Co.
527 Axminister Dr
Fenton, MO 63026
800-776-2088
sales@lochheadvanilla.com
www.lochheadvanilla.com
Processor and exporter of vanilla extracts including pure, natural and artificial blends.
Co-Owner: John Lochhead
sales@lochheadvanilla.com
Co-Owner: George Lochhead
Estimated Sales: $10-20 Million
Number Employees: 10-19
Type of Packaging: Consumer, Private Label, Bulk

7502 Lockcoffee
6 Kilmer Road
Larchmont, NY 10538-2636
914-273-7838
Fax: 212-827-0945
Coffee
President: B Brown Lock
Estimated Sales: Under $500,000
Number Employees: 1-4

7503 Lockwood Vineyards
849 Zinfandel Lane
St. Helena, CA 94574
707-963-6925
Fax: 831-644-7829 info@lockwoodvineyard.com
www.lockwoodvineyard.com
Wines
Owner: Paul Toeppen
Estimated Sales: $2.5-5 Million
Number Employees: 5-9
Type of Packaging: Private Label

7504 Locustdale Meat Packing
377 Lavelle Road
Locustdale, PA 17945
570-875-1270
Sausage, kielbasa, ring bologna and roast chicken and turkey
Owner: Jack Holderman
Estimated Sales: $1-3 Million
Number Employees: 1-4

7505 Lodi Canning Co
307 Nestles St
PO Box 315
Lodi, WI 53555
608-592-4236
Fax: 608-592-4742 bob@lodicanning.com
www.lodicanning.com
Canned peas and creamed corn
President: Bob Goeres
bob@lodicanning.com
Estimated Sales: $2-5 Million
Number Employees: 100-249
Type of Packaging: Private Label
Brands:
  Day By Day
  Idol
  Lodi's

7506 Lodi Nut Company
1230 S Fairmont Ave
Lodi, CA 95240
209-334-2081
Fax: 209-369-6815 800-234-6887
Black walnut kernels and nut factory gourmet nuts; also, custom processor and co-packer of English walnut, almond and macadamia kernels
President/Sales & Marketing Director: Kelvin Suess
Executive VP: Virgil Suess
Contact: Harvey Borton
hdborton@lodiacademy.net
Plant Manager: Reuben Rodriguez
Estimated Sales: $7,001,000
Number Employees: 75
Square Footage: 160000
Type of Packaging: Consumer, Food Service, Private Label, Bulk

7507 Loew Vineyards
14001 Liberty Rd
Mt Airy, MD 21771-9524
301-831-5464
Fax: 301-831-5464 loewvineyards@comcast.net
www.loewvineyards.net
Wines
Owner: Lois Loew
l.loew@loewvineyards.net
Estimated Sales: $800,000
Number Employees: 1-4

7508 Loffredo Produce
500 46th St
Rock Island, IL 61201
309-786-0969
Fax: 309-786-0660 800-383-3767
lbeener@loffredo.com www.loffredo.com
Produce
President: Gene Loffredo
CFO: Mark Zimmerman
Operations Director: Jerry Moore
VP Sales: John Loffredo
VP, Purchase: Mike Loffredo
Estimated Sales: $5-10 Million appx.
Number Employees: 50-99
Parent Co: Lofredo Fresh Produce

7509 Log 5 Corporation
4 Glenberry Court
Phoenix, MD 21131
410-329-9580
Fax: 443-705-0223 www.log5.com
Food ingredients; pasteurization process
President: Joost De Koomen
Vice President: Jochem Dekker
Contact: Chaus Davids
cdavids@log5.com

7510 Log House Foods
700 Berkshire Lane N
Plymouth, MN 55441
763-546-8395
info@loghousefoods.com
www.loghousefoods.com
Ingredients manufacturer
Co-Founder: Mary Kosir
Exec. VP: Larry Phillips
Year Founded: 1947
Type of Packaging: Private Label

7511 Loghouse Foods
700 Berkshire Ln N
Minneapolis, MN 55441-5499
763-546-8395
Fax: 763-546-7339 info@loghousefoods.com
www.loghousefoods.com
Twice-baked cinnamon toast and biscotti, flaked coconut, European-style melting creams for dipping and coating desserts, chocolate chips, candy coatings, etc.
President: Alan Kasdan
akasdan@loghousefoods.com
VP Operations: Josh Kasdan
Estimated Sales: $17,000,000
Number Employees: 20-49
Type of Packaging: Consumer, Food Service, Private Label
Brands:
  Bella Crema
  Jacobsen's Toast
  Log House
  Log House Candiquik
  Plymouth Pantry

7512 Lola Granola Bar Corporation
PO Box 63
Croton Falls, NY 10519
914-617-8833
info@lolagranolabar.com
www.lolagranolabar.com
Manufacturer of granola bars and water.
Founder: Mary Molina
Contact: Ernie Molina
ernie@lolagranolabar.com
Brands:
  LOLA GRANOLA BAR

7513 Lola Savannah
1701 Commerce St.
Houston, TX 77002-2244
713-222-9800
Fax: 713-222-9802 888-663-9166
lola@lolasavannah.com lolacc.com
Roasted coffee and tea
Owner: Duke Furgh
Vice President: Michael Spencer
Contact: Michael Spencer
mcs@lolasavannah.com
Operations Manager: Hank Segelke
Estimated Sales: Less than $500,000
Number Employees: 5-9
Type of Packaging: Consumer, Food Service, Private Label, Bulk

7514 Lolonis Winery
1930 Tice Valley Blvd
Walnut Creek, CA 94595-2203
925-938-8066
Fax: 925-938-8069
Wines
President: Petros Lolonis
Contact: Doreen Scallan
doreenscallan@yahoo.com
Estimated Sales: $600,000
Number Employees: 5-9
Brands:
  Ladybug White Old Vines

7515 Lombardi Brothers Meat Packers
1926 W Elk Pl
P.O. Box 11277
Denver, CO 80211
303-458-7441
lombardibrothers.com
Beef, pork, lamb and veal; importer of wild game.
President & Owner: Victoria Phillips
General Manager: Jeff Harvey
Year Founded: 1947
Estimated Sales: $30 Million
Number Employees: 60
Square Footage: 30000
Type of Packaging: Food Service

Food Manufacturers / A-Z

Other Locations:
Lombardi Brothers Meat
Fridley MN
Lombardi Brothers Meat
Le Mars IA

7516 Lombardi's Bakery
177 E Main St
Torrington, CT 06790-5432
860-489-4766
Fax: 860-489-4766
Baked goods
Owner: Camillo Lombardi
Estimated Sales: Less Than $500,000
Number Employees: 1-4
Brands:
Lombardi's

7517 Lombardi's Seafood
1152 Harmon Avenue
Winter Park, FL 32789
407-628-3474
Fax: 407-240-2562 800-879-8411
quality@lombardis.com www.lombardis.com
Processor, importer and wholesaler/distributor of fresh and frozen seafood; serving the food service market
Owner: Vince Lomabardi
VP: Vince Lombardi
Contact: James Carr
jamescarr@lombardis.com
Supervisor: Mike Lombardi
Estimated Sales: $10-20 Million
Number Employees: 100-249
Type of Packaging: Food Service

7518 Lombardi's Seafood Inc
1888 W Fairbanks Ave
Winter Park, FL 32789-4502
407-628-3474
Fax: 407-628-5165 quality@lombardis.com
www.lombardis.com
Fresh and frozen seafood and shellfish
President: Anthony Lomabardi
Vice President: Tony Lombardi
Estimated Sales: $1 Million
Number Employees: 10-19

7519 Lone Pine Enterprise Inc
121 Durkee St
Carlisle, AR 72024
870-552-3217
Processor and exporter rice and soybeans
President: Jason Smith
Estimated Sales: Less Than $500,000
Number Employees: 1-4
Type of Packaging: Consumer, Food Service, Bulk

7520 Lone Star Bakery
106 W Liberty St
Round Rock, TX 78664-5122
512-255-7268
Fax: 512-255-6405 www.roundrockdonuts.com
Processor and exporter of pre-baked and frozen buttermilk biscuits, muffins, cinnamon rolls, brownies, sheet cakes, fruit cobblers, pie shells, pecan and fruit pie, and portioned cookie and dough
Owner: Dale Cohrs
VP: Bill Scott
Sales: Rick Perrett
Operations: Damon Smith
Plant Manager: Fred Alexander
Purchasing: Clint Scott
Estimated Sales: $450000
Number Employees: 50-99
Square Footage: 600000
Type of Packaging: Food Service, Private Label, Bulk
Brands:
Lone Star

7521 Lone Star Consolidated Foods Inc.
1727 North Beckley Avenue
Dallas, TX 75203
214-946-2185
Fax: 214-946-2286 800-658-5637
Manufacturer of baked sweet rolls, doughnuts, cinnamon rolls, fritters and hushpuppies.
CEO/COO: Dolores Burdines
Contact: Kevin Murray
kevin@lonestarfunfoods.com
Year Founded: 1950
Estimated Sales: $20-50 Million
Number Employees: 100-249
Number of Brands: 2

Brands:
Babycakes
Lone Star

7522 Lone Wolf Farms
99 Ordway Avenue
PO Box 317
Minto, ND 58261
701-248-3482
Fax: 701-248-3508 www.lonewolffarms.com
Supplier of potatoes
President: Keith Bjorneby
VP: Dean Bjorneby
Sales Manager: Chris Bjorneby
Office Manager: Suzi Tibert
Production Manager: Chris Bjorneby
Estimated Sales: $10-20 Million
Number Employees: 16
Type of Packaging: Consumer, Bulk

7523 Long Food Industries
709 Rock Beauty Road
Fripp Island, SC 29920-7344
843-838-3205
Fax: 843-838-3918 www.longfoodindustries.com
Shrimp, cooked/diced chicken, clam (meat and broth), beef (diced/cooked), lobster, fish and pork
President: Leon Long
Estimated Sales: $10-20 Million
Number Employees: 1
Type of Packaging: Food Service

7524 Long Grove Confectionary
333 Lexington Dr
Buffalo Grove, IL 60089-6542
847-459-3100
Fax: 847-459-4871 800-373-3102
linda_gadas@longgrove.com www.longgrove.com
Confectionery items including chocolates, molded chocolate, apples, novelties, custom molded logos and holiday boxes.
President: John Mangel
maureen_herrington@longgrove.com
Vice President: David Mangel
Marketing: Linda Gadas
Site Manager: Maureen Herrington
maureen_herrington@longgrove.com
Estimated Sales: $5-10 Million
Number Employees: 50-99
Square Footage: 100000
Type of Packaging: Consumer, Food Service, Private Label, Bulk
Brands:
Chicago Mints
Long Grove Confections
Myrties
Myrtles
Ultimate Apple

7525 Long Island Cauliflower Assn
139 Marcy Ave
Riverhead, NY 11901-3099
631-727-2212
Fax: 631-727-4295 www.licassoc.com
Cauliflower
President/CEO: Carl Key
Estimated Sales: $5-10 Million
Number Employees: 10-19

7526 Long Trail Brewing Co Inc
5520 US Route 4
Bridgewater Cors, VT 05035-9600
802-672-5011
Fax: 802-672-5012 www.longtrail.com
Brewers of beer and ale.
Founder: Andy Pherson
Operations Manager: Matt Quinlan
Facility Manager: Billy Gault
Estimated Sales: $10-20 Million
Number Employees: 50-99
Number of Brands: 14
Brands:
Culmination
Cranberry Gose
Double Bag
Green Blaze IPA
Harvest
Imperial Pumpkin
India Pale Ale
Limbo IPA
Long Trail Ale
Mostly Cloudy
Sick Day
Stand Out

Summer Ale
Unearthed

7527 Long Vineyards
1535 Sage Canyon Rd
St Helena, CA 94574-9628
707-963-2496
Fax: 707-963-5016
Wines
Co-Owner/President: Robert Long
Co-Owner: Zelma Long
Marketing/PR Director: Pat Perini Long
Winemaking Operations Director: Sandi Belcher
Estimated Sales: $500,000-$1 Million
Number Employees: 1-4
Brands:
Johannisberg Riesling
Sangiovese

7528 Longacres Modern Dairy Inc
1445 Route 100
PO Box 69
Barto, PA 19504
610-845-7551
Fax: 610-845-2041 info@longacresdairy.com
Dairy
President: Daniel T Longacre Jr
longacre@longacresicecream.com
VP: Newton T Longacre
Treasurer: Kathryn Longacre
CFO: Timoty T Longacre
Sales Exec: Timothy Longacre
Plant Engineer: Daniel Longacre
Estimated Sales: Below $5 Million
Number Employees: 10-19
Brands:
Longacre

7529 Longbottom Coffee & Tea Inc
4893 NW 235th Ave # 101
Hillsboro, OR 97124-5835
503-648-1271
Fax: 503-681-0944 800-288-1271
info@longbottomcoffee.com
www.longbottomcoffee.com
Processor and importer of specialty coffees including certified organics, espresso, flavored, regionals and blends; wholesaler/distributor of espresso machines and fine teas
Owner: Jody Baccelleri
Marketing Director: Lisa Walker
Sales Director: Gabrielle Paeson
jbaccelleri@medicalteams.org
Manufacturing/Operations Director: Tom Brandon
Estimated Sales: $8 Million
Number Employees: 50-99
Square Footage: 112000
Type of Packaging: Consumer, Food Service, Private Label, Bulk

7530 Longford-Hamilton Company
17885 SW Tualatin Valley Hwy
Beaverton, OR 97006
503-642-5661
Fax: 503-649-1321 oldmillrum.com
Imported specialty foods and confectionery products
President: Malarkey Wall
Sales Director: Jan Rudolph
Estimated Sales: Below $5 Million
Number Employees: 1-4
Number of Brands: 1
Number of Products: 20
Type of Packaging: Consumer
Brands:
Old Mill Brand

7531 Longleaf Plantation
78 Baker Rd
Purvis, MS 39475
601-794-6001
Fax: 601-794-5052 800-421-7370
reeceholford@longleafplantation.net
www.longleafplantation.net
Manufacturers of pecans
President: Warren Hood Jr
reeceholford@longleafplantation.net
Sales Exec: Reece Holford
Estimated Sales: $5-10 Million
Number Employees: 20-49
Brands:
Longleaf Plantation

Food Manufacturers / A-Z

7532 Longmeadow Building Dept
20 Williams St
Longmeadow, MA 01106-1950
413-565-4153
Fax: 413-565-4112 www.longmeadow.org
Specialty sauces
Manager: Mark Denver
General Manager: Suzie Barton
Manager: Paul Healy
Estimated Sales: $2.5-5 Million
Number Employees: 5-9

7533 Longo's Bakery Inc
138 W 21st St
Hazleton, PA 18201-1909
570-454-5825
Fax: 570-454-6246 www.longosbakery.com
Breads, rolls, pizza shells
President: James N Capriotti
Estimated Sales: $500,000-$1 000,000
Number Employees: 20-49

7534 Longreen Corp.
5077 Walnut Grove Ave
San Gabriel, CA 91776
626-287-4700
bd@lgreenhealth.com
www.lgreenhealth.com
Health product manufacturer
Year Founded: 2010
Type of Packaging: Private Label
Brands:
　Longreen

7535 Longview Meat & Merchandise Ltd
PO Box 173
Longview, AB T0L 1H0
Canada
403-558-3706
Fax: 403-558-3708　866-355-3759
Beef jerky, wholesaler of bavarian style sausage and pepperonis
President/Owner: Peter Lawson
Plant Manager: Jacky Lau
Estimated Sales: $1 Million
Number Employees: 12
Square Footage: 26000
Type of Packaging: Consumer, Food Service, Private Label, Bulk

7536 LonoLife
1722 South Coast Hwy
Suite 4
Oceanside, CA 92054
855-843-8566
contact@lonolife.com www.lonolife.com
Bone broth, keto broth, snack broth, collagen, protein coffee, cleanse drink powder, plant based protein
Co-Founder: Jesse Koltes
Co-Founder: Craig Leslie

7537 Look Lobster Co
32 Old House Point Rd
Jonesport, ME 04649-3385
207-497-2353
Fax: 207-497-5559 looklobster@myfairpoint.net
www.lookslobster.com
Lobster
President: Bert Sid Look
Vice President, Sales & Logistics: William Look
Estimated Sales: $.5-1 million
Number Employees: 5-9

7538 Lopez Foods
6016 NW 120th Ct
Oklahoma City, OK 73162-1729
405-603-7500
Fax: 405-603-6120 sales@lopezfoods.com
www.lopezfoods.com
Manufacturer of frozen ground beef patties, partially cooked and fully-cooked sausage patties and sliced Canadian-style bacon.
President: John C Lopez
jlopez@lopezfoods.com
Co-Owner, Chairman: John Lopez
CEO: Ed Sanchez
Number Employees: 20-49
Square Footage: 460192
Type of Packaging: Food Service
Brands:
　Carneco Foods
　Lopez Foods

7539 LorAnn Oils
4518 Aurelius Rd
Lansing, MI 48910
517-882-0215
800-862-8620
www.lorannoils.com
Oils, flavors, colors and specialty ingredients.
CEO: John Grettenberger
National Sales Manager: Troy Sprague
COO: Carl Thelen

7540 Lora Brody Products Inc
91 Edgewater Dr
Waltham, MA 02453-2405
781-899-3910
Fax: 617-558-5383 lora@lorabrody.com
www.lorabrody.com
Bread dough enhancer
President: Lora Brody
lora@lorabrody.com
Estimated Sales: $160,000
Number Employees: 1-4
Brands:
　Dough Relaxer
　Lora Brody Bread Dou
　Sourdough Bread Enha

7541 Lord's Sausage & Country Ham
310 S Line St
Dexter, GA 31019-3967
478-875-3101
Fax: 478-875-3039　800-342-6002
www.lordssausage.com
Fresh and smoked pork sausage and cured country ham
President: Roger Lord
wayne@lordsausage.com
VP: Britt Lord
Estimated Sales: $10-20 Million
Number Employees: 20-49
Square Footage: 60000
Type of Packaging: Consumer, Food Service, Private Label, Bulk
Brands:
　Lord's

7542 Loretta's Authentic Pralines
1100 N Peters St # 9
Stall #9
New Orleans, LA 70116-2629
504-529-6170
Fax: 504-945-5912 lorettas@nocoxmail.com
www.lorettaspralines.com
Pralines and confections
Owner: Loretta Harrison
Estimated Sales: $1-2.5 Million
Number Employees: 1-4

7543 Lorina, Inc.
2655 S Le Jeune Rd
Suite 904
Coral Gables, FL 33134
305-779-3085
Fax: 305-779-4949 lorina.us@lorina.com
us.lorina.com
French lemonade
President: Jean-Pierre Barjon
Estimated Sales: $17 Million
Number Employees: 5-9

7544 Lorissa's Kitchen
110 N 5th St
Suite 700
Minneapolis, MN 55403-1618
715-466-2234
Fax: 715-466-5151 lorisskitchen.com
Meat jerky

7545 Loriva Culinary Oils
1192 Illinois Street
San Francisco, CA 94107
415-401-0080
Fax: 415-401-0087　866-972-6879
www.worldpantry.com
Processor and exporter of specialty oils including roasted, infused and toasted sesame, peanut, safflower, walnut, garlic, olive, avocado, hazelnut, macadamia, etc.; also, kosher varieties available
President: Patrick Lee
CEO: David Miller
Consumer Relations: Liz Scatena
Number Employees: 10-19
Parent Co: NSpired Natural Foods
Type of Packaging: Consumer, Food Service, Private Label, Bulk
Brands:
　Loriva
　Loriva Jazz Roasted Oils
　Loriva Supreme Flavored Oils
　Loriva Supreme Oils

7546 Los Altos Food Products
450 N Baldwin Park Blvd.
City Of Industry, CA 91746
626-330-6555
Fax: 626-330-6755 www.losaltosfoods.com
Mexican and Swiss cheeses
President: Raul Andrade
Co-Founder, Vice President: Gloria Andrade
Quality Control Manager: Sergio Mares
Director Sales & Marketing: William Finicle
Contact: Alin Andrade
aandrade@losaltosfoods.com
VP Operations: Alin Andrade
Estimated Sales: $21.5 Million
Number Employees: 1-4
Square Footage: 38000
Type of Packaging: Consumer, Food Service

7547 Los Amigo Tortilla Mfg Co
251 Armour Dr NE
Atlanta, GA 30324-3979
404-876-8153
Fax: 404-876-8102　800-969-8226
ruben@losamigos.com
Corn and flour tortillas and chips
President: Ruben N. Rodriguez, Jr
tom@losamigo.com
General Manager: Ruben Rodriguez
Sales Exec: Tom Gibbs
Operations: Tom Gibb
Plant Supervisor: Carlos Perez
Estimated Sales: Below $5 Million
Number Employees: 50-99

7548 (HQ)Los Angeles Nut House Brands
1601 E Olympic Blvd
Los Angeles, CA 90021-1936
213-481-0134
Fax: 213-481-0084
Nuts
Executive Director: Azuka Uzoh
Sales Director: Terry McClean
Purchasing Manager: Jon Anderson
Estimated Sales: $.5-1 million
Number Employees: 6
Type of Packaging: Private Label

7549 Los Angeles Smoking & Curing Company
1100 West Ewing Street
Seattle, WA 98119
213-628-1246
Fax: 213-614-8857 info@oceanbeauty.com
www.oceanbeauty.com
Herring, kippers, lox, roe, cod, mackerel, salmon, shad, caviar and whitefish
President: Howard Klein
VP Sales/Marketing: Richard Schaeffer
Contact: Glen Stein
gstein@oceanbeauty.com
Number Employees: 100-249
Parent Co: Ocean Beauty
Type of Packaging: Consumer, Food Service
Brands:
　Kodikook
　Lascco

7550 Los Chileros
309 Industrial Ave NE
Albuquerque, NM 87107-2232
505-768-1100
Fax: 505-242-7513 www.sfgfoods.com
Chiles, corn products, salsa, rubs and mixes
Manager: Charles Waghorne
chuck@loschileros.com
Estimated Sales: $1 Million
Number Employees: 5-9

7551 Los Gatos Brewing Company
130 N Santa Cruz Ave.
Los Gatos, CA 95030
408-395-9929
Fax: 408-395-2769 www.lgbrewingco.com
Restaurant and brewing center

Food Manufacturers / A-Z

Owner: Andy Pavicich Jr
Director Manufacturing: Jeff Alexander
General Manager: Randall Bertho
Estimated Sales: $2.5-5 Million
Number Employees: 100-249
Brands:
    Hefeweizen
    Los Gatos Lager
    Nut Brown Ale

7552 Los Gatos Tomato Products
PO Box 429
Huron, CA 93234
    559-945-2700
Fax: 559-945-2661 info@losgatostomato.com
www.losgatostomato.com
Tomato concentrates
CEO: Reuben Peterson
Controller: Linda Labandeira
Manager, Customer Service/Field Ops: Lance Dami
Estimated Sales: $7 Million
Number Employees: 20
Square Footage: 35000
Type of Packaging: Bulk

7553 Los Pericos Food Products
2301 Valley Blvd.
Pomona, CA 91768
    909-623-5625
Fax: 909-623-5486 sales@lospericosfood.com
www.lospericosfood.com
Mexican tostada shells
Partner: Marcelino Ortega
Owner: Guadalupe Ortega
Partner: Luis Ortega
Contact: Jesse Ortega
jesse@lospericosfood.com
Estimated Sales: $3.9 Million
Number Employees: 46
Brands:
    Tostada

7554 Lost Coast Brewery
1600 Sunset Dr
Eureka, CA 95503
    707-267-9651
www.lostcoast.com
Brewery
President: Barbara Groom
Sales Director: Briar Bush
Year Founded: 1986
Estimated Sales: $20-50 Million
Number Employees: 50-99
Number of Products: 14
Type of Packaging: Private Label
Brands:
    8-Ball Stout
    Alleycat Amber
    Arrgh! Pale Ale
    Downtown Brown
    Fogcutter Double IPA
    Great White
    Indica India Pale Ale
    Raspberry Brown
    Sharkinator
    Tangerine Wheat Ale
    Winterbraun

7555 Lost Coast Roast
550 G Street
Unit 36
Arcata, CA 95521
    lostcoastroast.com
Organic cold brew coffee
Co-Founder: Dusty Miller
Co-Founder: Lucas Miller
Co-Founder: Jonny Miller
Co-Founder: Dylan Miller

7556 Lost Mountain Winery
2958 Lost Mountain Rd
Sequim, WA 98382
    360-683-5229
Fax: 360-683-7572 888-683-5229
www.lostmountain.com
Wine
Co-Owner/Winemaker: Steve Conca
Co-Owner/Winemaker: Sue Conca
Estimated Sales: Less than $500,000
Number Employees: 1-4
Brands:
    Lost Mountain Winery

7557 Lost Trail Root Beer
PO Box 670
Louisburg, KS 66053-0670
    913-837-5202
Fax: 913-837-5762 800-748-7765
lcmill@micoks.net www.louisburgcidermill.com
Processor, wholesaler/distributor and exporter of apple cider and root beer; also, apple butter
President/Owner: Tom Schierman
Estimated Sales: $500,000-$1 Million
Number Employees: 5-9
Square Footage: 40000
Type of Packaging: Consumer, Private Label
Brands:
    Lost Trail
    Louisburg

7558 (HQ)Losurdo Creamery
20 Owens Rd
Hackensack, NJ 07601-3297
    201-343-6680
Fax: 201-343-8078 888-567-8736
info@losurdofoods.com www.losurdofoods.com
Cheeses, romano, parmesan, parmaroma, ricotta, mozzarella, provolone.
President: Michael Losurdo Sr
Marketing Head: Dincenva Tulibutz
VP: Mark Losurdo
Estimated Sales: $20-50 Million
Number Employees: 100-249
Type of Packaging: Consumer, Food Service
Other Locations:
    Losurdo Creamery
    Heuvelton NY
Brands:
    Losurdo

7559 Lotsa Pasta
1762 Garnet Ave
San Diego, CA 92109
    858-581-6777
Fax: 858-581-6783 chef@lotsapasta.com
Pasta
Owner: Carol Blomstrom
Estimated Sales: Below $5 Million
Number Employees: 20-49
Brands:
    Lotsa Pasta

7560 Lotte USA Inc
5243 Wayne Rd
Battle Creek, MI 49037-7323
    269-963-6664
Fax: 269-963-6695 lotteusa-inc@yahoo.com
Cream-filled cookies, throat drops and chewing gum
President: T Kaneko
Marketing Manager: Julie Fanning
Sales Manager: Frank Deleo
Manager: Robin Bailey
rbailey@lotteusainc.com
Operations Manager: Dick Thomason
Purchasing Manager: Ron Parsons
Estimated Sales: $15,000,000
Number Employees: 10-19
Type of Packaging: Consumer, Food Service
Brands:
    Full Blast Gum
    Koala No March Cookie

7561 Lotus Bakery
3336 Industrial Dr
Santa Rosa, CA 95403
    707-526-1520
Fax: 415-526-6377 800-875-6887
sales@lotusbakery.com
Bread, cookies and energy bars
Owner: Mark Menning
Estimated Sales: $400,000
Number Employees: 10-19
Type of Packaging: Private Label
Brands:
    Spirulina Bee Bar
    Spirulina Trail Bar

7562 Lotus Brands
PO Box 325
Twin Lakes, WI 53181
    262-889-8561
Fax: 262-889-2461 800-824-6396
lotusbrands@lotuspress.com
www.lotusbrands.com
Teas and herbal supplements
President: Santosh Krinsky
Year Founded: 1992
Estimated Sales: $1-2.5 Million
Number Employees: 50-99
Number of Brands: 16
Number of Products: 1000
Square Footage: 152000
Type of Packaging: Consumer, Private Label, Bulk
Brands:
    Ancient Secrets
    Blue Pearl Incense
    Dragon Eggs
    Eco-Dent
    Fuchs Tooth Brushes
    Life Tree Products
    Light Mountain
    Nature's Alchemy
    Neem Aura
    Nirvana
    Paul Penders
    Rainforest Remedies
    Sai Baba Nag Champa
    Smile Brite
    Tifert Aromatherapy
    Yakshi Fragrances

7563 Lotus Foods
5210 Wall Avenue
Richmond, CA 94804
    510-525-3137
Fax: 510-525-4226 info@lotusfoods.com
www.lotusfoods.com
Rice products
President/Partner: Kenneth Lee
CEO: Caryl Levine
Partner/VP: Caryl Levine
Marketing Director: Caryl Levine
Contact: Vivian Baker
vivian.baker@lotusfoods.com
Year Founded: 1995
Estimated Sales: $170,000
Number Employees: 3
Type of Packaging: Consumer, Food Service, Bulk
Brands:
    Forbidden Rice

7564 Lotus Manufacturing Company
529 San Pedro Avenue
San Antonio, TX 78212-5057
    210-223-1421
Fax: 210-223-1273
Breads and other bakery products
President: Germino Trevino
Estimated Sales: $1-2.5 Million
Number Employees: 1

7565 Lou Pizzo Produce
9660 NW 67th Pl
Parkland, FL 33076
    954-941-8830
Fax: 954-941-8870
Produce
President: Louis Pizzo
VP: Angelina Pizzo
Estimated Sales: Below $5 000,000
Number Employees: 1-4
Brands:
    Lou Pizzo

7566 Lou-Retta's Custom Chocolates
3764 Harlem Rd
Buffalo, NY 14215
    716-833-7111
Fax: 716-689-8113
Chocolate laced popcorn, chocolate pretzel nuggets dusted with gold dust and flavored with fresh ground coffee
President: Loretta Kaminsky
VP Marketing: Ellen Bradbury
Estimated Sales: Below $5 Million
Number Employees: 15
Type of Packaging: Private Label
Brands:
    Buffalo Gold
    Espresso Gold

7567 Lougheed Fisheries
539 2nd Avenue E
Owen Sound, ON N4K 2G5
Canada
    519-376-1586
Fax: 519-376-1589
Fresh and frozen fish and seafood
President: Greg Lougheed
Number Employees: 10-19

Food Manufacturers / A-Z

Type of Packaging: Bulk

7568 Louie's Finer Meats
Highway 63 North
2025 Superior Avenue
Cumberland, WI 54829
715-822-4728
Fax: 715-822-3150 800-270-4297
lfm@louiesfinermeats.net
www.louiesfinermeats.com
Smoked sausages
Owner/President: Louie Muench Sr
VP: Louie Muench Jr
Number Employees: 4

7569 Louis Dreyfus Company Citrus Inc
355 9th St.
Winter Garden, FL 34787
407-656-1000
www.ldc.com
Frozen fruit juice concentrates, citrus oils, pulp and purees.
CEO: Ian McIntosh
Head, Juice Platform: Murilo Parada
Year Founded: 1851
Estimated Sales: G
Number Employees: 100-249
Type of Packaging: Consumer, Food Service, Private Label, Bulk
Brands:
 Sunshine State
 Whole Sun
 Winter Gold

7570 Louis Dreyfus Company LLC
40 Danbury Rd.
Wilton, CT 06897
203-761-2000
www.ldc.com
International agribusiness spanning production, refining, transport and merchandizing.
CEO: Ian McIntosh
Head, North America Region: Adrian Isman
Year Founded: 1851
Estimated Sales: K
Number Employees: 500-999
Parent Co: Louis Dreyfus Company B.V.

7571 (HQ)Louis Dreyfus Corporation
Westblaak 92
3012
Rotterdam,
Netherlands
www.ldc.com
International agribusiness spanning production, refining, transport and merchandizing.
Non-Executive Chairperson: Margarita Louis-Dreyfus
CEO: Ian McIntosh
CFO: Patrick Treuer
COO: Michael Gelchie
Year Founded: 1851
Estimated Sales: $36.5 Billion
Number Employees: 22,000+
Type of Packaging: Food Service, Private Label, Bulk
Brands:
 Delta Rose
 Missouri's Finest
 Showboat

7572 Louis J Rheb Candy Co
3352 Wilkens Ave
Baltimore, MD 21229-4678
410-644-4321
Fax: 410-646-0327 800-514-8293
www.rhebcandy.com
Chocolate candy
President: Wynn Harger
rhebcandycl@comcast.net
Estimated Sales: $5-10 Million
Number Employees: 20-49
Type of Packaging: Consumer

7573 Louis M Martini Winery
254 Saint Helena Hwy S
St Helena, CA 94574-2203
707-968-9403
Fax: 707-963-8750 800-321-9463
www.louismartini.com
Wines
President: Michael Martini
michael.martini@louismartini.com
Sales Director: Bob Matheny
VP Operations/Winemaker: Michael Martini
Plant Manager: Michael Mullen
Number Employees: 100-249
Parent Co: E&J Gallo Winery
Type of Packaging: Consumer

7574 Louis Maull Co
219 N Market St
St Louis, MO 63102-1523
314-241-8410
Fax: 314-241-9840 www.maulls.com
Sauces including barbeque, worcestershire and steak
President: David Ahner
maulliv@maull.com
Estimated Sales: $5-10 Million
Number Employees: 10-19
Brands:
 Maull's Barbecue Sauce

7575 Louis Sherry Premium Chocolate and Tins
3537 W North Avenue
Chicago, IL 60647-4808
212-849-2862
www.louis-sherry.com
Ice cream and frozen desserts
Director Operations: Israel Gonzalez

7576 Louis Swiss Pastry
400 Aabc
Aspen, CO 81611-2545
970-925-8592
Fax: 970-925-1269
Bread and bakery products
Owner: Felix Tornare
Owner: Karse Simon
Estimated Sales: $10-20 000,000
Number Employees: 10-19

7577 Louisa Food Products Inc
1918 Switzer Ave
St Louis, MO 63136-3779
314-868-3000
Fax: 314-868-3014
Frozen Italian foods including ravioli, cannelloni, tortellini and sauces
Owner: Tom Baldetti
CEO: John Baldetti
Sales Executive: Rob Foskett
Human Resources Manager: Gerry Balassi
tom.baldetti@louisafoods.com
Operations Executive: Pete Baldetti
Head of Purchasing: Sarah Schaefer
Estimated Sales: $14.1 Million
Number Employees: 10-19
Square Footage: 80000
Type of Packaging: Consumer, Food Service, Private Label, Bulk
Brands:
 Louisa Pastas

7578 Louisburg Cider Mill
14730 K68 Hwy
Louisburg, KS 66053-8223
913-837-2143
Fax: 913-837-5762 800-748-7765
info@louisburgcidermill.com
www.louisburgcidermill.com
Cider, beverages and a variety of gift items
President: Shelly Schierman
Vice President: Tom Schierman
Estimated Sales: Less Than $500,000
Number Employees: 10-19
Type of Packaging: Private Label
Brands:
 Lost Trail Root Beer
 Louisburg Cider
 Louisburg Farms

7579 Louise's
1700 Isaac Shelby Drive
Shelbyville, KY 40065-9172
502-633-9700
Fax: 502-633-3543
Fat free potato chips and crisps
Quality Assurance Manager: John Lindle
Estimated Sales: $5-9.9 000,000
Number Employees: 40

7580 Louisiana Fish Fry Products
5267 Plank Rd
Baton Rouge, LA 70805-2700
225-356-2905
Fax: 225-356-8867 800-356-2905
www.louisianafishfry.com
Cajun food mixes, breadings, seasonings and sauces.
President: William Pizzolato
Founder: Tony Pizzolato
Partner: Cliff Pizzolato
cliff@louisianafishfry.com
VP, Sales & Marketing: John Deutschman
Quality Assurance Manager: Tana Pittman
Marketing Brand Manager: Richard Rees
National Sales Manager: Patrick Murray
Purchasing Manager: Lisa Fox
Estimated Sales: $10-20 Million
Number Employees: 100-249
Number of Brands: 2
Type of Packaging: Consumer
Brands:
 Louisiana Fish Fry
 Tony's Seafood

7581 Louisiana Gourmet Enterprises
222 S Hollywood Rd
Houma, LA 70360
985-783-2446
Fax: 985-783-6079 800-328-5586
www.mampapauls.com
Cajun/Creole sauces, gumbo, piquante, seasonings and mixes including rice, dinner, cake and frosting
President: Nancy Wilson
Number Employees: 5-9
Type of Packaging: Consumer, Private Label, Bulk
Brands:
 Lemon Velvet
 Mam Papaul's
 Mama Papaul's
 Mardi Gras King
 Red Velvet

7582 Louisiana Oyster Processors
10557 Cherry Hill Ave
Baton Rouge, LA 70816-4115
225-291-6923
Fax: 626-571-0613
Fresh oysters
Owner: Chester Williams
Estimated Sales: $5-10 Million
Number Employees: 10-19
Type of Packaging: Consumer, Food Service

7583 Louisiana Packing Company
501 Louisiana St
Westwego, LA 70094
504-436-2682
Fax: 504-436-1585 800-666-1293
www.lapack.com
Processor, importer and exporter of breaded, cooked and IQF shrimp
President: David Lai
CEO: John Mao
Plant Manager: David Lai
Estimated Sales: $500,000-$1 Million
Number Employees: 1-4
Square Footage: 132000
Type of Packaging: Consumer, Food Service, Private Label, Bulk
Brands:
 Bayou Segnette
 Fresh Sea Taste
 Sea Ray
 White Premium

7584 Louisiana Pride Seafood
2021 Lakeshore Drive Suite 300
New Orleans, LA 70122
504-286-8736
Fax: 504-286-8738
http://www.louisianaseafood.com
Seafood
President: Anthony Lama

7585 Louisiana Rice Mill
4 S Avenue D
PO Box 490
Crowley, LA 70526-5657
337-783-9777
Fax: 337-783-3204 contact@laricemill.com
www.laricemill.com
Long grain milled rice
President: William A Dore
bill.dore@supremerice.com

Food Manufacturers / A-Z

Estimated Sales: $11.9 Million
Number Employees: 50-99
Square Footage: 39732
Brands:
   Sofgrain
   Supreme

7586 (HQ)Louisiana Seafood Exchange
428 Jefferson Highway
Jefferson, LA 70121
   504-283-9393
Fax: 504-834-5633 800-969-9394
bmiller@louisianaseafoodexchange.net
www.louisianaseafoodexchange.net
Seafood including bass, garfish, catfish, trout, amberjack, crab, shark and snapper
Owner/General Manager: Benny Miller
Sales: Steve Shonkoff
Estimated Sales: $20-50 Million
Number Employees: 50-99
Type of Packaging: Consumer, Food Service, Private Label, Bulk

7587 Louisiana Seafood Exchange
3790-D I-55 South
Jackson, MS 39212
   601-853-4554
Fax: 601-853-4554
ray@louisianaseafoodexchange.net
www.louisianaseafoodexchange.net
Seafood including bass, garfish, catfish, trout, amberjack, crab, shark and snapper
Sales: Ray Hopkins
Type of Packaging: Consumer, Food Service, Private Label, Bulk

7588 Louisiana Seafood Exchange
11975 Lake Park Blvd.
Baton Rouge, LA 70809
   225-756-5225
Fax: 225-756-5237 800-314-5225
robwalker@louisianaseafoodexchange.net
www.louisianaseafoodexchange.net
Seafood including bass, garfish, catfish, trout, amberjack, crab, shark and snapper
Sales: Robert Walker
Type of Packaging: Consumer, Food Service, Private Label, Bulk

7589 Louisiana Seafood Promotion & Marketing Board
051 North Third Street
3rd Floor
Baton Rouge, LA 70802
   225-342-0552
Fax: 504-286-8738 info@louisianaseafood.com
www.louisianaseafood.com
Shrimp
President: Gerard Thomassie
Executive Director: Ewell Smith

7590 Louisiana Seafoods
2021 Lakeshore Dr
Suite 310
New Orleans, LA 70122
   504-286-8736
Fax: 504-286-8738 info@louisianaseafood.com
www.louisianaseafood.com
Frozen alligator meat, blue crabmeat, crawfish meat, cooked crawfish
President/CEO: Gregory Benhard
Executive Director: Ewell Smith
CFO: Jorge Benhard
Chairman: Harlon Pearce
Marketing Specialist: John Folse
Communications Manager: Ashley Roth
Administrative Assistant: Krystal Cox
Brands:
   Louisiana Premium Seafoods

7591 Louisiana Sugar Cane Co-Op Inc
6092 Resweber Hwy
St Martinville, LA 70582-6804
   337-394-3785
Fax: 337-394-3787
Manufacturer of raw sugar.
President: Mike Melancon
mike@lasuca.com
Estimated Sales: $20-50 Million
Number Employees: 100-249
Type of Packaging: Consumer

7592 Louisiana Sugar Cane Cooperative
6092 Resweber Hwy
St Martinville, LA 70582-6804
   337-394-3785
Fax: 337-394-5692 www.lasuca.com
Raw cane sugar and black strap molasses
President/General Manager: Michael Melancon
Vice President: Ross Harper
Grower Relations: John Hebert
Purchasing Manager: John La Vasseur
Human Resources: Neil Melancon
Plant Manager: Glenn Judice
Estimated Sales: $30-50 Million
Number Employees: 50-99
Brands:
   St. Martin

7593 Louisville Dairy
4420 Bishop Ln
Louisville, KY 40218-4598
   502-451-9111
Fax: 502-459-7858 www.deanfoods.com
Milk, dairy products
Manager: Steve Gurley
Estimated Sales: $20-50 Million
Number Employees: 100-249
Parent Co: Dean Foods Company

7594 (HQ)Lounsbury Foods
11 Wiltshire Avenue
Toronto, ON M6N 2V7
Canada
   416-656-6330
Fax: 416-656-6803 lounsbury@lounsbury.ca
Vinegar, beet relish, mustard and sauces including regular and extra hot horseradish, seafood cocktail, mint, tartar, hot and barbecue. Founded in 1962.
Manager: Tim Higgins
Vice President: David Higgins
Number Employees: 15
Type of Packaging: Consumer, Food Service, Private Label, Bulk
Brands:
   Cedarvale

7595 Love Beets
3 Bala Plz W
Suite 116
Bala Cynwyd, PA 19004-3402
   856-692-1740
abbie@lovebeets.com
www.lovebeets.com
Beets and beet products
General Manager: George Shropshire
Controller: Chris Lauersen
Marketing Director: Natasha Lichty
National Director of Sales: Chris Horrell

7596 Love Creek Orchards
13558 Highway 16 N
13495 State Hwy 16 North
Medina, TX 78055
   830-589-2588
Fax: 830-589-2880 800-449-0882
adamsapples@lovecreekorchards.com
www.lovecreekorchards.com
Grower of apples; processor of apple cider, jams, jellies, butter, sauce and gourmet flavored coffee
Owner: Brian Hutzler
b.hutzler@apple.com
Estimated Sales: Less Than $500,000
Number Employees: 1-4
Square Footage: 8000
Type of Packaging: Consumer, Food Service, Private Label, Bulk
Brands:
   Apple Strudel Coffee Beans
   Love Creek Orchards

7597 Love Good Fats
8 Market St
Suite 600
Toronto, ON M5E 1M6
Canada
   info@lovegoodfats.com
www.lovegoodfats.com
Snack bars
Founder & CEO: Suzie Yorke

7598 Love Grown Foods
3455 Ringsby Ct
Suite 94
Denver, CO 80216
   855-328-5683
lovegrown.com
Cereals

7599 Love Quiches Desserts
178 Hanse Ave
Freeport, NY 11520-4698
   516-623-8800
Fax: 516-623-8817 info@loveandquiches.com
www.loveandquiches.com
Frozen layer cakes, mousses, tarts, pies, cheesecakes and quiches; exporter of cakes, cheesecakes and brownies.
Chairwoman/Founder: Susan Axelrod
CEO: Andrew Axelrod
CFO: Jeffrey Appleman
VP: Bonnie Warstadt
VP, R&D: Michael Goldstein
Director of Quality Assurance: Ellen Lazzaro
EVP, Sales & Marketing: Karen Sullivan
Estimated Sales: $37 Million
Number Employees: 100-249
Number of Brands: 2
Square Footage: 40000
Brands:
   Sweet Singles
   Gourmet Grab & Go

7600 Love The Wild
4720 Table Mesa Dr
Suite E200
Boulder, CO 80305
   844-424-9875
sayhello@lovethewild.com lovethewild.com
Seafood kits and microwaveable bowls
Principal: Jacqueline Claudia

7601 Love You Foods
1650 S Plaza Way
Suite 2
Flagstaff, AZ 86001
   844-693-2662
support@fatbomb.com www.dropanfbomb.com
Snacks, cheese crisps, nut butters and oils
Co-Founder: Kara Taylor
Co-Founder: Ross Taylor

7602 Love'n Herbs
70 Deerwood Lane
Apt 8
Waterbury, CT 06704-1665
   203-756-4932
Fax: 203-756-4932 lovenherbs@aol.com
Distributors of all natural salad dressings and marinades that contain Canola oil, vineger, herbs and spices. No salt, no sugar, no MSG or preservatives. Also pure canola oil
President: Maria Klanko
Treasurer: Donald Klanko
VP: Peter Klanko
Estimated Sales: Under $300,000
Number Employees: 1-4
Square Footage: 4000
Parent Co: DaSilva-Klanko
Type of Packaging: Consumer
Brands:
   All Natural Herbal
   Love'n Herbs

7603 Love's Bakery
P.O.Box 294
911 Middle St
Honolulu, HI 96819-2317
   808-841-0397
Fax: 808-841-2646 www.lovesbakeryhawaii.com
Breads
President: Mike Walters
Vice President, Sales/Marketing: Byron Chone
Estimated Sales: $10-19 Million
Number Employees: 250-499

7604 Lovebiotics LLC
Los Osos, CA
   wholesale@thecoconutcult.com
www.thecoconutcult.com
Dairy-free, probiotic-infused coconut yogurt in various flavors
Founder: Noah Simon-Wadell

Food Manufacturers / A-Z

Number Employees: 11-50
Number of Brands: 1
Number of Products: 3
Type of Packaging: Consumer, Private Label
Brands:
    The Coconut Cult

7605 Lovin Oven Cakery
2207 N IL Route 83
Round Lake Beach, IL 60073-4907
    847-231-4700
Fax: 847-231-4250   888-775-0099
www.lovinovencakery.com
Homemade gingerbread cookies
Owner: Ken Slove
lovinovencakery@gmail.com
Estimated Sales: Less than $500,000
Number Employees: 20-49

7606 Low Country Produce
1919 Trask Parkway
Lobeco, SC 29931
    800-935-2792
Fax: 800-985-0405   800-935-2792
info@lowcountryproduce.com
www.lowcountryproduce.com
Pickles, chutneys & relishes, soups & sauces, salsas & dips, jellies & preserves
Contact: Maggie Radzwiller
maggie@lowcountryproduce.com
Estimated Sales: Under $500,000
Number Employees: 1-4

7607 Lowcountry Produce
Raleigh, NC
    800-935-2792
www.lowcountryproduce.com
Manufacturer of granola, sundries, canned goods, and baked goods.
Owner: Noel Garrett

7608 Lowcountry Shellfish Inc
7195 Bryhawke Circle
Charleston, SC 29418
    843-767-9600
Fax: 843-552-6560   800-999-2503
l.brooks@lowcountryshellfish.com
www.ipswichshellfish.com
Seafood
Sales Manager: Paul Filo
Number Employees: 300
Parent Co: Ipswich Shellfish Company, Inc.

7609 Lowell Farms
4 N Washington St
El Campo, TX 77437
    979-543-4950
Fax: 979-541-5655   888-484-9213
www.lowellfarms.com
Organic jasmine rice
Owner: Linda Raun
VP: Linda Raun
Estimated Sales: Below $5 Million
Number Employees: 5-9
Type of Packaging: Consumer, Bulk
Brands:
    Lowell Farms

7610 Lowell-Paul Dairy
14332 County Road 64
Greeley, CO 80631-9317
    970-353-0278
Fax: 970-353-0338
Fluid milk, cream and related products
President: Margaret Paul
Estimated Sales: $5-10 Million
Number Employees: 20-49

7611 Lower Foods, Inc.
700 South 200 West
Richmond, UT 84333
    435-258-2449
Fax: 800-395-5691   800-295-7898
charliejcms@aol.com   www.llranch.com
Sliced & shredded meats, poultry, hispanic items, pork, pot roast, pickled raw corned beef, oven roasted corned beef, smoked pastrami, prime rib, roast beef, and Angus beef
President: Alan Lower
VP/Accounting: Lori Howells
Director of Sales & Marketing: Vicki Boilesen
Director of Foodservice Sales: Charles Johnson
Customer Service: Stacy Knight
Estimated Sales: $120,000

Type of Packaging: Consumer

7612 Lowery's Home Made Candies
6255 W Kilgore Ave
Muncie, IN 47304-4794
    765-288-7300
Fax: 765-747-9662   800-541-3340
www.loweryscandies.com
Confectionery including caramel, taffy, chocolate, chocolate covered nuts and chocolate covered cherries
President: Michael Brown
Owner: Thelma Brown
Owner: Donald Brown
Contact: Vicki Good
orders@loweryscandies.com
Estimated Sales: $7 Million
Number Employees: 20-49
Type of Packaging: Consumer

7613 Lowery's Premium Roast Gourmet Coffee
P.O.Box 1858
Snohomish, WA 98291
    360-668-4545
Fax: 360-863-9742   800-767-1783
www.loweryscoffee.com
Coffee and wholesale and custom roasters, espresso machines, espresso accessories
President: Donald Lowery
CFO: Jeanette Zimmerman
Marketing: Mike Lowery
Contact: Don Lowery
dlowery@loweryscoffee.com
Roast/Operations Manager: Jerry Lowery
Estimated Sales: Below $5 Million
Number Employees: 20-49
Number of Brands: 2
Number of Products: 100
Square Footage: 20000
Type of Packaging: Private Label
Brands:
    Lowery's Coffee
    Pasano's Syrups

7614 Lowland Seafood
569 Kelly Watson Rd
Lowland, NC 28552-9653
    252-745-3751
Fax: 252-745-5040
Fish, shrimp, crabs and scallops
President: Carol Potter
Estimated Sales: $1,500,000
Number Employees: 25
Type of Packaging: Consumer, Food Service, Bulk

7615 Lt Blender's Frozen Concoctions
1202 Post Office St
Galveston, TX 77550-5041
    409-765-5666
Fax: 409-966-1581   info@ltblender.com
www.ltblender.com
Frozen concoction drinks in a bag: margarita; strawberry daiquiri; pina colada; mudslide; hurricane; mojito; peach bellini wine freezer; sangria wine freezer; strawberry wine freezer; and margarita wine freezer.
Founder/President: Ralph McMorris
Vice President Marketing: Scott Treadaway

7616 Luban International
9900 NW 25th St
Doral, FL 33172
    305-629-8730
Fax: 305-629-8740
Cereals
Owner: Luis Banegas
xbanegas@gmail.com

7617 Lubbers Family Farm
862 Luce Strett SW
Grand Rapids, MI 49534
    616-453-4257
info@lubbersfarm.com
Pork, beef, dairy, eggs, and fresh breads
President: Andy Lubber

7618 Lubrizol Corp
29400 Lakeland Blvd
Wickliffe, OH 44092
    440-943-4200
www.lubrizol.com
Synthetic food colors, natural food colors, secondary blends, lakes, solutions

Chairman, President & CEO: Eric Schnur
Treasurer, CVP & CFO: J Brian Pitts
CVP, Operations & Supply Chain: Mike Vaughn
Year Founded: 1928
Estimated Sales: Over $1 Billion
Number Employees: 5,000-9,999

7619 Lucas Meyer
765 E Pythian Ave
Decatur, IL 62526-2412
    217-875-3660
Fax: 217-877-5046   800-769-3660
Lecithin and soy flour
President: Peter Rohde
VP: Scott Hagerman
Director Sales/Marketing: Scott Hagerman
Sales Manager: Jack Chenault
Estimated Sales: $600000
Number Employees: 10-19

7620 Lucas Vineyards & Winery
3862 County Road 150
Interlaken, NY 14847-9805
    607-532-4825
Fax: 607-532-8580   800-682-9463
info@lucasvineyards.com
www.lucasvineyards.com
Wines
President, General Manager and Founder: Ruth Lucas
Vice President of Administration: Ruthie Crawford
Vice President of Retail Sales: Stephanie Lucas Houck
Office Manager: Jessica Siurano
Winemaker: Jeffrey Houck
Plant Manager: Ruthie Lucas
Estimated Sales: $5-10 Million
Number Employees: 10-19
Type of Packaging: Consumer, Food Service
Brands:
    Lucas

7621 Lucas Winery
18196 N Davis Rd
Lodi, CA 95242-9280
    209-368-2006
Fax: 209-368-4900   info@lucaswinery.com
www.lucaswinery.com
Fine wines
Owner: David Lucas
david@lucaswinery.com
Estimated Sales: Less than $500,000
Number Employees: 1-4
Type of Packaging: Private Label
Brands:
    Lucas

7622 Lucerne Foods
5918 Stoneridge Mall Road
Pleasanton, CA 94588
Canada
Fax: 925-226-9510   877-232-4271
www.lucernefoods.com
Baked goods, crackers, carbonated beverages, ice cream, juices and waters.
President: Dan Gott
Number Employees: 100-249

7623 Lucero Olive Oil Mfr
2120 Loleta Ave
Corning, CA 96021-9696
    530-824-2190
Fax: 530-824-1243   877-330-2190
mail@luceroliveoil.com   www.luceroliveoil.com
Olive oils
Owner: Bpb Crane
mail@luceroliveoil.com
Number Employees: 20-49

7624 Lucero Olive Oil Mfr
2120 Loleta Ave
Corning, CA 96021-9696
    530-824-2190
Fax: 530-824-1243   mail@luceroliveoil.com
www.luceroliveoil.com
Olive oils
Owner: Bpb Crane
mail@luceroliveoil.com
Vice President: Anthony Lucerno
Operations Manager: Pete Johnston
Number Employees: 20-49

Food Manufacturers / A-Z

7625 Lucia's Pizza Co
10989 Gravois Industrial Ct
St Louis, MO 63128-2032
314-843-2553
Fax: 314-843-3576
Processor and wholesaler/distributor of frozen pizza
President: Darrell Long
sean@luciaspizza.com
Sales Exec: Sean Lynch
Estimated Sales: $1,600,000
Number Employees: 20-49
Square Footage: 50000
Type of Packaging: Consumer, Private Label
Brands:
    Lucia's

7626 Lucich Santos Farms
12631 Rogers Rd
Patterson, CA 95363-8511
209-892-6500
Fax: 209-892-2446 www.blossomhillapricots.com
Processor and exporter of table grapes
Owner: Pete Lucich
Owner/Partner: David Santos
Sales Manager: Jim Lucich
blossomhill@inreach.com
Estimated Sales: $10.6 Million
Number Employees: 100-249
Square Footage: 23064
Parent Co: Stevco Inc.
Type of Packaging: Consumer, Bulk
Brands:
    Sall-N-Ann

7627 Lucile's
2124 14th St
Boulder, CO 80302-4804
303-442-4743
Fax: 303-939-9848 800-727-3653
info@luciles.com www.luciles.com
Creole seasonings and French roast blend coffee
Owner: Josh Mcillwain
Sales Manager: Jennifer Fowler
jmcillwain@lucilleslist.com
Estimated Sales: $500,000-$1 Million
Number Employees: 20-49
Square Footage: 16000
Type of Packaging: Consumer, Food Service, Bulk
Brands:
    Lucile's

7628 Lucille's Own Make Candies
156 Route 72 E
Manahawkin, NJ 08050
609-597-7300
Fax: 609-597-7393 800-426-9168
Candy and confections
President: Nathaniel Eismann
VP Sales: Janice Eismann
Estimated Sales: $500,000-$1 Million
Number Employees: 5-9

7629 Lucini Italia Company
601 22nd Street
San Francisco, CA 94107
866-972-6879
Fax: 415-401-0087 888-558-2464
www.lucini.com
Extra virgin olive oil
President: Renee Frigo
Estimated Sales: Less than $500,000
Number Employees: 5-9

7630 Lucky Foods
11847 SW Itel Street
Tualatin, OR 97062
503-612-1300
info@luckyfood.com
www.luckyfood.com
Korean foods

7631 Lucky Nutrition
1801 N Military Trl
Suite 120
Boca Raton, FL 33431-1810
Fax: 561-405-3158 800-928-4882
pickyeatersrule.com
Protein bars
Founder: Jamie Oberweger
Brands:
    Luckybars

7632 Lucky Seafood Corporation
6203 Jonesboro Road
Morrow, GA 30260-1723
770-960-9889
Fax: 770-968-9400
Seafood
President: David Ng

7633 Lucky Spoon Bakery LLC
32 Dartmoor Pl
Salt Lake City, UT 84103-2275
USA
801-824-0624
www.luckyspoon.com
Baked goods, cookies, cupcakes, muffins
Contact: Pam Schulte
pam.schulte@luckyspoon.com
Estimated Sales: 250,000
Number Employees: 10

7634 Lucky You
3167 Commercial Street
San Diego, CA 92113
619-450-6700
Fax: 619-450-6701 customerservice@yldinc.com
www.yldinc.com
Chocolates and other candy.
Marketing: Deborah Roberts
Contact: Deborah Roberts
droberts@yldinc.com

7635 Lucy's Foods
408 Longs Rd
Latrobe, PA 15650-3506
724-539-1430
Fax: 724-532-0525 nzappone@aol.com
www.lucyshealthfoods.com
Frozen Italian foods, pasta and sausage
President: Nicky Zappone
lucyfoods@aol.com
Estimated Sales: $6 Million
Number Employees: 1-4
Type of Packaging: Consumer
Brands:
    Delgrosso
    Denunzio
    Lotito
    Rizzo's
    Rosie's

7636 Lucy's Sweet Surrender
20314 Chagrin Blvd
Beachwood, OH 44122-4973
216-752-0828
Fax: 216-767-0735 info@lucyssweetsurrender.com
www.lucyssweetsurrender.com
Hungarian pastries and custom European baked goods
President: Michael Feigenbaum
Estimated Sales: Less Than $500,000
Number Employees: 5-9

7637 Ludfords
3038 Pleasant St
Riverside, CA 92507-5554
951-823-0306
Fax: 909-948-0597 support@ludfordsinc.com
www.ludfordsinc.com
Processor, importer and exporter of fresh, frozen and canned fruit juices including orange, apple, grape, etc
President: Paul Ludford
Contact: Matt Real
matt@ludfordsinc.com
Estimated Sales: Below $5,000,000
Number Employees: 1-4
Square Footage: 40000
Type of Packaging: Consumer, Food Service, Private Label
Brands:
    Ludford's

7638 Ludo LLC
5325 Naiman Pkwy Ste G
Solon, OH 44139
440-542-6000
Fax: 440-542-9555 info@ludollc.com
Candy
Manager: Stephanie Holmes
Estimated Sales: $300,000-500,000
Number Employees: 1-4
Brands:
    Bubble Candy

7639 Ludwick's Frozen Donuts
3217 3 Mile Rd NW
Grand Rapids, MI 49534-1223
616-453-6880
Fax: 616-453-1930 800-366-8816
Frozen doughnuts, fresh cookies, and seafoam candy frozen pastries.pies,cakes.
President: Thomas Ludwick
CEO: Jack Brown
Director of Sales: Jim Glupker
Contact: Sarah Trocke
sarahjtrocke@gmail.com
Estimated Sales: $5-10 Million
Number Employees: 10-19
Type of Packaging: Consumer, Food Service, Private Label, Bulk
Brands:
    Kneadin the Dough

7640 Ludwig Dairy Product
1270 Mark St
Elk Grove Vlg, IL 60007-6708
847-860-8646
Fax: 847-860-5657 info@ludwigdairy.com
www.ludwigfoods.com
Dairy products
Owner: Mirek Gebka
ludwigdairy@gmail.com
Assistant Plant Manager: Duane Hadaway
VP Manufacturing: Mario Jedwabrik
Maintenance Manager: Rich Majewiski
Plant Manager: Michael Imel/ Ed Tomasziewicz
Estimated Sales: $410 K
Number Employees: 5-9
Type of Packaging: Private Label

7641 Ludwig Fish & Produce Company
409 Michigan Ave
La Porte, IN 46350
219-362-2608
Fax: 219-325-8311 800-362-2608
www.ludwigfishproduce.com
Wholesaler/distributor of frozen food, general line products, produce, provisions/meats and seafood; serving the food service market
President: Harold Robinson
Estimated Sales: $3,800,000
Number Employees: 20-49

7642 Luhr Jensen & Sons Inc
400 Portway Ave
Hood River, OR 97031-1192
541-386-3811
Fax: 541-386-4917 info@luhrjensen.com
www.luhrjensen.com
Sausage and brine mixes and seasonings and spices; also, sausage making kits, electric smokers and wood flavor fuels
President: Philip Jensen
philipjensen@luhrjensen.com
Customer Service: Linda Gordon
Estimated Sales: $10-20 Million
Number Employees: 250-499
Square Footage: 100000

7643 Lukas Confections
231 W College Ave
York, PA 17401-2103
717-843-0921
Fax: 717-854-9743 sales@warrellcorp.com
www.classiccaramel.com
Processor and exporter of sugarless and regular caramel toffee, taffy nougat and caramel including liquid; also salt water taffy and nutraceuticals
President/CEO: Robert Lukas
angie@classiccaramel.com
CFO: G Mark Zelinski
angie@classiccaramel.com
Contact: Angela Smith
angie@classiccaramel.com
Operations Manager: Joseph Stuck
Estimated Sales: $4 Million
Number Employees: 50
Number of Brands: 4
Number of Products: 110
Square Footage: 208000
Type of Packaging: Consumer, Private Label, Bulk
Brands:
    Caramel Milk Roll
    Classic
    Dark Fruit Chews
    Dorks
    Flipsticks

Food Manufacturers / A-Z

7644 Luke's Organic
Santa Cruz, CA 95060
www.lukesorganic.com
Organic potato chips and tortilla chips
Founder: Jaap Langenberg
VP, Sales and Marketing: Steve Kneepkens

7645 Lumar Lobster
297 Burnside Ave
Lawrence, NY 11559
516-371-0083
Live lobster
President: Stanley Jassem
Estimated Sales: Less than $500,000
Number Employees: 1-4
Type of Packaging: Food Service

7646 Lumen
Oakland, CA 94607
www.drinklumen.com
Hemp elixir
Founder & CEO: Jacob Freepons
Co-Founder: Kris Taylor
Co-Founder: Yasir Kashim

7647 Luna & Larry's Coconut Bliss
PO Box 288
Eugene, OR 97440
541-345-0020
www.coconutbliss.com
Manufacturer of non-dairy ice cream.
Co-Founder: Larry Kaplowitz
Co-Founder: Luna Marcus
Quality Assurance Manager: Kate Campbell
Director of Marketing: Kim Clark
Director of Sales: Marc Donofrio
Contact: Karen Campbell
kate@coconutbliss.com
Purchasing Agent: J Luna
Brands:
  Coconut Bliss

7648 Luna's Tortillas
8524 Harry Hines Blvd
Dallas, TX 75235-3013
214-747-2661
Fax: 214-747-5862 info@lunastortillas.com
www.lunastortillas.com
Mexican food products including corn tortillas, flour tortillas, tostadas, taco shells, nacho chips, tamales, hot sauce, pico de gallo, beans, chorizo, masa and hojas.
President: Fernando Luna
fernando@lunastortillas.com
Sales/Marketing Executive: Fernando Luna
Purchasing Agent: J Luna
Estimated Sales: $1,200,000
Number Employees: 10-19
Square Footage: 30000
Type of Packaging: Consumer, Food Service
Brands:
  Luna's

7649 Lund's Fisheries
997 Ocean Dr
Cape May, NJ 08204
609-884-7600
Fax: 609-884-0664 info@lundsfish.com
www.lundsfish.com
Frozen cod, flounder, mackerel, squid, sturgeon, tuna, herring and shad.
Owner & Chairman: Jeffery Reichle
Owner & President: Wayne Reichle
wreichle@lundsfish.com
Director, Compliance & Quality Assurance: Marty Martinez
Director, Sales & Marketing: Randy Spencer
Director, Government Affairs: Jeff Kaelin
Year Founded: 1954
Estimated Sales: $219 Million
Number Employees: 250-499
Type of Packaging: Consumer, Food Service

7650 Lundberg Family Farms
5311 Midway
PO Box 369
Richvale, CA 95974
530-538-3500
Fax: 530-882-4500 info@lundberg.com
www.lundberg.com
Rice products
CEO: Grant Lundberg
VP Sales: Tim O'Donnell
Regional Sales Manager: Benjamin Strazze
Estimated Sales: Less Than $500,000
Number Employees: 1-4
Type of Packaging: Consumer, Food Service, Private Label, Bulk
Brands:
  Evergood
  Lundberg

7651 Lupi-Marchigiano Bakery
169 Washington Ave
New Haven, CT 06519-1618
203-562-9491
Fax: 203-562-5456
Baked goods
President: Pete Lupi
pete_lupi@lupis.com
Estimated Sales: Below $5 000,000
Number Employees: 20-49

7652 Lusty Lobster
10 Portland Fish Pier
Suite A
Portland, ME 04101-4620
207-773-2829
Fax: 207-774-3956
Lobster
President: Doug Douty
Estimated Sales: $10-20 Million
Number Employees: 10-19

7653 (HQ)Luv Yu Bakery
3410 Bashford Avenue Ct # 1
Louisville, KY 40218-3182
502-451-4511
Fax: 502-451-5510 luvyubrand@aol.com
www.luvyu.com
Chocolate-dipped, buffet and organic cookies, unique snacks, rice crackers and shrimp chips
President: Abel Yu
luvyubrand@aol.com
Vice President: Serena Yu
Number Employees: 10-19
Square Footage: 100000

7654 Luvo Inc.
Blaine, WA 98230
844-880-5886
luvofoods.com
Frozen meals
CEO: Christine Day
Type of Packaging: Consumer
Brands:
  LUVO STEAM IN POUCH
  LUVO FLIPPED BOWL
  LUVO BOWL
  LUVO PLANTED

7655 (HQ)Luxco Inc
5050 Kemper Ave
St Louis, MO 63139-1106
314-772-2626
Fax: 314-772-6021 contactus@luxco.com
www.luxco.com
Manufacturer, bottler, importer and exporter of quality destilled spirits and wines.
Chairman/CEO: Donn Lux
President/COO: David Bratcher
VP Finance/CFO: Steve Soucy
Chief Marketing Officer: Steve Einig
Director, Corporate R&D: John Rempe
EVP Sales: Dan Streepy
Contact: Tina Aebi
t.aebi@luxco.com
Warehouse Manager: Douglas Finkeldey
Estimated Sales: $23.8 Million
Number Employees: 1-4
Square Footage: 200000
Type of Packaging: Private Label
Brands:
  American
  Andrew's Long Island Iced Tea
  Arrow
  Azteca
  Baron's
  Bellows
  Black Duck
  Boord's
  Bourbon Supreme
  Brookside Reserve
  Burke & Barry
  Cachaca 61
  Caffe Lolita
  Calvert
  Canada House
  Canadian Deluxe
  Canadian Reserve
  Canadian Springs
  Carlos
  Chapala
  Colonial Club
  Conway's
  Coronado
  Country Club
  Crystal Clear
  Dan Tucker
  Dark Eyes
  David Nicholson 1843
  Daviess County
  Delacour
  Dimitri
  Dos Gusanos
  Dos Trianos
  El Mayor
  Everclear
  Exotico
  Expresso
  Ezra Brooks
  Fonda Blanca
  Gavilan
  Getreide
  Glaros
  Gold Award
  Golden Grain
  Governor's Club
  Grand Muriel
  Gusano Rojo
  Hawkeye
  Henri Philipe
  Highland Light
  Highland Piper
  Hot Shot
  Hound Dog
  Juarez
  Kentucky's Choice
  Kiev
  Korski
  Lady Bligh
  La Prima
  La Salle
  Lightning
  Limonce
  Lord Ansley
  Macalister
  Pearl
  Piping Rock
  Rebel Yell
  Pearl
  Piping Rock
  Rebel Yell
  Saint Brendan's
  Salvador's
  Yago Sant'Gria

7656 Luxor California Exports Corp.
3659 India Street
2nd Floor
San Diego, CA 92103-4767
619-465-7777
Fax: 619-692-4292 rkafaji@aol.com
Supplier and exporter of agricultural commodities closeouts including dry beans, grains, oils, yeast, dry milk, butter, etc
President: Ray Kafaji
Marketing Director: Holland Clem
Estimated Sales: $1000000
Number Employees: 5
Type of Packaging: Bulk

7657 Luxury Crab
64 Airport Rd
Unit 2
St John's, NL A1A 4Y3
Canada
709-739-6668
info@whitecapseafoods.com
www.luxurycrab.com
Frozen crab and crab claws.
Chief Executive Officer: Randolph Bishop
Technical Director: Brian Cuff
Project Manager: Brad Hookey
Estimated Sales: $40 Million
Number Employees: 25
Other Locations:
  Toronto ON
  Winnipeg MB
  Calgary AB
  Vancouver BC
  Danvers MA
  Seattle WA

Food Manufacturers / A-Z

Brands:
　　Atlantic Queen
　　Classic
　　Luxury

7658 Luyties Pharmacal Company
4200 Laclede Street
Saint Louis, MO 63108
　　　　　　　　　　　　314-533-9600
　　Fax: 314-535-9600 800-325-8080
　　　　　　　　info@1800homeopathy.com
Processor and exporter of vitamins and homeopathic products
Director Marketing: Michael Smith
Number Employees: 50-99
Parent Co: Manola Company
Brands:
　　Luyties

7659 Lve & Raymond Vineyards
849 Zinfandel Ln
St Helena, CA 94574-1645
　　　　　　　　　　　　707-963-0869
　　Fax: 707-963-8498 800-525-2659
　　customerservice@raymondvineyards.com
　　　　　　　　www.lvecollection.com
Wines
President/Owner: Jean Charles Boisset
Winemaking Director: Stephanie Putman
Vineyard Manager: Eric Pooler
Assistant Winemaker: Kathy George
Manager: Craig Raymond
craymond@raymondwine.com
Number Employees: 20-49
Type of Packaging: Private Label
Brands:
　　Raymond Vineyard

7660 Lynard Company
15 Maple Tree Ave
Stamford, CT 06906
　　　　　　　　　　　　203-323-0231
　　Fax: 203-323-0231 lynardco@aol.com
Chocolates, candies, pretzels, nuts, popcorn, cookies, dried fruits, honey package designing
President: Lillian Flaster
Vice President: Howard Flaster
Contact: Lilian Flaster
lynardco@aol.com
Estimated Sales: Less than $200,000
Number Employees: 5-9

7661 Lynch Foods
72 Railside Road
North York, ON M3A 1A3
Canada
　　　　　　　　　　　　416-449-5464
　　Fax: 416-449-9165 www.lynchfoods.ca
Dessert toppings, chocolate syrup, corn syrup, mincemeat, condiments, sauces, Asian sauces, marinades, drink mixes.
President/Board Member: Scott Lynch
Chairman: Walker Lynch
VP Marketing: Peter Henderson
VP Sales: Scott Lynch
Estimated Sales: $16 Million
Number Employees: 140
Square Footage: 240000
Type of Packaging: Consumer, Food Service, Private Label, Bulk

7662 Lyndell's Bakery
720 Broadway
Somerville, MA 2144
　　　　　　　　　　　　617-625-1793
　　　　　　　　　　　　lyndells.com
Baked goods
Founder: Birger Lindahl
Contact: Adam Bagarella
abagarella@lyndells.com

7663 Lynden Meat Co
1936 Front St
Lynden, WA 98264-1708
　　　　　　　　　　　　360-354-2449
　　　　　　Fax: 360-354-7687
Livestock slaughtering services, herd managemnt, livestock breeding and grooming, livestock management, livestock selection, ice cube makers, ice block makers, industrial freezers.
Owner: Rick Biesheuvel
Estimated Sales: $3-5 Million
Number Employees: 5-9
Type of Packaging: Consumer

7664 Lynfred Winery Inc
15 S Roselle Rd # 14
Roselle, IL 60172-2043
　　　　　　　　　　　　630-529-9463
　　Fax: 630-529-4971 wineinfo@lynfredwinery.com
　　　　　　　　www.lynfredwinery.com
Wines
President: Fred Koehler
Manager: Allen Adomite
wineinfo@lynfredwinery.com
Estimated Sales: $8-20 Million
Number Employees: 50-99
Number of Brands: 1
Number of Products: 50
Square Footage: 24000
Type of Packaging: Private Label
Brands:
　　Lynfred

7665 Lynn Dairy Inc
W1929 US Highway 10
Granton, WI 54436-8899
　　　　　　　　　　　　715-238-7129
　　Fax: 715-238-7130 info@lynndairy.com
　　　　　　　　www.lynndairy.com
Milk, cheese and other dairy products.
President: William L Schwantes
lynndairy@fibernetcc.com
Marketing Director: Rick Beilke
Estimated Sales: $5-10 Million
Number Employees: 100-249
Type of Packaging: Bulk
Brands:
　　Lynn Dairy
　　Lynn Protiens

7666 Lynn Springs Water LLC
4325 1st Ave # 562
Tucker, GA 30084-4498
　　　　　　　　　　　　770-572-5928
Water
President: Tandrias Thomas
CEO: Jocelyn Facen
CFO: Al Thomas
Vice President: Derrick Smith
Estimated Sales: $1-2 Million
Number Employees: 20-49
Number of Brands: 1
Number of Products: 1
Square Footage: 12000
Type of Packaging: Bulk

7667 Lyo-San
500 Boul De L Aeroparc
C P 598
Lachute, QC J8H 4G4
Canada
　　　　　　　　　　　　450-562-8525
　　Fax: 450-562-1433 800-363-3697
　　lyo-san@lyo-san.ca www.lyo-san.ca
Manufacturer and exporter of freeze-dried yogurt cultures and bifido-bacteria; custom freeze-drying available. Founded in 1983.
President/Owner: Celine St-Pierre
Number Employees: 10-19
Square Footage: 180000
Type of Packaging: Consumer, Food Service, Private Label, Bulk
Brands:
　　Yogourmet

7668 Lyoferm & Vivolac Cultures
3862 E Washington St
Indianapolis, IN 46201-4470
　　　　　　　　　　　　317-356-8460
　　　　　　　　www.iquest.net
Cultures including dairy, meat and bakery starter, freeze dried/lyophilized and food fermentation
President/Vice President: Ethel Sing
Vice President: Edmond Sing
Estimated Sales: $2 Million
Number Employees: 23
Brands:
　　Lyoferm
　　Vivolac

7669 (HQ)Lyons Magnus
3158 E Hamilton Ave
Fresno, CA 93702-4163
　　　　　　　　　　　　559-442-5077
　　Fax: 559-233-8249 800-344-7130
　　　　　　　　www.lyonsmagnus.com
Fruit and flavor preparations for use in frozen desserts, cultured or beverage products, as well as fountain syrups and toppings, aseptic juices, beverage bases, fruit fillings, and breakfast condiments
President: Robert Smittcamp
CEO: Edward Carolan
CFO: Nasrim Fletcher
Research & Development: Lisa Balesteri
VP Quality Assurance: Steve Tweet
SVP Marketing: Jim Davis
VP Sales: Vince Veneziano
Manager: Eddie Ogualo
Director of Operations: Ken Atkins
Operations/Production Assistant: Monica Romero
Plant Manager: Noa Nguyen
VP of Purchasing: Don Savino
Estimated Sales: $47.7 Million
Number Employees: 250-499
Type of Packaging: Food Service, Private Label, Bulk
Other Locations:
　　Lyons-Magnus Plant Facility
　　Walton KY

7670 Lyons Magnus
95 Richwood Rd.
Walton, KY 41094
　　　　　　Fax: 859-485-7546 859-485-7546
　　　　　　　　www.lyonsmagnus.com
Fruit and flavor preparations for use in frozen desserts, cultured or beverage products, as well as fountain syrups and toppings, aseptic juices, beverage bases, fruit fillings, and breakfast condiments
Type of Packaging: Food Service, Private Label, Bulk

7671 M & B Fruit Juice Co
955 Home Ave
Akron, OH 44310-4121
　　　　　　　　　　　　330-253-7465
　　　　　　Fax: 330-253-8401
Fruit drink concentrates including orange, lemonade, pink lemonade, grape, cherry, lime, loganberry, iced tea and punch; also, vanilla and strawberry syrups
President: James Stone
jimbbstone@aol.com
Estimated Sales: $1-3 Million
Number Employees: 1-4
Square Footage: 40000
Type of Packaging: Consumer, Food Service, Private Label, Bulk
Brands:
　　Magic-Mix
　　Party Punch
　　Super-Mix
　　Trim-Lite
　　Wiz

7672 M & B Products Inc
8601 Harney Rd
Tampa, FL 33637-6605
　　　　　　　　　　　　813-988-2211
　　Fax: 813-980-6596 800-899-7255
　　　　　　　　www.mbproducts.com
Juice including orange, apple, orange/pineapple, grape, etc.; also, milk, milkshakes and frozen fruit juice bars
President: Allyson Hostetler
allyson@tidewell.org
CFO: Howard Hutchinson
Estimated Sales: $10-20 Million
Number Employees: 10-19
Type of Packaging: Consumer

7673 M & CP FARMS
3986 County Road Nn
Orland, CA 95963-9810
　　　　　　　　　　　　530-865-9810
　　Fax: 530-865-9793 greatolives@greatolives.com
　　　　　　　　www.greatolives.com
Olive spreads, mixes, cured olives, olive oil, stuffed olives, in addition to spicy beans, and sweet/sour pickles.
President: Maurice Penna
maurice@greatolives.com
Secretary/Treasurer: Cynthia Penna
Estimated Sales: $5 Million
Number Employees: 10-19
Square Footage: 60000
Parent Co: D. Beccaris
Type of Packaging: Consumer, Food Service, Private Label, Bulk
Brands:
　　Loam Ridge
　　M&Cp Farms

Food Manufacturers / A-Z

7674 M & M Label Co
380 Pearl St
Malden, MA 02148-6607
781-321-2737
Fax: 781-322-9065 800-637-6628
info@mmlabel.com www.mmlabel.com
Packaging.
Owner: Linda Difiore
ldifiore@mmlabel.com
Estimated Sales: $1.2 Million
Number Employees: 10-19

7675 M & S Tomato Repacking Co Inc
1026 Bay St
Springfield, MA 01109-2427
413-737-1308
Fax: 413-736-6433
Packer of tomatoes
Owner: Laurie Chruscieo
Treasurer: Laurie Chruscieo
Estimated Sales: $4 Million
Number Employees: 10-19
Type of Packaging: Consumer

7676 M Buono Beef Co
3650 S 3rd St
Philadelphia, PA 19148-5398
215-463-3600
Fax: 215-463-3481
Frozen portion-controlled beef and pork
Owner: Mike Buono
Estimated Sales: $2.9 Million
Number Employees: 10-19
Brands:
Colonial Beef

7677 M J Barleyhoppers Sports Bar
621 21st St
Lewiston, ID 83501-3285
208-748-1008
Fax: 208-799-1000 800-232-6730
ewilson@redlionlewiston.com
www.mjbarleyhoppers.com
Ale, stout and lager
Principal: Lee Duncan
Estimated Sales: $230,000
Number Employees: 10-19
Parent Co: Impact Restaurants
Type of Packaging: Consumer, Food Service
Brands:
Oktoberfest

7678 M S Walker Inc
20 3rd Ave
Somerville, MA 02143-4404
617-776-6700
Fax: 617-776-5808
Processor and importer of brandy, liqueurs, wines and spirits
President: Harvey Allen
CEO: Richard Sandler
rsandler@mswalker.com
CEO: Richard Sandler
Estimated Sales: $1-3 Million
Number Employees: 100-249

7679 M&H Erickson Ranch
3916 County Road Mm
Orland, CA 95963-9702
530-865-9587
Fax: 530-865-8637
Co-Owner: Heidi Erickson
Co-Owner: Merritt Erickson

7680 M&L Gourmet Ice Cream
2524 E Monument St
Baltimore, MD 21205-2539
410-276-4880
Fax: 410-525-8320
Processor and exporter of kosher ice cream
Owner: Chris Napfel
Estimated Sales: Less than $500,000
Number Employees: 1-4
Type of Packaging: Consumer, Food Service

7681 M&L Ventures
1471 W. COMMERCE COURT
Tucson, AZ 85746-6016
520-884-8232
Fax: 520-770-9649 sales@meritfoods.net
www.meritfoods.net
Products include produce and groceries, eggs and cheese, deli meats and salad dressings.
President: Matt Sadowsky
Secretary/Treasurer: Lynn Sadowsky
Manager: Bob Richter
Manager: Paul Rosthenhausler

7682 M&M Food Distributors/Oriental Pride
3322 Virginia Beach Blvd
Virginia Beach, VA 23452-5608
757-499-5676
Fax: 757-499-0807
Ethnic foods
President: Joan Mallen

7683 M-CAP Technologies
3521 Silverside Rd
Wilmington, DE 19810-4900
302-695-5329
Fax: 302-695-5350 jdoncheck@lakefield.net
Processor and exporter of industrial ingredients including bromate replacers, additives and preservatives; also, temperature release vitamins and minerals
President: Ernie Porta
VP Technology: James Doncheck
Number Employees: 5
Parent Co: DuPont Chemical
Brands:
Baker's Label

7684 M. Licht & Son
PO Box 507
Knoxville, TN 37901
865-523-5593
Fax: 865-523-0270
Processor and exporter of liquid artificial sweeteners
President: Richard M Licht
VP: Karen McGuire
Estimated Sales: $5-10 Million
Number Employees: 5-9
Square Footage: 12800
Type of Packaging: Food Service
Brands:
Smoky Mountain

7685 M. Marion & Company
422 Larkfield Center
Suite 253
Santa Rosa, CA 95403-1408
707-836-0551
Wines
President: M Dennis Marion
Estimated Sales: $500,000-$1 Million
Number Employees: 1-4

7686 M.A. Hatt & Sons
405 Hwy 324
Lunenburg, NS B0J 2C0
Canada
902-634-8407
Fax: 902-634-8407
Sauerkraut
President: Ralph Hatt
VP: Gladys Hatt
Number Employees: 5-9
Type of Packaging: Consumer, Food Service, Bulk
Brands:
Tan Cook

7687 M.A. Johnson Frozen Foods
1912 E Monroe Pike
Marion, IN 46953-2610
317-664-8023
Frozen foods
President: S Allen Johnson
Estimated Sales: $5-10 Million
Number Employees: 10

7688 M.A. Patout & Son LTD
3512 J. Patout Burns Rd.
Jeanerette, LA 70394
337-276-4592
Fax: 337-276-4247 ggilmore@mapatout.com
Sugar cane ingredients such as raw sugar, cane syrup and blackstrap molasses.
President/CEO: Craig Caillier
CFO: Randall Romero
Year Founded: 1825
Estimated Sales: $184 Million
Number Employees: 250-499
Square Footage: 150000
Type of Packaging: Bulk

7689 M.E. Franks Inc.
175 Strafford Ave
#230
Wayne, PA 19087
610-989-9688
Manufacturer of milk products.
President: Don Street
Estimated Sales: $1-2.5 Million
Number Employees: 10-19

7690 M.E. Swing Company
612 S Pickett St # D
Alexandria, VA 22304-4620
703-370-5050
Fax: 703-370-7286 800-485-4019
www.swingscoffee.com
Roasted coffee
Owner: Mark Woarmuth
Executive Vice President: Dwayne Walker
VP Marketing: Dwayne Walker
Contact: Carl Dodge
roaster@swingscoffee.com
Director of Operations: Darren Dimisa
Estimated Sales: Less than $500,000
Number Employees: 5-9
Square Footage: 12000
Type of Packaging: Consumer, Food Service, Bulk

7691 M.H. Greenebaum
64 Campbell Avenue
Airmont, NY 10901-6407
973-538-9200
Fax: 973-538-3599
Cheese, cheese products
President: Rasmus Andersen
Estimated Sales: $10-20 000,000
Number Employees: 5-9

7692 M/S Smears
490 Old U.S. Highway 74
P.O. Box 467
Chadbourn, NC 28431-0467
910-654-5163
Fax: 910-654-4734 www.sweetpotatoes.com
Pies
CEO: George Wooten
CFO: Stuart Hill
Opeartion Manager: Adam Wooten
Production Scheduler: Nicky Herring

7693 (HQ)MAFCO Worldwide
300 Jefferson St
Camden, NJ 08104
856-986-4050
Fax: 856-964-6029
magnasweet@mafcolicorice.com
mafco.com
Licorice products and other ingredients, including sweeteners
President & COO: Lucas Bailey
Global Research & Development Director: Mark Hines
SVP Strategy & Business Development: Jeff Robinson
Year Founded: 1902
Estimated Sales: $36 Million
Number Employees: 230
Type of Packaging: Bulk
Brands:
Magnasweet

7694 MAK Enterprises
37315 26th Street E
Palmdale, CA 93550-6414
661-272-1867
makenterprisesllc.com
Salsa and hot sauces
President/Owner: Mike Klumpp
CEO: Mark Taylor
CFO: Renee Taylor
Underground Operations Mgr: Doug Nestle
Number Employees: 20-49
Brands:
Hell's Furry Fire Hot Sauce
The Salsa Addiction

7695 MAK Wood Inc
1235 Dakota Dr # E
Unit E
Grafton, WI 53024-9477
262-387-1200
Fax: 262-387-1400 info@makwood.com
www.makwood.com

Food Manufacturers / A-Z

Novelty sugars, cranberry, probiotics, lactobacillus and bifidobacterium. Supplier of L-arabinose, L-fucose, L-rhamnose, lactates, and of other probiotics.
Owner: Mark Brudnak
Secretary/Treasurer: Joseph Brudnak
Sr Executive VP: Mark Brudnak
Manager, Technical Sales Services: Eric Baer
mark@makwood.com
Estimated Sales: $380,000
Number Employees: 5-9
Type of Packaging: Private Label, Bulk

7696 MALK Organics
8211 Dunlap St
Houston, TX 77074
281-974-3251
malkorganics.com
Almond, pecan and cashew milks
Founder & CEO: August Vega
Co-Owner: Justin Brodnax
Co-Owner: Joel Canada
Number of Brands: 2
Number of Products: 5
Type of Packaging: Consumer
Brands:
 MALK
 MALK COFFEE

7697 MATI Energy
201 W Main St
Suite 103
Durham, NC 27701
866-924-8005
www.matienergy.com
Energy drinks
President/Owner: Tatiana Birgisson
Number of Brands: 1
Number of Products: 6
Type of Packaging: Consumer
Brands:
 MATI

7698 MFI Food Canada
70 Irene Street
Winnipeg, MB R3T 4E1
Canada
204-992-8200
Fax: 204-475-7740 www.michaelfoods.com
Egg products including egg whites and yolks, scrambled egg mix, omelettes and egg patties.
Human Resources Manager: Darren Luke
Plant Manager: Mark Driedger
Estimated Sales: $37 Million
Number Employees: 200
Number of Brands: 1
Parent Co: Michael Foods, Inc.
Type of Packaging: Food Service
Brands:
 Papetti's

7699 MG Fisheries
7 Norman Road
Grand Manan, NB E5G 2G5
Canada
506-662-3471
Fax: 506-662-3779
Products include sea urchin, scallops, shark, monkfish, flounder, pollock-dried, cod-dried, pollock-salted, hake-dried, hake-salted, lobster-live, and cod-salted.
President: Maurice Green
Number Employees: 10-19
Type of Packaging: Consumer, Food Service

7700 MGP Ingredients Inc
100 Commercial St
Atchison, KS 66002-2514
913-367-1480
Fax: 913-367-0192 800-255-0302
www.mgpingredients.com
Process starches and specialty wheat proteins for food and non-food applications.
President/CEO: Tim Newkirk
CEO: Augustus C Griffin
augustus.griffin@mgpingredients.com
Vice President of Technical Services: Clodualdo Maningat
Vice President of Sales and Marketing: David Dykstra
Number Employees: 250-499

7701 MI-AL. Corp
27 Carpenter St
Glen Cove, NY 11542-2398
516-759-0652
Fax: 516-759-5752
Pasta
President/CFO: O. Michael Zara
Estimated Sales: $120,000
Number Employees: 4
Type of Packaging: Food Service, Private Label, Bulk
Brands:
 Papagallo

7702 MIC Foods
8701 SW 137th Avenue
#308
Miami, FL 33183
786-507-0540
Fax: 786-507-0545 800-788-9335
info@micfood.com www.micfood.com/
Processor and importer of frozen plaintains, yuca, cassava and frozen fruit products.
President: Alfredo Lardizabal
Sales VP: Maria Krogh
maria@micfood.com
Estimated Sales: $5-10 Million
Number Employees: 5-9
Brands:
 Big Banana
 Costa Clara
 Tio Jorge

7703 MKE Enterprises LTD
375 5th Avenue
New York, NY 10016-3323
212-447-0051
Fax: 212-447-0068 mkegroupltd@gmail.com

7704 MO Air International
183 Madison Avenue
Suite 1202
New York, NY 10016
212-792-9400
Fax: 212-490-1763 800-247-3131
www.moair-usa.com
Manager: Sherry Kawabe
Parent Co: Mitsui & Co.

7705 MODe Sports Nutrition
1599 Superior Ave
Unit B-2
Costa Mesa, CA 92627
949-274-9948
info@myfitmode.com
myfitmode.com
Cold-pressed energy shots, energy bars, and protein and electrolyte powders
Co-Founder & CEO: Tammo Walter
VP, Sales: Beau Clark
Co-Founder & COO: Nikki Halbur
Type of Packaging: Consumer
Brands:
 MODE

7706 MSRF, Inc.
2501 N Elston Ave
Chicago, IL 60618
773-227-1115
Fax: 773-227-2031 www.msrf.com
Gourmet food gifts
President: David Reich
National Sales Manager: Scott Nejman
Contact: Fred Beegun
fred@msrf.com
Operations: Claire Danieleski
Estimated Sales: $7-19 Million
Number Employees: 20-49
Brands:
 Msrf

7707 MUD
247 Beach 136th St
Belle Harbor, NY 11694-1323
516-507-0212
hello@eatmud.co
www.eatmud.co
Non-dairy frozen desserts.
CEO: Sam Friedman
Brands:
 MUD

7708 MUSH Foods
Vista, CA 92081
hello@eatmush.com
eatmush.com
Overnight oats
Co-Founder & CEO: Ashley Thompson
Co-Founder & COO: Katherine Thomas

7709 MXO Global
220 Appin Ave
Mount Royal, QC H3P 1V8
Canada
tolerantfoods.com
Legume pasta
Founder: Tom Friedmann
Brands:
 Tolerant

7710 MYNTZ!
19016 72nd Ave S.
Kent, WA 98032
425-656-9076
Fax: 425-656-8059 800-800-9490
www.myntz.
MYNTZ! is a confection company that manufactures, packages and distributes up-scale consumer breath mints in a variety of flavors that include vanillamyntblast sugar-free, tropical fruit and orchard fruit.
President/CEO: David Parker
National Sales Director: Robert Kingsley
Customer Service: Diana Klein
Number Employees: 50-99
Brands:
 Dropz
 Myntz! Breath Mints
 Myntz! Instastripz
 Myntz! Lip Balm
 Sqyntz! Supersourz

7711 Maat Nutritionals
1875 Century Park East
6th Floor
Los Angeles, CA 90067
310-407-8608
Fax: 310-407-8618 888-818-6228
info@e-maat.com www.e-maat.com
Dietary supplements, vitamins and minerals
President: Rick Mandell

7712 Maberry & Maberry BerryAssociates
729 Loomis Trail Rd
Lynden, WA 98264
360-354-7708
Fax: 360-354-3906 www.maberrys.com
Fresh and frozen blueberries, strawberries and raspberries
President: Curt Maberry
Director, Sales: Carl Swartz
Contact: Marlys Lange
marlys@maberrys.com
Estimated Sales: $2.5-5 Million
Number Employees: 20-49
Type of Packaging: Private Label, Bulk

7713 Mac Farms Of Hawaii Inc
89-406 Mamalahoa Hwy
Captain Cook, HI 96704-8941
808-328-2435
Fax: 808-328-8081 sales@macfarms.com
www.macfarms.com
Macadamia nuts, flavored macadamia nuts, chocolate covered macadamia nuts and macadamia nut cookies
President: Nicole Knight
sales@macfarms.com
Executive Vice President: Scott Wallace
VP Sales: Brian Loader
Manager: Rick Vigden
Estimated Sales: $20-50 Million
Number Employees: 100-249
Parent Co: Blue Diamond Growers
Type of Packaging: Consumer, Private Label, Bulk
Brands:
 Macfarms of Hawaii

7714 Mac Knight Smoke House Inc
550 NE 185th St
Miami, FL 33179-4513
305-651-3323
Fax: 305-655-0039 sales@macknight.com
www.macknight.com
Processor and importer of smoked and fresh fish

Food Manufacturers / A-Z

President: Jonathan Brown
General Manager: Alex McMorran
Estimated Sales: $10-20 Million
Number Employees: 20-49
Square Footage: 20000
Type of Packaging: Consumer, Food Service, Private Label, Bulk

7715 Mac's Donut Shop
2698 Brodhead Rd
Aliquippa, PA 15001-2768
724-375-6776
Fax: 724-378-2961
Baked goods including doughnuts, cakes, pastries, cookies, muffins, brownies
Owner: Twila Mc Kittrick
VP: Twila McKittrick
Estimated Sales: $1.1 Million
Number Employees: 20-49
Type of Packaging: Consumer

7716 Mac's Farms Sausage Co Inc
209 Raleigh St
Newton Grove, NC 28366
910-594-0095
Fax: 910-594-1812 macfarms@intrstar.net
Sausage
Owner: Scott Mc Lamb
CEO: Scott McLamb
Estimated Sales: $700,000
Number Employees: 5-9
Type of Packaging: Bulk
Brands:
  Double D
  Mac's

7717 Mac's Meats Inc
1761 W Hadley Ave
Las Cruces, NM 88005-4122
575-524-2751
Fax: 575-526-3826
Meat including pork and beef
President: Al Guerrero
Estimated Sales: $10-20 Million
Number Employees: 5-9
Type of Packaging: Consumer, Food Service

7718 Mac's Oysters
414 Emerton Rd
Fanny Bay, BC V0R 1W0
Canada
250-335-2233
Fax: 250-335-2065 gordy@macsoysters.com
www.macsoysters.com
Clams and fresh shucked oysters
Managing Director: Gordon McLellan
Office Manager: Sally Kew
Number Employees: 50-99
Type of Packaging: Consumer, Food Service, Private Label, Bulk

7719 Mac's Snacks
615 N Great Southwest Pkwy
Arlington, TX 76011-5465
817-640-5626
Fax: 817-649-7832
Manufacturer of pork skins and cracklings.
Manager: David Sparesus
Plant Manager: David Sparesus
Estimated Sales: $10-20 Million
Number Employees: 20-49
Parent Co: Evans Food Products
Type of Packaging: Private Label, Bulk

7720 MacEwan's Meats
9620 Elbow Drive SW
Calgary, AB T2V 1M2
Canada
403-228-9999
Fax: 403-228-9999 www.macewansmeats.com
Meat pies including chicken, steak and scotch
President: John Hopkins
VP: Lynne Hopkins
Number Employees: 1-4
Square Footage: 6000
Type of Packaging: Consumer, Food Service, Bulk
Brands:
  Macewan's

7721 MacGregors Meat & Seafood
265 Garyray Drive
Toronto, ON M9L 1P2
Canada
416-746-5951
888-383-3663
www.macgregors.com
Poultry, seafood and meat products; importer of beef and seafood
CFO: Ed de Vries
Vice President: John Hercus
VP of Sales, National Accounts: Rob Simpson
Number Employees: 180
Square Footage: 184000
Brands:
  44th Street
  Center-of-the-Plate Specialists
  Certified Angus Beef
  Niman Ranch
  North Country Meat & Seafood
  Organic Ocean
  The Store

7722 MacKay's Cochrane Ice Cream
220 1st Street W
Cochrane, AB T4C 1A5
Canada
403-932-2455
Fax: 403-932-2455
generalinfo@mackaysicecream.com
www.mackaysicecream.com
Ice cream, frozen yogurt, sherbet and sorbet
Manager: Robyn MacKay
Production Manager: Rhona Mackay
Number Employees: 1-4
Type of Packaging: Consumer, Food Service
Brands:
  Mackay's

7723 MacKinlay Teas
1289 Waterways Dr
Ann Arbor, MI 48108-2783
734-846-0966
Fax: 734-747-9193
Teas
President: Davinder Singh
Estimated Sales: $2.9 Million
Number Employees: 1-4
Type of Packaging: Private Label
Brands:
  Mackinlay Tea's
  Queen Jasmine
  White Tiger Rice
  Wild Blend Rice

7724 Macabee Foods
250 West Nyack Road
West Nyack, NY 10994
845-623-1300
Fax: 845-623-7649 www.macabeefoods.com
Kosher frozen pizza
President: Marvin Kochansky
VP: Jeffery Schmelzer
Number Employees: 5-9
Square Footage: 16000
Type of Packaging: Consumer, Food Service, Private Label
Brands:
  Macabee

7725 Macaron Paris LLC
750 Third Ave.
New York, NY 10017
212-465-0510
www.macaroncafe.com
Manufacturer of macarons.
Public Relations: Cecile Cannone
Brands:
  Macaron Cafe

7726 Macco Organiques
100 rue Mc Arthur
Valleyfield, QC J6S 4M5
Canada
450-371-1066
Fax: 450-371-5519 macco@macco.ca
www.macco.ca
Processor and exporter of food preservatives including: calcium acetate; calcium chloride dihy; calcium propionate; potassium acetate; potassium benzoate; sodium acetate anh; sodium benzoate; sodium diacetate; and sodium propionate.

President: Robert Briscoe
VP: Jacques Rochon
General Manager: Simon Rinella
Estimated Sales: 9.27 Million
Number Employees: 60

7727 Macfarlane Pheasants
2821 S US Highway 51
Janesville, WI 53546-8945
608-757-7881
Fax: 608-757-7884 800-345-8348
info@pheasant.com www.pheasant.com
Producer of high quality, young, pheasants; available fresh, frozen, smoked as whole birds or cut down sized products.
Owner: Bill Mac Farlane
CFO: Brad Lillie
Sales: Sarah Pope
Shipping Manager: David Lennox
Plant Manager: Bryan Carter
Estimated Sales: $1-3 Million
Number Employees: 50-99
Square Footage: 20000
Type of Packaging: Food Service

7728 Machias Bay Seafood
503 Kennebec Rd
Machias, ME 04654
207-255-8671
Fax: 207-255-8243
Seafood
Owner: Randy Ramsdell
Estimated Sales: $1-3 Million
Number Employees: 1-4

7729 Mack's Bill Ice Cream
3890 Carlisle Rd
Dover, PA 17315-4418
717-292-1931
Ice cream including chocolate, vanilla, oreo cookie, peanut butter, raspberry, banana, caramel, strawberry, etc. Founded in 1993.
Owner: Todd Mc Daniel
Finance Executive: Amy McDaniel
Estimated Sales: $500,000-$1 Million
Number Employees: 20-49
Type of Packaging: Consumer
Brands:
  Bill Mack's

7730 Mack's Homemade Ice Cream
2695 S. Queen St.
York, PA 17402
717-741-2027
Fax: 717-747-0065
Owner: Walt Bloss
walt@macksicecream.com
Estimated Sales: $1-2.5 Million
Number Employees: 20-49
Parent Co: Bill Macks Homemade Ice Cream

7731 Mackenzie Creamery
6722 Pioneer Trl
Hiram, OH 44234-9714
330-569-3368
Fax: 330-569-3387 info@mackenziecreamery.com
www.mackenziecreamery.com
Organic Artisan goat cheeses
Founder/President: Jean Mackenzie
jeanniegoat@yahoo.com
Estimated Sales: Less Than $500,000
Number Employees: 10-19

7732 Mackie International, Inc.
#719 Palmyrita Avenue
Riverside, CA 92507-1811
951-346-0530
Fax: 951-346-0541 800-733-9762
www.mackieinternational.net
Ice pops, fruit flavored drinks and jellies
President: Ernesto Dacay
Sales/Marketing: Carmel Canete
Contact: Amando Briones
a.briones@mackieinternational.net
Estimated Sales: $10 Million
Number Employees: 50-99
Square Footage: 240000
Type of Packaging: Private Label, Bulk
Brands:
  Berry Cool
  Snowtime

Food Manufacturers / A-Z

7733 Macrie Brothers
750 S 1st Rd
Hammonton, NJ 08037-8407
609-561-6822
Fax: 609-561-6296 bluebuck@bellatlantic.net
Blueberries
Owner/CEO: Paul Macrie III
Superviser: Al Macrie
Operations: Nicholas Macrie
Production: Michael Macrie
Estimated Sales: Below $5 Million
Number Employees: 5
Square Footage: 120000
Type of Packaging: Consumer, Food Service, Private Label, Bulk
Brands:
　Blue Buck

7734 Mad Chef Enterprise
PO Box 321
Mentor, OH 44061-0321
440-951-0846
Fax: 440-269-2387 800-951-2433
Sauces, seasonings, rubs. Additional products include aprons, grilling mitts, basting brushes, grill lighters, spatulas, grilling baskets, salt & pepper mills, skewers, and mugs
President: Michael D'Amico

7735 Mad River Farm Kitchen
100 Ericson Ct # 140
Arcata, CA 95521-8940
707-822-0248
Fax: 707-822-4441 contact@mad-river-farm.com
www.mad-river-farm.com
Gourmet food products such as sunshine marmalade, lemon marmalade, plum orange jam with brandied raisins and wild huckleberry jam
Owner: Robin Bartlett
bartlettmrf@gmail.com
Vice President: Steven Ulrich
Administration: Marika Myrick
Production and Shipping: Mike Myrick
Estimated Sales: Below $5 Million
Number Employees: 1-4
Number of Brands: 1
Number of Products: 25
Square Footage: 4000
Type of Packaging: Consumer, Food Service, Private Label, Bulk
Brands:
　Mad River Farm

7736 Mad Scientist Nuts
3303 Airline Blvd
Suite 3A
Portsmouth, VA 23701-2635
757-288-6539
www.pizootz.com
Peanuts
CEO: Bo Perry
Brands:
　Pizootz

7737 Mad Will's Food Company
2043 Airpark Ct Ste 30
Auburn, CA 95602
530-823-8527
Fax: 530-823-1756 888-275-9455
www.madwills.com
Barbecue sauces, salsas, salad dressings, mustards, marinades, marinara sauces, hot sauces, other sauces and specialty food sauces; private label and contract packaging
President: Kim Sullivan
Marketing Director: Tim Sullivan
Operations Manager: Roy Ballard
VP Purchasing: Vanessa Johnson
Estimated Sales: $2.7 Million
Number Employees: 20
Number of Products: 70
Square Footage: 84672
Type of Packaging: Private Label

7738 Mada'n Kosher Foods
128 SW 3rd Ave
Dania, FL 33004
954-925-0077
Fax: 954-921-8739
Frozen kosher foods including beef, fish and poultry
President: Samuel Weiss
VP: Richard Marsico
Director Operations: Richard Anthony
Estimated Sales: $210000
Number Employees: 10-19
Square Footage: 14000
Parent Co: Mada'n Corporation
Type of Packaging: Consumer, Food Service

7739 Madani Halal
100-15 94th Ave
Ozone Park, NY 11416
718-323-9732
info@madanihalal.com
www.madanihalal.com
Halal goat, lamb, and poultry
President & CEO: Imran Uddin
Year Founded: 1996

7740 Maddalena Restaurant-Sn
737 Lamar St
Los Angeles, CA 90031-2514
323-223-1401
Fax: 323-221-7261 800-626-7722
info@sanantoniowinery.com
Wines
Owner/Manager: Anthony Riboli
anthony@sanantoniowinery.com
President/VP: Santo Riboli
Owner/President/Marketing Director: Steve Riboli
Sales Manager: Rick Rechetnick
HR & Finance Director/Purchasing Agent: Tony Tse
Estimated Sales: $12.7 Million
Number Employees: 100-249
Square Footage: 930000
Type of Packaging: Consumer, Food Service
Brands:
　Bodega De San Antonio Sangria
　Kinderwood
　La Quinta
　Maddalena
　Opaque
　Riobli Family Wine Estates
　San Antonio California Champagne
　San Antonio Dessert
　San Antonio Sacramental
　San Antonio Specialty
　San Antonio Winery
　San Simeon
　Stella Rosa Moscato D'Asti
　Windstream Windbreak

7741 Maddy & Maize
61 Winifred Street West
Saint Paul, MN 55107
612-405-9155
info@maddyandmaize.com
www.maddyandmaize.com
Popcorn
CEO & Founder: Brett Striker
Estimated Sales: $1 Million
Brands:
　Maddy & Maize

7742 Made In Nature
2500 Pearl St
Suite 315
Boulder, CO 80302
800-906-7426
www.madeinnature.com
Organic dried and fresh fruits and vegetables as well as pizza.
Founder & CEO: Doug Brent
Estimated Sales: $2.6 Million
Number Employees: 16
Square Footage: 2200
Type of Packaging: Consumer
Brands:
　Made In Nature

7743 Made Rite Foods
2229 Sunnybrook Dr
Burlington, NC 27215-4856
336-229-5728
Fax: 336-545-1880
Salads and sandwiches
President: Jerry McMasters
Plant Manager: Alan Harder
Number Employees: 100-249
Parent Co: Made Rite Foods
Type of Packaging: Consumer, Food Service, Private Label, Bulk
Brands:
　Made Rite
　Sedgefield

7744 Made-Rite Sandwich Co
5828 Main St
Ooltewah, TN 37363-8714
423-238-5492
Fax: 423-238-5844 800-343-1327
contact@greatamericandeli.com
www.greatamericandeli.com
Products include sandwiches, cakes, Hot 2 Go sandwiches, burritos, pocket sandwiches and rollergrill products.
President: Earl R Sullivan
Finance Controller: Randall Desha
Purchasing Manager: Daryl Marsh
Estimated Sales: $20-49 Million
Number Employees: 100-249

7745 Madecasse
Brooklyn, NY 11201
917-382-2020
info@madecasse.com
madecasse.com
Chocolate bars, vanilla beans and vanilla extract
VP: Perry Abbenante
Brands:
　Mad,casse

7746 Madelaine Chocolate Company
9603 Beach Channel Dr
Rockaway Beach, NY 11693-1398
718-945-1500
800-322-1505
service@madelainechocolate.com
www.madelainechocolate.com
Chocolate in various colors, and shapes, such as butterflies, flowers, hearts, its a boy/girl, chocolate coins and cigars, seasonal and holiday chocolates and truffles.
President & CEO: Jorge Farber
jfarber@madelainechocolate.com
VP, Sales & Marketing: Joan Sweeting
VP, Production: Sam Farber
Year Founded: 1949
Estimated Sales: $49.8 Million
Number Employees: 100-249
Square Footage: 200000
Type of Packaging: Private Label, Bulk
Brands:
　Madelaine
　Duets
　Hatchers
　Love & Kisses
　Gooey Ghouls
　Fiesta
　Penny Lanes
　Grand Estate Collection

7747 Madera Enterprises Inc
32565 Avenue 9
Madera, CA 93636-8346
559-431-1444
Fax: 559-674-8214 800-507-9555
maderaent@aol.com
Processor and exporter of custom fruit juice concentrates and purees including grape, apple, strawberry, plum, prune, date, raisin, pomegranate, etc.; also, dried fruits and vinaigrettes
President: Susan Nury
maderaent@aol.com
Marketing: Rosanna Andrews-White
Estimated Sales: $3-5 Million
Number Employees: 5-9
Type of Packaging: Bulk
Brands:
　Mina
　Zary

7748 (HQ)Madhava Natural Sweeteners
4665 Nautilus Court S
Suite 301
Boulder, CO 80301
800-530-2900
madhavasweeteners.com
Organic sweeteners, including honey, agave nectar and coconut sugar
CEO: Colin Sankey
Estimated Sales: $710,000
Number Employees: 20-49
Square Footage: 8974
Type of Packaging: Consumer, Food Service, Private Label, Bulk
Other Locations:
　Madhava Honey
　Parachute CO

Food Manufacturers / A-Z

Brands:
    Agave Nectar
    Ambrosia Honey
    Mountain Gold Honey

7749 Madhouse Munchies
20 San Remo Drive
South Burlington, VT 05403
802-655-6662
Fax: 802-655-7711 888-323-4687
info@madhousemunchies.com
www.madhousemunchies.com
Low-fat, hand-cooked potato chips
President: J Ehlen
Sales/Marketing Associate: Eric Bleckner
Contact: Brad Hall
bhall@madhousemunchies.com
Estimated Sales: $740,000
Number Employees: 10
Brands:
    Madhouse Munchies

7750 Madison Foods
238 Chester St
Saint Paul, MN 55107
651-265-8212
Fax: 651-297-6286 madisonfoodsmt.com
Butter substitutes; also, contract packager of retail and food service sauces
President: Steve Anderson
Estimated Sales: $.5-1 million
Number Employees: 1-4
Type of Packaging: Consumer, Food Service, Private Label, Bulk
Brands:
    Better

7751 Madison Park Foods
PO Box 320
Brookside, NJ 07926
800-963-3540
madisonparkfoods.com
Rubs, seasonings and heirloom popcorn.
President: Christine Myers

7752 Madison Vineyard
HC 72 Box 490
Ribera, NM 87560
575-421-8028
Fax: 575-421-8028 madison@plateautel.net
Wines
Owner: Bill Madison
william.madison@madison.lib.oh.us
Partner: Elise Madison
Director: Shirley Flint
Estimated Sales: $190,000
Number Employees: 3

7753 Madonna Estate Winery
5400 Old Sonoma Rd
Napa, CA 94559-9708
707-255-8864
Fax: 707-257-2778 866-724-2993
mail@madonnaestate.com
www.madonnaestate.com
Wines include Chardonnay, Pinot Noir, Due Ragazze, Pinot Noir Riserva, Merlot, Cabernet Sauvignon.
President: Andrea Bartolucci
mail@madonnaestate.com
Marketing: Ron Arata
Public Relations: Brette Bartolucci
Vineyard Manager: Andrea Bartolucci
Estimated Sales: $2.5-5 Million
Number Employees: 5-9
Brands:
    Madonna Estate Mont St John
    Poppy Hill

7754 Madrange
85 Division Avenue
PO Box 409
Millington, NJ 07946
908-647-6485
Fax: 908-646-8305 800-899-6689
mkessler@charter.net www.fromartharie.com
Products include cooked hams, goat cheese, dips, butter, and pates/mousse.
General Manager: Ron Schinbeckler
Vice President: Richard Kessler
Regional Manager: Jim Gregori
Number Employees: 10-19
Type of Packaging: Private Label, Bulk

7755 Madrinas Coffee
St. Louis, MO 63042
madrinascoffee.com
Fair trade organic coffee
President/Owner: Justin Davis

7756 Madrona Specialty Foods LLC
18300 Cascade Ave S # 260
Suite 260
Seattle, WA 98188-4746
425-656-2997
Fax: 206-577-3406 info@madronafoods.com
www.madronaspecialtyfoods.com
Chocolate almond toffee, chcolate shapes, caramels, holiday candies, cookies, and hot cocoa
Owner: Paul Piggott
antonio@lapanzanella.com
Marketing: Erin Cammarano
Estimated Sales: $3.4 Million
Number Employees: 20-49
Type of Packaging: Private Label, Bulk
Brands:
    Elegant Sweets
    Hannah's Delight
    Kingsley's Caramels

7757 Madrona Vineyards
PO Box 454
2560 High Hill Road
Camino, CA 95709
530-644-5948
Fax: 530-644-7517
winery@madronavineyards.com
www.madronavineyards.com
Wines
President: Richard Bush
Contact: Leslie Bush
leslie@madronavineyards.com
Estimated Sales: Below $5 Million
Number Employees: 20
Type of Packaging: Consumer

7758 Madys Company
1555 Yosemite Ave
San Francisco, CA 94124-3268
415-822-2227
Fax: 415-822-3673
Herbal, medicinal and regular teas; also, vitamins, ginseng root
Owner: Sandy Su Wing
General Manager: Marian Hong
Number Employees: 10-19
Square Footage: 13600
Parent Co: Azeta Brands
Type of Packaging: Consumer, Food Service, Private Label, Bulk
Brands:
    Butterfly
    Evergreen
    Madys
    Weiloss

7759 Madyson's Marshmallows
2211 W 3000 S # D
Suite D
Heber City, UT 84032-4520
435-315-0045
info@madysonsmarshmallows.com
Manufacturer of chocolate dipped marshmallows, stuffed marshmallows, s'mores kits, and beverage toppers.
CEO & Founder: Breeze Wetzel

7760 Maebo Noodle Factory Inc
711 W Kawailani St
Hilo, HI 96720-3155
808-959-8763
Fax: 808-959-4404 877-663-8667
sales@one-ton.com www.one-ton.com
Chinese foods including noodles, wonton chips and saimin
President/Manager: Blane Maebo
VP: Rachel Maebo
Contact: Maxine Hao
maxine@one-ton.com
Estimated Sales: $550000
Number Employees: 10-19
Type of Packaging: Consumer, Bulk
Brands:
    Maebo Noodle Factory, Inc.

7761 Maggie Lyon Chocolatiers
6000 Peachtree Industrial Blvd
Norcross, GA 30071
770-446-1299
Fax: 770-446-2191 800-969-3500
sales@maggielyon.com www.maggielyon.com
Products include gourmet chocolates, truffles, toffee, caramels, bark and nut clusters, toffee, special occassion and gift baskets, easter selections, bulk chocolates, and promotional products.
President: Jeffery Pollack
Cfo: Linda Pollack
VP: Michael Pollack
Estimated Sales: $1.8 Million
Number Employees: 15
Type of Packaging: Private Label
Brands:
    Connie's Handmade Toffee

7762 Maggie's Salsa
1303 Turley Rd
Charleston, WV 25314
304-550-5460
Fax: 304-881-0289
Salsa
President/Owner: Maggie Cook

7763 Maggiora Baking Co
1900 Garden Tract Rd
Richmond, CA 94801-1219
510-235-0274
Fax: 510-235-2427 info@maggiorabaking.com
Products include sourdoughs, french breads, focaccia, bread sticks, pesto dinner roll clusters, garlic rounds, Hawaiian bread/dinner rolls, Greek rings, egg bread and dinner rolls, and various specialty breads.
President: Dennis Maggiora
Sales Director: Robert Maggiora
Contact: Don Jones
don@maggiorabaking.com
General Manager: Don Maggiora
Estimated Sales: Less Than $500,000
Number Employees: 5-9

7764 Magic Gumball Intl
9310 Mason Ave
Chatsworth, CA 91311-5201
818-716-1888
Fax: 818-341-4234 800-576-2020
info@magicgumball.com www.magicgumball.com
Candy
Owner: Guy Hart
Estimated Sales: $5-10 Million
Number Employees: 50-99

7765 Magic Ice Products
1326 Ethan Ave
Cincinnati, OH 45225-1810
513-541-2645
800-776-7923
magiciceproducts@gmail.com
www.magiciceproducts.com
Processor and exporter of gourmet coffee flavor, slush and ice syrups; importer of shave ice machines and equipment
President: Shirley Weist
Number Employees: 5-9
Type of Packaging: Consumer, Food Service, Private Label
Brands:
    Flavor Magic
    Magic Ice

7766 Magic Seasoning Blends
720 Distributors Row
Po Box 23342
New Orleans, LA 70123-3208
504-731-3590
Fax: 504-731-3576 800-457-2857
www.magicseasoningblends.com
Dry spices, rubs, bottled sauces and marinades.
Owner: Paul Prudhomme
pprudhomme@chefpaul.com
President/CEO: Shawn McBride
CFO: Paula LaCour
R&D Director: Sean O'Meara
VP Sales/Marketing: John McBride
Director of Sales and Marketing: Anna Zuniga
pprudhomme@chefpaul.com
Human Resources Director: Naomi Roundtree
Director of Operations: Joey Duplechain
Vice President of Manufacturing: David Hickey
Purchasing Director: Patricia Cantrelle

Food Manufacturers / A-Z

Estimated Sales: $9.6 Million
Number Employees: 50-99
Number of Brands: 3
Number of Products: 29
Square Footage: 260000
Type of Packaging: Consumer, Food Service, Private Label, Bulk
Brands:
- Barbecue Magic
- Blackened Redfish Magic
- Blackened Steak Magic
- Breading Magic
- Gravy & Gumbo Magic
- Magic Pepper Sauce
- Magic Sauce & Marinades
- Meat Magic
- Pizza & Pasta Magic
- Pork & Veal Magic
- Poultry Magic
- Salmon Magic
- Seafood Magic
- Shrimp Magic
- Sweetfree Magic
- Vegetable Magic

7767 Magic Valley Growers
375 W Avenue D
Wendell, ID 83355-5512
208-536-6693
Fax: 208-536-6695 www.magicvalleygrowers.com
Grower and packer of specialty onions including pearl, boiler, peeled pearl and sets; exporter of pearl and boiler onions
President: Robert Reitveld
onions@magicvalleygrowers.com
VP: James Kelly
Estimated Sales: $1.1 Million
Number Employees: 20-49
Square Footage: 212400
Type of Packaging: Consumer, Private Label, Bulk
Brands:
- Dutch Boiler
- Dutch Girl
- Top Hat

7768 Magic Valley Quality Milk
1756 S Buchanan St
P.O. Box 507
Jerome, ID 83338-6146
208-324-7519
Fax: 208-324-7554 www.mvqmp.com
Cooperative selling raw milk to food processors
General Manager: Alan Stutzman
Estimated Sales: $.5-1 million
Number Employees: 20-49

7769 Magna Foods Corporation
16010 Phoenix Drive
City of Industry, CA 91745-1623
626-336-7500
Fax: 626-336-3999 800-995-4394
magnafoods@aol.com
Processor and exporter of confectionery, candy, cookies, crackers and cocoa products
President: Yogi Atmadja
VP: Peter Surjadinata
Estimated Sales: $1.5 Million
Number Employees: 25
Square Footage: 20000
Parent Co: IBIS
Brands:
- Coffeego
- Danisa
- Roma Marie

7770 Magnanini Farm Winery
172 Strawridge Rd
Wallkill, NY 12589-3905
845-895-2767
Fax: 845-895-9458 www.magwine.com
Wines
Owner: Richard Magnanini
rickmagnanini@gmail.com
CEO: Galba Magnanini
Estimated Sales: $500,000-$1 Million
Number Employees: 1-4
Type of Packaging: Private Label

7771 Magnetic Springs
1917 Joyce Ave
Columbus, OH 43219-1029
614-421-1780
Fax: 614-421-1681 800-572-2990
contact@magneticsprings.com
www.magneticsprings.com
Drinking, distilled, spring, artesian and infant water
President: Jeff Allison
jeff@magneticsprings.com
Plant Manager: Tim VanSickle
Estimated Sales: $11.9 Million
Number Employees: 50-99
Square Footage: 200000
Type of Packaging: Consumer, Food Service, Private Label, Bulk
Brands:
- Magnetic Springs

7772 Magnificent Muffin
64 Toledo St
Farmingdale, NY 11735-6628
631-454-8022
Fax: 631-454-8574
Muffins and baked goods
Owner: Jon Schreckinger
Estimated Sales: Below $150,000
Number Employees: 1-4
Type of Packaging: Consumer, Bulk

7773 Magnolia Bakery
New York, NY
855-622-5379
info@magnoliabakery.com
Baked cupcakes, cookies, brownies and bars.
Co-owner: Steve Abrams
Co-owner: Tyra Abrams

7774 Magnolia Citrus Assn
1014 E Teapot Dome Ave
Porterville, CA 93257-9766
559-784-4455
Fax: 559-781-9182 www.tcoe.org
Processor, packer and exporter of Valencia and navel oranges
Manager: Dominick Arcure
Manager: Larry Fultz
Manager: Dominick Arcure
Estimated Sales: $10-20 Million
Number Employees: 10-19
Type of Packaging: Private Label, Bulk
Brands:
- Magnolia
- Malta
- Memory

7775 Magnolia Meats
2013 Dutch Valley Rd
Knoxville, TN 37918
865-546-7702
Beef, pork and chicken
President: E Dean
Contact: Rob Noyes
robnoyes8@yahoo.com
Estimated Sales: $3-5 Million
Number Employees: 5-9
Type of Packaging: Consumer, Food Service, Bulk

7776 (HQ)Magnotta Winery Corporation
271 Chrislea Road
Vaughan, ON L4L 8N6
Canada
905-738-9463
Fax: 905-738-5551 800-461-9463
mailbox@magnotta.com www.magnotta.com
Wines and wine baskets, ice wines, sparking wines, various beers, and liquors
President/Ceo: Rossana Magnotta
Chief Financial Officer: Fulvio De Angelis
Estimated Sales: $23 Million
Number Employees: 107
Square Footage: 60000
Type of Packaging: Consumer
Other Locations:
- Magnotta Winery Corp.
- Scarborough ON
Brands:
- Magnotta

7777 Magnum Coffee Roastery
1 Java Blvd
Nunica, MI 49448-9462
616-837-0333
Fax: 616-837-0777 888-937-5282
4sales@magnumcoffee.com
www.magnumcoffee.com
Coffee roasting and quality packaging services
Owner: Kevin Kihnke
kevin@magnumcoffee.com
General Manager: Nick Andres
Estimated Sales: $2.5-5 Million
Number Employees: 20-49
Type of Packaging: Private Label
Brands:
- Island Trader
- Magnum Exotic

7778 Magrabar Chemical Corp
6100 Madison Ct
Morton Grove, IL 60053-3216
847-965-7550
Fax: 847-965-7553 www.magrabar.com
Manufactures additives, release agents and viscosity modifiers
President: Susan Jenkins
sijenkins@magrabar.com
Chairman of the Board: Sandy Roy
Vice President: Dale Roy
Technical Director: Jeffrey Conrad
Estimated Sales: $3.4 Million
Number Employees: 10-19

7779 Mah Chena Company
1416 W Ohio St
Chicago, IL 60642-7156
312-226-5100
Fax: 312-277-7170
Chinese frozen foods
President: Heather Shadur
Sales Manager: Jeffrey Hoffman
Plant Manager: Willis Yee
Number Employees: 10-19

7780 Mahantongo Game Farm
559 Flying Eagle Rd
Dalmatia, PA 17017-7003
570-758-6284
Fax: 570-758-2095 800-982-9913
mgf@tds.net www.pagamebirds.com
Processor and exporter of game birds including pheasants and partridges
Owner: Troy Laudenslager
mgf@tds.net
Estimated Sales: $360,000
Number Employees: 20-49

7781 Maher Marketing Services
1616 Corporate Ct # 140
Irving, TX 75038-2209
972-751-7700
Fax: 972-751-7777 mmaher@mahermark.com
www.mahermark.com
Cheeses, dairy products, frozen entrees, specialty snacks, crackers and cookies
President: Dan Vines
CEO: Mike Maher
CFO: Anne Maher
Marketing Manager: April Tieken
Estimated Sales: $5-10 Million
Number Employees: 5-9
Type of Packaging: Bulk

7782 Mahoning Swiss Cheese Cooperative
24060 Route 954 Highway N
Smicksburg, PA 16256-3428
814-257-8884
Fax: 724-286-9259
Cheese and butter
President: John Schablach
Plant Manager: Ralph Juart
Estimated Sales: Below $1 Million
Number Employees: 10

7783 Maid-Rite Steak Company
105 Keystone Industrial Park
Dunmore, PA 18512
800-233-4259
sales@mr-specialty.com www.mr-specialty.com
Portioned controlled meat products, including quick frozen beef, ground beef, pork, veal, and lamb products.
Executive Vice President: Michael Bernstein

Food Manufacturers / A-Z

Estimated Sales: $41.5 Million
Number Employees: 255
Square Footage: 115000
Type of Packaging: Consumer, Food Service, Private Label, Bulk
Brands:
    Chef Italia
    Maid-Rite
    Minit Chef
    Polarized

7784 Main Squeeze
28 S 9th St
Columbia, MO 65201-4814
573-817-5616
goodfood@main-squeeze.com
www.main-squeeze.com
Juice concentrates and bar mixes
Owner: Leigh Lockhart
leigh@main-squeeze.com
Estimated Sales: $500,000-$1 Million
Number Employees: 20-49

7785 Main Street Gourmet
170 Muffin Ln
Cuyahoga Falls, OH 44223
330-929-0000
800-678-6246
www.mainstreetgourmet.com
Gourmet fresh and frozen bakery items including an extensive selection of muffins and muffin batter, cookies, brownies and bars, granola, loaf cakes, cakes and baked goods and toppings.
CEO: Harvey Nelson
Manager, Quality Assurance: Angela Stoughton
Estimated Sales: $69 Million
Number Employees: 100-249
Square Footage: 65000
Parent Co: Clover Capital Partners LLC
Type of Packaging: Consumer, Food Service, Private Label, Bulk

7786 Main Street Ingredients
2340 Enterprise Avenue
La Crosse, WI 54603-1713
608-781-2345
Fax: 608-781-4667 800-359-2345
ingredients@agropur.com
www.mainstreetingredients.com
Hydrocolloids, stabilizers, and dairy ingredients including whey proteins, milk proteins, and milk powders serving the dairy, bakery and nutrition industries; also a private-label contract manufacturer
President: Bill Schmitz
Founder: Dave Clark
VP/Sales: Aaron Macha
Contact: Ellen Lusk
ellen.l@msing.com
VP/Operations: Rudy Rott
Number Employees: 125
Square Footage: 320000
Parent Co: Agropur
Brands:
    Keystone
    Cornerstone
    Capstone
    Gemstone

7787 Maine Coast Nordic
133 Smalls Point Rd
Mahiasport, ME 04655-3231
207-255-6714
Fresh salmon
President: Glen Cooke
g.cooke@cookeaqua.com
VP: William Groom
Estimated Sales: $760,000
Number Employees: 10
Parent Co: Nordic Enterprises
Type of Packaging: Bulk

7788 Maine Coast Sea Vegetables
3 George's Pond Rd
Franklin, ME 4634
207-565-2907
Fax: 207-565-2144 info@seaveg.com
www.seaveg.com
Edible seaweed products including sea vegetables, seasonings, snack bars, and chips. Wholesaler/distributor of seaweed including whole and ground
President/CEO: Shepard Erhart
President/CEO: Linnette Erhart
Treasurer/CFO: Carl Karush
Contact: Aaron Brown
aaron@seaveg.com
Operations Manager: Mary Ellen Lasell
Production Manager: Hannah Russell
Estimated Sales: $2 Million
Number Employees: 20
Number of Products: 40
Square Footage: 18000
Type of Packaging: Consumer, Bulk
Brands:
    Maine Coast Crunch
    Maine Coast Sea Vegetables
    Sea Cakes
    Sea Chips
    Sea Seasonings
    Sea Vegetables
    Wild Crafted Food From the Gulf Of

7789 Maine Lobster Outlet
360 US Route 1
York, ME 03909-1631
207-363-4449
Fax: 207-363-0613 info@mainelobsteroutlet.com
Lobster
Owner: Sheila Barnes
sbarnes@mainelobsteroutlet.com
Estimated Sales: $1-3 Million
Number Employees: 10-19

7790 Maine Mahogony Shellfish
8 Johnson Ln
Addison, ME 04606
207-483-2865
Fax: 207-483-4389
Wholesale and retail products include lobster, clams, crab, halibut, mussels, and a wide variety of shellfish.
Manager: Robert Johnson

7791 Maine Seaweed Company
P.O. Box 57
Steuben, ME 04680
207-546-2875
Fax: 207-546-2875 hanson.larch@gmail.com
www.theseaweedman.com
Dried seaweeds, including kelp, alaria, digitata, dulse, bladderwrack, irish moss & ascophyllum nodosum.
President: Larch Hanson
Type of Packaging: Consumer

7792 Maine Wild Blueberry Company
320 Ridge Rd.
Cherryfield, ME 04622-0128
207-546-7573
Fax: 207-546-2713 800-243-4005
www.oxfordfrozenfoods.com
Canned, dehydrated and frozen wild blueberries
President/CEO: John Bragg
Co-CEO: Dave Hoffman
Chief Operating Officer: Ragnar Kamp
Treasurer: Geoff Baldwin
VP, Sales: Matthew Bragg
Director/Manufacturing: Milton Wood
Year Founded: 1997
Estimated Sales: $27 Million
Number Employees: 20-49
Square Footage: 100000
Parent Co: Oxford Frozen Foods
Brands:
    Maine Wild

7793 Maisie Jane's California Sunshine
3764 Hegan Ln
Chico, CA 95928
530-899-7909
Fax: 530-895-3949 nuts@maisiejanes.com
www.maisiejanes.com
Nuts and nut butters
Founder: Maisie Jane Hurtado
Grower: Isidro Hurtado
Number of Brands: 1
Type of Packaging: Consumer
Brands:
    MAISIE JANE'S

7794 Maison Riviera
1625, boul Lionel-Boulet
Suite 203
Varennes, QC J3X 1P7
Canada
Fax: 450-746-0993 800-363-0092
info@riviera1920.com riviera1920.com
Yogurts, desserts, cheeses, butters and goat milk products
Executive Vice President: Alain Chalifoux

7795 Majestic Coffee & Tea Inc
2027 San Carlos Ave
San Carlos, CA 94070-1929
650-591-5678
Coffee, tea
President: Bob Gard
Contact: Robert Gard
bobgard@aol.com
Estimated Sales: Less Than $500,000
Number Employees: 1-4
Brands:
    Majestic Coffee and Tea

7796 Majestic Foods
33 Walt Whitman Rd
Suite 304
Huntington, NY 11746
631-424-9444
Fax: 631-424-5874 majesticfoods@sbcglobal.net
www.majesticfoods.net
Fruit concentrates, blends, essences and purees, canned fruits and vegetables, frozen fruits, dried fruits, nuts, vegetables and natural colors
President: Phil Maguire
Estimated Sales: $20-50 Million
Number Employees: 10-19

7797 Maju Superfoods
1455 Frazee Rd
Suite 500
San Diego, CA 92108
619-736-0622
www.majusuperfoods.com
Superfoods and supplements including black seed oil, hemp extract, spirulina, mushrooms, and powders
Co-Founder: Ryan Rigney
Co-Founder: Gunawan Wiyono
Year Founded: 2014

7798 Makana Beverages Inc.
Oxnard, CA
www.thebukombucha.com
Organic, raw, non-GMO, gluten-free and vegan kombucha in various flavors
Founder: Gary Hawes
CEO: Ryan Mason
Number of Brands: 1
Number of Products: 5
Type of Packaging: Consumer, Private Label
Brands:
    TheBu Kombucha

7799 Make It Simple
8362 Tamarack Village
Suite 119-444
Woodbury, MN 55129
connect@makeitsimpledrinks.com
www.drinkpeptalk.com
Caffeinated sparkling water
Brands:
    Pep Talk

7800 Maker Oats
844-782-5374
www.makeroats.com
Overnight oatmeal
Co-Founder: Jess Price
Co-Founder: Barry Nalebuff
Number of Brands: 1
Number of Products: 3
Type of Packaging: Consumer
Brands:
    MAKER OVERNIGHT OATS

7801 Maker's Mark DistilleryInc
3350 Burkes Spring Rd
Loretto, KY 40037-8027
270-865-2881
Fax: 270-865-2196 www.makersmark.com
Processor and exporter of whiskey
President/COO: Rob Samuels
Manager: Victoria Mc Rae-Samuels

Food Manufacturers / A-Z

Estimated Sales: $25-49 Million
Number Employees: 50-99
Parent Co: Beam Suntory Inc.
Type of Packaging: Consumer
Brands:
  Makers Mark

7802 Malabar Formulas
28537 Nuevo Valley Dr
Nuevo, CA 92567
909-866-3678
Milk digestants and activated enzyme concentrate
Owner: Shirley Partito

7803 Malcolm Meats Co
2665 Tracy Rd
Northwood, OH 43619-1006
419-666-0702
Fax: 419-666-2619 800-822-6328
www.sysco.com
Fine portion cut meat products including pork, lamb, veal, and poultry
President: Andrew Malcolm
Executive Vice President: Jeff Savage
Senior Vice President: Jerry Pasquale
Year Founded: 1982
Estimated Sales: $20-50 Million
Number Employees: 100-249

7804 Malibu Beach Beverage
885 Woodstock Rd
Roswell, GA 30075-2277
770-998-7204
877-825-0655
info@malibubev.com
Nutritional fruit flavored drinks including malibu mango; sunset strawberry; redondo raspberry; oceanside orange; beach peach; and tropical tea.
Chief Financial Officer: William Wager
Vice President Corporate Development: Jeff Glattstein
Chief Operations Officer: Patrick Doran

7805 Malie Kai Hawaiian Chocolates
PO Box 1146
Honolulu, HI 96807
808-599-8600
Fax: 808-599-8600 info@maliekai.com
www.maliekai.com
Chocolate bars
President/Owner: Nathan Sato

7806 Mallard's Food Products
708 L Street
Modesto, CA 95354-2320
209-522-1018
Fax: 209-577-8364
Fully-cooked entrees and pasta products
President/CEO: Dan Costa
CFO: Scott Wheeler
VP Sales: Steven Lay
Contact: Danita Thomson
danita.thomson@tyson.com
Plant Manager: Douglas Louis
Number Employees: 100-249
Parent Co: Tyson Foods

7807 Maloney Seafood Corporation
PO Box 690109
Quincy, MA 02269-0109
617-472-1004
Fax: 617-472-7722 800-566-2837
info@maloneyseafood.com
www.maloneyseafood.com
Importers of frozen seafood.
President: Thomas Maloney
Contact: Frank Maloney
frank@maloneyseafood.com
Estimated Sales: $10-20 Million
Number Employees: 5-9
Type of Packaging: Consumer, Food Service

7808 Malt Diastase Co
141 Lanza Ave # 31
Bldg 31
Garfield, NJ 07026-3539
973-772-2103
Fax: 973-772-0623 800-772-0416
Processor and exporter of flavoring extracts and syrups
President: Art Levy
Contact: Barry Kirsch
b_kirsch@maltproducts.com

Estimated Sales: $10-20 Million
Number Employees: 1-4
Type of Packaging: Food Service, Bulk

7809 Malt Diastase Co
88 Market St
Saddle Brook, NJ 07663
Fax: 201-845-0028 800-526-0180
www.maltproducts.com
Malt, molasses, natural sweeteners
Owner/President: Amy Targan
VP of Sales: John Johansen
Number Employees: 20-49
Type of Packaging: Bulk
Brands:
  MaltRite
  Nuvert

7810 Malteurop North America
3830 W Grant St
Milwaukee, WI 53215
414-671-1166
www.malteurop.com
Processor and exporter of malt, also offers several modes of commercial collaboration, as well as consulting, engineering, and training services.
CEO: Olivier Parent
President, North America: Kevin Eikerman
Chief Commercial & Innovation Officer: Alain Caekaert
Year Founded: 1984
Estimated Sales: $31.5 Million
Number Employees: 100-249
Parent Co: Malteurop
Type of Packaging: Food Service, Bulk

7811 Mama Amy's Quality Foods
5715 Coopers Avenue
Mississauga, ON L4Z 2C7
Canada
905-456-0056
Fax: 905-456-1536
Pizza and broccoli and cheese sticks, calzones, jambalaya
Sales/Marketing Director: Aldon Reed
Number Employees: 30
Square Footage: 28000
Type of Packaging: Consumer, Food Service, Private Label, Bulk
Brands:
  Mama Amy's

7812 Mama Del's Macacroni
420 Main St
East Haven, CT 06512-2838
203-469-6255
Fax: 203-469-6255
Homemade pasta
Owner: Edward Cole
Estimated Sales: Less than $200,000
Number Employees: 1-4
Type of Packaging: Consumer, Food Service, Bulk
Brands:
  Mama Del's

7813 Mama Lil's Peppers
5331 SW Macadam Ave.
Portland, OR 97239
503-206-6746
Fax: 503-961-7486 mamalils@zipcon.net
www.mamalils.com
Peppers in oil
President/Owner: Howard Lev

7814 Mama Maria's Tortillas
125 W 7200 S
Midvale, UT 84047-1011
801-566-5150
Fax: 801-566-7116 mamamarias@mtcon.net
Tortillas and tamales
President: Norbert Martinez
VP: Kenny Martinez
Estimated Sales: Below $5 Million
Number Employees: 20

7815 Mama Mary's
Fairforest, SC 29336
800-813-7574
info@mamamarys.com www.mamamarys.com
Pizza crusts, packaged pepperoni slices and pizza sauces.
President: Ken Romanzi
EVP, Sales & Marketing: Vanessa Maskal
EVP, Operations: William Herbes

Estimated Sales: $51 Million
Number Employees: 204
Number of Brands: 1
Square Footage: 50000
Parent Co: B&G Foods
Type of Packaging: Consumer
Brands:
  Mama Mary's

7816 Mama O's Premium Kimchi
630 Flushing Ave
Suite 810
Brooklyn, NY 11206-5026
917-326-1557
mamaos@kimchirules.com
www.kimchirules.com
Manufacturer of kimchi.
Founder: Kheedim Oh
Estimated Sales: Less Than $500,000
Number Employees: 1-4

7817 Mama Rap's & Winery
PO Box 247
Gilroy, CA 95020-8029
408-842-5649
Fax: 408-842-8353 800-842-6262
info@rapazziniwinery.com
www.rapazziniwinery.com
Wine
Owner: Charles Larson
Estimated Sales: $1-2.5 Million
Number Employees: 5-9

7818 Mama Rose's Gourmet Foods
P.O. Box 36852
Phoenix, AZ 85067
602-477-8333
Fax: 602-477-8338 855-809-2848
tonya@mamarosefoods.com
www.mamarosefoods.com
Sixteen years producing gourmet packaged foods ie.. salsa, hot sauce ,jams, jellies, marinara and pizza sauce, pickled olives, prickly pear products, importing italian pasta and olive oil. Private label and co-packaging specialists
President: Tonya Greenfield
VP: Al Greenfield
Sales/Marketing Manager: Al Greenfield
Estimated Sales: $5-9.9 Million
Number Employees: 6
Brands:
  Mama Rose's

7819 Mama Rosie's Ravioli
10 Dorrance St
Charlestown, MA 02129-1027
617-242-4300
Fax: 617-242-4208 888-246-4300
www.mamarosies.com
Frozen pastas as well as filled pasta products including Cheese Ravioli, Tortellini, Cheese Manicotti, Stuffed Shells, and more.
President: Brian McNulty
CEO: Nicholas Sardo
Estimated Sales: $5-10 000,000
Number Employees: 50-99
Brands:
  Mama Rosie's

7820 Mama Tish's Italian Specialties
4800 S Central Avenue
Chicago, IL 60638-1500
708-929-2023
Fax: 708-458-0027
Italian ice cream and frozen desserts
President/CEO: M Rudasil
Marketing Director: M Wenzell
VP Sales: Fergal Mulchrone
Plant Manager: I Bidiman
Estimated Sales: $5-10 Million
Number Employees: 5

7821 Mama Vida's Inc
9631 Liberty Rd # N
Ste N
Randallstown, MD 21133-2434
410-521-0742
Fax: 410-521-0785 877-521-0742
nila@mamavida.com www.mamavida.com
Vegetarian chili, eggplant spread, dressings, mustard, sauces, soups, black bean dip, marinade, salsas, tapenades

Owner: Toto Mechali
toto@mamavida.com
President: Albert Toto
Chief Financial Officer: Miki Mechali
Quality Control: Heidi Czakny
Director of Marketing: Nila Mechali
Estimated Sales: $1 Million
Number Employees: 1-4
Number of Brands: 30
Number of Products: 18
Type of Packaging: Consumer, Food Service, Private Label, Bulk
Brands:
   Toto's Gourmet Products

7822 Mamie's Pies
3701 Sacramento St
PO Box 119
San Francisco, CA 94118
                                  415-870-0390
                          kiki@mamiespies.com
                                 mamiespies.com
Frozen pocket pies
CEO: Kara Romanik
Operations: Peter Scherr
Number of Products: 3

7823 Mamma Chia
5205 Avenida Encinas
Suite E
Carlsbad, CA 92008
                                  855-588-2442
                             www.mammachia.com
Chia seeds and beverages
Founder & CEO: Janie Hoffman
janie@mammachia.com
Brands:
   Mamma Chia

7824 Mamma Lina Ravioli Company
6491 Weathers Pl
San Diego, CA 92121-2935
                                  858-535-0620
                            Fax: 858-535-5993
Pasta products including ravioli and frozen lasagna
President: Chick Massullo
Estimated Sales: Less than $500,000
Number Employees: 10-19
Type of Packaging: Consumer, Food Service

7825 Mamma Lombardi's All Natural Sauces
877 Main Street
Holbrook, NY 11741
                                  631-471-6609
                    infovilla@villalombardis.com
Sauces

7826 Mamma Says
49 Lincoln Road
Butler, NJ 07405-1801
                                  973-283-4463
              Fax: 973-283-2799   877-283-6282
Gourmet biscotti in almond pistachio and chocolate macadamia
VP: Jason Cohen
Brands:
   Mamma Says

7827 Mammoth Creameries
Austin, TX 78732
                    info@mammothcreameries.com
                     www.mammothcreameries.com
Keto ice cream
Co-Founder: Tim Krauss
Co-Founder: Susan Krauss
Number of Products: 2

7828 Manassero Farms
5405 Alton Pkw.
Ste. A-622
Irvine, CA 92604
                                  949-554-5103
          Fax: 949-551-6784 info@manasserofarms.com
                         www.manaserofarms.com
Various fresh produce, canned veggies, specialty jams and spreads, olive oils, raw organic honey, and specialty sauces.
Owner & CEO: Dan Manassero
Owner & Farm Chef: Anne Manassero
Year Founded: 1922
Type of Packaging: Consumer, Private Label

7829 Mancan Wine
1455 W 29th St
Cleveland, OH 44113-2970
                                  216-367-2928
              Fax: 216-927-3772 mancanwine.com
Wine in a can
Ohio Sales Manager: Alexander Feighan

7830 Manchac Seafood Market
131 Bait Alley
Ponchatoula, LA 70454
                                  985-370-7070
                            Fax: 985-386-2762
Seafood
President: Duke Robin

7831 Manchester Farms
8126 Garners Ferry Rd
Columbia, SC 29209-9402
                                  803-783-9024
              Fax: 803-227-3103   800-845-0421
              customerservice@manchesterfarms.com
                         www.manchesterfarms.com
Quail and bacon wrapped chicken; Franks-in-a-blanket; mini stuffed potato skins.
President: Brittney Miller
VP: Steve Odom
Total Quality Manager: Liz Benson
Marketing Manager: Matt Miller
Sales: Heather Ivey
Sales: Angela Covington
Director of Operations: Michael Davis
Plant Manager: Jennifer Alexander
Estimated Sales: Less Than $500,000
Number Employees: 1-4
Square Footage: 88000
Type of Packaging: Consumer, Food Service, Private Label
Brands:
   Manchester Farms

7832 Mancini Packing Co
3500 Mancini Pl
Zolfo Springs, FL 33890-4710
                                  863-735-2000
              Fax: 863-735-1172   800-741-1778
                       rmancini@mancinifoods.com
                         www.mancinifoods.com
Peppers and olive oil
Chairman/President: Frank Mancini
fmancini@mancinifoods.com
VP: Alan Mancini
Estimated Sales: $11 Million
Number Employees: 50-99
Type of Packaging: Consumer, Food Service, Private Label, Bulk
Brands:
   Mancini

7833 Mancuso Cheese Co
612 Mills Rd # 1
Joliet, IL 60433-2897
                                  815-722-2475
              Fax: 815-722-1302 pfalbo@mancusocheese.com
                         www.mancusocheese.com
Cheese including ricotta, mozzarella, etc.; exporter of pizza supplies; importer of pasta, olive oil, olives and anchovies; wholesaler/distributor of frozen foods, produce, meats, baked goods, general merchandise, etc.
President: Dominic Mancuso
mberta@mancusocheese.com
VP: Philip Falbo
Sales Exec: Mike Berta
Estimated Sales: $6 Million
Number Employees: 20-49
Square Footage: 80000
Type of Packaging: Consumer, Food Service, Bulk
Brands:
   Mancuso

7834 (HQ)Manda Fine Meats Inc
2445 Sorrel Ave
Baton Rouge, LA 70802-4252
                                  225-344-7636
              Fax: 225-344-7647   800-343-2642
                     kcambre@mandafinemeats.com
                         www.mandafinemeats.com
Processor of smoked sausages, cajun andouille, boudin, bacon, cracklins and deli meats, including cooked roast beef, spiced turkey breasts and smoked hams.
President: Tommy Yarborough
CEO: Bobby Yarborough
Sales Director: Steve Yarborough
Plant Manager: Ronny Webb
Year Founded: 1947
Estimated Sales: $20-50 Million
Number Employees: 250-499
Number of Brands: 1
Number of Products: 20
Type of Packaging: Consumer, Food Service, Private Label, Bulk
Brands:
   Manda

7835 Mandarin Noodle Manufacturing Company
3715 D Edmonton Trail NE
Calgary, AB T2E 3P3
Canada
                                  403-265-1383
              Fax: 403-264-3038 info@mandarinnoodle.com
                         www.mandarinnoodle.com
Rice and wonton noodles, rice rolls and wonton and egg roll wraps
President: Hang Trinh
Estimated Sales: $1.7 Million
Number Employees: 20
Type of Packaging: Consumer, Food Service

7836 Mandarin Soy Sauce Inc
4 Sands Station Rd
Middletown, NY 10940-4415
                                  845-343-1505
              Fax: 845-343-0731 info@wanjashan.com
                         www.wanjashan.com
Soy sauce, asian sauce, rice and vinegar
President: Alvin Lam
alvin.c.lam@chase.com
VP: Mike Shapiro
Estimated Sales: $165 Million
Number Employees: 20-49
Square Footage: 170000
Brands:
   Wan Ja Shan

7837 Manderfield's Home Bakery
811 Plank Rd
Menasha, WI 54952-2923
                                  920-882-6500
              Fax: 920-725-7958 www.manderfieldsbakery.com
Bakery products
President: Jerry Manderfield
manderfieldshb@aol.com
Estimated Sales: $1-2.5 Million
Number Employees: 20-49

7838 Mando Inc
16 Humphrey St
Englewood, NJ 07631-3445
                                  201-568-9337
                            Fax: 201-568-9426
Dumplings
President: Kyo Lee
Contact: Kyn Lee
jameschoi21@hotmail.com
Estimated Sales: $2.5-5,000,000
Number Employees: 5-9
Type of Packaging: Consumer, Food Service, Bulk
Brands:
   Mandoo

7839 Mane Inc.
2501 Henkle Dr.
Lebanon, OH 45036
                                  513-248-9876
              Fax: 513-248-8808 requests@mane.com
                         www.mane.com
Flavors and seasoning blends
President/CEO: Jean Mane
President: Michell Mane
Executive Vice President: Kent Hunter
Contact: James Abel
james.abel@mane.com
Year Founded: 1871
Estimated Sales: 20-50 Million
Number Employees: 50-99
Square Footage: 65000

7840 Mange
PO Box 311
Somerville, MA 02143-0009
                                  917-880-2104
                 Service@FreshFruitVinegars.com
                     www.freshfruitvinegars.com

Food Manufacturers / A-Z

Manufacturer of fruit vinegars.
Mange: Christopher Spivak

7841 Manger Packing Corp
124 S Franklintown Rd
Baltimore, MD 21223-2036
410-233-0126
Fax: 410-362-8065 800-227-9262
Manufacturer and packer of meat including pork, beef, chicken, lamb, veal and smoked ham; exporter of beef sausage
Owner: A Manger
Estimated Sales: $9 Million
Number Employees: 10-19
Type of Packaging: Consumer, Bulk

7842 Mangia Inc.
23166 Los Alisos Blvd
Suite #228
Mission Viejo, CA 92691
949-581-1274
Fax: 949-581-2906 866-462-6442
info@mangiainc.com www.mangiainc.com
Canned San Marzano tomato products, originally produced in Italy, with no preservatives or added salt
President: Matt Maslowski
Manager: Morgan Patterson
VP: Bob Maruca
Contact: Rosa Borrelli
rosacinzia@mangiainc.com
Estimated Sales: $1.3 Million
Number Employees: 12
Number of Brands: 1
Number of Products: 7
Type of Packaging: Consumer, Food Service
Other Locations:
   Conditalia
   Nocera Superiore, Italy
Brands:
   Carmelia

7843 Manhattan Bagel Company
246 Industrial Way W
Eatontown, NJ 07724-2206
732-544-0155
Fax: 732-544-1315
Frozen bagel dough
President/CEO: Jason Genussa
Chairman of the Board: Jack Grumet
Plant Manager: B Hanley
Estimated Sales: $25-49.9 Million
Number Employees: 100-249
Parent Co: New York Coffee & Bagels

7844 Manhattan Beach BrewingCompany
124 Manhattan Beach Blvd
Manhattan Beach, CA 90266
310-798-2744
Fax: 310-798-0365
Coffee
President: David Zislis
Director Manufacturing: Karol Kmeto
Estimated Sales: $1-2.5 Million
Number Employees: 20-49
Brands:
   Dominator Wheat
   Rat Beach Red
   Strand Amber

7845 Manhattan Food Brands, LLC
31 Bridge Street
Metuchen, NJ 08840
732-906-2168
Fax: 630-628-0385
Organic snack foods including corn cheese puffs, chocolate covered butter toffee and tortilla, reduced-fat potato chips, kettle cooked potato chips, peller snacks and popcorn products
President: Michael Season
Sales Director: Kelly Garrigan
Operations Manager: Mark Ruchti
Estimated Sales: $1.3 Million
Number Employees: 5-9
Number of Brands: 2
Number of Products: 35
Square Footage: 48000
Type of Packaging: Consumer, Food Service, Private Label, Bulk
Brands:
   Butter Toffee Covered Popcorn
   Chocolate Covered Potato Chips
   Chocolate Covered Toffee Popcorn
   Michael Season's Cheese Curls
   Michael Season's Cheese Puffs
   Michael Season's Kettle Potatoes
   Michael Season's Organically Grown
   Michael Season's Sensations
   Sweet Organics

7846 Manhattan Special Bottling
342 Manhattan Ave
Brooklyn, NY 11211-2404
718-388-4144
Fax: 718-384-0244 www.manhattanspecial.com
Pure Espresso, sodas and iced coffee drinks
President: Aurora Passaro
apassaro@manhattanspecial.com
Estimated Sales: $2.5-5 Million
Number Employees: 5-9

7847 Manildra Milling Corporation
4210 Shawnee Msn Pkwy Ste 312a
Fairway, KS 66205
913-362-0777
Fax: 913-362-0052 800-323-8435
info@manildrausa.com www.manildrausa.com
Processor, exporter and importer of wheat gluten; processor of wheat starch
President: Gerry Degnan
Vice President of Business Development: Tom McCurry
Engineering Manager: Deryl Hancock
Number Employees: 10-19
Parent Co: Manildra Group
Type of Packaging: Bulk
Brands:
   Gembond
   Gemstar

7848 Manischewitz Co
80 Avenue K
Newark, NJ 07105-3803
201-553-1100
Fax: 201-333-1809
deborah.ross@manischewitz.com
www.manischewitz.com
Manufacturer and exporter of kosher foods including matzoth, crackers, cereals, wine, bagel mixes, candy, pickles, gefilte fish, borscht, doughnut mixes, bagel mixes and egg noodles.
President & CEO: David Sugarman
Contact: Bankier Alain
bankier.alain@manischewitz.com
Number Employees: 400
Number of Brands: 12
Type of Packaging: Consumer, Food Service, Private Label
Brands:
   Manischewitz
   Guiltless Gourmet
   Season Brand
   Mishpacha
   Rokeach
   Goodman's
   Mrs. Adler's
   Mother's
   Horowitz Margareten
   Carmel
   Croyden House
   Jason

7849 Manischewitz Wine Co.
1740 E 13th Street
Brooklyn, NY 11229-1902
718-339-0547
Fax: 718-336-1904 www.manischewitzwine.com
Kosher wine.
President & CEO: Rob Sands
Parent Co: Constellation Brands
Brands:
   Manischewitz

7850 Manitoba Harvest Hemp
100 S Fifth Street
Suite 1085
Minneapolis, MN 55402-1204
800-665-4367
manitobaharvest.com
Hemp products
Co-Founder: Mike Fata
Brands:
   Manitoba Harvest

7851 Manitok Food & Gifts
PO Box 97
Highway 59 Main Street
Callaway, MN 56521-0097
218-375-3425
Fax: 218-375-4765 800-726-1863
Products include handmade jewelry, dolls, quilts, birch bark baskets, canoes, trays, corporate gift baskets filled with hand-harvested and handmade food products, wild rice, berry jellies and syrups.
Manager: Dave Reinke
Estimated Sales: $5-9.9 Million
Number Employees: 4

7852 Manley Meats Inc
302 S 400 E
Decatur, IN 46733-9095
260-592-7313
Fax: 260-592-6731 manleymeats@adamwells.com
www.manleymeats.com
Canned and frozen beef, pork and chicken
President: Amanda Ogg
aogg@manleymeats.com
Vice President: Ronald Manley
Estimated Sales: $10-20 Million
Number Employees: 20-49
Type of Packaging: Consumer, Food Service

7853 Mann Packing Co
1250 Hansen St
Salinas, CA 93901-4552
831-422-0270
Fax: 831-422-1131 800-285-1002
www.veggiesmadeeasy.com
Fresh vegetables supplier.
Owner: Jose Areas
jose.areas@mannpacking.com
Number Employees: 500-999
Type of Packaging: Consumer, Food Service, Bulk
Brands:
   Broccoli Wokly
   Sugar Valley
   Sunny Shores
   Sunny Shores Broccoli Wokly

7854 Mannhardt Inc
3209 S. 32nd Street
Sheboygan Falls, WI 53082
920-467-1027
Fax: 773-625-5639 800-423-2327
mannhardt1@aol.com mannhardtice.com
Ice storage dispensers and bagging equipment
President: John Williams
Sales: Lori Justinger
Number Employees: 10-19

7855 Manns Sausage Company
125 N Main Street
Suite 500 #109
Blacksburg, VA 24060
540-605-0867
Fax: 540-953-0032 info@mannssausage.com
www.mannssausage.com
Sausages
Contact: Nathaniel Haile
nathaniel@mannssausage.com

7856 Mansmith's Barbeque
600 Mission Vineyard Rd
P.O.Box 247
San Jn Bautista, CA 95045
831-623-4981
Fax: 831-623-2150 800-626-7648
info@mansmith.com www.mansmith.com
Barbecue products including sauces, seasonings, pastes and grilling spices
Owner/President: Jon Mansmith
Owner/Secretary/Treasurer: Juanita Mansmith
Estimated Sales: Less Than $500,000
Number Employees: 1-4
Parent Co: Mansmith Enterprises
Type of Packaging: Consumer, Food Service, Private Label
Brands:
   Mansmith's Gourmet

7857 Mantrose-Haeuser Co Inc
1175 Post Rd E
Westport, CT 06880-5431
203-454-1800
Fax: 203-227-0558 800-344-4229
info@mantrose.com www.mantrose.com
Edible coatings and glazes.

President: William Barrie
wbarrie@mantrose.com
VP/Controller: Sue O'Rourke
SVP, Research & Development: Stephen Santos
Estimated Sales: $10-20 Million
Number Employees: 100-249
Number of Brands: 12
Type of Packaging: Private Label
Brands:
    Certicoat
    Certified
    Certiseal
    Crystalac
    Mantrocel
    Mantroclear
    NatureSeal
    Poly-Soleil
    Poly-Tresse
    Reducit
    TEALAC
    VerdeCoat

7858 Manuel's Mexican-American Fine Foods
2007 S 300 W
Salt Lake City, UT 84115-1808
801-484-1431
Fax: 801-484-1440 800-748-5072
Tortilla chips, taco shells, corn tortilla, tostada shells and pre-cut tortillas
President: Orlando Torres
VP: Mike Torres
VP/Sales Exec: Paul Torres
Estimated Sales: Below $5 Million
Number Employees: 40
Type of Packaging: Consumer, Food Service, Private Label, Bulk

7859 Manuel's Odessa Tortilla
1915 E 2nd St
Odessa, TX 79761-5311
432-332-6676
Fax: 432-332-6699 800-753-2445
www.manuelstamales.com
Mexican foods including tortillas, and tamales.
President: Manuel Gonzalez
mangoniii@aol.com
Vice President: Evelyn Gonzalez
Year Founded: 1946
Estimated Sales: $1.1 Million
Number Employees: 10-19
Square Footage: 24000
Type of Packaging: Consumer, Food Service, Bulk
Brands:
    Manuel's
    Mito's

7860 Manzana Products Co.
9141 Green Valley Rd
Sebastopol, CA 95472
707-823-5313
Fax: 707-823-5218 northcoast.organic
Apple sauce, apple juice, apple cider and apple cider vinegar
CEO: Jean-Jacques Ducom
Year Founded: 1922
Estimated Sales: $6.2 Million
Number Employees: 100-249
Square Footage: 364000
Type of Packaging: Consumer, Private Label, Bulk
Brands:
    North Coast

7861 Maola Milk & Ice Cream Co.
844-287-1970
emailus@maolamilk.com www.maolamilk.com
Fluid milk, flavored milk, cream, and egg nog.
Year Founded: 1920
Estimated Sales: $100 Million
Number Employees: 250-499
Square Footage: 7
Parent Co: Maryland & Virginia Producers Cooperative Association, Inc.
Type of Packaging: Consumer, Food Service, Private Label, Bulk
Brands:
    Maola

7862 Maola Milk & Ice Cream Co
305 Avenue C
New Bern, NC 28560-3113
252-638-1131
Fax: 252-638-2268 800-476-1021
consumerservice@maolamilk.com
www.maolamilk.com
Dairy, Ice Cream
Owner: G D Currin
Manager: Alan Bentley
alanb@securewave.com
Estimated Sales: $.5-1 million
Number Employees: 250-499
Parent Co: Maola Milk & Ice Cream Company

7863 Maple Acres Inc
13910 Campbell Rd
Kewadin, MI 49648-9148
231-264-9265
Fax: 231-264-8532
Pure Northern Michigan maple syrup in 1/2 pint to one gallon jugs; private label available
President: Michael Luchenbill
President: Leta Luchenbill
Number Employees: 10-19
Square Footage: 12000
Type of Packaging: Consumer, Food Service, Private Label, Bulk
Brands:
    Maple Acres

7864 Maple Donuts
3455 E Market St
York, PA 17402-2696
717-757-7826
Fax: 717-755-8725 800-627-5348
www.mapledonuts.com
Yeast raised, cake style, fresh and frozen doughnuts, as well as unbaked pie shells, fritters, cinnamon buns and other pastries.
President: Charles Burnside
charliemaple@aol.com
CEO: Nathaniel Burnside
VP/General Manager: Ralph Wooten
VP, Sales & Marketing: Damian Burnside
Sales & Marketing Manager: Luke Burnside
Maintenance Manager: Frank Stefano
Plant Manager: Garry Rausch
Estimated Sales: $40-50 Million
Number Employees: 100-249
Square Footage: 80000
Parent Co: Maple Donuts LLC
Type of Packaging: Private Label

7865 Maple Donuts Inc
10307 Hall Ave
Lake City, PA 16423-1226
814-774-3131
Fax: 814-774-3136 877-774-3668
Frozen donuts, pie shells, unfinished donuts, waffles
Chairman: Bruce MacLeod
CEO: Nat Burnside
Vice President: Patrick Riha
Estimated Sales: $10-20 Million
Number Employees: 50-99

7866 Maple Grove Farms Of Vermont
1052 Portland St
St Johnsbury, VT 05819-2041
802-748-5141
Fax: 802-748-9647 www.maplegrove.com
Pure maple syrup, fruit flavored syrups, sugar free syrup, specialty salad dressings, pancake & waffle mixes, gluten free products, maple candies & spreads.
Owner: Jim Schiller
Director, Finance: Jeffrey Donley
Plant Manager: Mark Bigelow
Estimated Sales: $11 Million
Number Employees: 100-249
Number of Brands: 4
Square Footage: 250000
Parent Co: B&G Foods
Type of Packaging: Consumer, Food Service, Private Label, Bulk
Brands:
    Cozy Cottage
    Maple Grove Farms of Vermont
    Up Country Naturals
    Vermont Sugar Free

7867 Maple Hill Creamery
5 Hudson St
Kinderhook, NY 12106
518-758-7777
Fax: 315-266-1269 maplehillcreamery.com
Milk, cheese and yogurt.
Co-Founder: Laura Joseph
Co-Founder: Tim Joseph
Brands:
    Maple Hill(c)

7868 Maple Hill Farms
12 Burr Rd
Bloomfield, CT 06002-2204
860-242-9689
Fax: 860-243-2490 800-842-7304
www.mhfct.com
Dairy products
President: William Miller
info@maplehillfarm.com
Marketing Director: Scott Miller
Estimated Sales: $5-10 Million
Number Employees: 10-19

7869 Maple Hollow
W1887 Robinson Dr
Merrill, WI 54452-9543
715-536-7251
Maple syrup and sugar; wholesaler/distibutor of maple syrup processing machinery
Owner: Joe Polak
Vice President: Barbara Polak
Estimated Sales: $1 Million
Number Employees: 5-9
Number of Brands: 5
Number of Products: 4
Square Footage: 40000
Type of Packaging: Consumer, Private Label
Brands:
    Forest Country
    Maple Gardens
    Maple Hollow

7870 Maple Island
3497 Seventh Avenue E
Suite 105
Saint Paul, MN 55109-2907
651-773-1000
Fax: 651-773-2155 800-369-1022
info@maple-island.com www.maple-island.com
Processor and packager of food powders and dairy products; agglomerate, blend and package into pouches and canisters.
President: Greg Johnson
Founder: John Stoltze
Sales Manager: David Doebler
Director, Operations: Randy Biebl
Plant Manager: Scott Larson
Estimated Sales: $28.7 Million
Number Employees: 10-19
Type of Packaging: Consumer, Food Service, Private Label, Bulk
Brands:
    Bounce
    Diet Freeze
    Maple Island
    Shakequik

7871 Maple Leaf Bakery
PO Box 55021
Montreal, QC H3G 2W5
Canada
416-926-2020
Fax: 416-926-2018 800-268-3708
Mediahotline@mapleleaf.com www.mapleleaf.ca
Bakery products
President/CEO: Michael McCain
Corporate Director: Robert Stewart
Chief Financial Officer: Michael H. Vels
SVP, Finance: Debbie Simpson
VP, Corporate Engineering: Peter Smith
CFSO and SVP, Six Sigma and Quality: Randall Huffman
Chief Marketing Officer: Stephen Graham
SVP, Communications: Lynda Kuhn
Chief Operating Officer: Richard A. Lan
SVP, Logistics and Purchasing: Bill Kaldis
Estimated Sales: $4,406,000
Number Employees: 18,000
Brands:
    California Goldminer
    Eurofresh
    Home Fresh
    Maple Leaf

Food Manufacturers / A-Z

7872 Maple Leaf Cheesemakers
554 Frst Street
New Glarus, WI 53574
608-527-2000
Fax: 608-527-3050 888-624-1234
mapleleafl@tds.net
www.mapleleafcheeseandchocolatehaus.com
Cheese including monterey jack and gouda, fudge and chocolates
Owner: Barbara Kummerfeldt
Estimated Sales: $500,000-$1 Million
Number Employees: 20-49
Type of Packaging: Consumer, Food Service, Private Label, Bulk
Brands:
 Maple Leaf

7873 Maple Leaf Consumer Foods
7840 Madison Ave # 135
Fair Oaks, CA 95628-3591
916-967-1633
Fax: 916-967-1690 800-999-7603
www.mapleleaf.com
Ham and bacon
General Manager: Charles Brougher
Estimated Sales: $5-10 Million
Number Employees: 10-19
Parent Co: Maple Leaf Foods
Type of Packaging: Consumer, Food Service, Private Label, Bulk

7874 Maple Leaf Farms
101 E Church
P.O. Box 167
St Leesburg, IN 46538
574-453-4455
800-348-2812
cturk@mapleleaffarms.com
www.mapleleaffarms.com
Duck products.
Co-President: John Tucker
Co-President: Scott Tucker
Chief Executive Officer: Terry Tucker
CFO & COO: Scott Reinholt
Year Founded: 1958
Estimated Sales: $45.3 Million
Number Employees: 1100
Type of Packaging: Consumer, Food Service, Private Label, Bulk
Brands:
 C&D
 C&D
 Chef Tang
 Ech
 Fch
 Gold Label
 Maple Leaf

7875 Maple Leaf Foods
1 Warman Drive
Winnipeg, NB R2J 4E5
Canada
204-231-4114
Fax: 204-231-2944 800-564-6253
www.mapleleaf.com
Pork
CEO: Michael H McCain
CFO: Michael H Vels
Plant Manager: Jeff Parsons
Number Employees: 250-499
Parent Co: Schneider's Dairy
Type of Packaging: Food Service
Brands:
 Burns
 California Goldminer
 Hygrade
 Maison-Cousin
 Nutriwhip
 Shopsy's
 Tenderflake

7876 (HQ)Maple Leaf Foods International
5160 Yonge St
Suite 300
North York, ON M2N 6L9
Canada
416-480-8900
Fax: 416-480-8950 800-268-3708
www.mapleleaf.ca
Processor, importer and exporter of fresh and frozen meat, seafood, dairy products, produce, potato products and specialty grains
President: Michael Detlefsen
Senior Vice President, Transactions and: Rocco Cappuccitti
Executive VP/Chief Strategy Officer: Douglas Dodds
Chief Information Officer: Patrick Ressa
Chief Financial Officer: Michael Vels
Estimated Sales: $6.4 Million
Number Employees: 23,000
Square Footage: 42000
Type of Packaging: Consumer, Food Service, Private Label, Bulk
Other Locations:
 Maple Leaf Foods Internationa
 Chatham NJ
Brands:
 Bittner's
 California Goldminer
 Dempster's
 Hot & Crusty
 Hudrage
 Maison Cousin
 Maple Leaf
 Medallion Naturally
 Nature's Gourmet
 Olivieri
 Prime Naturally
 Prime Turkey
 Ready Crisp
 Shopsy's
 Slo-Roast Deli
 Tender Flake
 Top Dogs

7877 Maple Leaf Meats
PO Box 55021
Mctreal, QC H3G 2W5
Canada
204-233-2421
Fax: 204-233-5413 800-268-3708
www.mapleleaf.com
Meat products
Director Corporate: James F Hankinson
President: Chaviva M Hosek
Controller: John Main
CEO: Chaviva M Hosek
Number Employees: 400
Square Footage: 1036000
Parent Co: Maple Leaf Foods
Type of Packaging: Consumer, Food Service, Private Label, Bulk
Brands:
 Maple Leaf
 Royale

7878 Maple Leaf Pork
P.O. Box 55021
Montreal, QC H3G 2W5
Canada
403-328-1756
Fax: 403-327-9821 800-268-3708
www.mapleleaf.ca
Processor and exporter of fresh and frozen pork including carcass, boxed and by-products
President: Michael McCain
Sales: Wilf Fiebich
General Manager: Ralph Miller
Plant Manager: Dave Wood
Number Employees: 100-249
Parent Co: Maple Leaf Foods
Type of Packaging: Consumer, Bulk

7879 Maple Products
1500 Rue De Pacifique
Sherbrooke, QC J1H 2G7
Canada
819-569-5161
Fax: 819-569-5168
Processor and exporter of maple syrup and sugar; also, kosher grades available
Production Manager: Ghislain Pare
Number Employees: 10-19
Parent Co: Citadelle
Type of Packaging: Food Service, Bulk
Brands:
 Pride of Canada

7880 Maple Ridge Farms
975 S Park View Cir
Mosinee, WI 54455
Canada
715-693-4346
www.mapleridge.com
Processor for the production and extraction of essential oils and their fractions. Including caraway seed, cilantro (coriander foliage), dill seed and foliage. One hundred tons annually. Serving the bio-organic industry and ingredientmanufacturers
President: Martin Gareau

7881 Maple Valley Cooperative
919 Front St
P.O. Box 153
Cashton, WI 54619
608-654-7319
Fax: 877-579-5073
customerservice@maplevalley.coop
www.maplevalleysyrup.coop
Organic maple syrup, maple candy, maple sugar, and maple cream
Founder/President: Cecil Wright
General Manager: Renee Miller
Year Founded: 2007

7882 Maple's Organics
881 Route 1
Yarmouth, ME 04096-6930
207-846-1000
Manufacturer of gelato.
Co-Founder: Rachel Williams
Co-Founder: David Williams
Estimated Sales: Less Than $500,000
Number Employees: 5-9

7883 Maplebrook Farm
PO Box 966
Bennington, VT 05201-8005
802-440-9950
Fax: 802-440-9956 meri@maplebrookvt.com
www.maplebrookvt.com
Cheese.
Owner: Mike Scheps
Marketing: Meri Spicer

7884 Maplegrove Foods
1261 W State St
Ontario, CA 91762
909-545-6075
info@omasownfoods.com
omasownfoods.com
Noodle cups and fruit chips
President/Owner: Raj Sukul
Brands:
 Oma's Own

7885 Maplehill Creamery
285 Allendale Rd W
Stuyvesant, NY 12173-2611
USA
518-758-7777
contact@maplehillcreamery.com
Yogurt, cheese
President: Tim Joseph
Director Of Marketing & Communications: Sara Talcott
Contact: Glenn Haakonsen
ghaakonsen@lenel.com
Estimated Sales: Less Than $500,000
Number Employees: 5-9

7886 Maplehurst Bakeries LLC
50 Maplehurst Dr
Brownsburg, IN 46112
800-428-3200
info@maplehurstbakeries.com
www.maplehurstbakeries.com
Bread and other bakery products including; rolls, cakes, donuts, pies, and danishes.
President: Luc Mongeau
Supply Chain Director: Craig Myers
Year Founded: 1967
Estimated Sales: $107.2 Million
Number Employees: 1,000-4,999
Parent Co: George Weston Ltd.
Type of Packaging: Food Service, Private Label, Bulk
Brands:
 Freed's Bakery
 Granny's Kitchen
 La Baguetterie
 Plush Pippin

7887 Maplehurst Farms
936 S Moore Rd
Rochelle, IL 61068-9789
815-562-8723
Fax: 815-562-7543 www.maplehurstfarms.com

Milk and cottage cheese
General Manager: Jim Black
Vice President: Steve Garish
Year Founded: 1909
Estimated Sales: $100-400 Million
Number Employees: 50-99
Parent Co: Dean Foods Company

7888 Mapleland Farm
647 Bunker Hill Rd
Salem, NY 12865-1716
518-854-7669
www.maplelandfarms.com
Manufacturer of pure maple products.
Co-Founder: David Campbell
Co-Founder: Terry Campbell
Estimated Sales: Less Than $500,000
Number Employees: 1-4

7889 Mar-Jac Poultry Inc.
1020 Aviation Blvd.
Gainesville, GA 30501
770-531-5000
Fax: 770-531-5015 info@marjacpoultry.com
www.marjacpoultry.com
Fresh and frozen chicken; whole birds (with or without giblets), fast food (8, 9, or 6 pieces), splits, or quarters, boneless butterflies, tenders, filets, or thigh meat, and parts; split breasts, drums, thighs, whole legs, legquarters, whole wings, cut wings, gizzards, livers, paws.
CFO: Tanveer Papa
Vice President, Operations: Joel Williams
Year Founded: 1954
Estimated Sales: $284 Million
Number Employees: 1000-4999
Number of Brands: 2
Square Footage: 300000
Type of Packaging: Food Service, Private Label
Brands:
 M-J
 Mar-Jac Brands

7890 Mar-Key Foods
PO Box 603
Vidalia, GA 30475
912-537-4204
Fax: 912-537-2542
Soft drink concentrates, pre-sweetened drink mixes and freeze pops
President: Louie Powell
Secretary: Diane Collins
Estimated Sales: $110,000
Number Employees: 20-49
Type of Packaging: Consumer, Food Service, Bulk
Brands:
 Jolly Aid
 Jolly Pops

7891 (HQ)Maramor Chocolates
1855 E 17th Ave
Columbus, OH 43219
614-291-2244
Fax: 614-291-0966 800-843-7722
Processor and exporter of kosher boxed chocolates, chocolate covered bagel chips and mints; packaged for racks and fund raising purposes; contract manufacturing available
President: Michael Ryan
Sales: Scott Sher
Contact: Crystal Burchett
cburchett@maramor.com
Estimated Sales: $1.6 Million
Number Employees: 20-49
Square Footage: 120000
Type of Packaging: Consumer, Private Label, Bulk
Brands:
 Maramor

7892 (HQ)Marantha Natural Foods
1192 Illinois Street
San Francisco, CA 94107
415-401-0080
Fax: 415-401-0087 866-972-6879
customerservice@worldpantry.com
www.worldpantry.com
Organic and regular nut and seed butters, trail mixes and dry roasted nuts and seeds; importer of cashews and sesame seeds; exporter of organic and regular nut and seed butters and trail mixes
President: Patrick Lee
CEO: David Miller

Estimated Sales: $10-20 Million
Number Employees: 20-49
Square Footage: 28000
Type of Packaging: Consumer, Food Service, Private Label, Bulk
Other Locations:
 Marantha Natural Foods
 San Leandro CA
Brands:
 Marantha
 Nuttin' Butter

7893 Marathon Cheese
1000 Progressive Ave
Medford, WI 54451-1698
715-748-4500
Custom packager of cheese
Contact: Mike Mathias
mmccallum@mcheese.com
Plant Manager: John Wanish
Number Employees: 250-499
Type of Packaging: Consumer, Food Service, Private Label, Bulk

7894 (HQ)Marathon Cheese Corp
304 East St
PO Box 185
Marathon, WI 54448-9643
715-443-2211
Fax: 715-443-3843
Custom packager of cheese
President: Dan Zastoupil
CEO: John Skoug
jskoug@mcheese.com
Director: Gene Land
Director Sales/Marketing: Mike Mathias
Corporate Controller: Amy Janke
Systems Manager: Arlin Bradfish
Plant Manager: Lisa Trace
Number Employees: 500-999
Type of Packaging: Consumer, Food Service, Private Label, Bulk
Other Locations:
 Marathon Cheese
 Mountain Home ID
 Marathon Cheese
 Medford WI
 Marathon Cheese
 Booneville MS

7895 Marathon Enterprises Inc
9 Smith St
Englewood, NJ 07631-4607
201-569-2915
Fax: 201-935-5693 800-722-7388
info@sabrett.com www.sabretthotstuff.com
Hot dogs including; all beef natural casing, pork and beef natural casing, or all beef skinless, available in cocktail size up to foot long franks, and condiments such as sauerkraut, mustard, relish and onions in sauce
President: Boyd G Adelman
VP Sales: Mark Rosen
Plant Manager: Herb Tetens
Number Employees: 250-499
Type of Packaging: Consumer, Food Service, Private Label, Bulk
Brands:
 Sabrett

7896 Marathon Packing Corp
1000 Montague St
San Leandro, CA 94577-4332
510-895-2000
Fax: 510-895-2022 www.marathonpacking.com
Cooking oils and shortening
Chief Executive Officer: Cecilia Chan
Contact: Brendan Chan
brendan.chan@marathonpacking.com
Plant Manager: Luis Salazar
Estimated Sales: $10-20 000,000
Number Employees: 10-19

7897 Marburger Farm Dairy
1506 Mars Evans City Road
Evans City, PA 16033
724-538-4800
Fax: 724-538-3250 800-331-1295
www.marburgerdairy.com
Bottled milk and dairy products.
President: James Marburger
VP: Craig Marburger
Maintenance Manager: Larry Byers
Plant Manager: Garrie Wearing

Estimated Sales: $10-20 Million
Number Employees: 50-99
Number of Brands: 1
Type of Packaging: Private Label
Brands:
 Marburger

7898 Marcel et Henri Charcuterie Francaise
415 Browning Way
South San Francisco, CA 94080
650-871-4230
Fax: 650-871-5948 800-227-6436
marcelethenri@sbcglobal.net
French pate and sausage.
President: Henri Lapuyade
Estimated Sales: $3 Million
Number Employees: 10-19
Number of Brands: 1
Number of Products: 50
Square Footage: 60000
Type of Packaging: Consumer, Food Service, Bulk
Brands:
 Marcel Et Henri

7899 Marcho Farms Inc
176 Orchard Ln
Harleysville, PA 19438-1681
215-721-7131
Fax: 215-721-9719 ltufft@marchofarms.com
Grower and packer of milk fed veal. Processing primal, fresh cuts, portion control, precooked meatballs, meat loaf, bacon and philly steaks
President: Wayne A Marcho
wmarcho@marchofarms.com
Number Employees: 100-249

7900 Marconi Italian Specialty Foods
710 W Grand Ave
Chicago, IL 60654-5574
312-421-0485
Fax: 312-421-1286 sales@marconi-foods.com
www.marconi-foods.com
Manufacturers a variety of specialty Italian foods including cheeses; coffees; salad dressings; meats; olive oils; pasta; salads; sauces; seafoods; spices, and vinegars.
President/CEO/Co-Owner: Robert Johnson
Co-Owner: Sue Formusa
Estimated Sales: $5-10 Million
Number Employees: 5-9
Parent Co: V Formusa Company

7901 Mardale Specialty Foods
1120 Glen Rock Avenue
Waukegan, IL 60085-5458
845-299-0285
Fax: 847-336-5030
Portion controlled condiments including salad dressing, syrup, jam and mayonnaise
President: Ronald Tarantino
Plant Manager: Jim Streiff
Number Employees: 20-49
Type of Packaging: Food Service

7902 Mardi Gras
150 Bloomfield Ave
Verona, NJ 07044-2711
973-857-3777
Fax: 973-857-8884 maria@mardigrasfoods.com
www.mardigrasfoods.com
Gourmet fresh and frozen foods
Manager: Maria Carrozza
VP: Kim Newman
Estimated Sales: Below $5 Million
Number Employees: 10-19
Square Footage: 9600
Type of Packaging: Consumer

7903 Margarita Man
10818 Gulfdale St
San Antonio, TX 78216-3607
210-979-7191
Fax: 210-979-0718 800-950-8149
info@margaritamansa.com
www.margaritamansa.com
Frozen drink mixes; wholesaler/distributor of frozen beverage machines
President: Chris Murphy
ncmargman@nc.rr.com
Plant Manager: Steve Snyder
Estimated Sales: $1 Million
Number Employees: 5-9
Number of Brands: 1

Food Manufacturers / A-Z

Number of Products: 15
Square Footage: 10000
Brands:
    Go Bananas
    Go Mango
    Just Add Tequila
    Razzmatazzberry
    The Margarita Man

7904 Mari's Candy
2266 S Blue Island Ave
Chicago, IL 60608-4345
773-254-3351
Fax: 773-254-3581

Mexican-style coconut candy
Owner: Raul Hernandez
VP/CEO: Maris Elena
VP of Retail: Raul Hernandez Jr.
VP of General Market: Maria Hernandez
VP of Wholesale: Rodrigo Hernandez
Estimated Sales: Less Than $500,000
Number Employees: 1-4
Type of Packaging: Consumer

7905 Mari's New York
115 4th Ave Apt 8a
Suite C5
New York, NY 10003-4909
Fax: 615-622-0281 support@marisny.com
Brownies

7906 MariGold Foods
16693 Coaltown Rd
Willis, TX 77378
936-344-0444
www.marigoldbars.com
Gluten free, organic, non-GMO protein bars
Co-Owner: Mari Ann Lisenbe
Co-Owner: Steve Lisenbe
Year Founded: 2012

7907 Maria & Son
4201 Hereford St
St Louis, MO 63109-1798
314-481-9009
Fax: 314-481-9109 866-481-9009
Frozen Italian pastas and sauces
President: John Ard
Estimated Sales: $5-10 000,000
Number Employees: 10-19
Brands:
    Maria & Son
    Tita's

7908 Maria and Ricardo's
320 Turnpike St
Canton, MA 02021
800-881-7040
info@harbar.com www.mariaandricardos.com
Tortillas, wraps and tortilla crisps
VP, Sales: Tom Stacey
Number of Brands: 2
Number of Products: 20
Type of Packaging: Consumer
Brands:
    MARIA AND RICARDO'S
    ARTESANO

7909 Maria's Premium
www.mariaspremium.com
Flavored popcorn
Number of Brands: 1
Number of Products: 3
Type of Packaging: Consumer
Brands:
    MARIA'S PREMIUM

7910 Mariani Nut Co
28306 County Road 90a
Winters, CA 95694
530-795-1546
Fax: 530-795-2681 www.marianinut.com
Processor and exporter of walnuts and almonds
President & CEO: Jack Mariani
Co-Owner: Gus Mariani
Partner: Martin Mariani
Vice President: Dennis Mariani
VP Marketing & Ecommerce: Matt Mariani
Marketin Mgr, VP Operations/Sales: John Martin
Estimated Sales: $5.5 Million
Number Employees: 10-19
Square Footage: 120000
Type of Packaging: Consumer, Bulk
Brands:
    Mariani

7911 Mariani Packing Co.
500 Crocker Dr.
Vacaville, CA 95688-8706
707-452-2800
Fax: 707-452-2973 productinfo@mariani.com
www.mariani.com
Fresh dried fruit including; plums, apricots, cranberries, raisins, cherries, apples, and sun dried tomatoes.
President: George Sousa
Chairman/CEO: Mark Mariani
CFO: Forrest Chandler
Director Internet Sales: Stephen Sousa
Year Founded: 1906
Estimated Sales: $150 Million
Number Employees: 250-499
Square Footage: 10773
Type of Packaging: Consumer, Private Label, Bulk
Brands:
    Mariani

7912 Marich Confectionery
2101 Bert Dr
Hollister, CA 95023-2562
831-634-4700
Fax: 831-634-4705 800-624-7055
weborders@marich.com www.marich.com
Candy including chocolate cherries, apricots, blueberries, strawberries and nut mixes; also, mints, toffee and maltballs.
President: Bradley Van Dam
CEO: Steve Atwood
satwood@marich.com
Executive VP/COO: Troy Van Dam
VP Marketing/Sales: Michelle Van Dam
Sales Manager: Ellen Filberman
Plant Manager: Victor Moreno
Estimated Sales: Below $5 Million
Number Employees: 20-49
Type of Packaging: Consumer
Brands:
    Holland Mints
    Marich
    Wallabeans

7913 Marie Brizard Wines & Spirits
849 Zinfandel Lane
St. Helena, CA 94574
800-878-1123
Fax: 415-979-0305 info@boisset.com
www.boissetamerica.com
Processor, importer and exporter of alcoholic beverages including vodka, bourbon, tequila, scotch, brandy, cognac, schnapps, gin, rum, cordials, wines and champagne
President: Jean-Charles Boisset
VP/Director Marketing: Michael Avitable
VP/Director Sales: Robert Bermudez
Director Operations: Hubert Surville
Number Employees: 20-49
Square Footage: 26000
Parent Co: Marie Brizard Wines & Spirits USA
Brands:
    Marie Brizard

7914 Marie Callender's
27101 Puerta Real # 260
Suite 260
Mission Viejo, CA 92691-8538
949-448-5300
Fax: 949-582-7358 800-776-7437
www.mariecallenders.com
Cornbread mixes, desserts, pie glazes, muffin mixes and much more
CEO: Ron Bidinost
ron.bidinost@prkmc.com
Estimated Sales: $1-3 Million
Number Employees: 1000-4999

7915 Marie Callender's Gourmet Products/Goldrush Products
491 San Carlos Street
San Jose, CA 95110-2632
408-288-4090
Fax: 408-279-3742 800-729-5428
www.mccornbread.com
Kosher sourdough baking mixes including pancake, biscuit, cornbread, nine-grain and wholewheat bread, etc
President: Henry Down
Contact: Jim Musante
jim@commissary.com
Number Employees: 20-49
Parent Co: International Commissary Corporation
Type of Packaging: Consumer, Private Label, Bulk
Brands:
    Goldrush

7916 Marie F
123 Denison Street
Markham, ON L3R 1B5
Canada
905-475-0093
Fax: 905-475-0038 800-365-4464
fmarie@ca.inter.net
Beef, butcher supplies and sausage and sheep casings; importer of sausage casings, butcher suppliers and cures; exporter of sausage casings
President: Sandra Marie Rundle
Plant Manager: Alaister Sears
Estimated Sales: $4 Million
Number Employees: 25
Square Footage: 60000
Type of Packaging: Food Service

7917 Marie's Quality Foods
PO Box 1105
Brea, CA 92822
800-339-1051
www.maries.com
Salad dressing
President: Richard D Orr
VP Sales/Marketing: Richard Orr
Operations Manager: Drew Orr
Number Employees: 20-49
Square Footage: 400000
Type of Packaging: Consumer, Food Service, Private Label

7918 MarieBelle
484 Broome St
New York, NY 10013
212-925-6999
mariebelle.com
Chocolate
President & Founder: Maribel Lieberman
Type of Packaging: Private Label

7919 Maries Candies
311 Zanesfield Rd
West Liberty, OH 43357-9563
937-465-3061
Fax: 937-465-3336 866-465-5781
info@mariescandies.com www.mariescandies.com
Candy including turkins, peanut brittle, toffee, butter creams, peppermint chews and melt-aways
Owner: Jay R King
info@mariescandies.com
Co-Owner: Kathy King
Estimated Sales: $1,200,000
Number Employees: 20-49
Type of Packaging: Consumer

7920 Marietta Cellars
22295 Chianti Rd
Geyservill, CA 95441
707-433-2747
Fax: 707-857-4910 www.mariettacellars.com
Producer of wines the list of which includes Angeli Cuvee, Petit Sirah, Cabernet Sauvignon and Zinfandel.
President/CEO: Chris Bilbro
Office Manager: Suzie Buchignani
Bookkeeper: Judy Summary
Marketing Manager: Jake Bilbro
Contact: Will Hunter
will@mariettacellars.com
Facilities Manager: Sarah Herrerra
Cellar/Bottling Manager: Roman Cisneros
Estimated Sales: $1.5 Million
Number Employees: 15

7921 Marika's Kitchen
106 Old Route 1
Hancock, ME 04640-3448
207-422-2300
Fax: 207-422-2300 800-694-9400
marika_gauchi@hotmail.com
Almond and walnut baklava and Greek biscota
Owner: Gloria Day
Vice President: Michael Savoy
Number Employees: 1-4
Square Footage: 5000

Food Manufacturers / A-Z

Type of Packaging: Food Service, Bulk

7922 Marimar Torres Estates
11400 Graton Rd
Sebastopol, CA 95472-8901
707-823-4365
Fax: 707-823-4496 info189@marimarestate.com
www.sanfranciscobayarealimo.com
Wines
Proprietor/Winegrower: Marimar Torres
marimar@marimarestate.com
National Sales Manager: Kyle Ray
Cellar Master: Tony Britton
Vineyard Manager: Venutra Albor
Estimated Sales: $850,000
Number Employees: 5-9
Type of Packaging: Private Label
Brands:
    Marimar Torres Estate

7923 Marin Brewing Co
1809 Larkspur Landing Cir
Larkspur, CA 94939-1801
415-461-4677
Fax: 415-461-4688 brendan@marinbrewing.com
www.marinbrewing.com
Beer
Proprietor: Brendan Moylan
brendan@marinbrewing.com
Brew Master: Arne Johnson
Marketing Manager: Ryan Purtill
Sales Manager: Curtis Cassidy
Estimated Sales: Below $5 Million
Number Employees: 100-249
Brands:
    Albion Amber Ale
    Marin Weiss
    Miwok Weizen Bock
    Mt. Tom Pale Ale
    Old Dipsea Barley Wine
    Point Reyes Porter
    Raspberry Trail Ale
    San Quentin's Breakout Stout

7924 Marin Food Specialties
14800 Highway 4
Byron, CA 94505-2236
925-634-6126
Fax: 925-634-4647
Processor, importer and exporter of specialty foods including cookies, fig and fruit bars, pasta, trail mixes, marinated vegetables, almond butter, spices and candy; gift baskets available
President: Joseph Brucia
VP: Fred Vuylsteke
Estimated Sales: $1-3 Million
Number Employees: 50 to 99
Square Footage: 60000
Type of Packaging: Consumer, Private Label, Bulk
Brands:
    Marin
    Spanky's

7925 Marin French Cheese Co
7500 Red Hill Rd
Petaluma, CA 94952-9438
707-762-6001
Fax: 707-762-0430 800-292-6001
cheesefactory@marinfrenchcheese.com
www.marinfrenchcheese.com
Cheeses including camembert cheese, breakfast cheese, brie cheese, schloss cheese and specialty flavored bries; also gift boxes available.
Owner: Teresa Gordon
tgordon@santiagocorp.com
Finance Manager: Candice Millhouse
Marketing: Maxx Sherman
Estimated Sales: $1.6 Million
Number Employees: 20-49
Type of Packaging: Consumer, Bulk
Brands:
    Rouge Et Noir

7926 Marin Kombucha
Novato, CA 94925
415-496-5441
info@marinkombucha.com
marinkombucha.com
Kombucha
CFO: Kevin Igersheim

7927 Marina Foods
11125 NW 124th Street
Medley, FL 33178-3173
786-888-0129
Fax: 786-888-0134 info@marinafoods.com
www.marinafoods.com
Packers of edible oils, shortenings and related products.
President: John Ioannou
Contact: George Ioannou
george@marinafoods.com
Estimated Sales: $20 Million
Number Employees: 20-49
Number of Brands: 3
Type of Packaging: Consumer, Food Service, Private Label, Bulk
Brands:
    Chef's Recipe
    DiMarco
    Marina

7928 Marine MacHines
3 Strawberry Hill Road
Bar Harbor, ME 04609-1206
207-288-0107
Fax: 207-288-0462
Sea urchin procesing technology and equipment.
President: Mickey Kestner

7929 Mariner Neptune Fish & Seafood Company
472 Dufferin Avenue
Winnipeg, NB R2W 2X6
Canada
204-589-5341
Fax: 204-582-8135 800-668-8862
www.marinerneptune.com
Distributor of fish, seafood and protein food products
President: John Alexander
VP: Russell Page
Marketing: Evan Page
Sales: Doug Chandler
Plant Manager: Chris Juerson
Estimated Sales: $16 Million
Number Employees: 42
Number of Products: 2000
Type of Packaging: Consumer, Food Service
Brands:
    King Neptune
    Mariner-Neptune

7930 Mariner Seafood LLC
86 Macarthur Dr.
New Bedford, MA 02740-7221
774-202-4121
Fax: 714-202-6605 www.marinerseafood.com
Fresh and frozen cod, hake, flounder, lobster and crab
President & CEO: Jack Flynn
jackflynn@marinerseafood.com
Estimated Sales: Less Than $500,000
Number Employees: 1-4
Type of Packaging: Consumer, Food Service, Private Label, Bulk
Brands:
    Mariner Seafoods

7931 Mario Camacho Foods
2502 Walden Woods Dr
Plant City, FL 33566-7167
813-305-4534
Fax: 813-305-4546 800-293-9783
info@mariocamachofoods.com
www.mariocamachofoods.com
A leading manufacturer and distributor of olives, olive oil and other specialty food products
President: Shawn Kaddoura
CEO: Michelle Andersen
andersenm@mariocamachofoods.com
CEO: Bret Milligan
Marketing: Jeff Hanneken
Sales: Jon Horoquist
Production: Bob Fidoelke
Estimated Sales: $10-20 Million
Number Employees: 20-49
Square Footage: 375000
Parent Co: Angel Camacho S.A.
Type of Packaging: Consumer, Food Service, Private Label, Bulk
Brands:
    Christos
    Fragata
    Pride of Spain
    The Jug

7932 Mario's Gelati
88 E 1st Avenue
Vancouver, BC V5T 1A1
Canada
604-879-9411
Fax: 604-879-0435 info@mariosgelati.com
www.mariosgelati.com
Processor, importer and exporter of ice cream
President: Mario Loscerbo
Vice President: Chris Loscerbo
Estimated Sales: $5.4 Million
Number Employees: 30
Square Footage: 120000
Brands:
    Mario's Gelati

7933 Marion's Smart Delights
1515 North Harrison Street
Arlington, VA 22205
703-593-3450
Dairy-free, gluten-free, kosher, nut-free, organic/natural, vegetarian, baking mixes and ingredients.
Marketing Director: Marion Braswell

7934 Marion-Kay Spice Co
1351 W US Highway 50
Brownstown, IN 47220
812-358-3000
Fax: 812-358-3400 800-627-7423
info@marionkay.com www.marionkay.com
Spice blends and extracts
Estimated Sales: $2500000
Number Employees: 20-49
Type of Packaging: Consumer, Food Service, Bulk
Brands:
    Claudia Sanders
    Cream of Vanilla
    The House of Flavors

7935 Maritime Pacific Brewing Co
1111 NW Ballard Way
Seattle, WA 98107-4639
206-782-6181
Fax: 206-782-0718 marpac@maritimebrewing.com
www.maritimebrewery.com
Micro-brewery
President: George Hancock
Estimated Sales: Below $5 Million
Number Employees: 20-49

7936 Marjie's Plantain Foods, Inc.
PO Box 1211
New York, NY 10002
908-627-5627
Fax: 718-383-3337
info@marjiesplantainfoods.com
www.marjiesplantainfoods.com
Gluten-free, other lifestyle, vegetarian, frozen baked goods, other snacks.
Marketing: Majorie Gaston

7937 Marjon Specialty Foods Inc
3508 Sydney Rd
Plant City, FL 33566-1185
813-752-3482
Fax: 813-754-4974
www.marjonspecialtyfoods.com
Sprouts (bean, alfalfa and others), salad dressings, fresh ginger stir-fry sauce, tofu
Vice President: Pedro Agenjo
pagenjo@pb-santander.com
VP: Marcia Miller
Director of R&D: Jim Martin
Human Resources Manager: Joe Miller
pagenjo@pb-santander.com
Operations Manager: Martha Clingenpeel
Office Manager, Director of Sales & Purc: Lisa Minnes
Estimated Sales: $11 Million
Number Employees: 100-249
Square Footage: 21000

7938 Mark West Wines
7000 Trenton-Healdsburg Rd
Forestville, CA 95436
707-544-4813
www.markwestwines.com
Pinot Noir

Food Manufacturers / A-Z

7939 Market Fisheries
7129 S State St
Chicago, IL 60619-1017
773-483-3233
Fax: 773-483-0724
Seafood
President: Haim Brody
haim@centerstagechicago.com
Estimated Sales: $3-5 Million
Number Employees: 10-19

7940 Market Square Food Co.
444 Old Skokie Rd
Park City, IL 60085
847-599-6070
Fax: 847-599-6512 800-232-2299
info@marketsquarefood.com
www.marketsquarefood.com
Specialty food gift items
Founder: James Lockhart
Founder: David Lockhart
Estimated Sales: $2.5-5 Million
Number Employees: 5-9
Brands:
   Animal Crackers
   Happy Snacks

7941 Markham Vineyards
2812 Saint Helena Hwy N
P.O.Box 636
St Helena, CA 94574-9655
707-963-5292
Fax: 707-963-4616 info@markhamvineyards.com
www.markhamvineyards.com
Processor and exporter of wines
President: Bryan Del Bondio
bdelbondio@markhamvineyards.com
Winemaker: Kimberlee Nicholls
Associate Winemaker: James Coughlin
General Manager: Kathryn Fowler
Estimated Sales: $5-10 Million
Number Employees: 20-49

7942 Markko Vineyard
4500 S Ridge Rd W
Conneaut, OH 44030-9712
440-593-3197
Fax: 440-599-7022 800-252-3197
markko@suite224.net www.markko.com
Wines
Owner: Arnulf Esterer
markko@suite224.net
Owner: Tim Hubbard
Estimated Sales: $500,000-$1 Million
Number Employees: 1-4

7943 Marks Meat
N6586 McCurdy Rd,
Holmen, WI 54636
608-526-6058
www.marksmeats.net
Beef, pork and lamb; custom slaughtering services available
President: Kristie Akin
Estimated Sales: $110,000
Number Employees: 5-9
Type of Packaging: Consumer

7944 Marley Orchards Corporation
2820 River Rd
Yakima, WA 98902
509-248-5231
Fax: 509-248-7358
Produce including apples
Chief Financial Officer: Stanley Bostrom
President/Sales & Marketing Staff: William Gammie
Sales Representative: Tony Bishop
Contact: Angela Deaton
adeaton@jackfrostfruit.com
Estimated Sales: $2.8 Million
Number Employees: 75
Type of Packaging: Consumer, Food Service, Bulk

7945 Marlow Candy & Nut Co
65 Honeck St
Englewood, NJ 07631-4125
201-569-3725
Fax: 201-569-9533 www.marlowcandy.net
Wholesaler of packaged candy and nuts
President: Eric Lowenthal
rickyl@marlowcandy.net
Office Manager: Alden Kirk
Estimated Sales: $10-20 Million
Number Employees: 20-49

7946 Marlow Wine Cellars
Highway 41a-64
Monteagle, TN 37356
931-924-2120
Fax: 931-924-2587
Manufactuer of fine wines
President/Wine Maker: Joe Marlow
Sales Manager: Gena Stevens
Estimated Sales: $1-2.5 Million
Number Employees: 1-4

7947 Marlyn Nutraceuticals
4404 E Elwood St
Phoenix, AZ 85040-1909
480-991-0200
Fax: 480-991-0551 800-899-4499
Processor and exporter of health foods and natural vitamins, minerals and food supplements including B-complex and C-combination formulas, fish oils, fiber blends, multi-vitamins and enzymes
Owner: Joe Lehmann
Export Sales Manager: Mark Wojick
VP Sales: Don Haygood
lehmannj@naturallyvitamins.com
Estimated Sales: $5-10 Million
Number Employees: 50-99
Square Footage: 80000
Type of Packaging: Food Service, Private Label, Bulk
Brands:
   All B-100
   All B-50
   Body-Fuel
   Fiber
   Fiber-7
   Ginsen-Rgy
   Hi C-Plex
   Little Vab
   Max-C-Plex
   Mega C-Bio
   Special C-500
   Super Epa
   Super Stress
   Super Vab
   Supreme B 150
   Un-Fad Diet Packs
   Vit-A-Boost

7948 Marnap Industries
225 French Street
Buffalo, NY 14211
716-897-1220
Fax: 716-897-1306 www.flavorchem.com
Processor and exporter of essential oils, spice blends, seasonings, flavor compounds and oleoresins; importer of essential oils and oleoresins
President: Dennis J Napora
VP: Kevin Martin
Sales: Joanne Evans
Production: J Cogley
Estimated Sales: $3-5 Million
Number Employees: 5-9
Number of Products: 100+
Square Footage: 48000
Parent Co: Flavorchem Corp.
Type of Packaging: Bulk
Brands:
   Marnap-Trap

7949 Marquez Brothers International
101 South 11th Ave
Hanford, CA 93230-5043
408-960-2700
Fax: 408-960-3213 800-858-1119
www.marquezbrothers.com
Gelatin, sweet and sour cream, Mexican cheese and liquid yogurt
CEO: Gustave Marquez
VP: Juan Marquez
Contact: Gloria Castillo
gcastillo@marquezbrothers.com
Plant Manager: Juan Luis De La Torre
Estimated Sales: $1 Million
Number Employees: 10-19
Parent Co: Marquez Brothers International
Type of Packaging: Consumer, Food Service

7950 Marquis
600 St. Paul Ave
Suite 102
Los Angeles, CA 90017-2038
213-250-7414
drinkmarquis.com
Organic energy drinks
President/Owner: Danny Huang
CEO: Christopher Lai
Number of Brands: 1
Number of Products: 3
Type of Packaging: Consumer
Brands:
   MARQUIS

7951 Marroquin Organic Intl.
303 Potero St
Suite 18
Santa Cruz, CA 95060
831-423-3442
Fax: 831-423-3432 info@marroquin-organics.com
www.marroquin-organics.com
Organic and non-GMO ingredients
President: Grace Marroquin
Vice President: Mark Nelson
Organic Ingredient Specialist: Helen Hudson
Contact: Ciaran Cooney
ccooney@paypal.com
Estimated Sales: $4-5 Million
Number Employees: 5-9

7952 Mars Inc.
6885 Elm St.
McLean, VA 22101
703-821-4900
www.mars.com
Pet products, chocolate, chewing gum, beverages, food and health products.
CEO: Grant Reid
CFO: Claus Aagaard
Vice President/General Counsel: Stefanie Straub
President, Innovation: Jean-Christophe Flatin
Global President, Mars Food: Fiona Dawson
Mars Wrigley: Andrew Clarke
Year Founded: 1911
Estimated Sales: $35 Billion
Number Employees: 100,000
Number of Brands: 74
Type of Packaging: Consumer, Bulk
Brands:
   API
   AQUARIAN
   Banfield
   BluePearl
   Cesar
   DREAMIES
   Eukanuba
   IAMS
   NUTRO
   PEDIGREE
   Pet Partners
   Royal Canin
   SHEBA
   TEMPTATIONS
   WALTHAM
   WHISKAS
   WHISTLE
   WISDOM PANEL
   M&M's
   Wrigley's
   SNICKERS
   TWIX
   Skittles
   DOVE
   3 MUSKETEERS
   5 Gum
   Altoids
   AMERICAN HERITAGE
   AMICELLI
   BALISTO
   Big Red
   Bounty
   CELEBRATIONS
   COMBOS
   Doublemint
   Eclipse
   Ethel M
   GALAXY
   goodnessKNOWS
   Hubba Bubba
   Juicy Fruit
   Life Savers
   Maltesers
   MARS
   MILKY WAY
   Orbit
   Extra
   Freedent
   Starburst
   Winterfresh
   Wrigley's Spearminti

Food Manufacturers / A-Z

Abu Siouf
DOLIMO
Ebly
KAN TONG
MASTERFOODS
MIRACOLI
PAMESELLO
RARIS
Royco
SEEDS OF CHANGE
Suzi Wan
Tasty Bite
UNCLE BENS
CocoVia
CocoVia

7953 Marsa Specialty Products
5511 Long Beach Ave
Vernon, CA 90058
323-587-2288
Fax: 323-587-6729 800-628-0500
Dietetic products including syrups and ketchup
President: Helga Hanlein
Secretary/Treasurer: Allen Brown
Sales Director: James Hanelin
Estimated Sales: $1 Million
Number Employees: 10-19
Type of Packaging: Food Service

7954 (HQ)Marsan Foods
106 Thermos Road
Toronto, ON M1L 4W2
Canada
416-755-9262
Fax: 416-755-6790 sean@marsanfoods.com
www.marsanfoods.com
Processor and exporter of single-series frozen entries and bowls, family size entries, control and private label. Processor and exporter of specialty meal components for healthcare settings
President: James Jewett
Director Sales/Marketing: Sean Lippay
Number Employees: 100
Number of Products: 160
Square Footage: 300000
Type of Packaging: Consumer, Food Service, Private Label
Brands:
  Balanced Cuisine
  Puree Marsan

7955 Marshall Durbin Companies
2830 Commerce Blvd
P.O. Box 100755
Birmingham, AL 35210
205-380-3251 800-768-2456
Fax:
sales@marshalldurbin.com
www.marshalldurbin.com
Chicken eggs, chicken hatchery, raising, slaughtering and processing of chickens, wholesale poultry.
President: Melissa Durbin
Plant Manager: Allen Butler
Year Founded: 1939
Estimated Sales: $121.5 Million
Number Employees: 1,900
Other Locations:
  Feed Mill
  Haleyville AL
  Feed Mill
  Waynesboro MS
  Hatchery
  Moulton AL
  Hatchery
  Waynesboro MS
  Broiler Office
  Delmar AL
  Processing Plant
  Hattiesburg MS
  Processing Plant
  Jasper AL
  Laboratory
  Jackson MS
  Distribution Center
  Tarrant AL

7956 Marshall Ingredients
5740 Limekiln Rd
Wolcott, NY 14590
800-796-9353
cbones@marshallingredients.com
Fruits and vegetables in different forms such as fiber, pellet, whole, diced, sliced, powder, seeds, pomace
National Sales Manager: Casey Koehnlein
Contact: Scott Edwards
sedwards@marshallingredients.com

Type of Packaging: Bulk

7957 Marshall's Biscuit Company
T. Marzetti Company
380 Polaris Parkway, Suite 400
Westerville, OH 43082
251-679-6226
www.sisterschuberts.com
Breads, rolls
Branch Manager: Harris Morrisette
Estimated Sales: $10-20 Million
Number Employees: 50-99
Parent Co: T. Marzetti

7958 Marshallville Packing Co
50 E Market St
Marshallville, OH 44645
330-855-2871
Fax: 330-855-7991 www.marshallville-meats.com
Beef, pork including sausage, luncheon meats, poultry and cheese
President: Frank Tucker
Assistant Manager: John Tucker
Estimated Sales: $3 Million
Number Employees: 20-49
Square Footage: 81000
Type of Packaging: Consumer, Food Service, Bulk

7959 Martens Fresh
1323 Towpath Rd
Port Byron, NY 13140
315-776-8821
Fax: 315-776-8201 www.spudsrus.com
Potatoes
Owner: Timothy Martens
tim@spudsrus.com
Estimated Sales: $5-10 Million
Number Employees: 20-49
Square Footage: 25000
Type of Packaging: Consumer, Food Service, Private Label, Bulk

7960 Martha Olson's Great Foo
PO Box 66.
Sutter Creek, CA 95685-0066
209-234-5935
Fax: 209-223-7071 800-973-3966
www.marthasallnatural.com
All natural baking mixes including pancake, muffin, waffle, bread, cake and scone; also, chocolate sauce
Owner: Martha Olson
CEO: Margaret Brown
Marketing/National Accounts: Roylene Brown
Production Manager: Harvey Archer
Estimated Sales: $2.5-5 Million
Number Employees: 1-4
Brands:
  Martha's All Natural
  Martha's All Natural Baking Mixes

7961 Martha's Garden
475 Horner Avenue
Toronto, ON M8W 4X7
Canada
416-251-6112
Fax: 416-251-8443 866-773-2887
Fresh onions, cabbage, lettuce, celery, broccoli, cucumbers, carrots, cauliflower, tomatoes, zucchini, eggplant
President: Gus Arrigo, Jr.
Quality Assurance Manager: Jefery Musumi
Sales Manager: Richard Sabourin
Number Employees: 20-49

7962 Martin & Weyrich Winery
P.O.Box 1330
Templeton, CA 93465
805-239-1640
Fax: 805-238-0887 sales@martinweyrich.com
This winery produces a wide selection including Pinot Grigio, Moscato Allegro, Nebbiolo, Nebbiolo Vecchio, Insieme, Zinfandel La Primitiva, Cabernet Etrusco, Vin Santo, in addition to having a fine coffee selection including cappuccino, espresso, latte and mochas.
Manager: Katie Stemper
Marketing Director: Larry Persinger
Production Manager: Craig Reed
Purchasing Manager: Cynthia Reed
Estimated Sales: $5-10 Million
Number Employees: 20-49
Square Footage: 24

7963 Martin Bauer Group
300 Harmon Meadow Blvd
Suite 510
Sacaucus, NJ 07094
201-659-3100
Fax: 201-659-3180
welcome@martin-bauer-group.us
www.martin-bauer-group.us
Tea and botanical extracts, herbal and fruit infusions, powders, flavors, phytopharmaceutical ingredients and nutritional supplements.
President & CEO: Ennio Ranaboldo
Managing Director: Albert Ferstl
Chief Financial Officer: William Nicholas
Year Founded: 1980
Estimated Sales: $20 Million
Number Employees: 3
Type of Packaging: Consumer
Brands:
  Life Savers
  Planters

7964 Martin Brothers SeafoodCo
133 Westbank Expy
Westwego, LA 70094-4213
504-341-2251
Fax: 504-341-2251
Frozen crabmeat and gumbo crabs
President: William Martin
Owner: Donna Martin
Estimated Sales: Less Than $500,000
Number Employees: 1-4
Type of Packaging: Consumer, Food Service, Bulk

7965 Martin Coffee Co
1633 Marshall St
Jacksonville, FL 32206-6011
904-355-9661
Fax: 904-355-9673 info@martincoffee.com
www.martincoffee.com
Coffee
President: Ben Johnson
benjohnson@martincoffee.com
VP: Harold Johnson
VP Sales/Marketing: Ben Johnson
Estimated Sales: $15 Million
Number Employees: 5-9
Type of Packaging: Consumer, Food Service, Private Label
Brands:
  Martin

7966 Martin Farms
4021 Redman Road
Brockport, NY 14420
585-637-3636
Fax: 585-637-6852 877-838-7369
info@martinfarms.com www.martinfarms.com
Sliced, diced and halved sun-dried tomatoes; available in bags and oil
Owner: Joseph Martin
Contact: David Martin
david@martinfarms.com
Estimated Sales: Less Than $500,000
Number Employees: 1-4

7967 Martin Ray Winery
2191 Laguna Rd
Santa Rosa, CA 95401-3705
707-823-2404
Fax: 707-829-6151 tiffany@martinraywinery.com
www.martinraywinery.com
Wines
Owner: Courtney Benham
Director, Sales/Marketing: Tiffany Zolli
Vice President of Sales: Ken Mulligan
info@martinray-winery.com
Estimated Sales: $10-20 Million
Number Employees: 20-49
Square Footage: 360000
Type of Packaging: Consumer
Brands:
  Fountain Grove
  Martini & Prati

7968 Martin Rosols
45 Grove St
New Britain, CT 06053-4198
860-223-2707
Fax: 860-229-6690 orders@martinrosols.com
www.martinrosolsinc.com
Cold cuts, hot dogs and kielbasa

Food Manufacturers / A-Z

President: Karen Rosol
karen@martinrosolsinc.com
CEO: Eugene Rosol
Vice President: Sarah Rosol
Estimated Sales: $2 Million
Number Employees: 20-49
Type of Packaging: Consumer, Private Label

7969 Martin Seafood Company
7901 Oceano Avenue, Units 46, 48, 50 &
P.O.Box 220
Jessup, MD 20794
410-799-5822
Fax: 410-799-3545
Frozen breaded seafood products; wholesaler/distributor of raw frozen seafood products; serving the food service market
Owner: Billy Martin
Secretary: Shawn Isaac
Estimated Sales: $3 Million
Number Employees: 20-49
Square Footage: 100000
Type of Packaging: Consumer, Food Service

7970 Martin's Potato Chips
5847 Lincoln Hwy W
PO Box 28
Thomasville, PA 17364
717-792-3565
Fax: 717-792-4906 800-272-4477
info2@martinschips.com
Manufacturer of potato chips, popcorn and distributor of pretzels.
President & CEO: Ken Potter
Director of Sales & Marketing: David Potter
Contact: Derek Bennett
derek.bennett@martinschips.com
Year Founded: 1941
Estimated Sales: $34 Million
Number Employees: 200
Square Footage: 75000
Type of Packaging: Consumer, Food Service, Bulk

7971 Martino's Bakery
335 N Victory Blvd
Burbank, CA 91502-1841
818-842-0715
Fax: 818-842-5111 www.martinosbakery.com
Breads, cakes and related products
Owner: Mario Corradi
response@martinosbakery.com
CEO: Andy Horvatch
Controller: Kathy Prince
Purchasing Agent: Diana Wang
Estimated Sales: Less than $500,000
Number Employees: 10-19

7972 Martins Famous Pastry Shoppe
1000 Potato Roll Ln
Chambersburg, PA 17202-8897
717-263-9580
Fax: 717-263-6687 800-548-1200
info@potatorolls.com www.potatorolls.com
Bread and roll manufacturer in the heart of "Pennsylvania Dutch" country.
President: Jim Martin
Estimated Sales: G
Number Employees: 250-499
Type of Packaging: Consumer, Food Service, Private Label
Brands:
  Mr. C'S
  Mr. G'S
  Nibble With Gibble's

7973 Marubeni America Corp.
375 Lexington Ave.
New York, NY 10017
212-450-0100
Fax: 212-450-0700 www.marubeniamerica.com
Marubeni exports grains, meat, sugar and other foodstuffs to Asia.
President/CEO: Fumiya Kokubu
Year Founded: 1951
Estimated Sales: $273,000
Parent Co: Marubeni Corporation

7974 Maruchan Inc
15800 Laguna Canyon Rd
Irvine, CA 92618
949-789-2300
www.maruchan.com
Asian foods including wonton soup and instant ramen noodles.

President & Chairman: Mutsuhiko Oda
muoda@maruchaninc.com
Year Founded: 1953
Estimated Sales: $33.2 Million
Number Employees: 500-999
Parent Co: Toyo Suisan Kaisha
Type of Packaging: Consumer

7975 Marukai Market
1740 W Artesia Blvd # 114
Gardena, CA 90248-3238
310-660-6300
Fax: 310-660-6301 info@marukai.com
Established in 1965. Manufacturer, importer, and exporter of Japanese food products.
President: Masataka Hattori
Estimated Sales: $41 Million
Number Employees: 100-249
Parent Co: Marukai Corporation
Other Locations:
  Marukai Corporation
  Honolulu HI

7976 Marukan Vinegar USA Inc.
16203 Vermont Ave
Paramount, CA 90723-5042
562-630-6060
Fax: 562-630-0330 www.marukan-usa.com
Natural rice vinegars
President: John Tanklage
jtanklage@marukan-usa.com
CEO: Junichi Oyama
VP Sales/Marketing: Jon Tanklage
Sales/Marketing: Tom McReynolds
Operations: Tosh Zamoto
Production: Toru Saito
Production: Michitsugu Ogawa
Estimated Sales: $7-10 Million
Number Employees: 20-49
Square Footage: 60000
Parent Co: Marukan Vinegar Co, Ltd
Type of Packaging: Consumer, Food Service, Private Label, Bulk
Brands:
  Marukan

7977 Marukome USA Inc.
17132 Pullman Street
Irvine, CA 92614
949-863-0110
Fax: 949-863-9813 www.marukomeusa.com
Miso manufacturer
President: Shigeru Sharasaka
Secretary: Tetsuhiko Iijima
Marketing: (Fred) Teruo Yamanaka
Contact: Toshio Abe
tabe@marukomeusa.com
Number Employees: 17

7978 Marva Maid Dairy
5500 Chestnut Ave
Newport News, VA 23605-2118
757-245-3857
800-768-6243
dlovell@marvamaid.com
Milk and specialty food products, including; milk, buttermilk, egg nog and orange juice
President: David Grogan
Owner: Dennis Bailey
Finance Manager: Jan Pass
Chief Engineer/Vice President: W Gross
Procurement & Plan Supervisor: Peter Natale
Marketing Manager: Scott Garrett
Sales Mgr/Dir of Product Management: Ed Boyd
Human Resources Director: Ruby Jones
Operations Manager: Bruce Matson
Plant Manager: Walter Auman
Purchasing Agent: Andrea Lopez
Number Employees: 100-249
Square Footage: 406728
Parent Co: Maryland & Virginia Milk Producers Coop Assoc, Inc.
Type of Packaging: Consumer
Brands:
  Harvest Fresh
  Marva Maid
  Slendo

7979 Marwood Sales, Inc
6901 Shawnee Mission Pkwy
Overland Park, KS 66202
913-722-1534
Fax: 913-262-9132 800-745-2881
info@marwoodsales.com www.marwoodsales.com

Producer of dairy products such as natural, processed, and imitation cheese.
President: Mark Woodard
Domestic & International Sales: Larry Johnson
Estimated Sales: $8.2 000,000
Number Employees: 11-50
Brands:
  Marwood

7980 Marx Brothers Inc
3100 2nd Ave S
Birmingham, AL 35233-3097
205-251-3139
Fax: 205-324-6322 800-633-6376
www.marxbrothersinc.com
Sweetened coconut
President: Edgar Marx
emarx@marxbrothersinc.com
Sales Exec: Edgar B Marx
Estimated Sales: $3 Million
Number Employees: 20-49
Type of Packaging: Consumer, Food Service, Private Label, Bulk

7981 Mary Ann's Baking Co Inc
8371 Carbide Ct
Sacramento, CA 95828-5636
916-681-7444
Fax: 916-681-7470 www.maryannsbaking.com
Danish and pastries
President: George Demas
Manager: Robert Burzinski
bob@maryannsbaking.com
General Manager: Bob Burzinski
Plant Manager: Don Lavelle
Estimated Sales: $10-20 Million
Number Employees: 100-249
Type of Packaging: Consumer

7982 Mary of Puddin Hill
512 N John St
Palestine, TX 75801
903-455-2651
Fax: 903-723-2889 800-545-8889
customerservice@puddinhill.com
www.puddinhill.com
Pecan fruit cakes and chocolate candy.
Owner: Ken Bain
Year Founded: 1839
Estimated Sales: $1.3 Million
Number Employees: 10-50
Type of Packaging: Private Label

7983 Mary's Gone Crackers
100 Kentucky St
Gridley, CA 95948
888-258-1250
info@marysgonecrackers.com
www.marysgonecrackers.com
Organic, gluten-free and vegan crackers, pretzels and cookies
CEO: John Sheptor
Estimated Sales: $6.5 Million
Number Employees: 50-99
Type of Packaging: Consumer
Brands:
  MARY'S GONE CRACKERS

7984 MarySue.com
2600 Georgetown Rd
Baltimore, MD 21230
800-662-2639
info@marysue.com www.marysue.com
Manufacturer and importer of gourmet chocolate candy. Founded in 1948
President: William Buppert
VP Production: Mark Berman
Estimated Sales: $10 Million
Number Employees: 5-9
Square Footage: 204000
Type of Packaging: Consumer, Private Label, Bulk

7985 Maryland & Virginia Milk Producers Cooperative
1985 Isaac Newton Square W.
Suite 200
Reston, VA 20190-5094
703-742-6800
Fax: 757-952-2370 info@mdvamilk.com
www.mdvamilk.com
Milk.
President: Dwayne Myers
Director, Milk Marketing: Cooper Troye
tcooper@mdvamilk.com

Food Manufacturers / A-Z

Year Founded: 1920
Estimated Sales: $1.4 Billion
Type of Packaging: Consumer
Brands:
   Marva Maid
   Maola

7986 Marzetti
PO Box 29163
Columbus, OH 43229-0163
        614-846-2232
Fax: 614-848-8330 tmoje@marzetti.com
www.marzetti.com
Salad dressings
President: Bruce Rosa
CIO: Kevin Moran
EVP: Gary Thompson
Controller: Steve Evans
VP Sales: Tim Tate
SVP Operations: Doug Fell
Year Founded: 1896
Number Employees: 100-249
Parent Co: T. Marzetti Company
Type of Packaging: Consumer, Private Label
Brands:
   Marzetti's
   Pfeiffer's

7987 Marzetti Foodservice
380 Polaris Parkway
Suite 400
Westerville, OH 43082
        515-967-4254
Fax: 515-967-4147   800-247-4194
info@marzetti.com www.marzettifoodservice.com
Noodles, pasta, flatbreads, breads, rolls, dressings, sauces, dips, croutons, and dairy products
President: Carl Stealey
CEO: David Ciesinski
Vice President: Steven Hill
Estimated Sales: $20-50 Million
Number Employees: 100-249
Type of Packaging: Bulk
Brands:
   Marzetti
   Marzetti Frozen Pasta
   Sister Schuberts
   New York Bakery
   Flatout Flatbread
   Cardini's

7988 Marzipan Specialties Inc
1513 Meridian St
Nashville, TN 37207-0861
        615-226-4800
Fax: 615-226-4882
Marzipan candy
Owner: Karl Schoenperger
Contact: Merika Schoenenberger
arzipan@isdn.net
Estimated Sales: Below $5 Million
Number Employees: 5-9
Type of Packaging: Consumer

7989 Masala Chai Company
PO Box 8375
Santa Cruz, CA 95061-8375
        831-475-8881
Fax: 831-475-5967 masala@masalachaico.com
www.masalachaico.com
Processor and importer of chai teas including bottled and ready-to-drink, Indian spiced, regular, decaf and energy tonics
Co-Owner: Raphael Reuben
Co-Owner: Susan Beardsley
Estimated Sales: $240000
Number Employees: 1-4
Square Footage: 6000
Type of Packaging: Consumer, Food Service, Private Label, Bulk
Brands:
   Aphroteasiac Chai
   Masala Chai

7990 Masienda
11515 W Pico Blvd
Los Angeles, CA 90064
www.masienda.com
Red, blue and heirloom corn tortillas
Founder & CEO: Jorge Gaviria
VP, Marketing & Brand: Jackie Rangel
Retail Sales Manager: Darien Brown
VP, Operations: Danielle Dahlin
Number of Brands: 1
Number of Products: 3
Type of Packaging: Consumer, Food Service
Brands:
   MASIENDA BODEGA

7991 Mason County Fruit Packers Cooperative
409 Wood St
Hart, MI 49420-1351
        231-873-7504
Apple juice, applesauce, cherries, flavored juices, frozen fruits, plums and slice apples.
President: Roy Hackert
CEO: Doyle Fenner
Plant Manager: Joe Bates
Estimated Sales: $1 Million
Square Footage: 4000000
Type of Packaging: Consumer, Bulk

7992 Mason Dixie Biscuit Co.
PO Box 26155
Washington, DC 20003
        202-880-2315
info@masondixiebiscuits.com
www.masondixiebiscuits.com
Frozen biscuits
CEO: Ayesha Abuelhiga
Executive Chef: Jason Gehring
COO: Ross Perkins
Number of Brands: 1
Number of Products: 4
Type of Packaging: Consumer
Brands:
   MASON DIXIE

7993 Mason Jar Cookie Company
2240 W Woolbright Rd
Suite 402
Boynton Beach, FL 33426-6367
Fax: 212-202-6437   855-968-2536
masonjarcookiecompany.com
Cookie, brownie, granola, muffin, pancake, scone and hot cocoa mixes.
VP, Operations: Rachel Scarrett

7994 Massel USA
898 Carol Ct
Carol Stream, IL 60188
        704-573-2299
info@massel.com
massel.com
Bouillon and seasonings
National Sales Manager: Marc Migdal
Type of Packaging: Consumer
Brands:
   MASSEL

7995 Massimo Zanetti Beverage USA
1370 Progress Rd
Suffolk, VA 23434
        888-246-2598
www.mzb-usa.com
Coffee manufacturer
Founder: Massimo Zanetti
Estimated Sales: Less Than $500,000
Number Employees: 1-4
Type of Packaging: Food Service, Private Label
Brands:
   KAUAI COFFEE
   Chock full o' Nuts
   HILLS BROS
   HILLS BROS CAPPUCINO
   MJB
   CHASE & SANBORN COFFEE
   Segafredo ZANETTI
   BRODIES
   SM La San Marco

7996 Mastantuono Winery
2720 Oakview Rd
Templeton, CA 93465-8798
        805-238-0676
Fax: 805-238-9257
Wine
Owner: Pasquale Mastantuono
Operations Manager: Pasquale Mastantuono
Estimated Sales: Below $5 Million
Number Employees: 5-9
Brands:
   Mastantuono Wines

7997 Master Brew
PO Box 1508
3550 Woodhead Dr
Northbrook, IL 60065
        847-564-3600
Fax: 847-564-2317
Coffee and tea
President: Ronald Weber
CEO: Joseph Weber
Estimated Sales: $9 Million
Number Employees: 120

7998 Master Mix
181 W Orangethorpe Avenue
Placentia, CA 92870-6931
        714-524-1698
Fax: 714-524-8540
Processor and exporter of powdered mixes including soft serve, shake and yogurt; also, syrups, toppings, water soluable ginseng extract and drink bases
President: Pat Lagraffe
VP: Jim LaGraffe
Estimated Sales: $1-3 Million
Number Employees: 1-4
Square Footage: 20000
Type of Packaging: Consumer, Food Service, Private Label, Bulk
Brands:
   Chalet Gourmet
   Dairy's Pride
   Master Mix

7999 Masters Gallery Foods Inc
328 County Road Pp
Plymouth, WI 53073-4143
        920-893-8431
Fax: 920-893-6075   800-236-8431
dmacphee@mastersgalleryfoods.com
www.mastersgalleryfoods.com
Cheese
President and CEO: Jeff Giffin
jgiffin@mastersgalleryfoods.com
CFO: Catherine Schwartz
Executive Vice-President: Jeff Jeff Gentine
Vice President of Retail Sales: Dan MacPhee
Estimated Sales: Less Than $500,000
Number Employees: 5-9

8000 Masterson Co Inc
4023 W National Ave
Milwaukee, WI 53215-1000
        414-647-1132
Fax: 414-647-1170 www.mastersoncompany.com
Premium fudge and caramel toppings, fruit toppings, shake bases, fountain syrups, marshmallow creme toppings, ice cream cone dips and coatings.
President: Mike Masterson
CEO: Nancy Albro
nancy.albro@mastersoncompany.com
Year Founded: 1848
Number Employees: 100-249
Type of Packaging: Food Service, Bulk
Brands:
   Masterson

8001 Matador Processors
1820 N Council Rd
Blanchard, OK 73010
        405-485-2597
Fax: 405-485-2597   800-847-0797
matador@matadorprocessors.com
www.matadorprocessors.com
Frozen foods including chile rellenos (stuffed peppers), stuffed jalapenos and breaded hors d'oeuvres including cheese bites, mushrooms, desserts, etc.; exporter of chile rellenos, stuffed jalapenos and mozzarella sticks
Owner: Betty Wood
CFO: Richard Clark
VP: Ron W Diggs
R&D: Debbie Funderburk
Plant Manager: Debbie Funderburk
Estimated Sales: $3 Million
Number Employees: 50-99
Square Footage: 108000
Type of Packaging: Food Service, Private Label
Brands:
   Clif's
   Matador

Food Manufacturers / A-Z

8002 Matangos Candies
S 15th & Catherine St
Harrisburg, PA 17101
717-234-0882
www.matangoscandies.com
Candy and other confectionery products
Owner/President: Peter Matangos
Estimated Sales: $100,000
Number Employees: 1-4
Type of Packaging: Consumer
Brands:
  Matangoes

8003 Matanzas Creek Winery
6097 Bennett Valley Rd
Santa Rosa, CA 95404-8570
707-528-6464
Fax: 707-571-0156 800-500-6464
info@matanzascreek.com
www.matanzascreek.com
Wine
General Manager: Patrick Connelly
Estimated Sales: $7-20 Million
Number Employees: 5-9
Number of Brands: 2
Square Footage: 20
Type of Packaging: Private Label
Brands:
  Journey
  Matanzas Creek Winery

8004 MatchaBar
256 W 15th St
New York, NY 10011
212-627-1058
matchabarnyc.com
Matcha
President & Co-Founder: Max Fortgang
CEO & Co-Founder: Graham Fortgang

8005 Materne North America
20 W 22nd St
12th Fl.
New York, NY 10010
212-675-7881
www.gogosqueez.com
Applesauce snacks
President/Owner: Ivan Giraud
CEO: Michel Larroche
CFO: Carole Larson
VP, Quality: Mark Baumgarten
CMO: Helene Caillate
COO: Stephane Jacquet
Plant Manager: Don Tomaszewski
Brands:
  GoGo squeeZ

8006 Mathews Packing
950 Ramirez Rd
Marysville, CA 95901-9444
530-743-9000
Fax: 530-742-6625
Dried prunes, pitted prunes, rice
Owner: Ed Mathews
VP/Marketing: Mark Mathews
Estimated Sales: $1-$2.5 000,000
Number Employees: 1-4
Type of Packaging: Private Label

8007 Matilija Water Company
1026 Santa Barbara Street
Santa Barbara, CA 93101
805-963-7873
Fax: 805-966-9811 www.getpurewater.com
Bottled water; also, wholesaler/distributor of water purification systems; serving the food service market
Sales Manager: Eric Berumen
Estimated Sales: $1-3 Million
Number Employees: 10-19
Type of Packaging: Consumer, Food Service

8008 Matouk International USA Inc
3801 N University Dr
#32
Sunrise, FL 33351
954-742-2204
Fax: 954-742-2533
Chutney/relish, full-line condiments, other condiments, other soups, stews, beans, BBQ sauce, ethnic sauces (soy, curry, etc.), herbs.
Manager: Riad Boulos
Estimated Sales: $100,000
Number Employees: 2

8009 Matrix Health Products
9316 Wheatlands Road
Santee, CA 92071-5644
619-448-7550
Fax: 619-448-2995 888-736-5609
info@earthsbounty.com www.matrixhealth.com
Manufacturer, importer and exporter of nutritional and herbal supplements including tablets, liquids, powders and capsules-also kosher & organic products. Teas, coffee & vanilla and nonjuice
President: Steven Kravitz
Number Employees: 10-19
Type of Packaging: Consumer, Private Label, Bulk
Brands:
  Colloidal Silver
  Dhea
  Earth's Bounty
  Melatonin
  Meno-Select
  Noni
  Oxy-Caps
  Oxy-Cleanse
  Oxy-Max
  Oxy-Mist
  Prosta-Forte
  Woman's Select

8010 Matson Fruit Co
201 N Railroad Ave
Selah, WA 98942
509-697-7100
matsonfruit.com
Processor and exporter of apples and pears.
President & General Manager: Rod Matson
on@matsonfruit.com
Estimated Sales: $25 Million
Number Employees: 100-249
Square Footage: 18000
Type of Packaging: Consumer, Food Service

8011 Matson Vineyards
10584 Arapaho Dr
Redding, CA 96003-7638
530-222-2833
lynette@matsonvineyards.com
www.matsonvineyards.com
Wines
Owner/Winemaker: Oscar Matson
Analyst /Marketing Manager: Kdiko Goto
Owner: Roger Matson
Marketing Manager: Lynette Shaw
Estimated Sales: Under $500,000
Number Employees: 1-4

8012 Matt's Cookies
482 N Milwaukee Ave
Wheeling, IL 60090-3067
847-537-3888
www.mattscookies.com
Cookies and fig bars
Year Founded: 1979
Number of Brands: 1
Number of Products: 10
Type of Packaging: Consumer
Brands:
  MATT'S COOKIES

8013 Matthew's Bakery
71 W Broad St
Stamford, CT 06902-3713
203-316-9392
info@matthewsbakery.com
Breads, cakes, pastries, pies and desserts.

8014 Matthews 1812 House
250 Kent Road
P.O.Box 15
Cornwall Bridge, CT 06754-0015
860-672-0230
Fax: 860-672-1812 800-662-1812
info@matthews1812house.com
www.matthews1812house.com
All-natural cakes including apple crumb torte, brandied apricot, chocolate raspberry liqueur, chocolate rum, country spice, fruit and nut, fudge brownie torte, lemon rum, cookies, bar cookies, chocolate explosion brownies
President: Deanna Matthews
dm@matthews1812house.com
Corporate Secretary: Blaine Matthews
Manager: Cheryl Cass
Estimated Sales: $1 Million
Number Employees: 10-19
Square Footage: 8000
Type of Packaging: Consumer, Food Service, Private Label
Brands:
  Matthews 1812 House

8015 Matthiesen's Deer & Custom
3357 252nd St
De Witt, IA 52742-9223
563-659-8409
mikkie@365adventure.com
Meat products including, beef, lamb, venison, pork and mettwurst
President: Sandy Matthiesen
Estimated Sales: $500,000-$1 Million
Number Employees: 5-9
Type of Packaging: Consumer

8016 Mattingly Foods Of Louisville
2055 Nelson Miller Pkwy
Louisville, KY 40223-2185
502-253-2000
Fax: 502-253-2020
Prime choice steaks
President: Thomas M Dawson
Number Employees: 50-99
Parent Co: Mattingly Foods
Type of Packaging: Food Service

8017 Maui Bagel
200 Dairy Rd
Kahului, HI 96732-2978
808-270-7561
Fax: 808-270-7919 www.mauicounty.gov
Bread, rolls, bagels, donuts, sandwiches
Manager: Jeff Murray
Number Employees: 250-499

8018 Maui Coffee Roasters Wholesale
360 Papa Pl # D2
Kahului
Kahului, HI 96732-2464
808-877-7780
Fax: 808-871-2684 800-645-2877
info@hawaiiancoffee.com www.superpages.com
Roasted coffee
President: Nick Matichyn
mauideveloper@gmail.com
CFO: Mike Vaki
Marketing Manager: Cark Musto
VP Sales: Mike Okazaki
Purchasing Manager: Nicky Matichyn
Estimated Sales: $1-2.5 Million
Number Employees: 1-4
Type of Packaging: Private Label, Bulk

8019 Maui Gold Pineapple Company
PO Box 880190
Pukalani, HI 96788
808-877-3805
info@pineapplemaui.com
www.pineapplemaui.com
Whole fresh, canned and fresh-cut pineapple; also, pineapple juice and concentrates
President: Darren Strand
CFO: Michael Hotta
Estimated Sales: $78 Million
Number Employees: 1,000
Square Footage: 10000
Type of Packaging: Consumer, Food Service, Private Label, Bulk
Brands:
  Hawaiian Gold
  King of Hawaii

8020 Maui Potato Chip Factory
295 Lalo St
Kahului, HI 96732-2915
808-877-3652
Fax: 808-877-3652
Potato chips
President: Mark Kobayashi
Estimated Sales: $150,000
Number Employees: 1-4
Type of Packaging: Consumer
Brands:
  Original Maui Kitch'n Cook'd

8021 Maui Soda & Ice Works
918 Lower Main St
Wailuku, HI 96793-2007
808-244-7951
Fax: 808-244-4108 mauisoda.com
Beverages, soda

Food Manufacturers / A-Z

President: Robyn Taylor
robyn.taylor@mauisoda.com
Chairman: David Nobriga
Number Employees: 50-99

8022 Maui Wine
14815 Pillani Hwy
HC 1 Box 953
Kula, HI 96790
808-878-6058
Fax: 808-876-0127 877-878-6058
info@mauiwine.com www.mauiwine.com
Specialty, grape, and pineapple wines
President: Paula Hegele
Winemaker: Mark Beaman
Winery & Vineyard Engineer: Bill Long
Marketing & Branding Manager: Joe Hegele
Sales & Analytics Manager: Henry Hegele
Operations Manager: Ian Baldridge
Cellar Master: Keone Labuanan
Year Founded: 1974
Estimated Sales: $20-50 Million
Number Employees: 32
Type of Packaging: Private Label
Brands:
  Maui Blanc
  Maui Blush
  Maui Brut
  Maui Splash
  Maui Ulupalakua Red

8023 Maurice Carrie Winery
34225 Rancho California Rd
Temecula, CA 92591
951-676-1711
Fax: 951-676-8397 800-716-1711
info@mauricecarriewinery.com
www.mauricecarriewinery.com
Wines
Owner: Budd VanRoekel
Owner: Maurice VanRoekel
Sales: Jana Prais
Accounting Manager: LaDawn Allen
Winemaker: Gus Vizgirda
Type of Packaging: Consumer

8024 Maurice French Pastries
4949 W Napoleon Ave
Metairie, LA 70001-2249
504-455-0830
Fax: 504-885-1527 888-285-8261
sales@mauricefrenchpastries.com
www.mauricefrenchpastries.com
Mardi Gras cakes
Owner: John Luc
Estimated Sales: Less Than $500,000
Number Employees: 5-9
Brands:
  Maurice French Pastries

8025 Maverick Brands, LLC
990 Commercial St.
Palo Alto, CA 94303
424-571-7230
info@cocolibre.com
www.cocolibre.com
Manufacturer of coconut water.
CEO: Candace Crawford
Founder: Mark Shaw
Contact: Frank Hudson
frank@maverickbrands.com
Brands:
  Coco Libre

8026 Mavuno Harvest
Philadelphia, PA
www.mavunoharvest.com
Organic dried fruit and nuts
Number of Brands: 1
Number of Products: 9
Type of Packaging: Consumer
Brands:
  MAVUNO HARVEST

8027 Maxfield Candy
1050 S 200 W
Salt Lake City, UT 84101
801-355-5321
Fax: 801-355-5546 800-288-8002
Boxed chocolates, nut logs, cream sticks, holiday novelties, salt water taffy, cordial cherries, mint sandwiches, etc.; exporter of boxed chocolates
President: Taz Murray
Contact: Judy Adams
jadams@maxfieldcandy.com
Estimated Sales: $5-10 Million
Number Employees: 5-9
Square Footage: 424000
Parent Co: Alpine Confections
Type of Packaging: Consumer
Brands:
  Maxfield

8028 (HQ)Maxim's Import Corporation
2719 NW 24th Street
Miami, FL 33142-7005
915-577-9228
Fax: 91- 57- 921 800-331-6652
info@maximsimports.com maximsimports.com
Processor, importer and exporter of shrimp; processor of packaged fish; exporter of frozen chicken, duck, turkey, pork and beef; wholesaler/distributor of shrimp, pork, beef, poultry, fish, produce and frozen, specialty and healthfoods
President: Luis Chi
CEO: Jeo Chi
Contact: Joe Chi
luis.chi@hotmail.com
Estimated Sales: $4.1 Million
Number Employees: 22
Square Footage: 140000
Type of Packaging: Bulk
Other Locations:
  Maxim's Import Corp.
  Salvador
Brands:
  Airex
  Alpromar
  Caribe
  De La Marca
  Fish House
  Flodi Pesca
  Golden Star
  Golfo Mar
  Gulf Garden
  Inter Ocean
  Ocean Pac
  Pacific Pride
  Pesaca
  Stefan Mar

8029 Maxin Marketing Corporation
92 Argonaut, Suite #170
Aliso Viejo, CA 92656-5318
949-362-1177
Fax: 949-362-0449
Snack foods
President: Terry Kroll
Estimated Sales: Less than $500,000
Number Employees: 1-4
Number of Brands: 2
Number of Products: 10
Type of Packaging: Consumer, Private Label, Bulk
Brands:
  Health Creation Caramel Pretzels
  Health Creation Onion Pretzels
  Pocket Pretzels

8030 Maxine's Heavenly
Los Angeles, CA 90035
info@maxinesheavenly.com
www.maxinesheavenly.com
Gluten-free cookies
Co-Founder & CEO: Robert Petrarca
Marketing: Rachel Carmichael
Sales: Jeff Resnick
Founder & VP, Operations: Tim Miller
Number of Brands: 1
Number of Products: 4
Type of Packaging: Consumer
Brands:
  MAXINE'S HEAVENLY

8031 Maxwell House & Post
800 Westchester Ave
Rye Brook, NY 10573-1354
914-335-2500
Fax: 914-335-2706
Coffee and breakfast foods
President: Ann Fudge
Estimated Sales: Under $500,000
Number Employees: 1-4
Parent Co: Kraft Foods

8032 Maxwell's Gourmet Food
3208 Wellington Ct # L
Raleigh, NC 27615-4121
919-878-4321
Fax: 919-878-4325 800-952-6887
Peanuts, peanut brittle, chocolate dipped peanut brittle, pecans, chocolate-dipped pecans, pecan brittle, chocolate dipped pecan brittle, cashews
Owner: Paxton Kemps
CEO: Don Kempf
CFO: Shelia Kempf
Director Of Marketing: David Chapman
Director of Sales: Amy Kempf
Production Manager: Ana Arrendondo
Estimated Sales: $500,000-$1 Million
Number Employees: 5-9
Brands:
  Maxwell's Extraordinary

8033 Maya Kaimal
PO Box 700
Rhinebeck, NY 12572
845-876-8200
Fax: 845-876-8212 info@mayakaimal.com
www.mayakaimal.com
Indian meals, snacks and sauces
Founder: Maya Kaimal
CEO: Meena Mansharamani
CFO: Sunil Surana
Co-Founder: Guy Lawson
VP, Marketing: Michael Krishnan
Director of Operations: Elaine Delsol

8034 Mayacamas Fine Foods
20590 Palmer Avenue
Suite A
Sonoma, CA 95476
707-291-3024
Fax: 707-938-8350 800-826-9621
info@mayacamasfinefoods.com
www.mayacamasfinefoods.com
Processor and exporter of dehydrated soups, salad dressings, pasta sauces, gravies and seasonings
President: Vicki Webber
VP: Walter Rahrau
Contact: Craig Parrott
craig@mayacamasfinefoods.com
Estimated Sales: $2.4 Million
Number Employees: 1-4
Square Footage: 72000
Type of Packaging: Consumer, Food Service, Private Label

8035 Mayacamas Vineyards & Winery
1155 Lokoya Rd
Napa, CA 94558-9566
707-224-4030
Fax: 707-224-3979 www.mayacamas.com
Processor and exporter of wines including cabernet sauvignon, chardonnay, sauvignon blanc and pinot noir
Owner: John Fisher
johnf@mayacamas.com
Marketing Director: Trina Vaught
Estimated Sales: $88000
Number Employees: 10-19
Brands:
  Mayacamas Vineyards

8036 Mayakaimal Fine Indian Foods
6384 Mill St # 2
Rhinebeck, NY 12572-1497
845-876-8200
Fax: 845-876-8212 info@mayakaimal.com
www.mayakaimal.com
Simmer sauces and spicy ketchup
President/Owner: Maya Kaimal
maya@mayakaimal.com
Sales Manager: Erica Chapman
Number Employees: 5-9

8037 Mayer Bros
3300 Transit Rd
Buffalo, NY 14224-2525
716-668-1787
Fax: 716-668-2437 800-696-2928
info@mayerbrothers.com www.mayerbrothers.com
Bottled spring water, apple cider and juices including orange, grapefruit, grape and apple; also, concentrates including fruit punch, orange, grape, iced tea and lemonade
Owner: John Mayer
Controller: Linda Tryka
HR Manager: Deborah Schasel

Food Manufacturers / A-Z

Estimated Sales: $28 Million
Number Employees: 100-249
Number of Brands: 1
Type of Packaging: Consumer, Food Service, Private Label, Bulk
Brands:
  Mayer Bros.

8038 Mayer's Cider Mill
PO Box 347
Webster, NY 14580-347
 Fax: 585-671-5269 800-543-0043
Cider, apples and apple pies; also, beer, grape juice and wine-making supplies
Owner: David N Bower
Estimated Sales: Less than $500,000
Number Employees: 10-19
Parent Co: Mayer's Cider Mill
Type of Packaging: Consumer, Bulk

8039 Mayfield Dairy Farms LLC
806 E Madison Ave
Athens, TN 37303-3858
 423-745-2151
Fax: 423-745-9118 800-362-9546
 www.mayfielddairy.com
Dairy products such as; ice cream, sherbert, cottage cheese, dip, sour cream, milk, whip cream and juices
President: C S Mayfield Jr
Cmo: Robbie Roberts
rroberts@deanfoods.com
Number Employees: 1000-4999
Parent Co: Dean Foods
Type of Packaging: Consumer, Food Service
Other Locations:
  Braselton GA

8040 Mayfield Farms and Nursery
257 Highway 307
Athens, TN 37303
 423-746-9859
 mayfieldfarmandnursery@hotmail.com
Apple products including processed slices, dices, dumplings, fibre powder and juice, strawberries, squash, potatoes, peppers, and pumpkins.
Founder: Jesse Mayfield
Number Employees: 5-9
Type of Packaging: Consumer, Food Service

8041 Mayorga Coffee
15151 Southlawn Ln
Rockville, MD 20850-1385
 301-315-8093
Fax: 301-315-8094 877-526-3322
 info@mayorgacoffee.com
Coffee
President: Martin Mayorga
martin@mayorgacoffee.com
VP Finance/Administration: Lorena Herrada
VP Sales/Marketing: Jennifer Rogers
Vice President of Operations: Roger Fransen
Estimated Sales: $8.4 Million
Number Employees: 10-19
Square Footage: 24000

8042 Maysville Milling Company
661 Martin Luther King Boulevard
Maysville, NC 41056-7510
 606-759-8789
Feed and cornmeal
President: Edward Trott
General Manager: William Lamkin
Estimated Sales: $2 Million
Number Employees: 7
Brands:
  Mayco

8043 Maytag Dairy Farms Inc
2282 E 8th St N
Newton, IA 50208-8775
 641-792-1133
Fax: 641-792-1567 800-247-2458
 www.maytagdairyfarms.com
Cheeses including blue, cheddar, Swiss, edam, brick and cold pack
President: Chase Ashby
chaseashby@maytagblue.com
VP Operations/Production Manager: Jim Stevens
Plant Supervisor: Robert Wrdzinski
Estimated Sales: $4.6 Million
Number Employees: 20-49
Type of Packaging: Consumer

8044 Mayway Corp
1338 Mandela Pkwy
Oakland, CA 94607-2055
 510-208-3023
Fax: 510-208-3069 800-262-9929
 info@mayway.com www.mayway.com
Herbal health foods
President: Eva Lau
Estimated Sales: Below $5 Million
Number Employees: 20-49

8045 Maywood International Sales
PO Box 9292
Sante Fe, NM 87504
 505-982-2700
Fax: 505-982-9780 805-500-5500
Oilseed manufacturer
Sales: Jacques Brazy
Sales: Peter Connick

8046 Mazelle's Cheesecakes Concoctions Creations
9016 Garland Road
Dallas, TX 75218
 214-328-9102
Fax: 214-328-5202 sales@mazelles.com
 www.mazelles.com
Cheesecakes and cheesecake petit fours vanilla, chocolate decadence, raspberry cassis, chocolate marble, turtle-praline chocolate chip, pumpkin, strawberries nad cream, keylime margarita, amaretto
CEO: Gina Roidopoulos
Estimated Sales: $3-5 Million
Number Employees: 10-19
Type of Packaging: Consumer, Food Service
Brands:
  Mazelle's

8047 Mazzetta Company
P.O. Box 1126
Highland Park, IL 60035
 847-433-1150
Fax: 847-433-8973 seamazz@mazzetta.com
 www.mazzetta.com
Seafood and fish such as orange roughy fillets, whiting fillets, greenshell mussels, raw and cooked shrimp, lobster tails, Chilean sea bass fillets, squid and crab meat.
President: Thomas Mazzetta
Contact: Dominic Benedetto
dominic@mazzetta.com
Estimated Sales: $1-3 Million
Number Employees: 10-19

8048 Mazzocco Vineyards
1400 Lytton Springs Road
Healdsburg, CA 95448
 707-433-3399
Fax: 707-431-2369 800-501-8466
 vino@mazzocco.com www.mazzocco.com
Wines
President: Thomas Mazzocco
Sales/Marketing Manager: Ned Carton
Contact: Karen Clarke
karen@mazzocco.com
Winemaker, General Manager: Antoine Favero
Estimated Sales: $1-2.5 Million
Number Employees: 5-9

8049 Mc Glaughlin Oil Co
3750 E Livingston Ave
Columbus, OH 43227-2282
 614-231-2518
Fax: 614-231-7431 teresa@mcglaughlinoil.com
 www.faslube.com
Oils, flavored and pure
Owner: Steve Theodor
steve@faslube.com
Estimated Sales: $5-10 Million
Number Employees: 10-19
Brands:
  Petrol

8050 Mc Lure's Honey & MapleProd
46 N Littleton Rd
Littleton, NH 03561-3814
 603-444-6246
Fax: 603-444-6659 info@mclures.com
Pure honey and maple syrup
Founder: Ralph Gamber
Manager: Gordon Hartford
ghartford@mclures.com
Number Employees: 20-49
Parent Co: Dutch Gold Honey

8051 Mc Steven's Coca Factory Store
5600 NE 88th St
Vancouver, WA 98665-0971
 360-944-5788
Fax: 360-944-1302 800-547-2803
 sales@mcstevens.com
Beverage mixes including white chocolate, regular and sugar-free cocoa, lemonade, cappuccino, chai, and apple cider; exporter of cocoa mixes
Owner: Brent Houston
brent@mcstevens.com
VP Marketing: Dave Demsky
VP Operations: Brent Huston
Estimated Sales: $500,000-$1 Million
Number Employees: 20-49
Type of Packaging: Consumer, Food Service, Private Label, Bulk

8052 (HQ)McAnally Enterprises
32710 Reservoir Rd
Lakeview, CA 92567
 951-928-1935
Fax: 951-928-1947 800-726-2002
Processor and exporter of cartoned, frozen and liquid eggs and egg products
President: Carlton Lofgren
Rep. (S.W.): Glenn Lemley
Vice President: Don Brown
Marketing Director: John Klien
Operations Manager: Tom McAnally
Number Employees: 100-249
Square Footage: 80000
Type of Packaging: Food Service
Other Locations:
  McAnally Enterprises
  Phoenix AZ

8053 McArthur Dairy LLC
6851 NE 2nd Ave.
Miami, FL 33401-7724
 561-659-4811
Fax: 561-659-1763 www.mcarthurdairy.com
Dairy products including buttermilk, regular, chocolate, low-fat and skim milk.
Director/CEO, Dean Foods: Ralph Scozzafava
Executive VP/CFO, Dean Foods: Jody Macedonio
Year Founded: 1929
Estimated Sales: $150-199 Million
Number Employees: 100-249
Parent Co: Dean Foods Company
Type of Packaging: Consumer, Food Service, Private Label, Bulk

8054 (HQ)McCain Foods Ltd.
439 King St W
5th Floor
Toronto, ON M5V 1K4
Canada
 416-955-1700
 www.mccain.com
Frozen french fries, potato products, appetizers, pizzas, pizza products, and desserts
President/CEO: Max Koeune
Chief Financial Officer: Pierre Danet
Chief Human Resources Officer: Alison DeMille
Chief Research & Development Officer: David Stewart
Chief Legal Officer: David Chad Hutchison
Chief Agricultre Officer: Han Van Den Hoek
Chief Growth Officer: Mauro Pennella
Year Founded: 1957
Estimated Sales: $6.8 Billion
Number Employees: 19,000
Type of Packaging: Consumer, Food Service
Other Locations:
  Corporate Executive Headquarters
  Toronto, Ontario, Canada

8055 McCain Foods USA Inc.
One Tower Ln.
11th Floor
Oakbrook Terace, IL 60181
 800-938-7799
 communications.usa@mccain.com
 www.mccainusafoodservice.com
Frozen potato products including French fries, slices, dices, formed and private label brands. Also manufacturer of breaded and battered appetizers
Regional President, The Americas: Paolo Picchi
Year Founded: 1952
Estimated Sales: $632 Million
Number Employees: 3,800
Number of Brands: 6
Square Footage: 100000
Parent Co: McCain Foods Limited

Type of Packaging: Private Label
Other Locations:
  Othello WA
  Burley ID
  Rice Lake WI
  Plover WI
  Appleton WI
  Fort Atkinson WI
  Easton ME
  Grand Island NE
  Lisle IL
  Lodi NJ
  Colton CA
Brands:
  Anchor
  Brew City
  Harvest Splendor
  McCain
  Moore's
  Ore-Ida

8056 **McCain Produce Inc.**
8734 Main Street
Florenceville-Bristol, NB E7L 3G6
Canada
506-392-3036
www.mccainpotatoes.ca
Potato grower and processor
Parent Co: McCain Foods Ltd.
Type of Packaging: Consumer, Food Service

8057 **(HQ)McCleskey Mills**
197 Rhodes Street
PO Box 98
Smithville, GA 31787-0098
229-846-2003
Fax: 229-846-4805 mmi@mccleskeymills.com
www.mccleskeymills.com
Manufacturer and exporter of shelled peanuts, seed peanuts, and peanut hulls
President: Keith Chandler
Chairman & CEO: Jerry Chandler
Vice President & CFO: Billy Marshall
VP, MIS: Cleve McRee
Accounting Manager & Quality Assurance: Robert Hamlin
Executive Vice President Sales: Joe West
Contact: Tyler Carlisle
tcarlisle@mccleskeymills.com
Plant Manager: James Champion
Estimated Sales: $2 Million
Number Employees: 9
Square Footage: 72000
Type of Packaging: Consumer, Bulk

8058 **McClure's Pickles LLC**
8201 Saint Aubin St
Detroit, MI 48211-1330
USA
248-837-9323
Fax: 866-796-9679
picklehelp@mcclurespickles.com
www.mcclurespickles.com
Pickles, chips, chutney, relish
Owner: Bob McClure
Co-Owner: Joe McClure
Contact: Mike Daronco
mike@mcclurespickles.com

8059 **McConnell's Fine Ice Cream**
835 E Canon Perdido St
Santa Barbara, CA 93103
805-963-8813
Fax: 805-965-3764 info@mcconnells.com
mcconnells.com
Manufacturer and exporter of ice cream
Owner: Jimmy Young
Contact: Mike Vierra
mvierra@mcconnells.com
Year Founded: 1949
Estimated Sales: Below $5 Million
Number Employees: 5-9
Type of Packaging: Consumer, Food Service

8060 **McConnell's Fine Ice Creams**
The Old Dairy
835 East Canon Perdido St
Santa Barbara, CA 93103
805-963-8813
info@mcconnells.com
mcconnells.com
Ice cream

President: Charley Price
cprice@mcconnells.com
Owner: Michael Palmer
Owner: Eva Ein
Year Founded: 1949

8061 **McCormick & Company**
24 Schilling Rd
Hunt Valley, MD 21031
410-527-6189
www.mccormickcorporation.com
Dessert products, honey, flavors and sauces.
Chairman/President/CEO: Lawrence Kurzius
lawrence_kurzius@mccormick.com
CAO: Malcolm Swift
Executive VP/CFO: Mike Smith
VP/General Counsel: Jeffrey Schwartz
Year Founded: 1889
Estimated Sales: $5.3 Billion
Number Employees: 12,400
Number of Brands: 32
Type of Packaging: Consumer, Food Service, Private Label, Bulk
Brands:
  Aeroplane
  Billy Bee
  Brand Aromatics
  Cattlemen's BBQ Sauce
  Club House
  Drogheria & Alimentari
  Ducros
  El Guapo
  Frank's RedHot
  French's
  Giotti
  Gourmet Garden
  Kamis
  Kitchen Basics
  Kohinoor
  Lawry's
  Margao
  McCormick
  Old Bay
  Schwartz
  Silvo
  Simply Asia
  Stubb's
  Thai Kitchen
  Vahine
  Wuhan Asia-Pacific Condiments
  Zatarain's

8062 **McCormick Distilling Co**
1 McCormick Ln
Weston, MO 64098-9558
816-640-2276
Fax: 816-640-3082   888-640-3082
www.mccormickdistilling.com
Distiller of vodkas, tequilas, whiskey, and irish creams
President: Mick Harris
CFO: Chris Fernandez
cfernandez@mccormickdistillingco.com
VP Marketing: Patrick Fee
VP Sales: Shawn Scott
Estimated Sales: $20-50 Million
Number Employees: 100-249
Type of Packaging: Consumer, Private Label
Brands:
  Tequila Rose
  Broker's Gin
  360 Vodka
  Hussong's Tequila
  Platte Valley Corn Whiskey
  Triple Crown Whiskey
  Tarantula
  Keke
  Five Farms Irish Cream
  McCormick
  Viaka
  Pancho Villa
  Montego Bay Rum
  Ron Rio
  Prince Alexis Vodka

8063 **McCoy Matt Frontier International**
362 Capistrano Avenue
Pismo Beach, CA 93449-1907
805-773-2994
Fax: 805-773-0378
President: Mat McCoy
Estimated Sales: Under $500,000
Number Employees: 1-4

8064 **McCrea's Candies**
202 Neponset Valley Pkwy
Hyde Park, MA 02136
617-276-3388
Fax: 617-276-3380 www.mccreascandies.com
Caramels
Founder: Jason McCrea
Marketing & Product Development: Kate McCrea
Operations: Jim LaFond-Lewis

8065 **McDaniel Fruit**
965 E Mission Rd
Fallbrook, CA 92028
760-728-8438
Fax: 760-728-4898 www.mcdanielavocado.com
Processor, importer and exporter of avocados
Owner: Kay Ahrend
kay@mcdanielavocado.com
VP Sales/Marketing: Rankin McDaniel
General Sales Manager: Laurie Johnson
Secretary: Larry McDaniel
Estimated Sales: $9.3 Million
Number Employees: 20-49
Square Footage: 40000
Type of Packaging: Consumer, Food Service, Private Label, Bulk
Brands:
  Linda-Vista

8066 **McDowell Valley Vineyards & Cellars**
PO Box 449
Hopland, CA 95449-0449
707-744-1774
Fax: 707-744-1826
Wine
Owner, Winemaker: Bill Crawford
CEO: Gary Leonard
Sales Director: Bernadette Byrne
Estimated Sales: $1-2.5 Million
Number Employees: 5-9
Brands:
  McDowell

8067 **McDuffies Bakery**
9920 Main St
PO Box 427
Clarence, NY 14031-2043
716-759-8510
Fax: 716-759-6082   800-875-1598
info@mcduffies.com www.mcduffies.com
Shortbread cookies and biscotti
President: Dave Thomas
VP: Brian Thomas
Operations: Duston Peace
Estimated Sales: $2 Million
Number Employees: 20
Square Footage: 40000
Type of Packaging: Food Service, Private Label

8068 **McEvoy Ranch**
5935 Red Hill Rd
PO Box 341
Petaluma, CA 94952-9437
707-778-2307
Fax: 707-778-0128   866-617-6779
www.mcevoyranch.com
Extra virgin olive oil, tapenades, bruschettas, vinegars, jams & spreads, olives, wine
Owner, Chairman, CEO: Nion McEvoy
President: Samantha Dorsey
CFO: Dana Breaux
Winemaker: Byron Kosuge
Consulting Winemaker & Agronomist: Maurizio Castelli
Marketing Director: Christina Cavallaro
Orchard Manager: Shari DeJoseph
Farming Manager: Ria D'Aversa
Culinary Director: Jacquelyn Buchanan
Estimated Sales: $20-50 Million
Number Employees: 20-49

8069 **McFarland Foods**
PO Box 460
Riverton, UT 84065-0460
801-254-5009
Fax: 801-254-0432   800-441-9596
info@dsi1968.com
Chicken and turkey products
President: Stephen Mcfarland
CFO: Barbara McFarland
Quality Control: Justin McFarland
Sales Director: Thomas Mathias

Number Employees: 20-49
Number of Brands: 1
Number of Products: 25
Square Footage: 48000
Type of Packaging: Consumer, Food Service, Private Label, Bulk

8070 McGraw Seafood
3113 Main St
Tracadie Sheila, NB E1X 1G5
Canada
506-395-3374
Fax: 506-395-2821
Fresh and frozen crab, scallops, cod, smelt, mackerel, herring and lobster
General Manager: Paul Boudreau
Number Employees: 100-249
Type of Packaging: Consumer, Food Service, Private Label, Bulk
Brands:
 Mc Graw

8071 McHenry Vineyard
330 11th Street
Davis, CA 95616
530-756-3202
Fax: 530-756-3202 lmchenry@dcn.org
Wines
Operations Manager: Henry McHenry
Vineyard Manager: Linda McHenry
Estimated Sales: $45,000
Number Employees: 2
Type of Packaging: Private Label

8072 McIlhenny Company
Hwy. 329
Avery Island, LA 70513
800-634-9599
www.tabasco.com
Pepper sauces.
President/CEO: Harold Osborn
Year Founded: 1868
Estimated Sales: $1 Billion
Number Employees: 200
Type of Packaging: Food Service, Bulk
Brands:
 TABASCO

8073 McIntosh's Ohio Valley Wines
2033 Bethel New Hope Rd
Bethel, OH 45106-9691
937-379-1159
Fax: 973-379-1962
Wine
President: Edward Covert
Estimated Sales: $1-2.5 000,000
Number Employees: 1-4

8074 McJak Candy Company LLC
1087 Branch Road
Medina, OH 44256
330-722-3531
Fax: 330-723-4793 800-424-2942
ljohns@mcjakcandy.com www.mcjakcandy.com
Produces fudge and lollipops
President: Larry Johns
Contact: W David
dsmith@mcjakcandy.com
Estimated Sales: $3-5 Million
Number Employees: 10-19
Number of Products: 20
Type of Packaging: Consumer, Private Label, Bulk

8075 McKaskle Family Farm
PO Box 10
Braggadocio, MO 63826
573-752-5001
info@mckasklefamilyfarm.com
www.mckasklefamilyfarm.com
Organic rice and popcorn.
Owner: Steve McKaskle
Owner: Kaye McKaskle
Brands:
 Braggadocio
 Texas Best
 Hard Bargain

8076 McKee Foods Corp.
10260 McKee Rd.
PO Box 750
Collegedale, TN 37315
423-238-7111
Fax: 423-238-7127 800-522-4499
www.mckeefoods.com
Cookies, crackers, snack and granola bars, snack cakes and cereal.
President/CEO: Michael McKee
mike_mckee@mckee.com
CFO: Andrew Lang
Chairman/Chief Administrative Officer: R. Ellsworth McKee
Corp. Communications/Public Relations: Mike Gloekler
Year Founded: 1934
Estimated Sales: $1 Billion
Number Employees: 5,800
Number of Brands: 4
Type of Packaging: Consumer, Food Service, Private Label
Other Locations:
 McKee Foods
 Gentry AR
 Stuarts Draft VA
 Kingman AZ
 Chattanooga TN
Brands:
 Fieldstone Bakery
 Drake's
 Little Debbie
 Sunbelt

8077 McKee Foods Corp.
10260 McKee Road
Collegedale, TN 37315
800-522-4499
www.mckeefoods.com
Snack foods and desserts
President: Mike McKee
Year Founded: 1934
Number Employees: 6,300
Number of Brands: 5
Brands:
 DRAKE'S
 FIELDSTONE BAKERY
 HEARTLAND BRANDS
 LITTLE DEBBIE
 SUNBELT BAKERY

8078 McKinlay Vineyards
7120 NE Earlwood Road
Newberg, OR 97132-7010
503-625-2534
Fax: 503-625-2534
Wines
Contact: Matt Kinne
mkinne@monroecounty.gov
Estimated Sales: $67,000
Number Employees: 1

8079 McKnight Milling Company
15 CR 138
Hickory Ridge, AR 72347
870-697-2504
Fax: 870-697-2525 800-287-2383
hessmilling@yahoo.com
www.mcknightmilling.com
Basmati rice
Owner: Deloss Mc Knight
Plant Manager: Walter Pierce
Estimated Sales: $2.5 Million
Number Employees: 1-4
Square Footage: 11520
Type of Packaging: Consumer, Food Service, Private Label, Bulk
Brands:
 Cache River

8080 McLane's Meats
5710 56 Ave
Wetaskiwin, AB T9A 2Y9
Canada
780-352-4321
Fax: 780-352-8522
www.shop-alberta.com/wetaskiwin/mclanes-meats.htm
Beef and pork sausage and wild game including deer, elk and moose; custom slaughtering services available
Owner: Robin McLane
Number Employees: 10-19
Type of Packaging: Private Label

8081 McNasby's Seafood Market
723 2nd Street
Annapolis, MD 21403-3323
410-295-9022
Fax: 410-280-3707
Seafood

8082 McNeil Nutritionals
7050 Camp Hill Rd
Fort Washington, PA 19034
215-273-7000
Fax: 908-874-1120 www.splenda.com
Artificial sweetners
President: Peter Luther
Vice President: Sheila Bergey
Contact: Joan Anton
janton@mcnus.jnj.com
Estimated Sales: $10-20 Million
Parent Co: Johnson & Johnson

8083 McNeil Specialty Products Company
PO Box 2400
501 George St.
New Brunswick, NJ 08903-2400
732-524-3799
Fax: 732-524-3303
artifical sweetners.such as sucralose.
President: Stephen Fanning
Director Sales (North America): Jim Thornton
Director International Sales: Joseph Zannoni
Contact: Donna Fernandez
donna@sucralose.com
Estimated Sales: $10-25million
Number Employees: 20-49
Parent Co: Johnson & Johnson

8084 McSteven's
5600 NE 88th St
Vancouver, WA 98665
360-816-5259
Fax: 360-944-1302 800-838-1056
mcstevens.com
Cocoa, drink mixes and bulk tea.
Type of Packaging: Private Label, Bulk

8085 Mccadam Cheese Co Inc
39 Mccadam Ln
Chateaugay, NY 12920-4306
518-497-6644
Fax: 518-497-3297 800-639-4031
info@mccadam.com www.mccadam.coop
A variety of cheeses including aged and waxed cheddars; flavored and reduced fat cheddars; muenster cheese; monterey jack cheese, and extra sharp cheddar cheese in addition to smoked cheeses.
Chairman: Carl Peterson
Chief Executive Officer: Paul Johnston
EVP/Finance & Administration: Margaret Bertolino
SVP/Information Services: Ralph Viscomi
SVP/Economics & Legislative Affairs: Robert Wellington
Director International Sales: Peter Gutierrez
Communications Director: Douglas DiMento
EVP/Chief Operating Officer: Richard Wellington
Plant Manager: Ron Davis
Estimated Sales: $10-20 Million
Number Employees: 100-249
Parent Co: Agri-Mark Inc

8086 Mccall Farms
6615 S Irby St
Effingham, SC 29541-3577
843-662-2223
Fax: 843-665-5234 800-277-2012
customerservice@mccallfarms.com
www.margaretholmes.com
Canned garbanzo, green and lima beans, collard greens, kale, spinach, okra, tomatoes, corn, peas, squash, succotash and peanuts
Owner: Jimmy Kremidas
Regional Sales Manager: Woody Swink
Sales Manager: David Wold
Vice President of Sales: Mark Tarkenton
jimmykremidas@gmail.com
Director Engineering: Jerry Gulledge
Estimated Sales: $5-10 Million
Number Employees: 100-249
Type of Packaging: Consumer, Food Service
Brands:
 Canned Southern Vegetables
 Lord Chesterfield
 Margret Holmes

8087 Mccartney Produce Co
211 S Fentress St
Paris, TN 38242-4032
731-642-2362
Fax: 731-642-6681 www.mccartneyproduce.com
Fruit and vegetables

Food Manufacturers / A-Z

Cio/Cto: Mccartney Pierce
mpierce@mccartneyproduce.com
Chief Financial Officer: Debbie Woodard
Director, Sales/General Manager: Raymon Randolph
Estimated Sales: $10-20 000,000
Number Employees: 100-249

8088 Mcclancy Seasonings Co
1 Spice Rd
Fort Mill, SC 29707-9501
803-548-2366
Fax: 803-548-6273 800-843-1968
info@mcclancy.com www.mcclancy.com
Processor and exporter of spices, seasonings and dry food mixes including salad dressing, dips, breadings, batters, gravies, soups, sauces and meat marinades, snack food seasonings, nut and pretzel coatings, whole and ground spices;custom blending available.
President: Reid Wilkerson
Estimated Sales: G
Number Employees: 100-249
Type of Packaging: Consumer, Food Service, Private Label, Bulk
Brands:
  Southern Sweetener(c)
  Continental Chef(c)
  Spice Trader(c)

8089 Mccreas Candies
202 Neponset Valley Pkwy
Hyde Park, MA 02136-2410
617-276-3388
Fax: 617-276-3380 www.mccreascandies.com
Manufacturer of candy and caramel.
CEO and Founder: Jason McCrea
Operations Manager: Jim LaFond-Lewis
Number Employees: 5-9

8090 (HQ)Mccullagh Coffee Roasters
245 Swan St
Buffalo, NY 14204
800-753-3473
sales@mccullaghcoffee.com
www.mccullaghcoffee.com
Processor, importer and exporter of coffee, tea, non-dairy creamer and hot chocolate
President: Warren Emblidge
VP of Sales and Marketing: Paul Zanghi
Estimated Sales: $9 Million
Number Employees: 50-99
Brands:
  Alterra Coffee Roasters
  Bigelow
  Ecoverde Coffee
  Folgers
  Harney & Sons
  illy
  Lavazza
  Lipton
  McCullagh Coffee Roasters
  Mighty Leaf Tea
  Nespresso
  Seattle's Best Coffee
  Starbucks

8091 Mccutcheon Apple Products
13 S Wisner St
P.O. Box 243
Frederick, MD 21701-5625
301-662-3261
Fax: 301-663-6217 800-888-7537
www.mccutcheons.com
Products include apple juice, apple cider, fruit butters, preserves, jellies, juice sweetened fruit spreads, salad dressings, relishes, hot sauces and more.
President: Robert J Mc Cutcheon
VP Sales: Vanessa Smith
Estimated Sales: $10-20 Million
Number Employees: 20-49
Square Footage: 189000
Type of Packaging: Consumer, Private Label
Brands:
  McCutcheons

8092 Mcfadden Farm
16000 Powerhouse Rd
Potter Valley, CA 95469-8771
707-743-1122
Fax: 707-743-1126 800-544-8230
mcfaddenfarm@pacific.net
www.mcfaddenfarm.com
Processor and exporter of organic herbs including garlic braids and wild rice

Owner: Eugene Mc Fadden
mcfaddenfarm@pacific.net
Estimated Sales: $1.5 Million
Number Employees: 20-49
Square Footage: 4000
Type of Packaging: Consumer, Food Service, Bulk

8093 Mcfarling Foods Inc
333 W 14th St
Indianapolis, IN 46202-2204
317-635-2633
Fax: 317-687-6844 www.mcfarling.com
Wholesaler/distributor of groceries, provisions/meats, frozen foods, produce and seafood; serving the food service market
President: Len Mcfarling
lmcfarling@mcfarling.com
CFO: Frank Chandler
Vice President: Jeffery Hillis
Quality Control Manager: Christopher Davis
Director of Marketing: Sue Sorley
VP Sales & Marketing: Jerry Ward
Procurement Manager: Len McFarling
Estimated Sales: $48 Million
Number Employees: 100-249
Square Footage: 120000

8094 Mcgraths Seafood
1 Elizabeth Pl
Streator, IL 61364-1192
815-672-2654
Fax: 815-672-3474
Frozen food
Owner: Kevin Gaede
Estimated Sales: Less Than $500,000
Number Employees: 1-4

8095 (HQ)Mcgregor Vineyard Winery
5503 Dutch St
Dundee, NY 14837-9746
607-292-3999
Fax: 607-292-6929 800-272-0192
info@mcgregorwinery.com
www.mcgregorwinery.com
Premium vinifera wines
Owner: Dan Jimerson
djimerson@mcgregorwinery.com
Estimated Sales: $5-10 Million
Number Employees: 10-19
Type of Packaging: Consumer, Food Service

8096 Mckenzie Country Classic's
160 Flynn Ave
Burlington, VT 05401-5400
802-864-4585
Fax: 802-651-7335 800-426-6100
Meats and cheeses for the food service industry.
Manager: Greg Rouliie
greg.rouliie@mckenziecountryclassics.com
Number Employees: 10-19
Type of Packaging: Consumer, Food Service

8097 Mclaughlin Seafood
728 Main St
Bangor, ME 04401-6810
207-942-7811
Fax: 207-947-9176 800-222-9107
www.mclaughlinseafood.com
Products include seafood in addition to cookbooks, clothing and kitchenware.
Owner: Reid Mc Laughlin
reid@mclaughlinseafood.com
Estimated Sales: Less than $500,000
Number Employees: 1-4

8098 Mclemores Abattoir Inc
1912 Center Dr
Vidalia, GA 30474-9317
912-537-4476
Beef and pork
President: Eugene Mc Lemore
Owner: Gene Mc Lemore
Estimated Sales: $1.3 Million
Number Employees: 10-19
Type of Packaging: Consumer

8099 (HQ)Mcredmond Brothers
919 Massman Dr
Nashville, TN 37217-1205
615-361-8997
Fax: 615-361-5645 800-251-5930
Meat and blood meal

President: Linda Mc Redmond
mcredmond@bellsouth.net
VP: Charlie Sheridan
Plant Manager: Josh Rice
Estimated Sales: $570,000
Number Employees: 5-9
Type of Packaging: Consumer, Bulk

8100 Mctavish Shortbread
10234 NE Glisan St
Portland, OR 97220-4061
503-253-9394
Fax: 503-254-6616 800-256-9844
info@McTavishShortBread.com
www.mctavishshortbread.com
Shortbread cookies
Owner: Denise Pratt
denise@mctavishshortbread.com
Co-Owner: Bill Pratt
Estimated Sales: Less than $500,000
Number Employees: 10-19
Type of Packaging: Consumer, Food Service, Bulk
Brands:
  McTavish

8101 Me & the Bees Lemonade
PO Box 40098
Austin, TX 78704
www.meandthebees.com
Honey-sweetened lemonade
CEO: Mikaila Ulmer
Number of Brands: 1
Number of Products: 4
Type of Packaging: Consumer
Brands:
  ME AND THE BEES LEMONADE

8102 Me At Corral
3695 Thompson Bridge Rd
Gainesville, GA 30506-1515
770-536-9188
Fax: 918-622-8003
Meats
President: Richard Webb
Estimated Sales: $3-5 Million
Number Employees: 5-9

8103 Mead Johnson Nutrition
225 North Canal St.
25th Floor
Chicago, IL 60606
312-466-5800
www.meadjohnson.com
Infant and child nutrition.
President/CEO: Peter Kasper Jakobsen
EVP/CFO: Michel Cup
EVP, Infant & Child Nutrition: Aditya Sehgal
Chief Scientific Officer: Dirk Hondmann
Year Founded: 1905
Estimated Sales: $4 Billion
Number Employees: 7,500
Number of Brands: 8
Parent Co: Reckitt Benckiser
Brands:
  Enfamil
  Enfagrow
  Enfakid
  Enfapro A+
  Choco Milk
  Nutramigen
  Lactum
  Sustagen

8104 Meadow Brook Dairy Co
2365 Buffalo Rd
Erie, PA 16510-1459
814-899-3191
Fax: 814-464-9152 800-352-4010
www.meadowbrookdairy.com
Milk including whole, skim, 1% and 2%
CAO: Myrna Heise
myrna_heise@deanfoods.com
Marketing Director: Marty Schwartz
VP Sales/Marketing: Joseph Martin
Plant Manager: Rhett Flanders
Number Employees: 100-249
Parent Co: Dean Foods Company
Type of Packaging: Consumer, Food Service
Brands:
  Flavortight
  Milk Chugs
  Swiss Premium Drinks

Food Manufacturers / A-Z

8105 (HQ)Meadow Gold
www.meadowgold.com
Dairy products including milk, sour cream, cottage cheese, cream cheese, yogurt, butter solid & quarters, flavored ice cream, flavored sherbert and fruit drinks.
Year Founded: 1901
Estimated Sales: $62.8 Million
Number Employees: 100-249
Parent Co: Dean Foods
Type of Packaging: Consumer, Food Service, Private Label, Bulk
Brands:
   Meadow Gold
   Private Labels
   Tampico
   Viva

8106 Meadowbrook Farm
2338 Hermany Avenue
Bronx, NY 10473-1198
                                718-828-6400
                       Fax: 718-828-8110
Dairy products
Manager: Phil Carlson
Contact: Bill Schwartz
mbrkfarms@aol.com
Estimated Sales: $2.5-5 000,000
Number Employees: 50-99
Brands:
   Meadowbrook

8107 (HQ)Meadowbrook Meat Company
2641 Meadowbrook Rd.
Rocky Mount, NC 27801
                                252-985-7200
Fax: 252-985-7247 www.mbmfoodservice.com
Manufacturer & distributor of frozen foods
Chairman, President & CEO: Jerry Wordsworth
CFO: Jeffrey Kowalk
Exective Vice President & COO: Jim Sabiston
Business Development Manager: Kristine Newton
Director of Quality Assurance: Samuel Richardson
Contact: Mike Amodeo
mamodeo@mbmfoodservice.com
Executive Director of Operations: Andy Blanton
Distribution Manager: Earl Smith
Director of Purchasing: Mitch Brantley
Number Employees: 3,000
Square Footage: 800000
Type of Packaging: Consumer, Food Service
Other Locations:
   MBM Corp.
   Fort Worth TX

8108 Meadows Country Products
811 Scotch Valley Road
Hollidaysburg, PA 16648-9693
                                814-693-9714
Fax: 814-693-4625   888-499-1001
Refrigerated desserts, deli salads
President: James Meadows
Owner: Margie Meadows
Secretary/Treasurer: Margie Meadows
Quality Assurance/Plant Manger: Todd Hill
General Manager: Jon Thayer
Sales Manager: Norm Tucker
Office Manager: Eileen Snyder
Operations Manager: Jeff Meadows
Purchasing Director: Mike Ricker
Estimated Sales: Below $5 Million
Number Employees: 15
Number of Brands: 1
Number of Products: 60
Square Footage: 48000
Type of Packaging: Food Service, Private Label, Bulk
Brands:
   Meadows Country Products

8109 Meadowvale Inc
109 Beaver St
Yorkville, IL 60560-1797
                                  630-553-0202
Fax: 630-553-0262   800-953-0201
                                Wlsn75@aol.com
Ice cream, shake and soft serve mixes
President: Steve Steinwart
ssteinwart@meadowvale-inc.com
Sales Executive: Jason Leslie
Plant Manager: Thomas Schuch

Estimated Sales: $3 Million
Number Employees: 10-19
Square Footage: 60000
Type of Packaging: Consumer
Brands:
   Dairy Queen

8110 Meals-In-A-Minute
19751 E. Mainstreet, R2
Parker, CO 80138
                                303-601-5992
                           mealsinaminute.com
Sauces, dips, marinades, rubs, jams, spices

8111 Meat & Fish Fellas
5036 N 54th Ave # 7
Suite 7
Glendale, AZ 85301-7509
                                623-931-6190
Fax: 623-931-2960 www.meatandfishfellas.com
Meat and seafood
Owner: J T Tarbell
Partner: Marty Menter
Partner: Inyol Kim
Estimated Sales: $3-5 Million
Number Employees: 20-49

8112 Meat & Supply Co
New York, NY 10009
                                646-864-0967
                           info@harryandidas.com
                       www.harryandidas.com
Sandwich counter and general store carrying locally sourced and in-house prepared goods. Also, catering services available.
Co-Founder: Will Horowitz
Co-Founder: Julie Horowitz
Year Founded: 2015
Estimated Sales: Less than $500,000
Number Employees: 5-10
Type of Packaging: Consumer, Food Service

8113 Meat Center
3035 Fm 822
Edna, TX 77957-5033
                                361-782-3776
Meat packer
Owner: Eli Salinas
Estimated Sales: Less Than $500,000
Number Employees: 1-4
Type of Packaging: Consumer, Bulk

8114 Meat-O-Mat Corp
592 Pacific St # B
Suite B
Brooklyn, NY 11217-2077
                                718-965-7250
Fax: 718-832-1027 mickfat@aol.com
                           www.meatomat.com
Processor of frozen meats including hamburger, beef and turkey patties.
President/Owner: Ronald Fatato
General Manager: Tony Quaranta
Vice President: Michael Fatato
Estimated Sales: $20-50 Million
Number Employees: 10-19
Number of Brands: 4
Type of Packaging: Consumer, Food Service, Bulk
Brands:
   El Sol
   Meat-O-Mat
   The Big O
   Top Kut

8115 Meatco Sales Ltd.
5315 54th Street
Mirror, AB T0B 3L0
Canada
                                403-788-2292
Fax: 403-788-2294 www.meatcosales.com
Fresh and frozen beef, pork, wild game and sausage
Manager: Chris Pfisterer
Manager: Steven Pfisterer
Owner: Herman Pfisterer
Number Employees: 1-4
Type of Packaging: Consumer, Food Service, Private Label, Bulk

8116 Meatcrafters
3900 Ironwood Pl
Landover, MD 20785
                                240-764-7653
Fax: 240-764-7653 info@meatcrafters.com
                       www.meatcrafters.com
Sausages and salamis
Marketing: Debra Moser
Sales: Mitchell Berliner
Production: Stanley Feder

8117 Meating Place
185 Grant St
Buffalo, NY 14213-1607
                                716-885-3623
Fax: 716-885-6328 www.meatingplace.com
Meat products including pork sausage and beef patties
President: Mark Lefens
Chairman: Jim Franklin
Vice President of Information Systems: Annica Burns
Information Technology Manager: Benjamin Isidore
Director of Marketing: Laurie Hachmeister
Sales Support Manager: Dawn Batchelder
Office Manager: Robert Wilborn
Production Manager: Shirleen Kajiwara
Estimated Sales: $4 Million
Number Employees: 20-49
Type of Packaging: Consumer, Food Service

8118 Meatland Packers
3326 15th Avenue SW
Medicine Hat, AB T1B 3W5
Canada
                                403-528-4321
                       Fax: 403-529-5986
Fresh and frozen beef, pork, lamb and wild game including elk, moose and deer
President: Frank Noel
Number Employees: 3
Type of Packaging: Consumer, Food Service, Private Label, Bulk

8119 Medallion InternationalInc
233 W Parkway
Pompton Plains, NJ 07444-1028
                                973-616-3401
Fax: 973-616-3405 www.medallionint.com
Flavors: natural and artificial; edible and essential oils
President: Michael Boudjouk
VP Business Development: William Lulum
Director Sales/Marketing: Paula Boudjouk
Plant Manager: Gwen Kenyon
Estimated Sales: $2 Million
Number Employees: 10-19
Type of Packaging: Consumer, Food Service, Private Label, Bulk

8120 Medeiros Farms
4365 Papalina Rd
Kalaheo, HI 96741
                                808-332-8211
                     Fax: 808-332-8211
Grass fed, free range beef.
President: Bernard M Medeiros
VP/Secretary: Natalie Silve
Estimated Sales: $10-20 Million
Number Employees: 5-9
Type of Packaging: Consumer

8121 Meditalia
P.O.Box 1393
New York, NY 10113-1393
                                212-616-3006
                     Fax: 212-616-3005
Dairy and egg-free jarred sauces
Founder/CEO: Daniel Lubetzky
VP/New Product Development & Marketing: Sasha Hare
VP/Sales: Rami Leshem
VP/Operations: Doris Rivera
Parent Co: PeaceWorks

8122 Mediterranean Gyro Products
1102 38th Ave
Long Island City, NY 11101-6041
                                718-786-3399
Fax: 718-786-8518 yani@mediterraneanpita.com
                     www.mediterraneanpita.com
Wholesaler/distributor of Greek specialty items; processor of pita bread
President: Vasilios Memmos
Contact: Sophia Maroulis
smaroulis@corfufoods.com
Purchasing Agent: Sophia Maroulis
Estimated Sales: $24 Million
Number Employees: 20-49

Food Manufacturers / A-Z

8123 Mediterranean Pita Bakery
9046 132 Avenue NW
Edmonton, AB T5E 0Y2
Canada
780-476-6666
Pita bread
Manager: Ahmed Hagar
Number Employees: 5-9
Type of Packaging: Consumer, Food Service

8124 Mediterranean Snack Food Co
708 Main St
Boonton, NJ 07005-1450
973-402-2644
Healthy, non-GMO and gluten-free snacks such as chips and crackers
President: Vincent James
vincent@mediterraneansnackfoods.com
Vice President: Franck Le Berre
Estimated Sales: Less Than $500,000
Number Employees: 1-4

8125 Medlee Foods
319 S Jefferson St
Suite 300
Chicago, IL 60661-5616
312-442-0406
medleefoods.com
Seasoned butter
President & CEO: Alberto Valdes
Number of Brands: 1
Number of Products: 4
Type of Packaging: Consumer
Brands:
  MEDLEE

8126 Medterra CBD
9801 Research Dr
Irvine, CA 92618
800-971-1288
support@medterracbd.com www.medterracbd.com
CBD gel capsules
CEO: Jay Hartenbach

8127 Meduri Farms
P.O. Box 866
Dallas, OR 97338
877-388-8800
Fax: 800-310-4270
customerservice@meduriworlddelights.com
www.meduriworlddelights.com
Dried cherries, blueberries and strawberries; also, infused cherries with raspberry juice
President: Joe Meduri
Sales: Mike Meduri
Year Founded: 1984
Estimated Sales: Less Than $500,000
Number Employees: 5-9
Parent Co: Meduri Farms
Type of Packaging: Food Service, Private Label, Bulk
Brands:
  Razzcherries

8128 Meelunie America
26105 Orchard Lake Rd Ste 210
Farmington Hills, MI 48334
248-473-2100
Fax: 248-473-2114 www.meelunie.com
Starch products: potatoes, corn and wheat
Owner: William Lauer
Contact: Renee Barlow
renee.barlow@meelunie.com
Estimated Sales: $3-5 Million
Number Employees: 1-4

8129 Mega Pro Intl
251 W Hilton Dr # 100
St George, UT 84770-2201
435-673-1001
Fax: 435-673-1007 800-541-9469
info@mega-pro.com www.mega-pro.com
Processor, importer and exporter of nutritional supplements including vitamins for weight gain and loss
President: Dave Smith
megapro@mega-pro.com
Estimated Sales: $1.8 Million
Number Employees: 20-49

8130 MegaFood
Manchester, NH 03108
800-848-2542
questions@megafood.com www.megafood.com
Dietary supplements
Chief Executive Officer: Robert Craven
Quality Assurance Manager: Dale Bates
Marketing Communications Manager: Jamila Lasante
Customer Exeprience Manager: Amy Keronen
Year Founded: 1973
Estimated Sales: $20-50 Million
Number Employees: 50-99
Type of Packaging: Consumer
Brands:
  Daily Foods
  Essentials
  MegaFood
  Nutritional Therapeutix

8131 Megatoys Inc
6443 E Slauson Ave
Commerce, CA 90040-3107
323-887-8138
Fax: 323-887-8135 888-999-9168
www.megatoys.info
Toy company
President: Peter Woo
peter@megatoys.com
CEO: Charlie Woo
Finance: Teresa Chun
VP: Dennis Paris
Sales: Jackie Chanemougam
Estimated Sales: Less Than $500,000
Number Employees: 1-4
Brands:
  M&M Easter Baskets
  Peeps Easter Baskets

8132 Megpies
53 7th Ave
4th Fl
Brooklyn, NY 11217-3607
347-218-2971
Fax: 347-338-2559 www.megpies.com
Tarts
Owner: Meghan Ritchie
Year Founded: 2012

8133 Mehaffies Pies
3013 Linden Ave
Dayton, OH 45410-3053
937-253-1163
Fax: 937-254-4977 800-289-7437
www.mehaffiespies.com
Cheesecake, fresh and frozen pies
President: Greg Hay
greghay@mehaffiespies.com
Co-Owner: Jim Columbus
Sales: Mark Berry
Estimated Sales: $500,000-$1 Million
Number Employees: 10-19
Square Footage: 16000
Type of Packaging: Consumer, Food Service, Private Label, Bulk

8134 Mei Shun Tofu Products Company
523 W 26th St
Chicago, IL 60616-1803
312-842-7000
Fax: 312-791-9429
Canner and exporter of tofu
Owner: Yim Sung
Estimated Sales: Less than $500,000
Number Employees: 5 to 9
Type of Packaging: Consumer, Food Service, Private Label, Bulk

8135 Meier's Wine Cellars Inc
6955 Plainfield Rd
Cincinnati, OH 45236-3793
513-891-2900
Fax: 513-891-6370 800-346-2941
www.meierswinecellars.com
Juice, jams, jellies
President: Ralph Belling
r.belling@drinkmeiers.com
CEO: Bob Szabo
Controller: Barbara Boyd
Chairman: Robert Gottesman
Quality Manager: Dan Schuchter
Marketing Director: Lyn Lubin
Retail marketing & PR/ Advertising: Heather Friebus
Operations Manager: Ralph Belling
Bottling Manager: Mike Dooley
Estimated Sales: $5-10 Million
Number Employees: 20-49
Brands:
  Breckenridge Farm Sparkling Juices
  Meier's
  Meier's Sparkling Ju

8136 Meier's Wine Cellars Inc
6955 Plainfield Rd
Cincinnati, OH 45236
513-891-2900
Fax: 513-891-6370 800-346-2941
info@meierswinecellars.com
www.meierswinecellars.com
Fruit juices and wine
President: Paul Lux
Quality Manager: Dan Schuchter
Winemaker: Robert Distler
Estimated Sales: $4.1 Million
Number Employees: 20-49
Square Footage: 80000
Type of Packaging: Consumer

8137 Meijer Inc
2929 Walker Ave NW
Grand Rapids, MI 49544-9428
616-453-6711
Fax: 616-791-2572 www.meijer.com
Supermarket chain with 190 plus stores, half are in Michigan and the rest are spread across the states of Ohio, Kentucky, Illinois, and Indiana. Has two manufacturing facilities for their products listed below.
Co-Chairman/CEO: Hank Meijer
Co-Chairman: Doug Meijer
Vice Chairman: Paul Boyer
Estimated Sales: Over $1 Billion
Number Employees: 10000+
Square Footage: 400000
Other Locations:
  Dairy Manufacturing
  Holland MI
  Dairy/Meat Manufacturing
  Carlinville IL
Brands:
  Meijer
  Meijer Gold
  Meijer Organic
  Meijer Natural
  Meijer Ecowise
  Meijer Elements

8138 Meister Cheese Company
1050 E Industrial Dr
Muscoda, WI 53573
608-739-3134
Fax: 608-739-4348 800-634-7837
grandpa@meistercheese.com
www.meistercheese.com
Cheese
President: Scott Meister
Partner: Vicki Thingbold
Sales/Marketing: Dan Meister
Contact: Rt Hardy
rhardy@meistercheese.com
Estimated Sales: $5-10 Million
Number Employees: 20-49
Type of Packaging: Private Label

8139 (HQ)Mel-O-Cream Donuts Intl
5456 International Pkwy
Springfield, IL 62711-7086
217-483-7272
Fax: 217-483-7744
Doughnuts and doughnut holes; frozen pre-formed and frozen pre-fried dough.
President/CEO: David Waltrip
CEO: Dave Waltrip
dwaltrip@mel-o-cream.com
CFO: David Drendel
Director, Operations: Dan Alewelt
Estimated Sales: $10-20 Million
Number Employees: 50-99
Number of Brands: 1
Number of Products: 200+
Square Footage: 65000
Type of Packaging: Food Service, Bulk
Brands:
  Mel-O-Cream

8140 Mel-O-Cream Donuts Intl
5456 International Pkwy
Springfield, IL 62711-7086
217-483-7272
Fax: 217-483-7744 800-500-5414
Donuts

Food Manufacturers / A-Z

Owner: Robert Stevenson
CEO: Dave Waltrip
dwaltrip@mel-o-cream.com
General Manager: Lois Stevenson
Operations Manager: David Waltrip
Production Manager: Dan Alewelt
Estimated Sales: $1-2.5 Million
Number Employees: 50-99
Parent Co: Mel-O-Cream Donuts International

8141 Melba's Old School Po Boys
1525 Elysian Fields Avenue
New Orleans, LA 70117
504-267-7765
eatatmelbas.com
Prepared meals including shrimp & catfish platters, BBQ ribs, red bean, cabbage, baked chicken, bell pepper, roasted beef, rice, pork chops, bourbon chicken teriyaki plates, hamburgers, ham, sausage, turkey, vegetables, chicken or fishfillet platters, corn bread, gumbo, soups, desserts, salads, and prepared snack trays.
Founder/President & CEO: Scott Wolfe Sr.
Year Founded: 2005
Number Employees: 18
Type of Packaging: Consumer, Food Service, Bulk

8142 Melchers Flavors of America
5600 W Raymond Street
Indianapolis, IN 46241-4343
513-858-6300
Fax: 513-858-3110 800-235-2867
Food flavorings; including kosher, extracts, syrups and drink mixes
President: Hellmuth Starnitzkey
COO/VP: Wolfgang Boehmer
Purchasing Agent: Claudia Slaughter
Purchasing Manager: Kellie Hall
Estimated Sales: $5-9.9 Million
Number Employees: 20
Type of Packaging: Food Service, Bulk

8143 Mele-Koi Farms
787 Alderwood Drive
Newport Beach, CA 92660-7157
949-660-9000
Fax: 949-660-9000
Manufacturer and exporter of powdered tropical drink mixes
Owner: Lloyd L Aubert Jr
Estimated Sales: $400,000
Number Employees: 1 to 4
Number of Brands: 1
Number of Products: 1
Type of Packaging: Consumer
Brands:
    Mele-Koi Hawaiian Coconut Snow

8144 Meleddy Cherry Plant
1952 Shiloh Rd
Sturgeon Bay, WI 54235
920-743-2858
Frozen red tart cherries
President: Melvin Selvick
VP: Eddy Selvick
Estimated Sales: $5-10 000,000
Number Employees: 20-49

8145 Meli's Monster Cookies
Austin, TX 78746
www.meliscookies.com
Cookie mixes
Co-Founder: Melissa Blue
Co-Founder: Melissa Mehall
Number of Brands: 1
Number of Products: 4
Type of Packaging: Consumer

8146 Melitta USA Inc
13925 58th St N
Clearwater, FL 33760-3721
727-535-2111
Fax: 727-535-7376 888-635-4880
consumerrelations@melitta.com www.melitta.com
Processor, importer and exporter of coffee; also, coffee machines and filters

President & CEO: Martin Miller
CEO: Marty Miller
mmiller@melitta.com
Senior Product Manager: Kerrie Tobin
Quality Assurance Manager: Mark Kiczalis
Marketing Director: Chris Hillman
VP Sales: Edward Mitchell
National Sales Manager: Thomas Best
Plant Manager: Matthias Bloedorn
Estimated Sales: $27 Million
Number Employees: 100-249
Square Footage: 104000
Type of Packaging: Consumer, Food Service
Brands:
    Melitta

8147 Mellace Family Brands
6195 El Camino Real
Carlsbad, CA 92009
760-448-1940
Fax: 760-448-1945 866-255-6887
mrunion@mfbrands.com
Functional (antioxidants), kosher, organic/natural, vegetarian, nuts, other snacks, dried fruit, private label.
Marketing: Mike Runion
Contact: Chuck Amoura
camoura@mfbrands.com

8148 Mellos North End Mfr
63 N Court St
Fall River, MA 02720-2701
508-673-2320
Fax: 508-675-0893 800-673-2320
info@melloschourico.com
www.melloschourico.com
Processor and exporter of sausage patties, links and pork
Owner: Eduardo Rego
Sales Manager: Diane Rego
Contact: Dan Rego
dan@melloschourico.com
Estimated Sales: $500,000-$1 Million
Number Employees: 1-4
Type of Packaging: Consumer, Food Service, Bulk

8149 Meluka Honey
Santa Clarita, CA 91350
salesusa@melukahoney.com
www.melukahoney.com
Australian honey
Brands:
    Meluka

8150 Melville Candy Corp
70 Finnell Dr # 16
Unit 16
Weymouth, MA 02188-1153
781-331-2005
Fax: 800-466-0516 jmelville8878@aol.com
www.melvillecandycompany.com
Gourmet hard candy lollipops
Owner: Sarah Delory
sarah@melvillecandycompany.com
CFO: Debra Katz
Marketing: Joe Melville
Manufacturing Staff: Liz Mazzilli
Number Employees: 100-249

8151 Mememe Inc
1470 Birchmont Road
Toronto, ON M1P 2G1
Canada
416-972-0973
Fax: 416-972-9592
Organic/natural, other baked goods, other condiments, pudding.
Marketing: Marcy Mihalcheon

8152 Memphis Meats
Berkeley, CA
founders@memphismeats.com
www.memphismeats.com
Meat products including chicken, beef and duck.
Co-Founder: Uma Valeti
Co-Founder: Nicholas Genovese
Year Founded: 2015

8153 Mendocino Brewing Co Inc
1601 Airport Rd
Ukiah, CA 95482-6456
707-463-2627
Fax: 797-744-1910 questions@mendobrew.com
www.mendobrew.com

Beer, stout, ale and lager
President, Chief Executive Officer: Yashpal Singh
yashpal@mendobrew.com
CFO: Jerome Merchant
CEO: Vijay Mallya
Marketing Director: Michael Lovett
Estimated Sales: $4.3 Million
Number Employees: 50-99
Square Footage: 260000
Type of Packaging: Consumer, Food Service
Brands:
    Black Hawk
    Blackhawk Stout
    Blue Heron
    Blue Heron Pale Ale
    Eye of the Hawk
    Eye of the Hawk Select Ale
    Peregrine Golden
    Peregrine Pale Ale
    Red Tail
    Red Tail Ale
    Springtide Ale
    Yuletide Porter

8154 Mendocino Mustard
1260 North Main Street
Suite 11
Fort Bragg, CA 95437
707-964-2250
Fax: 707-964-0525 800-964-2270
info@mendocinomustard.com
mendocinomustard.com
Specialty mustards including hot/sweet and spicy seeded with ale. Foods available in fat-free and sodium-free
Founder: Devora Rossman
Production Manager: Kathy Silva
Estimated Sales: $255000
Number Employees: 1-4
Number of Brands: 1
Number of Products: 2
Square Footage: 6400
Type of Packaging: Consumer, Food Service
Brands:
    Mendocino
    Seeds & Suds

8155 Menehune Mac
707 Waiakamilo Rd
Honolulu, HI 96817-4312
808-841-3344
Fax: 808-841-3344 sales@menehunemac.com
www.menehunemac.com
chocolate-covered macadamia nuts. They are known for their Menehune Milk Chocolate.
President: Neal Arakaki
neala@menehunemac.com
Estimated Sales: $5-10,000,000
Number Employees: 20-50

8156 Menemsha Fish Market
54 Basin Rd
Chilmark, MA 2535
508-645-2282
Fax: 508-645-9783
menemshafishmarket@yahoo.com
www.menemshafishmarket.net
Fresh and prepared seafood; fish, crabs, scallops and shellfish
Owner: Stanley Larsen
menemshafishmarket@yahoo.com
Estimated Sales: Less Than $500,000
Number Employees: 1-4
Type of Packaging: Consumer, Food Service, Private Label, Bulk
Brands:
    Menemsha Bites
    Poole's

8157 Menghini Winery
1150 Julian Orchards Dr
Julian, CA 92036
760-765-2072
Fax: 760-765-2072
Wines
Owner: Toni Menghini
mmenghini@gmail.com
Estimated Sales: Less Than $500,000
Number Employees: 1-4
Type of Packaging: Private Label
Brands:
    Menghini

Food Manufacturers / A-Z

8158 Mennel Milling Company
319 S Vine Street
Fostoria, OH 44830
419-435-8151
Fax: 419-436-5150 800-688-8151
info@mennel.com www.mennel.com
Processor of flour used in cake mixes, cookies, snack crackers, breadings, batters, gravies, soups, ice cream cones, pretzels and oriental noodles.
President: D. Ford Mennel
Controller: Lori Kitchen
Senior Technical Advisor: C J Lin
Vice President of Operations: David Marty
Corp Milling Engineer: Joel Hoffa
Year Founded: 1886
Estimated Sales: Below $5 Million
Number Employees: 100-249
Type of Packaging: Bulk

8159 Meramec Vineyards
600 State Route B
St James, MO 65559-1000
573-265-7847
Fax: 573-265-3453 877-216-9463
www.meramecvineyards.com
Natural grape juice
President: P Meagher
Manager: Phyllis Meagher
Estimated Sales: $3-5 Million
Number Employees: 5-9
Type of Packaging: Consumer, Food Service
Brands:
 Meramec

8160 Merb's Candies
4000 S Grand Blvd
St Louis, MO 63118-3466
314-832-7117
Fax: 314-832-0146
Candy including chocolates and novelties
President: Teri Bearden
tbearden@merbscandy.com
Estimated Sales: $500,000-$1 Million
Number Employees: 10-19
Type of Packaging: Consumer

8161 Mercado Latino
245 Baldwin Park Blvd
City Of Industry, CA 91746-1404
626-333-6862
800-432-7266
www.mercadolatinoinc.com
Manufacturer, importer and distributor of authentic Latin products with nine distribution centers in the western United States.
Estimated Sales: Less Than $500,000
Number Employees: 1-4
Brands:
 Brillasol
 Faraon
 Milpas
 Ola Blanca
 Payaso
 Siesta
 Sol-Mex
 Sun Sun

8162 Mercer Foods
1836 Lapham Dr
Modesto, CA 95354
209-529-0150
Fax: 209-526-3406 www.mercerfoods.com
Freeze-dried fruits and vegetables
CEO: David Noland
Brands:
 Natural Heaven

8163 Mercer Processing
1836 Lapham Drive
Modesto, CA 95354
209-529-0150
Fax: 209-526-3406 sales@mercerfoods.com
www.mercerfoods.com
Freeze dried fruits, vegetables, and dairy products.
CEO: David Noland
Quality Manager: Cynthia Apodaca
Contact: Hannah E Silva
hsilva@mercerfoods.com
Estimated Sales: $12.9 Million
Number Employees: 75
Number of Brands: 3
Square Footage: 160000
Type of Packaging: Private Label

Brands:
 AquaFruit
 Mercer
 Truth in Snacks

8164 Mercer's Dairy
13584 NYS Rt 12
Boonville, NY 13309
315-942-2611
Fax: 315-942-5315 866-637-2377
mercersdairy@gmail.com www.mercersdairy.com
Gluten-free, kosher, organic/natural, milk, yogurt, ice cream/sorbet, co-packing, private label.
Marketing: Dalton Givens

8165 Merci Spring Water
11570 Rock Island Ct
Maryland Heights, MO 63043-3522
314-872-9323
Fax: 314-872-9544
Processor and exporter of water including spring, purified and distilled; also, concentrated juices
President: Don Schneeberger
Estimated Sales: Under $500,000
Number Employees: 1-4
Square Footage: 90000

8166 Mercon Coffee Group.
2333 Ponce de Leon Blvd.
Suite 600, Coral Gables
Miami, FL 33134
786-254-2300
Fax: 201-418-0306 traders@merconcoffee.com
www.merconcoffee.com
Green coffee
Founder: Duilio Baltodano
President: Andreas Enderlin
CFO/Treasurer: Salvador Rodriguez
Sales Manager: Richard Etkin
Number Employees: 20-49
Brands:
 Mercon

8167 Meredith & Meredith
2343 Farm Creek Rd
Toddville, MD 21672
410-397-8151
Fax: 410-397-8130
Frozen soft shell crabs, refrigerated blue crabmeat, oysters
President: Jennings Tolley
VP: Morgan Tolley
Estimated Sales: Below $5 000,000
Number Employees: 20-49
Type of Packaging: Consumer
Brands:
 Meredith's

8168 Meredyth Vineyard
RR 628
Route 626
Middleburg, VA 20118
540-687-6277
Fax: 540-687-6288
Wine
Partner: Archie Smith

8169 Meridian Beverage Company
2255 Button Gwinnett Dr
Atlanta, GA 30340
770-248-9315
Fax: 770-263-6960 800-728-1481
Naturally flavored noncarbonated spring water beverages
President: Steve Lovinger
Convenience Store Manager: Ralph Grasso
Sales Manager: Marilyn Hunter
Number Employees: 20-49

8170 Meridian Foods New Inc
201 W Babb Rd
Eaton, IN 47338
765-396-3344
Fax: 765-396-3430 info@edenfoods.com
www.edenfoods.com
Processor and canner of organic dry beans.
Manager: Terry Evans
Quality Assurance Manager: Katie Henry
Estimated Sales: $10-20 Million
Number Employees: 20-49
Number of Brands: 1
Square Footage: 45000
Parent Co: Eden Foods
Type of Packaging: Private Label

Brands:
 Eden

8171 Meridian Trading Co.
1136 Pearl Street
Suite 201
Boulder, CO 80302
303-442-8683
Fax: 303-379-5199 info@meridiantrading.com
www.meridiantrading.com
Herbal products, spices, organics
President: David Black
Estimated Sales: $5 Million
Number Employees: 1

8172 Meridian Vineyards
555 Gateway Dr.
P.O. Box 4500
Napa, CA 94558
707-259-4500
Fax: 707-259-4542 800-226-7133
inquiries@meridianvineyards.com
Wine including Cabernet Sauvignon, Chardonnay, Merlot, Moscato, Pinot Grigio, Pinot Noir, Ros,, Santa Barbara Chardonnay, Sauvignon Blanc
Winemaker: Lee Miyamura
Estimated Sales: $20-50 Million
Number Employees: 120
Parent Co: Treasury Wine Estates
Type of Packaging: Private Label, Bulk

8173 Merisant
33 N Dearborn Street
Suite 200
Chicago, IL 60602
312-840-6000
Fax: 312-840-5541 www.merisant.com
Artifical sweeteners
Chief Executive Officer, President: Paul Block
CFO: Julie Wool
VP/General Counsel/Secretary: Jonathan Cole
Quality Assurance Manager: Lonnie Morgan
Contact: Dan Beck
dan.beck@merisant.com
VP/COO: Richard Mewborn
Number Employees: 437
Square Footage: 52600
Type of Packaging: Consumer, Food Service
Brands:
 Canderel
 Equal
 Pure Via

8174 Merkley & Sons Packing Co Inc
3994 W 180n
Jasper, IN 47546-8498
812-482-7020
Fax: 812-482-7033
Meat products including beef and pork
President: Dave Merkley
Treasurer: Selma Merkley
VP: David Merkley
Estimated Sales: $10-20 Million
Number Employees: 20-49
Type of Packaging: Consumer, Bulk

8175 Merlin Candies
5635 Powell St
Harahan, LA 70123
504-733-5553
Fax: 504-733-5536 800-899-1549
Processor, importer and exporter of confectionery products including custom molded and sugar-free chocolates, seasonal candies and chocolate trolls
President: Jean La Hoste
VP: Mary Crowley
Contact: Raymond Brinson
rbrinson@merlincandies.com
Estimated Sales: $1 Million
Number Employees: 5-9
Type of Packaging: Consumer, Food Service, Private Label
Brands:
 Merlin's

8176 Merlino Italian Baking Company
19016 72nd Avenue South
Kent, WA 98032
425-656-9076
Fax: 425-656-8059 800-800-9490
info@merlinobaking.com
www.merlinobaking.com
Italian bakery goods, specialty cookies, soy products, organic products, health foods, etc

Food Manufacturers / A-Z

President: Greg Merlino
Vice President: Basel Nassar
Marketing: Margaret Domer
Plant Manager: Aurelio Coria
Estimated Sales: $3 Million
Number Employees: 20-49
Number of Brands: 3
Number of Products: 50
Square Footage: 20000
Parent Co: Seattle Gourmet Foods
Type of Packaging: Consumer, Food Service, Private Label
Brands:
   Merlino Signature Brands

8177 Merlinos
1330 Elm Ave
Canon City, CO 81212-4499
719-275-5558
Fax: 719-275-8980 www.den-air.com
Fruit juices including cider-apple, cherry, apple-strawberry, blackberry, red raspberry and grape
President: Michael A Merlino
Estimated Sales: $1,127,516
Number Employees: 50-99
Type of Packaging: Consumer, Food Service, Private Label, Bulk

8178 Mermaid Spice Corporation
5702 Corporation Cir
Fort Myers, FL 33905
239-693-1986
Fax: 239-693-2099
Processor and importer of herbs, spices, seasonings, salt substitutes, rices, soup bases and salad dressings; exporter of spices and soup bases; also, custom blending available
General Manager: Mike Asaad
Estimated Sales: $1-3 Million
Number Employees: 1-4
Square Footage: 72000
Type of Packaging: Food Service
Brands:
   Mermaid Spice

8179 Merrill Meat Co
813 WY 230
Encampment, WY 82325
307-327-5345
Meat
Owner: Cade Merrill
Estimated Sales: $500,000-$1 000,000
Number Employees: 1-4

8180 Merrill Seafood Center
6213 Merrill Rd
Jacksonville, FL 32277
904-744-3132
Seafood
President: Agostinho Arco
Estimated Sales: $500,000-$1 000,000
Number Employees: 1-4

8181 Merrill's Blueberry Farms
176 High Street
PO Box 149
Ellsworth, ME 04640-3141
207-667-9750
Fax: 207-667-4052 800-711-6551
merrblue@merrillwildblueberries.com
www.merrillwildblueberries.com
Wild blueberries
Estimated Sales: $1-3 Million
Number Employees: 10-19
Number of Brands: 1
Number of Products: 1
Square Footage: 200000
Type of Packaging: Private Label, Bulk
Brands:
   Merrill's

8182 Merrimack Valley Apiaries
96 Dudley Rd
Billerica, MA 01821-4131
978-667-2337
Fax: 978-318-0881 www.mvabeepunchers.com
Honey
President: Andy Card Jr
Number Employees: 1-4

8183 Merritt Estate Winery Inc
2264 King Rd
Forestville, NY 14062-9703
716-965-4800
Fax: 716-965-4800 888-965-4800
nywines@merrittestatewinery.com
www.merrittestatewinery.com
Processor and exporter of table wines including red, white, rose, dry, sweet and sparkling
President: William T Merritt
Director of Marketing, Branding & Events: Michael J. Ferguson
Wholesale Sales: Mike Burkland
Manager: Jason Merritt
nywine@merritwestawinery.com
Estimated Sales: $$1-2.5 Million
Number Employees: 1-4
Square Footage: 28000
Type of Packaging: Consumer, Food Service, Private Label
Brands:
   Merritt

8184 Merritt Pecan Co
Highway 520
Weston, GA 31832
229-828-6610
Fax: 229-828-2061 800-762-9152
merritt@merritt-pecan.com
Processor and exporter of shelled and in-shell pecans
Owner: Tammy Merritt
merritt@merritt-pecan.com
President: Richard Merritt
Estimated Sales: $2 Million
Number Employees: 20-49
Square Footage: 54000
Type of Packaging: Consumer, Bulk
Brands:
   Merritt Pecan Co.

8185 Merryvale Vineyards
1000 Main St
St Helena, CA 94574-2011
707-963-7777
Fax: 707-963-1949 800-326-6069
info@merryvale.com www.merryvale.com
Wines
President: Rene Schlatter
rschlatter@merryvale.com
Proprietor/CEO: Ren, Schlatter
Estimated Sales: $10-20 Million
Number Employees: 50-99
Number of Brands: 1
Brands:
   Merryvale

8186 Mertz Sausage Co
619 Cupples Rd
San Antonio, TX 78237-4329
210-433-3263
Fax: 210-433-3218
Smoked, fresh and Italian sausage; also, Mexican chorizo
President: Alejandro P Pena
Manager: Terri Millmeyer
tmillmeyer@sarodeo.com
Estimated Sales: $250,000-$290,000
Number Employees: 1-4
Type of Packaging: Consumer
Brands:
   Mertz Sausage

8187 Mesa Salsa
Santa Barbara, CA 93109
805-448-3836
info@mesasalsa.com
www.mesasalsa.com
Salsas
Co-Founder: Anne Altamirano
Co-Founder: Ali Altamirano

8188 Mesquite Organic Beef LLC
13808 E Greenwood Dr
Aurora, CO 80014-3952
303-680-1028
888-480-2333
Certified organic grass-fed beef producer.
CEO: Steve Atchley
satchley@mesquiteorganicbeef.com
Estimated Sales: Less Than $500,000
Number Employees: 1-4

8189 Messina Hof Winery & Resort
4545 Old Reliance Rd
Bryan, TX 77808-8995
979-778-9463
Fax: 979-778-1729 marketing@messinahof.com
www.messinahof.com
Wines
President/CEO: Paul Bonarrigo
owners@messinahof.com
CFO: Merrill Bonarrigo
Estimated Sales: $10-20 Million
Number Employees: 20-49
Type of Packaging: Private Label, Bulk

8190 MetaBall
General Nathan Cooper House
401 Route 24
Chester, NJ 07930
908-879-0880
800-247-6580
www.metaballenergybites.com
Energy bites
Founder: Susie Abramson

8191 Metabolic Nutrition
10450 W McNab Rd
Tamarac, FL 33321
800-626-1022
info@metabolicnutrition.com
www.metabolicnutrition.com
Processor and exporter of general and sports nutritional supplements
President/CEO: Murray Cohen
VP Marketing/CFO: Brian Cohen
VP/Sales: Jay Cohen
jay@metabolicnutrition.com
Estimated Sales: $1-2.5 Million
Number Employees: 5-9
Number of Products: 15
Square Footage: 56000
Type of Packaging: Private Label
Brands:
   Advantage
   Cgp
   Hydravax
   Protizyme
   Synedrex
   Tag

8192 Metafoods LLC
2970 Clairmont Rd NE # 510
Brookhaven, GA 30329-4418
404-843-2400
Fax: 404-843-1119 www.metafoodsllc.net
Frozen foods, beef, pork, poultry, frozen seafood, canned goods
President: Joe Wright
sales@metafoodsllc.com
CFO: Patricia Smith
Estimated Sales: $5-10 Million
Number Employees: 20-49

8193 Metagenics, Inc.
25 Enterprise
Aliso Viejo, CA 92656
949-366-0818
Fax: 949-366-0853 800-692-9400
www.metagenics.com
Vitamins, supplements and sports nutrition products
Founder: Jeff Katke
President & CEO: Brent Eck
VP of Research & Development: Matthew Tripp
Chief Science Officer: Jeffrey Bland
VP of Sales: Tim Katke
Contact: Laura Ajera
lauraajera@metagenics.com
Estimated Sales: $22.4 Million
Number Employees: 500-999
Square Footage: 88000
Brands:
   Ethical Nutrients
   Metagenics
   Unipro

8194 (HQ)Metarom Corporation
11 School Street
Newport, VT 05855
802-334-0117
Fax: 514-375-7953 888-882-5555
accueil@metarom.fr
Natural and artificial flavors and colors; natural extracts

President: Andre Bilodeau
General Manager: Pierre Miclette
CFO: Fernande Dubois
Vice President: John Murphy
Quality Control: Alain Gauther
Estimated Sales: Less than $500,000
Number Employees: 1-4
Parent Co: Metarom Canada
Other Locations:
  Metarom Corporation
  Granby PQ

8195 Metompkin Bay Oyster Company, Inc
101-105 Eleventh Street
P.O. Box 671
Crisfield, MD 21817
410-968-0662
Fax: 410-968-0670 metbay@verizon.net
www.metompkinseafood.com
Fresh and frozen seafood
President: Casey Todd
Co-Owner: Mike Todd
Executive VP: Michael Todd
Sales Manager of Purchasing: Brenda Thomas
Estimated Sales: $5-10 Million
Number Employees: 100-249
Type of Packaging: Private Label

8196 Metro Mint
PO Box 885462
San Francisco, CA 94188
415-979-0781
Fax: 415-543-2749 www.metromint.com
Pure water, real mint, no sweeteners
President/Owner: Rio Miura
Controller: Elena Korsakova
Sales Manager: David Kennedy
Operations Manager: Evan Campbell

8197 Metrohm USA
9250 Camden Field Parkway
Riverview, FL 33578-8653
281-810-4355
Fax: 813-316-4900 info@metrohmusa.com
www.metrohm.com
Laboratory and testing equipment for research and development and quality control for the food and beverage industry.
President & CEO: Edward Colihan
CFO: E.V. Bosque
VP Marketing: Michael Allen
VP Sales: Robert Harshbarger
Contact: Frank Allers
frankallers@verizon.net
Estimated Sales: $40 Million
Number Employees: 50-99

8198 Metropolitan Bakery
262 S 19th St
Philadelphia, PA 19103-5707
215-545-6655
Fax: 215-985-1605 877-412-7323
wsborn@gmail.com www.metropolitanbakery.com
Breads
President/Owner: Jim Lily
President: Wendy Born
mail@metropolitanbakery.com
Number Employees: 20-49

8199 Metropolitan Baking Co
8579 Lumpkin St
Hamtramck, MI 48212-3622
313-875-7246
Fax: 313-875-7792 www.metropolitanbaking.com
Producer of bread, buns and rolls.
General Manager: Michael Zrimec
Cmo: George Kordas
gkordas@metropolitanbaking.com
Estimated Sales: $10-20 Million
Number Employees: 50-99
Number of Brands: 1
Type of Packaging: Food Service
Brands:
  Metropolitan

8200 Metropolitan Gourmet
2 Cranberry Rd
Unit A-1A
Parsippany, NJ 07054-1053
973-588-5858
Fax: 973-588-5857
info@metropolitan-gourmet.com
www.metropolitan-gourmet.com
Gourmet baked goods
International Sales: David Park
Number Employees: 5-9

8201 Metropolitan Sausage Manufacturing Company
2908 Alexander Cres
Flossmoor, IL 60422-1704
708-331-3232
Fax: 708-798-2929
Meat and sausage
President: Willard Payne
Estimated Sales: $1-2.5 000,000
Number Employees: 1-4

8202 Metropolitan Tea Company
60 Industrial Pkwy
Suite 776
Cheektowaga, NY 14227
416-588-0089
Fax: 416-588-7040 800-388-0351
sales@metrotea.com www.metrotea.com
Bagged teas, loose teas, gift boxes, tea pots and mugs, tea presses, tea infusers, spoons and squeezers
President: Gerry Vandergrift

8203 Metzer Farms
26000 Old Stage Rd
Gonzales, CA 93926-9480
831-679-2355
Fax: 831-679-2711 800-424-7755
metzinfo@metzerfarms.com
www.metzerfarms.com
Asian duck egg products including incubated, salted and fresh; also, whole Chinese geese
President: John Metzer
metzer@metzerfarms.com
Estimated Sales: $3-5 Million
Number Employees: 10-19
Number of Products: 45
Square Footage: 124000
Type of Packaging: Consumer, Private Label
Brands:
  Balut Sa Puti

8204 Metzger Popcorn Co
24197 Road U20
Delphos, OH 45833-9343
419-692-2494
Fax: 419-692-0890 800-819-6072
mail@metzgerpopcorn.com
www.metzgerpopcorn.com
Processor and exporter of popcorn
Owner: Bob Metzger
b.metzger@metzgerpopcorn.com
Estimated Sales: Less Than $500,000
Number Employees: 1-4
Square Footage: 40000
Type of Packaging: Consumer, Food Service, Private Label, Bulk
Brands:
  Indian Creek
  Mello-Krisp
  Metzger Popcorn Co.

8205 Metzger Specialty Brands
250 W 57th St
Suite 1005
New York, NY 10107
212-957-0055
Fax: 212-957-0918 info@tillenfarms.com
www.tillenfarms.com
Asparagus (spicy and white), crunchy carrots, dilly beans, hot and spicy beans, maraschino cherries, snappers (snap peas), sweet bells (bell peppers), sunnysides (tomatoes), v-packed green beans
President/Owner: Tim Metzger
t_metzger@tillenfarms.com
Human Resources Manager: Tony Palacios
Warehouse Manager: Robert Stuckey
Estimated Sales: $2 Million
Number Employees: 2

8206 Mex America Foods LLC
1037 Trout Run Rd
St Marys, PA 15857-3124
814-781-1447
Fax: 814-834-9042
Tortillas including flour, whole wheat and corn; also, tortilla chips including white, yellow, blue and red
CEO: Mike Renaud
dstrikler@honnen.com
President, Chief Executive Officer: Ray Gunn
Quality, Training, Food Safety Manager: Toni McGill
Sales Manager: Ed Jurgielewicz
Vice President of Plant Operations: Tom Kornacki
Purchasing, Inventory and Scheduling Mgr: Margaret Hanes
Estimated Sales: $5 Million
Number Employees: 20-49
Number of Brands: 3-4
Number of Products: 1
Square Footage: 80000
Type of Packaging: Consumer, Food Service, Private Label, Bulk
Brands:
  Mexamerica

8207 Mexi-Frost Specialties Company
37 Grand Avenue
Brooklyn, NY 11205-1309
718-625-3324
Fax: 718-852-8699
Frozen West Indian, Mexican, Caribbean, Chinese and Italian foods including chicken, meat pies, tamales, burritos, egg rolls
President: Gonzalo Armendariz Jr
VP: Gonzalo Armendariz, Jr.
VP Sales: Mark Armendariz
Plant Manager: Gonzaol Armendariz, Jr.
Estimated Sales: $5-10 Million
Number Employees: 20-49
Type of Packaging: Consumer, Food Service, Private Label, Bulk
Brands:
  Gonzo's Little Big Meat
  La Jolla
  La Joya
  Mexi-Frost

8208 Mexican Accent
16675 W Glendale Dr
New Berlin, WI 53151
262-784-4422
Fax: 262-784-5810
Processor and exporter of flour and corn tortillas; processor of tortilla chips; private labeling available
President: Mike Maglio
Contact: Steve Carew
scarew@mexicanaccent.com
Estimated Sales: $13 Million
Number Employees: 150
Square Footage: 240000
Type of Packaging: Consumer, Food Service, Private Label, Bulk
Brands:
  Manny's
  Mexican Accent
  Rio Real

8209 Mexican Corn Products
238 Corduroy Rd
Vars, ON K0A 3H0
Canada
613-274-2872
mexicancornproducts@gmail.com
mexicancornproducts.com
Tortilla chips
Founder: Gabriela Godinez-Laverty
Co-Founder: Jos, Godinez Del Toro
Co-Founder: Jos, Godinez Luna

8210 Meyenberg Goat Milk
PO Box 934
Turlock, CA 95381
800-891-4628
info@meyenberg.com meyenberg.com
Goat milk
President: Robert Jackson
CFO: Doug Buehrle
Vice President: Carol Jackson
COO/Marketing: Tracy Plante-Darrimon
Plant Manager: Frank Fillman
Estimated Sales: $18-20 Million
Number Employees: 50
Number of Products: 25
Type of Packaging: Consumer, Bulk
Brands:
  Meyenberg
  Professional Preference

Food Manufacturers / A-Z

8211 Meyer Brothers Dairy
5130 Industrial St Ste 400
Maple Plain, MN 55359
952-473-7343
Fax: 952-473-8522
Products include milk, breakfast items, yogurt, pizza, meat, juices, eggs and bacon, coffee, bottled water, appetizers, produce and vegetables, butter and margarine, cheese and bakery items.
Manager: Jim Otis
Quality Control Manager: Tom Janas
Contact: Greg Hanson
gregh@meyerbro.com
Estimated Sales: $2.5-5 Million
Number Employees: 20-49

8212 Meyer's Bakeries
10491 W Battaglia Dr
Casa Grande, AZ 85293-7715
520-466-5491
Fax: 520-466-5996 800-528-5770
http://www.meyersbakeries.com
English muffins
Manager: Eric Robinson
Contact: Kathy Adair
kathy.adair@freshstartbakeries.com
Plant Manager: Frank Benefiel
Estimated Sales: $10-20 Million
Number Employees: 50-99
Square Footage: 160000
Parent Co: Meyers Bakeries
Type of Packaging: Food Service, Private Label, Bulk

8213 Mezza
222 E Wisconsin Avenue
Suite 300
Lake Forest, IL 60045-1723
847-735-2516
Fax: 415-727-4471 888-206-6054
Suppliers to the finest kitchens in America with a worldwide selection of gourmet pantry items.
Type of Packaging: Food Service, Private Label

8214 Mi Mama's Tortilla Factory Inc
828 S 17th St
Omaha, NE 68108-3115
402-345-2099
Fax: 402-345-1059 www.mimamas.com
Corn and flour tortillas.
General Manager: Paul Sharrar
Manager: Art Velasquez
pats@mimamas.com
Estimated Sales: $10-20 Million
Number Employees: 20-49
Number of Brands: 1
Type of Packaging: Food Service
Brands:
   Mi Mama's

8215 Mi Ranchito Foods
P.O. Box 6008
Phoenix, AZ 88023
602-272-3949
Fax: 602-278-6415
Frozen tamales; also, tortillas, chili and chili con carne
President: Joe Ramirez
Contact: Delia Cabrera
dcabrera@mi-ranchito.com
Estimated Sales: $17 Million
Number Employees: 5 to 9
Type of Packaging: Consumer, Food Service, Private Label, Bulk
Brands:
   Mi Ranchito

8216 Mi Rancho
425 Hester St
San Leandro, CA 94577
510-553-0444
www.mirancho.com
Organic tortillas
President/Owner: Manuel Berber

8217 Mia Products
1520 N Keyser Ave
Scranton, PA 18504-9737
570-207-5328
Fax: 570-457-0915
Frozen juice bars
General Manager: T Cousins
President: Gerald Shriber
VP: Ernest Fogle
Number Employees: 1-4
Parent Co: J&J Snack Foods Company
Type of Packaging: Food Service
Brands:
   Mia

8218 Miami Beef Co
4870 NW 157th St
Miami Lakes, FL 33014-6486
305-621-3252
Fax: 305-620-4562 info@miamibeef.com
Steaks, hamburgers, meat, beef, chicken, lamb, pork, sausage, roast beef, veal, prime rib, patties, stew, sirlion, tenderloim, soy, ground beef, breaded, cooked, hoagie, palomolla, pepper, salisbury, t-bone, sliced sandwich sirloinskirt steak, cubed steak, filet mignon
President: Michael Young
miamibeef@bellsouth.net
Head Sales: Barry Dean
Plant Manager: Russ Milina
Estimated Sales: $10.8 Million
Number Employees: 50-99
Type of Packaging: Consumer, Food Service, Private Label, Bulk
Brands:
   Miami Beef

8219 Miami Crab Corporation
10815 NW 33 Street
Miami, FL 33172
305-470-1500
Fax: 305-470-1502 800-269-8395
mail@miamicrab.com www.miamicrab.com
Crabmeat products
Estimated Sales: $5-10 Million
Number Employees: 5-9
Type of Packaging: Consumer, Food Service
Brands:
   Flamingo
   Jackpot
   Windy Shoal

8220 (HQ)Miami Purveyors Inc
7350 NW 8th St
Miami, FL 33126-2922
305-262-6170
Fax: 305-262-6174 800-966-6328
www.miamipurveyors.com
Manuafacturer and exporter of frozen foods including beef, pork, ham, poultry, seafood, fruits and vegetables
Owner: Rick Rothenberg
rick@miamipurveyors.com
Chief Financial Officer: Kaly Rosenberg
Estimated Sales: $14.1 Million
Number Employees: 50-99
Type of Packaging: Food Service

8221 Micalizzi Italian Ice
712 Madison Ave
Bridgeport, CT 06606-5511
203-366-2353
JAYICE712@aol.com
www.micalizzis.com
Italian ice and ice cream
Owner: Lucille Piccirillo
Co-Owner: Jay Piccirillo
Estimated Sales: Less Than $500,000
Number Employees: 1-4
Type of Packaging: Consumer, Food Service, Bulk

8222 Miceli Dairy Products Co
2721 E 90th St
Cleveland, OH 44104-3396
216-791-6222
Fax: 216-231-2504 www.miceli-dairy.com
Maker of Italian cheeses.
CEO: Joe Miceli
Year Founded: 1923
Number Employees: 100-249
Brands:
   Miceli's

8223 Michael Angelo's Inc
200 Michael Angelo Way
Austin, TX 78728
877-482-5426
customerservice@michaelangelos.com
www.michaelangelos.com
Frozen italian entrees, lasagnas, stuffed pasta, snacks and appetizers, protein dishes
President & CEO: Michael Pugliese
Estimated Sales: $100+ Million
Number Employees: 250-499
Number of Brands: 1
Number of Products: 100
Square Footage: 132000
Type of Packaging: Consumer, Food Service, Bulk
Brands:
   Michael Angelo's

8224 Michael David Winery
4580 W Highway 12
Lodi, CA 95242-9529
209-368-7384
Fax: 209-368-5801 888-707-9463
vintage@michaeldavidwinery.com
www.lodired.com
Wines
Partner: Mike Phillips
Partner: Dave Phillips
Estimated Sales: Below $5 Million
Number Employees: 100-249
Brands:
   Michael David Vineyards

8225 Michael Foods, Inc.
301 Carlson Pkwy.
Suite 400
Minnetonka, MN 55305
952-258-4000
info@michaelfoods.com
www.michaelfoods.com
Processed egg and potato products.
President: Mark Westphal
Year Founded: 1987
Estimated Sales: $1.5 Billion
Number Employees: 3,500
Number of Brands: 6
Type of Packaging: Consumer, Food Service, Private Label, Bulk
Other Locations:
   Michael Foods
   Minneapolis MN
Brands:
   Papetti's
   Simply Potatoes
   Abbotsford Farms
   Dakota Growers Pasta Co
   Davidson's
   Bob Evans Farms

8226 Michael Granese & Company
640 E Main Street
Norristown, PA 19401-5123
610-272-5099
Fax: 610-272-1995 elio.camilotto@grande.com
Italian cheeses including ricotta, mozzarella, scamorza and cream twist
President: John Carfagno
Estimated Sales: $2.9 Million
Number Employees: 10
Square Footage: 8000
Type of Packaging: Consumer, Bulk
Brands:
   Michael Granese Co.

8227 Michael Mootz Candies
1246 Sans Souci Pkwy
Hanover Twp, PA 18706-5230
570-823-8272
Fax: 570-826-1045 michaelmootzcandies.com
Confectionery products including chocolate coated creams, caramels and nuts, chocolate and chocolate chunks
President: Michael Mootz
Estimated Sales: $3-5 Million
Number Employees: 10-19
Type of Packaging: Consumer, Private Label

8228 Michael's Cookies
2205 6th Ave. S
Clear Lake, IA 50428
641-454-5577
Fax: 641-954-5451 800-822-5384
info@michaelscookies.com
www.michaelscookies.com
Frozen pre-portioned cookie doughs
COO/CFO: Scott Summeril
Quality Assurance: Myrkantra Dorlean
SVP Sales: Don Smith
Estimated Sales: $20-50 Million
Number Employees: 20-49
Number of Brands: 1
Number of Products: 1
Square Footage: 30000

Food Manufacturers / A-Z

Type of Packaging: Food Service, Private Label, Bulk
Brands:
  Bonzers

8229 Michael's Finer Meats/Seafoods
3775 Zane Trace Dr
Columbus, OH 43228
800-282-0518
www.michaelsmeats.com
Processor and wholesaler/distributor of meat including beef, pork, lamb, veal and wild game
President: Jonathan Bloch
Vice President of Sales: Jeff Goebel
Number Employees: 100-249
Square Footage: 240000
Type of Packaging: Consumer, Food Service, Bulk

8230 Michael's Gourmet Coffee
PO Box 350003
Ft. Lauderdale, FL 33335
954-567-4500
888-346-4646
neverstopmike@yahoo.com
www.michaelscoffee.com
Manufacturer of coffee.
Founder and CEO: Michael Mistretta

8231 Michael's Naturopathic Prgms
6003 Randolph Blvd
San Antonio, TX 78233-5719
210-661-8311
Fax: 210-661-8048 800-845-2730
www.michaelshealth.com
Vitamins, minerals and herbal supplements
Owner: Michael Schwartz
michael@michaelshealth.com
Director: Roxanne Llewellyn
Estimated Sales: $6.8 Million
Number Employees: 20-49
Square Footage: 44180
Brands:
  Michael's Health Products

8232 Michael's Provision Co
317 Lindsey St
Fall River, MA 02720-1132
508-672-0982
Fax: 508-672-1307
michaelschourico@hotmail.com
Meat products including Portuguese sausage
President: Ronald Miranda
info@michaelschourico.com
Owner: Joseph Miranda
Estimated Sales: $3-5 Million
Number Employees: 5-9
Type of Packaging: Consumer, Food Service, Bulk

8233 Michaelene's Gourmet Granola
7415 Deer Forest Ct
Clarkston, MI 48348-2734
248-625-0156
Fax: 248-625-8521
michaelenes@gourmetgranola.com
www.gourmetgranola.com
Granola
President: Michaelene Hearn
michaelenes@gourmetgranola.com
Estimated Sales: Below $5 Million
Number Employees: 5-9
Type of Packaging: Bulk
Brands:
  Michaelene's Gourmet
  Michaelene's Gourmet Granola
  Michaelene's Granola

8234 Michel de France
2020 South Haven Ave
Ontario, CA 91761
909-923-5205
Fax: 909-923-7804 info@micheldefrance.com
www.micheldefrance.com
European-style crepes and wafers.
Founder: Michel de France

8235 Michel et Augustin
98 4th St
Brooklyn, NY 11231
646-820-0935
micheletaugustin.com
Cookies

8236 Michel's Bakery
5698 Rising Sun Ave
Philadelphia, PA 19120-1698
267-345-7914
Fax: 215-745-1058 info@michelsbakery.com
www.michelsbakery.com
Danishes, cinnamon rolls, muffins, cakes, brownies and pies.
President: Jon Liss
CFO: Alan Stack
VP/General Manager: Stan Walulek
Purchasing Manager: Flo Collington
Year Founded: 1898
Estimated Sales: $20-30 Million
Number Employees: 100-249
Number of Brands: 2
Type of Packaging: Food Service, Private Label
Brands:
  Michel's Family Bakery
  Sensible Options

8237 Michel's Magnifique
34 N Moorie St
New York, NY 10003-2437
212-431-1070
Pates, mousses and sausage including saucisson
President: Ken Blanchette
Operations Manager: Allan Moss
Number Employees: 5-9
Type of Packaging: Consumer, Food Service

8238 Michel-Schlumberger Wine Est
4155 Wine Creek Rd
Healdsburg, CA 95448-9112
707-433-7427
Fax: 707-433-0444 800-447-3060
www.michelschlumberger.com
Wine
President: Jacques Schlumberger
CEO: Jerry Craven
President: Jacques Schlumberger
General Manager: Gary Brown
Public Relations: Joy Henderson
VP Operations/Production: Fred Payne
Estimated Sales: Below $5 Million
Number Employees: 20-49
Type of Packaging: Private Label
Brands:
  25 Imports From France
  Domaine Michel
  Michel-Schlumberger

8239 Michele Foods
16117 LA Salle St
South Holland, IL 60473-2064
708-331-7453
Fax: 708-862-5347 www.michelefoods.com
Honey-based syrups
Owner: Michelle Hoskins
michele@michelefoods.com
VP: Paul Walk
Estimated Sales: $1 Million
Number Employees: 10-19
Square Footage: 400
Type of Packaging: Consumer, Food Service
Brands:
  Michele's Honey Creme

8240 Michele's Chocolate Truffles
14704 SE 82nd Dr
Clackamas, OR 97015-9607
503-656-0220
Fax: 503-656-0440 800-656-7112
Gourmet hand dipped chocolate truffles, chews, nut clusters, cordials, toffee and caramel
Owner: Todd Davis
Estimated Sales: $3-5 Million
Number Employees: 5-9
Number of Brands: 1
Number of Products: 50
Square Footage: 10000
Type of Packaging: Consumer, Food Service, Private Label, Bulk
Brands:
  Michele's Chocolate Truffles
  Vicki's Rocky Road

8241 Michele's Family Bakery
2731 S Queen St
York, PA 17402
717-741-2027
Fax: 717-747-0065 www.macksicecream.com
Ice cream

Owner: Walt Bloss
Manager: Bill Lenick
Estimated Sales: $5-9.9 Million
Number Employees: 20-49

8242 Michelle Chocolatiers
122 N Tejon Street
Colorado Springs, CO 80903-1406
719-633-5089
Fax: 719-633-8970 888-447-3654
Processor, importer and exporter of ice creams and candy including chocolates and gold coins
VP: Jim Michopoulos
Estimated Sales: $5-10 Million
Number Employees: 20-49
Type of Packaging: Consumer, Private Label
Brands:
  Gremlin
  Michelle

8243 Michelle's RawFoodz
319 S Jefferson St
Suite 300
Chicago, IL 60661-5616
312-442-0406
medleefoods.com
Seasoned butter
President & CEO: Alberto Valdes
Number of Brands: 1
Number of Products: 4
Type of Packaging: Consumer
Brands:
  MICHELLE'S RAWFOODZ

8244 Michelle's RawFoodz
1111 Finch Ave W
Toronto, ON M3J 2E5
Canada
info@rawfoodz.com
michellesrawfoodz.com
Dressings and dips
Co-Founder: Michelle Cass
Number of Brands: 1
Number of Products: 11
Type of Packaging: Consumer

8245 Michigan Celery Cooperative
PO Box 306
Hudsonville, MI 49426
616-669-1250
Fax: 616-669-2890 www.michigancelery.com
Fresh celery including sliced and diced
General Manager: Gary Wruble
gwruble@michigancelery.com
Year Founded: 1951
Estimated Sales: Less Than $500,000
Number Employees: 1-4
Type of Packaging: Bulk

8246 Michigan Dairy LLC
29601 Industrial Rd
Livonia, MI 48150-2012
734-367-5390
Fax: 734-367-5391 www.thekrogerco.com
Dairy products including pasteurized milk, ice cream, yogurt, cottage cheese and sour cream
Manager: Jack Housley
Manager: Willow Brown
willow.brown@kroger.com
Plant Manager: Art Shank
Number Employees: 250-499
Parent Co: Kroger Company
Type of Packaging: Consumer

8247 Michigan Desserts
10750 Capital St
Oak Park, MI 48237-3134
248-544-4574
Fax: 248-544-4384 800-328-8632
sales@midasfoods.com www.midasfoods.com
Sweet dry mix items
President: Richard Elias
relias@midasfoods.com
Sr VP Sales/Marketing: Gary Freeman
Estimated Sales: $7 Million
Number Employees: 20-49
Square Footage: 180000
Parent Co: Midas Foods India
Type of Packaging: Consumer, Food Service, Private Label, Bulk
Brands:
  American Savory
  Michigan Dessert
  Sin Fill

Food Manufacturers / A-Z

8248 Michigan Farm Cheese Dairy
4295 E Millerton Rd
Fountain, MI 49410-9583
231-462-3301
Fax: 231-462-3805 877-624-3373
cheese@andrulischeese.com
www.andrulischeese.com
Cheese including feta and farmer
President: Lu Andrulis
Marketing Director: Amanda Andrulis-Preston
Production Manager: Jim Stankowski
Estimated Sales: $1 Million
Number Employees: 10-19
Type of Packaging: Consumer
Brands:
   Andrulis Farmers Cheese

8249 Michigan Freeze Pack
835 S. Griswold
P.O.Box 30
Hart, MI 49420
231-873-2175
Fax: 231-873-3025
msutton@michiganfreezepack.com
www.michiganfreezepack.com
Processor and exporter of asparagus, zucchini squash, celery, broccoli, peppers, carrots and eggplant
President: Gary Dennert
VP Sales/Finance: John Ritche
Contact: Ray Drum
rdrum@michiganfreezepack.com
Production Manager: Ronald Clark
Estimated Sales: $1 Million
Number Employees: 10
Square Footage: 400000
Type of Packaging: Food Service, Bulk

8250 Michigan Milk Producers Assn
41310 Bridge St
PO Box 8002
Novi, MI 48376-1302
248-474-6672
Fax: 248-474-0924 Burkhardt@mimilk.com
www.mimilk.com
Milk products include standardized milks, condensed whole milk, condensed skim milk, sweet condensed milks, instant nonfat dry milk, dried buttermilk, sweet cream butter, standardized cream, ice cream mixes, nonfat dry milk and driedwhole milk
President: Kenneth Nobis
nobis@mimilk.com
CEO: Joe Diglio
CFO: Josep Barenys
Director Quality: Sudeep Jain
Sr. Director Sales: Jim Feeney
Member Relations/Public Affairs: Sheila Burkhardt
General Manager: Clayton Galarneau
Estimated Sales: $20-50 Million
Number Employees: 100-249

8251 Michigan Sugar Company
122 Uptown Drive
Suite 300
Bay City, MI 48706
989-686-0161
Fax: 989-671-3719 www.michigansugar.com
Beet sugar
President/CEO: Mark Flegenheimer
CFO: Brian Haraga
Executive Vice President: Jim Ruhlman
VP Sales & Marketing: Pedro Figueroa
Vice President of Operations: Jason Lowry
Number Employees: 10-19
Type of Packaging: Consumer, Food Service, Private Label, Bulk
Other Locations:
   Michigan Sugar Factory
   Bay City MI
   Michigan Sugar Factory
   Caro MI
   Michigan Sugar Factory
   Croswell MI
   Michigan Sugar Factory
   Sebewaing MI
Brands:
   Big Chief
   Pioneer Sugar

8252 MicroSoy Corporation
300 Microsoy Dr
Jefferson, IA 50129
515-386-2100
Fax: 515-386-3287
Processor and exporter of microsoy flakes used in soy milk, tofu and other soy based foods
President/CEO: Terry Tanaka
CFO: Mike Mumma
Estimated Sales: $3.5 Million
Number Employees: 15
Square Footage: 115200
Parent Co: Mycal Corporation
Type of Packaging: Bulk
Brands:
   Microsoy Flakes

8253 Mid Atlantic Vegetable Shortening Company
125 Sanford Ave
Kearny, NJ 07032-5918
201-467-0200
Fax: 201-991-0765 800-966-1645
jhulihan@midatlanticveg.com
www.midatlanticveg.com
Shortenings, oils, margarines, pan releases, zero trans fat shortening and margarines, and specialty products such as lecithin, garlic spread and spice products
President: Calvin Theobald
CEO: Perry Theobald
VP Sales/Marketing: James Hulihan
Regional Sales Manager: Sara Theobald
Estimated Sales: $5-10 Million
Number Employees: 20-49

8254 Mid Kansas Co-Op Assn
117 N Edwards Ave
Moundridge, KS 67107-8826
620-345-6361
Fax: 620-345-8817 800-864-4428
webmaster@mkcoop.com www.mkcoop.com
Cooperative offering grains
President: Dave Christianson
Manager: Kelly Reed
kreed@mkcoop.com
Estimated Sales: Less Than $500,000
Number Employees: 1-4

8255 Mid Valley Nut Co
2065 Geer Rd
PO Box 987
Hughson, CA 95326-9614
209-883-4491
Fax: 209-883-2435 info@midvalleynut.com
www.midvalleynut.com
Processor and importer of walnuts
President: Regina Arnold
mheskin@belkorpag.com
Sales: Mary Valdez
Production Manager: Billy Casazza
Estimated Sales: $4.6 Million
Number Employees: 100-249
Type of Packaging: Consumer, Private Label, Bulk

8256 Mid-Atlantic Foods Inc
8978 Glebe Park Dr
Easton, MD 21601-7004
410-822-7500
Fax: 410-822-1266 800-922-4688
sales@seaclam.com www.seawatch.com
Canned and frozen clams and seafood chowders, sauces and soups, clam juice
President: Bob Brennan
CEO: Steve Gordon
Marketing Director: Brian Shea
Contact: Betty Bain
bbain@seaclam.com
Estimated Sales: Less Than $500,000
Number Employees: 10-19
Square Footage: 33000
Type of Packaging: Consumer, Food Service, Private Label
Brands:
   Gordon's Chesapeake Classics
   Mid-Atlantic
   Pot O' Gold
   Tucker's Cove
   Worcester

8257 Mid-Eastern Molasses Company
701 Seafarer Cir
Jupiter, FL 33477-9042
561-624-2843
Fax: 561-624-7060 memcomolas@aol.com
Molasses

8258 Mid-Pacific Hawaii Fishery
Old Airport Road
Hilo, HI 96720
808-935-6110
Fax: 808-961-6859
Processor and exporter of fresh tuna, marlin and shark
Owner: John Romero
Estimated Sales: $2.5-5 Million
Number Employees: 7
Type of Packaging: Consumer, Food Service
Brands:
   Mid Pacific

8259 Mid-South Fish Company
P.O.Box 185
Aubrey, AR 72311-0185
870-295-5600
Fax: 870-295-3559
Owner: Algie Jolly
Estimated Sales: $.5-1 million
Number Employees: 1-4

8260 Midamar
1105 60th Ave SW
Cedar Rapids, IA 52404-7212
319-362-3711
Fax: 319-362-4111 800-362-3711
info@midamar.com www.midamar.com
Halal food products including crescent chicken, ethnic sauces, beef, lamb, shawarma, turkey and pizzas.
President: Bill Aossey
baossey@midamar.com
Estimated Sales: $20-50 Million
Number Employees: 50-99

8261 Midas Foods Intl
10750 Capital St
Oak Park, MI 48237-3134
248-544-4574
Fax: 248-544-4384 877-728-2379
sales@midasfoods.com www.midasfoods.com
Dry mix foods and bases including gravies, sauces, cheese sauce, soup bases, batter products .They manufacturer dry powdered mixes for food processing and national restauraunt chains.
Owner: Richard Elias
relias@midasfoods.com
Number Employees: 10-19
Square Footage: 180000
Parent Co: MiDAS Foods International
Type of Packaging: Food Service, Bulk
Brands:
   American Saucery

8262 Middlebury Cheese Company
11275 W 250 N
Middlebury, IN 46540-7708
574-825-9511
Fax: 574-825-1102 800-262-2505
www.heritageridgecreamery.com
Cheeses including cheddar, colby, colby jack, monterey jack, pepper jack
President: Dick Bylsma
dbylsma@agropur.com
CEO: Richard Guggisber
CEO: Dick Bylsma
Plant Manager: David Gall
Year Founded: 1979
Estimated Sales: $20-50 Million
Number Employees: 50-99

8263 Middlefield Cheese House
15815 Nauvoo Rd
Middlefield, OH 44062-8501
440-632-5228
Fax: 440-632-5604 800-327-9477
shop@middlefieldcheese.com
www.rothenbuhlercheesemakers.com
Swiss cheese, cheese spreads, apple butters and jams, maple syrup and maple popcorn, beef sticks, summer sausage, beef jerky
President: Ann Rothenbuhler
Contact: Blake Andres
blake@ddcclinic.org
Plant Manager: Steve Ilg
Estimated Sales: $130,000
Number Employees: 10-19
Square Footage: 8000
Type of Packaging: Bulk
Brands:
   Middlefield

Food Manufacturers / A-Z

8264 Middleswarth Potato Chips
181 E State St
Kingston, PA 18704-1097
570-288-2447
Fax: 570-288-1381 toddhestor@hotmail.com
www.middleswarthchips.com
Potato chips including regular, barbecue, waffle style, sour cream and onion and salt and vinegar
President: Bob Middleswarth
VP: Anna Middleswarth
Manager: Jim Cobern
Estimated Sales: $3.3 Million
Number Employees: 10-19
Square Footage: 240000
Type of Packaging: Consumer, Food Service, Bulk

8265 Midwest Blueberry Farms
13720 Tyler St
Holland, MI 49424-9418
616-399-2133
Fax: 616-399-2133
Blueberries
Owner: Richard Keil
Estimated Sales: Under $300,000
Number Employees: 5-9
Brands:
  Midwest Blueberry Farms

8266 Midwest Food
3100 W 36th St
Chicago, IL 60632-2304
773-927-8870
Fax: 773-927-8715 admin@midwestfoods.com
Canned spaghetti dinners and stew including beef, chicken and meatball
President: Erin Fitzgerald
Number Employees: 100-249
Parent Co: Owatonna Canning Company
Type of Packaging: Food Service, Private Label

8267 Midwest Foodservice News
2736 Sawbury Boulevard
Columbus, OH 43235-4579
614-336-0710
Fax: 614-336-0713
A regional food service publication with more than 28,000 readers in Ohio, Michigan, Indiana, Kentucky, Pennsylvania, and West Virginia

8268 Midwest Frozen Foods, Inc.
2185 Leeward Ln
Hanover Park, IL 60133-6026
630-784-0123
Fax: 630-784-0424 866-784-0123
Midwest Frozen Foods provides in house and private label frozen fruits and vegetables to the retail, food services and industrial manufacturing sectors.
President: Zafar Iqbal
VP: Athar Siddiq
Operations: Rob Linchesky
Production: Jose Manjarrez
Estimated Sales: $5 Million
Number Employees: 18
Number of Brands: 2
Number of Products: 100+
Square Footage: 20000
Type of Packaging: Food Service, Private Label, Bulk

8269 Midwest Nut Co
3105 Columbia Ave NE
Minneapolis, MN 55418-1896
612-781-6596
Fax: 612-781-6728 800-328-5502
Snack foods including salty and trail mixes and roasted and raw seeds including pumpkin and sunflower; also, confections
President: Laure Rockman
laurerockman@qwestoffice.net
Plant Manager: Tim Fischer
Estimated Sales: $3 Million
Number Employees: 10-19
Square Footage: 160000
Type of Packaging: Consumer, Food Service, Private Label, Bulk
Brands:
  Aristo Snacks
  Dijon Crunch
  Fun Foods
  Giant Cashews
  Hokey Pokey
  Midwest

8270 Midwest Seafood
5500 Emerson Way
Suite A
Indianapolis, IN 46226-1477
317-466-1027
Fax: 317-466-1033
Estimated Sales: $1-3 Million
Number Employees: 5-9

8271 Miesse Candies
118 N Water St # 102
Lancaster, PA 17603-5597
717-392-6011
Fax: 717-392-3898 miessecandies@gmail.com
www.miessecandies.com
Hard, soft and chocolate candy
Owner: Tracy Artus
miessecandies@gmail.com
Estimated Sales: Below $5 Million
Number Employees: 10-19

8272 Mighty Leaf Tea
136 Mitchell Blvd
San Rafael, CA 94903
415-491-2650
Fax: 415-472-1780 877-698-5323
www.mightyleaf.com
Whole-leaf tea blends
CEO: Gary Shinner
Contact: Rafael Chacon
rafael@mightyleaf.com
Estimated Sales: Below $5 Million
Number Employees: 5-9

8273 Mighty Soy Inc
1227 S Eastern Ave
Los Angeles, CA 90022-4809
323-266-6969
Fax: 323-266-3844 www.mightysoy.com
Soy milk
President: Maung Myint
VP/Secretary: Gin Lee
Estimated Sales: $486,000
Number Employees: 10-19
Square Footage: 16000

8274 Mignardise
1963 Patrick Farrar
Suite 200
Chambly, QC J3L 4N7
Canada
450-447-0777
info@mignardise.ca
www.mignardise.ca
Cakes/pastries, cookies.
Marketing: Joan Cartier

8275 Miguel's Stowe Away
17 Town Farm Ln
Stowe, VT 05672
802-253-8900
Fax: 802-253-3946 800-448-6517
mexicanfoods@miguels.com
Processor and exporter of Mexican food products including salsa cruda, blue and white corn tortilla chips, red chili sauce, flavored salsa and smoked jalapeno
President: Christopher Pierson
Regional Sales Manager: Tim Couture
Estimated Sales: $3-5 Million
Number Employees: 1-4
Square Footage: 20000
Type of Packaging: Consumer, Food Service, Bulk
Brands:
  Miguel's

8276 Mikaela's Simply Divine
288 Route 46
Dover, NJ 07801
Fax: 866-648-7530 866-659-1553
info@sdbiscotti.com mikaelassimplydivine.com
Gluten-free biscotti
President & CEO: Mikaela Rae
CFO: Mark Leone
Operations: Christine Gold
Number of Brands: 1
Number of Products: 6
Type of Packaging: Consumer
Brands:
  MIKAELA'S SIMPLY DIVINE

8277 Mikawaya LLC
5563 Alcoa Ave
Vernon, CA 90058-3730
323-587-5504
Fax: 213-625-0943 Sales@mikawayausa.com
Japanese pastries and ice cream
President: Frances Hashimoto
CEO: Jerry Bucan
jerry@mikawayausa.com
CFO: Joel Friedman
Estimated Sales: $5-10 Million
Number Employees: 20-49
Type of Packaging: Private Label
Brands:
  Mikawaya
  Mochi Ice Cream

8278 Mike & Jean's Berry Farm
16234 Kamb Rd.
Mt Vernon, WA 98273-8865
360-424-7220
Fax: 360-424-7225 mike@mikeandjeans.com
www.mikeandjeans.com
Fresh cauliflower, strawberries and raspberries; also, frozen strawberries and raspberries
Owner: Michael Youngquist
Co-Owner: Jeanne Youngquist
Manager: Mike Youngquist
mike@mikeandjeans.com
Year Founded: 1889
Estimated Sales: $20-50 Million
Number Employees: 20-49
Type of Packaging: Food Service, Private Label

8279 Mike's Beverage Company
249 Dufferin St.
Toronto, ON M6K 1Z5
Canada
647-428-3123
Subsidiary of Labatt Breweries of Canada. The company also sells coolers, ciders and flavoured malt beverages, including Palm Bay, Mike's Hard, Okanagan Cider, American Vintage Hard Iced Teas and Bud Lime-a-Ritas
Director of Marketing: Sung Kang
Senior Sales Manager: Mark Haynes
Parent Co: Labatt Brewing Company
Brands:
  American Vintage Hard Iced Teas
  Bud Lime-a-Ritas
  Mike's Hard
  Okanagan Cider
  Palm Bay

8280 Mike's Hot Honey
67 West St
Suite 202
Brooklyn, NY 11222
347-450-4722
mikeshothoney.com
Chili pepper-infused honey
Founder: Michael Kurtz
Year Founded: 2011

8281 Mike's Mighty Good
PO Box 2205
Woodland, CA 95776-2205
530-669-6870
Fax: 530-669-6875 www.rightfoods.com
Soups, prepared salads and hot cereals.
Brand Manager: Carolyn Vinnicombe
Brands:
  Dr. McDougall's Right Foods(c)

8282 Mikesell's Potato ChipCompany
330 Leo Street
Po Box 115
Dayton, OH 45404
937-228-9400
Fax: 937-461-5707 www.mikesells.com
Mike-Sell's Potato Chips include original, groovy, old fashiioned, reduced fat, and assorted flavors including barbecue, cheddar and sour cream, sour cream, green onion, salt and vinegar and smoked bacon. Additional products include pretzels, regular and cheese puffcorn, cheese curls, corn chips, tortilla chips, pork rinds and salsa dip.
President & CEO: Charles Shive
CFO: Paul McNiel
Executive VP, Sales: Phil Kazar
Marketing Director: Luke Mapp
Estimated Sales: $25-49 Million
Number Employees: 270
Number of Brands: 1

Food Manufacturers / A-Z

Type of Packaging: Consumer, Food Service
Brands:
    Mikesell's

8283 Mikey's
Scottsdale, AZ 85254
eatmikeys.com
English muffins, muffin tops, sliced bread, pizza crust, pockets and tortillas

8284 Mikey's
480-696-2483
info@mikeysmuffins.com
www.eatmikeys.com
Gluten-free, dairy-free, soy-free, and paleo English muffins, muffin tops, sliced bread, pizza crusts, tortillas, and pizza pockets
Founder/CEO: Michael Tierney
Year Founded: 2014

8285 Miko Meat
230 Kekuanaoa Street
Hilo, HI 96720-6427
808-935-0841
Fax: 808-935-2781
Sausages and hot dogs
President: Ernest Matsumura
General Manager: Matt Asano
Estimated Sales: $620 K
Number Employees: 5-9

8286 Milan Provision Co
10815 Roosevelt Ave
Corona, NY 11368-2538
718-899-7678
Fax: 718-335-3354
Mexican meat
Owner: Salvatore Laurita
milanprovisions@aol.com
Estimated Sales: $1-3 Million
Number Employees: 10-19
Type of Packaging: Consumer, Food Service, Private Label, Bulk

8287 Milani
2905 Highway 61 N
Muscatine, IA 52761
800-442-5242
www.precisionfoods.com
Seasonings, salad dressings, sugar replacements, salt substitutes and base mixes
CEO: Gage Kent
CFO: Mark Dunsmore
Manager of Milani Foods: Linda Fortino
Number Employees: 1-4
Parent Co: Kent Precision Foods Group
Type of Packaging: Consumer, Food Service, Bulk

8288 Milano Bakery Inc
433 S Chicago St
Joliet, IL 60436-2268
815-727-2253
Fax: 815-727-3116 milanobakery@comcast.net
www.milanobakery.com
Italian bread, buns and rolls, wedding cakes and other speciality cakes, fruit cakes, strudels and coffee.
President: Mario DeBenedetti
Vice President: Darin DeBenedetti
Estimated Sales: $1-10 Million
Number Employees: 50-99

8289 Milano's Of New York City
56 Little West 12th St.
New York, NY 10014
800-643-6328
info@milanosausage.com
www.milanosausage.com
Manufacturer of cured meats.
Founder and CEO: Michael Milano

8290 Milat Vineyards Winery
1091 Saint Helena Hwy S
St Helena, CA 94574-2268
707-963-0758
Fax: 707-963-0168 800-546-4528
Wines including Chenin Blanc, Chardonnay, Merlot, Cabernet Sauvignon, Zinfandel, Zivio and dessert wines.
Owner: Mike Milat
mike@milat.com
Estimated Sales: $1-2.5 Million
Number Employees: 1-4
Brands:
    Milat Vineyards

8291 Mild Bill's Spices
PO Box 1303
Ennis, TX 75120
972-875-2975
http://www.mildbills.com/
Processor and exporter of chili powder, seasoning blends and barbecue spices, salsa, relish
Owner: Bill Dees
Co-Owner: Tamara Dees
Type of Packaging: Consumer, Food Service
Brands:
    Big Bruce's Gunpowder Chili
    Fire Marshall's Cajun

8292 Milea Estate Vineyard
40 Hollow Circle Rdl
Staatsburg, NY 12580
845-264-0403
Fax: 845-389-0313 info@mileaestatevineyard.com
www.mileaestatevineyard.com
Pinot Noir, Riesling, Chardonnay, Vignoles, Traminette, Ros, and sparkling wine
Co-Founder: Barry Milea
Co-Founder: Ed Evans
Co-Founder: Bruce Tripp
Year Founded: 2015
Number of Brands: 1
Number of Products: 10
Type of Packaging: Consumer, Private Label
Brands:
    Milea Estate Vineyard

8293 Miles of Chocolate
Austin, TX
milesofchocolate.com
Baked chocolate dessert
Co-founder: Miles Compton
Co-founder: Ben Welch

8294 Miljoco Corp
200 Elizabeth St
Mt Clemens, MI 48043-1643
586-777-4280
Fax: 586-777-7891 888-888-1498
info@mijoco.com www.miljoco.com
Manufacturers standard and custom thermometers.
President: Howard M Trerice
htrerice@miljoco.com
Reaserch Development: Heath Trerice
Quality Control: Bruce Trerice
Marketing: Mike Mroz
Sales: Tom Adams
Public Relations: Mike Mroz
Plant Manager: Alex Jakob
Purchasing: Kimberly Trerice
Estimated Sales: $10-20 Million
Number Employees: 20-49
Square Footage: 94000
Brands:
    Miljoco

8295 Milk Specialties Global
7500 Flying Cloud Dr
Suite 500
Eden Prairie, MN 55344
952-942-7310
Fax: 952-942-7611 www.milkspecialties.com
Dairy protein ingredients
President/Owner: Eddie Wells
CEO: Dave Lenzmeier
davelenzmeier@milkspecialties.com
Estimated Sales: $35 Million
Number Employees: 500-999

8296 MilkBoy Swiss Chocolate
605 Montgomery St
Brooklyn, NY 11225
www.milkboy.com
Swiss chocolate
Number of Brands: 1
Number of Products: 10
Type of Packaging: Consumer
Brands:
    MILKBOY

8297 Milkadamia
8100 S Madison St
Burr Ridge, IL 60527
630-861-2105
hello@milkadamia.com
www.milkadamia.com
Macadamia milk

8298 (HQ)Milky Way Jersey Farm Inc
220 Hidden Hills Rd
Starr, SC 29684-8809
864-352-2014
www.scmilkywayfarm.com
Milk
Co-Owner: Sherrie Peeler
Co-Owner: Lloyd Peeler
Manager: Davis Peeler
Number Employees: 1-4

8299 Milky Whey Inc
910 Brooks St # 203
Suite 203
Missoula, MT 59801-5784
406-542-7373
Fax: 406-542-7377 800-379-6455
dairy@themilkywhey.com
www.themilkywhey.com
Whey proteins and dry dairy ingredients including nonfat dry milk, whole milk, whey powder, butter, buttermilk powder, caseinates, lactose, nondairy creamers, whey protein concentrates and isolates, and cheese powders
President: Curt Pijanowski
curt@themilkywhey.com
CFO: Steve Schmidt
Vice President: Dan Finch
Operations Manager: Carla Messerly
Reception: Tony Cavanaugh
Estimated Sales: $1.2 Million
Number Employees: 10-19
Type of Packaging: Consumer, Private Label, Bulk

8300 Mill Cove Lobster Pound
381 Barters Island Rd
Trevett, ME 4571
207-633-3340
Fax: 207-633-7206 www.millcovelobster.com
Processor and wholesaler/distributor of seafood including lobster, shrimp, frozen cod, ocean perch, pollack, clams and oysters
President: Jeff Lewis
mclobster@roadrunner.com
Estimated Sales: $4-5 Million
Number Employees: 10-19
Type of Packaging: Consumer

8301 Mill Creek Vineyards
P.O.Box 758
Healdsburg, CA 95448
707-431-2121
Fax: 707-431-1714 877-349-2121
brian@mcvonline.com www.millcreekwinery.com
Wines
Proprietor: William Kreck
kreck@millcreekwinery.com
General Manager: Yvonne Kreck
Winemaker: Jeremy Kreck
Wholesale Sales: John Miller
Wine Club, Director of Retail Operations: Bruce Thomas
Bookkeeper: Julie Ricetti
IT: Brian Kreck
Estimated Sales: Below $5 Million
Number Employees: 10-19
Type of Packaging: Private Label
Brands:
    Felta Springs
    Mill Creek Vineyards
    Reflections

8302 Mill Haven Foods LLC
211 Leer St
New Lisbon, WI 53950-1170
608-562-6455
brian@millhavenfoods.com
www.millhavenfoods.com
Dairy
President: Hollie Slater
Partner: Brian Slater
brian@millhavenfoods.com
Vice President: Bruce Ritchart
Quality Assurance Manager: Chris Faber
Owner/Sales: Brian Slater
International Sales: Chris Dart
Number Employees: 20-49

Food Manufacturers / A-Z

8303 Millbrook Vineyards
26 Wing Rd
Millbrook, NY 12545-5017
845-677-8383
Fax: 845-677-6186   800-662-9463
millbrookwinery@millwine.com
www.millbrookwine.com
Wine
Owner: John Dyson
millbrookwinery@millwine.com
CFO: Eric Grans
General Manager/Sales Manager: Gary Goddard
Director of Marketing: Stacy Hudson
Director of Sales: Scott Koster
Estimated Sales: $5-10 Million
Number Employees: 10-19
Type of Packaging: Private Label
Brands:
 Millbrook

8304 Mille Lacs Gourmet Foods
P.O.Box 8919
Madison, WI 53590
608-837-8535
Fax: 608-825-6463   800-843-1381
wjones@millelacs.com   www.millelacs.com
Gourmet cheeses and chocolates
President: Jay Singer
VP: John Manzer
President: Jay Singer
Sales Director: David Sandorn
Estimated Sales: $5-10 Million
Number Employees: 20-49
Brands:
 Degeneve
 Heart of Wisconsin
 Mille Lacs

8305 Mille Lacs Wild Rice Corp
25300 Paddy Ave
PO Box 200
Aitkin, MN 56431
218-927-2740
800-626-3809
info@canoewildrice.com   www.canoewildrice.com
Processor and exporter of kosher wild rice
President: Chris Ratuski
Estimated Sales: $2.5 Million
Number Employees: 10-19
Type of Packaging: Consumer, Food Service, Private Label, Bulk
Brands:
 Canoe

8306 Millen Fish
PO Box 864
Millen, GA 30442-864
478-982-4988
Fax: 912-982-1746
Fish and fish products
President: David McMillian
Estimated Sales: $3-5 Million
Number Employees: 10-19

8307 Miller Baking
1415 North 5th St
Milwaukee, WI 53212
414-347-2300
www.pretzilla.com
Pretzel bread, buns and snacks
Owner: Brian Miller

8308 Miller Brothers PackingCompany
1118 Highway 82 East
Sylvester, GA 31791
229-776-2014
Fax: 229-776-4728
Beef, sausage, pork, lamb and ostrich including emu and rhea; slaughtering services available
President/Co-Owner: Otis Miller
VP/Co-Owner: Dan Miller
Estimated Sales: $5-10 Million
Number Employees: 10-19
Type of Packaging: Food Service, Bulk
Brands:
 Daeab
 Gold Nugget

8309 Miller Johnson Seafood
4310 Heron Bay Loop Road S
Coden, AL 36523-3714
251-873-4444
Fax: 252-729-1427
Seafood
Owner: Miller Johnson

8310 Miller's Cheese Corp
196 28th Street
Brooklyn, NY 11232
718-965-1840
Fax: 718-965-0979
customerservice@millerscheesecorp.com
Kosher cheese. Founded in 1898.
Owner: Meyer Thurm
Marketing Director: Yudi Sherer
Sales: Sruly Sherer
Estimated Sales: $5 Million
Number Employees: 1-4
Type of Packaging: Consumer

8311 Miller's Country Hams
7110 Highway 190
Dresden, TN 38225-2276
731-364-3940
Fax: 731-364-5338   800-622-0606
millersham@crunet.com   http://www.crunet.com
Country ham
President: Jan Frick
Quality Control: Mark Mash
Vice President: Mark Mash
CFO: Sharon Burress
Production Manager: Linda Burcham
Plant Manager: Barry King
Estimated Sales: $5-10 Million
Number Employees: 20-49
Brands:
 Miller's Country Ham

8312 Miller's Meat Market
1524 S Main St
Red Bud, IL 62278-1316
618-282-3334
Fax: 618-282-7799   meatman@htc.net
www.yahoo.com
Fresh and cured meats including beef, pork, elk, buffalo, sausage, etc.; also, slaughtering services available
Owner: Kevin Miller
meatman@htc.net
Estimated Sales: $300,000-500,000
Number Employees: 5-9
Square Footage: 20000
Type of Packaging: Consumer, Food Service, Private Label

8313 Miller's Mustard LLC
139 Golfview Dr.
Gibsonia, PA 15044
412-894-7172
Fax: 412-894-7143   info@millersmustard.com
www.millersmustard.com
Manufacturer of mustard.
Co-Founder: Robb Miller
miller2@zoominternet.net
Co-Founder: Carol Miller

8314 Millflow Spice Corp.
60 Davids Dr
Hauppauge, NY 11788
Fax: 631-231-5500   866-227-8355
info@castellaimports.com
www.millflowspicecorp.com
Food colors, flavoring extracts, spices, seasonings and sauces including pesto, Worcestershire, soy, barbecue, hot and smoke
President: Zane Moses
Estimated Sales: $2.6 Million
Number Employees: 21
Parent Co: Regal Extract Company
Type of Packaging: Consumer, Food Service, Private Label, Bulk
Brands:
 Bonton
 Growers Company
 Millflow
 Regal

8315 Milliaire Winery
276 Main St
Murphys, CA 95247-9564
209-728-1658
Fax: 209-736-1915   wines@milliairewinery.com
www.milliairewinery.com
Wines
Manager: Jana Nadler
Manager: Liz Millier
lmillier@goldrush.com
Estimated Sales: $160,000
Number Employees: 5-9
Brands:
 Milliaire Winery

8316 Millie's Pierogi
129 Broadway
Chicopee Falls, MA 01020
413-594-4991
800-743-7641
ann@milliespierogi.com   www.milliespierogi.com
Fully cooked pierogies including cabbage, potato and cheese, cheese, prune and blueberry.
President: Ann Kerigan
Estimated Sales: Less than $500,000
Number Employees: 5-9
Brands:
 Millie's Pierogi

8317 Milligan & Higgins
PO Box 506
Johnstown, NY 12095
518-762-4638
Fax: 518-762-7039   info@milligan1868.com
www.milligan1868.com
Manufacturer, importer and exporter of kosher edible and technical gelatins.
Year Founded: 1868
Parent Co: Hudson Industries Corporation
Type of Packaging: Bulk

8318 Milling Sausage Inc
629 S 10th Street
Milwaukee, WI 53204
414-645-2677
www.millingsausage.com
Sausages and frankfurters
Owner: Kate Mikolic
kmikolic@milwauke.org
Number Employees: 1-4
Number of Products: 10
Type of Packaging: Bulk

8319 Millrose Restaurant
45 S Barrington Rd
South Barrington, IL 60010-9508
847-382-7673
Fax: 847-382-7693   800-464-5576
manager@millroserestaurant.com
Beer
Owner: William Rose
COO: Mike Sheridan
Director Manufacturing: Thomas Sweeney
Estimated Sales: $5-10 Million
Number Employees: 100-249

8320 Mills Brothers Intl
16000 Christensen Rd
Suite 300
Seattle, WA 98188-2967
206-575-3000
Fax: 206-957-1362   mbi@millsbros.com
www.millsbros.com
Specialty and organic grains, dried peas, dried beans, lentils, millet rice and corn products including popcorn kernels, flour, grits, meal and starch
President: Eric Mills
Year Founded: 1982
Estimated Sales: $36306000
Number Employees: 50-99
Square Footage: 26000
Type of Packaging: Consumer, Food Service, Private Label, Bulk
Brands:
 Cascade
 Mills Brothers International

8321 Mills Coffee Roasting Co
1058 Broad St
Providence, RI 02905-1600
401-781-7860
Fax: 401-781-7978   888-781-5282
www.thequeenbean.com
Coffee
President: David Mills
millscoffee@aol.com
Plant Manager: Mike Candy
Estimated Sales: Below $5 Million
Number Employees: 10-19
Type of Packaging: Private Label

Food Manufacturers / A-Z

8322 Mills Seafood Ltd.
5 Mills Street
Bouctouche, NB E4S 3S3
Canada
506-743-2444
Fax: 506-743-8497 millsseafood.ca
Seafood processor
Owner: Steven Mills
Vice President: Marie Allain
Quality Control: George Robichaud
Plant Manager: Laurie Allain
Number Employees: 50-99
Type of Packaging: Food Service

8323 Millstream Brewing Co
835 48th Ave
Amana, IA 52203-8122
319-622-3672
Fax: 319-622-6516
Beers, ales and lagers
Owner: Chris Priebe
chris@millstreambrewing.com
Estimated Sales: Below $5 Million
Number Employees: 10-19
Type of Packaging: Consumer, Food Service
Brands:
 Millstream

8324 Milmar Food Group
One 6 1/2 Station Road
Goshen, NY 10924
845-294-5400
Fax: 845-294-6687 www.milmarfoodgroup.com
Frozen foods including breakfast selections, vegetarian, chicken, burrito, and pre-plated meal products
President: Martin Hoffman
EVP: Dov Peikes
Marketing Director: Rita O'Connor
Sales Director: Cindy Cohen
Purchasing: Barry Werk
Year Founded: 2000
Estimated Sales: $30 Million
Number Employees: 250
Number of Brands: 3
Number of Products: 100
Square Footage: 60000
Type of Packaging: Consumer, Food Service, Private Label, Bulk
Brands:
 Mrs. Veggies
 No Forks Required
 Spring Valley

8325 Milne Fruit Products Inc
804 Bennett Ave
P.O. Box 111
Prosser, WA 99350-1267
509-786-2611
Fax: 509-786-1724 selkins@milnefruit.com
www.milnefruit.com
Processes fruit juice, fruit juice concentrates, purees, custom blends and nutritional ingredients. Flavors include concord grape, strawberry, cranberry, raspberry, blueberry and cherry and others
President: Randy Hageman
rhageman@milnefruit.com
General Manager: Randall Hageman
Research & Development: Eric Johnson
Quality Control: Eric Johnson
Sales Director: Shannon Elkins
Number Employees: 20-49
Parent Co: Ocean Spray Cranberries
Type of Packaging: Bulk

8326 Milnot Company
120 W Saint John Street
Litchfield, IL 62056-2169
217-324-2146
800-877-6455
www.milnot.com
Dairy products.
President: Christoph Rudolph
Number Employees: 20-49
Parent Co: Milnot Company
Type of Packaging: Consumer, Private Label, Bulk

8327 Milnot Company
1 Strawberry Ln.
Orrville, OH 44667
888-656-3245
www.milnot.com
Milk and dairy products.
CEO, Eagle Family Foods: Bernard Kreilmann
Year Founded: 1912
Estimated Sales: $100-500 Million
Number Employees: 250-499
Number of Brands: 1
Parent Co: Eagle Family Foods Group LLC
Type of Packaging: Consumer, Private Label
Brands:
 Milnot

8328 Milone Brothers Coffee Co
1413 Lone Palm Ave
Modesto, CA 95351-2860
209-526-0865
Fax: 209-526-1652 800-974-8500
mbc@milone.com www.milone.com
Fresh roasted whole bean highest grade coffees. Custom blending/roasting, espresso and coffee machine experts
Owner: Joe Milone
joe@milone.com
Estimated Sales: $1 Million
Number Employees: 5-9
Square Footage: 12000
Type of Packaging: Food Service, Bulk
Brands:
 Milone Brothers

8329 Milos
125 West 55th Street
New York, NY 10019
212-245-7400
Fax: 212-245-4828 newyork@estiatoriomilos.com
www.milos.ca
Frozen potato cakes
Owner: Costas Spiliadis
Contact: Billy Mack
billy@firstcoastal.com
Estimated Sales: $2.5-5 Million
Number Employees: 10-19

8330 Milos Whole World Gourmet
94 Columbus Rd
Athens, OH 45701-1312
740-589-6456
Fax: 740-594-9151 866-589-6456
info@miloswholeworld.com
www.gourmetyourway.biz
Pasta sauces and salad dressings
President/Owner: Jonathan Milo
Wholesale Sales Manager: Maryjane Burch
Production Manager: Mark Temple
Estimated Sales: Less Than $500,000
Number Employees: 1-4

8331 Milroy Canning Company
100 South Railroad Street
PO Box 125
Milroy, IN 46156
765-629-2221
Fax: 765-629-2645
Canned tomatoes
President: Robert Tobian
Vice President: Andrew Tobian
Estimated Sales: $10-20 Million
Number Employees: 20-49
Type of Packaging: Consumer

8332 Milsolv Corporation
PO Box 444
Butler, WI 53007-0444
262-252-3550
Fax: 262-252-5250 800-558-8501
Beverages, confectionery, canned foods, processed cheese, bakery, meat, seafood, dairy
Chairman: Ed mills
Sales: Mark Hartung
Brands:
 Milsolv

8333 Milton A. Klein Company
PO Box 363
New York, NY 10021-0006
516-829-3400
Fax: 516-829-3427 800-221-0248
President: Irene Klein
VP: Allen Klein
Number Employees: 15
Square Footage: 6800

8334 Milton's Local
PO Box 1293
Hopewell, VA 23860-1293
804-925-2644
info@miltonslocal.com
miltonslocal.com
Sausages and bacon
Marketing Coordinator: Kelsey Ducker

8335 Milwhite Inc
5487 Padre Island Hwy
Brownsville, TX 78521-8300
956-547-1970
Fax: 956-547-1999 800-442-0082
www.milwhite.com
Manufacturer and importer of clay, talcs, calcium carbonate, barium sulfate, attapulgite, bentonite and other nonmetallic minerals; exporter of aflatoxin binders.
President: Mike Hughes
mhughes@milwhite.com
Accounting & Financial Manager: Hector Guerrero
Director, Health Science Division: Dr Orlando Osuna
Quality Assurance: Steve Lopez
Customer Service: Paola Tella
Estimated Sales: $20-50 Million
Number Employees: 20-49
Number of Brands: 5
Type of Packaging: Private Label, Bulk
Brands:
 Blanca
 Gel B
 Milsorb
 Super Gel B
 Tdm

8336 Mimac Glaze
271 Glidden Road
Unit 17
Brampton, ON L6W 1H9
Canada
905-457-7737
Fax: 905-457-9828 877-990-9975
dave@mimacglaze.com www.mimacglaze.com
Icing stabilizers and ready-to-use icings
President: W David Miles
Secretary/Treasurer: Marion Miles
Production Manager: Werner Barduhn
Estimated Sales: $975,000
Number Employees: 6
Square Footage: 26400
Type of Packaging: Consumer, Food Service
Brands:
 Paragon
 Supreme

8337 Mimi's Mountain Mixes
120 Chadwick Ave
Suite 16
Hendersonville, NC 28792
937-380-5600
info@mimismixes.com
www.mimismountainmixes.com
Bread, cake, candy, cookie, donut, pancake and soft pretzel mixes.
President: Lin Johnson-Carlson

8338 Mims Meat Company
12634 E Freeway
Houston, TX 77015-5614
713-453-0151
Fax: 713-453-6714
Meat products including beef, pork, poultry, lamb, veal and wild game meats.
President & CEO: Dan Mims
danmims@mimsmeatcompany.com
Treasurer & CFO: Mary Mims
Human Resources: James Mercer
Warehouse Operations Manager: Derek Woods
Estimated Sales: $43.36 Million
Number Employees: 110
Parent Co: Glazier Foods

8339 Min Tong Herbs
318 7th St
Oakland, CA 94607-4112
510-873-8677
Fax: 510-873-8671 800-562-5777
mintongherbs@hotmail.com www.mintong.com.tw
Processor and importer of Chinese herbal extracts

Food Manufacturers / A-Z

President: Charles Chang
mintongherbs@aol.com
Vice President: Susan Chang
Sales: Tiffany Zhon
Estimated Sales: $500,000-$1 Million
Number Employees: 10-19
Number of Brands: 1
Type of Packaging: Consumer, Private Label, Bulk
Brands:
   Min Tong

8340 Minas Purely Divine
1355 Rock Mountain Blvd
Stone Mountain, GA 30083-1536
404-508-6222
www.minasgf.com
Allergy-free, gluten free baked goods
Owner: Moses Julbe
mosesjulbe@minasgf.com
Number Employees: 5-9

8341 Mincing Overseas Spice Company
K N Building
10 Tower Road
Dayton, NJ 08810
732-355-9944
Fax: 732-555-9964 mail@mincing.com
www.mincing.com
Importers, processor of spices, seeds and aromatic herbs
President: Manoj Rupaerlia
CFO: K Jobanputra
Quality Controol: Nagy Beskal
Sales: Dorothy Hollomay
Plant Manager: Charles Armgnti
Purchasing: H Ruparelia
Estimated Sales: $.5-1 million
Number Employees: 1-4
Square Footage: 200000
Parent Co: Mincing Trading Corporation

8342 MindFull, Inc.
Hutto, TX 78634
info@mindfull.com
mindfull.com
Organic and electrolyte teas
President/Owner: Grant Burgess
CEO: Matt Jimenez

8343 Mindo Chocolate Makers
11061 Trinkle Rd
Dexter, MI 48130-9443
734-660-5635
info@mindochocolate.com
www.mindochocolate.com
Chocolate
Co-founder: Jose Meza
Co-founder: Barbara Wilson
Number Employees: 1-4

8344 Minerva Cheese Factory
430 Radloff Avenue
PO Box 60
Minerva, OH 44657
330-868-4196
Fax: 330-868-7947 jackie@minervadairy.com
www.cheesehere.com
Dairy products including butter, whey and cheese
Owner: Phillip Muller
VP: Adam Muller
Contact: Venae Banner
vbanner@minervacheese.com
Estimated Sales: $6 Million
Number Employees: 40
Type of Packaging: Consumer, Food Service, Private Label, Bulk

8345 Minerva Dairy Inc
430 Radloff Ave
PO Box 60
Minerva, OH 44657-1400
330-868-4196
Fax: 330-868-7947 www.minervadairy.com
Producer of various cheeses, cheese gift boxes, spreads, butters, meats and condiments.
President: Adam Mueller
CEO: Phil Mueller
phil@minervadairy.com
Treasurer: Venae Watts
Operations Manager: Dave Saling
Purchasing Manager: Anthony Aslanes
Estimated Sales: $25-49.9 Million
Number Employees: 20-49
Number of Brands: 2

Type of Packaging: Consumer, Food Service, Private Label, Bulk
Brands:
   Amish Gourmet
   Minerva

8346 Mingo Bay Beverages
721 Seaboard Street
Myrtle Beach, SC 29577-6520
843-448-5320
Fax: 843-448-4162 mingomoe@aol.com
Processor and exporter of coffee, tea and fruit bases, mixes and concentrates
President: Larry Moses
Estimated Sales: $1-5 Million
Number Employees: 8
Square Footage: 320000
Type of Packaging: Consumer, Food Service, Private Label, Bulk
Brands:
   Mingo Bay Beverages

8347 Mingo River Pecan Company
2005 Babar Ln
P.O. Box 2030
Florence, SC 29503
843-662-2452
Fax: 843-664-2338   800-440-6442
swise@youngplantations.com
www.mingoriverpecans.com
Flavored pecans
Executive Director: Chenen Harvey
Estimated Sales: $20-50 Million
Number Employees: 100-249

8348 Minh Food
1303 W Harris Ave
Pasadena, TX 77506
713-475-1970
Fax: 713-740-7272
Egg rolls
President: Chi Nguyen
COO: William Hirsch
Number Employees: 100-249
Parent Co: Schwann's Sales

8349 Minh Food Corporation
1251 Scarborough Ln
Pasadena, TX 77506
713-740-7200
Fax: 713-740-7205   800-344-7655
Frozen Asian foods
Manager: Cole Lewis
CEO: Ron Minist
Executive VP: Mike Minist
Number Employees: 10-19
Parent Co: Schwann's Sales
Type of Packaging: Consumer, Food Service, Private Label

8350 Mini Pops Inc
208 Tosca Dr
Stoughton, MA 02072-1506
781-436-5864
Fax: 781-533-9033 info@minipopsinc.com
Flavored gluten free, organic, popped sorghum snack
Contact: Chrissy Conti
chrissy.conti@myminipops.com
Number Employees: 1-4

8351 Minn-Dak Farmers Co-Op
7525 Red River Rd.
Wahpeton, ND 58075
701-642-8411
Fax: 701-642-6814 www.mdf.coop
Beet sugar manufacturer.
President/CEO: Kurt Wickstrom
Vice President, Agriculture: Tom Knudsen
Executive VP/CFO: Rick Kasper
Information Technology Director: John Wieser
Vice President, Human Resources/Safety: Sheila Klose
Vice President, Operations: Paul Fry
Year Founded: 1972
Estimated Sales: $214.31 Million
Number Employees: 766
Type of Packaging: Bulk
Other Locations:
   Minn-Dak Farmers Coop.
   Wahpeton ND

8352 Minn-Dak Growers LTD
4034 40th Ave N
PO Box 13276
Grand Forks, ND 58203-3818
701-746-7453
Fax: 701-780-9050 info@minndak.com
www.minndak.com
Buckwheat, mustard, safflower and sunflower
Owner/President/General Manager: Harris Peterson
harris.peterson@minndak.com
Principal/CFO: Mona Kozojed
R&D Director: Mohammad Badaruddin
Quality Control Manager: Liz Carruth
Marketing Director: Kristin Sharp
Sales: Harris Peterson
Public Relations Director: Jaci Peau
Manufacturing Supervisor: Bruce Sondreal
Estimated Sales: $11 Million
Number Employees: 20-49
Number of Brands: 3
Number of Products: 9
Square Footage: 180000
Type of Packaging: Consumer, Food Service, Bulk
Brands:
   Mdgl
   Mdm
   Minn-Dak

8353 Minn-Dak Yeast Co Inc
18175 Red River Rd W
Wahpeton, ND 58075-9697
701-642-3300
Fax: 701-642-1908 www.dakotayeast.com
Fresh bakers' yeast
EVP: Scott Miller
Manager: Richard Ames
rames@mdf.coop
Plant Manager: Richard Ames
Purchasing Director: John Nyquist
Estimated Sales: $9.5 Million
Number Employees: 20-49
Square Footage: 88000
Parent Co: Minn-Dak Farmers Cooperative
Brands:
   Dakota Yeast

8354 Minnehaha Spring Water Company
1906 E 40th Street
Cleveland, OH 44103-3557
216-431-0243
Bottled natural spring water
President: Michael Wright
Number Employees: 20-49
Type of Packaging: Consumer, Food Service, Private Label, Bulk

8355 Minnesota Dehydrated Veg Inc
915 Omland Ave N
PO Box 245
Fosston, MN 56542-1001
218-435-1997
Fax: 218-435-6770 info@mdvcorp.com
www.mdvcorp.com
Dehydrated vegetables
Manager: Jim Noise
Marketing Director: Jam Moyes
ic@mdvcorp.com
CFO: Jim Noyes
CFO: Jordy Alson
Site Manager: Karla Holm
ic@mdvcorp.com
Estimated Sales: $5-10 Million
Number Employees: 50-99
Brands:
   Minnesota Dehydrated Vegetables

8356 Minnesota Hemp Farms
14530 90th St S
Hastings, MN 55033
877-205-4367
www.mnhempfarms.com
Hemp products
President/Owner: John Strohfus
Year Founded: 2016

8357 Minnestalgia Foods LLC
41640 State Highway 65
PO Box 86
Mcgregor, MN 55760-1407
218-768-4917
Fax: 218-768-2543   800-328-6731
minnestalgia.com

Food Manufacturers / A-Z

Wild berry syrups, jams, jellies and sauces, maple syrup, honey and whipped honey; also, wild rice pancake mix and organic wild, cultivated long grain and broken wild rice
Owner: Jay Erckenbrack
minnestalgiawinery@citilink.net
General Manager: Lori Gordon
Estimated Sales: $700,000
Number Employees: 1-4
Square Footage: 6400
Type of Packaging: Consumer, Food Service, Private Label, Bulk
Brands:
 Minnesota Wild

8358 Minnestalgia Foods LLC
41640 State Highway 65
PO Box 86
Mcgregor, MN 55760-1407
218-768-4917
Fax: 218-768-2543 800-328-6731
minnestalgia@citlink.net www.minnestalgia.com
Wines, soup and pancake mixes, berry and maple syrups, honeys, gift baskets and more!
President: Jay Erckenbrack
minnestalgiawinery@citilink.net
Estimated Sales: $1-3 Million
Number Employees: 1-4

8359 Minor Fisheries
176 West Street
Port Colborne, ON L3K 4E2
Canada
905-834-9232
Fax: 905-834-5662 catch@minorfisheries.net
www.minorfisheries.net
Whole, dressed, filleted, fresh and frozen fresh water fish including yellow perch, yellow pickerel, white perch, whitefish, smelt, rock bass, silver bass and lingcod. Founded in 1974
President: Rod Minor
Director: Dan Minor
Estimated Sales: $2.8 Million
Number Employees: 7
Square Footage: 8400
Type of Packaging: Consumer, Bulk

8360 Minsa Corp
4401 82nd St
Suite 1150
Lubbock, TX 79424-3396
806-799-3757
Fax: 806-799-3783 800-852-8291
Specialty corn flour for mixes, available in white, yellow, blue, red and purple corn. Organic, Non-Gmo or Conventional Gluten Free Whole Fiber Certified.
CEO: Rodrigo Ariceaga
CFO: Hubert Torres
Quality Assurance Manager: Sergio Gonzalez
Sales: Ricky Rodriguez
Contact: Penny Blackerby
penny.blackerby@minsa.com
Plant Manager: Jesus Ayala
Estimated Sales: $20-40 Million
Number Employees: 855

8361 Minsley, Inc.
989 S Monterey Ave
Ontario, CA 91761
909-458-1100
Fax: 909-458-1101 info@minsley.com
www.minsley.com
Organic grain bowls and cups
Number of Brands: 1
Number of Products: 10
Type of Packaging: Consumer
Brands:
 MINSLEY

8362 Mint Savor
PO Box 13009
Jersey City, NJ 07303
info@mintsavor.com
www.mintsavor.com
Mints
Sales: Christina Nitsa
Brands:
 Mint Savor
 TEAKS

8363 Minterbrook Oyster Co
12002 114th Street Court Kp N
PO Box 432
Gig Harbor, WA 98329-5058
253-857-5251
Fax: 253-857-5521 www.minterbrookoyster.com
Processor and exporter of fresh and frozen oysters, Manila clams and mussels
President: Harold E Wiksten
COO: Erica Wiksten
mntrerka@aol.com
Sales Manager: Mike Paul
Estimated Sales: $8.6 Million
Number Employees: 5-9
Square Footage: 280
Type of Packaging: Consumer, Food Service, Private Label
Brands:
 Minterbrook

8364 Minus the Moo
196 Quincy St
Dorchester, MA 02121-1996
703-999-7183
minusthemoo.com
Lactose-free ice cream
Co-Founder: Gwen Burlingame

8365 (HQ)Minute Maid Company
PO Box 1734
Atlanta, GA 30301
800-520-2653
www.minutemaid.com
World's leading marketer of premium fruit juices and drinks. Processor of chilled, aseptic and frozen concentrated juices, punches and lemonades including orange, grape, grapefruit, tangerine, lemon, lime, etc.; also, citrus oils
President: Mike Saint John
CEO: E Neville Isdell
Number Employees: 500-999
Parent Co: Coca-Cola Company
Type of Packaging: Consumer, Food Service
Other Locations:
 Minute Maid
 Dinuba CA
 Minute Maid
 Apopka MI
 Minute Maid
 Northampton MA
 Minute Maid
 Paw Paw MI
 Minute Maid
 Waco TX
 Minute Maid
 Petersborough ON
 Minute Maid
 Mississauga ON
Brands:
 Minute Maid
 Minute Maid Juice to Go
 Minute Maid Just 15
 Minute Maid Sparkling

8366 Mira International Foods
1200 Tices Ln Ste 203
East Brunswick, NJ 08816
732-846-5410
Fax: 732-613-7206 800-818-6472
www.miramango.com
Tropical nectars
President: Ramses Awadalla
CEO: Mark Awadalla
Vice President: Pancy Awadalla
Marketing Director: Mariam Gandour
Sales Director: Joseph Awadalla
Public Relations: Mark Awadalla
Estimated Sales: $5-10 Million
Number Employees: 5-9
Square Footage: 96000
Type of Packaging: Private Label
Brands:
 Mira Mango Nectar

8367 Miracapo Pizza
2323 Pratt Blvd
Elk Grove Village, IL 60007
847-631-3500
miracapopizza.com
Premium pizzas, gourmet sandwiches, wraps, paninis, grab-n-go items, breakfast items and desserts. Gluten-free options.
VP, Finance: Dan Hoffman
VP, R&D and Quality Assurance: Lynn Waldman

Year Founded: 1984
Estimated Sales: $200 Million
Number Employees: 200-500
Square Footage: 150000
Brands:
 Bravissimo!
 Connie's Pizza
 Little Lady
 Primerro
 Tenaro

8368 Miracle Noodle
8606 Santa Monica Blvd.
Suite 6920
Los Angeles, CA 90069
800-948-4205
Fax: 310-496-0651 www.miraclenoodle.com
Manufacturer of noodles, rice, and matcha.
President: Jonathan Carp
Vice President: Jill Goldstein

8369 Miracle Tree
Miami, FL 33139
888-590-1555
info@miracletree.org www.miracletree.org
Moringa tea
CEO: Kunal Mirchandani

8370 Miramar Fruit Trading Company
2300 Nw 92nd Ave
Doral, FL 33172-4814
305-883-4774
Fax: 305-883-4773 miramarfruit.4t.com
Canned guava pulp, mango pulp, grated coconut, papaya chunks, guava shells, orange shells, pina colada mix, black beans, green pigeon peas
President: Carlos Unanue
Manager: Maria Miguel
Estimated Sales: $2.5-5 Million
Number Employees: 11
Brands:
 Ancel

8371 Miramar Pickles & Food Products
200 NW 20th Avenue
Fort Lauderdale, FL 33311
954-463-0222
Sauerkraut, pickles, pickled tomatoes
Estimated Sales: $100 Thousand
Number Employees: 1-4
Number of Brands: 1
Brands:
 Miramar

8372 Mirasco
900 Circle 75 Pkwy SE # 1660
Atlanta, GA 30339-3095
770-956-1945
Fax: 770-956-0308 atlanta@mirasco.com
www.mirasco.com
Supplier of meats, poultry and seafood
President: Sami Rizk
sami.rizk@mirasco.com
Estimated Sales: $4.5 Million
Number Employees: 20-49
Type of Packaging: Food Service, Private Label, Bulk

8373 Misfit Juicery
Washington, DC 20036
703-465-5355
Fax: 703-243-6410 misfitjuicery.com
Juices made from imperfect fruits and vegetables
Founder: Elyse Cohen
Number of Brands: 1
Number of Products: 7
Type of Packaging: Consumer
Brands:
 MISFIT

8374 Mishawaka Brewing Company
408 W Cleveland Rd
Granger, IN 46530
574-256-9993
misbrew@aol.com
Seasonal beer, ale, stout, lager and porter
Owner: Thomas R Schmidt
Estimated Sales: $1-2.5 Million
Number Employees: 20-49
Type of Packaging: Consumer, Food Service
Brands:
 Four Horsemen

Food Manufacturers / A-Z

8375 Mishler Packing Co
5680 W 100 N
Lagrange, IN 46761-8605
260-768-4156
Fax: 260-768-4354 800-860-4156
www.mishlersmeats.com
Established in 1947. Manufacturer of pork burger patties.
Co-Owner: Dennis Monson
Co-Owner: Jonathan Monson
Estimated Sales: $20 Million
Number Employees: 20-49
Type of Packaging: Consumer

8376 Mishrun
Edison, NJ 08820
347-495-4320
contactmishrun@gmail.com
www.mishrun.com
Chutneys and relishes
Founder: Rashmi Mehndroo

8377 Miss Ginny's Orginal Vermont Pickle Works
655 N Main Street
Northfield, VT 05663-6829
802-485-3057
Fax: 802-485-3057
Pickles

8378 Miss Jenny's Pickles
6104 Old Orchard Road
Kernersville, NC 27284-3296
336-978-0041
jenny@missjennyspickles.com
www.missjennyspickles.com

8379 Miss Jones Baking Co.
5900 Hollis St
Suite W
Emeryville, CA 94608
www.missjones.co
Clean-label baking mixes
Founder & CEO: Sarah Jones Garibaldi
Number of Brands: 1
Number of Products: 18
Type of Packaging: Consumer
Brands:
  MISS JONES BAKING CO.

8380 Miss Meringue
1709 LA Costa Meadows Dr
San Marcos, CA 92078-5105
760-471-4978
Fax: 760-712-7814 800-561-6516
Meringues and cookies
Owner: Roland D'Abel
CFO: Rick Lamb
Quality Control: Rom William
Estimated Sales: $5-10 Million
Number Employees: 100-249
Brands:
  Miss Meringue
  Splenda(r)

8381 Miss Scarlett's Flowers
1845 Anka St
Juneau, AK 99801-7211
907-586-1766
Fax: 907-586-6545 800-345-6734
Pickled fruits, olives and vegetables; mushrooms, artichokes, asparagus, eggplant, baby corn, green beans, carrots, Brussel sprouts, snow peas, snap peas, zucchini pickles, sweet baby onions, pickled garlic, cocktail tomatoes, babyokra, cap
Owner: Samra Green
missscarletts@gci.net
Co-Owner: Ralph Luper
Estimated Sales: Less Than $500,000
Number Employees: 1-4
Type of Packaging: Private Label
Brands:
  Miss Scarlett

8382 Miss Tea Brooklyn Inc
184 Eagle St
Suite 5A
Brooklyn, NY 11222-1570
718-389-9090
Manufacturer of a variety of teas.
Co-Founder: Nir Kahan
Contact: Revital Shoua
revital@miss-tea.com
Estimated Sales: Less Than $500,000
Number Employees: 1-4

8383 Mission Foods
5860 S Ash Ave
Tempe, AZ 85283-5100
480-491-2511
www.missionfoods.com
Mexican tortillas and tortilla chips
Estimated Sales: $50-100 Million
Number Employees: 250-499
Parent Co: Gruma Corporation
Type of Packaging: Consumer, Food Service, Private Label, Bulk

8384 (HQ)Mission Foods Corp.
1159 Cottonwood Ln.
Suite 200
Irving, TX 75038
214-583-5113
www.missionfoods.com
Authentic Mexican food products, such as tortillas, salas, tostadas, and more.
CEO: Craig Leonard
Year Founded: 1977
Estimated Sales: $1.7 Billion
Number Employees: 5,700
Parent Co: Gruma Corporation
Type of Packaging: Consumer, Food Service, Private Label, Bulk
Brands:
  Diago's
  Diane's
  Guerrero
  Mission

8385 Mission Foods Corp.
5601 Executive Dr.
Irving, TX 75038
972-232-5200
www.missionfoods.com
Corn chips, salsa, tortillas and barbecue sauce
Estimated Sales: $25-49.9 Million
Number Employees: 100-249
Parent Co: Gruma Corporation
Type of Packaging: Consumer, Food Service, Private Label, Bulk

8386 Mission Foods Corp.
5505 E Olympic Blvd
Commerce, CA 90022
323-803-1400
www.missionfoods.com
Mexican food products
Estimated Sales: $20-50 Million
Number Employees: 250-499
Parent Co: Gruma Corporation
Type of Packaging: Consumer, Food Service, Private Label, Bulk

8387 Mission Foodservice
PO Box 2008
Oldsmar, FL 34677-7008
800-443-7994
Fax: 800-272-5207 mission@answers-sys.com
Manufacturer and exporter of Mexican foods including flour and corn tortillas, tortilla chips, pastries, taco and tostada shells
SVP/GM: Robert Smith
Marketing Director: Robin Tobor
VP Sales: Tom Daley
Number Employees: 1,000-4,999
Square Footage: 1680000
Type of Packaging: Consumer, Food Service, Private Label, Bulk
Brands:
  Diago
  Dianes
  Guerrero
  Marias
  Mission

8388 Mission Mountain Winery
82420 US Hwy 93
PO Box 100
Dayton, MT 59914
406-849-5524
Fax: 406-849-5524
info@missionmountainwinery.com
www.missionmountainwinery.com
Wines
President: Thomas Campbell
Estimated Sales: $690,000
Number Employees: 10-19
Brands:
  Mission Mountain

8389 Mission Pharmacal Company
10999 Interstate Hwy. 10 W.
Suite 1000
San Antonio, TX 78230-1355
210-696-8400
Fax: 210-696-6010 www.missionpharmacal.com
Vitamins and nutritional supplements.
President/CEO: Neil Walsdorf
Chairman: Neil Walsdorf
Executive VP/COO: James Walsdorf
Year Founded: 1946
Estimated Sales: $157 Million
Number Employees: 461
Number of Brands: 17
Square Footage: 31000
Type of Packaging: Consumer
Other Locations:
  Commercial Office
  Doylestown PA
  Manufacturing, Distribution & R&D
  Boerne TX
  Specialty Manufacturing & Printing
  San Antonio TX
Brands:
  Aquoral
  Avar-e
  Avar
  Binosto
  CitraNatal
  Eletone
  Ferralet
  Glyderm
  Hyophen
  Liquid KI
  Lithostat
  Oncovite
  Ovace
  Texacort
  Uribel
  UROCKIT-K
  Utira-C

8390 Mission Valley Foods
43032 Christy St
Fremont, CA 94538
408-254-9387
General grocery
Owner: Jayant Patel
Estimated Sales: $990,000
Number Employees: 25
Type of Packaging: Private Label
Brands:
  Brickenridge
  Chef Martin

8391 Mississippi Cheese Straw
741 E Eighth St
Yazoo City, MS 39194-3309
662-746-7171
Fax: 662-746-7162 800-530-7496
info@mscheesestraws.com
www.mscheesestraws.com
Cheese, lemon, and chopped pecan and cinnamon straws and Mississippi mud puppies, cookies, chocolate chip, oatmeal, pecan
President: Hunter Yerger
hyerger@mscheesestraws.com
VP: Robbie Yerger
Estimated Sales: $2.5 Million
Number Employees: 10-19
Square Footage: 40000
Type of Packaging: Consumer
Brands:
  Mississippi Cheese Straws
  Mississippi Mud Pupp
  Original Lemon Straw

8392 Missouri Wine & Gift
2167 W Terra Ln
O Fallon, MO 63366-2366
636-639-9858
missouriwineandgift@centurytel.net
Distributor/wholesaler of wines and wine accessories
Owner: Judy Evans
missouriwineandgift@centurytel.net
Estimated Sales: $110,000
Number Employees: 1-4

Food Manufacturers / A-Z

8393 Mister Bee Potato ChipsCo
512 West Virginia Ave
Parkersburg, WV 26101-1647
304-428-6133
Fax: 304-428-1291 info@misterbee.com
www.misterbee.com
Established in 1951. Manufacturer of potato chips.
Co-Owner: Mary Anne Ketelsen
Co-Owner: Douglas Ketelsen
Co-Owner: James Barton
Co-Owner: Gregory Barton
Co-Owner: Gregory Reed
Sales Exec: Douglas Klein
info@misterbee.com
Estimated Sales: $20-50 Million
Number Employees: 20-49
Type of Packaging: Consumer, Food Service, Bulk
Brands:
  Mister Bee

8394 Mister Cookie Face
One Ice Cream Drive
PO Box 1318
Dunkirk, NY 14048
732-370-5533
Fax: 732-370-4015 800-333-0305
webmaster@fieldbrookfoods.com
www.cookieface.com
Novelty ice cream
President/ CEO: Kenneth Johnson
Controller & VP: Ronald Odebralski
Director Quality: Jack Lockwood
SVP Marketing & Sales: James Masood
Contact: Jack Lindstrand
jack.lindstrand@cookieface.com
Director Operations: Kevin Grismore
VP Purchasing: Robert Griewisch
Estimated Sales: $12.2 Million
Number Employees: 100-249
Square Footage: 80000
Type of Packaging: Consumer, Private Label, Bulk
Brands:
  Mr. Cookie Face

8395 Mister Fish Inc.
288 Rolling Mill Rd
Baltimore, MD 21224-2033
410-288-2722
Fax: 410-288-4757 ed@misterfishinc.com
www.misterfishinc.com
Seafood
Owner: Frank Petilo
Estimated Sales: $1-3 Million
Number Employees: 20-49

8396 Mister Pickle's Inc
540 Auburn Ravine Rd
Auburn, CA 95603-3954
530-885-1000
www.mrpickles.com
Pickles
Owner: Alan Neihaus
Vice President: Scott Wiseman
Estimated Sales: Below $5 Million
Number Employees: 10-19

8397 Mister Snacks Inc
500 Creekside Dr
Amherst, NY 14228-2109
716-691-1500
Fax: 716-210-1010 800-333-6393
www.mistersnacks.com
Snacks, trail mixes, yogurt, candy and chocolate coated items.
President: Michael Stern
VP, Sales: Stephen Stern
VP, Operations: Ed Lilly
Estimated Sales: $10-20 Million
Number Employees: 20-49
Number of Brands: 2
Square Footage: 14
Type of Packaging: Private Label, Bulk
Brands:
  Stone Mountain Snacks
  Sunbird Snacks

8398 Mister Spear
2900 E Harding Way
Stockton, CA 95205-3577
209-464-5365
Fax: 209-464-3846 800-677-7327
misterspear@misterspear.com
www.misterspear.com
Shiitake mushrooms, artichokes, asparagus, avocados, sugar snap peas, tomatoes, bi-color corn, bing cherries, Fuji apples
President: Chip Arnett Jr
Estimated Sales: Less Than $500,000
Number Employees: 1-4
Type of Packaging: Consumer, Food Service
Brands:
  Msi
  Mister Spear

8399 Misty Islands Seafoods
P. O. Box 201 Lepreau
Dipper Harbour, NB E5J 2T1
Canada
506-659-2781
Fax: 506-659-3113
www.mistyharbourseafood.com
Seafood
Manager: Robert Melovidov
Manager: Richard Tremaine
Estimated Sales: $3-5 Million
Number Employees: 1-3
Parent Co: Coastal Enterprises

8400 Misty's Restaurant & Lounge
6235 Havelock Ave
Lincoln, NE 68507-1279
402-466-7222
Fax: 402-466-7222 www.mistyslincoln.com
All-purpose seasonings and Bloody Mary mix
Owner: Reece Hummell
Sales Representative: Dave Walbrecht
Director Operations: Brian Tones
Estimated Sales: $3.8 Million
Number Employees: 50-99
Type of Packaging: Consumer, Food Service

8401 Mitch Chocolate
300 Spagnoli Rd
Melville, NY 11747-3507
631-777-2400
Fax: 631-777-1449 www.misschocolate.com
Hard candy lollypops; wholesaler/distributor of salt water taffy and fundraising boxed chocolates
President: Lawrence Hirsihheimer
VP Operations: Martin Bloomfield
Estimated Sales: $3-5 Million
Number Employees: 5-9
Square Footage: 16000
Type of Packaging: Consumer, Private Label
Brands:
  Frolic

8402 Mitchel Dairies
1591 E 233rd Street
Bronx, NY 10466-3336
718-994-6655
Fax: 718-994-6113
Dairy products including fluid milk
President: Philip Tulotta
Treasurer: Linda Tulotta
Estimated Sales: $110 K
Number Employees: 1

8403 (HQ)Mitchell Foods
80 Mitchell Foods Ln
Barbourville, KY 40906-7683
606-545-6677
Fax: 606-546-4190 888-202-9745
sales@mitchellfoods.com
Fresh marinated boneless pork chops, rib eyes, chicken breast, meat loaf and barbecue products; also, chili and beer cheese
President: Greg Mitchell
sales@mitchellfoods.com
Owner: Jim Mitchell
VP Quality Control: Greg Mitchell
Estimated Sales: $1-3 Million
Number Employees: 10-19
Square Footage: 60000
Type of Packaging: Consumer, Food Service, Private Label, Bulk
Other Locations:
  Mitchell Foods
  Lexington KY
Brands:
  Mitchell Foods

8404 Mitchum Potato Chips
P.O.Box 36639
Charlotte, NC 28236
704-372-6744
Fax: 704-339-0066
Potato chips
President: John Wilson
Marketing Director: Henry Pully
COO: Tommy Thompson
Contact: Randy Hardin
rhardin@mitchumchips.com
Estimated Sales: $10-20 000,000
Number Employees: 1-4
Type of Packaging: Bulk
Brands:
  Mdi
  Mitchum Rices
  Savealot
  Tiggly Wiggly
  Ukrop

8405 Mitsubishi Chemical Holdings
655 3rd Ave # 15
New York, NY 10017-9135
212-672-9400
Fax: 914-761-0108 webapid@m-chem.com
www.mitsubishichemical.com
Bacteriostatic emulsifiers; also, calcium suspension, confectionery including chocolate, low-fat spreads, dairy product analogs and fruit coatings
President: Tats Iwai
ageless@mgc-a.com
Sales: Takazumi Kanekiyo
Number Employees: 1000-4999
Parent Co: Mitsubishi Chemical Coorporation
Type of Packaging: Bulk
Brands:
  Ryoto Sugar Ester

8406 (HQ)Mitsubishi Intl. Corp.
520 Madison Avenue
Floor 18
New York, NY 10022-4327
212-759-5605
Fax: 212-605-1810 800-442-6266
Food commodities: coffee, cocoa, dairy products, fruits, vegetables and frozen juice concentrates. Food ingredients, enzymes, emulsifiers, baking agents.
President: James Brumm
CFO: Yasuyuki Sugiura
Executive VP/COO: Yoshihiko Kawamura
Sales/Purchasing Representative: Patrick Welch
Contact: Keigo Ando
keigo.ando@mitsubishicorp.com
Number Employees: 250-499
Other Locations:
  Seattle WA

8407 Mix-A-Lota Stuff LLC
4828 N Kings Hwy
Suite 424
Fort Pierce, FL 34951
727-365-7328
brendassauces@aol.com
www.mixalotastuff.com
Sauce
President: Brenda Chinn

8408 Mixallogy
Ponte Vedra Beach, FL 32082
mixallogy.com
Cocktail mixes
Founder & CEO: Gwen Manto
Co-Founder: Monica Pina Alzugaray
VP, Sales: Steve Manto

8409 Mixerz All Natural Cocktail Mixers
100 Cummings Center
Suite 220B
Beverly, MA 01915
978-922-6497
All natural cocktail mixers
Marketing: Christina Pesente

8410 Mixes by Danielle
615 Pelvedere Street
Warren, OH 44483
330-856-5190
Fax: 330-856-3386 800-537-6499
Urban spices
President: Trissa McClerry

8411 Mixon Fruit Farms Inc
2525 27th St E
Bradenton, FL 34208-7467
941-748-5829
Fax: 941-748-1085 800-608-2525
info@mixon.com www.mixon.com

Manufacturer, packer and exporter of citrus fruits, vegetables, fudge, honey, jellies, marmalades and spreads, salsa, dips, pickles and nuts
President: Dean Mixon
Estimated Sales: $3.43 Million
Number Employees: 50-99
Square Footage: 360000
Brands:
    Mixon

8412   Miyako Oriental Foods Inc
4287 Puente Ave
Baldwin Park, CA 91706-3420
                                  626-962-9633
          Fax: 626-814-4569 877-788-6476
                    joearai@coldmountainmiso.com
                    www.coldmountainmiso.com
Miso in different flavors and colors. Used in making sauces, soups, marinades, dressings, dips and main dishes.
Vice President: Teruo Shimizu
shimizu@coldmountainmiso.com
VP: Teruo Shimizu
Marketing/Sales/Quality Assurance Mgr: Joe Arai
Estimated Sales: $3 Million
Number Employees: 10-19
Square Footage: 72000
Type of Packaging: Consumer, Food Service, Private Label, Bulk
Brands:
    Cold Mountain
    Kanemasa
    Yamaizumi
    Yamajirushi

8413   Miyoko's Kitchen
2086 Marina Ave
Petaluma, CA 94954
                                  415-521-5313
                    info@miyokoskitchen.com
                    miyokoskitchen.com
Vegan cheese
Founder & CEO: Miyoko Schinner
CFO: John Breen
COO: Billy Bramblett
Quality Assurance Manager: Matt Smith
Square Footage: 30000

8414   Mizkan Americas Inc
2400 Nicholson Ave
Kansas City, MO 64120
                                  800-323-4358
                    info@mizkan.com www.mizkan.com
Flavored vinegars, mustards, and cooking wines.
Executive VP: Clarice Moore
Marketing Director: Tom Matthews
Operations Manager: Mike Cole
Plant Manager: Wayne Towe
Purchasing Manager: Phyllis Conover
Number Employees: 10-19
Type of Packaging: Consumer, Food Service, Private Label, Bulk
Brands:
    Cushing
    Lincoln
    Ozark
    Rogers
    Speas
    Springdale

8415   (HQ)Mizkan Americas Inc
1661 Feehanville Dr
Suite 300
Mount Prospect, IL 60056
                                  800-323-4358
                    info@mizkan.com www.mizkan.com
Flavored vinegars, mustards, and cooking wines.
President & Chief Operating Officer: Kevin Ponticelli
Chief Executive Officer: Koichi Yuki
Chief Financial Officer: Tommy Isshiki
Director, Information Technology: Mohammad Adnan
VP, Quality & Food Safety: Shen-Youn Chang
EVP, Retail Sales & Marketing: Mike Smith
VP, Marketing: Dan O'Leary
SVP, Sales: Paul Callahan
VP, Operations: Kevin Culver
Director, Operations: Alan Schmoldt
Director, Procurement: Penny Philp
Year Founded: 1804
Estimated Sales: $20 Million
Number Employees: 50-99

Brands:
    Nakano
    Holland House
    Mitsukan
    Barengo
    World Harbors
    Angostura
    El Diablo

8416   Mizkan Americas Inc
176 First Flight Dr
Auburn, ME 04210
                                  800-323-4358
                    info@mizkan.com www.mizkan.com
Flavored vinegars, mustards, and cooking wines.

8417   Mizkan Americas Inc
247 West Ave
Lyndonville, NY 14098
                                  800-323-4358
                    info@mizkan.com www.mizkan.com
Flavored vinegars, mustards, and cooking wines.

8418   Mizkan Americas Inc
7673 Sodus Center
Sodus, NY 14551
                                  800-323-4358
                    info@mizkan.com www.mizkan.com
Flavored vinegars, mustards, and cooking wines.

8419   Mizkan Americas Inc
445 N Dakota
Lake Alfred, FL 33850
                                  800-323-4358
                    info@mizkan.com www.mizkan.com
Flavored vinegars, mustards, and cooking wines.

8420   Mizkan Americas Inc
526 Interstate Dr
Crossville, TN 38555
                                  800-323-4358
                    info@mizkan.com www.mizkan.com
Flavored vinegars, mustards, and cooking wines.

8421   Mizkan Americas Inc
3290 7th Street Rd
Shively, KY 40216
                                  800-323-4358
                    info@mizkan.com www.mizkan.com
Flavored vinegars, mustards, and cooking wines.

8422   Mizkan Americas Inc
702 Kiddville Rd
Belding, MI 48809
                                  800-323-4358
                    info@mizkan.com www.mizkan.com
Flavored vinegars, mustards, and cooking wines.

8423   Mizkan Americas Inc
410 Seymour Court
Green Bay, WI 54306
                                  800-323-4358
                    info@mizkan.com www.mizkan.com
Flavored vinegars, mustards, and cooking wines.

8424   Mizkan Americas Inc
7331 Ben Frederick Rd
Abbeville, LA 70510
                                  800-323-4358
                    info@mizkan.com www.mizkan.com
Flavored vinegars, mustards, and cooking wines.

8425   Mizkan Americas Inc
4647 Bronze Way
Dallas, TX 75236
                                  800-323-4358
                    info@mizkan.com www.mizkan.com
Flavored vinegars, mustards, and cooking wines.

8426   Mizkan Americas Inc
9860 S Hwy 478
Vado, NM 88072
                                  800-323-4358
                    info@mizkan.com www.mizkan.com
Flavored vinegars, mustards, and cooking wines.

8427   Mizkan Americas Inc
4065 J St SE
Deming, NM 88030
                                  800-323-4358
                    info@mizkan.com www.mizkan.com
Flavored vinegars, mustards, and cooking wines.

8428   Mizkan Americas Inc
10037 E 8th St
Rancho Cucamonga, CA 91730
                                  800-323-4358
                    info@mizkan.com www.mizkan.com
Flavored vinegars, mustards, and cooking wines.

8429   Mizkan Americas Inc
46 Walker St
Watsonville, CA 95076
                                  800-323-4358
                    info@mizkan.com www.mizkan.com
Flavored vinegars, mustards, and cooking wines.

8430   Mizkan Americas Inc
1901 Ragu Dr
Owensboro, KY 42303
                                  800-323-4358
                    info@mizkan.com www.mizkan.com
Flavored vinegars, mustards, and cooking wines.

8431   Mizkan Americas Inc
1400 Waterloo Rd
Stockton, CA 95205
                                  800-323-4358
                    info@mizkan.com www.mizkan.com
Flavored vinegars, mustards, and cooking wines.

8432   Mj Kellner Co
5700 International Pkwy
Springfield, IL 62711-4052
                                  217-483-1700
          Fax: 217-483-1771 mjk@mjkellner.com
                    www.mjkellner.com
Wholesaler/distributor of groceries, meats, produce, frozen foods, baked goods, equipment and fixtures, general merchandise and seafood; serving the food service market
Owner: William Kellner
Founder: Maurice Kellner
CFO: Kathy Dierkes
kathyd@mjkellner.com
Sales Manager: Bill Barris
Director of Sales & Marketing: Gary Boston
Number Employees: 50-99

8433   Mo Hotta Mo Betta
2822 Limerick St
Savannah, GA 31404-4172
                                  912-748-2766
          Fax: 912-748-1364 www.mohotta.com
Processor and exporter of hot sauces
President: Jim Kelley
jimkelley@mohotta.com
Estimated Sales: $110,000
Number Employees: 20-49
Type of Packaging: Consumer, Food Service
Brands:
    Hot Sauce For Cool Kids
    Mo Hotta-Mo Betta

8434   Mobile Bay Seafood
11801 Old Shipyard Rd
Coden, AL 36523
                                  251-973-0410
                        Fax: 706-538-6850
Seafood
President: Bob Omainsky

8435   Mobile Processing
PO Box 501187 Mobile Al 36605
2201 Perimeter Rd Ste A
Mobile, AL 36615-1130
                                  251-438-6944
                        Fax: 251-438-6948
Fresh and frozen seafood including shrimp
Owner/President: James Higdon
Estimated Sales: $2 Million
Number Employees: 50-99

8436   Moceri South Western
4909 Pacific Hwy
San Diego, CA 92110-4005
                                  619-297-7900
                        Fax: 619-297-8900
Beverages and bottling
President: Grace Moceri
Estimated Sales: $10-20 000,000
Number Employees: 10-19
Type of Packaging: Private Label

Food Manufacturers / A-Z

8437 Mod Squad Martha
1202 Gregorie Commons
Johns Island, SC 29455
615-476-3696
melissa@modsquadmartha.com
modsquadmartha.com
Marinades, dressings and sauces.
Founder: Melissa Ann Barton

8438 Model Dairy LLC
500 Gould St
Reno, NV 89502-1466
775-788-7900
Fax: 775-788-7951 800-433-2030
Processor and wholesaler/distributor of a full line of dairy products including ice cream
Cmo: Derrick Alby
derrick_@deanfoods.com
VP/General Manager: Jim Breslin
Controller: Peggy Baker
Manager: Jim Breslin
Number Employees: 100-249
Square Footage: 100000
Parent Co: Suiza Dairy Group
Type of Packaging: Food Service

8439 Modena Fine Foods Inc
158 River Rd
Clifton, NJ 07014-1571
973-470-8499
Fax: 201-842-9001 www.modenafinefoods.com
Balsamic products, including balsamic vinegar, specialty wine vinegars, and balsamic condiments
President: Fred Mortadi
Vice President: Michael Giaimo
michael@modenafinefoods.com
Estimated Sales: $720,000
Number Employees: 10-19

8440 Modern Day Masala, LLC
Po Box 682374
Marietta, GA 30068-0040
866-611-3757
Fax: 866-611-1596
Gluten-free, organic/natural, USDA, full-line spices, spices, foodservice, private label.
Owner: Vikas Khanna
Marketing: Kristin Sharma

8441 Modern Gourmet Foods
18011 Mitchell S
Suite B
Irvine, CA 92614-6007
949-250-3129
sales@shonfelds.com
Designs, produces and manufactures gourmet food products that are sold straight to retailers. Company originally began as Shonfeld's USA, Inc. and was located in New Jersey.
Founder/Chairman: Boaz Shonfeld
President: Mark Greenhall
Vice President Sales, National Accounts: Jason Hoffman
Product Development: Yaron Bart
Estimated Sales: $15.5 Million
Number Employees: 10-19
Type of Packaging: Private Label

8442 Modern Italian Bakery of West Babylon
301 Locust Ave
Oakdale, NY 11769-1652
631-589-7300
Fax: 631-589-7383
Italian baked goods
President/CEO: James Turco
Estimated Sales: $20-49 Million
Number Employees: 100-249
Square Footage: 60000

8443 Modern Macaroni Co LTD
1708 Mary St
Honolulu, HI 96819-3103
808-845-6841
Fax: 808-845-6841 www.modernmacaroni.net
Dry Asian noodles, shrimp flakes and soybean flour
Owner: Darrell Siu
Estimated Sales: $900,000-$1 Million
Number Employees: 10-19
Square Footage: 4800
Type of Packaging: Consumer, Food Service
Brands:
 Hula

8444 Modern Oats
9600 Research Dr
Irvine, CA 92618
888-662-2334
support@modernoats.com modernoats.com
Instant oatmeal
President/Owner: Richard Principale
Year Founded: 2013
Number of Brands: 1
Number of Products: 10
Type of Packaging: Consumer
Brands:
 MODERN OATS

8445 Modern Packaging
3245 N Berkeley Lake Rd NW
Duluth, GA 30096
770-622-1500
Fax: 770-814-0046
www.modernpackaginginc.com
Contract packager of condiments and liquid food items; warehouse providing dry, cooler and humidity-controlled storage of foodstuffs, liquid packaging products and seasonal sales items; also, pick and pack and rail siding available
President: Herb Sodel
VP: Nancy Sodel
Estimated Sales: $3.6 Million
Number Employees: 50-99
Square Footage: 400000

8446 Modern Pod Co.
63 Baker St
Providence, RI 02905
info@modpodco.com
www.modpodco.com
Hummus snacks
General Manager: Levon Kurkjian
Number of Brands: 1
Number of Products: 4
Type of Packaging: Consumer
Brands:
 HUMMUS POD

8447 Modern Pop
Laguna Beach, CA 92651
themodernpop.com
Frozen fruit bars
CEO: Julie Podolec
Number of Brands: 1
Number of Products: 12
Type of Packaging: Consumer
Brands:
 MODERN POP

8448 Modern Products Inc
6425 W Executive Dr
Mequon, WI 53092-4478
262-242-2400
Fax: 262-242-2751 800-877-8935
modernfearn@aol.com www.modernfearn.com
Seasonings, spices, bake mixes, natural products and soy products
President: Gaylord G Palermo
modernfearn@aol.com
CEO & Chairman: Anthony Palermo
Secretary: Petronella Palermo
Quality Control Manager: Jim Kohnke
Estimated Sales: $2.5 Million
Number Employees: 20-49
Type of Packaging: Consumer, Food Service
Brands:
 Classique Fare
 Rearn Naturefresh
 Spice Garden
 Spike
 Swiss Kriss
 Vegeful
 Vegit

8449 Modern Table
Walnut Creek, CA 94597
www.moderntable.com
Plant-based pastas and prepared meals
Marketing: Jennifer Eiseman
National Sales Manager: Jeff Schonhoff
Number Employees: 1,000-4,999
Number of Brands: 1
Number of Products: 12
Type of Packaging: Consumer

8450 Modern Tea Packers
P.O.Box 370708
Brooklyn, NY 11237-0708
718-417-1060
Fax: 718-417-6405
Tea and tea bags
Owner: Julius Medwin
CEO: Julius Neumann
Estimated Sales: $5-9.9 000,000
Number Employees: 20-49

8451 Modesto WholeSoy
PO Box 1277
Ceres, CA 95301
209-523-5119
Fax: 209-523-5519
Produces the highest quality liquid soybase for use in soymilk, yogurt, smoothies, ice cream and other dairy-like products.
CEO: Ken Norquist
CFO: Henry Gloasser
Plant Manager: Frank Gasca
Estimated Sales: $290,000
Number Employees: 3
Square Footage: 7668

8452 Moet Hennessy USA
85 10th Ave
New York, NY 10011
212-251-8200
www.mhusa.com
Wines and spirits.
President & CEO: Jim Clerkin
Managing Director: Jo Thornton
Year Founded: 1980
Estimated Sales: $884.58 Million
Number Employees: 3,452
Other Locations:
 New Jersey
 Massachusetts
 Illinois
 Florida
 Georgia
 Texas
 California
Brands:
 10 Cane
 Ardbeg
 Belvedere
 Cape Mentelle Vineyards
 Capezzana
 Chandon
 Chateau Cheval Blanc
 Chateau D'Yquem
 Chateau De Sancerre
 Chateau La Nerthe
 Cheval Des Andes
 Chopin
 Cloudy Bay Vineyards
 Dom Perignon
 Esperto
 Glenmorangie
 Grand Marnier
 Green Point
 Hennessy
 Krug
 Lapostolle
 Livio Felluga
 Moet & Chandon
 Monsanto
 Navan
 Newton Vineyard
 Numanthia
 Ruinart
 Terrazas De Los Andes
 Veuve Clicquot

8453 Mogen David Wine Corp
85 Bourne St
Westfield, NY 14787
716-326-3151
www.mogendavid.com
Kosher and nonkosher wines including white, rose and red.
President: E. Schwartz
Year Founded: 1933
Estimated Sales: $200-500 Million
Number Employees: 100-249
Parent Co: The Wine Group
Type of Packaging: Consumer

Food Manufacturers / A-Z

8454 Mohn's Fisheries
1144 Great River Rd
Harpers Ferry, IA 52146-7565
563-586-2269
Fax: 563-423-1579
Seafood
Owner: Diane Mohn
Estimated Sales: $300,000-500,000
Number Employees: 1-4

8455 Mokk-a
Oostmaaslaan 628
Rotterdam, 3063 DJ
Netherlands
info@mokk-a.com
mokk-a.com
Coffee
Owner: Karen Glavimans-Hawa
Estimated Sales: A
Number Employees: 1
Parent Co: Danish Koffie Connection

8456 Moledina Commodities
5501 Muirfield Court
Flower Mound, TX 75028
817-490-1101
Fax: 817-490-1105 mohamed@moledina.com
Manufacturer of quality green coffees from throughout the work, with a strong emphasis on East African Coffees.
President: Mohamed Moledina
VP: Fidahusein R Moledina
fidahusein@moledina.com
Brands:
 Moledina

8457 Molinaro's Fine Italian Foods Ltd.
2345 Stanfield Rd
Unit 50
Mississauga, ON L4Y 3Y3
Canada
905-281-0352
www.molinaros.com
Processor, importer and exporter of pizza, fresh and frozen pizza shells, fresh pasta, flatbread, focaccia, pasta sauce, fresh and frozen pasta entrees, meat, vegetable and cheese lasagna, panzerottis and calzones.
President: Vince Molinaro
CEO: Gino Molinaro
Sales/Marketing: Catherine Pyman
Purchasing Manager: Frank Molinaro
Number Employees: 140
Square Footage: 304000
Type of Packaging: Consumer, Food Service, Private Label, Bulk
Brands:
 Famosa
 Molinaro's
 Supremo

8458 Molli
Dallas, TX
info@mollisauces.com
mollisauces.com
Mexican sauces and marinades.
Co-Founder: Rodrigo Salas
Co-Founder: Leticia Castellanos
Brands:
 Molli(c)

8459 (HQ)Molson Coors Beverage Company
250 South Wacker Dr.
Chicago, IL 60606
800-645-5376
www.molsoncoors.com
Brews and beer.
President/CEO, Molson Coors: Gavin Hattersley
President, Molson Coors Canada: Frederic Landtmeters
CFO: Tracey Joubert
President, Emerging Growth: Pete Marino
Chief Strategy Officer: Rahul Goyal
Chief People & Diversity Officer: Dave Osswald
Chief Marketing Officer: Michelle St. Jacques
President, U.S. Sales: Kevin Doyle
Chief Communications Officer: Adam Collins
Chief Legal & Government Affairs Officer: E. Lee Reichert
Chief Supply Chain Officer: Brian Erhardt
Estimated Sales: $6.7 Billion
Number Employees: 17,000
Number of Brands: 100
Type of Packaging: Consumer
Other Locations:
 Molson Coors Canada
  Montreal QC
 Molson Coors Europe
  Prague, Czech Rep.
 Molson Coors International
  New Delhi, India
 MillerCoors
  Chicago IL
Brands:
 Blue Moon
 Carling
 Coors
 Molson
 Molson Canadian
 Apatinsko
 Astika
 Barmen
 Bergenbier
 Black Horse
 Black Ice
 Bohemian
 Borsodi
 Branik
 Burgasko
 Caffreys
 Cobra
 Colorado Native
 Creemore Springs
 Crispin
 Extra Gold Lager
 Franciscan Well
 Granville Island Brewing
 Henry Weinhard's
 Herman Joseph's Private Reserve
 Hop Valley
 Icehouse
 India Beer
 Jelen
 Kamenitza
 Keystone
 Laurentide
 Leinenkugel's
 Mad & Noisy
 Mad Jack
 Magnum
 Mickey's
 Miller
 Milwaukee's Best
 Niksicko
 Noroc
 Old Style Pilsner
 Old Vienna
 Olde English 800
 Ostravar
 Ozujsko
 Red Dog
 Revolver Brewing
 Rickard's
 Saint Archer
 Sharp's
 Smith and Forge
 Sparks
 Standard Lager
 Staropramen
 Steel Reserve
 Terrapin
 Tomislav
 Vratislav
 Wanderoot
 Winterfest
 Worthington's
 Zima
 Cool

8460 Molson Coors North America
250 South Wacker Dr.
Chicago, IL 60606
800-645-5376
www.molsoncoors.com
Brews and beer; North American operating division of Molson Coors Beverage Company.
President/CEO, Molson Coors: Gavin Hattersley
President, U.S. Sales: Kevin Doyle
Chief Supply Chain Officer: Brian Erhardt
Year Founded: 2008
Estimated Sales: K
Number Employees: 10,000+
Parent Co: Molson Coors Beverage Company
Type of Packaging: Consumer
Other Locations:
 Brewery
  Albany GA
 Brewery
  Eden NC
 Brewery
  Elkton VA
 Brewery
  Fort Worth TX
 Brewery/Corporate Office
  Golden CO
 Brewery
  Irwindale CA
 Brewery/Corporate Office
  Milwaukee WI
 Brewery
  Trenton OH
 Corporate Headquarters
  Chicago IL
 Watertown Hops Company
  Watertown WI
Brands:
 Aguila
 Arnold Palmer Spiked Half & Half
 Barmen
 Blue Moon
 Colorado Native
 Coors
 Crispin Cider
 Cristal
 Cusquena
 Extra Gold Lager
 Foster's
 George Killian's Irish Red
 Grolsch Premium Lager
 Hamm's
 Hnery Weinhard's
 Herman Josheph's Private Reserve
 Hop Valley
 Icehouse
 Keystone
 Lech Premium
 Leinenkugel's
 Magnum
 Mickey's
 Miller
 Milwaukee's Best
 Molson Canadian
 Old Vienna
 Old English
 Peroni
 Pilsner Urquell
 Red Dog
 Redd's
 Revolver
 Saint Archer
 Sharp's
 Smith & Forge Hard Cider
 Sol Cerveza
 Sparks
 Steel Reserve
 Terrapin
 Tyskie Gronie

8461 Mom N' Pops Inc
834 Brooks St
New Windsor, NY 12553
845-567-0640
Fax: 845-567-0652
Wholesale manufacturers of candy and lollipops.
President: Barbara Regenbaum
Sales Director: Stacy Zagon
Estimated Sales: $2.5-5 Million
Number Employees: 10-19
Number of Brands: 1
Type of Packaging: Bulk
Brands:
 MOM 'N POPS

8462 Mom's Bakery
1703 N Woods St
Sherman, TX 75092-3629
903-893-7585
Fax: 404-969-1144 txgina1@aol.com
www.momsbakerysherman.com
Buttermilk and yeast raised biscuits
Owner: Gina Adams
VP: Daniel Kay
Estimated Sales: Less Than $500,000
Number Employees: 5-9
Square Footage: 225000
Type of Packaging: Food Service, Bulk

8463 Mom's Famous
145 NW 20th St
Boca Raton, FL 33431
561-750-1903
Fax: 561-750-4105
Baked goods
President: Tony Danesh

Food Manufacturers / A-Z

Estimated Sales: $575,000
Number Employees: 10-19
Brands:
   Mom's Famous

8464 Mom's Food Company
Post Office Box 97
Osterville, MA 02655
   508-648-0188
   800-969-6667
Frozen meatballs and sauce
President: Laurie Gardella
Estimated Sales: $1.1 Million
Number Employees: 23
Square Footage: 48000
Type of Packaging: Consumer, Food Service, Private Label, Bulk
Brands:
   Mom's

8465 Mom's Gourmet, LLC
17594 Walnut Trail
Chagrin Falls, OH 44023-6428
   440-564-9702
   skoepke@momsgourmet.net
   www.momsgourmet.net
Dairy-free, gluten-free, lactose-free, organic/natural, sugar-free, vegetarian, full-line spices, rubs.
Marketing: Sally Koepke

8466 Momence Packing Company
PO Box 906
Sheboygan Falls, WI 53085
   815-472-6485
   Fax: 815-472-2459 888-556-2728
Frozen sausage
President: Patrick Garinger
Contact: Kirsten Mueller
kmueller@johnsonville.com
Estimated Sales: Below $5,000,000
Number Employees: 250-499
Type of Packaging: Consumer, Private Label

8467 Mon Ami Restaurant
3845 E Wine Cellar Rd
Port Clinton, OH 43452-3704
   419-797-4446
   Fax: 419-797-9171 800-777-4266
   info@monamiwinery.com
   www.monamiwinery.com
Champagne
Owner: John Kronberg
info@monamiwinery.com
Estimated Sales: $500,000-$1 Million
Number Employees: 50-99
Brands:
   Mon Ami

8468 Mona Lisa Foods
600 West Chicago Ave
Suite 860
Chicago, IL 60654
   312-496-7300
   Fax: 312-496-7399 866-443-0460
   www.monalisadecorations.com
Gourmet chocolate products
CEO: Antoine de Saint-Affrique
CEO & President, Americas: Peter Boone
CFO: Remco Steenbergen
Year Founded: 1987
Estimated Sales: $20-50 Million
Number Employees: 20-49
Number of Products: 50
Square Footage: 32000
Parent Co: Barry Callebaut

8469 Monaco Baking Company
14700 Marquardt Avenue
Santa Fe Springs, CA 90670
   562-404-5028
   Fax: 562-229-0963 800-569-4540
Manufacturer of gingerbread and shortbread cookies, shortbread and gingerbread cookie mixes.
Executive Director: Philip Moreau
Contact: Sonia Orozco
sonia@monacobaking.com
Year Founded: 1994
Estimated Sales: $20-50 Million
Number Employees: 20-49
Type of Packaging: Private Label

8470 Monarch Beverage Company
3630 Peachtree Road NE
Suite 775
Atlanta, GA 30326
   404-262-4040
   Fax: 404-262-4001 800-241-3732
   info@monarchbeverages.com
   www.monarchbeverages.com
Manufacturer and exporter of concentrates including sports and energy drinks, healthy fruit beverages, enhanced waters, ready-to-drink beverages, ready-to-drink coffees and soft drinks. Beverage brand franchisor.
CEO: Jacques Bombal
COO: Didier Arnaud
Estimated Sales: $3.2 Million
Number Employees: 30
Type of Packaging: Bulk
Brands:
   Acute Fruit
   American Cola
   Comotion
   Kickapoo Joy Juice
   Ntrinsic
   Planet Cola
   Reaktor
   Rush! Energy

8471 Monarch Seafoods Inc
515 Kalihi St
Honolulu, HI 96819-3268
   808-841-7877
   Fax: 808-847-3930 www.monarchseafoods.com
Seafood and seafood products
President: Thomas Mukaigawa
Estimated Sales: $.5-1 million
Number Employees: 10-19

8472 Monastary Mustard
840 South Main Street
Angel, OR 97362
   503-949-6321
   Info@MonasteryMustard.com
   monasterymustard.com
Mustard
Mustard Flavor Creator: Sister Terry Hall

8473 Monastery Fruitcake
130 N Queen St
Martinsburg, WV 25401
   304-596-2024
   Fax: 304-264-3698
   orders@monasteryfruitcake.org
   monasteryfruitcake.org
Trappist monks at Holy Cross Abbey produce fruitcake and creamed honey.

8474 Mondelez International
100 Deforest Ave
East Hanover, NJ 07936
   855-535-5648
   www.mondelezinternational.com
Snacks
Chairman & CEO: Dirk Van De Put
President, North America: Glen Walter
Executive VP & CFO: Luca Zaramella
Estimated Sales: $25.9 Billion
Number Employees: 83,000
Brands:
   OREO
   Ritz
   Trident
   Halls
   Chips Ahoy!
   Triscuit
   Dentyne
   Green & Black's
   Toblerone
   belVita

8475 Mondial Foods Company
P.O.Box 75036
Los Angeles, CA 90075-0036
   213-383-3531
Processor and exporter of pineapple and other tropical juices
President: Ben Gattegno
Estimated Sales: $210000
Number Employees: 20-49
Type of Packaging: Food Service, Bulk

8476 Mondiv/Division of Lassonde Inc
3810 Alfred Laliberte
Boisbriand, QC J7H 1P8
Canada
   450-979-0717
   Fax: 450-979-0279 infomondiv@mondiv.com
   www.mondiv.com
Tapenades, bruschetta, glass jar gravy, specialty sauces and dips, glass jar soups and stews, meat-based pasta sauce, pasta sauce (non-meat), organic pasta sauces, organic glass jar soups, glass jar (ready-to-serve) meals, pestos andchutneys
President/Owner: Vito Monopoli

8477 Money's Mushrooms
#800-1500 W Georgia Street
Vancouver, BC V6G 2Z6
Canada
   604-669-3741
   Fax: 604-669-9732 800-669-7992
   www.calbur.com
Processor, grower and exporter of canned and pickled mushrooms
President: Keith Potter
CFO: Cliff Lillicrop
VP Sales/Marketing: Dean Fleming
Number Employees: 900
Type of Packaging: Consumer, Food Service, Private Label, Bulk
Brands:
   Moneys

8478 Monin Inc.
Clearwater, FL
   855-352-8671
   www.monin.com
Manufacturer and exporter of flavored syrups, smoothie mixes and purees, sauces, cocktail mixes, and sweeteners.
CEO: Bill Lombardo
Owner: Olivier Monin
VP of Marketing: Suzanna Geel

8479 Monini North America
6 Armstrong Rd # 4
Shelton, CT 06484-4722
   203-513-2685
   Fax: 203-513-2863 info@monini.us
   www.monini.us
Oils
Chairman: Marco Petrini
Manager: Elizabeth Brooks
e.donovan@silkroutestrategists.com
Estimated Sales: Less than $200,000
Number Employees: 5-9
Type of Packaging: Private Label
Brands:
   Amabile Umbro
   Granfruttato
   Ii Monello
   Il Poggiolo
   Monini

8480 Monkey Media
78 East 2nd Avenue
Vancouver, BC V5T 1B1
Canada
   604-215-2163
   Fax: 604-708-8747 877-666-6539
   mike@monkeymedia.net
Software for the food industry
CEO: Steve Izen
CFO: Erle Dardick
Sales Director: Mike Tyler
Operations Manager: Marrianne Zakure
Estimated Sales: $1.5 Million
Number Employees: 13
Number of Products: 4
Square Footage: 2400
Parent Co: Monkey Media Software
Brands:
   Monkey Baking
   Monkey Catering
   Monkey Party

8481 Monks' Specialty Bakery
3258 River Rd
Piffard, NY 14533
   monksbread@gmail.com
   monksbread.com
Bread and specialty foods.

Food Manufacturers / A-Z

8482 Monogram Food Solutions
530 Oak Court Drive
Suite 400
Memphis, TN 38117
901-685-7167
Fax: 901-259-6671 www.monogramfoods.com
Bacon, smoked meats
Contact: Spencer Mcclure
spencer.mcclure@pilottravelcenters.com

8483 Monsanto Co
304 Center St
West Fargo, ND 58078-1209
701-282-7338
Fax: 701-282-8218 800-437-4120
info@interstateseed.com
Soybean seeds
President: Bruce Hovland
Cmo: Jim Johnson
jim.m.johnson@monsanto.com
Marketing Coordinator: Gerri Leach
Sales Director: Bill Webber
Operations Manager: Vic Nordstrom
Estimated Sales: $2.5-5 Million
Number Employees: 20-49

8484 Monsoon Kitchens
159 Memorial Dr
Suite G
Shrewsbury, MA 01545
508-842-0070
Fax: 617-629-0160 info@monsoonkitchens.com
monsoonkitchens.com
Indian foods
Co-Founder: Swati Elavia
Type of Packaging: Consumer, Food Service

8485 Monster Beverage Corp.
1 Monster Way
Corona, CA 92879
800-426-7367
info@monsterbevcorp.com
www.monsterbevcorp.com
Energy drinks.
President/Vice Chair/COO: Hilton Schlosberg
Chairman/CEO: Rodney Sacks
Year Founded: 2002
Estimated Sales: $3.3 Billion
Number Employees: 1,991
Number of Brands: 7
Parent Co: The Coca-Cola Company
Type of Packaging: Consumer, Food Service
Brands:
  Monster Energy
  Burn
  NOS
  Full Throttle
  Relentless
  Mother
  Reign
  Predator

8486 Monster Cone
8500 Delmeade
Montreal, QC H4T 1L6
Canada
541-636-2022
Fax: 514-342-0346 800-542-9801
info@monstercone.com
Processor and exporter of waffle bowls and cones including plain and chocolate dipped
President: Daniel Mardinger
Number Employees: 50-99
Square Footage: 80000
Type of Packaging: Consumer, Food Service, Private Label, Bulk
Brands:
  Monster Cone

8487 Mont Blanc Gourmet
2925 E Colfax Ave
Denver, CO 80206
303-755-1100
Fax: 303-283-1100 800-877-3811
Chocolate syrup, cocoa powders, chai mixes, cappuccino, mocha mixes, and powdered hot cocoa mix. Flavoring: chocolate, white chocolate, caramel, kahlua
Chocolatier & Co-Founder: Michael Szyliowicz
Certified Executive Chef: Charles V Heaton
Senior Lab Technologist: Lauren Yoon
Contact: Rebecca Gelston
rebecca@montblancgourmet.com

Estimated Sales: $1-$3 Million
Number Employees: 8
Brands:
  Mont Blanc Chocolate Syrups

8488 (HQ)Montana Coffee Traders
5810 US Highway 93 S
Whitefish, MT 59937-8414
406-862-7628
Fax: 406-862-7680 800-345-5282
www.coffeetraders.com
Fresh roasted coffee and tea.
Owner: R C Beall
Estimated Sales: Less Than $500,000
Number Employees: 1-4
Other Locations:
  Whitefish Coffeehouse
  Whitefish MT
  Columbia Falls Cafe
  Columbia Falls MT
  Kalispell Cafe
  Kalispell MT

8489 Montana Flour & Grains
2225 Montana Hwy 223
Fort Benton, MT 59442
406-622-5436
Fax: 406-622-5439 800-622-5790
info@montanaflour.com www.montanaflour.com
Manufactures flour and other grain mill products specializing in organic flours
President: Andre Giles
andre@montanaflour.com
Estimated Sales: Below $5 Million
Number Employees: 10-19
Number of Brands: 3
Number of Products: 15
Type of Packaging: Food Service, Private Label, Bulk

8490 Montana Mex
PO Box 11255
Bozeman, MT 59719
hello@montanamex.com
www.montanamex.com
BBQ sauces, seasonings and oils
Chef & Co-Founder: Eduardo Garcia
Type of Packaging: Consumer
Brands:
  MONTANA MEX

8491 Montana Monster Munchies
PO Box 10711
Bozeman, MT 59719-0711
406-388-3077
Fax: 406-388-2063 info@mtmonstermunchies.com
www.montanacookiecompany.com
Gluten free baked goods, cookies
Owner: Rich Powell
Estimated Sales: Less Than $500,000
Number Employees: 10-19

8492 Montana Mountain Smoked Fish
10 Elkhorn View Dr
Montana City, MT 59634
800-649-2959
Fax: 406-449-4755 800-649-2959
smkfishqueen@aol.com
Smoked salmon, sockeye salmon, keta salmon, rainbow trout, halibut and salmon spread. All natural, no preservatives
President: Kim Waltee
Estimated Sales: Less than $500,000
Number Employees: 1-4
Type of Packaging: Private Label

8493 Montana Naturals
1400 Kearns Blvd
Park City, UT 84060-6725
800-650-9597
www.mtnaturals.com
Processor and exporter of dietary supplements
General Manager: Sterling Gabbitas
Number Employees: 50-99
Square Footage: 104000
Parent Co: HealthRite
Type of Packaging: Consumer, Private Label
Other Locations:
  Montana Naturals by HealthRit
  Arlee MT
Brands:
  Pure Energy

8494 Montana Ranch Brand
PO Box 2036
Billings, MT 59103
406-294-2333
Fax: 406-294-2336 www.montanaranchbrand.com
Natural Piedmontese beef, ranch beef, pioneer pork, prairie lamb, and heritage bison
President/Owner: Ralph Peterson
Number Employees: 3

8495 Montana Specialty Mills LLC
701 2nd St S # 5
P.O.Box 2208
Great Falls, MT 59405-1852
406-761-2338
Fax: 406-761-7926 800-332-2024
www.mtspecialtymills.com
Primary agricultural processor providing contracting, origination, storage and processing of grain and oilseed-based products to secondary food manufacturers
President: Steve Chambers
steve@mtspecialtymills.com
Controller: Cecil Swensen
General Manager: Gordon Svenby
Operations: Robert Bender
Conrad Plant Manager: Gordon Mattern
Estimated Sales: Below $5 Million
Number Employees: 20-49
Square Footage: 80000

8496 Montana Tea & Spice Trading
2600 W Broadway St
Missoula, MT 59808-1624
406-721-4882
Fax: 406-543-1126 montanatea@msn.com
www.montanatea.com
Tea and herbal tea blending, spice blending. Wholesale, retial and mail order
Owner: Sherri Lee
Estimated Sales: $750,000
Number Employees: 5-9
Number of Brands: 2
Number of Products: 300+
Square Footage: 16000

8497 Montchevre-Betin, Inc
4030 Palos Verdes Drive North
Suite 201
Rolling Hills Estates, CA 90274
310-541-3520
Fax: 310-541-3760 www.montchevre.com
Goat cheese
Owner: Arnaud Solandt
Estimated Sales: $1-3 Million
Number Employees: 5-9

8498 Monte Cristo Trading
14 Harwood Ct
Scarsdale, NY 10583-4121
914-725-8025
Fax: 914-725-0869
General grocery
President: Anton Derosa
aderosa@montecristo.com.au
Estimated Sales: $530,000
Number Employees: 1-4
Type of Packaging: Consumer, Food Service, Bulk

8499 Monte Vista Farming Co
5043 N Montpelier Rd
Denair, CA 95316-9608
209-874-1866
Fax: 209-874-2024 www.montevistafarming.com
Processor and exporter of almonds
President: Jonathan Hoff
jhoff@montevistafarming.com
CFO: Bob McClain
VP Sales: Dan Whisenhunt
Operations Manager: Renee Crozier
Estimated Sales: $1.3 Million
Number Employees: 50-99
Square Footage: 8000

8500 Montebello Kitchens
PO Box 610
Gordonsville, VA 22942
800-743-7687
Fax: 270-209-1371
Spices and rubs, dressing and marinades, sauces, Virginia peanuts, coups and milled grains.
Owner: Steven Lynch
selynch@montebellokitchens.com

Food Manufacturers / A-Z

8501 Montebello Packaging
1036 Aberdeen St
Hawkesbury, ON K6A 1K5
Canada
613-632-7096
Fax: 613-632-9638 bpilon@montebellopkg.com
www.montebellopkg.com
Aluminum aerosol cans & aluminum/laminate tubes
President: Betty Pilon
Chief Financial Officer: Greg Labuschagne
Vice President, Sales: Tom Zopf
Director of Information Technology: Jean-Francois Leclerc
Director of Quality Operations: Fred Long
Director of Sales: John Iorii
Estimated Sales: $20-50 Million
Number Employees: 240
Parent Co: The Jim Pattison Group
Brands:
 M-Bond
 M-Purity Ring
 M-Purity Seal

8502 Montelle Winery
201 Montelle Dr
PO Box 147
Augusta, MO 63332-1518
636-228-4464
Fax: 636-228-4754 888-595-9463
info@montelle.com www.montelle.com
In the late 1960s and early 1970s, a few pioneering souls began to refurbish the old vineyards and winery buildings of Missouri's premier wine-growing regions
Owner: Tony Kooyumjian
Founder: Clayton Byers
Vineyard Manager: Paul Hopen
Cellar Master: Mark Nienhueser
Manager: Brian Obermark
manager@montelle.com
Estimated Sales: Less Than $500,000
Number Employees: 1-4
Number of Products: 15

8503 Montello Inc
6106 E 32nd Pl # 100
Tulsa, OK 74135-5495
918-665-1170
Fax: 918-665-1480 800-331-4628
www.montelloinc.com
Importer and distributor of emulsifiers and gums
President: Allen Johnson
allenj@montelloinc.com
VP: Leo Wooldridge
Estimated Sales: $6 Million
Number Employees: 5-9

8504 Monterey Fish Company
950 S Sanborn Rd
Salinas, CA 93901
831-771-9221
Fax: 831-775-0156 mntyfish@redshift.com
www.montereyfishcompany.com
Canned and frozen herring, anchovies, herring roe, mackerel, sardines and squid
President: Carmelo J Trinqali
VP: Sal Trinquali
Contact: Mary Brand
mbrand@cityofslt.us
VP Operations: Anthony Trinqali
Plant Manager: Joseph Tringali
Estimated Sales: $1-$2.5 Million
Number Employees: 1-4
Type of Packaging: Consumer, Food Service, Private Label
Brands:
 Bono
 Seawave

8505 Monterey Mushrooms Inc
260 Westgate Dr
Watsonville, CA 95076
Fax: 831-763-2300 800-333-6874
www.montereymushrooms.com
Manufacturer and exporter of canned, frozen and refrigerated mushroom stems/pieces, slices and buttons
President & CEO: Shah Kazemi
shah.kazemi@montmush.com
VP of Sales & Marketing: Mike O'Brien
Number Employees: 1000-4999
Type of Packaging: Consumer, Food Service, Private Label, Bulk
Other Locations:
 Multi Site Fresh Operation Farms
 Orlando FL
 Multi Site Fresh Operation Farms
 Princeton IL
 Multi Site Fresh Operation Farms
 Royal Oaks CA
 Multi Site Fresh Operation Farms
 Las Lomas CA
 Multi Site Fresh Operation Farms
 Morgan Hill CA
 Multi Site Fresh Operation Farms
 San Miguel, Mexico
 Multi Site Fresh Operation Farms
 Vancouver, BC Canada
 Multi Site Fresh Operation Farms
 Arroyo Grande CA
 Multi Site Fresh Operation Farms
 Madisonville TX
 Multi Site Fresh Operation Farms
 Loudon TX
 Multi Site Fresh Operation Farms
 Temple PA
 Monterey Processing Facility
 Bonne Terre MO
 Monterey Product Development
 Royal Oaks CA
Brands:
 Let's Blend

8506 Monterey Vineyard
800 S Alta St
Gonzales, CA 93926
831-675-4000
Fax: 831-675-4019
Wines
General Manager/President: Ken Greene
Operations Manager: Ken Greene
Winemaker: Chris Mallar
Production Manager: Noel Vofter
Estimated Sales: Less than $500,000
Number Employees: 5-9

8507 Monterrey Products
803 S Zarzamora St
San Antonio, TX 78207-5363
210-435-2872
Fax: 210-435-2877 monpro@sbcglobal.net
www.montereyproducts.com
Mexican products including mole sauce, candy, spices, chili powder and dry chili mixes
Owner: Ernest DE Los Santos
Vice President: Sylvia De Los Santos
Estimated Sales: $2 Million
Number Employees: 10-19
Type of Packaging: Consumer, Food Service

8508 Monterrey Products
803 S Zarzamora St
San Antonio, TX 78207-5363
210-435-2872
Fax: 210-435-2877 800-872-1652
monpro@sbcglobal.net
www.montereyproducts.com
Spices, salsa and praline candies
Owner: Ernest DE Los Santos
Estimated Sales: Below $5 Million
Number Employees: 10-19
Brands:
 Monterrey

8509 Montevina Winery
20680 Shenandoah School Road
Plymouth, CA 95669
209-245-6942
Fax: 209-245-6617 info@montevina.com
www.montevina.com
Wine
CEO: Louis Trinchero
VP: Jeff Meyers
Estimated Sales: $2.5-5 Million
Number Employees: 10-19

8510 Monticello Canning Company
PO Box 3509
Crossville, TN 38557
monticello.c@usa.net
monticellocanning.tripod.com
Canned vegetables including sweet red and green peppers, pimientos
President: Earl Dean
Treasurer: Alton Tabor
Vice-President: Warren Dean
Qualtity Control: Kevin Dean
General Manager: Greg Barnwell
Estimated Sales: $3-5 Million
Number Employees: 5-9
Type of Packaging: Consumer, Food Service, Private Label, Bulk
Brands:
 Betty Ann

8511 Monticello Vineyards-Corley
4242 Big Ranch Rd
Napa, CA 94558-1301
707-253-2802
Fax: 707-253-1019
Wine@CorleyFamilyNapaValley.com
www.corleyfamilynapavalley.com
Wine and champagne
President: John Corley
john@monticellovineyards.com
Chairman: Jay Corley
Trade and Direct-to-Consumer Marketing: Leslie McCain
Sales & Marketing and Administration: Stephen Corley
Winemaker: Chris Corley
Estimated Sales: $1.3 Million
Number Employees: 10-19
Type of Packaging: Consumer

8512 Montione's Biscotti & Baked Goods
215 South Worcester St
Norton, MA 02766
508-285-4777
Fax: 508-285-4465 800-559-1010
www.montionesbiscotti.com
Baked goods, biscotti
President: Mary Montione
CFO: Dan Mahoney
Estimated Sales: $1 Million
Number Employees: 5-9
Type of Packaging: Private Label

8513 Montmorenci Vineyards
2989 Charleston Hwy
Aiken, SC 29801
803-649-4870
Fax: 803-642-1834
Wine
Owner/Winemaker: Robert Scott
Owner: Elaine Scott
General Manager: Stephanie Scott
Estimated Sales: $500,000-$1 Million
Number Employees: 1-4
Type of Packaging: Private Label
Brands:
 Blanc Du Bois
 Chambourcin
 De Caradeuc White
 Melody
 Savannah White
 Vin Eclipser

8514 Montreal Chop Suey Company
2100 Moreau Street
Montreal, QC H1W 2M3
Canada
514-522-3134
Fax: 514-522-8074
Chinese food products including fresh bean and alfalfa sprouts, fresh & frozen egg roll and wonton paste, fresh fried noodles and soya sprouts.
President: Bill Lee
Vice President: David Lee
VP: Robert Lee
Production Manager: Marc Comtols
Number Employees: 20
Square Footage: 140000
Type of Packaging: Consumer, Bulk
Brands:
 Montreal Chop Suey

8515 Monument Farms Dairy
2107 James Rd
Middlebury, VT 05753-9525
802-545-2119
Fax: 802-545-2117
Milk and other dairy products
President: Robert James
bj@gmavt.net
VP: Peter James
Secretary/Treasurer: Millicent Rooney
VP/Plant Manager: Jonathan Rooney
Estimated Sales: $3.7 Million
Number Employees: 20-49
Type of Packaging: Private Label

Food Manufacturers / A-Z

8516 Monument Farms Dairy
2107 James Rd
Middlebury, VT 05753-9525
802-545-2119
Fax: 802-545-2117
Milk products
President: Robert James
bj@gmavt.net
Co-Owner: Jon Rooney
Co-Owner: James Rooney
Estimated Sales: $10-24.9 000,000
Number Employees: 20-49
Brands:
  Monument Dairy Farms

8517 Moo Chocolate/Organic Children's Chocolate LLC
PO Box 271
Cos Cob, CT 06807-0271
203-561-8864
Fax: 203-869-7040 jackie@moochocolates.com
www.moochocolates.com
Gluten-free, kosher, organic/natural, chocolate bars.
Marketing: Jackie Eckholm

8518 Mooala
2633 McKinney Ave
Suite 130
Dallas, TX 75204
214-206-1902
info@mooala.com
www.mooala.com
Almond and banana milks
CEO: Jeff Richards
Number of Brands: 1
Number of Products: 4
Type of Packaging: Consumer
Brands:
  MOOALA

8519 Moody Dunbar Inc
2000 Waters Edge Dr # 21
Johnson City, TN 37604-8312
423-952-0100
Fax: 423-952-0289
customerservice@moodydunbar.com
www.moodydunbar.com
Processor of bell peppers, pimientos and sweet potatoes, products are certified Kosher
CEO: Stanley Dunbar
CFO: Christy Dunbar
R&D/Quality Assurance Manager: Katie Rohrbacher Nixa
Vice President of Sales & Marketing: Ed Simerly
Estimated Sales: $37,000,000
Number Employees: 20-49
Number of Brands: 11
Type of Packaging: Consumer, Food Service, Private Label
Other Locations:
  Saticoy Foods Corporation
  Santa Paula CA
  Dunbar Foods Corporation
  Dunn NC
Brands:
  CAL-SUN
  CANNON
  DUNBARS MARINATED ROASTED PEPPERS
  DUNBARS ROASTED PEPPERS
  DUNBARS SWEET POTATOES
  DROMEDARY
  SUNSHINE
  OSAGE
  DUNBARS CANDIED YAMS
  NATURE'S PRIDE SWEET POTATOES
  DUNBARS

8520 Moon Dance Baking
625 Martin Ave Ste 5
Rohnert Park, CA 94928-7535
USA
707-588-0800
Fax: 707-588-0804 info@hollybaking.com
www.moondancebaking.com
Cookies, biscotti
President: Debby Dyar
ddyar@hollybaking.com
Estimated Sales: G
Number Employees: 10-19

8521 Moon Rabbit Foods
267 Route 89
Savannah, NY 13146
828-273-6649
www.moonrabbitfoods.com
Manufacturer of baked desserts.
CEO: Candace Crawford
Founder: Mark Shaw

8522 Moon Shot Energy
208-411 Brazos St
Austin, TX 78701-3635
512-387-4703
www.moonshotenergy.com
Energy drinks
President: John Lee

8523 Moon's Seafood Company
461 N.
Harbor City Blvd
Melbourne, FL 32935
321-775-0552
Fax: 321-259-5958 800-526-5624
info@moonseafood.com www.moonseafood.com
Shrimp, scallops, clams and crabs
President: Jay Moon
Vice President: Rick Madrigal
Estimated Sales: $1-3 Million
Number Employees: 1-4
Brands:
  Moon's Seafood

8524 Moonlight Brewing Company
2218 Laughlin Road
PO Box 6
Windsor, CA 95492-8213
707-528-2537
www.moonlightbrewing.com
Beer
President: Brian Hunt
Estimated Sales: $1-3 Million
Number Employees: 1-4
Brands:
  Death and Taxes Black Beer
  Full Moon Light Ale
  Moonlight Pale Lager
  Santa's Tipple
  Twist of Fate Bitter Ale

8525 Moonlight Co
17719 E Huntsman Ave
Reedley, CA 93654-9205
559-638-7799
Fax: 559-638-7199
sales@moonlightcompanies.com
www.moonlightcompanies.com
Grapes and other summer fruit
President: Russ Tavlan
russ.tavlan@moonlightcompanies.com
Estimated Sales: $3-5 Million
Number Employees: 100-249
Type of Packaging: Consumer, Food Service, Private Label, Bulk
Brands:
  Caliente
  California Collection
  Moonlight
  Royal
  The Ripe Stuff

8526 Moonlight Gourmet
PO Box 9686
Tyler, TX 75711-2686
903-581-1228
Fax: 903-581-1098 victoria@txmoon.com
www.txmoon.com
Milk chocolate pecans

8527 Moonlight Mixes LLC
2321 Cantrell Rd
Little Rock, AR 72202-2111
501-374-2244
www.wickedmixes.com
Manufacturer of coconut water.
President: Stan Roberts
Founder & CEO: Brent Bumpers
brent@wickedmixes.com
Sales Manager: Alex Robinson
Number Employees: 5-9

8528 Moonlite Bar-B-Q Inn
2840 W Parrish Ave
Owensboro, KY 42301-2689
270-684-8143
Fax: 270-684-8105 800-322-8989
pbosley@moonlite.com www.moonlite.com
Barbecue meats including mutton, pork and beef; also, bean soup, sauces and chili
President: Fred Bosley
fbosley@moonlite.com
VP: Ken Bosley
Marketing Director: Pat Bosley
Estimated Sales: $3 Million
Number Employees: 100-249
Number of Brands: 1
Number of Products: 48
Type of Packaging: Private Label
Brands:
  Moonlite Bbq Inn

8529 Moonshine Sweet Tea
PO Box 500188
Austin, TX 78750
888-793-3883
info@moonshinesweettea.com
moonshinesweettea.com
Ready-to-drink and concentrated sweet tea
Founder: Joele Porter
CEO: Remmy Castillo
Year Founded: 1946
Number of Brands: 1
Number of Products: 7
Type of Packaging: Consumer, Food Service
Brands:
  MOONSHINE SWEET TEA

8530 Moonstruck Chocolate Co
6600 N Baltimore Ave
Portland, OR 97203-5403
503-247-3448
Fax: 503-247-3450 800-557-6666
www.moonstruckchocolate.com
Manufacturer of chocolate.
Co-Owner: Sally Bany
Co-Owner: Dave Bany
dbany@moonstruckchocolate.com
Number Employees: 50-99

8531 Moore Organics
9047 Sutton Place
Hamilton, OH 45011
513-881-7144
Fax: 513-881-7145 sdagnillo@amtodd.com
Creates and manufactures natural and certified organic specialty ingredients.
Inside Sales Representative: Susan D'Agnillo
Contact: Galliano Enrique
galliano.enrique@moorelab.com

8532 Moore's Candies
3004 Pinewood Avenue
Baltimore, MD 21214
410-836-8840
Fax: 410-426-7073
Handcrafted chocolates and candy including truffles, almond crunch, chocolate-covered potato chips and pretzels, holiday and wedding chocolate items and specialty items
Co-Owner: Jim Heyl Jr
Co-Owner: Lois Heyl
VP: Dana Heyl
Estimated Sales: $3 Million
Number Employees: 5-9
Square Footage: 5000
Type of Packaging: Consumer, Food Service, Private Label, Bulk
Brands:
  Moores

8533 (HQ)Mooresville Ice Cream Co
172 N Broad St
PO Box 118
Mooresville, NC 28115-3182
704-664-5456
Fax: 503-370-8516 800-304-7172
www.delux.com
Ice cream, low fat & no sugar added, sherbet, and novelties including ice cream sandwiches, flavored bars, and the infamous nutty cone.

Food Manufacturers / A-Z

President: Bob Stamey
Accounting: Tracy Potts
Manager: Marcus Ireland
Sales: Don Ashley
Manager: Brett French
brett@deluxe1924.com
Number Employees: 10-19
Type of Packaging: Consumer, Food Service, Private Label, Bulk
Brands:
  Deluxe
  Snickers
  Twix
  M&M
  Dove
  Klondike
  Rich's

8534 Moorhead & Company
PO Box 1799
Rocklin, CA 95677
818-787-2510
Fax: 916-624-1604   800-322-6325
order@moorAgar.com   www.mooragar.com
Manufacturer and importer of stabilizers including agar
President: Deborah Nichols
Sales/Marketing: Brenda Franklin
Estimated Sales: $180000
Number Employees: 3
Type of Packaging: Bulk
Brands:
  Agarich
  Agarloid
  Agarmoor

8535 Moosehead Breweries Ltd.
89 Main St W
St. John, NB E2M 3H2
Canada
www.moosehead.ca
Processor and exporter of beer.
President & CEO: Andrew Oland
Executive Chairman: Derek Oland
CFO: Patrick Oland
VP, Supply Chain: Matthew Oland
Quality Control Technician: Jeanann Fairweather
Director of Marketing & Communications: Karen Cousins
Retail Operations Manager: Stephen Buckley
Special Projects Manager: Mary Gardner
Year Founded: 1867
Estimated Sales: $263.8 Million
Number Employees: 400
Type of Packaging: Consumer, Food Service
Brands:
  Moosehead Lager

8536 Morabito Baking Co Inc
757 Kohn St
Norristown, PA 19401-3739
610-275-5419
Fax: 610-275-0358   800-525-7747
www.morabitobaking.com
Sourdough breads and Spoletti rolls
President: Aaron Chanthakoune
aaron@morabito.com
Marketing Manager: Joanna Morabito
Director of Sales: Marc Knox
Director of Human Resources: Cassandra Morabito
Estimated Sales: $10 Million
Number Employees: 100-249
Square Footage: 140000
Type of Packaging: Consumer, Food Service, Private Label, Bulk
Brands:
  Morabito

8537 Moravian Cookies Shop
224 S Cherry St
Winston Salem, NC 27101-5231
336-924-1278
Fax: 336-924-9470   800-274-2994
sales@salembaking.com
Cookies and baked goods
President/Owner: Dewey Wilkerson
Contact: Brooke Smith
b.smith@salembaking.com
Operations Manager: Vincent Pellegrino
Estimated Sales: $2.30 Million
Number Employees: 25

8538 More Than Gourmet
929 Home Ave
Akron, OH 44310-4107
330-762-6652
Fax: 330-762-4832   800-860-9385
info@morethangourmet.com
www.morethangourmet.com
Stocks and sauces
Owner: Brad Sacks
bsacks@morethangourmet.com
CFO: Scott Bonnette
Marketing: Todd Hohman
Estimated Sales: $500,000-$1 Million
Number Employees: 20-49
Type of Packaging: Consumer, Food Service
Brands:
  Demi-Glace Veal Gold
  Glace De Poulet Gold
  Veggie Glace Gold

8539 Morehouse Foods Inc
760 Epperson Dr
City Of Industry, CA 91748-1336
626-854-1655
Fax: 626-854-1656   888-297-9800
info@morehousefoods.com
www.morehousefoods.com
Yellow mustard, dijon mustard, stoneground mustard, honey spice mustard, spicy brown mustard, horseradish mustard, distilled vinegar and horseradish.
President: David Latter
davesr@morehousefoods.com
Year Founded: 1898
Estimated Sales: $20-50 Million
Number Employees: 20-49
Square Footage: 80000
Type of Packaging: Consumer, Food Service, Private Label, Bulk
Brands:
  Chalif
  El Rey
  Morehouse
  Redwood Empire
  Rhinegeld

8540 Moretti's Poultry
2124 Tremont Ctr
Columbus, OH 43221-3110
614-486-2333
Fax: 614-486-2333   www.morettisofarlington.com
Fresh chicken and turkey
Owner: Tim Moretti
Estimated Sales: $1-3 Million
Number Employees: 20-49
Type of Packaging: Food Service, Bulk

8541 Morey's Seafood Intl LLC
1218 Highway 10 S
Motley, MN 56466-8209
218-352-6345
Fax: 218-352-6523   800-808-3474
www.moreysmarkets.com
Processor, importer and exporter of fresh and frozen fish including marinated salmon, marinated tilapia and marinated smoked fish and other speciality products.
President: Jim Walstrom
CFO: Gary Ziolkowski
Plant Manager: Patti Zahler
VP of Purchasing: Greg Frank
Year Founded: 1937
Estimated Sales: $20-50 Million
Number Employees: 10-19
Square Footage: 52000
Parent Co: Morey's Seafood International
Brands:
  Morey's

8542 Morgan Foods Inc
90 W Morgan St
Austin, IN 47102
812-794-1170
888-430-1780
mfi-web@morganfoods.com
www.morganfoods.com
Canned foods including condensed soups, baked and refried beans, gravies, condiments and sauces.
SVP & Chief Financial Officer: Dan Slattery
dan.slattery@morganfoods.com
CEO & Chairman: John Morgan
Vice Chairman: Kelly Morgan Maciejak
Regional Sales Manager: Monty Craig
VP, Sales & Marketing: Bryan Flowers
VP, Human Resources: Phillip Bundy
Production Manager: Richard Miller
Year Founded: 1899
Estimated Sales: $48.5 Million
Number Employees: 250-499
Square Footage: 1000000
Type of Packaging: Consumer, Food Service, Private Label
Brands:
  American Beauty
  Royal Gem
  Scott Country

8543 Morgan Mill
P.O.Box 525
Cherokee, NC 28719-0525
828-497-9227
Fax: 828-497-4330
Rainbow trout
Owner: Dale Owen
Estimated Sales: Less than $200,000
Number Employees: 1-4

8544 Morgan Winery
590 Brunken Ave
Suite C
Salinas, CA 93901
831-751-7777
Fax: 831-751-7780   www.morganwinery.com
Wine
Propietors: Donna Lee
Propietors: Dan Lee
Wine Maker: Giane Abate
Marketing Coordinator: Jason Auxier
Director of Sales: Jim McAllister
Contact: Jason Auxier
jason.auxier@morganwinery.com
Production Team: Carmen Maldonado
Estimated Sales: $850000
Number Employees: 5-9

8545 Morii Foods, Inc.
8215 SW Tualatin Sherwood Rd.
Tualatin, OR 97062-8441
503-691-7007
Fax: 503-692-5388
Rice noodles, instant short rice pasta, organic non-fried wheat noodles, vermicelli noodles
Vice President: Hideki Ogino
Estimated Sales: $32.33 Million
Number Employees: 1-4
Type of Packaging: Private Label, Bulk

8546 Morinaga Nutritional Foods, Inc.
3838 Del Amo Blvd
Suite 201
Torrance, CA 90503
310-787-0200
Fax: 310-787-2727   info@morinu.com
www.morinu.com
Tofu products
President & CEO: Hiroyuki Imanishi
Estimated Sales: $3-5 Million
Number Employees: 10-19
Square Footage: 20000
Parent Co: Morinaga Milk Company
Type of Packaging: Consumer, Food Service, Private Label
Other Locations:
  Morinaga Nutritional Foods
  Tualatin OR
Brands:
  Mori-Nu

8547 Morning Glory Dairy
3399 S Ridge Rd
De Pere, WI 54115-9522
920-336-4206
Fax: 920-336-7317   www.deanfoods.com
Dairy
Manager: Calvin Rose
Plant Manager: Wally Hel
Estimated Sales: $10-20 Million
Number Employees: 100-249
Parent Co: Dairy Farmers of America

Food Manufacturers / A-Z

8548 Morning Star Foods
8 Joanna Court
East Brunswick, NJ 08816-2108
800-237-5320
Fax: 732-432-3928
Manufacturer and marketer of consumer packaged goods
President/CEO: Herman Graffinder
CFO: Craig Miller
Sr. VP Marketing: Toby Purdy
Sr. VP Operations: Samuel Hillin
Parent Co: Dean Foods Company
Type of Packaging: Private Label, Bulk

8549 MorningStar Coffee Company
207-E, Carter Drive
West Chester, PA 19382
888-854-2233
Fax: 610-701-7032 888-854-2233
www.morningstarcoffee.us
Specialty coffee roasters
President: Charles Streitwieser
cmarks@citymission.org
Estimated Sales: $450,000
Number Employees: 5-9
Type of Packaging: Private Label, Bulk
Brands:
 Morning Star
 Numit

8550 Morningland Dairy Cheese Company
6248 County Road 2980
Mountain View, MO 65548
417-855-0588
Fax: 417-469-5086 morninglanddairy@gmail.com
Gourmet health and raw milk cheeses
President: James Reiners
Estimated Sales: $3-5 Million
Number Employees: 5-9
Type of Packaging: Consumer, Food Service, Private Label, Bulk
Brands:
 Morningland Dairy
 Ozark Hills

8551 Morningstar Farms
1675 Fairview Rd
Zanesville, OH 43701-8890
740-453-5501
Fax: 740-453-7789 800-535-5644
www.morningstarfarms.com
Canned and frozen vegetarian foods
CEO/President: Dale Twomley
VP Finance/CFO: William Kirkwood
HR Executive: Don Michalenko
don.michalenko@kellogg.com
Plant Manager: Gene Fluck
Estimated Sales: $5-10 Million
Number Employees: 250-499
Square Footage: 800000
Parent Co: Kellogg Company
Type of Packaging: Consumer, Food Service
Brands:
 Loma Linda
 Morningstar Farms
 Worthington

8552 Morningstar Foods
13448 Volta Rd
Los Banos, CA 93635
209-826-8000
Fax: 209-826-8266 www.morningstarco.com
Tomatoes and tomato paste
President: Chris Rufer
Sales & Marketing: Jennifer Ingram
Year Founded: 1970
Estimated Sales: $200-249 Million
Number Employees: 100-249

8553 Moroni Feed Company
15 E. 1900 S. Feed Mill Rd.
Moroni, UT 84646
435-436-8202
Fax: 435-436-8101 norbest@norbest.com
Fresh and frozen turkeys.
President/CEO, Norbest: Matt Cook
mcook@norbest.com
Estimated Sales: $125 Million+
Number Employees: 850
Parent Co: Norbest, LLC
Type of Packaging: Private Label
Brands:
 Norbest

8554 Morre-Tec Ind Inc
1 Gary Rd
Union, NJ 07083-5527
908-686-0307
Fax: 908-688-9005 sales@morretec.com
www.morretec.com
Manufacturer, importer and exporter of magnesium chloride, food grade and potassium bromate; importer and wholesaler/distributor of low sodium substitutes and licorice, spray, dried and powder
Owner: Rachel Abenilla
rachela@morretec.com
Marketing Director: Michael Fuchs
Operations Manager: Norm Cantoe
Estimated Sales: $10-20 Million
Number Employees: 20-49
Number of Products: 150
Square Footage: 50000
Type of Packaging: Consumer, Bulk

8555 Morreale John R Inc
216 N Peoria St
Chicago, IL 60607-1706
312-421-3664
Fax: 312-421-8928 morrealemeat@aol.com
www.jrmorreale.com
Distributor of beef and pork products. Provides custom trimmed beef cuts and fresh beef trimmings.
President: Mike Magrini
President: Steve Hurckes
President: Jerry Schomer
Sales: Bob Apato
General Manager: Steve Hurckes
tfrigo@jrmorreale.com
Production Manager: Ramiro Corral
Estimated Sales: $25,000,000
Number Employees: 50-99
Number of Products: 1
Square Footage: 100000
Type of Packaging: Bulk

8556 Morris J Golombeck Inc
960 Franklin Ave
Brooklyn, NY 11225-2403
718-284-3505
Fax: 718-693-1941 golspice@aol.com
www.golombeckspice.com
Processor, importer and exporter of herbs and spices including basil, cassia, cayenne, garlic, ginger, paprika, etc
Owner: Hy Golombeck
mail@golombeckspice.com
Vice President: Sheldon Golombeck
Estimated Sales: $5-10 Million
Number Employees: 10-19
Square Footage: 480000
Type of Packaging: Bulk

8557 Morris Kitchen
Brooklyn, NY
347-457-6994
info@morriskitchen.com
www.morriskitchen.com
Manufacturer of cocktail syrup and mixers.
Founder: Kari Morris

8558 Morris National
760 Mckeever Ave
Azusa, CA 91702
626-385-2000
Fax: 626-969-8670 info@morrisnational.com
www.morrisnational.com
Truffles, licorice, hard candy and liquor-filled chocolates.
VP, Manufacturing: Claude Douessin
Year Founded: 1974
Parent Co: Morris National Canada

8559 Morrison Farms
R.R. 1 Box 50A
Clearwater, NE 68726
402-887-5335
Fax: 402-887-4709
morrison@nebraskapopcorn.com
www.morrisonfarms.com
High quality popcorn and dry, edible bean products
President: Frank Morrison
Estimated Sales: $300,000-500,000
Number Employees: 1-4

8560 Morrison Lamothe
5240 Finch Avenue East
Unit 2
Toronto, ON M1S 5A2
Canada
416-291-6762
Fax: 416-291-5046 877-677-6533
info@morrisonlamothe.com
www.morrisonlamothe.com
Frozen prepared beef, chicken and turkey pot pies, empanadas, puff pastry appetizers, strudels and wellingtons. Also offers single serve pasta frozen meals, compartment dinners, breakfast products, and bowl entrees.
President/CEO: J.M. Pigott
Estimated Sales: $45 Million
Number Employees: 350
Number of Brands: 4
Square Footage: 38000
Type of Packaging: Consumer, Private Label
Brands:
 Cliffside
 Holiday Farms
 Pub Pies
 Savarin

8561 Morrison Meat Packers
738 NW 72nd St
Miami, FL 33150-3695
305-836-4461
Fax: 305-836-2750 800-330-4267
gilda@morrisonmeat.com www.morrisonmeat.com
Processor of ham, ham products, and sausages.
President: Claudio Rodriguez
Vice President: Gilda Rodriguez
Year Founded: 1966
Estimated Sales: $20-50 Million
Number Employees: 50-99
Type of Packaging: Consumer

8562 Morrison Meat Pies
3403 S 1400 W # C
West Valley, UT 84119-4050
801-977-0181
Fax: 801-977-0448 www.morrisonmeatpies.com
Meat pies and frozen meat pie crust
Owner: Eugene Tafoya
Vice President, Manager: Susan Tafoya
Contact: Susan Tafoya
tafoya@morrisonmeatpies.com
Production Manager: Richard Gunther
Estimated Sales: $3-5 Million
Number Employees: 1-4
Type of Packaging: Consumer

8563 Morrison Milling Co
319 E Prairie St
Denton, TX 76201-6109
940-387-6111
Fax: 940-566-5992 800-531-7912
humanresources@morrisonmilling.com
www.morrisonmilling.com
Flour, processed corn, cornmeal, frosting mixes, soups, and gravies
President & CEO: Dale Tremblay
Operations Director: James Williams
Estimated Sales: $20-50 Million
Number Employees: 100-249
Parent Co: CH Guenther & Son
Type of Packaging: Private Label
Brands:
 Morrison Brand

8564 Morse's Sauerkraut
3856 Washington Rd
Waldoboro, ME 04572-5502
207-832-5569
Fax: 207-832-2297 866-832-5569
morses@roadrunner.com
www.morsessauerkraut.com
Salsa, beet relish, pickled beets and sauerkraut
Owner: James Gammon
james@morsessk.com
Estimated Sales: Below $5 Million
Number Employees: 10-19
Type of Packaging: Consumer, Food Service
Brands:
 Morse's

Food Manufacturers / A-Z

8565 Mortgage Apple Cake
677 Ramapo Rd
Teaneck, NJ 07666-1807
201-692-9538
angela@maccakes.com
www.maccakes.com
Manufacturer of apple cakes.
Founder: Angela Logan
Contact: Brenda Allen
brendaa@maccakes.com
Estimated Sales: Less Than $500,000
Number Employees: 1-4

8566 Mortillaro Lobster Company
65 Commercial St
Gloucester, MA 01930-5047
978-282-4621
Fax: 978-281-0579
Lobster
President: Vincent Mortillaro
Estimated Sales: $5-10 Million
Number Employees: 20-49

8567 Mortimer's Fine Foods
5341 John Lucas Drive
Burlington, ON L7L 6A8
Canada
905-336-0000
Fax: 905-336-0909
customerservice@mortimers.com
www.mortimers.com
Processor and exporter of frozen beef, prepared and vegetarian entrees and meat pies
VP Sales: Karim Talakshi
Type of Packaging: Consumer, Food Service, Private Label, Bulk
Brands:
  Mortimer Fine Foods

8568 Morton & Bassett Spices
1400 Valley House Dr
Suite 100
Rohnert Park, CA 94928
415-883-8530
Fax: 415-883-0813 www.mortonbassett.com
Spices and seasonings
Founder: Morton Gothelf
mgothelf@mortonbassett.com
Estimated Sales: Below $5 Million
Number Employees: 10-19
Number of Products: 70
Brands:
  M B Spices

8569 Morton Salt Inc.
123 North Wacker Dr.
Chicago, IL 60606-1743
312-807-2000
Fax: 312-807-2899 800-725-8847
www.mortonsalt.com
Salt including food grade and rock salt.
Chief Executive Officer: Christian Herrmann
Vice President/CFO: Tim McKean
Vice President/General Counsel: Chad Walker
Vice President, Human Resources: Nicole Turner
Vice President, Operations: Jennifer McCormick
Year Founded: 1848
Estimated Sales: $429.7 Million
Number Employees: 2,900
Square Footage: 95838
Parent Co: K+S AG
Type of Packaging: Consumer, Food Service, Private Label, Bulk
Other Locations:
  Morton Salt Distribution
  Newark CA
  Grantsville UT
  Perth Amboy NJ
  Port Canaveral FL
Brands:
  Morton Salt
  Morton Rock Salt
  Morton Evaporation Salt
  Morton Solar Salt

8570 Mosby Winery
9496 Santa Rosa Rd
Buellton, CA 93427-9482
800-706-6729
info@mosbywines.com mosbywines.com
Wines, oils and balsamics.
Estimated Sales: $2.5-5 Million
Number Employees: 4
Type of Packaging: Private Label

8571 Mosher Products Inc
4318 Hayes Ave
Cheyenne, WY 82001-2349
307-632-1492
Fax: 307-632-1492 info@wheatandgrain.com
www.wheatandgrain.com
Organic grain
President: Leonard O Mosher
leonard@wheatandgrain.com
Estimated Sales: Below $5 Million
Number Employees: 20-49
Square Footage: 240000
Other Locations:
  Bushnell NE
Brands:
  Mosher Products

8572 Moss Creek Winery
6015 Steele Canyon Rd
Napa, CA 94558-9634
707-252-1295
Fax: 707-254-9327 info@mosscreekwinery.com
www.mosscreekwinery.com
Wines
Owner: Ann Moskowite
Owner: George Moskowite
gmoskowite@mosscreekwinery.com
Winemaker: Nils Venge
Estimated Sales: Less Than $500,000
Number Employees: 1-4
Brands:
  Moss Creek

8573 Mossholder's Farm Cheese Factory
4017 N Richmond Street
Appleton, WI 54913-9704
920-734-7575
Cheese
Co-Owner: Larry Mossholder
Co-Owner: Lois Mossholder
Estimated Sales: Less than $500,000
Number Employees: 1-4

8574 Mosti Mondiale/Gourmet Mondiale
6865 Route 132
Ste-Catherine, QC J5C 1B6
Canada
450-638-6380
Fax: 450-638-7049
nino.piazza@mostimondiale.com
www.gourmetmondiale.com
Wine, olive oil, balsamic vinegar
Marketing: Nino Piazza

8575 Mother Earth Enterprises
15 Irving Place
New York, NY 10003-2316
212-777-1250
Fax: 212-614-8132 866-436-7688
denis@hempnut.com
Wholesaler/distributor of hempnuts; hemp oil, meal and flour; and toasted, sterilized and roasted grain hemp (seed). Highly adaptable for baking and cooking needs
President: Denis Cicero
Type of Packaging: Food Service

8576 Mother Murphy's
2826 South Elm-Eugene Street
Greensboro, NC 27406
336-273-1737
Fax: 336-273-0858 800-849-1277
www.mothermurphys.com
Flavor manufacturer serving the baking, beverage and tobacco industries.
President: David Murphy
Contact: Yuhong Chen
ychen@mothermurphys.com
Year Founded: 1920
Number of Products: 500
Square Footage: 210000
Type of Packaging: Private Label, Bulk

8577 Mother Nature's Goodies
13378 California St
Yucaipa, CA 92399-5106
909-795-6018
Fax: 909-795-0748
www.mothernaturesgoodies.com
Granola, seven grain bread, frozen pies and candy sundrops
President: Albert G Goude
Manager: Ronn Neish
CFO: Learner Guode
Estimated Sales: $3-5 Million
Number Employees: 10-19
Square Footage: 16000
Type of Packaging: Private Label
Brands:
  Mother Nature's Goodies

8578 Mother Parker's Tea & Coffee
2530 Stanfield Road
Mississauga, ON L4Y 1S4
Canada
905-279-9100
Fax: 905-279-9821 800-387-9398
www.mother-parkers.com
Processor and exporter of ground and whole bean coffees and teas including orange pekoe, regular, decaffeinated, black and herbal; importer of green coffee and teas
Co-CEO: Michael Higgins
Co-CEO: Paul Higgins, Jr.
Sr. VP/Finance/Administration: Brian Goard
Vice President: Chris Bklecki
Number Employees: 280
Type of Packaging: Consumer, Food Service, Private Label, Bulk
Brands:
  Blue Ribbon
  Higgins & Burke
  Mother Parkers

8579 Mother Raw
Toronto, ON M3J 2E5
Canada
855-464-0117
info@motherraw.com motherraw.com
Plant-based dressings, dips and condiments
Founder: Michelle Kopman

8580 Mother Shucker's Original Cocktail Sauce
900 Gregg Street, 1A
Columbia, SC 29201-3913
803-261-3802
Fax: 803-779-3444
mothershuckersauce@gmail.com
www.mothershuckersauce.com
Other condiments, other sauces, seasonings and cooking enhancers.
Marketing: Mary Sparrow

8581 Mother Teresa's
700 W Plantation Dr
Clute, TX 77531-5248
979-265-7429
Fax: 979-297-0932 888-265-7429
motTfinefoods@cs.com
www.motherteresasfinefoods.com
Vegetables, sauces and dressings
Owner: Teresa Polimano
mottfinefoods@cs.com
Estimated Sales: Less Than $500,000
Number Employees: 5-9
Brands:
  Mother Teresa's Fine Foods

8582 Mother's Mountain Pantry
2 Mustard Hollow
Falmouth, ME 04105
207-781-4658
Fax: 207-781-2121 800-440-9891
sales@mothersmountain.com
www.mothersmountain.com
Mustard, horseradish, ketchup, dill, chili sauce, creamy horseradish sauce and hot pepper sauce. Just added-jams and jellies!
President: Carrol Tanner
CFO: Dennis Proctor
Estimated Sales: Below $5 Million
Number Employees: 6

8583 Mother-In-Law's Kimchi
Long Island City, NY 11101
www.milkimchi.com
Manufacturer of kimchi and gochujang
Owner: Lauryn Chun

Food Manufacturers / A-Z

8584 **Motherland International Inc**
8822 Flower Road
Suite 202
Rancho Cucamonga, CA 91730
909-596-8882
Fax: 909-596-8870 800-590-5407
www.motherlandinc.org
Processor and exporter of herbs and vitamins in powder and extract forms used in nutritional supplements; contract manufacturing available
President: Jackson Wen
Marketing: Michael Pinson
Estimated Sales: $1-3 Million
Number Employees: 20-49
Square Footage: 100000
Parent Co: Motherland International
Type of Packaging: Consumer, Food Service, Private Label, Bulk

8585 **Mott's**
PO Box 869077
Plano, TX 75086-9077
972-673-8088
800-426-4891
www.motts.com
Apple products that include apple sauce and apple juice.
CEO, Keurig Dr Pepper: Robert Gamgort
Year Founded: 1842
Estimated Sales: $228 Million
Number Employees: 1000
Number of Brands: 2
Parent Co: Dr. Pepper Snapple Group
Type of Packaging: Consumer, Food Service
Brands:
  Mott's
  Mott's for Tots
  Mott's Sensibles
  Mott's Fruit Flavoured Snacks

8586 **(HQ)Mott's LLP**
P.O. Box 869077
Plano, TX 75086-9077
Fax: 914-612-4100 800-426-4891
www.motts.com
Applesauce, cooking wine, cocktail mixes, fruit drinks, lime juice, apple juice, tomato-clam cocktail, fruit drinks, apple juice, tomato-clam cocktail, molasses
President/Sales: Michael McGrath
CFO: Dave Gerics
CEO: Jack Belsito
Estimated Sales: $300,000-500,000
Number Employees: 1-4
Parent Co: Cadbury Schweppes PLC
Type of Packaging: Consumer, Food Service, Bulk
Brands:
  Clamato
  Grandma's Molasses
  Hawaiian Punch
  Holland House
  Ibc
  Mauna La'i
  Mott's
  Mott's Fruitsations
  Mr & Mrs T
  Realemon
  Reallime
  Rose's
  Ypp-Hoo

8587 **Motto**
Milton, MA
617-848-9248
orders@milkimchi.com
www.drinkmotto.com
Manufacturer of sparkling matcha tea.
Co-Founder: Tom Olcott
Co-Founder: Henry Cosby

8588 **Mound City Shelled Nut Inc**
7831 Olive Blvd
St Louis, MO 63130-2039
314-725-9040
Fax: 314-725-9044 888-338-6887
sales@moundcity.com www.moundcity.com
Chocolate candy, nut meats, shelled nuts, peanuts
President: Byron Smyrniotis
byron.smyrniotis@nutsgifts.com
Vice President: Stacy Smyrniotis
Estimated Sales: $1.8 Million
Number Employees: 1-4
Type of Packaging: Private Label

Brands:
  Jordan Almonds

8589 **Mount Franklin Foods**
1800 Northwestern Dr
El Paso, TX 79912
Fax: 888-880-9154 800-351-8178
www.mountfranklinfoods.com
Candy and fruit-flavored snack manufacturer and nut processor
President & CEO: Gary Ricco
COO: Jay David
Number of Brands: 1
Number of Products: 7
Type of Packaging: Consumer, Private Label

8590 **Mount Mansfield Maple Products**
450 Weaver St
Suite 18
Winooski, VT 05404
802-497-1671
www.vermontpuremaple.com
Maple syrup
Co-Owner: Chris White
Co-Owner: Lindsay White

8591 **Mount Olympus Waters**
800-782-5508
www.mountolympuswater.com
Manufacturer and supplier of bottler spring water, cups, water coolers and coffee brewers
President: Dave Muscato
CEO: Tom Harrington
CFO: Jerry Hoyle
General Manager: Mike Garrity
Estimated Sales: $5-10 Million
Number Employees: 50-99
Parent Co: DS Services of America
Type of Packaging: Consumer, Food Service, Private Label, Bulk

8592 **Mount Palomar Winery**
33820 Rancho California Road
Temecula, CA 92591
951-676-5047
Fax: 951-676-8928 800-854-5177
info@mountpalomar.com
www.mountpalomarwinery.com
Manufacturer of fine wines.
President: Peter Poole
General Manager: Carol Darwish
Accounting Manager: Tara Ruth
Director, Operations: Kris May
Year Founded: 1969
Estimated Sales: $20-50 Million
Number Employees: 50-99
Number of Brands: 2
Brands:
  Castelletto
  Mount Palomar

8593 **Mountain City Coffee Roasters**
285 Beaverdam Rd
Enka, NC 28728
828-667-0869
Fax: 828-667-0869 888-730-0869
roastmaster@mountaincity.com
www.mountaincity.com
Coffee
Owner: Randall Sluder
Co-Owner/President: Debra Furr Sluder
Estimated Sales: Less Than $500,000
Number Employees: 1-4
Type of Packaging: Consumer, Bulk
Brands:
  Mountain City

8594 **Mountain Cove Vineyards**
1362 Fortunes Cove Ln
Lovingston, VA 22949-2226
434-263-5392
Fax: 434-263-8540 aweed1@juno.com
www.mountaincovevineyards.com
Wines
President: Albert C Weed II
Estimated Sales: $1-3 Million
Number Employees: 1-4

8595 **Mountain Fire Foods**
2850 Main Road
Huntington, VT 05462-9608
802-434-2685
Fax: 802-434-2685
Marinades and ketchup

Owner: Karyl Kent

8596 **Mountain High Organics**
9 South Main St
New Milford, CT 06776
860-210-7805
Fax: 860-210-7837 mountainhighorganics.com
Organic pastas and oils
Founder: Joanne Fellin
Type of Packaging: Bulk

8597 **Mountain High Yogurt**
PO Box 9452
Minneapolis, MN 55440
303-761-2210
Fax: 763-764-8330 866-964-4878
www.mountainhighyoghurt.com
Original and honey style yogurt
President: Greg Bngles
Plant Manager: Ralph Lee
Number Employees: 20-49
Parent Co: Borden
Type of Packaging: Consumer, Food Service, Private Label
Brands:
  Mountain High

8598 **Mountain Organic Foods**
920 Country Club Dr, Suite 1A
Moraga, CA 94556
925-377-0119
www.morfoods.com
Organic fruit bars.
Co-Owner: Ken Newman
Co-Owner: Craig Gass
Estimated Sales: $180,000
Number Employees: 2
Type of Packaging: Consumer
Brands:
  BEAR FRUIT BAR

8599 **Mountain Rose Herbs**
35859 Highway 58
Pleasant Hill, OR 97455-9651
541-741-7307
Fax: 510-217-4012 800-879-3337
customerservice@mountainroseherbs.com
www.mountainroseherbsmercantile.com
Organic herbal products.
Owner: Julie Baily
Vice President: Shawn Donnille
Laboratory/Quality Control Manager: Steven Yeager
Marketing Director: Irene Wolansky
Terms Department Manager: Ray Sammartano
julie@mountainroseherbs.com
Public And Media Relations: Kori Rodley
Operations Manager: Jennifer Gerrity
Production Manager: Julie DeBord
Warehouse Manager: Kim Christenson
Purchasing Manager: Peggy Hall
Estimated Sales: Less Than $500,000
Number Employees: 5-9
Type of Packaging: Consumer, Bulk

8600 **Mountain States Pecan**
2830 N. Sycamore St.
Roswell, NM 88201
575-623-2216
Fax: 505-625-0126 farm@pecan.com
www.pecan.com
Grower and processor of pecans; gift tins available
Owner: Bruce Haley
Operations Manager: Reba Haley
Estimated Sales: $2.5-5 Million
Number Employees: 5-9

8601 **(HQ)Mountain States Rosen**
355 Food Center Dr # C16
C-16
Bronx, NY 10474-7053
718-842-4447
Fax: 718-617-4096 800-872-5262
info@rosenlamb.com
www.mountainstatesrosen.com
Lamb and veal
CEO: Dennis Stiffler
EVP: David Gage
Number Employees: 100-249
Type of Packaging: Food Service
Other Locations:
  Mountain States Rosen, LLC
  Greeley CO
Brands:
  Cedar Springs Lamb

Food Manufacturers / A-Z

Cedar Springs Natural Veal
Shepherd's Pride

8602 Mountain Sun Pubs & Breweries
1535 Pearl St
Boulder, CO 80302-5408
303-546-0886
Fax: 303-413-1312 jess@mountainsunpub.com
www.longspeakpub.com
Beer
Owner: Kevin Daly
General Manager: Jessica Candalaria
Estimated Sales: $500,000-$1 Million
Number Employees: 20-49
Brands:
Colorado Kind Ale
Quinn's Golden Ale
Thunderhead Stout

8603 Mountain Valley Poultry
631 S Kansas Avenue
PO Box 6967
Brandon, FL 72766-6967
813-689-2616
Fax: 479-751-0506 www.mvpmarketing.com
Further processed poultry products including de-boned, cooked, etc
Owner: Don Walker
Estimated Sales: $.5-1 million
Number Employees: 1-4

8604 Mountain Valley Products Inc
108 East Blaine Avenue
PO Box 246
Sunnyside, WA 98944-0246
509-837-8084
Fax: 509-837-3481 www.valleyprocessing.com
Processor and exporter of fruit juice concentrates including apple and grape; also, apple juice
President: Mary Ann Bliesner
VP Operation: Kelly Bliesner
Maintenance Manager: Jay Fanciullo
Sales Manager: Terry Bliesner
Maintenance Supervisor: Mark Mulford
Production/Personnel: David Perez
Estimated Sales: $1.2 Million
Number Employees: 20-49
Square Footage: 180000
Type of Packaging: Bulk

8605 (HQ)Mountain Valley Spring Company
150 Central Avenue
Hot Springs, AR 71901-3528
501-624-1635
Fax: 501-623-5135 800-643-1501
www.mountainvalleyspring.com
Spring water
Chief Executive Officer: Breck Speed
CFO: Brad Frieberg
Retail: Taylor Cronor
HOD Sales: John Speed
Contact: Melanie Breeding
mbreeding@mountainvalleyspring.com
Estimated Sales: $10-20 Million
Number Employees: 100-249
Type of Packaging: Consumer, Food Service, Private Label
Brands:
Carolina Mountain Spring Water
Diamond Spring Water
Mountain Valley Spring Water

8606 Mountain Valley Spring Water
299 Haywood Rd
Asheville, NC 28806-4545
828-254-9848
Fax: 828-252-1528 800-627-1062
springwater@mountainvalleywaterasheville.com
www.mountainvalleywaterasheville.com
Manufacturers of bottled water
President: Don Freeman
Estimated Sales: $1-3 Million
Number Employees: 10-19
Type of Packaging: Private Label, Bulk
Brands:
Natural Mountain Water

8607 Mountain View Fruit Sales
4275 Avenue 416
Reedley, CA 93654-9141
559-637-9933
Fax: 559-637-9733
rataide@mountainviewfruit.com

Necatrines, peaches and plums
Owner: Mike Thurlow
Sales Manager: Mike Thurlow
mthurlow@mountainviewfruit.com
Number Employees: 100-249

8608 Mountainbrook of Vermont
P.O.Box 39
Jeffersonville, VT 05464
802-644-1988
Fax: 802-644-6795
Dipping oils, fruit spreads, dressings, packaged dry mixes, mustards, and gift packs.
Owner: Lisa Bryan
Estimated Sales: $1-3 Million
Number Employees: 1-4
Type of Packaging: Consumer

8609 Mountainside Farms Inc
55724 State Highway 30
Roxbury, NY 12474-1324
607-326-4161
Produces hormone and antibiotic free milk and cage free eggs.
Manager: Stacy Palamtier
stacyp@msfdairy.com
Estimated Sales: $10-50 Million
Number Employees: 1-4
Number of Brands: 2
Parent Co: Elmhurst Dairy
Type of Packaging: Consumer
Brands:
Mountainside Farms

8610 Mountaire Corporation
P.O. Box 1320
Millsboro, DE 19966
302-934-1100
877-887-1490
www.mountaire.com
Poultry.
Chairman/CEO: Ronald Cameron
CFO: Craig Lair
Year Founded: 1914
Estimated Sales: $630 Million
Number Employees: 7,000
Brands:
Mountaire

8611 Mountanos Family Coffee & Tea Co.
1331 Commerce St.
Petaluma, CA 94549
707-462-6333
800-624-7031
info@mfct.com www.mfct.com
Coffee, tea, and accessories
Director of Operations: Erik Bianchi
Number Employees: 50-99

8612 Moutanos Brothers Coffee Company
380 Swift Ave
Suite 13
South San Francisco, CA 94080
650-952-5446
Fax: 650-871-4845 800-624-7031
info@mountanosbros.com
www.mountanosbros.com
Coffee
President: Michael Mountanos
Contact: Dora Gomez-Loeza
dora@mountanosbros.com
Estimated Sales: Less than $500,000
Number Employees: 20-49
Brands:
Lindsay's Teas
Shade Grown Organic
Straight Coffees

8613 Movie Breads Food
225 Industrial Blouevard
Chateauguay, QC J6J 4Z2
Canada
450-692-7606
Fax: 450-692-1810 trmblaykein05@hotmail.com
Grocery
Brands:
Shei Brand
Tradewinds

8614 Moweaqua Packing Plant
601 N Main St
Moweaqua, IL 62550-3695
217-768-4714
Meatpackers@frontiernet.net
www.mowpackingplant.com
Beef and pork
Owner: Terry Yoder
meatpackers@frontiernet.net
Co-Owner: Don Baker
Estimated Sales: Less Than $500,000
Number Employees: 1-4
Type of Packaging: Consumer

8615 Moyer Packing Co.
741 Souder Rd.
Elroy, PA 18964
Fax: 970-346-4611 800-967-8325
www.mopac.com
Boxed and ground beef, and fresh and frozen boxed beef.
Year Founded: 1877
Estimated Sales: Less Than $500,000
Parent Co: JBS USA
Type of Packaging: Consumer, Private Label, Bulk
Brands:
Mopac

8616 Mozzarella Co
2944 Elm St
Dallas, TX 75226-1509
214-741-4072
Fax: 214-741-4076 800-798-2954
mozzcomanager@aol.com www.mozzco.com
Manufacturer of cheese.
Founder: Paula Lambert
mozzco@aol.com
Number Employees: 10-19

8617 Mozzicato De Pasquale Bakery
329 Franklin Ave
Hartford, CT 06114-1890
860-296-0426
Fax: 860-296-8129 info@mozzicatobakery.com
www.mozzicatobakery.com
Bread, pizza, cakes, cookies and ice cream
Owner: Gisella Mozzicato
President: Luigi Mozzicato
COO: Gina Mozzicato
Estimated Sales: $1.5 Million
Number Employees: 20-49

8618 Mr Dell Foods
300 W Major St
Kearney, MO 64060-8550
816-628-4644
Fax: 816-628-4633 mrdells@mrdells.com
www.mrdells.com
Various styles of hash browns, shredded potatoes, O'Brien potatoes, and souther style potatoes.
President: Tommy Baker
tbaker@mrdells.com
VP: Kurt Johnsen
Marketing/Sales Director: Tom Sherrer
Operations Manager: Rick Wilkins
Plant Manager: John Duncan
Estimated Sales: $8445651
Number Employees: 20-49
Square Footage: 160000
Type of Packaging: Consumer, Food Service, Bulk
Brands:
Mr. Dell's I.Q.F. Country Potatoes
Mr. Dell's I.Q.F. Hash Browns
Mr. Dell's I.Q.F. Herb & Garlic
Mr. Dell's I.Q.F. Santa Fe

8619 Mr Espresso
696 3rd St
Oakland, CA 94607-3560
510-287-5200
Fax: 510-287-5204 info@mrespresso.com
www.mrespresso.com
Roasted coffee.
President/CEO: Carlo Di Ruocco
info@mrespresso.com
CFO: Marie-Francoise Di Ruocco
Quality Control Supervisor: John Di Ruocco
VP, Sales/Director, Marketing: Luigi Di Ruocco
Director, Warehouse Operations: Alex Zambrano
Estimated Sales: $10-20 Million
Number Employees: 20-49
Number of Brands: 2
Type of Packaging: Private Label

Food Manufacturers / A-Z

Brands:
  Faema
  Mr. Espresso

8620 Mr Jay's Tamales & Chili
11200 Alameda St
Lynwood, CA 90262-1725
310-537-3932
Fax: 310-537-3938
Chili and tamales
President: Patricia Lang
Owner: Pat Lang
Estimated Sales: Less than $500,000
Number Employees: 1-4
Type of Packaging: Consumer
Brands:
  Chicken Link
  Chilly

8621 Mr. C's
7021 South 220th St
Kent, WA 98032
253-867-6130
888-929-2378
info@calsonindustries.com
www.calsonindustries.com/mrC
Cocktail mixes
President: Sadru Kabani
Parent Co: Calson Industries

8622 Mr. Green Tea Ice Cream
42 E Front St
Keyport, NJ 07735
732-446-9800
www.mrgreentea.com
Ice cream
Purchasing: Lori Emanuele
Year Founded: 1968

8623 Mr. Mak's
32 East Broadway
Suite 501
New York, NY 10002
888-953-9209
hello@mrmaks.com mrmaks.com
Chinese ginger and ginseng tea
Number of Brands: 1
Number of Products: 3
Type of Packaging: Consumer
Brands:
  GINBAO

8624 Mrs Annie's Peanut Patch
1019 B St
Floresville, TX 78114-1947
830-393-7845
Fax: 830-393-9605 www.mrsanniescandy.com
Home-made peanut brittle, jalapeno peanut brittle, pecan brittle, peanut patties, pecan chewies, pecan pralines, flavored peanuts, all natural peanut butter and raw peanuts
Vice President: Mary Ann Sanchez
VP: Mary Ann Sanchez
Estimated Sales: Less Than $500,000
Number Employees: 1-4

8625 Mrs Auld's Gourmet Foods Inc
572 Reactor Way # B4
Reno, NV 89502-4133
775-856-3350
Fax: 775-856-3351 800-322-8537
john@mrs-aulds.com
Gourmet foods including brandied cherries, sweet and spicy pickles, marmalades, preserves, pancake, scone and soda bread mix, salsa, pasta sauce and bean, red corn and barbeque chips, chili sauce, pesto sauce, chestnuts
Owner: John Auld
Sales Manager: Teresa West
Estimated Sales: $1-3 Million
Number Employees: 5-9
Square Footage: 12000

8626 (HQ)Mrs Baird's
PO Box 976
Horsham, PA 19044
800-984-0989
www.mrsbairds.com
Bread, buns, donuts, cinnamon rolls, honey buns, applie pie and chocolate cup cakes
President, Grupo Bimbo: Fred Penny
Parent Co: Bimbo Bakeries USA
Type of Packaging: Consumer, Food Service, Private Label, Bulk

Other Locations:
  Mrs Baird's Bakeries
  Abilene TX
  Mrs Baird's Bakeries
  Fort Worth TX
  Mrs Baird's Bakeries
  Lubbock TX
  Mrs Baird's Bakeries
  Waco TX
  Mrs Baird's Bakeries
  Houston TX
  Mrs Baird's Bakeries
  San Antonio TX
Brands:
  Mrs Baird's(c)

8627 (HQ)Mrs Clark's Foods
740 SE Dalbey Dr
Ankeny, IA 50021-3908
515-964-8036
Fax: 515-964-8397 800-736-5674
info@mrsclarks.com www.mrsclarks.com
Shelf-stable beverages, sauces and dressings
President: Ron Kahrer
QC: Ned Williams
Sales: Julie Southwick
Plant Manager: John Weber
Purchasing: Ron Mathis
Estimated Sales: $450,000
Number Employees: 100-249
Number of Brands: 12
Number of Products: 50
Square Footage: 240000
Parent Co: AGRI Industries
Type of Packaging: Consumer, Food Service, Private Label
Brands:
  Alljuice
  Nature's Choice

8628 Mrs Fisher's Potato Chips
1231 Fulton Ave
Rockford, IL 61103-4025
815-964-9114
Fax: 815-964-3880 www.mrsfisherschips.com
Potato chips including barbecue and sour cream and onion
Owner: Marilyn Blume
mblume@aa.com
VP: Chuck Diventi
Estimated Sales: $780,000
Number Employees: 10-19
Square Footage: 40000
Type of Packaging: Consumer
Brands:
  Mrs. Fisher
  Vita-Sealed

8629 Mrs Grissom's Salads Inc
2500 Bransford Ave
Nashville, TN 37204-2810
615-255-4137
Fax: 615-251-9763 800-255-0571
www.mrsgrissoms.com
Prepared salad
President: Grace G Grissom
CEO: Kenneth Funger
kfunger@xspedius.net
CEO: Kenneth Funger
Plant Manager: Jack McGhee
Estimated Sales: $3.1 Million
Number Employees: 50-99
Square Footage: 160000
Type of Packaging: Consumer

8630 Mrs Mazzula Food Products Inc
240 Carter Dr
Edison, NJ 08817-2097
732-248-0555
Fax: 732-248-0442
Sun dried tomatoes, zucchini, salsa, peppers
President: Christopher Lotito
President: Christopher Lotito
Estimated Sales: Less than $500,000
Number Employees: 20-49
Type of Packaging: Bulk

8631 Mrs Prindables
6300 W Gross Point Rd
Niles, IL 60714-3916
847-588-2900
Fax: 847-588-0392 888-215-1100
customerservice@mrsprindables.com
www.mrsprindables.com
Gourmet caramel apples

President: Tami Gray
tgray@affytapple.com
Number Employees: 50-99

8632 Mrs Rios Corn Products
215 W Avenue N
San Angelo, TX 76903-8434
325-653-5640
Fax: 325-657-0825
Producer of flour and corn tortillas
President: Armando Martinez
mrsrios@zipnet.net
Estimated Sales: $20-50 Million
Number Employees: 20-49

8633 Mrs Stratton's Salads Inc
380 Industrial Ln
Birmingham, AL 35211-4462
205-940-9640
Fax: 205-940-9650 www.mrsstrattons.com
Fresh salads including pimiento, potato, cole slaw, chicken and tuna
President: George Bradford
gbradford@mrsstrattons.com
President: R Vance Fulkerson
Director: Martha Bradford
Estimated Sales: $19 Million
Number Employees: 50-99
Type of Packaging: Consumer, Food Service, Private Label
Brands:
  Mrs. Stratton

8634 Mrs Sullivan's Pies
256 Preston St
Jackson, TN 38301-4967
731-427-2101
Fax: 731-422-1045 info@mrssullivans.com
www.mrssullivans.com
Brownies and pies including coconut, chocolate and pecan
Vice President: Rodney Myrick
rodney@mrssullivans.com
Vice President: Rodney Myrick
rodney@mrssullivans.com
Operations/Manufacturing Director: Melvin Coope
Estimated Sales: $10-20 Million
Number Employees: 20-49
Square Footage: 36000
Type of Packaging: Consumer
Brands:
  Mrs. Sullivan's

8635 Mrs. Denson's Cookie Company
120 Brush St
Ukiah, CA 95482
707-462-2272
Fax: 707-462-2283 800-219-3199
Processor and exporter of fruit juice and honey sweetened cookies including energy, reduced fat, fat-free, vegan and organic
President/Owner: Mike Bielenberg
Vice President: Desi Ringor
Number Employees: 50-99
Square Footage: 100000
Type of Packaging: Consumer, Food Service, Private Label, Bulk
Brands:
  Monster Cookies
  Mrs. Denson's
  Total Fit

8636 Mrs. Dog's Products
PO Box 6872
Grand Rapids, MI 49516-6872
616-970-2677
800-267-7364
mrsdogsorders@comcast.net www.mrsdogs.com
Processor and exporter of gourmet mustard, Jamaican jerk marinade and habanero pepper sauces; also, shelled green chile pistachio nuts
Owner: Julie Curtis Applegate
Estimated Sales: Less than $500,000
Number Employees: 1-4
Type of Packaging: Consumer
Brands:
  Mrs. Dog's

8637 Mrs. Field's Hot Cocoas
PO Box 617
Farmington, UT 84025-0617
801-934-1000
Fax: 801-451-6118 800-845-2400
Hot cocoa

Food Manufacturers / A-Z

8638 Mrs. Fields Original Cookies
Bloomfield, CO
800-266-2547
www.mrsfields.com
Cookies and baked goods.
CEO: Dustin Lyman
Year Founded: 1977
Estimated Sales: $100-129 Million
Number Employees: 4,000
Parent Co: Z Capital Partners

8639 Mrs. Fly's Bakery
608 W Main St
Collegeville, PA 19426-1925
610-489-7288
Fax: 610-489-7488
Bakery products
President: Richard Landis
Estimated Sales: $1-2.5 000,000
Number Employees: 1-4

8640 (HQ)Mrs. Kavanagh's EnglishMuffins
145 North Broadway
Rumford, RI 02916-2801
401-434-0551
Fax: 401-438-0542 800-556-7216
bids@homesteadbaking.com
www.homesteadbaking.com
Breads, rolls and English muffins.
President: Peter Vican
Vice President: Bill Vican
Sales Manager: Vinny Palmiotti
vikramsimha@vitalimages.com
Transportation Director: Jimmy Amaral
Estimated Sales: $5-10 Million
Number Employees: 20-49
Number of Brands: 2
Square Footage: 40000
Type of Packaging: Food Service, Private Label, Bulk
Brands:
  Matthew's All Natural
  Mrs. Kavanagh's

8641 Mrs. Lauralicious
19363 Willamette Drive
Suite 234
West Linn, OR 97068
866-658-8267
Fax: 888-656-6839
Fruit treats
Contact: Laura Becker
mrslauralicious@gmail.com

8642 Mrs. Leeper's Pasta
1000 Italian Way
Excelsior Springs, MO 64024
816-502-6000
Fax: 816-502-6722 800-848-5266
Flavored dry pasta including shapes, fettucine, angel hair, wheat-free, gluten-free, bulk, organic, kosher and private label
President: Michelle Muscat
VP/Director,Sales and Marketing: Ed Muscat
Number Employees: 700
Number of Brands: 6
Type of Packaging: Consumer, Food Service, Private Label, Bulk
Brands:
  Eddie's Spaghetti Organic
  Fortune Macaroni
  Michelle's Organic
  Mrs Leeper's Wheat/Gluten Free

8643 Mrs. Malibu Foods
23852 Pacific Coast Highway
Suite 372
Malibu, CA 90265-4876
310-589-2777
Fax: 310-589-9898 800-677-6254
Food
President/Owner: Debra Root
Estimated Sales: $500,000-$1 Million
Number Employees: 5-9
Type of Packaging: Private Label
Brands:
  Mrs Malibu

8644 Mrs. May's Naturals
860 E 238th Street
Carson, CA 90745-6212
310-830-3130
Fax: 310-830-3045 877-677-6297
Vegan, non-GMO, cholesterol free, dairy free, wheat free, gluten free, 0 trans fat and contain no artificial colors or flavors, nut crunches and bars
President/Owner: Augustine Kim
mrsmay@mrsmay.com
Estimated Sales: $18 Million
Number Employees: 6

8645 Mrs. McGarrigle's Fine Foods
311 St Lawrence Street
PO Box 163
Merrickville, ON K0G 1N0
Canada
613-269-3752
Fax: 613-269-2736 877-768-7827
info@mustard.ca www.mustard.ca
Gourmet mustards, chutneys, preserves and seasonings
Owner: Janet Campbell

8646 Mrs. Miller's Homemade Noodles
110 Crawford Street
Fredericksburg, OH 44627
330-695-2393
Fax: 330-695-6900 800-227-4487
jim@mrsmillersnoodles.com
www.mrsmillersnoodles.com
Dairy-free, kosher, organic/natural, pasta (dry).
Marketing: Jim Gray
Contact: Jennifer Wiles
jenniferwiles@mrsmillersnoodles.com

8647 Mrs. Smiths Bakeries
5055 S Royal Atlanta Dr
Tucker, GA 30084-3097
770-723-6180
Fax: 770-939-6632
Baked goods, pies
President: James Allen
Estimated Sales: $20-50 Million
Number Employees: 100-249
Parent Co: Mrs. Smiths Bakeries

8648 Mrs. Ts Pierogies
600 E Centre St
PO Box 606
Shenandoah, PA 17976-0606
570-462-2745
Fax: 570-462-3299 800-743-7649
consumercontact@pierogies.com
www.pierogies.com
Low-fat pierogies
President: Tom Twardzik
Vice President: Tim Twardzik
IT Manager: Ted Twardzik
VP Marketing: Gary Loverman
VP Sales: Ron Suchecki
Estimated Sales: $10-20 Million
Number Employees: 100-249
Type of Packaging: Consumer, Food Service
Brands:
  Mrs. T'S

8649 Mrs. Willman's Baking
3732 Canada Way
Burnaby, BC V5G 1G4
Canada
604-434-0027
Fax: 403-250-8706 http://www.mrswillmans.com
Sandwiches, donuts, pastries and sausage rolls
CEO: Winston Haffat
President: Eric Olsen
Parent Co: Beaumont Select Corporation
Type of Packaging: Consumer, Food Service
Brands:
  Abm
  Coral Food
  Golden Crust
  Prestige

8650 Mt Baker Vineyards
4298 MT Baker Hwy
Everson, WA 98247-9422
360-592-2300
Fax: 360-592-2526
mountbakervineyards@frontier.com
www.mountbakervineyards.com
Produces red, white, sparkling, dessert and plum wines. As of late 2016, the owners were looking to sell the company.
President: Randy Finley
mountbakervineyards@frontier.com
Manager: Philippe Renaud
Vice President: Patricia Clark-Finley
Sales: Randy Finley
Estimated Sales: $280 Thousand
Number Employees: 10-19
Number of Brands: 1
Type of Packaging: Consumer, Food Service, Private Label
Brands:
  Mount Baker Vineyards & Winery

8651 Mt Bethel Winery
5014 Mount Bethel Dr
Altus, AR 72821-8878
479-468-2444
Fax: 479-468-2444 sales@mountbethel.com
www.mountbethel.com
Wines
Owner: Eugene Post
Estimated Sales: $300,000
Number Employees: 5-9

8652 (HQ)Mt Capra Products
279 SW 9th St
Chehalis, WA 98532-3313
360-748-4224
Fax: 360-748-3099 800-574-1961
www.mtcapra.com
Processor and exporter of dehydrated powder whey product and cheese including cheddar, feta and raw goat milk with no salt
Owner: Frank Stout
frank@mtcapra.com
Key Account Manager: Arny Davis
Estimated Sales: $$1-2.5 Million
Number Employees: 20-49
Square Footage: 20000
Other Locations:
  Mount Capra Cheese
  Chehalis WA

8653 Mt Claire Beverages
160 Perkins St
Torrington, CT 06790-6846
860-489-3804
Fax: 860-496-9425 888-525-2473
Water and soft drinks
Owner/CEO: Timothy Flynn
Manager: Bob Cox
bcox@lccc.wy.edu
Estimated Sales: Less Than $500,000
Number Employees: 5-9

8654 Mt Eden Vineyards
22020 Mount Eden Rd
Saratoga, CA 95070-9729
408-867-9587
Fax: 408-867-4329 info@mounteden.com
www.mounteden.com
Wines
President: Jeffrey Patterson
info@mounteden.com
Co-Owner/President: Ellie Patterson
CEO: Neil Hagen
Business Manager: Eleanor Davis Patterson
Operations Manager: Andrea Kyle
Estimated Sales: Below $5 Million
Number Employees: 5-9
Type of Packaging: Private Label
Brands:
  Mount Eden Vineyards

8655 Mt Franklin Foods
1800 Northwestern Dr
El Paso, TX 79912-1122
915-877-1173
Fax: 915-877-1198 800-685-1475
customerservice@mountfranklinfoods.com
www.azarnutco.com
Candies and nuts
Vice President: Barbara Powell
Chief Operating Officer: Gary Ricco
Chief Financial Officer: Richard Salazar
Vice President: Barbara Powell
Quality Control: Oscar Moreno
Sr Marketing Manager: Beth Podol
Sr Vice President/Sales/Marketing: Dave Barnett
Public Relations Manager: Beth Podol
Estimated Sales: A
Number Employees: 5-9

Food Manufacturers / A-Z

8656 Mt Nittany Vineyard & Winery
300 Houser Rd
Centre Hall, PA 16828-8002
814-466-6373
Fax: 814-466-2766 sales@mtnittanywinery.com
www.mtnittanywinery.com
Wines
Owner: Joe Carroll
sales@mtnittanywinery.com
VP: Betty Carroll
Estimated Sales: $1-2.5 Million
Number Employees: 5-9
Brands:
Mount Nittany

8657 Mt Olive Pickle Co
1 Cucumber Blvd
PO Box 609
Mt Olive, NC 28365-1210
919-581-4760
Fax: 919-658-6296 800-672-5041
mrcrisp@mtolivepickles.com
www.mtolivepickles.com
Pickles, relishes and peppers
President & CEO: Bobby Frye
Executive Chairman: William Hardy Bryan
CFO: Dan Bowen
Director of Marketing: Keith Britt
VP Operations: Doug Brock
Production Supervisor: Jolene Borst
Procurement Manager: Phil Denlinger
Estimated Sales: $46.7 Million
Number Employees: 500-999
Number of Products: 80
Square Footage: 400000
Brands:
Mt. Olive

8658 Mt Pleasant Winery
3125 Green Mountain Dr
Branson, MO 65616-3817
417-336-9463
Fax: 417-336-9167 800-467-9463
mailto@mountpleasant.com
www.mountpleasant.com
Wines
President: Phillip Dressel
Manager: Kay Driden
Estimated Sales: Below $5 Million
Number Employees: 5-9

8659 Mt Sterling Co-Op Creamery
505 Diagonal St
Highland, WI 53543
608-734-3151
Fax: 608-734-3810 866-289-4628
mtsterling@mwt.net buymtsterlinggoatcheese.com/
Raw goat's milk cheeses including cheddar, feta, pasteurized country jack and pasteurized no salt cheddar
Marketing Director: Patricia Lund
Manager: Shannon Adams
mtsterlingcoop@centurytel.net
Office Manager: Shannon Adams
Head Cheesemaker: Bjorn Unseth
Plant Manager: Al Bekkum
Estimated Sales: $2 Million
Number Employees: 10-19
Number of Brands: 1
Number of Products: 13
Square Footage: 9800
Type of Packaging: Consumer, Food Service, Private Label, Bulk
Brands:
Kickapoo of Wisconsin
Mt. Sterling Cheese Co.

8660 Mt. Konocti Growers
2550 Big Valley Road
Kelseyville, CA 95451
707-279-4213
Fax: 707-279-2251 www.mtkonoctiwines.com
Grower, packer and exporter of bartlett pears
Manager: Robert Gayaldo
Number Employees: 5-9
Square Footage: 170000
Type of Packaging: Bulk
Brands:
Lady of the Lake
Lake Cove
Mt. Konocti

8661 Mt. Olympus Specialty Foods
65 W Main St
Westminster, MD 21157
410-848-7080
Gourmet and specialty foods
President: Harry Sirinakis
VP: Rebecca Sirinakis
Contact: Jay Rutherford
jrutherford@mtolympustech.com
Estimated Sales: $1.3 Million
Number Employees: 35

8662 Mt. Olympus Specialty Foods
1601 Military Road
Buffalo, NY 14217-1205
716-874-0771
Fax: 716-839-4006
Processor and exporter of meat, poultry and fish marinades, Greek salad dressings, pasta sauces and appetizers, gourmet foods, salsa, hot sauce and seasonings
CEO/President: George Bechakas
Executive VP: Nick Bechakas
Estimated Sales: $1-3 Million
Number Employees: 20-49

8663 Mt. View Bakery
18 1319 Old Volcano Rd.
Mountain View, HI 96771
808-968-6353
Bread, cookies, pies, donuts, rolls, muffins
President: Robert Kotomori
Estimated Sales: Less than $500,000
Number Employees: 5-9
Type of Packaging: Consumer
Brands:
Mt. View Bakery

8664 Mucci Food Products LTD
7676 Ronda Dr
Canton, MI 48187-2430
734-453-4555
Fax: 734-453-1722 www.mamamuccispasta.com
Fresh, dry and frozen filled pastas.
President: Vince Mucci
Estimated Sales: $10-20 Million
Number Employees: 10-19
Number of Brands: 1
Type of Packaging: Private Label
Brands:
Mama Mucci

8665 Mucke's Meat Products
2326 Main St
Hartford, CT 06120
860-246-5609
Fax: 860-541-6403 800-726-5598
www.muckes.com
Meat products including sausage, kielbasa, frankfurters, salami and liverwurst
President: Ernest Mucke
Estimated Sales: $5-10 Million
Number Employees: 20-49
Type of Packaging: Consumer, Food Service, Private Label
Brands:
Circle M

8666 Mucky Duck Mustard Company
1505 Bonner St
PO Box 250441
Ferndale, MI 48220-1973
248-544-4610
Fax: 248-544-4610 zilkod@aol.com
Gourmet marinades, salad dressings, mustard, ketchup, and BBQ sauces
President: Dave Zilko
Estimated Sales: Less than $500,000
Number Employees: 1-4
Type of Packaging: Consumer, Food Service
Brands:
American Connoisseur Gourmet
American Moir's
American Mucky Duck
American Special Edition
Mucky Duck

8667 Muffin Revolution
1080 Marina Way South
Richmond, CA 94804
510-859-7655
info@muffinrevolution.com
muffinrevolution.com
Muffins
Co-Founder: Marirose Piciucco
Co-Founder: Christy Kovacs
Number of Brands: 1
Number of Products: 6
Type of Packaging: Consumer
Brands:
MUFFIN REVOLUTION

8668 Muir Copper Canyon Farms
951 S 3600 W
Salt Lake City, UT 84104-4587
801-908-6091
Fax: 801-908-6176 800-564-0949
ldehaan@coppercanyonfarms.com
www.coppercanyonfarms.com
Packer and exporter of potatoes, onions and frozen ready-to-process cherries; wholesaler/distributor of fresh fruits and vegetables; serving the food service market in the Salt Lake City metropolitan area
President/CEO: Phil Muir
VP/Chief Financial Officer: Chuck Madsen
Controller: Adam Jensen
Sales: John Marsh
Manager: Andy Salmon
asalmon@coopercanyonfarms.com
Operations Manager: Andy Salmon
Estimated Sales: $16.6 Million
Number Employees: 50-99
Square Footage: 400000
Type of Packaging: Food Service, Private Label, Bulk
Brands:
Big M

8669 Muirhead Canning Co
5267 Mill Creek Rd
The Dalles, OR 97058-8501
541-298-1660
Fax: 541-298-4158 www.muirheadcanning.com
Canned fruits including apricots, cherries, peaches, pears and plums
President: Jenny Loughmiller
jtloughmiller@gmail.com
Co-Owner: Dawn Barrett
President: Russell Loughmiller
Estimated Sales: $5-10 Million
Number Employees: 20-49
Square Footage: 48000
Type of Packaging: Consumer
Brands:
Hoodcrest

8670 Muirhead of Ringoes, NJ, Inc.
43 Highway 202/31
Ringoes, NJ 08551
908-782-7803
Fax: 908-788-4221 800-782-7803
info@muirheadfoods.com
www.muirheadfoods.com
Specialty foods
President: Edward Simpson
Vice President: Doris Simpson
Marketing Director: Barbara Simpson
Estimated Sales: $500,000 appx.
Number Employees: 5-9
Number of Brands: 1
Number of Products: 25
Square Footage: 6000
Type of Packaging: Consumer
Brands:
Dragon's Breath
Hazel's
Muirhead

8671 Mullens Dressing
211 S Main St
Palestine, IL 62451
618-586-2727
Fax: 618-586-2718 mullens11@frontier.com
www.mullensdressing.com
Salad dressings and BBQ sauces
Owner: Jeffrey Shaner
mullens11@frontier.com
Estimated Sales: $300,000-500,000
Number Employees: 1-4
Square Footage: 30000
Type of Packaging: Consumer, Food Service
Brands:
Mullen's

Food Manufacturers / A-Z

8672 Muller-Pinehurst Dairy
2110 Ogilby Rd
Rockford, IL 61102-3400
815-968-0441
Fax: 815-961-1625 www.xta.com
Dairy products
President: Neal Rosinsky
CEO: Raymond Bikulcius
mullers@xta.com
Marketing Executive: Renee Florent
Sales Executive: Tom Erb
General Manager: Neal L Rosinsky
Estimated Sales: Less than $500,000
Number Employees: 100-249
Parent Co: Prairie Farms Dairy
Type of Packaging: Consumer

8673 Mulligan Sales
14314 Lomitas Ave
City of Industry, CA 91746
626-968-9621
Fax: 626-369-8452 mulligansales@yahoo.com
Distributor and processor of dairy products.
President: Jeff Mulligan
VP: Susan Kukta
Safety Manager: Madalyn Hochenedel
Human Resources Manager: Pam Hartnett
Estimated Sales: $4 Million
Number Employees: 23

8674 Mullins Cheese Inc
598 Seagull Dr
Mosinee, WI 54455-9551
715-693-3205
Fax: 715-693-2682 jobs@mullinscheese.com
www.mullinswhey.com
Cheese
President: Donald Mullins
donald.mullins@paradisesolutions.net
Number Employees: 50-99

8675 Mullins Food Products
2200 S. 25th Ave.
Broadview, IL 60155
708-344-3224
Fax: 708-344-0153 www.mullinsfood.com
Sauces, including barbecue, sweet & sour, mustard, ketchup, dressings, mayonnaise, salsa & picantes, pizza sauces, marinara, cocktail, tartar, teriyaki, Asian, icings, horseradish, buffalo & hot sauces, tzatziki, cheese sauces, steaksauces, coleslaw base, specialty blends, syrups, and spoonable dressings.
Owner: Jeanne Gannon
jgannon@mullinsfoods.com
Year Founded: 1934
Estimated Sales: $105 Million
Number Employees: 250-499
Square Footage: 325000
Type of Packaging: Consumer, Food Service, Private Label

8676 Multi Marques
4650 Rue Notre-Dame O
Montreal, QC H4C 1S6
Canada
514-934-1866
Fax: 514-934-1866 www.multimarques.com
Manufacturer and distributor of bread, rolls, fruit cake and sponge cake
Regional Plant Director: Francine Henderson
Number Employees: 2
Square Footage: 14984
Parent Co: Canada Bread
Type of Packaging: Consumer, Food Service
Brands:
  Bon Matin
  Cuisine Nature
  Diana
  Durviage
  Gailuron
  Maison Cousin
  Petite Donceur
  Pom

8677 (HQ)Multiflex Company
18 Utter Ave
Hawthorne, NJ 07506-2127
973-636-9700
marzipanco@aol.com
Processor and exporter of confectionery items including marzipan, icing decorations, edible Easter eggs, chocolate dessert cups, chocolate liqueur cups, lollypops, sugar decorations and decorated chocolate covered sandwich cookies
President: Rita Keller
Vice President: Rozie Keller
VP Sales: Royce Keller
Estimated Sales: $120,000
Number Employees: 2
Square Footage: 30000
Type of Packaging: Food Service, Private Label, Bulk
Brands:
  Biermann
  Crescent Confections
  Keller's
  Panorama Easter Eggs
  Swissart
  Ultra Dark Rondo Kosher

8678 Multigrains Bread Co
117 Water St
Lawrence, MA 01841-4720
978-691-6100
Fax: 978-373-4801 www.multigrainsbakeries.com
Multigrain breads
President: Joseph Faro
joseph@multigrainsbakeries.com
EVP/Director R&D: Chuck Brandano
Director of Quality: Adam Gabour
Director of Purchasing: Darren Gaiero
Number Employees: 100-249

8679 Mung Dynasty
2200 Mary St
Pittsburgh, PA 15203-2160
412-381-1350
Asian foods, specialty products
Owner: Chris Wahlberg
Estimated Sales: $1-2.5 Million
Number Employees: 1-4
Square Footage: 20000
Brands:
  Mori-Nu Tofu
  Mung Dynasty

8680 Munk Pack
Greenwich, CT 06830
munkpack.com
Protein cookies and oatmeal fruit squeezes
Co-Founder: Tobias Glienke
VP, Sales: Joseph DiBenedetto
Number of Brands: 2
Number of Products: 9
Type of Packaging: Consumer
Brands:
  MUNK PACK
  OATMEAL FRUIT SQUEEZE

8681 Munkijo
Irvine, CA 92618
949-861-2798
www.munkijo.com
Coconut products
President/Owner: Sonny Sisante
Number of Brands: 1
Number of Products: 10
Type of Packaging: Consumer
Brands:
  MUNKIJO

8682 Munsee Meats
1701 W Kilgore Ave
P.O. Box 2843
Muncie, IN 47304-4997
765-288-3645
Fax: 765-282-8076 800-662-8001
www.munseemeats.com
Fresh and frozen beef products
President: Allysan Luczak
big_ds_girl8986@yahoo.com
CEO: Steve Hendrixson
Chief Financial Officer: Jeannie Bates
Sales: Carey Clark
Sales: Rick Allred
Sales: Mike Grubbs
Production: Frank Pease
Foreman: Rick Walsh
Production: Jeff Wray
Production: Terry Miller
Estimated Sales: $2.73 Million
Number Employees: 20-49
Brands:
  Munsee Meats

8683 Munson's Chocolates
174 Hopriver Rd
Bolton, CT 06043-7444
860-649-4332
Fax: 860-649-7209 888-686-7667
munsons@munsonschocolates.com
www.munsonschocolates.com
Chocolate candy
Owner: Robert Munson
munsons@munsonschocolates.com
CEO: Karen Munson
Estimated Sales: $10-20 Million
Number Employees: 20-49
Square Footage: 105000
Type of Packaging: Consumer, Food Service, Private Label, Bulk
Brands:
  Munson's

8684 Muntons Ingredients
2018 156th Ave NE, Ste 230
Bellevue, WA 98007
425-372-3082
terry.mcneill@muntons.com
www.muntons.com
Manufacture of grain malts and related ingredients
Executive Chairman: Tom Wells
MMI Inc, Vice President Sales: Terry McNeill
Parent Co: Muntons Malt

8685 Muqui Coffee Company
3398 Grossmont Drive
San Jose, CA 95132-3010
408-272-8471
Coffee roasters
President: Clyde McMorrow

8686 Murakami Farms
1431 SE 1st St
PO Box 9
Ontario, OR 97914
541-889-3131
Fax: 541-889-2933 800-421-8814
murakamionions.com
Packer and exporter of dry fresh yellow, red and white onions
President: Grant Kitamura
VP: David Murakami
Plant Manager: Paul Hopper
Estimated Sales: $2.5 Million
Number Employees: 25
Square Footage: 12000
Type of Packaging: Consumer, Food Service, Private Label

8687 Murdock Farm Dairy
62 Elmwood Rd
Winchendon, MA 01475
978-297-2196
Dairy products
Estimated Sales: $500,000-$1 000,000
Number Employees: 1-4

8688 Murphy Goode Estate Winery
4001 Highway 128
Geyserville, CA 95441
707-431-7644
Fax: 707-431-8640
general@murphygoodewinery.com
www.murphygoodewinery.com
Wine
Vice President: David Ready
Estimated Sales: $10-20 Million
Number Employees: 10-19
Number of Brands: 2
Type of Packaging: Private Label
Brands:
  Goode & Ready
  Murphy Goode

8689 Murray Cider Co Inc
103 Murray Farm Rd
Roanoke, VA 24019-8102
540-977-9000
Fax: 540-977-1336 info@murraycider.com
Apple juice and cider, also cherry-flavored apple cider
President: Robert Murray
info@murraycider.com
VP: Joe Murray
Estimated Sales: $100,000
Number Employees: 10-19
Square Footage: 240000

Food Manufacturers / A-Z

Type of Packaging: Consumer, Food Service, Private Label, Bulk
Brands:
   Murray's

8690 Murray's Chickens
5190 Main St
South Fallsburg, NY 12779
845-436-5001
Fax: 845-436-5001   800-588-5051
www.murrayschicken.com
All-natural chicken burgers and marinated chicken breasts
President/Owner: Murray Bresky
murrayb@murrayschicken.com
VP Operations: Dean Koplik
Number Employees: 250-499
Brands:
   Nature's Kitchen

8691 Murvest
5390 NW 12th Ave
Fort Lauderdale, FL 33309-3153
954-772-6440
Fax: 954-772-7728   murvest@msn.com
Pate's and sausages
President: John Murphy
Estimated Sales: Below $5 Million
Number Employees: 10-19
Brands:
   Murvest

8692 Musco Family Olive Co
17950 Via Nicolo
Tracy, CA 95377
866-965-4837
Fax: 209-836-0518   800-523-9828
sales@muscoolive.com   www.olives.com
Processor and exporter of canned olives including California stuffed green, Sicilian-style, black ripe and deli, and specialty olives and frozen ripe olives
President: Nicholas Musco
nicholasm@olives.com
CEO: Felix Musco
Director of Brand and Product Management: Tracy Wood
Director of Operations: Janet Mitchell Edwards
Director of Technical Services: Ben Hall
Year Founded: 1922
Number Employees: 250-499
Number of Brands: 7
Type of Packaging: Consumer, Food Service, Private Label
Brands:
   Early California
   Pearl's

8693 Mushroom Co
902 Woods Rd
Cambridge, MD 21613
410-221-8971
Fax: 410-221-8952
custserv@themushroomcompany.com
www.themushroomcompany.com
Canned, refrigerated, froze, organic, Kosher, seasoned, sauteed and sauced quality mushrooms.
President: Dennis Newhard
dnewhard@mushroomcanning.com
National Sales Manager: Ruth Newhard
Sales Representative: Fred Lister
Year Founded: 1931
Estimated Sales: $20 Million
Number Employees: 50-99
Square Footage: 150000
Type of Packaging: Consumer, Food Service, Private Label, Bulk
Brands:
   Mga
   Mother Earth
   Mushroom Canning Company
   Snocap

8694 Mushroom Harvest
PO Box 584
Athens, OH 45701
740-448-7376
Fax: 740-448-8007   info@mushroomharvest.com
www.mushroomharvest.com
Organic mushroom powder and capsules.
Owner: George Vaughan

8695 Mushroom Wisdom, Inc
1 Madison St
Bldg F6
East Rutherford, NJ 07073
973-470-0010
Fax: 973-470-0017   800-747-7418
www.mushroomwisdom.com
Processor and exporter of nutritional mushroom supplements and teas
President & CEO: Mike Shirota
VP: Joe Carroll
R&D: Dr. Cun Shuang
VP Marketing: Donna Noonan
Contact: Martin Agurto
martin.a@mushroomwisdom.com
Production: Masashi Ohara
Estimated Sales: $3-5 Million
Number Employees: 10-19
Number of Brands: 2
Number of Products: 24
Square Footage: 18000
Type of Packaging: Consumer, Food Service, Private Label, Bulk
Other Locations:
   Maitake Products
   Ridgefield Park NJ
Brands:
   Grifron
   Grifron D-Fraction
   Grifron Mushroom Emperors
   Grifron Prost Mate
   Mai Green Tea
   Mai Tonic Tea
   Mushroom Wisdom

8696 (HQ)Music Mountain Water Company
305 Stoner Avenue
Shreveport, LA 71101
Fax: 318-221-6650   800-349-6555
info@musicmountain.com
www.musicmountain.com
Bottled spring water
President: Marcus Wren
Plant Manager: Sean Mccaskill
Estimated Sales: $1-3 Million
Number Employees: 20
Other Locations:
   Music Mountain Spring Water
   Alexandria VA
   Music Mountain Spring Water
   Monroe VA
   Music Mountain Spring Water
   Lake Charles VA
   Music Mountain Spring Water
   Ruston VA
   Music Mountain Spring Water
   Lafayette VA
   Music Mountain Spring Water
   Natchitoches VA
   Music Mountain Spring Water
   Austin TX
   Music Mountain Spring Water
   Tyler TX
   Music Mountain Spring Water
   Longview TX
   Music Mountain Spring Water
   Marshall TX
   Music Mountain Spring Water
   Alto TX
   Music Mountain Spring Water
   Crockett TX
   Music Mountain Spring Water
   Glenwood AR

8697 Musicon Deer Farm
385 Scotchtown Rd
Goshen, NY 10924
845-294-6378
Fax: 516-239-8915
Glatt kosher and venison
President: Norman Schlaff
Estimated Sales: $500,000-$1 Million
Number Employees: 1-4
Type of Packaging: Private Label

8698 Mustard Seed
203 Sanders Road
Central, SC 29630-9349
864-639-1083
877-621-2591
sheltoncj@aol.com
Natural, organic, vegetarian, whole grain, high fiber, gourmet, heart healthy burger and protein replacement mixes, burger n' a bag
Owner: Jane Shelton
Brands:
   Burgers N'A Bag

8699 Mutchler's Dakota Gold Mustard
511 W Jackson Blvd.
Spearfish, SD 57783
605-642-8166
Fax: 605-642-0708   info@blackhills.com
www.blackhills.com
Mustard
President: Kelly Hitson
CEO: Betty Lenners

8700 Muth's Candy Store
630 E Market St
Louisville, KY 40202-1117
502-582-2639
Fax: 502-582-2639   www.muthscandy.com
Candy including chocolate, caramel and peanut brittle
President: Martha Vories
shop@muthscandy.com
Assistant Manager: Kimberly Bennett
Estimated Sales: Under $500,000
Number Employees: 5-9
Type of Packaging: Consumer
Brands:
   Kentucky Tavern
   Mojeska's
   Muth's Kentucky

8701 Mutual Fish Co
2335 Rainier Ave S
Seattle, WA 98144
206-322-4368
Fax: 206-328-5889   www.mutualfish.com
Fresh seafood including salmon, halibut, catfish, cod, sea bass, and oysters
Estimated Sales: $1.5 Million
Number Employees: 20-49
Square Footage: 60000

8702 My Boy's Baking LLC
1466 Hampton Rd
Allentown, PA 18104-2018
610-759-4552
Fax: 610-759-4525   robert@myboysbaking.com
www.myboysbaking.com
Biscotti, cookies and rugelach
Marketing: Robert Levine

8703 My Brother Bobby's Salsa
PO Box 3659
Poughkeepsie, NY 12603
845-462-6227
mbbsalsa@aol.com
www.mbbsalsa.com
Kosher, preservative-free salsas and ready-made bruschetta topping
Owner/CEO: Robert Gropper
Year Founded: 1993
Number of Brands: 1
Number of Products: 4
Type of Packaging: Consumer, Private Label
Brands:
   My Brother Bobby's Salsa

8704 My Brother's Salsa
1003 Beau Terre Dr
Suite 200
Bentonville, AR 72712
479-271-9404
www.mybrotherssalsa.com
Salsas and tortilla chips
Founder: Helen Lampkin

8705 My Cup of Cake
32 Woodland Drive
Port Washington, NY 11050
516-767-5137
sales@mycupofcake.com
Individual servings of cakes served in mugs.
Founder: Sharon Tracy

8706 My Daddy's Cheesecake
265 S Broadview St
265 S. Broadview
Cape Girardeau, MO 63703-5756
573-335-6660
800-735-6765
sales@mydaddyscheesecake.com
www.mydaddyscheesecake.com
Processor and exporter of confectionery items, cheesecakes, desserts, wedding and birthday cakes and gourmet cookies

Food Manufacturers / A-Z

Owner: Susan Stanfield
Estimated Sales: Less Than $500,000
Number Employees: 10-19
Square Footage: 10000
Type of Packaging: Consumer, Food Service, Private Label
Brands:
 Cookie Wedgies
 My Daddy's Cheesecake

8707 My Favorite Jerky
2000 5th Street
Apt C
Boulder, CO 80302-4948
 303-444-2846
 Fax: 303-444-9049
Beef jerky
President: James David
Brands:
 My Favorite Jerky

8708 My Grandma's Coffee Cake
1636 Hyde Park Ave
Hyde Park, MA 02136-2458
 617-364-9900
 Fax: 617-364-0505 800-847-2636
 www.mygrandma.com
Coffeecakes in a variety of flavors including Granny Smith Apple, Golden Raspberry, Cappuccino, New England Blueberry, Chocolate, Banana Walnut and Cape Cod Cranberry
President: Robert Katz
bmills@mygrandma.com
Controller: Seth Anapolle
EVP: Bruce Willis
VP of Marketing and Operations: Bruce Mills
Distribution Sales Manager: Gail Molino
VP Operations: Will Weeks
Estimated Sales: $5-6 Million
Number Employees: 20-49
Square Footage: 35600
Brands:
 My Grandma's of New England

8709 My Own Meals Inc
400 Lake Cook Rd # 107
5410 W Roosevelt Rd
Deerfield, IL 60015-4929
 847-948-1118
 Fax: 847-948-0468 sales@myownmeals.com
 www.myownmeals.com
Certified, halal and dhabiha halal meals, rations and food products
President: Mary Jackson
mary.jackson@myownmeals.com
CEO: Mary Anne Jackson
Manager: Robert Barnes
Estimated Sales: $.5-1 million
Number Employees: 5-9
Type of Packaging: Private Label
Brands:
 J&M

8710 My Sweet
57 Porter Ave
Brooklyn, NY 11237
 347-689-4402
 info@mysweet.com
 mysweet.com
Brigadeiros
Founder: Paula Barbosa

8711 My/Mo Mochi Ice Cream
5563 Alcoa Ave
Vernon, CA 90058-3730
 323-587-5504
 Fax: 323-587-5355 www.mymomochi.com
Ice cream
CEO: Ralph Denisco
Chief Financial Officer: Craig Berger
Chief Marketing Officer: Russell Barnett
Vice President, Sales: Thomas Bulowski
Production Manager: Tama Letuli
Number Employees: 51-200
Brands:
 my/mo Mochi Ice Cream

8712 MySuperfoods Company
Summit, NJ 07901
 www.mysuperfoodscompany.com
Superfood snacks
Co-Founder: Silvia Gianni
Co-Founder: Katie Jesionowski

8713 Myers Frozen Food Provisions
405 W Dorsey St
St Paul, IN 47272-9569
 765-525-6304
 Fax: 765-525-9635 info.myers@aol.com
 www.myersfrozenfood.com
Frozen foods
President: Tony Myers
Sales Manager: Dan Gindling
Production Manager: Mike Myers
Estimated Sales: $3-5 000,000
Number Employees: 5-9
Brands:
 Myers Frozen Food

8714 Mylk Labs
City of Industry, CA 91748
 info@mylklabs.com
 www.mylklabs.com
Oatmeal cups
Founder: Grace Cheng
Number of Brands: 1
Number of Products: 3
Type of Packaging: Consumer
Brands:
 MYLK LABS

8715 Myron's Fine Foods, Inc.
Rrenovator's Old Mill
One River Street
Millers Falls, MA 01349
 413-659-0247
 Fax: 413-659-0249 800-730-2820
 www.chefmyrons.com
Natural and kosher cooking sauces including tsukeyaki, soy sauce, szechuan, teriyaki, yakitori, ponzu, wild game and fish
President: Myron Becker
CFO: Lisa Richardson
Vice President: Kathy Becker
Production Manager: Steve Gambino
Plant Manager: Dawn Kennaway
Estimated Sales: Below $5 Million
Number Employees: 5-9
Number of Products: 9
Type of Packaging: Consumer, Food Service, Private Label, Bulk
Brands:
 Chef Myron's Original #1 Yakitori
 Chef Myron's Ponzu
 Chef Myron's Premium
 Chef Myron's Tsukeya
 Myron's 20 Gauge

8716 Mystic Coffee Roasters
8 Steamboat Wharf
Mystic, CT 06355-2544
 860-536-2999
 www.mysticcoffeeroaster.com
Coffee, tea
President/Treasurer: Bruce Carpenter
greenmarbleman@aol.com
Estimated Sales: Less Than $500,000
Number Employees: 1-4

8717 Mystic Lake Dairy
24200 NE 14th Street
Sammamish, WA 98074
 425-868-2029
 Fax: 425-868-0553
Organic dairy products including goats milk
President: Gary Wallace
CEO: Nellie Wallace
Number Employees: 2
Brands:
 Mystic Lake Dairy

8718 N A P Engineering
10965 Harborside Dr
Largo, FL 33773-4428
 727-544-3118
 www.napengineering.com
Manufacturer of Rotary Fillers and Sealers, Inline Tray Fillers and Sealersand Specialty Parts.
President: Paul Desocio
glouli@tampabay.rr.com
Estimated Sales: Less Than $500,000
Number Employees: 1-4

8719 N D Labs
202 Merrick Rd
Lynbrook, NY 11563-2622
 516-612-4900
 Fax: 516-504-0289 888-263-5227
 sales@ndlabs.com www.nutritionaldesignsinc.com
Nutritional supplements and foods, including fiber and soy products, soy proteins, high-fiber cookies, vegetarian entrees, etc
Vice President: Beth Beller
beth@ndlabs.com
Vice President: Beth Beller
Marketing/Sales: Michael Allen
Public Relations: Sherry Shah
Estimated Sales: Less Than $500,000
Number Employees: 1-4
Number of Brands: 10
Type of Packaging: Consumer, Food Service, Private Label, Bulk
Brands:
 Fiber 7
 Fiber Supreme
 Life Savy
 Nana Flakes
 Soy-Liccous Meals
 Soypro

8720 N.B.J. Enterprises
3950 Demetropolis Rd
Mobile, AL 36693
 251-661-2285
 Fax: 251-661-6198
Seafood
Owner: Toni Gulsby
Estimated Sales: $1-3 Million
Number Employees: 10-19

8721 N.Y.K. Line (North America)
377 E Butterfield Rd
Lombard, IL 60148-5615
 630-435-7800
 Fax: 630-435-3110 888-695-7447
Contact: Kathleen Sarullo
kathy.sarullo@na.nykline.com
Estimated Sales: $.5-1 million
Number Employees: 5-9

8722 NAR
75 Hawthorne Village Road
Nashua, NH 03062
 603-888-5420
 Fax: 603-888-5419 bahar@nargourmet.com
 www.nargourmet.com
Condiments, olive oil, other vinegar, spices, canned or preserved vegetables/fruit, dried fruit
Marketing: Bahar Ayasli
Contact: Asli Aksoy
asli@nargourmet.com

8723 NOKA
Pacific Palisades, CA
 hello@nokaorganics.com
 www.nokaorganics.com
Superfood smoothies
Co-Founder: Ryan Werner
Co-Founder: Adam Steiner
Number of Products: 6

8724 NORPAC Foods Inc
3225 25th St SE
Salem, OR 97302
 consumeraffairs@norpac.com
 www.norpac.com
Frozen vegetables, fruits and juices.
President & CEO: Shawn Campbell
Research & Development Manager: Kim Claggett
Director of Marketing: Brad Burden
VP of Operations: Mark Croeni
Year Founded: 1924
Estimated Sales: $476.3 Million
Number Employees: 1,500
Type of Packaging: Consumer, Food Service, Private Label, Bulk
Other Locations:
 Lake Oswego OR
 Salem OR
 Hermiston OR
 Quincy WA
Brands:
 Flav-R-Pac
 Westpac
 Santiam
 Grande Classics Island Blends
 Grande Classics
 Connoisseur Collection

Food Manufacturers / A-Z

Soup Supreme
Chili Supreme
Pasta Perfect
Fruit Topping
Flame Roasted Vegetables
Norpac
Scratch Recipe

8725 NOW Foods
244 Knollwood Dr.
Bloomingdale, IL 60108
888-669-3663
www.nowfoods.com
Vitamins, healthy foods, natural personal care and sports nutrition products.
CEO: Jim Emme
CFO: Andy Kotlarz
General Counsel: Beverly Reid
VP, Quality/Regulatory Affairs: Aaron Secrist
VP, Global Sales/Marketing: Dan Richard
Vice President, Human Resources: Michelle Canada
COO: Ernest Shepard
Year Founded: 1968
Estimated Sales: $100 Million
Number Employees: 100-249
Number of Brands: 9
Number of Products: 1500
Square Footage: 203000
Type of Packaging: Consumer, Private Label, Bulk
Brands:
  Better Stevia
  Living Now
  Now Real Tea
  Now Real Food
  Ellyndale Foods
  Coconut Infusions
  Nutty Infusions
  Q Cups
  Sugarless Sugar

8726 NPC Dehydrators
11761 Highway 770 E
Eden, NC 27288
336-635-5190
Fax: 336-635-5193
Dry brewers yeast
President: R Dean Fullmer
Executive: Max Selty
Sales Director: Mike Morales
Public Relations: Charles Setlif
Estimated Sales: $5-10 Million
Number Employees: 30
Type of Packaging: Private Label
Brands:
  Sonic Dried Yeast

8727 NPC Dehydrators
P.O.Box B
Payette, ID 83661-0017
208-642-4471
Fax: 208-642-4473
Dry brewers yeast
Manager: Vicki Swank
Estimated Sales: Less than $500,000
Number Employees: 1-4

8728 NSG Transport Inc
115 W 16th St
Gothenburg, NE 69138-1302
308-537-7191
Fax: 308-537-7193 www.nsgco.com
Processor and exporter of corn
President: Norman Geiken
wade@nsgco.com
Sales Exec: Wade Geiken
Estimated Sales: $3-5 Million
Number Employees: 20-49
Type of Packaging: Bulk

8729 Nabisco
7 Campus Dr
Parsippany, NJ 07054-0311
973-682-5000
Fax: 973-503-2153 www.snackworks.com
Baked goods including cookies and crackers
President/CEO: James Kilts Jr.
EVP/CFO: James Healey
EVP/CIO: Doreen Wright
Contact: Lois Collum
lois.collum@mdlz.com
Plant Manager: Larry Campbell
Purchasing Manager: Mike Swift
Parent Co: Kraft Foods
Type of Packaging: Consumer, Food Service
Brands:
  100 Calorie Packs
  Belvita
  Chips Ahoy!
  Barnum's Animals Crackers
  Cameo
  Nabisco Classics
  Kraft Handi-Snacks
  Easy Cheese
  Flavor Originals
  Ginger Snaps
  Honey Maid
  Kraft Cheese Nips
  Mixers
  Mallomars
  Newtons
  Nabisco 12 Packs
  Nutter Butter
  Nilla Wafers
  Premium
  Oreo
  Ritz Bits Sandwiches
  Ritz
  Snackwells
  Red Oval Farms Stoned Wheat Thins
  Toasted Chips
  Teddy Grahams
  Triscuit
  Wheat Thins
  Wheatsworth

8730 Nacan Products
60 West Drive
Brampton, ON L6T 4W7
Canada
905-454-4466
Fax: 905-454-5207
Modified starches derived from corn, waxy maize and tapioca
President: Roland Sirois
Vice-Chairman: Jim Grieve
Business Director: Bill Ruderman
Executive VP: John Morrell
Parent Co: National Starch & Chemical Company
Brands:
  Nacan

8731 NadaMoo
5555 N Lamar Blvd
Suite K111
Austin, TX 78751
nadamoo.com
Dairy-free frozen dessert
President & CEO: Daniel Nicholson
Number of Brands: 2
Number of Products: 18
Type of Packaging: Consumer
Brands:
  NADAMOO
  NADAMOO ORGANIC

8732 Nagasako Fish
800 Eha St
Suite 12
Wailuku, HI 96793
808-242-4073
Fax: 808-244-7020
Seafood
Owner: Darryl Flinton
Estimated Sales: $5-10 Million
Number Employees: 10-19

8733 Nagase America Corp.
546 Fifth Ave
16th Fl
New York, NY 10036
212-703-1343
nagaseamerica.com
Functional ingredients for the food and beverage industries.

8734 Nahmias et Fils
201 Saw Mill River Rd. #C
Yonkers, NY 10701
914-294-0055
www.nahmiasetfils.com
Whiskey, fig-flavored distilled spirits
Founder: Dorit Nahmias
Year Founded: 2010
Number of Brands: 1
Number of Products: 3s
Type of Packaging: Consumer, Private Label
Brands:
  Nahmias et Fils

8735 Naji's Pita Gourmet Restaurant
166 W Valley Ave
Birmingham, AL 35209-3620
205-945-6001
Fax: 205-945-6021 www.pita.net
Plain and wheat pita bread
Owner; President: Naji Constantine
naji@pita.net
Estimated Sales: Less Than $500,000
Number Employees: 10-19
Square Footage: 24000
Brands:
  Pito

8736 Najila's
PO Box 74
Binghamton, NY 13905-0074
607-722-4287
Fax: 607-773-9012
Gourmet cookies
President/CEO: Najla Aswad
Type of Packaging: Food Service, Bulk
Brands:
  Najla Gone Chunky

8737 Najla's Specialty FoodsInc
8007 Vine Crest Ave # 3
Suite 3
Louisville, KY 40222-8607
502-412-4420
Fax: 502-412-4421 877-962-5527
cookies@najlas.com www.najlas.com
Kosher, cookies, toffee, frozen bars, nuts, gift packs.
Owner: Najla R Aswad
cookies@najlas.com
Marketing: Najla Aswad
Estimated Sales: Less Than $500,000
Number Employees: 5-9

8738 Nakano Foods
55 E Euclid Ave
Mt Prospect, IL 60056-1283
847-290-0730
Fax: 847-590-0482 800-323-4358
dan_baron@nakanofoods.com
Wine and organic vinegars
Number Employees: 50-99

8739 Naked Bacon
Ste. Genevieve, MO
nakedbaconco.com
Gluten-free bacon
Founder: John Kreilich
Number of Brands: 1
Number of Products: 6
Type of Packaging: Consumer
Brands:
  NAKED BACON

8740 Naked Infusions LLC
23679 Calabasas Rd.
Calabasas, CA 91302
818-239-9058
info@nakedinfusions.com
www.nakedinfusions.com
Manufacturer of salsa.
Founder: Selene Kepila
selene@nakedinfusions.com

8741 Naked Juice Company
Monrovia, CA 91016
877-858-4237
www.nakedjuice.com
Fruit juices and smoothies
Parent Co: Pepsico

8742 Naked Mountain Winery Vineyard
2747 Leeds Manor Rd
Rt. 688
Markham, VA 22643-1715
540-364-1609
drinknaked@nakedmtnwinery.com
www.nakedmtnwinery.com
Wines
Owner: Randall Morgan
drinknaked@nakedmtnwinery.com
Co-Owner: Meagan Morgan
Office Manager: Sandy Coleman
Marketing/Sales Manager: Drew Hauser
Assistant Winemaker: Don Oldham
Office Manager: Darlene Call
Estimated Sales: Below $5 Million
Number Employees: 1-4

Food Manufacturers / A-Z

Type of Packaging: Private Label
Brands:
 Naked Mountain

8743 Naleway Foods
233 Hutchings Street
Winnipeg, MB R2X 2R4
Canada
 204-633-6535
 Fax: 204-694-4310 800-665-7448
 sales@naleway.com www.naleway.com
Processor and exporter of frozen foods including pierogies and panzarotti
Sales: W Halley
Number Employees: 100-249
Type of Packaging: Consumer, Food Service

8744 Nalle Winery
2385 Dry Creek Rd
Healdsburg, CA 95448-9796
 707-433-1040
 Fax: 707-433-6062 www.nallewinery.com
Wines
Co-Owner: Lee Nalle
Co-Owner: Doug Nalle
doug@nallewinery.com
Winemaker: Doug Nalle
Winemaker: Andrew Nalle
Number Employees: 1-4
Number of Brands: 1
Brands:
 Nalle

8745 Namaste Foods
P.O. Box 3133
Coeur d'Alene, ID 83816
 866-258-9493
 admin@namastefoods.com
 www.namastefoods.com
Gluten free foods
Owner: Daphne Taylor

8746 Nan Sea Enterprises of Wisconsin
900 Gale St
Waukesha, WI 53186-2515
 262-542-8841
 Fax: 262-542-4356
Manufacturer and distributor of fresh frozen king, dungeness, golden and snow crab; also, lobster and lobster claws
President: Eric Muehl
VP: Robert Nell
Estimated Sales: $10-20 Million
Number Employees: 5-9
Type of Packaging: Food Service, Private Label

8747 Nana Mae's Organics
708 Gravenstein Highway North, #174
Sebastopol, CA 95472
 707-829-7359
 Fax: 707-829-7356 www.nanamae.com
Organic apple juice and sauce and vinegar and honey
Owner: Paul Kolling
Sales: Kendra Kolling
Estimated Sales: $1,000,000
Number Employees: 15
Number of Brands: 1
Number of Products: 15
Square Footage: 1056000
Type of Packaging: Consumer, Food Service, Private Label, Bulk

8748 Nana's Cookie Co.
4901 Morena Blvd
San Diego, CA 92117
 800-836-7534
 www.nanascookiecompany.com
Gluten-free cookies
President/Owner: Miriam Diamond
Year Founded: 1992
Number of Brands: 3
Number of Products: 17
Type of Packaging: Consumer
Brands:
 NANA'S
 NANA'S NO GLUTEN
 NANA'S COOKIE BARS

8749 Nanci's Frozen Yogurt
4722 E Ivy St #108
Mesa, AZ 85205
 480-834-4290
 Fax: 480-834-4271 800-788-0808
 info@nancis.com www.nancis.com
Soft-serve dessert mixes including frozen yogurt, fruit freezer sorbet, non-dairy soft serve, no-sugar-added mixes, smoothie base mixes, granita mixes and more than 90 flavors
President/CEO: John Wudel
Spokesperson: Nanci Wudel
Estimated Sales: $1-3 Million
Number Employees: 10-19
Type of Packaging: Food Service, Bulk
Brands:
 Nanci's

8750 Nancy's Candy
2684 Jeb Stuart Highway
PO Box 860
Meadows Of Dan, VA 24120
 276-952-2112
 Fax: 276-952-1042 800-328-3834
 nancyscandy@embarqmail.com
 www.nancyscandycompany.com
Fudge, chocolates, nut brittles and more
Marketing: Nancy Galli
Contact: Nancy Galli
ngfudge@yahoo.com

8751 Nancy's Probiotic Foods
Eugene, OR 97402
 nancysyogurt.com
Organic yogurt, kefir, cottage cheese, and sour cream
General Manager & CFO: Sue Kesey
Number of Brands: 1
Number of Products: 11
Type of Packaging: Consumer
Brands:
 NANCY'S

8752 Nancy's Shellfish
91 Falmouth Rd
Falmouth, ME 04105-1841
 207-774-3411
 Fax: 207-780-0044
Shellfish, seafood
President: Joe Scola
Estimated Sales: $1.4 Million
Number Employees: 5-9

8753 Nancy's Specialty Foods
6500 Overlake Pl
Newark, CA 94560
 510-494-1100
 Fax: 510-494-1140 www.nancys.com
Processor and exporter of frozen appetizers, entrees and desserts.
President: Bob Kroll
markus.bahr@wellsfargo.com
CFO: Adam Ferris
Marketing/Communications Director: Diane DiMartini
VP Sales: R L Booth
VP Operations: David Joiner
Plant Manager: Rick Shepherd
Estimated Sales: $19.8 Million
Number Employees: 325
Square Footage: 172000
Type of Packaging: Consumer, Food Service, Private Label, Bulk
Brands:
 Nancy's

8754 Nanka Seimen Company
3030 Leonis Blvd
Vernon, CA 90058
 323-585-9967
 Fax: 323-585-9969
Japanese-style and egg noodles, chow mein, wontons, egg rolls and gyoza skins
President: Shoi Chi Sayano
VP: Toshiaki Yoshida
Estimated Sales: $5-10 Million
Number Employees: 18
Square Footage: 80000
Type of Packaging: Consumer, Food Service
Brands:
 Golden Dragon
 Nanka Udon

8755 Nanocor
1500 W Shure Dr
Arlington Hts, IL 60004-1443
 847-851-1918
 Fax: 847-851-1919 www.nanocor.com
Manager: Tie Lin
Contact: Tie Lan
tie.lan@amcol.com
Number Employees: 100-249
Parent Co: AMCOL International Corp.

8756 Nantong Acetic Acid Chemical Co., Ltd.
PO Box 1447
Hilliard, OH 43026
 614-947-0249
 Fax: 866-521-7624 gord@ntacf.com
 www.ntacf.com
Food additives and dye and pigment intermediates, as well as organic chemical raw materials
Sales Manager: Gord Chu
gchu@ntacf.com
General Manager: Caifeng Ding
Vice-General Manager: Qing Jiu
Type of Packaging: Bulk

8757 Nantucket Pasta Company, Inc.
20 Young's Way
Nantucket, MA 02584-2272
 508-494-5209
 www.nantucketpastagoddess.com
Pasta (fresh).
Marketing: Liliana Dougan

8758 Nantucket Tea Traders
P.O.Box 179
Nantucket, MA 02554-0179
 508-325-0203
 Fax: 508-325-0203
Processors of teas
President: Judy Kales
Sales: Paul Kales
Estimated Sales: $120,000
Number Employees: 1
Brands:
 Nantucket Tea Trader

8759 Nantucket Vineyard
5 Bartlett Farm Rd
Nantucket, MA 02554-4341
 508-228-9235
 Fax: 508-325-5209 jay@ciscobrewers.com
Wine
Owner: Randy Hudson
Founder/Co-Owner: Dean Long
Estimated Sales: $5-9.9 Million
Number Employees: 1-4
Parent Co: Cisco Brewers
Type of Packaging: Private Label
Brands:
 Nantucket Vineyard

8760 Nantze Springs Inc
156 W Carroll St
Dothan, AL 36301-4316
 334-794-4218
 Fax: 334-712-2899 800-239-7873
 www.nantzesprings.com
Water
President: Malone Garrett
mgarrett@nantzesprings.com
Estimated Sales: $3-5 Million
Number Employees: 10-19
Brands:
 Nantze Springs

8761 Napa Barrel Care
1075 Golden Gate Dr
Napa, CA 94558-6187
 707-254-1985
 Fax: 707-254-2092 info@barrelcare.com
 www.barrelcare.com
Manufacturing and storage of wine barrels
President/Winemaker: Mike Blom
mike@barrelcare.com
Warehouse Manager: Jorge Vargas
Estimated Sales: Less Than $500,000
Number Employees: 1-4

Food Manufacturers / A-Z

8762 Napa Cellars
7481 Saint Helena Hwy
Napa, CA 94558-9400
707-944-2565
Fax: 707-944-9749 800-535-6400
info@napacellars.com www.napawineco.com
Wines
Manager: Dean Slattery
Winemaker: Rob Lawson
General Manager: Sheldon Parker
Estimated Sales: $1.6 Million
Number Employees: 5-9
Type of Packaging: Private Label
Brands:
 Napa Wine

8763 Napa Hills
Chicago, IL 60614
nick@napahills.com
napahills.com
Sparkling water
Founder & CEO: Ellona Jarvis

8764 Napa Valley Kitchens
564 Gateway Dr
Napa, CA 94558-7517
707-254-3700
Fax: 707-259-0219
Manufacturer and exporter of flavored oils, marinades, and dressings
Chairman: John Foraker
Cfo: Dale Eagle
Vice President of R&D: Bob Kaake
Senior Vice President of Marketing: Sarah Bird
Sales Director: Terry Dudley
Production Manager: Mark Osborne
Estimated Sales: $10 Million
Number Employees: 75
Type of Packaging: Consumer
Brands:
 Consorzio
 Napa Valley Mustard Co.

8765 Napa Wine Company
7830-40 St. Helena Hwy.
Oakville, CA 94562
707-944-8669
Fax: 707-944-9749 800-848-9630
moreinfo@napawineco.com www.napawineco.com
Custom crush wine production
Managing Partner: Andrew Hoxsey
General Manager: Sheldon Parker
Winemaker: Rob Lawson
Estimated Sales: $5 Million
Number Employees: 20-49
Type of Packaging: Consumer, Private Label
Brands:
 Napa Wine Company

8766 Napoleon Locker
3536 W Napoleon Wilson Street
Napoleon, IN 47034
812-852-4333
Beef and pork; slaughtering services available
Owner: Matt Brancamp
Co-Owner: Kimberly Brancamp
Estimated Sales: $.5-1 million
Number Employees: 10-19
Type of Packaging: Private Label

8767 Napoli Pasta Manufacturers
9719 S Dixie Hwy # 8
Miami, FL 33156-2834
305-666-1942
Fax: 305-254-6139 npmgroup@aol.com
www.worldtrade.org
Pasta products
President: Charlotte Gallogly
Plant Manager: Patricia Matuk
Estimated Sales: $5-9.9 Million
Number Employees: 1-4

8768 Naraghi Group
20001 Mchenry Ave
Escalon, CA 95320-9614
209-579-5253
Fax: 209-551-4544
Processor and exporter of grapes, peaches, apples, walnuts, pistachios and almonds
Owner: Miguel Lizarraga
miguel@naraghifarms.com
Owner: Wendell Naraghi
Plant Manager: Isidro Vaca
Number Employees: 1-4

8769 Nardi Breads
45 Glendale Rd
South Windsor, CT 06074-2415
860-289-5458
Fax: 860-289-9012
Bread and rolls
Founder: Pasquale Nardi
President: Charles Nardi
Estimated Sales: $5-9.9 Million
Number Employees: 10-19

8770 Nardone Brothers
420 New Commerce Blvd
Hanover Twp, PA 18706-1445
570-823-0141
Fax: 570-823-2581 800-822-5320
vjn1@att.net nardonebros.com
Pizza manufacturer serving the school and institutional food service markets nationwide since 1942.
President: Vince Nardone
CFO: Louis Nardone
VP: Frank Nardone
Manufacturing/Operations Director: Mario Nardone
Estimated Sales: $24.4 Million
Number Employees: 100-249
Type of Packaging: Consumer, Food Service
Brands:
 Nardone Bros.
 Vincenzo's

8771 Naron Mary Sue Candies
2600 Georgetown Rd
Baltimore, MD 21230-1302
410-467-9932
Fax: 410-467-1649 800-662-2639
www.marysue.com
Chocolate and soft candy
Owner: Bill Buppert
CFO: Mike Wiss
R & D: Mark Berman
Estimated Sales: $5-10 Million
Number Employees: 5-9

8772 Nash Produce
6160 S NC Highway 58
Nashville, NC 27856-8642
252-443-6011
Fax: 252-443-6746 800-334-3032
info@nashproduce.com www.nashproduce.com
Sweet potatoes and cucumbers
President: Thomas Joyner
thomasjoyner@nashproduce.com
VP: Richard Joyner
Director of Marketing: Tami Long
Sales Director: Don Sparks
Director of Accounting and Business: Sarah Payne
Estimated Sales: $40 Million
Number Employees: 100+
Type of Packaging: Consumer, Food Service, Private Label, Bulk
Brands:
 Mr. Yam
 Cajan Gold
 Nash's Pride
 Nash's Gold
 Oh So Sweet

8773 Nashoba Valley Winery
100 Wattaquadock Hill Rd
Bolton, MA 01740-1238
978-779-5521
Fax: 978-779-5523 nashoba.winery@gte.net
www.nashobawinery.com
Wines
President: Richard Pelletier
rpelletier@nashobavalleywinery.com
VP: Cindy Rowe Pelletier
Estimated Sales: Below $5 Million
Number Employees: 20-49
Type of Packaging: Private Label

8774 Nasonville Dairy
10898 Hwy
10 West
Marshfield, WI 54449
715-676-2177
Fax: 715-676-3636
mailorder@nasonvilledairy.com
www.nasonvilledairy.com
Cheese, cheese products
Owner: Kim Heiman
Estimated Sales: Below $5 Million
Number Employees: 20-49

8775 Nasoya Foods
1 New England Way
Ayer, MA 01432-1514
978-772-6880
Fax: 978-772-6881 800-848-2769
info@vitasoy-usa.com www.myvitasoy.com
All-natural organic and all-natural tofu, wraps, noobles, spreads
Vice President: Susan Rolnick
srolnick@vitasoyusa.com
Vice President: Susan Rolnick
srolnick@vitasoyusa.com
Number Employees: 100-249

8776 (HQ)Nassau Candy Distributors
530 W John St
Hicksville, NY 11801-1039
516-433-7100
Fax: 516-433-9010 sales@nassaucandy.com
www.nassaucandy.com
Manufacturer, importer and distributor of confectionery items and gourmet foods.
President: Barry Rosenbaum
Chairman & CEO: Lesley Stier
Vice President: Carol Baca
carol.baca@nassaucandy.com
Number Employees: 100-249
Other Locations:
 Nassau Candy Co.
 Deer Park NY

8777 Natalie's Orchid Island Juice Co.
330 North U.S. Highway One
Ft. Pierce, FL 34950
772-465-1122
Fax: 772-465-4303 800-373-7444
www.oijc.com
Fresh-squeezed fruit juices
Owner/CEO: Marygrace Sexton
COO: Frank Tranchilla
EVP: John Martinelli
Quality Assurance/Food Safety Manager: Brian Christensen
Director of Marketing: Natalie Sexton
Director of Customer Service/Logistics: David Cortez
Contact: Keith Camara
kcamara@oijc.com
Director of Operations: Jim Zurbey
Senior Production Manager: Peter Binns
Estimated Sales: $20-50 Million
Number Employees: 50-99
Number of Brands: 1
Type of Packaging: Consumer, Food Service
Brands:
 Natalie's Orchid Island

8778 Natchez Pecan Shelling Company
P.O.Box 100
Taylorsville, MS 39168-0100
601-785-4333
Pecans
Owner: Harold Bynum
Estimated Sales: Less than $500,000
Number Employees: 1-4

8779 Natchitoches Crawfish Company
1205 Texas Street
Natchitoches, LA 71457
318-352-2194
Fax: 318-379-2816 mcfctr@bellsouth.net
natchitochescrawfish.com
Owner: Jimmy Strickland

8780 Natierra
7535 Woodman Pl
Van Nuys, CA 91405-1545
310-559-0259
Fax: 310-559-0289 www.natierra.com
Seeds; dried berries; cacao powder; and beets.
President/CEO: Thierry Olivier
Media Relations: Holly Franklin

8781 Nation Pizza & Foods
601 E Algonquin Rd
Schaumburg, IL 60173-3803
847-397-3320
Fax: 847-397-9456 www.nationpizza.com
Pizza crusts, pizzas, sauces, sandwiches, appetizers, hispanic foods, sweets, packaging
President: Richard Auskalnis
CFO: Joe Giglio
SVP: Jack Campolo
Quality Assurance: Teresa Martinez

Food Manufacturers / A-Z

Estimated Sales: $20-50 Million
Number Employees: 50-99
Parent Co: OSI Group
Type of Packaging: Consumer
Brands:
    Father & Son
    My Father's Best
    Nation

8782 Nation Wide Canning Ltd.
324 Essex County Road 34 East
PO Box 227
Cottam, ON N0R 1B0
Canada
    519-839-4831
Fax: 519-839-4993 www.cottamgardens.com
Canned and crushed tomatoes, mushrooms, potatoes, pie fillings, kidney beans and spaghetti and pizza sauce; also, private labeling available
President and CFO: H Finaldi
Office Manager: Irene Finaldi
Number Employees: 55
Square Footage: 200000
Type of Packaging: Private Label
Brands:
    Cottam Gardens

8783 National Beef Packing Co LLC
12200 N. Ambassador Dr.
Suite 500
Kansas City, MO 64163
    800-449-2333
www.nationalbeef.com
Fresh, chilled and processed beef products.
CEO: Timothy Klein
tklein@nationalbeef.com
Year Founded: 1992
Estimated Sales: $7.3 Billion
Number Employees: 8,200
Number of Brands: 5
Type of Packaging: Consumer, Food Service, Private Label, Bulk
Other Locations:
    HQ
    Kansas City MO
    Dodge City KS
    Liberal KS
    Hummels Wharf PA
    Moultrie GA
    National Beef Leathers
    St. Joseph MO
    International Office
    Chicago IL
Brands:
    Black Canyon Angus
    Black Canyon Premium Reserve
    Certified Angus Beef
    Certified Hereford Beef
    Natural Angus Beef
    Certified Premium Beef
    National Beef Prime
    Corned Beef
    Heritage Farms

8784 National Beverage Corporation
8100 SW 10th Streeet
Suite 4000
Fort Lauderdale, FL 33324
    954-581-0922
Fax: 954-473-4710 877-622-3499
salesteam@nationalbeverage.com
www.nationalbeverage.com
Canned and bottled beverages including soft drinks, juice and spring water
President: Joseph Caporella
Chairman/CEO: Nick Caporella
SVP Finance: George Bracken
EVP/Procurement: Edward Knecht
Executive Director/IT: Raymond Notarantonio
SVP/Chief Accounting Officer: Dean McKay
Senior Director/Consumer Marketing: Brent Bott
Director/Strategic Brand Management: Vanessa Walker
Senior Director/Beverage Analyst: Gregory Kworderis
Type of Packaging: Consumer, Food Service
Other Locations:
    National Beverage Corp.
    Hayward CA
Brands:
    Asante
    Big Shot
    Cascadia Only 2 Calories
    Cascadia Sparkling Cider
    Clearfruit
    Crystal Bay
    Everfresh
    Faygo
    Lacroix
    Mr Pure
    Mt. Shasta
    Ohana
    Rip It
    Ritz
    Shasta
    St. Nick's

8785 National Fish & Oyster
5028 Meridian Rd NE
Olympia, WA 98516-2339
    360-491-5550
Fax: 360-438-3681 www.nationaloyster.com
Processor and exporter of fresh and frozen oysters
President: James Bulldis
VP: George Bulldis
Plant Manager: Catherine Gylys
Estimated Sales: $5-10 Million
Number Employees: 20-49
Square Footage: 12000
Type of Packaging: Consumer
Brands:
    Sea Pearl

8786 National Fish & SeafoodInc
11-15 Parker St # 4
Gloucester, MA 01930-3017
    978-282-7880
Fax: 978-282-7882 800-229-1750
comments@nationalfish.com
www.nationalfish.com
Seafood
President: Jack Ventola
jventola@nationalfish.com
Number Employees: 20-49

8787 (HQ)National Fish & Seafood Inc
11-15 Parker St # 4
Gloucester, MA 01930-3017
    978-282-7880
Fax: 978-282-7882 800-229-1750
manager@nationalfish.com www.nationalfish.com
Seafood and seafood products
President & COO: Todd Provost
CFO: Ana Crespo
VP: Rick Waltzer
Purchasing Manager: Jason Brown
Estimated Sales: $20-50 Million
Number Employees: 20-49
Square Footage: 3500
Type of Packaging: Consumer, Food Service, Private Label
Brands:
    National Fisheries

8788 National Flavors
1206 E Crosstown Pkwy
Kalamazoo, MI 49001-2563
    269-344-3640
Fax: 269-344-1037 800-525-2431
national@nationalflavors.com
www.nationalflavors.com
Manufacturer of syrups, flavoring extracts, processed fruits and oils. Purchased land in 2015 to expand manufacturing facilities, due to be opened in late 2017.
President: Dan Hinkle
national@nationalflavors.com
Director of Research & Development: Polly B
Director of Sales & Marketing: Tony Overmyer
Director of Human Resources: Ann Woolley
Production Coordinator: Michael Visser
Estimated Sales: $4.8 Million
Number Employees: 20-49

8789 National Food Co LTD
3109 Koapaka St # C
Unit C
Honolulu, HI 96819-1998
    808-839-1118
Fax: 808-839-6866
Owner: Teresa Goo
teresa.goo@nfcegypt.com
Estimated Sales: $5-10 Million
Number Employees: 1-4

8790 National Food Corporation
728-134th St. SW
Suite 103
Everett, WA 98204
    425-349-4257
Fax: 425-349-4336 www.natlfood.com
Eggs and egg products including; yolks only, whole eggs, whites, and whole egg blends
President: Brian Bookey
VP Marketing: Roger Deffner
Sales Director: Gerry Wigren
Estimated Sales: $23.2 Million
Number Employees: 500
Type of Packaging: Consumer, Food Service

8791 National Foods
1414 S West Street
Indianapolis, IN 46225-1548
    317-634-5645
    800-683-6565
Processor and exporter of portion cut meat and frankfurters
President: Steve Silk
Senior VP/General Manager: Martin Silver
Sales/Marketing Executive: Mark Kleinman
Number Employees: 600
Square Footage: 720000
Parent Co: ConAgra Refrigerated Prepared Foods
Type of Packaging: Consumer, Food Service
Other Locations:
    National Foods
    Indianapolis IN

8792 National Foods
PO Box 20046
Kansas City, MO 64195-0046
    620-624-1851
Fax: 800-449-1333 www.nationalbeef.com
General grocery
President: John Miller
Sales Manager: Mike Sheehan
Parent Co: ConAgra Refrigerated Prepared Foods

8793 National Foods
600 Food Center Drive
Bronx, NY 10474-7037
    718-842-5000
Fax: 718-842-5664 800-683-6565
Processed meats, frankfurters, condiments and relishes. Kosher
President: Steve Silk
CFO: Bob Cahill
Executive VP: Marty Silver
Senior Marketing Manager: Leigh Platte
Sales Director: Scott Jacobs
Operations Manager: Henry Morris
General Manager: Robert Lichtman
Number Employees: 150
Parent Co: ConAgra Refrigerated Prepared Foods
Type of Packaging: Private Label

8794 National Frozen Foods Corp
1600 Fairview Ave E
Suite 200
Seattle, WA 98102
    206-322-8900
Fax: 206-322-4458 sales@nffc.com
www.nffc.com
Frozen foods including fruit and vegetable purees, vegetable blends, peas, corn, carrots, cooked squash, creamed corn, beans, pearl onions.
President & CEO: Dick Grader
Director of Chain Accounts: Sunshine Sang
Year Founded: 1912
Estimated Sales: $178.08 Million
Number Employees: 1,000-4,999
Square Footage: 12000
Type of Packaging: Consumer, Food Service, Private Label, Bulk
Other Locations:
    Albany OR
    Chehalis WA
    Moses Lake WA
    Quincy WA
Brands:
    Valamont

8795 National Fruit Flavor Co Inc
935 Edwards Ave
New Orleans, LA 70123-3124
    504-733-6757
Fax: 504-736-0168 800-966-1123
admin@nationalfruitflavor.com
www.nationalfruitflavor.com

Beverage concentrates, syrups and mixes. Manufacturer since 1917.
President: Gene Gamble
admin@nationalfruitflavor.com
Controller: Anthony Fulco
Vice President: Peter Gambel
Research and Development/Quality Control: Sharon Prados
Sales Manager: Avery Stirratt
Customer Service: Chris Rooks
Operations: Peter Gambel
Plant Manager: Giovanni Galvan
Purchasing: Michelle Adams
Estimated Sales: $10-20 Million
Number Employees: 20-49
Number of Brands: 6
Number of Products: 700
Square Footage: 41000
Type of Packaging: Consumer, Food Service, Private Label, Bulk
Brands:
  Gambelini
  National
  Old Comiskey
  Sno-Ball
  Tasty
  Zodiac

8796 National Fruit Product Co Inc
956 Poorhouse Rd
Winchester, VA 22603-3868
540-723-9614
Manufacturer of fruit products.
CEO and President: David Gum
Contact: Rhonda Alsberry
ralsberry@nfpc.com
Number Employees: 1-4
Brands:
  WHITEHOUSE FOODS

8797 National Grape Co-Op
2 S Portage St.
Westfield, NY 14787-1492
Fax: 716-326-5111 800-340-6870
www.welchs.com
Fruit and berry juices and jams.
President/CEO/Director: Bradley Irwin
Year Founded: 1952
Estimated Sales: $650 Million
Number Employees: 1000-4999
Brands:
  Welch's Fruit Juices
  Welch's Jams, Jellie & Spreads
  Welch's Fruit Fizz
  Welch's Sparkling
  Welch's Essentials
  Welch's Refrigerted Juice Cocktails
  Welch's Light
  Welch's Concentrates
  Welch's Natural Spreads
  Welch's Food & Snacks
  Welch's Chillers

8798 National Harvest
PO Box 26455
Kansas City, MO 64196-6455
816-842-9600
Fax: 816-531-3032 sales@nationalharvest.com
Baked potato meals and toppings
President: John Mueller
Estimated Sales: $1-3 Million
Number Employees: 5-9
Type of Packaging: Food Service, Private Label, Bulk
Brands:
  Super Stuffers

8799 National Importers
120-13100 Mitchell Road
Richmond, BC V6V 1M8
Canada
604-324-1551
Fax: 604-324-1553 888-894-6464
ussales@nationalimporters.com
www.nationalimporters.com
Importer of gourmet, Mexican, Chinese, Indian, Thai foods, candy and groceries
Owner: David Dueck
Marketing: Barbara Allen
Office Manager: Peggy Hunter

8800 National Meat & Provision Company
321 W 10th St
Reserve, LA 70084-6603
985-479-4200
Fax: 985-479-4205 www.natcofs.com
Beef, lamb, veal, pork, poultry, sausages, wild game, seafood, and dairy
President: Anne Babin
anne@natcofoodservice.com
Chairman: Leonard Lalla
CEO/Secretary: John Lalla
VP: Earline Lalla
Operations Manager: Joe Schwab
Manager: Sam Najm
Estimated Sales: $39.06 Million
Number Employees: 60
Square Footage: 85000

8801 National Pretzel Company
2060 Old Philadelphia Pike
Lancaster, PA 17602
800-732-0089
Pretzels

8802 National Raisin Co.
PO Box 219
Fowler, CA 93625
559-834-5981
Fax: 559-834-1055 info@nationalraisin.com
www.nationalraisin.com
Raisins, nuts and other dried fruits.
President/CEO: Lindakay Abdulian
Founder/Senior Advisor: Kenneth Bedrosian
kenneth.bedrosian@national-raisin.com
Accounts Payable Manager: Carlotta Bedrosian
Vice President: Bryan Bedrosian
Senior VP, Sales/Marketing: Jane Asmar
Vice President, Grower Relations: Michael Bedrosian
Year Founded: 1969
Estimated Sales: $140 Million
Number Employees: 500-999
Number of Brands: 1
Square Footage: 400000
Type of Packaging: Consumer, Food Service, Private Label, Bulk
Brands:
  Champion

8803 National Sign Corporation
1255 Westlake Ave N
Seattle, WA 98109-3531
206-282-0700
Fax: 206-285-3091 info@nationalsigncorp.com
www.nationalsigncorp.com
Manufacturing, installation and servicing of interior and exterior signage, including ADA signs.
President: Timothy Zamberlin
Estimated Sales: $5-10 Million
Number Employees: 35
Square Footage: 60000

8804 (HQ)National Starch Food Innovation
10 Finderne Ave
Bridgewater, NJ 08807
908-575-0178
Fax: 908-685-5355 800-743-6343
www.foodinnovation.com
Specialty starches for the food industry.
President: James Zallie
Contact: Bob Bacigalupo
kzizlercohen@citi-habitats.com
Parent Co: Ingredion Incorporated
Brands:
  Baka-Snack
  Batter BindS
  Capsul
  Capsul Ta
  Clearjel
  Colflo 67
  Crisp Coat Uc
  Crisp Film
  Crystal Gum
  Crystal Tex 627m
  Dry-Flo
  Elastigel 1000j
  Eliane
  Firm-Tex
  Frigex W
  Gel N Melt
  H-50
  Hi Flo
  Hi-Cap 100
  Hi-Maize 260
  Hi-Maize Whole Grain Flour
  Hi-Set 322
  Hi-Set C
  Homecraft Create
  Hylon Vii
  Instant Clearjel
  Instant Pure-Flo F
  Instant Textra
  K4484
  National
  N-Creamer 46
  N-Dulge
  N-Lok 1930
  N-Oil
  Novation
  N-Tack
  Nutriose
  N-Zorbit
  Paselli
  Perfectagel Mpt
  Perfectamyl
  Precisa
  Pure-Flo
  Purity Gum
  Purity
  Q-Naturale
  Textaid
  Textra
  Thermflo
  Thermtex
  Ultra Create
  Ultra-Crisp
  Ultra-Sperse
  Ultra-Tex

8805 National Steak & Poultry
301 E. 5th Ave.
Owasso, OK 74055
918-274-8787
www.nationalsteak.com
Marinated pre-portioned beef and poultry both fully cooked and fresh frozen.
President/CEO: Mike Wilson
Year Founded: 1980
Estimated Sales: $500 Million-$1 Billion
Number Employees: 500-999
Brands:
  National Steak

8806 (HQ)National Vinegar Co
1750 S Brentwood Blvd # 351
Suite 351
St Louis, MO 63144-1331
314-962-4111
Fax: 314-962-4115 www.natvin.com
Distilled vinegar, apple cider vinegar, corn sugar vinegar, colored distilled vinegar, apple-flavored distilled vinegar, burgundy cooking wine, and Sauterne cooking wine
President: John Placio
Vice President: David Wolff
Manager: Joan Weiner
Estimated Sales: $1-3 Million
Number Employees: 1-4
Type of Packaging: Consumer, Food Service, Private Label, Bulk
Other Locations:
  National Vinegar Company Plant
  Alton IL
  National Vinegar Company Plant
  Olney IL
Brands:
  Alton
  Garden Harvest
  Hardin

8807 National Wine & Spirits
Indianapolis, IN 46225
www.nwscorp.com
Alcoholic beverages, wine and spirits
Chairman, President, CEO & CFO: James LaCrosse
Corporate Controller & Treasurer: Patrick Trefun
VP, Information Systems: Dwight Deming
EVP & COO: John Baker
Year Founded: 1934
Estimated Sales: $100-500 Million
Number Employees: 1,600
Type of Packaging: Private Label

Food Manufacturers / A-Z

8808 National Wooden Pallet & Container Association
1421 Prince Street
Suite 340
Alexandria, VA 22314-2805
703-519-6104
Fax: 703-519-4720 palletcomm@aol.com
www.palletcentral.com
Manufacture, repair and distribute pallets and wood packaging in unit-load solutions.
President/CEO: Brent J. McClendon, CAE
Vice President of Operations and Events: Isabel Sullivan
Sales Director: Joni Leonardo
Contact: Patrick Atagi
patrick@palletcentral.com
Number Employees: 10-19

8809 Native American Herbal Tea
421 S Lincoln St
Aberdeen, SD 57401-4320
605-226-2006
Fax: 605-226-2414 888-291-8517
www.nativeamericantea.com
Coffee, tea
Manager: J Almon
nativeamericantea@yahoo.com
Estimated Sales: Below $5 Million
Number Employees: 5-9
Brands:
 Native American

8810 Native American Natural Foods
287 Water Tower Road
Kyle, SD 57752
800-416-7212
Fax: 605-455-2019 800-416-7212
mtilsen@tankabar.com
Dairy-free, gluten-free, lactose-free, nut-free, organic/natural, USDA, health, fitness and energy bars, food service

8811 Native Kjalii Foods
459 Fulton St Ste 205
San Francisco, CA 94102
415-522-5580
Fax: 510-686-1757
Fruit and vegetable salsas, vegetable hummus and tortilla chips
President/Co-Owner: Bret Jeremy
Marketing/Co-Owner: Julie Jeremy
Estimated Sales: $3-5 Million
Number Employees: 1-4
Square Footage: 16000
Type of Packaging: Consumer, Food Service, Bulk
Brands:
 Native Kjalii

8812 Native Scents
1040 Dea Ln
Taos, NM 87571-6277
575-758-9656
Fax: 575-758-5802 800-645-3471
Processor, importer and exporter of herbal teas and aromatic products, honey and essential oils, incense, bath products
President: Marlene Payfoya
CEO: Alfred Savinelli
nativescents@gmail.com
CEO: Alfred Savinelli
Estimated Sales: Less Than $500,000
Number Employees: 1-4
Number of Products: 127
Square Footage: 24000
Brands:
 Native Scents

8813 Native State Foods
201 Bicknell Ave
Suite 206
Santa Monica, CA 90405
866-647-2291
nativestatefoods.com
Cereals and snack cups
Co-Founder & Co-CEO: Claudio Ochoa
Co-Founder: Angela Palmieri
Year Founded: 2014
Type of Packaging: Consumer
Brands:
 PURELY PINOLE

8814 Natra US
2535 Camino Dek Rio South
Suite 355
Chula Vista, CA 91910
619-397-4120
Fax: 619-397-4121 800-262-6216
www.natrus.com
Importer and exporter of cocoa powder, butter and extract; also, chocolate, caffeine, theobromine and nutraceuticals
Manager: Maria Dominguez
Vice President: Martin Brabenec
Key Account Manager: Juan Carlos Vinolo
Estimated Sales: $650000
Number Employees: 1-4
Number of Brands: 2
Number of Products: 30
Parent Co: Natra S.A.
Type of Packaging: Consumer, Food Service, Bulk
Brands:
 Natra Cacao
 Natra Us
 Natraceutical

8815 Natrel
333 Lebeau Blvd
St. Laurent, QC H4N 1S3
Canada
800-501-1150
www.natrel.ca
Milk, butter, ice cream mix, chocolate milk and lemonade
President: Serge Serge Paquette
VP Marketing: Doug Kelly McGregor Gillespie
VP Finance/Administration: Eric Brunelle
Plant Manager: Gerry Verhoef
Number Employees: 100-249
Parent Co: Natrel
Type of Packaging: Consumer
Brands:
 Naterl
 Quebon
 Sealtest
 Silk Soy
 Ultra'cream

8816 Natren Inc
3105 Willow Ln
Thousand Oaks, CA 91361-4919
805-371-4737
Fax: 805-371-4742 800-992-3323
CustomerService@Natren.com www.natren.com
Yogurt starter and probiotic products
President: Natasha Trenev
CEO: Yordan Trenev
Contact: Diane Bassett
dianeb1@natren.com
Estimated Sales: $1.4 Million
Number Employees: 50-99
Brands:
 Bifido Factor
 Bifido Nate
 Bio-Nate
 D.F.A.
 Digesta-Lac
 Life Start
 Megadophilius
 Yogurt Starter

8817 (HQ)Natrium Products Inc
58 Pendleton Street
Cortland, NY 13045-2702
607-753-9829
Fax: 607-753-0552 800-962-4203
info@natrium.com www.natrium.com
Baking Soda/Sodium Biocarbonate
President: Tim Herman
herman@natrium.com
Estimated Sales: $10-20 Million
Number Employees: 20-49
Square Footage: 70000
Type of Packaging: Bulk
Brands:
 Natrium

8818 Natur Sweeteners, Inc.
11155 Massachusetts Avenue
Los Angeles, CA 90025
310-445-0020
Fax: 310-473-1086 stephenf@naturresearch.com
www.cweet.com
Natural intense sweetener; characteristics and other performance qualities similar to cane sugar

8819 Naturade Inc
1 City Blvd West
Suite 1440
Orange, CA 92868
714-535-9178
Fax: 714-935-9837 800-421-1830
customerservice@naturade.com
www.naturade.com
Soy protein powder shake mixes, herbal-based cough and cold formulas, and colostrum supplements
Founder: Nathan Schulman
Chief Executive Officer: Rick Robinette
Contact: Chuck Glona
cglona@naturade.com

8820 (HQ)Natural Balance
383 Inverness Pkwy # 390
Englewood, CO 80112-5864
303-688-6633
Fax: 303-688-1591 800-624-4260
service@naturalbalance.com
www.naturalbalance.com
Processor and wholesaler/distributor of natural nutrition supplements for energy, weight loss and sports
President: Mark Owens
Executive VP: Tim Hinricks
Sales Coordinator: Scott Smith
Contact: Steven Kahl
skahl@mai-architects.com
Plant Manager: John O'Brien
Purchasing Manager: Stephanie McArthur
Estimated Sales: $11.4 Million
Number Employees: 100-249
Square Footage: 50000
Other Locations:
 Natural Balance
 Castle Rock CO

8821 Natural Bliss
800-637-8534
www.coffee-mate.com
Cold-brew coffee and coffee creamer
Manager, RTD Coffee: Avantika Chakravorty
Number of Brands: 2
Number of Products: 15
Parent Co: Nestl,
Type of Packaging: Consumer
Brands:
 NATURAL BLISS
 NATURAL BLISS COLD BREW

8822 Natural By Nature
316 Markus Crt
Newark, DE 19713
302-455-1261
Fax: 302-455-1262 jayt@ndpc.net
www.naturalbynaturedairy.com
Milk, sour cream, yogurt and other dairy products.
President: Stephanie McVaugh
National Sales Manager: Jay Totman
Year Founded: 1994
Estimated Sales: $100-500 Million

8823 Natural Choice Distribution
5427 Telegraph Ave Ste U
Oakland, CA 94609
510-653-8212
Fax: 510-653-8163
info@naturalchoicedistribution.com
Salsa and sandwiches, distribution of natural food products
Owner: Steve Cutter
Contact: Douglas Gwosdz
douglasgwosdz@naturalchoicedistribution.com
Estimated Sales: Below $5 000,000
Number Employees: 18
Type of Packaging: Private Label

8824 Natural Company
8 W Hamilton St
Baltimore, MD 21201-5008
410-628-1262
Fax: 410-796-3977
info@thenaturalcompany.com.au
www.keeper.com.au
Health food, tofu
President: Joan Huang
Estimated Sales: Below $5 Million
Number Employees: 6
Brands:
 Moon Pads
 The Keeper

Food Manufacturers / A-Z

8825 Natural Earth Products
692 Thomas S. Boyland St
Brooklyn, NY 11212
718-552-2727
Fax: 718-552-2730 info@nepdistributors.com
nepdistributors.com
Olive oil, chia seeds, quinoa, kasha, turmeric and lollipops.
VP: Michael Gurevich

8826 Natural Enrichment Industries
1800 W Oak St
Herrin, IL 62948-2074
618-942-2112
Fax: 618-942-4112 lorip@neitcp.com
www.neitcp.com
Tricalcium phosphate from a domestically produced lime
Sales & Marketing Representative: Marci Swartz
Sales Manager: Mary Clark
Contact: Scott Fheeler
scotts@neitcp.com
Number Employees: 20-49

8827 Natural Exotic Tropicals
450 SW 12th Ave
Pompano Beach, FL 33069
954-783-4500
Fax: 954-783-8812 800-756-5267
Sugar-free fruit spreads, jellies, marmalades, butters and juices
President: Van Herrington
CFO: Jayne Herrington
Estimated Sales: $5-10 Million
Number Employees: 20-49
Brands:
  Natural Exotic Tropicals

8828 Natural Feast Corporation
PO Box 36
28 Old Farm Road
Dover, MA 02030-0036
508-785-3322
Fax: 508-984-1496
Frozen foods
President: Alan Attridge
Estimated Sales: $1-2.5 Million
Number Employees: 10

8829 Natural Flavors
268 Doremus Ave
Newark, NJ 07105-4879
973-589-1230
Fax: 973-589-0016 Flavorinfo@flavor.com
www.flavor.com
Natural and certified organic flavors
President: Herb Stein
Secretary: Joanne Hoffman
EVP: Julie Eisman
Director Quality Assurance: Robert Maxwell
E Commerce Manager: Josh Richards
National Sales Manager: Jeff Rakity
Manager: Isabel Couto
Estimated Sales: $2 Million
Number Employees: 10-19

8830 Natural Food Holdings
4241 US 75 Ave.
Sioux Center, IA 51250
800-735-7765
www.siouxpreme.com
Manufacturer and exporter of pork products.
CEO, Perdue Farms: Randy Day
Year Founded: 1969
Estimated Sales: $113 Million
Number Employees: 250-499
Square Footage: 50000
Parent Co: Perdue Farms
Type of Packaging: Consumer, Private Label, Bulk

8831 Natural Food Mill
2991 Doherty St
2991 Doherty Street
Corona, CA 92879-5811
951-279-5090
Fax: 951-279-1784 800-797-5090
www.foodforlife.com
Baked goods including sprouted grain breads
President: Jim Torres
Vice President: Charles Torres
Estimated Sales: $20-49,000,000
Number Employees: 50-99
Type of Packaging: Consumer

Brands:
  Ezekiel 4:9(c)
  Genesis 1:29(c)

8832 Natural Food Source
52 E Union Blvd
Bethlehem, PA 18017
610-997-0500
Fax: 610-954-9959 www.nimeks.com
Dried fruits, frozen vegetables, concentrates and purees.
VP: Kadir Veziroglu

8833 Natural Food Supplements Inc
8725 Remmet Ave
Canoga Park, CA 91304-1519
818-341-3375
Fax: 818-341-3376
Processor and contract packager of vitamins
President: Elmer Walters
Estimated Sales: $600,000
Number Employees: 5-9
Type of Packaging: Bulk
Brands:
  Sunshine Valley

8834 Natural Food World
6009 Washington Blvd
Culver City, CA 90232-7425
310-836-7770
Fax: 310-836-6454
Health and dietetic foods
President: Anne Stern
Estimated Sales: $5-10 000,000
Number Employees: 10

8835 Natural Foods Inc
3040 Hill Ave
Toledo, OH 43607-2983
419-537-1711
Fax: 419-531-6887 vip@bulkfoods.com
www.3qf.com
Wholesaler/distributor, importer and packer of food, candy, nuts, spices, fruit, and chocolates
Owner: Frank Dietrich
Estimated Sales: $5 Million
Number Employees: 20-49
Square Footage: 1800000
Type of Packaging: Food Service, Bulk

8836 Natural Formulas
2125 American Ave
Hayward, CA 94545-1803
510-372-1800
Fax: 510-782-9793 www.gnld.com
Powdered drink mixes
Founder: Jerry Brassfield
Quality Control: Ric Green
Executive Vice President of Product: Anjana Srivastava
Chief Operating Officer: Kevin Fox
Estimated Sales: $10-20 Million
Number Employees: 50-99

8837 Natural Fruit Corp
770 W 20th St
Hialeah, FL 33010-2430
305-887-7525
Fax: 305-888-8208 info@nfc-fruti.com
www.nfc-fruti.com
Processor and exporter of frozen fruit bars, cocktail mixes and ice cream novelties
Founder/President: Simon Bravo
Quality Assurance Director: Angelica Delia
EVP Operations/Founder: Jorge Bravo Sr
Plant Supervisor: Peter Infante
Estimated Sales: $14 Million
Number Employees: 20-49
Square Footage: 40000
Brands:
  Allison Jayne
  Chunks O'Fruit
  Fruti

8838 (HQ)Natural Group
505 South A Street
Second Floor
Oxnard, CA 93030
805-485-3420
Fax: 805-983-1428 www.naturalgroup.org
Soft drinks
Owner: Kanishka Lal
Executive VP: Judith Keer

Estimated Sales: $440,000
Number Employees: 7
Type of Packaging: Private Label
Brands:
  Ame
  Ame Celebration
  Apres
  Hildon Water
  Purdey's
  Yellow Gold Shelf St

8839 Natural Habitats USA
948 North St
Unit 7
Boulder, CO 80304
888-958-1967
info@natural-habitats.com
www.natural-habitats.com
Organic palm oil products
Managing Director: Neil Blomquist
Type of Packaging: Bulk

8840 Natural Ice Fruits
524 Mid Florida Dr
Suite 209
Orlando, FL 32824
407-270-9194
www.sofruitty.com
Vegan frozen fruit bars
Brands:
  So Fruitty

8841 Natural Intentions, Inc.
PO Box 6688
Folsom, CA 95763
www.thedailycrave.com
Veggie chips, organic veggie straws, quinia chips and lentil chips in various flavors
Number of Brands: 1
Type of Packaging: Consumer, Private Label
Brands:
  The Daily Crave

8842 Natural Nectar
196 E Main Street
Huntington, NY 11743
631-367-7280
Fax: 631-367-7282 www.natural-nectar.com
Baguette bites, Chocodream Fair Trade cookies and spreads, Cracklebred, Cracksnax, Mediterranean crackers, Mediterranean Sea Salt, Nectar Nugget Peanut Butter cup, natural Lady Fingers and organic biowafers
Contact: Vincent De Sartre
vincent@natural-nectar.com

8843 Natural Oils International
2279 Ward Ave
Simi Valley, CA 93065-1863
805-433-0160
Fax: 805-433-0182 www.naturaloils.com
Processor, importer and exporter of vegetable oils
President: Brendon Bonnar
Sales: Barbara Hardy
Sales: Jack Phillips
Estimated Sales: $1-3 Million
Number Employees: 1-4
Square Footage: 120000

8844 (HQ)Natural Ovens Bakery Inc
4300 County Road Cr
Manitowoc, WI 54220-9263
920-758-2500
Fax: 920-758-2594 800-558-3535
info@naturalovens.com www.naturalovens.com
Processor of bread, cookies, rolls and bagels.
CEO: Matt Taylor
CEO: Jim Irvin
jim.irvin@naturalovens.com
Year Founded: 1976
Estimated Sales: $20-50 Million
Number Employees: 100-249
Square Footage: 28000
Brands:
  100% Whole Grain
  Flax N' Honey
  Nutty All-Natural Wheat
  Sunny Millet

Food Manufacturers / A-Z

8845 Natural Products Inc
2211 6th Ave
Grinnell, IA 50112-2276
641-236-0852
Fax: 641-236-4835 npi@npisoy.com
www.npisoy.com
Roast and mill soybean, flour and grits for food industry
General Manager: Paul Lang
Quality Control: Ray Lang
Marketing Director: Jon Stratford
Estimated Sales: Below $5 Million
Number Employees: 20-49

8846 Natural Quick Foods
3737 NE 135th Street
Seattle, WA 98125-3831
206-365-5757
Fax: 206-365-5434
Vegan, organic pocket sandwiches
President: Larry Brewer
Estimated Sales: $5-10 Million
Number Employees: 5-9

8847 Natural Rush
PO Box 421753
San Francisco, CA 94142-1753
415-863-2503
Fax: 415-431-5763
Candy, confectionery and honey
President: Gilles Desaulniers
Estimated Sales: Under $500,000
Number Employees: 1-4
Type of Packaging: Private Label

8848 Natural Sins
New York, NY
naturalsinsonline.com
Baked fruit and vegetable chips
Co-Founder: Andres Dominguez
Number of Products: 6
Brands:
  Natural Sins

8849 Natural Spring Water Company
300 Boggs Ln
Johnson City, TN 37604
423-926-7905
Fax: 423-926-8210
Contract packager and bottler of noncarbonated mountain spring water
President: Bill Lizzio
Team Leader: John Gustke
Number Employees: 10-19
Square Footage: 24000
Type of Packaging: Consumer, Food Service, Private Label, Bulk
Brands:
  Laure Pristine

8850 Natural Value
1511 Corporate Way
Suite 100
Sacramento, CA 95831
916-836-3561
Fax: 916-914-2446 gary@naturalvalue.com
naturalvalue.com
Organic beans, lentils, tomatoes and condiments
President/Owner: Gary Cohen
CEO: Jody Cohen
Estimated Sales: $1-3 Million
Number Employees: 1-4
Number of Brands: 1
Number of Products: 200
Type of Packaging: Consumer, Food Service, Bulk
Brands:
  Natural Value

8851 Natural Way Mills Inc
24509 390th St NE
Middle River, MN 56737-9367
218-222-3677
Fax: 218-222-3408 naturalwaymills@wiktel.com
www.naturalwaymills.com
Organic wheat, seven-grain cereal, rye, flax seed, barley, millet, brown rice, flour and grits; custom milling available
Owner: Ray Juhl
rayjuhl@naturalwaymills.com
CEO: Helen Juhl
Quality Control: Aaron Pervis
Sales: Leigh Mott
rayjuhl@naturalwaymills.com
Plant Manager: Charles Knapp
Estimated Sales: $620,000
Number Employees: 5-9
Brands:
  7 Grain Cereal
  Gold N. White Bread Flour

8852 Naturalife Laboratories
20433 Earl St
Torrance, CA 90503-2414
310-370-1563
Fax: 310-370-7354 800-231-3670
info@ParagonLabsUSA.com
www.paragonlabsusa.com
Custom manufacturer of dietary supplements, vitamins, minerals, herbal products and nutritional supplements; available in tablets, capsules, powders and liquids
President: Jay Kaufman
President: Richard Kaufman
Estimated Sales: $10-20 Million
Number Employees: 50-99
Type of Packaging: Consumer, Private Label, Bulk

8853 Naturally Clean Eats
Manhattan Beach, CA
naturallycleaneats.com
All-natural snack bars
Founder: Jessica Luengo
Number of Brands: 1
Number of Products: 4
Type of Packaging: Consumer
Brands:
  NATURALLY CLEAN EATS

8854 Naturally Delicious Inc
1811 NW 29th St
Oakland Park, FL 33311-2123
954-485-6730
Fax: 954-485-6730 888-221-7352
info@naturally-delicious.com
www.naturally-delicious.com
Snack, natural cakes, cookies and brownies.
Owner/President: Arthur Price
aprice8945@aol.com
Estimated Sales: $750,000- 1 Million
Number Employees: 5-9
Square Footage: 20000
Brands:
  Naturally Delicious

8855 Naturally Homegrown
945 184 Street
Surrey, BC V3S 9R9
Canada
604-465-7751
Fax: 604-465-7727 info@hardbitechips.com
hardbitechips.com
Kettle chips and root vegetable chips
Number of Products: 18
Brands:
  Hardbite

8856 Naturally Nutty
P.O. Box 3151
Traverse City, MI 49685
888-224-9988
customerservice@naturallynutty.com
www.naturallynutty.com
Nut and seed butters
President: Katie Kearney
Year Founded: 2007

8857 Naturally Scientific
600 Willow Tree Road
Leonia, NJ 07605-2211
201-585-7055
Fax: 973-244-0044 888-428-0700
Liquid nutritional supplements and food and beverage ingredients
President/CEO: Frank Berger
Executive VP: Marc Pozner
Marketing Director: Douglas Lynch
Sales/Group Publisher: Jon Benninger
Contact: Rick Krupa
rkrupa@nsilabs.com
Estimated Sales: $1-3 Million
Number Employees: 5-9
Number of Products: 200
Type of Packaging: Consumer, Private Label

8858 Naturalmond Almond Butter
3400 W. Hospital Ave.
Unit 103
Chamblee, GA 30341
866-327-9301
www.naturalmond.com
Manufacturer of almond butter.
Founder and Owner: Jaime Foster
Brands:
  NaturAlmond

8859 Nature Cure Northwest
5271 NE Falcon Ridge Ln
Poulsbo, WA 98370-8923
360-697-8691
Fax: 360-697-7179 800-957-8048
Bottled bee pollen pills
Owner: Wasser Schmitt
Estimated Sales: 724,000
Number Employees: 1-4
Type of Packaging: Food Service
Brands:
  Nature Cure

8860 Nature Kist Snacks
5560 E. Slauson Ave.
Commerce, CA 90040
323-278-9578
Fax: 323-278-9579
Nut and seed trail mixes; private labeling available
President: Ronald L Mozingo
Office Manager: Nancy Freitas
Plant Manager: Rick Dorotheo
Estimated Sales: $10-20 Million
Number Employees: 20-49
Type of Packaging: Consumer, Private Label
Brands:
  Fresh Pak
  Nature Kist
  Holiday Bonus

8861 Nature Most Laboratories
Trigo Business Park
60 Trigo Drive
Middletown, CT 06457-6157
860-346-8991
Fax: 860-347-3312 800-234-2112
sales@naturemost.com
Manufacturer, importer and exporter of products, vitamins, oils, minerals, herbal supplements
President: Robert Trigo
Marketing: Sam Schwartz
Sales: Donna Platnum
Operations: Fred Wuschner
Estimated Sales: $5-10 Million
Number Employees: 20-49
Number of Brands: 3
Number of Products: 300
Square Footage: 80000
Type of Packaging: Consumer, Private Label
Brands:
  Naturemost Labs
  Trigo Labs

8862 Nature Nate's
2910 Nature Nate Farm
McKinney, TX 75071
469-452-4429
www.naturenates.com
Honey products
Founder: Nathan Sheets
Brands:
  Nature Nate's(c)

8863 Nature Quality
13805 Llagas Ave
San Martin, CA 95046
408-683-2182
Fax: 408-683-4249 natqual@aol.com
naturequality.com
Processor and exporter of IQF cut celery, olives, onions, garlic and peppers
President: Karen Ash
kash@naturesquality.com
Food Safety & Quality Assurance Manager: Nicole Kamath
Sales Manager: Melissa Guevara
Estimated Sales: $7 Million
Number Employees: 100-249
Square Footage: 40000
Type of Packaging: Food Service, Bulk

Food Manufacturers / A-Z

8864 Nature Soy Inc
713 N 10th St
Philadelphia, PA 19123-1902
215-765-3289
Fax: 215-765-3266 support@naturesoy.com
Manufacturer/supplier of healthy soy and vegetarian products to the ethnic market
President: Yat Wen
CEO: Gene He
he@naturesoy.com
EVP: Fenjin He
Estimated Sales: $2.4 Million
Number Employees: 20-49
Square Footage: 35000

8865 Nature Zen USA
159 River Rd
Essex Junction, VT 05452
info@nature-zen.com
www.nature-zen.com
Protein bars and powders
Number of Brands: 1
Number of Products: 7
Brands:
 NATURE ZEN

8866 Nature's Apothecary
244 Knollwood Drive
Suite 300
Bloomingdale, IL 60108
970-664-1600
Fax: 970-664-5106 888-669-3663
www.nowfoods.com
Processor and exporter of fresh organic, medicinal, botanical and herbal liquid extracts
President: Jim Emme
Engineering Manager: Dan Mirjanic
Sales Manager: Dan Richard
Type of Packaging: Consumer, Private Label, Bulk

8867 Nature's Bakery
425 Maestro Dr
Suite 101
Reno, NV 89511
naturesbakery.com
Fig bars and brownies
Co-Founder: Dave Marson
Co-Founder: Sam Marson
Year Founded: 2010
Estimated Sales: $100+ Million
Number of Brands: 1
Number of Products: 5
Other Locations:
 Manufacturing Location
 Hazelwood MO
 Manufacturing Location
 Carson City NV
 Commercial Office
 Pasadena CA
Brands:
 NATURE'S BAKERY

8868 Nature's Bandits
PO Box 541
Riverside, CT 06878-0541
203-571-2040
www.naturesbandits.com
Dried fruit and vegetable snacks.
Co-Founder: Tony Carvalho
Brands:
 Nature's Bandits(c)

8869 Nature's Best Inc
195 Engineers Rd
Hauppauge, NY 11788-4020
631-232-3355
Fax: 631-232-3320 800-345-2378
info@naturesbest.com
www.theisopurecompany.com
Processor and exporter of athletic supplements and sport drinks
President: Hal Katz
Estimated Sales: $1.5 Million
Number Employees: 5-9
Brands:
 Decades
 No Holds Bar
 Perfect 1100
 Perfect Aminos
 Perfect Carbs
 Perfect Rx

8870 Nature's Best Inc
195 Engineers Rd
Hauppauge, NY 11788-4020
631-232-3355
Fax: 631-232-3320 800-345-2378
info@naturesbest.com
www.theisopurecompany.com
Sport nutrition products
President: Hal Katz
Purchasing Manager: Ernie Geraci
Estimated Sales: $5-10 Million
Number Employees: 5-9
Number of Brands: 4
Number of Products: 150
Type of Packaging: Consumer
Brands:
 Decades
 Isopure
 No Holds Bar
 Perfect
 Perfect 1100
 Perfect Animos
 Perfect Carbs
 Perfect Rx
 Solid Protein

8871 Nature's Bounty Co.
2100 Smithtown Ave.
Ronkonkoma, NY 11779
631-200-2000
877-774-3361
consumeraffairsmgmt@nbty.com
www.naturesbountyco.com
Nutritional supplements and vitamins.
President/CEO: Paul Sturman
CFO: Ted McCormick
General Counsel/Chief Compliance Officer: Stratis Philipps
Estimated Sales: $3 Billion
Number Employees: 10,000+
Number of Brands: 19
Number of Products: 22K
Parent Co: KKR
Type of Packaging: Consumer, Private Label, Bulk
Brands:
 Pure Protien
 Nature's Bounty
 Sundown Naturals
 Solgar
 Body Fortress
 MET-Rx
 Puritan's Pride
 Ester-C
 Osteo Bi-Flex
 Dr. Organic
 Best Ever Bar
 Balance
 American Health
 Home Health
 Sisu

8872 Nature's Candy
632 Fm 2093
Fredericksburg, TX 78624-7149
830-997-3844
Fax: 830-997-6528 800-729-0085
Processor and wholesaler/distributor of natural and fruit-filled candy, maple-coated nuts and seasoned nuts and seeds
President: Michael Zygmunt
michael@beneficialfoods.com
Office Manager: Karen Gold
Estimated Sales: $482,000
Number Employees: 5-9
Type of Packaging: Consumer, Private Label, Bulk

8873 Nature's Dairy
5104 S Main St
Roswell, NM 88203-0822
575-623-9640
Fax: 575-622-1318 www.novabus.com
Milk, dairy products; noncheese
President: Edward Avitia
edward.avitia@volvo.com
Estimated Sales: $5-10 000,000
Number Employees: 20-49
Brands:
 Nature's Dairy

8874 Nature's Earthly Choice
Eagle, ID
208-898-4004
Fax: 208-939-2626 info@earthlychoice.com
www.earthlychoice.com
Manufacturer of quinoa.
President and Co-Founder: Chuck Watson
Brands:
 NATURE'S Earthly Choice

8875 Nature's Finest Products
PO Box 801326
Dallas, TX 75380-1326
773-489-2096
Fax: 972-960-8760 800-237-5205
Gourmet foods
President: Mike Griffin

8876 Nature's First Inc
58 Robinson Blvd # C
Orange, CT 06477-3647
203-795-8400
Fax: 203-795-8300 800-523-3752
sales@naturesfirst.com
Coffee, creamers, hot chocolates, cappuccinos and chai
Owner: Harjit Singh
sales@naturesfirst.com
Estimated Sales: Less Than $500,000
Number Employees: 1-4

8877 Nature's Fusions
1405 W 820 N
Provo, UT 84601
801-872-9500
www.naturesfusions.com
Essential oils and CBD
CEO: C.J. Peterson
Number of Brands: 1
Brands:
 NATURE'S FUSIONS

8878 Nature's Godfather
405 Waltham St
Suite 168
Lexington, MA 02421
339-970-9888
sales@belleandbella.com
www.belleandbella.com
Non-dairy yogurt starter and probiotics.
Managing Director: Ada Wong
Brands:
 belle + bella
 Probiology

8879 Nature's Guru
19416 Amhurst Ct
Cerritos, CA 90703-6787
949-478-4878
info@naturesguru.com
www.naturesguru.com
Chai
Brands:
 Nature's Guru(c)

8880 Nature's Habit Brand. Inc.
PO Box 522
Washago, ON
Canada
707-712-2826
www.natureshabit.com
Manufacturer of granola and granola trail mixes.

8881 Nature's Hand Inc
info@natureshand.com
www.natureshand.com
Manufacturer and exporter of drink mixes and puddings
Estimated Sales: $500,000-$1 Million
Number Employees: 5-9
Number of Brands: 1
Number of Products: 4
Type of Packaging: Consumer
Brands:
 Nature's Hand

8882 Nature's Herbs
PO Box 970
Merritt, BC V1K 1B8
Canada
250-378-8822
Fax: 250-378-8753 800-437-2257
www.naturesherbs.net/p/contact_us
Processor and exporter of dietary supplements and encapsulated herbs
President/CEO: Ross Blechman
Executive VP Sales: Dean Blechman
Estimated Sales: $5-10 Million
Number Employees: 250

Food Manufacturers / A-Z

Square Footage: 200000
Parent Co: Twin Laboratories
Type of Packaging: Consumer
Brands:
   Healthcare Naturals
   Herb Masters' Original
   Nature's Herbs
   Power Herbs

8883 Nature's Hilights
1608 Chico River Rd
Suite A
Chico, CA 95928
530-342-6154
Fax: 530-342-3130 800-313-6454
Baked products including rice crusts, bread, bread sticks, rice pizzas and frozen gluten-free desserts
President/CEO: Gayle Luna
Estimated Sales: $5-9.9 Million
Number Employees: 10-19
Type of Packaging: Food Service, Bulk

8884 Nature's Hollow
Probst Farms
3290 West 3500 South
Charleston, UT 84032
Fax: 435-216-9829 www.natureshollow.com
Sugar-free sauces and spreads
Number of Brands: 1
Brands:
   NATURE'S HOLLOW

8885 Nature's Kitchen
4651 Woodstock Rd
Suite 208-101
Roswell, GA 30075
678-845-6897
info@natureskitchn.com
www.thenatureskitchen.com
Rubs, marinade and saucinades.
Co-Founder: Rory Mitchell
Co-Founder: Archana Mitchell
Brands:
   Nature's Kitchen

8886 Nature's Legacy Inc.
417 S. Meridian Road
Hudson, MI 49247
517-448-2050
Fax: 517-448-2070 info@purityfoods.com
www.natureslegacyforlife.com
Organic pasta, flours, spelt granola, pretzels, sesame sticks, beans, grains, and seeds.
Owner/President: Donald Stinchcomb
Estimated Sales: $5.8 Million
Number Employees: 11
Square Footage: 24000
Type of Packaging: Consumer, Bulk
Brands:
   VITASPELT
   NATURE'S LEGACY
   PURITY FOODS

8887 Nature's Love
PO Box 745
Snyder, CO 80750
970-571-7959
info@natureslove.org
natureslove.org
Hemp extract
Number of Products: 18

8888 Nature's Nutrition
100 North Main St
Marysville, OH 43040
321-255-5505
Fax: 321-255-5881 800-242-1115
www.nothinbutherbs.com
Organic food and nutritional supplements including vitamins, amino acids, antioxidants and proteins; also, weight loss aids
President: Dee Corbitt
Estimated Sales: $500,000-$1 Million
Number Employees: 5-9
Square Footage: 20000
Brands:
   Harida
   The Capsule

8889 (HQ)Nature's Path Foods
205 H Street
Suite 275
Blaine, WA 98230
888-808-9505
naturespath@worldpantry.com
www.naturespath.com
Organic cereal products
President & Founder: Arran Stephens
Co-CEO & COO: Ratana Stephens
Executive VP Sales & Marketing: Arjan Stephens
Director of Human Resources: Jyoti Stephens
Year Founded: 1985
Estimated Sales: $145.87 Million
Number Employees: 60
Square Footage: 29999
Type of Packaging: Consumer, Private Label, Bulk
Other Locations:
   Nature's Path Foods
   Blaine WA
Brands:
   Nature's Path Organic
   Envirokidz Organic
   Optimum

8890 Nature's Plus
548 Broadhollow Rd
Melville, NY 11747-3722
631-293-0013
Fax: 800-688-7239 800-645-9500
salesinfo@naturesplus.com www.naturesplus.com
Processor and exporter of health products including protein weight loss supplements, vitamins and herbs
Director Marketing: Gerard McIntee
Estimated Sales: $15.1 Million
Number Employees: 5-9
Parent Co: Natural Organics

8891 (HQ)Nature's Products Inc
1301 Sawgrass Corporate Pkwy
Sunrise, FL 33323-2813
954-233-3300
Fax: 954-233-3301 800-752-7873
info@natures-products.com
Manufacturer and supplier of raw materials specializing in gelatin, flavors, active pharmaceuticals, botanicals and pharmaceutical additives. Providing import/export services, warehousing and freight forwarding to and from the United States and worldwide
President: Jose Minski
josem@npi-gmi.com
Number Employees: 100-249
Type of Packaging: Private Label, Bulk
Brands:
   Curt Georgi Flavors & Fragrances
   Gmi Gelatin
   Health Assure

8892 Nature's Provision Company
452 Krumville Rd
Olivebridge, NY 12461-5528
845-657-6020
Powdered health food supplements for circulatory improvement; wholesaler/distributor of pH balanced cleansers and lubricants
President: Clark Jung
Vice President: Ann Jung
Estimated Sales: $130,000
Number Employees: 2
Brands:
   Dr. Rinse Vita Flo Formula

8893 Nature's Select Inc
555 Cascade West Pkwy SE # 200
Grand Rapids, MI 49546-2105
616-956-1105
Fax: 616-956-0998 888-715-4321
naturesselect@aol.com www.natureselect.com
Dry roasted soynuts
President/Owner: Peter Assaly
naturesselect@aol.com
Estimated Sales: $500,000
Number Employees: 1-4
Number of Brands: 1
Number of Products: 9
Square Footage: 60000
Brands:
   Nature's Select

8894 Nature's Sunshine Products Company
2901 W. Blue Grass Blvd.
Lehi, UT 84043
800-223-8225
www.naturessunshine.com
Health products including vitamins, minerals and herbs.
CEO: Terrence Moorehead
Executive VP/CFO: Joseph Baty
Executive VP/General Counsel: Nathan Brower
Vice President, Human Resources: Tracee Comstock
Executive VP/COO: Sue Armstrong
Year Founded: 1972
Estimated Sales: $367.81 Million
Number Employees: 1,003
Square Footage: 63000
Type of Packaging: Consumer
Brands:
   Nature's Sunshine

8895 Nature's Touch
5105M Fisher St
Saint-Laurent, QC H4T 1J8
Canada
www.naturestouchfrozenfoods.com
Frozen fruit
Founder: John Tentomas
Year Founded: 2004
Number of Products: 9
Type of Packaging: Consumer, Private Label
Other Locations:
   Freezing and Packing Facility
   Abbotsford BC
   Packing Facility
   Front Royal VA
Brands:
   Nature's Touch

8896 (HQ)Nature's Way
825 Challenger Dr
Green Bay, WI 54311
Fax: 800-688-3303 800-962-8873
www.naturesway.com
Herbs, vitamins and minerals, oils and probiotics
CFO: Rich Jones
CEO: Randy Rose
Contact: Dustin Borneman
dustin.borneman@naturesway.com
Operations Manager: Brian Hufford
Production Manager: Greg Bone
Purchasing Manager: Dave Anderson
Estimated Sales: $100-500 Million
Number Employees: 100-249
Number of Brands: 8
Parent Co: Schwabe North America
Type of Packaging: Private Label
Brands:
   Alive!
   Boericke & Tafel
   Coconut Oil
   CranRx
   fortify
   Ginkgold
   Joint Movement
   MCT Oil
   NutraVege
   Primadophilus
   Remifemin
   sambucus
   Umcka ColdCare

8897 Naturel
9339 Foothill Blvd # A
Rancho Cucamonga, CA 91730-3548
909-987-0520
Fax: 909-390-5453 877-242-8344
Organic agave syrup prepared for 100% agave juice; natural fructose sweetener/flavor enhancer
Owner: Jong Kee Kim
National Sales Manager: Oscar Guerrero Whaley
Estimated Sales: Less than $500,000
Number Employees: 1-4
Parent Co: Industrializadora Integral Del Agave, SA DeCV

8898 Natures Sungrown Foods Inc
700 Irwin St # 103
Suite 103
San Rafael, CA 94901-3300
415-491-4944
Fax: 415-532-2233 hal@naturessungrown.com
www.naturessungrown.com

Manufacturer and exporter of natural beef and pork, organic foods (dried fruit, coffee, juice, sauce, tortilla chips, guacamole, jalapeno peppers and Mexican foods
President: Hal Shenson
hal@naturessungrown.com
Estimated Sales: $5-10 Million
Number Employees: 1-4
Number of Brands: 2
Type of Packaging: Consumer, Food Service, Private Label, Bulk
Brands:
  Nature's Sungrown Beef
  Vera Cruz Mexican Foods
  Tree of Life
  Sun Ridge Farms
  Spice Hunter
  Swiss Valley
  Joseph Farms
  Bar S
  Eberley
  Francesco Rinaldi
  La Victoria

8899 Naturex Inc
375 Huyler St
South Hackensack, NJ 07606
201-440-5000
www.naturex.com
Natural antioxidants, colors, herbs and spices oleoresins and essential oils, and botanical extracts for the food, flavor and nutraceutical industries.
Chief Procurement Officer: Serge Sabrier
Year Founded: 1992
Estimated Sales: $404.9 Million
Number Employees: 1,700
Square Footage: 14991
Parent Co: Naturex, France Avignon Headquarters
Type of Packaging: Bulk
Other Locations:
  Naturex, Inc. USA Chicago
  Chicago IL
  Naturex USA Atlanta Sales Office
  Marietta GA
  Naturex USA Californaia Sales Offic
  Costa Mesa CA
Brands:
  Stabil
  Arom
  Color
  Healthy
  Textur
  F&V
  Taste
  Colorenhance
  Osr
  Stabilenhance
  Wsr

8900 Naughty Noah's
201E-3211 Holiday Court
La Jolla, CA 92037
info@naughtynoahs.com
www.naughtynoahs.com
Instant Vietnamese pho noodles
CEO: JimmyTay Trinh
Number of Brands: 1
Number of Products: 3
Brands:
  NAUGHTY NOAH'S

8901 Naumes, Inc.
PO Box 996
Medford, OR 97501
541-772-6268
Grower of apples, plums, pears, pomegranates, persimmons, and Asian pears.
President and CEO: Michael Naumes
CFO: Annie Eadie
VP, Fresh Division Manager: Laura Naumes
Estimated Sales: $23.4 Million
Number Employees: 700
Square Footage: 8000
Type of Packaging: Consumer

8902 Navarro Pecan Co
2131 E State Highway 31
Corsicana, TX 75109
903-872-5641
Fax: 903-874-7143 800-333-9507
sales@navarropecan.com www.navarropecan.com
Processor and exporter of kosher certified shelled raw and roasted pecans used as ingredients.
Chief Information Officer: Linda Garza
lgarza@navarropecan.com
Year Founded: 1977
Estimated Sales: $20-50 Million
Number Employees: 250-499
Square Footage: 200000
Type of Packaging: Consumer, Bulk
Brands:
  Navarro

8903 Navarro Vineyards
5601 Highway 128
Philo, CA 95466-9513
707-895-3516
Fax: 707-895-3647 707-895-3686
office@navarrowine.com www.navarrowine.com
Wines
Owner: Deborah Cahn
Estimated Sales: $7 Million
Number Employees: 50-99
Type of Packaging: Private Label, Bulk

8904 Navas Instruments
105 Wind Tree Ln
Conway, SC 29526
843-347-1379
Fax: 843-347-2527 info@navas-instruments.com
www.navas-instruments.com
Laboratory instruments for testing ash and moisture in food, pet and animal feed, fertilizers, soils and wastewater
Contact: Pam Bailey
pbailey@navas-instruments.com

8905 Navitas Naturals
15 Pamaron Way
Novato, CA 94949
415-883-8116
Fax: 888-645-4282 888-645-4282
www.navitasorganics.com
Superfood shots, hot drink mixes, superfood ingredients, snack bars, seeds, nuts, and berries
Founder/CEO: Zach Adelman
z.adelman@navitasnaturals.com
Year Founded: 2003

8906 Naya
2030-340 Pie IX
Montreal, QC H1V 2C8
Canada
450-562-7911
Fax: 450-562-3654 info@naya.com
www.naya.com
Processor and exporter of bottled spring water
President: Anita Jarjour
Executive VP/COO: Stu Levitan
Director Sales Marketing: Raynald Brisson
VP Operations: Sylvain Mayrand
Number Employees: 100-249
Square Footage: 240000
Type of Packaging: Consumer, Food Service, Private Label
Brands:
  Naya

8907 Naylor Association Solutions
5950 NW 1st Pl
Gainesville, FL 32607-6060
352-332-1252
Fax: 352-331-3525 www.naylor.com
Publications
Manager: Jason Dolder
jdolder@naylor.com
Number Employees: 250-499

8908 Naylor Candies Inc
289 Chestnut St
Mt Wolf, PA 17347-9702
717-266-2706
Fax: 717-266-2706 www.naylorcandies.com
Processor and exporter of confectionery products including butter toffee peanuts, butter mints, cashew crunch, peanut crunch and honey roasted peanuts; importer of cashews and peanuts
Owner: Dennis Naylor
dennis@cannonfamily.4t.com
Estimated Sales: $750,000
Number Employees: 10-19
Square Footage: 32000
Type of Packaging: Consumer, Private Label, Bulk

8909 Naylor Wine Cellars Inc
4069 Vineyard Rd
Stewartstown, PA 17363-8478
717-993-2431
Fax: 717-993-9460 800-292-3370
info@naylorwine.com www.naylorwine.com
Wines
President: Richard Naylor
Winemaker: Ted Potted
Contact: Dick Naylor
dick@naylorwine.com
Estimated Sales: $2.5-5 Million
Number Employees: 10-19
Type of Packaging: Private Label, Bulk
Brands:
  Golden Grenadine
  Naylor

8910 Ne-Mo's Bakery Inc
416 N Hale Ave
Escondido, CA 92029-1496
760-741-5725
Fax: 760-741-0659 800-325-2692
customerservice@horizonfoodgroup.com
www.nemosbakery.com
Processor and exporter of baked goods including hand-wrapped cake squares, cake slices, cinnamon rolls, cookies, muffins, mini loaf cakes, danish, cake breads, coffee cakes, and specialty cakes
Cio/Cto: Darren Watson
dwatson@nemosbakery.com
Senior VP: Sam Delucca Jr
Estimated Sales: $10-20 Million
Number Employees: 100-249
Square Footage: 120000
Type of Packaging: Consumer, Food Service, Private Label, Bulk
Brands:
  Ne-Mo's

8911 Neal's Chocolates
2520 Lynwood Drive
Salt Lake City, UT 84109-1607
801-521-6500
Fax: 801-521-6555
Boxed chocolates
President: Neal Maxfield
Estimated Sales: Less than $500,000
Number Employees: 1-4

8912 Nealanders Food Ingredients
6980 Creditview Rd
Mississauga, ON L5N 8E2
Canada
905-812-7300
Fax: 905-812-7308 800-263-1939
www.nealanders.com
Oilseed manufacturer
President: Robert Leonard
CEO: Olav C. Caldenborgh
CFO: Jill Wuthmann
Parent Co: Nealanders International

8913 Near East Food Products
797 Lancaster Street
Leominster, MA 01453-4551
978-534-3338
800-822-7423
Thrirty different flavors and varieties of pilafs, couscous and grain dishes including tabouleh
General Manager: Philip Wiggin
Estimated Sales: $500,000
Number Employees: 50-99

8914 Neat Foods
244 North Queen St.
Lancaster, PA 17603
866-637-6328
www.eatneat.com
Manufacturer of plant-based meat alternatives.
Co-Founder and CEO: Phil Lapp
phillapp@eatneat.com
Brands:
  neat

8915 Nebraska Bean
85824 519th Ave
Clearwater, NE 68726-5239
402-887-5335
Fax: 402-887-4709 800-253-6502
brett@nebraskabean.com www.nebraskabean.com

Food Manufacturers / A-Z

Experienced grower, processor and packager of quality popcorn. The fully integrated operation offers microwave, bulk, private label and poly bags of popcorn
President: Brett Morrison
brett@nebraskabean.com
VP: Brett Morrison
Sales: Michelle Steskal
Estimated Sales: $10-20 Million
Number Employees: 20-49
Number of Brands: 1
Square Footage: 10000
Type of Packaging: Consumer, Food Service, Private Label, Bulk
Brands:
    Morrison Farms

8916 Nebraska Beef Council
1319 Central Ave
PO Box 2108
Kearney, NE 68847-6869
308-236-7551
Fax: 308-234-8701 800-421-5326
info@nebeef.org www.nebeef.org
Beef
CEO: Sallie Atkins
satkins@nebeef.org
CEO: Forrest Roberts
Director of Marketing: Adam Wegner
Director of Industry Relations: Doug Straight
Estimated Sales: $3.58 Million
Number Employees: 5-9

8917 Necco
135 American Legion Highway
Revere, MA 2151
800-225-5508
Confections, candy
Contact: Lena Florentino
lena@seeleycapital.com

8918 Nectar Island
56 5th Ave
St Paul, MN 55128
651-292-9963
Fax: 651-905-1958
Fruit drinks flavors which include: pommegranate; pommegranate blueberry; pommegranate raspberry; mango peach; tropical berries; and guava orange.
Owner: Scott Johnson

8919 Nedlog Company
92 Messner Dr
Wheeling, IL 60090
847-541-0924
Fax: 847-541-1046 800-323-6201
Manufactures and markets over 60 formulas of standard traditional and more exotic juice-based concentrates such as strawberry-apple. Also have an equipment program based on purchase of juice concentrates
CEO: Grant Golden
President/COO: Glenn Golden
CFO: Marilyn Dougal
Research & Development: Gennady Koyfman
Public Relations: Karyl Golden
Estimated Sales: $3-5 Million
Number Employees: 7
Type of Packaging: Food Service, Private Label
Brands:
    Berry Good
    Classic Blends
    Fiesta
    Hiline
    Nedlog 100
    Tropical Blends

8920 Neenah Springs
512 Fandrich Street
Oxford, WI 53952
608-586-5696
Fax: 608-586-4509
Bottler of artesian water
President: Thomas Rogers
VP: John McFarland
Marketing Director: Dan Revoy
Public Relations: Kathy Payter
Operations Manager: Chris Coates
Plant Manager: Barbara Ravenscroft
Purchasing Manager: Wendy Jankowski
Estimated Sales: $4.8 Million
Number Employees: 52
Square Footage: 80000
Type of Packaging: Consumer, Food Service, Private Label
Brands:
    Glacier Ice
    Great Glacier
    Mountain Mist
    Neenah Springs

8921 Neese Country Sausage Inc
1452 Alamance Church Rd
Greensboro, NC 27406-9430
336-275-9548
Fax: 336-275-0750 800-632-1010
info@neesesausage.com www.neesesausage.com
Processor and packager of country sausage, liver pudding, c-loaf, souse meat and scraple
President: Thomas Neese Jr
Plant Manager: Michael Garrett
Estimated Sales: $5-10 Million
Number Employees: 20-49
Type of Packaging: Consumer, Food Service

8922 Nehalem Bay Winery
34965 Highway 53
Nehalem, OR 97131-9329
503-368-9463
Fax: 503-368-5300 888-368-9463
nbwines@hotmail.com
www.nehalembaywinery.com
Wines including Niagara grape, rhubarb, apple, wildflower honey, Chardonnay, white table, Pinot Noir and Pinot Noir Blanc
Owner: Ray Schackelford
Estimated Sales: $3-5 Million
Number Employees: 5-9
Type of Packaging: Consumer

8923 Neighbors Coffee
3105 E Reno Ave
Oklahoma City, OK 73117
405-552-2100
Fax: 405-232-3729 800-299-9016
sales@neighborscoffee.com
www.neighborscoffee.com
Coffee; wholesaler/distributor of tea, cocoa and cappuccino
President: Steve Neighbors
Sales Manager: Phil Huggard
Contact: Todd Henson
thenson@executivecoffee.com
Estimated Sales: $100,000
Number Employees: 50-99
Type of Packaging: Consumer, Food Service, Private Label, Bulk
Brands:
    Neighbors

8924 Neil Jones Food Company
1701 W 16th Street
Vancouver, WA 98660-1067
360-696-4356
Fax: 360-696-0050 800-291-3862
sales@nwpacking.com
www.neiljonesfoodcompany.com
Manufacturer of canned fruits and vegetables
President/Owner: Matt Jones
CEO: L. Neil Jones
Estimated Sales: $500,000-$1 Million
Number Employees: 250-499
Type of Packaging: Consumer, Food Service, Private Label

8925 Neilly's Foods
1569 W King St
York, PA 17404-5656
717-668-3722
Fax: 717-885-5141 www.neillys.com
Frozen meals, appetizers, sauces, rice mixes and beans.
VP, Sales and Marketing: Julie Ndjee

8926 Nekta
PO BOX 1355
Auckland, 1140
New Zealand
649-250-2789
Fax: 649-573-7988 www.nekta.com
All-natural fruit carbohydrate derived from kiwifruit
Director: Adriana Tong
Director: Jonathan Wood

8927 Nell Baking Company
114 County Road 254
Kenedy, TX 78119-4267
830-583-3251
Fax: 830-583-9593 800-215-9190
nellbaking@yahoo.com
Biscotti in ten flavors, gourmet cookies and wafers
President: Lasca Arnold
Estimated Sales: $500,000
Number Employees: 10
Brands:
    Biscotti Di Lasca
    Cookies By Lasca

8928 Nello's Sauce
PO Box 80441
Raleigh, NC 27623
919-428-4338
Manufacturer of pasta sauce.
Founder: Neal McTighe
Contact: Neal Mctighe
nealmctighe@nellossauce.com

8929 Nellson Candies Inc
5800 Ayala Ave
Irwindale, CA 91706-6215
626-334-4508
www.nellsonllc.com
Manufacturer and exporter of custom formulated snack, diet/weight loss, sport nutrition and medical food nutrition bars
Processor: Hoa Nguyen
Estimated Sales: Less Than $500,000
Number Employees: 1-4
Square Footage: 89864
Type of Packaging: Consumer, Food Service, Private Label, Bulk

8930 (HQ)Nellson Nutraceutical LLC
5115 E LA Palma Ave
Anaheim, CA 92807-2018
714-765-7000
Fax: 714-765-7055 844-635-5766
www.nellsonllc.com
Powdered drinks including diet, muscle building and fiber
Principal: Richard Marconi
CEO: Jamie Better
Estimated Sales: G
Number Employees: 500-999

8931 Nelly's Organics
9811 Owensmouth Ave
Chatsworth, CA 91311
310-756-0738
info@nellysorganics.com
nellysorganics.com
Refrigerated organic candy bars
Founder: Carla Spiropulo
Number of Brands: 1
Number of Products: 7
Brands:
    NELLY'S ORGANICS

8932 Nelson Crab Inc
3088 Kindred Ave
Tokeland, WA 98590
360-267-2911
Fax: 360-267-2921 800-262-0069
Processor, importer and exporter of canned, fresh, smoked and frozen seafood including salmon steaks, shad, crabs, crab meat and shrimp
President: Kristi Nelson
kristi@nelsoncrab.com
Plant Manager: Les Candler
Estimated Sales: $10-20 Million
Number Employees: 50-99
Type of Packaging: Food Service, Private Label
Brands:
    Nelson Seatreats

8933 Nelson Ice Cream
920 Olive St W
Stillwater, MN 55082-5634
651-430-1103
www.nelsonsicecream.biz
Ice cream
Owner: Dave Najarian
dnajarian@nelsonsicecream.biz
Estimated Sales: $300,000-500,000
Number Employees: 20-49
Type of Packaging: Private Label

Food Manufacturers / A-Z

Brands:
 Nelson's
 Nelson's Dutch Farms

8934 Nema Food Distribution
18 Commerce Rd.
Suite D
Fairfield, NJ 07004
973-256-4415
Fax: 973-256-4442 www.nemahalal.com
Halal deli meat, beef, poultry, gyro, cheese, bread, heat & serve
President: Beyhan Nakiboglu
Year Founded: 2002

8935 Neo North America Inc.
San Francisco, CA
800-604-7051
www.neosuperwater.com
Manufacturer of water.
CEO and Founder: Ben Behrouzi
Brands:
 NEO WATER

8936 Nepco Egg Of Ga
469 Ronthor Dr SE
Social Circle, GA 30025
770-464-2652
Fax: 770-464-2998 www.goodegg.com
Processor and exporter of egg products including standard yolk, whole, whites and albumen
Manager: Brad Ginnane
Plant Manager: Terry Anglin
Estimated Sales: $1-3 Million
Number Employees: 1-4
Square Footage: 240000
Parent Co: Rose Acre Farms
Type of Packaging: Bulk

8937 Neptune Fisheries
802 Jefferson Ave
Newport News, VA 23607
757-245-3231
Fax: 757-893-9227 800-545-7474
Processor and importer of frozen, cooked, peeled and deveined shrimp and scallops; also, lobster tails
President: Robin West
CFO: Richard Costa
National Sales Manager: Aaron Cabral
Sales Director: Sam Weinstein
Plant Manager: Reuben Benkovitz
Number Employees: 5-9
Square Footage: 240000
Type of Packaging: Consumer, Food Service, Private Label, Bulk
Brands:
 Neptune

8938 Neptune Foods
4510 S Alameda St
Vernon, CA 90058-2011
323-232-8300
Fax: 323-232-8833 info@neptunefoods.com
www.neptunefoods.com
Frozen cod, perch, pollack, fish sticks, clams, lobster, oysters, scallops and shrimp
President: Howard Choi
info@neptunefoods.com
Marketing Manager: Kelly Osterhout
Controller/VP Human Resources: Martin Tsai
COO/Plant Manager: Barbara Letourneau
Estimated Sales: $29.8 Million
Number Employees: 250-499
Square Footage: 150000
Type of Packaging: Consumer, Food Service, Private Label, Bulk
Brands:
 Captain Neptune
 Mermaid Princess
 Neptune

8939 Nesbitt Processing
611 NE 7th Ave
Aledo, IL 61231-1061
309-582-5183
Processor and wholesaler/distributor of beef, pork, lamb, goat and deer; slaughtering services available
President/General Manager: Omar Deeds, Jr.
Secretary/Treasurer: Edith Nesbitt
Number Employees: 3
Type of Packaging: Consumer

8940 Neshaminy Valley Natural Foods
5 Louise Dr
Warminster, PA 18974-1542
215-443-5545
Fax: 215-443-7087 info@nvorganic.com
Gourmet foods
President: Philip S Margolis
info@nvorganic.com
COO/VP: Gene Margolis
VP: Gene Margolis
Estimated Sales: $4.5 Million
Number Employees: 20-49
Brands:
 Neshaminy Valley Natural

8941 Nest Eggs
411 W Fullerton Pkwy #1402W
Chicago, IL 60614-2849
773-525-4952
Fax: 773-525-5226 www.fact.com
Gourmet foods
Executive Director: Richard Wood
VP: Robert Brown
Sales Manager: Steve Roach
Estimated Sales: Below $5 Million
Number Employees: 5-9

8942 NestFresh
4340 Glencoe St
Denver, CO 80216
877-241-8385
nestfresh.com
Cage-free eggs
VP, Marketing: Nick Jioras
Year Founded: 1991
Brands:
 NESTFRESH

8943 Nestelle's, Inc.
3540 Brooks Ave NE
Salem, OR 97301
503-393-7056
Fax: 503-393-7091
Flavoring extracts and food colors
President: Kathi Jenks
Estimated Sales: $620,000
Number Employees: 5
Square Footage: 52000

8944 Nestle USA
150 Oak Grove Dr
Mt Sterling, KY 40353-9087
859-499-1100
Fax: 859-498-4363 www.nestleusa.com
Prepared frozen foods including stuffed sandwiches and croissants, pizza snacks and waffles
CEO: Paul Merage
CFO: Glenn Lee
VP: Larry Johnson
Research & Development: Phil Mason
V P Finance: Glenn Lee
Manufacturing Development Manager: John Spinner
Purchasing Director: George Turner
Purchasing Manager: Russ Shroyer
Plant Manager: Mike Crawford
Purchasing Manager: George Turner
Number Employees: 500-999
Type of Packaging: Consumer, Food Service

8945 Nestle USA Inc
800 N Brand Blvd
Glendale, CA 91203-3213
818-549-6210
Fax: 818-549-6952 800-225-2270
www.nestleusa.com
Baby foods, bottled water, cereals, chocolate & confectionery, coffee, culinary, chilled & frozen foods, dairy, drinks, foodservice, healthcare nutrition, ice cream, petcare, sports nutrition, and weight management
CEO: Paul Grimwood
paul.grimwood@us.nestle.com
CEO: Paul Bulcke
EVP & CFO: Wan Ling Martello
EVP, CTO, Head of Research & Development: Werner Bauer
EVP Marketing, Sales & Nespresso: Patrice Bula
Deputy EVP Human Resources & Admin.: Jean-Marc Duvoisin
EVP Operations, GLOBE: Jose Lopez
Estimated Sales: Over $1 Billion
Number Employees: 10000+
Square Footage: 1500000
Parent Co: Nestle S.A.
Type of Packaging: Consumer
Brands:
 Cerelac
 Gerber
 Graduates Toddler Foods
 Naturnes
 Nestum
 Nestle Pure Life Water
 Perrier
 Poland Spring
 S. Pellegrino
 Chocapic
 Cini Minis
 Cookie Crisp
 Estrelitas
 Fitness
 Nesquik
 Aero
 Butterfinger
 Cailler
 Crunch Bar
 Kitkat
 Orion
 Smarties
 Nestle Toll House
 Wonka
 Nescafe
 Nespresso
 Buitoni
 Digiorno
 Herta
 Hot Pockets
 Lean Cuisine
 Maggi
 Stouffer's
 Thomy
 Tombstone
 Carnation
 Coffee-Mate
 La Laitiere
 Nido
 Juicy Juice
 Nestea
 Milo
 Chef
 Chef-Mate
 Minor's
 Sjora
 Stouffer's
 Boost
 Nutren Junior
 Peptamen Af
 Resource
 Dreyer's
 Extreme
 Haagen-Dazs
 Movenpick
 Alpo
 Bakers
 Purina
 Beneful
 Cat Chow
 Chef Michael's
 Jenny Craig
 Powerbar
 Maggi Bouillion Cubes

8946 Neto's Market & Grill
1313 Franklin Street
Santa Clara, CA 95050
408-296-0818
Fax: 408-217-2603 888-482-6386
netosausage@msn.com netosmarketandgrill.com
Portuguese, Italian, Mexican, Spanish and chicken sausages
Owner: Deborah Costa
Estimated Sales: $2.5-5 Million
Number Employees: 10-19
Number of Brands: 3
Number of Products: 32
Square Footage: 64000
Type of Packaging: Consumer, Food Service, Private Label, Bulk
Brands:
 La Granada
 Neto
 Zorro

8947 Network Food Brokers
355 Lancaster Avenue
Haverford, PA 19041-1547
610-649-7210
Fax: 610-649-0747
Cheese

965

Food Manufacturers / A-Z

President: Nate Ostroff
Estimated Sales: $2.5-5 Million
Number Employees: 10

8948 NeuRoast
45 Wall St Ct
New York, NY 10005
info@neuroast.com
www.neuroast.com
Mushroom-enhanced coffee and coffee creamers
Founder: Alex Curtis

8949 Neuchatel Chocolatier
461 Limestone Rd
Oxford, PA 19363-1235
610-932-2706
Fax: 610-932-9036 800-597-0759
web_sales@neuchatelchocolates.com
www.neuchatelchocolates.com
Chocolate confections
Owner: Al Lauber
info@neuchatelchocolates.com
Estimated Sales: $1-3 Million
Number Employees: 20-49

8950 Neuman Bakery Specialties
1405 W Jeffrey Dr
Addison, IL 60101-4331
630-916-8909
Fax: 630-916-8919 800-253-5298
Wholesale bakery
President: George Neuman
gneuman@neumansbakery.com
CFO: Dan Neuman
R&D: James Neuman
Plant Manager: Bob Barrera
Estimated Sales: Below $5 Million
Number Employees: 10-19
Square Footage: 100000
Brands:
 Neuman

8951 Nevada Baking Company
299 West Charleston Blvd
Las Vegas, NV 89127-3911
702-384-8950
Bread and rolls
President: Jim Miller
COO: Robert Mayfield
Sales Manager: Scott Pollock
Estimated Sales: $10-25 Million
Number Employees: 50-99
Brands:
 Gail's
 Roman Meal
 Wholesome

8952 Nevada City Brewing
75 Bost Avenue
Nevada City, CA 95959-3024
530-265-2446
Fax: 530-265-2576 www.beerme.com
Beer
Co-Owner: Andy Sawdon
Co-Owner: Hans Schillinger
Director Manufacturing: Keith Downing
Estimated Sales: Under $500,000
Number Employees: 1-4
Brands:
 Broad St. Brown
 Fools Gold Ale

8953 Nevada City Winery
321 Spring St
Nevada City, CA 95959-2420
530-265-9463
Fax: 530-265-6860 800-203-9463
www.ncwinery.com
Wine
President: Dave Iorns
nccg@internet49.com
Director of Marketing: Rod Byers
Winemaker: Mark Foster
Estimated Sales: $2.5-5 Million
Number Employees: 10-19
Brands:
 Nevada City Winery

8954 Nevada County Wine Guild
11372 Winter Moon Way
Nevada City, CA 95959
530-265-3662
855-494-7025
reachus@ourdailyred.com

Wine
Owner: Tony Norskog
Contact: Donn Berdahl
donn@ourdailyred.com
Estimated Sales: Less than $500,000
Number Employees: 1-4
Brands:
 Our Daily Red

8955 New Age Beverages
1700 East 68th Ave
Denver, CO 80229
303-289-8655
newagebev.com
Natural, functional beverages, including RTD tea, energy drinks and premium bottled water
CEO: Brent Willis
Year Founded: 2003
Number of Brands: 5
Brands:
 COCO LIBRE
 XING
 BUCHA
 MARLEY BEVERAGE CO.
 ASPEN PURE

8956 New Bakery Company of Ohio
3005 E Pointe Dr
Zanesville, OH 43701
740-454-6876
Fax: 740-588-5860 800-848-9845
www.newbakerycompany.com
Hamburger buns
Manager: Sam McLaughlin
Contact: Tara Blackstone
tblackstone@newbakerycompany.com
Plant Manager: Doug Wendeler
Number Employees: 250-499
Square Footage: 100000
Parent Co: Wendy's International
Type of Packaging: Food Service
Brands:
 Sta Fresh
 Wendy

8957 New Barn
888-635-7102
hello@thenewbarn.com www.thenewbarn.com
Almond milk beverages and frozen dessert
CEO: Ted Robb
Chief Commercial Officer: Billie Thein
Number of Brands: 3
Brands:
 ALMONDMILK
 ALMONDCRÔME
 BARISTA ALMONDMILK

8958 New Barn Organics
1400 Valley House Dr
Suite 210
Rohnert Park, CA 94928
707-665-6307
888-635-7102
admin@newbarnorganics.com
www.newbarnorganics.com
Organic almond milk, non-dairy creamer, almond creme, almond dip, non-dairy buttery spread, single-serve coffee
Co-Founder: Dan Conrad
Co-Founder/CEO: Ted Robb
COO/CFO: Louis Kanganis
VP Innovation & Marketing: Darleen Scherer
VP Sales: Richard Tidrow
Year Founded: 2015
Number Employees: 20-49

8959 New Belgium Brewing Co
500 Linden St
Fort Collins, CO 80524
970-221-0524
888-622-4044
www.newbelgium.com
Beer
Co-Founder: Kim Jordan
Co-Founder: Jeff Lebesch
CEO: Steve Fechheimer
Year Founded: 1991
Estimated Sales: $58 Million
Number Employees: 500-999
Number of Brands: 8
Square Footage: 180000
Brands:
 CITRADELIC
 FAT TIRE
 HOF TEN DORMAAL
 GLUTINY
 SLOW RIDE IPA
 LIPS OF FAITH
 SNAPSHOT WHEAT
 RANGER IPA

8960 New Braunfels Smokehouse
1090 N. IH 35
New Braunfels, TX 78130
830-625-2416
Fax: 830-626-3785 800-537-6932
Emilio@nbsmokehouse.com
www.nbsmokehouse.com
Smoked meats including beef, pork, turkey, ham, chicken and venison; also, jerky
President: Susan Dunbar Snyder
CEO: Dudley Snyder
Vice President: Mike Dietert
Manager: Emilio Rodriquez
Estimated Sales: $5-10 Million
Number Employees: 120
Type of Packaging: Consumer, Food Service, Private Label, Bulk
Brands:
 Dunbar Ranch

8961 New Business Corp
444 Rutledge St
Gary, IN 46404-1011
219-885-1476
www.gourmetsupreme.com
Ketchup, barbecue, seafood and Worcestershire sauces
President: Ralph Shanabarger
ralph.shanabarger@student.ctuonline.edu
Secretary: Naomi Woods
Estimated Sales: Under $500,000
Number Employees: 5-9
Square Footage: 7200
Brands:
 Gourmet Slim #7
 Gourmet Slim Cuisine
 Gourmet Supreme

8962 New Canaan Farms
5916 W Highway 290
Dripping Springs, TX 78620
512-858-7669
Fax: 512-858-7513 800-727-5267
info@shopncf.com www.newcanaanfarms.com
Gourmet products including jams, salsa, dips and jellies: lemon fig, plum, peach, raspberry, strawberry, blackberry, etc.; also, mustards including jalapeno, honey and German and sauces including jalapeno shrimp, peach picantehabanero
President: Cindy Figer
cindy@shopncf.com
Production Manager: Patti Thurman
Estimated Sales: $1.2 Million
Number Employees: 10-19
Type of Packaging: Private Label

8963 New Century Snacks
5560 East Slauson Ave
City of Commerce, CA 90040
323-278-9578
Fax: 323-837-4699 800-688-6887
orders@NewCenturySnacks.com
www.energyclub.com
Hispanic snacks, candy, nuts, stoys, trail mix extra large packages, salty snacks, beef jerky, accessories and supplies
Owner: Miron Aviv
CEO: Tim Snee
CFO: Steve Deerwester
VP: Vincent Guiliano
Purchasing: Craig Hayman
Estimated Sales: $5-10 Million
Number Employees: 80
Number of Products: 300
Square Footage: 200000
Type of Packaging: Consumer, Private Label

8964 New Chapter
90 Technology Dr
Brattleboro, VT 05301-9180
802-257-0018
Fax: 802-257-0652 800-543-7279
info@newchapter.com www.newchapter.com
Whole food vitamins, organic herbal supplements, fish oil

Owner: Paul Schulick
CEO: Larry Allgaier
CFO: Ruth Austin
Executive Vice President: Herb Lewis
Quality Control Manager: Judy Mins
VP Marketing: Bob Lierle
National Sales Manager: Disa Pratt
info@new-chapter.com
Purchasing: Russ Thompson
Year Founded: 1982
Estimated Sales: $33.5 Million
Number Employees: 50-99
Square Footage: 93406

8965 (HQ)New City Packing Company
2600 Church Rd
Aurora, IL 60502-8732
630-851-8800
Fax: 630-898-3030
Purveyor of fine meats
President: Marvin Fagel
Vice President: Dave Aardema
National Sales: David McClendon
Estimated Sales: $6.6 Million
Number Employees: 30
Square Footage: 240000
Type of Packaging: Consumer

8966 New Direction Foods
16321 Gothard St
Suite C
Huntington Beach, CA 92647
562-606-8511
888-393-5590
curious@thecuriouscreamery.com
www.thecuriouscreamery.com
Ice cream mixes
Founder & CEO: Jareer Abu-Ali
VP, Business Development: Ron Tan

Brands:
 The Curious Creamery

8967 New Earth
565 Century Ct
Klamath Falls, OR 97601-7100
541-882-5406
Fax: 541-885-5458 www.newearth.com
Processor and exporter of blue green algae products
President: Jerry Anderson
COO: Justin Straus
VP Sales: Roger Martin
VP Marketing/Strategy: Victor Bond
Number Employees: 50-99
Square Footage: 1000000
Brands:
 Alpha Gold
 Elz Super Enzymes
 Omega Gold
 Omega Suro
 Planet Food
 Spectrabiotic
 Super Blue Green Enzymes
 Super Q10

8968 New England Country Bakers
15 Mountain View Rd
Watertown, CT 6795
860-945-9994
Fax: 860-945-9996 800-225-3779
Pound, no-sugar cheesecake and layer cakes, pies and tea breads including apple crumb, maple, banana, blueberry crumb, cranberry, pumpkin and zucchini nut
President: David Spivak
Director Marketing: Donna Spivak
General Manager: Gary Shields
Production: Andrew Kandefer
Estimated Sales: $2 Million
Number Employees: 20-49
Number of Brands: 1
Number of Products: 50
Square Footage: 48000
Type of Packaging: Food Service

8969 New England Cranberry
82 Sanderson Ave
Lynn, MA 01902-1974
781-596-0888
Fax: 781-596-0808 800-410-2892
info@newenglandcranberry.com
www.newenglandcranberry.com
Processor and exporter of naturally sweetened dried cranberries, premium suger sweetened dried cranberries, dried wild blueberries, dried cherries, frozen whole cranberries, cranberry jams and jellies, cranberry chutney and pepperjelly, and fine chocolates with sweet cranberries
President: Ted Stux
Sales: Arthur Stock
Estimated Sales: $530000
Number Employees: 10-19
Square Footage: 7400
Type of Packaging: Consumer, Food Service, Bulk
Brands:
 Fresh Pond
 New England Cranberry

8970 New England Muffin Co Inc
337 Pleasant St
Fall River, MA 02721-3000
508-675-2833
Fax: 508-675-2833
Fresh and frozen Portuguese muffins in various flavors
President: Filomena Botelho
Owner: Jose Martin
josemartin@island-candy.com
Estimated Sales: $980,000
Number Employees: 5-9
Type of Packaging: Food Service, Bulk

8971 New England Natural Bakers
74 Fairview St E
Greenfield, MA 01301
413-772-2239
Fax: 413-772-2936 800-910-2884
nenb@nenb.com www.nenb.com
Organic granola and trail mix
President & CEO: Pam Clark
pclark@nenb.com
CFO: Didi Foley
Quality Control: Dale Parda
Quality Assurance & IT Coordinator: Dale Prada
Brand Sales & Marketing Manager: Larry Cornick
Vice President Of Sales & Marketing: Pam Clark
Director Of Operations: Scott Johnson
Number Employees: 10-19
Number of Brands: 1
Number of Products: 50
Square Footage: 60000
Type of Packaging: Consumer, Food Service, Private Label, Bulk
Brands:
 New England Naturals

8972 New England Tea & Coffee Co
100 Charles St
Malden, MA 02148-6704
781-324-8094
Fax: 781-397-7580 800-225-3537
consumerrelations@necoffeeco.com
www.newenglandcoffee.com
Product line includes a variety of coffee, whole bean and ground, flavored and regular in addition to decaffeinated blends. Also available is tea, both regular and decaffeinated, flavored and non-flavored and a selection of gift itemsand gift baskets.
President/COO: James Kaloyanides
VP/Finance/Treasurer: Jamie Dostou
Vice President: Russell Ain
russell.ain@necoffeeco.com
VP/Product & Business Development: Michael Kaloyanides
VP/Operations & Human Resources: John Kaloyanides
VP/Purchasing: Stephen Kaloyanides
russell.ain@necoffeeco.com
Number Employees: 100-249

8973 New Era Canning Company
4856 1st St
New Era, MI 49446
231-861-2151
Fax: 231-861-4068
Canned fruits and vegetables including beans, asparagus, apples, and apple sauce
President/CEO: Rick Ray
CFO: Rick McClouth
Sales: Patrick Alger
Contact: Mike Aebig
maebig@gloryfoods.com
Production: Jim Merrill
Purchasing: Ron Fekken
Estimated Sales: $33 Million
Number Employees: 250
Number of Brands: 3
Number of Products: 65
Square Footage: 200000
Type of Packaging: Consumer, Food Service, Private Label
Brands:
 Good Taste
 Necco
 New Era

8974 New Generation Foods
7438 Elmonds Street
Burnaby, BC V 3N1A8
Canada
604-515-7438
Fax: 402-733-5755 danehodge@hotmail.com
Portion-controlled and breaded foods including beef, chicken, pork and turkey
CFO: Steve McCurdy
National Sales Manager: Dane Hodges
Plant Manager: John Schull
Number Employees: 15

8975 New Glarus Bakery & TeaRoom
534 1st St
PO Box 595
New Glarus, WI 53574-8908
608-527-2916
Fax: 608-527-5799 866-805-5536
Cookies, breads, pastries, donuts and desserts.
Owner: Casey Umhoefer
casey@beachbody.com
Co-Owner: Nancy Weber
Estimated Sales: $500,000-$1 Million
Number Employees: 10-19
Brands:
 New Glarus Bakery

8976 New Glarus Brewing CompaNy
2400 State Hwy 69
New Glarus, WI 53574
608-527-5850
Fax: 608-527-5855 www.newglarusbrewing.com
Beer
President: Daniel Carey
VP: Deborah Carry
Estimated Sales: Below $5 Million
Number Employees: 20-49

8977 New Grass Bison
PO Box 860033
Shawnee, KS 66286
866-422-5888
Natural and grassfed bison products

8978 New Harbor Fisherman's Cooperative
PO Box 125
New Harbor, ME 04554-0125
207-677-2791
Fax: 207-677-3835 866-883-2922
Lobster, crab and other seafood
Manager: Linda Vannah
Operations Manager: Ken Tonneson
Estimated Sales: $1 million
Number Employees: 1-4
Type of Packaging: Consumer, Bulk

8979 New Harmony Coffee & Tea Co.
505 S Main
New Harmony, IN 47631
812-682-4563
Coffee
Owner: Mary Webber
Brands:
 New Harmony

8980 New Harvest Foods
323 3rd Ave
PO Box 96503, #12998
Washington, DC 20090-6503
920-822-2578
info@new-harvest.org
www.new-harvest.org
Canned vegetables including peas, green beans, sweet corn, carrots, potatoes, sauerkraut and mixed vegetables
President: Timothy Grygield
Executive Director: Isha Datar
Production Manager: Tom Wojcik
Plant Manager: Robert Tetzlaff
Estimated Sales: $5-10 Million
Number Employees: 20-49
Square Footage: 140000

Food Manufacturers / A-Z

8981 New Holland Brewing Co
66 E 8th St
Holland, MI 49423-3504
616-355-6422
Fax: 616-355-2940 www.newhollandbrew.com
Beer
President: Elizabeth Aker
lizby1947@yahoo.com
Co-Owner/Head Brewer: John Haggerty
CFO/Co-Owner: Dave White
Owner/Partner: Jason Spaulding
Sales/Marketing Director: Fred Bueltmann
Estimated Sales: $3.3 Million
Number Employees: 50-99
Square Footage: 19486

8982 New Hope Mills Mfg Inc
181 York St
Auburn, NY 13021-9009
315-252-2676
Fax: 315-282-0720 store@newhopemills.com
www.newhopemills.com
Mixes including pancake, bread and cookie; also, milled flour including buckwheat, wheat and pancake
President/CEO: Dale Weed
sales@newhopemills.com
Sales Exec: Dale Weed
Estimated Sales: $1.3 Million
Number Employees: 20-49
Number of Products: 20
Square Footage: 90000
Type of Packaging: Consumer, Food Service, Private Label, Bulk

8983 New Hope Natural Media
1401 Pearl Street
Suite 200
Boulder, CO 80302
303-939-8440
Fax: 303-998-9020 info@newhope.com
Supplements and ingredients
Executive Director: Len Monheit
Sr Marketing Manager: Brad Mastrine
Sales: Kim Merselis
Contact: Nicole Aulik
naulik@newhope.com
Estimated Sales: $25 Million
Number Employees: 45
Square Footage: 60000

8984 New Hope Winery
6123 Lower York Rd
New Hope, PA 18938-9620
215-693-1568
Fax: 215-794-2341 800-592-9463
info@newhopewinery.com
www.newhopewinery.com
Red wine
Owner: Sandra Pizza
sandra@newhopewinery.com
Estimated Sales: $710,000
Number Employees: 5-9
Number of Products: 25

8985 New Horizon Farms
319 Hiawatha Ave.
P.O. Box 708
Pipestone, MN 56164
507-825-5462
Fax: 507-825-5877 800-906-7447
www.newhorizonfarms.com
Pork production.
Managing Partner: Bob Taubert
Partner & Production Manager: Jerry Bauman
CFO: Erin Musch
Year Founded: 1993
Number Employees: 100-249
Type of Packaging: Bulk

8986 New Horizon Foods
33440 Western Ave
Union City, CA 94587-3202
510-489-8600
Fax: 510-489-9797
Dough conditioners, bread bases, natural mixes, beverage, cake, muffin, pudding, meat spices, spice blends, snack and chip seasonings, custard, ice cream, waffle cone and sauce mixes and bases; exporter of dough conditioners and cakeand muffin mixes
Owner: Ken Crawford
kenc@newhorizonfoodsinc.com
Senior Vice President: Yael Melzer
Number Employees: 10-19
Parent Co: Tova Industries
Type of Packaging: Consumer, Food Service, Private Label, Bulk

8987 New Horizons Baking Co
700 W Water St
Fremont, IN 46737-2165
260-495-7055
Fax: 219-495-2307 www.newhorizonsbaking.com
Buns and English muffins
President: Tilmon Brown
Vice President: Bob Creighton
Quality Assurance Manager: Marsha Black
Vice President of Sales: Mike Porter
Manager: Mark Duke
VP/Director Operations: John Widman
Plant Manager: Aaron Brown
Estimated Sales: $3-5 Million
Number Employees: 50-99
Square Footage: 160000
Type of Packaging: Food Service, Private Label, Bulk
Other Locations:
 New Horizons Baking Company
 Norwalk OH

8988 New Jamaican Gold
3536 Arden Rd
Hayward, CA 94545
510-887-4653
Fax: 510-887-7466 800-672-9956
Ready-to-drink coffee/ice cappuccino
CEO: Kenneth Yeung
becky2snoop@gmail.com
Sales Director: Kimi Tom
Estimated Sales: $1+ Million
Number Employees: 10-19
Brands:
 Jamaican Gold

8989 New Land Vineyard
577 Lerch Rd
Geneva, NY 14456-9238
315-585-4432
Fax: 315-585-9844
Wines
Owner: Dale Nagy
Estimated Sales: Less than $500,000
Number Employees: 1-4

8990 New Mexico Green Chile Company
1807 Don Lewis Drive
Artesia, NM 88210
505-503-0996
stacy@greenchileco.com
www.greenchileco.com
Chile peppers, roasted tomatillos, dehydrated guajillo, red chile peppers, poblanos, and tamales
Manager: Samantha Lewis
Manager: Stacy Lewis
stacy@greenchileco.com

8991 New Nissi Corp.
529 E 39th St
Paterson, NJ 07504
973-278-4400
info@newnissi.com
www.nuttycrunchers.com
Natural nut and seed brittles
Founder: Steve Kim
steve.kim@newnissi.com
Year Founded: 1986
Number Employees: 1-4
Brands:
 Nutty Crunchers

8992 New Ocean
3077 Mccall Dr # 12
Suite 12
Doraville, GA 30340-2832
770-458-5235
Fax: 770-485-5235
Seafood, shrimp, scallops, king crab, lobster tails, snow crab
President: Mei Lin
Estimated Sales: Less Than $500,000
Number Employees: 5-9

8993 New Organics
600 Lawnwood Road
Kenwood, CA 95452
734-677-5570
Fax: 707-833-0105
Organic ingredient supplier-grains, sweetners, oils, soy powders
President: Jethren Phillips
Manager: Mathew Keegan
Estimated Sales: $17.5 Million
Number Employees: 74
Number of Brands: 3
Number of Products: 100
Square Footage: 25000
Type of Packaging: Bulk
Other Locations:
 American Health & Nutrition
 Eaton Rapids MI
Brands:
 Organic Garden
 Organic Harvest
 Soy-N-Ergy Soy Powders

8994 New Orleans Fish House II LLC
921 S Dupre St
New Orleans, LA 70125-1343
504-821-9700
Fax: 504-821-9011 800-839-3474
info@nofh.com www.neworleansfishhouse.com
Fresh and frozen catfish, tilapia, crawfish, softshell crabs, tuna, shark, red snapper, pompano, wahoo, drum, escalor and sheephead
Owner: Craig Borges
craig_b@nofishhouse.com
Owner/President: Bill Borges
VP Sales: Cliff Hall
Estimated Sales: $20-50 Million
Number Employees: 50-99
Type of Packaging: Consumer, Food Service, Private Label, Bulk

8995 New Orleans Food Co-op
2372 St. Claude Avenue
Suite 110
New Orleans, LA 70117
504-264-5579
Fax: 504-734-7684 800-628-4900
cook@bumblebee.com www.nolafood.coop
Canned shrimp, crab meat, oysters, clams, sardines, tuna and mackerel; also, bottled clam juice; exporter of canned shrimp; importer of canned seafood
VP Sales/Marketing: David Cook
Estimated Sales: $5-10 Million
Number Employees: 5-9
Type of Packaging: Consumer, Food Service, Private Label
Brands:
 Cutcher
 Dejean
 Gulf Belle
 Harris
 Marvelous
 Orleans

8996 New Orleans Gulf Seafood
509 Commerce Pt
New Orleans, LA 70123-3203
504-733-1516
Fax: 504-733-1517
Seafood
President: Albert Lin

8997 New Packing Company
1249 W Lake St
Chicago, IL 60607-1519
312-666-1314
Fax: 312-666-8698
Sausage
President: Kurt Kreuger
Estimated Sales: $1.8 Million
Number Employees: 19
Type of Packaging: Consumer

8998 New Salem Tea-Bread Company
837 Daniel Shays Hwy
New Salem, MA 01355
978-544-0294
Fax: 978-544-5643 800-897-5910
info@teabread.com
All natural, kosher tea breads. Flavors: lemon, banana orange cranberry, blueberry vanilla, pumpkin, carrot raisin, almond, apple cinnamon

Food Manufacturers / A-Z

Co-Owner: Steve Verney
Co-Owner: Kay Verney
Contact: Curran Tea
sales@teabreads.com

8999 New Season Foods Inc
2329 Yew St # A1
P.O. Box 157
Forest Grove, OR 97116-4401
503-357-7124
Fax: 503-357-0419 www.newseasonfoods.com
Drum-dried vegetable powders and other custom ingredients
CEO: Bruce McVean
Estimated Sales: $5-10 Million
Number Employees: 20-49
Square Footage: 600000
Type of Packaging: Bulk
Brands:
 Flavorland
 New Season Foods

9000 New Wave Cuisine
112 Schoolhouse Road
Mount Holly, NJ 8060
609-267-0276
Fax: 609-261-1949 800-486-0276
www.kaptainsketch.com
Frozen value-added poultry and seafood
President: Nash Cohen
Estimated Sales: $10-20,000,000
Number Employees: 20-49
Type of Packaging: Consumer, Food Service, Private Label
Brands:
 Herb's Five Star
 Kaptain's Ketch
 Westhampton Farms

9001 New World Pasta Co
85 Shannon Rd
Harrisburg, PA 17112-2787
717-526-2200
Fax: 717-526-2468 800-730-5957
mikehoar@nwpasta.com
Pasta
President: Bastian De Zeeuw
CEO: Peter Smith
CFO: Gregory Richardson
SVP and Sales Development: Shane Faucett
SVP Operatons: Brett Beckfield
Number Employees: 1000-4999
Square Footage: 1200000
Parent Co: New World Pasta
Type of Packaging: Bulk

9002 New York Apple Sales Inc
17 Languish Pl
Glenmont, NY 12077-4819
518-477-7200
Fax: 518-477-6770 888-477-6770
kaari@newyorkapplesales.com
www.newyorkapplesales.com
Apples and pears.
President: Kaari Stannard
kaari@newyorkapplesales.com
VP, Sales: John Cushing
Sales: Michael Harwood
Food Safety Coordinator: Colleen O'Brien
Production & Logistics Manager: Michael Shannon
Estimated Sales: $29 Million
Number Employees: 20-49
Type of Packaging: Consumer, Food Service, Bulk

9003 New York Bakeries Inc
261 W 22nd St
Hialeah, FL 33010-1521
305-883-0790
Fax: 305-883-0790
Manufacturer and exporter of bread, rolls, and cakes.
President: Sarah Zimmerman
Estimated Sales: $35 Million
Number Employees: 50-99
Parent Co: New York Bakeries
Type of Packaging: Consumer, Food Service, Private Label

9004 New York Bottling Co Inc
626 Whittier St
Bronx, NY 10474-6121
718-842-7416
Fax: 718-542-9004
Bottled and canned soft drinks, water, ice, alcohol free cocktails, drink mixes, sports drinks, spring/mineral water, powdered drink mixes, frozen juices, shelf stable juices, fresh juice, chocolate, malt and other hot beverages
Contact: Zvi Hold
info@naturale90.com
Estimated Sales: $5-10 Million
Number Employees: 1-4
Brands:
 La Pri Cranberry Apple Drink
 La Pri Grapefruit Dr
 La Pri Orange Drink

9005 New York Frozen Foods Inc
25900 Fargo Ave
Bedford, OH 44146-1369
216-292-5655
Fax: 216-292-5978 www.marzetti.com
Bread and rolls
President: Bruce Rosa
Executive Director: Mike Mahon
Controller: Mike Juhasz
Human Resource Executive: Vicki Verlato
Operations: Brian Millikin
Number Employees: 250-499
Parent Co: T. Marzetti Company
Type of Packaging: Consumer, Food Service

9006 New York Intl Bread Co
1500 W Church St
Orlando, FL 32805-2408
407-843-9744
Fax: 407-648-2785
Bread and baked products
CEO: Laura Masella
CEO: Laura Masella
Estimated Sales: $5-10 000,000
Number Employees: 50-99

9007 New York Pizza
725 E Internatl Speedway Blvd
Daytona Beach, FL 32118-4555
386-257-2050
www.nypizza.ru
Pizza
Owner: Richard Squillante
Estimated Sales: Less than $500,000
Number Employees: 1-4
Brands:
 New York Pizza

9008 New York Pretzel
200 Moore St
Brooklyn, NY 11206
718-366-9800
Fax: 718-821-4544 info@nypretzel.com
www.nypretzel.com
Soft pretzels
President: Themis Makkos
VP: Richard Berger
Contact: Ronald Orfinger
jack@nypretzel.com
Estimated Sales: $9.7 Million
Number Employees: 75
Brands:
 New York Pretzel

9009 New York Ravioli
12 Denton Ave S
New Hyde Park, NY 11040-4904
516-270-2852
Fax: 516-741-5289 888-588-7287
www.nyravioli.com
Ravioli and other products
President/Co-Founder: David Creo
VP/Co-Founder: Paul Moncada
Contact: Paul Moncada
paul@nyravioli.com
Estimated Sales: Less Than $500,000
Number Employees: 1-4
Type of Packaging: Food Service, Private Label, Bulk

9010 NewGem Products
3600-A Industry Drive East
Fife, WA 98424
253-896-3089
info@newgemfoods.com
www.newgemfoods.com
Fruit- and vegetable-based alternatives to seaweed wraps
CEO: Matthew De Bord
Corporate Executive Chef: Tracy Griffith
Number of Brands: 2
Brands:
 ORIGAMI WRAPS
 GEMWRAPS

9011 Newburg Corners Cheese Factory
Highway 33
Route 2
Bangor, WI 54614
608-452-3636
Fax: 608-452-3636
Cheese
Owner: Lowell Kitzmann
Owner: Mike Everhart
Number Employees: 1-4

9012 Newburgh Brewing Company
88 South Colden St.
Newburgh, NY 12550
845-569-2337
info@newburghbrewing.com
www.newburghbrewing.com
IPAs, American ales, sour beers, Belgian-style beers, stout
Founding Partner/Co-Owner: Christopher Basso
Year Founded: 2012
Number of Brands: 1
Number of Products: 14
Type of Packaging: Consumer, Private Label
Brands:
 Newburgh Brewing Company

9013 Newby Teas
333 Albert Ave
Suite 633
East Lansing, MI 48823
517-999-0590
www.newbyteas.us
Tea
Brand Ambassador: Raji Singh
Brands:
 Newby

9014 Newell Lobsters
72 Water St
PO Box 99
Yarmouth, NS B5A 4B1
Canada
902-742-6272
Fax: 902-742-1542
Processor and exporter of fresh herring roe and lobster
President: Robert Newell
Estimated Sales: $7.4 Million
Number Employees: 15
Type of Packaging: Consumer, Food Service, Private Label

9015 Newfound Resources
90 O'Leary Ave
Suite 203
St Josephs, NL A1B 2C7
Canada
709-579-7676
Fax: 709-579-7668 shrimp@nfld.com
www.newfoundresources.com
Processor and exporter of frozen shrimp
President: Brian McNamara
Controller: Bill Coady
Operations Manager: Jeff Simms
Estimated Sales: $6.6 Million
Number Employees: 60
Type of Packaging: Bulk

9016 (HQ)Newly Weds Foods Inc
2501 N Keeler Ave
Chicago, IL 60639-2131
773-489-6224
Fax: 773-489-2799 800-621-7521
nwfnorthamerica@newlywedsfoods.com
www.newlywedsfoods.com
Processor and exporter of breadings, batters, seasoning blends, marinades, glazes and capsicum products
President: Charles T. Angell
CFO: Brian Johnson
SVP Sales & Marketing: Bruce Leshinski
R&D: Jim Klein
Sales Director: Jim Chin
Contact: Mary Adderhold
madderhold@newlywedsfoods.com
VP Manufacturing: Mike Hopp
Plant Manager: Leo Vogler
Director of Purchasing: Tom Lisack

Food Manufacturers / A-Z

Estimated Sales: $959 Million
Number Employees: 1-4
Square Footage: 1500000
Other Locations:
  Newly Weds Foods
    Bethlehem PA
  Newly Weds Foods
    Chicago IL
  Newly Weds Foods
    Cleveland TN
  Newly Weds Foods
    Watertown MA
  Newly Weds Foods
    Yorkville IL
  Newly Weds Foods
    Horn Lake MS
  Newly Weds Foods
    Edmonton AB
  Newly Weds Foods
    Montreal QC
  Newly Weds Foods
    Toronto ON
Brands:
  Batter Blends
  Blended Breaders
  Newly Weds

9017 Newly Weds Foods Inc
437 S Mcclure Rd
Modesto, CA 95357-0519
209-491-7777
Fax: 209-575-1609 800-487-7423
www.newlywedsfoods.com
Seasonings and spices
Sales Manager: Bill McGlynn
General Manager: Coe Barnard
Plant Manager: Allen Holzman
Estimated Sales: $5-10 Million
Number Employees: 20-49
Parent Co: Heller Seasonings

9018 (HQ)Newman's Own
246 Post Rd E # 308
Suite 308
Westport, CT 06880-3615
203-222-0136
Fax: 203-227-5630 www.newmansown.com
Exporter of pizzas, complete skillet meals, salad dressings, sauces, salsas, marinades, beverages, cereals, popcorn, and wine
President & COO: Tom Indoe
CEO: Clea Newman
Business Development Manager: Steve Ripson
VP Marketing: Michael Havard
Director of Sales: Mark Tilley
Contact: M Anita
anita@newmansown.com
VP Operations: Bill Lee
Estimated Sales: $4.9 Million
Number Employees: 28
Square Footage: 16800
Type of Packaging: Consumer, Food Service
Other Locations:
  Newman's Own
    Aptos CA
Brands:
  Newman's Own
  Newman's Own Lemonade
  Newman's Own Pasta Sauces
  Newman's Own Popcorn
  Newman's Own Salad Dressing
  Newman's Own Salsa

9019 Newmarket Foods
2210 Pine View Way
Petaluma, CA 94954-5687
707-778-3400
Fax: 707-778-3434 www.newmarketfoods.com
VP Sales/Marketing: Tom Mierzwinski
Vice President: Thomas Mierzwinski
Estimated Sales: $1-2.5 Million
Number Employees: 1
Type of Packaging: Private Label
Brands:
  Butterscotch Bliss
  Chocolate Ecstasy
  Hot Fudge Fantasy

9020 Newmeadows Lobster Inc
60 Portland Pier
Portland, ME 04101-4713
207-775-1612
Fax: 207-874-2456 800-668-1612
Lobster
Owner: Patricia Burch
patriciaburch@newmeadowslobster.com

Estimated Sales: $5-10 Million
Number Employees: 10-19

9021 Newport Flavours & Fragrances
833 N Elm St
Orange, CA 92867-7909
714-744-3700
Fax: 714-771-3588 www.newportflavours.com
Flavor extracts, concentrates, fillings, icings, glazes, syrups, toppings, oils and fragrances; also, contract packaging available
President: Bill Sabo
customerservice@naturesflavors.com
VP: Jeanne Aragon
Estimated Sales: $3.6 Million
Number Employees: 10-19
Square Footage: 35200
Type of Packaging: Consumer, Food Service, Private Label, Bulk

9022 Newport Ingredients
5850 West 3rd St
Suite 142
Los Angeles, CA 90036
323-284-5959
Fax: 323-285-5352 sales@newportings.com
newportingredients.com
Natural ingredients
President/Owner: Israel Jaeger

9023 Newport Meat Co North
16691 Hale Ave.
Irvine, CA 92606
949-474-4040
info@newportmeat.com
www.newportmeat.com
Meats including; beef, poultry, pork, lamb, veal, seafood, foie gras, vegetables, potato products, and more
President: Pat Ansboury
pat@facciola.com
CEO: Robert Facciola
CFO: Robert Cruz
Vice President: Michael Nicholas
Quality Assurance Manager: Ambrosio Huasanoi
VP Human Resources: Krystal Martinez
Purchasing Manager: Bret Vanvoorhis
Estimated Sales: $30.3 Million
Number Employees: 100-249
Square Footage: 84000
Parent Co: Sysco

9024 Newport Vineyards & Winery
909 E. Main Rd (RT 138)
Middletown, RI 02842
401-848-5161
Fax: 401-848-5162 info@newportvineyards.com
www.newportvineyards.com
Wine
Owner, Vintner: John Nunes
Owner, Vineyard Manager: Paul Nunes
Winemaker: George Chelf
Estimated Sales: $5 Million
Number Employees: 19
Type of Packaging: Private Label
Brands:
  Newport

9025 Newton Candy Company
4912 Airline Dr # G
Houston, TX 77022-3078
713-691-6969
Fax: 713-691-6979
Candy
Manager: Muhammed Nazim
Estimated Sales: $2.5-5 000,000
Number Employees: 10-19

9026 Newton Vineyard
2555 Madrona Ave
St Helena, CA 94574-2300
707-204-7423
Fax: 707-963-5408 winery@newtonvineyard.com
www.newtonvineyard.com
Fine wines
President: Dr Su Hua Newton
CEO: Jean-Baptiste Rivail
Controller: Tim Lin
Winemaker: Alberto Bianchi
Assistant Winemaker: Andrew Holve
Estimated Sales: $20-50 Million
Number Employees: 1-4
Type of Packaging: Private Label

Brands:
  Newton Vineyard

9027 Newtown Foods USA Inc
6 Penns Trl # 215
Suite 215
Newtown, PA 18940-1889
215-579-2120
Fax: 215-579-2129 info@newtownfoods.com
www.newtownfoods.com
Cocoa ingredients, dehydrated fruit, natural extracts, banana puree, spray-dried ingredients
Owner: John Mc Donald
nfoodsusa@aol.com
Estimated Sales: Below $5 Million
Number Employees: 1-4
Brands:
  Duas Rodas Industrial
  Dutch Cocoa Bv
  Kievit
  Schoemaker

9028 Nexcel Natural Ingredients
PO Box 3483
2520 S Grand Ave East
Springfield, IL 62703
217-391-0091
Fax: 217-391-0096 www.nexcelfoods.com
Natural oils
President/Owner: Rob Kirby
VP, Sales & Business Development: Lynn Myers

9029 Nexira
15 Somerset St
Somerville, NJ 08876-2828
908-707-9400
Fax: 908-707-9405 800-872-1850
info-usa@nexira.com www.nexira.com
Nexira is a global leader in natural ingredients and botanical extracts for food nutrition and dietary supplements. Nexira built its reputation as the world leader in acacia gum and now manufactures a wide range of functional and nutritional ingredients, antioxidants, and active botanicals for weight management, sports nutrition, digestive and cardiovascular health. It manufactures the following ingredients for the food and health industry: acacia gum, botanical extracts and powders.
President: Stephane Dondain
heese@cnius.com
VP: Teresa Yazbek
Marketing/Logistics Specialist: Nina Segura
Sales: Bob Bremer
Estimated Sales: $14 Million
Number Employees: 10-19
Number of Brands: 25
Number of Products: 100
Type of Packaging: Bulk
Brands:
  FIBREGUM
  VINITROX
  EXOCYAN
  CACTi-NEA
  NEOPUNTIA
  ID-ALG
  INSTANTGUM
  SPRAYGUM
  EFICACIA
  EQUACIA
  THIXOGUM

9030 Nhs Labs Inc
11665 W State St
Star, ID 83669-5223
208-939-5100
Fax: 208-939-5100 888-546-8694
info@nutritionmanufacturer.com
www.nutritionmanufacturer.com
Private label sports drinks, supplements, and energy drinks
CEO: Larry Leach
Number Employees: 50-99
Square Footage: 74000

9031 Niagara Chocolates
3500 Genesee St
Buffalo, NY 14225-5015
716-634-0070
Fax: 716-634-4855 877-261-7887
info@sweetworks.net www.niagarachocolates.com
Chocolate novelties including bars, truffles and boxed

Food Manufacturers / A-Z

President: Schmassmann Christoph
CFO: Ralph Nicosia
Quality Assurance Manager: Marsha Koerner
Director of Marketing: Jeanne Palka
Director Sales: Jerry Tubbs
Plant Manager: Parha Paraj
Purchasing Manager: Bob Dunn
Estimated Sales: $36.5 Million
Number Employees: 100-249
Square Footage: 115000
Parent Co: SweetWorks, Inc.
Type of Packaging: Consumer
Other Locations:
  Oak Leaf Plant
  Toronto ON
Brands:
  Mercken's
  Mercken's Chocolate
  Sweet Works

9032 Niagara Foods
10 Kelly Ave
Middleport, NY 14105-1210
716-735-7722
Fax: 716-735-9076 www.agvest.com
Processor, importer and exporter of frozen vegetable products and fruit and vegetable powders and flakes; also, frozen and dehydrated fruits including apples, cherries, strawberries, cranberries and wild and cultivated blueberries
President: Barry Schneider
Contact: Bradley Devey
bradley@valley.net
General Manager: Bob Neuman
Estimated Sales: $14.9 Million
Number Employees: 50
Square Footage: 140000
Parent Co: Agvest
Type of Packaging: Consumer, Food Service, Private Label, Bulk
Brands:
  Agvest
  Quality

9033 NibMor
PO Box 6
Kennebunk, ME 04043
207-502-7541
info@nibmor.com
www.nibmor.com
Chocolate snacks
CEO: Ralph Chauvin
Operations Manager: Marcia Bell

9034 Nicasio Vineyards
14300 Nicasio Way
Soquel, CA 95073
831-423-1073
Wine
President: Dan Wheeler

9035 (HQ)Niche Import Co
45 Horsehill Rd # 106
Suite 106A
Cedar Knolls, NJ 07927-2009
973-993-8450
Fax: 973-898-0183 800-548-6882
mpersson@ourniche.com www.ourniche.com
Gourmet foods and beverages
President: Terri Nelson
tnelson@ourniche.com
Area Sales Manager: Matthew Nelson
Media Relations: Barbara Miele
Estimated Sales: $2.5-5 Million
Number Employees: 10-19
Type of Packaging: Private Label
Brands:
  Asbach Uralt
  Stroh
  Underberg Bitters

9036 Niche W&S
45 Horsehill Road
Suite 106A
Cedar Knolls, NJ 07927
973-993-8450
Fax: 973-898-0183 www.ourniche.com
Fine wines and spirits
President: Terri Nelson
Estimated Sales: $10-20 Million
Number Employees: 10-19
Parent Co: Niche Import Company

9037 Nichelini Family WineryInc
2950 Sage Canyon Rd
St Helena, CA 94574-9641
707-963-0717
Fax: 707-963-3262 mail@nicheliniwinery.com
www.nicheliniwinery.com
International wines and spirits
Manager: Toni Irwin
nichwine@nicheliniwinery.com
Treasurer: Richard Wainright
Wine Maker: Greg Boeger
Estimated Sales: Less Than $500,000
Number Employees: 1-4
Type of Packaging: Private Label

9038 Nichem Co
750 Frelinghuysen Ave
Newark, NJ 07114-2221
973-399-9810
Fax: 973-399-8818 sales@nichem.com
www.nichem.com
Processor and importer of ingredients including citric acid, vanillin and sodium citrate; exporter of citric acid
President: Peg Blue
sales@nichem.com
Estimated Sales: $700,000
Number Employees: 5-9
Square Footage: 80000
Type of Packaging: Consumer, Food Service

9039 Nichols Farms
Nichols Farms
13762 First Ave
Hanford, CA 93230
559-584-6811
Fax: 559-688-1603 info@nicholsfarms.com
www.nicholsfarms.com
Almonds, pistachios and mixes
President/Owner: Chuck Nichols
Brands:
  NICHOLS FARMS

9040 Nick Sciabica & Sons
2150 Yosemite Blvd
Modesto, CA 95354-3931
209-577-5067
Fax: 209-524-5367 800-551-9612
www.baginfusti.com
Extra-virgin olive oil; importer of olive oil, pasta and tomato products; wholesaler/distributor of wine vinegar, olive oil, canned tomatoes, olives and pasta
Partner: Jonathan Sciabica
Controller: Susan Ochoa
VP: Gemma Sciabica
Marketing Manager: Dean Cohan
Production Manager: Daniel Sciabica
Estimated Sales: $2.5 Million
Number Employees: 20-49
Number of Brands: 6
Number of Products: 150
Square Footage: 274912
Type of Packaging: Consumer, Food Service, Private Label, Bulk
Brands:
  Marsala
  Sciabica's Oil of the Olive

9041 Nick's Sticks
Wenzel's Farm
500 E 29th Street
Marshfield, WI 54449
715-257-0636
www.nicks-sticks.com
Beef snack sticks and jerky
Founder: Nick Wallace
Brands:
  NICK'S STICKS
  NICK'S JERKY

9042 Nickabood's Inc
1401 Elwood St
Los Angeles, CA 90021-2812
213-746-1541
Fax: 213-746-1542 bob@nickaboods.com
Health food products including sauces, honey, salad dressings, condiments seafood sauces, baked potato products, miso mayo, and frozen stuffed potatoes.
Vice President: Robert Abood
Estimated Sales: $700,000
Number Employees: 5-9
Number of Brands: 4
Number of Products: 15
Square Footage: 60000
Parent Co: Fisherman Wharf Foods
Type of Packaging: Private Label
Brands:
  Desert Gold
  Fisherman's Wharf
  So Good
  Spud King

9043 Nicky USA Inc
223 SE 3rd Ave
Portland, OR 97214-1006
503-234-4263
Fax: 503-234-8268 800-469-4162
info@nickyusa.com www.nickyusa.com
Distributor of natural game birds and meats including pheasant, poussin, quail, venison, buffalo, rabbit, ostrich, alligator, ducks and wild boar; also, sausage, veal, free-range lamb
Owner, President: Geoff Latham
glatham@nickyusa.com
VP: Melody Latham
Sales Office Manager: Ursula McVittie
Production Manager: Jace Hentges
Estimated Sales: $4 Million
Number Employees: 20-49
Square Footage: 20000
Type of Packaging: Consumer, Food Service, Private Label, Bulk
Brands:
  Cervera
  Country Game
  Nicky Usa

9044 Nicola International
4561 Colorado Blvd.
Los Angeles, CA 90039-0758
818-545-1515
Fax: 818-247-8585
Finest olives, olive oils and grape leaves for deli departments, bakeries and the pizza industry, salad manufacturers, custom marination and creative gourmet dishes
President: Nicola Khachatoorian
VP: Alice Toomanian
Contact: Adik Khachatoorian
adikk@nicolainternational.com
Purchasing Manager: Claudine Reyes
Estimated Sales: $1-10 Million
Number Employees: 25
Type of Packaging: Food Service, Private Label
Brands:
  Aiello

9045 Nicola Pizza
8 N 1st St
Rehoboth Beach, DE 19971-2116
302-226-2654
Fax: 302-226-3721 nicolapizza@comcast.net
www.nicolapizza.com
Spaghetti sauce
Owner: Nick Caggiano
VP: Nicolas Caggiano
CFO: Joan Caggiano
Estimated Sales: $1.2 Million
Number Employees: 20-49
Type of Packaging: Consumer, Food Service
Brands:
  Mama Nichola's Sago
  Nic-O-Boli

9046 Nicola Valley Apiaries
PO Box 1995
Merritt, BC V1K 1B8
Canada
250-378-5208
www.nicolavalleyhoney.com
Processor and packer of liquid, creamed, chunk and comb honey; also, beeswax
Partner: Alan Paulson
Partner: Margaret Paulson
Estimated Sales: $203,000
Number Employees: 2

9047 Nicole's Divine Crackers
1505 N Kingsbury Street
Chicago, IL 60642-2533
312-640-8883
Fax: 312-640-0988 nicolescrackers@msn.com
Crackers
President: Nicole Bergere
Estimated Sales: Below $5 Million
Number Employees: 5-9

Food Manufacturers / A-Z

9048 Niebaum-Coppola Estate Winery
1991 St Helena Highway
Rutherford, CA 94573
707-968-1100
Fax: 707-963-9084 800-782-4266
www.niebaum-coppola.com
Wines
Chairman: Francis Coppola
CEO: Jay Shoemaker
Estimated Sales: $5-10 Million
Number Employees: 20-49

9049 Nielsen Citrus ProductsInc
15621 Computer Ln
Huntington Beach, CA 92649-1607
714-892-5586
Fax: 714-893-2161 info@nielsencitrus.com
www.nielsencitrus.com
Processor and exporter of frozen, concentrated lemon and lime juice, lemon puree, lime puree, or-ange puree
President: Chris Nielsen
greg.hogue@verizon.net
Vice President: Earl Nielsen
Number Employees: 10-19
Square Footage: 40000
Type of Packaging: Consumer, Food Service, Private Label, Bulk
Brands:
Ez
Nielsen
Suntree

9050 Nielsen-Massey Vanillas Inc
1550 Shields Dr
Waukegan, IL 60085-8307
847-578-1550
Fax: 847-578-1570 800-525-7873
info@nielsenmassey.com nielsenmassey.com
Manufacturer of vanilla extracts and pure flavors
CEO: Kirk Trofholz
VP, Global Sales: Brent Allen
Director of Sales: Dan Fox
Year Founded: 1907
Estimated Sales: $20-50 Million
Number Employees: 20-49
Number of Brands: 1
Square Footage: 100500
Type of Packaging: Consumer, Food Service, Bulk
Other Locations:
Nielsen-Massey Vanillas Inter. B.V.
Leeuwarden, Netherlands
Brands:
Nielsen-Massey

9051 Niemuth's Steak & Chop Shop
715 Redfield St
Waupaca, WI 54981-1353
715-258-2666
www.niemuthssteakandchop.com
Processors of meat products including ham, bacon and sausage
President: Roger Niemuth
Owner: Robert Niemuth
Estimated Sales: $950,000
Number Employees: 10-19
Square Footage: 27000
Type of Packaging: Consumer

9052 Night Hawk Frozen FoodsInc
100 Nighthawk Cir
PO Box 867
Buda, TX 78610-9100
512-312-0757
Fax: 512-295-3988 800-580-4166
www.nighthawkfoods.com
Processor of frozen entrees including steak, beef and meatloaf dinners.
CEO: Leanne Logan
COO: Scott Logan
VP/Controller: Dale Reistad
VP Operations: Terrell Windham
Purchasing Manager: John Benites
Year Founded: 1939
Estimated Sales: $20-50 Million
Number Employees: 50-99
Number of Brands: 1
Number of Products: 18
Square Footage: 30000
Type of Packaging: Consumer, Food Service
Brands:
Night Hawk

9053 Nikken Foods
4984 Manchester Ave
St Louis, MO 63110-2010
314-881-5818
Fax: 502-292-3283 nikken@lilar.com
www.nikkenfoods.com
Processor, importer and exporter of soy sauce, fermented soy sauce powders, extracted seafood powders and concentrates and dehydrated mushrooms and oriental vegetables
Manager: Beth James
bethj@nikkenfoods.com
General Manager: Herb Bench
Number Employees: 10-19
Parent Co: Nikkens Foods Company
Type of Packaging: Bulk

9054 Nikki's Coconut Butter
Hudson, WI
nikki@nikkiscoconutbutter.com
www.nikkiscoconutbutter.com
Coconut butter spreads and chocolate bars
Owner: Andrew Frezza
Owner/CEO: Nikki Frezza

9055 Nikki's Cookies
2018 South 1st St
Milwaukee, WI 53207
414-481-4899
Fax: 414-481-5222 800-776-7107
customerservice@nikkiscookies.com
www.nikkiscookies.com
Processor and exporter of shortbreads and cookies
President: Nikki Taylor
Contact: Bill Danner
billdanner@nikkiscookies.com
Estimated Sales: Less than $500,000
Number Employees: 5-9
Square Footage: 120000
Type of Packaging: Consumer, Food Service
Brands:
English Toffee
Ladybug
Nikki's

9056 Nikola's Foods
8301 Grand Ave S
#110
Bloomington, MN 55420
952-229-4183
Fax: 952-253-5995 888-645-6527
sales@nikolasbakery.com www.nikolasbakery.com
A manufacturing and baking company that offers a full line of bakery products including muffins, cakes, dessert breads, cookies, croissants and macaroons; produces gluten free, organic and kosher products.
Director of Development and Innovation: Michael Itskovich
Contact: Gregory Noah
gnoah@nikolasbakery.com
Estimated Sales: $3.5 Million
Number Employees: 12
Type of Packaging: Consumer, Food Service

9057 Niman Ranch
1350 S Loop Rd # 102
Suite 120
Alameda, CA 94502-7081
510-995-8041
www.nimanranch.com
Meats
CEO: Jeff Swain
jeff.swain@nimanranch.com
Number Employees: 5-9

9058 Nimble Nectar
951-775-9543
info@nimblenectar.com
nimblenectar.com
Cocktail mixers
Co-Founder: Jason Joe
Co-Founder: Julie Joe
Sales: Noelle Arnzen
Brands:
NIMBLE NECTAR

9059 Nimeks Organics
52 E Union Blvd
Bethlehem, PA 18017
610-997-0500
Fax: 610-954-9959 www.nimeks.com
Dried fruits and nuts, frozen fruits and vegetables and fruit concentrates and purees

9060 Nina's Gourmet Dip
6305 Dunaway Court
Mc Lean, VA 22101-2205
703-356-1667
Fax: 703-356-8488
Gourmet and specialty foods
President: Bill Pournaras

9061 Ninety Six Canning Company
109 S Cambridge St
Ninety Six, SC 29666
864-543-2700
Canned barbecued hash
President/Owner: Jerry Gantt
Estimated Sales: $2.6 Million
Number Employees: 4
Type of Packaging: Consumer

9062 Ninth Avenue Foods
626-364-8722
steveg@ninthavenuefoods.com
www.ninthavenuefoods.com
Package dairy and nondairy products including flavored milks, protein fortified milks and beverages, organic blends, soy blends, nondairy creamers, nut and flax milk blends.
Director of Operations: Steve Goldenstein
Type of Packaging: Consumer, Private Label

9063 Nips Potato Chips
806 Pohukaina St
Honolulu, HI 96813
808-593-8549
donnachang@hotmail.com
Potato chips
CEO: Norman Nip
Estimated Sales: Less than $500,000
Number Employees: 1-4
Brands:
Nip's Potato Chips

9064 Nirvana Natural Spring Water
1 Nirvana Plaza
Forestport, NY 13338
315-262-8192
888-463-5675
www.nirvanawater.com
Bottled water

9065 Nirwana Foods
778 Newark Ave
Jersey City, NJ 07306
201-659-2200
Fax: 201-659-1260 www.nirwanafoods.com
Spices, almonds, cashews and tea.
President: Jimmy Singh
Brands:
Nirwana

9066 Nisbet Oyster Company
7081 Niawaukum St Hwy 101
P.O. Box 338
Bay Center, WA 98527-0338
360-875-6629
Fax: 360-875-6684 888-875-6629
sales@goosepoint.com www.goosepoint.com
Processor and exporter of Pacific and farm oysters; Pacific oyster farm operations; retail and food service products fresh and frozen
President, Owner: David Nisbet
Owner: Maureene Nisbet
Sales Manager: Josh Valdiz
Plant Manager: Kathleen Nisbet
Purchasing: Geoff Clarine
Estimated Sales: $10 Million
Number Employees: 75
Number of Brands: 1
Number of Products: 3
Square Footage: 12800
Brands:
Goose Point Oysters

9067 Nisshodo Candy Store
1095 Dillingham Blvd # I-5-109
Bldg I-5
Honolulu, HI 96817-4507
808-847-1244
mhirao@hawaiiantel.net
nisshodomochicandy.com
Candy
Number Employees: 5-9

Food Manufacturers / A-Z

9068 Nissin Foods USA Co Inc
2001 W Rosecrans Ave
Gardena, CA 90249-2994
310-327-8478
Fax: 323-515-3751 export@nissinfoods.com
www.nissinfoods.com
Asian noodles and noodle soup
President & CEO: Michael Price
b-barrett@mb1.nissinfoods.co.jp
CFO: Roy Shoemaker
Quality Control Director: Melinda Levinsky
VP Marketing: Carla Hunter
VP Sales: Terry McMartin
Human Resources Manager: Katrina Joy
b-barrett@mb1.nissinfoods.co.jp
Manufacturing Director: Mike Kirchner
Plant Manager: Don Babcock
Purchasing Manager: Billie Jo Dangro
Year Founded: 1948
Estimated Sales: $33.2 Million
Number Employees: 500-999
Square Footage: 64391
Parent Co: Nissin Foods USA Company
Type of Packaging: Private Label
Other Locations:
   Nissin Foods USA Company
   Fort Lee NJ
Brands:
   Cup O' Noodles
   Oodles of Noodles
   Top Ramen

9069 Nissley Vineyards & Winery
140 Vintage Dr
Bainbridge, PA 17502-9357
717-426-3514
Fax: 717-426-1391 800-522-2387
winery@nissley.com www.nissleywine.com
Wine
President: Judith Nissley
winery@nissleywine.com
Vice President: John Nissley
Winemaker: William Gulvin
Estimated Sales: $2.5-5 Million
Number Employees: 10-19
Type of Packaging: Private Label
Brands:
   Holiday White
   Niagara
   Rhapsody In Blue
   Topaz
   Whisper White

9070 Nita Crisp Crackers LLC
454 S. Link Lane
Fort Collins, CO 80524
970-482-9090
Fax: 970-482-1043 866-493-4609
www.nitacrisp.com
Artisan flatbreats in small batches or in bulk to natural grocers, specialty food stores, and restaurants from coast to coast
Managing Partner: Steve Landry
CEO: Paul Pellegrino
Customer Service / Sales: Michele Hattman
Estimated Sales: $170,000
Number of Products: 1
Square Footage: 5614
Type of Packaging: Consumer, Food Service, Bulk
Brands:
   Nita Crisp

9071 Nitta Casings Inc
141 Southside Ave
Bridgewater, NJ 08807-3256
908-218-4400
Fax: 908-725-2835 800-526-3970
info@nittacasings.com www.nittacasings.com
Meat and collagen casings
President & CEO: Rod Moore
Chief Financial Officer: Bruce Zacharias
Operations Manager: David Bensimon
Estimated Sales: $20-50 Million
Number Employees: 250-499

9072 Nitta Gelatin NA
598 Airport Blvd
Suite 900
Morrisville, NC 27560
919-238-3300
Fax: 919-238-3222 800-278-7680
www.nitta-gelatin.com
Gelatin
President: Guergen Gallert
Contact: Jeremy Anderson
j.anderson@nitta-gelatin.com
Office Manager: Tsutomu Takase
General Manager: Jurgen Gallert
Estimated Sales: $2.5-5 Million
Number Employees: 1-4
Parent Co: Nitta Gelatin
Type of Packaging: Bulk
Brands:
   Nitta Gelatin

9073 Niutang Chemical, Inc.
5181 Edison Ave
Chino, CA 91710
909-631-2895
Fax: 909-631-2309 sales@niutang.us
www.niutang.com
High-quality food additives and pharmaceutical intermediates including sucralose, aspartame and folic acid
President: Licheng Wang
Owner: Feng Lu
Director Technical & Quality Support: Kerry Kenny
Quality Manager: Sharon Bosch
Contact: Mandy Chen
mandy@niutang.us
Manager/Director: Jie Lin

9074 Nk Hurst Co Inc
230 W Mccarty St
Indianapolis, IN 46225-1234
317-634-6425
Fax: 317-638-1396 800-426-2336
www.nkhurst.com
Processor of dried beans.
President: Rick Hurst
Year Founded: 1938
Estimated Sales: $20-50 Million
Number Employees: 50-99
Number of Brands: 3
Type of Packaging: Consumer, Food Service, Bulk
Brands:
   Hurst Family Harvest
   Hurst's Brand Dry Beans
   Hurst's HamBeens

9075 No Cow
1526 Blake St
Suite 200
Denver, CO 80202
info@nocow.com
nocow.com
Non-dairy bars, butters and cookies
Founder: Daniel Katz
Number of Brands: 1
Number of Products: 3
Brands:
   NO COW

9076 No Evil Foods
PO Box 47
Asheville, NC 28801
828-367-1536
preach@noevilfoods.com
www.noevilfoods.com
Vegan plant meats
Co-Founder: Sadrah Schadel
Co-Founder: Mike Woliansky
Number of Brands: 1
Number of Products: 5
Brands:
   NO EVIL FOODS

9077 No Pudge! Foods
PO Box 387
Wolfeboro Falls, NH 03896-0387
603-230-9858
Fax: 504-539-5427 888-667-8343
customerservice@nopudge.com
www.nopudge.com
Fat-free brownie mix
Founder/President: Lindsay Frucci
Estimated Sales: $1-2.5 Million
Number Employees: 2
Type of Packaging: Food Service
Brands:
   No Pudge

9078 No Whey Foods
170 Oberlin Ave N
Suite 9
Lakewood, NJ 08701-4548
732-806-5218
www.nowheychocolate.com
Nut-free chocolates
Contact: Yochy Miller
Brands:
   No Whey Foods

9079 Noble Chocolates NV
Handelsstraat 5
Veurne, 8630
Belgium
contact@noble-chocolates.com
www.noble-chocolates.com
Chocolates, chocolate truffles
Number Employees: 20-49

9080 Noble Popcorn
401 N 13th St
PO Box 157
Sac City, IA 50583
712-662-4728
Fax: 712-662-4797 800-537-9554
info@noblepopcorn.com www.noblepopcorn.com
Popcorn including popped, unpopped and flavored
CFO: Rhonda Lines
Plant Manager: Dan Martin
Estimated Sales: $1-3 Million
Number Employees: 10-19
Square Footage: 32000
Type of Packaging: Consumer, Food Service, Private Label, Bulk
Brands:
   Cedar Creek
   Noble Popcorn

9081 Nobletree Coffee
499 Van Brunt St
Unit 3A
Brooklyn, NY 11231
718-643-6080
nobletreecoffee.com
Coffee
Managing Director: Eric Taylor
Operations Manager: Nina Nathel
Production Manager: Sky Swartout
Brands:
   Nobletree

9082 Nodine's Smokehouse Inc
65 Fowler Ave
PO Box 1787
Torrington, CT 06790-6529
860-489-3309
Fax: 860-496-9787 800-222-2059
nodinesmoke@optonline.net
www.nodinesmokehouse.com
Smoked hams, bacons, chicken, duck, turkey, goose, sausages, fish and cheeses
Owner: Ronald Nodine
VP: Johanne Nodine
Estimated Sales: $3-5 Million
Number Employees: 5-9
Type of Packaging: Consumer, Food Service

9083 Noel Corp
1001 S 3rd St
Yakima, WA 98901-3403
509-248-1313
Fax: 509-248-2843 www.noelcorp.com
Bottled and canned carbonated and noncarbonated beverages; also, bag-in-box juices including orange and apple
President: Rodger Noel
Controller: Martha Barman
VP: Justin Noel
Marketing Executive: Mike Sutton
Manager Sales: William Dalton
IT: Martha Berman
martha@noelcorp.com
Estimated Sales: $42.8 Million
Number Employees: 10-19
Square Footage: 200000
Type of Packaging: Consumer, Food Service, Private Label
Brands:
   Dr. Pepper
   Noel
   Pepsi
   Seven-Up

Food Manufacturers / A-Z

Squirt
Tap Juices

9084 Nog Incorporated
PO Box 162
Dunkirk, NY 14048
716-366-3322
Fax: 716-366-8487   800-332-2664
Ice cream ingredients including coatings, variegates and background flavors
President: Bruce Ritenburg
R&D Director: Bob Habich
Plant Manager: Rick Musso
Estimated Sales: $1-3 Million
Number Employees: 10-19
Square Footage: 96000
Type of Packaging: Bulk

9085 Noh Foods Of Hawaii
2043 S Beretania St # C
Honolulu, HI 96826-1344
808-944-0655
Fax: 808-944-0830   nohfoods@nohfoods.com
www.nohfoods.com
Seasonings and sauces
President: Raymond Noh
nohfoods@nohfoods.com
Estimated Sales: $3.5 Million
Number Employees: 10-19

9086 Nolechek Meats Inc
104 N Washington St
P. O. Box 599
Thorp, WI 54771-9239
715-669-5580
Fax: 715-669-7360   800-454-5580
nolechek@nolechekmeats.com
www.nolechekmeats.com
Smoked meats
Owner: William Nolechek Jr
nolechek@nolechekmeats.com
VP: Kelly Nolechek
Production: Leo Hawkeg
Estimated Sales: $1-3 Million
Number Employees: 5-9

9087 Nomi Snacks
Minneapolis, MN
www.nomisnacks.com
Fresh fruit and oat bars
Co-Founder: Will Handke
Number of Products: 6

9088 Nomolas Corp
999 Central Ave
Woodmere, NY 11598
516-569-3093
Health food
Chairman: Jay Salomon
Number Employees: 2

9089 Nona Lim
3310 Peralta St
Oakland, CA 94608
415-513-5328
www.nonalim.com
Noodle bowls, bone broths and soups
Founder: Nona Lim
Brands:
 NONA LIM

9090 Nona Vegan Foods
Toronto, ON
Canada
416-836-9387
info@nonavegan.com
www.nonavegan.com
Dairy free, gluten free, preservative free creamy pasta sauces including alfredo, cheesy, and carbonara styles
Founder: Kailey Gilchrist
Year Founded: 2013

9091 Nonna Pia's Gourmet Sauces
114-1330 Alpha Lake Rd
Whistler, BC V0N 1B1
Canada
604-938-8540
888-372-1534
info@nonnapias.com   nonnapias.com
Sauces, seasonings, cooking enhancers, vinegar, salad dressing
President: Natasha Strim
Director Of Sales: Kurt Koegler

9092 Nonni's Foods LLC
3920 E Pine St
Tulsa, OK 74115
918-621-1200
Fax: 918-560-4159   877-295-9604
info@nonnis.com   nonnis.com
Biscotti, crackers and cookies
Chief Executive Officer: Brian Hansberry
brianhansberry@nonnis.com
Estimated Sales: $150 Million
Number Employees: 100-249
Number of Brands: 2
Number of Products: 16
Type of Packaging: Private Label
Brands:
 Nonni's
 THINAddictives

9093 Nonpareil Farms
40 N 400 W
Blackfoot, ID 83221-5632
208-785-5880
Fax: 208-785-3656   800-522-2223
www.greenerfieldstogether.org
Grower of potatoes including potato flakes, hash browns, potato slices, diced potatoes, scalloped & au gratin, mashed potatoes, and flavored potatoes in casseroles and mashed.
CEO: Christopher Abend
Treasurer & Secretary: Ilene Abend
IT: Kent Nelson
knelson@gotspuds.com
Estimated Sales: $46.2 Million
Number Employees: 500-999
Type of Packaging: Consumer

9094 (HQ)Noon Hour Food Products Inc
215 N Desplaines St # 1
Floor One
Chicago, IL 60661-1072
312-382-1177
Fax: 312-382-9420   800-621-6636
Processor and importer of salted, canned and pickled fish, cheese and groceries
President: Paul Buhl
Executive VP: P Scott Buhl
Marketing Manager: Tyler Swanberg
Operations Manager: William Buhl
Estimated Sales: $6.7 Million
Number Employees: 20-49
Square Footage: 620000
Type of Packaging: Food Service
Other Locations:
 Noon Hour Food Products
 Minneapolis MN
Brands:
 Bond Ost
 Briny Deep
 De Mill
 I Will
 Lunds
 Noon Hour
 Swan
 Swan Island
 Viking

9095 Noosa Yoghurt
PO Box 403
Bellvue, CO 80512
844-800-4329
info@noosayoghurt.com   www.noosayoghurt.com
Australian-style yoghurt
Co-Founder: Koel Thomae
Co-Founder: Rob Graves
Number of Brands: 1
Number of Products: 12
Type of Packaging: Food Service
Brands:
 NOOSA

9096 Noosh Brands
4439 Ish Dr
Simi Valley, CA 93063
805-522-5744
nooshbrands.com
Almond protein powder, butter and oil
Brands:
 NOOSH

9097 Nootra Life
nootra.com
Probiotic smoothies and juice shots
Number of Brands: 1
Number of Products: 6
Brands:
 NOOTRA

9098 Noour Inc.
Huntington Beach, CA
Fax: 818-484-2202   800-621-1378
info@noour.com   noour.com
Date sugar, syrup and paste
Number of Brands: 1
Number of Products: 6
Type of Packaging: Bulk
Brands:
 ROYAL PALM

9099 Nor-Cliff Farms
888 Barrick Rd.
Port Colborne, ON L3K 6H2
Canada
905-835-0808
Fax: 905-892-4011   sales@norcliff.com
Processor and exporter of fresh, frozen and marinated fiddlehead greens; also, soup mix
President: Nick Secord
Vice President: Nina Dilorenzo Secord

9100 Nor-Tech Dairy Advisors
629 S Minnesota Ave
Sioux Falls, SD 57104-4874
605-338-2404
Fax: 605-338-0439   www.nortechdairy.com
Dairy products marketing and trading
President: Mike Hines
Estimated Sales: $6 Million
Number Employees: 1-4
Type of Packaging: Food Service, Private Label, Bulk
Brands:
 Nor-Tech

9101 Nora Snacks
13767 Milroy Place
Santa Fe Springs, CA 90670
562-404-9888
sales@norasnacks.com
www.norasnacks.com
Seaweed snacks
Co-Founder: Itthipat Peeradechapan
Co-Founder: Tim Minges

9102 Nora's Candy Shop
321 N DOXTATOR
Rome, NY 13440
315-337-4530
Fax: 315-339-4054   888-544-8224
customerservice@turkeyjoints.com
www.turkeyjoints.com
Candy and other confectionery products; also chocolate & cocoa products.
Owner: Spero Haritatos
Co-Owner: Sharon Haritatos
Estimated Sales: Less than $500,000
Number Employees: 5-9

9103 Norac Technologies
9110-23 Avenue
Edmonton Research Park
Edmonton, AB T6N 1H9
Canada
780-414-9595
Fax: 780-450-1016
Processor and exporter of spice extracts, egg yolk powder and essential, wheat germ and oat bran oils
President: Tom Evans
VP: Uy Nguyen
Plant Manager: Dan Moser
Number Employees: 10-19
Type of Packaging: Private Label, Bulk
Brands:
 Labex
 Sc

9104 Norben Co
38052 Euclid Ave # 209
Willoughby, OH 44094-6146
440-951-2715
Fax: 440-951-1366   888-466-7236
sales@norbencompany.com
www.norbencompany.com

Food Manufacturers / A-Z

Established in 1974. Supplier of chemicals and essential raw materials to the food, pharmaceutical and nutraceutical industries. Distributor of pea protien, pea starch, pea fiber, bamboo fiber, natural and GMO-free ingredients, nautralfibers, micronized products, low carbohydrate formulations, low fat formulations, custom blends, nautral flavor enhancers, probiotic and prebiotic ingredients, and seasoning blends.
President: B J Kresnye
bjkresnye@norbencompany.com
Estimated Sales: $6 Million
Number Employees: 5-9

9105 Norbest, LLC
PO Box 890
Moroni, UT 84646
Fax: 888-597-5416 800-453-5327
norbest@norbest.com www.norbest.com
Raw and cooked processed turkey products including roasts and deli breasts, and luncheon meats including ham, pastrami, salami, etc.
President/CEO: Matthew Cook
Year Founded: 1923
Estimated Sales: $100+ Million
Number Employees: 20-49
Type of Packaging: Consumer, Food Service, Private Label, Bulk
Brands:
   Norbest

9106 Nordic Group Inc
253 Summer St # 203
Boston, MA 02210-1114
617-423-3358
Fax: 617-423-2057 800-486-4002
Processor and importer of fresh and frozen Norwegian seafood including smoked salmon, cod, haddock and fillets
Owner: Salmon Bake
Finance/Administration VP: Joe Mara
Regional Sales Manager: Joe Scharon
sbake@nordicgroupusa.com
Estimated Sales: $500,000-$1 Million
Number Employees: 5-9
Parent Co: Nordic Group ASA
Type of Packaging: Food Service, Bulk
Brands:
   Fjord Fresh
   Troll

9107 Nordman Of California
4070 S Reed Ave
Sanger, CA 93657-9541
559-638-9923
Wines
President: James Hansen
Estimated Sales: $2 000,000
Number Employees: 5-9
Type of Packaging: Bulk
Brands:
   Grape Alpho

9108 Norfolk Hatchery
1000 East Omaha Avenue
PO Box 132
Norfolk, NE 68702-0132
402-371-5710
Fax: 402-371-5711 800-345-2449
www.norfolkhatchery.com
Poultry. Founded in 1926.
Owner/President: Paula Rasmussen
Estimated Sales: Less than $125,000
Number Employees: 2
Type of Packaging: Bulk

9109 Norfood Cherry Growers
383 Consession Rd 14 E
Simcoe, ON M3Y 4K3
Canada
519-426-5784
Fax: 519-426-7838 info@choosecherries.com
www.cherryprocessor.com
Frozen red pitted cherries
President: Drew Schuyler
Director: Marshall Schuyler
Estimated Sales: $500,000-1 Million
Number Employees: 5-9

9110 Norimoor Lic
4223 235th St
Flushing, NY 11363-1526
718-423-6667
Fax: 718-423-6668 info@norimoor.com
www.petselixir.com
Nature-made products for health, vitamins and toothpaste.
Owner: Karl Krupka
Estimated Sales: $500,000-$1 Million
Number Employees: 5-9
Brands:
   Norimoor
   Norivital Vitamins

9111 Norm's Farms
200 Washington St
Purdy, MO 65734
417-522-1375
normsfarms.com
Elderberry syrups and extracts

9112 Norpac Fisheries Inc
3140 Ualena St # 205
Honolulu, HI 96819-1965
808-528-3474
Fax: 808-537-6880 mjbudke@aol.com
Seafood-Live, fresh, frozen, manufactured
Owner: Michael Budke
mjbudke@aol.com
Estimated Sales: 10-20 Million
Number Employees: 5-9
Brands:
   Mikarla's Best

9113 Norpaco Inc
80 Bysiewicz Dr
Middletown, CT 06457-7564
860-632-2299
Fax: 860-632-2150 800-252-0222
www.norpaco.com
Manufacturer of Italian-style specialty food products.
Owner: Dean Spilka
dean@norpaco.com
CEO: Donald Spilka
Estimated Sales: F
Number Employees: 1-4
Type of Packaging: Consumer, Private Label, Bulk
Brands:
   Norpaco

9114 North Aire Market, Inc.
1157 Valley Park Drive
Suite #130
Shakopee, MN 55379-1964
952-496-2887
Fax: 952-496-3444 800-662-3781
sales@northairemarket.com
www.northairemarket.com
Dry soup mixes
Owner: Maggie Mortensen
maggie@northairemarket.com
Estimated Sales: Below $5 Million
Number Employees: 10-19
Type of Packaging: Consumer, Food Service, Private Label
Brands:
   North Aire Simmering Soups

9115 North American BeverageCo
901 Ocean Ave
Ocean City, NJ 08226-3540
609-399-1486
Fax: 609-399-1506
inquiry@northamericanbeverage.com
www.chocolatemoose.us
High energy, low fat premium chocolate dairy drinks
President: John Imbessi
jcimbesi@aol.com
Controller: Tom Repichi
Estimated Sales: $10-20 Million
Number Employees: 1-4
Brands:
   Chocolate Moose
   Chocolate Moose Energy
   Havana Cappucino
   Red Rose Ice
   Royal Mandalay Chai
   White Chocolate Moose

9116 North American Blueberry Council
80 Iron Point Circle
Folsom, CA 95630-8593
916-983-0111
Fax: 916-983-9370 800-824-6395
info@blueberry.org www.nabcblues.org
Blueberry products
Chairman: Dave Arena
Treasurer: Art Galletta
Vice President: Nell Moore
Secretary: Tom Bodtke
Contact: Whitney Mustin
wmustin@nabcblues.org
Executive Director: Mark Villata
Number Employees: 4
Brands:
   Blueberry Barbeque Sauce
   Harvest Bar
   Trader Joe's

9117 North American Breweries Inc.
445 Saint Paul St.
Rochester, NY 14605
585-546-1030
www.fifcousa.com
Brewed beer and ale.
CEO: Adrian Lachowski
Year Founded: 2009
Estimated Sales: $120 Million
Number Employees: 1,000-4,999
Parent Co: Florida Ice & Farm Co.
Type of Packaging: Consumer
Other Locations:
   Sales & Marketing
   Buffalo NY
Brands:
   Pura Still
   Genesee Brewing
   Labatt USA
   Cream Ale
   Friends Fun Wine
   Seagram'S Escapades
   Hemptails
   Magic Hat Brewing
   Pyramid Brewing
   Portland Brewing
   Honey Brown Lager
   Imperial
   GBH

9118 North American Coffees
1 Cattano Ave
Suite 2
Morriston, NJ 07960
973-359-0300
Fax: 973-359-0440
Coffee, tea
President: Michael Cahill
Estimated Sales: $1-10 Million
Number Employees: 25

9119 North American Enterprises
4330 N Campbell Ave Ste 256
Tucson, AZ 85718
520-885-0110
Fax: 520-298-9733 800-817-8666
www.capitanelli.com
Importer/distributor of olive oil, oil, balsamic vinegar, pasta sauces, salad dressings and biscotti; importer of Italian dry pasta and gourmet products
Owner: Joe Lovallo
VP Marketing: Grant Lovallo
National Sales Manager: Tim Champa
Contact: Joe Goodrich
jgoodrich@hazloc.net
Estimated Sales: $10-20 Million
Number Employees: 10-19
Square Footage: 4600
Type of Packaging: Consumer, Food Service
Brands:
   Capitanelli Fine Foods
   Capitanelli Specialty Foods
   Capitanelli's
   Loison Panetoni
   Rummo Gourmet Imported Pasta

9120 North American Reishi/Nammex
PO Box 1780
Gibsons, BC V0N 1V0
Canada
604-886-7799
Fax: 604-648-8954 info@nammex.com
www.nammex.com

Food Manufacturers / A-Z

Processor and exporter of standardized and certified organic mushroom extracts; also, whole dried mushrooms and mushroom mycelia
President: Jeffrey Chilton
Estimated Sales: $1.2 Million
Number Employees: 6
Type of Packaging: Bulk

9121 North American Water Group
8300 College Boulevard
Overland Park, KS 66210-1841
913-469-1156
Fax: 913-451-9418
Bottled water
President: Roger Hood
COO: Lee Dancer
Estimated Sales: $5-10 000,000
Number Employees: 1

9122 North Atlantic Inc
12 Portland Fish Pier # A
Portland, ME 04101-4620
207-774-6025
Fax: 207-774-1614 www.northatlanticseafood.com
President: Jerry Knecht
jerry@northatlanticseafood.com
Estimated Sales: $10-20 Million
Number Employees: 10-19

9123 North Atlantic Products
232 Buttermilk Ln
South Thomaston, ME 04858-3003
207-596-0331
Fax: 207-596-0532
Seafood

9124 North Atlantic Seafood
12a Portland Fish Pier
PO Box 682
Portland, ME 4101
207-774-6025
800-774-6025
info@northatlanticseafood.com
www.northatlanticseafood.com
Seafood including, bass, flounder, clams, cod, emperor, grouper, haddock, hake, halibut, lobster, mahi mahi, monk, mussels, oysters, perch, pollack, salmon, scallops, seabass, shark, shrimp, snapper, swordfish, tilapia, tuna andsole
Owner and Founder: Gerald Knecht
Chief Executive Officer: Terry Harriman
CFO: Stewart Wooden
VP & General Manager: Michael Norton
Quality Assurance Specialist: Jon Greenberg
Senior Sales Team Leader: Chris Bowker
Shipping/Receiving & Production Lead: Patrick Malia
Director of Procurement: Kevin Bolduc
Number Employees: 10-19

9125 North Bay Fisherman's Cooperative
Wharf Road
RR 4
Ballantyne's Cove, NS B2G 2L2
Canada
902-863-4988
Fax: 902-863-1112
Fresh and frozen lobster, scallops and groundfish; exporter of tuna
Manager: Kim MacDonald
Number Employees: 5-9
Type of Packaging: Consumer, Food Service, Private Label, Bulk

9126 North Bay Produce Inc
1771 N US Highway 31 S
Traverse City, MI 49685-8748
231-946-1941
Fax: 231-946-1902
marketing@northbayproduce.com
www.northbayproduce.com
Cooperative, importer and exporter of fresh produce including apples, asparagus, blueberries, cherries, peaches, plums, snow peas, sugar snaps, mangos, raspberries, blackberries, red currants, etc.; also, apple cider.
President: Mark Girardin
National Marketing Manager: Sharon Robb
Facilities & Compliance Manager: Jonathan Wall
Estimated Sales: $73 Million
Number Employees: 20-49
Number of Brands: 1
Square Footage: 15000
Type of Packaging: Consumer, Food Service, Private Label, Bulk
Other Locations:
North Bay Produce Warehouse Miami FL
North Bay Produce Warehouse Mascoutah IL
Brands:
North Bay

9127 North Bay Trading Co
13904 E US Highway 2
Brule, WI 54820-9038
715-372-5031
800-348-0164
borg@cheqnet.net www.northbaytrading.com
Organic and Canadian wild rice, heirloom beans, dehydrated vegetables, dry soup mixes
Owner: Greggar Isaksen
greggar@northbaytrading.com
Estimated Sales: $160,000
Number Employees: 5-9
Number of Brands: 2
Number of Products: 6
Type of Packaging: Consumer, Food Service, Bulk
Brands:
Brule Valley
North Bay Trading Company

9128 North Coast Farms
340 Woodpecker Ridge
Santa Cruz, CA 95060
831-426-3733
Fax: 831-426-5666 www.northcoastfarms.com
Processors of dressings: rasberry vinaigrette, maple dijon vinaigrette and apricot viniagrette, pancake and waffle mixes, wild rice, spices, seasoning, muffins

9129 North Coast Processing
5451 Avenida Encinas
Suite D
Carlsbad, CA 92008
814-725-9617
Fax: 814-725-4374 760-931-6809
info@northcoastphoto.com
www.northcoastphoto.com
Processor and contract packager of salad dressings, sauces, marinades and dry seasonings
President: Richard H Shute
Operations Manager: Tom Barnes
Plant Manager: Wilson Haller
Estimated Sales: $13 Million
Number Employees: 10-19
Square Footage: 50000
Type of Packaging: Consumer, Food Service, Private Label, Bulk
Brands:
Den
Garden Goodness

9130 North Country Natural Spring Water
P.O.Box 123
Port Kent, NY 12911
518-834-9400
Fax: 518-834-9429
Processor and importer of natural spring water
President: Roger Jakubowski
Estimated Sales: $1-3 Million
Number Employees: 10-19
Square Footage: 44000
Type of Packaging: Consumer, Food Service, Private Label, Bulk
Brands:
Loyola Springs
North Country

9131 North Country Smokehouse
471 Sullivan St
Claremont, NH 03743-5147
603-543-0234
Fax: 603-543-3016 800-258-4304
mike@ncsmokehouse.com
www.ncsmokehouse.com
Smoked hams, applewood bacon, smoked turkey, sausages, chicken and duck, brisket, cheeses and spreads and gifts
Owner: Mike Satzow
mike@ncsmokehouse.com
Estimated Sales: $6 Million
Number Employees: 20-49
Square Footage: 60000
Brands:
North Country Smokehouse

9132 North Dakota Mill & Elevator Assn.
1823 Mill Rd.
Grand Forks, ND 58208-3078
800-538-7721
ndm-store@ndmill.com www.ndmill.com
Flour including semolina, durum, wheat and high-gluten.
President/CEO: Vance Taylor
CFO: Ed Barchenger
Vice President, Grain Procurement: Jeff Bertsch
Vice President, Quality Assurance: Bob Sombke
Vice President, Sales: Russ Bischof
Vice President, Production Operations: Chris Lemoine
Year Founded: 1922
Estimated Sales: $262.66 Million
Number Employees: 100-249
Square Footage: 18000
Type of Packaging: Consumer, Food Service, Private Label, Bulk
Brands:
Dakota Maid

9133 North Lake Fish Cooperative
RR 1
Elmira, PE C0A 1K0
Canada
902-357-2572
Fax: 902-357-2386 www.gov.pe.ca/fard
Processor and exporter of fresh and frozen scallops, skate, silversides and lobster
President: Walter Bruce
CEO/General Manager: Mickey Rose
Number Employees: 100-249
Type of Packaging: Bulk

9134 North Pacific Seafoods Inc
4 Nickerson St
Suite 400
Seattle, WA 98109
206-726-9900
Fax: 206-352-7421
www.northpacificseafoods.com
Wild Alaska seafood products.
President: Hisashi Sugiyama

9135 North Peace Apiaries
RR1 Station Main
Fort St. John, BC V1J 4H5
Canada
250-785-4808
Fax: 250-785-2664
Processor and exporter of honey and bee pollen
President: Ernie Fuhr
Secretary/Treasurer: Rose Fuhr
Estimated Sales: $496,000
Number Employees: 3
Square Footage: 15120
Type of Packaging: Consumer

9136 North River Roasters
8 North Cherry St.
Poughkeepsie, NY 12601
845-418-2739
hello@northriverroasters.com
www.northriverroasters.com
Micro-roasted, small batch fair trade organic whole bean coffee; sourced from Mexico & Peru
Founder/Owner: Feza Oktay
Year Founded: 2015
Number of Brands: 1
Number of Products: 4
Type of Packaging: Consumer, Private Label
Brands:
North River Roasters

9137 North Shore Bottling Co
1900 Linden Blvd
Brooklyn, NY 11207-6806
718-272-8900
Fax: 718-649-2596 www.nsbottle.com
Soft drinks, juices, food, and household items
President: Eric Miller
eric@brooklynbottling.com
VP/General Manager: Tom Deluca
Marketing Director: Karen Miller
Estimated Sales: $20-50 Million
Number Employees: 50-99
Brands:
Ballantine Ale

Food Manufacturers / A-Z

Country Club Malt Liquor
Gold Crown Lager
Iberia Malt Liquor
Laser Malt Liquor
Pony Malta
Private Stock Malt Liquor
Tornado Malt Liquor

9138 North Taste Flavourings
71 Rte 320
Anse-Bleue, NB E8N 2B7
Canada
506-732-0010
Fax: 506-732-5370 joel.albert@northtaste.ca
www.northtaste.ca
All-natural seafood flavors for soups, bisques, chowders, spreads, dips, sauces, stuffings, and other seafood dishes
President: Julien Albert
Research & Production Manager: Dr. Eric Albert
Quality Control Supervisor: Johanne Doucet
VP Sales & Marketing: Joel Albert
VP US Sales & Product Development: Jerry Levine
Director of Asian Sales: K. Nunokawa
Square Footage: 56000

9139 North West Pharmanaturals Inc
1000 Beacon St
Brea, CA 92821-2938
714-529-0980
Fax: 714-577-0985
Dietary supplements and herbal products in tablet and capsule form; manufacturer of soft gelatin capsule machines and ancillary equipment; also, custom grinding and granulation available
President: Jack Brown
jack@northwestpn.com
Operations Manager: Margaret Haines
Estimated Sales: $$10-20 Million
Number Employees: 10-19
Square Footage: 40000
Type of Packaging: Private Label, Bulk

9140 North of the Border
PO Box 433
Tesuque, NM 87574
505-982-0681
Fax: 505-820-2108 800-860-0681
gaytherg@comcast.net
Salsa, chile sauce, chile seasoning, BBQ/Hot sauce, catchup, and soups
Owner: Gayther Gonzales
Estimated Sales: $.5-1 million
Number Employees: 1-4

9141 Northampton Brewing Company
11 Brewster Ct
Northampton, MA 01060
413-584-9903
Fax: 413-584-9972
info@northamptonbrewery.com
www.northamptonbrewery.com
Beer, ale, lager, stout and seasonal
Manager: Jessica Bellingham
Estimated Sales: Less than $500,000
Number Employees: 50-99
Type of Packaging: Consumer, Food Service
Brands:
  Northampton

9142 (HQ)Northeast Foods Inc
601 S Caroline St
Baltimore, MD 21231
800-769-2867
www.nefoods.com
Baked goods
President & CEO: Bill Paterakis
Year Founded: 1965
Number Employees: 100-249

9143 Northeast Kingdom Mustard Company
259 Derby Pond Road
Derby, VT 05829
802-766-2700
Fax: 802-766-2702 866-478-7388
wheeler@jedsmaple.com www.jedsmaple.com
Mustard, chutneys, jalapeno pepper jelly
Co-Owner: Steve Wheeler
Co-Owner: Amy Wheeler
Parent Co: Jed's Maple Products
Type of Packaging: Bulk

9144 Northeastern Products Company
P.O.Box 40
S Plainfield, NJ 07080
908-561-1660
Fax: 908-769-9200
Food flavorings
President: Paul Schiavi
CEO: Doug Connant
Controller: Tom Mathern
Marketing Director: Tina Hatten
Estimated Sales: Below $5 000,000
Number Employees: 50
Brands:
  Northeastern

9145 Northern Breweries
Sault Ste.
Marie, ON P3C 4P6
Canada
514-908-7545
Fax: 705-675-2926 info@northernbreweries.com
www.northernbreweries.com
Ale
President: William R Sharp
Manager: James Kaminski
Number Employees: 10-19
Parent Co: Northern Breweries
Type of Packaging: Consumer, Food Service
Brands:
  Northern

9146 Northern Dairy
3600 River Rd
Franklin Park, IL 60131-2152
847-671-2697
Dairy
President: Dick Bailey
CEO/Chairman: Howard Dean
VP Finance/CFO: William McManaman
Director Marketing/Advertising: Dave Rotunno
Corporate Purchasing: Jim Merret
Packing Buyer: Marvin Byrd
VP Frozen Desserts: Gary Cates
Parent Co: Dean Foods Company

9147 Northern Discovery Seafoods
E 5051 Grapeview Lp Rd
Grapeview, WA 98546
360-275-7246
Fax: 360-275-7245 800-843-6921
Seafood
President: Natalie Schonberg
VP: Kristian Schonberg
Number Employees: 3

9148 Northern Falls
7667 Spring Point Ct Ne
Rockford, MI 49341-8658
616-915-0970
Bottled water including caffeinated drinking, spring and flavored
Owner: John Neall
Estimated Sales: $1 Million
Number Employees: 25
Type of Packaging: Consumer, Private Label

9149 Northern Farmhouse Pasta LLC
65 Rockland Rd.
Roscoe, NY 12776
607-290-4064
northernfarmhousepasta@gmail.com
www.northernfarmhousepasta.com
Manufacturer of pasta.
Co-Founder: Bob Eckert

9150 Northern Feed & Bean Company
33278 Us Highway 85
Lucerne, CO 80646
970-352-7875
Fax: 970-352-7833 800-316-2326
mail@nfbean.com www.northernfeedandbean.com
Manufacturer and exporter of dried pinto beans
Manager: Larry Lande
Estimated Sales: $4.6 Million
Number Employees: 14
Square Footage: 27048
Type of Packaging: Consumer, Food Service, Private Label
Brands:
  Frontier

9151 Northern Flair Foods
3247 Gladstone Ln
Mound, MN 55364
952-472-2444
Fax: 952-472-7444 888-530-4453
markgoldberg@yahoo.com
Gourmet chocolate and candies
President: Mark Goldberg
CEO: Stacy Goldberg
Estimated Sales: $5-10 000,000
Number Employees: 5-9
Brands:
  Heavenly Bees
  Malto Bella

9152 Northern Keta Caviar
5720 Concrete Way
Juneau, AK 99801-7813
907-586-6095
Fax: 907-586-6094
Salmon caviar
President/CEO: Elisabeth Babich
VP: Sean Fansler
Production Manager: Sean Fansler
Plant Manager: Mark Hiermonymus
Estimated Sales: $1-10 Million
Number Employees: 25

9153 Northern Lights Brewing Company
1701 S Lawson
Airway Heights, WA 99001
509-242-2739
Beer
Owner: Mark Irvin
Head Chef: Lane Truesdell
Estimated Sales: $2.5-5 Million
Number Employees: 5-9
Brands:
  Chocolate Dunkel
  Crystal Bitter

9154 Northern Meats
163 E 54th Ave
Anchorage, AK 99518-1227
907-561-1729
Fax: 907-561-6848
Meats
President: Jerry Urling
Estimated Sales: $10-20 Million
Number Employees: 1-4

9155 Northern Neck
15725 Kings Highway
Montross, VA 22520
804-493-8051
Fax: 804-493-9109 804-493-8051
www.realgingerale.com
Soft drink bottling
President: John Adams
CEO: Gregory Purcell
Chief Marketing Officer: Charles B Fruit
Public Relations: Arthur Carver
Director Manufacturing: Richard Landon
Estimated Sales: $1-1.7 Million
Number Employees: 18
Brands:
  Alive
  Aquarious
  Carvers Original
  Diet Lift
  Fanta
  Finlay

9156 Northern Ocean Marine
7 Parker St
Gloucester, MA 01930-3025
978-283-0222
Fax: 978-283-5577
Seafood
Owner: Jim Lebouf
Sales & Marketing: Deke Fyrberg
Estimated Sales: $1.4 Million
Number Employees: 5-9

9157 Northern Orcharad Co Inc
537 Union Rd
Peru, NY 12972-4664
518-643-2367
Fax: 518-643-2751 northernorchard@verizon.net
www.northernorchard.com
Wholesaler/distributor, exporter and packer of macintosh apples and honey

Food Manufacturers / A-Z

President: Albert Mulbury
Contact: Samson Church
schurch@northernorchard.com
Estimated Sales: $1,950,266
Number Employees: 20-49
Type of Packaging: Consumer
Brands:
    Champlain Valley

9158 Northern Packing Company
2522 Rr 37
Brier Hill, NY 13614
    315-375-8801
    Fax: 315-375-8273
Packer of fresh and frozen beef
President: John Perretta
Estimated Sales: $3,300,000
Number Employees: 20
Type of Packaging: Consumer

9159 Northern Products Corporation
1932 1st Ave
Suite 705
Seattle, WA 98101-1040
    206-448-6677
    Fax: 206-448-9664 888-599-6290
Processor and exporter of frozen salmon, cod, halibut, flounder, pollock, squid, and rockfish
President: William Dignon
Plant Manager: Terry Barry
Estimated Sales: $1-3 Million
Number Employees: 1-4
Type of Packaging: Private Label, Bulk

9160 Northern Soy Inc
345 Paul Rd
Rochester, NY 14624-4925
    585-235-8970
    Fax: 585-235-3753 info@soyboy.com
    www.soyboy.com
All-natural organic tofu, organic tempeh and soy products
President: Norman Holland
norman@soyboy.com
Vice President: Andrew Schecter
Estimated Sales: $5-10 Million
Number Employees: 20-49
Number of Brands: 1
Number of Products: 24
Square Footage: 140000
Type of Packaging: Consumer, Food Service, Private Label, Bulk
Brands:
    Leaner Wiener
    Not Dogs
    Soyboy
    Tofu Lin

9161 Northern Utah Manufacturing
185 E 300 N
Wellsville, UT 84339
    435-245-4542
    Fax: 435-245-4542
Dry milk
Manager: David Bigelow
Estimated Sales: $2.5-5 Million
Number Employees: 20-49

9162 Northern Valley Baking Co
47 E Madison Ave
Dumont, NJ 07628-2417
    201-338-2812
    Fax: 201-338-2812 info@nvbaking.com
Manufacturer of macaroons and g'nache.
Co-Founder: Tricia Vanech
Co-Founder: Elyse Pressner
Co-Founder: Eve Megerle
Estimated Sales: Less Than $500,000
Number Employees: 1-4

9163 Northern Vineyards Winery
223 Main St N
Stillwater, MN 55082-5021
    651-430-1032
    Fax: 651-430-1331 info@northernvineyards.com
    www.northernvineyards.com
Wines
Manager: Cassie Pittman
VP: Ray Kenow
Manager: Robin Partch
robin@northernvineyards.com
Estimated Sales: Less than $500,000
Number Employees: 5-9
Type of Packaging: Private Label

Brands:
    Northern Vineyards

9164 Northern WIS Produce Co
1310 Clark St
Manitowoc, WI 54220-5109
    920-684-4461
    Fax: 920-684-4471
Cheese
Owner: Dave Litterman
Estimated Sales: $1-3 000,000
Number Employees: 10-19
Brands:
    Northern Wisconsin Cheese

9165 Northern Wind Inc
16 Hassey St
New Bedford, MA 02740-7209
    508-997-0727
    Fax: 508-990-8792 888-525-2525
    www.northernwind.com
Processor and exporter of fresh and frozen seafoods including; bay and sea scallops, farm-raised chilean mussels, farm-raised chilean atlantic salmon, hard shell north atlantic lobsters, monkfish, skate
Owner: Colleen Avila
CEO: Ken Melanson
VP: Betsy Borba
Sales Manager: Rick Moreno
sma1217@aol.com
Plant Manager: Michael Fernandes
Estimated Sales: $15.3 Million
Number Employees: 50-99
Number of Brands: 3
Number of Products: 3
Type of Packaging: Food Service, Private Label, Bulk
Brands:
    Captain's Call
    Mariner's Choice
    Ocean Request
    Sea Spray
    Bon Cuisine

9166 Northland Cranberries
20701 Main Street
Jackson, WI 53037
    262-677-2221
    Fax: 262-677-3647 866-719-5215
    www.northlandjuices.com
Fruit juices
Chairman/CEO: John Swendrowski
Plant Supervisor: Dave Carroll
Number Employees: 100-249
Square Footage: 768000
Type of Packaging: Consumer, Food Service, Private Label
Brands:
    Northland

9167 (HQ)Northland Juices
2 Seaview Blvd.
Port Washington, NY 11050
    608-252-4714
    Fax: 715-422-6800 866-719-5215
    www.northlandjuices.com
Fruit juice, juice concentrate, fresh and fozen
Chairman/CEO/Treasurer: John Swendrowski
President/COO: Ricke Kress
Number Employees: 218
Number of Brands: 5
Number of Products: 250
Type of Packaging: Consumer, Food Service, Bulk
Other Locations:
    Northland Cranberries
    Jackson WI
    Northland Cranberries
    Dundee NY
    Northland Cranberries
    Cornelius OR
    Northland Cranberries
    Wisconsin Rapids WI
Brands:
    Awake
    Meadow Valley
    Northland
    Seneca
    Treesweet

9168 Northridge Laboratories
20832 Dearborn St
Chatsworth, CA 91311
    818-882-5622
    Fax: 818-998-2815

Processor and exporter of vitamins, herbal supplements and protein powders
President: Brett Richman
CEO: Jane Richman
CFO: Charles Wands
Contact: Angie Armendariz
nrlabs@aol.com
Estimated Sales: $6400000
Number Employees: 50
Square Footage: 120000
Type of Packaging: Private Label

9169 Northside Bakery
149 N 8th St
Brooklyn, NY 11249-2001
    718-782-2700
    Fax: 718-782-7146
Breads and other baked goods
Owner: Richard Podedworny
info@oldpolandfoods.com
Co-Owner: Michael Hatcher
Estimated Sales: $480,000
Number Employees: 10-19

9170 Northumberland Dairy
256 Lawlor Lane
Miramichi, NB E1V 3M3
Canada
    506-627-7720
    800-501-1150
    info@northumberlanddairy.ca
    www.northumberlanddairy.ca
Dairy products including milk and cream; wholesaler/distributor of bottled water, ice cream, ice milk mix, fruit drinks and butter; serving the food service market
Director, Sales & Marketing: Paul Chiasson
Year Founded: 1942
Estimated Sales: $50 Million
Number Employees: 273
Number of Brands: 5
Square Footage: 79416
Parent Co: Agropur Dairy Co-Operative
Type of Packaging: Consumer, Food Service, Private Label
Brands:
    Frontier Water
    Jumbo Minisips
    Max Cranberry Cocktail
    Northshore Butter
    Northumberland

9171 (HQ)Northville Winery & Brewing Co
630 Baseline Rd
Northville, MI 48167-1265
    248-320-6507
    Fax: 248-349-1165 northvillewinery@gmail.com
    www.northvillewinery.com
Producer of ciders, wines and beers.
President: Diane Jones
Vice President: Cheryl Nelson
Estimated Sales: $180 Thousand
Number Employees: 1-4
Number of Brands: 1
Parent Co: Parmenter's Northville Cider Mill
Type of Packaging: Consumer, Food Service
Brands:
    Northville Winery

9172 Northwest Chocolate Factory
2162 Davcor Street SE
Salem, OR 97302-1510
    503-362-1340
    Fax: 503-362-0186 www.nwchocolate.com
Processor and exporter of chocolate covered hazelnuts
President: Sam Kaufman
General Manager: Dan Kaufman
Number Employees: 5-9
Square Footage: 40000
Type of Packaging: Consumer

9173 Northwest Fisheries
RR 1
Hubbards, NS B0J 1T0
Canada
    902-228-2232
    Fax: 902-228-2116
Processor and exporter of fresh lobster, cod and halibut
President: Olimpio Martins
Number Employees: 5-9

Food Manufacturers / A-Z

9174 Northwest Hazelnut Company
19748 Highway 99e
P.O.Box 276
Hubbard, OR 97032
503-982-8030
Fax: 503-982-8028
Vacuum-packed hazelnuts
President: Jeff Kenagy
Vice President: Lisa Pascoe
Contact: Verne Gingerich
verne.gingerich@nwhazelnut.com
Estimated Sales: $5-10 Million
Number Employees: 4
Type of Packaging: Consumer, Food Service, Private Label
Brands:
　Springhill

9175 Northwest Meat Company
440 N Morgan St
Chicago, IL 60642
312-733-1418
Fax: 312-733-1737
andrew@chicagowholesalemeats.com
www.chicagowholesalemeats.com
Beef, poultry, pork, veal, and lamb.
Owner: Stan Neva
Co-Owner: Lori Neva
Assistant/Office Manager: Audrey Ciota
Number Employees: 10-19

9176 Northwest Natural Foods
3805 56th Ave Ne
Olympia, WA 98506
360-866-9661
Fax: 360-866-0734
www.northwestnaturalfoods.com
Fresh and frozen fish/seafood
Owner: Gene Maltiziffs
President: Euegene Maltzess
Contact: Eugene Maltzeff
eugene.maltzeff@nwnatural.com
Estimated Sales: $300,000
Number Employees: 8
Square Footage: 20000
Type of Packaging: Private Label
Brands:
　Medallions

9177 Northwest Naturals LLC
11805 N Creek Pkwy S # 104
Bothell, WA 98011-8803
425-881-2200
Fax: 425-881-3063　nwn@nwnaturals.com
Processor, importer and exporter of concentrates including juice and iced coffee and fruit beverages and flavors
Vice President: Mike Marquand
mikem@nwnaturals.com
CEO: James
VP Sales and Administration: Mike Marquand
VP Operations: Danny Shaffer
Estimated Sales: $5-10 Million
Number Employees: 20-49
Number of Brands: 4
Number of Products: 50
Square Footage: 120000
Parent Co: Tree Top
Type of Packaging: Consumer, Food Service, Private Label, Bulk

9178 Northwest Packing Co
1701 W 16th St
PO Box 30
Vancouver, WA 98660-1067
360-696-4356
Fax: 831-637-7890　800-543-4356
www.neiljonesfoodcompany.com
Tomato products including ketchup, paste, sauce, stewed and cooked
President/COO: Matt Jones
CEO: L Neil Jones
Sales: David Watkins
Plant Manager: Mike Mullin
Estimated Sales: $20-50 Million
Number Employees: 100-249
Parent Co: Northwest Packing
Type of Packaging: Consumer, Food Service, Private Label, Bulk
Brands:
　San Benito

9179 Northwest Pea & Bean Co
6109 E Desmet Ave
Spokane Valley, WA 99212-1254
509-534-3821
Fax: 509-534-4350
Processor of lentils and green and yellow peas.
Manager: Brett Stauffer
Logistics Coordinator: Tim Kochel
Estimated Sales: $32 Million
Number Employees: 10-19
Number of Brands: 2
Parent Co: Cooperative Agricultural Producers
Type of Packaging: Food Service, Private Label, Bulk
Brands:
　Empire
　Speedy Cook'n

9180 Northwest Wild Products
354 Industry St.
Astoria, OR 97103
503-791-1907
amanda@northwestwildproducts.com
www.northwestwildproducts.com
Seafood including oysters, Dungeness crab, live lobster, Manila clams, Chinook salmon, coho salmon, wild sturgeon, razor clams, albacore tuna, ling cod, black cod, halibut, crayfish, dover sole, shrimp, scallops, sardines, mackerel, anchovies, squid, mussels, and red snapper; Also exotic meats
Co-Owner: Amanda Cordero
Co-Owner: Ron Neva
Number Employees: 1-4

9181 Northwestern Coffee Mills
20146 Soderlund Rd
Mason, WI 54856-6300
715-746-2100
Fax: 715-747-5405　800-243-5283
sales@northwesterncoffeemills.com
www.northwesterncoffeemills.com
Coffee, tea, spices
President: Harry Demorest
Estimated Sales: Less Than $500,000
Number Employees: 1-4
Type of Packaging: Private Label
Brands:
　American Breakfast Blend
　Apostle Islands Organic Coffee
　Brazil Serra Negra
　Ice Road Blend-Darkest
　North Coast Tea & Sp
　Northwestern Coffee

9182 Northwestern Coffee Mills
30950 Nevers Rd
Washburn, WI 54891
715-373-2122
Fax: 715-747-5405　800-243-5283
Processor, importer and exporter of coffee and tea
Owner: Harry Demorest
Estimated Sales: Under $300,000
Number Employees: 1-4
Square Footage: 8000
Type of Packaging: Consumer, Food Service
Brands:
　American Breakfast Blend
　Backsettler Blend
　Badger Blend
　Baker's Blend
　Broadway Red
　Fancy Dinner Blend
　Ice Road
　Island Blend
　Morning Sun
　North Coast
　Orange Rose
　Sleepeasy
　Stapleton

9183 Northwestern Extract
W194n11250 Mccormick Dr # 1
Germantown, WI 53022-3049
262-345-6900
Fax: 262-781-0660　800-466-3034
flavors@nwextract.com
www.northwesternextract.com
Flavorings and extracts
President: William Peter
CEO: Megan Bruzan
megan@nwextract.com
Marketing Director: Patricia Hein
Purchasing Manager: Michael Peter
Estimated Sales: $5-10 Million
Number Employees: 10-19
Square Footage: 40000
Type of Packaging: Consumer, Food Service, Private Label, Bulk
Brands:
　Northwestern
　Sparkle

9184 Northwestern Foods
1260 Grey Fox Road
Arden Hills, MN 55112
651-644-8060
Fax: 651-644-8248　800-236-4937
northwestern.n2ocompanies.com
Mixes including cocoa, cake, pancake, cappuccino, iced tea, power drinks and pizza dough
President: Kurt Kiaser
CEO: Bob Schafer
Vice President: Mimie Pollard
Sales Manager: Bob Freemore
Contact: Linda Petersen
lpetersen@n2ocompanies.com
Purchasing Manager: Nadine Vandeventer
Estimated Sales: $10-20 Million
Number Employees: 20-49
Square Footage: 48000
Type of Packaging: Consumer, Food Service, Private Label, Bulk

9185 Northwoods Candy Emporium
103 Branson Landing Blvd
Branson, MO 65616-2097
417-332-1010
info@northwoodscandy.com
www.northwoodscandy.com
Gourmet candy and cookies
Owner: Dennis Anderson
Production Manager: Al Hyde
Number Employees: 5-9
Brands:
　Espress-Umms
　Grandma's Recipe
　Northwest Espresso B

9186 Norwalk Dairy
13101 Rosecrans Ave
Santa Fe Springs, CA 90670
562-921-5712
Fax: 562-921-5573
Milk including whole, kosher, reduced, nonfat and chocolate
VP: Tanya Vanderham
President: John Vanderham
Estimated Sales: $500,000-$1,000,000
Number Employees: 5-9
Type of Packaging: Consumer, Food Service
Brands:
　Norwalk Dairy

9187 Nossack Fine Meats
7240 Johnstone Dr
Suite 100
Red Deer, AB T4P 3Y6
Canada
403-346-5006
Fax: 403-343-8066　www.nossack.com
Roast and corned beef, pastrami, sausage and ham; also, garlic rings and pizza products
President: Karsten Nossack
Manager of Finance: Ingrid Nossack
Estimated Sales: $27 Million
Number Employees: 70
Square Footage: 22000
Type of Packaging: Consumer, Food Service
Brands:
　Butcher's Pride
　Nossack

9188 Nostalgic Specialty Foods
399 S Federal Hwy
Boca Raton, FL 33432
561-391-8600
Gourmet and specialty foods
Owner: Leonard Felberbaum
Estimated Sales: $330,000
Number Employees: 6

Food Manufacturers / A-Z

9189 Nothin' But Foods
9 Bourmar Place
Elmwood Park, NJ 07407
203-557-8637
info@nothinbutfoods.com
www.nothinbutfoods.com
Snack bars and granola cookies.
Founder: Jerri Graham

9190 Nothing But The Fruit
300 Baker Ave
Suite 101
Concord, MA 01742-2131
978-341-1221
Fruit bites and fruit jerky
Brand Assistant: Olivia Dynan
Number of Brands: 1
Number of Products: 10
Brands:
　NOTHING BUT THE FRUIT

9191 Notre Dame Bakery
26 Wildwood Subdiv
Conception Harbour, NL A1X 7J8
Canada
709-535-2738
Fax: 709-535-3406
Bread products, pies, cookies and muffins
President: John Mullett
Owner: Larry Mullett
Owner/Sales: Paula Mullett
CEO: John Mullett
Estimated Sales: $531,000
Number Employees: 8
Brands:
　Humpty Dumpty Chips
　Nestle Chocolates

9192 Notre Dame Seafoods Inc.
PO Box 201
Comfort Cove, NL A0G 3K0
Canada
709-244-5511
Fax: 709-244-3451
jeveleigh@notredameseafoods.com
www.notredameseafoods.com
Processor and exporter of canned and frozen crab, cod, turbit, capelin, squid, mackerel, lumpfish, roe and lobster
President & COO: Jason Eveleigh
VP/General Manager: Rex Eveleigh
Number Employees: 250-499
Parent Co: Provincial Investments
Type of Packaging: Consumer, Food Service

9193 Nourishtea
222 Islington Ave
Suite 6C
Toronto, ON M8V 3W7
Canada
416-539-9299
info@nourishtea.ca
www.nourishtea.ca
Herbal tea, black tea, green tea
Year Founded: 2007

9194 Nouveau Foods
Mountain View, CA
www.lotuspops.com
Flavored, roasted lotus seeds
Number of Brands: 1
Number of Products: 6
Brands:
　LOTUS POPS

9195 Novozymes North America Inc
77 Perrys Chapel Church Rd
Franklinton, NC 27525-9677
919-494-3000
Fax: 919-494-3450 800-879-6686
enzymesna@novozymes.com
www.novozymes.com
Enzymes
President: Adam Monroe
ad@novozymes.com
EVP & CFO: Benny Loft
EVP & CSO: Per Falholt
Director Purchasing: Percy Taylor
Estimated Sales: $40 Million
Number Employees: 1000-4999
Parent Co: Novozymes
Type of Packaging: Bulk

9196 Now & Zen
908 Main St
Suite 130
Louisville, CO 80027-1867
720-508-3945
Fax: 303-530-6945 800-779-6383
www.now-zen.com
Whipped toppings including dairy-free, gluten-free and chocolate; also, vegan cookies, cakes, vegetarian turkey, steak, chicken and barbecue ribs
Founder & President: Steve McIntosh
Sales Director: Judy Stoffel
Operations Manager: Eleese Longino
Number Employees: 1-4
Number of Brands: 1
Number of Products: 15
Type of Packaging: Consumer, Food Service, Bulk
Brands:
　Bbq Unribs
　Chocolate Mousse Hip
　Hip Whip
　Unsteak-Out
　Unturkey

9197 Noyes, P J
89 Bridge St
Lancaster, NH 03584-3103
603-788-2848
Fax: 603-788-3873 800-522-2469
Liquids, tablets and capsules
President: David Hill
Quality Control Manager: Janet Christenson
Marketing Executive: Jim Hoverman
Sales/Marketing Manager: Jennifer Cusick
Contact: Alan Balog
alanb@pjnoyes.com
VP/COO: Dennis Wogaman
Production Manager: Steve Skinner
Estimated Sales: $10 Million
Number Employees: 5-9
Square Footage: 70000
Type of Packaging: Private Label, Bulk
Brands:
　Fishin' Chips
　Noyes Precision

9198 Nspired Natural Foods
4600 Sleepytime Dr
Boulder, CO 80301
800-434-4246
Dried fruits, nuts and trail mixes
Chairman: Charles Lynch
CEO: Gordon Chapple
Number Employees: 5-9
Square Footage: 40000
Other Locations:
　Nspired Natural Foods
　Melville NY

9199 Ntc Marketing
5680 Main St
Williamsville, NY 14221-5518
716-884-3345
Fax: 716-884-4680 800-333-1637
info@ntcmarketing.com
Processor and importer of canned products including pineapples, pineapple juice, tropical fruits, tropical fruit mix, mandarin orange
Owner/Principal: Michael Derose
mjderose@ntcmarketing.com
Human Resource Executive: Sue Godzala
Estimated Sales: $3.3 Million
Number Employees: 10-19
Square Footage: 40000
Type of Packaging: Consumer, Food Service, Private Label, Bulk
Brands:
　Libby's
　P/L
　Queen's Pride

9200 Nu Life Market
PO Box 105
Scott City, KS 67871
620-872-5236
Fax: 620-872-5019 866-962-5236
nulifemarket.com
Gluten-free sorghum flours, brans and grains
President/Owner: Earl Roemer
CFO: Kelsey Baker
VP, Sales & Marketing: Joshua Deschenes
Number of Brands: 1
Number of Products: 39
Brands:
　NU LIFE MARKET

9201 Nu Naturals Inc
2220 W 2nd Ave
Suite 1
Eugene, OR 97402-7112
541-344-9785
Fax: 541-343-0915 800-753-4372
info@nunaturals.com www.nunaturals.com
Health products including diet nutrients, odorless garlic, vitamins, minerals, amino acids, green tea, herbs, extracts, etc.
Owner & CEO: Warren Sablosky
warren@nunaturals.com
Estimated Sales: $6+ Million
Number of Brands: 17
Number of Products: 78
Square Footage: 32000
Type of Packaging: Consumer, Private Label, Bulk
Brands:
　Alcohol Free Stevia
　Brain Herbs
　Brain Well
　Calm Mind
　Clear Stevia
　Daily Energy
　Daily Soy
　Extra Energy
　Fast Asleep
　Gentle Change
　Joint Well
　Level Right
　Losweet
　Mellowmind
　Mental Energy Formula
　Preventin Green Tea
　Sweet 'n Healthy
　Sweet-X
　Throat Control Spray
　Travel Well
　Wellness Drops
　White Stevia

9202 Nu Products Co Inc
74 Louis Ct
South Hackensack, NJ 07606-1727
201-440-0065
Fax: 201-440-0096 800-836-7692
spice@aol.com www.nuproductsseasoning.com
Suppliers of food seasonings
Owner: Henry Goldstein
sirspice@aol.com
Marketing Director: Jim Sandler
CFO: Celia Hester
Estimated Sales: Below $5 Million
Number Employees: 20-49
Type of Packaging: Bulk
Brands:
　Nu

9203 Nu-Tek Food Science
5400 Opportunity Ct
Suite 120
Minnetouka, MN 55343
952-683-7580
Fax: 952-933-1396 info@nu-tekfoodscience.com
www.nu-tekfoodscience.com
Potassium chloride based sodium reduction products used for meat, cheese, poultry, bakery, snack foods, soups, sauces, gravies and spice blends. Salt reductions of 25-50%
President: Tom Yezzi
Director of Accounts Receivable/Payable: Kent McCoy
Director of Quality & Technical: Dustin Grossbier
Sr Director of Sales: John Musselman
Sr VP of Sales & Marketing: Dave Hickey
Contact: Dan Hagebak
dhagebak@nu-tekfoodscience.com
Sales Coordinator: Rob Manuel

9204 Nu-Way Potato Products
25 Colville Road
North York, ON M6M 2Y2
Canada
416-241-9151
Fax: 416-241-8274 joe@nuwaypotato.com
www.nuwaypotato.com
Fresh potatoes
President: Mike Sangiorgio
Office Manager: Nelson Ardon
Marketing Manager: Joe Montalbano
Office Manager: Nelson Ardon

Food Manufacturers / A-Z

Estimated Sales: $15 Million
Number Employees: 35
Type of Packaging: Consumer, Food Service

9205 Nu-World Amaranth Inc
552 S Washington St # 120
Suite #107
Naperville, IL 60540-6669
630-369-6851
Fax: 630-369-6851
customerservice@nuworldfoods.com
Manufacturer and exporter of amaranth-based products including popped, flour, pre-baked flat bread, sancks and cereal. Offers foods that are allergy free and gluten free foods
Founder/Co-Owner: Larry Walters
President: Susan Walters-Flood
CFO: Jim Behling
Vice President: Terry Walters
t.walters@nuworldamaranthinc.com
Manager/Co-Owner: Diane Walters
VP Production: Terry Walters
Estimated Sales: Under $500,000
Number Employees: 10-19
Number of Brands: 2
Number of Products: 15
Square Footage: 10800
Type of Packaging: Consumer, Private Label, Bulk
Brands:
   Nu-World Amaranth

9206 Nu-World Foods
552 S Washington Street
Suite 107
Naperville, IL 60540
630-369-6819
Fax: 630-369-6851 877-692-8899
Amaranth-based food products
Contact: Marissa Kopp
marissa@nuworldfoods.com

9207 NuGo Nutrition
520 Second St
Oakmont, PA 15139
412-828-4115
888-421-2032
www.nugonutrition.com
Dark chocolate-coated protein bars
President/Owner: David Levine
dlevine@nugonutrition.com
VP: Steven Smith
Director of Marketing: Alyssa Nard
Estimated Sales: $1.3 Million
Number Employees: 5-9
Type of Packaging: Consumer

9208 NuLeaf Naturals
1550 Larimer St
Suite 964
Denver, CO 80202
720-372-4842
contact@nuleafnaturals.com
nuleafnaturals.com
Organic CBD oil
President/Owner: Jaden Barnes
Year Founded: 2014

9209 NuNaturals
2220 West 2nd Ave
Eugene, OR 97402
Fax: 541-683-5268 800-753-4372
support@nunaturals.com www.nunaturals.com
Stevia sweeteners, baking goods and collagens
President/Owner: Jake Sablosky
Founder & CEO: Warren Sablosky
General Manager: Travis DeBacker
Number of Brands: 1
Brands:
   NUNATURALS

9210 NuPasta
55 Valleywood Dr
Markham, ON L3R 5L9
Canada
855-910-8800
www.nupasta.com
Konjac-based, gluten-free pasta
President/Owner: Stephen Cheung
Number of Brands: 1
Number of Products: 6
Brands:
   NUPASTA

9211 NuZee, Inc.
2865 Scott St
Suite 107
Vista, CA 92081
844-696-8933
coffeeblenders.com
Functional coffee beverages
President/Owner: Travis Gorney
Type of Packaging: Private Label
Brands:
   Coffee Blenders

9212 Nuchief Sales Inc
2710 Euclid Ave
Wenatchee, WA 98801-5914
509-663-2625
Fax: 509-662-0299 888-269-4638
nuchief@nwi.net
Grower, packer and exporter of apples and pears
President: Randy Steensma
randy@honeybear-nuchief.com
VP: Dave Battis
Quality Control: Ray Vespier
Sales: Joe Defina
Estimated Sales: $279.000
Number Employees: 5-9
Number of Brands: 5
Number of Products: 10
Type of Packaging: Consumer, Food Service
Brands:
   Big Check
   Crane & Crane
   Keystone

9213 Nueces Canyon Range
9501 Highway 290 W
Brenham, TX 77833-9138
979-289-5600
Fax: 979-289-2411 800-925-5058
nueces@nuescescanyon.com
www.nuescescanyon.com
Smoked meats including briskets, hams, quail, etc., also meat seasonings
Owner: Angele Caloudas
nueces@nuescescanyon.com
Estimated Sales: Less Than $500,000
Number Employees: 5-9
Square Footage: 40000
Parent Co: Nueces Canyon Ranch
Type of Packaging: Consumer, Food Service

9214 Nueske's Applewood Smoked Meat
203 N Genesee St
Wittenberg, WI 54499-9154
715-253-4000
Fax: 715-253-4021 800-720-1153
nueske@nueske.com www.nueskes.com
Smoked meats including bacon, ham, sausage and specialty items
President: Robert Nueske
Cmo: Gilbert Thompson
gthompson@nueske.com
VP: James Nueske
Marketing: Tanya Nueske
Number Employees: 100-249

9215 Nui Foods
112 E Orangethorpe Ave
Anaheim, CA 92801
support@eatnui.com
www.eatnui.com
Low carb, low sugar cookies
Co-Founder: Victor Macias
Co-Founder/CEO: Kristoffer Quiaoit
Research & Development Manager: Juan Altamirano
Marketing Manager: Valerie Bui
Year Founded: 2016

9216 Nulaid Foods Inc
200 W 5th St
Ripon, CA 95366-2793
209-599-2121
Fax: 209-599-5220 www.nulaid.com
Egg products
President: David Crockett
CEO: Christopher Barry
cbarry@bainbridge.com
CFO: Scott Hennecke
Number Employees: 50-99
Type of Packaging: Consumer, Food Service, Private Label, Bulk
Brands:
   Nulaid

9217 Numi Organic Tea
PO Box 20420
Oakland, CA 94620
888-404-6864
info@numitea.com www.numitea.com
Tea
Co-Founder & Chief Brand Officer: Reem Rahim
Co-Founder & CEO: Ahmed Rahim
Brands:
   Numi(c)

9218 Numo Broth
1630 Oakland Rd
Unit A110
San Jose, CA 95131
nulifemarket.com
Brew-it-yourself bone broth kits
Founder: Faye Luong
Number of Brands: 1
Number of Products: 2
Brands:
   NUMO BROTH

9219 Nunes Co Inc
930 Johnson Ave
Salinas, CA 93901
831-751-7500
Fax: 831-424-4955 employment@foxy.com
www.foxy.com
Grower and exporter of vegetables
Owner: Susan Canales
CFO: Mike Scarr
VP: David Nunes
VP Marketing: Matt Seeley
VP Sales: Mark Crossgrove
scanales@foxyproduce.com
Production Manager: Jim Nunes
Estimated Sales: $11,100,000
Number Employees: 100-249
Type of Packaging: Consumer, Food Service, Bulk
Brands:
   Foxy
   Nunes
   Tubby

9220 Nunes Farms Marketing
4012 Pete Miller Rd
Gustine, CA 95322-9507
209-862-3033
Fax: 209-862-1038 www.nunesfarms.com
Processor and exporter of roasted almonds, mixed nuts and pistachios. candies toffee caramel chews, chocolate almonds and toffee almonds
Owner: Maureen Nunes
maureen@nunesfarms.com
Estimated Sales: Under $500,000
Number Employees: 10-19
Brands:
   Almond Chews
   California Crunchies
   Caramel Chews
   Chocolate Toffee Almonds
   Foxy Salads

9221 Nuovo Pasta ProductionsLTD
125 Bruce Ave
Stratford, CT 06615-6102
203-380-4090
Fax: 203-336-0656 800-803-0033
www.nuovopasta.com
Frozen and fresh ravioli, tortelloni, gnocchi, pasta, and pasta sauces
President: Carl Zuanelli
CFO: Santa Vega
Marketing: Larry Montuori
Contact: Franco Dibattista
franco@nuovopasta.com
Production: Joe Dubee
Estimated Sales: Less Than $500,000
Number Employees: 5-9
Type of Packaging: Consumer, Food Service

9222 Nurture
28 S Waterloo Rd
Devon, PA 19333-1574
610-293-0718
Fax: 610-989-0991 888-395-3300
Ingredients for nutritional products
President: H Griffith
Contact: Sarah Mazzone
sarah@happyfamilybrands.com

Food Manufacturers / A-Z

Estimated Sales: $1,800,000
Number Employees: 5-9
Brands:
  Nurture

9223 Nurture Ranch
2770 Main St
Suite 234
Frisco, TX 75033
866-467-2624
www.nurtureranch.com
Grass-fed ground beef, sirloin and jerky
CEO: Rodney Mason

9224 Nush Foods
333 W Hope Ave
Salt Lake City, UT 84115
801-953-1370
contact@nushfoods.com
nushfoods.com
Keto-friendly snack cakes
Founder: Muffy Mead-Ferro
Number of Brands: 1
Number of Products: 3
Brands:
  NUSH

9225 Nustef Foods
2440 Cawthra Road #101
Mississauga, ON L5A 2X1
Canada
905-896-3060
Fax: 905-896-4349 877-306-7562
info@pizzellecookies.com
Processor and exporter of pizzelle cookies and polenta
President: Cesidio Nucci
Estimated Sales: $4 Million
Number Employees: 60
Square Footage: 48000
Type of Packaging: Consumer, Food Service, Private Label, Bulk
Brands:
  Gold'n Polenta
  Gold'n Treats
  Reko

9226 Nut Factory
PO Box 815
Spokane Valley, WA 99016-0815
509-926-6666
Fax: 509-926-3300 888-239-5288
nuts@TheNutFactory.com www.thenutfactory.com
Processor, packager and importer of nuts and dried fruits
President: Gene Cohen
gene_cohen@yahoo.com
Estimated Sales: $1700000
Number Employees: 5-9
Type of Packaging: Consumer
Brands:
  Big Value
  Old Fashioned
  Party Pak
  Sunburst

9227 NutRaw Foods
Delano, CA
info@nutrawbar.com
www.nutrawfarms.com
Pistachio nut bars, oils and butters
Number of Brands: 1
Number of Products: 14
Brands:
  NUTRAWBAR
  NUTRAW SNACKS
  NUTRAW BUTTER
  NUTRAW OIL

9228 Nutfield Brewing Company
P.O. Box 40
Derry, NH 03038
603-434-9678
Fax: 603-434-1042
Ale, lager and stout
President: Jim Killeen
Sales Manager: Geoff Tyson
Estimated Sales: Below $5 Million
Number Employees: 5-9
Type of Packaging: Consumer, Food Service
Brands:
  Nutfield Auburn Ale
  Nutfield's Classic Root Beer

9229 Nutiva
213 West Cutting Blvd
Richmond, CA 94804
800-993-4367
help@nutiva.com
nutiva.com
Oils, baking ingredients, seeds and spreads
Founder: John Roulac
CEO: Steven Naccarato
EVP, Global Sales: Chris Amsler
Contact: Diana Albus
Plant Manager: Dave Mehrer

9230 Nutmeg Vineyard
PO Box 146
Andover, CT 06232-0146
860-742-8402
Wines
Owner: Anthony Maulucci
Type of Packaging: Private Label

9231 Nutorious LLC
2057 Bellevue St
Green Bay, WI 54311-5619
920-288-0483
Fax: 866-703-6595
Nuts
President/Owner: Carrie Liebhauser
Contact: Carrie Leiderhouser
carrie@nutoriousnuts.com
Number Employees: 5-9

9232 Nutpods
15900 SE Eastgate Way
Building B, Suite 125
Bellevue, WA 98008
800-977-6094
customerservice@nutpods.com www.nutpods.com
Non-dairy creamer
Founder & CEO: Madeline Haydon
CFO: Geoff Haydon
Sales: Mark Nunn
Operations: Tara Foster
Number of Brands: 1
Number of Products: 4
Brands:
  NUTPODS

9233 Nutra Food Ingredients, LLC
4683 50th Street SE
Kentwood, MI 49512
616-656-9928
Fax: 419-730-3685
sales@nutrafoodingredients.com
www.nutrafoodingredients.com
Functional and nutritional ingredients supplier to the food, beverage, nutraceutical and cosmetics industries
President: Bryon Yang
Director of Business Development: Tim Wolffis
Quality Control: Monica Mylet
monica.mylet@nutrafoodingredients.com
Director of Sales and Marketing: Clarence Harvey
Year Founded: 2004
Estimated Sales: Under $500,000
Number Employees: 1-4
Other Locations:
  Distribution Center
  Edison NJ
  Distribution Center
  Carson CA

9234 Nutra Nuts
4528 E Washington Blvd
Commerce, CA 90040
323-260-7457
Fax: 323-260-7459 gocorny@nutranuts.com
www.nutranuts.com
Snack mixture of organic popcorn and soybeans flavored with sea salt or natural spices or coated with organic sugar
President: Mark Porro
CFO: Michael Porro
Estimated Sales: $300,000-500,000
Number Employees: 1-4
Number of Brands: 1
Number of Products: 3
Square Footage: 13200
Type of Packaging: Consumer, Food Service, Bulk
Brands:
  Grandpa Po's Slightly Spicy
  Grandpa Po's Slightly Sweet
  Grandpa Po's Slightly Unsalted
  Nutra Nuts

9235 NutraSun
6201 E Primrose Green Dr
Regina, SK S4V 3L7
Canada
306-751-2040
Fax: 306-751-2047 info@nutrasunfoods.com
www.nutrasunfoods.com
Organic and conventional, non-GMO flour
Director of Business Development: Kelvin Maloney

9236 NutraSweet Company
222 Merchandise Mart Plaza
Suite 936
Chicago, IL 60606
312-873-5000
Fax: 312-873-5050 800-323-5321
ordernow@nutrasweet.com www.nutrasweet.com
Sweeteners
CEO: Craig Petray
President/COO: William DeFer
CFO: James Stanley
SVP/Sales & Marketing: Kevin Bauer
Director Nutritional Science: Maureen Mackey
Purchasing Manager: James Pumphrey
Estimated Sales: $8.80 Million
Number Employees: 417
Parent Co: JW Childs Associates
Brands:
  Equal
  Nutrasweet

9237 Nutraceutical International
1777 Sun Peak Dr.
Park City, UT 84098
435-655-6000
800-669-8877
info@nutraceutical.com www.nutraceutical.com
Supplements.
CEO: Chad Clawson
Vice President/CFO: Cory McQueen
Cheif Marketing Officer: John D'Alessandro
Senior VP, Sales: David Bunch
COO: Camilla Shumaker
Year Founded: 1993
Estimated Sales: $188.07 Million
Number Employees: 810
Square Footage: 6103
Type of Packaging: Consumer, Food Service, Bulk
Brands:
  Solaray
  KAL
  Food Source
  Sunny Green
  VegLife
  Veglife
  Allvia
  Complimed
  bioAllers
  Herbs for Kids
  NatraBio
  Homeopathy for Kids
  NaturalCare
  Nutra BioGenesis
  Oakmont Labs
  Pioneer
  VAXA
  Zand
  Nature's Herbs
  Natural Balance
  Natural Sport
  BuckPower
  FunFresh Foods
  Dowd & Rogers
  Miztique
  Paleo Planet
  Refrigerator Fresh
  Sweet Moose
  Taste Waves
  World Berries
  The Real Food Trading Co.
  Zylicious
  Spring Drops
  Honey Gardens
  Montana Big Sky
  Premier One

9238 Nutraceutical International
1400 Kearns Blvd # 2
2nd Floor
Park City, UT 84060-7228
435-655-6000
Fax: 435-647-3802 800-669-8877
info@nutraceutical.com www.nutraceutical.com

Manufacturer and exporter of vitamins, minerals and nutritional supplements
President: Bruce R Hough
bruce.hough@nutraceutical.com
CEO/Director/Chairman: Frank W. Gay II
CFO/ VP: Cory J. McQueen
bruce.hough@nutraceutical.com
Executive Vice President: Gary M. Hume
VP Marketing/Sales: Christopher B. Neuberger
Vice President, Operations: Darren Peterson
Estimated Sales: $500,000-$1 Million
Number Employees: 500-999
Type of Packaging: Consumer, Private Label, Bulk
Brands:
   Fentinel
   Keep
   Natural Health
   Un-Soap

9239 Nutraceutical International
6704 Ranger Ave
Corpus Christi, TX 78415-5908
361-854-0755
Fax: 361-855-8031 800-338-4788
www.nutraceutical.com
Sublingual/liquid vitamins
Owner: Jerry Clure
COO: Gracie Villarreal
gvillarreal@nutriceuticalsolutions.com
Estimated Sales: $1.5 Million
Number Employees: 10-19
Type of Packaging: Consumer

9240 Nutraceutics Corp
2900 Brannon Ave
St Louis, MO 63139-1440
314-664-6684
Fax: 314-664-4639 877-664-6684
info@nutraceutics.com www.nutraceutics.com
Nutraceutical tablets, capsules, effervescents, tropicals and powers
President: Jennifer Cherry
jcherry@nutraceutics.com
Estimated Sales: $500,000-$1 Million
Number Employees: 20-49
Number of Brands: 50
Number of Products: 1000
Type of Packaging: Consumer, Private Label, Bulk
Brands:
   Dh3
   Dhea Plus
   Diet Dhea

9241 Nutralliance
23600 Via Del Rio
Suite B
Yorba Linda, CA 92887
714-694-1400
Fax: 714-694-1411 844-410-1400
info@nutralliance.com www.nutralliance.com
Manufacturer of ingredients for the food, nutritional, pet and pharmaceutical industries.
CEO: Brian Salerno
Executive Vice President: Michael Sodaro
Technical Director: Stephen O'Brien

9242 Nutranique Labs
398 Tesconi Court
Santa Rosa, CA 95401-4653
707-545-9017
Fax: 707-575-4611
Processor and exporter of broccoli sprouts and certified nutraceutical powders including spinach, wheat grass juice, tomato, broccoli, garlic, carrot, green tea, kale and cruciferous blends
General Manager: Mark Martindill
Director Sales/Marketing: Nancy Costa
Operations Manager: Tom Ikesaki
Number Employees: 1-4
Parent Co: FDP USA
Type of Packaging: Bulk
Brands:
   Nutranique Labs

9243 Nutraplex
658 Douglas Ave
Suite 1102
Altamonte Springs, FL 32714
www.nutraplex.com
Nutrition bars
Founder: Brad Fowler
Number of Brands: 1
Number of Products: 4

Brands:
   NUTRAPLEX

9244 Nutrex Hawaii Inc
73-4460 Queen Kaahumanu Hwy
Suite 102
Kailua Kona, HI 96740-2632
808-326-1353
Fax: 808-329-4533 800-453-1187
info@nutrex-hawaii.com www.nutrex-hawaii.com
Nutrient-rich dietary supplement
President: Gerald R Cysewski
CEO: Andrew Jacobson
ajacobson@cyanotech.com
Vice President: Glen Johnson
Vice President of Sales and Marketing: Bob Capelli
Sales: Agnes Prehn
Estimated Sales: $500-$1 Million
Number Employees: 50-99
Number of Brands: 2
Parent Co: Cyanotech Corporation
Type of Packaging: Consumer, Private Label, Bulk
Brands:
   Bioastin
   Spirulina Pacifica

9245 Nutri Base
3851 East Thunderhill Place
Phoenix, AZ 85044-6679
480-626-2025
Fax: 480-704-4116 877-223-5459
support@nutribase.com www.nutribase.com
Cereals
President: Sat Samtolch Khalsu
Owner: Guru Simran Singh Khalsa
Contact: Meredith Averill
maverill@nutritionsoftware.org
Type of Packaging: Private Label
Brands:
   Golden Temple
   Rainforest
   Wha Guru Chew

9246 Nutri Fruit
7510 SE Altman Rd
Gresham, OR 97080-8808
503-663-2680
Fax: 503-663-7095 nutrifruit@scenicfruit.com
Fruit
Owner: Maridean Eisele
maridean@scenicfruit.com
Estimated Sales: $1-2.5 Million appx.
Number Employees: 5-9
Brands:
   Nutri-Fruito

9247 Nutri-Bake Inc
1208 Rue Bergar
Laval, QC H7L 5A2
Canada
450-933-5936
Fax: 888-263-3208 info@nutri-bake.com
www.organic-baked-goods.com
Manufacturer and wholesaler of baked goods
President: Peter Tsatoumas

9248 Nutri-Cell
1915 Trade Center Way
Naples, FL 34109
866-953-2355
www.nutricell.com
Manufacturer and exporter of animal-free nutritional supplements
Medical Consultant: Dr Derrick De Silva
Medical Consultant: Dr William Judy
Medical Consultant: Dr Bruce Dooley
Number Employees: 1-4
Number of Brands: 2
Number of Products: 7
Square Footage: 12000
Type of Packaging: Consumer, Private Label
Brands:
   Nutri-Cell

9249 Nutri-Nation
1560 Broadway
Unit 1110
Port Coquitlam, BC V3C 2M8
Canada
604-552-5549
Fax: 604-941-0135 info@nutri-nation.com
www.nutri-nation.com
Private label manufacturer of energy and nutrition bars

Director of Business Development: Allison Cienciala
Type of Packaging: Private Label

9250 NutriFusion
10641 Airport Pulling Rd N
Suite 31
Naples, FL 34109-7330
239-300-9702
Fax: 866-393-1680 nutrifusion.com
Manufacturer of fruit and vegetable ingredients
CEO: William Grand
Executive Vice President: Myra Mackey
Director of Marketing: Eric Dunn

9251 Nutribiotic
PO Box 238
Lakeport, CA 95453
707-263-0411
Fax: 707-263-7844 800-225-4345
info@nutribiotic.com www.nutribiotic.com
Manufacturer and exporter of vitamins and supplements
President: Patrick Fourteau
CFO: Wendy Sexton
Sales Director: Teri Whitestone
Contact: Pam Lausten
sales@nutribiotic.com
Operations Manager: Wendy Brossard
Purchasing/Manufacturing Director: Kenny Ridgeway
Estimated Sales: Less Than $500,000
Number Employees: 1-4
Square Footage: 80000
Brands:
   Citricidal
   Fruitsnax
   Grapefruit Extract
   Jungle Juice
   Meta Boost
   Meta Rest
   Nutribiotic
   Prozone
   Spectrum Nutritional Shake

9252 Nutricepts
2208 E 117th St
Burnsville, MN 55337-1265
952-707-0207
Fax: 952-707-0210 800-949-9060
info@nutricepts.com www.nutricepts.com
Processor and exporter of calcium salts, oxygen consuming agents, oxygen scavengers, mold inhibitors, sodium lactate, humectants, flavor enhancers, etc
President: Mark Cater
mw.cater@nutricepts.com
Estimated Sales: $3-5 Million
Number Employees: 1-4
Type of Packaging: Bulk
Brands:
   Ampliflave
   Oxyvac
   Prop Whey
   Surface Guard

9253 Nutrilabs
1230 Market St
Suite 401
San Francisco, CA 94102-4801
415-235-6205
Fax: 415-707-2122 877-468-8745
www.nutrilabs.com
Private label manufacturer vitamins and supplements
Owner: Etty Motazedi
VP: Elsie Orell
Contact: Shahin Kashani
skashani@nutrilabs.com
Purchasing Director: Argee Davidovici
Estimated Sales: Less than $500,000
Square Footage: 11200
Type of Packaging: Consumer, Private Label, Bulk
Brands:
   Chromemate
   Citrimax
   Geri-Med
   Renuz-U
   Super B-12 Sublingual
   Valerian Extract
   Virility Plus

Food Manufacturers / A-Z

9254 Nutrilicious Natural Bakery
5446 Dansher Road
Countryside, IL 60525-3126
708-354-7777
Fax: 708-354-4797   800-835-8097
Cookies and doughnuts including plain, old-fashioned, spelt, whole wheat, low-fat baked and wheat-free spelt
President: Steve Maril
Contact: Gurbax Singh
singh@nutrilicious.com
General Manager: Joe Augelli
Number Employees: 12
Square Footage: 40000
Type of Packaging: Consumer, Food Service, Private Label

9255 Nutrisciences Labs
70 Carolyn Boulevard
Farmingdale, NY 11735
631-247-0600
855-492-7388
info@nutricaplabs.com   www.nutrasciencelabs.com
Nutritional supplements including vitamins, minerals, and sports supplements
President/Founder: Jason Provenzano
Chief Executive Officer: Jonathan Greenhut
VP Digital Marketing: Andrew Goldman
VP Sales: Blayney McEneaney
Operations Manager: Dana Roveto
Estimated Sales: $45 Million
Number Employees: 40
Parent Co: Twinlab Consolidation Corporation

9256 Nutrisoya Foods
4050 Av Pinard
Saint-Hyacinthe, QC J2S 8K4
Canada
450-796-4261
Fax: 450-796-1837   877-769-2645
www.nutrisoya.com
Processor and exporter of soy milk, rice milk and almond mil
President: Nicholas Feldman
Estimated Sales: $4.1 Million
Number Employees: 17
Square Footage: 40000
Type of Packaging: Consumer, Food Service, Private Label, Bulk
Brands:
  Natura
  Nutribio
  Nutrisoy
  Nutrisoya

9257 Nutrisport Pharmacal
200 North Church Rd
Franklin, NJ 07416
973-209-7200
Fax: 973-209-4422   833-403-2861
www.nutrisportpharmacal.com
Private labeler of nutritional supplements
President/Owner: Vincent Paternoster
VP, Operations: William DiBernard
Year Founded: 1997
Type of Packaging: Private Label

9258 Nutritech Corporation
719 E Haley St
Santa Barbara, CA 93103
805-963-9581
Fax: 805-963-0308   800-235-5727
www.all-one.com
All-in-one multi-vitamin and mineral amino acid powder including rice original and base, green phyto base, active seniors and fruit antioxidant formulas
President/CEO: Douglas Ingoldsby
VP Sales: Lori Herman
Contact: Ron Adams
ron.adams@nutritech.com
VP Operations: Carol Huerta
Estimated Sales: $1-3 Million
Number Employees: 5-9
Type of Packaging: Consumer
Brands:
  All One

9259 Nutrition 21 Inc
1 Manhattanville Rd
Purchase, NY 10577-2119
914-701-4500
Fax: 914-696-0860   www.nutrition21.com
Organic mineral nutrition includes chromium picolinate, selenium yeast and Cardea salt alternative compound
President: Joseph Weiss
CEO: Michael Satow
CFO: Whit Stearns Jr
Chief Science Officer: James Homorowski
VP Marketing: Sonny Stafford
VP Sales: Todd Spear
VP Operations: William Levi
Estimated Sales: $20-50 Million
Number Employees: 10-19
Brands:
  Chromax

9260 Nutrition Center Inc
PO Box 950
2132 E Richards St
Douglas, WY 82633-0950
307-358-5066
Fax: 307-358-9208   800-443-3333
info@nutriwest.com   www.nutriwest.net
Nutritional supplements
President: Tony White
tony@nutri-west.net
Marketing Director: Marcia White
Vice President: Tiffany Moore
Plant Manager: Glenn Goodell
Purchasing Manager: Marc Moore
Estimated Sales: $2.5-5 Million
Number Employees: 50-99
Square Footage: 240
Type of Packaging: Private Label
Brands:
  Nutri West

9261 Nutrition Supply Corp
317 Industrial Cir
Liberty, TX 77575-3447
936-334-0514
Fax: 800-671-3144   888-541-3997
nsc24@nsc24.com   www.nsc24.com
Processor and exporter of nutritional supplements, vitamins and encapsulated herbs
CEO: Frank Jordan
fjordan@healthinspirationministry.com
National Sales VP: Mark Campbell
Estimated Sales: Less than $500,000
Number Employees: 10-19
Square Footage: 60000
Type of Packaging: Consumer, Food Service
Brands:
  Nsc-100
  Nsc-24

9262 Nutritional Counselors of America
1267 Archie Rhinehart Pkwy
Spencer, TN 38585-4612
931-946-3600
Fax: 931-946-3602
Vitamins, minerals, herbs, herbal teas, nutritional supplements, and colon cleaners, neutraceuticals and probiotics
President/CEO: June Wiles
Estimated Sales: $3-$5 Million
Number Employees: 5 to 9
Square Footage: 10000
Type of Packaging: Consumer, Private Label
Brands:
  6-N-1
  K-Min
  Min-Col
  Nca

9263 (HQ)Nutritional Labs Intl
1001 S 3rd St W
Missoula, MT 59801-2337
406-273-5493
Fax: 406-273-5498   info@nutritionallabs.com
Nutritional and herbal supplements and nutraceuticals including tablets, and capsules
President & CEO: Terry Benishek
CEO: Peter Malecha
pmalecha@nutritionallabs.com
VP of Research & Development: Titut Yokelson
Director of Quality Assurance: Jera'le Smith
Director of Sales & Marketing: Doug Lefler
Sales Manager: Tito Flores
Director of Operations: Steve Dybdal
Estimated Sales: $21.4 Million
Number Employees: 50-99
Square Footage: 18000
Type of Packaging: Consumer, Private Label, Bulk

9264 (HQ)Nutritional Research Associates
407 E Broad St
South Whitley, IN 46787
260-723-4931
Fax: 260-723-6297   800-456-4931
pookjg@usa.net
Processor and exporter of vitamins including carotene, A, D and E
Manager: Jonathan Pook
Acting Manager: Jonathan Pook
Estimated Sales: $979000
Number Employees: 5-9
Square Footage: 40000
Type of Packaging: Consumer, Bulk
Brands:
  Carex
  Quintrex

9265 Nutritional Specialties
1967 N Glassell St
Orange, CA 92865-4320
714-634-9340
Fax: 714-634-9347   800-333-6168
www.lifetimevitamins.com
Herbal formulas and nutritional supplements; importer of chlorella powder and tablets; exporter of dietary supplements
President: Tom Pinkowski
VP: Tom Krech
VP: Sale Stauch
Estimated Sales: $10-20 Million
Number Employees: 20-49
Type of Packaging: Private Label, Bulk
Brands:
  Lifetime
  Tung Hai

9266 Nutriwest
P.O. Box 950
2132 E Richards St
Douglas, WY 82633
307-358-5066
Fax: 307-358-9208   800-443-3333
www.nutriwest.com
Vitamin products and food and sports drink supplements.
Year Founded: 1982
Estimated Sales: $20-50 Million
Number Employees: 20-49
Square Footage: 60000
Type of Packaging: Consumer, Private Label
Other Locations:
  Nutriwest
  Alliance NE
Brands:
  Nutriquest
  Nutriwest

9267 Nutro Laboratories
650 Hadley Road
South Plainfield, NJ 07080
908-754-9300
Fax: 908-754-5640   800-446-8876
Vitamins and other dietary supplements.
President: Michael Slade
Contact: Donna Cirullo
dcirullo@nbty.com
Estimated Sales: $25600000
Number Employees: 250-499
Type of Packaging: Consumer

9268 Nuts & Stems
PO Box 39
Rosharon, TX 77583-0039
281-464-6887
Fax: 281-464-7493
Gourmet flavored pistachios and cashews

9269 Nuts 'N More
10 Almeida St E
Providence, RI 02914
844-413-2344
questions@nuts-n-more.com   nuts-n-more.com
Almond and peanut butter spreads and powders
Founder & CEO: Peter Ferreira
Number of Brands: 1
Number of Products: 18

Food Manufacturers / A-Z

9270 Nuts + Nuts
68 Jay St
Greendesk Suite 201
Brooklyn, NY 11201-1189
347-513-9670
cyrilla@nutsplusnuts.com
www.nutsplusnuts.com
Owner: Cyrilla Suwarsa
Number Employees: 5-9

9271 Nuts About Granola
46 W Philadelphia St
York, PA 17401-5319
717-814-9648
orders@nutsaboutgranola.com
www.nutsaboutgranola.com
Manufacturer of granola.
Co-Founder: Sarah Lanphier
Co-Founder: Gayle Lanphier
gayle@nutsaboutgranola.com
Number Employees: 1-4

9272 Nuts About You
Los Angeles, CA 90036
hello@nutsaboutyoula.com
Flavored almonds
Brands:
NUTS ABOUT YOU

9273 Nuts For Cheese
London, ON
Canada
519-601-5070
info@nutsforcheese.com
www.nutsforcheese.com
Artisan cashew cheeses
Founder: Margaret Coons
Year Founded: 2015

9274 Nutty Bavarian
305 Hickman Dr
Sanford, FL 32771-6905
407-444-6322
Fax: 407-444-6335 800-382-4788
bruno@nuttyb.com www.nuttyb.com
Cinnamon nut glaze syrup and fresh roasted gourmet nuts; Manufacturer of nut roasting carts and warmers as well as paper and plastic cones and gift tins for nuts
Owner: David Brent
bruno@nuttyb.com
Customer Service Manager: Amber Stefanisko
Controller: Keya Morgan
Vice President of Sales: David Zangenberg
bruno@nuttyb.com
Production Manager: Ed Conrado
Estimated Sales: $500,000-$1 Million
Number Employees: 10-19
Square Footage: 28800
Type of Packaging: Consumer, Bulk
Brands:
Nbr 2000
Nutty Bavarian

9275 Nutty Goodness
1750 Signal Point Rd
Suite 2B
Charleston, SC 29412
info@nuttygoodness.com
nuttygoodness.com
Fruit and nut bites
Operations: Nathan Ouellette
Number of Brands: 1
Number of Products: 5
Brands:
NUTTY GOODNESS

9276 Nuttzo
3525 Del Mar Heights Rd
Unit 728
San Diego, CA 92130
888-325-0553
info@nuttzo.com
www.nuttzo.com
Nut and seed butters
Founder and President: Danielle Dietz-LiVolsi
Brands:
NuttZo

9277 Nuun Active Hydration
800 Maynard Ave S
Suite 102
Seattle, WA 98134
206-219-9237
Fax: 206-260-8732 855-426-6886
nuunlife.com
Hydration products
President & CEO: Kevin Rutherford
Year Founded: 2004
Number Employees: 51-200

9278 Nysco Products Inc
2350 Lafayette Ave
Bronx, NY 10473-1104
718-792-9000
Fax: 718-792-7732 Chuck@NYSCO.com
www.nysco.com
NYSCO Products LLC designs and manufactures custom and stock displays.
Owner: Barry Kramer
info@nysco.com
Senior Vice President: Chuck Levin
Number Employees: 50-99

9279 Nyssa-Nampa Beet Growers
525 Good Ave
Nyssa, OR 97913-3664
541-372-2904
Fax: 541-372-5063
Cooperative of sugar beet processors
President: Steve Martineau
Executive Director: Norma Burbank
VP: Tom Church
Executive Director: Rich Turner
Estimated Sales: $130,000
Number Employees: 1

9280 O & H Danish Bakery Inc
1841 Douglas Ave
Racine, WI 53402-4696
262-637-8895
Fax: 262-631-5395 www.ohdanishbakery.com
Danish and pastries
Owner: Mike Olesen
mike@ohdanishbakery.com
Founder: Christian Olesen
Co-Owner: Myrna Olesen
Estimated Sales: $2.5-5 Million
Number Employees: 50-99
Brands:
Kringle

9281 O C Schulz & Sons
401 4th St
P.O. Box 39
Crystal, ND 58222-4038
701-657-2152
Fax: 701-657-2425
Potatoes
Owner: David Moquist
Secretary/Treasurer: David Moquist
Sales: Dave Moquist
Plant Manager & Sales: Andy Moquist
Estimated Sales: $1 Million
Number Employees: 10-19
Square Footage: 150000
Type of Packaging: Consumer, Food Service

9282 O Olive Oil
1997 S McDowell Blvd
Petaluma, CA 94954
707-766-1755
Fax: 707-763-3782 888-827-7148
info@ooliveoil.com www.ooliveoil.com
Extra virgin citrus olive oils and oak-aged vinegars
President/Founder: Greg Hinson
National Director Sales/Marketing: Shelly Haygood
Estimated Sales: $2 Million
Number Employees: 4
Type of Packaging: Private Label
Brands:
O Olive Oil
O Vinegar

9283 O'Boyle's Ice Cream Company
6414 N Radcliffe St
Bristol, PA 19007
215-788-3882
Ice cream, frozen yogurt and frozen desserts
Componet: Beverly Boyle
Number Employees: 10-19
Type of Packaging: Consumer, Food Service, Bulk

Brands:
Country Creamery

9284 O'Brian Brothers Food
PO Box 42382
Cincinnati, OH 45242
513-791-9909
Fax: 513-791-9011
Barbecue sauce and salad dressings including French, Italian, honey mustard and ranch
President/CEO: John O'Brian
Estimated Sales: $500,000-$1 Million
Number Employees: 1-4
Type of Packaging: Consumer, Food Service, Private Label
Brands:
Beamons

9285 O'Brines Pickling
4103 E Mission Avenue
Spokane, WA 99202-4402
509-534-7255
Fax: 509-534-5564
Pickled products
President: James Moore
VP: Marsha Moore
Estimated Sales: $5-9 Million
Number Employees: 10-19

9286 O'Danny Boy Ice Cream
100 Prosperity Dr
Trotwood, OH 45426-2600
937-837-2100
Ice cream
Owner: Dannial Haas
Co-Owner: Kathleen Haas
Estimated Sales: $2.5-5 Million
Number Employees: 1-4

9287 O'Donnell Formulas Inc
1145 Linda Vista Dr # 110
San Marcos, CA 92078-3820
760-471-1182
Fax: 760-471-1878 800-736-1991
Health food supplements
President/CEO: Wanda O'Donnell
CFO: Angela Bongiorno
Estimated Sales: Less Than $500,000
Number Employees: 5-9
Type of Packaging: Food Service
Brands:
Flora-Balance
Latero-Flora

9288 O'Donnell-Usen
5024 Uceta Road
Tampa, FL 33619-3249
813-241-9200
Fax: 813-630-1200
Seafood
Estimated Sales: $480,000
Number Employees: 10-19
Parent Co: ConAgra Foods

9289 O'Doughs
320 Oakdale Rd
Toronto, ON M3N 1W5
Canada
416-342-5700
855-636-8447
eatwell@odoughs.com odoughs.com
Gluten-free baked goods
Owner: Ari Weinberg

9290 O'Garvey Sauces
1151 Madeline Street
New Braunfels, TX 78132-4725
830-620-6127
Fax: 830-620-6662
Hot and mild salsas
President: Norma Garvey
Estimated Sales: $150,000
Number Employees: 1-4
Type of Packaging: Consumer, Food Service, Private Label, Bulk
Brands:
Max's Salsa Sabrosa & Design

9291 O'Hara Corp
120 Tillson Ave # 1
Rockland, ME 04841-3450
207-594-4444
Fax: 207-594-0407 www.oharabait.com
Processor and exporter of seafood including frozen scallops

Food Manufacturers / A-Z

Owner: Frank O'Hara
foharajr@oharacooperative.com
Estimated Sales: $4100000
Number Employees: 50-99
Type of Packaging: Consumer, Food Service
Brands:
    Cape Ann
    Down East
    Tip Top

9292 O'Neal's Fresh Frozen Pizza Crust
122 E College Ave
Springfield, OH 45504-2505
    937-323-0050
    redparot@iapdatacom.net
Pizza crust including whole wheat
Manager: Brian O'Neill
Estimated Sales: $1-3,000,000
Number Employees: 20-49

9293 O'Neil's Distributors
110 S Iroquois Street
Goodland, IN 47948-8004
    219-297-4521
    Fax: 219-297-4625
Teas
Owner: Steven O'Neil
Estimated Sales: $2.5-5 000,000
Number Employees: 1-4

9294 O'Neill Coffee Co
20 Main Street Ext
West Middlesex, PA 16159-3478
    724-528-2244
    Fax: 724-528-1566 www.oneillcoffee.com
Coffee; wholesaler/distributor of teas and spices
President: Joseph Walsh
jwalsh@oneillcoffee.com
Account Manager: Neil Ostheimer
Estimated Sales: $1-3 Million
Number Employees: 10-19

9295 O'Sole Mio
4600, boul. Ambroise-Lafortune
Boisbriand, QC J7H 0G1
Canada
    844-696-8933
    info@osolemio.ca osolemio.ca
Pasta, sauces and prepared meals
President/Owner: Alfredo Napolitano

9296 O-At-Ka Milk Prods Co-Op Inc.
700 Ellicott St.
Batavia, NY 14020
    585-343-0536
    Fax: 585-343-4473 800-828-8152
    www.oatkamilk.com
Meal replacement beverages, pet milk replacers, dairy base liqueurs, RTD beverages, high protein products, infant formula, evaporated milk, milk powders, butter, bulk cream and skim milk concentrate.
General Manager: Larry Webster
CEO: Bill Schreiber
CFO: Michael Fuchs
Vice President, Human Resources: Donna Maxwell
Year Founded: 1959
Estimated Sales: $274.56 Million
Number Employees: 400+
Square Footage: 600000
Type of Packaging: Consumer, Food Service, Private Label, Bulk
Brands:
    Gold Cow
    Spring Farm

9297 OB Macaroni Company
    844-837-6259
    info@obmacaroni.com
    www.obmacaroni.com
Manufacturer of pasta
President: Jackie Krantz
Estimated Sales: $10-20 Million
Number Employees: 20-49
Square Footage: 50000
Type of Packaging: Consumer, Food Service, Private Label, Bulk
Brands:
    O.B.
    Q&Q
    Q&Q Fideo

9298 OCG Cacao
1 Plummers Cor
Whitinsville, MA 01588-2135
    508-234-5107
    Fax: 508-234-5495 888-482-2226
    ocggroup@aol.com
Dairy, bakery, confectionery products
President: Jean Chenal
General Manager: Roberta White
Estimated Sales: Below $5 Million
Number Employees: 1

9299 OH Chocolate
3131 E Madison Street
Seattle, WA 98112
Canada
    206-329-8777
    www.ohchocolate.com
Baked desserts and Belgian chocolates
President: Laurie Climan
Sales Manager: Mark Climan
Number Employees: 10-19
Type of Packaging: Consumer
Brands:
    L'Or Chocolatier
    Ott Chocolate

9300 OHi Food
750 Wesleyan Bay
Costa Mesa, CA 92626-6919
    808-281-7815
    www.ohifoodco.com
Superfood snack bar
Marketing Manager: Kayla Bittner
Number of Brands: 1
Number of Products: 4
Brands:
    OHI

9301 OK International Group
73 Bartlett Street
Marlborough, MA 01752
    508-303-8286
    Fax: 508-303-8207 sales@okcorp.com
    www.okcorp.com
Integrated packaging automation systems
Contact: Marcela Barragan
mbarragan@okcorp.com

9302 OLLI Salumeria Americana
1301 Rocky Point Dr
Oceanside, CA 92056
    877-655-4937
    info@olli.com www.olli.com
Artisanal cured meats
Founder and President: Oliviero Colmignolli

9303 OMG! Superfoods
2373 E Pacifica Pl
Rancho Dominguez, CA 90220
    855-664-3663
    omgsuperfoods.com
Superfood powders, including fruits, mushrooms and seeds

9304 OMGhee
24 Cedar St
Cedar Grove, NJ 07009
    973-931-3476
    mitul@omghee.com
    www.omghee.com
Ghee (clarified butter)
Owner: Mitul Parekh

9305 OMYA, Inc.
9987 Carver Rd
Suite 300
Cincinnatti, OH 45242
    513-387-4600
    800-749-6692
    www.omya.com
Fillers and pigments from calcium carbonate and dolomite, and distributor of chemical products.
President: Anthony Colak
CFO: Michael Phillips
Secretary: Leonard Eisenberg
Asst Sec: Patricia Kirkendall
Manager Technology Services: Michael Roussel
Sales Manager: Maria Burt
Contact: Hilary Allard
hilary.allard@omya.com
Manager: Scott McCalla
Manager Projects Engineering: Scott Schaffner
Director of Engineering: Rob Tikoft
Director Purchasing: Derrell Riley
Estimated Sales: $4.3 Million
Other Locations:
    Proctor VT
    Cincinnati OH
    Woodland WA
    Kingsport TN
    Lucerne Valley CA
    Johnsonburg PA
    Florence VT
    Hawesville KY
    Sylacauga AL
    Superior AZ
    Long Beach CA

9306 ONE Brands
5400 West W.T. Harris Blvd
Suite L
Charlotte, NC 28269
    888-231-2684
    one1brands.com
High protein snack bars
President & CEO: Peter Burns
Year Founded: 1999
Brands:
    ONE
    ONE BASIX

9307 ORB Weaver Farm
3406 Lime Kiln Road
New Haven, VT 05472
    802-877-3755
    marjorie@orbweaverfarm.com
    www.orbweaverfarm.com
Fresh fruits and vegetables, and fine cheeses
President: Marjorie Susman
marjorie@orbweaverfarm.com

9308 OSF Flavors Inc
40 Baker Hollow Rd
Windsor, CT 06095-2133
    860-298-8350
    Fax: 860-298-8363 800-466-6015
    sales@osfflavors.com www.osfflavors.com
Manufacturer of flavors for food and beverage products.
Marketing Director: Olivier de Botton
Financial Controller: Adam Feltman
Manager of Research & Development: Linda Faulkner
Sales: Susan Nasby
Manager: Doug Nasby
dnasby@osfflavors.com
Operations Manager: Doug Nasby
Production/Purchasing Manager: Vincent Lacocca
Estimated Sales: $12.5 Million
Number Employees: 10-19
Square Footage: 10000
Other Locations:
    OSF Europe
    Chambly, France
    OSF Asia
    Tangerang, Indonesia

9309 OWYN
100 Passaic Ave
Suite 100
Fairfield, NJ 07004
    833-533-7061
    liveowyn.com
Plant-based protein beverages
VP: Jeff Miller

9310 Oak Creek Brewing Company
2050 Yavapai Dr
Sedona, AZ 86336
    928-204-1300
    Fax: 520-204-1361 bestbrew@sedona.net
    www.oakcreekbrew.com
Seasonal beer, ale and lager
General Manager: Rita Kraus
Estimated Sales: $500,000-$1Million
Number Employees: 5-9
Type of Packaging: Consumer, Food Service

Food Manufacturers / A-Z

9311 (HQ)Oak Farm's Dairy
1148 Faulkner Ln
Waco, TX 76704
254-756-5421
Fax: 254-756-6987 www.oakfarmsdairy.com
Milk
President: Mackey Willims
CEO: Mickey Williams
General Sales Manager: Jerry Przada
Human Resources: Brad Patten
Estimated Sales: Less than $500,000
Number Employees: 100-249
Other Locations:
  Oak Farms Dairy
    Wichita Falls TX
  Oak Farms Dairy
    Weatherford TX
  Oak Farms Dairy
    Denison TX
  Oak Farms Dairy
    Paris TX
  Oak Farms Dairy
    Houston TX
  Oak Farms Dairy
    Beaumont TX
  Oak Farms Dairy
    Brenham TX
  Oak Farms Dairy
    San Antonio TX
  Oak Farms Dairy
    McAllen TX
  Oak Farms Dairy
    Waco TX
  Oak Farms Dairy
    Austin TX
  Oak Farms Dairy
    Tyler TX
Brands:
  Oak Farm's

9312 Oak Farms
PO Box 961447
El Paso, TX 79996
214-941-0302
Fax: 214-941-0309 800-395-7004
www.oakfarmsdairy.com
Processors of milk and cream
General Manager: Craig Roberts
General Sales Manager: Jerry Przada
General Manager: Micky Williams
Number Employees: 250-499
Parent Co: Suiza Dairy Group
Type of Packaging: Consumer, Food Service
Brands:
  Oak Farms

9313 Oak Grove Dairy
W10198 Oak Grove Rd.
Clintonville, WI 54929
715-823-6226
oakgrove@oakgrovedairy.com
www.oakgrovedairy.com
Milk, sour creams, yogurt, novelties, and cottage cheese
President: David Kust
Estimated Sales: $20-50 Million
Number Employees: 1000

9314 Oak Grove Orchards Winery
6090 Crowley Rd
Rickreall, OR 97371
541-364-7052
Wines
President: Carl Stevens
Estimated Sales: Under $500,000
Number Employees: 1-4

9315 Oak Grove Smoke House Inc
17618 Old Jefferson Hwy
Prairieville, LA 70769-3931
225-673-6857
Fax: 225-673-5757 www.oakgrovemix.webs.com
Seasoned and Cajun/Creole rice mixes, speciality spice mixes, breading and smoked meats
President: Robert Schexnailder
Estimated Sales: $500,000-$1 Million
Number Employees: 5-9
Number of Brands: 2
Number of Products: 15+
Square Footage: 51000
Type of Packaging: Consumer, Food Service, Bulk
Brands:
  Oak Grove Smokehouse
  Swamp Fire Seafood Boil

9316 Oak Hill Farm
15101 Hwy 12
Glen Ellen, CA 95442
707-996-6643
Fax: 707-935-6612 800-878-7808
info@oakhillfarm.net www.oakhillfarm.net
Sustainably grows over 200 varieties of vegetables, fruit, herbs and flowers.
Owner: Anne Teller
info@oakhillfarm.net
Estimated Sales: $780 Thousand
Number Employees: 20-49
Type of Packaging: Consumer

9317 Oak Island Seafood Company
PO Box 947
Portland, ME 04104-0947
207-594-9250
Fax: 207-594-9281
Seafood
President: Jay Trenholm

9318 Oak Knoll Dairy, Inc.
PO Box 443
Windsor, VT 05089
802-674-5426
Fax: 802-674-9166 oakknoll@earthlink.net
www.oakknolldairy.com
100% goats milk, 2% fat goats milk, chocolate goats milk, and half and half goats milk
Owner: George Redick
Owner: Karen Lindbo
Number Employees: 5-9
Square Footage: 30000
Brands:
  Oak Knoll

9319 Oak Knoll Winery
29700 SW Burkhalter Rd
Hillsboro, OR 97123-9245
503-648-8198
Fax: 503-648-3377 800-625-5665
info@oakknollwinery.com
www.oakknollwinery.com
Wines
President: William Ellsworth
william.ellsworth@adrian.k12.or.us
VP Sales/Marketing: John Vuylsteke
Sales Manager: Natalie Epler
Founder: Marj Vuylsteke
Cellar Master: Tom Vuylsteke
Office Manager: Martha Miller
Estimated Sales: Below $5 Million
Number Employees: 10-19
Number of Brands: 2
Number of Products: 8
Type of Packaging: Consumer, Private Label, Bulk
Brands:
  Oak Knoll

9320 Oak Leaf Confections
416-751-0740
Fax: 416-751-3656 877-261-7887
info@sweetworks.net sweetworks.net/oakleaf
Processor and exporter of confectionery products including malt balls, gum balls, bubble gum, hard candies and freeze pops
Owner/President: Philip Terranova
Number Employees: 300
Square Footage: 560000
Parent Co: SweetWorks Confections LLC
Type of Packaging: Consumer, Private Label, Bulk
Brands:
  Bubble King

9321 Oak Ridge Winery LLC
6100 E Victor Rd
Lodi, CA 95240-0804
209-369-4758
Fax: 209-369-0202 info@oakridgewinery.com
www.oakridgewinery.com
Produces a wide variety of wines.
President: Rudy Maggio
rmaggi@oakridgewinery.com
Vice President of Marketing and Sales: Stephen Bei
Director of International Sales: Stephen Merritt
Tasting Room Manager: Shelly Maggio-Woltkamp
Director of Winemaking/Production Manage: Chue Her
Estimated Sales: $10-20 Million
Number Employees: 50-99
Number of Brands: 8
Type of Packaging: Consumer, Food Service
Brands:
  Oak Ridge Winery
  OZW
  Old Soul
  3 Girls
  Maggio
  Helena Ranch
  Moss Roxx
  Lodi Estates

9322 Oak Spring Winery
2401 E Pleasant Valley Blvd
Altoona, PA 16601-8967
814-946-3799
Fax: 814-946-4245 oakspringwinery@verizon.net
www.oakspringwinery.com
Wines
Founder: Sylvia Schraff
President: Scott Schraff
oakspringwinery@keycon.net
Treasurer: John Schraff
Estimated Sales: $5-9 Million
Number Employees: 1-4
Brands:
  Oak Spring Winery

9323 Oak State Products Inc
775 State Route 251
PO Box 549
Wenona, IL 61377-7587
815-853-4348
Fax: 815-853-4625
Producer of soft cookies, cookie crumbs and toppings
Chairman & CEO: Rich Scalise
CFO & SVP, Finance: Fred Jasser
SVP, CCO: Chuck Metzger
SVP, Human Resources: Steve England
Year Founded: 1956
Estimated Sales: $22.8 Million
Number Employees: 250-499
Square Footage: 160000
Parent Co: Hearthside Food Solutions
Type of Packaging: Consumer, Bulk
Brands:
  Oak State Cookie Jar Delight

9324 Oak Street Manufacturing
255 Welter Dr
Monticello, IA 52310
319-465-4042
Fax: 877-465-4042 877-465-4344
www.oakstreetmfg.com
Manufacturer and distributor of restaurant furnishings
President/Owner: Cindy Bagge
Year Founded: 1995

9325 Oakhurst Dairy
364 Forest Ave.
Portland, ME 04101
207-772-7468
800-482-0718
info@oakhurstdairy.com www.oakhurstdairy.com
Milk and dairy products including fluid milk, cream, sour cream, cottage cheese, butter, ice cream mixes, juices, drinks and water.
President: John Bennett
Quality Control Assurance Manager: Jeff Connolly
Human Resources Manager: Darlene Cadorette-Levesque
Year Founded: 1921
Estimated Sales: $110 Million
Number Employees: 200
Type of Packaging: Consumer
Brands:
  Oakhurst

9326 Oakhurst Industries
2050 Tubeway Ave.
Commerce, CA 90040
818-502-1400
Fax: 818-502-1338
Bread and other bakery products
President: James Freund
Estimated Sales: $43.2 Million
Number Employees: 400
Square Footage: 81000

Food Manufacturers / A-Z

9327 Oakland Bean Cleaning & Storage
42445 County Road 116
Knights Landing, CA 95645-0518
530-735-6203
Fax: 530-735-6207
Dry, edible beans including kidney and pink
Operations Manager: Frank Anastasi
Estimated Sales: Less than $500,000
Number Employees: 1-4

9328 Oakland Noodle Co
10 W Main St
Oakland, IL 61943
217-346-2322
Fax: 217-346-2324
oaklandnoodle_company@yahoo.com
www.oaklandnoodle.com
Noodles
Owner: Clarence Ethington
Marketing Director: Stephanie Ethington
Estimated Sales: Under $500,000
Number Employees: 5-9
Square Footage: 2000
Brands:
  Oakland Noodle

9329 Oakrun Farm Bakery
58 Carluke Road West
PO Box 81070
Ancaster, ON L9G 3L1
Canada
905-648-1818
Fax: 905-648-8252 800-263-6422
customerservice@oakrun.com www.oakrun.com
Processor and exporter of English muffins, pastries, bagels, muffins, danish, tarts, crumpets, and cakes.
President: Roger Dickhout
COO: Tony Tristani
Research & Development: Maria Pais
Quality Control: Rita Fajardo
Marketing Director: Andra Zondervan
VP Sales: Dave MacPhail
Plant Manager: Chet Czerny
Purchasing: Christine Richer
Number Employees: 100-249
Square Footage: 1068000
Type of Packaging: Consumer, Food Service, Private Label

9330 Oasis Breads
440 Venture St
Escondido, CA 92029
760-747-7390
Fax: 760-747-4854 www.oasisbreads.com
Flourless sprouted whole grain breads and deli breads.
President: Jim Pickell
Estimated Sales: $1300000
Number Employees: 5-9
Square Footage: 40000
Type of Packaging: Consumer, Private Label
Brands:
  Oasis

9331 Oasis Coffee Co Inc
327 Main Ave
Norwalk, CT 06851-6156
203-847-0554
Fax: 203-846-9835 www.oasiscoffeect.com
Roasting coffee
President: Ralph Sandolo
oasiscoffeeco@yahoo.com
CEO: Veronica Sandolo
Vice President: Joseph Sandolo
Marketing Consultant: Martin Blank
Estimated Sales: $5-10 000,000
Number Employees: 5-9
Brands:
  Oasis Coffee

9332 Oasis Food Co
635 Ramsey Ave
Hillside, NJ 07205
908-964-0477
800-275-0477
foodservice.us@aak.com www.oasisfoodsco.com
Butter blends and substitutes, salad dressings, shortenings, margarine, edible oils, mayonnaise, sauces, pan and grill oil.
President: Anthony Alves
Year Founded: 1975
Estimated Sales: $100-500 Million
Square Footage: 300000
Type of Packaging: Consumer, Food Service, Private Label, Bulk
Brands:
  Olioro
  Ex-Seed
  Alpine Valley
  Golden Delicious
  Kleckner's
  Grill Blazin BBQ Sauce

9333 Oasis Mediterranean Cuisine
1520 W Laskey Rd
Toledo, OH 43612-2914
419-269-1516
Fax: 419-324-7777 info@omcfood.com
www.omcfood.com
Mediterranean vegetarian cuisine
Owner: Francois Hashem
Quality Control: Tonny Obid
Estimated Sales: $5-10 Million
Number Employees: 20-49
Brands:
  Non-Dairy Baklava

9334 Oasis Winery
14141 Hume Rd
Hume, VA 22639
540-635-7627
Fax: 540-635-4653 800-304-7656
Info@oasiswine.com www.oasiswine.com
Wines
Co-Founder: Tareq Salahi
Public Relations: Ann Runyon
Estimated Sales: $5-10 Million
Number Employees: 100-249
Type of Packaging: Private Label
Brands:
  Bleu Rock Vineyard Wines
  Fiery Rum Cellars
  Oasis Wines & Sparkling Wines

9335 Oatly
67 Irving Place
9th Floor
New York, NY 10003
info.us@oatly.com
us.oatly.com
Oat milk
General Manager, U.S.: Mike Messersmith
Number of Products: 4

9336 Oats Overnight
2420 W 14th St
Suite B
Tempe, AZ 85281
support@oatsovernight.com
www.oatsovernight.com
Flavored oatmeal
Number of Brands: 1
Number of Products: 3
Brands:
  OATS OVERNIGHT

9337 Oatworks
411 W. 14th St.
New York, NY 10014
646-624-2400
www.oatworks.com
Manufacturer of oat-powered fruit smoothies.
Founder: David Peters
Brands:
  oatworks

9338 Oberto Brands
7060 Oberto Dr.
Kent, WA 98032
877-453-7591
www.oberto.com
Beef & turkey jerky, beef sticks & beefsteak, tender cut and canister beef jerky, microwave pork rinds, and traditional beef jerky.
President, Premium Brands: George Paleologou
Year Founded: 1918
Estimated Sales: $75-99 Million
Number Employees: 500-999
Number of Brands: 3
Square Footage: 40000
Parent Co: Premium Brands
Type of Packaging: Consumer
Brands:
  Gentleman's Cut
  Oberto
  Pacific Gold

9339 Oberweis Dairy Inc
951 Ice Cream Dr # 1
North Aurora, IL 60542-1475
630-801-6100
Fax: 630-897-0562 866-623-7934
www.oberweis.com
Fluid dairy products, premium ice cream, and ice cream cakes, juice, meat products, crackers, cookies, salsas
Chairman: Jim Oberweis
President, Chief Executive Officer: Joe Oberweis
CFO: Jeff Wilhelm
jeff.wilhelm@oberweis.com
Vice President of Marketing: Bruce Bedford
VP Marketing: Mark Vance
VP, Sales: Lino Carrillo
VP, Operations: Mike McCarthy
VP Retail Operations: Elizabeth Craig
Estimated Sales: $1-2 Million
Number Employees: 100-249
Type of Packaging: Food Service, Private Label, Bulk

9340 (HQ)Obester Winery
12341 San Mateo Road
Half Moon Bay, CA 94019
650-726-9463
Fax: 650-726-7074 info@obesterwinery.com
www.obesterwinery.com
Wines
Owner: Kendyl Kellogg
kendyl.kellogg@mendonet.com
Estimated Sales: $3 Million
Number Employees: 5-9

9341 Obis One
Virginia Tech Corporate Research Center
1872 Pratt Dr, Suite 1375
Blacksburg, VA 24060
609-202-9766
pat@obisone.com
www.obisone.com
Black garlic
Founder: Patrick Lloyd
Brands:
  Obis One

9342 Oc Lugo Co Inc
15 Third St # 2
New City, NY 10956-4946
845-480-5121
Fax: 845-480-5122 info@oclugo.com
www.oclugo.com
Supplier of chemicals, vitamins, minerals, gelatins and food ingredients. OC Lugo's other division is Critical Filtration supplies
President: Richard Lugo
rlugo@oclugo.com
Estimated Sales: $830,000
Number Employees: 5-9

9343 Ocean Approved
PO Box 8129
Portland, ME 04104
www.oceanapproved.com
Fresh, frozen kelp
President/Owner: Paul Dobbins
Year Founded: 2006

9344 Ocean Beauty Seafoods Inc
1100 W Ewing St
Seattle, WA 98119
206-285-6800
800-365-8950
info@oceanbeauty.com www.oceanbeauty.com
Manufacturer and distributor of seafood.
President & CEO: Mark Palmer
CFO: Tony Ross
VP, Retail Sales: Ron Christianson
Year Founded: 1910
Estimated Sales: $409 Million
Number Employees: 1,000-4,000
Type of Packaging: Food Service
Other Locations:
  Ocean Beauty Seafood Facility
  Boston MA
  Ocean Beauty Seafood Facility
  Cordova AK
  Ocean Beauty Seafood Facility
  Alitak AK
  Ocean Beauty Seafood Facility
  Kodiak AK
  Ocean Beauty Seafood Facility
  Los Angeles CA
  Ocean Beauty Seafood Facility

Food Manufacturers / A-Z

Monroe AK
Ocean Beauty Seafood Facility
Naknek AK
Ocean Beauty Seafood Facility
Petersburg AK
Ocean Beauty Seafood Facility
Seattle WA
Ocean Beauty Seafood Facility
Nikiski AK
Brands:
  Pillar Rock
  Pink Beauty
  Icy Point
  Lascco
  Pirate
  Bay Beauty
  McGovern's Best
  Searchlight
  Nathan's Smoked Salmon
  Smoke It All
  Taste T Pacific Whiting
  Man of War Crab
  XIP-Salmon Cavier
  Sea Choice
  Port Clyde Sardines
  Neptune
  Echo Falls
  Ocean Beauty Brand

9345 Ocean Cliff Corp
362 S Front St
New Bedford, MA 02740-5745
508-990-7900
Fax: 508-990-7950
gregwhite@oceancliffcorporation.com
www.oceancliffcorporation.com
Fish and seafood liquid and powder extracts and spices including shrimp, clam, crab, fish, lobster and mussel
Owner: G White
Sales: Peter Shephard
gwhite@oceancliffcorporation.com
Estimated Sales: $2.5-5,000,000
Number Employees: 5-9
Square Footage: 40000
Type of Packaging: Bulk
Brands:
  Ocean Cliff

9346 Ocean Crest Seafoods
P.O. Box 1183
Gloucester, MA 01931
978-281-0232
Fax: 978-283-3211 800-259-4769
www.neptunesharvest.com
Seafood
President/CEO: Leonard Parco
Estimated Sales: $1-3 Million
Number Employees: 20-49

9347 Ocean Food Co. Ltd.
3 Turbina Ave
Toronto, ON M1V 5G3
Canada
416-285-6487
Fax: 416-285-4012 info@oceanfood.ca
www.oceanfood.ca
Fish cakes and imitation crab and lobster.
President: Joe Nishikaze
Estimated Sales: $1.4 Million
Number Employees: 10
Type of Packaging: Consumer, Food Service

9348 Ocean Fresh Seafoods
4241 21st Ave W # 306
Seattle, WA 98199-1250
206-285-2412
Fax: 206-283-3408
Fresh and frozen fish and seafood
President: Ted Otness
Contact: Nita Waller
nitaw@oceanfreshsea.com
Plant Manager: Bill Bryant
Estimated Sales: $1,100,000
Number Employees: 5-9
Type of Packaging: Food Service
Brands:
  Alaska Fresh

9349 Ocean Harvest
PO Box 60
Dennysville, ME 04628-0060
207-726-0609
Fax: 207-726-9571
Fish and seafood

Owner: Larry Matthews
Estimated Sales: $1-3 Million
Number Employees: 1-4

9350 Ocean King International
1680 S Garfield Avenue
Suite 202
Alhambra, CA 91801-5413
626-289-9399
Fax: 626-300-8177
Seafood
President/CEO: Jimmie Dang
CFO: Miling Shua
Vice President: Richard Mendelson
Secretary: Jorge Pardinas

9351 Ocean Mist Farms
10855 Ocean Mist Parkway
Castroville, CA 95012
831-633-2144
contactus@oceanmist.com
www.oceanmist.com
Spinach, cauliflower, celery, lettuce, artichokes, broccoli, etc.
CEO: Joe Pezzini
Sales Director: Tom Botelho
President of Production: Paul Scheid
Plant Manager: Mark Rensons
Estimated Sales: $9,200,000
Number Employees: 50-99
Type of Packaging: Consumer
Brands:
  Ocean Mist

9352 Ocean Pride Fisheries
136 Jacquard Rd
PO Box 402
Lower Wedgeport, NS B0W 2B0
Canada
902-663-4579
Fax: 902-663-2698 jules@oceanpridefisheries.com
www.oceanpridefisheries.com
Processor and exporter of smoked salmon, cod and haddock
President: Milton Leblanc
Chief Operating Officer: Jules Leblanc
Estimated Sales: $1.3 Million
Number Employees: 10
Type of Packaging: Consumer, Food Service, Bulk

9353 Ocean Pride Seafood
207 S Richard St
Delcambre, LA 70528
337-685-2336
Fax: 337-685-2339
Shrimp and crawfish
President: Denise Dooley
Contact: David Kunes
opbob@msn.com
Estimated Sales: $500,000-$1 Million
Number Employees: 1-4

9354 Ocean Select Seafood
10714 Highway 14
Delcambre, LA 70528
337-685-5315
Fax: 337-685-6079
Seafood
President: Mitch Polito
Estimated Sales: $5-$10 Million
Number Employees: 1-4

9355 Ocean Spray International
One Ocean Spray Dr.
Lakeville-Middleboro, MA 02349
800-662-3263
www.oceanspray.com
Manufacturer of bottled juices and fruit ingredient supplier.
Interim CEO: James White
Senior VP/CFO: Daniel Cunha
Global Chief Innovation Officer: Rizal Hamdallah
VP, Marketing Services: Yash Sikand
COO: Brian Schiegg
Year Founded: 1930
Estimated Sales: $2.2 Billion
Number Employees: 2,000
Number of Brands: 26
Square Footage: 99000
Type of Packaging: Consumer, Food Service
Other Locations:
  Middleboro MA
  Lehigh Valley PA
  Wisconsin Rapids WI
  Markham WA

Kenosha WI
Henderson NV
Sulphur Springs TX
Tomah WI
Lanco, Chile
Brands:
  Craisins
  Cranapple
  Crancherry
  Crangrape
  Cranicot
  Cranorange
  Ocean Spray
  Ocean Spray Apple Juice
  Ocean Spray Cranberries
  Ocean Spray Cranberry Cocktail
  Ocean Spray Fruit Punch
  Ocean Spray Fruit Punch Cooler
  Ocean Spray Grapefruit Juice
  Ocean Spray Jellied Cran. Sauce
  Ocean Spray Juice Blends
  Ocean Spray Kiwi Straq. Juice
  Ocean Spray Lemonade
  Ocean Spray Orange Juice
  Ocean Spray Pineapple Grapefruit
  Ocean Spray Pink Grapefruit Juice
  Ocean Spray Ruby Red & Mango
  Ocean Spray Ruby Red Grapefruit
  Ocean Spray Whole Berry Cranberries
  Wellfleet Farms
  Wellfleet Farms Cranberry Sauce
  Wellfleet Farms Specialty Foods

9356 Ocean Springs Seafood
608 Magnolia Ave
Ocean Springs, MS 39564
228-875-0104
Fax: 228-875-0117
Frozen, fresh, headless and peeled shrimp
President: Earl Sayard
VP: Ruby Fayard
Secretary: Linda Fayard
Estimated Sales: $1500000
Number Employees: 5-9
Square Footage: 6000000
Type of Packaging: Private Label
Brands:
  Surf Spray
  Tropic

9357 Ocean Union Company
2100 Riverside Pkwy
Suite 129
Lawrenceville, GA 30043-5927
770-995-1957
Fax: 770-513-8662
Seafood, snapper, grouper, lobster, crab, tuna, eel, mackerel
President: Jackie Tsai

9358 Ocean's Balance
343 Ocean House Rd
Cape Elizabeth, ME 04107
lscali@oceansbalance.com
www.oceansbalance.com
Seaweed products
President/Owner: Tollef Olson
CEO: Mitchell Lench
Director of Sales & Marketing: Lisa Scali

9359 Ocean's Halo
1424 Chapin Ave
Burlingame, CA 94010
650-642-5907
www.oceanshalo.com
Seaweed snacks, broths, sauces, noodles and noodle bowls
Co-Founder: Robert Mock
Co-Founder and President: Shin Rhee
Brands:
  Ocean's Halo

9360 Oceanfood Sales
1909 East Hastings Street
Vancouver, BC V5L 1T5
Canada
604-255-1414
Fax: 604-255-1787 877-255-1414
sales@oceanfoods.com www.oceanfoodsales.com
Processor and exporter of smoked salmon
VP: Robert Graham
VP, Controller: Louise Graham
Sales And Marketing Manager: Dave Slade
Customer Service: Dorothy Chaves
Production Manager: John Makowhichuk

Food Manufacturers / A-Z

Estimated Sales: $7.9 Million
Number Employees: 16
Type of Packaging: Consumer, Food Service, Private Label, Bulk

9361 Oceanledge Seafoods
138 Rankin Street
Rockland, ME 04841-2318
207-594-4955
Fax: 626-968-0196
Seafood
President: Steve Jonasson
Estimated Sales: $330,000
Number Employees: 2

9362 Oceans Prome Distributing
1413 Waukegan Rd
Glenview, IL 60025
847-998-5813
Fax: 847-729-5228
President: Jeffrey Burhop
Estimated Sales: $5-10 Million
Number Employees: 5-9

9363 Oceanside Knish Factory
3445 Lawson Blvd.
Oceanside, NY 11572
516-766-4445
Fax: 516-766-2319
Knishes
President: Leonard Model
knish1@aol.com
Estimated Sales: Below $5 Million
Number Employees: 20-49

9364 Ocena Wineary & Vineyards
4980 S. 52nd Ave
New Era, MI 49446
231-861-4657
renae@oceanawinery.com
www.oceanawinery.com
A family-operated winery specializing in estate wines made from French hybrid grapes, with a range from dry reds and whites to sweet, late harvest styles
Owner: Renae Goralski
Winemaker: Greg Goralski
Estimated Sales: Less than $500,000
Number Employees: 1-4

9365 Octavia Tea LLC
38w061 Tanglewood Drive
Batavia, IL 60510
866-505-6387
elizabeth@octaviatea.com
www.octaviatea.com
Tea.
Marketing: Elizabeth Stephano

9366 Odell Brewing Co
800 E Lincoln Ave
Fort Collins, CO 80524-2507
970-498-9070
Fax: 970-498-0706 cheers@odellbrewing.com
www.odellbrewing.com
Brewery
Founder: Doug Odell
CEO: Wynne Odell
Chief Financial Officer: Chris Banks
Chief Operating Officer: Brenden McGivney
Head of Human Resources: Corkie Odell
Estimated Sales: $20-50 Million
Number Employees: 100-249
Number of Brands: 55
Type of Packaging: Consumer, Food Service
Brands:
  90 Shilling
  Cutthroat Pale Ale
  Loose Leaf Session Ale
  India Pale Ale
  Myrcenary Double IPA

9367 Odell's
Reno, NV
800-635-0436
odellscustomerservice@venturafoods.com
www.popntop.com
Popping oils and popcorn toppings.
Co-owner: Arthur Anderson
Co-owner: Vikki Anderson

9368 Odom's Tennessee Pride Sausage Company
PO Box 1187
Madison, TN 37116-1187
615-868-1360
Fax: 615-860-4703 www.tnpride.com
Breakfast sausage including fresh and fully cooked, breakfast sandwiches, appetizers, and gravy.
President: Larry Odom
Chairman: Richard Odom
Year Founded: 1943
Estimated Sales: $185 Million
Number Employees: 700
Square Footage: 18000
Type of Packaging: Consumer, Food Service, Private Label, Bulk
Brands:
  Tennessee Pride Country Sausage

9369 (HQ)Odwalla
Sugar Land, TX
800-639-2552
consumers@odwalla.com www.odwalla.com
Almond milk, smoothies, juices and protein drinks
President/Owner: Alison Lewis
CEO: D. Stephen Williamson
CFO: James Steichen
SVP, Sales and Operations: Michael Cote
Contact: Monica Burns
burnsm@odshp.com
Estimated Sales: $25-49 Million
Number Employees: 60
Number of Brands: 1
Type of Packaging: Consumer
Brands:
  Odwalla

9370 Office General des EauxMinerales
5260 Avenue Notre-Dame-De-Grace
Montreal, QC H4A 1K9
Canada
514-482-7221
Fax: 514-482-7093 www.saintjustin.ca
Bottler and exporter of carbonated natural mineral water
President: Nicole Lelievre
Number Employees: 23
Type of Packaging: Food Service
Brands:
  Saint Justin

9371 Offshore Seafood Co
2586 25th Ave N
St Petersburg, FL 33713-3919
727-329-8848
www.offshoreseafood.com
Seafood including red grouper, gag grouper, red snapper, spiny FL Keys lobsters, stone crab claws, local wild caught shrimp and tuna
Co-Owner: Kent Sahr
Number Employees: 5-9
Type of Packaging: Food Service, Bulk

9372 Offshore Systems Inc
Mile 4 Captains Bay Rd
Dutch Harbor, AK 99692
907-581-1827
Fax: 907-581-1630
nreed@offshoresystemsinc.com
www.offshoresystemsinc.com
President: Daniel Roseta
Executive VP: Joey Willis
Director of Marketing: Wayne Bouck
Business Development Manager: Rick Wilson
Manager: Nick Reed
nreed@offshoresystemsinc.com
Operations Manager: Mike Peek
Number Employees: 20-49

9373 Ogeki Sake USA Inc
249 Hillcrest Rd
Hollister, CA 95023-4921
831-637-9217
Fax: 831-637-0953 question@ozekisake.com
www.ozekisake.com
Sake
President: Yasuo Umehara
yumehara@ozekisake.com
COO: Katsuyoshi Yoshida
Estimated Sales: $5-10 Million
Number Employees: 20-49
Type of Packaging: Private Label

9374 Oh Baby Foods, Inc.
21 West Mountain St., Suite 120
Fayetteville, AR 72701
800-788-1451
www.ohbabyfoods.com
Oh Baby Foods are all certified organic and non-GMO project verified. All ingredients are 100% US-grown and many are regionally raised.
Founder: Fran Free
Type of Packaging: Consumer

9375 Oh Yes! Foods
11420 Santa Monica Blvd
Suite 25966
Los Angeles, CA 90025
855-696-4937
www.ohyesfoods.com
Fruit- and vegetable-infused cheese pizza
Brands:
  OH YES!

9376 Oh, Sugar! LLC
1050 Northfield Ct
Suite 125
Roswell, GA 30076
678-393-6408
Fax: 678-393-6489 866-557-8427
info@namsbits.com
Cookies and candy
Marketing: Amanda Black

9377 Ohana Seafood, LLC
255 Sand Island Rd
Suite 2C
Honolulu, HI 96819-2292
808-843-1844
Fax: 808-843-1844
Seafood
President: Jeffrey Yee
Vice President: Jeffrey Yee
Estimated Sales: $570,000
Number Employees: 1-4

9378 Ohio Association Of Meat
6870 Licking Valley Rd
Frazeysburg, OH 43822-9563
740-828-9900
Fax: 740-828-2635 val@oamp.org
www.oamp.org
Meats
Executive Secretary: Valerie Parks Graham
Contact: Valerie Graham
val@oamp.org
Estimated Sales: $5-10 Million
Number Employees: 5-9
Square Footage: 88464
Parent Co: Instantwhip Foods
Type of Packaging: Food Service, Private Label
Brands:
  Instant Whip

9379 Ohio Mushroom Company
1893 N Dixie Hwy
Lima, OH 45801-3255
419-221-1721
Mushrooms
President: Robert Komminsk

9380 Ohta Wafer Factory
931 Hauoli St
Honolulu, HI 96826
808-949-2775
Puffed rice cakes and fortune and Japanese tea cookies
President: Herb Ohta
bran28@hotmail.com
Estimated Sales: $500,000-$1 Million
Number Employees: 1-4
Square Footage: 9000
Type of Packaging: Consumer, Food Service
Brands:
  Ohta's Senbei

9381 Oil & Olives Company
5975 Sunset Dr
Suite 603
Miami, FL 33143
305-670-0979
sales@oilandolives.es
www.oilandolives.es
Olives, olive oil and dried fruits.
President: Manuel Sala Lopez

Food Manufacturers / A-Z

9382 Oils Of Aloha
66-935 Kaukonahua Rd
Waialua, HI 96791-8706
808-637-5620
Fax: 808-637-6194 800-367-6010
info@oilsofaloha.com
Salad oils and cooking oils
Chairman/Owner: Dana Gray
President: Matthew Papania
Marketing: Barbara Gray
Plant Manager: Matthew Papania
Estimated Sales: $5-10 Million
Number Employees: 20-49
Number of Brands: 1
Square Footage: 60000
Type of Packaging: Consumer, Food Service
Brands:
  Oils of Aloha Macadamia Nut Oil

9383 Oilseeds International LTD
8 Jackson St
San Francisco, CA 94111-2022
415-956-7251
Fax: 415-394-9023 www.oilseedssf.com
Processes safflower oil, rice bran oil, and cottonseed cooking oil
President: John Gyulay
Vice President: Kenjiro Kondo
Marketing Director: Mickey Clements
Marketing: Roy Adam
Estimated Sales: $1-5 Million
Number Employees: 10-19
Type of Packaging: Bulk

9384 Oilseeds International LTD
8 Jackson St
San Francisco, CA 94111-2022
415-956-7251
Fax: 415-394-9023 sales@ricebranoil.biz
www.oilseedssf.com
Rice bran oil. Non-GMO and non-hydrogenated vegetable oil, meaning it contains no trans fats.
CFO: Akio Takami
Executive Vice President: Fumi Sugawara
Sales & Marketing: Collin Amon
Marketing Manager: Mickey Clements
Estimated Sales: $3.3 Million
Number Employees: 10-19
Type of Packaging: Bulk

9385 Ojai Cook
149 S Barrington Avenue
Los Angeles, CA 90049-3310
310-646-5001
Fax: 310-839-5135 886-571-1551
Condiments, sauces and beverages
President/CEO/Marketing Director: Joan Vogel
Brands:
  Cocktail Duet
  Prickly Pecans
  Puckers

9386 Ojai Cook LLC
1205 Maricopa Hwy
Ojai, CA 93023-3128
805-646-8020
Fax: 805-646-8020 888-657-1155
Condiments
Owner: Marty Folk
Estimated Sales: $300,000-500,000
Number Employees: 5-9

9387 Ojai Vineyard
10540 Encino Dr
Oak View, CA 93022-9257
805-649-1674
Fax: 805-649-4651 info@OjaiVineyard.com
www.ojaivineyard.com
Wine
Owner: John Anderson
johna@ojaivineyard.com
Estimated Sales: $590,000
Number Employees: 1-4
Brands:
  Ojai

9388 Ojeda USA
460 Southport Commerce Blvd
Spartanburg, SC 29306
864-574-6004
Fax: 864-574-6005 www.ojedausa.com
Commercial refrigeration equipment, specializing in novelty freezers and open air display cases
VP: Mark Thompson

Year Founded: 2005

9389 Ok Industries
PO Box 1787
Fort Smith, AR 72902
479-783-4186
Fax: 479-784-1358 800-635-9441
www.tenderbird.com
Fresh and frozen chicken.
President/CEO: Trent Goins
CFO: Scott Hunter
SVP, Supply Chain: Russ Bragg
Contact: Randall Goins
fgoins@okfoods.com
Estimated Sales: $20-50 Million
Number Employees: 100-249
Number of Brands: 2
Parent Co: OK Industries
Type of Packaging: Consumer, Food Service, Private Label
Brands:
  O.K. Foods
  TenderBird

9390 Okahara Saimin Factory LTD
1804 Waiola St
Honolulu, HI 96826-2698
808-949-0588
Fax: 808-949-0375 okaharasf001@hawaii.rr.com
www.buyimporter.com
Noodles
President: Kiyoko Okahara
okaharasf001@hawaii.rr.com
Estimated Sales: $1500000
Number Employees: 20-49
Type of Packaging: Consumer, Food Service

9391 Okanagan Spring Brewery
2808-27 Avenue
Vernon, BC V1T 9K4
Canada
250-542-2337
Fax: 250-542-7780 800-652-0755
info@okspring.com www.okspring.com
Beer, ale and stout
COO: Richardson Knudson
CEO: John Sleeman
Marketing Director: Paul Meehan
Managing Director: Rick Knudson
Parent Co: Seeman Brewing & Malting Company
Type of Packaging: Consumer, Food Service
Brands:
  Okanagan Spring
  Shastebury
  Sleeman
  Strohs Canada

9392 Oklahoma City Meat Co Inc
300 S Klein Ave
Oklahoma City, OK 73108-1495
405-235-3308
Fax: 405-235-9989 www.okcmeat.com
Beef, lamb and pork; wholesaler/distributor of chicken. Founded in 1957.
President: Tommy Saunders
office@okcmeat.com
Estimated Sales: $10-20 Million
Number Employees: 20-49
Type of Packaging: Food Service

9393 Okuhara Foods Inc
881 N King St
Honolulu, HI 96817-4554
808-848-0581
Fax: 808-841-5367
Pre-packaged frozen fish including salted butterfish, salmon and shellfish
President: James N Okuhara
okufoods@aol.com
Vice President: Satoru Okuhara
Estimated Sales: $10-20 Million
Number Employees: 20-49
Type of Packaging: Consumer, Bulk

9394 Ola Loa
1555 Burke Ave
Unit K
San Francisco, CA 94124
800-800-9550
www.olaloa.com
Vitamin beverage
Co-Founder: Gregory Kunin
Brands:
  OLA LOA

9395 Olam Spices
205 East River Park Pl
Suite 310
Fresno, CA 93720
559-447-1390
USA@olamnet.com
www.olamgroup.com
Edible nuts, cocoa, coffee, cotton and spices and vegetable ingredients
Co-Founder/Group CEO: Sunny Verghese
Year Founded: 2002
Estimated Sales: $13.9 Billion
Number Employees: 5,000+
Number of Products: 47
Parent Co: Olam International
Type of Packaging: Bulk
Other Locations:
  USA Head Office
  Fresno CA

9396 Oland Breweries
3055 Agricola Street
Halifax, NS B3K 4G2
Canada
902-453-1867
Fax: 902-453-3847 800-268-2337
www.olandbrewery.ca
Beer, ale, stout and lager
Marketing Director: Brent Qartermain
Number Employees: 100-249
Parent Co: Labatt Breweries
Type of Packaging: Consumer, Food Service
Brands:
  Labatt
  Oland

9397 Old Cavendish Products
93 Densmore Rd
Cavendish, VT 05142
802-226-7783
Fax: 802-226-7783 800-536-7899
fruitcakes@tds.net www.cavendishfruitcake.com
All natural fruitcake, mustard, herb vinegars
President: Mary Ormrod
COO: Andrew Leven
Estimated Sales: $200K
Number Employees: 2
Type of Packaging: Consumer, Food Service, Private Label, Bulk

9398 Old Chatham Sheepherding Co
155 Shaker Museum Rd
Old Chatham, NY 12136-2603
518-794-7733
Fax: 518-794-7641 888-743-3760
cheese@blacksheepcheese.com
Sheep's milk cheese
Owner: Stew Adams
stew@blacksheepcheese.com
Owner: Nancy Clark
Marketing/Sales: Lorie Appleby
Kleinpeter/Cheesemaker: Benoit Mailloil
Administrative Manager: Sandra Hoehneker
Estimated Sales: $5-10 Million
Number Employees: 20-49
Number of Brands: 1
Number of Products: 14

9399 Old Colony Baking Co Inc
PO Box 1111
Northbrook, IL 60065-1111
847-498-5434
Fax: 847-760-0707 info@ocolony.com
www.ocolony.com
Pastries and co-branded cookies
President/Owner: Jeffrey Kaufman
CEO: Ann Kaufman
Estimated Sales: $1-3 Million
Number Employees: 10-19
Type of Packaging: Private Label
Brands:
  Andes Chocolate Mint Chip Cookies
  Big Top Animal Cookies
  Chiquita Banana Cookies
  Diamond Walnut Shortbread Cookies
  Musselman's Apple Sauce Cookies
  Realemon Lemon Cookies

9400 Old Country Bakery
5350 Biloxi Avenue
North Hollywood, CA 91601-3531
818-838-2302
Fax: 818-838-2307
Cakes and pastry

Food Manufacturers / A-Z

General Manager: Chris Meyer

9401 Old Country Cheese
5510 Cty. Hwy. D
Cashton, WI 54619
608-654-5411
Fax: 608-654-5411 888-320-9469
info@oldcountrycheese.com
www.oldcountrycheese.com
Cheese and jams
President: Kevin Everhart
County Chief: Michael Everhart
Estimated Sales: $1-2.5 Million
Number Employees: 20-49
Type of Packaging: Consumer, Private Label, Bulk
Brands:
Old Country Cheese

9402 Old Country Meat & Sausage Company
811 W Washington St
San Diego, CA 92103-1894
619-297-4301
Sausages
CEO: Manfred Spenner
Marketing Manager: Manfred Spenner
Estimated Sales: Under $500,000
Number Employees: 5-9
Type of Packaging: Bulk
Brands:
Old Country

9403 Old Country Packers
318 River St
Duryea, PA 18642
570-655-9608
Fax: 570-457-1678
Horseradish including white and red beet, cocktail sauce, chicken wing sauce including mild, hot and honey, sauce and garlic in water and oil
President: Edwarded Orkwis
Estimated Sales: $1 million
Number Employees: 1-4
Square Footage: 8000
Type of Packaging: Consumer, Food Service, Private Label
Brands:
Old Country
Town Tavern

9404 Old Credit Brewing Co. Ltd.
1-75 Horner Ave
Toronto, ON M8Z 4X5
Canada
416-494-2766
Fax: 905-274-4154 info@ontariocraftbrewers.com
www.ontariocraftbrewers.com
Amber/red ale and pilsner
President: Aldo Lista
Brewer: Orrin Besko
Number Employees: 5-9
Square Footage: 24000
Type of Packaging: Consumer, Food Service
Brands:
Old Credit

9405 Old Creek Ranch Winery
10024 Old Creek Rd
Ventura, CA 93001-1002
805-649-4132
Fax: 805-649-9293 winery@oldcreekranch.com
www.oldcreekranch.com
Premium wines
President: John Whitman
jwhitman@oldcreekranch.com
Winemaker: Charles Branham
Estimated Sales: Below $5 Million
Number Employees: 5-9
Number of Products: 3
Square Footage: 16000
Type of Packaging: Private Label
Brands:
Old Creek Ranch Winery

9406 Old Dominion Peanut Corp
208 W 24th St
Norfolk, VA 23517-1355
757-622-1633
Fax: 757-624-9415 800-368-6887
sales@odpeanut.com
Candy including hard candies, fund raising, cashew and peanut brittle and chocolate covered and butter toffee peanuts
President/CEO: William Delchiaro
willd@odpeanut.com
Estimated Sales: $4500000
Number Employees: 50-99
Square Footage: 200000
Parent Co: The Virginia Food Group
Type of Packaging: Consumer, Food Service, Private Label, Bulk
Brands:
Old Dominion

9407 Old Dominion Spice Company
10990 Leadbetter Road
PO Box 249
Ashland, VA 23005
804-550-2780
Fax: 804-550-2868 www.olddominionspice.com
Dry blends used in condiments, marinades, seasonings, rubs, breaders, batters and other coating systems
President: Lindy Thackston
Founder/CEO: Milton Parma
Research & Development Manager: David Pauly
SVP Sales: H Guy Moyers
Contact: David Pauly
david@olddominionspice.com
Estimated Sales: $550,000
Number Employees: 8
Square Footage: 16600

9408 Old Dutch Foods LTD
Roseville, MN
customerservice@olddutchfoods.com
www.olddutch.com
Snack foods including potato chips, popcorn, pretzels, salsa and dips
President: Steve Aanenson
Year Founded: 1984
Estimated Sales: $107 Million
Number Employees: 500
Number of Brands: 10
Type of Packaging: Private Label
Brands:
Dutch Gourmet
Humpy Dumpty
Ringolos
Old Dutch
Ripples
Restaurant Style
Tiny Twists
Puffcorn
Bac'n Puffs

9409 (HQ)Old Dutch Mustard Company
98 Cuttermill Road
Suite 260 S
Great Neck, NY 11021-3010
516-466-0522
Fax: 516-466-0762
custservice@olddutchmustard.com
mustard flour, prepared mustard, vinegar, sauce and juice
President: Paul Santich
Sales Manager: Evan Dobkins
Contact: Susan Bruno
sbruno@pilgrimfoods.net
Number Employees: 70
Square Footage: 400000
Type of Packaging: Consumer, Food Service, Private Label, Bulk
Other Locations:
Brands:
Old Dutch

9410 Old Europe Cheese Inc
1330 E Empire Ave
Benton Harbor, MI 49022-2000
269-925-5003
Fax: 269-925-9560 mike@oldeuropecheese.com
www.oldeuropecheese.com
Producer of specialty cheeses, focusing on Brie, Camembert, Gouda, Edam, fontina and mantoro.
General Manager: Francois Capt
Manager: Mike Balane
mike@oldeuropecheese.com
Estimated Sales: $18 Million
Number Employees: 100-249
Number of Brands: 1
Square Footage: 50000
Parent Co: I.L.A.S.
Type of Packaging: Consumer, Food Service
Brands:
Remy Picot

9411 Old Fashioned Foods
650 Furnace St
Mayville, WI 53050-1248
920-387-7924
Fax: 920-387-7929 www.oldfash.com
Cheese spreads, cheese sauce, tex-mex, cheese dips, nacho cheese sauce, squeeze cheese, squeeze salsa, glass cheese spreads, cheese sticks, and aerosol and portion control pouches.
Owner/President: Bernard Youso
byouso@oldfash.com
Chairman: Gary Youso
Quality Control: Ben Lindstrom
Marketing: Bernie Youso
Sales: Jim Clark
Production/Maintenance: Cory Lenhardt
Purchasing: Kathy Emmer
Estimated Sales: $5-10 Million
Number Employees: 50-99
Brands:
Old Faishoned Foods

9412 Old Fashioned Kitchen Inc
1045 Towbin Ave
Lakewood, NJ 08701-5931
732-364-4100
Fax: 732-905-7352 info@oldfashionedkitchen.com
www.oldfashionedkitchen.com
Specialy frozen foods nationally
President: Jay Conzen
jayc@oldfashionedkitchen.com
SVP: Sal Mangiapane
Plant Manager: John Kercher
Year Founded: 1951
Estimated Sales: $20-50 Million
Number Employees: 50-99
Square Footage: 30000

9413 Old Fashioned Natural Products
2230 Cape Cod Way
Santa Ana, CA 92703-3582
714-835-6367
Fax: 714-835-4948 800-552-9045
alisha@lalifestyle.com www.lalifestyle.com
Vitamins and herbal teas and supplements; also, custom formulations and private labeling available
President: Patricia Logsdon
ofnp2@aol.com
VP: John Brown
Estimated Sales: $10-20 Million
Number Employees: 10-19
Square Footage: 32000
Type of Packaging: Private Label

9414 Old Firehouse Winery
5499 Lake Rd E
Geneva, OH 44041-9425
440-466-9300
Fax: 440-466-8011 800-362-6751
info@oldfirehousewinery.com
www.oldfirehousewinery.com
Ohio wines
Owner: Don Woodward
dave@oldfirehousewinery.com
Estimated Sales: $1-$3 Million
Number Employees: 5-9
Type of Packaging: Consumer

9415 Old Home Foods Inc
550 County Road D W # 18
Suite 18
New Brighton, MN 55112-3517
651-312-8900
Fax: 651-312-8901 info@oldhomefoods.com
www.oldhomefoods.com
Cultured dairy products like cottage cheese, sour cream, yogurt, dips, and salsa
CEO: Geoff Murphy
Estimated Sales: $20-50 Million
Number Employees: 10-19
Brands:
Old Home

9416 Old House Vineyards
18351 Corkys Ln
Culpeper, VA 22701-4413
540-423-1032
Fax: 540-423-1320 info@oldhousevineyards.com
www.oldhousevineyards.com
Wines
Owner: Patrick J Kearney
Winemaker: Doug Fabbioli
Estimated Sales: $3-5 Million
Number Employees: 1-4

Food Manufacturers / A-Z

9417 Old Kentucky Hams
PO Box 443
Cynthiana, KY 41031-0443
859-234-5015
Fax: 859-234-5015
Country hams and bacon
President: Nancy Hisle
Plant Manager: Elizabeth Hunt
Estimated Sales: $1-4.9 000,000
Number Employees: 1-4
Square Footage: 1
Type of Packaging: Private Label
Brands:
   Old Kentucky Hams
   Traditional Kentucky

9418 Old London Foods
Yadkinville, NC
www.oldlondonfoods.com
Low calorie snacks
President & CEO, B&G Foods: Robert Cantwell
Number Employees: 250
Parent Co: B&G Foods, Inc.

9419 Old Mansion Inc
3811 Corporate Rd
PO Box 1839
Petersburg, VA 23805
804-862-9889
800-476-1877
www.oldmansion.com
Quality spices, seasonings, coffee and teas
Sales: Tom Mullen
Number Employees: 20-49
Type of Packaging: Consumer, Food Service, Private Label, Bulk

9420 Old Mill Winery
403 S Broadway
Geneva, OH 44041-1844
440-466-5560
Fax: 440-466-2099 www.theoldmillwinery.com
Gourmet foods, wines
Owner: Dave Froelich
info@oldmillwinery.com
Winemaker: Bill Turgeon
Marketing Director: Shirley Barnett
Estimated Sales: $810,000
Number Employees: 10-19

9421 Old Monmouth Candies
627 Park Ave
Freehold, NJ 07728-2397
732-462-1311
Fax: 732-462-6820
Sales@OldMonmouthCandies.com
www.oldmonmouthcandies.com
Candy and confections
President: Hal Gunther
Manager: Steve Gunther
sgunther@oldmonmouthcandies.com
Estimated Sales: Below $5 Million
Number Employees: 10-19
Brands:
   Old Monmouth

9422 Old Neighborhood
37 Waterhill St
Lynn, MA 01905
781-595-1557
Fax: 781-595-7523
www.oldneighborhoodfoods.com
Meat including; hot dogs, sausage, fresh-cut deli, pre-cut deli, meat case, and shaved meat.
Chief Executive Officer: Tom Demakes
Year Founded: 1893
Estimated Sales: $45.1 Million
Number Employees: 250-499
Square Footage: 66000
Type of Packaging: Food Service
Brands:
   Thin 'n Trim
   Old Neighborhood

9423 Old Orchard Brands, LLC
1991 12 Mile Rd.
Sparta, MI 49345
800-330-2173
oldorchard.com
Bottled and frozen fruit juices.
President/Founder: Mark Saur
VP Sales: Craig Lampright
Year Founded: 1985
Estimated Sales: $103.3 Million
Number Employees: 50-99
Square Footage: 140000
Parent Co: Lassonde Industries
Type of Packaging: Consumer
Brands:
   Old Orchard

9424 Old Rip Van Winkle Distillery
113 Great Buffalo Trace
Frankfort, KY 40601
502-897-9113
Fax: 502-896-9989
pvanwinkle@oldripvanwinkle.com
www.oldripvanwinkle.com
Bourbon whiskey
Owner: Julian Van Winkle
Estimated Sales: $1-2.5 Million
Number Employees: 1-4
Brands:
   Old Rip Van Wrinkle

9425 Old Sacramento Popcorn Company
1011 St
Sacramento, CA 95814
916-446-1980
Fax: 916-442-2676 www.oslhp.net
Processor and exporter of popcorn
Owner: Jim Scott
Estimated Sales: Less than $150,000
Number Employees: 1-4

9426 Old South Winery
65 S Concord Ave
Natchez, MS 39120-6806
601-445-9924
Fax: 601-442-1215 mailus@newu.net
www.oldsouthwinery.com
Wines
Owner: Galbreath Edeen
edeeng@newu.net
Co-Owner: Edeen Galbreath
Winemaker: Scott Gallbreath
edeeng@newu.net
Estimated Sales: $500,000-$1 Million
Number Employees: 1-4
Type of Packaging: Private Label
Brands:
   Old South Winery
   Old South Muscadine

9427 Old Tavern Food Products Inc
230 S Prairie Ave
Waukesha, WI 53186-5937
262-542-5301
Fax: 262-542-5676 888-542-5317
Cheese, gift packs
President: Jill Strong
rdwgksgp@execpc.com
VP: Gail Strong
Estimated Sales: $500,000-$1 Million
Number Employees: 5-9
Type of Packaging: Private Label, Bulk
Brands:
   Old Tavern Club Cheese

9428 Old Time Candy Co
350 Commerce Dr E
Lagrange, OH 44050-9316
440-355-4345
Fax: 775-908-1995 www.oldtimecandy.com
Chocolate candy
Owner: Theresa Brunslik
Sales Manager: Lynn White
Estimated Sales: Less Than $500,000
Number Employees: 1-4
Type of Packaging: Consumer

9429 Old Tyme Mill Company
1517-21 S Kolmar Ave
Chicago, IL 60623
773-521-9484
Fax: 773-521-9486
Waffle, pancake and breading mix
President: John Pontikes
Treasurer: Dorothy Pontikes
Estimated Sales: $280,000
Number Employees: 4

9430 Old Wine Cellar
4411 220th Trl
Amana, IA 52203
319-622-3116
Fax: 319-622-6162
Wines
President: Les Aackermin
Estimated Sales: $1-2.5 Million
Number Employees: 5-9
Brands:
   Old Wine Cellar

9431 Old Wisconsin Food Products
950 West 175 Street
Homewood, IL 60430
708-798-0900
Fax: 708-798-3178 888-633-5684
www.buddig.com
Sausage
President: John Buddig
CFO: Roger Buddig
Plant Manager: Charles Belter
Estimated Sales: $200,000
Parent Co: Carl Buddig & Company
Brands:
   Carl Budding
   Old Wisconsin

9432 Old Wisconsin Sausage Inc
4036 Weeden Creek Rd.
Sheboygan, WI 53081
920-458-4304
Fax: 920-458-2716 877-451-7988
sales@oldwisconsin.com www.oldwisconsin.com
Smoked sausages
President: Tom Buddig
Manager: Bob Gielissen
Vice President: Tim Belter
belter@oldwisconsin.com
Plant Manager: Bob Gielissen
Year Founded: 1942
Estimated Sales: $20-50 Million
Number Employees: 100-249
Type of Packaging: Consumer
Brands:
   Ends and Curls
   Old Wisconsin Mug

9433 Old World Bakery
1933 W Galbraith Rd
Cincinnati, OH 45239-4767
513-931-1411
Fax: 513-931-3560 owb@fuse.net
www.oldworldbakery.com
Natural breads
Founder: Odette Skally
Public Relations: Cheryl Deleon
Number Employees: 50-99

9434 Old World Spices Inc
5320 College Blvd
Overland Park, KS 66211-1621
816-861-0400
Fax: 816-861-7073 800-241-0070
www.oldworldspices.com
Seasoning, spice and sauce packaging
Owner: John Jungc
sales@oldworldspices.com
Marketing: Kathy Wheat
Estimated Sales: $1-5 Million
Number Employees: 20-49
Brands:
   Old World Creations
   Party Creations
   Soups For One

9435 Olde Colony Bakery
519 Wando Ln
Mt Pleasant, SC 29464-8211
843-216-3232
Fax: 843-216-5553 800-722-9932
OCBenne@aol.com www.oldecolonybakery.com
Gourmet cookies and benne seed wafers
Owner: Peter Rix
Owner: Sheila Rix
ocbbenne@aol.com
Estimated Sales: Less than $500,000
Number Employees: 5-9
Brands:
   Olde Colony

9436 Olde Estate
782 Ne Harbour Drive
Boca Raton, FL 33431-6927
561-400-7444
Fax: 561-392-2204 denzykatz@aol.com
Classic rum cakes
President: Denise Katz

Food Manufacturers / A-Z

9437 Olde Heurich Brewing Company
1307 New Hampshire Avenue NW
Washington, DC 20036
202-333-2313
Fax: 202-333-9198 www.foggybottom.com
Beer
President: Gary Heurich
Estimated Sales: Below $5 Million
Number Employees: 5
Brands:
   Foggy Bottom Ale
   Foggy Bottom Lager
   Foggy Bottom Porter
   Olde Georgetown Beer
   Olde Heurich
   Senate Beer

9438 Olde Tyme Food Corporation
775 Benton Drive
East Longmeadow, MA 01028-3215
413-525-4101
Fax: 413-525-3621 800-356-6533
Snack foods including candy apples, cotton candy, waffles, waffle cones, peanuts
President: David Baker
Sales Director: David Wedderspoon
Estimated Sales: $1.7 Million
Number Employees: 21
Square Footage: 100000
Parent Co: Hampton Farms
Type of Packaging: Consumer, Food Service, Private Label, Bulk
Brands:
   Olde Tyme
   Ole Style Peanut Butter

9439 Olde Tyme Mercantile
1127 Mesa View Drive
Arroyo Grande, CA 93420-6542
805-489-7991
Fax: 805-481-5578
Gourmet products including olives, pickles, salad dressings, mustards, mayonnaise and candies
President: Larry Williams
CEO: Kevin Keim
Propietor: Diane Keim
Number Employees: 10-19
Square Footage: 8000
Type of Packaging: Consumer, Private Label
Brands:
   Scully
   Wah Maker

9440 Olds Products Co
10700 88th Ave
Pleasant Prairie, WI 53158
262-947-3500
Orders@OldsFitz.com
www.oldsproducts.com
Prepared mustard, specialty mustard blends, and vinegar
Supply Chain Manager: Brian Schnuckel
bschnuckel@oldsfitz.com
Estimated Sales: $6500000
Number Employees: 50-99
Parent Co: Olds Products Company
Type of Packaging: Consumer, Food Service, Private Label, Bulk
Brands:
   Koops' Mustard
   Fitzpatrick Bros

9441 Ole Salty's Potato Chips
1920 E Riverside Blvd
Loves Park, IL 61111
815-637-2447
www.olesaltys.com
Potato chips
Manager: Troy Wedeikand
Estimated Sales: Below $5 Million
Number Employees: 1-4
Brands:
   Ole Salty's

9442 Ole Smoky Candy Kitchen
642 Ski Mountain Rd
Gatlinburg, TN 37738
865-436-4716
Fax: 865-436-0268
Maggie@olesmokycandykitchen.com
www.olesmokycandykitchen.com
Candy
President: Esther J Dych
Manager: David Dych

Estimated Sales: Less Than $500,000
Number Employees: 5-9
Type of Packaging: Consumer

9443 Oley Distributing Company
PO Box 4660
Fort Worth, TX 76164-0660
817-625-8251
Fax: 817-626-7269
President: Patricia O'Neal
VP: Phil O'Neal, Jr.
General Manager: Bill Smith
Estimated Sales: $5-10 Million
Square Footage: 225000

9444 Oliva Verde USA
7413 Troy Avenue
Suite 157
Raleigh, NC 27615
919-846-9020
Fax: 919-844-1050
Olive oil

9445 Olive & Sinclair Chocolate Co
1628 Fatherland St
Nashville, TN 37206-2026
615-262-3007
info@oliveandsinclair.com
Manufacturer of chocolate and confections.
Founder: Scott Witherow
Production Manager: Jason Thompson
Number Employees: 1-4

9446 Olive Growers Council
4601 W School Ave
Visalia, CA 93291-5223
559-734-1710
Fax: 559-625-4847 olivecouncil@sbcglobal.net
www.olivecouncil.com
Bulk green olives
President: Adin A Hester
adin@goldstate.net
Estimated Sales: Less Than $500,000
Number Employees: 1-4
Type of Packaging: Private Label

9447 Olive Oil Factor
197 Huntingdon Ave
Waterbury, CT 06708-1413
475-235-2666
Fax: 860-945-8662 info@theoliveoilfactory.com
www.theoliveoilfactory.com
Oils including extra virgin olive, flavored and dipping, and balsamic vinegar
President: David Miller
david@theoliveoilfactory.com
Estimated Sales: $350,000
Number Employees: 20-49
Square Footage: 20000
Type of Packaging: Consumer, Food Service, Private Label

9448 Olive Oil Source
1833 Fletcher Way
Santa Ynez, CA 93460-9380
805-688-1014
sales@oliveoilsource.com
www.oliveoilsource.com
Olive oils
President: Shawn Addison
General Manager: Suzette Stahl
Accounting Manager: Joy Jonas
VP Operations: Antoinette Addison
Number Employees: 10-19

9449 Oliveo LLC
1717 Rice St
Rosenberg, TX 77471
281-633-9335
Fax: 713-334-9929 888-924-6687
Extra virgin olive oil
Estimated Sales: $300,000-500,000
Number Employees: 1-4

9450 Oliver Egg Products
9422 Hungarytown Road
Crewe, VA 23930-4125
804-645-9406
Fax: 804-645-7429 800-525-3447
www.jamieoliver.com
Frozen and refrigerated egg whites, whole eggs, yolks and scrambled egg mix
Owner: Bill Oliver
Type of Packaging: Food Service, Bulk

9451 Oliver Packaging & Equipment Co.
3236 Wilson Dr NW
Walker, MI 49534
616-356-2950
Fax: 616-233-1132 800-253-3893
oliver-info@oliverquality.com
www.oliverquality.com
Bakery and meal packaging equipment
President/Owner: Chadd Floria

9452 Oliver Winery
200 E Winery Rd
Bloomington, IN 47404-2400
812-876-5800
Fax: 812-876-9309 800-258-2783
admin@oliverwinery.com www.oliverwinery.com
Producer of wines, including semi-sweet, semi-dry, dry whites, dry reds, dessert and sparkling.
President: Julie Adams
CEO: Bill Oliver
boliver@oliverwinery.com
Executive Vice President: Kathleen Oliver
Vice President of Wholesale Sales: Chris Hibbert
Human Resources Director: Jessika Hane
VP of Operations, Director of Winemaking: Dennis Dunham
Vineyard Manager: Bernie Parker
Estimated Sales: $18.7 Million
Number Employees: 50-99
Number of Brands: 8
Type of Packaging: Consumer, Food Service, Bulk
Brands:
   Oliver
   Orchard Stand
   Bubblecraft
   Beanblossom Hard Cider
   Camelot Mead
   Creekbend
   Pilot Project
   Vine Series

9453 Olivia's Croutons
1423 North Street
New Haven, VT 05472
802-453-2222
Fax: 802-453-7722 888-425-3080
info@oliviascroutons.com
www.oliviascroutons.com
All natural specialty croutons: Butter and garlic, parmesan pepper, vermont cheddar and dill, multi grain with garlic, and gazapach lowfat croutons. Also roasted onion tostini and lemon parsley tostini
President: Francie Caccavo
info@oliviascroutons.com
Estimated Sales: Below $5 Million
Number Employees: 5-9
Type of Packaging: Consumer, Food Service, Private Label, Bulk

9454 Olivia's Kitchen
1580 Park Ave
New York, NY 10029-1853
917-374-0077
Baked goods
Founder: Olivia Marjoram
Brands:
   Olivia's Kitchen

9455 Olivier's Candies
2828 54th Ave SE
Calgary, AB T2C 0A7
Canada
403-266-6028
Fax: 403-266-6029 info@oliviers.ca
www.oliviers.ca
Chocolate, hard candy, brittles, barks
President: Wally Marcolin
Secretary: Rick Jeffrey
Number Employees: 10-19
Type of Packaging: Consumer, Bulk

9456 Olivina. LLC
4555 Arroyo Road
Livermore, CA 94550
925-455-8710
charles@theolivina.com
www.theolivina.com
Olive oils
President/Owner/CEO: Charles Crohare
charles@theolivina.com
General Manager: Alice Crohare
Estimated Sales: $25 Million
Number Employees: 20

Food Manufacturers / A-Z

9457 Olivio Premium Products
867 Boylston Street
Boston, MA 2116
customerservice@olivioproducts.com
www.olivio.com
Olive oil products
Contact: Ben Blier
bblier@motu.com

9458 Olomomo Nut Company
4760 Walnut St.
Boulder, CO 80301
877-923-6888
info@olomomo.com www.olomomo.com
Roasted & flavored nuts
Chairman & Founder: Justin Perkins
CEO: Mark Owens
VP Sales & Marketing: Justin Desiderio
Sales & Marketing Coordinator: Sarah Dhanraj
Production: Brian Starkman

9459 Olsen Fish Co
2115 N 2nd St
Minneapolis, MN 55411-2204
612-287-0838
Fax: 612-287-8761   800-882-0212
lutefisk@olsenfish.com www.olsenfish.com
Lutfisk and pickled herring
President: Chris Dorff
lutefisk@olsenfish.com
Estimated Sales: $3-5 Million
Number Employees: 10-19
Type of Packaging: Bulk
Brands:
    Olsen

9460 Olson Livestock & Seed
31921 Rd 711
Haigler, NE 69030-4006
308-297-3283
Fax: 308-297-3284
Popcorn
Owner: Jeff Olson
Owner: Scott Olson
Owner: Steve Olson
Estimated Sales: $3-5 Million
Number Employees: 5 to 9

9461 Olson Locker
917 Winnebago Ave
Fairmont, MN 56031-3614
507-238-2563
Fax: 507-238-2564
Meat and meat products
President: Mark Olson
mark@olsonfarms.com
Estimated Sales: $460,000
Number Employees: 1-4
Type of Packaging: Consumer

9462 Olymel
2200 Pratte Ave.
Suite 400
Saint-Hyacinthe, QC J2S 4B6
Canada
450-771-0400
Fax: 450-773-6436 www.olymel.com
Pork and poultry.
President/CEO: Rejean Nadeau
First VP: Paul Beauchamp
Senior VP, Sales/Marketing: Richard Davies
Year Founded: 1991
Estimated Sales: $3.6 Billion
Number Employees: 13,000
Number of Brands: 3
Type of Packaging: Private Label, Bulk
Brands:
    Olymel
    Flamingo
    Lafleur

9463 Olympia Candies
11606 Pearl Rd
Strongsville, OH 44136-3320
440-572-7747
Fax: 440-572-1819   800-574-7747
www.olympiacandy.com
Candied popcorn
Owner: Robert Mc Grath
sales@olympiacandy.com
Estimated Sales: $1-3 Million
Number Employees: 10-19

9464 Olympia International
2166 Spring Creek Road
Belvidere, IL 61008-9507
815-547-5972
Fax: 815-547-5973
pickles, mushrooms, horseradish, marinated peppers, beets and salads
President: Greg Bodak
Contact: Arturo Gonzalez
arturo@olympiaintl.com
Estimated Sales: $260,000
Number Employees: 1

9465 Olympia Oyster Co
1042 SE Bloomfield Rd
Shelton, WA 98584
360-426-3354
877-427-3193
info@olympiaoyster.com www.olympiaoyster.com
Oysters, clams, oyster soup bases
Estimated Sales: $1500000
Number Employees: 20-49
Type of Packaging: Consumer, Food Service

9466 Olympia Provisions
123 SE 2nd Ave
Portland, OR 97214-1002
503-894-8275
Fax: 503-894-8635 info@olympiaprovisions.com
www.olympiaprovisions.com
Salami, sausages, pft,, deli meats and pickles.
Controller: Jim Rowe
Contact: Michelle Cairo
Brands:
    Olympia Provisions

9467 Olympic Cellars
255410 Highway 101
Port Angeles, WA 98362-9200
360-452-0160
Fax: 360-452-3782 info@OlympicCellars.com
www.olympiccellars.com
Wines
Owner: Kathy Charlton
wines@olympiccellars.com
Co-Owner: Molly Rivard
Co-Owner: Libby Sweetser
Winemaker: Benoit Murat
Estimated Sales: Less Than $500,000
Number Employees: 1-4
Type of Packaging: Private Label
Brands:
    Olympic Cellars

9468 Olympic Coffee & Roasting
4907 119th Ave SE
Bellevue, WA 98006
206-244-8305
Fax: 206-244-8323   888-244-8313
Coffee
Director: Robert Doxsie
Estimated Sales: $5-10 Million
Number Employees: 5-9
Brands:
    Olympic Coffee

9469 Olympic Foods
5625 W Thorpe Rd
Spokane, WA 99224
509-455-8059
Fax: 509-455-8329
fruit juice
President: Doug Koffinke
CEO: Howard Chow
CFO: Richard Cook
Contact: Valerie Biladeau
jkskwilcox@msn.com
Estimated Sales: $1-2.5 Million
Number Employees: 12
Square Footage: 348000
Type of Packaging: Consumer, Food Service, Private Label
Brands:
    Albertson's
    Citrus Sunshine
    Dairyworld
    Minute Maid
    Newman's Own
    Tree Top
    Washington Natural
    Western Family

9470 Olympic Provisions Northwest
1632 NW Thurman St
Portland, OR 97209-2519
503-894-8136
info@olympiaprovisions.com
www.olympiaprovisions.com
cured and non-cured meats, pate, and pickles
Co-Owner: Elias Cairo
Co-Owner: Michelle Cairo
Manager: Travis Lewis
tlewis@olympiaprovisions.com
Number Employees: 20-49
Brands:
    OLYMPIA PROVISIONS

9471 Om Mushrooms
5931 Priestly Dr
Suite 101
Carlsbad, CA 92008
Fax: 760-798-8025   866-740-6874
info@ommushrooms.com ommushrooms.com
Organic mushroom powders
Co-Founder: Steve Farrar
Co-Founder: Sandra Carter

9472 Omaha Meat Processors
6016 Grover St
Omaha, NE 68106-4358
402-554-1965
Fax: 402-554-0224 omahameats@aol.com
Beef, pork steaks, sausage
President: David Kousgaard
omahameats@aol.com
Estimated Sales: $30 Million
Number Employees: 20-49
Square Footage: 9000
Type of Packaging: Food Service

9473 Omaha Steaks Inc
800-960-8400
www.omahasteaks.com
sausage, steak, veal and poultry; also desserts and wine
President: Bruce Simon
basimon@aol.com
Senior VP: Todd Simon
Number Employees: 1000-4999
Type of Packaging: Consumer, Food Service
Brands:
    Omaha Steaks International

9474 Omanhene Cocoa Bean Co
5441 S 9th St
Milwaukee, WI 53221-4417
414-744-8780
Fax: 414-744-8786   800-588-2462
www.omanhene.biz
Hot cocoa mixes, chocolate
President: Steven Wallace
Operations Manager: Mario Nissen
Number Employees: 20-49
Number of Brands: 1
Number of Products: 5
Type of Packaging: Consumer, Private Label, Bulk
Brands:
    Omanhene Cocoa

9475 Omar Coffee Co
41 Commerce Ct
Newington, CT 06111-2246
860-667-8889
Fax: 860-667-8883   800-394-6627
www.omarcoffee.com
Coffee carts and roasted coffee and tea.
Owner: Steve Costas
President: Diane Bokron
Year Founded: 1937
Estimated Sales: $30,900,000
Number Employees: 20-49
Number of Brands: 1
Square Footage: 30000
Type of Packaging: Consumer, Food Service
Brands:
    Omar Coffee

9476 Omega Foods
395 Pendant Drive
Unit 2
Mississauga, ON L5T 2W9
Canada
905-212-9252
Fax: 905-212-9484   877-212-9484
info@omega-foods.com www.omega-foods.com
Salmon, tuna, mahi mahi burgers

Food Manufacturers / A-Z

President/Owner: Patrick Sullivan
Director Marketing/Administration: Lisa Baker
Sales: Lori Johansen
Operations: Carl Nelson
Plant Manager: Dana Davis
Estimated Sales: $500,000
Number Employees: 9
Number of Brands: 1
Number of Products: 3
Type of Packaging: Consumer, Food Service, Bulk
Brands:
  Omega Foods

9477 **(HQ)Omega Nutrition**
6515 Aldrich Rd
Bellingham, WA 98226
Fax: 604-253-4228 800-661-3529
info@omeganutrition.com
www.omeganutrition.com
Organic oils: borage, flax, hazelnut, sesame, safflower, sunflower, pistachio, almond and canola; hazelnut flours
Owner: Bob Walbert
Marketing Director: Robert Gaffney
Contact: Simon Hatton
graphics@omeganutrition.com
Estimated Sales: $6.5 Million
Number Employees: 20-49
Square Footage: 64000
Type of Packaging: Food Service, Private Label
Other Locations:
  OMEGA Nutrition U.S.A.
  Vancouver BC
Brands:
  Efa Balanced
  Essential Balance
  Nutriflax
  Omegaflo
  Omegaplus Gla

9478 **Omega Produce Company**
PO Box 277
Nogales, AZ 85628
520-281-0410
Fax: 520-281-1010
cucumbers and bell peppers
President: George Gotsis
ggomega1@aol.com
Secretary/Treasurer, VP: Toru Fujiwara
Office Manager: Norah Romero
VP Sales: J Nick. Gotsis
Estimated Sales: $10-20 Million
Number Employees: 10-19

9479 **Omega Protein**
610 Menhaden Rd.
Reedville, VA 22539
804-453-6262
hq@omegaprotein.com
www.omegaprotein.com
Menhaden oil, red meat and fish.
President/CEO: Bret Scholtes
Executive VP/CFO: Andrew Johannesen
President, Animal Nutrition Division: Dr. Mark Griffin
Vice President, Operations: Montgomery Deihl
Year Founded: 1913
Estimated Sales: $168 Million
Number Employees: 546
Parent Co: Cooke Inc.

9480 **Omega Pure**
1851 Kaiser Avenue
Irvine, CA 92614
562-429-3335
Fax: 562-421-0920 jinman@omegapure.com
www.omegapure.com
Omega-3 fish oil
General Manager: Monty Deihl
Chairman: Blaine Altaffer
National Sales Manager: Julie Inman
Parent Co: Omega Protein

9481 **On The Verandah**
1536 Franklin Rd
Highlands, NC 28741-8557
828-526-2338
Fax: 828-526-4132 otv1@ontheverandah.com
Sauces
Executive Chef: Andrew Figel
Contact: A Figel
otv1@ontheverandah.com
General Manager: Marlene Figel
Estimated Sales: Less Than $500,000
Number Employees: 10-19

Type of Packaging: Food Service, Bulk
Brands:
  Alan's Maniac Hot Sauce

9482 **(HQ)On-Cor Frozen Foods**
www.on-cor.com
Frozen foods: chicken and noodles, hamburgers, lasagna, meat balls, stuffed peppers, stew, turkey and dumplings
Controller: John Statis
VP of Operations: Jim Bowen
Estimated Sales: $5.20 Million
Number Employees: 10-19
Type of Packaging: Consumer, Food Service
Brands:
  On-Cor Frozen Entrees

9483 **On-Cor Frozen Foods Redi-Serve**
1225 Corporate Blvd.
Aurora, IL 60505
920-563-6391
Fax: 920-563-3013 www.on-cor.com
Frozen prepared foods: meat balls, beef patties, chicken patties and breaded veal cutlets
VP, Operations: Jim Bowen

Estimated Sales: $49.5 Million
Number Employees: 250-499
Parent Co: Encore Frozen Foods
Type of Packaging: Consumer, Food Service, Private Label

9484 **Onalaska Brewing**
248 Burchett Road
Onalaska, WA 98570-9405
360-978-4253
Beer
Owner: David Moorehead
Estimated Sales: Under $500,000
Number Employees: 1-4

9485 **Once Again Nut Butter**
12 S State St
PO Box 429
Nunda, NY 14517
585-468-2535
Fax: 585-468-5995 888-800-8075
onceagainnutbutter.com
Organic peanut butter, nut and seed butters, roasted and raw nuts, honey
General Manager: Bob Gelser
rgelser@onceagainnutbutter.com
Chief Financial Officer: Bryan Fritz
VP: Bill Owen
Quality Assurance Manager: Jake Rawleigh
Director Of Sales: Lisa Blatz
Production Manager: Esther Hinrich
Director of Purchasing: Lloyd Kirwan
Estimated Sales: $1.5 Million
Number Employees: 50-99
Square Footage: 40000
Type of Packaging: Consumer, Food Service, Private Label, Bulk
Brands:
  Dawes Hill
  Once Again Nut Butter

9486 **Once Upon a Farm**
San Diego, CA
888-983-1606
care@uponafarm.com onceuponafarmorganics.com
Organic, cold-pressed baby foods
CEO: John Foraker

9487 **One Culture Foods**
1802 Santo Domingo Ave
Duarte, CA 91010-2933
646-650-2989
www.oneculturefoods.com
Noodle cups, sautés, marinades and dip
Founder: Hansen Shieh
Brands:
  One Culture Foods

9488 **One Degree Organic Foods**
PO Box 128
Stn A
Abbotsford, BC V2T 6Z5
Canada
855-834-2642
info@onedegreeorganics.com
onedegreeorganics.com
Cereal, granola, flour, bread, seeds and tortillas

President/Owner: Stan Smith
General Manager: Rickard Werner
Number of Brands: 1
Number of Products: 7
Brands:
  ONE DEGREE ORGANIC FOODS

9489 **One Potato Two Potato**
Womelsdorf, PA 19567
610-589-6500
www.onepotatosnacks.com
Chips
Sales Manager: Lauren Sweitzer
Brands:
  ONE POTATO TWO POTATO

9490 **One Source**
300 Baker Ave
Concord, MA 01742
978-318-4300
Fax: 978-318-4690 800-554-5501
www.onesource.com
Seasonings, spices
President: Philip J Garlick
Chief Executive Officer: Jonathan A. Flatow
Chief Financial Officer: Robert E. Bies
Chief Technology Officer: Hank Weghorst
Chief Marketing Officer: James Rogers
SVP, Global Sales and Services: Colleen Honan
Contact: Nicki Hunt
nicola_hunt@onesource.com
Estimated Sales: $1-2.5 Million
Number Employees: 100-249

9491 **One Vineyard and Winery**
3268 Ehlers Ln
Saint Helena, CA 94574
707-963-1123
Fax: 707-963-1123
Table wines
President: George Watson
Contact: Elaine Watson
ewatson@onewomanwines.com
Estimated Sales: Less than $500,000
Number Employees: 1-4
Type of Packaging: Private Label

9492 **One World Enterprises**
1401 Westwood Blvd
Suite 200
Los Angeles, CA 90024
310-802-4220
Fax: 310-477-7077 888-663-2626
www.onenaturalexperience.com
Nutritional beverages
Chief Executive Officer: Rodrigo Veloso

9493 **Oneonta Starr Ranch Growers**
One Oneonta Way
PO Box 549
Wenatchee, WA 98807
509-663-2191
Fax: 509-663-6333 www.oneonta.com
Apples, pears, cherries, stone fruit, grapes and citrus
President/Owner: Dalton Thomas
VP: Brad Thomas
Director of Food Safety: Mary Jo Gash
Marketing Director: Scott Marboe
Human Resources: Linda Edwards
General Manager: Brian Focht
Type of Packaging: Consumer

9494 **Oneonta Starr Ranch Growers**
One Oneonta Way
Wenatchee, WA 98801
509-663-2191
www.oneonta.com
Apples, pears, cherries, plums, nectarines, peaches, kiwifruit, potatoes, onions, citrus fruits, etc.
Director, Marketing: Scott Marboe
Chief Operating Officer: Shashin Ashraf
Year Founded: 1934
Estimated Sales: $9 Million
Number Employees: 37
Square Footage: 10000

9495 **Onnit Labs**
4401 Friedrich Ln
Suite 302
Austin, TX 78744
855-666-4899
help@onnit.com www.onnit.com
Health foods including supplements, protein powders, coffees and teas, and MCT oils, and snacks

Food Manufacturers / A-Z

Founder & CEO: Aubrey Marcus

9496 Ono Cones of Hawaii LLC
98-723 Kuahao Pl # B3
Pearl City, HI 96782-3103
808-487-8690
Fax: 808-486-5292
Ice cream cones
Owner: Wayne Howard
Marketing Manager: Colleen Howard
Operations Manager: Larry Howard
Estimated Sales: $500,000
Number Employees: 1-4
Brands:
Ono Cones

9497 Onoway Custom Packers
PO Box 509
Onoway, AB T0E 1V0
Canada
780-967-2727
Fax: 780-967-2727
Beef, pork, lamb, ostrich and bison
President: Court Skinner
General Manager: Dave Skinner
Number Employees: 25
Type of Packaging: Consumer, Food Service, Private Label, Bulk

9498 Ontario Foods
1 Stone Road West
Guelph, ON N1G 4Y2
Canada
519-826-3145
Fax: 519-826-3460 888-466-2372
ag.info.omafra@ontario.ca www.omaf.gov.on.ca
Dehydrated and packaged food mixes
President: David Clarke
Export Marketing Officer: Diana Campbell
Brands:
Ontario Foods

9499 Ontario Pork
655 Southgate Drive
Guelph, ON N1G 5G6
Canada
519-767-4600
Fax: 519-829-1769 877-668-7675
krobbins@ontariopork.on.ca
www.ontariopork.on.ca
Fresh pork
Executive Director: Jack Silbar
Director Financial/Operational Services: Lloyd Bauemhuber
Divisional Manager, Communications and C: Keith Robbins
Director Sales/Logistics: Andrew Marks
Estimated Sales: $10 Million
Number Employees: 45
Type of Packaging: Consumer, Food Service
Brands:
Ontario Pork

9500 Ontario Produce Company
PO Box 880
Ontario, OR 97914
541-889-6485
Fax: 541-889-7823
Red, yellow and white onions; dry storage for onions
President and CEO: Robert A Komoto
Office Manager & Transportation: Janet Komoto
Shed Foreman: Arturo Rodriguez
Inspector: Alan Lovitt
Estimated Sales: $5-10 Million
Number Employees: 20 to 49
Square Footage: 160000
Type of Packaging: Consumer, Food Service, Private Label, Bulk
Brands:
A Brand
Foppiano
Fox Mountain
Golden Bird
Real West
Riverside
Rodeo
Silver Spur
Wowie!

9501 Oogie's Snack LLC
1932 W 33rd Ave
Denver, CO 80211-3412
303-455-2107
Fax: 303-496-0153 comments@oogiesnacks.com
www.oogiesnacks.com
Flavored gourmet popcorn
Contact: Laurie Conklin
laurie@oogiesnacks.com
Number Employees: 1-4

9502 Oogolow Enterprises
2560 Dominic Drive
Suite A
Chico, CA 95928-7185
530-893-2646
Fax: 530-893-9344 800-816-6873
Chicken, turkey, beef, ham and vegetable flavored meat analogs, vegetarian tamales, vegan cokies and energy bars.
President: Michael Epperson
oogolow@gmail.com
Estimated Sales: Below $5 Million
Number Employees: 15
Square Footage: 16000
Type of Packaging: Consumer, Food Service, Private Label
Brands:
No Bones Wheat-Meat
Today's Tamales
Tofurky

9503 Ooh La La Candy
855-817-1896
Fax: 914-381-8068 www.oohlalacandy.com
Candies, candy cupcakes, cards, and candy tins
Marketing: Sara Stevens
Contact: Steven Zorowitz
sales@oohlalacandy.com

9504 Oorganik
PO Box 37305
Houston, TX 77237-7305
281-240-7992
Fax: 281-240-2304
Health and dietetic foods
President: N Peabody
Estimated Sales: Under $500,000
Number Employees: 1-4

9505 Opa! Originals
Po Box 25151
Rochester, NY 14625-0151
585-368-5623
anastasia@opaoriginals.com
Greek soda

9506 Opa's Smoked Meats
410 S Washington St
Fredericksburg, TX 78624-4637
830-997-3358
Fax: 830-997-9916 800-543-6750
www.opassmokedmeats.com
Smoked and fresh sausage, ham, beef jerky, beef, pork tenderloins and poultry products
President: Helen Wahl
COO: Michael Schandua
michael@fbg.com
Controller: Ken Wahl
Estimated Sales: $20-50 Million
Number Employees: 50-99
Type of Packaging: Consumer, Food Service
Brands:
Opa's

9507 Optima Wine Cellars
101 Grant Avenue
P.O. Box 1691
Healdsburg, CA 95448
707-431-8222
Fax: 707-431-7828 info@optimawinery.com
Wines
Owner/Winemaker: Mike Duffy
Owner: Nicol Duffy
Estimated Sales: Below $5 Million
Number Employees: 2
Brands:
Optima

9508 Optimal Automatics
120 Stanley St
Elk Grove Village, IL 60007
847-439-9110
Fax: 847-439-9115 www.autodoner.com
Vertical broiler manufacturer
President/Owner: John Georgis

9509 Optimal Nutrients
1163 Chess Dr Ste F
Foster City, CA 94404
707-528-1800
Fax: 707-349-1686
Vitamins and supplements: royal jelly, beta carotene, essential fatty acids
President: Tim Lally
Vice President: Darlene Angeli
darlenea@optinutri.com
Estimated Sales: $500,000-$1 Million
Number Employees: 5-9
Square Footage: 20000
Parent Co: Pegasus Corp

9510 Optimum Nutrition
Dept 75 Meridian Lake Drive
Aurora, IL 60504
630-236-0097
800-763-3444
consumer@optimumnutrition.com
www.optimumnutrition.com
Sports drinks, vitamins and supplements
Founder: Mike Costello
Co-Founder: Tony Costello
Estimated Sales: $1-2.5 Million
Number Employees: 1-4
Brands:
American Body Building
Optimum Nutrition
Science Foods

9511 Opus One
7900 St. Helena Highway
P.O. Box 6
Oakville, CA 94562
707-944-9442
Fax: 707-948-2496 800-292-6787
info@opusonewinery.com
www.opusonewinery.com
Wines
Manager: David Pearson
Director Sales/Marketing: Scotty Barbour
Contact: Aliye Melton
aliye.melton@opusonewinery.com
Winemaker: Timothy Mondavi
Estimated Sales: Below $5 Million
Number Employees: 20-49
Brands:
Opus One

9512 Orange Bakery
17751 Cowan
Irvine, CA 92614-6064
949-863-1377
Fax: 949-863-1932 orangebakery.com
Frozen pastries
Year Founded: 1978
Number Employees: 50-99
Type of Packaging: Consumer, Food Service, Private Label, Bulk

9513 Orange Bang Inc
13115 Telfair Ave
Sylmar, CA 91342-3574
818-833-1000
info@orangebang.com
www.orangebang.com
Fountain and fruit syrups and fruit beverage concentrates
President: David Fox
Finance Manager: Richard Stein
obang@aol.com
Estimated Sales: $4.9 Million
Number Employees: 20-49
Square Footage: 132000
Type of Packaging: Consumer, Food Service

9514 Orange County Distillery
19B Maloney Lane
Goshen, NY 10924
845-651-2929
info@orangecountydistillery.com
www.orangecountydistillery.com
Vodka, corn whiskey, flavored whiskey, single-malt whiskey, bourbon and gin
Founder/Co-Owner: John Glebocki
Founder/Co-Owner: Bryan Ensall
Number of Brands: 1
Number of Products: 12
Type of Packaging: Consumer, Private Label

Food Manufacturers / A-Z

Brands:
   Orange County Distillery

9515 Orange Cove-Sanger Citrus
180 South Ave
Orange Cove, CA 93646-9447
   559-626-4453
Fax: 559-626-7357 www.ocsca.com
Oranges
President: Lee Bailey
General Manager: Kevin Severns
kevin@orangecovesanger.com
Vice President: Shawn Stevenson
Sales Manager: Dave Christofferson
Plant Manager: Bob Johnson
Estimated Sales: $10 Million
Number Employees: 50-99
Type of Packaging: Consumer, Food Service

9516 Orange Peel Enterprises
2183 Ponce DE Leon Cir
Vero Beach, FL 32960-5337
   772-562-2766
Fax: 772-562-9848 800-643-1210
info@greensplus.com www.greensplus.com
Protein powders, energy bars
President: Ryan Deauville
ryan@greensplus.com
Director National Sales/Marketing: Todd Westover
Estimated Sales: $3.5 Million
Number Employees: 10-19
Square Footage: 60000
Type of Packaging: Consumer, Private Label
Brands:
   Fiber Greens
   Greens
   Pro-Relight
   Protein Greens

9517 Orangeburg Pecan Co
761 Russell St
Orangeburg, SC 29115
   803-534-4277
www.uspecans.com
Shelled pecans
Founder: Marion H Felder
Number Employees: 10-19
Type of Packaging: Consumer, Food Service, Bulk

9518 Orca Bay Foods
2729 6th Ave S
Suite 200
Seattle, WA 98134
   425-204-9100
Fax: 425-204-9200 800-932-6722
info@orcabayfoods.com orcabayseafoods.com
Frozen fish and seafood
President/CEO: Ryan Mackey
rmackey@orcabayfoods.com
VP/Finance: Jay Olsen
Senior Marketing Manager: Richard Mullins
National Sales Manager: Mark Tupper
Warehouse Manager: Troy Roy
Estimated Sales: $160 million
Number Employees: 200
Number of Brands: 1
Number of Products: 20
Square Footage: 70000
Type of Packaging: Consumer, Food Service, Private Label, Bulk
Brands:
   Orca Bay

9519 Orchard Heights Winery
6057 Orchard Heights Rd NW
Salem, OR 97304-9509
   503-391-7308
Fax: 503-364-1715
www.orchardheightswinery.com
Wines
CEO: Carol Wyscaver
cwyscaver@orchardheightswinery.com
Estimated Sales: $1-$2 Million
Number Employees: 1-4
Type of Packaging: Private Label
Brands:
   Island Princess
   Orchard Heights

9520 Orchard Pond
400 Cedar Hill Rd
Tallahassee, FL 32312
   850-894-0154
hello@orchardpond.com
www.orchardpond.com
Granola, honey and pesto
Brands:
   ORCHARD POND
   ORCHARD POND ORGANICS

9521 Orchid Island Juice Co
330 N US Highway 1
Fort Pierce, FL 34950-4207
   772-465-1122
Fax: 772-465-4303 800-373-7444
www.orchidislandjuice.com
Kosher, organic, natural juice and cider, non-alcoholic beverages, and full-line frozen products
CEO: Marygrace Sexton
Marketing: John Martinelli
Number Employees: 100-249

9522 (HQ)Ore-Cal Corp
634 Crocker St
Los Angeles, CA 90021-1002
   213-623-8493
Fax: 213-228-6557 800-827-7474
CustomerService@ore-cal.com www.ore-cal.com
Shrimp, pangasius, mahi mahi, swordfish, calamari, breaded shrimp, and ready mixed entree dishes such as; shrimp scampi, seafood gumbo, cioppino, shrimp pad thai, and shrimp torn kha soup.
President: William Shinbane
Human Resources: Josephine Davif
Controller/Vice President Finance: Mark Feldstein
Vice President: Mark Shinbane
Lab Director: Avito Moniz
Human Resources Compliance & Regulatory: Wendy Gomez
Manager of National Sales: Shelley Gee
Manufacturing Supervisor: Rick Kanase
Estimated Sales: $10.9 Million
Number Employees: 50-99
Number of Brands: 1
Number of Products: 11+
Square Footage: 240000
Type of Packaging: Consumer, Food Service, Private Label, Bulk
Brands:
   Harvest of the Sea

9523 Ore-Ida Foods
PO Box 57
Pittsburgh, PA 15230
   412-237-5700
800-255-5750
www.oreida.com
Frozen potato products
VP of Marketing: Fed Arreola
Estimated Sales: $20-50 Million
Number Employees: 400
Number of Brands: 12
Parent Co: H.J. Heinz Company
Type of Packaging: Consumer, Food Service
Brands:
   Creative Classics
   Crispers
   Crispy Crowns
   Crispy Crunchies
   Golden Crinkles
   Golden Fries
   Golden Patties
   Golden Twirls
   Pixie Crinkles
   Steam n' Mash
   Tater Tots
   Texas Crispers
   Zesties

9524 Oregon Bark
1400 NE 37th Ave
Portland, OR 97232
   mail@oregonbark.com
www.oregonbark.com
Vegan, gluten free candy including peanut butter flake candy and hazelnut rosemary crisp candy
Owner: Anne Smith
Year Founded: 2012

9525 Oregon Chai
1745 NW Marshall Street
Portland, OR 97209-2420
   503-221-2424
Fax: 503-796-0980 888-874-2424
nirvana@oregonchai.com www.oregonchai.com
Chai lattes, blends of tea, honey, vanilla and spices.
President: Cory Comstock
VP Finance: Kurt Peterson
Senior VP Marketing: Sean Ryan
VP Marketing: Lori Woolfrey
Sales Director: Tom Carl
Contact: Jeff Card
jeff.card@oregonchai.com
Production Manager: Emile Gaiera
Estimated Sales: $2.5-5 Million
Number Employees: 30
Square Footage: 36000
Type of Packaging: Consumer, Food Service
Brands:
   Oregon Chai

9526 Oregon Cherry Growers Inc
1520 Woodrow St NE
Salem, OR 97301
   Fax: 503-585-7710 sales@pcoastp.com
www.oregoncherry.com
Fresh, maraschino, froze, brined, glance, ingredient and canned cherries.
Chief Executive Officer: Tim Ramsey
tramsey@orcherry.com
VP, Human Resources & Communications: Michele Halverson
VP, Operations: Steve Travis
Year Founded: 1932
Estimated Sales: $46.1 Million
Number Employees: 100-249
Square Footage: 20000
Type of Packaging: Consumer, Food Service, Private Label, Bulk
Other Locations:
   The Dalles OR
   Salem OR

9527 Oregon Cherry Growers Inc
1st and Madison
P.O. Box 1577
The Dalles, OR 97058
Fresh, maraschino, froze, brined, glance, ingredient and canned cherries.
Chief Executive Officer: Tim Ramsey
Year Founded: 1932
Estimated Sales: $46.1 Million
Number Employees: 100-249
Type of Packaging: Consumer, Food Service, Private Label, Bulk

9528 Oregon Flavor Rack
   spice@spiceman.com
www.spiceman.com
Small, medium, large and extra large salt-free spice blends and gift sets.
President: David Johns
spice@spiceman.com
Year Founded: 1991
Estimated Sales: Less Than $500,000
Number Employees: 1-4
Brands:
   Spiceman's

9529 Oregon Freeze Dry, Inc.
525 W. 25th Ave. SW
Albany, OR 97322
   541-926-6001
Fax: 541-967-6527 customerservice@ofd.com
www.ofd.com
Kosher meats, poultry, seafood, sweetened fruits, vegetables, military rations, pet treats
President and COO: Jim Merryman
VP of Finance: Dale Bookwalter
VP: Fred Vetter
Manager, R&D: Norm Jager
VP Business & Technical Development: Walter Pebley
Contact: Kelvin Adams
kelvin.adams@ofd.com
Estimated Sales: $27.6 Million
Number Employees: 201-500
Square Footage: 29000
Type of Packaging: Consumer, Private Label
Other Locations:
Brands:
   Mountain House
   EasyMeal

Food Manufacturers / A-Z

9530 Oregon Fruit Products Co
150 Patterson St NW
PO Box 5283
Salem, OR 97304-4042
503-378-0255
Fax: 503-588-9519 800-394-9333
cooking@oregonfruit.com www.oregonfruit.com
Canned fruits and berries
President: Joe Peterson
joep@ofpc.com
Sales Director: Bryan Brown
Operations Manager: Patti Law
Estimated Sales: A
Number Employees: 100-249
Type of Packaging: Consumer, Food Service, Private Label, Bulk
Brands:
 Oregon Fruit

9531 Oregon Harvest
9348 N Peninsular Ave
Portland, OR 97217
503-249-0092
lillysfoods.com
Flavored hummus and salsas
Co-Founder: Lilly Moscoe
Number of Brands: 1
Number of Products: 9
Square Footage: 80000
Type of Packaging: Consumer
Brands:
 LILLY'S

9532 Oregon Hill Farms
32861 Pittsburg Rd
St Helens, OR 97051-9110
503-397-2791
Fax: 503-397-0091 800-243-4541
Specialty fruit jams, syrups, fruit butters and dessert toppings
President: Thomas Mcmahon
tom@oregonhill.com
Operations Manager: Carmen McMahon
Estimated Sales: $3-5 Million
Number Employees: 5-9
Square Footage: 68000
Type of Packaging: Consumer, Food Service, Private Label
Brands:
 Oregon Hill
 Swan's Touch

9533 Oregon Ice Cream Co.
13115 NE 4th St, Suite 220
Vancouver, WA 98684
360-713-6800
sales@oregonicecream.com
www.oregonicecream.com
Organic ice cream.
President: Tom Gleason
Brands:
 JULIE'S ORGANIC
 ALDEN'S ICE CREAM
 CASCADE GLACIER

9534 (HQ)Oregon Potato Co
650 E Columbia Ave
PO Box 169
Boardman, OR 97818
541-481-2715
Fax: 541-481-3443 800-336-6311
Potato products: flakes, flour, frozen, diced and fresh potatoes
Manager: Steve White
Director QA/Technical Services: Nick Ross
Director Global Sales: Barry Stice
Manager: Frank Tiegs
frank@ftiegs.com
Number Employees: 100-249
Square Footage: 400000
Type of Packaging: Private Label
Other Locations:
 Oregon Potato Co.
 Warden WA
Brands:
 Oergon Trail
 Regal Crest

9535 Oregon Potato Co
P.O. Box 3110
Pasco, WA 99302
509-545-4545
Fax: 509-545-4804 800-987-2726
customerservice@raderfarms.com
www.oregonpotato.com
Potatoes
President: Frank Tiegs
Sales: Jon Jardine
Sales: Steven DiNoia
Sales: Frank Simmons
Estimated Sales: $20-50 Million
Number Employees: 5-9
Brands:
 Brittany Acres
 Cajun Country
 Northland

9536 Oregon Pride
3400 Crates Way
The Dalles, OR 97058-3552
908-537-7539
Fax: 908-537-2582 888-697-4767
Gourmet kippered beefsteak and beef jerky
President: James Perkins
Estimated Sales: Below $5 Million
Number Employees: 10

9537 Oregon Raspberry & Blackberry Commission
4845 B SW Dresden Ave
Corvallis, OR 97333
541-758-4043
Fax: 541-758-4553 www.oregon-berries.com
Berries
Marketing Director: Darcy Kockis

9538 Oregon Seafoods
723 S 2nd St
Coos Bay, OR 97420-1502
USA
541-267-3474
www.seafarepacific.com
Seafood
President/Owner: Mike Babcock
mike@oregonseafoods.com
Number Employees: 10-19

9539 Oregon Spice Co Inc
13320 NE Jarrett St
Portland, OR 97230-1093
503-238-0664
Fax: 503-238-3872 800-565-1599
kevin@oregonspice.com www.oregonspice.com
Spices and seasoning blends
President: Patty Boday
patty@oregonspice.com
Chairman: Larry Black
Estimated Sales: Below $5 Million
Number Employees: 20-49
Brands:
 Oregon Spice

9540 Orfila Vineyards
13455 San Pasqual Rd
Escondido, CA 92025-7833
760-738-6500
Fax: 760-745-3773 info@orfila.com
www.orfila.com
Wines
Owner: Tom Blankenbeker
tom@orfila.com
Vice President: Leon Santoro
Estimated Sales: Below $5 Million
Number Employees: 20-49
Type of Packaging: Private Label
Brands:
 Mendoza Ridge
 Orfila Vineyards
 Quatre Lepages

9541 Organic Amazon
Key Biscayne, FL 33149
info@organicamazon.com
organicamazon.com
A‡ai sorbet snack
Co-Founder: Rodrigo Lima
Co-Founder: Jayson Fittipaldi
Brands:
 A‡ai To-Go

9542 Organic Gemini
68 33rd Street
4th Floor
Brooklyn, NY 11232
347-662-2900
hello@organicgemini.com
organicgemini.com
Tigernut snacks and beverages
Co-Founder: George Papanastasatos
Co-Founder: Mariam Kinkladze
Type of Packaging: Bulk

9543 Organic Germinal
8616 La Tijera Blvd
Suite 512
Los Angeles, CA 90045
310-846-5901
info@germinalorganic.com
www.germinalorganic.com
Organic crackers, bars and cookies
Owner: Emanuele Zuanetti
Number of Brands: 1
Number of Products: 10
Type of Packaging: Consumer
Brands:
 ORGANIC GERMINAL

9544 Organic Girl Produce
900 Work St
Salinas, CA 93901
831-758-7800
www.iloveorganicgirl.com
Organic salad greens, dressings and flavored teas and waters
Owner & Partner: Steve Taylor
Brands:
 ORGANICGIRL

9545 Organic Gourmet
14431 Ventura Blvd #192
Sherman Oaks, CA 91423
800-400-7772
Fax: 818-906-7417 scenar@earthlink.net
www.organic-gourmet.com
Organic vegetarian soups and stocks, yeast extract spreads, bouillon cubes and miso pastes
Founder & CEO: Elke Heitmeyer
Estimated Sales: $1-3 Million
Number Employees: 1-4
Number of Brands: 1
Number of Products: 16
Type of Packaging: Consumer, Food Service
Brands:
 Organic Gourmet

9546 Organic India USA
7088 Winchester Circle
Suite 100
Boulder, CO 80301
888-550-8332
organicindiausa.com
Herbal and organic teas
Contact: Marie Camille
marie@organicindiausa.com
Estimated Sales: $2.8 Million
Number Employees: 12

9547 Organic Liaison, LLC
1515 N University Dr #222
Coral Springs, FL 33071-6096
954-755-4405
Organic weight loss energy and vitamin pills
CEO: Peggy Crawford
Type of Packaging: Consumer

9548 Organic Milling
505 W Allen Ave
San Dimas, CA 91773
909-599-0961
Fax: 909-599-5180 info@organicmilling.com
www.organicmilling.com
Breakfast cereals and granola
President: Wolfgang Buehler
Vice President, Operations: Lupe Martinez
Year Founded: 1960
Number Employees: 100-249
Number of Products: 29
Type of Packaging: Private Label, Bulk
Other Locations:
 Warehouse & Distribution
 San Dimas CA
Brands:
 Nutritious Living
 StaySteady

999

Food Manufacturers / A-Z

Breakfast Choice
Vita-Crunch

9549 Organic Nectars LLC
PO Box 158
Malden On Hudson, NY 12453-0158
845-246-0506
info@organicnectars.com
www.organicnectars.com
Raw low-glycemic agave sweeteners and desert syrups, cashew creme gelato, extra virgin olive oil, gojiberries, and raw cocao products.
Co-Founder & President: Lisa Protter
Vice President: Steve Treccase
stevetrec@gmail.com
Number Employees: 1-4
Type of Packaging: Consumer

9550 Organic Olive Juice
2 Gold St
Suite 3612
New York, NY 10038-4860
info@organicolivejuice.com
www.organicolivejuice.com
Olive oil, spreads and sauces.
Owner: Giuseppe Damiani

9551 Organic Partners Intl.
2705 E Burnside St
Suite 210
Portland, OR 97214
503-445-1065
www.organic-partners.com
Organic ingredient supply company
Managing Partner: Jeff Vinson

9552 Organic Pastures
7221 S Jameson Ave
Fresno, CA 93706
877-729-6455
www.organicpastures.com
Raw milk and raw milk products, including cream, kefir, cheese and butter
President/Owner: Aaron McAfee
Brands:
 ORGANIC PASTURES

9553 Organic Planet
231 Sansome St # 3
San Francisco, CA 94104-2304
415-765-5590
Fax: 415-765-5922 www.organic-planet.com
Certified organic ingredients; edible seeds, dried fruits, tropical fruit, nuts, pulses, sweeteners
President: Hans Schmid
Sales: Carrie Hueseman
Estimated Sales: $20 Million
Number Employees: 5-9
Number of Brands: 1
Number of Products: 50
Brands:
 Organic Planet

9554 Organic RealBar
Diamond Bar, CA
888-622-8828
support@organicrealbar.com organicrealbar.com
Organic snack bars
Brands:
 RealBar

9555 Organic Wine Co Inc
1592 Union St # 350
San Francisco, CA 94123-4505
415-256-8888
Fax: 415-256-8883 888-326-9463
info@theorganicwinecompany.com
Organic wines
Owner: Veronique Raskin
vr@theorganicwinecompany.com
VP: Mike Jinoulhac
Vice President: Michelle Ginoulhac
Estimated Sales: $500,000-$1 Million
Number Employees: 1-4
Number of Products: 45
Brands:
 Bousquette
 Veronique

9556 Organically Grown Co
1800 Prairie Rd # B
Eugene, OR 97402-9722
541-689-5320
Fax: 541-461-3014 800-937-9677
davidl@organicgrown.com
www.organicgrown.com
Fruits and vegetables, tropical produce and dried fruit
CEO: Christopher Anderson
christopher.anderson@marriott.com
CEO: Josh Hinerfeld
Marketing Manager: Stacy Kraker
VP of Sales & Marketing: David Lively
Operations Manager: Anthony Seran
Purchasing/Inventory Director: David Amorose
Number Employees: 50-99
Other Locations:
 Clackamas OR
 Kent WA

9557 Organics Unlimited
8587 Avenida Costa Norte
Suite 2
San Diego, CA 92154
619-710-0658
info@organicsunlimited.com
www.organicsunlimited.com
Organic bananas, plantains, and coconuts
President/CEO: Mayra Velazquez de Leon
Director Operations: Marco Garcia Ojeda
Year Founded: 2000
Number Employees: 10-19

9558 Oriental Foods
2550 W Main Street
Suite 210
Alhambra, CA 91801-7003
626-293-1994
Fax: 626-293-1983
Seafood
President: Dr Venku Reddy
Estimated Sales: $1,300,000
Number Employees: 5

9559 Orientex Foods
1101 Railroad Ave
Pittsburg, CA 94565-2641
925-439-9009
Fax: 925-439-9242 800-660-0962
primoj@ramarfoods.com www.ramarfoods.com
Juice, cider, hors d'oeuvres, appetizers, ice cream, sorbet
CEO: Susan Quesada
susieq@raimerfood.com
Marketing: PJ Quesada
Number Employees: 50-99

9560 (HQ)Original American Beverage Company
74 Chester Main Road
North Stonington, CT 06359-1303
860-535-4650
Fax: 860-535-8545 800-625-3767
Old-fashioned soda and hard apple cider
President: Donald Benoit
Number Employees: 1-4
Square Footage: 20000
Type of Packaging: Consumer
Brands:
 Chester's
 Mystic Seaport

9561 Original Chili Bowl
4200 East Concours Dr.
Ontario, CA 91764
800-548-6363
www.theoriginalchilibowlfoodservice.com
Smoked barbecue meats and chili
COO: Bryan Cather
Technical Director: Robert Hastings
Plant Controller: Lil Green
Plant Manager: John Powers
Estimated Sales: $28600000
Number Employees: 50-99
Parent Co: Ajinomoto Windsor
Type of Packaging: Consumer, Food Service, Bulk
Brands:
 Cripple Creek
 Hickory Hollow

9562 Original Foods
701 Broad St East
Dunnville, ON N1A 1H2
Canada
905-701-7010
Fax: 418-527-3017 888-440-8880
service@originalfoods.com
www.originalfoods.com
Confectionery, syrups, pastry fillings
Assistant General Manager: Phillipe Canac-Marquis
Marketing & Logistics Manager: Kevin Tremblay
National Sales Manager: Dahna Weber
Customer Service: Chantal Langevin
Number Employees: 120
Brands:
 Original 1957

9563 Original Gourmet Food Co
52 Stiles Rd
Suite 201
Salem, NH 03079-4807
603-894-1200
Fax: 603-894-5400 www.ogfc.net
Lollipops and wafers
CEO: Richard Alimenti
EVP: Al Mosto
Estimated Sales: Less Than $500,000
Number Employees: 1-4
Brands:
 Original Gourmet

9564 Original Herkimer Cheese
2745 State Route 51
Ilion, NY 13357
315-895-7428
Fax: 315-895-4664 herkimer@cnymail.com
www.originalherkimercheese.com
Aged NY cheddar cheese, cheese balls & logs, cheese spreads, chocolate cheese fudge & other specialties.
President/Director Marketing: Michael Basloe
Estimated Sales: $3-5 Million
Number Employees: 20-49
Type of Packaging: Consumer, Food Service, Private Label, Bulk
Brands:
 Herkimer
 Ida Mae

9565 Original Juan
111 Southwest Blvd
Kansas City, KS 66103
913-432-5228
Fax: 913-432-5880 800-568-8468
Sauces, salsas, dips and snacks.
President & CEO: Joe Polo
VP, Sales: Greg Dennis
VP, Operations: Tom Clark
Year Founded: 1998
Number of Brands: 13
Number of Products: 1700
Square Footage: 60000
Type of Packaging: Consumer, Private Label
Brands:
 American Stockyard
 Cowtown BBQ
 Da'Bomb
 Fiesta Juan's
 Longhorn
 Mama Capri
 Original Juan's
 Pain 100%
 Pain Is Good
 Pancheros

9566 Original Tony Packo's
1902 Front St
Toledo, OH 43605-1226
419-691-6054
Fax: 419-691-8358 866-472-2567
shop@tonypacko.com www.tonypacko.com
Pickles, relishes
Owner: Tony Packo
Estimated Sales: Less than $500,000
Number Employees: 50-99
Brands:
 Tony Packo's

Food Manufacturers / A-Z

9567 Orinoco Coffee & Tea
8265 Patuxent Range Rd
Suite L
Jessup, MD 20794
410-312-5292
Fax: 240-636-5196 info@orinococoffeeandtea.com
www.orinococoffeeandtea.com
Coffe and tea
CEO: Pedro Ramirez
Master Roaster, R&D: Juan Carlos Ramirez

9568 Orlando Baking Co
7777 Grand Ave
Cleveland, OH 44104-3061
216-361-1872
Fax: 216-391-3469 800-362-5504
www.orlandobaking.com
Italian, French, Rye and Wheat breads, subs, hoagies, kaisers and hamburger buns, dinner rolls and Ciabatta bread
President: Chester Orlando
Marketing Director: Sharon Jones
VP Sales: Nick Orlando
sorlando@orlandobaking.com
Year Founded: 1872
Estimated Sales: G
Number Employees: 250-499
Number of Products: 250
Square Footage: 250000
Type of Packaging: Consumer, Food Service, Private Label
Brands:
  Orlando

9569 Orleans Packing Co
1715 Hyde Park Ave
Hyde Park, MA 02136-2457
617-361-6611
Fax: 617-361-2638 George@orleanspacking.com
www.orleanspacking.com
Olives
President: George Gebelein
george@orleanspacking.com
Vice President: Suzanne Gebelein
Estimated Sales: $1 Million
Number Employees: 10-19
Type of Packaging: Consumer, Food Service, Private Label, Bulk

9570 Orlinda Milling Company
9145 Highway 49 E
Orlinda, TN 37141-2025
615-654-3633
Fax: 615-654-4902
All-purpose and self-rising flour
President: Ricky Stark
Vice President: Bryant Stark
Secretary/Treasurer: Ronnie Stark
Estimated Sales: $470,000
Number Employees: 1-4
Type of Packaging: Consumer, Food Service
Brands:
  Crown Jewel
  Kwik Rize

9571 Ormand Peugeog Corporation
PO Box 227155
Miami, FL 33122-7155
305-624-6834
Fax: 305-624-0911
www.ormandpeugeog@aol.com
Wine and wine products
President: Paul Mirengoff.
CFO: Laura Robledo
Marketing Director: Olga Robledo
Plant Manager: Jose Robledo
Estimated Sales: $3 Million
Number Employees: 4
Square Footage: 240
Type of Packaging: Private Label
Brands:
  Cristal
  Frescas
  Gatomax
  Tai Bueno
  This Way Jose

9572 Orr Mountain Winery
355 Pumpkin Hollow rd.
Madisonville, TN 73754
423-442-5340
theorrs@usit.net
www.tnvacation.com
Wines
Manager: Susan Whitaker
Sales Director: Lee Curtis
Estimated Sales: $500,000-$1 Million
Number Employees: 1-4
Brands:
  Orr Mountain Winery

9573 Ortho-Molecular Products Inc
3017 Business Park Dr
Stevens Point, WI 54482-8835
715-342-9881
Fax: 715-342-9866 800-332-2351
www.discoverourstory.com
Vitamin supplements
President: Gary Powers
g.powers@ompimail.com
VP Sales: Jack Radloff
VP Operations: Dean Kramer
Estimated Sales: $5-10 Million
Number Employees: 50-99
Square Footage: 64000
Parent Co: Ortho Molecular Products

9574 Orto Foods
59 S Route 303
Congers, NY 10920-2470
516-725-5422
info@jicachips.com
www.jicachips.com
Jicama chips
Founder: Xin Wang
Brands:
  JicaChips(c)

9575 Orwasher's Bakery
308 E 78th St # 1
New York, NY 10075-2222
212-288-6569
Fax: 212-570-2706 www.orwashers.com
Breads and rolls: black pumpernickel, challah, cinnamon raisin, marble, potato, rye, sour dough, white, and whole wheat.
President: Aparm Orwasher
Owner: Keith Cohen
Estimated Sales: Less than $500,000
Number Employees: 20-49
Type of Packaging: Consumer, Food Service
Brands:
  Orwasher's

9576 Osage Pecan Co
909 W Fort Scott St
Butler, MO 64730
800-748-8305
sales@osagepecans.com www.osagepecans.com
Pecans and other nuts; also dried fruits
Estimated Sales: Less Than $500,000
Number Employees: 1-4
Number of Products: 100
Square Footage: 80000
Type of Packaging: Consumer, Food Service, Private Label, Bulk

9577 Oscar's Wholesale Meats
250 W 31st St
Ogden, UT 84401-3899
801-621-5655
Fax: 801-394-8113 oscarsmeat@live.com
www.oscarsmeat.comcastbiz.net
Steak, beef patties, poultry, bacon and roasts
Owner/President: Darrell Gardner
Estimated Sales: $25.5 Million
Number Employees: 10-19
Type of Packaging: Consumer, Food Service

9578 Osceola Farms Sugar Warehouse
1810 Old Dixie Highway
Pahokee, FL 33476
561-924-7156
Ground sugar, sugar cane, refining chocolate, sweeteners and confectionary products.
President: Jose Fanjul
VP: John Fanjul
Estimated Sales: $29000000
Number Employees: 1-4
Parent Co: Florida Crystals
Type of Packaging: Consumer

9579 Osem USA Inc
333 Sylvan Ave
Englewood Cliffs, NJ 07632-2724
201-871-4433
Fax: 201-871-8726 800-200-6736
Snacks
President: Izzet Ozdogan
robert@osemusa.com
Sales Exec: Robert Gatto
Estimated Sales: Below $5 Million
Number Employees: 5-9
Brands:
  Osem

9580 Oshkosh Cold Storage
1110 Industrial Ave
Oshkosh, WI 54901-1105
920-231-0610
Fax: 920-231-9441 800-580-4680
ocstg@vbe.com www.oshkoshcheese.com
Cheese, cheese products
Owner: Jordan Doemel
jordand@oshkoshcheese.com
Marketing Director: Stan Dietsche
Estimated Sales: $500,000-$1 Million
Number Employees: 5-9
Type of Packaging: Bulk

9581 Oskaloosa Food Products
543 9th Ave E
Oskaloosa, IA 52577-3901
641-673-3486
Fax: 641-673-8684 800-477-7239
info@oskyfoods.com www.oskyfoods.com
Dried, frozen and liquid egg products.
President: Blair Van Zetten
Controller: Brad Hodges
bhodges@oskyfoods.com
Sales/Purchasing Director: Jason Van Zetten
Human Resource Manager: Joyce Wilson
Estimated Sales: $10 Million
Number Employees: 50-99
Type of Packaging: Consumer, Food Service, Private Label, Bulk

9582 Oskar Blues Brewery
1800 Pike Road
Unit B
Longmont, CO 80501
303-776-1914
www.oskarblues.com
Beer
Owner: Dale Katichis
Marketing: Chad Melis
Contact: John Boetcher
jboetcher@bmhc.com
Estimated Sales: $1.2 Million
Number Employees: 47
Square Footage: 15352

9583 Oskri Corporation
528 E Tyranena Park Rd
Lake Mills, WI 53551
920-648-8300
info@oskri.com
www.oskri.com
Organic coffee, dried fruit and soup bases, teas and herbal products
Owner: Fekri Zainoba
Sales Director: Jen Fredrich
Contact: Tricia Blasing
tricia.kastrosky@gmail.com
Estimated Sales: $500,000-$1 Million
Number Employees: 5-9
Type of Packaging: Consumer, Private Label, Bulk

9584 Osowski Farms
33 Gillespie Ave
Minto, ND 58261
701-248-3341
Fax: 701-248-3341
Sugar beets, grain and dry beans
Owner: Dave Osowski
CEO: Rod Osowski
Marketing Director: Wayne Osowski
Estimated Sales: $1-3 Million
Number Employees: 1-4
Type of Packaging: Consumer, Food Service, Bulk
Brands:
  Wayne

9585 Ossian Smoked Meats
PO Box 405
Ossian, IN 46777-0405
260-622-4191
Fax: 260-622-4194 800-535-8862
www.ossianpackingcompany.com
Beef, pork, pork chops, sausage, steak, hamburger and ham
President: Peter Sorg

Food Manufacturers / A-Z

Estimated Sales: $10-20 Million
Number Employees: 15
Type of Packaging: Consumer, Food Service, Private Label, Bulk
Brands:
  Hoosier Pride
  Ye Olde Farm Style

9586 Osso Good, LLC
San Rafael, CA
hello@ossogoodbones.com
www.ossogoodbones.com
GMO-free, hormone-free and organic bone broth soups in various flavors; bone broth cleanse packages; Paleo diet-friendly soups
Co-Founder/CEO: Jazz Hilmer
Co-Founder/CEO: Meredith Cochran
Co-Founder/CFO: Toran Hilmer
Number of Brands: 1
Number of Products: 19
Type of Packaging: Consumer, Private Label
Brands:
  The Osso Good Co.

9587 (HQ)Ostrom Mushrooms
8322 Steilacoom Rd SE
Olympia, WA 98513
360-491-1410
info@ostromfarms.com
www.ostrommushrooms.com
Mushrooms
President: David Knudson
Type of Packaging: Consumer, Private Label, Bulk

9588 Ota Tofu
812 SE Stark St
Portland, OR 97214-1228
503-232-8947
Tofu
President: Eileen Ota
tofuupsidedowncake@integraonline.com
Estimated Sales: $770,000
Number Employees: 10-19
Type of Packaging: Consumer, Bulk

9589 Otafuku Foods
13117 Molette St
Santa Fe Springs, CA 90670
562-404-4700
info@otafukufoods.com
www.otajoy.com
Japanese sauces
President/Owner: Taka Ozawa
Type of Packaging: Private Label
Brands:
  OTAJOY

9590 (HQ)Otis Spunkmeyer
260 State St
Brockport, NY 14420
855-427-9982
ana.customercare@aryzta.com
www.otisspunkmeyer.com
Frozen cookie dough, fresh baked muffins, baked goods
President & CEO: John Schiavo
Year Founded: 1977
Estimated Sales: $500 Million
Parent Co: Aryzta AG
Type of Packaging: Private Label
Brands:
  Otis Spunkmeyer
  ARYZTA

9591 Otis Spunkmeyer
5855 Oakbrook Parkway
Suite F
Norcross, GA 30093-1838
770-446-1860
Fax: 770-446-2205 855-427-9982
Cookies, muffins, bagels and brownies
General Manager: Buck Hamillton
Contact: Chris Tralka
ctralka@spunkmeyer.com
Estimated Sales: $1-2.5 Million
Number Employees: 20-49
Parent Co: Otis Spunkmeyer
Type of Packaging: Consumer, Food Service
Brands:
  Otis Spunkmeyer

9592 Otsuka America Foods Inc
400 Oyster Point Blvd
Suite 534
San Francisco, CA 94080-1904
415-986-5300
Fax: 415-236-6341 www.otsuka-america.com
Frozen vegetables and purees
Number Employees: 5-9
Brands:
  Wild Veggie

9593 Ott Food Products Co
705 W Fairview Ave
Carthage, MO 64836-3724
417-358-2585
Fax: 417-358-4553 800-866-2585
www.ottfoods.com
Barbecue sauce and salad dressing: French, Italian, ranch and poppy seed
President: Jack Crede
jackc@ottfoods.com
Estimated Sales: $10-20 Million
Number Employees: 20-49
Type of Packaging: Consumer, Food Service
Brands:
  Louis Albert & Sons
  Ott's

9594 Ottawa Valley Grain Products
558 Raglan St S
Renfrew, ON K7V 1R8
Canada
613-432-3614
Fax: 613-432-6148 www.ovgp.ca
Milled, pearled and pot barley, wheat and barley flow
President/CEO: Ronald Wilson
Estimated Sales: $6.7 Million
Number Employees: 11
Number of Products: 7
Type of Packaging: Food Service, Bulk
Brands:
  Valley

9595 Ottenberg's Bakers
1413 Progress Way
Sykesville, MD 21784-0000
410-549-3362
Fax: 410-549-0383 800-334-7264
www.ottenbergs.com
Breads and rolls
Owner: Lee Ottenberg
President: Ray Ottenberg
Plant Manager: Shawn Wooleyhand
Estimated Sales: $20 Million
Number Employees: 5-9
Type of Packaging: Food Service

9596 Ottens Flavors
7800 Holstein Avenue
Philadelphia, PA 19153
215-365-7800
Fax: 215-365-7801 800-523-0767
www.ottensflavors.com
Spray dry flavorings, imitation and natural confectionery oils and spices
President: George Robinson
CEO: Richard Robinson
Eastern Manager: Sharon D'Alo
Contact: Philip Bafundo
philip@ottensflavors.com
COO: Rudy Dieperink
Estimated Sales: $11.5 Million
Number Employees: 50-99
Square Footage: 109500
Type of Packaging: Food Service, Private Label, Bulk

9597 Otto's Naturals
1802 St Rt 31N
Clinton, NJ 08833
732-654-6886
info@ottosnaturals.com
www.ottosnaturals.com
Cassava flour
COO: John Olsen
Brands:
  Otto's Naturals

9598 Ouachita Lumber Co
139 Syrup Mill Rd
West Monroe, LA 71291-7780
318-396-1960
Fax: 318-396-2560 info@ouachitalumber.com
www.ouachitalumber.com
Cane syrup
Owner: Fred Norris
Contact: Barbara Norris
barbara@ouachitalumber.com
Estimated Sales: $1.4 Million
Number Employees: 5-9
Type of Packaging: Consumer, Food Service, Private Label

9599 Ouhlala Gourmet
2655 S Le Jeune Rd
Suite 1011
Coral Gables, FL 33134-5803
305-774-7332
www.buddyfruits.com
Squeezable fruit to go
Owner: Jerome Lesur
jlesur@buddyfruits.com
Number Employees: 1-4

9600 Our Best Foods
170 Main St
Suite 210
Tewksbury, MA 01876-1762
978-858-0077
Fax: 978-858-0052 www.ourbestfoods.com
Hamburger patties, portabella mushrooms, corned beef, roast beef, pastrami, vegan burgers, bulk sliced trukey, meatballs, meatloaf, veal patties, and pepper steaks.
President: Micheal Naddif
Contact: Leon Berns
leon@naddif.com
Estimated Sales: $20-50 Million
Number Employees: 1-4
Type of Packaging: Food Service, Private Label
Brands:
  Our Best

9601 Our Cookie
13301 SW 132nd Avenue
Suite 109
Miami, FL 33186
305-238-1992
877-885-2715
Cookies

9602 Our Farms To You, LLC
7752 Middle Road
Middletown, VA 22645-6006
703-507-7604
ourfarmstoyou@gmail.com
Dairy-free, chocolate, breakfast cereals, granola
Marketing: Melinda Bremmer

9603 Our Lady of Guadalupe Trappist Abbey
9200 NE Abbey Rd
Carlton, OR 97111-9666
503-852-0103
Fax: 503-852-7748 dicklayton@trappistabbey.org
www.trappistabbey.org
Fruitcake, date-nut cake
Business Manager: Richard Laytlon
Estimated Sales: Under $500,000
Number Employees: 20

9604 Out of a Flower
657 Edgewood Dr
Lancaster, TX 75146
214-630-3136
Fax: 214-630-8797 800-743-4696
Edible flower based ice cream and sorbets
President: Jose Sanabria
Estimated Sales: $100,000
Number Employees: 1-4
Brands:
  Chiqui
  Out of a Flower
  Swiss Alp Mineral Water

9605 Outback Kitchens LLC
PO Box 153
Huntington, VT 05462
802-434-5262
Fax: 502-434-5262
Chutney

Food Manufacturers / A-Z

Estimated Sales: $300,000-500,000
Number Employees: 1-4

9606 Outer Aisle
103 Santa Felicia Dr
Galeta, CA 93117
805-242-9265
www.outeraislegourmet.com
Cauliflower-based bread alternatives
Founder: Jeanne David
Brands:
 Plantpower

9607 Outstanding Foods
Venice, CA
www.outeraislegourmet.com
Plant-based bacon alternative
Founder: Dave Anderson
Brands:
 PigOut

9608 Outta the Park Eats
PO Box 3422
Cary, NC 27519
919-462-0012
Fax: 800-341-8511 scottg@outtatheparksauce.com
www.outtatheparksauce.com
Gluten-free, organic and natural BBQ sauce
Marketing: Scott Granai

9609 Oven Arts
200 S Newman St
Hackensack, NJ 07601
Fax: 973-556-4824 855-354-4070
www.ovenarts.com
Brownies, cookies and dessert bars.
President: Betty Osmanoglu
Director, Sales & Marketing: Meghna Kashyap

9610 Oven Fresh Baking Company
250 N Washtenaw Ave
Chicago, IL 60612
773-638-1234
Fax: 773-638-1237
Croissants and muffins
President: George Spanos
gspanos@ovenfreshbaking.com
Marketing Director: Steve Sarsitis
Estimated Sales: $5-10 000,000
Number Employees: 100-249
Brands:
 Oven Fresh

9611 Oven Head Salmon Smokers
101 Oven Head Road
Bethel, NB E5C 1S3
Canada
506-755-2507
Fax: 506-755-8883 877-955-2507
ovenhead@xplornet.ca
www.ovenheadsmokers.com
Smoked Atlantic salmon, salmon pate and jerky
President: R Joseph Thorne
Vice President: Debra Thorne
Estimated Sales: $691,000
Number Employees: 5
Number of Brands: 1
Number of Products: 3
Brands:
 Oven Head

9612 Oven Poppers
99 Faltin Dr
Manchester, NH 03103-5755
603-644-3773
Fax: 603-669-8646
Frozen seafood entrees
President: Stacy Kimball
COO: Andy Desmarais
Plant Manager: James Carigran
Estimated Sales: $5-10 Million
Number Employees: 50-99
Type of Packaging: Consumer, Food Service
Brands:
 Oven Poppers

9613 Oven Ready Products
3-111 Watson Road
Guelph, ON N1E 6X7
Canada
519-767-2415
Fax: 519-823-2196
Frozen pastry food products, beef rolls, fruit turnovers
President: Jim Harrison

Number Employees: 1-4
Type of Packaging: Consumer, Food Service
Brands:
 Oven Ready

9614 Overhill Farms Inc
2727 E Vernon Ave
Vernon, CA 90058
323-582-9977
Fax: 323-582-6122 800-859-6406
sales@overhillfarms.com www.overhillfarms.com
Poultry, meat and seafood specialties; pastas, soups, sauces, vegetarian.
Chairman, CEO & President: James Rudis
Year Founded: 1968
Estimated Sales: $169.22 Million
Number Employees: 500-999
Square Footage: 25000
Type of Packaging: Consumer, Food Service, Private Label, Bulk
Brands:
 Overhill Farms

9615 Overlake Foods
PO Box 2631
Olympia, WA 98507-2631
360-352-7989
Fax: 360-352-8076 800-683-1078
Frozen blueberries, raspberries, strawberries, blackberries and peaches
COO: Rodney Cook
Sales: Paul Askier
Estimated Sales: $1 Million
Number Employees: 4
Square Footage: 5400
Parent Co: Producer Marketing Group
Type of Packaging: Bulk
Brands:
 Overlake

9616 Oversea Casing Co
601 S Nevada St
Seattle, WA 98108-1713
206-682-6845
Fax: 206-382-0883 info@overseacasing.com
www.overseacasing.com
Sausage casings
President: Mike Mayo
info@overseacasing.com
Sales Executive: David Mayo
Estimated Sales: $5.6 Million
Number Employees: 20-49
Square Footage: 31666

9617 Oversea Fishery & Investment
2752 Woodlawn Dr
Suite 5-110
Honolulu, HI 96822-1855
808-847-2500
Fax: 808-836-3308
Seafood
President: Francis Tsang
Estimated Sales: $3-5 Million
Number Employees: 1-4

9618 Owensboro Grain Co
822 E 2nd St
Owensboro, KY 42303
270-926-2032
Fax: 270-686-6509 800-874-0305
www.owensborograin.com
Refined soybean oil
President & CEO: Helen Cornell
CFO: Jeff Erb
Executive Vice President: John Wright
john.wright@owensborocatholic.org
Year Founded: 1906
Estimated Sales: $400 Million
Number Employees: 100-249

9619 Owl's Brew
135 W 29th St
Suite 602
New York, NY 10001-5104
212-564-0218
hoot@theowlsbrew.com
www.theowlsbrew.com
Cocktail teas
Founder and CEO: Jennie Ripps
President: Maria Littlefield
Number Employees: 10-19
Brands:
 Owl's Brew

9620 Oxford Frozen Foods
4881 Main Street
Po Box 220
Oxford, NS B0M 1P0
Canada
902-447-2100
Fax: 902-447-3245 sales@oxfordfrozenfoods.com
www.oxfordfrozenfoods.com
Frozen blueberries, carrots and onion rings
President and CEO: John Bragg
Co-CEO: David Hoffman
Vice President, Sales & Logistics: Matthew Bragg
Customer Service Coordinator: Kerri Baker
COO: Ragnar Kamp
Director of Manufacturing: Milton Wood
Number Employees: 250-499
Type of Packaging: Consumer

9621 Ozark Empire
2301 S 1st St
Rogers, AR 72758-6416
479-636-3313
Fax: 479-631-3895
Bread and buns
Manager: Mike Klingman
mike@harrisbaking.com
Estimated Sales: $21.1 Million
Number Employees: 100-249
Square Footage: 2000
Type of Packaging: Consumer
Brands:
 Best Choice
 Iga
 Ozark
 Tender Crust

9622 Ozarka Drinking Water
4718 Mountain Creek Pkwy
Dallas, TX 75236
817-354-9526
www.ozarkawater.com
Drinking water
Manager: Randy Payne
Estimated Sales: $20-50 Million
Number Employees: 100-249
Parent Co: Ozarka Houston Water Company

9623 Ozery Bakery
11 Director Ct
Vaughan, ON L4L 4S5
Canada
905-265-1143
888-556-5560
mail@ozerybakery.com ozerybakery.com
Pita breads and brioches
Co-President: Alon Ozery
Co-President: Guy Ozery
Estimated Sales: $18 Million
Number Employees: 110

9624 Ozery Bakery Inc
11 Director Court
Vaughan, ON L4L 4S5
Canada
905-265-1143
Fax: 905-265-1352
Kosher bread, biscuits, crackers
Marketing: Paul Vlahos

9625 Ozone Confectioners & Bakers Supplies
55 Bank St
Elmwood Park, NJ 07407-1146
201-791-4444
Fax: 201-791-2893
Licorice, almonds, nonpareil seeds
President: Patrick Lapone
VP: Louis Lapone
Estimated Sales: $3-5 Million
Number Employees: 10 to 19
Number of Brands: 1
Type of Packaging: Private Label
Brands:
 Lapone's Jordan

9626 Ozuna Food Products Corporation
1260 Alderwood Ave
Sunnyvale, CA 94089
408-400-0495
Fax: 408-400-0497 info@ozunafoodproducts.com
www.ozunafoodproducts.com
Corn and flour tortillas, tortilla chips

Food Manufacturers / A-Z

Owner: Vito Ozuna
Contact: Michael Ozuna
info@ozunafoodproducts.com
Estimated Sales: $300,000-500,000
Number Employees: 1-4
Square Footage: 225000
Type of Packaging: Consumer, Food Service, Private Label, Bulk

9627 PDEQ
PO Box 28511
Fresno, CA 93729
559-490-4412
hello@pdeq.net
pdeq.net
Tapioca-based cheese bread
President/Owner: Flavia Takahashi-Flores
Brands:
  PDEQ

9628 P & J Oyster Co
1039 Toulouse St
French Quarter
New Orleans, LA 70112-3425
504-523-2651
Fax: 504-522-4960 contact@oysterlover.com
www.oystercapitalofamerica.com
Oysters
President: Alfred Sunseri
asunseri@neworleansoysterfestival.org
Sales Manager: Sal Sunseri Jr
Office Manager: Merri Sunseri-Schneider
Estimated Sales: $1-2.5 Million appx.
Number Employees: 20-49
Brands:
  Gold Band Products

9629 P & L Poultry
3821 S Bates Court
Spokane, WA 99206-6348
509-892-1242
Fax: 509-892-1244
Chicken and turkey, frankfurters
President: John Singleton
Number Employees: 1-4
Type of Packaging: Consumer, Food Service, Private Label, Bulk

9630 P & M Staiger Vineyard
1300 Hopkins Gulch Rd
Boulder Creek, CA 95006-8632
831-338-0172
pmstaiger@msn.com
Wine
Owner: Paul Staiger
Estimated Sales: Under $300,000
Number Employees: 1-4

9631 P & S Food & Liquor
4910 W Irving Park Rd
Chicago, IL 60641-2619
773-685-0088
Fax: 773-685-0088
Wines
Owner: Edmund Sammando
Estimated Sales: $1 million
Number Employees: 1-4

9632 P & S Ravioli Co
1722 W Oregon Ave
Philadelphia, PA 19145-4726
215-339-9929
Fax: 215-465-3559 support@psravioli.com
www.psravioli.com
Pasta
Owner: Primo Di Giacomo
support@psravioli.com
Co-Owner: Secondo Ravioli
Plant Manager: Mariano DiGiacomo
Estimated Sales: Less than $500,000
Number Employees: 1-4
Brands:
  P&S Ravioli

9633 P & T Flannery Seafood Inc
45 Pier # B
San Francisco, CA 94133-1022
415-346-1303
Fax: 415-346-1304
Swordfish, tuna, seafoods
President/CEO: Terence Flannery
Vice President: Peter Flannery
Estimated Sales: $4,351,163
Number Employees: 5-9

Type of Packaging: Private Label

9634 P C Teas Co
882 Mahler Rd # 8
Burlingame, CA 94010-1604
650-697-8989
Fax: 650-697-9016 800-423-8728
teas4u@teastohealth.com www.teastohealth.com
Herbal tea
President: Sunny Wong
teas888@aol.com
Estimated Sales: Below $5 Million
Number Employees: 10-19
Type of Packaging: Private Label
Brands:
  Natural Green Leaf Brand

9635 P G Molinari & Sons
1401 Yosemite Ave
San Francisco, CA 94124-3321
415-822-5555
Fax: 415-822-5834 sales@molinarisalame.com
www.molinarisalame.com
Dry salami, sausage
President: Frank Giorgi
fg@molinarisalame.com
Sales Manager: Lou Mascola
Estimated Sales: Below $5 Million
Number Employees: 20-49
Type of Packaging: Food Service
Brands:
  Finocchiona
  Toscano Style

9636 P R Farms Inc
2917 E Shepherd Ave
Clovis, CA 93619-9152
559-299-0201
Fax: 559-299-7292 info@prfarms.com
www.prfarms.com
Almonds, olive oil, citrus, tree fruit, wine and raisin grapes
President: Pat Ricchiuti
Number Employees: 100-249
Type of Packaging: Consumer, Food Service, Private Label, Bulk
Other Locations:
  Headquarters
    Clovis CA
  Enzo Olive Oil Company
    Madera CA
  Almond Facility
    Madera CA
Brands:
  Bella Frutta
  P-R Farms
  Enzo

9637 P&E Foods
3077 Koapaka St
Suite 202
Honolulu, HI 96819-5105
808-839-9094
Fax: 808-834-8409
Frozen meats
President: Stephen S C Lee
Contact: Stephen Leong
sleong@avsupply.com
Manager: Harry Toywooka
Estimated Sales: $5-10 Million
Number Employees: 20-49

9638 P&H Milling Group
1060 Fountain Street North
Cambridge, ON N3E 0A1
Canada
519-650-6400
Fax: 519-650-6429 info@dovergrp.com
Baking ingredients and flours
President: Sheila LaLang

9639 P&L Seafood of Venice
401 Whitney Ave # 103
Gretna, LA 70056-2500
504-363-2744
Fax: 504-392-3334 www.chartwellsmenus.com
Seafood
Manager: John Duke

9640 P-Bee Products
31650 SR 20
Suite 3
Oak Harbor, WA 98277
949-586-6300
Fax: 649-586-6360 800-322-5572
www.pbeeproducts.com
Nutritional supplements
President: Raymond Guna
Founder: Steven Kramar
Vice President: Lacey Guna
Estimated Sales: $500,000-$1 Million
Number Employees: 1-4
Type of Packaging: Consumer, Bulk
Brands:
  P-Bee

9641 P. Janes & Sons
PO Box 10
Hant's Harbor, NL A0B 1Y0
Canada
709-586-2252
Fax: 709-586-2870
Seafood
Sales Director: Jeff Galliford
Purchasing Agent: Blair Janes
Type of Packaging: Consumer, Food Service, Private Label, Bulk

9642 P.A. Braunger Institutional Foods
900 Clark St
Sioux City, IA 51101
712-258-4515
Fax: 712-258-1130 www.braungerfoods.com
Frozen meats, general line products
President: Tony Wald
General Manager: J David
Estimated Sales: $10-20 Million
Number Employees: 50-99

9643 P.D.I Cone-Dutch Treat
69 Leddy St
Buffalo, NY 14210-2134
716-821-0698
www.pdicone.com
Sugar cones, candies and cookies
President: Michael Lichtenthal
Chief Executive Officer: James Lichtenthal
Office Administrator: Chrisanne Lichtenthal
Contact: Patrick Illig
pdi@pdicone.com
Plant Manager: Brian McMahon
Estimated Sales: Less Than $500,000
Number Employees: 5-9

9644 P.J. Markos Seafood Company
Eight Topsfield Road
Ipswich, MA 01938-2132
978-356-4347
Fax: 978-356-9380
Seafood
Estimated Sales: $1-3 Million
Number Employees: 5-9

9645 P.J. Merrill Seafood Inc
681 Forest Ave
Portland, ME 04103-4101
207-773-1321
Fax: 207-775-4160 www.pjmerrillseafood.com
Seafood
Owner: Paul Merrill
fpjmerri@maine.rr.com
Estimated Sales: $3-5 Million
Number Employees: 10-19

9646 P.M. Innis Lobster Company
P.O.Box 85
18 Yates Street
Biddeford Pool, ME 04006
207-284-5000
Fax: 207-283-3308 help@poollobster.com
www.poollobster.com
Lobster
Owner: Beth Baskin
Estimated Sales: $3-5 Million
Number Employees: 10-19

9647 P.T. Fish
10b Portland Fish Pier
Portland, ME 04101-4620
207-772-0239
Fax: 907-874-2072
Seafood
Owner: Michael Twiss

Food Manufacturers / A-Z

9648 (HQ)PAR-Way Tryson Co
107 Bolte Ln
St Clair, MO 63077-3219
636-629-4545
Fax: 636-629-8341 moreinfo@parway.com
www.parwaytryson.com
Food release coatings, bakery and seasoning sprays
President: Keyna Lowrey Klabzuba
Owner & CEO: Mandy Hanson
Contact: Mike Abts
mike@parwaytryson.com
Year Founded: 1948
Number Employees: 20-49
Type of Packaging: Food Service, Private Label, Bulk
Brands:
 Vegalene
 Bak-klene
 MallowCreme
 Saragosa Olive Oil
 PuriCit Odor Eliminator

9649 PB Leiner USA
PO Box 645
Plainview, NY 11803
516-822-4040
Fax: 516-465-0331 www.pbgelatins.com
Porcine gelatin
VP, Sales & Marketing: Cheryl Michaels
Contact: Kim Hildebrandt
kim.hildebrandt@pbleiner.com
Parent Co: Tessenderlo Group
Brands:
 SOLUGEL
 PEPTEIN

9650 PEI Mussel King
318 Red Head Road
P.O.Box 39 Prince Edward Island
Morrell, PE C0A 1S0
Canada
902-961-3300
Fax: 902-961-3366 800-673-2767
info@peimusselking.com www.peimusselking.com
Mussels, oysters and clams
President: Russell Dockendorff Sr
Co-Owner: Dorothy Dockendorff
Number Employees: 20-49
Type of Packaging: Consumer, Food Service, Private Label, Bulk
Brands:
 Pei Mussel King

9651 PET Dairy
800 E 21st St
Winston Salem, NC 27105-5354
336-784-1800
Fax: 336-784-1844 800-735-2050
www.petdairy.com
Ice cream, milk
Manager: Dennis Riggs
Division Sales Manager: Don Roland
Manager: Chris Richmond
Operations Manager: Mike Reid
Estimated Sales: $1 Million
Number Employees: 20-49
Parent Co: Dean Foods Company
Type of Packaging: Consumer
Other Locations:
 Spartanburg SC
 Portsmouth VA
 Florence SC

9652 PGP International
P.O. Box 2060
351 Hanson Way
Woodland, CA 95776
530-662-5056
Fax: 530-662-6074 800-233-0110
info@pgpint.com www.pgpint.com
Specialty ingredients: rice flour, breaders
CEO: Nicolas Hanson
Research & Development: Jennifer Eastman
Quality Control: Aman Das
Marketing Director: Cary Maigret-Saptiste
Operations Manager: Joe Holbrook
Number Employees: 100-249

9653 PJ's Coffee & Tea
109 New Camellia Blvd.
suite 201
Covington, LA 70433
985-792-5899
Fax: 985-792-1201 800-527-1055
www.pjscoffee.com
Coffee and tea
Manager: Tom Boudreaux
Owner: Phyllis Jordan
Accounts Manager: Tanya Mareno
Wholesale Manager: Felton Jones
Cafe Operations Manager: Mindy McKnight
Estimated Sales: $500,000-$1 Million
Number Employees: 5-9
Type of Packaging: Private Label
Brands:
 PJ's Coffee

9654 PLT Health Solutions Inc
119 Headquarters Plz
Morristown, NJ 07960-6834
973-984-0900
Fax: 973-984-5666 www.plthomas.com
Extracts for food, supplements and cosmeceuticals.
President & CEO: Paul Flowerman
Executive Vice President: Seth Flowerman
Contact: Jenson Chang
jensonchang@hotmail.com
Number Employees: 50-99
Brands:
 5-Loxin
 Ceamgel 1313
 Ecoguar
 Fenopure
 Glisodin
 Glocal
 Meganatural
 Nutralease
 Nutraveggie
 Nutricran
 Ultraguar

9655 PMC Specialties Group Inc
501 Murray Rd
Cincinnati, OH 45217-1014
513-242-3300
Fax: 513-482-7373 800-543-2466
davidsc@pmsg.com www.pmcsg.com
Saccharin, BHT, methyl anthranilate and benzonitrile
President: Michael Buchanan
Contact: Antaeus Kelly
antaeusk@pmcsg.com
Estimated Sales: $70 Milion
Number Employees: 250-499
Square Footage: 7500
Parent Co: PMC Global, Inc.

9656 PMP Fermentation Products
900 NE Adams St
Peoria, IL 61603-4200
309-637-0400
Fax: 309-637-9302 800-558-1031
info@pmpinc.com www.pmpinc.com
Sodium gluconate, erythorbate, calcium gluconate, gluconic acid, glucono-delta-lactone, sodium erythorbate, calcium potassium gluconate.
President/CEO: Randall Niedermeier
Director, Corporate Planning & Sales: Jim Zinkhon
Director, Administration: Dan Rudy
Year Founded: 1985
Estimated Sales: $25000000
Number Employees: 50-99
Parent Co: Fuso Chemical Company
Type of Packaging: Bulk
Brands:
 Eribate

9657 POG
PO Box 699
Grand Bend, ON N0M 1T0
Canada
519-238-5704
Fax: 519-238-6800
Onions
President/CEO: Nelson J Desjardine
Type of Packaging: Bulk

9658 POM Wonderful LLC
11444 W. Olympic Blvd.
Los Angeles, CA 90064
866-976-6999
pr.pom@wonderful.com www.pomwonderful.com
Pomegranates, fruit juices, extracts and more.
Owner: Lynda Resnick
Chief Executive Officer: Stewart Resnick
Chief Financial Officer: Marc Washington
Marketing Director: Molly Flynn
Year Founded: 2002
Estimated Sales: $762 Million
Number Employees: 100-249
Parent Co: The Wonderful Company
Type of Packaging: Bulk
Brands:
 POM

9659 POP Fishing & Marine
1133 N Nimitz Hwy
Honolulu, HI 96817
808-537-2905
Fax: 808-536-3225 sales@pop-hawaii.com
www.pop-hawaii.com
Seafood
President: Sean Martin
Owner: Jim Cook
Contact: Romeo Caban
romeo@pop-hawaii.com

9660 POPTime
200 Clifton Blvd
Clifton, NJ 07011
862-225-9549
www.poptimesnacks.com
Popcorn
CMO: Valentin Polyakov
Brands:
 POPTime

9661 (HQ)PR Bar
2350 E Germann Rd
Suite 31
Chandler, AZ 85286
480-963-4064
Fax: 858-576-9152 800-397-5556
customercare@prbar.com www.prbar.com
Nutritional drink mixes
CEO: Frank W Busch III
CFO/CPA, Director: Roger L Butterwick
Senior Advisor: Al Springer
VP, Sports Marketing: Anne Marie Berte
VP, Sales: Travis Goodwin
Number Employees: 50
Parent Co: Twinlab Corporation

9662 PS Seasoning & Spices
216 W Pleasant St
Iron Ridge, WI 53035-9665
920-387-2204
Fax: 920-387-2204 www.psseasoning.com
Seasoning and spices
Founder: Harold Hanni
Number Employees: 20-49

9663 PYCO Industries Inc
2901 Avenue A
Lubbock, TX 79404
806-747-3434
www.pycoindustriesinc.com
Cottonseed oil, whole cottonseed, meal, hulls and linters.
President: Robert Lacy
Chairman: Burt Heinrich
Burtaheinrich@gmail.com
VP, Finance: Tony Morton
VP, Marketing: Jerrod Drinnon
VP, Operations: Lewis Harvill
General Manager/Superintendent: Walt Stokes
Estimated Sales: $309 Million
Other Locations:
 Plainsman Switching Co.
 Lubbock TX

9664 (HQ)Pabst Brewing Company
Consumer Affairs Department
PO Box 792627
San Antonio, TX 78279
210-226-0231
Fax: 210-226-2512 800-947-2278
products@pabst.com www.pabst.com
Beers
Chairman: Dean Metropoulos
Co-CEO: Evan Metropoulos
Co-cEO: Daren Metropoulos
President: John Coleman
Chief Financial Officer: Brent Zachary
SVP/General Counsel: Jim Vieceli
Chief Marketing Officer: Daniel McHugh
VP Sales/National Accounts: Mark Beatty
Number Employees: 100-249
Type of Packaging: Consumer
Other Locations:
 Pabst Brewery Location
 San Antonio TX
 Pabst Brewery Location
 Milwaukee WI

Food Manufacturers / A-Z

Brands:
- Augsberger
- Big Bear
- Bull Ice
- Champale
- Clash Malt
- Colt 45
- Country Club
- Falstaff
- Goebel
- Ice Man
- Jacob Best
- Laser
- Old Milwaukee
- Olympia
- Pabst Blue Ribbon Beers
- Piels
- Piels Light
- Private Stock
- Red Bull Malt Liquor
- Red River
- Schaefer
- Schlitz
- Silver Thunder Malt Liquor
- Special Brew
- St. Ides Special Brew
- Stroh's
- White Mountain

9665 Paca Foods Inc
5212 Cone Rd
Tampa, FL 33610-5302
813-628-8228
Fax: 813-628-8426 800-388-7419
Spice blends, beverage mixes, flour based mixes, seasonings, industrial premixes, nutrition blends
President: Robert Cabral
Chief Executive Officer: Michael Shepardson
michael.shepardson@pacafoods.com
VP/CFO: Paul Pritchard
Quality Manager: Ken Crane
Chief Operating Officer: Matt Schneider
Estimated Sales: $5 Million
Number Employees: 20-49
Square Footage: 120000
Type of Packaging: Private Label

9666 Pacari Organic Chocolate
Boca Raton, FL
pacarichocolate.us
Organic Ecuadorian chocolate

9667 Pacheco Ranch Winery
235 Alameda Del Prado
Novato, CA 94949-6657
415-883-5583
Fax: 415-883-6992
contact@pachecoranchwinery.com
www.pachecoranchwinery.com
Wines
Owner: Herbert Rowland
contact@pachecoranchwinery.com
CFO: Debra Rowland
Quality Control: Jamie Mezes
Winemaker: Jamie Meves
Estimated Sales: $2.5-5 Million
Number Employees: 5-9
Brands:
- Pacheco Ranch

9668 Pacific American Fish Co Inc
5525 S Santa Fe Ave
Vernon, CA 90058-3523
323-587-3298
Fax: 323-319-1517 800-625-2525
pehuh@pafco.net www.pafco.net
Shrimp, fish fillets and calamari steaks, rings and strips
Chairman/CEO: Peter Huh
Vice Chairman/VP, Operations & Sales: Paul Huh
VP, New Venture Development: Jihee Huh
Estimated Sales: $37.8 Million
Number Employees: 50-99
Number of Brands: 4
Square Footage: 10600
Type of Packaging: Consumer, Food Service
Other Locations:
- San Francisco CA
- Boston MA

Brands:
- Oceankist
- Pacific Surf
- Pete's Seafood
- Snak N'Go

9669 Pacific Beach Peanut Butter
8691 LA Mesa Blvd
La Mesa, CA 91942-9503
USA
630-329-0792
info@pbpeanutbutter.com
www.pacificbeachpeanutbutter.com
Peanut Butter
President/Owner: Matthew Mulvihill
matthew@pbpeanutbutter.com
Number Employees: 1-4

9670 Pacific Chai
PO BOX 10
Farmington, UT 84025
801-939-9100
Fax: 801-939-9373 888-882-4248
customerservice@indulgentfoods.com
www.pacificchai.com
Chai Tea
Estimated Sales: $5-10 Million
Number Employees: 10-19

9671 Pacific Cheese Co
21090 Cabot Blvd
PO Box 56598
Hayward, CA 94545-1110
510-784-8800
Fax: 510-784-8846 info@pacificcheese.com
www.pacificcheese.com
Cheese
CEO: Stephen Gaddis
sgaddis@pacific-cheese.com
President & CEO: Steve Gaddis
Year Founded: 1973
Estimated Sales: $20-50 Million
Number Employees: 100-249
Square Footage: 45000
Other Locations:
- Excelpro Manufacturing Corp.
- Wellsville UT

9672 Pacific Choice Brands
4652 E. Date Ave.
Fresno, CA 93725
559-476-3581
Fax: 559-237-2096 sales@pacificchoice.com
www.pacificchoice.com
Maraschino cherries, garlic, grape leaves, peppers, olives, salsa, sauces, capers and sun dried tomatoes
President: Allan Andrews
CFO: Faith Buller
VP: Villalobos Boni
Plant Manager: Chris Rabago
Purchasing Manager: Mireille Akel
Estimated Sales: $39.5 Million
Number Employees: 275
Square Footage: 225000
Type of Packaging: Consumer, Food Service, Private Label
Brands:
- Durango Gold
- Orlando
- Pacific Choice

9673 Pacific Coast Brewing
906 Washington St
Oakland, CA 94607-4032
510-836-2739
Fax: 510-836-1987
Beer, ale, stout and porter
Owner: Steve Wolff
info@pacificcoastbrewing.com
Owner/Brewmaster: Don Gortemiller
Estimated Sales: Below $500,000
Number Employees: 20-49
Type of Packaging: Consumer, Food Service
Brands:
- Grey Whale
- Imperial
- Pacific Coast Brewing Co.

9674 Pacific Coast Fruit Co
201 NE 2nd Ave # 100
Portland, OR 97232-2993
503-234-6411
Fax: 503-234-0072 www.pcfruit.com
Frozen fruits, juice concentrates
President: Dave Nemarnik
Secretary/Treasurer: Ellen McIntyre
Accounting Manager: Jeff Rine
Vice President, Director: Don Daeges
Sales Manager: Bob Meikle
Vice President of Operations: Joe Santucci

Number Employees: 250-499
Type of Packaging: Bulk

9675 Pacific Coast Producers
631 N Cluff Ave
Lodi, CA 95240-0756
209-367-8800
Fax: 209-367-1084 877-618-4776
sales@pcoastp.com
Canned fruits and vegetables
President & CEO: Daniel Vincent
dvincent@pcoastp.com
Vice President, Finance & CFO: Matt Strong
Vice President, Sales & Marketing: Andrew Russick
Number Employees: 1000-4999
Type of Packaging: Consumer, Food Service

9676 Pacific Collier Fresh Company
925 New Harvest Rd
Immokalee, FL 34142
239-657-5283
Fax: 239-657-4924 800-226-7274
Beans, cabbage, cucumbers, potatoes, squash, tomatos
Manager: Jennifer Levy
Estimated Sales: $10-20 Million
Number Employees: 20-49
Parent Co: Heller Brothers
Brands:
- Sunripe

9677 Pacific Echo Cellars
8501 Highway 128
Philo, CA 95466
707-895-2065
Fax: 707-895-2758
Wines
Business manager: Mineille Guiliano
Manager: Walter Sawitsky
Winery Manager/Winemaker: Tex Sawyer
Vineyard Operations Manager: Bob Nye
Vineyard Manager: Tony Hortlig
Estimated Sales: $1-10 Million
Number Employees: 25
Type of Packaging: Private Label
Brands:
- Pacific Echo
- Scharffenberger

9678 Pacific Ethanol Inc.
400 Capitol Mall
Suite 2060
Sacramento, CA 95814
916-403-2123
Fax: 916-446-3937 info@pacificethanol.com
www.pacificethanol.net
Beverage alcohol, food grade yeast.
Co-Founder/CEO: Neil Koehler
Director/COO: Mike Kandris
CFO: Bryon McGregor
Vice President/General Counsel: Christopher Wright
Year Founded: 2003
Estimated Sales: $888 Million

9679 Pacific Farms
222 Juana Avenue
San Leandro, CA 94577
877-722-3276
Fax: 510-618-1605 info@pacificfarms.com
www.pacificfarms.com
Dehydrated and frozen vegetables
President: Garry Offenberg
CEO: Nate Offenberg
National Sales Manager: Lorrie Pullman
Operations Manager: Erleen Lum

9680 Pacific Foods
21612 88th Ave S
Kent, WA 98031-1918
253-395-9400
Fax: 253-395-3330 800-347-9444
Flavoring extracts, seasoning mixes, soup bases, baking powder, nuts and spices
President: James Hughs
Plant Manager: Brandan Caile
Vice President: Richard Weaver
Plant Manager: Mark Hendrickson
Estimated Sales: $5-10 Million
Number Employees: 50-99
Type of Packaging: Food Service, Private Label, Bulk
Brands:
- Chef Classic
- Crescent

Food Manufacturers / A-Z

9681 Pacific Foods of Oregon
19480 SW 79th Ave
Tualatin, OR 97062
503-692-9666
Fax: 503-692-9610 www.pacificfoods.com
Broths, stocks, soups, sauces, purees and non-dairy beverages.
Business Development Manager: Michael Mysels
Brands:
Pacific(c)

9682 Pacific Fruit Processors
7301 Ohms Lane
Suite 600, CA 55439
952-820-2518
Fax: 952-939-8106 pfpsalesorders@sunopta.com
Fruit ingredients
Prsident/CEO: Steve Bromley
COO: Frank Gonzalez
Estimated Sales: $93,000
Number Employees: 1
Square Footage: 7384
Type of Packaging: Food Service
Other Locations:
Pacific Fruit Processors
Lapham Co
Brands:
Lapham

9683 Pacific Gold Marketing
2109 E Division Street
Arlington, TX 76011
817-795-4671
Fax: 817-795-4673
Nuts, dried fruit and dark chocolate
President: Patricia Locktov
Estimated Sales: Below $5 Million
Number Employees: 100-249
Parent Co: GNS Foods
Brands:
Pacific Gold

9684 Pacific Gold Snacks
7060 South 238th Street
Kent, WA 98032
253-854-7056
pacificgoldsnacks.com
Beef jerky
President/Owner: Tom Hernquist
Parent Co: Oberto Sausage Co.
Brands:
PACIFIC GOLD
PACIFIC GOLD RESERVE

9685 Pacific Gourmet Seafood
26 Stine Road
Bakersfield, CA 93309-2011
661-533-1260
Fax: 805-831-9740
Seafood
Partner: Kelly Bowman
Partner: Patsy Bowman

9686 Pacific Grain & Foods
4067 W Shaw Ave
Suite 116
Fresno, CA 93722-6214
559-276-2580
Fax: 559-276-2936
www.pacificgrainandfoods.com
Beans, spices, seeds, chilies, edible nuts, dried fruit, rice and wheat.
President: Lee Perkins
lperkins@lightspeed.net
Sales Manager: Jose Alvarado
Number Employees: 10-19
Type of Packaging: Food Service, Private Label

9687 Pacific Harvest Products
13405 SE 30th Street
Bellevue, WA 98005-4454
425-401-7990
Dry blends, sauces, dressings, bases
Contact: Nicholas Ade
n.ade@pnb.org
Number Employees: 20-49
Type of Packaging: Consumer, Food Service, Private Label, Bulk
Brands:
Firmenich

9688 Pacific Hop Exchange Brewing Company
158 Hamilton Drive
Novato, CA 94949-5630
415-884-2820
Fax: 415-884-2820
Beer
President: Tom Whelan
CFO: Robert Ankrum
Brewer: Warren Stief
Estimated Sales: Under $500,000
Number Employees: 5-9
Square Footage: 3
Type of Packaging: Private Label
Brands:
06 Stout
Barbary Coast Barley
Gaslight Pale Ale
Graintrader Wheat Al
Holly Hops Spiced Al
I.P.A.
Irish Stout
Ol' Spout
St. Briogets Strong
Warren's Wonderful W

9689 Pacific Nutritional
6317 NE 131st Ave # 103
Vancouver, WA 98682-5879
360-896-2297
Fax: 360-253-6543
Tablet, capsule, powder and liquid nutritional formulations
President: Michael Schaesser
CEO: Tiffany Swett
CFO: Ron Golden
VP, Sales/Marketing: Tina Mori
COO: Scott Haugen
Estimated Sales: $27 Million
Number Employees: 50-99
Square Footage: 35000
Type of Packaging: Private Label

9690 Pacific Ocean Produce
105 Pioneer St
Santa Cruz, CA 95060-2159
831-423-2654
Fax: 831-423-2654
Dried seaweed
Owner: Matthew Hodel
Estimated Sales: $150,000
Number Employees: 2
Type of Packaging: Consumer, Bulk

9691 Pacific Poultry Company
PO Box 15851
1818 Kanakanui
Honolulu, HI 96830-5851
808-841-2828
Fax: 808-872-0872
Portion controlled poultry, barbecue sauce
President: Jaren Hancock
Treasurer: J Cuarisma
VP of Operations: Brent Hancock
Estimated Sales: $5-10 Million
Number Employees: 50-99
Square Footage: 41400
Type of Packaging: Consumer, Food Service, Private Label
Brands:
Ewa
Hawaii's Famous Huli Huli

9692 Pacific Salmon Company
21630 98th Ave W
Edmonds, WA 98020-3923
425-774-1315
Fax: 425-774-6856
Black cod, halibut, salmon, shark, smelt, squid, kosher foods and fish patties
Owner: John Mc Callum
Contact: James Chapa
johnmccallum@msn.com
Estimated Sales: $5-10 Million
Number Employees: 10 to 19
Brands:
Pacific

9693 Pacific Seafoods International
PO Box 401
Port Hardy, BC V0N 2P0
Canada
250-949-8781
Fax: 250-949-8781
Salmon fillets
President: Hardy Fish
CEO: Todd Harmon
Number Employees: 20-49
Square Footage: 48000
Type of Packaging: Consumer, Food Service, Private Label, Bulk
Brands:
St. Laurent
Treasure Island

9694 Pacific Soybean & Grain
411 Borel Ave
Suite 235
San Mateo, CA 94402-3512
650-525-0500
Fax: 415-433-9494 info@pacificsoy.com
www.pacificsoy.com
Oilseed: corn, soybean and sunflower
Manager: Lina Mesa
Contact: Dan Burke
burke@pacificsoy.com
Number Employees: 1-4

9695 Pacific Spice Co
6430 E Slauson Ave
Commerce, CA 90040-3108
323-890-0895
Fax: 323-726-9442 www.pacspice.com
Spices and herbs
President: Akiba Schlussel
akiba@pacspice.com
Estimated Sales: G
Number Employees: 100-249
Square Footage: 150000
Type of Packaging: Consumer, Food Service, Private Label, Bulk
Brands:
Pacific Natural Spices

9696 Pacific Standard Distributors
38954 Proctor Blvd
Suite 388
Sandy, OR 97055
760-479-1460
Fax: 800-741-2164 sales@modifilan.com
www.modifilan.com
Seaweed supplement capsules
Owner: Vladimir Bajanov
Contact: Michelle Arakaki
marakaki@modifilan.com
Estimated Sales: $1-3 Million
Number Employees: 1-4
Number of Products: 1
Type of Packaging: Consumer, Food Service, Bulk
Brands:
Modifilan

9697 Pacific Sun Olive Oil
22889 Gerber Road
PO Box 955
Gerber, CA 96035
530-385-1475
www.pacificsunoliveoil.com
Olive oils
President/Owner: Jane Flynn
General Manager: Brendon Flynn
Sales Manager: Leslie Stone
Estimated Sales: $15 Million
Number Employees: 15

9698 Pacific Trellis
1500 W Manning Ave
Reedley, CA 93654-9211
559-638-5100
Fax: 559-638-5400 www.pacifictrellisfruit.com
Stone fruits and grapes
Manager: Earl Mc Menamin
Contact: Tim Dayka
t.dayka@pacifictrellisfruit.com
Estimated Sales: $10-20 Million
Number Employees: 10-19

9699 Pacific Valley Foods Inc
2700 Richards Rd # 101
Bellevue, WA 98005-4200
425-643-1805
Fax: 425-747-4221 sales@pacificvalleyfoods.com
www.pacificvalleyfoods.com
French fries, frozen vegetables, frozen berries, tortillas, dried peas, lentils, chickpeas

Food Manufacturers / A-Z

Co-Owner/Co-Director: Scott Hannah
scott@pacificvalleyfoods.com
Co-Owner/Co-Director: Lynn Hannah
Executive VP: John Hannah
Estimated Sales: $2.7 Million
Number Employees: 5-9
Square Footage: 40000
Parent Co: Pacific Valley Foods
Type of Packaging: Consumer, Food Service, Private Label, Bulk
Brands:
  Basic Country Goodness
  Cedar Farms
  Great Gusto
  Hi West
  Lynden Farms
  Pacific Valley

9700 Pacific Westcoast Foods
3880 Sw 102nd Ave
Beaverton, OR 97005-3244
503-641-4988
Fax: 755-665-8610   800-874-9333
gourmet@teleport.com
Salad dressings, preserves, fruit syrups and fillings
President: Mark Roth
President: Gloria Sample
Estimated Sales: $280,000
Number Employees: 4
Square Footage: 20000
Type of Packaging: Consumer, Food Service, Private Label, Bulk

9701 Pacific Western Brewing Company
641 N Nechako Road
Prince George, BC V2K 4M4
Canada
250-562-2424
Fax: 250-562-0799   mail@pwbrewing.com
www.pwbrewing.net
Beer, lager and ale
CEO: Kazuko Komatfu
Marketing Director: Bruce Clark
Office Manager: Denise Vlanchette
Manager: Thomas Leboe
Estimated Sales: $2 Million
Number Employees: 50-99
Type of Packaging: Consumer, Food Service
Brands:
  Amberale
  Iron Horse
  Lager
  Pacific Pilsner

9702 Pacifica Culinaria
PO Box 507
Vista, CA 92085
760-727-9883
Fax: 951-727-9886   800-622-8880
sales@pacificaculinaria.com
www.pacificaculinaria.com
Infused avocado oils, infused vinegars, agave syrups, wasabi mayonnaise, spiced olives, mayan pearl fresh avacados

9703 Paciugo Distribution
1215 Viceroy Dr
Dallas, TX 75247
214-631-2663
info@paciugo
paciugo.com
Gelato, ingredients and beverage pouches
Contact: James Ludwick
james.ludwick@westhoustonent.com
Estimated Sales: $15 Million
Number Employees: 25

9704 Packaged Products Division
12395 Belcher Road S
Suite 350
Largo, FL 33773-3096
727-787-3619
Fax: 727-787-3619   888-833-2247
Snack foods
President: Roger Hoover
Vice President: Jason Brooks
Marketing Director: R Barry Williams
Sales Director: Pat Champagne
Public Relations: Angie Strother
Production Manager: Jerry Adams
Purchasing Manager: Jason Brooks
Estimated Sales: $3 Million
Number Employees: 25

9705 Pacsea Corporation
PO Box 898
Aiea, HI 96701-0898
808-836-8888
Fax: 808-836-7888
Seafood
President: Michael Li
Treasurer/Bookkeeper: Wendy Puampi
Vice-President: Gladis Li

9706 Paddack Enterprises
27052 State Highway 120
Escalon, CA 95320-9502
209-838-1536
Fax: 209-838-8063
Almonds
President: Vernon Paddack
Estimated Sales: $500,000 appx.
Number Employees: 5-9

9707 Paesana Products
101 Central Avenue
PO Box 709
East Farmingdale, NY 11735
631-845-1717
Fax: 631-845-1788   info@paesana.com
www.paesana.com
Pasta sauces, stuffed olives, peppers, artichokes, balsamic vinegars, garlic, mushrooms, olive oils, tomatoes, tuna
Contact: Edna Maniaci
ej@paesana.com

9708 Page Mill Winery
1960 S Livermore Ave
Livermore, CA 94550-9003
925-456-7676
info@pagemillwinery.com
www.pagemillwinery.com
Wines
Founder: Dick Stark
President: Michael Gibbs
Proprietor: Dane Stark
Sales Director: Gary Brink
Manager: Debbie Cristino
debbie@pagemillwinery.com
Operations Manager: Sue Swartz
Vineyard Manager: Leopoldo Gonzalez
Estimated Sales: Less than $500,000
Number Employees: 1-4

9709 Pahlmeyer Winery
811 Saint Helena Hwy S
St Helena, CA 94574-2266
707-255-2321
Fax: 707-255-6786   info@pahlmeyer.com
www.pahlmeyer.com
Wines
Founder: Jayson Pahlmeyer
info@pahlmeyer.com
Vice President: Michael Haas
Sales Manager: Camille Cox
Communications Director: Cleo Pahlmeyer
Controller: Lynn Gentry
Director of Winemaking-Napa Valley: Kale Anderson
Estimated Sales: $4 Million
Number Employees: 10-19
Type of Packaging: Private Label
Brands:
  Jayson
  Pahlmeyer

9710 Pahrump Valley Winery
3810 Winery Rd # 1
Pahrump, NV 89048-4898
775-751-7800
Fax: 775-751-7818   800-368-9463
pvwine@hotmail.com   www.pahrumpwinery.com
Wines
Manager: Bill Loken
Estimated Sales: $5-10 Million
Number Employees: 20-49
Brands:
  Pahrump Valley Winery

9711 Paisano Food Products
261 King Street
Elk Grove Village, IL 60007-1112
773-237-3773
Fax: 773-237-8114   800-672-4726
Dried beans, chicken
President: Paul Williams

Number Employees: 5-9
Parent Co: Cousin Foods
Type of Packaging: Food Service

9712 Paisley Farms Inc
38180 Airport Pkwy
Willoughby, OH 44094-8021
440-269-3923
Fax: 440-269-3929   800-474-5688
www.paisleyfarminc.com
vegetables and relishes
President: Kenneth Anderson
Estimated Sales: $24 Million
Number Employees: 20-49
Number of Brands: 1
Square Footage: 30000
Type of Packaging: Consumer, Food Service, Private Label, Bulk
Brands:
  Paisley Farm

9713 Paklab Products
1315 Gay-Lussac
Boucherville, QC J4B 7K1
Canada
450-449-1224
Fax: 450-449-3380   888-946-3233
Grape juice
President: Claudio Garuti
Finance Director: Assunta Marcone

9714 Palacios & Sons
1431 Greenway Dr
Suite 800
Irving, TX 75038-2574
469-449-2060
www.charras.com
Tostadas, tortilla chips and snacks.
General Manager: Raul Gonzalez
Brands:
  Charras(c)

9715 Paleo Powder Seasoning
979-540-9137
sales@paleopowderseasoning.com
www.paleopowderseasoning.com
Paleo-friendly, organic seasonings
Founder & Owner: Dustin Gersch
Brands:
  PALEO POWDER

9716 Paleo Prime Foods
PO Box 577451
Chicago, IL 60657
312-659-6596
hey@paleoprimefoods.com
www.paleoprimefoods.com
Grain-free protein cookies
Founder: Casey McMillin
Brands:
  PALEO PRIME

9717 Paleo Ranch
Lakeway, TX
www.paleoranch.com
Paleo-friendly protein snacks

9718 Palermo Bakery
1620 Fremont Blvd
Seaside, CA 93955-3607
831-394-8212
Fax: 831-394-0184   www.palermobakeryco.com
Breads
Owner: Rosario Zito
rosario.zito@palermobakery.com
Estimated Sales: $1.2 000,000
Number Employees: 10-19
Type of Packaging: Consumer, Food Service, Bulk
Brands:
  Palermo

9719 Palermo's Pizza
Villa Palermo
3301 Canal Rd
Milwaukee, WI 53208
414-643-0919
www.palermospizza.com
Frozen pizza
CEO: Giacomo Fallucca
Brands:
  PALERMO'S
  SCREAMIN' SICILIAN PIZZA CO.
  URBAN PIE PIZZA CO.
  CONNIE'S PIZZA

Food Manufacturers / A-Z

9720 Palm Beach Foods
352 Tall Pines Rd
Suite F
West Palm Beach, FL 33413-1737
561-242-9229
Fax: 561-584-5780   855-9GL-TEN
Cookies and snacks
Contact: Daniela Sujoy
dsujoy@palmbeachfoods.com
Estimated Sales: Less Than $500,000
Number Employees: 1-4

9721 Palme d'Or
228 Principale
Saint Louis de Gonzague, QC J0S 1T0
Canada
450-377-8766
www.palmedor.ca/en/
Duck foie gras

9722 (HQ)Palmer Candy Co
2600 N US Highway 75
Suite 1
Sioux City, IA 51105-2444
712-258-5543
Fax: 712-258-3224   800-831-0828
vicki@palmercandy.com
www.palmerspecialtyfoods.com
Bagged, multi-pack vending snacks
President: Martin Palmer
Director of Quality Control: Dawn Gorham
VP, Marketing: Bob O'Neill
VP, Operations: Bill Kennedy
Purchasing Manager: Jeff Wilkerson
Estimated Sales: $15.50 Million
Number Employees: 50-99
Square Footage: 420000
Type of Packaging: Consumer, Food Service, Private Label, Bulk
Other Locations:
   Palmer Candy Company
   Kansas City MO
Brands:
   Favorites
   King Bing
   Peanut Butter Bing
   Twin Bing

9723 Palmer Meat Packing Co
1315 S 100 E
Tremonton, UT 84337-8727
435-257-5329
Meat and jerky
Owner: George Palmer
Estimated Sales: $14 Million
Number Employees: 1-4
Type of Packaging: Consumer, Food Service

9724 Palmer Vineyards Inc
5120 Sound Ave
Riverhead, NY 11901-5533
631-722-5364
Fax: 631-722-5634   800-901-8783
palmervineyards@mail.com
www.palmervineyards.com
Wines
Owner: Alexandra Adams
alexandra@palmervineyards.com
Winemaker: Tom Drozd
Estimated Sales: $2.5-5 Million
Number Employees: 10-19
Type of Packaging: Private Label

9725 Palmetto Brewing Co
289 Huger St
Suite B
Charleston, SC 29403-4560
843-937-0903
Fax: 843-937-0092   www.palmettobrewery.com
Beer
President/Brewmaster: Louis Bruce
Brewer: Ed Falkenstein
Estimated Sales: Less than $500,000
Number Employees: 1-4
Brands:
   Palmetto

9726 Palmetto Canning
3601 US Highway 41 N
Palmetto, FL 34221
941-722-1100
pcrbaggs@tampabay.rr.com
palmettocanning.com
Canning and packaging sauces and beverage
Estimated Sales: $5-10 Million
Number Employees: 1-4
Square Footage: 128000
Type of Packaging: Consumer, Private Label
Brands:
   Palmalito

9727 Palmetto Pigeon Plant
335 Broad Street
Sumter, SC 29150
803-775-1204
Fax: 803-778-2896 www.palmettopigeonplant.com
Squab, chicken and poussin
President: Anthony Barwick
Office Manager: Sherry Cannon
Estimated Sales: $10-20 Million
Number Employees: 50-99
Square Footage: 32400
Type of Packaging: Consumer

9728 Palmieri Food Products
145 Hamilton St
New Haven, CT 06511-5837
203-624-0042
Fax: 203-782-6435   800-845-5447
sales@palmierifoods.com
Sauces
President: Mary Palmeri
sales@palmierifoods.com
Estimated Sales: $5-10 Million
Number Employees: 10-19
Type of Packaging: Consumer, Food Service, Private Label, Bulk
Brands:
   Andrews
   Palmieri
   Pinders

9729 Palmyra Bologna Co Inc
230 N College St
Palmyra, PA 17078-1697
717-838-6336
Fax: 717-838-5345   800-282-6336
www.seltzerslebanonbologna.com
Smoked bologna
President: Craig Seltzer
craig.seltzer@seltzerslebanonbologna.com
CFO: Peter Stanilla
Vice President, Sales: Perry Smith
Estimated Sales: $10 Million
Number Employees: 50-99
Type of Packaging: Consumer, Food Service, Private Label, Bulk
Brands:
   Penn Dutch
   Seltzers

9730 Pamela's Products
1 Carousel Ln
Ukiah, CA 95482-9509
707-462-6605
Fax: 707-462-6642   info@pamelasproducts.com
www.pamelasproducts.com
Cookies, bars, flours and baking mixes
President/Owner: Pamela Giusto-Sorrells
Estimated Sales: $450,000
Number Employees: 100-249
Type of Packaging: Consumer, Bulk
Brands:
   Pamela's
   Wheat-Free

9731 Pamlico Packing Company
66 Cross Road
P.O. Box 336
Grantsboro, NC 28529
252-745-3688
Fax: 252-745-3272   800-682-1113
kingcrab1@hotmail.com www.bestseafood.com
Scallops, shrimp, crabs, crabmeat, flounder, oysters, whiting and trout
President: Ed Cross
General Manager: Doug Cross
doug@bestseafood.com
Estimated Sales: $12 Million
Number Employees: 70
Type of Packaging: Consumer, Food Service, Bulk
Brands:
   Seafood People

9732 Pan American Coffee Co
500 16th St
Hoboken, NJ 07030-2336
201-963-2329
Fax: 201-659-1883   800-229-1883
www.panamericancoffee.com
Coffee
President: Roy Montes
Quality Control: Edili Jerridy
General Manager: Ruth Santuccio
ruth@panamericancoffee.com
Estimated Sales: $5-10 000,000
Number Employees: 20-49

9733 Pan De Oro Tortilla Chip Co
3478 Main St
Hartford, CT 06120-1138
860-724-7063
www.pandeoro.com
Tortilla chips
Co-Founder: Richard Stevens
Co-Founder: John Grikis
Vice President: Lief Dana
Contact: Beth Gabriele
gabrielebeth@severancefoods.com
Number Employees: 50-99

9734 Pan Pepin
PO Box 100
Bayamon, PR 00960-0100
787-787-1717
Fax: 787-740-2029   www.panpepin.com
Sandwiches, hamburgers, hot dog buns
CEO/President: Rafael Rovira
Marketing Director: Mario Somoza
VP Finance: Carolina Rodriguez
General Manager: Miguel Santiago
Number Employees: 300
Type of Packaging: Consumer
Brands:
   Healthy Juice
   Nature Zone
   Pan Pepin

9735 Pan's Mushroom Jerky
Vancouver, WA
hello@mushroomjerky.com
www.mushroomjerky.com
Mushroom jerky
President/Owner: Michael Pan

9736 Pan-O-Gold Baking Co.
444 E. Saint Germain St.
St. Cloud, MN 56304
320-251-9361
800-444-7005
info@panogold.com www.panogold.com
White and variety bread and buns, bagels, muffins, donuts, and rolls.
President: Howard Alton
Senior VP/CFO: Dennis Leisten
Vice President, Sales: Brent Schmaltz
Year Founded: 1911
Estimated Sales: $159.89 Million
Number Employees: 1,000-4,999
Number of Brands: 13
Square Footage: 190000
Type of Packaging: Consumer
Brands:
   Country Hearth
   Village Hearth
   Artisan Hearth
   Lakeland
   New England
   Frescados
   Holsum
   Pan-O-Gold
   Fiber Up
   Papa Pita
   Papa's Organic
   Bubba's Bagels
   Maya's Tortillas

9737 (HQ)Pandol Brothers Inc
33150 Pond Rd.
Delano, CA 93215-9598
661-725-3755
Fax: 661-725-4741   sales.domestic@pandol.com
Green, black, red and seeded grapes; persimmons, blueberries, cherries, apples, peaches, plums, nectarines

Food Manufacturers / A-Z

President & CEO: Cheri Diebel
Safety Manager: Andrew Pandol
Account Manager: Andrew Brown
Manager: Carlos Mendoza
Director, Global Operations: David Sudduth
Year Founded: 1923
Estimated Sales: $20-50 Million
Number Employees: 20-49

9738 Pandol Brothers Inc
1737 North Wenatche Ave.
Suite A
Wenatchee, WA 98801
509-662-3763
Fax: 509-663-8449 pandolWA@pandol.com
www.pandol.com
Green, black, red and seeded grapes; persimmons, blueberries, cherries, apples, peaches, plums, nectarines

9739 Pandol Brothers Inc
San Francisco de Asis
150 of 621
Santiago,
Chile
pandolCL@pandol.com
www.pandol.com
Green, black, red and seeded grapes; persimmons, blueberries, cherries, apples, peaches, plums, nectarines

9740 Panera Bread
3630 S. Geyer Rd.
Suite 100
Saint Louis, MO 63127
314-984-1000
www.panerabread.com
Breads, sandwiches, drinks, soups, salads, pastries.
President/CEO: Niren Chaudhary
Founder/Chairman: Ronald Shaich
Senior VP/Chief Financial Officer: Michael Bufano
SVP/Chief Legal & Francise Officer: Scott Blair
Senior Vice President, Marketing: Christopher Hollander
Executive VP/Chief Operating Officer: Charles Chapman III
Year Founded: 1987
Estimated Sales: $2.7 Billion
Number Employees: 50,000+
Brands:
  Panera(c)
  Saint Louis Bread Co.(c)
  Paradise Bakery & Cafe(c)

9741 Pangburn Candy Company
2000 White Settlement Road
Fort Worth, TX 76107-1467
817-332-8856
Fax: 940-887-4578
Candy
President: R Phillips
Estimated Sales: $2.5-5 Million
Number Employees: 50

9742 Panhandle Food Sales
1980 Smith Township State Rd
Burgettstown, PA 15021-2433
724-947-2216
Fax: 724-947-4940 info@panhandlefoodsales.com
www.panhandlefoodsales.com
Frozen pizza
Owner: Bill Dugas
Number Employees: 20-49

9743 Panhandle Milling
4805 FM809
Dawn, TX 79025
800-897-5226
www.panhandlemilling.com
Organic flours, whole wheat products and specialty grains
Brands:
  Panhandle Milling
  Ingredient Integrity
  Specialty Grains
  Specialty Blends

9744 Panoche Creek Packing
3611 W Beechwood Ave
Suite 101
Fresno, CA 93711-0648
559-449-1721
Fax: 559-431-9970 inquiry@panochecreek.com
www.panochecreek.com
Almonds
Owner: Estelle Holland
estelle@panochecreek.com
Vice President: John Blackburn
Marketing Manager: Ross Blackburn
Plant Manager: Jason Baldwin
Estimated Sales: Less than $500,000
Number Employees: 5-9
Type of Packaging: Private Label, Bulk
Brands:
  Golden

9745 Panola Pepper Co
1414 Holland Delta Rd
Lake Providence, LA 71254-5545
318-559-1774
Fax: 318-559-3003 800-256-3013
panola@bayou.com www.panolapepper.com
Spices, hot sauce
President: Grady W Brown
panola@bayou.com
CFO: Janne Brown
Vice President: John Bowers
Public Relations: Jim Byrant
Estimated Sales: Below $5 Million
Number Employees: 20-49
Type of Packaging: Private Label
Brands:
  Gourmet Pepper Sauce
  Panola
  Panola & Private Lab
  Pasta Salad
  Red Pepper Sauce
  Southern Spice
  Steak Sauce

9746 Panorama Foods Inc.
100 Messina Drive
Suite P
Braintree, MA 02184
781-592-1069
info@panoramafoods.com
www.panoramafoods.com
Crackers, drink mixes, and spices
President: Ken Meyers
Contact: Jan Siplon
jan.siplon@panoramafoods.com

9747 Panorama Meats
4325 W. Shaw Ave
Suite A
Fresno, CA 93722
707-765-6756
lori.carrion@panoramameats.com
www.panoramameats.com
Organic beef
Chief Executive Officer: Lori Carrion
Senior Advisor: Mack Graves
Sales Representative: Brian Graves
Contact: Darrell Wood
dwood@panoramameats.com
Vice President, Production: Wayne Langston

9748 Panos Brands
395 West Passaic St
Suite 240
Rochelle Park, NJ 07662
201-843-8900
Fax: 201-368-3575
customer.services@panosbrands.com
www.panosbrands.com
Cheese, Asian food, crackers, cookies, pastes, soy and rice powders, cakes, seafood, salsa
Member President: Kevin McGahren-Clemens
VP Sales: Steve Warner
VP Finance: John Lennan
Marketing: Steven Warner
Contact: Roger Valkenburgh
roger.vanvalkenburgh@panosbrands.com
Purchasing: Kathy Burkowski
Estimated Sales: $2.2 Million
Number Employees: 16
Brands:
  Amore(c)
  Andrew & Everett(c)
  Better Than Milk(c)
  Chatfield's(c)
  Downey's(c)
  KA-ME(c)
  MI-DEL(c)
  Mr.Spinkles
  Sesmark(c)
  Tap'n Apple(c)
  Yankee Clipper(c)
  Zapata(c)

9749 Panther Creek Cellars
110 SW Hwy 99E
Dundee, OR 97128
503-472-8080
Fax: 503-472-5667 info@panthercreekcellars.com
www.panthercreekcellars.com
Wines
Co-Owner: Linda Kaplan
Marketing Manager: Bill Hanson
Sales Manager: Mark Eggiman
Winemaker: Michael Stevenson
Estimated Sales: $750,000
Number Employees: 1-4
Type of Packaging: Consumer, Private Label

9750 Pantry Shelf/Mixxm
PO Box 613
Hutchinson, KS 67504
626-629-342
Fax: 620-662-9306 800-968-3346
Cakes, pastries, baking mixes, cocoa, baking chocolate, hot chocolate, alcoholic beverages, gift packs

9751 Papa Dean's Popcorn
999 East Basse Rd.
Suite 184
San Antonio, TX 78209-3827
877-855-7272
Fax: 210-822-2140 deanneu@aol.com
Flavored popcorn
Owner: Tara Zaglif
Contact: Martha Istueta
papadeans@me.com
Estimated Sales: Less than $500,000
Number Employees: 1-4
Number of Products: 25
Square Footage: 4800
Type of Packaging: Consumer, Food Service, Private Label, Bulk
Brands:
  Papa Dean's

9752 Papa Leone Food Enterprises
205 S Camden Dr
Beverly Hills, CA 90212-1660
310-552-1660
Italian and French sauces
President: Edmond Negari
Estimated Sales: $1 Million
Number Employees: 2
Square Footage: 8000
Type of Packaging: Consumer, Food Service, Private Label
Brands:
  Chef Alberto Leone
  Magic Gourmet

9753 Papas Chris A & Son Co
921 Baker St
Covington, KY 41011-2007
859-431-0499
Fax: 859-431-0499
Candy and confectionery
President: Carl Papas
cpapas@topiczinc.com
Vice President: Chris Papas
Estimated Sales: $1-2,500,000
Number Employees: 1-4
Number of Products: 15
Square Footage: 12000
Type of Packaging: Consumer, Private Label, Bulk
Brands:
  Chocolate Marshmallow
  It's a Boy
  It's a Girl
  Sugar Sticks

9754 Paper City Brewery
108 Cabot St
Holyoke, MA 01040
413-535-1588
Fax: 413-538-5774 info@papercity.com
www.papercity.com
Ale
President: Jay Hebert
Estimated Sales: Below $5 Million
Number Employees: 5-9
Brands:
  Paper City

Food Manufacturers / A-Z

9755 Papes Pecan House
101 S Highway 123 Byp
Seguin, TX 78155-5156
830-379-7442
Fax: 830-379-9665 888-688-7273
mrpetski@aol.com www.papepecan.com
Pecans
Owner: Kenneth Pape
papepecan@aol.com
Sales: Harold Pape
Estimated Sales: $8 Million
Number Employees: 10-19
Square Footage: 60000
Type of Packaging: Food Service, Private Label

9756 Pappardelle's Inc
3970 Holly St
Denver, CO 80207-1216
303-321-4222
Fax: 303-321-8554 800-607-2782
info@pappardellespasta.com
www.pappardellespasta.com
Pasta, ravioli, sauces and pestos
Owner: Adam Steinberg
adam@pappardellespasta.com
Vice President: Paula Steinberg
Estimated Sales: Below $1 Million
Number Employees: 10-19
Brands:
   Pappardelle's

9757 Pappy Meat Company
5663 E Fountain Way
Fresno, CA 93727-7813
559-291-0218
Fax: 559-291-5304 www.pappyschoice.com
Spices and seasonings
President: Marie Papulias
VP: Edward Papulias
Estimated Sales: $2 Million
Number Employees: 20-49
Type of Packaging: Consumer, Food Service, Private Label, Bulk
Brands:
   Pappy's Choice

9758 Pappy's Sassafras Tea
10246 Road P
Columbus Grove, OH 45830-9733
419-659-5110
Fax: 419-659-5110 877-659-5110
pappy@q1.net www.sassafrastea.com
Sassafras tea, green tea, raspberry tea and tea concentrate
President: Sandy Nordhaus
pappy@q1.net
VP: Don Nordhaus
Marketing & Sales: Jeff Nordhaus
Estimated Sales: $360,000
Number Employees: 5-9
Number of Brands: 1
Number of Products: 2
Square Footage: 45000
Type of Packaging: Consumer, Food Service, Private Label, Bulk
Brands:
   Pappy's

9759 Papy's Foods Inc
4131 W Albany St
Mchenry, IL 60050-8390
815-385-3313
Fax: 815-385-3367 www.papys.com
Spices, gravy mixes, seasoning mixes, noodles and sauce
President: Matt Gallimore
custservice@papys.com
Chairman: David Gallimore
Controller, VP Finance: Elizabeth Olson
Estimated Sales: $1.5 Million
Number Employees: 50-99
Square Footage: 260000
Type of Packaging: Consumer, Food Service

9760 Paradigm Foodworks Inc
5875 Lakeview Blvd
Suite 102
Lake Oswego, OR 97035-7347
503-595-4360
Fax: 503-595-4234 800-234-0250
sales@paradigmfoodworks.com
www.paradigmfoodworks.com
Sauces, salad dressings, bbq sauces, marinades, preserves, dessert sauces and mustards
President: Lynne Barra
lbarra@paradigmfoodworks.com
CFO: David Barra
Quality Control: Dr David Schultz
Marketing: Barb Reyer
Sales: Jud Barra
Operations: Sam Barra
Purchasing: Danette Cooper
Estimated Sales: $5-10 Million
Number Employees: 20-49
Square Footage: 80000

9761 Paradis Honey
PO Box 99
5023-50 Street
Girouxville, AB T0H 1S0
Canada
780-323-4283
Fax: 780-323-4238 info@paradishoney.com
www.paradishoney.com
Clover honey, beeswax and pollen
President/CEO: Michael Paradis
Marketing Manager: Jean Paradis
Secretary/Treasurer: Lisa Paradis
Number Employees: 10
Type of Packaging: Bulk
Brands:
   Honey

9762 Paradise Fruits NA
1504 Providence Highway
Suite 7B
Norwood, MA 02062
781-769-4900
Fax: 781-769-4910
jbrownbill@paradise-fruits.com
www.paradise-fruits.com
Frozen fruit and fruit ingredients
Sales Director: Jon Brownbill

9763 Paradise Inc
1200 W Dr. Martin Luther King Jr. blvd.
Plant City, FL 33563-5155
813-752-1155
Fax: 941-754-3168 paradisefruitco@hotmail.com
www.paradisefruitco.com
Candied fruits
Chairman/CEO: Melvin Gordon
President/Director: Randy Gordon
rgordon@paradisefruitco.com
Senior Vice President, Sales: Tracy Schulis
Executive Vice President: Mark Gordon
VP/Corporate Sales: Ron Peterson
Estimated Sales: $21 Million
Number Employees: 100-249
Number of Brands: 6
Square Footage: 275000
Type of Packaging: Consumer, Food Service, Private Label, Bulk
Brands:
   PARADISE
   PENNANT
   SUNRIPE
   MOR-FRUIT
   DIXIE BRAND
   WHITE SWAN

9764 (HQ)Paradise Island Foods
6451 Portsmouth Road
Nanaimo, BC V9V 1A3
Canada
250-390-2644
Fax: 250-390-2117 800-889-3370
lthomson@paradise-foods.com
www.paradise-foods.com
Muffin mixes, cheeses, pasta, yogurt, juice, candy, salad dressings and ethnic foods
President: Len Thomson
Vice President: Kevin Thomson
Estimated Sales: $15 Million
Number Employees: 60
Square Footage: 72000
Type of Packaging: Consumer, Private Label, Bulk

9765 Paradise Locker Inc.
405 W. Birch Street
Trimble, MO 64492
816-370-6328
Fax: 816-357-1229 info@paradisemeats.com
www.paradisemeats.com
Beef, pork and lamb
Owner & CFO: Teresa Fantasma
VP & CEO: Mario Fantasma
Marketing/Sales Director: Nick Fantasma
Plant Manager: Louis Fantasma
Estimated Sales: $2 Million
Number Employees: 21

9766 (HQ)Paradise Products Corporation
17851 Deauville Ln
Boca Raton, FL 33496-2458
Fax: 718-378-3521 800-826-1235
Marinated foods, condiments, olives, artichokes, pimientos, capers, cauliflower, cherries, corn, kumquats, mushrooms, olive oil, pickled onions, salsa, sauces
President: David Lax
Estimated Sales: $10-20 Million
Number Employees: 60
Square Footage: 450000
Type of Packaging: Consumer, Food Service, Private Label, Bulk
Brands:
   Juliana
   Paradise
   Three Star

9767 Paradise Tomato Kitchens
1500 S Brook St
Louisville, KY 40208-1950
502-637-1700
Fax: 502-637-8060 info@paradisetomato.com
www.paradisetomato.com
Pouched tomatoes, tomato paste, puree, sauce and pizza sauce
Owner: Diana Ammons
dammons@paradisetomato.com
Research & Development: Arlen Campbell
Quality Control: Justin Uhl
Purchasing Manager: Nathan Cosby
Estimated Sales: $10-20 Million
Number Employees: 100-249
Type of Packaging: Food Service, Private Label

9768 Paradise Valley Vineyards
4077 W Fairmount Avenue
Phoenix, AZ 85019-3620
602-233-8727
Fax: 602-233-8727
Wines
President: Mark William Stern
Vice President: Tom Dibecco
Sales Director: Jeff Cayton
Estimated Sales: $500-1 000,000 appx.
Number Employees: 1-4
Type of Packaging: Private Label
Brands:
   Paradise Valley Vineyards
   Paraiso Del Sol

9769 Paragon Fruits
8670 Monticello Lane N
Suite B
Maple Grove, MN 55369
763-559-0436
Fax: 763-447-3399 info@spectrumfruits.com
spectrumfruits.com
Fruit ingredients

9770 Paraiso Vineyards
38060 Paraiso Springs Rd
Soledad, CA 93960-9517
831-678-0300
Fax: 831-678-2584 info@paraisovineyards.com
www.smithfamilywines.com
Wines
Owner: Richard Smith
rrsmith@paraisovineyards.com
General Manager: Jason Smith
Marketing Director: Dave Muret
Hospitality Director: Jennifer Murphy-Smith
Production, Winemaker, Sales: David Fleming
Estimated Sales: $1-2.5 Million
Number Employees: 5-9
Number of Brands: 1
Number of Products: 10
Type of Packaging: Private Label
Brands:
   Paraiso

Food Manufacturers / A-Z

9771 Paramount Caviar
3815 24th St
Long Island City, NY 11101-3619
718-786-7747
Fax: 718-786-5730 800-992-2842
ladyofcaviar@aol.com www.paramountcaviar.com
Caviar and smoked salmon
Owner: Hossein Aimami
info@paramountcaviar.com
Vice President: Amy Aimani
Marketing: Amy Arrow
Estimated Sales: $1.4 Million
Number Employees: 5-9
Type of Packaging: Bulk
Brands:
  Canolla Truffles
  Fossen Smoked Salmon
  Manchurian Saffron
  Plantin Dried Mushro

9772 Paramount Coffee
130 N Larch St
Lansing, MI 48912-1244
517-372-5500
Fax: 517-372-2870 800-968-1222
www.paramountcoffee.com
Coffee
President: Jeff Poyer
Chairman and CEO: Angelo Oricchio
VP: Robert Morgan
Manager: Chris King
cking@paramountroasters.com
Estimated Sales: $5-10 Million
Number Employees: 100-249
Parent Co: Interstate Foods

9773 Paramount Distillers
3116 Berea Rd
Cleveland, OH 44111-1596
216-671-6300
Fax: 216-671-2299 800-821-2989
www.paramountdistillers.com
Spirits and liquors
Chairman & CEO: Robert Manchick
CFO: Robert Szabo
Director of Marketing: Lynn Lubin
VP Sales: John Pallo
Plant Manager: Dennis Fratiani
Estimated Sales: $27.8 Million
Number Employees: 337
Square Footage: 100000
Other Locations:
  Paramount Distillers
  Cincinnati OH
Brands:
  Korski
  Paramount
  La Prima
  Canadian Bay
  Gold Award
  Thunder 101
  Lightning 101
  Creme De Cacao
  Creme De Menthe
  Peppermint
  Triple Sec
  Davinia
  Sour Apple
  Peach
  Amaretto
  Butterscotch
  Lasalle
  Colonial Club
  Rock N Rye
  Glaros Ouzo
  Grand Muriel

9774 Parducci Wine Cellars
501 Parducci Rd
Ukiah, CA 95482-3015
707-463-5357
Fax: 707-462-7260 888-362-9463
info@mendocinowineco.com www.parducci.com
Wines
Manager: Tim Thornhill
timthornhill@mendocinowineco.com
Marketing: David Hance
Winemaker: Robert Swain
Estimated Sales: $2 Million
Number Employees: 20-49

9775 (HQ)Paris Foods Corporation
3965 Ocean Gateway
P.O. Box 121
Trappe, MD 21673
410-200-9595
sales@parisfoods.com
www.parisfoods.com
Fruits and vegetables
Sales Contact: Ward Cain
ward@parisfoods.com
Estimated Sales: $50 Million
Number Employees: 100
Square Footage: 67000
Type of Packaging: Consumer, Food Service
Other Locations:
  Paris Foods Forwarding Warehouse
  Walkerville MI
  Paris Foods Distribution Center
  Lexington NC
  Paris Foods Distribution Center
  Houston DE
  Cresco IA
  Pittsburgh PA
  Pennsauken NJ
  Hillsboro IL

9776 Paris Pastry
7008 Shoshone Ave
Van Nuys, CA 91406
310-474-8888
Fax: 310-470-2097 805-487-2227
Mousses, cookies
President: Raymond Lobjois
Executive Chef: Eric Westphal
Estimated Sales: $260,000
Number Employees: 10-19
Square Footage: 48000
Type of Packaging: Consumer, Food Service, Private Label, Bulk

9777 (HQ)Parish Chemical Company
P.O.Box 277
Orem, UT 84059-0277
801-226-2018
Fax: 801-226-8496
Nutritional food additives, acidulants and preservatives, ferulic acid, carboxyethylgermanium sesquioxide and indole-3-carbinol
President: W Wesley Parish
Marketing Director: Bill Ellenberger
Estimated Sales: $1 Million
Number Employees: 20-49
Square Footage: 100000
Type of Packaging: Bulk
Other Locations:
  Parish Chemical Co.
  Orem UT

9778 (HQ)Park 100 Foods Inc
326 E Adams St
Tipton, IN 46072-2001
765-675-3480
Fax: 765-675-3474 800-854-6504
www.park100foods.com
Soups, sauces, chili, side dishes, gravies, fruit toppings, dips, entrees, breaded meats, seafood, pasta and protein kits
Chairman: Jim Washburn
jwashburn@park100foods.com
President: Gary Meade
VP: David Alves
Project Manager/National Sales: Robert Orr
Sales: Mike Taft
Estimated Sales: $20-50 Million
Number Employees: 50-99
Square Footage: 100000
Other Locations:
  Kettle Processed Foods
  Morristown IN
  Kettle Processed Foods
  Kokomo IN
Brands:
  Park 100 Foods

9779 Park Avenue Bakery
44 South Park Ave
Helena, MT 59601
406-449-8424
www.parkavenuebakery.net
Breads, pastries, rolls, pizzas

9780 Park Cheese Company Inc
168 Larsen Drive
Fond Du Lac, WI 54937-8519
Fax: 920-923-8485 800-752-7275
Italian cheeses: asiago, aged provolone, romano, parmesan, pepato, fontina, Italian sharp, kasseri, and milk provolone.
President & COO: Eric Liebetrau
CEO: Alfred Liebetrau
Secretary/Treasurer: Lylia Liebetrau
Manager: Jason Blank
Director Sales & Marketing: Linda Cizek
Contact: Sue Behling
sueb@belgioioso.com
Plant Manager/General Manager: Steve Heard
Number Employees: 70
Square Footage: 80000
Type of Packaging: Consumer, Food Service, Private Label, Bulk
Brands:
  Casaro

9781 Parker Farm
9405 Holly Street
Suite B
Minneapolis, MN 55433
763-780-5100
Fax: 763-780-5104 800-869-6685
Cheese, peanut butter, cream cheese and salsa
President: Rick Etrheim
Estimated Sales: $5 Million
Number Employees: 20-49
Type of Packaging: Private Label

9782 Parker Fish Company
63 Cross Cedar Rd
PO Box 324
Wrightsville, GA 31096-5300
478-864-3406
Fax: 478-864-9417
Seafood
President: Jeff Powell
Manager: Dennis Moore
Estimated Sales: $5-10 Million
Number Employees: 10-19

9783 Parker Flavors Inc
1801 Portal Street
Baltimore, MD 21224
410-633-2230
Fax: 410-633-3530 800-336-9113
parkerflavors.com
Extracts, emulsions and flavors
CEO: Tim Parker
Type of Packaging: Consumer, Food Service, Private Label, Bulk
Brands:
  Parker

9784 Parker House Sausage Co
4605 S State St
Chicago, IL 60609-4699
773-538-1112
Fax: 773-285-0903 www.parkerhousesausage.com
Sausage
CEO: Sherlyn Alhambra
salhambra@parkerhousesausage.com
Number Employees: 20-49

9785 (HQ)Parker Products
3020 W. Lancaster Avenue
Fort Worth, TX 76107
817-336-7441
Fax: 817-877-1261 info@parkerproducts.com
www.parkerproducts.com
Desserts, candy, confectionery, ice cream toppings, fudge and flavors
President: Greg Hodder
Contact: Kim Ballinger
kim@parkerproducts.com
Estimated Sales: $10-19 Million
Number Employees: 30
Square Footage: 58000
Type of Packaging: Private Label, Bulk
Other Locations:
  Parker Products
  Andrews TX

9786 Parkers Farm
9405 Holly St NW
Suite B
Coon Rapids, MN 55433-5976
763-780-5100
Fax: 763-780-5104 800-869-6685
info@parkersfarm.com
Cheeses and bagel spreads
President: Rick Etrheim
Estimated Sales: $10-20 Million
Number Employees: 20-49

Type of Packaging: Consumer, Food Service, Private Label, Bulk

9787 (HQ)Parkside Candy Co
3208 Main St
Suite 1
Buffalo, NY 14214-1379
716-833-7540
Fax: 716-833-7560 www.parksidecandy.com
Lollipops, chocolates, fudge, pretzels
President: Phil Buffamonte
sales@parksidecandy.com
Estimated Sales: $14 Million
Number Employees: 20-49
Type of Packaging: Consumer, Food Service, Private Label, Bulk
Brands:
  Aunt Angies
  Old Fashioned

9788 Parma Sausage Products
1734 Penn Ave
Pittsburgh, PA 15222-4385
412-391-4238
Fax: 412-391-7717 877-294-4207
www.parmasausage.com
Sausage, prosciutto, coppa secca and salami, capicollo, mortadella, salami rosa, kolbassie, andouille, chorizo
President: Rina Edwards
darren@parmasausage.com
Vice President: Rita Spinabelli
Sales Exec: Darren Schumacher
Purchasing Manager: John Edwards
Estimated Sales: $1300000
Number Employees: 20-49
Type of Packaging: Consumer, Food Service, Private Label, Bulk
Brands:
  Gigi
  Parma

9789 Parmalat Canada
405 The West Mall
10th Floor
Toronto, ON M9C 5J1
Canada
800-563-1515
parmalat.ca
Milk, cheeses, spreads and yogurt.
CEO: Mark Taylor
Year Founded: 1997
Estimated Sales: $1.9 Billion
Number Employees: 3,500
Number of Brands: 10
Parent Co: Lactalis
Type of Packaging: Consumer, Food Service, Private Label, Bulk
Brands:
  Lactantia
  Beatrice
  Cracker Barrel
  Black Diamond
  Cheestrings
  Balderson
  Galbani
  Astro
  President
  Siggi's
  P'tit Quebec
  aMOOza!

9790 Parmela Creamery
Torrance, CA
310-584-7541
contact@parmelacreamery.com
www.parmelacreamery.com
Nut-based cheeses
Co-Founder: Laurice Do
laurice@parmelacreamery.com

9791 Parmenter's Northville Cider Mill
714 Baseline Rd
Northville, MI 48167
248-349-3181
Fax: 248-349-1165 info@northvillecider.com
www.northvillecider.com
Apple cider, preserves, donuts, maple products, apple products, specialty organic
President: Diane Jones
d_jones@northvillecider.com
Vice President: Cheryl Nelson
Estimated Sales: $250 Thousand
Number Employees: 50
Number of Brands: 1
Type of Packaging: Consumer
Brands:
  Parmenter's Northville Cider Mill

9792 Parmx
4117-16a Street SE
Calgary, AB T2G 3T7
Canada
403-237-0707
Fax: 403-264-2153
Parmesan cheese
President/CEO: Vincent Aiello
Production: Frank Aiello
Number Employees: 20-49
Type of Packaging: Consumer, Food Service
Brands:
  Parmx Cheese

9793 Parny Gourmet
390 NE 59th Terrace
Miami, FL 33137
305-798-5177
parny.gourmet@gmail.com
Sugar biscuits, candied hot pepper, pepper jam and sauce
Chef: Irene Brizard De Parny

9794 Parrish's Cake Decorating
225 W 146th St
Gardena, CA 90248-1803
310-324-2253
Fax: 310-324-8277 800-736-8443
Aluminum cake pans, cookie cutters, artificial icing, candy molds, plates and pillars, pastry bags, food colors and flavorings
President: Bob Parrish
customerservice@parrishsmagicline.com
VP: Norma Parrish
Estimated Sales: $1-3 Million
Number Employees: 10-19
Number of Products: 4000
Square Footage: 180000
Type of Packaging: Consumer, Food Service, Private Label, Bulk
Brands:
  Magic Line
  Magic Mist
  Magic Mold
  Perma-Ice

9795 Parthenon Food Products
226 S Main St
Ann Arbor, MI 48104-2106
734-994-1012
Fax: 734-994-7073 www.parthenonfoods.com
Greek salad dressings and marinades
President/Owner: Steve Gavas
CFO: John Gavas
Estimated Sales: $500,000
Number Employees: 10-19
Square Footage: 4000
Type of Packaging: Consumer, Food Service, Private Label, Bulk
Brands:
  Perthenon Greek Salad Dressing

9796 Particle Control
6062 Lambert Ave NE
Albertville, MN 55301-3919
763-497-3075
Fax: 763-497-1773 norm@particlecontrolinc.com
www.particlecontrolinc.com
Flavors, whey, oat flour, sugar
President: Bill Arns
bill@particlecontrolinc.com
Estimated Sales: $700,000
Number Employees: 5-9
Square Footage: 104000

9797 Particle Dynamics
2601 S Hanley Rd
Saint Louis, MO 63144
314-968-2376
Fax: 314-646-3761 800-452-4682
info@particledynamics.com
www.particledynamics.com
Vitamins, minerals, flavors, acidulants, colors, spices
President: Paul T Brady
Marketing: Andrea Keith
Sales VP: Richard Miller
Contact: Sonia Belotti
sonia.belotti@savannah.co.za
Purchasing: Jim Cronk
Estimated Sales: $3500000
Number Employees: 20-49
Square Footage: 180000
Parent Co: KV Pharmaceutical
Type of Packaging: Bulk
Brands:
  Descote
  Destab
  Micromask

9798 Partners Coffee LLC
4225 Westfield Dr SW
Atlanta, GA 30336-2651
404-344-5282
Fax: 404-349-6442 800-341-5282
Coffee
President: James Gilson
CEO: Mike Bacco
mjbacco@partnerscoffee.com
Sales/Marketing: Bert Kelly
Operations Manager: Gerry Larue
Production Manager: Bob Frazier
Purchasing Manager: Anne Gilson
Estimated Sales: $2559650
Number Employees: 10-19
Number of Brands: 3
Number of Products: 200
Square Footage: 80000
Type of Packaging: Consumer, Food Service, Private Label, Bulk
Brands:
  Casa Europa
  H&C
  Partners

9799 Partners: A Tasteful Choice
20232 72nd Avenue South
Kent, WA 98032
253-867-1580
Fax: 206-762-8424 800-632-7477
service@partnerscrackers.com
www.partnerscrackers.com
Crackers, granola, cookies
President & Owner: Marian Harris
Vice President, Sales, Owner: Cara Figgins
caraf@partnerscrackers.com
Estimated Sales: $500,000-$1 Million
Number Employees: 1-4
Square Footage: 48000
Brands:
  Blue Star Farms
  Cracker Snackers
  Get Movin Snack Packss
  Gourmet Granola
  Partners
  Wisecrackers

9800 Pascal Coffee
960 Nepperhan Ave
Yonkers, NY 10703-1726
914-969-7933
Fax: 914-969-8248 roaster@optonline.net
Coffee
Manager: Dean Peialteos
Estimated Sales: Below $5 Million
Number Employees: 20-49
Brands:
  Pascal Coffee

9801 Pascha Chocolate
1920 Yonge St.
Suite 200
Toronto, Ontario, M4S 3E6
CAN
855-472-7242
info@paschachocolate.com
paschachocolate.com
Organic chocolate
President & CEO: Simon Lester
Year Founded: 2013
Number Employees: 1-10

9802 Pascobel Inc
2066 De La Province
Longueuil, QC J4G 1R7
Canada
450-677-2443
Fax: 450-677-2899

Food Manufacturers / A-Z

Combolak, coverblak, viseolak, culurelak, fractolak and nonfat milk solids
President: Jean Guy Lauziere
Sales Manager: Guy Bouthillier
Technical Director: Pierre Combeaud
Number Employees: 20-49
Square Footage: 60000
Type of Packaging: Private Label, Bulk
Brands:
  Belcover
  Comboliak
  Coverlak
  Culturelak
  Fractolak
  Nollibel
  Viscolak

9803 Pasolivo Willow Creek Olive Ranch
8530 Vineyard Drive
Paso Robles, CA 93446
805-227-0186
Fax: 805-226-8809 info@pasolivo.com
www.pasolivo.com
Olive oils
General Manger: Jillian Pasolivo
Marketing: Joel Pasolivo

9804 Pasqualichio Brothers Inc
115 Franklin Ave
Scranton, PA 18503-1935
570-346-7115
Fax: 570-346-4610 800-232-6233
www.butchervangourmet.com
Beef, veal, lamb, turkey, chicken and pork
President: Michael Pasqualichio
Owner: Don Pasqualichio
VP: Patrick Pasqualichio
Plant Manager: William Pasqualichio
Estimated Sales: $10 Million
Number Employees: 10-19
Square Footage: 20000
Type of Packaging: Consumer
Brands:
  Pasqualichio

9805 Passage Foods LLC
30 Depot Street
PO Box 245
Collinsville, CT 06022
800-860-1045
Fax: 860-256-4559 info@passageusa.com
www.passagefoods.com
Ethnic sauces (soy, curry), grilling sauces, seasonings
Marketing: Mark Mackenzie
Contact: Chris Doutre
chris.doutre@passagefoods.com

9806 Passetti's Pride
923 Hotel Avenue
Hayward, CA 94541-4001
510-728-4969
Fax: 510-886-6909 800-521-4659
Sauces and marinades
Co-Owner: Valentino Passetti
Brands:
  Passetti's Pride

9807 Passport Food Group
2539 E Philadelphia St
Ontario, CA 91761
310-463-0954
customerservice@passportfood.com
www.passportfood.com
Noodles, appetizers, fortune cookies and tofu, egg roll, wonton and potsticker wrappers
Senior Vice President: Brian Dean
bdean@passportfood.com
VP, Sales & Marketing, Retail: Terry Girch
Broker Sales Manager: Rich Frankey
Territory Sales Manager: Jeffrey Tavares
Year Founded: 1978
Estimated Sales: $50 Million
Number Employees: 200-500
Number of Brands: 4
Type of Packaging: Consumer, Food Service, Private Label, Bulk
Brands:
  Wing Hing Gold Coin
  Wing Hing Panda

9808 Pasta Del Mondo
27 Seminary Hill Rd
Suite 27
Carmel, NY 10512-1928
845-225-8889
Fax: 845-225-0900 800-392-8887
Pasta
President: Frank Marrone
Production Manager: Brendan Conboy
Estimated Sales: $300,000-500,000
Number Employees: 9
Square Footage: 12000
Type of Packaging: Consumer, Food Service, Private Label, Bulk
Brands:
  Del Mondo

9809 Pasta Factory
11225 W Grand Ave
Melrose Park, IL 60164
847-451-0005
Fax: 847-451-6563 800-615-6951
Pasta
President: Michael Sica
VP: Irene Sica
Sales Manager/Marketing: Thomas Lichon
Contact: Brenda Sica
bsica@nova.edu
Operations/Purchasing Director: Joseph Sica
Estimated Sales: $2700000
Number Employees: 20-49
Square Footage: 64000
Parent Co: MAS Sales
Type of Packaging: Consumer, Food Service, Private Label, Bulk
Brands:
  Pasta Factory

9810 Pasta International
5715 Coopers Avenue
Mississauga, ON L4Z 2C7
Canada
905-890-5550
Fax: 905-890-8939
Pasta: linguine, fettuccine, spaghetti, ravioli, tortellini, lasagna and cannelloni
President: Massimo Liberatore
Number Employees: 5-9
Square Footage: 116000
Type of Packaging: Consumer, Food Service
Brands:
  Pasta International

9811 Pasta Mami
1600 Roswell St SE
Suite 12
Smyrna, GA 30080
770-438-6022
Fax: 770-438-9810
Pasta
President: Mark Portwood
Estimated Sales: $2.5-5 000,000
Number Employees: 10-19
Type of Packaging: Private Label
Brands:
  Pasta Mami

9812 Pasta Mill
12803 149th Street NW
Edmonton, AB T5L 2J7
Canada
780-454-8665
Fax: 780-454-8668
Pasta and pasta sauces
President: Steve Parsons
General Manager: Brien Plunkie
Estimated Sales: $284,000
Number Employees: 3
Type of Packaging: Consumer, Food Service
Brands:
  The Pasta Mill

9813 Pasta Montana
1 Pasta Pl
Great Falls, MT 59401-1377
406-761-1516
Fax: 406-761-1403 www.pastamontana.com
Pasta
President: Yasuhiko Harada
yasuhiko@costapasta.com
General Manager: Randy Gilbertson
Number Employees: 100-249
Square Footage: 30000
Type of Packaging: Consumer, Food Service, Private Label, Bulk
Brands:
  Pasta Montana
  Costa Pasta
  Amarone Pasta

9814 Pasta Prima
3909 Park Rd
Suite H
Benicia, CA 94510-1167
530-671-7200
www.pastaprima.com
Pasta
Contact: Aaron Garcia
agarcia@valleyfine.com
Estimated Sales: Less Than $500,000
Number Employees: 5-9

9815 Pasta Quistini
1700 Ormont Dr
Toronto, ON M9L 2V4
Canada
416-742-3222
Pasta
President: Elena Quistini
Vice President: Orlando Quistini
Estimated Sales: $3 Million
Number Employees: 18
Type of Packaging: Consumer, Food Service
Brands:
  Pasta Al Dente
  Pasta Quistini

9816 Pasta Shoppe
Nashville, TN
615-831-0016
Fax: 615-781-9335 800-247-0188
john@pastashoppe.com pastashoppe.com
Organic pastas and pasta sauce
President & Owner: John Aron
VP & Owner: Carey Aron
carey@pastashoppe.com
Estimated Sales: $2.7 Million
Number Employees: 25
Type of Packaging: Private Label, Bulk
Brands:
  Pastabilities
  Tailgate & Celebrate
  Pasta with Personality
  Divine Meringues

9817 Pasta Sonoma
640 Martin Ave
Suite 1
Rohnert Park, CA 94928-7994
707-584-0800
Fax: 707-584-2332 info@pastasonoma.com
www.pastasonoma.com
Pasta
President: Don Luber
luber@pastasonoma.com
Director of Sales: Dale Lucas
Manager: Cindy Riddle
Estimated Sales: $2 Million
Number Employees: 5-9
Type of Packaging: Private Label

9818 Pasta Valente
PO Box 2307
Charlottesville, VA 22902-2307
434-971-3717
Fax: 434-971-1511 888-575-7670
retail@pastavalente.com
Pasta and marinara sauces
President: Mary F Valente
Officer: Lois Pecavage
Estimated Sales: $370,000
Number Employees: 5

9819 Pastene Co LTD
330 Turnpike St
Suite 100
Canton, MA 02021-2703
781-298-3397
Fax: 781-830-8225 www.pastene.com
Cheese, sauces, oil and vinegar, vegetables, fish, olives, peppers, beans, bread sticks, pasta, rice and polenta
Owner: Mark Tosi
mtosi@pastene.com
Year Founded: 1848
Number Employees: 20-49
Type of Packaging: Consumer, Food Service

Food Manufacturers / A-Z

9820 Pastor Chuck Orchards
PO Box 1259
Portland, ME 04104
207-773-1314
Fax: 207-871-0117
Applesauce, salsa and apple butter
President: Charles Waite Maclin

9821 Pastorelli Food Products
162 N Sangamon St
Chicago, IL 60607-2210
312-666-2041
Fax: 312-666-2415 800-767-2829
www.pastorelli.com
Pizza sauces, crusts, pasta sauces, oils and vinegars
Owner: Richard Pastorelli
rpastorelli@pastorelli.com
Estimated Sales: $5-10 Million
Number Employees: 10-19
Square Footage: 244000
Type of Packaging: Consumer, Food Service, Private Label, Bulk
Brands:
  Italian Chef

9822 Pastori Winery
23189 Geyserville Ave
Cloverdale, CA 95425-9724
707-857-3418
Wines
Owner: Frank Pastori
frank@pedroncelli.com
Estimated Sales: $230,000
Number Employees: 1-4
Brands:
  Pastori

9823 Pastry Chef
112 Warren Avenue
Pawtucket, RI 02860-5604
401-722-1330
800-639-8606
Cakes and pies
President: Per Jensen
CEO: Paul Meunier
Number Employees: 20-49
Number of Brands: 3
Number of Products: 110
Square Footage: 80000
Parent Co: Pastry Chef
Type of Packaging: Food Service, Private Label
Brands:
  The Pastry Chef

9824 Pat LaFrieda Meat Purveyors
3701 Tonnelle Ave
North Bergen, NJ 07047-2421
201-537-8210
Fax: 201-864-2014 888-523-7433
info@lafrieda.com www.lafrieda.com
Meats
President: Mark Pastore
CEO: Pat LaFrieda
Number Employees: 1-4

9825 Pat's Meat Discounter
702 S 6th Ave
Mills, WY 82604-2532
307-237-7549
Meat
Owner: Patrick Keating
Estimated Sales: $500,000-$1 000,000
Number Employees: 1-4

9826 Patagonia Provisions
1750 Bridgeway
A100
Sausalito, CA 94965
415-729-9956
888-221-8208
marketing@patagoniaprovisions.com
www.patagoniaprovisions.com
Beef jerky, mussels, salmon, soups, chilis, sides, breakfast grains, snack bars, seeds, and beer
Founder: Yvon Chouinard
Managing Director: Birgit Cameron
Director of Sales: Erik Eaton
Number Employees: 20-49

9827 Path of Life
30W260 Butterfield Rd
Warrenville, IL 60555
844-248-9997
www.pathoflifebrand.com
Frozen prepared meals
Co-Owner: Jason Eckert
Co-Owner: Scott Schmidt
Brand Manager: Ashley Collins
Brands:
  Path of Life

9828 Pati-Petite Cookies Inc
1785 Mayview Rd
Bridgeville, PA 15017-1592
412-221-4033
Fax: 412-221-8711 800-253-5805
Cookies
President: Keith Graham
CEO: William Graham
william.graham@paychex.com
VP: Bruce Graham
Estimated Sales: $1,400,000
Number Employees: 20-49
Square Footage: 90000
Type of Packaging: Consumer, Food Service, Bulk

9829 Patience Fruit & Co.
Villeroy, QC
Canada
www.patiencefruitco.com
Trail mixes, dried berries, organic juices, fresh cranberries and snack bites
EVP & General Manager: Carl Blouin

9830 Patisserie Wawel
2543 Ontario East
Bureau A
Montreal, QC H2K 1W5
Canada
614-524-3348
Fax: 514-524-1266 patisseriewawel@videotron.ca
Sponge cake, butter strudel, breads, butter fillings
President: Peter Sowa
Manager: Alina Zych
Estimated Sales: $1.4 Million
Number Employees: 20
Square Footage: 14000

9831 Patric Chocolate
6601 Stephens Station Rd
Suite 109
Columbia, MO 65202-0011
573-814-7520
patric-chocolate.com
Chocolates
Head Chocolate Maker: Alan McClure
Estimated Sales: Less Than $500,000
Number Employees: 1-4

9832 Patricia Quintana
Los Angeles, CA
chefpatriciaquintana.com
Artisanal salsas and dressings
Chef: Patricia Quintana
Brands:
  Patricia Quintana

9833 Patrick Cudahy LLC
1 Sweet Applewood Ln
Cudahy, WI 53110
800-486-6900
www.patrickcudahy.com
Bacon, hams, lard, shortening, pepperoni, salami, bologna and sausage
President: Ken Sullivan
Year Founded: 1888
Estimated Sales: $200-300 Million
Number Employees: 1,000-4,999
Square Footage: 1000000
Parent Co: Smithfield Foods
Type of Packaging: Food Service, Private Label
Brands:
  Agar
  Appleblossom
  Danzig
  Golden Crisp
  Heat & Eat
  La Fortuna
  Patrick Cudahy
  Patricks Pride
  Pavone
  Realean
  Royalean

9834 Patriot Pickel Inc
20 Edison Dr
Wayne, NJ 07470-4713
973-709-9487
Fax: 973-709-0995
Pickles
Owner: Mc Bill
billmc@patriotpickle.com
Number Employees: 20-49

9835 Patsy's Brands
236 W 56 Street
New York, NY 10019
212-247-3491
Fax: 212-541-5071 www.patsys.com
Pasta sauces
Marketing: Russ Cahill

9836 Patsy's Candy
1540 S 21st St
Colorado Springs, CO 80904-4206
719-632-3733
Fax: 719-633-6970 866-372-8797
www.patsyscandies.com
Chocolates, mints, taffy, fudge, truffles, roasted nuts, candied popcorn and English toffee
Owner: Wes Niswonger
wes@patsyscandies.com
Estimated Sales: $5-10 Million
Number Employees: 20-49
Square Footage: 48000
Type of Packaging: Consumer, Food Service, Private Label, Bulk
Brands:
  Colorado Peanut Butter Nugget
  Preludes
  Rosecup Mints

9837 Patsy's Italian Restaurant
236 W 56th St
New York, NY 10019-4306
212-247-3491
Fax: 212-541-5071 sapatsys@aol.com
www.patsys.com
Sauces, marinaras, vegetables, olive oils and vinegars
President: Joseph Scognamillo
sapatsys@aol.com
Estimated Sales: $1-3 Million
Number Employees: 20-49
Brands:
  Patsy's

9838 PatsyPie
2496 rue Remembrance
Lachine, QC H8S 1X7
Canada
514-695-0707
Fax: 514-695-3191 877-695-0707
Pastries, breads
Founder: Pat Libling

9839 Patterson Frozen Foods
100 W. Las Palmas Avenue
Patterson, CA 95363-0114
209-892-2611
Fax: 209-892-2582
Vegetables, pasta, pesto sauces, blends, stir frys and fruits
CFO: Russell Kenerly
Information Technology Software: Gregg Skarmas
Sales Manager: Tom Ielmini
Contact: Vance Blade
vance.blade@pattersonfoods.com
Vice President of Operations: B Ingebretsen
Manager of Purchasing: Joe Ghisletta
Estimated Sales: $310,000
Square Footage: 10496
Type of Packaging: Consumer, Food Service, Bulk
Other Locations:
  Patterson Frozen Foods Plant
  Monte Alto TX
  Patterson Frozen Foods Plant
  Guatemala
Brands:
  Fair Acres
  Fresh Pact
  Microfresh
  Pat-Son
  Pour & Save
  Springtime
  Thrift-T-Pak

Food Manufacturers / A-Z

9840 Patterson Vegetable Company
100 W Las Palmas Avenue
Patterson, CA 95363
209-892-2611
Apricots, almonds, broccoli, spinach, tomatoes and peaches
CEO: Ray Walker
COO: Paul Fanelli
Number Employees: 600
Square Footage: 31964

9841 Patti's Plum Puddings
15020 Hawthorne Blvd
Suite C
Lawndale, CA 90260-1543
310-376-1463
Fax: 310-372-4132
Plum pudding and sauce
President/CEO: Patti Garrity
Estimated Sales: $50,000
Number Employees: 1-4
Number of Brands: 1
Number of Products: 2
Square Footage: 5340
Type of Packaging: Consumer
Brands:
 Patti's Plum Pudding

9842 Patty Palace Foods
595 Middlefield Road
Unit 16
Toronto, ON M1V 3S2
Canada
416-297-0510
Fax: 416-297-4024 info@pattypalace.net
www.pattypalace.net
Sandwiches
President: Michael Davidson
Estimated Sales: $3.6 Million
Number Employees: 30
Type of Packaging: Consumer, Food Service
Brands:
 Palace Foods
 Montego Bay
 Pieman and Montego

9843 Paul Piazza & Son Inc
1552 Saint Louis St
New Orleans, LA 70112-3254
504-524-6011
Fax: 504-566-1322 800-969-6011
kbaumer@paulpiazza.com www.paulpiazza.com
Shrimp, cod, perch and lobster
Owner: Luca Governale
Vice President, Sales: Andy Neely
lgovernale@paulpiazza.com
VP, Operations: Kathy Cooper
Plant Manager: Don Schwab
Estimated Sales: $10-20 Million
Number Employees: 20-49
Square Footage: 150000
Type of Packaging: Consumer, Food Service, Private Label, Bulk

9844 Paul Schafer Meat Products
343 N Charles St
Suite 3
Baltimore, MD 21201-4326
410-528-1250
Fax: 410-528-1059 FSIS.Outreach@usda.gov
www.fsis.usda.gov
Meat
Owner: Paul Schaefer
Director of Operations: Robert Fasulo
Estimated Sales: $1-2.5 Million
Number Employees: 5-9

9845 Paul Stevens Lobster
349 Lincoln St
Suite 32
Hingham, MA 02043-1609
781-740-8001
Fax: 781-749-2240
Fish and seafood; lobsters
Owner: Paul Stevens
Estimated Sales: $870,000
Number Employees: 1-4

9846 Paul's Candy Factory
434 South 300 West
Salt Lake City, UT 84101
801-363-8869
Fax: 801-359-4707 800-825-9912
www.westernut.com
Candy
President: Michael Place
Estimated Sales: Below $5 Million
Number Employees: 5-9
Brands:
 Paul's Candy

9847 Paulaur Corp
105 Melrich Rd
Cranbury, NJ 08512-3589
609-395-8844
Fax: 609-395-8850 sales@paulaur.com
www.paulaur.com
Confectionery toppings and inclusions, sweeteners, sugars, carbohydrates; custom blending, granulating, agglomerating, sizing and sieving services
CEO: Alex Martello
abiamonte@eldor.com
Number Employees: 100-249
Type of Packaging: Bulk

9848 Pauline's Pastries
50 Viceroy Road
Suite 7
Vaughan, ON L4K 3A7
Canada
905-738-5252
Fax: 905-738-0345 877-292-6826
www.paulinespastries.com
Pastries
President/CEO: Robyn Perlmutar
Marketing Director: Pauline Perlmutar
Estimated Sales: $5 Million
Number Employees: 25
Type of Packaging: Consumer, Food Service
Brands:
 Pauline's

9849 Paulsen Foods
748 Donald Hollowell Parkway
Atlanta, GA 30318
404-873-1804
paulsenfoods.com
Wholesale frozen breakfast, apetizers, entrees, and desserts.
Owner: Russell Paulsen
National Sales Manager: Tom Unverferth
Director of Operations: Mayra Vagras
Estimated Sales: $1-2.5 Million
Number Employees: 6
Square Footage: 80000
Type of Packaging: Consumer, Food Service, Private Label

9850 Paumanok Vineyards
1074 Main Road (Route 25)
P.O. Box 741
Aquebogue, NY 11931
631-722-8800
Fax: 631-722-5110 info@paumanok.com
www.paumanok.com
Wine
President: Charles Massoud
Estimated Sales: $1,400,000
Number Employees: 20-49
Brands:
 Paumanok Vineyards

9851 Pavel's Yogurt
14710 Wicks Blvd
San Leandro, CA 94577
510-352-1474
www.pavels.net
Russian-style artisanal yogurt
Owner: Donald Sortor
Director of Operations: Luke Sortor
Number of Products: 5
Brands:
 Pavel's Yogurt

9852 Pavero Cold Storage
10 North Rd
Highland, NY 12528-1017
845-691-2992
Fax: 845-691-2955 800-435-2994
applz25@aol.com www.paverocoldstorage.com
Apples and pears
President: Joseph Pavero
Cmo: Frank Sicolo
paveroapple@aol.com
Operations Manager: Jody Pavero
Estimated Sales: $8300000
Number Employees: 50-99

9853 Paw Paw Grape Juice Company
706 S Kalamazoo Street
Paw Paw, MI 49079-1558
269-657-3165
Fax: 269-657-4154 800-756-5357
www.warnerwines.com
Juices
President/CEO: James Warner
Estimated Sales: Under $500,000
Number Employees: 1-4
Parent Co: Warner Vineyards

9854 Pawelski Farm
736 Pulaski Hwy.
Goshen, NY 10924
845-772-2600
Yellow and red hybrid long-term storage onions
Contact: Chris Pawelski

9855 Payne Packing Co
704 W Richey Ave
Artesia, NM 88210-3434
575-746-2779
Beef, game and pork
President: Bob Yates
Estimated Sales: $260,000
Number Employees: 5-9
Type of Packaging: Consumer

9856 Pazdar Winery
6 Laddie Road
Scotchtown Branch, NY 10941-1708
845-695-1903
Fax: 845-695-1903 pazdar@citlink.net
www.pazdarwinery.com
Wines
President/CEO: David Pazdar
VP Marketing: Tracy Davis-Pazdar
Number Employees: 5-9
Parent Co: Pazdar Beverage Company
Type of Packaging: Consumer, Food Service
Brands:
 Pazdar Winery
 Sugary Wine

9857 Peaberry's Coffee & Tea
5655 College Ave
Oakland, CA 94618-1583
510-653-0450
Fax: 510-420-0260
peaberrys@rockridgemarkethall.com
Coffee and tea
Owner: Lynn Mallard
lynnmariemallard@gmail.com
Estimated Sales: Over $1 Million
Number Employees: 20-49
Type of Packaging: Private Label

9858 Peace Mountain Natural Beverages
PO Box 1445
Springfield, MA 01101-1445
413-567-4942
Fax: 413-567-8161
Bottled water, juices, nutraceuticals
Owner: J David
VP R&D: John Alden
Number Employees: 5-9
Type of Packaging: Private Label
Brands:
 Cardio Water
 Give Your Heart a Healthy Start
 Jana
 Miracle Ade
 Miracle Juice
 Miracle Juice Energy Drink
 Peace Mountain
 Skinny Water
 Sports Juice

9859 Peace River Citrus Products
582 Beachland Boulevard
Suite 300
Vero Beach, FL 32963
772-492-4050
Fax: 772-492-4056 www.peacerivercitrus.com
Citrus
President: Bill Becker
Contact: Dale Shaffer
dshaffer@google.com
Plant Manager: Romilio Herrera
Estimated Sales: $1 million
Number Employees: 100-249
Type of Packaging: Bulk

Food Manufacturers / A-Z

Other Locations:
  Peach River Citrus Products Plant
  Arcadia FL
  Peach River Citrus Products Plant
  Bartow FL

9860 Peace Village Organic Foods
76 Florida Avenue
Berkeley, CA 94707-1708
510-524-4420
info@peacevillage.net
www.peacevillage.net
Asian pasta and food ingredients
President: Joel Wollner
Type of Packaging: Consumer, Private Label

9861 Peaceful Bend Winery
1942 Highway T
Steelville, MO 65565-5067
573-775-3000
Fax: 573-775-3001 winery@peacefulbend.com
www.peacefulbendvineyard.com
Wine
Owner: Katherine Gill
CEO: Clyde Gill
vinic0com@gmail.com
Estimated Sales: $500,000-$1 Million
Number Employees: 1-4
Brands:
  Peaceful Bend

9862 Peaceful Fruits
330-356-8515
www.peacefulfruits.com
Organic fruit snacks
Founder/CEO: Evan Delehanty

9863 Peaceworks
PO Box 1393
Old Chelsea Station
New York, NY 10113
212-897-3985
www.peaceworks.com
Pesto and pasta sauces; tomato, olive and eggplant spreads
Founder: Daniel Lubetzky
Vice President, Sales: Rami Leshem
Sales Manager: Leah Majchel
leah@peaceworks.com
Estimated Sales: $1.3 Million
Number Employees: 5
Type of Packaging: Consumer, Food Service
Brands:
  Azteca Trading Co.
  Mediterranean Sprate
  Moshe & Ali's Sprat,
  Smoked Eggplant Sprat,
  Wafa

9864 Peak Foods
877 W Main St.
Suite 700
Boise, ID 83702
208-343-2602
800-727-9939
doug-oppenheimer@oppcos.com peakfoods.com
Ready to whip toppings
Contact: Larry Lipshultz
larry-lipschultz@golbon.com

9865 Peanut Butter & Co.
PO Box 2000
New York, NY 10101
212-677-3995
Fax: 212-677-6977 866-456-8372
info@ilovepeanutbutter.com
www.ilovepeanutbutter.com
Peanut butter, jams and jellies, snacks and fluff
Founder, President: Lee Zalben
info@ilovepeanutbutter.com
Marketing: Linda Grimard-Bender
Year Founded: 1998
Estimated Sales: $3 Million
Number Employees: 20-49

9866 (HQ)Peanut Corporation of America
2121 Wiggington Road
PO Box 10037
Lynchburg, VA 24506
434-384-7098
Fax: 434-384-9528 gbparnell@aol.com
www.peanutcorp.com
Peanuts
Owner/President: Stewart Parnell
Corporate Office Manager: Gloria Parnell
Sales Director: David Yoth
Estimated Sales: $3-$5 Million
Number Employees: 20-49
Type of Packaging: Consumer, Food Service, Bulk
Other Locations:
  Blakely GA
  Suffolk VA
  Plainview TX
Brands:
  Parnell's Pride

9867 Peanut Patch
4322 E County 13th St
Yuma, AZ 85365-4631
928-726-6292
Fax: 928-726-2433 800-872-7688
thepeanutpatch@thepeanutpatch.com
www.thepeanutpatch.com
Peanuts
Owner: Donna George
usapnut@peoplepc.com
Estimated Sales: $1-3 Million
Number Employees: 10-19

9868 Peanut Patch Gift Shop
27478 Southampton Pkwy
Courtland, VA 23837
757-653-2028
Fax: 757-653-9530 800-544-0896
customerservice@feridies.com
www.thepeanutpatchgiftshop.com
Peanuts and peanut candies
President: Jane Riddick-Fries
janerf@peanutpatch.com
CFO: Paul Sheffer
R&D: Ted Fries
Number Employees: 50-99
Type of Packaging: Consumer, Food Service, Private Label
Brands:
  Peanut Patch

9869 Peanut Processors Inc
7329 Albert St
Dublin, NC 28332
910-862-2136
Fax: 910-862-8076 800-330-3141
www.peanutprocessors.com
Peanuts
CEO: Houston Brisson
VP: Nile Brisson
Year Founded: 1962
Estimated Sales: $20-50 Million
Number Employees: 20-49

9870 Peanut Roaster
394 Zeb Robinson Rd
Henderson, NC 27537-8760
252-431-0100
Fax: 252-431-0224 800-445-1404
info@peanut.com www.peanut.com
Peanuts
President: John Monahan
monahanj@peanut.com
Marketing Director: Charles Penick
Quality Control: John William
Founder: Larry Monahan Sr.
Estimated Sales: Below $5 Million
Number Employees: 20-49
Brands:
  The Peanut Roaster

9871 Peanut Shop
8012 Hankins Industrial Park
Toano, VA 23168-9259
757-566-4030
Fax: 757-566-2992 800-637-3268
www.thepeanutshop.com
Peanuts
General Manager: Pete Booker
Operations Manager: Larry Winslow
Estimated Sales: Less Than $500,000
Number Employees: 1-4
Type of Packaging: Consumer, Food Service, Private Label, Bulk
Brands:
  Peanut Shop of Williamsburg
  Smithfield Tavern

9872 Pear's Coffee
901 Ft. Crook Rd., N.
Bellevue, NE 68005
402-934-8210
Fax: 402-934-8218 800-828-7688
rrb@hermansnuthouse.com
www.hermansnuthouse.com
Coffee, nuts
President: John Larsen
Operations Manager: Adam Gaines
Estimated Sales: Below $5 Million
Number Employees: 20-49
Type of Packaging: Bulk
Brands:
  Pear's Coffee

9873 Pearl Coffee Co
675 S Broadway St
Akron, OH 44311-1099
330-253-7184
Fax: 330-253-7185 800-822-5282
dianacoffee@aol.com
Coffee
President: John Economou
Vice President, Marketing: Johnna Economou
Estimated Sales: $9 Million
Number Employees: 10-19
Square Footage: 80000
Type of Packaging: Consumer, Food Service, Private Label
Brands:
  Diana

9874 Pearl Crop
1550 Industrial Dr
Stockton, CA 95206
209-808-7575
Fax: 209-254-9859 info@pearlcrop.com
pearlcrop.com
Walnut and almond processor
President/Owner: Gearry Davenport
CEO: Ulash Turkhan
Other Locations:
  Processing Plant
  Ripon CA
  Processing Plant
  Linden CA

9875 Pearl River Pastry & Chocolate
4 E Dexter Plz
Pearl River, NY 10965-2360
845-735-5100
Fax: 845-735-6434 800-632-2639
sales@prpastry.com www.prpastry.com
Chocolates, cakes and pastries
Owner: J Koffman
jkoffman@prpastries.com
Estimated Sales: $5-10 Million
Number Employees: 50-99

9876 Pearl Valley Cheese Inc
54775 Township Road 90
Fresno, OH 43824-9796
740-545-6002
Fax: 740-545-7703 www.pearlvalleycheese.com
Cheese
President: Charles Ellis
sellis@pearlvalleycheese.com
General Manager: Chuck Ellis
Number Employees: 20-49
Type of Packaging: Consumer, Food Service, Private Label, Bulk
Brands:
  Pearl Valley

9877 Pearson Candy Co
2140 W 7th St
St Paul, MN 55116-3199
651-698-0356
Fax: 651-696-2222
Candy: chocolate, multi-packs, mints, holiday novelties, vending, nut rolls and bun bars.
President & CEO: Michael Keller
Year Founded: 1909
Number Employees: 100-249
Type of Packaging: Consumer
Brands:
  Salted Nut Roll
  Bit-O-Honey
  Mint Patties
  Nut Goodie
  Bun Bar
  Coconut Patties

Food Manufacturers / A-Z

9878 Pearson's Berry Farm
34463 Range Rd 40
Site 24
Bowden, AB T0M 0K0
Canada
403-224-3011
Fax: 403-224-2096 www.pearsonsberryfarm.ca
Jams, pie fillings and dessert toppings
President: E Leonard Pearson
Sales Manager: Joyce Park
Number Employees: 20-49
Type of Packaging: Consumer, Food Service
Brands:
  Pearson's Berry Farm

9879 Pearson's Homestyle
Site 24 Box 1 RR 1
Bowden, AB T0M 0K0
Canada
403-224-3339
877-224-3339
Sauces, spices and seasonings, beverages
President: Duane Mertin
Production: Debbie Mertin
Number Employees: 10-19
Square Footage: 22000
Type of Packaging: Private Label
Brands:
  Gordo's

9880 Peas of Mind
2339 3rd Street
Unit 53-3R
San Francisco, CA 94107
415-504-2556
www.peasofmind.com
Baby food
Contact: Ron Parish
ron@peasofmind.com

9881 Pease's Candy
1701 S State St
Springfield, IL 62704-4098
217-523-3721
Fax: 217-523-7581 ILINI83@aol.com
www.peasescandy.com
Chocolates and nuts
Owner: Robert Flesher
Estimated Sales: $500,000-$1 Million
Number Employees: 5-9
Brands:
  Pease's

9882 Pecan Deluxe Candy Co
2570 Lone Star Dr
Dallas, TX 75212-6308
214-631-3669
Fax: 214-631-5833 800-733-3589
pdcc_info@pecandeluxe.com
www.pecandeluxe.com
Dessert and baked goods ingredients: toffees, nuts, chocolate coated items, flavor bases, sauces
President: Jay Brigham
Chairman of the Board: Bennie Brigham
bennie_brigham@pecandeluxe.com
Chief Financial Officer: Keith Hurd
Chief Operating Officer: Tim Markowicz
VP Quality Assurance: Rick Hintermeier
VP Operations: Mike Cavin
Inventory/Production Coordinator: Wayne Miller
Purchasing Manager: James Mitchell
Estimated Sales: $20-50 Million
Number Employees: 250-499
Number of Products: 2000
Square Footage: 63000
Type of Packaging: Bulk

9883 Peco Foods Inc.
1101 Greensoro Ave.
Tuscaloosa, AL 35401
205-345-4711
Fax: 205-366-4533 www.pecofoods.com
Deli and tray-pack chicken.
President/CEO: Mark Hickman
mhickman@pecofoods.com
Chairman: Denny Hickman
Chief Financial Officer: Patrick Noland
Director, Technical Services: Curtis Stell
Director, Human Resources: Bart Carter
Director, Sales & Marketing: Bobby Wilburn
Director, Live Operations: Roddy Sanders
Chief Operations Officer: Benny Bishop
Year Founded: 1937
Estimated Sales: $582.2 Million
Number Employees: 1000-4999
Square Footage: 6185
Type of Packaging: Consumer, Food Service
Other Locations:
  Peco Foods, Inc. Processing Plant
  Tuscaloosa AL
  Peco Foods, Inc. Processing Plant
  Bay Springs MS
  Peco Foods, Inc. Processing Plant
  Brooksville MS
  Peco Foods, Inc. Processing Plant
  Sebastopol MS
  Peco Foods, Inc. Processing Plant
  Canton MS
  Peco Foods, Inc. Processing Plant
  Batesville AR
  Peco Foods, Inc. Live Operations
  Gordo AL
  Peco Foods, Inc. Live Operations
  Bay Springs MS
  Peco Farms of Mississippi, LLC
  Sebastopol MS
  Peco Foods, Inc. Live Operations
  Piladelphia MS
  Peco Foods, Inc. Live Operations
  Batesville AR

9884 Peconic Bay Winery
P.O.Box 818
Cutchogue, NY 11935
631-734-7361
Fax: 631-734-5867
Wine
Manager: Matt Gillies
Co-Owner: Ursula Lowerre
Contact: James Silver
romina@martemultimedia.com
Winemaker: Gregory Gove
Estimated Sales: Below $5 Million
Number Employees: 20-49
Brands:
  Peconic Bay

9885 Pecoraro Dairy Products
287 Leonard St
Brooklyn, NY 11211-3618
718-388-2379
Fax: 315-339-3008 pcr2c1@aol.com
Cheeses
Owner: Ceasre Pecoraro
Operations: Ralph Parlato
Estimated Sales: Less Than $500,000
Number Employees: 1-4
Number of Brands: 4
Number of Products: 12
Square Footage: 14400
Type of Packaging: Consumer, Food Service, Private Label
Brands:
  Brown Cow Farm East
  Sweet Cheese, Queso Blanco

9886 Pecos Valley Spice Company
P.O.Box 2162
Corrales, NM 87048
505-243-2622
info@janebutelcooking.com
www.janebutelcooking.com
Chile, herbs, spices, corn & masa, barbecue, beans and nuts
Founder: Jane Butel

9887 Pede Brothers Italian Food
582 Duanesburg Rd
Suite 1
Schenectady, NY 12306-1096
518-356-3042
Fax: 518-355-7472 www.pedebrothers.com
Ravioli, lasagna sheets, manicotti, gnocchi, cavatelli, tortellini, stuffed shells, and rigatoni.
Owner: Romolo Pede
r.pede@pedebrothers.com
Year Founded: 1967
Estimated Sales: $20-50 Million
Number Employees: 20-49
Square Footage: 32000
Type of Packaging: Consumer, Food Service, Private Label

9888 Pederson's Natural Farms
1207 S Rice Street
Hamilton, TX 76531
pedersonsfarms.com
Fresh and smoked meat products
President/Owner: Cody Lane
Controller: Mark Wilson
VP: Neil Dudley
Marketing Director: Stacy Dudley
National Sales Manager: Brittany Hayes

9889 Pedrizzetti Winery
1645 San Pedro Ave
Morgan Hill, CA 95037
408-779-7389
Fax: 408-779-9083 wines@pedwines.net
Wines
President: Michael Sampognaro
Estimated Sales: $500,000-$1 Million
Number Employees: 1-4
Type of Packaging: Consumer, Private Label, Bulk
Brands:
  Barbera
  Sirah

9890 Pedroncelli J Winery
1220 Canyon Rd
Geyserville, CA 95441-9639
707-857-3531
Fax: 707-857-3812 800-836-3894
service@pedroncelli.com www.pedroncelli.com
Wines
Owner: Jim Pedroncelli
VP Marketing: Julie Pedroncelli St. John
VP Sales: Richard Morehouse
jim@pedroncelli.com
Estimated Sales: $1,500,000
Number Employees: 20-49
Type of Packaging: Private Label
Brands:
  Pedroncelli

9891 Peekskill Brewery
53 South Water St. # 57
Peekskill, N7 10566
914-734-2337
mail@peekskillbrewery.com
www.peekskillbrewery.com
IPAs, sour beer
Co-Owner: Kara Berardi
Co-Owner: Keith Berardi
Co-Owner: Morgan Berardi
Number of Brands: 1
Number of Products: 10
Type of Packaging: Consumer, Private Label
Brands:
  Peekskill Brewery

9892 Peeled Snacks
30 Martin St
Suite 3B
Cumberland, RI 02864
401-437-4386
customerservice@peeledsnacks.com
peeledsnacks.com
Puffed pea and dried fruit snacks
Founder: Noha Waibsnaider
Contact: Beth Kennedy
beth@peeledsnacks.com
Year Founded: 2004
Number Employees: 10-19

9893 Peeler's Jersey Farms
110 Newton Bridge Road
Athens, GA 30607-1163
706-543-7383
Fax: 706-543-2569
Milk and orange juice
President/CEO: Harvey Peeler, Sr.
Plant Manager: Vlaude Lollis
Estimated Sales: $25-49.9 Million
Number Employees: 50-99
Parent Co: Peeler's Jersey Farms

9894 Peer Foods Group Inc
1200 W 35th St
Chicago, IL 60609-1305
773-927-1440
Fax: 773-927-9859 800-365-5644
www.peerfoods.com
Bacon, hams and butts, pigs' feet, sausage and corned beef, pickled hocks
President: Larry O'Connell
CFO: Gary Radville
Director of Marketing: Harold Dangler
Director of Marketing: Gary Racine
Director Manufacturing: Bill Froula
Purchasing Manager: Brian Tooley

Food Manufacturers / A-Z

Estimated Sales: $10-20 Million
Number Employees: 100-249
Type of Packaging: Consumer, Food Service

9895 Peerless Coffee & Tea
260 Oak St
Oakland, CA 94607-4512
510-763-1763
Fax: 510-763-5026 800-310-5662
specialty@peerlesscoffee.com
www.peerlesscoffee.com

Coffee
President: Sonja Vukasin
CEO: George Vukasin
VP Administration General Counsel: Kristina Brouhard
Consultant: Michelle Thomas
Product Integrity & Quality Assurance: Stephanie Muljadi
Vice President of Marketing: Chris Browning
Director of Sales: Ruben Morales
Estimated Sales: $9.6 Million
Number Employees: 50-99
Square Footage: 260000
Type of Packaging: Consumer, Food Service

9896 Peet's Coffee
Berkeley, CA
510-594-2100
Fax: 510-594-2180 800-999-2132
customerservice@peets.com www.peets.com

Coffees, teas and coffee roasting equipment
CEO: Casey Keller
CFO: John Coletta
COO: Shawn Conway
Year Founded: 1966
Estimated Sales: $800 Million
Number Employees: 5,000
Square Footage: 60000
Parent Co: JAB Holding Company

9897 Peg's Salt
8354 Brooksville Rd
Greenwood, VA 22943-1721
434-249-2495
pegssalt.com

Salt
Contact: Cass Cannon
Brands:
  Peg's Salt(c)

9898 Peggy Lawton Kitchens
253 Washington St
East Walpole, MA 02032-1133
508-668-1215
Fax: 508-660-1636 800-843-7325

Brownies and cookies
President: William Wolf
bwolf@plkitchens.com
Office Manager: Robert Willis
Estimated Sales: $2-5 Million
Number Employees: 10-19
Number of Products: 10
Square Footage: 20000
Type of Packaging: Consumer, Food Service, Private Label, Bulk
Brands:
  Peggy Lawton

9899 Peju Province Winery
8466 Saint Helena Hwy
Rutherford, CA 94573
707-963-3600
Fax: 707-963-8680 800-446-7358
info@peju.com www.peju.com

Wines
Owner: Herta Behensky
hpeju@peju.com
Estimated Sales: Below $5 Million
Number Employees: 50-99
Brands:
  Peju

9900 Pekarna Meat Market
119 Water St
Jordan, MN 55352-1555
952-492-6101
info@pekarnameats.com
www.pekarnameats.com

Beef, pork, wild game and sausage
Owner: John Pekarna
CEO: Kenny Pekarna
Estimated Sales: $4 Million
Number Employees: 5-9
Type of Packaging: Consumer, Private Label

9901 Pekarski Sausage
293 Conway Rd
South Deerfield, MA 01373-9663
413-665-4537
www.pekarskis.com

Meat and poultry
Marketing Director: Mike Pekarskis
Estimated Sales: Less Than $500,000
Number Employees: 1-4
Brands:
  Pekarskis

9902 Peking Noodle Co Inc
1518 N San Fernando Rd
Los Angeles, CA 90065-1225
323-223-0897
Fax: 323-223-3211 info@pekingnoodle.com
www.pekingnoodle.com

Noodles, egg rolls, wontons, potsticker wraps, suey gow skins, fortune cookies and snack foods
Owner: Tony Li
chieffrank@yahoo.com
Vice President: Frank Tong
Plant Manager: Maria Gonzalez
Estimated Sales: $2200000
Number Employees: 50-99
Square Footage: 120000
Type of Packaging: Consumer, Food Service, Private Label, Bulk

9903 Pelican Bay Ltd.
150 Douglas Ave
Dunedin, FL 34698-7908
727-733-3069
Fax: 727-734-5860 800-826-8982
sales@pelicanbayltd.com www.pelicanbayltd.com

Baking and drink mixes, spice blends and gifts
Owner: Char Pfaelzer
char@pelicanbayltd.com
CEO: Jim Hubbard
Executive VP: David Pfaelzer
Plant Manager: Justin Pfaelzer
Purchasing: Greg Kathan
Estimated Sales: $4.7 Million
Number Employees: 20-49
Number of Brands: 1
Number of Products: 200
Square Footage: 120000
Type of Packaging: Consumer, Private Label, Bulk
Brands:
  Pelican Bay

9904 Pelican Seafoods
P.O.Box 110
Pelican, AK 99832-0110
907-735-2211
Fax: 907-735-2281

Seafood
Manager: Vance Ady'wirta
COO: Rusty Roessler
General Manager: Glen Woods
Plant Manager: Steve Pringle
Estimated Sales: $10-20 Million
Number Employees: 50-99
Parent Co: Kake Tribal Corporation

9905 Pellegrini Wine Co
4055 W Olivet Rd
Santa Rosa, CA 95401-3839
707-545-8680
Fax: 707-545-3709 800-891-0244
info@pellegrinisonoma.com
www.pellegrinisonoma.com

Wines
Financial Manager: Richard Pellegrini
Owner/manager: Robert Pellegrini
robert@pellegrinisonoma.com
Partner/Property Manager: Jeanne Pellegrini
Treasurer: Verna Rayala
Estimated Sales: $1 Million
Number Employees: 10-19
Type of Packaging: Private Label
Brands:
  Cloverdale Ranch
  Olivet Lane
  Pellegrini

9906 Pellman Foods Inc
122 S Shirk Rd
P.O. Box 337
New Holland, PA 17557
717-354-8070
Fax: 717-355-9944 info@pellmanfoods.com
www.pellmanfoods.com

Cakes, pies and tortes.
Controller: Michael Herr
VP, Sales & Marketing: Deryl Denlinger
Year Founded: 1973
Estimated Sales: $20-50 Million
Number Employees: 20-49
Number of Brands: 1
Number of Products: 30
Square Footage: 50000
Type of Packaging: Consumer, Food Service
Brands:
  Pellman

9907 Pemaquid Seafood
32 CO OP Rd
Pemaquid, ME 04558-4315
207-677-2801
Fax: 207-677-2818 866-864-2897
pemaquidcoop@yahoo.com

Seafood
Manager: Wayne Dighton
Manager: Tom Simmons
Estimated Sales: Less Than $500,000
Number Employees: 1-4

9908 Pemberton's Foods Inc
32 Lewiston Rd
Gray, ME 04039-7536
207-657-6446
Fax: 207-657-6453 800-255-8401
www.pembertonsgourmet.com

Sauces, mixes, pancake, scone, syrup, seasonings, salsa, relish, mustard, pickles, jams, jellies
Owner: David Fillinger
info@pembertonsgourmet.com
Estimated Sales: $1 million
Number Employees: 5-9
Square Footage: 14000

9909 Penauta Products
PO Box 155 RR2
4276 Betaesda Road
Stouffville, ON L4A 7Z5
Canada
905-640-1564
Fax: 905-640-7479

Jarred honey and bee pollen
President: Paul Nauta
General Manager: Henry Nauta
Production Manager: Martin Nauta
Estimated Sales: $130,000
Number Employees: 3
Square Footage: 24000
Type of Packaging: Consumer, Food Service, Private Label, Bulk
Brands:
  Ambrosia
  Meadowview

9910 Pender Packing Co Inc
4520 NC Highway 133
Rocky Point, NC 28457-9108
910-675-3311
Fax: 910-675-1625 penderpacking@aol.com
www.penderpacking.com

Smoked sausage, liver pudding, c-loaf, souse loaf, chitterling loaf, chorizo, fatback and pork barbecue
President: Danny L Baker
penderpacking@aol.com
Estimated Sales: $4,900,000
Number Employees: 20-49
Type of Packaging: Consumer

9911 Pendery's
1221 Manufacturing St
Dallas, TX 75207
800-533-1870
email@penderys.com www.penderys.com

Bay leaves, cinnamon, garlic, ginger, paprika, chile pepper and herb blends
Estimated Sales: $1-3 Million
Number Employees: 5-9
Square Footage: 92000
Type of Packaging: Consumer, Food Service, Private Label, Bulk
Brands:
  Chiltomaline

Food Manufacturers / A-Z

9912 Penguin Frozen Foods Inc
555 Skokie Blvd
Suite 440
Northbrook, IL 60062-2835
847-291-9400
Fax: 847-291-1588 800-323-1485
www.penguinfrozenfoods.com
Seafood and fish: shrimp, sole, turbot, fillets, lobster, crab meat
President: Ellen Paton
ellen@penguinfrozenfoods.com
Estimated Sales: $2,700,000
Number Employees: 10-19
Type of Packaging: Consumer, Food Service
Brands:
  Campeche Bay
  Dimo
  Texas Bay

9913 Penguin Natural Food Inc
4400 Alcoa Ave
Vernon, CA 90058-2412
323-727-7980
Fax: 323-727-7983 www.penguinfoods.com
Rice, baking mixes, potato mixes, cornbreads, pastas and rice blends.
President: Scott Nairne
Estimated Sales: $20-50 Million
Number Employees: 50-99
Type of Packaging: Consumer, Food Service, Private Label

9914 Penn Cheese
7199 County Line Rd
Winfield, PA 17889-9266
570-524-7700
Fax: 570-523-9691 jon.weber@penncheese.com
Swiss cheese
President: Michael Price
General Manager: Jonathan Weber
jonathan.weber@penncheese.com
Production Manager: Thomas P. Weber
Estimated Sales: $5 Million
Number Employees: 10-19
Number of Brands: 2
Number of Products: 2
Square Footage: 81200
Type of Packaging: Private Label, Bulk
Brands:
  Market Place
  Pennsylvania People

9915 Penn Dutch Meat & Seafood Market
3950 N 28th Ter
Hollywood, FL 33020-1179
954-921-7144
Fax: 954-921-7448 sueg@penn-dutch.com
www.penn-dutch.com
Meats and general groceries
President: Greg Salsburg
greg@penn-dutch.com
CEO: George Ronkin
Secretary/Treasurer: Paul Salsburg
Managing Director: Kara Boehly
Estimated Sales: $20-50 Million
Number Employees: 100-249

9916 Penn Dutch Meat & Seafood Market
3201 North State Road 7
Margate, FL 33063
954-974-3900
sueg@penn-dutch.com
www.penn-dutch.com
Meats and general groceries

9917 Penn Dutch Meat & Seafood Market
2301 North University Dr.
Sunrise, FL 33322
sueg@penn-dutch.com
www.penn-dutch.com
Meats and general groceries

9918 Penn Herb Co
10601 Decatur Rd
Suite 2
Philadelphia, PA 19154-3212
215-632-4430
Fax: 215-632-7945 800-523-9971
www.pennherb.com
Encapsulated herbs ginseng and golden seal root; vitamins and supplements
President: William Betz
wbetz@penton.com
President: Ronald Betz
Estimated Sales: $3500000
Number Employees: 20-49
Square Footage: 92000
Brands:
  Nature's Wonderland

9919 Penn Shore Winery Vineyards
10225 Lake Rd
Route 5
North East, PA 16428-2894
814-725-8688
Fax: 814-725-8689 www.pennshore.com
Wines
President: Jeffrey Ore
Vice President: Cheryl Ore
Estimated Sales: Less Than $500,000
Number Employees: 1-4
Number of Brands: 23
Type of Packaging: Bulk

9920 Penn Street Bakery
900 Hynes S.W.
Grand Rapids, MI 49507
616-241-2583
Fax: 616-241-6332 800-84-AKES
www.pennstreetbakery.com
Baked goods, cakes, cookies

9921 Pennacook Peppers
2207 Wake Forest St
Virginia Beach, VA 23451
757-663-8798
pennacookpeppers.com
Salsa, jelly and spice blends.
Operations: Kevin Oelhafen
Brands:
  Pennacook Peppers

9922 Pennfield Farms
1074 East Main St
Mt Joy, PA 17552
717-865-2153
Fax: 717-865-2186 800-732-0009
Eggs and chicken
President: Mark Mckay
Plant Manager: Bill Rahn
Number Employees: 400
Parent Co: Pennfield Corporation
Type of Packaging: Consumer, Bulk
Brands:
  Coleman

9923 Pennsylvania Brewing Company
800 Vinial St
Pittsburgh, PA 15212
412-237-9400
Fax: 412-237-9406 pennbrew@hotmail.com
www.pennbrew.com
Beer and ale
President: Tom Pastorius
Manager: Rick Brown
Contact: Sandy Cindrich
sandy@pennbrew.com
Estimated Sales: Below $5 Million
Number Employees: 20-49
Type of Packaging: Consumer, Food Service
Brands:
  Penn Dark
  Penn Gold
  Penn Maibok
  Penn Marzen
  Penn Pilsner
  Penn Weizen

9924 Pennsylvania Dutch: Birch Beer
5175 Cold Spring Creamert Rd
Suite 4
Doylestown, PA 18901
856-662-1869
dschwarz@daretogodutch.com
www.daretogodutch.com
Soft drinks
President: Michael Geehring
Chairman: Lincoln Warrell
VP Finance: L Lebo
VP: Dwayne Schwartz
Estimated Sales: $1-$2.5 Million
Number Employees: 2
Brands:
  Pennsylvania Dutch

9925 Pennsylvania Macaroni Company
2010-12 Penn Avenue
Pittsburgh, PA 15222
412-471-8330
Fax: 412-201-4751 800-223-5928
info@pennmac.com www.pennmac.com
Pasta, cheeses, deli meats and gift boxes
President: David Sunseri
Estimated Sales: $10-24 Million
Number Employees: 90

9926 Pennsylvania Renaissance Faire
2775 Lebanon Rd
Manheim, PA 17545-8711
717-664-0476
Fax: 717-664-3466 www.parenfaire.com
Wine
Vice President: Candace Smith
candace@parenfaire.com
VP: Barbara Lacek
Number Employees: 20-49
Brands:
  Mazza Vineyards

9927 Penny Lick Ice Cream Company
580 Warburton Ave.
Hastings, NY 10706
914-525-1580
www.pennylickicecream.com
Locally-sourced, natural ingredient small batch ice cream and sorbets in various fruit and seasonal flavors
Owner: Ellen Sledge
Year Founded: 2013
Number of Brands: 1
Number of Products: 27
Type of Packaging: Private Label
Brands:
  Penny Lick

9928 Penobscot Mccrum LLC
28 Pierce St
PO Box 229
Belfast, ME 04915-6648
207-338-4360
Fax: 207-338-5742 800-435-4456
www.penobscotmccrum.com
Potato pancakes, mashers, skins, and wedges.
Managing Partner: Jay McCrum
Managing Partner: David McCrum
Manager, JDR Transport, Inc.: Wade McCrum
Financial Analysis & Marketing: Nick McCrum
Manager, North Maine Farm Operations: Darrell McCrum
Estimated Sales: $33 Million
Number Employees: 100-249
Type of Packaging: Consumer, Food Service

9929 Penotti USA
4 Maplegrove Avenue
Westport, CT 06880-4917
203-341-9494
Fax: 203-277-0006 877-720-0896
www.penotti.com
Chocolate and nut spreads
President: Marcell Peteers
Contact: Stanley Rottell
stan@regattagingerbeer.com
Estimated Sales: $1 million
Number Employees: 1
Type of Packaging: Bulk

9930 Penta Manufacturing Company
50 Okner Pkwy
Livingston, NJ 07039-1604
973-740-2300
Fax: 973-740-1839 sales@pentamfg.com
www.pentamfg.com
Fructose, rice starch, nutraceuticals, food and flavor compounds, chemicals, cooking and essential oils, extracts, spices
Owner: Mark Esposito
SVP: George Volpe
Sales Manager: Christine Tavares
Contact: Fatima Jasmins
fatimaj@pentamfg.com
Estimated Sales: $10-20 Million
Number Employees: 20-49
Number of Products: 7000
Square Footage: 700000
Parent Co: Penta International Corporation

Food Manufacturers / A-Z

Type of Packaging: Food Service, Private Label, Bulk

9931 Penta Water
1601 E Steel Rd
Colton, CA 92324
800-531-5088
pentawater.com
Drinking water
Contact: Bill Austin
baustin@pentawater.com
New Media Relations: Joe Lupica
Square Footage: 220000

9932 People's Sausage Co
1132 E Pico Blvd
Los Angeles, CA 90021-2224
213-627-8633
Fax: 213-627-7767
info@peopleschoicebeefjerky.com
www.peopleschoicebeefjerky.com
Beef jerky
Owner: Brian Bianchetti
brian@peopleschoicebeefjerky.com
Estimated Sales: $3000000
Number Employees: 10-19
Square Footage: 20000
Type of Packaging: Consumer, Food Service, Private Label, Bulk

9933 Pepe's Inc
1325 W 15th St
Chicago, IL 60608-2190
312-733-2500
Fax: 312-733-2564 www.pepes.com
Mexican food
President: Betty Wright
b.wright@adm.com
General Manager: Mario Dovalina Jr
Number Employees: 1000-4999
Square Footage: 260000
Type of Packaging: Private Label, Bulk
Brands:
  Aventura Gourmet
  Pepe's

9934 Pepe's Mexican Restaurant
2429 W Ball Rd
Anaheim, CA 92804-5210
Canada
714-952-9410
Fax: 416-674-2805 www.pepesmexicanfood.com
Tortilla chips, flour tortillas, multi-grain snacks, burritos, jalapeno peppers, salsa and beans
Owner: Nathan Russi
Vice President: Ronaldo Sardelitti
VP Sales: Tom Reynolds
National Sales Manager: Tony Kent
Estimated Sales: Less Than $500,000
Number Employees: 5-9
Square Footage: 132000
Parent Co: Signature Brands
Type of Packaging: Consumer, Food Service
Brands:
  Casa Del Norte
  Gringos
  Pepes

9935 Pepper Creek Farms
1002 SW Ard St
Lawton, OK 73505-9660
580-536-1300
Fax: 580-536-4886 800-526-8132
info@peppercreekfarms.com
www.peppercreekfarms.com
Jellies, mustards, peppers, salsa, relish, syrup, mixes, and seasonings
Owner: Craig Weissman
craig@peppercreekfarms.com
Vice President: Marshall Weissman
Estimated Sales: $600,000
Number Employees: 10-19
Square Footage: 30000
Type of Packaging: Consumer, Food Service, Private Label
Brands:
  Jalapeno
  Jalapeno Tnt
  Wildfire

9936 Pepper Island Beach
PO Box 484
Lawrence, PA 15055-0484
724-746-2401
Fax: 724-746-1679
Hot sauce
President: Karen Hasak

9937 Pepper Mill Imports
P.O. Box 775
Seaside, CA 93955
831-899-2983
Fax: 831-899-2996 800-928-1744
sales@peppermillimports.com
www.peppermillimports.com
Olive oil, pepper and spice mills
President: William Sterling
Marketing: Amy Paris
Sales: Angel Geil
Estimated Sales: Below $5 Million
Number Employees: 10
Number of Brands: 2
Number of Products: 112
Square Footage: 120000
Type of Packaging: Consumer, Food Service, Private Label
Brands:
  Melina's

9938 (HQ)Pepper Source Inc
2720 Athania Pkwy
Metairie, LA 70002-5904
504-885-3223
Fax: 504-885-3187 www.peppersource.com
Sauces and glazes, dry blends, custome rubs and packaging services.
President: Joe Morse
Contact: Shannon Glover
sglover@peppersource.com
Vice President of Operations: Paul Liggio
Production Supervisor: Mike Bartels
Estimated Sales: $15 Million
Number Employees: 5-9
Type of Packaging: Food Service, Private Label, Bulk
Other Locations:
  Pepper Source
  Van Buren AR
  Pepper Source
  Rogers AR

9939 Pepper Source LTD
11103 N Old Wire Rd
Rogers, AR 72756-9871
479-246-1030
Fax: 479-246-1061 www.peppersource.com
Sauces, marinades and glazes
VP Marketing: John Bowerman
Manager: Mark Watson
mwatson@peppersource.com
Plant Manager: Brad Palmer
Estimated Sales: $5-10 Million
Number Employees: 50-99
Type of Packaging: Private Label

9940 Pepper Source, Rogers
5800 Alma Hwy
Van Buren, AR 72956-7202
479-474-5178
Fax: 479-474-4729 sales@peppersource.com
www.peppersource.com
Sauces, marinades and glazes.
President: Wanda Patton
w.patton@peppersource.com
Director Sales: Mark Watson
VP Operations: Paul Liggio
VP Purchasing: Steven Campbell
Estimated Sales: $5-10 Million
Number Employees: 100-249
Type of Packaging: Private Label

9941 Peppered Palette
PO Box 29003
Bellingham, WA 98228
919-468-7101
Fax: 360-306-5589 866-829-9151
Hot sauce
Owner: Todd Guiton
toadster@pepperedpalette.com
Estimated Sales: $300,000-500,000
Number Employees: 1-4
Brands:
  Toad Sweat

9942 Pepperidge Farm Inc.
595 Westport Ave.
Norwalk, CT 06851
203-846-7000
888-737-7374
www.pepperidgefarm.com
Desserts, pastries, breads and rolls
VP, Finance: Chris Dayton
Year Founded: 1937
Estimated Sales: $1 Billion
Number Employees: 5000-9999
Parent Co: Campbell Soup
Brands:
  Goldfish
  Milano
  Pepperidge Farm

9943 Pepperland Farms
41177 N. Thibodaux Rd.
Ponchatoula, LA 70454
985-956-6703
Fax: 877-296-8683 www.pepperlandfarms.com
Chili peppers
Owner: Dennis Hall

9944 Peppers
17601 Coastal Hwy
Unit 1
Lewes, DE 19958-6217
302-703-6355
Fax: 302-644-6901 800-998-3473
peppers@peppers.com www.peppers.com
Hot sauces, salsa, mustards & dips, marinades & cajun injectors, peppers, pickles & relishes, olives, bloody mary & mixers, chili, soups, pasta & coffee, seasoning & rubs, curry & chutney, nuts & snacks, jelly, preserves & peanutbutter
Owner: Luther Hearn
chip@peppers.com
Number Employees: 20-49
Type of Packaging: Consumer, Food Service, Private Label, Bulk

9945 PepsiCo.
700 Anderson Hill Rd.
Purchase, NY 10577
914-253-2000
www.pepsico.com
Global brands food, snack and beverage company.
Chairman/CEO: Ramon Laguarta
President, Global Foodservice: Anne Fink
Vice Chairman/CFO: Hugh Johnston
EVP/Chief Scientific Officer: Rene Lammers
Year Founded: 1898
Estimated Sales: $67.1 Billion
Number Employees: 263,000
Number of Brands: 54
Square Footage: 40000
Type of Packaging: Consumer
Brands:
  Pepsi
  Frito-Lay
  Quaker
  Tropicana
  Gatorade
  Pure Leaf
  Mountain Dew
  Bubly
  Naked
  Lipton
  Starbucks Frappacino
  Aquafina
  Brisk
  Kevita
  Life WTR
  Sierra Mist
  Stubborn Soda
  IZZE
  Propel
  O.N.E
  AMP ENERGY Organic
  SOBE
  Mug Root Beer
  Doritos
  Stacy's Pita Chips
  Bare
  Sabra
  Ruffles
  Smartfood
  Cheetos
  Tostitos
  Fritos
  Near East
  Maker

Food Manufacturers / A-Z

Imag!ne
Sun Chips
Off The Eaten Path
Rold Gold
Miss Vickies
Red Rock Deli
Cracker Jack
Nut Harvest
Life
Matador
Santitas
Funyuns
Cap'n Crunch
Pasta Roni
Rice A Roni
Maui Style
Sabritones
Munchos
Grandma's
Aunt Jemima

9946 Perdue Farms Inc.
31149 Old Ocean City Rd.
Salisbury, MD 21804
800-473-7383
www.perdue.com
Chicken, turkey and pork.
Chairman: Jim Perdue
CEO: Randy Day
Senior VP/CFO: Brenda Galgano
General Counsel: Herb Frerichs
Senior VP, Corporate Communications: Andrea Staub
Year Founded: 1920
Estimated Sales: $6.7 Billion
Number Employees: 21,000
Number of Brands: 8
Type of Packaging: Consumer, Food Service, Private Label, Bulk
Other Locations:
  Perdue Farms
  Monterey TN
Brands:
  Perdue
  Coleman Natural
  Harvestland
  Simply Smart Organics
  Draper Valley Farms
  Petaluma Poultry
  Prarie Grove Farms
  Niman Ranch
  Spot Farms
  Full Moon

9947 Pereg Gourmet Spices
6966 Main St
Flushing, NY 11367-1724
718-261-6767
Fax: 718-261-7688 gill@pereg-gourmet.com
www.pereg-gourmet.com
Spices, oils, salads and spreads, toppings, bread crumbs, quinoa, rice mixes, salt, basmati rice, couscous
Owner: Chim Pereg
pereg.usa@verizon.net
Marketing: Gill Schnieder
Estimated Sales: $1 Million
Number Employees: 10-19

9948 Perez Food Products
2826 Southwest Blvd
Kansas City, MO 64108-3613
816-931-8761
Fax: 816-931-2825 www.perfectoutput.com
Mexican food
Owner: Jesse Perez
Sales Manager: Daniel Perez
Estimated Sales: $2,500,000
Number Employees: 5-9
Type of Packaging: Consumer

9949 Perfect Addition
P.O.Box 8976
Newport Beach, CA 92658
949-640-0220
Fax: 949-640-0304 perfectadd@aol.com
Frozen foods
President: Constance Grigsby
CFO/VP: Jack Grigsby
CEO/VP Marketing: Connie Grigsby
Estimated Sales: Less than $200,000
Number Employees: 1-4
Type of Packaging: Consumer, Private Label
Brands:
  Perfect Addition Beef Stock
  Perfect Addition Chi
  Perfect Addition Fis
  Perfect Addition Veg

9950 Perfect Bite Co
747 W Wilson Ave
Glendale, CA 91203-2447
818-507-1527
Fax: 818-507-1376 joe@theperfectbiteco.com
www.theperfectbiteco.com
Appetizers: crisps, cookies.
President/CEO: Teri Valentine
CFO/Secretary: John Valentine
john@theperfectbiteco.com
Vice President: Joe Forristal
Estimated Sales: $300,000
Number Employees: 10-19

9951 Perfect Foods Inc
862 Pulaski Hwy
Goshen, NY 10924-6032
845-651-2012
Fax: 845-783-9683 800-933-3288
info@800wheatgrass.com
www.drsqueezejuicers.com
Wheat grass, sunflower, buckwheat greens, juice
President: Harley Matsil
harleymatsil@yahoo.com
Year Founded: 1982
Estimated Sales: $200,000
Number Employees: 10-19
Square Footage: 24000
Type of Packaging: Consumer
Brands:
  Green Gold Wheatgrass
  Perfect Foods Wheatgrass Juice

9952 Perfect Life Nutrition
380 Saint Cloud Ave
West Orange, NJ 07052
973-980-2298
pnuff.com
Vegan baked peanut puffs
Founder: Juan Salinas
Brands:
  P-nuff Crunch

9953 Perfect Puree of Napa Valley
2700 Napa Valley Corporate Dr
Suite L
Napa, CA 94558-7557
707-261-5100
Fax: 707-261-5111 info@perfectpuree.com
www.perfectpuree.com
Flavored purees
President: Tracy Hayward
thayward@perfectpuree.com
Marketing: Michele Lex
Estimated Sales: $1-3 Million
Number Employees: 10-19
Type of Packaging: Consumer, Bulk

9954 Perfect Snacks
3931 Sorrento Valley Blvd
Suite 100
Sorrento Valley, CA 92120
866-628-8548
perfectbar.com
Nut butter-based meal bars
CEO: Bill Keith

9955 Perfections by Allan
3 Old Creek Ct
Owings Mills, MD 21117
410-581-8670
Fax: 410-581-0877 800-581-8670
Dipping cookies and snacks
President: Allan Taylor
ataylor@perfectionsbyallan.com
Estimated Sales: Under $500,000
Number Employees: 1-4
Type of Packaging: Consumer, Private Label
Brands:
  Grandma Taylor's Gourmet Dip

9956 Perfetti Van Melle USA Inc
3645 Turfway Rd
Erlanger, KY 41018
859-283-1234
perfettivanmelleus.com
Candy and chewing gum.
President & CEO: Sylvia Buxton
CFO: Fred King
VP, Marketing: Rachel Chambers
VP, Sales: Dan Hamilton
VP, Manufacturing: Francisco Tello
VP, Supply Chain: James Biro
Estimated Sales: $50-100 Million
Number Employees: 100-249
Type of Packaging: Consumer
Brands:
  Airheads
  Alpenliebe
  Big Babol
  Center Fruit
  Chupa Chups
  Daygum
  Frisk
  Fruittella
  Golia
  Happydent
  Klene
  Look-O-Look
  Meller
  Mentos
  Morositas
  Smint
  StopNot
  Sula
  Vigorsol
  Vivident

9957 Performance Labs
5115 Douglas Fir Rd
Suite M
Calabasas, CA 91302-2597
818-591-9669
Fax: 818-591-2116 800-848-2537
Nutritional and herbal supplements, vitamins and garlic
Owner: Richard Burke
CEO: David Mercer, Jr.
Contact: Jon Ackland
cousteau@performancelab.co.nz
Purchasing Manager: Allan Suda
Estimated Sales: $3 Million
Number Employees: 20-49
Type of Packaging: Consumer
Brands:
  Cardiomax
  Garlimax
  Guardmax
  Immumax
  Relaxmax
  Vitalert

9958 Peri & Sons Farms
102 McLeod St.
Yerington, NV 89447
775-463-4444
Fax: 775-463-4028 www.periandsons.com
White, yellow, red, sweet and organic onions.
Owner: David Peri
Year Founded: 1979
Number Employees: 1000-5000
Type of Packaging: Private Label

9959 Perino's Inc
6850 Westbank Expy
Marrero, LA 70072-2523
504-347-5410
Fax: 504-341-2504 www.perinosseafood.com
Seafood
Manager: Mark Somme
Manager: Paul Ocrne
Estimated Sales: $3-5 Million
Number Employees: 10-19

9960 Perky Jerky
7400 E Crestline Cir
Suite 130
Greenwood Vlg, CO 80111-3655
720-389-7171
888-343-6113
perkyjerky.com
Meat jerkies
Founder: Brian Levin
Contact: Jessie Arellano
jessiearellano@perkyjerky.com
Number Employees: 10-19

Food Manufacturers / A-Z

9961 Perky's Pizza
4029 Tampa Rd
Oldsmar, FL 34677-3206
813-855-7700
Fax: 813-855-0014 800-473-7597
perky@perkys.com www.perkys.com
Pizza producer of Perky's pizza products, program and product sales
President: Jim Howell
CEO: Frank Rozel
R&D: Bill Sweet
Marketing Manager: Anne Reilley
Sales: Rick White
Contact: G Gable
g.gable@perkys.com
Estimated Sales: $2.5-5 Million
Number Employees: 10-19
Square Footage: 8000
Type of Packaging: Food Service, Private Label
Brands:
Perky's Fresh Bakery

9962 Perlarom Technology
9133 Red Branch Rd
Columbia, MD 21045-2029
410-997-5114
Fax: 410-964-9374 leif.kjargaard@danisco.com
Flavors and extracts
Executive VP: Soren Bjerre Nielsen
CEO: Tom Knutzen
Vice President: Philippe Lavielle
Executive VP: Mogens Granborg
Estimated Sales: $2.5-5 Million
Number Employees: 20-49

9963 Pernicious Pickling
350 Clinton St
Suite A
Costa Mesa, CA 92626-6028
714-794-9845
www.perniciouspickling.com
Pickled vegetables
Contact: Kendra Coggin

9964 Pernod Ricard USA
250 Park Ave.
New York, NY 10177
212-372-5400
Fax: 914-539-4550 www.pernod-ricard-usa.com
Spirits and wines.
Chairman/CEO: Paul Duffy
Chief Financial Officer: Guillaume Thomas
Senior Vice President: James Slack
Chief Marketing Officer: Jonas Tahlin
Chief Commercial Officer: Julien Hemard
Senior VP, Communications/Sustainability: Amandine Robin
Senior VP, New Brand Ventures: Jeff Agdern
Year Founded: 1980
Estimated Sales: $100+ Million
Number Employees: 1000-4999
Number of Brands: 30+
Parent Co: Pernod Ricard SA
Brands:
Aberlour Single Malt
Absolut(c)
Altos
Aura
Avion(c)
Azteca de Oro
Ballantine's
Beefeater(c)
Brancott Estate(c)
Campo Viejo
Chivas Regal(c)
Fris
G.H. Mumm
Graffigna & Jacob's Creek
Hiram Walker(c)
Jameson(c) Irish
Kahlua
Kenwood(c) Vineyards
Lillet(c)
Longmorn
Lot 40 and Pike Creek
Malibu(c)
Martell(c)
Midleton
Mumm Napa(c)
Pernod(c)
Perrier-Jouet(c)
Plymouth(c) Gin
Powers
Redbreast Irish
Ricard(c)
Seagram's Extra Dry Gin(c)
The Glenlivet(c) Single Malt
100 Pipers
Smithworks Vodka
Royal Salut
Green Spot
Vida
Monkey 47

9965 Perona Farms
350 Andover Sparta Rd
Andover, NJ 07821-5016
973-729-6161
Fax: 973-729-1097 800-750-6190
info@peronafarms.com www.peronafarms.com
Salmon, seafood
President: Tracey Giller
tracey@peronafarms.com
CFO: Mark Avondoglio
Executive Chef: Kirk Avondoglio
Estimated Sales: $2.5 Million
Number Employees: 100-249
Square Footage: 16400
Brands:
Perona Farms

9966 Perricone Juices
550 B St
Beaumont, CA 92223-2672
951-769-7171
Fax: 951-769-7176 www.perriconejuices.com
Juice: orange, tangerine, grapefruit, lemon, lime, lemonade, strawberry, pomegranate and apple
President: Bob Rovzar
CEO: Tom Carmody
tcarmody@perriconejuices.com
CFO: Joe Perricone
Director of Human Resources: Will Martin
Production Manager: Humberto Orellana
Estimated Sales: $15.8 Million
Number Employees: 50-99
Square Footage: 60000
Type of Packaging: Consumer, Food Service
Brands:
Perricone Farms

9967 Perrigo Nutritionals LLC
515 Eastern Ave
Allegan, MI 49010-9070
269-673-8451
www.perrigonutritionals.com
Infant formula
Vice President, Operations: Sean Walsh
Number Employees: 1-4

9968 Perry Creek Winery
7400 Perry Creek Rd
PO Box 350
Somerset, CA 95684-9207
530-620-5175
Fax: 215-699-8200 800-880-4026
www.perrycreek.com
Wines
Founder: Michael Chazen
Estimated Sales: $1-2.5 Million
Number Employees: 10-19

9969 Perry's Ice Cream Co Inc
1 Ice Cream Plz
Akron, NY 14001-1031
716-542-5492
Fax: 716-542-2544 800-873-7797
www.perrysicecream.com
Ice cream, custard, gelato, frozen yogurt, sherbet & sorbet
President: Michael Firth
CEO: Thomas Perry
EVP: Mike Calhoun
Quality Control Manager: Jim Marshall
VP Marketing: Diane Austin
VP Sales: Ken Kwarta
VP Operations: Michael Diem
Plant Manager: Tom Kowalski
Director Purchasing: Leigyh Menzel
Number Employees: 250-499
Type of Packaging: Consumer, Bulk
Brands:
Perry's
Perry's Deluxe
Perry's Free
Perry's Light
Perry's Pride

9970 Personal Edge Nutrition
275 White Tree Lane
Ballwin, MO 63011-3338
514-636-4512
Fax: 514-636-8356
Energy and protein bars, powdered soy beverages
Parent Co: DuPont Chemical
Brands:
Personal Edge Supro

9971 Pervida
PO Box 10175
Blacksburg, VA 24062
540-808-0800
www.pervida.net
Health drinks
Managing Partner: Debbie Custer
Brands:
Pervida(c)

9972 Pestano Foods
New Rochelle, NY 10801
info@drinktoma.com
www.drinktoma.com
Artisanal Bloody Mary cocktail mix
Founder/Owner: Alejandro Lopez
Number of Brands: 1
Number of Products: 1
Type of Packaging: Consumer, Private Label, Bulk
Brands:
Toma

9973 Pestos with Panache
176 Johnson Street
Suite 8E
Brooklyn, NY 11201
917-656-3082
Fax: 212-230-7404
Pesto
President/Owner: Lauren Stewart

9974 Petaluma Poultry
2700 Lakeville Hwy
Petaluma, CA 94954-5606
707-763-1904
Fax: 707-763-3924 800-556-6789
petalumareception@petalumapoultry.com
www.petalumapoultry.com
Organic chicken
President: Dick Krengal
CFO: Dave Martinelli
dmartinelli@petalumapoultry.com
Sales Manager: Brian Starr
Director of Manufacturing: Bob Wolfe
Estimated Sales: $20-50 Million
Number Employees: 100-249
Square Footage: 30000
Parent Co: Coleman Natural
Type of Packaging: Consumer
Brands:
Rocky Jr
Rocky the Range
Rosie Organic

9975 Pete & Joy's Bakery
121 E Broadway
Little Falls, MN 56345-3038
320-632-6388
Fax: 320-632-2740
Rolls, coffee, cake
Owner: Peter Kamrowski
petenjoy@charter.net
Estimated Sales: $8 Million
Number Employees: 10-19

9976 Pete and Gerry's Organic Eggs
140 Buffum Rd
Monroe, NH 03771
603-638-2827
800-210-6657
familyfarmteam@peteandgerrys.com
www.peteandgerrys.com
Organic free range eggs
Owner/CEO: Jesse Laflamme
CFO: Keith Fortier
COO: Erik Drake
VP Marketing: Paul Turbeville
Number Employees: 50-99

9977 (HQ)Pete's Brewing Company
14800 San Pedro Ave
San Antonio, TX 78232-3733
210-490-9128
Fax: 210-490-9984 800-877-7383

Food Manufacturers / A-Z

Beer
President: Scott Barnum
CEO: Jeffrey Atkins
CEO: Carlos Alvarez
VP Sales: Don Quigley
Contact: James Bolz
j.bolz@petes.com
Number Employees: 50-99
Parent Co: Miller Brewing Company
Brands:
    Pete's Wicked Ale

9978 Peter Cremer North America
3117 Southside Ave
Cincinnati, OH 45204-1215
    513-471-7200
Fax: 513-244-7775 877-901-7262
www.petercremerna.com
Oleochemicals: fatty alcohols, acids, biodiesel, esters, glycerin and care products
CEO: Robin Avedesian-Scol
ravedesianscol@petercremerna.com
Number Employees: 100-249
Parent Co: Cremer
Brands:
    Cremer Cunter

9979 Peter Michael Winery
12400 Ida Clayton Rd
Calistoga, CA 94515-9507
    707-942-4459
Fax: 707-942-0209 800-354-4459
retail@petermichaelwinery.com
Wines
Owner: Peter Michael
retail@petermichaelwinery.com
Vice President: Bill Vyenielo
Estimated Sales: $1-2.5 Million
Number Employees: 20-49
Brands:
    Peter Michael Winery

9980 Peter Pan Seafoods Inc.
3015 112th Ave. NE
Suite 100
Bellevue, WA 98004
    206-728-6000
Fax: 206-441-9090 sales@ppsf.com
www.ppsf.com
Seafood including crab, herring and surimi blends, canned salmon, swordfish, mahi mahi and tuna.
President/CEO: Barry Collier
barryc@ppsf.com
Controller/Treasurer: Adrian Yonke
Year Founded: 1912
Estimated Sales: $225 Million
Number Employees: 1,000-4,999
Number of Brands: 8
Parent Co: Maruha Capital Investment, Inc.
Type of Packaging: Consumer, Food Service, Private Label, Bulk
Brands:
    Deming's
    Double Q
    Gill Netter's Best
    Humpty Dumpty
    Peter Pan
    SeaBlends
    SeaKist
    Unica

9981 Peter Rabbit Farms
85810 Peter Rabbit Ln
Coachella, CA 92236
    760-398-0136
Fax: 760-398-0972 sales@peterrabbitfarms.com
www.peterrabbitfarms.com
Peppers, grapes, eggplant, leafy greens and Medjool dates
President/CEO: John Powell Jr
Controller: Stephanie Sibotka
stephanies@peterrabbitfarms.com
VP & COO: Steve Powell
Manager, Sales: John Burton
Number Employees: 100-249
Square Footage: 400000
Type of Packaging: Consumer, Food Service, Private Label, Bulk

9982 Peter's Mustards
PO Box 1036
Sharon, CT 06069-1036
    860-364-0842
Mustard

President: Richard Harris

9983 Petersen Ice Cream Company
1104 Chicago Ave
Suite 6
Oak Park, IL 60302
    708-386-6130
Fax: 708-386-6162 www.petersenicecream.com
Ice cream and frozen yogurt
President and CFO: Robert Raniere
Treasurer: D Raniere
Estimated Sales: $1-3 Million
Number Employees: 20-49
Type of Packaging: Consumer, Food Service

9984 Peterson & Sons Winery
9375 E P Ave
Kalamazoo, MI 49048-9762
    269-626-9755
Fax: 616-626-9755
Wine
Owner: Duane Peterson
Sales Manager: Tony Peterson
Estimated Sales: Less Than $500,000
Number Employees: 1-4

9985 Peterson Farms Inc
3104 W Baseline Rd
Shelby, MI 49455-9633
    231-861-0119
Fax: 231-861-2274 sarah@petersonfarmsinc.com
www.petersonfarmsinc.com
Fruit
CEO: Aaron Peterson
aaron@petersonfarmsinc.com
Chief Sales & Marketing Officer: Sarah Schlukebir
Director of Sales: Larry Hicks
Number Employees: 500-999
Brands:
    Peterson Farms

9986 Petit Pot
4221 Horton St
Emeryville, CA 94608
    650-488-7432
petitpot.com
Pot de crŠme, rice pudding and cookies.
CEO: Maxime Pouvreau
Brands:
    Petit Pot(c)

9987 Petra International
1260 Fewster Drive
Unit 1
Mississauga, ON L4W 1A5
Canada
    905-629-9269
Fax: 905-542-2546 800-261-7226
petra@petradecor.com www.petradecor.com
Gum paste flowers
President: Ham Go
Parent Co: Indomex Foods
Type of Packaging: Consumer, Private Label, Bulk
Brands:
    Petra

9988 Petrofsky's Bakery Products
16647 Annas Way
Chesterfield, MO 63005-4509
    636-519-1613
Dough and bagels
President: Jerry Shapiro
Vice President: Robert Petrofsky
Estimated Sales: $10-20 Million
Number Employees: 20-49
Parent Co: Maplehurst Bakeries
Type of Packaging: Consumer, Food Service

9989 Petschl's Quality Meats
1150 Andover Park E
Tukwila, WA 98188-3903
    206-575-4400
Fax: 206-575-4463 info@petschls.com
Beef, lamb, pork, veal and chicken
Owner: Shelley Greene
shelley@petschls.com
Vice President: Nancy Kvinge
Estimated Sales: $9 Million
Number Employees: 20-49
Type of Packaging: Consumer, Food Service, Private Label, Bulk

9990 Pett Spice Products Inc
4285 Wendell Dr SW
Atlanta, GA 30336-1632
    404-691-5235
Fax: 404-691-5237 orders@pettspice.net
Seasonings for marinades, glazes, salad dressings, soups, sauces, snack foods and breading
Owner: Ben Calhoun
bcalhoun@pettspice.net
Plant Manager: Mike Foley
Estimated Sales: $500,000-$1 Million
Number Employees: 5-9
Brands:
    Pett Spice

9991 Pez Candy Inc
35 Prindle Hill Rd
Orange, CT 06477-3616
    203-795-0531
Fax: 203-799-1679
Candy and dispensers
President: Joseph Vittoria
CEO: Christian Jegen
jegen@pezcandyinc.com
CFO: Brian Fry
VP Marketing: Peter Vandall
VP Sales: Dan Silliman
VP Operations: Mark Morrissey
Estimated Sales: $3,100,000
Number Employees: 100-249
Type of Packaging: Consumer
Other Locations:
    PEZ Candy
    Orange CT
Brands:
    Pez

9992 Pfanstiehl Inc
1219 Glen Rock Ave
Waukegan, IL 60085-6249
    847-623-0370
Fax: 847-623-9173
Lactic acid
Chairman: Jim Breckenridge
President: Cynthia Kerker
VP, Sales & Marketing: Chris Wilcox
VP, Research & Development: Trevor Calkins
Quality Control Chemist: Jimmy Moshopoulos
Contact: Jessica Bakutis
jessica.bakutis@pfanstiehl.com
Year Founded: 1919
Estimated Sales: $23.9 Million
Number Employees: 10-19
Parent Co: Med Opportunity Partners
Type of Packaging: Bulk

9993 Pfefferkorn's Coffee Inc
1200 E Fort Ave
P.O. Box 27007
Baltimore, MD 21230-5105
    410-727-3354
Fax: 410-547-1652 800-682-4665
www.pfefferkornscoffee.com
Coffee
President: Louis Pfefferkorn
pfefferkornscoffee@verizon.net
VP/Owner: Samuel Pfefferkorn
Operations Manager: Charles Pfefferkorn
Estimated Sales: $.5-1 million
Number Employees: 10-19
Type of Packaging: Consumer
Brands:
    Pfefferkorn's

9994 Pfeil & Holding Inc
5815 Northern Blvd
Woodside, NY 11377-2297
    718-545-4600
Fax: 718-932-7513 800-247-7955
info@cakedeco.com www.cakedeco.com
Bakers' equipment and utensils, cake decorations, pastry bags, pans, tubes, tier separators, flavors and ingredients
President: David Gordils
davidg@cakedeco.com
CEO: Sy Stricker
Sales Director: Jenn Covalluzzi
Estimated Sales: $5-10 Million
Number Employees: 20-49
Number of Products: 7000
Square Footage: 200000
Brands:
    PFEIL

Food Manufacturers / A-Z

9995 Pfizer
235 E 42nd St
New York, NY 10017-5703
212-573-3115
Fax: 212-309-0896 800-879-3477
www.pfizer.com
Chewing gum and breath mints
Trade Development Manager: Larry Roche
CEO: Ian C. Read
CFO: Frank D'Amelio
EVP: Rady Johnson
President: Mikael Dolsten, M.D
Sales/Marketing Executive: Michael Soriano
Estimated Sales: $1-3 Million
Number Employees: 1-4
Parent Co: Pfizer
Type of Packaging: Consumer, Food Service
Brands:
  Bubbilicious
  Certs
  Chiclets
  Clorets
  Cool Mint Drops
  Dentyne Ice
  Mint*A*Burst
  Trident
  Vichy

9996 Phamous Phloyd's Barbecue
2998 S Steele St
Denver, CO 80210-6948
303-757-3285
Fax: 303-757-3373 800-497-3281
phloyd@4edisp.net www.phloyds.com
Condiments, Bloody Mary mixes, marinades, sauces, mustards and dry rubs
President/Owner: Mary Ellen Baran
Estimated Sales: Under $500,000
Number Employees: 1-4
Type of Packaging: Consumer, Bulk
Brands:
  Phamous Phloyd's

9997 Pharmachem Laboratories
265 Harrison Ave
Kearny, NJ 07032-4315
201-246-1000
Fax: 201-991-5674 800-526-0609
www.pharmachemlabs.com
Ingredients: proteins, extracts, acids
President: David Holmes
CEO: Andrea Bauer
andrea.bauer@pharmachem.com
Number Employees: 50-99
Brands:
  Berry-Max
  Celadrin(c)
  Cran-Max(c)
  Enderma
  Lactium(c)
  Phase 2(c)
  Prenulin(c)
  Reducol

9998 Pharmavite LLC
8510 Balboa Blvd
Suite 100
Northridge, CA 91325-3581
818-221-6200
Fax: 818-221-6618 800-276-2878
www.pharmavite.com
Vitamin tablets and ingredients
President: Brent Belly
CEO: Connie Barry
Executive VP Marketing: Catherine Mardesich
Estimated Sales: $300,000-500,000
Number Employees: 5-9
Parent Co: Pharmavite Corporation
Type of Packaging: Bulk
Brands:
  Nature Made
  Nature's Resources

9999 Pharmco Aaper
58 Vale Rd
Brookfield, CT 06804-3984
203-740-3471
Fax: 203-740-3481 www.pharmcoaaper.com
Ethanol, solvents & custom sterile blends
President: Paul Demarco
paul@pharmco-prod.com
Manager of Domestic Sales: Amanda Cedeno
Number Employees: 50-99
Parent Co: GreenField

10000 Phat Fudge
578 Washington Blvd
Marina del Rey, CA 90292
www.phatfudge.com
Performance food
Founder/CEO: Mary Shenouda
Year Founded: 2016

10001 Pheasant Ridge Winery
3507 E County Road 5700
Lubbock, TX 79403-6962
806-746-6033
Fax: 806-746-6750 billgipson@aol.com
www.pheasantridgewinery.com
Wines
Manager: Bill Blackman
Owner: William Gibson
Estimated Sales: Below $5 Million
Number Employees: 5-9
Brands:
  Proprietor's Reserve

10002 Phenomenal Fudge Inc
4668 VT Route 74 W
Shoreham, VT 05770-9689
802-897-7300
Fax: 802-897-7300 800-430-5442
info@pfudge.com www.pfudge.com
Fudge
Owner/Fudgemaker: Steve Jackson
Estimated Sales: Less Than $500,000
Number Employees: 1-4

10003 Philadelphia Baking Company
2550 Grant Ave
Philadelphia, PA 19114
215-464-4242
Fax: 215-464-5701
Breads
Manager: Rich Toney
Estimated Sales: $25-49.9 Million
Number Employees: 100-249
Parent Co: North East Foods

10004 Philadelphia Candies Inc
1546 E State St
Hermitage, PA 16148-1823
724-981-6341
Fax: 724-981-6490 pc@phillyc.com
Confectionery: marshmallow, dietetic, mints, creams, nougats, nuts, fruits and chocolates
President: Spyros Macris
pc@phillyc.com
Vice President: Georgia Macris
Estimated Sales: $1,100,000
Number Employees: 50-99
Type of Packaging: Bulk
Brands:
  Loving Bunny

10005 Philadelphia Cheese Steak
520 E Hunting Park Ave
Philadelphia, PA 19124-6009
215-423-3333
Fax: 215-423-3131 800-342-9771
marketinginfo@phillycheesesteak.com
www.phillycheesesteak.com
Cheese and chicken steaks
President & CEO: John Karamatsoukas
Director of Quality Control: Caitlin Anderson
Year Founded: 1981
Estimated Sales: Less Than $500,000
Number Employees: 1-4
Parent Co: Tyson Foods
Type of Packaging: Consumer, Food Service
Brands:
  Philadelphia Cheese Steak

10006 Philadelphia Macaroni Co
760 S 11th St
Philadelphia, PA 19147-2614
215-923-3141
Fax: 215-925-4298 www.philamacaroni.com
Pasta and noodles.
Director of Sales/Marketing: Joe Viviano
EVP Sales: Bill Stabert
Customer Service: Fran Pickel
Estimated Sales: $20-50 Million
Number Employees: 10-19
Type of Packaging: Food Service, Private Label, Bulk

10007 Philip R's Frozen Desserts
750 Main Street
Winchester, MA 01890
781-721-6330
Fax: 781-721-4590
philipjr@icecream-desserts.com
www.icecream-desserts.com
Ice Cream
President: Phil Rotundo
Estimated Sales: $770,000
Number Employees: 10

10008 Philip Togni Vineyard
3780 Spring Mountain Rd
St Helena, CA 94574-9580
707-963-3731
Fax: 707-963-9186 tognivyd@wildblue.net
www.philiptognivineyard.com
Cabernet wine
Owner: Philip Togni
tognivyd@wildblue.net
Partner: Birgitta Togni
Partner/Winemaker: Lisa Togni
Estimated Sales: $500,000-$1 Million
Number Employees: 1-4
Brands:
  Philip Togni

10009 Phillip's Candy House
818 William T Morrissey Blvd
Dorchester, MA 02122-3404
617-282-2090
Fax: 617-288-4280 info@phillipschocolate.com
www.phillipschocolate.com
Candy
Owner: Maryann Nagle
Estimated Sales: $2,600,000
Number Employees: 10-19
Type of Packaging: Consumer, Private Label

10010 Phillips Beverage Company
500 Washington Ave South
Suite 1000
Minneapolis, MN 55415
612-362-7500
Fax: 612-362-7501 www.phillipsdistilling.com
Cordials and liqueurs
President: Dean Phillips
CEO: Edward Phillips
Estimated Sales: $10-20 Million
Number Employees: 6
Type of Packaging: Consumer, Food Service

10011 Phillips Candies
217 Broadway St
Seaside, OR 97138-5805
503-738-5402
Fax: 503-738-8326 candy@seasurf.net
www.phillipscandies.com
Saltwater taffy, chocolates and fudge
President: Steven C Phillips
Estimated Sales: $1-2.5 000,000
Number Employees: 10-19
Brands:
  Phillips Candies

10012 Phillips Foods
3761 Commerce Dr
Suite 413
Baltimore, MD 21227
888-234-2722
comments@phillipsfoods.com
www.phillipsfoods.com
Seafood
President & CEO: Steve Phillips
Senior Vice President: John Knorr
Director, Global Quality Control: Bobby Love
Vice President Sales: Scott Miller
Controller: Bob Banks
bbanks@phillipsfoods.com
Director, Restaurant Operations: Larry McAllister
Logistics Manager: Dave Ehly
Year Founded: 1914
Estimated Sales: $47.2 Million
Number Employees: 223
Square Footage: 270000
Type of Packaging: Consumer, Food Service, Bulk
Brands:
  Phillips

Food Manufacturers / A-Z

10013 Phillips Gourmet Inc
1011 Kaolin Rd
PO Box 190
Kennett Square, PA 19348-2605
610-925-0520
Fax: 610-925-0527 info@phillipsgourmet.com
www.phillipsmushroomfarms.com
Mushrooms
President: Marshall Phillips
marshall@phillipsgourmet.com
Number Employees: 100-249
Parent Co: Phillips Mushroom Farms
Type of Packaging: Consumer, Food Service
Brands:
   Bella

10014 Phillips Seafood
1418 Sapelo Ave NE
Townsend, GA 31331-5732
912-832-4423
Fax: 912-832-6228 www.sapeloseafarms.com
Seafood
President: Myron Phillips
Number Employees: 1-4

10015 Phillips Syrup Corp
28025 Ranney Pkwy
Cleveland, OH 44145-1159
440-835-8001
Fax: 440-835-1148 800-350-8443
info@PhillipsSyrup.com www.phillipssyrup.com
Chocolate, sugar-free, sno-cone, slush and maple syrups, sundae toppings, fountain drinks, bar mixes and concentrates
President: Maggie Gillanders
m.gillanders@phillipssyrup.com
Public Relations: Raisa Hawal
Production/Plant Manager: Joseph Mazak
Purchasing Manager: Susan Connerton
Estimated Sales: $7000000
Number Employees: 10-19
Number of Products: 200
Square Footage: 60000
Type of Packaging: Food Service, Private Label
Brands:
   Fundae
   Phillips

10016 Phin & Phebes
Brooklyn, NY
718-383-4300
yum@phinandphebes.com
Ice cream
Co-Founder: Jess Eddy
Co-Founder: Crista Freeman

10017 Phipps Desserts
1875 Leslie St
Unit 21
North York, ON M3B 2M5
Canada
416-391-5800
Fax: 416-391-0182 www.phippsdesserts.com
Desserts and pastries
Proprietor: Janet Schriber
Estimated Sales: $205,000
Number Employees: 3
Type of Packaging: Consumer, Food Service
Brands:
   Phipps

10018 Phivida Organics
600 B Street
Level 3
San Diego, CA 92101
844-744-6646
enquiries@feeloki.com feeloki.com
Hemp-infused water, and hemp oil and capsules
CEO: James Bailey

10019 Phoenicia Patisserie
PO Box 13128
Arlington, TX 76094-0128
817-261-2898
Fax: 817-274-3942
Pastries
Owner: Amer Hamedi

10020 Phoenician Herbals
P.O.Box 28381
Scottsdale, AZ 85251
480-368-8144
Fax: 480-368-2912 800-966-8144
Vitamins, supplements and teas
Owner: Redgie Hansen
Estimated Sales: $440,000
Number Employees: 5-9
Brands:
   Phoenician Herbals

10021 Phoenix Agro-IndustrialCorporation
521 Lowell St
Westbury, NY 11590
516-334-1194
Fax: 516-338-8647
Frozen foods and groceries
President: Tomipor Pasto
Marketing: Julianna Edlyn
Purchasing Director: Neone Din
Estimated Sales: $3-5 Million
Number Employees: 5-9
Square Footage: 40000
Type of Packaging: Consumer, Private Label, Bulk
Brands:
   Citizen Foods

10022 Phoenix Foods
1030 Reserve Dr
Canton, TX 75103-4947
903-287-9166
food@phoenixfoodco.com
phoenixfoodco.com
Dry mixes for soups, desserts and dips
Founder: Kenneth Johnsen
kjohnsen@homemadegourmet.com
Number Employees: 100-249
Brands:
   Homemade Gourmet
   Just In Time
   Modern Pantry

10023 Phoenix Laboratories
200 Adams Boulevard
Farmingdale, NY 11735-6615
516-822-1230
Fax: 516-822-1252 800-236-6583
Vitamins
President: Mel Rich
VP: Steven Stern
Contact: Cynthia Marshall
cmarshall@phoenixlaboratories.com
Number Employees: 50-99

10024 Phranil Foods
3900 E Main Avenue
Spokane, WA 99202-4737
509-534-7770
Fax: 509-534-4244
Pies
Owner: Fran Bessermin
Controller: Bob Clements
Estimated Sales: $1-2.5 000,000
Number Employees: 20-49

10025 Phyter Foods
245 W Roosevelt Rd
Bldg 14-143
West Chicago, IL 60185
630-206-3701
phyterfood.com
Organic plant-based snack bars
Owner and Partner: Gloria Athanis
Chef, Owner and Partner: David Choi
Owner and Partner: Jeff Adeszko

10026 Phyto-Technologies
107 Enterprise Dr
Woodbine, IA 51579
712-647-2755
Fax: 712-647-2885 877-809-3404
extracts@phyto-tech.com www.phyto-tech.com
Nutritional and herbal supplements, extracts and blends
Founder/President: Albert Leung
albert.leung@photo-tech.com
Sales/Marketing: Terry Jinks
Estimated Sales: Below $5 Million
Number Employees: 10-19
Square Footage: 80000
Parent Co: Earth Power
Type of Packaging: Consumer, Private Label
Brands:
   Earth Power's All American
   Earthpower's Phytochi

10027 Phytotherapy Research Laboratory
W Fourth S
PO Box 627
Lobelville, TN 37097-0627
931-593-3780
Fax: 931-593-3782 800-274-3727
Herb extracts
President: Brent Davis
Estimated Sales: $500,000-$1 Million
Number Employees: 1-4
Square Footage: 50000
Type of Packaging: Private Label
Brands:
   Forest Center
   Hahg
   Prl

10028 (HQ)Piantedosi Baking Co Inc
240 Commercial St
Malden, MA 02148-6709
781-321-3400
Fax: 781-324-5647 800-339-0080
www.piantedosi.com
Bread
President: Michelle Dalton
michelle.dalton@nttdata.com
Executive Vice President & Co-Owner: Joe Piantedosi
Number Employees: 100-249
Type of Packaging: Consumer, Food Service, Private Label, Bulk
Other Locations:
   Piantedosi Baking Co.
   Malden MA
Brands:
   Piantedosi

10029 Piazza's Seafood World LLC
205 James Dr W
St Rose, LA 70087-4036
504-602-5050
Fax: 504-602-1555 info@cajunboy.net
www.cajunboy.net
crawfish, alligator, catfish, shrimp, squid, crabmeat and softshell crabs
Manager: Jennifer Champagne
CFO: Mike Sabolyk
Manager: Jarrod Champagne
jarrod@cajunboy.net
Estimated Sales: $5-10 Million
Number Employees: 10-19
Number of Products: 20
Type of Packaging: Food Service, Private Label
Brands:
   Cajun Boy

10030 Picaflor
4745 Walnut St
Suite D
Boulder, CO 80301
720-442-3816
aaron@picaflor.co
www.picaflor.co
Pepper sauces and flakes
Chef and Farmer: Marcus McCauley
Year Founded: 2015

10031 (HQ)Picard Peanuts
447 Dundas Street E
Waterdown, ON L0R 2H1
Canada
905-690-1888
Fax: 519-426-0571 888-244-7688
www.picardpeanuts.com
Potato chip covered peanuts
President: James Picard Sr
CFO: John Picard
R & D: Lincoln Reid
CFO: John David
Quality Control: Michael Newsome
Estimated Sales: $3.8 Million
Number Employees: 23
Square Footage: 128000
Type of Packaging: Consumer, Bulk
Other Locations:
   Picard Peanuts Ltd.
   Waterford ON
Brands:
   Chipnuts

Food Manufacturers / A-Z

10032 Pickle Cottage
12989 Windy Road
Bucklin, KS 67834-8807
316-826-3502
Fax: 316-826-3866
Snack foods and pickles
President: Barry Stimpert
Estimated Sales: $500,000-$1 000,000
Number Employees: 10-19

10033 Pickled Pink
6649 Peachtree Industrial Blvd
Suite G
Norcross, GA 30092
770-998-1500
jim@pickledpinkfoods.com
pickledpinkfoods.com
Pickled fruits and vegetables
Contact: Jim Lawlor

10034 Pickled Planet
225 Water St
Ashland, OR 97520
541-201-2689
pickledplanet@gmail.com
pickledplanet.com
Organic fermented vegetables
Founder: Courtlandt Jennings

10035 Picklesmith Inc
300 Green Ave
Taft, TX 78390-2708
361-528-4953
Fax: 830-885-4560 800-499-3401
Pickles and olives
President: David Smith
Estimated Sales: $1-3 Million
Number Employees: 1-4
Square Footage: 10000
Type of Packaging: Consumer, Food Service
Brands:
A.P. Smith Canning Co.
Picklesmith

10036 Pickwick Catfish Farm
4155 Highway 57
Counce, TN 38326
731-689-3805
Smoked catfish
Owner: Betty Knussmann
Co-Owner: Quentin Knussman
Estimated Sales: Less than $500,000
Number Employees: 5-9
Brands:
Pickwick Catfish

10037 Picnik
Austin, TX
picnikaustin@gmail.com
picnikaustin.com
Butter coffee
Founder & CEO: Naomi Seifter
Co-Founder: Kevin Ward

10038 Pictsweet Co
10 Pictsweet Dr
Bells, TN 38006-4274
731-663-7600
Fax: 731-663-7639 mailbox@pictsweet.com
www.pictsweet.com
Asparagus, beans, broccoli, brussels sprouts, carrots, cauliflower, turnip, mustard and collard greens, okra, peas, spinach, squash, succotash
President: Billy Ennis
Chairman/Ceo: James Tankersley
jtankersley@pictsweet.com
Marketing Director: Julia Wells
Director Manufacturing: Frank Tankersley
Estimated Sales: $10-20 Million
Number Employees: 500-999
Number of Products: 100
Parent Co: Pictsweet
Type of Packaging: Consumer, Food Service, Private Label
Brands:
Dulany
Everfresh
Pictsweet
Prime Froz-N
Tennessee
Winter Garden

10039 Pidy Gourmet Pastry Shells
90 Inip Dr
Inwood, NY 11096-1011
516-239-6057
Fax: 516-239-9306 www.pidy.com
Tart shells, chocolate, desserts
CEO: Jerome Haussoullier
Parent Co: Biscuits Bouvard
Type of Packaging: Consumer, Food Service
Brands:
Aperi-Coeur
Aperiquiche
Barquette
Crescentgarniture
Croustade 4cm
Croustade 5cm
Croustade 7cm
Escarcoque
Fishka
Fleurette
Gaurmande
Mignardise
Mini-Croustade
Mini-Croustade Shell
Mini-Easre
Mini-Roulet
Mint Shell
Puff Pastry Tartlet
Quiche
Roulet
Zakouski

10040 Pie Piper Products
654 South Wheeling Road
Wheeling, IL 60090
847-459-3600
Fax: 630-595-1551 800-621-8183
www.distinctivefoods.com
Cheesecakes, brownies, quiche and beef frankfurters
President: Josh Harris
joshh@distinctivefoods.com
Chief Financial Officer: Ron Buck
Vice President: Daniel Mager
Quality Control: Jay Trujillo
Marketing/Sales/Public Relations: Stephanie Jacobs
Engineer: Jim Howard
Production Manager: Mike Lopardo
Purchasing: Araeeli Ocampo
Estimated Sales: $10-20 Million
Number Employees: 40
Square Footage: 32000
Parent Co: Vienna Manufacturing Company
Type of Packaging: Consumer, Food Service, Private Label
Brands:
Pie Piper
Vienna Bageldog
Wunderbar

10041 Pied-Mont/Dora
176 Saint-Joseph
Anne Des Plaines, QC J0N 1H0
Canada
450-478-0801
Fax: 450-478-6381 800-363-8003
info@piedmontdora.com www.piedmontdora.com
Vegetable and fruit dips, jams, jellies and marmalades; chocolate spreads, pie fillings, syrups and drink crystals
President/Board Member: Louis Limoges
Marketing: Justin Bart
Estimated Sales: $6.9 Million
Number Employees: 40
Brands:
Bensons
Clancy
Dora
Mondial
Pied-Mont

10042 Piedmont Candy Co
404 Market St
PO Box 1722
Lexington, NC 27292-1293
336-248-2477
Fax: 336-248-5841
customerservice@piedmontcandy.com
www.piedmontcandy.com
Candy
President: Kelly Dunn
kellydunn@piedmontcandy.com
VP: Chris Reid
Estimated Sales: $2,556,054
Number Employees: 50-99
Type of Packaging: Consumer

10043 Piedmont Vineyards & Winery
PO Box 286
Middleburg, VA 20118
540-687-5528
Fax: 540-687-5777
Wines
President: Gerhard Von Finck
Estimated Sales: Below $5 Million
Number Employees: 5-9
Type of Packaging: Private Label
Brands:
Piedmont

10044 Piedra Creek Winery
6425 Mira Cielo
San Luis Obispo, CA 93401-8395
805-541-1281
Fax: 805-782-0648 www.piedracreek.com
Wines
Co-Owner: Margaret Zuech
Owner/Winemaker: Romeo Zuech
info@piedracreek.com
Estimated Sales: Less Than $500,000
Number Employees: 1-4
Brands:
Piedra Creek Winery

10045 Piemonte Bakery Co
1122 Rock St
Rockford, IL 61101-1431
815-962-4833
Bread, dinner rolls and po-boys
Owner: Steve McKebebaer
Secretary: Irene McKeever
Estimated Sales: $2,600,000
Number Employees: 10-19
Type of Packaging: Private Label
Brands:
Piemonte

10046 Pierceton Foods Inc
127 N First St
Pierceton, IN 46562-9336
574-594-2344
Fax: 574-594-2344
Porkfritters, cheeseburgers, steaks, beef and tender loins
President: Jerry Wagoner
Plant Manager: Ben Bunyan
Estimated Sales: $1,040,000
Number Employees: 5-9
Number of Brands: 1
Square Footage: 12000
Type of Packaging: Food Service
Brands:
Paul's

10047 Pierino Frozen Foods
1695 Southfield Rd
Lincoln Park, MI 48146-2275
313-928-0950
Fax: 313-928-5410 info@pierinofrozenfoods.com
www.pierinofrozenfoods.com
Pasta, sauce and gnocchi
Founder: Pierino Guglielmetti
Operations Manager: Gianni Guglielmetti
Plant Manager: Silvana Gugliemetti
Estimated Sales: $1 Million
Number Employees: 20-49

10048 Pierre's French Bakery
PO Box 14280
Portland, OR 97293-0280
503-233-8871
Fax: 503-233-5060
Bakery products
President: Larry McDonald
Estimated Sales: $1-2 000,000
Number Employees: 50

10049 Pierre's French Ice Cream Inc
6200 Euclid Ave
Cleveland, OH 44103-3724
216-432-1144
Fax: 216-432-0001 800-837-7342
icecream@pierres.com www.pierres.com
Ice cream, yogurt, sherbet, sorbet and smoothies
President: Shelly Roth
sroth@pierres.com
Director Marketing: Laura Hindulak
Operations: John Pimpo

Food Manufacturers / A-Z

Year Founded: 1932
Estimated Sales: $20-50 Million
Number Employees: 100-249
Number of Products: 235
Square Footage: 30000
Type of Packaging: Consumer
Brands:
   Pierre's

10050 Pierz Cooperative Association
315 Edward St S
Pierz, MN 56364
   320-468-6655
Fax: 320-468-2773 www.pierzcoop.com
Animal feed
Manager: Randy Sullivan
Estimated Sales: $9,032,630
Number Employees: 10-19
Brands:
   Farmer Seed

10051 (HQ)Piggie Park Enterprises
1600 Charleston Hwy
West Columbia, SC 29169-5050
   803-791-5887
Fax: 803-791-8707 800-628-7423
mail@piggiepark.com www.piggiepark.com
Barbecue sauce and meat
President: Maurice Bessinger
mbessinger@piggie.com
Estimated Sales: $4.3 Million
Number Employees: 20-49
Type of Packaging: Consumer, Food Service, Bulk
Brands:
   Maurice's

10052 Pike Brewing Co
1415 1st Ave
Seattle, WA 98101-2017
   206-622-6044
Fax: 206-622-8730 info@mdv-beer.com
www.pikebrewing.com
Beer, ale, stout and porter
Owner: Rosann Finkel
rfinkel@pikebrewing.com
General manager: Kim Brusco
Director Manufacturing: Allen Fal
Estimated Sales: $2.5-5 Million
Number Employees: 50-99
Brands:
   Pike

10053 Pikes Peak Vineyards
3901 Jenitell Road
Colorado Springs, CO 80917-5351
   719-576-0075
Fax: 719-226-0639
Wine
President: Bruce McClaughlin
Vice President: Taffy McCloughlen
General Manager: Frankie Tuft
Estimated Sales: Less than $300,000
Number Employees: 1-4
Brands:
   Pikes Peak Vineyards

10054 Piknik Products Company
3806 Day Street
P.O. Box 9388
Montgomery, AL 36108-1720
   334-240-2218
Fax: 334-265-9490
Mayonnaise, mustard and salad dressing
President: Herman Loeb
Estimated Sales: $29 Million
Number Employees: 205
Type of Packaging: Consumer, Food Service, Private Label
Brands:
   Ol' South
   Piknik
   Salad Queen
   Stewart's

10055 Pilgrim Foods
98 Cuttermill Rd
Suite 260S
Great Neck, NY 11021-3036
   516-466-0522
Fax: 516-466-0762
CustService@Olddutchmustard.com
Juice, vinegar, mustard
President: Mycala Blanchard
mblanchard@pilgrimfoods.net
Estimated Sales: $5-10 Million
Number Employees: 1-4
Type of Packaging: Bulk

10056 Pilgrim's Pride Corp.
1770 Promontory Cir.
Greeley, CO 80634
   970-506-8000
www.pilgrims.com
Chicken.
Global CEO: Jayson Penn
Year Founded: 1946
Estimated Sales: $10 Billion
Number Employees: 35,700
Number of Brands: 11
Parent Co: JBS S.A.
Type of Packaging: Consumer, Food Service, Private Label, Bulk
Other Locations:
   WLR Foods
   Broadway VA
Brands:
   Pilgrim's
   Pierce Chicken
   Gold Kist Farms
   Country Pride
   Savoro
   Just BARE Chicken
   Gold'n Plump
   Moy Park
   Del Dia
   O'Kane
   To-Rico's

10057 Piller Sausages & Delicatessens
443 Wismer Street
Waterloo, ON N2K 2K6
Canada
   519-743-1412
Fax: 519-743-7111 800-265-2628
www.pillers.com
Sausage and processed meats
President: William Huber, Jr.
Number Employees: 100-249
Type of Packaging: Consumer, Food Service, Private Label, Bulk

10058 Piller's Fine Foods
443 Wismer Street
Waterloo, ON N2K 2K6
Canada
   519-743-1412
   800-265-2627
www.pillers.com
Pork, beef, poultry, chubs and sticks, hot dogs and franks, luncheon meat, sausages, pate and coils
CEO: Willy Huber
VP of Innovation & Business Development: Gerhart Huber
VP of Sales & Marketing: Sean Moriarty
Number Employees: 200
Type of Packaging: Private Label
Brands:
   Piller's
   Piller's Turkey Bites

10059 (HQ)Pillsbury
PO Box 9452
Minneapolis, MN 55440
   800-775-4777
Fax: 763-764-8330
consumer.services-pillsburycs@genmills.com
www.pillsbury.com
Bakery mixes and cake flour
General Manager: Alan Rodrigues
Mix Plant Manager: Ray Beckman
Number Employees: 100-249
Parent Co: General Mills
Type of Packaging: Consumer, Food Service, Bulk

10060 Pilot Meat & Sea Food Company
405 N Pilot Knob Road
Galena, IL 61036-8803
   319-556-0760
Fax: 319-556-4131
Meat and seafood
CEO: Randall Sirk
Accountant: Ted Kipper
Estimated Sales: $1.2 Million
Number Employees: 7

10061 Pindar Vineyards
37645 Main Road
Route 25
Peconic, NY 11958
   631-734-6200
Fax: 631-734-6205 info@Pindar.net
www.pindar.net
Wines
Owner: Herodotus Damianos
Chief Executive Officer: Kathy Krejci
Sales Manager: Steve Ciuffo
Estimated Sales: $5-10 Million
Number Employees: 20-49
Brands:
   Spring Splendor
   Summer Blush

10062 Pine Point Seafood
350 Pine Point Rd
Scarborough, ME 04074-9236
   207-883-4701
Fax: 207-883-4797 www.maine-lobster.com
Lobster, lobster tails, clams and steaks
President: B Michael Thurlow
Estimated Sales: $1-3 Million
Number Employees: 5-9

10063 Pine Ridge Vineyards
5901 Silverado Trail
Napa, CA 94558-9417
   707-252-9777
Fax: 707-253-1493 800-575-9777
info@pineridgewine.com
www.pineridgevineyards.com
Wines
President & CEO: Erle Martin
Vineyard Manager: Gustavo Avina
General Manager/Winemaker: Michael Beaulac
Assistant Winemaker: Michael Conversano
Enologist: Colleen Fitzgerald
Year Founded: 1978
Estimated Sales: $20-50 Million
Number Employees: 50-99
Brands:
   Pine Ridge Winery

10064 Pine River Cheese & Butter Company
RR 4
Ripley, ON N0G 2R0
Canada
   519-395-2638
Fax: 519-395-4066 800-265-1175
info@pinerivercheese.com
www.pinerivercheese.com
Cheese
President: Ian Courtney
Number Employees: 30
Square Footage: 96000
Type of Packaging: Consumer, Bulk

10065 Pine River Pre-Pack Inc
10134 Pine River Rd
Newton, WI 53063-9613
   920-726-4216
Cheese and cheese spreads, chocolate confections
CEO: Philip Lindemann
Marketing Associate: Mary Lindenann
Contact: Ian Behm
ian@pineriver.com
Estimated Sales: $3004699
Number Employees: 10-19
Square Footage: 94800
Type of Packaging: Consumer, Private Label
Brands:
   Pine River

10066 Pineland Farms
15 Farm View Drive
New Gloucester, ME 04260
   207-688-4539
Fax: 207-688-4531 www.pinelandfarms.org
Salsa, dips, cheese, spreads and syrup
Principal: Sarah Hunt
Marketing: Neal Kolterman
Contact: Matt Anderson
manderson@pinelandfarms.com
Estimated Sales: $69,000
Number Employees: 51-200

Food Manufacturers / A-Z

10067 Pines International
1992 E 1400 Rd
Lawrence, KS 66044-9303
785-841-6016
Fax: 785-841-1252   800-697-4637
pines@wheatgrass.com   www.wheatgrass.com
Grass: wheat, barley, rye and oat; powders and tablets; alfalfa
President: Ron Seibold
rseibold@wheatgrass.com
CEO: Steve Malone
Sales/Marketing: Allen Levine
Purchasing Director: Jeff Richards
Year Founded: 1976
Estimated Sales: $3,635,158
Number Employees: 20-49
Square Footage: 160000
Type of Packaging: Consumer, Private Label, Bulk
Brands:
   Mighty Greens
   Pines

10068 Pino's Pasta Veloce
1903 Clove Road
Staten Island, NY 10304-1607
718-273-6660
Fax: 718-720-5906
Pasta sauce, pasta heaters
Manager Marketing: Joe Klaus
VP Operations: Al Cappillo
Estimated Sales: $2.5-5,000,000
Number Employees: 1-4
Parent Co: AEI
Type of Packaging: Consumer, Food Service
Brands:
   Pino's Pasta Veloce

10069 Pinocchio Italian Ice Cream Company
12814 163 Street NW
Edmonton, AB T5V 1K6
Canada
780-455-1905
Fax: 780-455-1906
Ice cream and sorbets
President: Salvatore Ursino
VP: Tom Ursino
Number Employees: 1-4
Type of Packaging: Consumer, Food Service
Brands:
   Pinocchio

10070 Pinter's Packing Plant
193 S Front St
Dorchester, WI 54425-9559
715-654-5444
Fax: 715-654-5522   www.pinterspackingplant.com
Steak, roast, sausage and buffalo
Owner: Al Pinter
Estimated Sales: $180000
Number Employees: 10-19
Square Footage: 25600
Type of Packaging: Consumer

10071 Pinty's Premium Foods
5063 North Service Rd
Burlington, ON L7L 5H6
Canada
905-319-5300
Fax: 905-688-1222   800-263-7223
Retailsales@pintys.com   www.pintys.com
Chicken fryers, nuggets, burgers, meat balls, wings, breasts; pierogies and pizza fingers
Chairman: Fred Williamson
Vice-Chairman: Ken Thorpe
Director: Randy Kane
VP Marketing: Jon Pintwala
Sales Manager: W Greer
Estimated Sales: $4.8 Million
Number Employees: 49
Type of Packaging: Consumer, Food Service
Brands:
   Pinty's

10072 Pintys Delicious Foods
5063 North Service Road
Suite 101
Burlington, ON L7L 5H6
Canada
905-835-8575
Fax: 905-834-5093   800-263-9710
humanresources@pintys.com   www.pintys.com
Poultry
President/Owner: Phil Kudelka
CEO: Aba Vanderlaan
CFO: Patricia Bowman
VP Operations: Jack Vanderlaan
Sales: Greg Fox
General Manager: Doug Bowman
Number Employees: 100-249
Square Footage: 360000
Type of Packaging: Food Service, Bulk
Brands:
   Pintys Delicious Foods

10073 Pioneer Dairy
214 Feeding Hills Rd
Southwick, MA 01077
413-569-6132
Fax: 413-569-3762
Milk, cream, and ice cream
President: A Colson
Vice President: Paul Colson
Estimated Sales: $5-10 000,000
Number Employees: 30
Number of Brands: 2
Type of Packaging: Food Service, Private Label, Bulk
Brands:
   Meadowbrook Creamery
   Pioneer Dairy

10074 Pioneer Foods Industries
P.O. Box 1248
Stuttgart, AR 72160
870-673-4444
Fax: 870-355-2507   www.producersrice.com
Soups
President/CEO: Keith Glover
Executive Assistant: Lana Flowers
VP, Finance and Administration: Kent Lockwood
Vice President Marketing: Gary Reifeiss
Senior VP, Rice Sales and Marketing: Marvin Baden
Vice President of Operations: Kenny Dryden
Estimated Sales: Under $500,000
Number Employees: 10-19

10075 Pioneer Frozen Foods
627 Big Stone Gap Rd
Duncanville, TX 75137
972-298-4281
www.chg.com
Biscuits
President & CEO: Dale Tremblay
SVP & CFO: Justin Grubbs
SVP & COO: Eric Stockl
Estimated Sales: $92 Million
Number Employees: 100-249
Number of Brands: 1
Parent Co: C.H Guenther & Son, Inc.
Brands:
   Pioneer

10076 Pioneer Growers
227 NW Avenue L
Belle Glade, FL 33430-1935
229-243-9306
Fax: 561-996-5703   www.pioneergrowers.com
Chinese cabbage, carrots, celery, corn and radishes
Vice President, General Manager: Gene Duff
Vice President of Quality Assurance: James Jacks
Sales/ Marketing: Jon Browder
Sales Exec: J D Poole
Number Employees: 20-49
Type of Packaging: Consumer, Bulk
Brands:
   Frontier
   Team
   Well's Ace

10077 Pioneer Live Shrimp
2801 Meyers Road
Oak Brook, IL 60523-1623
630-789-1133
Fax: 312-226-7376
Shrimp
President: David Wong
VP: Chun Wah
Secretary: Esther Wong
Estimated Sales: $2.8 Million
Number Employees: 14
Square Footage: 56000

10078 Pioneer Marketing International
188 Westhill Drive
Los Gatos, CA 95032-5032
408-356-4990
Fax: 408-356-2795   www.pioneer.com
Corn, soybeans, alfalfa, canola, wheat, sunflowers; marketing, sales and product promotion
Partner: Russ Tritomo
Director Sales: Ed DeSoto
Estimated Sales: $1-5 Million
Number Employees: 4
Brands:
   Pioneer(c)
   Encirca(c)
   Nutrivail

10079 Pioneer Nutritional Formula
304 Shelburne Center Rd
Shelburne Falls, MA 01370-9779
413-625-8627
Fax: 413-625-9619   800-458-8483
customerservice@pioneernutritional.com
www.pioneernutritional.com
Nutritional supplements
Manager: Sara Rowan
CEO: Jim Lemkin
Manager: Sarah Rhone
Estimated Sales: Less Than $500,000
Number Employees: 5-9
Number of Brands: 1
Number of Products: 23
Brands:
   Pioneer

10080 Pioneer Packing Co
510 Napoleon Rd
PO Box 171
Bowling Green, OH 43402-4821
419-352-5283
Fax: 419-352-7330   wcontris@aol.com
www.pioneerpacking.com
Bacon, smoked meats and pork sausage
President: Jason Blower
jasonb@pioneersantaana.net
Estimated Sales: $5 Million
Number Employees: 20-49
Square Footage: 150000
Type of Packaging: Consumer, Bulk
Brands:
   Amish
   Country
   Pioneer

10081 Pioneer Snacks
30770 Northwestern Highway
Suite 300
Farmington Hills, MI 48334-2594
248-862-1990
Fax: 248-862-1991
Meat sticks, beef jerky, sausage, beef steak, meat & cheese and turkey jerky
Marketing Manager: Craig Thomas
Type of Packaging: Consumer
Brands:
   Hog Wild Pork Jerky

10082 Piper & Leaf
2211 Seminole Dr SW
Suite 151
Huntsville, AL 35805
256-929-9404
info@piperandleaf.com
piperandleaf.com
Teas and tisanes.
Owner: Caleb Christopher

10083 Piper Meat Processing
430 N Main St
Andover, OH 44003-9665
440-293-7170
Beef and pork
Owner: Terry Orahood
Estimated Sales: Less Than $500,000
Number Employees: 1-4
Type of Packaging: Consumer, Bulk

10084 Pippin Snack Pecans
1332 Old Pretoria Rd
PO Box 3330
Albany, GA 31721-8696
229-432-9316
Fax: 229-435-0056   800-554-6887
treypippen@gmail.com
Pecans

Food Manufacturers / A-Z

Manager: Trey Pippin
Estimated Sales: $7 Million
Number Employees: 50
Square Footage: 80000
Type of Packaging: Consumer, Food Service, Private Label, Bulk
Brands:
   Pippin Snack

10085 Pipsnacks
1580 Park Ave
Suite 2
New York, NY 10029-1802
   973-723-4246
   pipsnacks.com

Popcorn
Co-Founder: Jen Martin
Brands:
   Pipcorn

10086 Piqua Pizza Supply Co Inc
1727 W High St
Piqua, OH 45356-9325
   937-773-0699
Fax: 937-773-6096   800-521-4442
   www.piquapizza.net

Pizza crust
President: Paul Creager
ppsi-paulc@onecalmmail.com
Production Manager: Tom Fahestrock
Estimated Sales: $10-20 Million
Number Employees: 20-49
Type of Packaging: Consumer, Food Service, Private Label, Bulk
Brands:
   Diana's

10087 Pita King Bakery
2210 37th St
Everett, WA 98201-4509
   425-258-4040
Fax: 425-258-3366

Pita bread
President: Hauss Alaeddine
j_alaeddine@hotmail.com
CEO: Jason Aladdine
Number Employees: 10-19
Square Footage: 40000
Brands:
   Pita Products
   PitaSnax

10088 Pita Pal
3100 Canal St
Houston, TX 77003-1602
   713-777-7482
   comments@pitapal.com
   www.pitapal.com

Hummus, salsa, salads, falafels
Contact: James Grimes
jgrimes@pitapal.com
Estimated Sales: Less Than $500,000
Number Employees: 5-9

10089 Pita Products
30777 Northwestern Highway
Suite 3200
Farmington Hills, MI 48334-2549
   734-367-2700
Fax: 734-367-2701   800-600-7482

Pita chips
Type of Packaging: Consumer

10090 Pitbull Energy Products
20600 Belshaw Ave
Carson, CA 90746-3508
   310-604-9100
Fax: 818-686-6009   800-686-3697

Energy drinks
President/CEO: Mr Roscoe
Contact: Tamara Clark
tclark@hiphopbev.com
Number Employees: 5-9
Brands:
   Pit Bull

10091 PITTSBURGH BREWING Co
3340 Liberty Ave
Pittsburgh, PA 15201-1394
   412-682-7400
Fax: 412-682-2379   www.pittsburghbrewing.com
Beer
President/CEO: Eddie Lozano
CEO: Brian G Walsh
bwalsh@pittsburghbrewingco.com
Director of Sales & Marketing: David Sykes
Operations Manager: Melissa O'Dell
Brew master: Michael Carota
Plant Manager: Bill St Leger
Estimated Sales: $13 Million
Number Employees: 100-249
Square Footage: 27000
Parent Co: ICB Holdings, LLC
Type of Packaging: Consumer
Brands:
   IC Light Mango
   Iron City
   Iron City Light

10092 Pittsfield Rye Bakery
1010 South St
Pittsfield, MA 01201-8225
   413-443-9141
Fax: 413-499-5331   info@pittsfieldrye.com
   www.pittsfieldrye.com

Bread and rolls
President: Arnold Robbins
Owner: Rick Robbins
Estimated Sales: $5-10 Million
Number Employees: 10-19

10093 Piveg, Inc.
11760 Sorrento Valley Rd
Suite L
San Diego, CA 92121
   858-688-3070
Fax: 858-436-3071   ruben.angulo@piveg.com
   www.piveg.com

Mexican chili flavors, powders and flakes, mole paste blends, lutein esters, zeaxanthin, beta carotene
President: Roberto Espinoza
Estimated Sales: $12 Million
Number Employees: 220
Type of Packaging: Private Label, Bulk

10094 Pizza Products
38300 W 10 Mile Road
Farmington Hills, MI 48335-2804
   248-474-1601
Fax: 248-474-1608   800-600-7482
   www.pizzahut.com

Pizza
Manager: Dave Sabol
Marketing Director: Norman Wainwright
Estimated Sales: Below $5 Million
Number Employees: 1-4

10095 Pizzey's Milling & Baking Company
121 4th Ave. S.
Twin Falls, ID 83301
Canada
   208-733-7555
Fax: 204-773-2317   www.glanbiafoods.com

Flaxseed
President: Linda Pizzey
Vice President: Glenn Pizzey
Vice President of Business Development: Dave Snyder
Business Development Manager: Shawn Harrison
Estimated Sales: $10-20 Million
Number Employees: 20-49
Square Footage: 80000
Parent Co: Glanbia Nutritionals
Type of Packaging: Consumer, Food Service, Private Label, Bulk

10096 Plaidberry Company
830 Mimosa Ave
Vista, CA 92081
   760-727-5403
   dennisdickson@cs.com

Jams, muffins, pie and cake fillings, juices, confections, yogurt bases
President/Owner: Dennis Dickson
plaidberry@yahoo.com
Estimated Sales: Below 5 Million
Number Employees: 4
Number of Products: 6
Square Footage: 74000
Type of Packaging: Consumer, Bulk

10097 Plainfield Winery & Tasting Rm
6291 Cambridge Way
Plainfield, IN 46168-7905
   317-837-9463
Fax: 317-837-8464   888-761-9463
   info@chateauthomas.com
   www.chateauthomas.com

Wines
President: Charles Thomas
Manager: Sheila Cavanaugh
info@chateauthomas.com
Purchasing Manager: Tommy England
Estimated Sales: $5-10 Million
Number Employees: 20-49
Type of Packaging: Private Label
Brands:
   Chateau Thomas

10098 Plains Dairy Products
300 N Taylor St
Amarillo, TX 79107
   806-374-0385
   800-365-5608
   www.plainsdairy.com

Milk, buttermilk, cottage cheese and yogurt
President & CEO: Dub Garlington
Controller: James Wood
Marketing Manager: Michael Holliman
mholliman@plainsdairy.com
Year Founded: 1934
Estimated Sales: $173.2 Million
Number Employees: 100-249
Number of Brands: 2
Brands:
   Plains Dairy
   Shurfine

10099 (HQ)Plainview Milk Products
130 2nd St SW
Plainview, MN 55964-1394
   507-534-3872
Fax: 507-534-3992   800-356-5606
   www.plainviewmilk.com

Butter, whey and milk; custom agglomeration and spray drying
General Manager: Dallas Moe
dmoe@plainviewmilk.com
Controller: Janna Van Rooyen
Sales Manager: Darrell Hanson
Plant Manager: Donny Schreiber
Number Employees: 50-99
Square Footage: 18060
Type of Packaging: Consumer, Food Service, Private Label, Bulk
Brands:
   Greenwood Prairie

10100 Plainville Farms
304 S Water St
PO Box 38
New Oxford, PA 17350-9688
   717-624-2191
Fax: 717-624-5121   800-724-0206
   mail@plainvillefarms.com
   www.plainvillefarms.com

Turkeys and specialty dishes
Estimated Sales: $20-50 Million
Number Employees: 50-99
Brands:
   Heart Liteo
   Veggie Growno

10101 Plam Vineyards & Winery
80125 Miramonte Lane
La Quinta, CA 92253
   760-972-4465
   ken@plam.com
   www.plam.com

Wine
Co-Owner: Ken Plam
Co-Owner: Shirley Plam
Estimated Sales: Below $5 Million
Number Employees: 2
Type of Packaging: Private Label
Brands:
   Plam Vineyards

10102 Planet Oat
Lynnfield, MA
   800-242-2423
   planetoat.com

Oat milk
VP, Marketing: Christopher Ross

Food Manufacturers / A-Z

10103 Plant Based Foods
21011 St. Louis Rd.
PO Box 1841
Middleburg, VA 20117
540-687-8432
Fax: 540-687-8434 info@plantbasedfoods.com
www.plantbasedfoods.com
Dip mixes and seasonings
Co-Founder: Matt Webb
Co-Founder: Alecia Webb

10104 Plantation Candies
4224 Old Bethlehem Pike
Telford, PA 18969
215-723-6810
Fax: 215-723-6834 888-678-6468
chuck@plantationcandies.com
www.plantationcandies.com
Bulk hard candy
Owner/President: Charles Crawford
chuck@plantationcandies.com
Estimated Sales: $1500000
Number Employees: 5-9
Type of Packaging: Consumer, Food Service, Private Label, Bulk
Brands:
  Chocolate Straws
  Dainties
  Golden Crunchies
  Jinglebits
  Misty Mints

10105 Plantation Pecan & GiftCompany
HC-62 Box 139
Waterproof, LA 71375
318-749-5188
Fax: 318-749-5535 800-477-3226
www.plantationpecan.com
Pecans, pies, pralines and fudges
President: Harrison Miller
Co-Owner: Carol Miller
Estimated Sales: Less than $500,000
Number Employees: 1-4
Brands:
  Plantation Pecan

10106 Plantation Products Inc
202 S Washington St
Norton, MA 02766
508-285-5800
www.plantationproducts.com
Vegetable seeds, seed packets
President & CEO: Michael Pietrasiewicz
Estimated Sales: $50-99.99 Million
Number Employees: 20-49
Number of Brands: 6
Square Footage: 200000
Other Locations:
  Warehouse/Distribution
  West Bridgewater MA
  Livingston Seeds
  Columbus OH
  International Headquarters
  Brandon, Canada MB
Brands:
  American Seed(c)
  Ferry-Morse(c)
  Livingston Seed
  McKenzie
  NK Lawn & Garden(c)
  Jiffy(c)

10107 Platte Valley Creamery
1005 E Overland
Scottsbluff, NE 69361-3702
308-632-4225
Ice cream and desserts
President: Ron Smith
Estimated Sales: $1-3 Million
Number Employees: 1-4
Type of Packaging: Consumer

10108 Plaza House Coffee
339 Lincoln Avenue
Staten Island, NY 10306-5001
718-979-9555
Fax: 718-667-4394 plazahouse@aol.com
Coffee
President: Salvatore Rosso
Estimated Sales: Less than $500,000
Number Employees: 1-4

10109 Plaza Sweets Bakery
521 Waverly Ave
Mamaroneck, NY 10543-2235
914-698-0233
Fax: 914-698-3712 800-816-8416
Cakes
Owner: James Ward
Pres/CEO: Rodney Holden
Manager: Kathy Dumas
Estimated Sales: $5.8 Million
Number Employees: 20-49
Square Footage: 60000
Type of Packaging: Consumer, Food Service
Brands:
  Plaza Sweets

10110 Plaza de Espana Gourmet
100 Kings Point Drive
Apt 1004
Sunny Isles Beach, FL 33160-4729
305-971-3468
Fax: 305-971-5004
Spanish foods, olive oil, artichokes, asparagus, piquillo peppers, wine and ham
President: Jesus Metias, Sr.
Vice President: Serafina Atalaya
Estimated Sales: $2.5-5 Million
Number Employees: 5-9
Parent Co: Plaza De Espana Gourmet Foods
Type of Packaging: Consumer, Food Service, Private Label, Bulk
Brands:
  Cielo Azul
  Plaza De Espana
  Vega Fina
  Vega Metias

10111 Pleasant Grove Farms
PO Box 636
Pleasant Grove, CA 95668
916-655-3391
Fax: 916-655-3699 info@pleasantgrovefarms.com
www.pleasantgrovefarms.com
Almonds, wheat, beans, popcorn and rice
President: Thomas Sills
VP Sales: Edward Sills
Estimated Sales: $1,100,000
Number Employees: 5-9
Number of Products: 9
Square Footage: 20000
Parent Co: Sills Farms
Type of Packaging: Bulk

10112 Pleasant Valley Wine Co
8260 Pleasant Valley Rd
Hammondsport, NY 14840-9514
607-569-6111
Fax: 607-569-6135 info@pleasantvalleywine.com
www.pleasantvalleywine.com
Wines, champagnes, ports and sherries
President: Michael Doyle
Estimated Sales: $19 Million
Number Employees: 50-99
Square Footage: 1440000
Type of Packaging: Consumer, Food Service, Private Label, Bulk
Brands:
  Great Western
  Millennium
  Pleasant Valley

10113 Pleasant View Dairy
2625 Highway Ave
P.O. Box 1949
Highland, IN 46322-1614
219-838-0155
Fax: 219-838-1801
Milk, buttermilk and sour cream
President: Kenneth Leep
kenneth@pleasantviewdairy.com
Estimated Sales: Less than $500,000
Number Employees: 20-49
Square Footage: 160000
Type of Packaging: Consumer

10114 Pleasoning Gourmet Seasonings
2418 South Avenue
PO Box 2701
La Crosse, WI 54601
608-787-1030
Fax: 608-787-1030 800-279-1614
pleason@pleasoning.com www.pleasoning.com
Seasoning
President: Paul Boarman
Vice President: Lenore Italiano
Marketing Director: Kathy Boarman
Estimated Sales: $500,000-$1 Million
Number Employees: 1-4
Number of Brands: 1
Number of Products: 30
Square Footage: 12000
Type of Packaging: Consumer, Food Service, Bulk
Brands:
  Pleasoning Gourmet Seasoning

10115 Plehn's Bakery Inc
3940 Shelbyville Rd
Louisville, KY 40207-3170
502-896-4438
Fax: 502-897-9176 www.plehns.com
Breads, cookies, doughnuts, pastries, pies, cakes and ice cream
President: Nathan Hoy
nhoy@missionit.com
Vice President: Theodore Bowling
Estimated Sales: $1.5 Million
Number Employees: 20-49
Type of Packaging: Consumer

10116 Plentiful Pantry
265 West Plymouth Ave
Salt Lake City, UT 84115
801-977-9077
www.plentifulpantry.com
Prepared meals, soups, desserts and hot chocolate.
Co-Founder: Debbie Chidester
Co-Founder: Jody Chidester
Year Founded: 1992

10117 Plenty
570 Eccles Ave.
San Francisco, CA 94080
650-735-3737
plenty.ag
Leafy greens including baby arugula, kale, beets, tatsoi, and mizuna.
Founder & CEO: Matt Barnard
Year Founded: 2013
Number Employees: 250-500
Type of Packaging: Private Label

10118 Plenus Group Inc
101 Phoenix Ave
Lowell, MA 01852-4930
978-970-3832
Fax: 978-441-2528 info@plenus-group.com
www.pgifoods.com
Soups, sauces, chowders, bisques, seafood appetizers and entrees
President: Joseph Jolly
jhjolly@plenus-group.com
VP/CFO/VP Operations/Production: Jennifer Jolly
Sales Manager/Coordinator: Jamie Crane
Estimated Sales: $10.5 Million
Number Employees: 20-49
Brands:
  Boston Chowda Co
  East Coast Gourmet

10119 Plochman Inc
1333 N Boudreau Rd
Manteno, IL 60950
815-468-3434
800-843-4566
plochman@plochman.com www.plochman.com
Mustards
Estimated Sales: $6.9 Million
Number Employees: 50-99
Type of Packaging: Consumer, Food Service, Private Label, Bulk
Brands:
  Kosciusko
  Plochman's

10120 Plocky's Fine Snacks
15 Spinning Wheel Rd
Suite 314
Hinsdale, IL 60521
630-323-8888
Fax: 630-323-8988 info@plockys.com
www.plockys.com
Tortilla chips, hummus chips, hummus, kettle chips, dip strips, salsa, potato sticks and nut mixes
President: Paul Cipolla
Marketing: Diane Cipolla
Contact: Esther Neal
esther@plockys.com

Food Manufacturers / A-Z

Estimated Sales: $9.3 Million
Number Employees: 16
Brands:
   Nature Star
   Ploccy's Apple Chips

10121 Pluester Quality Meat Co
Batchtown Rd
Hardin, IL 62047
618-396-2224
Meat, slaughtering services
President: Irene Pluester
Manager: Suzanne Pluester
Estimated Sales: $1-3 Million
Number Employees: 1-4
Type of Packaging: Bulk

10122 Plum Creek Winery
3708 G Rd
Palisade, CO 81526-9603
970-464-7586
Fax: 970-464-0457 www.plumcreekwinery.com
Wines
Manager: Jenne Baldwin
Marketing Director: Sue Phillips
Manager: Jenne Eaton
info@plumcreekwinery.com
Estimated Sales: Below $5 Million
Number Employees: 5-9
Brands:
   Plum Creek

10123 Plum Organics
1485 Park Ave
Emeryville, CA 94608
877-914-7586
www.plumorganics.com
Organic baby food, formula, and kids snacks
Founder/CEO: Neil Grimmer
Product Innovation Manager: Meg Verdeyen
SVP Brand Marketing & Innovation: Ben Mand
Year Founded: 2005
Number Employees: 100-249

10124 Plumrose USA
651 W. Washington Blvd.
Suite 302
Chicago, IL 60661
800-526-4909
consumer@plumroseusa.com
www.plumroseusa.com
Deli meats, bacon, BBQ products, food service, specialty.
CEO: Dave Schanzer
Year Founded: 1932
Estimated Sales: $580 Million
Number Employees: 1,160
Number of Brands: 4
Square Footage: 5282
Parent Co: JBS USA
Type of Packaging: Consumer, Food Service
Other Locations:
   Sliced Deli Meats
   Booneville MS
   Bacon
   Elkhard IN
   Barbecue Items & Ribs
   Swanton VT
   Deli Meats & Bacon
   Council Bluffs IA
   Customer Service Dist. Center
   Tupelo MS
   Sales Office
   Bentonville AR
   Sales Office
   Upland CA
Brands:
   DAK
   Naked Meats
   Plumrose
   Knockout Meats

10125 Plus CBD Oil
10070 Barnes Canyon Rd
Suite 100
San Diego, CA 92121
855-758-7223
help@pluscbdoil.com pluscbdoil.com
CBD oil
CEO: Joseph Dowling
CFO: Joerg Grasser
Operations: Michael Mona

10126 Plus Pharma
2460 Coral St
Vista, CA 92081-8430
760-597-0200
Fax: 760-597-0734 info@pluspharm.com
www.pluspharm.com
Herbs, gelatin and vegetarian capsules
President: Bill Roberts
Estimated Sales: Less Than $500,000
Number Employees: 1-4

10127 Plush Puffs Marshmallows
3811 W Magnolia Blvd
Burbank, CA 91505-2820
USA
818-784-2931
Fax: 818-474-7816 www.plushpuffs.com
Marshmallow dessert toppings
President: Ann Hickey
Quality Coordinator: Darien Camacho

10128 Plyley's Candy
909 S Poplar St
Lagrange, IN 46761-2412
260-463-3351
Fax: 260-463-7011 877-665-2778
plyley@kuntrynet.com
Candy
President: Jack Plyley
jplyley@yahoo.com
VP: Willard Plyley
Estimated Sales: Below $500,000
Number Employees: 5-9

10129 Plymouth Artisan Cheese
106 Messer Hill Rd.
Plymouth Notch, VT 05056
802-672-3650
www.plymouthartisancheese.com
Cheese
President: Jesse Werner

10130 Plymouth Beef Co.
3585 Food Center Drive
Bronx, NY 10474
718-589-8600
Fax: 718-860-8930 info@plymouthbeef.com
www.plymouthbeef.com
Beef
Chairman: Gerald Sussman
Ceo/President: Andrew Sussman
Estimated Sales: $5 Million
Number Employees: 25
Type of Packaging: Consumer, Food Service

10131 Plymouth Cheese Counter
PO Box 517
Plymouth, WI 53073-0517
920-892-8781
Fax: 920-893-5986 888-607-9477
plychzct@excel.com www.cheesecapital.com
Cheese and gift baskets
Owner: Kris Hummes
Estimated Sales: Less Than $500,000
Number Employees: 5-9
Type of Packaging: Consumer

10132 Plymouth Colony Winery
56 Pinewood Rd
Plymouth, MA 02360
508-747-3334
Fax: 508-747-4463
Wine
Owner: Charles Caranci
General Manager: Lydia Carey
Estimated Sales: $10,950,985
Number Employees: 1-4
Type of Packaging: Private Label
Brands:
   Plymouth Colony Winery

10133 Plymouth Lollipop Company
P.O. Box 413
Westford, MA 1886
888-662-4948
Fax: 508-866-0822 800-777-0115
Lollipops and confection ingredients
President: Bill Johnson
Estimated Sales: Less than $500,000
Number Employees: 1-4
Brands:
   Plimouth Lollipop

10134 Pocas International
19 Central Blvd
South Hackensack, NJ 07606
201-941-7900
Fax: 201-941-9707
contact@pocasinternational.com
www.pocasinternational.com
Coconut water and aloe vera drink.
Brands:
   Pocas
   Ramun,
   Poca's Tacos
   OKF
   Pocasville
   Splash
   Pearl Royal
   Toucan

10135 Poche's Smokehouse
3015 Main Hwy
Suite A
Breaux Bridge, LA 70517-6347
337-332-2108
Fax: 337-332-5051 800-376-2437
support@pochesmarket.com
www.pochesmarket.com
Meat
Owner: Floyd Poche
Owner: Karen Poche
Estimated Sales: $5-10 Million
Number Employees: 20-49

10136 Pocino Foods
14250 Lomitas Ave
City Of Industry, CA 91746-3096
626-968-8000
Fax: 626-330-8779 800-345-0150
onlythebest@pocinofoods.com
www.pocinofoods.com
Deli meats (Italian and Mexican style), pizza toppings
CEO: Jason Katsuki
Vice President: Jim Pierson
National Sales Director: Karen Barro
Regional Sales Manager: Ramona Shope
Estimated Sales: $32 Million
Number Employees: 100-249
Number of Brands: 1
Type of Packaging: Private Label
Brands:
   Pocino

10137 Poco Dolce
2419 3rd St
San Francisco, CA 94107-3110
USA
415-255-1443
Fax: 415-255-1743 www.pocodolce.com
Chocolate bars, truffles, toffee
Owner: Kathy Wiley
Manager: James Amendolagine
james.amendolagine@roku.com
Number Employees: 1-4

10138 Pocono Cheesecake Factory
HC 1 Box 95
Swiftwater, PA 18370
570-839-6844
Fax: 570-839-6844
Cheesecakes
Manager: Alferd Johnson
Estimated Sales: $300,000
Number Employees: 10-19
Square Footage: 12000
Brands:
   Pocono Cheesecake

10139 Pocono Mountain Bottling Company
57 W Chestnut Street
Wilkes Barre, PA 18705-1751
570-822-7695
Bottled water and carbonated beverages
President/Treasurer: Veronica Iskra
Estimated Sales: $580,000
Number Employees: 5
Brands:
   Pocono Mountain

Food Manufacturers / A-Z

10140 Pocono Spring Company
1545 Industrial Park Drive
PO Box 787
Mt Pocono, PA 18344-0787
570-839-2837
Fax: 570-839-6705 800-634-4584
Bottled water
President/CEO: Michael Melnic
CFO: Bill Fraser
Operations Manager: Tim Fitzgerald
Estimated Sales: $1-2.5 000,000
Number Employees: 20-49
Brands:
  Pocono Spring

10141 (HQ)Point Group
1790 Highway A1a
Suite 103
Satellite Beach, FL 32937-5446
321-777-7408
Fax: 321-777-9777 888-272-1249
Coffee, tea, fruit extracts and juices
President: Gary Trump
VP: Roger Koltermann
Type of Packaging: Consumer, Food Service, Private Label, Bulk
Brands:
  Mingo Bay Beverages, Inc.

10142 Point Judith Fisherman's Company
P.O.Box 730
Narragansett, RI 02882-0730
401-782-1500
Fax: 401-782-1599
Fish
Manager: Larry Rainey
Sales Manager: John McLaughlin
Estimated Sales: $10-20 000,000
Number Employees: 50-99

10143 Point Lobster Co
1 St. Louis Ave
Point Pleasant Beach, NJ
732-892-1729
Fax: 732-892-3928 info@pointlobster.com
pointlobster.com
Lobster

10144 Point Reyes Farmstead Cheese Co.
14700 Hwy 1
Po Box 9
Point Reyes Station, CA 94956
415-663-8880
Fax: 415-663-8881 800-591-6787
lynn@pointreyescheese.com
www.pointreyescheese.com
Cheese
President: Bob Giacomini

10145 Point Saint George Fisheries
PO Box 1386
Santa Rosa, CA 95402-1386
707-542-9490
Seafood
General Manager: Rich Amundson
Estimated Sales: $1-2.5 000,000 appx.
Number Employees: 1

10146 Poiret International
7866 Exeter Boulevard E
Tamarac, FL 33321-8797
203-926-3700
Fax: 954-721-0110 800-237-9151
Preserves and organic jams
CEO/Purchasing: Ed Kerzner
CFO: Sheila Kerzner
Marketing Director: Stan Margulese
Plant Manager: Frank Bilisi
Number Employees: 20-49
Square Footage: 100000
Parent Co: Siroper/E. Meurens SA
Type of Packaging: Consumer, Food Service, Private Label, Bulk
Brands:
  Delice
  Meurens
  Poiret

10147 Poison Pepper Company
7310 E Shadywoods Court
Floral City, FL 34436-5732
888-539-5540
Fax: 727-894-5540 888-539-5540
Sauces
President: Tom Dahl

10148 Pok Pok Som
1222 Se Gideon St
Portland, OR 97202-2417
USA
503-235-0004
Fax: 503-232-0293 www.pokpoksom.com
Drinking vinegar
Owner: Andy Ricker

10149 Pokanoket Ostrich Farm
177 Gulf Rd
South Dartmouth, MA 02748
508-992-6188
Fax: 508-993-5356 pokanokets@aol.com
Ostrich meat
President: Alan Weinshel
National Sales Manager: Mike Yokemick
Contact: Gail Weinshel
pokanokets@aol.com
Estimated Sales: Below $5 Million
Number Employees: 1-4
Type of Packaging: Consumer, Food Service, Private Label
Brands:
  Pokanoket Farm

10150 Pokonobe Industries
2701 Ocean Park Blvd
Suite 208
Santa Monica, CA 90405-5247
310-392-1259
Fax: 310-392-3659 www.pokonobe.com
Oils: almond, grapeseed, soy, sunflower, sesame, walnut, corn, olive, linseed, wheat germ, safflower, rice bran, avocado, pumpkinseed, flaxseed, hazelnut, macadamia nut, coconut, palm
President: David Nagley
General Manager: Larry Kronenberg
Contact: Robert Grebler
info@pokonobe.com
Estimated Sales: $5-10 Million
Number Employees: 5-9
Square Footage: 7948
Type of Packaging: Bulk
Other Locations:
  Pokonobe Industries
  Santa Monica CA
Brands:
  Pokonobe

10151 Polar Beverages Inc.
1001 Southbridge St.
Worcester, MA 01610
800-734-9800
customerservice@polarbev.com
polarbeverages.com
Soft drinks and water.
President/CEO: Ralph Crowley
CFO/COO: Michael Mulrain
Executive Vice President: Christopher Crowley
ccrowley@polarbev.com
Year Founded: 1882
Estimated Sales: $120.3 Million
Number Employees: 500-999
Square Footage: 350000
Type of Packaging: Consumer, Food Service, Private Label
Brands:
  A&W
  Adirondack Beverages
  Adirondack Clear N' Natural
  Cape Cod Dry
  Diet Rite3
  Polar
  Royal Crown
  Seagrams
  Seven-Up
  Silver Spring
  Squirt
  Sunkist Country Time
  Waist Watcher

10152 Polar Water Company
45 Noblestown Rd
Carnegie, PA 15106
412-429-5550
Fax: 770-739-1884
Bottled water
Manager: Woody Godby
Number Employees: 20-49
Parent Co: Sontory Water Group

10153 Polarica USA, Inc.
5702 Marsh Drive
Suite G
Pacheco, CA 94553
415-647-1300
Fax: 888-502-7650 800-426-3872
sales@polaricausa.com www.polaricausa.com
Beef and specialty products
President: Carlos Tabeira
Manager: Mitch Niayesh
Estimated Sales: $5-10 Million
Number Employees: 5-9
Brands:
  Polarica

10154 Polka Home Style Sausage
8753 S Commercial Ave
Chicago, IL 60617
773-221-0395
Sausage
President: Paul Szczepkowski
Owner: Ed Szczepkowski
Estimated Sales: Less than $500,000
Number Employees: 1-4
Type of Packaging: Consumer, Food Service
Brands:
  Polka

10155 Pollio Dairy Products
8596 Main St
Campbell, NY 14821-9636
607-527-3621
Fax: 607-527-8060
Cheese
Manager: Dee Gibbs
Manager: Brian Smith
Manager: Mike Gracia
mgracia@kraft.com
Number Employees: 250-499
Type of Packaging: Consumer, Food Service

10156 Pollman's Bake Shop
750 S Broad St
Mobile, AL 36603-1197
251-438-1511
Fax: 251-438-9461
Cakes, pies and breads
Co-Owner: Charles Pollman
Co-Owner: Fred Pollman
Estimated Sales: $1-3 Million
Number Employees: 20-49
Type of Packaging: Consumer
Other Locations:
  Pollman's Bake Shops
  Mobile AL

10157 Polly's Gourmet Coffee
4606 E 2nd St
Long Beach, CA 90803-5307
562-433-2996
Fax: 562-439-4119 www.pollys.com
Coffee and tea
Owner: Mike Sheldrake
pollys@pollys.com
Estimated Sales: Under $500,000
Number Employees: 10-19
Brands:
  Celebes Kalosi
  Colombian Excelso
  Colombian Supremo
  Ethiopian Moka
  Jamaica Blue Mountain
  Java Estate
  Kenya Aa
  Kona Hawaii
  La Minita Tarrazu
  Sumatra Mandheling
  Tanzanian Peaberry

10158 Polypro International Inc
7300 Metro Blvd
Suite 570
Edina, MN 55439-2346
952-835-7717
Fax: 952-835-3811 800-765-9776
polypro@polyprointl.com www.polyprointl.com
Guar and cellulose gums
President: Mark Kieper
polypro@polyprointl.com
Controller: Jennifer Jansson
Senior Account Manager, Sales/Technical: Louise Polizzotto
Customer Service/Logistics: Janet Burger

Food Manufacturers / A-Z

Estimated Sales: $2.5-5 Million
Number Employees: 1-4
Type of Packaging: Bulk
Brands:
    Procol
    Progum
    Viscol

10159 Pommeraie Winery
10541 Cherry Ridge Road
Sebastopol, CA 95472-9644
    707-823-9463
Fax: 707-823-9106
Wine
President: Judith Johnson
Estimated Sales: $500-1 000,000 appx.
Number Employees: 1-4

10160 Pomodoro Fresca Foods
16 Bleeker Street
Millburn, NJ 07079
    973-467-6609
Fax: 973-467-3070
Sauces
President: Nancy Battista
Estimated Sales: $71,000
Brands:
    Fresca Foods

10161 Pompeian Inc
4201 Pulaski Hwy
Baltimore, MD 21224-1699
    410-276-6900
Fax: 410-276-3764 800-766-7342
www.pompeian.com
Spanish olive oil, vinegar and cooking wines.
President: Frank Patton
sales@pompeian.com
Chief Executive Officer: David Bensadoun
Year Founded: 1906
Estimated Sales: $20-50 Million
Number Employees: 50-99
Number of Brands: 4
Type of Packaging: Consumer, Food Service, Bulk
Brands:
    Avallo
    Laco
    Pompeian Olive Oil
    Romanza

10162 Pon Food Corp
101 Industrial Park Blvd
Ponchatoula, LA 70454-8306
    985-386-6941
Fax: 985-386-6755 info@ponfoodcorp.com
www.ponchatoula.com
Groceries, frozen foods, meats, dairy products and seafood
President: Pam Barado
pbarado@ponfoodcorp.com
Co-owner: Michael Berner
Estimated Sales: $7.7 Million
Number Employees: 20-49
Square Footage: 72000

10163 Pond Brothers Peanut Company
426 County Street
Suffolk, VA 23434-4704
    757-539-2356
Fax: 757-539-3995
Raw peanuts
President: Richard L Pond Jr
CEO: Jeffrey G Pond
Controller: Ernest Wyatt
Estimated Sales: $5-10 000,000
Number Employees: 1-4

10164 Pond Pure Catfish
14429 Market St
Moulton, AL 35650
    256-974-6698
Fax: 403-252-3918
Catfish
Owner: Bobby Norwood
Estimated Sales: $300,000-500,000
Number Employees: 1-4

10165 Ponderosa Valley Vineyard
3171 Highway 290
Ponderosa, NM 87044-9716
    575-834-7487
Fax: 505-834-7073 800-946-3657
winemaker@ponderosawinery.com
www.ponderosawinery.com
Wines
Owner: Henry Street
Owner: Mary Street
Estimated Sales: $150,000
Number Employees: 1-4
Number of Products: 21
Square Footage: 4000
Type of Packaging: Consumer
Brands:
    Chamisa Gold
    Jemez Blush
    Jemez Red
    N.M. Riesling
    Ponderosa Valley Vineyards
    Summer Sage
    Vino De Pata

10166 Pondini Imports
PO Box 5250
Somerset, NJ 08875-5250
    732-545-1255
Fax: 732-246-7570 spond@pondini.com
www.pondini.com
Coffee, olive oil, vinegar, cheese, pasta and rice
President/Owner: Matteo Panini
CEO: Seymour Pond
spond@pondini.com
Number Employees: 1-4

10167 Pontchartrain Blue Crab
38327 Salt Bayou Rd
Slidell, LA 70461-1103
    985-649-6645
Fax: 504-781-5064
pbcinfo@pontchartrainbluecrab.com
www.pontchartrainbluecrab.com
Seafood
President/CEO: Gary Bauer
garyb@pontchartrainbluecrab.com
Estimated Sales: $5,000,000
Number Employees: 5-9

10168 Ponti USA
5 West 19th St
New York, NY 10011
www.ponti.com
Vinegars, pasta sauces, pickled vegetables and olives.
Brands:
    Ponti

10169 Pontiac Coffee Break
2252 Dixie Hwy
Waterford, MI 48328
    248-332-6333
Fax: 248-335-0525 info@coffeebreakinc.com
www.coffeebreakinc.com
Coffee
President: Robert Smith
Estimated Sales: $500,000-$1 Million
Number Employees: 10-19

10170 Pontiac Foods
PO Box 25469
Columbia, SC 29224
    803-699-1600
Fax: 803-699-1649
Coffee
Manager: John Masa
General Manager: Joe Girone
Purchasing Manager: Stan Wilson
Estimated Sales: Under $500,000
Number Employees: 100-249
Brands:
    Kroger
    Pontiac Foods

10171 Pony Boy Ice Cream
211 Middle Road
Acushnet, MA 02743-2017
    508-994-4422
Fax: 508-995-9459
Ice cream and frozen yogurt
President: Raymond White
Estimated Sales: $10-20 000,000
Number Employees: 10-19
Brands:
    Pony Boy

10172 Ponzi Vineyards
19500 SW Mountain Home Road
Sherwood, OR Sherwood
    503-628-1227
Fax: 503-628-1808 info@ponziwines.com
www.ponziwines.com
Wines
President: Richard Ponzi
Accountant: Jeff Newlin
Marketing/Sales Director: Maria Ponzi Fogelstrom
President/Director of Sales and Marketin: Anna Ponzi
Chief Executive Officer: Michel Ponzi
Winemaker: Luisa Ponzi
Estimated Sales: $1-3 Million
Number Employees: 10-19
Type of Packaging: Private Label
Brands:
    Ponzi's

10173 Poore Brothers
5415 E High St
Suite 350
Phoenix, AZ 85054
    623-932-6200
Fax: 602-522-2690 www.inventurefoods.com
Chips
Vice President, Sales: Russell Law
Parent Co: Inventure Foods Inc
Brands:
    Bob's Texas Style
    Boulder Canyon
    Cinnabon
    Poore Brothers
    Tgi Friday's
    Tato Skins

10174 Pop & Bottle Inc.
San Francisco, CA
www.popandbottle.com
Plant-based lattes
Co-Founder: Blair Fletcher-Hardy
Co-Founder: Jash Mehta

10175 Pop Art Snacks
PO Box 9614
Salt Lake City, UT 84109
    801-983-7470
info@popartsnacks.com
www.popartsnacks.com
Flavored organic popcorn
Owner: Venessa Dobson
Owner: Mike Dobson
mike@popartsnacks.com

10176 Pop Gourmet LLC
13400 Interurban Ave S
Tukwila, WA 98168-3330
    206-397-3896
www.popgourmetpopcorn.com
Popcorn and chips
CEO: David Israel
Number Employees: 5-9
Brands:
    POP

10177 Pop Zero
3528 W 200 S
Units 1 & 2
Salt Lake City, UT 84104
    801-456-5757
info@popzeropopcorn.com
www.popzeropopcorn.com
Flavored popcorn
Co-Founder: Josh Brownlow

10178 Popchips
550 Montgomery St
Suite 925
San Francisco, CA 94111-6500
    415-391-2211
Fax: 415-391-2779 866-217-9327
sales@popchips.com www.popchips.com
Popped potato chips
Ceo: Patrick Turpin
Ceo: Keith Belling
Vice President: Martin Basch
Contact: Kristen Abbott
kristen@popchips.com
Estimated Sales: $500,000
Number Employees: 50-99

Food Manufacturers / A-Z

10179 Popcorn Connection
7615 Fulton Avenue
North Hollywood, CA 91605-1805
818-764-3279
Fax: 818-765-0578 800-852-2676
Popcorn and nuts
Owner: Kevin Needle
VP: Ross Wallach
Estimated Sales: $300,000
Number Employees: 3
Number of Products: 20
Square Footage: 14000
Type of Packaging: Consumer, Food Service, Private Label, Bulk
Brands:
  Corn Appetit
  Corn Appetit Ultimate
  Fruit Corn Appetit
  Video Munchies

10180 Popcorn Popper
6323 N 150 E
Monon, IN 47959
219-253-6607
Fax: 219-253-8172 800-270-2705
www.popcornpopper.com
Popcorn and gift baskets
President: Dani Paluchniak
Vice President: Joe Dold
Sales Manager: Steve Dold
Estimated Sales: $4041306
Number Employees: 5-9
Parent Co: Felknor International
Type of Packaging: Consumer
Brands:
  Theater Ii
  Wasbash Valley Farm
  Whirley Pop

10181 Popcorn World
520 S Ohio Ave
Sedalia, MO 65301-4450
660-826-9975
Fax: 660-359-4475 800-443-8226
Popcorn
Owner: Pam Kaduce
CEO: Keith Kaduce
Estimated Sales: $1-3 Million
Number Employees: 20
Type of Packaging: Consumer, Food Service, Private Label, Bulk

10182 Popcorner
1429 N Illinois Street
Swansea, IL 62226-4234
618-277-2676
Fax: 618-236-9420
Popcorn
Owner: Connie Kimble
Number Employees: 1-4
Square Footage: 1200
Type of Packaging: Consumer, Private Label, Bulk

10183 Popcornopolis LLC
3200 E. Slauson Ave
Vernon, CA 90058
310-414-6700
800-767-2489
customerservice@popcornopolis.com
www.popcornopolis.com
Popcorn and gift baskets
Co-Founder: Kathy Arnold
karnold@popcornopolis.com
Co-Founder: Wally Arnold
Number Employees: 100-249

10184 Popkoff's
18901 Railroad St.
City of Industry, CA 91748
844-767-5633
service@popkoffs.com
www.popkoffs.com
Pasta and pierogies
Founder: Peter Popkoff
Square Footage: 60000
Type of Packaging: Private Label

10185 Poppa's Granola
473 Grout Road
Perkinsville, VT 05151-9682
802-263-5342
Granola
Co-Owner: Angela Page
Co-Owner: Jacquelin Antonivich

Type of Packaging: Consumer, Food Service, Bulk

10186 Poppers Supply Company
PO Box 90187
Allentown, PA 18109
503-239-3792
Fax: 503-235-6221 800-457-9810
info@poppers.com www.poppers.com
Popcorn and fountain syrup
President: Vernon Ryles Jr
Sales Manager: Jody Riggs
Estimated Sales: $1.4 Million
Number Employees: 10
Type of Packaging: Consumer, Food Service
Brands:
  Allans
  Poppers

10187 Poppie's Dough
2600 W 35th St
Chicago, IL 60632-1602
312-949-0404
Fax: 312-949-0505 888-767-7431
info@poppiesbakeshop.com
www.poppiesdough.com
Cookies
President: Mark Cwiakala
mcwiakala@poppiesdough.com
President: Ronnie Himmel
Marketing: Yesenia Mendez
Estimated Sales: $2.4 Million
Number Employees: 5-9
Brands:
  Poppie's

10188 Poppies International
6610 Corporation Pkwy
Battleboro, NC 27809
252-442-4309
www.poppies.com
Bakery products and frozen desserts.
Contact: Pieter-Jan Buydaert
Brands:
  Poppies
  Delizza
  d'Haubry
  Rita

10189 Poppilu
Chicago, IL 60611
info@poppilu.com
www.poppilu.com
Antioxidant lemonade
Founder: Melanie Kahn

10190 Poppin Popcorn
933 4th Avenue N
Naples, FL 34102-5814
941-262-1691
Fax: 941-262-1691
Popcorn and maize
President: Mark Webb
Estimated Sales: Less than $500,000
Number Employees: 1-4

10191 Poppingfun Inc
1344 Constitution Dr
Neenah, WI 54956-1647
920-486-7210
Fax: 920-273-6013 Sales@poppingfun.com
www.poppingfun.com
Carbonated crystals
CEO: Julie Hesson
Founder/President: Lynn Hesson
Key Accounts: Mike Rieth
Executive Vice President: David Hesson
Technical Manager: Krista Bauman
Manager Quality/Research & Development: Lori Cramer
Contact: Keith Gray
keith@poppingfun.com
Production Manager: Chris Roebke
Number Employees: 10-19
Type of Packaging: Private Label, Bulk

10192 Poppy Hand-Crafted Popcorn
640 Merrimon Ave
Suite 201
Asheville, NC 28804
828-552-3149
www.poppyhandcraftedpopcorn.com
Flavored popcorn
Owner: Ginger Frank

Brands:
  Poppy Hand-Crafted Popcorn

10193 Popsalot
PO Box 7040
Beverly Hills, CA 90212-7040
USA
213-761-0156
Fax: 562-200-7910 www.popsalot.com
Popcorn
President/Owner: Noah Sheray
Estimated Sales: $2-5 Million
Number Employees: 10-19

10194 Porinos Gourmet Food
280 Rand St
Central Falls, RI 02863-2512
401-273-3000
Fax: 401-273-3232 800-826-3938
porinos@aol.com
Pasta and sauces, salad dressings, marinades and pickled pepper
Owner: Michael Dressler
VP Operations: Marshall Righter
Estimated Sales: $1.9 Million
Number Employees: 10-19
Square Footage: 120000
Type of Packaging: Consumer, Food Service, Private Label

10195 Pork Shop of Vermont
631 N Pasture Road
Charlotte, VT 05445-9254
802-482-3617
Fax: 802-482-2801 800-458-3441
Sausage and ham
President: Joseph Keenan
Estimated Sales: $5-9.9 000,000
Number Employees: 7

10196 Porkie Company of Wisconsin
3113 E Layton Ave
Cudahy, WI 53110-1309
414-483-6562
Fax: 414-483-6561 800-333-2588
www.porkiesofwisconsin.com
Pork rinds and cracklings, beef jerky, corn, peanuts, pistachios and cashews, olives, pickles, pretzels, potato chips and cheese curls, pigs' feet, pork hocks and Polish sausage
President: Richard Rydeski
porkieone@aol.com
Executive VP: Thomas Rydeski
Production: Dan Rydeski
Plant Manager: Mike Sodemann
Estimated Sales: $1600000
Number Employees: 20-49
Number of Products: 50
Square Footage: 200000
Brands:
  Jack's All American
  Porkies
  Snak Sales
  Vinegar Joe

10197 Porky's Gourmet Foods
644 Blythe Ave
Gallatin, TN 37066-2226
615-230-7000
Fax: 615-230-2800 800-767-5911
flavor@porkysgourmet.com
www.porkysgourmet.com
Sauces, seasonings, relishes and jellies
President: Ron Boyle
flavor@porkysgourmet.com
Estimated Sales: $5-10 Million
Number Employees: 10-19
Type of Packaging: Consumer, Food Service, Private Label

10198 Port City Pretzels
PO Box 631
Portsmouth, NH 03802
603-502-7946
info@portcitypretzels.com
www.portcitypretzels.com
Pretzels
Owner: Suzanne Foley

Food Manufacturers / A-Z

10199 Port Lobster Co Inc
122 Ocean Ave
Kennebunkport, ME 04046-6302
207-967-2081
Fax: 207-967-8419 800-486-7029
www.portlobster.com
Lobster
President: Kenneth Hutchins
portlob@gwi.net
Estimated Sales: $1-3 Million
Number Employees: 5-9
Type of Packaging: Consumer

10200 Port Royal Seafood
1948 Sea Island Pkwy
PO Box 1008
St. Helena, SC 29920
843-812-0257
Shrimp
Owner: William Gay
Estimated Sales: $210,000
Number Employees: 3
Brands:
Royal Seafood

10201 Porter Creek Vineyards
8735 Westside Rd
Healdsburg, CA 95448-8335
707-433-6321
Fax: 707-433-4245
info@portercreekvineyards.com
www.portercreekvineyards.com
Wine
President: George Davis
dijon1@sonic.net
Estimated Sales: Under $1 Million
Number Employees: 5-9
Brands:
Procter Creek

10202 Porter's Pick-A-Dilly
Stew Industrial Park
Stowe, VT 05672
802-253-6338
Fax: 802-253-6852
Produce
President: Lynn Porter
Estimated Sales: Under $500,000
Number Employees: 1-4

10203 Portier Fine Foods
436 Waverly Ave
Mamaroneck, NY 10543
914-899-9006
Fax: 914-381-4045 800-272-9463
portier.finefoods@verizon.net
Salmon, trout, scallops, shrimp, caviar, game, birds and Belgian chocolates
President: Sean Portier
Sales Director: Patrick Portier
Estimated Sales: Below $5 Million
Number Employees: 10-19
Parent Co: Chenoceaux, Inc
Type of Packaging: Consumer, Food Service

10204 Portland Creamery
PO Box 12071
Portland, OR 97212
503-616-4443
info@portlandcreamery.com
www.portlandcreamery.com
Goat cheese
Owner/Chessemaker: Liz Alvis

10205 Portland Shellfish Company
92 Waldron Way
Portland, ME 04103
207-799-9290
Fax: 207-799-7179 www.portlandshellfish.com
Crab and lobster
President: Jeff Holden
Human Resources: John Maloney
john@pshellfish.com
Estimated Sales: $9 Million
Number Employees: 100-249
Square Footage: 48000
Type of Packaging: Consumer, Food Service, Private Label, Bulk
Brands:
Portland Lighthouse

10206 Portland Specialty Seafoods
12 Portland Fish Pier
Suite A
Portland, ME 04101-4620
207-775-5765
Fax: 207-774-1614
Seafood
Manager: Ethan Court
ethan@northlanticseafood.com
Administrator: Jessica Burton
Estimated Sales: $10-20 Million
Number Employees: 20-49

10207 Portlandia Foods
12665 NE Marx St
Portland, OR 97230
833-739-3663
portlandiafoods.com
Organic condiments
Co-Owner & Founder: Jeff Bergadine
CEO: Rian Hanneman
Brands:
Portland

10208 Porto Rico Importing
201 Bleecker St
Suite A
New York, NY 10012-1446
212-477-5421
Fax: 212-979-2303 www.portorico.com
Coffee and tea
President: Peter Longo
Manager: Kate Reilly
kate@portorico.com
Estimated Sales: $5-10 Million
Number Employees: 10-19

10209 Portsmouth Chowder Co
124 Heritage Ave
Suite 1
Portsmouth, NH 03801-8655
603-431-3132
Fax: 603-431-3132 877-616-7631
info@portsmouthchowder.com
www.portsmouthchowder.com
Chowder and seafood
Owner: Rob Lincoln
rob@portsmithchowder.com
Estimated Sales: Below $5 000,000
Number Employees: 1-4
Brands:
Portsmouth Chowder Company

10210 Portuguese Baking Company
P.O.Box 5550
Newark, NJ 07105-0550
973-589-8875
Fax: 973-589-6510
Portuguese rolls
President: Marvin Everseyke
CFO/VP: Louis Pereira
CEO: Steve Latner
Estimated Sales: Under $500,000
Number Employees: 250-499
Type of Packaging: Private Label, Bulk
Brands:
Austin Company
Portuguese Baking Company

10211 Poseidon Enterprises
3516 Green Park Circle
Charlotte, NC 28217-2854
704-944-1164
Fax: 704-405-0018 800-863-7886
Seafood, salmon, tuna, swordfish, grouper, snapper, live lobster
President: Richard Lavecchia

10212 Positively 3rd St Bakery
1202 E 3rd St
Duluth, MN 55805-2319
218-724-8619
Fax: 218-724-4185 3rdstreetbakery@gmail.com
Cookies, bagels, granola and bread
Owner: Paul Steklin
Estimated Sales: Less than $500,000
Number Employees: 10-19
Type of Packaging: Consumer, Food Service, Bulk

10213 Post Consumer Brands
20802 Kensington Blvd.
Lakeville, MN 55044
800-431-7678
www.postconsumerbrands.com
Cereal and grain products
CEO: William Stiritz
Year Founded: 2015
Estimated Sales: $750 Million
Number Employees: 3,500
Number of Brands: 24
Parent Co: Post Holdings
Type of Packaging: Consumer, Food Service, Private Label, Bulk
Other Locations:
Asheboro NC
Coppell TX
Grove City OH
Northfield MN
Salt Lake City UT
St. Ansgar IA
Tremonton UT
Brands:
Alpha-Bits
Better Oats
Bran Flakes
Chips Ahoy! Cereal
Coco Wheats
Farina Mills
Golden Crisp
Golden Oreo's
Grape Nuts
Great Grains
Honey Bunches of Oats
Honey Maid S'Mores
Honeycomb
Post Hostess Cereal
Malt-O-Meal
Nilla Banana Pudding
Nutter Butter Cereal
Oh's
Oreo O's
Pebbles
Post Shredded Wheat
Raisin Bran
Sour Patch Kids Cereal

10214 Post Familie Vineyards
1700 Saint Marys Mountain Rd
Altus, AR 72821-9001
479-468-2741
Fax: 479-468-2740 800-275-8423
info@postfamilie.com www.arkansaswine.com
Wines, grape juices, jellies, champagne and grapes
President: Mathew J Post
VP/Director Marketing: Paul Post
Number Employees: 10-19
Type of Packaging: Consumer, Private Label, Bulk
Brands:
Aesop's Fable
Ozark Mountain Vineyards
Post Familie Vineyards

10215 Postum
Charlotte, NC
704-221-5587
info@postum.com
postum.com
Coffee alternative
Senior VP: Peter Hwang
Brands:
Postum

10216 Poteet Seafood Co
107 Speedy Tostensen Blvd
Brunswick, GA 31520-3149
912-264-5340
Fax: 912-267-9695
Seafood
Owner: Speedy Tostensen
poteetseafood@bellsouth.net
Estimated Sales: $350,000
Number Employees: 1-4

10217 Potlicker Kitchen
192 Thomas Road
Stowe, VT 05672
802-760-6111
potlickerkitchen@gmail.com
potlickerkitchen.com
Beer jelly, wine jelly and artisan jam
Owner: Nancy Warner
Year Founded: 2009
Estimated Sales: $7.4 Million
Number Employees: 38
Brands:
Potlicker

Food Manufacturers / A-Z

10218 Potomac Farms Dairy Inc
300 W Industrial Blvd
Cumberland, MD 21502-4156
301-722-4410
Fax: 301-722-8433 www.galliker.com
Milk
President: David W Gilles
Estimated Sales: $10-20 000,000
Number Employees: 50-99

10219 Pots de Creme
4954 Paris Pike
Lexington, KY 40511-9400
859-299-2254
Fax: 859-299-4638 www.kyagr.com
Produce, herbs, prawns, trout and tilapia
President: Susan Harkins
Director of Operations: Benson Bell
Number Employees: 1-4
Parent Co: Duntreath Farm
Brands:
 Dubbasue and Company

10220 Potter Siding Creamery Company
P.O.Box 494
Tripoli, IA 50676-0494
319-882-4444
Baked goods and creams
Owner: Kurt Kortbein
Estimated Sales: Less than $500,000
Number Employees: 1-4

10221 Powder Pure
250 Steelhead Way
The Dalles, OR 97058-3570
541-298-4800
Fax: 888-765-1720 info@powderpure.com
www.powderpure.com
Fruit and vegetable powders
CEO: Mark Savarese
Contact: Skip Benner
skip@powderpure.com
Number Employees: 100
Square Footage: 140000
Type of Packaging: Bulk

10222 Powell & Mahoney Ltd.
39 Norman St
Salem, MA 01970
978-745-4332
info@powellandmahoney.com
www.powellandmahoney.com
Cocktail mixers
Marketing: Mark Mahoney

10223 Power Crunch
Irvine, CA
powercrunch.com
Protein powders and bars
Founder: Kevin Lawrence

10224 Power of 3
P.O. Box 434
Tenants Harbor, ME 04860
888-211-7911
info@powerof3nutrition.com
powerof3nutrition.com
Health foods

10225 PowerBar
Premier Nutrition
P.O. Box 933
Kings Mountain, NC 28086
800-587-6937
www.powerbar.com
Energy bars and sports drinks
President & CEO: Rob Vitale
SVP & CFO: Jeff Zadoks
Estimated Sales: $175 Million
Number Employees: 50-99
Parent Co: Post Holdings Inc
Type of Packaging: Private Label
Brands:
 PowerBar(c) 10-12g Protein Snack Bar
 PowerBar(c) 20-30g Proteinplus
 PowerBar(c) Clean Whey Protein Bar
 PowerBar(c) Clean Whey Protein Drink
 PowerBar(c) Energy Blasts
 PowerBar(c) Energy Gels
 PowerBar(c) Performance Energy Bar
 PowerBar(c) Protein Plus
 PowerBar(c) Protein Shakes
 PowerBar(c) Variety Packs

10226 Powerful Foods
1828 Bay Rd
Suite 201
Miami, FL 33139
305-779-2449
info@powerful.co
powerful.co
Greek yogurt and yogurt drinks, oatmeal, smoothies and snack bites
Controller: Daniela Koch
Marketing Manager: Laura Peimer
Brands:
 Powerful Yogurt

10227 Powers Baking Company
7771 W Oakland Park Blvd
Miami, FL 33167-3705
305-381-7000
Fax: 305-769-1185
Breads, rolls and buns, cakes, pies, doughs, biscuits, baking mixes, supplies and cookies
President: Dolphus Powers
Estimated Sales: $5 Million
Number Employees: 80

10228 Prager Winery & Port Works
1281 Lewelling Ln
St Helena, CA 94574-2235
707-963-3720
Fax: 707-963-7679 800-969-7678
ahport@pragerport.com www.pragerport.com
Wine
Owner: Jim Prager
ahport@pragerport.com
CFO: Katie Rooney
Estimated Sales: $1-4.9 Million
Number Employees: 5-9
Brands:
 Prager Winery & Port

10229 Praim Co
92 Jackson St
Salem, MA 01970-3068
978-745-9100
Fax: 978-745-9150 800-970-9646
sales@praimgroup.com www.praimgroup.com
Chocolate, toffee and truffles
CEO: Paul Pruett
Estimated Sales: Less Than $500,000
Number Employees: 1-4
Square Footage: 60000
Brands:
 ChoxCard
 Seapoint Edamama
 Friendlys
 Warhol
 Bloomsberry & Co.
 Mary Phillips
 Rescue Bar
 Anne Taintor
 Bosco
 Bubble Chocolate
 Eric Condren
 PAN AM
 The Mensch On a Bench
 GK Communications
 Zone
 Praim Confections
 Waldo
 Garfield
 French Bull
 Build-A-Bear
 Dreamworks
 Boss Baby
 Trolls
 Happiness Sell Sheet

10230 Prairie Berries Inc.
PO Box 21
Keeler, SK S0H 2E0
Canada
306-788-2018
Fax: 306-788-4811 prairieberries@sasktel.net
www.prairieberries.com
Saskatoon berries
President: Sandra Purdy
Number Employees: 5-9
Type of Packaging: Consumer, Food Service

10231 Prairie Cajun Wholesale
5966 Highway 190
Eunice, LA 70535
337-546-6195
Seafood and exotic meats; alligator and nutria
President: Jeffery Derouen
Estimated Sales: $1-2 Million
Number Employees: 10-19
Type of Packaging: Consumer, Food Service

10232 Prairie City Bakery
100 N Fairway Dr
Suite 138
Vernon Hills, IL 60061-1859
847-573-9640
Fax: 847-573-9643 800-338-5122
customerservice@pcbakery.com
www.pcbakery.com
Danish, cookies, muffins and cakes
Owner: Bill Skeens
bskeens@pcbakery.com
Estimated Sales: $2,200,000
Number Employees: 5-9
Type of Packaging: Consumer, Food Service, Bulk
Brands:
 Prairie City

10233 (HQ)Prairie Farms Dairy Inc.
3744 Staunton Rd.
Edwardsville, IL 62025
618-659-5700
info@prairiefarms.com
www.prairiefarms.com
Cottage cheese, milk, sour cream, yogurt, ice cream, orange juice and fruit drinks.
CEO: Edward Mullins
emullins@prairiefarms.com
VP/CFO: Jason Geminn
Year Founded: 1938
Estimated Sales: $3 Billion
Number Employees: 5,700
Type of Packaging: Consumer, Food Service, Private Label, Bulk
Brands:
 Prairie Farms
 Swiss Valley Farms

10234 Prairie Malt
PO Box 1150
Biggar, SK S0K 0M0
Canada
306-948-3500
Fax: 306-948-5038 david_klinger@cargill.com
www.prairiemaltltd.com
Barley malt
President: Doug Eden
Number Employees: 50-99
Parent Co: Cargill, Incorporated
Type of Packaging: Bulk

10235 Prairie Mills Products LLC
401 E 4th St
P.O. Box 97
Rochester, IN 46975-1105
574-223-3177
Fax: 574-223-3414 www.prairiemills.com
Flour and cereal
President: Erik Bruun
Managing Director, CEO: John Cory
jcory@prairiemills.com
National Sales Manager: Gary Swaim
Estimated Sales: Less Than $500,000
Number Employees: 1-4
Type of Packaging: Private Label
Brands:
 Amaizen Crunch
 Prairie Star

10236 Prairie Mushrooms
52557 Range Road 215
Ardrossan, AB T8E 2H6
Canada
780-467-3555
Fax: 780-467-3893 info@prairiemushrooms.com
www.prairiemushrooms.com
Mushrooms
President: George DeRuiter
Marketing Manager: John Kostelyk
Sales: Kevin Christman
General Manager: Terry Uppal
Production: Don Kostelyk
Estimated Sales: $5-10 Million
Number Employees: 100-249
Type of Packaging: Consumer, Food Service
Brands:
 Prairie Mushrooms

Food Manufacturers / A-Z

10237 Prairie Thyme LTD
4363 Center Pl
Unit 3
Santa Fe, NM 87507-1823
505-473-1945
Fax: 505-473-0363 800-869-0009
prairiethyme@worldpantry.com
www.prairiethyme.com
Condiments; vinegars, cooking oils, fruit salsas and chutneys
President/Owner: Gary Hall
prairiethyme@aol.com
Estimated Sales: Less Than $500,000
Number Employees: 1-4
Number of Brands: 1
Number of Products: 4
Square Footage: 6400
Parent Co: WorldPantry.com Inc.
Type of Packaging: Consumer, Food Service, Private Label, Bulk
Brands:
  Prairie Thyme

10238 Prana
1440 Blvd Jules Poitras
Ville St Laurent, QC H4N 1X7
Canada
Fax: 514-276-5858 844-447-7262
www.pranasnacks.com
Trail mixes, organic nuts, chocolate barks and chia seeds

10239 Prayon Inc.
1610 Marvin Griffin Rd.
Augusta, GA 30906
206-213-5572
www.prayon.com
Phosphates and phosphoric acid.
Chairman: Olivier Vanderijst
CEO: Y. Caprara
Director of Finance: P. Schils
Director, Research: A. Germeau
Director, Sales & Marketing: V. Renard
Year Founded: 1882
Estimated Sales: $786 Million
Number Employees: 1,115
Parent Co: Prayon
Type of Packaging: Bulk
Brands:
  Prayphos
  Kasomel
  Carfosel
  Praylev

10240 Precise Food Ingredients
1432 Wainwright Way
Suite 150
Carrollton, TX 75007
972-323-4951
garrett.miller@precisefood.com
www.precisefood.com
Dry packaging and blending of seasonings for custom, industrial clients
President: Scott Miller
salesinfo@precisefood.com
VP of Sales & Marketing: Kevin Loiselle
Purchasing Agent: Linda Ransom
Year Founded: 1997
Estimated Sales: $6 Million
Number Employees: 20-49
Type of Packaging: Bulk

10241 Precision Blends
13460 Brooks Drive
Baldwin Park, CA 91706-2292
626-960-9939
Fax: 626-962-2570 800-836-9979
Blend spices
President: Charles Angell
Sales Manager: David Alnamva
Purchasing Manager: Charles Nordell
Estimated Sales: Under $500,000
Number Employees: 20-49
Type of Packaging: Private Label

10242 Preferred Brands Inc
9 W Broad St
Suite 5
Stamford, CT 06902-3734
203-348-0030
Fax: 203-348-0029 800-827-8500
comments@tastybite.com www.tastybite.com
Indian, Thai, vegetarian, vegan, kosher and gluten free rice, noodles, and entrees.

President/Owner: Ravi Nigam
CEO: Ashok Vasudevan
CFO: Sohel Shikari
EVP Sales & Marketing: Meera Vasudevan
VP Sales & Marketings: Hans Taparia
Estimated Sales: $5.7 Million
Number Employees: 10-19

10243 Preferred Meal Systems Inc
4135 Birney Ave
Moosic, PA 18507-1397
570-457-8311
Fax: 570-457-9241 www.preferredmeals.com
Portion control lunches
Executive Director: Bob Keen
Director Technology Services: Richard Ludt
Estimated Sales: $4,800,000
Number Employees: 250-499
Square Footage: 200000
Type of Packaging: Food Service, Private Label

10244 (HQ)Preferred Popcorn
1132 9th Rd
Chapman, NE 68827-2753
308-986-2526
Fax: 308-986-2626 info@preferredpopcorn.com
www.preferredpopcorn.com
Popcorn, salts and oils
CEO: Norm Krug
Estimated Sales: $30 Million
Number Employees: 20-49
Type of Packaging: Consumer, Food Service, Private Label, Bulk
Brands:
  Widman's Country

10245 Premier Beverages
5301 Legacy Drive
Plano, TX 75024-3109
972-547-6295
Beverages
COO: Robert O'Brien
VP Sales: Scott Corridean
Estimated Sales: Under $500,000
Number Employees: 1-4

10246 Premier Juices
19321 US Highway 19 N # 405
Suite 405
Clearwater, FL 33764-3142
727-533-8200
Fax: 727-533-8500 info@premierjuices.com
www.premierjuices.com
Fruit juices
President: Jody Marshburn
jody@premierjuices.com
Estimated Sales: $2.5-5 Million
Number Employees: 1-4

10247 Premier Malt Products Inc
25760 Groesbeck Hwy
Suite 103
Warren, MI 48089-1589
586-443-3355
Fax: 586-443-4580 800-521-1057
Malt extracts, fungal amylase and sequestrants
President: Pat Maison
pat@premiermalt.com
Estimated Sales: $1500000
Number Employees: 10-19
Type of Packaging: Consumer, Food Service, Bulk
Brands:
  Diamalt
  Premose

10248 Premier Meat Co
5030 Gifford Ave
PO Box 58183
Vernon, CA 90058-2726
323-277-5888
Fax: 323-277-9100 800-555-5539
www.premiermeats.com
Beef, veal and pork
Owner: Manuel Hernandez
manuel.hernandez@premiermeats.com
Controller: Richard Orosco
Vice President: Eldad Hadar
Operations Manager: Orner Greenberg
Production Supervisor: Maricela Romero
Number Employees: 50-99
Type of Packaging: Consumer, Food Service, Bulk

10249 Premier Organics
810 81st Avenue
Oakland, CA 94621
510-632-8612
Fax: 510-380-6942 866-237-8688
Raw nut and seed butters
Contact: Santiago Cuenca-Romero
santiago@premierorganics.org
Type of Packaging: Consumer, Bulk
Brands:
  ARTISANA

10250 Premier Pacific Seafoods Inc
333 1st Ave W
Seattle, WA 98119-4103
206-286-8584
Fax: 206-286-8810 www.prempac.com
Fish
President: Tom Coryell
tom@prempac.com
Estimated Sales: Under $500,000
Number Employees: 10-19
Type of Packaging: Bulk
Brands:
  Ocean Phoenix
  Premiere Pacific

10251 Premier Protein
5905 Christie Ave
Emeryville, CA 94608-1925
415-442-4343
Fax: 415-442-4347 888-836-8977
info@premiernutrition.com
www.premierprotein.com
Nutritional shakes, drinks, powders and bars
Owner: Karry Law
CEO: David Ritterbush
david@jointjuice.com
CFO: David Cooper
VP of Innovation and R&D: Ron Osbourne
VP of Marketing: Darcy Horn
VP of Sales: Lee Partin
VP of Operations: Stewart Irving
Estimated Sales: $5-10 Million
Number Employees: 10-19
Type of Packaging: Consumer, Private Label, Bulk
Brands:
  Odyssey
  Premier Nutrition
  Premier Shots
  Rocket Shot
  Twisted Brand

10252 Premier Smoked Fish Company
3185 Tucker Rd
Bensalem, PA 19020
215-639-4569
Fax: 305-625-5528 800-654-6682
Fish; salmon, cured and herring
Owner: J Purner
COO: David Donahue
Controller: John Cicero
Plant Manager: David Sperry
Estimated Sales: $5200000
Number Employees: 5-9
Square Footage: 96000
Parent Co: SeaSpecialties
Brands:
  Mama's
  Seaspecialties

10253 Premiere Packing Company
PO Box 815
Greenacres, WA 99016-0815
509-926-6666
Fax: 509-926-3300 888-239-5288
nuts@thenutfactory.com www.thenutfactory.com
Snack foods, nuts, chocolates
President: Gene Cohen
Estimated Sales: Below $5 Million
Number Employees: 5-9

10254 Premiere Seafood
257 Midland Avenue
Lexington, KY 40508-1978
606-259-3474
Fax: 606-389-9390
Seafood
President: Rex Webb

Food Manufacturers / A-Z

10255 Premium Brands
PO Box 785
Bardstown, KY 40004-0785
502-348-0081
Fax: 502-348-5539
kentuckybourbon@bardstown.com
www.kentuckybourbonwhiskey.com
Liquor, whiskeys
President: Even Kulsveen
Estimated Sales: Less than $1 Million
Number Employees: 10

10256 Premium Chocolatiers LLC
170 Oberlin Ave N
Suite 9
Lakewood, NJ 08701-4548
USA
732-806-5218
www.premiumchocolatiers.com
Chocolate
Owner: Yochonon Miller
Estimated Sales: 260,000
Number Employees: 5

10257 Premium Gold Flax Products & Processing
1321 12th Ave. NE
Denhoff, ND 58430-9611
866-570-1234
info@premiumgoldflax.com
www.premiumgoldflax.com
Flaxseed
Co-Owner: Deborah Miller
tupper1956@yahoo.com

10258 Premium Ingredients International US, LLC
285 E Fullerton Ave
Carol Stream, IL 60188-1886
630-868-0300
Fax: 630-868-0310 info@prinovausa.com
Food ingredients and aroma chemicals
President: Donald Thorp
CEO: Richard Thorp
CFO: Donald Cepican
VP: Daniel Thorp
Research/Development Director: Suzanne Johnson
VP Sales/Marketing: Richard Calabrese
Contact: Kim Sean
kim.sean@prinovausa.com
Estimated Sales: $30-35 Million
Number Employees: 100
Parent Co: AMC Chemicals
Other Locations:
  Premium Ingredients International
  Holladay UT
  Premium Ingredients International
  Ellisville MO
  Premium Ingredients International
  Cranford NJ
  Premium Ingredients Int'l(UK)
  London, England

10259 Premium Meat Co
1100 W 600 N
Brigham City, UT 84302-4423
435-723-5944
www.premiummeatcompany.com
Beef, pork and lamb
Owner: Doug Price
Sales Manager: David Wells
Estimated Sales: $3-5 Million
Number Employees: 5-9

10260 Premium Water
7810 N W 100th Street
Kansas City, MO 64153
816-801-6900
800-332-3332
www.premiumwaters.com
Bottled water
President: Peter Johnson
Contact: Dawn Andresen
dawn.andresen@premiumwaters.com
GM: Bob McBride
Estimated Sales: $5-10 Million
Number Employees: 50-99
Square Footage: 80000
Type of Packaging: Consumer, Food Service, Private Label
Brands:
  Acappella

10261 Prescott Brewing Co
130 W Gurley St
Suite A
Prescott, AZ 86301-3603
928-771-2795
Fax: 928-771-1115 angpbc1@cableone.net
www.prescottbrewingcompany.com
Beer
President: John Nielsen
pbc1@frontiernet.net
CFO: Roxanne Nielsen
Sales Director: Dave Jacobson
Estimated Sales: $1-5 Million
Number Employees: 50-99
Brands:
  Liquid Amber
  Lodgepole Light
  Petrified Porter

10262 President's Choice
1 President's Choice Circle
Brampton, ON L6Y 5S5
Canada
888-495-5111
www.presidentschoice.ca
Cookies, cola, biscuits, lasagna, turkey, pizza, coffee, poultry, ice cream and juice
President, Loblaw Companies Limited: Sarah Davis
Number Employees: 14
Square Footage: 20000

10263 Presque Isle Wine Cellars
9440 W Main Rd
North East, PA 16428-2699
814-725-1314
Fax: 814-725-2092 800-488-7492
info@piwine.com www.piwine.com
Wines and wine-making supplies
Owner: Doug Moorhead
doug@piwine.com
Co-Owner: Laury Bouttcher
Estimated Sales: Below $5 Million
Number Employees: 10-19
Type of Packaging: Private Label
Brands:
  Presque Isle Wine

10264 Pressery
2401 W 6th Avenue
Denver, CO 80204
info@pressery.com
www.pressery.com
Ramen kits, bone broth and cold-pressed juices
Founder & CEO: Ian Lee
Year Founded: 2013

10265 Prestige Proteins
1101 South Rogers Circle
Suite 1
Boca Raton, FL 33487-2748
561-997-8770
Fax: 561-997-8786 casein@casein.com
www.casein.com
Caseinate: calcium, sodium and potassium
Owner: Hue Henly
Sales Manager: Tina Thimlar
Estimated Sales: $1-2.5 Million
Number Employees: 1-4
Square Footage: 200000
Type of Packaging: Consumer, Food Service, Private Label, Bulk
Brands:
  Prestige Proteins

10266 (HQ)Prestige Technology
1101 S Rogers Cir
Suite 1
Boca Raton, FL 33487-2748
561-997-8770
Fax: 561-997-8786 888-697-4141
casein@casein.com
Sodium and calcium caseinates
President: Hugh Henley
casein@gate.net
Director of Sales: Tina Thimlar
Estimated Sales: $18 Million
Number Employees: 10-19
Square Footage: 20000
Other Locations:
  Prestige Technology Corp.
  Minsk
Brands:
  Prestige Proteins
  Qualcoat

10267 Presto Avoset Group
PO Box 1086
Claremont, CA 91711-1086
909-399-0062
Fax: 909-399-1162
Nondairy toppings and icings
Brands:
  Pastry Pride
  Pastry Pro
  Pour N' Performance
  Pour N' Whip
  Pride
  Qwip
  Tres Cremas

10268 Preston Farms Popcorn
1000 Zane Street
Louisville, KY 40210
502-813-3207
Fax: 502-813-3219 866-767-7464
Hybrid popcorn
CEO: Raymond Preston
President: Leigh Anne Preston
Private Label Sales: Charles Shacklette
Contact: Kermit Highfield
kermit@prestonfarms.com
Estimated Sales: $300,000-500,000
Number Employees: 10-19
Number of Products: 60
Type of Packaging: Private Label
Brands:
  America's Premium
  Gettelfinger Select
  Heartland U.S.A.
  Ky Poppers
  Spee-Dee Pop

10269 Preston Premium Wines
502 E Vineyard Dr
Pasco, WA 99301
509-545-1990
Fax: 509-545-1098 info@prestonwines.com
Wines
President: Brett Preston
Estimated Sales: $5-9.9 Million
Number Employees: 20-49
Brands:
  Preston Premium Wines

10270 Preston Vineyards & Winery
9282 W Dry Creek Rd
Healdsburg, CA 95448-9134
707-433-3372
Fax: 707-433-5307 800-305-9707
Wine, olives, produce and baked goods
Owner: Lou Preston
mail@prestonvineyards.com
Co-Owner: Susan Preston
Winemaker: Matt Norelli
Vineyard Manager: Jesus Arzate
Estimated Sales: $5-10 Million
Number Employees: 10-19
Brands:
  Kuchen

10271 Pretzel Perfection
215 E Reserve St
Suite 101
Vancouver, WA 98661
USA
360-635-3886
www.pretzelperfection.com
Pretzels, chocolates
Chief Executive Officer/Founder: Amy Holyk
Contact: Roysan Biscieglia
rbiscieglia@pretzelperfection.com

10272 Pretzel Pete
130 Domorah Dr.
Montgomeryville, PA 18936
877-857-1727
www.pretzelpete.com
Pretzels and other snacks
President: Karl Brown

10273 Pretzelmaker
1346 Oakbrook Drive
Suite 170
Norcross, GA 30093
470-388-6170
877-639-2361
customerservice@gfgmanagement.com
www.pretzelmaker.com
Soft pretzels

Food Manufacturers / A-Z

10274 Pretzels Inc
123 W Harvest Rd
Bluffton, IN 46714-9007
260-824-4838
Fax: 260-824-0895 800-456-4838
www.pretzels-inc.com
Pretzels, cheese curls, corn puffs and cheese balls
President: William Huggins
CEO: William Mann
Marketing Director: Chip Manneson
Sales Director: Marvin Sparks
Operations Manager: John Sommer
Purchasing Manager: Steve Huggins
Number Employees: 250-499
Square Footage: 800000
Type of Packaging: Consumer, Food Service, Private Label, Bulk
Brands:
  Harvest Road
  William's Corn

10275 (HQ)Price Co
370 Breaum Rd
Yakima, WA 98908-8931
509-966-4110
Fax: 509-966-2988 www.priceapples.com
Apples and pears
President: Bob Price
bob@priceapples.com
CFO: Adam Hill
Number Employees: 100-249
Type of Packaging: Consumer, Food Service, Private Label, Bulk
Brands:
  Gold Medal
  Moon
  Naches
  Panda
  Price
  Priceless

10276 Price Seafood
650 Water Street
Havre De Grace, MD 21078
410-939-2782
Shrimp and crabs
Owner: Norris Price
Principal: Susan Price
Estimated Sales: $500,000- 1Million
Number Employees: 15
Square Footage: 32800
Brands:
  Louisiana
  Louisiana Cajun
  Ocean Blue

10277 Price's Creameries
600 N Piedras St
El Paso, TX 79903-4023
915-565-2711
Fax: 915-562-8232 www.pricescreameries.com
Milk, ice cream, sherbet, mellorine, cream and ice milk mixes.
Director of Export & ESL Expansion: Gene Carrejo
Cmo: Irene Pistella
irene.pistella@deanfoods.com
Year Founded: 1906
Number Employees: 100-249
Parent Co: Dean Foods Company
Type of Packaging: Consumer
Brands:
  Price's

10278 Pride Dairies
517 Thompson St
Bottineau, ND 58318-1205
701-228-2216
Fax: 701-228-3426 pride@utma.com
www.pridedairy.com
Butter, milk and ice cream
President: Jeff Beyer
Vice President: Floyd Slaughbaugh
Marketing: Shelly Spang
Estimated Sales: $10-20 Million
Number Employees: 5-9
Type of Packaging: Consumer, Food Service, Bulk
Brands:
  Pride

10279 Pride Enterprises Glades
500 Orange Avenue Cir
Belle Glade, FL 33430-5221
561-996-1091
Fax: 561-996-8559
Sugarcane
Facility Manager: Peter Venables
Estimated Sales: Under $500,000
Number Employees: 5-9

10280 Pride of Dixie Syrup Company
217 Co Op Drive
Bono, AR 72416-8181
870-935-2252
Fax: 870-935-9325 800-530-7654
Pancake syrups: maple, honey and crystal white flavors
President: Troy Coleman
Estimated Sales: $180,000
Number Employees: 4
Square Footage: 15000
Type of Packaging: Consumer, Food Service, Private Label
Brands:
  Craft's
  Pride of Dixie

10281 Priester's Pecans
208 Old Fort Rd E
Fort Deposit, AL 36032-4012
334-227-4301
Fax: 334-227-4294 866-477-4736
customerservice@priesters.com
www.priesters.com
Pecan candies, pies, cakes, brownies, chocolates and cheese straws.
President: Thomas Ellis
priesters@aol.com
Owner: Ellen Burkett
CFO: Faye Hood
Plant Manager: Robert Hunter
Year Founded: 1935
Estimated Sales: $20-50 Million
Number Employees: 50-99
Number of Brands: 2
Type of Packaging: Food Service, Private Label, Bulk
Brands:
  Cloverland Sweets
  Priester's Pecans

10282 Prifti Candy Company
106 Green St
Worcester, MA 01604
508-754-5143
Fax: 508-754-0325 800-447-7438
Candies
Owner: Nick Prifti
Estimated Sales: Less than $500,000
Number Employees: 1-4
Brands:
  Prifti Candy

10283 Prima Foods International
PO Box 2208
Silver Springs, FL 34489
352-732-9148
Fax: 352-732-0625 800-774-8751
Syrup, cocktail mixes, fruit purees and concentrates, drink bases and milk replacers
President: Hector Viale
Vice President: Celeste Viale
VP Sales: Mary Lou Sharp
Estimated Sales: $1 Million
Number Employees: 8
Square Footage: 40000
Type of Packaging: Food Service, Private Label, Bulk
Brands:
  Flat Wood Farm
  Prima Naturals

10284 Prima Kase
W6117 County Road C
Monticello, WI 53570
608-938-4227
Fax: 608-938-1227 kase@madison.tds.net
Cheeses
CEO: Steve McKeon
Estimated Sales: $2.5-5 Million
Number Employees: 5-9
Type of Packaging: Consumer, Food Service, Private Label, Bulk
Brands:
  Prima Kase

10285 Prima Wawona
7108 N Fresno St
Suite 450
Fresno, CA 93720
559-787-8780
prima.com
Tree fruits, including peaches, plums, nectarines and apricots.
President & CEO: Dan Gerawan
Retail Sales Manager: Ben Vived
Estimated Sales: Over $1 Billion
Number Employees: 500-999
Brands:
  Sweet 2 Eat

10286 Primal Essence
1351 Maulhardt Ave
Oxnard, CA 93030-7963
805-981-2409
Fax: 805-981-2419 877-774-6253
sales@primalessence.com
www.primalessence.com
Botanical extracts
President And General Manager: Mark Smythe
mark.smyth@mac.com
Number Employees: 5-9
Type of Packaging: Consumer, Food Service, Bulk

10287 Primal Kitchen
Oxnard, CA
888-774-6259
info@primalkitchen.com www.primalkitchen.com
Condiments, dressings, marinades, oils and protein bars
Founder: Mark Sisson

10288 Primal Nutrition
23805 Stuart Ranch Rd
Suite 145
Malibu, CA 90265
310-317-4414
888-774-6259
info@primalkitchen.com www.primalkitchen.com
Drink mixes, bars, oils and salad dressings.
Owner: Mark Sisson
Brands:
  Primal Kitchen

10289 Prime Cut Meat & Seafood Company
2601 N. 31st Ave.
Phoenix, AZ 85009-1522
602-455-8834
800-277-1054
www.primecutusa.com
Meat, seafood
President: David Poppen
dpoppen@primemalta.com
VP/Treasurer: Linda Poppen
Estimated Sales: $17 Million
Number Employees: 50-99

10290 Prime Food Processing Corp
300 Vandervoort Ave
Brooklyn, NY 11211-1715
718-963-2323
Chinese dumplings and egg rolls
President: Yee Chan
Quality Control Director: Laymont Dofon
Estimated Sales: $13 Million
Number Employees: 50-99
Number of Brands: 1
Square Footage: 10000
Type of Packaging: Consumer, Food Service, Private Label, Bulk
Brands:
  Prime Food

10291 Prime Ingredients Inc
280 N Midland Ave
Saddle Brook, NJ 07663-5721
201-791-6655
Fax: 201-791-4244 888-791-6655
www.primeingredients.com
Dessert, dips and sauces, cheese, creamers, mixes, glazes, oils, margarines and olive oil
Director: Christopher Walsh
chris@primeingredients.com
Estimated Sales: Below $5 Million
Number Employees: 5-9
Square Footage: 80000
Type of Packaging: Bulk

Food Manufacturers / A-Z

10292 Prime Ostrich International
8702a 98th Street
Morinville, AB T8R 1K6
Canada
780-939-3804
Fax: 780-939-4888 800-340-2311
Ostrich meat and meat pies
President: James Danyluik
Marketing Director: Michelle Danyluik
Number Employees: 5-9
Type of Packaging: Consumer, Food Service, Private Label, Bulk

10293 Prime Pak Foods Inc
2076 Memorial Park Dr
Gainesville, GA 30504-5802
770-536-8708
Fax: 770-536-1638 info@primepakfoods.com
www.primepakfoods.com
Beef, pork, veal, poultry and barbecue meat products
President: Todd Robson
CFO: Christy Phillips
Vice President: Milton Robson
Year Founded: 1972
Estimated Sales: $23.5 Million
Number Employees: 100-249

10294 Prime Pastries
370 North Rivermed Road
Concord, ON L4K 3N2
Canada
905-669-5883
Fax: 905-669-8655 smuchnik@primus.ca
www.primepastries.ca
Pastries
President: Steven Muchnik
CFO: Ashley Berman
Brands:
　Prime Pastries

10295 Prime Produce
350 N Cypress St
Orange, CA 92866-1028
714-771-0718
Fax: 714-771-0728
Avocados
President: Avi Crane
Business Development Manager: Yair Crane
Sales Manager: Gahl Crane
Operations/Ripening Manager: Miguel Guzman
Estimated Sales: $5-10 Million
Number Employees: 20-49
Type of Packaging: Consumer, Food Service, Private Label, Bulk

10296 Prime Smoked Meats Inc
220 Alice St
Oakland, CA 94607-4394
510-832-7167
Fax: 510-832-4830
Pork
Owner: Dave Andes
Sales Manager: Tina DeMello
dave.andes@primesmoked.com
Office Manager: Elsie Jorstad
Production Manager: Jose Garcia
Estimated Sales: $5897842
Number Employees: 20-49
Square Footage: 48000
Type of Packaging: Consumer, Food Service, Private Label, Bulk
Brands:
　James
　Prime

10297 (HQ)Primer Foods Corporation
612 South 8th Street
PO Box 373
Cameron, WI 54822-0373
715-458-4075
Fax: 715-458-4078 800-365-2409
tkunz@primerafoods.com www.primerafoods.com
Egg products
President/CEO: Ron Ashton
Chief Executive Officer: John Ashton
Quality Control: Kristen Zuzek
Contact: Barry Eisen
eisen@primerafoods.com
Estimated Sales: $100 Million
Number Employees: 118
Square Footage: 105000
Other Locations:
　Primera Foods
　Penham MN
　Primera Foods
　Stockton IL
　Primera Foods
　Hayfield MN
　Primera Foods
　Faribault MN
　Primer Foods
　Altura MN
Brands:
　Eggstreme Bakery Mix 100
　Eggstreme Options
　Eggstreme Yolk
　Eggstreme-We 300
　Insta Thick
　Malta Gran
　Prime Cap
　Rice Complete
　Rice Pro 35
　Rice Trin
　Tapi
　Tomato Max

10298 Primera Meat Service
21649 N Stuart Place Rd
Harlingen, TX 78552-1962
956-423-3721
Fax: 956-423-3085
Meat products
Owner: Javier Abundiz
primerameats@gmail.com
Estimated Sales: $3-5 Million
Number Employees: 5-9

10299 Primex International Trading
5777 W Century Blvd
Suite 1485
Los Angeles, CA 90045
310-410-7100
Fax: 310-568-3336 info@primex.us
www.primex-usa.com
Pistachios, dried fruits and nuts.
Owner & CEO: Ali Amin
Quality System Director: Tiffany Weldin
Grower Relations Representative: Bob Engleman
Plant Manager: Mike Vasilescu
Year Founded: 1989
Estimated Sales: $184.5 Million
Number Employees: 10-19

10300 Primitive Feast
11693 San Vicente Blvd
Suite 488
Los Angeles, CA 90049
844-807-7688
info@primitivefeast.com primitivefeast.com
Frozen entr‚es
Co-Founder: Betty Morin
Co-Founder: Yin Goh
Co-Founder: Scott Fennel
Co-Founder: Rick Friedman

10301 Primo Foods
56 Huxley Rd
Toronto, ON M9M 1H2
Canada
416-741-9300
Fax: 416-741-3766 800-377-6945
website@primofoods.ca www.primofoods.ca
Primo pasta, tomatoes, beans, sauces
VP: Tony Gucciardi
Sales: Phil Ulias
Square Footage: 200000
Type of Packaging: Consumer, Food Service, Private Label

10302 Primo Foods
606 Morse Street
Oceanside, CA 92054
760-439-8711
Fax: 760-439-3664 www.primofoodsinc.com
Fish, meats, poultry, dairy, vegetables, spices, seasonings, baking supplies, rices, grains, cheese, kosher and organic foods
Plant Manager: Gabe Soffiaturo
Parent Co: Nabisco
Type of Packaging: Consumer, Food Service

10303 Primo Water Corporation
101 N Cherry St
Suite 501
Winston-Salem, NC 27101
844-237-7466
primowater.com
Water dispensers, purified bottled water, self-service refill drinking water.
Chief Executive Officer: Jerry Fowden
Chief Financial Officer: Jay Wells
Chief Accounting Officer: Jason Ausher
VP/General Counsel/Secretary: Marni Morgan-Poe
SVP/Global Human Resources: Steve Edman
Estimated Sales: K
Number Employees: 10,000+
Type of Packaging: Consumer, Food Service, Private Label, Bulk
Other Locations:
　Cliffstar Manufacturing Plant
　East Freetown MA
　Cliffstar Manufacturing Plant
　Fontana CA
　Cliffstar Manufacturing Plant
　Fredonia NY
　Cliffstar Manufacturing Plant
　Greer SC
　Cliffstar Manufacturing Plant
　Joplin MO
　Cliffstar Manufacturing Plant
　N East PA
　Cliffstar Manufacturing Plant
　Walla Walla WA
　Cliffstar Manufacturing Plant
　Warrens WI
　Cott Beverage Manufacturing Plant
　Calgary, Alberta, Canada
　Cott Concentrate Manufacturing
　Columbus GA
Brands:
　ALHAMBRA
　ATHENA
　BELMONT SPRINGS
　CRYSTAL SPRINGS
　DEEP ROCK WATER
　HINCKLEY SPRINGS
　KENTWOOD SPRINGS
　SIERRA SPRINGS
　SPARKLETTS
　CANADIAN SPRINGS
　JAVARAMA
　STANDARD COFFEE
　TERRAZA
　S&D COFFEE & TEA
　AIMIA FOODS
　RCCI

10304 Primos Northgate
2323 Lakeland Drive
Flowood, MS 39232-9514
601-936-3398
Fax: 601-936-3797 www.primoscafe.com
Baked goods: pies, tarts, cupcakes, brownies and cookies
Owner: Don Primos
President: Peter Primos
Estimated Sales: $500,000 appx.
Number Employees: 20-49
Type of Packaging: Consumer
Brands:
　Primos

10305 Primrose Candy Co
4111 W Parker Ave
Chicago, IL 60639-2176
773-276-9522
Fax: 773-276-7411 800-268-9522
support@primrosecandy.com
www.primrosecandy.com
Salt water taffy, lollipops, popcorn, sugar-free candies, and hard and chewy confections.
President/CEO: Mark Puch
mvp@primrosecandy.com
VP Sales/Marketing: Richard Griseto
Estimated Sales: $27,800,000
Number Employees: 100-249
Number of Brands: 2
Square Footage: 95000
Type of Packaging: Consumer, Food Service, Private Label, Bulk
Brands:
　Primrose
　Rockin' Rods

10306 Prince Michel
154 Winery Ln
Leon, VA 22725-2511
540-547-3707
Fax: 540-547-3088 800-869-8242
www.princemichel.com
Wine
Owner: Kristin Holzman
kholzman@princemichel.com
Estimated Sales: $5-10 Million
Number Employees: 20-49

Food Manufacturers / A-Z

10307 Prince of Peace
3536 Arden Rd
Hayward, CA 94545-3908
510-887-1899
Fax: 510-887-1799 800-732-2328
popsf@popus.com www.princeofpeacecharity.org
Ginseng tea
Vice President: Lolita Lim
lolita@popus.com
VP Finance: Agnes Tsang
National Sales Manager: Mike Jarrett
Purchasing: Maria Wong
Estimated Sales: $11,200,000
Number Employees: 20-49
Square Footage: 145548
Brands:
  Gx Power
  Hazelnut
  Jamaican Gold
  Mocha
  Nature Soothe
  New Jamaican Gold Cappuccino
  Prince of Peace
  Prince of Peace Hawaiian
  Tiger Balm Analgesic Ointments

10308 Principe Foods USA
3605 Long Beach Blvd
Suite 200
Long Beach, CA 90807
310-680-5500
Fax: 559-272-6183
Deli meats
Brands:
  Principe

10309 Prinova
285 Fullerton Ave
Carol Stream, IL 60188-1886
630-868-0300
Fax: 630-868-0310 info@prinovausa.com
www.prinovausa.com
Ascorbic acid, B vitamins and amino acids
Owner: Donald Thorp
sales@premiumingredients.com
Number Employees: 10-19

10310 (HQ)Printpack Inc.
2800 Overlook Pkwy. NE
Atlanta, GA 30339
404-460-7000
info@printpack.com
www.printpack.com
Printed, coated, laminated and flexible film, rolls, sheets and heat sealing paper; also, candy bar and meat wrappers.
Chairman & CEO: Jimmy Love
Senior VP & CFO: Tripp Seitter
Year Founded: 1956
Estimated Sales: Over $1 Billion
Number Employees: 1000-4999

10311 Private Harvest
5009 Windplay Dr
Suite 2
El Dorado Hills, CA 95762-9316
916-933-7080
Sauces and spreads.
President: Lynn Lok
Manager: Bonnie Ewing
Estimated Sales: $5-10 Million
Number Employees: 10
Parent Co: Private Harvest
Type of Packaging: Private Label
Brands:
  Bobby Flay
  Private Harvest
  Private Harvest Bobby Flay
  Private Harvest Tuscan Hills
  Tuscan Hills

10312 Private Label Foods
P.O.Box 60805
Rochester, NY 14606
585-254-9205
Fax: 585-254-0186 info@privatelabelfoods.com
www.privatelabelfoods.com
Sauces, salad dressings, salsa and marinades
President: Frank Lavorato
VP: Bonnie Lavorato
Estimated Sales: $4 Million
Number Employees: 10-19
Square Footage: 200000
Type of Packaging: Food Service, Private Label

10313 Private Spring Water
13240 Llagas Ave
San Martin, CA 95046-9562
408-681-1500
Fax: 408-686-2100 877-664-1500
info@privatespringwater.com
www.privatespringwater.com
Bottled water
Owner: Ken Churchill
ken@privatespringwater.com
Number Employees: 10-19

10314 Pro Form Labs
PO Box 626
Orinda, CA 94563
707-752-9010
Fax: 707-752-9014 info@proformlabs.com
www.proformlabs.com
Nutritional powders and vitamins; weight control and sports nutrition tablets, capsules and powders
President: Doug Gillespie
Customer Service: Kellie Henry
Purchasing Agent: Alex Gillespie
Estimated Sales: $3-5 Million
Number Employees: 1-4
Square Footage: 100000
Parent Co: Gillespie & Associates
Type of Packaging: Consumer, Food Service, Private Label, Bulk
Brands:
  Healthbody
  Juice-Mate
  Naturslim

10315 Pro Pac Labs
P.O.Box 9691
Ogden, UT 84409
801-621-0900
Fax: 801-621-0930 888-277-6722
Herbs, vitamins and minerals
President: Lew Wheelwright
CEO: Kim Wheelwright
Contact: Lauri Christiansen
lchristiansen@propaclabs.com
Estimated Sales: $9 Million
Number Employees: 100
Type of Packaging: Consumer, Private Label, Bulk

10316 Pro Portion Food
217 N Main Street
Sayville, NY 11782-2512
631-567-4494
Fax: 631-567-1636
Health and dietetics foods
President: Rhoda Rubin
Estimated Sales: $5-10 000,000
Number Employees: 15

10317 Pro-Source Performance Prods
2231 Landmark Pl
Manasquan, NJ 08736-1026
732-528-3260
Fax: 320-763-7996 www.prosource.net
Bodybuilding and nutritional supplements
Director: Donald Crank
Contact: Tom Chinery
tomc@prosource.net
Estimated Sales: $2.5-5 Million
Number Employees: 5-9
Brands:
  Prosource

10318 ProFormance Foods
99 Meserole St
Apt 1
Brooklyn, NY 11206-2014
703-869-3413
info@eatprotes.com
eatprotes.com
Chips
Contact: Ryan Wiltse
Brands:
  Protes

10319 Proacec USA
1158 26th Street
Suite 509
Santa Monica, CA 90403-4621
310-996-7770
Fax: 310-996-7772 www.proacec.com
Olives and olive oil
President: Paul Short
Estimated Sales: Below $5 Million
Number Employees: 10

Number of Brands: 4
Number of Products: 30
Square Footage: 2000
Type of Packaging: Consumer, Food Service, Bulk
Brands:
  Caroliva
  Don Quixate
  El Carmen
  Plantio Del Condado

10320 Probar
190 N Apollo Rd.
Salt Lake City, UT 84116
Fax: 801-456-8880 800-921-2294
info@theprobar.com www.theprobar.com
Plant based food products including snack bars, energy bites, and nut butters
President: Jules Lambert
Founder/CEO: Jeff Coleman

10321 Procell Polymers
PO Box 33
Baton Rouge, LA 70821-0033
225-978-8069
Fax: 866-860-1269
Cellulose gum, guar gum, xanthan gum and other specialty products.
Manager: David Hatcher
Manager: Harry Steeghs
Type of Packaging: Bulk

10322 Produce Buyers Company
7201 W Fort St
Suite 93
Detroit, MI 48209
313-843-0132
Produce
President: Salvatore Cipriano
Estimated Sales: $1-3 Million
Number Employees: 1-4

10323 Producer Marketing Overlake
700 N Capitol Way
Olympia, WA 98512
360-352-9096
Fax: 360-352-8076
info@olympiafarmersmarket.com
www.olympiafarmersmarket.com
Blueberries, strawberries, sliced peaches, Marion blackberries, raspberries
President: Rod Cook
Sales: Paul Askier
General Manager: Bill Whaley
Estimated Sales: $5-10 Million
Number Employees: 5-9
Parent Co: Overlake Farms
Type of Packaging: Consumer, Food Service, Private Label, Bulk
Brands:
  Bee Sweet
  Overlake

10324 Producers Cooperative
1800 N Texas Ave
Bryan, TX 77803-1831
979-778-6000
Fax: 979-778-0243
producers@producerscooperative.com
www.producerscooperative.com
Pinto beans
Manager: Bob Beyer
Manager: Martin Jackson
martin.jackson@nestle.com
General Manager: Eob Beyer
Number Employees: 5-9
Square Footage: 40000
Type of Packaging: Private Label
Brands:
  Cowboy
  Hub of the Uncompaghre

10325 Producers Cooperative Oil Mill
6 SE 4th St
Oklahoma City, OK 73129-1000
405-232-7555
Fax: 405-236-4887 www.producerscoop.net
Cottonseed
President/Chief Executive Officer: Gary Conkling
gary.conkling@producerscoop.net
Director, Health, Safety & Environment: Becky Mosshammer
Estimated Sales: $15 Million
Number Employees: 50-99
Number of Products: 1

Food Manufacturers / A-Z

10326 Producers Dairy Foods Inc
250 E Belmont Ave
Fresno, CA 93701
559-264-6583
Fax: 559-457-4683
customer.service@producersdairy.com
www.producersdairy.com
Milk, yogurt, cottage cheese, ice cream, eggs, butter, water and juice
President: Scott Shehadey
Director of Sales & Marketing: Richie Shehadey
Year Founded: 1932
Estimated Sales: $100 Million
Number Employees: 20-49

10327 Producers Peanut Company
PO Box 250
Suffolk, VA 23434
757-539-7496
Fax: 757-934-7730   800-847-5491
pntkid@producerspeanut.com
www.producerspeanut.com
Peanuts and peanut butter
CEO: James Pond
Estimated Sales: $800,000
Number Employees: 20-49
Square Footage: 144000
Type of Packaging: Food Service, Private Label, Bulk
Brands:
   Peanut & Tree Nut
   Peanut Kids Company Store

10328 Producers Rice Mill Inc.
PO Box 1248
Stuttgart, AR 72160
870-673-4444
Fax: 870-673-7394   info@producersrice.com
www.producersrice.com
Rice and soybeans.
President/CEO: Keith Glover
kglover@producersrice.com
Chairman: Jerry Hoskyn
Year Founded: 1943
Estimated Sales: $550 Million
Number Employees: 500-999
Square Footage: 30000
Type of Packaging: Consumer, Food Service

10329 Productos Del Plata
71st 8040 NW
Miami, FL 33166
786-357-8261
Fax: 786-331-7500   info@pdpgroup.us
www.pdpgroup.us
Cookies, tea, baked goods, pasta, sauces and dessert toppings
Marketing: Mauricio Montero

10330 Produits Alimentaire
1186 Rue Du Pont
St Lambert De Lauzon, QC G0S 2W0
Canada
418-889-8080
Fax: 418-889-9730   800-463-1787
Flour, food colors, confectionery and syrup
Director: Michel Blouin
Number Employees: 20-49
Square Footage: 32000
Type of Packaging: Consumer, Food Service, Private Label, Bulk
Brands:
   Blouin
   Maltee
   Pacha
   Supreme

10331 (HQ)Produits Alimentaire
1805 Berlier St
Laval, QC H7L 3S4
Canada
514-334-5503
Fax: 514-334-3584   800-361-9326
www.berthelet.com
Flavorings, seasonings, puddings, soup bases, sauces, jams, food colorings, jelly powder, pie fillings, beverage syrups, bouillon bases, concentrates, sundae toppings and beverage crystals
Special Advisor: Guy Berthelet
Sales Manager: Pierre Berthelet
Operations & Human Resources Director: Dany Miville
Planning & Purchasing Manager: Roger Tremblay

Type of Packaging: Consumer, Food Service, Private Label, Bulk
Other Locations:
   Produits Alimentaires Berthel
   Blainville PQ
Brands:
   Berthelet
   Juwong
   Le Saucier
   McLean
   Pasta Fiesta
   Privilege
   St. Hubert
   5 Fourchettes

10332 Produits Belle Baie
10 rue du Quai
Caraquet, NB E1W 1B6
Canada
506-727-4414
Fax: 506-727-7166   info@bellebaie.com
Herring, shrimp and crab
President: Alie Lebouthiller
Vice President: Valmond Chaison
Quality Control: Georges Boudreau
Marketing & Sales Director: Fernand Brideaux
Production Manager: Georges Foulem
Estimated Sales: $10 Million
Number Employees: 150
Type of Packaging: Consumer, Food Service

10333 Produits Ronald
200 St Joseph Street
St. Damase, QC J0H 1J0
Canada
450-797-3303
Fax: 450-797-2389   800-465-0118
Canned corn-on-the-cob, marinades, sauces, baked beans, bouillons and fondue
President: Jean Messier
Vice President/General Manager: Bernard Belanger
Quality Assurance Manager: Lucie Labbe
Plant Manager: Louis Richard
Purchasing Manager: David Lussier
Number Employees: 100-249
Square Footage: 160000
Parent Co: A. Lassonde
Type of Packaging: Consumer, Food Service
Brands:
   Camino Del Sol
   Canton
   Madelaine
   Mont-Rougr
   Rougemont

10334 Profood International
670 W Fifth Ave
Suite 116
Naperville, IL 60563
630-428-2386
Fax: 630-527-9905   888-288-0081
support@profoodinternational.com
www.profoodinternational.com
Preservatives, emulsifiers, enzymes, texturizers and acids
Contact: Dave Shi
daves@profoodinternational.com

10335 Progenix Corporation
7566 N 72nd Ave
Wausau, WI 54401
715-675-7566
Fax: 715-675-4931   800-233-3356
Ginseng, whole root, fiber, prong, powder and extract; capsules, teas and gift packaging
President: Robert Duwe
Number Employees: 20-49
Square Footage: 26000
Type of Packaging: Consumer, Food Service, Bulk
Brands:
   Ameriseng
   Wiscon
   Wisconsin American Ginseng

10336 Progressive Flavors
409 E. Main
Madison, WI 53703
608-257-4626
Fax: 805-383-2644   800-827-0555
Flavors
President: Norma Schwarz
Estimated Sales: $5-10 Million
Number Employees: 4
Type of Packaging: Food Service, Bulk

10337 Progresso Quality Foods
500 W Elmer Rd
Vineland, NJ 08360-6314
856-691-1565
Fax: 856-794-1574   www.generalmills.com
Canned soups, bread crumbs, cooking oils and spaghetti sauce
CEO: John Komer
Estimated Sales: $61 Thousand
Number Employees: 20-49
Number of Brands: 1
Square Footage: 600000
Parent Co: General Mills
Type of Packaging: Consumer
Brands:
   Progresso

10338 Prohibition Distillery, LLC
10 Union St.
Roscoe, NY 12776
917-685-8989
www.prohibitiondistillery.com
Vodka, gin, whiskey
Co-Founder: Brian Facquet
Co-Founder: John Walsh
Number of Brands: 1
Number of Products: 3

10339 Project 7
302 N El Camino Real
Suite 216
San Clemente, CA 92672
949-891-0729
Fax: 949-613-7170   info@project7.com
project7.com
Specialty candy and gum
President: Tyler Merrick
Controller: Paul Luster
Contact: Anoush Alexanian
alexanian@project7.com
Year Founded: 2008
Number Employees: 6

10340 Prolimer Foods
104 Liberte Avenue
Candiac, QC J5R 6X1
Canada
450-635-4631
Fax: 450-635-4637   877-535-4631
Hors d'oeuvres, appetizers, ready meals, pizza, soup, seafood, vegetables, fruit and olives
Marketing: Nicolas Bergeron

10341 Prolume
163 W. White Mountain Blvd
Lakeside, AZ 85929-7004
928-367-1200
Fax: 928-367-1205   info@prolume.com
www.prolume.com
Bioluminescence ingredients
CEO: Bruce Bryan
Brands:
   Prolume

10342 (HQ)Promised Land Dairy
Colorado Springs, CO 80907
877-520-2479
consumercare@promisedlanddairy.com
www.promisedlanddairy.com
Milk products
General Sales Managers: Gordon Kuenemann
Director of Operations: Dene Smith
Year Founded: 1987
Estimated Sales: $50-100 Million
Square Footage: 35167
Type of Packaging: Consumer

10343 Prommus Brands
Chicago, IL
www.prommus.com
Hummus
Founder: Anthony Brahimsha
Year Founded: 2014

10344 (HQ)Promolux Lighting
Box 40
Shawnigan Lake, BC V0R 2W0
Canada
250-743-1222
Fax: 250-743-1221   800-519-1222
info2@promolux.com   www.promolux.com
Lighting for food display cases

1043

Food Manufacturers / A-Z

President: Mark Granfar
Quality Control: Trevor Brien
Marketing: Lyn Rose
Sales: Scott Werhun
Purchasing: Michael Vankesteron
Estimated Sales: $10-20 Million
Number Employees: 20
Number of Products: 3
Square Footage: 4000
Parent Co: Samark SA
Type of Packaging: Private Label
Brands:
    Econofrost
    Lighting
    Long Life
    Mr16
    Multichrome
    Promolux

10345 Promotion in Motion Companies
PO Box 558
Closter, NJ 07624-0558
    201-784-5800
    800-369-7391
mail@promotioninmotion.com
www.promotioninmotion.com
Brand name confections, fruit snacks and other fine foods
President/CEO: Michael Rosenberg
mrosenberg@promotioninmotion.com
Executive Director: Frank McSorley
COO: Basant Dwivedi
Number Employees: 250-499
Type of Packaging: Private Label

10346 Proper-Chem
46 Arbor Ln
Dix Hills, NY 11746
    631-420-8000
    Fax: 631-420-8003
Vitamins and supplements
President: Emil Backstrom
Estimated Sales: $3-5 Million
Number Employees: 10-19
Square Footage: 40000
Type of Packaging: Consumer, Private Label
Brands:
    Goubaud
    Proper-Care

10347 Prosperity Organic Foods
475 West Main Street
Boise, ID 83702
    208-429-9800
    Fax: 208-854-0907 888-557-5741
www.meltbutteryspread.com
Organic butter and spread substitutes.
Founder: Cynthia Rapp
Consumer Products Leader: Meg Carlson
Contact: John Horne
john@meltorganic.com
Type of Packaging: Consumer
Brands:
    MELT ORGANIC

10348 Protano's Bakery
2301 N 22nd Ave
Hollywood, FL 33020-2003
    954-925-3474
    Fax: 954-925-3488 guy@protano.com
www.protanosbakery.com
Bakery products
Owner: Guy Protano Jr
greg@underweb.com
Plant Manager: Bob Woodmancy
Estimated Sales: $5-10 Million
Number Employees: 100-249

10349 Protein Research
1852 Rutan Dr
Livermore, CA 94551-7635
    925-243-6300
    Fax: 925-243-6308 800-948-1991
info@proteinresearch.com
www.proteinresearch.com
Amino acid, vitamin and mineral supplements
Owner: Robert Matheson
robert@proteinresearch.com
Director: Theodore Aarons
VP Operations: Daniel Aarons
Estimated Sales: $5-10 Million
Number Employees: 50-99
Number of Products: 12
Square Footage: 132000
Type of Packaging: Private Label, Bulk

10350 Protica Inc
1002 MacArthur Rd
Whitehall, PA 18052-7052
    610-832-2000
    Fax: 978-975-4325 800-776-8422
www.protica.com
Hydrolyzed proteins and fish gelatin
President: Peter Noble
Sales: Chris Gorski
Contact: Bill Dillon
wdillon@protica.com
Type of Packaging: Bulk

10351 Protient
PO Box 64101
St Paul, MN 55164-0101
    651-481-2068
    Fax: 507-334-8695 800-328-9680
www.landolakesinc.com
Dry cream powders, margarine and spreads
President: Christopher Policinsky
Contact: Steve Fiedler
sfiedler@landolakes.com
Number Employees: 50-99
Parent Co: Land O'Lakes
Type of Packaging: Consumer

10352 Protient
351 Hanson Way
Woodland, CA 95776
    651-638-2600
    Fax: 651-697-0997
Whey and soy proteins, hydrolysates and blends.
President: K Kachadurian
Chief Executive Officer: Nicolas Hanson
CFO: Tent Macoy
CEO: Todd Watson
Quality Control: Tom Yezzi
Market Development Specialist: Cheryl Reid
Sr Sales Manager: Kris Hanson
Estimated Sales: $5-10 Million
Number Employees: 20-49
Brands:
    Protient

10353 Protos Inc
449 Glenmeade Rd
Greensburg, PA 15601-1170
    724-836-1802
    Fax: 724-836-3895 protos@protos-inc.com
www.protos-inc.com
Ostrich meats
President: Logan Dickerson
Number Employees: 20-49
Type of Packaging: Food Service, Private Label, Bulk
Brands:
    Ostrim #1 Sports Meat Snack
    Ostrim Ostrich Saute

10354 Prova
100 Conifer Hill Drive
Suite 208
Danvers, MA 01923
    978-739-9055
    Fax: 978-739-4044 877-776-8287
contact@provaus.com www.prova.fr
Flavors: vanilla, cocoa, coffee and caramel.
Vice President of Sales, North America: M. William Graham
Contact: Muriel Acat-Vergnet
muriel.acat-vergnet@provaus.com
Parent Co: Prova SAS
Type of Packaging: Bulk

10355 Providence Cheese
49 Rotary Dr
Johnston, RI 02919
    401-421-5653
    Fax: 401-421-3870
Pasta, cheese
President/Owner: Wayne Wheatley
irwind@highlands.k12.fl.us
Estimated Sales: Less than $500,000
Number Employees: 1-4
Type of Packaging: Private Label

10356 Provimi Foods
W2103 County Road VV
Seymour, WI 54165
    920-833-6861
    Fax: 920-833-9850 800-833-8325
info@provimifoods.com www.provimifoods.com
Veal and sauces
President: Dan Schober
CFO: Rod Mackenzie
Contact: Bruce Achten
achten@provimifoods.com
Year Founded: 1982
Type of Packaging: Consumer, Food Service, Private Label, Bulk
Brands:
    Provimi

10357 Provitas LLC
5204 Blackhawk Dr
Plano, TX 75093-4901
    972-767-8867
    Fax: 972-793-8639 www.provitasllc.com
Vitamin powders, emulsions and oils
President: Mac Weber
Manager: Jenny Weber
Number Employees: 10-19
Type of Packaging: Bulk

10358 Provost Packers
5340 49th Avenue
PO Box 570
Provost, AB T0B 3S0
Canada
    780-753-2415
    Fax: 780-753-2413
Beef, pork and sausage
President: Bernard Bouma
Sales Manager: Lyle Bouma
Estimated Sales: $1-2 Million
Number Employees: 10-19
Square Footage: 328000
Type of Packaging: Consumer, Food Service, Private Label, Bulk
Brands:
    Dutch Brothers
    Provost Packers

10359 Pruden Packing Company
1201 North Main Street
Suffolk, VA 23434-5814
    757-539-8773
    Fax: 757-925-4971
Ham and pork shoulder
President: Peter Pruden
General Manager: K Jones
Plant Superintendent: Terry McNitt
Estimated Sales: $3.0 Million
Number Employees: 5-9
Parent Co: Smithfield Companies
Brands:
    Champon
    Peanut City
    Pruden

10360 Psycho Donuts
2006 Winchester Blvd
Suite C
Campbell, CA 95008-3400
    408-378-4540
    www.psychodonuts.com
Donuts
Owner: Web Granger
psychodonuts@gmail.com
Number Employees: 5-9

10361 Psyllium Labs
1701 E Woodfield Road
Suite 636
Schaumburg, IL 60173
    888-851-6667
info@psyllium.com www.psylliumlabs.com
Psyllium, chia and quinoa
Operations Executive: Drew West
Other Locations:
    Manufacturing Facility
    North Gujarat, India
    Manufacturing Facility
    Santa Cruz, Bolivia

10362 Publix Super Market
PO Box 407
Lakeland, FL 33802-0407
    800-242-1227
    www.publix.com
Groceries, produce, meat, seafood, deli, floral, beer, wine and dairy.
President/CEO: Todd Jones
Chairman: William Crenshaw
CFO: David Phillips

Year Founded: 1930
Estimated Sales: $38.1 Billion
Number Employees: 197,000
Other Locations:
  Bakery Manufacturing
  Atlanta GA
  Dairy/Fresh Foods Manufacturing
  Deerfield Beach FL
  Fresh Foods Manufacturing
  Jacksonville FL
  Bakery/Deli/Dairy Manufacturing
  Lakeland FL
  Dairy Manufacturing
  Lawrenceville GA

10363 Puebla Foods Inc
75 Jefferson St
Passaic, NJ 07055-6551
973-473-0201
Fax: 973-473-3854   pueblafoods@aol.com
Mexican products: tortillas, chips and taco shells, jalapenos, hot sauces, dried peppers, tomatillos and sodas
President: Felix Sanchez
VP: Carmen Sanchez
Contact: Martha Acevedo
macevedo@pueblafoods.com
General Manager: Gabriela Molina
Estimated Sales: Less Than $500,000
Number Employees: 1-4
Square Footage: 30000
Brands:
  El Ranchito
  Mipueblito
  Pueblafood

10364 Pulakos 926 Chocolate
2530 Parade St
Erie, PA 16503-2034
814-452-4026
Fax: 814-456-4876   www.pulakoschocolates.com
Chocolates
Owner: Michael Noel
mnoel@pulakoschocolates.com
VP/Treasurer: J Pulakos
Plant Manager: Pete Skelton
Estimated Sales: $1300000
Number Employees: 20-49
Square Footage: 64000
Type of Packaging: Consumer, Food Service, Private Label

10365 Pulmuone Foods USA Inc.
2315 Moore Ave.
Fullerton, CA 92833
800-588-7782
inquiry@pulmuone.com
www.pulmuonefoodsusa.com
Pastas, sauces, meat, chicken and vegetable patties, soybean products.
CEO: Hyo-Yul Lee
VP, Food Safety & Compliance: Jung Han
Manager, Product Excellence Insights: Faye Lee
Director, Marketing: Sean Kim
Director, Engineering & Technology: Brian Seong-Jun Kim
Year Founded: 1981
Estimated Sales: $1.5 Billion
Number Employees: 110
Number of Brands: 5
Parent Co: Pulmuone Co., Ltd.
Type of Packaging: Consumer, Food Service, Private Label, Bulk
Brands:
  Monterey Gourmet Foods
  Wildwood
  Emerald Valley Kitchen
  Pulmuone
  Nasoya

10366 Puratos Canada
520 Slate Dr
Mississauga, ON L5T 0A1
Canada
905-362-3668
Fax: 905-362-0296   info@puratos.ca
www.puratos.com
Dough conditioners, bases and mixes, custards, fruit compounds and fillings, glazes, chocolate products and ganache
President: Eddy Van Belle
Number Employees: 20-49
Square Footage: 160000
Parent Co: Puratos NV

10367 Pure Batch
Hillsborough, NJ
609-373-2015
info@pure-batch.com
www.pure-batch.com
Cookies
Year Founded: 2015

10368 Pure Dark
800 High Street
Hackettstown, NJ 07840
973-856-1899
dawn.gallagher@effem.com
www.puredark.com
Cocoa, baking chocolate, chocolate bars and gift packs.
Marketing: Dawn Gallagher

10369 Pure Extracts Inc
59 Remington Blvd
Suite D
Ronkonkoma, NY 11779-6991
631-588-9727
Fax: 631-588-9729
Herbs and oils
Chairman/President: Gurjeet Bajwa
Owner/Sales Exec: Joe Singh
Manager: Nat Patel
pureextracts@yahoo.com
Estimated Sales: $500,000
Number Employees: 1-4
Square Footage: 3000

10370 Pure Flo Water Co
7737 Mission Gorge Rd
Santee, CA 92071-3399
619-448-5120
Fax: 619-596-4154   800-787-3356
www.pureflo.com
Bottled water: purified, fluoridated and spring; water filtration system services
CEO: Brian Grant
bgrant@pureflo.com
General Manager: Leslie Alstad
Director of Marketing & Technology: Damon Grant
Accounting Manager: Bernadette Meyer
Estimated Sales: $13 Million
Number Employees: 100-249
Number of Brands: 1
Square Footage: 9000
Type of Packaging: Consumer, Bulk
Brands:
  Pure Flo Water

10371 Pure Food Ingredients
514 Commerce Pkwy
Verona, WI 53593
608-845-9601
Fax: 608-845-9628   800-355-9601
stan@itis.com
Canned tomatoes, chiles, jalapenos and olives; beeswax and honey
President: Stanley Kanter
Estimated Sales: $1,000,000
Number Employees: 5-9
Square Footage: 40000
Type of Packaging: Consumer, Food Service, Private Label, Bulk

10372 (HQ)Pure Foods
32533 Cascade View Drive
Sultan, WA 98294-7733
360-793-2241
Fax: 360-793-2485
Molasses and honey
President: Michael Ingalls
CEO: Denice Ingalls
Contact: Brian Albans
balbans@purefoodsco.com
Plant Manager: Dan Johnson
Estimated Sales: $5,000,000
Number Employees: 20 to 49
Square Footage: 36000
Type of Packaging: Consumer, Food Service, Private Label, Bulk
Brands:
  Bear Mountain
  Heins
  Miller's
  Pure Gold

10373 Pure Foods Meat
10 Shorncliffe Rd
Unit 5, Suite 202
Toronto, ON M9B 3S3
Canada
416-236-1163
consumercare@purefoodsmeat.ca
purefoodsmeat.ca
Pork
President: David Schwartz
VP, Business Development & Marketing: Anita Gravelle
Production Manager: Sol Colacci
Purchasing & Inventory Manager: Carla Verissimo
Year Founded: 1927
Estimated Sales: $86.05 Million
Number Employees: 600
Number of Brands: 1
Square Footage: 154591
Type of Packaging: Consumer, Food Service, Private Label, Bulk
Brands:
  Legacy Pork

10374 Pure Gourmet
719 Bridle Road
Glenside, PA 19038-2005
215-609-4219
Fax: 763-322-7035
kellymacleod@puregourmetfoods.com
Ice cream and sorbet
Manager: Kelly Macleod
kellymacleod@puregourmetfoods.com
Estimated Sales: $150,000
Number Employees: 2

10375 Pure Ground Ingredients
2535 Business Pkwy
Minden, NV 89423
775-297-4047
info@puregroundingredients.com
puregroundingredients.com
Organic herbal ingredients
Founder: Kevin Lindseth
Sales Manager: Stacy Kixmiller

10376 Pure Indian
PO Box 296
Princeton Jct., NJ 08550
609-785-9100
Fax: 302-371-3081   877-588-4433
info@pureindianfoods.com
www.pureindianfoods.com
Ghee, oils and spices
Co-Founder: Sandeep Agarwal
Co-Founder: Nalini Agarwal
Year Founded: 2008

10377 Pure Inventions LLC
64 Grant Pl
Suite 3H
Little Silver, NJ 07739-1042
732-842-5777
Fax: 732-842-8422   info@pureinventions.com
www.pureinventions.com
Nutritional extracts and supplements
Member: Lori Mulligan
Member: Lynne Gerhards
Manager: Debbie Potts
info@pureinventions.com
Manager: Johanna Cerliglione
Estimated Sales: $2 Million
Number Employees: 10-19

10378 Pure Life Organic Foods
6625 W Sahara Ave
Suite 1
Las Vegas, NV 89146
708-990-5817
info@purelifeorganicfoods.com
www.purelifeorganicfoods.com
Organic sugars, coconut milk and coconut oil
Managing Director: Pradeep Mathur
Sales and Marketing Head: Sayida Bano
Parent Co: Pure Diets Intl. Ltd.
Type of Packaging: Bulk

Food Manufacturers / A-Z

10379 Pure Milk & Ice Cream Company
1819 Rutland Dr
Austin, TX 78758-5423
512-837-2685
Fax: 512-339-0677 www.oakfarmsdairy.com
Dairy
Manager: Patrick Cummins
Production Manager: Terry Welty
Estimated Sales: $5-10 Million appx.
Number Employees: 50-99
Parent Co: Pure Milk Company

10380 Pure Planet
2610 Homestead Pl
Rancho Dominguez, CA 90220
562-951-5040 800-695-2017
Fax: 562-951-5040
info@pureplanet.com pureplanet.com
Organic plant powders
CEO: David Sandoval
dsandoval@organicbynatureinc.com
President: Amy Sandoval
General Sales Manager: Gerry Wong
Estimated Sales: $5.6 Million
Number Employees: 50-99
Brands:
 Organic By Nature

10381 Pure Sales
660 Baker St
Suite 367
Costa Mesa, CA 92626-4470
714-540-5455
Fax: 714-540-5974 puresales@aol.com
Pasta
President: James Silver
puresales@aol.com
Estimated Sales: Under $500,000
Number Employees: 1-4

10382 Pure Source LLC
9750 NW 17th St
Doral, FL 33172-2753
305-477-8111
Fax: 305-477-4002 800-324-6273
info@thepuresource.com www.thepuresource.com
Vitamins, antioxidants, raw materials and packaging services
Owner: Joel Meyer
sylvia@thepuresource.com
Estimated Sales: Below $5 Million
Number Employees: 100-249
Square Footage: 280000
Type of Packaging: Consumer, Food Service, Private Label, Bulk
Brands:
 Pure Source

10383 Pure Sweet Honey Farms Inc
514 Commerce Pkwy
Verona, WI 53593-1841
608-845-9601
Fax: 608-845-9628 800-355-9601
map007@earthlink.net www.puresweethoney.com
Honey, maple syrup and molasses
President: Stanley Kanter
stan@chorus.net
Sales Director: Mark Pelka
Estimated Sales: $470000
Number Employees: 5-9
Square Footage: 80000
Type of Packaging: Consumer, Food Service, Private Label, Bulk
Brands:
 Springhill

10384 Pure's Food Specialties
2929 S 25th Ave
Broadview, IL 60155-4529
708-344-8884
Fax: 708-344-8703 www.puresfood.com
Cookies
President: Elliot Pure
epure@puresfood.com
Estimated Sales: Below $5 Million
Number Employees: 20-49
Type of Packaging: Bulk

10385 Pure7 Chocolate
82 Sanderson Ave
Lynn, MA 01902
844-547-8737
info@pure7chocolate.com pure7chocolate.com
Chocolate
Founder & CEO: Julie MacQueen
COO: Dennis Mehiel
Brands:
 Pure7

10386 PureCircle USA
200 W Jackson Blvd
8th Floor
Chicago, IL 60606
630-361-0374
info.usa@purecircle.com
purecircle.com
Stevia
CEO: Lai Hock Meng
CFO: Lim Kian Thong
Year Founded: 2001
Estimated Sales: $127 Million
Parent Co: PureCircle Limited
Type of Packaging: Bulk

10387 PureForm CBD
Los Angeles, CA
www.pureformglobal.com
Manufacturer of non-hemp-based CBD for consumer brands
President/Owner: Jake Cormier

10388 Purely American
5635 Raby Road
Suite H
Norfolk, VA 23502
757-466-1312
Fax: 757-466-3041 800-359-7873
www.purelyamerican.com
Mixes, sauces and marinades, and peanuts.
President: Ray Leard
Estimated Sales: $500,000
Number Employees: 5
Type of Packaging: Private Label
Brands:
 Peter's Beach Sauces
 Purely American

10389 Purely Elizabeth
3200 Carbon Pl
Suite 101
Boulder, CO 80301-6135
720-242-7525
Fax: 888-586-9485 support@purelyelizabeth.com
purelyelizabeth.com
Gluten-free baking mixes, granola, oatmeal and superfood bars
Founder & CEO: Elizabeth Stein
elizabeth@purelyelizabeth.com
Director of Finance: Tracy Baumann
Marketing: Paige Mitchum
Operations: Garrett McBride
Estimated Sales: Less Than $500,000
Number Employees: 10-19
Brands:
 Purely Elizabeth

10390 Purely Pecans
Valdosta, GA
800-627-6630
purelypecans.com
Grain-free granola and nut butters
Founder: Jeff Worn

10391 Puritan/ATZ Ice Cream
301 E Wayne St
Kendallville, IN 46755-1457
260-347-2700
Fax: 260-347-2652
Ice cream
GM: Terry Atz
GM: Jeff Atz
Estimated Sales: $5-10 Million
Number Employees: 10-19
Type of Packaging: Consumer, Food Service

10392 Purity Candy Co
422 Market St
Lewisburg, PA 17837-1422
570-524-0823
Fax: 570-524-7793 800-821-4748
www.puritycandy.com
Candy and chocolates
Owner: Margaret Burfeindt
m.burfeindt@purity.com
President: Theodore Roosevelt
General Manager Production: Sharon Weiser
Estimated Sales: Less Than $500,000
Number Employees: 1-4
Brands:
 Purity Candy

10393 Purity Dairies LLC
360 Murfreesboro Pike
Nashville, TN 37210-2816
615-244-1900
Fax: 615-242-8547 www.puritydairies.com
Milk, ice cream, yogurt, cottage cheese, juice, sour cream and heavy cream
President: Mark Ezell
Cmo: Tim White
tim_white@deanfoods.com
Sales Manager: Mike Payne
Number Employees: 500-999
Parent Co: Dean Foods Company
Type of Packaging: Consumer, Food Service

10394 Purity Factories
96 Blackmarsh Rd
St. John's, NL A1C 5M9
Canada
709-579-2035
Fax: 709-738-2426 800-563-3411
orderdesk@purity.nf.ca www.purity.nf.ca
Jams, fruit syrups and biscuits
General Manager: Doug Spurrell
Sales Manager: Gerry Power
Type of Packaging: Consumer, Food Service, Private Label, Bulk

10395 Purity Farms
One Organic Way
La Farge, WI 54639
303-647-2368
Fax: 303-647-9875 877-211-4819
purityfarmsorganic@gmail.com
Organic butter
President: Kathy Feldenkreis
Number Employees: 1-4
Type of Packaging: Consumer, Food Service, Private Label, Bulk
Brands:
 Purity Farms Ghee

10396 Purity Foods Inc
417 S Meridian Rd
Hudson, MI 49247-9709
517-448-2050
Fax: 517-448-2070 800-997-7358
info@purityfoods.com
www.natureslegacyforlife.com
Beans, grains, seeds, cereals, cookbooks, flours, granola, pastas, pretzels and sesame sticks.
President: Donald Stinchcomb
Regional Sales Manager: Hezeden Graye
Manager: Gabby Williamson
gabby.williamson@purityfoods.com
Estimated Sales: Less Than $500,000
Number Employees: 1-4
Square Footage: 60000

10397 Purity Ice Cream Co
700 Cascadilla St
Suite A
Ithaca, NY 14850-3255
607-272-1545
Fax: 607-272-1546 purityice@aol.com
Ice cream
Owner: Heather Lane
blane@purityicecream.com
Estimated Sales: $1000000
Number Employees: 20-49
Type of Packaging: Consumer, Food Service

10398 Purity Organic
405 14th Street
Suite 1000
Oakland, CA 94612
415-440-7777
info@purityorganic.com
purityorganic.com
Ready-to-drink juice, tea and coconut water
CEO: Douglas Abrams
Contact: Demian Flores
demian@purityorganic.com

10399 Purity Products
200 Terminal Dr
Plainview, NY 11803-2312
516-767-1967
Fax: 516-767-1722 800-256-6102
customercare@puritypproducts.com
www.puritypgoducts.com

Food Manufacturers / A-Z

Sauces, mayonnaise, vinegar, mustard, salad dressings, vegetable oils, jellies, pickles
President: William Schroeder
President, Chief Executive Officer: Jahn Levin
jahn@purityproducts.com
CFO: Bruce Morecroft
Vice President of Quality Assurance: Richard Conant
Marketing: Al Rodriquez
Operations: Ricky Montejo
Purchasing Director: Charles Menezes
Estimated Sales: Less Than $500,000
Number Employees: 20-49
Square Footage: 400000
Parent Co: Sea Specialties Company
Type of Packaging: Food Service, Private Label, Bulk
Brands:
    Chef's Choice
    Cheryl Lynn
    Ideal
    Purity

10400 Puroast Coffee Co Inc
1221 Commerce Ave
Woodland, CA 95776-5902
530-668-0976
Fax: 530-668-0989 877-569-2243
info@puroast.com www.puroast.com
Low acid coffee
President: Carrie Vannuci
CEO: Kerry Sachs
Public Relations: Beth Goldstene
Operations Manager: Victor Quero
Production Manager: Sally Lopez
Purchasing Manager: Wendy Dial
Estimated Sales: $5-10 Million
Number Employees: 10-19
Type of Packaging: Private Label
Brands:
    Puroast

10401 Putney House Trading LLC
P.O. Box 2520
New London, NH 03257
603-526-2336
Fax: 603-526-2386 sales@cavedonibalsamic.com
cavedonibalsamic.com
Vinegar; balsamic condiments
President/Owner: Paolo Cavedoni
Year Founded: 1860
Type of Packaging: Private Label
Brands:
    Cavedoni Balsamic

10402 Putney Pasta
28 Vernon St
Suite 434
Brattleboro, VT 05301-3668
802-257-4800
Fax: 802-875-3322 800-253-3683
Pastas: tortellini, ravioli, agnolotti, fettucine, linguine, angel hair and gnocchi; sauses.
President: Rick McKelzey
carol@putneypasta.com
Estimated Sales: $3 Million
Number Employees: 1-4
Number of Brands: 1
Number of Products: 35
Square Footage: 168000
Type of Packaging: Consumer, Food Service, Private Label
Brands:
    Putney Pasta

10403 Puueo Poi Shop
265 Kekuanaoa St
Suite D
Hilo, HI 96720-4396
808-935-8435
Fax: 808-934-7762
Hawaiian food: poi, lau-lau and kalua
Owner: Gilbert Chang
VP: Okyo Chang
Business Manager: Shirlene Rayoan
Estimated Sales: $500,000
Number Employees: 1-4
Square Footage: 11000
Type of Packaging: Consumer, Food Service, Private Label, Bulk
Brands:
    Puueo Poi

10404 Pyramid Alehouse-Seattle
1201 1st Ave S
Seattle, WA 98134-1238
206-682-3377
Fax: 206-621-8483 host@pyramidbrew.com
www.pyramidbrew.com
Beer and soda
Manager: Alex Krallis
CFO: Eric Peterson
j.schaller@pyramidbrew.com
CFO: Wayne Drury
Chairman: George Hancock
Chairman: Martin Kelly
Site Manager: Jack Schaller
j.schaller@pyramidbrew.com
Estimated Sales: Under $500,000
Number Employees: 100-249
Type of Packaging: Private Label
Brands:
    Amber Wheat Beer
    Best Brown Ale
    Hart
    Thomas Kemper

10405 Pyramid Juice Company
160 Helman Street
Ashland, OR 97520-1720
541-482-2292
Fax: 541-482-1002
Organic fruit and vegetable juices
President/CEO: Judd Pindell
VP: Kim Kemske
Estimated Sales: $5-9.9 Million
Number Employees: 8
Square Footage: 14000
Brands:
    Mind's Eye Smart Drinks
    Pyramid Juice

10406 Pyrenees French Bakery
717 E 21st St
Bakersfield, CA 93305-5240
661-322-7159
Fax: 661-322-6713 888-898-7159
www.pyreneesbakery.com
Bread and rolls: sour dough, French, nine-grain, squaw, rye and whole wheat.
Owner: Marianne Laxague
order@pyreneesbakery.com
CEO: Juanita Laxague
Estimated Sales: Below $5 Million
Number Employees: 20-49
Square Footage: 86000
Brands:
    Pyrenees
    Sara Lee

10407 Pyure Brands
5405 Taylor Rd
Suite 10
Naples, FL 34109
305-509-5096
pyureorganic.com
Organic sweeteners
Founder & CEO: Ben Fleischer
Year Founded: 2008
Type of Packaging: Consumer, Bulk

10408 Q Bell Foods
PO Box 652
Nyack, NY 10960
845-358-1475
Fax: 845-353-5680
Chocolate wafer rolls and bars
Marketing: Bahram Shirazi
bshirazi@qbelfoods.com
Estimated Sales: $130,000
Number Employees: 2

10409 Q Drinks
45 Main St.
Brooklyn, NY 39425
718-398-6642
info@qdrinks.com
www.qdrinks.com
Sodas
Founder: Jordan Silbert
Contact: Meryll Cawn
meryll@qdrinks.com

10410 Q Mixers
45 Main St
Brooklyn, NY 11201
718-398-6642
info@qmixers.com
www.qdrinks.com
Bar mixers
Co-Founder & President: Ben Karlin
Founder & CEO: Jordan Silbert
Executive Vice President: Ted Roman
VP, Marketing: Jaron Berkhemer

10411 Q's Nuts
349 Highland Ave.
Somerville, MA 02144
617-764-3741
www.qsnuts.com
Roasted nuts
Co-Founder: Brian Quinn
Co-Founder: Beth Quinn

10412 Q.E. Tea
533 Washington Ave
Suite 100
Bridgeville, PA 15017
412-221-4444
800-622-8327
qetea@aol.com
Coffees and teas
President: Paul Rankin
Marketing Manager: Peter Shaffalo
Estimated Sales: $500,000-$1 Million
Number Employees: 5-9
Square Footage: 24000
Brands:
    Hedley's
    Q.E.

10413 QBI
500 Metuchen Road
South Plainfield, NJ 07080-4810
908-668-0088
Fax: 908-561-9682
Bioflavonoids, botanical powders, herbs, nutraceuticals, antioxidants, diet and sports supplements, fruit and vegetable powders, extracts and bee pollen
President: Joseph Schortz
VP Finance: Carlos Mendez
Marketing: Joan Naso
Sales Director: Allen Lovitch
International Account Executive: Rena Strauss-Cohen
Plant Manager: Donald Andrejewski
Number Employees: 50-99
Number of Products: 500
Square Footage: 224000
Type of Packaging: Bulk
Brands:
    Phytoflow Direct Compression Herbs

10414 QST Ingredients
9734-40 6th Street
Rancho Cucamonga, CA 91730
909-989-4343
Fax: 909-989-4334 www.qsting.com
Seasonings, ingredients and sausage casings
Office Manager: Jill Mauleon

10415 Quady Winery
13181 Road 24
Madera, CA 93637-9087
559-673-8068
Fax: 559-673-0744 800-733-8068
info@quadywinery.com www.quadywinery.com
Wines
President: Andrew Quady
Chief Financial Officer: Laurel Quady
Assistant Marketing Manager: Colin Hugh
Winemaker: Darin Peterson
Number of Products: 7
Brands:
    Electra
    Elysium
    Essensia
    Starbound
    Sweet Dessert Wine

10416 Quail Ridge Cellars & Vineyards
1155 Mee Lane
Saint Helena, CA 94574-9792
707-963-9783
Fax: 707-963-3593 800-706-9463
retail@ruthbench.com

Food Manufacturers / A-Z

Wine
President and CEO: Phillip Wade
CFO: Anthony Bell
Marketing Director: Michael Stedman
Public Relations: Victoria Olson
Production Manager: Jenel Hageman
Estimated Sales: $2.5-5 Million
Number Employees: 10-19
Type of Packaging: Private Label
Brands:
    Bell Cellars
    Fox Brook
    Quail Creek

10417 Quaker Bonnet
175 Allen St
Buffalo, NY 14201-1515
    716-884-0435
Fax: 716-885-7245 800-283-2447
liz@quakerbonnet.com www.quakerbonnet.com
Cookies and pastries
President: Liz Kolken
Vice President: Benjamin Kolken
Estimated Sales: Less than $500,000
Number Employees: 5-9
Square Footage: 17200
Type of Packaging: Consumer, Food Service, Private Label
Brands:
    Banana Moon Snack Line
    Buffalo Chips
    Quaker Bonnet

10418 Quaker Maid Meats
610 Morgantown Rd.
Reading, PA 19611
    610-376-1500
Fax: 610-376-2678 www.quakermaidmeats.com
Beef steaks, hamburger and veal patties, veal steaks and meatballs.
President: Stanley Szortyka
CFO: Andrew Sims
VP: Nancy Rubin
Director of Marketing: Joey Piazza
VP Sales: Tom Robinson
Year Founded: 1960
Estimated Sales: $20-50 Million
Number Employees: 60
Type of Packaging: Consumer, Food Service, Private Label
Brands:
    Gina Lina's
    Mama Lucia's
    Quaker Maid

10419 (HQ)Quaker Oats Company
555 W. Monroe St.
Suite 1
Chicago, IL 60661
    312-821-1000
www.quakeroats.com
Cookies, oats, oatmeal, farina, granola bars, puffed wheat, puffed rice, barley, groats, shredded wheat, pancake syrups and mixes, flour, corn syrups, baking mixes, pasta and corn meal.
Senior VP/General Manager: Robbert Rietbroek
IT: Mike Lyons
mike.lyons@pepsi.com
Estimated Sales: Over $1 Billion
Number Employees: 10000+
Number of Products: 195
Parent Co: PepsiCo
Type of Packaging: Consumer, Food Service
Brands:
    Quaker
    Life

10420 Quaker Oats Company
14 Hunter Street E
Quaker Park
Peterborough, ON K9J 7B2
Canada
    705-743-6330
Fax: 705-876-4125 800-267-6287
www.quakeroats.ca
Breakfast cereal
Business Unit Leader: Timothy McLaren
Number Employees: 500-999
Parent Co: PepsiCo Canada
Type of Packaging: Consumer, Food Service
Brands:
    Quaker

10421 Quaker Sugar Company
432 Rodney St
Brooklyn, NY 11211-3482
    718-387-6500
Fax: 718-963-2767 info@quakersugar.com
www.quakersugar.com
Sugar
Owner: Harriet Gelfas
Contact: Ralph Balsamo
rbalsamo@quakersugar.com
Operations Manager: Adam Wechsler
Production Manager: Harry Wechsler
Estimated Sales: $1500000
Number Employees: 20-49
Type of Packaging: Consumer, Bulk
Brands:
    Diamond

10422 Quali Tech Inc
318 Lake Hazeltine Dr
Chaska, MN 55318-1093
    952-448-5151
Fax: 952-448-3603 800-328-5870
qtfood@qualitechco.com www.qualitechco.com
Food particulates, inclusions and pellets
President: Mike Hodgens
mikeh@qualitechco.com
CFO: Tom Halverson
Vice President of Business Development: Kye Ploen
Number Employees: 100-249
Square Footage: 180000
Type of Packaging: Bulk
Brands:
    Flav-R-Grain
    Flavor-Ettes
    Flavor-Lites
    Pell-Ettes
    Pepr
    Season-Ettes

10423 QualiGourmet
3780 rue La Verendrye
Boisbriand, QC J7H 1R5
Canada
    514-287-3530
Fax: 514-287-3510 info@qualigourmet.ca
www.qualigourmet.ca
Salmon, mackerel, foie gras, duck, trout, caviar, charcuterie, jellies, fruit and wild berries
General Manager: Cathy Sahut
Buyer: Steve Labonte
Number Employees: 5-9
Type of Packaging: Food Service

10424 Qualicaps Inc
6505 Franz Warner Pkwy
Whitsett, NC 27377-9215
    336-449-7300
Fax: 336-449-3333 800-227-7853
info@qualicaps.com www.qualicaps.com
Gelatin capsules
President: Greg Bowers
Sales: Matt Schappert
CFO: Dennis Stella
CEO: Herb Hugill
Quality Control: Schuck Waldroup
Estimated Sales: $5-10 Million
Number Employees: 100-249
Parent Co: Shionogi
Type of Packaging: Bulk

10425 Qualifresh Michel St. Arneault
4605 Thibault Avenue
St. Hubert, QC J3Y 3S8
Canada
    450-445-0550
Fax: 450-445-5687 800-565-0550
French fries
President: Michelle St. Arneaul
National Manager, Sales And Marketing: Marc Dumas
Number Employees: 50-99
Type of Packaging: Consumer, Food Service, Private Label
Brands:
    Golden Crop
    Qualifreeze
    Qualifresh

10426 Quality Bakery
Box 519
1305-7th Ave
Invermere, BC V0A 1K0
Canada
    Fax: 888-682-9977 888-681-9977
info@healthybread.com www.healthybread.com
Rye bread
President: Peter Banga
Estimated Sales: $1.1 Million
Number Employees: 6
Square Footage: 30000
Type of Packaging: Consumer, Food Service, Private Label, Bulk
Brands:
    Invermere
    Quality Bakery
    Yukon Sourdough Recipe

10427 Quality Bakery Products
14330 Interdrive W
Houston, TX 77032-3316
    281-449-4977
Fax: 281-449-7820 866-449-4977
www.qualitybakeryproducts.net
Bread crumbs, croutons and stuffings, cakes, fruit fillings, cake glazes, and cheese pies
Vice President: Mike Tills
mtills@qualitybakeryproducts.net
Purchasing Manager: Henry Wellborn
Estimated Sales: $2.5-5 Million
Number Employees: 20-49
Type of Packaging: Consumer, Food Service, Private Label, Bulk
Brands:
    Quality Hearth

10428 Quality Candy Company
525 S Lemon Avenue
DFL Warehouse
Walnut, CA 91789
    909-444-1025
Fax: 909-595-4181 customerservice@qcandy.com
www.qcandy.com
Candy
CEO: Pierre Redmond
Estimated Sales: $10-20 Million
Number Employees: 20-49
Brands:
    Choco-Starlight
    Spi-C-Mint

10429 Quality Crab Co Inc
177 Knobbs Creek Dr
Elizabeth City, NC 27909-7002
    252-338-0808
Fax: 252-338-6290 www.qualityseafoodco.com
Seafood
Owner: Billy Barclift
info@qualityseafoodco.com
VP: Roy Martin III
R&D Director: Rick Durren
Estimated Sales: $11,400,000
Number Employees: 50-99
Square Footage: 48000
Type of Packaging: Private Label
Brands:
    Jumbo Lump

10430 Quality Croutons
4031 S Racine Ave
Chicago, IL 60609
    773-890-2343
Fax: 773-927-8228 800-334-2796
Croutons and packaging services
President: David M Moore
Marketing/Sales: Deadra Ashford
Contact: Brandon Beavers
bbeavers@infomatrix.com
Production Manager: Keith Taylor
Estimated Sales: $1900000
Number Employees: 20-49
Square Footage: 140000
Type of Packaging: Food Service, Private Label, Bulk

10431 Quality Dairy Co
947 Trowbridge Rd
East Lansing, MI 48823-5217
    517-319-4114
www.qualitydairy.com
Milk, ice cream and fruit juices

Food Manufacturers / A-Z

Manager: Swadhyaya Bey
Director, Retail Operations & Marketing: Michael Kosloski
Estimated Sales: Below $5 Million
Number Employees: 5-9
Type of Packaging: Private Label

10432 Quality Fisheries
157 Arbor St
Niota, IL 62358-1005
217-448-4241
Fax: 217-448-4021 qualityfisheries@yahoo.com
www.niotafishmarket.com
Seafood
Owner: Kirby Marsden
k.marsden@mchsi.com
Estimated Sales: $1 Million
Number Employees: 5-9
Square Footage: 24000

10433 Quality Food Company
25 Bath Street
Providence, RI 2908
401-421-5668
Fax: 401-421-8570 877-233-3462
info@qualityfoodcompany.com
www.qualitybeefcompany.com
Ground beef and seafood
Secretary: William Catauro
billcatauro@qualityfoodcompany.com
Vice President: Vincent Catauro, III
Sales: Gary Flynn
Purchasing: Mark Engelhardt
Year Founded: 1931
Estimated Sales: $10-20 Million
Number Employees: 20-49
Type of Packaging: Food Service

10434 Quality Food Products Inc
172 N Peoria St
Chicago, IL 60607-2311
312-666-4559
Fax: 312-666-7133
Eggs
President: George Aralis
Owner: Jim Aralis
qfp@earthlink.net
Estimated Sales: $10-20 Million
Number Employees: 10-19

10435 Quality Foods
705 Memorial Avenue
Qualicum Beach, BC 90733-1385
Canada
250-752-9281
Fax: 310-833-5424 877-833-7890
www.qualityfoods.com
Ethnic cuisine, snacks, fried onions, spices, chutneys, teas, pastes, pickles, sauces, salsa, dressings, marinades, relishes, mustard and condiments
Director of Operations: Ken Schley
Estimated Sales: $1-2.5 Million
Number Employees: 5-9
Brands:
 California Cuisine
 Clara's Kitchen
 Cummings & York
 Hothothot
 Jewel of India
 Mariachi
 Nara
 Nonna D'S
 Samos
 Sarah's Garden
 Simple Nevada
 Simply
 Skull & Bones
 Tara Foods
 Tomales Bay
 Tombstone

10436 Quality Ingredients
14300 Rosemount Dr
Burnsville, MN 55306-6925
952-898-4002
Fax: 952-898-4421 info@qic.us
www.qic.us
Powders: shortening, cream, whip, cheese, lemon.
Services: spray drying, chilling and product development.
Director, Strategy/Marketing: Valorie Klemz
Manager: Stewart Flanery
sflanery@qic.us
Chief of Operations: Robert St.Louis

Estimated Sales: 19 Million
Number Employees: 50-99
Number of Brands: 2
Square Footage: 50000
Type of Packaging: Consumer, Food Service, Private Label, Bulk
Brands:
 QuIC-FLAVOR
 QuIC-CHEESE

10437 Quality Instant Teas
PO Box 1967
Morristown, NJ 07962-1967
973-257-9450
Fax: 973-257-9370 888-283-8327
Tea mixes and concentrates
President: Gary Vorsheim
Estimated Sales: $1 Million
Number Employees: 3
Type of Packaging: Private Label

10438 Quality Kitchen Corporation
204 Southern Blvd
Wyoming, DE 19934-1028
302-697-3118
officemail@salame.com
Juices and concentrates: grapefruit and orange
Sales: Jerry McGuire
Estimated Sales: $5,000,000
Number Employees: 20 to 49
Type of Packaging: Consumer, Food Service

10439 Quality Meats & Seafood
3239 39 St S
West Fargo, ND 58078
701-282-0202
Fax: 701-282-0583 800-342-4250
admin@qualitymeats.com www.qualitymeats.com
Portion cut beef, chicken, pork, sausage and seafood
President: Ron Jansen
CEO: Lee McCleary
CFO: Blair Kemmer
Estimated Sales: $20-50 Million
Number Employees: 50-99
Parent Co: Quality Boneless Beef Company
Type of Packaging: Consumer, Food Service, Bulk
Brands:
 Valley Maid

10440 Quality Naturally Foods
18830 San Jose Ave
City Of Industry, CA 91748-1325
626-854-6363
Fax: 626-965-0978 888-498-6986
www.qnfoods.com
Bakery mixes, icings, fillings, cappuccino and cocoa drinks
President: Frank Watase
fwatase@qnfoods.com
VP: Lincoln Watase
Sales Manager: Jerry Tuma
Number Employees: 1-4
Square Footage: 224000
Type of Packaging: Food Service, Private Label, Bulk

10441 Quality Nut Co
3006 Yosemite Blvd
PO Box 739
Modesto, CA 95354-4176
209-526-3590
Fax: 209-526-8110 www.qualitynut.com
Walnuts
Owner: George Allen
georgeallen@qualitynut.com
Year Founded: 1967
Estimated Sales: $1-3 Million
Number Employees: 50-99
Type of Packaging: Consumer, Food Service

10442 Quality Sausage Company
1925 Lone Star Dr
Dallas, TX 75212-3002
214-634-3400
Fax: 214-634-2296 www.qualitysausage.com
Meat products including meat balls, taco meat, patties, pizza toppings and pepperoni.
Chairman: Paul Birinyi
CEO: Skippers Adams
CFO: Steve O'Brien
Director of Food Safety: Mark Mar
VP Sales: Tim Burns
Year Founded: 1976
Estimated Sales: $41100000

Number Employees: 100-249
Square Footage: 100000
Parent Co: H.M. International
Type of Packaging: Food Service

10443 Quality Seafood
399 Market St
Apalachicola, FL 32320-1425
850-653-9696
Fax: 850-653-3375 staceki@yahoo.com
Shrimp
President: Robert B. Kirvin
Estimated Sales: $140,000
Number Employees: 1-4
Type of Packaging: Private Label
Brands:
 Quality

10444 Quality Snack Foods Inc
3750 W 131st St
Alsip, IL 60803
708-377-7120
Fax: 708-377-7125 sales@qsfinc.com
www.qsfinc.com
Custom packaging and manufacturing of pork rinds, and precooked bacon.
Owner: Gary Trepina
Plant Manager: Luis Esparza
Estimated Sales: $5600000
Number Employees: 5-9
Square Footage: 160000
Type of Packaging: Private Label
Brands:
 Prairieland

10445 Quality Snacks
New York, NY
Popcorn
Brands:
 New Pop(c)

10446 Quantum Energy Squares
Santa Monica, CA
quantumsquares.com
Coffee-infused energy bars

10447 Quebec Ministry of Agriculture
191 Peachtree Street N.E
Suite 3240
Atlanta, GE 30303
Canada
404-584-2995
Fax: 404-584-2089 www.foodsofquebec.com
Ice cider, berries, maple syrup, game, specialty, cheese, yogurt, pork, veal, baked goods and seafood

10448 Queen Ann Ravioli & Macaroni
7205 18th Ave
Brooklyn, NY 11204-5634
718-256-1061
Fax: 718-256-1189 queenannravioli@aol.com
www.queenannravioli.com
Italian pasta and ravioli
President: George Switzer
Estimated Sales: $5-10 Million
Number Employees: 5-9
Type of Packaging: Private Label

10449 Queen Anne Coffee Roaster
1908 Queen Anne Ave N
Seattle, WA 98109-3674
206-284-2530
info@metropolitan-market.com
www.metropolitan-market.com
Coffee
Manager: Jim Hill
Director: Eric Stone
Roaster: Susan Hamilton
Estimated Sales: Less than $500,000
Number Employees: 100-249
Brands:
 Queen Anne

10450 Queen Bee Gardens
262 E Main St
Lovell, WY 82431-2102
307-548-7994
Fax: 307-548-6721 800-225-7553
queenbee@queenbeegardens.com
Confectionery: truffles, pralines, toffee, mints and turtles
President: Clarence Zeller
Partner: Von Zeller
Vice President: Gene Zeller
Executive Secretary: Bessie Zeller

Food Manufacturers / A-Z

Estimated Sales: $3-5 Million
Number Employees: 10-19
Square Footage: 80000
Type of Packaging: Consumer, Private Label, Bulk
Brands:
　Honey Essence
　Q-Bee

10451 Queen City Coffee Company
9267 Cincinnati Dayton Rd
West Chester, OH 45069-3839
　　　　　　　　　　513-755-1095
　　Fax: 513-777-5204　800-487-7460
　　　　　　　　　　qcccorb@aol.com
Coffee beans and gift items
President: Robert Badura
Estimated Sales: $2.5-5 Million
Number Employees: 1-4
Type of Packaging: Consumer, Food Service, Private Label

10452 Queen City Sausage & Provision
1136 Straight St
Cincinnati, OH 45214-1736
　　　　　　　　　　513-541-5581
　　Fax: 513-541-6182　877-544-5588
　　　　　　www.queencitysausage.com
Sausage and luncheon meats, bologna and Dutch loaves
President: Elmer Hensler
ejhensler@queencitysausage.com
Marketing Manager: Mark Balasa
Sales Manager: Patrick Miller
Estimated Sales: $5200000
Number Employees: 20-49
Type of Packaging: Consumer, Food Service, Bulk

10453 Queen International Foods
300 S Atlantic Blvd
Suite 201d
Monterey Park, CA 91754-3228
　　　　　　　　　　626-289-0828
　　Fax: 626-289-7283　800-423-4414
Mexican food: burritos, tacos, taquitos, enchiladas and chimichangas
Owner: Liza Tang
Controller: Patricia Thistlewhite
National Sales Manager: Douglas Werner
Estimated Sales: $11,100,000
Number Employees: 1-4
Parent Co: La Reina
Type of Packaging: Consumer, Private Label
Brands:
　Anita's
　Maria's

10454 Queen of America
3220 SE County Hwy 484
Belleview, FL 34420
　　　　　　　　　　352-245-3600
　　Fax: 877-402-9523　www.queenofamerica.com
Honey, spreads and energy drinks
Type of Packaging: Consumer, Food Service, Bulk
Brands:
　BeeBad
　Mr. Honey & Mrs. Fruit
　Queen of America

10455 (HQ)Queensboro Farm Products
4 Rasbach St
PO Box 227
Canastota, NY 13032-1496
　　　　　　　　　　315-687-6133
　　　　　Fax: 315-697-8267
Cottage cheese, ice cream mix, butter and sour cream, milk
President: Steven Miller
General Manager: Don Landry
Estimated Sales: $10-20 Million
Number Employees: 50-99
Square Footage: 27800
Type of Packaging: Consumer
Brands:
　Queensboro

10456 Queensboro Farm Products
152-02 Liberty Avenue
Jamica, NY 11433
　　　　　　　　　　718-658-5000
　　　　　Fax: 718-658-0408
　　　　www.queensborofarmproducts.com
Dairy
President/CEO: Allen Miller
Controller: Andrew Flitt
Estimated Sales: $33 Million
Number Employees: 80
Number of Products: 80
Type of Packaging: Consumer, Food Service

10457 Queensway Foods Company
1611 Adrian Rd
Burlingame, CA 94010
　　　　　　　　　　650-871-7770
　　Fax: 650-697-9966　info@qfco.com
　　　　　　　www.qfco.com
Chicken powder, rice sticks, peanuts, sugar, vegetable oils, preserved fruits, candy
Owner: May Huang
Contact: Ashly Grzyb
ashly.grzyb@redtri.com
Manager: Tim Yuen
Estimated Sales: $5-10 Million
Number Employees: 5-9
Brands:
　American Queen
　Ameriqueen Brand
　Auntie Liu's
　Chic Jiang
　San Gallio
　Tang Hoi Kee
　White Rabbit

10458 Quelle Quiche
814 Hanley Industrial Court
Brentwood, MO 63144-1403
　　　　　　　　　　314-961-6554
Quiches: lorraine, spinach, broccoli and crab meat
President: Eric Victor Cowle
VP: G Daniella Cowle
Number Employees: 10-19
Square Footage: 34000
Parent Co: Renaissance Foods
Type of Packaging: Consumer, Food Service, Private Label
Brands:
　Les Petites
　Quelle

10459 Quetzal Internet Cafe
1234 Polk St
San Francisco, CA 94109-5542
　　　　　　　　　　415-800-7167
　　Fax: 415-673-4182　888-673-8181
Coffee beans
Owner: Wayne Newman
Estimated Sales: Less Than $500,000
Number Employees: 5-9
Type of Packaging: Private Label

10460 Quibell Spring Water Beverage
328 E Church Street
Martinsville, VA 24112-2909
　　　　　　　　　　540-632-0100
　　Fax: 540-344-0311　ieanne@quibell.com
Bottled water
President/Chairman: John Franck
Marketing Director: Dave Vandergrift
VP: Will Pannill
Plant Manager: Jeanne Staley
Estimated Sales: $1-2.5 Million appx.
Number Employees: 5
Square Footage: 288
Type of Packaging: Private Label
Brands:
　Quibell

10461 Quigley Industries Inc
38880 Grand River Ave
Farmington, MI 48335-1526
　　　　　　　　　　248-426-8600
　　Fax: 248-426-8607　800-367-2441
　　sales@quigleyind.com　www.quigleyind.com
Confections and lozenges
Owner: Carol Quigley
VP: David Hess
Marketing: Libby Moyer
Plant Manager: Tom Nissley
Purchasing Director: William Latsha
Estimated Sales: $9500000
Number Employees: 20-49
Square Footage: 72000
Parent Co: Joel
Type of Packaging: Consumer, Private Label, Bulk
Brands:
　Old Fashioned
　Simon
　Simons

10462 Quilceda Creek Vintners
11306 52nd St SE
Snohomish, WA 98290-5727
　　　　　　　　　　360-568-2389
　　Fax: 360-568-2389　info@quilcedacreek.com
　　　　　　www.quilcedacreek.com
Wine
Partner: Alexander Golitzin
Partner: Jeannette Golitzin
jeannette@quilcedacreek.com
Estimated Sales: $350,000
Number Employees: 5-9
Type of Packaging: Consumer
Brands:
　Quilceda Creek Vintners

10463 Quillin Produce Co
3120 Fresh Way SW
PO Box 225
Huntsville, AL 35805-6720
　　　　　　　　　　256-883-7374
　　　　　Fax: 256-883-7364
　　　　jimQuillin@quillinproduce.com
　　　　　www.quillinproduce.com
Whole and freshly cut produce
President: Jim Quillin
jimquillin@quillinproduce.com
Vice President: Wanda Quillan
Office Manager: Amanda Quillan
Comptroller: Tricia Quillan Morris
Buyer: Andy Quillan
Customer Service Manager: Jamie Thomas
Estimated Sales: $5-10 Million
Number Employees: 10-19

10464 Quillisascut Cheese Co
2409 Pleasant Valley Rd
Rice, WA 99167-9706
　　　　　　　　　　509-738-2011
　　　　loralea1@centurytel.net
　　　　　www.quillisascut.com
Goat cheese
Owner: Lora Misterly
loralea@quillisascut.com
Owner: Lore Lea
Number Employees: 20-49
Type of Packaging: Food Service
Brands:
　Quillisascut Cheese

10465 Quinault Pride
100 W Quinault St
Taholah, WA 98587
　　　　　　　　　　360-276-4431
　　　　　Fax: 360-276-4880
Salmon: precooked, canned and foil pouched
Manager: Alan Heather
sunderwood@quinault.org
CFO: William Parkshurst
Sales Exec: David Underwood
Estimated Sales: $5-10 Million
Number Employees: 20-49
Type of Packaging: Consumer, Food Service, Private Label, Bulk

10466 Quinn Snacks
Boulder, CO
　　　　　　　　　　303-927-6655
　　quinnpopcrew@quinnpopcorn.com
　　　　　www.quinnsnacks.com
Popcorn and pretzels
Co-Founder: Kristy Lewis
Co-Founder: Coulter Lewis
Brands:
　Quinn

10467 Quinoa Corporation
PO Box 279
Gardena, CA 90248
　　　　　　　　　　310-217-8125
　　Fax: 310-217-8140　quinoacorp@aol.com
Pasta and grains
President: Dave Schnorr
Contact: Tom Spielberger
toms@quinoa.net
Estimated Sales: Below $5 Million
Number Employees: 1-4
Type of Packaging: Bulk
Brands:
　Ancient Harvest Quinoa
　Supergrain Pasta

Food Manufacturers / A-Z

10468 Quintessential Chocolates
251 W Main St
PO Box 687
Fredericksburg, TX 78624-3709
830-990-9382
Fax: 830-997-0811 800-842-3382
www.liquidchocolates.com
Chocolates
President: Lecia Duke
lduke@chocolat-tx.us
Sales: Hib Shelton
Public Relations: Carolyn Debus
Operations: Aaron Beeman
Production: Kelly Sundheimer
Purchasing: Jo Baethge
Estimated Sales: Less than $500,000
Number Employees: 5-9
Brands:
  Canadian Blended Whisky Chocolates
  Cutty Sark(r) Scots Whisky Chocolates
  Jack Daniels
  Kentucky Bourbon Chocolates
  McCallan
  Sam Houston Bourbon(tm) Chocolates
  Whidbey's

10469 Quinzani Bakery
380 Harrison Ave
Boston, MA 02118-2281
617-426-2114
Fax: 617-451-8075 800-999-1062
Sandwich rolls, dinner rolls, French and Italian breads
President: Steven Quinzani
Purchasing Manager: Larry Quinzani
larryquinzani@quinzanisbakery.com
Estimated Sales: $10 Million
Number Employees: 50-99
Type of Packaging: Consumer, Food Service
Brands:
  Quinzani

10470 (HQ)Quirch Foods
2701 S Le Jeune Rd.
12th Fl.
Coral Gables, FL 33134
800-458-5252
info@quirchfoods.com www.quirchfoods.com
Beef, pork, poultry, seafood, and deli meats.
President: Frank Grande
Year Founded: 1967
Type of Packaging: Private Label

10471 Quivira Vineyards & Winery
4900 W Dry Creek Rd
Healdsburg, CA 95448-9721
707-431-8333
Fax: 707-431-1664 800-292-8339
quivira@quivirawine.com www.quivirawine.com
Wines
Manager: Kris Cuneo
Co-Founder: Henry Wendt
Vineyard Manager: Tony Castellanos
Winemaker/General Manager: Grady Wann
National Sales Manager: Bill Wiebalk
Direct Sales & Inventory: Denise Rose
Assistant Tasting Room Manager: Jana Aitken
Concierge Relations: Pam Jorgensen
Winemaker: Steven Canter
COO: Denise Sanders
Cellar Master: Adam Armstrong
Accounting Manager: Sheila Williams
Office Administrator: Lori-Jo Martin
Estimated Sales: Below $5 Million
Number Employees: 10-19
Type of Packaging: Private Label
Brands:
  Quivira

10472 Quong Hop & Company
40 Airport Blvd
S San Francisco, CA 94080
650-553-9900
Fax: 650-952-3329
Soy deli tofu, tofu burgers, hummus and tempeh
President/CEO: Frank Stephens
Estimated Sales: $3.1 Million
Number Employees: 42
Square Footage: 40000
Type of Packaging: Consumer, Food Service, Private Label, Bulk
Brands:
  Quong Hop
  Raquel's
  Soy Deli

10473 Quorn Foods
PO Box 10789
Chicago, IL 60610
customer.services@quornfoods.com
www.quorn.us
Vegetarian frozen meats
CEO: Kevin Brennan

10474 R & D Sausage Co
15714 Waterloo Rd
Cleveland, OH 44110-1660
216-692-1832
Sausage
Owner: Joseph Zuzak
Estimated Sales: Less Than $500,000
Number Employees: 1-4
Type of Packaging: Consumer, Bulk

10475 R & R Seafood
801 1st Ave
Tybee Island, GA 31328
912-786-5504
Fax: 912-786-5504
Seafood
Owner: Robbie Robertson
Estimated Sales: Less than $100,000
Number Employees: 1-4

10476 R & S Mexican Food
5818 W Maryland Ave
Glendale, AZ 85301-3909
602-272-2727
Fax: 623-435-1377 www.rsmexfoods.com
Mexican foods: fruits, vegetables, canned goods, spices, tacos, tamales and tortillas
President: Danny Franks
contact@rsmexfoods.com
Sales/Marketing Manager: Mila Cano
Plant Manager: Francisco Ramirez
Estimated Sales: $4415000
Number Employees: 50-99
Square Footage: 140000
Type of Packaging: Consumer, Food Service

10477 R C Fine Foods Inc
139 Stryker Ln
Hillsborough, NJ 08844-1930
908-359-5500
Fax: 908-359-6957 800-526-3953
cs@rcfinefoods.com www.rcfinefoods.com
Mixes: soup, gravy, specialty, salad dressing, dessert and sauce, spices, seasonings, extracts, colors; dietetic products
Owner: Gary Cohen
gcohen@rcfinefoods.com
CEO: Anthony Todaro
Director Sales: Robert Dixon
Estimated Sales: $5,500,000
Number Employees: 50-99
Square Footage: 96000
Type of Packaging: Food Service
Brands:
  RC Fine Foods

10478 R D Laney Family Honey Co
25725 New Rd
North Liberty, IN 46554-9379
574-656-8701
Fax: 574-656-8603 info@laneyhoney.com
www.laneyhoney.com
Honey, nuts
President: Dave Laney
Co-Owner: Kay Laney
Estimated Sales: Below $500,000
Number Employees: 5-9
Type of Packaging: Consumer
Brands:
  Apple Blossom
  Autumn Wildflower
  Basswood
  Blueberry Blossom
  Buckwheat
  Clover
  Cranberry Blossom
  Michigan Star Thistle
  Orange Blossom
  Spring Blossom
  Wild Blackberry
  Wildflower

10479 R Four Meats
24 2nd St SW
Chatfield, MN 55923-1208
507-867-4180
Fax: 507-867-4180
Deer, beef, pork and lamb
Owner: Jeff Remme
connie.r4@myclearwave.net
Estimated Sales: $1-2.5 Million
Number Employees: 5-9
Type of Packaging: Consumer

10480 R I Provision Co
5 Day St
Johnston, RI 02919-4301
401-831-0815
Fax: 401-274-5508 sales@littlerhodyhotdogs.com
www.littlerhodyhotdogs.com
Sausages, franks and toppings
President: Ed Robal
sales@littlerhodyhotdogs.com
Estimated Sales: $1-2.5 Million
Number Employees: 1-4
Number of Brands: 1

10481 R L Schreiber Inc
2745 W Cypress Creek Rd
Suite B
Ft Lauderdale, FL 33309
954-972-7102
Fax: 954-972-4406 800-624-8777
www.rlschreiber.com
Soup bases, sauces, gravies, spices, spice blends, custom blending and specialty items
Chairman: Tom Schreiber
COO: Tina Michel
Estimated Sales: $5-10 Million
Number Employees: 100-249
Square Footage: 125000
Type of Packaging: Food Service, Private Label

10482 R M Felts' Packing Co
35497 General Mahone Blvd
Ivor, VA 23866-2859
757-859-6131
Fax: 757-859-6381
customerservice@feltspacking.com
www.shopvafinest.com
Smoked ham and picnic hams
President: Robert M Felts Jr
CEO: Charles Stallard
Vice President: Robbie Feuts
Estimated Sales: $3-5 Million
Number Employees: 20-49
Square Footage: 68000
Type of Packaging: Consumer, Food Service, Private Label
Brands:
  Southampton

10483 R M Lawton Cranberries Inc
221 Thomas St
Middleboro, MA 02346-3321
508-947-7465
Fax: 508-947-0280
Cranberries
Manager: Mark Di Carlo
Estimated Sales: $300,000-$375,000
Number Employees: 1-4
Type of Packaging: Food Service, Bulk
Brands:
  R.M. Lawton Cranberries

10484 R T Foods Inc
11333 N Scottsdale Rd
Suite 105
Scottsdale, AZ 85254-5186
480-596-1089
Fax: 480-596-3315 888-258-4437
www.rtfoods.com
Tempura and breaded shrimp
Owner: Jeff Krause
jeff@rtfoods.com
Number Employees: 1-4

10485 R Torre & Co
233 E Harris Ave
S San Francisco, CA 94080-6807
650-875-1200
Fax: 650-875-1600 800-775-1925
www.torani.com
Italian flavoring syrups and fruit bases

Food Manufacturers / A-Z

Principal & Owner: Paul Lucheta
CEO: Melanie Dulbecco
CFO: Scott Triou
VP Research, Development & Innovation: Don Birnbaum
VP Marketing: Julie Garlikov
Director of Human Resources: Ro Carbone
Estimated Sales: $19.7 Million
Number Employees: 100-249
Square Footage: 330000
Type of Packaging: Consumer, Food Service
Brands:
    Torani

10486 R Weaver Apiaries
16495 County Road 319
Navasota, TX 77868-6513
    936-825-2333
Fax: 936-825-3642 www.beeweaver.com
Honey
Owner: Richard Weaver
Office Manager: Risa Davis
Estimated Sales: Less Than $500,000
Number Employees: 5-9
Square Footage: 40000
Type of Packaging: Consumer, Food Service, Private Label, Bulk
Brands:
    Weaver's

10487 R&A Imports
1439 El Bosque Ct
Pacific Palisades, CA 90272
    310-454-2247
Fax: 310-459-3218 zonevdka@gte.net
Vodka
President: Veronica Pekarovic
Estimated Sales: $1-$2.5 Million
Number Employees: 1 to 4
Brands:
    Zone

10488 R&J Farms
9800 West Pleasant Home Road
West Salem, OH 44287
    419-846-3179
Fax: 419-846-9603 rjfarms@rjfarms.com
www.rjfarms.com
Soy beans, sesame and sunflower seeds, grains, flour, microwaveable popcorn, chips and pretzels, garbanzo beans
Owner: Todd Driscoll
Number Employees: 5-9
Square Footage: 80000
Type of Packaging: Consumer, Private Label, Bulk
Brands:
    Country Grown
    Whole Earth

10489 R&J Seafoods
16050 Sterling Hwy
Ninilchik, AK 99639
    907-567-3222
Fax: 907-567-7400 www.rjseafoods.com
Seafood
Plant Manager: Glen Guffey

10490 R&R Homestead Kitchen
2399 Loxley Ct
Saumico, WI 54173
    920-544-5221
Fax: 920-227-4147 888-779-8245
fudge@randrhomestead.com www.rnrfudge.com
Fudge toppings
Owner: Richard Roffers

10491 R.C. McEntire & Company
P.O.Box 5817
Columbia, SC 29250-5817
    803-799-3388
Fax: 803-254-3540
Tomatoes, peppers, lettuce, onions, cabbage and salads
Owner: Buddy McEntire
Estimated Sales: $10-20 Million
Number Employees: 10-19
Square Footage: 150000
Type of Packaging: Consumer, Food Service, Private Label, Bulk
Brands:
    Dinner Reddi
    Micro Fast
    Salad Pak
    Veg Fresh

10492 R.D. Offutt Farms
15357 US-71
Park Rapids, MN 56470
    218-732-1461
www.rdoffuttfarms.com
Potatoes
President: Keith McGovern
Number Employees: 500+

10493 R.E. Meyer Company
4611 W Adams Street
Lincoln, NE 68524-1444
    402-474-8500
Fax: 402-470-4380 888-990-2333
onlineorders@meyerfoods.com
Beef and pork
Owner: Robert Meyer
Number Employees: 100-249
Parent Co: Meyer Holdings
Type of Packaging: Food Service, Private Label, Bulk

10494 R.H. Phillips
26836 County Rd 12A
Esparto, CA 95627
    530-662-3504
Fax: 530-662-2880
Wines
Head Winemaker: Barry Bergman
Quality Control: David Keim
Public Relations: Lane Giguiere
Plant Manager: Ken Lazzaroni
Estimated Sales: 21,720,000
Number Employees: 100-249
Type of Packaging: Private Label
Brands:
    R.H. Phillips

10495 R.J. Corr Naturals
14028 S McKinley Avenue
Posen, IL 60469
    708-389-4200
Fax: 708-389-4294
Juice blends, sodas and mineral water
President: Robert Corr
General Manager: James Corr
VP Operations: Thomas Mann
Number Employees: 10-19
Square Footage: 64000
Brands:
    Gear Up
    Ginseng Rush
    Natures Flavors
    North Star
    Rj Corr
    Robert Corr

10496 R.L. Albert & Son
2001 W. Main Street
Suite 155
Stamford, CT 069020
    203-622-8655
Fax: 203-622-7454 www.albertscandy.com
Candy
CEO: Robert Katz
Sales/Marketing Manager: Jorge La Sada
Estimated Sales: $7 Million
Number Employees: 12
Brands:
    Big Baby
    Big Bol
    Fortune Bubble
    Fun Fruit
    Gum Time
    Ice Cubes
    Mint Balls
    Moritz Ice Cubes
    Neon Lasers
    Pnut Jumbo
    So Joao
    Stardrops

10497 R.L. Zeigler Company
1 Plant St.
Selma, AL 36703
    205-758-3621
Fax: 205-758-0185 800-392-6328
zeigler@zmeats.com www.zmeats.com
Lunch meats, bacon and frankfurters
Chairman/Director: James Hinton
CEO/Director: W Lackey
CFO: Ken Fitzgerald
Contact: Spencer Harris
spencerharris@zmeats.com
Year Founded: 1927
Estimated Sales: $35 Million
Number Employees: 20-49
Square Footage: 100000
Type of Packaging: Consumer, Food Service, Private Label
Brands:
    Talmadge Farms
    Zeigler

10498 R.M. Palmer Co.
77 S. 2nd Ave.
West Reading, PA 19611
    610-372-8971
sales@rmpalmer.com
www.rmpalmer.com
Confectionery items, such as chocolates.
President: Richard Palmer
Treasurer/CFO: Charles Shearer
Year Founded: 1948
Estimated Sales: $150-200 Million
Number Employees: 850
Number of Products: 500
Square Footage: 330230
Type of Packaging: Consumer, Bulk
Brands:
    R.M. Palmer

10499 R.W. Frookies
PO Box 1649
Sag Harbor, NY 11963-0060
    800-913-3663
    800-913-3663
Cookies and baked goods
President: Ned Parkhouse
Estimated Sales: Under $500,000
Number Employees: 1-4

10500 R.W. Garcia
100 Enterprise Way
Suite C230
Scotts Valley, CA 95066
    408-287-4616
Fax: 408-287-7724 rwgarcia.com
Tortilla chips and crackers
Owner: Robert Garcia
Sales Manager: Jake Stenton
robert_garcia@bd.com
Estimated Sales: $10-20 Million
Number Employees: 100-249
Square Footage: 60000
Parent Co: R.W. Garcia Company
Type of Packaging: Private Label
Brands:
    Santa Cruz

10501 RAB Food Group
80 Avenue K
Newark, NJ 07105-3803
    201-553-1100
Fax: 201-333-1809
deborah.ross@manischewitz.com
www.rabfoodgroup.com
Kosher foods: baked goods, pastas, soups, gefilte fish, grape juice and borscht.
President/CEO: Jeremy Fingerman
Vice President Sales: Kevin O'Brien
Contact: Monica Ruiz
mruiz@rabfoodgroup.com
Administrator: Deborah Ross
Number Employees: 1-4

10502 RAJB Hog Foods Inc
60 Amity St
Jersey City, NJ 07304-3510
    201-395-9400
Fax: 201-395-9409 suzymody@rajbhog.com
www.rajbhog.com
Hors d'oeuvres, appetizers, ice cream and sorbet
President: Sanjeev Modi
Vice President: Sachin Mody
Marketing & Sales Manager: Suzy Mody
Number Employees: 1-4
Square Footage: 72000

10503 RC Bottling Company
1100 Independence Ave
Evenasville, IN 47714
    812-424-7978
www.rcbeverage.com
Processor of soft drinks.
Vending Manager: Chris Blake

Food Manufacturers / A-Z

Year Founded: 1950
Estimated Sales: $20-50 Million
Number Employees: 300
Type of Packaging: Consumer, Food Service
Other Locations:
    Mayfield KY
    Vincennes IN
    Marion IL
    Scott City MO
    Beaver Dam KY
    Bowling Green KY

10504 RE Botanicals
Boulder, CO
303-214-2118
www.rebotanicals.com
Hemp-infused coconut oil
Founder: John Roulac

10505 REBBL
5900 Hollis St
Suite L
Emeryville, CA 94608
855-732-2500
info@rebbl.co rebbl.co
Coconut milk-based herb beverages
Co-Founder: Palo Hawken
CEO: Sheryl O'Loughlin
Controller: Ryan McKillop
Operations: Janaye Pohl

10506 REDCLAY Gourmet
678 Blue Rock Ct
Winston-Salem, NC 27103
336-575-3360
lance@redclaygourmet.com
www.redclaygourmet.com
Pimento cheese spreads
Owner: Michele Sawyer
Estimated Sales: Under $500,000
Number Employees: 9
Brands:
    REDCLAY Gourmet

10507 REED'S Inc
13000 S Spring St
Los Angeles, CA 90061-1634
310-217-9400
Fax: 310-217-9411 800-997-3337
info@reedsgingerbrew.com www.reedsinc.com
Ginger soft drinks, candy and ice cream
President & CEO: Christopher Reed
Estimated Sales: $10-15 million
Number Employees: 50-99
Type of Packaging: Consumer
Brands:
    China Cola
    Reed's
    Virgil's Root Beers

10508 RENFRO Foods Inc
815 Stella St
Fort Worth, TX 76104-1495
817-336-3849
Fax: 817-336-7910 jc@interstargroup.com
www.renfrofoods.com
Relishes, sauces, peppers and salsas
President: Doug Renfro
CEO: Bill Renfro
bill.renfro@renfrofoods.com
Vice President: Becky Renfro
Marketing: Dan Fore
InterStar PR: Jane Cohen
VP Production: James Renfro
Estimated Sales: $3.3 Million
Number Employees: 50-99
Number of Products: 27
Type of Packaging: Consumer, Food Service, Private Label
Brands:
    Mrs Renfro's

10509 REX Pure Foods
2121 Chartres St
New Orleans, LA 70116
504-525-7305
800-344-8314
info@rexfoods.com www.rexfoods.com
Seafood spices and seasonings, sauces, blends, vinegar and mustard; packaging services
President: J Geldart
CEO: Jenni Ratliff
VP, Chief Marketing Officer: Gene Ratliff
Estimated Sales: $2.5 Million
Number Employees: 1-4
Type of Packaging: Consumer, Food Service, Bulk
Brands:
    Rex

10510 RFS Limited
576 Colonial Park Dr
Suite 130
Roswell, GA 30075-3794
770-993-0030
Fax: 770-993-0792
Frozen broccoli, carrots, cauliflower, zucchini and squash
CEO: Fred Everett
fred.everett@rfs.com
National Sales Manager: Rob Rickerby
Estimated Sales: $1-2,500,000
Number Employees: 5-9
Type of Packaging: Food Service, Private Label, Bulk
Brands:
    Roca

10511 RFi Ingredients
300 Corporate Dr
Suite 14
Blauvelt, NY 10913-1162
845-358-8600
Fax: 845-358-9003 800-962-7663
trishad@rfiingredients.com
www.rfiingredients.com
Antioxidants, antimicrobials, preservatives, natural colors; fruit, vegetable and botanical extracts
President & CEO: Jeff Wuagneux
jeffw@rfiingredients.com
Vice President, R&D: Ginny Bank
Executive Vice President: Trisha Devine
Chief Operating Officer: Drew Luce
Estimated Sales: $4-5 Million
Number Employees: 50-99
Number of Brands: 5
Type of Packaging: Bulk
Brands:
    Colorpure
    Oxyphyte
    Phytbac
    Phytonutriance
    Stabilenhance

10512 RISE Brewing Co.
Cos Cob, CT
hello@risebrewingco.com
risebrewingco.com
Cold brew coffee
Co-Founder & CEO: Grant Gyesky

10513 RJ Balson and Sons Inc
PO Box 8153
Asheville, NC 28814
321-281-9473
contact@balsonbutchers.com
www.balsonbutchers.com
Bangers and bacon
President/CEO: Oliver Balson
oliver.balson@balsonbutchers.com

10514 RM Heagy Foods
227 Granite Run Drive
Suite 200
Lancaster, PA 17601
717-569-1032
Cheese, ice cream and sorbets, butters, dips and sauces, charcuterie meats.
CEO: Chuck Kukic
Chief Financial Officer: Douglas Hilliard
Sales & Marketing Manager: Abigail Heagy
Production Manager: Auston Martzall
Estimated Sales: $20-50 Million
Number Employees: 5-9

10515 RP's Pasta Company
1133 East Wilson Street
Madison, WI 53703
608-257-7216
Fax: 608-257-7267 freshpasta@rpspasta.com
www.rpspasta.com
Pasta
CEO & Master Pasta Maker: Peter Robertson
VP, General Counsel: Stephen Ciurczak
Quality Assurance Manager: Margo King
Estimated Sales: $5 Million
Number Employees: 50+
Type of Packaging: Food Service, Private Label
Brands:
    RPs PASTA

10516 RPM Total Vitality
18032 Lemon Drive
Suite C
Yorba Linda, CA 92886-3386
714-524-8864
Fax: 714-524-3247 800-234-3092
Antioxidants: pollen and dimethylaminoethanol
Owner: Pat McBride
pat@rpmtv.com
Co-Owner: Roger McBride
Number Employees: 1-4
Square Footage: 4000
Brands:
    Letan

10517 RW Delights
50 Division Ave
Suite 44
Millington, NJ 07946
917-301-5231
866-892-1096
info@heavenlysouffle.com
www.heavenlysouffle.com
Souffle and creme brulee desserts
President: Roxanne Kam
CEO: Wendy Friedman

10518 RW Garcia
521 Parrott St.
San Jose, CA 95112
408-287-4616
rwgarcia.com
Tortilla chips and crackers
President: Bob Garcia
Sales & Marketing Coordinator: January Riss
Snack Food Manufacturing: Allan Perkins
Year Founded: 1982
Estimated Sales: $40 Million
Number Employees: 50-200
Brands:
    RW Garcia

10519 RXBAR
225 W Ohio
Suite 500
Chicago, IL 60654
312-624-8200
support@rxbar.com
www.rxbar.com
Protein bars
CEO & Co-Founder: Peter Rahal
Chief Marketing Officer: Lindsay (Rubin) Levin
Chief Sales Officer: Sam McBride
Year Founded: 2013
Estimated Sales: $2.2 Million
Number Employees: 50-200
Brands:
    RXBAR

10520 Raaka Chocolate
64 Seabring St
Brooklyn, NY 11231
855-255-3354
help@raakachocolate.com
www.raakachocolate.com
Unroasted dark chocolate
Founder & CEO: Ryan Cheney
Co-Founder: Nathan Hodge
Estimated Sales: $2.4 Million
Number Employees: 11-50
Number of Brands: 1
Number of Products: 14
Brands:
    Raaka

10521 Rabbit Barn
630 W Clausen Rd
Turlock, CA 95380-9703
209-632-1123
Fax: 209-632-1123 www.littlerabbitbarn.com
Rabbit meat
Owner: Larry Sigafoos
CEO: Sherri Sigafoos
Estimated Sales: $1-3 Million
Number Employees: 1-4
Square Footage: 8000
Type of Packaging: Private Label
Brands:
    Rabbit Barn

Food Manufacturers / A-Z

10522 Rabbit Creek
903 N Broadway St
Po Box 1059
Louisburg, KS 66053-3541
913-837-2757
Fax: 913-837-5760 800-837-3073
rcreek@mokancomm.net
www.rabbitcreekgourmet.com
Mixes: muffin, dip, soup, scone, bread, brownie and cookie
President: Donna Cook
rcreek@mokancomm.net
Estimated Sales: $1-2.5 Million
Number Employees: 10-19
Number of Brands: 1
Number of Products: 120
Type of Packaging: Consumer, Private Label
Brands:
  Rabbit Creek

10523 Rabbit Ridge Winery
1172 San Marcos Rd
Paso Robles, CA 93446-7343
805-467-3331
Fax: 805-467-3339 rabbitridgewines@yahoo.com
www.rabbitridgewinery.com
Wines
Founder/Winemaker: Erich Russell
President: Joanne James Russell
Compliance/Operations Manager: Sandy James
Director Paso Vineyard Operations: Robert Pierce
Paso Robles Office Manager: Jacqueline Pierce
Paso Robles Assistant to the Director: Mike Sanford
Healdsburg Operations Director: Linda Garwood
Healdsburg Warehouse Manager: Craig Wisdom
Manager: Sandy James
jessica@rabbitridgewinery.com
Estimated Sales: Below $5 Million
Number Employees: 5-9
Brands:
  Rabbit Ridge

10524 Raber Packing Co
1413 N Raber Rd
Peoria, IL 61604-4790
309-673-0721
Fax: 309-673-6308 800-331-0543
www.raberpacking.com
Meat
President: Carroll Wetterauer
raberpacking@comcast.net
Year Founded: 1954
Estimated Sales: $3 Million
Number Employees: 20-49
Square Footage: 60000
Type of Packaging: Consumer

10525 Raceland Raw Sugar Corporation
175 Mill St.
PO Box 159
Raceland, LA 70394
985-537-3533
Fax: 985-537-7779 www.racelandrawsugar.com
Raw sugar and molasses
President: Daniel Duplantis
Estimated Sales: $33 Million
Number Employees: 100-249
Parent Co: M.A. Patout & Son
Type of Packaging: Bulk

10526 Rachael's Smoked Fish
150 Switzer Ave
Springfield, MA 01109
800-327-3412
rachaelsfoodcorp.com
Kosher foods: cream cheese, pickled herring, smoked fish and whitefish, salmon and herring salads
Plant Manager: Alan Axler
Number Employees: 38275
Square Footage: 24000
Type of Packaging: Consumer, Food Service, Private Label, Bulk
Brands:
  Axler's
  Springfield

10527 Racine Danish
2529 Golf Ave
Racine, WI 53404-1657
262-633-1819
Fax: 262-633-3036 customerservice@kringle.com
www.kringle.com
Pastries: danish
Owner: Mike Heyer
mheyer@kringle.com
Number Employees: 20-49

10528 Radanovich Vineyards & Winery
3936 Ben Hur Road
Mariposa, CA 95338-9466
209-966-3187
Wines
President: George Radanovich
Estimated Sales: $500,000-$1 000,000
Number Employees: 1-4

10529 Radlo Foods
313 Pleasant St
Watertown, MA 02472
617-926-7070
Fax: 617-923-6440 800-370-1439
Eggs and egg products
President & CEO: David Radlo
Contact: Jim Leroy
jiml@radlo.com
Estimated Sales: $2-5 Million
Number Employees: 1-4
Type of Packaging: Consumer, Food Service, Private Label, Bulk
Brands:
  Born Free
  Grown Free

10530 Raffield Fisheries Inc
1624 Grouper Ave
Port St Joe, FL 32456-5144
850-229-8494
Fax: 850-229-8782 eugene@raffieldfisheries.com
www.raffieldfisheries.com
Atlantic herring, black drum, roe, bluefish, blue runner, Jack Crevalle, ladyfish, Spanish sardines, butterfish, goatfish, croakers and crawfish
President: Harold Raffield
harold@raffieldfisheries.com
Secretary/Treasurer: Danny Raffield
Estimated Sales: $10-20 Million
Number Employees: 50-99
Type of Packaging: Consumer, Food Service, Private Label, Bulk

10531 Ragersville Swiss Cheese
2199 Ragersville Rd SW
Sugarcreek, OH 44681
330-897-3055
Fax: 330-897-0415
Swiss cheese
President/Owner: Richard Hicks
Estimated Sales: $3-5 Million
Number Employees: 1-4
Square Footage: 40000
Type of Packaging: Consumer

10532 Ragold Confections
516 NW 20th St
Wilton Manors, FL 33311
954-566-9092
Fax: 954-427-0413 rs@ragold.com
www.ragold.com
Candy
Chairman of the Board: Rainer Schindler
CFO: Arthur Pauly
Estimated Sales: $1.5 Million
Number Employees: 10-19
Type of Packaging: Private Label
Brands:
  Dilbert Mints&Gummies
  Juicefuls Hard Candy

10533 Ragozzino Foods Inc
10 Ames Ave
Meriden, CT 06451-2912
203-238-2553
Fax: 203-235-5158 800-348-1240
nancy@ragozzino.com www.ragozzino.com
Soups, pastas, sauces, entrees, side dishes and dips.
President: Nancy Ragozzino
CEO: Gloria Ragozzino
gloria@ragozzino.com
VP: John Ragozzino
VP Product Development: Susan Ragozzino
VP Purchasing/Distribution: Ellen Ragozzino
Estimated Sales: $23 Million
Number Employees: 100-249
Number of Brands: 1
Square Footage: 65000
Type of Packaging: Consumer, Food Service, Private Label
Brands:
  Sugo

10534 Ragsdale-Overton Food Traditions
PO Box 1626
Smithfield, NC 27577-1626
919-284-6700
Fax: 919-284-6706 888-424-8863
Condiments, chutneys, sauces
Partner: Sue Overton
Public Relations: Carolyn Ragsdale
Estimated Sales: Under $500,000
Number Employees: 1-4
Type of Packaging: Private Label
Brands:
  B-17
  Raggy-O

10535 Rahr Malting Co
800 1st Ave W
Shakopee, MN 55379-1148
952-445-1431
info@rahr.com
www.rahr.com
Malt and brewing supplies
CEO: Gary Lee
Contact: April Abbott
aabbott@rahr.com
Year Founded: 1847
Estimated Sales: $43.6 Million
Number Employees: 1-4
Type of Packaging: Bulk

10536 Rainbow Hills Vineyards
26349 Township Road 251
Newcomerstown, OH 43832-9631
740-545-9305
www.ravensglenn.com
Wines
Owner: Lee Wyse
rainbowhillsvineyards@gmail.com
Estimated Sales: Below $5 Million
Number Employees: 5-9
Brands:
  Rainbow Hill Vineyards

10537 Rainbow Light Nutritional Systems
125 McPherson St
Santa Cruz, CA 95060-5818
831-429-9089
Fax: 831-429-0189 800-635-1233
www.rainbowlight.com
Supplements and herbal extracts
President: Linda Kahler
Senior Director of Research: Marci Clow
Director of Marketing: Tisha Brady
Vice President of Sales: Ray Petrick
Contact: Barbara Apps
barbaraa@rlns.com
Vice President of Operations: Sharon Minski
Production Manager: Mark Keller
Purchasing Manager: Dee Dee Barrios
Estimated Sales: $6000000
Number Employees: 20-49
Number of Products: 150
Type of Packaging: Consumer
Brands:
  Just Once Natural Herbal Extras
  Rainbow Light
  Rainbow Light Herbal

10538 Rainbow Pops
45 Benbro Dr
Cheektowaga, NY 14225-4805
716-685-4340
Fax: 716-685-0810 800-879-7677
Lollipops
President: Roe Baran
Number Employees: 20-49
Brands:
  Popstop
  Premium Rainbow Drops
  Premium Rainbow Pops
  Rainbow Pops

10539 Rainbow Seafood Market
4303 Maine Ave
Suite 107
Baldwin Park, CA 91706-2395
626-962-6888
Fax: 626-962-3677
Seafood

Owner: David Tran
Estimated Sales: $800,000
Number Employees: 1-4
Type of Packaging: Consumer

10540 Rainbow Seafoods
422a Boston St
Topsfield, MA 01983
978-887-9121
Fax: 978-887-9125 www.rainbowseafood.com
Seafood
President: Frank Powell
Sales: Neil Murphy
Estimated Sales: $2,500,000
Number Employees: 9
Brands:
 Alda
 North Breeze
 Rainbow

10541 Rainbow Valley Frozen Yogurt
9444 W Shady Grove Ct
White Lake, MI 48386
248-355-1095
Fax: 248-353-3466 800-979-8669
Frozen yogurt mix
President: William Boyda
VP/Treasurer: Laurel Boyda
Estimated Sales: $500,000-$1,000,000
Number Employees: 5-9
Square Footage: 48000
Type of Packaging: Consumer, Food Service, Private Label, Bulk

10542 Rainforest Company
141 Millwell Dr
Maryland Heights, MO 63043
314-344-1000
Fax: 314-344-3044
michaelm@the-rainforest-co.com
Snacks: cashew and Brazil nut bars, popcorn, salad dressings, salsas, marinades and hot sauces
President: Rick Drevet
Controller: Sherry Dawes
Number Employees: 35
Square Footage: 80000
Brands:
 Jungle Munch
 Rainforest Crunch
 River Bank

10543 Rainsweet Inc
1460 Sunnyview Rd. NE
P.O. Box 7079
Salem, OR 97301
503-363-4293
Fax: 503-585-4657 800-363-4293
linda@rainsweet.com www.rainsweet.com
Frozen blackberries, blueberries, black and red raspberries, boysenberries, IQF and puree cane berries, mushrooms, peppers, onions and bean sprouts
CEO: Rich Brim
richb@rainsweet.com
Quality Assurance Manager: Ian Bennet
Fruit Sales & Customer Service: Linda Ervin
Vegetable Sales: Chantal Wright
Field Manager: Bill Dinger
Estimated Sales: $30.4 Million
Number Employees: 100-249
Square Footage: 130000
Type of Packaging: Consumer, Food Service, Private Label, Bulk
Brands:
 Rainsweet

10544 Rallis Whole Foods
2886 Riviera Drive
Windsor, ON N9E 3A4
Canada
519-796-9712
theo@rallisoliveoil.com
www.icepressed.com
Olive oils
Marketing: Theo Rallis

10545 Ralph Sechler & Son Inc
5686 SR 1
St Joe, IN 46785-0152
260-337-5461
Fax: 260-337-5771 800-332-5461
showroom@sechlerspickles.com
www.sechlerspickles.com
Pickles and peppers

Owner: Max Troyer
VP Technical Services: Karen Sechler-Linn
Sales Manager: Mark Decker
Estimated Sales: $10-20 Million
Number Employees: 20-49
Square Footage: 180000
Type of Packaging: Consumer, Food Service, Bulk
Brands:
 Sechler's

10546 Ralph's Famous Italian Ices
11 Cooper St
Babylon, NY 11702-2901
631-893-5646
info@ralphsices.com
www.ralphsices.com
Italian ices
Manager: Stephen Lazarra
Owner: Lawerence Silvestro
Owner: Michael Scolaro
Estimated Sales: $300,000-500,000
Number Employees: 10-19
Brands:
 Ralph's Italian Ices

10547 Ralph's Packing Co
500 W Freeman Ave
Perkins, OK 74059
405-547-2464
Fax: 405-547-2364 800-522-3979
comments@ralphspacking.com
www.ralphspacking.com
Fresh and smoked meat products available to consumers and wholesalers.
President: Gary Crane
garycrane@ralphspacking.com
Year Founded: 1959
Estimated Sales: $4 Million
Number Employees: 20-49
Square Footage: 39200
Type of Packaging: Consumer, Food Service, Private Label
Brands:
 Big Nasty
 Lil' Momma Nasty

10548 Ramona's Mexican Foods
13633 S Western Ave
Gardena, CA 90249
310-323-1950
Fax: 310-323-4210 sales@ramonas.com
ramonas.com
Frozen tortillas, burritos, tamales and Mexican dinners
Co-Founder: Ramona Acosta Banuelos
Co-Founder: Alejandro Banuelos
President & CEO: Martin Accosta Torres
Type of Packaging: Consumer, Food Service, Bulk
Brands:
 Ramona's

10549 Ramos Orchards
9192 Boyce Rd
Winters, CA 95694-9625
530-795-4748
Fax: 530-795-4148
Walnuts, prunes and almonds
Owner: Fred Ramos
Estimated Sales: $4 Million
Number Employees: 20-49
Type of Packaging: Bulk
Brands:
 Ramos Orchards

10550 Ramsen Inc
17725 Juniper Path
Lakeville, MN 55044-9482
952-431-0400
Fax: 952-431-8470 dbreuer@ramsendairy.com
www.ramsendairy.com
Dry dairy
Owner: Tim Krieger
Partner: John Baetty
jbaetty@ramsendairy.com
Marketing Director: Kathy Stevens
Sales Manager: Dennis Breuer
Estimated Sales: $10-20 Million
Number Employees: 10-19
Square Footage: 3600
Type of Packaging: Consumer, Food Service

10551 Ramsey Popcorn Co Inc
5645 Clover Valley Rd NW
Ramsey, IN 47166-8252
812-347-2441
Fax: 812-347-3336 800-624-2060
info@ramseypopcorn.com www.cousinwillies.com
Microwaveable popcorn
President: Wilfred Sieg
will@ramseypopcorn.com
Controller: Pat Smith
VP Operations: Daniel Sieg
Estimated Sales: $5 Million
Number Employees: 20-49
Type of Packaging: Consumer, Food Service, Private Label, Bulk
Brands:
 Cousin Willie's

10552 Ranaldi Bros. Frozen Food Products
960 Greenwich Ave
Warwick, RI 02886-4513
401-737-5130
Fax: 401-738-4446
Frozen dough, stuffed breads, kosher dairy pastries
President: Gary Ranaldi
Vice President: Raymond Ranaldi
Sales Director: Robin Capraro
Purchasing Manager: Joseph O'Neil
Estimated Sales: $2,500,000
Number Employees: 30
Number of Products: 100
Square Footage: 130000
Type of Packaging: Consumer, Food Service, Private Label, Bulk
Brands:
 Puff Dough

10553 Ranch Oak Farm
3005 Bledsoe St
Fort Worth, TX 76107-2905
817-877-3330
Fax: 817-877-3742 800-888-0327
info@RanchOak.com www.ranchoak.com
Smoked meats
President: Tom Misfeldt
info@ranchoak.com
Estimated Sales: Below $5 Million
Number Employees: 1-4
Type of Packaging: Private Label
Brands:
 Ranch Oak Farm

10554 Rancho De Philo Winery
10050 Wilson Ave
Rancho Cucamonga, CA 91737-2314
Fax: 909-987-4208 909-987-4208
Dessert wine
President: Alan Tibbetts
Co-Owner: Janine Tibbetts
janinetibbetts@earthlink.net
Estimated Sales: Less Than $500,000
Number Employees: 1-4
Type of Packaging: Private Label
Brands:
 Rancho De Philo
 Triple Cream Sherry

10555 Rancho Sierra
42 W Market St
Salinas, CA 93901-2653
831-422-3629
Fax: 831-422-3629 800-398-2929
Tortillas and Mexican food
President: Pamela Mills
Estimated Sales: $4 Million
Number Employees: 40
Square Footage: 140000
Type of Packaging: Consumer, Food Service, Private Label, Bulk
Brands:
 El Aguilia

10556 Rancho Sisquoc Winery
6600 Foxen Canyon Rd
Santa Maria, CA 93454-9656
805-934-4332
Fax: 805-937-6601 sisquoc@ranchosisquoc.com
www.ranchosisquoc.net
Wines
Manager: Mary Holt
COO: Edward Holt
Estimated Sales: Below $5 Million
Number Employees: 10-19

Food Manufacturers / A-Z

Brands:
Rancho Sisquoc

10557 Rancho's
1910 Madison Ave
Suite 724
Memphis, TN 38104-2620
901-276-8820
Fax: 901-744-0514
Sauces
Owner: Deborah Reinach
Estimated Sales: Less than $500,000
Number Employees: 1-4

10558 Randal Optimal Nutrients
1595 Hampton Way
Santa Rosa, CA 95407-6844
707-528-1800
Fax: 650-349-1686   800-221-1697
info@randaloptimal.com www.randaloptimal.com
Vitamins, minerals and nutritional supplements
President: Dan Brinker
dan@randaloptimal.com
Director Marketing/Technical Services: Donald Burns
Estimated Sales: $3200000
Number Employees: 20-49
Square Footage: 88000
Type of Packaging: Consumer, Private Label, Bulk
Brands:
Nuturpractic
Vimco

10559 Randall Food Products
8050 Hosbrook Road
Cincinnati, OH 45236
513-793-6525
www.randallbeans.com
Dry beans
President: W Mashburn
Office Manager: John Alyward
Estimated Sales: $5 Million
Number Employees: 20
Type of Packaging: Consumer, Private Label
Brands:
Randall

10560 Randall Foods Inc
2905 E 50th St
Vernon, CA 90058-2919
323-585-2094
Fax: 323-586-1587   800-372-6581
CS@RandallFoods.com www.randallfarms.com
Beef, chicken and pork
Owner: Ron Totin
ron@ranchofoods.com
Director Human Resources: Donna Zuchowski
Number Employees: 100-249
Square Footage: 336000
Brands:
Randall Foods

10561 Randazzo's Honest To Goodness Sauces
P.O. Box 901
Glen Rock, NJ 07452
201-543-1195
rochelle@randazzossauces.com
www.randazzossauces.com
Sauces: marinara, plum tomato, basil, tomato and pesto
Founder: Rochelle Randazzo
Estimated Sales: $5-10 Million
Number Employees: 10-19
Brands:
Randazzo's Honest to Goodness

10562 Randolph Packing Co
403 W Balfour Ave
Asheboro, NC 27203-3247
336-672-1470
Fax: 336-672-6545 www.randolphpacking.com
Meat
Owner: Don Garner
Estimated Sales: $30 Million
Number Employees: 50-99
Type of Packaging: Consumer

10563 Randy's Donuts
805 W Manchester Blvd
Inglewood, CA 90301-1524
310-645-4707
Donuts
Owner: Larry Weintraub
randysdonuts@yahoo.com
Number Employees: 10-19

10564 Randy's Frozen Meats
1910 5th St NW
Faribault, MN 55021-4606
507-334-7177
Fax: 507-334-9210 www.randysfoods.com
Pizzas
Co-Owner: Randy Creasman
Number Employees: 20-49
Type of Packaging: Consumer, Food Service, Private Label, Bulk

10565 Ranieri Fine Foods
278 Metropolitan Ave
Brooklyn, NY 11211-4006
718-599-9520
Fax: 718-599-6457
Dairy, cheese, meat, sauces and seasonings, baked goods, candy, grains and cereal, pasta, soups and stews.
President: Steven Shlopak
Estimated Sales: Under $500,000
Number Employees: 2-10
Brands:
Berni
Campi del Sole
Capretta
FIDA
Facino
Fatina-Murano
Fattoria Italia
Frumage
Galbusera
HAG
La Vallata
Madre Sicilia
Mellin
Osella
P.L.A.C
Pasta Campo
Ranieri
and more

10566 Rao's Specialty Foods Inc
17 Battery Pl
Suite 610
New York, NY 10004-1190
212-269-0151
Fax: 212-344-1680 info@raos.com
www.raos.com
Pasta and sauces, roasted peppers, olive oil & vinegars, marindaes & dressings, canned tomatoes and coffee
Owner: Ruby Briscol
rbriscol@raos.com
Owner: Lynn Iovino
Vice President: Jay Kuder
Marketing Manager: Ron Straci
Sales Manager: Peter Ardigo
Estimated Sales: $3.3 Million
Number Employees: 10-19
Number of Brands: 1
Number of Products: 20
Type of Packaging: Private Label
Brands:
RAO'S

10567 Rapazzini Winery
4350 Monterey Rd
Gilroy, CA 95020-8029
408-842-5649
Fax: 408-842-8353   800-842-6262
info@rapazziniwinery.com
www.rapazziniwinery.com
Wine, cooking wines, garlic, jelly, mustard, mayonnaise, spices, salsas and chips
Owner: Charles Larson
info@rapazzini.com
Owner: Alex Larson
Estimated Sales: Less Than $1Million
Number Employees: 5-9
Brands:
Rapazzini Winery

10568 Rapunzel Pure Organics
1455 Broad Street
4th Floor
Bloomfield, NJ 07003
973-338-1499
Fax: 973-338-1485   800-225-1449
info@rapunzel.com www.rapunzel.com
Organic sugar, chocolate, soups and bouillons, salt, vegetable juices, cocoa powder and spreads
President: Eckhart Kiesel
Director Sales/Marketing: Dale Kamibayashi
Sales Director: Jim Douglas
Number Employees: 5-9
Square Footage: 20000
Type of Packaging: Consumer, Food Service, Bulk
Brands:
A. Vogel
Bambu Juices
Biotta Juices
Faqs
Herbamare Juices
Rapunzel Pure Organi

10569 Raquelitas Tortillas
3111 Larimer St
Denver, CO 80205-2312
303-296-1672
Fax: 303-296-3008 www.raquelitas.com
Tortillas
Owner: Rich Schneider
rschneider@raquelitas.com
Number Employees: 10-19

10570 Rare Hawaiian Honey Company
66-1250 Lalamilo Farm Rd
Kamuela, HI 96743
888-663-6639
info@rarehawaiianhoney.com
www.rarehawaiianhoney.com
Organic honey
Commercial Director: Amy Domeier
Year Founded: 1982
Estimated Sales: Under $500,000
Number Employees: 8
Brands:
Rare Hawaiian

10571 Ratners Retail Foods
138 Delancey St
New York, NY 10002-3325
212-677-5588
www.nycfoods.com/ratners
Dairy
President: Harold Zankel
VP: Robert Hirmatz
Estimated Sales: $2.5-5 Million
Number Employees: 50-99

10572 Raven Creamery Company
3303 NE M L King Boulevard
Portland, OR 97212-2057
503-288-5101
Fax: 503-288-5103
Butter
President: Henry Turner
Marketing Director: Tom Hughes
Estimated Sales: $5-10 000,000
Number Employees: 10-19

10573 Ravenswood Winery
18701 Gehricke Rd
Sonoma, CA 95476-4710
707-938-1960
Fax: 707-933-2383   866-568-3946
customerservice@ravenswoodwinery.com
www.preferredlimousineservice.com
Wines
Founder: Joel Peterson
Chairman & CEO: W. Reed Foster
Chief Financial Officer: Callie Konno
Executive Vice President: Justin Faggioli
Estimated Sales: $625 Thousand
Number Employees: 50-99
Number of Brands: 1
Parent Co: Constellation Brand, Inc.
Brands:
Ravenswood

10574 Ravico USA
PO BOX 19
Riderwood, MD 21139-0019
443-921-8025
Fax: 443-921-8030 ravicousa@comcast.net
www.ravico.com
Chocolates, pastry shells and desserts
Owner: Jamie Fineran
Retail Sales Director: Erin Murdock Clark
Estimated Sales: Under $500,000
Number Employees: 1-4
Brands:
Ravico

Food Manufacturers / A-Z

10575 Ravioli Store
4344 21st St
Long Island City, NY 11101-5002
212-925-1737
877-727-8269
www.raviolistore.com
Pasta and sauces
Owner: Donna Seeherman
donna@raviolistore.com
Estimated Sales: $300,000-500,000
Number Employees: 20-49
Number of Brands: 52
Type of Packaging: Consumer, Food Service

10576 Raw Bite
10 Technology Dr
Suite 40
Hudson, MA 01749
844-729-2483
Organic fruit and nut bars
Number of Brands: 1
Number of Products: 5
Type of Packaging: Consumer
Brands:
  RAWBITE

10577 Raw Rev
PO Box 359
Hawthorne, NY 10532
914-326-4095
rawrev.com
Plant-based superfood bars
Founder & President: Alice Benedetto

10578 RawFusion
1650 E Gonzales Rd
Suite 282
Oxnard, CA 93030
888-852-3350
info@rawplantprotein.com rawplantprotein.com
Plant-based protein powder and bars

10579 Rawmantic Chocolate
12 West 57th Street
Suite 807
New York, NY 10019
212-247-2229
info@rawmanticchocolate.com
rawmantic-chocolate.myshopify.com
Chocolates, protein bars and nut butters
Founder: Kasia Bosne
Brands:
  Rawmantic Chocolate

10580 Ray's Sausage Co
3146 E 123rd St
Cleveland, OH 44120-3179
216-921-8782
Fax: 216-921-4736 www.rayssausage.com
Pork and beef sausage and links, souse and cheese
President: Renee Cash
CFO: Leslie Cash Lester
Vice President: Raymond Cash, Jr.
Marketing/Sales: Raymond Hardin
Estimated Sales: $600000
Number Employees: 5-9
Square Footage: 2800
Type of Packaging: Consumer, Food Service
Brands:
  Ray's Headcheese
  Ray's Italian Links
  Ray's Sausage
  Ray's Souse

10581 Raye's Mustard
83 Washington Street
P.O. Box 2
Eastport, ME 04631
800-853-1903
mustards@rayesmustard.com
www.rayesmustard.com
Mustard and mustard sauces
Owner: Karen Raye
Estimated Sales: $5-10 Million
Number Employees: 5-9
Type of Packaging: Consumer, Food Service, Bulk

10582 Raye's Old Fashioned Gourmet Mustard
83 Washington St
PO Box 2
Eastport, ME 04631
800-853-1903
mustards@rayesmustard.com
www.rayesmustard.com
Mustards
Owner: Kevin Raye
Owner: Karen Raye
Estimated Sales: $410,000
Number Employees: 6

10583 Raymond-Hadley Corporation
89 Tompkins St
Spencer, NY 14883
607-589-4415
Fax: 607-589-6442   800-252-5220
www.raymondhadley.com
South and Central American and African foods: barley, beans, bran, flour, cereal, dried fruit, grains, rice, spices, starches, vegetables and corn meal
President: Lori Maratea
Founder: Arthur B. Raymond
Founder: Francis E. Hadley
Vice President of Sales: Tracy McCutcheon
President: Elliot Dutra
Number Employees: 20-49
Square Footage: 204000
Type of Packaging: Bulk

10584 Reading Coffee Roasters
316 W Main St
Birdsboro, PA 19508-1900
610-582-2243
Fax: 610-582-3615   800-331-6713
www.thecoffeegourmet.com
Coffee
Owner: Albert Van Maanen
Co-Owner: Rosemary Hartigan
rdgcofrstr@aol.com
Estimated Sales: $300,000-500,000
Number Employees: 5-9
Type of Packaging: Private Label
Brands:
  Jazzy Java Custom Flavored Gourmet
  Oscars Flavoring Syrups
  Reading Coffee Roast

10585 Ready Foods Inc
2645 W 7th Ave
Denver, CO 80204-4112
303-892-5861
Fax: 303-629-6148   800-748-1218
info@readyfoods.biz www.readyfoods.biz
Mexican food
Owner: Marco Abarca
mabarca@readyfoods.biz
Estimated Sales: $.5-1 million
Number Employees: 10-19
Type of Packaging: Food Service, Private Label, Bulk
Brands:
  Marcos

10586 Ready Pac Foods Inc
4401 Foxdale St
Irwindale, CA 91706
800-800-4088
info@bfa.bonduelle.com www.readypac.com
Bag salads and fruit, vegetables and bistro bowls.
CEO: Mary Thompson
Chief HR Officer: Katie Lopez
Chief Manufacturing Officer: Mike Gomes
Chief Supply Chain Officer: Scott McGuire
Chief Procurement Officer: Scott Wilkerson
Year Founded: 1969
Estimated Sales: $50-100 Million
Number Employees: 1,000-4,999
Number of Brands: 1
Other Locations:
  Processing Facility
  Florence NJ
  Processing Facility
  Swedesboro NJ
  Processing Facility
  Jackson GA
Brands:
  Ready Pac

10587 Real Aloe Company
7470 Dean Martin Drive
Suite 102
Las Vegas, NV 89139
877-301-8296
Fax: 702-462-5880   800-541-7809
www.realaloeinc.com
Aloe vera gel, juice and beverages
Owner: Frank Mundell
VP: M Mundell
Operations Manager: Dan Mundell
Estimated Sales: $1,100,000
Number Employees: 5-9
Square Footage: 21000
Type of Packaging: Consumer, Food Service, Private Label, Bulk
Brands:
  Cal-Aloe Co.
  Real Aloe Co.

10588 Real Coconut Co. Inc., The
www.therealcoconut.com
Gluten-free and dairy-free coconut flour tortillas and snack chips
Founder/President: Daniella Hunter
Number of Brands: 1
Number of Products: 6
Type of Packaging: Consumer, Private Label
Brands:
  The Real Coconut

10589 Real Cookies
3212 Hewlett Avenue
Merrick, NY 11566-5505
516-221-9300
Fax: 516-221-9561   800-822-5113
Cookie dough and mixes: oatmeal raisin, mocha almond, ginger, macadamia, white chocolate, pecan and chocolate chip
President: Ellyn Knigin
CFO: Leonard Knigin
Vice President: Marian Knigin
Estimated Sales: $500,000-$1 Million
Number Employees: 5-9
Type of Packaging: Consumer, Food Service, Private Label, Bulk
Brands:
  Grandma's Cookie Mix
  Real Cookies

10590 Real Food Marketing
201 Wyandotte St
Suite 402
Kansas City, MO 64105
816-221-4100
Fax: 913-671-8083
Desserts, breads, meat pastries, ethnic breads, brownies, cookies, muffins, cakes, dietetic foods and pies.
President: John Fallucca
CFO: Tara Cupps
R&D: Bob Deal
Operations: Bill Scott
Purchasing: Clint Scott
Estimated Sales: $1-3 Million
Number Employees: 1-4
Number of Products: 50
Square Footage: 3600
Type of Packaging: Consumer, Food Service, Private Label, Bulk

10591 Real Kosher Sausage Company
9 Euclid Ave
Newark, NJ 07105-4527
973-690-5394
Fax: 212-598-9011
Kosher meats, sausage and deli
President/CEO: Jacob Hill
Estimated Sales: $750,000
Number Employees: 10
Square Footage: 60000
Type of Packaging: Consumer, Food Service, Private Label, Bulk
Brands:
  999
  Real Kosher

10592 Real Sausage Co
2710 S Poplar Ave
Chicago, IL 60608-5909
312-842-5330
Fax: 312-842-5414 nmakowski@realsausage.com
www.realsausage.com
Sausage

Food Manufacturers / A-Z

President: Nicole Makowski
Estimated Sales: Below $5 000,000
Number Employees: 20-49
Brands:
   Real Sausage

10593 Real Torino
PO Box 448
Brookside, NJ 07926-0448
973-895-5420
Fax: 973-895-8824 peteritaly@aol.com
www.pasta.com
Bread, biscuits, cakes, pastries, cookies, crackers and pasta.
Marketing: Peter Carolan
Estimated Sales: $1.4 Million
Number Employees: 10

10594 Realsalt
475 West 910 South
Heber City, UT 84032
Fax: 435-654-3329   800-367-7258
Darrylb@realsalt.com   www.realsalt.com
Kosher, stocks, spices, sea salt and minerals.
Quality Control Manager: Tiffany Riding
Sales Manager: Darrlyl Bosshaedt
Contact: Rhett Roberts
rhettr@redmondinc.com
Plant Manager: Dennis Schindler
Purchasing Manager: Delvon Julonder
Number Employees: 250
Parent Co: Redmond Inc.

10595 Rebec Vineyards
2229 N Amherst Hwy
Amherst, VA 24521-4378
434-946-5168
Fax: 804-946-5168 winery@rebecwinery.com
www.rebecwinery.com
Wines
Manager: Svetlozar Kanev
winery@rebecwinery.com
Estimated Sales: Below $500,000
Number Employees: 1-4
Type of Packaging: Private Label

10596 Rebecca-Ruth Candy Factory
116 E 2nd St
Frankfort, KY 40601-2902
502-223-7475
Fax: 502-226-5854   800-444-3866
office@rebeccaruth.com
Candy
President: Charles Booe
booe@rebeccaruth.com
Estimated Sales: Less Than $500,000
Number Employees: 5-9
Type of Packaging: Consumer, Private Label, Bulk
Brands:
   100 Bourbon Whiskey
   Buffalo Trace
   Butter Creams
   Classic Liquor Cremes
   Creme De Menthe
   Rebecca-Ruth

10597 Rebound
1 Pepsi Way
Newburgh, NY 12550-3921
845-562-5400
Fax: 845-562-7840
Bottled water
Owner: Tim Tenney
Estimated Sales: $5-10 Million
Number Employees: 5-9

10598 Reckitt Benckiser LLC
399 Interpace Pkwy.
PO Box 225
Parsippany, NJ 07054
973-404-2600
Fax: 973-404-5700 www.rb.com
Household cleaning and specialty food products.
CEO: Laxman Narasimhan
CFO: Adrian Hennah
Senior VP/General Counsel: Rupert Bondy
Year Founded: 1999
Estimated Sales: $14 Billion
Number Employees: 40,000
Number of Brands: 18
Square Footage: 139500
Type of Packaging: Consumer, Food Service, Bulk
Brands:
   Dettol
   Durex
   Mucinex
   Nurofen
   Scholl
   Strepsils
   Veet
   Clearasil
   Gaviscon
   Lysol
   Harpic
   Air Wick
   Cillit Bang
   Mortein
   Vanish
   Woolite
   Finish
   Calgon

10599 Rector Foods
2280 N Park Drive
Brampton, ON L6S 6C6
Canada
905-789-9691
Fax: 905-789-0989   888-314-7834
Seasoning blends
President: Eoin Connell
VP Sales: Michael Parry
Number Employees: 50
Square Footage: 212000

10600 Red Arrow Products Co LLC
633 S 20th St
Manitowoc, WI 54220-3816
920-769-1100
Fax: 920-769-1281 www.redarrowusa.com
Smoke and grill flavors; specialty browning
President: Jerald Kowalski
jerald@redarrow.com
Marketing Coordinator: Kayla Sommer
Sales: Mark Crass
Number Employees: 50-99
Type of Packaging: Food Service, Private Label, Bulk
Other Locations:
   Red Arrow Products Co.
   Manitowoc WI
Brands:
   Aro-Smoke
   Char Dex
   Char Oil
   Char Sol
   Char Zyme
   Grillin'
   Maillose
   Toastin
   True Gold

10601 Red Baron
115 W College Dr
Marshall, MN 56258-3799
507-532-3274
Fax: 507-537-8333   800-769-7980
Pizza
Owner: Greg Flack
Contact: Randy Brooks
r.brooks@redbaron.com
Director Manufacturing: Guy Hinton
Estimated Sales: Under $500,000
Number Employees: 5-9
Parent Co: Schwann's Sales

10602 Red Brick Brewing Company
2323 Defoor Hills Road
Atlanta, GA 30318
404-355-5558
Fax: 404-350-0127   800-475-5417
info@atlantabrewing.com
www.redbrickbrewing.com
Seasonal beer, ale, stout, lager and pilsner
President: Robet Budd
Sales: Robert Fowler
Contact: Tyler Cates
tylercates@atlantabrewing.com
Estimated Sales: $10-20 Million
Number Employees: 10-19
Type of Packaging: Consumer, Food Service
Brands:
   Red Brick

10603 Red Chamber Co
1912 E Vernon Ave
Vernon, CA 90058
323-234-9000
Fax: 323-231-8888 info@redchamber.com
www.redchamber.com
Seafood
CEO: Ming Bin Kou
CFO: Ming Shin Kou
VP: Andro Chen
VP, Food Innovation and R&D: Wales Yu
Year Founded: 1973
Estimated Sales: $100-500 Million
Number Employees: 100-249
Brands:
   Aqua Star
   Kitchens of the Oceans
   Mid-Pacific Seafoods
   Neptune Foods
   Singleton Seafoods
   Tampa Bay Fisheries
   and more

10604 Red Creek Marinade Company
P.O.Box 19875
Amarillo, TX 79114-1875
806-358-3531
Fax: 806-358-1587   800-687-9114
Mesquite-flavored marinades
Partner: Lawrence E New
Contact: Ginger New
redcreek@arn.net
Estimated Sales: $1-3 Million
Number Employees: 1-4
Number of Brands: 1
Number of Products: 3
Type of Packaging: Consumer, Food Service, Bulk
Brands:
   Red Creek

10605 Red Deer Lake Meat Processing
226 Avenue West
Calgary, AB T2J 5G5
Canada
403-256-4925
Fax: 403-256-8882 rdlmeats@telus.net
www.rdlmeats.ab.ca
Beef, hamburgers, pork, bacon, lamb, goat and sausage
President/General Manager Sales: Brian Barrett
CEO: Georgina Walker
Estimated Sales: $2-5 Million
Number Employees: 20-49
Type of Packaging: Consumer, Food Service, Private Label, Bulk
Brands:
   Rdl (Red Deer Lake)

10606 Red Diamond Coffee & Tea
400 Park Ave
Moody, AL 35004
800-292-4651
qcdept@reddiamond.com www.reddiamond.com
Coffee, tea pods and coffee brewers.
VP, Sales Development: John Padgett
VP, Manufacturing: Joe George
Year Founded: 1906
Estimated Sales: $45.9 Million
Number Employees: 100-249
Square Footage: 195000
Type of Packaging: Consumer, Food Service, Private Label, Bulk
Brands:
   Red Diamond Coffee & Tea

10607 Red Duck Foods
1515 SE Water Ave
Suite 103
Portland, OR 97214
USA
530-219-0150
www.redduckfoods.com
Artisanal ketchup, and BBQ, seafood and taco sauces
Marketing/Co-Founder: Jessica Hilbert
Operations/Co-Founder: Shannon Oliver
shannon@redduckfoods.com
Business Development: Karen Bonner
Number Employees: 5-9

10608 Red Gold Inc.
PO Box 83
Elwood, IN 46036
765-557-5500
Fax: 765-557-5501   866-729-7187
www.redgold.com
Sauces: tomato, pizza, taco, barbecue, chili, seafood, marinara and spaghetti; tomatoes
President/CEO: Brian Reichart
Senior VP/CFO: Tim Ingle

Food Manufacturers / A-Z

Year Founded: 1942
Estimated Sales: $750 Million
Number Employees: 2,100
Number of Brands: 5
Square Footage: 1000000
Type of Packaging: Consumer, Food Service, Private Label, Bulk
Other Locations:
  Red Gold
  Orestes IN
  Red Gold
  Geneva IN
Brands:
  Red Gold
  Tuttorosso
  Red Pack
  Sacramento
  Tuong Ot Sriracha

10609 Red Hat Cooperative
809 Broadway Avenue E
Redcliff, AB T0J 2P0
Canada
403-548-6208
Fax: 403-548-7255 sales@redhatco-op.com
www.redhatco-op.com
Vegetables
President: Albert Cramer
CEO: Lyle Aleman
Quality Control: Cassandra Cadrmin
Sales Manager: Blaine Andres
Operations: Tim Donnelly
Purchasing: Crystal McHargue
Number Employees: 180
Type of Packaging: Consumer, Food Service

10610 Red Hot Chicago
2501 N Damen Ave
Chicago, IL 60647-2101
312-829-3434
Fax: 312-829-2704 800-249-5226
info@redhotchicago.com www.redhotchicago.com
Chicago style hot dogs, buns and condiments.
President: Billy Ladany
billy@redhotchicago.com
Estimated Sales: $1-2 Million
Number Employees: 5-9
Type of Packaging: Food Service, Bulk
Brands:
  Red Hot Chicago

10611 Red Hot Foods
820 E Railroad Avenue
Santa Paula, CA 93060
805-258-3450
Fax: 805-525-6000 redhotfoods2003@yahoo.com
Condiments, relishes, salsas, sauces, olive oil, pesto, bean and chowder mixes.
President: Butch Baselite
Type of Packaging: Consumer, Food Service, Private Label, Bulk

10612 Red Lion Spicy Foods Company
420 W Broadway
Red Lion, PA 17356
717-309-8303
Fax: 717-244-7348 chip@redlionspicyfoods.com
www.redlionspicyfoods.com
Chili mixes and powder, dry rub, salsa, hot sauce, pepper pickles and garlic dills
President: Chip Welsh
Type of Packaging: Consumer

10613 Red Monkey Foods
6751 W Kings St
Springfield, MO 65802
417-319-7300
Fax: 314-754-9755 www.redmonkeyfoods.com
Spices, herbs, sauces, seasonings, cooking enhancers and rubs
President/Owner: Jeff Brinkhoff
CEO: Scott Bolonda
Contact: Tom Casey
tom.casey@redmonkeyfoods.com
Square Footage: 80000
Type of Packaging: Private Label

10614 Red Pelican Food Products
5650 Saint Jean Street
Detroit, MI 48213-3415
313-881-4095
Mustard, horseradish, relish, sauerkraut, vinegar, cheese, Belgian chocolate and sauce
President: Bernard Cornillie
Sales Manager: D Cornillie

Number Employees: 5-9
Square Footage: 56000
Type of Packaging: Consumer, Food Service, Private Label, Bulk

10615 Red Plate Foods
Bend, OR
541-550-7676
redplatefoods.com
Gluten-free baked goods
Co-Founder: Becca Williams
Co-Founder: Chell Williams

10616 Red River Commodities Inc
501 42nd St N
Fargo, ND 58102-3952
800-437-5539
contact@redriv.com www.redriv.com
Sunflower seeds, beans, millet, flax, soybeans and organics.
President & CEO: Eric Christianson
VP, Finance: Randy Wigen
Estimated Sales: $105.6 Million
Number Employees: 100-249
Square Footage: 140000
Type of Packaging: Food Service, Private Label, Bulk
Brands:
  Brown Flax
  Confection Sunflower Seed
  Goldtex

10617 Red River Foods Inc
9020 Stony Point Pkwy
Suite 380
Richmond, VA 23235-1944
804-320-1800
Fax: 804-320-1896 www.redriverfoods.net
Nuts, seeds, dried foods and snack foods
President: James Phipps
Controller: Keith Dickerson
Vice President: Jack Bousfield
Estimated Sales: $10-49.9 Million
Number Employees: 10-19
Number of Products: 30

10618 Red Rocker Candy
92B Industrial Drive
Suite 6
Troy, VA 22974
434-589-2011
Fax: 434-589-3649
sue.charney@redrockercandy.com
www.redrockercandy.com
Candy
Manager: Sue Charney
Estimated Sales: $250,000
Number Employees: 5

10619 Red Rose Trading Company
520 N Charlotte St
Lancaster, PA 17603
717-293-7833
Granola, pancake, baking and gluten-free mixes and blends
Owner: J Leichter
Estimated Sales: $3-5 Million
Number Employees: 10-19
Square Footage: 56000
Type of Packaging: Consumer, Food Service, Private Label, Bulk

10620 Red Smith Foods Inc
4145 SW 47th Ave
Davie, FL 33314-4006
954-581-1996
Fax: 954-581-6775 www.redsmithfoods.com
Pickled eggs, sausage and pigs' feet
President: Stephen Foster
bburton@redsmithfoods.com
COO: Jon Foster
CFO: Tim Foster
Executive VP: David Foster
Marketing & Sales Director: Brian Burton
Plant Manager: Michael Sandy
Estimated Sales: $8 Million
Number Employees: 20-49
Number of Brands: 2
Number of Products: 6
Square Footage: 48000
Parent Co: Red Smith of Florida, Inc.
Type of Packaging: Consumer

Brands:
  Big John
  Red Smith

10621 Red Star Yeast
P.O. Box 737
Milwaukee, WI 53201-0737
414-271-6755
Fax: 414-347-4795 800-445-4746
www.redstaryeast.com
Yeast, fermentation products
President & CEO: John Riesch
CFO: Geoff O'Connor
Director of Sales: Dean Modglin
Year Founded: 1882
Estimated Sales: $20-50 Million
Number Employees: 1,000-4,999
Brands:
  Red Star

10622 Red Steer Meats
3812 W Clarendon Ave
Phoenix, AZ 85019-3718
602-272-6677
Fax: 602-484-7381
Meat
President: Richard Barton
Vice President: Judy Barton
Estimated Sales: $5-10 000,000
Number Employees: 5-9
Type of Packaging: Private Label

10623 Red V Foods
1665 Heraeus Blvd
Buford, GA 30518
770-729-8983
Fax: 770-729-9428 info@redvfoods.com
www.redvfoods.com
Coconut products
Square Footage: 110000

10624 Red White & Brew
223 Ashley Ct
Redding, CA 96001-3656
530-222-5891
www.rwbaz.com
Beer
President: Bill Ward
Estimated Sales: $120,000
Number Employees: 3
Brands:
  Red White & Brew

10625 Red's All Natural
803 N Derby Ln
North Sioux City, SD 57049
605-956-7337
www.redsallnatural.com
Frozen burritos
Founder & CEO: Mike Adair

10626 Redd Superfood Energy Bars
R.e.d.d., Inc.
PO Box 15388
Portland, ME 04112
207-370-4433
www.reddbar.com
Energy bars
Founder & Chairman: Alden Blease
CEO: Peter Van Alstine
Marketing: Reed Allen
Number Employees: 2-10
Brands:
  Redd

10627 (HQ)Reddy Ice
5720 LBJ Freeway
Suite 200
Dallas, TX 75240
214-526-6740
800-683-4423
information@reddyice.com www.reddyice.com
Packaged ice products including cubes, blocks, and dry; Cold storage warehouse
Chairman: Bill Corbin
CEO: Deborah Conklin
CFO: Steven Janusek
COO: Paul Smith
Contact: Karen Apperson
kapperson@reddyice.com
Year Founded: 1927
Estimated Sales: $300 Million
Number Employees: 1000-4999

Food Manufacturers / A-Z

10628 Redhawk Vineyard & Winery
2995 Michigan City Rd NW
Salem, OR 97304-9704
503-362-1596
Fax: 503-585-4657 www.redhawkwine.com
Wines
Owner: John Pataccoli
jpatwine@aol.com
Estimated Sales: $350,000
Number Employees: 1-4
Type of Packaging: Private Label
Brands:
   Redhawk

10629 Redhook Brewery
929 North Russell St.
Portland, OR 97227
503-331-7270
redhook@redhook.com
www.redhook.com
Beer and ale
President: David Mickelson
redhook@redhook.com
CFO & Treasurer: Mark Moreland
Sales & Marketing Manager: Tim Oneill
Marketing Manager: Nelson Ray
Operations Manager: Naomi Graf
Estimated Sales: $20.4 Million
Number Employees: 10-19
Parent Co: Craft Brew Alliance
Type of Packaging: Consumer, Food Service
Brands:
   Ballard Bitter
   Black Hook
   Double Black
   Esb
   Hefeweizen
   Rye
   Wheatbrook
   Winterhook

10630 Redmond Minerals Inc
475 W 910 S
Heber City, UT 84032-2494
435-657-3600
Fax: 435-529-7486 866-312-7258
mail@redmondminerals.com
www.redmondinc.com
Sea salt
CEO: Rhett Roberts
Estimated Sales: $20-50 Million
Number Employees: 30
Type of Packaging: Consumer, Food Service, Private Label, Bulk

10631 Redondo Iglesias USA
67 New Hook Rd.
Suite 2E
Bayonne, NJ 11530-1631
201-455-5266
Fax: 201-455-5268 www.redondousa.com
Spanish hams: Serrano and Iberico
Sales & Marketing: Kate Whittum
Brands:
   Redondo Iglesias

10632 Redondo's LLC
94-140 Leokane St
Waipahu, HI 96797-2280
808-671-5444
Fax: 808-676-7009 www.redondos.com
Sausages
President: Hitoshi Okada
hitoshi@redondos.com
VP/General Manager: Yoshi Shinanti
VP: Toshiyuki Murakane
Owner: Frank Redondo
Estimated Sales: $5-10 Million
Number Employees: 20-49
Brands:
   Pipikaula

10633 Redwood Hill Farm
2064 Gravenstein Hwy N
Bldg. 1, Suite 130
Sebastopol, CA 95472
707-823-8250
Fax: 707-823-6976 877-238-3543
contact@redwoodhill.com redwoodhill.com
Goat milk yogurt, cheeses and kefir
Manager: Jennifer Bice
Marketing Director: Sharon Bice
Accounting Manager: Andrew Malmanis
Quality Control Manager: Ann Caswell
Owner: Jennifer Lynn Bice
Estimated Sales: $1-2.5 Million
Number Employees: 20-49
Type of Packaging: Private Label
Brands:
   Redwood Hill Farm

10634 Reed Lang Farms
118 W Colorado Ave
Rio Hondo, TX 78583
956-748-2354
Fax: 956-748-2888
Ruby Red and Rio Red grapefruits, navel oranges, Lula avacados, pecans, almonds and citrus blossom honey
President/Owner: Violet Lang
Estimated Sales: $50,000
Number Employees: 16
Square Footage: 44100
Type of Packaging: Private Label

10635 Reed's, Inc.
Los Angeles, CA
www.drinkreeds.com
Ginger beer

10636 Reeve Wines
PO Box 380
Healdsburg, CA 95448
707-235-6345
kelly@reevewines.com
www.reevewines.com
Wines
Co-Founder: Noah Dorrance
Co-Founder: Kelly Dorrance

10637 Refresco Beverages US Inc.
Tampa, FL 33614
813-313-1800
888-260-3776
ConsumerAffairs.NA@refresco.com
www.refresco-na.com
Soft drinks, sports and energy drinks, tea, and sparkling and flavoured water.
CFO, North America: Bill McFarland
COO, North America: Brad Goist
Estimated Sales: Over $1 Billion
Number Employees: 3,600
Type of Packaging: Consumer, Food Service, Private Label, Bulk
Brands:
   RC Cola
   RC Q
   Mulberry Farms
   Ben Shaws
   red rain
   Vit20
   Orient Emporium
   Vess
   Vintage
   Stars & Stripes
   So Clear
   Clear Choice
   Chadwick Bay
   Harvest Classic
   eXact

10638 Regal Crown Foods Inc
41 Mason St
Worcester, MA 01610-3203
508-752-2679
Fax: 508-831-0775
Vinegar pickles
Owner: William McEntee
regalcrownfoods@aol.com
Public Relations: Monica Freund Kaufman
Plant Manager: David Giorgio
Estimated Sales: $1-3 Million
Number Employees: 1-4
Number of Brands: 12
Number of Products: 6
Type of Packaging: Food Service, Private Label

10639 Regal Food Service
13206 Advance Dr
Houston, TX 77065-1102
281-477-3683
Fax: 713-222-2549
Sandwiches and spreads
Manager: Charles Smith
Estimated Sales: $10 Million
Number Employees: 50-99
Type of Packaging: Consumer, Food Service

10640 Regal Health Food
3705 W Grand Ave
Chicago, IL 60651-2236
773-252-1044
Fax: 773-252-0817 info@regalsnacks.com
www.regalsnacks.com
Dried fruits and nuts
President: Gregory Piatigorsky
regalgourmetfoods@gmail.com
VP Marketing/Sales: Igor Piatigorsky
Estimated Sales: $10-20 Million
Number Employees: 10-19
Square Footage: 54000
Type of Packaging: Consumer, Food Service, Private Label, Bulk
Brands:
   Regal

10641 Regatta Craft Mixers
63 Forest Ave
Locust Valley, NY 11560
info@regattacraftmixers.com
www.regattacraftmixers.com
Craft bar mixers
Acting CMO: Doug Metchick
Year Founded: 2006
Number of Products: 5

10642 Regco
46 Rogers Rd
Haverhill, MA 01835-6957
978-521-4370
Fax: 978-372-4371
Pitas
President: Regina Ragonese
pitadiva@regenies.com
Broker Sales Representative: Sheryl Makaron
Public Relations Director: Peter Ash
Production Supervisor: Guy Minnick
Number Employees: 20-49
Brands:
   Regenie's

10643 Regenie's Crunchy Pi
46 Rogers Rd
Haverhill, MA 01835-6957
978-521-4370
877-734-3643
info@regenies.com www.regenies.com
Pita chips
President/Owner: Regina Ragonese

10644 Regennas Candy Shop
10 Maple Lane
Myerstown, PA 17067
717-866-1873
www.clearcandy.com
Candy

10645 Regez Cheese & Paper Supply
N2603 Coplien Rd
Monroe, WI 53566
608-325-3417
Fax: 608-325-3499
Cheese
President: Michael Einbeck
Estimated Sales: $530,000
Number Employees: 1-4

10646 Reggie Balls Cajun Foods
501 Bunker Rd
Lake Charles, LA 70615-3875
337-436-0291
Fax: 337-433-9851 www.ballscajunfoods.com
Cajum seasonings and mixes; Contract packaging and private labeling
Owner/President: Reginald Ball
Estimated Sales: Less Than $500,000
Number Employees: 1-4
Type of Packaging: Private Label

10647 Reggie's Roast
1501 West Blancke Street
Linden, NJ 07036
908-862-3700
Fax: 908-862-3711 www.reggiesroast.com
Coffee.
President: Reggie Chungloy
Estimated Sales: $260,000
Number Employees: 4

Food Manufacturers / A-Z

10648 Reginald's Homemade LLC
Manakin Sabot, VA 23103
804-972-4040
www.reginaldshomemade.com
Nut butters
Owner: Andrew Broocker

10649 Register Meat Co
3160 Willow St
Cottondale, FL 32431-3334
850-352-4269
Fax: 850-352-2628
Pork and sausage
President: Al Kaempfer
Estimated Sales: $10 Million
Number Employees: 10-19
Type of Packaging: Consumer, Bulk

10650 Registry Steak & Seafood
7661 S 78th Ave
Unit B
Bridgeview, IL 60455-1271
708-458-3100
Fax: 708-458-3103
Meat, seafood
President: Tony Migacz
ynotshrimp@yahoo.com
Senior Vice President: Anthony S Migacz
Estimated Sales: $10 Million
Number Employees: 20-49
Square Footage: 5000
Type of Packaging: Food Service, Private Label, Bulk

10651 Rego Smoked Fish Company
6980 75th St
Flushing, NY 11379
718-894-1400
Fax: 718-894-9100
Smoked salmon, sturgeon, trout, sablefish and whitefish
President: Jason Spitz
Manager: Sheldon Spitz
Owner: Conrad Spitz
Estimated Sales: $500,000-$1 Million
Number Employees: 1-4
Square Footage: 28000
Type of Packaging: Consumer, Bulk
Brands:
  Spibro

10652 Reheis Co
235 Snyder Ave
Berkeley Heights, NJ 07922-1150
908-464-1500
Fax: 908-464-7726 rduffy@reheis.com
www.reheis.com
Potassium chloride
VP R&D: J C Parekh
VP Sales: D Fondots
VP Operations: J Bogan
Plant Manager: Gerry Kirwan
Estimated Sales: Less Than $500,000
Number Employees: 1-4
Brands:
  Kci

10653 Rehemond Farm Inc
232 Pottle Hill Rd
Minot, ME 04258-4802
207-345-5611
Fax: 207-345-5611
Poultry
Owner: Noella Hemond
Number Employees: 5-9
Brands:
  Oak Hurst Dairy

10654 Reid Foods
PO Box 406
Gurnee, IL 60031
847-625-7912
Fax: 847-625-7913 888-295-8478
reidfoods@yahoo.com www.reidfoods.com
Jams, dessert toppings, salsas, soups, pasta, pasta sauces, dips and chili
President: Maria Reid
Estimated Sales: $190,000
Number Employees: 3

10655 (HQ)Reilly Dairy & Food Company
6603 S Trask Avenue
Tampa, FL 33616
813-839-8458
Fax: 813-839-0394
Cheese, dairy, butter
President: Gerald Reilly
rdfjerry@gmail.com
Human Resources Director: Brenda Reilly
Estimated Sales: $16,000,000
Number Employees: 70
Square Footage: 36000
Type of Packaging: Consumer, Food Service, Private Label, Bulk
Brands:
  Dixie Fresh
  Wisconsin Gold

10656 Reilly's Sea Products
PO Box 149
South Bristol, ME 04568-0149
207-644-1400
Fax: 207-644-8192
Seafood
President: Terry Reilly
Estimated Sales: $5-10 Million
Number Employees: 20-49

10657 Reily Foods Company
400 Poydras St
10th Floor
New Orleans, LA 70130
Fax: 504-539-5427 800-535-1961
service@reilyproducts.com
www.reilyproducts.com
Coffee, tea, cake flour, sauces, chili seasonings, salad dressings, bean soups and brownie mixes.
President & COO: Mark Reed
Plant Manager: Duane Montague
Year Founded: 1902
Estimated Sales: $101.7 Million
Number Employees: 500-999
Square Footage: 500000
Type of Packaging: Consumer, Food Service, Private Label, Bulk
Brands:
  Blue Plate Mayonnaise
  Carroll Shelby Chili Kits
  Cdm Coffee & Chicory
  French Market Coffee
  Jfg Coffee and Tea
  La Martinique
  Luzianne
  No Pudge! Brownie Mix
  Old Dutch
  Presto
  Swans Down Cake Flour
  Try Me Sauces/Seasonings
  Wick Fowler Chili Kits

10658 Reimann Food Classics
1304 E Cooper Drive
Palatine, IL 60074-7284
847-991-1366
Fax: 847-359-7528
Pancake and waffle mixes
President: E Reimann
Number Employees: 5-9
Type of Packaging: Consumer

10659 Reinhart Foods
235 Yorkland Blvd
Suite 1101
Toronto, ON M2J 4Y8
Canada
416-645-4910
Fax: 888-519-0079 cs@reinhartfoods.com
www.reinhartfoods.com
Vinegar, maraschino cherries, glace fruit, dates, raisins, coconut, mince meat, pie fillings, apples and pineapples
President/CEO: Jeff King
Director of Sales/Bus. Dev./Marketing: Michael J.
Parent Co: Reinhart Vinegars
Type of Packaging: Consumer, Food Service, Private Label, Bulk
Brands:
  Allen's
  Daltons
  Jaffa

10660 Reinhold Ice Cream Company
800 Fulton St
Pittsburgh, PA 15233-2119
412-321-7600
Fax: 412-321-8456
Ice cream and frozen yogurt
President: Robert Mandell
Vice President: Michael Mandell
Salesman: Diane Beckerman
Contact: Joseph Olsavsky
joseph.olsavsky@philips.com
Plant Manager: Craig Metzgar
Estimated Sales: $7,400,000
Number Employees: 190
Type of Packaging: Consumer, Food Service, Private Label, Bulk

10661 Reist Popcorn Co
113 Manheim St
Mt Joy, PA 17552-1317
717-653-8078
Fax: 717-653-4121 reistpopcorn.com
Popcorn
President: David Reist
dreist@reistpopcorn.com
Estimated Sales: Less Than $500,000
Number Employees: 5-9
Type of Packaging: Private Label, Bulk
Brands:
  Dutch Country
  Hi-Pop

10662 Reiter Affiliated Companies
730 S A St.
Oxnard, CA 93030
805-483-1000
info@berry.net
www.berry.net
Strawberries, raspberries, blueberries and blackberries
President & CEO: Hector Lujan Valladolid
Year Founded: 1900
Number Employees: 10,000+
Type of Packaging: Private Label

10663 Reiter Dairy
216 E 11th St
Newport, KY 41071
859-431-7553
Fax: 859-431-0349 800-544-6455
www.reiterdairy.com
Juice and dairy
General Manager: Bill Riley
Cmo: Dan Smith
dan_smith@deanfoods.com
Year Founded: 1933
Number Employees: 250-499
Square Footage: 100000
Parent Co: Suiza Foods
Type of Packaging: Consumer, Food Service, Private Label, Bulk

10664 Reiter Dairy LLC
1961 Commerce Circle
Springfield, OH 45504
937-323-5777
Fax: 937-323-2420
www.deanfoods.com/brands/reiter-dairy/
Orange juice, bottled water, dairy, cheese, ice cream and sour cream.
Sales Executive: Steve Paasch
General Manager: Mike Allen
mike_allen@deanfoods.com
Year Founded: 1933
Estimated Sales: $100-124.9 Million
Number Employees: 100-249
Number of Brands: 3
Square Footage: 25000
Parent Co: Dean Foods Company
Type of Packaging: Consumer, Food Service
Brands:
  Jersey Farms
  Louis Trauth
  Reiter

10665 Rejuvila
PO Box 21447
Boulder, CO 80308
877-480-4402
info@rejuvila.com
Supplements
Founder: Myra Michelle Eby
Contact: Alene Bourcier
arlene@rejuvila.com

Food Manufacturers / A-Z

Type of Packaging: Consumer

10666 Remarkable Liquids
2 Van Buren Blvd, NE Industrial Park
Altamont, NY 12009
518-861-5351
www.remarkableliquids.com
Craft beers, ciders, and meads.
General Manager: Spencer Noakes
Partner: Matt Hartman
VP, Operations: Chad Farrington
Operations Manager: Jason Napoleon
Year Founded: 2012
Estimated Sales: $11 Million
Number Employees: 52
Number of Brands: 67
Brands:
  12% IMPORTS
  ABANDON BREWING CO.
  AGAINST THE GRAIN BREWERY
  ALMANAC BEER CO.
  ANCHORAGE BREWING CO.
  ARGUS CIDERY
  B. NEKTAR MEADERY
  BEAU'S ALL-NATURAL BREWING
  BREWMASTER JACK
  BROUWERIJ ST. BERNARDUS
  BROUWERIJ VERHAEGHE
  CLARDERA BREWING
  CAPTAIN LAWRENCE BREWING CO.
  CIDER CREEK HARD CIDER
  COLONY MEADERY
  COMMUNITY BEAR WORKS
  CROOKED STAVE
  DARK HORSE BREWING
  EVIL TWIN
  FINBACK BREWERY
  FOLEY BROTHERS BREWING

10667 Rembrandt Foods
1521 18th Street
Spirit Lake, IA 51360
877-344-4055
contactus@rembrandtinc.com
www.rembrandtfoods.com
Egg
President: David Rettig
Number Employees: 50-99
Type of Packaging: Food Service

10668 Renaissance Vineyard & Winery
12585 Rices Crossing Rd
Oregon House, CA 95962
530-692-2248
Fax: 530-692-2497 800-655-3277
www.renaissancewinery.com
Wine
President: Greg Holman
Vice President: Hagit Raubach
Sales: John Brooks
Office Manager: Sharon Shelton
Estimated Sales: $5-10 Million
Number Employees: 10-19
Number of Brands: 1
Type of Packaging: Consumer, Food Service
Brands:
  Renaissance

10669 Renard's Cheese
248 County Rd S
Algoma, WI 54201-9444
920-487-2825
Fax: 920-487-5042 orders@renardscheese.com
www.renards.com
Cheese
Owner: Tina Renard
renards@renards.com
Proprietor: Gary Renard
Vice President: Chris Renard
Estimated Sales: $5-9.9 Million
Number Employees: 10-19
Type of Packaging: Private Label

10670 Renault Winery
72 N Bremen Ave
Egg Harbor City, NJ 08215
609-965-2111
www.renaultwinery.com
Vermouth and wine
Estimated Sales: $3649539
Number Employees: 100-249
Type of Packaging: Consumer

10671 Rendulic Meat Packing Corp
800 Manning Ave
Mckeesport, PA 15132-3699
412-678-9541
Fax: 412-678-8891 info@nemahalal.com
www.nemahalal.com
Meat: bologna, suckling pig, veal and lamb
President: Beyhan Nakiboglo
Estimated Sales: $3300000
Number Employees: 10-19
Type of Packaging: Consumer

10672 Rene Produce Dist
895 E Frontage Rd
Rio Rico, AZ 85648-9675
520-281-0806
Fax: 520-281-2933 reneprod@dakotacom.net
www.reneproduce.com
Cucumbers, eggplant, squash, tomatoes and peppers
President: Rene Carrillo
carrillo@reneproduce.com
Sales Manager: David Kennedy
Sales: George Quintero
Estimated Sales: $3-5 Million
Number Employees: 10-19
Type of Packaging: Consumer, Food Service
Brands:
  Rene

10673 Rene Rey Chocolates Ltd
1119 West 14th Street
North Vancouver, BC V7P 1J9
Canada
604-985-0949
Fax: 604-985-0395 888-985-0949
sales@renerey.com www.renerey.com
Chocolate, candy
President: Rene Rey
Director Of Marketing: Gerald Pinton
Square Footage: 40000
Brands:
  Maple Nuts
  Nature Canada
  Sun Moon Stars

10674 Renfro Foods
PO Box 321
Fort Worth, TX 76101
800-332-2456
www.renfrofoods.com
Condiments and dips
President/Owner: Doug Renfro
CEO: Bill Renfro
COO: Jack Renfro
Brands:
  Mrs. Renfro's

10675 Renwood Mills
P.O. Box 350
Newton, NC 28658
828-464-1611
info@renwoodmills.com
www.renwoodmills.com
Processor of flour, corn meal, biscuit flour and baking mixes.
CEO: Bill Mackin
Commercial Business Manager: Steve Arndt
Year Founded: 1935
Estimated Sales: $271 Million
Number Employees: 100-249
Type of Packaging: Consumer, Food Service, Private Label, Bulk
Brands:
  Redimix
  Southern Biscuit
  Tenda Bake

10676 Renwood Winery
12225 Steiner Rd
Plymouth, CA 95669-9502
209-245-6979
Fax: 916-245-6013 800-348-8466
www.renwood.com
Wines
President: Robert Smerling
info@renwood.com
CFO: Bob Moore
VP Marketing: Joe Cusimano
Manager: Abby Bishop
Operations Manager: Bryan Wilkinson
Estimated Sales: $5-10 Million
Number Employees: 10-19
Square Footage: 72
Type of Packaging: Private Label
Brands:
  Renwood Wines
  Santino Wines

10677 Republic of Tea
5 Hamilton Landing
Suite 100
Novato, CA 94949-8703
415-382-3400
Fax: 415-382-3401 800-298-4832
info@republicoftea.com www.republicoftea.com
Tea and teaware
President: Ronald Rubin
CFO: Steve Lohmann
VP: Tod Rubin
Contact: Elizabeth Anderson
elizabeth@elizabeth-haley.com
Operations: Eva Wong
Estimated Sales: $2.5-5 Million
Number Employees: 25
Brands:
  Daily Green Teas
  Red Tea
  Republic of Tea

10678 Republica Del Cacao LLC
3780 Kilroy Airport Way
Suite 200
Long Beach, CA 90806
932-256-1320
Fax: 562-256-7001
Cocoa & baking chocolate, baking mixes and ingredients; chocolate bars
Manager: Bernard Duclos
Member: Ganzano Chieiboga
Estimated Sales: $74,000
Number Employees: 3

10679 Request Foods Inc
3460 John F Donnelly Dr
Holland, MI 49424-9569
616-786-0900
Fax: 616-786-9180 800-786-0900
info@requestfoods.com www.requestfoods.com
Frozen entrees and dinners
President: Jack Dewitt
jacdew@requestfoods.com
CFO: Bill Rysdyk
R & D: Jurgen Becker
Quality Control: Tom Muntter
Operations Director: Merle DeWitt
Purchasing Agent: Larry Vanderkolk
Estimated Sales: $31 Million
Number Employees: 250-499
Square Footage: 350000
Type of Packaging: Consumer, Food Service, Private Label

10680 Research Products Co
1835 E North St
Salina, KS 67401-8567
785-825-2181
Fax: 785-825-8908 800-234-7174
www.researchprod.com
Flour bleaching and maturing premixers; vitamins and minerals
President: Monte White
montewhite@researchprod.com
Estimated Sales: $10-20 Million
Number Employees: 50-99
Parent Co: McShares
Brands:
  Kurolite
  Oxylite

10681 Reser's Fine Foods Inc
P.O. Box 8
Beaverton, OR 97075
503-643-6431
800-333-6431
www.resers.com
Frozen dinners: cold salads, tortillas, salsas, smoked meats
President & CEO: Mark Reser
CFO & Treasurer: Paul Leavy
EVP, Sales, Marketing and R&D: Peter Sirgy
VP, Supply Chain: Pete Shepard
Year Founded: 1950
Estimated Sales: $310 Million
Number Employees: 3,000
Parent Co: Belletieri Company
Brands:
  Reser's American Classics
  Reser's Sensational Sides

Food Manufacturers / A-Z

Baja Cafe
Stonemill Kitchens

10682 Resource Trading Company
72 Commercial Street
Portland, ME 04104-1698
207-772-2299
Fax: 207-772-4709
Lobster, scallops and shrimp
President: Spencer Fuller
Domestic Sales: Tom Keegan
International Sales: Irene Ketalaar-Moon
Type of Packaging: Bulk
Brands:
  Arctic Pride
  Claw Island
  Northern Lights

10683 Restaurant Data
1 Bridge St
Irvington, NY 10533-1560
732-667-5885
Fax: 914-591-5494 800-346-9390
info@netsoftsolutions.com restaurantdata.com
Cashew and other nuts; Co-packing services
President: James Santo
R&D: Paul Mlynar
Contact: Jeff Kydd
jeff@foodservicereport.com
Purchasing Director: Joe Di Donato
Estimated Sales: $1-2 Million
Number Employees: 1-4
Number of Brands: 1
Number of Products: 12
Square Footage: 48000
Type of Packaging: Consumer, Private Label, Bulk
Brands:
  Nutsco

10684 Restaurant Lulu GourmetProducts
816 Folsom Street
San Francisco, CA 94107
415-495-5775
Fax: 415-495-7810 888-693-5800
Olive tapenade, honey, vinegars, seasonings, sauces and tomato
Manager: Tom Ratcliff
Sales Director: Leslie Wilson
Estimated Sales: $2.5-5 Million
Number Employees: 1-4
Square Footage: 16000
Type of Packaging: Private Label

10685 Restaurant Systems International
1000 South Avenue
Staten Island, NY 10314-3430
718-494-8888
Fax: 718-494-8776
Frozen yogurt
CEO: Richard Nicotra
Contact: Joe Giannetti
jgiannetti@restsys.com
Number Employees: 20-49
Square Footage: 40000

10686 Reter Fruit
3100 S Pacific Hwy
Medford, OR 97501-8758
541-772-9560
Fax: 541-772-5258
Pears
President: F Baker
Estimated Sales: $380000
Number Employees: 50-99
Type of Packaging: Consumer
Brands:
  Maltese Cross
  Sun-Sugared

10687 Rethemeyer Coffee Company
1711 N Broadway
St Louis, MO 63102
314-231-0990
Coffee
President: A Rethemeyer
Estimated Sales: Less than $500,000
Number Employees: 1-4
Brands:
  Rethemeyer

10688 Retzlaff Vineyards
1356 S Livermore Ave
Livermore, CA 94550-9505
925-447-8941
Fax: 925-447-9641 retzlaffwinery@gmail.com
www.retzlaffvineyards.com
Wines
Owner: Gloria Taylor
retzlaffwinery@gmail.com
Marketing Manager: Connie Vander Vouter
Estimated Sales: Below $5 Million
Number Employees: 10-19
Brands:
  Retzlaff Estate Wines

10689 Reutter Candy & Chocolates
4665 Hollins Ferry Road
Baltimore, MD 21227-4601
800-392-0870
Fax: 410-510-1222
Candy, chocolate
International Sales: Karl Heigold
Brands:
  Choco Berries
  Fine Mints
  The Mint

10690 Reva Foods
Saint Petersburg, FL 33732
727-692-1292
www.revafoods.com
Sauces, salsas, relish, ketchups, rubs, and seasonings.
President: Kathy Varricchio

10691 Revel, Gelato
Huntington Beach, CA
866-203-9145
www.revelegelato.com
Whipped gelato

10692 Revive Kombucha
101 2nd St
Suite 190
Petaluma, CA 94952
707-536-1193
thirsty@revivekombucha.com
www.revivekombucha.com
Kombucha beverages
Founder & CEO: Sean J. Lovett
Executive Assistant: Leah Burke
Director of Operations: Rebekah Lovett
Number Employees: 11-50
Brands:
  Revive Kombucha

10693 Revonah Pretzel LLC
507 Baltimore St Rear
Hanover, PA 17331-3396
717-630-2883
Fax: 717-632-3328 www.revonahpretzel.com
Pretzels and potato chips
Owner: Kevin Bidelspach
kevinb@revonahpretzel.com
Estimated Sales: $3900000
Number Employees: 5-9
Square Footage: 96000
Type of Packaging: Consumer, Food Service, Private Label, Bulk
Brands:
  Bickel
  Sam & Nick's
  Tom Sturgis

10694 Reynolds Sugar Bush
188572 W Maple Road
Aniwa, WI 54408
715-449-2057
Fax: 715-449-2879
Maple syrup
President: Juan Reynolds
Estimated Sales: Below $5 000,000
Number Employees: 4
Type of Packaging: Private Label

10695 Rezolex LLC
3 E Fort Selden Rd
Radium Springs, NM 88054
575-527-1730
Fax: 575-527-0221 www.rezolex.com
Seasonings
President: Louis Biad
rezolex.com@zianet.com
Plant Manager: Robert Stomp

Estimated Sales: Below $5 000,000
Number Employees: 20-49

10696 Rhino Foods Inc
79 Industrial Pkwy
Burlington, VT 05401-5435
802-862-0252
Fax: 802-865-4145 info@rhinofoods.com
www.rhinofoods.com
Ice cream, brownies, cookie dough batter, cakes, truffles, pie squares and baking inclusions.
President/Owner: Ted Castle
tcastle@rhinofoods.com
Director of Finance & Administration: Jayne Magnant
Research & Development Specialist: Rob Douglas
Quality Assurance Manager: Lauren Weber
Director of Marketing: Dan Kiniry
Marketing Manager/Demand Planner: Gillian Bell
Director of Operations: Gene Steinfeld
Year Founded: 1981
Estimated Sales: $25 Million
Number Employees: 100-249
Number of Brands: 2
Square Footage: 29000
Type of Packaging: Consumer, Food Service, Private Label, Bulk
Brands:
  Chessters
  Vermont Velvet

10697 Rhodes Bean & Supply Co-Op
24710 S Bird Rd
Tracy, CA 95304-9339
209-835-1284
Fax: 209-835-1304 ken@beanplant.com
www.beanplant.com
Dried beans
General Manager: Ken Kirsten
ken@beanplant.com
Estimated Sales: $500,000-$1 Million
Number Employees: 10-19
Type of Packaging: Bulk
Brands:
  Rhodes-Stockton Bean

10698 Rhodes International Inc
5121 S Murray Blvd
Salt Lake City, UT 84123-4602
801-972-0122
Fax: 801-972-0286 800-876-7333
customersatisfaction@rhodesbread.com
www.rhodesbread.com
Bread rolls
President & CEO: Ken Farnworth
Year Founded: 1932
Estimated Sales: $20-50 Million
Number Employees: 50-99
Square Footage: 30000
Type of Packaging: Consumer, Food Service, Private Label
Brands:
  Dakota Hearth
  Rhodes

10699 Rhythm Superfoods
PO Box 41345
Austin, TX 78704
512-441-5667
rhythmsuperfoods.com
Kale, beet and sweet potato chips
Co-Founder/President & CEO: Scott Jensen
Co-Founder & Creative Director: Keith Wahrer
CFO: Jeff Tusa
Controller: Alison White
Marketing Director: Sarah Caddell
VP Of Sales: Calvin Daily
Contact: Sarah Alexander
salexander@rhythmsuperfoods.com
Operations Director: Becky Conces
Type of Packaging: Consumer
Brands:
  Rhythm Superfoods

10700 Rib Rack
Birmingham, MI
www.theribrack.com
BBQ sauce
VP, Sales: Rich Gustafson

1063

Food Manufacturers / A-Z

10701 Riba Foods
P.O.Box 630461
Houston, TX 77263-0461
713-975-7001
Fax: 713-975-7036 800-327-7422
info@ribafoods.com www.ribafoods.com
Salsas, pickles, jalapeno peppers, mustards, sauces and bean dips
President: Miguel Barrios
Manager Sales/Marketing: Richard Wall
Contact: Misael Avellaneda
misael@ribafoods.com
Estimated Sales: $5-10 Million
Number Employees: 10-19
Number of Brands: 3
Number of Products: 45
Square Footage: 80000
Type of Packaging: Consumer, Food Service, Private Label
Brands:
   Arriba
   NortenA
   Texas Pepper Works

10702 Ribble Production
1601 Mearns Road
Warminster, PA 18974-1115
215-674-1706
Fax: 215-674-0123
Decorative toppings, nonpareils, jimmies and mixes; custom manufacturing and packaging
VP: Joseph Van Houten
Number Employees: 20-49
Type of Packaging: Consumer, Food Service, Private Label, Bulk

10703 Ribus Inc.
10900 Manchester Rd
Suite 206
St. Louis, MO 63122
314-727-4287
Fax: 314-727-1199 info@ribus.com
www.ribus.com
Rice-based food ingredients, emulsifiers and extrusion aids
President: Steve Pierce
steve@ribus.com
Finance Supervisor: Michelle Kyle
Technical Manager: Neal Hammond
Manager, Global Marketing: Laurie Wittenbrink
Sales: Jim Goodall
Director of Operations: Peggy Vorwald
Estimated Sales: $720000
Number Employees: 1-4
Square Footage: 40000
Type of Packaging: Food Service, Private Label, Bulk
Other Locations:
   RIBUS
   Sabetha KS
Brands:
   Nu-RICE
   Nu-MAG
   Nu-FLOW
   Nu-FLAC
   Nu-BAKE
   Nu-BIND

10704 Rice Company
11140 Fair Oaks Blvd
Suite 101
Fair Oaks, CA 95628
916-784-7745
Fax: 916-784-7681 jobs@riceco.com
www.riceco.com
Rice, popcorn, rice flour, sugar, beans, peas, lentils and ginger
Owner: Duane Kistner
President: J Kapila
Operations Manager: Vicki Manzoli
Estimated Sales: $4500000
Number Employees: 50-99
Type of Packaging: Consumer, Food Service, Private Label, Bulk

10705 Rice Foods
826 Harrington St.
Mount Vernon, IL 62864-3923
618-242-0026
Fax: 618-242-3109
Rice
CEO: Lynn Withworth

10706 Rice Fruit Co
2760 Carlisle Rd
Gardners, PA 17324-9684
717-677-9842
Fax: 717-677-9842 800-627-3359
info@ricefruit.com www.ricefruit.com
Apples, peaches and pears.
President: David Rice
david.rice@ricefruitcompany.com
Sales: John Rice
Number Employees: 50-99
Type of Packaging: Consumer, Food Service, Bulk

10707 Rice Hull Specialty Products
1304 Highway
Spur 146
Stuttgart, AR 72160
870-673-8507
Fax: 870-673-2116 www.ricehull.com
Parboiled rice hulls
President: John Moore
Sales Manager: Greg Crawford
Estimated Sales: $1600000
Number Employees: 10-19

10708 Rice Innovations
13112 Santa Ana Ave
Unit A2-A3
Fontana, CA 92337
Canada
909-823-8230
Fax: 909-823-2708
Rice, potato pastas, beverages
General Manager: Raj Sukul
R&D: Ly Hung
Customer Service: Sally Chee
Estimated Sales: $100,000
Number Employees: 1-4
Type of Packaging: Private Label
Brands:
   Body Fuel
   Cafe Bonjour
   Celifibr
   Herb Science
   Macariz
   Medicea
   Pastariso
   Pastato
   Rice Reality
   Ying Yang

10709 RiceBran Technologies
6720 N Scottsdale Road
Suite 390
Scottsdale, AZ 85253
602-522-3000
Fax: 602-522-3001 info@ricebrantech.com
www.ricebrantech.com
Rice bran and rice bran oil
CEO: W. John Short
CFO: J. Dale Belt
Sales & Marketing: Mark McKnight
Contact: Robert Smith
rsmith@ricebrantech.com
Manufacturing & Supply Chain: Robert DePaul
Estimated Sales: $40 Million
Number Employees: 278
Other Locations:
   Arbuckle CA
   Dillon MT
   Irving TX
   Mermentau LA
   Corporate Headquarters
   Phoenix AZ
   West Sacramento CA
   Pelotas, Brazil
Brands:
   Proryza P-35
   Proryza Platinum
   Proryza PF-20/50
   RiBran

10710 Riceland Foods Inc.
PO Box 927
Stuttgart, AR 72160
870-673-5500
855-742-3929
riceland@riceland.com www.riceland.com
Rice and rice bran oils.
CEO: Danny Kennedy
Estimated Sales: $1.3 Billion
Number Employees: 1,500
Type of Packaging: Consumer, Food Service, Private Label, Bulk
Other Locations:
   Newport AR
   Weiner AR
   Knobel AR
   Holly Grove AR
   Tuckerman AR
   Corning AR
   Stuttgart AR
   Des Arc AR
   Hazen AR
   Wheatley AR
   Dumas AR
   Griffithville AR
Brands:
   Riceland

10711 Rices Potato Chips
9407 Boyette Rd
Biloxi, MS 39532-8143
228-396-5775
Fax: 228-396-5775
Potato chips
President: Martha Vergunst
Estimated Sales: Less than $250,000
Number Employees: 2
Type of Packaging: Private Label

10712 Ricetec
1925 Fm 2917 Rd
PO Box 1305
Alvin, TX 77512
281-756-3300
Fax: 281-393-3532 800-580-7423
CustomerService@ricetec.com www.ricetec.com
Rice: Indian-style, basmati and American jasmine; rice mixes
President: John Nelson
jnelson@ricetec.com
CEO: Mike Gumina
EVP Business Development: Ken Fearday
VP Research & Development: Jose Re
Director Quality: Tim Williamson
Director Sales & Technical Services: Van McNeely
Estimated Sales: $33.4 Million
Number Employees: 50-99
Type of Packaging: Consumer, Food Service, Private Label, Bulk
Brands:
   Chefs Originals
   Jasmati
   Kasmati
   Texmati

10713 Ricex Company
1241 Hawks Flight Court
El Dorado Hills, CA 95762-9648
916-933-3000
Fax: 916-933-3232
Rice bran and rice bran fiber
President: Terrence Barber
CEO: Bradley Edson
CFO: Todd Crow
Contact: Terry Leclair
terry@inquira.com
Estimated Sales: $3511295
Number Employees: 12
Square Footage: 80000
Type of Packaging: Bulk
Brands:
   Ricex

10714 (HQ)Rich Products Corp
1 Robert Rich Way
Buffalo, NY 14213-1701
716-878-8000
Fax: 716-878-8266 800-828-2021
www.richs.com
Baked goods, dough, nondairy creamers, whipped toppings and Italian foods
President & CEO: Bill Gisel
Chief Financial Officer: Jim Deuschle
jdeuschle@rich.com
Chief Operating Officer: Richard Ferranti
Estimated Sales: Over $1 Billion
Number Employees: 5000-9999
Parent Co: Rich Products Corporation
Type of Packaging: Consumer, Food Service, Private Label, Bulk
Brands:
   Allen
   Avoset
   Bahama Blast(tm)
   Byron's Barbecue
   Casa Dibertacchi
   Coffee Rich

Food Manufacturers / A-Z

Farm Rich
Gold Label Plus Dairy
Jon Donaire
Mother's Kitchen
Presto
Rich's Eclairs
Seapak
Tres Riches

10715 Rich Products Corp
1910 Gallagher Dr
Vineland, NJ 08360-1545
856-696-5600
Fax: 856-696-3341 800-818-9261
info@richs.com www.richs.com
Italian meat balls, pasta and sausage
Estimated Sales: $20-50 Million
Number Employees: 100-249
Square Footage: 100000
Parent Co: Rich Products Corporation
Type of Packaging: Consumer, Food Service

10716 Rich's Ice Cream Co Inc
2915 S Dixie Hwy
West Palm Beach, FL 33405-1585
561-833-7585
Fax: 561-655-1952 www.richicecream.com
Ice cream, cream puffs, chocolate eclairs and cakes
CEO: Jhon Rich
Controller: Bob Thomas
Marketing Director: Randy Rich
randyice@bellsouth.net
Number Employees: 100-249
Type of Packaging: Consumer, Food Service
Brands:
  Rich Ice Creams

10717 Richard Bagdasarian Inc
65500 Lincoln St
Mecca, CA 92254-6500
760-396-2168
Fax: 760-396-2801 CBriones@mrgrape.com
www.mrgrape.com
Table grapes, citrus and vegetables
Owner: Mike Bozick
mbozick@mrgrape.com
VP/Manager: Nick Bozick
VP/Manager: Franz DeKlotz
VP/Manager: Bill Spidell
Number Employees: 10-19
Type of Packaging: Food Service

10718 Richard E. Colgin Company
2230 Valdina St
Dallas, TX 75207-6106
214-951-8687
Fax: 214-951-8668 888-226-5446
sales@colgin.com www.colgin.com
Liquid smoke flavorings
CEO: Kerry Thornhill
President: Elizabeth Thornhill
CFO: Sarah Johnson
Contact: Elizabeth Gardner
elizabeth@colgin.com
Estimated Sales: $2 Million
Number Employees: 20
Type of Packaging: Private Label
Brands:
  Chigarid
  Colgin

10719 Richard Green Company
1827 South Meridian St.
Indianapolis, IN 46225
317-972-0941
Fax: 317-972-1201 www.thepeanutking.com
Popcorn and nuts
President: Richard Green
Contact: Richard Byrd
rick@thepeanutking.com
Estimated Sales: $500,000-$1 Million
Number Employees: 5-9
Square Footage: 96000
Type of Packaging: Consumer, Private Label

10720 Richard L. Graeser Winery
255 Petrified Forest Rd
Calistoga, CA 94515
707-942-4437
Fax: 707-942-4437 www.graeserwinery.com
Wines
Owner: Richard Graeser
Estimated Sales: $500,000-$1 Million
Number Employees: 5-9

Type of Packaging: Private Label
Brands:
  Graeser

10721 Richard's Gourmet Coffee
124 Turnpike St
Suite 10
West Bridgewater, MA 02379
508-587-0800
Fax: 508-587-8139 800-370-2633
sales@richardsgourmet.com
www.richardsgourmet.com
Coffees and teas, lemonade, cappuccino, cocoa and spiced cider
President: Richard Salzman
sales@richardsgourmet.com
Estimated Sales: Below $5 Million
Number Employees: 10-19
Type of Packaging: Private Label
Brands:
  Richard's Gourmet

10722 Richards Maple Products
545 Water St
Chardon, OH 44024-1142
440-286-4160
Fax: 440-286-7203 800-352-4052
sales@richardsmapleproducts.com
www.richardsmapleproducts.com
Maple candy and syrup
Marketing Director: Debbie Richards
CFO: Annette Polson
Estimated Sales: Under $1 Million
Number Employees: 5-9
Square Footage: 16640
Type of Packaging: Consumer, Private Label, Bulk
Brands:
  Richards' Maple Candy
  Richards' Maple Syrup

10723 Richards Natural Foods
15213 S Hinman Road
Eagle, MI 48822-9703
517-627-7965
Natural and organic foods
President: Richard Osterbeck
EVP: Janet Splicer
Sales/Marketing: George Waite
Estimated Sales: Under $500,000
Number Employees: 1-4

10724 Richardson Brands Co
101 Erie Blvd
Canajoharie, NY 13317-1148
518-673-3553
Fax: 518-673-2451 www.richardsonbrands.com
Confectionery
Owner: Richard P Anderson
Supply Chain Manager: Rebecca Woodruff
Sr Traffic Controller: Marion Darrach
Senior VP Sales & Marketing: Michael Smith
Estimated Sales: $20 Million
Number Employees: 100-249
Type of Packaging: Consumer, Food Service, Private Label, Bulk
Brands:
  Dryden & Palmer
  Bogdon's
  Gravy Master
  Beechies

10725 Richardson International
2800 One Lombard Pl.
Winnipeg, MB R3B 0X8
Canada
204-934-5961
866-217-6211
communications@richardson.ca
www.richardson.ca
Grains and oilseed.
President/CEO: Curt Vossen
Year Founded: 1857
Estimated Sales: $28.6 Billion
Number Employees: 2,500
Type of Packaging: Consumer, Food Service, Private Label, Bulk

10726 Richardson Vineyards
2711 Knob Hill Road
Sonoma, CA 95476-9560
707-938-2610
Wines
President/CEO: Dennis Richardson

Estimated Sales: Less than $100,000
Number Employees: 1

10727 Richardson's Ice Cream
156 S Main St
Middleton, MA 01949-2452
978-774-5450
Fax: 978-777-6863
info@richardsonsicecream.com
www.richardsonsicecream.com
Ice cream
President: Dave Daniels
Estimated Sales: $5 Million
Number Employees: 10-19
Number of Brands: 1
Number of Products: 1
Type of Packaging: Consumer, Bulk
Brands:
  Richardson's Ice Cream

10728 Richelieu Foods Inc
222 Forbes Rd
Suite 4400
Braintree, MA 02184
781-786-6800
Fax: 781-843-1784 info@richelieufoods.com
www.richelieufoods.com
Pizzas, salad dressings, marinades, crusts and salsas
President & CEO: Ric Alverez
Chief Growth Officer: Chris Dugan
Year Founded: 1862
Estimated Sales: $100 Million
Number Employees: 500-999
Type of Packaging: Private Label
Brands:
  Caterer's Collection
  Chef Antonio
  Grocer's Garden
  Willow Farms

10729 Richland Beverage Association
2415 Midway Rd
Suite 115
Carrollton, TX 75006-2500
214-357-0248
Fax: 214-357-9581 sales@texasselectna.com
Nonalcoholic malt beverages and beer
President: Martha Zelzer
sales@hphardware.com
Sales: John Rule
Sales: Dana Verrill
Estimated Sales: Less than $500,000
Number Employees: 1-4
Square Footage: 22800
Parent Co: Richland Corporation
Type of Packaging: Consumer, Food Service, Private Label
Brands:
  Texas Select

10730 (HQ)Richmond Baking Co
520 N 6th St
P.O. Box 698
Richmond, IN 47375
765-962-8535
Fax: 765-962-2253 www.richmondbaking.com
Cracker and cookie crumbs, cracker meal and cookies.
President: Bill Quigg
billq@richmondbaking.com
Treasurer: Rob Quigg
Vice President, Sales: Don Lindeman
Year Founded: 1855
Estimated Sales: $20.2 Million
Number Employees: 100-249
Type of Packaging: Consumer, Food Service, Private Label, Bulk
Other Locations:
  McMinnville OR
Brands:
  Butternut
  Butternut Baked Goods

10731 Richmond Baking Co
135 Industrial Dr
P.O. Box 744
Alma, GA 31510
912-632-7213
Fax: 912-632-7215 www.richmondbaking.com
Cracker and cookie crumbs, cracker meal and cookies.
Square Footage: 340000
Type of Packaging: Consumer, Food Service, Private Label, Bulk

Food Manufacturers / A-Z

10732 Rick's Chips
524 San Anselmo Avenue
Suite 210
San Anselmo, CA 94960
415-420-8151
Fax: 415-532-1526 rick@rickschips.com
Chips
Owner: Rick Hirsch
Estimated Sales: $500,000-1,000,000
Number Employees: 1-4
Brands:
  Rick's Chips

10733 Rick's Picks
117 Grattan Street
Suite 319
Brooklyn, NY 11237
212-358-0428
Fax: 212-358-0231 www.rickspicks.com
Pickles
Owner: Richard Field
info@rickspicksnyc.com
Marketing: Jin Kim
Estimated Sales: Less Than $500,000
Number Employees: 1-4

10734 Rico Foods Inc
578 E 19th St
Paterson, NJ 07514-2711
973-278-0589
Fax: 973-278-0378 info@expreco.com
www.ricofood.com
Hispanic foods
President: Emilio Hernandes
emilio@ricofood.com
Vice President: Madeline Fernandez
Production Manager: Christine Hernandez
Estimated Sales: Below $5 Million
Number Employees: 20-49
Square Footage: 40
Type of Packaging: Private Label
Brands:
  Delicia
  Rico

10735 Ricos Candy Snack & Bakery
740 W 28th St
Hialeah, FL 33010-1220
305-885-7392
Fax: 305-885-7376
Candy, pork rinds and fried dough
President: Albertina Padron
VP: Steven Laderman
Estimated Sales: Less Than $500,000
Number Employees: 1-4
Type of Packaging: Consumer

10736 Riddles' Sweet Impressions
6311 Wagner Road NW
Edmonton, AB T6E 4N4
Canada
780-465-8085
Fax: 780-468-5929 riddles@telusplanet.net
Candy
President: Bill Agnew
VP Sales: Dave Read
Production Manager: Wendy Agnew
Number Employees: 30-50
Square Footage: 48000
Type of Packaging: Consumer, Food Service, Private Label, Bulk
Brands:
  Riddle's

10737 Ridge Vineyards Inc
17100 Montebello Rd
Cupertino, CA 95014-5435
408-867-3233
Fax: 408-868-1350 www.ridgewine.com
Wines
Chairman: Paul Draper
CEO: Mark Vernon
mvernon@ridgewine.com
Chief Operating Officer: Eric Baugher
Estimated Sales: $10-24.9 Million
Number Employees: 20-49
Number of Brands: 1
Parent Co: Otsuka America, Inc.
Type of Packaging: Private Label
Brands:
  Ridge Vineyards

10738 Riega
3517 Enterprise Dr
Suite C
Kansas City, MO 64129
816-744-8260
Fax: 816-533-7099 riegafoods.com
Sauce, dip and seasoning mixes, and organic flatbreads
President/Owner: Brad Gampper
Brands:
  Le Pain des Fleurs

10739 Rier Smoked Salmon
224 County Rd
Lubec, ME 04652-3611
207-733-8912
Fax: 207-733-8986 888-733-0807
Salmon, salmon pate and lox; chicken
Owner: Vinny Gartmayer
Sales/Marketing: Frank Rier
Estimated Sales: $450,000
Number Employees: 5-9
Square Footage: 14000

10740 Riffel's Coffee Company
10821 E 26th St N
Wichita, KS 67226-4524
316-269-4222
Fax: 316-269-1361 888-399-4567
Arabica beans, Italian syrup, coffee jellies
Administrator: Linda Price
General Manager: Paul Hawley
Plant Manager: Lewis Lusk
Purchasing Manager: Chuck Anderson
Estimated Sales: Below $5 Million
Number Employees: 10-19
Number of Products: 700
Square Footage: 20000
Type of Packaging: Consumer, Food Service, Private Label, Bulk
Brands:
  Riffels Gourmet Coffees

10741 Righetti Specialties Inc
7476 Graciosa Rd
Santa Maria, CA 93455-6110
805-937-2402
Fax: 805-937-7243 800-268-1041
susieq@susieqbrand.com www.susieqbrand.com
Beans, seasonings, pie mix, sauces & salsas, beef jerky, grilling wood.
Founder: Susan Righetti
susan@susieqbrand.com
VP: Renee Fowler
Estimated Sales: Below $5 Million
Number Employees: 5-9
Brands:
  Righetti Specialty

10742 Rigoni Di Asiago
3449 NE 1st Avenue
Suite L-32
Miami, FL 33137
305-470-7583
Fax: 800-887-9023 info@rigonidiasiago-usa.com
rigonidiasiago-usa.com
Chocolate, honey, jams and preserves.
Marketing: Alberto Carli
Contact: Giacomo Cera
giacomo.cera@rigonidiasiago.com

10743 Rill Specialty Foods
11442 N Thorp Hwy
Thorp, WA 98946-9505
509-964-2520
Fax: 509-964-2075 www.rillsonline.com
Soup mixes, corn bread, muffins
Owner: Ninon Wheatley

10744 Rinehart Meat Processing
133 Bell Road
Branson, MO 65616-9169
417-869-2041
Fax: 417-334-2059
Lean ground beef, bacon and ham, sausage and beef jerky
President: Jack Harris
Plant Manager: Tim Stewart
Estimated Sales: $10-20 Million
Number Employees: 20-49

10745 Rio Grande Valley SugarGrowers
P.O. Boz 459
Santa Rosa, TX 78593
956-636-1411
Fax: 956-636-1449 www.rgvsugar.com
Sugar cane, raw sugar and molasses.
President & CEO: Randy Rolando
AG Manager: Jerry Lara
Year Founded: 1913
Estimated Sales: $12 Million
Number Employees: 190
Type of Packaging: Bulk

10746 Rio Naturals
5050 Robert J. Mathews Pkwy
Suite 200
El Dorado Hills, CA 95762
916-719-4514
Fax: 916-941-3690
Sweeteners
President: Jack Mortelli
Brands:
  Riosweet

10747 Rio Syrup Co
2311 Chestnut St
St Louis, MO 63103-2298
314-436-7700
Fax: 314-436-7707 800-325-7666
flavors@riosyrup.com www.riosyrup.com
Syrups, extracts and concentrates, slush flavors and bases, fountain syrups and liquid food colors
President: Phillip Tomber
phil@riosyrup.com
Estimated Sales: $500,000-$1 Million
Number Employees: 5-9
Number of Products: 1200
Square Footage: 92000
Type of Packaging: Consumer, Food Service, Bulk
Brands:
  Rio

10748 Rio Trading Company
4924 Campbell Blvd
Suite 120
Baltimore, MD 21236-5909
443-384-2500
Fax: 443-384-2525
Owner: Michael Sruanis
Estimated Sales: $500,000-$1 Million
Number Employees: 1-4
Brands:
  Rio Trading

10749 Rio Valley Canning Co
225 S 13th St
Donna, TX 78537-3304
956-464-7843
Fax: 956-464-2538
Canned beans, peas, tomatoes, peppers and picante sauce
President: Robert Ault
Estimated Sales: $5-10 Million
Number Employees: 50-99
Type of Packaging: Consumer, Food Service, Private Label
Brands:
  Rio Valley

10750 Rip Van
Brooklyn, NY
415-529-5403
www.ripvan.com
Wafel cookies
Co-CEO: Rip Pruisken
Co-CEO: Marco De Leon

10751 Ripensa A/S
5781 Lee Boulevard
Unit 208
Lehigh Acres, FL 33971-6339
941-561-5882
Fax: 941-561-5885
Baked goods, cookies, biscuits, tray packs, containers and acrylic jars
President: Steen Thy Jensen
CEO: Richard Recchia
Estimated Sales: Less than $500,000
Number Employees: 1-4
Type of Packaging: Private Label
Brands:
  Ripensa

Food Manufacturers / A-Z

10752 Ripon Pickle Co Inc
1039 Beier Rd
Ripon, WI 54971-9063
920-748-7110
Fax: 920-748-8092 rpi@riponpickle.com
www.riponpickle.com
Celery, chili peppers, egg plant, onions, sauerkraut, green and red peppers
President: Darwin Wiese
Site Manager: Troy Gustke
tgusky@riponpickleco.com
Estimated Sales: $6.6 Million
Number Employees: 50-99
Square Footage: 280000
Type of Packaging: Consumer, Food Service, Private Label, Bulk
Brands:
  Pickle O'Pete
  Wisconsin Pride

10753 Ripple
Berkeley, CA
info@ripplefoods.com
www.ripplefoods.com
Plant-based milk alternative
Founder: Neil Renninger
Founder: Adam Lowry

10754 Ripple Brand Collective
225 North Route 303
Suite 101
Congers, NY 10920
845-353-1251
Fax: 845-353-5276 hello@barkthins.com
www.barkthins.com
Dark chocolate covered snacks
Founder and CEO: Scott Semel
Brands:
  barkTHINS

10755 Rippons Seafood
11911 Coastal Hwy
Suite 120
Ocean City, MD 21842-2621
410-723-0056
www.ripponsseafood.com
Oysters, crab and shrimp.
Owner: Chan Rippons
Estimated Sales: $21 Million
Number Employees: 5-9
Type of Packaging: Consumer, Food Service, Private Label

10756 Rise Bar
16752 Millikan Ave
Irvine, CA 92606
800-440-6476
cs2@risebar.com www.risebar.com
Protein bars
Founder & CEO: Peter Spenuzza
Year Founded: 2011
Number Employees: 20-49

10757 Rishi Tea
427 E Stewart St
Stop 5
Milwaukee, WI 53207-1200
414-747-4001
Fax: 414-747-4008 866-747-4483
inquiries@rishi-tea.com www.rishi-tea.com
Tea
Owner: Joshua Kaiser
joshua@rishi-tea.com
Estimated Sales: $1.3 Million
Number Employees: 20-49
Square Footage: 64000
Type of Packaging: Consumer, Food Service, Private Label, Bulk

10758 Rising Dough Bakery
8135 Elder Creek Rd
Sacramento, CA 95824
916-387-9700
Fax: 877-349-8900
Cakes, pies, muffins, croissants and strudels
Owner: Colette Jamet
cs@risingdough.com
Estimated Sales: Below $5 Million
Number Employees: 20-49
Brands:
  Rising Dough

10759 Rising Sun Farms
5126 S Pacific Hwy
Phoenix, OR 97535-6606
541-535-8331
Fax: 541-535-8350 800-888-0795
elizabeth@risingsunfarms.com
www.risingsunfarms.com
Oils, mustard, pesto sauces, dried tomatoes, vinegars, salad vinaigrettes, cheese tortas and marinades
Owner: Kim Allen
Coo: Jeff Williams
VP: Richard Fujas
Sales: Jenn Woodward
kim@risingsunfarms.com
Public Relations: Jim Woodward
Operations: Chris Hanry
Plant Manager: Richard Fujas
Purchasing Director: Lynn Perkins
Estimated Sales: $3.2 Million
Number Employees: 20-49
Type of Packaging: Consumer, Food Service, Private Label, Bulk
Brands:
  Rising Sun

10760 Risvold's Inc.
1234 W. El Segundo Blvd.
Gardena, CA 90247
323-770-2674
Fax: 323-770-0800 tbrandon@risvolds.com
risvolds.com
Prepared salads, pasta salads, desserts, speads and dips
President/Sales: Kristie Brandon-Brown
CEO: Tim Brandon
Quality Control/Research And Development: Wendy O'Neill
Sales/Customer Service: Mary DeNava
Production Manager: Brock O'Neill
VP, General Manager And Purchasing: Jon Lew
Year Founded: 1937
Type of Packaging: Consumer, Food Service, Bulk
Brands:
  LA COCINA MEXICANA
  FUN-N-SUN
  SEDONA BAKING COMPANY

10761 Rita's Italian Ice
2929 N. Rock Road
Wichita, KS 67226
316-440-4896
www.ritasice.com
Ice snacks and frozen custards
Senior Director, Franchise Sales: Gina Moughty

10762 Ritchey's Dairy
2130 Cross Cove Rd
Martinsburg, PA 16662-7619
814-793-2157
Fax: 814-793-0099 800-296-2157
ritcheysdairy@hotmail.com
www.ritcheysdairy.com
Milk, fruit drinks and ice tea
President: Ray Ritchey
rayr@ritcheysdairy.com
Estimated Sales: Below $5 Million
Number Employees: 50-99
Type of Packaging: Private Label
Brands:
  Ritchey

10763 Ritchie Creek Vineyard
4024 Spring Mountain Rd
St Helena, CA 94574-9773
707-963-4661
Fax: 707-963-4936 www.ritchiecreek.com
Wines
President: R Minor
Co-Owner: Peter Minor
Estimated Sales: Below $5 Million
Number Employees: 5-9

10764 Rito Mints
1055, rue Laverendrye
PO Box 312
Trois Rivieres, QC G9A 5GA
Canada
819-379-1449
Fax: 819-379-0344 info@ritomints.com
www.ritomints.com
Candy: mints, hearts and lozenges
President: Morris Masif
General Manager: Peter Nassif
Number Employees: 15
Square Footage: 64000
Type of Packaging: Consumer, Food Service, Private Label, Bulk
Brands:
  Rito
  Sweet Notes
  Ghost Talk

10765 Ritual Coffee Roasters
1026 Valencia St
San Francisco, CA 94110-2406
415-641-1011
info@ritualroasters.com
www.ritualroasters.com
Coffee
Manager: Briana Rognlin
briana@ritualroasters.com
Estimated Sales: Less Than $500,000
Number Employees: 5-9

10766 Rivard Popcorn Products
2870 Yellow Goos Road
Lancaster, PA 17601-6705
717-898-7131
Fax: 171-898-7265
Flavored popcorn, extruded corn, rice curls and puffs
President: Robert Rivard
National Sales Manager: Joe Guasco
Number Employees: 50-99
Type of Packaging: Consumer

10767 Rivella USA
3100 NW Boca Raton Boulevard
Suite 410
Boca Raton, FL 33431
561-417-5810
Fax: 561-417-5811
Soft drink
President: Franz Rieder
Vice President: Christian Mom
Estimated Sales: $1.1 Million
Number Employees: 8
Type of Packaging: Food Service, Bulk

10768 River Hills Harvest
3520 E 33Rd St
Minneapolis, MN 55406-2160
573-326-9454
855-662-3779
info@riverhillsharvest.com riverhillsharvest.com
Elderberry juice
President & CEO: Christopher Patton
Brands:
  River Hills

10769 River Market Brewing Company
P.O.Box 901898
Kansas City, MO 64190-1898
816-471-6300
Fax: 816-471-5562 www.rivermarketbrews.com
Beer, ale, lager, stout and seasonal
President: David Pecha
Estimated Sales: $1-2.5 Million
Number Employees: 20-49
Type of Packaging: Consumer, Food Service

10770 River Road Coffee
PO Box 252
Lake Clear, NY 12945-0252
315-769-9941
Fax: 315-769-7130
Coffee
President: David Copeland
General Manager: Michelle Yadon
Estimated Sales: $2.5-5 000,000
Number Employees: 20

10771 River Run Vintners
65 Rogge Ln
Watsonville, CA 95076-9418
831-726-3112
Fax: 831-726-3112 riverrun@cruzio.com
www.riverrunwine.com
Wines
Manager: J P Pawloski
Estimated Sales: Less Than $500,000
Number Employees: 1-4
Brands:
  River Run

Food Manufacturers / A-Z

10772 River Town Foods Corp
4601 Mcree Ave
St Louis, MO 63110-2239
314-776-5646
Fax: 314-776-6468 800-844-3210
mona@rivertownfoods.ccm
www.rivertownfoods.com
Salsas & Mexican sauces, marinades, dressings and spice blends.
President: Jeff Endraske
jeff@rivertownfoods.com
CEO: John Schnoebelen
General Manager: Monica Holtgreven
Estimated Sales: $500,000-$1 Million
Number Employees: 5-9
Number of Products: 153
Type of Packaging: Consumer, Food Service, Private Label, Bulk
Brands:
  River Town Foods Rib Rub
  Super Smokers Barbecue Sauces
  Taste of The Hill

10773 Riverdale Fine Foods
919 N Main St
Dayton, OH 45405-4694
937-743-4377
Fax: 937-223-9456 800-548-1304
info@daytonnut.com www.riverdalefinefoods.com
Chocolates, nuts, snack mixes, cookie mixes and candy
President: Stanley Maschino
Estimated Sales: $3-5 Million
Number Employees: 10-19
Number of Brands: 5
Brands:
  Candy Farm
  Dayton's
  Friesinger's
  Minute Fudge
  Yuletide

10774 Riverside Natural Foods
2720 Steeles Ave West
Bldg 4
Vaughan, ON L4K 4N5
Canada
416-360-8200
info@riversidenaturals.com
riversidenaturalfoods.com
Granola snackers
President/Owner: Nima Fotovat
Marketing: Janice Harada
Operations: Sahba Fotovat
Brands:
  MadeGood

10775 Riverton Packing
2515 E Monroe Ave
Riverton, WY 82501-6104
307-856-3838
Meat
Owner: Rod Baltes
Estimated Sales: Less than $500,000
Number Employees: 1-4
Type of Packaging: Consumer, Food Service

10776 Riverview Foods
1360 Bethleham Road
PO Box 765
Warsaw, KY 41095
859-567-5211
Fax: 859-567-5213
Smoked meats, barbecue and tomato sauces; research and development services
President: Bob Weldon
VP Sales/Marketing: Robert Schroeder
General Manager: Mike Benton
Number Employees: 50-99
Square Footage: 100000
Type of Packaging: Consumer, Food Service, Private Label, Bulk
Brands:
  Riverview Foods Authentic

10777 Riviana Foods Inc.
PO Box 2636
Houston, TX 77252
713-529-3251
sales@riviana.com
www.riviana.com
Rice and pasta.
President/CEO: Bastiaan de Zeeuw
bdezeeuw@riviana.com
Senior VP/CFO: Michael Slavin
Senior VP, Operations: Brett Beckfield
Senior VP, Marketing: Sandra Kim
Senior VP, Human Resources: Gerard Ferguson
Year Founded: 1965
Estimated Sales: $500 Million
Number Employees: 1,000-4,999
Number of Brands: 28
Parent Co: Ebro Foods, S.A.
Type of Packaging: Consumer, Food Service, Private Label, Bulk
Other Locations:
  Corporate Office
  Houston TX
  Plant
  Brinkley AR
  Plant
  Carlisle AR
  Plant
  Clearbrook MN
  Plant
  Hazen AR
  Plant
  Memphis TN
Brands:
  Mahatma
  Carolina
  Minute
  Success
  AA Brand
  Adolphus
  Blue Ribbon Rice
  Colusa Rose
  Comet Rice
  Gourmet House
  Pear Blossom
  Rice Select
  River Rice
  Sello Rojo
  Water Maid
  Wonder
  Ronzoni
  American Beauty
  No Yolks
  Skinner
  Creamette
  Light 'n Fluffy
  Mrs. Weiss'
  New Mill
  Prince
  San Giorgio
  Wacky Mac

10778 Riviera Ravioli Company
643 Morris Park Ave
Bronx, NY 10460
718-823-0260
Fax: 718-823-0344 rivrav@verizon.net
Macaroni and pasta
President: Joseph Giordano
Plant Manager: Michael Somereve
Estimated Sales: $10-20 Million
Number Employees: 10-19
Brands:
  Riviera

10779 RoRo's Baking Company
2201 Tucker St.
Suite 107
Dallas, TX 75214
972-897-2315
www.rorosbakingcompany.com
Baked goods
Co-Owner: Amy Collins
Co-Owner: Lauren Collins

10780 Road's End Organics
2160 Mountain Road
Suite 5
Carpinteria, CA 93014
805-684-8500
Fax: 805-684-8220 877-247-3373
http://www.roadsendorganics.com
Dairy free pasta and dip
President: Matthew Koch
Estimated Sales: $3-5 Million
Number Employees: 1-4
Parent Co: Edward & Sons Trading Company, Inc.

10781 Roadrunner Seafood Inc
548 E Crawford St
Colquitt, GA 39837-5200
229-758-6098
Fax: 229-758-3991 rrsfd@surfsouth.com
Seafood: catfish, conch, croaker, flounder, mullet, oysters and shrimp
President: James Stovall
Finance Executive: Amy Stovall
Number Employees: 20-49

10782 Roanoke Apple Products
844 Union St
Salem, VA 24153-5121
540-375-3782
Fax: 540-375-3782
Vinegar, apple cider, white and red wine
President: Glenn Dunville
Marketing Director: Deborah Dunville
Plant Manager: Randy Kesler
Estimated Sales: $1,100,000
Number Employees: 11
Square Footage: 66000
Type of Packaging: Food Service, Private Label, Bulk
Brands:
  Bandana
  Heidecker
  Old Kettle

10783 Roasterie Inc
1204 W 27th St
Kansas City, MO 64108-3555
816-931-4000
Fax: 816-931-4040 800-376-0245
info@theroasterie.com www.theroasterie.com
Coffee
Owner: Gwyneth Bowen
gwynethmaree@gmail.com
Customer Service Manager: Stacy Barter
Quality Control: Norm Killnorm
CFO: Bill Molini
CFO: Carla O'Neill
CFO: Chris Mikuls
Estimated Sales: $1-2.5 Million
Number Employees: 20-49
Brands:
  Roasterie

10784 Rob Salamida Co Inc
71 Pratt Ave
Suite 1
Johnson City, NY 13790-2255
607-729-4868
Fax: 607-797-4721 800-545-5072
info@spiedie.com www.hunterspideusa.com
Marinades, barbecue sauces and spice blends.
President: Robert Alan Salamida
sweethavens@msn.com
Estimated Sales: $4.2 Million
Number Employees: 1-4
Type of Packaging: Consumer, Food Service, Private Label
Brands:
  Pinch
  Spiedie Sauce
  State Fair

10785 Robbie's Natural Products
8002 NE Hwy 99
Suite 78
Vancouver, WA 98665
360-433-2325
Fax: 626-457-8705
Ketchup, salsa, fruit syrup and sauces
President: Robbie Roberts
Sales Manager: Roberta Fleischer
Estimated Sales: $3-5 Million
Number Employees: 1-4
Type of Packaging: Consumer, Food Service

10786 Robbins Packing Company
229 Stockyard Row
Statesboro, GA 30458-4375
912-764-7503
Fax: 912-489-2823
Pork, beef, sausage and smoked meats
President: Wayne Paulk
President/Managing Partner: Rodney Poole
Sales Executive: Tom Collins
Sales Manager: Glen Brown
Plant Manager: Jack Kasses

Food Manufacturers / A-Z

Estimated Sales: $1-3 Million
Number Employees: 1-4
Square Footage: 210000
Type of Packaging: Consumer, Food Service, Private Label, Bulk

10787 Roberian Vineyards
12614 King Rd
Forestville, NY 14062
716-679-1620
roberian@fairpoint.net
Wines
President: Bob Roach
Wine Maker: Maryann Roach
Estimated Sales: Under $500,000
Number Employees: 1-4

10788 Robert & James Brands
950 E Maple Road
Birmingham, MI 48009-6408
248-646-0578
Fax: 248-646-6040
Condiments and relishes
Owner: Robert Arnold
Estimated Sales: $1-2.5 000,000
Number Employees: 5

10789 Robert F Pliska & Company Winery
101 Cantwell Court
Purgitsville, WV 26852
304-289-3493
Fax: 304-289-3900 877-747-2737
VineyardHome@frontiernet.net
www.vineyardhome.org
Wines
Owner & Wine Maker: Robert F Pliska
Purchasing Manager: TC McGee
Estimated Sales: $1-3 Million
Number Employees: 1-4
Parent Co: Piterra Farms
Type of Packaging: Consumer
Brands:
　101 Piterra Place
　Assumption Wines
　Mt. Betty
　Mt. Mama

10790 Robert Keenan Winery
3660 Spring Mountain Rd
St Helena, CA 94574-9677
707-963-9177
Fax: 707-963-8209 rkw@keenanwinery.com
www.keenanwinery.com
Wines
Owner: Michael Keenan
rkw@keenanwinery.com
General Manager: Matt Gardner
Wine Maker: Niles Venge
Estimated Sales: $1-2.5 Million
Number Employees: 5-9
Brands:
　Robert Keenan Winery

10791 Robert Mondavi Winery
7801 Saint Helena Highway
Oakville, CA 94562
707-226-1395
Fax: 707-251-4110 888-766-6328
www.robertmondaviwinery.com
Wines
CEO: Greg Evans
Winemaker: Genevieve Janssens
genevieve@robertsinskey.com
VP Marketing: Kevin Conner
Vice President, Operations: Karen Egan
Estimated Sales: $42 Million
Number Employees: 600
Number of Brands: 1
Square Footage: 5000
Other Locations:
　Woodbridge Winery
　Acampo CA
Brands:
　Mondavi

10792 Robert Mueller Cellars
6301 Starr Rd
Windsor, CA 95492-9653
707-837-7399
Fax: 707-431-8365 www.muellerwine.com
Wines
President: Robert Mueller
CEO: Bruce E Ollodart

Estimated Sales: $1-2.5 Million
Number Employees: 1-4
Brands:
　Mueller

10793 Robert Pecota Winery
P.O.Box 303
Calistoga, CA 94515
707-479-7770
Fax: 707-942-6671 www.robertpecotawinery.com
Wines
Co-Owner & Partner: Robert Pecota
Co-Owner & Partner: Kara Pecota Dunn
Co-Owner & Partner: Andrea Pecota White
Operations Director/Guest Services: Brenda Wild
Consulting Winemker: Marco DiGiulio
Estimated Sales: $1-2.5 Million
Number Employees: 5-9
Type of Packaging: Private Label
Brands:
　Robert Pecota

10794 Robert Rothschild Farm
3015 E Kemper Rd
Cincinnati, OH 45241
Fax: 888-907-8090 800-222-9966
info@davidevansfoods.com
www.robertrothschild.com
Sauces, dips, condiments and preserves
Chairman: Robert Rothschild
CEO: Andrew Deister
Chief Financial Officer: Shara Vross
Director of Product Development: Bridget Sherman
Quality Manager: Mercedes Grome
Marketing Director: Ryan Husted
Vice President of Sales: Dan Carley
Director of Specialty Sales: Patti Walters
Vice President of Operations: Mike Maloy
Supply Chain Manager: John Eagle
Estimated Sales: $16.5 Million
Number Employees: 50-99
Number of Brands: 1
Square Footage: 45000
Type of Packaging: Consumer
Brands:
　Robert Rothschild

10795 Robert Sinskey Vineyards Inc
6320 Silverado Trl
Napa, CA 94558-9747
707-944-9090
Fax: 707-944-9097 800-869-2030
rsv@robertsinskey.com www.robertsinskey.com
Wines
Owner & Founder: Robert Sinskey
Winemaker: Jeff Virnig
Culinary Director: Maria Helm Sinskey
Sales Manager: Meg Bartley
National Wholesale Manager: Eric Sother
Vineyard Manager: Kirk Grace
Sales Manager: Meg Goddess
rsv@robertsinskey.com
Estimated Sales: Below $5 Million
Number Employees: 10-19
Type of Packaging: Private Label
Brands:
　Rsv

10796 Robert's Bakery
17516 Minnetonka Boulevard
Minnetonka, MN 55345-1000
612-473-9719
Fax: 612-473-1835
Baked goods
President: Robert Larson
Estimated Sales: $5-9.9 000,000
Number Employees: 20

10797 Robertet Flavors
10 Colonial Dr.
Piscataway, NJ 08854
732-981-8300
Fax: 732-981-1717
robertetFlavors@robertetUSA.com
www.robertet.com
Flavorings.
Chairman/CEO: Philippe Maubert
Head of the Flavourings Division: Olivier Maubert
CFO: Gilles Audoli
Managing Director, Flavourings Division: Antoine Kastler
Director, Industrial Operations: Herve Bellon
Year Founded: 1850
Estimated Sales: $524.9 Million

Number Employees: 1,800
Number of Brands: 5+
Square Footage: 16805
Parent Co: Robertet SA
Type of Packaging: Food Service
Other Locations:
　Robertet Culinary
　Schoten, Belgium
Brands:
　Citra-Next
　Natur-Cell
　Flavour Sensations
　Smart Flavours
　Accord Flavours

10798 Roberto A Cheese Factory
7465 Lincoln Street SE
East Canton, OH 44730-9439
330-488-1551
Fax: 330-488-1552
Cheese
President: Angelo Roberto
Co-Owner: Armand Babbo
Estimated Sales: $500,000-$1 000,000
Number Employees: 10-19
Brands:
　Roberto Cheese

10799 Roberts Ferry Nut Co
20493 Yosemite Blvd
Waterford, CA 95386-9506
209-874-3247
Fax: 209-874-3707
www.robertsferrynutcompany.com
Almonds and popcorn
Owner: Brigitte Hayat
brigitteh@pjcc.org
Partner: Dorothy Mallory
Estimated Sales: $3135592
Number Employees: 20-49
Type of Packaging: Consumer, Bulk
Brands:
　Roberts Ferry

10800 Roberts Seed
982 22 Rd
Axtell, NE 68924-3618
308-743-2565
Fax: 308-743-2048 robertsseed@gtmc.net
www.robertsseed.com
Grain, soybeans, popcorn kernels, wheat, corn and beans
President: Joe Roberts
robertsseed@gtmc.net
Estimated Sales: $950,000
Number Employees: 1-4
Square Footage: 30000
Type of Packaging: Private Label, Bulk

10801 Robertson's Country Meat Hams
P.O.Box 56
Finchville, KY 40022-0056
502-834-7952
Fax: 502-834-7095 800-678-1521
www.finchvillefarms.com
Country ham
President: William Robertson
Chief Financial Officer: Margaret Davis
Marketing Director: Jim Robertson
Estimated Sales: Below $5 Million
Number Employees: 10-19
Type of Packaging: Private Label, Bulk
Brands:
　Finchville Farms

10802 Robin & Cohn Seafood Distributors
3225 Palmisano Boulevard
Chalmette, LA 70043-3633
504-277-1679
Fax: 504-277-1679
Seafood
President: Fay Cohn

10803 Robinson Distributing Co
701 Robinson Rd
London, KY 40741-9018
606-864-2914
Fax: 606-864-3252 800-230-5131
www.robinsonmeats50.com
Meats: hog sausage and deli
President: Jimmy Robinson
robinson@mis.net

1069

Food Manufacturers / A-Z

Estimated Sales: $5,500,000
Number Employees: 20-49
Square Footage: 40000
Type of Packaging: Private Label

10804 Robinson's No 1 Ribs
940 Madison St
Oak Park, IL 60302-4430
    708-383-8452
Fax: 708-383-9486 800-836-6750
charlie@rib1.com www.rib1.com
Barbecue sauces
Owner: Charlie Robinson
sales@rib1.com
Vice President: Helen Robinson
Marketing Director: Cordell Robinson
Operations Manager: Bruce Swerdlow
Estimated Sales: $500,000-$1 Million
Number Employees: 20-49
Square Footage: 40000
Parent Co: Robinson's #1 Ribs Restaurants
Type of Packaging: Consumer, Food Service, Bulk
Brands:
    Charlie Robinson's

10805 Robller Vineyard Winery
275 Robller Vineyard Rd
New Haven, MO 63068-2142
    573-237-3986
Fax: 573-237-3985
Wine
Owner: Robert Miller
robller@fidnet.com
Owner: Lois Mueller
Estimated Sales: Less than $200,000
Number Employees: 1-4
Brands:
    Robller Vineyard and Winery

10806 Rocca's Italian Foods Inc
520 S Mill St
New Castle, PA 16101-4007
    724-654-3344
Fax: 724-654-4954 www.roccapasta.com
Pasta
President: Anthony Rocca
roccafoods@aol.com
Estimated Sales: Below $5 000,000
Number Employees: 10-19
Brands:
    Roccas

10807 Roche Caneros Estate Winery
122 West Spain Street
Sonoma, CA 95476-9700
    707-935-7115
Fax: 707-935-7846 800-825-9475
info@rochewinery.com www.rochewinery.com
Wines
President: Joseph Roche
CFO: Kerstin Kohlstrom
Account Manager: Carrie MacDonough
Contact: Jennifer Brons
brons@rochewinery.com
Estimated Sales: $5-9.9 Million
Number Employees: 10-19
Type of Packaging: Private Label
Brands:
    Roche

10808 Roche Fruit LLC
601 N 1st Ave
Yakima, WA 98902-2127
    509-248-7200
Fax: 509-453-3835 michaelroche@jewelapple.com
www.rochefruit.com
Apple slices
Owner/Sales Manager: Michael Roche
michaelroche@rochefruit.com
Quality Assurance Manager: Marina Britt
Customer Service: Janet McKay
Operation Manager, Sales: Mike Hanses
Estimated Sales: $19 Million
Number Employees: 250-499
Parent Co: Roche Fruit
Type of Packaging: Private Label

10809 Rochester Cheese
4219 N Frontage Rd.
Rochester, MN 55901-6672
    507-288-6678
Fax: 507-288-6175 888-246-6678
tomf@rochestercheese.com
Cheese

Plant Financial & Operational Director: Tom Ferris
Year Founded: 1976
Estimated Sales: $20-50 Million
Number Employees: 10-19
Parent Co: Prairie Farms Dairy
Type of Packaging: Private Label

10810 Rock Bottom Restaurant & Brewery
1001 16th St
Suite 100
Denver, CO 80265-0100
    303-534-7616
Fax: 303-534-2129
www.rockbottom.com/denver-downtown
Beer, ale and stout
Manager: Jim Maresca
Managing Partner: Bennett Ponder
Managing Partner: Jessica Buesing
Manager: John Clure
jmcclure@rockbottom.com
Estimated Sales: $10-20 Million
Number Employees: 100-249
Parent Co: CraftWorks Restaurants & Breweries
Type of Packaging: Consumer, Food Service, Bulk
Brands:
    Falcon Pale
    Red Rock

10811 Rock Point Oyster Company
1733 Dabob Post Office Rd
Quilcene, WA 98376
    360-765-3765
Fax: 360-765-3676
Oysters
President: Marshall Hinton
CEO: Dick Steele
Estimated Sales: Less than $500,000
Number Employees: 5

10812 Rock-N-Roll Gourmet
15 Outrigger St
Apt 302
Marina Del Ray, CA 90292
    424-228-4901
Fax: 310-751-6397 800-518-3891
Potato chips, cookies and popcorn
President/Owner: Jean Ehrlich
CEO: Dan Ehrlich
CFO: Peter Vermeulen
Number Employees: 10

10813 Rockbridge Vineyard
35 Hillview Ln
Raphine, VA 24472-2403
    540-377-6204
Fax: 888-511-9463 rockbridgewines@gmail.com
www.rockbridgevineyard.com
Wines
Onwer: Shepherd Rouse
Estimated Sales: $1-3 Million
Number Employees: 1-4
Type of Packaging: Consumer
Brands:
    Dechiel
    Rockbridge Vineyard

10814 Rocket Fizz
2619 Ventura Blvd
PO Box 3663
Camarillo, CA 93010-6647
    805-987-7632
info@rocketfizz.com
www.rocketfizz.com
Soda and candy
Manager: Angela Morgan
Number Employees: 5-9

10815 Rocket Products Company
PO Box 565
Fenton, MO 63026
    636-343-9110
Fax: 636-343-0897 800-325-9567
betty@rocketproducts.com
www.rocketproducts.com
Fruit concentrates
President/Founder/CEO: Charles Lazier, Jr.
General Manager: Michael Martin
Operations Director: Betty Honaker
Purchasing Director: Patty Bunse
Estimated Sales: $5-10 Million
Number Employees: 9
Number of Brands: 3

Number of Products: 11
Square Footage: 15000
Brands:
    Dair-E Lite
    Apache
    Wild Rocket

10816 Rockland Bakery
94 Demarest Mill Rd W
Nanuet, NY 10954-2989
    845-623-5800
Fax: 845-623-6921 800-734-4376
contactus@rocklandbakery.com
www.rocklandbakery.com
Bread, rolls, bagels, cakes, pies and challah
President: Sal Battaglai
battaglais@rocklandbakery.com
Director of Sales: Mike Battaglia
COO: Anthony Battaglia
Estimated Sales: $27 Million
Number Employees: 250-499
Type of Packaging: Consumer, Food Service

10817 Rockport Lobster Co
54 Commercial St
Gloucester, MA 01930-5025
    978-281-0225
Fax: 978-281-8578
Lobster
Owner: Craig Babinski
Estimated Sales: Less Than $500,000
Number Employees: 1-4

10818 Rockview Farms
7011 Stewart and Gray Rd
Downey, CA 90241
    562-927-5511
Fax: 562-928-9765 800-423-2479
www.rockviewfarms.com
Milk, butter, other dairy products and juices
VP, Sales & Marketing: Curt DeGroot
VP, Operations: Joe Lunzer
Estimated Sales: $135 Million
Number Employees: 300
Type of Packaging: Bulk

10819 Rocky Mountain Chocolate Factory
Durango, CO
    888-525-2462
www.rmcf.com
Chocolate
Square Footage: 53000

10820 Rocky Mountain Coffee Roasters
P.O. Box 2609
Jasper, Alberta T0E 1E0, AB
Canada
    780-852-4280
Fax: 780-852-5910 800-666-3465
www.rockymountainroasters.com
Coffee retail/wholesale/roaster
General Manager of Sales: Les Chorley
CFO: Brad Woods
Vice President: Andy Johnsen
VP Marketing: Andy Johnsen
Operations Manager: Jonathan Kitchensa
Estimated Sales: Under $500,000
Number Employees: 5-9
Brands:
    Clipper Foods
    Whitney Distributing

10821 Rocky Mountain Honey Company
642 N Pugsley St
Salt Lake City, UT 84103-1329
    801-355-2054
Fax: 801-355-2054
Beeswax and honey
President: Floyd Meyer
Partner: Melvin Meyer
Estimated Sales: $1-3 Million
Number Employees: 1-4
Parent Co: Meyer Honey Company
Type of Packaging: Consumer, Food Service, Private Label, Bulk

10822 Rocky Mountain Meats
4803 43rd St.
PO Box 459
Rocky Mountain House, AB T4T 1A4
Canada
    403-845-3434
Fax: 780-845-7418

1070

Fresh beef, pork and wild game including deer, elk, moose and bear
Owner: Rudi Koller
Co-Owner/Office Admin: Stefanie Koller
Sales & Administrative Manager: Hauke Theirfelder
Estimated Sales: C
Number Employees: 10-19
Type of Packaging: Consumer, Food Service, Private Label, Bulk
Brands:
　Rocky Mountain

10823 Rocky Mountain Natural Meats
9757 Alton Way
Henderson, CO 80640-8496
　　　　303-287-7100
Fax: 303-287-7272　800-327-2706
bison@greatrangebison.com
Meat distributor solely focusing on bison products.
CEO: Bob Dineen
bob@greatrangebison.com
Chief Financial Officer: Sharon Novacek
Safe Quality Food Practitioner: Mattie Hummel
Vice President, Sales & Marketing: Paul Bernardo
Estimated Sales: $20-49 Million
Number Employees: 100-249
Number of Brands: 1
Square Footage: 50000
Type of Packaging: Consumer, Food Service
Brands:
　Great Range Brand Bison

10824 Rocky Mountain Packing Company
500 1st Street
Havre, MT 59501
　　　　406-265-3401
Fax: 406-265-3401
Meat products
Owner/President: David Swallow
Owner/CEO: Linda Swallow
Estimated Sales: $100,000-$120,000
Number Employees: 1-4
Type of Packaging: Consumer

10825 Rocky Point Shrimp Association
429 West Madison Street
Phoenix, AZ 85003
　　　　602-254-8041
Fax: 602-523-9637
Shrimp
Estimated Sales: $3-5 Million
Number Employees: 5-9

10826 Rocky Ridge Maple
1258 Route 249
Middlebury Center, PA 16935
　　　　607-742-9566
sales@rockyridgemaple.com
rockyridgemaple.com
Maple syrup
Founder: Joshua C. Bronson
Estimated Sales: Under $500,000
Number Employees: 1-4
Type of Packaging: Private Label, Bulk
Brands:
　Rocky Ridge Maple

10827 Rocky Top Country Store
4201 Wears Valley Rd
Sevierville, TN 37862-8153
　　　　865-428-7311
Fax: 865-428-7524　866-260-0670
Fudge
Owner: Robert Glenn
Manager: Marni Sotomayor
Estimated Sales: $300,000-500,000
Number Employees: 1-4
Type of Packaging: Consumer

10828 Rocky Top Farms
11486 Essex Rd
Ellsworth, MI 49729-9650
　　　　231-599-2251
Fax: 231-599-2352　800-862-9303
sales@rockytopfarms.com www.rockytopfarm.com
Processor and exporter of preserves including raspberry, cherry, strawberry, blackberry and black raspberry; also, butter toppings
President: Tom Cooper
tomcooper@rockytopfarm.com
Estimated Sales: $3-5 Million
Number Employees: 5-9
Type of Packaging: Consumer, Bulk

10829 Rod Golden Hatchery Inc
85 13th St. NE
Cullman, AL 35055
　　　　256-734-0941
Broiler, fryer, and roaster chickens.
President: Forrest Ingram
Estimated Sales: $34 Million
Number Employees: 1010
Square Footage: 2000
Parent Co: Ingram Farms
Type of Packaging: Consumer, Food Service, Private Label, Bulk

10830 Rodda Coffee Company
PO Box 290
Yachats, OR 97498-0290
　　　　541-547-4132
Fax: 888-919-2722
Coffee
President: Tom Rodda
Estimated Sales: Under $500,000
Number Employees: 10-19
Brands:
　Rodda Coffee

10831 Rodelle Inc
3461 Precision Dr
Fort Collins, CO 80528-4545
　　　　970-482-8845
Fax: 970-482-4236　800-898-5457
www.customblendinginc.com
Vanilla, baking essential, herbs and spices
Owner: John Conway
jconway@customblendinginc.com
Number Employees: 20-49

10832 Rodgers' Puddings
1410 Poindexter Street
Chesapeake, VA 23324
　　　　757-543-9290
reggie@rodgerspuddings.com
www.rodgerspuddings.com
Puddings: banana, coconut, guava and blueberry.
Owner: Reggie Rodgers
Estimated Sales: Under $500,000
Number Employees: 1-4
Type of Packaging: Food Service
Brands:
　Rodgers'

10833 Rodney Strong Vineyards
11455 Old Redwood Hwy
Healdsburg, CA 95448-9523
　　　　707-431-1533
Fax: 707-433-0939　800-474-9463
info@rodneystrong.com
Wines
Proptietor: Tom Klein
tklein@rodneystrong.com
VP, Director of Winemaking: Rick Sayre
Estimated Sales: $.5-1 million
Number Employees: 100-249
Type of Packaging: Private Label
Brands:
　Rodney Strong

10834 Roelli Cheese Co
15982 State Road 11
Shullsburg, WI 53586-9748
　　　　608-965-3779
Fax: 608-965-4510　800-575-4372
www.roellicheese.com
Cheese
Owner: Paul Roelli
VP: Gary Roelli
Estimated Sales: $1-3 Million
Number Employees: 10-19
Brands:
　Balderson
　Bingham Hill Cheeses

10835 Roger Wood Foods Inc
7 Alfred St
Savannah, GA 31408
　　　　912-652-9600
　　　　800-849-9272
info@rogerwoodfoods.com
www.rogerwoodfoods.com
Sausage, franks, turkey and pork products.
President: David Solana
dsolana@rogerwoodfoods.com
Vice President: Mark Solana
Plant Manager: Matthew Lumley
Year Founded: 1936
Estimated Sales: $50 Million
Number Employees: 100-249
Square Footage: 100000

10836 Roger's Recipe
518 Perron Hl
Glover, VT 05839-9735
　　　　802-525-3050
Brittle made with maple syrup
Owner: Michael Rogers
Estimated Sales: $300,000-500,000
Number Employees: 1-4
Type of Packaging: Consumer

10837 Rogers Sugar Inc.
4026 Notre-Dame St. East
Montreal, QC H1W 2K3
Canada
　　　　514-527-8686
www.lanticrogers.com
Icing sugar, liquid sugar and soft sugar. Molasses is sold as a by-product of the refining operation.
President: John Holliday
Chief Financial Officer/VP/Secretary: Manon Lacroix
Year Founded: 2008
Estimated Sales: $805 Million
Number Employees: 487
Number of Brands: 1
Square Footage: 7050
Type of Packaging: Consumer, Food Service, Bulk
Other Locations:
　Rogers Sugar Limited
　Alberta, Canada
Brands:
　Roger's

10838 Rogers Sugar Inc.
123 Rogers St.
Vancouver, BC V6B 3N2
Canada
　　　　604-253-1131
www.lanticrogers.com
Granulated sugar of various grist sizes, sugar cubes, icing sugar, liquid sugars, soft sugars.
President/CEO: John Holliday
VP, Finance/CFO: Manon Lacroix
Vice President, Sales/Marketing: Mike Walton
VP, Operations/Supply Chain: Patrick Dionne
Year Founded: 2008
Estimated Sales: $805.2 Million
Number Employees: 700
Type of Packaging: Consumer, Food Service, Bulk
Brands:
　Rogers
　Lantic

10839 Rogers Sugar Inc.
5405 64th St.
Taber, AB T1G 2C4
Canada
　　　　403-223-3535
www.lanticrogers.com
Granulated sugar of various grist sizes, icing sugar, and liquid sugar. Beet molasses and beet pulp are produced as by-products.
President/CEO: John Holliday
Estimated Sales: $805 Million
Number Employees: 205-499
Type of Packaging: Consumer, Food Service, Bulk

10840 Rogers' Chocolates Ltd
4253 Commerce Circle
Victoria, BC V8Z 4M2
Canada
　　　　250-727-6851
Fax: 250-384-5750　800-663-2220
info@rogerschocolates.com
www.rogerschocolates.com
Processor and exporter of confectionery products including boxed cream-filled and dark chocolates, chocolate mint wafers, almond brittles, caramel nutcorn, fudge, etc
President: Steve Parkhill
Estimated Sales: $10 Million
Number Employees: 130
Square Footage: 87000
Type of Packaging: Consumer, Private Label
Brands:
　Rogers Imperials
　Victoria Creams

Food Manufacturers / A-Z

10841 Rogue Ales Brewery
748 SW Bay Blvd
Newport, OR 97365-4836
541-265-3188
Fax: 541-265-7528 www.rogue.com
Processor and exporter of ale, lager and barley wine
President: Jack Joyce
CEO: Jack Choice
jack@rogue.com
CEO: Jack Choice
Estimated Sales: $5-10 Million
Number Employees: 50-99
Type of Packaging: Consumer, Food Service

10842 Rogue Creamery
311 N Front St
Central Point, OR 97502
541-665-1155
Fax: 541-665-1133 866-396-4704
wholesale@roguecreamery.com
www.roguecreamery.com
Handmade cheese
Owner: David Gremmels
david@roguecreamery.com
CEO/Cheesemaker: Cary Bryant
Controller: Tyler Bare
Quality Control: Emily Aldrich
Marketing: Marguerite Merritt
Sales: Chelsea Faris
Production Manager: Brian Moss
Year Founded: 1933
Estimated Sales: $16 Million
Number Employees: 20-49
Type of Packaging: Consumer, Food Service, Private Label, Bulk

10843 Roha USA LTD
5015 Manchester Ave
St Louis, MO 63110-2011
314-289-8300
Fax: 314-531-0461 888-533-7642
roha.usa@rohagroup.com www.roha.com
Global manufacturer of color ingredients for food, beverage, pet food, cosmetic and industrial applications.
Estimated Sales: $10-20 Million
Number Employees: 50-99
Parent Co: ROHA Dyechem Pvt. Ltd.

10844 Rohrbach Brewing Co
3859 Buffalo Rd
Rochester, NY 14624-1103
585-594-9800
Fax: 585-594-1960 info@rohrbachs.com
Seasonal beer, ale, stout and lager
Owner: John Urlaub
jurlaub@rohrbach.com
CFO: Sam Fletcher
Sales Manager: Larry Schultz
Estimated Sales: $1-2.5 Million
Number Employees: 20-49
Type of Packaging: Consumer, Food Service

10845 Rokeach Food Corp
80 Avenue K
Newark, NJ 07105-3803
973-589-1472
Fax: 973-589-5298
Ethnic foods
CEO: Victor Ostreicher
Estimated Sales: Less than $500,000
Number Employees: 10-19
Brands:
 Jericho Canyon Red
 Rokeach Food

10846 Roland Machinery
816 N Dirksen Pkwy
Springfield, IL 62702-6115
217-789-7711
Fax: 217-744-7314 800-325-1183
Breadings, batters, baking powder, fermentation additives, dough conditioners, sausage/meat binders, chocolate milk, baking and cake mixes, etc.; exporter of baking mixes
CEO: Ray Roland
rroland@rolandmachinery.com
COO: Ian MacEwan
Vice President: Terry McGuire
Plant Manager: Keith Gill
Purchasing Manager: Mary Gajewski
Number Employees: 20-49
Square Footage: 280000
Parent Co: Abitec Corporation
Type of Packaging: Private Label, Bulk
Brands:
 Best O' the Wheat
 Choice Foods
 Gold N Good
 Golden Meal
 Heritage Hearth

10847 Roland Seafood Co
1790 Mayport Rd
Atlantic Beach, FL 32233-1931
904-246-9443
Fax: 904-241-0645
Fish and shrimp
President: Brad Roland
Estimated Sales: Less Than $500,000
Number Employees: 1-4
Type of Packaging: Consumer, Food Service, Bulk
Brands:
 Roland Star

10848 Rolet Food Products Company
70 Scott Ave
Brooklyn, NY 11237
718-497-0476
Fax: 718-497-0137
Producer of meat snacks & potato chips.
President: Mark Turetsky
Executive Vice President: Charles Littman
Contact: Raul Candelaria
raul@rolets.com
Operations Manager: Miles Turetsky
Estimated Sales: $5-10 Million
Number Employees: 50-99
Type of Packaging: Consumer

10849 Rolling Pin Bakery
119 5th Avenue W
Bow Island, AB T0K 0G0
Canada
403-545-2434
Fax: 403-545-2167
Bread, doughnuts, cakes and pastries
Partner: John Sytsma
Partner: Ineke Sytsma
Proprietor: Russell Dueck
Estimated Sales: $149,000
Number Employees: 3
Square Footage: 5500
Type of Packaging: Consumer, Food Service

10850 Rolling Pin Bakery
2211 Washington Street
Great Bend, KS 67530-2454
620-793-5381
Baked goods
President: Dave Cooley
Estimated Sales: $500,000
Number Employees: 5

10851 Rollingstone Chevre
27349 Shelton Rd
Parma, ID 83660-6731
208-722-6460
Fax: 208-722-6460 chevre@mac.com
Goat cheese
Owner: Karen Evans
chevre@mac.com
Owner: Charles Evans
Estimated Sales: Less Than $500,000
Number Employees: 1-4
Type of Packaging: Consumer, Bulk

10852 Roma & Ray's Italian Bakery
45 Railroad Ave
Valley Stream, NY 11580-6030
516-825-7610
Fax: 516-887-6866
Italian baked goods
President: Dario DE-Giovanni
robertde-giovanni@crhamilton.com
Estimated Sales: $10-20 000,000
Number Employees: 10-19

10853 Roma Bakeries
523 Marchesano Dr
Rockford, IL 61102-3596
815-964-6737
Fax: 815-964-6057
Rolls, bread, danish and pies
President: John Bowler
CFO: Gene Bowler
Vice President: Marilyn Bowler
Estimated Sales: $500,000-$1 Million
Number Employees: 10-19
Type of Packaging: Consumer
Brands:
 Roma Bakeries

10854 Roma Packing Company
2266 Pawtucket Avenue
East Providence, RI 02914-1710
401-228-7170
Fax: 401-228-7178
Sausage including Italian and Polish
President: Steven Lombardi
Owner: Marsha Caputo
Estimated Sales: $3-5 Million
Number Employees: 5-9
Type of Packaging: Consumer, Private Label, Bulk

10855 Roman Packing Company
2001 S 13th Street
Norfolk, NE 68701-6615
402-371-5990
Fax: 402-371-5639 800-373-5990
Meat products including dressed beef, pork, sausage and luncheon meats
President: Wendell Newcomb
Estimated Sales: $10-20 Million
Number Employees: 20-49
Type of Packaging: Consumer

10856 Roman Sausage Company
1810 Richard Avenue
Santa Clara, CA 95050-2818
408-988-1222
Fax: 408-988-0546 800-497-7462
Processor and importer of patties including sausage, salmon and tuna; also, salmon fillets
President: Amir Kanji
akanji@biomeddiagnostics.com
Estimated Sales: $1,100,000
Number Employees: 10
Square Footage: 32000
Brands:
 Prima Brands

10857 Romanian Kosher SausageCo
7200 N Clark St
Chicago, IL 60626-2416
773-761-4141
Fax: 773-761-9506
www.romaniankoshersausage.com
Sausages
President: Arnold Loeb
romaniankosher@gmail.com
Estimated Sales: Below $5 000,000
Number Employees: 20-49

10858 Rombauer Vineyards
3522 Silverado Trl N
St Helena, CA 94574-9663
707-963-5170
Fax: 707-963-5752 800-622-2206
info@rombauer.com www.rombauer.com
Winery
President: Koerner Rombauer
Chief Financial Officer: Tory Sims
Director, Marketing & Consumer Relations: Brandye Alexander
National Sales Manager: Alan Cannon
Chief Operating Officer: Robert Knebel
Estimated Sales: $40.5 Million
Number Employees: 20-49
Number of Brands: 1
Type of Packaging: Consumer, Food Service
Brands:
 Rombauer Vineyards

10859 Romero's Food Products Inc
15155 Valley View Ave
Santa Fe Springs, CA 90670-5323
562-802-1858
Fax: 562-921-7240 800-719-2690
orders@romerosfood.com www.romerosfood.com
Mexican sweet bread, tortillas, taco and tostada shells and tortilla chips
President: Leon Romero
CEO: Richard Scandalito
General Manager: Robert Romero
Vice President: Raul Romero
Sales: Sam Valenzuela
Operations Manager: Alfonso Valcarcel
Estimated Sales: $20-30 Million
Number Employees: 100-249

Type of Packaging: Consumer, Food Service, Private Label, Bulk
Brands:
   Romero's

10860 (HQ)Ron Son Foods Inc
81 Locke Ave
PO Box 38
Swedesboro, NJ 08085-1059
   856-241-7333
Fax: 856-241-7338 jim@ronsonfoods.com
www.ronsonfoods.com
Manufacturer, importer and importer of canned mushrooms, olives, olive oil, Italian pasta, anchovies, roasted peppers and artichokes
Owner: Ron Son
ron@ronsonfoods.com
CEO: James Bianco
CEO: James Bianco
Chief Marketing Officer: Peter Goldsberry
VP Sales: James Bianco
ron@ronsonfoods.com
Estimated Sales: $2-4 Million
Number Employees: 5-9
Square Footage: 200000
Type of Packaging: Consumer, Food Service, Private Label, Bulk
Brands:
   Ghigi
   Leone Bianco
   Ron Son
   Trifoglio

10861 Ron's Home Style Foods
4614 Perry St
Houston, TX 77021-3439
   713-747-9666
Fax: 713-640-2085 800-856-3131
service@ronsfoods.com www.ronsfoods.com
Refrigerated prepared foods: salads, spreads, desserts and frozen entrees
Number Employees: 20-49

10862 Ron's Wisconsin Cheese LLC
124 Main St
Luxemburg, WI 54217-1102
   920-845-5330
Fax: 920-845-9423 ronscheese@centurytel.net
www.ronscheese.com
Cheese spreads
Co-Owner: Ron Renard
Co-Owner: Terry Renard
ronscheese@centratel.net
Estimated Sales: Less Than $500,000
Number Employees: 10-19
Type of Packaging: Private Label, Bulk

10863 Rondo Specialty Foods LTD
118 Quigley Blvd
New Castle, DE 19720-4104
   302-325-1145
Fax: 800-876-7971 800-724-6636
info@rondofoods.com
Bread, biscuits, cakes, pastries, cookies, baking mixes and ingredients, coffee, chocolate bars and other chocolate.
Marketing: Robert Dundas
Contact: Robert Dundas
robert.dundas@rondofoods.com
Number Employees: 1-4

10864 Ronnoco Coffee Co
618 S Boyle Ave
St Louis, MO 63110-1628
   314-371-5050
Fax: 314-371-5056 800-428-2287
info@ronnoco.com www.ronnoco.com
Coffee
President: Frank Guyol
Estimated Sales: Below $5 Million
Number Employees: 100-249
Brands:
   Ronnoco

10865 Ronny Brook Farm Dairy
310 Prospect Hill Rd
Ancramdale, NY 12503
   518-398-6455
Fax: 518-398-6464 800-772-6455
info@ronnybrook.com www.ronnybrook.com
Milk, half & half, cream, chocolate milk, coffee milk, strawberry milk, drinkable yogurts, yogurt, ice cream and butter

Owner: Ronald Osofsky
info@ronnybrook.com
Estimated Sales: $1-2.5 Million
Number Employees: 10-19
Type of Packaging: Consumer, Private Label

10866 Ronzoni
PO Box 5400
Largo, FL 33779
   800-730-5957
www.ronzoni.com
Pastas, including gluten free, vegetable based, and whole grain varieties
President/CEO: Bastiaan de Zeeuw
Senior VP/CFO: Michael Slavin
Senior VP/COO: Enrique Zaragoza
Number Employees: 75
Parent Co: Riviana Foods Inc.
Type of Packaging: Consumer, Food Service
Brands:
   Ronzoni
   Ronzoni Garden Delight
   Ronzoni Gluten Free
   Ronzoni Healthy Harvest
   Ronzoni Homestyle
   Ronzoni Organic
   Ronzoni Smart Taste
   Ronzoni SuperGreens
   Ronzoni Thick and Hearty

10867 Roode Packing Company
P.O.Box 510
Fairbury, NE 68352
   402-729-2253
Fax: 402-477-5743
Beef, sausage and pork including smoked and cured
President: Tom Roode
Plant Manager: Dwayne Hasselbring
Estimated Sales: $3,250,000
Number Employees: 33
Type of Packaging: Consumer, Food Service

10868 Rooibee Red Tea
1102 Lyndon Lane, Suite B
Louisville, KY 40222
   502-749-0800
rooibee@rooibeeredtea.com
www.rooibeeredtea.com
Rooibee Red Tea, made from the South African rooibos bush and USDA-certified organic, offers all the benefits of red tea in five flavors: watermelon mint, peach, unsweetened, cranberry pomegranate, and vanilla chai. Naturally caffeinefree.
Chief Tea Officer: Heather Howell
Director Of Sales: Mike Fulkerson
Contact: Bryon Evans
bryon@rooibeeredtea.com
Logistics Coordinator: Gary Jacobs
Type of Packaging: Consumer

10869 Roos Foods
P.O.Box 310
Kenton, DE 19955
   302-653-0600
Fax: 302-653-8458 800-343-3642
rcastillo@roosfoods.com
Cheese, sour cream, exotic drinks, drink mixes, soy base drinks, and BBQ snacks
President: Anna Roos
Controller: Tammy Benini
Operations Manager: Alex Martin
Plant Manager: Roque Lopez
Estimated Sales: $4,900,000
Number Employees: 20-49
Number of Brands: 8
Number of Products: 98
Type of Packaging: Consumer, Food Service, Private Label
Brands:
   Amigo
   Mexicana
   Roos
   Santarosa
   Snyapa
   Wally's

10870 Root Cellar Preserves
9 Avon Road
Wellesley, MA 02482
   781-864-7440
Fax: 530-326-6104
info@RootCellarPreserves.com

Gluten-free, kosher, organic/natural, vegetarian, full-line condiments, salsa/dips, canned or preserved fruits/vegetables, pickles & pickled vegetables
Founder: Susan Jones
Founder: Lorne Jones
info@rootcellarpreserves.com
Estimated Sales: $100,000
Number Employees: 2

10871 Roquette America Inc.
2211 Innovation Dr.
Geneva, IL 60134
   630-463-9430
Fax: 319-526-2542 www.roquette.com
Corn, wheat and potato food ingredients including modified starches, proteins and high fructose and maltose syrups.
President/Chief Executive Officer: Dominique Baumann
CFO: Eric Loges
Year Founded: 1933
Estimated Sales: $100 Million
Number Employees: 8,400
Square Footage: 19107
Parent Co: Roquette Freres

10872 Rosa Brothers Milk Co Inc
10090 2nd Ave
Hanford, CA 93230-9370
   559-685-8825
info@rosabrothers.com
www.rosabrothers.com
Milk and milk products
President: Noel Rosa
Director of Sales & Marketing: Kathleen Johnson
Year Founded: 1953
Estimated Sales: $20-50 Million
Number Employees: 1-4
Type of Packaging: Consumer, Food Service

10873 Rosa Food Products
2750 Grays Ferry Ave
Philadelphia, PA 19146-3801
   215-467-2214
Fax: 215-467-6850 rosa@rosafoods.com
Manufacturer and wholesaler of pastas, sauces, cooking ingredients, condiments, etc.
President: Jack Foti
CEO: Giacomo Foti
mfoti@rosafoods.com
Chief Financial Officer: Leonardo Foti
Manager: Mary Foti
Estimated Sales: $11 Million
Number Employees: 10-19
Number of Brands: 9
Square Footage: 68000
Type of Packaging: Consumer, Food Service, Private Label, Bulk
Brands:
   Rosa
   Rita
   Leonardo
   Luna
   Pavilion
   Cassino
   Angela
   He Man
   Keller's

10874 Rosa Mexicano
846 7th Ave
5th Floor
New York, NY 10019-5221
   212-757-5447
Fax: 212-397-3003 mpolton@rosamexicano.com
Salsa/dips, soups/broths, other sauces, seasonings and cooking enhancers, chips.
President, Chief Executive Officer: Howard Greenstone
Vice President: Louis Alvarez
Contact: Amanda Morlock
amorlock@babylonbeachhouse.com
Vice President of Operations: Christian Plotczyk
Estimated Sales: $92,000
Number Employees: 10-19

10875 Rosa's Horchata, LLC
655 Deerfield Road
Suite 100
Deerfield, IL 60015
   847-267-0570
Fax: 847-729-7231 www.rosashorchata.com

Food Manufacturers / A-Z

Produces a bottled version of a traditional Mexican beverage, horchata, with a shelf stable (refrigeration not required). Available flavors include original with the taste of cinnamon rice and a hint of vanilla, Strawberry/Fresa with the taste of fresh berries, Melon with the taste of ripe cantaloupe & honeydew melons, and Chocolate Mexicano with the rich taste of Mexican chocolate and a hint of cinnamon.
Co-Founder: Marvin Berger
Co-Founder & Sales Representative: Edward Noeh

10876 Rosalind Candy Castle Inc
1301 5th Ave
New Brighton, PA 15066-2117
724-843-1144
Fax: 724-847-2008 www.rosalindcandy.com
Confectionery including chocolates
President: James Crudden
orders@rosalindcandy.com
Estimated Sales: Less Than $500,000
Number Employees: 1-4
Type of Packaging: Consumer

10877 Rosanna Imports Warehouse
6755 E Marginal Way S
Seattle, WA 98108-3406
206-329-1881
Fax: 206-264-7637 877-343-3779
info@rosannainc.com www.rosannainc.com
Manufacturer of food products.
Founder and President: Rosanna Bowles
info@rosannainc.com
Number Employees: 10-19

10878 Rosati Italian Water Ice
201 E Madison Ave
Clifton Heights, PA 19018-2690
610-626-1818
Fax: 610-626-0706 855-476-7284
srrosati@aol.com www.rosatiice.com
Italian water ice
President: Rich Trotter
VP: Al Everets
Estimated Sales: $700,000
Number Employees: 10-19
Type of Packaging: Consumer

10879 Rose Acre Farms
911 N 1200 W
Wolcott, IN 47995
765-258-4015
Fax: 812-497-3311 ajackson@goodegg.com
www.goodegg.com
Eggs
President: Lois Rust
Director of Sales: Amanda Jackson
Manager: Kim Allman
kallman@goodegg.com
Plant Manager: Nick Cary
Commodities Purchasing: Joe Easton
Estimated Sales: $5-10 Million
Number Employees: 50-99
Parent Co: Rose Acre Farms
Type of Packaging: Food Service, Bulk

10880 Rose Acre Farms Inc
6874 N Base Rd
Seymour, IN 47274-8934
812-497-2557
Fax: 812-497-3311 800-356-3447
info2003@goodegg.com www.goodegg.com
Producer of fresh shell eggs and egg products
President: Lois Rust
lrust@goodegg.com
VP: Mark Whintington
Marketing Manager: Greg Hinton
Production Manager: Victor Ritteink
Number Employees: 1000-4999
Type of Packaging: Consumer, Food Service, Private Label

10881 Rose City Pepperheads
16285 SW 85th Ave # 403
Suite 403
Tigard, OR 97224-5424
503-443-3873
Fax: 503-443-3873
susan@rosecitypepperheads.com
www.rosecitypepperheads.com
Flavored pepper jellies.
Owner: Susan Mc Cormick
rosecitypepperheads@gmail.com
Estimated Sales: $300,000-500,000
Number Employees: 1-4

Type of Packaging: Consumer

10882 Rose Creek Vineyards
226 East Ave N
Hagerman, ID 83332
208-837-4353
Fax: 208-837-6405
Wines
Manager: Katie Owsley
Treasurer: Susan Martin
Vice President: Stephanie Martin
Estimated Sales: $1-4.9 000,000
Number Employees: 1-4

10883 Rose Frozen Shrimp
741 Ceres Avenue
Los Angeles, CA 90021-1515
213-626-8251
Fax: 213-626-4802
Shrimp
President: Ken Takiguchi
Estimated Sales: $10-20 000,000
Number Employees: 20

10884 Rose Hill Distributors
81 Rose Hill Road
Branford, CT 06405-4015
203-488-7231
Fax: 203-488-2100
Poultry
President/CEO: Frank Vastola
Estimated Sales: $5-10 000,000
Number Employees: 20

10885 Rose Hill Seafood
2621 Hamilton Rd
Columbus, GA 31904
706-322-1269
Fax: 562-220-1575
Frozen foods, canned foods goods, dry goods, poultry, seafood, and produce
Owner: Jeff Lundsford
Estimated Sales: $1-3 Million
Number Employees: 20-49

10886 (HQ)Rose Packing Co Inc
65 S Barrington Rd
South Barrington, IL 60010-9589
847-381-5700
Fax: 847-381-9424 800-323-7363
postmaster@rosepacking.com
www.rosepacking.com
Meat products including; canadian bacon, hams, boneless turkey, pork loin, sausages, meatballs, pork shoulder, toppings, fresh/frozen meats, pizza toppers, and zip-packs.
President & CEO: Dwight Stiehl
williamrose@rosepacking.com
CFO: James O'Hara
Executive Vice President: Jim Vandenbergh
Director of Information Systems: Marty Strickler
Quality Assurance Manager: Sean R. Tuftedal
Dir of Marketing & Advertising: Erik W. Vandenbergh
Retail Sales Manager: Larry Null
Lab Director: Maria Maris
Director of Operations: Michael Reiter
Director of Product Development: Peter D. Rose
Plant Superintendent: Joseph Mihalov
Purchasing Manager: Bob Jones
Number Employees: 500-999
Type of Packaging: Consumer, Food Service
Other Locations:
  Rose Packing Company Plant
  Chicago IL

10887 Rose Randolph Cookies, LLC
PO Box 1117
Wappingers Falls, NY 12590-8117
917-834-2310
barbara@roserandolphcookies.com
Manufacturer of cookies and baking mixes.
Founder: Barbara Demosthene
bdemosthene@roserandolphcookies.com

10888 Rosebrand Corp
585 Berriman St
Brooklyn, NY 11208-5203
718-257-2058
Fax: 718-257-2058 800-854-5356
Batch ice cream flavoring, fruit sundae toppings and fountain syrups. Founded in 1926.
President: Elliot Keller
ekeller@rosebrand.com
Customer Development: Elliot Keller

Estimated Sales: $3-5 Million
Number Employees: 10-19
Type of Packaging: Food Service

10889 Rosebud Creamery
Route 3
354 Cornelia Street
Plattsburgh, NY 12901
518-561-5160
Fax: 518-561-6068
Dairy
President: Frederick Perras
Estimated Sales: $500-1 000,000 appx.
Number Employees: 1-4
Brands:
  Rosebud Creamery

10890 Roseland Manufacturing
119 Harrison Ave
Roseland, NJ 07068
973-228-2500
www.dialpestcontrol.com
Jams, jellies and perserves
Chief Executive Officer: Jerry Smith
Chief Operating Officer: Steven Adams
Estimated Sales: $500,000-$1 Million
Number Employees: 5-9

10891 Roselani Tropics Ice Cream
PO Box 1170
Wailuku, HI 96793-6170
808-244-7951
Fax: 808-244-4108 info@roselani.com
www.roselani.com
Carbonated beverages and ice cream
Manager: Todd Assmann
Sales Manager: Mike Nobriga
Estimated Sales: $15,151,351
Number Employees: 50-99
Type of Packaging: Consumer, Food Service

10892 Rosemark Bakery
258 Snelling Ave S
St Paul, MN 55105-2045
651-698-3838
Fax: 651-698-0828
Baked goods
Owner: Carol Rosemark
General Manager: Irv Gertz
Estimated Sales: $5-10 Million
Number Employees: 10-19

10893 Rosen's Diversified Inc.
1120 Lake Ave.
PO Box 933
Fairmont, MN 56031
507-238-6001
Fax: 507-238-9966
ContactUs@RosensDiversified.com
www.rosensdiversifiedinc.com
Agribusiness, beef processing, pet foods and carrier services.
CEO: Tom Rosen
trosen@riw2000.com
Year Founded: 1946
Estimated Sales: $3.2 Billion
Number of Brands: 7
Brands:
  Rosen's Inc.
  America's Heartland Beef
  Long Prairie Packing Company
  Great American
  Skylark
  Big City Reds
  Sheboygan Sausage Company

10894 Rosenberger's Dairies
847 Forty Foot Rd
PO Box 901
Hatfield, PA 19440-2870
800-355-9074
Fax: 215-855-6486 800-355-9074
info@rosenbergers.com
Dairy products including eggs, milk, cream, sour cream and cheese; also, beverages including apple juice, iced tea and fruit drinks
President: Marty Margherio
VP: Marcus Rosenberger
Production Manager: Jeffery Rosenberger
Plant Manager: Gerry Whiting
Number Employees: 250-499
Square Footage: 432268
Type of Packaging: Consumer

Food Manufacturers / A-Z

Brands:
    Rosenbergers

10895 Rosenblum Cellars
2900 Main St Ste 1100
Alameda, CA 94501
510-865-7007
Fax: 510-865-9225 www.rosenblumcellars.com
Wines
President: Kent Rosenblum
CFO: Tim Allen
Quality Control: Les Horton
Marketing Director: Kathy Coi
Operations Manager: Ron Pieretti
Estimated Sales: $5-9.9 Million
Number Employees: 20-49
Number of Brands: 1
Number of Products: 40
Square Footage: 232000
Other Locations:
    Rosenblum Cellars
    Healdsburgh CA
Brands:
    Rosenblum

10896 Roses Ravioli
219 E Walnut Street
Oglesby, IL 61348-1203
815-883-8011
Fax: 815-883-8409
Ravioli, tortellini and pasta sauce
President: Barbara Shields
Owner: Rose Causa
Estimated Sales: $2.5-5 000,000
Number Employees: 1-4

10897 Rosetti's Fine Foods Biscotti
3 Railroad Ave
Clovis, CA 93612-1219
559-323-6450
Fax: 559-323-2022 www.rosettis.com
Biscotti, bark confections
President: Diane Rosetti
rosetti@pacbell.net
Secretary/Treasurer: Dan Rosetti
Estimated Sales: $500,000-$1 Million
Number Employees: 5-9
Brands:
    Rosetti Fine Foods

10898 Roseville Corporation
120 Plum Ct
Mountain View, CA 94043-4899
650-255-9278
Fax: 650-592-8966 888-247-9338
www.bigsmiley.com
Candy
President: Enrique Ganitsky
Brands:
    Betty Twist & Match Chocolate Candy
    Big Smiley

10899 Rosina Food Holdings Inc
170 French Rd
Buffalo, NY 14227-2777
716-668-0123
Fax: 716-668-1132 888-767-4621
gsetter@rosina.com www.rosina.com
Italian foods including; appetizers, pastas, pizza toppings, meatballs, eggplant, specialty sausages, and entrees for consumers, industrial, foodservice and international markets.
President & CEO: Russell Corigliano
rcorigliano@rosina.com
Chairman: James Corigliano
CFO/COO: Roger Palczewski
VP: Joseph Corigliano
Manager Product Development: Nicholas Arbore
Quality Assurance Manager: Dan Etzinger
VP Marketing: Frank Corigliano
Communications Director: Nick Lukasiewicz
VP Engineering: Viren Sitwala
Estimated Sales: $32.4 Million
Number Employees: 250-499
Square Footage: 60000
Type of Packaging: Food Service
Brands:
    Rosina
    Celentano
    San Rallo Gourmet Italian
    Italian Village
    Floresta

10900 Rosmarino Foods/R.Z. Humbert Company
16216 Turnbury Oak Drive
Odessa, FL 33556-2870
813-926-9053
Fax: 813-920-0734 888-926-9053
Speciality award winning foods such as all natural salad dressings, hearty pasta sauces, flavorful marinades, great grilling sauces, tangy BBQ sauces, and fiery hot sauces
President: Rosemary Humbert
VP Marketing: Roger Humbert
Number Employees: 8
Number of Brands: 3
Number of Products: 50
Square Footage: 260000
Type of Packaging: Consumer, Food Service, Private Label, Bulk
Brands:
    Bonnies
    Luna Rossa
    Rosmarino

10901 Ross Fine Candies
4642 Elizabeth Lake Rd
Waterford, MI 48328-2831
248-682-5640
Fax: 248-682-0457
Candy and other confectionery products
President: Janet Greaves
Estimated Sales: $300,000
Number Employees: 5-9
Type of Packaging: Consumer, Private Label
Brands:
    Ross Fine

10902 Ross-Smith Pecan Company
107 Plantation Oak Dr
Thomasville, GA 31792-3540
229-859-2225
Fax: 229-859-2382 800-841-5503
Manufacturer and exporter of nuts including shelled pecans
President: Betty McDuffie
Estimated Sales: Less than $500,000
Number Employees: 23

10903 Rossi Pasta LTD
106 Front St
Marietta, OH 45750-3123
740-373-5155
Fax: 740-373-5310 800-227-6774
info@rossipasta.com www.rossipasta.com
Gourmet handmade pasta products and sauces
President: John Hammat
Chairman: Frank L Christy
Estimated Sales: Below $5 Million
Number Employees: 1-4
Type of Packaging: Private Label

10904 Rostov's Coffee & Tea Co
1618 W Main St
Richmond, VA 23220-4633
804-355-1955
Fax: 804-355-6963 800-637-6772
www.rostovs.com
Coffee and tea
Owner: Tammy Rostov
Founder: Jay Rostov
Estimated Sales: Below $5 Million
Number Employees: 10-19
Type of Packaging: Consumer
Brands:
    Rostov's Coffee Tea

10905 Rotella's Italian Bakery Inc.
6949 S. 108th St.
La Vista, NE 68128
402-592-6600
Fax: 402-592-2989 info@rotellasbakery.com
Hamburger buns, hoagies, bread loaves, dinner rolls and bread sticks, hot dog buns and brat buns, and specialty breads.
Controller: Dean Jacobsen
Sales Executive: Jim Rotella
jrotella@rotellasbakery.com
Year Founded: 1921
Estimated Sales: $133 Million
Number Employees: 250-499
Square Footage: 65000
Type of Packaging: Consumer, Food Service
Brands:
    Rotella's

10906 Roth Cheese USA
5525 Nobel Dr.
Suite 100
Fitchburg, WI 53711
608-285-9800
Fax: 608-328-2120 info@emmirothusa.com
www.rothcheese.com
Havarti, gouda, blue, muenster and commodity cheeses
President: Tim Omer
CEO: Stephen McKeon
Quality Manager: Alecia Vermeern
SVP Sales & Marketing: Anthony Salathe
SVP Supply Chain & Operations: Ty Brannen
Estimated Sales: $25-49.9 Million
Number Employees: 20-49
Type of Packaging: Consumer, Food Service, Bulk
Brands:
    Grand Cru Raclette
    Grand Crue
    Kronenost
    Pesto Havarti
    Rofumo
    Roth Kase
    Roth Kase
    Ustenborg
    Vangogh

10907 Rothbury Farms
PO Box 202
Grand Rapids, MI 49501-0202
616-574-5757
877-684-2879
www.rothburyfarms.com
Dry wheat-based products, including croutons, stuffing, and bread crumbs.
President: Robert Roskam
Manager: Janet Lennon
Year Founded: 1923
Estimated Sales: $128 Million
Number Employees: 1,000
Number of Brands: 2
Type of Packaging: Food Service, Private Label, Bulk
Brands:
    Rothbury Farms
    Grandpa's Oven

10908 Rothman's Food Inc
4718 Delmar Blvd
St Louis, MO 63108-1706
314-367-5448
Ethnic foods
Owner: A Rothman
Estimated Sales: Below $5 000,000
Number Employees: 5-9

10909 Rotteveel Orchards
6183 Reddick Ln
Dixon, CA 95620-9731
707-678-1495
Fax: 707-678-1446
Processor and exporter of almonds
President: Neil Rotteveel
info@rotteveel.com
Estimated Sales: $500,000-$1 Million
Number Employees: 5-9
Type of Packaging: Bulk

10910 Roudon-Smith Vineyards
13809 Serra Oaks Court
Saratoga, CA 95070
831-438-1244
Fax: 831-438-4374 sales@roudonsmith.com
www.roudonsmith.com
Wines
Owner: Annette Hunt
Owner: David Hunt
Estimated Sales: $1-2.5 Million
Number Employees: 1-4
Brands:
    Roudon Smith Vineyards

10911 Rougie Foie Gras
1661 Rue Marcoux
Marieville, QC J3M 1E8
Canada
450-460-2107
Fax: 450-460-2963 www.rougie.ca
Foie gras (duck) and lobster

Food Manufacturers / A-Z

CEO: Benoit Cuchet
Sales & Marketing Manager: Thomas Delannoy
Customer Service: Sandra Ratelle
sandra.ratelle@euralis.ca
Processing: C,dric Martineau
Brands:
  Rougie

10912 Round Hill Vineyards
1680 Silverado Trl S
St Helena, CA 94574-9542
707-963-5252
Fax: 707-963-0834 800-778-0424
info@rutherfordwine.com
www.roundhillwines.com
Wines
Owner: Morgan Zaninovich
morganz@roundhillwines.com
VP: Mark Fedorchak
Chairman: Erne Van Asperen
President: Virginia Van Asperen
Public Relations: Bonnie Zimmerman
Production Manager: Keith Groves
Plant Manager: Bob Iacampo
Estimated Sales: Below $5 Million
Number Employees: 50-99
Type of Packaging: Private Label
Brands:
  Round Hill Vineyards
  Rutherford Ranch
  Van Asperen Vineyard

10913 Round Rock Honey Co, LLC
1308 Chisholm Tr
Suite 107
Round Rock, TX 78681
512-828-5416
Fax: 512-828-5416 www.roundrockhoney.com
Honey

10914 Rousseau Farming Co
102 S 95th Ave
Phoenix, AZ 85043
623-936-7100
Fax: 623-936-7386 admin@rfcaz.com
www.rousseaufarming.com
Fruits and vegetables
President: David Rousseau
Partner: Jean Biggs
jeanb@rfcaz.com
Estimated Sales: $1-2,500,000
Number Employees: 250-499

10915 Rousselot Inc
1231 S Rochester St # 250
Suite 250
Mukwonago, WI 53149-9031
262-363-6050
888-455-3556
gelatin.usa@rousselot.com www.rousselot.com
Global gelatin and collagen manufacturer.
Contact: James Mcdermott
james.mcdermott@rousselot.com
Number Employees: 5-9
Number of Brands: 4
Parent Co: Darling Ingredients
Type of Packaging: Bulk
Other Locations:
  Sales Office
  Mukwonago WI
  Production
  Dubuque IA
  Production
  Peabody MA
Brands:
  Rousselot
  Synergy Systems
  ProTake
  Peptan

10916 Route 11 Potato Chips
11 Edwards Way
Mount Jackson, VA 22842-2037
540-477-9664
Fax: 540-869-0176 800-294-7783
sales@rt11.com www.rt11.com
Handcooked potato chips, sweet potato chips, mixed vegetable chips and potato chip cookies.
President/CEO: Sarah Cohen
sarah@rt11.com
Year Founded: 1992
Estimated Sales: $20-50 Million
Number Employees: 20-49
Brands:
  Route 11 Potato Chips

10917 Routin America
955 NW 17th Avenue
Suite F
Delray Beach, FL 334452516
export@routin.com
www.1883.com
Flavored syrups and sauces.
President: Jean Clochet
Estimated Sales: $1.5 Million
Number Employees: 2
Number of Brands: 1
Parent Co: Routin SA
Type of Packaging: Private Label
Brands:
  1883

10918 (HQ)Rovira Biscuit Corporation
619 La Ceiba Ave
Ponce, PR 00717-1901
787-844-8585
Fax: 787-848-7176
customerservice@rovirabiscuits.com
www.rovirabiscuits.com
Crackers and biscuits; exporter of crackers
President and Director: Rafael Rovira
President, Rovira Foods: Frances Rovira
Executive VP and General Manager: Carlos Rovira
Quality Control: Carla Traverso
Export Sales Manager: Roberto Ponce
Estimated Sales: $50 Million
Number Employees: 300
Square Footage: 180000
Other Locations:
  Rovira Biscuit Corp.
  Pueblo Viejo PR

10919 (HQ)Rowena
758 W 22nd St
Norfolk, VA 23517-1925
757-627-8699
Fax: 757-627-1505 800-627-8699
rowena@rowens.com www.rowenas.com
Processor and exporter of gourmet pound cakes, jams, curds, dry mixes and sauces
Founder, President: Rowena Fullinwider
General Manager: Joan Place
Sales: Ann Cole
Contact: Tamikka Doman
tamikka@rowenas.com
Production: Renee Satterfield
Warehouse Manager: Dom Tamikk
Estimated Sales: $620000
Number Employees: 20-49
Square Footage: 52000
Type of Packaging: Consumer, Food Service, Private Label, Bulk
Brands:
  Rowena's
  Rowena's Gourmet Sauces
  Rowena's Jams & Jellies
  Rowena's Pound Cake

10920 Rowland Coffee RoastersInc.
P.O.Box 520845
Miami, FL 33152-0845
305-592-7302
Fax: 305-592-9471 866-318-0422
www.javacabana.com
Processor, importer and exporter of coffee; importer and wholesaler/distributor of coffee equipment and supplies including filters
President: Jose Souto
General Manager of Sales: Angeo Soupo
Estimated Sales: $2.5-5 Million
Number Employees: 50-99
Square Footage: 50000
Parent Co: Tetley USA
Type of Packaging: Consumer, Food Service, Private Label
Brands:
  Cafe Bustelo

10921 Roy Dick Company
152 Harris Street
Griffin, GA 30223-7017
770-227-3916
Fax: 770-227-3916
Catfish, shrimp, oysters, chicken
Owner: Roy Dick

10922 Royal Atlantic Seafood
2 Carrie Lane
Gloucester, MA 01930-2328
978-281-6373
Fax: 978-283-7185
Seafood
President: Anne Mortillaro

10923 Royal Baltic LTD
9829 Ditmas Ave
Brooklyn, NY 11236-1925
718-385-8300
Fax: 718-385-4757
Manufactures smoked fish products; distributes gourmet foods, such as seafood delicacies, cheese, juice, feta, coffee, chocolate candy and sauces.
President: Alex Kaganovsky
alexkaganovsky@royalbaltic.com
Finance Manager: Alex Kaganovsky
Estimated Sales: $10-20 Million
Number Employees: 50-99
Type of Packaging: Consumer

10924 (HQ)Royal Caribbean Bakery
620 S Fulton Ave
Mt Vernon, NY 10550-5012
914-668-6868
Fax: 914-668-5700 888-818-0971
info@royalcaribbeanbakery.com
www.royalcaribbeanbakery.com
Jamaican baked goods and specialty foods
President/CEO: Jeanette Hosang
CEO: Vincent Hosang
Estimated Sales: $5-10 Million
Number Employees: 50-99
Square Footage: 240000
Type of Packaging: Consumer, Food Service, Private Label, Bulk
Other Locations:
  Royal Caribbean Bakery
  Orlando FL

10925 Royal Caviar Inc
4551 San Fernando Rd # 110
Glendale, CA 91204-3234
818-546-5858
Fax: 818-546-5856 www.royalcaviar.com
Caviar
President: Robert Khatchatrian

10926 Royal Center Locker Plant
104 S Chicago St
Royal Center, IN 46978-7029
574-643-3275
Fax: 574-643-3031
Meat products including beef, pork and lamb
Owner: Steve Layer
Estimated Sales: $12 Million
Number Employees: 10-19
Type of Packaging: Consumer

10927 Royal Crest Dairy
350 S Pearl St
Denver, CO 80209-2098
303-777-3055
Fax: 303-744-9173 888-226-6455
hr@royalcrestdairy.com www.royalcrestdairy.com
Milks, cream, butter, eggs, juices, water, bread, cheese, cottage cheese, sour cream, dips, yogurt and various seasonal items.
President: Ryan Bontrager
Founder: Paul Miller
CFO: Howard Lutz
VP Operations: Grady Cleckler
Estimated Sales: $20-50 Million
Number Employees: 100-249
Brands:
  Royal Crest

10928 Royal Cup Coffee
PO Box 170971
Birmingham, AL 35217-0971
800-366-5836
webjava@royalcupcoffee.com
www.royalcupcoffee.com
Coffee, tea, and coffee equipment.
CEO: Bill Smith
Chief Financial Officer: William Wann

Year Founded: 1896
Estimated Sales: $100-$500 Million
Number Employees: 859
Number of Brands: 4
Square Footage: 260000
Type of Packaging: Food Service

Other Locations:
   Royal Cup
   Birmingham AL
Brands:
   Prideland
   Royal Cup
   ROAR
   H.C. Valentine

10929 Royal Food Products
2322 E Minnesota St
Indianapolis, IN 46203
   317-782-2660
Fax: 317-782-2680 sales@royalfp.com
www.royalfp.com
Salad dressings, mayonnaise, mustard and sauces
President: Brian King
CEO: John Heidt
Director: James Heidt
Contact: Nancy Davidian
nancydavidian@royalfoodproducts.com
Estimated Sales: $8.5 Million
Number Employees: 55
Type of Packaging: Food Service
Brands:
   Royal

10930 Royal Foods & Flavor
2456 American Ln
Elk Grove Vlg, IL 60007-6204
   847-595-9166
Fax: 847-595-9690
Flavors, seasonings, yeast extracts and hydrolyzed vegetable proteins
Owner: Harry Gadhvi
harry.gadhvi@royalgoldribbonfoods.com
Estimated Sales: $730,000
Number Employees: 10-19
Type of Packaging: Bulk

10931 Royal Foods Inc
215 Reindollar Ave
Marina, CA 93933-3804
   831-582-2495
Fax: 831-582-2495 800-551-5284
info@gingerpeople.com www.gingerpeople.com
Ginger
President/Owner: Bruce Leeson
Marketing Coordinator: Nicole DeCarli
Contact: Abbie Leeson
abbiel@gingerpeople.com
Estimated Sales: $9.5 Million
Number Employees: 10-19

10932 Royal Gourmet Caviar
27 Blake Ave
Lynbrook, NY 11563-2505
   516-612-7407
Fax: 516-612-7408
Caviar, nuts and dried fruits
Distribution Manager: Donna Powers Bowe
Year Founded: 2000
Estimated Sales: Under $500,000
Number Employees: 1-4
Brands:
   Royal Gourmet Caviar

10933 Royal Harvest Foods Inc
90 Avocado St
Springfield, MA 01104-3304
   413-737-8392
Fax: 413-731-9336 sales@royalharv.com
www.royalharv.com
Poultry processing facility.
President: Jim Vallides
Sales Manager: Frank McNamara
Estimated Sales: Less Than $500,000
Number Employees: 1-4
Number of Brands: 1
Square Footage: 40000
Type of Packaging: Consumer, Food Service, Private Label
Other Locations:
   Royal Harvest Foods
   Marion AL
Brands:
   Royal Harvest

10934 Royal Hawaiian OrchardsLP
24901 Dana Point Harbor Dr
#A-210
Dana Point, CA 92629-2930
   949-661-6304
Fax: 949-487-0242
www.royalhawaiianorchards.com
Nuts
President: Scott Wallace
Senior Vice President: Randolph Cabral
Estimated Sales: 2,000,000.00

10935 Royal Home Bakery
160 Pony Drive
Newmarket, ON L3Y 7B6
Canada
   905-715-7044
Baked goods including bread, buns, biscuits, tarts, cakes and Jamaican patties
Owner: Harold Chin
Manager: Doris Chin
Sales Manager: Hope Chin
Estimated Sales: Under $300,000
Number Employees: 1-4
Square Footage: 16000

10936 Royal Ice Cream Co
27 Warren St
Manchester, CT 06040-6500
   860-649-5358
Fax: 860-647-7376 800-246-2958
sales@royalicecream.com
www.royalicecream.com
Portion packed spumoni, nut roll, tartufo, fruit sorbet, tortoni, bombe, etc.; also, ice cream cakes and pies
President: J Orfitelli
jso@royalicecream.com
VP: Cindy Orfitelli
Estimated Sales: $2000000
Number Employees: 10-19
Square Footage: 60000
Type of Packaging: Food Service, Private Label

10937 Royal Lagoon Seafood Inc
5208 Mobile South St
Theodore, AL 36582-1604
   251-653-1975
Fax: 251-653-1972 800-844-6972
john@royallagoonseafood.com
www.royallagoonseafood.com
Seafood
Owner: Valmon Hammond
Sales: Tanya Hammond
val@valssfd.com
Estimated Sales: $5,000,000
Number Employees: 5-9

10938 Royal Madera Vineyards
7770 Road 33
Madera, CA 93636-8307
   559-486-6666
Fax: 559-661-1427
www.royalmaderavineyards.com
Frozen foods
President: Steve Volpe
rmv@onemain.com
Estimated Sales: $10-20 Million
Number Employees: 10-19

10939 Royal Medjool Date Gardens
1203 Perez Rd
Bard, CA 92222
   760-572-0524
Fax: 760-572-2292
Grower and exporter of dates and date trees.
General Manager: David Nelson
Estimated Sales: $3 Million
Number Employees: 75
Brands:
   Medjool
   Royal

10940 Royal Oak Peanuts
13009 Cedar View Rd
Drewryville, VA 23844-2001
   434-658-9500
Fax: 703-991-8922 800-608-4590
info@royaloakpeanuts.com
www.royaloakpeanuts.com
Peanut and peanut products
President: Stephanie Pope
royaloakpeanuts@royaloakpeanuts.com
Sales/Marketing: Stephanie Pope
Number Employees: 1-4

10941 Royal Pacific Coffee Co
PO Box 6277
Scottsdale, AZ 85261-6277
   480-951-8251
Fax: 480-951-0092 royalpacific@syspac.com
www.royalpacificintl.com
Tea
CEO: Art Gartenberg
Manager: Grace Hatter
grace@royalpacificintl.com
Estimated Sales: Less Than $500,000
Number Employees: 5-9
Type of Packaging: Private Label
Brands:
   Royal Pacific Coffee
   Royal Pacific Tea

10942 Royal Pacific Fisheries
Mi 14.5 Kalifornsky Beach Rd
Kenai, AK 99611
   907-283-9370
Fax: 907-283-5974
Fresh, frozen and canned seafood
President: Marvin Dragseth
Estimated Sales: $5-9.9 Million
Number Employees: 5-9

10943 Royal Palate Foods
960 E Hyde Park Blvd
Inglewood, CA 90302-1708
   310-330-7701
Fax: 310-330-7710
Processor, exporter and wholesaler/distributor of kosher foods including chicken, beef, soups, sauces, frozen entrees, hors d'oeuvres, etc.; serving the food service market; importer of canned vegetables and fruits
President: William Pinkerson
Estimated Sales: $500,000-$1 Million
Number Employees: 10-19
Square Footage: 32000
Type of Packaging: Food Service, Bulk
Brands:
   Royal Palate
   Sierra Spring Foods

10944 Royal Palm Popcorn Company
100 McGaw Dr
Edison, NJ 08837-3725
   732-225-0200
Fax: 732-225-6363 800-526-8865
Gourmet popcorn
President: Michael Spitz
Number Employees: 10-19
Brands:
   Joons Chocolate Popcorn
   Park Avenue Gourmet
   Rainbow Popcorn

10945 Royal Products
P.O.Box 13628
Scottsdale, AZ 85267-3628
   480-948-2509
Fax: 480-951-0835 www.royalprod.com
Health vitamins and supplements
President: Johnny Shannon
CEO: David Stuart
Estimated Sales: Less than $100,000
Number Employees: 1-4
Type of Packaging: Food Service

10946 Royal Resources
PO Box 24001
New Orleans, LA 70184-4001
   504-283-9932
Fax: 504-283-2620 800-888-9932
rrbanfos@bellsouth.net
Salad dressing, jellies, salsas, dessert toppings, hot sauces and cake mix

10947 Royal Ridge Fruits
13215 Road F SW
Royal City, WA 99357
   509-346-1520
Fax: 509-346-2098 info@stoneridgeorchards.com
www.stoneridgeorchards.com
Frozen and dried fruits
Estimated Sales: $5-10 Million
Number Employees: 20-49
Square Footage: 200000
Type of Packaging: Private Label

Food Manufacturers / A-Z

10948 Royal Rose Syrups, LLC
14 Maine St.
Brunswick, ME 04011
718-303-0750
info@royalroseny.com
www.royalrosesyrups.com
Manufacturer of syrup for cocktails.
Co-Founder: Emily Butters
Co-Founder: Forrest Butler

10949 Royal Seafood Inc
2257 E 16th St
Brooklyn, NY 11229-4424
718-769-1517
Fax: 831-373-8336 www.netcostmarket.com
Frozen and fresh fish including cod, flounder, herring, mackerel, perch, salmon, sole, squid and tuna
Owner: Edward Schneider
edward.schneider@netcostmarket.com
Owner/VP: Elaine Pennisi
Estimated Sales: $800,000
Number Employees: 1-4
Type of Packaging: Consumer, Food Service
Brands:
- Black Cod (Sablefish
- Ca Halibut
- Channel Rockfish (Thornyheads
- Dover Sole

10950 Royal Touch Foods
315 Humberline Drive
Etobicoke, ON M9W 5T6
Canada
416-213-1077
Fax: 416-213-1055
Pork and beef sandwiches
President: Domenic Ruso
Estimated Sales: $5.6 Million
Number Employees: 50
Parent Co: J.M. Schneider
Type of Packaging: Food Service
Brands:
- Hamish & Enzo
- Royal Touch

10951 Royal Vista Marketing Inc
126 W Center Ave
Visalia, CA 93291-6228
559-636-9198
Fax: 559-636-9637 info@royalvista.com
Grower and exporter of table grapes, kiwifruit, stone fruit and figs; importer of stone fruit, kiwifruit and table grapes
Owner: Todd Steele
Sales Manager: Patrick Allen
todd@royalvista.com
Estimated Sales: $84000
Number Employees: 10-19
Square Footage: 96000
Parent Co: Atalanta
Type of Packaging: Consumer, Food Service, Bulk
Other Locations:
- Alkop Farms
- Chico CA

10952 Royal Wine Corp
63 Lefante Dr
Bayonne, NJ 07002-5024
718-384-2400
Fax: 718-388-8444 info@royalwines.com
www.royalwine.com
Manufacturer, importer and distributor of premium kosher wines, spirits and liquors. Affiliate of Kedem Food Products International.
President: David Herzog
CEO: Mordy Herzog
Chief Financial Officer: Sheldon Ginsberg
Executive Vice President: Sheldon Ginsberg
SVP: Phillip Herzog
Executive Vice President of Sales: Nathan Herzog
Estimated Sales: $49.5 Million
Number Employees: 200
Number of Brands: 61
Square Footage: 184000
Parent Co: KayCo
Type of Packaging: Consumer, Food Service
Brands:
- Alexander Winery
- Alfasi
- Barkan Winery
- Bartenura Wines
- Bazelet ha Golan Winery
- Binyamina
- Binyamina Winery
- Carmel Winery
- Casa De Corca
- Cave Winery
- Celler De Capcanes
- Covenant Winery
- Domaine du Castel
- Domaine Netofa
- Don Alfonso
- Elvi Winery
- French Wines
- Gamla
- Goose Bay Winery
- Hagafen Winery
- Bokobsa Wines
- Herzog Selection
- Herzog Wine Cellars
- Jeunesse Wines
- Kedem
- Flam Winery
- Baron Edmond De Rothschild
- Laufer Winery
- Legend of Kremlin
- Los Arango
- Morad Winery
- Pacifica
- Porto Cordovero
- Psagot Winery
- Ramon Cardova Winery
- Rashi Winery
- S'forno Winery
- Segal Winery
- Shiloh Winery
- Teal Lake Winery
- Tio Pepe Winery
- Tomintoul
- Tulip Winery
- Tzuba Winery
- Weinstock Wine Cellars
- Yatir Winery
- Zion
- Zachlawi
- (in)
- 1848 Winery
- Altoona Hills
- Chateau Rollan De By
- Clos Mesorah
- Matar by Pelter
- Montefiore Winery
- Or Haganuz Winery
- Padis Vineyards
- Teperberg Winery
- Terra di Seta
- Titora Winery
- Villa Cape Winery

10953 Royale Brands
5315 Tremont Ave
Davenport, IA 52807
563-386-5222
Fax: 563-386-1352 royale@netexpress.net
royalebrands.com
Produce and market frozen beverage products and equipment
President: Joe Colombari
Estimated Sales: Less than $500,000
Number Employees: 10-19
Number of Brands: 13
Number of Products: 250
Type of Packaging: Food Service
Brands:
- Cruisin Cool
- Energy Ice
- Royale Smoothie

10954 Royce C. Bone Farms
2913 Sandy Cross Road
Nashville, NC 27856-8633
252-443-3773
Fax: 252-937-4990 www.ncsweetpotatoes.com
Sweet potatoes, romaine, tomatoes and pickles
Director: David Godwin
Co-Owner: Fay Bone
Vice President: Dewey Scott
Number Employees: 10-19
Brands:
- Jean Sweet Potatos

10955 Rpac LLC
21490 Ortigalita Rd
Los Banos, CA 93635-9793
209-826-0272
Fax: 209-826-3882 info@rpacalmonds.com
www.rpacalmonds.com
Processor and exporter of almonds
Owner: Dave Parreira
dave@arpacalmonds.com
Partner: David Parreira
Shipping Manager: Janet Martin
Plant Manager: James Smith
Estimated Sales: $4500000
Number Employees: 20-49
Type of Packaging: Bulk

10956 Ruark & Ashton
1548 Taylors Island Road
Woolford, MD 21677-1327
410-221-6076
Fax: 410-221-6076 800-725-5032
Seafood
President: Terry Vinson
Estimated Sales: Under $500,000
Number Employees: 1-4

10957 Rubashkin
4308 14th Ave
Brooklyn, NY 11219-1428
718-436-5511
Fax: 718-435-4295
Kosher butcher
President: AA Rubashkin
Estimated Sales: $1-3 000,000

10958 Rubicon Food Products
180 Brodie Drive
Suite 1
Richmond Hill, ON L4B 3K8
Canada
905-883-1117
feedback@rubiconexotic.ca
rubiconexotic.ca
Tropical fruit juice
Financial Analyst: Ocean Yang Jiang
Quality Assurance Executive: Mohammad Bashar
Operation Director: Yuan Robin
Year Founded: 1982
Brands:
- Rubicon

10959 Rubino's Seafood Company
735 W Lake St
Chicago, IL 60661
312-258-0020
Fax: 312-258-0028
Seafood
President: James Rubino
Estimated Sales: $1-3 Million
Number Employees: 5-9
Type of Packaging: Food Service

10960 Rubschlager Baking Corp
800-661-7246
CCC@westonfoods.com
www.rubschlagerbaking.com
Processor and exporter of rye breads.
President: Luc Mongeau
CFO: Tina Murrin
Number Employees: 1-4
Number of Brands: 2
Number of Products: 45
Parent Co: Weston Foods
Type of Packaging: Consumer, Food Service
Brands:
- Rubschlager

10961 Ruby Rockets
55 Broadway
3rd Floor
New York, NY 10036
855-543-7677
www.rubyrockets.com
Frozen fruit and veggie pops
Founder: Wendy Makkena

10962 Rubys Apiaries
711 5th Ave
Milnor, ND 58060-4113
701-427-5200
Condiments and relishes
President: Dick Ruby
CEO: Doug Ruby
Estimated Sales: Less than $500,000
Number Employees: 1-4

10963 Rudd Winery
500 Oakville Xrd
Oakville, CA 94562
707-944-8577
Fax: 707-968-3807 info@ruddwines.com
www.ruddwines.com

Wines
President: Leslie Rudd
leslie@ruddwines.com
COO: Stephen Girard Jr
Marketing Director: Ellen Hunt
Estimated Sales: $5-10 Million
Number Employees: 20-49
Brands:
Bacigalupi Chardonnay
Jericho Canyon Red
Library Wines
Oakville Estate Red

10964 Rude Custom Butchering
6194 W Pines Rd
Mt Morris, IL 61054-9755
815-946-3795
Fax: 815-946-2333
Meats
President: Kevin Rude
Estimated Sales: $10-20 000,000
Number Employees: 20-49

10965 Rudi's Organic Bakery
3300 Walnut St # C
Unit C
Boulder, CO 80301-2529
303-447-0495
Fax: 303-447-0516 877-293-0876
www.rudisbakery.com
Fresh and frozen certified organic baked bread, buns, english muffins, bagels, and soft pretzels.
CEO: Jane Miller
aartzer@charterbaking.com
CFO: Mile Aufiero
Senior Marketing Manager: Maggie Garner
VP Sales: Tom Nash
Director Human Resources: Connie Dietsch
Site Manager: Andy Artzer
Purchasing Manager: Suzie Murphy
Estimated Sales: $20.7 Million
Number Employees: 50-99
Square Footage: 40000
Parent Co: Charter Baking Co.
Type of Packaging: Consumer, Food Service, Bulk
Brands:
Certified Organic Breads
Certified Organic Buns
Certified Organic Rolls

10966 (HQ)Rudolph Foods Co
6575 Bellefontaine Rd
Lima, OH 45804
419-648-3611
www.rudolphfoods.com
Manufacturer and exporter of pork rinds and related snacks
President: Richard Rudolph
VP, Sales & Marketing: Mark Singleton
Year Founded: 1955
Estimated Sales: $50 Million
Number Employees: 400
Number of Brands: 4
Square Footage: 110000
Type of Packaging: Consumer, Private Label, Bulk
Brands:
Grandpa John's
Pepe's
Rudolph's
Southern Recipe

10967 Rudolph's Market & Sausage
2924 Elm St
Dallas, TX 75226-1509
214-741-1874
Fax: 214-761-2017 www.rudolphsmeatmarket.com
Smoked meats and sausage
President: Justine M Andreason
Estimated Sales: $5-10 Million
Number Employees: 10-19
Type of Packaging: Consumer

10968 Rudolph's Specialty Bakery
390 Alliance Avenue
Toronto, ON M6N 2H8
Canada
416-763-4315
Fax: 416-763-4317 800-268-1589
www.rudolphsbakeries.com
Processor and exporter of rye and flat breads, tortillas and flan cakes
President: George Paech
Type of Packaging: Consumer, Food Service, Private Label

Brands:
Casa Jorge
Masala Roti
Roti & Chapati
Rudolph's
Taj Mahal
Wwrapps

10969 Rudy's Tortillas
2115 E Belt Line Rd.
Carrollton, TX 75006
214-634-7839
Fax: 214-638-5317 800-878-2401
www.rudystortillas.com
Tortillas, chalupas, tostadas, tacos, flavored wraps, shells and blue, red, yellow and white chips
President: Nansi Acevedo
nacevedo@rudystortillas.com
CEO: Louis Guerra
Vice President: Joe Guerra
Estimated Sales: $30 Million
Number Employees: 250-499
Brands:
Rudy's Tortillas

10970 Ruef's Meat Market
538 1st St
PO Box 251
New Glarus, WI 53574-8908
608-527-2554
bruef@charter.net
www.ruefsmeatmarket.com
Smoked meats and cheese
Owner: Willy Ruef
bruef@charter.net
CEO: Annette Ruef
Estimated Sales: Less than $300,000
Number Employees: 1-4
Type of Packaging: Consumer, Food Service, Bulk
Brands:
Ruef's Meat Market

10971 Ruffner's
704 W Lancaster Ave
Wayne, PA 19087-2515
610-687-9800
Fax: 610-687-9800 hhtp://www.supercuts.com
Cocktail drink mixes, green tomato salsa
Manager: Steve Costa
Estimated Sales: $300,000-500,000
Number Employees: 1-4
Brands:
Supercuts

10972 Rufus Teague
13410 W 73rd St
Shawnee, KS 66216-4182
913-706-3814
Fax: 913-562-9980 www.rufusteague.com
BBQ sauce, grilling sauce, rubs, spices
Owner: John McCone
Contact: Tony Munson
tony@rufusteague.com
Estimated Sales: 500,000
Number Employees: 10-19

10973 Ruger LLC
Bethesda, MD 20814
301-675-2398
www.rugerwafers.com
Manufacturer of wafers and wrapped candies.
Founder: Amir Frydman

10974 Ruggiero Seafood
474 Wilson Ave
Po Box 5369
Newark, NJ 07105-4833
973-344-2282
Fax: 973-589-5690 866-225-2627
info@ruggieroseafood.com
www.ruggieroseafood.com
Processor, importer and exporter of fresh, frozen and breaded calamari and calamari entrees
President: Rocco Ruggiero
rocco@ruggieroseafood.com
Controller: Connie Dasaliva
Vice President: Frank Ruggiero
Sales Manager: Steve Clemente
Manager Operations: Anthon Trimarche
Plant Manager: Marcos Fontana
Estimated Sales: $387,000
Number Employees: 20-49
Square Footage: 100000
Type of Packaging: Consumer, Food Service, Bulk

Brands:
Atlantic Coast
Fisherman's Pride
Fruit of the Sea
Northwind
Ocean Tide

10975 (HQ)Ruiz Flour Tortillas
1200 Marlborough Ave
Riverside, CA 92507
909-947-7811
Fax: 909-947-2338 info@ruizflourtortillas.com
www.ruizflourtortillas.com
Traditional and specialty, ethnic and gourmet flour tortillas serving food manufacturers, foodservice industry, restaurant distributors, retail food brokers, and specialty retail outlets
Founder: Edward Ruiz
CFO: Uriel Maciaf
Vice President: Vickie Salgado
R&D: David Rodriguez
Manager: Maria Lopez
Contact: Oscar Figari
oscarfigari@ruizflourtortillas.com
Purchasing: Carmen Sandoval
Type of Packaging: Food Service, Private Label, Bulk

10976 (HQ)Ruiz Food Products Inc.
501 S. Alta Ave.
PO Box 37
Dinuba, CA 93618
800-477-6474
contactus@ruizfoods.com www.ruizfoods.com
Frozen Mexican foods including burritos, enchiladas, tamales, soft tacos, chili rellenos, flautas and taquitos.
President/CEO: Rachel Cullen
Senior VP/CFO: John Landis
Year Founded: 1964
Estimated Sales: $276.2 Million
Number Employees: 3,500+
Number of Brands: 4
Square Footage: 200000
Type of Packaging: Consumer, Food Service, Private Label, Bulk
Brands:
El Monterey
Tornados
Artisan Bistro
Three Bold Brothers

10977 Rule Breaker
291 Union ST
Suite Phb
Brooklyn, NY 11231-4477
646-820-8074
Fax: 718-228-8455 hello@rulebreakersnacks.com
www.rulebreakersnacks.com
Bean-based brownies
Founder & CEO: Nancy Kalish
Finance Director: Cassie Abrams
Director, Marketing & Regional Sales: Brittany Barton
Field Sales Manager: Tracy McKinney
Social Media Manager: Erin Smith
Operations Director: Dawn Techow
Number Employees: 2-10
Brands:
Rule Breaker

10978 Rumi Spice
1400 W 46th St
Chicago, IL 60609-3212
213-447-6112
info@rumispice.com
www.rumispice.com
Saffron and spice blends
Co-Founder: Emily Miller
Director of New Product Development: Laura Willis
Year Founded: 2014
Estimated Sales: $500,000-$1,000,000
Number Employees: 2-10
Brands:
RUMI SPICE

10979 Rumiano Cheese Co.
511 9th St
Crescent City, CA 95531-3408
707-465-1535
Fax: 707-465-4141 866-328-2433
www.rumianocheese.com
Cheese manufacturer

Food Manufacturers / A-Z

President: Baird Rumiano
joby@rumianocheese.com
Logistics: Gary Smits
Production & Markering: Joby Rumiano
Office Manager: Tana Bachmann
Chief Operating Officer: Kirk Olsen
Production Manager: Enrique Leal
Lab Technician: Juan Pablo Gonzalez
Estimated Sales: $12 Million
Number Employees: 20-49
Number of Brands: 1
Square Footage: 16000
Type of Packaging: Consumer, Food Service
Other Locations:
   Distribution & Packaging
   East Williows CA
Brands:
   Rumiano

10980 Rumiano Cheese Factory
1629 County Road E
Willows, CA 95988-9642
530-934-5438
Fax: 530-934-5114 866-328-2433
www.rumianocheese.com
Cheese manufacturer specializing in Dry Montery Jack and Peppato; products are kosher and non-GMO certified. Provides slicing, packaging and labelling services.
President: Baird Rumiano
Cmo: Bill Rhinehart
bill@rumianocheese.com
Chief of Finances: Tony Rumiano
Vice President: John Rumiano
Sales & Purchasing: Bill Rinehart
Sales: Richard Moore
Human Resources: Georgia Cruz
Customer Relations: Cathy Thidsouvanh
Cut & Wrap Manager: John Permann
Purchasing: Holly Myers
Estimated Sales: $12 Million
Number Employees: 100-249
Parent Co: Rumiano Cheese Company
Type of Packaging: Consumer, Food Service, Private Label

10981 (HQ)Run-A-Ton Group Inc
401 State Route 24 # 2
Suite 2
Chester, NJ 07930-2923
908-879-0880
Fax: 973-984-2424 800-247-6580
www.whollywholesome.com
Conventional and natural baked goods
President: Doon Wintz
CEO/Chairman: Robert Wintz
CFO: Linda Hendricks
Vice President: Lynn Nelson
Director Sales Development/Marketing: Janeen Ortega
Estimated Sales: $10-20 Million
Number Employees: 10-19
Number of Brands: 5
Number of Products: 1000
Square Footage: 10000
Type of Packaging: Consumer, Food Service, Private Label
Brands:
   Apple Valley Inn
   Buttery Baker
   Simple Elegance
   Wholly Wholesome
   Outrageoulsy Decadent Cookies
   Unique Belgique
   Patrina's Bake House

10982 Runamok Maple
293 Fletcher Dr
Fairfax, VT 05454
802-849-7943
info@runamokmaple.com
runamokmaple.com
Maple syrup
Co-Owner: Eric Sorkin
Co-Owner: Laura Sorkin
Operations Manager: Dean Parent
Brands:
   Runamok

10983 (HQ)Runk Candy Company
5141 Fischer Place
Cincinnati, OH 45217
513-641-2345
Fax: 513-641-2557 800-641-8551
sales@runkcandy.com www.runkcandy.com

Marshmallow-filled ice cream cones and specialty candies
President: Dan Runk
Vice President: Pamela Arbino
Estimated Sales: $5-9.9 Million
Number Employees: 20-49
Brands:
   Marpro

10984 Rural Route 1 Popcorn Co
105 E Tama St
Livingston, WI 53554-9537
608-943-8283
Fax: 608-943-8283 800-828-8115
www.prpopcornstore.com
Popcorn
President: Bradley Biddick
Marketing Director: Nick Solomon
nicks@ruralroute1.com
CFO: Bradley Biddick
Estimated Sales: Below $5 Million
Number Employees: 20-49
Brands:
   Almonds
   Creamy Medley of Popcorn
   Ivory Almond K'Nuckle

10985 Rus Dun Farms Inc
2295 Highway 57
Collierville, TN 38017-5329
901-853-0931
Fax: 901-853-0387 www.lakesofgreenbrier.com
Eggs
Owner: Mike Russell
Estimated Sales: Less Than $500,000
Number Employees: 1-4

10986 Ruskin Redneck Trading Company
1203 1st Street SW
Ruskin, FL 33570-5345
813-645-7710
Fax: 813-641-1979
Sauces
President: Sandra Council
Estimated Sales: $240,000
Number Employees: 2

10987 Russ & Daughters
179 E Houston St # 1
New York, NY 10002-1024
212-475-4880
Fax: 212-475-0345 800-787-7229
info@russanddaughters.com
www.russanddaughters.com
Smoked fish, caviar and specialty foods
Owner: Mark Federman
info@russanddaughters.com
Estimated Sales: Less than $500,000
Number Employees: 10-19

10988 Russell & Kohne Inc
149 Riverside Ave # B
Suite B
Newport Beach, CA 92663-4067
949-645-8441
Baked goods and breads.
Owner: Paul Kohne
Estimated Sales: $2.04 Million
Number Employees: 20-49

10989 Russell Breweries, Inc.
202-13018 80th Avenue
Surrey, BC V3W 2B2
Canada
604-599-1190
Fax: 604-599-1048 cheers@russellbeer.com
www.russellbeer.com
Ale
President/COO: Andrew Harris
CEO: Brian Harris
Number Employees: 1-4
Type of Packaging: Consumer, Food Service
Brands:
   Russell Cream Ale
   Russell Honey Blonde Ale
   Russell Lemon Wheat Ale
   Russell Oager
   Russell Pale Ale
   Russell Winter Ale

10990 Russell E. Womack, Inc.
P.O. Box 3967
Lubbock, TX 79452
806-747-2581
Fax: 806-747-2583 877-787-3559
rewi@casserolebean.com www.casserolebean.com
Dry pinto beans packed in poly and burlap sacks
Owner: Mike Byrne
Product Management/Quality Control: Mike Bryne
Director of Sales: Richard Byrne
Consumer Affairs: Walter James
warehouse Manager: Albert Rodriguez
Estimated Sales: $3800000
Number Employees: 20-49
Number of Brands: 1
Number of Products: 1
Square Footage: 144000
Type of Packaging: Consumer, Food Service

10991 Russell Stover Candies Inc.
4900 Oak St.
Kansas City, MO 64112-2702
800-777-4004
customerservice@russellstover.com
www.russellstover.com
Chocolate candy.
CEO: Andrew Deister
CFO: Dick Masinton
Year Founded: 1923
Estimated Sales: $600 Million
Number Employees: 5000-9999
Parent Co: Lindt & Sprungli
Type of Packaging: Consumer
Brands:
   Russell Stovers
   Whitman's
   Pangburn's

10992 Russian Chef
40 E 69th St
New York, NY 10021-5016
212-249-1550
Fax: 212-249-5451
Processor and packer of fresh and pasteurized kosher caviar including domestic salmon, whitefish, sturgeon, paddlefish, hackleback and lumpfish; also, Scottish smoked salmon, tuna and smoked trout; importer of caviar
President: Simon Kublanov
Vice President: Lenny Kuvykin
Estimated Sales: $1-3 Million
Number Employees: 5-9
Square Footage: 27000
Type of Packaging: Consumer, Food Service
Brands:
   Ivan the Terrible
   Poriloff
   Purepak
   Russian Chef's

10993 Russo Farms
1962 S East Ave
Vineland, NJ 08360-7198
856-692-5942
Fax: 856-692-8534 www.russofarms.com
Fruits and vegetables including green onions, cabbage, peppers, eggplant, cucumbers, leafy greens, etc
President: Damian Russo
Estimated Sales: $12046688
Number Employees: 20-49
Type of Packaging: Consumer
Brands:
   Pat's Best

10994 Russo's Seafood
201 E 40th St
Savannah, GA 31401-9120
912-234-5196
Fax: 912-234-5703 866-234-5196
www.russoseafood.com
Seafood
Manager: Nolan Mell
Manager: Bryan Gray
bcgray35@aol.com
Estimated Sales: $3-5 Million
Number Employees: 10-19

10995 Rustic Bakery Inc.
4324 Redwood Hwy
San Rafael, CA 94903-2103
415-479-5600
Fax: 415-479-5700 www.rusticbakery.com

Baked goods: cereal, cheese coins, cookies, flatbread
Vice President Of Sales: Scott Frank
scott@rusticbakery.com

10996 Rustic Crust Inc
31 Barnstead Rd
Pittsfield, NH 03263-3101
603-435-5119
info@rusticcrust.com
www.rusticcrust.com
All natural and organic ready-made pizza crusts, pizza sauce, and ciabatta flatbread.
Founder/President: Brad Sterl
Process and Quality Manager: Lynn Karam
Sales/Marketing Coordinator: Kathleen Carroll
VP Sales: Alan Witcher
Contact: Tammy Blinn
tblinn@rusticcrust.com
Estimated Sales: $8 Million
Number Employees: 10-19
Square Footage: 4699
Type of Packaging: Consumer

10997 Ruth Ashbrook Bakery
6445 NE Martin Luther King Jr Blvd
Portland, OR 97211-3031
503-240-7437
Fax: 503-289-7264
Snack cakes, pies, doughnuts and other goods
President: Gerald Martinson
Estimated Sales: $250,000
Number Employees: 4

10998 (HQ)Ruth Hunt Candy Co
550 Maysville Rd
Mt Sterling, KY 40353
859-498-0676
800-927-0302
Info@Ruthhuntcandy.com
www.ruthhuntcandy.com
Confectionary products including pulled cream candy, bourbon balls, caramels, assorted soft creams, and sugar free chocolates.
President: Larry Kezele
larry@ruthhuntcandy.com
Estimated Sales: $790000
Number Employees: 10-19
Number of Products: 70
Square Footage: 18000
Parent Co: Kezele Corporation
Type of Packaging: Consumer
Brands:
  Blue Monday
  Woodford Reserve

10999 Rutherford Hill Winery
200 Rutherford Hill Rd
Rutherford, CA 94573
707-963-1871
Fax: 707-963-1878 info@rutherfordhill.com
www.rutherfordhill.com
Wines
President: Anthony Terlato
VP: Willis Blakewell
Estimated Sales: $4500000
Number Employees: 20-49

11000 Rutter's Dairy
2100 N George St
York, PA 17404-1898
717-848-9827
Fax: 717-845-8751 800-840-1664
www.rutters.com
Milk and dairy products
President: Todd Rutter
CFO: Tom Jonson
Treasurer: Stewart Hartman
CEO: Scott Hartman
VP: Rey Sendy
Operations Manager: Todd Rutter
Plant Manager: Brett Garner
Number Employees: 500-999
Type of Packaging: Private Label
Brands:
  Rutter's

11001 Rv Industries
1665 Heraeus Booulevard
Buford, GA 30518
770-729-8983
Fax: 770-729-9428 sales@rvindustries.com
www.rvindustries.com
Processor, importer and exporter of desiccated, sweetened and toasted coconut, coconut milk powder, aseptic coconut milk and water
President: Andres E Siochi
General Manager: Bob Weschrek
CFO: Bharat Shah
Sales: Robert Santiago
Production Manager: Guillermo Pineiro
Estimated Sales: $14,000,000
Number Employees: 20-49
Square Footage: 120000
Parent Co: RV Industries
Type of Packaging: Consumer, Food Service, Private Label, Bulk
Brands:
  Fiesta
  Red V
  Tropical

11002 Ryals Bakery
135 S Wayne St
Milledgeville, GA 31061-3439
478-452-0321
www.ryalsbakery.dinehere.us
Breads, rolls, cakes
Owner: Jacob Ryals
Estimated Sales: Less Than $500,000
Number Employees: 5-9
Brands:
  Ryals Bakery

11003 Rye Fresh
147 Ethel Road West
Piscataway, NJ 08854
732-855-0008
Fax: 732-855-9436 office@mycupful.com
mycupful.com
Milk
President & CEO: Marek Pyrycz
Brands:
  Cupful

11004 Rygmyr Foods
1030 County Road EW
Suite 100
South Saint Paul, MN 55126-8153
612-292-8777
800-545-3903
Molded popcorn novelties
President: Paul Lattate
Estimated Sales: $10-20 Million
Number Employees: 30
Square Footage: 26000
Type of Packaging: Consumer, Private Label
Brands:
  Bumpy & Jumpy
  Cutie Cupid
  Itchy Witchy
  Rookie Spookie
  Santa Pop

11005 Ryke's Bakery
1788 Terrace St # 1
Muskegon, MI 49442-5699
231-726-2253
Fax: 231-728-2162 info@rykes.com
www.rykes.com
Cakes, cookies, pies, breads and pastries
President: Renee Rouwhorst
Co-Owner: Butch Rouwhorst
Estimated Sales: $720,000
Number Employees: 20-49
Square Footage: 24000
Type of Packaging: Consumer

11006 Rymer Foods
4600 S Packers Avenue
Suite 400
Chicago, IL 60609-3338
773-254-7530
Fax: 773-927-7278 800-247-9637
Hamburgers, steaks, pot roast and meat loaf; also, frozen chicken
CEO: P Edward Schenk
President: Edward Hebert
Marketing Director: John Bormann
Operations Manager: Jose Muguerza
Number Employees: 10-19
Type of Packaging: Food Service

11007 Rymer Seafood
125 S Wacker Drive
Chicago, IL 60606-4424
312-236-3266
Fax: 312-236-4169
Seafood
President: Mark Bailin
Estimated Sales: $.5-1 million
Number Employees: 1-4

11008 S & D Coffee Inc
300 Concord Pkwy S
Concord, NC 28027-6702
704-782-3121
Fax: 800-950-4378 800-933-2210
www.sndcoffee.com
S&D is a coffee, tea and extracts supplier to the foodservice industry.
Chairman, President & CEO: Ron Hinson
hinsonr@sndcoffee.com
Number Employees: 1000-4999
Type of Packaging: Food Service, Private Label

11009 S & E Organic Farms Inc
1716 Oak St # 4
Bakersfield, CA 93301-3040
661-325-2644
Fax: 661-325-2602 seorganic@aol.com
Grower of organic vegetables, dry beans, grains and alfalfa; processor of frozen purees
President: Ed Davis
CEO: Shelley Davis
Manager: Cali Cheek
Estimated Sales: $500,000-$1 Million
Number Employees: 10-19
Type of Packaging: Bulk

11010 S & L Produce Inc
601 Medlin Rd
Walnut Hill, IL 62893
618-532-8344
Fax: 618-533-0378 www.slproduce.com
Produce
President: Mark Palazzolo
markslproduce@hughes.net
Estimated Sales: $1.5 Million
Number Employees: 5-9
Square Footage: 6000
Type of Packaging: Consumer, Food Service, Bulk

11011 S & M Communion Bread Co
829 Gale Ln
Nashville, TN 37204-3011
615-292-1969
Fax: 877-762-7323 www.buycommunion.com
Communion bread
President: Barbara Reynolds
drmom6278@aol.com
Estimated Sales: $3-5 Million
Number Employees: 10-19
Type of Packaging: Consumer
Brands:
  S&M

11012 S & M Fisheries Inc
1272 Portland Rd US Route 1
Kennebunkport, ME 4046
207-985-3456
Fax: 207-985-3038 www.thelobsterco.com
Wholesale distributor of shellfish
President: Stephanie Nadeau
dcowan@lobsters.org
Office Manager: Josh Smail
Vice President, Operational VP: Michael Marceau
Estimated Sales: $2.3 Million
Number Employees: 10-19

11013 S A Carlson Inc
160 Camfield Rd
Yakima, WA 98908-9684
509-965-8333
Fax: 509-965-8311 sherm@sacarlson.com
www.sacarlson.com
Processed fruit ingredients including apple, pear, peach, grapes, berry fruits, etc.
President: Sherman Carlson
russell@sacarlson.com
Customer Service: Ruffell Carlson
Vice President: Russell Carlson
Sales: Russell Carlson
Estimated Sales: $5-10 Million
Number Employees: 1-4
Square Footage: 500000
Type of Packaging: Food Service, Bulk

Food Manufacturers / A-Z

Brands:
    Invertec
    Tastee

11014 S A L T Sisters
2124 W Wilden Ave
Building B
Goshen, IN 46528-1146
        574-971-8368
        Fax: 800-950-3205
Manufacturer of sugar, salt, dips, and other all-natural flavors.
Founder and CEO: Charmane Skillen
Number Employees: 5-9

11015 S B Global Foods Inc
1330 N Broad St # 1
PO Box 1322
Lansdale, PA 19446-1143
        215-361-9500
        Fax: 215-361-9323 877-857-1727
info@sbglobalfoods.com www.sbglobalfoods.com
Seasoned filled pretzel nuggets, chocolate covered peanut butter filled pretzel nuggets, and mini marshmellows.
President: Karl Brown
kbrown@sbglobalfoods.com
Estimated Sales: Below $5 Million
Number Employees: 5-9
Type of Packaging: Private Label
Brands:
    American Cookie Boy
    Pretzel Pete
    Rocky Mountain Marshmallows
    Rocky Mountain Popcorn

11016 S P Enterprises
1889 E Maule Ave # E
Las Vegas, NV 89119-4603
        702-736-4774
        Fax: 702-736-6180 800-746-4774
spcandy@msn.com www.espeezcandy.com
Candy
Owner: Sam Popowcer
spcandy@msn.com
CEO: Alan Popowcer
Estimated Sales: $3-5 Million
Number Employees: 5-9
Brands:
    Lillipos
    Money Candy

11017 S S Lobster LTD
691 River St
Fitchburg, MA 01420-2910
        978-342-6135
        Fax: 978-345-7341
Seafood (lobster, clams, shrimp)
President: Mark Strazdas
Estimated Sales: $10-20 Million
Number Employees: 20-49

11018 (HQ)S S Steiner Inc
655 Madison Ave # 1700
New York, NY 10065-8078
        212-838-8901
        Fax: 212-593-4238 sales@hopsteiner.com
        www.hopsteiner.com
Processor, importer and exporter of hops extracts, pellets and oils.
President/COO: Louis Gimbel
VP of Sales: Mike Sutton
Estimated Sales: $20-50 Million
Number Employees: 10-19
Number of Brands: 1
Type of Packaging: Food Service
Other Locations:
    Salem OR
    Yakima WA
Brands:
    Hopsteiner

11019 S T Specialty Foods Inc
8700 Xylon Ave N
Brooklyn Park, MN 55445-1817
        763-493-9600
        Fax: 763-493-9506
        contactus@stspecialtyfoods.com
        www.stspecialtyfoods.com
Manufacturer of dry pasta products including macaroni & cheese dinners, microwavable pasta dishes, boxed pasta side dishes, rice & vermicelli mixes and pasta salads

President/CEO: Dale Schulz
dschulz@stspecialtyfoods.com
VP of Quality, Research & Development: Mark Welken
Senior Vice President Sales & Marketing: Kevin Kollock
Vice President of Operations: Steve Favro
Estimated Sales: $14.8 Million
Number Employees: 50-99
Parent Co: TreeHouse Foods, Inc.
Type of Packaging: Consumer, Private Label
Other Locations:
    S.T. Specialty Foods
    Kenosha WI

11020 S Zitner Co
3120 N 17th St
Philadelphia, PA 19132-2357
        215-229-9828
        Fax: 215-229-9828 www.zitners.com
Confectionery products including caramel coated apples and Easter candy
Owner: Mc Murphy
mmurphy@szitnerco.com
Estimated Sales: $10-20 Million
Number Employees: 20-49
Square Footage: 300000
Type of Packaging: Consumer

11021 S&B International Corporation
2815 Dalemead St
Torrance, CA 90505-7039
        310-257-0177
        Fax: 310-543-2168
Seasonings
President: Richard Jones
Estimated Sales: $5-10 000,000
Number Employees: 1-4

11022 S&D Bait Company
PO Box 3525
Morgan City, LA 70381-3525
        504-252-3500
        Fax: 504-385-5412
Live bait

11023 S&N Food Company
1321 Woodthorpe Drive
Mesquite, TX 75181-3519
        972-222-1184
        Fax: 972-222-1184 sweetpotatodesserts@msn.com
Dessert mixes such as sweet potato pie, sweet potato muffins, sweet potato brownies, chocolate brownies, coffee & chocolate, pumpkin pie, pumpkin brownies, lemon pound cake, chocolate muffin & bread mix, chocolate pound cake, lemonsupreme muffin & bread mix, pumpkin pound cake, pumpkin pancake & waffle mix, sweet potato pound cake, sweet potato pancake & waffle mix, and spiced cider mix.
President: Shirley Peters
Estimated Sales: Below $500,000
Number Employees: 2
Type of Packaging: Consumer, Private Label
Brands:
    Shirley's

11024 S&P Marketing, Inc.
11100 86th Ave
Maple Grove, MN 55369
        763-559-0436
        Fax: 763-557-1318
Fruit ingredients including tropical and temperate fruit juices, purees, dried fruits, powders and more. Niche products include tamarind, coconut cream, alphonso mango puree, prickly pear juice, puree, powder, fiber and oil.
President: Chareonsri Srisangnam
Marketing/R&D: Vinod Padhye
om@snpmarketing.com
Contact: Om Padhye
om@snpmarketing.com
Type of Packaging: Food Service, Bulk

11025 S. Wallace Edward & Sons
PO Box 25
Surry, VA 23883-0025
        800-290-9213
        Fax: 757-294-5378 800-222-4267
        www.virginiatraditions.com
Virginia hams, sweet hams, bacon & sausage, soups & stews, specialty meats, desserts, poultry, snacks, seafood

President: Sammuel Edwards
carla@edwardsvaham.com
CEO: Wallace Edwards
Vice President: Amy Edwards Harte
Sales Director: Bob Unterbrink
Contact: Carla Drewry
carla@edwardsvaham.com
Operations Manager: Al Kadons
Number Employees: 22
Number of Brands: 2
Type of Packaging: Consumer
Brands:
    Colonial Williamsburg
    Edwards
    Surry

11026 S.A.S. Foods
3005 Center Pl
Suite 200
Norcross, GA 30093
        770-263-9312
        Fax: 770-446-9234
Oriental grocery items, seafood, fin fish, shellfish
President: Goro Iwami
Estimated Sales: $5-10 Million
Number Employees: 5-9

11027 S.D. Mushrooms
P.O.Box 687
Avondale, PA 19311-0687
        610-268-8082
        Fax: 610-268-8644
Processor and importer of mushrooms and mushroom sauce
President/Owner: John D'Amico
Estimated Sales: $450,000
Number Employees: 1-4
Type of Packaging: Consumer, Food Service, Private Label, Bulk

11028 S.L. Kaye Company
230 5th Ave
New York, NY 10001-7704
        212-683-5600
        Fax: 212-947-7664 kaye230@aol.com
        www.slkaye.com
Candy
President/Owner: Mitchell Katzman
Sales Manager: S Handy
Estimated Sales: $1-2.5 Million
Number Employees: 1-4
Brands:
    Eskimo Pie Coffeepeaks
    Eskimo Pie Miniatures
    Eskimo Pie Snowpeaks
    Needlers Jersey English Toffee
    Titanic Esm Mints

11029 S.T. Jerrell Company
802 Labarge Dr
Bessemer, AL 35022
        205-426-8930
        Fax: 205-426-8989 www.jerrellpackaging.com
Non-fat dry milk
CEO: John Lyon
Vice President: Barry Cornell
Estimated Sales: Below $5 Million
Number Employees: 10-19
Square Footage: 100000
Type of Packaging: Food Service, Private Label, Bulk
Brands:
    Cloverleaf Farms Peanut Butter
    S. T. Jerrell Nonfat

11030 S.W. Meat & Provision Company
2019 N 48th St
Phoenix, AZ 85008-3303
        602-275-2000
Sausage, ground beef and patties, portion cut steaks and aged beef sides
President: W David Hart
Estimated Sales: $1-2.5 Million
Number Employees: 5-9
Type of Packaging: Food Service

11031 (HQ)SADKHIN Complex
2306 Avenue U
Brooklyn, NY 11229-4917
        718-769-7771
        Fax: 718-769-8087 800-723-5446
        NYOffice@sadkhin.com
Seasonal herbal formulas and multi-vitamins

Food Manufacturers / A-Z

Owner: Daniel Radinsky
daniel@sadkhin.com
Estimated Sales: Less Than $500,000
Number Employees: 1-4
Square Footage: 8800
Type of Packaging: Consumer
Other Locations:
  Los Angeles CA
  San Francisco CA
  Boston MA
  Philadelphia PA
  Detroit MI
Brands:
  The Sadkhin Complex(r)

11032 SANGARIA USA
3142 Pacific Coast Hwy
Suite 208
Torrance, CA 90505-6796
310-530-2202
Fax: 310-530-5335 sangaria@msn.com
www.sangariausa.com
Manufacturer, importer and exporter of soft drinks: Ramune drink, green tea, oolong tea, iced coffee, energy drink, fruit juices, etc
Owner: Leona Singer
Estimated Sales: $300,000-500,000
Number Employees: 1-4
Square Footage: 500000
Parent Co: Japan Sangaria Beverage Company
Type of Packaging: Consumer, Food Service
Brands:
  Sangaria

11033 SAPNA Foods
1154 Oakleigh Drive
Atlanta, GA 30344
404-589-0977
Fax: 404-589-9711 info@sapnafoods.com
www.sapnafoods.com
Beans, chocolate, dried chilies and fruits, mushrooms, extracts and flavors, puree, nuts and seeds, teas, ginger, oils, saffron, spices and herbs.
President & CEO: Rishi A. Nagrani
rishi@sapnafoods.com
Vice President, Business Development: Jack Dahlheimer
Sales Representative: Evan Sowers
Director of Operations: William Sowers
Director of Purchasing: Neil Renfroe
Year Founded: 1997
Estimated Sales: $20 Million
Number Employees: 11-50
Type of Packaging: Food Service
Brands:
  SAPNA Foods

11034 SASIB Biscuits and Snacks Division
118 W Streetsboro Street
Suite 306
Hudson, OH 44236-2711
330-656-3317
Fax: 330-656-2822
Baked goods, biscuits, snacks

11035 SBK Preserves
1161 East 156th Street
Bronx, NY 10474-6226
718-589-2900
Fax: 718-589-8412 800-773-7378
info@sarabeth.com www.sarabeth.com
Processor and exporter of jams, preserves, fruit spreads, syrups and granola cereal
President: Charlie Apt
Finance Executive: Carlos Blanco
VP: Suzanne Levine
Estimated Sales: D
Number Employees: 10-19
Square Footage: 30000
Parent Co: Sarabeth's Kitchen
Other Locations:
  SBK Preserves
  New York NY
Brands:
  Sarabeth's

11036 SBS Americas
616 Corporate Way
Suite 2-5615
Valley Cottage, NY 10989
844-727-0827
Fax: 845-503-2379 www.bee-and-you.com
Honey, royal jelly and propolis
Food Production: Mustafa Bayraktar
Brands:
  Bee & You

11037 SC Enterprises
RR 5
Owen Sound, ON N4K 5N7
Canada
519-371-0456
Fax: 519-371-5944
Fresh and frozen fish and wild game and rainbow trout.
Manager: Winston Jones
Number Employees: 10-19
Square Footage: 36000

11038 SD Watersboten
119 Millcreek Rd
Ardmore, PA 19003
610-645-7572
contact@sdwatersboten.com
www.sdwatersboten.com
Mineral waters
President & CEO: Denise Shamro
Estimated Sales: Under $500,000
Number Employees: 1-4
Type of Packaging: Private Label
Brands:
  WATERSBOTEN

11039 SEW Friel
100 Friels Pl
PO Box 10
Queenstown, MD 21658-1674
410-827-8841
Fax: 410-827-9472 www.sewfriel.com
Processor, importer and exporter of canned corn.
President: Michael Foster
Number Employees: 20-49
Type of Packaging: Consumer, Food Service, Private Label, Bulk
Brands:
  Friel's
  Hudson
  Ole Wye

11040 SFP Food Products
348 Highway 64 E
Conway, AR 72032-9414
501-327-0744
Fax: 501-327-2808 800-654-5329
jballard@sfpfoods.com www.sfpfoods.com
Processor and exporter of waffle, pancake and cone mixes; manufacturer and exporter of waffle and cone irons
President: Jon Ballard
VP Marketing/Sales: Jon Ballard
VP Operations: Ray Ballard
Estimated Sales: $3-5 Million
Number Employees: 5-9
Square Footage: 60000
Type of Packaging: Food Service, Private Label

11041 SIGCO Sun Products
227 6th St N
Breckenridge, MN 56520
218-643-8467
Fax: 218-643-4555 800-654-4145
www.sunopta.com
Sunflower oil
Sales Manager: Nancy Nelson
Plant Manager: John Bontjes

11042 SJH Enterprises
2415 Parview Rd Ste 4
Middleton, WI 53562
608-831-3001
Fax: 608-831-3001 888-745-3845
Broker of organic grains and natural colors and flavors
Manager: Hank Zimmerman
Estimated Sales: $170,000
Number Employees: 1-4
Type of Packaging: Consumer, Food Service, Private Label, Bulk

11043 SJR Foods
49 Brook Street
New Bedford, MA 02746-1742
617-500-4516
Fax: 781-821-5666 info@sjrfoods.com
www.sjrfoods.com
Cream cheese filled bagels including plain, cinnamon raisin, sesame, poppy and onion
Owner: Larry Barras
Brands:
  Unholey Bagel

11044 SKW Nature Products
2021 Cabot Boulevard W
Langhorne, PA 19047-1810
215-702-1000
Fax: 215-702-1015
Cultures, enzymes, edible and industrial gelatins, hydrocolloids, flavors, fragrance raw materials and fruit systems
VP/General Manager: Kenneth Hughes
VP/General Manager: George Masson
Number Employees: 500-999
Parent Co: SKW

11045 SKW Nature Products
2350 Kerper Blvd
Dubuque, IA 52001
563-588-6244
Fax: 563-588-9063 info@degussa.com
www.degussa.com
Enzymes and flavor ingredients for food, beverage, dairy and specialties industries
Head Corporate Communications: Ralph Driever
Press Relations Officer: Hannelore Gantzer
Internal Communications: Markus Langer
Sales Manager: Jorge Martinez
Number Employees: 100-249

11046 SLT Group
303 Ridge Rd
Dayton, NJ 08810
732-837-3096
www.sltgroup.com
Basmati rice, lentils, beans, flour & spice
CEO: Sandip Patel
Estimated Sales: $38.9 Million
Number Employees: 9
Brands:
  Heritage Select Brand

11047 SONOCO
5450 W Main St
Houma, LA 70360-1282
985-851-0727
Fax: 985-872-2251 800-458-7012
www.sontheimeroffshore.com
Provide offshore catering for people on drilling rigs.
President: Kent Sontheimer
Vice President, Finance: Pam Toups
Safety Director: David Soileau
Vice President, Sales: Juan Cosenza
Personnel Manager: Al Robinson
Vice President, Operations: Mark Hepburn
Number Employees: 250-499

11048 SOPAKCO Foods
215 S Mullins St
Mullins, SC 29574-3207
843-464-0121
Fax: 423-639-7270 800-276-9678
www.sopakco.com
Pasta sauces; also, retortable pouch manufacturer, canner and contract packager of poultry, meat, fish, pasta, vegetable, bean, fruit and dessert products, flexible, semi-rigid and glass containers
CEO: Al Reitzer
CFO: Steve Keight
R&D: Jim Dukes
Quality Control: Phyllis Calhoun
General Manager: Wynn Pettibone
Plant Manager: Carl Whitmore
Purchasing Director: Beverly Stacey
Estimated Sales: $5-10 Million
Number Employees: 100
Square Footage: 400000
Parent Co: Unaka Corporation
Type of Packaging: Consumer, Food Service, Private Label

11049 SOPAKCO Packaging
118 S Cypress St
Mullins, SC 29574-3004
843-464-7851
Fax: 843-464-2096 www.sopakco.com
Sure pak emergency meals
President: Lonnie Thompson
VP: Bill McCreary
Plant Manager: Vera Hahn
Purchasing Manager: Stewart Clark
Estimated Sales: $20-50 Million
Number Employees: 250-499
Parent Co: Sopacko

Food Manufacturers / A-Z

Type of Packaging: Consumer, Food Service, Private Label
Brands:
   Sopakco

11050 SOUPerior Bean & Spice Company
3801 NE 109th Ave
Suite C
Vancouver, WA 98682-7779
   360-882-4500
Fax: 360-882-1152 800-878-7687
soupbean@aol.com
Spice blends and mixes including bean soup, pasta salad, bread and broth
Owner: Paul Dendy
VP: Duane Rough Jr
Estimated Sales: $5-10 Million
Number Employees: 5-9
Square Footage: 11400
Brands:
   Our Counrtry

11051 SP Enterprises, Inc.
1889 E Maule Ave
Suite E
Las Vegas, NV 89119
   702-736-4774
Fax: 702-736-6180 800-746-4774
spcandy@msn.com www.espeezcandy.com
Kid's novelty candy
President: Sam Popowcer
Estimated Sales: $3-5 Million
Number Employees: 5-9
Brands:
   Aunt Flo's Country Fudge
   Espeez
   Eye of the Dragon
   Gold Mine Gum
   Kid Wizard
   Money Mints
   Usa Mints
   Viper
   Viper Blast
   Viper Gum
   Viper Venom
   Viper Vials

11052 SPI West Port, Inc
377 Swift Ave
South San Fancisco, CA 94080
   info@alodrink.com
Aloe vera beverages
Brands:
   Alo

11053 SRA Foods
1608 10th Ave N
Birmingham, AL 35203
   205-323-7447
www.srafoods.com
Wholesale/distributor of meats to restaurants and grocery stores.
President: Anthony Anselmo
anthonya@srafoods.com
Estimated Sales: $50-100 Million
Number Employees: 50-99
Number of Brands: 14
Brands:
   Cargill
   Wayne Farms
   Tyson
   Peco
   National Beef
   Mountaire Fresh Young Chicken
   Key Farms
   Hormel Foods
   Smithfield
   Southeastern Meats
   Creekstone Farms
   Heartland
   Michigan Turkey Producers
   Kent Quality Foods

11054 STE Michelle Wine Estates
14111 NE 145th St
PO Box 1976
Woodinville, WA 98072-6981
   425-488-1133
Fax: 425-415-3657 800-267-6793
info@ste-michelle.com www.smwe.com
Processor, exporter and importer of wines
President/CEO: Ted Baseler
CEO: Melissa Cable
melissa.cable@colsolarevineyards.com
EVP/CFO: Sheila Newlands
SVP/General Counsel: Tom Rowland
SVP Marketing: Martin Johnson
EVP Sales: Glenn Yaffa
SVP Human Resources: Susan Reams
EVP Winemaking/Vineyards/Operations: Doug Gore
Estimated Sales: $10-20 Million
Number Employees: 250-499
Type of Packaging: Consumer, Food Service, Private Label, Bulk
Other Locations:
   Stimson Lane Vineyards
   Woodinville WA

11055 SVB Food & Beverage Company
717 Corning Way
Martinsburg, WV 25405
   304-267-8500
Fax: 540-636-4470 cs@svbfoods.com
www.svbfoods.com
Processor and exporter of sparkling cider
President: Ben R Lacy III
Manager: Richard Wadkins
Sales Manager: Debra Hunter
Contact: Ken Bookmyer
kbookmyer@svbfoods.com
Estimated Sales: $944,000
Number Employees: 20-49
Square Footage: 100000
Type of Packaging: Consumer
Brands:
   Alpenglow

11056 SWELL Philadelphia Chewing Gum Corporation
North Eagle & Lawrence
Havertown, PA 19083
   610-449-1700
Fax: 610-449-2557
Manufacturer and exporter of chewing bubble gum and candy
President: Edward Fenimore
Estimated Sales: $14.5 Million
Number Employees: 100-249
Square Footage: 600000
Type of Packaging: Private Label, Bulk
Brands:
   Swell

11057 SYFO Beverage Company of Florida
10033 Sawgrass Drive West
Suite 202
Ponte Vedra Beach, FL 32082
   904-381-9002
Fax: 904-381-9004
customerservice@syfobeverages.com
http://www.syfobeverages.com
Beverages
President: Cydelle Mendius
Estimated Sales: $1-2.5 Million
Number Employees: 1

11058 Saad Wholesale Meats
2814 Orleans St.
Detroit, MI 48207
   313-831-8126
saadmeats@yahoo.com
www.saadmeats.com
Halal meats including beef bologna, lunch meats, hot dogs, salami, chicken patties, hamburger patties, chicken nuggets, chicken strips, turkey bacon, beef bacon, hickory smoked bacon, beef snack sticks, and sausage
President: Aref Saad
CEO: Mohamed Saad
Year Founded: 1976
Estimated Sales: $5.8 Million
Number Employees: 48
Number of Brands: 1
Brands:
   Sharifa Halal

11059 Saag's Products LLC
1799 Factor Ave
San Leandro, CA 94577-5617
   510-352-8000
Fax: 510-352-4100 855-287-6562
www.saags.com
Sausages, condiments, frankfurters, luncheon meats and pates, roast beef, corned beef and pastrami, salamis and dry cured meats, smoked hams and pork products, turkey breasts
President: Timothy Dam
CEO/Owner: Kathi Mosle
kmosle@saags.com
CFO: Mike Tye
VP: Jerry Meyer
VP Marketing: Bernard Steinert
Estimated Sales: $11 Million
Number Employees: 50-99
Square Footage: 80000
Type of Packaging: Food Service, Private Label, Bulk
Brands:
   Wurstmeister

11060 Sabatino Truffles USA
135 Front Avenue
West Haven, CT 06516
   718-328- 412
Fax: 718-328- 412 888-444-9971
w.matos@sabatinostore.com
www.sabatinostore.com
Extra virgin olive oil, truffles, truffle butter, truffle oil, pasta, mushrooms, sauces and creams.
President: Frederico Balestra
Contact: Vincent Jeanseaume
vincent@sabatinostore.com
Estimated Sales: $1-3 Million
Number Employees: 7
Parent Co: SABATINO ITALIA SRL
Type of Packaging: Food Service, Private Label

11061 Sabinsa Corp
20 Lake Dr
East Windsor, NJ 08520-5321
   732-777-1111
Fax: 732-777-1443 info@sabinsa.com
www.sabinsa.com
Botanical extracts
Founder & Chairman: Muhammed Majeed
CEO, Sabinsa USA: Asha Ramesh
President, Worldwide: Shaheen Majeed
EVP Global Operations: Madhu Subramanian
President Research Development: N Kalyanum
Marketing Director: Liz Smith
Estimated Sales: $20-50 Million
Number Employees: 20-49
Brands:
   Ashwagandha
   Boswellin
   Citrin
   Citrin K
   Curlumin C3 Complex
   Digezyme
   Gugulidid
   Lactospore

11062 Sable & Rosenfeld Foods
12 Lawton Blvd
Toronto, ON M4V 1Z4
Canada
   416-929-4214
Fax: 416-929-6727 info@sableandrosenfeld.com
www.sableandrosenfeld.com
Cocktail garnishes, appetizers/condiments and sauces.
President: Myra Sable
VP: Kathy Smith
Sales: Mary O'Neill

11063 Sabor Mexicano
Berkeley, CA 94704
   www.sabormexicano.com
Tortilla chips and salsas
Marketing Specialist: Halliny Ferreira

11064 Sabra Blue & White FoodProducts
PO Box 66063
Dallas, TX 75266-0634
   718-389-3800
   888-957-2272
www.sabra.com
Mediterranean dips, spreads, appetizers and gourmet specialities. As of September 2005 Strauss-Elite LTD has acquired a 51% stake in Sabra Salads
CEO: Ronen Zohar
Estimated Sales: $20-50 Million
Type of Packaging: Consumer, Food Service
Brands:
   Sabra

Food Manufacturers / A-Z

11065 Sabra Dipping Company,LL
649 Benet Rd
Oceanside, CA 92058-1208
760-757-2622
Fax: 760-721-2600 800-748-5523
info@sbsalsa.com
Refrigerated salsa, shelf stable foods and sauces.
Co-packer of specialty foods.
President/Manager: Doug Pearson
Vice President/Upper Management: Jackie Watson
Quality Assurance Manager: Tatiana Miranda
Contact: Carlos Heras
cheras@sbsalsa.com
VP Purchasing: Patrick Hickey
Estimated Sales: $10-15 Million
Number Employees: 100
Square Footage: 38000
Type of Packaging: Consumer, Food Service
Brands:
    Chachies
    Con Gusto
    San Diego Salsa
    Santa Barbara Salsa
    Tio Tio

11066 Sabra-Go Mediterranean
PO Box 660634
Dallas, TX 75266-0634
631-694-9500
888-957-2272
www.sabra.com
Mediterranean style refrigerated dips and spreads that iclude hummus, eggplant dips, babaganoush spreads, and Mediterranean salsa
CEO: Ronen Zohar
CFO: Amit Anand
Executive VP/General Manager: Meiky Tollman
Chief Marketing Officer: Rodrigo Troni
Executive VP Sales: John McGuckin
Human Resources Director: Angela King
Executive VP Operations: Guy Nir
Parent Co: Strauss Holdings LTD

11067 Sacramento Baking Co
9221 Beatty Dr
Sacramento, CA 95826-9702
916-361-2000
Fax: 916-361-0117
Bakery items including cakes
Owner: Sam Alajou
Marketing Director: Sam Alaclu
Quality Control: Sam Elajou
Estimated Sales: $20-50 Million
Number Employees: 20-49
Brands:
    Sacramento Baking

11068 Sacramento Cookie Factory
3428 Auburn Blvd
Sacramento, CA 95821-1904
916-482-8222
Fax: 916-482-8222 877-877-2646
www.wafercookie.com
Wafer cookies
President: Jiri Knedlik
sacoksac@pacbell.net
Number Employees: 5-9

11069 Saddleback Cellars
7802 Money Rd.
Oakville, CA 94562
707-944-1305
Fax: 707-944-1325 info@saddlebackcellars.com
www.saddlebackcellars.com
Fine wines
Founder: Nils Venge
General Manager: Rick Wehman
Estimated Sales: $20-50 Million
Number Employees: 20-49

11070 Sadler's Smokehouse
1206 N Frisco St
PO Box 1088
Henderson, TX 75652-6924
903-657-5581
Fax: 903-655-8404 www.sadlerssmokehouse.com
Barbecued beef and pork, smoked poultry and barbecue sauce; wholesaler/distributor of meats/provisions
CFO: Wendy Frey
wendy.frey@sadlersbbq.com
Plant Manager: Saul Quintanilla
Purchasing: Jarrod Ferguson
Estimated Sales: $6.5 Million
Number Employees: 250-499
Square Footage: 720000
Type of Packaging: Consumer, Food Service, Private Label
Brands:
    Double S
    Sadler's Smokehouse

11071 Safe Catch
85 Liberty Ship Way
Suite 203
Sausalito, CA 94965
415-944-4442
888-568-4211
info@safecatch.com safecatch.com
Seasoned canned tuna and salmon
President & Founder: Sean Wittenberg
Vice President, Operations: Kevin McCay
Marketing Manager: Michelle Watson
National Sales Manager: Sarena Hines
Number Employees: 1-10
Brands:
    SafeCatch

11072 Safely Delicious
P.O. Box 26446
Overland Park, KS 66225
913-963-5140
safelydelicious@gmail.com
safelydelicious.com
Allergen-free snacks.
Founder: Lisa Ragan
Number Employees: 1-4
Brands:
    Safely Delicious

11073 (HQ)Safeway Inc.
5918 Stoneridge Mall Rd.
Pleasanton, CA 94588
877-723-3929
www.safeway.com
Supermarket products such as bakery items, dairy, deli meats, dry cleaning, frozen foods, fuel, grocery, pharmacy, produce, meants, snack foods, and more.
Executive Chairman/CEO: Robert Miller
robert.miller@safeway.com
Executive VP/CFO: Peter Bocian
Year Founded: 1915
Estimated Sales: Over $1 Billion
Number Employees: 10000+
Number of Brands: 12
Parent Co: Albertsons
Type of Packaging: Consumer
Brands:
    O Organics
    Open Nature
    Lucerne Dairy Farms
    Signature Cafe
    Signature Select
    Signature Farms
    Signature Care
    Primo Taglio
    debi lilly design
    waterfrontBISTRO
    Signature RESERVE
    Value Corner

11074 Safeway Milk Plant
1115 W Alameda Dr
Tempe, AZ 85282-3384
480-894-4391
Fax: 480-929-8025 www.safeway.com
Milk including half and half, skim, whole, 1% and 2%
Plant Manager: Jason Glober
Plant Manager: Jeff Fowler
Number Employees: 50-99
Parent Co: Safeway Stores
Type of Packaging: Consumer, Food Service, Private Label, Bulk

11075 Saffron Road
Stamford, CT 06905
203-961-1954
877-425-2587
info@saffronroad.com saffronroad.com
Frozen entr,es, bowls, hors d'oeuvres, sauces, broths, chips and chickpea snacks
CEO and Founder: Adnan Durrani
Executive Vice President: Jack Acree
Brands:
    Saffron Road

11076 Safie Specialty Foods
Chesterfield, MI
586-598-8282
info@safiefoods.com
safiefoods.com
Pickled products
Founder: Mary Safie
Contact: Anthony Latalla
alatalla@safiespecialtyfoods.com
Year Founded: 1994

11077 Sagawa's Savory Sauces
8292 SW Nyberg St
Tualatin, OR 97062-9457
503-692-4334
Fax: 503-691-0661
Hawaiian-style sauces including teriyaki, sweet and sour and Polynesian barbecue; salad dressings, seasonings and mixes.
President: Linda Rider
Estimated Sales: $540,000
Number Employees: 7
Square Footage: 21732
Type of Packaging: Consumer, Food Service
Brands:
    Baste & Glaze
    Sweet & Sassy

11078 Sage V Foods
1470 Walnut St
Suite 202
Boulder, CO 80302
303-449-5626
sales@sagevfoods.com
sagevfoods.com
Rice products
Owner: Pete Vegas
Controller: Whilma Aleman
Estimated Sales: $5-10 Million
Number Employees: 50-99
Type of Packaging: Food Service, Private Label, Bulk
Brands:
    RYZE
    Grain Trust

11079 Sagely Naturals
1811 Centinela Ave
Santa Monica, CA 90049
424-262-6614
info@sagelynaturals.com
www.sagelynaturals.com
CBD creams and capsules
Co-Founder: Kerrigan Behrens
Co-Founder: Kaley Nichol
Year Founded: 2015

11080 Saguaro Food Products
1319 N Main Ave
Tucson, AZ 85705
520-884-8049
Fax: 520-884-9704 800-732-2447
Southwest gourmet foods, potato, dips and sauces, tortilla and corn chips
General Manager: Ralph Cortese
Finance Manager: Laurie Cowan
Marketing Manager: Sue Heems
Operations Manager: Raul Ruiz
Estimated Sales: Below $500,000
Number Employees: 8

11081 Sahadi Fine Foods Inc
4215 1st Ave
Brooklyn, NY 11232-3300
718-369-0100
Fax: 718-369-0800 800-724-2341
pwhelan@sahadifinefoods.com
www.sahadifinefoods.com
Maufacturer of nuts and seeds. Importer of dried fruit, beans, nuts, olives, Mediterranean foods
Owner: Robert Sahadi
VP: Pat Whelan
Sales: Ashraf Bakhoum
rsahadi@sahadifinefoods.com
Operations: Kristin Fernandez
Production: Brian Whelan
Estimated Sales: $11 Million
Number Employees: 20-49
Square Footage: 174000

1085

Food Manufacturers / A-Z

11082 Sahadi Importing Company
187 Atlantic Ave
Brooklyn, NY 11201
718-624-4550
Fax: 718-643-4415 asahadi@aol.com
www.sahadis.com
Ethnic foods
President: Charles Sahadi
VP: Robert Sahadi
Contact: Audrey Sahadi
asahadi@sahadis.com
Estimated Sales: Below $5 Million
Number Employees: 20-49
Brands:
 Sahadi

11083 Sahagian & Associates
124 Madison St
Oak Park, IL 60302
708-848-5552
Fax: 708-386-5959 800-327-9273
sales@sahagianinc.com www.sahagianinc.com
Bubble gum, licorice, taffy, candy-coated chocolate malted balls, chocolate bites, almonds, chocolate and caramel popcorn; also, multi-colored and tri-colored popcorn, candy coated licorice, and chocolate dips
President: Linda G. Sahagian
greg@sahagianinc.com
Estimated Sales: $630,000
Number Employees: 11
Type of Packaging: Consumer, Private Label, Bulk
Brands:
 A Foot Of
 A Yard Of
 The Whole 9 Yards

11084 Sahalee of Alaska
PO Box 104174
Anchorage, AK 99510-4174
907-349-4151
Fax: 907-349-4161 800-349-4151
sahalee@aol.com
Seafood
President/CEO: Hank Lind
VP/Secretary/Treasurer: Christa Lind
Sales Director: Bill Haller

11085 Sahara Coffee
2081 Mountain Vista Way
Reno, NV 89519-6269
775-825-5033
Fax: 775-825-3190
Processor and packer of whole leaf loose teas, organic dates and specialty coffees
Owner: Charles Hubach
Estimated Sales: Less than $500,000
Number Employees: 1-4
Brands:
 Sahara

11086 Sahara Date Company
8456A Tyco Road
Vienna, VA 22182
703-745-7463
info@saharadate.com
www.saharadate.com
Dates
Co-Founder: Maile Ramzi
Co-Founder: Jean Houpert
Estimated Sales: $6.9 Million
Number Employees: 34
Brands:
 Sahara Date Company

11087 Sahara Natural Foods
14855 Wicks Blvd
San Leandro, CA 94577
510-352-5111
Fax: 510-532-3227
Rice products, soups and organic bulk products
National Manager: Al Caldwell

11088 Sahlen's
318 Howard St
Buffalo, NY 14206-2760
716-852-8677
Fax: 716-852-8684 800-466-8165
www.sahlen.com
Meat products that include sausage, ham, bacon, lard and hot dogs
President: Joseph Sahlen
jsahlen@sahlen.com
VP: Christopher Cauley
Estimated Sales: $18 Million
Number Employees: 50-99
Brands:
 Sahlen's

11089 Saint Albans Cooperative Creamery
138 Federal St.
Saint Albans, VT 05478
802-524-6581
www.stalbanscooperative.com
Milk, cream, skim and skim condensed milk, and dry/powdered milk.
CEO: Leon Berthiaume
CEO: Harold Howrigan

Year Founded: 1919
Estimated Sales: $361.29 Million
Number Employees: 70
Type of Packaging: Private Label, Bulk
Brands:
 Orbit

11090 Saint Armands Baking Company
2594 12th Street
Sarasota, FL 34237-2943
941-365-7377
Baked goods
Owner: Richard Tritschler
Estimated Sales: Under $500,000
Number Employees: 1-4
Parent Co: Suncoast Bakeries

11091 Sainte Genevieve Winery
6231 State Route C
Ste Genevieve, MO 63670
573-483-3500
Fax: 573-483-3526 800-398-1298
spcandy@msn.com
www.saintegenevievewinery.com
Wines
Manager: Elaine Mooney
CEO: Lineus Hoffmeister
Estimated Sales: $500,000-$1 Million
Number Employees: 1-4
Brands:
 Sainte Genevieve

11092 Saintsbury
1500 Los Carneros Ave
Napa, CA 94559-9742
707-252-0592
Fax: 707-252-0595 info@saintsbury.com
Wines
Managing Partner: Richard Ward
drdick@saintsbury.com
Managing Partner: David Graves
Partner: Richard Ward
drdick@saintsbury.com
Estimated Sales: Below $6 Million
Number Employees: 10-19
Brands:
 Saintsbury

11093 Sakeone Corp
820 Elm St
Forest Grove, OR 97116-3041
503-357-7056
Fax: 503-357-1014 800-550-7253
www.sakeone.com
Sake
Owner: Steve Vuilsteke
Tasting Room Manager: Jennifer Brownstein
Plant Manager: Scott Eagler
Sales Manager: Greg Lorenz
VP Sales: Jim Scalace
Director Marketing: Dewey Weddington
Estimated Sales: Below $5 Million
Number Employees: 20-49
Type of Packaging: Private Label
Brands:
 G
 Momokawa
 Moonstone

11094 Salad Depot
51 Romeo St
Moonachie, NJ 07074
201-507-1980
Fax: 201-507-9001
Vegetables
President/Owner: Dan Zeigler
Marketing Director: John Zeigler
Buyer: Doreen Congo
Estimated Sales: Below $5,000,000
Number Employees: 1-4
Brands:
 Salad Depot

11095 Salad Girl Inc
1165 Summit Ave
Mahtomedi, MN 55115-1511
651-653-9155
saladgirlinc@comcast.net
Artisan vinaigrettes made with organic ingredients: Curry & Fig, Crisp Apple Maple, Lemony Herb, Pomegranate Pear, Honey & Ginger, and Blueberry Basil.
Founder/CEO: Pamela Powell
Number Employees: 10-19
Type of Packaging: Consumer

11096 Salad Oils Intl Corp
5070 W Harrison St
Chicago, IL 60644-5141
773-261-0500
Fax: 773-261-7555 saladoiljohn@earthlink.net
www.saladoils.net
Edible oils
Vice President: John Pacente
saladoiljohn@earthlink.net
VP: John Pacente
Estimated Sales: $1.1 000,000
Number Employees: 5-9
Square Footage: 15000
Type of Packaging: Private Label
Brands:
 Irilla Extra Virgin O.O.
 Mi Best Soybean Oil
 Onte Verde O.O.
 Rgo Mace O.O.
 Rosa Canola Oil
 Rosa Corn Oil
 Rosa Peanut Oil

11097 Salamandre Wine Cellars
108 Don Carlos Dr
Aptos, CA 95003-2912
831-685-0321
newt@cruzio.com
www.salamandrewine.com
Wines
General Partner: Will Shoemaker
Winemaker: Wells Shoemaker
Estimated Sales: $170,000
Number Employees: 1-4
Brands:
 Salamandre Wine Cellars

11098 Salamatof Seafoods
Bridge Access Road Mp 1.5
PO Box 1450
Kenai, AK 99611-1450
907-283-7000
Fax: 907-283-8499
Fresh and frozen seafood including salmon, halibut, herring and cod
Chairman: Shane Morgan
Director Manufacturing: Roy Bertoglio
Estimated Sales: $20-50 Million
Number Employees: 100-249
Type of Packaging: Consumer, Food Service, Bulk

11099 Salba Smart Natural Prod LLC
6418 S Quebec St
Bldg 4
Centennial, CO 80111-4628
303-999-3996
info@salbasmart.com
www.salbasmart.com
Whole and ground chia seeds.
President: Rally Ralston
Partner: Judith Brooks
judith@organicfoodbrokers.com
National Sales Director: Staci Owens
Operations Manager: Kayleen Nichols
Number Employees: 5-9

11100 Salem Baking Company
224 S Cherry St
Winston Salem, NC 27101-5231
336-748-0230
Fax: 336-748-0501 800-274-2994
sales@salembaking.com
Cookies: moravian, spice, sugar, lemon, keylime, black walnut, tangerine-orange and double chocolate.

Food Manufacturers / A-Z

President: Guy Wilkerson
Contact: April Boone
april.boone@salembaking.com
Estimated Sales: $3.5 Million
Number Employees: 1-4
Parent Co: Dewey's Bakery
Type of Packaging: Consumer, Food Service
Brands:
   Moravian Hearth

11101 (HQ)Salem Oil & Grease Company
60 Grove St
Salem, MA 01970-2245
   978-745-0585
Fax: 978-741-4426
Processor and exporter of sulphonated castor oil
President: V Smith
VP Sales: J Donovan
VP Production: G Hanson
Estimated Sales: $10-20 Million
Number Employees: 20-49

11102 Salem Old Fashioned Candies
93 Canal St
Salem, MA 01970-4839
   978-744-3242
Fax: 978-745-9459
Candy including bagged, hard, lollypops, mints, rock and taffy
President: Freeman Corkum
Estimated Sales: $950,000
Number Employees: 10-19
Type of Packaging: Consumer
Brands:
   Chestnut Street
   Gems
   Jane Stewart
   Noah's Treats
   Sea Chest
   Seabreeze
   Spindrift

11103 Salemville Cheese
W4481 County Road Gg
Cambria, WI 53923-9304
   920-394-3431
Cheese
President: Henry Miller
CFO: William Schrock
Manager: Nelson Schrock
Plant Manager: Lavern Miller
Estimated Sales: $5-10 000,000
Number Employees: 20-49

11104 Sales Associates Of Alaska
1900 Phillips Field Rd
Fairbanks, AK 99701-2707
   907-452-2201
Fax: 907-452-2201 800-478-2371
service@qualitysales.net www.qualitysales.net
Wholesale grocers.
President: Gary Nance
don@qualitysales.net
Secretary/Treasurer: Carl Olson
Estimated Sales: $1 Million
Number Employees: 20-49

11105 Sales USA
220 Salado Creek Road
Salado, TX 76571-5783
   254-947-3838
Fax: 254-947-3338 800-766-7344
pompeii1@aol.com
Fruit and vegetable juices.
President: Rusty Justus
CEO: Ronald Cox
Plant Manager: Lee Simpkins
Estimated Sales: $1 Million
Number Employees: 4
Square Footage: 60000
Type of Packaging: Consumer, Food Service, Private Label, Bulk

11106 Salishan Vineyards
35011 NE North Fork Ave
La Center, WA 98629
   360-263-2713
Fax: 360-263-3675
Wine
President: Joan Wolverton
CFO: Lincoln Wolverton
Estimated Sales: Under $300,000
Number Employees: 1-4
Type of Packaging: Private Label
Brands:
   Salishan

11107 Sally Lane's Candy Farm
2215 Gum Springs Rd
Paris, TN 38242-6362
   731-642-5801
Candy including peanut and coconut brittle and hard and sugar-free candies
Owner: Bobby Freeman
bobf5801@hotmail.com
Co-Owner: Jean Peterson
Number Employees: 10-19
Square Footage: 12000
Type of Packaging: Consumer
Brands:
   Sally Lane's

11108 Sally Sherman
300 N MacQuesten Pkwy
Mt Vernon, NY 10550-1093
   914-664-6262
Fax: 914-664-2846 718-822-1100
www.sallyshermanfoods.com
Premium salads
Owner/Operator: Felix Endico
General Manager: Paul Cannillo
VP Operations: Marc Mazzarulli
Account Manager: Debra Gentile
Estimated Sales: $20-50 Million
Number Employees: 50-99
Brands:
   Endico
   Hellmans

11109 Salmans & Assoc
1126 W Chestnut St
Chicago, IL 60642-4111
   312-226-1820
Fax: 312-226-6806 sales@salmans.com
Cheese
President: Van Salmans
van@salmans.com
Estimated Sales: $650,000
Number Employees: 5-9
Brands:
   Salmans

11110 Salmolux Inc
34100 9th Ave S # A
Federal Way, WA 98003-7393
   253-874-6570
Fax: 253-874-4042 seafood@salmolux.com
Smoked seafood products, pates, spreads, salmon burgers, herring, flavored butters and canned seafood salads
President: George Kuetgens
Cmo: John Randisi
seafood@salmolux.com
National Sales Director: Kira Kuetgens
Plant Manager: Ray Crockett
Year Founded: 1988
Estimated Sales: $20 Million
Number Employees: 50-99
Square Footage: 60000
Type of Packaging: Consumer, Food Service, Private Label, Bulk
Brands:
   Salmolux Anti Pasta
   Salmolux Gourmet Smoked Salmon
   Salmolux Saute Butters

11111 Salmon River Smokehouse
PO Box 40
Gustavus, AK 99826-0040
   907-697-2330
Fax: 907-456-3889
Smoke a variety of fish products.

11112 Salonika Imports Inc
3509 Smallman St
Pittsburgh, PA 15201-1936
   412-682-2700
800-794-2256
www.salonika.net
Mediterranean culinary products
President/Owner: Chris Balouris
sales@salonika.net
Number Employees: 5-9

11113 Salsa God
447 W 56th St
Suite 1E
New York, NY 10019
   646-359-0573
danny@thesalsagod.com
www.thesalsagod.com
Salsa
Co-Founder: Danny Mayans
Co-Founder: Bella Mayans
Number Employees: 2
Brands:
   Salsa God

11114 Salt Lake Macaroni & Noodle Company
5405 W 4700 S
Salt Lake City, UT 84118-6352
   801-969-9855
Fax: 801-969-9856
Pasta
Manager: Mike Stover
Estimated Sales: $5-10 000,000
Number Employees: 5-9

11115 Salt River Lobster Inc
72 Tidewater Dr
Boothbay, ME 04537-4242
   207-633-5357
Fax: 207-633-5357 orders@salt-river-lobster.com
www.salt-river-lobster.com
Sells lobster, shrimp, fish, and various other shellfish.
Estimated Sales: Less Than $500,000
Number Employees: 1-4

11116 Salt of the Earth Bakery
630 Flushing Avenue
4th Floor
Brooklyn, NY 11206
   646-330-5089
info@saltoftheearthbakery.com
saltoftheearthbakery.com
Sea salt cookies and brownies
President: Haskel Rabbani
Estimated Sales: $1,000,000
Number Employees: 2-10
Brands:
   Salt of the Earth

11117 SaltWorks
16240 Wood-Red Rd NE
Woodinville, WA 98072
   425-885-7258
800-353-7258
info@seasalt.com www.seasalt.com
Seasalt

11118 Salty Girl Seafood
P.O. Box 6557
Santa Barbara, CA 93160
   805-699-5025
hello@saltygirlseafood.com
www.saltygirlseafood.com
Sustainable, traceable seafood
Co-Founder: Laura Johnson
Co-Founder: Norah Eddy

11119 Salty Road
Brooklyn, NY
   929-250-2615
wholesale@thesaltyroad.com
www.thesaltyroad.com
Manufacturer of taffy.
Owner: Marisa Wu
Brands:
   Salty Road

11120 Salty Wahine Gourmet Hawaiian Sea Salt
1-3529 Kaumualii Highway
Unit 2B
Hanapepe, HI 96716
   808-378-4089
Fax: 808-442-1230 www.saltywahine.com
Hawaiian sea salt
Owner and Founder: Laura Anderslan

11121 Salute Sante! Food & Wine
68 Coombs St # I-2
Napa, CA 94559-3966
   707-251-3900
Fax: 707-251-3939 info@grapeseedoil.com
www.grapeseedoil.com

Food Manufacturers / A-Z

Flavored and regular grapeseed oil
Founder, President: Valentin Humer
Estimated Sales: $690,000
Number Employees: 5-9
Type of Packaging: Consumer
Brands:
    Salute Sante! Grapeseed Oil

11122 Salvy Sousa Dealer Locator
11242 282nd Rd
Arkansas City, KS 67005-8300
    620-442-2700
Fax: 620-446-1362 jscarroll@salvysousa.com
    www.salvysousa.com
Manufacturer of sauces and marinades.
CEO: Janet Carroll
Number Employees: 5-9

11123 Salwa Foods
P.O. Box 490579
Lawrenceville, GA 30049
    770-263-8207
salwa@salwafoods.com
    www.salwafoods.com
Halal chicken and beef products
Owner: Mushtaq "Mike" Mistry
Year Founded: 2002

11124 Sam KANE Beef Processors Inc
9001 Leopard St
Corpus Christi, TX 78409
    800-242-4142
    www.kanebeef.com
Processor and exporter of fresh, frozen and boxed beef.
Owner: Sam Kane
CEO: Alfred Bausch
CAO & CMO: Chuck Jackson
Director of Regulatory Compliance: Brian Honigbaum
Operations Manager: Dwayne Hubenak
Year Founded: 1949
Estimated Sales: $100-500 Million
Number Employees: 500-999
Type of Packaging: Consumer, Food Service, Bulk

11125 Sam Mills USA
2400 High Ridge Rd
Suite 102
Boynton Beach, FL 33426-8710
    561-572-0510
Fax: 561-572-0511 info@sammillsusallc.com
    www.sammills.com
Granola bars, pasta, mac & cheese, cookies and pretzels
Director of Operations: Tom Lagomarsini
Estimated Sales: Under $500,000
Number Employees: 2-4
Parent Co: Sam Mills Srl.
Type of Packaging: Food Service
Brands:
    SamMills(c)

11126 Sam's Leon Mexican Food
5014 S 20th St
Omaha, NE 68107-2925
    402-733-3809
    www.samsleon.com
Tortillas, taco shells and hot sauce
Owner: David Murillo
Estimated Sales: Less than $500,000
Number Employees: 1-4
Type of Packaging: Food Service

11127 Samadi Sweets Cafe
5916 Leesburg Pike
Falls Church, VA 22041
    703-578-0606
Fax: 703- 57-8 17
Middle Eastern pastries
Owner: Nora Burgan
Estimated Sales: Less than $500,000
Number Employees: 5-9

11128 Sambazon
209 Avenida Fabricante
Suite 200
San Clemente, CA 92672
    949-498-8618
    877-726-2296
info@sambazon.com www.sambazon.com
Organic açaí products including frozen superfruit packs, frozen desserts, sorbet, fresh juices, and energy drinks
Co-Founder: Jeremy Black
Co-Founder/CEO: Ryan Black
CFO/COO: Ricardo Perdigao
CMO: Renee Junge
Year Founded: 2000
Number Employees: 150
Type of Packaging: Food Service

11129 Sambets Cajun Deli
8650 Spicewood Spgs Rd # 111
Austin, TX 78759-4323
    512-258-6410
Fax: 512-258-6284 800-472-6238
Cajun hot sauces, salsas and spices
Owner: Doug Slocombe
Estimated Sales: $300,000-500,000
Number Employees: 1-4

11130 Sambol Meat Company
PO Box 13376
Overland Park, KS 66282
    913-334-8404
Meat and meat products. Founded in 1929.
Owner: Don Sambol
CEO: Bill Kolich
Marketing Manager: Mark Fishman
Estimated Sales: $.5-1 million
Number Employees: 1-4
Type of Packaging: Consumer
Brands:
    Sambol

11131 Sampac Enterprises
551 Railroad Ave
S San Francisco, CA 94080-3450
    650-876-0808
Fax: 650-876-0338 sales@sampacent.com
    www.sampacent.com
Teas; wholesaler/distributor of herbs, teas, honey, bee pollen, etc
Owner: Sammy MA
sales@sampacent.com
Estimated Sales: $2.3 Million
Number Employees: 10-19
Square Footage: 80000
Type of Packaging: Private Label, Bulk

11132 Sampco
651 W Washington Blvd # 300
Chicago, IL 60661-2138
    312-346-1506
Fax: 312-346-8302 800-767-1689
    www.sampcoinc.com
Cooked beef products
President/CEO: David Morrison
gmorrison@sampcoinc.com
Vice President: Verna Macintosh
VP Industrial Sales: Rod McNally
Estimated Sales: $5-10 Million
Number Employees: 20-49
Type of Packaging: Private Label
Brands:
    Classico
    Sampco

11133 San Angelo Packing
4238 Sunset Dr
San Angelo, TX 76904
    325-949-9401
Fax: 325-658-7272
Packer of beef; slaughtering services available.
General Manager: Jarrod Stokes
Estimated Sales: Below $5,000,000
Number Employees: 250-499

11134 San Anselmo's Cookies & Biscotti
PO Box 2822
San Anselmo, CA 94979-2822
    415-492-1220
Fax: 415-492-1282 800-229-1249
Cookies and biscotti
Co-Owner: Jane Cloth Richman
VP Marketing: Jane Cloth-Richman
Estimated Sales: Below $5 Million
Number Employees: 20
Brands:
    San Anselmo's

11135 San Antonio Farms
1555 E Highway 151
Platteville, WI 53818
    800-236-1119
    www.sanantoniofarmsonline.com
Mexican fajita marinade, pico de gallo, salsa, enchilada and picante sauce and peppers including jalapeno, serrano and chile.
Parent Co: Bay Valley Foods, LLC
Type of Packaging: Consumer, Food Service, Bulk
Brands:
    Van De Walle Farms

11136 San Antonio Packing Co
1922 S Laredo St
San Antonio, TX 78207-7093
    210-224-5441
Fax: 210-224-6664 www.sanantoniopacking.com
Meats including beef, lamb and pork
President: Ollie Craft
ollie.craft@mrcglobal.com
Co-Owner: Jennifer Roe
Estimated Sales: $7.4 Million
Number Employees: 50-99
Square Footage: 120000

11137 San Bernardo Ice Cream
2805 N Commerce Pkwy
Miramar, FL 33025-3956
    954-322-2668
Fax: 954-441-9577
    www.sanbernardoicecream.com
Manufacturer of ice cream.
Founder: Bob Tammara
Estimated Sales: Less Than $500,000
Number Employees: 1-4

11138 San Diego Soy Dairy
1330 Hill St # B
El Cajon, CA 92020-5758
    619-447-8638
Fax: 619-447-2068 soydairy@att.net
    www.sandiegosoydairy.com
Soy products including milk, tofu, salads and salad dressings; also, herbal teas
Owner/CEO: Luke Yam
soydairy@aol.com
Estimated Sales: $500,000-$1 Million
Number Employees: 5-9
Square Footage: 13200
Type of Packaging: Consumer, Food Service
Brands:
    San Diego Soy Dairy
    Waterfall

11139 San Dominique Winery
I-17 & State Highway 169
Camp Verde, AZ 86322
    480-945-8583
Wines
President: William Staltari
Estimated Sales: Less than $500,000
Number Employees: 1-4
Brands:
    San Dominique

11140 San Francisco Bay Coffee
1731 Aviation Blvd
Lincoln, CA 95648
    916-258-8000
    800-829-1300
service@sfbcoffee.com sfbaycoffee.com
Roasted coffee
President: Jon Rogers
VP: Jim Rogers
VP: Barbra Rogers
VP, Sales & Marketing: Kristen Rogers
Operations Manager: Pete Rogers
Year Founded: 1979
Estimated Sales: $100-140 Million
Number Employees: 230
Number of Brands: 2
Type of Packaging: Private Label
Brands:
    San Francisco Bay
    Organic Coffee Company

11141 San Francisco Bay Coffee Company
1731 Aviation Blvd
Lincoln, CA 95648
    510-638-1300
Fax: 510-632-0839 800-829-1300
service@sfbcoffee.com
    www.sanfranciscobaycoffee.com
Coffee including ground, beans, decaffeinated and flavored; also, aromatic, herbal and flavored teas

Food Manufacturers / A-Z

President/CEO/Founder: Jon B Rogers
Vice President/Sales: Jim Rogers
Co-Founder: Barbara Rogers
Purchasing Manager: Tom Gerber
Estimated Sales: $20-50 Million
Number Employees: 100-249
Square Footage: 82000
Parent Co: JBR Gourmet Foods
Type of Packaging: Consumer, Food Service, Private Label, Bulk
Brands:
 East India Coffee & Tea Co.
 Pastarific Pasta Co.
 San Francisco Coffee

11142 San Francisco Fine Bakery
2537 Middlefield Rd
Redwood City, CA 94063-2825
    650-369-8573
 Fax: 650-369-8382 order@sffinebakery.com
Bakery products
Owner: Clifford Chen
clifford@sffinebakery.com
President, Chief Executive Officer: Daniel Huang
Estimated Sales: Below $5 Million
Number Employees: 20-49
Brands:
 San Francisco Fine Bakery

11143 San Francisco French Bread
580 Julie Ann Way
Oakland, CA 94621
    510-729-6232
Processor and exporter of sourdough bread, rolls and croutons
President: Tom Hofmeister
National Sales Manager: Terry McDonough
Contact: Norm Andrews
norm@asapwinetags.com
Number Employees: 5-9
Parent Co: IBC
Type of Packaging: Consumer, Food Service

11144 San Francisco Popcorn Works
1028 Revere Ave
San Francisco, CA 94124
    415-822-4744
 Fax: 415-822-3376 800-777-2676
 www.sanfranciscopopcornremoval.com
Popcorn
President: Joan Adler
Estimated Sales: Below $5 Million
Number Employees: 10
Square Footage: 8
Type of Packaging: Private Label
Brands:
 Naturfood
 San Francisco Popcorn
 Somewhat Sinful

11145 San Francisco Salt
30984 Santana St
Hayward, CA 94544
    510-477-9600
 Fax: 510-477-9621 800-480-4540
 customerservice@sfsalt.com sfsalt.com
Salts: Himalayan, bath, dead sea, Epsom, scented, flavored and gourmet
President: Lee Williamson
Director of Sales: Marilou Collins
Operations Manager: Siro Rivera
Year Founded: 2002
Estimated Sales: $46 Million
Number Employees: 11-50
Brands:
 Epsoak(c)
 Minera(c)
 San Francisco Salt Company(c)
 Sherpa Pink(c)

11146 San Francisco Spice Co.
1640 Tide Court
Woodland, CA 95776
    530-669-6703
 Fax: 650-583-6376 866-972-6879
 drmcdougalls@worldpantry.com
 www.rightfoods.com
Produces a variety of packaged foods including soups, oatmeals, and quinoa products; offer organic and gluten free products.

President: Mike Vinnicombe
Research & Development Manager: Maria Firmacion
Quality Assurance/Shippping Supervisor: Maresa Scofield
Estimated Sales: $6 Million
Number Employees: 25
Number of Brands: 1
Square Footage: 175000
Type of Packaging: Consumer
Brands:
 Dr. McDougall's Right Foods

11147 San Franola Granola
2440 Geary Blvd # C
San Francisco, CA 94115-3375
    415-506-9582
Manufacturer of granola bars.
Co-Founder: Matt Teichmann
Co-Founder: David Miskie

11148 San Gennaro Foods Inc
19255 80th Ave S
Kent, WA 98032-1135
    253-872-1900
 Fax: 253-872-1919 800-462-1916
 mail@polenta.net www.polenta.net
Pre cooked polenta. Also mayonnaise, barbeque sauces and salad dressings
President: Julio Jimenez
julio@polenta.net
Estimated Sales: $1-2.5 Million
Number Employees: 5-9
Type of Packaging: Private Label
Brands:
 Northwest Gourmet
 San Gennaro

11149 San Joaquin Figs Inc
3564 N Hazel Ave
PO Box 9547
Fresno, CA 93722-4912
    559-224-4963
 Fax: 559-224-4926 info@nutrafig.com
 www.nutrafig.com
Figs including dried, diced and paste; also, fig juice concentrate
President: Sara Guerrero-Martinez
saraguerrero-martinez@nutrafig.com
Estimated Sales: $5.6 Million
Number Employees: 20-49
Brands:
 California Classic
 San Joaquin Supreme
 The Nutra Fig

11150 San Joaquin Vly Concentrates
5631 E Olive Ave
Fresno, CA 93727-2708
    559-458-2500
 Fax: 559-458-2564 800-557-0220
 inquiries@sjvconc.com www.sjvconc.com
SJVC produces red and white juice concentrates, the grape seed extract ActiVin and is the world's largest supplier of anthocyanin colors.
Number Employees: 20-49
Brands:
 ActiVin

11151 San Jose Apartments
1500 Cunningham Ave
San Jose, CA 95122-2308
    408-347-8209
 Fax: 408-272-7118
Coffee
Manager: Thomasa Alpha
sanjoseapts@dkdpmco.com
Estimated Sales: $690,000
Number Employees: 5-9

11152 San Juan Coffee Roasting Co
18 Cannery Lndg
Friday Harbor, WA 98250
    360-378-4443
 Fax: 360-378-6658 800-624-4119
 www.rockisland.com/sjcoffee
Fresh coffee roasted daily
President: Irene Herring
Operations Manager: Steve Herring
Estimated Sales: Less Than $500,000
Number Employees: 5-9

11153 San Luis Valley Hemp Co.
570 Columbia Ave
PO Box 130
Del Norte, CO 81132
    719-299-5000
    slvhemp.com
Hemp products
Partner: Dion Oakes
Partner: Monte Robertson
Operations: Brandi Wright

11154 San Marco Coffee, Inc.
3120 Latrobe Dr
Suite 280
Charlotte, NC 28211-2186
    704-366-0533
 Fax: 704-366-0534 800-715-9298
 www.sanmarcocoffee.com
American coffee, espresso, cappuccino
Chief Executive Officer: Marc Decaria
marc@sanmarcocoffee.com
Number Employees: 5-9
Type of Packaging: Consumer, Food Service, Private Label
Brands:
 San Giorgio

11155 San Marzano Imports
116 West Fourth Street
Howell, NJ 07731
    732-364-1724
 Fax: 732-364-1724
Dried tomatoes and Turkish and Greek olives
Sales Manager: Nick Soccodato
Number Employees: 5-9
Square Footage: 40000

11156 San-Ei Gen FFI
630 5th Ave
Suite 3201
New York, NY 10111
    212-315-7850
 Fax: 212-974-2540 contact@saneigen.com
    www.saneigen.com
Food ingredients including coloring extracts and antioxidants.
President: Takashige Shimizu
Contact: Osamu Enomoto
oenomoto@saneigen.com
Estimated Sales: $5 Million
Number Employees: 1-4
Square Footage: 17600
Parent Co: San-El Gen FFI
Type of Packaging: Bulk

11157 San-J International Inc
2880 Sprouse Dr
Henrico, VA 23231-6072
    804-226-8333
 Fax: 804-226-8383 800-446-5500
 info@san-j.com www.san-j.com
Gluten free tamari, Asian cooking sauces and salad dressings, brown rice crackers, organic shoyu, and soups.
President: Ola Badaru
obaru@san-j.com
Quality Manager: Mark Mansfield
Maintenance Manager: Gary Dudley
Purchasing Manager: Ola Badaru
Estimated Sales: $5.3 Million
Number Employees: 20-49
Number of Brands: 1
Number of Products: 22
Square Footage: 88000
Parent Co: San Jirushi Corporation
Type of Packaging: Consumer, Food Service, Bulk
Brands:
 San-J

11158 San-J International Inc
2880 Sprouse Dr
Henrico, VA 23231-6072
    804-226-8333
 Fax: 804-226-8383 800-446-5500
 info@san-j.com www.san-j.com
Canned tomatoes, pasta, assorted olive oils, olives, beans, condiments, sauces, soy sauces and more
President: Ola Badaru
obaru@san-j.com
Number Employees: 20-49

Food Manufacturers / A-Z

11159 Sanarak Paper & PopcornSupplies
456 Hinman Ave
Buffalo, NY 14216
716-874-5662
Fax: 716-874-4737 sanarak001@yahoo.com
www.buffalofunfoods.com
Popcorn
President: Jim Rogers
Estimated Sales: $500,000-$1 000,000
Number Employees: 5-9

11160 Sanborn Sourdough Bakery
5230 S Valley View Blvd
Suite A
Las Vegas, NV 89118-1626
702-795-1030
Fax: 702-795-8518
Breads, rolls, and buns
President: Donald Sanborn
CFO: Brenda Portela
General Manager: Joe Lazi
Operations Manager: John Klessia
Estimated Sales: $20-50 Million
Number Employees: 50-99
Brands:
 Sanborn Sourdough Bakery

11161 Sanchez Distributors
9711 Mid Walk Dr
San Antonio, TX 78230-4075
210-341-1682
Fax: 210-341-7470
Ethnic foods
President: Roberto Sanchez
Sales Manager: Fernando Sanchez
Estimated Sales: $5-10 000,000
Number Employees: 1-4

11162 Sand Castle Winery
755 River Rd
Erwinna, PA 18920
610-294-9181
Fax: 610-294-9174 800-722-9463
info@sandcastlewinery.com
Wines
President: Paul Maxian
CEO: Joseph Maxian
winesand@epix.net
Marketing/Sales Manager: Stephanie Driver
Estimated Sales: $5-10 Million
Number Employees: 10-19
Type of Packaging: Private Label
Brands:
 Johannisberg Riesling
 Sand Castle Winery

11163 Sand Hill Berries
304 Deerfield Rd
Mt Pleasant, PA 15666-9150
724-547-4760
Fax: 724-547-7319 www.sandhillberries.com
Raspberries, blackberries, gooseberries, currants, jostaberries, jams, jellies, vinaigrettes, fruit sauce and vinegar
Owner: Susan Lynn
shberries@aol.com
Estimated Sales: Less Than $500,000
Number Employees: 1-4
Type of Packaging: Consumer, Private Label

11164 Sand Springs
160 Sand Springs Rd
Williamstown, MA 01267-2248
413-458-8281
Spring waters
Owner: Jennifer Morin
Estimated Sales: $2.5-5 000,000
Number Employees: 5-9

11165 Sandbar Trading Corp
408 S Pierce Ave
Louisville, CO 80027-3018
303-499-7480
Fax: 303-527-1727 www.snatea.com
Herbs and spices
President: Barry Cowper
Manager: Karen Harbour
kharbour@snat.com
Manager: Dave Halford
Number Employees: 1-4
Brands:
 Sandbar Trading

11166 Sandco International
151 Union Chapel Rd
Northport, AL 35473
205-339-0145
Fax: 205-339-8222 800-382-2075
Processor and exporter of vitamins and sports supplements, anti-aging
President: Linda Sandlin
sandco@uronramp.com
Research & Development: Richard Sandlin
Marketing: Linda Madison
Purchasing Manager: Linda Wells
Estimated Sales: $1,100,000
Number Employees: 5-9
Square Footage: 80000
Type of Packaging: Consumer, Private Label, Bulk

11167 Sanders Candy Inc
23770 Hall Rd
Clinton Twp, MI 48036-1275
586-468-4300
Fax: 586-468-9407 800-852-2253
www.sanderscandy.com
Cookies, bread & rolls, danishes, cakes and doughnuts
President/CEO: Judith Brock
CFO: Joseph Talmage
Marketing Specialist: Susan Leso
VP Sales/Marketing: John McGuckin
Plant Manager: Mike Koch
Estimated Sales: $500,000-$1 Million
Number Employees: 100-249
Parent Co: Country Home Bakers
Type of Packaging: Private Label
Brands:
 Sanders Brand Candy

11168 Sanders Meat Packing Inc
237 S. Main St.
Custer, MI 49405-0128
231-757-4768
Fax: 231-757-4786 800-968-5035
info@sandersmeats.com www.sandersmeats.com
Beef and pork products
Owner: Dale Sanders
Estimated Sales: $5-10 Million
Number Employees: 10-19
Type of Packaging: Consumer

11169 Sanderson Farms
P.O. Box 988
Laurel, MS 39441
800-844-4030
www.sandersonfarms.com
Poultry.
President/COO: Lampkin Butts
Chairman/CEO: Joe Sanderson
Treasurer/CFO: Mike Cockrell
Secretary/Chief Accounting Officer: Tim Rigney
Year Founded: 1955
Estimated Sales: $3.4 Billion
Number Employees: 17,000+
Square Footage: 11418
Type of Packaging: Consumer, Food Service, Private Label, Bulk
Brands:
 Sanderson Farms

11170 Sandia Shadows Vineyard & Winery
8740 4th Street NW
PO Box 92675
Albuquerque, NM 87199-2675
505-856-1006
Fax: 505-858-0859 sandiawine@aol.com
Wine
Owner: Phillippe Littot
Estimated Sales: Less than $500,000
Number Employees: 1-4
Brands:
 Sandia Shadows Vineyard & Wine

11171 Sandors Bakeries
2245 W Flagler St
Miami, FL 33135-1522
305-642-8484
Fax: 305-643-9358
Breads and other bakery products, except cookies and crackers
President: Orlando Sanchez
Estimated Sales: $237,263
Number Employees: 5-9

11172 Sandridge Food Corp
133 Commerce Dr
Medina, OH 44256-1333
330-725-2348
Fax: 330-722-3998 800-627-2523
www.sandridge.com
Refrigerated deli salads, sides, soups, sauces, and specialty dishes
President: William Frantz
CEO: Mark Sandridge
VP Finance: Rick Sisko
VP of Business Development: Frank Sidari
Sr Director, Food Safety & Quality: Joel Riegelmayer
VP Sales/Marketing: John Becker
Sr Director/Food Service Sales: Michael Sandridge
Manager of Customer Service: Lori Kyle
Operations Director: Barry Pioske
Purchasing Manager: Rich Graziosi
Estimated Sales: $20-50 Million
Number Employees: 250-499
Square Footage: 130000
Type of Packaging: Consumer, Food Service, Private Label, Bulk
Brands:
 Sandridge Salads Set Free

11173 Sandstone Winery
4505 220th Trl
Amana, IA 52203-8029
319-622-3081
sandwine@netins.net
Homemade wines
President: Elsie Mattes
Vice President: Thomas Mattes
Estimated Sales: $550,000
Number Employees: 1-4
Type of Packaging: Consumer, Food Service
Brands:
 Sandstone Winery

11174 Sandt's Honey Co
714 Wagener Ln
Easton, PA 18040-8253
610-252-6511
Fax: 610-252-9069 800-935-3960
www.sandtshoney.com
Processor and packer of all-natural and kosher certified honey
President: Lee Sandt
Vice President: Linda Sandt
Estimated Sales: $12 Million
Number Employees: 1-4
Type of Packaging: Consumer, Food Service, Private Label, Bulk
Brands:
 Sandt's

11175 Sandusky Filling & Brittle
1034 Hancock St
Sandusky, OH 44870-3616
419-626-8080
Fax: 419-626-8330 800-274-8853
Candy
Manager: Dennis Babb
Specialty Sales: John Cayten
Estimated Sales: $10-20 Million
Number Employees: 20-49

11176 Sandy Candy
77 Fairfield Lane
Chester Springs, PA 19425
610-321-7263
Fax: 610-524-5649 800-386-7263
info@sandycandy.com
Confectionary candy
Contact: Sally Solomon
sandcrafters@comcast.net

11177 Sanford Milling Co Inc
1310 Nicholas St
1310 S. Nicholas Street
Henderson, NC 27536-5329
252-438-4526
Fax: 252-492-3014 866-438-4526
Flour
President: Scott Hartness
sanfordmilling@nc.rr.com
Estimated Sales: $10-20 Million
Number Employees: 10-19
Type of Packaging: Food Service, Private Label, Bulk
Brands:
 Hartness Choice

Food Manufacturers / A-Z

Packers Blend
Snow Flake

11178 Sanford Winery
5010 Santa Rosa Rd # 6
Lompoc, CA 93436-9551
805-735-5900
Fax: 805-688-7381 800-426-9463
info@sanfordwinery.com www.sanfordwinery.com
Wines
Partner: Richard Sanford
CFO: Stuart Fries
Marketing Manager: Tom Prendiville
Manager: Anthony Terlato
Operations: Sharon Blewis
Purchasing Manager: Sharon Blewis
Estimated Sales: Below $5 Million
Number Employees: 5-9
Type of Packaging: Private Label
Brands:
Sanford

11179 Sangudo Custom Meat Packers
4920 47 Avenue
Sangudo, AB T0E 2A0
Canada
780-785-3353
Fax: 780-785-3111 888-785-3353
Frozen beef and pork, pepperoni, bacon and sausage
Owner: Kevin Meier
Owner: Jeff Senger
Number Employees: 1-4

11180 Sanitary Bakery
126 E Ridge St
Nanticoke, PA 18634-2813
570-735-6630
Fax: 320-632-2740 www.sanitarybakery.com
Cookies
Owner: Edward Kowalski
Estimated Sales: Under $500,000
Number Employees: 10-19

11181 Sanitary Tortilla Manufacturing Company
623 Urban Loop
San Antonio, TX 78204
210-226-9209
Fax: 210-226-9424
sanitarytortillacompany@gmail.com
www.sanitarytortillacompany.com
Tortillas and other corn products
Owner: Louis Garcia
General Manager: Garcia Luis
Estimated Sales: $8 Million
Number Employees: 10 to 19
Square Footage: 18000
Type of Packaging: Food Service

11182 Santa Barbara Bar
233 E Gutierrez Street
Santa Barbara, CA 93101
855-722-2701
sbbar.co
Nutritional snack bars
Founder & CEO: Peter Gaum
Number Employees: 2-10
Brands:
santa barbara BAR(c)

11183 Santa Barbara Olive Company
12477 Calle Real
Santa Barbara, CA 93117
805-562-1456
Fax: 805-562-1464 800-624-4896
info@sbolive.com www.sbolive.com
Gourmet olives, extra virgin olive oils, sauces, vegetables, condiments, salsas
President: Craig Makela
Vice President: Cindy Makela
Contact: Jason Pace
jason@sbolive.com
Estimated Sales: $10 Million
Number Employees: 17
Square Footage: 14000
Type of Packaging: Consumer, Food Service, Private Label, Bulk

11184 Santa Barbara PistachioCo
3380 Highway 33
Maricopa, CA 93252-9688
661-766-2485
Fax: 661-766-2436 800-896-1044
info@sbpistachios.com
www.santabarbarapistachios.com
Grower and packager of naturally organic pistachios brined with organic, kosher-certified ingredients. Manufacturer of pistachio flour and pistachio oil.
Owner: Gene Zannon
zannon@sbpistachios.com
Owner: Gail Zannon
Vice President: Mark Purcell
Vice President: Steve Bertrand
Estimated Sales: Less Than $500,000
Number Employees: 1-4
Square Footage: 8000
Type of Packaging: Consumer, Bulk
Brands:
Santa Barbara Pistachio

11185 Santa Barbara Roasting Co
321 Motor Way
Santa Barbara, CA 93101-3436
805-898-3700
Fax: 805-962-2590 800-321-5282
www.sbcoffee.com
Coffee
President: Corey Russell
corey@sbcoffee.com
Executive Director: Jami Dunlop
Director Operations: Matthew Moore
Estimated Sales: Below $5 Million
Number Employees: 20-49
Type of Packaging: Private Label
Brands:
Santa Barbara

11186 Santa Barbara Salsa
649 Benet Rd
Oceanside, CA 92058-1208
760-757-2622
Fax: 760-721-2600 800-748-5523
info@sbsalsa.com
Salsa and sauces
President: Doug Pearson
Estimated Sales: $2.5 Million
Number Employees: 10-19
Parent Co: California Creative Foods
Type of Packaging: Consumer, Bulk
Brands:
Chacies
Con Gusto
San Diego Salsa
Santa Barbara Salsa
Tio Tio

11187 Santa Barbara Salsa/California Creative
649 Benet Rd
Oceanside, CA 92058-1208
760-757-2622
Fax: 760-721-2600 800-748-5523
info@sbsalsa.com
Salsa Flavors: artichoke, key lime, garlic; peach; roasted garlic; mango peach; roasted chili; black bean; corn; cheese and salsa; hot pepper and marinades
President: Doug Pearson
Estimated Sales: $300,000-500,000
Number Employees: 1-4
Brands:
Chachies
Congusto
San Diego Salsa
Santa Barbara Salsa
Tio Tio

11188 Santa Barbara Winery
202 Anacapa St
Santa Barbara, CA 93101-1887
805-963-3633
Fax: 805-962-4981 wine@sbwinery.com
www.sbwinery.com
Wines
President/Production Manager: Bruce McGuire
Owner: Pierre Lafond
wine@sbwinery.com
CFO: Marty-Pooe Winnen
Dir. of Research & Development: Suzanne Fitzgerald
Quality Control Manager: Dan Cerepanya
Marketing Director: Michelle Lafond
Sales Manager: George Fakinos
Dir. of Public Relations: Suzanne Fitzgerald
Operations Manager: Dan Cerepanya
Site Manager: Pierre Lafond
Estimated Sales: Below $5 Million
Number Employees: 10-19
Brands:
Lafond
Santa Barbara Winery

11189 Santa Clara Nut Co
1590 Little Orchard St
San Jose, CA 95110-3599
408-298-2425
Fax: 408-298-0101 santaclaranut@aol.com
Manufacturer and exporter of shelled and in-shell walnuts
Owner/President: Jim Pusateri
santaclaranut@aol.com
VP: Salvatore Pusateri
Estimated Sales: $15 Million
Number Employees: 5-9
Number of Brands: 1
Number of Products: 1
Square Footage: 150000
Type of Packaging: Consumer, Food Service, Bulk
Brands:
Santa Clara

11190 Santa Cruz Chili & Spice
1868 E Frontage Rd
1868 E. Frontage Rd.
Tumacacori, AZ 85640
520-398-2591
Fax: 520-398-2592 sales@santacruzchili.com
www.santacruzchili.com
Chile paste, powder, sauces and spices
President: Jean Neubauer
santacruzchili@theriver.com
Sales Manager: Armida Castro
Estimated Sales: $500000
Number Employees: 1-4
Type of Packaging: Consumer

11191 Santa Cruz Mountain Brewing
402 Ingalls St # 27
Santa Cruz, CA 95060-5869
831-425-4900
Fax: 831-429-8915 anthony@scmbrew.com
www.scmbrew.com
Seasonal beer and lager
Owner/Brewer: Emily Thomas
Owner/Brewer: Chad Brill
chad@santacruzmountainbrewing.com
Brewhouse Operations/Brewer: Thomas Mills
Taproom Operations: Jenny Price
Sales and Distribution: Anthony Carlson
Number Employees: 1-4
Type of Packaging: Consumer, Food Service
Brands:
Pacific
Santa Cruz

11192 Santa Cruz Mountain Vineyard
P.O.Box 1592
Felton, CA 95018
831-426-6209
Fax: 831-335-4242
info@santacruzmountainvineyard.com
www.scmountainvineyard.com
Wines
Proprietor: Jeff Emery
Contact: Cynthia Bournellis
cynthia@santacruzmountainvineyard.com
Estimated Sales: Below $5 Million
Number Employees: 5-9
Brands:
Santa Cruz Mountain Vineyard

11193 Santa Elena Coffee Company
550 S Fm 1660
Suite
Hutto, TX 78634-4362
512-846-2908
Fax: 512-846-2710
Coffee

Food Manufacturers / A-Z

Owner: Linda Truong
VP/Plant Manager: Astrid Bernstorff
Marketing Director: Lissette Bernstorff
Purchasing Manager: Everardo Bernstorff
Number Employees: 5-9
Square Footage: 12000
Type of Packaging: Private Label
Brands:
   Santa-Elena Coffee

11194 Santa Fe Brewing Co
35 Fire Place # Tasting
Santa Fe, NM 87508-4493
        505-424-3333
Fax: 505-474-5573 info@santafebrewing.com
        www.santafebrewing.com
Beer
Owner: Scott Biram
scott@santafebrewing.com
Estimated Sales: $275,000
Number Employees: 1-4
Brands:
   Santa Fe Brewing

11195 Santa Fe Seasons
34 Uss Thresher Ln
Belen, NM 87002
        505-988-1515
Fax: 505-988-1300 800-866-4695
        www.santafeseasons.com
Salsa and seasonings
President: Greg Deneen
Vice President: Edith Deneen
Sales Director: Lisa Duck
Estimated Sales: Below $5 Million
Number Employees: 20
Brands:
   De Santa Fe
   Santa Fe Seasons

11196 Santa Fe Vineyards
18348 Us 84/285
Espanola, NM 87532
        505-753-8100
Fax: 505-753-8100
        www.estrelladelnortevineyard.com
Wines
Manager: Dan Doughtery
Estimated Sales: $500,000
Number Employees: 1-4
Brands:
   Santa Fe Vineyards

11197 Santa Maria Foods
10 Armthorpe Rd
Branpton, ON L6T 5M4
Canada
        905-790-1991
Fax: 416-675-7466
Prosciutto and mortadella, salami and cured meats, hams and specialty meats
President: Eddie Zilli
CEO: Frederick Jaques
CFO: Andrew Linley

11198 Santa Monica Seafood Co.
18531 S. Broadwick St.
Rancho Dominguez, CA 90220
        310-886-7900
Fax: 310-886-3333 800-969-8862
        info@smseafood.com
        www.santamonicaseafood.com
Fresh and frozen fish including halibut, salmon, sea bass and swordfish.
President: Anthony Cigliano
anthony@smseafood.com
Controlling Partner: Marisa Cigliano
Controlling Partner: John Cigliano
Executive VP/Co-Owner: Michael Cigliano
Year Founded: 1939
Estimated Sales: $400 Million
Number Employees: 20-49
Type of Packaging: Consumer, Food Service, Private Label, Bulk
Other Locations:
   Long Beach Seafoods
   Del Mar CA
Brands:
   Fan-Sea
   Stars Pride
   Stilwell's

11199 Santa Ynez Wine Corp
2922 Grand Ave
Los Olivos, CA 93441
        805-688-9665
Fax: 805-686-1690 800-824-8584
        www.arthurearl.com
Wines
Owner: Athuur White
Estimated Sales: $1-2.5 000,000
Number Employees: 5-9
Type of Packaging: Private Label
Brands:
   Los Olivos Vintners

11200 Santa's Smokehouse
2400 Davis Rd
Fairbanks, AK 99701-5700
        907-456-3885
Fax: 907-456-3889 800-478-3885
        order@santassmokehouse.com
Reindeer and buffalo meat and sausages
Owner: Janet Mc Cormick
Estimated Sales: $300,000-500,000
Number Employees: 5-9
Parent Co: Interior Alaska Fish Processors

11201 Santanna Banana Company
12 Kelker Street
Harrisburg, PA 17113
        717-238-8321
Fax: 717-238-4480
Bananas
President: Raymond Santanna
Vice President: David Santanna
Vice President: Richard Santanna
Estimated Sales: $16 Million
Number Employees: 41
Square Footage: 75000

11202 Sante Specialty Foods
491 Laurelwood Rd
Santa Clara, CA 95054-2416
        408-451-9585
Fax: 408-451-9485 www.santenuts.com
Nuts
Owner: Sara Tidhar
Director Of Sales: Navot Tidhar
Number Employees: 1-4

11203 Santini Foods
16505 Worthley Dr
San Lorenzo, CA 94580
        510-317-8888
Fax: 510-317-8343 800-835-6888
        www.santinifoods.com
Milk products, syrups, sauces, and ethnic and specialty foods
President/Owner: Vikram Chand
CFO: Tyler Abbott
Vice President: Christopher Quie
Quality Control: Hal Burgan
Operations: Roger Tan
Year Founded: 1987
Estimated Sales: $11 Million
Number Employees: 50-99
Square Footage: 400000
Type of Packaging: Consumer, Food Service, Private Label, Bulk
Brands:
   California Farms
   La Vava Blanca
   Lotus Bloom

11204 Santini Foods
16505 Worthley Dr
San Lorenzo, CA 94580-1811
        510-317-7755
Fax: 510-317-8343 800-835-6888
        www.santinifoods.com
Condensed milk, salad dressing, olive oil, syrup, jarred vegetables, mushrooms, pesto
Owner: Anna Liu
anna@santinifoods.com
Estimated Sales: $10-20 Million
Number Employees: 50-99
Parent Co: Corticella USA Organic Farms

11205 Sapore della Vita
West Country Club Drive N
Sarasota, FL 34243-3513
        941-914-4256
        kristine@saporedellavita.com
        www.saporedellavita.com
Italian products: caramels, jams, marmalades, nut butter, biscotti, oils, sauces and confectionery.
Co-Owner: Kristine Insalaco-Gaioni
Year Founded: 2009
Estimated Sales: Under $500,000
Number Employees: 11-50
Type of Packaging: Food Service, Private Label
Brands:
   Crema di Miele
   Lick My Spoon
   Marchesi
   Sapore Del Tartufo
   Villa Lan Franca

11206 Sapp Birch Water
40 E Chicago Ave
Suite 407
Chicago, IL 60611-2026
        708-351-7777
        info@sapplife.co
        www.sapplife.co
Birch water
Co-Founder & Director: John Kavchak
Brands:
   Sapp Birch Water

11207 Sappore Coffee Co Of Alaska
6436 Homer Dr # A
PO Box 221187
Anchorage, AK 99518-1900
        907-333-3626
Fax: 907-333-3690
        www.alaskacoffeecompany.com
Coffee
Owner: Lori Brewer
coffeequeen1@aol.com
Estimated Sales: $280,000
Number Employees: 10-19

11208 Sapporo USA, Inc.
11 E 44th St
Suite 705
New York, NY 10017
        212-922-9165
Fax: 212-922-9576 info@sapporousa.com
Processor and importer of beer. They also prepare dishes using beer as an ingredient.
President: Tsukasa Orui
Contact: Saori Potts
saori@sapporousa.com
Estimated Sales: G
Number Employees: 30
Square Footage: 2000
Type of Packaging: Consumer, Food Service

11209 Saputo Cheese USA Inc.
One Overlook Point
Suite 300
Lincolnshire, IL 60069
        847-267-1100
Fax: 847-267-1110 www.saputocheeseusa.com
Natural cheese products and exporter of whey.
President/COO: Terry Brockman
Year Founded: 1954
Estimated Sales: $430 Million
Number Employees: 250-499
Number of Brands: 15
Number of Products: 12
Square Footage: 270000
Parent Co: Saputo, Inc.
Type of Packaging: Consumer, Food Service, Bulk
Brands:
   Black Creek
   DCI Cheese
   Dragone
   Frigo Cheese
   Great Midwest
   Lorraine
   Organic Creamery
   Salemville
   Saputo
   Stella
   Treasure Cave
   Woolwich Dairy
   Joan of Arc
   Montchevre
   Nikos

Food Manufacturers / A-Z

11210 Saputo Dairy Division (Canada)
2365, Chemin de la CoTe-de-Liesse
Saint-Laurent, QC H4N 2M7
Canada
514-328-6663
800-672-8866
www.saputo.com
Dairy products.
President/COO: Frank Guido
Parent Co: Saputo, Inc.
Other Locations:
  Cheese Division
  Lincolnshire IL
  Dairy Division
  Dallas TX

11211 (HQ)Saputo Inc.
6869, Metropolitain Est
Montreal, QC H1P 1X8
Canada
514-328-6662
800-672-8866
www.saputo.com
Dairy products.
Chair of the Board/CEO: Lino Saputo
President/COO: Kai Bockmann
Chief Financial Officer: Maxime Therrien
Chief Human Resources Officer: Ga,tane Wagner
Year Founded: 1954
Estimated Sales: $11.2 Billion
Number Employees: 16,800
Number of Brands: 45
Brands:
  Alexis de Portneuf
  Armstrong
  Bari
  Baxter
  Baileys
  Cheese Heads
  Chevrai
  Cracker Barrel
  Dairyland
  Cogruet
  DuVillage 1860
  International Delight
  JOYYA
  Kingsey
  Milk2Go
  Mornington Dairy
  Neilson
  Nutrilait
  Saputo
  Scotsburn
  Stella
  Wholesome Goat
  Woolwich Dairy
  Black Creek
  DCI Cheese
  Dragone
  Frigo
  Stella
  Great Middwest
  Lorraine
  Organic Creamery
  Salemville
  Treasure Cave
  DairYStar
  Friendship Dairies
  La Paulina
  Molfino
  Ricrem
  Coon
  Devondale
  Great Ocead Road
  Liddells
  Mil Lel
  Sungold
  Warrnambool Cheese and Butter

11212 Sara Lee Coffee & Tea
1370 Progress Rd
Suffolk, VA 23434
757-538-8083
Fax: 757-215-7447
Roasts and packs coffee
CEO: Massino Zanetti
Manager: Chuck Gosstrom
Contact: Felix Venezuela
fvenezuela@saraleecoffee.com
Plant Manager: Buddy McGuire
Number Employees: 200
Brands:
  Chase & Sanborn
  Chock Full O'Nuts
  Hills Bros
  Mjb
  Segafredo Espresso

11213 Sara Lee Foodservice
PO Box 3901
Peoria, IL 61612
800-261-4754
800-641-4025
www.saraleefoodservice.com
Roasted coffee
President/CEO: Sean Connolly
Contact: Brenda Barnes
bbarnes@saraleefoodservice.com
Regional Manager: Stephen Flwoer
Purchasing Manager Assoc.: Steve McCreary
Estimated Sales: $500,000-$1 Million
Number Employees: 5-9
Type of Packaging: Consumer, Food Service
Brands:
  Cains
  Superior

11214 Sara Lee Frozen Bakery
PO Box 708
Kings Mountain, NC 28086
800-323-7117
saraleefrozenbakery@casupport.com
www.saraleefrozenbakery.com
Bakery items, including pies, cakes, muffins, cornbread, donoughts
CEO: Craig Bahner
Sales Administrator/Contact: Tara Washington
twashington@saraleefoodservice.com
Parent Co: Tyson Foods Inc.
Type of Packaging: Food Service
Brands:
  Bistro
  Chef Pierre
  Sara Lee

11215 Sara Snacker Cookie Company
41 Purdy Ave.
Suite 505
Rye, NY 10580
914-305-6363
Fax: 914-206-3635
Manufacturer of cookies.
CEO and Founder: Sara Leand

11216 Sarabeth's Office
1161 E 156th St
Bronx, NY 10474-6226
718-589-2900
Fax: 718-589-8412 800-773-7378
info@sarabeth.com www.sarabeth.com
Muffins, cakes, cookies, pastries, puddings, pies, croissants, brownies, tarts and frozen blintzes
Chief Executive Officer: William Levine
Executive VP: Jennifer Firestone
Vice President: David Case
david.case@sarabeth.com
Co-Owner: David Case
Estimated Sales: Below $5 Million
Number Employees: 10-19
Square Footage: 17200
Parent Co: Sarabeth's Kitchen
Type of Packaging: Consumer, Food Service
Other Locations:
  Sarabeth's Bakery Ltd.
  New York NY
Brands:
  Sarabeth's

11217 Sarah's Vineyard
4005 Hecker Pass Rd
Gilroy, CA 95020-8843
408-842-4278
Fax: 408-842-3252 sales@sarahsvineyard.com
www.sarahs-vineyard.com
Wines
Proprietor: Tim Slater
Estimated Sales: $500,000-$1 Million
Number Employees: 5-9
Brands:
  Sarah's Vineyard

11218 Saranac Brewery
830 Varick St
Utica, NY 13502
800-765-6288
www.saranac.com
Manufacturer, brewer and exporter of beer, ale, stout, lager and malt; also, soft drinks and juices
President: Fred Matt
Chairman & CEO: Nicholas Matt
Director of Operations: Jim Kuhr
Estimated Sales: $21 Million
Number Employees: 150
Number of Brands: 12
Square Footage: 360000
Type of Packaging: Consumer, Food Service, Private Label, Bulk
Brands:
  Adirondack Amber
  American Plsener
  Black and Tan
  Black Forest
  English Pale Ale
  Light
  Mountain Berry
  Saranac Diet Root Beer
  Saranac Ginger Beer
  Saranac Orange Cream
  Saranac Root Beer
  Traditional Lager

11219 Sarant International Cmmdts
213 Hallock Rd # 3b
PO Box 659
Stony Brook, NY 11790-3000
631-675-2875
Fax: 631-246-5257 psarant@aol.com
Processor and importer of dehydrated vegetables including tomatoes, celery, carrots and red and green bell peppers
President: Peter Sarant
Co-Secretary: Pamela Sarant
Number Employees: 1-4
Type of Packaging: Bulk

11220 Saratoga Food Specialties
771 W Crossroads Pkwy
Bolingbrook, IL 60490
800-451-0407
info@saratogafs.com www.saratogafs.com
Whole and ground spices, custom seasoning blends, seasoned rice, stuffing and gravy mixes.
President: Michael Marks
CFO: Ed Herbert
Vice President: Wade McGeorge
Research & Development: Paul Maki
Quality Control: Mark Beattie
Marketing Director: Kristi Freitager
Sales Director: George Rackos
Contact: Alan Ainsley
aainsley@saratogafs.com
Operations Manager: Jim Benja
Purchasing Manager: Ron Batzer
Estimated Sales: $30-40 Million
Number Employees: 100-249
Square Footage: 110000
Type of Packaging: Consumer, Food Service, Private Label, Bulk
Other Locations:
  Saratoga Specialties Co.
  Northlake IL

11221 Saratoga Peanut Butter Company
P.O. Box 5111
Saratoga Springs, NY 12866
888-967-3268
customerservice@saratogapb.com
www.yopeanut.com
Almond butter, peanut butter, and nut butter blends
Owner: Jessica Arceri
Marketing: Senia Fleming

11222 Saratoga Salad Dressing
5 Whitman Rd
Canton, MA 02021-2707
781-821-1010
Fax: 781-821-4303 www.saratogadressings.com
Pickled fruits and vegetables, vegetable sauces and seasonings, and salad dressings
Owner: Judy Pearlstein
jpearlstein@saratogadressings.com
Estimated Sales: $3,100,000
Number Employees: 20-49
Type of Packaging: Food Service, Private Label, Bulk
Brands:
  Saratoga

Food Manufacturers / A-Z

11223 (HQ)Saratoga Spring Water Co
11 Geyser Rd
Saratoga Springs, NY 12866-9048
518-584-6363
Fax: 518-584-0380 888-426-8642
www.sswc.com
Spring water, orange and grapefruit juice and smoothies
President: Robin Prever
rprever@saratogaspringwater.com
CFO: Robert Braks
Vice President: Andrew Cook
Production Manager: Mike Lawson
Estimated Sales: $300,000-500,000
Number Employees: 50-99
Type of Packaging: Consumer, Food Service, Private Label
Other Locations:
  Saratoga Beverage Group
  Azusa CA
Brands:
  Saratoga
  Saratoga Splash
  Saratoga Vichy

11224 Sardinha's Sausage
177 Lepes Rd
Somerset, MA 02726-2635
508-674-2511
Fax: 508-674-2511 800-678-0178
www.sardinhas.com
Gourmet smoked and fresh sausages including chourico, linguica, turkey dogs and kielbasa, breakfast and Italian sausage
President: Ed Sardinha
esardinha@sardinhas.com
Estimated Sales: Less Than $500,000
Number Employees: 1-4
Square Footage: 14400
Type of Packaging: Consumer, Food Service, Private Label, Bulk
Brands:
  Francisco's
  Portuguese Sausages
  Sardinha's
  Vincenza's

11225 Sardinia Cheese
312 Roosevelt Drive
Seymour, CT 06483-2128
203-735-3374
Fax: 203-732-3959 tmavuli@aol.com
Cheese
CEO/VP: Tony Mavuli
Estimated Sales: $5 000,000
Number Employees: 3
Type of Packaging: Private Label

11226 Sargent and Greenleaf
PO Box 930
Nicholasville, KY 40340-930
859-885-9411
Fax: 859-885-3063 800-826-7652
www.sglocks.com
Bottled and glass and plastic-packed pickled products including beets, cauliflower, onions, olives, pickles, peppers, gherkins, etc.; also, vinegar
Co-Owner: James Sargent
Co-Owner: Halbert Greenleaf
CEO: Jerry A Morgan
Director Sales: Richard Greenberg
Type of Packaging: Consumer, Food Service
Brands:
  Lion
  Supreme

11227 Sargent's Bear Necessities
321 Guay Farm Road
North Troy, VT 05859-9207
802-988-2903
Jams, jellies, pickles and relishes
Owner: Michelle Sargent
Number Employees: 1

11228 (HQ)Sargento Foods Inc
1 Persnickety Pl
Plymouth, WI 53073-3544
920-893-8484
Fax: 920-893-8399 800-243-3737
www.sargento.com
Natural and processed cheese manufacturer.
CEO: Louis Gentine
Executive VP: Karri Neils
karri.neils@sargentocheese.com

Estimated Sales: Over $1 Billion
Number Employees: 1000-4999
Type of Packaging: Consumer, Food Service, Private Label, Bulk
Brands:
  Sargento
  Snack Bites
  Chef Blends
  Artisan Blends
  Natural Blends
  Ultra Thin
  Balanced Breaks

11229 Sarliz LLC
7000 Fordland Drive
Raleigh, NC 27606-4499
860-355-9697
Fax: 860-210-1999
Flavored soup stocks
President: Robert Greene
Type of Packaging: Consumer, Food Service, Private Label, Bulk
Brands:
  Savory Basics

11230 Sarris Candies Inc
511 Adams Ave
Canonsburg, PA 15317-2103
724-745-4042
Fax: 724-745-5642 800-255-7771
www.sarriscandies.com
Candies
CEO: Josh Cas
jlucas@sarriscandies.com
Number Employees: 250-499

11231 Sartori Co
107 N Pleasant View Rd
PO Box 258
Plymouth, WI 53073-4948
920-893-6061
Fax: 920-892-2732
customercare@sartoricheese.com
www.sartoricheese.com
Cheese
Founder: Paolo Sartori
CEO: James C Sartori
info@sartorifoods.com
Sales Manager: Jim Tassielli
Number Employees: 20-49

11232 Sarum Tea Company
332 Main St
Lakeville, CT 06039
860-435-2086
Fax: 860-435-9304
Tea
President/CEO: W Harris
Manager: E Lloyd-Harris
Estimated Sales: Less than $500,000
Number Employees: 1-4
Brands:
  Sarum Tea

11233 Sassafras Enterprises Inc
1622 W Carroll Ave
Chicago, IL 60612-2502
312-226-2000
Fax: 312-226-0873 800-537-4941
info@sassafrasenterprises.com
www.sassafras-wholesale.com
Gourmet gift baskets, natural pizza and pasta sauces, spices, oils, spreads, bruschettas, mixes, pastas and bread mixes
Owner: Rob Joslyn
rob.joslyn@marriott.com
VP: Nancy Schwab
Operations Manager: Ron Cahill
Estimated Sales: $10 Million
Number Employees: 5-9
Type of Packaging: Private Label
Brands:
  Superstone

11234 Saticoy Foods Corp
554 Todd Rd
Santa Paula, CA 93060-9725
805-647-5266
Fax: 805-933-1523 www.moodydunbar.com
Processor of bell peppers, pimientos and sweet potatoes; products are certified kosher.
President: Jerry Hensley
CEO: Stanley Dunbar

Estimated Sales: $10-20 Million
Number Employees: 20-49
Parent Co: Moody Dunbar, Inc.

11235 Satiety Winery & Cafe
1027 Maple Ln
Davis, CA 95616-1720
530-757-2699
Fax: 530-668-9263
Wines, wine vinegars, table grapes, wine grapes
Owner: Sterling Chaykin
Estimated Sales: $270,000
Number Employees: 5-9
Brands:
  Ambrosia
  Satiety

11236 Satin Fine Foods
32 Leone Lane
Chester, NY 10918
contact@satinfinefoods.com
www.satinice.com
Gluten-free, dairy-free, nut-free, vegan, Kosher fondant and gum paste in various colors
Founder/CEO: Kevin O'Reilly
Year Founded: 2001
Number of Brands: 1
Number of Products: 4
Type of Packaging: Consumer, Private Label, Bulk
Brands:
  Satin Ice

11237 Sattwa Chai
17900 NE Lewis Rogers Ln
Newberg, OR 97132-6521
503-538-4715
Fax: 503-538-5125 www.sattwachai.com
Tea, chai
Owner: Juanita Crampton
juanita@sattwa.com
Owner: David Fields
CFO/VP Operations: Juanita Crampton
Purchasing Manager: Jan Rhine
Estimated Sales: $2.5-5 Million
Number Employees: 1-4
Parent Co: Sattwa Chai
Type of Packaging: Food Service, Private Label, Bulk
Brands:
  Black Tea Chai
  Sattwa Sun Chai
  Sattwa Chai Concentrate
  Sattwa Kovalam Spice Chai
  Sattwa Shanti Herbal Chai
  Sattwa Sun Chai

11238 Sau-Sea Foods
303 S Broadway
Suite 224
Tarrytown, NY 10591
914-631-1717
Fax: 914-631-0865
Shrimp and sauces including cocktail, tartar and horseradish
President: Antonio Estadella
estadella@csi.com
National Sales Manager: Edward Cauley
Estimated Sales: $1,300,000
Number Employees: 5-9
Type of Packaging: Consumer, Food Service, Private Label, Bulk
Brands:
  Sea Maid
  Seagull Bay

11239 Sauces N' Love
86 Sanderson Ave
Suite 130
Lynn, MA 01902
781-595-7771
Fax: 781-595-7799 info@saucesnlove.com
saucesnlove.com
Homemade pasta sauces
Contact: Paolo Volpati-Kedra
paolo@saucesnlove.com
Estimated Sales: $5-10 Million
Number Employees: 10-19

11240 Saucilito Canyon Vineyard
3080 Biddle Ranch Rd
San Luis Obispo, CA 93401-8320
805-543-2111
Fax: 805-543-2111 info@saucelitocanyon.com
www.saucelitocanyon.com

Wines
Founder, Owner: Bill Greenough
Owner: Nancy Greenbough
nancy@saucelitocanyon.com
Marketing/Sales Manager: Nancy Greenbough
Winemaker: Amy Freeman
Estimated Sales: Less than $500,000
Number Employees: 1-4
Type of Packaging: Private Label
Brands:
Saucelito Canyon

11241 Sauder's Eggs
570 Furnace Hills Pike
Lititz, PA 17543-0427
717-626-2074
Fax: 717-626-0493 800-233-0413
info@saudereggs.com www.saudereggs.com
Eggs
President: Paul Sauder
CEO: Mark Sauder
Customer Sales Manager: Brian Chmiel
Director of Operations: Joe Brussell
Estimated Sales: Under $500,000
Number Employees: 1-4
Type of Packaging: Food Service, Private Label
Brands:
Sauder's

11242 Saugy Inc.
9 Sachemor Rd
Cranston, RI 02920-4514
401-640-1879
Fax: 401-383-9374 866-467-2849
saugy@cox.net www.saugys.com
Frankfurters
President & CEO: Mary O'Brien
Estimated Sales: $900,000
Number Employees: 3
Type of Packaging: Consumer, Food Service, Private Label, Bulk

11243 Sausage Kitchen
36 Main St
Lisbon Falls, ME 04252-1507
207-353-5503
Fax: 207-353-8707 888-453-5503
www.sausagekitchen.com
Sausages
President: Maurice Bonneau
info@sausagekitchen.com
Plant Manager: David Parker
Estimated Sales: $350,000
Number Employees: 1-4

11244 Sausages by Amy
1141 W Lake St
Chicago, IL 60607
312-829-2250
Fax: 312-829-2098
Sausages
President: Amy Kurzawski
VP: Chico Kurzawski
Estimated Sales: $5-10 Million
Number Employees: 50-99

11245 Sausal Winery
7370 Highway 128
Healdsburg, CA 95448
707-433-2285
Fax: 707-433-5136 800-500-2285
Wines
President: David Demostene
Estimated Sales: Below $5 Million
Number Employees: 10-19
Brands:
Sausal Wines

11246 Saval Foods Corp
6740 Dorsey Rd
PO Box 8630
Elkridge, MD 21075-6205
410-379-5100
Fax: 410-379-8068 800-527-2825
www.savalfoods.com
Meats & poultry, refrigerated products, non-foods, produce, frozen foods, general grocery items, and seafood products available to the commercial restaurant segment of the foodservice industry.
President: Dennis Barry
dennisbarry@savalfoods.com
Vice President: Richard Hatcher
Marketing Manager: Bryan Bernstein
Human Resources Manager: Paul Self
dennisbarry@savalfoods.com
Operations/ Quality Control Manager: Ron Tew
Production Manager: Joe Savage
Number Employees: 100-249
Type of Packaging: Food Service, Private Label, Bulk
Brands:
Elite
Saval

11247 Savannah Bee Co.
211 Johnny Mercer Blvd
Savannah, GA 31410-2119
912-234-0688
Fax: 912-234-0125 800-955-5080
info@savannahbee.com savannahbee.com
Honey
President/Owner: Ted Dennard
info@savannahbee.com
Estimated Sales: $1.1 Million
Number Employees: 20-49

11248 Savannah Chanelle Vineyards
23600 Big Basin Way
Saratoga, CA 95070-9755
408-741-2934
Fax: 408-867-4824 www.savannahchanelle.com
Wines
President: Michael Ballard
tastingroom@savannahchanelle.com
Co-Owner: Kellie Ballard
Winemaker: Tony Craig
Estimated Sales: $5-10 Million
Number Employees: 10-19
Brands:
Savannah Chanelle Vineyards

11249 Savannah Cinnamon & Cookie Company
P.O.Box 20251
Bradenton, FL 34204
Fax: 912-233-3004 800-288-0854
www.savannahcinnamon.com
Cinnamon and other liquid flavors for coffee, tea and juices
Owner: Brian Wiggins
Estimated Sales: $1-2.5 Million
Number Employees: 10-19
Type of Packaging: Consumer
Brands:
Savannah Cinnamon Mix
Savannah Squares

11250 Savannah Food Co
575 Industrial Rd
PO Box 1000
Savannah, TN 38372-5977
731-925-1155
Fax: 731-925-1855 800-795-2550
info@savannahclassics.com
www.savannahclassics.com
Manufacturer and marketer of homestyle hushpuppies and authentic southern side dishes.
President: John Bryan
VP, Sales & Marketing: Jim Sisco
VP, Operations: Paul Stodard
Direction of Production: Lynn Austin
Year Founded: 1970
Number Employees: 50-99
Type of Packaging: Consumer, Food Service, Private Label
Other Locations:
Savannah Foods & Industries
Breman GA
Brands:
Neokura
San Like
San Orange
San Red
San Yellow
San-Ei

11251 Saveur Food Group
101 Central Park west
Suite 3C
New york, NY 10023
212-595-5425
Fax: 732-730-9913 abankier@saveurfood.com
Beef, potato pancakes, vegetable pancakes, maztoh balls
Co-President & CEO: Paul Bensabat
Co-President & CFO: Alain Bankier
Estimated Sales: $5-10 Million
Number Employees: 50-99
Brands:
Ratner's

11252 (HQ)Savino's Italian Ices
1126 S Powerline Road
Deerfield Beach, FL 33442-8121
954-426-4119
Frozen Italian ice fruit desserts
CEO: Sal Savino
Number Employees: 1-4
Type of Packaging: Bulk

11253 Savoia Foods
402 W Lincon Hwy
Chicago Heights, IL 60411
708-756-7600
Fax: 708-754-2133 800-867-2782
www.savoiafoods.com
Pasta, brands spaghetti, spinach spaghetti, inguine, fettucine and lasagne
President/Owner: Rudolph Bamonti
Sales Executive: Julia Bamonti
Estimated Sales: $2.5-5million
Number Employees: 10-19
Type of Packaging: Consumer, Food Service
Brands:
Savoia

11254 Savoie Industries
351 Highway 999
Belle Rose, LA 70341
225-473-9293
Fax: 225-473-9294
Blackstrap molasses and sugar
President/GM: Patrick Cancienne
Vice President: Paul Cancienne
Estimated Sales: $10-20 Million
Number Employees: 50-99
Type of Packaging: Consumer

11255 Savoie's Sausage and Food Products
1742 Highway 742
Opelousas, LA 70570-0549
337-942-7241
Fax: 337-948-9571 info@savoiesfoods.com
www.savoiesfoods.com
Sausage including hog's headcheese, boudin, andouille and tasso; also, barbecue sauce, roux and dressing mix
President/Owner: Eula Savoie
Vice President: Frieda Hunt
frieda@savoiesfoods.com
Marketing Manager: Frederick Lafleur
Operations Manager: Gerald Boullion
Estimated Sales: $9 Million
Number Employees: 50-99
Square Footage: 100000
Type of Packaging: Consumer, Private Label
Brands:
Cajun House
Real Cajun
Savoie's

11256 Savor Street
159 Spring Valley Rd
Unit 101
Reading, PA 19605
800-523-8253
www.savorstreet.com
Baked snacks
Marketing Communications Coordinator: Laura Unger

11257 Savory Foods
900 Hynes Ave SW
Grand Rapids, MI 49507-1091
616-241-2583
Fax: 616-241-6332 800-878-2583
www.pennstreetbakery.com
Processor and exporter of pork rinds
Owner: Dan Abraham
Safety Manager: Adam Dengel
VP Sales/Production: K Sanderlin
dan.abraham@savoryfoods.com
Production Manager: Ed Thompson
Plant Manager: Rigel Olmos

Food Manufacturers / A-Z

Number Employees: 20-49
Square Footage: 120000
Type of Packaging: Food Service, Private Label
Brands:
   Porkies
   Savory
   Southern Style

11258 Savoury Systems Inc
230 Industrial Pkwy # C
Branchburg, NJ 08876-3580
       908-526-2524
       888-534-6621
       savourysystems.com
Savory flavors manufacturer.
President: David Adams
customerservice@savourysystems.com
Vice President, Marketing: Jackie Sun
Vice President & Director of Sales: Kevin McDermott
Director of Operations: Alex Carillo
Estimated Sales: $12.6 Million
Number Employees: 10-19
Brands:
   Savorganic

11259 Sawtooth Winery
13750 Surrey Ln
Nampa, ID 83686-9128
       208-467-1200
Fax: 208-468-7934 www.sawtoothwinery.com
Wines
Winemaker/General Manager: Brad Pintler
President: Ken McCabe
Partner: Charles Pintler
Retail Manager/Events Coordinator: Ina DeBoer
Manager: Ken Mccabe
kmccabe@sawtoothwinery.com
Estimated Sales: $1-2.5 Million
Number Employees: 5-9
Brands:
   Sawtooth

11260 Saxby Foods
4120 98th Street NW
Edmonton, AB T6E 5A2
Canada
       780-440-4179
Fax: 780-440-4480
Frozen desserts including cakes and cheesecakes
President: Jonathan Avis
Quality Control: Ana Avalos
Public Relations: Thea Avis
Plant Manager: Sean Gillis
Purchasing: Rhys Amatori
Estimated Sales: F
Number Employees: 120
Square Footage: 100000
Type of Packaging: Private Label
Brands:
   Albertson's
   Safeway
   Walmart

11261 Saxon Chocolates
21 Coleville Rd
Toronto, ON M6M 2Y2
Canada
       416-675-6363
Fax: 416-675-2777 sales@saxonchocolates.com
       www.saxonchocolates.com
Belgian chocolates
President/Owner: Johan DeGrees
Estimated Sales: $2.3 Million
Number Employees: 20

11262 Saxon Creamery
855 Hickory Street
PO Box 206
Cleveland, WI 53015
       920-693-8500
Fax: 920-693-8400 info@saxoncreamery.com
       www.saxoncreamery.com
Cheeses
Plant Manager of Sales: Gerald Heimerl

11263 Sazerac Co Inc
101 Magazine St
5th Floor
New Orleans, LA 70130
       504-831-9450
Fax: 504-831-9452 info@sazerac.com
       www.sazerac.com
Distilled spirits

Marketing Services Director: Meredith Moody
PR Manager: Amy Preske
Year Founded: 1850
Estimated Sales: $50-100 Million
Number Employees: 14,800
Number of Brands: 36
Type of Packaging: Private Label
Brands:
   1792
   99 Brand
   Ancient Age
   Benchmark
   Bentley's
   Big House
   Blantons
   Bowman's
   Bowman's Small Batch
   Buckhorn
   Buffalo Trace
   Buffalo Trace Distillery Experiment
   Colonel Lee
   E.H. Taylor Jr.
   Eagle Rare
   Elmer T. Lee
   Firefly
   Flatboat
   George T. Stagg
   Hancock's
   Kentucky Gentleman
   Kentucky Tavern
   Old Charter
   Old Taylor
   Rockhill Farms
   SABI
   Setter
   Southern Comfort
   Ten High
   Tom Moore
   Two Stars
   Van Winkle
   Very Old Barton
   Virginia Gentlemen
   W.L. Weller
   Zackariah Harris

11264 Sazerac Company, Inc.
3850 N Causeway Blvd
Suite 1695
Metairie, LA 70002-3825
       866-729-3722
       info@sazerac.com
       www.sazerac.com
Manufacturer and exporter of bourbon, scotch, whiskey, gin and vodka; importer of scotch
President & CEO: Mark Brown
mbrown@bourbonwhiskey.com
Owner: Chaolai Wu
Partner: Scott Newitt
Vice President of Human Resources: Kathy Thelen
Marketing Services Director: Meredith Moody
VP Sales & Marketing: Steve Wyant
PR Manager: Amy Preske
Plant Manager: Byron Du Bois
Number Employees: 350
Square Footage: 360000
Brands:
   1792 Ridgemont Reserve Bourbon
   99 Schnapps
   Barton
   Glenmore
   Hartley Brandy
   Highland Mist Scotch
   House of Stuart Scotch
   Imperial Blent
   Inver House Scotch
   Jacques Bonet Brandy
   Kentucky Gentleman Bourbon-A-Blend
   Kentucky Tavern Bourbon
   Lauder's Scotch
   Meukow Cognac
   Monte Alban Mezcal
   Montezuma Blue
   Montezuma Tequila
   Montezuma Triple Sec
   Calypso Gold Rum
   Calypso Light Rum
   Canadian Host
   Canadian Ltd
   Canadian Supreme
   Capitan Gold Tequila
   Capitan Tequila & Triple Sec
   Capitan White Tequila
   Caravella
   Chi-Chi's Appletini

   Chi-Chi's Caribbean Mudslide
   Mr. Boston
   Northern Light Canadian
   Old Thompson Blend
   Pikeman Gin
   Sabroso Di Cafe Liqueur
   Amaretto De Sabroso
   Colonel Lee Bourbon
   Crystal Palace
   Czarina
   Di Amore
   Skol
   Ten High Bourbon
   Tom Moore
   Very Old Barton Bourbon
   Wave Flavored Vodkas
   Sambuca Di Amore
   El Toro Tequila
   Fleischmann's

11265 Scala-Wisell International Inc.
24 S Tyson Avenue
Suite 1
Floral Park, NY 11001
       516-437-8600
Fax: 516-437-8686 info@scala-wisell.com
       www.scala-wisellint.com
Manufacturer of candied fruit, sprinkles and toasted and sweetened coconut.
President: Carol Wisell
cwisell@scala-wisell.com
Type of Packaging: Bulk

11266 Scally's Imperial Importing Company Inc
4354 Victory Blvd
Staten Island, NY 10314-6733
       718-983-1938
Fax: 718-259-2195 scallyimperial@aol.com
Manufacturer and marketer of Mission San Juan 100% fruit juices and smoothies in single serve and multiserve containers.
President/Sales/Plant Manager: Alex Scarselli
CEO: Alessandro Scarselli
VP/Purchasing Director: Christine Scarselli
Estimated Sales: $5 Million
Number Employees: 1-4
Number of Brands: 3
Number of Products: 20
Square Footage: 10000
Type of Packaging: Consumer, Food Service, Private Label
Brands:
   Apple Brand Juices
   Fruit Ole Smoothies
   Mission San Juan Juices

11267 Scandia Seafood Company
130 Tillson Avenue
Rockland, ME 04841-3424
       207-596-7102
     Fax: 207-596-7105
Crabs, cold water shrimp, American lobster, Atlantic herring
President: Asger Jorgensen
Square Footage: 25000

11268 (HQ)Scandinavian Formulas Inc
140 E Church St
Sellersville, PA 18960-2402
       215-453-2500
Fax: 215-453-2508 800-288-2844
       www.scandinavianformulas.com
Manufacturer, importer and exporter of vitamins and supplements, chemicals and ingredients. Botanicals, extracts, oils, bulk tablets and soft gels.
President: Catherine Peklak
Marketing: Sylvie Millet
Sales/Purchasing: Mike Peklak
IT: Bob Blackledge
bob@scandinavianformulas.com
Estimated Sales: $1005000
Number Employees: 1-4
Number of Brands: 7
Number of Products: 7
Square Footage: 36000
Type of Packaging: Consumer, Private Label, Bulk
Other Locations:
   Scandinavian Natural Health
   Perkasie PA
Brands:
   Alkyrol
   Bilberry Extract
   Dhea

Food Manufacturers / A-Z

Lycopene
Melatonin
Salix Sst
Sincera Skin Care Products

11269 Scandinavian Laboratories
316 Front Street
Belvidere, PA 07823-1510
908-475-4754
Fax: 908-469-4912 866-623-2650
scanlabs@epix.net www.oceanaproducts.com
Nutritional products including shark liver and fish oils, essential fatty acids, effervescent tablets and liquid emulsions; importer and exporter of nutritional supplements including shark liver oils
President: Olav Sandnes
Contact: Susan Battillo
susan@oceanaproducts.com
Estimated Sales: $500,000
Number Employees: 5-9
Type of Packaging: Private Label, Bulk
Brands:
 Calcitrace
 Ecomega
 Glycomarine
 Oceana
 Pedia-Vit
 Promega
 Squalene

11270 Scenic Fruit Co
7510 SE Altman Rd
Gresham, OR 97080-8808
503-663-3434
Fax: 503-663-7095 877-927-3434
info@scenicfruit.com www.scenicfruit.com
Frozen berries
President: Judy England
CEO: Hugh Eisele
hugh.eisele@scenicfruit.com
Plant Manager: John Vasquez
Estimated Sales: $18 Million
Number Employees: 100-249
Type of Packaging: Food Service, Bulk

11271 Scenic Valley Winery
103 Coffee St
Lanesboro, MN 55949
507-259-4981
Fax: 507-467-2640
Wines
Owner: Karrie Ristau
Estimated Sales: $470,000
Number Employees: 5-9

11272 Schadel's Bakery
212 N Bullard Street
Silver City, NM 88061-5308
505-538-3031
Bakery
President/CEO: Dexter Seay
Estimated Sales: $500,000
Number Employees: 5-9

11273 Schaefers Market
411 Sinclair Lewis Ave
Sauk Centre, MN 56378-1350
320-352-6490
www.schaefersmarket.com
Frankfurters, bologna, sausage and poultry
Owner: Chris Lawinger
Estimated Sales: $17 Million
Number Employees: 10-19
Type of Packaging: Consumer

11274 Schaefers Market
411 Sinclair Lewis Ave
Sauk Centre, MN 56378-1350
320-352-6490
Fax: 320-352-2206 www.schaefersmarket.com
Meat packing and slaughtering
Owner: Chris Lawinger
Estimated Sales: Below $5,000,000
Number Employees: 10-19

11275 Schafer Fisheries Inc
2112 Sandridge Rd
Thomson, IL 61285-7709
815-259-4300
Fax: 815-259-4542 800-291-3474
Seafood
Owner: Mike Schafer
mike@schaferfish.com
Estimated Sales: $3-5 Million
Number Employees: 20-49

11276 Schaller & Weber Inc
2235 46th St
Astoria, NY 11105-1305
718-721-5480
Fax: 718-956-9157 800-847-4115
info@schallerweber.com www.winstonfarm.com
Ham and German-style sausage, poultry, cold cuts, cooked and smoked products, salami and cervelat and seafood
Owner: Ralph Schaller
jeremyschaller@gmail.com
Sales Exec: Jeremy Schaller
Estimated Sales: $12 Million
Number Employees: 50-99
Square Footage: 32000
Type of Packaging: Consumer

11277 Schaller's Bakery Inc
826 Highland Ave
Greensburg, PA 15601-4316
724-837-3660
Fax: 724-837-6764 800-241-1777
Baked goods
President: Warren Schaller
Contact: Weddell Schaller
donna.simmons@midohiodevelopment.com
Estimated Sales: $2 Million
Number Employees: 20-49
Square Footage: 63000
Type of Packaging: Consumer, Food Service, Private Label, Bulk

11278 Scharffen Berger Chocolate Maker
790 Tennessee St
San Francisco, CA 94107
866-608-6944
scharffenberger@worldpantry.com
www.scharffenberger.com
Dark chocolate
CEO: John Scharffenberger
CFO/COO: Jim Harris
Marketing: Norm Shea

11279 Schat's Dutch Bakeries
763 N Main St
Bishop, CA 93514-2427
760-873-7156
Fax: 760-872-4932 866-323-5854
schatsbakery@mindspring.com
Baked goods
Owner: Erick Schat
CFO: Mirika Marijke
Estimated Sales: Below $5 Million
Number Employees: 50-99
Brands:
 Erick Schat

11280 Schenk Packing Co Inc
1321 S 6th St
Mt Vernon, WA 98273-4919
360-336-2128
Fax: 360-336-3092 info@schenkpacking.com
www.schenkpacking.com
Processor and exporter of meat products; custom slaughtering available.
Owner/President: Steve Lenz
stevel@schenkpacking.com
Operations Managerr: Marcie Lenz
Number Employees: 20-49
Square Footage: 84672
Type of Packaging: Consumer, Food Service

11281 Schepps Dairy
3114 S Haskell Ave
Dallas, TX 75223
214-824-8163
Fax: 214-824-1526 800-395-7004
Dairy products including; fluid milk, buttermilk, cream, half & half, lactose free milk, cottage cheese, sour cream, orange juice, fruit drink, yogurt, creamers, cream cheese, ice cream mix, cream topping, butter, eggs
Director: Debra Bowen
Vice President: Pat Boyle
Sales Director: Steve Schenkel
Contact: Debra Drinane
debra_drinane@deanfoods.com
Parent Co: Dean Foods
Type of Packaging: Consumer, Food Service, Private Label, Bulk
Other Locations:
 Schepps Dairy
 Houston TX
Brands:
 Schepps Dairy
 Silk
 Horizon
 International Delight
 Oak Farms

11282 Schermer Pecan Co
811 S Veterans Blvd
Glennville, GA 30427-2800
912-654-2230
Fax: 912-654-2344 800-841-3403
losborne@leapfrogprco.com
www.schermerpecans.com
Manufacturer of pecans and pecan oil.
Owner: Putt Wetherbee
Manager: Melita Humphries
melita@schermerpecans.com
Number Employees: 100-249

11283 Schiavone's Casa Mia
1907 Tytus Avenue
Middletown, OH 45042-2367
513-422-8650
Fax: 513-422-8602
Sauces
President: Michael Schiavone
Estimated Sales: $500,000-$1 Million
Number Employees: 20-49

11284 Schiff Food Products CoInc
994 Riverview Dr
Totowa, NJ 07512-1129
973-237-1990
Fax: 973-237-1999 sales@schifffood.com
www.schifffoods.com
Manufacturer, importer and exporter of spices, seeds, herbs and dehydrated vegetables
President: David Deutscher
david.deutscher@schiffs.com
Estimated Sales: $15 Million
Number Employees: 20-49
Square Footage: 600000
Type of Packaging: Consumer, Private Label
Brands:
 Schiff Food

11285 Schiff Nutrition International
P.O. Box 224
Parsippany, NJ 07054-0224
415-433-3777
800-526-6251
www.schiffnutrition.com
Vitamins and nutritional supplements.
President/CEO: Tarang Amin
EVP/CFO: Joseph Baty
VP/General Counsel: Scott Milstein
VP Research/Development: Shane Durkee
Contact: Webster Jarom
websterj@schiffnutrition.com
SVP of Operations: Jon Fieldman
Brands:
 Move Free
 Schiff
 Megared
 Digestive Advantage
 Tiger's Milk
 Sustenex

11286 Schillinger Genetics Inc
4401 Westown Pkwy # 225
Suite 225
West Des Moines, IA 50266-6721
515-225-1166
Fax: 515-225-1177 866-769-7200
heartland@heartlandfields.com
www.schillgen.com
Manufacturer and exporter of soybeans
President: John Schillinger
Marketing/Sales Director: Karen Labenz
Estimated Sales: $10-20 Million
Number Employees: 10-19
Parent Co: Monsanto
Type of Packaging: Consumer, Bulk
Brands:
 Dekalb

Food Manufacturers / A-Z

11287 Schiltz Foods Inc
7 W Oak St
Sisseton, SD 57262-1440
605-698-7651
Fax: 605-698-7112 877-872-4458
jschiltz@schiltzfoods.com www.schiltzfoods.com
Processor and exporter of dressed geese and goose products
President: Richard Schiltz
richard.schiltz@schiltzfoods.com
VP/Director of Sales: James Schiltz
Estimated Sales: $2.1 Million
Number Employees: 100-249
Number of Brands: 4
Number of Products: 20
Square Footage: 136000
Type of Packaging: Consumer, Food Service, Private Label, Bulk
Brands:
  All American Holiday Goose
  Whetstone Valley

11288 Schimpffs Confectionery LLC
347 Spring St
Jeffersonville, IN 47130-3449
812-283-8367
Fax: 812-288-2229 info@schimpffs.com
www.schimpffs.com
Candy
Owner: Warren Schimpffs
info@schimpffs.com
Number Employees: 10-19

11289 Schirf Brewing Company
P.O. Box 459
250 Main Street
Park City, UT 84060-0459
435-649-0900
Fax: 435-649-4999 www.wasatchbeers.com
Beer
President: Greg Schirf
Contact: Paul Brown
paul@wasatchbeers.com
Estimated Sales: $20-50 Million
Number Employees: 50-99
Brands:
  Wasatch

11290 Schisa Brothers
1 Commerce Blvd
Syracuse, NY 13211
315-463-0213
Fax: 315-463-0248
Processes and manufactures meat and meat products.
President: Bruce Dew
Number Employees: 47
Type of Packaging: Consumer, Food Service

11291 Schlafly Tap Room
2100 Locust St
St Louis, MO 63103-1616
314-241-2337
Fax: 314-241-8101 gimmes@schlafly.com
www.schlafly.com
Beer, ale, lager, stout and seasonal beers
President: Tom Schlafly
CEO: James Pendegraft
CFO/COO: Keith Moszczenski
Marketing Director: Mitch Turner
Estimated Sales: $20-50 Million
Number Employees: 100-249
Parent Co: Saint Louis Brewery
Type of Packaging: Consumer, Food Service
Brands:
  Schlafly

11292 Schleswig Specialty Meats
Highway 59 South
Schleswig, IA 51461
712-676-3324
Fax: 712-676-3936
Manufacturer and packer of meats.
President: Richard Beatty
Plant Manager: Phil Smith
Estimated Sales: $5-10 Million
Number Employees: 25
Square Footage: 80000
Type of Packaging: Private Label

11293 Schloss Doepken Winery
9177 Old Route 20
Ripley, NY 14775-9510
716-326-3636
Wines
President: John Watso
schlossdoepkenwines@gmail.com
Estimated Sales: $500,000-$1 000,000
Number Employees: 1-4
Brands:
  Schloss Doepken

11294 Schlotterbeck & Foss Company
117 Preble St
Portland, ME 04101
207-772-4666
Fax: 207-774-3449 800-777-4666
www.schlotterbeck-foss.com
Spicy salsas, grilling and stir-fry sauces.
President: Peter Foss
CEO: Richard Foss
Founder: Augustus G. Schlotterbeck
Marketing Manager: Charles Foss
Sales Director: Arthur Kyncos
Contact: Ron Badgett
rbadgett@schlotterbeck-foss.com
Plant Manager: Richard Raymond
Purchasing Manager: Annmarie Bruns
Estimated Sales: $5200000
Number Employees: 20-49
Square Footage: 120000
Type of Packaging: Consumer, Food Service, Private Label, Bulk
Brands:
  Foss
  Mos-Ness

11295 Schlotzsky's
11401 Century Oaks Terrace
Suite 400
Austin, TX 78758
512-236-3600
800-846-BUNS
www.schlotzskys.com
Catering, prepared foods

11296 Schmidt Bros Inc
2425 S Fulton Lucas Rd
Swanton, OH 43558-9658
419-826-3671
Fax: 419-826-8696 800-200-7318
lawrence@schmidtbrosinc.com
www.schmidtbrosinc.com
Grower of produce including pumpkins
President: Bob Schmidt
bob@schmidtbrosinc.com
VP: Robert Schmidt
Marketing Manager: Kathy Judge
Sales Director: Allen Schmidt
Estimated Sales: $3.5 Million
Number Employees: 50-99
Square Footage: 1500000
Type of Packaging: Bulk

11297 Schneider Cheese
N4085 County Road M
Waldo, WI 53093
920-467-3351
Fax: 920-467-6184
Cheese
President: John Schneider
CFO: Thomas Paul
Quality Control: Jane Gau
Estimated Sales: $10-20 000,000
Number Employees: 130

11298 (HQ)Schneider Foods
321 Courtland Ave East
Kitchener, ON N2G 3X8
Canada
519-741-5000
Fax: 519-749-7400 www.schneiders.ca
Processor and exporter of frozen and refrigerated frankfurters, meat pies, sausage, ham, bacon, deli meats and poultry; fat and calorie reduced products available
President: Douglas Dodds
President (Cust. Foods): Paul Lang
VP Business: John Howard
Quality Control: Judy Tetker
R & D: Tim Gorgon
Number Employees: 5,500
Square Footage: 2920000
Type of Packaging: Consumer, Food Service, Private Label, Bulk
Other Locations:
  Schneider Corp.
  Ayr ON
Brands:
  Deli-Best
  Lifestyle
  Lunchmate
  Mini-Sizzlers
  Olde-Fashioned
  Red Hots
  Schneider's

11299 Schneider Foods
Perth County Road 139
Saint Marys, ON N4X 1C4
Canada
519-229-8900
Fax: 519-229-8953 800-567-1890
cwehniai@schneiderfoods.ca www.schneiders.ca
Frozen and fresh poultry
Founder: John Metz Schneider
Plant Manager: Cheryl Firby
Number Employees: 250-499
Parent Co: J.M. Schneider
Type of Packaging: Consumer, Food Service, Private Label

11300 Schneider Foods
550 Kipling Avenue S
Etobicoke, ON M8Z 5E9
Canada
416-252-5790
Fax: 416-252-6215 cwehniai@schneiderfoods.ca
www.schneiders.ca
Fresh and frozen beef
President/General Manager: Ron Flaury
CEO: Rick Young
Marketing Director: Doug Gingrich
Purchasing Agent: Carmela Cieri
Number Employees: 100-249
Parent Co: J.M. Schneider
Type of Packaging: Consumer, Food Service
Brands:
  Schneider Foods

11301 Schneider's Dairy Inc
726 Frank St
Pittsburgh, PA 15227
412-881-3525
Fax: 412-881-7722 www.schneidersdairy.com
Milk, buttermilk, fruit drinks, 100% juice, iced tea, fresh creams, sour cream, dips, and ice cream mix. Wholesaler of; butter, margarine, eggs, yogurt, cheese, cream cheese, cottage cheese, ice cream mix, bottled water. Serving schools, healthcare facilities, supermarkets, convenience stores, restaurants, and foodservice companies.
President: William Schneider
CEO: David Schneider
dschneider@schneidersdairy.com
Director: Joe Pysola
Year Founded: 1935
Estimated Sales: $73 Million
Number Employees: 250-499
Square Footage: 60000
Other Locations:
  Williamsport PA
  Seneca PA
  State College PA
  Washington PA

11302 Schneider-Valley Farms Inc
1860 E 3rd St
Williamsport, PA 17701-3923
570-326-2021
Fax: 570-326-2736
Milk including whole, low-fat, flavored and skim, buttermilk, ice cream products, sherbet, ice cream mixes, sour cream, dips, fruit juices/drinks and iced teas; wholesaler/distributor of whipped topping, cottage cheese, yogurt, butter etc
President: William Schneider
Director: Clyde Mosteller
Vice President: Ed Schneider
edjr@schneidervfdairy.com
VP Sales: Edward Schneider
Number Employees: 20-49
Parent Co: Schneider's Dairy
Type of Packaging: Food Service

11303 Schnuck Markets, Inc.
11420 Lackland Rd.
PO Box 46928
St. Louis, MO 63146
314-994-9900
800-264-4400
nourish.schnucks.com
Grocery, bakery, deli, dairy, seafood, meat, frozen foods, produce, floral, liquor, and more.
Chairman/CEO: Todd Schnuck

Year Founded: 1939
Estimated Sales: $3.1 Billion
Number Employees: 14,500
Brands:
  Valutime
  Schnucks
  Full Circle
  Top Care
  Schnucks
  Culinaria

11304 Schobert's Cottage Cheese Corporation
586 Seiberling Street
Akron, OH 44306-3237
                                          216-733-6876
Cottage cheese
President: Mike Barr
Estimated Sales: $2.5-5 000,000
Number Employees: 5

11305 Schoep's Ice Cream
514 Division St
Madison, WI 53704-5512
                                          608-249-6411
        Fax: 608-249-7900 800-236-4050
             www.schoepsicecream.com
Ice cream, frozen yogurt, light ice cream, frozen custard, sherbet and novelties.
President: Paul Thomsen
CFO: Amy Mueller
amueller@schoeps.us
Number Employees: 100-249
Type of Packaging: Consumer, Food Service, Private Label, Bulk
Brands:
  Schoep's

11306 Schoppaul Hill Winery atIvanhoe
301 S Locust Street
Denton, TX 76201-6055
                                          940-380-9463
                             Fax: 940-387-5471
Wines
President: John Anderson
CFO: Gary Anderson
Estimated Sales: $5-9.9 000,000
Number Employees: 3

11307 (HQ)Schramsberg Vineyards
1400 Schramsberg Rd
Calistoga, CA 94515-9624
                                          707-942-6668
            Fax: 707-942-4336 800-877-3623
          info1@schramsberg.com www.schramsberg.com
Sparkling wine
Owner: Sagir Ahmed
VP Sales & Marketing: Laurent Sarazin
Manager Public Relations: Matthew Levy
sahmed@phmhotels.com
Number Employees: 50-99
Number of Brands: 2
Number of Products: 7
Other Locations:
  Schramsberg Vineyards
  Alijo
Brands:
  J. Schram
  Mirabelle
  Schramsberg

11308 Schreiber Foods Inc.
400 N. Washington St.
Green Bay, WI 54301
                                          920-437-7601
        Fax: 920-437-1617 contact@schreiberfoods.com
                  www.schreiberfoods.com
Dairy products such as cheese, yogurt, milk, milk powders and more.
President/CEO: Ron Dunford
SVP/CFO: Matt Mueller
SVP, U.S. Operations: Tony Nowak
SVP, Information Services: Tom Andreoli
SVP, Quality & Innovation: Vinith Poduval
SVP & Chief Commercial Officer: Trevor Farrell
Year Founded: 1945
Estimated Sales: Over $1 Billion
Number Employees: 8,000
Type of Packaging: Consumer, Food Service, Private Label, Bulk
Other Locations:
  Tempe AZ
  Gainesville GA
  Carthage MO
  Clinton MO
  Monett MO
  Mt Vernon MO
  Ravenna NE
  Shippensburg PA
  Nashville TN
  Stephenville TX
  Logan UT
  Smithfield UT
  Wisconsin Rapids WI
Brands:
  American Heritage
  Clearfield
  Cooper
  Laferia
  Lov-It
  Menu
  Raskas
  Ready-Cut
  School Choice
  Schreiber

11309 Schug Carneros Estate Winery
602 Bonneau Rd
Sonoma, CA 95476-9749
                                          707-939-9363
        Fax: 707-939-9364 800-966-9365
        info@schugwinery.com www.schugwinery.com
Wines
President: Walter Schug
walter@schugwinery.com
Co-Owner: Gertrud Schug
Sales/Marketing Director: Alex Schug
Director of Retail Sales: David Cumming
Winery Chef: Kristine Schug
Winemaker: Michael Cox
Estimated Sales: $5-10 Million
Number Employees: 10-19
Brands:
  Schug

11310 Schuil Coffee Co
3679 29th St SE
Grand Rapids, MI 49512-1811
                                          616-956-6815
        Fax: 616-956-7928 sales@schuilcoffee.com
                 www.schuilcoffee.com
Coffee
President: Lori Sytsma
lori@schuilcoffee.com
Estimated Sales: $500,000-$1 Million
Number Employees: 20-49
Type of Packaging: Private Label
Brands:
  Coppets
  Ibc
  Schuil Coffee

11311 (HQ)Schulze & Burch BiscuitCo
1133 W 35th St
Chicago, IL 60609
                                          773-927-6622
                 www.schulzeburch.com
Formed, baked, chewy and crunchy bars, toaster pastries, fruit bars, wire cut, laminated, extruded or rotary molded cookies and crackers, blended, coated or bases cereal and ingredients
VP of Sales: Steve Podracky
VP of Operations: Paul Salina
Production Supervisor: James Doubek
Year Founded: 1896
Estimated Sales: $96 Million
Number Employees: 100-249
Number of Brands: 3
Square Footage: 400000
Type of Packaging: Consumer, Food Service, Private Label, Bulk
Brands:
  Pop Ups
  Snackin Fruits
  Toast'em

11312 (HQ)Schumacher Wholesale Meats
1114 Zane Ave N
Golden Valley, MN 55422-4679
                                          763-546-3291
            Fax: 763-546-0053 800-432-7020
Processor and wholesaler/distributor of meat
President: John F Schumacher
Sales/Marketing Manager: Matt Schumacher
Operations Manager: Bob Timm
Purchasing: Bob Timm
Estimated Sales: $6700000
Number Employees: 20-49

Type of Packaging: Consumer, Food Service, Private Label, Bulk
Brands:
  Crown
  Great Meats
  Valley

11313 Schuman Cheese
40 New Dutch Ln
Fairfield, NJ 07004
                                          800-888-2433
                 info@schumancheese.com
                 www.arthurschuman.com
Cheese
CEO: Neal Schuman
nschuman@arthurschuman.com
Strategy Analyst: Keith Schuman
National Account Manager: Allison Schuman
Business Manager: Ian Schuman
Year Founded: 1945
Estimated Sales: $20.9 Million
Number Employees: 100-249
Square Footage: 50400
Brands:
  Cello(c)
  Montforte

11314 Schuster Marketing Corporation
6251 W Forest Home Ave
Milwaukee, WI 53220-1916
                                          414-543-2999
            Fax: 414-543-5588 888-254-8948
Tablet pressed chewing gum with or without active ingredients such as nutraceuticals.
President: Stephen P Schuster
VP Sales: Heidi Schuster
Estimated Sales: $5-10 Million
Number Employees: 48
Brands:
  Blitz Power Mints

11315 Schwab Meat Co
1111 Linwood Blvd
Oklahoma City, OK 73106-7039
                                          405-235-2376
            Fax: 405-236-4694 800-888-8668
                 websales@schwabmeat.com
                 www.schwabmeat.com
Fresh and frozen beef and pork
Owner: Scott Schwab
scott@schwabmeat.com
Marketing Director: Ron Walton
CFO: Gail Anderson
Estimated Sales: $10-20 Million
Number Employees: 20-49
Type of Packaging: Consumer, Food Service, Private Label, Bulk
Brands:
  Schwab

11316 Schwan's Company
115 W. College Dr.
Marshall, MN 56258
                                          507-532-3274
                                          800-533-5290
                 questions@schwans.com
                 www.schwanscompany.com
Frozen foods including pizza, desserts and snacks. Serves restaurants and schools.
President, Schwan's Consumer Brands: Julie Francis
CEO: Dimitrios Smyrnios
Senior VP/Chief Information Officer: Kathy Persian
Senior VP, Product Innovation/Dvlp.: Stacey Fowler Meittunen
Year Founded: 1952
Estimated Sales: $3 Billion
Number Employees: 12,000
Number of Brands: 12
Number of Products: 300+
Type of Packaging: Consumer, Food Service, Private Label
Brands:
  RED BARON
  MAMA ROSA'S
  FRESCHETTA
  TONY'S
  SCHWAN'S
  SCHWAN'S CHEF COLLECTION
  MRS. SMITH'S
  EDWARDS
  PAGODA
  MINH
  BIG DADDY'S
  VILLA PRIME PIZZERIA

Food Manufacturers / A-Z

11317 Schwan's Food Service Inc.
115 W. College Dr.
Marshall, MN 56258
877-302-7426
questions@schwans.com
www.schwansfoodservice.com
Asian food, frozen pizza and desserts.
President, Schwan's Consumer Brands: Julie Francis
CEO: Dimitrios Smyrnios
Estimated Sales: $3 Billion
Number Employees: 12,000
Number of Brands: 12
Parent Co: Schwan's Company
Type of Packaging: Consumer, Food Service, Private Label, Bulk
Other Locations:
  Atlanta GA
  Crossville TN
  Montgomery AL
  Pembroke NC
Brands:
  Red Baron
  Tony's
  Freschetta
  Big Daddy's
  Mrs. Smith's
  Edwards
  Villa Prima
  Minh
  Coyote Grill
  Beacon Street Cafe
  Stilwell
  Schwan's

11318 Schwebel Baking Co.
965 E. Midlothian Blvd.
P.O. Box 6018
Youngstown, OH 44502
330-783-2860
Fax: 330-782-1774 800-860-2867
www.schwebels.com
White, wheat, whole and multigrain breads; deli buns, rolls and subs; bagels, light breads, pitas, flat bread and tortillas; cinnamon, italian, sour dough, potato, high fiber and raisin breads.
President/CEO: Steven Cooper
VP Marketing & Corporate Communications: Lee Schwebel
Senior VP, Sales: Alyson Winick
Year Founded: 1906
Estimated Sales: $130 Million
Number Employees: 1000-4999
Number of Brands: 6
Square Footage: 125000
Type of Packaging: Consumer, Food Service, Private Label, Bulk
Other Locations:
  Akron OH
  Saybrook OH
  Austintown OH
  Canton OH
  Cleveland OH
  Hilliard OH
  Reynoldsburg OH
  Mansfield OH
  Solon OH
  Struthers OH
  Euclid OH
  Erie PA
  Reno PA
Brands:
  Schwebel's
  Cinnabon
  Schwebel's Organic
  Schwebel's Selects
  Sun-Maid
  'taliano

11319 Scialo Brothers Bakery
257 Atwells Ave
Providence, RI 02903-1521
401-421-0986
Fax: 401-274-6117 877-421-0986
www.scialobakery.com
Italian bread, bakery products, pastries, cakes, pies, cookies and wedding cakes
Co-Owner: Lois Ellis
scialobakery@scialobakery.com
Co-Owner: Carol Gaeta
Estimated Sales: Less Than $500,000
Number Employees: 10-19

11320 Sconza Candy Co
1 Sconza Candy Ln
Oakdale, CA 95361-7899
209-845-3700
Fax: 510-638-5792 877-568-8137
customerservice@sconzacandy.com
www.sconza.com
Candy including brittles, panned, butterscotch, hard, filled, mints, butter toffee nuts and seasonal
President: James Sconza
jrsconza@sconzacandy.com
Executive Vice President: Ron Sconza
Estimated Sales: $6 Million
Number Employees: 100-249
Square Footage: 200000
Type of Packaging: Consumer, Food Service, Private Label, Bulk
Brands:
  Bean Heads
  Bruiser
  Fruit Breaker
  Jordanettes
  Meteorites
  Pip Squeaks
  Sconza
  Screamer
  Wizbanger
  Zoygs

11321 Scooty's Wholesome Foods
PO Box 18898
Boulder, CO 80308-1898
303-440-4025
Fax: 970-663-6013
Gourmet and specialty foods
President: Scott Silverman
Estimated Sales: Under $500,000
Number Employees: 1-4

11322 Scotian Gold
2900 Lovett Road
Coldbrook, NS B4R 1A6
Canada
902-679-2191
Fax: 902-679-4540 888-726-8426
scotiangold.com
Tree fruit cooperative with 30 grower members.
CEO: David Parrish
Director of Sales: Dennis MacPherson
Estimated Sales: $21 Million
Type of Packaging: Consumer, Private Label
Brands:
  Scotian Gold

11323 Scotsburn Ice Cream Co.
4600 Armand-Frappier St.
Saint-Hubert, QC J3Z 1G5
Canada
800-501-1150
www.scotsburn.com
By the scoop ice cream and frozen desserts.
Year Founded: 1900
Estimated Sales: $175 Million
Number Employees: 375
Number of Brands: 1
Number of Products: 5
Square Footage: 52786
Parent Co: Agropur Cooperative
Type of Packaging: Consumer, Food Service, Private Label

11324 Scott Adams Foods
288 Newton Sparta Rd
Newton, NJ 07860
973-300-2091
www.pdifoods.com
Vegan meat alternative and vegetarian wraps
President: Jack Parker
CEO: Scott Adams
Estimated Sales: $1-3 Million
Number Employees: 1-4
Parent Co: Parker Development, Inc
Type of Packaging: Private Label
Brands:
  Dilberito
  Protein Chef

11325 Scott Farms Inc
7965a Simpson Rd
Lucama, NC 27851-9357
919-284-4014
Fax: 919-284-4872 877-284-4030
info@scottfarms.com www.scottfarms.com
Grower and shipper of sweet potatoes
Owner: Linwood Scott
sales@scottfarms.com
Estimated Sales: Below $5 Million
Number Employees: 5-9
Brands:
  Sonny's Pride

11326 Scott Hams
1301 Scott Rd
Greenville, KY 42345-4683
270-338-3402
Fax: 270-338-6643 800-318-1353
scotthams@att.net
Country cured and fully cooked hams, bacon, smoked sausage, turkey, jams and fruit butters, sorghum molasses, honey, dried apples, relish, bean soup mix, biscuits, pork cracklins and dog biscuits
Owner: June Scott
scotthams@att.net
Estimated Sales: Less Than $500,000
Number Employees: 1-4
Brands:
  Scott's

11327 Scott's Auburn Mills
503 Dockins St
Russellville, KY 42276-2065
270-726-2080
mail@auburnkyusa.com
www.auburnkyusa.com
White and yellow corn meal and wheat flour
President: Ray Clark
Vice President: Dave Clark
Chief Miller: Joe Crain
Production: Robert Covington
Estimated Sales: $2 Million
Number Employees: 20-49
Square Footage: 80000
Type of Packaging: Consumer, Food Service, Private Label, Bulk

11328 Scott's Candy
819 South Veterans Blvd
Glennville, GA 30427
608-837-8020
Fax: 608-837-0763 800-356-2100
Processor and exporter of boxed and tinned chocolates
CEO: Gary Ricco
National Sales Manager: James Regan
Contact: Gary Ricco
gricco@wisconsincheeseman.com
Estimated Sales: $3-5 Million
Number Employees: 20-49
Parent Co: Wisconsin Cheeseman
Type of Packaging: Consumer, Private Label
Brands:
  Classic Choice
  Scott's

11329 Scott's Sauce Co Inc
1205 N William St
Goldsboro, NC 27530-2163
919-734-0711
800-734-7282
info@scottsbarbequesauce.com
www.scottsbarbecuesauce.com
Barbecue sauces
Owner: A Scott
ascott@scottsbarbecuesauce.com
Estimated Sales: Less Than $500,000
Number Employees: 5-9
Square Footage: 28000
Parent Co: Scott's Barbecue
Type of Packaging: Consumer
Brands:
  Scott's Barbeque Sauce

11330 Scott's of Wisconsin
301 Broadway Dr
Sun Prairie, WI 53590
608-837-8020
Fax: 608-837-0763 800-693-0834
customerservice@wisconsincheeseman.com
www.wisconsincheeseman.com
Cheese spreads, chocolate candy
CEO: Holly Berkenstadt
President: Jay Singer
Marketing Director: Charlie Kesler
Sales Director: Jim Regan
Purchasing Manager: Mark Pelton
Estimated Sales: $1-2.5 Million
Number Employees: 20-49
Type of Packaging: Private Label

Food Manufacturers / A-Z

Brands:
- Grace Rush
- Nutty Pleasures
- Pecanbacks
- Scott's
- Scott's of Wisconsin
- Scottie
- Trinkets

11331 Scott-Bathgate
149 Pioneer Avenue
Winnipeg, MB R3C 2M8
Canada
204-943-8525
Fax: 204-957-5902 800-216-2990
www.scottbathgate.com
Snack foods, food colorings, mustard, peanut butter, candy and shelled and in-shell sunflower seeds
National Director: Vic Homyshyn
Office/Credit Manager: D Sheridan
Production Manager: Jens Fieting
Type of Packaging: Food Service
Brands:
- Food Club
- Nutty Club

11332 Scotty Wotty's Creamy Cheesecake
216 Us Highway 206
Suite 14
Hillsborough, NJ 08844-4384
908-281-9720
Fax: 908-281-9720
Cheesecake
President: Scott Discount
Brands:
- Scotty Wotty's

11333 Scray's Cheese
2082 Old Martin Rd
De Pere, WI 54115-8015
920-336-8359
Fax: 920-336-0553 ScrayCheese@yahoo.com
www.scraycheese.com
Cheese
President: Jim Scray
Estimated Sales: $500,000-$1 000,000
Number Employees: 10-19
Type of Packaging: Private Label
Brands:
- Scray's Cheese

11334 Screamin' Onionz
399 Manchester Rd.
Poughkeepsie, NY 12603
www.loveonionz.com
Sliced, slow-cooked onions in flavoured sauces
Founder: Richard Romano
Year Founded: 2015
Number of Brands: 1
Number of Products: 3
Type of Packaging: Consumer, Private Label

11335 Scripture Candy
1350 Adamsville Industrial Pkw
Birmingham, AL 35224-3300
205-798-0701
Fax: 205-798-0702 888-317-7333
Info@scripturecandy.com
www.scripturecandy.com
Candy
Owner: Brian Adkins
badkins@scripturecandy.com
Number Employees: 10-19

11336 Sculli Brothers
622C Industrial Park Drive
Yeadon, PA 19050
215-336-1223
Fax: 215-336-1225 Scullibrothers@gmail.com
Ham, italian sausage, coteghino, and prosciuto
President: Robert Sculli
VP: Dawn Sculli
Estimated Sales: $150,000
Number Employees: 2
Square Footage: 11212
Type of Packaging: Private Label, Bulk
Brands:
- Bari

11337 Sea Bear Smokehouse
605 30th St
Anacortes, WA 98221-2884
360-293-4661
Fax: 360-293-4097 800-645-3474
Processor and exporter of smoked fish and seafoods
President: Mike Mondello
CEO: Michael Mondello
mikem@seabear.com
VP Direct to Consumer: Patti Fisher
Marketing Manager: Barb Hoenselaar
Director Operations: Cathy Hayward-Hughes
Estimated Sales: $10.8 Million
Number Employees: 20-49
Type of Packaging: Consumer, Bulk

11338 Sea Best Corporation
PO Box 753
Ipswich, MA 01938-0753
978-768-7475
Fax: 314-241-1377
Seafood

11339 Sea Breeze Fruit Flavors
441 Main Road
Towaco, NJ 07082-1201
973-334-7777
Fax: 973-334-2617 800-732-2733
info@seabreezesyrups.com
www.seabreezesyrups.com
Syrups including chocolate, pancake and milkshake; sundae toppings, bar mixes, juice concentrates, soda, iced tea, lemonade, fruit juice, flavored water and beverage dispensing equipment.
President: Steve Sanders
Vice President: Josh Sanders
Technical Director: Frank Maranino
Contact: George Apostolopoulos
george@seabreezesyrups.com
Production Manager: Paul Maranino
Estimated Sales: $25-49.9 Million
Number Employees: 50-99
Number of Brands: 6
Type of Packaging: Consumer, Food Service, Private Label
Brands:
- Bosco
- Joshua Miguel
- New York Bash
- Sea Breeze
- Toshimi
- Tropic Beach

11340 Sea Dog Brewing Company
1 Bowdoin Mill Island
Suite 100
Topsham, ME 04086
207-725-0162
Fax: 207-947-8720 www.seadogbrewing.com
Beer
General Manager: Larry Killam
General Manager: Seth Hale
Contact: Jess Choate
jessc@seadogbrewing.com
Number Employees: 35
Type of Packaging: Consumer, Food Service
Brands:
- Sea Dog

11341 Sea Farm & Farm Fresh Importing Company
855 Monterey Passage Road
Monterey Park, CA 91754
323-265-7075
Fax: 323-265-9578
Seafood products.
CEO: Hooi Eng Ooi
VP Operations: S Tan
Estimated Sales: $5-10 Million
Number Employees: 10-19

11342 Sea Fresh USA Inc
45 All American Way
PO Box 398
North Kingstown, RI 02852-2607
401-583-0200
Fax: 401-583-0222 mfox@seafreshusa.com
www.seafreshusa.com
Seafood including Rhode Island calamari, tuna, fluke, monkfish, skate, scup
Owner: James Fox
james@seafreshusa.com
Accounting: Cheryl Anyzaeski
Estimated Sales: $20-50 Million
Number Employees: 20-49

11343 Sea Gold Seafood Products Inc
38 Blackmer St
New Bedford, MA 02744-2614
508-993-3060
Fax: 508-993-3070 seagold01@msn.com
www.seagolddips.com
Dips including gourmet seafood and crab dip, buttered seafood and lobster dip, seafood and jalapeno crab dip, spicy shrimp dip, seafood and shrimp scampi dip, cajun seafood and crab dip, clams casino clam dip, and seafood newburgdip.
Owner: Micheal Trazzra
seagold1@aol.com
Operations Manager: Wendy Harwood
Estimated Sales: Below $5 Million
Number Employees: 10-19
Number of Brands: 1
Number of Products: 9
Square Footage: 20000
Type of Packaging: Consumer, Food Service
Brands:
- Sea Gold

11344 Sea Horse Wharf
245 W Point Rd
Phippsburg, ME 04562-5127
207-389-2312
Fax: 207-389-1005
Seafood
Owner: Douglas Scott
Estimated Sales: $300,000-500,000
Number Employees: 1-4

11345 Sea Lyons
9093 Springway Ct
Spanish Fort, AL 36527-5522
251-626-2841
Fax: 251-626-2841
Seafood.
President: Martha Lyons
Vice President: Wade Lyons

11346 Sea Pac Of Idaho Inc
4074 N 2000 E
Filer, ID 83328-5033
208-326-3100
Fax: 208-326-5935
Trout and salmon jerky, smoked rainbow trout, and salmon sausages
President/General Manager: Ken Ashley
aken@seapacofidaho.com
Estimated Sales: $7.10 M
Number Employees: 20-49

11347 Sea Pearl Seafood
14120 Shell Belt Rd
Bayou La Batre, AL 36509-2308
251-824-2129
Fax: 251-650-1321 800-872-8804
www.sea-pearl.com
Frozen and breaded shrimp and oysters
Owner: Joseph G Ladnier
info@sea-pearl.com
Plant Manager: Allen Mayfield
Estimated Sales: $3.3 Million
Number Employees: 20-49
Type of Packaging: Consumer, Food Service, Bulk
Brands:
- Neptune Delight
- Sea Pearl Seafood Co., Inc.

11348 Sea Ridge Winery
13404 Dupont Road
Occidental, CA 95465
707-874-1707
800-692-5780
info@broncowine.com www.broncowine.com
Wines
President: Dan Wickham
Estimated Sales: $500-1 Million
Number Employees: 1-4

11349 Sea Safari
785 E Pantego St
Belhaven, NC 27810
252-943-3091
Fax: 252-943-3083 800-688-6174
seasafari@beaufortco.com
Processor and exporter of frozen crawfish and crab meat; also, canned blue crab meat

Food Manufacturers / A-Z

President/Finance & Sales Executive: Topper Bateman
General Manager: Guinn Leverett
Director Marketing: Christine Costley
Sales Manager: Frances Williams
Contact: Bateman Topper
tbateman@seasafari.com
Estimated Sales: $400,000
Number Employees: 4
Square Footage: 160000
Parent Co: Sea Safari
Type of Packaging: Consumer, Food Service
Brands:
    Acadian Gourmet
    Ecrevisse Acadienne
    Louisianas Best

11350 Sea Salt Superstore
19004 Highway 99
Lynnwood, WA 98036
    Fax: 425-640-2500 866-999-7258
customerservice@seasaltsuperstore.com
www.seasaltsuperstore.com
Gourmet foods, exotic spices and hand crafted natural sea salts to the gourmet food customers.
Contact: Jenny Mackie
jenny@seasaltsuperstore.com

11351 Sea Salt Superstore
11604 Airport Rd
Suite D300
Everett, WA 98204
    425-249-2331
    Fax: 425-249-2334
customerservice@seasaltsuperstore.com
www.seasaltsuperstore.com
Flavored sea salt
President: Scott Mackie
Customer Service & Sales: Jenny Mackie
Estimated Sales: $1 Million
Number Employees: 2-10
Brands:
    Caravel Gourmet
    Healthy Himalaya
    Sealina Spa
    Sea Salt Superstore

11352 Sea Snack Foods Inc
914 E 11th St
Los Angeles, CA 90021-2091
    213-622-2204
    Fax: 213-622-7845
Processor and exporter of cooked IQF shrimp and seafood cocktails
President/CEO: Fred Ockrim
fred@seasnack.com
VP: Jeffrey Kahn
Sales Director: Peter Peterson
Plant Manager: Alfred Dolor
Estimated Sales: $7 Million
Number Employees: 50-99
Square Footage: 8000
Type of Packaging: Consumer, Food Service
Brands:
    O.K. Brand
    Restaurant Row
    Sea Snack
    Twin Harbors

11353 Sea Stars Goat Cheese
1122 Soquel Ave
Santa Cruz, CA 95062-2106
    831-423-7200
    Fax: 831-454-0838
Cheese
Owner: Nancy Gassney
Estimated Sales: $2.5-5 000,000
Number Employees: 10-19
Type of Packaging: Private Label

11354 Sea Veggies
5801 S Malt Ave
Suite 220
Commerce, CA 90040
    323-728-4762
    Fax: 323-728-4761 info@sea-veggies.com
www.sea-veggies.com
Seaweed snacks
Number of Products: 10

11355 Sea View Fillet Company
15 Antonio Costa Ave
New Bedford, MA 02740-7347
    508-984-1406
    Fax: 508-984-1411
Seafood
Manager: Sandy Harbick
Estimated Sales: $10-24.9 000,000
Number Employees: 50-99

11356 Sea Watch Intl
8978 Glebe Park Dr
Easton, MD 21601-7004
    410-822-7500
    Fax: 410-822-1266 sales@seaclam.com
www.seawatch.com
Canned and frozen clams, crab cakes, extruded calamari rings, blue crab meat, squid, shrimp, soups and seafood chowders.
Vice President: Bernie Carr
bernie@seaclam.com
Controller: Betty Bain
Director, Quality Assurance: Larry Hughes
Senior Vice President of Sales: Michael Wyatt
Year Founded: 1978
Estimated Sales: $36.1 Million
Number Employees: 250-499
Number of Brands: 4
Square Footage: 15000
Type of Packaging: Food Service, Private Label
Brands:
    American Original
    Cap'ns Catch
    Capt. Fred
    Eastern Shore Foods, Llc
    Mid-Atlantic Foods
    Mr Frosty
    Old Salt Seafood
    Sailor's Choice
    Seawatch
    Tucker's Cove

11357 Sea-Fresh Seafood Market
1432 Hillcrest Rd
Mobile, AL 36695
    251-634-8650
    Fax: 714-897-4090
Seafood
President: Patrick Meacham
CFO: Rusty Brennan

11358 SeaBear Wild Salmon
605 30th Street
Anacortes, WA 98221
    360-293-4661
    Fax: 888-487-6427 800-645-3474
smokehouse@seabear.com www.seabear.com
Smoked seafood: salmon, cod, crab, scallops and rainbow trout.
President: Mike Mondello
mikem@seabear.com
Sales & Strategic Communication: Christine Bondick
Chief Operating Officer: Patti Fisher
Year Founded: 1957
Estimated Sales: $3 Million
Number Employees: 50-200
Type of Packaging: Food Service
Brands:
    Gerard & Dominique
    Pacific Alaska
    SeaBear

11359 SeaPak Shrimp
1867 Demere Rd
Saint Simons Island, GA 31522
    888-732-7251
seapak.com
Shrimp, seafood

11360 SeaPerfect Atlantic Farms
PO Box 12139
Charleston, SC 29422-2139
    843-762-0022
    Fax: 843-795-6672 800-728-0099
Scallops and clams
President: Carlos Celle
Sales Director: Michelle Black
General Manager: Knox Grant
Estimated Sales: $2.3 Million
Number Employees: 45
Square Footage: 136000
Brands:
    Seaperfect

11361 SeaSpecialties
1111 NW 159th Dr
Miami, FL 33169-5807
    305-625-5112
    Fax: 305-625-5528 800-654-6682
Seafood
Quality Control: Irvin Norss
CFO: Michael Metzkes
Estimated Sales: $20-50 Million
Number Employees: 100-249

11362 Seaberghs Frozen Foods
200 Westchester Avenue
White Plains, NY 10601-4510
    914-948-6377
Frozen foods
President: Harry Rich
Estimated Sales: $1-2.5 000,000
Number Employees: 1-4

11363 Seaboard Foods
9000 W. 67th St.
Suite 200
Shawnee Mission, KS 66202
    800-262-7907
info@seaboardfoods.com seaboardfoods.com
Fresh, frozen and processed pork products.
President/CEO: Darwin Sand
Vice President, Marketing: Tom Blumhardt
Vice President, Plant Operations: Marty Hast
Year Founded: 1995
Estimated Sales: $38.8 Million
Number Employees: 4,986
Number of Brands: 5
Parent Co: Seaboard Corporation
Type of Packaging: Consumer, Food Service, Private Label, Bulk
Other Locations:
    Processing Plant
    Guymon OK
    Ham Deboning Plant
    Reynosa, MEXICO
    Mount Dora Farms Management
    Houston TX
    Live Production Operations
    Kansas
    Daily's Premium Meats Bacon Plant
    Salt Lake City UT
    Daily's Premium Meats Bacon Plant
    Missoula MT
    Live Production Operations
    Colorado
    Live Production Operations
    Texas
Brands:
    Daily's Premium Meats
    Prairie Fresh
    Seaboard Farms
    St. Joe Pork
    67th Street BBQ
    Quick Fire Premium Meats

11364 Seabreeze Fish
2311 R Street
Bakersfield, CA 93301-2986
    661-323-7936
    Fax: 805-323-7936
Seafood
Owner: Ben Kim
Estimated Sales: $300,000-500,000
Number Employees: 1-4

11365 (HQ)Seabrook Brothers & Sons
85 Finley Road
Seabrook, NJ 08302
    856-455-8080
    Fax: 856-455-9282 seabroc@seabrookfarms.com
www.seabrookfarms.com
Frozen vegetables
Procurement: Ivin Seabrook
Sales: Brian Seabrook
Customer Service: Keith Mount
Estimated Sales: $93 Million
Number Employees: 325
Number of Brands: 2
Number of Products: 150
Square Footage: 350000
Type of Packaging: Consumer, Food Service, Private Label, Bulk
Brands:
    Seabrook Farms
    Somerdale

Food Manufacturers / A-Z

11366 Seafare Market Wholesale
PO Box 671
Moody, ME 04054-0671
207-646-5160
Fax: 408-294-3948
Seafood
President: John Foye
Estimated Sales: $10-20 Million
Number Employees: 10-19

11367 Seafood Connection
841 Pohukaina St # I
Suite I
Honolulu, HI 96813-5332
808-591-8550
Fax: 808-591-8445 sales@seafood-connection.com
www.seafood-connection.com
Seafood and gourmet products
President: Stuart Simmons
Estimated Sales: $10-20 Million
Number Employees: 10-19

11368 Seafood Dimensions Intl
22343 LA Palma Ave # 106
Suite 106
Yorba Linda, CA 92887-3804
714-692-6464
Fax: 714-282-8997
Seafood
Owner: Christi Lang
Estimated Sales: $1.4 Million
Number Employees: 5-9
Number of Brands: 20
Number of Products: 50
Type of Packaging: Food Service
Brands:
  20th Century Foods
  Brooks Street Baking
  Harvest Farm
  Lil' Fisherman
  Midship
  Neptune
  Schoner

11369 Seafood Express
179 Rossmore Rd
Brunswick, ME 04011
207-729-0887
Fax: 207-721-9146
Seafood
Contact: Thida Pov
tpov@seafoodexpress.in

11370 Seafood Hawaii Inc
875 Waimanu St # 634
Suite 634
Honolulu, HI 96813-5265
808-597-1971
Fax: 808-538-1973
Seafood
President: Jed J Inouye
Estimated Sales: $5-10 Million
Number Employees: 20-49

11371 Seafood International
1051 Old Henderson Hwy
Henderson, LA 70517-7805
337-228-7568
Fax: 337-228-7573 www.seafoodfromnorway.com
Seafood
Owner: Roy Robert
seafoodintl@cox-internet.com
Estimated Sales: $3,300,000
Number Employees: 5-9

11372 Seafood Merchants LTD
900 Forest Edge Dr
Vernon Hills, IL 60061-3105
847-634-0900
Fax: 847-634-1351
sales@theseafoodmerchants.com
Seafood
President: Roy Axelson
bonnie@theseafoodmerchants.com
CEO: Bonnie Axelson
bonnie@theseafoodmerchants.com
Sales Exec: Bonnie Axelson
Estimated Sales: $10-20 Million
Number Employees: 20-49
Square Footage: 23000
Type of Packaging: Consumer, Food Service, Bulk

11373 Seafood Packaging Inc
2120 Poydras St
New Orleans, LA 70112-1339
504-522-6677
Fax: 504-522-9008 800-949-9656
ksharp@seafoodpackaging.com
www.seafoodpackaging.com
Seafood
Owner: Kent Sharp
ksharp@seafoodpackaging.com
Estimated Sales: $5-10 Million
Number Employees: 5-9
Type of Packaging: Consumer

11374 Seafood Plus Corporation
10860 Bear Island Avenue
Orland Park, IL 60467-5397
708-795-4820
Fax: 708-795-7719
Seafood
President: Harry A Davros

11375 Seafood Producers Co-Op
2875 Roeder Ave
Suite 2
Bellingham, WA 98225
360-733-0120
Fax: 360-733-0513 jreynolds@spcsales.com
www.spcsales.com
Processor and exporter of salmon, halibut, sablefish and rockfish.
Chief Executive Officer: Joe Morelli
VP, Sales & Marketing: Jeff Reynolds
Sales Manager: Kurt Sigfusson
Traffic & Logistics: Jessie Koehler
Plant Manager: Craig Shoemaker
Year Founded: 1944
Estimated Sales: $45 Million
Number Employees: 5-9
Type of Packaging: Food Service, Bulk
Brands:
  Alaska Gold
  Longliner
  Sitka Gold

11376 Seafood Services
49 Bromfield St
Newburyport, MA 01950-3003
508-999-6785
Fax: 508-993-4001
Seafood
President: David Horton
Contact: Dan Canavan
dcanavan@foodinno.com
Estimated Sales: $20-50 Million
Number Employees: 20-49

11377 Seafood Specialties
155 E Vienna St
Anna, IL 62906-1839
618-833-6083
Fax: 618-833-9433
www.seafoodspecialtiesonline.com
Seafoods
Owner: Al Bush
afishiebusiness@hotmail.com
Human Resources: Bridget Sprinkle
Estimated Sales: Under $500,000
Number Employees: 1-4

11378 Seajoy
6619 S Dixie Hwy
PO Box 344
Miami, FL 33143
305-669-0108
Fax: 302-663-0312 877-537-1717
www.seajoy.com
Shrimp including raw head-on whole shrimp, raw shell-on tails, raw shell-on E-Z peel meats, raw peeled & deveined tail on or off, uncut, raw peeled, butterfly meat, raw breaded shrimp meat, and raw peeled & deveined meat on skewers
Administrative President: Peder Jacobson
VP Sales & Operations: Brad Price
Estimated Sales: $220 Thousand
Brands:
  Seajoy
  Cjoy
  Bluefield
  Seabrook

11379 Sealand Lobster Corporation
PO Box 423
Tenants Harbor, ME 04860-0423
207-372-6247
Fax: 207-389-1819
Lobster

11380 Sealaska Corp
1 Sealaska Plz
Suite 400
Juneau, AK 99801
907-586-1512
Fax: 907-586-2304 corpcomm@sealaska.com
www.sealaska.com
Seafood
CEO: Anthony Mallott
CFO: Carrie Rorem
Vice President: David Aldrich
COO: Terry Downes
Year Founded: 1971
Estimated Sales: $100-200 Million
Number Employees: 20-49
Brands:
  Ocean Beauty Seafoods

11381 Seald Sweet
1991 74th Ave
Vero Beach, FL 32966-5199
559-636-4400
Fax: 772-569-5110 www.sealdsweet.com
Grower, importer and exporter of citrus products including oranges, grapefruit, lemons, clementines, minneolas, tangerines and tangeros.
President: Jeff Baskovich
jbaskovich@sealdsweet.com
CFO: Christine Wallace
VP: David E Mixon
Marketing Manager: Kim Flores
Estimated Sales: $5-10 Million
Number Employees: 50-99
Square Footage: 60000
Type of Packaging: Food Service, Bulk
Brands:
  Florigold
  Seald Sweet

11382 Seapoint Farms
20042 Beach Blvd
Suite 102
Huntington Beach, CA 92648-3702
714-374-9831
info@seapointfarms.com
www.seapointfarms.com
Edamame and seaweed products
CEO: Kevin Cross
kcross@seapointfarms.com
National Sales Manager: Tim Boyer
COO: Phil Siegel
Estimated Sales: 1.6 Millin
Number Employees: 5-9

11383 Seaside Ice Cream
PO Box 734
Pelham, NY 10803-0734
914-636-2751
Fax: 631-728-1653
Ice cream
Owner: Arthur Haas

11384 Season Brand
80 Avenue K
Newark, NJ 07105
201-553-1100
contact@seasonproducts.com
www.seasonproducts.com
Canned fish and specialty vegetables
Brand Manager: Isabel Hill
Brands:
  SEASON(c)

11385 Season Harvest Foods
4906 El Camino Real # 206
Suite 206
Los Altos, CA 94022-1444
650-968-2273
Fax: 877-413-3894 sales@seasonharvestfoods.com
www.seasonharvestfoods.com
Organic vegetable and spice supplier.

Food Manufacturers / A-Z

11386 Seatech Corporation
16825 48th Ave W Ste 222
Lynnwood, WA 98037
425-487-3231
Fax: 425-835-0367 johnw@seatechcorp.com
www.seatechcorp.com
Frozen shrimp, crab and scallops
President: John Wendt
j.wendt@seatech.com
CFO: Jim Schantz
ice President: Todd Wendt
Estimated Sales: $6 Million
Number Employees: 3
Number of Brands: 2
Square Footage: 4000
Type of Packaging: Consumer, Food Service, Private Label, Bulk
Brands:
 Clean Kitchen
 Chiquititos
 Seatech

11387 Seatrade Corporation
P.O.Box 421
Hoboken, NJ 07030-0421
201-963-5700
Fax: 201-963-0577
Seafood
VP/Sales Manager: Richard Mendelson

11388 Seattle Bar Company
3302 Wallingford Avenue N
Seattle, WA 98103-9039
206-601-4301
Fax: 206-282-3548
Owner: Beth Campbell
Number Employees: 1-4
Brands:
 Seattle Bar

11389 Seattle Chocolates
1180 Andover Park W
Tukwila, WA 98188-3909
425-264-2800
Fax: 425-264-2811 800-334-3600
info@seattlechocolates.com
www.seattlechocolates.com
Chocolate truffles and bars
President and CEO: Jean Thompson
VP Operations: Niel Campbell
Marketing Manager: Kirsty Ellison
Controller: Joe Slye
Estimated Sales: $10 Million
Number Employees: 10-19
Number of Brands: 1
Number of Products: 11
Type of Packaging: Consumer, Private Label, Bulk
Brands:
 Chick Chocolates
 Seattle Chocolates
 Skinny Truffles

11390 Seattle Gourmet Foods
18200 Segale Park Dr B
Tukwila, WA 98188
425-656-9076
Fax: 425-656-8059 800-800-9490
sales@seattlegourmetfoods.com
www.seattlegourmetfoods.com
Chocolate meltaways, coffee spoons, molasses chews, thin mints, pecan delights, panned nuts, jams, jellies, fruit toppings, whipped taffy
General Manager: Tom Means
Controller: Mary Bides
marybides@seattlegourmetfoods.com
Distribution & Logistics Manager: Mike Harris
Year Founded: 1993
Estimated Sales: $63 Million
Number Employees: 275
Number of Brands: 11
Brands:
 Anna's Honey
 Buckeye Beans and Herbs
 Biringer's Farm Fresh
 Coffaro's Baking Company
 Cucina Fresca
 Dilettante Chocolates
 FungusAmongUs
 Maury Island Farm
 Merlino Baking Co.
 Myntz Breathmints
 Quinn's

11391 Seattle Seasonings
3920 E Lidstrom Hill Rd
Port Orchard, WA 98366-4855
360-871-1511
Fax: 360-377-0642 contact@twosnootychefs.com
www.twosnootychefs.com
Seasonings, cooking enhancers, salts, rubs
Co-Owner: Gary Fuller
contact@twosnootychefs.com
Number Employees: 1-4

11392 (HQ)Seattle's Best Coffee
PO Box 3717
Seattle, WA 98124-8891
800-611-7793
customercare@seattlesbest.com
www.seattlesbest.com
Ground coffee and beans
Manager: James Strasbaugh
Contact: Donald Blankenship
don.blankenship@seattle.gov
Estimated Sales: $10.9 Million
Number Employees: 100-249
Type of Packaging: Consumer, Food Service

11393 Seaver's Bakery
719 East Center St
Kingsport, TN 37660
423-245-2441
Fax: 423-578-3434 www.seaversbakery.com
Baked goods
President: Ralph Coomer
President/CEO: Richard Seaver
Plant Manager: Richard McKinney
Estimated Sales: $250,000
Number Employees: 10-19
Type of Packaging: Consumer

11394 Seavey Vineyard
1310 Conn Valley Rd
St Helena, CA 94574-9610
707-963-8339
Fax: 707-963-0232 info@seaveyvineyard.com
www.seaveyvineyard.com
Wines
President: William Seavey
Director of Sales and Marketing: Alex Kajani
Manager: Dorie Seavey
dseavey@seaveyvineyard.com
Estimated Sales: $500,000-$1 Million
Number Employees: 5-9
Brands:
 Seavey Cabernet Sauvignon
 Seavey Chardonnay
 Seavey Marlot

11395 Seaview Lobster Co
43 Government St
Kittery, ME 03904-1652
207-439-1599
Fax: 207-439-1476 800-245-4997
orders@seaviewlobster.com
www.seaviewlobster.com
Seafood
Owner: Tom Flanagan
seaviewlob@comcast.net
Estimated Sales: $.5-1 million
Number Employees: 10-19

11396 Seawater Food & Beverage
1212 Dolton Dr
Suite 301B
Dallas, TX 75207-2114
214-537-5070
info@seawatersolutions.com
mediterraneaseawater.com
Cooking seawater, zumo juice and potato chips
National Sales Manager: Jerald Morris
Purchasing & Logistics Manager: Lorena Pierce
Brands:
 Mediterranea Seawater for Cooking
 Seawater Soaked Potato Chips
 Zumo Juices

11397 Seaway Company
PO Box 868
Fairhaven, MA 02719-0800
508-992-1221
Fax: 508-992-1253
Seafood
Owner: Steve Doonan
Estimated Sales: $1-3 Million
Number Employees: 1-4

11398 Sebastiani Vineyards
389 4th St E
Sonoma, CA 95476-5790
707-938-5532
Fax: 707-933-3390 855-232-2338
tastingroom@sebastiani.com
Wines
Proprietor: Bill Foley
President/CEO: Mary Ann Sebastiani Cuneo
COO: Emma Swain
Operations Manager: Paul Bergna
Sebastiani Vineyards & Winery Winemaker: Mark Lyon
Estimated Sales: $5-10 Million
Number Employees: 50-99
Type of Packaging: Consumer

11399 Sebastiano's
4448 Heatherdowns Blvd
Toledo, OH 43614-3113
419-382-0615
Fax: 419-382-0615
Ice cream, frozen desserts
Owner: Jonathan Sagaser
Vice President: Helane Stiebler
Estimated Sales: Less Than $500,000
Number Employees: 5-9

11400 Sechler's Fine Pickles
5685 State Road 1
Saint Joe, IN 46785
260-337-5461
Fax: 260-337-5771 800-332-5461
showroom@sechlerspickles.com
Pickles
Owner: David Sechler
General Manager: Max Troyer
Sales Executive: Mike Meyers
Estimated Sales: $4 Million
Number Employees: 32
Square Footage: 116000

11401 Sechrist Brothers
32 E Main St
Dallastown, PA 17313-2206
717-244-2975
Fax: 717-244-6532 sechristbrosmeats@gmail.com
www.sechristbros.com
Processor and packer of meat including bologna, smoked ham, frankfurters and sausage
President: George Sechrist
gssiii@earthlink.net
VP: Jacob Sechrist
Estimated Sales: $910,000
Number Employees: 5-9
Square Footage: 40000
Type of Packaging: Consumer

11402 Secret Garden
10989 County 14
PO Box 544
Park Rapids, MN 56470-2119
218-732-4866
Fax: 218-732-2007 800-950-4409
sgmorg@wcta.net www.secretgardengourmet.com
Gourmet wild rice, bread, entree and seasoning mixes
President: Anne Morgan
sgmorg@wcta.net
Sales/Marketing: Andrea Roberts
Estimated Sales: Less Than $500,000
Number Employees: 1-4
Square Footage: 24000
Type of Packaging: Consumer, Private Label
Brands:
 Anne's Country Gourmet
 Continental Cuisine
 Creole Classics
 Midhaven Farm Cafe
 Midheaven Farm
 Pastry Perfect
 Secret Garden
 Soup For Singles
 Swany White
 Swany White Certified Organic
 The Secret Garden

11403 Secret Tea Garden
5559 West Boulevard
Vancouver, BC V6M 3W6
Canada
604-261-3070
Fax: 604-261-3075 info@secretgardentea.com
www.secretgardentea.com

Special varieties of tea
President: Erin McBeath
VP: With Kathy
Estimated Sales: Less than $500,000
Number Employees: 5

11404 Sedlock Farm
1557 Knoxville Road
Lynn Center, IL 61262-8504
309-521-8284
Fax: 309-521-8284
Fresh asparagus and asparagus products including fettucine; also, vinegars, hot pepper and jellies
Owner/CEO: John Sedlock
VP Manufacturing: Patricia Sedlock
Estimated Sales: Under $300,000
Number Employees: 6
Type of Packaging: Consumer, Food Service, Bulk

11405 Sedona Baking Company
c/o Risvold's Inc.
1234 W. El Segundo Blvd.
Gardena, CA 90247
323-770-2674
Fax: 323-770-0800 tbrandon@risvolds.com
risvolds.com
Cakes, particularly espresso
Founder: Sally McIntyre
CEO, Risvold's Inc.: Tim Brandon
Year Founded: 1991

11406 See Smell Taste
315 Sutter Street
5th Floor
San Francisco, CA 94108
415-986-4216
Fax: 415-986-4217 info@seesmelltaste.com
www.seesmelltaste.com
Herbs and spices

11407 See's Candies
20600 South Alameda Street
Carson, CA 90810
Fax: 800-275-4733 800-347-7337
qdordering@sees.com www.sees.com
Confectionary and chocolates
President & CEO: Charles Huggins
CFO: Ken Scott
General Manager: Jane Wellsplant
Estimated Sales: $.5-1 million
Number Employees: 5-9
Square Footage: 880000
Parent Co: See's Candies
Type of Packaging: Consumer
Brands:
See's Candies

11408 Seed Enterprises Inc
679 19th Rd
West Point, NE 68788-4510
402-372-3238
Fax: 402-372-2627 888-440-7333
Soybeans
President: Conrad Reeson
Estimated Sales: $1-3 Million
Number Employees: 5-9
Square Footage: 70000
Brands:
Sunrise

11409 Seeds of Change
P.O. Box 4908
Rancho Dominguez, CA 90220
888-762-7333
www.seedsofchange.com
Organic, non-GMO seeds of herbs and vegetables
Co-Founder: Alan Kapuler
CEO: Andrew Behar
Year Founded: 1989
Estimated Sales: $58 Million
Number Employees: 120
Parent Co: Mars, Inc.

11410 Seenergy Foods
121 Jevlan Drive
Woodbridge, ON L4L 8A8
Canada
905-850-2544
Fax: 905-850-2563 800-609-7674
info@seenergyfoods.com www.seenergyfoods.com
Processor and exporter of frozen vegetables including vegetable patties and IQF (individually quick frozen) beans

President/CEO: Shreyas Ajmera
Marketing/Sales: Carl McLaughlin
Estimated Sales: $3.2 Million
Number Employees: 80
Type of Packaging: Consumer, Food Service, Private Label, Bulk
Brands:
Presidents Choice

11411 Segall Nathan Co Inc
1667 Federal Dr # 12
Montgomery, AL 36107-1103
334-279-3174
Fax: 334-279-1751
Produce
Manager: Reid Barnes
nathansegallco@bellsouth.net
Estimated Sales: $3-5 Million
Number Employees: 5-9

11412 Seger Egg Corporation
P.O. Box 265
Farina, IL 62838-0265
618-245-3301
Fax: 618-245-3552
Eggs
President: Larry Seger
Sales/Marketing: Larry Pemberton
Estimated Sales: $10-20 000,000
Number Employees: 50-99

11413 Seghesio Family Vineyards
700 Grove St
Healdsburg, CA 95448-4753
707-433-0545
Fax: 707-433-0545 seghesio@seghesio.com
www.seghesio.com
Winery, specializing in zinfadel and Italian varietals.
CEO/President: Eric Martin
Chief Financial Officer: Pat Delong
Grower Relations & Viticulture Manager: Ned Neumiller
Ambassador: Pete Seghesio
Chief Operating Officer: Pat Delong
Production Manager/Winemaker: Ted Seghesio
Estimated Sales: $3.4 Million
Number Employees: 5-9
Number of Brands: 1
Parent Co: Crimson Wine Group
Type of Packaging: Consumer, Food Service
Brands:
Seghesio

11414 Seitenbacher America LLC
11505 Perpetual Drive
Odessa, FL 33556
727-376-3000
Fax: 727-376-4662
seitenbacheramerica@verizon.net
www.seitenbacher.com
Grain mix, berry mix, Honey Chia Muesli, cooking oils, nuts, cookies, cereals
President: Willi Pfannenschwarz
Manager: Harry Pfannenschwarz
Sales: Debbie Roberts
Contact: Harry Pfannenschwarz
harryp@seitenbacher.com
Estimated Sales: $600,000
Number Employees: 15
Square Footage: 11200

11415 Sejoyia Foods
195 Ctc Blvd
Louisville, CO 80027-3144
855-293-5577
customerservice@sejoyia.com sejoyia.com
Cookies and snacks
Founder & CEO: Sequoia Cheney
Brands:
Brussel Bytes
Cocoroons
Snips

11416 (HQ)Select Food Products
120 Sunrise Avenue
Toronto, ON M4A 1B4
Canada
416-759-9316
Fax: 416-759-9310 800-699-8016
www.selectfoodproducts.com
Manufacturers and exporter of salad dressings, sauces, salsas, relishes, mustard, gravies, canned dinners, etc; importer of tomatoes and tomato paste
President: Paul Fredricks

Number Employees: 150
Square Footage: 464000
Type of Packaging: Consumer, Food Service, Private Label, Bulk
Brands:
Duthie
Horne's
Laing's
Oxford Inn
Select

11417 Select Harvest USA
14827 W Harding Rd
Turlock, CA 95380
209-668-2471
Fax: 209-668-4988 info@selectharvestusa.com
selectharvestusa.com
Almonds
CEO: Robert Nunes

11418 Select Origins
PO Box 1748
Mansfield, OH 44901-1748
419-924-5447
General groceries
National Sales Manager: Noel Thompson
Estimated Sales: $5-10 000,000
Number Employees: 20

11419 Select Supplements Inc
5800 Newton Dr
Carlsbad, CA 92008-7311
760-431-7509
Fax: 760-804-8073
hectorg@selectsupplements.com
www.selectsupplements.com
Nutraceuticlas and other dietary supplement products.
Vice President: Hector Gudino
heg@select-ssi.com
Executive VP: Toshifumi Asada
QA/QC Manager: David Dean
Production Supervisor: James Morales
Purchasing Supervisor: Cheryl Moore
Estimated Sales: $990,000
Number Employees: 5-9

11420 Selecto Sausage Co
7120 Canal St
Houston, TX 77011-2754
713-926-1626
Mexican products including sausage, spices and tortillas
President: Carlos Gonzalez
Estimated Sales: $3-5 Million
Number Employees: 5-9
Type of Packaging: Consumer

11421 Selina Naturally
4 Celtic Dr
Arden, NC 28704-9157
828-299-9005
Fax: 828-654-0529 800-867-7258
info@selinanaturally.com
www.selinanaturally.com
Flavored Celtic sea salt
President/CEO: Selina Delangre
selina@celtic-seasalt.com
CFO: Theresa Imhoff
Estimated Sales: $4 Million
Number Employees: 20-49
Square Footage: 38000

11422 Sells Best
PO Box 428
Mishawaka, IN 46546-0428
574-255-1910
Fax: 574-258-6162 800-837-8368
www.coravent.com
Bakery mixes including breads, doughnuts, cakes and muffins including low fat, no cholesterol or preservatives and sugar free
President: Gary Sells
Office Manager: Kathy Campole
VP Sales: Coleman Caldwell
Director Manufacturing: Steven Surmay
Purchasing Manager: James Allen
Estimated Sales: $9 Million
Number Employees: 5-9
Square Footage: 80000

Food Manufacturers / A-Z

11423 Selma Good Company
PO Box 101
Selma, AL 36702
334-412-4214
robert@selmagood.com
gmommas.com
Cookies
Founder & Owner: Robert Armstrong
Estimated Sales: Under $500,000
Number Employees: 2-10
Brands:
  G MOMMAS

11424 Selma's Cookies
2023 Apex Ct
Apopka, FL 32703-7720
407-884-9433
Fax: 407-884-6121 800-992-6654
www.selmas.com
Gourmet cookies, brownies and crispy rice treats.
President: Selma Sayin
selma@selmas.com
Estimated Sales: Less than $500,000
Number Employees: 50-99

11425 Selwoods Farm Hunting Preserve
706 Selwood Rd
Alpine, AL 35014-5431
256-362-7595
Fax: 256-362-3856 800-522-0403
www.selwoodfarm.com
Smoked turkey and hams, cakes, mustards, jams, cookkies, stone ground grits, and pancake mix
Owner: Dell Hill
Estimated Sales: $1-3 Million
Number Employees: 5-9
Type of Packaging: Consumer

11426 Semifreddi's Bakery
1980 N Loop Rd
Alameda, CA 94502-3540
510-596-9930
877-LOV-SEMI
www.semifreddis.com
Sourdough bakery
Contact: Michael Anderson
m.anderson@abbott.com
Number Employees: 50-99

11427 Seminis Vegetable SeedsInc
2700 Camino Del Sol
Oxnard, CA 93030-7967
805-485-7317
info@seminis.com
www.seminis.com
Hybrid vegetable seeds
VP Marketing: Jorge Christlieb
CEO: Bruno Ferrari
CFO: Gaspar Alvarez
IT: Erik Ackerman
erik.ackerman@seminis.com
Number Employees: 20-49
Parent Co: Seminis Vegetable Seeds
Brands:
  Petoseed
  Royal Sluis

11428 Seminole Foods
1966 Commerce Circle
P.O.Box 305
Springfield, OH 45501
Fax: 352-245-8534 800-881-1177
customerservice@seminolefoods.com
www.seminolefoods.com
Fresh ground horseradish and fine sauces
President: Robert Schneider
Contact: Mary Lerchen
marylerchen@seminolefoods.com
Estimated Sales: Below $5 Million
Number Employees: 10
Square Footage: 76000
Type of Packaging: Consumer, Food Service, Private Label
Brands:
  Seminole

11429 Sempio Foods
12928 Moore St.
Cerritos, CA 90703
562-207-9540
Fax: 562-207-5498 en.sempio.com
Soy sauce, noodles, seafood, yondu, Korean hot sauce, tea and vinegar.
President: Woong-kyu Lee
National Marketing Manager: Duffield Gary
HR Manager: Julie Lee
Year Founded: 1946
Estimated Sales: $2.5 Million
Number Employees: 5-9
Brands:
  Sempio

11430 Senape's Bakery Inc
222 W 17th St
Hazleton, PA 18201-2426
570-454-0839
sfpayer@erols.com
Bread and pizza dough
President: Mary Lou Marchetti
Marketing: Mary Lou Marchetti
Estimated Sales: Below $5 000,000
Number Employees: 20-49

11431 Senba USA
23447 Cabot Blvd
Hayward, CA 94545
510-264-5850
Fax: 510-264-0938 888-922-5852
aoki@senbausa.com www.senbausa.com
Liquid sauces including teriyaki, beef and tempura; also, miso soup bases; importer of spray dried alcohol powder and tea extract; also, contract packaging and dry blending available
Sales: Hiro Aoki
Contact: Fernando Garcia
fgarcia@senbausa.com
Estimated Sales: $4.2 Million
Number Employees: 20-49
Square Footage: 52000
Parent Co: Senba Foods Company
Type of Packaging: Consumer, Food Service, Private Label, Bulk

11432 Sencha Naturals
912 E 3rd Street
Building 101
Los Angeles, CA 90013
213-346-9470
Fax: 213-947-1723 888-473-6242
inquiry@senchanaturals.com
www.senchanaturals.com
Green tea mints and green tea bars
President: David Kerdoon
Contact: Noe Claros
noe.claros@senchanaturals.com
Operations Manager: Desiree Thomas
Number Employees: 15

11433 Seneca Foods Corp
606 S Tremont St
Princeville, IL 61559-9468
309-385-4301
Fax: 309-385-2696 www.senecafoods.com
Canned vegetables including asparagus, pumpkins, green beans, corn and peas; also, salads including German potato, bean and garden salads
Manager: Wally Hochsprung
Vice President: Van Riper
Manager: L Dallinger
ldallinger@chiquita.com
Plant Manager: David Stoner
Estimated Sales: $10-20 Million
Number Employees: 100-249
Square Footage: 480000
Parent Co: Owatonna Canning Company
Type of Packaging: Consumer, Food Service, Private Label

11434 (HQ)Seneca Foods Corp
3736 S Main Steet
Marion, NY 14505
315-926-8100
webmaster@senecafoods.com
www.senecafoods.com
Largest processor of fruits and vegetables in North America
President & CEO: Kraig H. Kayser
kkayser@senecafoods.com
Chairman: Arthur Wolcott
SVP Technology and Planning: Carl Cichetti
Sr VP of Sales & Marketing: Dean Erstad
Sr. VP & Chief Administrative Officer: Cynthia Fohrd
Exec. VP & COO: Paul Palmby
Year Founded: 1949
Estimated Sales: Over $1 Billion
Number Employees: 1000-4999
Number of Brands: 6
Square Footage: 7000
Type of Packaging: Consumer, Food Service, Private Label
Other Locations:
  Modesto CA
  Geneva NY
  Leicester NY
  Marion NY
  Buhl ID
  Payette ID
  Lebanon PA
  Princeville IL
  Dayton WA
  Yakima WA
  Arlington MN
  Blue Earth MN
  Glencoe MN
Brands:
  Aunt Nellie's
  Cherry Man
  Green Valley
  Libby's
  Read
  Seneca Snacks

11435 Seneca Juice
PO Box 997
Marion, NY 14505-0997
315-926-3228
Juice
President/CEO: Edward Lutten
Sales Manager: C Rothfuss
Sr. VP Operations: Ricke Kress
Estimated Sales: $5-10 Million
Number Employees: 50-99
Parent Co: Tree Top

11436 Senomyx Inc
4767 Nexus Center Dr
San Diego, CA 92121-3051
858-646-8300
Fax: 858-404-0752
Flavor ingredients.
President/CEO: John Poyhonen
john.poyhonen@senomyx.com
CFO/SVP: Tony Rogers
VP/General Counsel/Corporate Secretary: Catherine Lee
SVP/Chief Commercial Development Officer: Sharon Wicker
VP, Information Technology: Lorenzo Pena
Estimated Sales: $28 Million
Number Employees: 50-99
Number of Brands: 3
Brands:
  Bittermyx
  Savorymyx
  Sweetmyx

11437 Senor Felix's Gourmet Mexican
4265 Maine Ave
Baldwin Park, CA 91706-3312
626-960-2800
Fax: 626-560-2855 senorfelix@ffci.us
Mexican fresh and frozen food, including enchiladas, burritos, taquitos, tamales, salsa, guacamole dip, etc
Owner: Lulu Juco
Controller: Sam Tabani
VP Sales/Marketing: Don O'Neill
Estimated Sales: $.5-1 million
Number Employees: 50-99
Type of Packaging: Private Label
Brands:
  Delicioso
  Pacifico
  Senor Felix's

11438 Senor Murphy Candymaker
1904 Chamisa St
Santa Fe, NM 87505-3440
505-988-4311
Fax: 505-988-2050 877-988-4311
chocolate@senormurphy.com
www.senormurphy.com
Candy
Owner: Rand Levitt
chocolate@senormurphy.com
VP: Bob Murphy
Estimated Sales: $770000
Number Employees: 5-9
Type of Packaging: Consumer

Food Manufacturers / A-Z

11439 Senor Pinos de Santa Fe
2600 Camino Entrada
Santa Fe, NM 87507-0491
505-473-3437
Fax: 505-473-5808 senorpinos@aol.com
Blue-corn flour, southwestern specialties
Owner: Nate Pino
Estimated Sales: $1 Million
Number Employees: 30
Brands:
  Josie's Best Blue Tortilla Chips

11440 Sensational Sweets
355 Sweets Ln
Lewisburg, PA 17837-7759
570-524-4361
Fax: 570-524-5360 info@sensationalsweets.com
www.sensationalsweets.com
Gourmet fudge, fudge bites, drizzled popcorn, dipped pretzels, and lollypops
Owner: Virginia Feitner
sweets@dejazzd.com
Estimated Sales: Less than $500,000
Number Employees: 10-19

11441 Sensible Foods LLC
PO Box 7345
Santa Rosa, CA 95407
707-569-0170
Fax: 707-762-1635 888-222-0170
Dried fruit and vegetable snacks. 100% natural, gluten free, and GMO free.
President/CEO: David Baxes
db@sensiblefoods.com
Vice President: Alan Christie
Type of Packaging: Consumer, Bulk

11442 Sensible Portions
4600 Sleepytime Drive
Boulder, CO 80301
973-283-9220
Fax: 973-283-2799 800-913-6637
www.sensibleportions.com
All natural and portion control snacks such as multi grain crisps, mini multi grain crisps, soy crisps, mini soy crisps, pita crackers, and pita chips.
President: Jason Cohen

11443 Sensient Flavors and Fragrances
2800 W Higgins Road
Suite 900
Hoffman Estates, IL 60169
847-755-5300
Fax: 847-755-5350
corporate.communications@sensient.com
www.sensientflavorsandfragrances.com
Flavoring extracts and syrups.
President, Flavors & Fragrances Group: E. Craig Mitchell
Estimated Sales: $100-200 Million
Number Employees: 1,000-4,999
Parent Co: Sensient Technologies Corporation

11444 (HQ)Sensient Technologies Corp
777 E Wisconsin Ave
Milwaukee, WI 53202-5304
414-271-6755
www.sensient.com
Colors, flavors and fragrances.
Chair/President/CEO: Paul Manning
paul.manning@sensient-tech.com
Senior VP/CFO: Stephen Rolfs
President, Colors Group: Michael Geraghty
President, Flavors & Fragrances Group: E. Craig Mitchell
Year Founded: 1882
Estimated Sales: $1.46 Billion
Number Employees: 4,000
Brands:
  Sensient

11445 Sensus America Inc
100 Lenox Dr # 104
Suite 104
Lawrence Twp, NJ 08648-2332
646-452-6140
Fax: 646-452-6150 www.inspiredbyinulin.com
Supplier of ingredients to the food and beverage industries.
Sales Manager: Carol Malczan
Number Employees: 1-4
Parent Co: Sensus

Brands:
  Frutafit
  Frutalose

11446 Sentry Seasonings
928 N Church Rd
Elmhurst, IL 60126-1014
630-530-5370
Fax: 630-530-5385 wayne@sentryseasonings.com
www.sentryseasonings.com
Flavors and seasonings for food processing companies
President: Carla Staniec
carla@sentryseasonings.com
VP: Michael Staniec
Estimated Sales: $730000
Number Employees: 10-19
Square Footage: 120000
Type of Packaging: Consumer, Food Service, Private Label, Bulk

11447 Seppic Inc
30 Two Bridges Rd # 210
Fairfield, NJ 07004-1555
973-882-5597
Fax: 973-882-5178 877-737-7421
stephen.oneill@airliquide.com www.seppic.com
Ingredients, minerals and extracts
President: Jean Marc Giner
Marketing/Sales: Regis Cazes
Contact: Yves Bantec
y.bantec@seppic.com
Estimated Sales: $1-2.5 Million
Number Employees: 500-999
Parent Co: Seppic

11448 Sequoia Brewing Co
777 E Olive Ave
Fresno, CA 93728-3350
559-264-5521
Fax: 559-264-6033 scott@sequoiabrewing.com
Seasonal beer, ale, stout, lager and pilsner
President: Scott Kendall
scottk@sequoiabrewing.com
Operations Manager: Holly Bragg
Director Manufacturing: Kevin Cox
Estimated Sales: $1-2,500,000
Number Employees: 20-49
Type of Packaging: Consumer, Food Service
Brands:
  Bridalveil Ale
  San Joaquin Golden Ale
  Tower Dark Ale

11449 Sequoia Grove
8338 Saint Helena Hwy
PO Box 449
Napa, CA 94558-9729
707-944-2945
Fax: 707-963-9411 800-851-7841
info@sequoiagrove.com www.sequoiagrove.com
Wines
Owner: Brett Adams
brett@sequoiagrove.com
CFO: Robert Aldridge
Vice President: Casandra Knox
Marketing Director: Anthony Ankers
Estimated Sales: $1-$2.5 Million
Number Employees: 10-19
Type of Packaging: Private Label
Brands:
  Sequoia Grove

11450 Sequoia Specialty Cheese Company
7000 W Doe Ave # C
Visalia, CA 93291-8623
559-752-4106
Fax: 559-752-4108
Cheese
Administrator: Ray Chavez
Production Manager: Greg Moe
Estimated Sales: $1-23 000,000
Number Employees: 10-19
Number of Products: 10
Square Footage: 40000
Type of Packaging: Consumer, Food Service, Private Label
Brands:
  Mt. Whitney

11451 Serenade Foods
9179 N 200 E
Milford, IN 46542
574-658-4121
Fax: 219-658-2246
Poultry
Communications Manager: Janelle Deatsman
Contact: Eric Essig
eessig@mapleleaffarms.com
Number Employees: 100-249
Parent Co: Maple Leaf Foods
Type of Packaging: Consumer, Food Service, Private Label, Bulk

11452 Serendipitea
73 Plandome Rd
Manhasset, NY 11030-2330
516-365-7711
Fax: 516-365-7733 888-832-5433
tea@serendipitea.com www.serendipitea.com
Tea; premium grade loose leaf
Principal: Linda Villano
tea@serendipitea.com
Estimated Sales: Less than $500,000
Number Employees: 5-9
Number of Brands: 1
Number of Products: 100+
Square Footage: 12000
Type of Packaging: Consumer, Food Service, Private Label, Bulk

11453 Serendipity Cellars
15275 Dunn Forest Rd
Monmouth, OR 97361
503-838-4284
Fax: 503-838-0067
Wines
Owner: Glen Longshore
Estimated Sales: $500,000-$1 000,000
Number Employees: 1-4

11454 Serengeti Tea Co
351 W Redondo Beach Blvd
Gardena, CA 90248-2101
310-527-5278
Fax: 310-527-2154 888-604-2040
tea@serengetitea.com www.serengetitea.com
Iced teas
Owner: David Massey
Estimated Sales: $690,000
Number Employees: 5-9
Brands:
  Southern Breeze
  Ticolino

11455 Serious Foodie
4754 Mainsail Dr
Bradenton, FL 34208-9409
844-736-6343
shop@serious-foodie.com
serious-foodie.com
Ingredients: sauces, rubs, vinaigrettes and marinades
President & CEO: James M. Pachence
Estimated Sales: $4 Million
Number Employees: 21
Brands:
  Serious Foodie

11456 Serranos Salsa
632 Ralph Ablanedo Dr # 330
Austin, TX 78748-6619
512-328-9200
Fax: 512-328-3005 www.serranos.com
Soups, ensaladas, tortas
Owner: Adam Gonzales
Director: Eric Cross
Estimated Sales: $500-1 Million appx.
Number Employees: 5-9
Brands:
  Serranos Salsa

11457 Serro Foods LLC
36 Koeppel Ave
Catskill, NY 12414-2018
518-943-9255
Pasta, grilling sauces, marinades and pasta sauce.
Founder and Owner: Charlie Serro
Estimated Sales: Less Than $500,000
Number Employees: 1-4
Brands:
  Grandpa Pete's Sunday Sauce

Food Manufacturers / A-Z

11458 (HQ)Serv-Agen Corporation
1200 S Union Ave
Cherry Hill, NJ 8002
856-663-6966
Fax: 856-663-7016 cwslade1@msn.com
Food colors, flavorings, dehydrated vegetables, gravy and soup bases, spices, puddings and sauce mixes including soy and worcestershire
President: Barbara Pearlman
VP: Charles W Slade
Estimated Sales: $989,000
Number Employees: 5-9
Square Footage: 45000
Type of Packaging: Consumer, Food Service, Private Label, Bulk
Brands:
 Bennetts
 Clawson
 Heinle
 Key Lime
 Lem
 Lemon

11459 Serv-Rite Meat Co Inc
2515 N San Fernando Rd
Los Angeles, CA 90065-1325
323-227-1911
Fax: 323-227-9068 www.bar-m.com
Bacon, smoked ham and sausage
President: Nora Hizon
nhizon@bar-m.com
Marketing Manager: Anna Cornellius
Estimated Sales: $10-20 Million
Number Employees: 50-99
Square Footage: 160000

11460 Service Foods
4355 International Blvd
Suite 150
Norcross, GA 30093
770-446-3085
Fax: 770-446-3085 800-872-3484
Frozen food and freezer plans
Founder: Stan Sax
CEO: Keith Cantor
Assistant Marketing Manager: Deborah Zachary
Outside Sales Representative: Rene Elalouf
Customer Service: Stephanie Shaw
Estimated Sales: $5-10 Million
Number Employees: 20-49

11461 Service Packing Company
250 Southern Street
Vancouver, BC V6A 2P1
Canada
604-681-0264
Fax: 604-681-9309
Dates, currants, raisins, shredded coconut, chocolate chips, prunes and nuts including walnuts and almonds
President: Ron Huntington
Estimated Sales: $500,000-1,000,000
Number Employees: 1-4
Square Footage: 340000
Type of Packaging: Private Label
Brands:
 Martins

11462 Sesaco Corp
6201 E Oltorf St # 100
Suite 100
Austin, TX 78741-7511
512-389-0790
Fax: 512-389-0790 800-737-2260
www.sesaco.com
Sesame seeds including white hulled
Executive Director: Ray Langham
Administration: Tina Smith
Director of Production: Jerry Riney
jriney@sesaco.com
Estimated Sales: $3-5 Million
Number Employees: 1-4
Type of Packaging: Consumer, Bulk
Brands:
 Flour
 Hp-White Hulled Sesame Seeds
 Oil
 T2p-Light
 T4p-Medium Toasted Hulled Sesame
 T5p-Dark
 Tnp-Toasted Natural Sesame Seeds
 Tahini
 Wnp-Washed Natural Sesame Seeds

11463 Sesinco Foods
54 W 21st Street
New York, NY 10010-6908
212-243-1306
Fax: 212-243-2036
Frozen and canned foods, beverages, dairy products
President: Serbajit Singh
VP: Ann Gaudet
Estimated Sales: $1600000
Number Employees: 7
Type of Packaging: Consumer, Food Service

11464 Sessions Co Inc
801 N Main St
Enterprise, AL 36330-9108
334-393-0200
Fax: 334-393-0240
Peanut sheller and processor producing quality shelled peanuts and peanut seed. Also producers of crude peanut oil and peanut meal.
Principal: Mo Sessions
CFO: Jeff Outlaw
sesscom@frost.snowhill.com
Estimated Sales: $9.3 Million
Number Employees: 50-99
Square Footage: 40000
Type of Packaging: Consumer, Food Service, Private Label, Bulk

11465 Seth Ellis Chocolatier
5345 Arapahoe Ave Ste 5
Boulder, CO 80303
720-565-2462
Fax: 720-565-2462 hey@sethellischocolatier.com
Chocolate
President/Owner: Frederick Levine
Number Employees: 5

11466 Sethness Caramel Color
3422 W Touhy Avenue
Skokie, IL 60076
847-329-2080
Fax: 847-329-2090 mail@sethness.com
www.sethness.com
Producer of caramel color for beverage, bakery, nutritional, and other applications.
COO: Tom Schufreider
Type of Packaging: Food Service, Bulk
Other Locations:
 Corporate Office
 Skokie IL
 Eastern Office
 Avenel NJ
 U.S. Plant & Research Center
 Clinton IA
 France Plant
 Merville, France
 China Plant
 Lianyungang, China
 India Plant
 Ahmedabad, India

11467 Setton Farms
9370 Road 234
Terra Bella, CA 93270
559-535-6050
Fax: 559-535-6089 info@settonfarms.com
www.settonfarms.com
Pistachios, nuts, dried fruits and trail mixes
VP, Domestic Sales & Marketing: Joseph Setton
Other Locations:
 Sales Office
 New York NY
 European Sales Office
 The Netherlands
Brands:
 Farmer Focus

11468 Setton International Foods
85 Austin Blvd
Commack, NY 11725
631-543-8090
Fax: 631-543-8070 800-227-4397
info@settonfarms.com
www.settoninternational.com
Pistachios, cashews, almonds, apricots, candy and snack foods
President: Joshua Setton
VP, Domestic Sales & Marketing: Joseph Setton
Human Resources Coordinator: Kellie Shepard
Logistics Manager: Patrick Braddock
Production Manager: Henry Scott
Plant Manager: Jeffrey Gibbons
Estimated Sales: $64 Million
Number Employees: 250-499
Square Footage: 55000
Type of Packaging: Consumer, Food Service, Private Label, Bulk
Other Locations:
 Processing Facility
 Terra Bella CA
 European Sales Office
 Zutphen, The Netherlands

11469 Setton Pistachio
9370 Road 234
Terra Bella, CA 93270
559-535-6050
Fax: 559-535-6089 info@settonfarms.com
www.settonfarms.com
Pistachios
President: Joshua Setton
settoninfo@settonfarms.com
VP, Domestic Sales & Marketing: Joseph Setton
Human Resources Coordinator: Kellie Shepard
Logistics Manager: Patrick Braddock
Project Manager: Henry Scott
Plant Manager: Jeffrey Gibbons
Estimated Sales: $64 Million
Number Employees: 100-249
Number of Brands: 2
Square Footage: 300000
Parent Co: Setton International Foods, Inc.
Type of Packaging: Consumer, Food Service, Bulk
Other Locations:
 New York Sales Office
 Commack NY
 European Sales Office
 Zutphen, The Netherlands
Brands:
 Setton Farms
 Setton Farms Chewy Bites

11470 Seven Barrel Brewery
5 Airport Rd # 16
West Lebanon, NH 03784-1658
603-298-5566
Fax: 603-298-5715 sevenbarrelbrew@gmail.com
Seasonal beer, ale, stout, lager and pilsner
President: Nancy Noonan
Manager: Earl Locke
Number Employees: 20-49
Type of Packaging: Food Service
Brands:
 Seven Barrell

11471 Seven Hills Coffee Co
11094 Deerfield Rd
Blue Ash, OH 45242-4112
513-489-5220
Fax: 513-489-6888 www.sevenhillscoffee.com
Coffee
Owner: Michael Melzer
mmelzer@sevenhillscoffee.com
Operations Manager: Matthew Kasper
Estimated Sales: $2.5-5 000,000
Number Employees: 5-9

11472 Seven Hills Winery
212 N 3rd Ave
Walla Walla, WA 99362-1883
509-529-7198
Fax: 509-529-7918 877-777-7870
info@sevenhillswinery.com
www.sevenhillswinery.com
Wines
Founder/Winemaker: Casey McClellan
Estimated Sales: Below $5 Million
Number Employees: 5-9
Brands:
 Seven Hills

11473 Seven Keys Co Of Florida
450 SW 12th Ave
Pompano Beach, FL 33069-3504
954-946-5010
Fax: 954-946-5012
Processor and exporter of tropical jams, jellies, marmalades and coconut toast spreads
President: Henry Stevens
Estimated Sales: $3-5 Million
Number Employees: 5-9
Square Footage: 45000
Type of Packaging: Consumer, Food Service, Private Label
Brands:
 Lapham
 Seven Keys

Food Manufacturers / A-Z

11474 Seven Lakes Vineyard & Winery
1111 Tinsman Rd
Fenton, MI 48430-1679
810-373-6081
Wines
President: Chris Guest
Manager: Karen Irwin
Estimated Sales: Less Than $500,000
Number Employees: 1-4

11475 Seven Seas Seafoods
901 S Fremont Ave Ste 168
Alhambra, CA 91803
626-570-9129
Fax: 626-570-0079
Seafood
President: Christopher Lin
VP: Sean Lin
Estimated Sales: $5-10 Million
Number Employees: 5-9

11476 Seven Sundays, LLC
PO Box 19294
Minneapolis, MN 19294
612-562-5316
www.sevensundays.com
Manufacturer of muesli.
Co-Founder: Hannah Bamstable
Co-Founder: Brady Bamstable
Contact: Hannah Barnstable
hannah@sevensundays.com

11477 Severance Foods Inc
3478 Main St
Hartford, CT 06120-1138
860-724-7063
Fax: 860-527-2045 www.severancefoods.com
Tortilla chips and tortillas including flour and corn
President: Richard Stevens
rstevens@severancefoods.com
Founder: John Grikis
Founder: Richard Dana
Estimated Sales: $3.35 Million
Number Employees: 50-99
Square Footage: 112000
Type of Packaging: Consumer, Food Service, Private Label, Bulk
Brands:
   Pan De Oro

11478 Severino Pasta Mfg Co Inc
110 Haddon Ave
Westmont, NJ 08108-1000
856-854-3716
Fax: 856-854-6098 info@severinopasta.com
www.severinopasta.com
Pasta
Owner: Louis Severino
lseverino@severinopasta.com
VP/Partner: Louis Servino
Estimated Sales: Below $5 Million
Number Employees: 20-49

11479 Severn Peanut Co
413 Main St
Severn, NC 27877
252-585-1744
Fax: 252-585-1718 www.hamptonfarms.com
Peanuts
President: Dallas Barnes
Estimated Sales: $41.8 Million
Number Employees: 50-99
Square Footage: 10000
Parent Co: Meherrin Agriculture
Type of Packaging: Consumer, Bulk

11480 Seville Olive Company
663 S Anderson St
Los Angeles, CA 90023
323-261-2218
Fax: 323-261-1026
Olives, onions, cherries and peppers
President: Louis Pavlic Sr
loupav45@att.net
Estimated Sales: $10-20 000,000
Number Employees: 100-249

11481 Seviroli Foods
385 Oak St
Garden City, NY 11530
516-222-6220
Fax: 516-222-0534 www.seviroli.com
All natural frozen pasta products.
President: Anthony D'Orazio
adorazio@doraziofoods.com
CFO: Michael Romano
VP Sales/Marketing: Terry D'Ozario
VP Operations/COO: Frank D'Orazio
VP Production: Anthony D'Orazio
Estimated Sales: $8.4 Million
Number Employees: 50-99
Square Footage: 100000
Brands:
   Dorazio

11482 Seviroli Foods Inc
601 Brook St
Garden City, NY 11530-6431
516-222-6220
Fax: 516-222-0534
Italian foods. Manufactures frozen pasta including ravioli, tortellini, manicotti, gnocchi, and stuffed shells
President: Joseph Seviroli Sr
Quality Assurance Manager: Nel Reformina
Estimated Sales: $5-10 Million
Number Employees: 250-499
Square Footage: 100

11483 Sewell's Seafood & Fish Market
1178 Lee St
Rogersville, AL 35652-7816
256-247-1378
Fax: 718-617-6851
Seafood
Owner: Tana Springer
tanaspringer@aol.com
Public Relations: Tana Springer
Estimated Sales: $1-3 Million
Number Employees: 1-4

11484 Sexy Pop LLC
100 Roslyn Ave.
Sea Cliff, NY 11579
516-671-4411
877-476-2755
info@robsbrands.com
Manufacturer of popcorn.
Founder and CEO: Robert Ehrlich
Contact: Rt Ehrlich
rob@sexypop.us
Brands:
   Vegan Rob's
   Crunchy Rob's

11485 Seydel Co
244 John B Brooks Rd
Pendergrass, GA 30567
706-693-2266
Fax: 706-693-2074 customerservice@seydel.com
www.seydel.com
Starch, dextrin and protein.
Chairman & CEO: Scott Seydel, Sr.
President & COO: Scott Seydel, Jr.
Chief Financial Officer: Graham Marsh
Estimated Sales: $43.5 Million
Number Employees: 50-99
Parent Co: Seydel Company
Type of Packaging: Food Service, Bulk
Brands:
   Emdex
   Emflo
   Emgum
   Emjel
   Emox

11486 Seymour & Sons SeafoodsInc
3201 Saint Charles St
Diberville, MS 39540-5315
228-392-4020
Fax: 228-392-8028
Seafood including frozen catfish and lobster
President: Paul Seymour
Plant Manager: David Seymour
Estimated Sales: $1.2 Million
Number Employees: 5-9
Square Footage: 10000

11487 Sfoglia Fine Pastas & Gourmet
P.O.Box 921
Freeland, WA 98249
360-331-4080
Gourmet and specialty foods
President: Stephanie Jushinski
Estimated Sales: Less than $500,000
Number Employees: 1-4

11488 Sfoglini Pasta Shop
630 Flushing Avenue
2nd Floor
Brooklyn, NY 11206
917-338-5955
info@sfoglini.com
www.sfoglini.com
Pasta: durum semolina and grain
Co-Founder: Steve Gonzalez
Co-Founder, Marketing & Operations: Scott Ketchum
Estimated Sales: $4 Million
Number Employees: 35
Type of Packaging: Consumer, Private Label

11489 Shaanxi Jiahe PhytochemCo., Ltd.
140 Littleton Rd
Suite 200
Parsippany, NJ 07054
973-439-6869
Fax: 973-439-6879 info@jiaherbinc.com
jiaherb.com
Herbal extract and natural ingredients for the nutraceutical, pharmaceutical, cosmetic and food & beverage industries.
Vice President: Charlie Wang
Sales Manager: Scott Chen
Number Employees: 500

11490 Shabazz Fruit Cola Company
P.O. Box 835
Newark, NJ 07101
973-230-4641
Fax: 973-230-1651 info@shabazzfruitcola.com
Fruit flavored colas
CEO: Frank Shabazz

11491 Shady Grove Orchards
183 Shady Grove Road
Onalaska, WA 98570-9453
360-985-7033
Organic American chestnuts and chestnut flour, dried chestnut kernels and seedlings
Co-Owner: Annie Bhagwandin
Co-Owner: Omroa Bhagwandin
Brands:
   Shady Grove Orchards

11492 Shady Maple Farm
2585 Skymark Ave
Mississauga, ON L4W 4L5
Canada
905-206-1455
Fax: 905-206-1477 www.shadymaple.ca
Processor and exporter of pure maple syrup products
President/CEO: Robert Swain
CFO: Darren Brash
Marketing Director: Marlene Jolicoeur
Sales Director: Daniel Neale
Number Employees: 10-19
Square Footage: 220000
Type of Packaging: Consumer, Food Service, Private Label, Bulk

11493 Shafer Lake Fruit Inc
60643 Red Arrow Hwy
Hartford, MI 49057-9703
269-621-3194
Fax: 269-621-4170
Packers of apples, peaches, plums and asparagus
President: Dale Drake
d_drake@frontier.com
Estimated Sales: $3-5 Million
Number Employees: 20-49
Type of Packaging: Consumer, Bulk

11494 Shafer Vineyards
6154 Silverado Trl
Napa, CA 94558-9748
707-944-2877
Fax: 707-944-9454 info@shafervineyards.com
Cabernet sauvignon, chardonnay, merlot, cabernet savignon, sangiovese
Owner: John Shafer
info@shafervineyards.com
President: Doug Shafer
Winemaker: Elias Fernandez
Estimated Sales: $5-10 Million
Number Employees: 10-19
Brands:
   Firebreak
   Hillside
   Red Shoulder Ranch
   Shafer Vineyards

Food Manufacturers / A-Z

11495 Shafer-Haggart
1055 West Hastings Street
Suite 1038
Vancouver, BC V6E 4E2
Canada
604-669-5512
Fax: 604-669-9554 info@shafer-haggart.com
www.shafer-haggart.com
Processor and importer of canned mushrooms, tomatoes, peaches, tuna and salmon; exporter of frozen poultry and canned corn and fish products
President: Clive Lonsdale
Sr. VP: Brian Dougall
Estimated Sales: $2.5-5 Million
Number Employees: 20-49
Type of Packaging: Consumer, Food Service, Private Label

11496 Shah Trading Company
3451 McNicoll Avenue
Scarborough, ON M1V 2V3
Canada
416-292-6927
Fax: 416-292-7932 info@shahtrading.com
www.shahtrading.com
Rice, spices, beans, peas, and lentils, specialty flours and nuts and dried fruits.
Other Locations:
  Pulse and Canning Plant
  Scarborough ON
  Rice Plant
  Scarborough ON
Brands:
  Dunya Harvest

11497 Shaker Country Meadowsweets
35 Hillside Avenue
Hillside, NJ 07205
973-926-2300
Fax: 973-926-4440 800-524-1304
info@hillsidecandy.com www.hillsidecandy.com
Fruit flavored candy
Estimated Sales: $5-10 Million
Number Employees: 10-19

11498 Shaker Museum
707 Shaker Rd
New Gloucester, ME 04260-2652
207-926-4865
888-624-6345
usshakers@aol.com www.maineshakers.com
Herbal teas, culinary herbs, herb mixes
Executive Director: Leonard Brooks
Estimated Sales: Less than $200,000
Number Employees: 1-4
Type of Packaging: Consumer, Food Service, Bulk
Brands:
  United Society of Shakers

11499 Shaker Valley Foods
3304 W 67th Pl
Cleveland, OH 44102-5243
216-961-8600
Fax: 216-961-8077 www.shakervalleyfoods.com
Deli meats and cheeses, fresh cut quality meats including steaks, chops, roasts, stews, cutlets, sausages, ground and pattied products.
President: Dean Comber
Human Resources Manager: Kim Andreas
Year Founded: 1984
Estimated Sales: $20-50 Million
Number Employees: 20-49

11500 Shakespeare's
3840 W River Dr
Davenport, IA 52802-2412
563-383-0150
Fax: 563-383-0151 800-664-4114
Specialty chocolates
Owner: Elisa Shakespeare
Contact: Michael Anglese
mikea@shopshakespeares.com
Estimated Sales: Less than $500,000
Number Employees: 10-19

11501 (HQ)Shaklee Corp
4747 Willow Rd
Pleasanton, CA 94588-2763
925-924-2000
Fax: 925-924-2862 800-742-5533
www.shaklee.com
Nutritional supplements
Chairman/CEO: Roger Barnett
CEO: Etta Adams
adams@shaklee.net
CFO: Mike Batesole
Sr EVP & COO: Luiz Cerqueira
Research & Development, Chief Scientist: Dr. Carsten Smidt
adams@shaklee.net
Chief Marketing Officer: Brad Harrington
SVP, Sales & Field Development: Laura Hughes
Number Employees: 1000-4999
Parent Co: Ripplewood Holdings
Type of Packaging: Consumer
Other Locations:
  Shaklee Corporation
  Norman OK
Brands:
  Airsource
  Perfect Pitcher
  Shaklee Carotomax
  Shaklee Flavomax

11502 Shallon Winery
1598 Duane St
Astoria, OR 97103-3707
503-325-5978
paul@shallon.com
www.shallon.com
Fine wines including whey wines and chocolate wines
President: Paul C Vanderveldt
paul@shallon.com
Estimated Sales: Less Than $500,000
Number Employees: 1-4
Brands:
  Shallon Winery

11503 Shallowford Farms Popcorn, Inc.
3732 Hartman Road
Yadkinville, NC 27055-5638
336-463-5938
Fax: 336-463-2358 800-892-9539
amanda.booe@yahoo.com
Popcorn
President: Amanda Booe
Plant Manager: Caswell Booe
Estimated Sales: $500,000-$1 Million
Number Employees: 10-19
Square Footage: 84000
Type of Packaging: Consumer, Private Label, Bulk
Brands:
  Dennis
  Mr Snack

11504 (HQ)Shamrock Foods Co
3900 E. Camelback Rd.
Suite 300
Phoenix, AZ 85018
602-233-6400
800-289-3663
www.shamrockfoodservice.com
General line items, groceries, meats, produce, dairy products, frozen foods, baked goods, equipment and fixtures, general merchandise and seafood; serving the food service market.
President: Kent McClelland
CFO: Stephen Down
Year Founded: 1922
Estimated Sales: Over $1 Billion
Number Employees: 1000-4999
Number of Brands: 45
Type of Packaging: Food Service
Other Locations:
  Phoenix AZ
  Commerce City CO
  Albuquerque NM
  Eastvale CA
Brands:
  Fair Meadow
  Bountiful Harvest
  Brickfire Bakery
  Intros
  Cobblestreet Market
  Katy's Kitchen
  Pier Port
  Prarie Creek
  ProClean
  ProPak
  ProSystem
  ProWare
  Rejuv
  Trescerro
  Villa Frizzoni
  Vista Verde
  Shamrock Farms
  Gold Canyon Meat Co.
  Markon
  Jensen Foods
  Coffee Roasters Ridgeline
  Azar
  B&G Foods, Inc.
  Brown Paper Goods
  Bueno
  Cheese Merchants
  Custom Culinary
  Ecolab
  Florida's Natural
  Hormel Foods
  Kellogg's
  Kraft Heinz
  Lamb Weston
  Michael Foods Inc.
  Mission Foodservice
  NCCO
  Nestl, Professional
  Perdue
  Rema Foods Imports
  Rich's
  Roland
  Schreiber
  Smithfield Farmland
  Sugar Foods Corporation
  Tysom

11505 Shamrock Foods Co
Boise Foods Branch
1495 N Hickory Ave
Meridian, ID 83642
208-884-8400
www.shamrockfoodservice.com
Serves Idaho, Oregon and Utah.
Parent Co: Shamrock Foods Co

11506 Shamrock Foods Co
Colorado Foods Branch
5199 Ivy St
Commerce City, CO 80022
800-289-3595
coinfo@shamrockfoods.com
www.shamrockfoods.com
Serves Colorado, Western Kansas, Western Nebraska and Wyoming.
Senior VP: Kent Mullison
kent_mullison@shamrockfoods.com
Number Employees: 500-999
Parent Co: Shamrock Foods Company

11507 Shamrock Foods Co
Arizona Foods Branch
2540 N 29th Ave
Phoenix, AZ 85009-1682
602-233-6467
Fax: 928-537-3428 800-289-3663
azinfo@shamrockfoods.com
www.shamrockfoodservice.com
Estimated Sales: $100+ Million
Number Employees: 10-19
Parent Co: Shamrock Foods Company

11508 Shamrock Foods Co
Southern California Foods Branch
12400 Riverside Dr
Eastvale, CA 91752
855-664-5166
cainfo@shamrockfoods.com
www.shamrockfoodservice.com
Parent Co: Shamrock Foods Company

11509 Shamrock Foods Co
New Mexico Foods Branch
2 Shamrock Way NW
Albuquerque, NM 87120
877-577-1155
nminfo@shamrockfoods.com
www.shamrockfoodservice.com
Serves New Mexico and West Texas.
Parent Co: Shamrock Foods Company

11510 Shamrock Slaughter Plant
6400 US Highway 83
Shamrock, TX 79079-4408
806-256-3241
Meat products
Owner: Larry Cook
Estimated Sales: $500,000-$1 Million
Number Employees: 1-4
Type of Packaging: Consumer

Food Manufacturers / A-Z

11511 Shane Candy Co
110 Market St
Philadelphia, PA 19106-3006
215-922-1048
Fax: 215-940-0003 www.shanecandies.com
Candy including chocolate, holiday and hard
Owner: Ryan Berley
ryan@franklinfountain.com
Estimated Sales: $5-10 Million
Number Employees: 20-49
Square Footage: 28800
Type of Packaging: Consumer

11512 Shaner's Family Restaurant
193 Main St
South Paris, ME 04281
207-743-6367
Ice cream, frozen desserts
President: John Shaner
Estimated Sales: $1-2.5 000,000
Number Employees: 20-49

11513 Shanghai Co
2800 SE Division St
Portland, OR 97202-1350
503-235-2525
Fax: 503-235-3842
Canned Chinese noodles
Owner: Brandon Wang
Estimated Sales: $1.1 Million
Number Employees: 10-19
Type of Packaging: Consumer

11514 Shanghai Freemen
2035 Route 27
Suite 08817
Edison, NJ 08817
732-981-1288
info@shanghaifreemen.com
shanghaifreemen.com
Dietary supplements and food and beverage ingredients, such as vitamins, stevia, natural beta carotene, energy beverage ingredients, amino acids and joint health products; their collection includes glucosamine, chondroitin, hyaluronicacid, fish gelatin, collagen, ascorbic acid, natural vitamin E, green tea extract, L-Glutamine, L-Valine, melatonin, probiotics, bromelain, vanillin, Sopure Stevia and many more.
President: Hanks Li
Director, Business Development Eastern: Paul Niemann
Director, Business Development Western: Lottie Siann
VP, Sales & Marketing: Christine Balediata
Year Founded: 1995
Estimated Sales: $100 Million
Number Employees: 51-200
Parent Co: Zhucheng Haotian Pharm Co.
Type of Packaging: Bulk
Other Locations:
  Shanghai Freemen Europe B.V.
  The Hague

11515 Shank's Extracts Inc
350 Richardson Dr
Lancaster, PA 17603-4034
717-393-4441
Fax: 717-393-3148 800-346-3135
www.shanks.com
Supplier of extracts, flavors, colors, syrups, emulsions and sauces to industrial, private label and grocery customers.
President: Jeff Lehman
Vice President, Sales: Mark Freeman
Estimated Sales: G
Number Employees: 50-99
Square Footage: 110000
Type of Packaging: Consumer, Food Service, Private Label, Bulk
Brands:
  Gold Medal
  Taste-T

11516 Shanley Farms
2448 Atascadero Road
Morro Bay, CA 93442
805-323-6525
hello@shanleyfarms.com
www.shanleyfarms.com
Finger limes and pearls; avocados and coffee trees.
Owner: Jim Shanley
Sales & Marketing: Megan Shanley
Operations Manager: Jessica Kamper
Estimated Sales: $4.9 Million
Number Employees: 11-50
Brands:
  Citriburst Finger Limes

11517 Shape Foods
2001 Victoria Avenue E
Brandon, MB R7A 7L2
Canada
204-727-3529
Fax: 204-728-3529 info@shapefoods.com
Producer of conventional and organic flaxseed oil and meal.
Sales Manager: Dane Lindenberg
Square Footage: 70000
Type of Packaging: Private Label, Bulk
Brands:
  Heart Shape
  Royal Harvest
  Flax Country

11518 Shariann's Organics
4600 Sleepytime Dr.
Boulder, CO 80301
63- 73- 220
Fax: 631-730-2550 800-434-4246
consumeraffairs@hain-celestial.com
http://www.hain-celestial.com/
Organic food products
President and CEO: Irwin Simon
CFO: Ira Lamel
Chief Marketing Officer: Maureen Putman
Estimated Sales: $900 Million
Number Employees: 130
Brands:
  Shariann's Italian White Beans
  Shariann's Refried Beans
  Shariann's Spicy Vegetable

11519 Sharkco's
707 Jump Basin Rd
Venice, LA 70091-4351
504-534-9577
Fax: 504-534-2217
Seafood
Owner: Tuan Guyn
Estimated Sales: $5-10 Million
Number Employees: 10-19

11520 Sharon Mill Winery
5701 Sharon Hollow Rd
Manchester, MI 48158
734-971-6337
Fax: 734-971-6386 www.ewashtenaw.org
Wines
Director: Robert Tetens
Estimated Sales: $1-2.5 Million
Number Employees: 20-49

11521 Sharp Rock Farm B & B
5 Sharp Rock Rd
Sperryville, VA 22740-2333
540-987-8020
Fax: 540-987-9031 jeast@sharprockvineyards.com
www.sharprock.com
Wines
Owner: James East
Estimated Sales: $1-3 Million
Number Employees: 1-4

11522 Shashi Foods
55 Esandar Dr
Toronto, ON M4G 4H2
Canada
416-645-0611
Fax: 416-645-0612 866-748-7441
Spices, herbs, seasoning blends and specialty flours, also, custom grinding, blending, bottling, and bagging.
President: Sujay Shah
VP: Ajay Shah
Estimated Sales: $7.37 Million
Number Employees: 30
Brands:
  Elephant Brand
  Shashi
  King of Spice
  Patak's

11523 Shashy's Bakery & Fine Foods
1700 Mulberry St
Montgomery, AL 36106-1524
334-263-7341
Fax: 334-263-7343 www.shashysbakery.com
Baked goods
President: James Shashy
Owner: Jimmy Shashy
Estimated Sales: $500,000-$1 Million
Number Employees: 20-49
Type of Packaging: Consumer

11524 Shasta Beverages Inc
9750 Moravia Park Dr.
Baltimore, MS 21237-1090
510-783-3200
Fax: 510-783-8681 800-834-9980
www.shastapop.com
Flavored soft drinks including grape, cola, root beer, orange, kiwi/strawberry, black cherry, etc
Manager: Rick Reynolds
Controller: Charles Reisig
Executive VP: Miguel Abril
mabril@shastabeverages.com
Sales Executive: Michael Perez
Plant Manager: Dan Penrod
Estimated Sales: $20-50 Million
Number Employees: 1000-4999
Parent Co: National Beverage Company
Type of Packaging: Consumer, Food Service, Private Label
Brands:
  Shasta

11525 Shaw Baking Company
240 S Algoma Street
Thunder Bay, ON P7B 3C2
Canada
807-345-7327
Fax: 807-345-7895 http://www.tbaytel.net
Rolls, doughnuts, muffins, danish pastries and bread including white and whole wheat
President/General Manager: G Shaw
Sales Manager: Joe Spina
Number Employees: 100-249
Type of Packaging: Consumer, Food Service
Brands:
  Country Hearth
  Holsum
  Shaw

11526 Shaw's Southern Belle Frozen, Inc.
P.O. Box 28620
Jacksonville, FL 32226
904-768-1591
Fax: 904-766-3071 888-742-9772
info@shawsouthernbelle.com
www.shawsouthernbelle.com
Specialty seafood packer of full service deli & seafood, home meal replacement and frozen products.
Owner: Howard Shaw
CEO: John Shaw
Chief Financial Officer: Joanna Zimmerman
Executive Vice President: Sylvia Shaw
Restaurant Sales Executive: Howard "Bubba" Shaw
dgreer@shawsouthernbelle.com
Human Resources Executive: Leslie Faulk
Director of Systems & Processes: Heidi Bash
Purchasing Manager: John Shaw
dgreer@shawsouthernbelle.com
Estimated Sales: $10.5 Million
Number Employees: 100
Type of Packaging: Consumer, Food Service, Private Label
Other Locations:
  Shaw's Cold Storage
  Jacksonville FL

11527 Shawmut Fishing Company
PO Box 1986
Anchorage, AK 99508
709-334-2559
Fax: 709-596-7189
Frozen crabs
President: William Berry
VP: Thomas Caines
Type of Packaging: Consumer, Food Service, Bulk

11528 (HQ)Shawnee Canning Co
212 Cross Junction Rd
Cross Junction, VA 22625-2324
540-888-3429
Fax: 540-888-7963 800-713-1414
sales@shawneesprings.com
www.shawneesprings.com

Food Manufacturers / A-Z

Apple sauces, apples, peaches, ciders, preserves and jams, fruit butters, apple syrup, apple mixes, honey, pickles, salsa, dressings, relishes and fresh baked pies
President: William Whitacre
GM: Lisa Whitacre Johnson
Estimated Sales: $3 Million
Number Employees: 20-49
Square Footage: 39000
Type of Packaging: Consumer, Private Label
Brands:
  Shawnee Springs

11529 (HQ)Shawnee Milling Co
201 S Broadway Ave
PO Box 1567
Shawnee, OK 74801-8427
405-273-7000
Fax: 405-273-7333 lspears@shawneemilling.com
www.shawneemilling.com
Flour, cornmeal, complete mixes, custom mixes
President: William Ford
bford@shawneemilling.com
CEo: Debra Howe
Vice President: Joe Lloyd Ford
Regional Sales Manager: James Smith
Plant Manager: Doug Myer
Purchasing Manager: Caleb Winsett
Number Employees: 250-499
Type of Packaging: Consumer, Food Service, Private Label, Bulk
Brands:
  Shawnee Best
  Shawnee Mills

11530 Shawnee Milling Co
PO Box 1567
Shawnee, OK 74802-1567
405-273-7000
Fax: 405-273-7333 800-654-2600
www.shawneemilling.com
Supplier of mixes and flours
President: Joe Ford
Director of Quality Control: Matthew Salter
Number Employees: 250-499
Parent Co: Shawnee Milling Company
Type of Packaging: Consumer, Food Service

11531 Shearer's Foods Inc
100 Lincoln Way E
Massillon, OH 44646-6634
330-767-4030
Fax: 330-767-3393 info@shearers.com
www.shearers.com
Regular, rippled, flavored and kettle-cooked potato chips
President: Robert Shearer
CEO: Christopher Fraleigh
CFO: Fritz Kohnmann
EVP: Montgomery Pooley
SVP Sales and Marketing: Bill McCabe
Public Relations: Melissa Shearer
VP Operations: Randy Whisler
VP Manufacturing: Joe McCarthy
Estimated Sales: $10-20 Million
Number Employees: 1000-4999
Square Footage: 150000
Type of Packaging: Consumer, Food Service, Private Label, Bulk
Brands:
  Grandma Shearer's
  Grandma Shearer's Snacks

11532 Shedd Food Products
4151 Gladewater Rd
Dallas, TX 75216-6435
214-374-4751
Fax: 214-761-4565
Margarine
Owner: Sherman Shead
Plant Manager: John Preacher
Estimated Sales: $300,000-500,000
Number Employees: 1-4
Parent Co: Unilever USA

11533 Sheffa Foods
P.O.Box 644
New York, NY 10028
484-494-1249
Fax: 484-497-5436 800-494-1956
contact@sheffafoods.com www.sheffafoods.com
Snack bars, granola bars, mixes and salad sprinkles.
Co-Founder & Owner: Leslie Angle
Co-Founder: Amotz Geshury

Type of Packaging: Food Service
Brands:
  SHEFFA

11534 Sheila G Brands LLC
2253 Vista Parkway
Suite 8
West Palm Beach, FL 33411
561-688-1890
info@browniebrittle.com
www.browniebrittle.com
Manufacturer of brownie brittle snacks.
Founder and CEO: Sheila Mains
Contact: Justin Roberts
justinroberts@abssystems.net
Brands:
  Brownie Brittle

11535 Sheila Gs Brownie Brittle Co
2253 Vista Pkwy
West Palm Beach, FL 33411-2722
USA
561-557-1178
Fax: 561-584-5881 www.browniebrittle.com
Cookies
CEO/Founder: Sheila Mains
Vice President Marketing: Nancy Eichler
Estimated Sales: Less Than $500,000
Number Employees: 1-4

11536 Sheila's Select Gourmet Recipe
325 W 600 S
Heber City, UT 84032-2230
435-654-6415
Fax: 435-654-5449 800-516-7286
www.bearcreekfoods.com
Soups(bagged and canned), culinary bases, freezies, and salsas.
President: Kevin Ruda
CFO: Al Van Leeuwen
VP of Operations: Kevin Kowalski
Marketing Director: Jeff Hanson
Sales Manager: Steve White
Brands:
  Bear Creek Country Kitchens
  Sheila's Select Gourmet Recipes

11537 Sheinman Provision Co
4192 Viola St
Suite 96
Philadelphia, PA 19104-1093
215-473-7065
Fax: 215-473-7038
Sausage, bologna and corned and roast beef
President: Stan Rultenberg
Estimated Sales: $3 Million
Number Employees: 1-4
Square Footage: 14000
Type of Packaging: Consumer, Food Service, Private Label, Bulk
Brands:
  Philly Maid
  Sheinman

11538 Shekou Chemicals
24 Crescent Street
Waltham, MA 02453-4358
781-893-6878
Fax: 781-893-6881
Processor, importer and exporter of ingredients including citric acid, ascorbic acid, sodium benzoate, sodium propionate, calcium propionate, ammonium bicarbonate, sodium erythrobate, sodium citrate, potassium citrate and potassiumsorbate
System Staff: Herb Kimiatek
Sales/Marketing Executive: Judith Roiva
Purchasing Manager: Simon Altstein
Estimated Sales: $1.1 Million
Number Employees: 7
Square Footage: 40000
Type of Packaging: Bulk

11539 Shelburne Falls Coffee Roaster
1335 Mohawk Trl
Shelburne Falls, MA 01370-9303
413-625-2123
Fax: 413-625-1083 shfallscoffee@cs.com
www.ibuycoffee.com
Coffee
Owner: Curtis Rich
curtrich@earthlink.net
Estimated Sales: $3-5 Million
Number Employees: 1-4

11540 Shell Ridge Jalapeno Project
1432 Highway 35 S
Rockport, TX 78382-3918
512-790-8028
Ethnic foods
President: Kay Segura Christian
Estimated Sales: $500,000
Number Employees: 1-4
Brands:
  Kay's Hot Stuff

11541 Shelley's
700 Bergen Ave
Jersey City, NJ 07306-4890
201-433-2900
Fax: 201-433-4549
Provisions/meats including fresh and frozen beef, veal, lamb, pork and poultry
President: Shelley Geller
General Manager: Chuck Brennan
Estimated Sales: $11.3 Million
Number Employees: 20-49
Square Footage: 30000
Type of Packaging: Food Service

11542 Shelton's Poultry Inc
204 N Loranne Ave
Pomona, CA 91767
800-541-1833
www.sheltons.com
Free range poultry products; also, soups, chili, jerky, sausage, uncured frankfurters, meat balls, etc.
Chief Financial Officer: Lori Barragar
lbarrager@sheltons.com
Year Founded: 1924
Estimated Sales: $20-50 Million
Number Employees: 20-49
Type of Packaging: Consumer
Brands:
  Shelton's

11543 Shemper Seafood Co
367 Bayview Ave
Biloxi, MS 39530-2502
228-435-2703
Fax: 228-432-2104
Seafood, seafood products
President: Gary Shemper
CEO: Jeffrey Shemper
camelot@datasync.com
Estimated Sales: Less Than $500,000
Number Employees: 1-4
Brands:
  Shemper Seafood

11544 Shenandoah Mills
145 South Cumberland St
Lebanon, TN 37088-0369
615-444-0841
Fax: 615-444-0286 donya@shenandoahmills.com
www.shenandoahmills.com
Dry mixes including biscuit, pancake, corndog, apple fritters, corn meal, corn bread, gravy and hushpuppies; also, breadings including fish, chicken, pork, beef, etc
Founder, Owner, Chief Operating Officer: Dale Nunnery
VP: Danny Hodges
Plant Manager: Ike Sandy
Director Sales: George Stonesifer
Contact: Emily Drucker
emily@shenandoahmills.com
Estimated Sales: $4 Million
Number Employees: 25
Square Footage: 260000
Type of Packaging: Food Service
Brands:
  Shenandoah

11545 Shenandoah Vineyards
12300 Steiner Rd
Plymouth, CA 95669-9503
209-245-4455
Fax: 209-245-5156 www.sobonwine.com
Wines
President: Leon Sobon
CEO: Shirley Sobon
Estimated Sales: Below $5 Million
Number Employees: 10-19

Food Manufacturers / A-Z

11546 Shenk's Foods
1980 New Danville Pike
Lancaster, PA 17603-9615
717-393-4240
Fax: 717-393-4240
Cheese, butter spreads, jellies, mustards, preserves, relishes and fruit spreads
President: Karl Achtermann
karl@shenks.com
Estimated Sales: $2 Million
Number Employees: 1-4
Square Footage: 36000
Type of Packaging: Consumer, Private Label
Brands:
  Shenk's

11547 (HQ)Shepherd Farms Inc
9330 E 8th Rd
Hillsboro, IL 62049-3448
217-532-5268
Fax: 815-389-1997 800-383-2676
www.shepherdfarms.com
Processor and packer of popcorn including yellow, white and specialty hybrids packaged for microwave, air poppers and commercial poppers; also, soybeans and tofu; exporter of soybeans for tofu, miso, natto and shoyu, seed corn and seedsoybeans
Owner: Jim Shepherd
Estimated Sales: Less Than $500,000
Number Employees: 1-4
Square Footage: 80000
Type of Packaging: Consumer, Food Service, Private Label, Bulk
Other Locations:
  Shepherd Farms
  Beloit IL
Brands:
  Boone County Supreme
  Shepherd
  Shepherd Supreme

11548 Shepherdsfield Bakery
777 Shepherdsfield Rd
Fulton, MO 65251-5974
573-642-0009
Fax: 573-642-1439
Frozen gourmet waffles, muffins, breads and whole wheat pancake mixes, pies, cookies and flour
Religious Leader: Thomas Mahaney
CEO: Vicki Staudenmyer
Estimated Sales: Less Than $500,000
Number Employees: 1-4
Square Footage: 80000
Type of Packaging: Consumer, Private Label

11549 Sherbrooke OEM Ltd
262 rue P,pin
Sherbrooke, QC J1L 2V8
Canada
819-563-7374
Fax: 819-563-7556 866-851-2579
info@sherbrooke-oem.com
www.sherbrooke-oem.com
President: Alain Brasseur
VP: Bryan Sinram
Marketing: Sylvie Hertrich
Sales: Ian Levasseus
Purchasing Director: Bernard Gilbert
Number Employees: 1-4
Number of Brands: 2
Number of Products: 3
Brands:
  Jo Citrus
  Jomints
  M60 Energy Mints

11550 Sherm Edwards Candies
509 Cavitt Ave
Trafford, PA 15085-1060
412-372-4331
Fax: 412-373-8089 800-436-5424
Chocolate-covered candy
President: David Golembeski
Contact: Mark Edwards
mark@edwardmarc.com
Estimated Sales: $724000
Number Employees: 20-49
Type of Packaging: Consumer, Bulk

11551 Sherrill Orchards
3265 Valpredo Rd
Arvin, CA 93203
661-858-2035
Fax: 661-858-2035 soprus@aorldnet.att.com
Pomegranate juice, vinegar, apple cider and blends
President: Donna Sherril
Estimated Sales: $340,000
Number Employees: 5
Brands:
  Sherrill

11552 Sherwood Brands
120 Jersey Ave
New Brunswick, NJ 08901
973-249-8200
info@sherwoodbrands.net
sherwoodbrands.net
Manufacturer of chocolates, truffles, cookies, snacks, tea and cappuccino.
Type of Packaging: Consumer, Private Label
Brands:
  Candy Kaleidoscope
  Cap'n Poptoy
  Cherry & Berry Blast
  Creative Gourmet
  Tweety
  Tweety Pops
  Wan-Na-Bes

11553 Sherwood Brands of Rhode Island Inc
275 Ferris Avenue
Rumford, RI 02916-1033
401-726-4500
sherwoodbrands.net
Candy and candy novelties
Estimated Sales: $5-9.9 Million
Number Employees: 20-49
Parent Co: Sherwood Brands

11554 Sheryl's Chocolate Creations
11 Commercial St
Hicksville, NY 11801-5211
516-681-4060
Fax: 516-681-4189 888-882-2462
Hand-dipped chocolate chips, pretzel rods, pretzel twists, sourdough pretzels, mini pretzels, popcorn and assorted cookies
President: Sheryl Simon
Purchasing Manager: Ron Simon
Estimated Sales: $1-2.5 Million
Number Employees: 10-19
Square Footage: 16000
Type of Packaging: Consumer, Private Label, Bulk

11555 Shields Date Garden
80225 US Highway 111
Indio, CA 92201-6599
760-347-0996
Fax: 760-342-3288 800-414-2555
shieldate@aol.com
Nuts, dates and fruits including citrus and dried; also, mail order available
Owner: Greg Raumin
jeweldate@aol.com
Estimated Sales: $5-10 Million
Number Employees: 20-49
Type of Packaging: Consumer
Brands:
  Date Crystals

11556 Shiloh Farms
191 Commerce Drive
New Holland, PA 17557
800-362-6832
info@shilohfarms.com www.shilohfarms.com
Grains, fruits, nuts, potatoes

11557 Shine Companies
4014 Evening Trail Drive
Spring, TX 77388-4936
281-353-8392
Fax: 281-353-8937
Processor and exporter of specialty seasonings, artichoke dips and toppings and marinades, salsas and condiments; importer of chile purees
President: Michael Shine
Executive VP: Janet Williams
Number Employees: 6
Square Footage: 5000
Brands:
  Jazzie J
  Semdiero

11558 Shine Foods Inc
21100 S Western Avenue
Torrance, CA 90501-1700
310-533-6010
Fax: 310-328-2608 www.shinefood.com
Dim sum, pot stickers, dumplings, gyoza, shumai and spring rolls
President: Stephen Y Lee
VP: John Freschi
Marketing Manager: Tracy Lee
Estimated Sales: $300,000-500,000
Number Employees: 1-4
Type of Packaging: Private Label, Bulk

11559 Shining Ocean Inc
1515 Puyallup St
Sumner, WA 98390-2234
253-826-3700
Fax: 206-283-7079 800-935-6464
email@kanimi.com www.kanimi.com
Frozen surimi, imitation crab and shrimp
President: Robert Bleu
CFO: Howard Frisk
R & D: Tim Taylor
Quality Control: Raymond McReaey
Sales Coordinator: Yuji Ishii
Year Founded: 1985
Estimated Sales: $30-50 Million
Number Employees: 100-249
Type of Packaging: Consumer, Food Service, Private Label
Brands:
  Emerald Sea
  Heathy 1
  Kanimi-Tem
  Pacific Choice
  Sea Farer
  Shining Choice

11560 Shipley Do-Nut Franchise Co
5200 N Main St
Houston, TX 77009-3665
713-869-4636
Fax: 713-863-9623
Donuts
President: Christopher Halsey
bodner.michael@gmail.com
Number Employees: 10-19

11561 Shipyard Brewing Co
86 Newbury St
Portland, ME 04101-4274
207-761-0807
Fax: 207-775-5567 800-789-0684
www.shipyard.com
Processor and exporter of beer, ale, stout and root beer
Owner: Fred Forsley
fforsley@shipyard.com
Master Brewer: Alan Pugsley
Director of Sales And Marketing: Bruce Forsley
fforsley@shipyard.com
Director Manufacturing: Paul Henry
Estimated Sales: Under $500,000
Number Employees: 50-99
Number of Brands: 17
Type of Packaging: Consumer, Food Service
Brands:
  Blue Fin
  Chamberlain
  Goat Island Light
  Longfellow Winter
  Old Thumper Extra Special
  Prelude Christmas

11562 Shipyard Brewing Co
86 Newbury St
Portland, ME 04101-4274
207-761-0807
Fax: 207-775-5567 www.shipyard.com
Beer
Owner: Fred Forsley
fforsley@shipyard.com
Estimated Sales: Under $500,000
Number Employees: 50-99
Parent Co: Philip Morris Companies

11563 Shire City Herbals
703 W. Housatonic Street
Suite 120
Pittsfield, MA 01201
413-213-6702
info@firecider.com
firecider.com

Food Manufacturers / A-Z

Cider
Co-Owner: Amy Huebner
Co-Founder & CEO: Dana St.Pierre
Sales & Customer Service: Brian Huebner
Wholesale & Customer Service: Bethany Geiger
Number Employees: 11-50
Type of Packaging: Food Service
Brands:
    Fire Cider

11564 Shirer Brothers Meats
7805 Adamsville Otsego Rd
Adamsville, OH 43802-9732
    740-796-3214
Beef, beef products
Owner: Jon Shirer
Estimated Sales: $1-2.5 000,000
Number Employees: 1-4

11565 Shirley Foods
505 Walnut St
Shirley, IN 47384-1229
    765-738-6511
Fax: 765-738-6881 800-560-2908
www.shirleyfoods.com
Flour and corn tortillas
President: Gary Toth
gtoth@shirleyfoods.com
Estimated Sales: Less Than $500,000
Number Employees: 10-19
Brands:
    Shirley Foods

11566 Shirley J Ventures, LLC
1464 W 40 South
Lindon, UT 84042
    801-225-5073
Fax: 801-225-5616 www.shirleyj.com
Sauce, seasoning
President And CEO: Kelly Olsen
Contact: Joel Neilsen
joeln@shirleyj.com

11567 Shoei Foods USA Inc
1900 Feather River Blvd
Olivehurst, CA 95961
    530-237-1295
www.shoeifoodsusa.com
Pine nuts, pumpkin seeds, sunflower seeds, walnut kernels.
President & CEO: Brian Dunning
briand@shoeiusa.com
Manager, Quality Control & Assurance: Tom Roach
Director, Global Sales & Marketing: John Gaffney
Director, Operations: Dwight Davis
Estimated Sales: $50-100 Million
Number Employees: 100-249
Number of Brands: 2
Number of Products: 5
Square Footage: 30000
Type of Packaging: Consumer, Food Service, Private Label, Bulk
Brands:
    Shoei

11568 Shonan USA Inc
702 Wallace Way
Grandview, WA 98930-8844
    509-882-5583
Fax: 509-882-5890 www.shonan-flv.co.jp
Refrigerated fruit juice concentrates including apple, cherry, grape, pear, carrot, strawberry and red raspberry
President: Akira Nozaka
Controller: Douglas Foth
Estimated Sales: $7 Million
Number Employees: 50-99
Type of Packaging: Bulk
Brands:
    Shonan

11569 Shonna's Gourmet Goodies
320 W Center Street
West Bridgewater, MA 02379-1626
    508-580-2033
Fax: 508-580-2044 888-312-7868
Frozen hors d'oeuvres
Owner/President: Howard Sherman
Estimated Sales: Less than $500,000
Square Footage: 12000
Type of Packaging: Private Label

11570 Shooting Star Farms
4000 Wright Rd.
Bartlesville, OK 74006
    918-766-0800
Fax: 888-450-4004 888-850-8540
Dips, gourmet salsas, jellies
President: Jim Reali
Estimated Sales: $300,000-500,000
Number Employees: 1-4
Type of Packaging: Consumer

11571 Shore Seafood Distr
19424 Saxis Rd
Saxis, VA 23427
    757-824-5517
Fax: 757-824-5662 www.shoreseafoodinc.com
Seafood
President: Greg Linton
mlinton@shoreseafoodinc.com
Vice President: Andy Drewer
Estimated Sales: $5-10 Million
Number Employees: 20-49
Type of Packaging: Private Label
Brands:
    Chesapeake Bay Delight

11572 Shore Trading Co
665 Union Hill Rd
Alpharetta, GA 30004-5652
    770-998-0566
Fax: 770-998-0571
Seafood
Owner: Ron Williams
ron@shoretrading.net
Owner: Marty Klausner
Estimated Sales: $1 Million
Number Employees: 1-4

11573 Shoreline Chocolates
212 W Shore Rd
Alburg, VT 05440
    802-796-3730
Fax: 802-796-4725 800-310-3730
info@lakesendcheeses.com
Produces assorted homemade chocolates
Operator: Joanne James
Operator: Alton James
Estimated Sales: $300,000-500,000
Number Employees: 1-4

11574 Shoreline Fruit
10850 E Traverse Hwy
Suite 4460
Traverse City, MI 49684-1365
    231-941-4336
Fax: 231-941-4525 800-836-3972
cs@shorelinefruit.com www.shorelinefruit.com
Dried fruits, fruit juice and fruit concentrate
CEO: John Sommavilla
cs@shorelinefruit.com
Marketing Manager: Kristen Moravcik
Director, Sales & Marketing: Brian Gerberding
Number Employees: 10-19
Other Locations:
    Headquarters
    Traverse City MI
    Production & Storage
    Williamsburg MI

11575 Short's Brewing Co
121 N Bridge St
Bellaire, MI 49615-9509
    231-498-2300
www.shortsbrewing.com
Lagers and ales
Owner: Joseph Short
President: Leah Hannan
VP: Scott Bale
Estimated Sales: Less Than $500,000
Number Employees: 1-4
Square Footage: 56000

11576 Shreve Meats Processing
193 E Mcconkey Street
Shreve, OH 44676
    330-567-2142
Beef and pork
Co-Owner: Ray Haas
Co-Owner: Tim Morris
Estimated Sales: $140,000
Number Employees: 4

11577 Shrums Sausage & Meats
4703 42 Ave
Box 1495
Stettler, AB T0C 2L0
Canada
    403-742-1427
Fax: 403-742-1429
Fresh meats, processed meats, wild game, custom cutting & wrapping, pork, beef, and bison.
Manager: Randy Cherewko
Sales: Kelly Greenwood
Number Employees: 25
Type of Packaging: Consumer, Food Service

11578 Shuckman's Fish Co & Smokery
3001 W Main St
Louisville, KY 40212-1840
    502-775-6478
Fax: 502-775-6373
shuckmans@kysmokedfish.com
www.kysmokedfish.com
Smokers of fish & seafood products.
President: Lewis Shuckman
lshuckman@kysmokefish.com
Estimated Sales: $3-5 Million
Number Employees: 10-19

11579 Shuff's Meat Market
12247 Baugher Rd
Thurmont, MD 21788-2333
    301-271-2231
Fax: 301-271-1037
Meat products
Owner: Robin Shuff
Estimated Sales: $18 Million
Number Employees: 5-9

11580 Shur-Good Biscuit Co.
11677 Chesterdale Rd
Cincinnati, OH 45246-3917
    513-458-6200
Fax: 513-458-6212
Cookies
CFO: Nicola Melillo
Marketing Director: William Klump
Sales Director: Mark O'Toole
Public Relations: Kathy Coggeshall
Operations Manager: Peter Lowes
Manager: Jerry Wallman
Estimated Sales: $5-10 Million
Number Employees: 100-249
Parent Co: Parmalat Bakery Group North America
Type of Packaging: Consumer

11581 Sibu Sura Chocolates, LLC
PO Box 215
Myersville, MD 21773
    877-642-7872
www.sibusura.com
Manufacturer of chocolate, cocoa beans, and cocoa nib brew.
Owner: Julie McLean

11582 Sidari's Italian Foods
3820 Lakeside Ave E
Cleveland, OH 44114-3891
    216-431-3344
Fax: 216-431-6227
Salad and pasta products.
President: Joseph Sidari
Controller: Marty Goellnitz
HR Executive: Marty Goellintz
siditalian@aol.com
Sales Manager: Joe Falsone
Estimated Sales: $8.7 Million
Number Employees: 50-99

11583 Side Hill Farm
74 Cotton Mill Hl # A110
Brattleboro, VT 05301-8602
    802-254-2018
Fax: 802-254-3381 info@sidehillfarmjam.com
www.sidehillfarmjam.com
Manfacturer of jams
Owner: Kelt Naylor
Co-Owner: Caroline Naylor
Estimated Sales: $1-3 Million
Number Employees: 5-9
Number of Products: 14

Food Manufacturers / A-Z

11584 Sidehill Farm
PO Box 1558
Brattleboro, VT 05302
802-254-2018
Fax: 802-254-3381 info@sidehillfarmjam.com
Handmade jams, fruit butters and maple syrup.
Owner: Kelt Naylor
Year Founded: 1976
Estimated Sales: $1 Million
Number Employees: 2-10
Brands:
  Maple Apple Drizzle
  Sidehill Farm

11585 Sieco USA Corporation
9014 Ruland Rd
PO Box 55485
Houston, TX 77055-4612
713-464-1726
Olive oil, stuffed olives, vinegar and gift sets
President: Sherif Cheman
Marketing: Diann Fischer
Estimated Sales: B
Number Employees: 4
Number of Brands: 2
Number of Products: 11
Square Footage: 34400
Type of Packaging: Consumer, Food Service, Private Label, Bulk
Brands:
  Amber
  Sammy's

11586 Siegel Egg Co
90 Salem Rd # 3
North Billerica, MA 01862-2706
978-528-2010
Fax: 617-873-0824 info@siegelegg.com
www.siegelegg.com
Fresh and frozen eggs
Owner: Ken Siegel
kens@siegelegg.com
Office Manager: Amy Siegel
Plant Manager: Charlie Di Sciaca
Estimated Sales: $8.1 Million
Number Employees: 50-99
Square Footage: 36608
Type of Packaging: Consumer

11587 (HQ)Siemer Milling Co
111 W Main St
Teutopolis, IL 62467
217-857-3131
Fax: 217-857-3092 800-826-1065
www.siemermilling.com
Miller of wheat flours for applications from donuts to pretzels.
President: Richard Siemer
VP, Finance: Joyce Stock
VP, Grain Supply: Carl Schwinke
VP, Production: David Jansen
Year Founded: 1882
Estimated Sales: $75-99 Million
Number Employees: 170
Number of Brands: 3
Type of Packaging: Consumer, Food Service, Bulk
Other Locations:
  Mill
    Hopkinsville KY
  Mill
    Teutopolis IL
  Mill
    West Harrison IN
Brands:
  Don's Chuck Wagon
  Hodgson Mill
  Kentucky Kernel

11588 Siena Foods
16 Newbridge Road
Toronto, ON M8Z 2L7
Canada
416-239-3967
Fax: 416-239-2084 800-465-0422
Processor, importer and exporter of Italian style meat including Genoa salami, mortadella, cappicola, prosciutto and hot and mild sausage
General Manager: Enzo DeLuca
Number Employees: 50-99
Type of Packaging: Consumer, Food Service

11589 Sierra Cheese Mfg Co
916 S Santa Fe Ave
Compton, CA 90221-4392
310-635-1216
Fax: 310-639-1096 800-266-4270
www.sierracheese.com
Italian cheese including mozzarella, ricotta, string, tuma, scamorze, requeson, feta, etc
President: John Curran
sierracheese@aol.com
Vice President: Charlene Franco
Sales Director: Carlos Rivera
General Manager: Charlene Franco
Purchasing Manager: Vince Inga
Number Employees: 20-49
Square Footage: 60000
Type of Packaging: Consumer, Private Label, Bulk
Brands:
  Montebello
  Sierra

11590 Sierra Madre Coffee
191 University Blvd
Denver, CO 80206-4613
303-446-0050
Fax: 303-393-8208
Coffee
President: Mena Moran

11591 Sierra Nevada Cheese Co.
6505 County Rd
Suite 39
Willows, CA 95988
530-934-8660
Fax: 530-934-8670 info@sierranevadacheese.com
www.sierranevadacheese.com
Cow's and goat's milk products
Co-Founder: Ben Gregersen
Co-Founder: John Dundon

11592 Sierra Nevada Taproom &Rstrnt
1075 E 20th St
Chico, CA 95928-6722
530-893-3520
Fax: 530-893-9358 info@sierranevada.com
Seasonal beer, ale, stout, lager and pilsner
President: Brittany Adams
blebeladams@sierranevada.com
President: Terence Sullivan
Quality Control: Rebecca Newman
Production Manager: Cory Ross
Estimated Sales: $32 Million
Number Employees: 500-999
Type of Packaging: Consumer, Food Service
Brands:
  Porter & Stout
  Sierra Nevada Bigfoo
  Sierra Nevada Celebration
  Sierra Nevada Pale Ale
  Sierra Nevada Stout
  Sierra Nevada Summer

11593 Sierra Vista Winery
4560 Cabernet Way
Placerville, CA 95667-8410
530-622-7221
Fax: 530-622-2413 800-946-3916
www.sierravistawinery.com
Wines
Owner: John Mac Cready
Owner/Winery Office VP: Barbara MacCready
Estimated Sales: Below $5 Million
Number Employees: 1-4
Type of Packaging: Private Label
Brands:
  Sierra Vista

11594 Siete Family Foods
3571 Far West Blvd
Suite 200
Austin, TX 78731
sietefoods.com
Grain free tortillas and tortilla chips
Founder & President: Veronica Garza
Co-Founder & CEO: Miguel Garza
Brand Builder: Rebeca Palacios
Chief Operating Officer: Ben Ponder
Number Employees: 2-10
Brands:
  Siete

11595 Sifers Valomilk Candy Co
5112 Merriam Dr
Shawnee, KS 66203-2118
913-722-0991
Fax: 913-722-5016 russ@valomilk.com
www.valomilk.com
Valomilk candy cups
President: Russell Sifers
russ@valomilk.com
Estimated Sales: $2.5-5 Million
Number Employees: 5-9
Number of Brands: 1
Number of Products: 1
Type of Packaging: Private Label
Brands:
  Sifers Valomilk Candy Cups

11596 Siggi's Dairy
135 West 26th St
Suite 4C
New York, NY 10001
212-966-6950
www.siggisdairy.com
Icelandic-style yogurt
Founder and CEO: Siggi Hilmarsson
President: Bart Adlam
Contact: Virginia Wong
virginia.wong@skyr.com
Year Founded: 2004

11597 Siggi's Dairy
855-860-6683
siggis.com
A variety of yogurt products, uncluding cups, drinkables, and plant-based.
Founder: Siggi Hilmarsson
Year Founded: 2006
Parent Co: Lactalis
Type of Packaging: Private Label

11598 Signature Beverage
PO Box 695
Merrick, NY 11566-0695
516-867-8291
Fax: 516-377-1228 800-277-2755
signaturebeverage@gmail.com
signaturebeverage.net
Sparkling and spring water, root beer and black cherry and cream soda, diet root beer, diet black cherry, iced tea, lemonade, grape soda, raspberry lime rickey, orange soda
President: Mark Eisenberg
VP: Rebecca Scott
Sales Manager: Richard Stern
Estimated Sales: $1 Million
Number Employees: 5
Square Footage: 20000
Type of Packaging: Food Service, Private Label

11599 Signature Brands LLC
808 SW 12th St
Ocala, FL 34471-0540
352-622-3134
Fax: 352-402-9451 800-456-9573
info@signaturebrands.com
www.signaturebrands.com
Manufacturer, importer, and exporter of dessert decorating and specialty baking products. Importer of preserves.
Co-Founder: Louise Crawford
Co-Founder: Bobby Jones
Year Founded: 1951
Estimated Sales: $20-50 Million
Number Employees: 100-249
Square Footage: 80000
Parent Co: McCormick & Company
Type of Packaging: Consumer, Food Service, Private Label, Bulk
Brands:
  Betty Crocker
  Cake Mate
  PAAS
  Pumpkin Masters

11600 Signature Foods
73-D Enterprise Drive
Pendergrass, DR 30587
706-693-0098
Co-packer and support manufacturer for food companies
President: Oran B Talkington
Estimated Sales: $3.3 Million
Number Employees: 23

Food Manufacturers / A-Z

11601 Signature Fruit
1 Tiffany Point
Suite 206
Bloomingdale, IL 60108-2916
630-980-2481
Fax: 630-980-3211
Canned foods including fruits and vegetables
Director (Central Zone): Bruce Scheer
Business Manager (Midwest): Hank Gergovich
Estimated Sales: $3-5 Million
Number Employees: 1-4
Parent Co: Tri-Valley Growers
Type of Packaging: Consumer

11602 Signature Seafoods Inc
4257 24th Ave W
Seattle, WA 98199-1214
206-285-2815
Fax: 206-282-5938 www.signatureseafoods.com
Salmon
President: Gabriel Angelo
gangelo@signatureseafoods.com
Estimated Sales: $4,000,000
Number Employees: 5-9
Brands:
 H&G Chum
 King Salmon
 Silver Salmon

11603 Signore Winery
153 White Church Road
Brooktondale, NY 14817-9769
607-539-7935
Wines
Owner: Daniel Signore
Estimated Sales: $1-4.9 000,000
Number Employees: 1-5

11604 Signorello Vineyards
4500 Silverado Trl
Napa, CA 94558-1100
707-255-5990
Fax: 707-255-5999 info@signorellovineyards.com
www.signorellovineyards.com
Wines
Owner: Ray Signorello
National Sales Director: Chris Carmichael
Director Marketing: Bruce Donsker
Contact: Jeff Adams
jadams@signorelloestate.com
Winemaker: Raymond Signorello
jadams@signorelloestate.com
Wine Maker / Vineyard Manager: Pierre Birebent
Estimated Sales: Below $5 Million
Number Employees: 5-9
Brands:
 Signorello

11605 Sigona's
San Carlos, CA 94070
650-368-6992
helloFFT@sigonas.com
www.fruitforthought.com
Organic dried fruits
Brands:
 Fruit for Thought

11606 Silani Sweet Cheese
10 Roybridge Gate
Suite 100
Woodbridge, ON L4H 3M8
Canada
905-792-3811
Fax: 905-792-7693 feedback@silani.ca
www.silanicheese.com
Processor and importer of cheese
President: Michael Talarico
CEO/VP: Joe Lanzino
Number Employees: 185
Square Footage: 100000

11607 Silesia Flavors
5250 Prairie Stone Pkwy
Hoffman Estates, IL 60192-3709
847-645-0270
Fax: 847-645-0266 info.us@silesia.com
www.silesia-aroma.com
Manufacturers of liquid, powder and granulated flavorings for the food and beverage industries.
Vice President: Richard Bartoszewski
richard@silesiafl.com
Vice President: Richard Bartoszewski
richard@silesiafl.com
Number Employees: 10-19

Brands:
 Sil-A-Gran
 Silarom
 Silvanil

11608 Siljans Crispy Cup Company
23 Skyline Crest NE
Calgary, AB T2K 5X2
Canada
403-275-0135
Fax: 403-275-0061 4sale@siljanscrispycup.com
www.siljanscrispycup.com
Processor and exporter of edible cups for hors d'oeuvres and desserts
President: B Ersson
CEO: Christina Ersson
Estimated Sales: $500,000
Number Employees: 5
Number of Brands: 1
Number of Products: 1
Square Footage: 32000
Type of Packaging: Consumer, Food Service, Private Label, Bulk
Brands:
 Salmolux
 Siljans

11609 Sill Farm Market
50241 Red Arrow Hwy
Lawrence, MI 49064-8781
269-674-3755
Fax: 269-674-3756 www.sillfarms.com
Frozen and fresh sliced fruits
President: Lois Ross
lross@castleofspirits.com
Estimated Sales: $5-9.9 000,000
Number Employees: 20-49
Brands:
 Plowshares
 Sunshower

11610 Silva Farms
111 Alpine Dr
Gonzales, CA 93926
831-675-2428
Fax: 831-675-2375
Vegetables
Owner: Edward Skua Jr
Manager: Theresa Silva-Amaral
Estimated Sales: $500,000-$1 000,000
Number Employees: 100-249
Type of Packaging: Private Label, Bulk

11611 Silva International
523 N Ash St
Momence, IL 60954-1335
815-472-3535
Fax: 815-472-3536 silva-intl.com
Supplier of dehydrated vegetable, herb and fruit ingredients to the food industry.
President: Peter Schmidt
Vice President: Kent DeVries
Quality Assurance Manager: Ed Bove
General Manager: Steve DeYoung
Sales Manager: Darren VanEssen
Number Employees: 10-19
Other Locations:
 Headquarters
 Momence IL
 South American Procurement
 Santiago, Chile
 South American Sales
 Lima, Peru
 European Procurement
 Schwetzingen, Germany
 Asian Quality & Procurement
 Qingdao, China

11612 Silvan Ridge Winery
27012 Briggs Hill Rd
Eugene, OR 97405-9767
541-345-1945
Fax: 541-345-6174 info@silvanridge.com
Wines
Owner: Liz Chambers
CEO: Elizabeth Chambers
CFO: Jim Plumber
Quality Control: Bryan Wilson
Marketing: Phil Cowles
Sales: Ryan Shockley
liz@silvanridge.com
Public Relations: Angela Bennett
Operations: Haley Smith

Estimated Sales: Below $5 Million
Number Employees: 5-9
Number of Brands: 2
Brands:
 Hinman Vineyards
 Silvan Ridge

11613 Silvateam USA
3200 E Guasti Road
Suite 100
Ontario, CA 91761
909-635-2870
Fax: 909-635-2871 en.silvateam.com
Ingredient producers and manufacturers serving the food, beverage, feed and other industries.
Parent Co: Silvateam

11614 Silver Creek Distillers
134 North 3300 East
Rigby, ID 83442
208-754-0042
Fax: 208-754-4758
Beverage grade alcohol
Manager: Bill Scott
Contact: Gray Ottley
gray@waytogoidaho.com
Estimated Sales: $3.2 000,000
Number Employees: 5-9
Brands:
 Teton Glacier Vodka

11615 Silver Creek Farms
450 Locust St S
Twin Falls, ID 83301-7848
208-736-0829
Fax: 208-736-0725
Smoked fruit and salmon

11616 Silver Creek Specialty Meats
153 W 28th Ave
Oshkosh, WI 54902-7202
920-232-3581
Fax: 920-232-3589 800-729-2849
office@silvercreekspecialtymeats.com
www.silvercreekspecialtymeats.com
Natural casing sausage
President: William Kramlich Sr
CEO: Bill Kramlich Jr
Estimated Sales: $4.5 Million
Number Employees: 10-19
Type of Packaging: Food Service, Private Label, Bulk

11617 Silver Fern Chemical Inc
2226 Queen Anne Ave N # C
Seattle, WA 98109-2372
206-282-3376
Fax: 206-282-0105 866-282-3384
info@silverfernchemical.com
www.silverfernchemical.com
Food chemicals and ingredients
President: Sam King
sam@silverfernchemical.com
Number Employees: 1-4

11618 Silver Fox Vineyards
4683 Morning Star Ln
Mariposa, CA 95338-9361
209-966-4800
Fax: 209-966-4369 enjoy@sti.net
Wines
Co-Owner/Co-Operator: Marvin Silver
Co-Owner/Co-Operator: Karen Silver
Estimated Sales: Below $5 Million
Number Employees: 1-4
Brands:
 Silver Fox Vineyard

11619 Silver Lake Sausage Shop
80 Ethan St
Providence, RI 02909-5327
401-944-4081
Sausage
President: Erminia Santilli
Estimated Sales: Less Than $500,000
Number Employees: 1-4

11620 (HQ)Silver Lining Seafood
5303 Shilshole Ave. N.W.
PO Box 6092
Seattle, WA 98107-4000
206-783-3818
Fax: 206-782-7195 800-426-5490
www.tridentseafoods.com

Processor and exporter of fresh, smoked and canned seafood.
Plant Manager: Leigh Gerber
Estimated Sales: $500,000-$1 Million
Number Employees: 5-9
Type of Packaging: Consumer, Food Service, Bulk

11621 Silver Mountain Vineyards
PO Box 3636
Santa Cruz, CA 95063-3636
408-353-2278
Fax: 408-353-1898 info@silvermtn.com
www.silvermtn.com
Wine
President: Jerold O'Brien
info@silvermtn.com
Estimated Sales: Less Than $500,000
Number Employees: 1-4
Type of Packaging: Private Label
Brands:
Silver Mtn Vineyards

11622 Silver Oak
915 Oakville Cross Road
Oakville, CA 94562
707-944-8808
Fax: 707-944-2817 www.silveroak.com
Maker of Cabernet Sauvignon
President & CEO: David Duncan
CFO: Rickie Pina

11623 Silver Palate Kitchens
221 Knickerbocker Rd
Cresskill, NJ
201-568-0110
www.silverpalate.com
Vinegars, oils, chutneys, mustards, savories, sweet sauces, preserves, brandied fruits, salad dressings, pasta sauces, oatmeals and berry cereals.
President & CEO: Peter Harris
Estimated Sales: $20-50 Million
Number Employees: 20-49
Type of Packaging: Consumer, Food Service, Private Label, Bulk
Brands:
Silver Palate

11624 Silver Spoon
92 S Central Ave
Hartsdale, NY 10530-2301
914-328-1536
Fax: 914-694-5622
Manager: John Randall
Estimated Sales: Less than $500,000
Number Employees: 1-4
Parent Co: Armenia Coffee Corporation

11625 Silver Spring Foods
2424 Alpine Road
Eau Clair, MI 54703
715-830-9702 800-826-7322
info@bredefoods.com silverspringfoods.com
Processor and exporter of horseradish and horseradish sauce, as well as other specialty sauces including mustards, siracha, tartar, and wasabi sauces.
Chairman/CEO: Nancy Bartusch
Distribution & Warehouse Manager: Allyssa Fradette
Estimated Sales: $630,000
Number Employees: 5-9
Square Footage: 36000
Parent Co: Hunstinger Farms, Inc.
Type of Packaging: Consumer, Food Service, Private Label, Bulk
Brands:
Brede Old Fashioned
Farmers
Hi Praize
Old Fashioned
Poznanski

11626 Silver Springs Citrus Inc
25411 Mare Ave
Howey-in-the-Hills, FL 34737
610-793-0266
800-940-2277
bhughes@aol.com www.healthysqueezejuices.com
Manufacturer, importer and exporter of juices.
Treasurer: Michael Hall
Human Resources: Debra Fontaine
Operations Manager: Patrick Falcone
Purchasing Director: Pat Patrick
Estimated Sales: $35.1 Million
Number Employees: 100-249
Square Footage: 1260
Type of Packaging: Consumer, Food Service, Private Label, Bulk

11627 Silver Star Meats Inc
1720 Middletown Rd
PO Box 393
Mc Kees Rocks, PA 15136-1602
412-771-4064
Fax: 412-771-2253 800-548-1321
info@silverstarmeats.com
www.silverstarmeats.com
Hams, sausages, hotdogs, kielbasa, lunch meats
President: Robert Geromoy
Plant Manager: Dominic Bovalina
Estimated Sales: $11 Million
Number Employees: 1-4
Square Footage: 110000
Type of Packaging: Consumer, Food Service, Private Label
Brands:
Rzaca

11628 Silver State Foods Inc
3725 Jason St
PO Box 11505
Denver, CO 80211-2624
303-433-3351
Fax: 303-433-2883 800-423-3351
tom@silverstatefoods.com
www.silverstatefoods.com
Canned and frozen foods including prepared, spaghetti sauce and egg noodles
Manager: Tom Ernst
Manager: Pasqual Aiello
pasqual.aiello@silverstatefoods.com
Estimated Sales: $600,000
Number Employees: 1-4
Number of Brands: 2
Number of Products: 2
Square Footage: 22400
Type of Packaging: Consumer, Food Service, Private Label, Bulk
Brands:
Aiellos
Salvatore's

11629 Silver Streak Bass Co
1205 Frank Stubbs Dr
PO Box 499
El Campo, TX 77437-6164
979-543-6343
Fax: 979-543-8988 info@silverstreakbass.com
www.silverstreakbass.com
Producer of farm-raised hybrid striped bass
Owner: James Ekstrom
jekstrom@silverstreakbass.com
Estimated Sales: Less Than $500,000
Number Employees: 1-4
Parent Co: Ekstrom Enterprises
Type of Packaging: Bulk
Brands:
Silver Streak

11630 Silver Sweet Candies
522 Essex St
Lawrence, MA 01840-1242
978-688-0474
Fax: 978-683-6636
Candy and confections
Owner: Robert Burkinshaw
candyman1806@aol.com
Estimated Sales: Below $5 000,000
Number Employees: 10-19

11631 Silver Tray Cookies
6861 SW 196th Avenue
Suite 203
Fort Lauderdale, FL 33332-1628
305-883-0800
Fax: 305-888-8438
Cookies, sugar free pound cake and fruit flavored cream cakes
President: Perry Burk
Estimated Sales: Below $5 Million
Number Employees: 2
Brands:
Silver Tray Cookies

11632 Silverado Vineyards Inc
6121 Silverado Trl
Napa, CA 94558-9415
707-257-1770
Fax: 707-257-1538 800-997-1770
neliason@silveradovineyards.com
Processors of wine
Owner: Ron Miller
rmiller@silveradovineyards.com
Owner: Diane Miller
General Manager: Russ Weis
Winemaker: Jon Emmerich
Number Employees: 20-49

11633 Silverbow Honey Company
1120 E Wheeler Rd
Moses Lake, WA 98837
509-765-6616
Fax: 509-765-6549 866-444-6639
Specialty honey, table honey, gourmet honey, sweet mustard, hot honey mustard, honey butter, gift sets, beeswax, beeswax candles and both colored and natural beeswax.
President: Gary Grigg
Office Manager: Eric Peters
Estimated Sales: $7.2 Million
Number Employees: 20-49
Square Footage: 152000
Type of Packaging: Consumer, Food Service, Private Label, Bulk
Brands:
Silverbow

11634 Silverland Bakery
439 Des Plaines Ave
Forest Park, IL 60130
708-488-0800
Fax: 708-488-0894 info@silverlandbakery.com
silverlandbakery.com
Brownies, bars, cookies and cakes.
Owner & President: Athena Uslander
Type of Packaging: Consumer, Food Service, Private Label
Brands:
Silverland Desserts

11635 Silverleaf International Corp
5050 Knight Rd
Suite 230 #218
Rosharon, TX 77583-2608
281-495-1250
Fax: 281-499-5505 800-442-7542
www.4garlic.net
Marinated garlic hors d'oeuvres, blue cheese and feta cheese stuffed olives, olive oils, dips and salsa, spices and seasonings, jams and jellies, sauces, Italian pasta.
President: Neal McWeeney
VP: Adriane McWeeney
Estimated Sales: Less Than $500,000
Number Employees: 1-4
Number of Brands: 1
Number of Products: 50
Type of Packaging: Consumer, Private Label

11636 Silverston Fisheries
1507 N 1st St
Superior, WI 54880-1146
715-392-5551
Fax: 715-392-5586
Fish
Owner: Stuart Sivertson
Estimated Sales: $10-20 000,000
Number Employees: 20-49

11637 Simi Winery
16275 Healdsburg Ave
Healdsburg, CA 95448-9075
707-433-3686
Fax: 707-433-6253 www.simiwine.com
Wines
Owner: Peter Seghesio
VP Winemaker: Roger Coldschmidt
Executive VP: Steve Reeder
steve.reeder@simiwinery.com
Sales Director: Steve Messinger
Operations Manager: Jim Debonis
Estimated Sales: $20-50 Million
Number Employees: 50-99
Parent Co: Canandaigua Wine Company

Food Manufacturers / A-Z

11638 Simit + Smith
501 Broad Ave
Suite 6
Ridgefield, NJ 07657
201-699-0320
info@simitandsmith.com
simitandsmith.com
Simits, breads, pastries, breadsticks, biscotti and cookies
President & General Manager: Zulfikar Bekar

11639 (HQ)Simmons Foods Inc
601 N Hico St
Siloam Springs, AR 72761-2410
479-524-8151
Fax: 479-524-6562 888-831-7007
Chicken including; boneless skinless tenderloins and breasts, breaded tenderloins, chicken wings, fully cooked, ready to cook, frozen, fresh, marinated, glazed, grill marked, portioning and pack sizes
President: Tammy Bomar
tbomar@marykay.com
CFO: Mike Jones
Director Research & Development: Brian Davis
Marketing Manager: Joseph Meszaros
VP Sales: Chip Miller
Director of Public Relations: Mary Doyle
Plant Manager: Brian Burke
Number Employees: 100-249
Square Footage: 120000
Type of Packaging: Consumer, Food Service, Private Label, Bulk
Brands:
  Manu Maker
  Simmons
  Town & Country
  Water Valley Farms

11640 Simmons Hot Gourmet Products Corp.
22 Greenview Close
Lethbridge, AB T1H 4K8
Canada
403-327-9087
Fax: 403-328-9589 sales@firenbrimstone.com
www.firenbrimstone.com

11641 Simon Hubig Company
2417 Dauphine St
New Orleans, LA 70117
504-945-2181
Fax: 504-945-2328
Baked goods
President: Thomas Bowman
Owner: Otto Ramsey
Contact: Drew Ramsey
drew@hubigs.com
Production Manager: Mike Tricou
Estimated Sales: $2.3 Million
Number Employees: 40
Square Footage: 64000

11642 Simon Levi Cellars
9380 Sonoma Hwy
Kenwood, CA 95452-9032
707-833-5070
Fax: 707-833-1355 888-315-0040
info@slcellars.com www.slcellars.com
Wines
President: John Garaventa
j.garaventa@slcellars.com
Estimated Sales: $1-2.5 Million
Number Employees: 10-19
Brands:
  Maboroshi
  Slc

11643 Simon's Specialty Cheese
2735 Freedom Rd
Appleton, WI 54913-9315
920-788-6311
Fax: 920-788-1424 800-444-0374
www.simonscheese.com
Signature cheeses such as feta, extra sharp cheddar, and marbled cheeses.
President: Doug Simon
General Manager: David Sohrweide
Cheesemaker: Terry Lensmire
Operations/R&D: Chris Simon
Estimated Sales: $25-49.9 Million
Number Employees: 50-99
Type of Packaging: Private Label
Brands:
  Simon's

11644 Simpatica
355 Lantana St.
Suite 725
Camarillo, CA 93010
310-286-2236
simpatica.ag
Avocados
Founder: Jamie Johnson
CEO & Partner: Scott Bauwens
Year Founded: 2013
Number Employees: 5-10
Type of Packaging: Private Label

11645 Simple Foods
116 Killewald Ave
Tonawanda, NY 14150
716-743-8850
800-234-8850
Nuts and nut butter
President: Karen Pease
Estimated Sales: Under $500,000
Number Employees: 1-4
Type of Packaging: Consumer, Bulk
Brands:
  Annie's
  Magic Munchie

11646 Simple Mills
435 N LaSalle St
2nd Floor
Chicago, IL 60654
312-600-6196
info@simplemills.com
www.simplemills.com
Natural baking mixes and crackers
Founder & CEO: Katlin Smith
Quality Assurance & Compliance: Ryan Johnson
Vice President, Marketing: Michelle Lorge
Vice President, Sales: Bobbie Turco
Operations Manager: Megan Huber
Estimated Sales: $500,000-$1,000,000
Number Employees: 100
Brands:
  Simple Mills

11647 Simplot Food Group
PO Box 9386
Boise, ID 83707
208-336-2110
800-572-7783
jrs_info@simplot.com www.simplotfoods.com
Distributor of avocado pulp, frozen potatoes, frozen fruit, frozen vegetables and frozen cornados
Parent Co: J.R. Simplot Company
Type of Packaging: Food Service

11648 Simply 7 Snacks
PO Box 710543
Houston, TX 77271
877-682-2359
Fax: 877-682-2368
paul.albrecht@simply7snacks.com
www.simply7snacks.com
Hummus and Lentil chips
President: Rashim Oberoi
Contact: Paul Albrecht
palbrecht@simply7snacks.com

11649 Simply Auri
1111 Hope St.
Suite 8
Stamford, CT 06907
860-389-2265
info@simplyauri.com
simplyauri.com
Wood ear mushroom drink
Co-Founder: Wei Chien Liang
Number Employees: 2-10
Brands:
  Mad,casse

11650 Simply Delicious
8411 Highway N Carolina 86 N
Cedar Grove, NC 27231
919-732-5294
Fax: 919-732-5180
Sauces, dressings
President: John Troy

11651 Simply Divine
334 Amsterdam Ave
New York, NY 10023-8205
212-541-7300
Fax: 917-553-7510 info@simplydivine.com
www.simplydivine.com
Kosher gourmet soups, sauces, entrees, salads and desserts
Owner/President: Judith Geller Marlow
jmarlow@simplydivine.com
Estimated Sales: $500,000-$1 Million
Number Employees: 20-49
Type of Packaging: Consumer, Food Service
Brands:
  Simply Divine

11652 Simply Gourmet Confections
PO Box 50141
Irvine, CA 92619
714-505-3955
Fax: 714-505-3957 info@simplyscrumptious.com
www.simplyscrumptious.com
Gourmet confections and cookies
President/Owner: Debra Formaneck

11653 Simply Gum
270 Lafatette St
New York, NY 10012
info@simplygum.com
www.simplygum.com
All-natural chewing gum
Founder/CEO: Caron Proschan
Marketing: Kelsey Jones
Sales/Operations Coordinator: Elise Goree
Sr Operations Manager: Emanuel Storch
Year Founded: 2014

11654 Simply Incredible Foods
140 Market Ave
Port Edwards, WI 54469-1346
715-697-6232
Fax: 715-909-0060 www.cransations.com
Cranberry ingredients processor.
Contact: Christine Sohns
chrissohns@yahoo.com
Number Employees: 5-9
Brands:
  Freeze Dried Cransations
  Squozen Frozen
  Cransations
  RazzAronia

11655 Simply Panache
26 Towne Center Way
Suite 162
Hampton, VA 23666
800-313-5613
contact@amangoparty.com
www.amangoparty.com
Manufacturer of mango preserves.
Co-Founder: Tanecia Willis
Co-Founder: Lakesha Brown-Renfro
Co-Founder: Nzinga Teule-Hekima
Brands:
  Mango Mango

11656 Simply Scruptious Confections
PO Box 50141
Irvine, CA 92619
714-505-3955
Fax: 714-505-3957 info@simplyscrumptious.com
www.simplyscrumptious.com
White bark candy falvors include peppermint, lemon, raspberry, cafe latte, key lime, cookies and cream and orange cremesicle. Also tea cake cookies

11657 Simply Shari's Gluten Free
890 Hampshire Rd
Suite S
Thousand Oaks, CA 91361-2875
805-241-5676
Fax: 602-218-8409 info@simplysharis.com
Cookies, pasta meals
Owner: Shari Cole
Co-Owner: Larry Schneider
Operations Manager: Lia Lang

11658 SimplyFUEL, LLC
Leawood, KS
913-269-1889
info@simplyfuel.com
simplyfuel.com
Protein balls
Founder: Mitzi Dulan

Food Manufacturers / A-Z

11659 Simpson & Vail
3 Quarry Rd
Brookfield, CT 06804-1053
203-775-0240
Fax: 203-775-0462 800-282-8327
info@svtea.com www.svtea.com
Processor, exporter and importer of coffee and gourmet tea
President: Jim Harron Jr
CEO: Joan Harron
Estimated Sales: $.5-1 million
Number Employees: 5-9
Square Footage: 32000
Type of Packaging: Food Service

11660 Simpson Spring Co
719 Washington St
South Easton, MA 02375-1139
508-238-4472
Fax: 508-238-5691 www.simpsonspring.com
Flavoring extracts for carbonated beverages
Owner: Jim Bertarelli
webmaster@simpsonspring.com
Estimated Sales: $2.9 Million
Number Employees: 10-19

11661 Sims Wholesale
540 River St
Batesville, AR 72501
870-793-1109
Fax: 870-793-2230
Wholesaler/distributor of general line products; serving the food service market
General Manager: Kenneth Thornton
Manager: Mike Hanson

11662 Sinai Gourmet
Montreal, QC
Canada
844-887-4624
info@sinaigourmet.com
sinaigourmet.com
Hot pepper coulis: ghost pepper, habanero and jalapeno.
Founder: Laurence Isaac
Number Employees: 2-10
Brands:
  Sinai Gourmet

11663 Sinbad Sweets
2401 West Almond Avenue
Madera, CA 93637
559-298-3700
Fax: 559-298-9194 866-746-2232
www.sinbadsweets.com
Pastries including baklava, strudel, tarts and fillo; exporter of baklava
President: Michael Muhawir
CEO: Edwina Aquino Seidel
COO: Anita Reina
Vice President: John Seidel
Public Relations: Sascha Muhawi
Operations Manager: Larry Burrow
Production Manager: Klaus Gernet
Number Employees: 50-99
Square Footage: 120000
Type of Packaging: Consumer, Food Service, Private Label, Bulk
Brands:
  Oliver Twist
  Sinbad Sweets

11664 Singer Extract Laboratory
13301 Inkster Rd
Livonia, MI 48150-2226
313-345-5880
Fax: 313-345-8686
Extracts and flavorings, food colorings, bar specialties and syrups.
President: Mike Letourneau
Estimated Sales: Below $5 Million
Number Employees: 3
Number of Brands: 3
Number of Products: 50
Square Footage: 20000
Brands:
  4%
  Belmo
  Seely

11665 Singing Dog Vanilla
255 Wallis St
Suite 1
Eugene, OR 97402
541-343-2746
Fax: 541-610-1868 888-343-0002
www.singingdogvanilla.com
Vanilla products

11666 Singleton Seafood
P.O.Box 2819
Tampa, FL 33601-2819
813-719-6626
Fax: 813-247-1782 800-732-3663
info@tbfish.com
Frozen shrimp, breaded fish and shrimp, peeled and deveined shrimp, cooked shrimp, shrimp specialties
President: Dennis Reeves
CFO: Andrew Hawaux
Vice President: Rob Sharpe
Research & Development: Nina Burt
Quality Control: Don Toloday
Marketing Director: Dan Davis
Sales Director: Doug Knudsen
Production Manager: Bill Jacks
Plant Manager: Mike Pent
Purchasing Manager: Bill Stone
Estimated Sales: $300,000-500,000
Number Employees: 1-4
Number of Brands: 8
Number of Products: 200
Square Footage: 800000
Parent Co: ConAgra Foods
Type of Packaging: Consumer, Food Service, Private Label, Bulk

11667 Singleton Seafood Company
1804 Turkey Creek Road
Plant City, FL
813-241-1500
Seafood
President: Robert Patterson
Human Resources Manager: Alan Lewis
Contact: Bob Bruno
bob.bruno@singletonseafood.com
Estimated Sales: $20-49.9 Million
Number Employees: 350
Type of Packaging: Private Label

11668 Sini Fulvi U.S.A.
136 Mohawk St
Newark, NJ 07114-3314
973-274-0822
Fax: 718-361-6999 sinifulvi@aol.com
Importer of Italian, Spanish and Portuguese cheeses and Italian cured meats
President: Agostino Sini
Vice President: Pierluigi Sini
Marketing Director: Michele Buster
Estimated Sales: $.5-1 million
Number Employees: 4
Parent Co: Sini Fulvi
Type of Packaging: Consumer, Food Service, Bulk
Brands:
  Cacio De Roma
  Cacio De Roma Cheese
  Crotonese
  Drunken Goat Cheese
  Genuine
  Genuine Fulvi Romano Cheese
  I Buoonatarula Sini
  Pasture Sini
  Rustico Cheese
  Sfizio Crotonese
  Sini Fulvi
  Spizzico Pepato Aged
  Triggi

11669 Sioux Honey Assn.
301 Lewis Blvd
Sioux City, IA 51101-2237
712-258-0638
Fax: 712-258-1332 www.suebee.com
Honey collective with more than 300 members.
President & CEO: David Allibone
CEO: Lisa Hansel
lhansel@suebeehoney.com
Year Founded: 1921
Number Employees: 100-249
Type of Packaging: Consumer, Food Service, Private Label, Bulk
Other Locations:
  Processing Plant
  Sioux City IA
  Processing Plant
  Anaheim CA
  Processing Plant
  Elizabethtown NC
Brands:
  Aunt Sue's
  Sue Bee

11670 Sipp
Stamford, CT
866-222-4735
hello@enjoysipp.com
www.enjoysipp.com
Sodas.
Year Founded: 2009
Brands:
  Sipp

11671 Sir Kensington's
101 W 24th Street
Apartment 27H
New York, NY 10011
646-450-5735
Fax: 646-755-3765 hello@sirkensingtons.com
www.sirkensingtons.com
Condiments
Co-Founder: Mark Ramadan
Co-Founder: Scott Norton

11672 Sir Real Foods
50 Hazelton Drive
White Plains, NY 10605-3816
914-948-9342
Fax: 914-948-9342 www.sirreal.com
Juices, beverages
President: Michael Albert
Vice President: Douglas Albert
Estimated Sales: Under $500,000
Number Employees: 2
Brands:
  Americus Natural Spring Water

11673 Siren Snacks
San Francisco, CA
hello@sirensnacks.com
www.sirensnacks.com
Protein bites
Co-Founder: Elizabeth Gianuzzi
Co-Founder: Abby Gianuzzi

11674 Sirocco Enterprises Inc
228 Industrial Ave
New Orleans, LA 70121-2904
504-834-1549
Fax: 504-837-7762 www.siroccoenterprises.com
Manufacturer and exporter of ready-to-use liquid cocktail mixers
Vice President: Anthony Muto
VP: Anthony Muto
Production: Benny Peel
Estimated Sales: $1 Million
Number Employees: 10-19
Number of Brands: 1
Number of Products: 10
Square Footage: 52000
Type of Packaging: Food Service
Brands:
  Pat O'Brien's Cocktail Mixes

11675 Sisler's Ice & Ice Cream
102 South Grove Street
Ohio, IL 61349
815-376-2913
888-891-3856
sisler@sisler.com www.sislers.com
Ice, ice cream
Owner/Operator: Bill Sisler
Manager: Dan Thompson
Estimated Sales: $500,000-$1 Million
Number Employees: 5-9
Square Footage: 72000
Type of Packaging: Consumer, Food Service
Brands:
  Sisler's Dairy

11676 Sister River Foods
PO Box 5563
Central Point, OR 97502
541-665-0348
www.eatparma.com
Vegan cheese manufacturer

1119

Food Manufacturers / A-Z

11677 Sister's Gourmet
965 Patrick Industrial Ct
Winder, GA 30680-8336
770-338-1388
Fax: 770-338-1267 877-338-1388
www.sistersgourmet.com
Gourmet cookie mixes
Owner: Lisa Sorensen
Estimated Sales: $5-10 Million
Number Employees: 50-99

11678 Sister's Gourmet
965 Patrick Industrial Ct
Winder, GA 30680-8336
770-338-1388
Fax: 770-338-1267 www.sistersgourmet.com
Manufacturer of baking mixes.
President and Owner: Lisa Sorensen
Director of Sales and Marketing: Andy Dollar
Number Employees: 50-99
Type of Packaging: Consumer

11679 Sisters' Gourmet
PO Box 1550
Dacula, GA 30019-0027
216-292-7700
Fax: 216-292-7701 orders@brandcastle.com
www.sistersgourmet.com
Baking mixes: cookie and brownie
R&D Project Manager: Taylor Reagan
Marketing Services: Linda Bina
Number Employees: 11-50
Parent Co: Brand Castle
Type of Packaging: Consumer, Private Label
Brands:
  Magical Reindeer Food
  Sisters Gourmet

11680 Sivetz Coffee
349 SW 4th St
Corvallis, OR 97333-4622
541-753-9713
Fax: 541-757-7644
Roasted coffee beans, extracts, almond kernels, hazelnut kernels, and coffee roasting machines
President: Mike Sivetz
Number Employees: 1-4
Type of Packaging: Consumer, Bulk
Brands:
  Sivetz Coffee Essence

11681 Six Mile Creek Vineyard
1551 Slaterville Rd
Ithaca, NY 14850-6335
607-272-9463
Fax: 607-277-7344 800-260-0612
info@sixmilecreek.com www.sixmilecreek.com
Wine
Owner: Amy Renodin
info@sixmilecreek.com
Co-Owner: Roger Battistella
Estimated Sales: Less Than $500,000
Number Employees: 1-4
Type of Packaging: Private Label
Brands:
  Six Mile Creek

11682 Sjaak's Organic Chocolates
1340 Commerce St # D
Petaluma, CA 94954-8015
707-775-2434
www.sjaaks.com
Bite size chocolates available in small tubs, large tubs, and individually wrapped; box assortments; chocolate bars; corporate gifts; seasonal; and vegan. Organic, non-GMO ingredients.
Owner: Jacques Holten
Sales: Jessica Holten-Casper
Manager: Jessica Holten
jholten@sjaaks.com
Production: Leo Marrella
Number Employees: 1-4
Type of Packaging: Consumer, Private Label

11683 Skedaddle Maple
Florenceville-Bristol, NB
Canada
skedaddle-maple.com
Maple syrup
President: Adam Stone
Parent Co: Hilltop Farm Forestry Group
Brands:
  Skedaddle

11684 Skillet Street Food
6100 4th Avenue S
Suite 155
Seattle, WA 98115
425-998-9817
www.skilletstreetfood.com
Bacon jam spread
Owner: Josh Henderson
Contact: Erik Abdelbari
erikabdelbari@skilletstreetfood.com
Square Footage: 5240

11685 Skim Delux Mendenhall Laboratories
715 Morton St
Paris, TN 38242-4296
731-642-9321
Fax: 731-644-3398 800-642-9321
Processor and exporter of dairy analogs, formulas and flavors for calcium-fortified milk, juice and fruit drink beverages; also, chocolate milkshake mixes
Owner: David Travis
Sales Assistant: Melissa Taylor
Estimated Sales: $500,000-$1 Million
Number Employees: 5-9
Type of Packaging: Bulk

11686 Skimpy Cocktails LLC
1000 E Belt Line Rd
Ste 242
Carrollton, TX 75006-6201
469-892-7988
Fax: 469-568-2617 www.skimpymixers.com
Juice, cider, non-alcoholic beverages
Owner: Krista LaMothe
CEO: Megan Toole
Founder: Summer Lamons
Contact: Krista Lamothe
krista@skimpymixers.com
Estimated Sales: 200,000
Number Employees: 4

11687 Skinners' Dairy
24741 Deer Trace Drive
Ponte Vedra Beach, FL 32082-2114
904-733-5440
Milk, dairy products
President: Denny Gaultney
Estimated Sales: $10-20 000,000
Number Employees: 100

11688 Skinny Mixes LLC
2849 Executive Dr
Suite 210
Clearwater, FL 33762-5329
727-826-0306
Fax: 727-800-9959
customerservice@skinnymixes.com
www.skinnymixes.com
Non-alcoholic cocktail mixes
Owner: Jordan Engelhardt
jordan@skinnymixes.com
Estimated Sales: 790,000
Number Employees: 1-4

11689 Skinny Souping
Chicago, IL
skinnysouping.com
Single-serving soups
Founder: Alison Velazquez

11690 Skipping Stone Productions
1335 Railroad Street
Paso Robles, CA 93446
805-226-2998
Wine infused cookies with Italian origins
Estimated Sales: $130,000
Number Employees: 3
Square Footage: 7736

11691 Skjodt-Barrett Foods
5 Precidio Ct
Brampton, ON L6S 6B7
Canada
905-671-2884
Fax: 905-671-2885 877-600-1200
www.sbfoods.com
Sauces, marinades, jams, spreads, toppings & fillings, icings & glazes and savoury fillings manufacturer.
President/Owner: Thomas Dreher
Estimated Sales: $49.8 Million
Number Employees: 172
Type of Packaging: Food Service, Private Label, Bulk
Other Locations:
  Canadian Operation
  Brampton ON
  U.S. Operation
  Lebanon IN
Brands:
  Skjodt-Barrett

11692 Skratch Labs
2885 Wilderness Place
Unit B
Boulder, CO 80301
800-735-8904
info@skratchlabs.com www.skratchlabs.com
Sports nutrition products
Founder: Allen Lim

11693 Sky Haven Farm
4871 Shepherd Creek Rd
Cincinnati, OH 45223-1015
513-681-2303
Fax: 513-681-8305
Cured hams
Owner: Ed J Dreyer
skyhavenfarms@aol.com
Estimated Sales: $1-2.5 000,000
Number Employees: 1-4

11694 Sky Valley Foods
145 Cane Creek Blvd
Danville, VA 24540
lpayne@skyvalleyfoods.com
www.skyvalleyfoods.com
Condiments, sauces, salsas and sparkling beverages
Founder: Allen Lim
Brands:
  Sky Valley
  Organicville

11695 Sky Vineyards
4352 Cavedale Rd
Glen Ellen, CA 95442-9767
707-935-1391
Fax: 510-540-8442 www.skyvineyards.com
Wine
Owner: Lore Olds
COO: Linn Brinier
Manager of Sales: Matt Gerloff
Estimated Sales: $3-5 Million
Number Employees: 5-9
Brands:
  Sky Vineyards

11696 Skylark Meats
4430 S 110th St
Omaha, NE 68137-1235
402-592-0300
Fax: 402-592-1414 800-759-5275
skysales@americanfoodsgroup.com
www.skylarkmeats.com
Corned beef and liver.
President: Paul Weiss
Chief Executive Officer: James Leonard
jamesleonard@skylarkmeats.com
Quality Assurance Manager: Jack Warner
Marketing Manager: Steve Giroux
VP Sales: John O'Brien
Human Resources Manager: Shane Keith
Operations Executive: Brayton Howard
Production Manager: Ray Marquez
Purchasing Manager: Barb Bevington
Year Founded: 1970
Estimated Sales: $41.1 Million
Number Employees: 250-499
Square Footage: 175000
Parent Co: Rosen's Diversified
Type of Packaging: Consumer, Food Service

11697 Skyline Chili Inc
4180 Thunderbird Ln
Fairfield, OH 45014-2235
513-874-1188
Fax: 513-874-3591 www.skylinechili.com
Chili
Vice President: Charlie Harnist
charnist@skylinechili.com
Number Employees: 500-999

11698 SlantShack Jerky
123 Butler St
Brooklyn, NY 11231
201-632-1035
www.slantshack.com

Beef jerky
President/Owner: Joshua Kace
CEO: David Koretz
Year Founded: 2009

11699 Slap Ya Mama Cajun Seasoning
1103 W Main Street
Ville Platte, LA 70586
337-363-6904
Fax: 337-363-6608 800-485-5217
sales@slapyamama.com www.slapyamama.com
Seasonings
General Manager: James Westerfield
Contact: Jack Walker
jack@slapyamama.com

11700 Slate Quarry Winery
460 Gower Road
Nazareth, PA 18064-9219
610-746-3900
Fax: 610-746-9684
Wine
General Manager: M Eleanor Butler
Production Manager: Sidney Butler
Estimated Sales: $1-2.5 Million
Number Employees: 5-9

11701 Slathars Smokehouse
RR 1
Box 52bb
Lake City, MN 55041-9312
507-753-2080
Beef
President: Khalil Robinson
Estimated Sales: $300,000-500,000
Number Employees: 1-4

11702 Slather Brand Foods LLC
28 Arabian Drive
Charleston, SC 29407
843-513-1750
Fax: 843-769-4876 info@slatheriton.com
Sauces
Founder: Robin Rhea
Contact: Brandy Bates
batesbl@gmail.com
Estimated Sales: $87,000
Number Employees: 2
Square Footage: 4374

11703 Slawsa
PO Box 272
Cramerton, NC 28032
comments@slawsa.com
www.slawsa.com
Salsa relish
CEO: Julie Busha
Estimated Sales: $6.4 Million
Number Employees: 54
Brands:
  Slawsa

11704 Sleeman Breweries, Ltd.
551 Clair Rd W
Guelph, ON N1L 1E9
Canada
519-822-1834
800-268-8537
www.sleemanbreweries.ca
Beer, ale, & lager
President: Kenny Sadai
VP, Sales & Marketing: Greg Newbrough
Year Founded: 1834
Estimated Sales: $92.5 Million
Number Employees: 1,000
Square Footage: 98328
Parent Co: Sapporo Holdings Limited
Type of Packaging: Consumer, Food Service

11705 Slide Ridge LLC
PO Box 66
Mendon, UT 84325-0066
435-752-4956
www.honeywinevinegar.com
Honey, vinegar
Owner/Founder: Martin James
Sales And Marketing: Michael Morgan
Contact: Kelli Bess
kelli@slideridgehoney.com

11706 Slim Jim
Conagra Brands
222 W. Merchandise Mart Plz
Chicago, IL 60654
877-266-2472
www.slimjim.com
Meats and grain snack foods
EVP & CFO: David Marberger
EVP & Chief Customer Officer: Derek De La Mater
Estimated Sales: $50-100 Million
Number Employees: 20,900
Parent Co: ConAgra Foods

11707 Slingshot Foods
650 California St
7th Floor
San Francisco, CA 94108
415-423-2444
info@slingshotfoods.com
www.slingshotfoods.com
Breakfast granola
President/Owner: Will Hartley
Number of Products: 6

11708 Slo Roasted Coffee
1172 Los Olivos Ave
Los Osos, CA 93402-3231
805-528-7317
Fax: 805-528-1150 800-382-6837
www.sloroasted.com
Coffee
Owner: Chris Galloway
Owner: Joe Galloway
Estimated Sales: Less than $500,000
Number Employees: 10-19
Type of Packaging: Food Service

11709 Small Axe Peppers
514 51st Ave
Long Island City, NY 11101-5879
bronxhotsauce.com
Hot sauce
Co-Founder: John A. Crotty
Co-Founder: John Fitzgerald
Brands:
  The Bronx Hot Sauce

11710 Small Batch Organics
53B Manchester Valley Road
Manchester Center, VT 05255-1054
802-367-1054
Fax: 802-367-1152 smallbatchvt@gmail.com
smallbatchgranola.com
Granola
President: Lindsay Martin
Brands:
  Small Batch

11711 Small Planet Foods
PO Box 9452
Minneapolis, MN 55440
Fax: 763-764-8330 800-624-4123
Small Planet Foods, under the Cascadian Farm, Muir Glen, Larabar, and Small Planet brand labels, offers more than 100 products that are USDA-certified organic. Cascadian Farm products include breakfast cereals, frozen fruits and vegetables, fruit spreads, granola and granola bars. Muir Glen makes premium tomato products such as pasta sauces, soups, ketchup, salsa, and canned tomatoes. As part of its business, Small Planet Foods also makes and markets frozen smoothie mix kits.
CFO: Michael Shadrack
SVP: Daniel Lloyd
Director of Research & Development: Edward Greenheck
Quality and Regulatory Operations: Katrina Heinze
Marketing Manager: Matt McQuinn
Contact: Laura Arcieri
laura.arcieri@smallplanetfoods.com
VP Operations: Marv Shelby
Plant Manger: Barbara Nelson
Director of Purchasing: Peter Lecompte
Estimated Sales: $16.1 Million
Number Employees: 110
Parent Co: General Mills
Type of Packaging: Consumer
Brands:
  Cascadian Farm
  Muir Glen Organic
  Larabar
  Food Should Taste Good

11712 Smart Baking Co.
297 Power Ct
Sanford, FL 32771
407-915-5519
info@smartbakingco.com
smartbakingco.com
Gluten-free cakes and buns
COO: Joanne Walter

11713 Smart Flour Foods, LLC
4020 S Industrial Dr
Ste 110
Austin, TX 78744-1028
512-706-1775
Fax: 440-306-1775 www.smartflourfoods.com
Pizza, pizza crust, bread, pancake & waffle mix
CEO: Charlie Pace
Director Of Marketing: Sameer Shah
Sales Manager: Lauren Rohr
Estimated Sales: C

11714 Smart Juice
1139 Lehigh Ave
Suite 300
Whitehall, PA 18052
610-443-1506
Fax: 888-625-0295 smartjuice.us
Organic juices
Contact: Erdem Abdulhay
erdem@smartjuice.us

11715 SmartSweets
Vancouver, BC
Canada
hello@smartsweets.com
smartsweets.com
Sugar-free candy
CEO: Tara Bosch

11716 Smarties
1091 Lousons Rd
Union, NJ 07083-5029
908-964-0660
Fax: 908-964-0911 800-631-7968
www.smarties.com
Manufacturer of Smarties, the iconic Halloween candy.
Vice President, Management: Jessica Dee
Vice President, Communications: Liz Dee
Vice President, Operations: Sarah Dee
Estimated Sales: $10-20 Million
Number Employees: 100
Type of Packaging: Consumer
Brands:
  Smarties

11717 Smashmallow
153 W Napa Street
Sonoma, CA 95476
707-512-0605
hello@smashmallow.com
smashmallow.com
Flavored marshmallows
Founder & CEO: Jonathan Sebastiani
Estimated Sales: $8 Million
Number Employees: 30
Parent Co: Sonoma Brands
Brands:
  Smash Mallow

11718 Smeltzer Orchard Co
6032 Joyfield Rd
Frankfort, MI 49635-9163
231-882-4421
Fax: 231-882-4430 info@smeltzerorchards.com
www.smeltzerorchards.com
Processor and exporter of frozen apples, apple juice, asparagus and cherries; also, dried blueberries, cherries, apples, strawberries and cranberries
President: Tim Brian
info@smeltzerorchards.com
Plant Manager: Mike Henschell
Estimated Sales: $9.3 Million
Number Employees: 50-99
Type of Packaging: Food Service

11719 Smiling Fox Pepper Company
610 Cherrywood Drive
North Aurora, IL 60542-1032
972-754-2820
Fax: 630-337-3734 sfoxpepco@aol.com
Relishes and jellies
Co-Owner: Mary Patterson
Co-Owner: Scott Patterson

Food Manufacturers / A-Z

Type of Packaging: Consumer

11720 Smiling Hill Farm
781 County Rd
Westbrook, ME 04092-1910
207-775-4818
Fax: 207-775-3537 800-743-7463
Milk, dairy
Owner: David Knight
david.knight@hillsidelumber.com
Number Employees: 20-49

11721 Smirk's
17601 US Hwy 34
Fort Morgan, CO 80701
970-762-0202
Fax: 877-682-1065 www.smirksbrand.com
Dried fruits, nuts, grains, seeds, flour and bird food
President: Nicholas Erker
nerker@smirksbrand.com
Chief Financial Officer: Cindy Schmid
Director, Quality Assurance: Jesse Bellefeuille
Sales: Jason Strauch
Chief Operations Officer: Eric Nickell
Number Employees: 2-10
Type of Packaging: Bulk

11722 Smith & Salmon
110 Summit St
Burlington, VT 05401-3928
802-578-8242
sapmaplewater.com
Maple sap soda and seltzer
Co-Founder: Chas P. Smith
Brands:
  Sap Maple

11723 Smith & Sons Seafood
1033 Mcintosh Industrial Blvd
Darien, GA 31305-6202
912-437-6471
Fax: 912-437-3553 shrimp@darientel.net
www.smithseafood.com
Shrimp
Owner: Gean Smith
shrimp@darientel.net
Number Employees: 20-49

11724 Smith & Truslow
3225 East 42nd Ave
Denver, CO 80216
303-339-6967
www.smithandtruslow.com
Smith & Truslow specializes in freshly ground organic spices & herbs.
Co-Founder/Co-Owner: Jean Gleason
jgleason@smithandtruslow.com
Co-Founder/Co-Owner: Jenny Ross
Type of Packaging: Consumer

11725 Smith Dairy
230 N Vine St
Orrville, OH 44667-1644
330-682-6230
Fax: 330-683-1079 800-776-7076
www.smithdairy.com
Dairy products including; milk, eggnog, ice cream, seasonal products, shake mixes, juices and drinks, water, cottage cheese, sour cream and dips.
President: Steve Schmid
Product Development Specialist: Mindy Mencl
Director of Marketin: Penny Baker
VP Sales & Marketing: Brian DeFelice
Contact: Alisha Bellmore
alishabellmore@smithdairy.com
VP Manufacturing Operations: Ron Them
Director of Purchasing: Ken Stuter
Number Employees: 1-4
Square Footage: 180000
Type of Packaging: Consumer, Food Service, Private Label
Brands:
  Smith's
  White Oak
  Whale-Of-A-Pail
  Ruggles

11726 Smith Frozen Foods Inc
101 Depot St
Weston, OR 97886
541-566-3515
Fax: 541-566-3707 www.smithfrozenfoods.com
Frozen vegetables including baby lima beans, diced and sliced carrots, kernel corn, corn-on-the-cob and peas
President & CFO: Gary Crowder
Co-Owner: Sharon Smith
Co-Owner: Gordon Smith
Corporate Controller: Rebecca Hatley
Director, Business Development: Ken Porter
Director, Quality Control & Assurance: John Humble
VP, Sales & Marketing: Kent Perkes
Sales Office Manager: Shelly Hall
VP, Logistics & Packaging: Aaron Ware
Warehouse Operations: Kelly Hahn
Director, Purchasing: Sandra Stewart
Year Founded: 1919
Estimated Sales: $85 Million
Number Employees: 250-499
Number of Brands: 1
Type of Packaging: Consumer, Food Service, Private Label, Bulk
Brands:
  Smith

11727 Smith Meat Packing
2920 Riopelle
Detroit, MI 48207
313-833-1590
Fax: 313-832-0232 sales@lklpacking.com
www.smithmeatpacking.com
Packer of smoked and cured pork
President: Anthony Peters
Estimated Sales: $5-10 Million
Number Employees: 10-19
Square Footage: 60000
Type of Packaging: Bulk

11728 (HQ)Smith Packing Regional Meat
105-125 Washington Street
P.O. Box 520
Utica, NY 13503-0520
315-732-5125
Fax: 315-732-1166 sales@smithpacking.com
www.smithpacking.com
Meat: beef, pork, veal, lamb, chicken and turkey; eggs, ham, bacon, frankfurters, sausage, kielbasa and turkey breast
President: Wesley Smith
VP: Mark Smith
Estimated Sales: $12.6 Million
Number Employees: 1-4
Square Footage: 150000
Type of Packaging: Private Label
Brands:
  Evergood
  Honest John's

11729 Smith Provision Co Inc
1300 Cranberry St
Erie, PA 16501-1566
814-459-4974
Fax: 814-879-0998 800-334-9151
www.smithprovision.com
Smoked luncheon meats and ham, frankfurters, roast beef and sausage
Chairman of the Board: Magnus Weber
President: Michael Weber
mike.weber@smithhotdogs.com
VP: John Weber
Operations Manager: Travis Lindsay
Estimated Sales: $10 Million
Number Employees: 10-19
Square Footage: 51726
Type of Packaging: Consumer, Food Service, Private Label, Bulk
Brands:
  Smith's

11730 Smith Vineyard & Winery
13577 Dog Bar Rd
Grass Valley, CA 95949
530-273-7032
Fax: 530-273-0229
Wines
Manager: Christina Smith
Estimated Sales: $1 Million
Number Employees: 5-9

11731 Smith's Bakery
P.O.Box 16389
Hattiesburg, MS 39404-6389
601-288-7000
Fax: 601-584-6487 www.forrestgeneral.com
Bakery
President: William C Oliver
Estimated Sales: $1.5 Million
Number Employees: 1-4

11732 Smith-Madrone Vineyards & Winery
4022 Spring Mountain Rd
PO Box 451
St Helena, CA 94574-9773
707-963-2283
Fax: 707-963-2291 contact@smithmadrone.com
www.smithmadrone.com
Wines
Manager: Stuart Smith
nvhigh@aol.com
Winemaker: Charles Smith
Estimated Sales: $1-2.5 Million
Number Employees: 5-9
Brands:
  Smith-Madrone

11733 Smithfield Foods Inc.
200 Commerce St.
Smithfield, VA 23430
757-365-3000
www.smithfieldfoods.com
Pork processor and hog producer.
President/CEO: Kenneth Sullivan
kennethsullivan@smithfieldfoods.com
Executive VP/CFO: Glenn Nunziata
COO, U.S. Operations: Dennis Organ
Year Founded: 1936
Estimated Sales: Over $1 Billion
Number Employees: 54,000
Number of Brands: 14
Number of Products: 200
Parent Co: WH Group Limited
Type of Packaging: Consumer, Food Service, Private Label
Brands:
  Smithfield
  Eckrich
  Farmland
  Armour
  Cook's
  Gwaltney
  John Morrell
  Nathan's Famous
  Kretschmar
  Curly's
  Carando
  Margherita
  Healthy Ones
  Farmer John

11734 Smoak's Bakery & Catering Service
2058 Walton Way
Augusta, GA 30904-2302
706-738-1792
Fax: 706-733-8979 tomt3@bellsouth.net
Cakes, cookies and breads
President: Steve Pierce
General Manager: Audery Hawn
Owner: Dan Smoak
Estimated Sales: $1-2.5 Million
Number Employees: 20-49
Type of Packaging: Private Label

11735 Smoke & Fire Natural Food
35 Railroad Ave
Great Barrington, MA 01230-1510
413-528-8008
Fax: 413-528-7997
Smoked and flavored tofu
Owner: Robert Harvey
Co-Founder: Mona Young
Estimated Sales: Under $500,000
Number Employees: 5-9
Brands:
  Smoke & Fire

11736 Smoke House
20 Smokehouse Rd
Sagle, ID 83860-8698
208-263-6312
Fax: 208-762-8979
Smoked meats
Owner: Dick Struntz
Estimated Sales: $.5-1 million
Number Employees: 1-4

Food Manufacturers / A-Z

11737 Smoked Turkey Inc
6608 E Marshville Blvd
Marshville, NC 28103-1198
704-624-6628
Fax: 704-624-2510
info@stegallsmokedturkey.com
www.stegallsmokedturkey.com
Frozen hickory-smoked turkey and honey-glazed ham
Estimated Sales: $500,000-$1 Million
Number Employees: 1-4
Square Footage: 440000
Type of Packaging: Private Label
Brands:
  Stegall Smoked Turkey

11738 Smokehouse Winery
10 Ashby Rd
Sperryville, VA 22740-2243
540-987-3194
Fax: 540-987-8189
smokehousewinery@earthlink.net
Wines
Owner: John Hallberg
Estimated Sales: $300,000-500,000
Number Employees: 1-4

11739 Smokey Denmark Sausage Co
3505 E 5th St
Austin, TX 78702-4913
512-385-0718
Fax: 512-385-4843 info@smokeydenmark.com
www.smokeydenmark.com
Beef, pork and venison sausage
Owner: Jonathan Pace
jonathan@smokeydenmark.com
Quality Assurance Manager: Colby DeFriese
Estimated Sales: $2.5 Million
Number Employees: 20-49
Type of Packaging: Consumer

11740 Smolich Bros. Home MadeSausage
760 Theodore St
Crest Hill, IL 60403-2380
815-727-2144
www.smolichsausage.com
Sausage including hot, mild, smoked, pork and bratwurst
President: Rudy Smolich
Co-Owner: Joe Smolich
joe.smolich@smolichsausage.com
Estimated Sales: Less Than $500,000
Number Employees: 1-4
Type of Packaging: Consumer

11741 Smothers Brothers Tasting Room
1976 Warm Springs Rd
Glen Ellen, CA 95442-8717
707-833-1010
Fax: 707-833-2313 800-795-9463
www.smothersbrothers.com
Wines
President/Owner: Thomas Smothers
Owner: Marcy Smothers
Estimated Sales: Below $5 Million
Number Employees: 5-9
Brands:
  Smothers/Remick Ridge

11742 Smuggler's Kitchen
PO Box 570
Dundee, FL 33838-0570
800-604-6793
Dehydrated foods including Irish potato soup, vegetable dips, Cajun and chili sauces, etc
Co-Owner: Tom Nischan
Co-Owner: Pat Nischan
Number Employees: 1-4

11743 Smuttynose Brewing Co
225 Heritage Ave # 2
Portsmouth, NH 03801-8642
603-436-4026
Fax: 603-433-1247 info@smuttynose.com
www.smuttynose.com
Beer
President: Peter Egelston
Executive Brewer: David Yarrington
CFO: Gale Merrigan
Head Brewer: Greg Blanchard
Sales Manager: Kevin Love
National Sales Manager: Anka Jacobs
Marketing: Jaime Pruzansky
Office Manager: Deb Fitt
Contact: Robby Brondolo
robby.brondolo@smuttynose.com
Estimated Sales: Below $5 Million
Number Employees: 20-49
Type of Packaging: Private Label
Brands:
  Big Beer Series
  Old Brown Bag
  Portsmouth Lager
  Smuttynose Belgian W
  Smuttynose Robust Po

11744 Snack Factory
PO Box 3562
Princeton, NJ 08543-3562
609-683-5400
Fax: 609-683-9595 888-683-5400
info@pretzelcrisps.com www.pretzelcrisps.com
Pretzel crisps-all natural and fat free; available in garlic, original and everything flavors.
President: Warren Wilson
VP: Sara Wilson
Contact: Todd Grandt
todd@pretzelcrisps.com
Estimated Sales: $5 Million
Number Employees: 9
Square Footage: 800000
Type of Packaging: Consumer, Food Service, Private Label, Bulk
Brands:
  Snack Factory

11745 Snack Works/Metrovox Snacks
612 N. Eckhoff St
Orange, CA 92868
714-634-3478
Fax: 714-634-4424 800-783-9870
questions@giftbasketsupplies.com
www.giftbasketsupplies.com
Popcorn, pretzels, chocolates
Owner: Paul Voxland
Estimated Sales: $500,000-$1 Million
Number Employees: 5-9

11746 SnackMasters, LLC
8332 Lander Ave
Hilmar, CA 95324
209-537-9770
Fax: 209-669-3240 800-597-9770
jerky@snackmasters.com www.snackmasters.com
Producer of meat snacks, including beef, beef heart, chicken, pork and turkey jerky.
President: James Rekoutis
Contact: Blanca Delhi
bdelhi@snackmasters.com
Estimated Sales: $10-20 Million
Number Employees: 50-99
Number of Brands: 2
Type of Packaging: Consumer
Brands:
  Aubrey'S Jerky
  SnackMasters

11747 Snackerz
6351 Chalet Dr
Commerce, CA 90040-3705
562-928-0023
Fax: 562-928-8923 888-576-2253
www.snackerz.com
Candy and nuts
Owner: Ron Emrani
ron@snackerz.com
Estimated Sales: $10-20 Million
Number Employees: 20-49
Type of Packaging: Consumer

11748 (HQ)Snak King Corp
16150 Stephens St
City Of Industry, CA 91745-1718
626-336-7711
Fax: 626-336-3777 info@snakking.com
www.snakking.com
Snack foods, caramel corn, tortilla and corn chips, popcorn, beef jerky, pork rinds, cheese and rice puffs, nut meats and candy.
Chairman/CEO: Barry Levin
jpapiri@snakking.com
VP Sales & Marketing: Joe Papiri
Sales Exec: Joe Papiri
Number Employees: 250-499
Type of Packaging: Consumer, Food Service, Private Label, Bulk
Other Locations:
  Snak King Corp.
  City Industry CA
Brands:
  El Sabroso
  Granny Goose
  Jensen's Orchard
  Snak King
  The Whole Earth

11749 Snake River Brewing Company
265 S Millward St
Jackson, WY 83001-8582
307-739-2337
Fax: 307-739-2296
brewpub@snakeriverbrewing.com
www.snakeriverbrewing.com
seasonal beer, ale, stout, lager & pilsner.
Owner/President/CEO: Ted Staryk
Estimated Sales: $1.5 Million
Number Employees: 50-99
Type of Packaging: Consumer, Food Service
Brands:
  Snake River

11750 Snapdragon Foods
PO Box 14103
Oakland, CA 94614
877-881-7627
info@snapdragonfood.com
www.snapdragonfood.com
Importer and manufacturer of Asian prepared meals
President: David Sakamoto
CEO: Seth Jacobson
Vice President of Sales: Ron Dallara
Estimated Sales: $1-2.5 Million
Number Employees: 5-9

11751 Snappy Popcorn
610 Main St
Breda, IA 51436-8719
712-673-2347
Fax: 712-673-2347 800-742-0228
jon@snappypopcorn.com
www.snappypopcorn.com
Manufacturer, wholesaler/distributor and exporter of popcorn and supplies
President: Alan Tiefenthaler
alan@itien.com
Office Manager: Lori Steinkamp
VP Sales: Jon Tiefenthaler
Estimated Sales: $1-2.5 Million
Number Employees: 20-49
Square Footage: 100000
Type of Packaging: Food Service, Bulk

11752 Sneaky Chef Foods, The
c/o Action Brand Management
851 Broken Sound Pkwy. # 155
Boca Raton, FL 33487
561-757-6541
Fax: 866-920-6487 info@thesneakychef.com
www.thesnackbrigade.com
No-nut butters, prepared spreads with vegetable purees to appeal to children
Founder/President: Missy Chase Lapine
Number of Brands: 1
Number of Products: 8
Type of Packaging: Consumer, Private Label
Brands:
  The Sneaky Chef

11753 Snelgrove Ice Cream Company
850 E 2100 S
Salt Lake City, UT 84106-1832
801-486-4456
Fax: 801-486-3926 800-569-0005
Processor, exporter and wholesaler/distributor of ice cream and ice cream novelties
President: David Mutzel
Contact: Troy Luckart
troy.luckart@dreyers.com
Estimated Sales: Less than $500,000
Number Employees: 50-99
Parent Co: MKD Distributing
Type of Packaging: Consumer, Food Service, Private Label, Bulk

1123

Food Manufacturers / A-Z

11754 Snikiddy, LLC
2505 Walnut St.
Suite 100
Boulder, CO 80302
303-444-4405
www.snikiddy.com
Manufacturer of various types of snacks including veggie chips, popcorn, cheese puffs, and baked fries.
Founder: Mary Schulman
Contact: Erin Carrigan
erin.carrigan@snikiddy.com
Brands:
  SmashPop
  Baked Fries Sharing Packs
  Cheese Puffs Sharing Packs
  Eat Your Vegetables

11755 Sno Shack Inc
2774 N 4000 W
P.O. Box 1010
Rexburg, ID 83440-3106
208-359-0866
Fax: 208-359-1773 888-766-7425
sales@snoshack.com www.snoshack.com
Flavors, thickeners and sweeteners; also, shaved ice equipment including shavers, bottles, racks and yogurt flavoring, carts, concession trailers
Owner: Burt Hensley
Owner: Cheryl Lewis
Sales Director: Peter Orr
burt@snoshack.com
Manager: Bud Orr
Purchasing Manager: Brooke Anstine
Estimated Sales: Less Than $500,000
Number Employees: 1-4
Square Footage: 36000
Type of Packaging: Consumer, Food Service, Private Label
Brands:
  Carts
  Concessions
  Kiosks

11756 Sno Wizard Inc
101 River Rd
New Orleans, LA 70121-4222
504-832-3901
Fax: 504-832-1646 800-366-9766
information@snowizard.com www.snowizard.com
Snowball, snowcone and shaved ice machines and flavorings
President: Ronnie Sciortino
Estimated Sales: $5-10 Million
Number Employees: 10-19
Square Footage: 20000
Type of Packaging: Consumer, Food Service, Bulk
Brands:
  Ronald Reginald's
  Snolite
  Snowizard

11757 Sno-Co Berry Pak
1518 4th Street
Marysville, WA 98270-5012
360-659-3555
Fruit
President: Christie Monroe
Treasurer: Barbara Clark
Estimated Sales: $10-20 000,000
Number Employees: 20-49

11758 Sno-Pac Foods Inc
521 Enterprise Dr
Caledonia, MN 55921-1844
507-725-5281
Fax: 507-725-5285 800-533-2215
snopac@snopac.com www.snopac.com
Frozen organic vegetables including soy and edamame beans, green peas, whole kernel corn, cut green and mixed
President: Peter Gengler
VP: Darlene Gengler
Estimated Sales: $3.5 Million
Number Employees: 50-99
Type of Packaging: Consumer, Food Service, Bulk
Brands:
  Sno Pac

11759 Snokist Growers
10 W Mead Ave
Yakima, WA 98902-6326
509-453-5631
Fax: 509-453-9359 800-377-2857
Fresh apples, pears and cherries; also, canned apple rings and sauces, fruit purees, pears and plums
President: Jim Davis
CFO: Jim Davis
Sales Director: Rich Boldoz
Sales: Neil Galone
Purchasing Manager: Nancy Weaver
Estimated Sales: $100,000
Number Employees: 500-999
Number of Products: 10
Square Footage: 200000
Type of Packaging: Consumer, Food Service, Private Label, Bulk
Brands:
  Blue Ribbon
  Cohort
  Dear Lady
  Nu House
  Red Ribbon
  Snokist
  Tri Our

11760 Snow Beverages
928 Broadway # 504
Suite 504
New York, NY 10010-8144
212-353-3270
Fax: 646-219-7559
Natural soda plus vitamins
CEO: Stuart Strumwasser
Contact: Melanie Randall
melanie@snowbeverages.com
Number Employees: 1-4

11761 Snow Dairy Inc
119 W 800 S
Springville, UT 84663-9416
801-489-6081
Fax: 801-489-6081 www.dairysnow.com
President: Mark Snow
Estimated Sales: Less Than $500,000
Number Employees: 1-4

11762 Snow Monkey
1223 Wilshire Blvd
Suite 1825
Santa Monica, CA 90403-5406
kingdom@snow-monkey.com
snow-monkey.com
Ice cream
Co-Founder: Rachel Geicke
Co-Founder: Mariana Ferreira
Director of Impact & Partnerships: Katie Krell
Number Employees: 2-10
Brands:
  Snow Monkey

11763 Snow's Ice Cream Co Inc
80 School St
Greenfield, MA 01301-2410
413-774-7438
Fax: 413-774-5406 www.bartshomemade.com
Ice cream, sorbet and frozen yogurt: wholesaler/distributor of frozen food, candy, snack foods, sauces, mustards and salsa's
Owner: Gary Schaefer
gary@bartshomemade.com
Estimated Sales: Below $5 Million
Number Employees: 5-9
Square Footage: 64000
Parent Co: Another Roadside Attraction
Type of Packaging: Consumer, Food Service, Private Label, Bulk
Brands:
  Bart's Homemade
  Snow's Nice Cream

11764 SnowBird Corporation
379 Broadway
Bayonne, NJ 07002-3631
201-858-8300
Fax: 201-451-5000 800-576-1616
Bottled filtered, spring, and distilled water, coffee makers and hot foods; wholesaler/distributor of water fountains and bottled water coolers; repair services available
President: Diane Drey
Vice President: Gerald Giannangeli
Estimated Sales: $3-5 Million
Number Employees: 6
Square Footage: 264000
Brands:
  Snowbird

11765 Snowbear Frozen Custard
328 E State St
W Lafayette, IN 47906
765-746-2930
www.snowbear.com
Retailers of frozen desserts
Partner: Richard Lodde
Partner: Kirk Lodde
Partner: William Lodde
Partner: Tom Lodde
Estimated Sales: $500,000-$1 Million
Number Employees: 10-19
Number of Products: 50

11766 Snowcrest Packer
1925 Riverside Road
Abbotsford, BC V2S 4J8
Canada
604-859-4881
Fax: 604-859-1426 800-265-3686
info@snowcrest.ca www.snowcrest.ca
Processor and importer of frozen apples, blueberries, cherries, cranberries, raspberries, strawberries, asparagus, beans, broccoli, brussels, sprouts, cauliflowers, corn, peas, peppers, rhubarb, spinach, squash and turnips
President: Tom Smith
Quality Control: Lim Lee
Sales: Pascal Countant
Operations Manager: Rob Christl
Number Employees: 120
Square Footage: 440000
Parent Co: Omstead Foods
Type of Packaging: Consumer, Food Service, Private Label, Bulk
Other Locations:
  Snowcrest Packer Ltd.
  Burnaby BC
Brands:
  Bonniebrook
  Brentwood
  Delnor
  Pennysaver
  Snowcrest

11767 Snowizard Extracts
101 River Rd
New Orleans, LA 70121-4222
504-832-3901
Fax: 504-832-1646 800-366-9766
info@snowizard.com www.snowizard.com
Snoballs, snowcones and shaved ice
President: Ronnie Sciortino
Estimated Sales: $5-10 Million
Number Employees: 10-19
Type of Packaging: Private Label
Brands:
  Snowizard

11768 Snyder Foods
15350 Old Simcoe Road
P.O Box 750
Port Perry, ON L9L 1A6
Canada
905-985-7373
Fax: 905-985-7289
Processor and exporter of meat and fruit pies, sausage rolls, quiche, stuffed sandwiches and pie and tart shells
General Manager: Dave Jackson
Number Employees: 125
Square Footage: 220000
Type of Packaging: Consumer, Food Service, Private Label
Brands:
  J.M. Schneider
  Maple Leaf
  Marks & Spencer
  Pillsbury
  Red-L
  Richs

11769 Snyder's of Hanover
PO Box 32368
Charlotte, NC 28232
800-233-7125
www.snydersofhanover.com
Snack foods including pretzels, flavored pretzel pieces and potato, tortilla and corn chips.
Chairman: Michael Warehime
Year Founded: 1909
Estimated Sales: $652 Million
Number Employees: 2,400

Food Manufacturers / A-Z

Number of Products: 45
Square Footage: 37800
Type of Packaging: Consumer

11770 Snyder's-Lance Inc.
13515 Ballantyne Corporate Pl.
Charlotte, NC 28277
800-438-1880
www.snyderslance.com
Sandwich crackers, nuts and seeds, captain's wafers, cookies, popcorn, pretzels, snack cakes, and 100 calorie packs.
President/CEO: Brian Driscoll
Year Founded: 2010
Estimated Sales: $1.62 Billion
Number Employees: 5,900
Number of Brands: 15
Parent Co: Campbell Soup Company
Type of Packaging: Consumer
Other Locations:
  Lance
  Hyannis MA
Brands:
  Snyder's of Hanover
  Lance
  Cape Cod Potato Chips
  Kettle Brand
  Snack Factory Pretzel Chips
  Late July Snacks
  Emerald
  Pop Secret
  Tom's
  Stella D'oro
  O-Ke-Doke
  Krunchers!
  Jays
  EatSmart Snacks
  Archway

11771 So Delicious Dairy Free
1130 Shelley St
Springfield, OR 97477
541-338-9400
Fax: 541-338-9401 866-388-7853
info@turtlemountain.com
www.sodeliciousdairyfree.com
Processor and exporter of frozen nondairy desserts; also, fat-free
Founder, President, Chief Executive Offi: Mark Brawerman
Marketing: John Tucker
Contact: Michael Murray
mmurray@sodeliciousdairyfree.com
Director of Operations: Michael Dunteman
Estimated Sales: Under $500,000
Number Employees: 1-4
Type of Packaging: Consumer, Food Service, Private Label
Brands:
  Carb Escapes
  It's Soy Delicious
  Organic Lil Buddies
  Organic Soy Delicious
  Soy Delicious Purely Decadent
  Sweet Nothings

11772 SoBe Beverages
40 Richards Avenue
Norwalk, CT 06854-2327
203-899-7111
Fax: 914-253-2000 800-588-0548
www.sobebev.com
Healthy fruit and herb beverages with vitamins and minerals
General Manager: Scott Mossitt
Office Manager: Jessica Lee
Vice President, Marketing: Tom Smallhorn
Estimated Sales: $25-49.9 Million
Number Employees: 1,500
Number of Brands: 1
Parent Co: Pepsico
Brands:
  SoBe

11773 Sobaya
201 Rue Miner
Cowansville, QC J2K 3Y5
Canada
450-266-8808
Fax: 450-266-4750 800-319-8808
info@sobaya.ca www.sobaya.ca
Natural pasta, organic pasta, Kamut organic pasta and Spelt organic pasta
President: Jacques Petit
Vice President: William Swaney
Marketing/Sales: Sandra Prevost
Number Employees: 7
Number of Brands: 1
Number of Products: 14
Square Footage: 20000
Parent Co: Eden Foods
Type of Packaging: Consumer, Private Label, Bulk
Brands:
  Genmai Udon
  Soba
  Somen
  Udon

11774 Sobon Estate
12300 Steiner Rd
Plymouth, CA 95669
209-333-6275
Fax: 209-245-5156 info@sobonwine.com
www.sobonwine.com
Wine
Co-Owner: Leon Sobon
Co-Owner: Shirley Sobon
Winemaker & Vineyard Operations Manager: Paul Sobon
Coordinator of Computer/Business Systems: Robert Sobon
Sales/Marketing: Tom Quinn
Estimated Sales: $5-10 Million
Number Employees: 10-19
Brands:
  Shenandoah Vineyards
  Sobon Estate

11775 Society Hill Snacks
8845 Torresdale Ave
Philadelphia, PA 19136-1510
215-708-8500
Fax: 215-288-4117 800-595-0050
contact@societyhillsnacks.com
www.societyhillsnacks.com
Gourmet sweet roasted nuts, snack mixes and great munchies.
President: Ronna Schultz
Estimated Sales: $1-3 Million
Number Employees: 10-19
Type of Packaging: Consumer, Food Service, Private Label, Bulk
Brands:
  Afrique
  Cinnful Coco
  Cravin Asian
  Hot Stuff
  Loco Coco
  Love That
  Society Hill Gourmet Nut Company
  Tres Toffee
  Tropical Honey Glace

11776 Sofina Foods Inc
100 Commerce Valley Dr W
Markham, ON L3T 0A1
Canada
905-747-3333
855-763-4621
sales@sofinafoods.com www.sofinafoods.com
Pork, beef, turkey, chicken and fish
Executive Chairman: Michael Latifi
President/CEO: Robert Wilt
VP/Controller: Robert Andru
EVP/Chief Commercial Officer: Brent Quartermain
Estimated Sales: Over $1 Billion
Number of Brands: 9
Type of Packaging: Consumer, Food Service, Private Label
Brands:
  Cuddy
  Fletcher's
  Janes
  Lavazza
  Lilydale
  Mastro
  Rio Mare
  San Benedetto
  San Daniele

11777 Sofo Foods
253 Waggoner Blvd
Toledo, OH 43612-1952
419-476-4211
Fax: 419-478-6104 800-447-4211
www.sofofoods.com
Appetizers, meat toppings and flour products such as doughs, pasta, cheese blends, and tomatoes.
CEO: Michael Sofo
Chief Operating Officer: Cos Figliomini
Chief Information Officer: Chuck Winters
Director, Corporate Accounting: Roger Bly
Director, Sales: Jeff Peer
VP, Operations: Gary Tolles
Director, Logistics: Jon Steinmetz
Director, Purchasing: Rob Kaufman
Estimated Sales: $20-50 Million
Number Employees: 250-499
Number of Brands: 6
Type of Packaging: Food Service
Other Locations:
  New Albany IN
  Suwanee GA
  Houston TX
Brands:
  A&M Cheese
  Bellissimo
  Spendida
  Tolibia
  Vantaggio
  Vantaggio D'Oro

11778 Soft Cell Technology
6986 Bandini Blvd
Commerce, CA 90040-3326
323-726-7065
Fax: 323-726-7065 800-360-7484
sales@soft-gel.com www.soft-gel.com
Herbal and nutritional supplements
President: Ron Udell
ronu@soft-gel.com
VP Sales Administration: Diane Hembree
Number Employees: 10-19
Type of Packaging: Private Label, Bulk
Brands:
  Coqsol
  Sgti

11779 Soho Beverages
8075 Leesburg Pike
Suite 760
Vienna, VA 22182-2739
703-689-2800
Soft drinks
President: Tom Cox
Estimated Sales: $5-10 000,000
Number Employees: 5
Type of Packaging: Private Label
Brands:
  Soho Natural Lemonades
  Soho Natural Soda &

11780 Sokol Blosser Winery
5000 NE Sokol Blosser Ln
Dayton, OR 97114-7232
503-864-2282
Fax: 503-864-2710 800-582-6668
info@sokolblosser.com www.sokolblosser.com
Wine
President: Allison Sokol Blosser
Vice President: Michael Brown
michael@sokolblosser.com
Estimated Sales: Below $5 Million
Number Employees: 20-49
Number of Products: 7
Brands:
  Evolution
  Medetrina
  Sokol Blosser

11781 Solana Beach Baking Company
5927 Farnsworth Court
Carlsbad, CA 92008-7303
760-444-9800
Fax: 760-444-9883
Breads and baked goods
President: David Wells
Quality Control: Kim Hogan
R & D: David Mears
Estimated Sales: $30-50 Million
Number Employees: 5-9

11782 Solana Gold Organics
1830 Gravenstein Hwy S
Sebastopol, CA 95472-4841
707-829-1121
Fax: 707-829-4715 800-459-1121
solanag@pacbell.net
Organic apples and apple products including kosher, dried, sauce, vinegar, juice, etc

Food Manufacturers / A-Z

Owner: John Kolling
jkolling@solanagold.com
Vice President: Cathy Gonzalez
Estimated Sales: $3 Million
Number Employees: 10-19
Type of Packaging: Consumer, Private Label, Bulk
Brands:
   Solana Gold
   Solana Gold Organics

11783 Solazyme Inc
225 Gateway Blvd
S San Francisco, CA 94080-7019
   650-589-5883
Fax: 650-989-6700
Microalgae-based healthy food ingredients and oils. Microalgae-derived lipid, protein and fiber-based products for nutrition, taste, texture and functionality.
CEO: Jonathan Wolfson
CFO & COO: Tyler Painter
Contact: Annie Chang
achang@solazyme.com
Estimated Sales: Less Than $500,000
Number Employees: 1-4
Type of Packaging: Bulk
Other Locations:
   Global Headquarters
   San Francisco CA
   Midwestern Operations
   Peoria IL
   South American Operations
   Sao Paulo, Brazil

11784 Sole Grano LLC
16-00 Pollitt Dr
Suite 3
Fair Lawn, NJ 07410-2765
   201-797-7100
info@solegrano.com
www.solegrano.com
Dried fruits, nuts, trail mixes, granolas, grains, beans, seeds, peas, lentils, and confections.
President: Harun Ekici
Number Employees: 1-4
Type of Packaging: Private Label

11785 Solgar Vitamin & Herbal
500 Willow Tree Rd
Leonia, NJ 07605
   201-944-2311
Fax: 201-944-7351 877-765-4274
pr@www.solgar.com www.solgar.com
Natural dietary and nutritional supplements
President/CEO: Barry Skolnick
Year Founded: 1947
Estimated Sales: $100-500 Million
Number of Products: 400
Square Footage: 50000
Parent Co: NBTY
Type of Packaging: Consumer
Brands:
   Kangavites
   Natural Bouncin' Berry
   Nature's Bounty
   Solgar
   Sundown

11786 Solis Winery
3920 Hecker Pass Rd
Gilroy, CA 95020-8805
   408-847-6306
Fax: 408-847-5188 888-838-6427
www.soliswinery.com
Wines
President: David Vanni
VP/Owner: Valerie Vanni
Marketing Director: Steve Beck
Contact: Julie Vanni
julie@soliswinery.com
Plant Manager: Michael Vanni
Estimated Sales: $90,000 approx.
Number Employees: 5-9
Brands:
   Solis

11787 Solnuts
711 7th St
Hudson, IA 50643
   319-988-3221
Fax: 319-988-4647 800-648-3503
nnewton@kerrygroup.com
Dry roasted soy nuts and all natural full fat soy flour
Manager: Mike Patterson
Vice President: Michael Healy
Marketing Director: Jim Andrews
Sales/Marketing: Nancy Newton
Operations Manager: Dave Zanchetti
Production Manager: Mike Patterson
Plant Manager: Mike Devine
Estimated Sales: $3-5 Million
Number Employees: 5-9
Square Footage: 64000
Parent Co: B.V. Solnut
Type of Packaging: Food Service, Private Label, Bulk
Brands:
   Solnuts

11788 Solo Foods
5315 Dansher Road
Countryside, IL 60525
   800-328-7656
info@solofoods.com www.solofoods.com
Cake and pastry fillings, almond paste and marzipan, pie and dessery fillings, marshmallow and toasted marshmallow creme, fruit butters, Asian dipping sauces and marinades, seasoning mixes.
President: John Sokol Novak
COO: Ralph Pirritano
Contact: Sami Abdel-Malek
sabdel-malek@solofoods.com
Estimated Sales: $20-50 Million
Parent Co: Sokol and Company
Type of Packaging: Consumer, Food Service, Private Label
Brands:
   Baker
   Solo
   Simon Fischer
   Chun's

11789 Solo Worldwide Enterprises
5683 Columbia Pike Ste 100
Falls Church, VA 22041
   703-845-7072
Fax: 703-560-5744 soloworld@aol.com
General grocery
President, US Division: Eyob Mamo
Estimated Sales: $500,000-$1 000,000
Number Employees: 5-9
Brands:
   Solo

11790 Soloman Baking Company
3820 Revere St Ste A
Denver, CO 80239
   303-371-2777
Fax: 303-375-9162
Pita bread, bagel and pita chips, snack mixes and tortillas greek pita
President: Sam Soloman
CEO: Andy Soloman
CFO: Malik Soloman
Estimated Sales: $3 Million
Number Employees: 12
Number of Products: 8
Square Footage: 48000
Type of Packaging: Consumer, Private Label

11791 Soloman Baking Company
3820 Revere St Ste A
Denver, CO 80239
   303-371-2777
Fax: 303-375-9162
Bakery products
President: Sam Soloman
Marketing Director: Hian Soloman
CFO: Annas Soloman
Quality Control: Hiam Soloman
R & D: Max Soloman
Estimated Sales: $5-10 000,000
Number Employees: 5-9
Brands:
   Soloman

11792 SoluBlend Technologies LLC
11487 Amherst Ct
Frankfort, IL 60423
   815-534-5778
Fax: 815-463-5493
Dietary supplements and specialty ingredients.
Manager: Richard Staack
COO: Eric Kuhrts
Contact: Eric Kuhrts
ekuhrts@solublend.com

11793 Soluble Products Company
480 Oberlin Ave S
Lakewood, NJ 08701-6997
   732-364-8855
Fax: 732-364-6689 Sales@associatedbrands.com
Manufacture of supplements for every lifestyle, including diet, bodybuilding, sports nutrition, nutraceutical and children's products
CEO: Stephen Hoffman
VP: Stewart Hoffman
Sales Manager: Thomas A Flora
Sales Manager: Thomas Flora
Estimated Sales: $2.5-5 Million
Number Employees: 20-49
Square Footage: 200000
Type of Packaging: Private Label
Brands:
   Soluble Products

11794 Solvaira Specialties
50 Bridge St
North Tonawanda, NY 14120-6842
   716-693-4040
Fax: 716-693-3528 888-698-1936
info@ifcfiber.com www.ifcfiber.com
A leading manufacturer of dietry fiber.
President/CEO: Dan Muth
Executive VP: Peter Vogt
pvogt@ifcfiber.com
R&D: Jit Ang
Exec VP of Operations: Brian Finn
Purchasing Manager: Steve Couladis
Year Founded: 2000
Number Employees: 50-99
Number of Brands: 10+
Type of Packaging: Bulk
Brands:
   Just Fiber
   Solkafloc
   Fibrex
   Nutrafiber
   Keycel
   Qualflo
   Aplphacel
   Floam
   Vintnercel

11795 Somebody's Mother's Chocolate
5551 Cedar Creek Dr
Houston, TX 77056-2307
   713-627-3055
info@somebodysmothers.com
www.somebodysmothers.com
Dessert toppings, chocolate
Owner: Lynn Lasher
Manager: Dino Bulsza
dbulsza@somebodysmothers.com
Estimated Sales: Less Than $500,000
Number Employees: 1-4

11796 Somerset Syrup & Concessions
100 Mcgaw Dr
Edison, NJ 08837-3725
   732-225-0200
Fax: 732-225-6363 800-526-8865
www.eatfunfoods.com
Confection products
President: Robert Spitz
bspitz@somersetsyrup.com
Estimated Sales: Below $5 Million
Number Employees: 20-49

11797 Something Natural LLC
321 W. 2nd St.
Boston, MA 02127
   617-315-7169
www.drinksomethingnatural.com
Manufacturer of carbonated water.
Founder: Randy Shefshick
sheffo14@gmail.com
Brands:
   Something Natural

11798 Something Special Deli-Foods
224 Kaska Road
Sherwood Park, AB T8A 4G7
Canada
   780-467-4448
Fax: 780-449-1238 800-461-5892
talktous@somethingspecialdeli.com
www.somethingspecialdeli.com
Salsa, dips, tapenades, pepper spreads and jellies.
President: Gordon Salamandick
Customer Care: Lori Martin

Estimated Sales: $20-50 Million
Number Employees: 10-19
Brands:
  Something Special Gourmet Antipasto
  Pepper Jellies

11799 Sommer Maid Creamery Inc
6069 Kellers Church Rd
PO Box 350
Pipersville, PA 18947-1019
215-345-6160
Fax: 215-345-4945 info@sommermaid.com
www.sommermaid.com
Cheese, eggs, butter and margarine
President: Brett Sexton
CFO: John T Poprick
VP/General Manager: Harry Mattern
Estimated Sales: $.5-1 million
Number Employees: 20-49
Type of Packaging: Consumer, Food Service, Private Label, Bulk
Brands:
  State

11800 Sommer's Food Products
106 W 7th Street
Salisbury, MO 65281-1108
660-388-5511
Potato chips
President: Jack Richardson
Estimated Sales: $5-9.9 000,000
Number Employees: 7
Brands:
  Sommer's Food

11801 Sommers Organic
339 Messner Drive
Wheeling, IL 60090
847-229-8192
Fax: 847-229-8264 877-377-9797
info@sommersorganic.com
Organic beef products, chicken products, turkey products, and pork products.
Chairman: Walter Sommers
Type of Packaging: Consumer

11802 Sonne
896 22nd Ave N
Wahpeton, ND 58075-3026
701-642-3068
Fax: 701-642-9403 800-727-6663
www.dakotagourmet.com
Roasted sunflower seeds, trail mixes and toasted corn and soybeans
President: Steven Bromley
Contact: Heather Budke
h.budke@sunopta.com
Estimated Sales: $3 Million
Number Employees: 20-49
Square Footage: 82200
Type of Packaging: Consumer, Food Service, Private Label, Bulk
Brands:
  Dakota Gourmet
  Dakota Gourmet Heart Smart
  Dakota Gourmet Toasted Korn

11803 Sonoita Vineyards
290 Elgin Canelo Rd
Elgin, AZ 85611-8001
520-455-5893
Fax: 520-455-5893 winery@sonoitavineyards.com
www.sonoitavineyards.com
Wines
Founder: Gordon Dutt
General Manager: Mike Duppost
VP: Jack Strolline
Estimated Sales: $1-2.5 Million
Number Employees: 5-9

11804 Sonoma Creamery
21750 8th St E
Suite 1
Sonoma, CA 95476-9803
707-996-1000
Fax: 707-935-3535 info@sonomacreamery.com
sonomacreamery.com
Cheese crisps
President & CEO: John Crean
Vice President: Lou Biaggi
Year Founded: 1931
Number Employees: 10-19
Brands:
  Mr. Cheese O's
  Sonoma Creamery
  Sonoma Jack
  Sonoma Organics

11805 Sonoma Flatbreads
935 Taylor Station Rd
Columbus, OH 43230
info@sonomaflatbreads.com
sonomaflatbreads.com
Flatbread pizzas
Chairwoman: Jane Grote Abell

11806 Sonoma Gourmet
21787 8th St E Ste 7
Sonoma, CA 95476
707-939-3700
Fax: 707-939-3730
Specialty sauces and condiments
President and Owner: William Weber
Vice President: Roger Declercq
Contact: Pedro Andrade
pedro@sonomagourmet.com
Estimated Sales: $3.14 Million
Number Employees: 25
Number of Brands: 30
Number of Products: 200
Type of Packaging: Private Label
Brands:
  Pometta's
  Sonoma Gourmet

11807 Sonoma Seafoods
2 E Spain St
Sonoma, CA 95476-5729
707-996-1931
Fax: 707-935-8846 800-411-2123
Sonomaseafoods@sonomaseafoods.com
sonomaseafoods.com
Stuffed entree products include fish and stuffed seafood in addition to a recently introduced new product line including poultry, pork, beef and vegetables.
Owner: Pete Vivani
Partner: Scott Gray
Sales Manager: Georgine Drees
Estimated Sales: $5.9 Million
Number Employees: 20-49

11808 Sonoma Syrup Co. Inc.
PO Box 819
Sonoma, CA 95476-0819
707-996-4070
Fax: 707-935-6976 www.sonomasyrup.com
Dessert toppings, flavoring syrups
Owner: Karin Campion
Number Employees: 1-4

11809 Sonoma Wine Services
P.O.Box 207
Vineburg, CA 95487
707-996-9773
Fax: 707-996-0145
Wines: shipping, storage. Controlled environment bonded warehouse
President: Warren McCambridge
CFO: Denise McCambridge
Estimated Sales: Under $500,000
Number Employees: 1-4
Brands:
  Sonoma Wine

11810 Sonoma-Cutrer Vineyards
4401 Slusser Rd
Windsor, CA 95492
707-528-1181
Fax: 707-528-1561 wineclub@sonomacutrer.com
www.sonomacutrer.com
wines. Some of their titles include Founders Reserve, Late Harvest Chardonnay, Sonoma Coast, Owsley Pinot Noir, Russian River Valley and more.
Winemaking Director: Mick Schroeter
Winemaker: Cara Morrison
General Manager: David Perata
david_perata@sonomacutrer.com
Estimated Sales: $1-2.5 Million
Number Employees: 50-99
Brands:
  Alban Viognier
  Chateau Montelena
  Hartwell Cabernet
  Louis Roederer
  MacPhail Pinot
  Oberschulte Syrah
  Worthy Cabernet

11811 Soozy's Grain-Free
246 Fifth Ave, 3rd Floor
P.O. Box 20077
New York, NY 10001
hello@soozys.com
www.soozysgrainfree.com
Muffins that are paleo and free from grain, gluten, dairy, peanuts, and soy
President: Mason Sexton
CEO: Susan Chen
Year Founded: 2017
Parent Co: Mindful Foods

11812 (HQ)Sopakco Foods
118 South Cypress Street
Mullins, SC 29574-1047
843-464-7851
Fax: 843-464-2096 sfernald@sopakco.com
www.sopakco.com
Sauces, dressings
President/CEO: Lonnie Thompson
Contact: Phil Howard
phil.howard@precisioncolor.com
Manufacturing Director: William Pettibone
Plant Operations: Bill Jennings
Estimated Sales: $5-10 Million
Number Employees: 250-499

11813 Sopako Foods
P.O.Box 1047
Mullins, SC 29574-1047
843-464-7851
Fax: 843-464-2096
Military food rations
President: Lonnie Thompson
Estimated Sales: $5-10 Million
Number Employees: 250-499
Parent Co: Sopako Foods

11814 Sophia Foods
480 Wortman Ave
Brooklyn, NY 11208
718-272-1110
Fax: 718-272-1230 www.sophiafoods.com
Oil, vinegar, salt, vegetables, rice and grains, sauces and spreads, pasta, crackers, grissini, cakes and cookies, preserves and juices.
CEO: Candace Abitbul
candace@sophiafoods.com
Director of Sales & Business Development: Paul Berger
Year Founded: 1991
Estimated Sales: $2.4 Million
Number Employees: 11-50
Type of Packaging: Consumer, Food Service
Brands:
  Sophia

11815 Sophia's Sauce Works
2533 N Carson Street
Carson City, NV 89706-0147
916-315-3584
Fax: 916-315-9372 800-718-7769
All natural sauces, spreads and dressings
Chairman: Sophia Fridas
President: Jim Fridas
Number Employees: 5-9
Square Footage: 8000
Parent Co: Sophia's Sauce Works
Type of Packaging: Consumer
Brands:
  Sophia's Authentic
  Sophia's Sauce Works

11816 Sopralco
6991 W Broward Blvd
Plantation, FL 33317-2907
954-584-2225
Fax: 954-584-3271 sopralco@aol.com
Ready-to-drink espresso
Owner: Peter Marciante
VP: Arcelia De Battisti
Marketing: Ana Ordaz
Estimated Sales: $1,500,000
Number Employees: 1-4
Square Footage: 1250
Parent Co: Sopralco
Type of Packaging: Consumer, Food Service
Brands:
  Espre
  Espre-Cart
  Espre-Matic

Food Manufacturers / A-Z

11817 (HQ)Sorbee Intl.
9990 Global Rd.
Philadelphia, PA 19115
215-677-5200
Fax: 215-677-7736 800-654-3997
Confectionery items including sugar hard candy, low-fat candy bars and sugar-free items
CEO: Daniel Werther
CFO: Tom Keogh
VP Sales: Barry Sokol
Estimated Sales: $31 Million
Number Employees: 20-49
Other Locations:
 Sorbee International Ltd.
 Philadelphia PA
Brands:
 Dream Candy
 Global Brands
 Sorbee

11818 Sorrenti Family Farms
14033 Steinegull Road
Escalon, CA 95320
209-838-1127
Fax: 209-838-7809 888-435-9490
Wild rice, blended rices, quick-cook rice mixes, pasta and wild rice mixes, soup mixes, muffin mixes, focaccia mix and pizza kits
President/CEO: Hita Sorenti
Estimated Sales: Less than $1 Million
Number Employees: 1-4
Brands:
 Cucina Sorrenti
 Mighty Wild
 Rising Star Ranch
 Sorrenti Family Farm
 Urban Delights

11819 Sorrento Lobster
224 Ocean Ave
Sorrento, ME 04677
207-422-9082
Fax: 207-422-9033
Seafood.
Manager: Rick Freeman
Estimated Sales: $2,100,000
Number Employees: 5-9

11820 Soteria
180 Kite Lake Road
Fairburn, GA 30213-9608
404-768-5161
Fax: 404-768-3704
Natural and dry seasoning blends with no salt, MSG or calories
CEO: Lee Armstrong
Executive VP: Denise Armstrong
VP Operations: Keith Jackson
Number Employees: 1-4

11821 Souperb LLC
1350 Powell St
Emeryville, CA 94608-2506
415-685-8508
www.naturallysouperb.com
Soups, broths
Chef & Founder: Joanna Terry

11822 Soupergirl
314 Carroll St NW
Washington, DC 20012
202-609-7177
info@thesoupergirl.com
thesoupergirl.com
Vegan soups, salads, sandwiches, hummus, rolls and muffins, cookies and rice puddings.
Co-Founder: Sara Polon
Co-Founder: Marilyn Polon
Chief Operating Officer: Leslie Neviaser
Farmer: Georgia O'Neal
Estimated Sales: $3.6 Million
Number Employees: 41
Type of Packaging: Food Service
Brands:
 Soupergirl

11823 Source Food Technology
2530 Meridian Parkway
#200
Durham, NC 27713
919-806-4545
Fax: 919-806-4842 866-277-3849
Cholesterol-free shortenings, fats and oils; also, cholesterol reduced egg and dairy products
CEO: Henry Cardello
VP Sales: Patrick Halliday
Estimated Sales: B
Number Employees: 5-9

11824 Source Naturals
23 Janis Way
Scotts Valley, CA 95066
831-438-1144
800-815-2333
www.sourcenaturals.com
Dietary supplements
President, CEO & Owner: Ira Goldberg
irag@thresholdent.com
Year Founded: 1982
Estimated Sales: $52.9 Million
Number Employees: 500-999
Square Footage: 100000
Parent Co: Threshold Enterprises
Brands:
 Source

11825 Souris Valley Processors
641 Govt Road Allowance
Melita, MB R0M 1L0
Canada
204-522-8210
Fax: 204-522-8210
Beef and pork
President: Larry Danyluk
Estimated Sales: $1-2.5 Million
Number Employees: 5-9
Square Footage: 16000
Type of Packaging: Consumer, Food Service

11826 South Beach Coffee Company
PO Box 403003
Miami Beach, FL 33140
305-576-9696
Fax: 305-532-0409 info@discoverourtown.com
Coffee for wholesale and retail customers
President: Hagai Gringarten
Vice President: Droma Gringarten
Marketing Director: Karen Kong
Operations Manager: Ruben Meoqui
Estimated Sales: $1-5 Million
Number Employees: 13
Type of Packaging: Consumer, Private Label
Brands:
 Lincoln Road Blend
 Ocean Drive Blend
 Ocean Road Blend

11827 South Beach Novelties & Confectionery
44 Robin Rd
Staten Island, NY 10305-4799
718-727-4500
Fax: 718-448-4108
Tobacco, tobacco products and confectionary.
Owner: John Lagana
Estimated Sales: $18 Million
Number Employees: 11
Square Footage: 6000

11828 South Bend Chocolate Co
3300 W Sample St
Suite 110
South Bend, IN 46619-3077
574-233-2577
Fax: 574-233-3150 800-301-4961
orders@sbchocolate.com www.sbchocolate.com
Distinctive chocolates, dried fruits, cherry treats, fudges, sugar free, creams, crunches, chocolates by the pound, gold boxes and gift baskets
Owner: Mark Tarner
orders@sbchocolate.com
Marketing Director: Kristina Pier
Year Founded: 1991
Estimated Sales: $20-50 Million
Number Employees: 100-249
Brands:
 South Bend Chocolate

11829 South Ceasar Dressing Company
PO Box 612
Novato, CA 94948-0612
415-897-0605
Fax: 415-897-0605
Salad dressing
Partner: Shirley Lesley
Partner: Mark Lesley
Estimated Sales: Under $500,000
Number Employees: 1-4
Type of Packaging: Private Label
Brands:
 South Ceasar Dressing Company

11830 South County Creamery
955 S. Main Street
Great Barrington, MA 01230
413-528-8400
Fax: 413-528-8402 sococreamery.com
Ice cream, sorbet and gelato
Co-Owner: Danny Mazursky
Estimated Sales: $300,000-500,000
Number Employees: 5-9
Brands:
 Berkshire Ice Cream

11831 South Georgia Pecan Co
309 S Lee St
PO Box 5366
Valdosta, GA 31601-5723
229-244-1321
Fax: 229-247-6361 800-627-6630
info@georgiapecan.com www.georgiapecan.com
Esatblished in 1913. Manufacturer and exporter of shelled pecans and almonds.
Co-Owner: Jim Worn
Co-Owner: Ed Crane
Estimated Sales: $20-50 Million
Number Employees: 100-249
Type of Packaging: Consumer
Brands:
 Dasher Pecan

11832 (HQ)South Mill
649 West South Street
Kennett Square, PA 19348
610-444-4800
Fax: 610-444-1338 info@southmill.com
www.southmill.com
National mushroom supplier.
Contact: Iris Ayala
iayala@southmill.com
Year Founded: 1978
Number Employees: 1,000
Type of Packaging: Consumer, Food Service, Private Label, Bulk
Other Locations:
 Distribution
 Atlanta GA
 Distribution
 New Orleans LA
 Distribution
 Houston TX
 Distribution
 Dallas TX
Brands:
 Brown King
 South Mill Mushroom Sales

11833 South Shores Seafood
1822 E Ball Rd
Anaheim, CA 92805-5936
714-956-2722
Fax: 714-956-0277
Seafood
President: Michael Armstrong
Estimated Sales: $2,000,000
Number Employees: 5-9

11834 South Texas Spice Co LTD
2106 Castroville Rd
San Antonio, TX 78237-3516
210-436-2280
Fax: 210-436-6658
Spices
President: Ida Faenz
Estimated Sales: $390,000
Number Employees: 5-9
Brands:
 Menchaca
 South Texas Spice
 Yellow Rose

11835 South Valley Farms
15443 Beech Ave
Wasco, CA 93280-7604
661-391-9000
Fax: 661-391-9012 www.southvalleyfarms.com
Grower and exporter of almonds and pistachios; processor of hulled and shelled almonds
Vice President: Benjamin Barnes
ben.y.barnes@gmail.com
VP: Daryl Wilkendors
Processing Manager: Jonathan Meyer

Food Manufacturers / A-Z

Estimated Sales: $2.5-5 Million
Number Employees: 100-249
Square Footage: 320000
Parent Co: Farm Management Company
Type of Packaging: Bulk

11836 Southeast Dairy Processors Inc
3808 E Columbus Dr
Tampa, FL 33605-3221
813-620-1516
Fax: 813-626-1516
www.southeastdairyprocessors.com
Milk and dairy products
President: William Tiller
Estimated Sales: $5-10 Million
Number Employees: 5-9
Type of Packaging: Private Label

11837 Southeastern Fisheries Assn
1118 Thomasville Rd # B
Tallahassee, FL 32303-6238
850-224-0612
Fax: 850-222-3663 bobfish@aol.com
www.sfaonline.org
Hot sauces, fisheries
Executive Director: Robert P Jones
Chairman: Dennis Henderson
Executive Director: Robert Jones
Number Employees: 1-4

11838 Southeastern Grocers
8928 Prominence Parkway
Suite 200
Jacksonville, FL 32256
904-783-5000
800-967-9105
www.segrocers.com
Supermarket portfolio.
President/CEO: Anthony Hucker
Estimated Sales: $1.5 Billion
Number Employees: 45,000
Number of Brands: 4
Type of Packaging: Consumer, Food Service, Private Label
Brands:
  Bi-Lo
  Fresco y Mas
  Harveys Supermarket
  Winn-Dixie

11839 Southeastern Mills Inc
100 E 1st Ave
Rome, GA 30161
800-334-4468
www.semillsfoods.com
Flour, corn meal & grits, sauce & gravy mixes, specialty baking mixes, batters & breadings, seasonings & marinades.
Chief Executive Officer: Vernon Grizzard
vgrizzard@semills.com
Chief Financial Officer: Peter Hjort
VP, Business Development: George Manak
Director, Purchasing: Chris Wheeler
Year Founded: 1941
Estimated Sales: $37.5 Million
Number Employees: 100-249
Square Footage: 300000
Type of Packaging: Consumer, Food Service, Private Label, Bulk
Brands:
  Four Roses
  Good Loaf
  Southeastern Mills
  Stivers Best
  Strong Boy

11840 Southern Art Company, LLC
PO Box 500398
Atlanta, GA 31150
800-257-6606
info@southernartco.com
www.southernartco.com
Manufacturer of dressings and sauces.
Founder: Kelly Woo

11841 Southern Baking
49 Batesville Ct
Greer, SC 29650-4800
864-627-1380
Fax: 864-627-1381 www.southern-baking.com
Bread
President: Mario Romano
Estimated Sales: $500,000-$1,000,000
Number Employees: 10-19

11842 Southern Bar-B-Que
PO Box 206
Jennings, LA 70546
337-824-3877
Fax: 337-824-6678 866-612-2586
Bbq sauce, basting sauce, crawfish, shrimp and crab boil, frying oil, grill-n-que rub, grill-n-que sauce, pepper sauce, roux, salsa, seasoning and spray basters
Contact: Mary Kojis
mkojis@southernco.com

11843 Southern Belle SandwichCompany
1969 N Lobdell Blvd
Baton Rouge, LA 70806
225-927-4670
Fax: 225-928-5661 800-344-4670
www.southernbellesandwich.com
Fresh sandwiches
President: Lloyd Bearden Jr
lbearden@southernbellesandwich.com
VP: Homer Miller
Sales Manager: Rick Bearden
Estimated Sales: $5-10 Million
Number Employees: 100-249
Square Footage: 40000
Parent Co: Bearden Sandwich Company
Type of Packaging: Consumer

11844 Southern Beverage Packers Inc
6341 Natures Way
Appling, GA 30802-5541
706-541-9222
Fax: 706-541-1730 800-326-2469
www.southernbev.com
Water and marketer of crystalline soft drink and fruit drinks
President: David Byrd
dbyrd@southernbev.com
Vice President: Stephen Byrd
Marketing Director: Jeff Millick
Production Manager: Lynn Hebbard
Plant Manager/Purchasing: Richard Maddox
Estimated Sales: $7 Million
Number Employees: 20-49
Number of Brands: 2
Number of Products: 50
Type of Packaging: Consumer, Bulk
Brands:
  Carolina Choice
  Flowing Wells
  Flowing Wells Natural Water
  Kist
  Spingtime
  Springtime Natural Artesian Water

11845 Southern Brown Rice
8553 Raybourn Rd
Weiner, AR 72479
870-684-2354
Fax: 870-684-2239 800-421-7423
Organically grown rice bran and flour; also, long, medium and short grain rice including basmati, brown, wild and wild blend
Manager: Bill Weeks
office@hoguefarms.com
Estimated Sales: $740000
Number Employees: 20-49
Square Footage: 56000

11846 Southern California Brewing Company
216 South Alameda Street
Los Angeles, CA
213-622-1261
Fax: 310-516-7989 www.angelcitybrewing.com
Seasonal beer, ale, stout, lager and pilsner
President/CEO: Michael Bowe
Vice President: Ray Mathys
Estimated Sales: $550,000
Number Employees: 3
Type of Packaging: Consumer, Food Service
Brands:
  Bear Country Bavarian
  Bock
  California Light Blonde
  Old Red Eye
  Winter Wonder

11847 Southern Cotton Oil Co
2782 Chelsea Ave
Memphis, TN 38108-1705
901-452-3151
Fax: 901-452-8968 www.adm.com
Cottonseed oil mill
Contact: Gary Coleman
g_coleman@admworld.com
Number Employees: 100-249
Parent Co: Archer Daniels Midland Company
Type of Packaging: Bulk

11848 Southern Culture Foods
6400 Atlantic Blvd
Suite 135
Peachtree Corners, GA 30071
ebarrett@southernculturefoods.com
www.southernculturefoods.com
Pancake and waffle mix in flavors including banana pudding, birthday cake, gingerbread, lemon blueberry, red velvet, strawberry, sweet potato, vanilla, and bourbon salted pecan; Also stone ground grits, cornbread mix, fried chickenmix, and bacon rub
Founder & CEO: Erica Barrett
Year Founded: 2011

11849 Southern Delight Gourmet Foods
1621 Scottsville Rd
Bowling Green, KY 42104
270-782-9943
Fax: 270-843-7544 866-782-9943
Gourmet sauces, gourmet marinades, gourmet salsas, gourmet seasonings, gourmet gift sets
Owner: Bart Anderson
Estimated Sales: $3-5 Million
Number Employees: 1-4
Type of Packaging: Consumer

11850 Southern Farms Fish Processors
103 W 26th Avenue
Kansas City, MO 64116-3060
870-355-2594
Fax: 870-355-4024 800-264-2594
Frozen catfish fillets, nuggets, strips, tidbits and breaded
President: John Gentry
Type of Packaging: Consumer, Food Service
Brands:
  Springwater Farms

11851 Southern Fish & Oyster Company
1 Eslava St
Mobile, AL 36603
251-438-2408
Fax: 251-432-7773
Seafood, oysters
Owner: Ralph Atkins
Estimated Sales: $1-3 Million
Number Employees: 10-19

11852 (HQ)Southern Flavoring Co
1330 Norfolk Ave
Bedford, VA 24523-2223
540-586-8565
Fax: 540-586-8568 800-765-8565
service@southernflavoring.com
www.southernflavoring.com
Liquid food flavorings
Owner: Thomas Thornton
tthornton@southernflavoring.com
Vice President: John Messier
VP Marketing: John Messier
Estimated Sales: $5 Million
Number Employees: 10-19
Square Footage: 140000
Parent Co: Southern Flavoring
Type of Packaging: Consumer, Private Label, Bulk
Brands:
  Clapier Mill
  Happy Home
  Road Kill BBQ
  Aunt Erma's Frugal Foods

11853 Southern Gardens Citrus
1820 County Road 833
Clewiston, FL 33440-9222
863-983-3030
Fax: 863-983-3060 www.ussugar.com
Citrus juices, concentrates, blends and ingredients
President: Robert Baker Jr
Finance Executive: Ginny Pena
VP Marketing: Charles Lucas
Contact: Dan Casper
dcasper@southerngardens.com
Number Employees: 100-249
Parent Co: US Sugar Corporation
Type of Packaging: Bulk

Food Manufacturers / A-Z

11854 Southern Gold Honey Co
3015 Brown Rd
Vidor, TX 77662-7902
409-768-1645
Fax: 409-768-1009 808-899-2494
Honey and specialty items including pecan cream honey and fruit flavored honeys
Owner: Gretchen Horn
Estimated Sales: Less than $500,000
Number Employees: 1-4
Type of Packaging: Consumer, Private Label
Brands:
  Southern Gold Honey

11855 Southern Heritage Coffee Company
6555 E 30th St Ste F
Indianapolis, IN 46219
Fax: 317-543-0757 800-486-1198
kevin@heritage-coffee.com
www.coppermooncoffee.com
Processor, importer, exporter and contract roaster of coffee including house blends and gourmet, liquid concentrate, espresso, instant cappuccino, pads, hotel in-room filter packed coffees
Manager: Doug Bachman
CEO: Kevin Daw
Sales Director: Kevin Daw
Contact: Christophe Burt
cgutwein@coppermooncoffee.com
Operations Manager: Dick Middleton
Purchasing Manager: Tom Oldridge
Number Employees: 20-49
Square Footage: 208000
Type of Packaging: Consumer, Food Service, Private Label, Bulk
Brands:
  Coffee Scapes
  Espresso Caruso
  Espresso Maria
  Heritage Espresso Pods
  Heritage Select
  Mugshots
  Sorengeti Coffees
  Safari Blend Liquid Coffee
  Santa's Favorite
  Select Blend In-Room Coffee
  Southern Heritage
  World Coffee Safari Gourmet

11856 Southern Ice Cream Specialties
1058 King Industrial Dr
Marietta, GA 30062
770-428-0452
Fax: 770-426-5441
Ice cream novelties
Manager: Craig McDufie
Contact: William Boehm
wboehm@southernice.com
Plant Manager: Kevin Vondusaar
Number Employees: 100-249
Parent Co: Kroger Company
Type of Packaging: Consumer, Private Label
Brands:
  Healthy Indulgence
  Texas Gold

11857 Southern Minnesota BeetSugar Cooperative
83550 County Road 21
Renville, MN 56284
320-329-8305
Fax: 320-329-3252 info@smbsc.com
www.smbsc.com
Molasses, refined sugar, liquid sugar, granulated sugar, fruit sugar, liquid sucrose, baker's sugar.
President/CEO: Kelvin Thompsen
Chairman: Mark Arnold
Agricultural Research: Mark Bredehoeft
Year Founded: 1974
Estimated Sales: $474 Million
Number Employees: 850
Square Footage: 140000
Type of Packaging: Consumer, Bulk

11858 Southern Okie
PO Box 30261
Edmond, OK 73003-0005
405-657-7765
gina@southernokie.com
www.southernokie.com
Manufacturer of fruit spreads.
Founder and President: Gina Hollingsworth

11859 Southern Packing Corp
4004 Battlefield Blvd S
Chesapeake, VA 23322-2431
757-421-2131
Fax: 757-421-3633 sopaco@verizon.net
www.southernpacking.com
Processor and packer of beef, pork and veal
President/Senior Executive: Hyman Brooke
Secretary: Ronald Brooke
Treasurer: L.H. Brooke
Vice President/General Manager: B.B. Brooke
Estimated Sales: $4.1 Million
Number Employees: 20-49
Square Footage: 61200
Type of Packaging: Consumer, Food Service, Bulk
Brands:
  Cavalier

11860 Southern Peanut Co Inc
7329 Albert St
Dublin, NC 28332
910-862-2136
Fax: 910-862-8076 800-330-3141
www.peanutprocessors.com
Peanuts including in shell, raw shelled, blanched redskins, peanut granules, oil & dry roasted peanuts and peanut butter
President: Nile Brisson
nbrisson@peanutprocessors.com
Plant Manager: Luke Clearman
Estimated Sales: $12 Million
Number Employees: 5-9
Square Footage: 540000
Parent Co: Peanut Processors
Type of Packaging: Consumer, Food Service, Bulk

11861 Southern Popcorn Company
3157 Norbrook Drive
Memphis, TN 38118-6608
901-362-5238
Fax: 901-888-0230
Popcorn, jellies, dessert toppings
President: Murrey Watkins
Estimated Sales: $5-10 Million
Number Employees: 10-19

11862 Southern Pride Catfish Company
2025 1st Ave Ste 900
Seattle, WA 98121
Fax: 334-624-8224 800-343-8046
Processor and exporter of farm-raised catfish
President: Joe Glover
Quality Control: Alice Moore
VP Sales: Randy Rhodes
Public Relations: Mary Hand
Operations Manager: Bobby Collins
Number Employees: 500-999
Type of Packaging: Consumer, Food Service, Private Label
Brands:
  Southern Pride

11863 Southern Roasted Nuts
PO Box 508
Fitzgerald, GA 31750-0508
912-423-5616
Fax: 912-423-6550
Roasted nuts
President: Allen Conger
Estimated Sales: $10-24.9 000,000
Number Employees: 40

11864 Southern Season
201 S Estes Dr # 300
University Place
Chapel Hill, NC 27514-6118
919-929-7133
Fax: 919-942-9274 877-929-7133
customerservice@southernseason.com
www.southernseason.com
Chocolates, preserves, relishes, hams, cookware
President: Dave Herman
dherman@southernseason.com
VP Public Relations: Jay White
Year Founded: 1975
Estimated Sales: $25 Million
Number Employees: 250-499
Square Footage: 59000
Other Locations:
  A Southern Season
  Hillsborough NC
Brands:
  A Southern Season
  Alaska Smoked Salmon
  Ashby's
  Barbera Frantioia
  California Harvest
  Carolina Cupboard
  Crook's
  Frescobaldi Laudemio
  Godiva
  Johnston County Hams
  Lindt
  McEvoy Ranch
  My Grandma's of New England
  Nunez De Prado
  Sparrow Lane
  Terre D'Olivier

11865 Southern Shell Fish Company
501 Destrehan Avenue
Harvey, LA 70058-2737
504-341-5631
Fax: 504-341-5635
Processor, canner and exporter of crabmeat, oysters and shrimp
Manager: Dennis Skrmetta
Sales Manager: H Burke Jr
Plant Manager: Golden Boutte
Estimated Sales: $1,400,000
Number Employees: 1-4
Parent Co: Deepsouth Packing Company
Type of Packaging: Consumer, Food Service, Private Label
Brands:
  Blue Plate
  Dunbar
  Gulf Kist
  House of Windsor
  Pride New Orleans

11866 Southern Shellfish
120 Johnny Mercer Boulevard
Savannah, GA 31410-2142
912-897-3650
Fax: 912-897-6036
Seafood, shellfish

11867 Southern Snow
103 W W St
Belle Chasse, LA 70037-1111
504-393-8967
Fax: 504-393-0112
Manufacturer and exporter of artificial concentrates including colors and flavors; also, ice block shavers
Owner: Milton Wendling
info@flavorsnow.com
Marketing: Danielle Havnen
Estimated Sales: $1500000
Number Employees: 20-49
Square Footage: 40000
Brands:
  Southern Snow

11868 Southern Style Nuts
114 N Houston Ave
Denison, TX 75021-3013
903-463-3161
info@squirrelbrand.com
Roasted and blended nuts including snack mixes, hot and honey roasted peanuts, confectionery pecans and almonds and sweet and salty cashews
President: Michael Kurilecz
VP: Virgil Williamson
Estimated Sales: $54,000
Number Employees: 2
Type of Packaging: Consumer, Food Service, Private Label, Bulk
Brands:
  Roann's Confections
  Southern Style Nuts
  Squirrel Brand

11869 Southern Twist Cocktail
PO Box 23
Folly Beach, SC 29439-0023
843-343-9577
info@southerntwistcocktails.com
southerntwistcocktails.com
Cocktail infusions
Owner: Rochelle Jones
Brands:
  Southern Twist

Food Manufacturers / A-Z

11870 Southside Seafood Inc
1930 Pittston Ave # 1
Scranton, PA 18505-4497
570-969-9726
Fax: 570-961-5181 www.southsideseafood.net
Seafood
Owner: Carl Pazzaglia
Estimated Sales: $3-5 Million
Number Employees: 5-9

11871 Southwest Cheese Company
1141 Curry County Road
#4
Clovis, NM 88101
575-742-9200
bcochie@southwestcheese.com
www.southwestcheese.com
Cheese
Vice President, Sales: Dave Snyder
Cheese Sales Manager: Becky Pearson
Human Resources Director: Leah Jackson

11872 Southwest Foods
13157 US Highway 271
Tyler, TX 75708-2453
903-877-6800
Fax: 903-877-6903 888-937-3776
dennisprice@brookshires.com
www.brookshires.com
Baked goods
Manager: Sheila Vickery
Number Employees: 250-499
Brands:
  South West

11873 Southwest Specialty Food
700 N Bullard Ave
Goodyear, AZ 85338-2506
623-931-3131
Fax: 623-931-9931 800-536-3131
southwest@asskickin.com www.asskickin.com
Makers of gourmet hot sauce and other fine products such as hot sauces, salsas, snacks, gift sets, marinades/sauces, chili mixes/spices, beverages and condiments.
Owner: Jeff Jacobs
southwest@asskickin.com
Estimated Sales: Below $5 Million
Number Employees: 10-19
Type of Packaging: Private Label
Brands:
  Banditos Salsas
  Candy Ass
  Habanero Products From Hell
  Seasonings From Hell
  Spontaneous Combustion

11874 Southwest Spirit
701 Buford Drive
Socorro, NM 87801-4019
800-838-0773
Fax: 505-838-0177 info@swspirit.com
www.swspirit.com
Salsas
Co-Owner: Cynthia Fowler
Co-Owner: Jim Fowler
Type of Packaging: Consumer

11875 Sovena USA Inc
1 Olive Grove St
Rome, NY 13441-4815
315-797-7070
Fax: 315-797-6981
customerservice@sovenausa.com
www.sovenagroup.com
Domestic edible oils including olive, corn, soybean, peanut and salad; importer of olive oil
CEO: Steve Mandia
CFO: Dave Lofgren
VP: Bert Mandia
VP Sales/Marketing: Mark Mottit
Manager: Luis Gato
l.gato@sovenagroup.com
Estimated Sales: $12.7 Million
Number Employees: 1-4
Square Footage: 45000
Brands:
  Clio Pomace
  Clio Pure
  Gem 100%
  Gem Blended
  Gem Extra

11876 Sow's Ear Winery
303 Coastal Rd
Brooksville, ME 04617-3705
207-326-4649
www.uniquemainefarms.com
Wines
Owner: Tom Hoey
Estimated Sales: Less Than $500,000
Number Employees: 1-4

11877 Sowden Brothers Farm
8888 Township Road
Live Oak, CA 95953
530-695-3750
Fax: 530-695-1395 www.organicprunes.com
Prune concentrate and dried prunes including Ashlock pitted and whole
President: Richard Taylor
VP: John Taylor
Estimated Sales: $20-50 Million
Number Employees: 50
Square Footage: 25000
Type of Packaging: Food Service, Private Label, Bulk
Brands:
  Cal Gold
  California Gold
  Taylor Brothers Farms

11878 Soy Vay Enterprises
6223 Highway 9
Felton, CA 95018
831-335-3824
Fax: 831-335-3589 800-444-6369
support@soyvay.com www.soyvay.com
Teriyaki, salad dressing and marinade, hoisin and garlic-based sauce
President/Owner: Eddy Scher
Estimated Sales: $1-3 Million
Number Employees: 1-4
Type of Packaging: Consumer, Food Service, Private Label
Brands:
  Cha-Cha Chinese Chicken Dressing
  Chinese Marinade
  Island Teriyaki
  Soy Vay Veri-Veri Teriyaki

11879 SoyLife Division
3300 Edinborough Way # 712
Edina, MN 55435-5963
952-920-7700
Fax: 952-920-7704 www.soylife.com
Soy isoflavone, nutraceutical ingredients
President: Laurent Leduc
Chief Executive Officer: Ori Yehudai
Estimated Sales: Less than $500,000
Number Employees: 5-9

11880 SoyTex
609 Eagle Rock Ave
West Orange, NJ 07052-2903
973-243-1899
Fax: 973-243-0800 888-769-8391
soytex.com
Meat substitution products made from high quality soy protein concentrate using modern extrusion technology.
President: Joseph Nazarian
VP: Tirdad Zandieh

11881 Soyfoods of America
1050 17th Street NW
Washington, DC 20036
202-659-3520
Fax: 202-659-3522 www.soyfoods.org
Soy milk and yuba; also, regular and marinated tofu, cultured soy beverage, bulk soymilk
President/Owner: Kanin Lee
Estimated Sales: $3 Million
Number Employees: 27
Square Footage: 60000
Type of Packaging: Consumer, Food Service, Private Label, Bulk
Brands:
  Furama
  Soywise

11882 Soylent
555 Mateo St
Suite 227
Los Angeles, CA 90013
info@soylent.com
www.soylent.com
Meal replacement drinks and powders
CEO: Bryan Crowley
CFO: Demir Vangelov
VP Product Development & Innovation: Julie Daoust
VP Brand Marketing: Andrew Thomas
SVP Sales: Melody Conner
Year Founded: 2013
Number Employees: 50-99
Parent Co: Rosa Foods Inc.

11883 Soylent Brand
PO Box 165475
Irving, TX 75016-5475
972-255-4747
Salsa
President/CEO: Jack Veach
CFO: Fred Harper
Vice President: Morris Woodall
Research & Development: R Michael MacGregor
Quality Control: James Valikont, Jr.
Sales Director: Dana Davidson
Operations/Production: Lynne Wainman
Plant Manager: Robert Roggers
Number Employees: 10-19
Number of Brands: 1
Number of Products: 6
Square Footage: 22000
Parent Co: Solvent Interntional
Type of Packaging: Private Label
Brands:
  Guacamole Salad
  Salsa Picante
  Tex-Mex
  Verde

11884 Soynut Butter Co
4220 Commercial Way
Glenview, IL 60025-3597
847-635-9960
Fax: 847-635-6801
Peanut butter substitute, gluten, nut & peanut free snacks, gluten free corn crumbs.
President: Steve Grubb
s.grubb@soynutbutter.com
Number Employees: 5-9
Type of Packaging: Consumer, Food Service

11885 (HQ)Spangler Candy Co
400 N Portland St
PO Box 71
Bryan, OH 43506-1257
419-636-4221
Fax: 419-636-3695 888-636-4221
www.spanglercandy.com
Lollipops, candy canes and circus peanuts
President & CEO: Kirk Vashaw
Chairman: Dean Spangler
CFO: Bill Martin
VP Marketing: Jim Knight
VP Sales: Denny Gunter
VP Production: Steve Kerr
Number Employees: 500-999
Square Footage: 2000000
Other Locations:
  Spangler Candy Co.
  Bryan OH
Brands:
  Astro Pops
  Cane Classics
  Dum Dum Pops
  Picture Pops
  Saf-T-Pops
  Spangler Candy Canes
  Spangler Chocolates
  Spangler Circus Peanuts

11886 Spangler Vineyards
491 Winery Ln
Roseburg, OR 97471-9365
541-679-9654
Fax: 541-679-3888 info@spanglervineyards.com
www.spanglervineyards.com
Wine
Owner: Patrick Spangler
info@spanglervineyards.com
Co-Owner: Loree Spangler
Winemaker: Leonard Postles
Estimated Sales: Less than $500,000
Number Employees: 1-4
Type of Packaging: Private Label
Brands:
  Spangler Vineyards

Food Manufacturers / A-Z

11887 Spanish Gardens Food Manufacturing
2301 Metropolitan Ave
Kansas City, KS 66106
913-831-4242
Taco shells, sauce, spices, tortilla chips and corn and flour tortillas
President: Norma Jean Miller
Estimated Sales: $1300000
Number Employees: 20-49
Square Footage: 160000
Type of Packaging: Consumer, Food Service, Bulk

11888 Sparboe Foods Corp
900 N Linn Ave
New Hampton, IA 50659-1204
641-394-3040
info@sparboe.com
www.sparboe.com
Fresh and frozen eggs
President: Bob Sparboe
Vice President: Beth Fechnell
Manager: Warren Miller
Estimated Sales: $20-50 Million
Number Employees: 100-249
Square Footage: 50000
Type of Packaging: Food Service, Private Label, Bulk
Brands:
  Bes Tex
  Except Mix

11889 Sparkletts
200 Eagles Landing Boulevard
Lakeland, FL 33810
800-728-5508
www.water.com
Bottled water for retail and businesses, as well as bottle water dispensers and break room supplies
President: David Muscato
Estimated Sales: $5200000
Number Employees: 50-99
Parent Co: DS Services of America
Type of Packaging: Consumer, Food Service
Brands:
  Alhambra
  Crystal Springs
  Deep Rock Water
  Hinckley Springs
  Kentwood Springs
  Mount Olympus
  Sierra Springs

11890 Sparrow Lane
4110 Brew Master Dr
Ceres, CA 95307
209-538-7600
Fax: 209-538-7614 866-515-2477
sparrowlane.com
Wine and fruit vinegars
Chef: Jesse Layman

11891 Spaten North America Inc
4621 Little Neck Parkway
Little Neck, NY 11362
718-281-1912
Brewery
Number of Brands: 1
Parent Co: Spaten-Franziskaner-Brau
Brands:
  Spaten

11892 Spaulding & Assoc
8700 N 2nd St # 202
Brighton, MI 48116-1296
810-229-4166
Fax: 810-227-4218
Cheese
President: Pat Spaulding
Estimated Sales: Less Than $500,000
Number Employees: 1-4

11893 SpecialTeas
2 Reynolds Street
Norwalk, CT 06855-1015
203-866-1522
Fax: 203-375-6820 888-365-6983
Gourmet tea
Managing Director: Juergen Link
Estimated Sales: $5-10 Million
Number Employees: 5-9

11894 Specialities Importers & Distributers
85 Division Avenue
PO Box 409
Millington, NJ 07946
908-647-6485
Fax: 908-647-8305 800-899-6689
www.specialitiesinc.com
Deli: cheeses, cured meats and hams.
President: Ron Schinbeckler
r.schinbeckler@specialitiesinc.com
Vice President, Sales & Marketing: Richard Kessler
Year Founded: 1991
Type of Packaging: Food Service
Brands:
  Bellentani
  Carpuela
  Bayonne Ham
  Ermitage
  leBistro
  Solera(c)

11895 (HQ)Specialty Bakers
450 S State Rd
Marysville, PA 17053-1009
717-957-2131
Fax: 717-957-0156 800-233-0778
CustomerService@SpecialtyBakers.com
www.specialtybakers.com
Manufacturer and exporter of sponge, snack and angel food cakes, lady fingers, dessert shells, French twirls and jelly rolls
President: John Piotrowski
CEO: Hamani Abdou
habdou@specialtybakers.com
Plant Manager: Richard Sychterz
Estimated Sales: $14 Million
Number Employees: 50-99
Square Footage: 150000
Type of Packaging: Consumer, Private Label
Other Locations:
  Specialty Bakers
  Marysville PA
  Specialty Bakers
  Lititz PA
  Specialty Bakers
  Dunkirk NY
Brands:
  Specialty

11896 Specialty Cheese Co Inc
430 N Main St
Reeseville, WI 53579-9790
920-927-3888
Fax: 920-927-3200 800-367-1711
scci@specialcheese.com www.specialcheese.com
Cheese packaging
President: Paul Scharfman
CEO: Jacquelyn Austin
jacquelyn@specialcheese.com
Estimated Sales: $2.5-5 Million
Number Employees: 100-249
Type of Packaging: Private Label
Brands:
  Hem
  Lavacarica
  Rich Cow

11897 Specialty Coffee Roasters
1300 SW 10th St
Suite 2
Delray Beach, FL 33444
Fax: 800-805-4422 800-253-9363
Processor, packer and importer of gourmet coffees; exporter of gourmet coffees
President: Gabriela Harvey
Estimated Sales: $300,000
Number Employees: 3
Square Footage: 20000
Parent Co: MGH Holdings Corporation
Type of Packaging: Consumer, Food Service, Private Label, Bulk
Brands:
  Shalina

11898 Specialty Commodities Inc
1530 47th St N
Fargo, ND 58102-2858
701-282-8222
Fax: 701-264-5744
www.specialtycommodities.com
Manufacturer and importer of specialty ingredients for snack food, dairy, bakery, cereal, energy bar and confectionery. Products include dehydrated, dried fruit, legumes, nuts, seeds, spices and grains.
President: Ken Campbell
Vice President: Kevin Anderson
Number Employees: 10-19
Parent Co: Archer Daniels Midland Company
Type of Packaging: Private Label, Bulk
Other Locations:
  Corporate Office
  Fargo ND
  Processing Plant
  Lodi CA
  Processing Plant
  Stockton CA
  Processing Plant
  Modesto CA

11899 Specialty Food America Inc
5055 Huffman Mill Rd
Hopkinsville, KY 42240-9162
270-889-0017
888-881-1633
www.specialtyfoodamerica.com
Herbs and spices; cooking related supplies and contract packaging
Owner: Thomas L Marshall
specialtyfoodtom@gmail.com
Estimated Sales: Less Than $500,000
Number Employees: 1-4
Square Footage: 4800
Type of Packaging: Consumer, Private Label
Brands:
  Lucini Honestete
  Sonoma Syrups

11900 Specialty Food Association
136 Madison Ave
New York, NY 10016
646-878-0301
www.specialtyfood.com
Baby food, baked goods, baking mixes, beverages, condiments, confectionery, eggs, dairy, frozen food, meat and game, oils, snacks, seafood, soups, spreads and syrups, sauces, seasonings, grains and cereals, vegetables and fruits.
Contact: Equazia Cordero
equazia.cordero@xerox.com

11901 Specialty Food Magazine
136 Madison Ave
12th Floor
New York, NY 10016
212-482-6440
socialmedia@specialtyfood.com
www.specialtyfood.com
Food magazine
Sales Manager: Kathy Sackett
Publisher: Chris Crocker
ccrocker@specialtyfood.Com
Brands:
  Specialty Food Magazine

11902 (HQ)Specialty Foods Group Inc
6 Dublin Ln
Owensboro, KY 42301
270-926-2324
800-238-0020
www.specialtyfoodsgroup.com
Spices, lunch meats, turkey, and pork products including bacon, ham, and sausage.
Year Founded: 1914
Estimated Sales: $234 Million
Number Employees: 250-499
Number of Brands: 7
Type of Packaging: Consumer, Food Service, Private Label, Bulk
Other Locations:
  SFG Production Plant
  Owensboro KY
  SFG Production Plant
  Humboldt IA
  SFG Production Plant
  Chicago IL
  SFG Production Plant
  Williamston NC
Brands:
  Artisan Crafted Series
  Field
  Fischer's
  Kentuckian Gold
  Kentucky Legend
  Mickelberry's
  Scott Pete

Food Manufacturers / A-Z

11903 Specialty Foods South LLC
1023 Wappoo Rd # B37
Charleston, SC 29407-5960
843-766-2580
Fax: 843-766-2580 800-538-0003
Orders@foodforthesouthernsoul.com
www.foodforthesouthernsoul.com
Gourmet foods
Owner: James Hagood
jimmyhagood@foodforthesouthernsoul.com
Estimated Sales: Under $500,000
Number Employees: 5-9
Type of Packaging: Private Label, Bulk

11904 Specialty Ingredients
1130 W. Lake Cook Road
Suite 320
Buffalo Grove, IL 60089
847-419-9595
Fax: 847-419-9547 sales@ingredientsinc.com
www.ingredientsinc.com
Dehydrated/whole/starch potato products, soy based ingredients, dairy ingredients, food acids and salts, and frozen & dehydrated vegetables.
Chief Executive Officer, Owner: Debbie Stew
Sales: Jim Stewart

11905 Specialty Meats & Gourmet
1810 Webster St # 8
Hudson, WI 54016-9318
715-377-0734
Fax: 715-386-6613 800-310-2360
Marketer and processor of fresh and frozen farm raised game meat from alligator to yak; gourmet items, corporate gift boxes, etc.
Principal: Kent Phillips
Contact: Linda Janse
ljanse@smgfoods.com
Estimated Sales: Under $500,000
Number Employees: 1-4
Square Footage: 8000
Parent Co: Venison America
Type of Packaging: Consumer, Food Service

11906 Specialty Minerals Inc
35 Highland Ave
Bethlehem, PA 18017-9482
610-861-3496
Fax: 610-882-8726 800-801-1031
www.mineralstech.com
Manufacturer, sellers and exporters of food and pharmaceutical grades of precipitated calcium carbonate, ground limestone and talc
Chairman/CEO: Jospeh Muscari
CFO: Douglas Dietrich
Director: Gary Castagna
Sales: Jay Esty
Commercial Manager: Jay Esty
Number Employees: 50-99
Parent Co: Minerals Technologies Inc
Type of Packaging: Private Label
Other Locations:
  SMI Mineral Plant
  Adams MA
  SMI Mineral Plant
  Canann CT
  SMI Mineral Plant
  Barretts MT
  SMI Mineral Plant
  Lucerne Valley CA
Brands:
  Albaglos
  Jetcoat
  Opacarb
  Pcc

11907 Specialty Products
128 Rogers Street
Gloucester, MA 01930
216-362-1050
Fax: 216-362-6506 800-222-6846
luis.granja@gortons.com www.gortons.com
Processor and exporter of breading batter
Manager: Luis Granja
Controller: Sue Spisak
Plant Manager: Luis Granja
Estimated Sales: $10-20 Million
Number Employees: 20-49
Parent Co: Gorton's
Type of Packaging: Food Service, Private Label, Bulk

11908 Specialty Rice Inc
1000 W 1st St
Brinkley, AR 72021-9000
870-734-1235
Fax: 870-734-1237 800-467-1233
info@dellarice.com www.delroserice.com
Processor, miller and exporter of five types of rice
Manager: Ojus Ajmara
Manager: Glenda Hilsdon
glendah@dellarice.com
General Manager: Glenda Hilsdon
Estimated Sales: $800,000
Number Employees: 10-19
Square Footage: 32000
Brands:
  Della
  Della Gourmet Rice
  Gourmet Basmati Rice
  Jasmine

11909 Speco Inc
3946 Willow St
Schiller Park, IL 60176-2311
847-678-4240
Fax: 847-678-8037 800-541-5415
sales@speco.com www.speco.com
Manufacturer and exporter of meat cutting equipment including meat and mincer knives and bone collector systems
Vice President: Clarence Hoffman
clarence@speco.com
Office Manager: Sue Ryan
Sales Manager: Steve Jacob
Production Manager: Clarence Hoffman
Maintenance Supervisor: Ron Schulmeister
Estimated Sales: $7 Million
Number Employees: 50-99
Square Footage: 100000
Brands:
  Superior
  Triumph

11910 Spectrum Foods Inc
2520 South Grand Ave E
P.O. Box 3483
Springfield, IL 62703-5613
217-528-5301
Fax: 217-391-0096 lmyers@spectrum-foods.com
www.spectrum-foods.com
Offers natural and organic vegetable oil, organic soy products, and low sodium sea salt.
President: Rob Kirby
Chairman: Al Maiocco
VP Sales & Business Development: Lynn Myers
Manager: Karen Adamo
kglitter-adamo@spectrum-foods.com
Number Employees: 20-49
Type of Packaging: Bulk
Brands:
  NEXCEL
  NEXSOY

11911 Spelt Right Foods, LLC
961 Elton St.
Brooklyn, NY 11208
877-773-5801
Fax: 718-240-9041 info@speltright.com
www.speltright.com
Manufacturer of breads, doughs, and frozen baked goods made with spelt flour.
Co-Founder: Beth George
Co-Founder: Tim George
Contact: Menachem Delevkovitz
info@speltright.com

11912 Spence & Company
78 Campanelli Industrial drive
Brockton, MA 02301
508-427-5577
Fax: 508-427-5557 salmon@spenceltd.com
www.spenceltd.com
Smoked fish; importer of fish ingredients
President: Alan Spence
Estimated Sales: $4500000
Number Employees: 25
Type of Packaging: Consumer, Food Service

11913 Spencer Packing Company
PO Box 753
Washington, NC 27889-0753
252-946-4161
Fax: 252-946-4162
Processor and packer of pork
President: Harold Spencer

Estimated Sales: $1,250,000
Number Employees: 10-19

11914 Sperry Apiaries
15750 Highway 46
Kindred, ND 58051
701-428-3000
Honey
President: Mark Sperry
Estimated Sales: Under $500,000
Number Employees: 1-4
Number of Brands: 1
Number of Products: 1

11915 Spice & Spice
655 Deep Valley Drive
Ste 125
Rolling Hills Estates, CA 90274
310-265-2914
Fax: 310-265-2934 866-729-7742
info@spicenspice.com www.spicenspice.com
Bulk line of whole and ground spice products: black pepper, white pepper, cumin, cinnamon, crush chili, cinnamon stick, chili powder, granulated garlic, dry chili pods
Owner: Anthony Dirocco
CEO: Mukesh Thakker
R & D: Nitul Unekekett
Quality Control: Nina Lukamanje
Contact: Cindy Philips
cindy@calwind.com
Estimated Sales: $5-10 Million
Number Employees: 1-4
Number of Brands: 1
Number of Products: 25
Square Footage: 200000
Type of Packaging: Food Service, Bulk
Brands:
  Boat Brand

11916 Spice Chain
6c Terminal Way
Avenel, NJ 07001-2228
732-499-9070
Fax: 732-499-9139
Spices including basil, bay leaves, garlic, oregano, paprika, pepper, etc
President: Andrew Barna
andrew.barna@spice-co.com
VP: James Peterkin
Estimated Sales: $11 Million
Number Employees: 50-99
Type of Packaging: Consumer, Food Service, Private Label, Bulk
Brands:
  Pride of Malabar
  Pride of Shandung
  Pride of Szeged

11917 Spice Galleon
281 Commerce Street
Belgium, WI 53004-9408
262-285-4800
Fax: 262-285-4820 877-668-4800
Gourmet seasonings
President: Rick Boum
Estimated Sales: $1 Million
Number Employees: 25
Number of Brands: 5
Number of Products: 100
Square Footage: 40000
Type of Packaging: Consumer, Food Service, Private Label, Bulk

11918 Spice House International Specialties
47 Bloomingdale Road
Hicksville, NY 11801-1512
516-942-7248
Fax: 516-942-7249 www.spicehouseint.com
Spices and blends, specialty foods, hot sauces, dried fruits and nuts; serving the food service market from around the world
President: Anthony Provetto
Estimated Sales: $5-10 Million
Number Employees: 5-9
Square Footage: 18400
Type of Packaging: Consumer, Food Service, Private Label, Bulk

Food Manufacturers / A-Z

11919 Spice Hunter Inc
2000 W Broad St
Richmond, VA 23220-2006
804-359-5786
Fax: 805-544-9046 800-444-3061
www.spicehunter.com
Dried bean soups, entree seasonings, dips, salad seasonings, Asian soups, spices and drink mixes
President/CEO: Conrad Sauer
President: Lucia Cleveland
CFO: William Ulick
HR Executive: Karen Woodling
kwoodling@spicehunter.com
Estimated Sales: $17 Million
Number Employees: 50-99
Number of Products: 200
Square Footage: 226000
Parent Co: C.F. Sauer Company
Type of Packaging: Private Label, Bulk
Brands:
 Oriental Noodle Soup
 Quick & Natural Soup
 Quick Pot Pasta
 Savory Smoke
 Simmer Kettle
 Spice Hunter
 Spice Hunter Spices & Herbs

11920 Spice King Corporation
438 El Camino Dr
Beverly Hills, CA 90212
310-836-7770
Fax: 310-836-6454
Processor, importer and exporter of custom formulated natural spices and seasonings; also, dehydrated vegetables and fruits
General Manager: James Stephens
VP: A Stern
Marketing Director: Anne Stern
Number Employees: 20-49
Square Footage: 100000

11921 Spice Lab
4000 N. Dixie Highway
Pompano Beach, FL 33064
954-275-4478
brett@thespicelab.com
www.thespicelab.com
Sea salts

11922 Spice O' Life
PO Box 70406
Seattle, WA 98127-0406
206-789-4195
Fax: 206-782-9339 www.spiceolife.com
Custom blended spices
Owner: Scotty McDonell
Account Manager: Judith Jager
Advertising Manager: David Barker
Number Employees: 1-4

11923 Spice Of Life Co
15445 Ventura Blvd # 115
Suite 115
Sherman Oaks, CA 91403-3005
818-909-0052
info@spice-of-life.com
www.spice-of-life.com
Meatless meats and jerky
Co-Founder: Spice Williams-Crosby
Contact: Crosby Gregory
spiceoflife@earthlink.net
Number Employees: 1-4

11924 Spice Rack Chocolates
10908 Courthouse Rd
Suite 102 #264
Fredericksburg, VA 22408
540-847-2063
Fax: 416-757-5183
Dark chocolates infused with hers and spices
President/Owner: Mary Schellhammer
CFO: Paul Schellhammer

11925 Spice Time Foods
940 Monroe Street
Hoboken, NJ 07030-6429
201-792-1200
Fax: 201-792-9796
Spices
President: John Stapleton
Director Manufacturing: John Hybner
Plant Manager: Jim Maurice
Parent Co: Gambrinus Company

11926 Spice World Inc
8101 Presidents Dr
Orlando, FL 32809
sworld@spiceworldinc.com
www.spiceworldinc.com
Processor and exporter of garlic, custom seasoning blends and garlic including minced, chopped and packed in olive oil or water
Year Founded: 1949
Estimated Sales: $5-10 Million
Number Employees: 100-249
Number of Brands: 1
Square Footage: 480000
Type of Packaging: Consumer, Food Service, Private Label, Bulk
Brands:
 Spice World

11927 Spiceland
6604 W Irving Park Rd
Chicago, IL 60634-2435
773-736-1000
800-352-8671
Spices
Co-Owner: Doris Stockwell
Co-Owner: Jim Stockwell
Estimated Sales: Less than $500,000
Number Employees: 5-9
Brands:
 Spiceland

11928 Spicely
4180 Business Center Dr.
Fremont, CA 94538
510-440-1044
Fax: 510-440-1008 customerservice@spicely.com
www.spicely.com
Organic and natural foods; planet friendly packaging; encourage certified fair trade.
Contact: Clara Bonner
clara@spicely.com
Parent Co: American Natural & Organic Spices
Type of Packaging: Consumer

11929 (HQ)Spices of Life Gourmet Coffee
4135 Dr Mlk Blvd
Fort Myers, FL 33916
239-334-8004
Fax: 941-549-9041
Coffee
Owner: Cheryl Dejonghe
Vice President: Edward Miller
Estimated Sales: $300,000-500,000
Number Employees: 1-4

11930 (HQ)Spicetec Flavors & Seasonings
11 Conagra Drive
Omaha, NE 68102-5003
402-595-4000
Fax: 402-595-4707 800-921-7502
www.conagrafoods.com
Savory flavors, seasonings, food bases, advanced flavoring systems
Vice President/General Manager: Amy Patterson
Senior Director, R&D: Joanne Ferrara
Senior Quality Specialist: Lachelle Petty
Director of Operations: Paul Werner
Estimated Sales: $20-49.9 Million
Number Employees: 295
Number of Brands: 1
Number of Products: 3000
Square Footage: 104000
Parent Co: Givaudan
Type of Packaging: Bulk
Other Locations:
 Seasoning Blends Plant
 Carol Stream IL
 Seasoning/Culinary Bases Plant
 Cranbury NJ
Brands:
 Spicetec

11931 Spicy Sense
58 Jacobus Ave
Kearny, NJ 07032
718-790-0070
Coconut water
CEO: Sam Chawla

11932 Spiech Farms Fruit & Floral
61675 M 40
Paw Paw, MI 49079-9210
269-657-1980
Fax: 269-657-5023 www.spiechfarms
Concord grapes
President: Daniel Martinez
dmartinez@spiechfarms.com
Estimated Sales: $1 Million
Number Employees: 250-499
Square Footage: 36000

11933 Spike Seasoning Magic
6425 W Executive Dr
Mequon, WI 53092
262-242-2400
ModernFearn@aol.com
www.spike-it-up.com
Blended spices and seasonings.
Founder: Gayelord Hauser
Chairman/CEO: Anthony Palermo
Secretary: Petronella Palermo
Quality Assurance Manager: Jim Kohnke
Number Employees: 5-10
Parent Co: Modern Products
Type of Packaging: Consumer, Food Service

11934 (HQ)Spilke's Baking Company
590 Rocky Glen Rd.
Moosic, PA 18507
570-457-2400
Fax: 570-457-3626 arnold@macaroonking.com
www.macaroonking.com
Individually packaged macaroons and cakes including kosher
President: Arnold Badner
Estimated Sales: $10-20 Million
Number Employees: 10-19
Square Footage: 60000
Type of Packaging: Consumer, Food Service
Brands:
 Jennie
 Manhattan Gourmet
 Red Mill Farms

11935 Spinato's Fine Foods
1920 E 5th Street
Tempe, AZ 85281-2905
480-275-4319
Fax: 480-275-7288 www.spinatosfinefoods.com
Gluten-free pizza and sauces
National Director of Sales: Todd Niezgodzki

11936 Spindrift Beverage
260 Charles St
Waltham, MA 02453
617-391-0356
www.spindriftfresh.com
Fruity sparkling water
Founder: Bill Creelman
Brands:
 Spindrift Sparkling Water

11937 Spinelli Coffee Company
3100 Airport Way S
Seattle, WA 98134-2116
415-821-7100
Fax: 415-821-7199
Coffee
President: Christophe Calkins
Number Employees: 10

11938 Spinney Creek Shellfish
2 Howell Ln
Eliot, ME 3903
207-439-2719
Fax: 207-439-7643 877-778-6727
www.spinneycreek.com
Seafood
Owner: Tom Howell
Estimated Sales: $10-20 Million
Number Employees: 10-19

11939 Spitz USA
1775 Horseshoe Drive
Loveland, CO 80538-7201
970-613-9319
Fax: 970-613-9320
National Sales Manager: Roger Shantz

Food Manufacturers / A-Z

11940 Splendid Specialties
2198 South McDowell Blvd
Petaluma, CA 94954-5661
707-796-7800
Fax: 707-957-8022 info@tornranch.com
www.tornranch.com
Gourmet specialty foods that include the finest chocolates and baked goods, and famous dried fruit and nuts
President: Dean Morrow
CEO: Deana Kay
Estimated Sales: $20-50 Million
Number Employees: 50-99
Brands:
  Cafe Time
  Gigi Baking Company
  Mashuga Nuts & Cookies
  Splendid Specialties Chocolates

11941 Splendid Spreads
1483 Auburn Court
Eagan, MN 55122
877-632-1300
Fax: 651-688-7630 877-773-2374
http://splendidspreads.com
Gouret salmon spreads and toppings
President/Owner: Judy Tucker

11942 Spoetzl Brewery
603 E Brewery St
Shiner, TX 77984
361-594-3383
Fax: 361-594-4334 shiner@shiner.com
www.shiner.com
Brewery founded in Shiner, TX in 1909 producing the Shiner line of beers.
Manager: Carlos Alvarez
calvarez@shiner.com
Number Employees: 50-99
Parent Co: Gambrinus Company
Type of Packaging: Consumer
Brands:
  Shiner Blonde
  Shiner Bock
  Shiner Dunkelweizen
  Shiner Hefeweizen
  Shiner Kolsch
  Shiner Light

11943 Spohrers Bakeries
600 MacDade Boulevard
Collingdale, PA 19023-3804
610-532-9959
Fax: 610-532-8927
Pastries
Owner: David Olandi
Manager: Derek Everstyke
Brands:
  Spohrers Bakeries

11944 Spokandy
1412 W 3rd Ave
Spokane, WA 99201-7024
509-624-1969
Fax: 509-624-2017 www.spokandy.com
Chocolates, wedding mints, brittles, barks, saltwater taffy
President: Todd Davis
spokandy@spokandy.com
Plant Manager: Mary Ellithorp
Estimated Sales: $5 Million
Number Employees: 10-19
Type of Packaging: Private Label

11945 Spokane Seed Co
6015 E Alki Ave
Spokane Valley, WA 99212-1019
509-535-3671
Fax: 509-535-0874 800-359-8478
spokseed@spokaneseed.com
www.spokaneseed.com
Processor and exporter of peas and lentils
President: Peter Johnstone
CFO: Jeff White
Sales: Nelson Fancher
Estimated Sales: $3900000
Number Employees: 20-49
Type of Packaging: Consumer, Food Service, Bulk
Brands:
  Greenpod
  Rumba

11946 Spoonable
345 Clinton Avenue
#4G
Brooklyn, NY 11238
718-974-0653
info@spoonablellc.com
www.spoonablellc.com
Salty caramel sauce, butterscotch sauce, chewy sesame caramel sauce, spicy chili caramel sauce, flowery lavender caramel sauce, peppered orange caramel sauce
President/Owner: Michelle Lewis
mnlewis@spoonablellc.com
Number Employees: 4
Number of Brands: 1
Number of Products: 7
Type of Packaging: Consumer, Food Service, Private Label, Bulk

11947 Sportabs International
PO Box 492118
Los Angeles, CA 90049-8118
310-451-2625
Fax: 310-207-8526 888-814-7767
Processor and exporter of multi-vitamin tablets
President: Richard Griswold
Estimated Sales: $500,000
Number Employees: 1-4
Type of Packaging: Consumer
Brands:
  Spor Tabs

11948 Sporting Colors LLC
3630 S. Geyer Rd.
Suite 100
St. Louis, MO 63127
314-984-1000
Fax: 314-909-3300 888-394-2292
www.panerabread.com
President: William Moreton
CEO: S Jeff Schroeder
Senior Vice President: Liz Dunlap
Senior Vice President of Operations: Irene Cook
Estimated Sales: $1-3 Million
Number Employees: 20-49

11949 Sportsman's Paradise Whites Ranch
PO Box 129
Paradise, UT 84328
435-245-3053
Fax: 435-245-4603 www.whitesranch.com
Processor and canner of fresh rainbow trout
President: Grant White
Estimated Sales: $150000
Number Employees: 1-4
Type of Packaging: Consumer, Food Service

11950 Sportsmen's Cannery
381 Broadway
PO Box 1011
Winchester Bay, OR 97467-0800
541-271-3293
Fax: 541-271-9381 800-457-8048
orders@adventureinfood.com
www.sportsmenscannery.com
Gourmet canned seafood products including smokehouse and gift boxes
Manager: Brandy Roelle
Secretary: Mikyale Karcher
Estimated Sales: Below $1 Million
Number Employees: 10-19
Brands:
  Sportsmen's Cannery

11951 Sportsmen's Cannery & Smokehouse
182 Bayfront Loop
Winchester Bay, OR 97467
541-271-3293
Fax: 541-271-9381 800-457-8048
karch@presys.com www.sportsmenscannery.com
Processor and canner of salmon, albacore tuna, sturgeon and shellfish
Manager: Brandy Roelle
Owner: Mikayle Karcher
Number Employees: 1-4
Type of Packaging: Consumer, Private Label
Brands:
  Winchester

11952 Sportsmens Seafoods
1617 Quivira Rd
San Diego, CA 92109-7801
619-224-3551
Fax: 619-224-1646 www.sportsmensseafood.com
Canned fish including albacore, bonito, marlin, tuna and yellow tail
Owner: Joe Busalacchi
Estimated Sales: $300,000-500,000
Number Employees: 10-19

11953 Spotted Tavern Winery & Dodd's Cider Mill
PO Box 175
Hartwood, VA 22471-0175
540-752-4453
Fax: 540-752-4611
Wine, sparkling cider, Virginia hard cider and fresh apple cider in season.
Owner: Cathy Harris

11954 Spottswoode
1902 Madrona Ave
St Helena, CA 94574-2354
707-963-0134
Fax: 707-963-2886
spottswoode@spottswoode.com
www.spottswoode.com
Wine
President: Nicole Knoth
nicole@spottswoode.com
VP: Peah Armstrong
National Sales/Marketing: Lindy Novak Lahr
Consumer Sales/Tours: Shanyn McDaera
Winemaker: Rosemary Cakebread
Estimated Sales: Below $5 Million
Number Employees: 10-19

11955 Sprague Foods
385 College Street E
Belleville, ON K8N 5S7
Canada
613-966-1200
Fax: 613-962-8600 info@spraguefoods.com
Beans, soups, beans in sauce, pasta in tomato sauce, salad dressings
President: Roger Sprague
Number Employees: 20-49
Type of Packaging: Consumer, Food Service

11956 Sprecher Brewing Co
701 W Glendale Ave
Milwaukee, WI 53209-6509
414-964-7837
Fax: 414-964-2462 888-650-2739
beer@sprecherbrewery.com
www.sprecherbrewery.com
Hard sodas, ciders, and a wide variety of craft beers
President/Founder: Randal Sprecher
beer@sprecherbrewery.com
Brewmaster: Craig Burge
Production Manager: Tom Bosch
Year Founded: 1985
Estimated Sales: $20-50 Million
Number Employees: 50-99

11957 (HQ)Spreda Group
7410 New Lagrange Rd
PO Box 378
Louisville, KY 40222
502-426-9411
Fax: 502-423-7531
Fruit and vegetable powder, tomato paste, colors, spray and vacuum dried and dehydrated fruits and vegetables, apple pectin and apple juice concentrate
President: George Falk
VP: James Falk
Number Employees: 100-249
Type of Packaging: Food Service, Bulk
Brands:
  Elmasu
  Obi Pektin
  Puccinelli
  Spreda

11958 Spring Acres Sales Company
1280 Macedonia Rd
Spring Hope, NC 27882
252-478-5127
Fax: 252-478-5266 800-849-5436
Sweet potatoes including medium, large and jumbo

1135

Food Manufacturers / A-Z

President: Cindy S Joyner
Quality Assurance: Jordan L Jackson
Domestic & Int'l Sales: Chris Thompson
Contact: Charlie Lewis
charlie@springacres.com
Estimated Sales: $500,000-$1,000,000
Number Employees: 1-4
Type of Packaging: Bulk
Brands:
   Hernandez
   Spring Acres
   Tarheel

11959 Spring Creek Natural Foods
212 E Main St C
Spencer, WV 25276
   518-436-7603
Fax: 518-436-9035
Tofu
President: Donald Carpenter
President: Mark Bossert
Estimated Sales: $2.5 Million
Number Employees: 15

11960 Spring Glen Fresh Foods
PO Box 518
Ephrata, PA 17522
   717-733-2201
Fax: 717-721-6720 800-641-2853
www.springglen.com
Soup and stew including meat, poultry and seafood; also, potato, pasta and macaroni salad, coleslaw, entrees and desserts including cobblers, parfaits, cheese, puddings, gelatin and custards
President: John Warehime
VP General Manager: Steve Piechocki
Marketing Manager: Jeff Miller
Contact: David Karkosak
davidkarkosak@hanoverfoods.com
Plant Manager: Jeff Warehime
Purchasing Director: Rich Paulukow
Estimated Sales: $19 Million
Number Employees: 165
Square Footage: 90000
Parent Co: Hanover Foods Corporation
Type of Packaging: Consumer, Food Service, Private Label
Brands:
   Deli Direct
   Spring Glen

11961 Spring Grove Foods
312 S 3rd St
Miamisburg, OH 45342-2933
   937-866-4311
Fax: 937-866-1410
Cheese, beef, pepperoni, ham, salami, sausage and bologna
President: Jerry Beale
Estimated Sales: $10 Million
Number Employees: 5 to 9
Square Footage: 30000
Type of Packaging: Food Service, Private Label, Bulk

11962 Spring Hill Meat Market
207 N Frank St
Spring Hill, KS 66083-8905
   913-592-3501
Meat products
Owner: William Madison
Estimated Sales: Less Than $500,000
Number Employees: 1-4
Type of Packaging: Consumer

11963 Spring Hill Pure Water
136 Neck Rd
Haverhill, MA 01835-8028
   978-373-3481
Fax: 978-521-0870 www.springhillwater.com
Dairy products
Owner: Harold Rogers
hrogers@springhillwater.com
Estimated Sales: Below $5 Million
Number Employees: 20-49

11964 Spring Kitchen
101 Chartres St
Houston, TX 77002-2307
   713-222-0598
Fax: 713-222-0890 info@springkitchen.com
www.springkitchen.com
Spring rolls and eggrolls
Founder: Thu Do
Contact: Thu DO
thu@springkitchen.com
Number Employees: 5-9
Brands:
   Spring Kitchen

11965 Spring Ledge Farm Stand
37 Main St
New London, NH 03257-7800
   603-526-6253
Fax: 603-526-6679 info@springledgefarm.com
www.springledgefarm.com
Fresh grapes
President: Earl Andrews
Estimated Sales: $.5-1 million
Number Employees: 20-49

11966 Spring Mountain Vineyard
2805 Spring Mountain Rd
St Helena, CA 94574-1775
   707-967-4188
Fax: 707-963-2753 877-769-4637
info@springmtn.com
www.springmountainvineyard.com
Wine
President: Don Yannias
Co-Owner: John Nickel
Director, Customer Relations & Events: Leah Smith
Estimated Sales: $3 Million
Number Employees: 50-99
Brands:
   Chateau Chevalier

11967 Spring Street Bake Shop
400 Old Reading Pike
Pottstown, PA 19464
   484-624-8201
Cookies and biscotti
General Operations Manager: Richard Zayaitz

11968 Springbank Cheese Company
201 Winniett St
Woodstock, ON N4S 6A1
Canada
   519-539-7411
Fax: 519-539-0294 800-265-1973
spcheese@oxford.net www.springbankcheese.ca
Processor and packer of cheese
President: Tom Hemsworth
Estimated Sales: $2.6 Million
Number Employees: 10
Square Footage: 26000
Brands:
   Gjetost Ekte
   Wensleydale Blueberry

11969 Springdale Cheese Factory
19104 County Hwy Ee
Richland Center, WI 53581
   608-538-3213
Fax: 608-538-3212 ltorkelson@aol.com
Muenster and brick cheese
President: Thomas Torkelson
Contact: Tom Torkelson
ltorkelson@aol.com
Estimated Sales: $6100000
Number Employees: 35
Type of Packaging: Consumer, Food Service

11970 Springdale Ice Cream & Bev
11801 Chesterdale Rd
Cincinnati, OH 45246-3407
   513-671-2790
Fax: 513-671-2864 www.kroger.com
Ice cream
Human Resources: Stacey Rose
Plant Engineer: Mike Smith
Number Employees: 100-249

11971 Springfield Creamery Inc
29440 Airport Rd
Eugene, OR 97402-9537
   541-689-2911
Fax: 541-689-2915 sue@nancysyogurt.com
www.nancysyogurt.com
Manufacturer of yogurt, cultured soy yogurt, cream cheese, cottage cheese, sour cream, and kefir.
Owner: Joe Kesey
esther@nancysyogurt.com
Owner: Sue Kesey
Marketing: Sheryl Kesey Thompson
Operations: Kit Kesey
Estimated Sales: $22 Million
Number Employees: 50-99
Number of Brands: 1
Number of Products: 13
Square Footage: 40000
Type of Packaging: Consumer, Food Service, Private Label, Bulk
Brands:
   Nancy's

11972 Springhill Cellars
2920 NW Scenic Dr
Albany, OR 97321-9827
   541-928-1009
Fax: 541-928-1009 springhill@proaxis.com
www.springhillcellarswinery.com
Wines
President: Michael Lain
Contact: Mervin Anthony
manthony@springhillcellars.com
Estimated Sales: Less Than $500,000
Number Employees: 1-4
Brands:
   Springhill

11973 Springhill Farms
PO Box 10000
Neepawa, NB R0J 1H0
Canada
   204-476-3393
Fax: 204-476-3791
Fresh and frozen pork
General Manager: William Teichrow
Number Employees: 400
Type of Packaging: Bulk
Brands:
   Spring Hill Farms

11974 Springville Meat & ColdStorage
268 S 100 W
Springville, UT 84663-1804
   801-489-6391
Fax: 801-491-3399
Domestic and game meats including ground beef and patties, beef, poultry, lamb and buffalo; also, custom processing available
President: David Cope
VP: Ray Cope
Estimated Sales: $810,000
Number Employees: 10-19
Square Footage: 100000
Type of Packaging: Consumer, Food Service

11975 Sprinkles Cupcakes
780 Lexington Ave
New York, NY 10065-8169
   212-207-8375
   888-220-2210
eat@sprinkles.com www.sprinkles.com
Cupcakes
Contact: Michael Lin
michael@sprinkles.com
Number Employees: 20-49

11976 Sprout Creek Farm
34 Lauer Rd.
Poughkeepsie, NY 12603
   845-485-8432
info@sproutcreekfarm.org
www.sproutcreekfarm.org
Farm-made cow and goat milk cheese
President: Margot Morris
Year Founded: 1974
Number of Brands: 1
Number of Products: 7
Type of Packaging: Consumer, Private Label
Brands:
   Sprout Creek Farm

11977 Sprout House
17267 Sundance Dr
Ramona, CA 92065
   760-788-7979
Fax: 760-788-4800 800-777-6887
info@sprouthouse.com www.sprouthouse.com
Sprouting seeds
President: Richard Kohn
Marketing Director: Steve Meyerowitz
Estimated Sales: $500,000
Number Employees: 1-4
Type of Packaging: Private Label
Brands:
   Hemp Sprout Bag

Food Manufacturers / A-Z

Sprout House & Salad
Sproutman's Organic

11978 Sprout Nutrition
50 Chestnut Ridge Rd
Montvale, NJ 07645
877-704-8777
info@sproutfoods.com
www.sproutorganicfoods.com
Organic baby food

11979 Sprouts Farmers Market Inc.
5455 E. High St.
Suite 111
Phoenix, AZ 85054
www.sprouts.com
National grocery store chain specializing in fresh foods and health foods.
Chief Executive Officer: Jack Sinclair
Chief Financial Officer: Denise Paulonis
Chief Operating Officer: Dan Sanders
Year Founded: 2002
Estimated Sales: $5.2 Billion
Number Employees: 30,000
Brands:
  Country Kitchen Meals
  Henry's Heritage Bread
  Sprouts
  Sunflower

11980 Spruce Foods
800 S El Camino Real
Suite 210
San Clemente, CA 92672-4274
949-366-9457
Fax: 800-708-9775 800-326-3612
bobbreen@sprucefoods.com
www.sprucefoods.com
Importer of organic grocery products
President: Bob Breen
Estimated Sales: $5-10 Million
Number Employees: 4
Number of Brands: 3
Number of Products: 160
Brands:
  Lapas
  Massetti
  Montebello

11981 Spruce Lane Investments
37 Spruce Lane
Stratford, PE C1B 1M9
Canada
902-892-2600
Fax: 902-892-2620
Baked goods including danish, cinnamon rolls, bread, cookies, bagels, pies, rolls, etc
President/CEO: Robert DeBlois
Secretary/Treasurer: Elaine DeBlois
Estimated Sales: $1 Million
Number Employees: 20
Square Footage: 5200

11982 Spruce Mountain Blueberries
Mount Pleasant Road
PO Box 68
West Rockport, ME 04865-0068
207-236-3538
Fax: 207-236-8545
info@sprucemtnblueberries.com
Wild blueberry chutney, blueberry topping, cranberry chutney, conserves, jam, and blueberry vinegar
President: Molly Sholes
Estimated Sales: $75,000
Number Employees: 3
Number of Brands: 1
Number of Products: 7
Type of Packaging: Consumer, Food Service

11983 Sprucewood Handmade Cookie Company
PO Box 430
Warkworth, ON K0K 3K0
Canada
877-632-1300
Fax: 705-924-2626 email: sprucewoodbrands.com
www.sprucewoodbrands.com
Flavored shortbread cookies and nuts
President/Owner: Mark Pollard

11984 Spurgeon Vineyards & Winery
16008 Pine Tree Rd
Highland, WI 53543-9602
608-929-7692
Fax: 608-929-4810 800-236-5555
Wine in the following flavors; honey, cranberry, grape, sweet cherry, white and juice blend
Owner: Glen Spurgeon
spurgeon@mhtc.net
Co-Owner: Mary Spurgeon
Vice President: James Spurgeon
Estimated Sales: $1 Million
Number Employees: 1-4
Type of Packaging: Consumer, Private Label, Bulk
Brands:
  Spurgeon Vinyards

11985 Squab Producers of California
409 Primo Way
Modesto, CA 95358-5721
209-537-4744
Fax: 209-537-2037 squabbob@aol.com
www.squab.com
Processor and exporter of fresh and frozen squab, pheasant, quail, poussin and partridge
President: Robert Shipley
squabbob@aol.com
Sales Exec: Robert Shipley
Estimated Sales: $5-10 Million
Number Employees: 50-99
Square Footage: 40000
Type of Packaging: Consumer, Food Service, Private Label, Bulk
Brands:
  King-Cal
  Mendes Farms
  Sierra Gourmet

11986 Squair Food Company
1418 Newton Street
Los Angeles, CA 90021-2726
213-749-7041
Fax: 213-749-3591
http://www.sprucemtnblueberries.com
Mexican foods
President: Jerry Karrizer
Vice President: Morris Kharrazi
Estimated Sales: $5 Million
Number Employees: 1-4

11987 Square One Organics
PO Box 6549
River Forest, IL 60305
866-771-7138
info@squareoneorganics.com
www.squareoneorganics.com
Organic baby food.
Founder/Chief Executive Officer: Denise Henderson
Director of Accounting: Kathy Kruegger
Director of Communications: Mari Monaco Hynes
Director of Logistics: Jeffrey Henderson
Type of Packaging: Consumer

11988 Square-H Brands Inc
2731 S Soto St
Vernon, CA 90058-8026
323-267-4600
Fax: 323-261-7350 www.squarehbrands.com
Pork, sausage, ham and bacon
President/CEO: Henry Haskell
CEO: Edgar Borgja
edgar.borgja@sqhb.com
Quality Assurance Manager: Bill Parke
Sales Director: Kirk Kolden
Estimated Sales: $20-49.9 Million
Number Employees: 100-249
Number of Brands: 2
Number of Products: 200
Brands:
  Hoffy
  Bill Bailey's

11989 Squire Boone Village
406 Mount Tabor Rd
New Albany, IN 47150-2207
812-941-5900
Fax: 812-941-5920 888-934-1804
www.squireboone.com
Snacks
Owner: Rick Conway
ricksbv@aol.com
Number Employees: 100-249

11990 Squirrel Brand Company
113 Industrial Blvd Ste D
McKinney, TX 75069
214-585-0100
Fax: 214-585-0880 800-624-8242
info@squirrelbrand.com www.squirrelbrand.com
Nuts
President: Brent Meyer
Estimated Sales: $5-9.9 Million
Number Employees: 1-4
Square Footage: 160
Type of Packaging: Private Label
Brands:
  Coconut Zipper
  Squirrel
  Squirrel Nut Caramel
  Squirrel Nut Chew
  Squirrel Nut Zippers

11991 St Armands Baking Co
2811 59th Avenue Dr E
Bradenton, FL 34203-5334
941-753-7494
Fax: 941-751-1417 sales@sabc.cc
www.starbake.com
Bread, rolls and sweet goods
President: Bernard Vroom
bernard@starbake.com
Estimated Sales: $1-3 Million
Number Employees: 5-9

11992 St Arnold Brewing Co
2000 Lyons Ave
Houston, TX 77020-2028
713-686-9494
Fax: 713-686-9474 800-801-6402
brewery@saintarnold.com www.saintarnold.com
Seasonal beer, ale, stout, lager and pilsner
President: Brock Wagner
brewery@saintarnold.com
Sales Rep: Frank Mancuso
Estimated Sales: Below $5 Million
Number Employees: 50-99
Type of Packaging: Consumer, Food Service
Brands:
  Amber
  Brown
  Christmas
  Elissa Ipa
  Fancy Lawnmower
  Kristall Weizen
  Oktoberfest
  Root Beer
  Spring Bock
  Summer Pils
  Winter Stout

11993 St Charles Trading Inc
650 N Raddant Rd
Batavia, IL 60510-4207
630-377-0608
Fax: 630-406-1936
customerservice@stcharlestrading.com
Food ingredient distributor
President/VP Sales: Al Cicanci
CEO: William Manns
williammanns@stcharlestrading.com
Quality Assurance Officer: Dana Capes
Director of Operation: Janet Matthews
Estimated Sales: $15,000,000
Number Employees: 20-49
Square Footage: 40000

11994 St Clair Ice Cream Co
155 Woodward Ave # 7
Norwalk, CT 06854-4731
203-853-4774
Fax: 203-857-4099
Special occasion ice cream and sorbet molded into a variety of shapes.
Manager: Kay Gelsman
Estimated Sales: $5 Million
Number Employees: 5-9
Brands:
  St. Clair Ice Cream

11995 St Francis Winery & Vineyards
100 Pythian Rd
Santa Rosa, CA 95409-6529
707-833-4668
Fax: 707-833-1394 info@stfranciswine.com
www.stfranciswinery.com
Wine

Food Manufacturers / A-Z

President: Christopher Silva
csilva@stfranciswine.com
CFO: Patti Smith
CEO: Lloyd Canton
Marketing Director: Nan Fontaine
Production Manager: Dennis Borell
Estimated Sales: Below $5 Million
Number Employees: 100-249
Brands:
   Claret
   Reserve Cabernet Sauvignon
   Reserve Merlot
   Reserve Zinfandel

11996 St Innocent Winery
5657 Zena Rd NW
Salem, OR 97304-9722
   503-378-1526
Fax: 503-378-1041 www.stinnocentwine.com
Wine, still and sparkling
Owner: Mark Velossak
m_vlossak@stinnocentwine.com
Sales Manager: Felice Leonhardt
m_vlossak@stinnocentwine.com
Winemaker: Mark Vlossak
Estimated Sales: Below $5 Million
Number Employees: 10-19
Type of Packaging: Private Label
Brands:
   St. Innocent

11997 (HQ)St John's Botanicals
7711 Hillmeade Rd
Bowie, MD 20720-4571
   301-262-5302
Fax: 301-262-2489 www.stjohnsbotanicals.com
Spice blends, herb teas, essential oils, ginseng products, nutritional supplements
Owner: William Mussenden
Ceo: Sydney Vallentync
CFO: Patti Mussenden
Research/Dev: Diane Tolsen
Quality Control: Diane Tolsen
Marketing: Rayla Cuffey
Sales Manager: Rayla Cuffey
Pub Relations: Maria McCulvey
Operations Manager: Brandy Schwartz
Plant Manager: Diane Tolson
Purchasing: Sydney Vallentyne
Estimated Sales: Less Than $500,000
Number Employees: 5-9
Type of Packaging: Private Label, Bulk
Brands:
   Rose Hill
   Scent-O-Vac
   The Prefume Garden

11998 (HQ)St Julian Winery
716 S Kalamazoo St
Paw Paw, MI 49079-1558
   269-657-5568
Fax: 269-657-5743 800-732-6002
wines@stjulian.com www.stjulian.com
Processor and exporter of grape beverages including champagne, wine and juice
President: Kim Babcock
babcockk@stjulian.com
Executive VP: Charles Catherman
Marketing Director: Kim Babcock
VP Sales: Joe Zuiderueen
Wine Maker: David Miller, Ph.D.
Estimated Sales: $9 Million
Number Employees: 50-99
Type of Packaging: Consumer, Food Service

11999 St Laurent Brothers
1101 N Water St
Bay City, MI 48708-5625
   989-893-7522
Fax: 989-893-6571 800-289-7688
Peanuts including salted, roasted and candy coated; also, peanut butter
Owner: Keith Whitney
Co-Owner: Steve Frye
Estimated Sales: $2 Million
Number Employees: 20-49
Type of Packaging: Consumer, Food Service, Bulk

12000 St Mary Sugar Co-Op
20056 Highway 182 W
Jeanerette, LA 70544-8532
   337-276-6761
Fax: 337-276-4297 www.stmarysugar
Sugar and condiments

President: Raphael Rodriguez
Plant Manager: Ronald Guilotte Jr
Estimated Sales: $500,000-$1 000,000
Number Employees: 50-99

12001 St-Germain Bakery
1930 Dillingham Blvd
Honolulu, HI 96819-4021
   808-847-5396
Fax: 808-842-7056 www.stghi.com
Breads, rolls, bakery products
Manager: Lorraine Yamada
Marketing Division Manager: Norikazu Miyata
Manager: Yukikazu Sato
sato@stghi.com
Estimated Sales: $8,065,258
Number Employees: 50-99
Number of Brands: 1
Brands:
   Dee Lite

12002 (HQ)St. Amour Inc/French Cookies
2171 Grace Lane B
Costa Mesa, CA 92626
   714-754-1900
infofrenchcookies@gmail.com
www.healthycookiesdirect.com
Cookies including madelines, croquants and teethers; also, snack foods
Owner: Daniel De St Amour
Number Employees: 5-9
Brands:
   Rocks N' Rolls

12003 St. Clair Industries
3067 E Commercial Blvd
Ft Lauderdale, FL 33308
   954-491-0400
Fax: 954-351-9082
Processor and exporter of catalyst altered water
President: Saul Rubinoff
CEO: Anne Rubinoff
Vice President: Anne Rubinoff
Estimated Sales: Less than $100,000
Number Employees: 2
Square Footage: 10000
Type of Packaging: Consumer, Bulk
Brands:
   Briz
   Willard

12004 St. Croix Beer Company
363 Webster St
Saint Paul, MN 55102
   651-387-0708
Fax: 651-439-0221 info@stcroixbeer.com
www.stcroixbeer.com
Processor and wholesaler/distributor of lager and regular, maple and pepper ale
President: Tod Fyten
Estimated Sales: $86,000
Number Employees: 1-4
Type of Packaging: Consumer, Food Service
Brands:
   Serrano
   St. Croix

12005 St. Jacobs Candy Co.
180 Frobisher
Unit #2
Waterloo, ON N2J 4R8
Canada
   519-884-3505
Fax: 519-884-9854 contactus@brittles-n-more.com
www.brittles-n-more.com
Candy manufacturer; brittles, fudges, beernuts, caramel, turkish delight, sponge toffee, hard candy drops &'shapes, hard candy suckers and batter crunch.
President: Michael McEachern
Operations: Deana Pfanner
Production: Rhys Carter
Estimated Sales: $750,000
Number Employees: 25
Number of Products: 9
Square Footage: 5000
Type of Packaging: Consumer, Private Label, Bulk

12006 St. James Sugar Cooperative
5354 Saint James Coop St
Saint James, LA 70086
   225-265-4056
Fax: 225-265-4060
Blackstrap syrup and sugar

Sales Representative: Mr. Bourgeois
Estimated Sales: $10-20 Million
Number Employees: 50-99
Type of Packaging: Consumer

12007 St. James Winery
540 Sidney St
Saint James, MO 65559
   573-265-7912
Fax: 573-265-6200 800-280-9463
info@stjameswinery.com www.stjameswinery.com
Wine and grape juice
President: Andrew Hofherr
Chairman of the Board: Patricia Hofherr
Vice President: John Hofherr
Vice President of Sales: Dean Chalem
Chief Executive Officer: Peter Hofherr
Estimated Sales: $5-10 Million
Number Employees: 20-49
Square Footage: 1200
Type of Packaging: Bulk
Brands:
   St. James Winery

12008 St. Julien Macaroons
343 Main St.
Sandown, NH 03873-2101
   603-887-2233
   800-473-8869
www.macaroons.com
Manufacturer of macaroons.
Founder: James Price

12009 St. Lawrence Starch
141 Lakeshore Road E
Mississauga, ON L5G 1E8
Canada
   905-271-8396
Fax: 905-271-1258
Starches and corn sweeteners including glucose and fructose
President: Ian Gray
CEO: Nick Lacivita
Sales Manager: Howard Low
Parent Co: Cargill Foods

12010 St. Maurice Laurent
735 6e Rang N Ss 1
St-Bruno-Lac-St-Jean, QC G0W 2L0
Canada
   418-343-3655
Fax: 418-343-2996
Cheese and butter
President: Luc St Laurent
Number Employees: 25
Square Footage: 40000

12011 St. Ours & Company
1571 Commercial St
East Weymouth, MA 02189-3015
   781-331-8520
Fax: 781-331-8628 email@saintours.com
www.saintours.com
Processor of frozen shellfish, including lobster, crab, dehydrated clam and seafood broths; wholesaler and distributor of seafood and specialty foods.
President: Fred St. Ours
Marketing Manager: Sharon St. Ours
Sales: John Christian
Director of Manufacturing: Richard St. Ours
Estimated Sales: $3-5 Million
Number Employees: 5-9
Type of Packaging: Consumer, Food Service, Bulk
Brands:
   St. Ours

12012 St. Simons Seafood
130 Paradise Marsh Cir
Brunswick, GA 31525-2143
   912-265-5225
Fax: 912-264-3181
Seafood and fish
President: Chuck Egeland
Estimated Sales: $1,500,000
Number Employees: 5-9

12013 St. Stan's Brewing Company
1028 11th St.
Modesto, CA 95354-0837
   209-284-0170
Fax: 209-524-4827 info@ststans.com
www.ststans.com
Ales and lagers

Food Manufacturers / A-Z

President/CEO: Garith Helm
CFO: Romy Angle
VP, Co-Owner, COO: Richard Hodder
Plant Manager: Eric Kellner
Estimated Sales: $20-50 Million
Number Employees: 35
Type of Packaging: Private Label
Brands:
    Red Sky Ale
    St. Stan's Alt Beer

12014 Stacey's Famous Foods
10334 N Taryne Street
Hayden, ID 83835-9807
650-261-9912
800-782-2395
Frozen seafood, products such as; sauces, appetizers, quiches, pot pies, potatoe
Owner/President: Stacey James
Estimated Sales: Less than $500,000
Number Employees: 1-4
Brands:
    Stacey's

12015 Stacy's Pita Chip Co
663 North St
Randolph, MA 02368-4317
781-961-7799
Fax: 781-961-2830 888-332-4477
www.stacyssnacks.com
Manufacturer and distributor of pita and soy-based chips.
President: Sheryl Carbone
sheryl.carbone@stacyssnacks.com
CEO: Mark Andrus
Estimated Sales: $5-10 Million
Number Employees: 10-19

12016 Stadelman Fruit LLC
111 Meade St
Zillah, WA 98953-9419
509-829-5145
Fax: 509-829-5164 www.stadelmanfruit.com
Processor and exporter of produce including apples, cherries, nectarines, pears, plums and prunes
President: Peter Stadelman
CEO: Rob Stewart
Manager: Rob Stewart
Number Employees: 500-999
Type of Packaging: Consumer, Food Service, Private Label, Bulk

12017 Staff Of Life Natural Foods
1266 Soquel Ave
Santa Cruz, CA 95062-2108
831-423-8632
Fax: 831-423-8065 staflife@pacbell.net
www.staffoflifemarket.com
Natural foods
Owner: Anthony Blanco
staffoflifemeats@gmail.com
VP: Gary Bascou
Estimated Sales: $5-10 Million
Number Employees: 100-249
Brands:
    Beckmann
    Imagine Foods
    Natures Path
    R.W.Knudsen

12018 Stafford County Flour Mills Company
PO Box 7
108 Church Street
Hudson, KS 67545
620-458-4121
Fax: 620-458-5121 800-530-5640
www.hudsoncream.com
Flour
President: Alvin A Brensing
Manager: Reuel Foote
Estimated Sales: $25-30 Million
Number Employees: 20-49
Type of Packaging: Consumer
Brands:
    Hudson Cream Flour

12019 Stags' Leap Winery
6150 Silverado Trl
Napa, CA 94558-9748
707-944-1303
Fax: 707-944-9433 www.stagsleap.com
Winery

Manager: Robert Brittan
r.brittan@stagsleap.com
Winemaker: Christophe Paubert
Assistant Winemaker: Joanne Wing
Number Employees: 20-49
Number of Brands: 1
Parent Co: Treasury Wine Estates
Type of Packaging: Consumer, Food Service
Brands:
    Stags' Leap

12020 Stahlbush Island Farms Inc
3122 SE Stahlbush Island Rd
Corvallis, OR 97333-2709
541-757-1497
Fax: 541-754-1847 sif@stahlbush.com
www.stahlbush.com
Frozen fruits, vegetables, grains and legumes.
Owners: Bill & Karla Chambers
Number Employees: 100-249

12021 Stahmann Farms
22500 S Highway 28
La Mesa, NM 88044-9531
575-526-2453
www.stahmannpecan.com
Pecans
Owner: Sally Stahmann-Solis
Vice-CEO: Deane Stahmann
Estimated Sales: Less Than $500,000
Number Employees: 5-9
Type of Packaging: Bulk

12022 Stallings Head Cheese Co
2314 Portsmouth St
Houston, TX 77098-3902
713-523-1751
Headcheese and boudin
Owner: Fred Chu
Estimated Sales: $1-3 Million
Number Employees: 1-4
Square Footage: 6000

12023 Stampede Meat, Inc.
7351 S 78th Ave
Bridgeview, IL 60455
Fax: 888-376-9349 800-353-0933
stampedemeat.com
Beef, pork and chicken products
CEO & President: Brock Furlong
CFO: Vito Giustino
COO: Jim Scott
VP, Technical Innovation & Development: Dennis Gruber
VP, Food Safety & Quality Assurance: Adam Miller
Sr. VP, Sales & Marketing: Ray McKiernan
Director, Human Resources: Christina Hackney
VP, Production: Krys Harbut
Estimated Sales: $45.5 Million
Number Employees: 250-499
Square Footage: 140000
Type of Packaging: Consumer, Food Service
Other Locations:
    Cook Processing Facility
    Oak Lawn IL
Brands:
    Cro-Magnon
    Cro-Man
    Cro-Mag
    Stampede
    Mission Hill Bistro

12024 Stan-Mark Food Products Inc
1100 W 47th Pl
PO Box 09251
Chicago, IL 60609-4302
773-690-5086
Fax: 773-847-6253 800-651-0994
admin@Ingredients-USA.com
www.stanmarkfoods.com
Pickles, spices, grains and seeds, herring
General Manager: Mark Kongrecki
kongrecki@stanmark.biz
Estimated Sales: $20-50 Million
Number Employees: 20-49
Square Footage: 60000
Type of Packaging: Consumer, Private Label, Bulk

12025 Stanchfield Farms
73 Medford Rd
Milo, ME 04463
207-732-5173
Fax: 207-732-5173

Sweet and spicy pickles, pure fruit jams and jellies, bouron barbeque sauce and marinades, fruit chutneys, and pickled vegetables
Type of Packaging: Consumer

12026 Standard Bakery Inc
79-7394 Mamalahoa Hwy # 79
Kealakekua, HI 96750-7910
808-322-3688
Fax: 808-322-2462 standardbakery@gmail.com
www.standardbakeryhawaii.com
Cakes, pies and pastries
President: Lloyd Fujino
standardbakery@gmail.com
Estimated Sales: $1 Million
Number Employees: 10-19
Type of Packaging: Consumer, Food Service

12027 Standard Functional Foods Grp
715 Massman Dr
Nashville, TN 37210
615-889-6360
Fax: 615-889-7775 800-226-4340
www.sffgi.com
Manufacturer, exporter and contract packager of candy including bars, boxed, log rolls and caramel corn.
President & COO: Tom Drummond
Chief Executive Officer: Jimmy Spradley
VP Administration & Corporate Secretary: Dennis Adcock
Vice President: Neil Spradley
Director of Business Development: Bryan Lewis
Director of Quality Assurance: Scott Sherry
Marketing Manager: Joanne Barthel
Director of Corporate Procurement: Brian Hillman
Director of Human Resources: Carol Cooper
Director of Operations: Bill Hardin
Year Founded: 1901
Estimated Sales: $41.2 Million
Number Employees: 500
Square Footage: 96500
Type of Packaging: Private Label, Bulk
Brands:
    Coconut Waves
    Cumberland Ridge
    Goo Goo Cluster

12028 Standard Meat Co LP
5105 Investment Dr
Dallas, TX 75236-1420
972-283-8501
Fax: 214-561-0560 866-859-6313
www.standardmeat.com
Sausages and other prepared meats
Partner: Joseph Penshorn
Partner: William Rosenthal
Controller: Garry Custer
Food Safety & Research & Development: Scott Boleman
Quality Assurance: Jonathan Savell
Purchasing Manager: Sam Beede
Estimated Sales: $13.7 Million
Number Employees: 100-249
Square Footage: 195912

12029 Stangl's Bakery
572 Merchant St
Ambridge, PA 15003-2463
724-266-5675
stanglerbakery@yahoo.com
Baked goods
President: Lorianne Burgess
stanglsbakery@gmail.com
Estimated Sales: Less Than $500,000
Number Employees: 5-9

12030 Stanislaus Food Prod
1202 D St
Modesto, CA 95354-2407
209-548-3537
Fax: 209-527-0227 800-327-7201
freshpacktomato@stanislaus.com
Canned tomato paste and sauces
Owner: Tom Cortopassi
saintstanislaus@gmail.com
CFO: William Butler
VP Marketing: Cindy Brenon
SVP/Operations Executive: Mark Kimmel
Estimated Sales: $25 Million
Number Employees: 250-499
Square Footage: 50000
Type of Packaging: Food Service

Food Manufacturers / A-Z

Brands:
- 7/11
- 74-40
- 80-40
- Al Dente
- Alta Cucina
- Full Red
- Pizzaiolo
- Pizzaletto
- Pomarola
- Saporito
- Tomato Magic
- Trattoria
- Valoroso

12031 Stanley Orchards Sales, Inc.
2044 State Route 32
#6
Modena, NY 12548
845-883-7351
Fax: 845-883-5077 sales@stanleyorchards.com
www.stanleyorchards.com
Apple growing and storage/packing facility; importer of apples and pears; cold storage facility.
President/CEO: Ronald Cohn
Sales & Marketing: Jordan Cohn
Sales Manager: Anthony Maresca
Domestic Sales: Janine Skurnick
Controller: Susan Surprise
Import/Export Liason: Lorrie Hazzard
Estimated Sales: $293 Thousand
Number Employees: 8
Type of Packaging: Consumer, Food Service, Private Label, Bulk

12032 Stanley Provision Company
50 Batson Dr
Manchester, CT 6040
860-649-0656
888-688-6347
Sausage, kielbasa and ground beef
President: Stephen Wisniewski
Number Employees: 10-19
Square Footage: 30000
Type of Packaging: Consumer, Food Service

12033 Stanley's Best Seafood
7475 Patruski Road
Coden, AL 36523-3181
251-824-2801
Fax: 919-734-1201
Seafood
Owner: Robert Stanley

12034 Star Anise Foods
PO Box 591125
San Francisco, CA 94159
staranisefoods.com
Vietnamese food products
Co-Founder: Karen Cheng
Co-Founder: Thao Nguyen

12035 Star Fine Foods
2680 W Shaw Ln
Fresno, CA 93711
559-498-2900
Fax: 559-498-2910 starfinefoods.com
Olives, olive oil and vinegars
President & CEO: Jeff Freeman
jfreeman@borgesusa.com
Estimated Sales: $10-25,000,000
Number Employees: 20-49
Type of Packaging: Consumer, Food Service, Private Label, Bulk
Brands:
- STAR
- Cara Mia
- Borges

12036 Star Kay White Inc
85 Brenner Dr
Congers, NY 10920-1307
845-268-6304
Fax: 845-268-3572 800-874-8518
inquiry@starkaywhite.com www.starkaywhite.com
Syrups, candies, panned-items and extracts and flavors
Owner/President/CEO/Plant Manager: Walter Katzenstein
walter@starkaywhite.com
General Manager: Don Heffner
R&D: Richard Sroka
Marketing: Stephen Platt
VP/Sales Executive: James Taft
Manufacuturing Supervisor: George Granada
Purchasing Manager: Judy Beaman
Estimated Sales: $8 Million
Number Employees: 50-99
Number of Brands: 1
Number of Products: 750
Square Footage: 180000
Type of Packaging: Bulk

12037 Star Ravioli Mfg Co
2 Anderson Ave # 2
Moonachie, NJ 07074-1678
201-933-6427
Fax: 201-933-0484 sales@starravioli.com
www.starravioli.com
Producers of more than thirty varieties of ravioli, as well as other italian specialties including manicotti, stuffed shells, gnocchi, cavatelli, tortellini, fettuccini and much more.
President: Laurence Piretra
CFO: Laurence Piretra
R&D: Rick Pisani
Quality Control: Rick Pisani
Estimated Sales: $3-5 Million
Number Employees: 10-19
Square Footage: 48000
Type of Packaging: Consumer, Food Service, Private Label, Bulk

12038 Star Route Farms
95 Olema Bolinas Rd
Bolinas, CA 94924-9710
415-868-1658
Fax: 415-868-9530 warrenweber@earthlink.net
www.starroutefarms.com
Produce
Owner: Warren Weber
warrenweber@earthlink.net
Estimated Sales: Below $5 Million
Number Employees: 20-49

12039 Star Seafood
14160 Shell Belt Road
Bayou La Batre, AL 36509
251-824-3110
Fax: 251-824-4199
Seafood

12040 Star Snacks
105 Harbor Dr
Jersey City, NJ 07305-4505
201-200-9820
Fax: 201-200-9827 888-782-7688
info@starsnacks.net www.starsnacks.net
Nuts and dried fruit.
Owner: Mendel Brachfeld
Year Founded: 1992
Number Employees: 50-99
Type of Packaging: Food Service, Private Label, Bulk

12041 Star of the West Milling Co.
121 E. Tuscola St.
Frankenmuth, MI 48734
989-652-9971
Fax: 989-652-6358 www.starofthewest.com
Flour, cereal bran and wheat germ.
Chairman: Art Loeffler
CEO: Jim Howe
Vice President, Grain Marketing: Gary Kaufman
Year Founded: 1870
Estimated Sales: $445 Million
Number Employees: 100-249
Square Footage: 45000
Type of Packaging: Private Label, Bulk

12042 Starbucks
2401 Utah Ave. S.
Seattle, WA 98134
206-749-5925
Fax: 206-447-0828 800-782-7282
www.starbucks.com
Whole bean coffees and espresso beverages, a variety of pastries and confections, coffee-related accessories and equipment. Also ice cream and coffee drinks including blended and flavored and dairy-free blended juiced teas.
President/CEO: Kevin Johnson
Executive Chairman: Myron Ullman
Systems Analyst: Kris Aamot
kaamot@starbucks.com
Year Founded: 1971
Estimated Sales: $24.71 Billion
Number Employees: 291,000
Number of Brands: 8
Type of Packaging: Consumer, Private Label, Bulk
Brands:
- Starbucks Coffee
- Seattle's Best Coffee
- Teavana
- Tazo
- Evolution Fresh
- La Boulange
- Ethos Water
- Torrefazione Italia Coffee

12043 Starich
248 Montclair Loop
Daphne, AL 36526-7150
251-626-5037
Seafood

12044 (HQ)Stark Candy Company
135 American Legion Highway
Revere, MA 02151-2405
985-446-1354
Fax: 985-448-1627 800-225-5508
www.necco.com
Manufacturer and exporter of candy. Founded in 1847.
President: Dominic Antonellis
General Manager: Bobby Folfe
VP Sales: Tom Drummond
Number Employees: 30
Type of Packaging: Consumer

12045 Starkel Poultry
10524 128th Street East
Puyallup, WA 98373
253-845-2876
Fax: 253-841-1004
Processor and exporter of bagged poultry including fresh and frozen
President: Elsie Starkel
Vice President: Leona Starkel
Estimated Sales: $4400000
Number Employees: 45
Type of Packaging: Consumer, Bulk

12046 Starkist Co
225 N Shore Dr # 400
Suite 400
Pittsburgh, PA 15212-5860
412-231-0361
Fax: 412-222-4050 www.starkist.com
Processor, canner and exporter of tuna
President, CEO: In-Soo Cho
Marketing: Barry Shepard
Vice President Sales: Stephen L Hodge
SVP of Corporate Affairs and Human Resou: Melissa Murphy
Estimated Sales: $5 million
Number Employees: 5-9
Parent Co: Del Monte Foods
Brands:
- Chunk Light Tuna
- Gourmet's Choice Tuna Fillets
- Low Sodium Tuna
- Solid White Albacore Tuna
- Starkist Flavor Fresh Pouch
- Starkist Lunch To-Go
- Starkist Select
- Starkist Tuna Creations

12047 Starport Foods
2655 Judah St
San Francisco, CA 94122
415-731-0663
Fax: 415-731-0663 866-206-9343
sales@starportfoods.com www.starportfoods.com
Ethnic specialty sauces, dressings and seasonings
Owner/VP: Cheryl Tsang
Estimated Sales: $500,000-$1 Million
Number Employees: 5-9
Number of Products: 40
Type of Packaging: Consumer, Food Service, Private Label, Bulk

Food Manufacturers / A-Z

12048 Starr & Brown
10610 NW Saint Helens Road
Portland, OR 97231-1048
503-287-1775
Wine
President: Eric Brown
Estimated Sales: Less than $500,000
Number Employees: 1-4

12049 Starr Hill Winery & Vineyard
861 Bailey Rd
Curwensville, PA 16833-7174
814-236-0910
Fax: 800-326-9618 www.groundhogwinetrail.com
Wines
Owner: Kenneth R Starr
info@starrhillwinery.com
Estimated Sales: Under $500,000
Number Employees: 10-19

12050 Startupcandy Co
534 S 100 W
Provo, UT 84601-4505
801-373-8673
Fax: 801-373-7312 www.startupcandy.com
Candy and confectionery products
Owner: Jon Startup
startupcandy@gmail.com
Vice President: Jon Startup
Estimated Sales: $2,000,000
Number Employees: 5-9
Type of Packaging: Consumer

12051 Starwest Botanicals Inc
161 Main Ave # A
Sacramento, CA 95838-2080
916-638-8100
Fax: 916-853-9673 800-800-4372
www.starwest-botanicals.com
Processor, importer and exporter of herbs and herbal extracts, spices and essential and vegetable oils; also, custom milling, blending and formulating available
Founder, President: Van Joerger
CEO: Shirley Abrahamson
shirleyabrahamson@starwestherb.com
VP Finance: Mark Wendley
SVP R&D/Production Manager: Dawn Bennett
Marketing/Product Development: Daniela Nelson
VP Sales: Richard Patterson
Purchasing: Bonnie Sadkowski
Estimated Sales: $9.8 Million
Number Employees: 50-99
Square Footage: 200000
Type of Packaging: Bulk
Brands:
 Nature Actives
 Starwest

12052 Stasero International
7021 South 220th Street
Kent, WA 98032
253-867-6130
Fax: 206-324-4586 888-929-2378
info@calsonindustries.com
www.calsonindustries.com/stasero
Drink mixes, syrups, sauces, toppings, frappes, accessories, and tea concentrates.
President: Sadru Kabani
Year Founded: 1918
Estimated Sales: $20-50 Million
Number Employees: 20-49
Parent Co: Calson Industries
Type of Packaging: Private Label
Brands:
 Stasero

12053 Stash Tea Co
16655 SW 72nd Ave
Suite 200
Portland, OR 97224-7769
503-684-4482
Fax: 503-684-4424 800-547-1514
stash@stashtea.com www.stashtea.com
Tea: black, white, green, oolong, herbal, chais, Chinese & Japanese and iced teas.
President/CEO: Thomas Lisicki
CEO: Tom Lisicki
tom@stashtea.com
Quality Assurance Manager: Maria Lidiasari
VP Marketing: Dorothy Arnold
Sales Director: Kai Larsen
Human Resources Manager: Mitzi Bodine
Operations Manager: Jim Messina
Estimated Sales: $8,300,000
Number Employees: 50-99
Square Footage: 132000
Type of Packaging: Consumer, Food Service, Bulk
Brands:
 Exotica
 Stash
 Stash Premium Organic Teas
 Yamamotoyama 1690

12054 Stassen North America
408 S Pierce Ave
Louisville, CO 80027-3018
303-563-1016
Fax: 303-527-1702 sales@snatea.com
www.snatea.com
General grocery
President: Mike Fitzgerald
CEO: Barry Cooper
sales@snatea.com
Business Development Manager: Cecelia DesPortes
Estimated Sales: $2.5-5 Million
Number Employees: 10-19

12055 State Fish Distributors
39 S La Salle St.
Suite 1410
Chicago, IL 60603-1706
312-451-0800
Fax: 773-225-4660
Seafood
President: Donald Nathan

12056 State Garden Inc.
P.O. Box 6277
Chelsea, MA 02150
stategarden.com
Leafy greens, spinach, and celery.
Owner: Mark DeMichaelis
Year Founded: 1938
Number of Brands: 2
Type of Packaging: Private Label
Brands:
 Olivia's Organics
 Simple Beginnings

12057 State Of Maine Cheese Co
461 Commercial St
Rockport, ME 04856-4455
207-236-8895
Fax: 207-236-9591 800-762-8895
infoA@cheese-me.com www.cheese-me.com
Cheese
President: Cathe Morrill
c.morrill@cheese-me.com
Estimated Sales: $500,000-$1 Million
Number Employees: 5-9

12058 Statewide Meats & Poultry
211 Food Terminal Plz
New Haven, CT 06511
203-777-6669
Fax: 203-492-4073
Processor and wholesaler/distributor of meat
President: Stephen Falcigno
Estimated Sales: $7900000
Number Employees: 20-49

12059 Stauber Performance Ingrdients
4120 N Palm St
Fullerton, CA 92835-1026
714-441-3900
Fax: 714-441-3909 888-441-4233
customerservice@stauberusa.com
www.stauberusa.com
Leading supplier of bulk ingredients to the nutritional products, food, cosmetic and pet care industries.
President: Olivier Guiot
CEO: Sam Butler
sam.butler@viasat.com
COO & CFO: Steve Graham
Number Employees: 20-49
Type of Packaging: Bulk

12060 Stauffer Biscuit Co
P.O. Box 12002
York, PA 17402-0672
888-480-1988
www.stauffers.com
Cookies, crackers and snack products
President: Yujiro Kataoka
y.kataoka@stauffers.net
Vice President: Jim Biondolillo
Year Founded: 1871
Estimated Sales: $150 Million
Number Employees: 500-999
Parent Co: Meiji Co., Ltd.
Brands:
 Stauffer's

12061 Stauffer's
8670 Farnsworth Rd
Cuba, NY 14727-9720
585-968-2700
Fax: 585-968-2722
Manufacturers of cookies.
Manager: John Fletcher
Estimated Sales: $2.5-5,000,000
Number Employees: 20-49
Brands:
 Stauffer's

12062 Stavis Seafoods
212 Northern Ave
Suite 305
Boston, MA 02210-2090
617-897-1200
Fax: 617-897-1291 800-390-5103
fish@stavis.com www.stavis.com
Fresh and frozen seafood including cod, haddock, pollock, tuna, swordfish, mahi, snapper, grouper and seabass fillets, rockshrimp and baby scallops
President & CEO: Charles Marble
Chief Sustainability Officer: Richard Stavis
CFO: Mary Fleming
Executive Vice President: Stewart Altman
Director of Quality Assurance: Allison Roderick
VP Marketing: Michael Lynch
VP Sales: Stephen Young
VP Operations: Mohamad Fakira
Estimated Sales: $28.9 Million
Number Employees: 100-249
Square Footage: 10000
Type of Packaging: Food Service, Private Label, Bulk
Brands:
 Bos'n
 Boston Pride
 Foods From the Sea
 Prince Edward

12063 Stawnichy Holdings
PO Box 18
Mundare, AB T0B 3H0
Canada
780-764-3912
Fax: 780-764-3765 888-764-7646
shltd@telusplanet.net www.mundaresausage.com
Pepperoni, frankfurters, Ukrainian-style sausage, bologna, garlic rings, cooked and pressed ham, salami, ham and bacon loafs, macaroni and cheese loafs, corned beef, pastrami, beef jerky, bacon, veal cutlets, ground beef, pierogiesetc
VP/General Manager: E Stawnichy
Number Employees: 20-49
Square Footage: 46000
Brands:
 Stawnichy's

12064 Ste Chapelle Winery
19348 Lowell Rd
Caldwell, ID 83607-9502
208-453-7840
Fax: 208-453-7831 877-783-2427
www.stechapelle.com
Wines
Manager: Mary Sloyer
mary.sloyer@ascentiawines.com
Estimated Sales: Below $5 Million
Number Employees: 20-49
Parent Co: Canandaigua Wine Company
Type of Packaging: Private Label

12065 Steak-Umm Company
P.O. Box 350
Shillington, PA 19607-0350
860-928-5900
Fax: 860-928-0351 http://www.steakumm.com
Quick and easy to prepare and delicious in an endless variety of recipes.
President: Dennis Newnham
Estimated Sales: $14 Million
Number Employees: 120
Square Footage: 352000
Brands:
 Red.L
 Spare-The-Ribs

Food Manufacturers / A-Z

Steak-Umm
Steak-Umm Sandwich To Go

12066 Stearns Wharf Vintners
217 Stearns Wharf # G
Santa Barbara, CA 93101-3582
805-966-6624
Fax: 805-966-6624 www.stearnswharf.org
Wines
President: Candy Scott
Estimated Sales: $2.5-5 Million
Number Employees: 5-9
Brands:
Stearns Wharf

12067 Steckel Produce
905 State Highway 16
Jerseyville, IL 62052-2834
618-498-4274
Fax: 618-498-4780
Fruits and vegetables
Owner: Robert Steckel
rsteckel@sincsurf.net
Estimated Sales: $3 Million
Number Employees: 5-9

12068 Steel's Gourmet Foods, Ltd.
55 E Front St # D175
Bridgeport, PA 19405-1489
610-277-1230
Fax: 610-277-1228 800-678-3357
Processor and exporter of gourmet, sugar free dessert toppings, jams, sweetners, syrups and condiments; also organic salad dressings, condiments, fruit spreads and low sugar fudge sauces.
President, Owner: Elizabeth Steel
Contact: Anna Steel
annasteel@steelsgourmet.com
Plant Manager: Carlos Short
Estimated Sales: $2.5 Million
Number Employees: 8
Number of Products: 60
Square Footage: 40000
Parent Co: Clack-Steel
Type of Packaging: Consumer, Private Label
Brands:
Charlie Trotter Foods
Daven Island Trade
Steel's Gourmet

12069 Steep & Brew
855 E Broadway
Monona, WI 53716-4012
608-223-0707
Fax: 608-223-0355 800-876-1986
coffee@steepnbrew.com
www.steepandbrewcoffee.com
Coffee
Owner: Mark Ballering
mb@steepnbrew.com
VP/Sales Manager: Mark Mullee
Estimated Sales: Below $5 Million
Number Employees: 10-19
Type of Packaging: Private Label
Brands:
Cafe Fair

12070 Stefani Premium Foods
1033 W Van Buren St # 5
Chicago, IL 60607-3288
312-275-9000
Fax: 312-275-9024
Produces a variety of Italian food products including sauces, relishes, pizza toppings, cheeses, and gift sets.
Founder/President/CEO: Phil Stefani
Executive Chef: Marcello Petrini

12071 Stefano Foods
4825 Hovis Rd
Charlotte, NC 28208-1510
704-399-3935
Fax: 704-399-3930 800-340-4019
www.stefanofoods.com
Frozen foods for supermarkets and the foodservice industry. pizza, calzones, tuscanni hand-held pizza, stromboli, stuffed pizza rings, italian paninis, quiche, quesadilla, flatbread melts, and breakfast sandwiches.
President: Enrico Piraino
Director Finance: Linda Wortman
VP: Stefano Piraino
VP Sales: Alan Hammer
Operations Executive: Todd Sanderhouse
General Manager Special Products: Al Silva
Purchasing Manager: Lynn Huss
Estimated Sales: $8.5 Million
Number Employees: 100-249
Square Footage: 124000
Parent Co: Smithfield Foods, Inc.
Type of Packaging: Consumer, Food Service, Bulk
Brands:
Take & Bake Deli Pizza
Stefano's

12072 Stehlin & Sons Company
10134 Colerain Ave
Cincinnati, OH 45251
513-385-6164
Fax: 513-385-6165 800-352-7396
www.stehlinsmeatmarket.com
Beef and pork
President: John Stehlin
Estimated Sales: $1,300,000
Number Employees: 10-19
Type of Packaging: Consumer, Bulk

12073 Steiner Cheese
201 Mill St
Baltic, OH 43804
330-897-5505
Fax: 330-897-6911 888-897-5505
Swiss cheese
President: James Sommers
VP: Dale Lendon
Estimated Sales: $5-10 Million
Number Employees: 5
Type of Packaging: Consumer, Bulk

12074 Stella D'oro
8600 South Boulevard
Charlotte, NC 28273
800-995-2623
www.stelladoro.com
Manufacturer of Italian baked goods.
Type of Packaging: Consumer

12075 Stella Foods
PO Box 99
Hinesburg, VT 05461-0099
802-482-2121
Fax: 802-482-2115
Feta cheese
President/CEO: Joseph Keenan
Marketing Director: Lynn Park
Estimated Sales: $10-24.9 Million
Number Employees: 50-99
Parent Co: Stella Foods

12076 Stella Reedsburg
1120 Commercial Ave
Reedsburg, WI 53959-2132
608-524-8244
Fax: 608-524-8091 www.saputo.com
Mozzarella cheese
Marketing Director: Cindy Zirngible
Plant Manager: Kelley Ford
Estimated Sales: $25-49.9 Million
Number Employees: 50-99
Parent Co: Stella Foods

12077 Stellar Pasta Company
955 Main Street
Great Barrington, MA 01230-2106
413-528-2150
Fax: 530-348-7081
Pasta

12078 Stello Foods Inc
551 Mahoning St
Punxsutawney, PA 15767
814-938-8764
Fax: 814-938-8769 800-849-4599
stellofoods@hotmail.com www.stellofoods.com
Peppers, mustards, sauces, salsas, BBQ sauces, spreads, spaghetti sauces, hot sauces, marinades & dressings
President: Nickki L Stello
Vice President: James Stello
Estimated Sales: $2.5 Million
Number Employees: 20-49
Square Footage: 240000
Type of Packaging: Consumer, Food Service, Private Label, Bulk
Brands:
Pinks
Rapes
Rosie's

12079 Steltzner Vineyards
5 Financial Plz # 104
Napa, CA 94558-6418
707-944-2486
Fax: 707-252-2079 800-707-9463
wines@steltzner.com www.steltzner.com
Winery, procuding red, white and dessert wines.
Owner/Proprietor: Dick Steltzner
National Sales Director: Allison Steltzner
Controller: Rebecca Rose
Estimated Sales: $1-2.5 Million
Number Employees: 1-4
Number of Brands: 1
Type of Packaging: Consumer
Brands:
Steltzner

12080 Stengel Seed & Grain Co
14698 SD Highway 15
Milbank, SD 57252-5452
605-432-6030
Fax: 605-432-6064 gstengel@tnics.com
www.tnics.com
Organic grains. Services include cleaning, dehulling, packaging, warehousing and shipping.
President: Doug Stengel
stengelseed@tnics.com
Estimated Sales: Less than $500,000
Number Employees: 5-9
Square Footage: 60000

12081 Stepan Co.
22 W. Frontage Rd.
Northfield, IL 60093
847-446-7500
Fax: 847-501-2100 www.stepan.com
Surfactants, polymers and specialty products for industries including nutrition, food and beverage, and personal care.
Chairman/President/CEO: F. Quinn Stepan
Vice President/CFO: Luis Rojo
Vice President/General Counsel: David Kabbes
Year Founded: 1932
Estimated Sales: $1.925 Billion
Number Employees: 2,096
Type of Packaging: Bulk
Brands:
Neobee 1053
Neobee 1095
Neobee 895
Neobee M-20
Neobee M-5
Wecobee Fs
Wecobee M
Wecobee S

12082 Sterling Candy, Inc.
27 Ludy Street
Hicksville, NY 11801
516-932-1104
Fax: 516-932-8392
Candy manufacturer and wholesaler.
President/CEO: Edward Greenberg

12083 Sterling Caviar LLC
9149 E Levee Rd
Elverta, CA 95626-9559
916-991-4420
Fax: 916-991-4334 800-525-0333
info@sterlingcaviar.com www.sterlingcaviar.com
White sturgeon including fresh, cold smoked and frozen
Manager: Peter Struffenegger
CFO: Joeseph Ruffo
R&D: Richard Helfrich
Manager: Carl Beckham
cbeckham@sterlingcaviar.com
Estimated Sales: $10-20 Million
Number Employees: 20-49
Square Footage: 110000
Parent Co: Stolt Sea Farm Group
Type of Packaging: Food Service

Food Manufacturers / A-Z

12084 Sterling Caviar LLC
Sterling Sturgeon
Sacramento, CA
916-991-4420
Fax: 916-991-4334 800-525-0333
info@sterlingcaviar.com www.sterlingcaviar.com
Caviar
Manager: Peter Struffenegger
Type of Packaging: Private Label

12085 Sterling Extract Co Inc
10929 Franklin Ave # V
Franklin Park, IL 60131-1430
847-451-9728
Fax: 847-451-9745
www.sterlingextractcompany.com
Pure and artifical vanilla flavoring extracts, flavors for ice cream, candy and bakery products.
President: Kitty Greenwood
kgreenwood@sterlingextractcompany.com
Vice President: Lynn Wakefield
Marketing Director: John Wakefield
Sales Director: Deborah Pavone
Estimated Sales: $1,500,000
Number Employees: 5-9
Type of Packaging: Bulk
Brands:
   Bourbonil
   Star-Van
   Sterling Old Fashion Flavors
   Vanaleigh 6b

12086 Sterling Foods LLC
1075 Arion Pkwy
San Antonio, TX 78216-2883
210-490-1669
Fax: 210-490-7964 www.sterlingfoodsusa.com
Gourmet cakes, biscuits, breads and rolls, cookies and brownies, loaf cakes and muffins
CEO: John D Likovich
jlikovich@sterling-fd.com
CEO: John Likovich
CFO: Mark Kuehl
SVP Sales/Marketing: Fred Friend
Human Resources Director: Jim Kuehl
SVP/COO: Nick Davis
Plant Manager: Hugo Salinas
Purchasing Manager: Barry Daley
Estimated Sales: $7900000
Number Employees: 100-249
Square Footage: 340000

12087 Sterling Vineyards
1111 Dunaweal Ln
Calistoga, CA 94515-9799
707-942-3344
Fax: 707-942-3463 servicedesk.na@diageo.com
www.sterlingvineyards.com
Wines
VP: Mike Westrick
Director, Operations: Vince Bonotto
Estimated Sales: $25 Million
Number Employees: 100-249
Parent Co: Diageo Chateau & Estate Wines

12088 Sterzing Food Co
1819 Charles St
Burlington, IA 52601-2201
319-754-8467
Fax: 319-752-7195 800-754-8467
www.sterzingchips.com
Potato chips, sour cream and dip
Owner: Craig Smith
craig@sterzingchips.com
Estimated Sales: $2 Million
Number Employees: 20-49
Type of Packaging: Consumer
Brands:
   Sterzing's

12089 Steuk's Country Market & Winery
165 E Washington Row
Sandusky, OH 44870-2610
419-625-8324
Fax: 419-625-9007
Wines
President: Charles Sprigg
Estimated Sales: $2.5-5 000,000
Number Employees: 1-4

12090 Steve & Andy's Organics
630 Flushing Avenue
Brooklyn, NY 11206
718-499-7933
organic@steveandandys.com
steveandandys.com
Gluten-free cookies and candied orange peel.
Owner: Arjan Khiani
CEO: Michelle Schwartz
Business Development: Quinn Rhone
Estimated Sales: $2.2 Million
Number Employees: 51
Brands:
   Steve & Andy's

12091 Steve Connolly Seafood Co Inc
34 Newmarket Sq
Boston, MA 02118-2601
617-427-7700
Fax: 617-427-7697 800-225-5595
retail@steveconnollyseafood.com
www.steveconnollyseafood.com
Fresh and frozen seafood, lobster, shellfish, smoked fish, prepared foods
Chairman & CEO: Stephen Connolly
Executive Vice President: David Coombs
Estimated Sales: $28 Million
Number Employees: 50-99
Type of Packaging: Bulk
Brands:
   Steve Connolly

12092 Steve Mendez
16016 County Road 101
Woodland, CA 95776
530-662-0512
Fax: 530-662-9418
Condiments, beans and sprouts
President/Owner: Steve Mendez
Estimated Sales: $420,000
Number Employees: 10

12093 Steve's Authentic Key Lime Pies
204 Van Dyke Street
Brooklyn, NY 11231
770-333-0840
Fax: 770-436-4280 888-450-5463
inquiry@keylime.com www.keylime.com
Processor and exporter of key lime pies, pie filling, sorbet and novelty desserts
President: Kenneth Burts
Plt. Mgr.: K Michael Miller
Quality Control: Slorence Clay
Estimated Sales: $5-10 Million
Number Employees: 20-49
Square Footage: 48000
Type of Packaging: Food Service, Private Label
Brands:
   Kenny's
   Kenny's Island Style
   Kenny's Key Lime Crunch

12094 Steve's Doughnut Shop
4 Winslow Ave
Somerset, MA 02726-2318
508-672-0865
Doughnuts
Owner: Mario Gulinello
Estimated Sales: $1-2.5 000,000
Number Employees: 10-19

12095 Steve's Ice Cream, Craft Collective
630 Flushing Ave.
4th Floor
Brooklyn, NY 11206
718-412-9393
888-782-7688
www.stevesicecream.com
Manufacturer of ice cream and sorbets.
Owner: David Stein
Contact: Forbes Fisher
ffisher@stevesicecream.com

12096 Steve's Mom
200 Food Center Dr
Bronx, NY 10474
718-842-8090
Fax: 718-832-6302 800-362-4545
ruggiebake@aol.com
Kosher dessert strudels, vegetable strudels, rugelach, coconut macaroons, brownies, and cheesecake
President: Suellen Schussel
Vice President: Erwin Schussel
Estimated Sales: $664696
Number Employees: 5-9
Square Footage: 10000
Type of Packaging: Consumer, Food Service, Private Label, Bulk
Brands:
   Fudgeroons
   Scotcheroons
   Steve's Mom

12097 Steve's PaleoGoods
7800 Airport Hwy
Pennsauken, NJ 08109
856-356-2258
info@stevespaleogoods.com
www.stevespaleogoods.com
Paleo diet products
Founder: Steve Liberati

12098 Steven Roberts Originals
2780 Tower Rd
Aurora, CO 80011-3501
303-375-9925
info@originaldesserts.com
www.originaldesserts.com
Baked goods, cake pops, cake bars
President: Brian McGuire
CEO: Steven Fabos
Chairman: Charles Kosmont
HR Executive: Fran Adragna-Hayes
info@originaldesserts.com
Number Employees: 500-999

12099 Stevenot Winery
458 Main St # B
PO Box 978
Murphys, CA 95247-9353
209-728-3485
info@stevenotwinery.com
www.stevenotwinery.com
Wines
Owner: David Oliveto
david@stevenotwinery.com
Winemaker: Chuck Hovey
Estimated Sales: $5-10 Million
Number Employees: 5-9
Type of Packaging: Bulk
Brands:
   Shephard Ridge
   Stevenot Winery

12100 Stevens Creative Enterprises, Inc.
New York, NY
646-558-6336
www.oohlalacandy.com
Manufacturer of coffee, tea, candy, baking mixes, and cocoa.
Founder: Sara Stevens
President: Rebecca Zorowitz
Brands:
   Brew La La Coffee
   Brew La La Tea
   Ooh La La Candy
   Chef Ooh La La Baking Mixes
   Cocoa

12101 Stevens Point Brewery
2617 Water St
Stevens Point, WI 54481-5248
715-344-9310
Fax: 715-344-8897 800-369-4911
info@pointbeer.com www.pointbeer.com
Processor and exporter of beer and gourmet soda.
Founder: Frank Wahle
Founder: George Ruder
Co-Owner: Jim Wiechmann
Operating Partner: Joe Martino
Brewing: Gabe Hopkins
Director, Marketing: Julie Birrenkott
Year Founded: 1857
Estimated Sales: $20-50 Million
Number Employees: 20-49
Number of Brands: 2
Type of Packaging: Consumer, Private Label
Brands:
   Point Premium
   Point Special

12102 Stevens Sausage Co
3411 Stevens Sausage Rd
Smithfield, NC 27577-7539
919-934-3159
Fax: 919-934-2568 800-338-0561
tstev25536@aol.com www.stevens-sausage.com

Food Manufacturers / A-Z

Fresh ham, pork, frankfurters and sausage
President: Tim Stevens
tstev25536@aol.com
Marketing Executive: Tim Stevens
Estimated Sales: $11 Million
Number Employees: 50-99
Type of Packaging: Consumer, Food Service, Bulk

12103 Stevens Tropical Plantation
6550 Okeechobee Blvd
West Palm Beach, FL 33411-2798
561-683-4701
Fax: 561-683-4993
Processor and importer of syrups, fruit juices, nectar and beverage bases
President: Henry Stevens Jr
Estimated Sales: $1-3 Million
Number Employees: 5-9
Square Footage: 40000
Type of Packaging: Consumer, Food Service
Brands:
  Parkway
  Sunny Isle

12104 Stevenson-Cooper Inc
1039 W Venango St
PO Box 46345
Philadelphia, PA 19140-4391
215-223-2600
Fax: 215-223-3597 waxcooper@aol.com
Manufacturer and exporter of oils including cottonseed and palm oils; also, manufacturer of paraffin and sealing wax
President: Dennis Cooper
dcooper@stevensonseeley.com
R&D: Tammy Pullins
Estimated Sales: Below $5 Million
Number Employees: 5-9

12105 Stevison Ham Co
125 Stevison Ham Rd
PO Box 219
Portland, TN 37148-2037
615-325-7315
Fax: 615-325-5914 800-844-4267
sales@stevisonham.com
www.tennesseetraditions.com
Smoked ham, ribs, BBQ pork, beef, poultry
President: Michael Stevison
mstevison@stevisonham.com
VP Marketing: Sean Stevison
Vice President: John White
Customer Service: Lara Stevison
Estimated Sales: $20-30 Million
Number Employees: 50-99
Brands:
  Stevison's

12106 Stevita Naturals
7650 U.S. 287 Frontage Rd
Arlington, TX 76001
214-556-5933
800-577-8409
stevitanaturals.com
Candy, gum and cocoa sweetened with stevia
President/Owner: Oscar Rodes

12107 Steviva Ingredients
725 NW Flanders Street
Suite 402
Portland, OR 97209
310-455-9876
Fax: 310-388-5393 800-851-6314
sales@steviva.com www.stevivaingredients.com
Manufacturer of sweeteners for the food and beverage industries.
President & CEO: Thom King

12108 Stewart Candies
600 Haines Ave
Waycross, GA 31501-2202
912-283-1970
Fax: 912-284-0354 candy.stewartdistribution.com
Candy and confections
President: Sam Stewart
sams@stewartcandy.com
CEO: Jimmy Stewart
CFO: Deen J Stewart
Estimated Sales: $20-50 Million
Number Employees: 10-19

12109 Stewart's Beverages
900 King Street
rye Brook, NY 10573
914-397-9200
800-762-7753
www.drinkstewarts.com
Soft drinks
President: Samuel M Simpson
CFO: Myron D Stadler
Number Employees: 10-19
Parent Co: Triarc Companies
Type of Packaging: Consumer, Food Service

12110 Stewart's Private Blend Foods
4110 W Wrightwood Ave
Chicago, IL 60639-2172
773-489-2500
Fax: 773-489-2148 800-654-2862
info@stewarts.com www.stewarts.com
Processor, importer and exporter of coffees including flavored, decaffeinated and roasted; also, flavored and blended teas
President: Donald Stewart
CEO: Robert Stewart
Vice President: William Stewart Jr
Contact: Steve Blair
steve.blair@stewarts.com
Production Manager: Elita Pagan
Plant Manager: Ed Fabro
Estimated Sales: $2,000,000
Number Employees: 20-49
Square Footage: 192000
Type of Packaging: Consumer, Food Service, Private Label, Bulk
Brands:
  Stewarts

12111 Stewart's Shops Corp
2907 State Route 9
Ballston Spa, NY 12020-4201
518-581-1200
Fax: 518-581-1209 www.stewartsshops.com
Whole, 2% and skim milk; also, regular and low-fat ice cream
President: Gary Dake
gdake@stewartsshops.com
Estimated Sales: Over $1 Billion
Number Employees: 1000-4999
Type of Packaging: Consumer

12112 Stewarts Market
17821 State Route 507 SE
Yelm, WA 98597-9654
360-458-2091
Fax: 360-458-3150
Meat and homemade sausage
President: Dorthy Carlson
Vice President: Stewart Carlson
Estimated Sales: $3-5 000,000
Number Employees: 20-49

12113 Stewarts Seafood
8401 Highway 188
Coden, AL 36523-3059
251-824-7368
Fax: 251-824-7369
Seafood
President: Janice Stewart
Co-Owner: James O Stewart
Estimated Sales: $10-20 Million
Number Employees: 20-49

12114 Stichler Products Inc
1800 N 12th St
Suite 1
Reading, PA 19604-1545
610-921-0211
Fax: 610-921-0294 info@megacandyco.com
www.megabuttons.com
Confectionery products: candy, decorative and ornamental
President: Martin Deutschman
spicandy@aol.com
Vice President: Brad Deutschman
Public Relations: Rachel Buckholtz
Estimated Sales: $4700000
Number Employees: 20-49
Square Footage: 248000
Type of Packaging: Consumer, Food Service, Private Label, Bulk
Brands:
  Candy Farms

12115 Stickney & Poor Company
12 Reynolds Dr
Peterborough, NH 03458-1611
603-924-2259
Processor and exporter of portion-controlled products including ketchup, relish, nondairy coffee creamers, honey, artificial sweeteners, jams, jellies, marmalades, preserves, mayonnaise, mustard, salt, pepper, vinegar, salad dressingsand dipping sauces
President: H Sandy Brown
VP: Chuck Lavery
Number Employees: 50-99
Type of Packaging: Food Service, Private Label, Bulk
Brands:
  Harvest Selects
  Stickney & Poor

12116 Stickney Hill Dairy Inc
15371 County Road 48
Kimball, MN 55353-9771
320-398-5360
Fax: 320-398-5361 sales@stickneydairy.com
www.stickneydairy.com
Goat cheeses
General Manager: Cheryl Willenbring
Quality Assurance Manager: Kathy Ratka
Manager: Frankie Lenzmeier
flenzmeier@stickneydairy.com
Estimated Sales: $2 Million
Number Employees: 10-19

12117 Sticky Fingers Bakeries
1839 W Summit Pkwy
Spokane, WA 99201-6027
509-922-1985
Fax: 509-922-7102 800-458-5826
sales@stickyfingersbakeries.com
www.stickyfingersbakeries.com
English scones
Site Manager: Ted Vogelman
ted@stickyfingersbakeries.com
Estimated Sales: Less Than $500,000
Number Employees: 5-9

12118 Sticky Toffee Pudding Company
1313 W. 9 1/2 St.
Austin, TX 78703
512-472-0039
tracyclaros@stickytoffeepuddingcompany.com
www.stickytoffeepuddingcompany.com
Cakes, puddings, bars, and dessert sauces.
Founder: Tracy Wilkinson-Claros

12119 Stiebs
11767 Road 27«
Madera, CA 93637
559-661-0031
Fax: 559-661-0032 info@stiebs.com
www.stiebs.com
Fruit and vegetable juices, concentrates, purees, powders and extracts
Owner: Heather Chavez
hchavez@stiebs.com
Partner: Brad Miller
Sales Manager: Brian Nova
Number Employees: 1-4

12120 Stimo-O-Stam, Ltd.
70593 Bravo St
Covington, LA 70433
Fax: 985-845-1489 800-562-7514
laurie_sre@yahoo.com www.stimostam.com
Processor and exporter Supplements, Nutritional: Energy Mixes
Manager: Alan Lafferty
Estimated Sales: $300,000-500,000
Number Employees: 1-4
Square Footage: 40000
Type of Packaging: Consumer
Brands:
  Stim-O-Stam

12121 Stinking Rose, The
325 Columbus Ave
San Francisco, CA 94133-3907
415-781-7673
Fax: 415-781-2833 800-995-7674
sfcomments@thestinkingrose.com
www.thestinkingrose.com
Extra virgin olive oil, pickled garlic and garlic stuffed olives

Food Manufacturers / A-Z

Owner: Dante Serafini
comments@thestinkingrose.com
Owner: Jerry Dal Bozzo
Estimated Sales: $1-3 Million
Number Employees: 50-99

12122 Stirling Foods
P.O.Box 569
Renton, WA 98057
425-251-9293
Fax: 425-251-0251   800-332-1714
Processor and exporter of gourmet beverage flavors and syrups
President: Mark Greiner
CEO: Earl Greiner
Contact: Jeff Greiner
stirling@stirling.net
Estimated Sales: $1,300,000
Number Employees: 5-9
Type of Packaging: Consumer, Food Service, Private Label
Brands:
  Stirling Gourmet Flavors

12123 Stirrings
376 Nash Rd
New Bedford, MA 2746
866-646-4266
customercare@stirringsshop.com stirrings.com
Cocktail mixers, bar ingredients and rimmers
Contact: Laura Camara
lcamara@stirrings.com
Year Founded: 1997

12124 Stock Popcorn Ind Inc
304 Vine St
Lake View, IA 51450
712-657-2811
Fax: 712-657-2550 stockpop@netins.net
Processor and exporter of yellow and white popcorn including processed unpopped and microwaveable; also, feed sack fashion packaging for popcorn
Owner: Jim Stock
stockpop@netins.net
Number Employees: 5-9
Type of Packaging: Consumer, Private Label, Bulk
Brands:
  Lil' Chief
  Lil' Chief Popcorn

12125 Stock Yards Packing Company
2457 W North Ave.
Melrose Park, IL 60160
312-733-6050
Fax: 708-223-1257 877-785-9273
customerservice@stockyardscustomerservice.com
www.stockyards.com
Processor and exporter of beef, pork, veal and lamb
President: Dan Pollack
Plant Manager: Oscar Moore
Estimated Sales: $10-20 Million
Number Employees: 100-249
Square Footage: 180000

12126 Stockton Graham & Co
4320 Delta Lake Dr
Suite 199
Raleigh, NC 27612-7000
919-881-0746
Fax: 919-881-0746 800-835-5943
info@stocktongraham.com
www.stocktongraham.com
Wholesale specialty beverages
President: Jeff Vojta
vojta@stocktongraham.com
Estimated Sales: $500,000-$1 Million
Number Employees: 10-19
Brands:
  Stoktin Grahan

12127 Stokes Canning Company
18023 Peakview Place
Aurora, CO 80016-3152
303-292-4018
800-978-6537
www.stokeschile.com
Chile sauce
CEO: Jeffrey Nieder
Estimated Sales: $10-19 Million
Number Employees: 50-99
Parent Co: Centennial Specialty Food
Brands:
  Strokes

12128 Stoller Fisheries
1301 18th St
PO Box B
Spirit Lake, IA 51360
712-336-1750
Fax: 712-336-4681 800-831-5174
stollerfisheries@mchsi.com
www.kreativekosherfoods.com
Processor and exporter of fresh fish including carp, buffalo, sheepheads and suckers- Asian Corp.
President: Larry Stoller
lstoller@stollerfisheries.com
Controller: Mark Salzwedel
VP: Thomas Opheim
Quality Control: LaRonna Opheum
Estimated Sales: $4 Million
Number Employees: 20-49
Square Footage: 140000
Parent Co: Progressive Companies
Type of Packaging: Bulk

12129 Stone Brewing
1999 Citracado Pkwy
Escondido, CA 92029-4158
760-294-7899
Fax: 760-471-7690 email@stonebrew.com
www.ubermary.com
Beer
President: Steve Wagner
stevew@stonebrew.com
Chairman/CEO: Greg Koch
Senior Vice President: Alan Eustace
VP Sales: Arlan Arnsten
HR Manager: Kathy Loven
stevew@stonebrew.com
Senior Vice President of Operations: Laszlo Bock
Production Manager/Head Brewer: Mitch Steele
Number Employees: 100-249
Brands:
  Stone Pale Ale
  Stone Smoked Porter
  Stone Ipa
  Stone Sublimely
  Arrogant Bastard Ale

12130 Stone Crabs Inc
11 Washington Ave
Miami Beach, FL 33139-7395
305-534-8788
Fax: 305-532-2704 800-260-2722
Fresh and frozen stone crabs, whole lobsters and lobster tails
President: Stephen Sawitz
alopez@stonecrabsinc.com
CFO: Marc Fine
Marketing Director: Tracie Gordon
Operations Manager: James McClendon
Facilities: Alex Lopez
Plant Manager: Ron Pressley
Estimated Sales: $10-20 Million
Number Employees: 20-49
Type of Packaging: Consumer, Food Service
Brands:
  Sci

12131 (HQ)Stone Hill Winery
1110 Stone Hill Hwy
Hermann, MO 65041-1280
573-486-2221
Fax: 573-486-3828
hermann-info@stonehillwinery.com
www.stonehillwinery.com
Grape juice, wine and champagne
Co-Owner: James Held
Co-Owner: Betty Held
Director of Sales & Advertising: Thomas Held
General Manager: Jon Held
Number Employees: 100-249
Other Locations:
  Stone Hill Winery
  New Florence MO
  Stone Hill Winery
  Branson MO
Brands:
  Stone Hill Winery

12132 Stone Meat Processor
1485 Stonefield Way
Ogden, UT 84404
801-782-9825
Fax: 801-782-1109 Jared@stonemeats.com
www.stonemeats.com
Ground beef
President: Frank Stone
Marketing/Operations: Burke Stone
Estimated Sales: $10-20 Million
Number Employees: 20-49
Type of Packaging: Consumer, Food Service

12133 Stone Mountain Pecan Co
1781 Highway 78 NW
Monroe, GA 30655-5227
770-266-6659
Fax: 770-207-4403 800-633-6887
smpc1@mindspring.com
www.stonemountainpecan.com
Processors of pecans
President: Robby E Coker
smpc1@mindspring.com
Estimated Sales: $3200000
Number Employees: 10-19
Type of Packaging: Consumer, Food Service, Private Label, Bulk

12134 Stone Mountain Vineyards
1376 Wyatt Mountain Rd
Dyke, VA 22935-1371
434-990-9463
www.stonemountainvineyards.com
Wines
Founder: Alfred Breiner
General Manager & Assistant Winemaker: Kate Breiner
Estimated Sales: $3-5 Million
Number Employees: 1-4

12135 Stone's Home Made CandyShop
145 W Bridge St
Oswego, NY 13126-1495
315-343-8401
Fax: 315-343-8401 888-223-3928
Candy and confectionery products
Owner: Margaret Stachowicz
Estimated Sales: $300,000
Number Employees: 5-9
Square Footage: 9000
Type of Packaging: Consumer, Food Service

12136 StoneHammer Brewing
355 Elmira Rd N
Unit 135
Guelph, ON N1K 1S5
Canada
519-824-1194
Fax: 519-822-8201
Manufacturer and exporter of beer, lager and cask condition ale
CEO: Karen Cerniuk
General Manager: Brian Relly
Office Admin: Myriam Mullin
Sales & Service: Lee Ecclestone
Brewmaster: Charles MacLean
Brewery Manager: Brian Reilly
Estimated Sales: $382,000
Number Employees: 5
Type of Packaging: Consumer, Food Service
Brands:
  Eramosa Honey Wheat
  F and M Special Draft
  Macleans Cask Conditioned
  Macleans Pale
  Oac Gold
  Royal City
  Saint Andre Vienna
  Stone Hammer Pilsner

12137 Stonegate
2300 Lower Chiles Valley Rd
St Helena, CA 94574-9632
707-603-2203
Fax: 707-603-2209
Wines
President: Paul D Croft Croft
CFO: Cathy del Fava
Estimated Sales: $5-10 Million
Number Employees: 10-19

12138 Stoneridge Winery
13862 Ridge Rd
Sutter Creek, CA 95685
209-223-1761
Wines
Owner: Gary Porteous
gary.porteous@stoneridge.com
Estimated Sales: Below $5 000,000
Number Employees: 5-9

1145

Food Manufacturers / A-Z

12139 (HQ)Stonewall Kitchen
2 Stonewall Ln
York, ME 03909-1665
207-351-2713
Fax: 207-351-2715 800-826-1752
info@stonewallkitchen.com
www.stonewallkitchen.com
Specialty foods
CFO: Laurie King
Executive VP: Natalie King
nking@stonewallkitchen.com
Estimated Sales: $10-50 Million
Number Employees: 100-249
Square Footage: 60000
Type of Packaging: Consumer
Brands:
  Stonewall Kitchen

12140 Stonie's Sausage Shop
1507 Edgemont Blvd
Perryville, MO 63775-1230
573-547-2540
Fax: 573-547-1747 888-546-2540
contact@shopstonies.com www.shopstonies.com
Smoked meats and sausages
Owner: Roger Wibbenmeyer
contact@shopstonies.com
Co-Owner: Tyson Wibbenmeyer
Estimated Sales: $1-1.5 Million
Number Employees: 10-19
Square Footage: 60000
Type of Packaging: Food Service, Private Label

12141 Stonington Lobster Co-Op
Indian Point Rd
Stonington, ME 4681
207-367-2286
Fax: 207-367-2802
Lobster
Manager: Ronald Trundy
Manager: Steve Robins Iii
Estimated Sales: $5-10 Million
Number Employees: 5-9

12142 Stonington Vineyards
523 Taugwonk Rd
P.O. Box 463
Stonington, CT 06378-1805
860-535-1222
Fax: 860-535-2182 800-421-9463
info@stoningtonvineyards.com
www.stoningtonvineyards.com
Table wines including chardonnay, seaport white, fume vidal, white and bush, cabernet franc and gewurztraminer
Owner: Happy Smith
happy@stoningtonvineyards.com
General Manager/Winemaker: Mike McAndrew
Founder: Nick Smith
Founder: Happy Smith
Marketing Director: Nick Smith
Estimated Sales: $400000
Number Employees: 5-9
Square Footage: 40000
Type of Packaging: Consumer
Brands:
  Seaport Blush
  Seaport White
  Seaport Wines
  Stonington
  Stonington Vineyards

12143 Stony Hill Vineyard
3331 Saint Helena Hwy N
St Helena, CA 94574-9660
707-963-2636
Fax: 707-963-1831 info@stonyhillvineyard.com
www.stonyhillvineyard.com
Wines
Owner: Peter Mccrea
Office Manager: Willinda McCrea
Vineyard and Winery Operations: Mike Chelini
Vineyard Foreman: Alejandro Salomon
Customer Relations: Mary Burklow
Estimated Sales: $500,000-$1 Million
Number Employees: 10-19
Brands:
  Stony Hill Vineyard

12144 Stonybrook Mountain Winery
3835 State Highway 128
Calistoga, CA 94515-9739
707-942-5282
Fax: 707-942-5334 www.storybookwines.com
Wines
President: Jerry Seps
Contact: Norman Wu
nwu@apple.com
Estimated Sales: Less Than $500,000
Number Employees: 1-4
Brands:
  Storybook Mountain Winery

12145 Stonyfield Organic
10 Burton Dr
Londonderry, NH 03053-7436
603-437-4040
Fax: 603-437-7594 800-776-2697
www.stonyfield.com
Natural organic yogurt, frozen yogurt, smoothies, snacks, milk, cream, and baby food
Chairman/Co-Founder: Gary Hirshberg
President/CEO: Esteve Torrens
Director Operations/Finance: Rick Burleigh
VP Research & Development: Paul Rosethal
VP Marketing: Christopher Malnar
Senior Director Sales: Mark Murphy
VP Human Resources: Sue Melvin
COO: Diane Carhart
VP Sourcing & Product Development: Rolf Carlson
Year Founded: 1983
Estimated Sales: $370 Million
Number Employees: 400
Brands:
  Stonyfield Farm Frozen Yogurt
  Stonyfield Farm Ice Cream
  Stonyfield Farm Refrig Yogurt
  Yo Baby Yogurt
  Brown Cow

12146 Stop & Shop Manufacturing
104 Meadow Road
Readville, MA 02136-2349
508-977-5132
Processor and wholesaler/distributor of milk, juices and sodas
Marketing Director: William Sress
Estimated Sales: $3-5 Million
Number Employees: 20-49
Parent Co: Stop & Shop Supermarket Company
Type of Packaging: Consumer

12147 Storck Canada
100 City Centre Dr
PO Box 2103
Mississauga, ON L5B 3C6
Canada
905-272-4480
Fax: 905-272-6899 www.storck.com
Candy wholesaler
President & CEO: Ralph Hilpuesch
VP, Finance & Operations: Andrew Ruttgers
Brands:
  Campino
  Knoppers
  Merci
  Merci Crocant
  Merci Pur
  Mini Dickmann's
  Super Dickmann's
  Toffifee
  Werther's Original

12148 Storck U.S.A.
Suite 400
Chicago, IL 60654
312-467-5700
Fax: 312-467-9722 800-852-5542
www.storck.us
Confectionary products
President & CEO: Ralph Hilpuesch
VP, Finance & Operations: Andrew Ruttgers
Year Founded: 1903
Estimated Sales: $87 Million
Number Employees: 7,000
Number of Brands: 5
Brands:
  Werther's Original
  Merci
  Riesen
  Toffifay
  Mamba

12149 StoreHouse Foods
22431 Antonio Parkway
Suite B 160
Rancho Santa Margarita, CA 92688
www.storehousefoods.com
Gluten free portable meals
Founder: Yvonne Williams

12150 Storrs Winery
303 Potrero St # 35
Santa Cruz, CA 95060-2782
831-458-5030
Fax: 831-458-0464 salesmgr@storrswine.com
www.storrswine.com
Wines
President: Stephen Storrs
steves@storrswine.com
Owner/VP: Pamela Bianchini-Storrs
Operations Manager: Aaron Storrs
Production Manager: Morgan Storrs
Estimated Sales: $1-2.5 Million
Number Employees: 10-19
Brands:
  Storrs

12151 Story Winery
10525 Bell Rd
Plymouth, CA 95669-9516
209-245-6208
Fax: 209-245-6619 800-712-6390
www.storywinery.com
Wines
Owner: Robert Campbell
rob@zin.com
CEO: Jan Tichenor
Marketing Director: Jan Tichenor
Estimated Sales: $500,000-$1 Million
Number Employees: 10-19
Brands:
  Story Wine

12152 Story's Popcorn Company
P.O.Box 247
Charleston, MO 63834-0247
573-649-2727
Fax: 314-649-3374
Popcorn
President: A Story
Estimated Sales: $10-20 000,000
Number Employees: 1-4

12153 Stoudt Brewing Co
2800 N Reading Rd # 272
Adamstown, PA 19501
717-484-4386
Fax: 717-484-4182 jack@stoudtsbeer.com
www.stoudtsbeer.com
Seasonal beers, ale, stout, lager and pilsner
President: Carol Stoudt
CFO: Edward Stoudt
Estimated Sales: $6 Million
Number Employees: 50-99
Type of Packaging: Consumer, Food Service
Brands:
  American Pale Ale
  Stoudt Gold
  Scarlet Lady Ale
  Pilsener
  Fat Dog Stout
  Double India Pale Ale
  Triple
  Brewers Reserves
  Old Abominable Barkey Wine

12154 Stoutridge Vineyard
10 Ann Kaley Lane
Marlboro, NY 12542
www.stoutridge.com
Gin, whiskey, brandy, vodka, natural wines
Co-Owner: Stephen Osborn
Co-Owner: Kimberly Wagner
Year Founded: 2001
Number of Brands: 1
Type of Packaging: Consumer, Private Label
Brands:
  Stoutridge

12155 Strasburg Provision
1317 N Wooster Ave
Strasburg, OH 44680
330-878-5557
Fax: 330-878-5558 800-207-6009
Meat products and catering
President: Rudolf M Klapper
Sales: Herb Gritzan
Production: Frank H Klapper
Estimated Sales: $3000000
Number Employees: 20-49

Food Manufacturers / A-Z

Type of Packaging: Consumer, Food Service, Private Label, Bulk

12156 Strassburger Steaks
40 Broad St.
P.O. Box 465
Carlstadt, NJ 07072
201-842-8890
Fax: 201-842-8891 orders@strassburgersteaks.com
www.strassburgersteaks.com
Offers aged, cut and prime steaks, Berkshire pork, lamb, and veal.
CEO: Suzanne Strassburger Reidy
Type of Packaging: Consumer

12157 Strathroy Foods
PO Box 188
225 Lothian Avenue
Strathroy, ON N7G 3J2
Canada
519-245-4600
Fax: 519-245-3661
Processor and exporter of frozen vegetables including peas and carrots and other vegetable varieties
President: Craig Richardson
Estimated Sales: $20-50 Million
Number Employees: 200
Type of Packaging: Consumer, Food Service, Private Label
Brands:
 Red Valley

12158 Straub Brewery Inc
303 Sorg St
St Marys, PA 15857-1592
814-834-2875
Fax: 814-834-7628 straub@straubbeer.com
www.straubbeer.com
Brewer
President & CEO: Bill Brock
Vice President, Sales, Marketing & PR: Cathy Lenze
Number Employees: 20-49
Brands:
 Straub
 Straub Light

12159 Straub's
8282 Forsyth Blvd
Clayton, MO 63105
314-725-2121
Fax: 314-725-2123 888-725-2121
straubs@anet-stl.com www.straubs.com
Steaks, seafood including lobster tails and gift baskets
President: Jack Straub
Founder: William A Straub
CEO: Jack W Straub Jr
Contact: Roger Mcelroy
roger@straubs.com
Number Employees: 100-249
Brands:
 Straubs

12160 Straus Family Creamery
1105 Industrial Ave
Ste 200
Petaluma, CA 94952-1141
707-776-2887
Fax: 707-776-2888 800-572-7783
sfc@strausmilk.com
www.strausfamilycreamery.com
Producers of organic milk and dairy products.
President: Albert Straus
Quality Assurance Supervisor: Ian-Hero Serrano
Inside Sales Administrator: Carissa Biss
Director of People & Culture: Laurangelica Angel Lechon
Production Manager: Miguel Gonzales
Estimated Sales: Less Than $500,000
Number Employees: 5-9

12161 Strauss Bakery
5115 13th Ave
Brooklyn, NY 11219-3560
718-851-7728
Fax: 718-437-1882 tzvi@straussbakery.com
www.straussbakery.com
Bakery products
President: Elliot Berman
bakerellyb@aol.com
Sales Manager: John Macley
Estimated Sales: Less Than $500,000
Number Employees: 5-9

12162 Strauss Brands International
9775 S 60th St
Franklin, WI 53132
414-421-5250
info@straussbrands.com
straussbrands.com
Veal
CEO: Randy Strauss
VP, New Business Development: Lori Dunn
COO: Greg Martin
VP, International Operations: Steve Starnes
Estimated Sales: $50-100 Million
Number Employees: 200-500
Number of Brands: 5
Brands:
 Free Raised
 Strauss
 Chiappetti
 Musillami
 Dos Mamacitas

12163 Strawberry Hill Grand Delights
1901 Revere Beach Pkwy
Suite 4
Everett, MA 02149-5904
617-319-3557
www.strawberryhillcandy.com
Lollipops, sweeteners, tea candies, chocolate, and marshmallows.
Founder: Henry Zunino
Number Employees: 10-19

12164 Strebin Farms
28245 SE Division Dr
Troutdale, OR 97060-9486
503-665-8328
Fax: 503-669-7783
Fresh and frozen red raspberries
CEO: William P Strebin
williams@strebin.com
Marketing Director: William P Strebin
Estimated Sales: $5-10 Million
Number Employees: 50-99
Type of Packaging: Food Service
Brands:
 Strebin Farms

12165 Streblow Vineyards
PO Box 233
Saint Helena, CA 94574-0233
707-963-5892
Fax: 707-963-5835
Wine
President/Owner: Bruce Streblow
Co-Owner: Ana Canales
Brands:
 Streblow Vineyards

12166 Streit Carl & Son Co
703 Atkins Ave
Neptune, NJ 07753-5169
732-775-0803
Fax: 732-775-2274 www.carlstreit.com
Processor and wholesaler/distributor of poultry, Italian sausage and special cuts of beef, lamb, veal and pork
Owner: Jim Robinson Jr
VP: Judith Robinson
Estimated Sales: $10-20 Million
Number Employees: 5-9
Square Footage: 12000
Brands:
 Allen
 Hatfield

12167 Streit's
171 Rt 303
Orangeburg, NY 10962
845-359-9203
Fax: 845-359-9208 info@StreitsMatzos.com
www.streitsmatzos.com
Matzos and other kosher foods.
Executive VP: Aron Yagoda
Executive VP: Aaron Gross
Executive VP: Alan Adler
Estimated Sales: $5-10 Million
Number Employees: 50-99
Brands:
 Ethnic Delights
 Streits

12168 Stremick's Heritage Foods
4002 Westminster Ave
Santa Ana, CA 92703-1310
714-775-5000
Fax: 714-775-7677 800-371-9010
info@heritage-foods.com
www.stremicksheritagefoods.com
Milk, cheese and cream, organic milk and soy milk
President/CEO: Louis Stremick
CFO: Mike Malone
VP Foodservice Sales: Tom Gustafson
VP Quality Assurance: Jin Jo
VP Sales & Marketing: Dan Nolan
Sales Manager: Tom Gustafson
Estimated Sales: $45.5 Million
Number Employees: 100-249
Type of Packaging: Consumer, Food Service
Other Locations:
 Heritage Foods
 Riverside CA

12169 Stretch Island Fruit
P.O. Box 649
Solana Beach, CA 92075
800-700-9687
www.stretchislandfruit.com
Fruit snacks
Year Founded: 1976
Estimated Sales: $20-50 Million
Number Employees: 50-99
Square Footage: 12000
Type of Packaging: Consumer, Food Service
Brands:
 Stretch Island

12170 Stripling's General Store
1401 West Blvd
Moultrie, GA 31768-4223
229-985-4226
www.striplings.com
Beef and pork products including smoked sausage
President: Danny L Dunn
Number Employees: 5-9
Square Footage: 42000
Type of Packaging: Consumer
Other Locations:
 Stripling's General Store
 Cordele GA
Brands:
 Dunn's

12171 Stroh Brewery
100 River Place Dr # 100
Detroit, MI 48207-4278
313-446-2000
Fax: 313-446-2880
Beer
President/CEO: J Stroh
CEO: William L Henry
Sr Director Corporate Communications/PR: Lacey Logan
VP International Sales: Jovan Jovanovski
Contact: Stephen Ewing
estephen@skillman.org
Estimated Sales: $1-2.5 Million
Number Employees: 250-499
Parent Co: Pabst
Type of Packaging: Private Label

12172 Stroh's Beer
Detroit, MI
strohs-beer.com
Pilsners
Chairman & CEO: Eugene Kashper
CFO: Eric Tis
Chief Sales Officer: Brian Smith
Year Founded: 1850
Parent Co: Pabst Brewing Company

12173 Strong Roots
The Rootstock, Rm 3103
109 S 5th Street
Brooklyn, NY 11249
929-466-1639
hello@strongroots.com
www.strongroots.com
Plant-based prepared foods
CEO: Sam Dennigan

12174 Strossner's Bakery & Cafe
21 Roper Mountain Rd
Greenville, SC 29607-4125
864-233-2990
Fax: 864-232-2819
www.strossnerspoundcakes.com

Food Manufacturers / A-Z

Prepared European bread mixes, cakes, tortes, fancy pastries, danish and baked/partially baked breads
Owner: Richard Strossner
HR Executive: Carol Martin
info@strossners.com
Sales Manager: Mary Michalsky
Production Manager: Connie Jud
Estimated Sales: $2,000,000
Number Employees: 50-99
Square Footage: 56000
Type of Packaging: Consumer, Food Service

12175 Strub Pickles
100 Roy Boulevard
Brantford, ON N3R 7K2
Canada
519-751-1717
Fax: 519-752-5540 info@strubpickles.com
www.strubpickles.com
Sauerkraut, hot peppers, sweet pimientos, horseradish, herring, jalapeno peppers, kosher dill pickles and relish; exporter of pickles, refrigerated and shelf stable foods, zucchini relish and chili sauce
President: Leo Strub
CEO: Martin Strub
CFO: Arnold Strub
Vice President: Anoy Strub
Number Employees: 100-249
Number of Brands: 2
Number of Products: 250
Square Footage: 424000
Type of Packaging: Consumer, Food Service, Private Label, Bulk
Brands:
Strub's
Willie's

12176 Strube Celery & Vegetable Co
2404 S Wolcott Ave # 16
Unit 16-20
Chicago, IL 60608-5341
773-446-4000
Fax: 312-226-7644 www.strube.com
Wholesale fresh fruits & vegetable
President: David Watson
Chief Executive Officer: Janet Fleming
Chief Financial Officer: Lisa Strube
Executive Vice President: Sue Strube
Chief Technology Officer: Tom Davidson
Director, Sales: Suzy Trott
Estimated Sales: $30 Million
Number Employees: 50-99
Square Footage: 70000

12177 Stryker Sonoma
5110 Highway 128
Geyserville, CA 95441-9422
707-433-1944
Fax: 707-433-1948 800-433-1944
Wine
Owner: Craig Mac Donald
Owner: Karen Naley
Owner: Kat Stryker
Estimated Sales: Below $5 Million
Number Employees: 10-19
Brands:
Stryker Sonoma Winery Vineyards

12178 Stuart & CO
12 Mcguinness Blvd S
Apt 2B
Brooklyn, NY 11222-4995
347-292-7456
Fax: 212-202-3868
BBQ sauce, potato chips, spice blends and beef jerky
Founder: Michael Steifman
Type of Packaging: Food Service
Brands:
A-Salted
Bitchin'
Brooklyn Bourbon
Cherry Bomb
Dark & Moody
Lakehouse Lime & Chili
Marshall's Curry
Mr. Fancy's
No.5
Smoky's House

12179 Stuart Hale Co
4350 W Ohio St
Chicago, IL 60624-1051
773-638-1800
Fax: 773-638-1888 info@grandwarehouse.com
www.grandwarehouse.com
Bakers' supplies including bakery pan grease and pan and white mineral oils
President: David Schulman
support@stuarthale.com
General Manager: Stuart Schulman
Estimated Sales: $170000
Number Employees: 10-19
Type of Packaging: Private Label, Bulk

12180 Stubb's Legendary BBQ
811 Barton Springs Rd
Austin, TX 78704-8702
512-480-0203
Fax: 512-476-3425 800-227-2283
www.stubbsbbq.com
Rubs, sauces and marinades
Year Founded: 1968
Estimated Sales: $30 Million
Brands:
Stubb's

12181 Stumptown Coffee Roasters Inc
100 SE Salmon St
Portland, OR 97214-3370
503-230-7797
Fax: 503-230-7125 www.stumptowncoffee.com
Coffee
Owner: Duane Sorenson
Number Employees: 50-99

12182 Sturm Foods Inc
215 Center St
Manawa, WI 54949-9277
920-596-2511
Fax: 920-596-3040 800-347-8876
www.sturmfoods.com
Healthy drink mixes and supplements
President & CEO: Michael Upchurch
Manager: Rob Rugger
rrugger@sturminc.com
Number Employees: 250-499
Parent Co: TreeHouse Foods
Type of Packaging: Consumer, Food Service, Private Label, Bulk
Brands:
Vita Splash
Fulfill Fitness
Power Edge
Morning Spark
Replenish
Moo Magic
Frappe Creme
Cider Drink Mix
Mixer Stix Drink Mix
McCann's Irish Oatmeal
For Pet's Sake

12183 Stutz Candy Company
7306 Frankford Avenue
Philadelphia, PA 19136-3827
215-333-7323
888-692-2639
Candy including boxed chocolates
President: John Glaser
Estimated Sales: $3,100,000
Number Employees: 5 to 9
Square Footage: 42000
Type of Packaging: Consumer

12184 Subco Foods Inc
4350 S Taylor Dr
Sheboygan, WI 53081-8479
920-457-7761
Fax: 920-457-3899 800-473-0757
mkhan@subcofoods.com www.subcofoods.com
Contract packager/ Private label manufacturer products include: drink mixes, iced tea mixes, hot chocolate, gelatins, puddings, cappuccino mixes, coffee creamers, instant gravies, soup bases, spice/spice blends, cake mixes andnutraceuticals
President: Masroor Khan
Year Founded: 1925
Estimated Sales: $13,100,000
Number Employees: 50-99
Square Footage: 375000
Type of Packaging: Food Service, Private Label
Other Locations:
Subco Foods Inc
West Chicago IL
Brands:
New Image

12185 Sucesores de Pedro Cortes
Manuel Camunas #205, Tres Monjitas
PO BOX 363626
Hato Rey, PR 00918-1485
787-754-7040
Fax: 787-754-2650 cortesco@tld.net
www.chocolatecortes.com
Chocolate and cocoa products; private labeling available; importer of chocolate, milk drinks and crackers; wholesaler/distributor of confectionery items, beverages and biscuits
President: Ignacio Cortes Del Valle
VP: Ignacio Cortes Gelpi
Number Employees: 50-99
Number of Brands: 11
Square Footage: 150000
Type of Packaging: Consumer, Private Label, Bulk
Brands:
Chocolate Cortes
Choki
Semi-Industrialized

12186 SuckerPunch Gourmet
7525 W 99th Place
Bridgeview, IL 60455
708-784-3000
contact@suckerpunchgourmet.com
suckerpunchgourmet.com
Pickles, Bloody Mary mix and salsa
President & COO: Todd Francisco
tfrancisco@suckerpunchgourmet.com
Director of Finance: Jennifer Martens
Founder & Exec. VP: David van Alphen
Brands:
SUCKERPUNCH

12187 Sucre
3930 Euphrosine St
New Orleans, LA 70125-1309
504-708-4366
Fax: 504-708-4367 855-557-8273
info@shopsucre.com
Macarons, dark chocolate and chocolate gifts
Founder: Joel Dondis
Executive Pastry Chef: Tariq Hanna
Manager: Michelle Kuehne
Number Employees: 10-19

12188 Sucre
3930 Euphrosine St
New Orleans, LA 70125-1309
504-708-4366
info@shopsucre.com
Manufacturer of macarons, chocolates, confections, and cakes.
Founder: Joel Dondis
Executive Pastry Chef: Tariq Hanna
Manager: Michelle Kuehne
Number Employees: 10-19

12189 Sudbury Soups and Salads
40 Walker Farm Rd
Sudbury, MA 01776-2442
978-443-7715
Fax: 978-443-7715 888-783-7687
sudsoup@ultranet.com
Natural foods, dry soup mixes, lentils
CEO: Susan Sullivan
Brands:
Sudbury

12190 Sudlersville Frozen Food Locker
PO Box 203
Sudlersville, MD 21668-0203
410-438-3106
Fax: 410-438-3121
Frozen meat products including beef and pork
President: William Faust
Chairman: Ronald Ford
Bookkeeper: Marge Messner
Estimated Sales: Less than $500,000
Number Employees: 5-9
Type of Packaging: Consumer
Brands:
Sudlersville

Food Manufacturers / A-Z

12191 Sudwerk Privatbrauerei Hubsch
2001 2nd St
Davis, CA 95618-5474
530-758-8700
Fax: 530-753-0590 www.sudwerk.com
Beer
Owner: Tim Mc Donald
VP: Dean Unger
Quality Assurance: Candace Whalin
Marketing Director: Dave Sipes
Contact: Kb Brandl
kb@sudwerkbrew.com
Plant Manager/Purchasing Director: Neil Jensen
Estimated Sales: Below $5 Million
Number Employees: 50-99
Brands:
  Hubsch Doppel Bock
  Hubsch Dunkel
  Hubsch Lager
  Hubsch Marzen
  Hubsch Pilsener
  Suderwerk Doppel
  Suderwerk Dunkel
  Suderwerk Lager
  Suderwerk Mai Bock
  Suderwerk Marzen
  Suderwerk Pilsenser

12192 Sugai Kona Coffee
79-7098 Mamalahoa Hwy
Holualoa, HI 96725-8742
808-322-7717
Fax: 808-322-4008 kona@kona.net
www.sugaikonacoffee.com
Producers of Sugai Kona coffee
CEO: Lee Sugai
kona@kona.net
Estimated Sales: Less Than $500,000
Number Employees: 5-9
Number of Brands: 5
Number of Products: 30
Square Footage: 60000
Type of Packaging: Consumer, Food Service, Private Label, Bulk
Brands:
  Sugai Kona Grove Coffee
  Sugai Kona Coffee Emporium

12193 Sugar & Plumm
377 Amsterdam Ave
New York, NY 10024-6207
212-787-8778
Fax: 212-787-8780 info@sugarandplumm.com
www.sugarandplumm.com
Manufacturer of dark chocolate, truffles, boxed chocolate, macarons, and cookies.
Founder: Lamia Jacobs
CEO: Thierry Atlan
atlanthierry@sugarandplumm.com
Estimated Sales: Less Than $500,000
Number Employees: 1-4

12194 Sugar Bob's Smoked Maple Syrup
2564 Landgrove Rd
Londonderry, VT 05148
802-297-7665
sugarbobsfinestkind@gmail.com
www.sugarbobsfinestkind.com
Maple syrup
President & Sugarmaker: Robert F Hausslein
Estimated Sales: Under $500,000
Number Employees: 2-10
Brands:
  Sugar Bob's Finest Kind

12195 Sugar Bowl Bakery
1963 Sabre St
Hayward, CA 94545-1021
510-782-2118
Fax: 510-782-2119 888-688-1380
info@sugarbowlbakery.com
www.sugarbowlbakery.com
Baked goods, gourmet cakes and pastries.
Chief Executive Officer: Andrew Ly
Director of Finance: Peter Vermeulen
General Manager/Vice President: Michael Ly
Assistant General Manager: Kristine Trieu
Buyer: Urmi Mukherjee
Buyer: Paul Rivas
Director of Sales & Strategy: Pete Thomsen
Human Resources Manager: Theresa Martinez
Director of Operations: Frank Kieffer
navision@sugarbowlbakery.com
Chef/Process Manufacturing Manager: Kevin Ly
Purchasing Agent: Kevin Ly
Estimated Sales: $30-60 Million
Number Employees: 250-499
Square Footage: 120000

12196 Sugar Cane Growers Co-Op of Florida
1500 George Wedgworth Way
Belle Glade, FL 33430
561-996-5556
info@scgc.org
www.scgc.org
Sugar and blackstrap molasses.
Founder/Chair: George Wedgworth
CEO: Antonio Contreras
CFO: Brian Lohmann
Year Founded: 1960
Estimated Sales: $100 Million
Number Employees: 550
Number of Brands: 6
Type of Packaging: Consumer
Brands:
  Domino
  C&H
  Tate & Lyle
  Lyles Golden Syrup
  Sidul
  Sores

12197 Sugar Creek
2101 Kenskill Ave
Washington Ct Hs, OH 43160-9404
740-335-7440
Fax: 740-335-7443 800-848-8205
www.sugarcreek.com
Manufacturer of bacon and turkey bacon.
Chairman/CEO: John Richardson
COO: Michael Richardson
CFO: Tom Bollinger
tbollinger@sugar-creek.com
VP of Quality Assurance: Rob Howe
VP of Sales: Jim Coughlin
Plant Manager: Dan Sileo
Estimated Sales: $20 Million
Number Employees: 1000-4999
Number of Brands: 1
Type of Packaging: Consumer, Food Service, Bulk
Other Locations:
  Cincinnati OH
  Hamilton OH
  Frontenac KS
  Cambridge City IN
Brands:
  Sugar Creek

12198 Sugar Creek Winery
125 Boone Country Ln
Defiance, MO 63341-3103
636-987-2400
Fax: 636-987-2051 info@sugarcreekwines.com
www.sugarcreekwines.com
Wines
Owner: Ken Miller
kmiller@sugarcreekwines.com
President: Wesley Wissman
Estimated Sales: $5-10 Million
Number Employees: 20-49

12199 Sugar Flowers Plus
601 Vine St
Glendale, CA 91204
818-545-3592
Fax: 818-545-7459 800-972-2935
Cake decorations including gum paste flowers
Owner: Terry Becker
R&D: Anna Becker
Sales: Garrick Wright
Plant Manager: Gary Roundtree
Estimated Sales: $.5-1 million
Number Employees: 1-4
Type of Packaging: Consumer, Food Service
Brands:
  Sugar Flowers

12200 Sugar Foods Corp
9500 El Dorado Ave
Sun Valley, CA 91352-1339
818-768-7900
Fax: 818-768-7619 info@sugarfoods.com
www.sugarfoods.com
Contract packager and exporter of dry entrees, side dishes, mixes including snack, nondairy creamer, sugar and sugar substitutes and croutons in bags, pouches, cups, cartons and canisters
President: Stephen O'Dell
sodell@sugarfoods.com
Operations Manager: Brian Thomson
Estimated Sales: $8500000
Number Employees: 250-499
Square Footage: 1400000
Parent Co: Sugar Foods Corporation

12201 Sugar Foods Corp
950 3rd Ave
12st Fl
New York, NY 10022
info@sugarfoods.com
www.sugarfoods.com
Sweetners, non dairy creamers, croutons, stuffing mixes, crumbs/cracker meal, snacks & snack mixes, specialty items, and almonds.
Chairman & CEO: Donald Tober
COO: James Walsh
jwalsh@sugarfoods.com
Year Founded: 1948
Number Employees: 500-999
Type of Packaging: Consumer, Food Service
Brands:
  Almond Toppers
  Blue Diamond
  C&H
  Crisp 'n Fresh
  Fresh Gourmet
  Natrataste
  Non Dairy Toppings
  Sugar In the Raw
  Supersnax
  Sweet 'n Low
  True Lemon

12202 Sugar Plum
88 Dilley St # 2
Kingston, PA 18704-3437
570-288-0559
Fax: 570-288-1710 800-447-8427
customerservice@sugar-plum.com
Chocolate covered potato chips, chocolate covered pretzels and chocolate covered popcorn.
Owner: Frann Edley
frann@sugar-plum.com
Estimated Sales: Less Than $500,000
Number Employees: 1-4
Brands:
  Dip Sticks
  Get Popped
  Supremes

12203 Sugar Plum LLC
5756 W Main St
Houma, LA 70360-1745
985-872-9524
Fax: 985-872-9664
Designer cakes, wedding cakes, holiday cakes, confectionary, and various other desserts
Owner: Cindy Dugas
thesugarplum1@comcast.net
Number Employees: 10-19
Square Footage: 10000

12204 Sugar Sugar
465 S. Orlando Ave
#205
Maitland, FL 32751
877-784-2724
Fax: 877-249-6419 info@handmadelollies.com
www.handmadelollies.com
Candy lollipops

12205 SugarCreek
12021 Sheraton Lane
Cincinnati, OH 45246
479-968-1005
Fax: 479-968-5651 800-445-2715
sales@sugarcreek.com www.sugarcreek.com
Pork bacon, turkey bacon, chicken bacon, sausage links and patties, flat surface proteins, large scale sous vide, meatballs

Food Manufacturers / A-Z

Chairman & CEO: John G Richardson
Chief Operating Officer: Michael Richardson
Chief Financial Officer: Thomas J Bollinger
VP, Sales & Business Development: Alan Riney
Director of Sales: Jennifer Hutcheson
EVP, Operations: Mike Rozzano
Estimated Sales: $20-50 Million
Number Employees: 700
Square Footage: 25000
Type of Packaging: Private Label

12206 Sugarbush Farm
591 Sugarbush Farm Rd
Woodstock, VT 05091-8089
802-457-1757
Fax: 802-457-3269   800-281-1757
contact@sugarbushfarm.com
www.sugarbushfarm.com
Waxed cheeses and Pure Vermont Maple Syrup
President: Elizabeth Luce
sugarbsh@sover.net
Vice President: Jeff Luce
Estimated Sales: $.5-1 million
Number Employees: 5-9

12207 Sugardale Foods Inc
800-860-6333
www.sugardale.com
Bacon, ham, hot dogs, lunch meats and weiners.
VP of Corporate Sales: Mark Slaughter
Estimated Sales: $100-500 Million
Number Employees: 500-999

12208 Sugarman of Vermont
P.O.Box 1060
Hardwick, VT 05843
802-472-9891
Fax: 802-472-8526   800-932-7700
sales@sugarmanofvermont.com
www.sugarmanofvermont.com
Processor and exporter of jams, jellies, marmalades and preserves; processor and exporter of maple syrup
President: Anthony Sedutto
Contact: Marilyn Rogerson
m.rogerson@sugarmanofvermont.com
Number Employees: 20-49
Square Footage: 160000
Type of Packaging: Consumer, Food Service, Private Label, Bulk
Brands:
   Sugarman

12209 Sugarplum Desserts
20381 62nd Avenue
Building 5
Langley, BC V3A SE6
Canada
604-534-2282
Fax: 604-534-2280 info@sugarplumdesserts.com
www.sugarplumdesserts.com
Thaw and serve cheesecakes and thaw and bake cookies
President: Leslie Goodman
Number Employees: 15
Square Footage: 32000

12210 Sugarright
Fairless Hills, PA
215-486-2105
sales@sugaright.com
www.sugaright.com
Various types of sugar and syrups.
President: Paul Farmer
Year Founded: 2016
Type of Packaging: Food Service, Bulk

12211 Suity Confections Co
8105 NW 77th St.
P.O. Box 558943
Miami, FL 33166
305-639-3300
Fax: 305-593-7070 info@suity.com
www.suity.com
Candy, gum, chocolates, and cookies
VP: Jose Garrido Jr
garridojr@waltonpost.com
Quality Control: Luis Perez
Estimated Sales: $20-50 Million
Number Employees: 20-49
Brands:
   Bubble Gum
   Fruiticas Lollipops
   Fruity Ball

Party Snacks
Salty Snacks

12212 Suiza Dairy Corporation
131 Ave De Diego
San Juan, PR 00921
787-707-6500
earias@suizapr.com
www.suizapuertorico.com
Dairy Products
President: Carmen Marrero
Estimated Sales: $100-500 Million
Parent Co: Suiza Foods
Type of Packaging: Private Label

12213 Suja Juice
3831 Ocean Ranch Blvd
Oceanside, CA 92056
855-879-7852
info@sujajuice.com
www.sujajuice.com
Nutritious drinks
Co-Founder: Annie Lawless
CEO & Co-Founder: Jeff Church
Vice President, Sales: Jessica Pratt
Estimated Sales: $48.6 Million
Number Employees: 175
Brands:
   Suja

12214 Suji's Korean Cuisine
71 Columbia St
Suite 125
Seattle, WA 98104
206-985-6640
www.sujiskorean.com
Korean BBQ, meals and sauces
Founder: Suji Park

12215 Sukhi's Gourmet Indian Food
23682 Clawiter Rd
Hayward, CA 94545-1329
510-264-9265
Fax: 510-264-1236   888-478-5447
info@sukhis.com www.sukhis.com
Gourmet indian food
President/Owner: Sukhi Singh
Number Employees: 50-99

12216 Sullivan Harbor Farm
1545 U.S. Route 1
Hancock Village, ME 04640
207-422-2209
Fax: 207-422-8229   800-422-4014
sullivanharborfarm@verizon.net
www.sullivanharborfarm.com
Smoked salmon
Owner: Joel Franzman
Estimated Sales: $300,000-500,000
Number Employees: 1-4

12217 Sullivan Vineyards
1090 Galleron Rd
St Helena, CA 94574-9540
707-963-9646
Fax: 707-963-0377   877-244-7337
www.sullivanwine.com
Wines
CEO: Joanna C Sullivan
CFO: Sean Sullivan
VP Marketing: Kelleen Sullivan
Operations Manager: Ross Sullivan
Estimated Sales: Below $5 Million
Number Employees: 5-9
Type of Packaging: Private Label
Brands:
   Sullivan Cabernet Sauvignon
   Sullivan Chardonnay
   Sullivan Coeur De Vigne
   Sullivan Merlot

12218 Sulpice Chocolate
121 Barrington Commons Ct # A
Barrington, IL 60010-3256
630-301-2345
info@sulpicechocolat.com
www.sulpicechocolat.com
Manufacturer of dark chocolate bars.
Founder: Anne Shaeffer
anne.shaeffer@sulpicechocolat.com
Number Employees: 5-9
Brands:
   Sulpice

12219 Summer Fresh
334 Rowntree Dairy Rd
Woodbridge, ON L4L 8H2
Canada
905-856-8816
Fax: 905-856-9298   877-472-5237
social@summerfresh.com www.summerfresh.com
Salads, dips, snacks and hummus
President: Susan Niczowski
CFO: Gilles Hamel
VP, Sales: Lynn Sandell
Director, Operations: Dane Adams
Senior Manager, Production: Predrag Knezevic
Estimated Sales: $100 Million
Number Employees: 51-200
Type of Packaging: Private Label
Brands:
   Summer Fresh

12220 Summer Garden Food Manufacturing
500 McClurg Rd
Boardman, OH 44512
330-965-8455
Fax: 330-965-3864 info@summergardenfood.com
www.summergardenfood.com
Private label foods including Italian pasta sauces, cream based sauces, meat and fish sauces, specialty and finishing sauces, bbq and wing sauces, and salsas. Also, soups, simmer sauces, and marinades and dressings
Owner and CEO: Thomas R. Zidian
CFO: John Angelilli
VP: Anthony Larocca
Quality Control Manager: Sean Doering
Contact: John Angelilli
johna@summergardenfood.com
Manager: Rick Coradini
Estimated Sales: $1.3 Million
Number Employees: 20
Square Footage: 100000
Type of Packaging: Consumer, Private Label, Bulk

12221 Summer In Vermont Jams
686 Davis Rd
Hinesburg, VT 05461-9359
802-453-3793
Homegrown, homemade jams and jellies.
President: Norma Norris
Estimated Sales: $.5-1 million
Number Employees: 1-4

12222 Summerfield Farm Products
4206 Twymans Mill Rd
Orange, VA 22960-4850
540-547-9600
Fax: 540-547-9628   800-898-3276
www.summerfieldfarm.com
Free-range veal, venison, salmon and condiments
President: Jamie Nicoll
Marketing Manager: Mary Thornton
Financial Manager: Carolyn Mills
Accounts Receivable: Barbara Frazier
Estimated Sales: Below $5 Million
Number Employees: 10
Brands:
   Summerfield Farms

12223 Summerfield Foods
335 Shiloh Valley Ct
Santa Rosa, CA 95403-8085
707-579-3938
Fax: 707-579-8442 sales@summerfieldfoods.com
Contract packager and exporter of canned vegetarian foods including refried beans, soups and chili; also, cookies and cakes; private labeling available
President: Roland Au
roland@summerfieldfoods.com
Executive VP: John Stanghellini
Estimated Sales: $2000000
Number Employees: 5-9
Type of Packaging: Consumer, Private Label
Brands:
   Summerfield's

12224 Summerland Sweets
6206 Canyon View Road
Summerland, BC V0H 1Z7
Canada
250-494-0377
Fax: 250-494-7432   800-577-1277
summerlandsweets@telus.net
www.summerlandsweets.com

Canner of fruit candy/pectin jelly including apricot, cherry and apple; also, fruit leather, gourmet jam, fruit syrup and fruit pulp
President: Frances Beulah
Estimated Sales: $1,200,000
Number Employees: 10
Number of Brands: 2
Number of Products: 40
Type of Packaging: Food Service, Private Label

12225 Summit Brewing Company
910 Montreal Cir
Saint Paul, MN 55102
651-265-7800
Fax: 651-265-7801 info@summitbrewing.com
www.summitbrewing.com
Brewer of beer
President: Mark Stutrud
Contact: Derek Allmendinger
allmendinger.derek@summitbrewing.com
Operations Manager: Christopher Seitz
Production Manager: Jon Lindberg
Number Employees: 20-49
Square Footage: 232000
Brands:
Summit

12226 Summit Hill Flavors
21 Worlds Fair Drive
Somerset, NJ 08873
732-805-0335
Fax: 732-805-1994 www.summithillflavors.com
Natural flavorings for dry and liquid applications used for marinating meats and poultry. Flavorings for soups, gravies, sauces, food bases and pasta dishes.
Contact: Selvin Medina
medinaselvin@summithillflavors.com

12227 Summit Lake Vineyards
2000 Summit Lake Dr
Angwin, CA 94508-9778
707-965-2488
Fax: 707-965-2281
www.summitlakevineyards.securecheckout.com
Wines
Owner: Robert Brakesman
summitlake@summitlakevineyards.com
CEO: Heather Griffin
Marketing Director: Heather Griffin
Estimated Sales: $200,000-$300,000
Number Employees: 1-4
Number of Brands: 3
Number of Products: 3
Brands:
Clair Riley Zinfandel Port
Emily Kestral Cabern
Summit Lake Vinyards

12228 Sun Chlorella USA
3305 Kashiwa Street
Torrance, CA 90505-4022
310-891-0600
Fax: 310-891-0621 800-829-2828
www.sunchlorellausa.com
Ginseng and chlorella including tablets, liquid extract and green single cell algae with broken cell walls
President/CEO: Futoshi Nakayama
VP/Chief Financial Officer: Ellen Kubijanto
VP/Chief Operating Officer: Rose Straub
Marketing Manager: Susan Arboua
Public Relations: Janise Zantine
Estimated Sales: $24 Million
Number Employees: 61
Square Footage: 5000
Parent Co: YSK International Corporation
Brands:
Green Magician
Sun Chlorella
Sun Siberian Ginseng
Wakasa

12229 Sun Empire Foods
P.O.Box 376
Kerman, CA 93630-0376
559-846-8208
Fax: 559-846-9488 800-252-4786
Hand made coated delicacies
Co-Owner: Phil Dee
Co-Owner: Sandy Dee
Estimated Sales: $.5-1 million
Number Employees: 5-9
Number of Products: 100

Type of Packaging: Consumer

12230 Sun Garden Sprouts
1011 Volunteer Drive
Cookeville, TN 38506
931-400-2710
www.sproutnet.com
Bean sprouts
President: Robert Rust
Marketing: Kelly Warren
Estimated Sales: $5-10 Million
Number Employees: 20-49
Brands:
Sun Garden Sprouts

12231 Sun Glo Of Idaho
378 S 7th W
PO Box 300
Sugar City, ID 83448-5009
208-356-7346
Fax: 208-356-7351 bruce@sunglo-idaho.com
www.sungloidaho.com
Idaho potatoes
CEO: George M Crapo
george@sunglo-idaho.com
CEO: George Crapo
CFO: Bruce Crapo
VP Fresh Sales: Betty Miles
Human Resource Manager: Melissa Coles
Number Employees: 100-249
Type of Packaging: Consumer, Food Service, Private Label, Bulk
Brands:
Sun Supreme
Sun-Glo
Top Bakes

12232 Sun Grove Foods Inc
45 Tulip St
Passaic, NJ 07055-3133
973-574-1110
Fax: 973-574-1113 info@sungrovefoods.com
www.sungrovefoods.com
Olive oils.
Executive Vice President: Joanna Lacina
Contact: Ed Cekici
ecekici@sungrovefoods.com
Number Employees: 5-9

12233 Sun Groves Inc
3393 State Road 580
Safety Harbor, FL 34695-4931
727-726-8484
Fax: 727-726-7158 800-672-6438
www.sungroves.com
Citrus fruits, gift baskets, preserves, and fudge
Owner: Michelle Urbanski
Estimated Sales: $20-50 Million
Number Employees: 20-49
Brands:
Sun Groves

12234 Sun Harvest Foods Inc
6201 Progressive Dr # 400
Suite 400
San Diego, CA 92154-6651
619-661-0909
Fax: 619-690-1173 www.productosfrugo.com.mx
Processor, importer and exporter of IQF entrees, canned vegetables, jalapenos, tomatillo, sauces, salsa, broccoli, cauliflower, vegetable blends and fruit; kosher items available
President: Jorge Gonzalez
Sales & Marketing: Art Sanchez
Estimated Sales: $1.4 Million
Number Employees: 1-4
Square Footage: 640000
Parent Co: Productos Frugo S.A. de C.V.
Type of Packaging: Consumer, Food Service, Private Label, Bulk
Brands:
Secret Sun

12235 Sun Noodle
1933 Colburn St
Honolulu, HI 96819-3248
808-841-5808
Fax: 808-842-7622 info@sunnoodle.com
www.sunnoodle.com
Japanese style noodles
President: Hidehito Uki
Contact: Kenshiro Uki
kenshiro@sunnoodle.com

Estimated Sales: $2.5-5 Million
Number Employees: 5-9

12236 Sun Noodle New Jersey
40 Kero Road
Carlstadt, NJ 07072
201-530-1100
www.sunnoodle.com
Ramen noodles, yakisoba, udon, and soba noodles, ramen soup.
CEO: Hidehito Uki
Number Employees: 80
Square Footage: 10000

12237 Sun Olive Oil Company
4668 Town Crossing Drive
Suite 109
Jacksonville, FL 32246
904-645-6630
Fax: 805-434-0626 www.sunoliveoil.com
Olive oil
President: Rory Muniz
Brands:
Sun Olive Oil

12238 Sun Opta Inc.
2233 Argentia Rd.
Sutie 401
Mississauga, ON L5N 2X7
Canada
952-820-2518
info@sunopta.com
www.sunopta.com
Organic, non-GMO raw materials such as soy, corn, sunflower and coconut.
CEO: Joseph Ennen
CAO: Jill Barnett
CFO: Scott Huckins
Chief Information Officer: Rob Duchscher
Chief Quality Officer: David Largey
SVP, Supply Chain: Christopher Whitehair
Year Founded: 1973
Estimated Sales: $1,3 Billion
Number Employees: 1,300+
Type of Packaging: Consumer, Food Service, Bulk
Brands:
Sunrich Naturals
Nature's Finest
Pure Nature

12239 Sun Orchard INC
1200 S 30th St
Haines City, FL 33844-9099
863-422-5062
Fax: 863-422-5176 877-875-8423
www.sunorchard.com
Manufacturer of citrus fruits and juices.
President/CEO: Marc Isaacs
CFO: Thomas Spielberger
SVP, Strategy & Planning: Peter Maulbeck
Manager: Tom Winter
Estimated Sales: $20-50 Million
Number Employees: 100-249
Number of Brands: 4
Parent Co: Sun Orchard, Inc.
Type of Packaging: Food Service, Private Label
Brands:
EPIC
fOMZ
Fruit 66
Sun Orchard

12240 Sun Orchard Inc
2 South Biscayne Blvd.
Miami, FL 33131
786-646-9200
800-505-8423
info@sunorchard.com www.sunorchard.com
Juices including orange, grapefruit, lemon and lime; also, apple cider, lemonade, margarita mix and granita slushes
President/CEO: Marc Isaacs
CFO: Carl Colletti
SVP Sales: Bob Corlett
VP, Product Innovation: Tony Decastro
VP, Purchasing: Chris Hess
Estimated Sales: $20-50 Million
Number Employees: 50-99
Square Footage: 40000
Type of Packaging: Consumer, Food Service, Private Label, Bulk
Brands:
Sun Orchards Labels

Food Manufacturers / A-Z

12241 (HQ)Sun Pac Foods
10 Sun Pac Boulevard
Brampton, ON L6S 4R5
Canada
905-792-2700
Fax: 905-792-8490
Processor and contract packager of canned fruit juices, drinks and concentrates, bread crumbs, croutons and tortilla chips; importer of canned seafood and mandarin orange sections; exporter of juices and drinks
President: J Riddell
VP Finance: Vince McEwan
VP Imports/Exports: Cathy Knowles
Number Employees: 135
Square Footage: 1420000
Type of Packaging: Consumer, Food Service, Private Label, Bulk
Brands:
 Featherweight
 Fiesta
 McDowell Ovens
 Saico
 Sun Crop
 Sun Pac

12242 Sun Pacific
1095 E Green St
Pasadena, CA 91106
213-612-9957
customercare@sunpacific.com
www.sunpacific.com
Grower, exporter and shipper of produce
Founder: Berne Evans
berneevans@sunpacfic.com
Estimated Sales: $120,000
Number Employees: 20-49
Square Footage: 2310
Brands:
 Cuties(c)
 Mighties

12243 Sun Ray International
1260 Lake Blvd
Davis, CA 95616
530-297-1688
Fax: 530-758-0089 sales@sunraygroup.net
www.sunraygroup.net
Agricultural food ingredients such as dehydrated onion, garlic, tomato and other vegetable products.
Contact: Jihua Lui
jihua.lui@sunraygroup.net

12244 Sun Rich Fresh Foods USA Inc
515 E Rincon St
Corona, CA 92879-1391
951-735-3800
Fax: 951-735-3322 800-735-3801
customerservice@sun-rich.com www.sunrich.com
Fresh cut fruit
Vice President: Roxanne Emmerling
roxannee@sun-rich.com
EVP/CFO: Neville Israel
Vice President of Supply Chain: Jeff Pitchford
Quality Assurance Technician: Daysi Aleman
Sales/Marketing Coordinator: Lisa Ten Heggeler
Vice President of Sales and Marketing: Cam Haygarth
HR Manager: Sylvia Del Rio
roxannee@sun-rich.com
VP Operations: Dan O'Connell
Senior Production Manager: Javier Lopez
Number Employees: 100-249
Square Footage: 66000
Type of Packaging: Consumer, Food Service
Other Locations:
 Vancouver, Canada
 Los Angeles CA
 Toronto, Canada
 Reading PA

12245 Sun State Beverage
2442 Pleasant Hill Rd
Atlanta, GA 30349
770-451-3990
Fax: 770-813-0065
Beverages
President: John Son
Estimated Sales: $2.5-5 000,000
Number Employees: 1-4

12246 Sun States
PO Box 25965
Charlotte, NC 28229-5965
704-821-0615
Fax: 704-821-0616
Cheese
Marketing Director: Marty Crosby

12247 Sun Sun Food Products
14415 115th Avenue NW
Edmonton, AB T5M 3B8
Canada
780-454-4261
Fax: 780-453-1728
Oriental foods including bean sprouts, steamed noodles and wonton and egg roll wrappers
Manager: Ken Nhan
Type of Packaging: Food Service
Brands:
 Sun Sun

12248 Sun Tropics Inc
2430 Camino Ramon
Suite 111
San Ramon, CA 94583-4214
925-380-6324
Fax: 925-202-2223 www.suntropics.net
Juice, cider, ice cream, sorbet
President: Sharon Sy
Contact: Rhonda Lowry
rlowry@suntropics.net
Estimated Sales: 2,200,000
Number Employees: 5-9

12249 Sun Valley Mustard
731 1st Ave N
Hailey, ID 83333-5024
208-578-0078
Fax: 208-785-0216 800-628-7124
bstuns@cs.com www.sunvalleymustard.com
Mustard
President: Latham Williams
General Manager: Barbara Stuns
Estimated Sales: Under $500,000
Number Employees: 1-4
Brands:
 Sun Valley Mustard

12250 Sun Valley Packing
7381 Avenue 432
Reedley, CA 93654-9016
559-591-1515
Fax: 559-591-1616 sunvaly@mobynet.com
Plums, peaches and nectarines
Owner: Walter Jones
wjones@sunvalley.com
Number Employees: 250-499
Brands:
 Kay Pak

12251 Sun Valley Raisins Inc
9595 S Hughes Ave
Fresno, CA 93706-9731
559-233-8070
Fax: 559-233-8075 info@sunvalleyraisins.com
www.sunvalleyraisins.com
Premium raisins from California's Central Valley for over 70 years.
Manager: Charles Degeneres
chuck@sunvalleyraisins.com
Number Employees: 5-9
Type of Packaging: Bulk
Brands:
 Sun Valley

12252 Sun West
2281 W 205th Street
Torrance, CA 90501-1450
310-320-4000
Fax: 310-320-8444
Distributor of rice based sweetners and rice based proteins
President: Qasim Habib
Estimated Sales: $2.5-5 Million
Number Employees: 5

12253 Sun West Foods
1550 Drew Avenue
Suite 150
Davis, CA 95618-7852
530-758-8550
Fax: 530-758-8110 nor-calrice@saber.net
www.sunwestfoods.com
Grower/packer of processed wild rice; developer of proprietary wild rice varieties and specialty rices; processor of quick-cook wild and brown rice. Specializes in ingredient sales to packers and ingredient users
President: James Errecarte
Contact: Rebecca Baxter
rbaxter@sunwestfoods.com
Estimated Sales: $5-10 Million
Number Employees: 10-19
Square Footage: 92000
Type of Packaging: Food Service, Private Label, Bulk
Brands:
 Nor-Cal

12254 (HQ)Sun World Intl LLC
73161 Fred Waring Dr
Suite 200
Palm Desert, CA 92260
760-398-9450
www.sun-world.com
Fresh fruits and vegetables ranging from apricots, peaches, nectarines and grapes to tangerines, grapefruit, lemons and oranges to sweet colored peppers and seedless watermelon. Also Medjool dates and Deglet Noor dates.
President: David Marguleas
EVP & CFO: Keith Mitchell
EVP, Business Development: Jeff Jackson
Marketing Manager: Dan, Joubert
Year Founded: 1976
Estimated Sales: $231.70 Million
Number Employees: 200-499
Type of Packaging: Private Label

12255 Sun-Brite Canning
1532 County Rd 34
Kingsville, ON N0P 2G0
Canada
519-326-9033
Fax: 519-326-8700 www.sun-brite.com
Tomato canners
President: Henry Iacobelli
Director of Sales: John Iacobelli
Plant Manager: Sam Lopez
Number Employees: 50-99
Type of Packaging: Consumer, Food Service, Private Label

12256 Sun-Maid Growers of California
13525 S Bethel Ave
Kingsburg, CA 93631-9232
559-896-8000
Fax: 559-897-2362 info@sunmaid.com
www.sunmaid.com
Sun-dried fruits including raisins, peaches, apricots and pears; raisin paste and juice concentrate
President & CEO: Harry Overly
Number Employees: 500-999
Type of Packaging: Consumer, Food Service, Private Label, Bulk
Brands:
 Sun-Maid

12257 Sun-Re Cheese Co
178 Lenker Ave
Sunbury, PA 17801-2902
570-286-1511
Fax: 570-286-5123
Italian cheeses including pizza, mozzarella and ricotta
Owner: Thomas Aiello
thomas@strausmilk.com
Plant Manager: Gary Deates
Estimated Sales: $6.4 Million
Number Employees: 50-99
Square Footage: 224000
Type of Packaging: Consumer, Food Service, Private Label, Bulk

12258 Sun-Rise
3423 Casa Marina Road NW
Alexandria, MN 56308-9058
320-846-5720
Beverages
President: John Sherman
Brands:
 Sun-Rise Beverages

Food Manufacturers / A-Z

12259 Sun-Rype Products
1165 Ethel St
Kelowna, BC V1Y 2W4
Canada
888-786-7973
www.sunrype.com
Juice and fruit snacks and also organic fruit snacks.
President & CEO: Lesli Bradley
Manager, Strategic Growth: Cindy Wilker
Year Founded: 1946
Estimated Sales: $148 Million
Number Employees: 335
Square Footage: 123602
Type of Packaging: Consumer, Food Service, Private Label, Bulk
Brands:
  Energy-To-Go
  Fruit-To-Go
  Sun-Rype

12260 SunButter
PO Box 3022
Fargo, ND 58108
Fax: 701-282-5325 877-873-4501
sunbutter.com
Sunbutter, a nut spread made from sunflower seeds; whole sunflower seeds and trail mixes.
CEO: Rob Majkrzak
CFO: Randy Wigen
VP: Dan Hofland
VP Marketing: Dan Hofland
Contact: Nick Deutz
nickd@sunbutter.com
Operations Manager: Brad Newton
Number Employees: 200
Type of Packaging: Consumer, Food Service, Private Label, Bulk

12261 SunFed Ranch
203 Court St
Woodland, CA 95695
530-723-5373
sunfedranch.com
Beef products
President/Owner: Matt Byrne

12262 (HQ)SunWest Foods, Inc.
1550 Drew Avenue
Suite 150
Davis, CA 95618
530-758-8550
Fax: 530-758-8110 www.sunwestfoods.com
Processor and exporter of regular, organic and wild rice; also, walnuts, almonds, pistachios and pecans.
Contact: Jess Errecarte
jess@sunwestfoods.com
Year Founded: 1991
Brands:
  Nutririte
  Sunnuts
  Sunwest

12263 SunWest Organics
1550 Drew Ave
Suite 150
Davis, CA 95618-7852
530-758-8550
Fax: 530-758-8110 www.sunwestfoods.com
Organic brown, pilaf, wild mix, wild and crisp rice
President: James Errecarte
Estimated Sales: $20-50 Million
Number Employees: 10-19
Square Footage: 30000

12264 Sunburst Foods
1002 Sunburst Dr
Goldsboro, NC 27534
919-778-2151
Fax: 919-778-9203
Processor and wholesaler/distributor of prepacked sandwiches
President: Ray Lewis
Chairman: B Darden
Vice President: Lori Moss
Maintenance Manager: Bill Sugg
Estimated Sales: $13 Million
Number Employees: 150
Square Footage: 150000
Type of Packaging: Consumer

12265 Sunburst Trout Farms
314 Industrial Park Drive
Waynesville, NC 28786
800-673-3051
www.sunbursttrout.com
Trout fillets, caviar and gift baskets
CEO: Sally Eason
Chief Financial Officer: Benjamin Eason
Marketing & HR Director: Anna Eason
Sales & Processing Manager: Wes Eason
Office Manager: Stephanie Strickland
Year Founded: 1948
Number Employees: 11-50
Type of Packaging: Food Service
Brands:
  Sunburst Trout Farms

12266 Sunchef Farms
4722 Everett Avenue
Vernon, CA 90058-3133
323-588-5800
Fax: 323-588-2285
Portion-controlled chicken including marinated and flavored products
President: Steve Tsatas

12267 Sunco & Frenchie
489 Getty Avenue
Clifton, NJ 07011
Fax: 973-478-1063 973-478-1011
www.sunconatural.com
Dried fruits, nuts, granola, raw sugar, quick oats, corn meal, and juice.
Co-Owner: Joel Ammar
Year Founded: 2009
Estimated Sales: $1-5 Million
Number Employees: 15
Brands:
  Frenchie(c)
  Sunbest(c)
  Sunco(c)

12268 Suncrest Farms
1336 Bethany Church Rd.
Princeton, KY 42445-5259
973-595-0214
Fax: 973-595-0214 www.suncrestfarms.com
Ham
Owner: E L Scott
Estimated Sales: Less than $500,000
Number Employees: 1-4
Brands:
  Suncrest Farms

12269 Sundance Industries
P.O.Box 1446
Newburgh, NY 12551-1446
845-565-6065
Fax: 845-562-5699 sundanceind@verizon.net
www.sundanceind.com
Wheateena wheatgrass juicers.
President/CEO: Alden Link
Office Manager: Valerie Lynn
Estimated Sales: $1-3 Million
Number Employees: 1-4
Number of Brands: 1
Number of Products: 9
Square Footage: 56000
Type of Packaging: Consumer
Brands:
  Wheateena

12270 Sunday House Foods
Sunco Avenue
Fredericksburg, TX 78624
830-997-2136
Fax: 830-997-6056
Smoked Turkey Products
President: Richard Dillow
CFO: Dan Mittel
Vice President: Steve Foucort
VP Sales: Michael Quint
Operations Manager: Larry Wray
Purchasing Manager: Ross Allen
Estimated Sales: $25-49.9 Million
Number Employees: 250-499
Parent Co: Granada Foods Corporation
Type of Packaging: Private Label
Brands:
  Hill Country
  Sunday House

12271 Sundia Corp
70 Washington St # 425
Suite 425
Oakland, CA 94607-3705
415-762-0600
sales@sundiacorp.com
www.sundiafruit.com
Fruit cups
Vice President: Mark Sherburne
mark@sundiacorp.com
CEO: Jim Watkins
VP Finance: Alex Auseklis
Founder/Chairman: Bradford Oberwager
VP Sales: Mark Sherburne
Chief Operating Officer: James Kairos
Estimated Sales: $7 Million
Number Employees: 10-19
Square Footage: 3200

12272 Sundial Herb Garden
59 Hidden Lake Rd
Higganum, CT 06441-4441
860-345-4290
Fax: 860-345-3462 sundial9@localnet.com
www.sundialgardens.com
Spices, herb blends, tea cake and scone mixes including hazelnut, pumpkin-ginger, cranberry and traditional; importer of rare and herbal teas
Owner: Ragna Goddard
VP: Thomas Goddard
Estimated Sales: Less Than $500,000
Number Employees: 1-4
Square Footage: 10000
Type of Packaging: Consumer
Brands:
  Ceylon Teas
  China Teas
  Herbal Teas
  India Teas
  Mulling Cider
  Sundial Blend Teas
  Sundial Gardens

12273 Sunergia Soyfoods
1125 Little High St
Charlottesville, VA 22902
434-970-2798
Fax: 801-437-3484 800-693-5134
Seasoned tofu. Includes ten delicious flavors such as italian herb, savory portabella, peanut & ginger, indian masala, spicy thai, garlic shitake, porcini herb, spinach jalapeno, pesto and spicy indian.
President: Jon Kessler
Vice President: John Raphaelidis
Sales Manager: Marsha Burger
Operations Manager: Jon Kessler
Estimated Sales: $200,000
Number Employees: 3
Number of Brands: 2
Number of Products: 13
Type of Packaging: Consumer, Food Service, Private Label, Bulk
Brands:
  More-Than-Tofu
  Sunergia Breakfast Style Sausage
  Sunergia More Than Tofu Garlic
  Sunergia More Than Tofu Herbs
  Sunergia More Than Tofu Porcinis
  Sunergia More Than Tofu Savories
  Sunergia More-Than-Tofu
  Sunergia Organic Soy Sausage
  Sunergia Smoked Portabella Sausage

12274 Sunfood
1830 Gillespie Way
Suite 101
El Cajon, CA 92020-0922
619-596-7979
Fax: 619-596-7997 888-729-3663
support@sunfood.com www.sunfood.com
Goji berries, raw cacao, goldenberries, and maqui.
President: Doug Harbison
CEO: Matt Alonso
matt.alonso@sunfood.com
CFO: Deion Stromenger
Chief Marketing Officer: Eric Cutler
Sales Executive: Sara Thompson
Operations Director: Jack Wortman
Facilities Manager: Jerome Fodor
Number Employees: 20-49
Type of Packaging: Consumer, Bulk

Food Manufacturers / A-Z

12275 Sunfresh Beverages Inc.
111 Oxmoor Road
Birmingham, AL 35209
706-324-0040
www.buffalorock.com
Producer of soft drinks and fruit beverages.
Chairman/CEO: James Lee
Estimated Sales: $5-9 Million
Number Employees: 50-99
Number of Brands: 1
Parent Co: Buffalo Rock Company
Type of Packaging: Consumer, Food Service
Brands:
 Sunfresh

12276 Sunfresh Foods
125 S Kenyon St
Seattle, WA 98108-4207
206-764-0940
Fax: 206-764-0960 800-669-9625
www.sunfreshjams.com
Uncooked freezer jams and fruit sauces
President: David Allison
david.allison@schwab.com
VP Marketing: Jerry Brozowski
Estimated Sales: Below $5 Million
Number Employees: 5-9
Type of Packaging: Food Service, Private Label
Brands:
 President's Choice
 Sunfresh Freezerves
 Western Classics

12277 Sunja's Oriental Foods
40 Foundry St # 1a
Waterbury, VT 05676-1554
802-244-7644
Fax: 802-244-6880 sunjas@madriver.com
www.sunjaskimchi.com
Oriental foods, kimchee, all natural sauces, frozen specialties, sushi
President: Sunja Hayden
sunjas@madriver.com
Estimated Sales: $5-10 Million
Number Employees: 5-9

12278 Sunland Inc/Peanut Better
PO Box 1059
Portales, NM 88130
575-356-6638
Fax: 575-356-6630
Peanuts, peanut butter and flavored infused peanut
President/CEO: Jimmie Shearer
Contact: Cheri Bostwick
cheri@sunlandinc.com

12279 Sunlike Juice
170 5th Avenue
Rougemont, QC J0L 1M0
Canada
416-297-1140
Fax: 416-297-5703 866-552-7643
www.alassonde.com
Processor and exporter of fruit juices and drinks including apple, apple/strawberry, cranberry cocktail, grapefruit, mango, orange juice, orange/pineapple, peach, pineapple, fruit punch, grape, papaya, pink lemonade, black cherry andiced tea
President/CEO: Jean Gattuso
EVP/General Manager of Sales: Pierre L Heureux
EVP/General Manager of Operations: Sylvain Mayrand
VP Marketing: Luc Prevost
VP Communications: Stefano Bertolli
Brands:
 Sunlike

12280 Sunny Avocado
20872 Deerhorn Valley Road
Jamul, CA 91935-7937
619-479-3573
Fax: 619-479-2960 800-999-2862
Provides extra chunky avocado pulp, original mild qualcomole and spicy blends; guac, salsa and guacamaya drink
President: Enrique Bautista
VP: Ana Rosa Bautista
VP Sales/Marketing: Michael Spinner
Estimated Sales: $120000
Number Employees: 2
Type of Packaging: Food Service, Private Label, Bulk
Brands:
 Sunny Avocado

12281 Sunny Delight Beverage Company
10300 Alliance Rd
Suite 500
Cincinnati, OH 45242
www.sunnyd.com
Fruit drinks
President: William Cyr
Year Founded: 1963
Estimated Sales: $341 Million
Number Employees: 800
Number of Brands: 3
Type of Packaging: Private Label
Brands:
 Fruit 2o
 Sunny D
 Veryfine

12282 Sunny Dell Foods Inc
135 N 5th St
Oxford, PA 19363-1502
610-932-5164
Fax: 610-932-9479 bestshroom@aol.com
www.sunnydell.com
Mushrooms, IQF, refrigerated, canned, marinated, pouch packs, organic, roasted red peppers, pepperoncini's, garlic, salsa's, sauces and custom product development.
Cmo: Bobby Fella
bestshroom@aol.com
Finance Manager: Lori Caligiuri
Sales Manager: Bobby Fella
Purchasing Manager: Monica Philistine
Estimated Sales: $14.5 Million
Number Employees: 100-249

12283 Sunny Fresh Foods
206 W Fourth St
Monticello, MN 55362-8524
763-271-5600
Fax: 763-271-5711 800-872-3447
usaeggs@cargill.com www.sunnyfreshfoods.com
Eggs including fresh, liquid, mixes, omelets, diced, hard-cooked and pre-cooked
President: Michael Luker
Director Sales/Marketing: Dale Jenkins
Marketing Manager: Rebecca Hanf
Contact: Dennis Darnell
dennis_darnell@cargill.com
Number Employees: 250-499
Parent Co: Cargill Foods
Type of Packaging: Food Service, Private Label

12284 Sunny South Pecan Company
31 E Olliff Street
Statesboro, GA 30458
912-764-5337
Fax: 912-489-1391 800-764-3687
Processor and grower of pecans
Owner: Garland L Nessmith
VP: Steve Rushing
Estimated Sales: $500,000-$1 Million
Number Employees: 1-4
Square Footage: 46800
Type of Packaging: Consumer
Brands:
 Savannah
 Sunny South

12285 Sunnydale Meats Inc
165 Hyatt St
Gaffney, SC 29341-1558
864-489-6091
Fax: 864-489-6092
Beef, pork, chicken, turkey, bacon, sausage and wieners
President: Anthony Hopper Jr
Estimated Sales: $15 Million
Number Employees: 10-19

12286 Sunnyland Farms
P.O.Box 8200
Albany, GA 31706-8200
229-317-4979
Fax: 229-888-8332 800-999-2488
www.sunnylandfarms.com
Nuts, mixed nuts, pecans, dried fruits and specialty products.
Sales Manager: Beverly Willson
Purchasing: Larry Willson
Estimated Sales: $10-20 Million
Type of Packaging: Consumer, Bulk
Brands:
 Sunnyland Farms

12287 Sunnyland Mills
4469 E Annadale Ave
Fresno, CA 93725-2221
559-233-4983
Fax: 559-233-6431 800-501-8017
mike@sunnylandmills.com
www.sunnylandmills.com
Leading manufacturer of premium quality organic and traditional bulgur wheat, pearled soft white wheat, and Grano
President: Steve Orlando
VP: Mike Orlando
Contact: Saso Danilovski
saso@sunnylandmills.com
Plant Manager: Steve Orlando
Number Employees: 10-19
Square Footage: 36000
Type of Packaging: Food Service, Bulk
Brands:
 Sunnyland

12288 Sunnyrose Cheese
Hwy 25
Diamond City, AB T0K 0T0
Canada
403-381-4024
Fax: 403-381-3838 www.milkingredients.ca
Cheeses including cheddar, colby, mozzarella, Monterey jack, gouda, havarti, marble, parmesan and specialty
President Sales: Emanuela Leoni
Number Employees: 10-19
Parent Co: Agropur
Type of Packaging: Consumer, Food Service
Brands:
 Sunnyrose Cheese

12289 Sunnyside Farms
PO Box 164
Neligh, NE 68756-0164
402-791-2210
Fax: 402-791-2210
Produce
President: James McNally
Estimated Sales: Under $500,000
Number Employees: 1-4

12290 Sunnyside Farms LLC
P.O.Box 478
Washington, VA 22747-0478
540-675-3669
Fax: 540-675-1135
Proceesor of beef
Owner: David Cole
Estimated Sales: $.5-1 million
Number Employees: 1-4

12291 Sunnyside Organics Seedlings
PO Box 478
Washington, VA 22747-0478
510-221-5050
Fax: 540-675-1135 sunnyside@organic.biz
www.organic.biz
Family owned farm that produces eggs, prime meats, and 200 kinds of fruits, vegetables and herbs.

12292 Sunnyside Vegetable Packing
730 Lebanon Road
Millville, NJ 08332-9773
856-451-5077
Fax: 856-451-4388
Vegetables
President: Vic Sammartano
Estimated Sales: Under $500,000
Number Employees: 50-99

12293 Sunray Food Products Corporation
3441 Kingsbridge Ave
Bronx, NY 10463-4003
718-548-2255
Fax: 718-548-2313
Nuts including cashews and pistachios; also, nut mixes, pumpkin and sunflower seeds
Manager: Agustine Morales
Manager: Dave Brechner
Estimated Sales: $423177
Number Employees: 10-19
Parent Co: Zenobia Company
Type of Packaging: Consumer, Food Service, Private Label, Bulk
Brands:
 Private Stock
 Zenobia

Food Manufacturers / A-Z

12294 (HQ)Sunrich LLC
3824 SW 93rd St
Hope, MN 56046-2010
507-451-4724
Fax: 507-451-2910 800-297-5997
sueklem@sunrich.com www.sunrich.com
Processor and exporter of soy products including milk, tofu powder and frozen green soybeans; also, corn products including grits and flour
President: Allan Routh
CFO: John Dietrich
Manager: Jon Meyer
john.meyer@sunopta.com
Estimated Sales: $9 Million
Number Employees: 20-49
Type of Packaging: Food Service, Private Label, Bulk
Other Locations:
  SunRich
  Cresco IA
Brands:
  Soy Supreme
  Sunrich
  Sweet Beans

12295 Sunridge Farms
423 Salinas Rd
Royal Oaks, CA 95076-5232
831-786-7000
Fax: 831-786-8618 info@sunridgefarms.com
www.sunridgefarms.com
Organic and all natural nuts & seeds, dried fruit, candies, and snacks & tril mixes.
CFO: Phillip Adrian
Vice President: Larry Cox
Quality Assurance: Robert Yebra
Assistant Marketing Director: Vivian Guajardo
Sales: Eric Birckner
Director of Operations: Don Blodget
Production and Food Safety Supervisor: Pat Ryan
Estimated Sales: $900 Million
Number Employees: 20-49
Type of Packaging: Consumer, Bulk
Brands:
  Sunridge Farms

12296 Sunridge Farms Inc
1582 Moffett St
Suite C
Salinas, CA 93905-3342
831-755-1530
Fax: 831-755-1429 info@coastlineproduce.com
www.coastlineproduce.com
Bulk and packaged organic and natural foods, snacks, dried fruits, nuts and trail mixes; natural candies; granolas and cereals; grain and bean blend; pastas
President/Owner: Steve Henderson
VP/Owner: Phil Adrians
phil@coastlinefamilyfarms.com
Owner: Larry Cox
Marketing Manager: Vivian Sotelo
Retail Sales Manager: Linda Kivlehan
Director of Operations: Don Blodget
Estimated Sales: $2.5-5 Million
Number Employees: 20-49
Type of Packaging: Consumer, Food Service, Bulk
Brands:
  Coastline

12297 (HQ)Sunrise Growers
701 W Kimberly
Suite 210
Placentia, CA 92870
714-630-6292
Fax: 714-630-0920 website@sunrisegrowers.com
www.sunrisegrowers.com
Manufacturer, exporter and importer of frozen strawberries and purees
President: Ed Haft
CEO: Edward Haft
CFO: Tim Graven
VP: Carl Lindgren
Sales Executive: Steve Cjrcle
Contact: Doyal Andrews
dandrews@sunrisegrowers.com
Estimated Sales: $10-20 Million
Number Employees: 250-499
Square Footage: 1000000
Type of Packaging: Consumer, Food Service, Private Label, Bulk
Other Locations:
  Frozsun Foods
  Oxnard CA
Brands:
  Frozsun

12298 Sunrise Markets
729 Powell St
Vancouver, BC V6A 1H5
Canada
604-253-2326
Fax: 604-251-1083 800-661-2326
www.sunrise-soya.com
Tofu and soy milk
President: Leslie Joe
Plant Manager: Jimmy Cuan
Estimated Sales: $16 Million
Number Employees: 160
Square Footage: 50000
Type of Packaging: Consumer, Food Service

12299 Sunrise Winery
1418 Shasta Avenue
San Jose, CA 95126-2531
408-741-1310
Wines
President: Rolayne Storz
Estimated Sales: $500-1 000,000 appx.
Number Employees: 1-4

12300 Sunset Farm Foods Inc
1201 Madison Hwy
Valdosta, GA 31601
Fax: 229-242-3389 800-882-1121
webinfo@sunsetfarmfoods.com
www.sunsetfarmfoods.com
Processor of smoked sausage, fresh sausage, smoked meats, cooked products (souse, chitterling loaf, liver pudding, chili).
Owner & President: Tom Carroll
t.carroll@sunsetfarmfoods.com
Plant Manager: Ricky Lightsey
Year Founded: 1918
Estimated Sales: $20-50 Million
Number Employees: 50-99
Number of Brands: 6
Number of Products: 250
Square Footage: 40000
Type of Packaging: Consumer, Food Service, Private Label, Bulk
Brands:
  Flavority
  George Maid
  Georgia Reds
  Georgia Special
  Queen of Dixie
  Southern Chef
  Sunset Farm

12301 Sunset Specialty Foods
PO Box 50, PMB 145
Lake Arrowhead, CA 92352
909-337-7643
Fax: 909-337-0963
Processor and exporter of specialty frozen items including pizza, chocolate chip cookies, etc
President/CEO: James Tolliver
Estimated Sales: $5-10 Million
Number Employees: 11-50
Square Footage: 108000
Type of Packaging: Consumer, Food Service, Private Label, Bulk
Brands:
  Amelia's
  Deli
  Dina
  Maestro Giovanni

12302 Sunshine Burger & Spec Food Co
701 Jones Ave
Fort Atkinson, WI 53538-2118
920-568-1100
Fax: 920-568-1504 info@sunshineburger.com
www.sunshineburger.com
Vegan burgers made with non-GMO, organic whole food ingredients. Varieties include Orginal, Garden Herb, BBQ, Falafel, Mushroom, Southwest, and Hemp & Sage.
Owner: Carol Debberman
Owner: John Hiler
Manager: Ann Adkins
aadkins@sunshineburger.com
Estimated Sales: $500,000-$1 Million
Number Employees: 5-9
Square Footage: 14000
Type of Packaging: Consumer

Brands:
  Organic Sunshine
  Sunshine

12303 Sunshine Dairy
584 Coleman Rd
Middletown, CT 06457
860-346-6644
Fax: 860-346-5246
Milk, dairy products
President: Nancy A Guida
nguida@sunshinedairyfoods.com
Estimated Sales: $10-20 000,000
Number Employees: 20-49
Brands:
  Guida

12304 Sunshine Dairy Foods Inc
801 NE 21st Ave
Portland, OR 97232-2280
503-234-7526
Fax: 503-233-9441 info@sunshinedairyfoods.com
Established in 1936. Processor of dairy products including ice cream, yogurt, fresh milk, and cultures.
President and CEO: Dirk Davis
CFO: Aaron Atkins
Chief Quality Officer: Michael Freudenthal
Sr. Manager of Sales: Chris Haines
Director of Operations: Scott Salisbury
West Plant Manager: Darin Quituqua
Estimated Sales: $20-50 Million
Number Employees: 100-249
Square Footage: 75000
Type of Packaging: Consumer, Food Service, Private Label, Bulk
Brands:
  Albertson's
  Quality Chekd
  Tillamook
  Western Family

12305 Sunshine Farm & Garden
696 Glicks Rd
Renick, WV 24966-6601
304-497-2208
Fax: 304-497-2698 barry@sunfarm.com
www.sunfarm.com
Processor, importer and exporter of organic fruits including apples and pawpaws; also, organic herbs and seeds
President: Barry Glick
barry@sunfarm.com
VP: Zak Glick
Estimated Sales: $400000
Number Employees: 20-49
Square Footage: 260000

12306 Sunshine Farms
N8873 Currie Rd
Portage, WI 53901-9218
608-742-2016
Fax: 608-742-1577 sunshine@jvlnet.com
www.jvlnet.com
Processor and wholesaler/distributor of cheese and goat milk; wholesaler/distributor of health foods
President: Daniel Considine
sunshine@jvl.net
Estimated Sales: $3-5 Million
Number Employees: 1-4
Type of Packaging: Consumer
Brands:
  Sunshine Farms

12307 Sunshine Food Sales
2900 NW 75th St Ste 305
Miami, FL 33147
305-696-2885
Processor and importer of fresh and frozen fish including mackerel, kingfish, lobster and crabs
President: Carlos Sanchez
Co-Owner: David Dossi
Plant Manager: Jesus Alonsa
Number Employees: 1-4
Type of Packaging: Bulk

12308 Sunshine Fresh
4425 Vandenberg Dr
North Las Vegas, NV 89081-2716
702-838-4698
Fax: 702-838-4691 800-832-8081
info@sunshinefresh.com www.majorproducts.com
Pickles; wholesaler/distributor of deli products; serving the food service market, manufactures and packs liquid food products.

Food Manufacturers / A-Z

President: Michael Rosenblum
Estimated Sales: $8100000
Number Employees: 5-9
Type of Packaging: Consumer, Food Service, Bulk

12309 Sunshine International Foods
26 Spruce St
Methuen, MA 01844-4336
978-837-3209
Fax: 978-837-3161 info@sunshinefood.com
www.sunshinefood.com
All natural tahini paste.
Owner: Emile Maroun
info@sunshinefood.com
Managing Director: George Maroun
Estimated Sales: $500,000
Number Employees: 10-19
Square Footage: 6640

12310 Sunshine Nut Company
16192 Coastal Highway
Lewes, DE 19958
210-732-9460
info@sunshinenuts.com
www.sunshinenuts.com
Walnuts, almonds and pecans
Contact: Don Larson
don@sunshinenuts.com
Parent Co: John B. Sanfilippo & Son

12311 Sunshine Seafood
PO Box 136
Stonington, ME 04681
207-367-2955
Fax: 207-367-6394
Fish, seafood and shellfish.
President: James Eaton
Estimated Sales: $2,600,000
Number Employees: 10-19

12312 Sunstone Vineyards & Winery
125 N Refugio Rd
Santa Ynez, CA 93460-9303
805-688-9463
Fax: 805-686-1881 800-313-9463
www.sunstonewinery.com
Wines
President: Geoff Alexander
geoff@filmsantabarbara.com
CEO: Linda Rice
VP: Ashley Rice
Marketing Director: Anna Rice
Estimated Sales: Less Than $500,000
Number Employees: 1-4

12313 Sunsweet Growers Inc.
901 N. Walton Ave.
Yuba City, CA 95993
800-417-2253
sunsweet@casupport.com www.sunsweet.com
Dried fruits including prunes, apricots and mangos, as well as prune juice. nuts and more.
President/CEO: Dane Lance
Vice President/CFO: Ana Klein
VP, Global Sales/Marketing: Brad Schuler
Year Founded: 1917
Estimated Sales: $281 Million
Number Employees: 500-999
Type of Packaging: Consumer, Food Service, Private Label, Bulk
Brands:
Sunsweet

12314 Sunterra Meats
233 North Rd
P.O. Box 309
Trochu, AB T0M 2C0
Canada
403-442-4202
Fax: 403-442-2771 www.sunterrameats.ca
Fresh and frozen pork
President: Ray Price
VP Sales & Marketing: Tony Martinez
Plant Manager: Richard Johnson
Estimated Sales: $46 Million
Number Employees: 115
Type of Packaging: Food Service

12315 (HQ)Suntory International
7 Times Sq.
21st Floor
New York, NY 10036
212-891-6600
Fax: 212-891-6601 www.suntory.com
Bottled water, beverages, and alcoholic beverages.
President/CEO: Takeshi Niinami
Year Founded: 1967
Estimated Sales: $840 Million
Number Employees: 2,199
Parent Co: Suntory
Brands:
Nature's Twist
Orangina
Jim Beam
Maker's Mark
Suntory Whisky
Yamazaki
Hakushu
Hibiki
Toki
Sauza Tequila
Courvoisier
Bowmore Islay
Laphroaig
Canadian Club
Roku
Chateau Lagrange
Chateau Beychevelle
Robert Weil

12316 Sunup Green Coffee
New York, NY
212-842-9767
info@sunupgreencoffee.com
www.sunupgreencoffee.com
Green coffee beverage
Area Manager: Colin Fickes
Brands:
Sunup

12317 Sup Herb Farms
300 Dianne Dr
Turlock, CA 95380-9523
209-633-3600
Fax: 209-633-3644 800-787-4372
www.superbfarms.com
Processors and marketers of culinary herbs and specialty products the selection of which includes fresh, frozen and freeze-dried varieties.
President: Mike Brem
EVP/Strategic Planning & CFO: Francis Contino
SVP/General Counsel & Secretary: Robert Skelton
VP/Human Relations: Cecile Perich
Number Employees: 100-249
Parent Co: McCormick & Company Inc

12318 SupHerb Farms
300 Dianne Dr
Turlock, CA 95380-9523
209-633-3600
Fax: 209-633-3644 800-787-4372
custserv@superbfarms.com
www.superbfarms.com
Frozen culinary herb and specialty vegetable ingredients
President & CEO: Matt Reid
VP Finance & Administration: Debbie Salcedo
Executive Corporate Chef: Scott Adair
VP Sales & Marketing: Don Douglas
National Account Manager: Stephanie Schutz
Human Resources Director: Patricia Silva
Plant Manager: Eduardo Luna
Estimated Sales: $3.4 Million
Number Employees: 100-249
Square Footage: 65190
Type of Packaging: Food Service, Bulk
Brands:
Supherb Farms

12319 Super Mom's LLC
625 2nd St
St Paul Park, MN 55071-1807
651-459-2253
Fax: 651-459-0804 800-944-7276
www.superamerica.com
Manufacturer of fresh and frozen bakery items (donuts, pastries, cookies, muffins, loaves. cupcakes, cakes, bread, and buns) and commissary items (pizza, hot meals, deli sandwiches, salads and wraps, vegetable trays, fruit cups andyogurt parfaits). Offers private label and co-packing services.
President: Doug Muchow
Estimated Sales: $14 Million
Number Employees: 250-499
Number of Brands: 1
Parent Co: Western Refining Inc.
Type of Packaging: Consumer, Private Label
Brands:
SuperMom's

12320 Super Nutrition Life Extension
1100 W Commercial Blvd # 100
Fort Lauderdale, FL 33309-3748
954-766-8433
Fax: 954-202-7745 800-678-8989
customerservice@lifeextension.com www.lef.org
Supplements including nutritional, anti-aging and sport supplements; also, vitamin formulas
Owner: William Flannon
Marketing/Design: Kathy Mooney
National Sales Manager: Michael Mooney

12321 Super Smokers Bar-B-Que
601 Stockell Dr
Eureka, MO 63025-1236
636-938-9742
Sauces
Number Employees: 10-19

12322 Super Snooty Sea Food Corporation
7 Fish Pier St E
Boston, MA 02210-2007
617-426-6390
Fax: 617-439-9144
Processor and wholesaler/distributor of frozen seafood including round and filleted flat fish
General Manager: Paul Sousa
Estimated Sales: $1-5 Million
Number Employees: 10-20
Type of Packaging: Consumer

12323 Super Stores Industries
2600 Spengler Rd
Turlock, CA 95380
209-668-2100
customersupport@savemart.com
www.ssica.com
Dairy products including milk, cottage cheese, yogurt and ice cream; orange juice.
President & CEO: Jay Simon
Year Founded: 1981
Estimated Sales: $50-100 Million
Number Employees: 100-249
Number of Brands: 3
Type of Packaging: Private Label
Brands:
Bayview Farms
Sunnyside Farms
Superstore

12324 SuperEats
205 West 10th St #GN
New York, NY 10014
802-760-7075
www.supereats.com
Chips
Co-Owner: Aaron Gailmor
Co-Owner: Charlie Ruehr
Brands:
SuperEats

12325 SuperFat
Beaverton, OR
hello@superfat.com
www.superfat.com
Nut butter snack pouches

12326 Superbrand Dairies
9 Wax Myrtle Ct
Montgomery, AL 36117-3770
334-277-6010
Fax: 334-279-6964
Frozen pizza
Owner: Dennis Houde
Plant Manager: J Parsons
Number Employees: 50-99
Parent Co: Winn Dixie
Type of Packaging: Private Label

12327 Superbrand Dairies
3000 NW 123rd Street
Miami, FL 33167-2517
305-769-6600
Fax: 305-783-2896
Milk and juice: orange, grapefruit and apple
Vice President: Pat Carraro
Number Employees: 50-99
Parent Co: Winn Dixie
Type of Packaging: Consumer

Food Manufacturers / A-Z

12328 Superior Bakery Inc
72 Main St
N Grosvenordale, CT 06255-1712
860-923-9555
Fax: 860-923-2087 www.superiorbakery.com
Italian bread and rolls-Italian sliced, vienna, grinder, pepper bisuits, torpedoes, round buns and pizza
VP Finance: Michael Faucher
General Manager: Victor Strama
Estimated Sales: $8.5 Million
Number Employees: 50-99
Square Footage: 120000
Type of Packaging: Consumer, Food Service, Private Label, Bulk
Brands:
 Green-Freedman
 Kasanofs's
 Superior

12329 Superior Baking Co
176 N Warren Ave
Brockton, MA 02301-3431
508-586-6601
Fax: 508-580-4056 800-696-2253
sbaking1@comcast.net www.superiorbakery.com
Breads, rolls, bagels, pastries and wraps
President: Michael Debenedictis
sbaking1@comcast.net
VP Sales: Joseph Ferrini
Vice President: Robert DeBenedictis
Estimated Sales: Below $5 000,000
Number Employees: 20-49
Square Footage: 16000
Type of Packaging: Consumer, Food Service, Private Label, Bulk

12330 Superior Bean & Spice Company
PO Box 753
Brush Prairie, WA 98606-0753
360-694-0819
Fax: 360-883-6915
Vegetables, soup mixes
President: Duane Rough

12331 Superior Cake Products
105 Ashland Ave
Southbridge, MA 1550
508-764-3276
Fax: 508-765-5344 www.superiorcake.com
Cakes and snack cakes including carrot spice rolls, Boston cream pie, etc
President: Chris Smith
VP Finance: Michael Faucher
VP: Karo Mc Hugh
Contact: Sonia Carrasco
scarrasco@superiorcake.com
VP Operations: Raymond Faucher Jr
Type of Packaging: Consumer, Food Service, Private Label
Brands:
 Superior Cake

12332 Superior Dairy
220 N Fulton St
Wauseon, OH 43567-1161
419-335-3553
Dairy products
President: Joseph Sorhnlen
President/COO: Daniel Sorhnlen
CEO: Joseph P Soehnlen
Sales Manager: Jeff Bouequin
Estimated Sales: $43,000
Number Employees: 2
Type of Packaging: Consumer, Private Label

12333 Superior Farms
2530 River Plaza Dr.
Sacramento, CA 95833
530-297-7299
Fax: 530-758-3152 800-228-5262
thiinc@superiorfarms.com
www.superiorfarms.com
Lamb, venison, buffalo and veal
CEO: Rick Stott
Chairman: Les Oesterreich
CFO: Jeff Evanson
VP Marketing & Brand Strategy: Bob Mariano
VP Sales: Kenneth Wilks
Human Resources Manager: Alfredo Saldivar
VP Operations: Shane MacKenzie
Plant Manager: Greg Ahart
Purchasing Manager: Brian Phelan
Estimated Sales: $34.5 Million
Number Employees: 250-499

Other Locations:
 Boston MA
 Chicago IL
 Denver CO
 Dixon CA
 Hawarden IA
 Vernon CA
Brands:
 Superior Farms

12334 Superior Foods
275 Westgate Dr
Watsonville, CA 95076-2470
831-728-3691
Fax: 831-722-0926 info@superiorfoods.com
www.superiorfoods.com
Global supplier and manufacturer of frozen fruits, vegetables and grains for the consumer, foodservice, club and industrial markets.
President & CEO: R. Neil Happee
Number Employees: 50-99
Type of Packaging: Consumer, Food Service
Brands:
 Asian Pride
 Garden Fresh
 Orchard Park
 Superior Foods
 Superior Pride

12335 Superior Meat Co
480 N 500 E
Vernal, UT 84078-1808
435-789-3274
www.superiormaintenanceservices.com
Meat products
Owner: D Reynolds
Sales Manager: D Reynolds
reynoldssno@msn.com
Estimated Sales: Less than $500,000
Number Employees: 1-4
Type of Packaging: Consumer, Food Service

12336 Superior Mushroom Farms
52557 Range Road
Suite 215
Ardrossan, AB T8E 2H6
Canada
780-922-2535
Fax: 780-922-2078 866-687-2242
Grower of fresh mushrooms
President/CEO: Brent Schwabe
Marketing/Sales Director: Wanda Ziober
Production Manager: Norman Schwabe
Estimated Sales: $5-10 Million
Number Employees: 76
Type of Packaging: Consumer, Food Service, Bulk

12337 (HQ)Superior Nut & Candy
1111 W 40th St
Chicago, IL 60609-2506
773-254-6000
Fax: 773-254-9171 800-843-2238
www.superiornutandcandy.com
Nuts including honey roasted, salted meats and trail mixes; also, fund raising programs available
Owner: Gary Chan
VP Finance: Ramona Mastrangelo
VP: Mona Mastrangelo
Director of Sales: Daniel Hathaway
gchan@superiornutandcandy.com
VP Operations: Richard Slayton
Purchasing: Leonard Shamoon
Estimated Sales: $16,068,865
Number Employees: 20-49
Square Footage: 102000

12338 Superior Nut Company
225 Monsignor Obrien Hwy
Cambridge, MA 02141
617-876-3808
Fax: 617-876-8225 800-251-6060
info@SuperiorNut.com www.superiornut.com
Nuts
President: Harry Hintlian
Estimated Sales: $1-2.5 Million
Number Employees: 1-4
Type of Packaging: Consumer, Food Service, Bulk
Brands:
 Superior Nut Company

12339 Superior Nutrition Corporation
601 N Market Street
Wilmington, DE 19801-3006
302-655-5762
Fax: 302-655-5760 info@sncorp.com
www.sncorp.com
Baked onion pieces
Chief Executive Officer: Fatih Ozmen
Estimated Sales: $2.5-5 Million
Number Employees: 1-4

12340 Superior Ocean Produce
4423 N Elston Ave
Chicago, IL 60630
773-283-8400
Fax: 773-561-0139 bill@fishguy.com
www.fishguy.com
Seafood
Owner: William Dugan
bdugan@fishguy.com
Estimated Sales: $1-3 Million
Number Employees: 10-19

12341 Superior Pasta Co
905 Christian St
Philadelphia, PA 19147-3807
215-627-3306
Fax: 215-922-7114 www.superiorpasta.com
Pasta products
Owner: Joe Lonanno
fundraiser@superiorpasta.com
Estimated Sales: Less than $1 Million
Number Employees: 5-9
Type of Packaging: Private Label

12342 Superior Pecans
317 N Orange Ave
Eufaula, AL 36027-1623
334-687-2031
Fax: 334-687-2075 800-628-2350
www.superiorpecans.com
Pecans
Owner: Dee Kellogg
superiorpecans@gmail.com
Estimated Sales: Less Than $500,000
Number Employees: 1-4
Square Footage: 72000
Type of Packaging: Consumer

12343 Superior Quality Foods
2355 E Francis St
Ontario, CA 91761
909-923-4733
Fax: 909-947-7065 800-300-4210
Soup bases, beef extracts, dried seasonings and sauce mixes
President: Linda Owen
Vice President: Bob Grizzard
National Sales Manager: Paul Smalley
Contact: Cindy Deets
cdeets@superiortouch.com
Estimated Sales: $22.3 Million
Number Employees: 63
Parent Co: Southeastern Mills, Inc.
Type of Packaging: Food Service, Bulk

12344 Superior Seafood
4338 Saint Charles Ave
New Orleans, LA 70115-4742
504-293-3474
Fax: 504-293-0596 info@superiorseafoods.com
www.superiorseafoodnola.com
Seafood
President/Executive Chef: Justin Fergusen
Manager: John Michael
johnm.superiorseafood@gmail.com
Estimated Sales: Less than $500,000
Number Employees: 10-19

12345 Superior Seafood & MeatCompany
623 S Olive Street
South Bend, IN 46619-3309
574-289-0511
Fax: 574-289-0919
Seafood and meat
President: Joe Neary Sr

12346 Superseedz
50 Devine St
North Haven, CT 06473-2244
203-407-0546
Fax: 203-281-3407 www.superseedz.com
Flavored pumpkin seeds

Food Manufacturers / A-Z

Owner/Founder: Kathie Pelliccio
Contact: Joe Lupica
joe@superseedz.com
Estimated Sales: 823,000
Number Employees: 9

12347 Suprema Specialties
14253 S Airport Way
Manteca, CA 95336-8641
209-858-9696
Fax: 209-858-9599
Milk, cheese, cheeses include mozzarella, parmesan, ramano, Monterrey jack and chedder cheese
Owner: Ming Shin-Kou

12348 Supreme Artisan Foods
#308-124, 4653 Carmel Mountain Rd.
San Diego, CA 92130
844-278-3663
www.supremeartisanfoods.com
Producer of cheeses such as Baked Brie en croute and Torta Cheese spreads. Some of their products include Cantar, Traditional Olive Tapenade, Cantar, Feta Olive Tapenade and Cantar, Red Pepper Tuscan Tapenade.
CEO: Olivier Fischer-Morelle
Purchasing Executive: Scott Colling
Estimated Sales: $7,6,000,000
Number Employees: 60
Brands:
  Cantar,

12349 Supreme Chocolatier
1150 South Ave
Suite 1
Staten Island, NY 10314-3404
718-761-9600
Fax: 718-761-5279 www.supremechocolatier.com
Chocolate novelties and gift baskets
Owner: George Biddle
george.biddle@supremechocolatier.com
VP Marketing: Wayne Stottmeister
Estimated Sales: $6,100,000
Number Employees: 50-99
Type of Packaging: Consumer
Brands:
  Superior Chocolatier
  Superior Confections, Inc.
  The Chocolate Factory

12350 Supreme Dairy Farms Co
111 Kilvert St
Warwick, RI 02886-1006
401-739-8180
Fax: 401-739-8230 www.supremedairyfarms.com
Processor and importer of tomato products; also, mozzarella and ricotta cheese
President: Paul Areson
Director: Bill Toll
Contact: Vincent Bruzzese
vincent@supremedairyfarms.com
Estimated Sales: $1.8 Million
Number Employees: 1-4
Square Footage: 56000
Type of Packaging: Food Service, Private Label
Brands:
  Avanti
  Supreme Dairy Farms

12351 Supreme Frozen Products
5813 W Grand Ave
Chicago, IL 60639
773-622-3777
Fax: 773-622-3350 store@supremetamale.com
www.supremetamale.com
Mexican food including tamales, chili, fajitas and burritos
President: John Paklaian
Estimated Sales: $1.2 Million
Number Employees: 10
Square Footage: 24800

12352 Supreme Frozen Products
1495 Brummel Avenue
Elk Grove Village, IL 60007
847-979-8480
www.supremetamale.com
Beef tamales, been and bean burritos, beeh chili with beans, crispy pizza fluffs
Owner: John Pak
Estimated Sales: $5-10 Million
Number Employees: 10-19

12353 Suram Trading Corporation
2655 Le Jeune Road
Suite 1006
Coral Gables, FL 33134
305-448-7165
Fax: 305-445-7185
Frozen seafood shrimp
President and CEO: Guido Adler
Controller: Carmen Artime
Marketing: Kristina Adler
Sales: Michael del Aguila
Contact: Michael Aguila
mdelaguila@suram.com
Operations Manager: Kenji Kurenuma
Estimated Sales: $20-49.9 Million
Number Employees: 10
Number of Brands: 1
Brands:
  Suram

12354 Sure-Fresh Produce Inc
1302 W Stowell Rd
Santa Maria, CA 93458-9730
805-349-2677
Fax: 805-349-2674 888-423-5379
www.surefreshproduce.com
Industrial frozen vegetable ingredient manufacturer of both conventional and organic bulk products
President: Robert Witt
robert@surefreshproduce.com
CFO: Renee Kolding
Quality Control: Corrie Landymore
Marketing Director: Matthew Johnson
Sales Representative: Armando Gonzalez
Estimated Sales: $10-20 Million
Number Employees: 50-99
Number of Products: 750
Square Footage: 100000
Type of Packaging: Food Service, Bulk
Brands:
  Sure Fresh

12355 Sure-Good Food Distributors
6361 Thompson Rd
Syracuse, NY 13206-1448
315-422-1196
Fax: 315-478-5220
Fresh and frozen poultry
President: Jerry Savlov
Estimated Sales: $10-20 000,000
Number Employees: 10-19

12356 Surface Banana Company
1272 Gihon Road
Parkersburg, WV 26101
304-485-2400
Fax: 304-589-7252
Bananas and tomatoes; importer of bananas
Owner: David Surface
Estimated Sales: $300,000-500,000
Number Employees: 1-4

12357 Surfing Goat Dairy
3651 Omaopio Rd
Kula, HI 96790-8871
808-878-2870
Fax: 808-876-1826 info@surfinggoatdairy.com
Goat milk products: Milk, cheese, soaps
Number Employees: 1-4

12358 Surgital America
2805 North Commerce Parkway
Miramar, FL 33025
954-538-6891
customerservice@surgital.com
www.pastificiobacchini.com
Pasta
Marketing (Italy): Anna Baccarani
Type of Packaging: Food Service, Private Label
Brands:
  Pastificio Bacchini

12359 Surlean Foods
1545 S San Marcos
San Antonio, TX 78207-7033
210-227-4370
Fax: 210-226-4208 800-999-4370
mcannon@surleanfoods.com
www.surleanfoods.net
Meats, soups, sauces, marinades and more

President: Daryl Scott
dscott@surleanfoods.com
Director of National Accounts: Bill McKenna
VP Sales & Marketing: Mike Cannon
Plant Manager: Ryan Scott
VP of Sales & Procurement: Chad Wilhite
Estimated Sales: $110,000
Number Employees: 250-499
Type of Packaging: Food Service

12360 Susie's Smart Cookie
333 Hook Rd.
Katonah, NY 10536
914-740-1007
susie@susiesmartcookie.com
www.susiesmartcookie.com
Manufacturer of healthy cookies.
President: Susan Allport
Contact: Susie Aliport
susie@susiesmartcookie.com
Brands:
  Susie's Smart Cookie

12361 Susie's South Forty Confection
401 S Marienfeld St
Midland, TX 79701-5002
432-570-4040
Fax: 432-682-4040 800-221-4442
CustService@susiessouthforty.com
www.susiessouthforty.com
Toffee, pralines, fudge, gift baskets, gift tins
President/Owner: Susie Hitchcock-Hall
cust@susiessouthforty.com
Estimated Sales: $3-5 Million
Number Employees: 50-99
Type of Packaging: Consumer

12362 Susquehanna Valley Winery
802 Mount Zion Dr
Danville, PA 17821
570-275-2364
Fax: 570-275-5813
Wine
Owner: Miklos Latranyi
Partner: Mark Latranyi
Marketing Manager: Hildegard Latranyi
Estimated Sales: Below $5 000,000
Number Employees: 1-4
Brands:
  Susquehanna Valley

12363 Suss Sweets
5 Columbia Ave
Nashua, NH 03064-1607
603-864-8563
Fax: 603-864-8621 www.susssweets.com
Candy caramels
Owner/Founder: Tammy Fahey
Number Employees:

12364 Sustainable Sourcing
PO Box 900
Great Barrington, MA 01230
413-528-5141
Fax: 413-528-5172 sales@himalasalt.com
www.himalasalt.com
Himalayan sea salt. Ethically Sourced, Kosher Certified, and Green-e Certified (made by 100% renewable wind and solar energy, sustainably packaged), with 5% of profits going to the environment and back to the source community.
Founder, CEO, President: Melissa Kushi
Estimated Sales: $1.5 Million
Number Employees: 10
Type of Packaging: Consumer

12365 Suter Co Inc
258 May St
Sycamore, IL 60178-1395
815-895-9186
Fax: 815-895-4814 800-435-6942
www.suterco.com
Processor of canned and refrigerated salads including tuna, chicken, ham, egg and seafood; also, shelf stable lunch kits, deviled egg kits.
President: Tim Suter
tsuter@suterco.com
Year Founded: 1925
Number Employees: 100-249
Type of Packaging: Consumer, Food Service, Private Label, Bulk
Brands:
  Alaska Bay

Food Manufacturers / A-Z

Suter
Sycamore Farms

12366 Sutherland's Foodservice
16 Forest Pkwy
Building K
Forest Park, GA 30297-2015
404-366-8550
Fax: 404-366-8599 cservice@suthfood.com
www.suthfoodservice.com
Dairy, frozen foods, fresh and frozen meat, fresh and frozen poultry, fresh and frozen seafood, dry grocery, nonfood, and produce
CIO/CTO: Bonnie Wilson
bwilson@suthfood.com
Marketing Coordinator: Callie Crowe
Sales Manager: Drew Wilson
Estimated Sales: $20-50 Million
Number Employees: 100-249

12367 Sutter Buttes Olive Oil
2204 California St
Sutter, CA 95982-2445
530-763-7921
sales@sutterbuttesoliveoil.com
www.sutterbuttesoliveoil.com
Oils, spices, sauces, rubs, and salt.
Founder: Alka Kumar
Product Manager: Arek Kazimierczak
Number Employees: 20-49

12368 Sutter Foods LLC
1973 Barry Rd
Yuba City, CA 95993-9501
530-682-7776
Organic prunes. Wholesale only.
Estimated Sales: Less Than $500,000
Number Employees: 1-4

12369 Sutter Home Winery
277 Saint Helena Hwy S
St Helena, CA 94574-2202
707-963-3104
800-967-4663
info@sutterhome.com www.sutterhome.com
Processor and exporter of wines
President: Larry Dizmang
CEO: Sandra Barros
sbarros@tfewines.com
CFO: George Schofield
Public Relations Director: David Foster
Production Manager: Scott Harvey
Purchasing Agent: Marc Norwood
Number Employees: 100-249
Square Footage: 58624
Brands:
  Sutter Home

12370 Sutton Honey Farms
285 Conns Ln
Lancaster, KY 40444-9706
859-792-4277
Fax: 859-792-4277 www.suttonhoneyfarm.com
Processor and packer of nonfiltered and creamed honey with fruit and cinnamon
President: Rick Sutton
VP: Dianne Sutton
Estimated Sales: A
Number Employees: 1-4
Square Footage: 16000
Type of Packaging: Consumer, Private Label, Bulk
Brands:
  Sutton's

12371 Suzanna's Kitchen
4025 Buford Hwy
Peachtree Cor, GA 30096-4137
770-476-9900
Fax: 770-476-8899 www.suzannaskitchen.com
Foodservice partner manufacturing frozen heat-and-serve meat products including pork, veal, beef, turkey, barbecue, ribs, corn dogs and chicken breasts, breast strips, chicken patties and wings.
Founder: Barbara Howard
CEO: Brad Howard
bradh@suzannaskitchen.com
CFO: David Ashton
Director of Operations: Nelson Rodriguez
Number Employees: 100-249
Number of Products: 100+
Type of Packaging: Food Service, Private Label
Brands:
  Suzanna's

12372 Suzanne's Specialties
411 Jersey Ave
New Brunswick, NJ 08901
732-828-8500
Fax: 732-828-8563 800-762-2135
info@suzannes-specialties.com
suzannes-specialties.com
Organic sweeteners and sugar alternatives including brown rice syrup, agave syrup and evaporated cane juice
President/Owner: Susan Morano
VP, Operations: Jim Morano
Number Employees: 20-49
Type of Packaging: Consumer, Food Service, Bulk
Brands:
  Rice Nectar
  Sunrice
  Sunshine's
  Suzanne's Conserves

12373 Suzanne's Sweets
9 Comanche Ct
Katonah, NY 10536-2917
Fax: 914-232-1291
Rugelach

12374 Suzhou-Chem Inc
396 Washington St
Suite 318
Wellesley, MA 02481
781-433-8618
Fax: 781-433-8619 info@suzhouchem.com
www.suzhouchem.com
Food and beverage ingredients including ascorbic acid, sodium ascorbate, calcium ascorbate, sodium saccharin granular, sodium saccharin dehydrate, sodium saccharin powder, calcium saccharin, insoluble saccharin, acesulfame-kaspartame, caffeine, potassium, sorbic acid, etc.
President: Joan Ni
Estimated Sales: $302 Million
Number Employees: 5-9
Type of Packaging: Bulk

12375 Svenhard's Swedish Bakery Inc
335 Adeline St
Oakland, CA 94607-2519
510-834-5035
Fax: 510-839-6797 800-705-3379
ccare@svenhards.com www.svenhards.com
Pastries such as; cinnamon rolls and danishes
President & CEO: Ronny Svenhard
CEO: Norman Andrews
norman@svenhards.com
Director of Manufacturing: Allen Herman
Estimated Sales: $19.2 Million
Number Employees: 250-499
Square Footage: 79768
Type of Packaging: Consumer, Food Service
Other Locations:
  Svenhard's Swedish Bakery
  Exeter CA
Brands:
  Svenhards

12376 Svzusa Inc
1700 N Broadway Ave
Othello, WA 99344-8918
509-488-6563
Fax: 509-488-2631 info@svz-usa.com
www.svz.com
Liquid fruit and vegetable concentrates, proteins and blends.
President: Doug Granitz
doug.granitz@svz.com
CFO: Roger Wilson
Sales & Marketing Manager: Timothy Jaeger
Human Resources: Agatha Willis
Estimated Sales: $6.3 Million
Number Employees: 50-99
Parent Co: SVZ Industrial Products B.V.
Type of Packaging: Bulk

12377 Swagger Foods Corp
900 Corporate Woods Pkwy
Vernon Hills, IL 60061-3155
847-913-1200
Fax: 847-913-1263 info@swaggerfoods.com
Supplying the industrial, food service and retail markets as a manufacturer of seasonings, functional foods with vitamins, minerals, omega-3, other micronutrients/nutraceuticals, salt substitutes, soup mixes/bases, rubs, marinadesgravy/sauce mixes, dip/dressing mixes, drink mixes, side dish mixes and other dry blends including Ethnic.
President: Terry R Shin
terry.shin@swaggerfoods.com
Number Employees: 10-19
Type of Packaging: Consumer, Food Service, Private Label, Bulk
Brands:
  Bits O' Butter
  Fancy Pantry
  Health-Fu'd
  Spice So Rite
  Swagger

12378 Swanson Vineyards & Winery
PO Box 459
Rutherford, CA 94573
707-944-0905
Fax: 707-967-3505 800-942-0809
www.swansonvineyards.com
Wines
Owner: W Clarke Swanson
Sales Manager: Michael Opdegraff
Contact: Chris Cutler
chris@chriscutler.com
Winemaker: Marco Capell
Estimated Sales: $5-9.9 Million
Number Employees: 20-49
Brands:
  Swanson Vineyards & Winery

12379 Swany White Flour Mills LTD
206 2nd St SE
PO Box 214
Freeport, MN 56331-9036
320-836-2174
Fax: 320-836-2477 swanywhiteflour.com
White flours
President: Sharon Thelen
sa_thelen@hotmail.com
Number Employees: 1-4

12380 Swapples
Washington, DC
info@swapfoods.com
www.swapfoods.com
Paleo, vegan, and gluten free waffles in both sweet and savory flavors
Founder/CEO: Rebecca Peress
Year Founded: 2016

12381 Swatt Baking Co
222 Homer St
Olean, NY 14760-1132
716-372-9480
Fax: 716-373-6019 800-370-6656
www.lacinnamonbread.com
Rolls, regular and cinnamon bread and cinnamon bread sauce
President: Leonard Anzivine
VP: Lee Anzivine
lacinnamonbread@aol.com
Estimated Sales: $700000
Number Employees: 10-19
Square Footage: 37600
Type of Packaging: Food Service, Bulk
Brands:
  L.A. Cinnamon

12382 Swedish Hill Vineyard & Winery
4565 State Route 414
Romulus, NY 14541-9769
607-403-0029
Fax: 315-549-8477 888-549-9463
info@swedishhill.com www.swedishhill.com
Winery, producing red, white, rose, sparkling and dessert wines.
President: Richard Peterson
CEO: Dave Peterson
Finance Manager: Amanda Fitzgerald
Director of Operations: Jean Peterson
Winemaker: Derek Wilber
Winemaker: Zach Pegram
Estimated Sales: $6 Million
Number Employees: 50-99
Number of Brands: 3
Type of Packaging: Consumer, Food Service
Other Locations:
  Swedish Hill Lake Placid

1159

Food Manufacturers / A-Z

Lake Placid NY
Swedish Hill Saratoga Springs
Saratoga Springs NY
Goose Watch Winery
Romulus NY
Goose Watch Lake Placid
Lake Placid NY
Penguin Bay
Hector NY
Brands:
  Swedish Hill
  Goose Watch
  Penguin Bay

12383 Sweeney's Gourmet Coffee Roast
671 Middlegate Road
Suite C
Henderson, NV 89011-2628
702-558-0505
Fax: 702-558-3799
Coffee
President: Robert Sweeney
Estimated Sales: $2.5-5 Million
Number Employees: 1
Type of Packaging: Private Label, Bulk

12384 Sweenors Chocolates
21 Charles St
Wakefield, RI 02879-3621
401-783-4433
Fax: 401-783-9340 800-834-3123
www.sweenorschocolates.com
Chocolates, hard candies, fudge and mints
President: Brian Sweenor
Vice President: Brian Sweenor
Estimated Sales: $5-10 Million
Number Employees: 10-19
Type of Packaging: Consumer, Private Label, Bulk

12385 Sweet & Sara
4331 33rd St # 4
Suite 4
Long Island City, NY 11101-2316
718-707-2808
sara@sweetandsara.com
sweetandsara.com
Vegan treats
Owner: Sara Sohn
Number Employees: 10-19

12386 Sweet & Saucy Inc
5974 S Pennsylvania St
Centennial, CO 80121-2252
303-807-5132
Fax: 303-798-8258 jane@sweetandsaucy.net
www.sweetandsaucy.net
21 flavors of gourmet caramel and chocolate sauces.
President: Jane Jones
jane@sweetandsaucy.net
Vice President: Erin Jones
CMO: Robert Jones
COO: Brent Jones
Estimated Sales: Less Than $500,000
Number Employees: 1-4
Number of Brands: 1
Number of Products: 21
Type of Packaging: Consumer, Food Service
Brands:
  Sweet & Saucy Caramel Sauces
  Sweet & Saucy Chocolate Sauces

12387 Sweet Additions
4440 PGA Boulevard
Suite 600
Palm Beach Gardens, NY 33410
561-472-0178
Fax: 561-472-0548
customerservice@sweetadditions.com
www.sweetadditions.com
Manufacturer of organic sweeteners and sugar alternatives for the food and beverage industries.
President & CEO: Ken Valdivia
sweetadditions@gmail.com
Other Locations:
  Corporate Headquarters
  Palm Beach Gardens FL
  Manufacturing Facility
  Cameron WI
Brands:
  CaneSweet
  SweetDex
  GrainSweet

12388 Sweet Baby Ray's
PO Box 31250
Chicago, IL 60631-0250
877-729-2229
service@sweetbabyrays.com
www.sweetbabyrays.com
Barbecue sauces, original, honey, hickory and brown sugar, sweet and spicy, chipotle, and sweet vidalia onion.
Founder: Dave Raymond
Operations Manager: Larry Duce Raymond
Estimated Sales: $20-50 Million
Number Employees: 5-9
Parent Co: Ken's Foods
Type of Packaging: Consumer, Food Service
Brands:
  Sweet Baby Ray's

12389 Sweet Blessings
23805 Stuart Ranch Rd
Malibu, CA 90265-4856
310-317-1172
Fax: 310-317-1132
Chocolates
President: Dave Singelyn
CEO/Owner: B Wayne Hughes
VP Sales: Mark Bontempo
Estimated Sales: $3-5 Million
Number Employees: 5-9
Brands:
  Noahs Buddies
  Sweet Blessings

12390 Sweet Breath
950 3rd Ave
New York, NY 10022-2705
212-755-9300
Fax: 212-755-9305 877-673-9777
customercare@sweetbreath.com
www.sweetbreath.com
Breath fresheners, energy strips, vitamin strips and cough and cold strips instant energy for your body and mind
Founder/President: Jeffrey Hirschman
National Account Manager: David Hirschman
Vice President Marketing: Roger Mascall
Contact: Roger Mascall
roger.mascall@sweetbreath.com
Number Employees: 5-9
Brands:
  Ice Chews
  Ice Chips
  Ice Chunks
  Sweet Breath Xtreme Intense Breath

12391 Sweet Candy Company
3780 West Directors Row
Salt Lake City, UT 84104
801-886-1444
Fax: 801-886-1404 855-772-7720
mail@sweetcandy.com www.sweetcandy.com
Confectionery products including brittles, chocolates, holiday novelties, filled items, jellies, hard candies, jelly beans, marshmallows, mints, nougats, glazed nuts, taffy, etc.; also, in bags
Founder/President: Leon Sweet
Contact: Jacki Arevalo
arevaloj@sweetcandy.com
Type of Packaging: Consumer, Bulk

12392 Sweet Christine's Bakery
503 Orchard Avenue
Kennett Square, PA 19348
610-444-5542
www.sweetchristinesglutenfree.com
Gluten free baked goods
Contact: Kevin Mccann
kevin@sweetchristinesglutenfree.com

12393 Sweet City Supply
5820 Ward Ct
Virginia Beach, VA 23455
757-456-0800
Fax: 757-456-9980 888-793-3824
A contract manufacturer and national distributor of imported and domestic bulk and packaged candy, nuts, and confections.
President: Ronald Bublick
Type of Packaging: Food Service, Bulk

12394 Sweet Corn Products Co
124 N Broadway St
Bloomfield, NE 68718-4406
402-373-2211
Fax: 402-373-2219 877-628-6115
www.no-nobirdfeeder.com
Processor and exporter of sweet corn products including dry mature for tortilla chips and toasted nuts
General Manager: Raymon Lush
ray@sweetcornproducts.com
Estimated Sales: $2000000
Number Employees: 1-4
Square Footage: 92000
Type of Packaging: Consumer, Food Service, Private Label, Bulk
Brands:
  Ugly Nut

12395 Sweet Designs Chocolatier Inc
16100 Detroit Ave
Lakewood, OH 44107-3715
216-226-4888
info@sweetdesigns.com
www.sweetdesigns.com
Manufacturer of assorted chocolates, truffles, and freshly dipped fruit.
Founder: Ines Rehmer
Estimated Sales: Less Than $500,000
Number Employees: 1-4

12396 Sweet Earth Foods
3080 Hilltop Rd
Moss Landing, CA 95039
831-375-8673
Fax: 831-375-3441 800-737-3311
zenfarmer@sweetearthfoods.com
www.sweetearthfoods.com
Vegetarian foods including soups, salads, burritos, salad dressings, salsa, hummus, vegeburgers, sweet bars, pies and seitan(wheat-meat)
Owner: Russell Hicks
sweetearth@pacbell.net
Co-Owner: Caren Hicks
Estimated Sales: $3-5 Million
Number Employees: 10-19
Square Footage: 8000
Type of Packaging: Consumer, Food Service, Bulk
Brands:
  Awaken Foods
  Fiesta Rice
  Grand Life Seitan
  Heat-N-Eat
  Sweet Earth Natural Foods

12397 Sweet Endings Inc
1220 Okeechobee Rd
West Palm Beach, FL 33401-6947
561-655-0334
Fax: 561-209-1901 888-635-1177
swtend@aol.com www.sweetendingsdesserts.com
Processor and exporter of cakes, pies, tortes and crumbles including sugar and fat-free
Owner: Dalanna Browning
dalannabrowning@sweetendingsdesserts.com
Estimated Sales: $3-5 Million
Number Employees: 20-49
Square Footage: 12000
Type of Packaging: Food Service, Private Label

12398 Sweet Fortunes of America
783a Yerry Hill Road
Woodstock, NY 12498
845-679-7327
Fax: 845-679-7327
Gourmet and specialty foods
President: Carol Lieberman

12399 Sweet Gallery Exclusive Pastry
2312 Bloor St W
Toronto, ON M6S 1P2
Canada
416-766-0289
Fax: 416-766-7965
Processor of sponge cakes, butter cream tortes, pastries, croissants, wedding cakes, danishes and European cakes and pastries
President: Radi Jelenic
President: Lydia Jelenic
Number Employees: 10
Square Footage: 20000
Type of Packaging: Consumer

Food Manufacturers / A-Z

12400 Sweet Grass Dairy
19635 US Highway 19 N
Thomasville, GA 31792-9060
229-227-0752
Fax: 229-227-0752 sweetgrassdairy.com
Cow's milk cheese
Estimated Sales: Less Than $500,000
Number Employees: 1-4

12401 Sweet Harvest Foods
15100 Business Parkway
Rosemount, MN 55068
507-263-8599
Fax: 651-322-1229 info@sweetharvestfoods.com
www.sweetharvestfoods.com
Natural and organic honey and peanut butter.
President: Curt Riess
Quality Manager: Gary Stromley
COO: Brian McGregor
Plant Manager: Brian Pleschourt
Estimated Sales: $4.8 Million
Number Employees: 20-49
Type of Packaging: Consumer, Food Service, Private Label
Brands:
  MEL-O HONEY
  JOHN MOUNTAIN ORGANIC

12402 Sweet Jubilee Gourmet
273 Mulberry Drive
Suite 14
Mechanicsburg, PA 17050
717-691-9782
Fax: 717-691-0228 877-691-9732
diane@brittlebark.com
www.sweetjubileegourmet.com
Brittle candy made with assorted nuts, dried fruits and premium chocolate.
President/Owner: Diane Krulac
Estimated Sales: $750,000
Number Employees: 13
Square Footage: 10000

12403 Sweet Lady Jane
8360 Melrose Ave
Los Angeles, CA 90069
323-653-7145
Fax: 323-662-8950 www.sweetladyjane.com
Baked goods
Owner/Founder: Jane Lockhart
Contact: Oscar Gomez
ogomez@sweetladyjane.com
Estimated Sales: 500,000
Number Employees: 1-4

12404 Sweet Leaf Tea Company
515 S Congress Ave Ste 700
Austin, TX 78704
512-328-7775
Fax: 512-328-7725 www.sweetleaftea.com
Teas, lemonades, mixers and fixers
Founder/CEO: Clayton Christopher
CFO/COO: Brian Goldberg
Marketing Director: Adi Wilk
Co-Founder/VP of Sales: David Smith
Contact: Genevieve Court
vieve@sweetleaftea.com
VP Operations: Robert Walker
Production/Logistics Manager: Brian Selensky
Estimated Sales: $1.1 Million
Number Employees: 10

12405 Sweet Life Enterprises
2350 Pullman St.
Santa Ana, CA 92705
714-256-8900
Cinnamon rolls and cookies inluding chocolate chip, double fudge chocolate, oatmeal raisin, sugar, peanut butter, white chocolate, snickerdoodle, etc
President & CEO: Mike Gray
Quality Assurance Manager: Derek Osato
Marketing Manager: Stephanie Easterday
Vice President Sales: Lori Gray
Contact: Ryan Anita
ryan.anita@freshstartbakeries.com
VP Operations: Scott Fitzgerald
Estimated Sales: 20.9 Million
Number Employees: 115
Other Locations:
  North America Support Offices
  Santa Ana CA
Brands:
  The Sweet Life

12406 Sweet Loren's
60 Broad Street
Floor 24
New York, NY 10004
646-257-5700
Fax: 646-930-5757 hello@sweetlorens.com
sweetlorens.com
Cookies
Founder & CEO: Loren Brill
Consumer Marketing Manager: Lindsey Tauer
Vice President, Sales: Yvette Baumgarten Borrack
Operations Manager: Melania Macko
Estimated Sales: $6.4 Million
Number Employees: 36
Brands:
  Sweet Loren's

12407 Sweet Mavens, LLC
128B Addison Rd.
Glastonbury, CT 06033
860-490-1407
Fax: 860-568-6145 info@sweetmavens.com
www.sweetmavens.com
Manufacturer of biscotti, pecans, and almonds.
Founder: Anite Carpene
Contact: Anita Carpene
a.carpene@sweetmavens.com

12408 Sweet Megan Baking Company
234 Holland Rd.
Southampton, PA 18966
267-288-5080
www.glutenfreesweetmegan.com
No preservatives, all natural baked goods

12409 Sweet Mountain Magic
2131 N Larrabee Street
Apt 6205
Chicago, IL 60614-4422
773-755-4539
Fax: 703-437-1031
Ice cream
President: Stephen Kleiman
VP Marketing: Ehtel Hammer

12410 Sweet Peas Floral Design
6231 Pacific Ave # A2
Stockton, CA 95207-3700
209-472-9284
Fax: 209-472-9284
Marinades and barbecue sauces
Owner: Katie Wendland
Estimated Sales: $300,000-$500,000
Number Employees: 1-4
Square Footage: 7200
Type of Packaging: Consumer, Food Service
Brands:
  Delta
  Riverboat

12411 Sweet Pillar
Newport Beach, CA
310-913-7261
www.sweetpillar.com
Manufacturer of chocolate covered dates and mamool cookies.
Founder: Nadia Hubbi

12412 Sweet Sams Baking Corp
1261 Seabury Ave
Bronx, NY 10462-5526
718-822-0599
Fax: 718-409-0309 richardsklar@hotmail.com
www.sweetsams.com
Premium all butter bakery products
President: David Grogan
david.grogan@sweetsams.com
Estimated Sales: Less Than $500,000
Number Employees: 1-4

12413 Sweet Sensations
201 Humber Ave
Labrador City, NL A2V 2V3
Canada
709-944-2660
Fax: 709-944-2656
Chocolate and candies, also nuts and glazed nuts
Owner: Andrea Cormier
Estimated Sales: $1 Million

12414 Sweet Shop USA
1316 Industrial Rd
Mt Pleasant, TX 75455-2614
903-575-0033
Fax: 817-336-9169 888-957-9338
customercare@sweetshopusa.com
www.sweetshopusa.com
Chocolates, truffles, caramels and fudge.
President: Michael Moss
CEO: Jim Webb
jim@sweetshopusa.com
Chief Financial Officer: Matt Kelley
Lead Customer Service Representative: Sherry Bostick
Manager: Ashlyn Reynolds
Estimated Sales: $4.5 Million
Number Employees: 50-99
Number of Brands: 3
Square Footage: 66000
Type of Packaging: Consumer
Brands:
  Mrs. Weinstein's Toffee
  Price's Fine Chocolates
  Sweet Shop USA

12415 Sweet Street Desserts
722 Hiesters Ln
Reading, PA 19605-3095
610-921-8113
Fax: 610-921-8195 800-793-3897
ussales@sweetstreet.com www.sweetstreet.com
Variety of coffee bar and desserts: hazelnut cappucino torte, apple crumb cake, chocolate chip crumb cake, sour cream coffee cake
President: Sandy Solmon
sandys@sweetstreet.com
Estimated Sales: $39400000
Number Employees: 500-999
Type of Packaging: Consumer, Food Service
Brands:
  Sweet Street

12416 Sweet Sue Kitchens
106 Sweet Sue Drive
Athens, AL 35611-2181
256-216-0500
Fax: 256-216-0531
Processor and exporter of canned poultry products including chicken broth, chunks, stew and dumplings
Sales/Marketing Executive: Shirley Brown
Plant Manager: Bob Mahan
Purchasing Agent: Carol Moore
Parent Co: Sara Lee Corporation
Type of Packaging: Consumer, Food Service, Private Label

12417 Sweet Swiss ConfectionsInc
7821 W Electric Ave
Spokane, WA 99224-9000
509-838-1334
Fax: 509-456-0824 chocologos@sweetsswiss.com
www.sweetswiss.com
Chocolate truffles, marzipan and personalized chocolate logos
President: Matt Phillipson
inquire@sweetswiss.com
Controller: Pam Martin
Vice President: Phina Phillipson
Estimated Sales: Below $5 Million
Number Employees: 5-9

12418 Sweet Traders
5362 Oceanus Dr # C
Suite C
Huntington Beach, CA 92649-1000
714-903-6800
Fax: 714-892-4345 info@sweettraders.com
www.sweettraders.com
Wine, chocolate, baked goods, and gift baskets; including chocolate wrapped wines and ciders, champagnes and nonalcoholic beverages
Owner: R Louw
rflouw@yahoo.com
Estimated Sales: Less Than $500,000
Number Employees: 1-4
Square Footage: 10000
Type of Packaging: Consumer, Private Label

Food Manufacturers / A-Z

12419 Sweet Water Brewing Co
195 Ottley Dr NE
Atlanta, GA 30324-3924
404-691-2537
Fax: 404-691-0936 Steve@sweetwaterbrew.com
www.sweetwaterbrew.com
Ale and stout
Owner: Fredrick Bensch
Sales: Dave Guender
Estimated Sales: $2.5-5 Million
Number Employees: 20-49
Type of Packaging: Consumer, Food Service
Brands:
 Sweetwater
 Sweetwater 42
 Sweetwater Blue

12420 Sweet Water Seafood
369 Washington Ave
Carlstadt, NJ 07072-2805
201-939-6622
Fax: 201-939-4014 www.sweetwaterseafood.net
Frozen shellfish including squid, conch, clams and mussels
Manager: Teri Niece
Chairman: Robert Inglese
Manager: Theresa Niece
tniece@sweetwaterseafood.net
Estimated Sales: Less Than $500,000
Number Employees: 1-4
Square Footage: 132000
Type of Packaging: Consumer, Food Service, Private Label, Bulk
Brands:
 Mussel King
 Plumpy

12421 Sweet Whispers
6031 Crimson Ct
Mclean, VA 22101-0000
954-328-5079
info@sweetwhispers.store
sweetwhispers.store
Meringue filling
Co-Founder: Maria Umana
Co-Founder: Liliana Guerra
Year Founded: 2016
Brands:
 Sweet Whispers

12422 Sweet'N Low
2 Cumberland St
Brooklyn, NY 11205
www.sweetnlow.com
Manufacturer of artificial sweeteners.
Chairman: Marvin Eisenstadt
President/CEO: Steven Eisenstadt
Estimated Sales: $100+ Million
Number Employees: 400
Number of Brands: 1
Parent Co: Cumberland Packing Corp.
Type of Packaging: Consumer
Brands:
 Sweet'n Low

12423 SweetWorks Inc
3500 Genesee Street
Buffalo, NY 14225
716-634-0880
Fax: 716-634-4855 www.sweetworks.com
Chocolates, candy and gum products
Owner: Philip Terranova
CFO: Ralph Nicosia
Marketing Director: Jeanne Palka
Sales Director: Jerry Tubbs
Contact: Pascal Bieri
pbieri@sweetworks.net

12424 Sweetaly
Sweetaly Dolceria
Oceanside, CA 92056
760-539-2196
info@sweetaly.us
sweetaly.us
Italian desserts: mousse, tiramisu and panna cotta.
Co-Founder: Oliviero Colmignoli
Type of Packaging: Consumer, Private Label
Brands:
 Sweetaly

12425 Sweetcraft Candies
PO Box 15
Timonium, MD 21094-0015
410-252-0684
Fax: 410-252-0352
Candy
President: George George

12426 Sweetener Supply Corp
9501 Southview Ave
Brookfield, IL 60513-1529
708-588-8400
Fax: 708-588-8460 888-784-2799
sweetenersupply.com
Manufacturer and distributor of sweeteners for the food, beverage and confectionery industries.
Number Employees: 20-49
Number of Brands: 5
Brands:
 Delicious
 Ridgeland
 Ambersweet
 Sur Sweet
 Ultraclear

12427 Sweeteners Plus Inc
5768 Sweeteners Blvd
Lakeville, NY 14480-9741
585-346-3193
Fax: 585-346-2310 www.sweetenersplus.com
Manufacturer and distributor of liquid and dry sweeteners including white and brown sugar, organic and kosher products, fructose, maltitol, corn syrup, and invert syrups. Also bottling, custom blending, and liquid fondants. Shipped regionally long haul by rail and short haul by trucks and nationally by distribution products
President & CEO: Carlton Myers
Quality Assurance Manager: Mark Rudolph
VP Sales: Mark Whitford
Operation Manager: Bill Devine
Estimated Sales: $14.7 Million
Number Employees: 1-4
Type of Packaging: Food Service, Bulk

12428 Sweetery
1814 E Greenville St
Anderson, SC 29621-2035
864-224-8394
Fax: 864-224-8469 800-752-1188
www.thesweetery.net
Cakes, cheesecakes and pies
President: Jane Jarahian
jjarahian@sweetery.com
Estimated Sales: Under $500,000
Number Employees: 20-49
Type of Packaging: Consumer, Private Label
Brands:
 Southern Special
 Uggly Cake

12429 Sweetleaf Co
1203 W San Pedro St
Gilbert, AZ 85233-2406
480-921-2160
Fax: 480-966-3805 www.sweetleaf.com
Tea, extracts, sweetners
President: Carol May
cmay@wisdomnaturalbrands.com
Chief Executive Officer: James May
Number Employees: 20-49

12430 Sweetleaf Co
1203 W San Pedro St
Gilbert, AZ 85233-2406
480-921-2160
Fax: 480-966-3805 800-899-9908
info@wisdomnaturalbrands.com sweetleaf.com
Manufacturer of award-winning stevia sweetener.
President: Carol May
cmay@wisdomnaturalbrands.com
Number Employees: 20-49
Number of Brands: 5
Brands:
 SweetLeaf Stevia
 Sweet Drops
 Water Drops
 SugarLeaf
 Organic SweetLeaf Stevia

12431 Sweetstacks LLC
PO Box 33227
San Diego, CA 92163-3227
619-997-1097
www.sweetstacks.com
Pancake mixes, baking mixes, fruit spreads, syrups
President: Elaine Babauta
Estimated Sales: C

12432 Sweetwater Spice Company
3800 N Lamar Blvd
Suite 730-155
Austin, TX 78756
800-531-6079
Fax: 512-857-0083 www.sweetwaterspice.com
Sauces and marinades
Contact: Scott Sapire
ssapire@mac.com

12433 Sweetwood Cattle Co
2670 Copper Ridge Cir
Suite 3
Steamboat Spgs, CO 80487-9492
970-879-7456
Fax: 970-870-7980 www.sweetwood.com
Meats
CEO: Ryan Wood
Vice President: Caitlin Colgan
Manager: Jeremiah Jackson
jeremiah@sweetwood.com
Operations Director: Rebecca Fix
Estimated Sales: Less Than $500,000
Number Employees: 5-9

12434 Sweety Novelty
633 Monterey Pass Rd
Monterey Park, CA 91754
626-282-4482
Fax: 626-282-2482
Frozen fruit bars and ice cream including red bean, mango, green tea, durian, peanut and taro; also, mocha ice cream including green tea, vanilla, strawberry, mango and taro
President: Tracy Lee
Manager: Patty Lee
Estimated Sales: $870,000
Number Employees: 10-19
Square Footage: 32000
Type of Packaging: Consumer, Food Service

12435 Swerseys Chocolate
63 Flushing Ave.
Brooklyn, NY 11205
718-497-8800
Fax: 718-497-8100 info@swerseys.com
www.swerseys.com
Manufacturer of chocolate, dried fruit and mixed nuts.
Owner: Jack Levy

12436 Swerve Sweetener
1000 S. Rendon
New Orleans, LA 70125
504-309-9280
Fax: 504-309-9287 888-979-3783
hello@swervesweetener.com
www.swervesweetener.com
Natural sweetener
President & CEO: Andress Blackwell
Marketing Manager: Natalia Matallana
Estimated Sales: $1-2 Million
Number Employees: 2-10
Brands:
 Swerve

12437 (HQ)Swiss American Inc
4200 Papin St
St Louis, MO 63110-1736
314-533-2224
Fax: 314-533-0765 800-325-8150
Packer, importer and distributor of cheese and fine foods
President: Joseph Hoff
CEO: R Weil
VP: D Boyd
Contact: Chris Biscan
chris.biscan@swissamerican.com
Operations VP: David Boyd
Estimated Sales: Less Than $500,000
Number Employees: 1-4
Square Footage: 180000
Type of Packaging: Consumer, Bulk
Other Locations:
 Swiss-American
 North Charleston SC

Food Manufacturers / A-Z

Brands:
- Capricorn
- Dutch Garden
- Dutch Garden Super Swiss
- Epic
- Fire Jack
- Freshwrap Cuts
- Freshwrap Slices
- Mr. Sharp
- Saint Louis
- Verdaccio

12438 (HQ)Swiss Chalet Fine Foods
9455 NW 40th Street Rd
Doral, FL 33178-2941
305-592-0008
Fax: 305-592-1651 800-347-9477
info@scff.com www.scff.com
A wide range of quality gourmet products from sweets to savories
CFO: Donna Croup
donna@scff.com
Estimated Sales: $300,000-500,000
Number Employees: 5-9
Brands:
- Felchlin-Swiss
- Haco
- Hero

12439 Swiss Dairy
12171 Madera Way
Riverside, CA 92503
951-898-9427
Fax: 951-734-3786
Milk
Office Manager: Lorry Olson
Contact: John Schneider
john_schneider@deanfoods.com
Estimated Sales: $.5-1,000,000
Number Employees: 5-9
Parent Co: Suiza Dairy Group
Type of Packaging: Consumer, Food Service

12440 Swiss Food Products
4333 W Division St
Chicago, IL 60651
312-829-0100
Fax: 773-394-6475 www.swissfoodproducts.com
Manufacturer and exporter of bases including soup, gravy, browning, seasoning and sauce; also, flavors
Estimated Sales: $5-10 Million
Number Employees: 10-19
Square Footage: 100000
Type of Packaging: Consumer, Food Service, Private Label, Bulk
Brands:
- Swiss

12441 Swiss Heritage Cheese Inc
114 E Coates Ave
Monticello, WI 53570-9828
608-938-4455
Fax: 608-938-1325 www.tdsnet.com
Cheese
President/Treasurer: Paul Rufener
Estimated Sales: $1,600,000
Number Employees: 10-19
Brands:
- Swiss Heritage Cheese

12442 Swiss Premium Dairy Inc
2401 Walnut St
Lebanon, PA 17042-9444
717-273-2658
Fax: 717-273-2794 800-222-2129
www.deanfoods.com
Milk including 2% and skim; also, chilled orange juice, iced tea and fruit drinks
General Manager: Mike Eiceman
mike_eiceman@deanfoods.com
Plant Manager: John Wengert
Year Founded: 1931
Estimated Sales: B
Number Employees: 100-249
Square Footage: 120000
Parent Co: Dean Foods
Type of Packaging: Consumer, Food Service, Private Label
Other Locations:
- Wengert's Dairy
- Camp Hill PA
Brands:
- Swiss 2
- Swiss Premium
- Swiss Premium

12443 Swiss Way Cheese
1315 Us Highway 27 N
Berne, IN 46711-1031
260-589-3531
Fax: 219-589-3843 swoss@swissway.com
Cheese
President: Tim Ehlerding
Operations Manager: Russ Reimer
Estimated Sales: $2.5 Million appx.
Number Employees: 5-9
Type of Packaging: Private Label
Brands:
- Berne Baby Swiss
- Berne Swiss Lace

12444 Swiss-American Sausage Company
251 Darcy Pkwy
Lathrop, CA 95330
209-858-5555
Fax: 209-858-1102
Processor and exporter of meat pizza toppings including pepperoni, salami, ham, linguica and raw and cooked sausage
President/CEO: Theodore Arena
Human Resources: Heidi Moore
Sales Manager: Paul Sheehan
Estimated Sales: $300,000-500,000
Number Employees: 50-99
Square Footage: 360000
Type of Packaging: Food Service, Private Label
Brands:
- Capo Di Monte

12445 Swisser Sweet Maple
6242 Swiss Road
Castorland, NY 13620-1244
315-346-1034
Fax: 315-346-1662
Pure NY maple syrup, pure maple cream spread, maple candies, maple lollipops, maple granulated sugar, gift arrangements, wedding party favors and corporate gifts. Retail, wholesale and bulk.
Co-Owner: Barbara Zehr
Co-Owner: Jason Zehr
Number Employees: 6
Type of Packaging: Consumer, Private Label, Bulk
Other Locations:
- Swisser Sweet Maple
- Casta-Land NY

12446 Swissland Milk
4310 South US Hwy 27
Berne, IN 46711
260-589-2761
Fax: 260-589-2761
Milk and yogurt
General Manager: Kirk Johnson
Estimated Sales: $1-2.5 Million
Number Employees: 10-19

12447 Switch Beverage
381 Post Rd
Darien, CT 06820
203-202-7383
Fax: 203-202-7386 www.switchbev.com
Juice
President/Owner: Mike Gilbert

12448 Switzer's Inc
209 S Belt E
Belleville, IL 62220
618-234-2225
Fax: 618-271-6339
bellevilleswitzerfoods@gmail.com
Frozen foods, groceries, provisions/meats and general merchandise; serving the food service market
President: Carolyn Hundley
switzerfoods@gmail.com
Estimated Sales: $20-50 Million
Number Employees: 20-49

12449 Sycamore Vineyards
PO Box 410
Saint Helena, CA 94574-0410
707-963-9694
Fax: 707-963-0554 800-963-9698
wineinfo@freemarkabbey.com
www.freemarkabbey.com
Wines
Director Winemaking: Ted Edwards
Winemaker: Tim Bell
Estimated Sales: $1.9 Million
Number Employees: 20

12450 Sylvin Farms Winery
24 N Vienna Ave
Egg Harbor City, NJ 08215-3245
609-965-1548
Sylvinfarms@comcast.net
www.sylvinfarmswinery.com
Wines
Proprieter: Frank Salek
Vineyard Manager: Franklin Salek
Estimated Sales: $500,000-$1 000,000
Number Employees: 1-4
Brands:
- Sylvin Farms

12451 Symms Fruit Ranch Inc
14068 Sunny Slopes Rd
Caldwell, ID 83607
208-459-4821
Fax: 208-459-6932 www.symmsfruit.com
Produce including apples, cherries, peaches and plums, necatrines, pluots, pears, wine grapes, asparagus, onions and potatoes.
Partner: Jim Mertz
jim@symmsfruit.com
Year Founded: 1914
Estimated Sales: $20 Million
Number Employees: 100-249
Square Footage: 150000
Type of Packaging: Consumer, Food Service, Bulk
Brands:
- Sss

12452 Symons Frozen Foods
619 Goodrich Rd
Centralia, WA 98531-9336
360-736-1321
Fax: 360-736-6328
Processor and exporter of frozen fruits and vegetables including blackberries, blueberries, red and black raspberries, corn, peas, peas/carrots and succotash
Owner: Bill James
bjames@symonsfrozenfoods.com
Production Manager: Howard McLoughlin
Estimated Sales: $18,200,000
Number Employees: 50-99
Type of Packaging: Consumer, Food Service, Private Label, Bulk

12453 Symphony Foods
1685 Short Street
Berkeley, CA 94702-1231
510-845-8275
Fax: 510-558-9255
General groceries
Owner: Alan Finkelstein
Number Employees: 1-4
Type of Packaging: Private Label

12454 Symrise Inc.
300 North St.
Teterboro, NJ 07608
201-288-3200
Fax: 201-462-2200 www.symrise.com
Global fragrance and flavorings company.
CEO: Dr. Heinz-Jürgen Bertram
CFO: Olaf Klinger
President, Scent & Care: Achim Daub
President, Nutrition: Dr. Jean-Yves Parisot
President, Flavor: Heinrich Schaper
Year Founded: 2003
Estimated Sales: $3.1 Billion
Number Employees: 9,649
Number of Products: 30K
Parent Co: Symrise AG
Other Locations:
- Customer Service
- Saddle Brook NJ
- Engineering, Purchasing, Production
- Branchburg NJ
- Production
- Elyria OH
- Chemical Production
- Goose Creek SC

12455 Synergy
2279 Resource Blvd
Moab, UT 84532-3406
435-259-5366
Fax: 435-259-2328 800-804-3211
customer-service@synergy-co.com
www.thesynergycompany.com
Organic nutritional supplements, vitamins, juice powder, and honey.

Food Manufacturers / A-Z

Founder/CEO: Mitchell May
CFO: Terry May
Quality Control Assurance: Tim Harkwright
Director of Sales: Sarah Muhlbradt
Contact: Steven Lattey
steven@synergyhc.com
Manager of Purchasing: Leslie Warren
Estimated Sales: Less Than $500,000
Number Employees: 1-4
Type of Packaging: Consumer

12456 Synergy Flavors Inc
1500 Synergy Dr
Wauconda, IL 60084-1073
847-487-1011
Fax: 847-487-1066
Global flavorings manufacturer.
Number Employees: 20-49
Type of Packaging: Consumer, Food Service, Bulk
Other Locations:
 U.S. Headquarters
 Wauconda IL
 U.K. Headquarters
 High Wycombe, UK
 Hamilton OH
 Rochester NY
 Ballineen, Ireland
 Sao Paulo, Brazil
 Samut Prakan, Thailand

12457 Synergy Plus
500 Halls Mill Rd
Freehold, NJ 07728-8811
732-308-3000
Fax: 732-761-2878
Vitamins
Manager: Barb McCleer
Vice President, General Counsel, Secreta: Ellen Chiniara
Sales Coordinator: Arthur Edell
Estimated Sales: Under $500,000
Number Employees: 250-499

12458 Synthite USA Inc.
840 South Oak Park Avenue
Suite 212
Oak Park, IL 60304
708-446-1716
synthiteusa@synthite.com
www.synthite.com
Global premium ingredients company headquartered in India with operations in Sri Lanka, China, Brazil and the USA.
Contact: Joseph Jesus
josephj@synthite.com

12459 Syracuse Casing Co
528 Erie Blvd W
Syracuse, NY 13204-2323
315-475-0309
Fax: 315-475-8536 makincasin@aol.com
Natural sausage casings
President: Peter Frey Sr
Estimated Sales: $2200000
Number Employees: 5-9
Square Footage: 60000
Type of Packaging: Food Service, Private Label, Bulk

12460 T G Lee Dairy
315 N Bumby Ave
Orlando, FL 32803-6029
407-894-4941
Fax: 407-896-4757 800-432-4872
www.tgleedairy.com
Citrus juices and milk including low-fat, chocolate, whole, skim, 1% and 2%; also, cream and ice cream cones, sandwiches and dixies
Manager: Billy Giovanetti
billy_giovanetti@deanfoods.com
CEO: Howard Dean
VP Sales/Marketing: Bill Giovanetti
Manager: Billy Giovanetti
billy_giovanetti@deanfoods.com
Number Employees: 500-999
Parent Co: Dean Foods Company
Type of Packaging: Consumer, Food Service, Private Label, Bulk
Brands:
 T.G. Lee Foods

12461 T Hasegawa USA Inc
14017 183rd St
Cerritos, CA 90703-7000
714-522-1900
Fax: 714-522-6800 www.thasegawa.com
Processor, importer and exporter of custom blended flavors and seasonings for beverages, cuisine, dairy, salad dressings, sauces and prepared foods
President: Mark Scott
mscott@thasegawa.com
President: Michiru Waku
Sales Manager (Western): Jeff Carlson
Sales Manager (Eastern): Robert Taylor
Estimated Sales: $8300000
Number Employees: 50-99
Square Footage: 216000
Parent Co: T. Hasegawa Company
Other Locations:
 T. Hasegawa U.S.A.
 Northbrook IL

12462 T M Duche Nut Co
1502 Railroad Ave
Orland, CA 95963-2035
530-865-5511
Fax: 530-865-7864 www.duchenut.com
Processor and exporter of almonds
President: Mosha Schwartz
CFO: Tim Gray
Manager: John Wilson
barbara.pruitt@pmi.org
Estimated Sales: $1-2.5 Million
Number Employees: 20-49
Type of Packaging: Consumer, Food Service, Private Label, Bulk

12463 T O Williams Inc
300 Wythe St
Portsmouth, VA 23704-5208
757-397-0771
Fax: 757-397-5702 towi@bellatlantic.net
Meat packer
Owner: Pete Chay
p.chay@towilliamsinc.com
CEO: Diane Chay
VP: Peter J Chay
President: Hyun J Chay
Marketing: Bridgette McClung
Estimated Sales: $1,600,000
Number Employees: 20-49
Square Footage: 39000
Type of Packaging: Food Service
Brands:
 Blue Ribbon Hot Sausage
 Diane's Italian Sausage
 H.C. Smoked Sausage
 Virginia Smoked Sausage

12464 T Sterling Assoc
121 W 4th St
Jamestown, NY 14701-5005
716-483-0769
Fax: 716-664-9508
Cheese marketing
Manager: Spring Martin
lakewoodcheeseny@windstream.net
Estimated Sales: $.5-1 000,000
Number Employees: 1-4
Type of Packaging: Private Label

12465 T&T Seafood
14550 Brown Rd
Baker, LA 70714
225-261-5438
Fax: 225-261-5260
Seafood
President: John Tourere
Estimated Sales: $2 Million
Number Employees: 1-4

12466 T'Lish Dressings and Marinades
904 5th Ave
Opelika, AL 36801-4133
205-503-8603
www.tlish.com
Salad dressings and marinades
Owner: Tiffany Denson
Brands:
 T'Lish vinaigrette & marinade

12467 T. Marzetti Company
380 Polaris Pkwy.
Suite 400
Westerville, OH 43082
614-846-2232
Fax: 614-848-8330 800-999-1835
www.marzetti.com
Bread and rolls, caviar, croutons, dairy products, dips, dressings and sauces, noodles and pasta, and specialty products.
President: David Ciesinski
Director, Marketing: Irene Castle
Year Founded: 1896
Estimated Sales: $922.9 Million
Number Employees: 2,700
Number of Brands: 14
Square Footage: 28000
Type of Packaging: Food Service, Private Label, Bulk
Brands:
 Marzetti
 New York Brand
 Sister Schubert's
 Flatout
 Girard's
 Amish Kitchens
 Chatham Village
 Marshall's
 Cardinis Salad Dressing
 Reames
 Inn Maid
 Romanoff
 Angelic Bakehouse
 What's For Dinner?

12468 T.B. Seafood
450 Commercial St
Portland, ME 04101-4636
207-871-2420
Fax: 207-871-0906
Seafood
President: Roderick Wintle Jr

12469 T.J. Blackburn Syrup Works
108 East Lafayette
Jefferson, TX 75657
903-665-2541
Fax: 903-665-1128 800-657-5073
Established in 1972. Manufacturer of jams, jellies and syrups.
President: Jeffrey Fuquay
Chief Information Officer: Sean Fuquay
Chief Operating Officer: Ronnie Bullard
Purchasing Executive: Troy Hunter
Estimated Sales: $40 Million
Number Employees: 50-99
Type of Packaging: Consumer, Bulk
Brands:
 Blackburn's

12470 T.J. Kraft
1535 Colburn St
Honolulu, HI 96817-4905
808-842-3474
Fax: 808-842-3475 tkraft@norpacexport.com
Various types of fresh Hawaiian seafood
President: Thomas Kraft
Estimated Sales: $10-20 Million
Number Employees: 10-19

12471 T.L. Herring & Company
2101 Old Stantonsburg Road
P.O. Box 3186
Wilson, NC 27893
252-291-1141
Fax: 252-291-1142 TLHERRINGCO@yahoo.com
www.tlherring.com
Processor and packer of hot dog chili, fresh pork sausage, souse meat, cooked chitterlings, all with Southern flavorings
President: Thomas Mark
CFO: Jean Herring
Vice President: Mike Herring
Estimated Sales: $5-10 Million
Number Employees: 10 to 19
Square Footage: 44700

12472 T.S. Smith & Sons
8887 Redden Rd
Bridgeville, DE 19933
302-337-8271
Fax: 302-337-8417 www.tssmithandsonsfarm.com

Food Manufacturers / A-Z

Apples, peaches, nectarines, sweet corn, asparagus, strawberries, soybeans, wheat, barley and broiles; exporter of apples
President: Matthew Smith
Sales (Wholesale/Retail): Thomas Smith
Production Manager: Charles Smith
Estimated Sales: $3-5 Million
Number Employees: 20-49
Type of Packaging: Consumer, Bulk
Brands:
    T.S. Smith & Sons

12473 T.W. Garner Food Company
614 W 4th St
Winston Salem, NC 27101-2730
    336-661-1550
Fax: 336-661-1901   800-476-7383
www.twgarnerfoodservice.com
Manufacturer of hot sauces, wing sauces and seafood sauces; sriracha sauces, salsa and tortilla strips.
CEO: Ann Garner Riddle
Chief Financial Officer: Matt Mccollum
Chief Marketing Officer: Glenn Garner
Chief Operating Officer: Heyward Garner
Estimated Sales: $17.7 Million
Number Employees: 27
Number of Brands: 3
Type of Packaging: Consumer, Food Service
Other Locations:
    T.W. Garner Production Facility
    Winston-Salem NC
Brands:
    Garner Jams & Jellies
    Green Mountain Gringo
    Texas Pete

12474 T.W. Garner Food Company
4045 Indiana Ave
Winston-Salem, NC 27105
    336-661-1550
www.texaspete.com
Manufacturer of hot sauces, wing sauces and seafood sauces; sriracha sauces, salsa and tortilla strips.
CEO: Ann Garner Riddle
Chief Financial Officer: Matt Mccollum
Chief Marketing Officer: Glenn Garner
Chief Operating Officer: Heyward Garner
Number Employees: 65
Number of Brands: 3
Parent Co: T.W. Garner Food Company
Type of Packaging: Consumer, Food Service

12475 TBJ Gourmet
1554 Paoli Pike
Suite 254
West Chester, PA 19380
    856-222-2000
info@tbjgourmet.com
tbjgourmet.com
Bacon jams
Managing Partner: Michael Oraschewsky
Estimated Sales: $1-2 Million
Type of Packaging: Food Service
Brands:
    TBJ Gourmet

12476 TCHO Ventures
Pier 17
San Francisco, CA 94111
    415-981-0189
Fax: 415-723-7497 info@tcho.com
www.tcho.com
Chocolate
President/Owner: Louis Rossetto
Director of Finance: Sam Christian
Contact: Chris Bell
c.bell@apple.com
Estimated Sales: $1.3 Million
Number Employees: 20

12477 TH Foods, Inc.
2134 Harlem Rd.
Loves Park, IL 61111
    815-636-9500
Fax: 815-636-8400 sales@thfoods.com
www.thfoods.com
Manufacturer of crackers, snack crips and chips.
President: Ken Takao
Brands:
    Crunchmaster
    Harvest Stone

12478 TIC Gums
4609 Richlynn Drive
Belcamp, MD 21017
    410-273-7300
Fax: 410-273-6469   800-899-3953
info@ticgums.com   www.ticgums.com
Manufacturer of texture and stabilization ingredients for the food industry.
Contact: Philip Abecket
pabecket@ticgums.com
Number Employees: 50-100
Type of Packaging: Bulk

12479 TMI Trading Co
7 Bushwick Pl
Brooklyn, NY 11206-2815
    718-821-5052
Fax: 718-821-6841 www.tmitrading.com
Asian-style beverages, snacks, and food.
Contact: Todd Abramson
todd@tmitrading.com
Number Employees: 5-9

12480 TNT Crust
P.O.Box 8929
Green Bay, WI 54308
    920-431-7240
Fax: 920-431-7249 tntcrust@tyson.com
www.tntcrust.com
Processor and exporter of pre-made, partially baked pizza crusts including thin, thick and raised edge; also, fresh and frozen pizza dough.
President: Roger Lebreck
Vice President: Shreenivas Manthana
VP Sales/Marketing: Larry Kropp
Sales Director: Larry Kropp
VP Operations: Kent Reschke
VP Engineering: Phil Vangsnes
Number Employees: 100-249
Parent Co: FoodBrands America
Type of Packaging: Food Service

12481 TODDS Enterprises Inc
2450 White Rd
Irvine, CA 92614-6250
    949-250-4080
Fax: 949-724-1338   800-568-6337
ed.stokes@us.hjheinz.com www.toddsfoods.com
Processor and exporter of soups, sauces, chili and salad dressings
Marketing Director: Ed Stokes
Contact: Carole Hoffman
Number Employees: 100-249
Type of Packaging: Food Service, Private Label
Brands:
    Todd's

12482 TOST Beverages LLC
54 Elizabeth St. # 110
Red Hook, NY 12571
info@tostbeverages.com
www.tostbeverages.com
Sparkling, non-alcoholic fruit-flavored beverage
CEO: Brooks Addington
Number of Brands: 1
Number of Products: 1
Type of Packaging: Consumer, Private Label
Brands:
    TOST

12483 TRC Corp
12320 E Skelly Dr
Tulsa, OK 74128-2414
    918-437-7310
Fax: 918-492-9546   800-258-5028
customerservice@reachforlife.com
Super oxygenated drinking water
President: Rocky Heinrich
rockyh@trccorp.com
CEO: Elmer Heinrich
Vice President: Shirley Heinrich
Estimated Sales: $7.5 Million
Number Employees: 20-49
Type of Packaging: Consumer
Brands:
    Liquidlise
    Super Oxy-Pure

12484 Tabard Farm Potato Chips
PO Box 351
Middletown, VA 22645-0351
    540-869-0104
Fax: 540-869-0176
Potato chips
Sales Manager: Sarah Cohen
Plant Manager: Chris Miller
Estimated Sales: $5-9.9 Million
Number Employees: 20-49
Parent Co: Tabard Corporation

12485 Tabatchinick Fine Foods
1230 Hamilton St
Somerset, NJ 08873-3343
    732-247-6668
Fax: 732-247-6555 info@tabatchnick.com
www.tabatchnick.com
Homemade soups, sorbets, icepops and cheese
Owner: Ben Tabatchinick
ben@tabatchinick.com
CFO: Robert Ingebretsen
VP/National Food Service: Peter Hans
Institutional Sales: Marc Blake
Chief Engineer: Bud Barry
Retail Sales Cooordinator: Claudia Davila
Commodities Coordinator: Barbara Slicner
Customer Relations: Michelle Kopitman
Plant Manager: Cezar Capalong
Estimated Sales: Below $5 Million
Number Employees: 20-49

12486 Tabco Enterprises
1906 W Holt Ave
Pomona, CA 91768-3351
    909-623-4565
Fax: 909-623-2605
Processor and exporter of nutritional food supplements including deep sea fish oil, shark cartilage, multivitamins and minerals, grape seed extract, herbal products, spirulina, garlic, etc
President: Bruce Lin
Financial Officer: Rebecca Lin
Estimated Sales: $5-10 Million
Number Employees: 20-49
Square Footage: 80000
Parent Co: Essential Pharmaceutical
Brands:
    Eden Life
    Essential Elite
    Wonderful Life

12487 Table De France
2020 S Haven Ave
Ontario, CA 91761-0735
    909-923-5205
Fax: 909-923-7804 info@micheldefrance.com
www.micheldefrance.com
Authentic French-Style Crepes, soy wraps, fan wafers, butter wafer cookies, rolled wafers and filled rolled wafers, Paillette Feuilletine and Parisian cakes.
Owner: Ovi Constantine
Owner/CFO: Philip Bayon
Quality Control: Teresa Aguire
Sales Director: Erwan Le Bayon
ovi@micheldefrance.com
Plant Manager: Philippe Le Bayon
Estimated Sales: $820,000
Number Employees: 10-19
Number of Products: 4
Square Footage: 120000
Type of Packaging: Food Service, Private Label
Other Locations:
    Table De France
    Ontario CA
Brands:
    Krazy
    Michel De France
    Table De France

12488 Table Talk Pies Inc
120 Washington St # 1
Worcester, MA 01610-2751
    508-798-8811
Fax: 508-798-0848
customerservice@tabletalkpie.com
www.tabletalkpie.com
4, 6, 8, 9, and 10 inch pies in a variety of dessert and fruit flavors
Director of Sales/Marketing: Bob Littlefield
Inside Sales: Tara Tula
Sales/Marketing: Louise Lindberg
Logistics: Valdemar Siqueira
Estimated Sales: $40 Million
Number Employees: 50-99
Brands:
    Table Talk

Food Manufacturers / A-Z

12489 Tabor Hill Winery & Restaurant
185 Mount Tabor Rd
Buchanan, MI 49107-8326
269-422-1161
Fax: 269-422-2787 800-283-3363
info@taborhill.com www.taborhill.com
Winery producing reds, whites, sparkling, dessert and non-alcoholic wines.
President: Linda Upton
CEO: Mike Merchant
Winemaker: Michael Merchant
Estimated Sales: $5.3 Million
Number Employees: 50-99
Number of Brands: 3
Type of Packaging: Consumer, Food Service
Other Locations:
  Tabor Hill Champagne Celler
  Bridgman MI
  Tabor Hill Wine Port
  Saugatuck MI
Brands:
  Michael Merchant Winemaker
  Tabor Hill
  Grand Mark

12490 Tadin Herb & Tea Co
3345 E Slauson Ave
Vernon, CA 90058-3914
323-728-5100
Fax: 323-582-8687 800-838-2346
support@tadincorp.com
Tea bags and cellophane-packaged herbs and capsules and herbal remedies
Owner: Laura Alvarez
Sales Manager: Davor Hervas
lalvarezparra@tadin.com
Estimated Sales: $5-10 Million
Number Employees: 50-99
Brands:
  Tadin

12491 Taffy Town Inc
55 W 800 S
Salt Lake City, UT 84101-2912
801-355-4637
Fax: 801-355-7664 800-765-4770
worlds_best_taffy@taffytown.com
www.taffytown.com
Salt water taffy
President: Jason Glade
worlds_best_taffy@taffytown.com
VP Marketing: Jason Glade
VP Manufacturing: Derek Glade
Estimated Sales: $1-2.5 Million
Number Employees: 20-49

12492 Taft Street Winery
2030 Barlow Ln
Sebastopol, CA 95472-2555
707-823-2049
Fax: 707-823-8622 www.taftstreetwinery.com
Wines consisting of Sauvignon Blancs, Chardonnays, Zinfadel, Russian river, PEKA Pinot Noir
President: Michael Tierney
miket@taftstreetwinery.com
General Manager/CEO: Mike Martini
Account Manager: Clayton SmithKey
Winemaker: Kent Barthman
Assistant Winemaker: Megan Baccitich
Cellar Master: Joel Rabune
Estimated Sales: $5-10 Million
Number Employees: 10-19
Type of Packaging: Private Label, Bulk

12493 Taftsville Country Store
2706 E Woodstock Rd
PO Box 2
Taftsville, VT 05073
802-457-1135
800-854-0013
clwilson@taftsville.com
Supplier of camembert, brie, stilton, gruyere and parmesan cheese, Vermont maple syrup, Vermont gourmet foods
President: Rebecca Loftus
Estimated Sales: $300,000-500,000
Number Employees: 1-4
Type of Packaging: Consumer
Brands:
  Blythedale

12494 Tahana Confections LLC
PO Box 4314
Portsmouth, NH 03802-4314
603-498-6246
www.tahanaconfections.com
Candy: Caramel
Owner/Founder: Amanda Telford
amanda@tahanaconfections.com
Estimated Sales: 83,000
Number Employees: 5-9

12495 Tahitian Gold
23883 Madison St
Torrance, CA 90505-6008
310-465-0856
Fax: 310-465-0857 info@tahitianvanilla.com
www.tahitianvanilla.com
Dessert toppings, baking & mixing ingredients, extracts
Owner: Manu Martin
Sales Manager: Caryn Briedis
pacificislandimports@yahoo.com
Operations Manager: Eddie Kikuchi
Number Employees: 1-4

12496 Taif Inc
600 Kaiser Dr # A
Folcroft West Business Park
Folcroft, PA 19032-2122
610-522-0122
Fax: 610-522-5305 info@tallutos.com
www.tallutos.com
Frozen pasta and related items
President: Joseph A. M. Talluto
joseph_talluto@taifinc.com
VP: Gus De Nicola
Number Employees: 5-9
Square Footage: 54000
Type of Packaging: Food Service
Brands:
  Talluto's

12497 Tait Farm Foods
179 Tait Rd
Centre Hall, PA 16828-7806
814-466-2386
Fax: 814-466-6561 800-787-2716
info@taitfarmfoods.com www.taitfarmfoods.com
Specialty jams, jellies, conserves, chutneys, scone and pan cake mixes, colonial fruit shrubs, international fruit sauces and herbal oils.
Wholesale Manager: Karen Myford
Estimated Sales: $80,000
Number Employees: 7
Type of Packaging: Private Label
Brands:
  Raspberry Teriyaki
  Tait Farm Foods

12498 Taiyo International Inc.
5960 Golden Hills Dr
Minneapolis, MN 55416-1040
763-398-3003
Fax: 763-398-3007 sales@taiyoint.com
www.taiyointernational.com
Manufacturer of functional ingredients for the food and pharmaceutical industries.
President: Nagahori Yamazaki
Executive Vice President: Yoshiki Yamazaki
Number Employees: 5-9
Brands:
  Sunphenon
  Organic Matcha Powder
  Teavigo

12499 Taj Gourmet Foods
4600 Sleepytime Dr.
Boulder, CO 80301
610-692-2209
800-434-4246
www.ethnicgourmet.com
Processor and exporter of ethnic entrees including Thai, Indian and Italian
President: Paul Jaggi
VP: Sangeeta Jaggi
VP Operations: Harmeet Shanhu
Estimated Sales: $5-10 Million
Number Employees: 25
Square Footage: 120000
Brands:
  Bravissimo
  Taj
  Thai Chef

12500 Takara Sake USA Inc
708 Addison St
Berkeley, CA 94710-1925
510-540-8250
Fax: 510-486-8758 info@takarasake.com
Manufacturer of sake, plum wine, mirin and sake kasu; importer of sake and shochu.
President: Yoshihiro Naka
yoshihiro@takarasake.com
Vice President: Hidetaka Iinuma
Regulations & Project Development: William Giddens
Senior Sake Tasting/Marketing Manager: Izumi Motai
Sales Manager: Samuel Geniella
Estimated Sales: $6.5 Million
Number Employees: 20-49
Number of Brands: 8
Square Footage: 15000
Parent Co: Takara Group
Type of Packaging: Consumer, Food Service
Other Locations:
  Takara Sake USA New York (Sales)
  Fort Lee NJ
  Takara Sake USA Los Angeles (Sales)
  Torrance CA
Brands:
  Sho Chiku Bai
  Hana
  Yuki Nigori
  Shirakabe Gura
  Takara
  Takara Plum
  Kinsen Plum
  Koshu Plum

12501 (HQ)Takasago International Corp
4 Volvo Dr
Rockleigh, NJ 07647-2508
201-767-9001
Fax: 201-784-7277 www.takasago.com
Flavors for soft drinks, desserts, confections, dairy products, and savory. Also food materials like fruit juices, coffee extracts, and tea extracts.
President & CEO: Satoshi Masumura
SVP, President USA Div.: Hisaya Fujiwara
VP Flavor Division: Takashi Matsuo
VP Research & Development Division: Takashi Miura
EVP Sales: Haruo Nakanishi
VP Public Relations: Hideki Saito
SVP Production: Kazuhiko Tokoro
Estimated Sales: $41.3 Million
Number Employees: 100-249
Square Footage: 50000
Other Locations:
  Northvale NJ
  Teterboro NJ
  New York NY
  Crystal Lake IL

12502 Takeiya USA
214 5th St # 204
Huntington Beach, CA 92648-8191
714-374-9900
Fax: 714-374-9925 www.takeyausa.com
Tea
CEO: John Lown
jlown@takeyausa.com
Vice President: Patrice Gerber
Customer Marketing Manager: Kristi Labrenz Galvan
Estimated Sales: D
Number Employees: 5-9

12503 Taku Smokehouse
550 S Franklin St
Juneau, AK 99801-1330
907-463-4617
Fax: 907-463-4644 800-582-5122
mailorder@takusmokeries.com
www.takustore.com
Processor and exporter of Alaskan salmon, halibut, crab and cod including frozen, portion cut, fillet, smoked, salted and packed
President: Sandro Lane
Smokehouse Manager: Jeremy LaPierre
General Manager: Eric Norman
CEO: Giovanni Gallizio
Contact: Laura Powers
lpowers@takusmokeries.com
Estimated Sales: Less than $500,000
Number Employees: 100-249
Square Footage: 200000

Type of Packaging: Consumer, Food Service, Private Label, Bulk
Brands:
   Taku

12504 Talbott Farms
3800 F-1/4 Road
Palisade, CO 81526
   970-464-5656
   talbottfarms.com
Peach and wine grape grower.
Brands:
   Mountain Gold
   Talbott's

12505 Talbott Teas
6475 Christie Avenue,
Suite 150
Emeryville, CA 94608
   Fax: 773-404-6420 855-850-6309
   www.talbottteas.com
Teas, including gourmet, green, black, white, rooibos
CEO: Shane Talbott
Contact: Steven Nakisher
steven@talbottteas.com
Number Employees: 5

12506 Talbott Vineyards
1380 River Rd
Salinas, CA 93908
   831-675-3000
   Fax: 831-675-3120 www.talbottvineyards.com
Wines-specializing in Chardonnay and Pinot Noir
General Manager of Sales: Dan Karlsen
dan@talbottvineyards.com
VP Sales and Marketing: Matt Viotto
General Manager: Sam Balderas
Marketing Coordinator: Andy Abraham
Marketing Manager: Ross Allen
Manager: Dan Karlsen
dan@talbottvineyards.com
Estimated Sales: Below $5 Million
Number Employees: 10-19
Number of Brands: 3
Number of Products: 7
Parent Co: E&J Gallo Winery
Type of Packaging: Consumer
Other Locations:
   Sleepy Hollow Vineyard
   Gonzales CA
   River Road Vineyard
   Sant Lucia Highlands CA
   Del Mar Vineyard
   Dalinas Valley CA
Brands:
   Kali Hart Chardonnay
   Logan Chardonnay
   Talbott Chardonnay
   Talbott Diamond T Chardonnay

12507 Talenti Gelato e Sorbetto
Dallas, CA
   www.talentigelato.com
Gelato and sorbetto.
Parent Co: Unilever

12508 Talisman Foods
3324 S 200 E
Salt Lake City, UT 84115
   801-487-6409
   Fax: 801-487-6409
Turkey
President: Chad Maddox
VP: Ben Maddox
Estimated Sales: $1-2,500,000
Number Employees: 5-9

12509 Talk O'Texas Brands Inc
1610 Roosevelt St
San Angelo, TX 76905-6235
   325-655-6077
   800-749-6572
   customerservice@talkotexas.com
   www.talkotexas.com
Pickled okra, liquid hickory smoked flavor
President/CEO: Larry Ricci
CEO: Russell Brown
VP: Lisa Ricci
VP Operations: Dan Herrington
Number Employees: 50-99
Square Footage: 180000
Type of Packaging: Consumer

12510 Talking Rain Beverage Co
30520 SE 84th St
Preston, WA 98050
   425-222-4900
   Fax: 425-222-4901 800-734-0748
   events@talkingrain.com www.talkingrain.com
Spring water, oxygenated water, sparkling water, diet flavored non-carbonated water and flavored non-carbonated water, enhanced with fruit flavors, enriched with natural herbal supplements and infused with vitamins.
Owner: Doug Mac Lean
Technical Service: James Fecteau
VP Marketing/R & D: Nina Morrison
VP: Michael Fox
Quality Control: Sam Samia
VP Sales: Wayne King
National Accounts Manager: John Stevens
Plant Manager: Chuck Park
Purchasing Manager: Monica Runyon
Estimated Sales: $5-10 Million
Number Employees: 50-99
Brands:
   Diet Ice Botanicals
   Sparkling Ice
   Talking Rain
   Talking Rain Biotonical

12511 Tall Grass Toffee Co
14406 W 100th St
Lenexa, KS 66215-1155
   913-599-2158
   Fax: 913-599-2160 877-344-0442
   www.tallgrasstoffee.com
Toffee and chocolate specialties
Owner: James Ladd
Estimated Sales: Less Than $500,000
Number Employees: 1-4

12512 Tall Talk Dairy
11961 S Emerson Road
Canby, OR 97013-9311
   503-266-1644
Dairy products
Marketing Director: Harlent Peterson
Sales Director: Esther Peterson

12513 Talley Farms
2900 Lopez Dr
Arroyo Grande, CA 93420-4999
   805-489-5400
   Fax: 805-489-5201 www.talleyfarms.com
Grower and exporter of produce including sugar peas, bell peppers, nappa, cabbage, romaine lettuce, zucchini, Blue Lake beans, spinach and cilantro
President: Brian Talley
btalley@talleyfarms.com
Sales: Todd Talley
Sales Director: Jeff Halfpenny
Operations Manager: Ryan Talley
Plant Manager: Arturo Ibarra
Estimated Sales: $10-20 Million
Number Employees: 250-499
Number of Brands: 2
Number of Products: 12
Type of Packaging: Consumer, Food Service, Bulk
Brands:
   Arroyo Grande
   Talley Farms

12514 Talley Vineyards
P.O. Box 360
Arroyo Grande, CA 93421-0360
   805-489-2508
   Fax: 805-489-5201 info@talleyvineyards.com
   www.talleyfarms.com
Estate wines such as Chardonnay and Pinot Noir
President: Don Talley
Marketing Director: David Block
CFO: Brain Caley
Contact: Brian Fiorentino
brian@talleyvineyards.com
Estimated Sales: Below $5 Million
Number Employees: 10-19
Brands:
   Talley Vineyards

12515 Tallgrass Beef Company
400 West Erie
Suite 500
Chicago, IL 60654
   312-846-1361
   tallgrassbeef.com
Beef

12516 Tamarack Farms Dairy
1701 Tamarack Rd
Newark, OH 43055-1390
   740-522-8181
   Fax: 740-522-9235 866-221-4141
   investors@kroger.com www.kroger.com
Milk and juices including fruit and vegetable
Chairman/CEO: David B Dillon
VP Operations: Mark Prestidge
Plant Engineer: Tony Neely
Number Employees: 100-249
Parent Co: Kroger Company
Type of Packaging: Consumer, Food Service, Private Label, Bulk
Brands:
   City Market
   Dillons
   Food4less
   Gerbes
   King Soopers
   Owen's
   Qfc
   Ralphs
   Smith's

12517 Tamarind Tree
518 Justin Way
Neshanic Station, NJ 8853
   908-369-6300
   800-432-8733
All-natural and preservative, wheat and gluten-free Indian vegetarian entrees, snack foods, condiments and spicy lentil crisps
President: Harshad Parekh
Number Employees: 1-4
Square Footage: 4000
Brands:
   Pappadums
   The Taste of India

12518 Tamashiro Market Inc
802 N King St
Honolulu, HI 96817-4513
   808-841-8047
   Fax: 808-845-2722 www.tamashiromarket.com
Japanese foods
President: Cyrus Tamashiro
Estimated Sales: $10-20 Million
Number Employees: 20-49

12519 Tampa Bay Fisheries Inc
3060 Gallagher Rd
Dover, FL 33527-4728
   813-752-8883
   Fax: 813-752-3168 800-732-3663
   info@tbfish.com www.tbfish.com
Variety of fresh and frozen shrimp, crab, clams, scallops, lobster tails, squid, mussels, frog legs, oysters.
President: Robert Patterson
CFO: Tom Tao
VP Sales/Marketing: Robert Hatcher
Human Resources Director: Sandi Fail
Operations Manager: Fred Godbold
Plant Manager: Mary Brown
Purchasing Director: Brenda Newman
Estimated Sales: $25 Million
Number Employees: 500-999
Square Footage: 18562
Type of Packaging: Consumer, Food Service

12520 Tampa Maid Foods Inc
1600 Kathleen Rd
Lakeland, FL 33805-3435
   863-687-4411
   Fax: 863-683-8713 800-237-7637
   info@tampamaid.com www.tampamaid.com
Processor, importer and exporter of frozen prepared seafood including breaded, peeled and deveined shrimp, stuffed flounder, oysters, scallops and appetizers
President/CEO: George Watkins
CFO: Dave Cordy
dcordy@tampamaid.com
Data Processing: Gene Gerstmeier
Production Manager: Kevin Stallworth
Purchasing Manager: Tim Moore
Number Employees: 250-499
Square Footage: 560000
Type of Packaging: Consumer, Food Service, Private Label, Bulk
Brands:
   Beer'n Batter
   Cap'n Joe
   Dipt'n Dusted

Food Manufacturers / A-Z

Grand Bayou
Oven Ready
Shrimp Jammers
Tampa Maid
Tropic Isle
Shrimp Teazers
Crab Teazers

12521 Tampico Beverages Inc
3106 N Campbell Ave
Chicago, IL 60618-7921
773-296-0190
Fax: 773-296-0191 877-826-7426
comments@tampico.com www.tampico.com
Processor, exporter and importer of beverage bases and citrus blends
CEO: John Carson
CEO: Scott Miller
VP Marketing: Tracey Schroeder
Number Employees: 50-99
Type of Packaging: Bulk
Brands:
Tampico Punches

12522 Tampico Spice Co
5941 S Central Ave
Los Angeles, CA 90001-1128
323-235-3154
Fax: 323-232-8686 info@tampicospice.com
www.tampicospice.com
spices and seasoning blends.
Vice President: Gabriel Martinez
National Sales Manager: David Martinez
Operations: Eduardo Freiwald
Estimated Sales: $6 Million
Number Employees: 20-49
Type of Packaging: Consumer, Food Service, Private Label, Bulk
Brands:
Tampico

12523 Tamuzza Vineyards
111 Cemetry Road
Hope, NJ 07844
908-459-5878
Fax: 908-459-5560 856-896-0619
winemaker@tamuzzavineyards.com
www.tamuzzavineyards.com
Wines
President: Al Ivory
Owner: Paul Tamuzza
Winemaker: Paul Tamuzza
Estimated Sales: $5-9.9 Million
Number Employees: 10

12524 Tanglewood Farms
297 Riverdale Rd
Warsaw, VA 22572
804-394-4505
Fax: 804-333-0422
Produce products such as cantaloupe, squash, tomatoes
President: Earl Lewis
VP: John E Lewis
Marketing: Ken Taylor
Estimated Sales: $2.5-5 000,000
Number Employees: 5-9

12525 (HQ)Tanimura Antle Inc
1 Harris Rd
Salinas, CA 93908-8608
831-455-2950
Fax: 831-455-3913 800-772-4542
www.taproduce.com
Processor and exporter of cauliflower, broccoli, broccoflower, celery, lettuce, scallions, green onions and value-added products.
Executive Vice President: Gary Tanimura
CEO: Rick Antle
rick@taproduce.com
Executive Vice President: Mike Antle
Number Employees: 100-249
Type of Packaging: Consumer
Other Locations:
Tanimura & Antle
Salinas CA
Brands:
Brian
Salad Time
T & A
Tanbro

12526 Tank's Meats Inc
3355 S State Route 51
Elmore, OH 43416-9799
419-862-3312
www.tanksmeats.com
Beef and pork
President: Al Amstutz
al@tanksmeats.com
Estimated Sales: $5-10 Million
Number Employees: 10-19
Type of Packaging: Consumer, Food Service, Bulk

12527 Tantos Foods International
15 Josiah Court
Markham, ON L3R 9A1
Canada
905-943-9993
Fax: 905-943-9943 info@tantos.com
Processor, exporter and importer of hot sauce, frozen fruit pulp, plantain, cassava and taro chips, annatto seeds, powder norbixin and ackees
President: Sultanali Ajani
Manager: Konrad Lutz
Estimated Sales: $390,000
Number Employees: 3
Square Footage: 28000
Parent Co: Mejores Alimentos de Costa Rica/Alina Foods C.A.
Type of Packaging: Consumer, Food Service, Private Label, Bulk
Brands:
Banana Gold
Tantos

12528 Tanzamaji USA
5602 Hummingbird Lane
Fairview, TX 75069
info@tanzamaji.com
tanzamaji.com
Bottled water
Managing Director: Beda Ruefer
Brands:
Smart Harvest

12529 Taos Brewing Supply
20 ABC Mesa Road
El Prado, NM 87571
575-779-0449
info@taosmesabrewing.com
www.taosmesabrewing.com
Producer of beer
President: Jonathan Riebli
Number Employees: 5-9
Square Footage: 16000

12530 Taos Mesa Brewing Co
20 Abc Mesa Rd
El Prado
El Prado, NM 87529
575-758-1900
www.taosmesabrewing.com
Specialty beers
Owner: Dan Irion
dan@taosmesabrewing.com
Founder: Jayson Wylie
Founder: Peter Kolshorn
Founder: Dan Irion
Number Employees: 5-9
Brands:
Taos

12531 Tapatio Hot Sauce
4685 District Blvd
Vernon, CA 90058-2731
323-587-8933
Fax: 323-587-5266 info@tapatiohotsauce.com
www.tapatiohotsauce.com
Processor and exporter of hot sauce
Owner/President: Luis Saavedra
Manager: Jose Saavedra
Estimated Sales: $2 Million
Number Employees: 20-49
Type of Packaging: Consumer, Food Service
Brands:
Tapatio

12532 Taqueria El Milagro
1927 S Blue Island Ave
Chicago, IL 60608-3014
773-579-2410
Fax: 773-650-4690 elmilagro@el-milagro.com
www.el-milagro.com
Mexican foods

President: Rafael Lopez
Marketing/Sales: Raulinda Fierria
Estimated Sales: Less Than $500,000
Number Employees: 5-9

12533 Tara Foods
801 Virginia Ave
Atlanta, GA 30354-1913
404-559-0605
Fax: 404-559-9090 www.tarafoodsindia.com
Peanut butter and flavoring extracts-nut spreads
Owner: Debra Theall
VP: Julie Davis
Plant Manager: Richard Barnhill
Estimated Sales: $300,000-500,000
Number Employees: 5-9
Parent Co: Kroger Company
Type of Packaging: Consumer, Food Service, Private Label
Brands:
Tara Foods

12534 Tarara Winery
13648 Tarara Ln
Leesburg, VA 20176-5236
703-771-7100
Fax: 703-771-8443 www.tarara.com
Wine specialties such as Chardonnay, Pinot Gris, Viognier, Cabernet Franc
Executive Director: Heather Akers
Manager: David Gwilliam
david.gwilliam@tarara.com
Operations Manager: Margaret Russell
Production Manager: Daniel Alcorso
Winemaker: Rob Warren
Estimated Sales: $5-10 Million
Number Employees: 20-49
Number of Products: 12
Brands:
Varietals
Viognier

12535 Tarazi Specialty Foods
13727 Seminole Dr
Chino, CA 91710-5515
909-628-3601
Fax: 909-590-4869 www.tarazifoods.com
Tahini and falafel dry mix
Owner: Ernest Busby
ernestbusby@tarazifoods.com
CFO: J Huleis
VP: J Huleis
Estimated Sales: $2-5 Million
Number Employees: 5-9
Square Footage: 47200
Type of Packaging: Consumer, Food Service, Private Label, Bulk
Brands:
Tarazi

12536 Tarazi Specialty Foods
13727 Seminole Dr
Chino, CA 91710-5515
909-628-3601
Fax: 909-590-4869 info@tarazifoods.com
www.tarazifoods.com
Sesame seeds-raw or roasted, Garbanzo beans, Tahini-a savory sesame paste, Falafel mix, and Tabouli
Owner: Rocco Fiore
rfiore@tarazifoods.com
CFO: Christine Huleis
Estimated Sales: $3 Million
Number Employees: 5-9
Brands:
Falafel Dry Mix
Tabouli
Tahini

12537 Target Flavors Inc
7 Del Mar Dr
Brookfield, CT 06804-2401
203-775-4727
Fax: 203-775-2147 800-538-3350
info@targetflavors.com www.targetflavors.com
Processor and exporter of flavorings and extracts
Owner: John Mac Lean
info@targetflavors.com
General Manager: Bill McLean
Estimated Sales: $2100000
Number Employees: 10-19
Square Footage: 100000

Food Manufacturers / A-Z

12538 Tartine Bakery
600 Guerrero St
San Francisco, CA 94110-1528
415-487-2600
Fax: 415-487-2605 info@tartinebakery.com
www.tartinebakery.com
Baked goods
Owner: Miranda Gomez
miranda.gomez@wellsfargo.com
General Manager: Suzanne Yacovetti
Estimated Sales: Less Than $500,000
Number Employees: 5-9

12539 Tase-Rite Co
1211 Kingstown Rd
Wakefield, RI 02879-2441
401-783-7300
Fax: 401-789-2889
General grocery and meats
President: Wesley Lessard
Marketing Director: Gary Lessard
Vice President: Gary Lessard
CFO: Wesley Lessard
Estimated Sales: $5-10,000,000
Number Employees: 5-9

12540 Taste It Presents Inc
200 Sumner Ave
Suite A
Kenilworth, NJ 07033-1319
908-241-0672
Fax: 908-241-9410 sales@tasteitpresents.com
www.tasteitpresents.com
Ethnic pastries
Vice President: Paula Perlis
andrew@tasteitpresents.com
Vice President: Larry Dimurro
Estimated Sales: $7.5 Million
Number Employees: 20-49
Type of Packaging: Consumer, Food Service, Private Label

12541 Taste Maker Foods
1415 E Mclemore Ave
Memphis, TN 38106-3470
901-274-4407
Fax: 901-272-1088   800-467-1407
custsvc@tastemakerfoods.com
Spcies, seasonings, bakery mixes and dry blends
Owner: Buford Tomlinson
stomlinson@tastemakerfoods.com
VP: Justin Reed
Quality Control: Stacey Castleman
Director Operations: Bill Tomlinson
Plant Manager: Justin Dukes
Estimated Sales: $5-10 Million
Number Employees: 20-49
Square Footage: 100000
Parent Co: Reed Food Technology
Type of Packaging: Consumer, Food Service, Private Label, Bulk
Brands:
   Old Hickory
   Taste Maker

12542 Taste Teasers
6910 Northwood Rd
Dallas, TX 75225
214-750-6334
Fax: 214-696-3316   800-526-1840
Processor and exporter of jalapeno based condiments and confections
President: Susanne Hilou
VP: Eddie Michel
Estimated Sales: $100,000
Number Employees: 1-4
Type of Packaging: Consumer, Food Service, Bulk
Brands:
   Hot Chocolate-Fine Chocolate
   Pepper Chicks

12543 Taste Traditions Inc
9097 F St
Omaha, NE 68127-1305
402-339-7000
Fax: 402-339-1579   800-228-2170
www.tastetraditions.com
Packer and exporter of precooked roast beef, pastrami, corned beef, smoked meats, frozen prepared soups, entrees, Mexican foods and home meal replacements
President: Harold Mann
CEO: Jeff Souba
jeffsouba@tastetraditions.com
VP: Linda Mann
VP Marketing: John Shipp
Sales Executive: Lewis Marshall
Plant Manager: Bruce Hamilton
Estimated Sales: $11.2 Million
Number Employees: 50-99
Brands:
   El Hombre Hambre
   Gourmet International
   Mann's International

12544 Taste Weavers
PO Box 189
Urbana, OH 43078-0189
937-206-0388
Fax: 866-388-0784   888-810-8365
contact@tasteweavers.com   www.tasteweavers.com
Manufacturer of dips, salsa, and grilling sauces.
Co-Founder: Robin Coffey
Co-Founder: Susan Neiswander

12545 Taste Wine Co
50 Third Ave
New York, NY 10003
212-461-1708
www.tastewineco.com
Winery
Year Founded: 2015
Estimated Sales: Less than $500,000
Number Employees: 2-10
Type of Packaging: Consumer, Private Label

12546 Taste of Gourmet
36 Sunflower Rd
Indianola, MS 38751
662-887-6760
Fax: 662-887-5547   800-833-7731
jennifer@tasteofgourmet.com
www.tasteofgourmet.com
Processor and exporter of catfish pate and capers; also, fudge and lemon pie mixes including fat-free
President: Evelyn Roughton
Estimated Sales: $885603
Number Employees: 20-49
Type of Packaging: Consumer
Brands:
   Antique Crown Foods
   Mississippi Delta Fudge
   Mississippi Mousse
   The Crown Restaurant Gourmet

12547 Taste of Nature Inc.
2828 Donald Douglas Loop North
Suite A
Santa Monica, CA 90405
310-396-4433
Fax: 310-396-4432 info@candyasap.com
www.candyasap.com
Candy
Manager: Scott Samet
Estimated Sales: $3-5 Million
Number Employees: 5-9
Brands:
   Care Bears Gummi Bears
   Cat In the Hat Cotton Candy
   Cat In the Hat Sour Gummies
   Cookie Dough Bites
   Cotton Candy Swirl
   Hulk Candies
   Jolt Cola Energy Rush
   Muddy Bears
   Shari Candies
   Sour Cotton Candy Swirl
   Spiderman Cotton Candy
   Spiderman Sour Gummi Mutant Spiders
   Sqwiggles
   Tiny Tarts

12548 Tastebuds Popcorn
208 N Main Street
Belmont, NC 28012
704-461-8755
mail@tastebudspopcorn.com
tastebudspopcorn.com
Popcorn
President: Jay Pithwa
General Manager: Jen Colangelo
Estimated Sales: $4 Million
Number Employees: 11-50
Brands:
   Tastebuds Popcorn

12549 Tastee Apple
60810 County Road 9
Newcomerstown, OH 43832-9638
740-498-8316
Fax: 740-498-6108   800-262-7753
customerservice@tasteeapple.com
www.tasteeapple.com
Apple products including chocolate covered apples; caramel apples; apple cider; and apple powder, in addition to jelly apples, candy apples and wild apples.
President: Greg Hackenbracht
greg@tasteeapple.com
Number Employees: 250-499
Type of Packaging: Consumer, Food Service, Private Label, Bulk
Brands:
   Tastee

12550 Tastepoint
10801 Decatur Rd
Philadelphia, PA 19154
215-632-3100
Fax: 215-637-3920   800-363-5286
customerrequest@tastepoint.com
www.tastepoint.com
Flavors including beef extract replacement, savory, nut, fruit, vanilla extract and raisin juice concentrate; also, stabilizers. Formerly known David Michael & Co.
Chairman & CEO: Andreas Fibig
EVP/General Counsel/Corp Secretary: Anne Chwat
EVP, Operations: Francisco Fortanet
Group President, Flavors: Matthias Haeni
Group President, Fragrances: Nicolas Mirzayantz
EVP/Global Scientific & Sustainability: Dr. Gregory Yep
EVP & Chief Financial Officer: Richard O'Leary
EVP & Chief Human Resources Officer: Dr. Susana Suarez Gonzalez
Year Founded: 1896
Estimated Sales: $22.2 Million
Number Employees: 100-249
Square Footage: 66000
Parent Co: International Flavors & Frangrances Inc.
Type of Packaging: Consumer, Private Label, Bulk
Brands:
   Beefmate
   Cocoamate
   Dm Choice
   Dm Ole
   Fairway
   Gorilla Vanilla
   Honeymate
   Michaelok
   Michtex
   Premier
   Raisinmate
   Super Supreme
   Supervan
   Supreme

12551 Tasty Baking Company
Navy Yard Corporate Center
#200, 3 Crescent Dr
Philadelphia, PA 19112
215-221-8500
800-248-2789
www.tastykake.com
Baked goods and snack cakes.
Research & Development: Shelley McDonnough
Year Founded: 1914
Estimated Sales: $250+ Million
Number Employees: 1,000-4,999
Parent Co: Flowers Foods
Brands:
   Butterscotch Krimpets(c)
   Chocolate Juniors(c)
   Chocolate Kandy Kakes(c)
   Cinnamon Mini Donuts
   Coconut Juniors(c)
   Creme Filled Butterscotch Krimpets(c)
   Dreamies
   Iced Fudge Cookies Bars
   Jelly Krimpets(c)
   Koffee Kake Juniors(c)
   Peanut Butter Kandy Kakes(c)
   Pretzel Rods
   Rich Frosted Mini Donuts
   Swirly Cups
   and many more

Food Manufacturers / A-Z

12552 Tasty Brand Inc
24003 Ventura Blvd # A
Calabasas, CA 91302-3926
818-225-9000
Manufacturer of gummies, fruit snacks, and cookies.
CEO: Liane Weintraub
CEO: Candace Ciongoli
candace@tastybrand.com
Number Employees: 5-9

12553 Tasty Mix Quality Foods
88 Walworth St
Brooklyn, NY 11205-2808
718-855-7680
Fax: 718-855-7681 tastymx@aol.com
www.tastyblend.com
Dough conditioners and stabilizers for the pasta and bakery industries
President: Salvatore Ballarino
Manager: Sal Ballarino Jr
Estimated Sales: $500,000
Number Employees: 5-9
Square Footage: 20000
Type of Packaging: Consumer, Food Service, Private Label, Bulk
Brands:
 Dough Stabilizer
 Gold-Tex Flour
 Shelf-Aid

12554 Tasty Seeds Ltd
130 Market Street
Winkler, NB R6W 4A3
Canada
204-331-3480
Fax: 204-325-6832 888-632-6906
Salted, seasoned and cajun sunflower seeds, and pumpkin seeds
Owner: Wayne Nestibo
Owner: Bryan Tyerman
Owner: Sales/Marketing Manger: Brad Edwards

12555 Tasty Selections
350 Creditston Road
Suite 102
Concord, ON L4K 3Z2
Canada
905-760-2353
Fax: 905-660-4585 www.tastyselections.com
Processor/manufacturers of frozen proportioned cookie dough, frozen muffin batters and a broad selection of thaw and serve cakes.
President: Alan Greenspoon
Owner: John Allenson
Estimated Sales: $2.3 Million
Number Employees: 60
Square Footage: 100000
Type of Packaging: Consumer, Food Service, Bulk

12556 Tasty Tomato
PO Box 6984
San Antonio, TX 78209-0984
210-822-2443
Fax: 210-822-2538 www.worldtrade.org
Spaghetti sauce
President: Charlotte Gallogly
Estimated Sales: $2.5-5 Million
Number Employees: 5

12557 Tasty Toppings Inc
2804 13th St
Columbus, NE 68601-4919
402-564-1347
Fax: 402-563-1469 800-228-4148
www.dorothylynch.com
Salad dressings
President: Gordon M Hull
Secretary: Joann Johnson
Number Employees: 20-49
Square Footage: 8000
Type of Packaging: Consumer, Food Service, Private Label
Brands:
 Dorothy Lynch Home Style

12558 Tastybaby
26880 Pacific Coast Hwy
#748
Malibu, CA 90265
310-457-6040
Fax: 310-317-4404 866-588-8278
info@tastybaby.com
Frozen organic baby food
President/Co-Founder: Shannan Swanson
CEO/Co-Founder: Liane Weintraub

12559 Tata Tea
1001 Dr Martin L King Jr Blvd
Plant City, FL 33563-5150
813-754-2602
Fax: 813-754-2272 www.tata.com
Tea
President: Ashok Bhardwha
Chairman: Patrick McGoldrick
Quality Control: Ivey Campbell
Estimated Sales: $2.5-5 Million
Number Employees: 20-49
Brands:
 Tata Tea

12560 Tatangelo's Wholesale Fruit & Vegetables
80 Hanlan Road
Unit 12
Woodbridge, ON L4L 3P6
Canada
905-850-0545
Fax: 905-850-2241 877-328-8503
Frozen fruit and vegetables
President: Rocco Tatangelo
Vice President: John Tatangelo
Estimated Sales: $6 Million
Number Employees: 14
Type of Packaging: Food Service
Brands:
 Tatangelo

12561 Tate & Lyle PLC
5450 Prairie Stone Pkwy.
Hoffman Estates, IL 60192
847-396-7500
www.tateandlyle.com
Specialty and bulk ingredients manufacturer serving the food, beverage and animal feed industries.
Chairman: Dr. Gerry Murphy
Chief Executive: Nick Hampton
Chief Financial Officer: Imran Nawaz
Executive VP/General Counsel: Lindsay Beardsell
Estimated Sales: $3.9 Billion
Number Employees: 4,162
Type of Packaging: Bulk
Brands:
 Avenacare Oat Beta Glucan
 CLARIA Starches
 DOLCIA PRIMA Allulose
 PrOatein
 PROMITOR Dietary Fiber
 PromOat Beta Glucan
 PUREFRUIT Monk Fruit Extract
 SODA-LO Salt Microspheres
 SPLENDA Sucralose
 STA-LITE Polydextrose
 TASTEVA Stevia Sweetener

12562 Tate's Bake Shop
43 North Sea Rd.
Southampton, NY 11968
631-283-9830
Fax: 631-283-9844 info@tatesbakeshop.com
www.tatesbakeshop.com
Cookies, bars, brownies, pies, cakes and gift baskets
Founder: Kathleen King
CEO: Maura Mottolese
Chief Financial Officer: Thomas Pawluk
Customer Service Manager: Jill Jenkins
Vice President, Operations: Ralph Palotta
Estimated Sales: $5 Million
Number Employees: 51-200
Brands:
 Tate's Bake Shop

12563 Tatra Herb Co
222 Grove St
Morrisville, PA 19067-1235
215-295-5476
Fax: 215-736-3089 888-828-7248
www.tatraherb.com
Herbal teas
CEO: George Zofchak
Estimated Sales: Less Than $500,000
Number Employees: 1-4
Type of Packaging: Consumer

12564 Tavalon Tea
100 Louis Street
Unit G
South Hackensack, NJ 7606
800-282-5051
tavalon.com
Tea
Contact: John-Paul Lee
john-paul@tavalon.com

12565 Taylor Cheese Corp
508 N Mill St
Weyauwega, WI 54983-9046
920-867-2337
Fax: 920-867-2360
Custom cheese cut, slice and wrap services for private label or conversion needs. Shingled slice packaging gift box components.
President: Robert Ehrenberg
Marketing Director: Bob Ehrenberg
Estimated Sales: Below $5 000,000
Number Employees: 10-19

12566 Taylor Farms
911 Blanco Cir Ste B
Salinas, CA 93901
831-754-0471
Fax: 831-794-0473 www.taylorfarms.com
Fresh cut fruit and vegetables including cantaloupe, honeydew, pineapple, onions, lettuce, peppers, garlic, cabbage and tomatoes
Chairman/CEO: Bruce Taylor
CFO: Tom Brain
Food Safety Department: Marshall Braga
Harvest Operations: Carson Braga
VP Production: Vikki Chandley
Number Employees: 5,000-9,999
Square Footage: 200000
Type of Packaging: Consumer, Food Service, Private Label, Bulk

12567 Taylor Farms Pacific
1820 N Macarthur Dr # 200
Suite 200
Tracy, CA 95376-2831
209-830-1086
www.taylorfarms.com
Salads, fruits and vegetables.
Manager: Oneyda Garcia
Contact: Christina Larkin
clarkin@taylorfarms.com
Purchasing Manager: Christina Larkin
Estimated Sales: $20-49 Million
Number Employees: 10-19
Number of Brands: 1
Square Footage: 80000
Parent Co: Taylor Fresh Foods
Type of Packaging: Consumer
Brands:
 Taylor Farms

12568 Taylor Lobster Co
32 Route 236
Kittery, ME 03904-5525
207-439-1350
Fax: 207-763-3861 info@taylorlobster.com
www.taylorlobster.com
Lobster
Owner: Bret Taylor
Estimated Sales: $1 Million
Number Employees: 10-19

12569 Taylor Meat Co
2211 W 2nd St
Taylor, TX 76574-2130
512-352-6357
Fax: 512-352-9426 info@taylormeat.com
www.taylormeat.com
Smoked meat company founded in 1947.
President: Ron Ivy
customerservice@taylormeat.com
Number Employees: 20-49
Type of Packaging: Consumer, Food Service, Bulk
Brands:
 Tip Top

12570 Taylor Orchards
1665 E Fall Line Fwy
Highway 96 West
Reynolds, GA 31076-2707
478-847-5963
Fax: 478-847-4464 www.taylororchards.com
Processor, packer and exporter of peaches

Food Manufacturers / A-Z

Owner: Jeff Wainwright
gafruit@pstel.net
Owner/Sales Manager: Walter Wainwright
Estimated Sales: $7215000
Number Employees: 100-249
Square Footage: 16000
Type of Packaging: Consumer, Bulk

12571 Taylor Precision Products
2311 W 22nd St # 200
Oak Brook, IL 60523-5625
  630-954-1250
  Fax: 630-954-1275   866-843-3905
  info@taylorusa.com   www.taylorusa.com
Manufactures thermometers, scales and related measurement devices.
CFO: Donald Robinson
VP: Donald Robinson
Director Sales/Marketing: Kent Beaverson
Contact: Elvira Abate
eabate@taylorusa.com
Estimated Sales: $1-2,500,000
Number Employees: 10-19
Type of Packaging: Consumer, Food Service, Private Label, Bulk

12572 Taylor Provisions Company
63 Perrine Ave
Trenton, NJ 08638-5114
  609-392-1113
  Fax: 609-392-1354
Meat products. Founded in 1939.
President: John T Cumbler
VP: George Cumbler
Estimated Sales: $10 Million
Number Employees: 75

12573 (HQ)Taylor Shellfish Farms
130 SE Lynch Rd
Shelton, WA 98584-8615
  360-426-6178
  Fax: 360-427-0327   Marcelle@taylorshellfish.com
  www.taylorshellfishfarms.com
Fresh and frozen oysters, clams, mussels, scallops and crabs
President: Jeff Pearson
Human Resources: John Fogo
Estimated Sales: $16 Million
Number Employees: 500-999
Type of Packaging: Consumer
Other Locations:
  Taylor Shellfish Farms
  Bow WA
Brands:
  Taylor Shellfish

12574 Taylor Wine Company
10223 Middle Rd
Hammondsport, NY 14840-9582
  607-868-3245
  Fax: 607-868-3246
Wines
Manager: Matt Doyle
Estimated Sales: $1-3 Million
Number Employees: 10-19
Parent Co: Canandaigua Wine Company

12575 Taylor's Mexican Chili Co Inc
116 S West St
Carlinville, IL 62626-1758
  217-854-8713
  800-382-4454
  www.taylorschili.com
Chili, sauce, beans
Owner: Joe Gugger
CEO: David Tucker
dave@taylorschili.com
Operations VP: Dave Tucker
Production VP: Dave Tucker
Estimated Sales: Less Than $500,000
Number Employees: 5-9
Brands:
  Taylor's Mexican Chili

12576 Taylor's Poultry Place
4701 Augusta Rd
Lexington, SC 29073-9197
  803-356-3431
  www.taylorssteakhouse.com
Poultry
President: Luther Taylor
jwetzel@sumter-sc.com
Estimated Sales: Less than $500,000
Number Employees: 1-4

12577 Taylor's Sausage Co
1822 N Grand Blvd
St Louis, MO 63106-1299
  314-652-3476
Sausages
President: John Taylor
Estimated Sales: Below $5 000,000
Number Employees: 5-9

12578 Tayse Meats
1979 W 25th St # C6
Cleveland, OH 44113-3435
  216-664-1799
Beef
Owner: Keith Tayse
Estimated Sales: Less than $500,000
Number Employees: 1-4

12579 Taza Chocolate
561 Windsor St
Suite B206
Somerville, MA 02143-4189
  617-623-0804
  Fax: 617-716-2085   info@tazachocolate.com
  www.tazachocolate.com
Chocolate, chocolate bars, cocoa, baking chocolate
Owner: Charles Braman
cbraman@aerotek.com
Founder: Kathleen Fulton
Estimated Sales: C
Number Employees: 50-99

12580 Taziki's Cafe
Birmingham, AL
  www.tazikis.com
Greek and Mediterrian cuisine. Dishes include gyros, sandwiches, soups, and salads.
Founder: Keith Richards
CEO: Dan Simpson
CFO: Billy Magruder
VP, Marketing & Growth: Rachel Layton
COO: Mike Smith
Year Founded: 1998
Type of Packaging: Consumer

12581 Tazo Tea
Kent, WA
  855-829-6832
  www.tazo.com
Premium teas, bottled tea and juice, organic chai and full leaf teas.
CEO, Unilever: Alan Jope
Year Founded: 1994
Estimated Sales: $1 Billion+
Number Employees: 60
Parent Co: Unilever
Type of Packaging: Consumer, Food Service

12582 Tea Aura
234 Dunview Avenue
Toronto, ON M2N 4J2
Canada
  416-225-8868
Shortbread cookies infused with tea
President: Susan Ho

12583 Tea Beyond
PO Box 1911
West Caldwell, NJ 07007
  973-226-0327
  Fax: 973-226-0327   info@teabeyond.com
  www.teabeyond.com
Authentic teas

12584 Tea Forte
23 Bradford St # 8
Concord, MA 01742-2971
  978-369-1598
  Fax: 978-369-3427   info@teaforte.com
  www.teaforte.com
Whole leaf teas with rough-cut herbs and flowers
President/Owner: Peter Hewitt
phewitt@teaforte.com
Estimated Sales: $10 Million
Number Employees: 20-49

12585 Tea Needs Inc
3000 Banyon Road
Boca Raton, FL 33432
  561-237-5237
  877-832-8289
  mark@teaneeds.com

Disposable instant cup of tea with teabag inside each cup. Three lines are available: tea, fruit tea, and Chinese herb tea.
President & Owner: Mark Reiman
VP: Alla Kartel
Marketing: Ed Camargo
Operations: Joyce Liang
Estimated Sales: $10 Million
Number Employees: 20-49
Number of Brands: 6
Number of Products: 18
Square Footage: 10000
Type of Packaging: Consumer, Private Label, Bulk
Brands:
  Happy Cup Tea

12586 Tea Room
130 Doolittle Dr
Units 2 and 13
San Leandro, CA 94577-1028
  510-567-8868
  Fax: 707-561-7081   info@thetearoom.biz
  www.rimann.com
Loose leaf tea, drinking chocolate, macarons, truffles, and tea infused chocolate.
CEO and President: Heinz Rimann
Number Employees: 1-4
Brands:
  TeaRoom

12587 Tea-n-Crumpets
252 Coleman Dr
San Rafael, CA 94901
  415-457-2495
  Fax: 415-457-1893
Organic crumpets, teas, jams, tea accessories and gift items from around the world.
President: Norman Barahona
CEO: Jena Rose
Estimated Sales: $1-3 Million
Number Employees: 1-4

12588 Teapigs
117 Grattan Street
Suite 320
Brooklyn, NY 11237
  212-705-8723
  info@teapigs.com
  www.teapigs.com
Matcha green tea
Associate Marketing Manager: Emily Spring
General Manager: Matthew Wood
Number Employees: 11-50
Type of Packaging: Bulk
Brands:
  teapigs

12589 Tearrific Ice Cream
480 Barnum Ave.
3rd Floor
Bridgeport, CT 06608
  203-354-9805
  info@tearrificicecream.com
  www.tearrificicecream.com
Manufacturer of ice cream infused with tea.
Founder: Mario Leite
sleite@tearrificicecream.com

12590 Teasdale Quality Foods Inc
901 Packers St
PO Box 814
Atwater, CA 95301-4614
  209-358-5616
  Fax: 209-357-5239
  customerservice@teasdalefoods.com
  www.teasdalefoods.com
Mexican foods, beans and sauces.
CEO: Kenneth Ancalade
kennetha@teasdale.net
CEO: Alberto Bandera
Estimated Sales: $20-49 Million
Number Employees: 100-249
Number of Brands: 2
Square Footage: 250000
Type of Packaging: Consumer, Food Service, Private Label
Brands:
  Aunt Penny's
  Teasdale

Food Manufacturers / A-Z

12591 Teawolf LLC
25 Riverside Dr # 7
Pine Brook, NJ 07058-9391
973-575-4600
Fax: 973-575-4601 info@teawolf.com
www.teawolf.com
Manufacturer of coffee, tea, vanilla, chocolate, botanical and specialty products for the food, beverage and nutritional supplement industries.
Owner: Gambrell Bill
bgambrell@teawolf.com
Estimated Sales: $5-10 Million
Number Employees: 5-9
Type of Packaging: Private Label

12592 Tebay Dairy Company
Lubeck Road
Parkersburg, WV 26101-7761
304-863-3705
Fax: 304-863-8712
Dairy products including ice cream
Owner: Robert Kent Tebay
Owner: Bob Tebay
Estimated Sales: $3,200,000
Number Employees: 10-19
Type of Packaging: Consumer
Brands:
  Tebay

12593 Techno Food IngredientsCo., Ltd
236 W Clary Ave
San Gabriel, CA 91776
626-288-8478
Fax: 626-288-8479 sales@techno-fi.com
Food ingredients specializing in sucralose.
Owner: Helena Xue
Number Employees: 200-500

12594 Techno USA
236 W Clary Avenue
San Gabriel, CA 91776
626-288-8478
Fax: 626-288-8479 sales@techno-fi.com
www.techno-fi.com
Sucralose
Owner: Helena Xue
Marketing Manager: Peter Zou
Estimated Sales: $370,000
Number Employees: 3
Parent Co: Techno Food Ingredients Co., Ltd.
Other Locations:
  Headquarters
  Guangzhou, China
  Manufacturing Plant
  Yongan, Fujian, China
  San Gabriel CA
  Vancouver, Canada
  Hong Kong

12595 Technology Flavors & Fragrances
10 E Edison St
Amityville, NY 11701
631-789-8228
Fax: 631-842-8332
Natural and artificial flavors for the beverage and food industries
CFO: Joseph A Gemmo
Chairman/CEO: Phil Rosner
CEO: Philip Rosner
Marketing Director: Virginia Bonofligio
Sales Director: Gary Frumberg
Contact: Richard Cerniglia
cerniglia@tffi.com
Operations/Production: Ronald Dintemann
Plant Manager: Joseph Piazza
Purchasing Manager: Rose Marotta
Estimated Sales: $15,587,285
Number Employees: 50-99
Number of Products: 1200
Square Footage: 104000

12596 Tecumseh Poultry, LLC
13151 Dovers St.
Waverly, NE 68462
402-786-1000
www.smartchicken.com
Air-chilled chicken products including whole chickens, boneless skinless breasts, tenderloins, thin sliced breasts, boneless skinless thighs, drumsticks, thighs, and wings. Also, pre-cooked chicken sausage products includingfrankfurters; and chicken broth.
President: Kevin Siebert
Year Founded: 1998
Number Employees: 600
Number of Brands: 1
Type of Packaging: Private Label
Brands:
  Smart Chiken

12597 Ted Drewes Frozen Custard
6726 Chippewa St
St Louis, MO 63109-2533
314-481-2652
Fax: 314-481-4241 www.teddrewes.com
Frozen custard
President: Ted Jr Drewes
Manager: Travis Dillion
tdrewes@teddrewes.com
Estimated Sales: Below $5 Million
Number Employees: 50-99

12598 Ted Shear Assoc Inc
1 West Ave # 210
Larchmont, NY 10538-2471
914-833-0017
Fax: 914-833-0233 ted.shear@verizon.net
Honey and vanilla extracts
President: Ted Shear
katestanley@avis.com
Estimated Sales: $1-3 000,000
Number Employees: 1-4
Type of Packaging: Private Label

12599 Teddy's Tasty Meats
6123 Mackay St
Anchorage, AK 99518-1739
907-562-2320
Fax: 907-562-1919
Meat
President: Ted Kouris
Secretary/Treasurer: Barbara Kouris
Vice President: Steven Kouris
Number Employees: 20-49

12600 Tee Pee Olives, Inc.
411 Theodore Fremd Avenue
Suite 120
Rye, NY 10580
914-925-0450
Fax: 914-925-0458   800-431-1529
lucy.teepeeolives@verizon.net
www.teepeeolives.com
Importer and packer of bulk Spanish green olives in the US.
Pres/CEO/Mktg/Purchasing: Lucy Landesman
CFO: William Barrett
VP/Quality Control: Robert Cory PhD
VP Sales: Deborah Eklund
COO: Joseph Fairchild
Plant Manager: Robert Roaden
Purchasing Manager: Emil Cairo
Estimated Sales: $10-20 Million
Number Employees: 50
Type of Packaging: Consumer, Food Service, Private Label, Bulk

12601 Teeccino
1015 Cindy Ln # A
Carpinteria, CA 93013-2905
805-966-0999
Fax: 805-966-0855   800-498-3434
info@teeccino.com www.teeccino.com
Herbal coffee, tea, and cereal.
President/Founder: Caroline MacDougall
CEO: Caroline Macdougall
caroline@teeccino.com
CFO: Jerry Isenberg
Marketing Communications: Danielle Edberg
Sales Manager: Devon Garnsey
Operations Manager: John Magee
Warehouse Manager: Eddie Bolvito
Estimated Sales: $1,000,800
Number Employees: 10-19
Number of Brands: 1
Number of Products: 7
Type of Packaging: Consumer, Food Service, Private Label, Bulk
Brands:
  Balanced Coffee
  Teeccino Caffeine-Fr

12602 Teelee Popcorn
101 W Badger St
Shannon, IL 61078-9020
815-864-2363
Fax: 815-864-2388   800-578-2363
Processor and exporter of microwaveable popcorn
Owner: Gary Armstrong
VP/Sales: Ken Weaver
garyarmstrong@teeleepopcorn.com
Estimated Sales: $2 Million
Number Employees: 20-49
Square Footage: 100000
Type of Packaging: Consumer, Private Label, Bulk
Brands:
  Prime Time
  Tee Lee

12603 Teeny Foods Inc
3434 NE 170th Pl
Portland, OR 97230-5072
503-252-3006
Fax: 503-254-3004 info@teenyfoods.com
www.teenyfoods.com
Producer of hand held entrees, filled breadmakers, pizza crust, flatbread.
President: Rick Teeny
rick.teeny@teenyfoods.com
General Manager: Darryl Abram
VP Finance: Don Parsons
VP: Debbi Teeny
Marketing Manager: Janna Woodgate
VP Sales: Darryl Abram
VP Operations: Michel Layonn
Plant Manager: Dave Hermanson
Purchasing: Ken Martin
Estimated Sales: $15-20 Million
Number Employees: 100-249
Square Footage: 116000
Brands:
  Teeny Foods

12604 Teeny Tiny Spice Company of Vermont LLC
PO Box 1113
Shelburne, VT 05482
802-598-6800
Fax: 603-768-4247 info@teenytinyspice.com
www.teenytinyspice.com
Organic spice blends.
Owner: Thora Pomicter
Owner: Ed Pomicter

12605 Teff Co
7 9th Ave N
Nampa, ID 83687-3354
208-465-0987
Fax: 208-459-0481   888-822-2221
questions@teffco.com www.teffco.com
Whole grain and flour
President: Wayne Carlson
Marketing Director: Elizabeth Carlson
Manager: Gareth Carlson
Number Employees: 5-9
Brands:
  Maskal Teff

12606 Teixeira Farms, Inc.
2600 Bonita Lateral
Santa Maria, CA 93458
805-928-3801
Fax: 805-928-9405 info@teixeirafarms.com
Grower of lettuce, broccoli, cabbage, and celery.
Co-Owner: Dean Teixeira
Co-Owner: Glenn Teixeira
Co-Owner: Marvin Teixeira
Co-Owner: Allan Teixeira
Co-Owner: Norman Teixeira
Contact: Dan Cooper
dan@teixeirafarms.com
Estimated Sales: $20-50 Million
Number Employees: 300
Type of Packaging: Consumer, Private Label, Bulk
Brands:
  Teixeira

12607 Tejon Ranch Co
4436 Lebec Rd
Lebec, CA 93243-9705
661-248-3000
Fax: 661-248-6209 bzoeller@tejonranch.com
www.tejonranch.com
Processor and exporter of pistachios, walnuts, almonds and wine grapes

President/CEO: Robert Stine
CEO: Gregory S Bielli
bielli@tejonranch.com
CFO/VP/Corporate Secretary: Allen Lyda
Vice President, Controller: Abel Guzman
Vice President of Corporate Communicatio: Barry Zoeller
Vice President of Operations: Brian Grant
Estimated Sales: Less than $500,000
Number Employees: 100-249
Type of Packaging: Consumer, Private Label, Bulk

12608 Tekita House Foods
6848 El Paso Drive
El Paso, TX 79905-3336
915-779-2181
Fax: 915-775-1857
Mexican food products, including tortillas, tostadas, pico de gallo salsa, chorizo, tamales, chiles rellenos, taco roll, flautas and pork crackling
President: Nelson Guerra
Estimated Sales: $500,000 appx.
Number Employees: 10-19

12609 Tell City Pretzel Company
1315 Washington Street
Tell City, IN 47586
812-548-4499
Fax: 812-548-4434 www.tellcitypretzel.com
Hard pretzels
Owner: Craig Kendall
Plant Manager: Betty Beard
Estimated Sales: $110000
Number Employees: 3
Type of Packaging: Consumer, Bulk

12610 Temo Candy
495 W Exchange St
Akron, OH 44302-1403
330-376-7229
Confectionery products
President: Lawrence Temo
Estimated Sales: $344,051
Number Employees: 5-9
Square Footage: 30000
Parent Co: Temo's
Type of Packaging: Consumer
Brands:
    Temo's

12611 Tempest Fisheries LTD
38 Hassey St
New Bedford, MA 02740-7209
508-997-0720
Fax: 508-990-2117
Fish and seafood
President: Timothy Mello
tempest01@rcn.com
Estimated Sales: $5-10 Million
Number Employees: 5-9

12612 Templar Food Products
571 Central Avenue
New Providence, NJ 7974
908-665-9511
Fax: 908-665-9122 800-883-6752
info@icedtea.com www.icedtea.com
Templar Food Products manufactures private-label tea using black, green, and oolong sourced from around the world. Tea mixture and flavor is customized according to customer preference.
President/Founder: Edward D Reeves
Manager of Laboratory: Trudy Genna
Sales Manager: Spencer Griffith
Contact: Michael Eagan
michael@icedtea.com
VP, Operations: Michael Murray
Estimated Sales: $870,000
Number Employees: 10-19
Type of Packaging: Private Label
Brands:
    Perfect Choice

12613 Temptee Specialty Foods
2011 E 58th Ave
Denver, CO 80216
303-292-1577
Fax: 303-292-1701 800-842-1233
info@tempteeco.com tempteeco.com
Portion controlled deli meats including beef; also, specialty processing available
President: Jack Lowe
Sales Manager: Jim Mayworm

Estimated Sales: $3,616,653
Number Employees: 20-49
Square Footage: 40000

12614 Ten Ren Tea & Ginseng Co Inc
75 Mott St
New York, NY 10013-4812
212-349-2286
Fax: 212-349-2180 800-292-2049
tenrenusa@aol.com
Tea
President: Mark Lee
Founder: Ray Ho Lee
Estimated Sales: Below $5 Million
Number Employees: 10-19
Brands:
    Ten Ren's Tea

12615 Tenayo
250 West Broadway
5th Floor
New York, NY 10013
917-677-7607
hello@tenayo.com
www.tenayo.com
Salsa
Founder: Arturo Cruz
Chief Marketing Officer: Andrew Bourke
Estimated Sales: $7 Million
Number Employees: 1-10
Brands:
    Tenayo

12616 Tennessee Bun Company
2975 Armory Dr.
Nashville, TN 37204
615-256-6500
Fax: 615-256-2084 888-486-2867
www.buncompany.com
Hamburger buns
President: Joe Waters
Chief Executive Officer: Cordia Harrington
CFO: Tom Harrington
VP Operations: Dave Nemecheck
Contact: Katie Austin
katie.austin@buncompany.com
Estimated Sales: Below $5 Million
Number Employees: 50-99
Brands:
    Tennessee Bun

12617 Tennessee Valley Packing Co
307 1/2 Carter St
Columbia, TN 38401-2925
931-388-2623
Fax: 931-388-2624
Meat products including sausages, frankfurters and bologna
President: Richard Jewell Jr
Estimated Sales: $3-5 Million
Number Employees: 5-9
Type of Packaging: Consumer

12618 Tenth & M Seafoods
1020 M St
Anchorage, AK 99501-3317
907-272-6013
Fax: 907-272-1685 800-770-2722
tenmsea@alaska.net www.10thandmseafoods.com
Processor, exporter and wholesaler/distributor of salmon, halibut, shrimp and king crab and scallops. Also operates under the name Alaska Sea Pack, Inc
President: Skip Winfree
tenmsea@alaska.net
Vice President: Rob Winfree
Sales Manager: Dannon Southall
Estimated Sales: $8 Million
Number Employees: 20-49
Type of Packaging: Consumer, Food Service

12619 Terlato Kitchen
2401 Waukegan Rd
Bannockburn, IL 60015-1505
855-805-7221
info@terlatokitchen.com
www.terlatokitchen.com
Pomodoro sauces, preserves and baking mixes
Sales Manager: Taylor Young
General Manager: Ann Kidd
Estimated Sales: Under $500,000
Number Employees: 2-10
Brands:
    Terlato Kitchen

12620 Terra Botanica Products
92 Waycaster Circle
Dahlonega, GA 30533
Canada
770-718-9340
sales@terrabotanica.com
Homeopathics, botanical extracts, capsules, gels and vitamins
president: John Miller
CEO: Connie Miller
Marketing Director: John Miller
Sales Director: Paul Peterson
Contact: Greg Grabowski
ggrabowski@terrabotanica.com
Number Employees: 10,000+
Type of Packaging: Private Label

12621 Terra Flavors & Fragrances
45 W 34th Street
Suite 1103
New York, NY 10001
212-244-1181
Fax: 212-681-9813 info@terraflavors.com
www.terraflavors.com
Manufacturer of essential oils, natural flavors, synthetic aromas and botanical extracts.
Type of Packaging: Food Service

12622 Terra Ingredients
730 2nd Ave. S
Minneapolis, MN 55402
612-486-3954 888-497-3308
Fax: hello@terraingredients.com
www.terraingredients.com
Beans, cereal, corn, flax, fonio, oilseeds including soybeans and chia, grains including quinoa and buckwheat, lintels, peas, and chickpeas.
Co-Founder & CEO: Rolf Peters
Co-Founder & COO: Tim Carlson
CFO: Bill Hren
Year Founded: 2000
Number Employees: 50-200
Type of Packaging: Private Label

12623 Terra Ingredients LLC
Minneapolis, MN
Fax: 612-486-3954 855-497-3308
hello@terraingredients.com
www.terraingredients.com
Whole organic ingredients for feed and consumer products, including flax, beans and lentils, corn, quinoa, millet, buckwheat, oats, rye, barley, wheat, soybeans, chia seeds and complete feed ingredient blends
Year Founded: 2000
Number of Brands: 1
Type of Packaging: Private Label, Bulk

12624 Terra Origin, Inc.
Hauppauge, NY 11788
631-300-2306
info@terraorigin.com
www.terraorigin.com
Health supplements and powders, including superfood powder blends, whey protein powder, bone broth protein, plant-based protein and antioxidant formula capsules
Year Founded: 2017
Number of Brands: 1
Number of Products: 21
Type of Packaging: Consumer, Private Label
Brands:
    Terra Origin

12625 Terra Sol Chile Company
9415 Burnet Road 106
Austin, TX 78758
512-836-3525
Fax: 512-533-9388
Chili
Founder: Alexandra Weeks

12626 Terra's
PO Box 265
Perham, MN 56573-0265
218-346-4100
Beef
President: Rod Osvold
Estimated Sales: Under $500,000
Number Employees: 1-4

Food Manufacturers / A-Z

12627 Terrace At J Vineyards
11447 Old Redwood Hwy
Healdsburg, CA 95448-9523
707-431-5400
Fax: 707-431-5410 800-885-9463
info@jwine.com www.jwine.com
Wines
President: Judy Jordan
judy.jordan@jwine.com
Regional Sales Manager: Brandon Vorst
Public Relations: Robin Oden
Winemaker: Lisa Kashin
Estimated Sales: $5-9.9 Million
Number Employees: 50-99
Parent Co: E&J Gallo Winery
Type of Packaging: Private Label
Brands:
  J Nicole Vineyard Pinot Noir
  J Russian River Vall
  J Sparkling Wine

12628 Terranettis Italian Bakery
844 W Trindle Rd
Mechanicsburg, PA 17055-4095
717-697-5434
Fax: 717-697-6815 www.terranettis.com
Baked goods manufacturer.
President: Terry McMahon
Number Employees: 20-49
Type of Packaging: Consumer, Food Service
Brands:
  Terranetti's

12629 Terrapin Ridge
1208 S Myrtle Ave
Clearwater, FL 33756-3425
727-442-3663
800-999-4052
www.terrapinridge.com
Dips, dressings, extracts, jams, jellies, mustards, sauces, sweet toppings
Co-Owner: Brian Coughlin
Co-Owner: Mary O'Donnell
Co-Founder: Susan Furst
Number Employees: 5-9
Type of Packaging: Consumer, Private Label

12630 Terrell Meats
1211 E Main St
Delta, UT 84624
435-864-2600
Fax: 435-864-2600
Beef jerky, beef, pork and lamb
Partner: Clark Terrell
Estimated Sales: $1,200,000
Number Employees: 6
Type of Packaging: Consumer, Food Service

12631 Terrell's Potato Chip Co
218 Midler Park Dr
Syracuse, NY 13206-1819
315-437-2786
Fax: 315-437-2069 terrellschip@msn.com
Potato chips including regular, barbecue, onion and sour cream; also, salsa
President: Jack Terrell
terrellschip@msn.com
Estimated Sales: $6500000
Number Employees: 100-249
Type of Packaging: Consumer
Brands:
  Bachman
  Keystone

12632 Terressentia Corp.
3525 Iron Horse Rd # 104
Suite 104
Ladson, SC 29456-4331
843-225-3100
Fax: 843-225-3107 simon.burch@terressentia.com
www.terressentia.com
Distilled spirits
CEO: Joseph Bosco
joe@terressentia.com
CEO: Earl Hewlette
Number Employees: 10-19

12633 (HQ)Terri Lynn Inc
1450 Bowes Rd
Elgin, IL 60123-5539
847-741-1900
Fax: 847-741-7791 800-323-0775
sales@terrilynn.com www.terrilynn.com
Manufacturer and wholesaler of nuts, dried fruits and coated nuts.
President: Terri Graziano
Estimated Sales: $5-10 Million
Number Employees: 100-249
Number of Brands: 1
Number of Products: 600
Square Footage: 108000
Type of Packaging: Food Service, Private Label, Bulk
Other Locations:
  Terri Lynn-Pecan Shelling Operation
  Cordele GA

12634 Terry Brothers, Inc
5039 Willis Wharf Dr
Willis Wharf, VA 23486
757-442-6251
Fax: 757-824-3461 infoat@terrybrothers.com
www.terrybrothers.com
Clams and oysters
President: N Terry Jr
Estimated Sales: $2.5-5 Million
Number Employees: 5-9
Type of Packaging: Consumer, Food Service
Brands:
  Sewansecott
  Terry Brothers

12635 Terry Foods
Genesis Centre, 18 Innovation Way
North Staffs Business Park
Stoke-on-Trent, ST6 4BF
UK
enquiries@terryfoods.com
www.terryfoods.com
Ingredients wholesaler
CEO: John Gardiner
CFO: Nikolai Terry
Sales Manager: Larry Haws
Estimated Sales: $5-10 Million

12636 Tessemae's All Natural
8805 Kelso Dr.
Essex, MD 21221
855-698-3773
customerhappiness@tessemaes.com
www.tessemaes.com
Salad dressings, condiments, and marinades. Keto, vegan, and gluten free options available
Co-Founder: Brian Vetter
Co-Founder/CEO: Greg Vetter
Director Marketing: Keri Nwosu
EVP Sales & Strategy: Shawn McLaughlin
VP National Accounts: Mike Shields
Year Founded: 2009
Number Employees: 50-99

12637 Tessenderlo Kerley Inc
2255 N 44th St # 300
Phoenix, AZ 85008-3279
602-889-8300
Fax: 602-889-8430 800-669-0559
info-tki@tkinet.com www.tkinet.com
Producer of high quality gelatins for the food, pharmaceutical and photoghaphic industry, operating worldwide
Vice President: Larry Tryon
ltryon@tkinet.com
CEO: Jordan Burns
Estimated Sales: $3-5 Million
Number Employees: 50-99
Type of Packaging: Private Label
Brands:
  Cryogel
  Instagel
  Solgel
  Swiftgel

12638 Test Laboratories Inc
7121 Canby Ave
Reseda, CA 91335-4304
818-881-4251
Fax: 818-881-6370 rob@testlabinc.com
www.testlabinc.com
Processor and exporter of enzymes, flavors and ingredients.
President: Rob Brewster
Estimated Sales: $1,100,000
Number Employees: 20-49
Square Footage: 4000
Brands:
  Brewster Nutrition
  Testlab
  Vitalfa

12639 Testamints Sales-Distribution
41 Lakeside Blvd
Hopatcong, NJ 07843-1339
226-946-3677
Fax: 973-895-3742 888-879-0400
orders@testamints.net www.testamints.net
Confections
President: Al Poe
Contact: Mark Bontempo
markbontempo@testamints.net
Estimated Sales: Less Than $500,000
Number Employees: 1-4
Brands:
  Promise Pops
  Testamints Chewing Gum
  Testamints Fruit Flavored Candy
  Testamints Sour Fruit Mints
  Testamints Sugar Free Mints
  Testamints Sugar Mints

12640 Teti Bakery
27 Signal Hill Avenue
Etobicoke, ON M9W 6V8
Canada
416-798-8777
Fax: 416-798-8749 800-465-0123
www.tetibakery.com
Pizza, pizza crusts and Italian flat bread; exporter of pizza crusts
President: Franco Teti
VP: Dino Teti
Sales Manager: Tony Saldutto
Estimated Sales: $2 Million
Number Employees: 50
Square Footage: 56000
Type of Packaging: Consumer, Food Service, Private Label, Bulk
Brands:
  San Mario
  Teti

12641 (HQ)Tetley Tea
890 Mountain Avenue
Suite 105
New Providence, NJ 07974
203-929-9200
Fax: 203-925-0512 800-728-0084
info@tetleyusa.com www.tetleyusa.com
Tea, coffee and tea bags
President: John Petrizzo
President: Glynne Jones
CFO: John Petrizzo
Sr. VP, Supply Chain: Dan Smith
Number Employees: 500-999
Parent Co: Tata Tea Ltd
Type of Packaging: Private Label
Brands:
  Tetley Teas

12642 Tetley USA
1090 King Georges Post Road
Bldg 1
Edison, NJ 08837-3701
732-738-5599
Fax: 732-225-8469 800-728-0084
tetleyusa@worldpantry.com
Tea
VP Field Sales: Ann Rowe
Parent Co: Tetley Tea

12643 Tetley USA
1267 Cobb Industrial Dr
Marietta, GA 30066
770-428-5555
Fax: 770-427-7019 www.tetleyusa.com
Tea
President: Marty Kushner
CEO: Bruce Klodt
VP Sales: Elaine Meyers
Plant Manager: L Griffen
Estimated Sales: $20-50 Million
Number Employees: 100-249
Parent Co: Tetley Tea

12644 Teton Waters Ranch LLC
3301 Lawrence St. # 3
Denver, CO 80205
720-340-4590
www.tetonwatersranch.com
100% grass-fed and grass-finished beef frankfurters and sausages in various flavors
Founder: Jeff Russell
CEO: Walt Freese

Food Manufacturers / A-Z

Year Founded: 2008
Number of Brands: 1
Number of Products: 11
Type of Packaging: Consumer, Private Label
Brands:
  Teton Waters Ranch

12645 Tex-Mex Cold Storage
6665 Padre Island Hwy
Brownsville, TX 78521-5218
956-831-9433
Fax: 956-831-9572
info@texmexcoldstorage.bzzp.net
www.texmexcoldstorage.bzzp.net
Seafood including shrimp; warehouse providing freezer and dry storage
President: Emilio Sanchez
VP: Norma Sanchez
Plant Manager: Nick Sato
Estimated Sales: $6,307,658
Number Employees: 225
Square Footage: 620000
Type of Packaging: Private Label, Bulk

12646 Tex-Mex Gourmet
201 W First Street
Brenham, TX 77833
979-836-4701
Fax: 713-784-7616 888-345-8467
info@texmexgourmet.com
www.texmexgourmet.com
Sauces
Number Employees: 10-19
Type of Packaging: Consumer, Private Label
Brands:
  Los Tios
  Tuldy's

12647 TexaFrance
525 Round Rock
Round Rock, TX 78681
512-246-2500
Fax: 512-246-2716 800-776-8937
info@texafrance.com www.texafrance.com
Processor and co-packer of natural pasta and pesto sauces, salad dressings, mustards, chutneys and jellies; private labeling available
President: Jean Parant
Vice President: David Griswold
VP Purchasing: David Griswold
Estimated Sales: $.2 Million
Number Employees: 7
Square Footage: 32000
Type of Packaging: Consumer, Private Label

12648 Texas Beach
Richmond, VA
757-403-3598
texasbeachllc@gmail.com
www.texasbeachbloodymary.com
Bloody Mary mix
President: Austin Green
CEO: Greg White
Number Employees: 2-10
Brands:
  Texas Beach

12649 Texas Chili Co
3313 N Jones St
Fort Worth, TX 76106-4339
817-626-0983
Fax: 817-626-9105 800-507-0009
sales@texaschili.com www.texaschili.com
Frozen chili, taco filling and chili sauce
President: Danny Owens
sales@texaschilicompany.com
Plant Manager: Rebbca Marlvo
Estimated Sales: Below $10 Million
Number Employees: 5-9
Type of Packaging: Private Label
Brands:
  Texas Chili

12650 Texas Coffee Co
3297 S M L King Jr Pkwy
Beaumont, TX 77705-2513
409-835-3434
Fax: 409-835-4248 800-259-3400
texjoy@texjoy.com www.texjoy.com
Tea, coffee, extracts, spices and seasonings; importer of coffee and tea
President/Operations: Carlo Busceme
cbusceme@texjoy.com
VP: Donald Fertitta

Estimated Sales: $10-20 Million
Number Employees: 20-49
Square Footage: 135000
Type of Packaging: Consumer, Food Service, Private Label, Bulk
Brands:
  Seaport
  Texjoy

12651 Texas Coffee Traders Inc
1400 E 4th St
Austin, TX 78702-3808
512-476-2279
Fax: 512-476-3617 800-343-4875
www.texascoffeetraders.com
Coffee, teas, candies, syrups, chocolate
President: Robert Beall
rc@texascoffeetraders.com
Marketing Director: Michael Gomez
Service Manager: Brad Nevens
Production Manager: Steven Kerner
Estimated Sales: Less than $500,000
Number Employees: 20-49
Parent Co: Montana Coffee Traders

12652 Texas Crumb & Food Products
3250 Towerwood Dr
Farmers Branch, TX 75234
972-243-8443
Fax: 972-484-9315 800-522-7862
info@dasbrot.com www.dasbrot.com
Bread crumbs, batters, breadings and stuffing and seasoning mixes
President: S Holtsclaw
Vice President: W Holtsclaw
Contact: Diana Podowski
dianapodowski@dasbrot.com
Estimated Sales: $900000
Number Employees: 5-9
Square Footage: 64000
Parent Co: Das Brot
Type of Packaging: Food Service, Private Label, Bulk

12653 Texas Heat
P.O.Box 33246
San Antonio, TX 78265
210-656-4328
Fax: 210-656-5916 800-656-5916
Picante sauce, chili mix and cheese dip
President: Robert Delgado
Estimated Sales: $1-3 Million
Number Employees: 1-4
Type of Packaging: Consumer, Food Service

12654 Texas Reds Steak House
400 E Main St
Red River, NM 87558-0111
575-754-2922
Fax: 575-754-2309 www.texasreds.com
Steak
President: William Gill
VP: Richard Gill
CFO: Deanna Tapia
Estimated Sales: $1-2.5 Million
Number Employees: 35
Brands:
  Texas Red

12655 Texas Sausage Co
2915 E 12th St
Austin, TX 78702-2401
512-472-6707
Fax: 512-472-9360 www.texashotsausage.com
Processor and wholesaler/distributor of sausage; serving the food service market
President: Gary Tharp
hotlinks1@yahoo.com
Estimated Sales: $.5-1 million
Number Employees: 5-9
Type of Packaging: Consumer, Food Service

12656 Texas Spice Co
2709 Sam Bass Rd
Round Rock, TX 78681-1811
512-255-8816
Fax: 512-255-4189 800-880-8007
contact@texas-spice.net www.texas-spice.net
Wholesale and retail custom blending, spices, seasoning blends, bases, extracts, flavors, coffee & tea
Owner: Beckie Forsyth
Contact: Jason Spangler
spangler@texas-spice.net

Estimated Sales: Less Than $500,000
Number Employees: 1-4
Type of Packaging: Food Service
Brands:
  Texas Spice

12657 Texas Tamale Co
9087 Knight Rd
Houston, TX 77054-4305
713-795-5500
Fax: 713-795-5534 info@texastamale.com
www.texastamale.com
Tamales, chili, and sauces.
COO and Co-Owner: Shirley Bailey
Number Employees: 10-19

12658 Texas Tito's
P.O. Box 12847
Austin, TX 78711
512-463-7476
Fax: 210-250-5055 877-99 -OTEX
www.gotexan.org
Texas regional food
President: Hiroshi Shimizu
State Marketing Coordinator: Susan Dunn
Coordinator for Marketing: Lindsay Dickens
Estimated Sales: $500,000-$1 Million
Number Employees: 250-499
Brands:
  Go Texan

12659 Texas Toffee
5 Santa Fe Pl
Odessa, TX 79765
972-596-1031
Fax: 915-563-4105 800-599-2133
www.texastoffee.com
Processor and exporter of toffee including milk and white chocolate, bittersweet, peanut, butterscotch and sugar-free
President: Susan Leshnower
Number Employees: 1-4
Square Footage: 64
Type of Packaging: Consumer, Food Service, Private Label, Bulk
Brands:
  Texas Toffee

12660 Texas Traditions Gourmet
PO Box 2705
Georgetown, TX 78627-2705
512-863-7291
Fax: 512-869-6212 800-547-7062
www.texastraditions.com
Processor and exporter of foods with Texas heritage, inlcuding mesquite smoke, jalapeno pepper, country-style German and black peppercorn mustard, jalapeno and red chile pepper, prickly pear cactus jelly, hot salt, seasoning blends anddry dip mixes
Founder, CEO: Dianna Howard
Estimated Sales: $300,000-500,000
Number Employees: 10-19
Brands:
  Texas Hot Salt
  Texas Traditions

12661 Thackrey & Co
660 Horseshoe Hill Rd
Bolinas, CA 94924
415-868-9543
Fax: 415-868-1781 www.wine-maker.net
Gourmet foods
President: Sean Thackery
Estimated Sales: Under $500,000
Number Employees: 1-4
Brands:
  Thackrey

12662 Thanasi Foods LLC
PO Box 4307
4745 Walnut St Ste A
Boulder, CO 80306-4307
720-570-1065
Fax: 720-570-1064 866-558-7379
goneal@thanasi.com www.thanasifoods.com
Meats, nuts
Founder And CEO: Justin Havlick
Director of Marketing: Greg O'Neal
Sales Support Manager: Kimmee Helbak
Estimated Sales: C

Food Manufacturers / A-Z

12663 Thanksgiving Coffee Co
19100 S Harbor Dr
Fort Bragg, CA 95437-5718
707-964-0118
Fax: 707-964-0351 800-462-1999
www.thanksgivingcoffee.com
Vacuum packed coffee including certified organic, shade grown, regular, decaffeinated and flavored
Owner: Susan Coy
kristina.robertson@va.gov
Secretary, Treasurer: Joan Katzeff
Plant Manager: David Gillette
Estimated Sales: $4741877
Number Employees: 20-49
Type of Packaging: Consumer, Food Service, Private Label, Bulk
Brands:
   Aztec Harvest
   Grand Slam
   Inca Harvest
   Mayan Harvest
   Pony Express
   Royal Garden Tea
   Song Bird
   Thanksgiving
   Zip

12664 That's How We Roll, LLC
100 Passaic Ave. # 155
Fairfield, NJ 07004
973-602-3011
info@thwroll.com
www.thwroll.com
Snack crisps and cookies made with wholesome ingredients
Chief Operating Officer: Samuel Kestenbaum
Number of Brands: 3
Number of Products: 2
Type of Packaging: Consumer, Private Label
Brands:
   Mrs. Thinsters
   Kitchen Table Bakers
   Party 'Tizers

12665 That's It Nutrition
834 S Broadway
8th Floor
Los Angeles, CA 90014-3501
213-892-1505
Fax: 888-782-8040 888-862-5235
support@thatsitfruit.com www.thatsitfruit.com
Fruit bars, truffles
Founder/CEO: Lior Lewensztain
Vice President, Sales: Rachelle Minteer
Chief Operating Officer: Miriam Lewensztain
Year Founded: 2012
Number Employees: 20-49
Type of Packaging: Bulk
Brands:
   That's it(c)

12666 Thatcher's Gourmet Specialties
1201 Minnesota St
San Francisco, CA 94107-3407
415-643-9945
Fax: 415-643-9948 800-926-2676
sales@tgsp.com www.tgsp.com
Gourmet popcorn and snacks
President: Gus Ghassan
Vice President: Ghada Ghassan
Manager: Joe Eidson
Estimated Sales: Less Than $500,000
Number Employees: 1-4
Type of Packaging: Private Label
Brands:
   Joy's Gourmet Snacks
   Thatcher's
   Thatcher's Special Popcorn

12667 The Amazing Chickpea
1600 Hwy. 100 South # 500A
St. Louis Park, MN 55416
612-548-1099
contact@theamazingchickpea.com
www.theamazingchickpea.com
Gluten-free chickpea butter spread in various flavors
Contact: Sunil Kumar
Year Founded: 2016
Number of Brands: 1
Number of Products: 4
Type of Packaging: Consumer, Private Label
Brands:
   The Amazing Chickpea

12668 The Ardent Homesteader
PO Box 44
Arden, NY 10910
www.ardenthomesteader.com
Handmade, all-natural caramel sauce
Founder/Owner: Kristin Nelson
Year Founded: 2010
Number of Brands: 1
Number of Products: 1
Type of Packaging: Consumer, Private Label
Brands:
   Cara-Sel

12669 The Art of Broth, LLC
818-715-9320
info@theartofbroth.com
www.theartofbroth.com
Sippable chicken, beef and vegan vegetable-flavored broth; broths are vegan, Kosher, non-GMO and gluten-free
Number of Brands: 1
Number of Products: 3
Type of Packaging: Consumer, Private Label
Brands:
   The Art of Broth

12670 The Bauman Family
118 Hoffmansville Road
P.O. Box 210
Sassamansville, PA 19472-0210
610-754-7251
Fax: 610-754-7251 baumans@baumanfamily.com
www.baumanfamily.com
Apple butter

12671 The Bites Company
PO Box 122
Westport, CT 06881
203-296-2482
www.thebitescompany.com
Bite-size biscotti
Owner/Baker: Dina Upton

12672 The Boisset Collection
849 Zinfandel Ln
St. Helena, CA 94574
707-967-7667
customerservice@boisset.com
www.boissetcollection.com
Wines
President: Jean Charles Boisset
VP, Marketing & Communications: Patrick Egan
Director, Public Relations: Caroline de Laurens
caroline.delaurens@baccarat.fr
COO: Lisa Heisinger
Estimated Sales: $50-74,999,999
Number Employees: 40
Number of Brands: 17
Brands:
   Bouchard Aine Fils
   Boisset Classic
   Boisset Mediterranee
   Charles De Fere
   Christophe Cellars
   Evoluna Estate
   Fog Mountain
   J Moreau Fils
   Jean-Claude Boisset
   Joliesse Vineyards
   Les Domaines Bernard
   Lyeth Estate
   Oceana Coastal
   Ropiteall
   Summerlake
   Vienot
   William Wheeler Winery

12673 The Brooklyn Salsa Co LLC
1717 Troutman Street
Suite 254
Ridgewood, NY 11385
347-470-5493
Fax: 347-435-2436 www.bksalsa.com
Salsa.
Co-founder: Matt Burns
matt@bksalsa.com
Co-founder/CEO: Rob Behnke
Operations Manager: Casey Gilbertson

12674 The Bruss Company
3548 N. Kostner Ave.
Chicago, IL 60641
773-282-2900
customer.bruss@tyson.com
www.bruss.com
Portion controlled steaks, pork, and veal.
Year Founded: 1937
Estimated Sales: $175 Million
Number Employees: 250-499
Number of Brands: 1
Square Footage: 52000
Parent Co: Tyson Foods
Type of Packaging: Consumer, Food Service
Brands:
   Golden Trophy Steaks

12675 The Chalet Market
6410 Jackrabbit Lane
Belgrade, MT 59714
406-388-4687
800-752-1029
www.chaletmarket.com
Specialty deli, prepared foods

12676 The Chili Lab
Brooklyn, NY
info@thechililab.com
Manufacturer of chili salts and do-it-yourself hot sauce kits.
Founder: Thomas Kelly

12677 The Coffee Bean & Tea Leaf
1945 S La Cienega Blvd
Los Angeles, CA 90034
310-237-2326
877-653-1963
officecoffee@coffeebean.com
www.coffeebean.com
Coffee, tea and blended drinks
President and Chief Executive Officer: John Dawson
CEO: Sunny Sassoon
CFO: Karen Kate
VP of Store Development: William (Bill) Robards
Sr.Dir of Coffee Roasting&Manufacturing: Jay Isais
VP of Marketing: Diane Kuyoomjian
Sr.VP Sales & Supply Chain: Paul Balzer
Contact: Patrice Anderson
patricea@johnnycreates.com
Vice President of Operations: Jeff Schroeder
Estimated Sales: $300,000-500,000
Number Employees: 10-19

12678 The Cookie Dough Cafe
1701 E Empire St
Suite 360
Bloomington, IL 61704-7900
309-539-4585
Fax: 309-539-4585 www.thecookiedoughcafe.com
Cookie dough
Co-Owner: Joan Pacetti
Brands:
   the cookie(c) dough cafe

12679 The Coromega Company
PO Box 131135
Carlsbad, CA 92013-1135
760-599-6088
Fax: 760-599-6089 877-275-3725
www.coromega.com
Flavored Omega-3 fish oil gel supplements and gummy supplements
Chief Operating Officer: Andrew Aussie
Year Founded: 1999
Number of Brands: 1
Number of Products: 6
Type of Packaging: Consumer, Private Label
Brands:
   Coromega

12680 The Crispery
2728 Sterling Point Dr.
Portsmouth, VA 23703
501-224-8947
valerie@thecrispery.com
www.thecrispery.com
Marshmallow snacks.
Co-Owner: Judy Soldinger
Co-Owner: Steven Soldinger
Brands:
   CRISPYCAKESTM

Food Manufacturers / A-Z

12681 The Daphne Baking Company, LLC
300 E 77th Street
Suite 21B
New York, NY 10075
212-517-7626
Fax: 646-349-4164
Frozen tarts, shells and cakes
Marketing: Bo Bartlett
Number Employees: 5

12682 The Dow Chemical Company
2211 H.H. Down Way
Midland, MI 48674
989-636-1000
Fax: 989-832-1456   800-331-6451
www.dow.com
Cooking oils and fat replacements
President & CFO: Howard Ungerleider
Chairman & CEO: Jim Fitterling
SVP of Operations & Manufacturing: Peter Holicki
Estimated Sales: $50-100 Million
Number Employees: 250-499
Type of Packaging: Private Label, Bulk

12683 The Eli's Cheesecake Company
6701 W. Forest Preserve Drive
Chicago, IL 60634
773-308-7000
Fax: 773-736-1169   800-999-8300
info@elicheesecake.com   www.elicheesecake.com
Cheesecake
President: Marc S. Schulman

12684 The Food Collective
1882 McGraw Ave, Suite A
Irvine, CA 92614
949-797-0014
Fax: 949-797-0041   866-328-8638
Organic gourmet heat-n-serve frozen foods.
Owner: Stephen Moore
Type of Packaging: Consumer
Brands:
  HELEN'S KITCHEN
  ORGANIC BISTRO

12685 The Good Bean
2980 San Pablo Ave
Berkeley, CA 94702-2471
USA
561-243-7773
Fax: 510-295-2424   www.thegoodbean.com
Chips, chickpea snacks, fruitbars
Owner: Sarah Wallace
Owner: Suzanne Slatcher
Number Employees: 5-9

12686 The Good Crisp Company
www.thegoodcrispcompany.com
Gluten-free potato crisps in various flavors
Director, Sales/Marketing: Matt Parry
Number of Brands: 1
Number of Products: 3
Type of Packaging: Consumer, Private Label
Brands:
  The Good Crisp Company

12687 The Great San Saba River Pecan Company
234 West Highway 190
San Saba, TX 76877
325-372-6078
Fax: 325-372-5852   800-621-8121
info@greatpecans.com   www.greatpecans.com
Pecan preserves, pies, cakes, breads, candies, spreads, toppings and pecan praline popcorn
Co-Owner/President: Larry Newkirk
Type of Packaging: Consumer
Brands:
  Great San Saba River Pecan

12688 The Great Western Tortilla Co.
1761 E 58th Ave.
P.O. Box 16346
Denver, CO 80216-0346
303-298-0705
Fax: 303-298-0216
Tortilla chips in a variety of stone-ground and natural flavors, salsa and hot sauce
President: William A Ralston
Estimated Sales: $20-50 Million
Number Employees: 50-99

Brands:
  Buffalo Bill's
  Wild West

12689 The Hampton Popcorn Company
999 S Oyster Bay Rd
Bethpage, NY 11714
888-947-6726
www.hamptonpopcorn.com
Popcorn
Chairman Of The Board: Robert Gutman
Estimated Sales: 82,000
Number Employees: 2

12690 The Healthy Beverage Company
329B S Main Street
Doylestown, PA 18901
215-321-8330
Fax: 866-642-9179   800-295-1388
info@steaz.com   www.steaz.com
All-natural, organic and fair trade tea-based beveraged in product lines that include iced tea, sparkling green tea and energy drinks.
Owner: Eric Schnell
Director of Finance: Linda Flagler
VP Marketing: Lee Brody
Director of Operations: Carlos Valdes
Estimated Sales: $1-2.5 Million
Number Employees: 5-9
Type of Packaging: Consumer
Brands:
  STEAZ

12691 The Honest Stand
PO Box 100742
Denver, CO 80250
chat@thehoneststand.com
www.thehoneststand.com
Plant-based, certified organic, dairy- and gluten-free cheese style dips in various flavors
Co-Founder: Alexandra Carone
Co-Founder: Jeremy Day
Year Founded: 2014
Number of Brands: 1
Number of Products: 5
Type of Packaging: Consumer, Private Label
Brands:
  The Honest Stand

12692 The Humphrey Co
Po Box 832
Lockport, NY 14094
716-597-1974
Fax: 716-804-6881
Soft drinks, candy, full-line snacks, nuts, and popcorn.
President: Wendy Farnsworth
Marketing: Cyd Cehulik

12693 The Invisible Chef
1818 Hopple Ave SW
Canton, OH 44706-1909
USA
330-880-5223
Fax: 330-880-4749
contactus@theinvisiblechef.com
www.theinvisiblechef.com
Baking mixes
Co-Owner: Jill Mccauley
Estimated Sales: D
Number Employees: 10-19

12694 The Jam Stand
Brooklyn, NY
718-218-5194
info@thejamstand.com
thej.am
Jams.
Co-Founder: Jessica Quon
Co-Founder: Sabrina Valle

12695 The Jersey Tomato Company
38 Buff Ln
Suite 101
Hillsdale, NJ 07642-1101
dave@jerseytomatoco.com
jerseytomatoco.com
Tomato sauces
Marketing & Advertising: David Stoff
Brands:
  The Jersey Tomato Co.

12696 The Junket Folks
One Hansen Island
Little Falls, NY 13365
877-248-2477
800-556-6674
info@junketdesserts.com   www.junketdesserts.com
Desserts, custard, ice cream mix, tablets

12697 The King's Kitchen
129 W. Trade Street
Charlotte, NC 28202
704-375-1990
kingskitchen.org
Prepared foods

12698 The Konery
630 Flushing Ave
Suite 6N
Brooklyn, NY 11206-5026
917-750-4147
hello@thekonery.com
www.thekonery.com
Waffle cone
Cone Expert & Founder: Kristine Tonkonow
Number Employees: 1-50
Type of Packaging: Food Service
Brands:
  Konery

12699 The Kroger Co.
300 N Lp Miller St
Murray, KY 42071
270-762-5100
Fax: 270-759-1919   800-632-6900
tcolson@kroger.com   www.kroger.com
Hot chocolate mixes, breakfast drinks, instant teas and oatmeal; also, canned nuts
Manager: Bob Beuhler
bob.beuhler@kroger.com
Number Employees: 10,000
Parent Co: Kroger Company
Type of Packaging: Consumer, Private Label
Brands:
  Kenlake Foods

12700 The Lancaster Food Company
Lancaster, PA
Certified organic and allergen-free breads and cookies
Co-Founder/CEO: Charlie Crystle
Co-Founder/Chief Product Offucer: Craig Lauer
Vice-President, Operations: Polly Lauer
Year Founded: 2014
Number of Brands: 1
Number of Products: 7
Type of Packaging: Consumer, Private Label
Brands:
  The Lancaster Food Company

12701 The Little Kernel
400 Madison Ave.
Manalapan, NJ 07726
732-607-3880
info@thelittlekernel.com
Olive-oil popped popcorn with no artificial ingredients, in various flavors
Co-Founder: Christopher Laurita
Co-Founder: Andy Epstein
Year Founded: 2016
Number of Brands: 1
Number of Products: 6
Type of Packaging: Consumer, Private Label
Brands:
  The Little Kernel

12702 The Lobster Place
75 Ninth Avenue
Chelsea Market
New York, NY 10011
212-255-5672
info@lobsterplace.com
lobsterplace.com
Lobster, seafood
President: Brendan Hayes
CEO: Ian MacGregor
Lead Sales Executive: Joe Cooper
Contact: Renee Alevras
ralevras@lobsterplace.com
Operations Manager: Christian Quintana
Purchasing Manager: Mark Grobman

Food Manufacturers / A-Z

12703 The Lollipop Tree, Inc
181 York St
Auburn, NY 13021
315-252-2676
Fax: 315-282-0720   800-842-6691
www.lollipoptree.com
Baking mixes, pepper jellies, grilling sauces, hot chocolate mixes. Experienced in certified organic, sprouted wheat and spelt, low-carb, low/no sugar mixes and more.
President: Robert Lynch
CEO/Chairman/Founder: Laurie Lynch
CFO: Bob Lynch
Contact: Steve Wellauer
it@newhopemills.com
Estimated Sales: D
Number Employees: 20-49
Number of Products: 90
Square Footage: 237000
Type of Packaging: Consumer, Private Label
Brands:
 Harborside
 Lollipop Tree
 Quick Loaf
 The Lollipop Tree
 Good Simple Food

12704 The Long Life Beverage Company
P.O.Box 7802
Mission Hills, CA 91346-7802
661-259-5575
800-848-7331
Processor, importer and exporter of organic herbal black and green teas, over 40 boxed varieties and 11 ready to drink bottled iced teas, and a variety of enhanced waters
Owner: Troy Long
Estimated Sales: $7.5 Million
Number Employees: 1-4
Number of Brands: 3
Number of Products: 52
Square Footage: 44000
Parent Co: Consac Industries
Type of Packaging: Consumer, Private Label
Brands:
 Enhance Vitamin/Waters
 Long Life Black Teas
 Long Life Green Teas
 Long Life Herbal Teas
 Long Life Iced Teas

12705 The Lovely Candy Company LLC
1725 Kilkenny Ct
Woodstock, IL 60098-7437
USA
801-824-0624
www.lovelycandyco.com
Fruit chews, caramels, licorice, fudge rolls
CEO/Founders: Jackie & Mike Nakamura
Vice President Of Marketing: Brian Heiser
Contact: Brian Heiser
brianheiser@lovelycandyco.com

12706 The Maple Guild
One Sweet Tree Ln
Island Pond, VT 05846
802-723-6753
info@mapleguild.com
www.mapleguild.com
Maple syrup and maple syrup-infused tea and water
CEO: Mike Argyelan
Number of Brands: 2
Number of Products: 14
Type of Packaging: Consumer
Brands:
 THE MAPLE GUILD
 TAPT

12707 The Mapled Nut Co.
P.O. Box 303
Morrisville, VT 05661
802-888-9559
Fax: 80- 88- 955   800-726-4661
Gourmet maple sugar cashews, almonds, pecans and walnuts
Owner: Marsha Phillips
Estimated Sales: $.5-1 million
Number Employees: 1-4

12708 The Matzo Project
575 Union St
3rd Floor
Brooklyn, NY 11215-1024
929-276-2896
hello@matzoproject.com
www.matzoproject.com
Matzo
Co-Owner: Ashley Albert
Co-Owner: Kevin Rodriguez
Brands:
 The Matzo Project

12709 The Meeker Vineyard
5377 Dry Creek Road
Healdsburg, CA 95448
707-431-2148
Fax: 707-431-2549   www.meekerwine.com
Wines the selection of which includes Chardonnay, Dry Rose, Zinfandel, Petite Sirah, Cabernet Sauvignon and Merlot, in addition to others.
President: Charles Meeker
VP Marketing/Operations: John Burtner
Contact: Julia Berman
julia@meekerwine.com
Estimated Sales: Less than $500,000
Number Employees: 1-4

12710 The Murphs Famous Inc.
395 Summit Point Drive
Suite One
Henrietta, NY 14467
888-281-6400
Fax: 585-321-9906   www.murphsfamous.com
Manufacturer of bloody mary mix.

12711 The Naked Edge, LLC
3020 Carbon Place #103
Boulder, CO 80301
888-297-9426
www.wildmadesnacks.com
Organic, non-GMO Veggie-Go's dried fruit & vegetable snack; available in strips or bites
Co-Founder: John McHugh
Co-Founder: Lisa McHugh
Number of Brands: 1
Type of Packaging: Consumer, Private Label
Brands:
 Veggie-Go's

12712 The New Primal
3690 Old Charleston Hwy
Johns Island, SC 29455-7826
866-723-1386
meat@thenewprimal.com
thenewprimal.com
Beef and turkey jerky
Founder & CEO: Jason Burke
Senior Marketing Manager: Samantha Blatz
Director of Sales: David Paul Miller
Director of Operations: Ashley Zager
Estimated Sales: $9.6 Million
Number Employees: 10-50
Brands:
 The New Primal

12713 The Pantry Club
2054 Weaver Park Dr.
Clearwater, FL 33765
877-335-8842
www.thepantryclub.com
Manufacturer of gourmet dip mixes and seasonings.
Co-Founder: Matt Webb
Co-Founder: Alecia Webb

12714 The Peanut Butter Shop of Williamsburg
8012 Hankins Industrial Park Road
Toano, VA 23168
757-566-0930
Fax: 757-566-1605   800-831-1828
info@thepeanutshop.com
www.thepeanutshop.com
Virginia peanuts and specialty nut meats, cocoa mixes including chocolate, raspberry, traditional and chocolate hazelnut
VP: Pete Booker
Marketing: Michael McDonald
Sales Director: Jeff Armbruster
Plant Manager: Larry Winslow
Number Employees: 20-49
Type of Packaging: Consumer
Brands:
 Amber Brand Deviled Smithfield Ham
 Colonial Williamsburg
 King's Arms Tavern
 Nut Case Collection
 Peanut Shop of Williamsburg
 Smithfield Tavern

12715 The Perfect Pita
7653 Fullerton Rd
Springfield, VA 22153
703-644-0004
info@theperfectpita.com
theperfectpita.com
Pita falafel, BLT sandwhich, hummus, pizza, homemade soup, salads and desserts.
Director of Catering Sales: Michael Tam
Estimated Sales: $600,000
Number Employees: 10
Brands:
 The Perfect Pita

12716 The Pickle Juice Company
206 S Town East Blvd
Mesquite, TX 75149
972-755-0289
sales@picklepower.com
www.picklepower.com
Sports drink
Owner: Brandon Brooks
VP, Global Sales & Marketing: Filip Keuppens
Year Founded: 2001
Estimated Sales: $10 Million
Number Employees: 11-50
Brands:
 Extra Strength Pickle Juice Shots
 Pickle Juice Sport Drink

12717 The Pillsbury Company
100 Justin Dr
Chelsea, MA 02150-4032
617-884-9800
Fax: 617-889-0281   800-370-7834
www.pillsbury.com
Frozen and par-baked goods including French bread
President: David Baker
Contact: Michael Blight
michael.blight@signaturebreads.com
Number Employees: 100-249
Square Footage: 400000
Parent Co: General Mills Inc
Type of Packaging: Food Service, Private Label

12718 The Piping Gourmets
786-233-8660
info@thepipinggourmets.com
www.thepipinggourmets.com
Gluten free and vegan whoopie pies
Co-Founder: Leslie Kaplan
Co-Founder: Carolyn Shulevitz
Number Employees: 5-9

12719 The Poseidon Group
300 Park Ave
12th Fl
New York, NY 10022-7412
646-926-0206
www.drinkcham.com
Chamomile tea
CEO & Co-Founder: Niko Nikolaou
Number Employees: 2-10
Brands:
 cham cold brew tea

12720 The Power of Fruit
Po Box 456
Lebanon, NJ 08833-0456
908-450-9806
Fax: 908-566-3352
Dairy-free, gluten-free, kosher, nut-free, organic/natural, sugar-free, frozen desserts, foodservice.
Marketing: Ron Kazmierski
Contact: Scott Elser'
scott@powerOffruit.com

12721 The Procter & Gamble Company
1 P&G Plaza
Cincinnati, OH 45202
513-983-1100
Fax: 513-983-9369   800-692-0132
us.pg.com
Baby diapers, fabric care, feminine products, shampoos, paper towels, toilet paper, tissues, conditioners, dishwashing detergent, home cleaning products, razors, shaving gels, supplements, pregnancy tests, cough syrup, and more.

Food Manufacturers / A-Z

Chairman, President & CEO: David Taylor
CFO: Jon Moeller
Estimated Sales: $67.6 Billion
Number Employees: 97,000
Number of Brands: 57
Type of Packaging: Consumer
Brands:
  Always
  Ariel
  Luvs
  Pampers
  Tide
  Bounce
  Cheer
  Downy
  Dreft
  Era
  Gain
  Ace
  Rindex 3en1
  Bounty
  Charmin
  Puffs
  Always Discreet
  Tampax
  Head & Shoulders
  Aussie
  Herbal Essences
  Old Spice
  Pantene
  Cascade
  Dawn
  Febreeze
  Joy
  Mr. Clean
  Swiffer
  Salvo
  Ambi Pur
  Comet
  Braun
  Gillette
  Venus
  The Art of Shaving
  Align
  Clearblue
  Meta
  Pepto-Bismol
  Prilosec OTC
  Vicks
  ZzzQuil
  Crest
  Fixodent
  Oral-B
  Scope
  Ivory
  Olay
  Safeguard
  Secret
  Native
  Snowberry
  SK-II

12722 The Pur Company
23 Kodiak Crescent
Toronto, ON M3J 3E5
Canada
416-941-7557
info@thepurcompany.com
thepurcompany.com
Mints and gum
Founder & CEO: Jay Klein
Director of Sales & Marketing: John Kapralos
Sales Coordinator: Jenna Maislin
Director of People & Culture: Cerys Cook
Year Founded: 2010
Estimated Sales: $10-20 Million
Number Employees: 11-50
Brands:
  pur

12723 The Real Co
3613F Kirkwood Hwy.
Wilmington, DE 19808
347-433-8945
info@thereal.co
www.thereal.co
Single-origin, non-GMO food products: quinoa, raw coconut sugar, raw cane sugar, pink Himalayan salt and white basmati rice
Founder: Colin Carter
Chief Executive Officer: Belal El-Banna
Chief Commercial Officer: Mo Elkateb
Number of Brands: 1
Number of Products: 6
Type of Packaging: Consumer, Food Service, Private Label
Brands:
  The Real Co

12724 The Really Great Food Company
P.O. Box 2239
St. James, NY 11780
Fax: 631-382-8344 800-593-5377
orders@reallygreatfood.com reallygreatfood.com
Baking mixes

12725 The Roscoe NY Beer Company, Inc.
145 Rockland Rd.
Roscoe, NY 12776
607-290-5002
inquiries@roscoebeercompany.com
www.roscoebeercompany.com
IPAs, flavoured ale, rye beer, stout
Operations Manager: Josh Hughes
Director, Marketing and Events: Shannon Feeney
Year Founded: 2013
Number of Brands: 1
Number of Products: 11
Brands:
  Trout Town

12726 The Rubin Family of Wines
5220 Ross Rd
Sebastopol, CA 95472-2158
707-887-8130
Fax: 707-887-8160 wine@rubinfamilyofwines.com
rubinfamilyofwines.com
Wines
Founder: Ron Rubin
Winemaker: Joe Freeman
Estimated Sales: Under $500,000
Number Employees: 1-4
Type of Packaging: Private Label
Brands:
  River Road Vineyards

12727 The Safe + Fair Food Company
1 N LaSalle St.
Chicago, IL 60602
www.safeandfair.com
Allergy-safe snacks with allergen-free, gluten-free, and vegan options. Products include granola mix, popcorn, graham crackers, and chips.
Co-Founder: Dave Leyrer
Co-Founder: Pete Najarian
Number Employees: 10-50
Type of Packaging: Private Label

12728 The Saucey Sauce Company Inc.
196 Court St.
Suite 2
Brooklyn, NY 11201
646-648-0159
www.getsauceynow.com
Manufacturer of Vietnamese homestyle sauces.
Co-Founder: Toan Huynh
Co-Founder: Ken Huynh
Contact: Sarah Briguglio
briguglios@getsauceynow.com

12729 The Shed Saucery
7501 Hwy 57
Ocean Springs, MS 39565
228-875-9590
contact@theshedbbq.com
theshedbbq.com
Barbeque sauces and meats
Co-Founder & Owner: Brad Orrison
Co-Founder & Owner: Brooke Lewis
Co-Founder: Brad Orrison
Estimated Sales: $1.2 Million
Number Employees: 3
Brands:
  The Shed Barbeque & Blues Joint
  The Shed BBQ Sauces & Marinades

12730 The Sola Company
4203 Montrose Blvd. # 490
Houston, TX 77006
800-277-1486
hello@solasweet.com
www.solasweet.com
Low-carb and low-glycemic index yogurt, ice cream, granola, bread, nut bars and sweetener
Co-Founder: Ed Bosarge
Co-Founder: Ryan Turner
Year Founded: 2012
Number of Brands: 1
Number of Products: 6
Type of Packaging: Consumer, Private Label
Brands:
  Sola

12731 The Soulfull Project
Camden, NJ
megan@thesoulfullproject.com
www.thesoulfullproject.com
Vegan hot cereals; gluten free options available
Co-Founder: Megan Shea
Co-Founder: Chip Heim

12732 The Sprout House
874 Neighborhood Rd
Lake Katrine, NY 12499
800-777-6887
info@sprouthouse.com sprouthouse.com
Organic sprouting seeds, sprouters and wheatgrass juice supplies.
Brands:
  Vermont Sprout

12733 The Stephan Company
4829 East 7th Avenue
Tampa, FL 33605
954-971-0600
Fax: 954-971-2633 www.thestephanco.com
Flavoring extracts and over-the-counter pharmaceuticals
Office Manager: Rita Chlau
Plant Manager: Mike Henry
Number Employees: 50-99

12734 The Stroopie
105 Old Dorwart St
Lancaster, PA 17603-3677
717-875-3426
sales@stroopies.com
www.stroopies.com
Stroopwafel
Co-Founder: Ed McManness
Co-Founder: Dan Perryman
Type of Packaging: Bulk
Brands:
  Stroopies

12735 The Sunshine Tomato Company
149 Geary Avenue
New Cumberland, PA 17070
717-909-0844
www.sunshinepastasauce.com
Pasta sauce
President: Carla Noss
Brands:
  Sunshine Pasta Sauce

12736 The Swiss Bakery
Burke Town Plaza
9536 Old Keene Mill Rd
Burke, VA 22015
703-569-3670
Fax: 703-321-3673 info@theswissbakery.com
www.theswissbakery.com
Fresh baked goods, cakes, pastries, tarts

12737 The Tao of Tea
3430 SE Belmont St.
Portland, OR 97214
503-736-0119
Fax: 503-736-9232 info@taooftea.com
taooftea.com
Tea and tea ware
Owner: Veerinder Chawla
Year Founded: 1997
Estimated Sales: $7.3 Million
Number Employees: 11-50
Type of Packaging: Consumer, Food Service, Private Label

12738 The Tea Spot, Inc.
4699 Nautilus Ct. South # 504
Boulder, CO 80301
303-444-8324
www.theteaspot.com
A variety of white, green, oolong, black, pu'erh, mate, herbal and organic teas in various flavors and sampler packs
CEO: Maria Upenski
Number of Brands: 1
Type of Packaging: Consumer, Private Label
Brands:
  The Tea Spot

Food Manufacturers / A-Z

12739 The Toasted Oat Bakehouse
Columbus, OH
www.thetoastedoat.com
Gluten- and preservative-free all natural granola blends in various flavors
Founder: Erika Boll
Chief Financial Officer: Tom Kelley
Year Founded: 2013
Number of Brands: 1
Number of Products: 4
Type of Packaging: Consumer, Private Label
Brands:
　The Toasted Oat

12740 The Truffleist
3146 45th St
Apt Basment
Astoria, NY 11103-1651
917-325-3374
jkunz@truffleist.com
www.truffleist.com
Truffle based oils, butters and mustards
President: Jimmy Kunz
Estimated Sales: Under $500,000
Number Employees: 1-4
Type of Packaging: Food Service
Brands:
　The Truffliest

12741 The Valpo Velvet Shoppe
Downtown Valparaiso
55-57 W Monroe Street
Valparaiso, IN 46383
219-464-4141
Fax: 219-462-9785 www.valpovelvet.com
Ice cream, frozen yogurt and sherbet
President: Mike Brown
Treasurer: Elizabeth Brown
VP: Mark Brown
Secretary: Sue Cain
Estimated Sales: $810,000
Number Employees: 15
Square Footage: 6000
Parent Co: Valpo Velvet Ice Cream Company
Type of Packaging: Consumer, Food Service
Brands:
　Valpo Velvet

12742 The Van Cleve Seafood Company
6910 Fox Ridge Rd.
Spotsylvania, VA 22551
800-628-5202
vancleveseafood.com
Crab pie
President & CEO: Monica Van Cleve-Talbert
Chief Financial Officer: Allie Cushing
Estimated Sales: $4-5 Million
Number Employees: 44
Type of Packaging: Food Service
Brands:
　Girls With Crabs
　Seafood Sisters
　The Van Cleve Seafood Co.

12743 The Veri Soda Company
71 Fifth Ave.
4th Floor
New York, NY 10003-3004
203-409-3995
Manufacturer of organic sodas.
Founder: Leonard Freeke
Contact: Zeger Van Hcbvell
zeger@verisoda.com
Number Employees: 1-10

12744 The Vine
240 Main Street
PO Box 56
Manhasset, NY 11030-3928
516-365-8463
Fax: 516-869-0460 www.foodsofthevine.com
Marinara and salsa
Owner: Eve Durante
Co-Founder: Richard Mangione
Number Employees: 2-10
Brands:
　The Vine

12745 The Water Kefir People
Bend, OR
www.thewaterkefirpeople.com
Small-batch crafted non-GMO and non-dairy water kefir beverages in various flavors
President/Owner: Crystal Bossola
Year Founded: 2014
Number of Brands: 1
Number of Products: 6
Type of Packaging: Consumer, Private Label
Brands:
　The Water Kefir People

12746 The Wine RayZyn Company
3390 Mt Veeder Rd
Napa, CA 94558
707-251-1600
info@rayzyn.com
rayzyn.com
Wine grapes
Co-Founder: Andrew Cates
Estimated Sales: Under $500,000
Number Employees: 2-10
Brands:
　CabernayZyn
　ChardonayZyn
　MerlayZyn

12747 The Worlds Best Cheese
111 Business Park Dr
Armonk, NY 10504
914-273-1400
Fax: 914-273-2052　800-922-4337
sales@wbcheese.com　www.cheezwhse.com
Cheeses
Owner/President: Joseph Gellert
CEO: George Gellert
Marketing Director: Ellen Gellert
Sales Manager: Richard Rosenberg
Estimated Sales: $6.2 Million
Number Employees: 30
Other Locations:
　Manufacturing Facility
　Hauppauge NY

12748 Theo Chocolate
3400 Phinney Ave N
Seattle, WA 98103-8624
206-632-5100
Fax: 206-632-0413 info@theochocolate.com
www.theochocolate.com
Organic and Fair Trade bean-to-bar chocolate factory.
CEO: Joseph Whinney
jwhinney@theochocolate.com
CFO: Charles Horne
Vice President Sales and Marketing: Deborah Music
Number Employees: 50-99

12749 Theriault's Abattoir Inc
314 Hamlin Rd
Hamlin, ME 4785
207-868-3344
Fax: 207-868-2866
Meat products and hydrogenated fats
President: Reynold A Theriault
Estimated Sales: $36,000
Number Employees: 1-4
Type of Packaging: Consumer

12750 Thermice Company
1445 E Putnam Avenue
Old Greenwich, CT 06870-1379
203-637-4500
General grocery
President: Dave Herman
Estimated Sales: $.5-1 000,000
Number Employees: 5-9

12751 Thermo Pac LLC
1609 Stone Ridge Dr
Stone Mountain, GA 30083-1109
770-934-3200
www.thermopacllc.com
Wide range of thin-to-thick viscosity liquids including processed cheese sauces, tomato-based sauces and other savory or sweet sauces. Also peanut butter, in pouches, single serve cups and dried powder sticks.
Manager: Dave Barnes
Controller/Director: Leticia Simbach
IS Manager: Glenn Corbin
Administrative Assistant: Jean Williams
Plant Manager: John Stevens
Purchasing Manager: Buddy Wilson
Estimated Sales: $12.4 Million
Number Employees: 100-249
Square Footage: 120000
Parent Co: AmeriQual Group LLC
Type of Packaging: Consumer, Food Service, Private Label, Bulk

12752 Thiel Cheese & Ingredients
N7630 County Hwy BB
Attn: Kathy Pitzen
Hilbert, WI 54129
920-989-1440
Fax: 920-989-1288 kathyp@thielcheese.com
www.thielcheese.com
Manufacturer and custom formulator of processed cheeses that are used primarily as ingredients in other food products
President: Steven Thiel
Sales: Kathy Pitzen
Number Employees: 50-99
Type of Packaging: Consumer, Food Service, Private Label, Bulk
Brands:
　Thiel

12753 Think Jerky
500 N Michigan Ave
Suite 600
Chicago, IL 60611-3754
312-380-0039
hello@thinkjerky.com
www.thinkjerky.com
Jerky: beef and turkey
Founder & CEO: Ricky Hirsch
Marketing Manager: S. Baer Lederman
Sales Manager: Lauren LeCoq
Chef: Gale Gand
Estimated Sales: $10 Million
Number Employees: 2-10
Brands:
　Think Jerky(c)

12754 Thinkthin, LLC
Los Angeles, CA 90066
866-988-4465
customerservice@worldpantry.com
www.thinkproducts.com
Manufacturer of high protein snacks, smoothie mixes, and oatmeal.
Founder: Lizanne Falsetto
Brands:
　thinkThin

12755 Third Street Inc
408 S Pierce Ave
Louisville, CO 80027-3018
303-527-1700
800-636-3790
info@3rdstreetchai.com www.thirdstreetchai.com
Bottled chai, lemonade, and iced tea.
Contact: Lisa Ginsberg
lisa@takethirdstreet.com
Number Employees: 5-9
Type of Packaging: Consumer

12756 Thirs-Tea Corp
4611 N Dixie Hwy
Boca Raton, FL 33431-5030
561-948-5600
info@thirs-tea.com
www.thirs-tea.com
Processor of tea beverages amd concentrates.
President: Ray Welch
Year Founded: 1977
Estimated Sales: $500,000-$1 Million
Number Employees: 11-50
Type of Packaging: Consumer, Food Service, Private Label, Bulk
Brands:
　Thirs-Tea

12757 This Bar Saves Lives, LLC
Culver City, CA
310-730-5060
hello@thisbarsaveslives.com
www.thisbarsaveslives.com
Non-GMO, gluten-free healthy snack bar; with every purchase, the company gives food aid to a child in need from Haiti, the Democratic Republic of the Congo, South Sudan, the Philippines and/or Mexico
Co-Founder: Ryan Devlin
Co-Founder: Todd Grinnell
Co-Founder: Ravi Patel
Year Founded: 2013
Number of Brands: 1
Number of Products: 6
Type of Packaging: Consumer, Private Label
Brands:
　This Bar Saves Lives

Food Manufacturers / A-Z

12758 Thistledew Farm
Rr 1 Box 122
Proctor, WV 26055-9608
304-455-1728
Fax: 304-455-1740 800-854-6639
www.thistledewfarm.com
Honey, hot pepper butter, hot honey mustard, wild wing and rib sauce, garden gourmet salad dressing, original honey mustard, red raspberry, and red raspberry honey vinegar, candles, cosmetics, gift boxes and crates, baskets, and othergreat products.
President: Ellie Conlon
CEO: S Conlon
Estimated Sales: $200,000
Number Employees: 1-4
Number of Brands: 2
Number of Products: 7
Square Footage: 20000
Type of Packaging: Consumer, Food Service, Private Label, Bulk
Brands:
  Thistledew Farm's
  West's Best

12759 Tholstrup Cheese
6366 Norton Center Dr
Muskegon, MI 49441-6032
231-798-4371
Fax: 231-798-4374 800-426-0938
Cheese
Manager: Torben Siggaard
VP: Hans Lund
Vice President: Vincent Staiger
Plant Manager: Ernst Siggaard
Estimated Sales: $500,000 appx.
Number Employees: 20-49
Brands:
  Saga

12760 Thoma Vineyards
11975 Smithfield Rd
Dallas, OR 97338-9339
503-623-6420
Fax: 503-623-4310 800-884-1927
www.vanduzer.com
Wines
Manager: Jim Kakacek
Operations Manager: Marilynn Thoma
Estimated Sales: $300,000-500,000
Number Employees: 5-9

12761 Thomas Brothers CountryHam
1852 Gold Hill Rd
Asheboro, NC 27203-4291
336-672-0337
Fax: 336-672-1782 www.thomasbrothersham.com
Processor and packer of country hams; wholesaler/distributor of frozen and specialty foods and meats; serving the food service and retail markets in the southeast
President/CFO: Howard M Thomas
frank@thomasbrothersham.com
Quality Control: Don Thomas
Sales/Plant Manager: Don Thomas
Plant Manager: Don Thomas
Estimated Sales: $10-20 Million
Number Employees: 20-49
Number of Brands: 10
Number of Products: 300
Type of Packaging: Consumer, Private Label
Brands:
  Farmer Dons Country Ham
  Private Labels
  Thomas Brothers Country Ham

12762 Thomas Canning/Maidstone
Rural Route 1
Maidstone, ON N0R-1K0
Canada
519-737-1531
Fax: 519-737-7003
Processor and canner of tomatoes and tomato juice
President: Bill Thomas
Type of Packaging: Food Service, Private Label
Brands:
  Utopia

12763 Thomas Dairy
2096 US Route 7 N
Rutland, VT 05701-8701
802-773-6788
Fax: 802-747-7121 sales@thomasdairy.com
www.thomasdairy.com
Fluid milk
President: Richard Thomas
thomasdairy@aol.com
Founder: Orin Thomas
Marketing Director: John Thomas
Estimated Sales: $5-10 Million
Number Employees: 20-49
Brands:
  Thomas

12764 Thomas Fogarty Winery
19501 Skyline Blvd
Woodside, CA 94062
650-851-6777
Fax: 650-851-5840 800-247-4163
info@fogartywinery.com www.fogartywinery.com
Wines
Director of Sales and Marketing: Anne Krolczyk
anne@fogartywinery.com
Winemaker: Michael Martella
Director of Sales and Marketing: Anne Krolczyk
Office Administrator: Melissa Baker
Tasting Room Manager: Rick Davis
Assistant Winemaker: Nathan Kandler
Accounting Manager: Carrie Larkin
Events Coordinator: Dana Miller
Events Coordinator: Becky Thatcher
Estimated Sales: Below $5 Million
Number Employees: 10-19
Brands:
  Thomas Fogarty Winery

12765 Thomas Gourmet Foods
P.O.Box 8822
Greensboro, NC 27419-0822
336-299-6263
Fax: 336-299-7852 800-867-2823
info@thomasgourmetfoods.com
www.thomasgourmetfoods.com
Sauce, marinade, dressing, cocktail sauce, tartar sauce, Bloody Mary mix, marinara and pasta sauce
Owner: Dwight Thomas
CEO: Brian Thomas
Estimated Sales: $3-5 Million
Number Employees: 5-9
Number of Brands: 1
Type of Packaging: Consumer, Private Label, Bulk
Brands:
  Thomas

12766 Thomas Kemper Soda Company
6500 River Place Boulevard Building 1
Suite 450
Austin, TX 78730
206-381-8712
host@tksoda.com
Beverages
President: Thomas Kemper
Chairman: Laura Bracken-Clough
President: T Maxwell Clough
Estimated Sales: $5-10 Million
Number Employees: 1
Brands:
  Thomas Kemper Birch Soda
  Thomas Kemper Cola
  Thomas Kemper Cream

12767 Thomas Kruse Winery
3200 Dryden Avenue
Gilroy, CA 95020
408-842-7016
Fax: 408-842-7016 krusewine@aol.com
Manufacture of wine
President/CEO: Thomas Kruse
Marketing Director: Thomas Kruse
Contact: Karen Kruse
karenjkruse@aol.com
Estimated Sales: Below $5 Million
Number Employees: 1-4
Brands:
  Thomas Kruse Winey

12768 Thomas Lobster Co
45 Bar Rd
Little Cranberry Island
Islesford, ME 4646
207-244-5876
Fax: 808-244-7020 David@thomaslobster.com
Lobster
President: David Thomas
david@thomaslobster.com
Number Employees: 1-4

12769 Thomas Packing Company
4643 Farley Dr
Columbus, GA 31907-6342
706-689-3513
Fax: 770-227-2166 800-729-0976
jon@crouch.com
Processor and packer of meat products including cured ham, bacon, smoked, andouille and frankfurters; also, smoked turkeys and hams for holiday gift boxes
President: Lee Thomas
CEO: Billy Thomas
Estimated Sales: $.5-1 million
Number Employees: 5-9
Square Footage: 104000
Type of Packaging: Consumer, Food Service, Bulk
Brands:
  Thomas
  Treasure

12770 Thompson Packers
550 Carnation St
Slidell, LA 70460-1899
985-641-6640
Fax: 985-645-2112 800-989-6328
Began in 1953. Manufacturer and exporter of frozen beef, pork, veal and lamb; processor of frozen ground beef and hamburger patties.
Owner: Mary Thompson
thompson@thompack.com
Estimated Sales: $21 Million
Number Employees: 10-19
Square Footage: 50000
Type of Packaging: Consumer, Food Service, Private Label

12771 Thompson Seafood
66 Franklin St
PO Box 1057
Darien, GA 31305
912-437-4649
Shrimp, trout and flounder
Owner: Glenn Young
Estimated Sales: $575,000
Number Employees: 1-4
Type of Packaging: Food Service, Bulk

12772 Thompson's Fine Foods
5973 Pheasant Dr
Shoreview, MN 55126
651-481-0374
Fax: 651-482-1944 800-807-0025
muclijoh@msn.com
Mild/sweet, medium/spicy, hot/spicy and hot/hot barbecue dipping sauces for meats, sandwiches and appetizers
Owner/President: John Thompson
muclijoh@msn.com
Estimated Sales: Under $500,000
Number Employees: 1-4
Type of Packaging: Consumer, Food Service, Private Label, Bulk
Brands:
  Thompson's Black Tie

12773 Thomson Meats
618 Hamilton Avenue W
Melfort, SK S0E 1A0
Canada
306-752-2802
Fax: 306-752-4674
Value added meat products including fresh and frozen pork, beef and chicken
CEO: Paul Marciniak
CFO: Wendy Welsch
R&D: Daryl Durell
Marketing: Donna Walton
Sales: Ron Andrujek
Plant Manager: Gerard Kiefe
Number Employees: 42
Square Footage: 120000
Type of Packaging: Private Label, Bulk

12774 Thor Inc
1280 W 2550 S
Ogden, UT 84401-3238
801-393-3312
Fax: 801-621-3298 888-846-7462
Custom formulating and contract packaging for vitamins and supplements in liquids, capsules and powders
Owner: Whittle Allen
whittle.allen@thor.com

1181

Food Manufacturers / A-Z

Estimated Sales: $10-20 Million
Number Employees: 10-19
Type of Packaging: Private Label

12775 Thor-Shackel Horseradish Company
Po Box 360
2424 Alpine Road
Eau Claire, WI 54702-0360
800-826-7322
Fax: 715-832-9915 www.silverspringfoods.com
Fresh grated horseradish and sauces including cocktail, horseradish, etc
General Manager: Michael Dogan
General Manager: Joe Dogan
Estimated Sales: $3-5 Million
Number Employees: 10-19
Square Footage: 120000
Type of Packaging: Consumer, Food Service, Private Label, Bulk
Brands:
Thor's

12776 Thornton Foods Company
8590 Magnolia Trail
Suite 121
Eden Prairie, MN 55344
952-944-1735
Fax: 952-944-2083 thorntonfoods@aol.com
Low-fat and fat-free dairy based food products including pasta and cheese sauces
President/CEO: Barbara Thornton
Partner: John Lindahl
Estimated Sales: Under $500,000
Number Employees: 1-4
Type of Packaging: Consumer, Food Service, Private Label, Bulk
Brands:
Living Light
Living Light Dairy Blend

12777 Thornton Winery
32575 Rancho California Road
Temecula, CA 92589-9008
951-699-0099
Fax: 951-699-5536 info@thorntonwine.com
www.thorntonwine.com
Wines, champagne
President: John Thornton
Co-Owner: Steve Thornton
CFO: Tim Kelly
Quality Control: Cheryl Rolph
Public Relations Manager: Jan Schneider
Production Manager: Jon McPherson
Estimated Sales: $5-10 Million
Number Employees: 50-99
Brands:
Thornton

12778 Thorpe Vineyard
8150 Chimney Heights Blvd
Wolcott, NY 14590-9201
315-594-2502
Fax: 315-594-2502 info@thorpevineyard.com
www.thorpevineyard.com
Wine
President: Fumie Thorpe
Estimated Sales: Less Than $500,000
Number Employees: 1-4
Type of Packaging: Private Label
Brands:
Thorpe Vineyard

12779 Thoughtful Food
Lafayette, CA
510-910-2581
www.thoughtfulfood.net
Organic, gluten-free, dairy-free and vegan snack mix and granola
Founder/CEO: Jennifer Bielawski
Year Founded: 2009
Number of Brands: 2
Number of Products: 7
Type of Packaging: Consumer, Private Label
Brands:
Nosh Organic
Giddy Up & Go

12780 Three Acre Kitchen
154 Farrington Corner Road
Hopkinton, NH 03229
603-223-5985
Fax: 603-223-5985
Balsamic salad dressing and sauces

Contact: Nancy Brown
nancyspecialtyfoods@comcast.net

12781 Three Bakers Gluten Free Bakery
360 J & J Road
Moscow, PA 18444
570-689-9694
contact@threebakers.net
threebakers.com
Gluten free products: breads, rolls, pizzas

12782 Three Jerks Jerky
515 Spoleto Dr
Pacific Palisades, CA 90272-4517
424-703-5375
info@threejerksjerky.com
www.threejerksjerky.com
Filet Mignon beef jerky
Co-Founder: Jordan Barrocas
Co-Founder: Daniel Fogelson
Estimated Sales: $4.5 Million
Number Employees: 52
Brands:
Three Jerks

12783 Three Lakes Winery
6971 Gogebic St
Three Lakes, WI 54562-9058
715-546-3080
Fax: 715-546-8148 800-944-5434
www.tlwinery.com
Wine including cranberry, apricot, cranberry/apple, cranberry/raspberry, blackberry, strawberry, wild plum, strawberry-rhubarb, red raspberry, rhubarb, Italian plum and kiwi
President: Mark Mc Cain
info@fruitwine.com
Advertising/Marketing: Marla Shane
Sales/Distribution: Mark McCain
Wine Maker: Scott McCain
Production Manager: Scott Foster
Estimated Sales: $720000
Number Employees: 5-9
Square Footage: 16000
Type of Packaging: Consumer
Brands:
Fruit of the Woods

12784 Three Meadows Spirits LLC
139 Coleman Station Rd.
Millerton, NY 12546
845-702-3903
peonyvodka@gmail.com
www.peonyvodka.com
Five-times distilled vodka infused with botanicals
Founder/Principal: Leslie Farhangi
Year Founded: 2016
Number of Brands: 1
Number of Products: 1
Type of Packaging: Consumer, Private Label
Brands:
Peony Vodka

12785 Three Rivers Fish Company
168 Riverfront Drive
Simmesport, LA 71369-0668
318-941-2467
Fax: 318-941-2467
Fresh and frozen seafood/fish
Owner: William Arnouville
Estimated Sales: $730,000
Number Employees: 1-4

12786 Three Springs Farm
1367 Highway 32A
Oaks, OK 74359
918-868-5450
Fax: 804-574-7248
Processor and contract packager of garlic seed and elephant garlic cloves
Owner: Garrett Doering
Number Employees: 5-9
Type of Packaging: Consumer, Private Label, Bulk

12787 Three Trees Almondmilk
San Mateo, CA
855-863-8733
contact@threetrees.com www.threetrees.com
Organic, additive-free almond milk in unsweetened and vanilla varieties
Co-Founder: Jenny Eu
Number of Brands: 1
Number of Products: 2
Type of Packaging: Consumer, Private Label

Brands:
Three Trees

12788 Three Twins Ice Cream
419 1st St.
Petaluma, CA 94952
707-763-8946
www.threetwinsicecream.com
Ice cream, ice cream cones, and ice cream sandwiches.
Founder and CEO: Neal Gottlieb
VP: Scott Sowry
Chief Sales and Marketing Officer: Sarah Bird
Director of Operations: Matt Grebil
Plant Manager: Todd Pimentel

12789 ThreeWorks Snacks
259 Niagara St., ON M6J 2L7
Canada
hello@threeworks.ca
www.threeworks.ca
Gluten-free, non-GMO, nut-free, no sugar added dehydrated apple chips in various flavors
Founder/CEO: Michael Petcherski
Year Founded: 2016
Number of Brands: 1
Number of Products: 6
Type of Packaging: Consumer, Private Label
Brands:
ThreeWorks

12790 Thrive Farmers
215 Hembree Park Drive
Suite 100
Roswell, GA 30076
855-553-2763
Fax: 855-872-8475 connect@thrivefarmers.com
www.thrivefarmers.com
Farmers of coffee beans and tea leafs
Founder & CEO: Michael Jones
Founder & Chief Sustainability Officer: Kenneth Lander
President: Tom Matthesen
Chief Operating Officer: Bart Newman
Chief Origin Officer: Edgar Cabrera Cozza
Year Founded: 2011
Number Employees: 11-50

12791 (HQ)Thumann Inc.
670 Dell Rd
Carlstadt, NJ 07072
201-935-3636
Fax: 201-935-2226
customer.service@thumanns.com
www.thumanns.com
Ham, roast beef, corned beef, pastrami, turkey, liverwurst, bologna, hot dogs, breakfast meats and sausages, cheeses, soups, salads, condiments and frozen products
Owner: Robert Burke
Product Manager: John Zelekowski
Year Founded: 1949
Estimated Sales: $50 Million
Number Employees: 200
Square Footage: 130000
Brands:
Thumann's

12792 Thunderbird Real Food Bar
1101-West 34th St. # 229
Austin, TX 78705
512-383-8334
support@thunderbirdbar.com
www.thunderbirdbar.com
Gluten-free, non-GMO, vegan, no-sugar-added fruit and nut snack bars in various flavors
Chief Executive Officer: Mike Elhaj
Number of Brands: 1
Number of Products: 14
Type of Packaging: Consumer, Private Label
Brands:
Thunderbird

12793 Thyme & Truffles Hors d'Oeuvres
51 Kesmark
Dollard-Des-Ormeaux, QC H9B 3J1
Canada
514-685-9955
Fax: 514-685-2602 877-785-9759
www.thymeandtruffles.com
Frozen oven-ready hors d'oeuvres with assorted fillings including canapes; also, frozen vegetarian entrees

President: Rhonda Richer
QA/QC Specialist: Santi Vicente
Sales Manager: Tim Lipa
Director of Operations: Gino Giansante
Production Manager: Alfred Meth
Number Employees: 50-99
Number of Products: 40
Square Footage: 50000
Type of Packaging: Food Service, Private Label, Bulk
Brands:
Thyme & Truffles

12794 Thyme Garden Herb Co
20546 Alsea Hwy
Alsea, OR 97324-9714
541-487-8671
Fax: 817-558-3570 800-482-4372
herbs@thymegarden.com
www.thymegarden.com
Biscotti, teas and herbal vinegars and oils
Owner: Rolfe Hagen
herbs@thymegarden.com
CEO: Mary Doebbeling
Estimated Sales: Less Than $500,000
Number Employees: 1-4
Square Footage: 2000
Type of Packaging: Consumer, Food Service, Private Label, Bulk
Brands:
Our Thyme Garden

12795 Thymly Products Inc
1332 Colora Rd
Colora, MD 21917-1422
410-658-4826
Fax: 410-658-4824 877-710-2340
Manufacturer of dry food ingredients.
President: Trey Muller-Thym
CEO: Harry Muller-Thym
hmuller@thymlyproducts.com
Number Employees: 10-19
Type of Packaging: Private Label
Brands:
Baker's Cremes
Bread Glaze
Brew Buffers
Glalcto
Parve Plain Muffin

12796 Tichon Sea Food Corp
7 Conway St
New Bedford, MA 02740-7287
508-999-5607
Fax: 508-990-8271 info@tichonseafood.com
www.tichonseafood.com
Fresh and frozen fish including squid, scallops and fish sticks
President: Paul Saunders
paul@tichonseafood.com
VP: R Tichon
Executive VP: Ronald Tichon
Estimated Sales: $1,200,000
Number Employees: 20-49
Square Footage: 180000
Type of Packaging: Consumer
Brands:
Tichon

12797 Tideland Seafood Company
PO Box 99
Dulac, LA 70353
985-563-4516
Fax: 985-563-4296
Prepared fresh shrimp; fish & seafood canning and curing.
President: Judith Gibson
Estimated Sales: $5-10 Million
Number Employees: 5-9

12798 (HQ)Tierra Farm
2424 NY-203
Valatie, NY 12184
519-392-8300
Fax: 518-392-8304 info@tierrafarm.com
www.tierrafarm.com
Organic and gluten-free nut butters and nuts, raw and roasted seeds, dried fruit mixes, granolas, chocolate snacks and fair-trade coffee beans
Founder/President: Gunther Fishgold
Chief Executive Officer: Todd Kletter
Year Founded: 1999
Number of Brands: 1
Type of Packaging: Consumer, Private Label, Bulk

Brands:
Tierra Farm

12799 Tiesta Tea
213 West Institute Place # 310
Chicago, IL 60610
312-202-6800
customerservice@tiestatea.com
www.tiestatea.com
Loose leaf tea blends in various flavors; cold brew bottled tea
Co-Founder: Patrick Tannous
Co-Founder/Chief Executive Officer: Dan Klein
Year Founded: 2010
Number of Brands: 1
Number of Products: 50
Type of Packaging: Consumer, Private Label
Brands:
Tiesta Tea

12800 Tiger Meat & Provisions
1445 NW 22nd St
Miami, FL 33142-7741
305-324-0083
Fax: 305-324-1570
Packer of fresh pork
President: Jose Requejo
tiger_meat@bellsouth.net
Estimated Sales: $10-20 Million
Number Employees: 20-49
Type of Packaging: Food Service
Brands:
Tiger

12801 Tiger Mushroom Farm
PO Box 909
Nanton, AB T0L 1R0
Canada
403-646-2578
Fax: 403-646-2240
Mushrooms
President: Tiger Goto
Operations Manager: Jack Trinn
Estimated Sales: C
Number Employees: 20-49
Square Footage: 66000
Type of Packaging: Consumer, Food Service
Brands:
Tiger

12802 Tigo+
786-207-4772
info@tigosportsdrink.com
www.tigosportsdrink.com
Sports drink made with coconut water and amino acids, sweetened with Stevia; various flavors
Number of Brands: 1
Number of Products: 5
Type of Packaging: Consumer, Private Label
Brands:
Tigo+

12803 Tillamook Country Smoker
8335 North Hwy. 101
Bay City, OR 97107
www.tcsjerky.com
Beef jerky, steak cuts, nuggets, jerky sticks and other snacks
Co-Founder: Dick Crossley
Year Founded: 1975
Number of Brands: 1
Type of Packaging: Consumer, Private Label
Brands:
Tillamook Country Smoker

12804 Tillamook County Creamery Association
Tillamook, OR
503-842-4481
Fax: 503-842-6039 www.tillamook.com
Dairy butter, cheese, nonhygroscopic cheddar cheese whey powder and ice cream; exporter of dried whey, sour cream, yogurt, fluid milk.
Chief Executive Officer: Patrick Criteser
Chief Financial Officer: Linda Pearce
Director of R&D: Jill Allen
Vice President Sales & Marketing: Jay Allison
Plant & Facilities Manager: Rich Snyder
Year Founded: 1909
Estimated Sales: $49.4 Million
Number Employees: 250-499
Square Footage: 30000
Type of Packaging: Consumer, Food Service, Private Label, Bulk

Brands:
Tillamook

12805 Tillamook Meat Inc
405 Park Ave
Tillamook, OR 97141-2524
503-842-4802
Fax: 508-342-2330 www.tillamookmeat.com
Meat products including beef, lamb, pork and poultry, jerky
President/Co-Owner: Laurel Travis
VP/Co-Owner: Mark Travis
Estimated Sales: Less Than $500,000
Number Employees: 1-4
Type of Packaging: Consumer, Food Service, Bulk

12806 (HQ)Tiller Foods Company
967 Senate Dr
Dayton, OH 45459-4017
937-435-4601
Fax: 937-435-1408
Portion controlled dairy products including sour cream, half and half, nondairy creamers, whipped cream and toppings
President: Donald Tiller Jr
Sales Manager: David Yost
Estimated Sales: $5-10 Million
Number Employees: 5-9
Type of Packaging: Consumer, Food Service, Private Label, Bulk
Other Locations:
Tiller Foods Co.
Tampa FL

12807 Tillie's Gourmet
173 Ash Way
Doylestown, PA 18901
215-272-8326
Fax: 215-348-2192
Dressings, marinades and blue crab salsas

12808 Tim's Cascade Snacks
PO Box 2302
Auburn, WA 98071-2302
253-833-2986
Fax: 253-939-9411 800-533-8467
consumer_affairs@timschips.com
www.timschips.com
Snacks including original potato chips, jalapeno, sour cream and onion, cheddar. sea salt, dill picklie, onion ring chips, and popcorn.
President: Dennis M Mullen
COO: Jeff Leichleiter
Sales/Marketing Executive: George Masiello
Year Founded: 1986
Estimated Sales: $20-50 Million
Number Employees: 50-99
Square Footage: 130000
Parent Co: Agrilink Foods
Type of Packaging: Consumer, Food Service, Private Label

12809 Timber Crest Farms
4791 Dry Creek Rd
Healdsburg, CA 95448-9739
707-433-8251
Fax: 707-433-8255 888-766-4233
www.timbercrest.com
Organic and preservative free dried fruits, nuts, tomatoes and specialty food products
Co-Owner: Ronald Waltenspiel
Co-Owner: Ruth Waltenspiel
Public Relations: Ruth Waltenspiel
Estimated Sales: $4.5 Million
Number Employees: 250-499
Number of Brands: 2
Number of Products: 50
Square Footage: 120000
Type of Packaging: Consumer, Food Service, Private Label, Bulk
Brands:
Sonoma
Timber Crest Farm

12810 Timber Lake Cheese Company
PO Box A
Timber Lake, SD 57656
605-865-3605
Fax: 605-865-3605
Cheese
President: Virgil Johnson
Estimated Sales: Less than $500,000
Number Employees: 1-4

Food Manufacturers / A-Z

12811 Timber Peaks Gourmet
6180 Hollowview Ct
Parker, CO 80134-5808
303-841-8847
Fax: 303-805-0174 800-982-7687
www.timberpeaksgourmet.com
Cocoa, bean soups, dessert mixes, bread mixes, trail mixes, and dried salsa
President: Laurie Yankoski
laurie.yankoski@timberpeaksgourmet.com
Estimated Sales: Less Than $500,000
Number Employees: 1-4
Number of Brands: 1
Number of Products: 41
Square Footage: 6000
Type of Packaging: Consumer, Bulk
Brands:
  Mud
  Mountain House Kitchen

12812 Timeless Seeds
48 Ulm-Vaughn Rd
P.O. Box 331
Ulm, MT 59485
406-866-3340
Fax: 406-866-3341 orders@timelessfood.com
www.timelessfood.com
Organic lentils, peas, chickpeas, and heirloom grains
Founder/CEO: David Oien
Accounts: Heather Hadley
General Manager: Matthew Leardini
Year Founded: 1987
Number Employees: 10-19

12813 Tin Star Foods
Austin, TX
info@tinstarfoods.com
www.tinstarfoods.com
Grassfed cultured ghee; lactose- and casein-free
Founder/Chief Executive Officer: Hima Pal
Year Founded: 2014
Number Employees: 2-10
Number of Brands: 1
Number of Products: 1
Type of Packaging: Consumer, Private Label
Brands:
  Tin Star Foods

12814 Tin Whistle Brewing Co
954 Eckhardt Ave W
Penticton, BC V2A 2C1
Canada
250-770-1122
Fax: 250-770-1122
Ale
President: Lorraine Nagy
Number Employees: 5-9
Type of Packaging: Consumer, Food Service
Brands:
  Black Widow
  Coyote
  Ratle Snack

12815 Tincture Distillers
5521 27Th St N
Arlington, VA 22207-1773
888-658-6899
info@elementshrub.com
www.elementshrub.com
Shrub sodas
CEO & Founder: Charlie Berkinshaw
Estimated Sales: Under $500,000
Number Employees: 1-4
Brands:
  Element Shrub

12816 Tinkyada
120 Melford Drive, Unit 8
Scarborough
Ontario, Ca M1B 2X5
416-609-0016
Fax: 416-609-1316 iris@tinkyada.com
www.tinkyada.com
Herbs

12817 Tiny But Mighty Popcorn
3282 62nd St
Shellsburg, IA 52332
800-330-4692
connect@tinybutmightyfoods.com
tinybutmightyfoods.com
Popcorn
Owner: Gene Mealhow
Chief Marketing Officer: Linda Rosenberg
Sales Manager: LeeAnn Stevens
Operations: Lynn Mealhow
Production Manager: Mark Kluber
Estimated Sales: $4.3 Million
Number Employees: 49
Brands:
  Tiny But Mighty Popcorn

12818 Tiny Hero Foods
200 Kansas St. # 205
San Francisco, CA 94103
855-778-4662
www.tinyherofoods.com
Golden quinoa, quinoa and rice blends, quinoa side dishes, quinoa macaroni and cheese dish, quinoa breakfast packs
Chief Executive Officer: Aaron Jackson
Director, Marketing: Christine Lee
Year Founded: 2016
Number Employees: 2-10
Number of Brands: 1
Type of Packaging: Consumer, Private Label
Brands:
  The Tiny Hero

12819 Tio Gazpacho
115 W 18th Street
2nd Fl
New York, NY 10011
917-946-1160
hola@tiogazpacho.com
www.tiogazpacho.com
Vegan soup
Founder: Austin Allan
Production Manager: Pearl Wong
Number Employees: 2-10
Brands:
  tio gazpacho

12820 Tip Top Canning Co
505 S 2nd St
Tipp City, OH 45371-1753
937-667-3713
Fax: 937-667-3802 800-352-2635
info@tiptopcanning.com www.tiptopcanning.com
Producers of tomatoes and tomato products.
President: Randy Allen
rallen@tiptopcanning.com
Vice President: Scott Timmer
Sales Manager: Cynthia Timmer
Production Manager: Matt Timmer
Estimated Sales: $10-20 Million
Number Employees: 20-49
Number of Products: 60
Square Footage: 450000
Type of Packaging: Consumer, Food Service, Private Label, Bulk

12821 Tip Top Poultry Inc
327 Wallace Rd
Marietta, GA 30062-3573
770-973-8070
Fax: 770-973-6897 800-241-5230
www.tiptoppoultry.com
Processor and exporter of poultry
President: Evelyn Delong
evelyn.delong@regalpoultry.com
COO: Mike Brooks
CFO: Charlie Singleton
VP: Lee Bates
VP/Sales: Brian Tucker
Technical VP: Mitch Forstie
Production Manager: Steve Moore
Estimated Sales: $15 Million
Number Employees: 1000-4999
Type of Packaging: Consumer, Bulk

12822 Tipiak Inc
45 Church St
Suite 303
Stamford, CT 06906-1733
203-961-9117
Fax: 203-975-9081 sales@tipiak-e.com
www.tipiak.com
Specialty rices and beans, tapioca flour and pearls, frozen appetizers and desserts.
President: Laurent Chery
laurent.chery@tipiak-e.com
VP: Laurent Chery
Estimated Sales: Below $5 Million
Number Employees: 5-9

12823 Tipp Distributors Inc
500 W Overland Ave # 300
#300
El Paso, TX 79901-1086
915-594-1618
Fax: 915-590-1225 888-668-2639
Condiments and relishes
President: Ramon Carrasco
CEO: Luis Fernandez
consumer.relations@novamex.com
CFO: Thomas Deleon
Executive VP: Sanford Gross
Estimated Sales: $1-2.5 Million
Number Employees: 100-249
Brands:
  Chata
  Cholula
  D'Gari
  Ibarra
  Jarritos
  Mineragua
  Rogelio Bueno
  San Marcos
  Sangria Seorial
  Sidral Mundet
  Tuny

12824 Tirawisu
13705 Ventura Blvd
Sherman Oaks, CA 91423-3023
818-906-2640
Fax: 516-599-6540
Exporter and processor of Italian desserts including chocolate mousse, tiramisu, gelato, tartufo, tortoni and spumoni; importer of Italian cakes and pasta
Owner/President: Aldo Antonoacci
Contact: Peter Kastelan
peter@il-tiramisu.com
Estimated Sales: Less Than $500,000
Number Employees: 5-9

12825 Titan Farms
5 RW DuBose Rd.
Ridge Spring, SC 29129
803-685-5381
Fax: 803-685-5885 www.titanfarms.com
Grower of peaches, bell peppers, and broccoli.
President & CEO: Chalmers Carr, III
VP & Administrative Manager: Lori Anne Carr
VP, Sales & Marketing: Daryl Johnston
VP, Operations: Jason Rodgers
Production Manager: Dwight Harmon
Year Founded: 1999
Type of Packaging: Consumer, Private Label

12826 Titusville Dairy Products Co
217 S Washington St
Titusville, PA 16354-1660
814-827-1833
Fax: 814-827-2510 800-352-0101
www.titusvilledairy.com
Ice cream mixes, dairy products, juices, fruit drinks and bottled water
President: Charles Turner Jr
VP: William Schneider Jr
Manager: Ralph Kerr
rktdpc@zoominternet.net
Plant Manager: Chester Anthony
Estimated Sales: $4 Million
Number Employees: 20-49
Square Footage: 120000
Type of Packaging: Consumer, Private Label
Brands:
  Blossom Time
  Natural Harvest
  Titusville Dairy Products

12827 Tkc Vineyards
11001 Valley Dr
Plymouth, CA 95669
209-245-6428
Fax: 209-245-4006 888-627-2356
www.tkcvineyards.com
Family winery committed to the production of premium wines. Specialties include Zinfandel, Mourvedre and Cabernet
Owner/CEO: Harold Nuffer
VP/CFO: Monica Nuffer
Marketing Director: Monica Nuffer
Estimated Sales: Less Than $500,000
Number Employees: 1-4
Type of Packaging: Private Label
Brands:
  Tkc Vineyards

Food Manufacturers / A-Z

12828 To Market To Market
200 12th St SW # 130
Suite 130
Loveland, CO 80537-6393
970-278-1000
Fax: 503-655-3390 kathy@tomarket-tomarket.com
tomarket-tomarket.com
Natural spice blends
President: Kent Heusinkveld
kent@tomarket-tomarket.com
Estimated Sales: Less Than $500,000
Number Employees: 5-9
Type of Packaging: Consumer, Food Service

12829 To Your Health Sprouted Flour Co., Inc.
PO Box 898
Floyd, VA 24091
540-283-9589
customerservice@bluemountainorganics.com
www.organicsproutedflour.com
Manufacturer of seeds and nuts, nut butters, frozen desserts, grains, dired fruits, and granola.
CEO: Jeff Sutton

12830 Todd's
PO Box 4821
Des Moines, IA 50305
515-266-2276
Fax: 515-266-1669   800-247-5363
Variety of food products, wet and dry, kosher and organic certified.
President/CEO: Alan Niedermeier
Quality Control: Diana Burzloff
Public Relations: Alissa Douglas
Operations: Duane Hettkamp
Production: Jeff Sullivan
Plant Manager: John Routh
Purchasing: Danielle Robinson
Estimated Sales: $1-3 Million
Number Employees: 30
Number of Brands: 40
Number of Products: 200
Square Footage: 320000
Type of Packaging: Consumer, Food Service, Private Label, Bulk
Brands:
 Butcher's Friend
 Papa Joe's Specialty Food

12831 Todd's
6055 Malburg Way
Vernon, CA 90058
323-585-5900
Fax: 323-585-5900   800-938-6337
Processor, importer and exporter of nuts and nut meats, dried fruit, trail mixes, candy, etc
President: Todd Levin
Estimated Sales: $5-10 Million
Number Employees: 5-9
Type of Packaging: Consumer, Food Service, Private Label, Bulk
Brands:
 Dr Jerkyll & Mr Hide
 Huckleberry's Farm
 Just Snak-It
 Lucy's Sweets
 Todd's Treats

12832 Todd's Salsa
PO Box 7045
Bangor, ME 04402
844-328-7257
info@toddssalsa.com
www.toddsoriginalsalsa.com
Salsa
Owner: Todd Simcox
Type of Packaging: Food Service, Private Label
Brands:
 Inner Beauty Hot Sauce
 Todd's Salsa

12833 (HQ)Toddy Products Inc
803 W Kansas Ave
Midland, TX 79701-6121
713-225-2066
Fax: 713-225-2110 www.toddycafe.com
Processor and exporter of liquid concentrates including coffee, tea, mocha, chai, etc.; also, espresso pecan brittle; manufacturer of cold brew coffee makers
Owner: Strother Simpson
Vice President: Scott Schroer
Contact: Kathy Kat
kkat@toddycafe.com
Estimated Sales: $1500000
Number Employees: 5-9
Square Footage: 80000
Type of Packaging: Consumer, Food Service, Private Label, Bulk
Brands:
 Toddy
 Toddy Cappuccino
 Toddy Coffee Crunch
 Toddy Coffee Maker
 Toddy Gourmet Iced Tea Concentrate
 Toddy Mocha

12834 Todhunter Foods
222 Lakeview Avenue
Suite 1500
West Palm Beach, FL 33401-6174
561-655-8977
Fax: 561-655-9718   800-336-9463
www.todhunter.com
Cooking wines, powdered wine flavors, denatures spirits, vinegar and wine reductions.
President: Jay Maltby
CFO: Ezra Shashoua
Vice President: D Chris Mitchell
Sales Director: Jim Polansky
Plant Manager: Ousik Yu
Purchasing Manager: Frank Dibling
Number Employees: 410
Parent Co: Todhunter International
Type of Packaging: Consumer, Food Service, Private Label, Bulk

12835 Todhunter Foods
PO Box 1447
Lake Alfred, FL 33850-1447
863-956-1116
Fax: 863-956-3979 www.todhunter.com
Vinegar and cooking wine; contract packager of fruit juices and carbonated/flavored beverages; importer of alcoholic beverages and juice concentrates; exporter of alcoholic beverages and vinegar
President: Jay Maltby
Number Employees: 100-249
Square Footage: 1800000
Parent Co: Todhunter International
Type of Packaging: Consumer, Food Service, Private Label, Bulk

12836 Toe-Food Chocolates and Candy
2500 Milvia Street
Suite 216
Berkeley, CA 94704-2636
510-649-9250
Fax: 510-849-3810   888-863-3663
www.toefood.com
Chocolate and candy in the shape of feet.
Founder/CEO: Mark Wolpa
Estimated Sales: $300,000-500,000
Number Employees: 8
Brands:
 Toe-Rific Candy

12837 Toffee Boutique
11353 Pyrites Way
Suite 16
Rancho Cordova, CA 95670-4454
916-638-8462
www.toffeeboutique.com
Manufacturer of toffee.
Founder: Lisa Ferrato
Estimated Sales: Less Than $500,000
Number Employees: 1-4

12838 Toffee Co
359 N Post Oak Ln # 126
#126
Houston, TX 77024-5942
713-688-5531
Fax: 713-688-7602 BBurk924@aol.com
www.toffeeco.com
Toffee, candy
Owner: Ben Burkholder
bburk924@aol.com
Estimated Sales: Less Than $500,000
Number Employees: 1-4

12839 Tofield Packers Ltd
5020 50th Avenue
Tofield, AB T0B 4J0
Canada
780-662-4842
Fax: 780-662-4842
Fresh and processed meats including sausage and wild game; also, custom slaughtering available
President: Dale Erickson
Estimated Sales: C
Number Employees: 10-19
Type of Packaging: Consumer, Bulk

12840 Toft Dairy Inc
3717 Venice Rd
Sandusky, OH 44870-1640
419-625-4376
Fax: 419-621-2010   800-521-4606
info@toftdairy.com www.toftdairy.com
Milk, ice cream, frozen yogurt, fruit drinks, orange juice, cottage cheese and sour cream
Owner: Thomas Meisler
tmeisler@toft.com
VP: Thomas Meisler
Plant Manager: Dan Meisler
Estimated Sales: $17.8 Million
Number Employees: 50-99
Square Footage: 188000
Type of Packaging: Consumer, Food Service, Private Label, Bulk

12841 Tofu Shop Specialty Foods Inc
65 Frank Martin Ct
Arcata, CA 95521-8930
707-822-7401
Fax: 707-822-7401 info@tofushop.com
www.tofushop.com
Fresh tofu, smoked tofu, fresh soymilks, international spiced tofu, seasoned and baked tofu
President: Matthew Schmit
info@tofushop.com
Estimated Sales: $500,000
Number Employees: 20-49
Number of Products: 22
Square Footage: 18000
Type of Packaging: Consumer, Bulk
Brands:
 Snack Fu
 Tofu Shop

12842 Tofurky
PO Box 176
Hood River, OR 97031
Fax: 541-386-7754   800-508-8100
www.tofurky.com
Tofu products, vegan meat alternatives
Contact: Jaime Athos
jathos@tofurkey.com

12843 Tofutti Brands Inc
50 Jackson Dr
Cranford, NJ 07016-3504
908-272-2400
Fax: 908-272-9492 info@tofutti.com
www.tofutti.com
Processor and exporter of nondairy food products including imitation cream cheese, no-cholesterol egg products made of egg whites and tofu with added vitamins and minerals and frozen tofu desserts
CEO: Shana Joseph
sjoseph@tofutti.com
CEO: David Mintz
CFO: Steven Kass
Director: Neal Axelrod
Estimated Sales: $10-20 Million
Number Employees: 5-9
Type of Packaging: Consumer, Food Service, Bulk
Brands:
 Lite Lite Tofutti
 Tofutti
 Tofutti Better Than Cheesecake

12844 Tokunaga Farms
12019 S Highland Avenue
Selma, CA 93662-9003
559-896-0949
Farm products
President: George Tokunga

12845 Tolteca Foodservice
4305 Steve Reynolds Boulevard
Norcross, GA 30093
770-263-0490
800-541-6835
www.toltecafoods.com
A self-proclaimed one-stop shop for Mexican restaurants. A manufacturer of every kind of supplies a Mexican restaurant may need, including tortillas, spices, meats, dairy, oils, grains, fruit and vegetables, beverages, etc.

Food Manufacturers / A-Z

Estimated Sales: $1700000
Number Employees: 10-19
Number of Products: 2000
Square Footage: 50000
Type of Packaging: Consumer, Food Service, Private Label
Brands:
  Mexican Bear

12846 Tom & Dave's Coffee
3095 Kerner Blvd # A
San Rafael, CA 94901-5420
415-454-3064
Fax: 415-454-3281 800-249-5050
orders@novarosti.com www.tomanddaves.com
Coffee
Owner: Christopher Rygg
customerservice@tomanddaves.com
Estimated Sales: Below $5 Million
Number Employees: 1-4
Type of Packaging: Private Label
Brands:
  Columbian
  House Blend
  Moka-Java

12847 Tom & Sally's Handmade Chocolates
P.O.Box 600
Brattleboro, VT 05302-0600
802-254-4200
Fax: 802-254-5518 800-827-0800
Gourmet chocolate products including old-fashioned creams, foil-wrapped coins, spoons, nut patties, lollypops, almond bark, dessert toppings and molded
Chairman: Thomas E Fegley
Estimated Sales: $3-5 Million
Number Employees: 10-19
Square Footage: 46800
Type of Packaging: Consumer, Private Label
Brands:
  Cowlicks
  Dog-Gones
  Reindeer Pies
  Vermont Meadow Muffins
  Vermont Pasture Patties

12848 Tom Cat Bakery Inc
43-05 10th St
Queens, NY 11101
718-786-7659
Fax: 718-786-9046
customerservice@tomcatbakery.com
www.tomcatbakery.com
French and Italian breads, rolls, baguettes
VP & General Manager: James Rath
jamesrath@tomcatbakery.com
EVP & General Manager: Peter Sonenstein
R&D Manager: Leonardo Duran
VP, Sales: John Martinez
Production Manager: Laurie Williams
Year Founded: 1987
Estimated Sales: $50-100 Million
Number Employees: 50-99
Number of Brands: 1
Brands:
  Tom Cat Bakery

12849 Tom Farms
8542 N Harper Rd.
Leesburg, IN 46538
574-453-3300
Fax: 574-453-4787 www.tomfarms.com
Seed corn, corn and soybeans.
Co-Founder: Everett Tom
Co-Founder: Marie Tom
Managing Member: Kip Tom
CFO: Derrick Deardorff
Year Founded: 1952
Type of Packaging: Food Service, Bulk

12850 Tom Ringhausen Orchards
Route 16 & 100
PO Box 201
Hardin, IL 62047-0201
618-576-2311
800-258-6645
www.enjoycalhouncounty.com
Processor and grower of fruits and vegetables including apples, peaches, plums, pears, nectarines, blackberries, squash, pumpkins, melons and turnips. Also cider
President: Tom Ringhausen

Estimated Sales: Under $300,000
Number Employees: 400
Square Footage: 6000
Type of Packaging: Consumer
Brands:
  Tom Ringhausen

12851 Tom Sturgis Pretzels Inc
2267 Lancaster Pike
Reading, PA 19607-2498
610-775-0335
Fax: 610-796-1418 800-817-3834
csr@tomsturgispretzels.com
www.tomsturgispretzels.com
Pretzels
President: Bruce Sturgis
Founder: Tom Sturgis
tsturgis@tomsturgispretzels.com
Vice President: Barbara Sturgis
Sales Director: Timothy Snyder
Operations Manager: Jean Harms
Production Manager: David Amour
Plant Manager: Mike Kappenstein
Estimated Sales: $5 Million
Number Employees: 20-49
Number of Brands: 3
Square Footage: 300000
Type of Packaging: Private Label
Brands:
  Cousin Rachel Pretzels
  Mr. C'S Pretzels
  Tom Sturgis Pretzels

12852 Tom Tom Tamale & BakeryCo
4750 S Washtenaw Ave
Chicago, IL 60632-2096
773-523-5675
Tamales
President: Nick Petros
Estimated Sales: $500,000-$1 Million
Number Employees: 20-49
Type of Packaging: Consumer

12853 Tom's Foods
8600 South Blvd
Charlotte, NC 28273
877-309-6361
Snack foods including potato chips
Contact: Jack Warden
hr@tomsfoods.com
Plant Manager: John Rothenfluh
Parent Co: Snyders-Lance Inc.
Type of Packaging: Private Label

12854 Tom's Snacks Company
8600 S Boulevard
Charlotte, NC 28273
706-323-2721
Fax: 706-323-8231 800-995-2623
www.tomsfoods.com
Potato chips, thick and bold chips, thunder chips, cheezers, pork skins, rings, fries, corn and tortilla, bugles and mega twisters
Supply Chain VP, Lance Inc.: Blake Thompson
Contact: Marc Albers
malbers@tomsfoods.com
Estimated Sales: $.5-1 million
Number Employees: 50-99
Parent Co: Lance, Inc.
Type of Packaging: Consumer
Brands:
  Tom's

12855 Tomanetti Food ProductsInc
625-631 Allegheny Avenue
Oakmont, PA 15139-2003
412-828-3040
Fax: 412-828-2282 800-875-3040
tomanetti@aol.com www.tomanetti.com
Gourmet pizza products including cheese analogs, crusts and focaccia; also, whole wheat pizzas
President: George Michel
Sales Manager: Christopher Presutti
Customer Service Representative: Jessica Piccolino
Operations: Jerry Drolz
Administrative Manager: Tammy Carroll
Estimated Sales: $10-20 Million
Number Employees: 20-49
Parent Co: Tomanetti Foods
Type of Packaging: Consumer, Food Service, Private Label, Bulk
Brands:
  Graindance
  Soydance

12856 (HQ)Tomanetti Food Products
631 Allegheny Avenue
Oakmont, PA 15139
412-828-3040
Fax: 412-828-2282 800-875-3040
tomanetti@aol.com www.tomanetti.com
Pizza shells, breadsticks and focaccia.
President: George Michel
COO: Robert Finlay
Sales Manager: Chris Presutti
Production Supervisor: Bill Vidra
Plant Manager: Paul Sypolt
Estimated Sales: Below $5 Million
Number Employees: 30

12857 Tomanetti Food Products
625 Allegheny Ave
Oakmont, PA 15139
412-828-3040
Fax: 412-828-2282 tomanetti@tomanetti.com
www.tomanetti.com
Manufacturer and distributor of pizza crusts and flatbreads.
President: Rodney Butcher
Estimated Sales: Under $500,000
Number Employees: 20-49
Parent Co: Hollymead Capital
Brands:
  Graindance
  Soydance

12858 Tomaro's Bakery
411 N 4th St
Clarksburg, WV 26301-2004
304-622-0691
www.tomarosbakery.com
Bread, rolls and pizza crusts
President: Janice Brunett
Manager: Steve Schartiger
tomarosbakery@aol.com
Estimated Sales: $6 Million
Number Employees: 20-49
Type of Packaging: Consumer

12859 Tomasello Winery
225 N White Horse Pike
Hammonton, NJ 08037-1868
609-561-0567
Fax: 609-561-8617 800-666-9463
wine@tomasellowinery.com
www.tomasellowinery.com
Wines
President: Chris Curry
ccurry@tomasellowinery.com
Owner: Jack Tomasello
Vice President: Jack Tomasello
Estimated Sales: Below $5 Million
Number Employees: 5-9
Brands:
  Tomasello Winery

12860 Tomasso Corporation
20425 Clark Graham
Baie D'Urfe, QC H9X 3T5
Canada
514-325-3000
Fax: 514-457-5107 www.cordonbleu.ca
Frozen Italian entrees including meat lasagna, chicken lasagna, meat sauce, vegeatble lasagna, cannelloni, macaroni and cheese
Chairman/CEO: J-Rene Ouimet
CFO/Treasurer: Peter Tasgal
Number Employees: 120
Square Footage: 212000
Type of Packaging: Food Service, Private Label
Brands:
  Buona Cucina
  Gusto Italia
  Piazza Tomasso

12861 Tomer Kosher Foods
5340 Lincoln Avenue
Skokie, IL 60077
847-779-4870
matthew@rotemfoods.com
www.tomerkosher.com
Kosher beef and jerky
President: Justin Teten
justin@tomerkosher.com
Sales & Marketing: Matthew Sharos
Office Manager: Jennifer Morales
Brands:
  TK Tomer Kosher

Food Manufacturers / A-Z

12862 Tommy Tang's Thai Seasonings
PO Box 46700
Los Angeles, CA 90046-7512
818-442-0219
Seasonings, spices
President: Sandi Tang
Owner: Tommy Tang
sandi.arabia@gmail.com
Estimated Sales: $1-2.5 Million
Number Employees: 10-19

12863 Tommy's Jerky Outlet
8640 Mentor Ave
Mentor, OH 44060-6140
440-255-3994
Fax: 305-723-7686 866-448-6942
info@tommysjerky.com www.tommysjerky.com
Beef jerky and jerky spices
President: Thomas Stabosz
Production: Joe Muscarella
Number Employees: 5-9
Number of Brands: 1
Number of Products: 9
Parent Co: TFS
Type of Packaging: Consumer, Food Service, Private Label, Bulk
Brands:
  Gold Rush
  Grandpa Vals
  Toxic Tommy

12864 Tomorrow Enterprise
5918 Spanish Trl W
New Iberia, LA 70560
337-783-2666
Fax: 337-233-9514
Hot sauces
President: Tony Morrow

12865 Toms Moms Foods, LLC
5914 Grisby House Crt.
Centreville, VA 20120
614-716-9436
Manufacturer of homemade syrup.
Founder: Andy Humphries

12866 Tone Products Inc
2129 N 15th Ave
Melrose Park, IL 60160-1406
708-681-3660
Fax: 708-681-2368 800-536-8663
Processor and exporter of fountain beverages, energy drinks, fruit smoothies, pancake syrups, beverage concentrates, sauces and marinades.
President/CEO: Tim Evon
CEO: Timothy E Evon
timevon@toneproducts.com
Chief Financial Officer: William Hamen
Director, National Accounts: Tim Collins
VP, Sales: William Evon
Director, Operations: Greg Sperry
Director of Purchasing: Matt Claus
Estimated Sales: $12 Million
Number Employees: 50-99
Number of Brands: 9
Square Footage: 46000
Type of Packaging: Consumer, Private Label, Bulk
Brands:
  Balboa Bay
  Bonnie
  Bonnie Maid
  Evon's
  Golden Kettle
  Lost Lake
  Rainbo-Rich
  Sno-Bal
  Timber Trails

12867 Tonewood Maple
301 Glen View Rd
Waitsfield, VT 05673-4401
802-496-5512
info@tonewoodmaple.com
www.tonewoodmaple.com
Manufacturer of solid and liquid maple products.
Founder: Dori Ross
info@tonewoodmaple.com
Number Employees: 1-3

12868 Tonex
27 Park Row
Wallington, NJ 07057-1629
973-773-5135
Fax: 973-916-1091 tonexinc@aol.com
Cappuccino, nondairy creamers, instant coffee and tea and chocolate covered nuts; importer and exporter of beer, vodka, candy, fresh and dried fruits, tea, instant cappuccino, juice and juice concentrates, etc
Owner: Bogdan Torbus
President: Grace Torbus
Marketing Director: Angela Torbus
Type of Packaging: Consumer, Food Service, Private Label, Bulk
Brands:
  Chocolate Covered Nuts
  Instant Cappuccino
  Instant Tea

12869 Tony Chachere's Creole Foods
519 N Lombard St
Opelousas, LA 70570-6232
337-942-9303
Fax: 337-948-6854 800-551-9066
www.tonychachere.com
Seasonings and rice dinner mixes
President: Donald Chachere
Marketing Director: Christopher Roch
CFO: William Pollingue
CFO: Donald Chachere Jr
VP Sales: Mona Campbell Jr
Public Relations: Janice LeBlanc
Production Manager: Alex Chachere
Plant Manager: Carl Trahan
Estimated Sales: Below $1 Million
Number Employees: 50-99
Type of Packaging: Consumer, Food Service, Private Label, Bulk
Brands:
  Instant Roux & Gravy
  More Spice Seasoning
  Tony Chachere's Orig

12870 Tony Downs Foods
54934 210th Ln
Mankato, MN 56001
507-387-3663
Fax: 507-388-6420 866-731-4561
mdowns@downsfoodgroup.com
www.tonydownsfoods.com
Poultry fully cooked, diced-frozen and commercial and retail canned chicken.
President: Mike Downs
mdowns@downsfoodgroup.com
Vice President: Greg Cook
Director, Human Resources: David Ross
Year Founded: 1947
Estimated Sales: $22 Million
Number Employees: 20-49
Square Footage: 100000
Type of Packaging: Consumer, Food Service, Private Label, Bulk

12871 Tony Vitrano Company
7470 Conowingo Ave.
PO Box 2001
Jessup, MD 20794
410-799-7444
800-481-3784
dorothy@fruitiongifts.com
www.tonyvitranocompany.com
Established in 1934. Processor of apples, oranges, cucumbers, onions, lettuce, and squash.
President: Anthony Vitrano
Director of Marketing: Dorothy Vitrano
Contact: Dorothy Vitrano
dorothy@fruitiongifts.com
Estimated Sales: $20-50 Million
Number Employees: 51-200
Type of Packaging: Consumer, Food Service, Bulk
Brands:
  Dole
  Sunkist
  Ocean Spray

12872 Tony's Chocolonely
1355 Nw Everett
Suite 100
Portland, OR 97209-2655
503-388-5990
mailme@tonyschocolonely.com
www.tonyschocolonely.com
Chocolate bars
American Brand Builder: Maudi Admiraal
US Sales Manager: Peter Zandee
Operations & Finance: Heather Bright
Office Manager: Meredith McEntee
Estimated Sales: $6.3 Million
Number Employees: 11-50
Brands:
  Tony's Chocolonely

12873 Tony's Ice Cream Co
604 E Franklin Blvd
Gastonia, NC 28054-7111
704-867-7085
www.tonysicecream.com
Ice cream
President: Robert Coletta
Vice President: Louis Coletta
Manager: Cheryl Martin
Estimated Sales: Less Than $500,000
Number Employees: 5-9
Type of Packaging: Consumer

12874 Tony's Pizza
Marshall, MN
888-465-8324
Frozen pizza manufacturer.
Parent Co: Schwan's Company
Brands:
  Tony's(c)

12875 Tony's Seafood LTD
5215 Plank Rd
Baton Rouge, LA 70805-2730
225-357-9669
Fax: 225-355-3530 800-356-2905
www.tonyseafood.com
Seafood
Owner: Darren Pizzolato
darren.pizzolato@tonyseafood.com
Year Founded: 1959
Estimated Sales: $20-50 Million
Number Employees: 1-4

12876 Tonya's Gluten-Free Kitchen
167 Sinclair Road
Newmanstown, PA 17073
717-949-4175
tonya@tonyasglutenfree.com
www.tonyasglutenfree.com
Gluten free soft pretzels
Contact: Ben Bernard
tonya@tonyasglutenfree.com

12877 Too Cool Chix
Too Cool Chix
New York, NY 10001
929-244-3022
orders@toocoolchix.com
Ice cream sandwich
President & CEO: Sharon Monahan
s.monahan@toocoolchix.com
Co-Founder: Michele Elmer
Number Employees: 1-4
Brands:
  Too Cool Chix

12878 Too Good Gourmet
2380 Grant Ave
San Lorenzo, CA 94580-1806
510-317-8150
Fax: 510-317-8755 877-850-4663
info@toogoodgourmet.com
www.toogoodgourmet.com
Cookies
President: Jennifer Finley
jennifer@toogoodgourmet.com
Marketing/Sales: Katie Bidstrup
Estimated Sales: $5-10 Million
Number Employees: 50-99
Type of Packaging: Consumer, Food Service, Private Label, Bulk

12879 Toom Dips
Saint Paul, MN
651-447-8666
www.toomdips.com
Garlic dip made with all natural ingredients and based on Lebanese toum sauce, in various flavors
Founder/Chief Executive Officer: Matty Joyce
Number of Brands: 1
Number of Products: 4
Type of Packaging: Consumer, Private Label
Brands:
  Toom

Food Manufacturers / A-Z

12880 Tootsie Roll Industries Inc.
7401 S. Cicero Ave.
Chicago, IL 60629
773-838-3400
Fax: 773-838-3435 866-972-6879
tootsieroll@worldpantry.com www.tootsie.com
Candy.
President/CEO/Director: Ellen Gordon
VP Finance/CFO: G. Howard Ember
VP: George Rost
Year Founded: 1896
Estimated Sales: $550 Million
Number Employees: 2,201
Number of Brands: 23
Square Footage: 2375000
Type of Packaging: Consumer, Food Service, Bulk
Brands:
  Andes
  Caramel Apple Pops
  Candy Blox
  Candy Carnival
  Cella's Cherries
  Charleston Chew
  Charms
  Child's Play
  Cry Baby
  DOTS
  Dubble Bubble
  Fluffy Stuff
  Frooties
  Fruit Chews
  Junior Mints
  Mini Bites
  Nik-L-Nip
  Razzles
  Sugar Babies
  Sugar Daddy
  Tootsie Roll
  Wack-O-Wax

12881 Top Hat Co Inc
2407 Birchwood Ln
Wilmette, IL 60091-2349
847-256-6565
Fax: 847-256-6579 info@tophatcompany.com
www.tophatcompany.com
Sauces including raspberry, hot, mocha and mint fudges, butterscotch, caramel, double chocolate fondue and bittersweet chocolate
President: Marla Murray
Contact: Brandon Chillingworth
chillingworthbrandon@tophat.com
Estimated Sales: Less than $1,000,000
Number Employees: 5-9
Type of Packaging: Consumer, Food Service, Private Label, Bulk
Brands:
  Top Hat Dessert Sauces
  Mayan Legacy
  Prince of Orange
  Southern Sin

12882 Top Pot Doughnuts
609 Summit Ave E
Seattle, WA 98102-4821
206-323-7841
www.toppotdoughnuts.com
Donuts
Contact: Adam Clark
aclark@toppotdoughnuts.com
Estimated Sales: Less Than $500,000
Number Employees: 5-9

12883 Top Tier Foods Inc.
3737 Oak St.
Vancouver, BC V6H SM4
Canada
778-628-0015
hello@toptierfoods.com
www.toptierfoods.com
Ready-to-serve quinoa pilafs in various flavors; sushi quinoa
President: Blair Bullus
Year Founded: 2013
Number of Brands: 1
Type of Packaging: Consumer, Private Label
Brands:
  Quinoa Quickies

12884 Topaz Farm
17100 NW Sauvie Island Rd
Portland, OR 97231
503-708-0008
info@topazfarm.com
topazfarm.com
Pummpkins and berries
Owner: Kat Topaz
Estimated Sales: $3600000
Number Employees: 10-19

12885 Topco Associates LLC
150 Northwest Point Blvd.
Elk Grove Village, IL 60007
847-676-3030
Fax: 847-676-4949 consumerservices@topco.com
www.topco.com
Grocery, frozen, dairy, and bakery, branded meat, equipment and supplies, business services, world brands and diverting.
President/CEO: Randall Skoda
rskoda@topco.com
Executive VP/CFO: Thomas Frey
Senior VP & General Counsel: Andy Broccolo
Senior VP, Fresh: Scott Caro
Year Founded: 1944
Estimated Sales: $1 Billion
Number Employees: 250-499
Number of Brands: 21
Type of Packaging: Consumer, Food Service, Private Label
Other Locations:
  Visalia CA
  West Palm Beach FL
  Miami FL
  Quincy MA
  Yakima WA
Brands:
  Food Club
  Shur Fine
  Tippy Toes
  Paws
  Simply Done
  @Ease
  Sweet P's
  Buckley Farms
  Harvest Club
  Over the Top
  Cape Covelle
  Papa Enzo's
  CharKing
  Culinary Tours
  Top Care
  Full Circle
  Pure Harmony
  Wide Awake Coffee Co.
  Cow Belle Creamery's
  Valu Time
  Nostimo

12886 Topo Chico Mineral Water
5800 Granite Pkwy. # 900
Plano, TX 75024
888-456-4357
www.topochicousa.net
Sparkling mineral water in various flavors; bottled at source in Monterrey, Mexico
General Manager: Gerardo Galvan
Year Founded: 1895
Number of Brands: 1
Type of Packaging: Consumer, Private Label
Brands:
  Topo Chico

12887 Topolos at Russian River Vine
5700 Gravenstein Highway North
Forestville, CA 95436-0358
707-887-3344
Fax: 707-887-1399
www.russianrivervineyards.com
Wine and gourmet foods
President: Michael Topolos
Estimated Sales: $1 Million
Number Employees: 25
Brands:
  Topolos At Russian River Vine

12888 Topor's Pickle & Food Svc Inc
2800 Standish St
Detroit, MI 48216-1539
313-237-0288
Fax: 313-981-4249
Pickles, dill green tomatoes, hot pickles with red peppers, Hungarian hot banana peppers
President: Larry Topor
Estimated Sales: $3-5 000,000
Number Employees: 5-9

12889 Torani
233 East Harris Ave.
San Francisco, CA 94080
650-875-1200
855-972-0508
www.torani.com
Flavored syrups, sauces, and beverage bases.
CEO: Melanie Dulbecco
Contact: Christopher Bernardino
cbernardino@torani.com
Number Employees: 100

12890 Torie & Howard LLC
143 West St
Suite 121C
New Milford, CT 06776-3599
860-799-7772
www.torieandhoward.com
Candy.
Co-Founder: Torie Burke
info@torieandhoward.com
Co-Founder: Howard Slatkin
Number Employees: 1-4

12891 Torke Coffee Co
3455 Paine Ave
Sheboygan, WI 53081-8457
920-458-4114
Fax: 920-458-0488 800-242-7671
info@torkecoffee.com
www.torke-coffee.myshopify.com
Manufacturer of coffee and tea.
President: Jay Torke
Year Founded: 1941
Estimated Sales: $20-50 Million
Number Employees: 20-49
Brands:
  Torke

12892 Torkelson Cheese Co
9453 W Louisa Rd
Lena, IL 61048
815-369-4265
info@torkelsoncheese.com
www.torkelsoncheese.com
Manufacturer and wholesaler of cheeses, specifically Muenster, brick, quesadilla and asadero cheeses; lactose manufacturer.
Owner: Lindsey White
Head Cheesemaker: Jamie White
Year Founded: 1985
Estimated Sales: $50-100 Million
Number Employees: 20-49
Number of Brands: 3
Type of Packaging: Consumer, Food Service, Bulk
Brands:
  Torkelson Cheese Co.
  El Ganador del Premio
  Apple Jack Cheese

12893 Torn & Glasser
1769 Glendale Blvd
Los Angeles, CA 90026-1761
323-661-2332
Fax: 213-688-0941 800-282-6887
Nuts, dried fruit, seeds, granola, beans, rice, dry chili, candy, etc
Owner: Tony Tierno
VP: Greg Glasser
Purchasing Manager: Gus Gutmun
Estimated Sales: $300,000-500,000
Number Employees: 1-4
Type of Packaging: Consumer, Food Service, Private Label, Bulk

12894 Torn Ranch
23 Pimentel Ct
Suite B
Novato, CA 94949-5661
707-796-7800
Fax: 415-506-3002 info@tornranch.com
www.tornranch.com
Dried fruits, roasted nuts, snack foods and shortbreads.
President: Dean Morrow
Vice President: Sue Morrow
Quality Control: Robert Wagner
Contact: Rich Shaffer
shafcndy@aol.com
Estimated Sales: $5-10 Million
Number Employees: 50-99

Food Manufacturers / A-Z

Type of Packaging: Private Label
Brands:
- Cafe Time
- Gigi Baking Company
- Mashuga Nuts & Cookies
- Splendid Specialties Chocolate Co

12895 Torre Products Co Inc
479 Washington St
New York, NY 10013-1381
212-925-8989
Fax: 212-925-4627
Manufacturer, importer and exporter of flavoring extracts and essential oils
Owner: Liberty F Raho
Estimated Sales: $10-20 Million
Number Employees: 5-9
Square Footage: 33000
Brands:
- Flambe Holiday
- La Torinese
- Rum-Ba
- Soft Mac

12896 Torrefazione Barzula & Import
3117 Wharton Way
Mississauga, ON L4X 2B6
Canada
905-625-6082
Fax: 905-625-5741 866-358-5488
sales@barzula.com www.barzula.com
Processor, importer and exporter of coffee beans including green, espresso, Turkish and decaffeinated
President: Luigi Russignan
Treasurer: Gigliola Russignan
VP: Phil Cennova
Estimated Sales: $2.2 Million
Number Employees: 14
Number of Brands: 1
Number of Products: 12
Square Footage: 48000
Brands:
- Barzula

12897 Torrefazione Italia
2401 Utah Avenue South
Seattle, WA 98134
206-624-5773
Fax: 206-624-3262 800-827-2333
Gourmet/ specialty coffee
President/COO: Dick Holbrook
VP Marketing: Kim Beerli
CFO: Chris December
Founder: Umberto Bizzarri
Sales Director: Tom Danowski
Operations Manager: Jane Albright
Estimated Sales: Below $500,000
Number Employees: 2
Type of Packaging: Private Label
Brands:
- Torrefazione Italia

12898 Torreo Coffee Company
4950 Rhawn St
Philadelphia, PA 19136
215-333-1105
Fax: 215-333-6615 888-286-7736
torreo.com
Premium coffees
President: Eric Patrick
Vice President: H Patrick
Operations Manager: Howard Patrick
Estimated Sales: $500,000-$1 Million
Number Employees: 5-9
Square Footage: 38400
Parent Co: Torreo Coffee & Tea Company
Type of Packaging: Consumer, Private Label, Bulk
Brands:
- Torreo

12899 Tortillas Inc
2912 Norht Commerce Street
North Las Vegas, NV 89030-3945
702-399-3300
Fax: 702-399-2507 gus@tortillasinc.com
www.tortillasinc.com
Tortillas
Owner: Gus Gutierrez
Partner: Jose Gutierrez
Owner: Salvo Gutierrez
Estimated Sales: $2.5-5 Million
Number Employees: 20-49

12900 Totally Chocolate
2025 Sweet Rd
Blaine, WA 98230-9198
360-332-3900
Fax: 360-332-1802 800-255-5506
sales@totallychocolate.com
www.totallychocolate.com
Chocolate
President: Ken Strong
kstrong@totallychocolate.com
VP Sales: Matt Roth
Plant Manager: Steve Hocker
Estimated Sales: $5-10 Millions
Number Employees: 50-99
Type of Packaging: Private Label
Brands:
- Totally Chocolate

12901 Totino's
General Mills, Inc.
PO Box 9452
Minneapolis, MN 55440
800-248-7310
www.totinos.com
Pizza products and stuffed nachos.
President & COO, General Mills: Jeffrey Harmening
Chairperson & CEO, General Mills: Ken Powell
Estimated Sales: Under $500,000
Number Employees: 10-19

12902 Toucan Chocolates
RR 128
Box 72
Waban, MA 02468
617-964-8696
Fax: 800-816-8696
Chocolate
President: Michael Goldman

12903 Touche Bakery
384b Neptune Cr.
London, ON N6M 1A1
Canada
518-455-0044
Fax: 519-455-5843 aswartz@touchebakery.com
www.touchebakery.com
All natural, nut-free biscotti, cookies, and meringues
President: Peter Cuddy
President & CEO: Allan Swartz
Finance/Administration Manager: Pat Gauthier
Account Manager: Peggy Swartz
Administrative Assistant: Vickie Suter
Square Footage: 32000
Type of Packaging: Consumer, Food Service, Private Label

12904 Touche Bakery
384b Neptune Cr
London, ON N6M 1A1
Canada
519-455-0044
Fax: 519-455-5843 aswartz@touchebakery.com
www.touchebakery.com
Biscotti, meringues, cookies, brownies, frozen cookie dough, muffin and brownie batter
President/CEO: Allan Swartz
Estimated Sales: $1.2 Million
Number Employees: 20

12905 Toufayan Bakeries
175 Railroad Ave
Ridgefield, NJ 07657-2312
201-861-4131
Fax: 201-861-0392 msteve@toufayan.com
www.toufayan.com
Pita bread, flatbread, bagels, wraps, lavash, and bread sticks
Owner: Greg Toufayan
CFO, Controller: Kristine Toufayan
Vice President: Bob Thomas
VP & Treasurer: Suzanne Toufayan
VP Marketing: Karen Toufayan
VP Sales: Roy Peterson
Operations Manager: Chris Clark
Production Manager: Paul Steinbach
Purchasing Manager: James Bogosian
Estimated Sales: $26 Million
Number Employees: 20-49
Type of Packaging: Consumer, Food Service
Other Locations:
- Orlando FL
- Plant City FL

12906 Tova Industries LLC
P.O. Box 24410
Louisville, KY 40224
502-267-7333
Fax: 502-267-7119 888-532-8682
corporate@tovaindustries.com
www.tovaindustries.com
Dry mix food products, spices, table and beverage syrups
President: Zack Melzer
zackmelzer@tovaindustries.com
SVP: Yael Melzer
Year Founded: 1985
Estimated Sales: $100+ Million
Number Employees: 50-99
Number of Products: 1000
Type of Packaging: Consumer, Food Service, Private Label, Bulk
Other Locations:
- New Horizon Foods
- Union City CA
Brands:
- Heritage-the Essence of Tradition
- Lifesource Foods
- Stoneground Mills
- Superior Spices
- Superior Syrups
- Tova

12907 Townsend Farms Inc
23400 NE Townsend Way
Fairview, OR 97024-4626
503-666-1780
Fax: 503-618-8257 www.townsendfarms.com
Fresh and frozen blueberries, blackberries and strawberries; fresh black raspberries, mixed fruit, manoes, boysenberries, cherries, marionberries, red raspberries and pineapple; fresh raspberries
President: Tracy Casillas
tracyc@thecanbycenter.org
CEO: Jeff Townsend
CFO: Chris Valenti
Plant Manager: Reyes Pena
Purchasing: Mark Davis
Estimated Sales: $10-20 Million
Number Employees: 1000-4999
Square Footage: 4000
Type of Packaging: Consumer, Food Service, Private Label, Bulk

12908 Trace Minerals Research
1996 W 3300 S
West Haven, UT 84401-9774
801-731-6051
Fax: 801-731-3702 800-624-7145
infor@traceminerals.com www.traceminerals.com
Dietary supplements
President: Matt Kilts
mattk@traceminerals.com
Chairman: George Harris
Sales Director: Ryan Fisher
Estimated Sales: $4972329
Number Employees: 50-99
Number of Products: 100
Square Footage: 52000
Type of Packaging: Consumer, Food Service, Private Label, Bulk

12909 Tracy Luckey Pecans
110 N Hicks St
PO Box 880
Harlem, GA 30814
706-556-6216
Fax: 706-556-6210 800-476-4796
Shelled pecans and pecan products
President: Francis Tracy
VP/CEO: Ruth Tracy
Controller: Ed Wicker
VP Marketing/Sales: Ruth Tracy
Contact: Nancy Studdard
nancy@tracy-luckey.com
Plant Manager: Homer Gay
Estimated Sales: $120,000
Number Employees: 50-99
Square Footage: 320000
Type of Packaging: Bulk
Brands:
- Sunblet

12910 Trade Marcs Group
55 Nassau Ave
Brooklyn, NY 11222-3143
718-387-9696
Fax: 718-782-2471

Food Manufacturers / A-Z

General grocery
Manager: Andi Billow
Contact: Marc Greenberg
marc@cafelasemeuse.com
Estimated Sales: Less than $500,000
Number Employees: 1-4

12911 Trade Winds Pizza
1085 Parkview Road
Green Bay, WI 54304-5616
920-336-7810
Fax: 920-336-2942
Pizzas
Director Operations: Jim Peppich

12912 Trader Vic's Food Products
9 Anchor Dr
Emeryville, CA 94608
510-653-3400
Fax: 510-653-9384 877-762-4824
china@tradervics.com tradervics.com
Processor and exporter of nonalcoholic cocktail mixes, syrups, dry spices, sauces and salad dressings
CEO: Hans Richter
VP: Peter Seely
Estimated Sales: $540000
Number Employees: 6
Type of Packaging: Consumer
Brands:
  Trader Vic's

12913 Tradeshare Corporation
207 Flushing Avenue
Brooklyn, NY 11205
718-237-2295
Food preparation and general grocery
President: Robert Krasnor
Estimated Sales: $2.5-5 000,000
Number Employees: 10-19

12914 Tradewinds
3601 South Congress Ave
Austin, TX 78704
www.tradewindstea.com
Brewed teas in nine flavors
President: Kenneth Lichtendahl
Marketing Director: Christy Lichtendahl
Estimated Sales: $5-10 Million
Number Employees: 5-9
Parent Co: Sweet Leaf Tea
Brands:
  Concord Grape
  Granny Smith Apple
  Ice Tea
  Lemon Tea

12915 Tradewinds Coffee Company
5500 Atlantic Springs Rd Ste 106
Raleigh, NC 27616
919-878-1111
Fax: 919-878-0041 800-457-0406
Coffee and coffee flavored candy
President: Art Watkins
Co-Owner: Elaine Watkins
Estimated Sales: Below $5 Million
Number Employees: 10-19
Brands:
  Trade Winds Coffee

12916 Tradin Organics USA
100 Enterprise Way
Suite B 101
Scotts Valley, CA 95066
831-685-6565
info@tradinorganicsusa.com
tradinorganic.com
Fruits and berries.
VP, Sales & Procurement: Hendrik Rabbie
Contact: Jacqueline Chuang
jacqueline.chuang@tradinorganic.com
Parent Co: Tradin Organic

12917 Traditional Baking Inc
2575 S Willow Ave
Bloomington, CA 92316-3256
909-877-8471
Fax: 909-877-6728 admin@traditionalbaking.com
www.traditionalbaking.com
Cookies and sugar free cookies

CEO: Kathy Voortman
Research & Development Associate: Ruby Torres
Quality Assurance Manager: Trisha Winne
Account Manager: Mark Jordan
Human Resources Manager: Maria Prieto
Maintenance & Parts Manager: Fabian Galarza
Production Manager: Gerardo Perez
Warehouse Manager: Eli Valadez
Director of Procurement: Mike Shevette
Estimated Sales: Less Than $500,000
Number Employees: 1-4

12918 Traditional Medicinals Inc
4515 Ross Rd
Sebastopol, CA 95472-2250
707-823-8911
Fax: 707-823-1599 800-543-4372
www.traditionalmedicinals.com
Herb teas
Co- Founder, Chairman of the Board: Drake Sadler
Chief Executive Officer: Blair Kellison
President: Lynda Sadler
Vice President of Research and Developme: Josef Brinckmann
Vice President of Quality: Katie Huggins
Sales Coordinator: Brenda Hodges
Vice President of Sales: Darrick Blinoff
Contact: Liz Alber
lalber@tradmed.com
Estimated Sales: $3200000
Number Employees: 100-249
Brands:
  Traditional Med Ginger Energy
  Traditional Med Gypsy Cold Cure
  Traditional Med Organics

12919 Trafalgar Brewing Company
1156 Speers Road
Oakville, ON L6L 2X4
Canada
905-337-0133
Fax: 905-845-2246 www.alesandmeads.com
Beer, ale, lager and stout
President: Mike Arnold
Estimated Sales: Under $500,000
Number Employees: 1-4
Type of Packaging: Consumer, Food Service
Brands:
  Celtic
  Elora Esb
  Elora Grand Lager
  Elora Irish Ale
  Harbour Gold
  Paddy's Irish Red
  Port Side Amber
  Trafalgar

12920 Trail's Best Snacks
930 S. White Station Road
Memphis, TN 38017
Fax: 507-677-2478 800-852-1863
www.trailsbest.com
Manufacturer of meat snacks.
Chairman/CEO: Karl Schledwitz
Estimated Sales: $10-20 Million
Number Employees: 5-9
Number of Brands: 3
Parent Co: Monogram Foods
Type of Packaging: Consumer, Bulk
Brands:
  Happy Trails Meat Snack Sticks
  Team Realtree
  Trail's Best Snacks

12921 Trailblazer Foods
17900 NE San Rafael St
Portland, OR 97230-5930
503-666-5800
Fax: 503-666-6800 800-777-7179
customerserv@tbfoods.com
www.trailblazerfoods.com
Preserves, fruit products, quality foods, punches, marinades and syrups
President & CEO: Rob Miller
robm@tbfoods.com
CFO: Derek Lohrey
Quality Manager: Jeff Gleason
Marketing Director: Mike Miller
Director of Sales: Mike Post
VP Operations: Sebastian Pastore
Production Manager: Henry Catan
Estimated Sales: $20-50 Million
Number Employees: 20-49

Brands:
  Walls Berry Farm Preserves
  Walls Berry Farm Organic Preserves
  Nalley Lumberjack Table Syrup
  Portland Punch

12922 Traina Foods Inc
337 Lemon Ave
Patterson, CA 95363-9634
209-892-5472
Fax: 209-892-6231 info@traina.com
www.trainafoods.com
Sun dried fruit
President: Willie Traina
willie@traina.com
Number Employees: 100-249
Type of Packaging: Consumer, Food Service

12923 Tram Bar LLC
PO Box 1079
Victor, ID 83455
208-354-4790
www.katesrealfood.com
Organic energy bars.
Owner: Kate Schade
kate@katesrealfood.com
Marketing: Rachel Reich
Type of Packaging: Consumer

12924 Trans Pecos Foods
112 E Pecan St # 800
San Antonio, TX 78205-1578
210-228-0896
Fax: 210-228-0781 pjk@texas.net
www.transpecosfoods.com
Manufacturer, importer and exporter of frozen breaded vegetables
President: Patrick J Kennedy
Contact: Steven Skinner
steven.skinner@transpecosbanks.com
Plant Manager: Bruce Salcido
Estimated Sales: $3900000
Number Employees: 20-49
Parent Co: Anchor Food Products
Type of Packaging: Consumer, Food Service, Private Label, Bulk

12925 Trans-Ocean Products Inc
350 W Orchard Dr
Bellingham, WA 98225-1769
360-671-6886
Fax: 360-671-0354 800-290-2722
info@trans-ocean.com www.trans-ocean.com
Imitation crab, lobster and salmon meat
President: Robert Draper
robert.draper@deepwater.com
CFO: Allen Leaf
Research & Development Manager: Bill Ott
VP Sales & Marketing: Louis Shaheen
Procurement & Product Manager: Norio Yanagisawa
Number Employees: 100-249
Square Footage: 192000
Parent Co: Maruha Corporation
Type of Packaging: Consumer, Food Service, Private Label, Bulk
Other Locations:
  Trans-Ocean Products
  Williamsville NY
  Southeast Sales
  Chapel Hill NC
  Northwest Office/Shrimp Sales
  Lynnwood WA
Brands:
  Classic
  Pouch Pak
  Transocean

12926 Trans-Packers Svc Corp
419 Vandervoort Ave
Brooklyn, NY 11222-5313
718-963-0900
Fax: 718-486-6344 877-787-8837
sales@transpackers.com www.transpackers.com
Contract packager of food and nonfood products including powders, granules, solids and liquids in glass jars and bottles, etc
Owner: Monica Weiss
monica@transpackers.com
Vice President: Daniel Weiss
Plant Manager: Nester Serrano
Estimated Sales: $4900000
Number Employees: 100-249
Square Footage: 400000
Type of Packaging: Consumer, Food Service

Food Manufacturers / A-Z

12927 Transamerica Wine Corporation
120 Brooklyn Navy Yard
Brooklyn, NY 11201
718-875-4017
Fax: 718-625-1180
Wines
Manager: Yeshiah Schwartz
Estimated Sales: $5-10 Million
Number Employees: 10-19

12928 Transnational Foods
1110 Brickell Ave # 808
Suite 808
Miami, FL 33131-3138
305-415-9970
www.transnationalfoods.com
Global manufacturer and distributor of hundreds of consumer products in categories such as beverages, cereals, dressings and soups.
President & CEO: Marcelo Young
myoung@transnationalfoods.com
CFO: Juan Iribarne
COO: Americo Preneste
Number Employees: 20-49
Number of Brands: 5
Number of Products: 500+
Type of Packaging: Consumer, Private Label
Brands:
   Pampa(c)
   So Natural
   Ali's
   della Natura(c)
   TummyTreats

12929 Transpacific Foods Inc
2603 Main St # 730
Suite 730
Irvine, CA 92614-4264
949-975-9900
Fax: 949-975-9907 www.transpacificfoods.com
U.S. pineapple supplier
President: Septi Suwandi
Number Employees: 10-19
Type of Packaging: Consumer, Food Service

12930 Trappey's Fine Foods Inc
PO Box 13610
New Iberia, LA 70562-3610
337-365-8281
www.trappeys.com
Okra, pickled peppers, sauces and ethnic food
CEO: Edward Simmons
Estimated Sales: $10-20 Million
Number Employees: 50-100
Number of Brands: 1
Parent Co: B&G Foods
Brands:
   Trappey's

12931 Trappist Preserves
540 East 105th Street #115
Cleveland, OH 44108
Fax: 216-249-3387 800-472-0425
info@monasterygreetings.com
www.monasterygreetings.com
Jellies, jams and marmalades including apricot, peach, strawberry, grape, etc
President: Damian Carr
Purchasing Manager: Henry Scarborough
Estimated Sales: $16 Million
Number Employees: 95
Type of Packaging: Consumer
Brands:
   Trappist

12932 Trappistine Quality Candy
300 Arnold St
Wrentham, MA 02093
Fax: 215-922-1335 866-549-8929
info@trappistinecandy.com
www.trappistinecandy.com
Candy
Number Employees: 20-49

12933 Trattore Farms
7878 Dry Creek Road
Geyserville, CA 95441
707-431-7200
info@trattorefarms.com
www.trattorefarms.com
Wines, vinegars, and olive oils
President: Tim Boucher
CEO: Michelle Robson
Vice President: Mary Louise Bucher

Estimated Sales: $20 Million
Number Employees: 18
Other Locations:
   Los Angeles CA
   Lodi CA
   South Kearney NJ
   Chicago IL
   Minneapolis MN
   San Francisco CA
   Portland OR
   Seattle WA
   Miami FL

12934 Travel Chocolate
PO BOX 4668 PMB59369
New York, NY 10163-4668
718-841-7030
Fax: 718-841-7030 info@travelchocolate.com
Organic chocolate bars

12935 (HQ)Travis Meats Inc
7210 Clinton Hwy
PO Box 670
Powell, TN 37849-5216
865-938-9051
Fax: 865-938-9211 800-247-7606
www.travismeats.com
Frozen veal and pork; also beef, including meat loaf, pot roast and hamburger patties.
CEO: W Travis
Vice President: Dale Travis
Customer Service: Margie McWhorter
Marketing: Jeanine Stanley
VP of Sales & Marketing: Larry King
Estimated Sales: $20-50 Million
Number Employees: 100-249
Square Footage: 110000
Type of Packaging: Consumer, Food Service
Other Locations:
   Knoxville TN

12936 Treasure Foods
2500 S 2300 W # 11
West Valley, UT 84119-7676
801-974-0911
Fax: 801-975-0553 treasurefoods@hotmail.com
Processor and exporter of whipped honey butter, flavored fruit honey, scones; wholesaler/distributor of frozen foods and general line items; serving the food service market
Owner: Amin Motilla
CFO: Zarina Motiwala
Vice President: Mohamed Motiwala
Marketing Director: Amin Motiwala
Public Relations: Amin Motiwala
Production Manager: Fawad Motiwala
Plant Manager: Fawad Motiwala
Purchasing Manager: Amin Motiwala
Estimated Sales: $450,000
Number Employees: 5
Number of Brands: 3
Number of Products: 3
Square Footage: 14400
Parent Co: Algilani Food Import & Export
Type of Packaging: Food Service, Private Label, Bulk
Other Locations:
   Treasure Foods
   Salt Lake City UT
Brands:
   Honey Butter Topping
   Raspberry Honey Butter Topping
   Scones

12937 Treasury Wine Estates
555 Gateway Dr.
P.O. Box 4500
Napa, CA 94558
707-259-4500
Fax: 707-259-4542 www.tweglobal.com
Wine
President-Americas: Victoria Snyder
Managing Director & CEO: Michael Clarke
CFO: Matt Young
Chief Marketing Officer: Michelle Terry
Chief People & Legal Officer: Linnsey Caya
COO: Tim Ford
Estimated Sales: $34.6 Million
Number Employees: 3400
Number of Brands: 44
Brands:
   19 Crimes
   Acacia Vineyard
   Annie's Lane
   Beaulieu Vineyard

   Belcreme de Lys
   Beringer Vineyards
   Blossom Hill
   Cavaliere d'Oro
   Chateau St. Jean
   Coldstream Hills
   Devil's Lair
   emBRAZEN
   Etude
   Fifth Leg
   Greg Norman Estates
   Heemskerk
   Hewitt Vineyard
   Ingoldby
   Jamieson's Run
   Killawarra
   Leo Buring
   Lindeman's
   Maison de Grand Esprit
   Matua
   Meridian
   Metala
   Penfolds
   Pepperjack
   Provenance Vineyards
   Rawson's Retreat
   Samuel Wynn & Co.
   Seppelt
   Shingle Peak
   Sledgehammer
   Squealing Pig
   St Huberts
   Stags' Leap Winery
   Stellina di Notte
   Sterling Vineyards
   T'Gallant
   The Walking Dead Wine
   Wolf Blass
   Wynns Coonawarra Estate
   Yellowglen

12938 Treat Ice Cream Co
11 S 19th St
San Jose, CA 95116-2202
408-292-9321
Fax: 408-298-5859 treat@treaticecream.com
www.treaticecream.com
Gourmet ice cream
Owner: Alfred Mauseth
treat@treaticecream.com
Vice President: Bob Mauseth
Estimated Sales: $3-5 Million
Number Employees: 5-9
Square Footage: 16000
Type of Packaging: Consumer, Private Label, Bulk
Brands:
   Treat

12939 Treats Island Fisheries
PO Box 21
Scaly Mountain, NC 28775-0021
207-733-4580
Fax: 207-733-4880
Seafood
President: James English

12940 Treatt USA Inc
4900 Lakeland Commerce Pkwy
Lakeland, FL 33805
863-668-9500
www.treatt.com
Food additives including essential oils and aromatic chemicals.
Chairman: Tim Jones
CEO: Daemmon Reeve
CFO: Richard Hope
Year Founded: 1886
Estimated Sales: $116 Million
Number Employees: 370
Parent Co: Treatt PLC
Type of Packaging: Bulk
Brands:
   Citreatt
   Treattarome

12941 Tree Ripe Products
53 S Jefferson Rd
Whippany, NJ 07981-1082
973-463-0777
800-873-3747
www.1800treeripe.com
Processor and exporter of nonalcoholic cocktail mixes
President: Joel Fishman

Food Manufacturers / A-Z

Estimated Sales: $3,000,000
Number Employees: 20-49
Square Footage: 20000
Type of Packaging: Consumer, Food Service
Brands:
    Frothee Creamy Head
    Lem-N-Joy
    Tree-Ripe

12942 Tree Top Inc
220 E Second St
Selah, WA 98942
    509-697-7251
    faq@treetop.com
    www.treetop.com
Grape juice and concentrate, apple juice, apple sauce, apple concentrate and blended juices.
President & CEO: Tom Hurson
CFO: Craig Green
VP, Information Services & CIO: Dwaine Brown
VP, Fruit Procurement & Growth Services: Cris Hales
VP, Quality & Technical Service: Ken James
VP, Supply Chain: Monica Taylor
VP, Human Resources: Scott Washburn
VP, Operations: Gary Price
Year Founded: 1960
Estimated Sales: $399 Million
Number Employees: 1,008
Square Footage: 74000
Type of Packaging: Consumer, Food Service, Private Label, Bulk
Brands:
    Tree Top

12943 TreeHouse Foods, Inc.
2021 Spring Rd.
Suite 600
Oak Brook, IL 60523
    708-483-1300
    info@treehousefoods.com
    www.treehousefoods.com
Cereals, snack foods, condiments, frozen baked goods and frozen prepared meals.
President/CEO: Steven Oakland
Executive VP/CFO: William Kelley
Senior VP/COO: C. Shay Braun
Estimated Sales: $6.3 Billion
Number Employees: 13,489
Number of Brands: 4
Type of Packaging: Consumer, Private Label
Brands:
    Bay Valley Foods
    TreeHouse Private Brands
    Flagstone Foods
    E.D. Smith

12944 Treehouse Farms
116 Camino Agave
Elgin, AZ 85611
    559-757-5020
    Fax: 559-757-0510
Processor and exporter of almonds including natural, blanched, sliced, roasted, diced and slivered
President: David Fitzgerald
Executive Director: Jacob Carter
Sales Manager: Carol Coffey
Number Employees: 250-499
Square Footage: 400000
Parent Co: Yorkshire Foods
Type of Packaging: Private Label, Bulk
Brands:
    Treehouse Farms

12945 Treesweet Products
16825 Northchase Drive
Suite 1600
Houston, TX 77060-6099
    281-876-3759
    Fax: 281-876-2643
Orange juice and products
President: Jeffrey Rosenberg
Estimated Sales: $500,000-$1 000,000
Number Employees: 5-9
Brands:
    Awake
    Orange Plus
    Treesweet Products

12946 Trefethen Family Vineyards
1160 Oak Knoll Ave # 3
Napa, CA 94558-1398
    707-255-7700
    Fax: 707-255-0793 winery@trefethen.com
    www.trefethen.com
Producer and exporter of wine
Owner: John Trefethen
VP Finance: Gerald Bush
VP: David C Whitehouse Jr
Marketing: Terry Hall
Sales Director: Betty Calvin
jtrefethen@trefethen.com
Public Relations: Terry Hall
Operations Manager: Richard De Garmo
Estimated Sales: $5 Million
Number Employees: 20-49
Square Footage: 16000
Brands:
    Trefethen Vineyards

12947 Trega Foods
105 E 3rd Ave
Weyauwega, WI 54983
    920-867-2137
    Fax: 920-867-2249
Cheese such as cheddar, feta, mozzarella, mozzarella sticks, provolone and dairy ingredients
President: Doug Simon
VP: Richard Wagner
Contact: Kirsten Slocum
kirsten.slocum@agropur.com
Estimated Sales: $5-10 Million
Number Employees: 5-9
Type of Packaging: Consumer, Food Service
Other Locations:
    Trega Foods Processing Plant
    Little Chute WI
    Trega Foods Processing Plant
    Luxemburg WI
Brands:
    Trega

12948 Treier Popcorn Farms
16793 County Line Rd
Bloomdale, OH 44817
    419-454-2811
    Fax: 419-454-3983 ptreier@wcnet.org
Popcorn including bagged, natural, buttered and microwaveable; wholesaler/distributor of commercial popcorn poppers and other concession supply equipment; serving the food service market
President: Don Treier
Secretary/Treasurer: Peggy Treier
Estimated Sales: $500,000-$1 Million
Number Employees: 15
Number of Brands: 2
Number of Products: 6
Square Footage: 12000
Parent Co: Treier Family Farms
Type of Packaging: Consumer, Food Service, Bulk
Brands:
    Lake Plains
    Pelton's Hybrid Popcorn

12949 Tremblay's Sweet Shop
10569 Main St
Hayward, WI 54843-6658
    715-634-2785
    Fax: 715-634-7830
Candy
President: Dennis Tremblay
Quality Control: Charles Tremblay
Manager: Charles Tremblay
Estimated Sales: Below $5 000,000
Number Employees: 20-49

12950 Trentadue Winery
19170 Geyserville Ave
Geyserville, CA 95441-9528
    707-473-9338
    Fax: 707-433-5825 888-332-3032
    info@trentadue.com www.trentadue.com
Wines
Owner: Leo Trentadue
info@trentadue.com
Proprietor: Evelyn Trentadue
Proprietor, Vineyard Manager: Victor Trentadue
Winemaker: Miroslav Tcholakov
Estimated Sales: $5-10 Million
Number Employees: 10-19
Type of Packaging: Private Label
Brands:
    Trentadue

12951 Trenton Bridge Lobster Pound
1237 Bar Harbor Rd
Trenton, ME 04605-6021
    207-667-2977
    Fax: 207-667-3412 www.trentonbridgelobster.com
Lobster
President: Anthony Pettegrow
info@trentonbridgelobster.com
Estimated Sales: $3-5 Million
Number Employees: 10-19

12952 Trenton Processing Ctr
120 W Broadway
Trenton, IL 62293-1306
    618-224-7383
    Fax: 618-224-9038 800-871-7675
    tp1pork@sbcglobal.net
    www.trentonprocessingcenter.com
Meat products
Owner: Gary Schwend
Founder: Calvin Schwend
Founder: Loretta Schwend
Purchasing Manager: Judy Kuhn
Estimated Sales: $5-10 Million
Number Employees: 10-19
Type of Packaging: Consumer

12953 Treo Brands
106 Calvert St
Harrison, NY 10528
    914-341-1850
    info@drinktreo.com
    www.drinktreo.com
Flavored birch water
President: Brian O'Byrne
CEO: Bob Golden
Brand Manager: Zoe McElligott
Brands:
    Treo

12954 TresOmega
9 S Main St
New Milford, CT 06776
    860-210-7805
    info@tresomega.com
    www.tresomega.com
Coconut flour, pasta, chia seed, and coconut oil
Parent Co: Mountain High Organics, Inc.

12955 Tri State Beef Co
2124 Baymiller St
Cincinnati, OH 45214-2208
    513-579-1722
    Fax: 513-579-1739
CEO: Robert Runtz
Secretary/Treasurer: Betty Stout
Marketing Manager: Robert Runtz
Number Employees: 50-99
Parent Co: DaeKyung Oil and Transportation Co.
Type of Packaging: Consumer, Food Service, Bulk
Brands:
    Soauthter

12956 Tri-Boro Fruit Co
2500 S Fowler Ave
Fresno, CA 93725-9308
    559-486-4141
    Fax: 559-486-7627
Grape grower
President: Chris Fazio
Executive: Tony Fazio
Estimated Sales: $5-10 000,000
Number Employees: 10-19

12957 Tri-Counties Packing Company
845 Vertin Ave
Salinas, CA 93901
    831-422-7841
    Fax: 831-422-7856
Celery and celery hearts
President/Owner: Jack Baillie
Sales: John Baillie
john@celeryhearts.com
Estimated Sales: $5 Million
Number Employees: 20-49
Number of Brands: 3
Number of Products: 1
Square Footage: 184000
Type of Packaging: Consumer
Other Locations:
    Tri-Counties Packaging Coompany
    Oxnard CA
Brands:
    Candy Stick

Snappy
Tri-Sign

12958 Tri-State Dairy
120 West Jefferson Boulevard
Fort Wayne, IN 46802
256-534-8464
Fax: 256-534-6259 www.tristatedairy.osu.edu
Milk, dairy products
Marketing Director: D Fitch
Estimated Sales: Under $500,000
Number Employees: 100-249
Parent Co: Dean Foods Company

12959 Tri-State Ingredients
6147 Western Row Rd
Mason, OH 45040-2459
513-573-0057
Fax: 513-573-0870 800-622-1050
www.techfood.com
Herbal extracts
Owner: Lloyd Makstell
CEO: Edward Makstell
CFO: Nadine Whitsell
Estimated Sales: $5 Million
Number Employees: 10-19
Number of Products: 42
Square Footage: 203000
Parent Co: Technical Food Sales Inc
Type of Packaging: Bulk

12960 Tri-State Logistics Inc
3156 Spring Valley Road
Dubuque, IA 52001-1531
563-690-0926
Fax: 775-417-6709 866-331-7660
www.tri-statelogistics.com
Energy drink and power cool drink
President: Evan Fleisher
VP: Randy Sirk
Estimated Sales: C
Number Employees: 5-9
Square Footage: 3500
Type of Packaging: Private Label
Brands:
  Rox Energy Drink

12961 Tri-Sum Potato Chip Company
80 Julian Dr
Leominster, MA 01453
978-697-2447
www.tri-sum.com
Potato chips, popcorn and cheese puffs
COO: Richard Gates
Contact: Richard Duchesneau
richard@tri-sum.com
Number Employees: 20-50
Type of Packaging: Consumer, Food Service, Private Label, Bulk
Brands:
  Jp's
  Suncrisp

12962 Triangle Seafood
212 Adams Street
Louisville, KY 40206-1862
502-561-0055
Fax: 502-561-0096
Seafood
President: J Shannon Bouchillon

12963 Tribali Foods
2275 Huntington Dr. # 342
San Marino, CA 91108
310-592-5420
hello@tribalifoods.com
www.tribalifoods.com
Organic, grass-fed Mediterranean style beef patties and Umami beef patties; organic, free-range chicken patties
Founder/Owner: Angela Bicos Mavridis
Year Founded: 2016
Number of Brands: 1
Number of Products: 3
Type of Packaging: Consumer, Private Label
Brands:
  Tribali Foods

12964 Tribe 9 Foods
2901 Progress Rd
Madison, WI 53716
608-257-7216
www.tribe9foods.com
Fresh pasta, gluten free pasta, bars, cookies, and nut butters
Chairman & CEO: Brian Durst
President & CFO: Richard Ciurczak
Quality Assurance Manager: Margo King
VP Operations: William Ciurczak
Number Employees: 20-49
Brands:
  Ona
  RP's Pasta Company
  Yumbutter
  Taste Republic

12965 Tribe Mediterranean
110 Prince Henry Dr
Taunton, MA 02780-7385
774-961-0000
800-848-6687
info@tribehummus.com www.tribehummus.com
Processor and exporter of hummus dips/spreads
President/Ceo: Carlos Canals
Cfo: Charles Webster
Number Employees: 100-249
Square Footage: 240000
Type of Packaging: Consumer, Food Service, Private Label, Bulk
Brands:
  Nathan's
  Rite

12966 Tribeca Oven
447 Gotham Pkwy
Carlstadt, NJ 07072-2409
201-935-8800
Fax: 201-935-6685 www.tribecaoven.com
Breads including rye, white, wholewheat, etc
Manager: Jesse Kirsch
mcruz@tribecaoven.com
Facilities: Mario Cruz
Number Employees: 1-4
Type of Packaging: Consumer, Food Service

12967 Trickling Springs Creamery
2330 Molly Pitcher Hwy
Chambersburg, PA 17202-9299
717-709-0711
Fax: 717-709-0885
www.tricklingspringscreamery.com
Dairy
Co-Founder: Torie Burke
Co-Founder: Howard Slatkin
Sales Exec: Fred Rodes
tscmilkday@yahoo.com
Number Employees: 20-49

12968 (HQ)Trident Seafoods Corp
5303 Shilshole Ave NW
Seattle, WA 98107
206-783-3818
Fax: 206-782-7195 800-426-5490
humanresources@tridentseafoods.com
www.tridentseafoods.com
Seafood from Alaska and the Pacific Northwest.
Founder/Chairman: Chuck Bundrant
Chief Executive Officer: Joe Bundrant
Year Founded: 1973
Estimated Sales: $2.4 Billion
Number Employees: 1000-4999
Number of Brands: 3
Type of Packaging: Consumer, Food Service, Bulk
Brands:
  Trident
  Louis Kemp Crab Delights
  Pure Alaska Omega

12969 Trident Seafoods Corp
P.O. Box 908
641 Shakes Street
Wrangell, AK 99929
907-874-3346
Fax: 907-874-3035
Processor and exporter of canned, fresh and frozen shrimp, crab, halibut, herring and salmon
Type of Packaging: Food Service, Bulk

12970 Trigo Corporation
PO Box 2369
Toa Baja, PR 00951-2369
787-794-1300
Fax: 787-794-3110
Rum, vodka, liquor and wine
Executive Director: Benigno Trigo
Marketing Director: Mariella Algarin
Marketing: Eunice Miranva
Number Employees: 20-49
Type of Packaging: Consumer
Brands:
  Ponte Vecckio

12971 Triland Foods Inc
311 8th St
Sergeant Bluff, IA 51054-8516
712-943-7675
Fax: 712-943-6776 866-943-7675
www.trilandfoods.com
Pork products: pork rind pellets and pork crackling pellets
President: Joe Rieger
info@trilandfoods.com
Number Employees: 20-49

12972 Trinidad Benham Company
PO Box 427
Bridgeport, NE 69336
308-262-1361
Fax: 308-586-1058
Dry beans
President: Bill McCormack
Contact: Dale Eirich
deirich@trinidadbenham.com
Area Operations Manager: Dale Eirich
Estimated Sales: $3-5 Million
Number Employees: 25
Type of Packaging: Consumer, Food Service
Brands:
  Benco Peak
  Cookquick'
  Evans
  Jack Rabbit
  Kings
  Ranch Wagon
  Royal Wrap
  Shamrock

12973 Trinidad Benham Corporation
3650 S Yosemite, Suite 300
P.O. Box 378007
Denver, CO 80237
303-220-1400
Fax: 303-220-1490 info@trinidadbenham.com
www.trinidadbenham.com
Dry beans, rice, popcorn, and peas
Vice President: Steve Dipasquale
Estimated Sales: $36.3 Million
Number Employees: 500
Square Footage: 35000
Type of Packaging: Consumer, Food Service, Private Label, Bulk
Brands:
  Jack Rabbit
  Siler's
  Green Earth Organics
  Budget Buy
  Everyday Chef
  Wonder Foil
  Peak
  Master Wrap
  Solfresco
  Diamond
  Cookquik Ranch Wagon
  Sabor Del Campo

12974 Trinity Fruit Sale Co
7571 N Remington Ave # 104
Suite 104
Fresno, CA 93711-5799
559-433-3777
Fax: 559-433-3790 sales@trinityfruit.com
www.trinityfruit.com
Fresh cherries, apricots, peaches, plums, nectarines, kiwi, grapes, apples and pears
President: David White
Marketing Director: John Hein
Sales: Vance Uchiyama
Number Employees: 20-49

12975 Trinity Spice
901 W Florida Ave
Suite B
Midland, TX 79701
915-683-8333
Fax: 915-683-8338 800-460-1149
Gourmet Southern spice blends
President: S Floyd
Estimated Sales: $150,000
Number Employees: 1
Type of Packaging: Consumer, Food Service, Private Label, Bulk

Food Manufacturers / A-Z

Brands:
Southern Dynamite

12976 Trio's Original ItalianPasta Co.
32 Auburn Street
Chelsea, MA 02150-1825
617-884-5211
Fax: 617-884-2563   800-999-9603
Fresh and frozen pasta, sauces
President: Paul Stevens
Sales/Marketing: Kathy Burinskas
Director Operations: Steve Lagasse
Plant Manager: Jim Dee
Purchasing Manager: George Hachey
Estimated Sales: $5-9.9 Million
Number Employees: 35
Type of Packaging: Private Label

12977 Triple D Orchards Inc
8310 W Stormer Rd
Empire, MI 49630-9480
231-326-5174
Fax: 231-326-5480
Processor and exporter of canned and frozen sweet cherries
President: TJ Keyes
Year Founded: 1973
Estimated Sales: $20-50 Million
Number Employees: 100-249
Type of Packaging: Consumer, Food Service, Private Label, Bulk
Brands:
Glen Lake

12978 Triple H Food Processors Inc
5821 Wilderness Ave
Riverside, CA 92504-1004
951-352-5700
Fax: 951-352-5710 tharris3@triplehfoods.com
Barbecue sauces, bar mixes, oils, relishes, lemon juices, cajun sauces, citrus punches, spaghetti sauces, sno cone syrups, spices, dry rubs, preserves, hot sauces, salad dressings, jellies, oriental sauces, maple syrup, and salsas.
Vice President: Richard J Harris
rharris@triplehfoods.com
General Manager: Tommy Harris
Controller: Charles Richards
VP: Richard J Harris
Quality Assurance: Guillermo Loaiza-Aponte
Customer Service: Merilyn Ewart
Production Planner: Mike Elsman
Plant Manager: Ken Lujan
Purchasing: Greg Bourdon
Estimated Sales: $10-20 Million
Number Employees: 50-99
Type of Packaging: Private Label
Brands:
Triple H

12979 (HQ)Triple K Manufacturing Company, Inc.
4193 200 Street
PO Box 219
Shenandoah, IA 51601
712-246-4376
Fax: 712-246-4010 webmaster@x-tra-touch.com
www.xtratouch.com
Processor and exporter of baking flavorings; dry seasonings; salad dressings; sauces; dietary foods and cleaning products. Contract packaging and private label services also available.
President/Manager: Charles Maxine
Estimated Sales: $1.30 Million
Number Employees: 11
Square Footage: 15600
Type of Packaging: Consumer, Food Service, Private Label
Brands:
Drops O'Gold
X-Tra-Touch

12980 Triple Leaf Tea Inc
434 N Canal St # 5
S San Francisco, CA 94080-4667
650-588-8255
Fax: 650-588-8406   800-552-7448
triple@tripleleaf-tea.com
Processor and exporter of authentic, traditional Chinese medicinal teas including green, ginger, ginseng, diet and medicinal; also, American ginseng capsules
President: Johnson Lam
Estimated Sales: $450.00k
Number Employees: 5-9

Number of Brands: 1
Number of Products: 18
Square Footage: 20000
Type of Packaging: Consumer, Food Service, Private Label
Brands:
Triple Leaf Tea

12981 Triple Rock Brewing Co Brkly
1920 Shattuck Ave
Berkeley, CA 94704-1022
510-843-2739
Fax: 510-843-6920 reservations@triplerock.com
www.triplerock.com
Brewery
Co-Owner: Reid Martin
Co-Owner: John Martin
Manager: Jesse Sarinana
jessesarinana@triplerock.com
Head Brewer: Jeff Kimpe
Estimated Sales: $20-50 Million
Number Employees: 20-49
Type of Packaging: Consumer, Food Service

12982 Triple Springs Spring Water Co
199 Ives Ave # 1
Meriden, CT 06450-7179
203-235-8374
Fax: 203-686-0200
Natural spring water
President: George Kuchle
Estimated Sales: $9 Million
Number Employees: 10-19
Type of Packaging: Consumer, Bulk
Brands:
Triple Springs Spring Water

12983 Triple U Enterprises
26314 Tatanka Rd
Fort Pierre, SD 57532
605-567-3624
Fax: 605-567-3625 uuubuff@gwtc.net
Fresh, smoked, dried and frozen buffalo meat including portion cut
President: Kaye Ingle
CEO: Clint Amiotte
Estimated Sales: $700,000
Number Employees: 1-4
Type of Packaging: Consumer, Bulk

12984 Triple XXX Root Beer Co.
S.R. 26 W & Salisbury
West Lafayette, IN 47906
765-743-5373
Fax: 713-780-8764
contact@triplexxxrootbeer.com
www.triplexxxrootbeer.com
Soft drinks
President: Lee Lydick
Estimated Sales: Below $5 Million
Number Employees: 1-4
Brands:
Triple Xxx

12985 Triple-C
8 Burford Road
Hamilton, ON L8E 5B1
Canada
905-573-7900
Fax: 905-573-7867   800-263-9105
VP Sales/Marketing: Harry Scholtens
Brands:
Gummy Guy
Rachel's
Sour Simon

12986 Tripoli Bakery Inc
106 Common St
Lawrence, MA 01840-1633
978-682-7754
Fax: 978-687-8455 www.tripolibakery.com
Breads, rolls
President: Rosario Zappala
Estimated Sales: $1-2.5 000,000
Number Employees: 20-49

12987 Tripper Inc
PO Box 51440
Oxnard, CA 93031-1440
805-988-8851
Fax: 805-988-2992 www.tripper.com

Processor and importer of kosher & spices including pepper, nutmeg, cinnamon, and ginger; also, ingredients including vainilla beans and extracts; organic available
Owner: Francois Bervard
frab@tripper.com
Estimated Sales: $1-2.5 Million
Number Employees: 1-4
Square Footage: 60000
Type of Packaging: Food Service, Private Label, Bulk
Brands:
Alligator Pepper
Bullfrog Lavander
Chameleon Pepper
Cobra Vanilla
Dragon Cinnamon
Elephant Ginger
Flamingo Pepper
Gorilla Cloves
Leopard Cardamon
Orangutan Mace
Panther Pepper
Rhino Nutmeg
Tiger Pepper
Toro Safron
Tripper

12988 Tristao Trading
116 John St Rm 500
New York, NY 10038
212-285-8120
Fax: 212-964-1735 admin@tristaousa.com
Coffee
Manager: Liz Wagner
President: Ricardo Tristao
Contact: Joao Carollo
jcarollo@tristao.com
Estimated Sales: $5-10 000,000
Number Employees: 1-4

12989 Triton Seafood Co
7301 NW 77th St
Medley, FL 33166-2205
305-888-0051
Fax: 305-888-1485
All-natural conch chowder and conch fritters
CEO: Alfredo Alvarez
asa@tritonsfd.com
Marketing Director: Yvonne Conde
Estimated Sales: $1700000
Number Employees: 10-19
Type of Packaging: Food Service, Private Label
Brands:
Neptune's

12990 Triumph Brewing Co
138 Nassau St # A
Princeton, NJ 08542-7011
609-924-7855
Fax: 609-924-7857 www.triumphbrewing.com
Seasonal beer, ale, stout and pilsner
Manager: Doug Bork
General Manager: Eric Nutt
Estimated Sales: Below $5 Million
Number Employees: 50-99
Type of Packaging: Consumer, Food Service

12991 Triumph Foods, LLC
5302 Stockyards Espressway
St. Joseph, MO 64506
816-396-2700
800-262-7907
info@triumphfoods.com triumphfoods.com
Pork and pork products
Chief Executive Officer: Mark Campbell
SVP & Chief Financial Officer: Kevin Wedeking
VP, Finance & Accounting: Josh Kleinlein
VP, Human Resources & Communication: Kevin Neal
VP, Genetics & Livestock Procurement: Jerry Lehenbauer
EVP & Chief Operating Officer: Matt England
Year Founded: 2003
Estimated Sales: $1.6 Billion
Number Employees: 2,800
Square Footage: 11000
Type of Packaging: Consumer

Food Manufacturers / A-Z

12992 Trophy Nut Co
320 N 2nd St
Tipp City, OH 45371-1912
937-667-8478
Fax: 937-667-4656   800-219-9004
customercare@trophynut.com   www.trophynut.com
Dry and oil roasted nuts
President: Mike Bhagmath
mbhagmath@loraincounty.us
CEO: Dave Henning
QA/QC Manager: Phyllis Nieter
VP Sales/Plant Manager: Bob Wilke
Operations Manager: Chrissy Wagner
Purchasing: Dawn Akers
Year Founded: 1968
Estimated Sales: $24 Million
Number Employees: 50-99
Square Footage: 110000
Type of Packaging: Consumer, Food Service, Private Label, Bulk
Brands:
   Nut Barrel
   Trophy Gold Nut Barrel
   Trophy Nut
   True Measures Baking Nuts

12993 Tropic Fish Hawaii LLC
2312 Kamehameha Hwy E-5
Honolulu, HI 96819
808-591-2936
Fax: 808-591-2934   sales@tropicfishhawaii.com
www.tropicfishhawaii.com
Tuna, billfish, bottomfish, open ocean fish
President & COO: Shawn Tanoue
CEO: Charles Umamoto
General Manager: Daryl Yamaguchi
VP Sales: Toby Arakawa
VP Operations: Shannon Tanoue
Estimated Sales: $20-50 Million
Number Employees: 100-249

12994 Tropical Açaí LLC
587 East Sample Rd. # 263
Pompano Beach, FL 33064
917-699-1923
855-550-2224
www.tropicalacai.com
Organic açai berry packs, açai sorbets
General Manager: Renata Nogueria
Number of Brands: 1
Number of Products: 10
Type of Packaging: Consumer, Private Label
Brands:
   Tropical Açai

12995 Tropical Blossom Honey Co
106 N Ridgewood Ave
Edgewater, FL 32132-1714
386-428-9027
Fax: 386-423-8469
Honey
Vice President: Michael Hauger
m.hauger@tropicbeehoney.com
VP: John Ginnis
Estimated Sales: $1.3 Million
Number Employees: 10-19

12996 Tropical Cheese
452 Fayette St
Perth Amboy, NJ 08861
732-442-4898
Fax: 732-442-8227   888-874-4928
admin@tropicalcheese.com
www.tropicalcheese.com
Hispanic specialty food products, including cheese products, tortillas, beverages, meat products, other dairy products and desserts.
President & Founder: Rafael Mendez
Vice President of Opertions: Alejandro Lopez
Production Manager: Alex Quiles
Year Founded: 1983
Number of Brands: 5
Type of Packaging: Consumer
Brands:
   Authentic Latino Flavor
   Flavor of Mexico
   Flavor of Central America
   Flavor of South America
   Tropical

12997 Tropical Commodities
9230 Nw 12th Street
Miami, FL 33172
305-471-8120
Fax: 305-471-9825   tropicom@direcway.com
Fresh habanero chili peppers and mash as well as other varieties of chili peppers.
President: D Douglas Bernard
Vice President: Robert Kholer
Marketing: Alberto Beers
Estimated Sales: $1.3-1.5 Million
Number Employees: 5-9
Number of Products: 10
Square Footage: 60000
Type of Packaging: Private Label, Bulk
Brands:
   Caribbean Hot Peppers

12998 Tropical Foods
350 Riverside Pkwy
Lithia Springs, GA 30122-3865
770-438-9950
Fax: 770-435-1371   800-544-3762
info@tropicalfoods.com   www.tropicalfoods.com
Processor and importer of candy, dried fruits, nuts, seeds, Asian rice snacks and dessert toppings
President: David Williamson
President: John Bauer
Sales Director: Debbie Ponton
Manager: Peter Njuguna
njuguna@tropical.com
Operations Manager: William Stapleton
Estimated Sales: $10-20 Million
Number Employees: 10-19
Parent Co: Tropical
Type of Packaging: Food Service, Private Label, Bulk

12999 (HQ)Tropical Foods
1100 Continental Blvd
PO Box 7507
Charlotte, NC 28273-6380
704-588-0400
Fax: 704-588-3092   800-438-4470
info@tropicalfoods.com   www.tropicalfoods.com
Snack mixes, dried fruits, roasted nuts, seeds, candy and confectionery, spices and specialty foods including oils, vinegars, mustards, artichoke hearts, roasted bell peppers and pasta
Owner/CEO: Angela Bauer
Chief Operating Officer: John Bauer
Director of Marketing: Chad Hartman
Director of Human Resources: Juan Gomez
Purchasing Manager: Bryan Keeton
Year Founded: 1977
Estimated Sales: $24600000
Number Employees: 100-249
Square Footage: 72000
Type of Packaging: Consumer, Food Service, BulkTropical Memphis
   Memphis TN
   Tropical Landover
   Landover MD
Brands:
   Christille Bay

13000 Tropical Foods
350 Riverside Pkwy.
Lithia Springs, GA 30122
800-544-3762
info@tropicalfoods.com   www.tropicalfoods.com
Snack mixes, dried fruits, roasted nuts, seeds, candy and confectionery, spices and specialty foods including oils, vinegars, mustards, artichoke hearts, roasted bell peppers and pasta
Type of Packaging: Consumer, Food Service, Bulk

13001 Tropical Foods
1160 Mustang Dr.
Suite 400
DFW Airport, TX 75261
866-847-6987
info@tropicalfoods.com   www.tropicalfoods.com
Snack mixes, dried fruits, roasted nuts, seeds, candy and confectionery, spices and specialty foods including oils, vinegars, mustards, artichoke hearts, roasted bell peppers and pasta
Type of Packaging: Consumer, Food Service, Bulk

13002 Tropical Foods
1650 Shelby Oaks Dr.
Suite 1
Memphis, TN 38134
800-223-8171
info@tropicalfoods.com   www.tropicalfoods.com
Snack mixes, dried fruits, roasted nuts, seeds, candy and confectionery, spices and specialty foods including oils, vinegars, mustards, artichoke hearts, roasted bell peppers and pasta
Type of Packaging: Consumer, Food Service, Bulk

13003 Tropical Foods
3368 Bartlett Blvd.
Orlando, FL 32811
800-749-8869
info@tropicalfoods.com   www.tropicalfoods.com
Snack mixes, dried fruits, roasted nuts, seeds, candy and confectionery, spices and specialty foods including oils, vinegars, mustards, artichoke hearts, roasted bell peppers and pasta
Type of Packaging: Consumer, Food Service, Bulk

13004 Tropical Foods
573-A Commerce Dr.
Upper Marlboro, MD 20774
800-220-0125
info@tropicalfoods.com   www.tropicalfoods.com
Snack mixes, dried fruits, roasted nuts, seeds, candy and confectionery, spices and specialty foods including oils, vinegars, mustards, artichoke hearts, roasted bell peppers and pasta
Type of Packaging: Consumer, Food Service, Bulk

13005 Tropical Illusions
1436 Lulu Street
PO Box 338
Trenton, MO 64683-1819
660-359-5422
Fax: 660-359-5347   tropical@tropicillusions.com
Processor and exporter of frozen drinks mixes including: cocktail, slush and granita, cream base, and smoothies.
President: Vance Cox
Vice President: Carrol Baugher
Estimated Sales: $590,000
Number Employees: 6
Square Footage: 200000
Type of Packaging: Food Service, Private Label
Brands:
   Captain Space Freeze
   Elmeco
   Tropical Illusions

13006 Tropical Link Canada Ltd.
7668 Winston St.
Burnaby, BC
Canada
778-379-3510
Fax: 778-379-3511   www.tropicallinkcanada.ca
Organic cinnamon powder, cinnamon sticks, turmeric powder, coconut sugar, coconut oil, coconut vinegar, prepared fruit dips, rice blends, bulk dried fruit
Director: Sudhani Perera
Number of Brands: 2
Number of Products: 20
Type of Packaging: Consumer, Private Label, Bulk
Brands:
   Snow Farms
   Wild Tusker

13007 Tropical Nut & Fruit Co
3368 Bartlett Blvd
Orlando, FL 32811-6482
407-841-8273
Fax: 407-843-4340   800-749-8869
nutsnorl@aol.com
Custom snack mixes, freshly roasted nuts and seeds, baking items, candies, spices, dried fruit, grains and minibar items.
President: John Baller
david@tropicalnutandfruit.com
Estimated Sales: $6000000
Number Employees: 50-99
Type of Packaging: Consumer, Food Service, Private Label, Bulk

13008 Tropical Nut Fruit & Bulk Cndy
350 Riverside Pkwy
Lithia Springs, GA 30122-3865
770-438-9950
Fax: 770-435-1371   800-544-3762
info@tropicalfoods.com   www.tropicalfoods.com

Food Manufacturers / A-Z

Nut candy, caramels, sesame sticks, soup mixes and dried fruits
President: David Williamson
Manager: Peter Njuguna
njuguna@tropical.com
Estimated Sales: $10-20 Million
Number Employees: 10-19
Square Footage: 56000
Type of Packaging: Consumer, Food Service, Bulk

13009 Tropical Preserving Co Inc
1711 E 15th St
Los Angeles, CA 90021-2715
213-748-5108
Fax: 213-748-4998 sales@tropicalpreserving.com
www.tropicalpreserving.com
Processor and exporter of jams, jellies and apple butter
President: Ronald Randall
Estimated Sales: $12,000,000
Number Employees: 20-49
Type of Packaging: Consumer, Private Label
Brands:
 Market's Best

13010 Tropical Treets
130 Bermondsey Road
North York, ON M4A 1X5
Canada
416-759-8777
Fax: 416-759-7782 888-424-8229
www.tropicaltreets.com
Tropical ice cream; wholesaler/distributor of tropical food products, drinks and juices
CEO: Rumi Keshavjee
VP Sales/Marketing: Zahir Keshavjee
Estimated Sales: $471,000
Number Employees: 5
Square Footage: 24000

13011 Tropical Valley Foods
32 Powerdam Way
Dock 30
Plattsburgh, NY 12901
Fax: 518-478-8838 877-756-6831
www.nextchocolates.com
Chocolate coated fruits and nuts
President & Owner: Eric Bertheau
Quality Control: Darrell Clark
Marketing & HR Coordinator: Elizabeth LaRosa
elizabeth@tropical-valley-foods.com
Sales Consultant: Armand Langevin
Director of Operations: Amanda Gokey
Production Manager: Warren Caswell
Estimated Sales: $3.7 Million
Number Employees: 25
Brands:
 next organics(c)

13012 (HQ)Tropicana Products Inc.
555 W. Monroe St.
Chicago, IL 60661
800-237-7799
www.tropicana.com
Orange and grapefruit juices, as well as frozen concentrates.
Chairman/CEO, PepsiCo: Ramon Laguarta
Year Founded: 1947
Estimated Sales: $431.9 Million
Number Employees: 1000-4999
Square Footage: 100000
Parent Co: PepsiCo
Type of Packaging: Consumer, Food Service
Brands:
 Trop50
 Tropicana
 Tropicana Essentials
 Tropicana Kids
 Tropicana Twister

13013 Troppers
P.O.Box 50211
Santa Barbara, CA 93150-0211
805-969-4054
Baked goods
Manager: Diane Tourney
Estimated Sales: $.5-1 000,000
Number Employees: 1-4

13014 Trotter Soft Pretzels
1880 N Penn Road
Hatfield, PA 19440-1950
215-855-2197
Fax: 215-855-0725

Soft Pretzels, snack foods
Plant Manager: Wayne Childs
Estimated Sales: $10-20 Million
Number Employees: 20-49
Parent Co: J&J Snack Foods Company

13015 Trout Lake Farm
PO Box 181
Trout Lake, WA 98650
509-395-2025
Fax: 509-395-2749 800-655-6988
www.troutlakefarm.com
Processor, exporter and importer of certified organically grown medicinal and beverage tea herbs and spices including garlic, oregano, peppermint and spearmint
CEO: Lloyd Scott
Sales Manager: Martha-Jane Hylton
Contact: Sharon Frazey
sharon.frazey@troutlakefarm.com
Operations Manager: Gary Vollema
Estimated Sales: $3500000
Number Employees: 50
Square Footage: 160000
Type of Packaging: Bulk
Brands:
 1st Sneeze Echinacea
 Camus Prarie Tea
 Florased Valerian
 Trout Lake Farm

13016 Troverco
727 N 1st Street
St. Louis, MO 63102
Fax: 314-925-4099 800-468-3354
Manufacturer and distributor of prepared meals and snack foods.
CEO: Joseph Trover
Contact: Rodney Gordon
rodney.gordon@troverco.com
Type of Packaging: Consumer, Food Service, Private Label
Brands:
 Deli Maid
 Landshire

13017 Troy Foods Inc
404 E US Highway 40
Troy, IL 62294-2205
618-667-6332
www.troyfoodsinc.us
Meat including home cured ham and bacon, frankfurters, bologna and sausage
President: Don Nihiser
dnihiser@troyfoodsinc.com
Estimated Sales: $2,000,000
Number Employees: 5-9
Type of Packaging: Consumer

13018 Troy Pork Store
158 4th St
Troy, NY 12180
518-272-8291
Fax: 518-272-8291
Fresh, smoked and pickled pork and beef
Owner: Carmen Amedeo
Estimated Sales: $500,000-$1 Million
Number Employees: 1-4
Type of Packaging: Consumer

13019 Troyer Foods Inc
17141 State Road 4
PO Box 608
Goshen, IN 46528-6674
574-533-0302
Fax: 574-533-3851 800-876-9377
www.troyers.com
Brand Director/President: Paris Ball-Miller
Executive Director: Tony Swihart
CFO & Controller: Neal Yoder
Executive Director: Donald Hixenbaugh
Director of Marketing: Beth Rodick
Director of Sales: Terry Blythe
Operations Manager: Frank Herbes
Production Manager: Steve Gile
Number Employees: 100-249
Other Locations:
 Central Warehouse Troyer Foods
  Bloomington IN
 South Warehouse Troyer Foods
  Grandview IN

13020 Tru Chocolate
PO Box 317
Medford, MA 02155
855-878-2462
info@tru-chocolate.com
tru-chocolate.com
Dark chocolate covered almonds, raisins and pretzels
CEO: Michael F. Gilmore
Chief Financial Officer: David Dahn
Brands:
 TRU Chocolate(c)

13021 Tru Fru, LLC
1546 S 4650 W # 200
Salt Lake City, UT 84104
888-437-2497
info@trufru.com www.trufru.com
Freeze-dried, dark chocolate-covered fruits
Co-Founder: Taz Murray
National Sales Director: Dion Rasmussen
Year Founded: 2015
Number of Brands: 1
Number of Products: 6
Type of Packaging: Consumer, Private Label
Brands:
 TruFru

13022 Tru-Blu Cooperative Associates
PO Box 5
New Lisbon, NJ 08064-0005
609-894-8717
trublucoop@aol.com
Fresh and frozen blueberries
General Manager: Dennis Doyle
Number Employees: 1-4
Type of Packaging: Consumer

13023 TruBrain
Santa Monica, CA
650-241-8372
team@trubrain.com
www.trubrain.com
Drinks and bars to improve brain function; ketones
Founder/CEO: Chris Thompson
Finance & Strategy: Gary Epper
Lead Neuroscientist: Dr. Andrew Hill
Product Research & Development: Garrett Ruhland
Marketing: Bill Mackay
Analytics/Operations: Tomas Ferrari
Product Management: Celso Ferrari

13024 TruMoo
P.O. Box 961447
El Paso, TX 79996
800-395-7004
www.trumoo.com
Flavored milk and protein shakes.
CEO, Dean Foods Company: Ralph Scozzafava
Parent Co: Dean Foods Company
Type of Packaging: Consumer, Private Label

13025 TruVibe Organics
Santa Monica, CA
www.truvibeorganics.com
Organic superfood blends (raw cacao nibs, goji berries, chia seeds) and superfood meal replacement drinks
Co-Founder: Anand Dani
Co-Founder: Jason Dekker
Year Founded: 2013
Number of Brands: 1
Number of Products: 10
Type of Packaging: Consumer, Private Label
Brands:
 Eat Clean Organic
 TruVibe

13026 Truan's Candies
13716 Tireman St
Detroit, MI 48228
313-584-3400
800-584-3004
Chocolate
President: Mark Truan
Estimated Sales: $5-10 Million
Number Employees: 10-19
Type of Packaging: Private Label

13027 Truchard Vineyards
3234 Old Sonoma Rd
Napa, CA 94559-9701
707-253-7153
Fax: 707-253-7234

Food Manufacturers / A-Z

Wine
Owner: Anthony Truchard
truchard@aol.com
Estimated Sales: $5-10 Million
Number Employees: 20-49
Brands:
 Truchard Vineyards

13028 Truckee River Winery
11467 Brockway Rd
Truckee, CA 96161-2115
530-587-4626
Fax: 530-550-8809 russ@truckeeriverwinery.com
www.truckeeriverwinery.com
Wines
Owner: Russ Jones
russ@truckeeriverwinery.com
Co-Owner: Joan Jones
Sales Manager: Kate Shaw-Outside
russ@truckeeriverwinery.com
Estimated Sales: Under $300,000
Number Employees: 1-4
Type of Packaging: Private Label
Brands:
 Truckee River

13029 Truco Enterprises
2727 Realty Rd
Carrollton, TX 75006
972-869-4600
ontheborderproducts.com
Manufacturer of authentic Mexican-style chips, salsas and queso dips.
President & CEO: Jeff Partridge
CFO: Nicki Wolpmann
Contact: Kimberly Slone
kslone@pilgrims.com
Senior VP, Operations: Steve Slack
Brands:
 On The Border(c)

13030 True Beverages
2001 East Terra Lane
O Fallon, MO 63366-4434
636-240-2400
Fax: 636-272-7546 800-325-6152
truefood@truemfg.com www.truemfg.com
Beverages
Owner: Bill Smith
Contact: Russel Gledstone
rgledstone@truemfg.com
Brands:
 True Beverages

13031 True Blue Farms
9548 County Road 215
Grand Junction, MI 49056-9214
269-434-6112
Fax: 269-434-8192 877-654-2400
www.truebluefarms.com
Blueberries including fresh, frozen and puree
Owner: Shelly Hartmann
CEO: Myron Brady
Secretary: Evelyn Farmer
Marketing Manager: Juana Chavez
Sales: Ronald Benson
truebluefarms@btc-bci.com
Office Manager: Lee Erickson
Estimated Sales: Less Than $500,000
Number Employees: 5-9
Type of Packaging: Consumer, Food Service, Private Label, Bulk

13032 True Jerky
226 Union St
Suite A
San Francisco, CA 94123
858-336-2005
www.madebytrue.com
Flavored beef jerky, jerky snack mix and biltong
Chief Executive Officer: Jess Thomas
Year Founded: 2015
Number of Brands: 2
Number of Products: 12
Type of Packaging: Consumer, Private Label
Brands:
 True Jerky
 Made by True

13033 True Nopal Cactus Water
8255 East Raintree Dr. # 300
Scottsdale, AZ 85260
480-636-8044
info@truenopal.com
www.truenopal.com
All-natural cactus water
Number of Brands: 1
Number of Products: 1
Type of Packaging: Consumer, Private Label
Brands:
 True Nopal

13034 True Organic Product Inc
20225 W Kamm Ave
Helm, CA 93627
559-866-3001
Fax: 559-866-3003 800-487-0379
info@trueorganicproducts.net
Processor and exporter of organic juices including orange, apple, pineapple, grape, tangerine, lime, watermelon, blackberry, soursop, lulo and pineapple blends
President/CEO: Jake Evan
CEO: Jake Evans
jevans@trueorganicproducts.net
Estimated Sales: $3-5 Million
Number Employees: 20-49
Square Footage: 48000
Brands:
 True Organic

13035 True Story Foods
San Francisco, CA
888-277-1171
hi@truestoryfoods.com www.truestoryfoods.com
Organic, GMO-free deli meats, sausages, hot dogs and fresh pork
Founder/Chief Executive Officer: Phil Gatto
Number of Brands: 1
Number of Products: 34
Type of Packaging: Consumer, Private Label
Brands:
 True Story Foods

13036 True World Foods LLC
24 Link Dr
Rockleigh, NJ 07647-2504
201-750-0024
Fax: 201-750-0025 info@trueworldfoods.com
www.trueworldfoods.com
Fresh seafood
President: Jackie Madsuka
CEO: Takeshi Yashiro
yashiro@trueworldfoods.com
Estimated Sales: $20-50 Million
Number Employees: 100-249

13037 Truffle Treasures
314 Richmond Road
Ottawa, ON K1Z 6X6
Canada
613-761-3859
www.truffletreasures.com
Handmade candies and chocolates including truffles, chocolate bars, brittle, dipped fruits, coffees & teas, cookies and other candies
Owner: Lara Vaarre

13038 Truitt Bros Inc
1105 Front St NE
PO Box 309
Salem, OR 97301-1034
503-362-3674
Fax: 503-581-5912 800-547-8712
truittbros@truittbros.com www.truittbros.com
Canned green beans, cherries, pears and plums; also, shelf stable entrees
Founder and CEO: David Truitt
davidt@truittbros.com
Estimated Sales: $20-50 Million
Number Employees: 500-999
Type of Packaging: Consumer, Food Service, Private Label
Brands:
 Truitt Bros.

13039 Trumark
830 E Elizabeth Ave
Linden, NJ 7036
908-486-5900
Fax: 908-486-5900 800-752-7877
Processor and exporter of sodium and potassium lactate and lactate and acetate blends

President: Mark Satz
CEO: Jeff Wales
Contact: Kathy Moraglia
kathy@tru-mark.com
Estimated Sales: $780,000
Number Employees: 10-19

13040 Trumps Food Interest
646 Powell St
Vancouver, BC V6A 1H4
Canada
604-732-8473
Fax: 604-732-8433 info@trumpsfood.com
www.trumpsfood.com
Manufacturer of dessert products.
Managing Director: Heather Angel
Number of Products: 200+

13041 Truth Bar LLC
260 Charles St. # 210
Waltham, MA 02453
888-886-8959
www.truthbar.com
Various flavors of energy bars with prebiotics and probiotics
Co-Founder: Sean Fay
Co-Founder: Diana Stobo
Year Founded: 2014
Number of Brands: 1
Number of Products: 5
Type of Packaging: Consumer, Private Label
Brands:
 Truth Bar

13042 Tsar Nicoulai Caviar LLC
60 Dorman Ave
San Francisco, CA 94124-1807
415-543-3007
Fax: 415-543-5172 800-952-2842
info@tsarnicoulai.com www.tsarnicoulai.com
Caviar and smoked fish
President/CEO: Mats Engstrom
Co-Owner: Dafne Engstrom
Manager: Marian Mahone
concierge@tsarnicoulai.com
Estimated Sales: $500,000-$1 Million
Number Employees: 20-49
Type of Packaging: Private Label
Brands:
 Tsar Nicoulai Caviar

13043 Tu Me Beverage Company
818-237-5105
info@tumewater.com
www.drinktume.com
Turmeric-infused, naturally-sweetened flavored water
Co-Founder: Shaina Zaidi
Number of Brands: 1
Number of Products: 5
Type of Packaging: Consumer, Private Label
Brands:
 Tu Me

13044 Tualatin Estate Vineyards
10850 NW Seavey Rd
Forest Grove, OR 97116-7703
503-357-5005
Fax: 503-357-1702 tualatinestate@yahoo.com
www.tualatinestate.com
Processor and exporter of table wines including chardonnay, pinot noir, pinot blanc, gewurztraminer, riesling and semi-sparkling muscat
Founder: Jim Bernau
Vice President: William L Fuller
Operations Manager/Winegrower: Stirling Fox
Winemaker: Joe Dobbes
Estimated Sales: $600000
Number Employees: 10-19
Square Footage: 80000
Parent Co: Willamette Valley Vineyards
Type of Packaging: Consumer
Brands:
 Tualatin Estate

13045 Tucker Cellars
70 Ray Rd
Sunnyside, WA 98944
509-837-8701
Fax: 509-837-8701 wineman@televar.com
www.tuckercellars.net
Wines and pickled vegetables
Co-Owner: Rose Tucker
Co-Owner: Randy Tucker

Food Manufacturers / A-Z

Estimated Sales: $1-2.5 Million
Number Employees: 5-9
Brands:
　Tucker

13046 Tucker Packing Co
955 N Mill St
Orrville, OH 44667
　　　　　　　　　　330-683-3311
　　　http://www.marshallville-meats.com/
Fresh and frozen beef, pork and lamb
President: John Tucker
Plant Manager: Leon Hilty
Estimated Sales: $1,600,000
Number Employees: 10-19
Type of Packaging: Consumer, Food Service, Bulk

13047 Tucker Pecan Co
350 N Mcdonough St
Montgomery, AL 36104-3652
　　　　　　　　　　334-262-4470
　　Fax: 334-262-4690　800-239-6540
　　sales@tuckerpecan.com www.tuckerpecan.com
Processor and wholesaler/distributor of pecans
President: David Little
sales@tuckerpecan.com
Operations Manager: David Little
Estimated Sales: $450,000
Number Employees: 10-19
Square Footage: 13436
Type of Packaging: Consumer, Food Service, Bulk

13048 Tucson Tamale Company
Tucson, AZ
　　　　　　　　　　520-398-6282
　　　　　www.tucsontamale.com
Handmade tamales with various meat, cheese and bean fillings; organic hot sauce; oregano and seasoning mixes
Founder/Owner: Todd Martin
Year Founded: 2008
Number of Brands: 1
Type of Packaging: Consumer, Private Label
Brands:
　Tucson Tamale

13049 Tudal Winery
1015 Big Tree Rd
St Helena, CA 94574-9711
　　　　　　　　　　707-963-3947
　　Fax: 707-968-9691 www.tudalwinery.com
Wines
Owner: Alma Tudal
matt@tudalwinery.com
Vice President: John Tudal
Marketing Director: Susan Greene
Estimated Sales: Less than $500,000
Number Employees: 1-4
Type of Packaging: Private Label
Brands:
　2001 Estate Cabernet Sauvignon
　Flat Bed Red
　Tractor Shed Red

13050 Tufts Ranch
27260 State Highway 128
Winters, CA 95694-9066
　　　　　　　　　　530-795-4144
　　　　Fax: 530-795-3844
Grower and packer of apricots, prunes, kiwifruit and persimmons. Broker of walnuts and almonds
General Manager: Stan Tufts
Office Manager: Brad Graf
Estimated Sales: $5-10 Million
Number Employees: 50 to 99

13051 Tularosa Vineyards
23 Coyote Canyon Rd
Tularosa, NM 88352-9404
　　　　　　　　　　575-585-2260
　　Fax: 505-585-2260　800-687-4467
　　　　　www.tularosavineyards.com
Wines
Owner: David Wickham
wine@nmex.com
Estimated Sales: $250,000
Number Employees: 5-9
Brands:
　Tularosa Wines

13052 Tulkoff's Food Products Inc
2229 Van Deman St
Baltimore, MD 21224-6604
　　　　　　　　　　410-327-6585
　　Fax: 443-524-0148　800-638-7343
　　　　　　www.tulkoff.com
Condiment, sauce and ingredient manufacturer.
Owner: Phil Tulkoff
dave@tulkoff.com
Number Employees: 50-99
Type of Packaging: Consumer, Food Service, Private Label, Bulk
Brands:
　Snap-Back
　Top
　Tulkoff

13053 Tull Hill Farms Inc
2264 Hugo Rd
Kinston, NC 28501-7173
　　　　　　　　　　252-523-8052
　　　　Fax: 252-523-8052
Grower of sweet potatoes
Vice President: Michael Hill
the98@esn.net
Sales: Kendall Hill
Sales: Rob Hill
Estimated Sales: $1-2.5 Million
Number Employees: 20-49
Brands:
　Hill's

13054 Tulocay Cemetery
411 Coombsville Rd
P.O.Box 7
Napa, CA 94558-3957
　　　　　　　　　　707-252-4727
　　Fax: 707-252-8375　888-627-2859
　　　　　www.tulocaycemetery.org
Baking mixes, balsamic & champagne vinegars, dessert sauces, dipping and flavored oils, everyday classics, vinaigrettes & dressings, global herbed rubs, herbed rubs, marinades & glazes, mustards, savory sauces, tapenades & savory condiments, gift sets, and fruit condiments
Manager: Peter Manasse
Director Manufacturing: William Cadman
Estimated Sales: Less than $500,000
Number Employees: 10-19

13055 Tumai Water
PO Box 1751
Martinsburg, WV 25402
　　　　　　　　　　304-264-1466
　　　　　　　　　　866-948-8624
Bottled spring water
Owner/President/CEO: Bob Downey
Estimated Sales: $32,000
Number Employees: 2
Square Footage: 4768
Parent Co: Spero Group
Type of Packaging: Consumer

13056 Tumbador Chocolate
34 34th St
Unit 6
Brooklyn, NY 11232-2020
　　　　　　　　　　718-788-0200
　　Fax: 718-788-3179 sales@tumbadorchocolate.com
　　　　　www.tumbadorchocolate.com
Chocolates and spreads
CEO: Michael Altman
Sales Manager: Carolyn Barwicki
Estimated Sales: $2-5 Million
Number Employees: 11-50
Type of Packaging: Consumer, Food Service, Private Label
Brands:
　Brooklyn Born Chocolate(c)
　Tumbador(c) Chocolate

13057 Tumericalive Healing Enterprise
39 Broadway
Suite 1110
New York, NY 10006
　　　　　　　　　　347-559-6760
　　　　　info@templeturmeric.com
　　　　　www.templeturmeric.com
Manufacturer of turmeric-based beverages.
Founder and CEO: Daniel Sullivan
Contact: Michelle Tyler
michelle@tumericalive.com
Number Employees: 11-50

13058 Tuna Fresh
401 Whitney Ave # 103
Gretna, LA 70056-2500
　　　　　　　　　　504-363-2744
　　Fax: 504-392-3324 www.chartwellsmenus.com
Tuna
Manager: John Duke

13059 Tundra Wild Rice
PO Box 263
Pine Falls, NB R0E 1M0
Canada
　　　　　　　　　　204-367-8651
　　　　Fax: 204-367-8309
Processor and exporter of Canadian lake wild rice
President: Denis Pereux
Sales/Marketing: Ed Thibedeau
Number Employees: 4
Square Footage: 11360
Type of Packaging: Private Label, Bulk
Brands:
　Tundra

13060 Turano Baking
6501 Roosevelt Rd
Berwyn, IL 60402-1100
　　　　　　　　　　708-788-9220
　　Fax: 708-788-3075 info@turano.com
　　　　　　www.turano.com
Fresh and frozen breads, rolls and pastries
President: Turano Co
aturano@turano.com
Chairman & CEO: Renato Turano
VP: Umberto Turano
EVP Sales & Marketing: Giancarlo Turano
EVP Production & Operations: Tony Turano
Estimated Sales: $6.76 Million
Number Employees: 250-499
Square Footage: 280000
Type of Packaging: Consumer, Food Service, Private Label
Brands:
　Turano

13061 Turano Baking
6501 Roosevelt Rd
Berwyn, IL 60402-1100
　　　　　　　　　　708-788-9220
　　Fax: 708-788-3075 info@turano.com
　　　　　　www.turano.com
Baked goods, bread
Co-Owner/President: Turano Umberto
Co-Owner/Chief Executive Officer: Renato Turano
Vice President, Finance/Controller: Sandra Battersby
Executive VP Sales/Marketing: Giarcarto Turano
Estimated Sales: $46,000,000
Number Employees: 250-499
Type of Packaging: Private Label

13062 Turk Brothers Custom Meats Inc
1903 Orange Rd
Ashland, OH 44805-1399
　　　　　　　　　　419-289-1051
　　Fax: 419-281-8280　800-789-1051
　　　　　www.turkbrothersmeats.com
Processor and wholesaler/distributor of beef, pork and lamb; wholesaler/distributor of frozen foods, equipment and fixtures and seafood; serving the food service market; also, slaughtering services available
Owner: Roy M Turk
VP: Kevin Turk
Estimated Sales: $5-10 Million
Number Employees: 10-19
Square Footage: 33684
Type of Packaging: Consumer, Food Service, Bulk

13063 Turkey Creeks Snacks Inc
1286 Thurston School Rd
Thomaston, GA 30286-7636
　　　　　　　　　　706-647-8841
　　Fax: 706-647-3978　800-329-8875
　　　　info@turkeycreeksnacks.com
　　　　www.turkeycreeksnacks.com
Pork rinds, hard cracklings and hot sauce
Owner: Laddie Fulcher
Estimated Sales: $3-5 Million
Number Employees: 20-49
Square Footage: 100000
Type of Packaging: Consumer, Food Service, Private Label, Bulk
Brands:
　Deli Style

Food Manufacturers / A-Z

Sunrise Farms
Turkey Creek

13064 Turkey Hill Dairy Inc
2601 River Rd
Conestoga, PA 17516-9341
717-872-5461
Fax: 717-872-4130 800-693-2479
careers@turkeyhill.com www.turkeyhill.com
Ice cream, sherbet, frozen yogurt and drinks
President: Edison Abreu
edison.abreu@turkeyhill.com
Executive Vice President: John Cox
Number Employees: 500-999
Square Footage: 428000
Type of Packaging: Consumer, Private Label, Bulk
Brands:
  Turkey Hill

13065 Turkey Hill Sugarbush
10 Waterloo Street
PO Box 160
Waterloo, QC J0E 2N0
Canada
450-539-4822
Fax: 450-539-1561 www.turkeyhill.ca
Processor and exporter of maple products including syrups, cookies, chocolates, coffee, tea, fudge, caramels, butter, soft and hard candies
President/Board Member: Michael Herman
Chairman: Brian Herman
Estimated Sales: $10-20 Million
Number Employees: 35
Number of Brands: 1
Number of Products: 85
Square Footage: 70000
Type of Packaging: Consumer, Private Label, Bulk
Brands:
  Turkey Hill

13066 Turkey Store
116 4th Ave NW
Faribault, MN 55021
507-334-5555
Fax: 507-332-5349 www.jennieo.com
Fresh and frozen whole turkeys
Director Operations: Steve Williams
Manager Distribution: Pete Vikeras
Estimated Sales: Less Than $500,000
Number Employees: 1-4
Type of Packaging: Consumer, Private Label

13067 Turlock Fruit Co
500 S Tully Rd
Turlock, CA 95380-5121
209-634-7207
Fax: 209-632-4273 www.turlockfruit.com
Processor and exporter of honeydew melons
President: Donald Smith
Treasurer: Stephen Smith
Secretary: Stuart Smith
Estimated Sales: $500,000-$1 Million
Number Employees: 20-49
Type of Packaging: Consumer, Bulk
Brands:
  King O' The-West
  Oak Flat
  Peacock
  Sycamore

13068 Turnbull Bakeries
523 First Street
New Orleans, LA 70130-2004
504-581-5383
Fax: 504-581-6115 www.turnbullbakeries.com
Bread sticks, bread crumbs, and melba toast
Owner: Wayne Turnbull
Sales/Marketing: Steven Wolf
Sales/Marketing: Andrew Ford
Director of Sales: Frank LeCourt
Contact: Elizabeth Turnbull
turnbula@bellsouth.net
Chief Operating Officer: John Riddell
Plant Manager: Wes Stone
Number Employees: 10,000
Type of Packaging: Food Service, Private Label, Bulk

13069 Turnbull Cone Baking Company
PO Box 6248
Chattanooga, TN 37401-6248
423-265-4551
Fax: 423-624-8724
Ice cream cones and wafers; also, melba toast

President: Wayne W Turnbull
Director Sales: Deris Bagli
Number Employees: 100-249
Parent Co: Turnbull Bakeries
Type of Packaging: Private Label

13070 Turner & Pease Company
1519 Elliott Avenue W
Seattle, WA 98119-3129
206-282-9535
Fax: 206-282-9633
Butter
President: Milton Turner
National Sales: Bill Bowen
Number Employees: 25
Square Footage: 72000
Type of Packaging: Consumer, Food Service, Private Label, Bulk
Brands:
  Creamerie Classique
  Golden West
  Meadowbrook

13071 Turner Dairy Farms Inc
1049 Jefferson Rd
Pittsburgh, PA 15235-4700
412-372-2211
Fax: 412-372-0651 800-892-1039
info@turnerdairy.net www.turnerdairy.net
Milk, premium ice teas, fruit drinks, juices, cultured dairy, cream, ice cream mixes, butter and eggs
President: Chuck Turner
Management: Jim Turner
Controller: Robin Turner
Year Founded: 1930
Estimated Sales: $20-50 Million
Number Employees: 100-249

13072 Turri's Italian Foods
16695 Common Rd
Roseville, MI 48066-1901
586-773-6010
Fax: 586-773-6851 www.turrisitalianfoods.com
A full line of Italian specialities including Ravioli, lasagna, manicotti, tortellini and other fine pastas
Vice President: John Turri
gail.turri@turrisitalianfoods.com
Secretary & Treasurer: Mary Derlicki
Executive Vice President: John Turri
Research & Development Manager: Jennifer Kaupp
Quality Assurance Manager: Andrea DeBusschere
VP National Sales & Marketing: Joe Morano
National Sales Manager: Joe Batayeh
Office Manager: Nora Allor
Plant Manager: Tom Dam
Purchasing Manager: Kevin Najor
Estimated Sales: $6.4 Million
Number Employees: 100-249
Square Footage: 140000
Type of Packaging: Consumer, Food Service, Private Label, Bulk
Brands:
  Turris

13073 Turtle Island Foods
601 Industrial St
PO Box 176
Hood River, OR 97031-2006
541-386-7766
Fax: 541-386-7754 800-508-8100
info@tofurky.com
Processor, importer and exporter of soy meat analos including tempeh, tofurkey, deli slices, sausages, franks
President: Seth Tibbott
sue@tofurky.com
CFO: Sue Tibbott
VP: Bob Tibbott
Quality Assurance Manager: James Athos
Production Manager: Graciela Pulido
Plant Manager: Graciela Pulido
Estimated Sales: $2,398,946
Number Employees: 20-49
Number of Brands: 2
Number of Products: 25
Square Footage: 40000
Type of Packaging: Consumer, Food Service, Private Label, Bulk
Brands:
  Super Burgers
  Tofurky
  Vegetaballs

13074 Turtle Island Foods
601 Industrial St
Hood River, OR 97031-2006
541-386-7766
Fax: 541-386-7754 800-508-8100
info@tofurky.com
Cheese and vegetable based soups
Founder: Seth Tibbott
sue@tofurky.com
CFO: Sue Tibbott
Production Manager: Graciela Pulido
Estimated Sales: Less than $500,000
Number Employees: 20-49
Brands:
  Superburgers
  Tempeh
  Tofurky

13075 Turtle Island Herbs
4735 Walnut St # F
Boulder, CO 80301-2553
303-546-6362
Fax: 303-546-0625 800-684-4060
island@earthnet.net www.earthnet.net
Processor and wholesaler/distributor of organic herbal extracts and syrups
President: Feather Jones
CEO: Bahman Saless
VP Operations: Peter Danielson
Estimated Sales: $300,000-500,000
Number Employees: 1-4
Square Footage: 6000

13076 Turveda
www.turveda.com
Turmeric protein powder, turmeric capsules, turmeric tea K-cups, turmeric sparkling tonics in various flavors
Founder: Dev Chakrabarty
Number of Brands: 1
Number of Products: 12
Type of Packaging: Consumer, Private Label
Brands:
  Turveda

13077 Tuscan Bakery
12831 NE Airport Way
Bldg 8
Portland, OR 97230-1030
503-256-2099
Fax: 503-256-1929 800-887-2261
Biscotti
Owner: Mike Lisac
VP: Wayne Winter
Estimated Sales: Less Than $500,000
Number Employees: 1-4
Square Footage: 12000
Type of Packaging: Consumer, Food Service
Brands:
  Lawman's

13078 Tuscan Dairy Farms
117 Cumberland Blvd
Burlington, NJ 08016-9722
609-499-2600
800-648-0135
www.tuscandairy.com
Dairy, milk, Skinny cow, chocolate milk
Site Manager: Brian Kornfiend
brian_kornfiend@deanfoods.com
Number Employees: 20-49

13079 Tuscan Eat/Perdinci
3003 S Tamiami Trl
Sarasota, FL 34239-5108
941-565-7382
www.perdinci.com
Italian foods
Owner & President: Lorenzo Masolini
Estimated Sales: Under $500,000
Number Employees: 6
Brands:
  Perdinci

13080 Tuscarora Organic Growers Cooperative
22275 Anderson Hollow Rd
Hustontown, PA 17229
814-448-2173
Fax: 814-448-2333 www.tog.coop
Cooperative providing fresh fruits and vegetables including certified organic

1199

Food Manufacturers / A-Z

Bookkeeping/Sales: Sherry Meuser
Office Manager: Christine Treichler
Contact: Jeff Taylor
jeff@tog.coop
Operations Manager: Teresa Showalter
Number Employees: 1-4
Type of Packaging: Bulk
Brands:
 Tuscarora Organic

13081 Tusitala
12400 Creel Rd
PO Box 189
Grand Bay, AL 36541

251-865-4353
Fax: 251-865-3763

Herbs and herbal supplements
President: George E. Spellmeyer
Secretary: Norma Jean Spellmeyer

13082 Tuthilltown Spirits
14 Grist Mill Lane
Gardiner, NY 12525

845-255-1527
distillery@tuthilltown.com
www.tuthilltown.com

Gin, vodka, flavored liqueur, corn whiskey, bourbon, rye, bitters
Co-Founder: Ralph Erenzo
Co-Founder: Brian Lee
Year Founded: 2005
Number of Brands: 5
Number of Products: 13
Type of Packaging: Consumer, Private Label
Brands:
 Tuthilltown
 Indigenous
 Half Moon
 Hudson New York
 Basement Bitters

13083 Tutti Gourmet
76 Rue Cameron
Hudson, QC J0P 1H0
Canada

450-458-0911
inquiries@tuttigourmet.com
tuttigourmet.com

Biscotti, crackers and bites
President: Michael Kachani
tuttigourmet@hotmail.com
Brands:
 Tutti Gourmet

13084 Tuv-Taam Corp
502 Flushing Ave
Brooklyn, NY 11205-1616

718-855-2207
Fax: 718-802-1872

Appetizers, entrees and dinners
President: Aaron Nutovics
hmaraldo@campusdirectory.com
Number Employees: 50-99

13085 Twang Partners LTD
6255 Wt Montgomery
San Antonio, TX 78252-2227

210-226-7008
Fax: 210-226-4040 800-950-8095
info@twang.com www.twang.com

Processor and importer of flavored salts including lemon-lime, traditional and colored margarita, beer, pickle and chili; also, Bloody Mary toppings
Owner: Roger Trevino Sr
VP Finance: Patrick Trevino
Sales/Marketing: Roger Trevino Jr
Estimated Sales: $10-20 Million
Number Employees: 20-49
Number of Brands: 10
Number of Products: 15
Square Footage: 24000
Type of Packaging: Consumer, Food Service, Private Label, Bulk
Brands:
 Kid-Tastic
 Texican
 Twang

13086 Twenty First Century Snacks
921 S 2nd St
Ronkonkoma, NY 11779-7203

631-588-8000
Fax: 631-467-3995 800-975-2883

Assortment of nuts, candy and dried fruit

President: Eddie Bell
Estimated Sales: $1-2.5 000,000
Number Employees: 10-19
Type of Packaging: Consumer, Food Service, Private Label, Bulk

13087 Twenty Rows
880 Vallejo St
Napa, CA 94559-1823

707-265-7750
Fax: 707-944-0145 800-620-7697
tim@vinoce.com www.vinoce.com

Wines
President: Timothy Nuss
Manager: Tim Nuss
tim@vinoce.com
Number Employees: 5-9

13088 Twenty-First Century Foods
30 Germania St # 2
Jamaica Plain, MA 02130-2312

617-522-7595
Fax: 617-522-8772 www.21stcenturyfood.com

Soy products including tofu and tempeh; exporter of tempeh starter
Owner: Rudy Canale
rudy@cantinabostonia.com
Estimated Sales: $.5-1 million
Number Employees: 1-4
Square Footage: 3800
Brands:
 Tofu Cream Chie
 Tofu Pudding

13089 Twenty-Two Desserts
236 Livingston St
Apt 10F
Brooklyn, NY 11201

917-979-3438
info@malai.co
www.malai.co

Ice cream sorbet
Founder & CEO: Pooja Bavishi
Brands:
 Malai

13090 Twin City Bagels
130 Hardman Ave South
South St Paul, MN 55075-2453

651-554-0200
Fax: 651-554-8383

Fresh and refrigerated bagels
Chief Financial Officer: Shimon Harosh
Chief Executive Officer: Michel Rouache
Vice President: Steve Hughes
Research & Development: Mark Heckel
Quality Control: Mark Heckel
Marketing Director: Steve Hughes
Sales Director: Steve Hughes
Contact: Josh Duncanson
duncansonj@cintas.com
Operations Manager: Steve Hughes
Production Manager: Jason Holt
Number Employees: 100-249
Type of Packaging: Consumer, Private Label

13091 Twin City Foods Inc.
10120 269th Pl. NW
PO Box 699
Stanwood, WA 98292

206-515-2400
Fax: 206-515-2499 www.twincityfoods.com

Frozen vegetables including; corn, peas, green beans, carrots, and baby lima beans.
President/COO: John Lervick
Chairman/CEO: Roger Lervick
rogerl@twincityfoods.com
Vice President, Finance: Thomas Hofbauer
Executive Vice President: Mark Levrick
Year Founded: 1943
Estimated Sales: $135 Million
Number Employees: 500-999
Square Footage: 10000
Type of Packaging: Consumer, Food Service, Private Label, Bulk
Other Locations:
 Stanwood WA
 Arlington WA
 Ellensburg WA
 Pasco WA
 Kennewick WA
 Lake Odessa MI

13092 Twin County Dairy
2206 540th Street SW
Kalona, IA 52247

319-656-2776

White cheddar cheese
President/Owner: John A Roetlin Jr
Estimated Sales: $9 Million
Number Employees: 5 to 9
Type of Packaging: Consumer, Private Label, Bulk

13093 Twin Hens
P.O.Box 439
Princeton, NJ 08543

908-925-9040
Fax: 908-281-9908

Chicken pot pies and gluten free beef pot pies
President/Owner: Linda Twining
VP: Kathy Herring

13094 Twin Marquis
7 Bushwick Place
Brooklyn, NY 11206-2802

718-386-6868
Fax: 718-821-6841 800-367-6868
info@twinmarquis.com www.twinmarquis.com

Processor and importer of Asian foods including buns, dumplings, sauces, soups, and noodles; also organic pasta and instant coffee and cappuccino
President: Joseph Tang
Executive Director: Terry Tang
Vice President: Alan But
Contact: Alan But
alan@twinmarquis.com
Estimated Sales: $3-4 Million
Number Employees: 50-99
Square Footage: 88000
Brands:
 Chef One
 Twin Marquis

13095 Twin Oaks Community
138 Twin Oaks Rd
Louisa, VA 23093-6337

540-894-5141
Fax: 540-894-4112 www.twinoaks.org

Tofu, soy milk, tofu salads, herbal spreads and vegetarian burgers
President: Sam Weinreb
Contact: Jeffrey Porter
mccune@twinoaks.org
Estimated Sales: Under $500,000
Number Employees: 50-99
Type of Packaging: Consumer

13096 Twin Valley Developmental Services
427 Commercial
P.O.Box 42
Greenleaf, KS 66943-0042

785-747-2251
Fax: 785-747-2278 800-748-7416
www.twinvalleythriftshop.com

Popped and flavored popcorn and related products
CEO: Ed Henry
VP Marketing: Nate Wirrick
Contact: Barbara Mccord
bmccord@tvds.org
Operations Manager: Carolyn Pinnick
Estimated Sales: $500-1 000,000 appx.
Number Employees: 20-49
Type of Packaging: Private Label

13097 Twinlab Corporation
4800 T-Rex Ave
Boca Raton, FL 33431

800-645-5626
product@twinlab.com www.twinlab.com

Processor and importer of vitamins and nutritional supplements.
Quality Assurance Manager: Mary Baum
mbaum@twinlab.com
Year Founded: 1968
Estimated Sales: $30 Million
Number Employees: 400
Type of Packaging: Consumer
Other Locations:
 American Fork UT
 Grand Rapids MI
 Farmingdale NY
Brands:
 Alvita
 Metabolife
 Nature's Herbs
 Twinlab Bariatric Support

Food Manufacturers / A-Z

Twinlab Fuel
Twinlab Nutrition
Cheramino
Animal Friends
B-12 Dots
Allerdophilus Caps
Colon Care
Fibersol Capsules
Cal-Quick
Cellmins
Gaba Plus
Power Herbs

13098 (HQ)Two Chefs on a Roll
18201 Central Ave
Carson, CA 90746
310-436-1600
Fax: 310-436-1722 800-842-3025
www.twochefsonaroll.com
Dips, sauces, bakery, soups, pasta, salads and appetizers
President & CEO: Jeffrey Goh
Founder: Lori Daniel
CFO: Richard Tansley
Founder: Eliot Swartz
VP Research & Development/Quality Assur.: Kathy Ware
Director of Quality Assurance: Gerson Espindola
VP of Sales & Marketing: Dawn Rasmussen-Hickey
Contact: Joe Alonso
jalonso@twochefsonaroll.com
VP of Operations: Humberto Villagomez
Estimated Sales: $31.9 Million
Number Employees: 175
Square Footage: 100000
Parent Co: Bakkavor
Type of Packaging: Food Service, Private Label
Brands:
  Two Chefs on a Roll

13099 Two Chefs on a Roll
46 Alberigi Dr.
Jessup, PA 18434
570-483-3000
Fax: 570-383-9806 www.twochefsonaroll.com
Dips, sauces, bakery, soups, pasta, salads and appetizers
Parent Co: Bakkavor
Type of Packaging: Food Service, Private Label

13100 Two Chicks and a Ladle
401 Second Avenue
14g
New York, NY 10010
212-251-0025
Fax: 914-631-1738 lisafood@aol.com
Fat-free cheesecakes
Co-owner: Cathy Golup
Co-owner: Lisa Adler

13101 Two Friends Chocolates
16 Depot Road
Boxborough, MA 01719
978-264-1949
contact@twofriendschocolates.com
www.twofriendschocolates.com
Chocolate truffles
Director: Neethu Viswanath
Type of Packaging: Private Label
Brands:
  Two Friends

13102 Two Guys Spice Company
2404 Dennis Street
Jacksonville, FL 32204-1712
949-248-1269
Fax: 904-791-9330 800-874-5656
www.twoguysgrilling.net
Broker and wholesaler/distributor of dehydrated onions, garlic and vegetables; also, spices and industrial ingredients
President: Michael Simmons
Vice President: Guy Simmons
Estimated Sales: $2.4 Million
Number Employees: 1-4
Number of Brands: 1
Number of Products: 500
Square Footage: 20800
Type of Packaging: Food Service, Private Label, Bulk

13103 Two Leaves & A Bud Inc
23400 Two Rivers Rd
Suite 45
Basalt, CO 81621-9239
970-927-9911
Fax: 970-927-9917 866-631-7973
support@twoleavesandabud.com
www.twoleavestea.com
Teas
President/Owner: Richard Rosenfeld
richard@twoleavesandabud.net
Estimated Sales: $1 Million
Number Employees: 5-9

13104 Two Moms In The Raw
1200 S Fordham St # B
Longmont, CO 80503-7759
720-221-8555
Fax: 720-524-4094 info@twomomsintheraw.com
www.soulsprout.com
Manufacturer of raw snack foods like granolas bars, crackers, and nut bars.
Founder: Shari Leidich
Number Employees: 20-49

13105 TyRy Inc
4041 Alvis Court
Rocklin, CA 95677-7799
916-624-6050
Fax: 916-624-1604 800-322-6325
info@tyry.com
Manufacturer and exporter of health, backpacking, self-heating and emergency prepared foods, freeze-dried and no cooking required foods including; pre-packed beans, cereals, desserts, dried fruits and vegetables, grains and meatsubstitutes
President: Don Gearing
donald@tyry.com
Square Footage: 200000
Parent Co: TyRy, Inc
Type of Packaging: Consumer, Private Label, Bulk
Brands:
  Alpineaire
  Gourmet Reserves

13106 Tyee Wine Cellars
26335 Greenberry Rd
Corvallis, OR 97333-9534
541-753-8754
Fax: 541-753-0807 merrilee@storypages.com
www.tyeewine.com
Wine
Owner: Margaret Buchanan
tyeewine@peak.org
Co-Founder: Nola Moiser
Co-Founder: David Buchanan
Co-Founder: Margy Buchanan
Winemaker: Barney Watson
Estimated Sales: Less than $300,000
Number Employees: 1-4
Type of Packaging: Private Label
Brands:
  Tyee

13107 Tyler Candy Co LLC
4337 DC Dr
Tyler, TX 75701-8416
903-561-3046
Fax: 903-581-8030 tylercandyco@aol.com
www.tylercandles.com
Hard candy
Manager: Ron Sumibek
ron@tylercandy.com
Estimated Sales: $5-10 000,000
Number Employees: 20-49
Type of Packaging: Consumer, Private Label
Brands:
  Dickies

13108 Tyler Packing Co
2209 E Erwin St
Tyler, TX 75702-6420
903-593-9592
Fax: 903-593-1273
Beef, pork and veal
Owner: H C Buie
Estimated Sales: $3-5 Million
Number Employees: 5-9
Type of Packaging: Bulk

13109 (HQ)Tyson Foods Inc.
2200 W. Don Tyson Pkwy.
Springdale, AR 72762
479-290-4000
www.tysonfoods.com
Chicken, beef and pork products.
CEO: Noel White
President/Director: Dean Banks
Executive VP/CFO: Stewart Glendinning
Executive VP/General Counsel: Amy Tu
Executive VP/Chief Customer Officer: Scott Rouse
Estimated Sales: $40 Billion
Number Employees: 122,000
Number of Brands: 41
Type of Packaging: Consumer, Food Service, Bulk
Brands:
  Tyson
  Jimmy Dean
  Hillshire Farm
  Hillshire Snacking
  Ball Park
  Wright
  Aidells
  State Fair
  Bonici
  Bosco's Pizza Co.
  The Bruss Company
  Chairman's Reserve
  Advance Pierre Foods
  Gallo Salame
  Barber Foods
  IBP Trusted Excellence
  Lady Aster
  Mexican Original
  Open Prairie Natural Angus
  Russer
  Star Ranch Angus
  Supreme Tender
  Big AZ
  Fast Fixin'
  Hot 'n' Ready
  Wunderbar
  Sara Lee
  Golden Island
  Nature Raised Farms
  PB Jamwich
  Landshire
  Steakeze
  Original Philly Cheesesteak Co.
  Bryan
  True Chews
  Top Chews
  Nudges
  Reuben

13110 Tyson Foods Inc.
P.O. Box 2020
Springdale, AR 72765
800-233-6332
www.tyson.com
Meats including smoked, cured, pork, ham, beef, hot dogs and cold cuts
Group President, Poultry: Chad Martin
Group President, Prepared Foods: Noelle O'Mara
Year Founded: 1935
Type of Packaging: Consumer, Food Service, Private Label
Brands:
  American Favorite
  Black Forest
  Fresh Cut
  Wilson Continental D

13111 U Okada & Co LTD
1000 Queen St
Honolulu, HI 96814-4116
808-597-1102
Fax: 808-591-6634
Wholesaler/distributor of frozen foods, provisions/meats and seafood; serving the food service market
President: Dexter Okada
dexter@uokada.com
President: Saneo Okada
Estimated Sales: $10-20 Million
Number Employees: 20-49
Square Footage: 60000

13112 U Roast Em Inc
16778 W US Highway 63
Hayward, WI 54843-7214
715-634-6255
Fax: 715-934-3221 info@u-roast-em.com

Food Manufacturers / A-Z

Supplier of green coffee beans, bulk teas, home roasting supplies and coffee flavorings
Manager: Terry Wall
info@u-roast-em.com
Number Employees: 1-4
Type of Packaging: Consumer
Brands:
  Bodum
  Fresh Beans

13113 U.S. Range
1177 Kamato Rd
Mississauga, ON L4W IX4
Canada
905-624-0260
800-424-2411
www.garland-group.com
Manufacturer of cooking systems.

13114 UBC Food Distributors
12812 Prospect St
Dearborn, MI 48126-3652
877-846-8117
Fax: 313-846-8118 info@wellmadefood.com
www.wellmadefood.com
Honey, chocolates, cookies, juices, and snacks
Sales Manager: Hassan Houssami
Estimated Sales: $10-12 Million
Number Employees: 10
Other Locations:
  East Coast NJ
  West Coast CA
Brands:
  Wellmade Honey

13115 UBF Food Solutions
2200 Cabot Dr Ste 200
Lisle, IL 60532
630-955-5394
www.unileverfoodsolutions.com
Sauces, dressings
Managing Director: Tracey Rogers
Estimated Sales: $25-49.9 Million
Number Employees: 250-499
Parent Co: Unilever

13116 UFL Foods
450 Superior Boulevard
Mississauga, ON L5T 2R9
Canada
905-670-7776
Fax: 905-670-7751
Processor and exporter of custom formulated and blended ingredients including milk replacers, mustard, seasonings, meat binders, curing preparations, etc.; also, pasta and rice sauce mixes, soup and sauce bases, batters andbreadings
VP: Jack Conway
Number Employees: 100-249
Square Footage: 440000
Parent Co: Newly Weds Foods
Type of Packaging: Food Service, Private Label, Bulk

13117 ULDO USA
10 Dewey Road
Lexington, MA 02420-1018
781-860-7800
Fax: 781-863-1973 productinfo@bakenjoy.com
Baked goods
Contact: Arlene Kolovson
imaginatemundo@hotmail.com
Brands:
  Baken Joy

13118 UNOI Grainmill
Route 13-A
Seaford, DE 19973-5749
302-629-4083
Miller of whole wheat flour, white and yellow corn meal, buckwheat, etc
Owner: Janice Griffith
Manager: Charles Willoughby
Estimated Sales: Under $300,000
Number Employees: 3
Square Footage: 40000
Parent Co: United Nation of Islam
Type of Packaging: Private Label
Brands:
  Hearn & Rawlins
  White Dove

13119 US Chocolate Corp
4801 1st Ave
Brooklyn, NY 11232-4208
718-788-8555
Fax: 718-788-3311 uschoc@aol.com
Processor and exporter of kosher liquid marble chocolate and white parve coatings, fudge bases and flavors.
President: David Rosenberg
abe@uschoc.com
Estimated Sales: $10-20 Million
Number Employees: 10-19
Square Footage: 81000
Brands:
  U.S. Brand

13120 US Distilled Products Co
1607 12th St S
Princeton, MN 55371-2311
763-389-4903
Fax: 763-389-2549 info@usdp.com
www.usdp.com
Alcoholic beverages
President: Bradley P Johnson
CFO: Pat Pelzer
Production Manager: Kevin Issendorf
Purchasing Manager: Todd Rhode
Year Founded: 1981
Estimated Sales: $20-30 Million
Number Employees: 250-499
Square Footage: 250000
Brands:
  Athena Test
  Black Eagle
  Blanks
  Cactus Bills
  California Crest
  California Ltd
  English Guard
  Gionelli
  Karkov
  Kingston
  Marrone
  McAdams
  Mothers
  Petri
  The Antiquary
  Tomatin
  Trader Vics
  Wakefield

13121 US Durum Products LTD
1812 William Penn Way
P.O.Box 10126
Lancaster, PA 17601-5831
717-293-8698
Fax: 717-293-8699 866-268-7268
wross@usdurum.com www.usdurum.com
Couscous
President: Wendy Ross
wross@usdurum.com
Estimated Sales: $2.5-5 Million
Number Employees: 10-19

13122 US Foods & Pharmaceuticals Inc
313 W Beltline Hwy # 182
Suite 182
Madison, WI 53713-2682
608-278-1293
Fax: 608-278-9042 800-362-8294
Milk minerals, dairy formulations, enhanced dairy products and formulations, nutritional products, nutraceuticals
President: Tammi Ceballos
tammi.ceballos@usfood.com
VP: James Henderson
Marketing Director: Richard Nelson
Public Relations: Kalle Smith
Operations Manager: Jay Zahom
Estimated Sales: $1,500,000
Number Employees: 5-9
Square Footage: 20000
Type of Packaging: Consumer
Brands:
  Dari-Cal
  Infalac
  My-Baby

13123 US Ingredients
P.O.Box 9207
Naperville, IL 60567-0207
630-820-1711
Fax: 630-820-1883
Seasonings and food flavoring products

Owner: Eric Maul
Executive Vice President of Network Serv: Jim OBrien
Estimated Sales: $5-10 Million
Number Employees: 5-9

13124 US Mills
401 E City Ave Ste 220
Bala Cynwyd, PA 19004-1117
Fax: 781-444-3411 800-422-1125
Processor and exporter of natural/organic foods including ready-to-eat and hot cereals and graham crackers.
Executive VP: Cynthia Davis
Director of Marketing: Daniel Wiser
Sales: William Bunn
Number Employees: 6
Number of Brands: 5
Number of Products: 45
Type of Packaging: Consumer
Brands:
  Erewhon
  Farina Mills
  New Morning
  Skinner's
  Uncle Sam Cereal

13125 US Sugar Company
111 Ponce de Leon Ave.
Clewiston, FL 33440
863-983-8121
info@ussugar.com
www.ussugar.com
Granulated, brown and powdered sugars; sugar and artificial sweetener packets; and orange juice.
President: William McDaniel
VP: Steve Ward
Contact: Sunil Abey
sabey@ussugar.com
VP Operations: Tom Moran
Plant Manager: Avery Foy
Estimated Sales: $25 Million
Number Employees: 20-49
Number of Brands: 30
Number of Products: 20
Square Footage: 300000
Type of Packaging: Consumer, Food Service, Private Label
Brands:
  Private Label
  Us Sugars

13126 US Wellness Meats
P.O. Box 249
Canton, MO 63435
877-383-0051
eathealthy@grasslandbeef.com
grasslandbeef.com
Meats
Owner: John Wood
Year Founded: 2000
Estimated Sales: $7,300,000
Number Employees: 9
Brands:
  Grassland Beef

13127 USA Beverage
1410a E Old Us Highway 40
Warrenton, MO 63383-1316
636-456-5468
Fax: 636-456-3422
Wines
President: Hugh White
CFO: Thomas Nittler
Marketing Director: Darrell Wiss
Production Manager: Terre Novell
Plant Manager: Hugh White
Estimated Sales: $500,000
Number Employees: 20-49
Type of Packaging: Private Label
Brands:
  Usa Beverages

13128 USA Laboratories Inc
1438 Highway 96
Burns, TN 37029-5030
615-441-1521
Fax: 615-446-3788 800-489-4872
usalabs@usalabs.com www.usalabs.com
Processor and exporter of vitamins, minerals, nutritional supplements and weight loss aids

President/Owner: Charles Stokes
CEO: Charles Stokes
R&D: David Bethshears
yumyum1969@live.com
Quality Control: Brad Stokes
Marketing Director: Erica White
Sales Director: Shelby Bethsheard
Contact: Suzzane Guire
yumyum1969@live.com
Operations: Ted Sanders
Estimated Sales: $4.7 Million
Number Employees: 1-4
Number of Brands: 5
Number of Products: 1000
Square Footage: 400000
Parent Co: USA Laboratories
Brands:
   Burn Off
   Jewel Laboratories
   Nutrceuticals
   Power Rangers Chewable Vitamins
   Usa Best
   Usa Laboratories Nutrients
   Usa Sports Labs

13129 UTZ Quality Foods Inc.
900 High St.
Hanover, PA 17331
717-637-6644
Fax: 717-634-5890 800-367-7629
info@utzsnacks.com www.utzsnacks.com
Potato chips, pretzels, popcorn, tortilla chips, cheese curls, pub fries, pork rinds, etc.
President/COO: Tom Flocco
CEO: Dylan Lissette
Executive VP/CFO: Jay Thompson
Executive VP/Chief Customer Officer: Mark Schreiber
Year Founded: 1921
Estimated Sales: $215 Million
Number Employees: 2,500
Number of Brands: 9
Square Footage: 550000
Type of Packaging: Consumer, Food Service, Bulk
Other Locations:
   Utz Distribution Centers
   East Hartford CT
   Patterson NY
   Laurel DE
   Newark DE
   Auburn ME
   West Springfield MA
   North Easton MA
   South Yarmouth MA
   Wilmington MA
   Shrewsbury MA
   Cumberland MD
   Waldorf MD
   Hanover PA
Brands:
   Bachman
   Golden Flake
   Dirty
   Zapp's Potato Chips
   Good Health
   Snikiddy
   Boulder Canyon
   TGI Fridays Snacks
   TORTIYAHS!

13130 (HQ)Uas Laboratories
9953 Valley View Rd
Eden Prairie, MN 55344
952-935-1707
Fax: 952-935-1650 800-422-3371
info@uaslabs.com
Manufacturer and exporter of nutritional supplements
President: S K Dash
Quality Control: Scot Elert
Marketing Director: Raj Dash
Operations Manager: Steven Shack
Estimated Sales: $3 Million
Number Employees: 10-19
Number of Products: 12
Square Footage: 21600
Type of Packaging: Consumer, Private Label, Bulk
Brands:
   Dds
   Dds Acidophilus
   Dds Junior
   Dds Plus
   Uas Activin Plus
   Uas Coenzyme Q10
   Uas Joint Formula

13131 Ubons Sauce LLC
801 Jerry Clower Blvd.
Yazoo City, MS 39194
662-716-7100
info@ubons.net
ubonsbbq.com
Bloody mary mix and sauces.
Founder: Leslie Scott
Contact: David Rosen
david@ubons.net

13132 Udi's Gluten-Free Foods
1600 Pearl Street
Suite 300
Boulder, CO 80302
201-421-3970
udisglutenfree.com
Gluten free foods

13133 Udi's Granola
12000 E. 47th Avenue
Suite 400
Denver, CO 80239
303-657-6366
Fax: 303-657-5373 www.udisgranola.com
Flavored granola
Founder: Udi Baron

13134 Ugo Di Lullo & Son
1004 Edgewater Ave
Westville, NJ 08093-1246
856-456-3700
Fax: 856-456-7161
Canned goods
President: Ugo Di Lullo
Estimated Sales: $5-10 Million
Number Employees: 5-9

13135 Uhlmann Co
4801 Main St # 550
Suite 550
Kansas City, MO 64112-2544
816-221-8200
Fax: 816-221-5504 866-866-8627
www.heckerseresota.com
All-purpose unbleached and whole wheat flour
President: Judi Rasmussen
judi@heckerseresota.com
Retail Sales: Wesley Fehsenfeld
Estimated Sales: $10-20 Million
Number Employees: 10-19
Square Footage: 60000
Type of Packaging: Consumer, Food Service
Brands:
   Ceresota
   Heckers

13136 Uinta Brewing Co
1722 S Fremont Dr
Salt Lake City, UT 84104-4215
801-467-0909
Fax: 801-463-7151 info@uintabrewing.com
www.uintabrewing.com
Beer
President: William Hamill
Vice President: Steve Kuftinec
skuftinec@uintabrewing.com
Public Relations Officer: Steve Kustinec
Estimated Sales: $5-10 Million
Number Employees: 20-49
Square Footage: 104000
Type of Packaging: Private Label
Brands:
   Uinta

13137 Ultima Health Products Inc.
3284 Niles-Cortland Rd.
Cortland, OH 44410
Fax: 330-638-5500 888-663-8584
www.ultimareplenisher.com
Electrolyte-balanced energy drink without sugar, carbs or calories
Vice-President, Sales: Skeet Freeman
Year Founded: 1996
Number of Brands: 1
Type of Packaging: Consumer, Private Label
Brands:
   Ultima

13138 Ultimate Bagel
1226 State Street
Santa Barbara, CA 93101
805-845-2511
ultimatebagel@gmail.com
Bagels
President: Carol Kozak
Estimated Sales: $230,000
Number Employees: 6
Square Footage: 8000
Type of Packaging: Consumer, Food Service

13139 Ultimate Biscotti
1000 S Bertelsen Road
Suite 10
Eugene, OR 97402-5448
541-344-8220
Fax: 541-344-8357
Biscotti including ginger, hazelnut chocolate, citrus, etc.; also, wheat and gluten-free available
President: Heather Kent
Number Employees: 5-9
Square Footage: 24000
Type of Packaging: Consumer, Food Service, Bulk
Brands:
   Ultimate Biscotti

13140 Ultimate Foods
P.O. Box 1008
Linden, NJ 07036
908-486-0800
Fax: 908-486-2999 www.ultimatefoodsservice.com
Offer a full line of fresh and frozen seafood, produce, meats, oils, pastas, canned tomatoes, and other grocery and specialty items.
General Manager: Scott Greisman
Seafood Buyer/Quality Control: John Parisi
Produce Buyer/Quality Control: Albert Sindoni
Road Sales Manager: Al Ferrentino
Operations Manager: Anthony Stropoli
Dry Goods Buyer: James Boniface
Estimated Sales: $3.6 Million
Number of Brands: 1
Type of Packaging: Food Service, Bulk
Brands:
   ULTIMATE

13141 Ultimate Gourmet
12 Ilene Ct
Hillsborough, NJ 8844
908-359-4050
Fax: 908-359-2494
contact@ultimate-gourmet.com
www.ugbrands.com
Bar mixes, jellies, jams, sauces, brandied fruit, barbacue sauces, marinades and rubs
President: Tali Almagor
holly@altimate-gourmet.com
Estimated Sales: Less Than $500,000
Number Employees: 1-4
Type of Packaging: Consumer, Food Service, Private Label, Bulk
Brands:
   Club Tahity
   Cramore
   Creamy Head
   Firehouse
   Giroux
   Milem
   Proud Mary
   Raffetto
   Tahiti

13142 Ultimate Nut & Candy Company
6333 West 3rd Street
Los Angeles, CA 90036
800-767-5259
Candy, nuts
President: Steve Turner
Quality Control: Theresa Malgonadio
Marketing Manager: Steve Turner
Number Employees: 20-49
Type of Packaging: Private Label
Brands:
   Studio Confections
   Ultimate Confections

13143 Ultimate Nutrition
161 Woodford Avenue
Farmington, CT 06034-0643
860-409-7100
Fax: 860-793-5006 www.ultimatenutrition.com
Food processor and exporter of food supplements including capsules, tablets, powders and protein bars
President: Victor Rubino
Advertising: Seth Darvick
VP Sales: Dean Caputo
Type of Packaging: Consumer

Food Manufacturers / A-Z

13144 Ultimate Salsa
PO Box 47343
Charlotte, NC 28247
704-847-4857
888-827-2572
Salsa
Co-Owner: Ellen Siegler
President: Tom Siegler
Brands:
  Iguana Tom's

13145 Ultra Dairy
40236 State Highway 10
Delhi, NY 13753-3289
607-746-2141
Fax: 607-746-3725
Milk
Manager: Liz Van Buren
Senior VP: Fred Bruzzese
Estimated Sales: $10-24.9 Million
Number Employees: 100-249
Parent Co: Tuscan/Lehigh Valley Dairies
Brands:
  Actic Splash
  Lehigh Valley Dairies
  Tuscan

13146 Ultra Enterprises
14108 Lambert Rd
Whittier, CA 90605-2427
562-945-4833
Fax: 562-698-7362 800-543-0627
b.kaliultra@verizon.net www.ultraent.com
Processor and sports nutrition of granulars
President/CEO: Bud Thompson
Vice President: Mary Thompson
Number of Products: 50
Type of Packaging: Consumer
Brands:
  Sports Nutrition
  Ultra Rain Glandulars

13147 Ultra Seal
521 Main St
New Paltz, NY 12561-1609
845-255-2490
Fax: 845-255-3553 info@ultra-seal.com
www.ultra-seal.com
Contract packager of portion controlled products including ketchup, mustard, powder lemonade, fruit juice, iced tea mix, etc
President: Dennis Borrello
dennisb@ultra-seal.com
Manager: Christine Downs
Executive: Terry Murphy
Estimated Sales: $5-10 Million
Number Employees: 100-249
Square Footage: 104000
Type of Packaging: Consumer, Food Service, Private Label, Bulk

13148 Umanoff & Parsons
1704 Boone Ave
Bronx, NY 10460-5400
212-219-2240
Fax: 718-684-7978 800-248-9993
Fresh and frozen all natural kosher dairy cakes, pies, quiches and tarts
President: Simon Seaton
Estimated Sales: $5,200,000
Number Employees: 20-49
Square Footage: 26000

13149 Umpqua Dairy
333 SE Sykes Ave
P.O. Box 1306
Roseburg, OR 97470
541-672-2638
Fax: 541-673-0256 888-672-6455
info@umpquadairy.com www.umpquadairy.com
Processor and exporter of ice cream, milk, cottage cheese, sour cream and butter
President: Douglas Feldkamp
Director, Sales & Marketing: Marty Weaver
COO: Steve Feldkemp
Year Founded: 1931
Estimated Sales: $50.2 Million
Number Employees: 100-249
Type of Packaging: Consumer, Food Service, Private Label

13150 Umpqua Oats
2980 Sunridge Heights Pkwy
Suite 130
Henderson, NV 89052
877-303-8107
brysonb@umpquaoats.com
umpquaoats.com
Oatmeal
Owner: Mandy Holborow
Co-Owner: Sheri Price
Sales & Marketing Manager: Bryson Buck
Co-Owner & Purchasing: Chris Holborow
Estimated Sales: $10-20 Million
Number Employees: 1-10
Brands:
  Umpqua Oats

13151 UnReal Brands
Boston, MA
hi@getunreal.com
www.getunreal.com
Non-GMO, fair trade, gluten-free, artificial ingredient-free dark and milk chocolate peanut butter cups, chocolate-coated quinoa and chocolate-covered nuts
Co-Founder: Nicky Bronner
Co-Founder: Kristopher Bronner
Year Founded: 2010
Number of Brands: 1
Number of Products: 6
Type of Packaging: Consumer, Private Label
Brands:
  UnReal

13152 Uncle Andy's Cafe
171 Ocean St
South Portland, ME 04106-3623
207-799-7199
Fax: 207- 79-9 34
Baked goods
Owner: Dennis Fogg
Estimated Sales: Less Than $500,000
Number Employees: 1-4

13153 Uncle Charley's Sausage
1135 Industrial Park Rd
Vandergrift, PA 15690-6050
724-845-3302
Fax: 724-845-3174 www.unclecharleys.com
Pork, pork products
President: Charles Armitage
CEO: Frances Armitage
charley@unclecharleyssausage.com
Vice President: Charles Armitage Jr
Estimated Sales: $5-10 Million
Number Employees: 20-49

13154 Uncle Dougie's
Chicago, IL
www.originaluncledougies.com
Preservative- and GMO-free barbecue sauces, marinades, seasonings, rubs, hot sauces and drink mixes in various flavors
Founder: Doug Tomek
Year Founded: 1989
Number of Brands: 1
Number of Products: 19
Type of Packaging: Consumer, Private Label
Brands:
  Uncle Dougie's

13155 Uncle Fred's Fine Foods
209 N Doughty Street
Rockport, TX 78382-5322
361-729-8320
www.unclfred.com
Processor and importer of habanero ketchup, jelly, hot sweet mustard and chips, salsa, spices, meat rubs and sauces including cocktail, pepper and barbecue
President: Fred Franklin
VP/Co-Owner: Pat Marsh
Manager: Judith Jecmen-Fuhrman
Number Employees: 1-4
Square Footage: 6400
Parent Co: Island Enterprises
Type of Packaging: Consumer
Brands:
  Uncle Fred's Fine Foods

13156 Uncle Lee's Tea Inc
11020 Rush St
South El Monte, CA 91733-3547
626-350-3309
Fax: 626-350-4364 800-732-8830
www.unclelee.com
Processor, exporter and importer of teas including herb, spiced, traditional and dieter's; co-packing and private label available
Vice President: Tim Carter
tim.carter@health.net
Chairman: Lee Rieho
Vice President: Jonason Lee
Sales Director: James O'Young
Public Relations: Patty Gillno
Plant Manager: Joe Villegas
Estimated Sales: $1400000
Number Employees: 20-49
Parent Co: Ten Ren Tea Company
Brands:
  Uncle Lee's Tea

13157 Uncle Matt's Organic
PO Box 120187
Clermont, FL 34712
833-729-8625
Fax: 352-394-1003 media@unclematts.com
www.unclematts.com
Organic orange, grapefruit, apple juices; organic lemonade; organic probiotic waters in various flavors
Founder/Owner: Matt McLean
Year Founded: 1999
Number of Brands: 1
Number of Products: 11
Type of Packaging: Consumer, Private Label
Brands:
  Uncle Matt's Organic

13158 Uncle Ralph's Cookies
801 N East St # 5
Frederick, MD 21701-4652
301-695-6224
Fax: 301-695-6327 800-422-0626
sales@uncleralphscookies.com
www.uncleralphscookies.com
Gourmet cookies, brownies, crumb cakes, pound cakes, and quick breads
Owner: Ed Riffle
Founder: Peggy Wight
Sales Director: Jamie Mater
eriffle@uncleralphscookies.com
Estimated Sales: $3-5 Million
Number Employees: 50-99
Square Footage: 120000
Type of Packaging: Consumer, Food Service, Private Label
Brands:
  Uncle Ralph's

13159 Uncle Ray's Potato Chips
14245 Birwood St
Detroit, MI 48238
313-834-0800
Fax: 313-834-0443 800-800-3286
www.unclerays.com
Potato chips, nacho chips, popcorn, snack foods
President & COO: Brian Gaggin
CFO: Sandra Subotich
General Manager: Joseph Dilly
Year Founded: 1965
Estimated Sales: $20-30 Million
Number Employees: 200-499
Parent Co: AmeriFoods
Brands:
  Unclerays

13160 Uncommon Grounds Coffee
2813 Seventh Street
Berkeley, CA 94710-2702
510-764-1211
Fax: 510-868-1841 800-567-9183
uncommon@uncommongrounds.net
www.uncommongrounds.net
Coffee
President/CEO: Kim Moore
CFO: Derek Lantner
Contact: Skip Blakely
skip.blakely@uncommongrounds.net
Operations Manager: Kim Moore
Production Manager: James Spottn
Estimated Sales: $2.3 Million
Number Employees: 14
Parent Co: Berkeley Coffee and Tea
Type of Packaging: Private Label
Brands:
  Double Star Espresso
  El Salvador Finca Las Nubes
  Ethiopian Organic
  Molta Roba

Food Manufacturers / A-Z

13161 Une-Viandi
505 Industriel Boulevard
St. Jean Sur Richelieu, NB J3B 5Y8
Canada
450-347-8406
Fax: 450-347-8142   800-363-1955
Processor, importer and exporter of meat products including bone-in and boneless beef, lamb and veal
President: Claude Berni
Export Manager: Lloyd Arshinoff
Number Employees: 50-99
Square Footage: 88000
Type of Packaging: Consumer, Food Service, Private Label, Bulk

13162 Ungars Food
9 Boumar Pl
Elmwood Park, NJ 07407-2615
201-773-6846
Fax: 201-703-9333   webquery@drpraegers.com
www.drpraegers.com
Veggie burgers, pancakes, breaded fish fillets, fillet fish sticks
Owner: Larry Praeger
larry@drpraegers.com
CFO: Jeff Coher
Estimated Sales: $2.5-5 Million
Number Employees: 50-99

13163 (HQ)Ungerer & Co
4 Bridgewater Ln
Lincoln Park, NJ 07035-1491
973-706-7381
Fax: 973-628-0251   www.ungererandcompany.com
Manufacturer, importer and exporter of natural and artificial fruit flavors and essential oils including lemon, orange, peppermint, spearmint, ginger, lime and dill
President: Casey Annicchiarico
cannicchiarico@ungererandcompany.com
Estimated Sales: $10 Million
Number Employees: 100-249
Type of Packaging: Consumer, Private Label, Bulk
Other Locations:
   Ungerer & Company Plant
   Bethlehem PA
   Ungerer & Company Plant
   Oaxaca, Mexico

13164 Unibroue/Unibrew
80 Rue Des Carrišres
Chambly, QC J3L 2H6
Canada
450-658-7658
Fax: 450-658-9195   info@unibroue.com
www.unibroue.com
Gourmet beer including black currant, apple, and chambly blonde
Brewing Supervisor: Martin Gagn,
Year Founded: 1990
Estimated Sales: $21million
Number Employees: 250
Parent Co: Sapporo
Type of Packaging: Consumer, Food Service
Brands:
   Unibrew
   Unibroue

13165 Unica
23w101 Kings Ct # 100
Glen Ellyn, IL 60137-7215
630-790-8107
Fax: 630-790-8117
Sugar free confectionary
President: Peter Zeuthen
Contact: Leif Pedersen
leif@unicable.com
Estimated Sales: $5-10 Million
Number Employees: 5-9
Brands:
   Unica

13166 Unified Food Ingredients
145 Vallecitos DE Oro # 208
San Marcos, CA 92069-1459
760-744-7225
Fax: 760-744-7215
Processor, exporter and importer of dehydrated vegetables including bell peppers, carrots, celery, peas, corn, mushrooms, garlic, etc
Owner: Dan Stouder
VP: Dan Stouder
Sales Manager: Simone Grunewald
Customer Service: Kris Cannan
Operations Manager: Melissa Coetzee
Estimated Sales: $1-3,000,000
Number Employees: 1-4
Square Footage: 20000
Type of Packaging: Bulk

13167 Unilever Canada
160 Bloor St. East
Suite 1400
Toronto, ON M4W 3R2
Canada
416-415-3000
www.unilever.ca
Food products, personal care, and home products.
Director, Customer Development: Bruce Findlay
VP, Brand Strategy & Innovation: Margaret McKellar
Year Founded: 1949
Estimated Sales: $466 Million
Number Employees: 3,400
Square Footage: 80912
Parent Co: Unilever US
Type of Packaging: Consumer, Food Service
Brands:
   Becel
   Breyers
   Hellmann's
   Knorr
   Lipton
   Red Rose
   Slim-Fast

13168 Unilever Food Solutions
800 Sylvan Ave
Englewood Cliffs, NJ 07632
foodsolutions@unilever.com
www.unileverfoodsolutions.us
Bases and bouillons, dressings and condiments, mayonnaise, sauces and gravies, seasonings, soups, teas and beverages.
President, Foods & Refreshment: Hanneke Faber
Number Employees: 250-499
Parent Co: Unilever USA
Type of Packaging: Consumer, Food Service, Private Label, Bulk
Brands:
   Becel
   Bertolli
   Blue Band
   Flora

13169 Unilever US
800 Sylvan Ave
Englewood Cliffs, NJ 07632
800-298-5018
www.unileverusa.com
Food products, personal care, and home products.
President, North America: Amanda Sourry
CEO: Alan Jope
CFO: Graeme Pitkethly
Chief R&D Officer: Richard Slater
VP, Human Resources, North America: Mike Clementi
Estimated Sales: $18 Billion
Number Employees: 5000-9999
Parent Co: Unilever N.V. & Unilever plc
Type of Packaging: Consumer, Food Service
Brands:
   Hellmann's
   Knorr
   Lipton
   Magnum
   Talenti
   Ben & Jerry's
   Breyers
   Good Humor
   Klondike
   Popsicle

13170 Union
14522 Myford Rd
Irvine, CA 92606-1000
714-734-2200
Fax: 714-734-2223   800-854-7292
Processor and exporter of Oriental ramen noodles
President: Sang Mook Lee
CEO: Victor Sim
Sales Manager: Bob Hicks
Estimated Sales: $10,900,000
Number Employees: 100-249
Square Footage: 200000
Type of Packaging: Consumer, Private Label
Brands:
   Noodle Plus
   Smack Cup-A-Ramen
   Smack Ramen
   Snoodles

13171 Union Fisheries Corp
6186 N Northwest Hwy
Chicago, IL 60631-2126
773-738-0448
Fax: 773-763-8775
Prepared fresh or frozen fish and seafood
Owner: Jim Gubrow
Estimated Sales: $3-5 Million
Number Employees: 5-9

13172 Union Seafoods
2100 W McDowell Rd
Phoenix, AZ 85009-3011
602-254-4114
Fax: 602-254-4117
Seafood
President: Ernest Linsenmeyer
Estimated Sales: $4,000,000
Number Employees: 1-4

13173 Union Square Wines & Spirits
140 Fourth Ave
New York, NY 10003
212-675-8100
Fax: 212-675-8663   info@unionsquarewines.com
www.unionsquarewines.com
wines and spirits
Sales Manager: David Hatzopoulos
Wine Director: Jesse Salazar
Sales General Manager: Katherine Moore
Year Founded: 1995
Estimated Sales: $500,000-$900,000
Type of Packaging: Consumer, Private Label

13174 Union Wine Co
19600 SW Cipole Rd
Tualatin, OR 97062
info@unionwinecompany.com
www.unionwinecompany.com
Wine
Founder & Owner: Ryan Harms
Director of Finance/Accounting: Eric Harms
VP Sales: Adam Coremin
Director of Winemaking: JP Caldcleugh
Year Founded: 2005
Number Employees: 20-49
Brands:
   Underwood
   Kings Ridge
   Alchemist

13175 Unique Beverage Company
PO Box 2246
Everett, WA 98213-0246
425-267-0959
Fax: 425-353-5600
customerservice@cascadeicewater.com
www.cascadeicewater.com
Sodium-free, caffeine-free, sugar-free flavored sparkling water; organic varieties available
Chief Executive Officer: Mark Christensen
Number of Brands: 1
Type of Packaging: Consumer, Private Label

13176 Unique Foods
3221 Durham Dr # 107
Raleigh, NC 27603-3507
919-779-5600
Fax: 919-779-3766
Canned and exotic mushrooms
President: Louis J Deangelis Sr.
CEO: Louis De Angelis
VP: Louis J Deangelis Jr.
Marketing Head: Louis De Angelis
Contact: Gina Bissette
gina@uniquefoodcompany.com
Operations Manager: Bryan Parrish
Estimated Sales: $3,700,000
Number Employees: 20-49
Square Footage: 15000

13177 Unique Ingredients LLC
6460 S Mountainside Dr
Gold Canyon, AZ 85118-2900
480-983-2498
Fax: 509-653-1992   oly@werunique.com
www.werunique.com

Food Manufacturers / A-Z

Dried apples in a variety of cuts, styles and varieties; offering air dried, drum dried and upon request, freeze dried fruits and vegetables, specializing in apples, apricots, cherries, peaches, plums, raisins, bananas and all tropical fruits
Founder: Dave Olsen
Finance and Accounting: Karen Bentz
Sales: Matt Gibbs
Contact: Delrae Blanchard
delrae@werunique.com
Operations: Becky Cornwall
Estimated Sales: $3 Million
Number Employees: 5-9
Number of Brands: 1
Number of Products: 100
Square Footage: 500
Type of Packaging: Private Label, Bulk
Brands:
    Unique Ingredients

13178 Unique Pretzel Bakery, Inc.
215 East Bellevue Ave.
Reading, PA 19605
    610-929-3172
Fax: 610-929-3444
Hard-baked pretzel "splits"; pretzel shells, chocolate-covered pretzels
Number of Brands: 1
Type of Packaging: Consumer, Private Label
Brands:
    Unique

13179 Unique Vitality Products
29215 Hillrise Dr
Agoura Hills, CA 91301-1533
    818-889-7739
Fax: 818-889-4895
Processor and exporter of vitamins
Owner: Pierre Van Wessel
uvppierre@extreme.com
CEO: Robert Van Wessel
CFO: Wendy Van Wessel
Quality Control: Ashwin Patel
Production: Hasmuck Patec
Estimated Sales: $.5-1 million
Number Employees: 1-4
Square Footage: 800000
Type of Packaging: Private Label, Bulk
Brands:
    Hypo Form
    Kidney Rinse
    Liver Rinse
    Unique Colonic Rinse
    Vascustrem

13180 Uniquely Together
Apt 3
2000 W Estes Ave
Chicago, IL 60645-2452
    847-675-1555
Fax: 847-675-4049 800-613-7276
Cocktail biscuit collection, line of chocolates, line of sandwich creme cookies; all natural
Owner: Mark Callahan
Owner: Anne Callahan
Number Employees: 5-9
Number of Brands: 1
Number of Products: 22
Square Footage: 22000
Type of Packaging: Consumer, Private Label
Brands:
    Heavenly Cluster
    Heavenly Clusters Collection
    Martini Biscuit
    Sweet Savory Cocktai

13181 United Apple Sales
124 Main St Ste 5
New Paltz, NY 12561
    585-765-2460
Fax: 585-765-9710 uasales@aol.com
www.unitedapplesales.com
Grower, importer and exporter of apples
COO: Chuck Andola
Domestic/Export Sales: Dean Decker
Estimated Sales: $360,000
Number Employees: 1-4
Type of Packaging: Consumer, Food Service
Brands:
    America's Fruit
    Storm King

13182 United Canadian Malt
843 Park Street South
Peterborough, ON K9J 3V1
Canada
    705-876-9110
Fax: 705-876-9118 800-461-6400
Processor, exporter and importer of dried and custom liquid brewing extracts, malt syrups and liquid malt
President/General Manager: Monte Smith
Estimated Sales: $500,000-999,999
Number Employees: 15
Square Footage: 499600
Type of Packaging: Bulk
Brands:
    Bru-Mix
    Canadian Grand
    Master Baker
    Master Brewer

13183 United Canning Corporation
12505 South Ave
North Lima, OH 44452
    216-549-9807
Fax: 216-549-9809
Canned mushrooms
Owner: Andrew Dibacco
Plant Manager: Richard Innocenzi
Number Employees: 10-19
Square Footage: 135000
Type of Packaging: Consumer, Food Service, Private Label
Brands:
    Frankies
    Masterbrand
    Sno-Top

13184 United Citrus
244 Vanderbilt Ave # 1
Norwood, MA 02062-5052
    781-769-7300
Fax: 781-769-9492 800-229-7300
www.unitedcitrus.com
Bulk dry blends and liquid food products including: cocktail mixes, cocktail rimmers, beverage juices, energy drinks, hydration beverages, frozen carbonated beverages, superfruit beverages and dry blended specialty desserts
President: Richard Kates
rkates@unitedcitrus.net
VP/General Manager: Christopher Fernandes
R&D: Linda Halik
Quality Control: Cheryl Senato
Purchasing: Kristen Burbank
Estimated Sales: $5 Million
Number Employees: 10-19
Type of Packaging: Consumer, Food Service, Private Label, Bulk
Brands:
    All-In-One
    Best Way
    Florida's Own
    Good Spirits
    Jollie Juan
    Sir Citrus
    The Last Word

13185 United Dairy Farmers Inc.
3955 Montgomery Rd.
Cincinnati, OH 45212
    866-837-4833
consumerrelations@udfinc.com www.udfinc.com
Ice cream and dairy drinks.
President/CEO: Brad Lindner
blindner@udfinc.com
CFO: Marilyn Coleman
Year Founded: 1940
Estimated Sales: $500-$900 Million
Number Employees: 1000-4999
Number of Brands: 1
Brands:
    UDF

13186 United Dairy Inc.
300 N. 5th St.
Martins Ferry, OH 43935
    740-633-1451
800-252-1542
drinkunited.com
Full line of dairy products including fluid milk, low fat milks, chocolate, skim, half & half, buttermilk, dairy smart, ultra skim, juices and drinks. Also, cottage cheese, sour cream and dips, sterile products, yogurt and icecream.
CEO: Brad Lindner
Chief Financial Officer: George Wood
Year Founded: 1954
Estimated Sales: $145 Million
Number Employees: 250-499
Square Footage: 20000
Type of Packaging: Consumer
Other Locations:
    Distribution Center
    Lancaster OH
    Distribution Center
    Fairmont WV
    United Dairy, Pennsylvania
    Uniontown PA
    United Dairy, West Virginia
    Charleston WV
    Distribution Center
    West Portsmouth OH
    Distribution Center
    Paintsville KY
    Distribution Center
    Salem VA
    Distribution Center
    Beckley WV
    Distribution Center
    Galax VA

13187 United Dairymen of Arizona
2008 S. Hardy Dr.
Tempe, AZ 85282-1211
    480-966-7211
www.uda.coop
Milk, butter and powdered dairy products.
Chief Executive Officer: Keith Murfield
CFO: Mark H.
VP, Quality Assurance: Heidi M.
VP, Operations: Steve B.
Year Founded: 1960
Estimated Sales: $780 Million
Number Employees: 300
Square Footage: 9000

13188 United Fishing Agency LTD
1131 N Nimitz Hwy # 8
Honolulu, HI 96817-4522
    808-536-2148
Fax: 808-526-0137
Seafood
Manager: Frank Goto

Estimated Sales: $20-50 Million
Number Employees: 50-99

13189 United Foods USA
23447 Cabot Blvd
Hayward, CA 94545-1665
    510-264-5850
Fax: 510-264-0938 www.ufiusa.com
Sauce, seasoning and dry mixes
Vice President: Hiro Aoki
aoki@sebbausa.com
Number Employees: 5-9

13190 United Intertrade Corporation
PO Box 821192
Houston, TX 77282-1192
    713-827-7799
Fax: 713-827-7881 800-969-2233
info@mitalenacoffee.com
www.mitalenacoffee.com
Processor and canner of green and roasted coffee beans
President: Bob Ajouz
VP: Misako Ajouz
Number Employees: 5-9
Square Footage: 40000
Type of Packaging: Private Label, Bulk
Brands:
    Bluebonnet
    Cafe Dontedro
    Cafe Orleans
    Cafe Unico
    Imperial Choice
    Mediterranean

13191 United Intratrade
1139 Brittmoore Rd
Houston, TX 77043-5003
    713-827-7799
Fax: 713-827-7881 713-827-7799
info@mitalenacoffee.com
www.mitalenacoffee.com
Coffee
President: Misako Ajouz
majouz@donpedrocoffee.com
VP/CFO: Misako Ajouz

Food Manufacturers / A-Z

Estimated Sales: $1 Million
Number Employees: 5-9
Type of Packaging: Private Label
Brands:
- Bluebonnet Coffee
- Cafe Don Pedro
- Cafe Orleans-Coffee
- Cafe Unico-Espresso
- Divian Coffee
- Diwan Coffee
- Imperial Choice Coff
- Mediterranean Coffee
- Mitalena Coffee
- Unico

13192 United Juice Companies of America
505 66th Ave. SW.
Vero Beach, FL 32968
772-562-5442
Fax: 888-562-9229 dan@unitedjuice.com
www.unitedjuice.com
Manufacturer of fresh squeezed and pasteurized juice.
President and CEO: Steve Bogen
COO: Marc Craen
VP of Food Service Sales: Dan Petry
Contact: Randy Plair
randy@lambethgroves.com
Type of Packaging: Private Label
Brands:
- Lambeth Groves
- Always Sweet
- Froze-Fresh
- Fresh Blendz

13193 United Marketing Exchange
215 Silver St
Delta, CO 81416-1517
970-874-3332
Fax: 970-874-9525
Processor and exporter of fresh fruits and onions
President: Harold Broughton
Sales Manager: Mike Gibson
mike@umefruit.com
Estimated Sales: $1089000
Number Employees: 1-4
Parent Co: Hi Quality Packing
Type of Packaging: Consumer
Brands:
- Burrow
- Owl
- Tom-Tom

13194 United Meat Company
1040 Bryant St.
San Francisco, CA 94103
415-864-2118
Fax: 415-703-9061
Manufacturer, exporter, and importer of frozen portion controlled lamb, venison, veal and beef.
President: Phil Gee
Finance Executive: Bill Gee
Sales Executive: Leonard Gee
Contact: Philip Gee
philjr77@yahoo.com
Estimated Sales: $20-50 Million
Number Employees: 20-49
Square Footage: 19430
Type of Packaging: Food Service
Brands:
- Umc

13195 United Noodle Manufacturing Company
3077 S 300 W
Salt Lake City, UT 84116-3414
801-485-0951
Chinese noodles and fortune cookies
Owner: Rufus Spraug
Estimated Sales: $$1-2.5 Million
Number Employees: 1-4
Type of Packaging: Consumer, Food Service

13196 (HQ)United Pickles
4366 Park Ave
Bronx, NY 10457-2494
718-933-6060
Fax: 718-367-8522 picklebiz@aol.com
www.unitedpickle.com
Pickle, sauerkraut and relish maker.
Owner: Steve Leibowitz
sleibowitz@unitedpickle.com
Number Employees: 1-4
Type of Packaging: Consumer, Food Service, Bulk
Other Locations:
- United Pickle Products Corp.
  Rosenhayn NJ
Brands:
- Leibo
- Leibowitz
- Nathan's Famous
- Teddy's
- United
- United Brand
- Upco
- Upzo

13197 United Pies Of Elkhart Inc
1016 Middlebury St
Elkhart, IN 46516-4510
574-294-3419
Baked products including pies
President: Blanche Nichols
VP of Sales: Kari Nichols
Estimated Sales: $10 Million
Number Employees: 5-9
Type of Packaging: Consumer

13198 United Provision Meat Company
156 S Ohio Ave
Columbus, OH 43205
614-252-1126
Fax: 614-252-1127 unitedmeats@cs.com
Portion control meats including cooked prime rib, meatballs, meatloaf, beef roasts, pork roasts, london broil, chicken, turkey, geese, duck, cornish hens, sloppy joes and corned beef and pastrami
President: Allen Scott
Estimated Sales: $5 Million
Number Employees: 5-9
Square Footage: 48000
Type of Packaging: Food Service

13199 United Pulse Trading Inc
1611 E Century Ave # 102
Suite 102
Bismarck, ND 58503-0780
701-751-1623
Fax: 701-751-1626 info@uspulses.com
www.agtfoods.com
Red split lentils, yellow split peas, green split peas, chickpeas, laird/eston/richlea lentils, whole red lentils, kabuli chickpeas and split desi chickpeas
President/Owner: Murad Katib
CFO: Lory Island
VP: Gaepan Bourassa
Manager: Eric Bartsch
agtfoods@agtfoods.com
Estimated Sales: Less Than $500,000
Number Employees: 1-4

13200 United Salt Corp
4800 San Felipe St
Houston, TX 77056-3908
713-877-2600
Fax: 713-877-2609 800-554-8658
uscinfo@tum.us www.unitedsalt.com
Processor and exporter of salt including plain, iodized, agricultural and water conditioning
President: Jim O'Donnell
VP: Theresa Feldman
Contact: Ashley Baker
abaker@aquasalt.com
Estimated Sales: $16,100,000
Number Employees: 10-19
Parent Co: Texas United Corporation
Type of Packaging: Consumer, Food Service, Private Label, Bulk
Brands:
- Flavor House
- Gulf
- Ranch House

13201 United Supermarkets
2206 114th St
Lubbock, TX 79423-7235
806-745-9667
Fax: 806-745-9653 praterscontact@praters.com
www.praters.com
Smoked meats, breadings, frozen entrees, stuffings, gravies and casseroles
Owner: Chip Chenowetch
Sales Manager: Benny Cousatte
Purchasing Manager: Daryl Halsey
Estimated Sales: $10-20 Million
Number Employees: 20-49
Type of Packaging: Consumer

13202 United Valley Bell Dairy
508 Roane St
Charleston, WV 25302-2091
304-344-2511
Fax: 304-344-2518
Fluid milk
Manager: John Duty
Marketing Director: Halan Varley
Estimated Sales: Less than $500,000
Number Employees: 100-249
Type of Packaging: Private Label

13203 United With Earth
2833-7th St.
Berkeley, CA 94710
510-210-4359
Fax: 510-984-0538 www.unitedwithearth.com
Medjool dates, coconut and almond date rolls, pitted dates, California golden figs, Mission figs, Persian cucumbers
Number of Brands: 1
Type of Packaging: Consumer, Private Label, Bulk
Brands:
- United With Earth

13204 Universal Beef Products
3511 Canal St
Houston, TX 77003-1835
713-224-6043
Fax: 713-224-0716 www.universalbeef.net
Beef products
President: Neil Brody
Estimated Sales: $2.5-5 000,000
Number Employees: 20-49

13205 Universal Beverages Inc
10033 Sawgrass Dr W # 202
Ponte Vedra Bch, FL 32082-3550
904-280-7795
Fax: 904-280-7794 ubisyfocorp@aol.com
www.syfobeverages.com
Processor and exporter of bottled water including purified and sodium free; also, regular and flavored seltzer and naturally sparkling water
CEO: Jonathan Moore
Plant Manager: Justin Jones
Estimated Sales: $$2.5-5 Million
Number Employees: 20-49
Square Footage: 400000
Parent Co: Universal Beverages Holding Corporation
Type of Packaging: Consumer, Food Service, Private Label
Brands:
- Syfo

13206 (HQ)Universal Beverages Inc
3301 W Main St
Leesburg, FL 34748-9714
352-315-1010
Fax: 352-315-1009
Bottled water
Manager: Justin Jones
universalbeverages@yahoo.com
Site Manager: Justin Jones
Estimated Sales: $1.6 Million
Number Employees: 10-19
Type of Packaging: Private Label
Brands:
- 100% Purified Non Carbonated Water
- Naturally Flavored S
- Syfo Brand Original

13207 Universal Formulas
7136 E N Ave
Kalamazoo, MI 49048-9758
269-373-2930
Fax: 616-383-3449 800-342-6960
Enzymes, minerals and herbs. Founded in 1984.
President: Ralf Ostertag
CEO: Andrew Bruex
andrew@ilconline.com
Estimated Sales: $$2.5-5 Million
Number Employees: 5-9

13208 Universal Impex Corporation
780 Fenmar Drive
Toronto, ON M9L 2T9
Canada
416-743-7778
info@universalimpexcorp.com
www.universalimpexcorp.com

Food Manufacturers / A-Z

Seasonings and spices, sugars, baking products, flavors, fruit jams, condiments, sauces, marinades and dips, sweeteners, drinks (sodas, nectars, energy drink), coconut oil, coconut milk and plantain chips.
Operations Manager: Paul Bridgemohan
Estimated Sales: $5.7 Million
Number Employees: 15
Brands:
   British Class
   Cool Runnings
   Mekong

13209 Universal Nutrition
3 Terminal Rd
New Brunswick, NJ 08901
732-545-3130
Fax: 732-509-0458 800-872-0101
info@universalusa.com
Bodybuilding supplements including aminos, bars, fat burners, joint support, proteins, vitamins, and minerals
President: Danny Keller
VP: Robert Gluckin
Chief Sales & Marketing Officer: Tim Tantum
Chief Creative & Strategy Officer: Phil K
Product Director: Jason Budsock
Year Founded: 1977
Number Employees: 250-499

13210 Universal Poultry Company
1769 Old West Broad Street
Athens, GA 30606-2867
706-546-6767
Fax: 706-546-6790
Poultry
Manager: Robert Harris
Estimated Sales: $500,000-$1 000,000
Number Employees: 5-9

13211 Universal Preservachem Inc
60 Jiffy Rd
Somerset, NJ 08873-3438
732-568-1266
Fax: 732-568-9040 mravitz@upichem.com
www.upichem.com
Wholesaler/distributor of chemicals and ingredients. Vitamins sweeteners preservatives, antioxidants, acidulants, etc
Chairman of the Board: Herbert Ravitz
President: Dan Ravitz
Vice President: Michael Ravitz
Manager: Daniel Ravitz
dan@upichem.com
Estimated Sales: Less Than $500,000
Number Employees: 10-19
Square Footage: 240000
Type of Packaging: Private Label, Bulk

13212 Unna Bakery
1510 Lexington Ave
Apt 17E
New York, NY 10029-7171
917-543-8133
ulrika@unnabakery.com
www.unnabakery.com
Cookies
Founder & CEO: Ulrika Pettersson
Year Founded: 2015
Estimated Sales: Under $500,000
Number Employees: 1-4
Brands:
   UNNA

13213 Up Mountain Switchel
295 Clinton Ave
Apt F14
Brooklyn, NY 11205-4747
315-939-3085
switcheldrink@gmail.com
drinkswitchel.com
Nutritious beverage
Co-Founder: Ely Key
Co-Founder: Garrett Riffle
Number Employees: 2-10
Brands:
   Up Mountain Switchel

13214 Upcountry Fisheries
85 Kino Pl
Makawao, HI 96768-8891
808-871-8484
Fax: 808-871-6071
Seafood
Owner: Richard Samsing
Estimated Sales: $.5-1 million
Number Employees: 1-4

13215 Upper Crust Bakery USA
3655 W Washington St
Phoenix, AZ 85009-4759
602-255-0464
Fax: 602-255-0433 info@ucbakery.com
www.uppercrustbakeryusa.com
Baked goods including bread, rolls, pastries, cakes, croissants, muffins, and danishes
Chairman & CEO: Tab Navidi
Sales/Marketing: Pat Navidi
Year Founded: 1980
Estimated Sales: $20-50 Million
Number Employees: 10-249
Square Footage: 130000
Type of Packaging: Private Label

13216 Upper Crust Biscotti
P.O.Box 203
Pismo Beach, CA 93448-203
800-676-1691
Fax: 805-543-1284 866-972-6879
uppercrustbiscotti@worldpantry.com
Flavored regular and tiny biscotti, cookies and crostini
Owner: Terez Tyni
President: Tracey Amuiller
Estimated Sales: $500,000-$1Million
Number Employees: 11
Square Footage: 18000
Brands:
   Itty-Bittie Biscotti
   Itty-Bittie Cookies
   Upper Crust Biscotti

13217 Upstate Farms
25 Anderson Rd
Buffalo, NY 14225
716-896-3156
foodservice@upstatefarms.com
upstatefarms.com
Dairy products, including yogurt and sour cream.
Chief Executive Officer: Larry Webster
Chief Operating Officer: Joe Duscher
Number Employees: 10-19
Parent Co: Upstate Niagara Cooperative Inc.
Type of Packaging: Consumer

13218 Upstate Niagara Co-Op Inc.
25 Anderson Rd.
Buffalo, NY 14225
716-892-3156
Fax: 716-892-3157 emailus@upstateniagara.com
www.upstateniagara.com
Dairy products including; milk, cream, flavored milks, butter, egg nog, yogurt, orange juice, iced tea, lemonade.
CEO: Larry Webster
CFO: Edward Luongo
Chief Operating Officer: Lawrence Webster
Year Founded: 1965
Estimated Sales: $719 Million
Number Employees: 500-999
Number of Brands: 5
Square Footage: 12468
Type of Packaging: Consumer, Food Service, Private Label, Bulk
Other Locations:
   Fluid Milk Processing Plant
   Buffalo NY
   Fluid Milk Processing Plant
   Rochester NY
   Distribution Center
   Syracuse NY
   Cultured Product Processing Plant
   Seneca NY
   Cultured Product/North Country
   North Lawrence NY
   O-At-Ka Milk Products Coop
   Batavia NY
Brands:
   Upstate Farms
   Intense Flavored Milks
   Bison
   Valley Farms
   Milk For Life

13219 Uptime Energy, Inc.
7930 Alabama Ave.
Canoga Park, CA 91304
www.uptimeenergy.com
Energy drink with caffeine, coenzyme Q10, Ginkgo Biloba and ginseng; capsules also available
Chief Executive Officer: Benjamin Kim
Year Founded: 1985
Number Employees: 10-50
Number of Brands: 1
Type of Packaging: Consumer, Private Label
Brands:
   Uptime

13220 Upton's Naturals
2054 West Grand Ave.
Chicago, IL 60612
info@uptonsnaturals.com
www.uptonsnaturals.com
Pre-packaged, marinated jackfruit and seitan; prepared vegan side dishes
Co-Founder: Nicole Sopko
Year Founded: 2006
Number of Brands: 1
Number of Products: 19
Type of Packaging: Consumer, Private Label
Brands:
   Upton's Naturals

13221 Uptown Bakers
5335 Kilmer Pl
Hyattsville, MD 20781-1034
301-864-1500
Fax: 301-864-7744 info@uptownbakers.com
www.uptownbakers.com
European pastries and breads including scones, cinnamon bread, muffins, cookies, danish and cakes rolls
Owner: Michael Mc Cloud
orders@uptownbakers.com
CFO: Elliot Person
Estimated Sales: $13.4million
Number Employees: 100-249
Type of Packaging: Consumer, Food Service

13222 Urban Accents
4241 N Ravenswood Ave
Suite 1
Chicago, IL 60613-1199
773-528-9515
Fax: 773-528-9533 877-872-7742
mail@urbanaccents.com www.urbanaccents.com
Snack crackers and distinctive spices
President: Tom Knibbs
info@urbanaccents.com
Vice President: Jim Dygas
Estimated Sales: Below $5 Million
Number Employees: 5-9
Type of Packaging: Private Label
Brands:
   Bloody Mary Blend

13223 Urban Foods LLC
PO Box 302
Sacramento, CA 95691
916-372-3663
info@urbanfoods.com
www.urbanfoods.com
All natural, gluten-free superfood snack bites and flavored seed blends
Co-Founder: Greg Durst
Co-Founder: Regan Durst
Year Founded: 2016
Number of Brands: 1
Number of Products: 8
Type of Packaging: Consumer, Private Label
Brands:
   Urban Foods

13224 Urban Moonshine
Burlington, VT
802-428-4707
customerservice@urbanmoonshine.com
www.urbanmoonshine.com
Herbal supplements and bitters
Founder/Chief Executive Officer: Jovial King
Director, Sales: Megan Foster
Chief Operating Officer: Lexie Donovan
Year Founded: 2008
Number of Brands: 1
Type of Packaging: Consumer, Private Label
Brands:
   Urban Moonshine

Food Manufacturers / A-Z

13225 Urban Oven
2431 N Arizona Ave
Suite 4
Chandler, AZ 85225-1391
480-921-2476
Fax: 480-921-2477 866-770-6836
gene@urbanoven.com www.urbanoven.com
Crackers
Owner: Gene Williams
gene@urbanoven.com
Director of Sales: Patty Clark
Number Employees: 10-19

13226 Urgasa
2655 S Le Jeune Rd.
Suite 810
Coral Gables, FL 33134
786-543-6693
sales@urgasa.us
urgasa.us
Quail meat and eggs
Director: David Lourenco
Brands:
 URGASA

13227 Ursula's Island Farms Company
6321 Corgiat Drive S
Suite A
Seattle, WA 98108-2862
206-762-3113
Fax: 206-762-0658
Dried fruit
Owner: Ursula Blackburn

13228 Us Spice Mill Inc
4537 W Fulton St
Chicago, IL 60624-1609
773-378-6800
Fax: 773-378-0077 www.usspice.com
Manufacturer and importer of spices
President: Nick Patel
usspice@gmail.com
Estimated Sales: $600000
Number Employees: 5-9

13229 Utah Coffee Roasters
2375 S West Temple
South Salt Lake, UT 84115-2633
801-486-3334
Fax: 801-486-9714 888-486-3334
www.silverbeancoffee.com
The largest coffee roaster in Utah. We also produce; hot cocoa mixes, powder coffee creamers and powdered shake mixes
Owner: Dave Brog
dave@brog.com
Sales/Marketing Manager/EVP: Anton Broq
Estimated Sales: $500,000-$1 Million
Number Employees: 10-19

13230 Utzy, Inc.
PO Box 248
Lake Geneva, WI 53147
877-307-6142
care@utzy.com www.utzy.com
Herbal wellness supplements
Director, Digital Marketing: Daniel Powers
Year Founded: 2016
Number Employees: 2-10
Number of Brands: 1
Type of Packaging: Consumer, Private Label
Brands:
 Utzy Naturals

13231 Uvalde Meat Processing
508 S Wood St
Uvalde, TX 78801-5653
830-278-6247
Fax: 830-278-6245
Sausage, venison, goat, beef, lamb and pork; also, game birds; slaughtering services available
Owner: Heather Mock
hmock@twu.edu
VP/Co-Owner: Gail Jackowski
Estimated Sales: $1-3 Million
Number Employees: 10-19

13232 V & E Kohnstamm Inc
882 3rd Ave # 7
Brooklyn, NY 11232-1902
718-788-1776
Fax: 718-768-3978 800-847-4500
flavorinfo@virginiadare.com
www.virginiadare.com
Flavors, masking agents, bases, extracts, vanilla, orange oils and colors
President: Howard Smith Jr
VP Finance: Bobby Corcoran
VP Research Dev/Quality Assurance: Michael Springsteen
VP Operations: Frederic Thor
Year Founded: 1835
Estimated Sales: $21100000
Number Employees: 100-249
Type of Packaging: Private Label, Bulk
Brands:
 Veko

13233 V & V Supremo
2141 S Throop St
Chicago, IL 60608
Fax: 888-301-2244 888-887-8773
customerrelations@vvsupremo.com
www.vvsupremo.com
Cheddar cheeses
President: Gilberto Villaseñor II
VP of Marketing: Anne Marie Splitstone
Estimated Sales: $60 Million
Number Employees: 160
Number of Brands: 6
Parent Co: V & V Supremo Foods

13234 V Chocolates
440 Lawndale Dr
Salt Lake City, UT 84101
801-269-8444
Fax: 801-269-8449 vmail@vchocolates.com
www.vchocolates.com
Chocolates
Contact: Mark B Nelson
nelson@vchocolates.com
Number Employees: 12

13235 V L Foods
70 W Red Oak Lane
White Plains, NY 10604-3602
914-697-4851
Fax: 914-697-4888
President: Paul Pruzan
Brands:
 Piccadeli

13236 V Sattui Winery
1111 White Ln
St Helena, CA 94574-1599
707-963-7774
Fax: 707-963-4324 info@vsattui.com
www.vsattui.com
Manufacturer of fine wines
President: Tom Davies
Director of Winemaking: Brooks Painter
Year Founded: 1882
Estimated Sales: G
Number Employees: 100-249
Type of Packaging: Consumer

13237 V.W. Joyner & Company
PO Box 387
Smithfield, VA 23431-0387
757-357-2161
Fax: 757-357-0184
Processor and exporter of smoked cured country hams, picnics and bacon for distribution to wholesale, retail and restaurant markets
VP/General Manager: Larry Santure
Plant Manager: R Howell
Number Employees: 10-19
Square Footage: 160000
Parent Co: Smithfield Companies
Type of Packaging: Consumer, Food Service, Private Label, Bulk
Brands:
 Joyner's
 Red Eye Country Picnic
 V.W. Joyner Genuine Smithfield

13238 VCPB Transportation
600 Meadowlands Pkwy # 138
Secaucus, NJ 07094-1637
201-770-0070
Fax: 201-770-0102 info@vcpbtrans.com
www.vcpbtrans.com
Importers and distributors of a wide range of food ingredients, supplying food manufacturers, bakeries and food service companies throughout the USA
Owner: Fredric Israel
fisrael@vcpbtrans.com
Number Employees: 5-9
Type of Packaging: Food Service, Bulk

13239 VIP Food Svc
74 Hobron Ave
Kahului, HI 96732-2106
808-877-5055
Fax: 808-877-4960 www.vipfoodservice.com
Foodservice distributor on Hawaiian island of Maui with two stores that are also open to the public.
President: Nelson Okumura
Contact: Brian Tokeshi
btokeshi@vipfoodservice.com
Number Employees: 5-9
Type of Packaging: Consumer, Food Service

13240 (HQ)VIP Foods
1080 Wyckoff Ave
Flushing, NY 11385
718-821-5330
Fax: 718-497-7110 vipfoods@aol.com
Processor and exporter of soups, instant lunches, low-calorie sweeteners and mixes including dessert, pasta, tea, hot chocolate, pasta, pudding, cake and cake mixes, sauce and chicken coating
Owner: Mendel Freund
Sales Manager: Esther Freund
esther@vipfoodsinc.com
Estimated Sales: $10-20 Million
Number Employees: 20-49
Square Footage: 90000
Type of Packaging: Consumer, Food Service, Private Label, Bulk
Brands:
 Kojel
 Minute Lunch
 Soup Bowl
 Vip

13241 VIP Sales Company
2395 American Ave
Hayward, CA 94545
918-252-5791
Fax: 918-254-1667 866-536-8008
sbeck@vipfoods.com www.vipfoods.com
Packer and exporter of frozen fruits, vegetables and Chinese entrees and prepared foods; importer of raspberries, blueberries and broccoli
President: Guy Lewis
Sr. VP/COO: Lee Turman
VP Sales/Marketing: Steve Beck
Public Relations: Mick Lewis
Plant Manager: Don Avera
VP Purchasing: Fred Meyer
Estimated Sales: $5900000
Number Employees: 30
Number of Brands: 5
Number of Products: 180
Type of Packaging: Consumer, Food Service, Private Label, Bulk
Brands:
 Basic Value
 Food Pac
 Food Trend
 Tai Pan
 Vip

13242 VLR Food Corporation
610 Oster Lane
Vaughan, ON L4K 2B9
Canada
905-669-0700
Fax: 905-669-9829 800-387-7437
Phylo dough, puff dough, vegetarian entrees, kosher products, hors doeuvres
General Manager: Jean-Marie Ouellette
Vice President: Rhys Quin
Estimated Sales: $21 Million
Number Employees: 250
Number of Brands: 3
Number of Products: 20
Type of Packaging: Food Service
Brands:
 Jonathan T.
 Tgf

13243 VOD Gourmet
3 Stormy Circle
PO Box 4922
Greenwich, CT 6830
203-531-5172
Fax: 203-532-4883 ulla@vodkacheese.com
Swedish cheese with peppercorn vodka, juniper berries, pre-cooked/frozen
Founder: Ulla Nylin

Food Manufacturers / A-Z

Estimated Sales: $130,000
Number Employees: 1-4
Type of Packaging: Private Label, Bulk
Brands:
  Vod

13244 Vacaville Fruit Co
2055 Cessna Dr # 200
Vacaville, CA 95688-8838
707-447-1085
Fax: 707-447-1085 info@vacavillefruit.com
www.vacavillefruit.com
Processor importer and exporter of kosher dried fruit and fruit pastes; serving the food service market
President: Richard Nola
HR Executive: Nichole Nolz
info@vacavillefruit.com
Director Sales/Marketing: Nicole Nola
Plant Superintendent: Gary De La Rosa
Estimated Sales: $4200000
Number Employees: 50-99
Type of Packaging: Consumer, Food Service, Bulk

13245 Val Verde Winery
100 Qualia Dr
Del Rio, TX 78840-7697
830-775-9714
Fax: 830-775-5394 www.valverdewinery.com
Wines
Owner: Thomas Qualia
Operations Manager: Thomas Qualia
Estimated Sales: $300,000
Number Employees: 1-4
Type of Packaging: Private Label
Brands:
  Val Verde Winery

13246 Val's Seafood
3437 Winford Drive
Mobile, AL 36619-4309
251-639-2570
Fax: 251-639-1198
Seafood
President: Val Hammond
Estimated Sales: $632,000
Number Employees: 1-4

13247 Valdez Food Inc
1815 N 2nd St
Philadelphia, PA 19122-2305
215-634-6106
Fax: 215-634-8645
Chinese food products including wonton soup, chow mein, fish cakes, shrim, egg & pizza rolls.
Owner: Perfecto Valdez
Treasurer: Juanito Valdez
Estimated Sales: $500,000-$1 Million
Number Employees: 10-19
Square Footage: 9000
Type of Packaging: Consumer

13248 Valentine Chemicals
129 Valentine Dr
Lockport, LA 70374-3969
985-532-2541
Fax: 985-532-6806 www.valentinechemicals.com
Sugar
President: Hugh Caffery
hugh@valentinechemicals.com
Estimated Sales: $500,000-$1 Million
Number Employees: 20-49
Type of Packaging: Consumer
Brands:
  Valentine Sugars

13249 Valentine Enterprises Inc
1291 Progress Center Ave
Lawrenceville, GA 30043-4801
770-995-0661
Fax: 770-995-0725 info-sales@veiusa.com
www.veiusa.com
Powdered products including diet meal replacements, protein, fiber, sport fitness products, lecithin granules, etc
President & CEO: Alan Smith
Estimated Sales: $30 Million
Number Employees: 100-249
Square Footage: 50000

13250 Valhalla Winery
23785 Highway 126
Veneta, OR 97487-9101
541-935-9711
info@valhallawinery.com
www.valhallawinery.com
Winery; recently rebranded from Domaine Meriwether.
Owner: Eric Norman
Owner: Lori Norman
Estimated Sales: $160 Thousand
Number Employees: 1-4
Number of Brands: 1
Type of Packaging: Consumer, Food Service
Brands:
  Valhalla Winery

13251 Valhrona
1801 Avenue of the Stars
Suite 600
Los Angeles, CA 90067-5908
310-277-0401
Fax: 310-277-7304
Candy and baking chocolate
President: Bernard Duclos
Founder: Monsieur Guironnet
Estimated Sales: $300,000-500,000
Number Employees: 1-4
Type of Packaging: Private Label
Brands:
  Valrhona

13252 Valley Bakery
4058 Hastings Street
Burnaby, BC V5C 2H9
Canada
604-291-0674
valleybakery@shaw.ca
Cookies, breads, rolls and pastries
Owner: Ted Triezenberg
Estimated Sales: $150,000
Number Employees: 20-49
Type of Packaging: Consumer

13253 Valley Farms LLC
1860 E 3rd St
Williamsport, PA 17701
570-326-2021
Fax: 570-326-2736 www.valleyfarmsdairy.com
Milk
Chief Executive Officer: Larry Webster
Chief Operating Officer: Joe Duscher
Year Founded: 1962
Parent Co: Upstate Niagara Cooperative Inc
Type of Packaging: Consumer, Private Label

13254 Valley Fig Growers
2028 S 3rd St
Fresno, CA 93702-4156
559-237-3893
Fax: 559-237-3898 info@valleyfig.com
www.valleyfig.com
Fig growers cooperative exports dried figs worldwide.
President: Gary Jue
gjue@valleyfig.com
CFO: Jim Gargiulo
Operations Manager: Darin Ciotti
Number Employees: 50-99
Type of Packaging: Consumer, Food Service, Private Label, Bulk
Brands:
  Blue Ribbon Orchard Choice
  Sun-Maid

13255 Valley Grain Products
3599 W Menlo Avenue
Fresno, CA 93711-0854
559-675-3400
Fax: 559-675-0723
Corn flour, tortilla chips and taco shells
Manager: Barry Runyon
Number Employees: 2

13256 Valley Lahvosh
502 M St
Fresno, CA 93721-3013
559-485-0173
Fax: 559-485-0173 800-480-2704
customerservice@valleylahvosh.com
www.valleylahvosh.com
Crackerbreads, wraps and flatbreads
Owner: Rikki Aidoo
Vice President: Agnes Saghatelian
Marketing Coordinator: Jenni Bonsignore
Sales Director: Chip Muse
rikkia@valleylahvosh.com
Operations Manager: Danny Olosa
Production Manager: Brian Sperling
Estimated Sales: $3877239
Number Employees: 20-49
Number of Products: 33
Square Footage: 160000
Type of Packaging: Consumer, Food Service
Brands:
  Calley Lahvosh
  Hearts
  Lahvosh
  Round Lahvosh
  Soft Square
  Stone Street
  Valley Bakery
  Valley Lahvosh Crackerbread
  Valley Lahvosh Flatbread
  Valley Wraps

13257 Valley Meat Company
217 Daly Ave
Modesto, CA 95354
209-544-8950
Fax: 209-522-5892 800-222-6328
Hamburger patties and ground beef
Owner, Chief Executive Officer: Russell Heffner
Estimated Sales: $10 Million
Number Employees: 20-49
Type of Packaging: Consumer, Food Service, Bulk

13258 Valley Meats
2302 1st St
PO Box 69
Coal Valley, IL 61240-9408
309-517-6639
Fax: 309-799-7633 info@valleymeatsllc.com
www.valleymeatsllc.com
Fresh and frozen steaks, pork chops, beef patties, ground beef, pork and veal products; also, breaded beef, pork, chicken and veal
President: Sandy Belshouse
belshouse@valleymeatsllc.com
Regional Manager: Adam Jobe
Quality Assurance Manager: Sandy Belshause
VP Sales/Marketing: Randy Ehrlich
Regional Manager: Adam Jobe
Estimated Sales: $1.3 Million
Number Employees: 50-99
Type of Packaging: Consumer, Food Service

13259 Valley Milk Products
412 E King St
Strasburg, VA 22657
540-465-5113
Fax: 540-645-4042
Milk and specialty dried food ingredients
President: Don Utz
CFO: Jeff Mank
Estimated Sales: $10-24.9 000,000
Number Employees: 35

13260 Valley Queen Cheese Factory
200 E Railway Ave
Milbank, SD 57252-1813
605-432-4563
Fax: 605-432-9383 cheese@vqcheese.com
www.vqcheese.com
Whey and cheese
CEO: Mark Leddy
mleddy@vqcheese.com
Co-CEO: Dave Gonzenbach
Vice President: Max Gozenbach
Quality Control: Jody Kuper
Plant Engineer: Dave Gozenbach
Operations Manager: Lance Johnson
Estimated Sales: $10-20 Million
Number Employees: 100-249
Type of Packaging: Consumer
Brands:
  Valley Queen

13261 Valley Sun Products Inc
3324 Orestimba Rd
Newman, CA 95360
Fax: 209-862-1100 800-426-5444
ranaya@valleysun.com www.valleysun.com
Sun-dried tomatoes, plain and in oil

Food Manufacturers / A-Z

Office Manager, HR & Administration: Rosie Anaya
ranaya@valleysun.com
Quality Assurance: Yolanda Padilla
Sales: Robert Young
Operations & Sales: Cesar Corona
Production Supervisor: Frank Lua
Estimated Sales: $11 Million
Number Employees: 250-499
Square Footage: 25000
Type of Packaging: Consumer, Food Service, Private Label, Bulk

13262 Valley Tea & Coffee
1101 W Valley Blvd Ste 103
Alhambra, CA 91803
        626-281-5799
      Fax: 626-281-5799
Tea and coffee
Manager: Ted Lee
CEO: Ted Lin
Estimated Sales: Under $300,000
Number Employees: 1-4
Type of Packaging: Food Service

13263 Valley View Blueberries
21717 NE 68th St
Vancouver, WA 98682-9060
        360-892-2839
      valley.view@comcast.net
Dried blueberries and strawberries, jams, syrups, glazes, honeys, trail mixes, pancake and corn bread mixes and chocolate covered blueberries; also, no-sugar products available
President: Vicki Duchesneau
valley.view@comcast.net
Estimated Sales: $86,000
Number Employees: 1-4
Square Footage: 8000
Type of Packaging: Consumer, Food Service, Private Label, Bulk
Brands:
 Valley View Blueberries

13264 Valley View Cheese Co Inc
6028 Route 62
Conewango Valley, NY 14726-9730
        716-296-5821
  Fax: 716-296-5822 www.valleyviewcheese.com
Cheese
President: Rick Binder
Marketing Manager: Linda Bates
Plant Manager: Linda Bates
Estimated Sales: Less Than $500,000
Number Employees: 5-9
Brands:
 Valley View Cheese

13265 Valley View Packing Co
7547 Sawtelle Ave
PO Box 3540
Yuba City, CA 95991-9514
        530-673-7356
  Fax: 530-673-9432 info@sacramentopacking.com
      www.valleyviewfoods.com
Manufacturer and exporter of dried fruits and fruit juices and concentrates
Owner: Dennis Serger
serger@valleyviewpacking.com
Estimated Sales: $17 Million
Number Employees: 10-19
Type of Packaging: Consumer, Food Service, Private Label, Bulk

13266 Valley View Winery
1000 Upper Applegate Rd
Jacksonville, OR 97530-9175
        541-899-8468
    Fax: 541-899-8468 800-781-9463
      www.valleyviewwinery.com
Wines
President: Mark Wisnovsky
CFO: Mark Wisnovsky
Vice President: Michael Wisnovsky
Estimated Sales: Less Than $500,000
Number Employees: 1-4
Type of Packaging: Private Label
Brands:
 Anna Maria
 Valley View

13267 Valley of the Moon Winery
P.O.Box 1951
Glen Ellen, CA 95442
        707-996-6941
      Fax: 707-996-5809
luna@valleyofthemoonwinery.com
www.valleyofthemoonwinery.com
Wines
Manager: Randy Meyer
Marketing Manager: Paul Young
President: Harold Duncan
Production Manager: Pat Henderson
Estimated Sales: $10-20 Million
Number Employees: 20-49
Brands:
 Valley of the Moon

13268 Vallos Baking Co
1800 Broadway
Bethlehem, PA 18015-3802
        610-866-1012
      Fax: 610-866-1012
Bread, donuts and rolls
Owner: Tina Hanushack
Co-Owner: Gus Skoutelas
Estimated Sales: $10-20 000,000
Number Employees: 10-19
Type of Packaging: Consumer, Food Service

13269 Van Der Heyden Vineyards
4057 Silverado Trl
Napa, CA 94558-1113
        707-257-0130
    Fax: 707-257-3311 800-948-9463
Wine
Manager: Andrea Vander Heyede
Estimated Sales: $1-2.5 Million
Number Employees: 1-4
Type of Packaging: Private Label
Brands:
 Van Der Heyden

13270 Van Drunen Farms
300 W 6th St
Momence, IL 60954-1136
        815-472-3100
  Fax: 815-472-3850 sales@vandrunen.com
      www.vandrunenfarms.com
Manufacturer of fruit, vegetable and herb ingredients.
President: Edward Van Drunen
evandrunen@vandrunen.com
Sales Manager: Irv Dorn
Estimated Sales: $25-100 Million
Number Employees: 50-99
Type of Packaging: Consumer, Food Service, Private Label, Bulk
Brands:
 Van Drunen Farms

13271 Van Dyke Ice Cream
145 Ackerman Ave
Ridgewood, NJ 07450-4205
        201-444-1429
      www.vandykes.com
Ice cream, frozen desserts and novelty
Owner: Demetrios Kotrokas
Estimated Sales: $2.5-5 000,000
Number Employees: 10-19

13272 Van Eeghen International Inc
750 Rue Gougeon
St Laurent, QC H4T 4L54
Canada
        514-332-6455
    Fax: 514-332-6475 www.vaneeghen.com
Dehydrated vegetables, culinary herbs and spices.
Director: Willem Van Eeghen
Account Manager: Tim Dias
Estimated Sales: $5 Million
Number Employees: 31
Square Footage: 20904

13273 Van Hees Gmbh
2500 Regency Pkwy
Cary, NC 27518-8549
        919-654-6862
  Fax: 919-654-6864 info@vanheesinc.com
      www.van-hees.com
Premier manufacturer of functional ingredients tailored specifically to the meat industry.
President: W.D. (Dave) Pierce
Dir. of Technical Sales: Deanna Hofing
Contact: Frank Averta
faverta@vanheesinc.com
Parent Co: VAN HEES GmbH
Brands:
 Bombal
 Zartin
 Sominus

13274 Van Leer Chocolate Corporation
600 W Chicago Ave.
Suite 860
Chicago, IL 60654
        201-798-8080
    Fax: 201-798-0138 800-225-1418
      www.vanleerchocolate.com
Chocolate for baking, compounds, fountains, sugar-free, glazes and ice creams
Manager: Scott Applegate
CFO: Anthony Forns
Operations Manager: Robert Mohn
Plant Manager: Tom Jones
Year Founded: 1949
Estimated Sales: $25-49.9 Million
Number Employees: 100-249

13275 Van Leeuwen
56 Dobbin St
Brooklyn, NY 11222-3110
        718-701-1630
    hello@vanleeuwenicecream.com
     www.vanleeuwenicecream.com
Ice cream and sobert
Co-Founder: Laura O'Neill
Co-Founder: Benjamin Van Leeuwen
Co-Founder: Peter Van Leeuwen
Wholesale Manager: Matt McKenna
Year Founded: 2008
Number Employees: 8
Type of Packaging: Consumer, Food Service

13276 Van Oriental Food Inc
4828 Reading St
Dallas, TX 75247-6705
        214-630-0111
  Fax: 214-630-0473 feedback@vaneggrolls.com
      www.vaneggrolls.com
Frozen foods including regular and low-fat egg rolls, fried wontons, crab rangoon, enchiladas, burritos and spring rolls
President: Kimberly Nguyen
Co-Owner: Gretchen Perrenot
Corporate Treasurer: Theresa Motter
Sales Manager: Carl Motter
Contact: David Duval
david@vanfoods.com
Plant Engineer: Apollo Nguyen
Estimated Sales: $8.9 Million
Number Employees: 10-19
Square Footage: 224000
Type of Packaging: Consumer, Food Service, Private Label, Bulk

13277 Van Otis Chocolates
341 Elm St
Manchester, NH 03101-2708
        603-668-1603
    Fax: 603-627-0781 800-826-6847
      www.vanotis.com
Chocolates
Owner: Mark Amiet
Co-Owner: Frank Bettencourt
Estimated Sales: Less Than $500,000
Number Employees: 1-4
Square Footage: 80000
Type of Packaging: Private Label
Brands:
 Foiled Chocolate
 Swiss Fudge Sampler Tier
 Van Otis Swiss Fudge

13278 Van Peenans Dairy
978 Valley Rd
Wayne, NJ 07470-2997
        973-694-2551
      Fax: 973-696-3854
Dairy
Owner: Tunis Van Peenan
Estimated Sales: $5-10 000,000
Number Employees: 20-49

1211

Food Manufacturers / A-Z

13279 Van Roy Coffee Co
4569 Spring Rd
Cleveland, OH 44131-1023
216-749-7069
Fax: 216-749-7039 877-826-7669
www.vanroycoffee.com
Roasted coffee and tea; also, spices
President: Jeff Miller
jeffm@vanroycoffee.com
Vice President: John Schanz
Estimated Sales: $1,400,000
Number Employees: 10-19
Square Footage: 152000
Type of Packaging: Food Service, Private Label, Bulk
Brands:
 De-Kaffo
 Van Roy

13280 Van Tone Creative
200 Metro Dr
Terrell, TX 75160-9169
972-563-2600
Fax: 972-563-2640 800-856-0802
Food, ice cream, bakers, dairy and beverage flavoring concentrates, food colors, slush concentrates and syrups including sno-cone, FCB, granita, smoothie, fruit drink and fountain
Vice President: Joe Gibbs
jgibbs@vantonecf.com
Vice President: Joe Gibbs
jgibbs@vantonecf.com
VP Marketing: Steve Myrlin
VP Sales: Joe Gibbs
Estimated Sales: $3494044
Number Employees: 20-49
Square Footage: 144000
Type of Packaging: Food Service, Private Label, Bulk
Brands:
 Allez
 Cyclone
 Van Tone

13281 Van Waters & Roger
PO Box 446
Summit, IL 60501-0446
708-728-6830
Fax: 708-728-6801
Distributor of chemicals and food ingredients
President: Terry Irvine
President: James Lacey
Chief Marketing Department: Mark Buntin
Head Sales Department: Mike Clary
Number Employees: 250-499
Brands:
 Van Waters & Roger

13282 Van de Kamps
Po Box 3900
Peoria, IL 61612
800-798-3318
www.vandekamps.com
Processor and exporter of pies, fish and vegetables
Plant Manager: James Frey
Number Employees: 100-249
Parent Co: Van de Kamps
Type of Packaging: Consumer, Food Service, Private Label
Brands:
 Van De Kamp

13283 Van's International Foods
20318 Gramercy Pl
Torrance, CA 90501
310-320-8611
Fax: 310-320-8805 customerservice@vansintl.com
Round, square, toaster, mini and jumbo frozen waffles including original, whole grain, wheat-free, organic and gluten-free
President: James Kelly
Sales Director: Kim Fernandez
Contact: Gus Conde
gus.conde@vansintl.com
Operations Manager: Frank Copenhaver
Estimated Sales: $4600000
Number Employees: 40
Square Footage: 40000
Type of Packaging: Private Label
Brands:
 Van's

13284 Van-Lang Food Products
5227 Dansher Rd
Countryside, IL 60525-3123
708-588-0800
Fax: 708-588-0801 info@vanlangfoods.com
Frozen hors d'oeuvres and appetizers
President: Hien Lam
Estimated Sales: Below $5 Million
Number Employees: 50-99
Type of Packaging: Food Service
Brands:
 Van-Lang

13285 Vana Life Foods
Seattle, WA 98104-2205
347-446-6504
info@vanalifefoods.com
www.vanalifefoods.com
Green chickpea-based, pre-packaged superfood bowls in various flavors
Founder/Chief Executive Officer: Krishan Walia
Year Founded: 2015
Number of Brands: 1
Number of Products: 4
Type of Packaging: Consumer, Private Label
Brands:
 Vana Life Foods

13286 (HQ)Vance's Foods
2129 Harrison St.
PO Box 627
San Francisco, CA 94110
800-497-4834
Fax: 800-497-4329 415-621-1171
info@vancesfoods.com
Processor and exporter of nondairy and fat-free potato-based milk substitutes including dry and liquid, and dry soy-based milk substitutes
President: Vance Abersold
VP: Glenn Abersold
Director Marketing: Frederick Mattos
Type of Packaging: Consumer, Food Service, Bulk
Brands:
 Notmilk
 Sno-E Tofu
 Vance's Darifree

13287 Vanco Trading Inc
50 Old Kings Hwy N # 101
Suite 101
Darien, CT 06820-4609
203-656-2800
Fax: 203-655-8307 www.vancotrading.com
Food chemicals and ingredients
Owner: J Vaneck
janvaneck@vancotrading.com
Estimated Sales: $500,000-$1 Million
Number Employees: 1-4
Brands:
 Quinine

13288 Vancouver Island Brewing Company
2330 Government Street
Victoria, BC V8T 5G5
Canada
250-361-0007
Fax: 250-360-0336 800-663-6383
www.vanislandbrewery.com
Brewer of lager and ale
President: Barry Fisher
General Manager: Jim Dodds
Number Employees: 20-49
Square Footage: 112000
Parent Co: Island Pacific Brewing Company
Type of Packaging: Consumer
Brands:
 Blonde Ale
 Hermann's Dark Lager
 Hermannator Ice Bock
 Piper's Pale Ale
 Vancouver Islander Lager
 Victoria Lager
 Wolf's Scottish Cream Ale

13289 Vande Walle's Candies Inc
400 N Mall Dr
Appleton, WI 54913-8569
920-738-7799
Fax: 920-738-3280 800-738-1020
info@vandewallecandies.com
www.vandewallecandies.com
Candy including boxed, fund raising, Easter, Valentine, bars, brittles, caramels, chocolates, toffee, fudge, caramel corn and popcorn specialties
President: Steve Vande Walle
jaydv@aol.com
President: Thomas Walle
Vice President: Donald Walle
Estimated Sales: $3 Million
Number Employees: 20-49
Square Footage: 160000

13290 Vanee Foods Co
5418 Mcdermott Dr
Berkeley, IL 60163-1299
708-449-7300
Fax: 708-449-2558 jackridge@vaneefoods.com
www.vaneefoodscompany.com
Roasted gravies, broths, breakfast entrees, dinner entrees, chilis, meats, sauces and soups.
President: Al Van Eekeren
ronvanee@vaneefoods.com
CFO: Ron Van Eekeren
R&D Director: Robert Benson
Quality Assurance Director: Jack Ridge
VP Sales/Marketing Director: Michael Vanee
Human Resource Director: Beatrice Kemphel
President/Operations Director: Al Vanee
Purchasing Director: Dan Vanee
Estimated Sales: $17,000,000
Number Employees: 250-499
Square Footage: 850000
Type of Packaging: Food Service

13291 Vanilla Corp Of America LLC
2273 N Penn Rd
Hatfield, PA 19440-1952
215-996-1978
Fax: 215-996-9867
Grain and field bean merchant wholesalers
President: Doug Daugherty
vanillacorp@aol.com
Estimated Sales: $500,000-1 Million
Number Employees: 5-9
Type of Packaging: Food Service, Bulk

13292 Vanlab Corporation
86 White Street
Rochester, NY 14613
585-232-6647
Fax: 585-232-6168 bmarchetti@vanlab.com
Flavoring supplies, flavors
President: David A Patton
VP: Diane Merritt
R & D: Florent Montagne
VP: Jim Abraham
Marketing/Sales: Kim Kubach
Contact: Joette Astifan
jastifan@vanlab.com
Operations/Production: Jim Abraham
Plant Manager: Hank Rankowsky
Estimated Sales: $10-20 Million
Number Employees: 30-50
Square Footage: 35000
Type of Packaging: Food Service, Private Label, Bulk

13293 Vanmark Equipment
300 Industrial Pkwy
Creston, IA 50801-8102
641-782-6575
Fax: 641-782-9209 800-523-6261
www.vanmarkequipment.com
Manufacturer of industrial food processing for a wide range of produce products.
Manager: Tom Mathues
Sales: Tom Jones
Manager: Jason Davis
Operations: Rich Shafar
Estimated Sales: $5-10 Million
Number Employees: 20-49
Square Footage: 120000
Brands:
 Vanmark

13294 Vanns Spices LTD
1716 Whitehead Rd
Suite A
Gwynn Oak, MD 21207-4029
410-944-3888
Fax: 410-944-3998 800-583-1693
sales@vannsspices.com www.vannsspices.com
Spices, seasonings and extracts

President: Meg Whitlock
meg@vannsspices.com
CEO: Erhan Kuran
Executive VP: Erhan Kurany
Estimated Sales: $3.6 Million
Number Employees: 1-4
Square Footage: 30000
Type of Packaging: Private Label, Bulk

13295 Vantage Foods
4000-4 St SE
Unit 225
Calgary, AB T2G 2W3
Canada
403-215-2820
Fax: 403-215-2830 info@vantagefoods.net
www.vantagefoods.net
Case-ready fresh meats including ground and sausage products
CEO: Gary Haley
President & COO: Leonal Kilgore
CFO: Don Finsstad
US Corporate Controller: Kelly Kuhn
Year Founded: 1997
Estimated Sales: $72 Million
Number Employees: 800

13296 Varco Brothers
1832 N Burling Street
Chicago, IL 60614-5104
312-642-4740
Noodles, spaghetti and macaroni
President: John Varco
Estimated Sales: $1-2.5 000,000
Number Employees: 1-5

13297 Varda Chocolatier
41 S Spring St
Elizabeth, NJ 07201-2608
908-354-9090
Fax: 908-354-9091 800-448-2732
www.vardachocolatier.com
Chocolate confectionery products including truffles, dessert cups, novelties and creative chocolate presentation
Owner: Varda Shandan
sales@vardachocolatier.com
Officer: Sue Hughes
Estimated Sales: $6.5 Million
Number Employees: 50-99

13298 Varet Street Market
89 Varet St
Brooklyn, NY 11206
718-302-0560
Fax: 718-302-0560
Tropical fruit
President: Alfonzo Estevez
CEO: Lely Estevez
Estimated Sales: Less than $400,000
Number Employees: 1-4
Type of Packaging: Food Service, Bulk
Brands:
 Reyes Mares

13299 Varied Industries Corp
905 S Carolina Ave
Mason City, IA 50401-5813
641-423-1460
Fax: 641-423-0832 800-654-5617
www.vi-cor.com
Manufacturer and exporter of lactic acid fermentation and yucca extracts for food, feed and litter products
President: Mark Holt
VP/ Controller: Michael Lunning
Vice President: Gerry Keller
PD & Research Coordinator: Sangita Jalukar Ph. D.
Quality Manager: Julie Sanchez
VP/ Director of Marketing: Jodi Ames-Peterson
Exec. VP International BD: Roger Beers
Contact: Charlie Elrod
celrod@vicor.com
Vice President Operations: Henry Savoy
Production Supervisor Benjamin Facility: Robert Barber
Estimated Sales: $7.6 Million
Number Employees: 10-19
Square Footage: 60000
Parent Co: International Whey Technics
Brands:
 Desert Gold Dry

 Kulactic
 Kulsar

13300 Varni Brothers/7-Up Bottling
400 Hosmer Avenue
Modesto, CA 95351-3920
209-521-1777
Fax: 209-521-0877 water@noahs7up.com
www.noahs7up.com
Manufacturer of soft drinks, spring water and other beverages.
President/CEO: Tony Varni
Contact: Deshawn Black
blackd@noahs7up.com
Estimated Sales: $17 Million
Number Employees: 60
Number of Brands: 4
Square Footage: 120000
Parent Co: Dr. Pepper/7-UP Bottling Companies
Type of Packaging: Food Service, Private Label
Brands:
 Nella Bella
 Noah's Water
 Cock'n Bull
 Cheerwine

13301 Vaughn Rue Produce
1217 Peachtree Rd NW
Wilson, NC 27896-2058
252-237-6710
Fax: 252-237-7662 800-388-8138
Sweet potatoes, butternut squash and pickles
President: Vaughn Rue
Estimated Sales: Below $5,000,000
Number Employees: 20-49
Brands:
 Rue's Choice
 Steakhouse

13302 Vaughn-Russell Candy Kitchen
401 Augusta Street
Greenville, SC 29601
864-271-7786
Fax: 704-484-8326 info@vaughnrussell.com
www.vaughnrussell.com
Confectionary manufacturer; original makers of "Incredible Edibles" and "Mint Pecans."
Owner: Chris Beard
Plant Manager: Ashton Beard
Estimated Sales: 500,000
Number Employees: 4
Type of Packaging: Consumer, Food Service, Bulk
Brands:
 Vaughn Russell

13303 Vauxhall Foods
PO Box 430
Vauxhall, AB T0K 2K0
Canada
403-654-2771
Fax: 403-654-2211
Processor and exporter of dehydrated potato granules
President: Frank Gatto
CFO: Frank Inaba
Research & Development: Gordon Packer
General Manager: Ken Tamura
Production Manager: Ken Franz
Number Employees: 50-99
Square Footage: 200000
Type of Packaging: Food Service, Private Label, Bulk
Brands:
 Chipper
 Gourmet
 V.G. Blue

13304 Vaxa International
4801 George Rd
Suite 190
Tampa, FL 33634
813-870-2904
Fax: 888-734-4154 877-622-8292
Customerservice@vaxa.com www.vaxa.com
Dietetic chocolate and vanilla powdered shake mixes
President: Bill Harper
VP: Chris Behan
Contact: Vicky Chaleff
vicky@vaxa.com
Estimated Sales: $1-3 Million
Number Employees: 20-49
Parent Co: Direct Access Network

Type of Packaging: Consumer, Private Label, Bulk
Brands:
 Vaxa

13305 VegGuide.org
7122 S Jeffery Blvd
Chicago, IL 60649
773-363-3939
Fax: 773-363-7101
Frozen foods with soy products
General Manager: Cheryl Simms
Estimated Sales: Less than $500,000
Number Employees: 5-9
Type of Packaging: Private Label
Brands:
 Natural Harvest
 Vegetarian Cornmeal
 Vegetarian Tamale

13306 Vega Food Industries Inc
80 Stamp Farm Rd
Cranston, RI 02921-3400
401-942-0620
Fax: 401-942-5760 800-973-7737
www.vegapeppers.com
Gourmet stuffed and sliced cherry peppers, olives, peppers and packed salads in oil and garlic
Owner: Dennis Christofaro
vegafoods@aol.com
VP: Anthony Cippola
Operations Manager: Frank Bisignano
Plant Manager: Carrie Zamborano
Estimated Sales: $1900000
Number Employees: 5-9
Square Footage: 20000
Type of Packaging: Consumer, Food Service, Private Label, Bulk
Brands:
 Vega's Gourmet

13307 Vegan Metal FabricatorsCo
2045 State Route 339 E
Sedalia, KY 42079-9604
270-328-8980
Fax: 270-328-8983 veganmetal@wk.net
Metal Fabricators for food industry
Office Manager: Sherry Nelson
Estimated Sales: $.5-1 million
Number Employees: 1-4

13308 Vegan Rob's
100 Roslyn Ave
Sea Cliff, NY 11579-1274
516-671-4411
info@robsbrands.com
veganrobs.com
Vegan snacks
Founder & CEO: Robert Ehrlich
Eastern Regional Sales Manager: David Curtis
Number Employees: 11-50
Brands:
 Rob's Brands

13309 Vegan Treats
1444 Linden St # 1
Bethlehem, PA 18018-2600
610-861-7660
info@vegantreats.com
www.vegantreats.com
Vegan baked goods
Manager: Laurence Koch
info@vegantreats.com
Number Employees: 20-49

13310 Vege USA
1425 S. Myrtle Avenue.
Monrovia, CA 91016
626-386-0800
Fax: 626-386-0900 888-772-8343
sales@vegeusa.com vegeusa.com
Vegetarian entrees; vegan protein, snacks and teas.
National Sales Director: Brian Schick
Office Manager: Hea-Jin Yoon
Year Founded: 1998
Estimated Sales: Under $500,000
Number Employees: 1-4
Type of Packaging: Food Service
Brands:
 Vegetarian Plus(c)
 VeriSoy(c)
 Myrtle Greens

Food Manufacturers / A-Z

13311 (HQ)Vege-Cool
802 Inyo Ave
Newman, CA 95360
209-862-2360
Lima beans and peas
Owner: William Cerutti
Manager: Steve Lewis
Estimated Sales: $400,000
Number Employees: 3
Type of Packaging: Bulk

13312 Vegetable Juices Inc
7400 S Narragansett Ave
Chicago, IL 60638-6022
708-924-9500
Fax: 708-924-9510 888-776-9752
shvizdos@vegetablejuices.com
Natural and fresh ingredient products that deliver culinary and functional solutions to the food and beverage industry.
CEO: James Hurley
President, Chief Executive Officer: Elizabeth Doyle
Sr VP Sales/Marketing: Barry Horne
VP of Innovation and Research: Anthony Popielarz
Quality Control: Paul Bollinger
Director of Marketing: Dawn Molski
Vice President of National Sales: Mark Witowski
Operations: Mike O'Hara
Estimated Sales: $6 Million
Number Employees: 50-99
Square Footage: 700000
Type of Packaging: Food Service, Bulk

13313 Vegetarian Traveler
8362 Tamarack Village
Suite 119
Woodbury, MN 55125
vegetariantraveler.com
Salad toppers
Co-Founder: Chuck Krejci
Co-Founder & CEO: Christy Krejci

13314 Veggie Grill
Irvine, CA
www.veggiegrill.com
Vegetable based dishes. Gluten-free options. Available for catering.
CEO: Steve Heeley
Year Founded: 2006
Type of Packaging: Consumer

13315 Veggie Land
222 New Rd # 3
Parsippany, NJ 07054-5626
973-808-1540
Fax: 973-882-3030 888-808-5540
info@veggieland.com www.veggiburger.com
Processor and exporter of vegetarian foods including burgers, meat balls, frankfurters, sausage, sandwiches and chili
Executive VP: Len Torine
Estimated Sales: Below $5 Million
Number Employees: 20-49
Square Footage: 64000
Brands:
 Veg-T-Balls
 Veggieland

13316 Vegi-Deli
17 Paul Dr Ste 104
San Rafael, CA 94903
415-883-6100
Fax: 415-526-1453 888-473-3667
Vegetarian meat alternative deli products including pepperoni, cold cuts and pizza toppings and vegi-jerky, pepperoni snack sticks.
General Manager: Debra Ventura
Estimated Sales: $3-5 Million
Number Employees: 8
Square Footage: 24000
Type of Packaging: Consumer, Food Service, Private Label
Brands:
 Quick Stix
 Vegetarian Slice of Life

13317 Vegy Vida
1100 Sycamore Street
6th Floor
Cincinnati, OH 45202
513-659-0781
info@vegyvida.com
vegyvida.com
Salsa and dips for kids
Founder: Josh Young
Estimated Sales: Under $500,000
Number Employees: 17
Brands:
 Vegy Vida

13318 Velatis
8408 Georgia Ave # B
Silver Spring, MD 20910-4442
301-578-8612
888-483-5284
www.velatis.com
Caramel
Owner: Tim Beyer
VP: Janet Beyer
Estimated Sales: $500,000-$1 Million
Number Employees: 5-9
Brands:
 Vatore's

13319 Velda Farms
3634 South Vineland Road
Orlando, FL 32811
407-849-6202
Fax: 305-651-2766 800-795-4649
Processor of dairy products including milk, cream and ice cream
Principal: Janet Hill
CEO: Gregg Tanner
VP/CFO: Chris Bellairs
COO: Ralph Scozzafava
Year Founded: 1940
Estimated Sales: $10 Million
Number Employees: 35
Number of Brands: 2
Parent Co: Dean Foods
Type of Packaging: Consumer, Food Service, Private Label, Bulk
Brands:
 Sunnydell
 Velda

13320 Vella Cheese Co
315 2nd St E
Sonoma, CA 95476-5710
707-938-3232
Fax: 707-938-4307 800-848-0505
vella@vellacheese.com www.vellacheese.com
Cheese including Monterey jack, asiago, cheddar, dry jack and Italian-style table
President: Sarah Vella
Manager: Chicke Vella
Estimated Sales: $2,000,000
Number Employees: 10-19
Square Footage: 42960
Type of Packaging: Consumer
Brands:
 Asiago
 Bear Flag
 Dry Sack
 High Moisture Fresh Jack
 Mezzo
 Seasoned Cheddar Cheese
 Seasoned Jack Cheese
 Sello
 Vella

13321 Velvet Creme Popcorn Co
4710 Belinder Rd
Westwood, KS 66205-1883
913-236-7742
Fax: 913-236-9631 888-553-6708
customerservice@velvetcremepopcorn.com
www.velvetcremepopcorn.com
Popcorn
President: Barbara Odle
staff@velvetcremepopcorn.com
Estimated Sales: $1 Million-1.5
Number Employees: 10-19
Square Footage: 120000
Type of Packaging: Consumer
Brands:
 Velvet Creme

13322 Velvet Ice Cream Co Inc
11324 Mount Vernon Rd
Utica, OH 43080-7703
740-892-3921
Fax: 740-892-4339 800-589-5000
info@velveticecream.com
www.velveticecream.com
Ice cream and frozen desserts.

President: Kayla Allen
kallen@columbuscrewsc.com
CFO: Dave Elwell
VP: Mike Bearsohio
Foodservice Director: Joanne Dager
Treasurer: Tatla Dager
VP Marketing: Mike Dager
Marketing Assistant: Nathan Arnold
Plant Engineer: Jeff Belford
Number Employees: 100-249
Square Footage: 164000
Type of Packaging: Consumer

13323 Vending Nut Co
2222 Montgomery St
Fort Worth, TX 76107-4519
817-737-3071
Fax: 817-377-1316 800-429-9260
www.vendingnutco.com
Nuts wholesaler
President: Johnny Minshew
Estimated Sales: $4 Million
Number Employees: 10-19

13324 Venice Baking Co
134 Main St
El Segundo, CA 90245-3801
310-322-7357
contact@venicebakery.com
www.pizzaandiamo.com
Gluten free baked goods
Owner: James Desisto
jimmy@venicebakery.com
Number Employees: 20-49

13325 Ventana Vineyards Winery
2999 Monterey-Salinas Highway
Community Box #10
Monterey, CA 93940
831-372-7415
Fax: 831-375-0797 800-237-8846
Wines
Owner: Randy Pura
VP/Marketing Director: LuAnn Meador
Bookkeeper: Christy Florez
Vineyard Foreman: David Rodriguez
Production Manager: Reggie Hammond
Winemaker: Miguel Martinez
National Sales Manager: Terry Lannon
California Sales Manager: Sarah Robinson
Sales/Marketing: Gerre Calderon
Tasing Room Manager: Rosemary Hermans-Walls
Estimated Sales: $1-3 Million
Number Employees: 10-19
Type of Packaging: Private Label
Brands:
 Ventana Wines

13326 Ventre Packing Company
P.O. Box 6487
Syracuse, NY 13217
315-463-2384
Fax: 315-463-5897
Manufacturer and packager of spaghetti sauces and salsas; production plant bought by Giovanni Food Company Inc in 2010.
Chairman: Marty Ventre
President/CEO: Martin Ventre
Number of Brands: 1
Parent Co: Giovanni Food Company Inc.
Type of Packaging: Consumer, Food Service, Private Label
Brands:
 ENRICO'S

13327 Ventura Coastal LLC
2325 Vista Del Mar Dr
Ventura, CA 93001-3700
805-653-7000
Fax: 805-653-7777 sales@vcoastal.com
www.venturacoastal.com
Manufacturer and exporter of citrus concentrates and single strength juices; contract packager of frozen pectin products
President: William Borgers
borgens@vcoastal.com
EVP, Sales & Marketing: Rick Torres
Estimated Sales: $44 Million
Number Employees: 50-99
Type of Packaging: Consumer, Food Service, Private Label, Bulk
Other Locations:
 Visalia CA
 Tipton CA

Food Manufacturers / A-Z

13328 Ventura Foods LLC
40 Pointe Dr
Brea, CA 92821
714-257-3700
800-421-6257
www.venturafoods.com
Produces extensive line of branded and private label products, inlcuding: syrups, mayonnaise, salad dressings, oils, shortenings, and sauces. It also provides contract packaging services for a variety of products sold to retail andfoodservice customers.
President/CEO: Christopher Furman
cfurman@venturafoods.com
Executive VP & CFO: Erika Noonburg-Morgan
Executive VP, Sales & Marketing: John Buckles
Chief Administrative Officer: Andy Euser
Parent Co: CHS Inc
Type of Packaging: Consumer, Food Service, Private Label, Bulk
Brands:
  Classic Gourmet
  LouAna
  Odell's
  Hidden Valley
  Marie's
  Churn Spread
  Grandioso
  Pride
  Smart Balance
  Sunglow
  Sauce Craft
  Smokehouse 220
  Extend
  Mel-Fry
  Phase
  White Cap
  Deans
  Gold 'N Soft

13329 Venture Vineyards
8830 Upper Lake Rd
Lodi, NY 14860
607-582-6774
888-635-6277
venturev@capital.net
Grower of asparagus, raspberries and grapes including concord, Niagara, Catawaba, and Delaware. Also a processor of grape juice and importer and exporter of concord grapes
President: Melvin Nass
VP: Phyllis Nass
Operations Manager: Andrew Nass
Number Employees: 5-9
Square Footage: 40000
Brands:
  Venture For the Best

13330 Venus Wafers Inc
100 Research Rd
Suite 3
Hingham, MA 02043-4345
781-740-1002
Fax: 781-740-0791 800-545-4538
www.venuswafers.com
Crackers
CFO: Edward Barmakian
Manager: James Anderko
jranderko@aol.com
Estimated Sales: $5-10 Million
Number Employees: 20-49
Type of Packaging: Consumer
Brands:
  Deli-Catessen
  Old Brussels
  Venus Wafers

13331 VerMints Inc.
PO Box 850473
Braintree, VT 02184
781-340-4440
Fax: 617-765-4761 800-367-4442
wholesale@vermints.com www.vermints.com
All natural breath mints
Estimated Sales: $300,000-500,000
Number Employees: 1-4
Parent Co: Ohare Enterprises

13332 Veramar Vineyard
905 Quarry Rd
Berryville, VA 22611-4222
540-955-5510
Fax: 540-955-0404 jamesbogaty@veramar.com
www.veramar.com
Wines
Owner: Jim Bogaty
info@veramar.com
Co-Owner: Della Bogaty
Number Employees: 5-9

13333 Verdant Kitchen
1745 Corporate Drive
Suite 215
Norcross, GA 30093
912-349-2958
info@verdantkitchen.com
www.verdantkitchen.com
Ginger based products: baked goods, candies, cocktail syrups, infused honey and ginger ales
President & CEO: Ross Harding
Business Developer: Emma Evans
Estimated Sales: Under $500,000
Number Employees: 7
Brands:
  Verdant Kitchen

13334 Verday
270 Lafayette St.
New York, NY 10012
hello@drinkverday.com
www.drinkverday.com
Flavored chlorophyll water
Founder/Chief Executive Officer: Randy Kohana
Number of Brands: 1
Number of Products: 4
Type of Packaging: Consumer, Private Label
Brands:
  Verday

13335 Verde Farms, LLC
300 Trade Center # 3540
Woburn, MA 01801
617-221-8922
Fax: 617-221-8923 info@verdefarms.com
www.verdefarms.com
Organic, free range, hormone-free and grass-fed beef for retail, wholesale, foodservice and ingredient customers
Co-Founder/Chief Executive Officer: Dana Ehrlich
Vice-President, Marketing: Pete Lewis
Co-Founder/Director of Operations: Pablo Garbarino
Year Founded: 2005
Number of Brands: 1
Type of Packaging: Food Service, Bulk
Brands:
  Verde Farms

13336 Verdure Sciences
1250 Conner St # 201
Suite 201
Noblesville, IN 46060-2900
317-776-3600
Fax: 317-776-3650 888-656-4364
info@vs-corp.com www.thymocid.com
Boswellia Serrata Extract
Owner/President/CEo: Ajay Patel
R&D: Dr Lal Hingorani
Marketing Director: Sonya Bucklew
Sales Director: Nipen Lavingia
Estimated Sales: $.5-1 million
Number Employees: 10-19
Number of Brands: 2
Number of Products: 30
Brands:
  Wokvel

13337 Verhoff Alfalfa Mill Inc
1188 Sugar Mill Dr
Ottawa, OH 45875-8518
419-523-4767
Fax: 419-523-5715 800-834-8563
ags@alfagreen.us.com
www.alfagreensupreme.com
Dehydrated alfalfa
President: Constance Verhoff
verhoffalfalfa@embarqmail.com
Chief Executive Officer, Manager: Ken Vaupel
Vice President: Donald Verhoff
Operations Quality Control Manager: Michael Wood
Estimated Sales: $2274776
Number Employees: 20-49
Type of Packaging: Bulk

13338 Verifine Dairy
P.O.Box 879
Sheboygan, WI 53082-0879
920-457-7733
Fax: 920-457-5372 www.deanfoods.com
Milk
Manager: Steve Weinreich
Contact: Dale Aherns
dale_aherns@deanfoods.com
Plant Manager: Dale Ahrens
Estimated Sales: $10-24.9 Million
Number Employees: 50-99
Parent Co: Dean Foods Company

13339 Veritas Chocolatier
1816 Johns Drive
Glenview, IL 60025
847-729-8787
Fax: 847-729-8879 800-555-8331
Chocolate truffles
VP Marketing: Chris Samuel
VP Sales: Michael Gordon

13340 Veritas Vineyard
151 Veritas Ln
Afton, VA 22920-2342
540-456-8000
Fax: 540-456-8483 contact@veritaswines.com
www.veritaswines.com
Wines
Owner: Andrew Hodson
andrew.hodson@veritaswines.com
Estimated Sales: $3-5 Million
Number Employees: 10-19

13341 Verlasso
786-522-8418
www.verlasso.com
Farm-raised sustainable salmon
Year Founded: 2011
Number of Brands: 1
Number of Products: 1
Brands:
  Verlasso

13342 Vermilion Packers Ltd
4825-47 Avenue
Vermilion, AB T9X 1J4
Canada
780-853-4622
Fax: 780-853-4623
vermillionpacker@hotmail.com
Fresh and cured meats including sausage
President: Rick Bozak
Estimated Sales: Below $5 Million
Number Employees: 14
Type of Packaging: Consumer, Food Service
Brands:
  Vermilion

13343 Vermont Bread Co
80 Cotton Mill Hl
Brattleboro, VT 05301-8681
802-254-4600
Fax: 802-257-0165 info@vermontbread.com
All-natural, organic and premium bread
Ceo: Lisa Lorimer
Vice President: J Rogers
Plant Manager: Susan Vitelly
Estimated Sales: $10 Million
Number Employees: 50-99
Square Footage: 44000
Type of Packaging: Consumer, Food Service, Private Label
Brands:
  Vermont
  Windham Hearth

13344 Vermont Chocolatiers
9 East St
Northfield, VT 05663
802-485-5181
Fax: 802-485-5191 877-485-4226
Chocolate and shortbread
Co-Owner: Walter Delia
Co-Owner: Jane Delia
Estimated Sales: $300,000-500,000
Number Employees: 1-4

Food Manufacturers / A-Z

13345 Vermont Coffee Co
1197 Exchange St # 3
Suite 3
Middlebury, VT 05753-4463
802-398-2776
888-308-5099
friends@vermontcoffeecompany.com
www.vermontcoffeecompany.com
Manufacturer of coffee beans.
President: Paul Ralston
paul@vermontcoffeecompany.com
Number Employees: 10-19

13346 Vermont Confectionery
1541 West Rd (Rt 9)
Bennington, VT 05262-0380
80- 44- 261
Fax: 802-447-2610 800-545-9243
vtcandy@sover.net www.vermontcandy.com
Chocolate
Owner: George Mc Cain
Estimated Sales: $3-5 Million
Number Employees: 5-9

13347 Vermont Country Naturals
PO Box 238
Charlotte, VT 05445-0238
802-425-5445
Fax: 866-528-7091 800-528-7021
sales@vermontcountrynaturals.com
www.vermontspecialtyfoods.org
Kosher, wildcrafted maple sugar (powder and granules) and maple syrup
President: Joan Savoy
CEO: Jeffrey Madison
Estimated Sales: $300,000-500,000
Number Employees: 3
Square Footage: 14000
Parent Co: Vermont Country Maple Mixes
Brands:
  Maple Sprinkles

13348 Vermont Creamery
40 Pitman Rd
Websterville, VT 5678
802-479-9371
Fax: 802-479-3674 info@vermontcreamery.com
www.vermontcreamery.com
Cheeses
Co-Founder: Allison Hooper
awolf@vermontcreamery.com
Co-Founder: Bob Reese
Accounting Manager: Matt Reese
General Manager: Adeline Druart
Quality Control Supervisor: Andrew Schmitt
Marketing Coordinator: Hilary Schwoegler
Sales Exec: Allison Wolf
Estimated Sales: $6.6 Million
Number Employees: 20-49

13349 Vermont Creamery
20 Pitman Rd.
PO Box 95
Websterville, VT 05678
802-479-9371
Fax: 802-479-3674 800-884-6287
www.vermontcreamery.com
Cream, butter, and cheese.
Co-Founder and CEO: Allison Hooper
Co-Founder and CEO: Bob Reese
President: Adeline Druart
Marketing Manager: FM Munoz
Director of Sales: Michele Haram

13350 Vermont Food Experience
PO Box 943
Shelburne, VT 05482-0943
802-985-8101
Fax: 802-885-2040
Gourmet and specialty foods
President: Richard Hurlburt
Estimated Sales: Under $500,000
Number Employees: 1-4

13351 Vermont Harvest Spec Food LLC
1799 Mountain Rd
Stowe, VT 05672-4389
802-253-7138
Fax: 802-253-7139 800-338-5354
info@vtharvest.com www.vtharvest.com
Jams, jellies, chutneys and breads
Owner: Whip Burks
whip@vtharvest.com
Estimated Sales: $1-3 Million
Number Employees: 1-4

13352 Vermont Liberty Tea
1 Derby Ln # 4
Waterbury, VT 05676-8926
802-244-6102
Fax: 802-244-6102
Herbal, green and black tea
Owner: John Mcconnell
vermontlibertytea@myfairpoint.net
Estimated Sales: $.5-1 million
Number Employees: 1-4

13353 Vermont Made Richard's Sauces
471 Bushey Rd
St Albans, VT 05478-9604
802-524-3196
Fax: 802-524-4224 sauce@vtmadebbqu.com
www.vtmadebbqu.com
BBQ sauce, game sauce and marinades, gift favors and hot sauce.
Owner: Steve Rocheleau
sauce@vtmadebbqu.com
Co-Owner: Martha Rocheleau
Estimated Sales: $150,000+
Number Employees: 1-4
Number of Products: 5
Type of Packaging: Consumer, Food Service, Private Label, Bulk

13354 Vermont Natural Co
201 VT Route 112
Jacksonville, VT 05342-9634
802-368-2231
Fax: 802-368-7556
www.vermontnaturalcoatings.com
Gourmet and specialty foods
Principal: Robert Moses
Manager: Annmary Block-Reed
ablock@vermontnaturalcoatings.com
Estimated Sales: $300,000-500,000
Number Employees: 12
Square Footage: 17
Type of Packaging: Private Label

13355 Vermont Nut Free Chocolates
10 Island Cir
Grand Isle, VT 05458-4408
802-372-4654
Fax: 802-372-4654 888-468-8373
customerservice@vermontnutfree.com
www.vermontnutfree.com
Nut free chocolates
Owner: Mark Elvidge
vtnutfree@aol.com
Estimated Sales: $1-3 Million
Number Employees: 20-49

13356 Vermont Pretzel & Cookie Co.
25 Rockingham Street
Bellows Falls, VT 05101
802-460-4600
Fax: 802-869-2837 888-671-4774
Stuffed and soft pretzels, cookies and bars
President: Christine Holtz

13357 Vermont Signature Sauces
PO Box 667
Saxtons River, VT 05154
802-869-5000
info@vermontsignaturesauces.com
Manufacturer of gourmet finishing sauces.
Founder: Karen Whitman

13358 Vermont Smoke and Cure
Hinesburg, VT
802-482-4666
www.vermontsmokeandcure.com
Smoked meats and meat snacks.
CEO: Chris Bailey

13359 Vermont Specialty Food Association
Freedom Foods
24 Pleasant Street
Randolph, VT 05060
802-728-0070
Fax: 802-728-0071
Fruit infused maple syrups, gift baskets, mustards, granola & mixes
Square Footage: 16000

13360 Vermont Sweetwater Bottling Co
1075 VT Route 30 N
Poultney, VT 05764-9633
802-287-9897
Fax: 802-287-9897 800-974-9877
york@sover.net
Soda
Co-Owner: Robert Munch
Co-Owner: Richard Munch
york@sover.net
Estimated Sales: $3-5 Million
Number Employees: 5-9

13361 Vermont Tea & Trading Co Inc
43 Court St
43 Court Street
Middlebury, VT 05753-1454
802-388-4005
Fax: 802-388-4005 888-255-9327
Loose leaf teas
Co-Owner: Curron Malhotra
Co-Owner: Bruce Malhotra
b.malhotra@vermonttea.com
Estimated Sales: $1-3 Million
Number Employees: 1-4

13362 Vermont Tortilla Company
22 Sage Court
Shelburne, VT 05482
802-999-4823
info@vttortillaco.com
www.vttortillaco.com
Tortillas
Co-Founder & Owner: April Moulaert
Chief Tortilla Officer: Azur Moulaert
Year Founded: 2015
Number Employees: 2-10
Brands:
  Vermont Tortilla

13363 Vermont Village
698 South Barre Rd.
Barre, VT 05641
www.vermontvillage.com
Raw, organic apple cider sipping vinegar and vinegar shots; organic malt vinegar; organic flavored apple sauce; organic spiced apple butter
Owner: Joseph Shepherd
Number of Brands: 1
Type of Packaging: Consumer, Private Label

13364 Vern's Cheese
312 W Main St
Chilton, WI 53014-1312
920-849-7717
Fax: 920-849-7883 info@vernscheese.com
www.vernscheese.com
Cheeses
President: Vern Knoespel
info@verncheese.com
Estimated Sales: $20-50 Million
Number Employees: 20-49

13365 Veronica Foods Inc
1991 Dennison St
Oakland, CA 94606-5225
510-535-6833
Fax: 510-532-2837 800-370-5554
info@evoliveoil.com www.evoliveoil.com
Olive oil manufacturers and importers
President: Michael Bradley
CEO: Mike Bradley
mbradley@evoliveoil.com
CFO: Leah Bradley
VP: Veronica Bradley
Marketing: Arnie Kaufman
VP Retail Sales: Arnie Kaufman
Operations: Fred Johnson
Production: Myron Manown
Plant Manager: Dave Fitzgerald
Purchasing: Fred Johnson
Estimated Sales: $16,200,000
Number Employees: 50-99
Square Footage: 684000
Brands:
  Dainty Pak
  Delizia
  Italia
  Panther
  Purn Life

Food Manufacturers / A-Z

13366 Veronica's Treats
31 W Grove St # C
Middleboro, MA 02346-1859
508-946-4438
Fax: 508-946-4460 866-576-1222
info@veronicastreats.com
www.veronicastreats.com
Personalized cookies, brownies, and cupcakes
Owner: Hilary Souza
veronicastreats@gmail.com
Number Employees: 10-19
Square Footage: 24000
Type of Packaging: Private Label

13367 Verve Coffee Roasters
816 41st Ave
Santa Cruz, CA 95062-4421
831-475-7776
sarah.a@vervecoffeeroasters.com
www.vervecoffeeroasters.com
Coffee
Site Manager: Chris Baca
chrisb@vervecoffeeroasters.com
Number Employees: 10-19

13368 Veryfine Products Inc
3900 Aero Dr
Mason, OH 45040
service.fin@sunnyd.com
veryfine.com
Fruit juice drinks
President & CEO: Bill Cyr
Year Founded: 1865
Estimated Sales: $150 Million
Number Employees: 5-9
Square Footage: 350000
Parent Co: Sunny Delight Beverage Company
Type of Packaging: Private Label
Brands:
  Veryfine Juices

13369 Vessey & Co Inc
1605 Zenos Rd
P.O. Box 28
Holtville, CA 92250-9603
760-356-0130
Fax: 760-356-0137 kevinolson@redshift.com
www.vessey.com
Grower of cabbage including red, green, bok choy and napa; also, red and yellow onions, red and yukon potatoes, sweet corn, cantaloupes and garlic including fresh, whole, peeled, minced and chopped; importer and exporter of garlic
President: Jon Vessey
Partner: Jack Vessey
jack@vessey.com
Sales Manager: David Grimes
Sales: Eric Pompa
Estimated Sales: $3100000
Number Employees: 10-19
Type of Packaging: Food Service, Bulk

13370 Vestergaard Farms
4408 S Wagner Rd.
Ann Arbor, MI 48103
734-929-2875
info@vestergaardfarms.com
www.vestergaardfarms.com
Various meat products including beef, pork, lamb, and poultry.
Owner: Michael Vestergaard
Year Founded: 2010
Type of Packaging: Private Label

13371 Vetter Vineyards Winery
8005 Prospect Station Rd
Westfield, NY 14787-9630
716-326-3100
Fax: 716-326-3100 wine@cecomet.net
Wines
Owner: Mark Lancaster
wine@fairpoint.net
Co-Owner: Barbara Lancaster
Estimated Sales: Less Than $500,000
Number Employees: 1-4
Type of Packaging: Private Label
Brands:
  Vetter Vineyards

13372 Via Della Chiesa Vineyards
413 Church Street
Raynham, MA 02767-1008
508-822-7775
Fax: 508-880-0500
Wines
President: Robert DiCroce
CFO: Sharon Tweedy
Marketing Manager: Kate Desmond
Public Relations Officer: Lidm Piwa
Winery Manager: Dolly Tulsiani
Production Manager: Matyas Vogel
Estimated Sales: Below $5 Million
Number Employees: 10
Type of Packaging: Private Label
Brands:
  Cranberry Blush Wine
  Dry-Atlantic Coastal
  Raspberry Rave Wine

13373 Viader Vineyards & Winery
1120 Deer Park Rd
Deer Park, CA 94576-9715
707-963-3816
Fax: 707-963-3817 www.viader.com
Wines
Owner: Delia Viader
delia@viader.com
Director of Operations: Alan Viader
Administrative Assistant: Valaree Martinez
Shipping Manager: Blanca Avina
Sales/Marketing Director: Janet Viader
Director of Operations: Alan Viader
Winemaker: Delia Viader
Number Employees: 5-9
Type of Packaging: Consumer, Food Service, Private Label
Brands:
  Viader

13374 Viano Vineyards
150 Morello Ave
Martinez, CA 94553-3522
925-228-6465
Fax: 925-228-5670 info@vianovineyards.com
www.vianovineyards.com
Wines
Owner: John Viano
President: Paula Viano
Estimated Sales: Less than $400,000
Number Employees: 1-4
Brands:
  Viano Winery

13375 Viansa Winery
25200 Arnold Dr
Sonoma, CA 95476-9222
707-939-0782
Fax: 707-935-5654 800-995-4740
ViansaService@viansa.com www.viansa.com
Wines
President: Austin Haynes
austinh@valleycom.org
CEO: Vicki Sebastiani
CFO: Russ Jay
Co. Founder: Sam Sebastiani
Winemaker: Michael Sebastiani
Estimated Sales: $5-10 Million
Number Employees: 50-99
Brands:
  Nebbiolo
  Vernaccia

13376 Viau Foods
6625 Ernest Cormier
Laval, QC H7C 2V2
Canada
450-665-6100
Fax: 450-665-7100 800-663-5492
www.viausila.com
Cooked or dry cured pepperoni, Italian cooked meats, sausages, pizza toppings and meatballs.

13377 Vic's Corn Popper
14935 Industrial Rd
Omaha, NE 68144-3232
402-932-0426
Fax: 402-331-2507 vic@vicspopcornomaha.com
www.vicspopcornomaha.com
Popcorn
President: Ken Nelson
Number Employees: 5-9
Brands:
  Vic's

13378 Vichy Springs Mineral Water
2605 Vichy Springs Rd
Ukiah, CA 95482-3507
707-462-9515
Fax: 707-462-9516 vichy@vichysprings.com
www.vichysprings.com
Processor and exporter of naturally carbonated bottled mineral water
President: Gilbert Ashoff
VP: Marjorie Ashoff
Estimated Sales: $500,000 appx.
Number Employees: 10-19
Square Footage: 28000
Type of Packaging: Private Label
Brands:
  Vichy Springs
  Vichy Springs Mineral Water

13379 Vickey's Vittles
16420 Gledhill St
North Hills, CA 91343-2807
818-841-1944
Fax: 818-841-1191 vickeysvittles@msn.com
Specialty cookies, bundt cakes, brownies, dessert bars, pies and cobblers; also, gift baskets, fat-fee and low-fat items available
President: Vickey Conover
Estimated Sales: $300,000-500,000
Number Employees: 5-9
Brands:
  Vickey's Vittles

13380 Vicky's Artisan Bakery
500 Alden Rd.
Unit 4
Markham, ON L3R 5H5
Canada
905-944-0940
info@artisanbakerycompany.com
artisanbakerycompany.com
Flatbreads
President: Richard Bedford
richard@artisanbakerycompany.com
Co-Founder: Vicky Min
Brands:
  Vicky's All Natural

13381 Victor Allen Coffee Company
1401 12th St NW
Albuquerque, NM 87104-2117
505-856-5282
Fax: 505-856-5588 800-662-2575
email@avaloncoffee.com victorallen.com
Coffee and tea
Manager: Aaron Simpson
Marketing Specialist: Kathryn Utterback
VP Sales: Liz Kollar
Operations Manager: Andy Wieczorek
Estimated Sales: Below $5 Million
Number Employees: 5-9
Type of Packaging: Private Label
Brands:
  Avalon Organic Coffee
  Bosque Tea Co
  High Desert Roasters
  Rio Grande Roasters

13382 Victor Allen's Coffee and Tea
1101 Moasis Dr
PO Box 307
Little Chute, WI 54140
920-788-1252
800-394-5282
www.victorallen.com
Manufacturer of coffee and teas
Owner: Scott Dercks
Principal: Nathan Impola
Contact: Kate Bons
kjanssen@victorallen.com
Year Founded: 1979
Estimated Sales: $20-50 Million
Number Employees: 5-9
Type of Packaging: Private Label

13383 Victor Ostrowski & Son
524 S Washington St
Baltimore, MD 21231-3030
410-327-8935
Fax: 410-252-9372
Polish garlic bologna, liver sausage, stuffed cabbage and horseradishes
Owner/President: John Ostrowski
Estimated Sales: $1-3 Million
Number Employees: 5-9

Food Manufacturers / A-Z

Type of Packaging: Consumer

13384 Victor Packing
11687 Road 27 1/2
Madera, CA 93637-9440
559-673-5908
Fax: 559-673-4225 www.victorpacking.com
Manufacturer, and exporter of currants and raisins including organic, natural, golden and seedless; also, raisin juice concentrate and raisin paste available
Owner: Victor Sahatjian
victor@victorpacking.com
VP: Margaret Sahatjian
Domestic Sales: Kristina Surabian
International Sales: Richard Burright
Year Founded: 1928
Estimated Sales: $10 Million
Number Employees: 50-99
Square Footage: 150000
Type of Packaging: Consumer, Food Service, Private Label, Bulk
Brands:
  Liberty Bell
  Madera
  Natural Thompson
  Victor

13385 Victor Preserving Company
6318 Ontario Center Rd
Ontario, NY 14519-9324
315-524-2711
Fax: 315-524-7040 onedavid@aol.com
Sauerkraut
President/CEO: David Tobin
Estimated Sales: $3-5 Million
Number Employees: 10 to 19
Square Footage: 135000
Type of Packaging: Private Label

13386 Victoria Amory & Co LLC
440 Riversville Rd
Greenwich, CT 06831-3257
203-220-6454
shop@victoriaamory.com
Manufacturer of flatbread crisps, condiments, sauces, and mayonnaise.
Founder: Victoria Amory
vamory@victoriaamory.com

13387 Victoria Fancy Sausage
6506 118th Avenue NW
Edmonton, AB T5W 1G6
Canada
780-471-2283
Fax: 780-477-5381
Fresh beef, pork, chicken and wild game including venison, elk and moose
President: John Snyder
Vice President: Alan Snyder
Estimated Sales: A
Number Employees: 1-4
Square Footage: 14000
Type of Packaging: Bulk
Brands:
  Victoria Fancy

13388 (HQ)Victoria Fine Foods
443 E 100th St
Brooklyn, NY 11236-2103
718-927-3000
Fax: 718-649-7069
victoria@victoriafinefoods.com
www.victoriafinefoods.com
Pasta and specialty sauces, condiments and gourmet spreads.
President: Brian Dean
CEO: Gerald Aquilina
Vice President, Finance: Robert Haberman
Executive VP, Sales: William Paskowski
Number Employees: 100-249
Type of Packaging: Consumer, Food Service, Private Label, Bulk
Brands:
  Victoria

13389 Victoria Gourmet Inc
17 Gill St
Unit 4
Woburn, MA 01801-1768
781-935-2100
Fax: 781-935-9979 800-403-8981
info@vgourmet.com www.vgourmet.com
Blended seasonings

Founder, President: Victoria Taylor
vtaylor@vgourmet.com
Estimated Sales: $500,000-$1 Million
Number Employees: 10-19

13390 Victoria's Catered Traditions
1240 Eastridge Place
Manteca, CA 95336
209-823-9015
Fax: 208-823-8213 877-272-5208
Chocolate covered popcorn
Owner Principal: Victoria Costa

13391 Victrola Coffee Roasters
310 E Pike St
Seattle, WA 98122-3610
206-325-6080
info@victrolacoffee.com
www.victrolacoffee.com
Coffee
Contact: Joshua Boyt
joshua@victrolacoffee.com
Number Employees: 5-9

13392 Vida Blend
1430 State Highway 5s
Amsterdam, NY 12010-8184
518-620-6216
Fax: 866-243-6216 www.vida-blend.com
Organic nutrients and ingredients
Director: Freddy Luna
Formulator: Jessica Ruedisuelli
Marketing: Yasmin Pacia
Global Sales Associate: Linda Gibeault
Number Employees: 10-19

13393 Vidalia Brands Inc
PO Box 2120
Reidsville, GA 30453-2120
912-654-2726
Fax: 912-654-9135 800-752-0206
info@vidaliabrands.com www.vidaliabrands.com
Vidalia sweet onions, gourmet treats, peach salsa, blossom kit, salad dressings, relishes, BBQ sauce, chow-chow
President/CEO: Sandra Bland
Marketing Director: Wendy Moore
Vice President: Sandra Bland
Marketing & Communications Manager: Greg Smith
Public Relations: Susan Lynch
Plant Manager: Mike Gulbranson
Number Employees: 50-99
Type of Packaging: Private Label
Brands:
  Vidalia

13394 (HQ)Vidalia Sweets Brand
818 Ga Highway 56 West
Lyons, GA 30436
912-565-8881
Fax: 912-565-0199
Fresh and pickled onions, onion relish, barbecue sauce, etc.; wholesaler/distributor of vidalia onions and specialty food products; serving the food service market
President: Jim P Cowart
Estimated Sales: $210000
Number Employees: 1-4
Type of Packaging: Consumer, Food Service
Brands:
  Vidalia Sweets

13395 Videri Chocolate Factory
327 W. Davie Street
Suite 100
Raleigh, NC 27601
919-755-5053
hello@viderichocolatefactory.com
viderichocolatefactory.com
Chocolate bars
Co-Founder & Head Chocolate Maker: Sam Ratto
Co-Founder & Public Engagement: Starr Sink
Manager: Chris Heavener
Estimated Sales: $3.3 Million
Number Employees: 65
Brands:
  Videri Chocolate Factory

13396 Vie De France Yamazaki Inc
2070 Chain Bridge Rd # 500
Suite 500
Vienna, VA 22182-2588
703-442-9205
Fax: 703-821-2695 800-446-4404
www.viedefrance.com
Baked goods including croissants, pastries, danish, breads and desserts.
President: Sadao Yasumura
Estimated Sales: $44.5 Million
Number Employees: 1000-4999
Square Footage: 30000
Type of Packaging: Consumer, Food Service, Bulk

13397 Vie-Del Co
11903 S Chestnut Ave
Fresno, CA 93725-9618
559-834-2525
Fax: 559-834-1348
Processor and exporter of fruit concentrates including grape; also, wine and brandy
President: Dianne Nury
dnury@vie-del.com
Vice President: Richard Watson
Customer Service: Janel Cook
Purchasing Manager: Robert Reiter
Estimated Sales: $18,800,000
Number Employees: 100-249

13398 Vienna Bakery
110 Maple Ave
Barrington, RI 02806-3520
401-245-2355
Fax: 401-247-5432 info@viennabakeryri.com
www.viennabakeryri.com
Gourmet bread and pastries
Owner: Joe Balasco
CEO: Bernie Jager
Marketing Manager: Bernie Jager
Number Employees: 20-49
Type of Packaging: Consumer, Food Service
Brands:
  Vienna

13399 Vienna Beef LTD
6033 Malburg Way
Vernon, CA 90058-3947
323-583-8951
Fax: 323-585-7580 800-733-6063
www.viennabeef.com
Pickles, cured meat, soups, kosher specialties and desserts.
CEO: James Eisenberg
CFO: Richard Steele
Vice President of Marketing: Keith Smith
SVP/Sales & Marketing: Thomas McGlade
VP/Human Resources: Jane Lustig
VP/Purchasing: Richard Ewert
Number Employees: 10-19
Type of Packaging: Consumer, Food Service, Private Label

13400 (HQ)Vienna Beef LTD
2501 N Damen Ave
Chicago, IL 60647
773-278-7800
800-366-3647
info@viennabeef.com www.viennabeef.com
Meats including hot dogs, Italian beef, Polish sausage and condiments
President: Tim O'Brien
Finance Director: Richard Steele
Project Engineer: Jack Bodman
VP, Quality Assurance: Kim Brown
Production Director: Henry Stepniak
Year Founded: 1893
Estimated Sales: $86 Million
Number Employees: 500-999
Number of Brands: 4
Square Footage: 100000
Type of Packaging: Consumer, Food Service
Brands:
  Bistro Soups and Chili
  Chipico
  Minaret
  Vienna

13401 Vienna Meat Products
170 Nugget Avenue
Scarborough, ON M1S 3A7
Canada
416-297-1062
Fax: 416-297-0836 800-588-1931

Food Manufacturers / A-Z

Processor and importer of ham, sausage, cold cuts, turkey products, roast beef, corned beef and pastrami.
President: Michael Latifi
Director Retail Sales: Vince Romano
Estimated Sales: $9.5 Million
Number Employees: 100
Brands:
  Austrian Crown
  Grand Chef De Paris
  Vienna

13402 Vietti Foods Co Inc
636 Southgate Ave
Nashville, TN 37203-5516
615-244-7864
Fax: 615-242-7055 www.viettichili.com
Processor and canner of pork and beef with barbecue sauce, chili spaghetti, regular chili and beef stew; also, sauces including hot dog, spaghetti and Creole.
President: Trent Baker
baker@viettifoodsinc.com
Vice President, R&D: Dee Folmar
Number Employees: 50-99
Parent Co: Zwanenberg Food Group BV
Type of Packaging: Consumer, Food Service, Private Label
Brands:
  Vietti
  Artisan Craft
  Butcher's Cut
  Southgate
  Zwanenberg

13403 Vigneri Chocolate Inc.
810 Emerson St
Rochester, NY 14613-1804
585-254-6160
Fax: 585-254-6872 877-844-6374
info@vigneri.com www.vigneri.com
chocolate tablets, filled chocolates, chocolate dipped products, novelty chocolates, chocolate covered products, drinking chocolate and wellness chocolate in the gifting, snacking, entertaining and decorating categories for our VigneriChocolate bran
CEO: Alexander Vigneri
Number Employees: 10+
Square Footage: 60000
Type of Packaging: Consumer, Food Service, Private Label, Bulk
Brands:
  Give Collection
  By Nature By Hand
  Surprizers!

13404 Vigo Importing Co
4701 W Comanche Ave
P.O. Box 15584
Tampa, FL 33614
800-282-4130
www.vigo-alessi.com
Processor and exporter of seasoned rice dinners, paella and bread crumbs; importer of olives, peppers, sundried tomatoes, olive oil, cheese, pasta, balsamic vinegar, bread sticks, pine nuts, coffee, vegetable pates, porcini mushroomsartichokes, etc.
General Manager: Sam Ciccarello
sam@vigo-alessi.com
Marketing Director: Laura De Lucia
VP, Sales: Alfred Alessi
Year Founded: 1947
Estimated Sales: $21.1 Million
Number Employees: 100-249
Square Footage: 165000
Type of Packaging: Consumer, Food Service, Private Label, Bulk
Brands:
  Vigo
  Alessi

13405 Viki's Montana Classics
801 Grand Dr
Bigfork, MT 59911-3532
406-837-5545
Fax: 406-837-5545 800-248-1222
Preserves and syrups
Owner: Viki Hoveland
Estimated Sales: $1-2.5 Million
Number Employees: 1-4
Parent Co: Canandaigua Wine Company

13406 Viking Distillery
1101 E Broad Ave
Albany, GA 31705-2872
229-436-0181
Fax: 229-434-1768 866-729-3722
info@sazerac.com www.sazerac.com
Bourbon blends, gin and vodka
President & CEO: Mark Brown
Vice President of Human Resources: Kathy Thelen
Marketing Services Director: Meredith Moody
Vice President of Sales & Marketing: Steve Wyant
PR Manager: Amy Preske
Plant Manager: Julius Drakes
Estimated Sales: $6 Million
Number Employees: 10-19
Parent Co: Barton Brands
Type of Packaging: Consumer

13407 Viking Seafoods Inc
50 Crystal St
Malden, MA 02148-5919
781-322-2000
Fax: 781-397-0527 800-225-3020
jcovelluzzi@vikingseafoods.com
Frozen seafood including fish cakes, fish and chips, cod, fish flake, halibut, perch, fish sticks, fish patties, scallops and shrimp; also, value-added products including Nordica and bake n'broil style.
President: Charles Gulino
CEO: James Covelluzzi
Sales Manager: Douglas Farrell
Contact: Leonard Abbene
abbene@vikingseafoods.com
Plant Manager: Joseph Novello
Estimated Sales: $8200000
Number Employees: 50-99
Type of Packaging: Consumer, Food Service
Brands:
  Kitchens of the Sea
  Viking

13408 Viking Trading
2375 John Glenn Dr
Suite 106
Atlanta, GA 30341
770-455-8630
Fax: 770-455-9632
Blue crab, caviar, conch, crab, crawfish, kingfish, lobster meat
President: Juan Vales
Principal: Frank Valdez

13409 Vikis Foods
999 South Oyster Bay Rd.
Suite 403
Bethpage, NY 11714
516-767-8700
Fax: 516-767-1300 info@vikisfoods.com
www.vikisfoods.com
Granola
President: Viktoria Sater
Vice President: Greg Gutsko
Director of Operations: Christine Busse
Estimated Sales: $1-5 Million
Number Employees: 11
Type of Packaging: Food Service
Brands:
  Viki's Granola

13410 Viktoria's Gourmet Foods, LLC
Bethpage, NY 11714
516-767-8700
www.vikisfoods.com
Manufacturer of soft-baked granola.
Owner and Founder: Viki Sater

13411 Villa Barone
21825 Jerusalem Grade Road
Middletown, CA
707-987-8823
Fax: 707-235-8613 info@thevillabarone.com
www.thevillabarone.com
Olive oils and olive oil products
President: Robert Lipari

13412 Villa Helena/Arger-Martucci Winery
1455 Inglewood Ave
St Helena, CA 94574-2219
707-963-4334
Fax: 707-963-4748 www.arger-martucci.com
Wines
President: Carol Martucci
Marketing Director: Katarena Arger
Estimated Sales: $500,000-$1 Million
Number Employees: 1-4
Type of Packaging: Private Label
Brands:
  Villa Helena

13413 Villa Milan Vineyard
7287 E County Road 50 N
Milan, IN 47031-8946
812-654-3419
Wines
President: John Garrett
CEO: Marc A McNeece
Estimated Sales: $2.5-5 Million
Number Employees: 10-19
Brands:
  Villa Milan

13414 Villa Mt. Eden Winery
8711 Silverado Trl S
Saint Helena, CA 94574
866-931-1624
Fax: 707-963-7840
Processor and exporter of wines
Manager: Jeff Mc Bride
j.mcbride@villamteden.com
Estimated Sales: $10-20 Million
Number Employees: 10-19
Parent Co: Stimson Lane
Type of Packaging: Consumer

13415 Village Roaster
9255 W Alameda Avenue
Lakewood, CO 80226-2802
303-238-8718
Fax: 303-233-4370 800-237-3822
contact@villageroaster.com
www.villageroaster.com
Coffee
President: Jim Curtis
VP: Kathleen Curtis
CFO: Kathleen Curtis
Contact: Melissa Charles
charles@villageroaster.com
Estimated Sales: Under $500,000
Brands:
  Village Roaster

13416 Villar Vintners of Valdese
4940 Villar Ln NE
Valdese, NC 28690
828-879-3202
Fax: 828-879-3202
Wines
President: Joel Talmas
CEO: Ernest Jahier
Estimated Sales: $3-5 000,000
Number Employees: 5-9
Brands:
  Villar Vintners

13417 Vilore Foods Co Inc
8220 San Lorenzo Dr
Laredo, TX 78045-8704
956-722-7190
Fax: 956-728-8383 info@vilore.com
www.vilore.com
Jalapeno peppers
President: Suzanna Almanza
salmanza@vilore.com
Estimated Sales: $200 Million
Number Employees: 20-49

13418 Vinalhaven Fishermens Co-op
PO Box 366
Camden, ME 04843-0366
207-236-0092
Fax: 207-236-7733 janetvhcoop@hotmail.com
vinalhavencoop.com
Seafood
Owner: John R Long
Estimated Sales: $1-3 Million
Number Employees: 5-9

13419 Vince's Seafoods
1105 Lafayette St
Gretna, LA 70053-6345
504-368-1544
Fax: 504-368-1545
Processor and exporter of frozen and boiled seafood; shrimp, crabs, oysters, crawfish, catfish, tuna, trout, flounder and tilapia. Also gumbo and soups
President: Barbara Jimenez
vdesalvojr@yahoo.com

Food Manufacturers / A-Z

Estimated Sales: $500,000-$1 Million
Number Employees: 1-4
Square Footage: 32000

13420 Vincent Arroyo Winery
2361 Greenwood Ave
Calistoga, CA 94515-1031
707-942-6995
Fax: 707-942-0895 info@vincentarroyo.com
www.vincentarroyo.com
Wines
President: Vincent Arroyo
arroyo707@aol.com
Estimated Sales: Less than $1 Million
Number Employees: 5-9
Type of Packaging: Bulk

13421 Vincent B Zaninovich & Sons
20715 Avenue 8
Richgrove, CA 93261
661-725-2497
Fax: 661-725-5153 www.vbzgrapes.com
Processor and exporter of grapes
Owner: Antone Zaninovich
Owner/President: Vincent Zaninovich
vincentz@vbzgrapes.com
VP: Andrew Zaninovich
Sales Team Member: Joe Butkiewicz
Human Resources Director: Mark Boyer
Estimated Sales: $11 Million
Number Employees: 10-19
Square Footage: 30900
Type of Packaging: Bulk
Brands:
  Mr Z
  Richgrove King
  Vbz

13422 Vincent Formusa Company
2150 Oxford Road
Des Plaines, IL 60018
847-813-6040
Fax: 312-421-1286 sales@marconi-foods.com
www.marconi-foods.com
Beans, salad dressings, giardiniera & peppers, olives, olive oils, pasta, Italian style salads, spices, tomatoes, vinegars
President: Robert Johnson
bob@marconi-foods.com
Estimated Sales: $830,000
Number Employees: 10
Square Footage: 100000
Type of Packaging: Consumer, Food Service, Bulk
Brands:
  Digiovanni
  Marconi

13423 Vincent Piazza Jr & Sons
5736 Heebe St
Harahan, LA 70123
504-734-0012
Fax: 504-734-8752 800-259-5016
packages@piazzaseafood.com
www.piazzaseafood.com
Shrimp; wholesaler/distributor of crab, crawfish, alligator, conch, octopus, clams, lobster, frog legs, scallops, turtle, gumbo, etc
Owner: Vincent Piazza Jr
Sales and Inventory Control: Nicholas Piazza
Contact: Bryan Piazza
bryanpiazza@piazzaseafood.com
Computer Systems and Purchasing: Bryan Piazza
Estimated Sales: $2.5-5 Million
Number Employees: 20-49
Square Footage: 24000
Type of Packaging: Food Service
Brands:
  Lucky Star
  Papa Piazza Brand
  Papa's Fresh Catch
  Tri Dragon

13424 Vincent's Food Corporation
179 Old Country Rd
Carle Place, NY 11514
516-481-3544
Fax: 516-742-4579
Sauces
President: Anthony Marisi
amarisi@vincentsclambar.com
Estimated Sales: $5-10 Million
Number Employees: 5-9

13425 Vincor Canada
441 Courtneypark Drive E
Mississauga, ON L5T 2V3
Canada
905-564-6900
Fax: 905-564-6909 800-265-9463
www.cbrands.com
Wine and vodka cooler importer, marketer and distributor.
President & CEO: Eric Morham
CFO: Don Dychuck
SVP Marketing, Canadian Portfolio: Steve Bolliger
Director Sales & Marketing, RJ Spagnols: Ellen Johnson
SVP Operations: Martin van der Merwe
Square Footage: 60655
Type of Packaging: Consumer, Food Service
Other Locations:
  Vincor Quebec
  Rougemont QC
Brands:
  Camarad
  Goundry Fine Wine
  Hogue
  Inniskillin
  Jackson-Triggs
  Kim Crawford Wines
  Kumala
  Loiseau Bleu
  Pallenque
  Toasted Head

13426 Vine Village Day
4059 Old Sonoma Rd
Napa, CA 94559-9702
707-255-4116
Fax: 707-255-8431 www.vinevillage.org
Wine
Executive Director: Michael Kerson
Estimated Sales: Below $5 Million
Number Employees: 20-49
Type of Packaging: Private Label
Brands:
  Carneros Chardonnay

13427 Vink & Beri
140 Domorah Dr
Montgomeryville, PA 18936
215-654-5252
info@vinkandberi.com
www.vinkandberi.com
Aloe vera juices and syrup, coconut water, orange juice
Chairman: Cornelis Gerardus Vink
CEO: Vipul Chander Beri
Sr. Regional Sales Manager: Brandon Hawes
Estimated Sales: $1-2 Million
Number Employees: 11-50
Parent Co: Tropical General Investment (TGI) Group
Brands:
  Alor
  Bare Nature

13428 Vino's Brew Pub
923 W 7th St
Little Rock, AR 72201-4005
501-375-8466
Fax: 501-375-8468 www.vinosbrewpub.com
Beer
President: Henry Lee
CEO: Dan O'Byrne
Estimated Sales: Below $5 Million
Number Employees: 20-49
Type of Packaging: Private Label
Brands:
  7th Street Pale
  Big House Ale
  Lazy Boy Stout

13429 Vinoklet Winery
11069 Colerain Rd
Cincinnati, OH 45252-1425
513-385-9309
Fax: 513-385-9379 vinokletwinery@fuse.net
www.vinokletwines.com
Wine manufacturer and restaurant service
Owner/Winemaker: Kreso Mikulic
vinokletwinery@fuse.net
Estimated Sales: $500,000 appx.
Number Employees: 10-19
Type of Packaging: Food Service
Brands:
  Vinoklet

13430 (HQ)Vinquiry Wine Analysis
7795 Bell Rd
Windsor, CA 95492-8519
707-838-6312
Fax: 707-838-1765 info@vinquiry.com
Wine industry yeasts and supplements
President: Jose Santos
Founder: Marty Bannister
mbannister@vinquiry.com
Sales Manager, Winemaking Products: Max Buiani
Director of Operations: Michelle Bowen
Estimated Sales: $5-10 Million
Number Employees: 20-49
Square Footage: 41600
Type of Packaging: Private Label, Bulk
Other Locations:
  Vinquiry Central Coast Office
  Santa Maria CA
  Vinquiry Napa Office
  Napa CA

13431 Vintage Bee Inc.
4020 Stirrup Creek Dr.
Suite 109
Durham, NC 27703
919-699-6788
Manufacturer of honey.
Co-Founder: Van Tapp
Co-Founder: Laura Tapp

13432 Vintage Italia
513 Main St.
Windermere, FL 34786
407-217-5910
Fax: 407-217-5911 info@pastachips.com
www.pastachips.com
Pasta based chips
Founder: Jerry Bello

13433 Vintage Plantations Chocolates
461 Frelinghuysen Ave
Newark, NJ 07114-1426
908-354-9304
Fax: 973-242-1998 800-207-7058
Chocolate
President: Pierrick Chouard
Operations Manager: Bryan Sargent
Estimated Sales: Below $5 Million
Number Employees: 5-9
Type of Packaging: Private Label
Brands:
  Dagoba Organic Chocolate
  Fritz Knipschildt

13434 Vintage Wine Estates
205 Concourse Blvd
Santa Rosa, CA 95403
877-289-9463
www.vintagewineestates.com
Producer and retailer of wines and champagnes
Founding Partner & CEO: Pat Roney
President: Terry Wheatley
CFO: Katherine DeVillers
COO: Jeff Nicholson
Estimated Sales: $69 Million
Number Employees: 100-249
Number of Brands: 1
Number of Products: 42
Type of Packaging: Consumer
Brands:
  Windsor Vineyards

13435 Viobin USA
226 W Livingston St
Monticello, IL 61856-1673
217-762-2561
Fax: 217-762-2489 888-473-9645
info@viobinusa.com www.viobinusa.com
Manufacturer of nutritional extract, defatted wheatgerm, and wheat germ oil.
CEO: Monte White
Marketing/Sales: Geni Heider
Manager: Bart Allen
sales@viobinusa.com
General Manager: Roger Mohr
Production: Kevin Stevens
Estimated Sales: $10-20 Million
Number Employees: 20-49
Number of Brands: 1
Parent Co: McShares, Inc.
Type of Packaging: Consumer, Bulk
Brands:
  Viobin

Food Manufacturers / A-Z

13436 Viola's Gourmet Goodies
P.O.Box 351075
Los Angeles, CA 90035
323-731-5277
Fax: 323-731-6898 violasgg@pacbell.net
Gourmet relish, jelly, zinger and rim shot
Owner: Nancy Rowland
violasgg@pacbell.net
Estimated Sales: $.5-1 million
Number Employees: 1-4
Type of Packaging: Bulk
Brands:
  Viola's

13437 Violet Packing Holdings LLC
123 Railroad Ave
Williamstown, NJ 08094-1699
856-629-7428
Fax: 856-629-6340 www.deiorios.com
Peppers, tomatoes and sauces including spaghetti and pizza
President: James Zhao
jamesz@genscript.com
VP Operations: Chip Sclafani
GM: Lou Sclafani
Estimated Sales: $10-20 Million
Number Employees: 50-99
Parent Co: Don Pepino Company
Type of Packaging: Consumer, Food Service
Brands:
  Don Pepino
  Sclafani
  Violet

13438 Violife
Thessaloniki,
Greece
info@violifefoods.com
www.violifefoods.com
Vegan, lactose-free, non-GMO, gluten-free dairy and meat alternatives in various flavors
Number of Brands: 1
Number of Products: 43
Type of Packaging: Consumer, Private Label
Brands:
  Violife

13439 Virgil's Root Beer
201 Merritt 7 Corporate Park
Norwalk, CT 06851
203-890-0557
Fax: 203-496-8883 800-997-3337
info@reedsinc.com www.virgils.com
Root beer in various flavors, including original, premium, extra, cherry, raspberry, spiced apple, plus ginger candy and ginger ice cream
CEO & Director: Val Stalowir
Chief Innovation Officer: Chris Reed
CFO: James Linesch
COO: Stefan Freeman
SVP Sales And Marketing: Neal Cohane
Contact: Peter Anton
panton@reedsgingerbrew.com
Estimated Sales: $20.38 Million
Number Employees: 20
Square Footage: 30000
Parent Co: Reed's Ginger Brew
Type of Packaging: Consumer, Food Service
Brands:
  Virgil's

13440 Virgin Raw Foods LLC
11645 Wilshire Blvd.
Los Angeles, CA 90025
424-322-0535
800-830-7047
cs@virginrawfoods.com www.virginrawfoods.com
Royal honey infused with herbs and superfoods
Founder/Owner: Monika Kozdrowiecka
Number of Brands: 1
Number of Products: 1
Type of Packaging: Consumer, Private Label
Brands:
  Bee Panacea

13441 Virginia & Spanish Peanut Co
260 Dexter St
Providence, RI 02907-2798
401-421-2543
Fax: 401-421-2557 800-673-3562
contact@vspnut.com www.vspnutco.com
Salted nuts, peanuts and peanut butter
President: Robert Kaloostian
vfpnutco@aol.com
VP/Treasurer: Candale Kaloostain
Estimated Sales: $10-20 Million
Number Employees: 5-9
Square Footage: 48000
Type of Packaging: Consumer, Food Service, Private Label, Bulk
Brands:
  Anchor
  Brown Bear

13442 Virginia Artesian Bottling Company
4300 Spring Run Rd
Mechanicsville, VA 23116-6639
804-779-7500
Fax: 866-291-9504 sales@virginiaartesian.com
www.virginiaartesian.com
Bottled water
Owner: Steven Brown
Sales Manager: Frank Atwood
Production Manager: Nick Brown
Year Founded: 2003
Estimated Sales: Under $500,000
Number Employees: 1-10
Type of Packaging: Food Service
Brands:
  Virginia Artesian(c)

13443 Virginia Chutney Company
113A Aileen Rd.
Flint Hill
Washington, VA 22627
540-675-1984
Fax: 540-675-1985 sales@virginiachutney.com
www.virginiachutney.com
Chutneys
Contact: Oliver Turner
oliver@virginiachutney.com

13444 Virginia Dare Extract Co
882 3rd Ave # 2
Brooklyn, NY 11232-1902
718-788-1776
Fax: 718-768-3978 flavorinfo@virginiadare.com
www.virginiadare.com
Flavor and extract company founded in 1835.
President: Howard Smith
hsmith@virginiadare.com
Number Employees: 100-249
Type of Packaging: Bulk
Brands:
  Contrasweet
  G-Brew
  Gourmet Brew
  Prosweet
  Superfex
  Superfreeze
  Tre Cafe
  Vidarome

13445 Virginia Diner Inc
322 W Main St
Wakefield, VA 23888
888-823-4637
www.vadiner.net
Peanuts, cashews, almonds, peanut brittle, nutty candies, chocolates and snacks.
President: Christine Epperson
Year Founded: 1929
Estimated Sales: $100+ Million
Number Employees: 250-499
Number of Brands: 4
Brands:
  Game Day Snacks
  Norman Rockwell
  Old Bay
  Virginia Diner

13446 Virginia Honey Company
P.O.Box 1915
Inwood, WV 25428
304-267-8500
Fax: 304-263-0946
Honey, salad dressings, including Vidalia Onion Vinagarette salad dressing, sauces, jams and jellies, herring products, salmon products, condiments, horseradish, cream cheese, party platters
CEO: Terry Hess
Parent Co: Vita Food Products
Type of Packaging: Consumer, Food Service, Private Label, Bulk
Brands:
  Virginia Brand
  Vita Brand

13447 Virginia Trout Co
5480 Potomac River Rd
Monterey, VA 24465-2257
540-468-2280
Fax: 540-468-2279 info@virginiatroutfarms.com
Fresh and frozen mountain trout
Owner: Bryan Plemmons
b.plemmons@virginiatroutfarms.com
Estimated Sales: Less Than $500,000
Number Employees: 5-9
Type of Packaging: Food Service
Brands:
  Allegheny
  Mountain Trout

13448 Visalia Citrus Packing Group
19743 Avenue 344
Woodlake, CA 93286
559-564-3351
Fax: 559-564-3865 vcpg@vcpg.com
Golden State Citrus Packers is a licensed commercial shipper of citrus products for Sunkist Growers, Inc.
President: George Lambeth
Manager: John Kalendar
johnkalendar@vcpg.com
Office Manager: Judith Jenkins
Plant Manager: Raul Gamez
Number Employees: 100-249
Parent Co: Visalia Citrus Packing Group
Type of Packaging: Food Service

13449 Visalia Produce Sales
201 W Stroud Ave
Kingsburg, CA 93631-9531
559-897-6652
Fax: 559-897-6650 george@visaliaproduce.com
www.visaliaproduce.com
California fruits and vegetables
Owner: Stan Shamoon
Sales Representative: Stan Shamoon
Sales Representative: Aron Gularte
Sales Representative: George Matoian
Estimated Sales: $1-10 Million
Number Employees: 20-49

13450 Vision Pack Brands
531 Main Street
Suite 513
El Segundo, CA 90245
877-477-8500
Fax: 866-825-1808 877-477-8500
visionpack@verizon.net
www.visionpackbrands.com
Gourmet crackers, snacks and dip, candy, confections and beverages

13451 Vision Seafood Partners
41 Summer Street
Kingston, MA 02364-1418
781-585-2000
Fax: 773-561-0139
Seafood

13452 Vista D'Oro Farms
346-208th Street
Langley, BC V2Z 1T7
Canada
604-514-3539
Fax: 604-514-3599 855-514-3539
info@thepreservatory.com thepreservatory.com
Preserves, wines, jams and jellies
Owner: Lee Murphy
Estimated Sales: Under $500,000
Number Employees: 1-10
Type of Packaging: Food Service
Brands:
  The Preservatory
  Vista D'Oro

13453 Vit-Best Nutrition
2802 Dow Ave
Tustin, CA 92780
714-832-9700
info@vit-best.com
www.vit-best.com
Nutritional supplements and vitamins.

Food Manufacturers / A-Z

CEO: Tom Mooy
CFO: Stacey Kato
VP, Quality: Rick Beatty
VP, Sales: John Altenberg
VP, Operations: Juliun Brabon
Estimated Sales: $20-50 Million
Number Employees: 200
Square Footage: 140000
Parent Co: Xiamen Kingdomway Group Co.
Type of Packaging: Consumer, Bulk

13454 Vita Food Products Inc
2222 W Lake St
Chicago, IL 60612
800-989-8482
www.vitafoodproducts.com
Pickled herring, lox & nova salmon, cream cheese with salmon, horseradish, cocktail and tarter sauces; gourmet sauces, marinades, salad dressings, dessert toppers, syrups & honey, salsa, drinks.
President & CEO: Clifford Bolen
Chief Financial Officer: R. Anthony Nelson
Vice President: William Zaikos
Production Manager: Henry Williams
Purchasing Manager: Doug Clark
Estimated Sales: $32 Million
Number Employees: 100-249
Square Footage: 82200
Type of Packaging: Consumer, Food Service
Brands:
  Vita
  Elf
  Jim Beam
  Grand Isle
  Virginia Brand
  Oak Hill Farms
  Biltmore
  Scorned Woman
  Sauza

13455 Vita Plus Corp
2514 Fish Hatchery Rd
P.O. Box 259126
Madison, WI 53713-2424
608-256-1988
Fax: 608-283-7990 608-256-1988
www.vitaplus.com
Dairy
Owner: Roop Rache
Co-Owner: Eddie Molina
CFO: Mike Miley
mmiley@vitaplus.com
Estimated Sales: $5-10 Million
Number Employees: 100-249
Brands:
  Cortilite
  Life Line Vita Plus
  Vita-Plus

13456 Vita-Pakt Citrus Products Co
203 E Badillo St
Covina, CA 91723-2116
626-332-1101
Fax: 626-966-8196 888-684-8272
www.vita-pakt.com
Citrus and kiwi processor.
Chairman & CEO: James Boyles
james.boyle@vita-paktcitrus.com
Number Employees: 50-99
Type of Packaging: Consumer, Food Service, Bulk

13457 Vita-Pure Inc
410 W 1st Ave
Roselle, NJ 07203-1047
908-245-1212
Fax: 908-245-1999 www.vitapuretech.com
Food/dietary supplements, vitamins, nutritional supplements
President: Achyut Sahasra
vitapureinc@yahoo.com
Vice President: Jaqueline Schauffler
Marketing Director: Joseph Campis
Operations Manager: Sheldon Tannebaum
Production Manager: Angelo Padilla
Estimated Sales: $5-10 000,000
Number Employees: 20-49
Square Footage: 17500
Type of Packaging: Private Label

13458 VitaThinQ Inc.
Davie, FL
info@vitathinq.com
www.essentialmints.com
Caffeinated peppermints for weight loss; peppermints with melatnonin for sleep aid
Number of Brands: 1
Number of Products: 3
Type of Packaging: Consumer, Private Label
Brands:
  Essential Mints

13459 Vitakem Neutraceutical Inc
811 West Jericho Turnpike
Smithtown, NY 11787
855-837-0430
www.vitakem.com
Vitamins and supplements
President/CEO: Bret Hoyt Sr
Contact: Aaron Berkman
aaron@vitakem.com

13460 Vital Choice
P.O. Box 4121
Bellingham, WA 98227
800-608-4825
www.vitalchoice.com
Wild fish, shellfish, canned fish, meats, omega-3s, supplements, and organic foods
Year Founded: 2001

13461 Vital Farms
3913 Todd Lane
Suite 505
Austin, TX 78744
877-455-3063
info@vitalfarms.com
vitalfarms.com
Eggs and butter
President & Chief Operating Officer: Russell Diez-Canseco
CEO & Owner: Matt O'Hayer
Chief Financial Officer: Jason Dale
Director of Marketing: Kathryn McKeon
Senior Director of Human Resources: Jennifer A. Gregg
Year Founded: 2007
Estimated Sales: $5.4 Million
Number Employees: 50-200
Brands:
  Certified Humane(c)
  Vital Farms(c)

13462 Vital Proteins LLC
545 Busse Rd.
Elk Grove Village, IL 60007
224-544-9110
info@vitalproteins.com
www.vitalproteins.com
Collagen supplements in various flavors
Co-Founder/Chief Executive Officer: Kurt Seidensticker
Number of Brands: 1
Type of Packaging: Consumer, Private Label
Brands:
  Vital Proteins

13463 Vitale Poultry Company
800 E Cooke Rd
Columbus, OH 43214
614-267-1874
Fax: 614-267-7824
Poultry processing
Co-Owner: Mark Cecutti
Co-Owner: Dan Cecutti
President: Rose Vitale
Estimated Sales: $5-9.9 000,000
Number Employees: 10-19

13464 Vitalicious
11 Broadway Ste 1155
New York, NY 10004
212-233-6030
Fax: 212-233-6031 877-848-2877
customerservice@vitalicious.com
www.vitalicious.com
100 calorie VitaTops, VitaMuffins, VitaBrownies, VitaMixes, VitaCakes
Contact: Ian Gillespie
ian.gillespie@vitalicious.com
Brands:
  Vitatops
  Vitamuffins
  Vitabrownies
  Vitamixes
  Vitacakes

13465 Vitality Life Choice
5350 Capital Court, Suite #109
PO Box 21133
Carson City, NV 89721-1133
775-882-7186
Fax: 775-882-6686 800-423-8365
Health and nutritional supplements
President: Gary Paulsen

13466 Vitality Works
8500 Bluewater Rd. NW
Albuquerque, NM 87121
505-268-9950
Fax: 505-268-9952 www.vitalityworks.com
Herbal, vitamin and nutraceutical supplements
Chief Executive Officer: Mitch Coven
Production Manager: Jackie Keepers
Year Founded: 1982
Number of Brands: 1
Type of Packaging: Private Label
Brands:
  Vitality Works

13467 Vitamer Laboratories
46 Corporate Park
Irvine, CA 92606
800-432-8355
customerservice@vitamer.com www.vitamer.com
Processor of dietary supplements and herbal products.
Year Founded: 1924
Estimated Sales: $20-50 Million
Number Employees: 100-249
Parent Co: Anabolic
Type of Packaging: Private Label

13468 Vitamilk Dairy
4141 Agate Road
Bellingham, WA 98226-8745
206-529-4128
Fax: 206-524-7070
Dairy products including milk, sour cream and ice cream
President: E Gerald Teel
VP Sales: Larry Burns
Plant Manager: Paul Nelson
Number Employees: 100-249
Type of Packaging: Consumer, Food Service, Private Label, Bulk

13469 (HQ)Vitaminerals
1815 Flower St
Glendale, CA 91201-2024
818-500-8718
Fax: 818-240-2785 800-432-1856
www.cryogel.tv
Processor and exporter of food supplements and vitamins
Owner: Michael Gorman
jgorman@vitamineralsinc.com
President: John Gorman
jgorman@vitamineralsinc.com
VP: Mike Gorman
National Sales Director: Charles DesVos
Estimated Sales: $5-10 Million
Number Employees: 20-49
Square Footage: 70000
Brands:
  Hampshire Laboratories
  Vitaminerals

13470 Vitamins
200 E Randolph Drive
Chicago, IL 60601-6436
312-861-0700
Fax: 312-861-0708
customerservice@vitamins-inc.com
www.vitamins-inc.com
Nutritional ingredients including defatted wheat germ, wheat germ oil and soluble vitamins
President: James Carozza
Vice President: Robert Lenburg
Contact: Bill Redwood
redwood@vitamins-inc.com
Number Employees: 1-4

13471 Vitarich Ice Cream
572 Highway 1
Fortuna, CA 95540-9711
707-725-6182
Fax: 707-725-6186 info@humboldtcreamery.com
www.humboldtcreamery.com
Ice cream, sherbet, frozen yogurt and ice cream mixes and novelties

Food Manufacturers / A-Z

President: Rich Ghilarducci
Number Employees: 20-49
Type of Packaging: Consumer, Food Service, Private Label, Bulk
Other Locations:
  Vitarich Ice Cream Co.
  Seattle WA
Brands:
  Vitarich

13472 (HQ)Vitarich Laboratories
4365 Arnold Ave
Naples, FL 34104
239-430-2266
Fax: 239-430-4930   800-817-9999
Processor, importer and exporter of vitamins, nutraceuticals and food supplements including herbal, whole leaf wheat, barley and algae
President: Kevin Thomas
Marketing: Bill Foley
Sales Director: Frank Guzzo
Contact: Steve Colligan
colligans@vitarichlabs.com
Estimated Sales: $.5-1 million
Number Employees: 5-9
Square Footage: 80000
Type of Packaging: Consumer, Private Label, Bulk
Other Locations:
  Vitarich Laboratories
  Bainbridge GA
Brands:
  Hydra-Green

13473 Vitasoy USA
57 Russell Street
Woburn, MA 01801
781-430-8988
Fax: 978-772-6881   800-848-2769
info@vitasoy-usa.com   www.vitasoy-usa.com
Tofu, asian noodles, fresh pasta wraps, vegan sandwich spreads, soymilks, juices and teas
President/Chief Executive Officer: Walter Riglian
Contact: Terry Arkinstall
terry.arkinstall@vitasoy-usa.com
Chief Executive Officer: Tom Perry
Research & Development: Fred Jewett
Quality Assurance Manager: Rick Baum
Vice President, Marketing: Tim Kenny
Sales Executive: Eugene Lye
Public Relations: Stella Lung
Vice President, Operations: John Wareham
Production Supervisor: Edgar Bonilla
Facility Manager: Peter Breed
Purchasing Manager: Heidi Bonasoro
Estimated Sales: $20 Million
Number Employees: 160
Number of Brands: 4
Square Footage: 21227
Type of Packaging: Consumer, Food Service, Private Label
Brands:
  Nasoya
  Azumaya
  San Sui
  Vita

13474 Vitatech Nutritional Sciences
2802 Dow Ave
Tustin, CA 92780-7212
714-832-9700
Fax: 714-731-8482   info@vit-best.com
www.vit-best.com
Vitamins
CEO: Thomas Mooy
VP Supply Chain: Katie Watts
Director of Technical Services: David Jiang
Estimated Sales: $20-50 Million
Number Employees: 100-249
Type of Packaging: Private Label

13475 Viterra, Inc
2625 Victoria Ave.
Regina, SK S4T 7T9
Canada
306-569-4411
Fax: 306-569-4708   866-647-4090
www.viterra.com
Grain and oilseeds.
President/CEO: Kyle Jeworski
Estimated Sales: $2.4 Billion
Number Employees: 190,000
Parent Co: Glencore plc
Type of Packaging: Consumer, Food Service, Private Label, Bulk

Brands:
  Dakota Growers Pasta
  Pasta Sanita
  Zia Briosa

13476 Vity Meat & Provisions Company
1418 N 27th Avenue
Phoenix, AZ 85009-3603
602-269-7768
Fax: 602-269-0044
Meats
President: Michael Brown
VP Finance: Gary Rasmussen
Estimated Sales: $.5-1 million
Number Employees: 1-4

13477 Viva Tierra
601 S 2nd St
Mt Vernon, WA 98273
360-855-0566
organic@vivatierra.com
www.vivatierra.com
Organic produce including apples, pears, peaches, and onions
President/CEO: Luis Acuna
EVP/CFO: Steve Mackey
Sales Manager: Matt Roberts
Organic Integrity & Logistics: Addie Pobst

13478 Vive Organic
2554 Lincoln Blvd. # 772
Venice, CA 90291
877-774-9291
contact@vive-organic.com   www.vive-organic.com
Organic wellness shots in various flavors
Co-Founder/Chief Executive Officer: Wyatt Taubman
Co-Founder/Vice-President, Sales: J.R. Simich
Co-Founder/Chief Executive Officer: Kyle Withycombe
Number of Brands: 1
Number of Products: 3
Type of Packaging: Consumer, Private Label
Brands:
  Vive Organic

13479 Vivienne Dressings
P.O.Box 16072
St Louis, MO 63105-0772
314-994-7549
Fax: 636-947-1123   800-827-0778
ttucker.vivienne@gmail.com   www.vivienne.com
Gourmet dressings and marinades
President: Thomas A Tucker
Estimated Sales: Below $5 Million
Number Employees: 1-4
Brands:
  Vivienne

13480 Vivolac Cultures Corporation
3862 E Washington St
Indianapolis, IN 46201
317-356-8460
Fax: 317-356-8450   sales@vivolac.com
www.vivolac.com
Manufacturer and exporter of dairy, meat and bread starter cultures in pelletized, frozen and freeze-dried form
President: Wesley Sing
Technical Sales Manager: Rossana Reyle
Chief Marketing Officer: Philip Reinhardt
Technical Sales: David Winters
Estimated Sales: $1.4 Million
Number Employees: 20-49
Type of Packaging: Private Label, Bulk
Brands:
  Bioflora
  Vivolac

13481 Vivoo
Via del Commercio 16
Verona, 37066
Italy
info@vivoo.it
www.vivoo-re-evolution.com
Organic raw chocolate bars, energy bites, energy bars; raw cacao powder, cacao butter and cacao beans
Founder: Giorgio Sergio
Number of Brands: 1
Type of Packaging: Consumer, Private Label
Brands:
  Vivoo

13482 Vivra Chocolate
24 Walpole Park S
Walpole, MA 02081-2541
800-359-8950
info@vivrachocolate.com
vivrachocolate.com
Chocolate bars
Founder: Robert Leavitt
Director of Sales: Jordan Phillips
Number Employees: 2-10
Brands:
  Vivra(c)

13483 Vixen Kitchen
Santa Cruz, CA
707-223-5627
info@vixenkitchen.co
www.vixenkitchen.co
Organic, natural, vegan- and paleo-friendly gelato in various flavors
Founder/Chief Executive Officer: Sundara Clark
Number of Brands: 1
Number of Products: 6
Type of Packaging: Consumer, Private Label
Brands:
  Vixen Kitchen

13484 Vocatura Bakery Inc
695 Boswell Ave
Norwich, CT 06360-2826
860-887-2220
Breads
President: John Vocatura
Manager: David Vochtura
Estimated Sales: $500,000-$1 000,000
Number Employees: 10-19
Brands:
  Vocatura

13485 Vogel Popcorn
21325 Hamburg Avenue
Lakeville, MN 55044
952-469-7482
Fax: 952-469-2152   www.vogelpopcorn.com
Popcorn
President: Gary Rodkin
EVP: Colleen Batcheler
Estimated Sales: $10-20 Million
Number Employees: 20-49
Parent Co: ConAgra Foods
Type of Packaging: Consumer, Private Label, Bulk

13486 Voget Meats Inc
2930 E St
Hubbard, OR 97032-9313
503-981-6271
Fax: 503-981-0220
Smoked meats, sausages
CEO: Merle Stutzman
Vice President: Grace Stuzman
Estimated Sales: $2.5-5 Million
Number Employees: 10-19
Type of Packaging: Private Label
Brands:
  Voget Meats

13487 Vogue Cuisine Foods
PO Box 70608
Sunnyvale, CA 94086-0608
310-391-1053
Fax: 310-390-0883   888-236-4144
inquiry@voguecuisine.com
www.voguecuisine.com
Natural dehydrated low sodium and organic instant soup bases and mixes including chicken, beef, onion and vegetable vegetarian-chicken
President: Clinton Helvey
CEO: Carol Schlanger
Vice President: Clinton Helvey
Public Relations: Carol Helvey
Estimated Sales: Less Than $500,000
Number Employees: 5-9
Type of Packaging: Private Label
Brands:
  Vogue Beef Base
  Vogue Chicken Base
  Vogue Onion Base
  Vogue Vegebase
  Vogue Vegetarian Chicken Base

Food Manufacturers / A-Z

13488 Volcano Island Honey Company
46-4013 Puano Rd
Honokaa, HI 96727
808-775-1000
Fax: 808-775-0412 888-663-6639
www.volcanoislandhoney.com
Gourmet honey
Manager: Candice Choy
candice@volcanoislandhoney.com
Estimated Sales: Under $500,000
Number Employees: 5-9
Brands:
  Rare Hawaiian

13489 Vollwerth & Baroni Companies
PO Box 239
Hancock, MI 49930-0239
906-482-1550
Fax: 906-482-0842 800-562-7620
topdog@vollwerth.com www.vollwerth.com
Sausage and meat products; wholesaler/distributor of hotel and restaurant supplies; serving the food service market
President: Robert Vollwerth
Vice President/General Manager: Jim Schaaf
Secretary/Treasurer: Mary Ann Berryman
Sales Representative: Richard Vollwerth
Contact: Mary Berryman
berryman@vollwerth.com
Packaging Manager: Don Hiltunen
Production Manager: Adam Manderfield
Estimated Sales: $3.5 Million
Number Employees: 35
Square Footage: 80000

13490 Volpi Foods
5263 Northrup Avenue
St Louis, MO 63110-3026
314-772-8550
Fax: 314-772-0411 800-288-3439
www.volpifoods.com
Italian specialty meats, salami, proscuitto ham, pancetta, coppa, rotola
President & CEO: Lorenza Pasetti
COO: Jim Fleming
Chief Marketing Officer: Tim Urban
Sales Director: Christine Illuminato
Estimated Sales: $20-50 Million
Number Employees: 100-349
Brands:
  Volpi

13491 Von Stiehl Winery
115 Navarino St
Algoma, WI 54201-1246
920-487-5208
Fax: 920-487-5108 800-955-5208
vonstiehl@vonstiehl.com www.vonstiehl.com
Wine
President: William Schmiling
VP: Sandra Schmiling
Estimated Sales: $5 Million
Number Employees: 20-49
Type of Packaging: Consumer

13492 Von Strasser
1510 Diamond Mountain Rd
Calistoga, CA 94515-9669
707-942-0930
Fax: 707-942-0454 888-359-9463
wines@vonstrasser.com www.lvvsw.com
Wines
Owner: Rudy Von Strasser
rudy@vonstrasser.com
Director National Sales/Marketing: John Schulz
Vice President: Rita Von Strasser
Vineyard Manager: Gerardo Alfaro
Assistant Winemaker: Jason Bull
Vineyard Manager: Gerardo Alfaro
Estimated Sales: $2.5-5 Million
Number Employees: 5-9
Type of Packaging: Private Label
Brands:
  Von Strasser
  Von Strasser

13493 Voodoo Doughnut
22 SW 3rd Ave
Portland, OR 97204-2713
503-241-4704
www.voodoodoughnut.com
Donuts
Estimated Sales: Less Than $500,000
Number Employees: 5-9

13494 Voortman Bakery
4475 N Service Rd
Suite 600
Burlington, ON L7L 4X7
Canada
800-808-5950
info@voortman.com www.voortman.com
Manufacturers a variety of cookies including pre-packaged family packs and seasonal cookies.
Co-Founder & President: Harry Voortman
VP, Sales: Stephane Musicka
Estimated Sales: $67 Million
Number Employees: 450
Number of Brands: 1
Square Footage: 23229
Type of Packaging: Consumer, Bulk
Brands:
  Voortman

13495 Vosges Haut-Chocolat
2950 N Oakley Ave
Suite 203
Chicago, IL 60618-8010
773-388-5560
Fax: 773-772-7917 888-301-9866
www.vosgeschocolate.com
Chocolate truffles and gourmet gifts
Owner: Katrina Markoff
katrina@vosgeschocolate.com
Number Employees: 100-249

13496 Vtopian Artisan Cheeses
Portland, OR
contact@vtopiancheeses.com
www.vtopiancheeses.com
Artisan cashew cheeses including peppercorn brie, port cheddar, aged white cheddar, sharp cheddar, and camembert
Founder, Co-Owner: Imber Lingard

13497 Vynecrest Winery
172 Arrowhead Ln
Breinigsville, PA 18031-1462
610-398-7525
Fax: 610-398-7530 800-361-0725
wines@vynecrest.com www.vynecrest.com
Wines
Co-Owner: Janice Landis
Co-Owner: John Landis
john@vynecrest.com
Estimated Sales: Less than $200,000
Number Employees: 1-4
Type of Packaging: Private Label
Brands:
  Vynecrest Vineyards

13498 Vyse Gelatin Co
5010 Rose Rd
Schiller Park, IL 60176-1023
847-678-4780
Fax: 847-678-0329 800-533-2152
sales@vyse.com www.vyse.com
Manufacturer, exporter and importer of food grade gelatins.
President: Gary Brunet
gbrunet@vyse.com
Estimated Sales: $2.5-5 Million
Number Employees: 10-19
Type of Packaging: Food Service, Private Label, Bulk
Brands:
  150 Bloom
  225 Bloom
  610-D
  710-D
  Atlas
  Celero
  Economix
  Finemix
  Flour Fine
  Hypowr
  Pbc-210
  Protector
  Seeclear
  Stabilo
  Superclear
  Superla
  Supertex
  Superwhip
  Textura
  Vee Gee
  Velvatex
  Viscomix
  X-Fine

13499 W & G Marketing Company
413 Kellogg Avenue
PO Box 1742
Ames, IA 50010
515-233-4774
Fax: 515-233-4773 www.wgmarketing.com
Processor and exporter of roasting pigs including whole and frozen; also, meat and poultry by-products and fully cooked barbecue turkey, beef and pork
President/Sales and Marketing: Darren Dies
ddies@wgmarketing.com
VP Operations: Robert Olinger
Estimated Sales: $5-10 Million
Number Employees: 5
Square Footage: 21928
Type of Packaging: Consumer, Food Service, Private Label
Brands:
  Hickory Grove
  W&G's

13500 W. Forrest Haywood Seafood Company
431 Messick Rd
Poquoson, VA 23662-1815
757-868-6748
Fax: 757-868-1111
Fresh crabmeat
President: Laura Hornsby
forrestseafoodva@aol.com
VP: Delores Forrest
Estimated Sales: $2.5-5,000,000
Number Employees: 1-4

13501 W.A. Beans & Sons
229 Bomarc Road
Bangor, ME 04401
207-947-0364
Fax: 207-990-4211 800-649-1958
sales@beansmeats.com www.beansmeats.com
Processor and wholesaler of meats, including smoked poultry, gourmet sausages, pork chops, bacon, fish, and hams.
Estimated Sales: Under $5 Million
Number Employees: 20-49
Square Footage: 16
Type of Packaging: Consumer, Food Service, Private Label, Bulk

13502 W.J. Stearns & Sons/Mountain Dairy
50 Stearns Road
Storrs Mansfield, CT 06268-2701
860-423-9289
Fax: 860-423-3486 www.mountaindairy.com
Processor and wholesaler/distributor of dairy products including cream and milk
President: W Stearns
Vice President: James Stearns
Estimated Sales: $3 Million
Number Employees: 35
Type of Packaging: Consumer, Private Label

13503 W.L. Petrey Wholesale Inc.
10345 Petrey Hwy
Luverne, AL 36049
334-230-5674
Fax: 334-335-2422 mail@petrey.com
www.petrey.com
Wholesaler/distributor of frozen food, general merchandise, general line products, provisions/meats and seafood
President: Bill Jackson
CEO: James Jackson
Contact: Kevin Argo
kargo@petrey.com
Number Employees: 500-999

13504 W.O. Sasser
135 Johnny Mercer Blvd
Savannah, GA 31410-2118
912-897-1154
Fax: 912-897-0331
Seafood
Owner: William Sasser
Estimated Sales: $.5-1 million
Number Employees: 5-9

13505 W.R. Delozier Sausage Company
12350 Chapman Highway
Seymour, TN 37865-6231
865-577-5907
Sausages
President: W Delozier

Estimated Sales: Less than $500,000
Number Employees: 1-4

13506 W.S. Wells & Sons
P.O. Box 109
Wilton, ME 04294-0109
207-645-3393
Fax: 207- 64-5 33
Canned fiddleheads and dandelions, green beans, baked beans, soup mixes
Owner: Adrian Wells
Estimated Sales: $2.5-5 000,000
Number Employees: 10-19

13507 W.T. Ruark & Company
2543 Hoopers Island Rd.
Fishing Creek, MD 21634
410-397-3133
Established in 1948. Manufacturer of seafood including oysters, crabs and crabmeat.
President: William Ruark
Estimated Sales: $21 Million
Number Employees: 20-49
Type of Packaging: Consumer

13508 W.T.I.
281 Martin Luther King Jr Ave
Jefferson, GA 30549
417-767-4790
Fax: 706-387-5159 800-827-1727
kevon@wtiinc.com www.wtiinc.com
Marinades and flavorings for meat.
Owner: Wolf Ludwig
Sr. Vice President: Michael Crump
Quality Assurance Manager: Jenni Rench
Director of Sales and Marketing: Kevon Ledgerwood
Director of Operations: Stephan Georg
Production Manager: Ertan Hyuseinov
Square Footage: 140000

13509 WACO Beef & Pork Processors
523 Precision Dr
Waco, TX 76710-6972
254-772-4669
Fax: 254-772-4579 www.holysmokedsausage.com
Fresh portion controlled beef, chicken and pork including sausage, chorizo and bratwurst; importer of beef skirts; wholesaler/distributor of meat and general merchandise; serving the food service market
Manager: Sara Jones
Estimated Sales: $2.2 Million
Number Employees: 5-9
Square Footage: 28000
Type of Packaging: Food Service
Brands:
   Precision

13510 WBM International
54 State Route 12
Flemington, NJ 08822-1540
973-350-8900
Fax: 973-350-8848 866-802-9366
support@wbminternational.com
wbminternational.com
Himalayan salt
Sales Representative: Juliana Mata
Director: Nafees Anjum
Estimated Sales: $7 Million
Number Employees: 35
Brands:
   Himalayan Chef
   Himalayan Glow
   WBM

13511 (HQ)WCC Honey Marketing
636 Turnbull Canyon Rd # A
City Of Industry, CA 91745-1107
626-855-3086
Fax: 626-855-3087
Processor and exporter of natural sweeteners, syrups and nutritional supplements including honey, comb honey, molasses, blackstrap molasses, corn syrup, agave nectar and royal jelly; importer of honey, barley malt sweetener, rice syrup and juice concentrate
Owner: Anthony Li
info@wcchoney.com
General Manager: Chuck Burkholder
National Sales Manager: Norma Robinson
info@wcchoney.com
Purchasing Manager: James Littlejohn
Estimated Sales: $5-10 Million
Number Employees: 5-9
Square Footage: 118800

Type of Packaging: Consumer, Food Service, Private Label, Bulk
Other Locations:
   Western Commerce Corp.
   Kansas City MO
Brands:
   Cucamonga
   El Panal
   Fruitsweet
   Hawaiian Gold
   Lo Han
   Pot O' Gold
   Powers

13512 WEIS Markets Inc.
1000 S. 2nd St.
PO Box 471
Sunbury, PA 17801
570-286-4571
866-999-9347
www.weismarkets.com
Grocery, bakery, deli, produce, floral, seafood, and more.
Chair/President/CEO: Jonathan Weis
jweis@weismarkets.com
Year Founded: 1912
Estimated Sales: $3.4 Billion
Number Employees: 18,000
Other Locations:
   Manufacturing Facility-Market St
   Sunbury PA
   Manufacturing Facility-N 4th St
   Sunbury PA
Brands:
   Weis Five Star
   Weis Quality
   Full Circle

13513 WG Thompson & Sons
2 Hyland Dr.
Blenheim, ON N0P 1A0
Canada
519-676-5411
Fax: 519-676-3185 800-265-5225
Agricultural products including soybeans, edible beans, and commercial grains to domestic and export markets.
President: Wes Thompson
Estimated Sales: $100 Million
Number Employees: 350
Type of Packaging: Consumer, Food Service, Private Label, Bulk
Brands:
   C&G
   Hyland

13514 WILD Flavors (Canada)
7315 Pacific Circle
Mississauga, ON L5T 1V1
Canada
905-670-1108
Fax: 905-670-0076 800-263-5286
www.wildflavors.com
Flavors, colors, seasonings, spray-dried ingredients, sauces, batters, coatings, marinades; also, custom blending; exporter of cheese powders
Acting Director: Tim Husted
Director Finance: Tamara Robichaud
R & D: Allison Berridge
Chief Operating Officer: Erik Donhowe
Plant Manager: Dave Oldroyd
Purchasing Manager: Leigh Bailey
Number Employees: 30-50
Number of Products: 200
Square Footage: 240000
Parent Co: WILD Flavors
Type of Packaging: Food Service, Bulk

13515 WK Eckerd & Sons
107 Speedy Tostensen Blvd
Brunswick, GA 31520-3149
912-265-0332
Fax: 912-261-8460 eckerd@thebest.net
Seafood
President: William Eckerd
Owner: Bill Eckerd
Estimated Sales: Below $5 Million
Number Employees: 1-4

13516 WSU Creamery
Po Box 641122
Pullman, WA 99164-1122
800-457-5442
Fax: 509-335-7525 800-457-5442
salvadalena@wsu.edu www.wsu.edu/creamery

Cheddar cheese and ice cream
Creamery Manager: Russ Salvadalena
Assistant Manager: John Haugen
Contact: Lynn Chelgren
lynn@wsu.edu
Number Employees: 50
Square Footage: 80000
Type of Packaging: Consumer, Food Service
Brands:
   Cougar Gold
   Viking

13517 Wabash Heritage Mfg LLC
2525 N 6th St
Vincennes, IN 47591-2405
812-886-0147
Fax: 812-895-0064 info@knoxcountyarc.com
www.knoxcountyarc.com
Spices, powders
President: Michael Carney
Vice President: Bobby Harbison
bharbison@knoxcountyarc.com
Research & Development: John TRUE
Quality Control: John TRUE
Plant Manager: Leroy Douffron
Number Employees: 20-49
Number of Brands: 1
Number of Products: 90
Square Footage: 480000
Type of Packaging: Consumer, Food Service, Private Label, Bulk
Brands:
   Wasbash Heritage

13518 Wabash Seafood Co
2249 W Hubbard St
Chicago, IL 60612-1613
312-733-5070
Fax: 312-733-2798 john@wabashseafood.net
www.wabashseafood.net
Seafood
President: John Rebello
john@wabashseafood.net
Estimated Sales: $10-20 Million
Number Employees: 20-49

13519 Wabash Valley Farms
6323 N 150 E
Monon, IN 47959-8010
219-232-4930
Fax: 219-253-1389 877-888-7077
Manufacturer of bagged popcorn, popcorn kernels, and popcorn makers.
President: Danielle Paluchniak
SVP of Sales: Tammy Luse
Contact: Trent Lehman
trent@intri-cut.com
Estimated Sales: Less Than $500,000
Number Employees: 1-4

13520 Wabash Valley Produce Inc
4886 E 450n
PO Box 127
Dubois, IN 47527-9660
812-678-3131
Fax: 812-678-5931
Bulk liquid egg products including pasteurized and raw whole eggs, egg whites and egg and salt yolks
President: Danielle Paluchniak
Chief Financial Officer/Sales: Andrew Seger
Vice President: Scott Seger
Human Resources Manager: Tom Seger
Purchasing Agent: Gene Bonifer
Estimated Sales: $24.5 Million
Number Employees: 100-249
Square Footage: 66000
Type of Packaging: Bulk

13521 Wabi Fishing Company
14608 Smokey Point Boulevard
Marysville, WA 98271-8946
360-659-9474
Fax: 360-659-9093 888-536-7696
Wild Pacific smoked salmon available in five flavors
President: Leo Palmer
Brands:
   King Nova
   Leo's
   Sockeye Nova

Food Manufacturers / A-Z

13522 Wachusett Brewing Co
175 State Rd E
Westminster, MA 01473-1208
978-874-9965
Fax: 978-874-0784 info@wachusettbrew.com
www.wachusettbrew.com
Flavored ales.
Owner: Ned La Fortune
Office Manager: Megan Graves
Director, Administration: Lesa Bourgeios
Director, Marketing & Sales: TJ Morse
Sales Manager: Peter Quinn
Account & PR: Kim Slayton
Director, Operations: Brad Dufour
Plant Engineer: Kevin Buckler
Estimated Sales: Less Than $500,000
Number Employees: 1-4
Type of Packaging: Consumer, Food Service
Brands:
 Wachusett

13523 Wachusset Potato Chip Co Inc
759 Water St
Fitchburg, MA 01420-6499
978-342-6038
Fax: 978-345-4894 800-551-5539
Potato chips, plain, salt and vinegar, rippled, barbeque, no salt added, ketchup, potato sticks, sour cream and onion, cheese twists, popcorn, cheese popcorn
President: Edward Krysiak
ed@wachusettchip.com
Estimated Sales: $10 Million
Number Employees: 50-99
Square Footage: 168000
Type of Packaging: Consumer, Food Service, Private Label
Brands:
 Wachusett

13524 Wackym's Kitchen
PO Box 180871
Dallas, TX 75218
214-327-7667
info@wackymskitchen.com
www.wackymskitchen.com
Cookies
Founder: Paul Wackym

13525 WaffleWaffle
43 River Rd
Nutley, NJ 07110-3411
201-559-1286
info@mywafflewaffle.com
mywafflewaffle.com
Waffles: Belgian-style, cones, doughs, mixes, and waffle irons.
Co-Founder: Justin Samuels
Co-Founder: Samuel Rockwell
Vice President, Business Development: Brian Samuels
Chief Marketing Officer: David Song
Vice President, Sales: Bracken Abrams
Director of Operations: Grant Ramsey
Estimated Sales: $2 Million
Number Employees: 12
Type of Packaging: Consumer, Food Service, Private Label
Brands:
 WaffleWaffle

13526 Wagner Excello Food Products
2625 Gardner Rd
Broadview, IL 60155
708-338-4488
Fax: 708-338-4495
Manufacturer of flavouring extracts and syrups.
Owner: Harry Berger

13527 Wagner Gourmet Foods
10618 Summit St
Lenexa, KS 66215
913-469-5411
Fax: 913-469-1367
customerservice@wagner-gourmet.com
www.hicks-ashby.com
Spices, preserves, jams, ice cream sauces, seasoned rice and gift pack assortments; importer of tea; wholesaler/distributor of snack foods including cookies
President: James T Baldwin
Estimated Sales: $3-5 Million
Number Employees: 5-9
Square Footage: 480000
Parent Co: Wagner Gourmet Foods
Type of Packaging: Consumer, Private Label

13528 Wagner Seafood
9626 S Pulaski Rd
Oak Lawn, IL 60453-3391
708-636-2646
Fax: 843-559-1156
www.wagnerseafood.dinehere.us
Seafood
Owner: Bob Wagner
Estimated Sales: Less Than $500,000
Number Employees: 1-4

13529 Wagner Vineyards
9322 State Route 414
Lodi, NY 14860-9641
607-582-6450
Fax: 607-582-6446 866-924-6378
d.wagner@wagnervineyards.com
www.wagnervineyards.com
Wines and beer; exporter of wines
President: Stanley A Wagner
s.wagner@wagnervineyards.com
Retail Manager: Carol Voorhees
COO: John Wagner
Director of PR & Marketing: Katie Roller
Operations: John Wagner
Estimated Sales: $2,762,368
Number Employees: 50-99
Square Footage: 144000
Type of Packaging: Consumer
Brands:
 Wagner Brewing Co.
 Wagner Vineyards

13530 Wagshal's Imports
4845 Massachusetts Ave NW
Washington, DC 20016-2065
202-363-5698
Fax: 202-363-0893 feedback@wagshals.com
www.wagshals.com
Beef, seafood, produce, sauces & condiments, dairy, wines, iberico pork
Principal: Aaron Fuchs
Director of Sales: Ann Sayre
Estimated Sales: Under $500,000
Number Employees: 1-4
Brands:
 Wagshal's

13531 Wah Yet Group
28301 Industrial Blvd Ste C
Hayward, CA 94545-4429
510-887-3801
Fax: 510-887-3803 800-229-3392
Processor and exporter of diet and ginseng teas; importer of health drinks
President: Ying Lau
Manager: Judy Lau
Estimated Sales: $1-3 Million
Number Employees: 1 to 4
Square Footage: 4000
Type of Packaging: Consumer
Brands:
 Chinese Ginseng
 Green Leaf

13532 Wai Lana Snacks
5005 Raley Blvd.
Suite 1
Sacramento, CA 95838
888-924-5262
info@wailana.com www.wailana.com
Cassava chips, fruit and nut bars
Founder: Wai Lana
Number Employees: 11-50
Brands:
 Wai Lana

13533 Wainani Kai Seafood
2126 Eluwene St
Suite A
Honolulu, HI 96819
808-847-7435
Fax: 808-841-7536 lpang00@yahoo.com
Seafood
President: Lance Pang
lpang00@yahoo.com
Estimated Sales: $3-5 Million
Number Employees: 5-9

13534 Wainwright Dairy
13607 161st Rd
Live Oak, FL 32060-6539
386-776-2001
info@wainwrightdairy.com
www.wainwrightdairy.com
Dairy products
Manager: James Wainwright
Number Employees: 5-9

13535 Waken Meat Co
1015 Boulevard SE
Atlanta, GA 30312-3809
404-627-3537
Fax: 404-624-3191
Beef, pork, chicken, frozen seafood
President: Charles Waken
Estimated Sales: $300,000-500,000
Number Employees: 5-9

13536 Wakunaga Of America Co LTD
23501 Madero
Mission Viejo, CA 92691-2764
949-855-2776
Fax: 949-458-2764 800-421-2998
info@wakunaga.com www.kyolic.com
Nutritional supplements
President: Kenro Nakamura
CEO: Kazuhiko Nomura
Research & Development Manager: Justin Oshima
Quality Control: Vithia Monica Lee
Manager: Jay Levy
jlevy@wakunaga.com
Estimated Sales: $24 Million
Number Employees: 50-99
Number of Brands: 5
Number of Products: 70
Square Footage: 42000
Parent Co: Wakunaga Pharmaceutical
Brands:
 Besure
 Estro Logic
 Kyo-Chlorella
 Kyo-Dophilus
 Kyo-Green
 Kyo-Green Harvest Blend
 Kyolic
 Moducare
 Moduchol
 Moduprost

13537 Walcan Seafood
PO Box 429
Heroit Bay, BC V0P 1H0
Canada
250-285-3361
Fax: 250-285-3313 www.walcan.com
Seafood processing
Manager: William Perez

13538 Walden Farms
1209 W Saint Georges Ave
Linden, NJ 07036-6117
908-925-6020
Fax: 908-925-9537 800-229-1706
info@waldenfarms.com www.waldenfarms.com
Processor and exporter of salad dressings, dips, bbq sauces, pancake syrups, fruit spread jams and jellies, fruit syrups, ketchup and seafood sauces, bruschetta and chocolate syrup.
President: Mitchell Berko
mitchellburko@waldenfarms.com
Vice President: Paul Berko
Operations: Brian Sherwood
mitchellburko@waldenfarms.com
Number Employees: 50-99
Square Footage: 64000
Type of Packaging: Consumer, Food Service
Brands:
 Walden Farms

13539 Walden Farms
1209 W Saint Georges Ave
Linden, NJ 07036-6117
908-925-6020
Fax: 908-925-9537 800-229-1706
customerservice@waldenfarms.com
www.waldenfarms.com
Sauces
President: Mitchell Berko
mitchellburko@waldenfarms.com
Sales Director: Mitchell Berko
Operations Manager: V Naccarato

Estimated Sales: $500,000-$1 Million
Number Employees: 50-99
Type of Packaging: Private Label
Brands:
    Walden Farms

13540 Walden Foods
660 N Loudoun St
Winchester, VA 22601-4986
540-622-2800
Fax: 540-253-9807 800-648-7688
All natural and gourmet applewood smoked seafood, poultry and meats
President: John P Good Jr
VP Marketing: Christine Hyre
Number Employees: 20
Square Footage: 50000
Parent Co: Walden Foods Inc.
Type of Packaging: Consumer, Food Service
Brands:
    The Farm At Mt. Walden

13541 Walker Foods
237 N Mission Rd
Los Angeles, CA 90033-2103
323-268-5191
Fax: 323-268-7812 800-966-5199
info@walkerfoods.com www.walkerfoods.net
Producers of hot spicy tomato sauce and other tomato products
President: Robert Walker
Cmo: Fernando Montano
elpatowfi@aol.com
Director, Retail Sales: Andy Zahra
Production Manager: Alfred Heredia
Plant Manager: Fernando Montano
Estimated Sales: $10-20 Million
Number Employees: 50-99
Square Footage: 360000
Type of Packaging: Consumer, Food Service, Private Label, Bulk
Brands:
    El Pato
    Golden State

13542 Walker Meats
821 Tyus Carrollton Rd
Carrollton, GA 30117-9609
770-834-8171
Fax: 770-834-2208 800-741-3601
info@walkermeats.com www.walkermeats.com
Beef, pork, poultry, produce, seafood
President: Bill Walker
bill@walkermeats.com
Estimated Sales: $10-20 Million
Number Employees: 20-49

13543 Walker's Seafood
312 Southwest Sq
Jonesboro, AR 72401-5984
870-932-0375
Fax: 870-935-8697
Seafood
President: Darrell Walker
Secretary/Treasurer: Patricia Walker

13544 Walkers Shortbread
170 Commerce Dr
Hauppauge, NY 11788-3944
631-273-0014
Fax: 631-273-0438 800-521-0141
cs@walkersshortbread.com
us.walkersshortbread.com
Shortbread and cookies
President: Steve Dawson
CEO: Neil Apple
cs@walkersshortbread.com
CFO: Joseph Gadaleta
Marketing: Lisa Sherman
Estimated Sales: $2800000
Number Employees: 20-49
Parent Co: Walkers Shortbread
Type of Packaging: Consumer, Bulk
Brands:
    Duchy Originals
    Kambly
    Walker's
    Walkers

13545 Wall Meat Processing
21 N Creighton Rd
Wall, SD 57790
605-279-2348
Manufactures slab & sliced bacon and other meat products
Owner: Scott Carson
Estimated Sales: $1-3 Million
Number Employees: 1-4
Type of Packaging: Private Label

13546 Wallaby Yogurt Co
12002 Airport Way
Broomfield, CO 80021
707-553-1233
Fax: 707-553-1293 855-925-4636
info@wallabyyogurt.com www.wallabyyogurt.com
Organic yogurt, kefir, and sour cream
Founder: Jerry Chou
Marketing & Event Manager: Nicole Smith
Operations Manager: Tibi Molnar
Year Founded: 1995
Estimated Sales: $45 Million
Number Employees: 50-99
Parent Co: WhiteWave
Brands:
    Wallaby

13547 Wallace Edwards & Sons
11455 Rolfe Highway
PO Box 25
Surry, VA 23883
757-294-3121
Fax: 757-294-5378 800-200-4267
info@edwardsvaham.com
www.edwardsvaham.com
Virginia hams, hickory smoked bacon, dry cured duck, sausage, turkey, and Virginia peanuts
President/CEO: Bob Anderson

13548 Wallace Fisheries
PO Box 2046
Gulf Shores, AL 36547-2046
251-986-7211
Fax: 251-987-5127
Seafood

13549 Wallace Grain & Pea Company
4932 State Route 27
Pullman, WA 99163
509-878-1561
Fax: 509-878-1671
Processor and exporter of chickpeas, barley, lentils and peas
President: Joe Hulett
Assistant Manager: Gary Heaton
Estimated Sales: $500,000-$1 Million
Number Employees: 1-4
Type of Packaging: Consumer, Food Service, Private Label, Bulk
Brands:
    Palouse

13550 Wallace Plant Company
201 High St
Bath, ME 04530-1677
207-443-2640
Fax: 207-386-0268
Seafood
Owner: Wallace Plant
Estimated Sales: $1 Million
Number Employees: 5-9
Type of Packaging: Consumer

13551 Wallingford Coffee Co Inc
11401 Rockfield Ct
Cincinnati, OH 45241-1971
513-771-3131
Fax: 513-771-3138 800-533-3690
sales@wallingfordcoffee.com
www.wallingfordcoffee.com
Coffee, cappuccino and tea
President: Gary Weber
Controller: Michael Hoban
VP Operations: Gary Davis
Purchasing Manager: Brian Weber
Estimated Sales: $10-49 Million
Number Employees: 50-99
Number of Brands: 3
Brands:
    Wallingford
    White Castle
    Aroma Valley

13552 Wally Biscotti
4850 E 39th Ave
Denver, CO 80207-1010
303-320-9969
Fax: 303-320-9966 866-659-2559
wallybicotti@aol.com
Biscotti
President: Wally Friedlander
Marketing Manager: Wally Biscotti
Operations Manager: Jamey Biscotti
Estimated Sales: $1-$1.3 Million
Number Employees: 20-49
Type of Packaging: Consumer, Food Service, Private Label, Bulk
Brands:
    Wally Biscotti

13553 Walnut Acres
4600 Sleepytime Dr.
Boulder, CO 80301
800-434-4246
www.walnutacres.com
Soups, pasta sauces, salsas, juices and kid's snacks

13554 Walsh's Coffee Roasters
273 Baldwin Avenue
San Mateo, CA 94401-3914
650-347-5112
Fax: 650-347-0569
Coffee
Owner/President: John Walsh
Estimated Sales: Less than $500,000
Number Employees: 1-4

13555 Walsh's Seafood
RR 1
Gouldsboro, ME 04607
207-963-2578
Fax: 207-963-2578
Seafood
Owner: Craig Walsh

13556 Walter P Rawl & Sons Inc
824 Fairview Rd
Pelion, SC 29123
803-894-1900
www.rawl.net
Grower of peppers, beets, cilantro, collard, corn, green onion, jalapeno, kale, leeks, mustard, parsley, turnip, turnip root, yellow squash, zucchini.
President: Howard Rawl
Director, Accounting: Sue Elizabeth
Business Development Manager: Mark Haun
Senior Quality Assurance Manager: Nancy Shimabukuro
Marketing Manager: Christine Jackson
Director of Sales: Gary James
Director of Corp Strategy & HR: Tim Rabon
Operations Manager: Dale Clark
Director of Transportation: Jeff Pratt
Year Founded: 1920
Estimated Sales: Less than $500,000
Type of Packaging: Consumer, Food Service

13557 Waltham Beef Company
18 Food Mart Road
Boston, MA 02118-2802
617-269-2250
Fax: 617-269-8183
Processed beef, pork, poultry
President: Douglas Atamian
President: Wesley Atamian
Type of Packaging: Private Label

13558 Waltkoch Limited
1990 Lakeside Pkwy
Suite 240
Tucker, GA 30084
404-378-3666
Fax: 404-378-8492 www.waltkoch.com
Poultry frozen foods, meats, seafood.
Owner: Walter Koch
Partner: Sam Stanford
Chief Executive Officer: Keith Steinberg
Year Founded: 1950
Estimated Sales: $43 Million
Number Employees: 54
Type of Packaging: Consumer, Food Service

Food Manufacturers / A-Z

13559 Wampler's Farm Sausage Company
781 U.S. 70
Lenoir City, TN 37771
865-986-2056
Fax: 865-988-3280 800-728-7243
sales@wamplersfarm.com
www.wamplersfarm.com
Established in 1953. Processor, packer, and exporter of sausage.
Vice President: John Ed Wampler
Sales Manager: Doug Young
Operations Manager: Darrell Griffis
Plant Supervisor: Mike Marney
Plant Manager: Jim Wampler
Estimated Sales: $24000000
Number Employees: 100-249
Type of Packaging: Consumer, Food Service, Private Label, Bulk
Brands:
  Wampler's Farm

13560 Wan Hua Foods
804 6th Avenue South
PO Box 14075
Seattle, WA 98134
206-622-8417
Fax: 206-622-7088 info@wanhuafoods.com
www.wanhuafoods.com
Fresh cooked noodles including udon, yaki soba, miki and chow mein.
President: Sui-Ming Tam
Founder: Tony Tam
Founder: Judy Tam
Contact: Tai Chainarong
tai@wanhuafoods.com
Estimated Sales: C
Number Employees: 10-19
Square Footage: 48000
Brands:
  Miki
  Phillipino's
  U-Don
  Yakisoba

13561 Wanchese Fish Co Inc
2000 Northgate Commerce Pkwy
Suffolk, VA 23435-2142
757-673-4500
Fax: 757-653-4550 www.wanchese.com
Processor and exporter of fresh and frozen seafood including flounder, bass, scallops, tuna, scallops and shrimp.
President: Sam Daniels
sam@wanchese.com
CFO: Mark Palmer
VP: Kenny Daniels
Sales Manager: Gordon Craddock
Plant Manager: Chris Daniels
Estimated Sales: $6400000
Number Employees: 20-49
Square Footage: 1000000
Parent Co: Daniels Enterprises
Type of Packaging: Consumer, Food Service, Private Label, Bulk
Other Locations:
  Wanchese Fish Co.
  Hampton VA

13562 Wanda's Nature Farm
1700 Cushman Dr
Lincoln, NE 68512-1238
402-423-1234
Fax: 402-423-4586 800-735-6828
heartlandgourmet.com
Processor and exporter of natural mixes including bread, cake, muffin, pancake, pasta, pizza, bagels, etc
President: Susan Zink
Vice President: David Eisner
Marketing Director: Shari Rogge-Fidler
Estimated Sales: $2311332
Number Employees: 20-49
Type of Packaging: Consumer, Food Service

13563 Wandering Bear Coffee
162 W 13th St
Apt 142
New York, NY 10011-7813
929-251-3752
hello@wanderingbearcoffee.com
www.wanderingbearcoffee.com
Coffee
Co-Founder: Ben Gordon
Co-Founder: Matthew Bachmann
Number Employees: 2-10
Brands:
  Wandering Bear Coffee

13564 Wapsie Creamery
300 10th St NE
Independence, IA 50644-1220
319-334-7193
Fax: 319-334-4914 markn@wapsievalley.com
www.wapsievalley.com
Monterey and marble pepper jack, cheddar and colby cheese; processor and exporter of kosher reduced lactose whey, edible dried delactose and lactose.
President: Mark Nielsen
VP: Wilbur Nielsen
Estimated Sales: $20-50 Million
Number Employees: 50-99
Square Footage: 78000
Type of Packaging: Consumer, Private Label, Bulk

13565 Wapsie Produce
702 E Water St
Decorah, IA 52101
563-382-4271
Fax: 563-382-8210 info@capons.com
www.capons.com
Processor and exporter of frozen capons and fowl
President: Marc Nichols
Vice President: Paul Nichols
paul.nichols@capons.com
Estimated Sales: $9 Million
Number Employees: 100
Type of Packaging: Consumer, Private Label
Brands:
  Ioma
  Minowa
  Thrift

13566 War Eagle Mill
11045 War Eagle Rd
Rogers, AR 72756-7544
479-789-5343
Fax: 479-789-2972 866-492-7324
info@wareaglemill.com www.wareaglemill.com
Processor and miller of stone burr corn meal and wholewheat flour and mixes
President: Zoe Caywood
Contact: Barbara Allen
barbara@wareaglemill.com
Type of Packaging: Consumer

13567 Warbucks Seafood
1581 McDonald Avenue
Brooklyn, NY 11230
718-998-4900
Fax: 718-732-2884 info@warbucksseafood.com
www.blackdiamondcaviarnyc.com
Caviar
Co-Owner: Raymond Mizrahi
Estimated Sales: $1.5 Million
Number Employees: 6
Brands:
  Black Diamond Caviar

13568 Warden Peanut Company
620 E Lime St
Portales, NM 88130
575-356-6691
Fax: 575-359-0072
Snack foods
VP: Sam Rigsey
General Manager: Bill Owen
Plant Manager: Leonard Stanton
Estimated Sales: Under $500,000
Number Employees: 20-49

13569 Warner Candy
Ste A
1240 Don Haskins Dr
El Paso, TX 79936-7887
847-928-7200
Fax: 847-928-2115
Candy
Estimated Sales: $10-20 Million
Number Employees: 20-49

13570 (HQ)Warner Vineyards
706 S Kalamazoo St
Paw Paw, MI 49079-1558
269-657-3165
Fax: 269-657-4154 800-756-5357
www.warnerwines.com
Wines
President: Patrick Warner
patrickwarner@verizon.net
Estimated Sales: $500,000
Number Employees: 5-9
Type of Packaging: Consumer, Private Label
Brands:
  Warner Vineyards

13571 (HQ)Warner-Lambert Confections
810 Main St
Cambridge, MA 02139-3588
617-491-2500
Fax: 617-547-2381
Candy
President/CEO: J Craig
Plant Manager: Gerald Chesser
Estimated Sales: Under $500,000
Number Employees: 100-249

13572 Warrell Corp
1250 Slate Hill Rd
Camp Hill, PA 17011-8011
717-761-5440
Fax: 717-761-2206 844-234-3217
sales@warrellcorp.com www.warrellcorp.com
Processor, importer and exporter of confectionery products.
President: Kevin Silva
Executive VP, Sales & Marketing: Richard Warrell
Vice President, Operations: Robert Bard
Number Employees: 250-499
Type of Packaging: Consumer, Food Service, Private Label, Bulk
Brands:
  Pennsylvania Dutch Candies
  Bonomo Turkish Taffy
  Katharine Beecher
  Flipsticks
  Classic Caramel

13573 Warrell Corp
1250 Slate Hill Rd
Camp Hill, PA 17011-8011
717-761-5440
Fax: 717-761-2206 800-233-7082
sales@warrellcorp.com www.warrellcorp.com
Candy
President: Patrick Huffman
patrickh@warrellcorp.com
Number Employees: 250-499

13574 (HQ)Warrell Corp
1250 Slate Hill Rd
Camp Hill, PA 17011-8011
717-761-5440
Fax: 717-761-5702 800-233-7082
sales@warrellcorp.com www.warrellcorp.com
Candies and chocolates
President & CEO: Matthew Caiazza
CFO: Patricia Zwergel
Executive Vice President: Richard Warrell
VP Sales & Marketing: Steve Sullivan
VP Operations: Robert Bard
VP Administration: Susan Tandle
Year Founded: 1965
Estimated Sales: $20-50 Million
Number Employees: 250-499
Number of Brands: 3
Square Footage: 200000
Type of Packaging: Private Label, Bulk
Brands:
  Katherine Beecher
  Melster
  Pennsylvania Dutch Candies
  Flipsticks
  Classic Caramel
  Nut N But Natural

13575 Warren & Son Meat Processing
7585 State Route 821
Whipple, OH 45788-5164
740-585-2421
Fax: 740-585-2073
Beef, pork, lamb, specialty meats and smoked sausage and ham

Food Manufacturers / A-Z

Owner/Sales: Danny Warren
Marketing Director: Kathryn Warren
Estimated Sales: $3-5 Million
Number Employees: 1 to 4
Type of Packaging: Consumer, Bulk

13576 Warren Laboratories LLC
1656 Ih 35 S
Abbott, TX 76621-3014
254-580-9990
Fax: 254-580-9944   800-421-2563
karenk@warrenlabsaloe.com
www.georgesaloe.com
Refined aloe vera beverages
Manager: Tony Tustejovsky
Contact: George Arren
georgew@warrenlabsaloe.com
Estimated Sales: $2100000
Number Employees: 10-19

13577 Warwick Ice Cream
743 Bald Hill Rd
Warwick, RI 02886-0713
401-821-8403
Fax: 401-821-8404   info@warwickicecreamco.com
www.warwickicecreamco.com
Ice cream cakes, pies and popsicles
Owner: Gerard Bucci Sr
Estimated Sales: $1-3 Million
Number Employees: 20-49
Type of Packaging: Consumer, Food Service, Bulk

13578 Warwick Valley Winery & Distillery
114 Little York Rd.
Warwick, NY 10990
845-258-4858
www.wvwinery.com
Fruit liqueurs, hard fruit ciders, gin, red and white wines
Owner: Jason Grizzanti
Year Founded: 2001
Number of Brands: 2
Number of Products: 23
Type of Packaging: Consumer, Private Label
Brands:
 Warwick Winery
 Doc's Draft Hard Cider
 American Fruits
 Warwick Distillery

13579 Wasatch Meats Inc
926 S Jefferson St
Salt Lake City, UT 84101-2983
801-363-5747
Fax: 801-799-5511   800-631-8294
www.wasatchmeats.com
Processors of meat including beef, pork and poultry.
President: Richard Broadbent
richb@wasatchmeats.com
VP: Scott Rich
VP Marketing: Mark Broadbent
VP Sales: Mark Broadbent
Operations Manager: Roger Rausch
Production Foreman: Dave Burke
Estimated Sales: $15,914,424
Number Employees: 20-49
Type of Packaging: Food Service

13580 Washington Fruit & Produce Company
401 N 1st Ave
P.O.Box 1588
Yakima, WA 98907-1588
509-457-6177
Fax: 509-452-8520   information@washfruit.com
www.washfruit.com
Processor and exporter of fresh fruits including apples, pears, and cherries.
Manager: Tom Hanses
Contact: Lorri Denison
ldenison@neptunesociety.com
Estimated Sales: Less than $500,000
Number Employees: 1-4
Type of Packaging: Consumer, Bulk

13581 Washington Potato Company
1900 1st Ave West
PO Box 3110
Pasco, WA 99302
509-545-4545
Fax: 509-545-4804   800-897-2726
customerservice@oregonpotato.com
www.oregonpotato.com
Processor and exporter of frozen and dehydrated potatoes
President/CEO: Frank Tiegs
Director of Sales: Barry Stice
Sales: Don Smith
Plant Manager: Bob Bernard
Estimated Sales: $16.6 Million
Number Employees: 100
Square Footage: 10000
Parent Co: Oregon Potato
Type of Packaging: Food Service, Bulk

13582 Washington Rhubarb Grower Assn
16623 88th St E
Sumner, WA 98390-8149
253-863-7333
Fax: 253-863-2775   800-435-9911
Cooperative of Washington rhubarb growers; also, manufacturer of IQF rhubarb
President: Stacey Ota
wa_rhubarb@yahoo.com
General Manager: Cindy Moore
Estimated Sales: Less Than $500,000
Number Employees: 1-4
Square Footage: 36000
Type of Packaging: Bulk
Brands:
 First Pick
 Sumner

13583 Washington State Juice
10725 Sutter Ave
Pacoima, CA 91331-2553
818-899-1195
Fax: 818-899-6042
Manufactures and processes fruit concentrates, blends and natural flavors. Custom blending is available
President: Fred Farago
Estimated Sales: $.5-1 million
Number Employees: 100-249
Type of Packaging: Food Service, Private Label, Bulk

13584 Wasson Brothers Winery
17020 Ruben Ln
Sandy, OR 97055
503-668-3124
Fax: 503-668-3124
Wines
Partner: James Wasson
Partner: John Wasson
Estimated Sales: $1-2.5 Million
Number Employees: 1-4
Brands:
 Wasson

13585 (HQ)Water Concepts
561 Plate Drive
Suite 1
East Dundee, IL 60118
847-699-9797
Fax: 847-699-9889
Caffeine enchanced natural artesian water.
Owner: Steve Rodgers
Marketing: Joe Brumfield
Estimated Sales: $300,000-500,000
Number Employees: 1-4
Type of Packaging: Consumer, Food Service
Brands:
 Water Joe

13586 Waterfield Farms
500 Sunderland Road
Amherst, MA 01002-1038
413-549-3558
Fax: 413-549-9945   bioshelter@aol.com
Tilapia fish, basil, tomatoes and pesto sauces
President: John Reid
Vice President: Tracy Hightower
Director of Aquaculture: Dr Jose Llobrera
Estimated Sales: $500-1 Million appx.
Number Employees: 20-49
Type of Packaging: Consumer, Food Service
Brands:
 Hydroponic Sweet Basil
 Tilapia
 Waterfield Farms

13587 Waterfront Seafood
14358 Shell Belt Rd
Bayou La Batre, AL 36509-2330
251-824-2185
Fax: 251-824-4307
Seafood
Owner: Norowod Cain
Vice President: Nor Cain
Number Employees: 20-49

13588 Waterfront Seafood Market
2900 University Ave Ste A4
West Des Moines, IA 50266
515-223-5106
Fax: 515-224-9665   waterfrontseafood@msn.com
www.waterfrontseafoodmarket.com
Seafood
President: Ted Hanke
Estimated Sales: $3-5 Million
Number Employees: 50-99

13589 Watermark Innovation
400 Noyac Rd
Suite A-1
Southampton, NY 11968
631-259-2329
Fax: 631-259-2329
Flavored water
President: Patti Kelly

13590 Watershed Foods
202 N Ford St
Gridley, IL 61744-3902
309-747-3000
Fax: 309-747-4647
jill.legner@watershedfoods.com
Contract processor of yogurt, purees, fruits and other healthy snacks. Services include freeze drying and pumpable liquids and R&D test drying.
President & COO: Jeremy Zobrist
jeremy.zobrist@watershedfoods.com
CFO: Lynette Schick
Director of Food Quality & Safety: Craig Hammond
VP Sales & Marketing: Brandon Rinkenberger
VP & Director Operations: Marc Johnson
Manager: Jill Legner
Estimated Sales: $4.3 Million
Number Employees: 5-9

13591 (HQ)Watson Inc
301 Heffernan Dr
West Haven, CT 06516-4139
203-932-3000
Fax: 203-932-8266   800-388-3481
www.watson-inc.com
Ingredients manufacturer for the food and supplement industries.
President: James Watson
james.watson@watson-inc.com
Number Employees: 100-249
Type of Packaging: Bulk
Other Locations:
 Watson Foods Co.
 Rockville CT
Brands:
 Oven Spring

13592 Watson Inc
301 Heffernan Dr
West Haven, CT 06516-4139
203-932-3000
Fax: 203-932-8266   800-388-3481
info@watson-inc.com   www.watson-inc.com
Dietary supplements, gummy application, balery ingredients, nutrient premixe, spray dried nutrients, edible glitter, compressible sweeteners, hops
President: James Watson
james.watson@watson-inc.com
Estimated Sales: $20-50 Million
Number Employees: 100-249
Parent Co: Glanbia Nutritionals

13593 Watusee Foods
1368 Newton St NW
Apt A
Washington, DC 20010-3510
202-281-8245
hi@watuseefoods.com
watuseefoods.com
Chickpea snacks
Co-Founder & CEO: Jimmy Edgerton
Accountant: Miriam Discenza
Type of Packaging: Food Service
Brands:
 Watusee Foods

Food Manufacturers / A-Z

13594 Waugh Foods Inc
701 Pinecrest Dr
East Peoria, IL 61611-4894
309-427-8000
Fax: 309-694-3115
Wholesaler/distributor of frozen and refrigerated food, fresh dairy and produce.
President: John Waugh
CEO: Joe Waugh
VP Sales: Jim Susin
Operations Manager: Norm Ralph
VP Purchasing: Tim Waugh
Year Founded: 1948
Estimated Sales: $20 Million
Number Employees: 50-99
Square Footage: 51550
Type of Packaging: Food Service

13595 Wausau Paper Corp.
100 Paper Pl.
Mosinee, WI 54455
715-693-4470
866-722-8675
torkusa@essity.com www.wausaupaper.com
Towels, tissue, soap, wipers and dispensing system.
President/CEO, Essity: Magnus Groth
Year Founded: 1899
Estimated Sales: $822 Million
Number Employees: 870
Number of Brands: 12
Parent Co: Essity
Type of Packaging: Food Service
Brands:
  Artisan
  DublSoft
  DublNature
  EcoSoft
  Alliance
  Wave'n Dry
  Optiserv
  Optiserv Hybrid
  Optiserv accent
  Revolution
  DublServe
  OptiSource Convertible
  Silhouette
  Dubl-tough

13596 Waverly Crabs
3400 Greenmount Ave
Baltimore, MD 21218-2823
410-243-1181
Fax: 410-243-0348
Crab
Owner: Jane Gordon
jgordon@bcps.org
Estimated Sales: $3-5 Million
Number Employees: 10-19

13597 Wawa Inc
Red Roof
260 W Baltimore Pike
Wawa, PA 19063
610-358-8000
800-444-9292
www.wawa.com
Milk and dairy products.
President & CEO: Chris Gheysens
chris.gheysens@wawa.com
Chief Financial Officer: Kevin Wiggins
Chief Operating Officer: Jim Morey
Year Founded: 1803
Estimated Sales: $10.6 Billion
Number Employees: 31,000

13598 Wawona Frozen Foods Inc
100 W Alluvial Ave
Clovis, CA 93611-9176
559-299-2901
Fax: 559-299-1921 info@wawona.com
www.wawona.com
Processor and exporter of IQF and syrup packed frozen fruits including peaches, strawberries and mixed fruit; also a variety of fruit-based portion controlled products; importer of frozen fruits including melons, grapes and pineapple
President: Jose Barajas
joseb@wawona.com
CFO: Julie Olsen
Director Quality Assurance: Duncan Donaldbe
VP Sales & Marketing: Willian Astin
Director of Sales: Toni Lindeleaf
VP Operations: Pete Peterson
Production Supervisor: Jose Valdez
Purchasing Manager: Ken Cole
Estimated Sales: $23.3 Million
Number Employees: 250-499
Square Footage: 125000
Type of Packaging: Consumer, Food Service, Private Label, Bulk
Brands:
  Summer Prize
  Wawona Frozen Foods

13599 Wax Orchards
P.O.Box 25448
Seattle, WA 98165-2348
206-463-9735
Fax: 206-463-9731 800-634-6132
customerservice@waxorchards.com
www.waxorchards.com
Fat-free, fruit-sweetened preserves and toppings
President: Anna Sestrap
Estimated Sales: $400,000
Number Employees: 5
Square Footage: 60
Brands:
  Wax Orchards

13600 Way Better Snacks
800 Washington Ave N
Suite 207
Minneapolis, MN 55401-1148
612-314-2060
consumeraffairs@gowaybetter.com
gowaybetter.com
Crackers and tortilla chips
Founder & CEO: Jim Breen
Chief Financial Officer: Dan Wilkins
Vice President, Sales & Operations: Joe Lawer
Estimated Sales: $12-14 Million
Number Employees: 30
Brands:
  Way Better Snacks

13601 Wayco Ham Co
506 N William St
Goldsboro, NC 27530-2804
919-735-3962
Fax: 919-734-4080 800-962-2614
tworrell@waycohams.com www.waycohams.com
Country ham and smoked turkey
President: Tony Worrell
tworrell@waycohams.com
VP: George Howell
Estimated Sales: $4300000
Number Employees: 20-49
Type of Packaging: Consumer, Food Service, Private Label

13602 Wayfield Foods
5145 Wellcome All Road
Atlanta, GA 30349
404-559-3200
Fax: 404-559-3206 www.wayfieldfoods.com
General grocery items, frozen foods, meats, dairy, deli items, seafood, produce
President: Ronald Edenfield
Estimated Sales: G
Number Employees: 500-999

13603 Waymouth Farms Inc
5300 Boone Ave N
Minneapolis, MN 55428-4034
763-533-5300
Fax: 763-533-9890 800-527-0094
www.goodsensesnacks.com
Dried fruit, nuts, seeds, trail mixes, and other snacks.
President: Gerard Knight
gknight@goodsensesnacks.com
Quality Manager: Dean Giroux
Marketing Manager: Kathleen Vargas
Regional Sales Manager: Bob Cosgrove
Purchasing Manager: Melissa Boeser
Estimated Sales: $32 Million
Number Employees: 100-249
Number of Brands: 7
Square Footage: 16240
Type of Packaging: Consumer, Food Service, Private Label, Bulk
Brands:
  Good Sense
  Goodniks
  Kracker Nuts
  Nutty Corn
  Omega Munchies
  Pea Poppers
  Salad Pizazz!

13604 Wayne Dairy Products Inc
1590 NW 11th St
Richmond, IN 47374-1404
765-935-7521
Fax: 765-935-2184 www.smithdairy.com
Established in 1909. Processor of dairy products including milk, soft serve and hard ice cream, and shake mixes.
President: Steve Schmid
VP of Ice Cream: Pat Ruggles
VP of Sales: Brian DeFelice
Estimated Sales: $20-50 Million
Number Employees: 100-249
Parent Co: Smith Dairy
Type of Packaging: Consumer, Food Service, Private Label, Bulk
Brands:
  Smith Dairy

13605 Wayne E Bailey Produce Co Inc
490 Old US Highway 74
P.O.Box 467
Chadbourn, NC 28431-9510
910-654-5163
Fax: 910-654-4734 800-845-6149
info@sweetpotatoes.com
Sweet potatoes
CEO/Owner: George Wooten
COO: Andy Pope
CFO: Stuart Hill
CEO: George Wooten
Sales: Ronnie Mercer
Estimated Sales: $3-5 Million
Number Employees: 50-99
Brands:
  Girlwatcher
  Playboy
  Pride of Samspon

13606 Wayne Estay Shrimp Company
PO Box 946 Oak Street
Grand Isle, LA 70358-0946
504-787-2166
Fax: 504-787-3982 877-787-2166
Fish and seafood
President: Wayne Estay
Sales Manager: Wayne Estay
Estimated Sales: $300,000
Number Employees: 6

13607 Wayne Farms LLC.
4110 Continental Dr.
Oakwood, GA 30566
800-392-0844
www.waynefarms.com
Poultry producer.
President/CEO: J. Clinton Rivers
CFO/Treasurer: Courtney Fazekas
VP/General Manager, Prepared Foods: Tom Bell
VP, Quality Assurance & Food Safety: Bryan Miller
VP, Fresh Sales: Steve Clever
Year Founded: 1965
Estimated Sales: $2.2 Billion
Number Employees: 9,000
Number of Brands: 6
Parent Co: Continental Grain Company
Type of Packaging: Consumer, Food Service, Private Label
Other Locations:
  Albertville AL
  Danville AR
  Decatur AL
  Dobson NC
  Dothan AL
  Enterprise AL
  Laurel MS
  Pendergrass GA
  Union Springs AL
Brands:
  Wayne Farms
  Platinum Harvest
  Buffaloos
  Chef's Craft
  Crispy FlierS

Naked Truth
Ladybird
Quick Creations

13608 We Rub You
630 Flushing Ave
8th Fl.
Brooklyn, NY 11206
718-387-9797
eat@werubyou.com
www.werubyou.com
Korean BBQ marinades and sauces
Co-Founder: Ann Chung
Co-Founder: Janet Chung
Estimated Sales: $5.7 Million
Number Employees: 32
Type of Packaging: Food Service
Brands:
 We Rub You

13609 Weaver Brothers
417 Dearborn Street
Berne, IN 46711-2012
219-589-2869
Fax: 219-589-3038
Cheese
Marketing Director: Wayne Amstutz

13610 Weaver Nut Co. Inc.
1925 W Main St
Ephrata, PA 17522-1112
717-738-3781
Fax: 717-733-2226 800-473-2688
info@weavernut.com www.weavergourmet.com
Processor importer and distributor of nuts, dried fruits, candies, confectionery items, snack mixes, gourmet coffees and teas, beans and spices; custom roasting and contract packaging available
President: E Paul Weaver III
Vice President: Michael Reis
Sales Director: Tom Flynn
Manager: Lisa Weaver
retail@weavernut.com
Estimated Sales: $18,000,000
Number Employees: 20-49
Number of Products: 3500
Square Footage: 116000
Type of Packaging: Consumer, Private Label, Bulk
Brands:
 Arcor
 Asher's
 Hershey Chocolate
 Jaret
 Jelly Belly
 Nabisco
 Wilbur Chocolate

13611 Weaver Popcorn Co Inc
408 W Landess St
Van Buren, IN 46991
concessionsales@popweaver.com
www.popweaver.com
Regular and microwave popcorn; also, caramel popcorn specialties including caramel with almonds and pecans and fat-free
CFO: Brian Hamilton
National Sales Manager: Jim Labas
Year Founded: 1928
Estimated Sales: $20-50 Million
Number Employees: 100-249
Type of Packaging: Consumer, Food Service, Private Label, Bulk
Brands:
 Bonnie Lee
 Pop Weaver
 Weaver Original

13612 Webb's Candy
38217 Highway 27
Davenport, FL 33837-7886
863-422-1051
Fax: 863-422-6214 800-289-9322
www.citruscandy.com
Mints, lemon drops, taffy, toffee, nougats, glazed and coated nuts, fudge, vanilla and chocolate candies, etc
President: John Webb
john@citruscandy.com
Estimated Sales: $1200000
Number Employees: 10-19
Type of Packaging: Consumer, Food Service, Bulk

13613 Webbpak Inc
110 Railroad Ave
Trussville, AL 35173
205-655-3500
Fax: 205-655-3500 800-655-3500
Vinegar, syrups, sauces, drink mixes and flavorings
President: Peter Calzone
Estimated Sales: Less Than $500,000
Number Employees: 1-4
Square Footage: 40000
Type of Packaging: Consumer, Food Service, Private Label
Brands:
 Diamond Joe
 Farmers Favorite
 Flowing Gold
 Formula 18
 Johnny Boy Vanilla
 Webb's

13614 Weber Flavors
549 Palwaukee Dr
PO Box 546
Wheeling, IL 60090
800-558-9078
www.weberflavors.com
Family-owned flavoring manufacturer founded in 1902.
Contact: Mary Marvan
marym@weberflavors.com
Number of Brands: 6
Brands:
 Simply Natural
 Simply Natural-Like
 Whol-Bean
 HoMaid
 Waves
 Petran

13615 Webster City Custom Meats Inc
1611 E 2nd St
PO Box 280
Webster City, IA 50595-1741
515-832-1130
Fax: 515-832-5515
www.webstercitycustommeats.com
Smoked ham, smoked bacon, smoked turkeys, fresh sausage products, boneless ham roasts, and smoked pork loins.
President: Dean Bowden
VP Sales & Marketing: Phil Voge
Operations Manager: Chip Abbott
Estimated Sales: $20 Million
Number Employees: 100-249
Square Footage: 57000
Type of Packaging: Food Service, Private Label

13616 Webster Farms
5859 Highway 1
Unit 1
Cambridge, NS B0P 1G0
Canada
902-538-9492
Fax: 902-538-7662 800-507-8844
webfarm@eastlink.ca www.websterfarms.ca
Frozen strawberries and rhubarb; also, dry beans
President: Greg Webster
Number Employees: 20-49
Type of Packaging: Consumer, Food Service

13617 Wechsler Coffee Corporation
250 Central Avenue
Teterboro, NJ 07608-1861
201-994-1861
800-800-2633
Gourmet coffee, tea and drink bases; importer of green coffee; wholesaler/distributor of general merchandise and groceries including coffee and tea; serving the food service market
President: Mike O'Donnell
VP Finance: Jim Pypen
Estimated Sales: $300,000-500,000
Number Employees: 10-19
Square Footage: 200000
Parent Co: Superior Coffee & Foods
Type of Packaging: Food Service, Private Label

13618 Wedding Cake Studio
7373 Stanhope Kell Road
Williamsfield, OH 44093
440-667-1765
Fax: 440-293-5573
Cakes and candy
President: Craig Harvey

Estimated Sales: Under $500,000
Number Employees: 1-4
Brands:
 Ther Cake Loft

13619 Wedemeyer's Bakery
314 Harbor Way
S San Francisco, CA 94080-6900
650-873-1000
Fax: 650-873-3170
wedemeyer@wedemeyerbakery.com
www.wedemeyerbakery.com
Hearth bread, sliced bread and specialty rolls.
Owner/President: Laurence Strain
Estimated Sales: $1 Million
Number Employees: 20-49
Square Footage: 28636
Type of Packaging: Consumer, Food Service
Brands:
 Better Way

13620 Weetabix Canada
751 D'Arcy St.
Cobourg, ON K9A 4B1
Canada
800-343-0590
Fax: 905-372-7261 888-933-8249
www.weetabix.com
Breakfast cereals and ingredients.
President/CEO, Post Consumer Brands: Howard Friedman
Year Founded: 1975
Estimated Sales: $300 Million
Number Employees: 250+
Number of Brands: 4
Parent Co: Post Holdings, Inc.
Type of Packaging: Consumer, Food Service, Private Label, Bulk
Other Locations:
 Weetabix Food Company
 Burton Latimer
Brands:
 Alpen Dark Chocolate
 Alpen No Added Sugar
 Alpen Original Muesli
 Barbara's Baked Original
 Barbara's Baked White Cheddar
 Barbara's Chocolate Chip
 Barbara's Cinnamon
 Barbara's Cinnamon Crunch
 Barbara's Jalapeno
 Barbara's Oatmeal
 Barbara's Original
 Barbara's Peanut Butter
 Babara's Vanilla
 Barbara's Vanilla Blast
 Barbara's GrainShop
 Barbara's Weetabix

13621 Weetabix Food Co.
500 Nickerson Road
Marlborough, MA 01752
800-343-0590
www.weetabixusa.com
UK-based cereal manufacturer with a plant in Cobourg, Ontario, Canada that serves the North American market.
CEO, Weetabix North America: Steve Van Tassel
Contact: James Gillespie
jgille@weetabixna.com
Parent Co: Bright Food (Group) Co., Ltd
Type of Packaging: Consumer, Food Service, Private Label, Bulk
Brands:
 Weetabix
 Alpen
 Barbara's

13622 Wege Pretzel Company
PO Box 334
Hanover, PA 17331
717-843-0738
Fax: 717-633-3910 800-888-4646
info@wege.com www.wege.com
Producers of sourdough, whole wheat, organic, butter flavor and specialty pretzels.
President: Ike Laughman
Vice President: Edith Staub
VP Marketing: William Still
Estimated Sales: $8200000
Number Employees: 85
Square Footage: 440000
Parent Co: LDI
Type of Packaging: Consumer, Food Service, Private Label, Bulk

Food Manufacturers / A-Z

Brands:
- Dutchie
- Wege

13623 Wege of Hanover
PO Box 334
Hanover, PA 17331
717-843-0738
Fax: 717-633-3910   800-888-4646
info@wege.com   www.wege.com

Pretzels
Manager: Carol Arentz
VP: Tony Laughman
Estimated Sales: $500-1 Million appx.
Number Employees: 50-99
Type of Packaging: Private Label
Brands:
- Dutchie

13624 Wegmans Food Markets Inc.
1500 Brooks Ave.
PO Box 30844
Rochester, NY 14624-0844
800-934-6267
www.wegmans.com

Grocery, bakery, dairy, deli, floral, meat, produce, seafood, alcoholic beverages, and more.
President/CEO: Colleen Wegman
Chairman: Danny Wegman
daniel.wegman@wegmans.com
Senior VP: Nicole Wegman
Year Founded: 1916
Estimated Sales: $9.7 Billion
Number Employees: 50,000
Brands:
- Wegmans Gluten Free
- Wegmans Organic

13625 Wei-Chuan USA Inc
6655 Garfield Ave
Bell Gardens, CA 90201-1807
562-372-2020
Fax: 562-927-0780   info@weichuanusa.com
www.weichuanusa.com

Manufacturer and distributor of frozen Chinese foods.
President, Wei-Chuan USA: Steve Lin
stevel@weichuanusa.com
Year Founded: 1972
Number Employees: 250-499
Type of Packaging: Consumer, Food Service, Private Label
Other Locations:
- Manufacturing Facility Los Angeles CA
- Manufacturing Facility Murfreesboro TN

Brands:
- Farmer King
- Golden Foods
- Ho-Tai
- Lotus
- Wei-Chaun
- Wei-Chuan

13626 Weibel Vineyards
1 Winemaster Way # D
Suite D
Lodi, CA 95240-0860
209-365-9463
Fax: 209-365-9469   800-932-9463
www.weibel.com

Wines
President: Fred Weibel Jr
CFO: Bruce Baker
Sales: Douglas Richards
Manager: Liz West
liz@weibel.com
Operations Manager: Gary Habletzel
Estimated Sales: $4.5 Million
Number Employees: 20-49
Square Footage: 400
Type of Packaging: Private Label

13627 Weil's Food Processing
483 Erie Street N
PO Box 130
Wheatley, ON N0P 2P0
Canada
519-825-4572
Fax: 519-825-7337   email@weilsfood.ca
www.weilsfood.ca

Asparagus, canned tomatoes and potatoes
President: Henry Weil
Vice President/Board Member: Robert Weil
Sales: Mark Weil
Estimated Sales: $1-2.5 Million
Number Employees: 10-19
Type of Packaging: Consumer, Food Service, Private Label

13628 Weinberg Foods
11410 NE 124th Street
Suite 264
Kirkland, WA 98034-4305
800-866-3447
Fax: 310-230-9057   weinberg@weinbergfoods.com
www.bakingingredients.com

Kosher egg products, dry milk and vegetable powders; importer of kosher vegetable powders; exporter of kosher egg products
President: W Weinberg
Sales: Ashley Hester
Estimated Sales: $930,000
Number Employees: 4
Square Footage: 12000
Type of Packaging: Bulk

13629 Weisenberger Mills
2545 Weisenberger Mill Rd
Midway, KY 40347-9791
859-254-5282
Fax: 859-254-0294   800-643-8678
flourusa@te.net   www.weisenberger.com

Processor and exporter of wheat flour, cornmeal and baking mixes including biscuit, pancake, pizza dough, cornbread and hush puppies; exporter of fish batter breading
President: Ernest Weisenberger
sales@weisenberger.com
Vice President: Philip Weisenberger
Estimated Sales: $900000
Number Employees: 5-9
Square Footage: 64000
Type of Packaging: Consumer, Food Service, Private Label

13630 Weiser River Packing
531 Unity Lane
Weiser, ID 83672-5372
208-549-0200
Fax: 208-549-0503

Processor and exporter of onions
President: Calvin Hickey
Estimated Sales: $1,000,000
Number Employees: 20
Type of Packaging: Consumer, Food Service, Private Label, Bulk
Brands:
- Burger Buddies
- Head of the Class
- Sun Lovin
- Weiser River Whoppers

13631 Weiss Brothers Smoke House
132 Norton Rd
Johnstown, PA 15906-2906
814-539-4085
Fax: 814-536-3951

Smoked and Italian sausage, bacon, frankfurters and bologna
President: Walter Grata
Quality Control: Joseph Miller
Estimated Sales: Below $5 000,000
Number Employees: 5-9

13632 Weiss Homemade Kosher Bakery
5011 13th Ave
Brooklyn, NY 11219
718-438-0407
Fax: 718-438-1872   800-498-3477

Kosher breads, cakes, pastries, rugulach and wedding cakes
President: Abe Weiss
Estimated Sales: $1-3 Million
Number Employees: 20-49

13633 Weiss Noodle Company
31313 Aurora Road
Cleveland, OH 44139-2705
440-248-4550

Dry Pasta
President: James Price
Estimated Sales: $5-10 Million appx.
Number Employees: 20-49
Parent Co: Ideal Macaroni Company

13634 Welch Foods Inc
300 Baker Ave # 101
Suite 101
Concord, MA 01742-2731
978-371-1000
Fax: 978-371-3855   800-340-6870
www.welchs.com

Juice, jellies and jams and frozen concentrates
President & CEO: Brad Irwin
birwin@welchs.com
CMO: Tom Dixon
Number Employees: 1000-4999
Square Footage: 2120000
Type of Packaging: Consumer, Food Service

13635 Welch Foods Inc.
300 Baker Ave.
Suite 101
Concord, MA 01742
978-371-1000
Fax: 978-371-3855   800-340-6870
www.welchs.com

Jams, jellies, marmalades, preserves, beverage and frozen dessert bases, juice concentrates, frozen dessert pops and juice including grape, tomato, apple cider, cranberry and cranberry blends.
President/CEO/Director: Bradley Irwin
Vice President/Chief Financial Officer: Michael Perda
Year Founded: 1869
Estimated Sales: $650 Million
Number Employees: 1000-4999
Parent Co: National Grape Cooperative
Type of Packaging: Consumer, Food Service
Brands:
- Bama Fruit Spreads
- Welch's

13636 Welch's Global Ingredients Group
300 Baker Avenue
Suite 101
Concord, MA 01742
978-371-3692
www.welchsgig.com

Manufacturer of grape juice, purees, FruitWorx real fruit pieces and powders.
General Sales Manager: Justin White
Contact: Kate Boze
kboze@welchs.com
Parent Co: Welch's Food

13637 Welcome Dairy Inc
H4489 Maple Rd
Colby, WI 54421-9519
715-223-2874
Fax: 715-223-3958   www.welcomedairy.com

Manufacturer of processed cheese products.
President: Tollefson Amanda
tollefson@welcomedairy.com
Number Employees: 50-99
Number of Brands: 1
Number of Products: 7
Brands:
- Welcome

13638 Weldon Ice Cream Co
2887 Canal Dr
Millersport, OH 43046-9701
740-467-2400
mgmt@weldons.com
www.weldons.com

Ice cream including novelties, sandwiches, creamsicles and fudgecicles
Owner: David Pierce
david@weldons.com
Estimated Sales: $460000
Number Employees: 5-9
Type of Packaging: Consumer, Food Service, Bulk

13639 Well Dressed Food Company
96, Park Street
Tupper Lake, NY 12986
518-359-5280
Fax: 518-618-3147   sales@welldressedfoods.com
www.welldressedfoods.com

Breakfast mixes, sweet & savory jams, crunchy granola, dessert mixes, sauces/rubs and honey & toppings
President/Owner: David Tomberlin

Food Manufacturers / A-Z

13640 Well-Pict Inc
209 Riverside Rd
PO Box 973
Watsonville, CA 95076-3656
831-722-3871
Fax: 831-722-6041 sales@wellpict.com
www.wellpict.com
Strawberries, raspberries
Owner: Keith Bungo
kbungo@wellpict.com
CFO: George Schaaf
General Manager: Eric Miyasaka
Quality Control: Keith Bungo
Estimated Sales: $30-50 Million
Number Employees: 20-49

13641 Wella Bar
1403 MLK Jr. Industrial Blvd.
East Lockhart, TX 78644
877-725-7289
info@wellabar.com www.wellabar.com
Energy bars
Co-Founder: George Ghilarducci
Co-Founder: Deborah Nease
Brands:
  Lockhart Fine Foods
  Wella Bar

13642 (HQ)Wellesse
1441 W Smith Rd
Ferndale, WA 98248-8933
800-232-4005
Fax: 360-384-1140 800-232-4005
info@wellesse.com www.wellesse.com
Processor, exporter and contract packager of herbal and homeopathic food supplements in liquid form
President & CEO: Jim Thornton
COO & CFO: Shri Iyengar
Manager Research & Development: Mary Galloway
Quality Control Director: John Knight
VP Marketing/Product Management: Greg Andrews
VP Sales: Marc Kubota
Director Operations: Tim Schaafsma
Purchasing Manager: Scott Sticklin
Estimated Sales: $6 Million
Number Employees: 10-19
Square Footage: 181000
Type of Packaging: Consumer, Private Label
Brands:
  Bioallers
  Complimed
  Natrabio
  Nico-Rx
  Symtec
  Zand Hebs For Kids
  Wellesse

13643 Wellington Brewery
950 Woodlawn Road West
Guelph, ON N1K 1B8
Canada
519-837-2337
Fax: 519-837-3142 800-576-3853
mail@wellingtonbrewery.ca
www.wellingtonbrewery.ca
Beer, ale, lager and stout
President: Doug Dawkins
VP: Brent Davies
General Manager: Sarah Dawkins
Marketing: Paul Aquilina
Sales Representative: Scotty Baugh
Operations Manager: Christopher Sheppard
Production Manager: Ian Meredith
Purchasing: Sarah Dawkins
Estimated Sales: $3,500,000
Number Employees: 30
Type of Packaging: Consumer, Food Service
Brands:
  Beehive
  Black Knight
  Countryale
  Iron Uke
  Spa
  Trailhead

13644 Wellington Foods
1930 California Avenu
Corona, CA 92881
951-547-7000
Fax: 562-989-9322 www.wellingtonfoods.com
Health foods and institutional foods
Owner: Anthony Harnack Sr
Contact: Hal Amick
hal.amick@colingordon.com
Estimated Sales: $2.5-5 Million
Number Employees: 20-49
Brands:
  Wellington Foods

13645 Wells Enterprises Inc.
1 Blue Bunny Dr.
Le Mars, IA 51031
712-546-4000
Fax: 712-548-3800 www.wellsenterprisesinc.com
Ice cream and frozen novelty manufacturer.
President/CEO: Michael Wells
Executive VP/CFO: Jeremy Pinkerman
Senior VP/General Counsel: Erick Opsahl
Executive VP/COO: Liam Killeen
Year Founded: 1913
Estimated Sales: Over $1 Billion
Number Employees: 2,500+
Number of Brands: 4
Type of Packaging: Consumer, Food Service, Bulk
Other Locations:
  Ice Cream Plant
  St. George UT
Brands:
  Blue Bunny
  Blue Ribbon Classics
  Bomb Pop
  Chillycow

13646 Welsh Farms
1330 Main Ave
Clifton, NJ 07011-2215
973-772-2388
Fax: 973-403-0180
Ice cream and frozen yogurt
Owner: Atul Patel
anilkumar_290@msn.com
General Manager: Robert Pailillo
Plant Manager: Joe Marscovetta
Estimated Sales: Less Than $500,000
Number Employees: 1-4
Type of Packaging: Consumer, Food Service

13647 Welsh Farms
520 Main Avenue
Wallington, NJ 07057
973-777-2500
Fax: 973-249-3849 800-221-0663
wallington.questions@bordendairy.com
www.farmlanddairies.com
Powdered milk, buttermilk, ice cream and juice
President/CEO: Terri Webb
Estimated Sales: $1-2.5 Million
Number Employees: 20-49
Square Footage: 360000
Parent Co: Welsh Farms
Type of Packaging: Consumer, Food Service
Brands:
  Welsh Farms-Ice Cream
  Farmland Dairy
  Clinton
  Skim Plus
  School Milk

13648 Wenda America Inc
1823 High Grove Ln
Suite 103
Naperville, IL 60540
844-999-3632
sales@wendaingredients.com
www.wendaingredients.com
Global meat and poultry ingredients manufacturer and processor.
President: Chad Boeckman
chadb@wendaingredients.com
Year Founded: 1995
Estimated Sales: $200 Million
Number Employees: 200-500
Number of Brands: 7
Type of Packaging: Bulk
Brands:
  Wendaphos
  Prosur
  Novapro
  NatureBind
  Senor Paprika
  Koolgel
  SoyPura

13649 Wendysue & Tobey's
15530 Broadway Center St
Gardena, CA 90248-2137
310-516-9705
Fax: 310-516-0876
Bakery
President: John Roberts
info@wendysue-tobeys.com
Plant Manager: John Roberts
Estimated Sales: Below $5 Million
Number Employees: 20-49
Type of Packaging: Private Label

13650 Wenger Spring Brook Cheese Inc
12805 N Spring Brook Rd
Davis, IL 61019-9719
815-865-5612
Fax: 815-248-2450
Swiss and muenster cheeses
Owner: Fred S Wenger
wengers@state-isp.com
Vice President: John Wenger
Estimated Sales: $.5-1 million
Number Employees: 20-49
Type of Packaging: Consumer, Private Label, Bulk

13651 Wenger's Bakery
900 N 10th St
Reading, PA 19604-2302
610-372-6545
Buns, pies, cakes, breads, cookies and pastries
Owner: Javiar Martinez
Marketing Director: Peter Menicucci
Estimated Sales: Less Than $500,000
Number Employees: 1-4
Type of Packaging: Consumer

13652 Wenk Foods Inc
PO Box 368
Madison, SD 57042
605-256-4569
Fax: 605-256-3204 wfi@hcpd.com
Processor and exporter of frozen and dried egg products; also, frozen whole geese
President: William Wenk
Sales Director: Norbert Moldan
Number Employees: 50-99
Square Footage: 120000
Type of Packaging: Consumer, Food Service, Private Label, Bulk
Brands:
  Wenk

13653 Wenner Bakery
33 Rajon Rd
Bayport, NY 11705
Fax: 631-563-6546 800-869-6262
sales@wennerbread.com www.wennerbakery.com
Frozen unbaked bread products including egg twist rolls, Italian bread, bagels, hard rolls, challah and specialty breads; also, par-baked rolls and rolls.
CEO: Jeffrey Montie
Estimated Sales: G
Number Employees: 250-499
Square Footage: 72000
Type of Packaging: Food Service, Private Label, Bulk
Brands:
  Npn
  Swirl Onion
  Steakhouse Style
  Wenner
  Rustica

13654 Wente Family Estates
5565 Tesla Rd
Livermore, CA 94550
925-456-2305
info@wentevineyards.com
www.wentevineyards.com
Wines
CEO: Carolyn Wente
Senior Brand Manager: Aly Wente O'Neal
Estimated Sales: $50-100 Million
Number of Brands: 5
Brands:
  Wente
  Murrieta's Well
  entwine
  Hayes Ranch
  Double Decker

13655 Wenzel's Bakery
125 E Broad Street
Tamaqua, PA 18252-2007
570-668-2360
Baked goods
President: George Wenzel
Estimated Sales: $76,000
Number Employees: 3

Food Manufacturers / A-Z

Type of Packaging: Consumer

13656 Werling & Sons Slaughterhouse
100 S Plum Street
Burkettsville, OH 45310
937-338-3281
Fax: 419-375-0037 www.werlingandsons.com
Meat products and hydrogenated fats; custom slaughtering available
Owner/Marketing Manager: Edward Werling
VP Sales/Marketing: James Werling
Estimated Sales: $5-10 Million
Number Employees: 10
Square Footage: 17752
Type of Packaging: Consumer, Bulk

13657 Wermuth Winery
3942 Silverado Trl
Calistoga, CA 94515
707-942-5924
Cabernet sauvignon
Winemaker: Ralph Wermuth
Estimated Sales: A
Number Employees: 1-4

13658 Wessanan
420 W Broadway Avenue
Minneapolis, MN 55411
612-331-3775
Fax: 612-378-8398
Milk, dairy and non-cheese products
President: Tim Green
VP Sales: Pat Graiziger
Plant Manager: John Gronholm
Number Employees: 100-249
Brands:
Clover Leaf

13659 West Bay Fishing
RR 1
Box 752
Gouldsboro, ME 04607-9753
207-963-2392
Fax: 207-963-7403
Seafood
President: Richard Noble

13660 West Brothers Lobster
830 Pigeon Hill Rd
Steuben, ME 04680
207-546-3622
Fax: 207-255-3987
Lobster
Owner: Blair West
Estimated Sales: $300,000-500,000
Number Employees: 1-4

13661 West Coast Products
717 Tehama St
Orland, CA 95963-1248
530-865-3379
Fax: 530-865-1581 800-382-3072
www.westcoastproducts.net
Manufacturer and exporter of specialty olives and olive oil
President: Estelle Krackov
Manager: Dan Vecere
dan.vecere@westcoastproducts.net
Estimated Sales: $380,000
Number Employees: 10-19
Square Footage: 18608
Type of Packaging: Food Service, Bulk
Brands:
Olinda

13662 West Coast Seafood Processors Association
650 NE Holladay St
Suite 1600
Portland, OR 97232
503-227-5076
www.wcspa.com
Processor and exporter of frozen Pacific whiting
Manager: Tom Libby
Executive Director: Rod Moore
Contact: Rod Moore
tuna_1@charter.net
Estimated Sales: $10-20 Million
Number Employees: 100-249
Parent Co: California Shellfish
Type of Packaging: Bulk

13663 West Coast Specialty Coffee
71 Lost Lake Lane
Campbell, CA 95008
650-259-9308
Fax: 650-259-8024 rh@specialtycoffee.com
www.specialtycoffee.com
Coffee and coffee equipment and supplies
President: Robert Hensley
rh@specialtycoffee.com
Estimated Sales: $500,000
Number Employees: 2
Type of Packaging: Consumer, Food Service, Bulk

13664 West Liberty Foods LLC
207 W 2nd St
P.O. Box 318
West Liberty, IA 52776
888-511-4500
www.wlfoods.com
Ready-to-eat sliced processed meat, poultry and protein products.
CEO: Edward Garrett
President: Michael Quint
VP & CFO: Allen Hansen
VP & COO: Gerald Lessard
Quality Assurance: Chasity Abel
chasity.abel@wlfoods.com
Operations Manager: Chad Schnepper
Year Founded: 1996
Estimated Sales: $200-500 Million
Number Employees: 1,900
Square Footage: 175000
Parent Co: Iowa Turkey Growers Cooperative
Type of Packaging: Consumer, Food Service, Private Label
Other Locations:
West Liberty Foods Plant
Mt Pleasant IA
West Liberty Foods Plant
Sigourney IA

13665 West Pac
9671 N 5th E
Idaho Falls, ID 83401-5637
801-973-7400
Fax: 801-973-7436 800-973-7407
Cake mixes, barbecue sauces and spices; contract packager of liquid and dry mixes in cans, bottles and boxes
President: Hal Havens
Number Employees: 5-9
Square Footage: 80000
Type of Packaging: Consumer, Private Label
Brands:
Gourmet Spices

13666 West Pak Avocado Inc
38655 Sky Canyon Dr
Murrieta, CA 92563-2536
951-696-5845
Fax: 951-296-5744 800-266-4414
www.westpakavocado.com
Importer, exporter and packer of avocados; importer of Mexican and Chilean fruits; processor of persimmons and kumquats
President: Randy Shoup
randy.shoup@westpakavocado.com
Import Export Director: Dave Culpeper
VP/General Manager: Galen Newhouse
Estimated Sales: $3-5 Million
Number Employees: 50-99
Square Footage: 88000
Type of Packaging: Consumer, Food Service, Bulk
Brands:
Asian Star
West Pak

13667 West Park Wine Cellars
P.O.Box 280
West Park, NY 12493
845-384-6709
Fax: 845-384-6709
Wines
President: Louis Fiore
Estimated Sales: Under $300,000
Number Employees: 1-4
Type of Packaging: Private Label
Brands:
Full Service Caterin

13668 West Point Dairy Products
1715 East Road
West Point, NE 68788
402-372-5551
Fax: 402-372-5061 info@westpointdairy.com
www.westpointdairy.com
Dairy products including butter
Estimated Sales: $20-50 Million
Number Employees: 50-99
Type of Packaging: Private Label
Brands:
Country Cream Butter

13669 West Thomas Partners, LLC
4053 Brockton SE
Grand Rapids, MI 49512
616-755-8432
info@theglutenfreebar.com
www.theglutenfreebar.com
Gluten-free, non-GMO, soy-free and nut-free snack bars, energy bites and oats in various flavors
Co-Founder: Marshall Rader
Co-Founder: Elliott Rader
Year Founded: 2010
Number of Brands: 1
Number of Products: 17
Type of Packaging: Consumer, Private Label
Brands:
GFB: The Gluten Free Bar

13670 Westar Nutrition Corporation
350 Paularino Ave.
Costa Mesa, CA 92626
949-645-6100
Fax: 949-645-9131 800-645-1868
cs@vivalife.com www.vivalife.com
Nutraceuticals and nutritional supplements
President/CEO: David Fan
VP Sales & Business Development: May Chen
VP Regulatory/Business Affairs: Cheryl Cartwright
Director/Production: Joe Ramos
Estimated Sales: $29800000
Number Employees: 20-49

13671 Westbend Vinyards
5394 Williams Road
Lewisville, NC 27023-8278
336-945-5032
Fax: 336-945-5294 866-901-5032
Wine
Owner: Jack Kroustalis
Manager: Steve Shepard
Estimated Sales: $500,000-$1 Million
Number Employees: 10-19

13672 (HQ)Westbrae Natural Foods
58 S Service Rd
Melville, NY 11747
631-730-2200
Fax: 631-730-2550 800-434-4246
www.westbrae.com
Processor, importer and exporter of natural and organic soy and rice beverages, tortilla and potato chips, soups, beans, chili, condiments, sauces, rice cakes, popcorn, pretzels, licorice, cookies, spreads and Asian foods
President/CEO: Irwin Simon
CFO/EVP: Ira Lamel
Number Employees: 1,000-4,999
Square Footage: 156000
Parent Co: The Hain Celestial Group, Inc.
Type of Packaging: Consumer, Private Label
Brands:
Bearitos
Little Bear Organic
Westbrae Natural
Westsoy

13673 Westbrae Natural Foods
4600 Sleepytime Dr.
Boulder, CO 80301
800-434-4246
www.westbrae.com
Natural and organic beans, pastas, vegetables, japanese misos and condiments.
President & CEO: Irwin Simon
Estimated Sales: $10-20 Million
Number Employees: 20-49

Food Manufacturers / A-Z

13674 Westbrook Trading Company
3410b Odgen Road SE
Calgary, AB T2G 4N5
Canada
403-290-0860
Fax: 403-264-3017 800-563-5785
Processor and exporter of fresh, frozen and boxed beef and pork
President: Michael Nutik
Sales Manager: Daren Uens
Number Employees: 100-249
Type of Packaging: Consumer, Food Service, Bulk

13675 Westco-BakeMark
7351 Crider Avenue
Pico Rivera, CA 90660-3705
562-949-1054
Fax: 562-948-5506 www.yourbakemark.com
Processor, importer and exporter of baking ingredients and supplies, including mixes, fillings, icings and frozen products.
Chief Supply Chain Officer: Jim Parker
CFO/VP of Finance: Refugio Reynoso
Marketing Director: David Roccio
EVP of Sales: William Day
VP of Human Resources: Kenneth Sparks
Estimated Sales: $20-50 Million
Number Employees: 500-999
Number of Brands: 1
Parent Co: CSM Bakery Solutions
Type of Packaging: Food Service, Bulk
Other Locations:
  Union City CA
  Reno NV
  Phoenix AZ
  Seattle WA
Brands:
  Westco

13676 Westdale Foods Company
14541 S 88th Ave
Orland Park, IL 60462-2752
708-458-7774
Fax: 708-458-1298
Candy
Owner: Tom Vandervliet
Estimated Sales: $5-10 Million
Number Employees: 10-19
Brands:
  Sachers
  Schluckwerder
  Schumann's
  Schwarteau
  Siljans
  Simpkins
  Smooth & Melty
  Soldans

13677 Western Bagel Baking Corp
7814 Sepulveda Blvd
Van Nuys, CA 91405-1062
818-786-5847
Fax: 818-787-3221 wbinfo@westernbagel.com
www.westernbagel.com
Processor and exporter of fresh and frozen bagels.
President: Steve Ustin
Cmo: Corrie Ustin
custin@westernbagel.com
Vice President: Skip Scheidt
Operations Manager: Jim Schultz
Estimated Sales: $29280131
Number Employees: 250-499
Square Footage: 30000
Brands:
  Western

13678 Western Beef Jerky
7209 B 101 Avenue NW
Edmonton, AB T6A 0H9
Canada
780-469-4817
Fax: 780-468-5006 info@westernbeefjerky.ca
www.westernbeefjerky.ca
Beef jerky
President: Danny Ljubsa
Estimated Sales: A
Number Employees: 1-4
Type of Packaging: Consumer

13679 Western Buffalo Company
1015 E St. Patrick Street
PO Box 4185
Rapid City, SD 57709
605-342-0322
Fax: 605-342-5375 800-247-3263
kenwbc@rushmore.com
www.westernbuffalocompany.com
Meat including beef and buffalo
President: Bruce Anderson
Secretary: Gail Hise
Plant Manager: Al Holzer
Estimated Sales: $10-20 Million
Number Employees: 20-49
Square Footage: 24000
Type of Packaging: Consumer, Food Service, Private Label, Bulk

13680 Western Creamery
91 Delta Park Blvd
Unit 2
Brampton, ON L6T 5E7
Canada
905-458-8696
Fax: 905-458-8717 800-265-3230
info@westerncreamery.com
www.westerncreamery.com
Dairy products including cotage cheese, cream cheese, sour cream, yogurt, baker's special, and maslanka
Director General, Libert,: Martin Valiquette
Parent Co: Libert, Natural Foods Inc.
Brands:
  Western Creamery

13681 Western Meat Co
4101 Capitol Blvd SW
Tumwater, WA 98501-4069
360-357-6601
866-357-6601
info@westernmeats.comcastbiz.net
www.westernmeats.net
Beef and pork
President: Dennis Mydlar
Estimated Sales: $500,000-$1 Million
Number Employees: 5-9
Type of Packaging: Consumer, Food Service

13682 Western New York Syrup Corporation
3401 Rochester Road
Lakeville, NY 14480-0910
585-346-2311
Liquid sweeteners
Manager: Tim Calway
Assistant Manager: Lee Robinson
Estimated Sales: $5-10 Million
Number Employees: 1-4
Parent Co: Archer Daniels Midland Company
Type of Packaging: Bulk

13683 Western Pacific Oils, Inc.
201 S Anderson St
Los Angeles, CA 90033
213-232-5117
Fax: 213-232-5102 www.westpacoils.com
Palm oils and coconut oil.
Manager: Y Neman
Contact: Suraj Bhojwani
suraj@westpacoils.com
Estimated Sales: $900 Thousand
Type of Packaging: Food Service, Bulk
Brands:
  Golden Palm Shortening
  Golden Joma Palm Oil
  Golden Palm Margarine
  Golden Palm Cake & Icing
  Golden Coconut Oil

13684 Western Pacific Produce
36 W Gutierrez
Santa Barbara, CA 93101
805-568-1550
Fax: 805-884-9181 800-963-4451
sales@western-pacific.com
www.western-pacific.com
Grower and packer of broccoli and other fresh produce.
President & CEO: Mark Vestal
mark@western-pacific.com
VP & Chief Financial Officer: Diana Vestal
Sales Manager: Steve Bellandi
Chief Operating Officer: Bob Cordova
Year Founded: 1990
Estimated Sales: $20-50 Million
Number Employees: 250-499
Type of Packaging: Consumer, Food Service, Private Label, Bulk

13685 Western Sugar Cooperative
7555 E. Hampden Ave.
Suite 520
Denver, CO 80231
303-830-3939
Fax: 303-695-1093 800-523-7497
www.westernsugar.com
Beet sugar, including fine granulated sugar, powdered sugar, and light and dark brown sugar for retail or industrial use. Also sugar beet pressed pulp, molasses beet pulp pellets, HE molasses, and molasses desugarized solubles.
President/CEO: Rodney Perry
Senior VP/CEO: Jason Bridges
Vice President/General Counsel: Heather Luther
Vice President, Operations: Parker Thilmony
Year Founded: 1901
Estimated Sales: $350 Million
Number Employees: 1,000+
Number of Brands: 1
Square Footage: 6321
Type of Packaging: Consumer, Private Label, Bulk
Brands:
  GW

13686 Western Syrup Company
13766 Milroy Pl
Santa Fe Springs, CA 90670
562-921-4485
Fax: 562-921-5170
Processor and exporter of custom formulated beverage bases, concentrates, flavors and flavor emulsions for carbonated beverages, slushes, sno-cones, etc.; also, dessert toppings including chocolate syrup, fudge and fruit
President: Pushpa Sastry
Sales Director: Ken Molder
Plant Manager: Marlon King
Estimated Sales: $3-5 Million
Number Employees: 5-9
Square Footage: 110000
Parent Co: Western Syrup Company
Brands:
  Bartenders Pride
  High Mountains
  Rooster
  Western Syrup

13687 Westfield Farm
28 Worcester Rd
Hubbardston, MA 01452-1139
978-928-5110
Fax: 978-928-5745 877-777-3900
stetson222@verizon.net
www.westfield-farm.myshopify.com
Surface ripened and fresh goat cheese
Owner: Bob Stetson
Marketing Director: Debby Stetson
Sales Director: Bob Stetson\
stetson222@verizon.net
Estimated Sales: $500,000-$1 Million
Number Employees: 5-9
Square Footage: 12000
Type of Packaging: Consumer, Food Service
Brands:
  Capri
  Classic Blue
  Hubbardson Blue

13688 Westfield Foods
19 Lark Industrial Pkwy # F
Greenville, RI 02828-3003
401-949-3558
Fax: 401-949-3738
Dry soup and rice mixes; also, chili
President: John Pezzillo
Estimated Sales: $130000
Number Employees: 1-4
Square Footage: 34000
Type of Packaging: Consumer, Food Service
Brands:
  Millie's

Food Manufacturers / A-Z

13689 (HQ)Westin Foods
11808 W Center Rd # 1
Omaha, NE 68144-4435
402-691-8800
Fax: 402-691-7920   800-228-6098
jweese@westinfoods.com   www.westinfoods.com
Bacon bits, imitation bacon bits, lecithin, onion rings, breaded cheese, sunflower seeds, soy products, corn starch, salad dressings, sauces, etc.; importer of olives; exporter of frozen breaded vegetables
Chairman/Ceo: Richard Westin Sr
CEO/President: Scott Carlson
scarlson@westinfoods.com
Number Employees: 250-499
Type of Packaging: Consumer, Food Service, Private Label, Bulk
Other Locations:
  Westin
  Wahoo NE
Brands:
  Big Red
  Fairbury
  Feaster Foods
  Great American

13690 Westnut
401 N 26th Ave
Cornelius, OR 97113-8510
800-382-5339
www.westnut.com
Nuts, hazelnuts
Estimated Sales: $5-10 Million
Number Employees: 20-49
Parent Co: Wilco Farm Stores

13691 Weston Foods
1425 The Queensway
Etobicoke, ON M8Z 1T3
Canada
416-252-7323
Fax: 416-252-5553   www.westonfoods.ca
Manufacturer of fresh and frozen baked goods.
President: Luc Mongeau
Number Employees: 5,000
Parent Co: George Weston Ltd.
Type of Packaging: Consumer, Food Service
Brands:
  Weston
  Ready Bake
  Wonder
  D'Italiano
  Gadova
  Gadova MultiGo
  Country Harvest
  All But Gluten
  Fourn,e
  Flat Oven
  ACE
  Colonial

13692 Westport Locker LLC
707 S West St
Westport, IN 47283-9116
812-591-3033
877-265-0551
www.westportnow.com
Meat products including beef, lamb and pork
Owner: Ben Davis
Estimated Sales: $3-5 Million
Number Employees: 5-9

13693 Westport Rivers Vineyard
417 Hixbridge Rd
Westport, MA 02790-1316
508-636-3423
Fax: 508-636-4133   800-993-9695
retail@westportrivers.com
www.westportrivers.com
Wine jellies, wine ketchup, wine mustards, wines, champagne
Owner: Bob Russell
Vice President: Carol Russell
Owner: Carol Russell
Sales Director: Jan Potts
bob@westportrivers.com
Estimated Sales: $1.5 Million
Number Employees: 10-19
Number of Brands: 2
Number of Products: 15
Square Footage: 10800
Type of Packaging: Private Label
Brands:
  Westport Farms Sparkling
  Westport Farms Specialty Foods
  Westport Farms White & Rose
  Westport Rivers Vine

13694 Westtown Brew Works
236 Schefflers Rd.
Westtown, NY 10998
www.westtownbrewworks.com
Farm-brewed wheat ales
Founder/Owner: Rich Coleman
Number of Brands: 1
Number of Products: 5
Type of Packaging: Consumer, Private Label

13695 Westway Trading Corporation
365 Canal Street
Suite 2900
New Orleans, LA 70130
701-282-5010
Fax: 701-281-2695   www.westway.com
Processor and exporter of molasses
CEO: Gene McClain
CFO: Thomas Masilla
Estimated Sales: $5-10 Million
Number Employees: 10-19
Type of Packaging: Bulk

13696 Westwood Winery
11 E Napa St # 3
Suite 3
Sonoma, CA 95476-6765
707-933-7837
Fax: 707-935-3286   info@westwoodwine.com
www.westwoodwine.com
Wines
Founder: Umbert Urch
Co-Owner: Betty Urch
Estimated Sales: $210,000
Number Employees: 5-9
Brands:
  Stanley's
  Westwood Winery

13697 Wet Planet Beverage
7 Purcell Court
Monachie, NJ 07074
201-288-1999
www.wetplanet.com
Root beer, spring water and colas; also, sports, guaranas and ginseng drinks
CEO: Robert Clamp
CFO: Katherine Butkevich
Number Employees: 5-9
Type of Packaging: Consumer, Food Service
Brands:
  Blubotol
  Blue Bottle
  Cronk 2 O
  First Tec
  Jolt
  Jolt-Cola
  Pirate's Keg
  Pirates Keg
  Xtc

13698 Wetherby Cranberry Company
3365 Auger Rd
Warrens, WI 54666
608-378-4813
Fax: 608-378-3157   wetherby@mwt.net
www.freshcranberries.com
Cranberries
Owner: Nodji Van Wichen
Owner/CEO: James Van Wychen
Estimated Sales: $.5-1 million
Number Employees: 1-4
Type of Packaging: Consumer, Bulk
Brands:
  Wetherby

13699 Weyand's Fishery
471 Biddle Ave
Wyandotte, MI 48192-2703
734-284-0400
Fax: 734-284-2671   800-521-9815
david@weyandfish.com   www.weyandfish.com
Fresh, frozen and batter-dipped fish
Owner: David Blume
david@weyandfish.com
Vice President: Carolyn Smith
Plant Manager: Richard Weyand
Estimated Sales: $5932554
Number Employees: 5-9
Square Footage: 64000

Type of Packaging: Consumer, Food Service, Private Label, Bulk

13700 Weyauwega Star Dairy
109 N Mill St
P.O. Box 658
Weyauwega, WI 54983
920-867-2870
888-813-9720
www.wegastardairy.com
Cheese manufacturer, specializing in Parmesan, Asiago and Romanao; sting cheeses and curds; meat products; spreadable cheeses. Provide private label, shredding and packing services.
President: James Knaus
Contact: Gerard Knaus
gknaus@wegastardairy.com
Estimated Sales: $12.5 Million
Number Employees: 75
Number of Brands: 7
Type of Packaging: Consumer, Food Service, Private Label, Bulk
Brands:
  Weyauwega
  Star Dairy
  Alacreme
  Scott's
  Lakeside's
  Rose Cottage
  Fontina Cheese

13701 Whaler Vineyard
6201 Old River Rd
Ukiah, CA 95482-9657
707-462-6355
Fax: 707-462-6353   www.whalervineyard.com
Wines
President: Russ Nyborg
whalerzin@pacific.net
CFO: Tara Larwood
VP Marketing/VP Operations: Ann Nyborg
Estimated Sales: Less Than $500,000
Number Employees: 1-4
Type of Packaging: Private Label
Brands:
  Flagship Shiraz
  Flagship Zinfandel
  Whaler Vineyard Flag

13702 Whaley Pecan Co Inc
1113 S Brundidge Blvd
Troy, AL 36081
334-566-3504
Fax: 334-566-9336   800-824-6827
info@whaleypecan.com   www.whaleypecan.com
Processors of shelled pecans and some exports
Owner: Bob Whaley
whaleypecan@bellsouth.net
Estimated Sales: $5,000,000
Number Employees: 10-19
Square Footage: 160000
Type of Packaging: Consumer, Food Service, Bulk
Brands:
  Whaley's
  Whaley's Fancy Shelled

13703 Wharton Seafood Sales
43505 Belt Highway
PO Box 440
Paauilo, HI 96776-0440
808-776-1087
Fax: 877-591-8944   800-352-8507
Seafood
Owner/President: Bailey Wharton
wharton@aloha.net
Estimated Sales: Less than $100,000
Number Employees: 1-4

13704 What's Brewing
138 W Rhapsody Dr
San Antonio, TX 78216-3104
210-308-0062
Fax: 210-308-8883   877-262-7311
info@sacoffeeroasters.com
www.sacoffeeroasters.com
Coffee roasters
Owner: Tony Chbeir
tony@sacoffeeroasters.com
VP: Antoine Chebeir
Secretary/Treasurer: Pauline Chebeir
Estimated Sales: Less Than $500,000
Number Employees: 1-4

Food Manufacturers / A-Z

13705 Wheat Montana Farms Inc
10778 US Highway 287
Three Forks, MT 59752-9518
406-285-3614
Fax: 406-285-3749 800-535-2798
info@wheatmontana.com
www.wheatmontana.com
Grain, flour, bread
President: Dean Folkvord
Marketing Director: Rita DeAngelis-Kockl
National Sales Manager: Dan Scott
Estimated Sales: $5-10 Million
Number Employees: 100-249
Type of Packaging: Consumer, Food Service, Private Label, Bulk

13706 Wheeling Coffee & SpiceCo
13 14th St
Wheeling, WV 26003-2833
304-232-0141
Fax: 304-232-0162 800-500-0141
www.wheelingcoffeeco.com
Roast coffee and spices
President: Mary Martin
whgcoffee@wheelingcoffeeco.com
CEO: Stephanie Ann Lokmer
Estimated Sales: $5-9.9 Million
Number Employees: 10-19
Type of Packaging: Consumer, Food Service, Bulk
Brands:
   Paramount Coffee

13707 Whetstone Candy Company
1 Dolphin Drive
St. Augustine, FL 32080
904-825-1700
Fax: 904-825-1750
sales@whetstonechocolates.com
www.whetstonechocolates.com
Candy and confectionery
President: Virginia Whetstone
Estimated Sales: $500,000 Thousand
Number Employees: 5
Number of Brands: 1
Brands:
   Wheatstone

13708 Whetstone Chocolates
1 Dolphin Dr
St Augustine, FL 32080-4530
904-825-1700
Fax: 904-824-0436 877-261-7887
www.whetstonechocolates.com
Manufacturers, sells, and distributes chocolate, candy and gum products in the North American and worldwide confectionery markets.
Owner: Jose Lopez
CEO: Philip Terranova
VP Sales: Tom Fox
sales@whetstonechocolates.com
Number Employees: 10-19
Other Locations:
   Sweetworks
   Buffalo NY
   Sweetworks
   Toronto, Canada
Brands:
   Niagara Chocolates
   Oak Leaf Confections
   Whetstone Candy

13709 Whipped Pastry Boutique
37 Richards Street
Brooklyn, NY 11231
718-858-8088
info@whippedpastryboutique.com
whippedpastryboutique.com
Tarts, pastries, breads, cakes and cookies
President & Founder: Michelle Tampakis
michelle@whippedpastryboutique.com
Estimated Sales: $1-3 Million
Number Employees: 10-20
Type of Packaging: Food Service, Private Label
Brands:
   Whipped Pastry Boutique

13710 Whistler Brewing Company
1045 Miller Creek Road
Whistler, BC V0N 1B1
Canada
604-731-2900
Fax: 604-932-7293 tours@whistlerbeer.com
http://www.whistlerbeer.com
Processor and exporter of ale and lager
President: Trevor Khoe
Estimated Sales: F
Number Employees: 100-249
Type of Packaging: Consumer, Food Service

13711 Whistler Brewing Company
1045 Millar Creek Rd.
Whistler, BC V0N1B1
Canada
604-962-8889
www.whistlerbeer.com
Beer
President: David Beardsell
CFO: George Tetreau
Sales/Marketing: Brian Keast
General Manager: Eric Spence
Estimated Sales: $2.5 Million
Number Employees: 10-19
Number of Brands: 18
Number of Products: 18
Square Footage: 40000
Type of Packaging: Consumer, Food Service
Brands:
   Albino Rhino Ale
   Black Bear Ale
   Brown Bear Ale
   Brown Island Bitter
   Hemp Cream Ale
   Jow Stiff's Spiked Rootbeer
   Polar Bear Ale
   Rethink Beer

13712 Whitaker & Assoc Architects
1794 Charline Ave NE
Atlanta, GA 30306-3128
404-266-1265
Fax: 678-285-0547
Wholesale food manufacturing, dairy, beverage, bakery, meat, poultry, ingredients
Owner: Peggy Whitaker
Estimated Sales: Less Than $500,000
Number Employees: 1-4

13713 Whitcraft Winery
36 S Calle Cesar Chavez # A
Santa Barbara, CA 93103-3680
805-730-1086
Fax: 805-730-1086 info@whitcraftwinery.com
www.whitcraftwinery.com
Wines
Owner: Chris Whitcraft
cwhitcraft@whitcraftwinery.com
Estimated Sales: Less Than $500,000
Number Employees: 1-4
Number of Brands: 1
Number of Products: 12
Square Footage: 10000
Brands:
   Whitcraft Winery

13714 White Camel Foods Group
333 16th St
Carlstadt, NJ 07072-1921
201-848-1215
info@whitecamelfoods.com
www.whitecamelhummus.com
Hummus
President: Glenn Rice
Number Employees: 2-10
Brands:
   White Camel

13715 White Cap Fish Market
120 Main St # 1
Islip, NY 11751-3431
631-277-6577
Fax: 631-277-6578 info@whitecapfish.com
www.whitecapfish.com
Seafood including tuna
Owner: V Russo
Manager: Vinny Russo
info@whitecapfish.com
Estimated Sales: $1-3 Million
Number Employees: 20-49

13716 White Cloud Coffee
5089 Alworth St
Suite A
Boise, ID 83714
208-322-1166
Fax: 888-229-3249 888-229-3249
orders@whitecloudcoffee.com
www.whitecloudcoffee.com
Roasted coffee

CEO: Jerome Eberharter
Director Marketing: Ron Thompson
VP Sales/Operations: Roger Daub
Estimated Sales: $5-10 Million
Number Employees: 20-49
Brands:
   Buckaroo
   Cowboy
   Kona Island

13717 White Coffee Corporation
18-35 38th Street
Long Island City, NY 11105
718-204-7900
Fax: 718-956-8504 800-221-0140
info@whitecoffee.com www.whitecoffee.com
Cocoa, coffee, tea, gelatin, soup mixes and bases
President: Carole White
Executive Vice President: Jonathan White
Vice President: Gregory White
Plant Manager: Tom Tolfree
Estimated Sales: $18,800,000
Number Employees: 100-249
Brands:
   Melitta
   Parker House
   White House

13718 White Fence Farm
1376 Joliet Rd
Romeoville, IL 60446-4078
630-739-1720
Fax: 630-739-4466 wffchicago@yahoo.com
Poultry
President: Laura Hastert
wffchicago@yahoo.com
Estimated Sales: $5-10 Million
Number Employees: 250-499

13719 White Hall Vineyards
5282 Sugar Ridge Road
Crozet, VA 22932
434-823-8615
tastingroom@whitehallvineyards.com
www.whitehallvineyards.com
Wines
Co-Owner: Antony Champ
Co-Owner: Edith Champ
Contact: Michael Panczak
mpanczak@comclin.net
Estimated Sales: $3-5 Million
Number Employees: 5-9

13720 White House Foods
701 Fairmont Avenue
Winchester, VA 22601
540-662-3401
Fax: 540-665-4671 tbastas@nfpc.com
www.whitehousefoods.com
Apple products including apple juice, apple sauce, vinegar and apple slices.
Chairman & CEO: David Gum
VP of Food Service Div.: Mark Thomas
Brand Sales: Dave Durden
Director Private Label Retail: Charlie Wollbrinck
Type of Packaging: Consumer, Food Service, Private Label, Bulk
Other Locations:
   National Fruit Product Plant
   Winchester NC
   National Fruit Product Plant
   Lincolnton NC
Brands:
   Orchard Boy
   Shenandoah
   Skyland
   White House

13721 White Label Yerba Mate Soda
New York, NY
info@whitelabelmate.com
whitelabelmate.com
Soda
Co-Founder: Jesse Rudoy
Brands:
   White Label Yerba Mate Soda

13722 White Oak Farm and Table
161 Cross Highway
Westport, CT 06880
203-716-1577
Fax: 877-236-4528
whiteoakfarmandtable@gmail.com
www.whiteoakfarmandtable.com

Food Manufacturers / A-Z

Pasta sauces, mustards, ketchups, fruit preserves, apple sauces, salad dressings, grilling sauces, salsas and tapenades.
President: Renee Hooper
Marketing Communications Manager: Bastien Huet
Estimated Sales: $1.4 Million
Number Employees: 33
Brands:
    White Oak Farm and Table(c)

13723 White Oak Farms Inc
343 Main St
Sandown, NH 03873-2101
    603-887-2233
Fax: 603-887-2880 800-473-8869
www.macaroons.com
Macaroons
President: James Price
info@macaroons.com
Estimated Sales: Below $5 Million
Number Employees: 5-9
Brands:
    St. Julien Macaroons

13724 White Oak Pastures
101 Church St.
Bluffton, GA 39824
    229-641-2081
www.whiteoakpastures.com
Grassfed beef, goat, and lamb; pastured beef, pork, turkey, chicken, duck, goose, guinea, and rabbit; organic vegetables including cabbage and kale.
Owner: Will Harris
Year Founded: 1866
Number Employees: 155+
Type of Packaging: Consumer, Private Label

13725 White Oak Vineyards & Winery
7505 Highway 128
Healdsburg, CA 95448-8020
    707-433-8429
Fax: 707-433-8446
tastingroom@whiteoakwinery.com
www.whiteoakwinery.com
Wines
Owner: Bill Meyers
Marketing Director: Jerry Baker
CEO: Don Grogh
Public Relations: Denise Gill
Production Manager: Steve Ryan
Estimated Sales: $180,000
Number Employees: 10-19
Type of Packaging: Private Label
Brands:
    White Oak Chardonnay
    White Oak Merlot
    White Oak Sauvignon

13726 White Oaks Frozen Foods
2525 Cooper Ave
Merced, CA 95348-4313
    209-725-9492
Fax: 209-725-9441
www.whiteoakfrozenfoods.com
Reduced Moisture (RM) vegetable ingredients processor.
President: Jack Sollazzo
CEO: Suvan Sharma
Vice President, Sales: Dan Wilkinson
Number Employees: 1-4
Parent Co: Cascade Specialties, Inc.

13727 White Packing Company
1965 Jefferson Davis Highway
Fredericksburg, VA 22401
    540-373-9883
Bacon producer.
President: Karl White
Year Founded: 1971
Estimated Sales: $21 Million
Number Employees: 150
Type of Packaging: Consumer

13728 White Rock Products Corp
14107 20th Ave # 403
Flushing, NY 11357-3045
    718-746-3400
Fax: 718-767-0413 800-969-7625
info@whiterockbev.com
www.whiterockbeverages.com
Processor and exporter of carbonated and noncarbonated soft drinks; also, mixes, iced teas, fruit drinks and spring water
President: Larry Bodkin
lbodkin@whiterockbev.com
Marketing Director: Larry Bodkin
Estimated Sales: Less Than $500,000
Number Employees: 5-9
Number of Brands: 6
Type of Packaging: Consumer, Food Service
Brands:
    Chocolate Delight
    Delicious
    Kentucky Nip
    Kentucky Nip Cherry Julep
    La Cascade Del Cielo
    Lemon Licious Lemonade
    Punch 'n Fruity
    Pure Rock
    Rock Pop Carbonated Beverages
    Sarsaparilla
    Sioux City
    Sioux City Sarsaparilla
    Southern Swirl
    Tnt Chocolate
    Tealicious Iced Tea
    Western Style Soft Drinks
    White Rock
    White Rock Orchards
    Workout Energy Drinks

13729 White Rock Vineyards
1115 Loma Vista Dr
Napa, CA 94558-9752
    707-257-7922
Fax: 707-257-7922
caves@whiterockvineyards.com
www.whiterockvineyards.com
Wines
Owner: Terra Albee
terra@whiterockvineyards.com
Winemaker: Christopher Vandendriessche
Estimated Sales: $450,000
Number Employees: 5-9
Brands:
    White Rock Vineyards
    White Rock Vineyards

13730 White Stokes International
3615 South Jasper Place
Chicago, IL 60609
    773-523-7540
Fax: 773-523-0767 800-978-6537
Quality ingredients for bakery, confectionary, and ice cream. Founded in 1906.
President: Nicholas Tzakis
Vice President: George Tzakis
Number Employees: 26

13731 White Toque
11 Enterprise Ave N
Secaucus, NJ 07094-2505
    201-863-6699
Fax: 201-863-2886 800-237-6936
r.rullo@whitetoque.com www.whitetoque.com
Importer of IQF fruits and vegetables and specialty and broad-line food service distributors with a wide selection of imported European high quality frozen and dry goods
Owner: Didier Amiel
Sales Director: Graham Taylor
d.amiel@whitetoque.com
Number Employees: 10-19

13732 White's Meat Processing
23867 N 7 Mile Rd
Fort Gibson, OK 74434-6237
    918-478-2347
Beef, pork and lamb
Owner: Brad White
Estimated Sales: $490,000
Number Employees: 1-4
Type of Packaging: Consumer, Bulk

13733 White-Stokes Company
1821 North Clybourn
Suite 3
Chicago, IL 60609-1399
    773-254-5000
Fax: 773-523-7445 800-978-6537
www.whitestokes.com
Pie fillings; also, marshmallow, butterscotch and bittersweet hot fudge toppings, nougats, caramel creams, pectin, coconut paste, etc
President/CEO: Nicholas Tzakis
VP: George Tzakis
Customer Relations: Melissa Pagan
Estimated Sales: $1400000
Number Employees: 20-49
Type of Packaging: Bulk

13734 WhiteWave Foods
1225 Seventeenth Street
Suite 1000
Denver, CO 80202
    303-635-4000
Fax: 303-443-3952 800-488-9283
www.whitewave.com
WhiteWave Foods Company makes and sells branded plant-based foods and beverages, coffee creamers and beverages, and premium products.
President: Blaine E. McPeak
Chief Executive Officer: Gregg L. Engles
Chief Financial Officer: Kelly J. Haecker
Contact: Katie Hofmann
khofmann@linkedin.com
Number of Products: 40
Square Footage: 60000
Type of Packaging: Consumer
Brands:
    Silk
    Alpro
    International Delight
    Mini Moo's
    Land O'Lakes Half & Half
    Horizon Organic

13735 Whitecliff Vineyard & Winery
331 McKinstry Rd.
Gardiner, NY 12525
    845-255-4613
www.whitecliffwine.com
Chardonnay, Riesling, Merlot, Malbec, Traminette, Ros,, other wine blends
Co-Founder/Co-Owner: Michael Migliore
Co-Founder/Co-Owner: Yancey Stanforth-Migliore
Year Founded: 1979
Number of Brands: 1
Number of Products: 19
Type of Packaging: Consumer, Private Label
Brands:
    Whitecliff

13736 Whitehall Lane Winery
1563 Saint Helena Hwy S
St Helena, CA 94574-9775
    707-963-9454
Fax: 707-963-7035 greatwine@whitehalllane.com
www.whitehalllane.com
Wines
Owner: Thomas Leonardini
greatwine@whitehalllane.com
Winemaker: Dean Sylvester
Estimated Sales: Below $5 Million
Number Employees: 10-19
Brands:
    Whitehall Lane

13737 Whitehall Specialties Inc
36120 Owens St
P.O. Box 677
Whitehall, WI 54773
    715-538-2326
    888-755-9900
www.whitehall-specialties.com
Imitation cheese, cheese food slices, blended cheese products, dried, grated
President & CEO: Steve Snyder
CFO: Mike Berg
Director, International Sales: Federico Noltenius
Year Founded: 1994
Estimated Sales: $50-100 Million
Number Employees: 100-249
Number of Brands: 2
Square Footage: 50
Type of Packaging: Food Service, Private Label, Bulk
Brands:
    Ridgeview Farms
    Whitehall

13738 Whitewave Foods Company
12002 Airport Way
Broomfield, CO 80021
    303-635-4000
Fax: 303-635-5504 www.whitewave.com
Dairy products
President: Blaine McPeak
SVP: Roger Theodoredis
Contact: James Blumberg
melissa.gillespie@gsk.com

Food Manufacturers / A-Z

Number Employees: 350

13739 Whitey's Ice Cream Inc
2525 41st St
Moline, IL 61265-5017
309-762-2175
Fax: 309-762-0053 888-594-4839
whiteys@whiteysicecream.com
www.whiteysicecream.com
Ice cream, ice milk, frozen yogurt and novelties
CEO: Elizabeth Knoche
eknoche@whiteysicecream.com
Owner/CEO: Jon Tunberg
Owner/VP: Jeffrey Tunberg
Human Resources Director: Kirsten Runburg
Operations Director: Scott Larson
Plant Manager: Gary Neer
Purchasing Manager: Tom Hendrickx
Estimated Sales: $7500000
Number Employees: 250-499
Square Footage: 100000
Type of Packaging: Consumer, Private Label

13740 Whitfield Foods Inc
1101 N Court St
Montgomery, AL 36104
334-263-2541
800-633-8790
www.whitfieldfoods.com
Maple products including butter, syrup, and honey; juices; vitamin waters; greem teas.
President & CEO: Joe Friday
VP, Quality & Technical Services: Ed Watkins
Estimated Sales: $23.9 Million
Number Employees: 100-249
Square Footage: 225000
Type of Packaging: Consumer, Food Service, Private Label
Brands:
  Alaga
  Plow Boy
  Yellow Label

13741 Whitford Cellars
4047 E 3rd Ave
Napa, CA 94558
707-942-0840
Fax: 707-942-0840 www.whitfordcellars.com
Winery of chardonnay, pinot noir and syrah
Co-Owner: Duncan Haynes
Co-Owner: Patricia Haynes
Contact: Patricia Haynes
whitford@napanet.net
Estimated Sales: $500-1 Million appx.
Number Employees: 1-4
Number of Brands: 2
Number of Products: 4
Square Footage: 10000
Type of Packaging: Private Label
Brands:
  Old Vines
  Whitford

13742 Whitley Peanut Factory Inc
2371 Hayes Rd
Hayes, VA 23072-3516
804-642-7688
Fax: 804-642-7658 800-470-2244
customercare@whitleyspeanut.com
www.whitleyspeanut.com
Peanuts, almonds, cashews, mixed nuts, pecans and honey-roasted, brazil nuts and filberts; Virginia hams.
President: Craig Smith
VP Sales: James Scannell
Estimated Sales: $590000
Number Employees: 20-49
Type of Packaging: Consumer, Food Service, Private Label, Bulk
Brands:
  Flavor Crunch
  The Peanut Factory

13743 Whitney & Sons Seafood
13326 US Highway 19
Hudson, FL 34667-1658
727-869-3728
Fax: 727-862-8283
www.whitneyandsonseafoods.com
Seafood
Owner: Mark Whitney
marksr@whitneyandsonseafoods.com
Vice President: Mark Whitney

Estimated Sales: $5-10 Million
Number Employees: 20-49

13744 Whitney Foods Inc
15504 Liberty Ave
Jamaica, NY 11433-1038
718-291-3333
Fax: 718-291-0560 www.steubenfoods.com
Dairy products
President: Mike Brown
mbrown@steubenfoods.com
Marketing Director: Bill Masterson
VP Sales: Robert Zak
Marketing: Brian Lee
Estimated Sales: $2.5-5 000,000
Number Employees: 20-49
Brands:
  Whitney Yogurt

13745 Whole Earth Bakery
130 Saint Marks Pl
Suite 1009
New York, NY 10009-5843
212-677-7597
Fax: 212-677-7067
Baked goods
Owner: Peter Slyvestri
Estimated Sales: $110,000
Number Employees: 1-4

13746 Whole Herb Co
19800 8th St E
Sonoma, CA 95476-3805
707-935-1077
Fax: 707-935-3447 sales@wholeherbcompany.com
www.berjeinc.com
Raw material supplier of herbs, spices, botanicals, spice blends, extracts and essential oils.
Manager: Holly Sherwood
Number Employees: 20-49
Square Footage: 50000
Parent Co: Berj, Inc.
Type of Packaging: Food Service, Bulk
Brands:
  Jasmine Green
  Mango Sunrise Tea
  Peach Ambrosia
  Somaguard
  Somaguard Premium Grape Extract
  Summer Berry Delight

13747 Whole Life Nutritional Supplements
13340 Saticoy St Ste B
North Hollywood, CA 91605
818-255-5357
Fax: 818-255-5307 800-748-5841
wholelife2@aol.com
Wholesaler/distributor and contract packager of vitamins
Manager: Rajen Patel
Director Sales: Irma Arroyo
Contact: Zenit Simmons
wholelife2@aol.com
Estimated Sales: $1-3 Million
Number Employees: 5-9
Square Footage: 10000
Type of Packaging: Private Label

13748 Whole in the Wall
S. Washington St. Binghamton
Binghamton, NY 13903
607-722-5138
Fax: 607-722-4237 www.wholeinthewall.com
Premium quality natural pesto, whole wheat bread and bagels, mushroom soup.
President: Elliot Fiks
CFO: Stacey Gould
Estimated Sales: Less than $500,000
Number Employees: 10-19
Type of Packaging: Consumer, Food Service, Private Label, Bulk

13749 WholeMe
3255 Spring St NE
Suite 150
Minneapolis, MN 55413-4530
612-247-9728
hello@wholeme.com
www.wholeme.com
Granola snacks: coconut clusters, peanut chocolate clusters and more.

Co-Founder & CEO: Mary Kosir
Director of Sales: Dennis Lider
Co-Founder & Chief Operating Officer: Krista Steinbach
Year Founded: 2013
Estimated Sales: $500,000
Number Employees: 1-4
Brands:
  WholeMe(c)

13750 Wholesome Bakery
299 Divisadero St
San Francisco, CA 94117
415-343-5414
info@wholesomebakery.com
www.wholesomebakery.com
Gluten-free, dairy free, egg free, soy free, trans fat free & low glycemic baked goods
Founder/CEO: Mandy Harper
Year Founded: 2009

13751 Wholesome!
14141 Southwest Freeway
Suite 160
Sugar Land, TX 77478
800-680-1896
wholesomesweet.com
Fair trade, organic sweeteners.
CEO: Nigel Willerton
Contact: Dawn Archer
dawn.archer@wholesomesweet.com
Number Employees: 50
Parent Co: Arlon Group
Type of Packaging: Food Service, Bulk
Brands:
  Sucanat
  Wholesome Foods

13752 Wholesum Family Farms
2811-3 N Palenque Ave
Nogales, AZ 85621
520-281-9233
Fax: 520-281-4366 marketing@wh.farm
www.wh.farm
Organic produce including tomatoes, cucumbers, peppers, eggplants, and squash
Chief Commercial Officer: Ricardo Crisantes
VP Business Development: Steve Lefevre
Quality Assurance: Rebeca Rabago
Marketing Specialist: Joanna Jaramillo
Sales Manager: Kristina Luna
Year Founded: 1928
Number Employees: 50-99

13753 Wholly Wholesome
General Nathan Cooper House
401 Route 24
Chester, NJ 07930
908-879-0880
800-247-6580
info@runaton.com www.whollywholesome.com
Organic and gluten-free pie shells, cakes, pies, and waffles
President/Owner: Doon Wintz
Contact: Lisa Colao
lisa.colao@runaton.com

13754 Wiards Orchards Inc
5565 Merritt Rd
Ypsilanti, MI 48197-9367
734-390-9211
Fax: 734-482-7753 www.wiards.com
Cider and apples
President: Jay Wiard
Vice President: Brandon Wiard
Events Coordinator: Rose Timbers
Estimated Sales: Less Than $500,000
Number Employees: 5-9

13755 Wiberg Corporation
931 Equestrian Court
Oakville, ON L6L 6L7
Canada
905-825-9900
Fax: 905-825-0070 info@wiberg.ca
Unitized ingredients, seasoning blends, natural spices, ASTA quality pepper, phosphates, casings and food additives.
President: Richard Welzel
Estimated Sales: $13 Million
Number Employees: 75
Square Footage: 91020

Food Manufacturers / A-Z

13756 Wichita Fish Co
1601 W Douglas Ave
Wichita, KS 67213-4022
316-265-3474
Fax: 316-262-7770 www.wichitafishcompany.com
Owner: Larry Towns
info@360wichita.com
Estimated Sales: Less Than $500,000
Number Employees: 5-9

13757 Wichita Packing Co Inc
340 N Oakley Blvd
Chicago, IL 60612-2216
312-763-3965
Fax: 312-421-0696
information@wichitapacking.com
www.wichitapacking.com
Incorporated in 1963. Manufacturer, packer and distributor of pork ribs.
Owner: Robert Golang
robertgolang@wichitapacking.com
Executive Vice President: Mark Guon
Number Employees: 20-49

13758 (HQ)Wick's Pies Inc
217 SE Greenville Ave
PO Box 268
Winchester, IN 47394-1714
765-584-8401
Fax: 765-584-3700 800-642-5880
www.wickspies.com
Frozen pies and pie shells
President: Mike Wickersham
wickspies@wickspies.com
VP: Clark Loney
Quality Control: Sue Bone
Marketing/Sales: Marsha Welch
Purchasing: Steve Burge
Estimated Sales: $9 Million
Number Employees: 50-99
Square Footage: 80000
Type of Packaging: Consumer, Food Service
Brands:
  Wick's

13759 Wicked Crisps
209 Citation Ct
Greensboro, NC 27409-9026
www.wickedcrisps.com
Crisps
Founder: Phil Kosak
Brands:
  Chad's Carolina Corn
  Wicked Crisps

13760 Wicked Mix
2321 Cantrell Rd
Little Rock, AR 72202
501-374-2244
www.wickedmixes.com
Snack mix
President: Stan Roberts
stan@wickedmixes.com
Founder & CEO: Brent Bumpers
Sales Manager: Alex Newberry Robinson
Estimated Sales: $0.5-2 Million
Number Employees: 2-10
Brands:
  Wicked Mix(c)

13761 Wicked Whoopies
621 Maine Ave
Farmingdale, ME 04344
Fax: 207-582-7007 877-447-2629
customerservice@wickedwhoopies.com
www.wickedwhoopies.com
Baked goods: whoopie pies, cake

13762 Wickers Food Products Inc
501 Main St
Hornersville, MO 63855-8501
573-737-2416
Fax: 573-737-2113 800-847-0032
wickers09@att.net www.wickersbbq.com
Marinades
Manager: Misty Edmonston
Estimated Sales: Less Than $500,000
Number Employees: 5-9
Brands:
  Wicker

13763 Wicklund Farms
3959 Maple Island Farm Rd
Springfield, OR 97477
541-747-5998
Fax: 541-747-7299
Processor and exporter of spiced green beans and bean relish
President: Larry Wicklund
Estimated Sales: $1600000
Number Employees: 6
Type of Packaging: Consumer, Food Service, Private Label, Bulk

13764 Widman's Candy Shop
116 S Broadway
Crookston, MN 56716-1955
218-281-1487
Chocolate-covered potato chips, peanut butter candy, cow pies
President: George Widman
Estimated Sales: Less Than $500,000
Number Employees: 1-4

13765 Widmer's Cheese CellarsInc
214 W Henni St
P.O.Box 127
Theresa, WI 53091-9803
920-488-2503
Fax: 920-488-2130 888-878-1107
info@widmerscheese.com
www.widmerscheese.com
Brick, colby cheese and extra sharp cheddar
President: Joseph Widmer
joew@widmerscheese.com
Estimated Sales: Below $5 Million
Number Employees: 10-19
Number of Brands: 1
Number of Products: 10
Square Footage: 64000
Type of Packaging: Consumer, Bulk
Brands:
  Widmer's Cheese

13766 Widmers Wine Cellars
116 Buffalo St
Canandaigua, NY 14424
585-374-6311
Fax: 585-374-3266
Wines
President: Clenn Curtiss
COO: Jake Makepeace
Director Engineering: Mack Baxter
Estimated Sales: $20-50 Million
Number Employees: 100-249
Parent Co: Canandaigua Wine Company

13767 Widoffs Modern Bakery
129 Water St
Worcester, MA 01604-5080
508-752-7200
Fax: 508-756-6365
Bakery products
President: Jerry Ducas
Contact: Daniel Ducas
danducas@gmail.com
Estimated Sales: Below $5 000,000
Number Employees: 20-49
Brands:
  Hearth

13768 Widow's Mite Vinegar Company
1309 P Street NW
Apt 6
Washington, DC 20005-3750
202-462-3669
Fax: 202-462-3669 877-678-5854
Salad dressing mix and Creole vinegar
President: John Allen Franciscus
Vice President: James Franciscus
Type of Packaging: Consumer, Bulk

13769 Wiederkehr Wine CellarsInc
3324 Swiss Family Dr
Altus, AR 72821-9037
479-468-2611
Fax: 479-468-4791 800-622-9463
info@wiederkehrwines.com
www.wiederkehrwines.com
Winery, producing white, rose, red, dessert, sparkling and alcohol-free wines.
WineMaster: Al Wiederkehr
wiederkehr@centurytel.net
President: Gary Wiederkehr
Vice President & National Sales Manager: Dennis Wiederkehr
Chief Financial Officer: Beverly Morrow
Estimated Sales: $4 Million
Number Employees: 50-99
Number of Brands: 1
Brands:
  Wiederkehr Wine

13770 Wiegardt Brothers
3215 273rd Street
Nahcotta, WA 98637
360-665-4111
Fax: 360-665-4950
Manufacturer and exporter of fresh oysters
President: Fritz Wiegardt
Estimated Sales: $10-20 Million
Number Employees: 50-99
Type of Packaging: Consumer
Brands:
  Jolly Roger
  Tidepoint

13771 Wilbur Chocolate Candy
48 N Broad St
Lititz, PA 17543-1005
717-626-3249
Fax: 717-626-3487 888-294-5287
www.360lancaster.com
Chocolate confectionery
President: W Shaughnessy
Sales Director: Mickey Radigan
Estimated Sales: Less Than $500,000
Number Employees: 1-4
Parent Co: Cargill Foods

13772 Wilbur Chocolate Candy
45 N Broad St
Lititz, PA 17543
888-294-5287
chocolate@cargill.com www.wilburbuds.com
Chocolate and cocoa products including cocoa powder, ice cream coatings, chocolate drops, cream coatings, confectionary coatings, chocolate coatings, sugar-free chocolate, chocolate chunks, compound drops, cocoa butter and chocolateliquor
President: Bryan Wurscher
Estimated Sales: Less Than $500,000
Parent Co: Cargill Incorporated
Brands:
  Wilbur

13773 Wilbur Packing Company
PO Box 3598
Yuba City, CA 95992
530-671-4911
Fax: 530-671-4905 sales@wilburpacking.com
www.wilburpacking.com
California prunes and walnuts
Owner/President/Sales Manager: Richard Wilbur
VP: Randy Baucom
Plant Manager: Brad Meinen
Number Employees: 350
Square Footage: 121300
Type of Packaging: Consumer

13774 Wilcox Farms
40400 Harts Lake Valley Rd
Roy, WA 98580
360-458-7774
customerservice@wilcoxfarms.net
www.wilcoxfarms.com
Eggs and milk.
Co-Owner: Andy Wilcox
Co-Owner: Brent Wilcox
Co-Owner: Chris Wilcox
Year Founded: 1909
Estimated Sales: $100-500 Million
Number Employees: 100-249
Type of Packaging: Food Service, Bulk
Brands:
  Wilcox

13775 Wild Aseptics, LLC
1261 Pacific Avenue
Erlanger, KY 41018
859-342-3600
Fax: 859-342-3610 877-787-7221
www.wildflavors.com

Bulk blending, ingredient processing and filling for the food and beverage industries, including high acid liquid ingredients for use in ready-to-use concentrates
Owner: Dr Hans Peter
CEO/President: Michael Ponder
CFO: Gary Massie
Quality Control: Karen Eberts
Sales: Kevin Farrell
Contact: Billie Davila
bdavila@wildflavors.com
Plant Manager: David Devine
Purchasing: Luke Seibert
Number Employees: 50-99
Square Footage: 130000
Parent Co: Rudolf Wild GmbH & Co. KG
Type of Packaging: Consumer, Food Service, Private Label, Bulk

13776 Wild Bill's Foods
200 Knauss Ave
Martinsville, VA 24112
276-656-3500
Fax: 717-295-9722 800-848-3236
www.wildbillsfoods.com
Beef jerky
General Manager/Public Relations: Michael Kane
CFO: Steve Woelkers
CEO: Phil Clemmens
R&D/Quality Control: Greg Rhinier
Marketing Director: John Connell
Sales Manager: Teresa Musser
Operations/Plant Manager: Steve Groff
Production Manager: Armando Torres
Estimated Sales: $10-15 Million
Number Employees: 20-49
Parent Co: Clemens Family Corporation
Type of Packaging: Consumer, Bulk

13777 Wild Blueberries
PO Box 100
Old Town, ME 04468
207-570-3535
Fax: 207-581-3499 wildblueberries@gwi.net
www.wildblueberries.com
Frozen wild blueberries.

13778 Wild Fruitz Beverages
270 Ridings Way
Ambler, PA 19002-5246
718-909-0819
Fax: 973-742-7634 888-688-7632
sales@wildfruitz.com www.wildfruitz.com
Carbonated natural fruit juices
President, CEO: Trev Warshauer
trev@wildfruitz.com
Chairwoman: Sally Watt
CFO: Jon Jensen
Estimated Sales: $3.3 Million
Number Employees: 6
Brands:
　Wild Fruitz

13779 Wild Hibiscus Flower Company
PO Box 246
Richford, VT 05476-0246
800-499-8490
northamerica@wildhibiscus.com
www.wildhibiscus.com
Hibiscus, rose and butterfly pea flowers and extracts, teas and salts
Founder & Managing Director: Lee Etherington
Co-Owner: Jocelyn Etherington
Estimated Sales: $4.4 Million
Number Employees: 44
Type of Packaging: Food Service, Private Label
Brands:
　b'Lure
　Heart Tee
　Wild Hibiscus Flowers

13780 Wild Hog Vineyard
30904 King Ridge Rd
Cazadero, CA 95421
707-847-3687
Fax: 707-847-3160 info@wildhogvineyard.com
www.wildhogvineyard.com
Wine
Owner: Daniel Schoenfeld
Co-Owner: Marion Schoenfeld
Estimated Sales: Less Than $500,000
Number Employees: 1-4
Square Footage: 8000
Brands:
　Wild Hog Vineyard

13781 Wild Horse Winery & Vineyards
1437 Wild Horse Winery Ct
Templeton, CA 93465-8449
805-434-2541
Fax: 805-434-3516 info@wildhorsewinery.com
www.wildhorsewinery.com
Winery, producing red and white wines.
Senior Winemaker: Todd Ricard
Winemaker: Kip Lorenzetti
Estimated Sales: $10-20 Million
Number Employees: 20-49
Number of Brands: 1
Type of Packaging: Consumer, Food Service
Brands:
　Wild Horse

13782 Wild Leaf Active Tea
Sparta, NJ 07871
888-605-7564
Tea
Founder: Susan Parnell
Year Founded: 2016
Estimated Sales: Under $500,000
Number Employees: 11-50
Type of Packaging: Food Service
Brands:
　WildLeaf

13783 Wild Planet Foods
1585 Heartwood Drive
Suite F
McKinleyville, CA 95519
707-840-9116
Fax: 707-839-3260 800-998-9945
elizabeth@wildplanetfoods.com
www.wildplanetfoods.com
Seafood
President/Owner: Bill Carvalho
CEO: Terry Hunt
Vice President, Co-Founder: Bill McCarthy
Sales: Justin Desiderio
Contact: Suzie Blaney
suzie@wildplanetfoods.com

13784 Wild Poppy
2355 Westwood Blvd
Suite 413
Los Angeles, CA 90064-2109
310-384-1004
info@wildpoppyjuice.com
wildpoppy.life
Poppy juice and soda
Co-Founder & CEO: George Bryson
Director of Sales: Michael Thorne
Operations: Steve Altes
Estimated Sales: $4.5 Million
Number Employees: 30-60
Brands:
　Wild Poppy

13785 (HQ) Wild Rice Exchange
1277 Santa Anita Ct
Woodland, CA 95776
530-669-0150
Fax: 530-668-9317 800-223-7423
thewildriceexch@aol.com www.wildrice.org
Processor, importer and exporter of wild rice, products and blends including basmati, arborio, red gourmet rices, organic, brown and polished white; also, quick-cook, frozen and pre-mixed pilaf; large line of specialty beans
Manager: Carlos Zambello
Sales: Carlos Zambello
Production: Golnar Emam
Type of Packaging: Consumer, Food Service, Private Label, Bulk
Brands:
　Gourmet Valley
　Gourmet Valley Foods
　Great Valley

13786 Wild Things Snacks
115 N 36th St
Unit B
Seattle, WA 98103-8663
720-231-9196
getskinnydipped.com
Chocolate covered almonds
Co-Founder: Val Griffith
Co-Founder & CEO: Breezy Griffith
Chief Sales Officer: Chrissy Haller
Estimated Sales: Under $500,000
Number Employees: 1-4
Brands:
　Skinny Dipped almonds

13787 Wild Thyme Cottage Products
127-B Donegani
Pointe Claire, QC H9R 5E9
Canada
514-695-3602
Fax: 514-695-3602
Processor and exporter of jams, jellies, marmalades, relishes and chutneys
President: David Ranlings
Number Employees: 1-4
Number of Brands: 1
Number of Products: 50
Square Footage: 2800
Type of Packaging: Consumer, Food Service
Brands:
　Wild Thyme Cottage Products

13788 Wild Thymes Farm Inc
643 County Route 403
Greenville, NY 12083-1703
518-966-5990
Fax: 845-266-8395 845-266-8387
www.wildthymes.com
Chutneys, salad dressings, fruit spreads, sauces/marinades, mustards, balsamic vinegars
Owner: Enid Stettner
Owner: Ann Stettner
ann@wildthymes.com
Quality Control: Enid Stettner
Marketing Director: Ann Stettner
Estimated Sales: Less Than $500,000
Number Employees: 1-4
Number of Brands: 1
Number of Products: 50
Type of Packaging: Consumer, Food Service, Private Label, Bulk

13789 Wild West Spices
P.O. Box 471
Cody, WY 82414-0471
307-587-8800
Fax: 307-587-8800 888-587-8887
Western-style spice blends, grilling spices and rubs, all natural dry mixes and dips
President: Bonnie Dallinger
b.dallinger@wildwestspices.com
Estimated Sales: Less than $500,000
Number Employees: 1-4
Brands:
　Wild West Spices, Inc.

13790 Wild Zora Foods
325 E 4th St.
Loveland, CO 80537
970-541-9672
support@wildzora.com
www.wildzora.com
Paelo foods including meat & veggie snack bars, soups, teas, and prepared meals
Founder/Owner: Zora Tabin
Content Marketing Manager: Hanna Jensen
Wholesale Manager: Lorenzo Moreno Jr
Project Manager: Michael Arden Conley
Year Founded: 2014
Number Employees: 20-49

13791 Wildcat Produce
PO Box 5224
McGrew, NE 69353
308-783-2438
Fax: 308-783-1054
Cucumbers, green beans, onions, potatoes and pumpkins
President: Mike Chrisman
CEO: Ruftin Rahmig
Brands:
　Wildcat Produce Garden

13792 Wilde Brands
2705 Spruce St.
Boulder, CO 80302
720-328-0843
hello@wildebrands.com
www.wildebrands.com
Chips made from chicken
Founder/CEO: Jason Wright
EVP/CFO: Jerome Metivier
National Marketing Manager: Braden Bingham

Food Manufacturers / A-Z

Year Founded: 2014
Number Employees: 5-9

13793 Wildhurst Vineyards
3855 Main St
P.O.Box 1310
Kelseyville, CA 95451-7430
707-279-4302
Fax: 707-279-1913   800-595-9463
www.wildhurst.com
Wines
President: Myron Holdenried
info@wildhurst.com
Winemaker: Mark Burch
Estimated Sales: Below $5 Million
Number Employees: 5-9
Type of Packaging: Private Label
Brands:
  Reserve Chardonnay
  Reserve Fume Blanc
  Wildhurst Cabernet F
  Wildhurst Chardonnay
  Wildhurst Merlot
  Wildhurst Zinfandel

13794 Wildlife Cookies Co
2025 Forest Ridge Rd
St Charles, IL 60174-1482
630-377-6196
Fax: 630-377-6321   sales@wildlifecookie.com
www.wildlifecookie.com
Cookies
President: Kenneth Smith
Estimated Sales: Less Than $500,000
Number Employees: 1-4

13795 Wildly Delicious
114A Railside Rd
Toronto, ON M3A 1A3
Canada
416-444-2011
Fax: 416-444-0010   888-545-9995
feedback@wildlydelicious.com
www.wildlydelicious.com
Dip, mix and spread, seasoning, spices and salts, premium oils and vinegars, gourmet sauces, pastes and mustards.
COO: Austin Muscat
CEO: Michelle Muscat
Operations: Austin Muscat

13796 Wildly Organic
99 Edison Blvd
Silver Bay, MN 55614
218-220-5030
Fax: 218-220-5030   800-945-3801
help@wildlyorganic.com   www.wildlyorganic.com
Coconut oil, cacao powders, nuts, sweeteners, herbs, dressings, popcorn, rice and grains, spices, seasonings and teas.
President: Fischer Annette
CEO: Chris Toal
Chief Financial Officer: Thomas Noll
Vice President, Sales & Marketing: Roxana C. Lopez
Director of Operations: Alex Bethke
Year Founded: 2000
Estimated Sales: $5 Million
Number Employees: 25
Brands:
  Wilderness Family Naturals

13797 Wildtime Foods
1061 W 2nd Ave
Eugene, OR 97402-4947
541-747-1654
Fax: 541-747-5067   800-356-4458
info@wildtime.com
Bulk and packaged cereals
President: Genevieve Averill
Marketing Director: Whit Hemphill
Manager: Patrick Schoenherr
patrick@grizzliesbrand.com
Estimated Sales: Below $5 Million
Number Employees: 20-49
Square Footage: 18000
Brands:
  Grizzliesh

13798 Wildtree
55 Jefferson Blvd.
Warwick, RI 2886
800-672-4050
Fax: 615-884-3359   rc@wildtree.com
Grapeseed oils, dressings and sauces

13799 Wildway
10203 Kotzebue St
Suite 101
San Antonio, TX 78217-4447
512-677-9965
info@wildwayoflife.com
www.wildwayoflife.com
Granola
Co-Founder: Kyle Koehler
Co-Founder: Kelli Koehler
Estimated Sales: Under $500,000
Number Employees: 1-10
Brands:
  Wildway

13800 Wileman Brothers & Elliott Inc
40232 Road 128
Cutler, CA 93615-2104
559-528-4772
Fax: 559-528-2456   info@mr-sunshine.com
Offers a full line of California citrus products
President: Frank Elliott III
CEO: Tommy Elliott
CFO: Brian Johnson
brian@mr-sunshine.com
Research & Development: Brad McCord
Quality Control: Raul Lopez
Sales Manager: Andrew Felts
Public Relations: Truman McGuire
Operations Manager: Manuel Guillen
Production Manager: Mark Savage
Plant Manager: Jon Hornburg
Estimated Sales: $930,000
Number Employees: 100-249
Square Footage: 16110
Type of Packaging: Consumer, Food Service, Private Label, Bulk

13801 Wilhelm Foods
8951 NE Saint Paul Hwy
Newberg, OR 97132-7132
503-538-2929
Fax: 503-538-1992
Fruit syrups and toppings
President: Charles Cox
Estimated Sales: $5-10 Million
Number Employees: 10-19

13802 Wilke International Inc
14321 W 96th Ter
Lenexa, KS 66215-4709
913-438-5544
Fax: 913-438-5554   800-779-5545
whw@wilkeinternational.com
www.wilkeinternational.com
Processor, importer, exporter and wholesaler/distributor of lactic acid, lactates, sports nutrition and dietary supplements
President: Wayne Wilke
wwilke@wilkeinternational.com
Director Administration: John Veazey
General Manager: James France
Estimated Sales: $5-10 Million
Number Employees: 10-19
Type of Packaging: Bulk
Brands:
  Createam
  Nutrasense

13803 (HQ)Wilkins Rogers Inc
27 Frederick Rd
Ellicott City, MD 21043-4759
410-465-5800
Fax: 410-750-0163   consumer@wrmills.com
www.wrmills.com
Processor and exporter of flour, corn meal, baking mixes, breading and batters
President: Samuel Rogers
Joint CEO: Samuel Rogers
Joint CEO: Tom Rogers
black@wrmills.com
CEO: Sam Rogers Jr
General Manager: James Koehnlein
Director Sales/Marketing: Steve Friesner
Director/Operations: Aaron Black
Estimated Sales: $27,900,000
Number Employees: 100-249
Square Footage: 180000
Type of Packaging: Consumer, Food Service, Private Label, Bulk
Brands:
  Crutchfield
  Indian Head
  Raga Muffins
  Spanglers
  Velvetx
  Washington

13804 Wilkinson-Spitz
705 Bronx River Road
Suite 204
Yonkers, NY 10704-1752
914-237-5000
Fax: 914-237-7295
Candy
Manager: Joel Miller
VP: Jim Koehlein
Sales Director: Leon Gleaves
Estimated Sales: $1-2.5 000,000 appx.
Number Employees: 1

13805 Will-Pak Foods
3350 Shelby Street
Suite 200
Ontario, CA 91764-5556
909-945-4554
Fax: 909-899-7822   800-874-0883
taste_adv@earthlink.net   www.tasteadventure.com
All-natural foods including soups, beans, chilies, and side dishes
President: Gary Morris
Estimated Sales: $990,000
Number Employees: 10
Square Footage: 40000
Type of Packaging: Food Service, Private Label, Bulk
Brands:
  Taste Adventure

13806 Willamette Valley Pie Co
2994 82nd Ave NE
Salem, OR 97305
503-362-8857
info@wvpie.com
www.wvpie.com
Pies, cobblers, packaged fruit, jams, and syrups
CEO: Jeff Dunn
CFO/Controller: Michael Schelske
QA Manager: Scott Lemke
Warehouse Manager: Tom Parsons
Year Founded: 1999
Number Employees: 50-99

13807 Willamette Valley Walnuts
475 NE 17th Street
PO Box 1007
McMinnville, OR 97128-3326
503-472-3215
Fax: 503-472-3294
wine@walnutcitywineworks.com
www.walnutcitywineworks.com
Processor and exporter of shelled walnuts and English walnut meats
Owner: Zac Spence
VP: Todd Heidgerken
Brand Manager: Andrew Minor
General Manager: John Gilpin
Winemakers: John Davidson
Estimated Sales: $500,000-$1 Million
Number Employees: 1-4
Type of Packaging: Consumer, Food Service, Private Label, Bulk

13808 Willcox Meat Packing House
3266 N Fort Grant Rd
Willcox, AZ 85643-3020
520-384-2015
Meat products including beef, lamb and pork
Owner: David Harris
Manager: Scott Harris
Estimated Sales: $870,000
Number Employees: 5-9
Type of Packaging: Consumer, Food Service, Private Label, Bulk

13809 William Bounds
3737 W. 240th Street
Torrance, CA 90505-6003
310-375-0505
Fax: 310-375-0756   800-473-0504
support@wmbounds.com
Spices, flavored chocolate, colored sugars.
President: Helen Bounds
Contact: Bill Bounds
billb@wmboundsltd.com

Food Manufacturers / A-Z

Estimated Sales: Below $5 Million
Number Employees: 20-49

13810 William E. Martin & Sons Company
55 Bryant Avenue
Suite 300
Roslyn, NY 11576
516-605-2444
Fax: 516-605-2442 mail@martinspices.com
www.martinspices.com
Processor, wholesaler/distributor, exporter and importer of spices, seasonings, salts, herbs and herbal supplements, seeds, powders and raisins. Wholesaler/distributor of dehydrated onion and garlic products, full line of ground spices and bakery seeds
Owner: William Martin Jr
Contact: Martin Spencer
spencer@martinspices.com
Estimated Sales: $10-20 Million
Number Employees: 22
Number of Brands: 1
Square Footage: 60000
Type of Packaging: Bulk
Brands:
   W.E.M.

13811 William Grant & Sons
300 Spectrum Center St
Suite 1150
Irvine, CA 92618
www.williamgrant.com
Distiller
CEO: Simon Hunt
CFO: Jim Heaton
Regional Director: Michel Aboujawdeh
michel.aboujawdeh@wgrant.com
Year Founded: 1887
Estimated Sales: $120 Million
Number Employees: 2,800
Type of Packaging: Private Label
Brands:
   Armida
   Balvenie
   Berentzen
   Borgianni
   Brolio
   Castello Di Volpaia
   Clan Macgregor
   Colombo
   Dry Sack
   Fonterutoli
   Frangelico Liqueur
   Glenfiddich
   Grant's
   Licor 43
   Luis Felipe Edwards
   Marques De Murrieta
   McDowell
   Metaxa

13812 William Harrison Winery LLC
1443 Silverado Trl S
St Helena, CA 94574-9798
707-963-8762
Fax: 707-963-4552 800-913-9463
info@harrisonvineyards.com www.whwines.com
Garlic dill pickles
Manager: Bruce Bradley
CEO: Lyndsey Harrison
Manager: Scott Morrison
Hospitality Manager: Shelly Zanoli
Winemaker: Scott Morrison
Estimated Sales: Less than $500,000
Number Employees: 1-4
Type of Packaging: Consumer
Brands:
   Aceto D'Oro
   Kirk and Glotzer New
   New York Deli

13813 William Harrison Winery LLC
1443 Silverado Trl S
St. Helena
St Helena, CA 94574-9798
707-963-8762
Fax: 707-963-8762 info@whwines.com
www.whwines.com
Wines
Owner: William Harrison
Marketing/Sales: Rob Monaghan
Manager: Scott Morrison
Winemaker/General Manager: Bruce Bradley
Number Employees: 1-4

Brands:
   Mario Perelli-Minetti
   Miriam

13814 William Hill Estate Winery
1761 Atlas Peak Rd
Napa, CA 94558-1251
707-224-4477
Fax: 707-224-4484 707-265-3024
www.williamhillwinery.com
Winery
Contact: Celina Marcus
celina.marcus@williamhill.com
Head Winemaker: Mark Williams
Estimated Sales: $2.2 Million
Number Employees: 20-49
Number of Brands: 1
Parent Co: E&J Gallo Winery
Type of Packaging: Consumer, Food Service
Brands:
   William Hill

13815 William Poll Inc
1051 Lexington Ave
New York, NY 10021-3294
212-288-0501
Fax: 212-288-2844 800-993-7655
wpollny@aol.com www.williampoll.com
Baked potato thins, dips, sauces
President: Stanley Poll
wpollny@aol.com
Estimated Sales: Less than $500,000
Number Employees: 5-9
Type of Packaging: Consumer
Brands:
   Baked Potato Thins
   Dip Indulgence

13816 Williams & Bennett
1815 Cypress Lake Dr.
Orlando, FL 32837
561-276-9007
sales@williamsandbennett.com
www.williamsandbennett.com
Cookies, barks, toffees, brittles, pretzels, marshmallows and graham crackers
Co-Founder: Becky Gardner
Co-Founder: Bill Gardner
Year Founded: 1992
Estimated Sales: $10-20 Million
Number Employees: 2-10
Type of Packaging: Food Service, Private Label
Brands:
   Nutter Butter
   Oreo

13817 Williams Candy Co
1230 Perry St
Chesapeake, VA 23324-1334
757-545-9311
Candy
Owner: Lillie Williams
Estimated Sales: $220,000
Number Employees: 5-9

13818 Williams Candy Company
18 Main St
Somerville, MA 02145
617-776-0814
Fax: 617-776-0816
Chocolate candy
President: Ron Cataldo
Estimated Sales: Below $5 000,000
Number Employees: 5-9
Type of Packaging: Bulk

13819 Williams Institutional Foods
1325 Bowens Mill Rd SW
Douglas, GA 31533-3933
912-384-5270
Fax: 912-384-0533 info@williams-foods.com
www.williams-foods.com
Groceries, meat, frozen foods, bakery goods, equipment and general merchandise
President/Sales Manager: Craig McCrary
CEO/Purchasing: Bob Williams
bobwilliams@williams-foods.com
Marketing: Karen Williams
Sales: George Smith
Year Founded: 1951
Estimated Sales: $37000000
Number Employees: 50-99

13820 Williams Pork
551 Joe Brown Hwy N
Chadbourn, NC 28431-7202
910-654-0204
Fax: 910-628-0081 910-654-0204
www.williamsbluehut.com
Bacon, hams, sausages, pork chops, ribs

13821 Williams Selyem Winery
7227 Westside Rd
Healdsburg, CA 95448-8357
707-433-6425
Fax: 707-431-4862 contact@williamsselyem.com
www.williamsselyem.com
Wines
Manager: Bob Cabral
contact@williamsselyem.com
Proprietor: Kathe Dyson
Director of Marketing: Mark Malpiede
Director of Winemaking & General Manager: Bob Cabral
Winemaker: Lynn Krausmann
Assistant Winemaker: Mark Ray
Estimated Sales: $1-2.5 Million
Number Employees: 10-19
Brands:
   Williams-Selym Winery

13822 Williams-R J
998 N Huron Rd
PO Box 249
Linwood, MI 48634-9219
989-697-5183
Fax: 989-697-4203 800-968-4492
dave@williamscheese.com
www.williamscheese.com
Cheese and cheese spreads
President, CEO, CFO: Michael Williams
mhw@williamscheese.com
Quality Assurance Manager: Toni Lorenz
Sales, Marketing & Public Relations: Pat Meehleder
Regional Head Of Sales: Dave Williams
Purchasing Director: Ladd Williams
Estimated Sales: $10-19 Million
Number Employees: 50-99
Number of Brands: 2
Square Footage: 16000
Brands:
   Williams
   Amish Country

13823 Williams-R J
998 N Huron Rd
Linwood, MI 48634-9219
989-697-5183
Fax: 989-697-4203 800-968-4462
mhw@williamscheese.com
www.williamscheese.com
Processed and flavored cheese
CEO: Michael H Williams
mhw@williamscheese.com
Marketing Manager: Jay Williams
Sales Director: Todd Williams
Operations Manager: Mike Williams Sr
Estimated Sales: $9 Million
Number Employees: 50-99
Square Footage: 80
Type of Packaging: Private Label
Brands:
   Amish Country
   Cheese Rounds and Bricks
   Cheese Spreads
   Williams

13824 Williamsburg Chocolatier
P.O.Box 1712
Williamsburg, VA 23187
757-253-1474
Fax: 804-966-9025 wmsbgchoc@aol.com
Confectionery products, pound cakes, chocolate lollypops, dessert toppings, fudge and seasonal chocolate specialties
Owner: Maryann Boho
Marketing: Lee Boho
Estimated Sales: Under 500,000
Number of Products: 50
Square Footage: 4800
Type of Packaging: Consumer

13825 Williamsburg Winery LTD
5800 Wessex Hundred
Williamsburg, VA 23185-8063
757-229-0999
Fax: 757-229-0911 wine@wmbgwine.com

Food Manufacturers / A-Z

Wines
President: Patrick Dufseler
pdufseler@wmbgwine.com
Estimated Sales: $3.7 Million
Number Employees: 50-99
Type of Packaging: Private Label
Brands:
   Donmir Wine Cellars
   La Donaings De Franc
   Williamsburg Winery

13826 Willie's Smoke House LLC
562 S Main St
Harrisville, PA 16038-1626
                                    724-735-4184
     Fax: 724-735-4184 800-742-4184
             www.smokedspecialtymeats.com
Hickory smoked meat products including ham, bacon, sausage, poultry, dried beef, jerky, pork loins, etc
Owner: John Mc Kee
williessmokehouse@gmail.com
Estimated Sales: $500,000 appx.
Number Employees: 5-9
Square Footage: 3800
Type of Packaging: Consumer

13827 Willmar Cookie & Nut Company
1118 U.S 12
Willmar, MN 56201-0088
                                    320-235-0600
                                    800-426-7845
                      www.gurleysfoods.com
Cookies and crackers. Salted and roasted nuts and seeds
Estimated Sales: $10-24.9 Million
Number Employees: 100-249
Number of Brands: 1
Square Footage: 140000
Type of Packaging: Private Label
Brands:
   Gurley's

13828 Willmark Sales Company
33 Nassau Ave
Brooklyn, NY 11222-3132
                                    718-388-7141
                         Fax: 718-963-3924
Processor and exporter of bakery ingredients
President: Robert Leibowitz
willmark01@aol.com
VP: Edward Leibowitz
Estimated Sales: $5-10 Million
Number Employees: 50-99

13829 Willoughby's Coffee & Tea
550 E Main St # 27
Branford, CT 06405-2948
                                    203-481-1700
     Fax: 203-481-1777 800-388-8400
                  www.willoughbyscoffee.com
Coffee
President: Barry Levine
CEO: Robert Williams
Manager: Merisa Mangano
merisa@willoughbyscoffee.com
Estimated Sales: $500,000-$1 Million
Number Employees: 10-19
Brands:
   Willoughby's

13830 Willow Foods
7774 SW Nimbus Ave
Beaverton, OR 97008
                                    503-641-6602
     Fax: 503-641-6899 800-338-3609
     info@luckyfood.com www.luckyfood.com
Chinese and Vietnamese cuisine, spring rolls, pot stickers and potato rolls.
Owner: Tammy Jo
CFO: Bonnie Tompkins
Sales Director: Peter Yu
Contact: Tanya Ramos
tammyjo@luckyfood.com
Estimated Sales: $1.35 Million
Number Employees: 20
Number of Brands: 1
Number of Products: 20
Square Footage: 40000
Type of Packaging: Consumer, Food Service, Private Label, Bulk
Brands:
   Willow

13831 Willow Tree Poultry Farm Inc
997 S Main St # 2
Attleboro, MA 02703-6299
                                    508-222-3621
    Fax: 508-222-8258 info@willowtreefarm.com
                      www.willowtreefarm.com
Poultry products
President/CEO: Chester Cekala
CEO: Robert Arobian
rarobian@willowtreefarm.com
Estimated Sales: $14,500,000
Number Employees: 50-99

13832 WillowOak Farms
611 Hartless Road
Amherst, VA 24521
                                    434-942-7104
     Fax: 530-662-0907 888-963-2767
                    wiloakfarm@aol.com
    www.willowoakfarmhorsetraining.com
All-natural hors d'oeuvre spreads, sauces and salad dressings
President: Kevin Sanchez
Research & Development: Massimo Di Sciullo
Director of Marketing: Kevin Sanchez
Contact: Willow Farm
millerfrm@gmail.com
Estimated Sales: $1-2.5 Million
Number Employees: 1-4
Number of Brands: 3
Number of Products: 30
Square Footage: 80000
Type of Packaging: Consumer, Food Service
Brands:
   L'Ortolano
   Willow Oak Farms

13833 Willowcroft Farm Vineyards
38906 Mount Gilead Rd
Leesburg, VA 20175-6721
                                    703-777-8161
    Fax: 703-777-8157 willowine@aol.com
                    www.willowcroftwine.com
Wine
Owner: Lewis Parker
willowwine@aol.com
Estimated Sales: Less Than $500,000
Number Employees: 1-4

13834 Wilson Candy Co
408 Harrison Ave
Jeannette, PA 15644-1997
                                    724-523-3151
    Fax: 724-523-5959 www.wilsoncandy.com
Boxed and bulk chocolates
President: Doug Wilson
VP: Kay Wilson
Production Manager: Rob Kane
Estimated Sales: $870,000
Number Employees: 10-19
Square Footage: 28800
Type of Packaging: Consumer, Private Label, Bulk
Brands:
   Wunder Bar

13835 Wilson's Fantastic Candy
384 Greenway Rd
Memphis, TN 38117-4338
                                    901-767-1900
                       Fax: 901-398-1375
Candy including caramels, chocolates, coconut, fudge, corn, bagged, fundraising, theater and vending; also, fat-free and sugar-free cookies and glazed nuts
Owner: Robert Wilson
VP/General Manager: Jerry Adams
Number Employees: 5-9
Square Footage: 60000
Parent Co: Kemmons Wilson Companies
Type of Packaging: Consumer, Bulk
Brands:
   Wilson Foods

13836 Wilsons Oysters
1981 S Van Ave
Houma, LA 70363
                                    985-857-8855
   Fax: 985-857-8139 wilson@wilsonsoysters.com
Oysters
Owner: Toby Voisin
tobyvoisin@yahoo.com
Estimated Sales: $5-10 Million
Number Employees: 20-49

13837 Wimberley Valley Winery
2825 Lone Man Mountain Rd
Driftwood, TX 78619-9313
                                    512-847-2592
                       Fax: 281-288-8298
Wines
Vice President: Dean Valentine
wimberleyvalleywinery@wvwtx.com
VP: Dean Valentine
Estimated Sales: $500,000-$1 Million
Number Employees: 5-9
Type of Packaging: Bulk
Brands:
   Wimberley Valley

13838 Winans Chocolates & Coffees
121 West High Street
Piqua, OH 45356
                                    937-381-0247
  Fax: 937-773-2388 www.winanscandies.com
Candy
President: Joe Reiser
Estimated Sales: $10-20 Million
Number Employees: 20-49
Type of Packaging: Consumer

13839 Winchell's Donut House
18830 San Jose Ave
City Of Industry, CA 91748-1325
                                    626-964-1478
                     Fax: 626-912-2779
    wincustservdept@winchells.com
                      www.winchells.com
Donuts
IT Executive: Henry Lau
hlau@yumyumdonuts.com
Number Employees: 1000-4999

13840 Winchester Cheese Company
32605 Holland Rd
Winchester, CA 92596
                                    951-926-4239
                     Fax: 951-926-3349
Gouda cheese
Manager: Jeff Floot
Estimated Sales: Less than $500,000
Number Employees: 5-9
Square Footage: 14600
Type of Packaging: Consumer, Food Service, Private Label, Bulk
Brands:
   Cumin Gouda
   Herb Gouda
   Jalapeno Gouda
   Mild Gouda
   Sharp Gouda
   Super Aged Gouda

13841 Winchester Farms Dairy
675 Rolling Hills Ln
Winchester, KY 40391-8102
                                    859-745-5500
    Fax: 859-745-5547 www.winchester.us
Milk including chocolate, 2%, whole and skim; also, buttermilk
President: Bill McCarthy
CFO: Mike McGuire
VP: Michael Schlotman
Manager: Bruce Abbot
bruce.abbot@kroger.com
Estimated Sales: $500,000-$1 Million
Number Employees: 100-249
Parent Co: Kroger Company
Type of Packaging: Consumer, Private Label
Brands:
   Kroger

13842 Windcrest Meat Packers
1350 Scugog 3rd Line
Port Perry, ON L9L 1B3
Canada
                                    905-985-7267
     Fax: 905-985-9393 800-750-2542
Meat products including beef, pork, lamb, goat and veal
President: Victor Diminno
Estimated Sales: $1-2.5 Million
Number Employees: 10-19
Type of Packaging: Consumer, Private Label

13843 Windmill Candies
810 Prentice Street
Granite Falls, MN 56241
                                    877-771-8892

Food Manufacturers / A-Z

Candy
President: Tom Aus
Vice President: Laurie Aus
Estimated Sales: Under $500,000
Number Employees: 6

13844 Windmill Water Inc
2042 Old US 66
P. O. Box 2174
Edgewood, NM 87015-6740
505-281-9287
Fax: 505-286-9669 Windmillwater@comcast.net
www.windmillwater.com
Bottled spring water
President: Leon Ricter
Plant Manager: Leon Ricter
Estimated Sales: Less Than $500,000
Number Employees: 5-9

13845 Windsor Confections
4632 Telegraph Ave
Oakland, CA 94609-2022
510-653-3703
Fax: 510-653-3755 800-860-0021
Chocolate confections including chocolate dipped strawberries and gift baskets
President: Jeff White
Estimated Sales: $5-10 Million
Number Employees: 10-19
Parent Co: California Autism Foundation
Brands:
  Anytime Candy
  Break Up
  California Finest
  Chewey Kisses
  Chocolate Jollies
  Hoopee Doops
  My Selection
  Old Fashioned
  Patio Squares
  Royal Gift
  Smooth and Melties

13846 Windwalker Vineyards & Winery
7360 Perry Creek Rd
Somerset, CA 95684-9207
530-620-4054
Fax: 530-620-5224 windwalkerinfo@gotsky.com
www.windwalkervineyard.com
Wines
Owner: Jim Taff
windwalkervineyard@gotsky.com
Operations: Alanna Taff
Estimated Sales: More than $500,000
Number Employees: 5-9
Brands:
  Windwalker

13847 Windy City Organics
3320 Commercial Ave.
Northbrook, IL 60062
800-925-0577
info@windycityorganics.com
www.windycityorganics.com
Chocolate, nut butters, snacks and supplements
CEO: Alex Malinsky
Social Marketing & Brand Communications: Anna Speaks
Sales & Account Management: Adam Fohrman
Estimated Sales: $3 Million
Number Employees: 25
Type of Packaging: Consumer, Private Label
Brands:
  Sun Biotics
  Rawmio
  RawGuru
  Dastony
  Veggimins

13848 Wine Country Chef LLC
PO Box 1416
Hidden Valley Lake, CA 95461
707-322-0406
Fax: 800-306-2660
Organic spice blends and all natural marinades & sauces
President/Owner: Harold Imbrunetti
chef@winecountrychef.net
Estimated Sales: $250,000
Number Employees: 2
Number of Brands: 4
Number of Products: 4
Type of Packaging: Consumer, Food Service, Bulk

Brands:
  Wine Country Chef Gourmet Marinade
  Wine Country Chef Lemon Pepper Rub
  Wine Country Chef Spiced Mustard
  Wine Country Chief Spiced Bbq Rub

13849 Wine Country Kitchens
511 Alexis Ct
Napa, CA 94558-7526
707-252-9463
Fax: 707-252-9424 866-767-9463
info@winecountrykitchens.com
www.winecountrykitchens.com
Gourmet oils, wine vinegars, pasta suaces and salad dressings
Owner: Michele Channels
Controller: Debbie Azevedo
Vice President: D Mark Wilson
VP Business Development: Jack Harkins
Year Founded: 1995
Estimated Sales: $20-50 Million
Number Employees: 20-49
Type of Packaging: Private Label
Brands:
  Napa Valley Barbeque Co.
  Napa Valley Harvest
  Wine Country Kitchens

13850 Wine Country Pasta
201 W Napa St
Sonoma, CA 95476-6643
707-935-1366
www.winecountry.com
Pasta
Owner: Zepe Devito
zdevito@winecountry.com
Estimated Sales: Below $5 000,000
Number Employees: 1-4

13851 Wine Group
315 Montgomery St
San Francisco, CA 94104
415-986-8700
Fax: 415-986-4305
Wines
Chairman: Arthur Ciocca
CEO: David Kent
Contact: Ashlee Bennick
ashlee.bennick@thewinegroup.com
Number Employees: 5-9
Type of Packaging: Consumer
Brands:
  Franzia Wine
  Glen Ellen
  Mg Vallejo
  Mogen David

13852 Wine-A-Rita
2011 Mall Drive
Suite 2
Texarkana, TX 75503
903-832-7309
Fax: 903-838-7803 info@wineglace.com
www.wineglace.com
Cocktail mixes
President: Donna Griffin
donna@wineglace.com
CEO: Judy Smith

13853 Winfrey Fudge & Candy
42 Newburyport Turnpike
Rowley, MA 01969-2106
978-948-7448
Fax: 978-948-7088 888-946-3739
info@winfreys.com www.winfreys.com
Chocolates and fudge
Owner: Chris Winfrey
Owner: Christine Winfrey
Estimated Sales: Below $5 Million
Number Employees: 10-19
Brands:
  Winfrey's

13854 Wing It Inc
174 Queen St # 4f
Falmouth, MA 02540-3222
508-540-9860
Fax: 508-540-9861 Sales@Wingit.com
www.wingit.com
Buffalo wing sauce
President: Steven Robinson
sales@wingit.com
Estimated Sales: Less Than $500,000
Number Employees: 1-4

Type of Packaging: Consumer, Food Service, Private Label, Bulk
Brands:
  Wing It

13855 Wing Nien Food
30560 San Antonio St
Hayward, CA 94544-7102
510-487-8877
Fax: 510-489-6666 ghall@wnfoods.com
www.wnfoods.com
Processor and packager of sauces, oils, salsa, mustard and syrups; exporter of organic oils and sauces; also, custom blending and packaging in portion packs, glass bottles and plastic containers available
Manager: Linda Lee
Manager: Margaret Liang
mliang@wnfoods.com
Plant Superintendent: Jon Choy
Estimated Sales: $10-20 Million
Number Employees: 20-49
Square Footage: 135000
Parent Co: US Enterprise Corporation
Type of Packaging: Consumer, Food Service, Private Label
Other Locations:
  Wing Nien Co.
  Vancouver BC

13856 Wing Seafood Company
1133 W Lake St
Chicago, IL 60607-1618
312-421-8686
Fax: 312-942-0391
Seafood
Owner: Wing Ng
Estimated Sales: $1.2 Million
Number Employees: 5-9

13857 (HQ)Wing Sing Chong Company
152 Utah Avenue
Suite 140
S San Francisco, CA 94080-6718
415-552-1234
Fax: 415-552-3812
Manufacturer, importer and wholesaler/distributor of Asian foods
Owner: Roberta Woo
Estimated Sales: $15 Million
Number Employees: 1-4
Square Footage: 150000
Brands:
  Lantern

13858 (HQ)Wing's Food Products
50 Torlake Crescent
Toronto, ON M8Z 1B8
Canada
416-259-2662
Fax: 416-259-3414 custserv@wings.ca
www.wings.ca
Portioned controlled foods including ketchup, mustard, relish, vinegar, soy and plum sauce and steam cooked noodles; manufacturer of egg roll wrappers
President: Jennifer Chan
General Manager: Neal Lee
Finance Manager: Cynthia Lee
Number Employees: over 275
Parent Co: Wing's Food Products
Type of Packaging: Food Service, Private Label, Bulk
Other Locations:
  Wing's Food Products
  Edmonton AB
Brands:
  Wing's

13859 Wing-Time
85 Exchange Street
Suite #330
Lynn, MA 01901
781-592-1069
Fax: 970-871-1215 info@wingtime.com
www.wingtime.com
Buffalo wing and barbecue sauces available in six varieties
President: Terence Brown
Estimated Sales: Below $5 Million
Number Employees: 1-4
Number of Brands: 1
Number of Products: 6
Type of Packaging: Consumer, Food Service, Private Label

Food Manufacturers / A-Z

13860 (HQ)Winger Cheese
P.O.Box 238
Towner, ND 58788
701-537-5463
Fax: 701-537-5854
Cheese
Owner: Pete Winger
Number Employees: 1-4
Type of Packaging: Food Service, Bulk
Brands:
　Winger

13861 Wings Foods of Alberta Ltd
2959 Parsons Road
Edmonton, AB T6N 1A3
Canada
780-433-6406
Fax: 780-431-1026 www.wings.ca
Noodles, condiments and fortune cookies
President: Barry Lee
Sales Manager: Doug Petrie
Production Manager: Chris Hambley
Number Employees: 50-99
Square Footage: 340000
Type of Packaging: Private Label
Brands:
　Pc
　Wing's

13862 Wink Frozen Desserts
P.O. Box 111375
Stamford, CT 06911
516-323-5283
info@winkfrozendesserts.com
www.winkfrozendesserts.com
Fat free, sugar free ice cream
CEO: Gabriel Wolff
CMO: Jordan Pierson
Year Founded: 2012

13863 (HQ)Winmix/Natural Care Products
7466 Cape Girardeau Street
Englewood, FL 34224-8004
941-475-7432
Fax: 941-475-7432
Processor and exporter of soft serve ice cream and sorbets, meat analogs, fruit juice and beverage bases, low-fat replacers and nonfat mixes. Importer of juice and coffee bases.
Board of Directors: Winsor Eveland
Owner: Martha Efird
Estimated Sales: $100000
Number Employees: 2
Number of Products: 350
Square Footage: 8000
Type of Packaging: Consumer, Food Service, Private Label, Bulk
Brands:
　Multy Grain Foods
　Soy Flax 5000
　Winmix

13864 Winn-Dixie Stores
5050 Edgewood Ct.
Jacksonville, FL 32254-3699
904-783-5000
800-967-9105
info@winndixie.com www.winndixie.com
Supermarket chain.
President/CEO, Southeastern Grocers: Anthony Hucker
Year Founded: 1925
Estimated Sales: $10 Billion
Number Employees: 41,000
Parent Co: Southeastern Grocers
Other Locations:
　Manufacturing Facility
　　Baldwin FL
　Manufacturing Facility
　　Jacksonville FL
　Manufacturing Facility
　　Orlando FL
　Manufacturing Facility
　　Miami FL
　Manufacturing Facility
　　Hammond LA
　Manufacturing Facility
　　Montgomery AL
Brands:
　Astor
　Thrifty Maid
　Winn & Lovett
　Winn-Dixie
　Topcare
　Paws
　Fisherman's Wharf
　Chex
　Prestige
　Valutime

13865 (HQ)Winning Solutions Inc
3810 Conflans Rd
Irving, TX 75061-3915
972-986-5355
Fax: 972-986-5337　800-899-2563
info@miracleofaloe.com www.miracleofaloe.com
Processor and exporter of aloe vera gel drinks, juice blends, etc
Owner: Jess Clarke
winninginc@aol.com
Estimated Sales: $500,000-$1 Million
Number Employees: 10-19
Square Footage: 8000
Type of Packaging: Consumer, Food Service
Other Locations:
　Winning Solutions
　Westport CT

13866 Winona Foods
1552 Lineville Road
Green Bay, WI 54313
920-662-2184
Fax: 920-662-2195 www.winonafoods.com
Cheese
President: Terry Steinmann
Marketing & Social Media: Nathan Meyer
Director of Human Resources: Chris Cohorst
Production Manager: Chad Koerten
Estimated Sales: $4-5 Million
Number Employees: 51-200
Type of Packaging: Consumer, Food Service

13867 Winona Packing Company
152 Highway 407
Winona, MS 38967
662-283-4317
Fax: 662-283-4799
Beef and pork; also, fresh and smoked sausage
President: Bill Graves Jr
Vice President: Vicky Stiemann
Estimated Sales: $10-20 000,000
Number Employees: 20-49
Type of Packaging: Consumer, Food Service

13868 Winsor SB Dairy
18 Clinton St
Johnston, RI 02919-4121
401-231-7832
Fax: 401-231-7832
Milk and dairy products
Owner: Albert Winsor
Estimated Sales: $2.5-5 000,000
Number Employees: 1-4

13869 Winter Harbor Co-Op Inc
23 Pendleton Rd
Winter Harbor, ME 04693-3233
207-963-5857
Fax: 207-963-7275
randy@winterharborlobster.com
www.winterharborlobstercoop.com
Whole fish and seafood
President: Michael Sargeant
Manager: Randy Johnson
Estimated Sales: $600,000
Number Employees: 5-9

13870 Winter Park Farm
4501 Howell Branch Rd
Winter Park, FL 32792-7359
407-671-5888
Cheese@WinterParkDairy.com
Dairy products
Estimated Sales: Less Than $500,000
Number Employees: 1-4

13871 Winter Sausage Manufacturing Company
22011 Gratiot Ave
Eastpointe, MI 48021
586-777-9080
Fax: 586-777-7996　800-321-2987
www.wintersausage.com
Sausages, premium deli meats and spiral hams. Proprietary and private label
President: Rosemary Wuerz
Founder: Eugene Winter
VP/Sales: Ron Eckert
R&D/Marketing: Dorianne Wuerz
Quality Control: Mary Ellen Menard
Sales Manager: Kevin McCauslin
Contact: Gary Taylor
wintersausage@aol.com
Production/Purchasing Director: Eugene Wuerz
Plant Manager: Greg Van Hazenbrouck
Estimated Sales: $4.7 Million
Number Employees: 40
Type of Packaging: Consumer, Private Label, Bulk
Brands:
　Farmer Jack
　Kroger
　Lipary

13872 Winterbrook Beverage Group
2000 Schenley Place
Greendale, IN 47025-1593
812-537-7348
Bottled water
President: Raymond Smith
Brands:
　Cascadia
　Lacroix
　Winterbrook

13873 Wintergreen Winery
462 Winery Lane
P.O. Box 648
Nellysford, VA 22958
434-361-2519
Fax: 434-361-1510 www.wintergreenwinery.com
Wine
Co-Owner: Jeff Stone
Co-Owner: Tamara Stone
Estimated Sales: $1-3 Million
Number Employees: 1-4

13874 Wisconsin Cheeseman
3650 Milwaukee Street
Madison, WI 53714-2399
608-837-5166
Fax: 608-837-5493　800-693-0834
customerservice@wisconsincheeseman.com
www.wisconsincheeseman.com
Food gifts company, products include; cheese, sausage, chocolates, fruitcakes, candy, nuts & snacks, sugar free items
CFO: Jay Singer
VP: Francis Cremer
VP Sales & Marketing: Bret Jenkin
Type of Packaging: Consumer, Food Service, Private Label, Bulk

13875 Wisconsin Dairyland Fudge Company
743 Superior Street
Wisconsin Dells, WI 53965
608-254-7771
Fax: 608-254-4859 www.dellsfudge.com
Dairy farm products
Manager: Roj Rosen
Estimated Sales: Below $5 Million
Number Employees: 20-49
Brands:
　Dairyland
　Swiss Made

13876 Wisconsin Farmers Union
117 W Spring St
Chippewa Falls, WI 54729-2391
715-723-5561
Fax: 608-943-6769　800-272-5531
info@wisconsinfarmersunion.com
www.midwestcsa.com
Aged, curd, fresh cheese; gift boxes are available
President: Sheri Reinhart
sheri.reinhart@alghs.k12.wi.us
Plant Manager/Production: Tim Tehl
Treasurer: Mark Liebaert
Vice President : Craig Myrhe
Estimated Sales: $500,000-$1 Million
Number Employees: 5-9
Brands:
　Montforte

Food Manufacturers / A-Z

13877 Wisconsin Milk Mktng Board Inc
8418 Excelsior Dr
PO Box 182
Madison, WI 53717-1931
608-836-8820
Fax: 608-836-5822 800-589-5127
info@eatwisconsincheese.com
www.eatwisconsincheese.com
Cream cheese spreads; shredded mozzarella and cheddar cheeses
President: Jeff Laack
CEO: James Robson
VP: Mark Laack
Estimated Sales: $10-20 Million
Number Employees: 50-99
Square Footage: 50000
Type of Packaging: Consumer, Food Service, Private Label, Bulk
Brands:
   Laack's Finest

13878 Wisconsin Packaging Corp
104 E Blackhawk Dr
PO Box 28
Fort Atkinson, WI 53538-1152
920-563-9363
Fax: 920-563-0222 www.wisconsinpackaging.com
Hamburger patties, chili and diced beef
President: Fred Negus
fnegus@wisconsinpackaging.com
VP Sales/Operations: Frank Vignieri
Plant Manager: Rick Chamber
Number Employees: 50-99
Square Footage: 280000
Type of Packaging: Consumer, Food Service, Private Label, Bulk

13879 Wisconsin Specialty Protein
222 West Washington Ave. # 250
Madison, WI 53703
info@teraswhey.com
Organic flavored whey protein powder; flavored fatty acid health oil
Founder: Tera Johnson
Number of Brands: 1
Type of Packaging: Consumer, Private Label
Brands:
   tera's

13880 Wisconsin Spice Inc
478 S Industrial Park Rd
PO Box 190
Berlin, WI 54923-2241
920-361-3555
Fax: 920-361-0818 info@wisconsinspice.com
www.unclephilsmustard.com
Manufacturer and exporter of gourmet spices and herbs, seasoning blends, dry mustard products and prepared liquid mustards
President: Phillip Sass
wispice@wisconsinspice.com
VP Marketing: John Clausen
VP Sales: Phillips Sass
Estimated Sales: $7 Million
Number Employees: 20-49
Type of Packaging: Consumer, Food Service, Private Label, Bulk
Brands:
   Uncle Phil's

13881 Wisconsin Whey International
N2689 County Road South
Juda, WI 53550-9714
608-233-5101
Fax: 608-934-1044
Processor and exporter of kosher and HALAL approved whey products including edible lactose and whey protein concentrate
President/CEO: Nicolas Hanson
Sales Manager: Doug Clairday
Number Employees: 50-99
Square Footage: 95600
Type of Packaging: Bulk
Brands:
   Lactose Pharma
   Wisconsin Whey International
   Wpc 34
   Xl 2000
   Xl 440
   Xl 480

13882 Wisconsin Wilderness Food Products
11 North Skoikie Hwy
Suite 207
Lake Bluff, IL 60044
847-735-8661
Fax: 847-735-8673 800-359-3039
Bread and dessert mixes including cranberry cinnamon, date nut and apple crisp; also, cranberry mustard and chutney, honey mustard and preserves
President: Margaret Gunn
Plant Manager: Christina Grohmann
Estimated Sales: $1000000
Number Employees: 10-19
Number of Brands: 2
Number of Products: 30
Square Footage: 84000
Type of Packaging: Consumer, Food Service, Private Label, Bulk

13883 Wisdom Natural Brands-Uani
1203 W San Pedro St
Gilbert, AZ 85233-2406
480-921-1373
Fax: 480-966-3805 800-899-9908
wisdom@wisdomnaturalbrands.com
www.wisdomnaturalbrands.com
Herbal teas
President: James May
jmay@wisdomnaturalbrands.com
Vice President: Steve May
Quality Control: Mike Small
Operations Manager: Mike Small
Estimated Sales: $1-3 Million
Number Employees: 20-49
Type of Packaging: Consumer, Private Label, Bulk
Brands:
   La Merced Organic
   Stevia Products
   Sweet and Slender Natural Sweetener
   Sweet Leaf
   Wisdom Nutrition
   Wisdom of the Ancients Herbal Teas

13884 Wise Foods Inc
228 Raseley St
Berwick, PA 18603
888-438-9473
www.wisesnacks.com
Pretzels, chips, cheese doodles, tortilla chips, dips, popcorn and pork rinds.
Controller & Director, Human Resources: Ken Krakosky
Year Founded: 1921
Estimated Sales: $20-50 Million
Number Employees: 500-999
Parent Co: Arca Continental
Type of Packaging: Consumer
Brands:
   Bravos Tortilla Chips
   Cheez Doodles
   Cottage Cuts Potato Chips

13885 Wise Mouth
691 Main St
Warren, RI 02885
wisemouthtea.ma.us@gmail.com
www.wise-mouth.com
Tea
Owner & Founder: Lei Nichols
Brands:
   Wise Mouth

13886 Wish Farms
P.O. Box 1839
Plant City, FL 33564
813-752-5111
info@wishfarms.com
wishfarms.com
An assortment of berries including strawberries, blueberries, backberries, and raspberries.
Owner: Gary Wishnatzki
VP, Marketing: Nick Wishnatzki
VP, Fresh Sales: James Peterson
VP, Accounting: Stephen Cramer
Year Founded: 1922
Type of Packaging: Private Label

13887 Wishnev Wine Management
2125 Oak Grove Rd Ste 120
Walnut Creek, CA 94598
925-930-6374
Fax: 925-930-6388
Wines
Owner: Sanford Wishnev
Estimated Sales: $300,000-500,000
Number Employees: 1-4
Type of Packaging: Private Label

13888 Wisteria Candy Cottage
39961 Old Highway 80
Boulevard, CA 91905
619-766-4453
800-458-8246
www.wisteriacandycottage.com
Candy
Owner: Dana Eascobellis
Co-Owner: LuzCelia Rankin
Estimated Sales: Less Than $500,000
Number Employees: 1-4
Type of Packaging: Private Label

13889 Witness Tree Vineyard LTD
7111 Spring Valley Rd NW
Salem, OR 97304-9777
503-585-7874
Fax: 503-362-9765 888-478-8766
info@witnesstreevineyard.com
www.witnesstreevineyard.com
Wines
CEO: Carolyn Devine
carolyn@witnesstreevineyard.com
Vice President: Dennis Devine
Marketing Manager: Carolyn Devine
Sales Director: William Rosser
Winemaker/Vineyard Manager: Steven Westby
Estimated Sales: $2.5-5 Million
Number Employees: 10-19
Type of Packaging: Private Label
Brands:
   Witness Tree Vineyard

13890 Wixon Inc.
1390 E. Bolivar Ave.
St. Francis, WI 53235
414-769-3000
Fax: 414-769-3024 800-841-5304
service@wixon.com www.wixon.com
Manufacturer of food and beverage seasonings and flavor systems.
President: Peter Gottsacker
Chief Financial Officer: Peter Caputa
Year Founded: 1907
Estimated Sales: $100 Million
Number Employees: 100-249
Number of Brands: 3
Square Footage: 400000
Type of Packaging: Consumer, Food Service, Private Label, Bulk
Brands:
   Wix-Fresh
   Mag-nifique
   Redi-Flow

13891 Wixson Honey Inc
4937 Lakemont Himrod Rd
Dundee, NY 14837-8820
607-243-7301
Fax: 607-243-7143 800-363-8209
www.wixsonhoney.com
Manufacturer and importer of honey including clover, buckwheat, orange, beeswax and fall flower
Owner: Jerald Howell
jerry@wixsonhoney.com
Estimated Sales: $3-5 Million
Number Employees: 5-9
Type of Packaging: Consumer, Food Service, Private Label, Bulk

13892 Wizards Cauldron, LTD
878 Firetower Road
Yanceyville, NC 27379
336-694-5665
Fax: 336-664-5284
Manufacturer and exporter of natural and organic salad dressing and sauces including barbecue, steak, soy, poultry, stir-fry, hot, table and vegetable
President: Sean Kearney
CEO: John Troy
Administration: Glenda Smith
Research & Development: Tina Toney
Quality Control: Jason Dawson
VP Sales and Marketing: Ron Rash
Contact: Steve Bailey
steve@wizardscauldron.com
Purchasing Manager: Sean Kearney

Food Manufacturers / A-Z

Number Employees: 5-9
Square Footage: 40000
Parent Co: Wizard's Cauldron
Type of Packaging: Consumer, Food Service, Private Label, Bulk
Brands:
    Flavor of the Rainforest
    Simply Delicious
    Troys

13893 Wockenfuss Candy Co
6831 Harford Rd
Parkville, MD 21234-7716
    410-483-4414
Fax: 410-485-6512 800-296-4414
info@WockenfussCandies.com
www.wockenfusscandies.com
Chocolate and old-fashioned candies
Manager: Wockenfuss Company
janice.wmotter@gmail.com
Number Employees: 100-249

13894 Woeber Mustard Mfg Co
1966 Commerce Cir
PO Box 388
Springfield, OH 45504-2012
    937-323-6281
Fax: 937-323-1679 800-548-2929
raywoeber@woebermustard.com
www.woebermustard.com
Condiments and sauces including mustard, sandwich spreads, dips, vinegars, lemon juice, and garlic and horseradish products.
President: Ray Woeber
Vice President: Dick Woeber
Director, Quality Control: Randy Weyant
National Sales Manager: Wally Miller
Human Resources Manager: Judy Finnegan
Operations Manager: Christopher Woeber
Logistics Manager: Bob Sharp
Director, Purchasing: Nate Golden
Estimated Sales: $40 Million
Number Employees: 100-249
Number of Brands: 7
Type of Packaging: Consumer, Food Service, Private Label, Bulk
Brands:
    Crowning Touch
    Mayo Gourmet
    Mister Mustard
    Sandwich Pals
    Simply Supreme Organic
    Supreme Dips
    Woeber's

13895 Wohlt Cheese Corp
1005 Orville Dr
P.O. Box 203
New London, WI 54961-9398
    920-982-9000
Fax: 920-982-6288
Manufacturer of processed cheeses (including American cheese, cheese food, cheese spread and other cheese products); available in loaves and blocks, flavoured varities, custom blends and various melts. Offer shredding and dicingservices.
President: Marilyn Taylor
Quality Manager: Frederick Ladenburger
Production Manager: Mark Gelhausen
Estimated Sales: $19.6 Million
Number Employees: 50-99
Square Footage: 20000
Type of Packaging: Consumer, Food Service, Private Label, Bulk

13896 Wohrles Foods
1619 East St
Pittsfield, MA 01201-3857
    413-442-1518
Fax: 413-442-6024 800-628-6114
jon@wohrlesfoods.com www.wohrlesfoods.com
Meat products, distribute food services
President: Walter Pickwell
info@wohrlesfoods.com
VP Marketing: Jon Pickwell
Sales Exec: John Pickwell
Estimated Sales: Less than $500,000
Number Employees: 20-49
Type of Packaging: Consumer, Private Label, Bulk

13897 Wolf Canyon Foods
27880 Dorris Dr Ste 200
Carmel, CA 93923
    831-626-1323
Fax: 831-626-1325 info@wolfcanyon.com
www.wolfcanyon.com
Processor and exporter of freeze-dried fruits, vegetables, meat, seafood and dairy products
Founder: James Mercer
VP: Marybeth Frearson
Sales Manager: Carlos Forte
Estimated Sales: Under $500,000
Number Employees: 3
Square Footage: 320000
Type of Packaging: Bulk

13898 Wolf Creek Winery
2637 S Cleveland Massillon Rd
Barberton, OH 44203-6417
    330-666-9285
Fax: 330-665-1445 800-436-0426
sara@wineryatwolfcreek.com
www.troutmanvineyards.com
Wine
Owner: Andy Troutman
andy@wineryatwolfcreek.com
Estimated Sales: $5-10 Million
Number Employees: 10-19
Number of Brands: 1
Number of Products: 15

13899 Wolferman's
2500 S Pacific Hwy
Medford, OR 97501-8724
    800-798-6241
Fax: 800-999-7548 800-798-6241
service@wolfermans.com www.wolfermans.com
Fresh and frozen English muffins, crumpets and tea and toasting bread
President: Micheal Dubois
CFO: Shane Jarvis
CFO: Gary Strub
Contact: Sue Brown
sbrown@williamsfoods.com
Estimated Sales: $3-5 Million
Number Employees: 1-4
Square Footage: 440000
Parent Co: 1-800-Flowers.com
Type of Packaging: Consumer
Brands:
    Charlie Trotter's
    Wolferman's

13900 Wolfgang Puck Food Company
1250 4th Street
Suite 310
Santa Monica, CA 90401-1304
    310-432-1350
Fax: 310-451-5595
Frozen California style pizzas, pastas, canned soups and gourmet specialities
President: Terry Hall
Number Employees: 1-4

13901 Wolfies Roasted Nut Co
1718 N Romick Parkway
Findlay, OH 45840
    419-423-1355
info@wolfiesnuts.com
www.wolfiesnuts.com
Dry roasted and crisp-coated nuts including cashews, peanuts, almonds and mixes
President: Bill Wolf
Estimated Sales: Less Than $500,000
Number Employees: 11-50
Square Footage: 24000
Type of Packaging: Consumer, Food Service, Private Label

13902 Wolfson Casing Corp
700 S Fulton Ave
Mt Vernon, NY 10550-5014
    914-668-5754
Fax: 914-668-6900 800-221-8042
Processor, exporter and importer of sausage casings.
CEO: Phiil Schartz
tschartz@dccasing.com
Executive VP: David Gordon
Estimated Sales: $26300000
Number Employees: 50-99
Square Footage: 40000

13903 Wollersheim Winery
7876 State Rd 188
Prairie Du Sac, WI 53578-0087
    608-643-6515
Fax: 608-643-8149 800-847-9463
info@wollersheim.com www.wollersheim.com
Wines
President: Philippe Coquard
CFO: Jo Ann Wollersheim
Marketing Director: Julius Coquard
Operations Manager: Phil Coquard
Estimated Sales: Below $5 Million
Number Employees: 20-49
Type of Packaging: Private Label
Brands:
    Wollersheim Winery

13904 Wolverton Seafood
PO Box 1721
Houlton, ME 04730-5721
    506-276-4629
Fax: 506-276-1803
Seafood
Owner: Margaret Wolberton

13905 Wonder Natural Foods Corp
30 Blank Ln
Water Mill, NY 11976-2134
    631-726-4433
Fax: 631-726-4433
Low fat, low calorie peanut butter spread
Owner: Stewart Lasdon
slx30@aol.com
Vice President: Stuart Lasdon
Estimated Sales: Under $500,000
Number Employees: 1-4
Type of Packaging: Private Label
Brands:
    Peanut Wonder

13906 Wonderful Citrus
4000 E Goodwin Rd.
Mission, TX 78574
    956-205-7300
contact.citrus@wonderful.com
www.wonderfulcitrus.com
Citrus fruit including grapefruit, manderins, lemons, limes, and oranges.
President: Zak Laffite
Number of Brands: 12
Type of Packaging: Private Label
Brands:
    Wonderful Halos
    Wonderful Sweet Scarletts
    Paramount Citrus
    Texas Grown Red Grapefruit
    Ultimate
    Kashu Gold Oranges
    Gold Buckle Oranges
    Satin Oranges
    Blue Goose Minneolas
    Belt Oranges

13907 (HQ)Wonderful Pistachios & Almonds
13646 Hwy 33
Lost Hills, CA 93249
    661-797-6500
www.wonderfulpistachiosandalmonds.com
Grower and processor of almonds and pistachios.
President: Stewart Resnick
Co-Founder: Lynda Resnick
CFO: Mike Hohmann
VP, Domestic Sales: Michael Celani
Media Contact: Steven Bram
steven.bram@Wonderful.Com
Estimated Sales: $111 Million
Number Employees: 20-49
Square Footage: 15000
Other Locations:
    Plant and Farming Facility
    Lost Hills CA
Brands:
    Everybody's Nuts
    Paramount Farms
    Sunkist

13908 Wong Wing
Florenceville-Bristol, NB E7L 1B2
Canada
    866-622-2461
www.wongwing.ca
Frozen Chinese food

EVP: Peter Pope
Quality Assurance: Jeanette Sprague
Marketing/Sales: Shelly Bronnum
Number Employees: 100
Square Footage: 132000
Parent Co: McCain Foods Ltd.
Type of Packaging: Consumer, Food Service, Private Label, Bulk
Brands:
    Belleisle

13909 Wonton Food
220-222 Moore St
Brooklyn, NY 11206-3744
718-628-6868
Fax: 718-628-1028 800-776-8889
goldenbowl@wontonfood.com
www.wontonfood.com
Producer of fortune cookies, eggroll and wonton skins, dry and fresh noodles including chow mein, lo mein, spinach and wonton; Importer of oriental canned and dry goods
President: Sing Lee
CEO: Norman Wong
CFO: Weilik Chan
Sales/Marketing Manager: Danny Zeng
Year Founded: 1984
Estimated Sales: $20-50 Million
Number Employees: 100-249
Type of Packaging: Consumer, Food Service, Private Label

13910 Wonton Food
1045 Firestone Parkway
La Vergne, TN 97086
615-501-8898
www.wontonfood.com
Producer of fortune cookies, eggroll and wonton skins, dry and fresh noodles including chow mein, lo mein, spinach and wonton; Importer of oriental canned and dry goods
Type of Packaging: Consumer, Food Service, Private Label

13911 Wonton Food
2902 Caroline St.
Houston, TX 77004
832-366-1280
www.wontonfood.com
Producer of fortune cookies, eggroll and wonton skins, dry and fresh noodles including chow mein, lo mein, spinach and wonton; Importer of oriental canned and dry goods
Type of Packaging: Consumer, Food Service, Private Label

13912 Wood Brothers Inc
3023 Augusta Rd
West Columbia, SC 29170-2864
803-796-5146
Fax: 803-796-5291 info@thewoodbrothers.com
www.woodbrothersfinefoods.com
Mayonnaise, barbecue and tartar sauces, mustard and salad dressings including Thousand Island, French, Italian, blue cheese and slaw
Vice President: Katrina Drew
kdrew@woodbrothersfinefoods.com
VP: Douglas Wood
Production Manager: James Wood
Estimated Sales: $110,000
Number Employees: 10-19
Type of Packaging: Food Service, Private Label, Bulk
Brands:
    Capital
    Cardinal
    Carolina Chef
    Glenwood
    Holland

13913 Wood Sugarbush
N7845 170th St
Spring Valley, WI 54767-8101
715-772-4656
Fax: 715-772-4665 info@woodssugarbush.com
www.woodssugarbush.com
Certified organic maple syrup, cream and granulated sugar
President: Scott Wood
Partner: Scott Wood
Number Employees: 10-19
Number of Brands: 1
Number of Products: 4
Square Footage: 14000
Type of Packaging: Consumer, Food Service, Private Label, Bulk

13914 Woodbine
729 Pecan Point Rd
Norfolk, VA 23502-3416
757-461-2731
Fax: 757-461-4704
Beef and pork. Full distribution of food service items
President: Ray Lister
Production Manager: Aubrey Lister
Estimated Sales: $3-5 Million
Number Employees: 10-19
Type of Packaging: Food Service

13915 Woodbury Vineyards
3215 S Roberts Rd
Fredonia, NY 14063-9417
716-679-9463
Fax: 716-679-9464 866-691-9463
info@WoodburyVineyards.com
www.woodburyvineyards.com
Winery
President: Joseph Carney
Retail Sales Manager: Virginia Bragg
Manager: Lindsey Alfred
lindsey@woodburyvineyards.com
Estimated Sales: $1,700,000
Number Employees: 5-9
Brands:
    Woodbury Vineyards

13916 Wooden Valley Winery
4756 Suisun Valley Rd
Fairfield, CA 94534-3114
707-864-0730
Fax: 707-864-6038 info@woodenvalley.com
www.woodenvalley.com
Wines
President: Adrienne Lanza
adrienne.lanza@woodenvalley.com
Vice President: Ron Lanza
Estimated Sales: $1-2.5 Million
Number Employees: 5-9
Brands:
    Wooden Valley

13917 Woodfield Fish & OysterCompany
P.O.Box 259
Galesville, MD 20765-0259
410-897-1093
Fax: 410-867-3423
Packaged ice and oyster
Owner: Bill Woodfield
Treasurer: Shirley Day
Vice President: Bill Woddfield
Plant Manager: David Loftice
Purchasing Manager: Ray Hardesty
Estimated Sales: Less than $500,000
Number Employees: 1-4
Type of Packaging: Private Label
Brands:
    Woodfield Fish & Oyster
    Woodfield Ice

13918 Woodie Pie Company
110 S 13th Street
Artesia, NM 88210
575-746-2132
Baked goods including pies
President: D Balencia
Estimated Sales: $500,000-$1 Million
Number Employees: 1-4
Type of Packaging: Consumer
Brands:
    Woodie Pie

13919 Woodlake Ranch
21730 Avenue 332
Woodlake, CA 93286
559-564-2161
Fax: 559-564-8120
Grower of olives
President: Everett Kracov
Manager: Randy Childrsh
Estimated Sales: Less than $300,000
Number Employees: 1-4
Type of Packaging: Food Service, Private Label, Bulk

13920 Woods Smoked Meats Inc
1501 Business Highway 54 W
Bowling Green, MO 63334-1030
573-324-2247
Fax: 573-324-2249 800-458-8426
Meats including ham, bacon, sausage, poulty, snack food, fresh sausage, exotic meats, game processing, cajun products, private labeling, federal inspection.
President: Ed Woods
wsmeats@yahoo.com
Co-Owner: Regina Woods
Estimated Sales: $5-10 Million
Number Employees: 10-19
Number of Brands: 2
Number of Products: 80
Square Footage: 64000
Type of Packaging: Consumer, Private Label, Bulk
Brands:
    Sweet Betsy From Pike
    Woods

13921 Woodside Vineyards
205 Constitution Dr
Menlo Park, CA 94025-1108
650-851-3144
Fax: 650-847-1490 info@woodsidevineyards.com
www.woodsidevineyards.com
Wines
Founder/President: Robert Mullen
bob@woodsidevineyards.com
Estimated Sales: $1,400,000
Number Employees: 5-9
Type of Packaging: Private Label
Brands:
    Woodside Vineyards

13922 Woodsmoke Provisions
1240 Menlo Dr NW
Atlanta, GA 30318-4163
404-355-5125
Fax: 404-355-6850 www.woodsmoke.com
Salmon and trout
President: Mitchell Gallant
m.gallant@woodsmoke.com
Estimated Sales: $3-5 Million
Number Employees: 20-49

13923 Woodstock Farms Manufacturing
96 Executive Ave
Edison, NJ 08817
800-526-4349
www.woodstockfarmsmfg.com
Importer, processor, packager, and wholesale distributor of nuts, dried fruit, seeds, trail mixes, natural and organic products, and confections.
President: Bob Kaufman
VP, Sales & Customer Service: Matt Mellet
Square Footage: 100000
Parent Co: United Natural Foods
Type of Packaging: Consumer, Food Service, Private Label, Bulk
Brands:
    Expressnacks
    Woodfield Farms

13924 Woodward Canyon
11920 W Highway 12
Touchet, WA 99360-9710
509-525-4129
Fax: 509-522-0927 info@woodwardcanyon.com
www.woodwardcanyon.com
Wine
Owner: Rick Small
info@woodwardcanyon.com
Production Director: Rick Small
Estimated Sales: Below $5 Million
Number Employees: 5-9

13925 Woodworth Honey & Bee Co
8503 4th St SW
Halliday, ND 58636-9239
701-938-4647
Fax: 701-938-4657 bon@ndsupernet.com
www.ndsupernet.com
Processor and exporter of honey
Owner: Brent Woodworth
brentwoodworth@ndsupernet.com
Chief Executive Officer: Bruce Boynton
Estimated Sales: $10-20 Million
Number Employees: 10-19
Square Footage: 18000
Type of Packaging: Bulk

Food Manufacturers / A-Z

13926 Woody's Bar-B-Q Sauce Company
PO Box 66
Waldenburg, AR 72475-0066
870-579-2251
Fax: 870-579-2241   888-747-9229
Barbeque sauce
President: William Wood
CEO: Cecelia Wood
Estimated Sales: $300,000-500,000
Number Employees: 5-9
Number of Products: 7
Type of Packaging: Consumer, Food Service, Private Label, Bulk

13927 Woolwich Dairy
425 Richardson Road
Orangeville, ON L9W 4Z4
Canada
519-941-9206
Fax: 519-941-9349   877-438-3499
gerhard@woolwichnova.com
www.woolwichdairy.com
Goat's milk cheeses including cheddar, whole and crumbled feta, mozzarella, gouda, cream and brie
CEO: Tony Dutra
VP Marketing: Michael Domingues
VP Sales: Liz Long
Year Founded: 1983
Estimated Sales: $24 Million
Number Employees: 97
Number of Brands: 7
Number of Products: 109
Square Footage: 4000
Parent Co: Saputo
Type of Packaging: Consumer, Food Service, Private Label, Bulk
Brands:
  Chevrai
  Gourmet Goat
  Madame Chevre

13928 Worden
7217 W Westbow Boulevard
Spokane, WA 99224-5668
509-455-7835
Fax: 509-838-4723 wordenwine@aol.com
Wine
President: Ken Barrett
CEO: Rebecca Chateaubriand
Estimated Sales: $1 000,000+
Number Employees: 10
Square Footage: 13000
Type of Packaging: Private Label, Bulk

13929 World Art Foods
702 S 53rd St
Temple, TX 76504-5113
254-774-8322
Fax: 254-773-7339 oneworld@vvm.com
Spreads, sauces, dressing and ketchup
President: Pat Guillen
Estimated Sales: $300,000-500,000
Number Employees: 5-9

13930 World Casing Corp
4706 Grand Ave
Maspeth, NY 11378-3007
718-628-3800
Fax: 718-628-5800   800-221-4887
casings@worldcasing.com www.worldcasing.com
Natural sausage casings
Owner: Irwin Feinstein
ifeinstein@wolfsoncasing.com
VP: Paul LoPiccolo
Estimated Sales: $2.5 Million
Number Employees: 20-49

13931 World Cheese Inc
178 28th St
Brooklyn, NY 11232-1604
718-965-1700
Fax: 718-965-0979
customerservice@worldcheeseco.com
www.worldcheeseco.com
World Cheese Company is the largest kosher cheese manufacturer in the United States.
Owner: Leo Thurm
lthurm@allkoshercheese.com
Year Founded: 1937
Number Employees: 20-49
Type of Packaging: Consumer, Food Service, Bulk
Brands:
  Haolam
  Ko-Sure
  Migdal
  Miller's
  Schmerling
  Taam Tov

13932 World Citrus West
130 W Santa Fe Avenue
Fullerton, CA 92832
714-870-6171
Fax: 714-871-4100
Processor and bottler of chilled citrus drinks and juices including orange and grapefruit
CEO: Stephen M Caruso
Sales Manager (Retail): Rod Adamson
Number Employees: 250-499
Parent Co: Florida's Natural Growers'
Type of Packaging: Consumer, Food Service, Private Label, Bulk
Brands:
  Daily Sun
  Donald Duck
  Supersocco

13933 World Confections Inc
14 S Orange Ave # A
South Orange, NJ 07079-1754
718-768-8100
Fax: 718-499-4918 Info@worldconfections.com
www.worldconfections.com
Manufacturer and exporter of confectionery products including gum, bagged, bars, boxed chocolates, caramels, lollypops, jaw breakers, peppermint and lemon twists, seasonal, etc
President: Mathew Cohen
Contact: Devin Abbott
devina@worldconfections.com
Estimated Sales: $10 Million
Number Employees: 50-99
Type of Packaging: Consumer, Private Label, Bulk

13934 World Cup Coffee & Tea
1740 NW Glisan St
Portland, OR 97209-2225
503-228-5503
Fax: 503-228-3489 www.worldcupcoffee.com
Processor and exporter of coffee and teas; also, roasting and water filltration services available
Owner: Dan Welch
info@worldcupcoffee.com
Number Employees: 20-49
Square Footage: 50000
Type of Packaging: Consumer, Food Service, Bulk
Brands:
  World Cup

13935 World Famous Buffalo Wing Sauce
PO Box 66
Buffalo, NY 14209-0066
716-912-9068
Fax: 716-853-2011 www.buffalowing.com
Produces buffalo wings, a variety of sauces, and gift novelty items.
Executive: Joanne Will
Estimated Sales: Below $5 Million
Number Employees: 6
Brands:
  Frank & Teressa's Original Anchor
  Frank & Teressa's Wing Sauce

13936 World Flavors Inc
76 Louise Dr
Warminster, PA 18974-1588
215-672-4400
Fax: 215-672-4405 www.worldflavors.com
Custom formulated, manufactured and packaged ingredients for food processors including liquid and ground spices, meat, poultry and seafood seasonings, flavors, breadings, salad dressings and meat binders, extenders and tenderizingcompounds
President: M Donna
donna_m@worldflavors.com
VP Sales: Thomas Holmquist
Estimated Sales: $4900000
Number Employees: 50-99
Type of Packaging: Food Service, Private Label, Bulk

13937 World Ginseng Ctr Inc
825 Kearny St
San Francisco, CA 94108-1303
415-362-2255
Fax: 415-362-0801   800-747-8808
info@worldginsengcenter.com
www.worldginsengcenter.com
Manufacturer and exporter of ginseng and frozen seafood
President: Raymond Chao
Manager: William Nghe
Treasurer: Jane Chao
Estimated Sales: Less Than $500,000
Number Employees: 1-4
Type of Packaging: Consumer, Food Service, Private Label, Bulk

13938 World Harbors
176 First Flight Dr
Auburn, ME 04210-9055
207-786-3900
Fax: 207-786-3900   800-355-6221
Gourmet specialty foods, sauces and marinades
President: Steven Arthurs
CFO: Karen Foust
Quality Control: Mike Murphy
Estimated Sales: $5-10 Million
Number Employees: 5-9
Parent Co: Angostura International
Type of Packaging: Consumer, Food Service
Brands:
  Acadia Naturals
  Angostura
  World Harbors

13939 World Herbs Gourmet
165 Boston Post Rd
Old Saybrook, CT 06475
860-388-3781

13940 World Nutrition, Inc.
Scottsdale Seville
7001 N Scottsdale Rd
Scottsdale, AZ 85253-3666
480-921-1188
Fax: 480-921-1471   800-548-2710
customerservice@worldnutrition.info
www.worldnutrition.info
Processor and importer of vitamins, minerals, organic grains, fruits, vegetables and dehydrated fruits and vegetable juices
President: Ryuji Hirooka
CEO: Chuck Eberhardt
Marketing Manager: Robert Nisenfeld
Operations Executive: Andy Rodriguez
Plant Manager: Tony Negrete
Purchasing Agent: Rhonda Poe
Estimated Sales: $1.9 Million
Number Employees: 18
Square Footage: 34000

13941 World Of Chantilly
4302 Farragut Rd
Brooklyn, NY 11203-6520
718-859-1110
Fax: 718-859-1303 info@chantilly.com
www.chambordesserts.com
Kosher desserts including cakes, pies, brownies, tiramisu, tortes, etc
Owner: Daniel Faks
danny@chantilly.com
Owner/President: Alberto Faks
Estimated Sales: $1800000
Number Employees: 10-19
Square Footage: 40000

13942 World Of Coffee
328 Essex St
Stirling, NJ 07980-1302
908-647-1218
Fax: 908-647-7827   800-543-0062
www.worldofcoffee.biz
Coffee
Owner: Avi Greenfield
avigreenfield@worldofcoffee.biz
Estimated Sales: Less Than $500,000
Number Employees: 5-9

13943 World Organics Corporation
5242 Bolsa Ave Ste 3
Huntington Beach, CA 92649-1054
714-893-0017
Fax: 714-897-5677 plicata@prodigy.net

Vitamins, food supplements, herbal extracts and capsules and chlorophyll liquid and capsules
Owner: Paul Licata
CEO: Al Licata
Director of Sales: Bernie Lucich
Estimated Sales: Under $500,000
Number Employees: 12
Number of Brands: 4
Number of Products: 300
Square Footage: 16000
Type of Packaging: Private Label
Brands:
    Natural's Concept
    Nu-Vista
    Poma Noni Berry
    Seafood
    Vita-Vista

13944 World Spice
223-235 Highland Parkway
Roselle, NJ 07203
908-245-0600
Fax: 908-245-0696 800-234-1060
sales@wsispice.com www.wsispice.com
Spices, seasonings, herbs and dehydrated vegetables
President: Bela Lowy
Vice President: J Lefbowitz
Estimated Sales: $2 Million
Number Employees: 5-9
Square Footage: 60000
Type of Packaging: Food Service, Bulk
Brands:
    Wsi

13945 World of Chia
26310 Oakridge Dr
Suite 38
The Woodlands, TX 77380
800-251-6973
Fax: 281-609-0654 sales@worldofchia.com
www.worldofchia.com
Chia fruit spread
President: Fernando Ramirez Ocampo
Year Founded: 2009
Estimated Sales: $4-5 Million
Number Employees: 50
Parent Co: Space Enterprises
Brands:
    World of Chia

13946 World of Spices
328 Essex St
Stirling, NJ 07980-1302
908-647-1218
Fax: 908-647-7827
Spices
President: Charles Newman
Estimated Sales: $2.5-5 000,000
Number Employees: 5-9

13947 World's Best Donuts
10 E Wisconsin St
P.O. Box 1272
Grand Marais, MN 55604
218-387-1345
bestdonuts@boreal.org
www.worldsbestdonutsmn.com
Donuts
Vice President: Stacey Hawkins
skizzle@boreal.org
Vice President: Stacey Hawkins
skizzle@boreal.org
Number Employees: 10-19

13948 World's Finest Chocolate Inc
4801 S Lawndale Ave
Chicago, IL 60632-3062
773-847-4600
Fax: 773-847-4006 888-821-8452
www.worldsfinestchocolate.com
Chocolate manufacturer serving the North American fundraising and promotional/gift markets.
Owner: Rodney Amison
rodney.amison@worldsfinestchocolates.com
CEO: Eddie Opler
Number Employees: 500-999
Type of Packaging: Consumer
Brands:
    Queen Anne
    World's Finest Chocolate

13949 World's Greatest Ice Cream
P.O. Box 190646
Miami Beach, FL 33119-0646
305-538-0207
Fax: 305-538-1026 info@thefrieze.com
www.thefrieze.com
Ice cream
President: Lisa Warren
Estimated Sales: $500,000-$1 Million
Number Employees: 10-19

13950 Worldwide Specialties In
2421 E 16th St Unit 1
Los Angeles, CA 90021
323-587-2200
Fax: 323-587-0050 800-437-2702
Gourmet specialty produce; importer and exporter of baby squash, French beans and fresh herbs
President: Horacio Belloflore
Treasurer: Nora Belloflore
Contact: Bruce Hoffman
bruce@californiaspecialtyfarms.com
Estimated Sales: $10,000,000
Number Employees: 126
Brands:
    California Specialty Farms

13951 Wornick Company
4700 Creek Rd.
Cincinnati, OH 45242
800-860-4555
www.wornick.com
Convenience foods and military rations to restaurant chains, consumer product goods companies, and the U.S. government, including kids meals, sides, sauces, and breakfast.
President/Chief Executive Officer: John Kowalchik
VP Marketing/Business Development: Randy Newbold
Year Founded: 1970
Estimated Sales: $100-500 Million
Number Employees: 500-999
Square Footage: 600000
Type of Packaging: Food Service, Private Label
Other Locations:
    Wornick Co.
    McAllen TX

13952 Worthington Foods
P.O. Box CAMB
Battle Creek, MI 49016
614-885-9511
Fax: 614-885-2594 800-962-1413
Vegetarian foods
President/CEO: Dale Twomley
CFO: William Kirkwood
VP Sales: Jay Robertson
Merchandise Support Manager: Randy Wollert
Sales Director: David Schwantes
Public Relations: Veronica Peita
Estimated Sales: Less than $500,000
Number Employees: 1-4
Parent Co: Kellogg Company
Type of Packaging: Private Label

13953 Worthmore Food ProductsCo
1021 Ludlow Ave
Cincinnati, OH 45223-2687
513-559-1473
Fax: 513-559-0286 866-837-7687
worthmore@fuse.net www.worthmorefoods.com
Canner of food products including chili con carne, mock turtle soup, spaghetti sauce, pizza sauce and mushroom steak sauce
President: Phil Hock III
worthmore@fuse.net
Number Employees: 5-9
Type of Packaging: Consumer, Food Service, Private Label

13954 Wow! Factor Desserts
174 cree Road
Sherwood Park, AB T8A 3X8
Canada
780-464-0303
Fax: 780-467-3604 800-604-2253
www.wowfactordesserts.com
Baked goods including cheesecakes, cakes, tortes and pies for the food service sector
President: Bryan Yaakov
VP: Joanne Yaakov
Purchasing Manager: Dean McMullen
Estimated Sales: D
Number Employees: 50-99
Type of Packaging: Consumer, Food Service

13955 Wrawp
862 Towne Center Dr.
Suite A
Pomona, CA 91767
909-447-1800
855-972-9748
customerservice@wrawp.com www.wrawp.com
Organic, gluten-free veggie wraps, coconut wraps, and pizza crusts
Founder/CEO: Elena Semenova
Co-Founder: Kraig Dooman
Accounting: Iris Medina
Marketing & Brand Partnerships: Daniel Bauer
Operations Manager: Bioncia Martin
Production Manager: Anastasiia Lewis
Engineer: Vadim Kan
Year Founded: 2012
Number Employees: 20-49

13956 Wrench Mints
333 North Michigan Avenue
Suite 400
Chicago, IL 60601
312-496-3690
Fax: 312-496-3691
Mint candies
President: Angela Moran

13957 Wright Brand Oysters
9216 Faith St
Coden, AL 36523-3007
251-824-7880
Fax: 251-824-7880
Processor and distributor of oysters
President: Stanley Wright
Estimated Sales: $1-3 Million
Number Employees: 10-19

13958 Wright Enrichment Inc
6428 Airport Rd
PO Box 821
Crowley, LA 70526-1604
337-783-3096
Fax: 337-783-0724 800-201-3096
chris@wenrich.com www.thewrightgroup.net
Processor and exporter of custom vitamin, mineral and amino acid premixes, microencapsulates and direct compressed granulations
Owner: Grant Bergstrom
Marketing Manager: Chris Hebert
Regional Sales Manager: John Miller
grant@wenrich.com
Estimated Sales: $10-20 Million
Number Employees: 100-249
Type of Packaging: Bulk

13959 Wright's Ice Cream Co
3570 N State Road 63
Cayuga, IN 47928-8156
765-492-3454
Fax: 765-492-4915 800-686-9561
Ice cream and frozen desserts, dairy products, dried or canned, and candy and other confectionery products.
President: Ned Wright
Marketing Director: Ned Wright
Estimated Sales: Less Than $500,000
Number Employees: 1-4
Type of Packaging: Consumer
Brands:
    Wright Delicious

13960 Wrigley
1132 W. Blackhawk St.
Chicago, IL 60642
312-794-6000
www.mars.com/made-by-mars/mars-wrigley
Gum, mints, hard and chewy candy and lollipops.
CEO: Martin Radvan
Year Founded: 1891
Estimated Sales: $5.3 Billion
Number Employees: 16,000
Number of Brands: 15
Parent Co: Mars, Incorporated
Brands:
    Juicy Fruit
    Wrigley's Spearmint
    Altoids
    Orbit
    Extra
    Starburst
    Doublemint

Food Manufacturers / A-Z

Skittles
Freedent
5 Gum
Life Savers
Eclipse
Winterfresh
Big Red
Hubba Bubba

13961 Wunder Creamery
New York, NY
844-986-3371
www.wundercreamery.com
Yogurt made from low-fat curd cheese
Co-Founder: Kamilya Abilova
Number of Brands: 1
Number of Products: 6
Type of Packaging: Consumer
Brands:
  WUNDER CREAMERY

13962 Wuollet Bakery
3608 W 50th St
Minneapolis, MN 55410-2014
612-922-4341
Fax: 612-922-4041   info@wuollet.com
www.woulletbakery.com
Bakers of cakes, desserts, breads and pastries.
Owner: Jim Jurmu
info@woullet.com
CEO: Jim Jurmu
Operations Manager: Doug Wuollet
Estimated Sales: Less Than $500,000
Number Employees: 5-9

13963 Wurth Dairy
8805 Maple Avenue
Caseyville, IL 62232-2135
217-271-7580
Dairy
President: Albert Wurth
Estimated Sales: Under $500,000
Number Employees: 1-4

13964 (HQ)Wyandot Inc
135 Wyandot Ave
Marion, OH 43302-1595
740-383-4031
Fax: 740-382-5584   800-992-6368
www.wyandotsnacks.com
Private label snack foods including baked cheese puffs and chips including potato, tortilla, nacho and corn.
President & CEO: Rob Sarlls
CEO: Nick Chilton
nick.chilton@wyandotsnacks.com
CFO: Bob Wentz
Number Employees: 250-499
Type of Packaging: Consumer, Food Service, Private Label, Bulk
Brands:
  Grandaddy's
  Muchmates
  Munchrights
  Wyandot

13965 Wyandotte Winery LLC
4640 Wyandotte Dr
Gahanna, OH 43230-1258
614-476-3624
Fax: 614-934-5035   877-906-7464
info@wyandottewinery.com
www.wyandottewinery.com
Wines
Owner: Robin Coolidge
info@wyandottewinery.com
CEO: Joe Reardon
Marketing Director: Valerie Coolidge
Winemaker: Robin Coolidge
Estimated Sales: $500,000-$1 Million
Number Employees: 1-4
Brands:
  Wyandotte Graystone Winery
  Wyandotte Winery

13966 Wynnewood Pecan Company
301 S Washita Avenue
Wynnewood, OK 73098-7823
405-665-4102
Fax: 405-682-2503   800-892-4985
Pecans
President: Jeff Earles
Estimated Sales: Less than $500,000
Number Employees: 1-4

13967 Wysong Corp
7550 Eastman Ave
Midland, MI 48642-7809
989-631-0009
Fax: 989-631-8801   800-748-0188
wysong@wysong.net
www.grain-free-dog-food.com
Trail mixes, vitamins and potato chips; also, organic soy, wheat and rice baking items
Owner: Randy Wysong
wysong@wysong.net
Estimated Sales: $3100000
Number Employees: 20-49
Brands:
  Wysong

13968 Xena International
910 S Division Avenue
Polo, IL 61064
815-946-2626
Fax: 815-946-2752
customerservice@xenainternational.com
www.xenainternational.com
Importer and manufacturer of dry and liquid ingredients.
President: Richard Sikorski
Contact: Nick Livingston
nick@xena.biz

13969 Ximena's Latin Flavors
21300 Hwy. 71 West
Suite 100
Spicewood, TX 78669
817-821-3246
ximena@latinflavors.net
Salsa, marinades, salad dressings and dips
Founder: Ximena Guerra
Brands:
  Salsa Criolla

13970 Xochitl
17304 Preston Rd
Suite 1240
Dallas, TX 75252
214-800-3551
Fax: 214-800-3547   866-595-8917
info@salsaxochitl.com
Salsas, queso dips and corn chips
President: Carlos Salinas

13971 Xooz Gear
2831 El Dorado Parkway
Suite 103-139
Frisco, TX 75033
214-206-1222
info@sierramadrehoney.com
sierramadrehoney.com
Honey
General Manager: Alex Lopez
Type of Packaging: Food Service
Brands:
  Sierra Madre Honey Co.

13972 Y & T Packing Co
1129 Taintor Rd
Springfield, IL 62702-1760
217-522-3345
Fax: 217-522-6395   www.turaskymeats.com
Packer/processor of meat
President: Joseph Turasky
Co-Owner: Joe Turasky
bradturasky@turaskymeats.com
Sales Manager: Tom Reilly
Estimated Sales: $1800000
Number Employees: 10-19
Type of Packaging: Consumer

13973 Y Not Foods
1322 SE 46th Lane
Suite 102
Cape Coral, FL 33904
608-222-2860
Fax: 239-205-6133   tony@ynotfoods.com
www.ynotfoods.com
Frozen sauce and smoothie chips for the prepared foods industry.
Contact: Aaron Steinmann
aarons@ynotfoods.com

13974 Y Z Enterprises Inc
1930 Indian Wood Cir # 100
Maumee, OH 43537-4001
419-893-8777
Fax: 419-893-8825   800-736-8779
info@almondina.com   www.almondina.com
Processor and exporter of natural almond cookies including low-calorie, no-cholesterol, no-salt, kosher and parve
Owner: Yuval Zaliouk
CFO: Susan Zaliouk
Contact: Niwedita Bakshi
niwedita.bakshi@macys.com
Estimated Sales: Less Than $500,000
Number Employees: 5-9
Square Footage: 66000
Type of Packaging: Consumer
Brands:
  Almondina

13975 Y Z Enterprises Inc
1930 Indian Wood Cir # 100
Maumee, OH 43537-4001
419-893-8777
Fax: 419-893-8825   800-736-8779
almondina@worldpantry.com
www.almondina.com
Cookies, biscuits. No artificial colors, flavors or preservatives.
Founder: Yuval Zaliouk
Contact: Mike Connors
mconnors@almondina.com
Estimated Sales: Less Than $500,000
Number Employees: 5-9
Type of Packaging: Consumer, Food Service, Private Label
Brands:
  Almondina Biscuits

13976 Y&W Shellfish
8725 Us Highway 17
Woodbine, GA 31569
912-729-4814
Fax: 912-729-1143
Seafood
Owner: Richard Roberts

13977 Y.M.C. Corp.
481 W 26th St
Chicago, IL 60616
312-842-4900
Fax: 312-225-2262
Chinese foods and noodles
President: Harry Moy
harry.moy@ymcinc.com
Secretary: Tom Moy
Secretary: James Moy
Estimated Sales: $1,500,000
Number Employees: 17

13978 YB Meats of Wichita
798 N West St
Wichita, KS 67203
316-942-1213
Fax: 316-942-1419   www.yodermeatsks.com
Meat products
President: Ellsworth Kauffman
CEO: Erik Kaufmann
Marketing Director: Erik Kaufmann
Manager: Brad Warzeka
Estimated Sales: $500,000-$1 Million
Number Employees: 5-9
Type of Packaging: Consumer

13979 Ya-Hoo Baking Co
5302 Texoma Pkwy
Sherman, TX 75090-2112
903-893-8151
Fax: 903-893-5036   888-869-2466
customerservice@yahoocake.com
www.yahoocake.com
Dessert cakes, cobblers, cookies, cake and pie fillings, bread, frozen dough; custom work is our specialty
President: Chelsea Lanehart
clanehart@boongroup.com
R&D: Monette Wible
Director Sales/Marketing: David Millican
Sales Administrator: Tanda Wall
Purchasing Manager: Becky Roberts
Number Employees: 50-99
Square Footage: 180000
Type of Packaging: Consumer, Food Service, Private Label, Bulk

Food Manufacturers / A-Z

Brands:
  Ya-Hoo!

13980 Yai's Thai
3047 Larimer St.
Suite 202
Denver, CO 80205
info@yaisthai.com
www.yaisthai.com
Thai curries, almond sauce, ginger lime sauce, garlic hot sauce, relish, and salsa. Products are paleo, vegan, and gluten free
Co-Founder/CEO: Leland Copenhagen
Co-Founder/COO: Sarah Hughes
VP Sales: Aaron Barnholt
Year Founded: 2016

13981 Yakima Chief-Hopunion LLC
306 Division St.
Yakima, WA 98902
509-453-4792
Fax: 509-453-1551 hops@ychhops.com
www.yakimachief.com
Processor and exporter of hops and hops products.
Contact: Stephen Carpenter
stephen.carpenter@hopunion.com
Year Founded: 1869
Estimated Sales: $140 Million
Number Employees: 20
Square Footage: 75000
Type of Packaging: Bulk

13982 Yakima Craft Brewing Company
2920 River Rd
Suite 6
Yakima, WA 98902-7332
509-654-7357
www.yakimacraftbrewing.com
Processor and exporter of ales, stout and porter
President: Jeff Winn
CEO/Founder: Chris McCoy
Director of Marketing: Sheldon Weddle
Contact: Chris Swedin
chris@yakimacraftbrewing.com
Estimated Sales: $500,000-999,999
Number Employees: 5-9
Square Footage: 162000
Type of Packaging: Consumer
Brands:
  Bert Grant's

13983 Yakima Fresh
111 University Pkwy # 101
P.O. Box 1709
Yakima, WA 98901-1471
509-248-5770
Fax: 509-457-6137 steve.smith@yakimafresh.com
www.yakimafresh.com
Manufacturer and exporter of apples, cherries and pears
Quality Control Manager: Brian Mortimer
VP Marketing & Business Development: Tom Papke
Sales Manager: Randy Eckert
Manager: Steve Smith
steve.smith@yakimafresh.com
General Manager: Steve Smith
Estimated Sales: $2 Million
Number Employees: 20-49
Square Footage: 16452
Type of Packaging: Consumer, Food Service, Bulk
Other Locations:
  Yakima Fresh Warehouse
  Wapato WA
  Yakima Fresh Warehouse
  Zillah WA
  Yakima Fresh Warehouse
  Hood River OR

13984 Yakima River Winery
143302 West North River Road
Prosser, WA 99350-8228
509-786-2805
Fax: 509-786-3203
redwine@yakimariverwinery.com
Wine
Co-Owner: John Rauner
redwine@yakimariverwinery.com
Co-Owner: Louise Rauner
Winemaker: John Rauner
Estimated Sales: $500,000-$1 Million
Number Employees: 1-4
Type of Packaging: Private Label
Brands:
  Yakima Valley

13985 Yamamotoyama of America
122 Voyager St
Pomona, CA 91768-3252
909-594-7356
Fax: 909-595-5849 info@yamamotoyama.com
www.yamamotoyama.com
Loose green, black, herbal, and flavored teas
Chairman: Kahei Yamamoto
Administration Manager/Purchasing: William Yu
Senior VP: Kazumi Ikeda
Contact: Kazuya Aburano
aburano@yamamotoyama.com
Estimated Sales: $20-50 Million
Number Employees: 100-249

13986 Yamasa Corp USA
3500 Fairview Industrial Dr SE
Salem, OR 97302-1154
503-363-8550
Fax: 503-363-8710 www.yamasausa.com
Soy sauce
President: Masura Ogura
Number Employees: 500-999
Square Footage: 83000
Parent Co: Yamasa Corporation
Type of Packaging: Consumer, Food Service, Bulk
Brands:
  Yamasa

13987 Yamasa Fish Cake Co
515 Stanford Ave
Los Angeles, CA 90013-2189
213-626-2211
Fax: 213-627-9018 www.yamasafishcake.com
Fresh and frozen fish cakes
President: Frank Kawana
dwatanabe@yamasafishcake.com
Sales Exec: Doug Watanabe
Estimated Sales: $2,900,000
Number Employees: 20-49
Type of Packaging: Consumer, Food Service

13988 Yamasho Inc
750 Touhy Ave
Elk Grove Village, IL 60007-4916
847-981-9342
Fax: 847-981-9347 info@yamashoinc.com
www.yamashoinc.com
Japanese products
President: Kunio Iwadate
Estimated Sales: $20-50 Million
Number Employees: 5-9

13989 Yamate Chocolatier
320 Cleveland Ave
Highland Park, NJ 08904
732-249-4847
Fax: 732-545-4494 800-433-2462
Chocolate and confections
Co-Owner: Diane Yamate
Co-Owner: John Cunnell
Estimated Sales: $500,000-$1 Million
Number Employees: 1-4

13990 Yamhill Valley Vineyards
16250 SW Oldsville Rd
Mcminnville, OR 97128-8546
503-843-3100
Fax: 503-843-2450 800-825-4845
www.yamhill.com
Wines
President: Stephen Cary
info@yamhill.com
General Manager: David Anderson
Sales Exec: Sandi Kolb
Estimated Sales: $5-10 Million
Number Employees: 20-49
Brands:
  Yamhill Wines

13991 Yancey's Fancy
857 Main Road
Corfu, NY 14036
www.yanceysfancy.com
Artisan cheese
Contact: Daniel Alidoust
dalidoust@yanceysfancy.com

13992 Yankee Specialty Foods
22 Fish Pier St W
Boston, MA 02210-2008
617-951-0740
Fax: 617-951-9907 800-688-9904
info@bayshorechowders.com
www.yankeespecialtyfoods.com
Processor and exporter of chili, soup, gumbo and chowder
Owner: Sara Giargiari
saragiargiari@yankeespecialtyfoods.com
Estimated Sales: $300000
Number Employees: 5-9
Type of Packaging: Consumer, Private Label
Brands:
  Bay Shore

13993 (HQ)Yarmer Boys Catfish International
5192c Fannett Road
Beaumont, TX 77705-4202
409-842-1962
Fax: 409-842-1212 vsj42@aol.com
Shrimp
CEO: Glenda Jones
President: Vicky Jones
Sales Director: Trudy Verdine
Number Employees: 100-249
Type of Packaging: Private Label
Brands:
  Fishermans Rees

13994 Yaupon Tea
143 Telfair Rd
Savannah, GA 31415-1604
912-596-1506
info@drinkasi.com
www.yaupontea.com
Tea
Founder: Lou Thomann
Accounting & Administration: Kelli Ventling
Lead Harvester: Elliott Day
Number Employees: 11-50
Brands:
  ASI Yaupon Tea

13995 Yaya's
515 Acacia Avenue
Corona Del Mar, CA 92625-1906
949-675-7708
Organic and fat-free caramel popcorn
CEO/President: Bob George
VP: Patty George
Estimated Sales: Under $500,000
Number Employees: 1-4
Type of Packaging: Private Label

13996 Yayin Corporation
12725 Hatteras Street
Valley Village, CA 91607-1408
707-829-5686
Fax: 707-829-0993
Wines
President: Craig Winchell
Estimated Sales: $500,000-$1 000,000
Number Employees: 1-4

13997 Ye Olde Pepper Co
122 Derby St
Salem, MA 01970-5646
978-745-2744
Fax: 978-557-1017 866-526-2376
www.peppercandy.net
Hard and soft candy, chocolates
President: Robert Burkinshaw
candyman1806@aol.com
Estimated Sales: Below $5 Million
Number Employees: 20-49
Brands:
  Black Jacks
  Salem Gibralters

13998 (HQ)Yellow Emperor Inc
510 Conger St
Eugene, OR 97402-2718
541-485-6664
Fax: 541-485-0039 877-485-6664
office@yellowemperor.com
www.yellowemperor.com
Custom herbal extracts, ginseng, teas, tea concentrates and herbal honey
President: Andrew Levine
andy@yellowemperor.com

Food Manufacturers / A-Z

Estimated Sales: Less than $500,000
Number Employees: 1-4
Square Footage: 9600
Type of Packaging: Consumer, Private Label, Bulk
Brands:
  Honeymoon
  Inner Force
  Oregon Natural Sportstonic
  Phytotherapy
  Wild American Herb Co.
  Yellow Emperor

13999 Yeomen Seafoods Inc
30 Western Ave # 201
Gloucester, MA 01930-3664
978-283-7422
Fax: 978-283-7522
Whole frozen seafood
Owner: Tim Kennedy
yeomen@gis.net
Estimated Sales: $4.7 Million
Number Employees: 1-4

14000 Yerba Prima
740 Jefferson Ave
Ashland, OR 97520-3743
541-488-2228
Fax: 541-488-2443 800-488-4339
yerba@yerba.com www.yerbaprima.com
Processor and exporter of high quality dietary supplements, specializing in dietary fiber, internal cleansing aids and herbal products.
CEO: John Jung
yerba@yerba.com
Marketing Manager: Shelley Matteson
Estimated Sales: $5-10 Million
Number Employees: 10-19
Type of Packaging: Consumer, Private Label
Brands:
  Aloe Falls
  Yerba Prima

14001 Yerba Santa Goat Dairy
6850 Scotts Valley Rd
Lakeport, CA 95453
707-263-8131
Fax: 707-263-8131
Dairy products
Owner: Javier Salmon
Marketing Director: Chris Twohy
Contact: Christopher Twohy
yerbasanta44@hotmail.com
Estimated Sales: Below $5 000,000
Number Employees: 1-4

14002 (HQ)Yergat Packing Co
5451 W Mission Ave
Fresno, CA 93722-5074
559-276-9180
Fax: 559-276-2841 info@yergatpacking.com
www.yergatpacking.com
Processor and exporter of grapevine leaves
President: Kirk Yergat
Contact: Thao Duong
thaod@yergatpacking.com
Number Employees: 5-9
Parent Co: Yergat Packing Company
Type of Packaging: Consumer, Private Label

14003 Yick Lung Company
3015 Koapaka Street
Honolulu, HI 96819-1936
808-841-3611
Fax: 808-842-4763
Chips, candy and sunflower seeds
President: Patricia Ching
Chairman: Gertrude Lee
COO: Daniel King
Estimated Sales: $5-9.9 000,000
Number Employees: 20-49
Brands:
  Yick Lung

14004 Ying Leong Look Funn Factory
1028 Kekaulike St
Honolulu, HI 96817-5007
808-537-4304
Ethnic foods
Owner: Fooying Chee
Estimated Sales: $2.5-5 000,000
Number Employees: 10-19

14005 Ying's Kitchen
485 Park Ave
Suite 1
Lake Villa, IL 60046-6547
847-403-7078
ying@yingskitchen.com
www.yingskitchen.com
Asian sauces, rubs and mixes
President & Owner: Ying Stoller
Estimated Sales: Under $500,000
Number Employees: 2-10
Type of Packaging: Food Service
Brands:
  Ying's

14006 Yo Mama's Foods
9130 SW 51st Rd
Gainesville, FL 32608
support@yomamasfoods.com
www.yomamasfoods.com
Salad dressings, pasta sauces and marinades
Founder: David T. Habib
Year Founded: 2017
Estimated Sales: Under $500,000
Number Employees: 1-10
Type of Packaging: Food Service
Brands:
  Yo Mama's

14007 YoFiit
167 Applewood Cr
Vaughan, ON L4K 4K7
Canada
647-997-7846
info@yofiit.com
yofiit.com
Fiber and energy bars; cereal; milk substitutes; quinoa; nutritional shakes.
Co-Founder: Marie Amazan
Year Founded: 2015
Number Employees: 5-9
Type of Packaging: Private Label

14008 Yoakum Packing Co
500 Front St
Yoakum, TX 77995-3009
361-293-3541
Fax: 361-293-2261 800-999-6997
www.farmpac.com
Smoked and cured pork, beef and poultry
President: Glen Kusak
glen@farmpac.com
Estimated Sales: $7,226,707
Number Employees: 50-99
Square Footage: 120000
Type of Packaging: Consumer, Food Service, Private Label, Bulk
Brands:
  Farm Pac
  Ranch Pac

14009 Yoder Dairies
1620 Mount Pleasant Rd
Chesapeake, VA 23322-1219
757-482-4068
Fax: 757-497-3510
Milk including standard homogenized, low-fat, skim, half/half and chocolate; also, cream buttermilk, whipping cream, eggs, eggnog, spring water and orange, grapefruit and apple juices, as well as ice cream.
President: Kenneth Miller
VP: L Miller
General Manager: Maria Dlah
Plant Manager: Lester Miller
Estimated Sales: $4.3 Million
Number Employees: 31
Type of Packaging: Consumer

14010 Yogavive
6 Beach Road #863
Tiburon, CA 94920
415-366-6226
Fax: 415-366-1750 info@yogavive.com
www.yogavive.com
Apple and mango chips in sweet and savory flavors. Certified Organic, Fair Trade, non-GMO, Gluten Free, Vegan, Kosher, and Halal.
President: Beau Giannini
beau@yogavive.com
VP Sales And Marketing: Michael Blicher
VP Operations: Richard Turner
Type of Packaging: Consumer

14011 Yogi Tea
950 International Way
Springfield, OR 97477
800-964-4832
yogitea.customerservice@yogiproducts.com
www.yogiproducts.com
Tea
Square Footage: 200000
Parent Co: Yogi Tea
Type of Packaging: Consumer, Food Service, Private Label, Bulk
Other Locations:
  Tea Business Sales
  Portland OR
Brands:
  Ancient Healing Formulas
  Golden Temple
  Herb Technology
  Rain Forest
  Sweet Home Farm
  Yogi Tea

14012 Yogurtland Franchising Inc
17801 Cartwright Rd
Irvine, CA 92614-6216
949-265-8000
Fax: 949-265-8000 www.yogurt-land.com
Yogurt
CEO: Phillip Chang
phillip.chang@yogurt-land.com
Number Employees: 20-49

14013 (HQ)Yohay Baking Co
146 Albany Ave
Lindenhurst, NY 11757-3628
631-225-0300
Fax: 631-225-4277
Processor, importer and exporter of wafer rolls, specialty cookies, biscotti, and fudge mix, kosher and all natural products. Retail packaging available
Owner: Michael Soloman
solomanyohay@aol.com
Number Employees: 20-49
Type of Packaging: Consumer, Food Service, Private Label, Bulk
Brands:
  Fudge Gourmet
  Gourmet Cookie Place
  Sweetheart Fudge

14014 Yokohl Packing Co
125 S Mount Vernon Ave
Lindsay, CA 93247-2442
559-562-1327
Fax: 559-562-6732
Packer of oranges
Manager: Henry Howison
henry@yokohlvalley.com
Sales: Tim Bentley
Estimated Sales: $10-20 Million
Number Employees: 50-99
Type of Packaging: Bulk

14015 Yonkers Brewing Company LLC
92 Main St.
Yonkers, NY 10701
914-226-8327
info@yonkersbrewing.com
www.yonkersbrewing.com
Craft lagers, IPAs and ales
Co-Founder: John Rubbo
Co-Founder: Nick Califano
Number of Brands: 1
Number of Products: 12
Type of Packaging: Consumer, Private Label
Brands:
  Yonkers Brewing Company

14016 Yoo-Hoo Chocolate Beverage Company
600 Commercial Ave
Carlstadt, NJ 7072
201-933-0070
Fax: 201-933-5360
consumer.relations@brandspeoplelove.com
www.drinkyoo-hoo.com
Chocolate drinks
President: Brian O'Byrne
Marketing Manager: Christine Karumpe
Contact: Brian O''Byrne
brian.obyrne@orangina.com
Plant Manager: Bill Pedeto

Estimated Sales: $16,500,000
Number Employees: 20-49
Parent Co: Yoo-Hoo Chocolate Beverage
Type of Packaging: Consumer

14017 Yoplait
5825 Explorer Drive
Mississauga, ON L4W 5P6
Canada
800-516-7780
www.yoplait.ca
Dairy products including regular and drinkable yogurt
Chairman/CEO: Jeffrey Harmening
CFO: Kofi Bruce
Chief Marketing Officer: Ivan Pollard
Number Employees: 4000
Parent Co: General Mills
Type of Packaging: Consumer
Brands:
 Creamy
 Minigo
 Source
 Tubes
 Yop

14018 York Mountain Winery
7505 York Mountain Road
Templeton, CA 93465
805-237-7575
hreed@martinweyrich.com
Red and white wine, dry sherry, champagne and salad dressing
Owner: David Weyrich
Manager: Suzanne Redberg
Wine Maker: Steve Goldman
Estimated Sales: $920000
Number Employees: 5-9
Square Footage: 12000
Type of Packaging: Consumer
Brands:
 Suzanne's Salad Splash
 York Mountain

14019 Yorktown Baking Company
1500 Front St Ste 7
Yorktown Heights, NY 10598
914-245-9319
Fax: 914-243-7138 800-235-3961
Fresh and frozen batter including muffin, scone and cookie. Prepared flour mixes and doughs
Owner: Emil Gold
Estimated Sales: $2,600,000
Number Employees: 20-49
Type of Packaging: Consumer, Food Service
Brands:
 Yorktown Baking Company

14020 Yoshida Food Products Co
8338 NE Alderwood Rd
Suite A
Portland, OR 97220-6809
503-284-1114
Fax: 503-284-0004 800-653-1114
info@yfintl.com www.yfintl.com
Non MSG, nonfat and cholesterol-free sauces, marinades, drippings and coatings
President: Matt Guthrie
CFO: Tim Sether
CEO: Junki Yoshida
Quality Control: John Hunter
VP Sales/Marketing: John Moran
Sales Director: Andy Moberg
Public Relations: Marti Lucich
Operations Manager: Eric Rinearson
Production Manager: Frank Heuschkel
Purchasing Manager: Ken Hamilton
Estimated Sales: $8 Million
Number Employees: 5-9
Square Footage: 260000
Parent Co: Heinz
Type of Packaging: Consumer, Food Service, Private Label, Bulk
Brands:
 Benihana
 Yoshida Foods International

14021 Yost Candy Co Inc
51 S Cochran St
Dalton, OH 44618-9602
330-828-2777
Fax: 330-828-8296 800-750-1976
info@yostcandy.com
Processor and exporter of lollypops and Halloween candy
President: Earl Yost
Vice President: Joe Yost
Sales Director: Earl Yost
Estimated Sales: $2000000
Number Employees: 10-19
Type of Packaging: Consumer, Private Label, Bulk
Brands:
 Kiddi Pops
 Licklers
 Lil Kiddies

14022 Young Pecan
2455 Entrada Del Sol
Las Cruces, NM 88001
575-524-4321
Fax: 575-525-3432
Bagged and boxed pecans
Manager: Paul Koenig
Contact: Michael Cabezas
mcabezas@youngpecan.com
Purchasing Agent: Malcolm Burdett
Estimated Sales: $2.5-5 Million
Number Employees: 50-99
Parent Co: Young Pecan Company
Type of Packaging: Bulk

14023 (HQ)Young Pecan, Inc.
2005 Babar Ln
Florence, SC 29501
800-729-6003
www.youngplantations.com
Pecans
President & CEO: James Swink
Executive Vice President: Helen Watts
Estimated Sales: $75-99 Million
Number Employees: 183
Number of Brands: 3
Square Footage: 150000
Parent Co: King Ranch
Type of Packaging: Consumer, Food Service, Bulk
Other Locations:
 Las Cruces NM
 Los Angeles CA
 Salem OR
 Seattle WA
 Detroit MI
 Mason OH
 Elizabeth NJ
 Milwaukee WI
Brands:
 Goodbee
 Indian Creek
 Schermer

14024 (HQ)Young Winfield
1700 Brampton Street
Hamilton, ON L8H 3S1
Canada
905-893-2536
Fax: 416-544-4390 youngwinfield.com
Onion oil, cajun spice, salt and vinegar seasonings
President/Contact: Amirali Sunderji
Estimated Sales: $3-5 Million
Number Employees: 12
Square Footage: 108000
Type of Packaging: Consumer, Food Service, Private Label, Bulk
Brands:
 Simply Spice
 You Win

14025 Young's Bakery
67 S Gallatin Ave
Uniontown, PA 15401-3540
724-437-6361
Cakes and cookies
President: Dino Palermo
Marketing Director: Ruth Palermo
Estimated Sales: Less than $500,000
Number Employees: 1 to 4
Type of Packaging: Food Service

14026 Young's Jersey Dairy
6880 Springfield Xenia Rd
Yellow Springs, OH 45387-9610
937-325-0629
Fax: 937-325-3226 cows@youngsdairy.com
www.youngsdairy.com
Milk, ice cream, rolls, bread and donuts
President: Robert Young
robertyoung@youngsdairy.com
Human Resource Manager: Ben Young
Sales Manager: Cathy Young
Estimated Sales: Below $5 Million
Number Employees: 100-249

14027 Young's Lobster Pound
4 Mitchell Street
Belfast, ME 04915
207-338-1160
Fax: 207-338-3498
Processor, exporter and importer of fresh and frozen seafood including crabs, lobster, live and shucked clams and mussels, scallops and shrimp; wholesaler/distributor of fresh and frozen seafood
Owner: Raymond Young
Co-Owner: Claire Young
Manager; Owner: Raymond Young
Estimated Sales: $3-5 Million
Number Employees: 20-49
Square Footage: 10944
Type of Packaging: Consumer, Food Service
Brands:
 Young's Lobster Pound

14028 Young's Noodle Factory Inc
1635 Liliha St
Honolulu, HI 96817-3154
808-533-6478
Fax: 808-536-6533
Noodles
President/Treasurer: Erwin Young
Owner: Gordon Kwan
Estimated Sales: $1,000,000
Number Employees: 10-19
Type of Packaging: Food Service

14029 Your Bar Factory
7232 Coroner
LaSalle, QC H8N 2W8
Canada
514-364-0258
Fax: 514-364-2229 888-366-0258
info@yourbarfactory.com
www.yourbarfactory.com
Manufacturer rice crispy squares, and manufacturer of private label bars for various customers profiles including major retailers and smaller accounts
Chief Executive Officer: Martin Joyal
VP: Daniel Levesque
R&D: Melanie Carre
Quality Control: Celine Boiniere
Sales: Myrian Ang
Vice President of Operations: Chantal Glenisson
Purchasing: Anilcar Parraga
Estimated Sales: $10 Million
Number Employees: 60
Square Footage: 30000
Parent Co: Rapid Snack
Type of Packaging: Food Service, Private Label, Bulk

14030 Yum Yum Donut Shops Inc
18830 San Jose Ave
City Of Industry, CA 91748-1325
626-964-1478
Fax: 626-912-2779 www.yumyumdonuts.com
Donut shop chain on U.S. West Coast.
President: Lincoln Watase
Number Employees: 10-19

14031 Yum Yum Potato Chips
40 Du Moulin
Warwick, QC J0A 1M0
Canada
819-358-3600
Fax: 819-358-3687 800-567-5792
yumyum@yum-yum.com www.yum-yum.com
Snack foods including potato chips, cheese sticks, onion rings and fries
President: Pierre Riverd
Director Production: Guy Trudel
Number Employees: 200
Type of Packaging: Consumer, Private Label

14032 Yvonne's Gourmet Sensations
404 Berkshire Way
Marlton, NJ 08053-4222
856-985-7677
Fax: 856-810-3798
Gourmet chocolate pretzels, chocolate cookies, chocolate grahams, chocolate waffles
Marketing Manager: Gary Greenberg
Brands:
 Yvonne's Gourmet

Food Manufacturers / A-Z

14033 Z Foods Inc.
9537 Road 29 1/2
Madera, CA 93637
559-673-6368
Fax: 559-673-7508 888-400-1015
Dried fruits
President: Daniel Villanueva
VP: Nina Zoria
Number Employees: 2

14034 Z Specialty Food, LLC
1250 Harter Ave # A
Woodland, CA 95776-6106
530-668-0660
Fax: 530-668-6061 800-678-1226
tasty@zspecialtyfood.com
www.ZSpecialtyfood.com
Processor and exporter of gourmet chocolate and vanilla nut butters cremes, honey and honey products including fruit spreads and honey straws, bee pollen, bees wax, royal jelly and propolis; also, gift packs
Co-Owner: Ishai Zeldner
Square Footage: 16000
Type of Packaging: Consumer, Food Service, Private Label, Bulk
Brands:
 Chocolate & Vanilla Nut Spread
 Gourmet Butters & Spreads
 Gourmet Honey Collection
 Honey Fruit Spreads
 Honey In the Straw
 Moonshine Trading

14035 Z&S Distributing
7090 N. Marks Avenue
Suite 104
Fresno, CA 93711
559-432-1777
Fax: 559-432-2888 800-467-0788
Fruits and vegetables.
President: Martin Zaninovich
Estimated Sales: $7,700,000
Number Employees: 10-19
Type of Packaging: Consumer
Brands:
 Just-Ripe

14036 Z-Trim Holdings, Inc
1101 Campus Drive
Mundelein, IL 60060
847-549-6002
Fax: 847-549-6028 customerservice@ztrim.com
Ingredients
Sales Director: Rick Harris
VP Sales/Applications: Lynda Carroll
Applications Project Manager: Aili Young
Research Chef: Erin Ryan

14037 Zabiha Halal Meat Processors
1715 Cortland Ct
Addison, IL 60101
630-620-5000
Fax: 630-620-5013 info@fatimabrand.com
www.fatimabrand.com
Meats, poultry, and seafood
Co-Founder: Mohammed Yousuf Khan
Co-Founder: Laila Khan
Team Member: Sajid Khan
Year Founded: 1987
Number of Brands: 1
Brands:
 Fatima

14038 Zaca Mesa Winery
6905 Foxen Canyon Rd
Los Olivos, CA 93441
805-688-9339
Fax: 805-688-8796 800-350-7972
info@zacamesa.com www.zacamesa.com
Wines
President/CEO: Brook Williams
CFO: Susan English
susan@zacamesa.com
VP Sales/Marketing: Jim Fiolek
Estimated Sales: $6.3 Million
Number Employees: 20-49
Brands:
 Roussanne
 Syrah
 Z Gris Dry Rose
 Zcuvee

14039 Zachary Confections Inc
2130 W State Road 28
Frankfort, IN 46041-8771
765-659-4751
Fax: 765-659-1491 800-445-4222
www.zacharyconfections.com
Processor and exporter of confectionery products including caramels, boxed chocolates, marshmallows, mints, nougats and holiday novelties.
President: Jack Zachary
Number Employees: 250-499
Type of Packaging: Consumer, Private Label, Bulk
Brands:
 Zachary

14040 Zachys Wine
39 Westmoreland Ave
White Plains, NY 10606
914-448-3026
Fax: 914-313-2350 866-647-9075
cs@zachys.com www.zachys.com
wines & spirits
President: Jeff Zacharia
Year Founded: 1944
Number Employees: 51-200

14041 (HQ)Zacky Farms
2020 S East Ave
Fresno, CA 93721-3328
559-443-2700
Fax: 559-443-2778 800-888-0235
zfsales@zacky.com
Turkey
President: Richard Zacky
richardzacky@zacky.com
Estimated Sales: $500,000-$1 Million
Number Employees: 500-999
Type of Packaging: Consumer
Brands:
 Culinary Classic Breast of Turkey N
 Culinary Classic Slices Breast of T

14042 Zarda Bar-B-Q & Catering Company
214 N 7 Highway
Blue Springs, MO 64014
816-229-9999
Fax: 816-224-3171 800-776-7427
info@zarda.com www.zarda.com
Barbecue sauce and baked beans
President: Michael Zarda
Quality Control Manager: Brian Packer
Marketing Director: Terry Hyer
Plant Manager: Ron Dorris
Estimated Sales: $10-24.9 Million
Number Employees: 50-99
Brands:
 Zarda

14043 (HQ)Zartic Inc
438 Lavender Dr NW
Rome, GA 30165
706-234-3000
Fax: 706-291-6068 800-241-0516
www.pierrefoods.com
Full service beef, poultry, veal and pork further processor
President: Anthony Schroder
CEO: James Mauer
jmauer@zetec.com
CFO: Robert Miles
Vice President of Technical Services: Bill Theis
Vice President of Research and Developme: Bernie Panchot
Sales VP: Mike Wilson
Senior Vice President of Operations: Mike Zelkind
Purchasing Agent: Ken Fries
Number Employees: 50-99
Type of Packaging: Consumer
Other Locations:
 Zartic Inc (Beef Division)
 Cedartown GA
 Zartic Inc (Poultry Division)
 West Rome GA
 Zartic Inc (Pork Division)
 Hamilton AL
Brands:
 Circle Z
 Crispy Steaks
 Fryz
 Jim's Country Mill Sausage
 Shurtenda
 Spicy Wings
 Vittles
 Z-Bird
 Zartic
 Zartic Beef Bakeables
 Zartic Chicken Bakeables
 Zartic Chicken Fried Beef Steaks
 Zartic Chicken Fryz Flavorz
 Zartic Chicken Tenderloins
 Zartic Circle Z Beef Burgers
 Zartic Crispy Steaks
 Zartic Homestyle Meatloaf
 Zartic Honey Hugged Chicken
 Zartic Pork Bakeables
 Zartic Pork Sausage Sampler
 Zartic Rockin' Roasted Chicken
 Zartic Veal Entree Legends
 Zartic Veal Specialties

14044 Zayante Vineyards
420 Old Mount Rd
Felton, CA 95018-9054
831-335-7992
Fax: 831-335-5770
Wines
Owner: Prashant Kanhere
pkanhere@zayantevineyards.com
Co-Owner: Marion Nolten
Co-Owner: Kathleen Starkey-Nolten
Vineyard Manager: Greg Nolten
Estimated Sales: Less Than $500,000
Number Employees: 1-4
Type of Packaging: Private Label
Brands:
 Zayante

14045 Zazi Baking Company
1360 Industrial Ave
Petaluma, CA 94952-6521
707-778-1635
Fax: 707-778-6991
Biscotti and cookies
President: Celeste Longo
VP: Debby Dyar
Estimated Sales: $5-10 Million
Number Employees: 10-19
Square Footage: 24000
Type of Packaging: Food Service, Private Label, Bulk
Brands:
 Cookie Brittle
 Mrs. Little's
 Running Rabbit
 Spendido Nuggets
 Splendido Biscotti
 Zazi Organics

14046 Zazubean
1529 W 6th Ave
Vancouver, BC V6J 1R1
Canada
604-801-5488
info@zazubean.com
www.zazubean.com
Organic fair trade chocolate
Co-Founder: Tiziana Ienna
Co-Founder: Tara Gilbert
Year Founded: 2007
Number Employees: 2-9

14047 Zd Wines
8383 Silverado Trl
Napa, CA 94558-9436
707-963-5188
Fax: 707-963-2640 800-487-7757
info@zdwines.com www.zdwines.com
Processor and exporter of wines including chardonnay, pinot noir and cabernet sauvignon
President/Partner: Brett DeLeuze
CEO/Partner: Robert DeLeuze
CFO: Julie De Leuze
Marketing Coordinator: Elyse Chambers
VP Sales: Teresa d'Aurizio
Winemaker: Chris Pisani
Estimated Sales: $5-10 Million
Number Employees: 20-49
Number of Brands: 2
Number of Products: 8
Square Footage: 90928
Type of Packaging: Consumer, Food Service
Brands:
 Abacus
 Z.D. Wines

Food Manufacturers / A-Z

14048 Zebra Technologies Corporation
3 Overlook Point
Lincolnshire, IL 60069
847-634-6700
Fax: 847-913-8766 866-230-9494
www.zebra.com
Bar code equipment including printers, supplies and software for point-of-application labeling and performance thermal transferring.
Chief Executive Officer: Anders Gustafsson
Chief Financial Officer: Olivier Leonetti
Senior VP, Corporate Development: Michael Cho
Senior VP/General Counsel/Secretary: Cristen Kogl
Chief Marketing Officer: Jeff Schmitz
Senior VP, Global Sales: Joachim Heel
Year Founded: 1969
Estimated Sales: $3.7 Billion
Number Employees: 7,400
Square Footage: 167600
Brands:
  Zebra
  Zebra Value-Line
  Zebra Xii

14049 Zego Foods
912 Cole St.
Suite 294
San Francisco, CA 94117
415-706-8094
info@zegofoods.com
www.zegofoods.com
Seed & fruit snack bars, protein, oats, and muesli
Founder/CEO: Colleen Kavanagh
COO: Brian Jansen
Customer Relations: Danielle Schnake
Year Founded: 2013

14050 Zeigler's
1513 N Broad St
Lansdale, PA 19446-1111
215-855-5161
Fax: 215-855-4548 customerservice@zeiglers.com
Apple cider, lemonades, teas, juices and spices.
General Manager: Art Balzereit
a.balzereit@zeiglers.com
Estimated Sales: $20-50 Million
Number Employees: 50-99
Number of Brands: 1
Square Footage: 60000
Parent Co: LiDestri Food & Beverage
Type of Packaging: Consumer, Food Service, Private Label, Bulk
Brands:
  Zeigler's

14051 Zelda's Sweet Shoppe
4113 Main St
Skokie, IL 60076-2753
847-679-0033
Fax: 847-679-0030 888-449-3532
www.zkgourmet.com
Baked goods, cakes, cookies
Owner: Linda Neiman
linda@zeldas.net
Number Employees: 10-19

14052 Zemas Madhouse Foods Inc.
P.O. Box 823
Highland Park, IL 60035-0823
847-910-4512
Fax: 847-780-3178 zemasfoods.com
Gluten-free cookies and baking mixes.
President: Jill Motew
Marketing Manager: Tricia Goldfarb
Year Founded: 2010
Estimated Sales: Less than $500,000
Number Employees: 2
Type of Packaging: Private Label

14053 (HQ)Zenobia Co
5774 Mosholu Ave # B
Bronx, NY 10471-2200
347-843-8080
Fax: 718-548-2313 866-936-6242
Processor, importer and exporter of pistachios, cashews, pumpkin and sunflower seeds, organic dried fruits, etc
President: Kenneth Bobker
National Sales Manager: Donald DiMatteo
Estimated Sales: $5-10 Million
Number Employees: 1-4
Square Footage: 100000
Type of Packaging: Consumer, Food Service, Private Label, Bulk
Other Locations:
  Zenobia Co.
  Bronx NY
Brands:
  Indian
  Zenobia

14054 Zentis Sweet Ovations
1741 Tomlinson Rd
Philadelphia, PA 19116-3847
215-676-3900
Fax: 215-613-2115 800-223-7073
Processor and exporter of fruit preparations
CEO: Kevin Daugherty
Plant Manager: Corey Arrick
Number Employees: 100-249
Parent Co: Systems Bio-Industries

14055 (HQ)Zephyr Hills
6403 Harney Rd
Tampa, FL 33610-9349
813-630-5763
Fax: 813-620-6862 800-950-9398
www.zephyrhillswater.com
Coffee and bottled spring and distilled water
President: Kim Jefferies
Quality Control Manager: Winnie Louie
Marketing/Sales Development Manager: Monica Kelley
Number Employees: 20-49
Parent Co: Nestl, Waters North America
Type of Packaging: Consumer
Brands:
  Deer Park
  Zephyrhillis

14056 Zephyrhills Bottled Water Company
6403 Harney Rd
Tampa, FL 33610-9349
813-630-5763
Fax: 813-620-6862 800-950-9398
Bottled water
President: Kim Jeffery
Marketing Director: John Bryan
Sales Manager: Monica Kelley
Operations Manager: Eddie Edmunds
Estimated Sales: $.5-1 million
Number Employees: 1-4
Parent Co: Perrier Group of America
Type of Packaging: Private Label

14057 Zerna Packing
2231 Highway 100
Labadie, MO 63055-2000
636-742-4190
Meat; smoking and curing available
Owner: Carl Zerna Sr
Estimated Sales: $1-3 Million
Number Employees: 1-4
Type of Packaging: Consumer, Food Service

14058 Zeroodle
Richmond Hill, ON L4B 1C9
Canada
905-889-9880
help@zeroodle.com
zeroodle.com
Bean pasta

14059 Zest Tea LLC
1100 Wicomico St
Suite 321
Baltimore, MD 21230-2063
636-579-1809
zesttea.com
Tea
Co-Founder: James Fayal
Co-Founder: Rickey Ishida
Chief Marketing Officer: Karyn Vilbig
Year Founded: 2013
Estimated Sales: Less than $500,000
Number Employees: 1-4
Type of Packaging: Food Service, Private Label

14060 Zesty Z: The Za'atar Company
630 Flushing Ave
Brooklyn, NY 11206
917-740-5241
zesty-z.com
Mediterranean inspired spreads and condiments.
Co-Founder: Alexander Harik
Co-Founder: Lorraine Harik

Year Founded: 2016
Number Employees: 1-4
Type of Packaging: Private Label

14061 Zevia
10200 Culver Blvd
Culver City, CA 90232
310-202-7000
855-469-3842
sales@zevia.com www.zevia.com
Soda
Principal Director: Derek Newman
Chief Executive Officer: Paddy Spence
VP Sales: Jeff Taylor
Contact: Nancy Aguilar
nancy@zevia.com
Operations Manager: Michael Spain
Estimated Sales: $500,000-1 Million
Number Employees: 10-19

14062 Zhena's Gypsy Tea
6041 Triangle Dr
Commerce, CA 90040-3642
323-767-0300
Fax: 805-646-4262 800-448-0803
info@gypsytea.com
Teas
Contact: Jeanne Cloutier
cloutier@gypsytea.com
Number Employees: 5-9

14063 Ziegenfelder Ice Cream Co
87 18th St
Wheeling, WV 26003-3756
304-232-6360
Fax: 304-232-6368 800-322-3642
info@twinpops.com www.budgetsaver.com
Manufacturer of ice cream pops.
President and CEO: Lisa Allen
budgetsaver@twinpops.com
Estimated Sales: $20-50 Million
Number Employees: 100-249
Type of Packaging: Consumer

14064 Zimmerman Cheese Inc
6853 State Road 78
South Wayne, WI 53587-9724
608-968-3414
Fax: 608-968-3425 paul@zimmermancheese.com
Cheese
President: Mark Witke
zimcheese@pcmli.com
Marketing Director: Linda Moe
Estimated Sales: $10-24.9 000,000
Number Employees: 5-9

14065 Zinda Products
104 avenue Libert,
Candiac, QC J5R 6X1
Canada
450-635-6664
Fax: 450-635-6632 888-867-6664
info@zindaproducts.com zindaproducts.com
Couscous
President & Founder: Majid Jamal Eddine
Quality and R&D Director: Marouane Abdellaoui
Estimated Sales: $9,721,564
Number Employees: 40
Type of Packaging: Private Label

14066 Zink & Triest Company
150 Domorah Dr
Montgomeryville, PA 18936-9633
215-469-1950
Fax: 215-628-8651 800-537-5070
Suppliers of vanilla beans, vanillin and ethyl vanillin
President: Henry Todd
Sales Manager: Amie Briethaupt
Contact: Tammy Adgalane
tadgalane@amtodd.com
Estimated Sales: $10-20 Million
Number Employees: 10-19

14067 Zippy's Inc
1765 S King St
Honolulu, HI 96826-2190
808-973-0880
Fax: 808-973-0888 customerservice@zippys.com
www.zippys.com
Chili manufacturing
President: Paul Yokota
pyokota@foodsolutionshi.com
Number Employees: 1000-4999

Food Manufacturers / A-Z

Brands:
　Napolean's Bakery
　Zippys

14068　Zitos Specialty Foods
129 Cousley Drive SE
Port Charlotte, FL 33952-9149
　　　　　　　　　941-625-0806
Gourmet and specialty foods
Owner: David Smith
Co-owner: Christine Smith
Brands:
　Zitos

14069　Zoe's Meats
2445 Bluebelle Dr
Santa Rosa, CA 95403-2548
　　　　　　　　　707-545-9637
　　Fax: 707-542-9601　sales@zoemeats.com
　　　　　　　　www.zoemeats.com
Cured meats; cheese; eggs; spices; jams; canned vegetables; pickles and pickled vegetables.
Founder/CEO: George Gravros
Co-Founder/Partner: Charlie Hertz
Year Founded: 2006
Type of Packaging: Food Service, Private Label
Brands:
　Daphne's Creamery
　Emmy's Pickles & Jams
　Yioryo
　Zoe'S Meats

14070　Zoelsmann's Bakery & Deli
912 E Abriendo Ave
Pueblo, CO 81004
　　　　　　　　　719-543-0407
　　　　　　Fax: 719-543-4083
Bread, cakes, pies and hard and sweet rolls
Owner: Ron Petkosek
Estimated Sales: $500,000-$1 Million
Number Employees: 5-9
Type of Packaging: Consumer, Food Service, Bulk

14071　Zone Perfect Nutrition Company
625 Cleveland Ave
Columbus, OH 43215
　　　　　　　　　614-624-7485
　　Fax: 614-624-9001　800-390-6690
　ansupport@abbott.com　www.zoneperfect.com
Nutrition products, bars, meals, drinks and supplements
Chairman and Chief Executive Officer: Miles D. White
EVP, Finance and Chief Financial Officer: Thomas C. Freyman
EVP, Corporate Development: Richard W. Ashley
SVP, Chief Marketing Officer: Paul K. Magill
EVP, Human Resources: Stephen R. Fussell

Number Employees: 1,000-4,999
Parent Co: Abbott Laboratories

14072　Zotter Chocolates
10120 Ne Pine Island Rd
Suite 302
Cape Coral, FL 33909
　　　　　　　　　239-214-7883
　　　　　　schokolade@zotter.at
　　　　　　　　zotter.at
Chocolate
Founder: Josef Zotter
Manager: Ulrike Zotter
Year Founded: 1987
Estimated Sales: Less than $500,000
Number Employees: 5-9

14073　Zoup! Fresh Soup Co LLC
28290 Franklin Rd
Southfield, MI 48034-1659
　　　　　　　　　248-663-1111
　　　　　　support@zoup.com
　　　　　　　　www.zoup.com
Soup
CEO: Christine Bessert
christine@zoupco.com
Number Employees: 10-19

14074　Zuccaro Produce
455 37th Avenue NE
Columbia Heights, MN 55421
　　　　　　　　　612-333-1122
　　Fax: 612-333-7611　zp@zuccarosproduce.net
　　　　　　　zuccarosproduce.site123.me
Provides fruit, produce, dry and canned goods, paper and plastic products, and cleaning supplies to restaurants, food trucks, consession stands, and homes.
Year Founded: 1937
Estimated Sales: $2.5-5 Million
Number Employees: 20-49

14075　Zummo Meat Co
3705 Saint James Blvd
Beaumont, TX 77705-1143
　　　　　　　　　409-842-1810
　　Fax: 409-842-5491　zummo@zummo.com
　　　　　　　　zummomeat.com
Meats including sausage and boudin
Owner: Frank Zummo
VP: Greg Zummo
Estimated Sales: $5-10 Million
Number Employees: 50-99
Type of Packaging: Consumer
Brands:
　Zummo

14076　Zuni Foods
13838 Jones Maltsberger Road
San Antonio, TX 78247-3904
　　　　　　　　　210-481-3600
　　Fax: 210-481-3603　800-906-3876
Mild table salsa
Owner: John Warlow
Brands:
　Zuni Fire Roasted Salsa
　Zuni Zalsa Verde

14077　Zurheide Ice Cream Company
816 Michigan Avenue
Sheboygan, WI 53081-3438
　　　　　　　　　920-458-4581
Ice cream, ice milk, sherbert and frozen yogurt
President: John Zurheide
VP Sales: Wendy Kohl
Contact: Ralph Allen
wally@moosetracks.com
Plant Manager: Nate Dehne
Estimated Sales: $2.5-5 Million
Number Employees: 10-19

14078　Zweigle's Inc
651 Plymouth Ave N
Rochester, NY 14608-1689
　　　　　　　　　585-546-1740
　　Fax: 585-546-8721　info@zweigles.com
　　　　　　　　www.zweigles.com
Processor of meat including sausages, pork, beef, chicken, deli meats and hot dogs.
President: Julie Camardo-Steron
Director, Marketing & Sales: Steve Vacanti
Sales Manager: Jim Vacanti
Year Founded: 1880
Estimated Sales: $20-50 Million
Number Employees: 50-99
Number of Brands: 1
Square Footage: 38500
Type of Packaging: Consumer, Food Service, Private Label, Bulk
Brands:
　Zweigle's

Brand Name Index

Numeric

-196 C, 1120
06 Stout, 9688
1-2-3 Gluten Free, 1
10, 2738
10 Barrel Brewing Co., 571
10 Cane, 8452
100 Anos®, 1120
100 Bourbon Whiskey, 10596
100 Calorie Packs, 8729
100 Grande, 2132
100 Pipers, 9964
100% Flaked Wheat, 6917
100% Purified Non Carbonated Water, 13206
100% Whole Grain, 8844
101 Pitterra Place, 10789
12% Imports, 10666
14'er Esb, 838
150 Bloom, 13498
1710, 5331
1792, 11263
1792 Ridgemont Reserve Bourbon, 11264
18 Rabbits, 5
1848 Winery, 10952
1855®, 6391
1857 Spirits, 1023
1859 Porter, 2911
1883, 10917
19, 3447
19 Crimes, 12937
1950 127 Brand, 4591
1st Sneeze Echinacea, 13015
2 Gingers®, 1120
2-Mix, 783
2001 Estate Cabernet Sauvignon, 13049
20th Century Foods, 11368
225 Bloom, 13498
24 Super Amino Acids, 131
24-Hour Royal Jelly, 1914
25 Imports From France, 8238
3 George, 4969
3 Girls, 9321
3 Musketeers®, 7952
3 Musketeersc, 2132
3 Springs, 11
34 Degrees, 13
35, 2257
360 Nutrition, 15
360 Vodka, 8062
3pm Bites, 16
3v Classic™, 17
3v Fresh™, 17
4%, 11664
4-Grain™, 2031
40 Fathoms®, 5844
409, 2766
44th Street, 7721
479 Degrees, 19
4c Beverages, 20
4c Foods, 20
4pure, 21
4th & Heart, 22
4th of July Cola, 6310
5 Fourchettes, 10331
5 Gum®, 7952, 13960
5 Star®, 6391
5-Alive, 2815
5-Loxin, 9654
51fifty, 25
5lung Re-Leaf, 5789
5th Avenue, 2847, 5818
6-In-1, 4111
6-N-1, 9262
610-D, 13498
67th Street Bbq™, 11363
7 Grain Cereal, 8851
7-Keto, 6236
7/11, 12030
710-D, 13498
74-40, 12030
7th Street Pale, 13428
7up®, 3725, 6818
8 Seconds Canadian Whiskey, 4658
8-Ball Stout, 7554
80-40, 12030
9 Lives, 6380
90 Shilling, 9366
98% Fat-Free, 4668
99 Brand, 11263
99 Schnapps, 11264
999, 10591

A

A & M Cookie, 2886
A & S Brewing, 1592
A Brand, 9500
A Dose of Good Fortunes, 5160
A Foot Of, 11083
A Nonini, 57
A Southern Season, 11864
A Taste of China, 551
A Taste of India, 551
A Taste of Thai, 551
A Yard Of, 11083
A&C, 51
A&D Water Care, 3469
A&J Brand, 849
A&M Cheese, 11777
A&W, 554, 10151
A&W Root Beer®, 3725, 6818
A'Guania, 6776
A-1 Pickle, 53
A-Salted, 12178
A-Treat, 54
A. Bauer's, 1086
A. Gagliano, 55
A. Rafanelli, 58
A. Thomas Meats, 4321
A. Vogel, 67, 10568
A.C. Calderoni, 60
A.C. Larocco Vegetarian Pizza, 63
A.P. Smith Canning Co., 10035
A/D/F, 4687
Aa Brand®, 10777
Aaland, 108
Aangamik Dmg, 4575
Aarsh, 2763
Aasan, 2096
Abacus, 14047
Abandon Brewing Co., 10666
Abb, 4150
Abba-Zabbac, 583
Abbey Well, 2815
Abbotsford Farms®, 8225
Abbotsford Growers Co-Op, 112
Abbott's Candy, 115
Abbotts Meat, 116
Abbuland, 118
Abby's Better Nut Butter, 117
Abc, 4804
Abc Tea (A Better Choice), 72
Abc Carrier, 6211
Abe's, 120
Aberlour Single Malt, 9964
Abg, 4827
Abita, 125
Abita Golden, 6797
Abita Purple, 6797
Abita Root Beer, 6797
Abita Seasmals, 6797
Abita Springs®, 3319
Abita Turboday, 6797
Abm, 8649
Abn, 4150
Absente, 3165
Absolutc, 9964
Absolute Fruit, 1766, 1767
Absolute Nutrition, 4150
Absolutely Almond, 2604
Absolutenergy, 6310
Absopure, 129
Abu Siouf®, 7952
Abuelita, 130
Abunda Body, 131
Ac'cent Sa-Son®, 864
Ac'cent®, 864
Acacia, 132
Acacia Vineyard, 12937
Acadia Naturals, 13938
Acadian Gourmet, 11349
Acai Roots, 136
Acappella, 10260
Acconon®, 126
Accoquat®, 126
Accord® Flavours, 10797
Accufitness, 4150
Ace, 12721, 13691
Ace Bandito, 5648
Ace-Hi, 7142
Aces, 6364
Aceto D'Oro, 13812
Acg, 343
Acg Broadcast Gypsum, 343

Acidoplius Pearls, 4086
Ackerman, 7463
Ackerman's Wild, 6184
Acme, 151
Acremax®, 3775
Act Ii, 2935
Act Ii®, 2939, 2940
Actic Splash, 13145
Action Ade, 5362
Activia, 3377, 3379
Activin Energy, 6310
Activin™, 11150
Acute Fruit™, 8470
Adagio®, 6818
Adam Matthews, 161
Adam's Ranch, 167
Adams, 166, 6380
Adams & Brooks, 163
Adams & Brooks, Inc, 2132
Adelsheim Vineyard, 173
Adf, 451
Adironack, 174
Adirondack Amber, 11218
Adirondack Beverages, 10151
Adirondack Cheese, 3
Adirondack Clear N' Natural, 10151
Adirondack Maple Farms, 175
Adkin's, 176
Adkin's Royal Blue, 176
Adluh, 178
Admiral Nelson's Spiced Rum, 5720
Adolphus®, 10777
Adrenal Cleanse, 5682
Advance, 1891
Advance Pierre Foods®, 13109
Advanced, 192
Advantage, 8191
Adventure Foods, 194
Aep, 81
Aerion, 4736
Aero®, 8945
Aeroplane, 8061
Aeros, 5189
Aesop's Fable, 10214
Affiorato, 3236
Afrique, 11775
After Byrne Recovery Drink, 1902
After Dark, 743
After Shock®, 1120
Ag Co-Op, 201
Agalima, 439
Agar, 9833
Agarich, 8534
Agarloid, 8534
Agarmoor, 8534
Agassiz Amber, 4466
Agave Dream, 203
Agave Nectar, 7748
Agavero, 3165
Agavestix, 5073
Agisyn™, 3320
Aglio Di Mirabellac, 170
Agp Grain Ltd, 81
Agp Grain Marketing, 81
Agricom, 5036
Agripac, 216
Aguardiente Caldas, 3545
Aguila, 71
Aguila®, 8460
Agvest, 9032
Ah!Laska®, 1484
Ah-So, 345
Ahlgren Vineyard, 229
Aidell's, 232
Aidells®, 13109
Aiello, 9044
Aiellos, 11628
Aim, 2666
Aimia Foods, 10303
Air Wick®, 10598
Airex, 8028
Airheads, 2132, 9956
Airlie, 235
Airship, 4387
Airsource, 11501
Ajilys®, 239
Ajinomoto®, 237, 238
Ajipro®-L, 239
Ak Mak, 241
Aketta, 244
Akulon®, 3320

Al Cohen's, 2862
Al Dente, 247, 12030
Al Dente Pasta Selecta, 247
Al Dente Sure Success, 247
Al Gelato, 248
Al Pete, 249
Al Safa Halal, 251
Al's, 252
Al's Best, 2051
Al-Rite, 253
Alacreme, 13700
Aladdin, 256
Alaga, 13740
Alamo, 259
Alamos®, 3834
Alan's Maniac Hot Sauce, 9481
Alaska Bay, 12365
Alaska Fresh, 9348
Alaska Gold, 11375
Alaska Jack's, 264
Alaska Smoked Salmon, 11864
Alaska Smokehouse, 270
Alaska Tea Traders, 264
Alaska Wild Teas, 263
Alaskan, 268
Alaskan Amber, 271
Alaskan Boreal Bouquet, 263
Alaskan Fireweed, 263
Alaskan Freeride Apa, 271
Alaskan Gold, 263
Alaskan Gourmet, 272
Alaskan Hopothermia, 271
Alaskan Icy Bay Ipa, 271
Alaskan Imperial Red, 271
Alaskan Kicker Session Ipa, 271
Alaskan Leader Fisheries, 273
Alaskan Stout, 271
Alaskan Summer Ale, 271
Alaskan White, 271
Alaskan Winter Ale, 271
Alati-Casserta, 275
Alba, 277
Alba Botanica, 5505
Albaglos, 11906
Alban Viognier, 11810
Albergo, 4942
Albers, 2971
Alberta Premium®, 1120
Albertson's, 9469, 11260, 12304
Albino Rhino Ale, 13711
Albion Amber Ale, 7923
Albunate, 4430
Alcalase, 1692
Alchemist, 13174
Alcohol Free Stevia, 9201
Alcoholado Baluarte, 3545
Alcoholado Superior 70, 3545
Alcolec, 468
Alcosa, 5555
Alda, 10540
Alden's Ice Cream, 9533
Alden's Organic, 283
Alder Cove, 3394
Alder Ridge, 2909
Alder Springs, 284
Alderfer, 285
Alebrta, 4025
Ales & Lagers, 1789
Alesia, 209
Alessi, 13404
Alessi Bakery, 289
Alewel's Country Meats, 290
Alex & Dani's Biscotti, 1397
Alexander Keith's India Pale Ale, 7123
Alexander Valley, 6375
Alexander Winery, 10952
Alexander's Gourmet Tea, 291
Alexia®, 2939, 2940
Alexis Bailly, 296
Alexis De Portneuf®, 11211
Alfasi, 10952
Alfonso Gourmet Pasta, 298
Alfred & Sam's, 299
Alfredo, 303
Alfredobuds, 1880
Algonquin Honeybrown, 1702
Algood Blue Label, 305
Algood Jelly, 305
Algood Marmalade, 305
Algood Old Fashioned, 305
Algood Preserves, 305
Algood Red Label, 305

1259

Brand Name Index

Alhambra, 10303
Alhambra®, 3220, 3319, 11889
Ali's, 12928
Alicante Bouschet, 2637
Alien Pop, 6158
Alien Poppin' Pops, 6158
Align, 12721
Alimony Ale, 1837
Alive, 9155
Alive & Radiant, 315
Alive & Well, 314
Alive!, 8896
Alkinco, 316
Alkyrol, 11268
All American, 318
All American Afternoon Delight, 319
All American Holiday Goose, 11287
All American Precious Stones, 319
All American White Trash, 319
All B-100, 7947
All B-50, 7947
All But Gluten, 13691
All Fresh, 340
All Natural, 4904
All Natural Herbal, 7602
All One, 9258
All Round Foods, 322
All Season's Kitchen, 4665
All Soft, 1735
All Sport®, 3725
All-American Sports Pasta, 4794
All-American Squeeze-Salsa, 3957
All-Bran, 6766
All-Bran®, 6765
All-In-One, 13184
All-Q™, 3320
Allan, 5818
Allans, 10186
Alldrin, 328
Alleghanys, 330
Allegheny, 13447
Allegrini, 3834
Allegro, 333, 334
Allegro Coffee, 332
Allegro Tea, 332
Allen, 10714, 12166
Allen's, 56, 337, 10659
Allens, 336, 338, 4499
Aller Bee-Gone, 1914
Aller-7, 6236
Allerdophilus® Caps, 13097
Allertonic, 5791
Alley Kat Amber, 339
Alleycat Amber, 7554
Allez, 13280
Alliance®, 13595
Alligator Pepper, 12987
Allirich, 672
Allison Jayne, 8837
Alljuice, 8627
Allvia®, 9237
Alma, 338
Almanac Beer Co., 10666
Almark, 352
Almarla Black Lightning, 353
Almarla Soul Train, 353
Almased, 354
Almaviva, 1006
Almond Breeze, 1471
Almond Chews, 9220
Almond Ingot, 5140
Almond Joy, 2132, 5818
Almond Toppers, 1471, 12201
AlmondcrOMe, 8957
Almondina, 13974
Almondina Biscuits, 13975
Almondmilk, 8957
Almonds, 10984
Alnose, 5474
Alo, 89
Alo®, 11052
Aloe Burst, 359
Aloe Falls, 14000
Aloe Farms, 358
Aloe Gloe, 7036
Aloe Labs, 359
Aloe'ha, 360
Aloevine, 6400
Aloha, 396
Aloha Maid, 6327
Alor, 13427
Alouettec, 368

Alpaflor®, 3320
Alpen, 13621
Alpen Cellars, 369
Alpen Dark Chocolate, 13620
Alpen No Added Sugar, 13620
Alpen Original Muesli, 13620
Alpen Sierra, 370
Alpendough, 371
Alpenglow, 11055
Alpenliebe, 9956
Alpenrose, 373
Alpha Glutamine, 1377
Alpha Gold, 8967
Alpha-Bits, 10213
Alphabet Cookies, 3343
Alphadim, 463
Alpine, 380, 2718, 2971
Alpine Coffee, 379
Alpine Lace, 7198
Alpine Start, 382
Alpine Valley, 384, 9332
Alpine Valley Bakery, 4529
Alpineaire, 13105
Alpo®, 8945
Alpro, 13734
Alpromar, 8028
Alsum Farms & Produce, 386
Alsum Organics, 386
Alta, 389, 390
Alta Cucina, 12030
Alta Dena, 3442
Alta Dena Classic, 387
Altanta Dairy, 4290
Altbier, 1507
Alterra Coffee Roasters, 8090
Altima, 7107
Alto Rey, 394
Altoids, 2132
Altoids®, 7952, 13960
Alton, 8806
Altoona Hills, 10952
Altos, 9964
Altria, 541
Alube, 137
Alvarado Street Bakery, 397
Alvita, 13097
Alvita Tea, 398
Always, 12721
Always Discreet, 12721
Always Sweet, 13192
Amabile Umbro, 8479
Amador Foothill, 403
Amafruits, 404
Amaizen Crunch, 10235
Amana Meats, 409
Amanda Hills, 410
Amano, 414
Amano Jenbrana, 412
Amano Ocumare, 412
Amara, 415
Amaretti Virginia, 3381
Amaretto, 9773
Amaretto De Sabroso, 11264
Amarone Pasta, 9813
Amazake, 5248
Amazin' Raisin, 419
Amazing Herbs, 420
Amazing Meals, 329
Amazingly Tasty, 4668
Amazon Pepper Products, 6015
Amazonas, 2719
Ambake, 416
Amban, 416
Amber, 11585, 11992
Amber Ale, 1097
Amber Brand Deviled Smithfield Ham, 12714
Amber Farms, 6409
Amber Light, 7330
Amber Wheat Beer, 10404
Amberale, 9701
Amberg Wine Cellars, 422
Amberhill, 1543
Ambersweet, 12426
Ambi Pur, 12721
Ambootia, 424
Ambretta, 1524
Ambrosia, 9909, 11235
Ambrosia Honey, 7748
Amburst, 416
Ame, 8838
Ame Celebration, 8838

Amelia Bay, 917
Amelia's, 12301
Amelia's Sugar Free Shoppe, 5140
Ameri Color, 494
America, 5660
America Almond, 438
America's Best, 2389
America's Catch, 436
America's Choice, 6126
America's Classic Foods, 437
America's Fruit, 13181
America's Heartland Beef®, 10893
America's Heartland Organic Beef, 457
America's Northwest, 2905
America's Premium, 10268
American, 2750, 7655
American Lamb, 2313
American Almond, 438
American Bbq Company, 5141
American Beauty, 648, 6126, 8542
American Beauty™, 10777
American Body Building, 9510
American Breakfast Blend, 9181, 9182
American Cheesemen, 446
American Chef Larry Forgione's, 485
American Classic Tea, 2437
American Classics, 7446
American Cola®, 8470
American Connoisseur Gourmet, 8666
American Cookie Boy, 11015
American Creamery, 437
American Culinary Gardens, 450
American Dietary, 4063
American Favorite, 13110
American Food, 455
American Fruit Butters, 485
American Fruit Toppings, 485
American Fruits, 13578
American Grana, 1174
American Health & Herbs Ministry, 393
American Health®, 8871
American Heritage, 11308
American Heritage™, 7952
American Licorice Co., 2132
American Micronutrients, 471
American Moir's, 8666
American Mucky Duck, 8666
American Naturals, 393
American Original, 11356
American Pale Ale, 1507, 12153
American Plsener, 11218
American Pride®, 5844
American Queen, 10457
American Salad Dazzlers, 485
American Saucery, 8261
American Savory, 8247
American Seedc, 10106
American Shiitake, 5583
American Special Edition, 8666
American Spoon Foods, 485
American Spoon Fruits, 485
American Stockyard, 9565
American Tradition Reserve, 4353
American Tuna, 487
American Vintage Hard Iced Teas, 8279
American Yeast, 7173
Americana, 492
Americandy, 431
Americus Natural Spring Water, 11672
Amerigift Sweet Tooth Originals, 434
Ameripure, 495
Ameriqueen Brand, 10457
Ameriseng, 10335
Amgrain, 416
Amhurst Kitchens, 2964
Ami, 2313
Amicelli™, 7952
Amick Farms Poultry, 500
Amigo, 947, 4891, 10869
Amigos, 501
Aminoplus, 81
Amir, 6255
Amish, 10080
Amish Country, 13822, 13823
Amish Farm, 5420
Amish Gourmet, 8345
Amish Kitchens, 12467
Amish Valley Farms, 1851
Amma's Kitchen, 6026
Ammonia Guard, 4479
Amooza, 6976
Amooza!, 9789

Amore Bianco, 7111
Amorec, 9748
Amoretti, 507
Amoroso's Hearth Baked, 508
Amoy®, 237, 238
Amp Energy Organic®, 9945
Amphisol®, 3320
Amphora, 509
Ampliflave, 9252
Amport Foods, 462
Amrita, 514
Amwell Valley Vineyard, 518
Amy & Brian, 519
Amy's, 498
Amylu, 523
Amys Kitchen, 522
Ana's, 524
Anabol Naturals, 526
AnAi To-Go, 9541
Ananda Hemp, 528
Ancel, 8370
Anchor, 13441
Anchor Porter, 531
Anchor Small, 531
Anchor Steam, 531
Anchor®, 4552, 8055
Anchorage Brewing Co., 10666
Ancient Age, 11263
Ancient Harvest, 534
Ancient Harvest Quinoa, 10467
Ancient Healing Formulas, 14011
Ancient Nutrition, 535
Ancient Secrets, 7562
And Many More, 648, 5489, 12551
And More, 2010, 4353, 10565, 10603
Andechs, 1702
Andersen'sc Soup, 187
Anderson Dairy, 545
Andes Chocolate Mint Chip Cookies, 9399
Andes®, 12880
Andre Prost, Inc., 2132
Andre®, 3834
Andrew & Everettc, 9748
Andrew's Long Island Iced Tea, 7655
Andrews, 557, 9728
Andrulis Farmers Cheese, 8248
Andy Boy, 3301
Andy Capp's®, 2939, 2940
Andy Roo's, 2019
Andy's Cajun Fish Breading, 560
Andy's Golden Fish Batter, 560
Andy's Hot 'n' Spicy Breading, 560
Andy's Mild Chicken Breading, 560
Andy's Red Fish Breading, 560
Andy's Seasoned Salt, 560
Andy's Shrimp Tempura Batter, 560
Andy's Vegetable Breading, 560
Andy's Yellow Fish Breading, 560
Anejo, 914
Angel, 2042
Angel Food, 6912
Angela, 10873
Angelic Bakehouse, 563, 12467
Angelo & Franco, 565
Angels Creek, 6290
Angie's Boomchickapop®, 2939, 2940
Angostura, 13938
Angostura®, 8415
Angry Orchard, 569
Angry Orchard®, 1592
Angy's, 570
Animal Crackers, 2903, 7940
Animal Friends®, 13097
Animal Pak, 572
Anis Paloma, 3545
Anisi, 5964
Anita's, 573, 10453
Anke Kruse Organics, 5089
Anna Maria, 13266
Anna's, 6255
Anna's Honey, 11390
Anne Taintor, 10229
Anne's Chicken Base, 5634
Anne's Country Gourmet, 11402
Anne's Dumpling Squares, 5634
Anne's Dumpling Strips, 5634
Anne's Flat Dumplings, 5634
Anne's Old Fashioned, 5634
Anne's Pot Pie Squares, 5634
Annie Chun's, 1953
Annie Pie's, 1233
Annie's, 5936, 11645

Brand Name Index

Annie's Lane, 12937
Annie's Macaroni & Cheese, 591
Annie's Naturals, 592
Annie's Naturals Magic Sauces, 592
Annie's Naturals Salad Dressings, 592
Annie's Organic Foods, 591
Annie's Supreme, 2964
Annie's®, 4947
Anniversary Bock, 1702
Ansac Cognac, 5720
Answer, 2666
Antelope Valley, 593
Anthony's, 465
Anthony-Thomas Chocolates, 596
Anti Oxidant Edge, 1532
Antico, 56
Antique Crown Foods, 12546
Antler Hill, 1358
Antoine's, 46
Antonella, 4028
Antoni Ravioli, 598
Antonia, 7069
Antonio, 2012
Anysweetplus™, 4837
Anytime, 7150
Anytime Candy, 13845
Ao Vodka, 1120
Apache, 10815
Apatinsko, 8459
Apco, 615
Aperi-Coeur, 10039
Aperiquiche, 10039
Aperoi, 2114
Aperossimo, 5405
Apg, 741
Aphroteasiac Chai, 7989
Api®, 7952
Apiterra, 605
Aplets, 7410
Aplphacel™, 11794
Apollinaris, 2815
Apollo, 6986
Apollo®, 750
Apostle Islands Organic Coffee, 9181
Apothic®, 3834
Appeteasers, 183
Apple & Eve, 56, 608
Apple Blossom, 10478
Apple Brand Juices, 11266
Apple Cinnamon Pecan Cake, 2881
Apple Delight, 5362
Apple Jack Cheese, 12892
Apple Pears, 6880
Apple Ridge, 6415
Apple Royal, 5362
Apple Sidra, 3045
Apple Snax, 7282
Apple Strudel Coffee Beans, 7596
Apple Time, 6923
Apple Valley Inn, 10981
Appleblossom, 9833
Applecreek Orchards, 612
Appledore, 2981
Applegate Farms, 614
Applegate®, 6000
Applerazzi, 3311
Appletiser, 2815
Appleton, 615
Applewood Winery, 618
Apres, 8838
Apricot Ale, 2911
Apricot Pecan Cake, 2881
Aprikat, 339
Apro™, 4119
Aqua Best, 3545
Aqua Blox®, 154
Aqua Clara, 620
Aqua Star, 10603
Aquabona, 2815
Aquacuisine, 622
Aquafina®, 9945
Aquafruit, 8163
Aqualon, 1692
Aqualon Benecel, 1692
Aqualon Klucel, 1692
Aquamax™, 3775
Aquarian®, 7952
Aquarious, 9155
Aquarius, 2815
Aquavits, 3165
Aquila D'Ora, 7428
Aquoral®, 8389

Ara Real, 100
Arapahoe, 5304
Arbor Crest, 627
Arbor Hill Wine, 628
Arbuckle, 633
Arbutus Flour, 6917
Arcadia, 635
Archie Moore's, 640
Archway, 11770
Arco, 101
Arcor, 13610
Arcor Premium Hard Filled Candies, 643
Arcor Value Line Hard Candies, 643
Arctic Blast, 6338
Arctic Pride, 10682
Arctica Gardens, 2260
Ardbeg, 8452
Ardmore, 650
Ardmore Farms®, 3083
Ardmore®, 1120
Argiano®, 3834
Argo Corn Starch, 73
Argus Cidery, 10666
Argyle Brut, 659
Aria, 3540
Ariel, 663, 12721
Ariel Blanc, 663
Ariel Brut Cuve, 663
Ariel Cabernet, 663
Ariel Chardonnay, 663
Ariel Merlot, 663
Ariel Rouge, 663
Ariel White Zinfandel, 663
Arista, 666
Aristo Snacks, 8269
Arizona, 670, 4566
Arizona Iced Tea, 4342
Arizona Ranch Fresh, 5837
Arizona Vineyards, 677
Arjuan Berry Farm, 5036
Arm & Hammer, 2666
Armanino, 680
Armeno, 683
Armida, 13811
Armistead Citrus Products, 684
Armon, 346
Armour, 11733
Armour Star®, 2939, 2940
Armstrong®, 11211
Arnite®, 3320
Arnitel®, 3320
Arnold Palmer, 388
Arnold Palmer Spiked Half & Half, 8460
Arnold's Meats, 690
Arnold®, 1359
Arnorld, 892
Arns, 691
Aro-Smoke, 10600
Arol, 833
Arom®, 8899
Aroma, 7107
Aroma Cuisiner's Choice, 692
Aroma Mi Amore, 56
Aroma Southern Maison, 692
Aroma Turkish, 692
Aroma Valley, 13551
Aroma Vera, 695
Aroma-Life, 696
Aromahop, 6554
Aromi D'Italia, 700
Arox, 833
Arra, 5036
Arracado, 5036
Arrgh! Pale Ale, 7554
Arriba, 10701
Arrid, 2666
Arrogant Bastard Ale, 12129
Arrow, 703, 7655
Arrowhead Mills, 5505
Arrowood, 706
Arroyo Grande, 12513
Art Coco, 707
Art Fidos Cookies, 707
Art Topo, 707
Art's Mexican Products, 708
Art's Tamales, 709
Arte Nova, 56
Artesano, 7908
Artezin, 5820
Artho Life, 4127
Arthrimin Gs™, 6449
Artisan, 13595

Artisan Bistro®, 10976
Artisan Blends®, 11228
Artisan Craft, 13402
Artisan Crafted Series, 11902
Artisan Hearth®, 9736
Artisan Kettle, 715
Artisana, 10249
Artuso, 718
Aruero, 3857
Aryzta, 9590
Arz, 6719
Asahi, 5427
Asante, 8784
Asbach Brandy, 3570
Asbach Uralt, 9035
Ascend, 5139
Ashby's, 11864
Ashby's Iced Teas, 2848
Ashby's Teas of London, 2848
Asher, 431
Asher's, 13610
Ashland, 728, 729, 1692
Ashoka, 6185
Ashwagandha, 11061
Asi Yaupon Tea, 13994
Asiago, 13320
Asian Gourmet®, 1484
Asian Pride, 12334
Asian Star, 13666
Ask Foods, 103
Asp, 4769
Aspen Pure, 8955
Aspen Ridge®, 6391
Aspi-Cor, 5683
Associates, 3765
Assumption Wines, 10789
Astazanthin, 5682
Astica, 4677
Astika, 8459
Astor, 13864
Astra, 2089
Astro, 745
Astro Pops, 11885
Astro®, 9789
@Ease®, 12885
Athena, 10303
Athena Test, 13120
Athena®, 3220, 3319
Athenian, 5341
Athenos, 2667
Athens, 749, 6986
Athens®, 750
Atkins, 753, 754
Atkins Elegant Desserts, 847
Atkinson's, 757
Atlanta Bread, 758
Atlanta Burning, 759
Atlantic, 773
Atlantic Blueberry, 764
Atlantic Capes, 765
Atlantic Coast, 10974
Atlantic Meat, 770
Atlantic Queen, 7657
Atlantic Seasonings, 778
Atlas, 13498
Atlas Peak, 781
Atomic Fireball, 1417, 2132, 4345
Atripla®, 1721
Attiki, 6986
Attnetion Span, 5883
Atwater, 785, 786
Atwater Dried Fruits, 786
Au Printemps Gourmet, 789
Au Quotidien, 56
Au'some, 2132
Aubrey's Jerky, 11746
Auchentoshan, 1120
Audisio & Lori, 6255
Auer, 846
Augsberger, 9664
August's Fried, 794
Aunt Aggie De's Pralines, 799
Aunt Angies, 9787
Aunt Bertie's, 2250
Aunt Erma's Frugal Foods, 11852
Aunt Flo's Country Fudge, 11051
Aunt Gussie's Cookies & Crackers, 801
Aunt Hattie's, 5917
Aunt Hattie's Quality Breads, 5917
Aunt Jayne's, 890
Aunt Jemima, 811
Aunt Jemima®, 2939, 2940, 9945

Aunt Kitty's, 805, 5555
Aunt Lizzie's, 806
Aunt Millie's, 807
Aunt Nellie's, 11434
Aunt Patty's, 5073
Aunt Penny's, 12590
Aunt Sally's Creamy Pralines, 808
Aunt Sally's Gourmet, 808
Aunt Sue's®, 11669
Aunt Zelda's, 4854
Auntie Annie's, 6338
Auntie Liu's, 10457
Aura, 9964
Aura Cacia, 4752
Auribella, 1174
Aurora Angus Beef, 813
Aussie, 4891, 12721
Aussie Sauce, 4891
Austex Products, 805
Austin, 6766
Austin Blues Bbq®, 6000
Austin Company, 10210
Austinuts, 819
Austrian Crown, 13401
Authentic Latino Flavor®, 12996
Authentico®, 1200
Author's Choice, 1610
Autin's, 823
Autocrat, 4407
Autumn Ale, 1687
Autumn Fest, 3746
Autumn Wildflower, 10478
Avagel, 833
Avalanche, 621
Avalanche Ale, 1687
Avallo, 10161
Avalon, 650
Avalon Organic Coffee, 13381
Avalon Organics, 5505
Avanti, 12350
Avapol, 833
Avar-E®, 8389
Avar®, 8389
Avatar, 833
Avatech, 833
Avenacare™ Oat Beta Glucan, 12561
Aventura Gourmet, 9933
Avera Sport, 357
Avery, 166, 838
Aviator Ale Micro Brew Mustards, 1034
Avila, 2719, 7133
Avionc, 9964
Avitae, 840
Avitae Xr, 840
Aviva, 2096
Avo, 488
Avo-King, 841
Avolov, 842
Avon, 2260
Avoset, 10714
Avox, 833
Avri Companies, 845
Awake, 9167, 12945
Awaken Foods, 12396
Award Auer/Blaschke, 846
Award Crunchy Dunkers, 846
Awesome, 6882
Awesome Orange, 5362
Awestruck Ciders, 5286
Awrey's Maestro, 847
Axler's, 10526
Ayurveda, 5679
Az-One, 5682
Azactam®, 1721
Azalea, 4969
Azar®, 11504
Azo, 6107
Aztec Harvest, 12663
Azteca, 7655
Azteca De Oro, 9964
Azteca Trading Co., 9863
Azteca®, 855
Azumaya, 13473

B

B 3 R, 1647
B C Natural, 1647
B&B, 1925
B&B/Benedictine, 914
B&G Foods, Inc.®, 11504

Brand Name Index

B&G®, 864
B&K Coffee, 874
B&K Manufacturing, 1903
B&M Baked Beans, 1867
B&M®, 864
B'Lure, 13779
B-12 Dots™, 13097
B-17, 10534
B. King, 6858
B. Nektar Meadery, 10666
B.Bob's Foods, 7073
B2b, 2060
B5000, 1735
Ba-Tampte, 1079
Baba Foods, 907
Baba Ghannouj, 128
Babara's Vanilla, 13620
Babe, 571
Babe Farms, 910
Babe's, 911
Babu's Pocket Sandwiches, 3465
Baby Cakes, 2226
Baby Dino Eggs, 6851
Baby Ruth, 2132
Baby's Breakfast Roast, 912
Baby's Private Buzz, 912
Baby's Wrelker's Roa, 912
Baby-D™, 6449
Babycakes®, 7521
Bac'n Puffs, 9408
Bacala Rico, 2122
Bacardi Breezers, 914
Bacardi Limon, 914
Bacardi Rum, 914
Bacardi Spice, 914
Bachelor's Brew, 5217
Bachman, 916, 12631, 13129
Bacigalupi Chardonnay, 10963
Back Country Emu Products, 3612
Back To Basics, 918
Back To Nature, 864, 919
Backer's, 921
Backsettler Blend, 9182
Backus Vineyard, 6603
Bacon 1®, 6000
Bad Frog Amber Lager, 925
Bad Frog Bad Light, 925
Bad Frog Micro Malt, 925
Bad Seed, 926
Badger, 928
Badger Blend, 9182
Badia Canned Vegetables, 930
Badia Hot Sauces, 930
Badia Nuts & Seeds, 930
Badia Seasoning Blends, 930
Badia Spices, 930
Badia Teas, 930
Bafos, 1089
Bagel Bites, 6976
Bagel By Bell, 936
Bagel King, 5590
Bagels, 3353
Baggywrinkle, 2691
Bahama, 5539
Bahama BlastÖ, 10714
Bahama Mama®, 5929
Bahl Baby, 2255
Bahlsen, 4592
Bai®, 3725, 6818
Baier's, 940
Bailey's, 2691
Bailey's Irish Cream, 4986
Baileys™, 11211
Baily, 944
Baja Cafe®, 10681
Bajoz, 3545
Bak-Klene®, 9648
Baka-Snack®, 8804
Bakalars, 948
Bake Crafters, 950
Bake Lite All Soy, 2796
Bake Lite Soy/Cotton, 2796
Bake Packers, 194
Bake-Rite H & R, 2389
Bake-Soft, 463
Bakeable, 3353
Baked Classics, 2728
Baked Fries Sharing Packs, 11754
Baked Potato Thins, 13815
Bakemark, 954
Baken Joy, 13117
Baken-Ets, 4741

Bakeology, 958
Bakeqwik, 955
Baker, 962, 5105, 11788
Baker Boy, 959
Baker Boys Baked Goods, 960
Baker Supreme, 965
Baker's, 5105, 6976
Baker's Best, 166
Baker's Blend, 9182
Baker's Cremes, 12795
Baker's Gold, 4025
Baker's Joy®, 6792
Baker's Joys®, 864
Baker's Label, 7683
Baker's Rib Inc, 970
Baker's®, 1120
Bakerhaus Veit, 971
Bakers Beauties, 965
Bakers®, 8945
Bakery Feeds, 3390
Bakerycorp, 978
Bakesense, 955
Bakesmart®, 190
Bakon Seasonings, 981
Bakon Yeast, 981
Balagna Winery, 983
Balance, 984
Balance®, 8871
Balanced Breaks®, 11228
Balanced Coffee, 12601
Balanced Cuisine, 7954
Balboa Bay, 12866
Balderson, 10834
Balderson®, 9789
Baldinger, 987
Baldwin, 989, 2430
Bali's Best, 4804
Balisto®, 7952
Ball Park, 992
Ball Park®, 1359, 13109
Ballantine, 993
Ballantine Ale, 9137
Ballantine's, 5892, 9964
Ballantine's Finest, 3024
Ballard Bitter, 10629
Ballas, 995
Ballatore®, 3834
Balsamic and Herb Dipping Oil, 869
Balsamic Vinegar of Modena, 869
Balthazar's Blend, 2860
Baltimore Tea, 3893
Balut Sa Puti, 8203
Balvenie, 13811
Bama, 1935
Bama Fruit Spreads, 13635
Bambu Juices, 10568
Ban, 1692
Banana Gold, 12527
Banana Moon Snack Line, 10417
Bananitas, 100
Bandana, 10782
Bandersnatch Milk Stout, 2653
Banditos Salsas, 11873
Banfield®, 7952
Bankers Club, 7146
Banquet, 6395
Banquet Better Foods, 7166
Banquet Butter, 7166
Banquet Cheese, 7166
Banquet®, 2939, 2940
Bansi, 3465
Banza, 1012
Bar Harbor Ginger Ale, 1015
Bar Harbor Peach Ale, 1015
Bar S, 5917, 8898
Bar-B-Q Fiesta, 3695
Bar-B-Q Treat, 3695
Bar-Pak, 7363
Bar-Snitz, 1064
Baraclude®, 1721
Barbara's, 13621
Barbara's Baked Original, 13620
Barbara's Baked White Cheddar, 13620
Barbara's Bakery, 1020
Barbara's Chocolate Chip, 13620
Barbara's Cinnamon, 13620
Barbara's Cinnamon Crunch, 13620
Barbara's Grainshop, 13620
Barbara's Jalapeno, 13620
Barbara's Oatmeal, 13620
Barbara's Original, 13620
Barbara's Peanut Butter, 13620

Barbara's Vanilla Blast, 13620
Barbara's Weetabix, 13620
Barbary Coast Barley, 9688
Barbecue Magic, 7766
Barber Foods, 1022
Barber Foods®, 184, 13109
Barber's, 3442
Barbera, 7238, 9889
Barbera Frantioia, 11864
Barbours, 4820
Barbousville Vineyards, 1026
Barcardi, 913
Barcelona, 1027
Barclay's, 3024
Bare, 1029
Bare Nature, 13427
Bare®, 9945
Barefoot Bubbly®, 3834
Barefoot®, 3834
Barely Bread, 1031
Barengo®, 8415
Bargetto, 1033
Bari, 11336
Bari®, 11211
Barilla Pasta, 1037
Barilla Pronto™, 1037
Barilla Proteinplus™, 1037
Barista Almondmilk, 8957
Barista Bros®, 6818
Barista Prima, 6819
Barista Prima Coffeehouse®, 6818
Baristatude, 2009
Baristella, 507
Barkan Winery, 10952
Barkeater Chocolates, 1038
Barkthins, 10754
Barley Wine Ale, 1401
Barmen, 8459
Barmen™, 8460
Barnacles Snack Mix, 1470
Barnes, 1045
Barney Flats Oatmeal Stout, 549
Barney's Town & Country, 4244
Barnum's Animals Crackers, 8729
Barnwood, 7133
Baron, 1050
Baron De Ley, 4677
Baron Edmond De Rothschild, 10952
Baron's, 7655
Baronet Coffees, 1792
Barq's, 2811, 6338
Barquette, 10039
Barrel Head, 252
Barrel O'Fun, 1052
Barrie House, 1053
Barrington Estate, 1054
Barrington Gold, 1054
Barrister, 7146
Barrows, 1055
Barry Callebaut, 1056
Bart's Homemade, 11763
Bartenders Pride, 13686
Bartenura Wines, 10952
Bartles & Jaymes®, 3834
Bartlett, 2737
Bartlett Dairy, 1060
Barton, 11264
Bartons, 1638
Barzi, 6210
Barzula, 12896
Basement Bitters, 13082
Basf, 1692
Basic American Foods, 1069
Basic American Frozen Foods, 4222
Basic Country Goodness, 9699
Basic Promotions, 2132
Basic Research, 4150
Basic Value, 13241
Basics Plus, 7423
Basil Hayden's®, 1120
Basilic Pistou, 4148
Basitan's, 4839
Baskin Robbins, 1075
Baskin-Robbins®, 3803
Bass, 7123
Bass Ale, 5427
Bassett's, 1078
Basso, 5034
Basswood, 10478
Baste & Glaze, 11077
Batchpak™, 342
Batiste Dry Shampoo, 2666

Batter Bind™S, 8804
Batter Bites®, 6374
Batter Blends, 9016
Batter-Moist, 4039
Battistoni, 1084
Battle Creek, 2909
Bau Maniere, 5405
Bauducco, 1085
Bauza, 5036
Bavarian Brand Sausage, 2162
Baxter®, 11211
Baxters Old Nauvoo, 1093
Bay Beauty, 9344
Bay Shore, 1101, 5608, 13992
Bay State Chowda, 1593
Bay Valley Foods, 12943
Bay Valley™, 1103
Bayard's, 4645
Bayhawk Ipa, 1097
Bayhawk Stout, 1097
Bayonne Ham, 11894
Bayou Land Seafood, 1110
Bayou Segnette, 7583
Bayview Farms, 12323
Baywood Cellars, 1112
Bazelet Ha Golan Winery, 10952
Bazzini, 1114
Bbq Shack, 888
Bbq Unribs, 9196
Bbq'n Fools, 889
Bbs Bodacious, 890
Be Happy 'n Healthy Snacks, 5562
Bea's Best, 2708
Beach, 4668
Beach Blonde, 1097
Beacon Drive-In Iced Tea, 1118
Beacon Street Cafe™, 11317
Beamons, 9284
Bean Brothers, 3177
Bean Coffee, 881
Bean Forge, 1123
Bean Heads, 11320
Beanblossom Hard Cider, 9452
Beanfields, 1124
Beanos's, 2958
Bear Claw, 6796
Bear Country Bavarian, 11846
Bear Creek Brand, 1127
Bear Creek Country Kitchens, 1126, 11536
Bear Creek®, 864
Bear Flag, 13320
Bear Flag®, 3834
Bear Fruit Bar, 8598
Bear Meadow Farm, 1129
Bear Mountain, 10372
Bear River, 1677
Bearitos, 1133, 5505, 13672
Beartooth Kitchens, 6861
Beatrice®, 9789
Beau's All-Natural Brewing, 10666
Beaulieu Vineyard, 12937
Beaver, 1147
Beaver Falls, 5643
Beaver Pop, 7279
Bebeto, 6810
Because Cookie Dough, 1142
Becel, 13167, 13168
Bech, 6381
Beck Cafe, 1143
Beck Flavors, 1143
Beck's, 71, 689, 7123
Beck's Dark, 689
Beck's For Oktoberfest, 689
Beckman's, 1147
Beckmann, 12017
Beckmann's, 1148
Becks Ice Cream, 1144
Beddy By, 1600
Bedell Cellars, 1152
Bee & You, 11036
Bee Gee, 2719
Bee My Honey, 6821
Bee Panacea, 13440
Bee Pollen, 1164
Bee Propolis, 1914
Bee Raw, 1159
Bee Sting, 5304
Bee Supreme, 3411
Bee Sweet, 10323
Beebad, 10454
Beech-Nut, 1161
Beech-Nut Organic, 1161

Brand Name Index

Beechies, 10724
Beef International, 4244
Beef Master, 3262
Beef Not, 3633
Beefeater, 5892
Beefeater Dry, 3024
Beefeaterc, 9964
Beefmate, 12550
Beefsteak®, 1359
Beefsteakc, 1359
Beehive, 1720, 13643
Beehive Botanicals, 1164
Beer Nutsc, 1168
Beer'n Batter, 12520
Beesting, 5516
Beetnik, 1169
Beetroot Delights, 1170
Beik's Esb, 549
Beirmeister, 7428
Beit Hashita, 2096
Bekal, 4877
Bekaplus®, 898
Bel Normande - Spritzers, 4148
Belcolade, 1175
Belcover, 9802
Belcreme De Lys, 12937
Belgian Ale, 1401
Belgioioso, 1174
Bell & Evans the Excellent Chicken, 1178
Bell 'orto, 4111
Bell Bialy, 936
Bell Cellars, 10416
Bell Mini Bagel, 936
Bell' Agio, 1006
Bell's Scotch, 3570
Bella, 10013
Bella Crema, 2848, 7511
Bella Famiglia®, 1484
Bella Festa, 4153
Bella Frutta, 9636
Bella Italia, 223
Bella Mercato, 4005
Bella Ravioli, 1189
Bella Rosa, 4111
Bella Sera®, 3834
Bella Sun Luci, 1190
Bella Union, 4258
Bella Vista, 1191
Bellarico's, 541
Bellatoria, 1248
Belle + Bella, 8878
Belle Gueule, 7380
Belle Mead, 5566
Belle of Piru, 4387
Belle River, 1195
Belleisle, 13908
Bellentani, 11894
Bellerose, 1197
Belleweather, 4362
Bellissimo, 11777
Bellocq, 1201
Bellows, 7655
Bellringer, 4658
Bellwether, 1205
Belmo, 11664
Belmont Springs, 10303
Belmont Springs®, 3220, 3319
Belt Oranges, 13906
Belvedere, 3024, 8452
Belvita, 8474, 8729
Belvoir Fruit Farms, 1661
Ben & Jerry, 5137
Ben & Jerry's, 1212, 13169
Ben & Jerry's Frozen Smoothies, 1212
Ben & Jerry's Ice Cream, 1212
Ben Shaws, 10637
Ben's®, 2121
Benbow's, 1217
Bencheley, 4422
Benchmark, 11263
Benco Peak, 12972
Beneflex, 7331
Beneful®, 8945
Benevita, 5819
Beni Di Batasiolo, 1543
Benihana, 14020
Benley's Irish Creme, 5596
Bennett's, 1221
Bennetts, 11458
Bennetts®, 1103
Bensdorp, 1056
Bensons, 10041

Bent Arm Ale®, 6374
Bent's, 4832
Bentley's, 11263
Benzel's Brand, 1224
Ber Boreale, 7379
Berentzen, 13811
Bergenbier, 8459
Bergeron, 6395
Berghoff Family, 1231
Beringer Vineyards, 12937
Berk-Cap, 1238
Berkeley Farms, 3442
Berkley & Jensen, 6126
Berks, 1235
Berkshire Ale, 1237
Berkshire Bark, 1236
Berkshire Ice Cream, 11830
Berkwood Farms, 4321
Bermuda Dunes, 3565
Bernadette's Biscotti, 1241
Bernadette's Biscotti Soave, 1241
Bernadette's Cookies, 1241
Bernard, 1244
Bernard Fine Foods, 3441
Bernard Pradel Cabernet, 5189
Bernardi®, 237, 238
Bernardo, 1246
Bernardus, 1247
Berne Baby Swiss, 12443
Berne Swiss Lace, 12443
Bernheim Original Wheat Whiskey, 5720
Berni, 10565
Bernstein's®, 2939, 2940
Berri Pro, 1253
Berry Cool, 7732
Berry Good, 8919
Berry Weiss, 7330
Berry White, 6590
Berry-Max, 9997
Berrylicious, 6222
Bert Grant's, 13982
Bertha's, 4362
Berthelet, 10331
Bertman Raddish Sauce, 6532
Bertoli®, 2939, 2940
Bertolli, 13168
Bes Tex, 11888
Bessie, 1391
Best Bar Ever, 4150
Best Brown Ale, 10404
Best Choice, 4891, 9621
Best Ever Bar®, 8871
Best Foods, 1267
Best Maid, 1270
Best O' the Wheat, 10846
Best of Health, 416
Best of Luck, 6082
Best of Luck Horseshoe Chocolates, 6082
Best Way, 3811, 13184
Besure, 1659, 13536
Beta Stab, 6554
Beta-Care, 1244
Beth's, 1275
Beth's Baking Basics, 1275
Bethune, 7006
Betsy's Best, 1277
Bette's Oceanview Diner, 1280
Better, 7750
Better Bakery™, 184
Better Buy, 2419
Better Made, 1286
Better Oats, 10213
Better Stevia®, 8725
Better Than, 1288
Better Than Milkc, 9748
Better Way, 13619
Better'n Eggs, 3211
Betty, 6590
Betty Ann, 8510
Betty Crocker, 11599
Betty Crocker®, 4947
Betty Lou's, 1291
Betty Twist & Match Chocolate Candy, 10898
Between Friends Promotional Candy, 4884
Beverly, 4539
Beverly Hills, 6310
Beverly International, 1297
Bevnet, 10311
Beyond Better, 1620
Beyond Meat, 1299
Beyond Vodka, 4658

Bfp, 463
Bhu Fit, 1302
Bi-Lo, 11838
Bialy, 6970
Bianchi Vineyards, 1306
Biazzo Brand, 1308
Bib Ulmer Spatz, 954
Bibigo, 1953
Bick's, 6380
Bickel, 10693
Bickel's, 1309, 5555
Bickford, 1312
Bickle Snacks, 1310
Biena Chickpea Snacks, 1317
Biermann, 8677
Biery, 1320
Bifido Factor, 8816
Bifido Nate, 8816
Big Az®, 184, 13109
Big B, 1324
Big Babol, 9956
Big Baby, 10496
Big Banana, 7702
Big Bear, 9664
Big Beer Series, 11743
Big Ben, 2311
Big Blue, 54
Big Blue, 1339
Big Bol, 10496
Big Boy, 604
Big Bruce's Gunpowder Chili, 8291
Big Check, 9212
Big Chief, 1327, 2019, 8251
Big Chunks Salsa, 4587
Big City Reds, 457, 1328
Big City Reds®, 10893
Big Daddy's, 11316
Big Daddy's™, 11317
Big Dipa, 2763
Big Dipper, 1329
Big Fork, 4321
Big Horn Premium, 2653
Big House, 11263
Big House Ale, 13428
Big Hunkc, 583
Big Island Candies, 1333
Big John, 10620
Big League Chew, 2132
Big M, 8668
Big Nasty, 10547
Big Onion, 300
Big Papa, 6353
Big Peach ®, 1339
Big Pineapple ®, 1339
Big Ram, 5409
Big Red, 5294, 13689
Big Red Vanilla Float ®, 1339
Big Red®, 3725, 6818, 7952, 13960
Big Shot, 8784
Big Sky Ipa, 1344
Big Smiley, 10898
Big Tea, 5612
Big Time, 2172
Big Top Animal Cookies, 9399
Big V, 6354
Big Value, 9226
Big Y, 570
Big Yummy, 2947
Bigelow, 1350, 7124, 8090
Bigger Better, 5590
Bigs®, 2939, 2940
Biladi, 3615
Biladi Tohina, 3615
Bilberry Extract, 11268
Bill Bailey's, 11988
Bill Mack's, 7729
Bill's, 4158
Billingsgate, 1355
Billy Bee, 8061
Billy Bock, 1837
Bilopage, 2426
Biltmore, 1358, 13454
Bimbo®, 1359
Bin 36, 5499
Bin Chxn, 1951
Bindi, 1360
Bingham Hill Cheeses, 10834
Binosto®, 8389
Binyamina, 10952
Binyamina Winery, 10952
Bio K, 1368
Bio-Familia, 6279

Bio-Foods, 1366
Bio-Nate, 8816
Bio-Tech Pharmacal, 1370
Bioallers, 13642
Bioallers®, 9237
Bioastin, 9244
Bioastin Natural Astaxanthin, 3281
Biobest, 745
Biochem, 3080
Bioflora, 13480
Biomega, 783
Bionate®, 3320
Bionova, 5475
Bionutrient, 641
Biopur, 10366
Biospan®, 3320
Biotta Juices, 10568
Biovelop, 1692
Birch Bark, 2108
Birch Logs, 2108
Birchwood Foods, 6790
Bird Brine, 2019
Bird-In-Hand, 1385
Birdie Pak, 1386
Birds Eye C&W, 2939, 2940
Birds Eye Voila, 2939, 2940
Birds Eye®, 1389, 2939, 2940
Birdseye, 1388
Biringer's Farm Fresh, 11390
Bis Train, 2833
Bisca, 6279, 6774
Biscotti Di Lasca, 8927
Biscotti Di Roma, 846
Biscotti Di Suzy™, 1395
Biscotti Toscani, 7111
Bison, 7443
Bison®, 13218
Bisquick®, 4947
Bissett's, 1403
Bisto, 2115
Bistro, 11214
Bistro 36, 6790
Bistro Faire, 3232
Bistro Favorites, 7197
Bistro Soups and Chili®, 13400
Bisurkey, 7443
Bit-O-Honey, 9877
Bitburger, 1208
Bitchin', 12178
Bitchin' Sauce, 1406
Bite Fuel, 1407
Bite-Size Bakery, 1408
Bites, 2580
Bits O' Butter, 12377
Bits'n'pops, 525
Bittermyx®, 11436
Bitterroot Extra Special Bitter, 4466
Bittner's, 7876
Bitzels, 7424
Bixby Bar, 1414
Bj Beer, 897
Black, 5323
Black & Gold, 1977
Black & Tan, 1208
Black & White, 3570
Black and Tan, 11218
Black Bear Ale, 13711
Black Butte, 3533
Black Canyon® Angus, 8783
Black Canyon® Premium Reserve, 8783
Black Cat, 7006
Black Cherry Royal, 5362
Black Cod (Sablefish, 10949
Black Cow, 756
Black Creek®, 11209, 11211
Black Diamond Caviar, 13567
Black Diamond®, 9789
Black Duck, 7655
Black Eagle ®, 13120
Black Forest, 11218, 13110
Black Forest Organic, 1417, 4345
Black Hawk, 8153
Black Hook, 10629
Black Horse, 8459
Black Ice, 8459
Black Jacks, 13997
Black Jewell®, 1420
Black Knight, 13643
Black Label Bacon®, 6000
Black Licorice Vines, 469
Black Mesa, 1422
Black Prince, 1423

Brand Name Index

Black Ranch Gourmet Grains, 1424
Black Roberts, 4515
Black Silk, 4543
Black Swamp, 5402
Black Tea Chai, 11237
Black Tie, 2108
Black Widow, 12814
Black Wolf Blend, 5794
Blackbird Porter, 4466
Blackburn's, 12469
Blackened Redfish Magic, 7766
Blackened Steak Magic, 7766
Blackening Spice, 2499
Blackhawk Stout, 8153
Blackheart Premium Spiced Rum, 5720
Blackjack Pasture Cabernet, 4862
Blackjack Porter, 7310
Blackout Stout, 5314
Blair's, 1431
Blake's®, 2939, 2940
Blanc De Noirs, 3661
Blanc Du Bois, 8513
Blanca, 8335
Blanchard & Blanchard, 6279
Bland Farms, 5132
Blanks ®, 13120
Blanton's, 1438
Blantons, 11263
Blaser's, 1440, 4028
Blasting Powder, 2947
Blazing Star, 180
Blazzin, 1442
Blend Pak, 1443
Blended Breaders, 9016
Blends With Benefits, 15
Blendsure™, 4837
Blenheim, 1447
Blenjavas, 5819
Blessing's Mustard, 4587
Bletsoe's Cheese, 1449
Bleu Rock Vineyard Wines, 9334
Bliss Bar, 5221
Blissfully Better, 1453
Blitz Power Mints, 11314
Blonde Ale, 13288
Blood Building Broth, 131
Blood Building Powder, 131
Blood Cleanse, 5682
Blood Red, 3746
Bloody Mary Blend, 13222
Bloody Mary Juice Burst, 5460
Bloom, 1457
Bloombuilder, 4374
Bloomfield Farms, 1443
Bloomington Brewing, 1460
Bloomsbury & Co., 10229
Blossom Hill, 3815, 12937
Blossom Time, 12826
Blossom Water, 1463
Blouin, 10330
Blount, 1464
Blow Hard Mustard, 6054
Blubotol, 13697
Blue Band, 13168
Blue Barn, 726
Blue Bell Dairy, 1465
Blue Bell Ice Cream, 1465
Blue Bonnet®, 2939, 2940
Blue Bottle, 13697
Blue Boy, 2657
Blue Buck, 7733
Blue Buffalo®, 4947
Blue Bunny®, 13645
Blue Chip Baker, 1506
Blue Chip Group, 1506
Blue Crab Bay, 1470
Blue Curacao, 3545
Blue Diamond, 1471, 12201
Blue Diamond Almonds, 1471
Blue Diamond Hazelnut, 1471
Blue Diamond Macadamias, 1471
Blue Evolution, 1473
Blue Fin, 11561
Blue Gold, 1474
Blue Goose Minneolas, 13906
Blue Green Organics, 1476
Blue Heron, 8153
Blue Heron Pale Ale, 8153
Blue Hill, 1479
Blue Hill Bay, 151
Blue Jay Orchards, 1481
Blue Light, 7123

Blue Monday®, 10998
Blue Moon, 8459
Blue Moon Tea, 1486
Blue Moon®, 8460
Blue Pearl Incense, 7562
Blue Plate, 11865
Blue Plate Mayonnaise, 10657
Blue Plumb Brandy, 2737
Blue Point Brewing Company, 571
Blue Ribbon, 7163, 8578, 11759
Blue Ribbon Classics®, 13645
Blue Ribbon Hot Sausage, 12463
Blue Ribbon Orchard Choice, 13254
Blue Ribbon Rice®, 10777
Blue Ribbon®, 6391
Blue Ridge Farms, 4244
Blue Ridge Teas, 1496
Blue Runner, 1497
Blue Seal, 2559
Blue Star, 1500, 7123
Blue Star Farms, 9799
Blue Star Mockiko, 6673
Blue Valley, 6702
Blue Willow, 1501
Blueberry Ale, 6283
Blueberry Barbeque Sauce, 9116
Blueberry Blossom, 10478
Blueberry King, 1171
Bluebird, 4662
Bluebird Restaurant, 1507
Bluebonnet, 13190
Bluebonnet Coffee, 13191
Bluefield®, 11378
Bluegrass, 5402
Bluegrass Bourbon™ Sauce, 1654
Bluepearl®, 7952
Blueprint Organic, 5505
Blume Honey Water, 1510
Blumer's Root Beer, 1231
Blythedale, 12493
Bnutty, 1513
Boar's Head, 4652
Boardwalk, 2172
Boat Brand, 11915
Bob Evans Farms®, 8225
Bob Evans®, 1516
Bob's, 1417, 4345
Bob's Big Boy, 6679
Bob's Red Mill, 1519
Bob's Texas Style, 10173
Bobalu Nuts, 1520
Bobby Flay, 10311
Bobo's, 1523
Boboli, 892
Boboli®, 1359
Boca Bons, 1526
Boca®, 1527
Bocconcino, 1896
Bock, 11846
Boddie, 757
Boddingtons Pub Ale, 7123
Bodega De San Antonio Sangria, 7740
Bodin's, 1531
Bodum, 1542
Body Fortress®, 8871
Body Fuel, 10708
Body-Fuel, 7947
Bodyguard™, 6449
Boericke & Tafel, 8896
Bogdon's, 10724
Boggiatto, 1538
Bogland, 1540, 2798
Bogland By the Sea, 1540, 2798
Boglandish, 1540
Bohemian, 1542, 8459
Bohemian Maid, 4654
Boisset Classic, 12672
Boisset Mediterranee, 12672
Boja's, 1545
Boja's Chef's Delight, 1545
Bokobsa Wines, 10952
Bola Pop's, 2947
Bold Beans, 3575
Bold Italiano™, 1654
Bomb Pop®, 13645
Bombal, 13273
Bombay, 56, 913, 914, 2922
Bombay Bites, 6026
Bombay Gold 100, 5467
Bombe Glaze, 5399
Bon & Viv Spiked Seltzer, 571
Bon Ca Ca, 2019

Bon Cuisine, 9165
Bon Matin, 8676
Bon Matin®, 2121
Bon Secour, 1550
Bon Ton, 1310
Bonafide Provisions, 1552
Bonaqua, 2815
Bonbon Barnier, 3381
Bond Ost, 9094
Bone Suckin', 1555
Bone Suckin' Sauce, 4587
Bongiovi Pasta Sauces, 1558
Bonici®, 13109
Bonk Breaker, 1559
Bonnie, 12866
Bonnie Blue, 2235
Bonnie Lee, 13611
Bonnie Maid, 12866
Bonniebrook, 11766
Bonnies, 10900
Bono, 8504
Bonomo, 2132
Bonomo Turkish Taffy®, 13572
Bonterra, 1567
Bonton, 8314
Bonzers, 8228
Bookbinder's, 1569
Boomchickapop, 567
Boone County Supreme, 11547
Boone's Farm®, 3834
Boont Amber, 549
Boord's, 7655
Boordy Vineyards, 1572
Boost®, 8945
Boot Scootin', 7364
Borden, 3862, 6760, 7137
Borden Dairy, 1576
Borden®, 1103
Borden® Cheese, 3335
Border Springs Farm Lamb, 4321
Borges, 12035
Borgianni, 13811
Borgogno, 1006
Born 3, 5138
Born Free, 10529
Bornstein, 1582
Bornt Family Farms, 1583
Borra, 1584
Borsodi, 8459
Bortilly, 56
Bos'n, 12062
Bosco, 1586, 10229, 11339
Bosco's Pizza Co.®, 13109
Bosell, 1759
Boskydel, 1589
Bosque Tea Co, 13381
Boss Baby, 5020
Boston America Corp, 2132
Boston Baked Beans, 1417, 4345
Boston Bakers Exchange, 2683
Boston Chowda Co, 10118
Boston Fruit Slices, 1596
Boston Pride, 12062
Boston Spices, 1598
Boswellin, 11061
Bottle Caps, 2132
Bottle Green, 1605
Botto's Genuine Italian Sausage, 1938
Bou, 1607
Bouchard Aine & Fils, 1543
Bouchard Aine Fils, 12672
Bouchard Family Farm, 1609
Boudin, 553
Boudreaux's, 1610
Boueka, 7344
Boulder Canyon, 1613, 10173, 13129
Boulder Cookie, 1614
Boulder Creek, 1615
Boulder Ice Cream, 1617
Boulder Sausage Products, 1619
Bouma, 1622
Bounce, 7870, 12721
Bountiful Harvest™, 11504
Bounty, 12721
Bounty®, 7952
Bourbon Deluxe®, 1120
Bourbon Excelso, 7107
Bourbon Supreme, 7655
Bourbonil, 12085
Boursin, 1172
Bousquette, 9555

Bove's of Vermont, 1629
Bow Valley, 1630
Bowie River, 4078
Bowl & Roll™, 6685
Bowlby's Bits, 525
Bowman's, 59, 11263
Bowman's Small Batch, 11263
Bowmore, 1120
Bowmore Islay, 12315
Bowness Baker, 1633
Boxer, 1638
Boyajian, 1635
Boyd's Coffee, 1636
Boyds' Kissa Bearhugs, 6291
Boyer, 1638
Bp Gourmet, 903
Bpi, 4150
Bpi®, 1163
Br-Lerie Mont Royal®, 6818
Br-Lerie St. Denis®, 6818
Brach's, 1417, 4345
Brad's Pretzel Dip, 6918
Bragg, 1652
Braggadocio, 8075
Brahm's Wine Country, 628
Brahma, 71
Brain Herbs, 9201
Brain Invigoration Powder, 131
Brain Vita, 5682
Brain Well, 9201
Brainstrong, 6107
Brakebush®, 1654
Bramble Berry Brew, 1139
Brami Beans, 904
Bran Flakes, 10213
Brancaia®, 3834
Brancott Estatec, 9964
Brand Aromatics, 8061
Brander, 1657
Brandt, 1662, 1957, 4244
Brandy, 2343
Brandywine, 5028
Branik, 8459
Braren Pauli, 1664
Brasal Bock, 1666
Brasal Legere, 1666
Brasal Special Amber, 1666
Brass Ladle, 1665
Brassica, 1667
Brassica Teas With Sgs, 1667
Brauhaus Pretzel, 6338
Braumeister, 1231
Braumeister Light, 1231
Braumeister Select Ipb, 5193
Braun, 12721
Brava, 7123, 7157
Bravard, 1672
Bravissimo, 12499
Bravissimo!, 8367
Bravos Tortilla Chips, 13884
Brazi Bites, 1673
Brazil Celebes, 761
Brazil Serra Negra, 9181
Brazos Legends, 1675, 6787
Bread & Biscuits, 4362
Bread & Chocolate, 1677
Bread Alone, 1678
Bread Glaze, 12795
Bread, Rice & Pasta Lovers Diet, 7422
Breadeli, 1524
Breading Magic, 7766
Breads of Venice, 5097, 5098
Break Up, 13845
Breakfast Choice, 9548
Breakstones, 6760
Breaktime, 3384
Breakwater, 1684
Breathsavers, 2132, 5818
Breckenridge Brewery, 571
Breckenridge Farm Sparkling Juices, 8135
Bred-Mate, 6340
Brede Old Fashioned, 11625
Breezy Hills, 7463
Breitenbach, 1688
Brekki, 1689
Bremner, 1690
Bremner Wafers, 1690, 3384
Brenntag, 1692
Brent & Sam's, 5477
Brentwood, 11766
Brer Rabbit®, 864
Breton, 3384

Brand Name Index

Breton Minis, 3384
Brew Buffers, 12795
Brew City, 530
Brew City®, 8055
Brew Dr., 1694
Brew House, 5294
Brew La La Coffee, 12100
Brew La La Tea, 12100
Brew Pub, 1248
Brew-A-Cup: Perfect Potfuls, 2848
Brewer's, 7404
Brewer's Crystals, 6211
Brewers Clarex®, 3320
Brewers Reserves, 12153
Brewmaster Jack, 10666
Brewski Snack, 1690
Brewster Nutrition, 12638
Breyers, 5137, 13167, 13169
Breyers Blasts®, 5165
Breyers®, 5165
Brian, 12525
Brick Premium, 1702
Brickenridge, 8390
Brickfire Bakery®, 11504
Bridalveil Ale, 11448
Bridgetown, 1706
Bridlewood Estate Winery®, 3834
Brie W/Garlic De Luxe, 2409
Briess, 1710
Brifisol®, 898
Brigham's, 1711
Bright Greens, 1712
Bright Harvest, 1713
Bright Leaf, 2245
Brighton Mills, 5466
Brill, 954
Brill's, 5482
Brillasol, 8161
Brimley Stone, 5245
Brimstone Hill, 1716
Briny Deep, 9094
Brisk, 1718
Brisk®, 9945
Brisling Sardines, 651
Bristle Ridge, 1719
Brita, 2766
British Class, 13208
Brittany Acres, 9535
Brittle Duet, 2881
Brittnia, 3336
Briz, 12003
Bro Egcellent, 1735
Bro White Sour, 1735
Broad Run Vineyards, 1726
Broad St. Brown, 8952
Broadleaf, 1730
Broadleaf Cervena, 1730
Broadway Red, 9182
Broccoli Wokly, 7853
Broccosprouts, 1667
Brock, 1732
Brodies, 7995
Broken Bow, 1734
Broken Rock Cellars, 5774
Broker's Gin, 8062
Broker's London Dry Gin, 5981
Broker's Whiskey, 5981
Brolio, 13811
Brolite Ia, 1735
Brooklyn, 1748
Brooklyn Baking Pumpernickel Bread, 1744
Brooklyn Baking Rye Bread, 1744
Brooklyn Bean Roastery, 1745
Brooklyn Born Chocolatec, 13056
Brooklyn Bourbon, 12178
Brooklyn Brine, 1749
Brooklyn Cider House, 1750
Brooklyn Java, 5012
Brooklyn Whatever, 1754
Brooks Street Baking, 11368
Brooks®, 2939, 2940
Brookshire's®, 1758
Brookside, 1759, 5818
Brookside Reserve, 7655
Brosoft, 1735
Brother Bru Bru's, 1762
Brotherhood, 1764
Brothers Ice Cream, 1766
Broths, 2115
Broughton®, 3442
Brouwerij St. Bernardus, 10666
Brouwerij Verhaeghe, 10666

Brown, 11992
Brown & Jenkins Fresh Roasted, 1772
Brown 'n' Serve, 833
Brown Ale, 556, 7310, 7315
Brown Bear, 13441
Brown Bear Ale, 13711
Brown Cow, 12145
Brown Cow Farm, 1774
Brown Cow Farm East, 9885
Brown Flax, 10616
Brown Island Bitter, 13711
Brown King, 11832
Brown Kwik, 1531
Brown Paper Goods®, 11504
Brown's Dairy, 1782
Brown's Dairy®, 3442
Brown's Ware, 1789
Brownberry®, 1359
Brownie Brittle, 1786, 11534
Brownies & Roses, 2903
Browns Best, 6761
Bru-Mix, 13182
Bruce Baking, 1791
Bruce Cost Ginger Ale, 1793
Bruce Foods, 2019
Bruce Tea, 1795
Bruce's® Mixes, 1794
Bruce's® Yams, 1794
Brucepac, 1796
Bruiser, 11320
Brule Valley, 9127
Brunkow Cheese, 1800
Bruno, 1802
Bruschetta, 4005
Brussel Bytes, 11415
Brut Classic, 3661
Brutal Bajan, 4895
Bryan, 6762, 13109
Bryan Products, 805
Bryant Autumn Blush, 1807
Bryant Country White, 1807
Bryant Dixie Blush, 1807
Bryant Festive Red, 1807
Bryant Vineyard, 1807
Bubba's Bagels, 9736
Bubba's Fine Foods, 1810
Bubbaganouj Ipa, 4466
Bubbies Homemade Ice Cream, 1812
Bubbilicious, 9995
Bubbilicious Bubble Gum, 1980
Bubble Candy, 7638
Bubble Chocolate, 10229
Bubble Gum, 12211
Bubble King, 9320
Bubble Yum, 5818
Bubblecraft, 9452
Bubblegum, 1591
Bubblegum Buddies, 6780
Bubbles, 1813
Bubblicious Bubble Gum, 2132
Bubly®, 9945
Buccaneer, 648, 5861
Bucha, 8955
Buck, 4658
Buckaroo, 13716
Buckeye, 1819
Buckeye Beans and Herbs, 11390
Buckhead Gourmet, 1821
Buckhorn, 11263
Buckingham, 1822
Buckley Farms™, 12885
Buckley's, 5140
Buckman's Best, 7346
Buckman's Best Snack, 7346
Buckpower™, 9237
Buckson, 340
Buckwheat, 10478
Bud Flo, 571, 7123
Bud Light Lime, 7123
Bud Lime-A-Ritas, 8279
Buddha Teas, 1826
Buddig Original, 2212
Buddy Fruits, 1827
Buddy Fruits & Veggies, 1827
Buddy Squirrel, 1828
Budget Buy, 12973
Budget Gourmet®, 1200
Budibar, 1830
Budweiser, 71, 571, 7123
Buena Ventura, 2122
Buena Vida®, 855
Buena Vida™, 864

Buena Vista Winery, 1543
Bueno, 1835
Bueno®, 11504
Bufalo®, 6000
Buffalo, 6211
Buffalo Bill's, 12688
Buffalo Bob's Everything Sauce, 4354
Buffalo Brew, 1837
Buffalo Chips, 10417
Buffalo Gold, 7566
Buffalo Maid, 576
Buffalo Ranchc, 5489
Buffalo Trace, 10596, 11263
Buffalo Trace Distillery Experiment, 11263
Buffaloos®, 13607
Bug Bites, 4060
Bugles®, 4947
Build-A-Bear, 10229
Buitoni®, 8945
Bulgarian Style, 1782
Bulk Co2, 7363
Bull and Barrel, 1841
Bull Ice, 9664
Bull's Eye, 6976
Bullfrog Lavander, 12987
Bulls Eye, 3060
Bumble Bee, 6267, 7331
Bumpy & Jumpy, 11004
Bun Bar, 9877
Bunker Hill, 805
Bunny, 3193
Bunny Bread, 4529
Bunny Pasta, 4794
Bunny®, 7402
Buon Giorno, 7428
Buona Cucina, 12860
Buona Vita, 1854
Burgasko, 8459
Burger Buddies, 13630
Burgers N'A Bag, 8698
Burgers Smokehouse, 1858
Burke & Barry, 7655
Burke®, 6000
Burkec, 1861
Burleson Pure Honey, 1863
Burlle Meats, 1940
Burma, 2966
Burn, 2815, 8485
Burn Off, 13128
Burnett's London Dry Gin, 5720
Burnett's Vodkas, 5720
Burnetti's, 1866
Burning River Pale Ale, 5314
Burnley Vineyards, 1868
Burns, 7875
Burrow, 13193
Burt's Bees, 2766
Busch, 571, 7123
Bush's Best Baked Beans, 1872
Bush's Canned Beans, 1872
Bush's Chili, 1872
Bush's Grilling Beans, 1872
Bushman's Best Mazavaroo, 5765
Bushwhacker's Mustard, 6054
Busseto, 1875
Busseto Special Reserve, 1875
Buster, 5517
Busy Bee, 1040, 1876
But-R-Creme™, 3412
Butcher Boy, 6881
Butcher Wagon, 5643
Butcher's Cut, 13402
Butcher's Friend, 12830
Butcher's Pride, 9187
Butler, 1878
Butter Creams, 10596
Butter Flo, 1880
Butter Grahams, 2903
Butter Kernel®, 4267
Butter Toffee Covered Popcorn, 7845
Butter-Krust Country, 1881
Butterball, 1882, 1883
Butterbuds, 1880
Butterfield, 338
Butterfinger, 2132
Butterfinger®, 8945
Butterfly, 7758
Buttermist, 1880
Butternut, 10730
Butternut Baked Goods, 10730
Butternut Breads, 4529

Butterscotch, 9773
Butterscotch Bliss, 9019
Butterscotch Krimpetsc, 12551
Buttery Baker, 10981
Buyer Label, 6622
Buzz Bars, 1914
Buzz Buttered Steaks, 1891
Buzzn Bee Farms, 1893
By Nature By Hand, 13403
Bybee's, 4374
Byblos, 1894
Byington, 1895
Byrd Cookies, 1897
Byrd Missouri Grown, 1899
Byrd's Famous Cookies, 1897
Byrd's Hoot Owl Pecan Ranch Pecans, 1899
Byrne Dairy, 1902
Byron's Barbecue, 10714

C

C & E Sugar, 1908
C Howard Co., 2132
C&D, 7874
C&G, 13513
C&H, 1911, 4517, 12201
C&H Sugar, 3666
C&H®, 12196
C&S, 1928
C&T, 1929
C.F. Burger, 1915
C.F. Sauer Company, 1935
C.P., 1922
C.V.P. Systems, 1968
Ca Bianca, 4677
Ca Donini, 4677
Ca Halibut, 10949
Cabana, 1310
Cabaret, 3384
Cabernayzyn, 12746
Cabernet Sauvignon, 4745
Cabernet Vinegar, 869
Cabin Air Filters, 3833
Cabin Fever Ale, 1237
Cabot, 211, 1972
Cabot Cheeses, 1972
Cacao Barry, 1056
Cachaca 61, 7655
Cache River, 8079
Cache Valley® Cheese, 3335
Cacio De Roma, 11668
Cacio De Roma Cheese, 11668
Cacique, 1977
Cacoco, 1978
Cacti-Nea, 9029
Cactu Life, 1979
Cactus Bills, 13120
Cactus Cooler®, 6818
Cadbury, 5818
Cadbury Chocolate, 1981
Cadbury Dairy Milk, 1981
Cadbury Dark, 1981
Cadbury Favourites, 1981
Cadbury Schweppes, 1294, 5975
Cadbury Thins, 1981
Cadillac Coffee, 1984
Cadillac Mountain Stout, 1015
Cady Creek Farms, 1985
Caesar's, 4244
Caesar's Kitchen, 1986
Caf, Bustelo, 6380
Caf, Classicsc, 187
Caf, Delight Certified Sweeteners, 3574
Caf, Delight Premium Drink Mixes, 3574
Caf, Escapes®, 6818
Caf, Punta Del Cielo®, 6818
Cafe Altura, 1987
Cafe Amigo, 947
Cafe Appassionato, 2005
Cafe Bodega, 1053
Cafe Bonjour, 10708
Cafe Bustelo, 10920
Cafe Caracolillo Decafe, 2192
Cafe Caracolillo Expresso, 2192
Cafe Caracolillo Gourmet, 2192
Cafe Caribe, 2847
Cafe Del Mundo, 1991
Cafe Don Pablo, 1859
Cafe Don Pedro, 13191
Cafe Dontedro, 13190
Cafe Du Monde, 1993

1265

Brand Name Index

Cafe El Marino, 3420
Cafe Escapes, 6819
Cafe Europa, 2885
Cafe Excellence, 1053
Cafe Extract, 1490
Cafe Fair, 12069
Cafe H®, 6000
Cafe La Semeuse, 1997
Cafe Latino, 2885
Cafe Orleans, 13190
Cafe Orleans-Coffee, 13191
Cafe Pick, 6497
Cafe Quisqueva, 2192
Cafe Regil, 2192
Cafe Rico Rico, 2192
Cafe Riquisimo, 2192
Cafe Supremo, 2847
Cafe Tequila, 2003
Cafe Tiamo, 6198
Cafe Time, 11940, 12894
Cafe Unico, 13190
Cafe Unico-Espresso, 13191
Caffarel, 3381
Caffe D'Oro Cappuccino & Cocoa, 2008
Caffe D'Vita, 2009
Caffe La Llave, 4202
Caffe Lolita, 7655
Caffe Trieste Coffee Beans, 2013
Caffreys, 8459
Cafix, 6279
Cailler®, 8945
Cain Concept, 2015
Cain Cuv,E, 2015
Cain Five, 2015
Cains, 4928, 11213
Caito, 2016
Cajan Gold, 8772
Cajohns, 2017
Cajun Aujus, 2023
Cajun Bayou, 1279
Cajun Bites, 1531
Cajun Blast, 2019
Cajun Boy, 10029
Cajun Boy's Louisiana, 2018
Cajun Brand Sausage, 2162
Cajun Chef, 2019
Cajun Country, 4232, 9535
Cajun Creole, 2021
Cajun Creole Coffee, 2021
Cajun Creole Coffee & Chicory, 2022
Cajun Creole Hot Nuts, 2021
Cajun Creole Jalapeanuts, 2021
Cajun Flip N Fry, 2019
Cajun Gourmet Magic, 7206
Cajun Hollar, 6334
Cajun House, 11255
Cajun Injector, 2023
Cajun Injector®, 1794
Cajun King®, 1794
Cajun Land, 2019
Cajun Poultry Marinade, 2023
Cajun Smoked Sausage, 2944
Cajunshake, 2023
Cake Mate, 11599
Cake-Mate, 6340
Cakebread, 2025
Cakezyme®, 3320
Cal Best, 5418
Cal Gold, 11877
Cal Harvest, 5036
Cal India, 2027
Cal-Aloe Co., 10587
Cal-Fruit, 2063
Cal-King, 2026
Cal-Quick®, 13097
Cal-Sun, 8519
Cal-Tex, 2032
Calabro, 2033
Calafia Wines, 2034
Calavo, 2037
Calcitrace, 11269
Calco, 6032
Calera, 2044
Calessence, 1692
Calgary Italian, 2045
Calgo, 2040
Calgon®, 10598
Calhoun Bend Mill, 2046
Calico Cottage Fudge Mix, 2048
Calico Jack®, 1120
Calido Chile Traders, 1279
Caliente, 8525

California Almond, 2053
California Champagne, 2637
California Churros, 6338
California Classic, 11149
California Classics, 2059, 2075
California Coast Naturals, 2058
California Collection, 8525
California Crest, 13120
California Crisps, 183
California Crunchies, 9220
California Cuisine, 5216, 10435
California Farms, 883, 11203
California Finest, 13845
California Gold, 11877
California Golden Pop, 6506
California Goldminer, 7871, 7875, 7876
California Grown, 7451
California Harvest, 5280, 11864
California Independent Brand, 2068
California Just Chile!, 6015
California Light Blonde, 11846
California Ltd ®, 13120
California Nuggets, 2072
California Nuts, 1471
California Pale Ale (Cpa), 1097
California Pantry, 6019
California Rabbit, 1543
California Ranch Fresh, 5837
California Special, 7125
California Specialty Farms, 13950
California Sunshine Dairy Pproducts, 5837
Calio Groves, 2085
Calise, 2086
Calistoga Food, 2087
Callaway, 2042
Calle Sabor, 5141
Callebaut®, 1056
Calley Lahvosh, 13256
Calm Mind, 9201
Calmar Bakery, 2094
Calona Vineyards, 555
Calorie Control, 1244
Calpro, 2095
Calrose, 1849
Calrose Rice, 4260
Calvert, 7655
Calypso, 6867
Calypso Caribbean, 7273
Calypso Gold Rum, 11264
Calypso Light Rum, 11264
Camarad, 13425
Camas, 2100
Cambozola, 2409
Cambria, 2101
Cambridge Food, 2103
Camellia, 2105, 7027
Camelot Mead, 9452
Cameo, 8729
Cameron, 2108
Cameron's, 2108
Camilla Pecan, 2110
Camino Del Sol, 10333
Camp, 2693
Camp Mixes, 3079
Camp Rite, 7150
Campaniac, 2010
Campari, 2114
Camparron, 3545
Campbells, 2116
Campbells Canada, 2116
Campbells Chunky, 2116
Campbells Foodservice, 2116
Campbells Ready To Enjoy Soups, 2115
Campbells Soup At Hand, 2115
Campeche Bay, 9912
Campesino Jamoneta, 2670
Campfire, 3713, 4891, 6267
Campfire Marshmallows, 6267
Campi Del Sole, 10565
Campino, 12147
Campo Lindoc, 187
Campo Viejo, 9964
Camrose, 2118
Camus Prarie Tea, 13015
Canada Dry, 252, 1294, 2811
Canada Dry®, 3725, 6818
Canada Gold, 2693
Canada Goose, 3950
Canada House, 7655
Canadian, 6901
Canadian Bay, 9773

Canadian Blended Whisky Chocolates, 10468
Canadian Club, 56, 3024, 5892, 12315
Canadian Club®, 1120
Canadian Deluxe, 7655
Canadian Gourmet, 2367
Canadian Grand, 13182
Canadian Harvest, 5138
Canadian Host, 11264
Canadian Jumbo Lake, 575
Canadian Ltd, 11264
Canadian Mist, 2124
Canadian Reserve, 7655
Canadian Springs, 7655, 10303
Canadian Supreme, 11264
Canadian Whiskey, 1784
Canadian Wild Rice, 4508
Canandaigua Blend, 4403
Canaplus, 1847
Canard Duchene, 3570
Candelari's, 2128
Candelita, 218
Canderel, 8173
Candle Cafe Vegan, 5505
Cando Pasta, 2129
Candoni De Zan, 652
Candurin®, 2370
Candy Activity, 418
Candy Art, 5160
Candy Ass, 11873
Candy Blox®, 12880
Candy Carnival®, 12880
Candy Climbers, 6780
Candy Club, 1114
Candy Farm, 3421, 10773
Candy Farms, 12114
Candy Flower Bouquets, 2134
Candy Kaleidoscope, 11552
Candy Stick, 12957
Candy Whistler, 4255
Candy Yams, 1856
Candy Yo-Yo, 790
Candyman Lane, 1027
Candyrific, 2132
Cane Classics, 11885
Canesweet™, 12387
Canine Carry Outs, 6380
Canned Southern Vegetables, 8086
Cannon, 8519
Cano Cosecha, 3545
Canoe, 4508, 8305
Canolean, 6395
Canoleo®, 864
Canolla Truffles, 9771
Cantar,, 12348
Cantatti, 3381
Canterbury Naturals, 2950
Cantisano, 7408
Canton, 56, 10333
Canvas, 71
Canvasback, 3779
Canyon Bakehouse, 4529
Canyon Oaks, 104
Canyon Oats, 4830
Canyon Road, 4992
Canyon Road®, 3834
Cap 'n Kid, 305
Cap'n Crunch®, 9945
Cap'n Joe, 12520
Cap'n Poptoy, 11552
Cap'ns Catch, 11356
Capalbo's, 2150
Capay Canyon Ranch, 2152
Cape Ann, 9291
Cape Cod, 2116, 2156, 2572
Cape Cod Clam Chowder, 2309
Cape Cod Cranberry C, 5477
Cape Cod Cranberry Candy, 2159
Cape Cod Dry, 10151
Cape Cod Lobster Bisque, 2309
Cape Cod Lobster Chowder, 2309
Cape Cod Potato Chips, 11770
Cape Covelle®, 12885
Cape May, 7054
Cape May Salt, 765
Cape Mentelle Vineyards, 8452
Cape Royal, 3891
Cape Sandy Vineyards, 3877
Capezzana, 8452
Capital, 13912
Capitan Gold Tequila, 11264
Capitan Tequila & Triple Sec, 11264

Capitan White Tequila, 11264
Capitanelli Fine Foods, 9119
Capitanelli Specialty Foods, 9119
Capitanelli's, 9119
Capitol Foods, 2164
Capmul®, 126
Capo Di Monte, 12444
Capol®, 2370
Capolla Foods, 2165
Capone Foods, 2166
Cappo, 2169
Cappuccine, 2171
Cappuccino Supreme, 464
Cappuccio, 1908
Capretta, 10565
Capri, 1080, 13687
Capri-Sun, 2815
Capric, 2010
Capriccio, 507, 4515
Capricorn, 12437
Caprimo, 1056
Caprisun, 6977
Caprol®, 126
Capstone®, 7786
Capsul®, 8804
Capsul® Ta, 8804
Capsule Works, 2179
Capsulong, 3948
Capt'n Don's, 2572
Capt'n Eds, 2572
Capt. Fred, 11356
Captain Bob's Jet Fuel, 2183
Captain Charlie, 2431
Captain Cook Coffee, 2184
Captain Jac, 6267
Captain Jack's, 6159
Captain Joey, 1357
Captain John's Derst's, 4529
Captain Ken's, 2186
Captain Lawrence Brewing Co., 10666
Captain Mike's, 1019
Captain Morgan, 3545
Captain Neptune, 8938
Captain Pierre, 5438
Captain Space Freeze, 13005
Captain Swain's Extra, 2691
Captain's Call, 9165
Captain's Choice Honey Brine, 2189
Captains, 7146
Captex®, 126
Cara Mia, 12035
Cara-Sel, 12668
Caramel Apple Pops®, 12880
Caramel Chews, 9220
Caramel Creams®, 5096
Caramel Milk Roll, 7643
Caramels, 6976
Caramilk, 1981
Carando, 11733
Carando Gourmet, 2193
Caraquet, 2194
Carat, 1175
Caravan, 954
Caravel Gourmet, 11351
Caravella, 11264
Carb Escapes, 11771
Carb Smart®, 5165
Carbernet Sauvignon, 1314
Carbmate, 357
Carbosil®, 3320
Cardi C, 2199
Cardiaslim, 6236
Cardinal, 13912
Cardinal Kettle, 2200
Cardinal Pale Ale, 2653
Cardini's, 7987
Cardinis Salad Dressing, 12467
Cardio Discovery, 7331
Cardio Life, 4127
Cardio Water, 9858
Cardiomax, 9957
Care Bears Gummi Bears, 12547
Carenero, 2617
Caretree, 7339
Carex, 9264
Carey's®, 864
Carfagna, 2275
Carfosel™, 10239
Cargill, 11053
Cariani Italian Dry Salami, 6326
Cariani Italian Specialty Loaves, 6326

Brand Name Index

Caribbean Chill, 387
Caribbean Condiments, 5516
Caribbean Hot Peppers, 12997
Caribbean Marketplace, 4894
Caribbean Red® Papaya, 1757
Caribe, 8028
Caribou Coffee®, 6818
Carl Buddig Meats, 2212
Carl Budding, 9431
Carling, 8459
Carlo Rossi®, 3834
Carlos, 7655
Carlsbad Oblaten, 846
Carlson, 6364
Carma®, 1056
Carmel, 209, 7848
Carmel Winery, 10952
Carmela's, 2220
Carmelia, 7842
Carmi Flavors, 2223
Carnation, 6380
Carnation®, 8945
Carneco Foods, 7538
Carneros, 1834, 2225
Carneros Chardonnay, 869, 13426
Carneros Creek, 2225
Carnival Cajun Classics, 2226
Carnivor®, 3834
Carocare®, 3320
Carol Lee, 2230
Carolan's, 4422
Carolans Irish Cream Liqueur, 5720
Carole's, 2232
Carole's Tops, 2232
Carolina Atlantic Seafood, 2233
Carolina Barbecue, 2416
Carolina Chef, 13912
Carolina Choice, 11844
Carolina Classics, 2237
Carolina Cupboard, 42, 11864
Carolina Gem, 178
Carolina Gold, 2248
Carolina Mountain Spring Water, 8605
Carolina Pride, 2246, 2247
Carolina Treet, 2250
Carolina®, 10777
Caroline's Sausage, 690
Caroliva, 10319
Carophyll®, 3320
Carousel, 2253, 4586
Carousel Cakes, 2252
Carousel Pop, 6158
Carpuela, 11894
Carr Valley, 2256
Carr's, 6766
Carriage House, 2258
Carriere, 2260
Carrington Tea, 2262
Carroll Shelby Chili Kits, 10657
Carson's, 3847
Cartcelt, 783
Cartilade, 783
Cartreuse Liqueur, 4677
Carts, 11755
Carve Cookie, 2266
Carvers Original, 9155
Casa Blanco, 3545
Casa De Carmen, 130
Casa De Corca, 10952
Casa De La Ermita, 3545
Casa Del Norte, 9934
Casa Dibertacchi, 10714
Casa Dilisio, 2269
Casa Europa, 9798
Casa Jorge, 10968
Casa Luca, 2012
Casa Maid, 5555
Casa Nuestra, 2271
Casa Primo, 7069
Casa Tinto, 3545
Casa Visco, 2274
Casabe Rainforest Crackers, 4607
Casafiesta®, 1794
Casale Degli Ulivi, 4386
Casanova, 1638
Casaro, 9780
Casbah, 5505
Cascade, 8320, 12721
Cascade Ale, 3533
Cascade Crest Organics, 2505
Cascade Fresh, 2283
Cascade Glacier, 9533

Cascade Specialties, 2285
Cascadia, 13872
Cascadia Only 2 Calories, 8784
Cascadia Sparkling Cider, 8784
Cascadian Farm, 2286, 11711
Cascadian Farm®, 4947
Case Farms Amish Country, 2288
Casey's, 2291
Cashew Critters, 7184, 7200
Cass, 71
Cass-Clay, 2295
Cassino, 10873
Castelet, 5405
Castellblanch, 4693
Castelletto, 8592
Castellini, 2298
Castello Di Volpaia, 13811
Castello Monachi, 4677
Castillo Rums, 914
Castle Beverages, 2300
Castle Carbonated Beverages, 2300
Castle Cheese, 2301
Castleberry Products, 805
Castor River Farms, 2304
Cat Chow®, 8945
Cat In the Hat Cotton Candy, 12547
Cat In the Hat Sour Gummies, 12547
Catawba Grape Juice, 5731
Catch of the Day®, 5844
Catelli, 6976
Cateraid, 2314
Catered Gourmet, 2314
Caterer's Collection, 10728
Cathay Foods, 2317
Catskill Brewery, 2321
Catskill Distilling Company, 2322
Cattail, 757
Cattaneo Brothers, 2324
Cattle Boyz, 2325
Cattleman's, 2326
Cattlemen's Bbq Sauce, 8061
Catuama, 127
Cavalier, 11859
Cavaliere D'Oro, 12937
Cave Winery, 10952
Cavedoni Balsamic, 10401
Caveman Foods, 4150
Cavendish Farms®, 2332
Cawy Cc, 2338
Cawy Lemon-Lime, 2338
Cawy Watermelon, 2338
Cayenne Kicker™, 1654
Caymus, 2339
Cb's Nuts, 1942
Cbs, 1945
Cbw, 1710
Ccff, 2060
Cdm Coffee & Chicory, 10657
Ceamgel 1313, 9654
Cecchetti Sebastiani Napa Valley, 2343
Cecchi, 1006
Cece's Veggie Noodle Co., 2344
Cedar Creek, 2345, 9080
Cedar Crest, 2404
Cedar Farms, 9699
Cedar Grove, 2347, 2351
Cedar Lake, 2350
Cedar Mountain, 2351
Cedar River Farms®, 6391
Cedar Springs Lamb, 8601
Cedar Springs Natural Veal, 8601
Cedar's, 2354
Cedarlane, 2355
Cedarvale, 2357, 7594
Cekol, 1962
Celadrinc, 9997
Celebes, 761
Celebes Kalosi, 10157
Celebration Libation, 2691
Celebrations®, 7952
Celebri Tea, 2360
Celebrity Cheesecakes, 2359
Celentano®, 10899
Celero, 13498
Celeste, 811
Celeste® Pizza For One, 2939, 2940
Celestial Seasonings, 5505, 5506, 6819
Celifibr, 10708
Celio, 223
Cell Charge®, 1377
Cella's Cherries®, 12880

Celler De Capcanes, 10952
Cellmins™, 13097
Celloc, 11313
Celluclast, 1692
Cellucor, 4150
Celsius Heat, 2364
Celsius Live Fit, 2364
Celtic, 12919
Cenprem, 2387
Centanni, 4386
Centennial, 2367
Center Fruit, 9956
Center-Of-The-Plate Specialists, 7721
Centra-Vit, 75
Central Coast, 2044
Central Coast Chardonnay, 2637
Central Market, 5473
Central Valley Creamery, 6719
Century Harvest Farms, 2385
Cereal Match, 3670
Cerelac®, 8945
Cerelose, 6211
Ceres®, 6869
Ceresota, 13135
Certi-Fresh, 2394
Certicoat®, 7857
Certified Angus Beef, 5141, 5338
Certified Angus Beef®, 6391, 7721, 8783
Certified Hereford Beef®, 8783
Certified Humanec, 13461
Certified Organic Breads, 10965
Certified Organic Buns, 10965
Certified Organic Rolls, 10965
Certified Piedmontese, 5327
Certified Premium Beef, 8783
Certified®, 7857
Certiseal®, 7857
Certo, 6976
Certs, 9995
Certs Breath Mints, 1980
Certs Cool Mint Drops, 1980
Certs Powerful Mints, 1980
Cervera, 9043
Cesar®, 7952
Cetus Textile Fabrics, 3833
Ceylon Classic, 2729
Ceylon Teas, 12272
Cg Supreme, 2964
Cgp, 8191
Cha-Cha Chinese Chicken Dressing, 11878
Chachies, 11065, 11187
Chacies®, 11186
Chad's Carolina Corn, 13759
Chaddsford, 2399
Chadwick Bay, 10637
Chai Bites, 6026
Chaidfontaine, 2815
Chairman's Reserve®, 13109
Chalet Gourmet, 7998
Chalif, 8539
Chalk Hill Estate Bottled, 2403
Chalk Hill Estate Selection, 2403
Challenge, 2404
Challenge Dairy Products, 2061
Challenge Danish, 2404
Cham Cold Brew Tea, 2406, 12719
Chamberlain, 11561
Chambord, 1784, 2407
Chambourcin, 8513
Chameleon Pepper, 12987
Chamisa Gold, 10165
Champ, 2413
Champ's Cola, 2338
Champagne Delight, 5030
Champagne Vinegar, 869
Champale, 9664
Champignon, 2409
Champion, 8802
Champlain Valley, 9157
Champon, 10359
Chandler Foods, 2416
Chandon, 8452
Chang Food, 2417
Channel, 2418
Channel Rockfish (Thornyheads, 10949
Chapala, 7655
Chappallet, 2423
Chaqwa, 2815
Char Crust, 2424
Char Dex, 10600
Char Oil, 10600
Char Sol, 10600

Char Zyme, 10600
Char-Wil, 2425
Chardonayzyn, 12746
Chardonnay, 1314, 3661, 4745
Chardonnay Barrel Select, 5989
Chardonnay Vinegar, 869
Charking®, 12885
Charles De Fere, 12672
Charles Krug, 2432
Charles Shaw, 1738
Charles Spinetta Barbera, 2435
Charles Spinetta Primitivo, 2435
Charles Spinetta Zinfanel, 2435
Charleston Chew, 2102, 2132
Charleston Chew®, 12880
Charlie Flint's Original Lager, 339
Charlie Palmer, 2439
Charlie Robinson's, 10804
Charlie Trotter Foods, 12068
Charlie Trotter's, 13899
Charlie's Salsa, 1141
Charlie's Specialties, 1903, 1904
Charmin, 12721
Charming Nancy, 1688
Charms Co., 2132
Charms®, 12880
Charrasc, 9714
Chas. W. Howeth & Bro., 2532
Chase & Sanborn, 11212
Chase & Sanborn Coffee, 7995
Chase Brothers, 2450
Chaser, 3707
Chata, 12823
Chateau, 2457, 5317
Chateau Beniot, 2905
Chateau Beychevelle, 12315
Chateau Boswell, 2454
Chateau Boswell Estate, 2454
Chateau Cellars, 1306
Chateau Cheval Blanc, 8452
Chateau Chevalier, 11966
Chateau D'Yquem, 8452
Chateau De Sancerre, 8452
Chateau Diana, 2456
Chateau Frank Champagne Cellars, 3724
Chateau Fuisse, 4677
Chateau Julien, 2459
Chateau La Nerthe, 8452
Chateau Lagrange, 12315
Chateau Montelena, 2461, 11810
Chateau Potelle, 2463
Chateau Rollan De By, 10952
Chateau Souverain, 2465
Chateau St. Jean, 12937
Chateau Thomas, 10097
Chatfield'sc, 9748
Chatham Village, 12467
Chatsworth, 5735
Chatter Creek, 7286
Chatz, 2472
Chaucers, 1033
Chaya, 932
Checkerbites, 3625
Checkers Cookies, 1394
Cheddar & Bacon Flavored Ranch, 5489
Cheddar Box Cheese, 2479
Cheemo, 5798
Cheer, 12721
Cheerios®, 4947
Cheerwine, 2234, 13300
Cheerwine Soft Drink, 2234
Cheese Heads®, 11211
Cheese Merchants®, 11504
Cheese Puffs Sharing Packs, 11754
Cheese Rounds and Bricks, 13823
Cheese Senasations, 530
Cheese Spreads, 13823
Cheese-Mor™, 342
Cheesebuds, 1880
Cheesecake Factory®, 2485
Cheesecake Slicer, 2881
Cheestrings®, 9789
Cheetos, 4741
Cheetos®, 9945
Cheez Doodles, 13884
Cheez Whiz, 6976
Cheez-It, 6766
Chef Alberto Leone, 9752
Chef Antonio, 10728
Chef Blends®, 11228
Chef Boyardee, 6267
Chef Boyardee Pastas, 6267

1267

Brand Name Index

Chef Boyardee®, 2939, 2940
Chef Classic, 9680
Chef Creole, 2226
Chef Gaston, 6395
Chef Hans, 2489, 6725
Chef Howard's Williecake, 6314
Chef Italia, 7783
Chef Martin, 8390
Chef Master, 207
Chef Merito, 2490
Chef Michael's®, 8945
Chef Myron's Original #1 Yakitori, 8715
Chef Myron's Ponzu, 8715
Chef Myron's Premium, 8715
Chef Myron's Tsukeya, 8715
Chef One, 13094
Chef Ooh La La Baking Mixes, 12100
Chef Paul Prudhomme's, 2491
Chef Pierre, 11214
Chef Pleaser, 5643
Chef Tang, 7874
Chef Vito Pasta Meals, 6410
Chef's Choice, 5928, 10399
Chef's Companion, 3574
Chef's Craft®, 13607
Chef's Exclusive®, 6391
Chef's Helper, 3989
Chef's Pastry, 2787
Chef's Pride, 2708
Chef's Recipe, 1087, 7927
Chef's Seasoning, 3574
Chef's Signature, 3653
Chef-A-Roni, 2503
Chef-Mate®, 8945
Chef®, 8945
Chefmaster, 1904
Chefs Originals, 10712
Chefs-In-A-Bag, 6334
Chefstyle, 5473
Cheiljedang, 1953
Chelsea, 51
Chelsea Market Baskets, 2507
Chelsea Spice, 2499
Chelten House, 2509
Cheolong, 3948
Cher-Make Sausage, 2511
Cheramino®, 13097
Cherchies, 2514
Cheri's Desert Harvest, 2515
Cherith Valley Gardens, 2517
Cherry & Berry Blast, 11552
Cherry Bomb, 12178
Cherry Central, 2518
Cherry Man, 11434
Cherry Mash, 2449
Cherrybrook Kitchen, 6049
Cherryman, 5288
Cheryl & Co., 2526
Cheryl Lynn, 10399
Chesapeake Bay Delight, 11571
Chesapeake Bay Ice, 868
Chesapeake Bay's Finest, 2291
Chesapeake Pride, 868, 3097
Chessters, 10696
Chester Farms, 2530
Chester Farms Popping Corn, 2530
Chester Fried Chicken, 2533
Chester's, 4741, 9560
Chesterfried, 2533
Chestertown, 2535
Chestnut Street, 11102
Cheval Des Andes, 8452
Chevalier Chocolates, 2537
Chevrai, 13927
Chevrai™, 11211
Chew-Ets, 5144
Chewels®, 1009
Chewey Kisses, 13845
Chewy Gooey Pretzel Sticks, 1018
Chewy's, 2538
Chex, 13864
Chex®, 4947
Chi-Chi's Appletini, 11264
Chi-Chi's Caribbean Mudslide, 11264
Chi-Chi's, 6000
Chianti Cheese, 6702
Chiappetti, 12162
Chiatai Conti Group, 2970
Chic Jiang, 10457
Chicago 58, 2541
Chicago Mints, 7524
Chicago Steak, 2549

Chicago Style, 5341
Chicama, 2551
Chick Chocolates, 11389
Chick-Fil-A®, 2552
Chick-O-Stick, 756
Chickadee Products, 6768
Chickapea, 2553
Chickapea Pasta, 2553
Chicken Link, 8620
Chicken Not, 3633
Chicken of the Sea, 2555
Chicken of the Sea Singles, 2555
Chicken of the Sea Tuna Salad Kit, 2555
Chicken-To-Go, 1444
Chickpea Chipotle, 6522
Chicle Chips, 1158
Chiclets, 9995
Chiclets Gum, 1980
Chicopee Provision, 2559
Chicory Stout, 3644
Chidester Farms, 6246
Chief Chelan, 2560
Chief Kahai™, 7402
Chief Supreme, 2560
Chief Wenatchee, 2560
Chief's Creations, 3623
Chieftainc, 2561
Chigarid, 10718
Chik'n Giggles®, 1654
Chik'n Gone Wild™, 1654
Chik'n Hoops®, 1654
Chik'n Pretzels™, 1654
Chik'n Stars™, 1654
Chik'n'zips®, 1654
Child's Play®, 12880
Chile, 3393
Chili Bowl®, 237, 238
Chili Dude, 2565
Chili Supreme, 8724
Chillee Snow Cones, 5333
Chilliman®, 4267
Chilly, 8620
Chillycow™, 13645
Chiltomaline, 9911
Chimay, 1748
Chimayo, 1835
China Bowl, 5717
China Boy, 4164
China Cola, 10507
China Collection Teas, 5155
China Mist, 2570
China Pack, 6665
China Pride, 345
China Teas, 12272
China White, 5861
China Yunnan Silver Tip Choice, 5228
Chinese Chicken Salad Dressing, 5143
Chinese Ginseng, 13531
Chinese Marinade, 11878
Chinese-Lady, 6665
Chino Valley, 2576
Chinoteaque, 2572
Chipico®, 13400
Chipnuts, 10031
Chipper, 13303
Chipper Beef Jerky, 2579
Chips Ahoy!, 8474, 8729
Chips Ahoy!® Cereal, 10213
Chips Deluxe, 6766
Chiqui, 9604
Chiquita Banana Cookies, 9399
Chiquita®, 2580
Chiquititos, 11386
Chitolean, 4575
Chivas Regalc, 9964
Chobani, 217
Choc Adillos, 7200
Choc'adillos, 7200
Choc-Adillos, 7184
Choc-Dip, 6340
Chocapic®, 8945
Chocatal, 6497
Chock Full O' Nuts, 7995
Chock Full O'Nuts, 2587, 11212
Choco Berries, 10689
Choco D' Lite, 3670
Choco Milk®, 8103
Choco Pals, 6780
Choco Rocks, 6851
Choco-Starlight, 10428
Chocolat Jean Talon, 2594

Chocolate & Vanilla Nut Spread, 14034
Chocolate By Design, 2598
Chocolate Charlie, 2712
Chocolate Cortes, 12185
Chocolate Covered Marshmallows, 2903
Chocolate Covered Graham Crackers, 6525
Chocolate Covered Nuts, 12868
Chocolate Covered Potato Chips, 7845
Chocolate Covered Pretzels, 6787
Chocolate Covered Toffee Popcorn, 7845
Chocolate Delight, 13728
Chocolate Dunkel, 9153
Chocolate Ecstasy, 9019
Chocolate Flavored Coffee Spoons, 6787
Chocolate Fortune Cookies, 6787
Chocolate Jollies, 13845
Chocolate Juniorsc, 12551
Chocolate Kandy Kakesc, 12551
Chocolate Marshmallow, 9753
Chocolate Masters™, 1056
Chocolate Milk Stout, 3746
Chocolate Mint Meltaways, 2604
Chocolate Moose, 9115
Chocolate Moose Energy, 9115
Chocolate Mousse Hip, 9196
Chocolate Oreos, 4253
Chocolate Pizza, 4253
Chocolate Porter, 1097
Chocolate Products, 5428
Chocolate Slicks, 7912
Chocolate Slim, 3753
Chocolate Stout, 1401
Chocolate Straws, 10104
Chocolate Street of Hartville, 2611
Chocolate Toffee Almonds, 9220
Chocolaterie Bernard Callebaut, 2614
Chocolates a La Carte, 2619
Chocolove, 2623
Chocomite, 3593
Chocovic, 1056
Choice, 2630
Choice Foods, 10846
Choice of Vermont, 2631
Choice Organic Teas, 2630
Choki, 12185
Cholesterol Solve, 131
Cholov Yisrael, 2312
Cholula, 12823
Chomper, 665
Chomps, 2632
Chooljian, 2634
Chop Block Breads, 3078
Chopin, 3024, 8452
Choppin N Block, 446
Chouinard Red, 2637
Chouinard Rose, 2637
Chowards, 1918
Choxcard, 10229
Choy Sun, 7296
Chr, 1947
Christian Brothers Brandies, 5720
Christie's Instant-Chef, 2647
Christille Bay, 12999
Christina's Organic, 4111
Christmas, 11992
Christmas Ale, 531, 1687, 5314
Christophe Cellars, 12672
Christopher Norman Chocolates, 2654
Christopher's, 6375
Christos, 7931
Christy Crops, 2657
Chromax, 9259
Chromemate, 6236, 9253
Chuckles, 1417, 2102, 2132, 4345
Chudleigh's, 2661
Chugwater Chili, 2662
Chummy Chums, 6780
Chun's, 11788
Chung's, 2665
Chunk a Chew, 4586
Chunk Light Tuna, 12046
Chunks O'Fruit, 8837
Chunky Ready To Go Bowls, 2115
Chunky Ready To Serve Soups/Chili, 2115
Chupa Chups, 9956
Churchills Ports, 4677
Churn Spread®, 13328
Chux, 2766
Ciao Bella, 2669
Ciao Bella Sorbet, 2669
Cider Creek Hard Cider, 10666
Cider Drink Mix, 12182

Ciel, 2814
Cielo Azul, 10110
Cien En Boca, 1581
Cillit Bang®, 10598
Cimarron Cellars, 2677
Cinchona Coffee, 2881
Cincy Style, 6410
Cinderella, 2680
Cinerator Hot Cinnamon Whiskey, 5720
Cini Minis®, 8945
Cinnabar Specialty Foods, 2681
Cinnabon, 10173, 11318
Cinnabon®, 6818
Cinnamon Bakery, 2683
Cinnamon Mini Donuts, 12551
Cinnamon Ridge, 2899
Cinnamon Toast Crunch®, 4947
Cinnful Coco, 11775
Cinzano, 2114, 3545
Cipriani's Classic Italian, 2684
Cipriani's Premium, 2684
Cirashine, 716
Circle a Brands Beef Patties, 770
Circle M, 8665
Circle R Gourmet Foods, 2686
Circle Z, 14043
Circlea Beef Patties, 770
Circus Man, 2689
Circus Sticks, 6780
Circus Wagon Animal Crackers, 3343
Citadelle, 2693
Citation, 833, 3424
Citizen Foods, 10021
Citra-Next®, 10797
Citradelic, 8959
Citranatal®, 8389
Citreatt, 12940
Citriburst Finger Limes, 11516
Citricidal, 9251
Citrico, 2694
Citrimax, 6310, 9253
Citrimax - French Diet Cola, 6310
Citrin, 11061
Citrin K, 11061
Citrus Pride, 2032
Citrus Punch Sugar-Free, 5460
Citrus Royal, 5362
Citrus Sunshine, 9469
Citterio, 2701
City Grillers, 1796
City Lager, 2705
City Light, 2705
City Market, 12516
City Slicker, 2705
Cizonin Vineyards, 3179
Cjoy®, 11378
Ck, 2487
Ck Mondavi, 2432
Clabber Girl®, 2711
Claeys Gourmet Cream Fudge, 2712
Claeys Gourmet Peanut Brittle, 2712
Claeys Old Fashion Hards Candies, 2712
Claiborne & Churchill, 2713
Clair Riley Zinfandel Port, 12227
Clamato, 8586
Clamato®, 3725, 6818
Clan Macgregor, 13811
Clancy, 10041
Clapier Mill, 11852
Clara's Kitchen, 10435
Clardera Brewing, 10666
Clarendon Hills®, 3834
Claret, 11995
Clarified Butter, 5679
Clasen, 2722
Clash Malt, 9664
Classic, 7643, 7657, 12925
Classic Banjo, 5819
Classic Blends, 8919
Classic Blue, 13687
Classic Bon Bons, 1767
Classic Caramel, 13574
Classic Caramel®, 13572
Classic Casserole, 1069, 1577
Classic Ceylon, 2729
Classic Choice, 11328
Classic Commissary, 2723
Classic Complements, 4543
Classic Confections, 3541
Classic Country, 3079
Classic Cream, 258

Brand Name Index

Classic Delight, 2726
Classic Gourmet®, 13328
Classic Liquor Cremes, 10596
Classic Malts, 3570
Classic Reserve, 5236
Classic Reserve Ext Sharp Cheddar, 5236
Classic Traditions, 3629
Classico, 6976, 6977, 11132
Classique, 1997
Classique Fare, 8448
Classy Delites, 2730
Claudia Sanders, 7934
Claussen, 6976, 6977
Clausthaler, 1361
Claw Island, 10682
Clawson, 11458
Claxton, 2732
Clayton Coffee & Tea, 2734
Clayton Farms, 5555
Clean Kitchen, 11386
Clean N' Natural, 4888
Clear 'n' Natural, 174
Clear Choice, 10637
Clear Coat, 2332
Clear Creek Grappas, 2737
Clear River Farms®, 6391
Clear Sailing, 338
Clear Springs Kitchen®, 2740
Clear Springs®, 2740
Clear Stevia, 9201
ClearùCuts®, 2740
Clearasil®, 10598
Clearblue, 12721
Clearbrook Frams, 2679
Clearfield, 5400, 11308
Clearfruit, 8784
Clearjel®, 8804
Clearly Canadian, 2742
Clearly Canadian O+2, 2742
Clearly Kombucha, 2743
Clement Pappas, 7236
Clements Pastry Shop, 2749
Clemson Bros., 2752
Clermont, 4968
Clif Bar, 2756, 4150
Clif Builder's, 2756
Clif Crunch, 2756
Clif Kid, 2756
Clif Mojo, 2756
Clif Shot, 2756
Clif's, 8001
Cliffside, 8560
Clifty Farm, 2758
Cline Cellars, 2759
Clinton, 13647
Clinton Victory, 2761
Clinton's, 4290
Clio Pomace, 11875
Clio Pure, 11875
Clipper, 6279
Clipper Foods, 10820
Clorets, 9995
Clorets Breath Freshener, 1980
Clorox, 2766
Clos Du Val, 2769
Clos Mesorah, 10952
Clos Normand, 4148
Clos Reserve, 4649
Close-Up, 2666
Cloud Nine, 2772
Cloud Nine All-Natural Chocolate, 2772
Cloudy Bay Vineyards, 8452
Clove Valley Farms, 5765
Clover, 10478
Clover Farms, 2778, 2782
Clover Hill, 2784
Clover Hill Cuvee, 2779
Clover Hill Pinot Noir, 2779
Clover Hill Rose, 2779
Clover Leaf, 6267, 13658
Cloverdale, 2783, 2787, 5233
Cloverdale Ranch, 9905
Cloverland, 2786
Cloverland Sweets, 10281
Cloverleaf Farms Peanut Butter, 11029
Club Caribe, 4515
Club Chef, 2298, 2789
Club House, 8061
Club Tahity, 13141
Clutters Indian Fields, 2790
Clyde's, 2791
Clyde's Soon To Be Famous, 922

Cm - 22, 4827
Cns, 1959
Co Yo, 1960
Co2 Hard Candy, 1343
Coach Farm, 2793
Coag-U-Loid, 2386
Coast, 4668
Coast Refined Lard, 2796
Coastal Gourmet, 2798
Coastline, 12296
Coastlog, 2805
Cobblestone Bread Co., 4529
Cobblestone Mill, 4662
Cobblestreet Market®, 11504
Cobra, 8459
Cobra Vanilla, 12987
Coby's Cookies, Inc., 2810
Coca-Cola, 2811, 2814, 2815
Coca-Cola Light/Diet, 2815
Coca-Cola Zero, 2814, 2815
Cochise Farms, 4373
Cocina De Mino, 2816
Cocinaware, 5473
Cock'n Bull, 13300
Cocktail Duet, 9385
Coco Libre, 8025, 8955
Coco Lopez, 2820
Coco Lopez, Usa, 4057
Coco Pops, 6766
Coco Rico, 5177
Coco Solo, 2338
Coco Well, 2202
Coco Wheats, 10213
Cocoa, 12100
Cocoa Amore, 2848
Cocoa Creations, 291
Cocoa Metro, 2822
Cocoa Replacers, 5462
Cocoalaska, 263
Cocoamate, 12550
Cocolalla, 2825
Cocomels, 2826
Coconut Beach, 2828
Coconut Bliss, 2829, 7647
Coconut Grove, 7170
Coconut Infusions™, 8725
Coconut Juniorsc, 12551
Coconut Oil, 8896
Coconut Patties, 9877
Coconut Waves, 12027
Coconut Zipper, 11990
Cocoroons, 11415
Cocovia®, 7952
Code, 1891
Coffaro's Baking Company, 11390
Coffee, 362
Coffee Bean, 4276
Coffee Beanery Franchise, 2838
Coffee Blenders, 9211
Coffee Brothers, 2839
Coffee Exchange, 2843
Coffee Express, 2844, 4324
Coffee House Roasters, 1636
Coffee Masters, 2848
Coffee People, 3591, 6819
Coffee People®, 6818
Coffee Rich, 10714
Coffee Rio, 163
Coffee Roasters Ridgeline®, 11504
Coffee Scapes, 11855
Coffee Time, 6683
Coffee-Mate®, 8945
Coffeego, 7769
Coffeehouse Porter, 1237
Cognizin, 7017
Cogruet™, 11211
Cohort, 11759
Colavita 25-Star Gran Riserva Vin., 2864
Colavita Balsamic Vinegar, 2864
Colavita Classic Hot Sauce, 2864
Colavita Extra Virgin Olive Oil, 2864
Colavita Fat Free Classic Hot Sauce, 2864
Colavita Fat Free Garden Style Sau., 2864
Colavita Fat Free Marinara Sauce, 2864
Colavita Fat Free Mushroom Sauce, 2864
Colavita Garden Style Sauce, 2864
Colavita Healthy Sauce, 2864
Colavita Marinara Sauce, 2864
Colavita Marinated Vegetables, 2864
Colavita Mushroom Sauce, 2864
Colavita Pasta, 2864
Colavita Pasta Plus, 2864

Colavita Puttanesca Sauce, 2864
Colavita Red Clam Sauce, 2864
Colavita White Clam Sauce, 2864
Cold Hollow Cider Mill, 2869
Cold Mountain, 8412
Cold River, 6139
Cold Stone Creamery, 2132
Cold/Hot Pack Tunnel Pasterized, 5027
Coldstream Hills, 12937
Colectivo Keg Company Beers, 2874
Coleman, 9922
Coleman Natural, 2875
Coleman Natural®, 9946
Coleman Organic, 2875
Colflo™ 67, 8804
Colgin, 2876, 10718
Colita, 5861
College Inn®, 3478
Collingwood Canadian Whisky, 1784
Colloidal Silver, 8009
Coloma, 2883
Colombian Excelso, 10157
Colombian Supremo, 10157
Colombina, 2132
Colombo, 13811
Colon Care™, 13097
Colon Cleanse, 5682
Colonel Lee, 11263
Colonel Lee Bourbon, 11264
Colonial, 13691
Colonial Beef, 7676
Colonial Club, 7655, 9773
Colonial International, 2885
Colonial Jacks, 6222
Colonial Williamsburg, 5285, 11025, 12714
Colonna, 2887, 3439
Colony Meadery, 10666
Color Blaster, 6158
Color Garden, 2890
Color®, 8899
Colorado Classic, 5945
Colorado Gold, 5409
Colorado Kind Ale, 8602
Colorado Native, 8459
Colorado Native™, 8460
Colorado Peanut Butter Nugget, 9836
Colorado Sunshine Honey, 5766
Colorado's Kernels, 7433
Colorenhance, 8899
Coloreze, 6261
Colorpure, 10511
Colors Gourmet Pizza, 2901
Colossal Crisp®, 7179
Colosseum, 4411
Colt 45, 9664
Colts Bolts, 2903
Columbia, 46
Columbia Empire Farms, 2905
Columbia Winery®, 3834
Columbian Pale Ale, 2911
Columbian, 761, 12846
Columbus®, 6000
Colusa Rose®, 10777
Comboliak, 9802
Combos®, 7952
Comeaux's Andouille Sausage, 2918
Comeaux's Crawfish Tails, 2918
Comeaux's Tasso, 2918
Comet, 12721
Comet Rice®, 10777
Comfortcoat®, 3320
Comic Animal, 163
Commodore Perry India Pale Ale, 5314
Common Folk Farm, Inc., 2924
Commonwealth, 4614, 5325
Community Bakeries, 2925
Community Bear Works, 10666
Community Coffee, 2926
Comotion®, 8470
Complan, 6977
Compleats®, 6000
Complimed, 13642
Complimed®, 9237
Con Gusto, 11065
Con Gusto®, 11186
Con Yeager Spices, 2936
Concannon Vineyard, 2941
Concessions, 11755
Concha Y Toro, 1006
Concord Foods, 2943
Concord Grape, 12914
Condado De Almara, 3545

Condex, 2386
Coney Island, 3695
Coney Island Classics, 7414
Confection Sunflower Seed, 10616
Confecto, 6261
Congusto, 11187
Conn's Bbq Pork Rinds, 2952
Conn's Bean Dip, 2952
Conn's Caramel Popcorn, 2952
Conn's Cheese Corn Popcorn, 2952
Conn's Cheese Curls, 2952
Conn's Cheese Dip, 2952
Conn's Corn Chips, 2952
Conn's Corn Pops Popcorn, 2952
Conn's Green Onion, 2952
Conn's Honey Bbq Jerky, 2952
Conn's Honey Mustard Dip, 2952
Conn's Jalapeno Dip, 2952
Conn's Nacho Tortilla Chips, 2952
Conn's Oat Bran Pretzels, 2952
Conn's Original, 2952
Conn's Original Beef Jerky, 2952
Conn's Party Mix, 2952
Conn's Picante Dip, 2952
Conn's Pork Rinds, 2952
Conn's Pretzel Rods, 2952
Conn's Pretzel Sticks, 2952
Conn's Pretzel Thins, 2952
Conn's Pretzel Twists, 2952
Conn's Restaurant Tortilla Chips, 2952
Conn's Round Tortilla Chips, 2952
Conn's Salsa Supreme Dip, 2952
Conn's Salt & Vinegar, 2952
Conn's Sour Cream, 2952
Conn's Wavy, 2952
Connemara®, 1120
Conners Best Bitter, 1702
Connie's Handmade Toffee, 7761
Connie's Pizza, 8367, 9719
Connoisseur Collection, 8724
Connoisseur Master Blend, 5228
Cono Sur, 1006
Conquest®, 6374
Conrad-Davis, 2956
Consenso, 781
Consorzio, 8764
Consumers, 2966
Contadina®, 3478
Conti, 2970
Continental Chefc, 8088
Continental Cuisine, 11402
Contiparaguay, 2970
Contrasweet, 13444
Convetual Franciscan Friars, 3597
Conway's, 7655
Conway's Irish Ale, 5314
Cook's, 11733
Cook's Pantry Organic, 2979
Cooked Perfect®, 5929
Cookie Art, 5160
Cookie Brittle, 14045
Cookie Crisp®, 8945
Cookie Cupboard, 3399
Cookie Dough Bites, 12547
Cookie Wedgies, 8706
Cookies, 2988
Cookies By Lasca, 8927
Cookietree Bakeries, 2986
Cookin' Cajun, 3147
Cookquick', 12972
Cookquik Ranch Wagon, 12973
Cooks Delight, 6234
Cool, 8459
Cool Beans Coffee, 3217
Cool Crisp, 5003
Cool Mint Drops, 9995
Cool Mountain Gourmet Soda, 2994
Cool Mule, 3180
Cool Natural Sodas, 2992
Cool Pops, 2136
Cool Quencher Sports, 2992
Cool Runnings, 13208
Cool Whip, 6976
Cool-E-Pops, 5752
Coombs Family Farms, 1067
Coon®, 11211
Cooper, 11308
Cooper's Craft, 1784
Coors, 5975, 8459
Coors®, 8460
Copa, 5499
Copa De Oro Coffee Liqueur, 5720

1269

Brand Name Index

Copes, 6551
Copper Ridge Vineyards®, 3834
Copperhead Pale Ale, 4959
Copperline Amber, 2236
Coppets, 11310
Coqsol, 11778
Coqui Cookies, 4137
Cora®, 6818
Coral Food, 8649
Corazonas' Heartbar, 6338
Corbett Canyon, 3545
Core Power, 2811
Corey Creek, 1152
Corfu, 3028
Corn Appetit, 1683, 10179
Corn Appetit Ultimate, 10179
Corn Flakes, 6766
Corn King, 2126
Corn Pops, 6766
Corn Pops®, 6765
Corned Beef, 8783
Cornell Beverages, 3036
Cornerstone®, 7786
Coromega, 12679
Corona, 71
Corona Extra, 4881, 7123
Corona Light, 4881
Coronado, 7655
Coronet Vsq Brandy, 5720
Corpora Agricola, 5036
Cortilite, 13455
Cortland Manor, 5753
Cosco Flavors, 3045
Cosmo's, 3048
Costa, 3051
Costa Clara, 7702
Costa Coffee, 2814
Costa Deano's, 3050
Costa Pasta, 9813
Costa Rica, 761, 1000
Costa's Pasta, 3053
Costadeanos Gourmet, 3052
Costello Banfi, 1006
Cote De Carneros, 2225
Cotlets, 7410
Cottage Bake, 6542
Cottage Cuts Potato Chips, 13884
Cottage Delight, 2507
Cottam Gardens, 8782
Cotton Candy Swirl, 12547
Cottonwood Canyon, 3057
Couch's Original, 2794
Cougar Gold, 13516
Cougar Mountain, 3059
Coumadin®, 1721
Country, 10080
Country Archer Beef Jerky, 3063
Country Blend Cereal, 5946
Country Boy, 2045
Country Choice, 3066
Country Classic, 6528
Country Club, 7655, 9664
Country Club Malt Liquor, 9137
Country Coffee, 3620
Country Cow, 5777
Country Cow Cocoa, 5777
Country Cream, 5282
Country Cream Butter, 13668
Country Creamery, 9283
Country Delight, 3070
Country Fair, 6352
Country Festival, 4262
Country Fresh, 3075, 3077
Country Fresh Farms, 3074
Country Fresh Fudge, 3075
Country Fresh™, 3442
Country Game, 9043
Country Gardens Blush Banquet, 1314
Country Gardens Cuisine, 2919
Country Golden Yolks, 5138
Country Grown, 10488
Country Grown Foods, 5040
Country Harvest, 13691
Country Hearth, 11525
Country Hearth®, 9736
Country Home Bakers, 3078
Country Home Bakery, 6338
Country Home Creations, 3079
Country Kitchen Meals, 11979
Country Krisp®, 1654
Country Life, 3080
Country Maid, 3081

Country Morning, 4078
Country Pasta, 3072
Country Pride®, 10056
Country Road, 6186
Country Select, 2961
Country Spice Tea, 2834
Country Style, 241, 2219
Country Time, 6976
Countryale, 13643
Countrymixes, 6821
Countryside Red, 1672
Courageous Captain's, 2419
Courtney's, 183
Courtney's Organic Water Crackers, 183
Courvoisier, 3024, 5892, 12315
Courvoisier®, 1120
Cousin Rachel Pretzels, 12851
Cousin Willie's, 10551
Covenant Winery, 10952
Covered Bridge Mills, 5331
Covey Run Winery®, 3834
Covi-Ox, 1692
Covitol, 1692
Cow Belle Creamery's™, 12885
Cow Lick, 1018
Cow Pie, 1018
Cow Tales®, 5096
Cow-Town and Rancher's, 5477
Cowboy, 10324, 13716
Cowboy Foods, 3099
Cowcium, 4914
Cowgirl Chocolates, 3100
Cowie, 3102
Cowlicks, 12847
Cowpuccino Toppers, 5777
Cowrageous!™, 6676
Cowtown Bbq, 9565
Coyote, 5442, 12814
Coyote Cocina, 3522
Coyote Grill®, 11317
Coyote Star, 5442
Coyote White, 6763
Coyote Wine, 1422
Cozy Cottage, 7866
Cplus®, 6818
Crab House Nuts, 1470
Crab Teazers, 12520
Cracker Barrel, 6976, 9789
Cracker Barrel®, 11211
Cracker Jack, 4741
Cracker Jack®, 9945
Cracker Snackers, 9799
Craft's, 10280
Crain Ranch, 3110
Craisins, 9355
Cram For Students, 131
Cramore, 13141
Cran-Maxc, 9997
Cranapple, 9355
Cranberry Blossom, 10478
Cranberry Blush Wine, 13372
Cranberry Gose, 7526
Cranberry Sweets, 3114
Crancherry, 9355
Crane & Crane, 9212
Crane's Aqua Line, 3115
Crane's Blue Line, 3115
Crane's Gray Line, 3115
Crane's Maroon Line, 3115
Crane's Red Line, 3115
Crangrape, 9355
Cranicot, 9355
Cranorange, 9355
Cranrx, 8896
Cransations™, 11654
Crater's Meats, 3117
Crave, 6976
Craven Crab, 3119
Cravin Asian, 11775
Crawfish Monica, 6687
Crayola, 2136, 6810
Crazy Cow, 387
Crazy Jerry's, 3123
Cream Ale, 9117
Cream of Peanut, 1151
Cream of the West, 3130
Cream of Vanilla, 7934
Cream of Weber, 4328
Cream of Wheat®, 864
Creamerie Classique, 13070
Creamette®, 10777

Creamland, 3131, 3442
Creamy, 14017
Creamy Head, 13141
Creamy Medley of Popcorn, 10984
Createam, 13802
Creation Nation, 3132
Creative Bakers, 4244
Creative Classics™, 9523
Creative Confections, 3133
Creative Foods, 3136
Creative Gourmet, 11552
Creative Snacks Co., 3139
Creative Spices, 3140
Creekbend, 9452
Creekside, 6290
Creekstone, 5492
Creekstone Farms, 11053
Creemore Springs, 8459
Creemore Springs Premium Lager, 3141
Creemore Springs Urbock, 3141
Crema De Cacao, 3545
Crema De Coco, 3545
Crema De Many, 1151
Crema Di Miele, 11205
Creme Curls, 3143
Creme D'Lite, 3144
Creme De Cacao, 9773
Creme De Menthe, 9773, 10596
Creme Filled Butterscotch Krimpetsc, 12551
Cremer Cunter, 9978
Cremes, 3145
Cremora®, 1103
Creole Classic, 4886
Creole Classics, 11402
Creole Delicacies, 3147
Creole Delights, 4886
Creole Rose, 4886
Crescent, 3151, 9680
Crescent Confections, 8677
Crescent Ridge Dairy, 3153
Crescentgarniture, 10039
Crest, 12721
Cricklewood Soyfoods, 3163
Crider, 3164
Crimson Jewell®, 1420
Crina®, 3320
Cripple Creek, 9561
Crisco, 6380
Crisp & Delicious, 6451
Crisp 'n Fresh, 12201
Crisp Coat™ Uc, 8804
Crisp Film®, 8804
Crispers®, 9523
Crispin, 8459
Crispin Cider®, 8460
Crispix®, 6765
Crispy Crowns®, 9523
Crispy Crunchies®, 9523
Crispy Fliers®, 13607
Crispy Steaks, 14043
Crispy-Lishus®, 1654
Crispycakestm, 12680
Crispycoat Fries, 7179
Cristal, 9571
Cristal®, 8460
Cristobal, 2122
Critchfield Meats, 3168
Critelli, 3169
Criterion, 3170
Cro-Mag, 12023
Cro-Magnon, 12023
Cro-Man, 12023
Croccantinic, 7098
Crock Pot®, 864
Crockett's, 3173
Crockpot, 2950
Crofter's, 3176
Crofter's Just Fruit, 3176
Crofter's Superfruit, 3176
Croissant De Paris, 5106
Cronk 2 O, 13697
Crook's, 11864
Crooked River Brewing, 3180
Crooked Stave, 10666
Crosby, 3185
Crosse & Blackwell, 6380
Crosset Company, 2298
Crotonese, 11668
Croustade 4cm, 10039
Croustade 5cm, 10039
Croustade 7cm, 10039
Crow Canyon, 104

Crowley, 3188
Crowley Ridge, 1727
Crown, 3195, 11312
Crown Jewel, 9570
Crown Prince Natural, 3194
Crown Prince Seafood, 3194
Crown's Pride, 4650
Crowning Touch, 13894
Croyden House, 7848
Cruisin Cool, 10953
Crunch 'n Munch, 6267
Crunch 'n Munch®, 2939, 2940
Crunch Pak®, 2505
Crunch'n'munch Glazed Popcorn, 6267
Crunch-A-Mame, 3200
Crunch® Bar, 8945
Cruncha Ma-Mec, 5376
Crunchmaster, 12477
Crunchsters, 3202
Crunchy Nut, 6766
Crunchy Rob's, 11484
Cruse Vineyards, 3204
Crush®, 3725, 6818
Crutchfield, 13803
Cruzan®, 1120
Cry Baby, 2132
Cry Baby®, 12880
Cryogel, 12637
Crystal, 1087, 3210
Crystal Bay, 8784
Crystal Bitter, 9153
Crystal Clear, 7655
Crystal Farms, 3211
Crystal Foods, 1662
Crystal Gum™, 8804
Crystal Lake, 3213
Crystal Light, 6976
Crystal Palace, 11264
Crystal R-Best, 1662
Crystal Rock Water, 3217
Crystal Springs, 3218, 10303
Crystal Springs®, 3220, 3319
Crystal Tex™ 627m, 8804
Crystal® Springs, 11889
Crystalac®, 7857
Cth, 3390
Cucamonga, 13511
Cucina & Amore, 3223
Cucina Fresca, 11390
Cucina Sorrenti, 11818
Cuddy, 11776
Cuetara, 5108
Cuisine Nature, 8676
Cuisine Solutions, 3229
Cuisiniers Choice, 692
Cuizina Italia, 3230
Culinaire, 3232
Culinaria, 11303
Culinary Classic Breast of Turkey N, 14041
Culinary Classic Slices Breast of T, 14041
Culinary Tours®, 12885
Culligan, 3239, 3469
Culmination, 7526
Cultured Red Neck T-Shirts, 6796
Culturelak, 9802
Culturelle, 6107
Culver City Meat, 5141
Culver Duck, 3244
Cumberland Dairy, 3247
Cumberland Gap, 3248
Cumberland Ridge, 12027
Cumin Gouda, 13840
Cummings & York, 10435
Cup O' Noodles, 9068
Cup-O-Gold, 163
Cupagranols, 3857
Cupful, 11003
Cupid, 4387
Cure 81®, 6000
Curlumin C3 Complex, 11061
Curly's, 3258, 11733
Curran Cheese, 3259
Currentc, 3184
Curry King, 3260
Curt Georgi Flavors & Fragrances, 8891
Curtis, 3262
Cusa Tea, 3263
Cusano's, 3265
Cushing, 8414
Cusquena®, 8460
Custom Coffee Plan, 4276
Custom Culinary™, 11504

Brand Name Index

Custom Lable, 6508
Custom Up Cakes, 3541
Customer's Bags, 6506
Cutcher, 8995
Cutie Cupid, 11004
Cutie Pies, 3276
Cutiesc, 12242
Cutthroat Pale Ale, 9366
Cutty Sark, 3545
Cutty Sarkr Scots Whisky Chocolates, 10468
Cutwater Spirits, 571
Cuvaison, 3280
Cuvee Sauvage, 4649
Cvc Specialsties, 1967
Cvf, 5643
Cvi Bulk Wines, 3161
Cybele's Free To Eat, 3282
Cycle, 4387
Cycles, 5499
Cyclone, 13280
Cygnet, 3285
Cylactin®, 3320
Cytosport, 4150
Czarina, 11264

D

D' Sol, 4687
D'Agostino, 6126
D'Eaubonne Vsop Napoleon, 3024
D'Gari, 12823
D'Haubry, 10188
D'Italiano, 13691
D'Italianoc, 1359
D'Oni Specialty Sauces, 4839
D-Max, 6629
D.F.A., 8816
D.J. Jardine, 6456
Da'bomb, 9565
Dab, 1361
Dacopa, 2071
Dad's, 6380
Dad's Old Fashioned®, 6483
Daddy Ray's, 6338
Daddy-Q, 3537
Dadex, 137
Daeab, 8308
Daedol, 137
Daejel, 137
Daelube, 137
Dagoba Organic Chocolate, 3306, 13433
Dahlicious, 3326
Dai Dairy, 345
Dai Juhyo, 1120
Daily Energy, 9201
Daily Foods, 3331, 8130
Daily Green Teas, 10677
Daily Made, 3330
Daily Multiple S/C, 75
Daily Soy, 9201
Daily Sun, 13932
Daily's® Premium Meats, 11363
Dainties, 10104
Dainty Pak, 13365
Dair-E Lite, 10815
Dairfair, 3386
Dairy Fresh, 3336
Dairy Group, 3337
Dairy House Chocolate Dairy Powderc, 6260
Dairy Housec Milk Flavors, 6260
Dairy Housec Stabalizers, 6260
Dairy Housec Vitamins, 6260
Dairy Maid, 3341
Dairy Maid Dairy, 3340
Dairy Maid Dairy®, 3335
Dairy Mart, 387
Dairy Pure, 7320
Dairy Pure®, 3442
Dairy Queen, 8109
Dairy's Pride, 7998
Dairyamerica, 2061, 3345
Dairyland, 13875
Dairyland®, 11211
Dairystar®, 11211
Dairytime, 7419
Dairyworld, 9469
Daisey Sour Cream, 3350
Daisy Brand Meat Products, 3121
Daisy Cottage Cheese, 3350

Daisy Light Sour Cream, 3350
Daisy Low Fat Cottage Cheese, 3350
Dak®, 10124
Daklinza™, 1721
Dakota, 3353
Dakota Gourmet, 11802
Dakota Gourmet Heart Smart, 11802
Dakota Gourmet Toasted Korn, 11802
Dakota Growers Pasta, 13475
Dakota Growers Pasta Co®, 8225
Dakota Hearth, 10698
Dakota Maid, 9132
Dakota Seasonings, 423
Dakota Yeast, 8353
Dalla, 3361
Dallis Bros. Coffee, 3362
Dallmayr, 1957, 3714
Daltons, 10659
Daminaide, 137
Daminco, 137
Daminet, 137
Damron, 3366
Dan Carter, 3367
Dan Tucker, 7655
Dan's Prize®, 6000
Danactive, 3379
Dancing Bull®, 3834
Dandies Marshmallows, 2550
Dandyc, 3781
Danesi, 3009
Daniel Orr, 4487
Danimals, 3377, 3379
Danisa, 7769
Dannon, 3377, 3379
Danzig, 9833
Daphne's Creamery, 3380, 14069
Dar Pro Bioenergy, 3390
Dar Pro Ingredients, 3390
Dar Pro Solutions, 3390
Darcia's Organic Crostini, 183
Dardenella, 1688
Dardimans, 3382
Dare Creme Cookies, 3384
Dare Realfruit Candies, 3384
Dari Pride, 6971
Dari-Cal, 13122
Darjceling Superb 6000, 5228
Dark & Moody, 12178
Dark Dog Organic, 3388
Dark Eyes, 7655
Dark Fruit Chews, 7643
Dark Horse Brewing, 10666
Dark Horse Chocolates, 5578
Dark Horse®, 3834
Dark Lager, 4139
Dark Roast, 1054, 5462
Dark Star, 2860
Dark Star Porter, 1507
Dark Tickle, 3389
Dasani, 2811, 2814
Dasher Pecan, 11831
Dastony, 13847
Date Crystals, 11555
Dave, 6590
Dave's Killer Bread, 4529
Daven Island Trade, 12068
David Beards, 5298
David Beards Texas Style, 5298
David Del Curto, 5036
David Nicholson 1843, 7655
David Rio, 2833
David Rio Chai, 3398
David's Cookies, 3399
David's Gourmet Coffee, 1601
David's Kosher, 1262
David® Seeds, 2939, 2940
Davidson's Inc, 3400
Davidson's®, 8225
Daviess County, 7655
Davinci, 6279
Davinci Gourmet, 2606
Davinci®, 3834
Davinia, 9773
Davis Bread, 3405
Davis Bynum, 3406
Davis Strait Fisheries Ltd, 3408
Davis®, 2711
Davy's Mix, 4521
Dawes Hill, 9485
Dawn, 12721
Dawn Glo, 5555
Dawn's Foods, 3413

Day By Day, 7505
Day-Lee Foods, 3416
Daybreak, 3417
Daybreak Classics, 1282
Daybreak Foods, 3418
Daygum, 9956
Dayton Nut Specialties, 3421
Dayton's, 10773
Dci Cheese®, 11209, 11211
Dds, 13130
Dds Acidophilus, 13130
Dds Junior, 13130
Dds Plus, 13130
De Bas Vineyard, 4815
De Beukelaer, 3433
De Caradeuc White, 8513
De Champaque Bakery Snacks, 3615
De Groen's, 999
De Kuyper Geneva, 3024
De L'Ora®, 3479
De La Marca, 8028
De Lescot, 5405
De Loach, 3509
De Lorimeir, 3510
De Mill, 9094
De Rose Vineyards, 2675
De Santa Fe, 11195
De Winkel®, 4552
De-Kaffo, 13279
De-Lish-Us, 3501
Dean, 3441
Dean & Deluca, 3440
Dean's, 3131
Dean's Country, 3443
Dean's™, 3442
Deans®, 13328
Dear Lady, 11759
Dearborn Sausage, 3446
Death and Taxes Black Beer, 8524
Death Valley Habanero, 6015
Deauville, 4515
Deaver Vineyards Wine, 3447
Debbie D'S, 3448
Debco, 3424
Debi Lilly™ Design, 11073
Deboles, 5505
Dec a Cake®, 864
Decacake, 73
Decadent Temptations, 387
Decades, 8869, 8870
Decatur Dairy, 3457
Dechiel, 10813
Decker Farms Finest, 3458
Deconna, 3461
Decovery®, 3320
Decoy, 3779
Dee Lite, 12001
Deen, 3463
Deep, 3465
Deep Chi Builder, 5791
Deep Cover, 7310
Deep Cover Brown, 7309
Deep Dairy, 3465
Deep Dish Pecan Pike, 2881
Deep Eddy Vodkas, 5720
Deep Purple, 5539
Deep Rich, 464
Deep River Snacks, 3466
Deep Rock Water, 10303, 11889
Deep Rock®, 3220, 3319
Deep Sleep, 5791
Deep Valley, 3467
Deer Creek, 3468
Deer Park, 14055
Deerfield, 3470
Deering, 4369
Deez Nutz, 4299
Degeneve, 8304
Degoede, 954
Dehydrates, 3474
Dei Fratelli, 5893, 5894
Deiorio's, 3427
Deja Blue®, 3725, 6818
Dejean, 8995
Dekalb, 11286
Dekuyper®, 1120
Del Campo, 3788
Del Cara, 2375
Del Dia®, 10056
Del Fuerte®, 6000
Del Grosso, 3494
Del Mar, 3477

Del Mondo, 9808
Del Monte, 56
Del Monte Fresh®, 3479
Del Monte®, 3478
Del Rio, 3481
Del Sol, 6177
Del Valle, 2814
Del's, 3482
Del's Italian Ices, 3482
Del's Lemonade, 3482
Delacour, 7655
Delallo, 3487
Delancey Dessert, 3488
Delaviuda, 3490
Delecto Chocolates, 4884
Delftree, 3493
Delgrosso, 7635
Deli, 12301
Deli Cuts, 2212
Deli Direct, 11960
Deli Express, 3836
Deli Flavor, 5391
Deli Maid, 13016
Deli Meats, 6000
Deli Sliced, 5039
Deli Style, 13063
Deli-Best, 11298
Deli-Catessen, 13330
Deli-Dogs, 2541
Deli-Fresh, 3336
Delicare, 2666
Delicato, 3497
Delice, 10146
Delicia, 10734
Delicioso, 11437
Delicious, 2750, 13728
Delicious™, 12426
Delico, 6945
Delighted By, 3504
Delights, 3189
Delishaved, 7197
Delizia, 13365
Delizza, 10188
Della, 11908
Della Gourmet Rice, 11908
Della Naturac, 12928
Delmonte, 4928
Delnor, 11766
Deloach, 1543
Delta, 12410
Delta Bay, 6290
Delta Foods, 3513
Delta Fresh, 3515
Delta Rose, 7571
Deluscious, 3438
Deluxe, 3480, 8533
Deluxe Fruitcake®, 2881
Delvo®Cheese, 3320
Delvo®Fresh, 3320
Delvotest®, 3320
Demaria Seafood, 3429
Dement's, 5029
Demi-Glace Veal Gold, 8538
Deming's, 9980
Demitasse After Dinner Tea, 5228
Demitri's Bloody Mary Seasonings, 3518
Dempster's, 7876
Dempster's®, 2121
Den, 9129
Denmark: Officer, 5108
Dennis, 11503
Dennison, 6267
Dennison's, 6267
Dennison's®, 2939, 2940
Denrado, 648
Dentyne, 2132, 8474
Dentyne Fire Gum, 1980
Dentyne Ice, 1980, 9995
Dentyne Tango, 1980
Denunzio, 7635
Denver, 2898, 5304
Denver Co, 4079
Dependable, 4681
Depiezac, 5791
Derco, 3530
Dermagest, 7422
Dermanex, 783
Des Coteaux, 4748
Descote, 9797
Desert Gardens Chile and Spice, 2919
Desert Gold, 9042
Desert Gold Dry, 13299

1271

Brand Name Index

Desert Pepper, 3537
Desert Pride, 1603
Desert Wonder, 1603
Designer Protein, 4150
Designer Whey, 3540
Desirable, 4387
Desolite® Supercoatings, 3320
Dessert Jewell, 462
Desserts By David Glass, 3544
Destab, 9797
Detoxwater, 3546
Dettol, 10598
Devil's Fire, 4928
Devil's Lair, 12937
Devils Backbone Brewing Company, 571
Devils Spring, 1423
Devine Nectar, 3550
Devon, 2960
Devondale™, 11211
Devonsheer®, 864
Devro, 3552
Dewar's Scotch, 914
Dewar's White Label, 3570
Dewied, 3554
Dextranase, 1692
Dextrozyme, 1692
Dh3, 9240
Dhagold™, 3320
Dhea, 746, 6107, 8009, 11268
Dhea Plus, 9240
Dhidow Enterprise 150x, 3558
Dhidow Enterprise 20x, 3558
Dhidow Enterprise 50x, 3558
Dhidow Enterprise Zero, 3558
Di Amore, 11264
Di Grazia Vineyards, 3597
Di-Mare Gold Label, 3565
Diabetiks, 5363
Diablo Ignited Sours, 1343
Diago, 8387
Diago's®, 8384
Diamalt, 954, 10247
Diamond, 726, 3572, 5409, 7118, 10421, 12973
Diamond Bakery, 3571
Diamond Cake, 1061
Diamond D, 7207
Diamond Green Diesel, 3390
Diamond Joe, 13613
Diamond K, 6673
Diamond Spring Water, 8605
Diamond Springs, 3469
Diamond Walnut Shortbread Cookies, 9399
Diana, 8676, 9873
Diana Sauce, 6976
Diana's, 10086
Diane's Italian Sausage, 12463
Diane's Sweet Heat, 3583
Diane's®, 8384
Dianes, 8387
Dibella, 3566
Dick & Casey's, 4981
Dick Servaes, 5428
Dickies, 13107
Dickinson Frozen Foods, 3588
Dickinson's, 6380
Dickson's Pure Honey, 3589
Diedrich Coffee, 3591
Diedrich Coffee®, 6818
Dieffenbach's, 3592
Diestel Turkey Ranch, 3594
Diet Big Red ®, 1339
Diet Chaser, 3707
Diet Cheerwine, 2234
Diet Clear Jazz, 5539
Diet Coke, 2814
Diet Dhea, 9240
Diet Double-Cola, 3707
Diet Freeze, 7870
Diet Ice Botanicals, 12510
Diet Lift, 9155
Diet Rite, 4521
Diet Rite3, 10151
Diet Rite®, 3725, 6818
Diet Ski, 3707
Dieters Tea, 131
Dietz & Watson, 3595
Difiore Pasta, 3563
Digesta-Lac, 8816
Digestive Advantage, 11285
Digestive Care™, 6449
Digezyme, 11061

Digiorno, 2667
Digiorno®, 8945
Digiovanni, 13422
Dijon Clone, 1128
Dijon Crunch, 8269
Dilberito, 11324
Dilbert Mints&Gummies, 10532
Dilettante Chocolates, 11390
Dillard's, 3600
Dillman Farm, 3601
Dillman's All Natural, 3601
Dillons, 12516
Dilusso Deli Company®, 6000
Dimarco, 7927
Dimitri, 7655
Dimo, 9912
Dina, 12301
Dinapoli, 2065
Dinatura, 6806
Dine-Meat Emu Products, 3612
Ding Gua Gua, 1478
Dingdongs®, 6013
Dinkel's, 3609
Dinkel's Famous Stollen, 3609
Dinkel's Sip'n, 3609
Dinkel's Southern Double, 3609
Dinner Reddi, 10491
Dinny Robb, 5717
Dinosaur Brand, 6880
Dinty Moore®, 6000
Dip Indulgence, 13815
Dip N' Joy, 5105
Dip Sticks, 12202
Dip-Idy-Dill, 6528
Dipasa Biladi, 3615
Dipasa De Champagne, 3615
Dipasa Usa, 3615
Dippin' Candy, 4507
Dippin' Dots, 3616
Dipt'n Dusted, 12520
Dirty, 13129
Discovery, 4575
Disney, 4659
Disney Princess, 4507
Distillata, 3621
Ditka, 1087
Diver's Hole Dunkelweizen, 7143
Divian Coffee, 13191
Divine Delights, 3625
Divine Meringues, 9816
Divine Organics, 3627
Diwan Coffee, 13191
Dixie, 3631
Dixie Brand, 9763
Dixie Crystals®, 6164
Dixie Fresh, 10655
Dl Geary Brewing, 3637
Dm Choice, 12550
Dm Ole, 12550
Dnx, 3329
DoA MarjA™, 6000
Dobake, 3639
Doc's Draft Hard Cider, 13578
Doctor Dread's, 3641
Doctor's Nutriceuticals, 5698
Doe Mill, 2044
Dog Bakery Products, 818
Dog-Gone Chik'n®, 1654
Dog-Gones, 12847
Dogflex, 3753
Dogsters, 6338
Dogwood, 3646
Dohlar, 4943
Dolce, 3009, 4258, 6806
Dolcea®, 3834
Dolcia Prima™ Allulose, 12561
Dole, 741, 7213, 12871
Dole® Soft Serve, 6792
Dolefam, 679
Dolimo®, 7952
Dolores, 3658
Dolphin Natural, 3659
Dom Perignon, 3570, 8452
Dom's, 3660
Domaine Armand Rousseau, 4677
Domaine Breton, 5417
Domaine De Canton, 5720
Domaine De La Vougeraie, 1543
Domaine Du Castel, 10952
Domaine Michel, 8238
Domaine Netofa, 10952

Domaine Noel, 1306
Domaine St. George, 3662
Domaine St. Vincent, 5413
Dominator Wheat, 7844
Dominex, 3664
Dominick's, 6126
Domino, 4517
Domino Sugar, 3666
Domino®, 12196
Don Alfonso, 3667, 10952
Don Bernardo, 7126
Don Francisco's, 4202
Don Hilario Estate Coffee, 3669
Don Jose Horchata, 3670
Don Manuel 100% Colombian, 2847
Don Miguel Gascon®, 3834
Don Miguel®, 6000
Don Pedro, 7219
Don Pedro Jamonada, 2670
Don Pepino, 13437
Don Pepino®, 864
Don Peppe, 223
Don Quixate, 10319
Don's Chuck Wagon, 5898, 11587
Don't Go Nuts, 3675
Donald Duck, 13932
Donatoni, 3679
Donettes®, 6013
Dong Dong Joo Rice Wine, 6968
Donita, 100
Donmir Wine Cellars, 13825
Donnelly Chocolates, 3685
Donq Anejo, 3545
Donq Coco, 3545
Donq Cristal, 3545
Donq Gold, 3545
Donq Grand Anejo, 3545
Donq Limon, 3545
Donq Mojito, 3545
Donq Pasion, 3545
Dontil, 5123
Donut House, 6819
Donut House Collection®, 6818
Donut Shop, 1053, 6819
Doodleberry, 2905
Door County Potato Chips, 3691
Door-Peninsula, 3692
Dopplerock, 5314
Dora, 10041
Dorado, 1423
Dorazio, 11481
Dorcheste, 2750
Doritos, 4741
Doritos®, 9945
Dorks, 7643
Dorothy, 3697
Dorothy Lynch Home Style, 12557
Dorset Tea, 5612
Dos Gusanos, 7655
Dos Mamacitas, 12162
Dos Trianos, 7655
Dots®, 12880
Double Bag, 7526
Double Black, 10629
Double D, 7716
Double Decker, 13654
Double Deep Fudge Pecan Pie, 2881
Double Dry Gingerale, 3707
Double Fruit, 6380
Double India Pale Ale, 12153
Double L, 3463
Double Q, 9980
Double R®, 2332
Double Red Provisions, 1658
Double S, 11070
Double Star Espresso, 13160
Double-Cola, 3707
Double-Dry Mixers, 3707
Doublemint®, 7952, 13960
Doublepure Distilled, 4462
Douce Provence, 3165
Dough Relaxer, 7540
Dough Stabilizer, 12553
Dough-To-Go, 3709
Dove, 8533
Dove®, 7952
Dove® Chocolate, 6483
Dover Sole, 10949
Dowd & Rogers™, 9237
Dowd and Rogers, 3718
Down East, 9291
Downeast, 3719

Downeast Candies, 3720
Downeast Coffee, 3722
Downey's, 5957
Downey'sc, 9748
Downtown After Dark, 6711
Downtown Brown, 7554
Downtown Sumatra, 6547
Downy, 12721
Doyle's, 377
Dpo, 833
Dr Cookie, 3730
Dr Jerkyll & Mr Hide, 12831
Dr Oetker, 3734
Dr Pepper, 2811
Dr Pepper®, 3725
Dr Praeger's, 3727
Dr Tima, 3740
Dr. Bronner's, 4988
Dr. Konstantin Frank, 3724
Dr. McDougall's, 3733
Dr. McDougall's Right Foods, 11146
Dr. McDougall's Right Foodsc, 8281
Dr. Organic®, 8871
Dr. Pepper, 2815, 9083
Dr. Pepper®, 6818
Dr. Pete's, 3726
Dr. Peter's Peppermint Crunch, 6525
Dr. Red Norland, 3216
Dr. Rinse Vita Flo Formula, 8892
Dragnet, 3743
Dragon Cinnamon, 12987
Dragon Eggs, 7562
Dragon's Breath, 8670
Dragone®, 11209, 11211
Drake's, 8077
Drake's®, 8076
Drakes Amber Ale, 3746
Drakes Blond Ale, 3746
Drakes Fresh, 3747
Drakes Hefe-Weizen, 3746
Drakes Ipa, 3746
Drangle, 3748
Draper Valley Farms®, 9946
Drayman's Porter, 1237
Dream, 4025, 5505
Dream Candy, 11817
Dream Greens, 195
Dream Pretzels, 3752
Dreamies, 12551
Dreamies®, 7952
Dreaming Cow, 3755
Dreamworks, 10229
Dreft, 12721
Dreidoppel, 954
Dreimeister, 3236
Drew's All Natural, 3758
Drewclar, 135
Dreyer Wine, 3759
Dreyer's, 3760
Dreyer's®, 8945
Drier Meats, 3763
Drinde®, 4119
Driscoll's, 3765
Drive Activated, 1343
Drizzls, 4976
Drogheria & Alimentari, 8061
Dromedary, 8519
Drops O'Gold, 12979
Dropz, 7710
Droxia®, 1721
Drsoy, 6279
Drunken Goat Cheese, 11668
Drusilla, 3770
Dry Creek, 3771
Dry N-3, 1692
Dry Sack, 13320, 13811
Dry-Atlantic Coastal, 13372
Dry-Flo®, 8804
Dryden, 3772
Dryden & Palmer, 2132, 10724
Dsa, 3765
Du Bouchett Liqueurs & Cordials, 5720
Du Crose, 4920
Du Glaze, 4920
Du Sweet, 4920
Duas Rodas Industrial, 9027
Dubbasue and Company, 10219
Dubbel Felix Caspian, 2691
Dubble Bubble, 2132
Dubble Bubble®, 12880
Dubl-Tough®, 13595
Dubleuet, 5405

Brand Name Index

Dublin's Pub, 56
Dublnature, 13595
Dublserve®, 13595
Dublsoft, 13595
Dubonnet Apperitifs, 5720
Dubreton Natural, 7387
Duchess, 2242
Duchy Originals, 13544
Duck Pond Cellars, 3778
Duckhorn Vineyards, 3779
Ducktrap, 3780
Ducros, 8061
Duet, 2761
Duets, 7746
Duff's, 5015
Duffy, 3695
Dufour Pastry Kitchens, 3783
Duke's, 3787
Duke's Mayonaise, 1935
Duke's Smoked Shorty, 3787
Duke's®, 2939, 2940
Dulany, 10038
Dum Dum Pops, 11885
Dum Dumsc Pops, 2132
Dummbee Gourmet, 3791
Dun-D, 3796
Dunaweal Vineyard, 2770
Dunbar, 11865
Dunbar Ranch, 8960
Dunbars, 8519
Dunbars Candied Yams, 8519
Dunbars Marinated Roasted Peppers, 8519
Dunbars Roasted Peppers, 8519
Dunbars Sweet Potatoes, 8519
Duncan, 3793
Duncan Hies Wilderness®, 2939, 2940
Duncan Hines, 811
Duncan Hines Comstock®, 2939, 2940
Duncan Hines®, 2939, 2940
Dundee, 3798
Dundee Brandied, 3794
Dundee Candy Shop, 3795
Dunkin Donuts, 2811, 6819
Dunkin' Donuts, 1075, 6380
Dunkin' Donuts®, 3803
Dunn, 3804
Dunn's, 12170
Dunn's Best, 5094
Dunya Harvest, 11496
Duplin, 3805
Dupont D'Isigny - Candies, 4148
Durango, 3807
Durango Gold, 9672
Durell Vineyard, 6892
Durex®, 10598
Durkee, 73
Durkee®, 864
Durviage, 8676
Dusty Miller, 1688
Dutch Ann, 3811
Dutch Boiler, 7767
Dutch Boy, 1537
Dutch Brothers, 10358
Dutch Choux, 1524
Dutch Cocoa Bv, 9027
Dutch Country, 10661
Dutch Delight, 6551
Dutch Farms, 5555
Dutch Garden, 12437
Dutch Garden Super Swiss, 12437
Dutch Girl, 7767
Dutch Gold, 3815
Dutch Gourmet, 9408
Dutch Henry, 3816
Dutch Kitchen, 3817
Dutch Quality House, 1891
Dutch Waffle, 6338
Dutchie, 13622, 13623
Duthie, 11416
Dutlettes, 3633
Dutton Ranch, 6892
Duvel, 1748
Duvillage 1860®, 11211
Dyc Whisky, 1120
Dylan's, 961
Dynamic Foods, 3830
Dynamic Trio, 1914
Dynamite Energy Shake, 5669
Dynamite Vites, 5669
Dyneema Purity®, 3320
Dyneema®, 3320

E

E&S, 344
E(Lm)Inate®, 5665
E-Gems, 6364
E-Z Keep, 446
E. Waldo Ward, 3838
E.D. Smith, 1103, 3844, 12943
E.H. Taylor Jr., 11263
E.O.C., 4479
Eagle, 7173
Eagle Brand, 3862
Eagle Lager, 71
Eagle Rare, 11263
Eagle River Brand, 6721
Earl Grey Superior Mixture, 5228
Early California, 8692
Early Times, 1784
Earnest Eats, 3866
Earth Balance, 3868
Earth Balance®, 2939, 2940
Earth Power's All American, 10026
Earth Song Whole Food Bars, 3872
Earth Unt Farm, 1548
Earth's Best, 3617
Earth's Best Organic, 5505
Earth's Bounty, 8009
Earthbound Farm, 3379
Earthpower's Phytochi, 10026
Easley's, 3877
East Coast Gourmet, 10118
East India Coffee & Tea Co., 11141
East India Coffee and Tea, 4229
East Wind, 3887
East Wind Almond, 3887
East Wind Cashew, 3887
East Wind Organic Peanut Butter, 3887
East Wind Peanut, 3887
East Wind Tahini, 3887
Easten Shore Tea, 1000
Eastern Shore Foods, Llc, 11356
Eastside Deli, 3896
Easy Cheese, 8729
Easy Squeeze Bottle, 5489
Easymeal, 9529
Eat a Bowl, 2497
Eat Clean Organic, 13025
Eat Natural, 4148
Eat Smart, 4242
Eat the Bear, 4150
Eat Your Coffee, 3904
Eat Your Vegetables, 11754
Eatem, 3908
Eatmor, 178
Eatsmart Snacks, 11770
Eau Galle Cheese, 3910
Eberley, 8898
Ebly®, 7952
Ebro, 3914
Ecclestone, 942
Ecco, 4107
Ecco Domani®, 3834
Ecco!, 6314
Ech, 7874
Echinacea, 4859
Echinacea Triple Source, 5791
Echinacea/Goldenseal Supreme, 4859
Echo Falls, 9344
Echo Farm Pudding, 3915
Eckrich, 11733
Eclipse, 4407
Eclipse®, 7952, 13960
Eco-Dent, 7562
Ecocaps®, 1009
Ecoguar, 9654
Ecolab®, 11504
Ecomega, 11269
Econofrost, 10344
Economix, 13498
Economy, 2384
Ecopaxx®, 3320
Ecosnax, 498
Ecosoft, 13595
Ecoson, 3390
Ecoverde Coffee, 8090
Ecrevisse Acadienne, 11349
Ed & Don's Chocolate Macadamias, 3927
Ed & Don's Macadamia Brittles, 3927
Ed & Don's Macadamia Chews, 3927
Ed-Vance, 3948
Eda Sugarfree Hard Candies, 3934
Eda-Zenc, 5376

Eddie's, 4919, 6279
Eddie's Spaghetti Organic, 8642
Edelweiss Dressings, 4839
Eden, 3940, 8170
Eden Farms, 5910
Eden Life, 12486
Eden Organic, 3940
Eden's, 3941
Edenbalance, 3940
Edenblend, 3940
Edensoy, 3940
Edensoy Extra, 3940
Edge City Ipa, 1720
Edge City Pilsner, 1720
Edgewood Estate, 3946
Edibowl, 3013
Edinburgh Gin, 4677
Edmund Fitzgerald Porter, 5314
Edna Foods, 3953
Edna Valley, 3952
Edna Valley Vineyard®, 3834
Eds, 3471
Edward&Sons, 3956
Edwards, 11025, 11316
Edwards®, 11317
Edy's, 3760
Eez-Out, 6261
Efa Balanced, 9477
Effen®, 1120
Efferve, 4148
Effervescent, 6449
Effi, 3851
Eficacia, 9029
Efx Sports, 4150
Egg Beaters®, 2939, 2940
Egg King, 5092
Egg Low Farms, 3966
Egg-Land's Best™, 2031
Egg-O-Lite, 1735
Eggland's Best, 3968
Eggo, 6766
Eggo®, 6765
Eggstreme Bakery Mix 100, 10297
Eggstreme Options, 10297
Eggstreme Yolk, 10297
Eggstreme-We 300, 10297
Egon Muller, 4677
Eidelweiss, 773
Eight O'Clock, 3974
Ein Prosit!, 339
Eisbock, 3171
Eisenberg, 6767
Eisenberg Beef Hot Dogs, 6773
Eisenberg Corned Bee, 6773
Eisenberg Pastrami, 6773
Eisenberg®, 5929
Eisrebe, 6603
Eiwa, 3852
El Aguilia, 10555
El Almendro, 3490
El Carmen, 10319
El Cerdito, 690
El Charro, 3978
El Condor, 5405
El Conquistador, 4351
El Coto De Rioja, 4677
El Diablo®, 8415
El Dorado Coffee Roasters, 3997
El Ganador Del Premio, 12892
El Guapo, 8061
El Gusto, 4910
El Hombre Hambre, 12543
El Isleno, 4741
El Jimador, 1784, 3545
El Matador Tortilla Chip, 3981
El Mayor, 7655
El Mino, 28
El Monterey®, 10976
El Orgullo De Mi Tierra, 1909
El Panal, 13511
El Paso, 2574
El Pato, 13541
El Peto, 3987
El Ranchito, 10363
El Rancho, 7064
El Rancho Bean Chips, 7064
El Rancho Salsa Fresca, 7064
El Rancho Tortilla Chips, 7064
El Rey, 2617, 8539
El Sabroso, 11748
El Salvador Finca Las Nubes, 13160
El Sol, 8114

El Taino, 4351
El Tesoro De Don Felipe®, 1120
El Toro Loco, 357
El Toro Tequila, 11264
Elan, 1711
Elasthane™, 3320
Elastigel™ 1000j, 8804
Elavida™, 3320
Eldorado, 3998
Eldorado Natural Spring Water, 3996
Eldorado Spring Water, 3996
Eleanor's Best, 3999
Electra, 10415
Elegant Sweets, 7756
Element Shrub, 12815
Elephant Brand, 11522
Elephant Ginger, 12987
Eletone®, 8389
Eleutherogen, 4827
Elf, 13454
Eli's, 4010
Eliane™, 8804
Elijah Craig Bourbons, 5720
Eliot's Adult Nut Butters, 4011
Eliquis®, 1721
Elisir Mp Roux, 3165
Elissa Ipa, 11992
Elite, 4039, 11246
Elite Bakery, 7358
Elizabeth's, 859
Elk Run, 3837
Ella's Kitchen, 5505
Ella's Oven®, 4024
Ellie's Brown, 838
Ellis Davis, 757
Ellison, 4024
Ellison's, 4025
Ello Raw, 4027
Ellsworth, 4028
Ellsworth Valley, 4028
Ellyndale Foods®, 8725
Elmasu, 11957
Elmeco, 13005
Elmer T. Lee, 11263
Elmhurst Milked, 4034
Elora Esb, 12919
Elora Grand Lager, 12919
Elora Irish Ale, 12919
Elvi Winery, 10952
Elwood, 4038
Elyon, 5123
Elysian Brewing, 571
Elysium, 10415
Elz Super Enzymes, 8967
Embasa®, 6000
Embassy, 4039
Embassy Wines, 4104
Embrace, 2761
Embrazen, 12937
Emdex, 11485
Emer'gen-C, 255
Emerald, 11770
Emerald Bay Coastak, 2459
Emerald Cove, 5306
Emerald Green, 932
Emerald Nuts, 3575
Emerald Sea, 11559
Emerald Valley Kitchen™, 10365
Emeril's®, 864
Emeril®, 6818
Emerils, 6819
Emflo, 11485
Emgum, 11485
Emile's, 5421
Emily Kestral Cabern, 12227
Emily's, 498
Emily's Gourmet, 3696
Eminence, 196
Emjel, 11485
Emkay, 4046
Emmy's Pickles & Jams, 14069
Emox, 11485
Empact, 4050
Emperor's Kitchen, 5306
Empire, 9179
Empire Kosher, 5505
Empire Kosher Poultry Products, 4052
Empire's Best, 4054
Empliciti™, 1721
Empower, 437
Empress Chocolates, 4058
Emsland, 466

1273

Brand Name Index

Enak, 6340
Encircac, 10078
Encirclec, 187
Endangered Species Chocolate Bars, 4060
Enderma, 9997
Endico, 11108
Endless Summer Gold, 6711
Endorphin, 4895
Ends and Curls, 9432
Endure, 6843
Ener Jet, 5682
Ener-G, 4062
Energique®, 4065
Energy Bars, 7419
Energy Brand, 1294
Energy Chews, 1559
Energy Ice, 10953
Energy Powder, 131
Energy Supplements, 5155
Energy-To-Go, 12259
Energyfruits, 6751
Energysmart®, 190
Energysource®, 190
Enerjuice, 7210
Enfagrow®, 8103
Enfakid®, 8103
Enfamil™, 8103
Enfapro A+®, 8103
Enfield Farms, 4068
English Batter, 4070
English Guard ®, 13120
English Pale Ale, 556, 11218
English Toffee, 9055
Enhance To Go, 3753
Enhance Vitamin/Waters, 12704
Enjoying Las Vegas, 5660
Enjoying San Francisco, 5660
Enjoymints, 6926
Enoferm, 7176
Enrico's, 13326
Enroute, 4258
Enstrom Candies, 4079
Entemanns, 892
Entenmann's®, 1359
Entericare®, 1009
Enterprise, 4081
Entree, 1006
Entwine, 13654
Enviroflight, 3390
Envirokidz Organic, 8889
Environments, 2772
Enzact, 3548
Enzeco®, 4087
Enzo, 9636
Enzo Organic Balsamic Vinegar, 4085
Enzo Organic Olive Oil, 4085
Enzo's Table, 4085
Enzose, 6211
Eola, 1202
Eos, 3857
Epi, 7254
Epi De France, 4091
Epi-Guide®, 3320
Epic, 12239, 12437
Epicure, 6358
Epsoakc, 11145
Equacia, 9029
Equal, 8173, 9236
Equire, 6586
Era, 12721
Eragrainc, 4102
Eramosa Honey Wheat, 12136
Erewhon, 13124
Eribate, 9656
Eric Condren, 10229
Erica's Rugelach, 4105
Erick Schat, 11279
Erie, 4107
Erin's Rock Amber and Stout, 2410
Erin's®, 2939, 2940
Erjuv-Powder, 5883
Ermitage, 11894
Erucical, 716
Esb, 10629
Escarcoque, 10039
Eskimo Pie Coffeepeaks, 11028
Eskimo Pie Miniatures, 11028
Eskimo Pie Snowpeaks, 11028
Espeez, 11051
Esper Deluxe, 4115
Esperto, 8452
Espre, 11816

Espre-Cart, 11816
Espre-Matic, 11816
Espress-Umms, 9185
Espresso, 1997
Espresso Blend, 6611
Espresso Caruso, 11855
Espresso Gold, 7566
Espresso Maria, 11855
Esprion, 4736
Essaic Formula, 131
Essen Smart Gluten Free, 4208
Essen Smart Single Cookie 2, 4208
Essen Smart Single Cookie 3, 4208
Essen Smart Soy Cookies, 4208
Essensia, 10415
Essential, 491, 7173
Essential 10, 3540
Essential Balance, 9477
Essential Elite, 12486
Essential Mints, 13458
Essentials, 8130
Essiac (Extract), 4126
Essiac (Powder), 4126
Estancia, 4649
Estate Cabernet Sauvignon, 4980, 7003
Estate Chardonnay, 7003
Estate Grown Olive Oil, 6603
Estate Merlot, 4980, 7003
Estate Syrah, 7003
Estate Viognier, 7003
Estate Zinfandel (Ce, 7003
Esteem Plus, 4127
Ester-C®, 8871
Esterlina, 4128
Estrelitas®, 8945
Estrella, 1738
Estrella Jalisco, 571
Estro Logic, 13536
Estroven, 6107
Etch-A-Sketch, 2136
Ethan's, 4132
Ethel M®, 7952
Ethel's Baking, 4134
Ethical Nutrients, 8193
Ethiopian Moka, 10157
Ethiopian Organic, 13160
Ethnic Delights, 12167
Ethnic Edibles, 4137
Ethos Water, 12042
Etna Ale, 4139
Etna Bock, 4139
Etna Doppelbock, 4139
Etna Oktoberfest, 4139
Etna Weizen, 4139
Etopophos®, 1721
Etude, 12937
Eugalan, 1369
Eukanuba, 726
Eukanuba®, 7952
Eureka, 6586, 7160
Eureka!®, 1359
Euro Chocolate, 4145
Eurobubblies, 4148
Eurofresh, 7871
European Bakers, 4529
European Gourmet Bakery, 6049
Eurosupreme, 4148
Evan Williams Bourbons, 5720
Evangeline, 2019
Evans, 12972
Evelyn Sprague, 6868
Ever Clean, 2766
Everclear, 7655
Evercrisp®, 1196
Everfresh, 56, 4163, 8784, 10038
Everglades, 4165
Everglades Heat, 4165
Everglades Original, 4165
Evergood, 7650, 11728
Evergreen, 7758
Everland, 4170
Everybody's Nuts, 13907
Everyday Chef, 12973
Everything But The..., 2525
Evian, 1661
Evian®, 6818
Evil Twin, 10666
Evo, 2085, 4453
Evo Coffee, 2845
Evo Hemp, 4174
Evol®, 2939, 2940
Evoluna Estate, 12672

Evolution, 11780
Evolution Fresh, 4176, 12042
Evolve™, 6000
Evon's, 12866
Evonik, 1692
Evotaz®, 1721
Ewa, 9691
Eward Marc Chocolatier, 3958
Ex-Seed, 9332
Exact, 10637
Excalibur, 5061
Excel, 6762
Exceldor Express, 4183
Excelle, 6240
Excelpro™, 4119
Excelpro™ Plus, 4119
Except Mix, 11888
Exo, 4186
Exocyan, 9029
Exotica, 12053
Exotico, 7655
Expedition, 3746
Explore Cuisine, 4187
Exporsevilla, 218
Export Lager, 4139
Express Delights, 2726
Express Load, 4515
Expressnacks, 13923
Expresso, 7655
Exquisita, 4189
Exquizita, 4769
Extend®, 13328
Extinguisher, 469
Extol, 137
Extra Energy, 9201
Extra Gold Lager, 8459
Extra Gold Lager®, 8460
Extra Strength Pickle Juice Shots, 12716
Extra Value, 1658
Extra®, 7952, 13960
Extreme, 3953
Extreme®, 8945
Exxtra-C™, 6449
Eye of the Dragon, 11051
Eye of the Hawk, 8153
Eye of the Hawk Select Ale, 8153
Ez, 9049
Ezekiel 4:9c, 8831
Ezra Brooks, 7655
Ezy Time, 1444

F

F and M Special Draft, 12136
F Domin and Sons, 2559
F&A, 4195
F&V™, 8899
F1-1 Soy Fibre, 4357
Fa!Rlife, 2814
Fabrianoc, 2010
Fabuless®, 3320
Fabulous Fiber, 7404
Face Twisters Sour Bubble Gum, 4793
Facies, 56
Facino, 10565
Faema, 8619
Fair Acres, 9839
Fair Meadow, 11504
Fairbury, 13689
Fairfield Farm, 4222
Fairlee, 56
Fairtime, 163
Fairview Swiss Cheese, 6557
Fairway, 1064, 12550
Fairwinds Coffee, 4229
Fairy Food, 1828
Falafel Dry Mix, 12536
Falcon, 4232
Falcon Orange Soda, 5539
Falcon Pale, 10810
Falcone's, 4233
Falcone's Baked Goods, 4233
Falcone's Cookies, 4233
Falcone's Flatbread, 4233
Falfurrias, 6760
Falk Salt, 2879
Fall Creek, 5282
Fall River, 2082, 4235
Falstaff, 9664
Family Farmer, 2347
Family Favorite, 386

Family Traditions, 1553
Famli, 4537
Famosa, 8457
Famous, 4243
Famous Amos, 6766
Famous Original Formula Staminex, 7404
Fan-Sea, 11198
Fancy Brand, 1801
Fancy Dinner Blend, 9182
Fancy Farm, 4245
Fancy Foods, 4244
Fancy Lawnmower, 11992
Fancy Lebanese Bakery, 4246
Fancy Pantry, 12377
Fancy's Finest, 4244
Fanestil, 4249
Fanny Farmer, 4250
Fanny May Fine Chocolates, 4250
Fanta, 2811, 2814, 2815, 9155
Fanta Still, 2815
Fanta Zero, 2815
Fantaisie, 4544
Fantasia, 721, 4244
Fantastic, 4252
Fantastic Foods, 2286
Fantastic World Foods®, 1484
Faqs, 10568
Far Niente, 4258
Far West Meats, 4259
Farallon Foods, 4261
Faraon, 8161
Farbest, 4263
Farbest Foods, 4262
Farina Mills, 10213, 13124
Farm Country, 3695
Farm Fed Veal, 779
Farm Fresh, 2789
Farm Pac, 14008
Farm Pantry®, 1654
Farm Rich, 10714
Farman's®, 1103
Farmer Brothers, 340, 4276
Farmer Dons Country Ham, 12761
Farmer Focus, 11467
Farmer Girl, 5555
Farmer Jack, 13871
Farmer John, 2776, 11733
Farmer John Meats, 2776
Farmer King, 13625
Farmer Seed, 10050
Farmer's Cheese, 7423
Farmers, 4279, 11625
Farmers Favorite, 13613
Farmers Hen House, 4278
Farmers Ice Cream, 2377
Farmers Market, 4242
Farmers Pride Natural, 1178
Farmers Way, 4286
Farmhouse, 4386
Farmhouse Culture, 4288
Farmhouse Originals Ceasar, 5489
Farmhouse Originals®, 6374
Farmhouse Saison, 1401
Farmhouse™, 2031
Farmland, 1891, 11733
Farmland Dairies, 4290
Farmland Dairies Special Request, 4290
Farmland Dairy, 13647
Farr, 722
Farrell Baking, 4298
Fast Asleep, 9201
Fast Eddy's, 2991
Fast Fixin'®, 184, 13109
Fastachi, 4301
Fasweet, 4302
Fat Boy, 2294
Fat Dog Stout, 12153
Fat Free®, 5165
Fat Snax, 4303
Fat Tea, 4303
Fat Tire, 8959
Fatal Attraction, 4804
Father & Son, 8781
Father Sam's Pocket Breads, 4306
Father Sam's Tortillas, 4306
Father Sam's Wraps, 4306
Fatima, 14037
Fatina-Murano, 10565
Fattoria Dell'ulivo, 4386
Fattoria Italia, 10565
Fatworks, 4310
Favorit Swiss Premium, 1957

Brand Name Index

Favorites, 9722
Favorites of Hawaii, 5660
Fawen, 4312
Faygo, 8784
Fazio's, 4316, 6535
Fch, 7874
Feaster Foods, 13689
Featherweight, 12241
Febreeze, 12721
Federal Pretzel, 4318
Federal Pretzel Baking Company, 6338
Fee Brothers, 4320
Felbro, 4324
Felchlin-Swiss, 12438
Feline Pine, 2666
Felix Roma, 4326
Felta Springs, 8301
Fendall's, 4328
Fenestra Winery, 4329
Fenopure, 9654
Fentinel, 9238
Fenulife, 137
Feridies, 4335
Ferlac, 7172
Fermaid, 491, 7173, 7176
Fermalife, 4336
Fernandes, 2815
Ferolito Vultaggio, 4342
Ferolito, Vultaggio & Sons, 670
Ferralet®, 8389
Ferrante, 4343
Ferrara, 4346, 6540
Ferrara Candy Co., 2132
Ferrigno, 4349
Ferris, 4351
Ferry-Morsec, 10106
Festal, 7161
Festejos, 4483
Festino, 2260
Festival, 1688
Festival Light Ale, 7143
Festy, 122
Fever Sours, 1735
Ff, 4374
Fiber, 7947
Fiber 7, 8719
Fiber Greens, 9516
Fiber One, 5103
Fiber One®, 4947
Fiber Plus, 6766
Fiber Supreme, 8719
Fiber Up®, 9736
Fiber-7, 7947
Fiberbond, 6211
Fibersol® Capsules, 13097
Fibregum, 9029
Fibrex, 11794
Fibrim, 3773
Fibrymid, 3550
Ficks, 4359
Fida, 10565
Fiddle Cakes, 4362
Fiddle Faddle, 3430
Fiddle Faddle®, 2939, 2940
Fiddlers, 4032
Fiddlers Green Farms, 4362
Field, 11902
Field Day®, 1484
Field Roast, 4364
Field Trip, 4366
Field's, 4367
Fieldgate, 4424
Fieldstone Bakery, 8077
Fieldstone™ Bakery, 8076
Fiery Fingers®, 1654
Fiery Rum Cellars, 9334
Fiesta, 1279, 1547, 7746, 8919, 11001, 12241
Fiesta Del Sol, 4375
Fiesta Del Sole, 4373
Fiesta Juan's, 9565
Fiesta Rice, 12396
Fifth Leg, 12937
Fig & Olive Tapenade, 6522
Fig Food Co., 4378
Figaro, 1087, 4381
Fighting Cock, 6796
Fighting Cock Bourbon, 5720
Figuerola, 4383
Figure-Maid, 1882
Fiji, 4384
Fiji Water ®, 5884

Filet of Chicken®, 6025
Filippo Berio, 4386
Filippo Berio Extra Virgin, 4386
Filippo Berio Green, 4386
Filippo Berio Olive, 4386
Fillo Factory, 4388
Finast, 570
Finback Brewery, 10666
Finchville Farms, 10801
Finding Home Farms, 4391
Fine Coat®, 2332
Fine Mints, 10689
Fine Spun, 1061
Fine Vines, 4396
Fine-Mix Dairy, 2764
Finemix, 13498
Finest Call, 439, 4401
Finest Honey Organic, 300
Finest Honey Selection, 300
Finger Lakes, 5057
Fingerlakes Wine Cellars, 6083
Finish®, 10598
Finlandia, 1784
Finlandia Frost, 1784
Finlandia Lappi, 4405
Finlandia Naturals, 4405
Finlandia Swiss, 4405
Finlay, 9155
Finley, 2815
Finocchiona, 9635
Fiori-Bruna, 4410
Fiorucci, 4411
Fire Braised Meats®, 6000
Fire Cider, 11563
Fire Jack, 12437
Fire Marshall's Cajun, 8291
Fire Nugget, 3393
Fireball Fat Burner, 5682
Firebreak, 11494
Firefly, 11263
Firehouse, 13141
Firenza, 5328
Firenzec, 2010
Fireside, 6267
Fireside Kitchen, 4417
Firm-Tex®, 8804
Firmenich, 9687
First Colony, 4422
First Crush, 1688
First Pick, 13582
First Response, 2666
First Roasters of Central Florida, 4429
First Tec, 13697
Fis-Chic Wonder Batter, 3769
Fischer & Wieser, 4432
Fischer's, 4433, 11902
Fish Brothers, 4436
Fish Crunchies, 2418
Fish House, 8028
Fisher, 6548
Fisher Boy®, 5844
Fisher Honey, 4443
Fisher Scones, 2950
Fisherman's Pride, 10974
Fisherman's Reef, 4448
Fisherman's Wharf, 9042, 13864
Fishermans Rees, 13993
Fishhawk, 4450
Fishin' Chips, 9197
Fishka, 10039
Fishmarket Seafoods, 4441
Fitmark, 4150
Fitness First, 5483
Fitness®, 8945
Fitpro Go, 4453
Fitzpatrick, 4455
Fitzpatrick Bros, 9440
Five Farms Irish Cream, 8062
Five Forces of Nature, 5883
Five Leaf, 3229
Five Roses, 6380
Five Star Bars, 7148
Fix, 1702
Fix Quix, 2212
Fixodent, 12721
Fizz Wiz, 2947
Fizzle Flat Farm, 4463
Fjord Fresh, 9106
Fla-Vor-Ice®, 6483
Flagship Shiraz, 13701
Flagship Zinfandel, 13701
Flagstone Foods, 12943

Flam Winery, 10952
Flambe Holiday, 12895
Flamboise, 2737
Flame Roasted Vegetables, 8724
Flamigni, 3381
Flamingo, 8219, 9462
Flamingo Pepper, 12987
Flamm's, 4469
Flapjacked, 4473
Flashgril'd, 80
Flat, 4207
Flat Bed Red, 13049
Flat Oven, 13691
Flat Wood Farm, 10283
Flatboat, 11263
Flatout, 7189, 12467
Flatout Flatbread, 7987
Flatzzza, 563
Flav'r Top, 4008
Flav-R-Grain, 10422
Flav-R-Pac, 8724
Flavolin, 4430
Flavor, 5027
Flavor 86, 4430
Flavor Aid, 6483
Flavor Burst Liquid Citrus Tea, 5460
Flavor Burst Liquid Sweet Tea, 5460
Flavor Burst Liquid Unsweet Tea, 5460
Flavor Charm, 1103
Flavor Crunch, 13742
Flavor Depot, 2223
Flavor Farmer, 6880
Flavor Fresh, 3574
Flavor House, 13200
Flavor King Blue, 2796
Flavor King Red, 2796
Flavor Magic, 7765
Flavor of Central America®, 12996
Flavor of Mexico®, 12996
Flavor of South America®, 12996
Flavor of the Rainforest, 13892
Flavor Originals, 8729
Flavor Pack, 2126
Flavor Safari, 4242
Flavor-Ettes, 10422
Flavor-Glow, 3441
Flavor-Lites, 10422
Flavor-Mate, 6806
Flavorbank, 4487
Flavorburst, 5460
Flavorganics, 4489
Flavority, 12300
Flavorland, 8999
Flavors of the Heartland, 4494
Flavortight, 8104
Flavour Sensations, 10797
Flavourcrisp®, 2332
Flavoured Milk, 2377
Flavourzyme, 1692
Flax Country, 11517
Flax N' Honey, 8844
Flb, 4246
Fleischann's, 4499
Fleischer's, 4498
Fleischmann's, 11264
Fleischmann's Baking Powder, 2711
Fleischmann's Yeast, 4500
Fleischmann's®, 2939, 2940
Fletcher's, 4501, 11776
Fletchers, 5391
Fleur De Carneros, 2225
Fleur De Mer®, 3834
Fleurette, 10039
Flex Able, 6107
Flip It, 5331
Flipsticks, 7643, 13574
Flipsticks®, 13572
Flo-Gard, 1692
Flodi Pesca, 8028
Floam ®, 11794
Floating Leaf, 4508
Flor-Essence, 4509
Flora, 4509, 13168
Flora Grow, 665
Flora-Balance, 9287
Floraglo, 6777
Floraglo® Lutein, 3320
Floraglow, 5475
Florased Valerian, 13015
Florecitas, 1581
Floresta®, 10899
Floria Julep, 6638

Florida Crystals, 3666, 4517
Florida Food Products, 4518
Florida Key Lime Pie, 2484
Florida Key West, 4520
Florida Old Reserve, 4515
Florida Pik't, 4714
Florida Straits Rum Runner, 4650
Florida's Gold Cocktail, 4650
Florida's Natural, 4523
Florida's Natural®, 11504
Florida's Own, 13184
Florida's Pride, 4650
Florigold, 11381
Florina, 6986
Florio, 1006
Flotta, 2065
Flour, 11462
Flour Brands, 955
Flour Fine, 13498
Flow Lite®, 342
Flower Crystals, 4718
Flowery Jasmine-Before the Rain, 5228
Flowing Gold, 13613
Flowing Wells, 11844
Flowing Wells Natural Water, 11844
Fluffy Stuff, 2132
Fluffy Stuff®, 12880
Flushield™, 6449
Flying Saucer, 6880
Foamation, 3536
Foch, 1672
Focus Foodservice, 4538
Focus Foodservice Bakeware, 4538
Fody, 4209
Fog Mountain, 1543, 12672
Fogcutter Double Ipa, 7554
Fogdog, 6603
Foggy Bottom Ale, 9437
Foggy Bottom Lager, 9437
Foggy Bottom Porter, 9437
Foiled Chocolate, 13277
Foley Brothers Brewing, 10666
Folger's Filter Pack, 4543
Folger's Flavor, 4543
Folger's Instant, 4543
Folger's Simply Smooth, 4543
Folgers, 6380, 8090
Folie a Deux, 4544
Folklore, 4545
Folklore Cream Soda, 4545
Folklore Gourmet Syrups, 4545
Folklore Sasaparilla, 4545
Folklore Sparkling Beverages, 4545
Follow Your Heart, 3870
Fomz™, 12239
Fonda Blanca, 7655
Fontanini®, 6000
Fonterutoli, 13811
Fontina Cheese, 13700
Food and Wine, 1034
Food and Wine Mustards, 1034
Food Blends, 2764
Food Club, 6126, 11331
Food Club®, 12885
Food Concentrate Corp., 4556
Food For Life, 4570
Food Mill, 4564
Food Pac, 13241
Food Pak, 6971
Food Reserves, 5159
Food Should Taste Good, 11711
Food Should Taste Good®, 4947
Food Source®, 9237
Food Tone, 4324
Food Trend, 13241
Food4less, 12516
Foodies, 4459
Foods From the Sea, 12062
Foodstirs, 4576
Fool Proof Gourmet, 4577
Fools Gold Ale, 8952
Foothill Farms®, 6792
Foppiano, 4579, 9500
For Pet's Sake, 12182
Forager Project, 4581
Forbidden Fruit, 4253
Forbidden Rice, 7563
Ford's Foods, 4587
Foremost®, 388
Forest Center, 10027
Forest Country, 7869
Forestville, 1738

Brand Name Index

Foret Noire, 5405
Forge Mountain, 4593
Formosa Draft, 1702
Formosa Oolong Champagne of Tea, 5228
Formost Farms Usa, 4591
Formula 18, 13613
Fort Pitt, 4732
Fortify, 8896
Fortii®, 3320
Fortitech® Premixes, 3320
Forto, 4608
Forto®, 6818
Fortress, 5767
Fortune, 6409
Fortune Bubble, 10496
Fortune Macaroni, 8642
Fortune's Catch, 4613
Fortunes, 4614
Forza, 572
Foss, 11294
Fossen Smoked Salmon, 9771
Foster Farms Always Natural, 4621
Foster Farms Fresh & Natural, 4621
Foster Farms Naturally Seasoned, 4621
Foster Farms Organic, 4621
Foster Farms Saut, Ready, 4621
Foster Farms Simply Raised, 4621
Foster's, 2908
Foster's®, 8460
Fountain Court, 4649
Fountain Grove, 7967
Fountain Shake, 4622
Four Horsemen, 8374
Four Peaks Brewing Co., 571
Four Roses, 11839
Four Sigmatic, 4628
Four Star, 4243
Four Star Beef®, 6391
Fourn,E, 13691
Fox, 5465
Fox Brook, 10416
Fox Hollow Farm Mustard, 4635
Fox Mountain, 4579, 9500
Fox N Hare, 4639
Fox Run, 4640
Fox's U-Bet, 5465
Fox-More Than a Mustard, 4635
Foxhollow, 1738
Foxtail, 4644
Foxy, 9219
Foxy Lady, 6083
Foxy Salads, 9220
Foy's B.B.Q. Sauce, 3292
Fpi ® Brand, 5844
Frac-Packs, 4152
Fractolak, 9802
Fractured Fortunes, 5160
Fragata, 7931
Fralinger's, 4645
Fran's Healthy Helpings, 4647
Francesco Rinaldi, 7408, 8898
Francesconi, 4386
Franciscan Oakville Estate, 4649
Franciscan Well, 8459
Francisco's, 11224
Franco's, 280
Franco's Margarita Salt Sombrero, 4650
Frangelico, 4422
Frangelico Liqueur, 13811
Frank & Dean's Cocktail Mixes, 4651
Frank & Teressa's Original Anchor, 13935
Frank & Teressa's Wing Sauce, 13935
Frank's Kraut, 4694
Frank's Redhot, 8061
Frankel's Homestyle, 1251
Frankford, 4659
Frankford Candy, 2132
Frankies, 13183
Franklin Crunch 'n' Munch, 6267
Franklin Street, 2236
Frankly Natural3, 4668
Frankly Organic, 4668
Franzia, 4670
Franzia Wine, 13851
Franziskaner Hefe-Weisse, 1208
Frappe Creme, 12182
Fratello, 4674
Frazier's Finest, 4675
Fred Imus Southwest, 6170
Fred Imus Turquoise, 6170
Fred Meyer, 3387
Fred's®, 237, 238

Freda Deli Meats, 246
Free Flow®, 342
Free Raised, 12162
Free Run, 1864
Free2b, 4679
Freebird, 5505
Freed's, 4681
Freed's Bakery, 7886
Freed, Teller & Fredd, 4681
Freeda, 4682
Freedent®, 7952, 13960
Freemark Abbey, 4688
Freerun, 5138
Freerun Omega 3, 5138
Freestone, 4689
Freestone Vineyards, 6603
Freeyumm, 4680
Freez-A-Pops, 7279
Freeze Dried Cransations™, 11654
Freeze-Thaw, 4008
Freezefridge®, 6374
Freezerta, 6971
Frei Brothers Reserve®, 3834
Freida's Kitchen, 903
Freidel's Finest, 6221
Freihofer's®, 1359
Freihoffer, 892
Freirich Porkette®, 4692
Freixenet Spanish Wines, 4693, 5069
Freixenet Wines, 4693, 5069
French Bull, 10229
French Chew, 3699
French Does, 7377
French Gourmet, 4699
French Market, 4700
French Market Coffee, 10657
French Paradox, 6310
French Rabbit, 1543
French Wines, 10952
French's, 73, 8061
French's Dry Spice Mixes, 73
Frenchie Winery, 1543
Frenchiec, 12267
Frenzi, 3233
Frenzy Mist, 2570
Fresca, 2811
Fresca Foods, 10160
Frescados®, 9736
Frescas, 9571
Freschetta, 11316
Freschetta®, 11317
Fresco Y Mas, 11838
Frescobaldi Laudemio, 11864
Fresh 'n Fruity®, 4552
Fresh Aland Beef and Pork, 7001
Fresh Beans, 13112
Fresh Bellies, 4708
Fresh Blendz, 13192
Fresh Cargo, 2719
Fresh Creations, 7168
Fresh Cut, 13110
Fresh Express, 4709
Fresh Express®, 2580
Fresh From the Deli, 3896
Fresh Gourmet, 12201
Fresh Harvest, 2026
Fresh Health, 3315
Fresh Health Kids, 3315
Fresh Ideas, 4712
Fresh Nature, 4717
Fresh Pact, 9839
Fresh Pak, 8860
Fresh Pik't, 4714
Fresh Pond, 8969
Fresh Samantha, 4722
Fresh Sea Taste, 7583
Fresh Step, 2766
Fresh Taste Fast!, 6520
Freshbakes, 951
Freshbox Farms, 3183
Freshcut, 2332
Freshdry, 3696
Freshman, 5479
Freshwrap Cuts, 12437
Freshwrap Slices, 12437
Friel's, 11039
Friendly's®, 3442
Friendlys, 10229
Friends Fun Wine, 9117
Friendship Dairies™, 11211
Friendship Diaries, 2559
Friesinger's, 10773

Friesinger's Fine Chocolates, 3421
Frigex® W, 8804
Frigo Cheese®, 11209
Frigo®, 11211
Frio, 4737
Fris, 9964
Frisches Brot, 1633
Frisk, 9956
Frito-Lay2go, 4741
Frito-Lay®, 9945
Fritos, 4741
Fritos®, 9945
Fritz, 6372
Fritz Knipschildt, 13433
Frolic, 8401
Froma-Dar, 4748
Frontera Foods, 4751
Frontera®, 2939, 2940
Frontier, 4752, 4753, 9150, 10076
Frontier Gold, 1324
Frontier Water, 9170
Froot Loops, 6766
Froot Loops®, 6765
Frooties, 2132
Frooties®, 12880
Froozer, 4754
Frost Fire, 1688
Frosted Flakes, 6766
Frosted Mini-Wheats, 6766
Frostee Snow Cones, 5333
Frostline® Frozen Treats, 6792
Frosty Pak, 7363
Frothee Creamy Head, 12941
Froze-Fresh, 13192
Frozfruit, 4757
Frozfruit All Natural Fruit Bars, 4757
Frozsun, 12297
Frs Company, 4150
Fruice, 3550
Fruigees, 4759
Fruit & Chia™, 3478
Fruit & Nadia, 2815
Fruit & Oats™, 3478
Fruit 2o, 12281
Fruit 66, 12239
Fruit Belt, 4761
Fruit Bliss, 4762
Fruit Breaker, 11320
Fruit By the Foot®, 4947
Fruit Chews®, 12880
Fruit Chocolates, 7410
Fruit Corn Appetit, 10179
Fruit Crystals, 4718
Fruit Delights, 7410
Fruit Drop, 56
Fruit Festives, 7410
Fruit Fiber, 131
Fruit For Thought, 11605
Fruit Hill White, 1672
Fruit N' Juice, 6159
Fruit of the Sea, 10974
Fruit of the Woods, 12783
Fruit Ole, 427
Fruit Ole Smoothies, 11266
Fruit Parfaits, 7410
Fruit Refreshers®, 3478
Fruit Rush™, 3442
Fruit Softees, 7410
Fruit Stripe, 1417, 4345
Fruit Topping, 8724
Fruit Tubes, 1827
Fruit Water, 4066
Fruit Wave H2o, 3279
Fruit-To-Go, 12259
Fruitcrown, 4769
Fruite, 56
Fruitflow®, 3320
Fruitful Juice Products, 3365
Fruitfull, 5562
Fruiticas Lollipops, 12211
Fruitini, 3479
Fruitland, 5767, 6985
Fruitopia, 2815
Fruitrim®, 190
Fruits De Mer, 5325
Fruitsavr®, 190
Fruitslim, 3753
Fruitsnax, 9251
Fruitsource®, 190
Fruitsweet, 13511
Fruittella, 9956
Fruity Ball, 12211

Frumage, 10565
Frutafit, 6163
Frutafitt®, 11445
Frutalose®, 11445
Fruti, 8837
Fry Foods, 1891, 4776
Fry Krisp, 4777
Fry Krisp Batter Mixes, 4777
Fry Stix™, 1654
Fryz, 14043
Fuchs Tooth Brushes, 7562
Fudge Gourmet, 14013
Fudgeroons, 12096
Fudgescotti, 1529
Fudgie Bears, 2604
Fuel Snacks, 4573
Fukusuke Rice, 4260
Ful-Flav-R, 4784
Fulfill Fitness, 12182
Full Blast Gum, 7560
Full Circle, 11303, 13512
Full Circle®, 1758, 12885
Full House, 7296
Full Moon Light Ale, 8524
Full Moon Pale Ale, 339
Full Moon Shrimp, 1916
Full Moon®, 9946
Full Power, 648
Full Red, 12030
Full Sail, 4786
Full Service Caterin, 13667
Full Throttle, 8485
Fulton Organic Free Range Chicken, 6770
Fulton Valley Farms, 6770
Fulton's Harvest Cream Liqueur, 5720
Fun Foods, 8269
Fun Fruit, 10496
Fun Fruits Fruit Snacks-Sunkist, 4884
Fun Pops, 258
Fun Stuff, 2947
Fun Whip, 258
Fun-N-Sun, 10760
Functional Teas, 5155
Fundae, 10015
Funfoods Holiday Pasta, 4794
Funfoods Premium, 4794
Funfresh Foods®, 9237
Fungamyl, 1692
Fungusamongus, 11390
Funny Farm, 4093
Funyun's, 4741
Funyuns®, 9945
Furama, 11881
Furstenberg, 5427
Fuse Burger™, 6000
Future Bakery, 4806
Fuze, 2811

G

G, 11093
G & W, 7146
G Blanchet, 6395
G Mommas, 11423
G-Brew, 13444
G.H. Cretors, 3862
G.H. Ford, 4833
G.H. Mumm, 9964
Gaba Plus™, 13097
Gabriella's Kitchen, 4854
Gabrielli, 2112
Gabrielli Winery, 2112
Gaby, 4854
Gadoua, 4856
Gadova, 13691
Gadova Multigo, 13691
Gaetano's, 4891
Gail's, 8951
Gailuron, 8676
Gain, 12721
Gaiser's, 4861
Galactic Grape, 5362
Galante Wines, 4862
Galassi, 4863
Galasso, 4864
Galaxy Desserts, 4866
Galaxy®, 7952
Galbani, 7126
Galbani Precious, 7126
Galbani Sorrento, 7126
Galbani®, 9789

Brand Name Index

Galbusera, 10565
Galena Cellars, 4869
Galilean, 4870
Galleano, 4872
Galliker's, 4873
Gallo Family Vineyards®, 3834
Gallo Salame®, 13109
Galloping Garlic, 6528
Gambelini, 8795
Game Day Snacks, 13445
Gamla, 10952
Gamma - E, 4827
Gandy's, 3442
Ganong Chicken Bones, 4884
Ganong Chocolates, 4884
Ganong Fruitfull, 4884
Ganong Sugar Confections, 4884
Garandina, 3545
Garcia Brand, 3818
Gardein, 4889
Gardein®, 2939, 2940
Garden Club, 2750
Garden Fresh, 12334
Garden Goodness, 9129
Garden Harvest, 8806
Garden Hearts, 1538
Garden of Eatin', 5505
Garden Path, 7028
Gardenburger, 6766
Gardenburgers, 3773
Gardennay, 2115
Gardetto's®, 4947
Garelick, 4904
Garelick Farms®, 3442
Garfield, 10229
Garland Ranch, 2459
Garli Garni, 4907
Garlic Festival, 4907
Garlic Galore, 6528
Garlic Gus, 6353
Garlic Juices, 4908
Garlic Parmesan Crouton Bites, 5489
Garlimax, 9957
Garner Jams & Jellies, 12473
Gartenbrau, 2160
Garvi Gujarat, 6026
Gaslight Pale Ale, 9688
Gastro-Ad, 7172
Gateway - Du Bake, 4920
Gateway®, 7402
Gatherings®, 6000
Gatomax, 9571
Gatorade, 4150
Gatorade®, 9945
Gatsby's/Pierre Koenig, 3381
Gaucho, 4922
Gaurmande, 10039
Gavilan, 7655
Gavina, 4202
Gaviscon®, 10598
Gavottes, 7499
Gbh, 9117
Ge - Oxy 132, 4827
Gear Up, 10495
Gedney, 4928
Geefree, 4929
Geevani, 5755
Gehl Gourmet, 4930
Gehl Mainstream Cafe, 4930
Gel B, 8335
Gel N Melt®, 8804
Gelati Celesti, 4933
Gelato, 2669
Gelato Fresco, 4935
Gelita, 4937
Gelite, 6396
Gem, 4829
Gem 100%, 11875
Gem Berry, 4828
Gem Blended, 11875
Gem Extra, 11875
Gem Gem, 1763
Gembond, 7847
Gems, 11102
Gemstar, 7847
Gemstone Gourmet Candies, 756
Gemstone Vineyard, 7490
Gemstone®, 7786
Gemwraps, 9010
Genarom, 4943
General Mills, 541, 1891
General Produce, 2298

Generation Farms, 5782
Genesee Beer, 4950
Genesee Brewing, 9117
Genesee Cream Ale, 4950
Genesee Ice, 4950
Genesee Light, 4950
Genesee N.A., 4950
Genesis 1:29c, 8831
Genisoy Soy Products, 4955
Genista, 783
Genivida®, 3320
Genmai Udon, 11773
Genova Tonno, 2555
Gentle Ben Winter Brau, 4959
Gentle Change, 9201
Gentleman's Cut®, 9338
Genu, 1962
Genu Plus, 1962
Genugel, 1962
Genuine, 11668
Genuine Fulvi Romano Cheese, 11668
Genuine Lager, 7123
Genulacta, 1962
Genutine, 1962
Genuvisco, 1962
George Dickel Whiske, 3570
George Killian's Irish Red®, 8460
George Maid, 12300
George T. Stagg, 11263
George's, 4970
Georgetown Farm Bison, 4973
Georgetown Farm Piedmontese, 4973
Georgia, 2814, 4974
Georgia Fruit Cake, 4974
Georgia Grinders, 4975
Georgia Moon Corn Whiskey, 5720
Georgia Reds, 12300
Georgia Special, 12300
Georgia's, 4976
Georgiana, 1856
Geraldine's Bodacious, 1528
Geraldo's, 4928
Gerard & Dominique, 11358
Gerber 1st Foods, 4982
Gerber 2nd Foods, 4982
Gerber 3rd Fodos, 4982
Gerber Cereal, 4982
Gerber Good Start, 4982
Gerber Graduates, 4982
Gerber®, 8945
Gerbes, 12516
Geri-Med, 9253
German, 5902
German Style Kolsch, 5515
Germany: Wessergold, 5108
Gerolsteiner, 5108
Gerrit J. Verburg Co., 2132
Get Movin Snack Packss, 9799
Get Popped, 12202
Getreide, 7655
Gettelfinger Select, 10268
Gevalia Kaffe, 6976
Geyser Peak, 4992
Gf Harvest, 4830
Gfa, 4831
Gfb: the Gluten Free Bar, 13669
Gg Unique Fiber, 5505
Ghiaccio, 4901
Ghiardelli, 2606
Ghiradelli, 6819
Ghiradelli Syrup, 2833
Ghirardelli, 434, 2971, 3009, 4422, 4994
Ghost Pines®, 3834
Ghost Talk, 10764
Giant, 6126
Giant Cashews, 8269
Giant Gourmet, 5590
Giants, 3354
Giardino, 6145
Gibbons, 5001, 7150
Gibbs, 5555
Giddy Up & Go, 12779
Gifford's, 5004
Gift Baskets By Carmela, 36
Gift of Bran, 6806
Gigi, 9788
Gigi Baking Company, 11940, 12894
Gila Caf,®, 6818
Gilbey's®, 1120
Gilda, 4244
Gill Netter's Best, 9980

Gillette, 12721
Gillies, 5012
Gilly's Hot Vanilla, 5013
Gilt Edge, 5016
Gimme, 5019
Gimme Lean, 7427
Gimme Organic, 5019
Gin Ultimate, 754
Gina Lina's, 10418
Gina Marie Cream Cheese, 5878
Ginbao, 8623
Ginebra Calvert, 3545
Ginger Ale, 7310
Ginger Kids, 3079
Ginger Shots, 5022
Ginger Snaps, 551, 8729
Gingerbread Ale, 1401
Ginkgold, 8896
Gino's, 831
Ginsen-Rgy, 7947
Ginseng 4x, 157
Ginseng Extract, 4859
Ginseng Rush, 10495
Ginseng Up, 5027
Gionelli ®, 13120
Giorgio, 5028
Giotti, 8061
Giovanni, 2012
Giovanni's, 5030
Girard's, 5032, 12467
Girls With Crabs, 12742
Girlwatcher, 13605
Giroux, 13141
Give Collection, 13403
Give Your Heart a Healthy Start, 9858
Gjetost Ekte, 11968
Gk Communications, 10229
Glac,Au Smart Water, 2814
Glac,Au Vitaminwater, 2814
Glace De Poulet Gold, 8538
Glaceau Smart Water, 2815
Glaceau Vitamin Water, 2815
Glaceau Vitaminwater, 4066
Glacier Caviar, 5309
Glacier Freeze, 5041
Glacier Ice, 1966, 8920
Glacier Salmon, 5309
Glacier Valley, 3084
Glacier Valley®, 3083
Glad Bags, 2766
Gladder's Gourmet Cookie, 5043
Gladiator, 5499
Gladstone Candies, 5398
Glalcto, 12795
Glanbia Foods, 5046
Glaros, 7655
Glaros Ouzo, 9773
Glen Ellen, 13851
Glen Garioch, 1120
Glen Grant, 2114
Glen Lake, 12977
Glen Ord Scotch, 3570
Glendale, 4078
Glendora Quiche Co., 5053
Glendronach, 3024
Glenfiddich, 13811
Glenglassaugh, 1784
Glenlivet, 3545
Glenmark, 1262
Glenmorangie, 8452
Glenmore, 11264
Glenny's, 5055
Glenora, 5057
Glenrothes, 3545
Glenwood, 13912
Glider, 4387
Glier's, 5058
Glisodin, 9654
Global, 5062
Global Botanical, 5061
Global Brands, 11817
Global Creations®, 1654
Global Food, 5063
Globe, 6211
Globe Artichoke, 4315
Globe Plus, 6211
Glocal, 9654
Gloria Ferrer, 4693
Gloria Jean's Coffees®, 6818
Gloria Jeans, 3591, 6819
Glorybee, 5073

Glossop's, 5074
Glow Pop, 6158
Gluconal, 5078
Glucophage®, 1721
Glucovance®, 1721
Glutamine, 4736
Gluten-Free Heaven, 5083
Glutino®, 2939, 2940
Glutiny, 8959
Gluzyme, 1692
Glycomarine, 11269
Glyderm®, 8389
Gmi Gelatin, 8891
Go Bananas, 7903
Go Lean, 6720
Go Mango, 7903
Go Matcha, 15
Go Raw, 5087
Go Salsa, 3522
Go Texan, 12658
Go Veggie, 4867
Go-Go Drinks, 4066
Go-Mex, 573
Goat Island Light, 11561
Goavo, 5088
Gobstopper, 2132
Godiva, 2115, 5092, 11864
Godiva Biscuits, 5092
Godiva Chocolate, 5092
Godshall's, 5093
Godwin, 5094
Godwin Produce, 5094
Godwin's Blue Ribbon, 5094
Goebel, 9664
Goelitz, 6485
Gogo Squeez, 8005
Gold, 362
Gold 'n Soft®, 13328
Gold Award, 7655, 9773
Gold Band Products, 9628
Gold Bond, 178
Gold Brick, 4032
Gold Buckle Oranges, 13906
Gold Canyon Meat Co.™, 11504
Gold Circle Farms, 5837
Gold Coast, 2450, 2796, 5098
Gold Coast Baking Company, 5097
Gold Cow, 9296
Gold Crown Lager, 9137
Gold Cup, 3
Gold Dollar, 5102
Gold Dollar Lemon, 5102
Gold Dollar/Monedade'oro, 5102
Gold Kist Farms®, 10056
Gold Label, 3269, 6544, 7874
Gold Label Plus Dairy, 10714
Gold Medal, 1891, 1935, 5103, 5233, 10275, 11515
Gold Medal®, 4947
Gold Mine Gum, 11051
Gold N Good, 10846
Gold N. White Bread Flour, 8851
Gold Nectar, 6065
Gold Nugget, 615, 8308
Gold Nugget Butter, 7166
Gold Nugget Cheese, 7166
Gold Peak, 2811
Gold Peak Tea, 2814
Gold Plus, 1718
Gold Premium, 6221
Gold Ribbon, 5643
Gold Rim, 3424
Gold Rush, 12863
Gold Seal, 262
Gold Spike Ale, 1237
Gold Standard, 5106
Gold Star, 3768, 5108
Gold Star Coffee, 1601
Gold'n Plump®, 10056
Gold'n Polenta, 9225
Gold'n Treats, 9225
Gold'n'spice®, 1654
Gold's, 5105
Gold-Tex Flour, 12553
Goldegg, 5138
Golden, 125, 953, 2530, 9744
Golden 100, 5113
Golden Amber, 932
Golden Bake, 2796
Golden Barrel, 5157
Golden Beauties, 965
Golden Bird, 9500

1277

Brand Name Index

Golden Brands, 70
Golden Circle, 6977
Golden Coconut Oil, 13683
Golden Crest, 4874
Golden Crinkles®, 9523
Golden Crisp, 530, 9833, 10213
Golden Crop, 10425
Golden Crunchies, 10104
Golden Crust, 8649
Golden Dawn, 347
Golden Delicious, 9332
Golden Dragon, 4311, 8754
Golden Dreams, 754
Golden Eagle, 5118, 5132
Golden Eagle Ale, 3519
Golden Farm Candies, 4779
Golden Flake, 5122, 13129
Golden Fluff, 5123
Golden Foods, 70, 13625
Golden Fries™, 9523
Golden Gate, 6451
Golden Glow, 5233
Golden Goodness, 5282
Golden Gourmet, 1310
Golden Gourmet Nuts, 3430
Golden Grain, 465, 7655
Golden Grenadine, 8909
Golden Grill, 1069, 1577
Golden Grower, 754
Golden Harvest, 2026
Golden Island, 5126
Golden Island®, 13109
Golden Joma Palm Oil, 13683
Golden Kernel, 5127
Golden Kettle, 12866
Golden Kola, 6943
Golden Life, 4127
Golden Loaf, 1950
Golden Magic, 7373
Golden Meal, 10846
Golden Moon Tea, 5129
Golden One, 5132
Golden Oreo's®, 10213
Golden Palm Cake & Icing, 13683
Golden Palm Margarine, 13683
Golden Palm Shortening, 13683
Golden Patties®, 9523
Golden Rich, 2045
Golden Ripe®, 3479
Golden River, 5132
Golden Road Brewing, 571
Golden Roast, 5462
Golden Rum Cake, 2881
Golden Star, 8028
Golden State, 13541
Golden State Hops, 4633
Golden Sun, 5132
Golden Temple, 6380, 9245, 14011
Golden Tiger®, 237, 238
Golden Touch, 6267
Golden Treasure, 6119
Golden Trophy Steaks, 12674
Golden Twirls®, 9523
Golden Valley, 5138
Golden Walnut, 5140
Golden West, 2381, 13070
Goldenberg's Peanut Chews®, 6641
Goldenbrook Farms®, 1758
Goldeneye, 3779
Goldfish, 2116
Goldfish®, 9942
Golding, 5146
Golding Farms, 5146
Golding Gourmand, 5146
Goldrush, 3216, 7915
Goldtex, 10616
Goldthread, 5148
Goldwater's, 5149
Goldwater's Taste of the Southwest, 5149
Golfo Mar, 8028
Golia, 9956
Golightly Sugar Free Candy, 5874
Gollots Brand Shrimp, 1916
Gomacro, 5090
Gonzo's Little Big Meat, 8207
Goo Goo Cluster, 12027
Good & Plenty, 5818
Good Buddies, 5362
Good Earth, 4537
Good Earth Teas, 5155
Good Food Made Simple, 5158
Good Fortunes, 5160
Good Friends, 6720
Good Health, 13129
Good Humor, 13169
Good Humor®, 5165
Good Karma, 5166
Good Loaf, 11839
Good Lovin' Foods, 5167
Good News Eggs, 3142
Good Planet Foods, 5170
Good Sense®, 13603
Good Simple Food, 12703
Good Spirits, 13184
Good Stuff Cocoa, 6821
Good Taste, 8973
Good Times, 597
Good Zebra, 5175
Goodart's, 5182
Goodbee, 14023
Goodbelly, 5178
Goodbelly Plusshot, 5178
Goodbelly Straightshot, 5178
Goodbites, 5179
Goodbites Cbd, 5179
Goode & Ready, 8688
Goodheart, 5183
Goodlife, 4501
Goodman's, 7848
Goodness Knows, 5185
Goodnessknows®, 7952
Goodniks®, 13603
Goodseed, 5186
Goodwheat™, 634
Goody Shake, 1915
Gooey Butter Bar, New!, 2903
Gooey Ghouls, 7746
Goose Bay Winery, 10952
Goose Hill, 965
Goose Isalnd, 571
Goose Point Oysters, 9066
Goose Watch, 12382
Goosecross, 5189
Gopi, 6719
Gorant & Yum Yum Chocolates, 5192
Gordo's, 9879
Gordon Biersch, 5193
Gordon's Chesapeake Classics, 8256
Gordon's Gin, 3570
Gordon's Vodka, 3570
Gorilla Cloves, 12987
Gorilla Vanilla, 12550
Gorton's Beer Battered Fillets, 5194
Gorton's Fish Sticks, 5194
Gorton's Grilled Tilapia, 5194
Gorton's Natural Catch, 5194
Gorton's Parmesean Crusted Cod, 5194
Gorton's Popcorn Shrimp, 5194
Gorton's Pub Style Cod, 5194
Gorton's Seafood Appetizers, 5194
Gorton's Shrimp Bowl, 5194
Gorton's Simply Bake Salmon, 5194
Gossner Foods, 5195
Gotham Dairy, 2669
Gotliebs, 5196
Goubaud, 10346
Goundry Fine Wine, 13425
Gourmet, 3336, 13303
Gourmet Baker, 721
Gourmet Basmati Rice, 11908
Gourmet Brew, 13444
Gourmet Butters & Spreads, 14034
Gourmet Cookie Place, 14013
Gourmet Deli, 5039
Gourmet Fare, 5280
Gourmet Foods Market, 5208
Gourmet French Chew, 3699
Gourmet Fresh, 5216
Gourmet Garden, 8061
Gourmet Goat, 13927
Gourmet Gold, 4907
Gourmet Grab & Go®, 7599
Gourmet Granola, 9799
Gourmet Honey Collection, 14034
Gourmet House®, 10777
Gourmet International, 12543
Gourmet Jose, 5396
Gourmet Lite, 5213
Gourmet Pepper Sauce, 9745
Gourmet Products, 5211
Gourmet Reserves, 13105
Gourmet Selections, 4543
Gourmet Slim #7, 8961
Gourmet Slim Cuisine, 8961
Gourmet Snack Bags, 3396
Gourmet Specialty Cookies, 5909
Gourmet Spices, 13665
Gourmet Stuffed Clams, 1464
Gourmet Supreme, 8961
Gourmet Treats, 5213
Gourmet Valley, 13785
Gourmet Valley Foods, 13785
Gourmet's Choice Tuna Fillets, 12046
Governor's Club, 7655
Goya®, 5223
Graber Olives, 1933
Grace Rush, 11330
Graceland Fruit, 5229
Graduates® Toddler Foods, 8945
Graeser, 10720
Graffigna & Jacob's Creek, 9964
Grafschafter, 1957
Graft Cider, 5235
Grafton Gold, 5236
Grafton Gold-Ext Aged Cheddar, 5236
Graham Dunks, 6787
Grain Belt, 796
Grain Millers, 214, 5243
Grain Place, 5244
Grain Trust, 11078
Grain-Pro, 5245
Grainaissance, 5248
Graindance, 12855, 12857
Graines De Vie, 4091
Grainful, 5249
Grainsfirst, 3384
Grainsweet™, 12387
Graintrader Wheat Al, 9688
Gram Dunks, 6787
Grand Archer, 706
Grand Bayou, 12520
Grand Champion, 6438
Grand Chef De Paris, 13401
Grand Cru, 1738
Grand Cru Raclette, 10906
Grand Crue, 10906
Grand Estate Collection, 7746
Grand Isle, 13454
Grand Life Seitan, 12396
Grand Mark, 12489
Grand Marnier, 8452
Grand Muriel, 7655, 9773
Grand Slam, 12663
Grand Teton, 7166
Grand Teton Brewing, 5255
Grand Teton Cheese, 7166
Grand-MSRe, 1661
Grandaddy's, 13964
Grande, 847
Grande Bravo Whey Protein, 5259
Grande Classics, 8724
Grande Classics Island Blends, 8724
Grande Gusto Natural Flavor, 5259
Grande Italia, 6238
Grande River Vineyards, 5260
Grande River Vineyards Everyday, 5260
Grande River Vineyards Meritage, 5260
Grande Ultra Nutritional Whey Prot., 5259
Grandioso®, 13328
Grandma Brown's, 5263
Grandma Shearer's, 11531
Grandma Shearer's Snacks, 11531
Grandma Sycamore's®, 1359
Grandma Taylor's Gourmet Dip, 9955
Grandma's, 4555, 4741
Grandma's Bake Shoppe, 1134
Grandma's Cookie Mix, 10589
Grandma's Fruit Cake, 1134
Grandma's Molasses, 8586
Grandma's Molasses®, 864
Grandma's Recipe, 9185
Grandma's®, 9945
Grandpa A'S, 290
Grandpa John's, 10966
Grandpa Pete's Sunday Sauce, 11457
Grandpa Po's Slightly Spicy, 9234
Grandpa Po's Slightly Sweet, 9234
Grandpa Po's Slightly Unsalted, 9234
Grandpa Vals, 12863
Grandpa's Choice, 3142
Grandpa's Oven, 10907
Grandpa's Secret Omega-3 Muesli, 3872
Grandpops Lollipops, 5269
Grandview Farms, 5270
Grandyoats, 5271
Granfruttato, 8479
Granny Cheescakes, 5297
Granny Cookies, 818
Granny Goose, 11748
Granny Smith Apple, 2637, 12914
Granny's, 1736, 6070
Granny's Kitchen, 7886
Granny's Oven, 1394
Granowska's, 5277
Grant County Foods, 2298
Grant's, 13811
Granum, 2630
Granville Island Brewing, 8459
Grape Alpho, 9107
Grape Nuts, 10213
Grapefruit, 883
Grapefruit Extract, 9251
Grapeking, 5036
Grapelets, 7410
Grapevine Trading Co., 5280
Grass Run Farms®, 6391
Grassland, 5282
Grassland Beef, 13126
Gratifica, 7428
Graves, 56, 2260
Graves Mountain, 5285
Gravy & Gumbo Magic, 7766
Gravy Master, 5287, 10724
Gravy Train, 6380
Gravymaster, 5287
Great, 3750
Great American, 13689
Great American Barbecue, 5295
Great American Hamburgers, 457
Great American®, 10893
Great Expectations, 5307
Great Glacier, 8920
Great Golden Ale, 4466
Great Grains, 10213
Great Grub Rubs, 4894
Great Gusto, 9699
Great Hill Blue, 5313
Great Lakes, 5316, 5318
Great Meats, 11312
Great Middwest®, 11211
Great Midwest®, 11209
Great Ocead Road™, 11211
Great Organic Hotdog, 614
Great Pacific, 5326
Great Plains, 5327
Great Pumpkin, 2763
Great Range Brand Bison, 10823
Great Recipes, 5328
Great San Saba River Pecan, 12687
Great Valley, 13785
Great Valley Mills, 5331
Great Valley Mixes, 5331
Great Western, 10112
Great Western Products Company, 5333
Great White, 7554
Great Whites, 4242
Greater Omaha, 5338
Greaves, 5339
Grebe's, 5340
Greek Yogurt Creamy Ceasar, 5489
Greek Yogurt Lemon Garlic, 5489
Greek Yogurt Ranch, 5489
Greek Yogurt Salad Dressing Mix, 5489
Greek Yogurt Spinach & Feta, 5489
Green & Black's, 8474
Green Bay Puddles, 1018
Green Blaze Ipa, 7526
Green Coffee, 6611
Green Dragon, 3921
Green Earth Orchards, 5348
Green Earth Organics, 12973
Green Essence, 5349
Green Gaint, 1548
Green Giant®, 4947
Green Giant™, 864
Green Gold Wheatgrass, 9951
Green Head, 3301
Green Leaf, 13531
Green Magician, 12228
Green Mountain, 816
Green Mountain Chocolate Truffle, 5354
Green Mountain Coffee, 6819
Green Mountain Coffee®, 6818
Green Mountain Creamery, 5356
Green Mountain Farms, 4665
Green Mountain Gringo, 6069, 12473
Green Point, 8452
Green Spot, 54, 5362, 9964

Brand Name Index

Green Star, 2570
Green Valley, 4872, 11434
Green Works, 2766
Green-Freedman, 12328
Green-Go, 5368
Green-T Energy Mints, 1343
Greene's, 1482
Greenfield, 5372, 6160
Greenpod, 11945
Greens, 9516
Greenwell Farms, 5377
Greenwood, 5379
Greenwood Prairie, 10099
Greeter's Pale Ale, 7143
Greg Norman Estates, 12937
Gregorio, 2012
Gremlin, 8242
Gremlins, 1290
Grey Goose, 913
Grey Poupon, 6977
Grey Whale, 9673
Grifron, 8695
Grifron D-Fraction, 8695
Grifron Mushroom Emperors, 8695
Grifron Prost Mate, 8695
Grill Blazin Bbq Sauce, 9332
Grill-In-A-Bottle, 4560
Grillin', 10600
Grillo's Pickles, 5389
Grimaud Farms, 5390
Grimaud Farms Muscovy Ducks, 5390
Grimmway, 5393
Grinch, 1591
Gringos, 9934
Gritstone, 3171
Grizzliesh, 13797
Grocer's Garden, 10728
Groeb Farms, 5396
Grolsch Premium Lager®, 8460
Grooner, 4677
Grote & Weigel, 5400
Grounds For Thought, 5402
Groundwork, 5404
Grouse Hunt Farms, 5406
Grove on the Go, 4840
Grove Sweet, 2699
Grove, Jr, 4840
Grow Gardens, 922
Grow-Pac, 5408
Grower Pete's Certified Organicc, 7480
Grower's Pack, 5663
Growers Company, 8314
Growers Fancy Juice, 7339
Growing Roots, 5411
Growler, 1208
Grown Free, 10529
Gruet Winery, 5413
Gsi, 194
Gtc, 5473
Gu, 4850
Guacamole Salad, 11883
Guardmax, 9957
Guayabita Best - Pasta De Guayaba, 3545
Guenoc, 5417
Guerrero, 8387
Guerrero®, 8384
Guflielmo Reserve, 5421
Guggisberg, 5420
Guglielmo, 5421
Guglielmo Vineyard Selection, 5421
Gugulidid, 11061
Guida, 12303
Guida's, 5422
Guida's Dairy, 3335
Guido & Sals Old Chicago, 1123
Guido's Serious, 5423
Guidparg Chocolates, 2833
Guiltless Gourmet, 5426, 7848
Guinness Extra Stout, 7123
Guinness Stout, 5427
Guinness®, 5427
Guittard, 2606, 3009
Gujarati, 3465
Gulden's, 6267
Gulden's®, 2939, 2940
Gulf, 3424, 13200
Gulf Belle, 8995
Gulf Central, 5430
Gulf Crown, 5432
Gulf Garden, 8028
Gulf Kist, 11865
Gulf Pride, 5438

Gulf Star, 5430
Gulf-Maid, 102
Gum Time, 10496
Gummi Alien Invaders, 790
Gummy Guy, 12985
Gumpert's, 5444
Gun Powder Pearl Pinhead Green Tea, 5228
Gurley's, 13827
Gurley's Candy, 5448
Gurley's Golden Recipe Nuts, 5448
Gurley's Natures Harvest, 5448
Guru, 4851
Gurunanda, 5449
Gusano Rojo, 7655
Gustafson's, 2346
Gusto Italia, 12860
Guy's, 5456
Guy's Tea, 4055
Guylian, 6540
Gw, 13685
Gwaltney, 11733
Gx Power, 10307
Gyros Usa, 3028

H

H&C, 9798
H&G Chum, 11602
H&K Packers, 5470
H&S Bread Crumbs, 5472
H-50, 8804
H-E-B, 5473
H-E-B Kitchen & Table, 5473
H-E-B Organics, 5473
H-E-B Select Ingredients, 5473
H-E-Buddy, 5473
H-O, 4831
H.C. Smoked Sausage, 12463
H.C. Valentine™, 10928
H.K. Anderson®, 2939, 2940
H2o, 5586
H2o To Go, 3469
H2rose, 5480
H3o, 5481
Haagen Dazs, 5137
Haagen-Dazs®, 4947, 8945
Haake Beck Non-Alcoholic, 689
Habanero Products From Hell, 11873
Habero, 7051
Habersham Estates, 5492
Habitant, 2115, 3844
Hacienda, 1738
Haco, 12438
Haddar, 4104
Haddon House®, 1484
Haddys, 1891
Hadley Date Gardens, 5494
Hafner, 5496
Hag, 10565
Hagafen Winery, 10952
Hagensborg Meltaways Truffles, 5497
Hagerty Foods, 5498
Haggen, 3387
Hahg, 10027
Hahn's, 4665
Haig, 3570
Haight Vineyard Wines, 5502
Haiku, 5306
Hail Merry, 5503
Hain Kidz, 3617
Hain Pure Foods, 5505
Haine Pure Foods, 5506
Haitoglou, 6986
Hakuna Banana, 5511
Hakushu, 12315
Halal Meats, 457
Hale's Celebration Porter, 5515
Hale's Cream, 5515
Hale's Dublin Style Stout, 5515
Hale's Pale American Ale, 5515
Hale's Special Bitter, 5515
Half Moon, 13082
Hallcrest Vineyards, 5524
Hallmark, 5525
Halls, 8474
Halo Top, 3939
Haloflex™, 3320
Halos, 4633
Ham Sausage, 2162
Hamburger Helper®, 4947
Hamish & Enzo, 10950

Hamm's®, 8460
Hammond's, 5534
Hammons, 5537
Hampshire Laboratories, 13469
Hamptom Farms, 5541
Hampton House, 6394
Hana, 12500
Hana-Nori, 135
Hancock's, 11263
Handy, 5547
Hang Ten, 2763
Hanna's, 5553
Hannah's Delight, 7756
Hannegan Seafoods, 444
Hanover, 5555
Hanover Farms, 5555
Hansen, 5558, 5559
Hansen-Norge, 5558
Haolam, 13931
Happiness Sell Sheet, 10229
Happy Cup Tea, 12585
Happy Day Pops, 5752
Happy Drinks, 258
Happy Heart Lollipops, 6158
Happy Herberts, 5569
Happy Hive, 5570
Happy Home, 5245, 11852
Happy Indulgence, 5562
Happy Indulgence Deladent Dips, 5562
Happy Snacks, 7940
Happy Trails Meat Snack Sticks, 12920
Happy Trails T-Shirts, 2903
Happydent, 9956
Harbor, 5579
Harbor Lighthouse Ale, 1015
Harborside, 12703
Harbour Gold, 12919
Hard Bargain, 8075
Hard Cookies, 5909
Hard-E Foods, 5582
Hardbite, 8855
Hardfast, 572
Hardin, 8806
Hargita, 5108
Hargrave Vineyards, 2299
Hari Om Farms, 5586
Haribo, 2132, 5587
Harida, 8888
Harlan Bakeries, 5590
Harlin Fruit, 5591
Harmless Harvest, 5594
Harmony, 4732
Harmony Bay, 5596
Harmony Cellars, 5597
Harmony Snacks, 3575
Harney & Sons, 5599, 8090
Harold Food Co., 5600
Harp Lager, 5427
Harper Seafood, 5603
Harpic®, 10598
Harpoon, 5606
Harrell Nut, 2110
Harrgate, 4148
Harris, 8995
Harris Farms, 5609
Harris Fresh, 5609
Harris Ranch, 5609, 5611
Harrisburg Dairies, 5613
Harrison, 5614
Harry & David, 5615
Harry London, 4250
Harry London Chocolates, 5616
Harry's Choice, 3629
Hart, 10404
Hart Winery, 5618
Hartford, 5619
Hartford Court, 5619
Hartford Farms®, 7402
Hartley Brandy, 11264
Hartley's, 5460
Hartness Choice, 11177
Hartwell Cabernet, 11810
Harvard, 474
Harvest, 7526
Harvest Ale British Esb, 3746
Harvest Bakery, 5628
Harvest Bar, 9116
Harvest Bay®, 1484
Harvest Classic, 10637
Harvest Club®, 12885
Harvest Delighta, 3366
Harvest Farm, 11368

Harvest Foods, 5630
Harvest Fresh, 7978
Harvest of the Sea®, 9522
Harvest Pasta, 4794
Harvest Road, 10274
Harvest Selects, 12115
Harvest Splendor®, 8055
Harvest Stone, 12477
Harvest Sweets, 2159
Harvest-Pac, 5637
Harvestland®, 9946
Harveys Supermarket, 11838
Hatchers, 7746
Hatfield, 2559, 5643, 12166
Hatties, 5753
Hatuey Beers, 914
Haus Barhyte Mustard, 1034
Havana Cappucino, 9115
Havoc Maker, 5652
Havren, 6460
Hawaii, 4493
Hawaii Coffee Company, 5654
Hawaii Coffee Roasters, 5659
Hawaii's Famous Huli Huli, 9691
Hawaiian Delight, 5660
Hawaiian Festives, 7410
Hawaiian Gold, 8019, 13511
Hawaiian Host, 4592
Hawaiian Hula Dressing, 6736
Hawaiian Island Crisp, 5653
Hawaiian Island Crisp Cookies, 5653
Hawaiian Joys, 5660
Hawaiian King, 5660
Hawaiian Majesty, 5660
Hawaiian Natural Water, 5661
Hawaiian Princess Smoke, 6303
Hawaiian Punch, 8586
Hawaiian Punch®, 3725, 6818
Hawaiian Snacks®, 2939, 2940
Hawaiian Sun, 427, 5662
Hawaiice, 918
Hawkeye, 7655
Hawkhaven, 5663
Hawthorne Valley Farm, 5666
Hayes Ranch, 13654
Haystack, 7310
Hazel Creek, 5670
Hazel's, 8670
Hazelnut, 10307
Hazle, 5672
Hazlitt, 5673
Hazyme®, 2370
Hb Batters, 6098
Hb Breadings, 6098
Hb Pastis, 3165
He Man, 10873
Head & Shoulders, 12721
Head Country, 5675
Head of the Class, 13630
Health Assure, 8891
Health Concerns, 5680
Health Cookie, 6442
Health Creation Caramel Pretzels, 8029
Health Creation Onion Pretzels, 8029
Health Is Wealth, 5687
Health Valley, 3617, 5505, 5684
Health-Fu'd, 12377
Healthbest, 5689
Healthbody, 10314
Healthcare Naturals, 8882
Healthee, 5691
Healthline, 2960
Healthnut, 1027
Healthseed, 4702
Healthy Choice®, 2939, 2940
Healthy Hemp, 4702
Healthy Himalaya, 11351
Healthy Indulgence, 11856
Healthy Juice, 9734
Healthy Life®, 7402
Healthy Ones, 11733
Healthy Partner Pet Snacks, 5139
Healthy Request Ready To Serve Soup, 2115
Healthy Skoop, 5699
Healthy Sleep™, 6449
Healthy To Go, 6049
Healthy'n Fit Nutritionals, 5698
Healthy™, 8899
Hearn & Rawlins, 13118
Heart, 3852
Heart Cleanse, 5682
Heart Liteo, 10100

1279

Brand Name Index

Heart of Tea, 5718
Heart of Wisconsin, 8304
Heart Right®, 1612
Heart Shape, 11517
Heart Tee, 13779
Heart To Heart, 6720
Hearth, 13767
Hearth & Kettle, 6868
Hearth Club, 2711
Heartland, 465, 5707, 11053
Heartland Brands, 8077
Heartland Chocolates, 5616
Heartland Mill, 5713
Heartland U.S.A., 10268
Heartland®, 1491
Hearts, 13256
Heartline, 194
Hearty Life®, 1491
Hearty Naturals, 5719
Hearty Originals, 4753
Heat & Eat, 9833
Heat & Serve, 4243
Heat-N-Eat, 12396
Heath, 2132, 5818
Heath & Heather, 4244
Heathy 1, 11559
Heaven Scent, 3924, 5721
Heaven Scent Butter, 5721
Heaven Scent Butter Cookies, 3924
Heaven Scent Croutons, 3924, 5721
Heaven Scent Fat Free Cookies, 3924
Heaven Scent Natural Foods, 3924
Heaven Scent Windmill Cakes, 5721
Heaven Scent Windmill Cookies, 3924
Heavenly Bees, 9151
Heavenly Cluster, 13180
Heavenly Clusters Collection, 13180
Heavenly Hash, 4032
Heavenly Light, 4405
Heavenly Little Cookies, 1275
Heavy Bran, 6917
Heavy Seas Marzen, 2763
Heavyweight Gainer 900, 2411
Hebrew National®, 2939, 2940
Hecker Pass, 5726
Heckers, 13135
Hedley's, 10412
Heemskerk, 12937
Hefe Proper, 1687
Hefe Weizen, 1097, 1139
Hefeweizen, 1237, 7551, 10629
Hefeweizer, 3107
Heidecker, 10782
Heifetz®, 1103
Heine's, 5108
Heineman's, 5731
Heiner's, 1359
Heini's Brand Cheese, 1851
Heinkel's, 5733
Heinle, 11458
Heins, 10372
Heinz Abc, 6977
Heinz Ketchup, 6976
Heise's, 5738
Heitz, 5739
Hela, 1957
Helen's Kitchen, 12684
Helena Ranch, 9321
Helena View, 5743
Hell on the Red, 5744
Hell's Furry Fire Hot Sauce, 7694
Helles Bock, 4950
Hellmann's, 1267, 13167, 13169
Hellmans, 11108
Hello Kitty, 2132, 3852, 4659
Hello Water, 5748
Hells Canyon, 5749
Helms, 5752
Helmut, 3714
Helmuth, 5753
Helshiron, 5754
Heluva Good Cheese, 5757
Helwa, 6279
Hem, 11896
Hemingway's Hair Of, 912
Hemp Bar, 5221
Hemp Cream Ale, 13711
Hemp Fusion, 5758
Hemp Sprout Bag, 11977
Hemp2o, 5761
Hemptails, 9117
Hen-Of-The-Woods, 5583

Hendon, 5765
Hengstenberg, 1957
Heniz, 4111
Hennessy, 8452
Hennessy Cognacs, 3570
Henninger Kaiser Pils, 1702
Henri Abele, 4693
Henri Merchant, 1080
Henri Philipe, 7655
Henri's®, 864
Henry Estate, 5772
Henry Weinhard's, 8459
Henry's Heritage Bread, 11979
Henry's Kettle, 5479
Hepac, 3390
Hepahop Gold, 6554
Herb Actives, 5065
Herb Alchemy, 4575
Herb Crystals, 4718
Herb Gouda, 13840
Herb Masters' Original, 8882
Herb Science, 10708
Herb Society of America, 5779
Herb Technology, 14011
Herb's Five Star, 9000
Herbal Essences, 12721
Herbal Nutrition, 665
Herbal Teas, 5155, 12272
Herbal Teazers, 291
Herbamare Juices, 10568
Herbco, 5782
Herbox®, 6000
Herbs America, 5790
Herbs For Kids®, 9237
Herbs Seafood, 5781
Herbs, Etc., 5791
Herdez®, 6000
Hereford Beef, 5338
Heritage, 4891, 5803
Heritage - the Essence of Tradition, 12906
Heritage Chipotle Roasted Salsa, 5795
Heritage Coffee, 5794
Heritage Espresso Pods, 11855
Heritage Fancy Foods, 3629, 5796
Heritage Farms®, 8783
Heritage Fresh Salsa, 5795
Heritage Garlic Mayo, 5795
Heritage Health Foods, 5799
Heritage Hearth, 10846
Heritage Ovens, 2227
Heritage Pride, 4262
Heritage Salmon, 5800
Heritage Select, 11855
Heritage Select Brand, 11046
Heritage Soups, 3956
Herkimer, 9564
Herlocher's Dipping Mustard, 5805
Herman Joseph's Private Reserve, 8459
Herman Joseph's Private Reserve, 8460
Hermann J. Wiemer, 5808
Hermann Pickle, 5809
Hermann's Dark Lager, 13288
Hermannator Ice Bock, 13288
Hermes, 1120, 6986
Hernandez, 11958
Hero, 71, 6540, 12438
Hero Jerky, 5139
Herr's®, 5815
Herradura, 1784
Hershey, 6540
Hershey Chocolate, 13610
Hershey's, 541, 5818
Hershey's Bliss, 5818
Hershey's Kisses, 5818
Hershey's Milkshake, 1782
Hershey'sc, 2132
Hershey®'s Ice Cream, 5819
Herta®, 8945
Herzog Selection, 10952
Herzog Wine Cellars, 10952
Hess Collection, 5820
Hess Estate, 5820
Hess Select, 5820
Hewitt Vineyard, 12937
Hey Nut, 5188
Heyday, 5822
Hf's Outstanding, 1140
Hi Ball Energy, 571
Hi C-Plex, 7947
Hi Flo®, 8804
Hi Praize, 11625

Hi West, 9699
Hi-Bak, 6768
Hi-C®, 6483
Hi-Cap® 100, 8804
Hi-Country, 5826
Hi-Maize® 260, 8804
Hi-Maize® Whole Grain Flour, 8804
Hi-Pop, 10661
Hi-Set® 322, 8804
Hi-Set® C, 8804
Hi0spring, 181
Hiawatha, 4928
Hibernation, 5304
Hibiki, 12315
Hiccuppin' Hot Sauce, 4587
Hickory, 4078
Hickory Baked, 5832
Hickory Farms, 5833
Hickory Grove, 13499
Hickory Harvest Foods, 5834
Hickory Hills, 3248
Hickory Hollow, 9561
Hickory Smoked Sausage, 2944
Hidden Valley, 2766
Hidden Valley®, 13328
Hidden Villa Ranch, 5837
Higgins & Burke, 8578
High Brew, 5840
High Brew Coffee®, 6818
High Country Gourmet, 5842
High Country Kombucha, 6049
High Desert, 1914
High Desert Roasters, 13381
High Impact, 4479
High Liner Culinary, 5844
High Liner®, 5844
High Meadows, 4244
High Moisture Fresh Jack, 13320
High Mountains, 13686
High Rollers Wheat, 549
High Tide Seafoods, 5850
High Valley Farm, 5832
Highland, 5852
Highland Estates, 5993
Highland Light, 7655
Highland Mist Scotch, 11264
Highland Piper, 7655
Highland Sugarworks, 5858
Highwood, 5861
Hilary's, 5864
Hilco Corporation, 2132
Hildon Water, 8838
Hiline, 8919
Hill & Valley, 6338
Hill Country, 12270
Hill Country Products, 5473
Hill Farms, 5520
Hill of Westchester, 1638
Hill's, 13053
Hillcrest, 5418
Hillcrest Orchard, 5869
Hillman, 7776
Hills Bros, 7995, 11212
Hills Bros Cappucino, 7995
Hillshire Farm®, 13109
Hillshire Snacking®, 13109
Hillside, 11494
Himalasalt, 5881
Himalayan Chef, 5882, 13510
Himalayan Glow, 13510
Hinckley Springs, 10303, 11889
Hinckley Springs®, 3220, 3319
Hine Cognac, 3570
Hinman Vineyards, 11612
Hinoichi, 6021
Hint Mint, 5886
Hinzerling, 5888
Hip Chick Farms, 5889
Hip Whip, 9196
Hippie Snacks, 5891
Hiram Walkerc, 9964
Hires®, 3725, 6818
Hnery McKenna Single Barrel, 5720
Hnery Weinhard's®, 8460
Ho Hos®, 6013
Ho-Tai, 13625
Hobby, 7160
Hobgoblin - Beer, 4148
Hodag, 716
Hodgson Mill, 5898, 11587
Hodo, 5899
Hoegaarden, 71, 571, 7123

Hof Ten Dormaal, 8959
Hoffman House®, 1103
Hoffmans, 2667
Hoffy, 11988
Hofmeister, 2409
Hofmeister Haus, 6553
Hog Heaven, 838
Hog Wild Pork Jerky, 10081
Hoghaus, 5903
Hogue, 13425
Hokey Pokey, 8269
Hol Grain, 2956
Hola, 1244
Holidale Barley Wine, 1237
Holiday Bonus, 8860
Holiday Farms, 8560
Holiday Pasta, 4794
Holiday Royal, 4689
Holiday White, 9069
Holland, 13912
Holland House, 8586
Holland House®, 8415
Holland Mints, 7912
Hollmans, 5910
Hollow Tree, 6747
Holly Hops Spiced Al, 9688
Holly Sugar®, 6164
Hollys Coffee®, 6818
Hollywood, 5505
Holopop, 7426
Holsom, 741
Holsum, 1881, 5917, 11525
Holsum Bread, 3056
Holsum®, 9736
Holy Moses White Ale, 5314
Holy Sheet, 2763
Holzofen, 3606
Homaid™, 13614
Homarus, 5924
Home Country, 4232
Home Fresh, 7871
Home Game, 2511
Home Health®, 8871
Home Kombucha, 5921
Home of Ramona, 4387
Home Pride, 4529
Home Run Inn, 5931
Home Style, 166, 2873
Homecraft® Create, 8804
Homemade Gourmet, 10022
Homemade In Minutes, 4753
Homeopathy For Kids®, 9237
Homestead, 1759, 5944
Homestead Mills, 5946
Homestyle, 103
Homestyle Italian Pasta Salad, 5489
Hometown Stars, 2216
Hommage Cabernet, 2770
Hommage Chardonnay, 2770
Honchos, 3466
Honees, 551
Honest, 2814
Honest John's, 11728
Honest Tea, 2811
Honey, 9761
Honey Acres, 5953
Honey Baked Ham, 5966
Honey Basil Ale, 1401
Honey Bbq Ranchc, 5489
Honey Bear Farms, 7339
Honey Blonde, 1097
Honey Brown, 3171
Honey Brown Lager, 9117
Honey Bunches of Oats, 10213
Honey Butter Topping, 12936
Honey Essence, 10450
Honey Fruit Spreads, 14034
Honey Gardens™, 9237
Honey In the Rough, 3815
Honey In the Straw, 14034
Honey Maid, 8729
Honey Maid® S'Mores, 10213
Honey Silk, 1164
Honey Stinger, 5963
Honey Weiss, 7330
Honey-Touched®, 1654
Honeybake Farms, 2501
Honeycomb, 10213
Honeyman & Wood, 5969
Honeymate, 12550
Honeymoon, 13998
Honeystix, 5073

1280

Brand Name Index

Honeywood Grande, 5969
Honeywood North American Grape, 5969
Honeywood Premium, 5969
Hongar Farms, 5147
Honig, 6977
Honkers, 5188
Hood®, 5486
Hoodcrest, 8669
Hoodsies®, 5486
Hoodsport, 5984
Hoody's, 5632
Hoopee Doops, 13845
Hoosier Pride, 9585
Hop Ottin' Ipa, 549
Hop Valley, 8459
Hop Valley®, 8460
Hope, 5990
Hopkins Inn Caesar Dressing, 5992
Hopkins Inn House Dressing, 5992
Hopkins Vineyard, 5993
Hopkins Westwind, 5993
Hoppin' Pops, 6158
Hopps Aux Pommes, 1666
Hopps Brau, 1666
Hopsteiner®, 11018
Horio, 6986
Horizon, 11281
Horizon Orangic, 5837
Horizon Organic, 3379, 13734
Hormel, 6762
Hormel Chili®, 6000
Hormel Foods, 1891, 11053
Hormel Foods®, 11504
Hormel Health Labs, 6000
Hormel Pepperoni®, 6000
Hormel Side Dishes, 6000
Hormel Taco Meats®, 6000
Hormel®, 6000
Horne's, 11416
Hornitos Sauza, 3024
Hornitos®, 1120
Horowitz Margareten, 7848
Horseshoe Brand, 6003
Horseshoe Cake, 6082
Horseshoes and Nails, 6082
Horton's, 2981
Hosmer Mountain Soft Drinks, 6009
Hospitality, 5015, 6010
Hospitality Mints, 2132
Hostess, 6555
Hostess Cupcakes®, 6013
Hostess®, 6483
Hot 'n' Ready®, 184, 13109
Hot & Crusty, 7876
Hot Chocolate Supreme, 464
Hot Chocolate-Fine Chocolate, 12542
Hot Fudge Fantasy, 9019
Hot Mama, 6353
Hot Mix, 3465
Hot Pockets®, 8945
Hot Sauce For Cool Kids, 8433
Hot Shot, 7655
Hot Stuff, 11775
Hot Tamales®, 6641
Hot Wachula's Gourmet Dips & Sauces, 6018
Hot Wok, 3465
Hot! Hot! Hot!, 6015
Hot'n Zesty Links, 6574
Hot-C-Pops, 5752
Hot-N-Coldpops, 5752
Hotel Bar, 6760
Hothothot, 10435
Hound Dog, 7655
House Blend, 3574, 12846
House Foods, 6021
House of Bazzini, 1114
House of Raeford, 6573
House of Raeford®, 6025
House of Stuart Scotch, 11264
House of Tsang®, 6000
House of Windsor, 11865
Howard Johnson, 4369
Howard's, 6034
Hoyt's Pure Honey, 6038
Hoyts, 6038
Hp - White Hulled Sesame Seeds, 11462
Hpnotiq, 5720
Hrd, 5981
Hub of the Uncompaghre, 10324
Hubba Bubba®, 7952, 13960
Hubba Bubbac, 2132

Hubbardson Blue, 13687
Huber, 1231
Huber Bock, 1231
Hubert's Lemonade, 2811
Hubsch Doppel Bock, 12191
Hubsch Dunkel, 12191
Hubsch Lager, 12191
Hubsch Marzen, 12191
Hubsch Pilsener, 12191
Huck's, 6046
Huckleberry, 3953
Huckleberry's Farm, 12831
Hudrage, 7876
Hudson, 11039
Hudson Cream Flour, 12018
Hudson New York, 13082
Hudson Valley, 6050, 6051
Hudson Valley Farms, 1153
Hudson Valley Homestead, 6054
Hudson Valley Malt, 6056
Hudsonville Ice Cream, 6057
Hugo Et Fils, 4677
Huisken, 1659
Hula, 8443
Hulk Candies, 12547
Humane Harvest, 2576
Humble Tea, 4820
Humbly Hemp, 6063
Humm, 6071
Hummel Meats, 6072
Hummer, 648
Hummos, 128
Hummus Pod, 8446
Hummustir, 6075
Humpty Dumpty, 9980
Humpty Dumpty Chips, 9191
Humpy Dumpty, 9408
Hung's Noodle House, 6079
Hungry Buddha, 1825
Hungry Jack, 1069
Hungry-Man®, 2939, 2940
Hunt Country Vineyards, 6083
Hunt's, 2939, 2940
Hunter's Sausage, 6973
Huntingcastle, 4769
Huntington, 5499
Hunts, 6084
Hurst Family Harvest®, 9074
Hurst's Brand Dry Beans®, 9074
Hurst's Hambeens®, 9074
Husman's, 6091
Husman's®, 2939, 2540
Hussong's Tequila, 8062
Hy Van, 3945
Hy-D®, 3320
Hybread, 6094
Hyde Vineyard, 6892
Hydra-Green, 13472
Hydravax, 8191
Hydrea®, 1721
Hydro-Kote®, 126
Hydrologix, 3469
Hydroponic Sweet Basil, 13586
Hydroxycut, 4150
Hye Delites, 6100
Hye Roller, 6100
Hygeia, 6101
Hygeia®, 3442
Hygrade, 1478, 7875
Hyland, 726, 13513
Hylon® Vii, 8804
Hyophen®, 8389
Hypo Form, 13179
Hypower, 6769
Hypowr, 13498
Hyskor, 5462
Hywave, 6387

I

I Buoonatarula Sini, 11668
I Flex, 6107
I Heart Keenwah, 6102
I Love Pasta, 4794
I Will, 9094
I'Ll Bring the Saladd, 4753
I'M Different, 6106
I-Cool, 6107
I.M. Good Snacks, 5834
I.P.A., 9688
I.W. Harper Bourbon, 3570

Iams®, 7952
Ibarra, 12823
Ibc, 1056, 8586, 11310
Ibc Root Beer®, 3725
Ibc®, 6818
Iberia Malt Liquor, 9137
Ibp, 3262
Ibp Trusted Excellence®, 13109
Icco Brand, 6126
Ice & Easy, 5334
Ice Beer, 7123
Ice Breakers, 2132, 5818
Ice Chews, 12390
Ice Chips, 6127, 12390
Ice Chunks, 12390
Ice Cream Joe, 4227
Ice Cubes, 10496
Ice Man, 9664
Ice Road, 9182
Ice Road Blend - Darkest, 9181
Ice Tea, 12914
Ice Tickles, 2050
Iced Fudge Cookies Bars, 12551
Icee, 2132, 6338
Icehouse, 8459
Icehouse®, 8460
Iceland: Armant, 5108
Icelandic, 1057
Icelandic Provisions, 6132
Icelandic Seafood®, 5844
Ichiban Delight®, 857
Ici, 6252
Icl Industrial Products, 1692
Icy Point, 9344
Id-Alg, 9029
Ida Mae, 9564
Idaho Lake Wild Rice, 575
Idaho Spud, 6134
Idaho Supreme, 6138
Idaho's Best, 6139
Idaho-Pacific, 6137
Idahoan, 6140
Iddian Hollow, 6186
Ideal, 10399
Idee, 3714
Idf, 6254
Idol, 7505
Idol Vodka, 1543
Iga, 9621
Iguana, 5516
Iguana Tom's, 13144
Igzu, 6114
Ii Biscotto Della Nonna, 4021
Ii Monello, 8479
Ii Sisters, 6115
Il Caffe, 2839
Il Hwa, 6116
Il Poggiolo, 8479
Illegal Mezcal, 4677
Illinois Prairie, 4753
Illy, 8090
Iltaco, 2542
Imag!Ne®, 9945
Imagine, 5505
Imagine Chocolate, 6150
Imagine Foods, 12017
Imagine Natural Creations, 6151
Imlak'esh Organics, 6153
Immaculate Baking®, 4947
Immaculate Consumption, 6155
Immordl, 6156
Immort Ale, 3644
Immumax, 9957
Immune Life, 4127
Immuno Force, 5883
Impact Confections, 2132
Imperial, 7309, 9117, 9673
Imperial Blent, 11264
Imperial Choice, 13190
Imperial Choice Coff, 13191
Imperial Ipa Black Pilsner, 3746
Imperial Ipa Pilsner, 3746
Imperial Pumpkin, 7526
Imperial Stout, 1237, 3746
Imperial Sugar®, 6164
Impress, 6232
Improved Meat, 6168
Imus Brothers Coffee, 6170
In the Raw, 6172
Inca Harvest, 12663
Inca Kola, 6943

Incognito, 4815
Incosity, 5246
India Beer, 8459
India House, 6653
India Pale Ale, 1139, 1401, 7526, 9366
India Teas, 12272
Indian, 14053
Indian Brown Ale, 3644
Indian Creek, 8204, 14023
Indian Head, 13803
Indian River Pride, 3314
Indian River Select, 6188
Indian Summer, 2518
Indiana Spud®, 7402
Indica India Pale Ale, 7554
Indigenous, 13082
Indigo, 6197
Induveca, 2670
Infalac, 13122
Inferno Wings®, 1654
Infinity®, 6374
Inglehoffer, 1141
Ingoldby, 12937
Ingot, 5140
Ingredient Integrity, 9743
Ingredionc, 6260
Inharvest, 6171
Inka Chips, 6214
Inka Corn, 6214
Inka Crops Kettle Chips, 6214
Inka Crops Seeds & Nuts, 6214
Inka Crops Veggie Chips, 6214
Inked Organics, 6215
Inn Maid, 12467
Inner Beauty Hot Sauce, 12832
Inner Force, 13998
Innerclean, 746
Innisfree, 6603
Inniskillin, 6223, 13425
Innkeeper's Own, 1134
Innkeepers Choice, 1718
Innovaphase™, 2711
Inscription White, 6763
Insignia, 6603
Insta Grains, 1710
Insta Thick, 10297
Instacafe, 1490
Instagel, 12637
Instant Cappuccino, 12868
Instant Clearjel®, 8804
Instant Indulgence, 2525
Instant Pure-Cote, 5246
Instant Pure-Flo® F, 8804
Instant Roux & Gravy, 12869
Instant Tea, 12868
Instant Textra®, 8804
Instant Whip, 9378
Instantgum, 9029
Instantwhip, 6233
Integrale, 3127
Intense™ Flavored Milks, 13218
Inter Ocean, 8028
Interial Stout, 7310
Intermountain Bison, 5139
Internation Seafood of Alaska, 6270
International Brownie, 6248
International Delight, 3379, 13734
International Delight®, 11281
International Delight™, 11211
Intros®, 11504
Introvigne's, 570
Inver House Scotch, 11264
Invermere, 10426
Invertec, 11013
Invertose Hfcs, 6211
Invisible Goodness, 463
Ioma, 13565
Iowa State, 1660
Ipa, 4950, 5188
Ipswich Ale, 6283
Iq Juice, 6122
Irilla Extra Virgin O.O., 11096
Irish Mist, 5892
Irish Mist Liqueur, 5720
Irish Stout, 9688
Irish Style Nut Brown Ale, 5515
Iron City, 10091
Iron City Light, 10091
Iron Horse, 9701
Iron Kettle, 6267
Iron Uke, 13643
Iron-Tek, 3080

1281

Brand Name Index

Isabo Hearts of Palm, 4607
Isahop, 6554
Island Blend, 9182
Island Fruit, 7373
Island Mist Iced Tea, 1636
Island Prince®, 1140
Island Princess, 6303, 9519
Island Queen®, 1140
Island Spring, 6309
Island Sweetwater, 6310
Island Teriyaki, 11878
Island Trader, 7777
Island Treasures Gourmet, 2296
Islander, 3765
Islander's Choice, 4362
Iso-Sport, 253
Isomalt, 1219
Isopure, 8870
Issimo Celebrations!, 6314
Issimo's Creme Br-L,, 6314
Istara, 7126
It's a Boy, 9753
It's a Girl, 9753
It's It, 6315
It's Soy Delicious, 11771
Italia, 6316, 13365
Italia D'Oro Coffee, 1636
Italian Chef, 9821
Italian Rose, 6322
Italian Village®, 10899
Italico, 1174
Itchy Witchy, 11004
Ithaca Cold-Crafted, 6325
Ititropicals, 6276
Itoen, 6327
Itty-Bittie Biscotti, 13216
Itty-Bittie Cookies, 13216
Ivan the Terrible, 10992
Ivanhoe, 6328
Ivanhoe Classics, 6328
Ivanhoe Fresh, 6328
Iveta Gourmet, 6329
Ivory, 12721
Ivory Almond K'Nuckle, 10984
Izze, 6124
Izze®, 9945

J

J & J, 4035
J Bar B, 6334
J Moreau Fils, 12672
J Nicole Vineyard Pinot Noir, 12627
J Russian River Vall, 12627
J Sparkling Wine, 12627
J Vineyards & Winery®, 3834
J&J Gourmet, 6451
J&M, 8709
J-Burger Seasoning, 795
J. Berrie Brown Wine Nuts, 4587
J. Crow's, 6371
J. Filippi, 6350
J. Schram, 11307
J.C. Rivers Gourmet Jerky, 5056
J.F. Braun, 6398
J.M. Schneider, 11768
J.Moreau & Fils, 1543
J.S. McMillan, 6387
J.T.M. Food Group, 6410
Jack Daniel's, 4422
Jack Daniel's Gentleman Jack, 6416
Jack Daniel's Old No. 7, 6416
Jack Daniel's Single Barrel, 6416
Jack Daniel's Tennessee Fire, 6416
Jack Daniel's Tennessee Honey, 6416
Jack Daniel's Tennessee Rye, 6416
Jack Daniel's®, 6416
Jack Daniels, 1784, 5141, 10468
Jack Link's, 541, 5141, 7449
Jack Links, 4150
Jack Mackerel, 2555
Jack Man, 7310
Jack Miller, 6417
Jack Rabbit, 12972, 12973
Jack's All American, 10196
Jack's Beans, 2879
Jackpot, 4232, 5409, 8219
Jackson's Honest, 6423
Jackson-Triggs, 13425
Jacob Best, 9664
Jacobs, 3714

Jacobsen's Toast, 7511
Jacquelynn Cuv'e, 2454
Jacquelynn Syrah, 2454
Jacques Bonet Brandy, 11264
Jaffa, 10659
Jaffer, 2096
Jager, 6433
Jake & Amos, 7193
Jake's Grillin, 6439
Jalapeanuts, 2021, 2022
Jalapeno, 9935
Jalapeno Gouda, 13840
Jalapeno Tnt, 9935
Jamaica Blue Mountain, 10157
Jamaica Bluemountain, 761
Jamaican Gold, 8988, 10307
James, 10296
James Chocolate Seal Taffy, 6445
James Cream Mints, 6445
James Harbour, 4515
James Salt Water Taffy, 6445
James', 4645
Jamesonc Irish, 9964
Jamieson's Run, 12937
Jamy's Three Dragon, 520
Jana, 9858
Jane Dough, 3709
Jane Stewart, 11102
Janes, 11776
Janes Family Favourites, 6451
Japone, 1120
Jar-Lu, 5738
Jaret, 13610
Jarritos, 12823
Jasmati, 10712
Jasmine, 11908
Jasmine Green, 13746
Jason, 5505, 7848
Jason & Son, 6461
Jason Pharmaceuticals, 6462
Jasper, 7463
Jasvine, 6460
Java Estate, 10157
Java Jelly, 5217
Javarama, 10303
Jaw Busters, 1417, 4345
Jays, 11770
Jayson, 9709
Jazz, 6310
Jazz Cola, 5539
Jazzie J, 11557
Jazzy Barbecue Sauce, 887
Jazzy Java Custom Flavored Gourmet, 10584
Jb's Extreme, 3279
Jc's Pie Bites, 6393
Jc's Pie Pops, 6393
Jcb By Jean-Charles Boisset, 1543
Jdk & Sons™, 1120
Jean Sweet Potatos, 10954
Jean-Claude Boisset, 12672
Jecky's Best, 6478
Jeff's Naturals, 6481
Jelen, 8459
Jell-O, 6976
Jello, 6977
Jelly Bean, 5017
Jelly Belly, 6485, 13610
Jelly Belly Candy Company, 4150
Jelly Krimpetsc, 12551
Jemez Blush, 10165
Jemez Red, 10165
Jemmburger, 1262
Jennie, 11934
Jennie-O Turkey®, 6000
Jenny Craig®, 8945
Jenny's, 6491
Jenny's Country Kitchen, 6490
Jensen Foods®, 11504
Jensen Solos™, 6492
Jensen's Orchard, 11748
Jeremiah's Pick, 6497
Jericho Canyon Red, 10845, 10963
Jermann®, 3834
Jerry's, 6500
Jersey Boardwalk, 5400
Jersey Farms, 10664
Jersey Shore®, 2332
Jersey Supreme, 4578
Jesben, 6505
Jess Jones Farms, 6506
Jessie Lord, Inc., 3078

Jet Tea, 3009
Jet-Puffed, 6976
Jetcoat, 11906
Jeunesse Wines, 10952
Jewel Laboratories, 13128
Jewel of India, 10435
Jfg Coffee and Tea, 10657
Ji Hao, 734
Jicachipsc, 9574
Jif, 6380
Jiffy Mix, 2508
Jiffy Pop, 6267
Jiffy Pop®, 2939, 2940
Jiffyc, 10106
Jila & Jols, 3381
Jilbert, 3442
Jim Beam, 3545, 12315, 13454
Jim Beam®, 1120
Jim Candy, 431
Jim's Country Mill Sausage, 14043
Jimmy Dean, 6520
Jimmy Dean®, 13109
Jinglebits, 10104
Jinja, 6523
Jk Sweet, 6402
Jmh Premium, 6405
Jo Citrus, 11549
Jo's Candies, 6525
Jo's Original, 6525
Joan of Arc®, 864, 11209
Jodar, 6527
Jody Maroni, 6529
Jody's, 6530
Joe Bertman's Ballpark Mustard, 6532
Joe Clark's Candies, Inc., 6533
Joe Corbi's, 6534
Joe Perry's, 730
Joey's, 6542
Johannisberg Riesling, 7527, 11162
John Morrell, 11733
John Mountain Organic, 12401
John O'S, 1553
John Wm. Macy's Cheesecrips, 6561
John Wm. Macy's Cheesesticks, 6561
John Wm. Macy's Sweetsticks, 6561
John Z'S Big City, 5402
Johnny Boy Vanilla, 13613
Johnny Walker Scotch, 3570
Johnson's Alexander Valley, 6569
Johnsonville Bratwur, 6574
Johnsonville Country, 6574
Johnston County Hams, 11864
Johnston's Winery, 6578
Johr®, 898
Joia All Natural Soda, 6579
Joint Cleanse, 5682
Joint Movement, 8896
Joint Well, 9201
JojÉ, 6580
Joker - Fruit Juice, 4148
Joker's Wild Energy, 3753
Joliesse Vineyards, 12672
Jollie Juan, 13184
Jolly Aid, 7890
Jolly Good, 6985
Jolly Llama, 6581
Jolly Pops, 7890
Jolly Rancher, 2132, 5818, 6483
Jolly Roger, 13770
Jolly Rogers, 3746
Jolly Time, 478
Jolt, 13697
Jolt Cola Energy Rush, 12547
Jolt-Cola, 13697
Jomints, 11549
Jon Donaire, 6583, 10714
Jonathan International Foods, 3953
Jonathan T., 13242
Jonathan's Organics, 6585
Jonathan's Sprouts, 6585
Jones, 6589
Jones Sausagest, 6587
Jones Soda Carbonated Candy, 1343
Jones Soda Carbonated Sours, 1343
Jones Soda Energy Boosters, 1343
Jones Sours, 1343
Jonnypops, 6592
Joons Chocolate Popcorn, 10944
Jordan Almonds, 8588
Jordanettes, 11320
Jose Cuervo Margarita Salt Sombrero, 4650
Jose Goldstein, 1279

Jose Ole®, 237, 238
Jose Pedro, 5029
Joseph Farms, 8898
Joseph Farms Cheese, 6600
Josh & John's Ice Cream, 6608
Joshua Miguel, 11339
Josie's Best Blue Tortilla Chips, 11439
Joullian Vineyards, 6612
Journey, 8003
Jow Stiff's Spiked Rootbeer, 13711
Joy, 6614, 6821, 12721
Joy Stick, 614
Joy Stiks, 2947
Joy's, 6615
Joy's Gourmet Snacks, 12666
Joyce Farms, 4321
Joyful Mind, 5883
Joyfuls, 6617
Joyner's, 13237
Joyya™, 11211
Jp's, 12961
Jr Buffalos®, 6374
Juanita's, 6619
Juarez, 7655
Jubilations, 6621
Jubilee, 6622
Juice Bowl, 3279
Juice Bowl Sparkling Juice, 3279
Juice Direct, 3365
Juice Plus, 6159
Juice-Mate, 10314
Juiceburst, 5460
Juicefuls Hard Candy, 10532
Juicemaster, 4521
Juicetyme Delites, 1292
Juicy Fruit®, 7952, 13960
Juicy Juice®, 6483, 8945
Juicy Orange, 6159
Juicy Whip, 6628
Juju, 7310
Juju Ginger, 7309
Jujyfruits, 1417, 4345
Julian's Recipe, 6630
Juliana, 9766
Julie's Organic, 9533
Julie's Real, 6632
Jumbo Flavors, 3707
Jumbo Lump, 10429
Jumbo Minisips, 9170
Jump Start, 2860
Jumping Black Beans, 4252
Juneau, 8474
Jungle Juice, 9251
Jungle Munch, 10542
Junior Mints,, 2102
Junior Mints®, 12880
Jupiler, 71
Jupina, 2338
Jus-Rol®, 4947
Just, 6649
Just - Ripe, 14035
Just Add Tequila, 7903
Just Bare Chicken®, 10056
Just Born, Inc, 2132
Just Born®, 6641
Just Chips, 6647
Just Crisps, 6647
Just Croutons, 6647
Just Date Syrup, 6643
Just Delicious, 6644
Just Fiber, 11794
Just Flatbread, 6647
Just Great Bakers, Inc., 2810
Just In Time, 10022
Just Juice, 3479
Just Meringues, 1751, 2599
Just Nuts, 4032
Just Once Natural Herbal Extras, 10537
Just Panela, 6648
Just Pik't, 4714
Just Right®, 6765
Just Snak-It, 12831
Just Whites, 3449
Justin, 6651
Justin Vineyard, 3545
Justin's®, 6000
Juwong, 10331
Jw Dundee's Honey Brown Lager, 4950
Jyoti, 6653

Brand Name Index

K

K&F, 6654, 6902
K&S, 6656
K-Cup Packs, 4543
K-Min, 9262
K4484, 8804
Ka-Mec, 9748
Kaboom, 2666
Kaffe Magnum Opus, 6683
Kaffree Roma, 772
Kagome, 6684
Kahiki, 6685
Kahlua, 5892, 9964
Kahl£A®, 6818
Kahns, 5792
Kaho Mai, 1849
Kaiseki Select, 2630
Kal®, 9237
Kalamazoo, 6690
Kalena, 6691
Kali Hart Chardonnay, 12506
Kaliber, 5427
Kalin Cellars, 6693
Kalmbach, 726
Kalsec, 6695
Kambly, 13544
Kamchatka®, 1120
Kamenitza, 8459
Kamis, 8061
Kammerude, 4028
Kamora, 3545
Kamora®, 1120
Kamut®, 6171
Kan Tong®, 7952
Kana Organics, 6700
Kandy Kookies, 6851
Kanemasa, 8412
Kanga Beans, 1909
Kangaroo®, 2939, 2940
Kangavites, 11785
Kanimi-Tem, 11559
Kanonkop, 4677
Kansas Sun, 2389
Kantner, 6702
Kaori Horoyoi, 1120
Kapiti®, 4552
Kaptain's Ketch, 9000
Kara, 6707
Karbach Brewing Company, 571
Karen's Fabulous Biscotti, 1397
Karenvolf, 6774
Kargher Chocolate Chips, 6708
Kari-Out, 6665
Karine & Jeff, 6709
Karkov ®, 13120
Karl Strauss, 6711
Karlsburger, 6714
Karm'l Dapples, 2050
Karma, 6716
Karoun, 6719
Kars, 4721
Kas, 6666
Kasanofs's, 12328
Kashi Cereals, 6720
Kashi Frozen Foods, 6720
Kashi Snacks, 6720
Kashruth, 6970
Kashu Gold Oranges, 13906
Kasilof Fish, 6721
Kasira, 6722
Kasmati, 10712
Kasomel™, 10239
Kasser, 7146
Kastin's, 7279
Katahna, 357
Kate Latters Chocolates, 6725
Kate's, 6726
Katharine Beecher®, 13572
Katherine Beecher, 13574
Kathi, 1957
Kathryn Kennedy, 6729
Kathy's Gourmet Specialties, 6730
Katy's Kitchen®, 11504
Katy's Smokehouse, 6733
Kauai Coffee, 6735, 7995
Kauai Kookie, 6736
Kaukauna, 1172
Kava, 6380
Kava Kava, 1285
Kava King Beverage Mixes, 6740
Kava King Chocolates, 6740

Kavli, 6279
Kay Foods, 6741
Kay Pak, 12250
Kay's Hot Stuff, 11540
Kayem®, 6744
Kci, 10652
Kedem, 6540, 10952
Keebler, 6747, 6766
Keegan Ales, 6748
Keenan Farms, 6749
Keenwa Krunch, 3906
Keep, 9238
Kefir, 7423
Kefir Starter, 7423
Kehr's Kandy, 6755
Keke, 8062
Kel-Yolk, 6768
Kelapo, 6756
Kelchner's, 6758
Kelcogel, 1962
Kelgum, 1962
Keller's, 6760, 8677, 10873
Keller's® Creamery Butter, 3335
Kelley's, 6762
Kellogg's, 6766
Kellogg's Corn Flakes®, 6765
Kellogg's Frosted Flakes, 6765
Kellogg's®, 11504
Kelly, 6767, 6769, 6771
Kelly Corned Beef, 6773
Kelly's, 6772
Kelson Creek, 6775
Keltrol, 1962
Kemach, 6776
Kemps®, 3335
Kenalog®, 1721
Kencraft Classics, 6780
Kendall Brook, 3780
Kenlake Foods, 12699
Kenny's, 12093
Kenny's Island Style, 12093
Kenny's Key Lime Crunch, 12093
Kent Foods, 6791
Kent Quality Foods, 11053
Kentuckian Gold, 11902
Kentucky Beer Cheese, 6795
Kentucky Bourbon Chocolates, 10468
Kentucky Bourbonq, 6796
Kentucky Farm, 3443
Kentucky Gentleman, 11263
Kentucky Gentleman Bourbon-A-Blend, 11284
Kentucky Kernel, 5898, 11587
Kentucky Legend, 11902
Kentucky Nip, 13728
Kentucky Nip Cherry Julep, 13728
Kentucky Tavern, 8700, 11263
Kentucky Tavern Bourbon, 11264
Kentucky's Choice, 7655
Kentucky's Old Reserve, 4515
Kentwood Springs®, 3220, 3319
Kentwood Springs, 10303
Kentwood® Springs, 11889
Kenwood Vineyards, 6798
Kenwoodc Vineyards, 9964
Kenya Aa, 1123, 10157
Kerleens, 5909
Kern Ridge, 6670
Kersen, 6119
Keto Cups, 3909
Kettle & Fire, 6813
Kettle Brand, 2116, 6814, 11770
Kettle Brand Krinkle Cut, 6814
Kettle Chips, 6918
Kettle Classics, 2728
Kettle Gourmet, 3696
Kettle Uprooted, 6814
Kevita®, 9945
Key Farms, 11053
Key Iii, 6823
Key Lime, 11458
Key Lime Cheesecake, 2881
Key Lime Pie Slices Dipped In Choco, 6825
Key Lime Pies Assorted Flavors, 6825
Key-E, 6364
Keycel ®, 11794
Keylime Graham Crackers, 4253
Keystone, 6829, 8459, 9212, 12631
Keystone®, 7786, 8460
Khatsa, 6831
Khg-7, 5683
Kia Ora, 2815

Kibbles 'n Bits, 6380
Kibun, 5483
Kickapoo Joy Juice®, 8470
Kickapoo of Wisconsin, 8659
Kid Cuisine®, 2939, 2940
Kid Wizard, 11051
Kid-Tastic, 13085
Kidalin, 5791
Kiddi Pops, 14021
Kiddie Kakes, 3404
Kidfresh, 6835
Kidney Cleanse, 5682
Kidney Rinse, 13179
Kids Cookie, 6836
Kids Klassics, 2728
Kids Klassics®, 1654
Kidsmania Inc, 2132
Kidz, 5061
Kidzels, 916
Kiev, 7655
Kievit, 9027
Kilbeggan®, 1120
Kill Cliff, 6843
Killawarra, 12937
Killer Joe, 912
Kilwons Foods, 6846
Kim & Scott's Gourmet Pretzels, 6338
Kim Crawford Wines, 13425
Kim's Simple Meals, 5799
Kimball, 6849
Kimco, 6869
Kimes, 6850
Kind Snacks, 4150
Kinderwood, 7740
King & Prince, 6855
King Bing, 9722
King Cole, 6860
King Cole Tea, 4820
King Conch, 4870
King Core, 5483
King Cove, 5483
King Floyd's, 6864
King Juice, 6867
King Lion, 466
King Neptune, 7929
King Nova, 13521
King O' The-West, 13067
King of Fish, 1355
King of Hawaii, 8019
King of Potato Pies, 4853
King of Spice, 11522
King Oscar, 6871
King Products, 6677
King Salmon, 11602
King Soopers, 12516
King's Arms Tavern, 12714
King's Choice, 4554
King's Delicious®, 6870
King's Hawaiian, 6874
King-Cal, 11985
Kingchem, 6875
Kingkold, 6868
Kings, 12972
Kings Choice, 5470
Kings Ford, 2766
Kings Old Fashion, 7163
Kings Ridge, 13174
Kingsey®, 11211
Kingsgate, 6901
Kingsley's Caramels, 7756
Kingston ®, 13120
Kinley, 2815
Kinnikinnick Foods, Inc., 6884
Kinsen Plum, 12500
Kiona, 6886
Kiosks, 11755
Kirigin Cellars, 6888
Kirin Beer, 6889
Kirin Ichiban, 6889
Kirin Lager, 6889
Kirk and Glotzer New, 13812
Kirschwasser (Cherry Brandy), 2737
Kiss Me Frog Truffles, 5497
Kiss of Burgundy, 4315
Kissling, 62
Kist, 11844
Kit Kat, 5818
Kit Katc, 2132
Kitchen Basics, 8061
Kitchen Bouquet, 2766
Kitchen Craft™, 6374
Kitchen Pride Farms, 6894

Kitchen Table Bakers, 12664
Kitchens of the Oceans, 10603
Kitchens of the Sea, 13407
Kite Hill, 6898
Kitkat®, 8945
Kiwa, 6903
Kiwa Kids, 6903
Kiwi Kiss, 6904
Kiwi Kola, 6310
Kix®, 4947
Kjeldsens, 6774
Klara's Gourmet, 6906
Kleckner's, 9332
Kleergum, 5017
Kleinpeter, 6909
Klement's, 6910
Klene, 9956
Klerzyme®, 2370
Klingshirn Winery, 6911
Klondike, 5137, 8533, 13169
Klondike®, 5165
Kloss, 6914
Klosterbrot, 3606
Klosterman, 6915
Kmc Citrus, 6672
Knack & Back®, 4947
Knapp, 6916
Knauss, 3847
Knaust Beans, 5479
Kneadin the Dough, 7639
Knickers Irish Cream Whiskey, 5981
Knight, 6919
Knob Creek®, 1120
Knockout Meats®, 10124
Knoppers, 12147
Knorr, 13167, 13169
Knott's, 6922
Knott's Berry Farm, 6380
Knott's Berry Farms, 1394
Knott's Meat Snacks, 6922
Knott's Novelty Candy, 6922
Knott's Salads, 6922
Knouse Food Service, 6923
Knudsen®, 388
Ko-Sure, 13931
Koala No March Cookie, 7560
Kobricks, 6928
Kobu Beverages, Llc, 6929
Koch's Golden Anniversary, 4950
Kodiak Cakes, 6932
Kodiak Seafood, 6270
Kodikook, 7549
Koffee Kake Juniorsc, 12551
Koffee Kup, 6936
Kogee, 4489
Kohinoor, 6939, 8061
Kohler Deli Meats, 246
Koia, 6941
Kojel, 13240
Kokanee, 7123
Kokanee Gold, 7123
Koko's Confectionery & Novelty, 2132
Kokopelli's Kitchen, 6942
Kokuho Rose, 6673, 6931
Kokushibori, 1120
Kola Champagne, 5177
Kollar, 6946
Komachi Premium Rice, 4260
Kombrewcha, 571
Kombucha Wonder Drink, 6948
Kona, 362, 5659
Kona Brewing, 6949
Kona Coast, 5039
Kona Coffee, 6953
Kona Hawaii, 10157
Kona Island, 13716
Konared, 6954, 7036
Konery, 12698
Konriko, 2956
Konto's, 6956
Kookie Kakes, 6780
Kool Pops, 6483
Kool-Aid, 6976, 6977
Koolgel®, 13648
Koops' Mustard, 9440
Kor Shots, 6963
Korbel, 1784
Korinek, 4654
Korski, 7655, 9773
Kosciusko, 10119
Koshu Plum, 12500
Kosmos Lager, 4881

1283

Brand Name Index

Koster Keunen, 1692
Kosto, 6971
Kowalski, 6973
Koyo™, 1484
Kozlowski Farms, 6974
Kozy Shack, 6676, 7198
Krackel, 5818
Kracker Nuts™, 13603
Kraft, 541, 1891
Kraft 100% Parmesan, 6976
Kraft Bbq Sauce, 6976
Kraft Cheese Nips, 8729
Kraft Dinner, 6976
Kraft Handi-Snacks, 8729
Kraft Heinz®, 11504
Kraft Macaroni & Cheese, 6977
Kraft Mayo, 6976
Kraft Peanut Butter, 6976
Kraft Salad Dressings, 6976
Kraft Singles, 6976
Kramer, 6979
Krave, 6766
Krave®, 6765
Krazy, 12487
Krema, 6983
Kretschmar, 11733
Kretschmer, 2971
Kringle, 9280
Krispy Kernels, 6987
Krispy Kreme®, 6818
Kristall Weizen, 11992
Kristian Regale, 6989
Kristin Hill, 6990
Kroger, 5797, 10170, 13841, 13871
Kron, 1638
Kronenost, 10906
Krug, 8452
Kruger, 6232
Krunchers!, 11770
Krunchie Wedges®, 6374
Krusovice, 1361
Krusteaz, 2971
Krusteaz Professional, 2971
Krystal, 2815
Ksc, 6919
Kt's Kitchens, 6679
Kubla Khan, 6998
Kuchen, 10270
Kuju Coffee, 7000
Kul, 2705
Kulactic, 13299
Kulana Foods, 7001
Kuli, 2815
Kulsar, 13299
Kum Chun Brand, 7296
Kumala, 13425
Kuner's®, 4267
Kura, 7005
Kurolite, 10680
Kuromaru, 1120
Kusmi Tea, 1661
Kutik's Honey, 7009
Kutztown, 7010
Kwai, 127
Kwik Rize, 9570
Kwik-Dish, 1244
Ky Poppers, 10268
Kyger, 7014
Kyo-Chlorella, 13536
Kyo-Dophilus, 13536
Kyo-Green, 13536
Kyo-Green Harvest Blend, 13536
Kyolic, 13536
Kyrol, 648

L

L & M Bakery, 7019
L'Esprit, 7033
L'Il Critters, 2666
L'Ombrelle, 5405
L'Or Chocolatier, 9299
L'Ortolano, 13832
L-Lysine, 239
L-Optizinc, 6236
L-Threonine, 239
L-Tryptophan, 239
L-Valine, 239
L.A. Cinnamon, 12381
L.B. Maple Treat, 7037
L.Mawby, 7029

La Baguetterie, 7886
La Boulange, 12042
La Boulangerie, 7040
La Buena Vida Vineyards, 7041
La Caboose, 7080
La Canasta, 7042
La Captive, 1543
La Cascade Del Cielo, 13728
La Chiquita, 7081
La Chiripada, 7044
La Choy, 6084
La Choy®, 2939, 2940
La Cocina Mexicana, 10760
La Creme, 3377
La Donaings De Franc, 13825
La Flor, 7091
La Follette, 7138
La Fortuna, 9833
La Fruta, 7423
La Granada, 8946
La Grande Folie, 4544
La Herencia®, 6391
La Jolla, 8207
La Joya, 8207
La Laitiere®, 8945
La Marca, 947
La Marca®, 3834
La Martinique, 10657
La Merced Organic, 13883
La Mexicana, 7051
La Mexicanita, 6244
La Minita Tarrazu, 10157
La Morella Nuts, 1056
La Napa, 5498
La Nova, 7097
La Pablanita, 3978
La Panzanellac, 7098
La Patisserie, 3953, 7056
La Paulina®, 11211
La Petite Folie, 4544
La Preferida, 7101
La Pri Cranberry Apple Drink, 9004
La Pri Grapefruit Dr, 9004
La Pri Orange Drink, 9004
La Prima, 7655, 9773
La Quinta, 7740
La Reina, 573, 7059
La Rocca Vineyards, 7060
La Romagnola, 7104
La Ronga Bakery, 7222
La Salle, 7655
La Saltena®, 4947
La San Marco, 6928
La Spiga Doro, 7108
La Superior, 7109
La Tang, 7110
La Tapatia, 7062
La Tonita, 4158
La Torinese, 12895
La Torre, 6244
La Tortilla Factory, 7063
La Vallata, 10565
La Vaquita®, 3335
La Vava Blanca, 11203
La Victoria, 7115, 8898
La Victoria Salsa Su, 7115
La Victoria®, 6000
La Vida, 7110
La Vigns, 7116
La Vina, 7065
La Yogurt, 6545
Laack's Finest, 13877
Labatt, 9396
Labatt 50, 7123
Labatt Blue, 7123
Labatt Crystal, 7123
Labatt Genuine Honey, 7123
Labatt Ice, 7123
Labatt Lite, 7123
Labatt Sterling, 7123
Labatt Usa, 9117
Labex, 9103
Labriola, 6338
Lacas, 7124
Lacey, 7125
Lacey Delite, 2387
Laco, 10161
Lacroix, 4163, 7117, 8784, 13872
Lacroix Sparkling Water, 5884
Lacrosse Lager, 2705
Lacrosse Light, 2705
Lactaid®, 5486

Lactalins, 5683
Lactantia®, 9789
Lacteeze, 4279
Lactiumc, 9997
Lacto, 1369
Lacto Stab, 6554
Lactoperoxidase, 4736
Lactose Pharma, 13881
Lactospore, 11061
Lactoval, 4736
Lactozym Pure, 1692
Lactum®, 8103
Lad's, 7129
Lady Aster®, 13109
Lady Bligh, 7655
Lady Genevieve, 1672
Lady In Red, 6796
Lady of the Lake, 8660
Lady Walton's, 7073
Lady's Choice, 2666
Ladybird®, 13607
Ladybug, 9055
Ladybug White Old Vines, 7514
Laetitia, 7133
Lafave, 953
Lafaza, 7135
Laferia, 11308
Laffy Taffy, 2132
Lafleur®, 9462
Lafond, 11188
Lager, 9701
Lagomarcino's, 7141
Laguna Beach Blinde, 7143
Laguna®, 3834
Lahvosh, 13256
Laing's, 11416
Laird Superfood, 7147
Laird's, 7146
Lake Blend, 4403
Lake Cove, 8660
Lake Plains, 12948
Lake Sonoma Winery, 7154
Lake States, 7155
Lakehouse Lime & Chili, 12178
Lakeland Dairies, 3574
Lakeland®, 9736
Lakeport, 7123
Lakeport Honey Lager, 7157
Lakeport Ice, 7157
Lakeport Light, 7157
Lakeport Pilsener, 7157
Lakeport Strong, 7157
Laker Family of Beers, 1702
Lakeridge, 7158
Lakeshore, 7159
Lakeside, 7160
Lakeside's, 13700
Lakeview Farms, 7168
Lakewood, 7170
Lakewood Vineyards, 7171
Lallemand, 7173
Laloo'sc, 4093
Lalvin, 7176
Lamagna, 7178
Lamb Weston®, 7179, 11504
Lamb's Navy, 3024
Lamb's Palm Breeze, 3024
Lamb's Seasoned®, 7179
Lamb's Supreme®, 7179
Lamb's White, 3024
Lambent, 7180
Lambert Bridge Winery, 7181
Lamberti, 4677
Lambeth Groves, 13192
Lambweston®, 4061
Lamchem, 716
Laminita, 761
Lamonica, 7054
Lamont's, 2628
Lancaster, 5818
Lance, 2116, 11770
Land O Lakes®, 3442
Land O'Frost, 7197
Land O'Lakes, 7198
Land O'Lakes Half & Half, 13734
Land O'Lakes™, 6792
Landmark Damaris Chardonnay, 7203
Landmark Grand Detou, 7203
Landmark Kastania Pi, 7203
Landmark Overlook Ch, 7203
Landry's, 7206
Landshark Lager, 571

Landshire, 13016, 13109
Landshire®, 184
Lanes Dairy, 7208
Lange Winery, 7212
Langers Juice, 7213
Langlois, 5325
Langtry, 5417
Lanky Franky, 2541
Lantana, 7214
Lantern, 13857
Lanthier, 7215
Lantic, 7216, 10838
Lapas, 11980
Lapham, 9682, 11473
Laphroaig, 3024, 12315
Laphroaig®, 1120
Lapone's Jordan, 9625
Lapostolle, 8452
Lapsang Souchong Smoky #1 Blend, 5228
Larabar, 11711
Larabar®, 4947
Larceny Bourbon, 5720
Laredo, 4232
Larios®, 1120
Larosa's Famous Biscotti, 7224
Larosa's Famous Cannoli, 7224
Larosa's Famous Cookies, 7224
Larry's Vineyards, 7228
Larsen Farms, 7229
Laru, 3390
Las Cruces, 7231
Las Palmas®, 864
Las Palomas Grandes, 7433
Las Rocas®, 3834
Lasalle, 9773
Lasanta Maria, 5034
Lascco, 7549, 9344
Laser, 9664
Laser Malt Liquor, 9137
Late Harvest, 2770
Late Harvest Zinfandel, 5989
Late July Snacks, 2116, 11770
Latero-Flora, 9287
Latina®, 4947
Latta, 7242
Latvia: Unda, 5108
Lauder's Scotch, 11264
Laufer Winery, 10952
Laughing Cow, 1172, 1173
Laughing Lab, 1720
Laughing Man®, 6818
Laura Chenel's, 7243
Laura Scudder's, 6380
Laura Secord®, 6818
Laura's, 7245
Laure Pristine, 8849
Laurel Hill, 773
Laurentide, 8459
Lavacarica, 11896
Lavazza, 7253, 8090, 11776
Lavazza Coffee, 1000
Lavita, 1033
Lavosh Hawaii, 183
Lawman's, 13077
Lawrence, 7256
Lawry's, 8061
Lawry's®, 7257
Laxmi, 6026
Lay's, 4741
Layman's, 7261
Lazy Boy Stout, 13428
Lazy Creek Vineyards, 7262
Lba, 7377
Le Belge Chocolatier, 743
Le Bleu Bottled Water, 7264
Le Chatelain, 7126
Le Pain Des Fleurs, 10738
Le Patron, 7104
Le Royal, 1056
Le Saucier, 10331
Le Sueur®, 864
Le Younghurt, 387
Lea & Perrins, 3844, 6976
Lea & Perrins®, 7277
Leader, 7279
Leaf Cuisine, 7280
Lean Cuisine®, 8945
Lean For Less, 5686
Lean on Me Naturally, 4839
Leaner Wiener, 9160
Leaves, 4244
Leaves Pure Tea, 7287

Brand Name Index

Lebanon Cheese, 7289
Lebistro, 11894
Lech Premium®, 8460
Lecitase, 1692
Lee Kum Kee, 7295, 7296
Lee Kum Kee Premium, 7296
Leech Lake, 7301
Leech Lake Wild Rice, 7302
Leelanau, 7303
Leeward, 7306
Leffe, 71, 7123
Lefrancias, 5917
Lefse House, 7308
Left Field Farms, 3379
Left Hand Black Jack, 7309
Legacy, 6919
Legacy Juice Works, 7313
Legacy Pork, 10373
Legacy Red Wine, 6375
Legand Brown, 7315
Legand Pilsner, 7315
Legatin, 2666
Legend of Kremlin, 10952
Legendary Foods, 7316
Legere, 7123
Legg's Old Plantation, 64
Lehi Roller Mills, 7318
Lehigh Valley Dairies, 13145
Lehigh Valley®, 3442
Leibo, 13196
Leibowitz, 13196
Leidenfrost Vineyards, 7325
Leidy's, 285, 7327
Leighton's, 7329
Leinenkugel Original, 7330
Leinenkugel's, 8459
Leinenkugel's®, 8460
Lejay Lagoute, 1120
Lem, 11458
Lem-N-Joy, 12941
Lemon, 11458
Lemon Creek Winery, 7338
Lemon Dew, 1600
Lemon Hart, 3024
Lemon Licious Lemonade, 13728
Lemon Poppy Seed Cake, 2881
Lemon Shortbread, 806
Lemon Splash, 2054
Lemon Tea, 12914
Lemon Twist, 7363
Lemon Velvet, 7581
Lemon-Lime, 883
Lemon-X, 7339
Lemon/Lime Thristaway, 5460
Lemonhead, 1417, 4345
Lemonkind, 7340
Lena Maid, 85
Lender's, 811
Lender's®, 2939, 2940
Lennox, 7349
Lenny's Bee Productions, 7351
Lenora, 1032
Leo Buring, 12937
Leo's, 13521
Leodoro Espresso, 6928
Leon's Sausage, 523
Leon's Texas Cuisine, 7360
Leona's, 7362
Leonard Mountain, 7364
Leonardo, 2012, 10873
Leone Bianco, 10860
Leonetti Cellar, 7366
Leonetti's, 7367
Leopard Cardamon, 12987
Leroux Creek, 7371
Leroux®, 1120
Leroy Hill, 7372
Les Bourgeois, 7378
Les Domaines Bernard, 12672
Les Moulins D'Haiti, 2970
Les Petites, 10458
Lesley Elizabeth, 7390
Lesley Elizabeth's Crisps, 7390
Lesley Elizabeth's Dipping Oils, 7390
Lesley Elizabeth's Dips, 7390
Lesley Elizabeth's Pesto, 7390
Lesley Elizabeth's Vinegarettes, 7390
Lesley Marinara, 7390
Lesoy, 137
Lesstanol, 4914
Let's Blend, 8505
Let's Do, 3956

Let's Do Organic, 3956
Letan, 10516
Letter of Marquee 2010, 2763
Letter of Marquee 2011, 2763
Letterbox Fine Tea, 2874
Level Right, 9201
Lewis Labs Rda, 7404
Lewis®, 7402
Lexington, 2327
Lexington Coffee Tea, 7406
Li'l Guy, 7407
Liano Farms, 5036
Libby's, 6267, 9199, 11434
Libby's Pecan Cookies, 806
Libby's®, 2939, 2940
Liberate Your Senses, 6831
Liberte®, 4947
Liberty Ale, 531
Liberty Bell, 13384
Liberty Creek®, 3834
Library Wines, 10963
Lick My Spoon, 11205
Lick-A-Pig, 1018
Licklers, 14021
Licor 43, 13811
Licorice Ropes, 469
Liddells™, 11211
Life, 10419
Life Force, 7413
Life Line Vita Plus, 13455
Life Savers, 7963
Life Savers®, 7952, 13960
Life Savy, 8719
Life Start, 8816
Life Tree Products, 7562
Life Wtr®, 9945
Life's Dha®, 3320
Life's™Ara, 3320
Life's™Gla, 3320
Life's™Omega, 3320
Life®, 9945
Lifeline, 773
Lifesource Foods, 12906
Lifestyle, 11298
Lifetime, 7419, 9265
Lifetime Fat Free Cheese, 7419
Lifetime Lactose/Fat Free Cheese, 7419
Lifetime Low Fat Cheese, 7419
Lifetime Low Fat Rice Cheese, 7419
Lifewise Ingredients, 7424
Lift, 2815
Light, 5489, 7330, 11218
Light & Fit, 3379
Light 'n Fluffy®, 10777
Light and Fit, 3377
Light Burgers, 7427
Light Mountain, 7562
Light Rock, 7425
Lighthouse, 1123
Lighthouse Gold, 3180
Lighting, 10344
Lightning, 7655
Lightning 101, 9773
Liguria, 7428
Lil Dutch Maid, 122
Lil Kiddies, 14021
Lil' Chicks™, 1654
Lil' Chief, 12124
Lil' Chief Popcorn, 12124
Lil' Fisherman, 11368
Lil' Lollies, 6780
Lil' Momma Nasty, 10547
Lil' Pepe, 6353
Lil'entrees, 4982
Lil'meals, 4982
Lilletc, 9964
Lilliday Pops, 6158
Lillipos, 11016
Lilly's, 9531
Lilt, 2815
Lily of the Desert, 7430
Lily's, 7431
Lilycake, 6314
Lilydale, 11776
Lilydale®, 7432
Limbo Ipa, 7526
Limited Edition, 1054
Limited Edition Presents, 7435
Limonce, 7655
Limpert Brothers, 7437
Lin Court Vineyards, 7438
Lincoln, 6923, 8414

Lincoln Road Blend, 11826
Linda's Little Lollies, 7440
Linda's Lollies, 7440
Linda-Vista, 8065
Lindeman's, 12937
Linden's, 7442
Lindor Truffles, 7446
Lindsay Farms, 7444
Lindsay Olives, 1185
Lindsay's Tea, 7445
Lindsay's Teas, 8612
Lindt, 2606, 11864
Lindt Chocolate, 7446
Ling Ling®, 237, 238
Linumlife, 137
Lion, 7451, 11226
Lion Coffee, 5654
Lionshead Light, 7450
Lionshead Pilsner, 7450
Lipary, 13871
Lipo - Serine, 4827
Lipo Butter, 5462
Lipopan, 1692
Lipozyme, 1692
Lips of Faith, 8959
Lipton, 8090, 13167, 13169
Lipton®, 9945
Liqueur, 362
Liquid Amber, 10261
Liquid Ki, 8389
Liquid Life Essential Day & Night, 5786
Liquid Plumr, 2766
Liquid Smoke, 2876
Liquidlise, 12483
Liquimax, 7331
Liquimul Black, 5462
Liquisoft™, 1009
Lisanatti, 7458
Lite, 3540
Lite Lite Tofutti, 12843
Lite-95, 1244
Litehouse, 4828
Lithostat®, 8389
Little Bear Organic, 13672
Little Debbie, 8077
Little Debbie, 8076
Little Duck Organics, 7466
Little Lady, 8367
Little Miss Muffin, 7469
Little Pig, 2750
Little Rhody Brand, 7473
Little River Seafood, 7475
Little Sizzlers®, 6000
Little Swan Lake, 7463
Little Vab, 7947
Livabec, 7375
Live a Little Dressings, 7479
Live Clean, 5505
Live Gourmetc, 7480
Live Love Pop, 7481
Live Plant Juice, 131
Live Soda, 7070
Liver Cleanse, 5682
Liver Detox Formula, 131
Liver Restore, 5786
Liver Rinse, 13179
Livia, 7375
Living Food Concentrates, 7421
Living Light, 12776
Living Light Dairy Blend, 12776
Living Now®, 8725
Livingston Cellars®, 3834
Livingston Seed, 10106
Livio Felluga, 8452
Lize Jamaican Style Gourmet Bbq, 1669
Lk Burman, 5555
Llord's, 1423
Lloyds Barbeque Co®, 6000
Lo Han, 13511
Loam Ridge, 7673
Lobster Chowder, 2309
Lockhart Fine Foods, 13641
Lockwood Vineyard, 1543
Loco Coco, 11775
Lodgepole Light, 10261
Lodi Estates, 9321
Lodi Zinfandel, 2637
Lodi's, 7505
Log Cabin, 811
Log Cabin®, 2939, 2940
Log House, 7511
Log House Candiquik, 7511

Logan Chardonnay, 12506
Logo Chocolates, 4253
Logyan's Garden, 1598
Logyn'S Garden Soups, 1598
Loiseau Bleu, 13425
Loison Panetoni, 9119
Lola, 218
Lola Granola Bar, 7512
Lollipals, 6780
Lollipop Paint Shop, 6158
Lollipop Tree, 12703
Lolly Lo's, 7279
Loma Linda, 772, 8551
Lombardi's, 7516
Lombardi's Italian Classics, 4665
London Classic Broil, 118
London Herb & Spice, 4614
Lone Creek Cattle Company, 5327
Lone Pine, 3033
Lone Pine Country, 4578
Lone Star, 7520, 7521
Lone Tree Farm, 4623
Long Beach Crude, 1208
Long Boys, 756
Long Grove Confections, 7524
Long Island Iced Tea, 5012
Long Life, 10344
Long Life Beverages, 3080
Long Life Black Teas, 12704
Long Life Green Teas, 12704
Long Life Herbal Teas, 12704
Long Life Iced Teas, 12704
Long Prairie Packing Company®, 10893
Long Sweet Red, 6763
Long Trail Ale, 7526
Longacre, 7528
Longaniza Cibao, 2670
Longfellow Winter, 11561
Longhorn, 9565
Longhorn Grill, 1244
Longhorns, 7184, 7200
Longleaf Plantation, 7531
Longliner, 11375
Longmorn, 9964
Longreen, 7534
Look!c, 583
Look-O-Look, 9956
Loose Cannon, 2763
Loose Leaf Session Ale, 9366
Looza, 6255
Lopez Foods, 7538
Lora Brody Bread Dou, 7540
Lord Ansley, 7655
Lord Chesterfield, 8086
Lord's, 7541
Lorina - Lemonade, 4148
Loriva, 7545
Loriva Jazz Roasted Oils, 7545
Loriva Supreme Flavored Oils, 7545
Loriva Supreme Oils, 7545
Lorraine®, 11209, 11211
Lorunita Extra, 4881
Los Arango, 10952
Los Cantores, 1348
Los Gatos Lager, 7551
Los Olivos Vintners, 11199
Los Tios, 12646
Lost Lake, 12866
Lost Mountain Winery, 7556
Lost Sailor India Pale Ale, 1237
Lost Trail, 7557
Lost Trail Root Beer, 7578
Losurdo, 7558
Losweet, 9201
Lot 40 and Pike Creek, 9964
Lotito, 7635
Lotsa Pasta, 7559
Lotta-Pop, 1660
Lotus, 13625
Lotus Bloom, 11203
Lotus Pops, 9194
Lou Pizzo, 7565
Louana®, 13328
Louis Albert & Sons, 9593
Louis Bernard, 1543
Louis Bouillot, 1543
Louis Kemp, 6267
Louis Kemp Crab Delights®, 12968
Louis M. Martini®, 3834
Louis Roederer, 11810
Louis Roederer - Remis, 3545
Louis Trauth, 10664

1285

Brand Name Index

Louisa Pastas, 7577
Louisburg, 7557
Louisburg Cider, 7578
Louisburg Farms, 7578
Louisiana, 10276
Louisiana Cajun, 10276
Louisiana Fish Fry, 7580
Louisiana Hot Sauce, 1794
Louisiana Mini, 4886
Louisiana Mixes, 2019
Louisiana Premium Seafoods, 7590
Louisiana® Gold, 1794
Louisiana® Wing Sauce, 1794
Louisianas Best, 11349
Lounsbury, 2357
Lov-It, 11308
Love & Kisses, 7746
Love Creek Orchards, 7596
Love Mints, 1343
Love That, 11775
Love'n Herbs, 7602
Loving Bunny, 10004
Low Fat Body Mueslix, 4214
Low Sodium Tuna, 12046
Lowat, 6236
Lowcoom, 5017
Lowell Farms, 7609
Lowenbrau, 7123
Lowery's Coffee, 7613
Loyola Springs, 9130
Lqd, 571
Lsc, 833
Lsk, 7072
Lucarotin, 1692
Lucas, 7620, 7621
Lucerne® Dairy Farms, 11073
Lucia's, 7625
Lucien Georgelin, 1661
Lucienne, 5499
Lucile's, 7627
Lucini Honestete, 11899
Luck's, 6267
Luck's Beans, 6267
Luck's®, 4267
Lucky Charms®, 4947
Lucky Lager, 7123
Lucky Leaf, 6923
Lucky Pasta, 4794
Lucky Seas, 6390
Lucky Star, 13423
Luckybars, 7631
Lucy's Sweets, 12831
Ludford's, 7637
Luigi Giovanni, 5029
Luigi Vitelli, 6126
Luigi's, 6338
Luis Felipe Edwards, 13811
Luisa's, 7168
Lumen, 194
Lumisolve, 716
Lumisorb, 716
Lumistor, 7017
Lumpy Logs, 2947
Lumpy Lous, 2947
Lumulse, 716
Luna, 2756, 10873
Luna Rossa, 10900
Luna's, 7648
Lunazul Tequilas, 5720
Lunchables, 6977
Lunchmate, 11298
Lundberg, 7650
Lunds, 9094
Lung Tonic, 5791
Lush, 3755
Luv'ya, 5036
Luvo Bowl, 7654
Luvo Flipped Bowl, 7654
Luvo Planted, 7654
Luvo Steam In Pouch, 7654
Luvs, 12721
Luxury, 465, 7657
Luyties, 7658
Luzianne, 10657
Luzianne Ready-To-Drink, 1782
Lvc, 7484
Lvo, 7411
Lw Private Reserve®, 7179
Lycomato, 5475
Lycopene, 11268
Lycovit, 1692
Lyeth Estate, 1543, 12672

Lyle's Golden Syrup, 3666
Lyles Golden Syrup®, 12196
Lymphatonic, 5791
Lynden Farms, 9699
Lynfred, 7664
Lynn Dairy, 7665
Lynn Protiens, 7665
Lynwood Farms, 1547
Lyoferm, 7668
Lysodren®, 1721
Lysol®, 10598

M

M & M'S, 2132
M and V, 6460
M B Spices, 8568
M&Cp Farms, 7673
M&M, 1357, 8533
M&M Cookies, 818
M&M Easter Baskets, 8131
M&M's®, 7952
M-Bond, 8501
M-J, 7889
M-Purity Ring, 8501
M-Purity Seal, 8501
M.Lawrence, 7029
M60 Energy Mints, 11549
Ma Baensch, 931
Ma Baensch Herring, 931
Maazo, 6026
Maboroshi, 11642
Mac's, 7716
Mac's Dumplings, 5634
Maca Magic, 5790
Macabee, 7724
Macalister, 7655
Macariz, 10708
Macaron Cafe, 7725
Macayo Mexican Foods, 4373
MacDonald's™, 864
Macedonian, 6986
Macewan's, 7720
Macfarms of Hawaii, 7713
Mack's, 6971
Mackay's, 7722
Mackinlay Tea's, 7723
Mackoly Rice Wine, 6968
Macleans Cask Conditioned, 12136
Macleans Pale, 12136
MacMurray Estate®, 3834
MacPhail Pinot, 11810
Macs, 4158
Mad & Noisy, 8459
Mad Cat, 730
Mad Dog Hot Sauce, 730
Mad Dragon, 4515
Mad Jack, 8459
Mad River Farm, 7735
Mad,Casse, 7745, 11649
Madame Chevre, 13927
Maddalena, 7740
Maddy & Maize, 7741
Made By True, 13032
Made In Nature, 7742
Made In the Shade, 608
Made Rite, 7743
Madegood, 10774
Madeira Farms, 5735
Madelaine, 7746, 10333
Madeleine, 56
Madera, 2074, 13384
Madhouse Munchies, 7749
Madonna Estate Mont St John, 7753
Madre Sicilia, 10565
Madria Sangria®, 3834
Madys, 7758
Maebo Noodle Factory, Inc., 7760
Maestro Giovanni, 12301
Mag-Nifique™, 13890
Mag® Melon, 3479
Magellin Gin, 3165
Maggi Bouillion Cubes®, 8945
Maggi®, 8945
Maggio, 9321
Magic Baking Powder, 6976
Magic Gourmet, 9752
Magic Hat Brewing, 9117
Magic Ice, 7765
Magic Line, 9794
Magic Mist, 9794

Magic Mold, 9794
Magic Mountain, 1600
Magic Munchie, 11645
Magic Pepper Sauce, 7766
Magic River, 7373
Magic Sauce & Marinades, 7766
Magic-Mix, 7671
Magical Reindeer Food, 11679
Magically Mexican, 6528
Magnasweet, 7693
Magnetic Springs, 7771
Magnificat, 4649
Magnifico Special, 648
Magnifoodsc, 1861
Magnolia, 784, 7774
Magnolia Bay, 5438
Magnotta, 7776
Magnum, 8459, 13169
Magnum Exotic, 7777
Magnum®, 8460
Maha Organic Hard Cider, 571
Maharishi, 5679
Mahatma®, 10777
Mahogany Black, 5462
Mai Green Tea, 8695
Mai Tonic Tea, 8695
Maibock Hefeweizen, 5193
Maid-Rite, 7783
Maier's®, 1359
Mailbock Lager, 1237
Maillose, 10600
Main Beach Brown, 7143
Maine Coast Crunch, 7788
Maine Coast Sea Vegetables, 7788
Maine Wild, 7792
Mainland®, 4552
Maisie Jane's, 7793
Maison Cousin, 7876, 8676
Maison De Grand Esprit, 12937
Maison-Cousin, 7875
Maizetos, 5122
Majestic Coffee and Tea, 7795
Make Out Mints, 1343
Make Your Own Gummies, 418
Maker Overnight Oats, 6282, 7800
Maker's Mark, 3024, 5892, 12315
Maker's Mark®, 1120
Maker®, 9945
Makers Mark, 7801
Mako, 5034
Malabar Gorld Premium, 6611
Malai, 13089
Malibu, 5892
Malibu Coconut Rum, 3024
Malibuc, 9964
Malk, 7696
Malk Coffee, 7696
Mallomars, 8729
Mallowcreme®, 9648
Malpotane, 5683
Malt Teenies, 4976
Malt-O-Meal, 10213
Malta, 7774
Malta Cawy, 2338
Malta Gran, 10297
Malta Rica, 2338
Malted Peanut, 1151
Maltee, 10330
Maltese Cross, 10686
Maltesers®, 7952
Malto Bella, 9151
Maltoferm, 1710
Maltogenase, 1692
Maltorose, 1710
Maltrin, 5246
Maltrin Qd, 5246
Maltrite®, 7809
Mam Papaul's, 7581
Mama, 6677
Mama Amy's, 7811
Mama Capri, 9565
Mama Del's, 7812
Mama Leone's, 7364
Mama Lina, 6316
Mama Linda, 4111
Mama Lucia's, 10418
Mama Mary's, 7815
Mama Mary's™, 864
Mama Mia, 1854
Mama Mucci, 8664
Mama Nichola's Sago, 9045
Mama Papaul's, 7581

Mama Ranne, 4550
Mama Rosa's, 11316
Mama Rose, 2983
Mama Rose's, 7818
Mama Rosie's, 7819
Mama's, 10252
Mamba, 12148
Mamma Chia, 7823
Mamma Says, 7826
Mammoth®, 4552
Man of War Crab, 9344
Mancakes, 4150
Manchester Farms, 7831
Manchurian Saffron, 9771
Mancini, 7832
Mancuso, 7833
Manda, 7834
Mandoo, 7838
Mango Mango, 11655
Mango Sunrise Tea, 13746
Manhattan Gourmet, 6489, 11934
Manischewitz, 7848, 7849
Manitoba Harvest, 7850
Mann's International, 12543
Mann's®, 3479
Manner, 1957
Mannings, 3097
Manny's, 8208
Mansion, 4387
Mansmith's Gourmet, 7856
Mantrocel, 7857
Mantroclear, 7857
Manu Maker, 11639
Manuel's, 7859
Manwich®, 2939, 2940
Maola, 7861, 7985
Maple Acres, 7863
Maple Apple Drizzle, 11584
Maple Gardens, 7869
Maple Grove Farms of Vermont, 7866
Maple Grove Farms of Vermont®, 864
Maple Hillc, 7867
Maple Hollow, 7869
Maple Island, 7870
Maple Leaf, 7871, 7872, 7874, 7876, 7877, 11768
Maple Melts, 5363
Maple Nuts, 10673
Maple Sprinkles, 13347
Mar-Jac Brands, 7889
Maramor, 7891
Maranatha, 5505
Marantha, 7892
Marathon, 1208
Marblehead Mints, 5578
Marburger, 7897
Marc Roman, 4677
Marcel Et Henri, 7898
Marcello, 5400
Marchesi, 11205
Marconi, 13422
Marcos, 10585
Mardi Gras King, 7581
Margao, 8061
Margaritaville®, 3725
Margherita, 11733
Margret Holmes, 8086
Margritaville®, 6818
Maria & Son, 7907
Maria and Ricardo's, 5573, 7908
Maria's, 10453
Maria's Premium, 7909
Mariachi, 10435
Mariani, 7910, 7911
Marias, 8387
Marich, 2606, 7912
Marie Brizard, 7913
Marie Callender's®, 2939, 2940
Marie McGhee's, 2903
Marie's, 13328
Mariebellec, 1011
Marimar Torres Estate, 7922
Marin, 7924
Marin Weiss, 7923
Marina, 7927
Marinade Bay, 2509
Marinela®, 1359
Mariner Biscuits, 1472
Mariner Seafoods, 7930
Mariner's Choice, 9165
Mariner-Neptune, 7929
Mario Perelli-Minetti, 13813

1286

Brand Name Index

Mario's Gelati, 7932
Mariquitas Classic, 100
Market Place, 9914
Market's Best, 13009
Markon®, 11504
Marks & Spencer, 11768
Marla, 3336
Marlboro Village, 1220
Marley Beverage Co., 8955
Marnap-Trap, 7948
Marotti Biscuits, 822
Marpro, 10983
Marquerite, 954
Marques De Murrieta, 13811
Marquis, 1517, 7950
Marquise, 847
Marrone, 13120
Mars, 541, 961
Mars, Inc, 2132
Mars®, 7952
Marsa, 4324
Marsala, 9040
Marshall's, 12467
Marshall's Curry, 12178
Marshmallow Fluff, 3810
Martellc, 9964
Martha's All Natural, 7960
Martha's All Natural Baking Mixes, 7960
Marthedal Berry Farms, 5036
Martin, 7965
Martin Codax®, 3834
Martin's Virginia Roast, 4239
Martini & Prati, 7967
Martini & Rossi, 913
Martini & Rossi Asti, 914
Martini & Rossi Vermouth, 914
Martini Biscuit, 13180
Martini Party, 2799
Martins, 11461
Marty Griffin Big Red, 5989
Marukan, 7976
Marushka, 5861
Maruyu, 1849
Marva Maid, 7978, 7985
Marvel, 2136, 4659
Marvelous, 8995
Marwood, 7979
Mary B'S, 6338
Mary Jo's Blueberries, 6599
Mary Jo's Fancy, 6599
Mary Kitchen®, 6000
Mary Phillips, 10229
Mary's, 3603
Mary's Gone Crackers, 7983
Maryland Chef, 5555
Marzen Lager, 1139
Marzetti, 7189, 7987, 12467
Marzetti Frozen Pasta, 7987
Marzetti's, 7986
Masa Mixta ®, 856
Masala Chai, 7989
Masala Craft, 6026
Masala Roti, 10968
Maseca ®, 856
Mashuga Nuts & Cookies, 11940, 12894
Masienda Bodega, 7990
Maskal Teff, 12605
Maso Canali®, 3834
Mason Dixie, 7992
Mass Transit, 1720
Massel, 7994
Massetti, 11980
Mastantuono Wines, 7996
Master, 6977
Master Baker, 13182
Master Brewer, 13182
Master Mix, 7998
Master of Mixes, 439, 4401
Master Wrap, 12973
Master's Mark, 1077
Master's Touch, 3269
Masterbrand, 13183
Mastercut, 2367
Masterfeeds, 81
Masterfoods®, 7952
Masterpiece, 2766
Masterson, 8000
Mastro, 11776
Matador, 4741, 8001
Matador®, 9945
Matangoes, 8002
Matanzas Creek Winery, 8003

Matar By Pelter, 10952
Matassini Seafoods, 6373
Materva, 2338
Mati, 7697
Matt's Cookies, 2985, 8012
Matthew's All Natural, 8640
Matthews 1812 House, 8014
Matthews All Natural, 5942
Matua, 12937
Matzo Meal, 6776
Maui Blanc, 8022
Maui Blush, 8022
Maui Brut, 8022
Maui Splash, 8022
Maui Style, 4741
Maui Style®, 9945
Maui Ulupalakua Red, 8022
Maull's Barbecue Sauce, 7574
Mauna La'i, 8586
Maurice French Pastries, 8024
Maurice's, 10051
Maury Island Farm, 11390
Maury's Cookie Dough, 2703
Mavuno Harvest, 8026
Max, 7409
Max Boost Coffee, 6976
Max Cranberry Cocktail, 9170
Max's, 4928
Max's Salsa Sabrosa & Design, 9290
Max-C-Plex, 7947
Max-Sea, 3998
Maxfield, 8027
Maxilact®, 3320
Maximo, 4677
Maxine's Heavenly, 8030
Maxinvert®, 2370
Maxiren®, 3320
Maxwell House, 6976, 6977
Maxwell's Extraordinary, 8032
Maya's Tortillas, 9736
Mayacamas Vineyards, 8035
Mayan Farm, 5573
Mayan Harvest, 12663
Mayan Legacy, 12881
Mayberry's Finest, 2628
Mayco, 8042
Mayer Bros., 8037
Mayfield Creamery™, 3442
Mayfield®, 3442
Mayo Gourmet, 13894
Maypo, 6267
Mazelle's, 8046
Mazza Vineyards, 9926
Mbpxl, 3262
Mc Graw, 8070
McAdams ®, 13120
McArthur Dairy®, 3442
McCadam, 211
McCaf,, 2811
McCain®, 4061
McCain™, 8055
McCallan, 10468
McCann's, 6279
McCann's Irish Oatmeal, 12182
McCann's®, 864
McCarthy's Oregon Single Malt, 2737
McClelland's, 1120
McConnell'sc, 1136
McCormick, 8061, 8062
McCrea Vineyard, 6892
McCullagh Coffee Roasters, 8090
McCutcheons, 8091
McDowell, 8066, 13811
McDowell Ovens, 12241
McEvoy Ranch, 11864
McGovern's Best, 9344
McKay's, 3619
McKenzie, 10106
McLean, 10331
McLure's Maple, 3815
McT Oil, 8896
McTavish, 8100
Mdgl, 8352
Mdi, 8404
Mdm, 8352
Me and the Bees Lemonade, 8101
Meadow Brook®, 3442
Meadow Gold, 8105
Meadow Gold®, 3442
Meadow Valley, 9167
Meadowbrook, 8106, 13070
Meadowbrook Creamery, 10073

Meadows Country Products, 8108
Meadowview, 9909
Meal Mart, 329
Meaning of Lifec, 2010
Meat Magic, 7766
Meat of Wheat, 6331
Meat-O-Mat, 8114
Medaglia D'Oro, 6380
Medallion Naturally, 7876
Medallions, 9176
Medeor® Matrix, 3320
Medetrina, 11780
Medford, 5643
Medford Farms®, 1484
Medicea, 10708
Medifast, 3773
Mediterranea Seawater For Cooking, 11396
Mediterranean, 2499, 13190
Mediterranean Coffee, 13191
Mediterranean Organic™, 1484
Mediterranean Sprate, 9863
Medjool, 10939
Medlee, 8125
Mee Tu, 345
Meg-3®, 3320
Mega C-Bio, 7947
Mega Cal™, 6449
Mega Warheads, 4589
Megace®, 1721
Megacrunch®, 6374
Megadophilius, 8816
Megafood, 8130
Meganatural, 9654
Megared, 11285
Meher, 2923
Meica, 1957
Meier's, 8135
Meier's Sparkling Ju, 8135
Meijer, 8137
Meijer Ecowise, 8137
Meijer Elements, 8137
Meijer Gold, 8137
Meijer Natural, 8137
Meijer Organic, 8137
Meinel, 5400
Meistermarken, 954
Mekach, 6776
Mekong, 13208
Mel's, 2843
Mel-Fry®, 13328
Mel-O Honey, 12401
Mel-O-Cream, 8139
Melatonin, 8009, 11268
Melcer, 1064
Mele-Koi Hawaiian Coconut Snow, 8143
Melina's, 9937
Melinda's, 4382
Meliora Organic, 5139
Melissa, 6986
Melitta, 8146, 13717
Meller, 9956
Mellin, 10565
Mello Joy, 2019
Mello Yello, 2811, 2814
Mello-Krisp, 8204
Mellow Corn Whiskey, 5720
Mellowmind, 9201
Melo-Glow, 5517
Melody, 8513
Melster, 13574
Melt Organic, 10347
Melt-N-Mold, 5428
Meluka, 8149
Memory, 7774
Menchaca, 11834
Mendes Farms, 11985
Mendocino, 8154
Mendocino Cty. Sauvignon Blanc, 869
Mendoza Ridge, 9540
Menehune Magic, 1123
Menemsha Bites, 8156
Menghini, 8157
Meno-Select, 8009
Mens Bread, 4702
Mental Energy Formula, 9201
Mentos, 2132, 9956
Menu, 11308
Menu a La Carte, 3989
Meow Mix, 6380
Mer, 2815
Meramec, 8159
Meratrim, 6236

Mercer, 8163
Merci, 12147, 12148
Merci Crocant, 12147
Merci Pur, 12147
Mercier Champagnes, 3570
Mercken's, 9031
Mercken's Chocolate, 9031
Merco, 703
Mercon, 8166
Merecol, 4773
Meredith's, 8167
Meretec, 4773
Merezan, 4773
Meridian, 12937
Meridian Foods, 5479
Merion Park Rye Bread, 508
Merita, 4529
Meritage, 3771
Merkts, 1172
Merlayzyn, 12746
Merlin's, 8175
Merlino Baking Co., 11390
Merlino Signature Brands, 8176
Merlot, 1314, 4745
Mermaid Princess, 8938
Mermaid Spice, 8178
Mermaid's Supreme Shrimp, 1916
Merrill's, 8181
Merritt, 8183
Merritt Pecan Co., 8184
Merryvale, 8185
Mertz Sausage, 8186
Meso Biomatrix®, 3320
Met-Max, 2411
Met-Rx®, 8871
Meta, 12721
Meta Boost, 9251
Meta Rest, 9251
Metabolife, 13097
Metabolol, 2411
Metagenics, 8193
Metala, 12937
Metaxa, 13811
Meteorites, 11320
Metropolitan, 8199
Metzger Popcorn Co., 8204
Meukow Cognac, 11264
Meurens, 10146
Mevgal, 6986
Mexamerica, 8206
Mexene® Chili, 1794
Mexi-Frost, 8207
Mexican Accent, 8208
Mexican Bear, 12845
Mexican Original®, 13109
Mexicana, 10869
Meyenberg, 8210
Meyer Natural Angus Beef, 457
Mezzetta, 5039
Mezzo, 13320
Mezzo Mix, 2815
Mg Vallejo, 13851
Mga, 8693
Mgm, 2350
Mi Best Soybean Oil, 11096
Mi Casa, 4529, 4662
Mi Mama's, 8214
Mi Ranchito, 8215
Mi-Delc, 9748
Mi-Kee, 7022
Mia, 8217
Mia's Mirror, 5473
Miami Beef, 8218
Mice-A-Fours, 3625
Miceli's, 8222
Michael Angelo's, 8223
Michael David Vineyards, 8224
Michael Foods Inc.®, 11504
Michael Granese Co., 8226
Michael Merchant Winemaker, 12489
Michael Season's Cheese Curls, 7845
Michael Season's Cheese Puffs, 7845
Michael Season's Kettle Potatoes, 7845
Michael Season's Organically Grown, 7845
Michael Season's Sensations, 7845
Michael Shea's Irish Amber, 4950
Michael's Health Products, 8231
Michaelene's Gourmet, 8233
Michaelene's Gourmet Granola, 8233
Michaelene's Granola, 8233
Michaelok, 12550
Michel De France, 12487

Brand Name Index

Michel De Francec, 1411
Michel Torino, 4677
Michel's Family Bakery, 8236
Michel-Schlumberger, 8238
Michele's Chocolate Truffles, 8240
Michele's Honey Creme, 8239
Michelina's Grande, 1200
Michelina's Lean Gourmet®, 1200
Michelina's Pizza Snack Rolls, 1200
Michelina's Signature®, 1200
Michelle, 8242
Michelle's, 4919
Michelle's Organic, 8642
Michelle's Rawfoodz, 8243
Michelo Ultra, 7123
Michelob Ultra, 571
Michigan Dessert, 8247
Michigan Fine Herbs, 5782
Michigan Made, 5951
Michigan Star Thistle, 10478
Michigan Turkey Producers, 11053
Michtex, 12550
Mickelberry's, 11902
Mickey Mouse, 4507
Mickey's, 8459
Mickey's®, 8460
Micro Basil Nutmeg, 4718
Micro Bmx Bike, 1158
Micro Cucumber, 4718
Micro Fast, 10491
Micro Mint Lime, 4718
Micro Mustard Dijon, 4718
Micro Radish Ruby, 4718
Micro Scooter, 1158
Micro Tangerine Lace, 4718
Micro Wasabi, 4718
Microfresh, 9839
Microgreens, 4718
Micromask, 9797
Microsoy Flakes, 8252
Mid Pacific, 8258
Mid-Atlantic, 8256
Mid-Atlantic Foods, 11356
Mid-Pacific Seafoods, 10603
Middlefield, 8263
Midhaven Farm Cafe, 11402
Midheaven Farm, 11402
Midleton, 9964
Midori, 5892
Midori Melon, 1120
Midship, 11368
Midtown Caff, 6547
Midwest, 8269
Midwest Blueberry Farms, 8265
Migdal, 13931
Mighties, 12242
Mighty Greens, 10067
Mighty Leaf Tea, 8090
Mighty Organic, 1963
Mighty Wild, 11818
Mignardise, 10039
Migration, 3779
Miguel's, 8275
Mihel, 2457
Mikaela's Simply Divine, 8276
Mikarla's Best, 9112
Mikawaya, 8277
Mike and Ike®, 6641
Mike's Hard, 8279
Mikesell's, 8282
Miki, 13560
Mil Lel™, 11211
Milano, 1881, 2116
Milano®, 9942
Milat Vineyards, 8290
Milcal, 4914
Milcal-Fg, 4914
Milcal-Tg, 4914
Mild Gouda, 13840
Milea Estate Vineyard, 8292
Milem, 13141
Miles River, 1098
Miljoco, 8294
Milk Bone, 6380
Milk Chugs, 8104
Milk Duds, 5818
Milk For Life®, 13218
Milk Stout, 7310
Milk-Free, 6340
Milk2go®, 11211
Milkboy, 8296
Milko, 6204

Milkshake Factory, 3958
Milky Way®, 7952
Milky Wayc, 2132
Mill Creek Vineyards, 8301
Millbrook, 5245, 8303
Mille Lacs, 8304
Millennium, 10112
Miller, 8459
Miller's, 3469, 10372, 13931
Miller's Country Ham, 8311
Miller®, 8460
Millflow, 8314
Milliaire Winery, 8315
Millie's, 13688
Millie's Pierogi, 8316
Mills, 2044
Mills Brothers International, 8320
Millstone, 3171, 6819
Millstream, 8323
Milnot, 3862, 8327
Milo's Kitchen, 6380
Milo®, 8945
Milone Brothers, 8328
Milpas, 8161
Milsolv, 8332
Milsorb, 8335
Milwaukee Seltzer Company, 6159
Milwaukee's Best, 8459
Milwaukee's Best®, 8460
Mimi's Muffins, 6291
Min Tong, 8339
Min-Col, 9262
Mina, 2276, 7747
Minaret™, 13400
Mind's Eye Smart Drinks, 10405
Minerac, 11145
Mineragua, 12823
Minerva, 6986, 8345
Minestrone, 2309
Ming Cha, 1600
Mingo Bay Beverages, 8346
Mingo Bay Beverages, Inc., 10141
Minh, 11316
Minh®, 11317
Mini Babybel, 1172, 1173
Mini Bites®, 12880
Mini Dickmann's, 12147
Mini Flower Crystals, 4718
Mini Herb Crystals, 4718
Mini Me's®, 1484
Mini Moo's, 13734
Mini Tubs, 5909
Mini-Croustade, 10039
Mini-Croustade Shell, 10039
Mini-Easre, 10039
Mini-Roulet, 10039
Mini-Sizzlers, 11298
Mini-Wheats®, 6765
Minigo, 14017
Minions, 2132
Minit Chef, 7783
Minn - Dak, 8352
Minnesaurus Dill Picklodon, 4928
Minnesota Dehydrated Vegetables, 8355
Minnesota Girl, 648
Minnesota Heartland, 4753
Minnesota Wild, 8357
Minor's®, 8945
Minowa, 13565
Minski, 4515
Minsley, 8361
Mint, 9995
Mint Balls, 10496
Mint Lumps, 5752
Mint Patties, 9877
Mint Puffs, 5752
Mint Savor, 8362
Mint Shell, 10039
Mint Twists, 756
Minterbrook, 8363
Minute Fudge, 10773
Minute Lunch, 13240
Minute Maid, 2811, 2814, 2815, 6338, 8365, 9469
Minute Maid Juice To Go, 8365
Minute Maid Just 15, 8365
Minute Maid Sparkling, 8365
Minute Menu, 3549
Minute®, 10777
Mio, 6976
Mipueblito, 10363
Mira Mango Nectar, 8366

Mirabel®, 5844
Mirabelle, 11307
Mirabo, 2409
Miracle, 255
Miracle Ade, 9858
Miracle Juice, 9858
Miracle Juice Energy Drink, 9858
Miracle Maize, 7465
Miracle Treec, 1549
Miracle Whip, 6976
Miracoli®, 7952
Miramar, 8371
Mirassou, 7103
Mirassou®, 3834
Mirch Masala, 3465
Mirror Pond Pale Ale, 3533
Miscela Bar, 6238
Miscela Napoli, 6238
Misfit, 8373
Mishpacha, 7848
Miso Master Organic, 5306
Miss Jones Baking Co., 8379
Miss Leone's, 7364
Miss Meringue, 8380
Miss Sally's, 2261
Miss Scarlett, 8381
Miss Vickie's, 4741
Miss Vickies®, 9945
Mission, 8387
Mission Foodservice®, 11504
Mission Hill Bistro, 12023
Mission Mountain, 8388
Mission San Juan Juices, 11266
Mission®, 3479, 8384
Mississippi Cheese Straws, 8391
Mississippi Delta Fudge, 12546
Mississippi Lime, 1692
Mississippi Mousse, 12546
Mississippi Mud Pupp, 8391
Missouri's Finest, 7571
Mister Bee, 8393
Mister Fudge, 2048
Mister Mustard, 13894
Mister Spear, 8398
Mistic, 1294
Mistic Iced Tea, 4521
Misto, 2012
Misto Dark, 2012
Misty Mints, 10104
Mitalena Coffee, 13191
Mitchell Foods, 8403
Mitchell's, 5555
Mitchum Rices, 8404
Mito's, 7859
Mitoku Macrobiotic, 2630
Mitsukan®, 8415
Mitsuko's Vineyard, 2770
Miwok Weizen Bock, 7923
Mix-Ups, 525
Mixer Stix Drink Mix, 12182
Mixers, 8729
Mixon, 8411
Miztique™, 9237
Mjb, 7995, 11212
Mlo Sports Nutrition, 4955
Mo Hotta - Mo Betta, 8433
Mocafe, 3009
Mocha, 10307
Mocha Mix®, 1103
Mocha Mud, 1665
Mocha Mud Cake Mix, 1665
Mochi, 5248
Mochi Ice Cream, 8277
Mode, 7705
Model Dairy, 3442
Modelo, 71, 7123
Modelo Especial, 4881
Modern Oats, 8444
Modern Pantry, 10022
Modern Pop, 8447
Moderna Alimentos, 2970
Modifilan, 9696
Modleo Especial, 4881
Moducare, 13536
Moduchol, 13536
Moduprost, 13536
Moet & Chandon, 8452
Moffett, 7490
Mogen David, 13851
Moisturlok®, 190
Mojeska's, 8700

Moka-Java, 12846
Moledina, 8456
Molfino®, 11211
Molinaro's, 8457
Molinos Champion S.A., 2970
Mollic, 8458
Molly McButter, 864
Molson, 8459
Molson Canadian, 8459
Molson Canadian®, 8460
Molta Roba, 13160
Mom 'n Pops, 8461
Mom's, 4432, 8464
Mom's Choice, 5637
Mom's Famous, 8463
Mommy's Choice, 437
Momokawa, 11093
Mon Ami, 8467
Mon Cheri, 4348
Mona Lisa, 1056
Monadnock Mountain Spring Water, 1480
Monarch, 5981
Monari Federzoni, 6279
Monasterio Sta. Ana Monte, 3545
Mondavi, 10791
Mondelez International, 541, 2132
Mondial, 10041
Money Candy, 11016
Money Mints, 11051
Money on Honey, 3767
Moneys, 8477
Monfort, 3262
Mongo, 4895
Mongoose, 7157
Monica's, 5140
Monin, 3009
Monini, 8479
Monique's Pasta Sauces, 247
Monkey 47, 9964
Monkey Baking, 8480
Monkey Catering, 8480
Monkey Party, 8480
Monkgold™, 4837
Monksweet™, 4837
Monsanto, 8452
Monsooned Malabar, 6611
Monster, 2947
Monster Chews, 2947
Monster Cone, 8486
Monster Cookies, 8635
Monster Energy, 2811, 2815, 8485
Monsters®, 4947
Mont Blanc Chocolate Syrups, 8487
Mont-Rougr, 10333
Montagnolo, 2409
Montana Big Sky™, 9237
Montana Mex, 8490
Montchevre®, 11209
Monte Alban Mezcal, 11264
Monte Carlo Bake Shop, 903
Montebello, 2075, 11589, 11980
Montefiore Winery, 10952
Montego Bay, 9842
Montego Bay Rum, 8062
Monterey Cabernet Sauvignon, 2637
Monterey Chardonnay, 2637
Monterey Gourmet Foods®, 10365
Monterey Petite Syrah, 2637
Monterrey, 8508
Montesierra, 3545
Montezuma Blue, 11264
Montezuma Tequila, 11264
Montezuma Triple Sec, 11264
Montforte, 11313, 13876
Montpellier, 1738
Montreal Chop Suey, 8514
Monument Dairy Farms, 8516
Moo & Oink, 1262
Moo Chew, 1018
Moo Magic, 12182
Moo-Calcium, 4914
Mooala, 8518
Moon, 10275
Moon Lake, 7339
Moon Mountain, 5743
Moon Pads, 8824
Moon's Seafood, 8523
Moonlight, 8525
Moonlight Pale Lager, 8524
Moonlite Bbq Inn, 8528
Moonpie, 2470
Moonshine Madness, 6796

Brand Name Index

Moonshine Sweet Tea, 8529
Moonshine Trading, 14034
Moonstone, 11093
Moor, 2691
Moore's, 530
Moore's®, 4061, 8055
Moores, 8532
Moose Drool Brown Ale, 1344
Moose Mountain, 1677
Moosehead Lager, 8535
Mopac, 8615
Mor-Fruit, 9763
Morabito, 8536
Morad Winery, 10952
Moravian Hearth, 11100
More Spice Seasoning, 12869
More-Than-Tofu, 12273
Morehouse, 8539
Morey's, 8541
Mori-Nu, 3773, 8546
Mori-Nu Tofu, 8679
Moritz Ice Cubes, 10496
Morn'n Fresh, 6670
Morning Cheer, 5517
Morning Glory, 1388
Morning Moo's, 1506
Morning Spark, 12182
Morning Star, 8549
Morning Star Farms, 6766
Morning Sun, 9182
Morningland Dairy, 8550
Morningstar Farms, 8551
Mornington Dairy®, 11211
Morositas, 9956
Morrison Brand, 8563
Morrison Farms, 8915
Morrison's, 1917
Morse's, 8564
Mortein®, 10598
Mortimer Fine Foods, 8567
Morton, 6661
Morton Evaporation Salt, 8569
Morton Rock Salt, 8569
Morton Salt, 8569
Morton Solar Salt, 8569
Mos-Ness, 11294
Moshe & Ali's Sprat,, 9863
Mosher Products, 8571
Moss Bay Extra Ale, 5515
Moss Bay Stout, 5515
Moss Creek, 8572
Moss Roxx, 9321
Mossy Bayou, 2019
Mostly Cloudy, 7526
Mother, 8485
Mother Earth, 7028, 8693
Mother Nature's Goodies, 8577
Mother Parkers, 8578
Mother Teresa's Fine Foods, 8581
Mother's, 166, 7848
Mother's Cookies, 6766
Mother's Kitchen, 10714
Mother's Prize, 3092
Mother's Pure Preserves, 3092
Mothers ®, 13120
Mothers Free Range, 2576
Mothers Maid, 1866
Mott's, 8585, 8586
Mott's For Tots®, 8585
Mott's Fruit Flavoured Snacks, 8585
Mott's Fruitsations, 8586
Mott's Sensibles™, 8585
Mott's®, 3725, 6818
Mou Cuisine, 329
Mounds, 5818
Mount Baker Vineyards & Winery, 8650
Mount Eden Vineyards, 8654
Mount Hagen, 6279
Mount Herman, 1121
Mount Nittany, 8656
Mount Olympus®, 3220, 3319
Mount Olympus™, 11889
Mount Palomar, 8592
Mountain Apple, 1812
Mountain Bar, 1771
Mountain Berry, 11218
Mountain City, 8593
Mountain Country, 2844
Mountain Dew®, 9945
Mountain Gold, 12504
Mountain Gold Honey, 7748
Mountain Grown, 4543

Mountain High, 8597
Mountain High®, 4947
Mountain House, 9529
Mountain House Kitchen, 12811
Mountain Mist, 8920
Mountain Trout, 13447
Mountain Valley, 4143, 4462
Mountain Valley Spring Water, 8605
Mountain Valley Spring Water ™, 5884
Mountain-Grown Fancy Ceylon, 5228
Mountainman, 2323
Mountainside Farms, 8609
Mountaire, 8610
Mountaire Fresh Young Chicken, 11053
Move Free, 11285
Movenpick®, 8945
Moxie, 2311
Moy Park®, 10056
Moyer®, 6391
Mozzaluna, 530
Mozzamia, 530
Mr & Mrs T, 8586
Mr Frosty, 11356
Mr Pure, 8784
Mr Snack, 11503
Mr Z, 13421
Mr. & Mrs. T®, 3725
Mr. Boston, 11264
Mr. C'S, 7972
Mr. C'S Pretzels, 12851
Mr. Cheese O'S, 11804
Mr. Clean, 12721
Mr. Cookie Face, 8394
Mr. Dell's I.Q.F. Country Potatoes, 8618
Mr. Dell's I.Q.F. Hash Browns, 8618
Mr. Dell's I.Q.F. Herb & Garlic, 8618
Mr. Dell's I.Q.F. Santa Fe, 8618
Mr. Egg Roll, 2040
Mr. Espresso, 8619
Mr. Fancy's, 12178
Mr. G'S, 7972
Mr. Honey & Mrs. Fruit, 10454
Mr. P'S, 4756
Mr. Sharp, 12437
Mr. Spice, 7210
Mr. Yam, 8772
Mr.Goodbar, 5818
Mr.Spinkles, 9748
Mr16, 10344
Mrs Baird's®, 1359
Mrs Baird'sc, 8626
Mrs Bairds, 892
Mrs Butterworth's, 811
Mrs Dash®, 864
Mrs Difilippo's, 3549
Mrs Fanings, 4831
Mrs Feldman's Desserts, 5322
Mrs Kavanagh's, 5942
Mrs Leeper's, 6279
Mrs Leeper's Wheat/Gluten Free, 8642
Mrs Malibu, 8643
Mrs Paul's, 811
Mrs Renfro's, 10508
Mrs Schlorers, 5157
Mrs Slaby's, 6971
Mrs. Adler's, 7848
Mrs. Asien, 5372
Mrs. Brahms, 628
Mrs. Campbells, 5146
Mrs. Crockett's, 3173
Mrs. Dash® Foodservice, 6792
Mrs. Denson's, 3635
Mrs. Dog's, 8636
Mrs. Filberts, 1935
Mrs. Fisher, 8628
Mrs. Freshley's, 4529
Mrs. Friday's, 6855
Mrs. Grimes®, 4267
Mrs. Kavanagh's, 8640
Mrs. Klein's, 6908
Mrs. Little's, 14045
Mrs. Powell's Gourmet, 4001
Mrs. Renfro's, 10674
Mrs. Richardson Toppings, 988
Mrs. Smith's, 11316
Mrs. Smith's®, 11317
Mrs. Stratton, 8633
Mrs. Sullivan's, 8634
Mrs. T'S, 8648
Mrs. T'S Pierogies, 747
Mrs. Thinsters, 12664
Mrs. Veggies, 8324

Mrs. Weinstein's Toffee, 12414
Mrs. Weiss'®, 10777
Mrs.Butterworth's®, 2939, 2940
Mrs.Paul's®, 2939, 2940
Ms. Kays, 557
Msi, 8398
Msrf, 7706
Mt Veeder, 4649
Mt. Betty, 10789
Mt. Harlan, 2044
Mt. Konocti, 8660
Mt. Mama, 10789
Mt. Olive, 8657
Mt. Shasta, 8784
Mt. Sterling Cheese Co., 8659
Mt. Tom Pale Ale, 7923
Mt. Veeder Blanc De Blancs, 3661
Mt. View Bakery, 8663
Mt. Vikos™, 1484
Mt. Whitney, 11450
Muchmates, 13964
Mucinex®, 10598
Mucky Duck, 8666
Mud, 7707, 12811
Muddy Bears, 12547
Mueller, 10792
Mueller's, 465
Muenchner/Stadtbrot, 3606
Muenster, 4405
Muffin Revolution, 8667
Mug Root Beer®, 9945
Muginoka, 1120
Mugshots, 11855
Muir Glen, 2286
Muir Glen Organic, 11711
Muir Glen®, 4947
Muirhead, 8670
Muirwood, 104
Mulberry Farms, 10637
Mullen's, 8671
Mulling Cider, 12272
Multichrome, 10344
Multiplex, 7421
Multirome®, 3320
Multy Grain Foods, 13863
Mumm Napac, 9964
Mumsey, 6445
Munchies, 4741
Munchos, 4741
Munchos®, 9945
Munchrights, 13964
Mung Dynasty, 8679
Munk Pack, 8680
Munkijo, 1120
Munkijo, 8681
Munroe Dairy, 32
Munsee Meats, 8682
Munson's, 8683
Murphy Goode, 8688
Murray Sugar Free Cookies, 6766
Murray's, 8689
Murrieta's Well, 13654
Murvest, 8691
Muscle Milk®, 6000
Muscle Nitro, 2411
Musette®, 1484
Museum, 4677
Mushroom Canning Company, 8693
Mushroom Meringue Cookies, 2599
Mushroom Wisdom, 8695
Musillami, 12162
Muslix®, 6765
Mussel King, 12420
Musselman's Apple Sauce Cookies, 9399
Mussleman's, 6923
Mustard, 6532
Mustard Pretzels, 972
Muth's Kentucky, 8700
Muy Frescoc, 187
Mvp, 3397
My Brother Bobby's Salsa, 8703
My Bubby's, 4021
My Country Sweet, 2274
My Daddy's Cheesecake, 8706
My Father's Best, 8781
My Favorite, 4369
My Favorite Jerky, 8707
My Grandma's of New England, 8708, 11864
My Hero, 6806
My Little Pony, 1591
My M&Ms, 2132

My Mom's Mixes, 3079
My Nana's, 7042
My Selection, 13845
My T Fine®, 6483
My Utapia®, 3319
My-Baby, 13122
My-Dol®, 857
My/Mo Mochi Ice Cream, 8711
Myco Curb, 6777
Myers, 5555
Myers Frozen Food, 8713
Mylk Labs, 8714
Myntz Breathmints, 11390
Myntz! Breath Mints, 7710
Myntz! Instastripz, 7710
Myntz! Lip Balm, 7710
Myrcenary Double Ipa, 9366
Myron's 20 Gauge, 8715
Myrties, 7524
Myrtle Greens, 13310
Myrtles, 7524
Mystic Lake Dairy, 8717
Mystic Mead, 7171
Mystic River, 7373
Mystic Seaport, 9560
Mythos, 6986
Myvacet, 137
Myverol, 137

N

N-Creamer 46, 8804
N-Dulge™, 8804
N-Lok ® 1930, 8804
N-Oil®, 8804
N-Tack®, 8804
N-Zorbit™, 8804
N.M. Riesling, 10165
Na Po'okela O Honaunau, 1908
Nabisco, 13610
Nabisco 12 Packs, 8729
Nabisco Classics, 8729
Nabob, 6976
Nacan, 8730
Naches, 10275
Nacho Grande, 4623
Nadamoo, 8731
Nadamoo Organic, 8731
Nahmias Et Fils, 8734
Nair, 2666
Najla Gone Chunky, 8736
Nakano®, 8415
Naked Bacon, 8739
Naked Flock, 618
Naked Meats®, 10124
Naked Mountain, 8742
Naked Truth®, 13607
Naked Wild Honey, 1040
Naked®, 9945
Nalle, 8744
Nalley Lumberjack Table Syrup, 12921
Nalley®, 1103, 2939, 2940
Nalu, 2815
Namp, 2313
Nana Flakes, 8719
Nana's, 8748
Nana's Cocina, 130
Nana's Cookie Bars, 8748
Nana's No Gluten, 8748
Nana's Own, 1069
Nance's Mustards, 988
Nanci's, 8749
Nancy's, 8751, 8753, 11971
Nanka Udon, 8754
Nanko, 1120
Nantucker Nectars®, 6818
Nantucket Nectars®, 3725
Nantucket Tea Trader, 8758
Nantucket Vineyard, 8759
Nantze Springs, 8760
Napa Ridge, 1738
Napa Syrah, 6603
Napa Valley, 1141, 2770, 4649
Napa Valley Barbeque Co., 13849
Napa Valley Harvest, 13849
Napa Valley Homemade, 5039
Napa Valley Mustard Co., 8764
Napa Wine, 8762
Napa Wine Company, 8765
Napolean's Bakery, 14067
Nara, 10435

Brand Name Index

Nardone Bros., 8770
Nascar Bottled Water, 7264
Nash's Gold, 8772
Nash's Pride, 8772
Nasim, 7007
Nasoya, 13473
Nasoya®, 10365
Nasty Tricks, 2947
Natalie's Orchid Island, 8777
Natcelt, 783
Natco, 1600
Nate Dog's, 2017
Naterl, 8815
Nathan's, 5105, 12965
Nathan's Famous, 11733, 13196
Nathan's Smoked Salmon, 9344
Nation, 8781
National, 8795, 8804
National Beef, 11053
National Beef® Prime, 8783
National Fisheries, 8787
National Gold, 5132
National One, 5132
National Poultry Company, 3479
National Steak, 8805
Native, 12721
Native American, 8809
Native Forest, 3956
Native Kjalii, 8811
Native Scents, 8812
Natives Pride, 741
Natra Cacao, 8814
Natra Us, 8814
Natrabio, 13642
Natrabio®, 9237
Natraceutical, 8814
Natragest, 7422
Natrataste, 12201
Natrium, 8817
Natur-Cell®, 10797
Natura, 100, 9256
Natural Angus Beef, 8783
Natural Balance Pet Foods, 6380
Natural Balance®, 9237
Natural Blends®, 11228
Natural Bliss, 8821
Natural Bliss Cold Brew, 8821
Natural Bouncin' Berry, 11785
Natural Certified Angus Beef, 3451
Natural Choice, 1766, 1767
Natural Choice®, 6000
Natural Country, 3084
Natural Country®, 3083
Natural Exotic Tropicals, 8827
Natural Gourmet Flavor Oil, 7409
Natural Green Leaf Brand, 9634
Natural Harvest, 12826, 13305
Natural Health, 9238
Natural Heaven, 8162
Natural Life, 7331
Natural Light, 571
Natural Mountain Water, 8606
Natural Ovens Bakery, 374
Natural Personal Care, 3080
Natural Sea™, 1484
Natural Sins, 8848
Natural Sport®, 9237
Natural Sterols, 572
Natural Thompson, 13384
Natural Value, 8850
Natural Vines, 469
Natural's Concept, 13943
Naturalcare®, 9237
Naturalcrisp®, 6374
Naturally Aloe, 357
Naturally Clean Eats, 8853
Naturally Delicious, 8854
Naturally Flavored S, 13206
Naturally Healthy, 5146
Naturalmond, 4975, 8858
Naturalvalves, 5061
Naturaselectc, 1861
Nature Actives, 12051
Nature Canada, 10673
Nature Cure, 8859
Nature Kist, 8860
Nature Made, 9998
Nature Nate'sc, 8862
Nature Raised Farms®, 13109
Nature Select, 4982
Nature Soothe, 10307
Nature Star, 10120

Nature Valley®, 4947
Nature Works, 127
Nature Zen, 8865
Nature Zone, 9734
Nature's Alchemy, 7562
Nature's Bakery, 8867
Nature's Banditsc, 8868
Nature's Beauty, 4888
Nature's Best, 1864, 6250
Nature's Bounty, 11785
Nature's Bounty®, 8871
Nature's Burger Mix, 4252
Nature's Choice, 1020, 8627
Nature's Dairy, 8873
Nature's Earthly Choice, 8874
Nature's Edge, 3919
Nature's Finest™, 12238
Nature's Fusions, 8877
Nature's Glory, 4888
Nature's Gold, 5987
Nature's Gourmet, 7876
Nature's Guruc, 8879
Nature's Hand, 8881
Nature's Harvest®, 1359
Nature's Herbs, 8882, 13097
Nature's Herbs®, 9237
Nature's Hollow, 8884
Nature's Kitchen, 8690, 8885
Nature's Legacy, 8886
Nature's Mist, 2190
Nature's Own, 1577, 4529, 4662
Nature's Own Potato Pearls, 1069
Nature's Path Organic, 8889
Nature's Plus, 5065
Nature's Pride, 1799
Nature's Pride Sweet Potatoes, 8519
Nature's Quest, 4162
Nature's Recipe, 6380
Nature's Resources, 9998
Nature's Select, 8893
Nature's Sungrown Beef, 8898
Nature's Sunshine, 8894
Nature's Touch, 8895
Nature's Twist, 12315
Nature's Wonderland, 9918
Naturebind®, 13648
Naturemost Labs, 8861
Natures Club, 1114
Natures Flavors, 10495
Natures Fountain, 1915
Natures Path, 12017
Naturesafe, 3390
Natureseal®, 7857
Naturessence, 1490
Naturfood, 11144
Naturnes®, 8945
Naturox, 6777
Naturslim, 10314
Natuures Partner®, 5036
Naughty Noah's, 8900
Navan, 8452
Navarro, 8902
Naya, 8906
Naylor, 8909
Nbr 2000, 9274
Nca, 9262
Ncco®, 11504
Ne-Mo's, 8910
Neal's, 7083
Near East®, 9945
Neat, 772, 8914
Nebbiolo, 13375
Necco, 2132, 8973
Nectarade, 4505
Nedlog 10, 8919
Needlers Jersey English Toffee, 11028
Neem Aura, 7562
Neenah Springs, 8920
Neera's, 2681
Negra Modelo, 4881
Negro Modelo, 4881
Nehi Cola®, 6818
Nehi Flavors, 4521
Neige, 1543
Neighbors, 8923
Neilson®, 11211
Nella Bella, 13500
Nelly's Organics, 8931
Nelson Seatreats, 8932
Nelson's, 1550, 8933
Nelson's Dutch Farms, 8933
Nem®, 6449

Neo Water, 8935
Neobee 1053, 12081
Neobee 1095, 12081
Neobee 895, 12081
Neobee M-20, 12081
Neobee M-5, 12081
Neocryl®, 3320
Neokura, 11250
Neon Lasers, 10496
Neopac™, 3320
Neopuntia, 9029
Neorad™, 3320
Neorez™, 3320
Neptune, 8937, 8938, 9344, 11368
Neptune Delight, 11347
Neptune Foods, 10603
Neptune's, 12989
Nerds, 2132
Nesbitts®, 1339
Nescafe, 816
Nescafe®, 8945
Neshaminy Valley Natural, 8940
Nespresso, 8090
Nespresso®, 8945
Nesquik, 1782
Nesquik®, 8945
Nestea, 1661, 2815
Nestea®, 8945
Nestfresh, 5837, 8942
Nestl,, 2132
Nestl, Professional®, 11504
Nestle, 541
Nestle Chocolates, 9191
Nestle® Pure Life Water, 8945
Nestle® Toll House, 8945
Nestum®, 8945
Neto, 8946
Neuhaus, 2592
Neuman, 8950
Neuro®, 6818
Neurosome™, 6449
Neutral Slush, 5460
Neutrase, 1692
Nevada City Winery, 8953
New Classics, 5211
New Day, 6338
New England, 5211
New England Cranberry, 8969
New England Farms Eggs, 2866
New England Naturals, 8971
New England Premium, 5942
New England®, 9736
New Englander, 6542
New Era, 8973
New Glarus Bakery, 8975
New Granola, 6222
New Harmony, 8979
New Harvest Foods, 1947
New Holstein Cheese, 1940
New Image, 12184
New Jamaican Gold Cappuccino, 10307
New Line Homemade, 4753
New Mill®, 10777
New Morning, 13124
New Popc, 10445
New Rinkel, 5371
New Season Foods, 8999
New Southern Tradition Teas, 1296
New World Home Cooking Co., 2323
New York Bakery, 7189, 7987
New York Bash, 11339
New York Brand®, 12467
New York Classics, 2587
New York Club, 5660
New York Deli, 13812
New York Flatbreads™, 864
New York Kosher Deli, 329
New York Pizza, 9007
New York Pretzel, 9008
New York Style Cheesecake, 2881
New York Style™, 864
Newburgh Brewing Company, 9012
Newby, 9013
Newly Weds, 9016
Newman's Own, 7124, 9018, 9469
Newman's Own Lemonade, 9018
Newman's Own Organic, 5612
Newman's Own Pasta Sauces, 9018
Newman's Own Popcorn, 9018
Newman's Own Salad Dressing, 9018
Newman's Own Salsa, 9018
Newmann's Own Organics®, 6818

Newmans Own, 6819
Newport, 9024
Newport Coffee Traders, 4407
Newton Vineyard, 8452, 9026
Newtons, 8729
Nexcel, 11910
Nexsoy, 11910
Next Organicsc, 13011
Niacin-Time, 6364
Niaga®, 3320
Niagara, 3171, 9069
Niagara Chocolates, 13708
Niagra Seed, 5610
Nibble With Gibble's, 7972
Nic-O-Boli, 9045
Nichols Farms, 9039
Nicholson's Bestea, 5467
Nicholson's Bottlers, 5467
Nicholson's Chok-Nick, 5467
Nick's Jerky, 9041
Nick's Sticks, 9041
Nickel & Nickel, 4258
Nickelodeon, 4659
Nicky Usa, 9043
Nico-Rx, 13642
Nicola, 6310
Nido®, 8945
Niederegger Lubeck, 1957
Nielsen, 9049
Nielsen-Massey, 9050
Night Hawk, 9052
Nik-L-Nip®, 12880
Nikki Bars, 985
Nikki's, 9055
Nikola's Biscotti, 3009
Nikos®, 11209
Niksicko, 8459
Nile Spice, 5505
Nilla Wafers, 8729
Nilla® Banana Pudding, 10213
Niman Ranch®, 7721, 9946
Nimble Nectar, 9058
Ninja Sticks, 2947
Nip's Potato Chips, 9063
Nirvana, 7562
Nirwana, 9065
Nita Crisp, 9070
Nitta Gelatin, 9072
Nk Lawn & Gardenc, 10106
No Bones Wheat-Meat, 9502
No Cow, 9075
No Evil Foods, 9076
No Forks Required, 8324
No Holds Bar, 8869, 8870
No Pudge, 9077
No Pudge! Brownie Mix, 10657
No Whey Foods, 9078
No Yolks®, 10777
No-Cal, 5465
No-Stick™, 342
No.5, 12178
Noah's Spring Water, 181
Noah's Treats, 11102
Noah's Water, 13300
Noahs Buddies, 12389
Nobadeer Ginger, 2691
Nobella, 5405
Noble Popcorn, 9080
Nobletree, 9081
Nochebuena, 1977
Nodark, 741
Noel, 9083
Nojo, 1373
Nolan Porter, 4959
Nollibel, 9087
Non Diary Toppings, 12201
Non-Dairy Baklava, 9333
Nona Lim, 9089
Noni, 8009
Noni Nonu, 1285
Nonna D'S, 10435
Nonni's, 9092
Noodle Delights, 2040
Noodle Plus, 13170
Noon Hour, 9094
Noosa, 9095
Noosh, 9096
Nootra, 9098
Noprthern Lites Pancakes, 5946
Nor-Cal, 12253
Nor-Tech, 9100
Norbest, 8553, 9105

Brand Name Index

Norchip, 3216
Norden, 2089
Nordic, 2815
Norimoor, 9110
Norivital Vitamins, 9110
Norma Lou, 6564
Norman Bishop, 4839
Norman Rockwell, 13445
Noroc, 8459
Norpac, 8724
Norpaco, 9113
Nortena, 10701
Norteno, 5479
North Aire Simmering Soups, 9114
North Atlantic, 2418, 2419
North Bay, 9126
North Bay Trading Company, 9127
North Breeze, 10540
North Coast, 7860, 9182
North Coast Tea & Sp, 9181
North Country, 9130
North Country Meat & Seafood, 7721
North Country Smokehouse, 9131
North Eastern, 226
North Pacific Seafood, 266
North River Roasters, 9136
North Star, 10495
Northampton, 9141
Northeast Family Farms, 3653
Northeastern, 9144
Northern, 9145
Northern Light Canadian, 11264
Northern Lights, 10682
Northern Pines Gourmet, 5451
Northern Pride, 5508
Northern Serenitea, 754
Northern Spirit, 754
Northern Vineyards, 9163
Northern Wisconsin Cheese, 9164
Northland, 56, 4928, 9166, 9167, 9535
Northshore Butter, 9170
Northumberland, 9170
Northville Winery, 9171
Northwest Espresso B, 9185
Northwest Gourmet, 2905, 11148
Northwestern, 9183
Northwestern Coffee, 9181
Northwind, 10974
Northwoods, 4928, 7330
Northwoods®, 1103
Norwalk Dairy, 9186
Nos, 2811, 8485
Nosferatu, 5314
Nosh Organic, 12779
Nossack, 9187
Nostalgic Creations, 6787
Nostimo®, 12885
Not Dogs, 9160
Not Just Jam, 6821
Not So Sloppy Joe®, 6000
Nothing But the Fruit, 9190
Notmilk, 13286
Notta Pasta, 551
Nottingham, 7028
Novamid, 3320
Novapro®, 13648
Novation®, 8804
Novella, 3857
Novelty Chocolates, 4253
Novelty Specialties, 2132
Novo Pro D, 1692
Novoshape, 1692
Novozym, 1692
Novozymes, 1692
Now & Later, 4345
Now and Later, 1417, 4345
Now Real Food®, 8725
Now Real Tea®, 8725
Noyes Precision, 9197
Nozimes, 3471
Npn, 13653
Nsc-100, 9261
Nsc-24, 9261
Ntrinsic™, 8470
Nu, 9202
Nu House, 11759
Nu Life Market, 9200
Nu-Bake, 10703
Nu-Bind, 10703
Nu-Flac, 10703
Nu-Flow, 10703
Nu-Mag, 10703

Nu-Rice, 10703
Nu-Vista, 13943
Nu-World Amaranth, 9205
Nucita, 122
Nudges, 13109
Nugget, 3275
Nugrape ®, 1339
Nuit, 2761
Nulaid, 9216
Nulojix®, 1721
Numantia, 8452
Numi Tea, 3009
Numi Teas, 6928
Numic, 9217
Numo Broth, 9218
Nunaturals, 9209
Nunes, 9219
Nunez De Prado, 11864
Nupasta, 9210
Nurofen, 10598
Nursery ®, 5884
Nursery®, 3220
Nursery® Water, 3319
Nurture, 9222
Nush, 9224
Nut Barrel, 12992
Nut Brown Ale, 1507, 2911, 7551
Nut Case Collection, 12714
Nut Club, 1114
Nut Goodie, 9877
Nut Harvest®, 9945
Nut N But Natural, 13574
Nut Thins, 1471
Nutellac, 2132
Nutfield Auburn Ale, 9228
Nutfield's Classic Root Beer, 9228
Nuthouse, 659, 4969
Nutpods, 9232
Nutra Biogenesis®, 9237
Nutra Nuts, 9234
Nutrafiber, 11794
Nutralease, 9654
Nutralin, 6163
Nutramer, 135
Nutramigen™, 8103
Nutranique Labs, 9242
Nutraplex, 9243
Nutrasense, 13802
Nutrasweet, 9236
Nutravege, 8896
Nutraveggie, 9654
Nutraw Butter, 9227
Nutraw Oil, 9227
Nutraw Snacks, 9227
Nutrawbar, 9227
Nutrceuticals, 13128
Nutren Junior®, 8945
Nutri Source, 918
Nutri Sperse®, 126
Nutri West, 9260
Nutri-Cell, 9248
Nutri-Fruito, 9246
Nutri-Grain, 6766
Nutri-Grain®, 6765
Nutribio, 9256
Nutribiotic, 9251
Nutricran, 9654
Nutriflax, 9477
Nutrifresh, 2576
Nutrilait®, 11211
Nutriose™, 8804
Nutriquest, 9266
Nutririte, 12262
Nutrisentials™, 6449
Nutrisoy, 9256
Nutrisoya, 9256
Nutritional Noodle, 4093
Nutritional Therapeutix, 8130
Nutritious Living, 9548
Nutrivail, 10078
Nutrivan, 463
Nutriwest, 9266
Nutriwhip, 7875
Nutro®, 7952
Nuts 'n' Fruit, 4472
Nuts 'n' Things, 4472
Nuts About, 4820
Nuts About You, 9272
Nuts'n'pops, 525
Nutsco, 10683
Nutter Butter, 8729, 13816

Nutter Butter® Cereal, 10213
Nuttin' Butter, 7892
Nutty All-Natural Wheat, 8844
Nutty Bavarian, 9274
Nutty Club, 11331
Nutty Corn®, 13603
Nutty Crunchers, 8991
Nutty Goodness, 9275
Nutty Infusions™, 8725
Nutty Pleasures, 11330
Nuttzo, 9276
Nuturpractic, 10558
Nutworld, 2905
Nuvert®, 7809
Nzmp™, 4552

O

O & C, 5555
O Olive Oil, 9282
O Organics®, 11073
O Vinegar, 9282
O'Bannon's, 1598
O'Boy, 2242
O'Brien Harvest Ale, 5515
O'Canada, 2693
O'Charley's, 2628
O'Kane, 10056
O'Mara's Irish Country Cream, 5720
O-Jay, 1292
O-Ke-Doke, 11770
O.B., 9297
O.C. Lager, 1097
O.K. Brand, 11352
O.K. Foods, 9389
O.N.E®, 9945
Oac Gold, 12136
Oak Creek, 9310
Oak Farm's, 9311
Oak Farms, 9312, 11281
Oak Farms Dairy, 3442
Oak Flat, 13067
Oak Grove Smokehouse, 9315
Oak Hill Farms, 13454
Oak Hurst Dairy, 10653
Oak Knoll, 9318, 9319
Oak Leaf Confections, 13708
Oak Ridge Winery, 9321
Oak Spring Winery, 9322
Oak State Cookie Jar Delight, 9323
Oak Valley Farms, 3980
Oakhurst, 9325
Oakland Noodle, 9328
Oakmont Labs®, 9237
Oakville, 4649
Oakville Estate Red, 10963
Oasis, 56, 2815, 9330
Oasis Coffee, 9331
Oasis Wines & Sparkling Wines, 9334
Oat-N-Bran, 4556
Oatbran & Brown Rice, 4362
Oatmeal, 5188
Oatmeal Fruit Squeeze, 8680
Oatmeal Stout, 1687
Oats Overnight, 9336
Oatwell®, 3320
Oatworks, 9337
Obe Sauce, 5967
Obe Sauce Mix, 5967
Oberschulte Syrah, 11810
Oberti, 2074
Oberto®, 9338
Obi Pektin, 11957
Obis One, 9341
Oboy's, 1691
Obsidian Stout, 3533
Obviously Onion, 6528
Ocean Beauty Brand, 9344
Ocean Beauty Seafoods, 11380
Ocean Blue, 10276
Ocean Cliff, 9345
Ocean Coffee Roasters, 3722
Ocean Dawn, 703
Ocean Deli, 4613
Ocean Drive Blend, 11826
Ocean Harvest, 2042
Ocean Leader, 1057
Ocean Mist, 9351
Ocean Organics, 1583
Ocean Pac, 8028
Ocean Phoenix, 10250

Ocean Prince Seafood, 3194
Ocean Request, 9165
Ocean Road Blend, 11826
Ocean Spray, 868, 2815, 3314, 9355, 12871
Ocean Spray Apple Juice, 9355
Ocean Spray Cranberries, 9355
Ocean Spray Cranberry Cocktail, 9355
Ocean Spray Fruit Punch, 9355
Ocean Spray Fruit Punch Cooler, 9355
Ocean Spray Grapefruit Juice, 9355
Ocean Spray Jellied Cran. Sauce, 9355
Ocean Spray Juice Blends, 9355
Ocean Spray Kiwi Straq. Juice, 9355
Ocean Spray Lemonade, 9355
Ocean Spray Orange Juice, 9355
Ocean Spray Pineapple Grapefruit, 9355
Ocean Spray Pink Grapefruit Juice, 9355
Ocean Spray Ruby Red & Mango, 9355
Ocean Spray Ruby Red Grapefruit, 9355
Ocean Spray Whole Berry Cranberries, 9355
Ocean Tide, 10974
Ocean's Halo, 9359
Oceana, 11269
Oceana Coastal, 12672
Oceanica, 1500
Oceankist, 9668
Oceanway Seafood, 6855
Oceen Fresh, 3336
Octacosanol Gf, 4914
Odell's®, 13328
Odense, 551
Odom's Tennessee Pride®, 2939, 2940
Odwalla, 2814, 9369
Odyssey, 10251
Oergon Trail, 9534
Off the Eaten Path®, 9945
Ogi's, 1736
Oh Canada, 4508
Oh Nuts, 5828
Oh So Sweet, 8772
Oh Yes!, 9375
Oh's, 10213
Ohana, 8784
Ohganics, 3315
Ohi, 9300
Ohta's Senbei, 9380
Oikos, 3379
Oil, 11462
Oils of Aloha Macadamia Nut Oil, 9382
Oishii, 2075
Ojai, 9387
Okanagan Cider, 8279
Okanagan Spring, 9391
Okf, 10134
Okio, 3107
Oktoberfest, 5314, 7330, 7677, 11992
Oktoberfest Lager, 1237
Ol' Smokey, 3537
Ol' South, 10054
Ol' Spout, 9688
Ola Blanca, 8161
Ola Loa, 9394
Oland, 7123, 9396
Olay, 12721
Old Abominable Barkey Wine, 12153
Old Bay, 8061
Old Bay®, 13445
Old Brookville, 1006
Old Brown Bag, 11743
Old Brussels, 13330
Old Cape Harbor, 1478
Old Charter, 11263
Old Chester, 5852
Old Chisholm Trail, 4432
Old Comiskey, 8795
Old Country, 9402, 9403
Old Country Cheese, 9401
Old Country Store, 2971
Old Credit, 9404
Old Creek Ranch Winery, 9405
Old Crow®, 1120
Old Dipsea Barley Wine, 7923
Old Dobbin, 5484
Old Dominion, 9406
Old Dutch, 1327, 9408, 9409, 10657
Old El Paso®, 4947
Old English®, 8460
Old Faishoned Foods, 9411
Old Faithful, 6134
Old Fashioned, 9226, 9787, 10461, 11625, 13845
Old Fashioned Way®, 6374

1291

Brand Name Index

Old Fitzgerald Bourbon, 5720
Old Folks, 4197
Old Forester, 1784
Old Grand-Dad®, 1120
Old Hickory, 12541
Old Home, 9415
Old Kentucky, 3248
Old Kentucky Hams, 9417
Old Kettle, 10782
Old Laredo, 5146
Old London®, 864
Old Mexico, 5861
Old Mill Brand, 7530
Old Milwaukee, 9664
Old Monmouth, 9421
Old Neighborhood, 9422
Old No.23, 1720
Old North State, 2236
Old Orchard, 56, 9423
Old Overholt®, 1120
Old Pueblo Ranch, 573
Old Red Eye, 11846
Old Rip Van Winkle, 9424
Old Salt Seafood, 11356
Old Smokehouse®, 6000
Old Soul, 9321
Old South, 1806
Old South Winery, 9426
Old South Muscadine, 9426
Old Southern, 4891
Old Spice, 12721
Old Style Pilsner, 8459
Old Tavern Club Cheese, 9427
Old Taylor, 11263
Old Thompson Blend, 11264
Old Thumper Extra Special, 11561
Old Town Roast, 912
Old Tyme, 387
Old Vienna, 8459
Old Vienna®, 8460
Old Vines, 13741
Old Wessex™, 1484
Old West Bar-B-Q Delight, 3695
Old Wine Cellar, 9430
Old Wisconsin, 2212, 9431
Old Wisconsin Mug, 9432
Old World, 4062, 5105
Old World Creations, 9434
Olde Colony, 9435
Olde Deuteronomy, 339
Olde English 800, 8459
Olde Fashioned, 2219
Olde Georgetown Beer, 9437
Olde Heurich, 9437
Olde Philadelphia, 5643
Olde Tyme, 9438
Olde-Fashioned, 11298
Ole Salty's, 9441
Ole Style Peanut Butter, 9438
Ole Wye, 11039
Ole' Henry's Nuthouse, 2110
Oled Desiccant, 3833
Oleocal, 716
Olf Foghorn, 531
Olinda, 13661
Olio Santo, 2085
Olioro, 9332
Olive Hill Cabernet Sauvignon, 869
Olive Hill Pinot Noir, 869
Olivenos, 530
Oliver, 9452
Oliver Twist, 11663
Olivet Lane, 9905
Olivia's Kitchen, 9454
Olivia's Organics, 12056
Olivier Leflaive, 4677
Olivieri, 7876
Olivir, 4827
Olsen, 9459
Olymel®, 9462
Olympia, 9664
Olympia Provisions, 9466, 9470
Olympic Cellars, 9467
Olympic Coffee, 9468
Oma's Own, 7884
Omaha Hereford, 5338
Omaha Natural Angus, 5338
Omaha Steaks International, 9473
Omanhene Cocoa, 9474
Omar Coffee, 9475
Omega, 3028
Omega Care, 7331

Omega Complete™, 6449
Omega Foods, 9476
Omega Gold, 8967
Omega Munchies®, 13603
Omega Pro, 1864
Omega Suro, 8967
Omega-3 Brain™, 6449
Omega-3 Calm™, 6449
Omega-3 Select™, 6449
Omegaflo, 9477
Omegaplus Gla, 9477
On the Borderc, 13029
On-Cor Frozen Entrees, 9482
Ona, 12964
Once Again Nut Butter, 9485
Oncovite™, 8389
One, 9306
One Basix, 9306
One Culture Foods, 9487
One Daily Essential With Iron, 75
One Degree Organic Foods, 9488
One Potato Two Potato, 9489
One World, 5306
Ono Cones, 9496
Ontario Foods, 9498
Ontario Pork, 9499
Onte Verde O.O., 11096
Oodles of Noodles, 9068
Oogly Eyes, 2947
Ooh La La Candy, 12100
Opa's, 9506
Opacarb, 11906
Opaque, 7740
Opdivo®, 1721
Open Country, 194
Open Nature®, 11073
Open Pit®, 2939, 2940
Open Prairie Natural Angus®, 13109
Optiberry, 6236
Optima, 9507
Optimum, 8889
Optimum Nutrition, 9510
Optimum®, 3775
Optiserv, 13595
Optiserv Accent®, 13595
Optiserv Hybrid®, 13595
Optisharp® Zeaxanthin, 3320
Optisource Convertible®, 13595
Optrix®, 3320
Opus One, 9511
Or Haganuz Winery, 10952
Ora-Plus, 5682
Orajel, 2666
Oral-B, 12721
Orange Blossom, 10478
Orange Blossom Special, 7329
Orange County Distillery, 9514
Orange Glo, 2666
Orange Honey Cream Ale, 4950
Orange Maison, 56
Orange Mist, 7363
Orange Paradise Cake, 2881
Orange Plus, 12945
Orange Rose, 9182
Orange Thirstaway, 5460
Orangina, 12315
Orangina®, 3725, 6818
Orangutan Mace, 12987
Orbit, 11089
Orbit Gum, 2132
Orbit®, 7952, 13960
Orbitz, 2742
Orca Bay, 9518
Orchard Boy, 13720
Orchard Heights, 9519
Orchard Hills, 498
Orchard Mills, 2046
Orchard Naturals, 2164
Orchard Park, 12334
Orchard Pond, 9520
Orchard Pond Organics, 9520
Orchard Pure™, 3442
Orchard Stand, 9452
Orchard Valley Harvest, 6548
Orchardpure, 7320
Ore-Ida, 6977
Ore-Ida®, 8055
Oregan Orchard, 5671
Oregon, 575, 6862
Oregon Berries, 3114
Oregon Brewers, 2036
Oregon Chai, 2606, 3009, 9525

Oregon Fruit, 9530
Oregon Hill, 9532
Oregon Natural Sportstonic, 13998
Oregon Spice, 9539
Orencia®, 1721
Oreo, 8474, 8729, 13816
Oreo Churros, 6338
Oreo O'S, 10213
Orfila Vineyards, 9540
Organic, 5138
Organic Altura, 2282
Organic Bistro, 12684
Organic By Nature, 10380
Organic Coffee, 332
Organic Coffee Co, 4229
Organic Coffee Company, 11140
Organic Country, 3956
Organic Cow, 5996
Organic Creamery®, 11209, 11211
Organic Extra Virgin Olive Oil, 869
Organic Flax Tempeh, 7427
Organic Garden, 8993
Organic Garden Veggie Tempeh, 7427
Organic Germinal, 9543
Organic Gourmet, 9545
Organic Guayaki Yerba Mate, 5416
Organic Harvest, 8993
Organic Lil Buddies, 11771
Organic Matcha™ Powder, 12498
Organic Mexican Altura, 2282
Organic Ocean®, 7721
Organic Pastures, 9552
Organic Planet, 5306, 9553
Organic Prairie, 1963
Organic Pro 30, 3540
Organic Shell Eggs, 1864
Organic Sierra Madre Blend, 2282
Organic Smoky Tempeh Strips, 7427
Organic Soy Delicious, 11771
Organic Soy Tempeh, 7427
Organic Sunshine, 12302
Organic Sweetleaf Stevia®, 12430
Organic Three Grain Tempeh, 7427
Organic Valley, 1963
Organic Wild Rice Tempeh, 7427
Organic/Fair Trade, 1054
Organicgirl, 9544
Organicville, 11694
Organipure™, 4837
Orient Emporium, 10637
Orient Express®, 6818
Oriental Noodle Soup, 11919
Origami Wraps, 9010
Original, 6532
Original 1957, 9562
Original Baby, 5420
Original Chocolates of Vermont, 7148
Original Gourmet, 9563
Original Habanero Pepper Sauce, 4382
Original Juan, 1279
Original Juan's, 9565
Original Lemon Straw, 8391
Original Maui Kitch'n Cook'd, 8020
Original Philly Cheesesteak Co., 13109
Original Ranch Dips Mix, 5489
Original Ranchc Homestyle, 5489
Original Ranchc Pasta Salad, 5489
Original Sesame Low Fat Crackers, 1472
Original Smoked Sausage, 2944
Orin Swift Cellars®, 3834
Oringer, 2942, 2943
Oriole, 4387
Orion®, 8945
Orlando, 9568, 9672
Orleans, 6267, 8995
Oro Glo, 6777
Orobianco-California Nv, 3181
Orogold, 6638
Oroweat®, 1359
Orowheat, 892
Orr Mountain Winery, 9572
Ortega, 864
Orv's, 1248
Orville Redenbacher, 6084
Orville Redencacher's®, 2939, 2940
Orwasher's, 9575
Osage, 8519
Oscar Mayer, 6976, 6977
Oscars Flavoring Syrups, 10584
Osella, 10565
Osem, 9579
Osr, 8899

Osseofit™, 3320
Osteo Bi-Flex®, 8871
Ostravar, 8459
Ostrim #1 Sports Meat Snack, 10353
Ostrim Ostrich Saute, 10353
Otajoy, 9589
Otis Spunkmeyer, 9590, 9591
Ott Chocolate, 9299
Ott's, 9593
Otter Pops®, 6483
Otter Valley, 6230
Ottimo, 6015
Otto's Naturals, 9597
Our Best, 9600
Our Counrtry, 11050
Our Daily Red, 8954
Our Famous Texas Chili, 4428
Our Thyme Garden, 12794
Out of a Flower, 9604
Out of Bounds, 838
Outrageoulsy Decadent Cookies, 10981
Ovace®, 8389
Ovacion, 3545
Ovation, 6603
Ovega-3, 6107
Oven Fresh, 9610
Oven Head, 9611
Oven Krisp Coating Mixes, 4777
Oven Lovin' Chik'n™, 1654
Oven Poppers, 9612
Oven Ready, 9613, 12520
Oven Spring, 13591
Over the Top®, 12885
Overhill Farms, 9614
Overlake, 9615, 10323
Ovn™, 3320
Owen's, 12516
Owl, 13193
Owl's Brew, 9619
Owl's Nest, 1172
Owner's Blend Premium Congou, 5228
Owyhee, 6134
Oxford Inn, 11416
Oxi - Gamma, 4827
Oxi - Grape, 4827
Oxi Pro Metabolol, 2411
Oxiclean, 2666
Oxy-Caps, 8009
Oxy-Cleanse, 8009
Oxy-Max, 8009
Oxy-Mist, 8009
Oxylite, 10680
Oxyphyte, 10511
Oxyvac, 9252
Ozark, 8414, 9621
Ozark Hills, 8550
Ozark Mountain Vineyards, 10214
Ozarka, 4143, 4462
Ozujsko, 8459
Ozw, 9321

P

PDeQ, 9627
P&S Ravioli, 9632
P'Tit Qu•Bec, 6976
P'Tit Quebec, 9789
P-Bee, 9640
P-Nuff Crunch, 9952
P-Nuttles, 163
P-Nuttles Butter Toffee Peanuts, 163
P-Proplus, 4837
P-R Farms, 9636
P.F. Chang's Home Menu, 2939, 2940
P.L.A.C, 10565
P/L, 9199
Paas, 11599
Pabst Blue Ribbon Beers, 9664
Pace, 2115, 2116
Pacha, 10330
Pacheco Ranch, 9667
Pacific, 1057, 9692, 11191
Pacific Alaska, 11358
Pacific Choice, 9672, 11559
Pacific Coast Brewing Co., 9673
Pacific Echo, 9677
Pacific Farms, 1141
Pacific Foods, 2116
Pacific Gold, 9683, 9684
Pacific Gold Reserve, 9684
Pacific Gold, 9338

1292

Brand Name Index

Pacific International, 1849
Pacific Natural Spices, 9695
Pacific Pilsner, 9701
Pacific Pride, 8028
Pacific Real Draft, 1702
Pacific Surf, 9668
Pacific Treasures, 666
Pacific Valley, 9699
Pacifica, 10952
Pacificc, 9681
Pacifico, 11437
Pacifico Clara, 4881
Pacifika, 1500
Pack of the Roses, 1882
Pack-Age, 3320
Package Bulk Key Lime Filling, 6825
Packers Blend, 11177
Packers Pride, 7213
Paddy's Irish Red, 12919
Padis Vineyards, 10952
Paesana, 7022
Pagoda, 11316
Pahlmeyer, 9709
Pahrump Valley Winery, 9710
Pain 100%, 9565
Pain Is Good, 9565
Paisley Farm, 4694, 9712
Pal-O-Mine Chocolate Bars, 4884
Palace Foods, 9842
Palace Pastry, 1061
Palasurance, 6777
Palatase, 1692
Pale American, 5515
Paleao, 3171
Paleo People, 4150
Paleo Planet, 9237
Paleo Powder, 9715
Paleo Prime, 9716
Paleothin, 6629
Palermo, 9718
Palermo's, 9719
Pallenque, 13425
Palm Bay, 8279
Palmalito, 9726
Palmetto, 9725
Palmieri, 9728
Palouse, 13549
Pam, 6267
Pam Cooking Spray, 6267
Pam, 2939, 2940
Pama Pomegranate Liqueur, 5720
Pamela's, 9730
Pamesello, 7952
Pampac, 12928
Pampers, 12721
Pampryl, 4148
Pan Am, 10229
Pan De Oro, 11477
Pan Ducale, 6255
Pan Pepin, 9734
Pan-O-Gold, 9736
Panache Cocoa and Blender Mix, 2834
Panache Gourmet Coffee, 2834
Panamore, 3320
Pancheros, 9565
Pancho Villa, 8062
Panda, 7295, 10275
Panda Brand, 7296
Pandora's Bock, 1687
Panera Bread, 6818
Panerac, 9740
Paneze, 833
Panforte, 7111
Pangburn's, 10991
Panhandle Milling, 9743
Panisgood, 1279
Pankote, 833
Pano, 6261
Panola, 9745
Panola & Private Lab, 9745
Panola Pepper Corp, 2019
Panorama Easter Eggs, 8677
Panroast, 3269
Pantene, 12721
Pantesin, 7017
Panther, 13365
Panther Pepper, 12987
Papa Dan's World Famous Jerky, 889
Papa Dean's, 9751
Papa Enzo's, 12885
Papa Joe's, 1547
Papa Joe's Downhome, 3075

Papa Joe's Specialty Food, 12830
Papa Piazza Brand, 13423
Papa Pita, 9736
Papa Presto, 1282
Papa Scotts, 2019
Papa's Fresh Catch, 13423
Papa's Organic, 9736
Papadina Pasta, 183
Papadini Hi-Protein, 183
Papagallo, 7701
Paper City, 9754
Papetti's, 7698, 8225
Pappadums, 12517
Pappardelle's, 9756
Pappy's, 7364, 9758
Pappy's Best Premimum Marinade, 6796
Pappy's Choice, 9757
Pappy's Xxx White Lightnin, 6796
Par, 2750
Paradigmox, 6777
Paradise, 2065, 9763, 9766
Paradise Bakery & Cafec, 9740
Paradise Bay, 6806
Paradise Valley Vineyards, 9768
Paraduxx, 3779
Paragon, 8336
Paraiso, 9770
Paraiso Del Sol, 9768
Paramount, 6267, 9773
Paramount Citrus, 13906
Paramount Coffee, 13706
Paramount Farms, 13907
Parampara, 4947
Parasite Annihilation Powder, 131
Pares Baltas, 3545
Pari, 7007
Pariolic, 2010
Park 100 Foods, 9778
Park Avenue Gourmet, 10944
Park Farm, 7463
Parkay, 2939, 2940
Parker, 9783
Parker House, 13717
Parker's Heritage Collection, 5720
Parkway, 12103
Parma, 9788
Parmenter's Northville Cider Mill, 9791
Parmesan Low Fat Crackers, 1472
Parmx Cheese, 9792
Parnell's Pride, 9866
Parrot Bay, 3545
Parrot-Ice, 6338
Parsol, 3320
Partetime, 4689
Partners, 9798, 9799
Party 'tizers, 12664
Party Creations, 9434
Party Favors By Astor, 743
Party Pak, 9226
Party Pretzels, 4253
Party Punch, 7671
Party Snacks, 12211
Party Time, 709
Parve Plain Muffin, 12795
Pasano's Syrups, 7613
Pascal Coffee, 9800
Pascal Jolivet, 4677
Paselli, 8804
Paso Robles Cabernet Sauvignon, 2637
Paso Robles Orange Muscat, 2637
Pasqualichio, 9804
Passetti's Pride, 9806
Passport, 5660
Pasta Al Dente, 9815
Pasta Campo, 10565
Pasta Della Festa, 4794
Pasta Factory, 9809
Pasta Fiesta, 10331
Pasta International, 9810
Pasta Maltagliati, 5034
Pasta Mami, 9811
Pasta Montana, 9813
Pasta Partners, 6246
Pasta Perfect, 8724
Pasta Pick Ups, 4982
Pasta Quistini, 9815
Pasta Roni, 9945
Pasta Salad, 9745
Pasta Sanita, 13475
Pasta Time, 4153
Pasta With Personality, 9816
Pastabilities, 9816

Pastarific Pasta Co., 11141
Pastariso, 5080, 10708
Pastato, 10708
Pastene, 6126, 9819
Pastificio Bacchini, 12358
Pastori, 9822
Pastry Essentials, 743
Pastry Perfect, 11402
Pastry Pride, 10267
Pastry Pro, 10267
Pasture Sini, 11668
Pat O'Brien's, 4650
Pat O'Brien's Cocktail Mixes, 11674
Pat's Best, 10993
Pat's Psyillium Slim, 5682
Pat-Son, 9839
Pata Negra, 3545
Patagonia, 71
Patagonia Cerveza, 571
Patak's, 73, 11522
Path of Life, 9827
Pathfinder, 6869
Pathmark, 6126
Patio, 6338
Patio Squares, 13845
Pationic, 463
Patissa, 1524
Patricia Green Cellars, 826
Patricia Quintana, 9832
Patrick Cudahy, 9833
Patricks Pride, 9833
Patrina's Bake House, 10981
Patriotic Pasta, 4794
Patsy's, 9837
Patti's Plum Pudding, 9841
Paul Penders, 7562
Paul's, 10046
Paul's Candy, 9846
Paul's Pintos, 1889
Paula, 2260
Paulaner, 1748
Pauline's, 9848
Paulines, 1545
Paumanok Vineyards, 9850
Pavel's Yogurt, 9851
Pavilion, 10873
Pavolami, 2670
Pavone, 9833
Paws, 13864
Paws Premium, 1758
Paws, 12885
Payaso, 8161
Payday, 5818
Payne Family Farms, 5036
Pazdar Winery, 9856
Pb 8, 2666
Pb Jamwich, 13109
Pb Jamwich, 184
Pbc-210, 13498
Pc, 13861
Pcc, 11906
Pdq Puncher, 233
Pea Poppers, 13603
Peace Mountain, 9858
Peace Tea, 2811
Peaceful Bend, 9861
Peach, 9773
Peach Ambrosia, 13746
Peach Gal, 2761
Peach Orchard Farms, 5057
Peach Ridge, 6415
Peach Royal, 5362
Peacock, 5525, 7318, 13067
Peak, 12973
Peanut & Tree Nut, 10327
Peanut Butter Bars, 756
Peanut Butter Bing, 9722
Peanut Butter Dream, 4253
Peanut Butter Kandy Kakesc, 12551
Peanut Butter Pretzels, 972
Peanut Chews, 5144
Peanut City, 10359
Peanut Crunchers, 6851
Peanut Kids Company Store, 10327
Peanut Patch, 9868
Peanut Paws, 7184
Peanut Shop of Williamsburg, 9871, 12714
Peanut Wonder, 13905
Pear Blossom, 10777
Pear Brandy, 2737
Pear's Coffee, 9872
Pearex, 2370

Pearl, 2729, 6187, 7655
Pearl Empress, 4804
Pearl Royal, 10134
Pearl Valley, 9876
Pearl's, 8692
Pearson, 2102
Pearson's Berry Farm, 9878
Pease's, 9881
Pebbles, 10213
Pecan Coffee Cake, 2881
Pecan Duet, 2881
Pecan Halves & Pieces, 2881
Pecan Street Sweets, 4840
Pecanbacks, 11330
Peco, 11053
Peconic Bay, 9884
Pectose-Standard, 6396
Pedia-Vit, 11269
Pedigree, 7952
Pedroncelli, 9890
Peekskill Brewery, 9891
Peel Away, 918
Peeps, 2136
Peeps Easter Baskets, 8131
Peeps, 6641
Peet's Coffee, 6818
Peets, 816, 1000
Peg's Saltc, 9897
Peggy Lawton, 9898
Pei Mussel King, 9650
Peju, 9899
Pekarskis, 9901
Pelican Bay, 9903
Pell-Ettes, 10422
Pellegrini, 9905
Peller Estates, 555
Pellman, 9906
Pelton's Hybrid Popcorn, 12948
Penafiel, 3725, 6818
Pendleton Whisky, 5981
Pendleton1910, 5981
Penelope's, 5954
Penfolds, 12937
Penguin, 6113
Penguin Bay, 12382
Penn Dark, 9923
Penn Dutch, 9729
Penn Gold, 9923
Penn Maibok, 9923
Penn Marzen, 9923
Penn Pilsner, 9923
Penn Weizen, 9923
Pennacook Peppers, 9921
Pennant, 5288, 9763
Pennsylvania Dutch, 465, 9924
Pennsylvania Dutch Candies, 13574
Pennsylvania Dutch Candies, 13572
Pennsylvania Dutch Foods, 5406
Pennsylvania Dutchman, 5028
Pennsylvania People, 9914
Penny Fogger, 1208
Penny Lanes, 7746
Penny Lick, 9927
Pennyroyal, 1672
Pennysaver, 11766
Pennysticks Brand, 1224
Penobscot Porridge, 4362
Penrose, 2939, 2940
Penta, 1367
Pentopan, 1692
Peony Vodka, 12784
Pep Fest, 4928
Pep Talk, 7799
Pepe Lopez, 1784
Pepe's, 9933, 10966
Pepe's Sauce, 6015
Peperoncino, 1174
Pepes, 9934
Pepogest, 783
Pepper Chicks, 12542
Pepper Jellies, 11798
Pepperdoux, 2019
Pepperidge Farm, 2115, 2116
Pepperidge Farm, 9942
Pepperjack, 12937
Peppermint, 9773
Pepperwood Grove, 2343
Pepr, 10422
Pepsi, 9083
Pepsi-Cola, 5975
Pepsi, 9945
Pepsodent, 2666

1293

Brand Name Index

Peptamen Af, 8945
Peptan, 3390
Peptan, 10915
Peptein, 9649
Peptide Fm, 4736
Pepto-Bismol, 12721
Peptopro, 3320
Perch Creek, 868
Perdinci, 13079
Perdue, 9946, 11504
Peregrine Golden, 8153
Peregrine Pale Ale, 8153
Perennial Sweets, 5578
Perfect, 8870
Perfect 1100, 8869, 8870
Perfect Addition Beef Stock, 9949
Perfect Addition Chi, 9949
Perfect Addition Fis, 9949
Perfect Addition Veg, 9949
Perfect Aminos, 8869
Perfect Animos, 8870
Perfect Answers, 1654
Perfect Carbs, 8869, 8870
Perfect Choice, 12612
Perfect Croutons, 7479
Perfect Foods Wheatgrass Juice, 9951
Perfect Italiano, 4552
Perfect Party Mixes, 3079
Perfect Pitcher, 11501
Perfect Rx, 8869, 8870
Perfect-O-Portion, 7196
Perfectagel Mpt, 8804
Perfectamyl, 8804
Perfection, 5334
Perfectly Free, 6176
Perky's Fresh Bakery, 9961
Perma-Ice, 9794
Pernodc, 9964
Pero, 6279
Perona Farms, 9965
Peroni, 8460
Perricone Farms, 9966
Perrier Jouet - Epernay, 3545
Perrier-Jouetc, 9964
Perrier, 8945
Perry's, 9969
Perry's Deluxe, 9969
Perry's Free, 9969
Perry's Light, 9969
Perry's Pride, 9969
Personal Edge Supro, 9970
Perthenon Greek Salad Dressing, 9795
Perugina, 6540
Pervidac, 9971
Pesaca, 8028
Pesto Havarti, 10906
Pet, 3862
Pet Partners, 7952
Pet, 3442
Petaluma Poultry, 9946
Pete's Pride, 249
Pete's Seafood, 9668
Pete's Wicked Ale, 9977
Peter Michael Winery, 9979
Peter Pan, 6084, 9980
Peter Pan, 2939, 2940
Peter Vella, 3834
Peter's Beach Sauces, 10388
Peter's Movie Time Products, 5333
Peterson Farms, 9985
Peterson's, 6870
Petit Potc, 9986
Petite Donceur, 8676
Petite Green Mixes, 4718
Petoseed, 11427
Petra, 9987
Petran, 13614
Petri , 13120
Petrified Porter, 10261
Petrol, 8049
Pett Spice, 9990
Pez, 961, 9991
Pez Candy, 2132
Pfefferkorn's, 9993
Pfeiffer's, 7986
Pfeil, 9994
Phamous Phlyod's, 9996
Pharmacist Formula, 7331
Pharmatose, 4736
Phase 2c, 9997
Phase, 13328
Philadelphia, 6976, 6977

Philadelphia Cheese Steak, 10005
Philip Togni, 10008
Phillipino's, 13560
Phillips, 5555, 10012, 10015
Phillips Candies, 10011
Philly Maid, 11537
Phillyswirl, 6338
Phipps, 10017
Phytbac, 10511
Phyto Foods, 5475
Phyto-Est, 783
Phytoflow Direct Compression Herbs, 10413
Phytonutriance, 10511
Phytotherapy, 13998
Piako, 4552
Piantedosi, 10028
Piazza Tomasso, 12860
Pica, 5405
Piccadeli, 13235
Pick O' the Bushel, 1600
Pickle Juice Sport Drink, 12716
Pickle O'Pete, 10752
Picklesmith, 10035
Pickwick, 5606
Pickwick Catfish, 10036
Pico Pica, 6619
Pictsweet, 10038
Picture Pops, 11885
Pie Piper, 10040
Pie Rite, 2386
Pieces, 5818
Pied-Mont, 10041
Piedmont, 10043
Piedra Creek Winery, 10044
Piels, 9664
Piels Light, 9664
Pieman and Montego, 9842
Piemonte, 10045
Pier Fresh, 1443
Pier Port, 11504
Pierce Chicken, 10056
Pieropan, 3834
Pierre's, 10049
Pierre, 184
Pigout, 9607
Pike, 10052
Pikeman Gin, 11264
Pikes Peak, 648
Pikes Peak Vineyards, 10053
Pikesville Straight Rye Whiskey, 5720
Piknik, 10054
Pikos Pikosos, 2490
Pilarcitas, 1116
Pilgrim's, 6391, 10056
Pillar Rock, 9344
Piller's Turkey Bites, 10058
Piller's, 10058
Pillsbury, 11768
Pillsbury, 4947
Pilon, 6380
Pilot Project, 9452
Pilsener, 1139, 12153
Pilsner Urquell, 8460
Pinah's, 7312
Pinch, 10784
Pinders, 9728
Pine Ridge Winery, 10063
Pine River, 10065
Pineapple Pecan Cake, 2881
Pines, 10067
Pink Beauty, 9344
Pinks, 12078
Pinnacle, 833, 6387
Pinnacle, 1120
Pino's Pasta Veloce, 10068
Pinocchio, 10069
Pinot Meunier, 3661
Pinot Noir, 3661
Pinot Noir Santa Barbara County, 4353
Pinty's, 10071
Pintys Delicious Foods, 10072
Pioneer, 1917, 10075, 10079, 10080
Pioneer Dairy, 10073
Pioneer French Bakery, 5097, 5098
Pioneer Sugar, 8251
Pioneer, 3775, 9237
Pioneerc, 10078
Pip Squeaks, 11320
Pipcorn, 10085
Piper's Pale Ale, 13288

Pipikaula, 10632
Piping Rock, 7655
Pippin Snack, 10084
Pirate, 5508, 9344
Pirate's Keg, 13697
Pirates Keg, 13697
Pirineo, 3545
Pirineos, 3545
Pit Bull, 10090
Pita, 3603
Pita Folds, 5341
Pita Products, 10087
Pitasnax, 10087
Pitch'r Pak, 5735
Pito, 8735
Pixie Crinkles, 9523
Pixy Stix, 2132
Pizazz, 2387
Pizootz, 7736
Pizza & Pasta Magic, 7766
Pizza Corner, 1248
Pizzaiolo, 12030
Pizzaletto, 12030
Pj's Coffee, 9653
Placido, 1006
Plains Dairy, 10098
Plainville Farms, 5505
Plam Vineyards, 10101
Planet Cola, 8470
Planet Food, 8967
Planet Harmony, 3575
Planet Harvest, 4093
Plank 1, 2763
Plant Power, 5786
Plantation, 345
Plantation Pecan, 10105
Planters, 6977, 7963
Plantin Dried Mushro, 9771
Plantio Del Condado, 10319
Plantpower, 9606
Plasmon, 6977
Platform Beer Co., 571
Platinum Harvest, 13607
Platte Valley Corn Whiskey, 8062
Plavix, 1721
Playboy, 13605
Playboy Mints, 1343
Plaza De Espana, 10110
Plaza Sweets, 10109
Pleasant Valley, 10112
Pleasoning Gourmet Seasoning, 10114
Plenish, 3775
Plentiful Pantry, 6246
Plimouth Lollipop, 10133
Ploccy's Apple Chips, 10120
Plochman's, 10119
Plough Boy, 1355
Ploughman's Pils, 5903
Plow Boy, 13740
Plowshares, 11609
Plue Grass, 5792
Plugra, 6760
Plugra Butter, 3335
Plum Creek, 10122
Plum Organics, 2116
Plume De Veau, 779
Plumpy, 12420
Plumrose, 10124
Plus and Moisturlok, 190
Plush Pippin, 7886
Plymouth Colony Winery, 10132
Plymouth Pantry, 7511
Plymouthc Gin, 9964
Pnut Jumbo, 10496
Poblanos, 4375
Poca's Tacos, 10134
Pocahontas, 3275
Pocas, 10134
Pocasville, 10134
Poche's, 2019
Pocino, 10136
Pocket Pretzels, 8029
Pocono, 1391
Pocono Cheesecake, 10138
Pocono Mountain, 10139
Pocono Spring, 10140
Pocos, 7064
Poe Brands, 2449
Poett, 2766
Poffenberger's Bellville, 1204
Point Judith, 1464
Point Pleasant, 896

Point Premium, 12101
Point Reyes Porter, 7923
Point Special, 12101
Point St. George, 5525
Poiret, 10146
Pokanoket Farm, 10149
Pokka, 5662
Pokonobe, 10150
Pol Roger, 4677
Poland Spring, 8945
Poland: Solidarnosc, 5108
Polaner, 864
Polar, 10151
Polar Bear Ale, 13711
Polar Ice Tassel, 3024
Polar Pak, 7363
Polar Sparkling Water, 5884
Polarica, 10153
Polarized, 7783
Poleeko Gold, 549
Polish Sausage, 2162
Polka, 10154
Polka Dot, 3834
Pollenergy, 1914
Polly Orchard, 1596
Polly-O, 2667
Poly-Soleil, 7857
Poly-Tresse, 7857
Polycal, 716
Polylacton, 7172
Polynesian, 345
Polynesian Pleasure, 4521
Pom, 8676
Pom Poms, 2102
Pom, 2121, 9658
Poma Noni Berry, 13943
Pomarola, 12030
Pometta's, 11806
Pomme De Coeur, 56
Pommeroy, 914
Pompeian Olive Oil, 10161
Ponderosa Valley Vineyards, 10165
Ponte Vecckio, 12970
Ponti, 10168
Pontiac Foods, 10170
Pony Boy, 10171
Pony Express, 12663
Pony Malta, 9137
Ponzi's, 10172
Poole's, 8156
Poore Brothers, 10173
Pop, 10176
Pop Candy, 961
Pop Magic, 790
Pop Rocks, 2132
Pop Secret, 11770
Pop Ups, 11311
Pop Weaver, 13611
Pop'n Snak, 7433
Pop-A-Bear, 6158
Pop-Ice, 6483
Pop-Out, 1882
Pop-Tarts, 6766
Pop-Tarts, 6765
Poparazzi, 3311
Popart, 7426
Popcorn Dippers, 3034
Popcorn, Indiana, 3862
Poplar Ridge Vineyards, 938
Poppers, 530, 10186
Poppie's, 10187
Poppies, 10188
Poppy Hand-Crafted Popcorn, 10192
Poppy Hill, 7753
Poppy's Pierogies, 2831
Poppycock, 3430
Poppycock, 2939, 2940
Popsicle, 13169
Popsicle, 5165
Popstop, 10538
Poptime, 9660
Poriloff, 10992
Pork & Veal Magic, 7766
Pork Clouds, 924
Pork Panko, 924
Porkies, 4158, 10196, 11257
Port, 7238
Port Clyde Sardines, 9344
Port Side Amber, 12919
Porter, 7315
Porter & Stout, 11592
Porter House, 3262

1294

Brand Name Index

Portland, 10207
Portland Brewing, 9117
Portland Lighthouse, 10205
Portland Punch, 12921
Porto Cordovero, 10952
Portola Hills, 3179
Portsmouth Chowder Company, 10209
Portsmouth Lager, 11743
Portuguese Baking Company, 10210
Portuguese Sausages, 11224
Posada, 237, 238
Positively Blueberry, 2232
Positively Pecan, 2604
Positively Pralines, 2232
Positively Strawberry, 2232
Post Familie Vineyards, 10214
Post Hostess Cereal, 10213
Post Shredded Wheat, 10213
Postum, 10215
Pot O' Gold, 8256, 13511
Potato Mity Red, 741
Potato Pancake Mix, 5946
Potato Pearls, 1069
Potato Pearls Excel, 1069
Potatoe Pearls, 1577
Potel Aviron, 4677
Potentiator Plus, 7424
Potlicker, 10217
Potomac Farms, 4873
Potomac River, 6828
Potomac River Brand, 6828
Pouch Pak, 12925
Poultry Magic, 7766
Pour & Save, 9839
Pour N' Performance, 10267
Pour N' Whip, 10267
Pow! Pasta, 534
Powder Hound Winter Ale, 1344
Power Crunch, 1377
Power Edge, 12182
Power Herbs, 8882
Power Herbs, 13097
Power Plus, 5786
Power Rangers Chewable Vitamins, 13128
Powerade, 2811, 2814, 2815
Powerbar, 8945
Powerbarc 10-12g Protein Snack Bar, 10225
Powerbarc 20-30g Proteinplus, 10225
Powerbarc Clean Whey Protein Bar, 10225
Powerbarc Clean Whey Protein Drink, 10225
Powerbarc Energy Blasts, 10225
Powerbarc Energy Gels, 10225
Powerbarc Performance Energy Bar, 10225
Powerbarc Protein Plus, 10225
Powerbarc Protein Shakes, 10225
Powerbarc Variety Packs, 10225
Powerful Yogurt, 10226
Powermate, 5363
Powerpuff Girls, 1591
Powers, 9964, 13511
Powersleep, 5363
Powervites, 5363
Poznanski, 11625
Ppeppers, 2490
Ppg, 1692
Prager Winery & Port, 10228
Praim Confections, 10229
Prairie City, 10232
Prairie Farms, 10233
Prairie Fresh, 11363
Prairie Mushrooms, 10236
Prairie Star, 10235
Prairie Sun, 1950, 4039
Prairie Thyme, 10237
Prairieland, 10444
Praline Pack, 5221
Praline Pecan Cheesecake, 2881
Prarie Creek, 11504
Prarie Grove Farms, 9946
Pravachol, 1721
Praylev, 10239
Prayphos, 10239
Pre-Seed, 2666
Precisa, 8804
Precision, 13509
Predator, 8485
Prego, 2116
Prelude Christmas, 11561
Preludes, 9836
Premier, 12550
Premier Coffee, 1601

Premier Fields, 1909
Premier Japan, 3956
Premier Nutrition, 10251
Premier One, 9237
Premier Shots, 10251
Premiere Pacific, 10250
Premium, 2384, 5323, 7197, 7206, 8729
Premium America, 5333
Premium Brand, 5138
Premium Chicken Breast, 6000
Premium Cuts, 5141
Premium Rainbow Drops, 10538
Premium Rainbow Pops, 10538
Premium Tea, 427
Premoroc, 1861
Premose, 10247
Prenatal Formula, 75
Prenulinc, 9997
Presedente, 571
President, 7126
President's Choice, 12276
President, 9789
Presidents Choice, 11410
Presidor, 4852
Presque Isle Wine, 10263
Prestige, 8649, 13864
Prestige Proteins, 10265, 10266
Presto, 10657, 10714
Preston Premium Wines, 10269
Pretzel Fillers, 6338
Pretzel Pete, 11015
Pretzel Rods, 12551
Pretzel Twisters, 5160
Pretzel Wands, 5160
Pretzeland, 1633
Pretzels, 6918
Preventin Green Tea, 9201
Price, 1172, 10275
Price Chopper, 6126
Price's, 3442, 10277
Price's Fine Chocolates, 12414
Priceless, 10275
Prickly Pecans, 9385
Pride, 3314, 10267, 10278
Pride New Orleans, 11865
Pride of Alaska, 4440, 6855
Pride of Canada, 7879
Pride of Dixie, 10280
Pride of Idaho, 4435
Pride of Malabar, 11916
Pride of Peace Vegetables, 5764
Pride of Samspon, 13605
Pride of Shandung, 11916
Pride of Spain, 7931
Pride of Szeged, 11916
Pride, 4267, 13328
Prideland, 10928
Priester's Pecans, 10281
Prifti Candy, 10282
Prilosec Otc, 12721
Prima Brands, 10856
Prima Kase, 10284
Prima Naturals, 10283
Prima Porta, 5643
Prima Quality, 313
Primadophilus, 8896
Primal Chocolate, 3909
Primal Kitchen, 10288
Primalthin, 6629
Primasamo Cubes, 530
Prime, 10296
Prime Cap, 10297
Prime Food, 10290
Prime Froz-N, 10038
Prime Naturally, 10237
Prime Pastries, 10294
Prime Pro Tex, 6168
Prime Time, 12602
Prime Turkey, 7876
Primel, 4148
Primellose, 4736
Primerro, 8367
Primivito Zinfandel, 5989
Primo, 4891
Primo Taglio, 11073
Primo, 4552
Primojel, 4736
Primos, 10304
Primrose, 10305
Primrose Oile, 5363
Prince Alexis Vodka, 8062
Prince Edward, 12062

Prince Gourmet Foods, 1832
Prince of Orange, 12881
Prince of Peace, 10307
Prince of Peace Hawaiian, 10307
Prince, 10777
Princess, 6567
Principe, 10308
Pringles, 6766
Priorato - Mas D' En Gil, 3545
Pristine, 463
Pritikin, 6279
Private Harvest, 10311
Private Harvest Bobby Flay, 10311
Private Harvest Tuscan Hills, 10311
Private Label, 223, 917, 1976, 2060, 3830, 13125
Private Label Products, 1619
Private Labels, 3931, 8105, 12761
Private Stock, 9664, 12293
Private Stock Malt Liquor, 9137
Privilege, 10331
Prize, 2634
Prl, 10027
Pro Mix, 317
Pro Plus, 5786
Pro Treats, 1785
Pro-Life, 2190
Pro-Relight, 9516
Pro-Shake, 15
Proatein, 1692
Proatein, 12561
Probase, 4119
Probio, 833
Probiology, 8878
Probiotic-2000, 7172
Prochill, 833
Proclean, 11504
Procol, 10158
Procon, 833
Procter Creek, 10201
Producer, 648
Produits Marguerite, 955
Proferm, 6211
Professional Preference, 8210
Proflavor, 4119
Progranola, 6629
Progresso, 10337
Progresso, 4947
Progum, 10158
Prokote, 833
Prolume, 10341
Promega, 11269
Promise Pops, 12639
Promitor Dietary Fiber, 12561
Promoat, 1692
Promoat Beta Glucan, 12561
Promolux, 10344
Prop Whey, 9252
Propak, 11504
Propel, 9945
Proper-Care, 10346
Prophecy, 3834
Prophos, 833
Proprietor's Reserve, 10001
Proryza P-35, 10709
Proryza Pf-20/50, 10709
Proryza Platinum, 10709
Prosource, 10317
Prosperity, 597
Prosta-Forte, 8009
Prostacare, 783
Prostate Cleanse, 5682
Prostavite, 783
Prostease, 6449
Prosur, 13648
Prosweet, 13444
Prosyn, 833
Prosystem, 11504
Protake, 10915
Protamex, 1692
Protech, 833
Protector, 13498
Protein Bonk Breaker, 1559
Protein Chef, 11324
Protein Greens, 9516
Protes, 10318
Protflan, 5629
Protient, 10352
Protizyme, 8191
Proto Whey, 1377
Protrolley, 833
Protykin, 6236

Proud Mary, 13141
Provago Wheels, 530
Provecho, 7081
Provenance Vineyards, 12937
Provimi, 10356
Provitamina, 6449
Provost Packers, 10358
Proware, 11504
Prozone, 9251
Pruden, 10359
Psagot Winery, 10952
Psycho Pops, 163
Psycho Psours, 163
Pub Pies, 8560
Puccinelli, 11957
Puckers, 9385
Pudliszki, 6977
Pueblafood, 10363
Puerto Vallarta, 4658
Puff Dough, 10552
Puff Pastry Tartlet, 10039
Puffcorn, 9408
Puffs, 12721
Pulmuone, 10365
Pumpkin Ale, 1837
Pumpkin Masters, 11599
Punch 'n Fruity, 13728
Pup-Peroni, 6380
Puppet Pals, 6780
Pur, 12722
Pura Still, 9117
Purdey's, 8838
Pure 'n Simple, 1040
Pure Alaska Omega, 12968
Pure Assam Irish Breakfast, 5228
Pure Brand Products, 4870
Pure Chocolate Whippet, 3384
Pure Energy, 8493
Pure Flo Water, 10370
Pure Fruit, 5165
Pure Fruite, 2737
Pure Gold, 6869, 10372
Pure Harmony Dakota Clover, 1040
Pure Harmony, 12885
Pure Leaf, 9945
Pure Maid, 3336
Pure Nature, 12238
Pure Protein, 4150
Pure Protien, 8871
Pure Rock, 13728
Pure Source, 10382
Pure Via, 8173
Pure-Bind, 5246
Pure-Cote, 5246
Pure-Dent, 5246
Pure-Flo, 8804
Pure-Gel, 5246
Pure-Li Natural, 5061
Pure7, 10385
Pureco, 126
Puree Marsan, 7954
Purefruit Monk Fruit Extract, 12561
Purekick, 6483
Purely American, 7364, 10388
Purely Elizabeth, 10389
Purely Pinole, 8813
Purepak, 10992
Purestv, 4837
Puricit Odor Eliminator, 9648
Purina, 726, 7198
Purina, 8945
Puritan, 1391
Puritan's Pride, 8871
Purity, 3442, 10399
Purity Candy, 10392
Purity Farms Ghee, 10395
Purity Foods, 8886
Purity Gum, 8804
Purity, 8804
Purn Life, 13365
Puroast, 10400
Purple Carrot, 6590
Purple Haze, 125
Pursil, 3320
Push Pop Candy, 2132
Put Me Hot, 6536
Putney Pasta, 10402
Puueo Poi, 10403
Py-O-My, 5015
Pyramid Brewing, 9117
Pyramid Juice, 10405
Pyrenees, 10406

1295

Brand Name Index

Pyromania, 4895
Pyure Brands, Llc, 1692

Q

Q Cups, 8725
Q&Q, 9297
Q&Q Fideo, 9297
Q-Bee, 10450
Q-Naturale, 8804
Q.E., 10412
Qc Fibers, 3126
Qfc, 12516
Qslic, 300
Quail Creek, 10416
Quaker, 10419, 10420
Quaker Bonnet, 10417
Quaker Maid, 10418
Quaker, 9945
Qualcoat, 10266
Qualflo, 11794
Quali-Tea, 7363
Quali-Carotene, 3320
Qualifreeze, 10425
Qualifresh, 10425
Quality, 226, 9032, 10443
Quality Bakery, 10426
Quality Candy, 1828
Quality Chef Foods, Inc., 5736
Quality Chekd, 4873, 12304
Quality Hearth, 10427
Quality Minded, 5436
Quarrymen Pale, 1460
Quatre Lepages, 9540
Quatro, 2343
Quebon, 8815
Queen Anne, 5288, 10449, 13948
Queen Helene, 5505
Queen Jasmine, 7723
Queen of America, 10454
Queen of Dixie, 12300
Queen's Pride, 9199
Queensboro, 10455
Quelle, 10458
Quencher, 2742
Quero, 6977
Queso Del Valle, 6719
Queso Triangulos, 530
Quest Nutrition, 4150
Questias, 5294
Quibell, 10460
Quic-Cheese, 10436
Quic-Flavor, 10436
Quiche, 10039
Quick & Natural Soup, 11919
Quick Acid, 300
Quick Chew, 300
Quick Coat, 300
Quick Creations, 13607
Quick Fibre, 300
Quick Fire Premium Meats, 11363
Quick Glanz, 300
Quick Gum, 300
Quick Lac, 300
Quick Loaf, 12703
Quick Oil, 300
Quick Peanut Porridge, 1151
Quick Pot Pasta, 11919
Quick Shine, 300
Quick Start, 1577
Quick Stix, 13316
Quick-Start Home Style Chili, 1069
Quickset, 7150
Quilceda Creek Vintners, 10462
Quillisascut Cheese, 10464
Quinabeer, 2338
Quinine, 13287
Quinn, 10466
Quinn's, 11390
Quinn's Golden Ale, 8602
Quinoa Krunch, 2452
Quinoa Quickies, 12883
Quintessa, 4649
Quintrex, 9264
Quinzani, 10469
Quivira, 10471
Quong Hop, 10472
Qwip, 10267

R

R&R Oatmeal Stout, 1139
R-Own Cola, 4521
R.H. Phillips, 10494
R.M. Lawton Cranberries, 10483
R.M. Palmer, 10498
R.M.Quiggs, 2956
R.W. Knudsen, 6380
R.W.Knudsen, 12017
Raaka, 10520
Rabbit Barn, 10521
Rabbit Creek, 10522
Rabbit Ridge, 10523
Rachel Ray Nutrish, 6380
Rachel's, 12985
Radeberger, 1361
Raffaello, 4348
Raffetto, 13141
Raft, 6167
Raga Muffins, 13803
Raggy-O, 10534
Rail Head Red Ale, 1139
Rain Blo, 1417
Rain Forest, 14011
Rainberry, 7170
Rainblo, 4345
Rainbo-Rich, 12866
Rainbow, 10540
Rainbow Hill Vineyards, 10536
Rainbow Light, 10537
Rainbow Light Herbal, 10537
Rainbow Organics, 386
Rainbow Popcorn, 10944
Rainbow Pops, 3415, 10538
Rainbow Springs, 6139
Rainforest, 9245
Rainforest Crunch, 10542
Rainforest Organic, 3956
Rainforest Remedies, 7562
Rainsweet, 10543
Raisin Bran, 10213
Raisin Bran, 6765
Raisin Royales, 6851
Raisinmate, 12550
Raison D'Etre, 3644
Ralph & Paula Adams Scrapple, 6587
Ralph's Italian Ices, 10546
Ralphs, 12516
Ramon Cardova Winery, 10952
Ramona's, 10548
Ramos Orchards, 10549
Ramsey Medium Rye, 648
Ramun,, 10134
Ranch House, 13200
Ranch Oak Farm, 10553
Ranch Pac, 14008
Ranch Style, 6267
Ranch Style Beans, 2939, 2940
Ranch Style Brand Beans, 6267
Ranch Wagon, 12972
Ranchero, 1977
Rancho De Philo, 10554
Rancho Galante Cabernet, 4862
Rancho Palm Springs, 3565
Rancho Sisquoc, 10556
Rancho Zabaco, 3834
Randall, 10559
Randall Foods, 10560
Randazzo's Honest To Goodness, 10561
Ranger Ipa, 8959
Ranieri, 11565
Rao's, 10566
Rapazzini Winery, 10567
Rapes, 12078
Rapidase, 2370, 3320
Raps Blue Ribbon, 6294
Rapunzel Pure Organi, 10568
Raquel's, 10472
Rare Hawaiian, 10570, 13488
Rare Teas, 3895
Raris, 7952
Rashi Winery, 10952
Raskas, 11308
Raspberry Barley Wine, 1237
Raspberry Brown, 7554
Raspberry Champagne Vinegar, 869
Raspberry Honey Butter Topping, 12936
Raspberry Rave Wine, 13372
Raspberry Teriyaki, 12497
Raspberry Trail Ale, 7923
Rat Beach Red, 7844

Rather Jolly Tea, 6378
Ratle Snack, 12814
Ratner's, 11251
Ravenswood, 10573
Ravico, 10574
Ravifruit, 3236
Raw Earth Organics, 167
Raw Live Soda, 7070
Raw Power, 5221
Rawbite, 10576
Rawguru, 13847
Rawmantic Chocolate, 10579
Rawmio, 13847
Rawson's Retreat, 12937
Ray's Headcheese, 10580
Ray's Italian Links, 10580
Ray's Sausage, 10580
Ray's Souse, 10580
Raymond Vineyard, 7659
Raymond Vineyards, 1543
Raynal, 3545
Razcal, 3187
Razzaronia, 11654
Razzcherries, 8127
Razzle Dazzle, 1600
Razzlenuts, 5140
Razzles, 12880
Razzmatazzberry, 7903
Razzykat, 339
Rc, 252
Rc Cola, 1283, 10637
Rc Cola, 3725
Rc Fine Foods, 10477
Rc Q, 10637
Rcci, 10303
Rdl (Red Deer Lake), 10605
Re-Natured, 5407
Read, 7161, 11434
Readi-Bake, 6338
Reading Coffee Roast, 10584
Ready Bake, 13691
Ready Cheese, 2387
Ready Crisp, 7876
Ready Crust, 6747
Ready Grains, 6676
Ready Leaf, 3442
Ready Pac, 10586
Ready-Cut, 11308
Readypac, 2789
Reaktor, 8470
Real, 4877
Real Aloe Co., 10587
Real Bacon Toppings, 6000
Real Cajun, 11255
Real Clean Protein, 1951
Real Cookies, 10589
Real Freshc, 187
Real Hydration, 1559
Real Kosher, 10591
Real Life, 4063
Real Sausage, 10592
Real West, 9500
Realbar, 9554
Realean, 9833
Realemon, 8586
Realemon Lemon Cookies, 9399
Realemon, 3725, 6818
Realime, 3725
Reallime, 8586
Reames, 12467
Rearn Naturefresh, 8448
Rebecca-Ruth, 10596
Rebel Yell, 7655
Rebound, 6310
Rebpure, 4837
Rebsweet, 4837
Red, 7330
Red & White Condensed Soups, 2115
Red Ale, 1401
Red Baron, 1702, 11316
Red Baron, 11317
Red Bird, 204
Red Brick, 10602
Red Bull Malt Liquor, 9664
Red Cap, 1702
Red Cat Amber, 4959
Red Creek, 10604
Red Diamond Coffee & Tea, 10606
Red Dog, 8459
Red Dog, 8460
Red Dragon, 6449
Red E Made, 2943

Red Eye, 1675
Red Eye Country Picnic, 13237
Red Gold, 1891
Red Gold, 10608
Red Hot Chicago, 10610
Red Hots, 1417, 11298
Red Label, 5909
Red Lasoda, 3216
Red Lobster, 2971
Red Mill Farms, 11934
Red Moon, 5141
Red Nectar, 6065
Red Oval Farms Stoned Wheat Thins, 8729
Red Pack, 10608
Red Parrot, 6822
Red Pepper Sauce, 9745
Red Pop, 5177
Red Rain, 10637
Red Ribbon, 11759
Red River, 9664
Red Rock, 10810
Red Rock Deli, 9945
Red Rock Winery, 3834
Red Rocket, 1720
Red Rooster, 555
Red Rooster Ale, 3519
Red Ropes, 469
Red Rose, 2381, 5612, 13167
Red Rose Hill Cabernet, 4862
Red Rose Ice, 9115
Red Shoulder Ranch, 11494
Red Sky Ale, 12013
Red Smith, 10620
Red Stag, 1120
Red Star, 10621
Red Tail, 8153
Red Tail Ale, 8153
Red Tea, 10677
Red Trolley Ale, 6711
Red V, 11001
Red Valley, 12157
Red Velvet, 7581
Red Vines, 469, 3204
Red White & Brew, 10624
Red-L, 11768
Red.L, 12065
Redbreast Irish, 9964
Redclay Gourmet, 10506
Redd, 10626
Redd's, 8460
Reddi-Wip, 2939, 2940
Reddy Glaze, 2942
Redhawk, 10628
Redhots, 4345
Redi Prep Strudel, 4244
Redi Shred, 1577
Redi-Flow, 13890
Redi-Shred, 1069
Redi-Shred Potato Cheese Bake, 1069
Redihop, 6554
Redimix, 10675
Redivivo Lycopene, 3320
Redneck, 7364
Redneck Gourmet, 5520
Redondo Iglesias, 10631
Redpath, 4517
Redpath Sugar, 3666
Redpoint, 838
Reducit, 7857
Reducol, 9997
Redwood Ale, 1615
Redwood Creek, 3834
Redwood Empire, 8539
Redwood Hill Farm, 10633
Reed, 2044
Reed's, 10507
Reedy Brew Teas, 1296
Reena's, 3465
Reese's, 5818
Reflections, 1891, 8301
Refrigerated Entre,S, 6000
Refrigerator Fresh, 9237
Regal, 3033, 8314, 10640
Regal Chef, 4692
Regal Crest, 9534
Regatta, 3771
Regenie's, 10642
Regent, 3480
Reggano, 6126
Regina, 864
Regional Recipe, 1577
Reign, 2811, 8485

Brand Name Index

Reindeer Pies, 12847
Reinhardt, 3381
Reiter, 10664
Reiter Dairy, 3442
Rejuv, 11504
Reko, 9225
Relax & Sleep, 6449
Relaxmax, 9957
Relentless, 8485
Relentless Energy Drink, 2815
Relora, 6236
Rema Foods Imports, 11504
Remeteas Detoxitea, 398
Remeteas Masculinitea, 398
Remeteas Pms Rescue, 398
Remeteas Visibilitea, 398
Remifemin, 4086, 8896
Remy Picot, 9410
Ren,E's, 6976
Renaissance, 4038, 10668
Renaissance Red, 7143
Renato Ratti, 3834
Rendac, 3390
Rene, 10672
Rene Barbier, 4693
Renee's Gourmet, 6240
Renew Life, 2766
Renuz-U, 9253
Renwood Wines, 10676
Rephresh, 2666
Replenish, 12182
Replens, 2666
Republic of Tea, 10677
Rescue Bar, 10229
Reser's American Classics, 10681
Reser's Sensational Sides, 10681
Reserve Brut, 3661
Reserve Brut Rose, 3661
Reserve Cabernet Sauvignon, 11995
Reserve Carneros Chardonnay, 869
Reserve Chardonnay, 13793
Reserve Fume Blanc, 13793
Reserve Merlot, 11995
Reserve Zinfandel, 11995
Resource, 8945
Respitose, 4736
Restaurant Quality, 1658
Restaurant Row, 11352
Restaurant Style, 9408
Restore, 6340
Resvida, 3320
Rethemeyer, 10687
Rethink Beer, 13711
Retzlaff Estate Wines, 10688
Reuben, 13109
Revelstoke, 3024
Revenge, 2411
Revive Kombucha, 10692
Revolution Hall, 1789
Revolution, 13595
Revolver Brewing, 8459
Revovler, 8460
Revv, 6818
Rex, 10509
Rex Coffee, 2711
Rex Hill, 48
Rexpo, 6395
Reyataz, 1721
Reyes Mares, 13298
Re_L Cocktail, 439
Rg's, 1659
Rgo Mace O.O., 11096
Rhapsody In Blue, 9069
Rhinegeld, 8539
Rhino Nutmeg, 12987
Rhodes, 10698
Rhodes-Stockton Bean, 10697
Rhum Barbancourt, 3165
Rhythm Superfoods, 10699
Rias Baixas, 3545
Ribera Del Duero, 3545
Ribran, 10709
Rica, 1581
Rica Malt Tonic, 2338
Ricardo, 9964
Rice a Roni, 9945
Rice Complete, 10297
Rice Crunchies, 4668
Rice Krispies, 6766
Rice Krispies Squares, 6765
Rice Krispies, 6765
Rice Nectar, 12372

Rice Pro 35, 10297
Rice Reality, 10708
Rice Select, 10777
Rice Trin, 10297
Rice's Products, 6105
Riceland, 10710
Ricex, 10713
Rich Cow, 11896
Rich Frosted Mini Donuts, 12551
Rich Ice Creams, 10716
Rich's, 8533
Rich's Eclairs, 10714
Rich's, 11504
Richard's Gourmet, 10721
Richards' Maple Candy, 10722
Richards' Maple Syrup, 10722
Richardson's Ice Cream, 10727
Riche, 3661
Richgrove King, 13421
Richly Deserved, 5346
Richmond Rye Bread, 508
Richs, 11768
Rick's Chips, 10732
Rickard's, 8459
Rico, 10734
Rico's, 100, 5168
Ricotta Con Latte, 1174
Ricrem, 11211
Riddle's, 10736
Ridge Vineyards, 10737
Ridgeland, 12426
Ridgeview Farms, 13737
Ridgways, 4614
Riesen, 12148
Riffels Gourmet Coffees, 10740
Righetti Specialty, 10741
Righteously Raw Chocolate, 3874
Riley's Beef Sausage, 5400
Rindex 3en1, 12721
Ring of Fire, 6015
Ringolos, 9408
Rinquinquin, 3165
Rio, 10747
Rio Caribe, 2617
Rio Grande, 345
Rio Grande Roasters, 13381
Rio Mare, 11776
Rio Real, 8208
Rio Trading, 10748
Rio Valley, 10749
Riobli Family Wine Estates, 7740
Rioja, 3545
Riojano, 28
Riosweet, 10746
Rip It, 8784
Ripensa, 10751
Ripples, 9408
Rips Toll, 4589
Rising Dough, 10758
Rising Moon Organics, 1484
Rising Star Ranch, 11818
Rising Sun, 10759
Rita, 10188, 10873
Ritas, 571
Ritchey, 10762
Rite, 12965
Rito, 10764
Rittenhouse Straight Rye Whiskey, 5720
Ritter, 4721
Ritz, 8474, 8729, 8784
Ritz Bits Sandwiches, 8729
Riunite, 1006
River Ale, 1237
River Bank, 10542
River Bend, 3406
River Hills, 10768
River Island, 3274
River Queen, 7288
River Rat Cheese, 3
River Rice, 10777
River Road, 1547, 1808
River Road Vineyards, 12726
River Run, 4242, 10771
River Town Foods Rib Rub, 10772
River Valley Farms, 3274
River West Stein, 7156
Riverbank, 5924
Riverboat, 12410
Riverside, 4579, 9500
Riverview Foods Authentic, 10776
Riviera, 5317, 10778
Rizzo's, 7635

Rj Corr, 10495
Rjreynolds, 541
Ro, 2939, 2940, 6267
Road Kill Bbq, 11852
Roadhouse, 2200
Roadhouse Red, 1688
Roann's Confections, 11868
Roar, 10928
Roasted Garlic Ranch, 5489
Roasterie, 10783
Roastworks, 6374
Rob's Brands, 13308
Robert Corr, 10495
Robert De Serbie, 5405
Robert Keenan Winery, 10790
Robert Pecota, 10793
Robert Rothschild, 10794
Robert Weil, 12315
Roberto Cheese, 10798
Roberts Ferry, 10799
Robin Hood, 6380
Robller Vineyard and Winery, 10805
Roca, 1771, 10510
Roccas, 10806
Roche, 6007, 10807
Rocher, 4348
Rock 'n Roll Chews, 2947
Rock N Rye, 9773
Rock Pop Carbonated Beverages, 13728
Rock River Cattle, 457
Rockbridge Vineyard, 10813
Rocket Shot, 10251
Rockhill Farms, 11263
Rockin' Rods, 10305
Rocklets, 643
Rocks N' Rolls, 12002
Rocky Jr, 9974
Rocky Mountain, 4578, 5448, 10822
Rocky Mountain Marshmallows, 11015
Rocky Mountain Popcorn, 4749, 11015
Rocky Mountain Products, 1619
Rocky Ridge Maple, 10826
Rocky Roadc, 583
Rocky the Range, 9974
Rodda Coffee, 10830
Roddenbery's, 1103
Rode Lee, 5297
Rodeo, 9500
Rodgers', 10832
Rodney Strong, 10833
Roederer Estate, 3545
Rofumo, 10832
Rogelio Bueno, 12823
Roger's, 10837
Rogers, 8414, 10838
Rogers Imperials, 10840
Rogue Valley, 1128
Rokeach, 7848
Rokeach Food, 10845
Roku, 12315
Roland Star, 10847
Roland, 11504
Rold Gold, 972, 4741
Rold Gold, 9945
Rollerbites, 5929
Rollers, 3931
Rolling Rock, 7123
Rolo, 5818
Roma, 1248
Roma Bakeries, 10853
Roma Marie, 7769
Roman Meal, 5917, 8951
Romance, 2761
Romanoff, 12467
Romanza, 10161
Rombauer Vineyards, 10858
Romeo, 1866
Romero's, 10859
Ron Carlos, 4515
Ron Granado, 3545
Ron Llave, 3545
Ron Palo Viejo, 3545
Ron Rico, 3545
Ron Rio, 8062
Ron Son, 10860
Ronald Reginald's, 11756
Ronco, 465
Rondele, 7126
Ronnoco, 10864
Ronozyme, 3320
Ronrico, 1120
Ronzoni, 6126

Ronzoni Garden Delight, 10866
Ronzoni Gluten Free, 10866
Ronzoni Healthy Harvest, 10866
Ronzoni Homestyle, 10866
Ronzoni Organic, 10866
Ronzoni Smart Taste, 10866
Ronzoni Supergreens, 10866
Ronzoni Thick and Hearty, 10866
Ronzoni, 10866
Ronzoni, 10777
Rookie Spookie, 11004
Roos, 10869
Rooster, 13686
Rooster Run, 431
Root Beer, 11992
Root To Health, 6040
Ropiteall, 12672
Ropiteau Freres, 1543
Rosa, 10873
Rosa Canola Oil, 11096
Rosa Corn Oil, 11096
Rosa Peanut Oil, 11096
Rosarita, 6084
Rosarita, 2939, 2940
Rose, 4539, 4649
Rose Cottage, 13700
Rose Hill, 11997
Rose's, 8586
Rose's, 3725, 6818
Rosebarb, 1688
Rosebud, 1950
Rosebud Creamery, 10889
Rosecup Mints, 9836
Roseen, 6777
Rosell, 7172
Rosellac, 7172
Rosen's Inc., 10893
Rosenbergers, 10894
Rosenblum, 10895
Rosetti Fine Foods, 10897
Rosie Organic, 9974
Rosie's, 7635, 12078
Rosina, 10899
Rosmarino, 10900
Rosport Blue, 2815
Ross Fine, 10901
Rostov's Coffee Tea, 10904
Rosy, 3479
Rotella Bread, 1940
Rotella's, 10905
Roth Kase, 10906
Rothbury Farms, 10907
Rothsay, 3390
Roti & Chapati, 10968
Roudon Smith Vineyards, 10910
Rouge Et Noir, 7925
Rougemont, 56, 10333
Rougette, 2409
Rougie, 10911
Roulet, 10039
Round Hill Vineyards, 10912
Round Lahvosh, 13256
Round the Clock, 5555
Roundpetal, 555
Roussanne, 14038
Rousselot, 3390
Rousselot, 10915
Route 11 Potato Chips, 10916
Rovimix, 3320
Rowena's, 10919
Rowena's Gourmet Sauces, 10919
Rowena's Jams & Jellies, 10919
Rowena's Pound Cake, 10919
Rox Energy Drink, 12960
Roy Rogers Happy Trails, 2903
Royal, 6211, 7007, 8525, 10929, 10939
Royal Bavarian, 2409
Royal Blend, 3564
Royal Borinquen Export, 1581
Royal Canadian, 2089
Royal Canin, 7952
Royal City, 12136
Royal Crest, 10927
Royal Crown, 10151
Royal Crown Cola, 6818
Royal Cup, 10928
Royal Dansk, 6774
Royal Delights, 6483
Royal Garden Tea, 12663
Royal Gem, 8542
Royal Gift, 13845
Royal Gourmet Caviar, 10932

1297

Brand Name Index

Royal Harvest, 10933, 11517
Royal Icing Decoration, 3460
Royal Jelly, 1164
Royal Kona Coffee, 5654
Royal Konaccino, 6953
Royal Mandalay Chai, 9115
Royal Pacific Coffee, 10941
Royal Pacific Tea, 10941
Royal Palate, 10943
Royal Palm, 9098
Royal Pastry, 4025
Royal Pollen Complex, 131
Royal Poultry, 5141
Royal Recipe, 3189
Royal Reef, 6267
Royal Reserve, 3024
Royal Salut, 9964
Royal Seafood, 10200
Royal Sluis, 11427
Royal Touch, 10950
Royal Wrap, 12972
Royal-T, 6211
Royal, 2711, 6483
Royale, 7877
Royale Smoothie, 10953
Royalean, 9833
Royco, 7952
Rp's Pasta Company, 12964
Rps Pasta, 10515
Rrogala, 7344
Rsv, 10795
Rt 66 Foods, 1129
Ru-Bee, 4374
Rubicon, 10958
Rubino & Vero, 6255
Rubschlager, 10960
Ruby Kist, 56
Rudis, 5505
Rudolph the Red Nosed Reindeer, 4507
Rudolph's, 10966, 10968
Rudy's Tortillas, 10969
Rue's Choice, 1403, 13301
Ruef's Meat Market, 10970
Ruffles, 4741
Ruffles, 9945
Ruggles, 11725
Ruinart, 8452
Rule Breaker, 10977
Rum-Ba, 12895
Rumba, 11945
Rumford, 2711
Rumi Spice, 10978
Rumiano, 10979
Rummo Gourmet Imported Pasta, 9119
Runamok, 10982
Running Rabbit, 14045
Rush! Energy, 8470
Russell Cream Ale, 10989
Russell Honey Blonde Ale, 10989
Russell Lemon Wheat Ale, 10989
Russell Oager, 10989
Russell Pale Ale, 10989
Russell Stovers, 10991
Russell Winter Ale, 10989
Russell's, 722
Russer, 13109
Russetts, 6882
Russian Caravan Original China, 5228
Russian Chef's, 10992
Russian Prince, 913
Russo's, 1998
Rustica, 13653
Rustico Cheese, 11668
Rustler Root Beer, 5539
Rutherford Ranch, 10912
Rutherford Vintners, 1738
Rutter's, 11000
Rw Garcia, 10518
Rwi Logistics, 2298
Rx Extreme Energy Shot, 670
Rxbar, 10519
Ryals Bakery, 11002
Rye, 10629
Ryoto Sugar Ester, 8405
Ryvita, 6279
Ryze, 11078
Rzaca, 11627

S

S & W Beans, 4267
S&D Coffee & Tea, 10303
S&M, 11011
S&W, 2847
S&W, 3478
S'Forno Winery, 10952
S. Pellegrino, 8945
S. Rosen's, 374
S. T. Jerrell Nonfat, 11029
S.O.S., 2766
Sabana, 5325
Sabi, 11263
Sabor Del Campo, 12973
Sabra, 11064
Sabra, 9945
Sabrett, 7895
Sabritones, 4741
Sabritones, 9945
Sabrosito, 2490
Sabroso Di Cafe Liqueur, 11264
Sachers, 3714, 13676
Sacramento Baking, 11067
Sacramento, 10608
Sacred Bond, 5720
Sadler's Smokehouse, 11070
Saf-T-Pops, 11885
Safari, 3570
Safari Blend Liquid Coffee, 11855
Safe-T-Salt, 6661
Safecatch, 11071
Safeguard, 12721
Safely Delicious, 11072
Safeway, 3387, 11260
Saffron Road, 11075
Safrante, 4560
Saga, 12759
Sage'n Pepper, 6574
Sagri, 4386
Sahadi, 11082
Sahale Snacks, 6380
Sahara, 6693, 11085
Sahara Date Company, 11086
Sahlen's, 11088
Sai Baba Nag Champa, 7562
Saico, 12241
Sail, 3889
Sailor's Choice, 11356
Saint Andre Vienna, 12136
Saint Archer, 8459
Saint Archer, 8460
Saint Brendan's, 7655
Saint Brigid's, 5304
Saint Clair Family Estate, 3834
Saint Geron, 1661
Saint Justin, 9370
Saint Louis, 12437
Saint Louis Bread Co.c, 9740
Sainte Genevieve, 11091
Saintsbury, 11092
Salad Crispinsc, 5489
Salad Dazzlers, 485
Salad Depot, 11094
Salad Expressions, 462
Salad Pak, 10491
Salad Pizazz!, 13603
Salad Queen, 10054
Salad Time, 12525
Salad Toppers, 7196
Salada, 5612
Salads of the Sea, 7168
Salamandre Wine Cellars, 11097
Salami Campesino, 2670
Salami Del Pueblo, 2670
Salami Sosua, 2670
Salapeno Salami, 2670
Salazar Farms, 5036
Salem Gibralters, 13997
Salemville, 11209, 11211
Salignac, 1120
Salishan, 11106
Salix Sst, 11268
Sall-N-Ann, 7626
Sallie's, 4839
Sally Lane's, 11107
Sally Sherman Foods, 4061
Salmans, 11109
Salmolux, 11608
Salmolux Anti Pasta, 11110
Salmolux Gourmet Smoked Salmon, 11110
Salmolux Saute Butters, 11110
Salmon Bay, 4440
Salmon Magic, 7766
Salmonberry, 1470
Salpica, 4751
Salsa Criolla, 13969
Salsa Del Rio, 3537
Salsa Del Sol, 5735
Salsa Diablo, 3537
Salsa Divino, 3537
Salsa God, 11113
Salsa Picante, 11883
Salt For Life, 3574
Salt Kriek Cherry Be, 7143
Salt of the Earth, 11116
Salted Nut Roll, 9877
Salty Road, 11119
Salty Snacks, 12211
Salute Sante! Grapeseed Oil, 11121
Salutti, 6400
Salvador's, 7655
Salvation, 838
Salvatore's, 11628
Salvo, 12721
Sam & Nick's, 10693
Sam Houston BourbonÖ Chocolates, 10468
Samai, 4607
Sambol, 11130
Sambuca Di Amore, 11264
Sambuca Molinari, 3545
Sambucus, 8896
Sammillsc, 11125
Sammy's, 11585
Sammye's Sumptuous, 890
Samos, 10435
Sampco, 11132
Sams Clams, 1464
Samsons, 4633
Samuel Adams, 1592
Samuel Smith, 1748
Samuel Wynn & Co., 12937
San Anselmo's, 11134
San Antonio California Champagne, 7740
San Antonio Dessert, 7740
San Antonio Sacramental, 7740
San Antonio Specialty, 7740
San Antonio Winery, 7740
San Benedetto, 11776
San Benito, 9178
San Daniele, 11776
San Diego Salsa, 11065, 11187
San Diego Salsa, 11186
San Diego Soy Dairy, 11138
San Dominique, 11139
San Francisco Bay Traders, 5660
San Francisco Coffee, 11141
San Francisco Fine Bakery, 11142
San Francisco Popcorn, 11144
San Francisco Salt Companyc, 11145
San Franciso Bay, 11140
San Gallio, 10457
San Gennaro, 11148
San Giorgio, 6126, 11154
San Giorgio, 10777
San Joaquin Golden Ale, 11448
San Joaquin Supreme, 11149
San Like, 11250
San Marcos, 12823
San Mario, 12640
San Orange, 11250
San Quentin's Breakout Stout, 7923
San Rallo Gourmet Italian, 10899
San Red, 11250
San Simeon, 7740
San Sui, 13473
San Yellow, 11250
San-Ei, 11250
San-J, 11157
Sanborn Sourdough Bakery, 11160
Sand Castle Winery, 11162
Sandbar Trading, 11165
Sandeman Character Oloroso, 3545
Sandeman Don Fino, 3545
Sanders, 3078
Sanders Brand Candy, 11167
Sanderson Farms, 11169
Sandhill, 555
Sandia Shadows Vineyard & Wine, 11170
Sandridge Salads Set Free, 11172
Sandstone Winery, 11173
Sandt's, 11174
Sandwhich Bros. of Wisconsin, 2939, 2940
Sandwich Naturals, 4405
Sandwich Pals, 13894
Sandwich Shop, 7196
Sanford, 11178
Sangaria, 11032
Sangiovese, 2469, 7527
Sangria Cola, 6310
Sangria Seorial, 12823
Sans Sucre, 1244
Santa Barbara, 11185
Santa Barbara Barc, 11182
Santa Barbara County, 4353
Santa Barbara Pistachio, 11184
Santa Barbara Salsa, 11065, 11187
Santa Barbara Salsa, 11186
Santa Barbara Winery, 11188
Santa Clara, 11189
Santa Cruz, 498, 10500, 11191
Santa Cruz Mountain Vineyard, 11192
Santa Cruz Organic, 6380
Santa Elena, 2970
Santa Fe Brewing, 11194
Santa Fe Seasons, 3522, 11195
Santa Fe Vineyards, 11196
Santa Marta, 5036
Santa Pop, 11004
Santa's Favorite, 11855
Santa's Tipple, 8524
Santa-Claus, 6310
Santa-Elena Coffee, 11193
Santaka Chili Pods, 191
Santarosa, 10869
Santiago, 1577
Santiago Beans, 1069
Santiam, 8724
Santino Wines, 10676
Santitas, 4741
Santitas, 9945
Sap Maple, 11722
Sapna Foods, 11033
Sapore Del Tartufo, 11205
Saporito, 12030
Sapp Birch Water, 11206
Saputo, 11209, 11211
Sara Lee, 541, 5792, 10406, 11214
Sara Lee, 1359, 13109
Sarabeth's, 2669, 11035, 11216
Saragosa Olive Oil, 9648
Sarah's Garden, 10435
Sarah's Vineyard, 11217
Saranac Diet Root Beer, 11218
Saranac Ginger Beer, 11218
Saranac Orange Cream, 11218
Saranac Root Beer, 11218
Sarantis, 6986
Saratoga, 11222, 11223
Saratoga Splash, 11223
Saratoga Vichy, 11223
Sardinha's, 11224
Sargento, 11228
Sarsaparilla, 13728
Sartori, 1006
Sarum Tea, 11232
Sasquatch Stout, 4466
Sathers, 1417, 4345
Satiety, 11235
Satin Ice, 11236
Satin Oranges, 13906
Satin White Flour, 6917
Satise, 6777
Satman Overseas, 6939
Sattwa Chai Concentrate, 11237
Sattwa Kovalam Spice Chai, 11237
Sattwa Shanti Herbal Chai, 11237
Sattwa Sun Chai, 11237
Sauce Craft, 13328
Sauce For Sissies, 6796
Saucelito Canyon, 11240
Saucy Susan, 345
Sauder's, 11241
Sauer's Everyday Spices, 1935
Sausage a La Carte, 4676
Sausal Wines, 11245
Sautene, 353
Sauvignon Blanc, 1314, 4745
Sauza, 5892, 13454
Sauza Commemorativo, 3024
Sauza Extra Gold, 3024
Sauza Margarita Salt With Juicer, 4650
Sauza Silver, 3024
Sauza Tequila, 12315
Sauza Triada, 3024
Sauza, 1120
Savage Energy, 2234
Saval, 11246
Savannah, 12284

Brand Name Index

Savannah Chanelle Vineyards, 11248
Savannah Cinnamon Mix, 11249
Savannah Gold, 6164
Savannah Squares, 11249
Savannah White, 8513
Savarin, 8560
Savealot, 8404
Savoia, 11253
Savoie's, 2019, 11255
Savorganic, 11258
Savorlok, 4430
Savoro, 10056
Savory, 2750, 11257
Savory Basics, 11229
Savory Smoke, 11919
Savorymyx, 11436
Sawtooth, 2909, 7309, 11259
Sb-3x, 6302
Sc, 9103
Sc Fibers, 3126
Scalfani, 864
Scanpro, 4119
Scapa Single Malt, 3024
Scape Goat Pale Ale, 1344
Scarlet Lady Ale, 12153
Scent-O-Vac, 11997
Schabers, 2274
Schaefer, 9664
Scharffenberger, 9677
Schell's, 796
Schepps Dairy, 11281
Schermer, 14023
Schiff, 11285
Schiff Food, 11284
Schlafly, 11291
Schlitz, 9664
Schloss Doepken, 11293
Schluckwerder, 13676
Schmerling, 13931
Schneider, 6379
Schneider Foods, 11300
Schneider's, 11298
Schnitzius, 1064
Schnucks, 11303
Scho-Ko-Lade, 1957
Schoemaker, 9027
Schoep's, 11305
Scholl, 10598
Schoner, 11368
School Chioce, 11308
School Milk, 13647
School Milk!, 4290
Schooner, 7123
Schrafft's, 1638
Schramsberg, 11307
Schreiber, 11308
Schreiber, 11504
Schug, 11309
Schuil Coffee, 11310
Schumann's, 13676
Schuss, 2815
Schwab, 11315
Schwan's, 11316
Schwan's Chef Collection, 11316
Schwan's, 11317
Schwarteau, 13676
Schwartz, 8061
Schwebel's, 11318
Schwebel's Organic, 11318
Schwebel's Selects, 11318
Schweppes, 3725, 6818
Schwepps, 2815
Sci, 12130
Sciabica's Oil of the Olive, 9040
Science Foods, 9510
Sclafani, 13437
Scones, 12936
Sconza, 11320
Scooby Doo, 1591
Scoop Away, 2766
Scoopy, 6614
Scope, 12721
Scora S.A., 1692
Scoralite, 1692
Scoresby Scotch, 3570
Scorned Woman, 5520, 13454
Scotch Ale, 4950
Scotcheroons, 12096
Scotian Gold, 11322
Scotsburn, 11211
Scott & Jon's, 2477
Scott Country, 8542

Scott Pete, 11902
Scott's, 11326, 11328, 11330, 13700
Scott's Barbeque Sauce, 11329
Scott's of Wisconsin, 11330
Scottie, 11330
Scottish, 1720
Scottsdale Mustard Co, 4839
Scotty Wotty's, 11332
Scramblettes, 3449
Scratch Recipe, 8724
Scray's Cheese, 11333
Screamer, 11320
Screamin' Sicilian Pizza Co., 9719
Scully, 9439
Sea Best, 1140
Sea Breeze, 11339
Sea Cakes, 7788
Sea Chest, 11102
Sea Chips, 7788
Sea Choice, 9344
Sea Cuisine, 5844
Sea Devils, 666
Sea Dog, 11340
Sea Farer, 11559
Sea Gold, 11343
Sea Maid, 11238
Sea Market, 6390
Sea Mist, 3097
Sea Pearl, 8785
Sea Pearl Seafood Co., Inc., 11347
Sea Ray, 7583
Sea Salad, 857
Sea Salt Superstore, 11351
Sea Seasonings, 7788
Sea Snack, 11352
Sea Spray, 9165
Sea Valley, 5479
Sea Vegetables, 7788
Sea View, 3565
Seabear, 11358
Seablends, 9980
Seaboard Farms, 11363
Seabreeze, 11102
Seabrook Farms, 11365
Seabrook, 11378
Seafest, 6267
Seafood, 13943
Seafood Magic, 7766
Seafood People, 9731
Seafood Sisters, 12742
Seafreez, 1057
Seagram's, 2815
Seagram's Escapades, 9117
Seagram's Extra Dry Ginc, 9964
Seagrams, 10151
Seagull Bay, 11238
Seajoy, 11378
Seakist, 9980
Seald Sweet, 6081, 11381
Sealicious, 5325
Sealina Spa, 11351
Sealtest, 6204, 8815
Seaman Orchard, 4506
Seapak, 10714
Seaperfect, 11360
Seapoint Edamama, 10229
Seaport, 12650
Seaport Blush, 12142
Seaport White, 12142
Seaport Wines, 12142
Seapro, 3891
Sear 'n Smoke, 5473
Searchlight, 9344
Seaside, 5479, 6508
Season Brand, 7848
Season Opener, 6880
Season-Ettes, 10422
Seasonc, 11384
Seasoned Cheddar Cheese, 13320
Seasoned Delux, 6486
Seasoned Jack Cheese, 13320
Seasonedcrisp, 6374
Seasoning Salt, 4148
Seasonings From Hell, 11873
Seaspecialties, 10252
Seassentials, 1500
Seastix, 5483
Seatech, 11386
Seattle Bar, 11388
Seattle Chocolates, 11389
Seattle's Best Coffee, 8090, 12042
Seavey Cabernet Sauvignon, 11394

Seavey Chardonnay, 11394
Seavey Marlot, 11394
Seawatch, 11356
Seawater Soaked Potato Chips, 11396
Seawave, 8504
Seaway, 3484
Sechler's, 10545
Second Nature, 1103
Secret, 12721
Secret Garden, 11402
Secret Sun, 12234
Secureflo, 342
Sedgefield, 7743
Seditol, 6236
Sedna, 6726
Sedona Baking Company, 10760
See's Candies, 11407
Seeclear, 13498
Seeds & Suds, 8154
Seeds of Change, 7952
Seely, 4626, 11664
Segafredo Espresso, 11212
Segafredo Zanetti, 7995
Segal Winery, 10952
Seghesio, 11413
Segura Viudas, 4693
Seitenbacher, 1957
Select, 11416
Select Blend In-Room Coffee, 11855
Select Origins, 6806
Select Recipe, 6374
Selecta , 856
Selleck, 2044
Sello, 13320
Sello Rojo, 10777
Seltzers, 9729
Semdiero, 11557
Semi-Industrialized, 12185
Seminole, 11428
Sempio, 11429
Senate Beer, 9437
Senators Club, 7146
Seneca, 9167
Seneca Blend, 4403
Seneca Snacks, 11434
Senor Cane, 5755
Senor Felix's, 11437
Senor Paprika, 13648
Senor Rico, 7168
Senorio De Lazan, 3545
Senorio De Los Llanos, 3545
Sensations, 6394
Sense, 3545
Sensible Carbs, 3836
Sensible Delights, 2726
Sensible Options, 8236
Sensible Portions, 5505
Sensient, 11444
Senza, 6806
Seppelt, 12937
Sequoia Grove, 11449
Serious Foodie, 11455
Serious Kick, 4820
Serrano, 12004
Serranos, 4375
Serranos Salsa, 11456
Server's Choice, 457
Sesa-Krunch, 5462
Sesame Birch Sticks, 2108
Sesame Seed, 5462
Sesame Street, 608
Sesamin, 3615
Sesmarkc, 9748
Session, 4786
Session Roasted Coffees, 2874
Setria, 7017
Setter, 11263
Setton Farms, 11469
Setton Farms Chewy Bites, 11469
Seven Barrell, 11470
Seven Hills, 11472
Seven Keys, 11473
Seven Seas, 498
Seven-Up, 181, 9083, 10151
Sevigny, 4198
Sewansecott, 12634
Sexpresso, 912
Seyval Blanc, 2761
Seyval Naturel, 2761
Sfizio Crotonese, 11668
Sgti, 11778
Shabadoo Black and Tan Ale, 1237

Shade Grown Organic, 8612
Shadow Mountain Foods, Inc., 2899
Shady Grove Orchards, 11491
Shafer Vineyards, 11494
Shake 'n Bake, 6976
Shaken Country Meadows Sweets, 5874
Shakequik, 7870
Shaklee Carotomax, 11501
Shaklee Flavomax, 11501
Shalina, 11897
Shallon Winery, 11502
Shamiana, 6026
Shamrock, 4143, 12972
Shamrock Farms, 11504
Shana Spice, 2499
Shandy, 1208
Shang Pin, 734
Shape Ups, 6338
Shari Candies, 12547
Shariann's Italian White Beans, 11518
Shariann's Refried Beans, 11518
Shariann's Spicy Vegetable, 11518
Sharifa Halal, 11058
Sharkinator, 7554
Sharp Cheddar Cheese, 806
Sharp Gouda, 13840
Sharp's, 8459
Sharp's, 8460
Shashi, 11522
Shasta, 8784, 11524
Shastebury, 9391
Shaw, 11525
Shaw's, 570
Shawnee Best, 11529
Shawnee Mills, 11529
Shawnee Springs, 11528
Shearer, 6928
Sheba, 7952
Sheboygan Sausage Company, 457
Sheboygan Sausage Company, 10893
Sheffa, 11533
Shei Brand, 8613
Sheila's Select Gourmet Recipes, 1126, 11536
Sheinman, 11537
Shelf-Aid, 12553
Shellac, 300
Shelly's Hair Care, 5682
Shelter Pale Ale, 3644
Shelton's, 11542
Shemper Seafood, 11543
Shenandoah, 11544, 13720
Shenandoah Vineyards, 11774
Shenk's, 11546
Shephard Ridge, 12099
Shepherd, 11547
Shepherd Supreme, 11547
Shepherd's Pride, 8601
Shephody, 3216
Sherpa Pinkc, 11145
Sherrill, 11551
Shiloh Winery, 10952
Shiner Blonde, 11942
Shiner Bock, 4881, 11942
Shiner Dunkelweizen, 11942
Shiner Hefeweizen, 11942
Shiner Kolsch, 11942
Shiner Light, 11942
Shiner Premium, 4881
Shingle Peak, 12937
Shining Choice, 11559
Shirakabe Gura, 12500
Shire Gate, 4321
Shirley Foods, 11565
Shirley's, 11023
Shitake Mushroom Soup Mixes (4), 6433
Shmolives, 1754
Shnuts., 1754
Sho Chiku Bai, 6673, 12500
Shock Top, 571
Shoei, 11567
Shonan, 11568
Shop Rite, 6126
Shopsy's, 7875, 7876
Shoreline Fruit, 786
Shortbread Housf, 2507
Shotball, 4515
Showboat, 7571
Showcase, 6391
Shpickles, 1754
Shrimp Butler, 6796
Shrimp Jammers, 12520

1299

Brand Name Index

Shrimp Magic, 7766
Shrimp Teazers, 12520
Shuckman's Fish Co. & Smokery, Inc., 4321
Shur Fine, 12885
Shurfine, 10098
Shurtenda, 14043
Sicao, 1056
Sick Day, 7526
Sid and Roxie's, 5364
Sideboard Sweets & Savories, 5140
Sidehill Farm, 11584
Sidewinders, 6374
Sidral Mundet, 12823
Sidul, 3666
Sidul, 12196
Sierra, 11589
Sierra Gourmet, 11985
Sierra Madre Brand, 3838
Sierra Madre Honey Co., 13971
Sierra Mist, 9945
Sierra Nevada, 1748
Sierra Nevada Bigfoo, 11592
Sierra Nevada Celebration, 11592
Sierra Nevada Pale Ale, 11592
Sierra Nevada Stout, 11592
Sierra Nevada Summer, 11592
Sierra Sausage Co., 6770
Sierra Spring Foods, 10943
Sierra Springs, 10303
Sierra Springs, 3220, 3319
Sierra Vista, 11593
Sierra Springs, 11889
Siesta, 8161
Siete, 11594
Sifers Valomilk Candy Cups, 11595
Siggi's, 9789
Sigma, 2839
Signal 369, 5363
Signature Cafe, 11073
Signature Care, 11073
Signature Farms, 11073
Signature Reserve, 11073
Signature Select, 11073
Signorello, 11604
Sil-A-Gran, 11607
Silarom, 11607
Siler's, 12973
Silfoam, 1692
Silhouette, 13595
Siljans, 11608, 13676
Silk, 3379, 11281, 13734
Silk Soy, 8815
Silk Tassel, 3024
Silvan Ridge, 11612
Silvanil, 11607
Silver, 6395
Silver Creek, 4506
Silver Fleece, 5893, 5894
Silver Fox Vineyard, 11618
Silver Label, 2708
Silver Label Cabernet Sauvigno, 869
Silver Lake, 4244
Silver Mtn Vineyards, 11621
Silver Palate, 11623
Silver Ridge, 1738
Silver Salmon, 11602
Silver Seyual, 1688
Silver Spring, 10151
Silver Spur, 9500
Silver Streak, 11629
Silver Thunder Malt Liquor, 9664
Silver Tray Cookies, 11631
Silverado Cellars, 2461
Silverbow, 11633
Silverland Desserts, 11634
Silvers, 4348
Silvo, 8061
Simi Ravenswood, 4649
Simmer Kettle, 11919
Simmonds, 5325
Simmons, 11639
Simon, 10461
Simon Fischer, 11788
Simon's, 3696, 11643
Simons, 10461
Simpkins, 13676
Simple Beginnings, 12056
Simple Eats, 5141
Simple Elegance, 10981
Simple Mills, 11646
Simple Nevada, 10435
Simple Smart, 5486

Simplesse, 1962
Simplot, 1891
Simplot Classic, 6374
Simplot Daily Pick, 6374
Simplot Good Grains, 6374
Simplot Harvest Fresh Avocados, 6374
Simplot Simple Goodness, 6374
Simplot Sweets, 6374
Simplot Thunder Crunch, 6374
Simply, 4741, 10435
Simply Asia, 8061
Simply Delicious, 13892
Simply Devine, 3550
Simply Divine, 11651
Simply Done, 12885
Simply Fresh, 4461
Simply Gold, 6374
Simply Lite, 5694
Simply Natural, 2509, 3945
Simply Natural-Like, 3945
Simply Natural-Like, 13614
Simply Natural, 13614
Simply Orange, 2814
Simply Organic, 4752
Simply Potatoes, 8225
Simply Ranch Classic Ranch, 5489
Simply Ranch Cucumber Basil, 5489
Simply Rich, 7424
Simply Saline, 2666
Simply Smart Organics, 9946
Simply Spice, 14024
Simply Supreme Organic, 13894
Simplywell, 6676
Sin Fill, 8247
Sinai Gourmet, 11662
Sinatra, 5717
Sinbad Sweets, 11663
Sincera Skin Care Products, 11268
Sincerity, 1006, 6869
Sinfire Cinnamon Whisky, 5981
Singel Serving Sundae, 3541
Singers Saving Grace, 5791
Single Origin, 1054
Single Serv, 3574
Singleton Seafoods, 10603
Singletree Farms, 6334
Sini Fulvi, 11668
Sioux City, 13728
Sioux City Sarsaparilla, 13728
Sip, 4081
Sip-N-Chew, 469
Sipp, 11670
Sipsmith, 1120
Sir Citrus, 13184
Sir Francis Stout, 3746
Sir George Fudge, 6787
Siracuse, 4148
Sirah, 9889
Sirius Ttr, 3833
Sisler's Dairy, 11675
Sister Schubert's, 7189, 12467
Sister Schuberts, 7987
Sisters Gourmet, 11679
Sisu, 8871
Sitka Gold, 11375
Sivetz Coffee Essence, 11680
Six Mile Creek, 11681
Sjora, 8945
Sk-Ii, 12721
Skedaddle, 11683
Ski, 3707
Skim Plus, 4290, 13647
Skincredibles, 6374
Skinner Bakery, 6448
Skinner's, 13124
Skinner, 10777
Skinny, 4957
Skinny Dipped Almonds, 13786
Skinny Sticks, 3862
Skinny Truffles, 11389
Skinny Water, 9858
Skinnygirl, 1120
Skinnygirl, 864
Skins, 3320
Skippy, 3574
Skippy, 6000
Skittles, 6483, 7952, 13960
Skjodt-Barrett, 11691
Skol, 11264
Skor, 5818
Skull, 961
Skull & Bones, 10435

Sky Valley, 11694
Sky Vineyards, 11695
Skyland, 13720
Skylark, 457
Skylark, 10893
Skyy, 2114
Skyy Vodka, 3545
Slane Irish Whiskey, 1784
Slap Ya Mama, 2019
Slater's 50/50 Bacon Burger, 6492
Slawsa, 11703
Slc, 11642
Sledgehammer, 12937
Sleeman, 9391
Sleepeasy, 9182
Sleepless In Seattle Coffee, 270
Slender, 6310
Slendo, 7978
Slide Pops, 4255
Slim, 5897
Slim 'n' Trim, 4873
Slim Diez, 6811
Slim Jim, 2939, 2940
Slim Shake, 15
Slim-Fast, 13167
Slimcado Avocado, 1757
Slimdown, 6449
Slinky Brand Candy, 2136
Slo Poke, 756
Slo-Roast Deli, 7876
Sloppy Joe, 4428
Slotkowski, 523
Slow Ride Ipa, 8959
Slush Puppie, 6338
Slush Puppie, 6483
Slushade, 6971
Sm La San Marco, 7995
Smack Cup-A-Ramen, 13170
Smack Ramen, 13170
Small Batch, 11710
Small Planet Foods, 2286
Small Talk Conversation Hearts, 4032
Smart Bacon, 7427
Smart Balance, 5837
Smart Balance, 1612, 2939, 2940, 13328
Smart Bbq, 7427
Smart Chiken, 12596
Smart Chili, 7427
Smart Cookies, 1409
Smart Crackers, 1409
Smart Cutlets, 7427
Smart Deli, 7427
Smart Dogs, 7427
Smart Gourmet, 4699
Smart Ground, 7427
Smart Harvest, 12528
Smart Kids, 5917
Smart Links, 7427
Smart Sausage, 7427
Smart Tenders, 7427
Smart Water, 4066
Smart Wings, 7427
Smart Flavours, 10797
Smartcake, 4957
Smartchocolates, 4795
Smartfood, 4741
Smartfood, 9945
Smartfruit, 17
Smartgels, 6676
Smarties, 11716
Smarties, 8945
Smartshapes, 1654
Smartwater, 2811
Smash Mallow, 11717
Smashpop, 11754
Smile Brite, 7562
Smint, 9956
Smith, 11726
Smith & Forge Hard Cider, 8460
Smith & Hook Winery, 5499
Smith and Forge, 8459
Smith Dairy, 13604
Smith Home Cured, 167
Smith's, 11725, 11729, 12516
Smith-Madrone, 11732
Smithfield, 11053, 11733
Smithfield Farmland, 11504
Smithfield Tavern, 9871, 12714
Smithworks Vodka, 9964
Smitten, 1196
Smoke & Fire, 11735
Smoke It All, 9344

Smoked Eggplant Sprat,, 9863
Smoked Habanero Pretzels, 3393
Smoked Porter, 339
Smoked Salmon, 2189
Smoked Spices, 2189
Smokehouse, 1471
Smokehouse 220, 13328
Smokehouse Favorite, 3177
Smokeless Blackened Seasoning, 2022
Smokey Mesquite, 2511
Smoky Mountain, 7684
Smoky Mountain Trail Rub, 6796
Smoky Valley, 2511
Smoky's House, 12178
Smooth & Creamy, 437
Smooth & Melty, 13676
Smooth and Melties, 13845
Smooth-N-Melty, 5428
Smoothie Sparkling Choc.Egg Cream, 2410
Smothers/Remick Ridge, 11741
Smucker's, 6380
Smucker's Natural, 6380
Smucker's Toppings, 6380
Smucker's Uncrustables, 6380
Smuttynose Belgian W, 11743
Smuttynose Robust Po, 11743
Snack Bites, 11228
Snack Factory, 11744
Snack Factory Pretzel Chips, 11770
Snack Factory Pretzel Crisps, 2116
Snack Fu, 12841
Snackin Fruits, 11311
Snackmasters, 11746
Snacknut, 1027
Snackwell'sD, 864
Snackwells, 8729
Snak King, 11748
Snak N'Go, 9668
Snak Sales, 10196
Snake River, 11749
Snap-Back, 13052
Snappers, 3958
Snapple, 1294, 5975
Snapple, 3725, 6818
Snappy, 12957
Snappy's, 5902
Snaps, 469
Snapshot Wheat, 8959
Snausages, 6380
Snickers, 8533
Snickers, 7952
Snikiddy, 13129
Snips, 11415
Sno Pac, 11758
Sno-Bal, 12866
Sno-Ball, 8795
Sno-E Tofu, 13286
Sno-Top, 6253, 13183
Snocap, 8693
Snokist, 11759
Snolite, 11756
Snoodles, 13170
Snow Cod, 6387
Snow Farms, 13006
Snow Flake, 11177
Snow Goose, 3033
Snow Monkey, 11762
Snow White, 833
Snow's Nice Cream, 11763
Snowberry, 12721
Snowbird, 11764
Snowcrest, 11766
Snowden, 3216
Snowite, 2123
Snowizard, 11756, 11767
Snowman, 1677
Snowqualmie Falls Lodge, 2971
Snowtime, 7732
Snyapa, 10869
Snyder's of Hanover, 2116, 11770
So Clear, 10637
So Delicious, 3379
So Fruitty, 8840
So Good, 9042
So Joao, 10496
So Natural, 12928
So-Good Bar-B-Q Delight, 3695
So-Good Pork Bar-B-Q, 3695
Soauthter, 12955
Soba, 11773
Sobe, 11772
Sobe, 9945

Brand Name Index

Soberdough, 1167
Sobon Estate, 11774
Soccer Pops, 6158
Sochu Distilled Rice, 6968
Societe, 7126
Society Hill Gourmet Nut Company, 11775
Sockeye Nova, 13521
Soda Fountain, 1966
Soda Pops, 6803
Soda-Lo Salt Microspheres, 12561
Sodex, 3404
Sofgels, 1009
Sofgrain, 7585
Soflet Gelcaps, 1009
Soft Bake, 6340
Soft Chews, 5017
Soft Cookies, 5909
Soft Mac, 12895
Soft Square, 13256
Soft White, 833
Soho Natural Lemonades, 11779
Soho Natural Soda &, 11779
Sokol Blosser, 11780
Sol Cerveza, 8460
Sol De Oro, 7062
Sol-Mex, 8161
Sola, 12730
Solae, 3773
Solait, 5629
Solana Gold, 11782
Solana Gold Organics, 11782
Solar, 4761
Solaray, 9237
Soldans, 13676
Soleil-Late Harvest Sauvignon, 3771
Solerac, 11894
Solero, 6288
Solfresco, 12973
Solgar, 11785
Solgar, 8871
Solgel, 12637
Solid Protein, 8870
Solid White Albacore Tuna, 12046
Solis, 11786
Solkafloc, 11794
Solnuts, 11787
Solo, 4976, 11788, 11789
Soloman, 11791
Soluble Products, 11793
Soluflex, 3753
Solugel, 9649
Solvatrol, 1009
Somaguard, 13746
Somaguard Premium Grape Extract, 13746
Somen, 11773
Somerdale, 11365
Something Natural, 11797
Something Special Gourmet Antipasto, 11798
Somewhat Sinful, 11144
Sominus, 13273
Sommer's Food, 11800
Sonac, 3390
Sonavavitch, 4515
Song Bird, 12663
Sonic Dried Yeast, 8726
Sonic, 6483
Sonny's Pride, 11325
Sonoma, 12809
Sonoma Brewing, 3519
Sonoma Coast, 6892
Sonoma County Classics, 6974
Sonoma County Zinfandel, 5989
Sonoma Creamery, 11804
Sonoma Cuvee, 1543
Sonoma Extra Virgin Olive Oil, 869
Sonoma Foie-Gras, 5390
Sonoma Gourmet, 11806
Sonoma Jack, 11804
Sonoma Organics, 11804
Sonoma Pacific, 4854
Sonoma Syrups, 11899
Sonoma Valley Merlot, 869
Sonoma Valley Zinfandel, 869
Sonoma Wine, 11809
Sonoma-Cutrer, 1784
Soo, 6347
Sootherbs, 6107
Sopakco, 11049
Sophia, 11814
Sophia's Authentic, 11815
Sophia's Sauce Works, 11815

Sophie Mae, 756
Sophisticated Chocol, 3396
Sorbee, 11817
Sorbet By Yo Cream, 3378
Sorengeti Coffees, 11855
Sorento, 280
Sores, 12196
Sorrell Flavours, 6115
Sorrenti Family Farm, 11818
Sorrento Valley Organics, 2772
Sotac, 6917
Souena, 7051
Sound Sea Vegetables, 2630
Sound Sleep, 7422
Soup Bowl, 13240
Soup For Singles, 11402
Soup Supreme, 8724
Soupergirl, 11822
Soups For One, 9434
Sour Apple, 9773
Sour Cotton Candy Swirl, 12547
Sour Patch Kids, 6338, 6483
Sour Patch Kids Cereal, 10213
Sour Pops, 6803
Sour Punch, 469
Sour Simon, 12985
Source, 11824, 14017
Source of Life, 5065
Sourdough Bread Enha, 7540
Sourz, 1120
South Beach, 5975
South Bend Chocolate, 11828
South Ceasar Dressing Company, 11829
South Hills, 5728
South Mill Mushroom Sales, 11832
South of the Border Chili, 5946
South Shore, 6537
South Side, 6537
South Texas Spice, 11834
South West, 11872
Southampton, 10482
Southeastern Meats, 11053
Southeastern Mills, 11839
Southern, 2019
Southern Biscuit, 10675
Southern Breeze, 11454
Southern Breeze, 5612
Southern Chef, 12300
Southern Comfort, 4422, 11263
Southern Dynamite, 12975
Southern Gold Honey, 11854
Southern Harvest, 5492
Southern Heritage, 11855
Southern Pride, 11862
Southern Ray's, 1850
Southern Recipe, 10966
Southern Select, 1654
Southern Sensations, 5520
Southern Sin, 12881
Southern Snow, 11867
Southern Special, 12428
Southern Spice, 9745
Southern Style, 6548, 11257
Southern Style Nuts, 11868
Southern Supreme, 6622
Southern Sweetenerc, 8088
Southern Swirl, 13728
Southern Twist, 11869
Southgate, 13402
Souverain, 3834
Soy Cheese, 7419
Soy Deli, 10472
Soy Delicious Purely Decadent, 11771
Soy Dream, 3009
Soy Flax 5000, 13863
Soy Products, 2764
Soy Roast, 3548
Soy Supreme, 12294
Soy Treat, 7423
Soy Vay Veri-Veri Teriyaki, 11878
Soy Water, 4066
Soy-Liccous Meals, 8719
Soy-N-Ergy Soy Powders, 8993
Soy-Sation, 7458
Soyboy, 9160
Soydance, 12855, 12857
Soyfine, 2764
Soygold, 81
Soylife, 137
Soymilk, 2764
Soynut Crunch Bar, 6442
Soynuts, 6442

Soypreme, 2355
Soypro, 8719
Soypura, 13648
Soywise, 11881
Spa, 13643
Spaghettios, 2116
Spam, 6000
Spangler Candy Canes, 11885
Spangler Chocolates, 11885
Spangler Circus Peanuts, 11885
Spangler Wineyards, 11886
Spanky's, 7924
Spare-The-Ribs, 12065
Spark Bites, 3062
Sparkle, 9183
Sparkletts, 10303
Sparkletts, 3220, 3319
Sparkling Avitae, 840
Sparkling Ice, 5884, 12510
Sparkling Live Drinking Vinegars, 7070
Sparks, 8459
Sparks, 8460
Sparrow Lane, 11864
Spaten, 11891
Speas, 8414
Special Brew, 9664
Special C-500, 7947
Special K, 6766
Special K, 6765
Special Old, 3024
Specialty, 11895
Specialty Blends, 9743
Specialty Farms, 406
Specialty Flour, 5946
Specialty Food Magazine, 11901
Specialty Grains, 9743
Specialty Minerals, 1692
Speckles, 4976
Spectrabiotic, 8967
Spectrum, 5505
Spectrum Nutritional Shake, 9251
Speedy Bird, 6025
Speedy Cook'n, 9179
Spendida, 11777
Spendido Nuggets, 14045
Spi-C-Mint, 10428
Spibro, 10651
Spice, 4362
Spice Bouquet, 1600
Spice Choice, 1547
Spice Garden, 8448
Spice Hunter, 8898, 11919
Spice Hunter Spices & Herbs, 11919
Spice Islands, 73, 4499
Spice Islands, 864
Spice Products, 4276
Spice Ranch, 1547
Spice So Rite, 12377
Spice Star, 1547
Spice Traderc, 8088
Spice World, 11926
Spiceland, 11927
Spicely, 473
Spiceman's, 9528
Spicery Shoppe Natural, 4488
Spicetec, 11930
Spicy and Hot Hickory Sausage, 2944
Spicy Olive, 6522
Spicy Wings, 14043
Spider-Man, 1591
Spiderman Cotton Candy, 12547
Spiderman Sour Gummi Mutant Spiders, 12547
Spiedie Sauce, 10784
Spike, 8448
Spin Blend, 4831
Spinbrush, 2666
Spindrift, 11102
Spindrift Sparkling Water, 11936
Spingtime, 11844
Spirithouse, 659
Spirulina Bee Bar, 7561
Spirulina Hawaiian Spirulina, 3281
Spirulina Pacifica, 9244
Spirulina Trail Bar, 7561
Spirutein, 5065
Spizzico Pepato Aged, 11668
Splash, 2054, 10134
Splash, 2740
Splenda Sucralose, 12561

Splendar, 8380
Splendid, 1962
Splendid Specialties Chocolate Co, 12894
Splendid Specialties Chocolates, 11940
Splendido, 6126
Splendido Biscotti, 14045
Splinter, 1517
Spohrers Bakeries, 11943
Spongebob Squarepants, 4659
Spontaneous Combustion, 11873
Spoon Fruit, 485
Spoon Toppers, 485
Spoonful of Flavors, 2134
Spoonty, 4148
Spor Tabs, 11947
Sport Shake, 3335
Sport Totoe 'ems, 4255
Sports Juice, 9858
Sports Nutrition, 13146
Sportsmen's Cannery, 11950
Spot Farms, 9946
Spraygum, 9029
Spreadable Fruit, 2679
Spreda, 11957
Spring Acres, 11958
Spring Blossom, 10478
Spring Bock, 11992
Spring Drops, 9237
Spring Farm, 9296
Spring Glen, 5555, 11960
Spring Glen Fresh Foods, 5555
Spring Hill Farms, 11973
Spring House, 4462
Spring Kitchen, 11964
Spring Splendor, 10061
Spring Tree, 864
Spring Valley, 8324
Springdale, 8414
Springerlies, 5756
Springfield, 10526
Springhill, 9174, 10383, 11972
Springtide Ale, 8153
Springtime, 9839
Springtime Natural Artesian Water, 11844
Springwater Farms, 11850
Sprite, 2811, 2814, 2815
Sprout Creek Farm, 11976
Sprout House & Salad, 11977
Sprouted, 563
Sproutman's Organic, 11977
Sprouts, 11979
Spruce Point, 3780
Sprycel, 1721
Spud King, 9042
Spudsters, 6374
Spurgeon Vinyards, 11984
Squalene, 11269
Square, 1120
Square One, 743
Squawkers, 1654
Sque'easy, 4592
Squeaks, 2347
Squealing Pig, 12937
Squeezers, 5735
Squirrel, 11990
Squirrel Brand, 6548, 11868
Squirrel Nut Caramel, 11990
Squirrel Nut Chew, 11990
Squirrel Nut Zippers, 11990
Squirt, 9083, 10151
Squirt, 3725, 6818
Squozen Frozen, 11654
Sqwiggles, 12547
Sqwincher, 6792
Sqyntz! Supersourz, 7710
Sriracha Ranchc, 5489
Ssips, 6545
Sss, 12451
St Huberts, 12937
St Peter's, 4148
St. Briogets Strong, 9688
St. Clair Ice Cream, 11994
St. Claire, 3925
St. Croix, 12004
St. Etienne, 5558
St. Hubert, 10331
St. Ides Special Brew, 9664
St. Innocent, 11996
St. James Winery, 12007
St. Joe Pork, 11363
St. Julien Macaroons, 13723
St. Laurent, 9693

1301

Brand Name Index

St. Martin, 7592
St. Nick's, 8784
St. Nicks Poter, 556
St. Ours, 12011
St. Paddy's, 339
St. Stan's Alt Beer, 12013
Sta Fresh, 8956
Sta-Lite Polydextrose, 12561
Stabil, 8899
Stabilenhance, 8899, 10511
Stabilo, 13498
Stablebond, 6211
Stacey's, 12014
Stacy's, 4741
Stacy's Pita Chips, 9945
Stadium Mustard, 3407
Stagg Chili, 6000
Stags' Leap, 12019
Stags' Leap Winery, 12937
Stahl Meyer, 4244
Stahl-Meyer, 4351
Stallion X Malt Liquor, 2410
Stam, 2615
Stamere, 4773
Stampede, 6310, 12023
Stan Barth Farms, 2152
Stand Out, 7526
Standard Coffee, 10303
Standard Coffee, 3319
Standard Formulation, 7172
Standard Lager, 8459
Stanley's, 7490, 13696
Stapleton, 9182
Star, 4243, 12035
Star Blend, 985
Star Caps, 985
Star Cross, 5894
Star Dairy, 13700
Star of David Pasta, 4794
Star Ranch Angus, 13109
Star Sucker Sour, 985
Star Suckers, 985
Star-Van, 12085
Starborough, 3834
Starbound, 10415
Starbucks, 8090
Starbucks Coffee, 12042
Starbucks Frappacino, 9945
Starbucks Hot Cocoa, 2950
Starburst, 7952, 13960
Starbursts, 6483
Starcross, 5893
Stardrops, 10496
Stargazer, 6711
Starkist Flavor Fresh Pouch, 12046
Starkist Lunch To-Go, 12046
Starkist Select, 12046
Starkist Tuna Creations, 12046
Staropramen, 8459
Starrey's Ion, 7490
Stars & Stripes, 6294, 10637
Stars Pride, 11198
Starters, 3696
Starwest, 12051
Stasero, 12052
Stash, 12053
Stash Premium Organic Teas, 12053
State, 11799
State Fair, 4928, 10784
State Fair, 13109
Static Guard, 864
Stauffer's, 12060, 12061
Stawnichy's, 12063
Stay Well, 3919
Staysteady, 9548
Steak Sauce, 9745
Steak-Eze, 184
Steak-Umm, 12065
Steak-Umm Sandwich To Go, 12065
Steakeze, 13109
Steakhouse, 13301
Steakhouse Style, 13653
Steakwich, 3549
Steakwich Lite, 3549
Stealth Fries, 7179
Steam & Serve, 6685
Steam N' Mash, 9523
Stearns & Lehman, 6806
Stearns Wharf, 12066
Steaz, 5693, 12690
Steel Creek, 104
Steel Rail Extra Pale Ale, 1237

Steel Reserve, 8459
Steel Reserve, 8460
Steel's Gourmet, 12068
Steeler Lager, 7157
Steen's Cane Cured Pheasant, 1924
Steens, 2019
Stefan Mar, 8028
Stefano's, 12071
Stegall Smoked Turkey, 11737
Steinfeld's, 1103
Stella, 6986
Stella Artois, 71, 571, 7123
Stella D'Oro, 11770
Stella Rosa Moscato D'Asti, 7740
Stella, 11209, 11211
Stellina Di Notte, 12937
Steltzner, 12079
Sterling Old Fashion Flavors, 12085
Sterling Vineyards, 12937
Sterling Vinyards, 3545
Sterotex, 126
Sterzing's, 12088
Steve & Andy's, 12090
Steve Connolly, 12091
Steve's Mom, 12096
Steven Smith Teamaker Teas, 6928
Stevenot Winery, 12099
Stevia Products, 13883
Steviacane, 6164
Stevison's, 12105
Stewart's, 4521, 10054
Stewart's, 6818
Stewarts, 252, 12110
Stewarts Honey, 4443
Stewarts, 3725
Stews and Sauces, 1598
Stickers, 2947
Stickney & Poor, 12115
Stilwell's, 11198
Stilwell, 11317
Stim-O-Stam, 12120
Sting Ray Bloody Mary Mixer, 1470
Stirfresh, 6685
Stirling Gourmet Flavors, 12122
Stirling Syrup, 2833
Stirring Sticks, 6787
Stivers Best, 11839
Stok, 3379
Stokely, 2260
Stoktin Grahan, 12126
Stolichnaya, 3024, 5892
Stolichnaya Razberi, 3024
Stolichnaya Red, 3024
Stolichnaya Vanil, 3024
Stone Cat Ale, 6283
Stone Hammer Pilsner, 12136
Stone Haven, 1006
Stone Hill Winery, 12131
Stone Ipa, 12129
Stone Mountain Snacks, 8397
Stone Pale Ale, 12129
Stone Smoked Porter, 12129
Stone Street, 13256
Stone Sublimely, 12129
Stone's, 1006
Stoned Classics, 2728
Stoneground Mills, 12906
Stonehedge, 1027
Stonemill Kitchens, 10681
Stonemill, 2121
Stonewall Kitchen, 12139
Stoney, 785
Stoney Hill, 1121
Stoney's, 6586
Stoney's Black & Tan, 6586
Stoney's Harvest Gold, 6586
Stoney's Light, 6586
Stoney's Non-Alcoholic Brew, 6586
Stonington, 12142
Stonington Vineyards, 12142
Stony Hill Vineyard, 12143
Stonyfield Farm Frozen Yogurt, 12145
Stonyfield Farm Ice Cream, 12145
Stonyfield Farm Refrig Yogurt, 12145
Stopnot, 9956
Storehouse Foods, 5159
Storm King, 13181
Storrs, 12150
Story Wine, 12151
Storybook Mountain Winery, 12144
Storypoint, 3834
Storytime, 1677

Stoudt Gold, 12153
Stouffer's, 8945
Stoutridge, 12154
Stove Top, 6976
Straight Coffees, 8612
Straight Up Tea, 3725, 6818
Strand Amber, 7844
Straub, 12158
Straub Light, 12158
Straubs, 12159
Strauss, 12162
Strawberry Blonde, 1208
Strawberry Colada Frozen Batter, 951
Strawberry Shortcake, 1591
Strebin Farms, 12164
Streblow Vineyards, 12165
Streits, 12167
Strendge Pasta, 3691
Strepsils, 10598
Stress Formula With Zinc, 75
Stressease, 6449
Stretch Island, 12169
Stroehmann, 1359
Stroh, 9035
Stroh's, 9664
Strohs Canada, 9391
Strokes, 12127
Strong Boy, 11839
Stroopies, 12734
Strub's, 12175
Strudelkins, 3603
Stryker Sonoma Winery Vineyards, 12177
Stubb's, 8061, 12180
Stubborn Soda, 9945
Stubi, 3236
Studio Confections, 13142
Stutz Olive Oil, 2085
Stylus, 4649
Suarez, 1357
Subsole, 5036
Sucanat, 13751
Success, 10777
Suckerpunch, 12186
Sudbury, 12189
Suderwerk Doppel, 12191
Suderwerk Dunkel, 12191
Suderwerk Lager, 12191
Suderwerk Mai Bock, 12191
Suderwerk Marzen, 12191
Suderwerk Pilsenser, 12191
Sudlersville, 12190
Sue Bee, 11669
Sugai Kona Coffee Emporium, 12192
Sugai Kona Grove Coffee, 12192
Sugar & Spice, 1856
Sugar Art, 5160
Sugar Babies, 2102
Sugar Babies, 12880
Sugar Bob's Finest Kind, 12194
Sugar Creek, 12197
Sugar Daddy, 2102
Sugar Daddy, 12880
Sugar Flowers, 12199
Sugar Foods Corporation, 11504
Sugar Free Cookies, 5909
Sugar Free Vines, 469
Sugar Grove, 7463
Sugar In the Raw, 12201
Sugar Mama, 2102
Sugar Sticks, 9753
Sugar Tree, 6880
Sugar Twin, 864, 6792
Sugar Valley, 7853
Sugardale, 4715
Sugarleaf, 12430
Sugarless Sugar, 8725
Sugarman, 12208
Sugary Wine, 9856
Sugo, 10533
Suja, 12213
Sul-Ray, 746
Sula, 9956
Sullivan Cabernet Sauvignon, 12217
Sullivan Chardonnay, 12217
Sullivan Coeur De Vigne, 12217
Sullivan Merlot, 12217
Sulpice, 12218
Sumatra Mandheling, 10157
Sumbeam, 807
Sumiwataru Umeshu, 1120
Summer Ale, 7526
Summer Beer, 531

Summer Berry Delight, 13746
Summer Blush, 10061
Summer Fresh, 12219
Summer Golden Ale, 556
Summer Harvest, 6870
Summer Honey Seasonal Ale, 1344
Summer Naturals, 4757
Summer of Lager, 2691
Summer Pils, 11992
Summer Prize, 13598
Summer Sage, 10165
Summer Song, 7170
Summer's Choice, 1190
Summerbright Ale, 1687
Summerfield Farms, 12222
Summerfield's, 12223
Summerlake, 12672
Summerripe, 4242
Summerset, 7463
Summit, 12225
Summit Lake Vineyards, 12227
Sumner, 13582
Sumptuous Ions, 1925
Sun Beauty, 861
Sun Biotics, 13847
Sun Chips, 4741
Sun Chips, 9945
Sun Chlorella, 12228
Sun Crop, 12241
Sun Drop, 3725, 6818
Sun Garden Sprouts, 12230
Sun Groves, 12233
Sun Leaf, 421
Sun Lovin, 13630
Sun Maid, 1394
Sun Moon Stars, 10673
Sun Olive Oil, 12237
Sun Orchard, 12239
Sun Orchards Labels, 12240
Sun Pac, 12241
Sun Ray, 2086
Sun Ridge Farms, 8898
Sun Siberian Ginseng, 12228
Sun Sun, 8161, 12247
Sun Supreme, 12231
Sun Valley Mustard, 12249
Sun Valley, 12251
Sun-Bird, 1917
Sun-Dried Tomato Str, 806
Sun-Glo, 12231
Sun-Maid, 11318, 12256, 13254
Sun-Ripe, 2386
Sun-Ripened, 1490
Sun-Rise Beverages, 12258
Sun-Rype, 12259
Sun-Sugared, 10686
Sunbeam, 2242, 4527, 4662
Sunbeam Bread, 4529
Sunbelt Bakery, 8077
Sunbelt, 8076
Sunbestc, 12267
Sunbird Snacks, 8397
Sunblet, 12909
Sunburst, 9226
Sunburst Trout Farms, 12265
Sunbursts, 6851
Suncoc, 12267
Suncrest Farms, 12268
Suncrisp, 12961
Sundance, 5132
Sunday House, 12270
Sundial Blend Teas, 12272
Sundial Gardens, 12272
Sundown, 11785
Sundown Naturals, 8871
Sunergia Breakfast Style Sausage, 12273
Sunergia More Than Tofu Garlic, 12273
Sunergia More Than Tofu Herbs, 12273
Sunergia More Than Tofu Porcinis, 12273
Sunergia More Than Tofu Savories, 12273
Sunergia More-Than-Tofu, 12273
Sunergia Organic Soy Sausage, 12273
Sunergia Smoked Portabella Sausage, 12273
Sunflo, 3084
Sunflower, 11979
Sunfresh, 12275
Sunfresh Freezerves, 12276
Sunfruit, 2059
Sunglo, 5333
Sunglow, 13328
Sungold, 11211
Sunkist, 252, 6483, 12871, 13907

Brand Name Index

Sunkist Citrus, 1343
Sunkist Country Time, 10151
Sunkist Flavour Bursts, 4884
Sunkist Fruit First Fruit Snacks, 4884
Sunkist, 3725, 6818
Sunland, 676
Sunlike, 56, 12279
Sunmeadow, 4813
Sunmed, 220
Sunnie, 5363
Sunnuts, 12262
Sunny Avocado, 12280
Sunny Boy, 1950
Sunny D, 12281
Sunny D, 6483
Sunny Farm, 2260
Sunny Fresh, 2205
Sunny Green, 9237
Sunny Isle, 12103
Sunny Lea, 3084
Sunny Millet, 8844
Sunny Morning, 5334
Sunny Shores, 7853
Sunny Shores Broccoli Wokly, 7853
Sunny South, 12284
Sunnyd, 6818
Sunnydale Farms, 4290
Sunnydell, 13319
Sunnyland, 12287
Sunnyland Farms, 12286
Sunnyrose Cheese, 12288
Sunnyside, 5555, 6567
Sunnyside Farms, 12323
Sunphenon, 12498
Sunrice, 12372
Sunrich, 12294
Sunrich Naturals, 12238
Sunridge Farms, 12295
Sunripe, 9676, 9763
Sunrise, 635, 1006, 1808, 11408
Sunrise Farm Fresh, 500
Sunrise Farms, 13063
Sunset Farm, 12300
Sunset Pink, 6763
Sunshine, 3540, 8519, 12302
Sunshine California, 7451
Sunshine Farms, 12306
Sunshine Pasta Sauce, 12735
Sunshine Snacks, 2960
Sunshine State, 7569
Sunshine Valley, 8833
Sunshine's, 12372
Sunshower, 11609
Sunspire, 5505
Sunsweet, 12313
Suntory Umeshu, 1120
Suntory Whisky, 1120, 12315
Suntree, 9049
Sunup, 12316
Sunvista, 4267
Sunwest, 12262
Sunwise, 5555
Suparossa, 1305
Super, 3695
Super Aged Gouda, 13840
Super Antioxidant Blend, 665
Super B-12 Sublingual, 9253
Super Blue Green Enzymes, 8967
Super Bowl Cleanse, 131
Super Bubble, 1417, 4345
Super Burgers, 13073
Super C Active, 131
Super Detox, 131
Super Dickmann's, 12147
Super Epa, 7947
Super Fabulous Fiber, 7404
Super Fat Burner, 5682
Super Fine, 5555
Super Gel B, 8335
Super Good, 6101
Super Green, 131
Super Juhyo, 1120
Super Kleaned Wheat, 6869
Super Kmh, 4124
Super Life, 4127
Super Oxy-Pure, 12483
Super Q10, 8967
Super Ropes, 469
Super Salad Oil, 131
Super Smokers Barbecue Sauces, 10772
Super Soynuts, 7297
Super Stress, 7947

Super Stuffers, 8798
Super Sucker, 790
Super Supreme, 12550
Super Thins, 2692
Super Tonic, 131
Super Vab, 7947
Super-1-Daily, 6364
Super-Mix, 7671
Superba, 243
Superburgers, 13074
Superc, 6483
Supercitrimax, 6236
Superclear, 13498
Supercol, 1692
Supercuts, 10971
Supereats, 12324
Superfex, 13444
Superfine, 5555
Superfreeze, 13444
Supergrain Pasta, 10467
Superior, 7006, 11213, 11909, 12328
Superior Cake, 12331
Superior Chocolatier, 12349
Superior Confections, Inc., 12349
Superior Farms, 12333
Superior Foods, 12334
Superior Nut Company, 12338
Superior Pride, 12334
Superior Source, 1967
Superior Spices, 12906
Superior Syrups, 12906
Superior's Brand, 4715
Superla, 13498
Supermom's, 12319
Superpretzel, 6338
Superpretzel Bavarian, 6338
Superseedz, 6728
Supersnax, 12201
Supersocco, 13932
Superstar Strawberry, 5362
Superstone, 11233
Superstore, 12323
Supertex, 13498
Supervan, 12550
Superwhip, 13498
Supherb Farms, 12318
Supper Topper, 191
Supreme, 2796, 7585, 8336, 10330, 11226, 12550
Supreme 7, 5786
Supreme B 150, 7947
Supreme Dairy Farms, 12350
Supreme Dips, 13894
Supreme Stuffers, 6338
Supreme Tender, 13109
Supremes, 12202
Supremo, 3127, 8457
Sur Sweet, 12426
Suram, 12353
Sure Fresh, 12354
Surebond, 6211
Sureflo, 342
Surefresh Foods, 2393
Surf Spray, 9356
Surface Guard, 9252
Surge, 2814
Surprizers!, 13403
Surry, 11025
Susan Winget, 6291
Sushi Chef, 1105
Sushi Sonic, 5306
Susie's Smart Cookie, 12360
Susquehanna Valley, 12362
Sustagen, 8103
Sustained Energy, 3540
Sustamine, 7017
Sustenex, 11285
Sustiva, 1721
Suter, 12365
Sutter Home, 12369
Sutton's, 12370
Suzanna's, 12371
Suzanne's Conserves, 12372
Suzanne's Salad Splash, 14018
Suzi Wan, 7952
Suzie's, 5161
Suzuki Eikodo, 3852
Svenhards, 12375
Swagger, 12377
Swamp Fire Seafood Boil, 9315
Swan, 9094
Swan Island, 9094

Swan Joseph, 6604
Swan's Touch, 9532
Swans Down Cake Flour, 10657
Swanson, 2116
Swanson Vineyards & Winery, 12378
Swany White, 11402
Swany White Certified Organic, 11402
Swedish Hill, 12382
Sweet & Sassy, 11077
Sweet & Saucy Caramel Sauces, 12386
Sweet & Saucy Chocolate Sauces, 12386
Sweet 'n Healthy, 9201
Sweet 'n Low, 12201
Sweet 2 Eat, 10285
Sweet and Slender Natural Sweetener, 13883
Sweet Baby Ray's, 12388
Sweet Basics, 3114
Sweet Beans, 12294
Sweet Betsy From Pike, 13920
Sweet Blessings, 12389
Sweet Blossoms, 2134
Sweet Breath Xtreme Intense Breath, 12390
Sweet Carolina, 5094
Sweet Cheese, Queso Blanco, 9885
Sweet Cloud, 5306
Sweet Cravings, 2159
Sweet Dessert Wine, 10415
Sweet Drops, 12430
Sweet Earth Natural Foods, 12396
Sweet Home Farm, 14011
Sweet Kiss, 7423
Sweet Leaf, 13883
Sweet Loren's, 12406
Sweet Meadow Farms, 4351
Sweet Moose, 9237
Sweet Notes, 10764
Sweet Nothings, 903, 11771
Sweet Occasion, 4032
Sweet Onion Low Fat Crackers, 1472
Sweet Organics, 7845
Sweet P'S, 12885
Sweet Pepper Low Fat Crackers, 1472
Sweet Pleasers Gourmet, 5735
Sweet Portion, 5735
Sweet Savory Cocktai, 13180
Sweet Seduction, 4804
Sweet Shells, 5578
Sweet Shop Usa, 12414
Sweet Singles, 7599
Sweet Sloops, 5578
Sweet Squeeze, 1893
Sweet Stirrings, 2947
Sweet Street, 4244, 12415
Sweet Stripes, 4345
Sweet Stuffers, 6338
Sweet Things, 7179
Sweet Treasures, 5346
Sweet Whispers, 12421
Sweet Works, 9031
Sweet'n Low, 12422
Sweet-Water, 4269
Sweet-X, 9201
Sweetaly, 12424
Sweetango , 2476
Sweetango Apples, 1196
Sweetcorn, 1882
Sweetdex, 12387
Sweetfire, 2860
Sweetfree Magic, 7766
Sweetheart Fudge, 14013
Sweetleaf Stevia, 12430
Sweetmyx, 11436
Sweetsting, 5516
Sweetwater, 12419
Sweetwater 42, 12419
Sweetwater Blue, 12419
Sweetzyme, 1692
Swell, 11056
Swerve, 12436
Swiffer, 12721
Swift Premium, 6391
Swift, 6391
Swiftgel, 12637
Swiftwater, 6267
Swing-A-Way, 4538
Swirl Onion, 13653
Swirly Cups, 12551
Swiss, 12440
Swiss 2, 12442
Swiss Alp Mineral Water, 9604
Swiss American Sausage Co., 1861

Swiss Colony Foods, 2888
Swiss Fudge Sampler Tier, 13277
Swiss Heritage Cheese, 12441
Swiss Kriss, 8448
Swiss Made, 13875
Swiss Miss, 6084
Swiss Party, 831
Swiss Premium, 388, 12442
Swiss Premium Drinks, 8104
Swiss Premium, 3442
Swiss Valley, 8898
Swiss Valley Farms, 10233
Swiss Whey D'Lite, 1506, 3074
Swissart, 8677
Sycamore, 13067
Sycamore Farms, 12365
Syfo, 13205
Syfo Brand Original, 13206
Sylvester, 7276
Sylvin Farms, 12450
Symbio, 4552
Symphony, 5818
Symphony Pastries, 3236
Symtec, 13642
Synature, 1490
Synedrex, 8191
Synergy Systems, 10915
Syrah, 2469, 7490, 14038
Syrah Santa Barbara County, 4353
Sysco Products, 3387
Sytrinol, 6236

T

T & A, 12525
T'Gallant, 12937
T'Lish Vinaigrette & Marinade, 12466
T.G. Lee, 3442
T.G. Lee Foods, 12460
T.H. Angermeier, 2386
T.O.P. Chops, 2635
T.S. Smith & Sons, 12472
T2p - Light, 11462
T4p - Medium Toasted Hulled Sesame, 11462
T5p - Dark, 11462
Taam Tov, 13931
Tab X-Tra, 2815
Tabasco, 8072
Tabernash, 7309
Tabiah Halal, 5141
Table De France, 12487
Table Joy, 7022
Table Talk, 12488
Table Two Entree, 6574
Tabor Hill, 12489
Tabouli, 12536
Tabouli Salad Mix, 4252
Tadin, 12490
Taffy Delight, 5017
Taffy Lite, 5017
Tag, 8191
Tahini, 11462, 12536
Tahini Crunch, 1791
Tahiti, 13141
Tahitian Treat, 6818
Tai Bueno, 9571
Tai Pan, 13241
Tai Pei, 237, 238
Tailgate, 118
Tailgate & Celebrate, 9816
Tait Farm Foods, 12497
Taj, 12499
Taj Mahal, 10968
Takara, 12500
Takara Plum, 12500
Take & Bake Deli Pizza, 12071
Take 5, 5818
Takohachi, 857
Taku, 12503
Tal-Furnar, 2960
Talapa Mezcal, 3165
Talbott Chardonnay, 12506
Talbott Diamond T Chardonnay, 12506
Talbott Vineyards, 3834
Talbott's, 12504
Talenti, 13169
Talking Rain, 12510
Talking Rain Biotanical, 12510
Tall-Boy, 1321
Talley Farms, 12513

Brand Name Index

Talley Vineyards, 12514
Talluto's, 12496
Talmadge Farms, 10497
Tamarind Tree, 591
Tamarindo Bay, 5516
Tambellini, 2312
Tampa Bay Fisheries, 10603
Tampa Maid, 12520
Tampax, 12721
Tampico, 8105, 12522
Tampico Punches, 12521
Tamxicos, 7076
Tan Cook, 7686
Tanbro, 12525
Tandoor Chef, 3465
Tandoori, 7273
Tang, 6976
Tang Hoi Kee, 10457
Tangerine Wheat Ale, 7554
Tangle Ridge, 1120
Tango, 947
Tangy Bang, 7210
Tanqueray Gin, 3570
Tantos, 12527
Tanzanian Peaberry, 1123, 10157
Taorminac, 2010
Taos, 12530
Tap Juices, 9083
Tap'n Applec, 9748
Tapatio, 12531
Tapi, 10297
Tappers, 1654
Taproom, 1789
Tapt, 12706
Tara Foods, 10435, 12533
Tarantula, 8062
Tarazi, 12535
Tarheel, 11958
Tasmanian Devil, 1837
Tassimo, 6976
Tast-T, 5048
Tast-T Tender, 5048
Taste Adventure, 13805
Taste Maker, 12541
Taste O'Spriing, 4970
Taste of Florida, 2801
Taste of Island Legends, 857
Taste of the Hill, 10772
Taste Pleasers Gourmet, 5735
Taste Republic, 12964
Taste T Pacific Whithing, 9344
Taste the Beauty of North Idaho, 4828
Taste the Beauty of the Rockies, 4828
Taste Waves, 9237
Taste-T, 11515
Taste, 8899
Tasteboost, 4837
Tastebuds Popcorn, 12548
Tastee, 11013, 12549
Tastemorr Snacks, 1071
Tasteva Stevia Sweetener, 12561
Tasty, 3028, 8795
Tasty Bakery, 1758
Tasty Bite, 7952
Tastykake, 4529
Tata Tea, 12559
Tatangelo, 12560
Tate & Lyle, 12196
Tate's Bake Shop, 12562
Tate+Lyle, 3666
Tater Pals, 6374
Tater Tots, 9523
Tato Skins, 10173
Tavern Traditions, 7179
Taxco, 2111
Taylor Brothers Farms, 11877
Taylor Country Farms, 6858
Taylor Farms, 12567
Taylor Jane's Raspberry Ale, 4959
Taylor Shellfish, 12573
Taylor's Mexican Chili, 12575
Taza Rica Mexican Spiced Cocoa, 6654
Tazarriba, 6902
Tazo, 12042
Tazo Teas, 6928
Tbj Gourmet, 12475
Tchibo, 3714
Tdm, 8335
Tea India , 5612
Tea of Life, 421
Tea Sickles, 6787
Tea Temptations, 4055
Tea Tibet, 6948
Tea Tyme Cookies, 6821
Teacher's Highland Cream, 3024
Teacher's, 1120
Teaks, 8362
Teal Lake Winery, 10952
Tealac, 7857
Tealicious Iced Tea, 13728
Team, 10076
Team Realtree, 12920
Teapigs, 12588
Teaports, 5108
Teardrop, 2783
Tearoom, 12586
Teasdale, 12590
Tease, 6821
Teatro, 450
Teavana, 12042
Teavigo, 12498
Teays Valley, 1891
Tebay, 12592
Techni-Brew, 1636
Teddie, 7288
Teddy Grahams, 8729
Teddy's, 1478, 13196
Tee Lee, 12602
Teeccino Caffeine-Fr, 12601
Teenee Beanee, 6641
Teenies, 4976
Teeny Foods, 12603
Teese Vegan Cheese, 2550
Teixeira, 12606
Tejas Sizzle, 4375
Temo's, 12610
Tempeh, 13074
Tempo, 2943
Tempt Hemp, 6049
Temptation Ice Cream, 2550
Temptations, 7952
Ten High, 11263
Ten High Bourbon, 11264
Ten Ren's Tea, 12614
Tenaro, 8367
Tenayo, 12615
Tenda Bake, 10675
Tender Crust, 9621
Tender Flake, 7876
Tender Plus, 5643
Tender Quick, 6661
Tenderbird, 9389
Tenderflake, 7875
Tendersweet, 7161
Tennessee, 10038
Tennessee Bun, 12616
Tennessee Pride Country Sausage, 9368
Tenuta Polvaro, 652
Teperberg Winery, 10952
Tequila Rose, 8062
Tera's, 13879
Terlato Kitchen, 12619
Termamyl, 1692
Terra, 5505
Terra Alba, 343
Terra Di Seta, 10952
Terra Origin, 12624
Terrafood, 4148
Terranetti's, 12628
Terrapin, 8459
Terrapin, 8460
Terraza, 10303
Terrazas De Los Andes, 8452
Terre D'Olivier, 11864
Terry Brothers, 12634
Testamints Chewing Gum, 12639
Testamints Fruit Flavored Candy, 12639
Testamints Sour Fruit Mints, 12639
Testamints Sugar Free Mints, 12639
Testamints Sugar Mints, 12639
Testlab, 12638
Teti, 12640
Tetley Teas, 12641
Teton, 5255
Teton Glacier Vodka, 11614
Teton Waters Ranch, 12644
Tetrahop Gold, 6554
Teuscher, 2592
Teva Foods, 5141
Tex-Mex, 11883
Tex-O-Gold, 4428
Tex-Pro, 1244
Texacort, 8389
Texan Wiener, 5400
Texas, 1064
Texas Bay, 9912
Texas Beach, 12648
Texas Best, 8075
Texas Brand, 4201
Texas Chewie, 7200
Texas Chewie Pecan Praline, 7184
Texas Chili, 12649
Texas Crispers, 9523
Texas Gold, 11856
Texas Grown Red Grapefuit, 13906
Texas Hot Salt, 12660
Texas Jack's Tex-Mex, 6410
Texas Lean, 2554
Texas Longhorn, 1279
Texas One Step, 4428
Texas Pepper Works, 10701
Texas Pete, 12473
Texas Red, 12654
Texas Select, 10729
Texas Smokehouse, 6334
Texas Spice, 12656
Texas Toffee, 12659
Texas Traditions, 12660
Texican, 13085
Texite, 4430
Texjoy, 12650
Texmati, 10712
Textaid, 8804
Textra, 8804
Textrion, 4736
Textron, 1692
Textur, 8899
Textura, 13498
Tezzatac, 1861
Tgf, 13242
Tgi Friday's, 10173
Tgi Fridays Snacks, 13129
Thackrey, 12661
Thai Chef, 12499
Thai Chicken, 7273
Thai Kitchen, 8061
Thai Sauce, 5143
Thank You Pops, 5752
Thanksgiving, 12663
That's Hollywood, 5660
That's Itc, 12665
Thatcher's, 12666
Thatcher's Special Popcorn, 12666
The Algonquin Tea Co, 304
The Amazing Chickpea, 12667
The Antiquary, 13120
The Art of Broth, 12669
The Art of Shaving, 12721
The Benriach, 1784
The Big O, 8114
The Bitter Housewife, 6167
The Blue, 1120
The Bronx Hot Sauce, 11709
The Brownie Baker, 1785
The Bruss Company, 13109
The Candy Tree, 1964
The Capsule, 8888
The Carolina Cracker, 2239
The Chocolate Factory, 12349
The City Bakery, 2703
The Cloud, 1658
The Coconut Collaborative, 2830
The Coconut Cult, 7604
The Coffee, 427
The Coffee Mill, 2850
The Colorado Spice Co., 2899
The Complete Cookie, 7350
The Cookiec Dough Cafe, 12678
The Crown Restaurant Gourmet, 12546
The Curious Creamery, 8966
The Daily Crave, 8841
The Dimple, 3570
The Epic Seed, 6049
The Epicurean, 779
The Essential Baking Company, 4121
The Famous Pacific Dessert Company, 270
The Farm At Mt. Walden, 13540
The Funnel Cake Factory, 6338
The Glendronach, 1784
The Glenlivetc Single Malt, 9964
The Good Crisp Company, 12686
The Greek Gods, 5505
The Grove, 4840
The Honest Stand, 12691
The House of Flavors, 7934
The Inn, 6221
The Jackfruit Company, 6420
The Jersey Tomato Co., 12695
The Jug, 7931
The Keeper, 8824
The Lancaster Food Company, 12700
The Last Word, 13184
The Little Kernel, 12701
The Living Apothecary, 7036
The Lollipop Tree, 12703
The Maple Guild, 12706
The Margarita Man, 7903
The Matzo Project, 12708
The Mensch on a Bench, 10229
The Mint, 10689
The Muscle Brownie, 7350
The Muscle Muffin, 7350
The Naked Grape, 3834
The New Primal, 12712
The Nutra Fig, 11149
The Organic Wine Work, 5524
The Original Donut Shop, 6818
The Original Ranchc, 5489
The Osso Good Co., 9586
The Pasta Mill, 9812
The Pastry Chef, 9823
The Peanut Factory, 13742
The Peanut Roaster, 9870
The Perfect Pasta, 6320
The Perfect Pita, 12715
The Pierson Company, 4063
The Prefume Garden, 11997
The Preservatory, 13452
The Pub, 184
The Real Co, 12723
The Real Coconut, 10588
The Real Food Trading Co., 9237
The Red Plane, 56
The Reverend, 838
The Ripe Stuff, 8525
The Sadkhin Complexr, 11031
The Salsa Addiction, 7694
The Secret Garden, 11402
The Shed Barbeque & Blues Joint, 12729
The Shed Bbq Sauces & Marinades, 12729
The Shrink, 56
The Sneaky Chef, 11752
The Spice Box, 2899
The Spice Co., 2899
The Spice Hunter, 1935
The Store, 7721
The Sushi Chef, 1106
The Sweet Life, 12405
The Taste of India, 12517
The Tea Spot, 12738
The Tiny Hero, 12818
The Toasted Oat, 12739
The Truffliest, 12740
The Unbeatable Eatable Egg, 3966
The Van Cleve Seafood Co., 12742
The Vine, 12744
The Walking Dead Wine, 12937
The Water Fountain, 3469
The Water Kefir People, 12745
The Whole 9 Yards, 11083
The Whole Earth, 11748
The Wright Pils, 5314
The Yogurt Stand, 3378
Theater Ii, 10180
Thebu Kombucha, 7798
Thel-Egg, 6768
Ther Cake Loft, 13618
Thera-M Multiple, 75
Theramune Nutritonals, 420
Theraplant, 1797
Thermflo, 8804
Thermo Slim, 5897
Thermo Tropic, 5065
Thermtex, 8804
Thick N' Juicy, 1658
Thiel, 12752
Thimble, 5140
Thin 'n Trim, 9422
Thinaddictives, 9092
Think Jerkyc, 12753
Thinkthin, 12754
Thirs-Tea, 12756
Thirsty Buddha, 1825
Thirty Bench, 555
This Bar Saves Lives, 12757
This Way Jose, 9571
Thistledew Farm's, 12758
Thixogum, 9029

Brand Name Index

Thixx, 1244
Thomas, 892, 12763, 12765, 12769
Thomas Brothers Country Ham, 12761
Thomas Fogarty Winery, 12764
Thomas Kemper, 10404
Thomas Kemper Birch Soda, 12766
Thomas Kemper Cola, 12766
Thomas Kemper Cream, 12766
Thomas Kruse Winey, 12767
Thomas', 1359
Thomasson's, 6589
Thomasson's Potato Chips, 6589
Thompson's Black Tie, 12772
Thomy, 8945
Thor's, 12775
Thornton, 12777
Thorpe Vineyard, 12778
Thousand Flowers, 5989
Thousand Steps Stout, 7143
Three Bold Brothers, 10976
Three Herb Ranch, 5489
Three Jerks, 12782
Three Star, 9766
Three Trees, 12787
Three-Pin Pale Ale, 4466
Threeworks, 12789
Thrift, 13565
Thrift-T-Pak, 9839
Thrifty Bee, 1040
Thrifty Maid, 13864
Thrifty Pak, 7363
Thrive, 5090
Throat Control Spray, 9201
Throughbred, 2688
Thumann's, 12791
Thunder 101, 9773
Thunder Hole Ale, 1015
Thunder McCloud, 353
Thunderbird, 12792
Thunderhead Stout, 8602
Thyme & Truffles, 12793
Tia Anita, 6619
Tia Rosa, 1359
Tib, 7409
Tic Tac, 4348
Tichon, 12796
Tick Stop, 5683
Ticolino, 11454
Tide, 12721
Tidepoint, 13770
Tierra Farm, 12798
Tiesta Tea, 12799
Tietolin, 4430
Tifert Aromatherapy, 7562
Tiffany Bagged Candy, 4884
Tiger, 12800, 12801
Tiger Balm Analgesic Oitments, 10307
Tiger Brand, 4386
Tiger Pepper, 12987
Tiger Tea, 5654
Tiger's Milk, 11285
Tiggly Wiggly, 8404
Tigo+, 12802
Tilapia, 13586
Tilda, 5505
Tilenus, 3545
Tilex, 2766
Tillamook, 12304, 12804
Tillamook Country Smoker, 3896, 12803
Timber Crest Farm, 12809
Timber Trails, 12866
Timothy's, 6818
Tin Star Foods, 12813
Tina's Las Campanas, 2111
Tiny But Mighty Popcorn, 12817
Tiny Tarts, 12547
Tiny Twists, 9408
Tio Franco, 5987
Tio Gazpacho, 12819
Tio Jorge, 7702
Tio Pepe Winery, 10952
Tio Pepe's Churros, 6338
Tio Tio, 11065, 11187
Tio Tio, 11186
Tip Top, 9291, 12569
Tip Top, 4552
Tippy Toes, 12885
Tisdale Vineyards, 3834
Tita's, 7907
Titanic Esm Mints, 11028
Titora Winery, 10952
Titusville Dairy Products, 12826

Tj Toad, 1423
Tk Tomer Kosher, 12861
Tkc Vineyards, 12827
Tnp - Toasted Natural Sesame Seeds, 11462
Tnt Chocolate, 13728
To-Rico's, 10056
Toad Sweat, 9941
Toast'em, 11311
Toasta Ma-Me, 5376
Toasted Buckwheat, 4362
Toasted Chips, 8729
Toasted Head, 13425
Toastin, 10600
Tobikko, 857
Toblerone, 8474
Today, 1636
Today's Tamales, 9502
Todd's, 12481
Todd's Salsa, 12832
Todd's Treats, 12831
Toddy, 6484, 12833
Toddy Cappuccino, 12833
Toddy Coffee Crunch, 12833
Toddy Coffee Maker, 12833
Toddy Gourmet Iced Tea Concentrate, 12833
Toddy Mocha, 12833
Toe-Rific Candy, 12836
Toffarassi, 3311
Toffifay, 12148
Toffifee, 12147
Tofu Burger Mix, 4252
Tofu Cream Chie, 13088
Tofu Lin, 9160
Tofu Pudding, 13088
Tofu Pups, 7427
Tofu Scrambler Mix, 4252
Tofu Shop, 12841
Tofurky, 9502, 13073, 13074
Tofutti, 12843
Tofutti Better Than Cheesecake, 12843
Toki, 12315
Toleftar Pilfen, 7310
Tolerant, 7709
Tolibia, 11777
Tom Cat Bakery, 12848
Tom Moore, 11263, 11264
Tom Ringhausen, 12850
Tom Sturgis, 10693
Tom Sturgis Pretzels, 12851
Tom's, 11770, 12854
Tom-Tom, 13193
Toma, 9972
Tomales Bay, 10435
Tomasello Winery, 12859
Tomatin, 13120
Tomato Magic, 12030
Tomato Max, 10297
Tombstone, 10435
Tombstone, 8945
Tomintoul, 10952
Tomislav, 8459
Tonalin, 1692
Tone's, 864
Tony Chachere's Orig, 12869
Tony Packo's, 9566
Tony's, 11316
Tony's Chocolonely, 12872
Tony's Seafood, 7580
Tony's, 11317
Tony'sc, 12874
Too Cool Chix, 12877
Toom, 12879
Tootsie Roll, 12880
Top, 13052
Top - the Oil Plant, 4854
Top Bakes, 12231
Top Banana, 100
Top Care, 11303
Top Care, 1758, 12885
Top Chews, 13109
Top Dogs, 7876
Top Hat, 7767
Top Hat Dessert Sauces, 12881
Top Kut, 8114
Top N Go, 4741
Top Notch, 340
Top Ramen, 9068
Top Sail Amber, 1208
Topaz, 1196, 9069
Topcare, 13864
Topiary Toffee, 5578

Topo Chico, 12886
Topolos At Russian River Vine, 12887
Toppik, 2666
Toptex, 6340
Torani, 10485
Torani Syrups, 6928
Torke, 12891
Torkelson Cheese Co., 12892
Tornado Malt Liquor, 9137
Tornados, 10976
Tornatore, 3834
Toro, 4232
Toro Safron, 12987
Torrefazione Italia, 12897
Torrefazione Italia Coffee, 12042
Torreo, 12898
Tortiyahs!, 13129
Toscal, 2815
Toscano Style, 9635
Toshimi, 11339
Tost, 12482
Tostada, 7553
Tostados, 5122
Tostitos, 4741
Tostitos, 9945
Total Fit, 8635
Total Man, 4127
Total Woman, 4127
Total, 4947
Totally Chocolate, 12900
Totally Egg, 3540
Tote 'ems, 4255
Totino's, 4947
Toto's Gourmet Products, 7821
Tott's, 3834
Toucan, 10134
Touchdown Nuggets, 1654
Tour Eiffel, 2426
Tout Fini Cocktail Mixes, 4650
Tova, 12906
Tova's Best, 1802
Tovli, 1251
Tower Dark Ale, 11448
Towie, 5288
Town & Country, 11639
Town House, 6766
Town Tavern, 9403
Townsend, 6352
Toxic Tommy, 12863
Toy Bus Animal Crackers, 3343
Toy Story, 4507
Tpp Tarts Kids Kandy, 2135
Tracey's, 2384
Tractor Shed Red, 13049
Trade Winds Coffee, 12915
Trademark Pale Ale, 1687
Trader Joe's, 9116
Trader Vic's, 12912
Trader Vics , 13120
Tradewinds, 8613
Tradition, 6395
Traditional, 6374
Traditional Kentucky, 9417
Traditional Lager, 11218
Traditional Med Ginger Energy, 12918
Traditional Med Gypsy Cold Cure, 12918
Traditional Med Organics, 12918
Traditional Stir Fry Sauce, 5143
Trafalgar, 12919
Trail's Best Snacks, 12920
Trailhead, 13643
Trancendim, 463
Transocean, 12925
Traou Mad, 7499
Trappey's, 12930
Trappey's, 864
Trappist, 12931
Trattoria, 12030
Trave Amaretto, 3545
Trave Amaretto - Decanter, 3545
Travel Well, 9201
Traverse Bay Fruit Co, 2518
Tre Cafe, 13444
Tre Stelle, 678, 787
Tre Vini Rossi, 229
Tre' Limone, 2742
Treasure, 12769
Treasure Bay, 5430
Treasure Cave, 11209, 11211
Treasure Chest Shrimp, 1916
Treasure Island, 9693
Treasure Pak, 6081

Treat, 916, 12938
Treat-Up, 54
Treattarome, 12940
Trebor, 1982
Tree of Life, 8898
Tree Ripe, 2519, 6545
Tree Top, 9469, 12942
Tree-Ripe, 12941
Treehouse Farms, 12944
Treehouse Private Brands, 12943
Treemont Farms, 3574
Treesweet, 9167
Treesweet Products, 12945
Trefethen Vineyards, 12946
Trega, 12947
Trentadue, 12950
Treo, 12953
Tres Cremas, 10267
Tres Generaciones, 3024
Tres Generaciones, 1120
Tres Riches, 10714
Tres Toffee, 11775
Trescerro, 11504
Trestle Creek, 5057
Tri Dragon, 13423
Tri Our, 11759
Tri-Motor, 7209
Tri-Sign, 12957
Tribal, 608
Tribali Foods, 12963
Trident, 8474, 9995
Trident, 12968
Trifoglio, 10860
Trigal Dorado, 955
Triggi, 11668
Trigo Labs, 8861
Trigone, 312
Trim & Firm Am/Pm, 4127
Trim Maxx, 1532
Trim-Lite, 7671
Trimalta, 2338
Trimino, 7036
Trimma, 3753
Trimspa, 5095
Trinkets, 11330
Trio of Cheesecake, 2881
Triple, 12153
Triple Berry Blast Frozen Batter, 951
Triple Chocolate Cake, 2881
Triple Cream Sherry, 10554
Triple Crown Whiskey, 8062
Triple H, 12978
Triple Leaf Tea, 12980
Triple Sec, 3545, 5861, 9773
Triple Springs Spring Water, 12982
Triple Xxx, 12984
Tripper, 12987
Triscuit, 8474, 8729
Triton Water, 258
Triumph, 11909
Trius Winery, 555
Trix, 4947
Trojan, 2666
Trokote, 833
Troll, 9106
Trolli, 1417, 4345
Trolls, 10229
Trop50, 13012
Trophic, 1467
Trophy Gold Nut Barrel, 12992
Trophy Nut, 12992
Tropi-Kool Smoothies, 5819
Tropic, 9356
Tropic Beach, 11339
Tropic D'Lite, 3144
Tropic Isle, 12520
Tropic Seafood, 1140
Tropical, 253, 11001, 12996
Tropical AnAi, 12994
Tropical Blends, 8919
Tropical Chile Co, 4894
Tropical Chips, 100
Tropical Coffee, 1601
Tropical Grove, 56
Tropical Honey Glace, 11775
Tropical Illusions, 13005
Tropical Mist, 7363
Tropical Pepper, 1484
Tropical Pleasure, 4521
Tropical Royal, 5362
Tropical Source, 2772
Tropical Source Dairy-Free Gourmet, 2772

1305

Brand Name Index

Tropical Source Organic, 2772
Tropical Wonders, 6926
Tropicana, 7213, 13012
Tropicana Essentials, 13012
Tropicana Kids, 13012
Tropicana Twister, 13012
Tropicana, 9945
Tropics, 6159
Troubadour Artisan Breads, 2874
Trout Lake Farm, 13015
Trout Slayer Ale, 1344
Trout Town, 12725
Troy's, 3956
Troys, 13892
Tru Blu, 122
Tru Chocolatec, 13020
Truchard Vineyards, 13027
Truckee River, 13028
True Beverages, 13030
True Blue, 1015, 3942
True Chews, 13109
True Citrus, 3574
True Fruit, 4394
True Gold, 10600
True Jerky, 13032
True Lemon, 12201
True Measures Baking Nuts, 12992
True Nopal, 13033
True North, 864
True Organic, 13034
True Recipe, 6374
True Story Foods, 13035
Truffini, 1733
Truffle Babies, 2903
Trufflecots, 3625
Truffles To Go, 5497
Trufru, 13021
Truitt Bros., 13038
Truly, 1592
Truly Dutch, 1385
Truly Radient, 2666
Truman's, 393
Trumoo, 3442, 7320
Trumoo Chocolate Milk, 388
Truroots, 6380
Truth Bar, 13041
Truth In Snacks, 8163
Truvibe, 13025
Try Me Sauces/Seasonings, 10657
Tsar Nicoulai Caviar, 13042
Tu Me, 13043
Tualatin Estate, 13044
Tubby, 9219
Tubes, 14017
Tucher, 1361
Tucker, 13045
Tucker's Cove, 8256, 11356
Tucson Blonde, 4959
Tucson Tamale, 13048
Tuesday Toffee, 2947
Tularosa Wines, 13051
Tuldy's, 12646
Tulelake, 1141
Tulip, 2251
Tulip Street Bakery, 1524
Tulip Winery, 10952
Tulkoff, 13052
Tullamore Dew, 3024
Tully's Coffe, 6818
Tumaro's, 1484
Tumbadorc Chocolate, 13056
Tummytreats, 12928
Tundra, 13059
Tung Hai, 9265
Tuny, 12823
Tuong Ot Sriracha, 10608
Turano, 13060
Turbodog, 125
Turkey, 7318
Turkey Creek, 13063
Turkey Hill, 13064, 13065
Turning Leaf, 3834
Turris, 13072
Turrisin, 898
Turtlerazzi, 3311
Turveda, 13076
Tuscan, 13145
Tuscan Hills, 10211
Tuscan Traditions Organic, 5029
Tuscan Traditions Premium, 5029
Tuscan, 3442
Tuscarora Organic, 13080

Tuthilltown, 13082
Tutti Gourmet, 13083
Tuttorosso, 10608
Tutus, 1812
Tuxedo, 6267
Twang, 13085
Tweety, 11552
Tweety Pops, 11552
Twin Bing, 9722
Twin Harbors, 11352
Twin Lake, 6537
Twin Marquis, 13094
Twinkies, 6013
Twinlab Bariatric Support, 13097
Twinlab Fuel, 13097
Twinlab Nutrition, 13097
Twist of Fate Bitter Ale, 8524
Twist Pops, 6780
Twisted Brand, 10251
Twisted Peaks, 5819
Twisted Tea, 1592
Twistix, 6780
Twisty Punch, 469
Twix, 8533
Twix, 7952
Twizzlers, 5818
Two Chefs on a Roll, 13098
Two Fingers Tequilas, 5720
Two Friends, 13101
Two Sicily's, 1282
Two Stars, 11263
Tyee, 13106
Tyrconnell, 1120
Tyskie Gronie, 8460
Tysom, 11504
Tyson, 11053
Tyson, 4061, 13109
Tzuba Winery, 10952

U

U-Bake, 4025
U-Don, 13560
U-Noc, 583
U.F.O., 5606
U.S. Brand, 13119
U.S. Zinc Votorantim Metals, 1692
Uas Activin Plus, 13130
Uas Coenzyme Q10, 13130
Uas Joint Formula, 13130
Ucii, 6236
Udderly Delightful, 7435
Udf, 13185
Udon, 11773
Udupi, 3465
Uggly Cake, 12428
Uglies, 3592
Ugly Dog Stout, 3519
Ugly Nut, 12394
Uinta, 13136
Ukraine: Chumak, Nektar, 5108
Ukrop, 8404
Ullr Nordic Libation, 5981
Ultima, 13137
Ultimate, 5017, 13140, 13906
Ultimate Apple, 7524
Ultimate Bartender, 2799
Ultimate Biscotti, 13139
Ultimate Confections, 13142
Ultimate Food Complex, 665
Ultimate Petite Pretzels, 2133
Ultimate Pretzel, 2133
Ultimate Pretzel Rods, 2133
Ultimate Pretzel Sculptures, 2133
Ultra Create, 8804
Ultra Dark Rondo Kosher, 8677
Ultra Rain Glandulars, 13146
Ultra Slim, 5897
Ultra Thin, 11228
Ultra'cream, 8815
Ultra-Crisp, 8804
Ultra-Pure Bestate, 5665
Ultra-Sperse, 8804
Ultra-Tex, 8804
Ultrabond, 6211
Ultraclear, 12426
Ultragrain Tortillas, 855
Ultraguar, 9654
Ultralac, 5665
Umc, 13194
Umcka Coldcare, 8896

Umpqua Oats, 13150
Un-Fad Diet Packs, 7947
Un-Soap, 9238
Uncle Bens, 7952
Uncle Dave's, 5105
Uncle Dougie's, 13154
Uncle Fred's Fine Foods, 13155
Uncle John's Pride, 3177
Uncle Lee's Tea, 13156
Uncle Luke's, 7037
Uncle Matt's Organic, 13157
Uncle Matt's, 3442
Uncle Phil's, 13880
Uncle Ralph's, 13158
Uncle Sam Cereal, 13124
Uncle Walter's, 4556
Uncle Waynes Fish Batter, 5946
Unclerays, 13159
Uncut Before the Butcher, 6492
Underberg Bitters, 9035
Underwood, 13174
Underwood, 864
Unearthed, 7526
Ungar's, 3727
Unholey Bagel, 11043
Uni, 1934
Unibrew, 13164
Unibroue, 13164
Unica, 9980, 13165
Unico, 13191
Unicorn Pops, 163
Unicum Zwack, 3165
Unidex, 6211
Unipro, 1891, 8193
Unique, 13178
Unique Belgique, 10981
Unique Colonic Rinse, 13179
Unique Ingredients, 13177
Unique Pretzels, 972
United, 13196
United Brand, 13196
United Society of Shakers, 11498
United With Earth, 13203
Unna, 13212
Unreal, 13151
Unsteak-Out, 9196
Unturkey, 9196
Unwrap & Roll, 1174
Up Country Naturals, 7866
Up Mountain Switchel, 13213
Upco, 13196
Upper Bay, 865
Upper Crust Biscotti, 13216
Upper Fingers, 1018
Upstate Farms, 13218
Uptime, 13219
Upton's Naturals, 13220
Upzo, 13196
Urban Bruce, 1796
Urban Delights, 11818
Urban Foods, 13223
Urban Moonshine, 13224
Urban Nomad Food, 6831
Urban Pie Pizza Co., 9719
Urban Special, 648
Urgasa, 13226
Urge, 2815
Uribel, 8389
Urockit-K, 8389
Us Cola, 883
Us Select, 883
Us Sugars, 13125
Usa, 5660
Usa Best, 13128
Usa Beverages, 13127
Usa Laboratories Nutrients, 13128
Usa Mints, 11051
Usa Sports Labs, 13128
Usg, 1692
Ustenborg, 10906
Utc, 3479
Utility, 2389
Utira-C, 8389
Utopia, 12762
Utzy Naturals, 13230
Uvaferm, 7176
Uvvw Decaff, 2854

V

V&V Supremo Cheeses & Meats, 7407

V.G. Blue, 13303
V.Pearl, 4947
V.W. Joyner Genuine Smithfield, 13237
V8, 2115
V8 Beverages, 2116
V8 Splash, 2115, 3773
V8 Vgo, 2115
Vachon, 2121
Vahine, 8061
Val Verde Winery, 13245
Valamont, 8794
Valbreso Feta, 7126
Valdiguie, 5989
Valentine Sugars, 13248
Valentino, 5405
Valerian, 746
Valerian Extract, 9253
Valhalla Winery, 13250
Valley, 9594, 11312
Valley Bakery, 13256
Valley Dairy, 4227
Valley Farms, 13218
Valley Fresh, 6000
Valley Gold, 2688
Valley King, 5517
Valley Lahvosh Crackerbread, 13256
Valley Lahvosh Flatbread, 13256
Valley Maid, 916, 10439
Valley of the Moon, 13267
Valley Pokt, 6221
Valley Queen, 13260
Valley Sun Organic Brown Rice, 4260
Valley View, 13266
Valley View Blueberries, 13263
Valley View Cheese, 13264
Valley Wraps, 13256
Valoroso, 12030
Valpo Velvet, 12741
Valrhona, 13251
Valu Time, 1758, 12885
Valu-Fil, 343
Value Corner, 11073
Value Glacier, 3218
Valutime, 11303, 13864
Van Asperen Vineyard, 10912
Van De Kamp, 13282
Van De Kamp's, 811
Van De Walle Farms, 11135
Van Der Heyden, 13269
Van Dierman, 1524
Van Drunen Farms, 13270
Van Holten, 6353
Van Houten Drinks, 1056
Van Houten Professional, 1056
Van Houtte, 6818
Van Otis Swiss Fudge, 13277
Van Roy, 13279
Van Tone, 13280
Van Waters & Roger, 13281
Van Winkle, 11263
Van's, 13283
Van-Lang, 13284
Vana Life Foods, 13285
Vanaleigh 6b, 12085
Vance's Darifree, 13286
Vancouver Islander Lager, 13288
Vandon Sea-Pack, 2659
Vangogh, 10906
Vanilla Imperial, 1581
Vanish, 10598
Vanleer, 1056
Vanmark, 13293
Vantaggio, 11777
Vantaggio D'Oro, 11777
Varietals, 11777
Vascustrem, 13179
Vassi Espresso, 6547
Vassilaros, 6547
Vat 69, 3570
Vatore's, 13318
Vaughn Russell, 13302
Vaxa, 13304
Vaxa, 9237
Vbm, 5036
Vbz, 13421
Vector, 6765
Vee Gee, 13498
Veet, 10598
Veg Con Beet, 4518
Veg Con Carrot, 4518
Veg Con Celery, 4518
Veg Fresh, 10491

Brand Name Index

Veg-A-Fed, 2576
Veg-A-Loid, 2386
Veg-T-Balls, 13315
Vega, 3379
Vega Fina, 10110
Vega Metias, 10110
Vega's Gourmet, 13306
Vegalene, 9648
Vegan Decadence, 4668
Vegan Gourmet, 3870
Vegan Rob's, 11484
Vegapure, 1692
Vege-Coat, 4914
Vegeful, 8448
Vegenaise, 3870
Vegetaballs, 13073
Vegetable Cocktail, 5555
Vegetable Magic, 7766
Vegetarian Cornmeal, 13305
Vegetarian Plusc, 13310
Vegetarian Slice of Life, 13316
Vegetarian Tamale, 13305
Vegetrates, 4063
Veggemo, 5064
Veggiballs, 4664
Veggiburger, 4664
Veggidogs, 4664
Veggie Fries, 4295, 5697
Veggie Glace Gold, 8538
Veggie Grownto, 10100
Veggie Ribs, 5629
Veggie Rings, 4295
Veggie Tots, 4295
Veggie-Deli Slices, 5358
Veggie-Deli, 5358
Veggie-DeliQuick Stick, 5358
Veggie-Go's, 12711
Veggie-Jerky, 5358
Veggieland, 13315
Veggimins, 13847
Vegginuggets, 4664
Vegit, 8448
Veglife, 9237
Vegolin Hvp, 4430
Vegy Vida, 13317
Veko, 13232
Velda, 13319
Vella, 13320
Velletric, 2010
Velvatex, 13498
Velveeta, 6976, 6977
Velvet Creme, 13321
Velvetop, 3412
Velvetx, 13803
Vemon Energy, 3725
Venezia, 4992
Venice Maid Products, 805
Ventana Wines, 13325
Venture For the Best, 13329
Venus, 6540, 12721
Venus Wafers, 13330
Ver-Mex, 2670
Vera Cruz Mexican Foods, 8898
Veramonte, 4649
Verdaccio, 12437
Verdant Kitchen, 13333
Verday, 13334
Verde, 11883
Verde Farms, 13335
Verdecoat, 7857
Verdegrass, 5663
Verdi Line, 6340
Verifine, 4185
Verisoyc, 13310
Verlasso, 13341
Vermilion, 13342
Vermont, 13343
Vermont Maid, 864
Vermont Meadow Muffins, 12847
Vermont Pasture Patties, 12847
Vermont Pure Water, 3217
Vermont Sprout, 12732
Vermont Sugar Free, 7866
Vermont Tortilla, 13362
Vermont Velvet, 10696
Vernaccia, 13375
Vernon Bc, 2301
Vernors, 3725, 6818
Veronique, 9555
Versatrol, 1009
Versilac, 98
Very Old Barton, 11263

Very Old Barton Bourbon, 11264
Veryfine, 12281
Veryfine Juices, 13368
Vess, 10637
Vetter Vineyards, 13371
Veuve Clicquot, 8452
Veuve Cliquot, 3570
Veza Sur Brewing Co., 571
Vg Buck California Foods, 2085
Via Roma, 2847
Viader, 13373
Viaggio Coffee, 1636
Viaka, 8062
Viano Winery, 13374
Vic's, 13377
Vicality Albafil, 1692
Vicenzi, 6255
Vichy, 9995
Vichy Springs, 13378
Vichy Springs Mineral Water, 13378
Vickey's Vittles, 13379
Vicki's Rocky Road, 8240
Vicky's All Natural, 13380
Vicks, 12721
Vicron, 1692
Victor, 13384
Victor's, 6160
Victoria, 71, 13388
Victoria Creams, 10840
Victoria E.S.B., 7143
Victoria Fancy, 13387
Victoria Lager, 13288
Victoria, 864
Vida, 9964
Vidalia, 13393
Vidalia Sweets, 13394
Vidarome, 13444
Video Munchies, 10179
Videri Chocolate Factory, 13395
Videx, 1721
Videyards, 3952
Vie De France, 1891
Vienna, 13398, 13401
Vienna Bageldog, 10040
Vienna Lager, 1139
Vienna, 13400
Vienot, 12672
Vietti, 13402
Vigne Regali, 1006
Vigo, 13404
Vigorsol, 9956
Vigorteen, 1151
Viki's Granola, 13409
Viking, 9094, 13407, 13516
Viking, 5844
Vilas Del Turbon, 2815
Villa Cape Winery, 10952
Villa Frizzoni, 11504
Villa Helena, 13412
Villa Lan Franca, 11205
Villa Mella, 2670
Villa Milan, 13413
Villa Prima, 11317
Villa Prime Pizzeria, 11316
Villa Quenchers, 6867
Villaformosa, 3545
Village, 7463
Village Hearth, 9736
Village Roaster, 13415
Villaggio, 2121
Villar Vintners, 13416
Vimco, 10558
Vin Eclipser, 8513
Vin Vault, 3834
Vinatopia, 5524
Vincenza's, 11224
Vincenzo's, 8770
Vincotto, 3236
Vine Series, 9452
Vineco, 555
Vinegar Joe, 10196
Vinitrox, 9029
Vinmar, 6460
Vino De Pata, 10165
Vinoklet, 13429
Vinta, 3384
Vintage, 3661, 10637
Vintage Port, 942
Vinter's Choice, 1080
Vintnercel, 11794
Vio, 2815
Vio Bio Limo, 2815

Viobin, 13435
Viognier, 2044, 6603, 12534
Viognier Santa Barbara County, 4353
Viola's, 13436
Violet, 13437
Violife, 13438
Vip, 13240, 13241
Vip, 237, 238
Viper, 11051
Viper Blast, 11051
Viper Gum, 11051
Viper Venom, 11051
Viper Vials, 11051
Virgil's, 13439
Virgil's Root Beers, 10507
Virginia, 2075
Virginia Artesianc, 13442
Virginia Beauty, 5752
Virginia Brand, 13446, 13454
Virginia Diner, 13445
Virginia Gentleman, 59
Virginia Gentlemen, 11263
Virginia Roast, 4239
Virginia Smoked Sausage, 12463
Virility Plus, 9253
Virture Cider, 571
Viscol, 10158
Viscomix, 13498
Viscozyme L, 1692
Vision, 3948
Visionary Vinegars, 982
Vista D'Oro, 13452
Vista Verde, 1306
Vista Verde, 11504
Vit-A-Boost, 7947
Vit20, 10637
Vita, 4822, 4942, 13454, 13473
Vita Brand, 13446
Vita Coco, 6818
Vita Plus, 1735
Vita Splash, 12182
Vita-Crunch, 9548
Vita-Curaid, 4430
Vita-Ex, 6340
Vita-Fresh, 2032
Vita-Most, 2032
Vita-Plus, 13455
Vita-Sealed, 8628
Vita-Vista, 13943
Vitaball, 6107
Vitabrownies, 13464
Vitacakes, 13464
Vitafusion, 2666
Vital Cuisine, 6000
Vital Farmsc, 13461
Vital K, 4807
Vital Life, 6905
Vital Proteins, 13462
Vitalert, 9957
Vitalfa, 12638
Vitaline Coq10, 4086
Vitality Works, 13466
Vitamin Classics, 4888
Vitamin Water, 2811, 4066
Vitaminerals, 13469
Vitamite, 3593
Vitamixes, 13464
Vitamuffins, 13464
Vitanat, 7172
Vitaphos, 4430
Vitarich, 13471
Vitaspelt, 8886
Vitatops, 13464
Vito's Bakery, 6410
Vittles, 14043
Viva, 2815, 8105
Viva Lard, 2796
Viva Manteca Mixta, 2796
Viva Retail Lard, 2796
Vivani, 6279
Vivant, 3384
Vive Organic, 13478
Vivident, 9956
Vivienne, 13479
Viviscal, 2666
Vivolac, 7668, 13480
Vivoo, 13481
Vivrac, 13482
Vivre Dans La Nuit, 56
Vivre Une Double Vie, 56
Vixen Kitchen, 13483

Vlaha, 6986
Vocatura, 13484
Vod, 13243
Vodka Nikolai, 3545
Vogel, 2935
Voget Meats, 13486
Vogue Beef Base, 13487
Vogue Chicken Base, 13487
Vogue Onion Base, 13487
Vogue Vegebase, 13487
Vogue Vegetarian Chicken Base, 13487
Volcano Wings, 3511
Volpi, 13490
Volpi Foods, 6560
Volvic, 1661
Von Strasser, 13492
Voortman, 13494
Voss Water, 5884
Vox, 1120
Vratislav, 8459
Vynecrest Vineyards, 13497

W

W&G's, 13499
W-R, 2389
W.E.M., 13810
W.L. Weller, 11263
Wachusett, 13522, 13523
Wack-O-Wax, 12880
Wacker, 1692
Wacky Mac, 10777
Wafa, 9863
Wafflewaffle, 13525
Wagner Brewing Co., 13529
Wagner Vineyards, 13529
Wagshal's, 13530
Wah Maker, 9439
Wahoo! Appetizers, 5294
Wai Lana, 13532
Waiker Conveyor Belt & Equipment, 2436
Waist Watcher, 174, 10151
Wakasa, 12228
Wakefield, 13120
Walden Farms, 13538, 13539
Waldo, 10229
Walker's, 13544
Walkers, 13544
Wallabeans, 7912
Wallaby, 13546
Wallaby Organic, 3379
Wallace, 5888
Wallingford, 13551
Walls Berry Farm Organic Preserves, 12921
Walls Berry Farm Preserves, 12921
Wally Biscotti, 13552
Wally Walleye, 1018
Wally's, 10869
Walmart, 11260
Walnut Acres, 5505
Walnut Crest, 1006
Wals Brut, 71
Waltham, 7952
Wampler's Farm, 13559
Wan Ja Shan, 7836
Wan-Na-Bes, 11552
Wanchai Ferry, 4947
Wanda's, 5711
Wandering Bear Coffee, 13563
Wanderoot, 8459
Wanko, 1120
Warfarers, 3953
Warheads, 6483
Warhol, 10229
Warme Bakker, 3078
Warner Vineyards, 13570
Warp Energy Mints, 1343
Warp Micro Hyper Charged Mints, 1343
Warren's Wonderful W, 9688
Warrnambool Cheese and Butter, 11211
Warwick Distillery, 13578
Warwick Winery, 13578
Wasatch, 11289
Wasbash Heritage, 13517
Wasbash Valley Farm, 10180
Washburn, 4198
Washington, 13803
Washington Natural, 9469
Wasson, 13584
Water & Health, 3469
Water Crackers, 3384

1307

Brand Name Index

Water Drops, 12430
Water Fountain of Edenton, 3469
Water Joe, 13585
Water Maid, 10777
Water Valley Farms, 11639
Waterfall, 11138
Waterfield Farms, 13586
Waterfrontbistro, 11073
Waterloo Dark, 1702
Waterpik, 2666
Watersboten, 11038
Watertyme, 1292
Watson Fine Teas, 1045
Wattie's, 6977
Watts Island Trading, 1470
Watusee Foods, 13593
Wave Flavored Vodkas, 11264
Wave'n Dry, 13595
Waves, 13614
Wawona Frozen Foods, 13598
Wax Orchards, 13599
Way Better Snacks, 13600
Wayne, 9584
Wayne Farms, 2970, 11053
Wayne Farms, 13607
Wayne Gretzky Estates, 555
Wber Seasonings, 73
Wbm, 13510
We Rub You, 13608
We're Talking Serious Salsa, 4587
Weat, 7310
Weaver, 2126, 4387
Weaver Original, 13611
Weaver's, 10486
Webb's, 13613
Weber's Horseradish Mustard, 5734
Weber's Hot Garlic M, 5734
Weber's Hot Piocacic, 5734
Weber's Spicy Dill Pickles, 5734
Weber's Sweet Pickle, 5734
Weber, 864
Wecobee Fs, 12081
Wecobee M, 12081
Wecobee S, 12081
Wee Heavy Winter Ale, 5515
Wee Willy, 7157
Weetabix, 1020, 13621
Wege, 1310, 13622
Wegmans Gluten Free, 13624
Wegmans Organic, 13624
Wei-Chaun, 13625
Wei-Chuan, 13625
Weigh Down, 7404
Weight Watchers Smart Ones, 6977
Weight Watchers Baked Goods, 3412
Weihnachtskatze, 339
Weiloss, 7758
Weingut Wittman, 4677
Weinstock Wine Cellars, 10952
Weir's, 730
Weis, 6126
Weis Five Star, 13512
Weis Quality, 13512
Weiser River Whoppers, 13630
Weiss, 7310
Welch's, 5694, 13635
Welch's Chillers, 8797
Welch's Concentrates, 8797
Welch's Essentials, 8797
Welch's Food & Snacks, 8797
Welch's Fruit Fizz, 8797
Welch's Fruit Juices, 8797
Welch's Jams, Jellie & Spreads, 8797
Welch's Light, 8797
Welch's Natural Spreads, 8797
Welch's Refrigerted Juice Cocktails, 8797
Welch's Sparkling, 8797
Welch's, 6483
Welchs, 4659
Welcome, 13637
Weldon, 2923
Well Seasoned Traveler, 194
Well Yes, 2116
Well's Ace, 10076
Wella Bar, 13641
Weller Bourbon, 3570
Wellesley, 68
Wellesse, 13642
Wellfleet Farms, 9355
Wellfleet Farms Cranberry Sauce, 9355
Wellfleet Farms Specialty Foods, 9355
Wellgate, 2666

Wellington Foods, 13644
Wellmade Honey, 13114
Wellness Drops, 9201
Welsh Farms, 4290
Welsh Farms - Ice Cream, 13647
Wenatchee Gold, 2560
Wenatchee Valley, 5826
Wendaphos, 13648
Wendy, 8956
Wenk, 13652
Wenner, 13653
Wensleydale Blueberry, 11968
Wente, 13654
Werther's Original, 12147, 12148
Wesson, 6084
West Bend, 4538
West Indian Kola, 5177
West Island, 6119
West Pak, 13666
West's Best, 12758
Westbrae Natural, 5505, 13672
Westco, 955, 13675
Western, 13677
Western Beauty, 965
Western Classics, 12276
Western Creamery, 13680
Western Family, 3387, 9469, 12304
Western Gold, 6267
Western Style Soft Drinks, 13728
Western Syrup, 13686
Westhampton Farms, 9000
Weston, 13691
Westpac, 8724
Westport Farms Sparkling, 13693
Westport Farms Specialty Foods, 13693
Westport Farms White & Rose, 13693
Westport Rivers Vine, 13693
Westsoy, 5505, 13672
Westwood Winery, 13696
Wetherby, 13698
Weyauwega, 13700
Wha Guru Chew, 9245
Whale's Tale, 2691
Whale-Of-A-Pail, 11725
Whaler Vineyard Flag, 13701
Whaley's, 13702
Whaley's Fancy Shelled, 13702
What's For Dinner?, 12467
Whatchamacallit, 5818
Wheat Nuts, 525
Wheat Thins, 8729
Wheat-Free, 9730
Wheatbrook, 10629
Wheateena, 12269
Wheatena, 6267
Wheaties, 4947
Wheatstone, 13707
Wheatsworth, 8729
Wheeler's, 6195
Whetstone Candy, 13708
Whetstone Valley, 11287
Which Ends, 6787
Whidbey's, 10468
Whip N Ice, 4483
Whip N Top, 4483
Whipped Pastry Boutique, 13709
Whirley Pop, 10180
Whiskas, 7952
Whiskey Run, 1123
Whisper Chocolate Bon Bons, 643
Whisper White, 9069
Whistle, 7952
Whitcraft Winery, 13713
White Buffalo, 1837
White Camel, 13714
White Cap, 1464
White Cap, 13328
White Castle, 13551
White Chocolate Moose, 9115
White Dove, 13118
White Horse, 3570
White House, 13717, 13720
White Label Yerba Mate Soda, 13721
White Lightning, 5861
White Mountain, 9664
White Oak Chardonnay, 13725
White Oak Farm and Tablec, 13722
White Oak Merlot, 13725
White Oak Sauvignon, 13725
White Oak, 11725
White Premium, 7583
White Rabbit, 10457

White Rascal, 838
White Riesling, 1314
White Rock, 1061, 13728
White Rock Orchards, 13728
White Rock Vineyards, 13729
White Satin, 407
White Stevia, 9201
White Swan, 5288, 9763
White Tiger Rice, 7723
White Wave, 3009
White Wings, 1917
Whitecliff, 13735
Whitefish, 5323
Whitehall, 13737
Whitehall Lane, 13736
Whitehaven, 3834
Whitehouse Foods, 8796
Whitewater, 5304
Whitey's, 237, 238
Whitford, 13741
Whitman's, 10991
Whitney Distributing, 10820
Whitney Yogurt, 13744
Whol-Bean, 13614
Whole Body Cleanse, 4086
Whole Earth, 10488
Whole Spectrum, 4125
Whole Sun, 7569
Wholefruit, 6338
Wholemec, 13749
Wholesome, 8951
Wholesome Foods, 13751
Wholesome Goat, 11211
Wholly Guacamole, 6000
Wholly Wholesome, 10981
Whoppers, 5818
Wick Fowler Chili Kits, 10657
Wick's, 13758
Wicked Crisps, 13759
Wicked Mixc, 13760
Wicked Weed Brewing, 571
Wicker, 13762
Wide Awake Coffee Co., 12885
Wide Shoulders Bakin, 7469
Widman's Country, 10244
Widmer Brothers, 3107
Widmer's Cheese, 13765
Wiederkehr Wine, 13769
Wigwam, 1061
Wilbur, 13772
Wilbur Chocolate, 13610
Wilcox, 13774
Wild & Ricey, 575
Wild American Herb Co., 13998
Wild and Mild, 1279
Wild Blackberry, 10478
Wild Blend Rice, 7723
Wild Crafted Food From the Gulf Of, 7788
Wild Fruitz, 13778
Wild Hibiscus Flowers, 13779
Wild Hog Vineyard, 13780
Wild Horse, 13781
Wild Huckleberry, 5323
Wild Jungle Animal Crackers, 3343
Wild Keta Salmon, 6494
Wild Man, 5520
Wild Olive, 2801
Wild Poppy, 13784
Wild Raspberry, 5304
Wild Red King Salmon, 6494
Wild Rocket, 10815
Wild Roots, 2971
Wild Springs, 1292
Wild Thyme Cottage Products, 13787
Wild Turkey, 2114
Wild Tusker, 13006
Wild Veggie, 9592
Wild Vines, 3834
Wild West, 12688
Wild West Spices, Inc., 13789
Wild White King Salmon, 6494
Wildcat Produce Garden, 13791
Wildcat Strong, 7123
Wildcraft, 4537
Wilderness Family Naturals, 13796
Wildfire, 9935
Wildflower, 10478
Wildfruit Fruit Snacks, 4884
Wildhurst Cabernet F, 13793
Wildhurst Chardonnay, 13793
Wildhurst Merlot, 13793
Wildhurst Zinfandel, 13793

Wildleaf, 13782
Wildway, 13799
Wildwood, 10365
Willard, 12003
William Hill, 13814
William Hill Estate, 3834
William Wheeler Winery, 12672
William's Corn, 10274
Williamette Valley Mustard, 1034
Williams, 1917, 13822, 13823
Williams-Selym Winery, 13821
Williamsburg Winery, 13825
Willie's, 12175
Willoughby's, 13829
Willow, 13830
Willow Farms, 10728
Willow Oak Farms, 13832
Wilson Continental D, 13110
Wilson Foods, 13835
Wiltshire, 2357
Wimberley Valley, 13837
Win You, 2750
Winchester, 11951
Wind & Willow Key Lime Cheeseball, 806
Windansea Wheat, 6711
Windham Hearth, 13343
Windsock, 7209
Windsor, 6661
Windsor Nature's Seasons, 6661
Windsor Vineyards, 13434
Windsor Half Salt, 6661
Windstream Windbreak, 7740
Windwalker, 13846
Windy Shoal, 8219
Wine Country, 6019
Wine Country Chef Gourmet Marinade, 13848
Wine Country Chef Lemon Pepper Rub, 13848
Wine Country Chef Spiced Mustard, 13848
Wine Country Chief Spiced Bbq Rub, 13848
Wine Country Kitchens, 13849
Wine Gift Packaging, 5280
Winemaker's Choice, 5498
Winemakers Reserve, 4649
Wines, 2343
Winexpert, 555
Winey Keemun English Breakfast, 5228
Winfield, 7198
Winfrey's, 13853
Wing Hing Gold Coin, 9807
Wing Hing Panda, 9807
Wing It, 13854
Wing's, 13858, 13861
Wing-Ditties, 1654
Winger, 13860
Winky Foods, 7168
Winmix, 13863
Winn & Lovett, 13864
Winn-Dixie, 11838, 13864
Winston, 4038
Winsuel, 5095
Winter Block, 5193
Winter Garden, 10038
Winter Gold, 7569
Winter Harbor, 3780
Winter Solstice, 549
Winter Stout, 11992
Winter Warlock, 1720
Winter Warmer, 1401
Winter Wonder, 11846
Winterbraun, 7554
Winterbrook, 13872
Winterfest, 8459
Winterfresh, 7952, 13960
Winterhook, 10629
Winters, 1638
Wintrex, 833
Wipe Out, 7143
Wiscon, 10335
Wisconsin American Ginseng, 10335
Wisconsin Gold, 10655
Wisconsin Lakeshore, 4753
Wisconsin Pride, 10752
Wisconsin Whey International, 13881
Wisdom & Warter, 1006
Wisdom Nutrition, 13883
Wisdom of the Ancients Herbal Teas, 13883
Wisdom Panel, 7952
Wise Mouth, 13885
Wisecrackers, 9799
Wiser's Deluxe, 3024

Brand Name Index

Wiser's Special Blend, 3024
Wiser's Very Old, 3024
Wisi Club, 1231
Wisnack, 3501
Wit, 5304
Witness Tree Vineyard, 13889
Wix-Fresh, 13890
Wiz, 7671
Wizards, 3956
Wizbanger, 11320
Wm. Wycliff Vineyards, 3834
Wnp - Washed Natural Sesame Seeds, 11462
Woeber's, 13894
Wok Menu, 3513
Wokvel, 13336
Wolf Blass, 12937
Wolf's Scottish Cream Ale, 13288
Wolferman's, 13899
Wolffs, 1391
Wollersheim Winery, 13903
Woman's Select, 8009
Womens Bread, 4702
Wonder, 4529, 6395, 13691
Wonder Bread, 3056, 6555
Wonder Foil, 12973
Wonder, 10777
Wonderful Halos, 13906
Wonderful Life, 12486
Wonderful Sweet Scarletts, 13906
Wonka, 4255
Wonka Pixy Stix Mixers, 4255
Wonka, 8945
Woodbury Vineyards, 13915
Woodchuck Draft Cider, 5355
Woodchuck Pear Cider, 1208
Wooden Valley, 13916
Woodfield Farms, 13923
Woodfield Fish & Oyster, 13917
Woodfield Ice, 13917
Woodford Reserve, 1784
Woodford Reserve, 10998
Woodie Pie, 13918
Woods, 13920
Woodside Vineyards, 13921
Woodstock Wheat, 5903
Woodstock, 1484
Woolite, 10598
Woolwich Dairy, 11209, 11211
Worcester, 8256
Workout Energy Drinks, 13728
World Berries, 9237
World Classics, 1758
World Coffee Safari Gourmet, 11855
World Cup, 13934
World Harbors, 13938
World Harbors, 8415
World Kitchen's, 1796
World of Chia, 13945
World's Best, 5590
World's Finest Chocolate, 13948
Worthington, 5799, 8551
Worthington's, 8459
Worthy Cabernet, 11810
Wos-Wit, 5406
Wowie!, 9500
Wpc 34, 13881
Wrap Arounds, 7063
Wrap'n Roll, 7252
Wrapitz, 7076
Wrappers, 7063
Wrappetizers, 530
Wrappy, 5573
Wright Delicious, 13959

Wright's, 864
Wright, 13109
Wrigley, 541
Wrigley's Spearmint, 13960
Wrigley's Spearminti, 7952
Wrigley's, 7952
Wsi, 13944
Wsr, 8899
Wu Wei, 1501
Wuhan Asia-Pacific Condiments, 8061
Wunder Bar, 13834
Wunder Creamery, 13961
Wunderbar, 10040
Wunderbar, 13109
Wundernuggets, 3109
Wurstmeister, 11059
Wuthrich, 5282
Wwrapps, 10968
Wyandot, 13964
Wyandotte Graystone Winery, 13965
Wyandotte Winery, 13965
Wychwood, 4148
Wye River, 5717
Wyler's, 6483
Wyler's Light, 6483
Wynns Coonawarra Estate, 12937
Wysong, 13967

X

X-Fine, 13498
X-Tra-Touch, 12979
X-Treme Freeze, 4901
Xanadu Exotic Tea, 2834
Xangold, 1692
Xing, 8955
Xip - Salmon Cavier, 9344
Xl 2000, 13881
Xl 440, 13881
Xl 480, 13881
Xtc, 13697
Xtra, 2666
Xtreme Nerds, 4255
Xxx Habanero, 3537

Y

Ya-Hoo!, 13979
Yago Sant'gria, 7655
Yakima Valley, 13984
Yakisoba, 13560
Yakshi Fragrances, 7562
Yamaizumi, 8412
Yamajirushi, 8412
Yamamotoyama 1690, 12053
Yamasa, 13986
Yamato Colony, 7489
Yamazaki, 12315
Yamazaki Aged Umeshu, 1120
Yamhill Wines, 13990
Yamic Yogurt, 792
Yankee Clipperc, 9748
Yanni, 6719
Yata, Pilta, Kapha Teas, 5679
Yatir Winery, 10952
Yaucono, 2004
Yazi Ginger Vodka, 5981
Ye Olde English, 1134
Ye Olde Farm Style, 9585
Yellow Emperor, 13998
Yellow Gold Shelf St, 8838
Yellow Label, 13740
Yellow Rose, 11834

Yellowglen, 12937
Yerba Prima, 14000
Yervoy, 1721
Yick Lung, 14003
Ying Yang, 10708
Ying's, 14005
Yioryo, 14069
Yiotis, 6986
Yo Baby Yogurt, 12145
Yo Cream, 3378
Yo Cream Smoothies, 3378
Yo Mama's, 14006
Yo-Goat, 2793
Yocream, 3379
Yocrunch, 3379
Yoder Dairies, 3469
Yogi Tea, 14011
Yogourmet, 7667
Yogurt Starter, 8816
Yohimbe, 1532
Yohimbe Bar, 572
Yoki, 4947
Yonique, 1977
Yonkers Brewing Company, 14015
Yoohoo, 3725
Yop, 14017
Yoplait, 4947
York, 5818
York Mountain, 14018
Yorktown Baking Company, 14019
Yoshida Foods International, 14020
You Win, 14024
Young's Breading, 3695
Young's Lobster Pound, 14027
Yowser!!, 4586
Yoyummy, 5356
Ypp-Hoo, 8586
Yu-Qui-Tas, 100
Yuccafoam, 1179
Yuengling, 3310
Yuki Nigori, 12500
Yukon Sourdough Recipe, 10426
Yule Tide, 2763
Yuletide, 10773
Yuletide Porter, 8153
Yum Yum Stix, 6685
Yumbutter, 12964
Yummy Fruit Company, 5036
Yumy Yumy, 6810
Yup!, 2811
Yutaka, 2719
Yves Veggie Cuisine, 3773, 5505
Yvonne's Gourmet, 14032

Z

Z Gris Dry Rose, 14038
Z-Bird, 14043
Z.D. Wines, 14047
Zachary, 14039
Zachlawi, 10952
Zackariah Harris, 11263
Zagnut, 5818
Zakouski, 10039
Zanae, 6986
Zand Hebs For Kids, 13642
Zand, 9237
Zany Pretzels, 3396
Zap'ems, 1200
Zapatac, 9748
Zapp's Potato Chips, 13129
Zarda, 14042
Zartic, 14043

Zartic Beef Bakeables, 14043
Zartic Chicken Bakeables, 14043
Zartic Chicken Fried Beef Steaks, 14043
Zartic Chicken Fryz Flavorz, 14043
Zartic Chicken Tenderloins, 14043
Zartic Circle Z Beef Burgers, 14043
Zartic Crispy Steaks, 14043
Zartic Homestyle Meatloaf, 14043
Zartic Honey Hugged Chicken, 14043
Zartic Pork Bakeables, 14043
Zartic Pork Sausage Sampler, 14043
Zartic Rockin' Roasted Chicken, 14043
Zartic Veal Entree Legends, 14043
Zartic Veal Specialties, 14043
Zartin, 13273
Zary, 7747
Zatarain's, 8061
Zatec Pilsner, 3746
Zayante, 14044
Zazi Organics, 14045
Zcuvee, 14038
Zebra, 14048
Zebra Value-Line, 14048
Zebra Xii, 14048
Zeelanco, 4081
Zefina, 2909
Zeigler, 10497
Zeigler's, 14050
Zeniht, 3753
Zenipro, 6777
Zenobia, 12293, 14053
Zephyrhillis, 14055
Zerit, 1721
Zero, 5818
Zespri, 5036
Zesties, 9523
Zia Briosa, 13475
Zico, 2811, 2814
Zima, 8459
Zinfandel, 4745
Zing, 3666
Zingers, 6013
Zingos Mints, 1771
Zion, 10952
Zip, 3696, 12663
Zipp, 2226
Zippity Doo-Wa Ditties, 1654
Zippy Pop, 5752
Zippys, 14067
Zito, 2059
Zitos, 14068
Zma, 6236
Zodiac, 8795
Zoe's Meats, 14069
Zoi Greek Yogurt, 792
Zone, 10229, 10487
Zoo Crew, 1654
Zoombees, 4374
Zorro, 8946
Zotz, 551
Zoygs, 11320
Zpasta, 6246
Zummo, 14075
Zumo Juices, 11396
Zuni Fire Roasted Salsa, 14076
Zuni Zalsa Verde, 14076
Zwanenberg, 13402
Zweigle's, 14078
Zychrome, 6236
Zylicious, 9237
Zzzquil, 12721

Ethnic Food Index / African

African
Honeydrop Beverages, 5967
Omanhene Cocoa Bean Co, 9474
Pots de Creme, 10219
Southern Heritage Coffee Company, 11855
Tantos Foods International, 12527

Arabic
Blue Pacific Flavors & Fragrances, 1490
Choice of Vermont, 2631
Dipasa USA Inc, 3615
East Wind Inc, 3887
Fillo Factory, The, 4388
Golden Platter Foods, 5131
Grounds For Thought, 5402
Marantha Natural Foods, 7892
Solo Foods, 11788
Tarazi Specialty Foods, 12535
Tribe Mediterranean, 12965
Victoria Fine Foods, 13388

Argentinean
Blue Pacific Flavors & Fragrances, 1490
Goodheart Brand Specialty Food, 5183

Asian
99 Ranch Market, 31
Ajinomoto Frozen Foods USA, Inc., 238
Ajinomoto Heartland Inc, 239
Alternative Health & Herbs, 393
AM Todd Co, 91
American Culinary Garden, 450
Associated Fruit Company, 739
Basic Food Flavors, 1070
Baycliff Co Inc, 1105
Boyajian LLC, 1635
Cathay Foods Corporation, 2317
Chang Food Company, 2417
Chinese Spaghetti Factory, 2573
Cinnabar Specialty Foods Inc, 2681
Clements Foods Co, 2750
Clofine Dairy Products Inc, 2764
Cricklewood Soyfoods, 3163
Delta Food Products, 3513
Discovery Foods, 3618
Dixie USA, 3633
Dong Kee Company, 3681
Eastern Tea Corp, 3894
Eckert Cold Storage, 3918
Eden Foods Inc, 3940
Edward & Sons Trading Co, 3956
Egg Roll Fantasy, 3967
Erba Food Products, 4104
Flavor House, Inc., 4481
Fmali Herb, 4537
Fortella Fortune Cookies, 4604
Frozen Specialties Inc, 4756
Fuji Foods Corp, 4781
Glacier Fish Company, 5041
Glennys, 5055
Gold Pure Food Products Co. Inc., 5105
Great Eastern Sun Trading Co, 5306
Harvest Food Products Co Inc, 5630
Hawaii Candy Inc, 5653
Health Concerns, 5680
Health is Wealth Foods, 5687
House Foods America Corp, 6021
Hsu's Ginseng Enterprises Inc, 6040
Hung's Noodle House, 6079
Indian Foods Company, Inc., 6185
Ito En USA Inc, 6327
JSL Foods, 6409
Kapaa Poi Factory, 6704
Kubla Khan Food Company, 6998
L & S Packing Co, 7022
Lawry's, 7257
Lee's Food Products, 7298
Mad Will's Food Company, 7737
Maine Seaweed Company, 7791
Mandarin Noodle Manufacturing Company, 7835
Mando Inc, 7838
Maruchan Inc, 7974
Metzer Farms, 8203
Millflow Spice Corp., 8314
Minh Food Corporation, 8349
Mo Hotta Mo Betta, 8433
Modern Macaroni Co LTD, 8443
Montreal Chop Suey Company, 8514
Morinaga Nutritional Foods, Inc., 8546
Myron's Fine Foods, Inc., 8715
Nanka Seimen Company, 8754
Naumes, Inc., 8901
Nikken Foods, 9053
Nissin Foods USA Co Inc, 9068
Nu Naturals Inc, 9201
Ota Tofu, 9588
Pacific Ocean Produce, 9690
Pacific Valley Foods, 9699
Paisley Farms Inc, 9712
Passport Food Group, 9807
Pearson's Homestyle, 9879
Peking Noodle Co Inc, 9902
Premier Pacific Seafoods Inc, 10250
Prince of Peace, 10307
Progenix Corporation, 10335
Quong Hop & Company, 10472
San Diego Soy Dairy, 11138
San-J International Inc, 11157
Schiff Food Products Co Inc, 11284
Senba USA, 11431
Shepherd Farms Inc, 11547
Shine Foods Inc, 11558
Shining Ocean Inc, 11559
Sno-Pac Foods Inc, 11758
Soyfoods of America, 11881
Spice Hunter Inc, 11919
St John's Botanicals, 11997
Sun Chlorella USA, 12228
Sun Sun Food Products, 12247
Sunrich LLC, 12294
Sunrise Markets, 12298
Sure-Fresh Produce Inc, 12354
Sweet Earth Foods, 12396
Talley Farms, 12513
Timber Crest Farms, 12809
Tofu Shop Specialty Foods Inc, 12841
Tofutti Brands Inc, 12843
Triple Leaf Tea Inc, 12980
Twenty-First Century Foods, 13088
Twin Marquis, 13094
Twin Oaks Community, 13095
Union, 13170
Van Oriental Food Inc, 13276
Vessey & Co Inc, 13369
Victoria Fine Foods, 13388
Vitasoy USA, 13473
Wah Yet Group, 13531
Wan Hua Foods, 13560
Wei-Chuan USA Inc, 13625
Westbrae Natural Foods, 13672
Willow Foods, 13830
Wing Nien Food, 13855
World Ginseng Ctr Inc, 13937
Yamasa Corp USA, 13986
Yellow Emperor Inc, 13998

Brazilian
Aryzta, 721
Blue Pacific Flavors & Fragrances, 1490
Country Smoked Meats, 3088
Crofton & Sons Inc, 3177
Kalustyan, 6696
KOZY Shack Enterprises Inc, 6676
Manuel's Odessa Tortilla, 7859
McCain Produce Inc., 8056
Nielsen Citrus Products Inc, 9049
Northwest Pea & Bean Co, 9179
Sprague Foods, 11955
Talk O'Texas Brands Inc, 12509

Cajun
Atlantic Seasonings, 778
Autin's Cajun Cookery, 823
Azar Nut Co, 854
Bayou Land Seafood, 1110
Bear Creek Country Kitchens, 1126
Blue Runner Foods Inc, 1497
Boudreaux's Foods, 1610
Cajun Boy's Louisiana Products, 2018
Cajun Crawfish Distributors, 2020
Cajun Creole Products Inc, 2021
Carnival Brands Mfg, 2226
Cheese Straws & More, 2482
Chef Hans' Gourmet Foods, 2489
Cooke Aguaculture, 2981
Hollman Foods, 5910
Hummingbird Kitchens, 6074
JD Sweid Foods, 6394
Kajun Kettle Foods, 6687
Louisiana Gourmet Enterprises, 7581
Magic Seasoning Blends, 7766
Mild Bill's Spices, 8291
Morey's Seafood Intl LLC, 8541
Oak Grove Smoke House Inc, 9315
Old Mansion Inc, 9419
Olde Tyme Mercantile, 9439
Raffield Fisheries Inc, 10530
REX Pure Foods, 10509
Savoie's Sausage and Food Products, 11255
Smuggler's Kitchen, 11742
SOUPerior Bean & Spice Company, 11050
Sunset Farm Foods Inc, 12300
Suzanna's Kitchen, 12371
Texas Crumb & Food Products, 12652
Uncle Fred's Fine Foods, 13155
Victoria Fine Foods, 13388
Woods Smoked Meats Inc, 13920
Yankee Specialty Foods, 13992
Zummo Meat Co, 14075

Chinese
Allied Old English Inc, 345
American Botanicals, 442
American Culinary Garden, 450
Basic Food Flavors, 1070
Calco of Calgary, 2040
Canton Noodle Corporation, 2144
Cathay Foods Corporation, 2317
Chang Food Company, 2417
Chelten House Products, 2509
Clements Foods Co, 2750
Creative Foodworks Inc, 3137
Delta Food Products, 3513
Dong Kee Company, 3681
Eckert Cold Storage, 3918
Eckroat Seed Company, 3921
Egg Roll Fantasy, 3967
Erba Food Products, 4104
Everfresh Food Corporation, 4164
Favorite Foods, 4311
Fine Choice Foods, 4393
Flavor House, Inc., 4481
Fortella Fortune Cookies, 4604
Frozen Specialties Inc, 4756
Gold Pure Food Products Co. Inc., 5105
Great Northern Products Inc, 5325
Green Gold Group LLC, 5351
Harvest Food Products Co Inc, 5630
Hawaii Candy Inc, 5653
Health Concerns, 5680
Hong Kong Noodle Company, 5970
Hormel Foods Corp., 6000
Hung's Noodle House, 6079
JR Laboratories, 6408
KARI-Out Co, 6665
Kelly Gourmet Foods Inc, 6770
L & S Packing Co, 7022
La Tang Cuisine Manufacturing, 7110
Lee Kum Kee, 7295
Lee's Food Products, 7298
Maebo Noodle Factory Inc, 7760
Mandarin Noodle Manufacturing Company, 7835
Mandarin Soy Sauce Inc, 7836
Marsan Foods, 7954
Maruchan Inc, 7974
Metzer Farms, 8203
Mexi-Frost Specialties Company, 8207
Millflow Spice Corp., 8314
Min Tong Herbs, 8339
Miyako Oriental Foods Inc, 8412
Montreal Chop Suey Company, 8514
Morinaga Nutritional Foods, Inc., 8546
Mung Dynasty, 8679
Nanka Seimen Company, 8754
Nikken Foods, 9053
Ohta Wafer Factory, 9380
Paradise Products Corporation, 9766
Peking Noodle Co Inc, 9902
Porkie Company of Wisconsin, 10196
Prime Food Processing Corp, 10290
Progenix Corporation, 10335
Rosmarino Foods/R.Z. Humbert Company, 10900
Schiltz Foods Inc, 11287
Shanghai Co, 11513
Shine Foods Inc, 11558
Soyfoods of America, 11881
Sure-Fresh Produce Inc, 12354
Texas Coffee Co, 12650
Triple Leaf Tea Inc, 12980
Union, 13170
United Noodle Manufacturing Company, 13195
Valdez Food Inc, 13247
Van Oriental Food Inc, 13276
Victoria Fine Foods, 13388
Wan Hua Foods, 13560
Wei-Chuan USA Inc, 13625
Willow Foods, 13830
Wing Nien Food, 13855
Wing Sing Chong Company, 13857
Wings Foods of Alberta Ltd, 13861
Wizards Cauldron, LTD, 13892
Wong Wing, 13908
Wonton Food, 13909
Yamasa Corp USA, 13986
Young's Noodle Factory Inc, 14028

Colombian
Barrie House Gourmet Coffee, 1053
Blue Pacific Flavors & Fragrances, 1490

Creole
Blue Runner Foods Inc, 1497
Carnival Brands Mfg, 2226
Chef Hans' Gourmet Foods, 2489
Conway Import Co Inc, 2975
Lucile's, 7627
Mama Amy's Quality Foods, 7811
Oak Grove Smoke House Inc, 9315
Vietti Foods Co Inc, 13402

Cuban
Aryzta, 721
Bacardi Canada, Inc., 913
Banana Distributing Company, 1004
Buffalo Trace Distillery, 1839
Casino Bakery, 2292
Central Bean Co, 2374
Corby Distilleries, 3024
Crofton & Sons Inc, 3177
Destileria Serralles Inc, 3545
Hanover Foods Corp, 5555
Highwood Distillers, 5861
Hiram Walker & Sons, 5892
Hood River Distillers Inc, 5981
Jack's Bean Co LLC, 6418
Kalustyan, 6696
KOZY Shack Enterprises Inc, 6676
Manuel's Odessa Tortilla, 7859
Marie Brizard Wines & Spirits, 7913
Northwest Pea & Bean Co, 9179
Sprague Foods, 11955
Tantos Foods International, 12527
Trigo Corporation, 12970
Victoria Fine Foods, 13388

Czech
HealthBest, 5689
Lake Erie Frozen Foods Co, 7152
McCain Foods Ltd., 8054
Mike & Jean's Berry Farm, 8278
Patterson Frozen Foods, 9839
Pines International, 10067
Victoria Fine Foods, 13388
Wallace Grain & Pea Company, 13549

Dutch
Baensch Food Products Co, 931
BlueWater Seafoods, 1502
Chase Brothers Dairy, 2450
Chicago 58 Food Products, 2541
Clofine Dairy Products Inc, 2764
Cloverland Dairy, 2785
Crowley Cheese Inc, 3188
Dairy Maid Dairy LLC, 3340
Farmdale Creamery Inc, 4275
Felix Custom Smoking, 4325
Gaudet & Ouellette, 4923
HP Hood LLC, 5486
Independent Packers Corporation, 6182
Inshore Fisheries, 6231
International Seafoods - Alaska, 6270
Island Marine Products, 6301
Kyler's Catch Seafood Market, 7015
Maytag Dairy Farms Inc, 8043
McArthur Dairy LLC, 8053

Ethnic Food Index / English/Scottish/Welsh

Menemsha Fish Market, 8156
North Pacific Seafoods Inc, 9134
Plainview Milk Products, 10099
Red Pelican Food Products, 10614
Reilly Dairy & Food Company, 10655
Schneider-Valley Farms Inc, 11302
Strub Pickles, 12175
Sunnyrose Cheese, 12288
Trident Seafoods Corp, 12969
Welsh Farms, 13647
Winchester Cheese Company, 13840
Winchester Farms Dairy, 13841
Yoder Dairies, 14009

English/Scottish/Welsh

AB InBev, 71
Adrienne's Gourmet Foods, 183
AleSmith Brewing Company, 286
Alley Kat Brewing Co, Ltd, 339
Amberland Foods, 423
Amsterdam Brewing Company, 517
Anchor Brewing Company, 531
Anderson Valley Brewing Co, 549
Aryzta, 721
Assets Grille & Southwest Brewing Company, 738
Atwater Block Brewing Company, 785
Bass Lake Cheese Factory, 1077
Baumer Foods Inc, 1087
Bay Hawk Ales, 1097
Bell's Brewery Inc, 1184
Berkshire Food Co Inc, 1237
Big Bucks Brewery & Steakhouse, 1326
Big Rock Brewery, 1340
Big Sky Brewing Co, 1344
BJ's Restaurants Inc., 897
Bloomington Brewing Co, 1460
Bluegrass Brewing Company, 1507
Bodega Chocolates, 1529
Bohemian Brewery, 1542
Boston Spice & Tea Company, 1598
Boulder Beer, 1611
Boulevard Brewing, 1621
Breadworks, 1682
Breckenridge Brewery, 1687
Brick Brewery, 1702
Bristol Brewing Co, 1720
Brooklyn Brewery, 1748
Brown-Forman Corp, 1784
Buffalo Bill Brewing Company, 1837
Cajun Brands, 2019
Calgary Italian Bakery, 2045
Campbell Soup Co., 2116
Capital Brewery & Beer Garden, 2160
Case Side Holdings Company, 2289
Cedarvale Food Products, 2357
Cisco Brewers, 2691
Clarkson Scottish Bakery, 2720
Claxton Bakery Inc, 2732
Clements Foods Co, 2750
Clipper City Brewing, 2763
Confectionately Yours LTD, 2947
Copper Tank Brewing Company, 3008
Creative Cotton, 3133
Criveller California Corp, 3171
Crooked River Brewing Company, 3180
David's Cookies, 3399
Deschutes Brewery, 3533
DG Yuengling & Son, Inc., 3310
Dogwood Brewing Company, 3646
Dundee Groves, 3797
E Waldo Ward & Son Marmalades, 3838
Eden Foods Inc, 3940
Erba Food Products, 4104
Fee Brothers, 4320
Felbro Food Products, 4324
Flying Dog Brewery, 4534
Fort Garry Brewing Company, 4601
Frazier Nut Farms Inc, 4675
Fresh Start Bakeries, 4724
Froma-Dar, 4748
Fudge Farms, 4779
Golden Valley Foods Ltd., 5138
Golden Walnut Specialty Foods, 5140
Goose Island Beer Co, 5188
Grand Teton Brewing Co, 5255
Gray's Brewing Co, 5290
Great Divide Brewing Co, 5304
Great Lakes Cheese Company, Inc., 5315
Great Northern Brewing Co, 5323
Great Western Brewing Company, 5332

Greaves Jams & Marmalades, 5339
Guinness Import Co, 5427
Hanover Foods Corp, 5555
Hawaii Star Bakery, 5656
Heartland Brewery, 5707
Heaven Hill Distilleries Inc., 5720
Heluva Good Cheese, 5757
High Liner Foods Inc., 5844
Hiram Walker & Sons, 5892
Hog Haus Brewing Company, 5903
Homestead Baking Co, 5942
Hood River Distillers Inc, 5981
Humboldt Brews LLC, 6065
Idaho Candy Co, 6134
Illes Seasonings & Flavors, 6146
Ipswich Ale Brewery, 6283
K & S Cakes, 6656
Karl Strauss Brewing Co, 6711
La Brasserie McAuslan Brewing, 7077
Labatt Brewery London, 7122
Lafayette Brewing Co, 7134
Laguna Beach Brewing Company, 7143
Lakeport Brewing Corporation, 7157
Lea & Perrins, 7277
Leader Candies, 7279
Left Hand Brewing Co, 7309
Legend Brewing Co, 7315
Les Brasseurs Du Nord, 7379
Les Brasseurs GMT, 7380
Lodi Nut Company, 7506
Lounsbury Foods, 7594
M J Barleyhoppers Sports Bar, 7677
MacEwan's Meats, 7720
Marich Confectionery, 7912
Maries Candies, 7919
Mary of Puddin Hill, 7982
Mendocino Brewing Co Inc, 8153
Mexi-Frost Specialties Company, 8207
Meyer's Bakeries, 8212
Millflow Spice Corp., 8314
Mishawaka Brewing Company, 8374
Morrison Meat Pies, 8562
Mrs Auld's Gourmet Foods Inc, 8625
Mrs. Kavanagh's English Muffins, 8640
Naylor Candies Inc, 8908
New Business Corp, 8961
New Horizons Baking Co, 8987
North American Breweries Inc., 9117
North Bay Produce Inc, 9126
Northampton Brewing Company, 9141
Northern Breweries, 9145
Nutfield Brewing Company, 9228
Oakrun Farm Bakery, 9329
Okanagan Spring Brewery, 9391
Oland Breweries, 9396
Old Credit Brewing Co. Ltd., 9404
Old Dominion Peanut Corp, 9406
Pacific Coast Brewing, 9673
Pacific Coast Fruit Co, 9674
Pacific Western Brewing Company, 9701
Paper City Brewery, 9754
Pastry Chef, 9823
Pecan Deluxe Candy Co, 9882
Pepper Creek Farms, 9935
Pete's Brewing Company, 9977
Pied-Mont/Dora, 10041
Pike Brewing Co, 10052
Queen Bee Gardens, 10450
R.M. Palmer Co., 10498
Red Brick Brewing Company, 10602
Redhook Brewery, 10629
Richardson Brands Co, 10724
River Market Brewing Company, 10769
Robbie's Natural Products, 10785
Rock Bottom Restaurant & Brewery, 10810
Rohrbach Brewing Co, 10844
Russell Breweries, Inc., 10989
Russian Chef, 10992
Sarabeth's Office, 11216
Saranac Brewery, 11218
Schlafly Tap Room, 11291
Sconza Candy Co, 11320
Sea Dog Brewing Company, 11340
Sequoia Brewing Co, 11448
Serv-Agen Corporation, 11458
Seven Barrel Brewery, 11470
Sierra Nevada Taproom & Rstrnt, 11592
Snake River Brewing Company, 11749
Southern California Brewing Company, 11846
St Arnold Brewing Co, 11992
St. Croix Beer Company, 12004

StoneHammer Brewing, 12136
Stoudt Brewing Co, 12153
Sundial Herb Garden, 12272
Sweet Water Brewing Co, 12419
Tin Whistle Brewing Co, 12814
Torn & Glasser, 12893
Trafalgar Brewing Company, 12919
Trappist Preserves, 12931
Treasure Foods, 12936
Triumph Brewing Co, 12990
Turkey Hill Sugarbush, 13065
Uptown Bakers, 13221
Vancouver Island Brewing Company, 13288
Wachusett Brewing Co, 13522
Webb's Candy, 13612
Wellington Brewery, 13643
Weston Foods, 13691
Whistler Brewing Company, 13710
Willamette Valley Walnuts, 13807
Wolferman's, 13899
Yakima Craft Brewing Company, 13982
Yorktown Baking Company, 14019

European

Adolf's Meats & Sausage Kitchen, 182
Beck's Waffles of Oklahoma, 1145
Cateraid Inc, 2314
Future Bakery & Cafe, 4806
Home Market Foods Inc., 5929
Mancini Packing Co, 7832
Milmar Food Group, 8324
Neto's Market & Grill, 8946
OH Chocolate, 9299
Orlando Baking Co, 9568
Patisserie Wawel, 9830
Pearson's Homestyle, 9879
Rubschlager Baking Corp, 10960
Strossner's Bakery & Cafe, 12174
Uptown Bakers, 13221
Vigneri Chocolate Inc., 13403

French

Alexian Pfts, 295
Aryzta, 721
Atlantic Seasonings, 778
Breadworks, 1682
Cafe Du Monde Coffee Stand, 1993
Carnival Brands Mfg, 2226
Cherchies, 2514
Creme Curls, 3143
Dufflet Pastries, 3782
Edelweiss Patisserie, 3938
Emkay Trading Corporation, 4046
Fiera Foods, 4371
Food Source Company, 4569
G Scaccianoce & Co, 4818
Galasso's Bakery, 4864
Gold Coast Bakeries, 5097
Hawaii Star Bakery, 5656
Heluva Good Cheese, 5757
Home Market Foods Inc., 5929
Kolb-Lena Bresse Bleu Inc, 6945
La Brea Bakery Inc, 7078
Laura's French Baking Co, 7245
Marcel et Henri Charcuterie Francaise, 7898
Mardi Gras, 7902
Marin French Cheese Co, 7925
Morabito Baking Co Inc, 8536
Nicky USA Inc, 9043
Old Fashioned Kitchen Inc, 9412
Out of a Flower, 9604
Palmetto Pigeon Plant, 9727
Papa Leone Food Enterprises, 9752
Piemonte Bakery Co, 10045
Piller's Fine Foods, 10058
Quelle Quiche, 10458
Rollingstone Chevre, 10851
Salmolux Inc, 11110
Sarabeth's Office, 11216
Savoie's Sausage and Food Products, 11255
Spring Glen Fresh Foods, 11960
Spruce Foods, 11980
The Pillsbury Company, 12717
Vie De France Yamazaki Inc, 13396

German

Amana Meat Shop & Smoke House, 409
Aryzta, 721
Athens Foods Inc, 750
Atwood Cheese Company, 787

August Schell Brewing Co, 796
Bay Valley Foods, 1103
Beaverton Foods Inc, 1141
Best Provision Co Inc, 1271
Big City Reds, 1328
Binkert's Meat Products, 1363
Boesl Packing Co, 1536
Clyde's Italian & German Sausage, 2792
Country Smoked Meats, 3088
Creme Curls, 3143
Culinary Institute Lenotre, 3235
Del Monte Foods Inc., 3478
Dimpflmeier Bakery, 3606
Dufflet Pastries, 3782
Elmwood Locker Svc, 4035
Far West Meats, 4259
Farmers Meat Market, 4282
Fillo Factory, The, 4388
Fischer & Wieser Spec Foods, 4432
Gouvea's & Purity Foods Inc, 5219
Hatfield Quality Meats, 5643
Hazle Park Quality Meats, 5672
Kilgus Meats, 6842
Koegel Meats Inc, 6934
Left Hand Brewing Co, 7309
Lightlife, 7427
Little Rhody Brand Frankfurts, 7473
Marin French Cheese Co, 7925
Matthiesen's Deer & Custom, 8015
Michigan Farm Cheese Dairy, 8248
Morse's Sauerkraut, 8564
New Canaan Farms, 8962
Organic Gourmet, 9545
P & L Poultry, 9629
R.L. Zeigler Company, 10497
Saag's Products LLC, 11059
Schaller & Weber Inc, 11276
Seneca Foods Corp, 11434
Shelton's Poultry Inc, 11542
Silver Star Meats Inc, 11627
Smith Provision Co Inc, 11729
Smithfield Foods Inc., 11733
Smolich Bros. Home Made Sausage, 11740
Stawnichy Holdings, 12063
Steve's Mom, 12096
Sunnydale Meats Inc, 12285
Thomas Packing Company, 12769
WACO Beef & Pork Processors, 13509
Whole Herb Co, 13746

Greek

A.C. LaRocco Pizza, 63
Agro Farma Inc., 217
Alimentare Whyte's Inc, 307
Athens Foods Inc, 750
Atlantic Seasonings, 778
Atwood Cheese Company, 787
Bob Gordon & Associates, 1517
Corfu Foods Inc, 3028
Cosmo Food Products, 3048
FAGE USA Dairy Ind Inc, 4203
Fantis Foods Inc, 4257
Fillo Factory, The, 4388
Grecian Delight Foods Inc, 5341
Hye Cuisine, 6099
Kalustyan, 6696
Kolb-Lena Bresse Bleu Inc, 6945
Konto's Foods, 6956
L & S Packing Co, 7022
Marika's Kitchen, 7921
Marsan Foods, 7954
Mediterranean Gyro Products, 8122
Mediterranean Pita Bakery, 8123
Morabito Baking Co Inc, 8536
Mt Capra Products, 8652
Mt. Olympus Specialty Foods, 8662
Nature's Legacy Inc., 8886
Naumes, Inc., 8901
Orleans Packing Co, 9569
Parthenon Food Products, 9795
Pearl Coffee Co, 9873
Pearson's Homestyle, 9879
San Joaquin Figs Inc, 11149
San Marzano Imports, 11155
Sinbad Sweets, 11663
Soloman Baking Company, 11790
Spruce Foods, 11980
Victoria Fine Foods, 13388
Woodlake Ranch, 13919

Hawaiian

Aloha Poi Factory Inc, 364
Ames International Inc, 498
Ann's House of Nuts, Inc., 580
AquaCuisine, 622
Barcelona Nut Co, 1027
Cyanotech Corp, 3281
Garden & Valley Isle Seafood, 4890
Hawaii Candy Inc, 5653
HealthBest, 5689
Healthmate Products, 5692
Honey Acres, 5953
Kapaa Poi Factory, 6704
Lodi Nut Company, 7506
Ocean Beauty Seafoods Inc, 9344
Prince of Peace, 10307
Puueo Poi Shop, 10403
Rio Grande Valley Sugar Growers, 10745
Sagawa's Savory Sauces, 11077
Setton International Foods, 11468
Torn & Glasser, 12893

Hispanic

Crown Candy Corp, 3189
Kokopelli's Kitchen, 6942
Nedlog Company, 8919
New Century Snacks, 8963
Romero's Food Products Inc, 10859
Sierra Cheese Mfg Co, 11589
Thiel Cheese & Ingredients, 12752
Tropical Cheese, 12996

Hungarian

Boesl Packing Co, 1536
Charlie's Country Sausage, 2440
Chicago 58 Food Products, 2541
Erba Food Products, 4104
Famous Specialties Co, 4244
Kajun Kettle Foods, 6687
Mucke's Meat Products, 8665
Olympia International, 9464
Stawnichy Holdings, 12063
Whole Herb Co, 13746
World Spice, 13944

Indian-Pakistani

Ann's House of Nuts, Inc., 580
Arizona Pistachio Company, 675
Bear Meadow Farm, 1129
Beetroot Delights, 1170
Blue Jay Orchards, 1481
California Fruit & Nut, 2063
California Fruit and Tomato Kitchens, 2065
Cinnabar Specialty Foods Inc, 2681
Commissariat Imports, 2922
Creative Foodworks Inc, 3137
Curry King Corporation, 3260
Deep Foods Inc, 3465
Eastern Tea Corp, 3894
Eckroat Seed Company, 3921
Ethnic Gourmet Foods, 4138
Ful-Flav-R Foods, 4784
Graves Mountain Lodge Inc., 5285
HealthBest, 5689
House Foods America Corp, 6021
House of Spices, 6026
In Harvest Inc, 6171
Indian Foods Company, Inc., 6185
Jardine Ranch, 6457
Jay Shah Foods, 6473
Jonathan's Sprouts, 6585
Jyoti Cuisine India, 6653
Kalustyan, 6696
Lang Pharma Nutrition Inc, 7210
Mando Inc, 7838
Marsan Foods, 7954
Masala Chai Company, 7989
McKnight Milling Company, 8079
Medallion International Inc, 8119
North Bay Produce Inc, 9126
Northumberland Dairy, 9170
Northwest Pea & Bean Co, 9179
Sahadi Fine Foods Inc, 11081
Schiff Food Products Co Inc, 11284
Setton International Foods, 11468
Silver Palate Kitchens, 11623
Southern Brown Rice, 11845
Specialty Rice Inc, 11908
Spice Hunter Inc, 11919
Spokane Seed Co, 11945
Spruce Mountain Blueberries, 11982
Sunray Food Products Corporation, 12293
SunWest Foods, Inc., 12262
Taj Gourmet Foods, 12499
Tamarind Tree, 12517
TexaFrance, 12647
Timber Crest Farms, 12809
Torn & Glasser, 12893
Victoria Fine Foods, 13388
Wallace Grain & Pea Company, 13549
Wonderful Pistachios & Almonds, 13907
World Spice, 13944
Zenobia Co, 14053

Indonesian

AM Todd Co, 91
Cricklewood Soyfoods, 3163
Eckroat Seed Company, 3921
House Foods America Corp, 6021
Jonathan's Sprouts, 6585
Lightlife, 7427
Morinaga Nutritional Foods, Inc., 8546
San Diego Soy Dairy, 11138
Shepherd Farms Inc, 11547
Sunrise Markets, 12298
Tantos Foods International, 12527
Tofu Shop Specialty Foods Inc, 12841
Tofutti Brands Inc, 12843
Twenty-First Century Foods, 13088
Twin Oaks Community, 13095
Vitasoy USA, 13473

Irish

Acadian Seaplants, 135
Alley Kat Brewing Co, Ltd, 339
Amberland Foods, 423
Anderson Valley Brewing Co, 549
Assets Grille & Southwest Brewing Company, 738
Bell's Brewery Inc, 1184
Big Bucks Brewery & Steakhouse, 1326
Big Rock Brewery, 1340
Big Sky Brewing Co, 1344
Bloomington Brewing Co, 1460
Bluegrass Brewing Company, 1507
Boulevard Brewing, 1621
Breadworks, 1682
Breckenridge Brewery, 1687
Bristol Brewing Co, 1720
Brooklyn Brewery, 1748
Brown-Forman Corp, 1784
Buffalo Bill Brewing Company, 1837
Capital Brewery & Beer Garden, 2160
Carando Gourmet Frozen Foods, 2193
Case Side Holdings Company, 2289
Center Locker Svc, 2369
Charlie's Pride, 2441
Copper Tank Brewing Company, 3008
Crooked River Brewing Company, 3180
Dehydrates Inc, 3474
Deschutes Brewery, 3533
DG Yuengling & Son, Inc., 3310
Dogwood Brewing Company, 3646
Dutterer's Home Food Service, 3821
Evergood Fine Foods, 4166
Goose Island Beer Co, 5188
Grand Teton Brewing Co, 5255
Gray's Brewing Co, 5290
Great Western Brewing Company, 5332
Guinness Import Co, 5427
Heaven Hill Distilleries Inc, 5720
HH Dobbins Inc, 5484
Hog Haus Brewing Company, 5903
Ipswich Ale Brewery, 6283
Labatt Brewery London, 7122
Laguna Beach Brewing Company, 7143
Legend Brewing Co, 7315
Les Brasseurs Du Nord, 7379
Les Brasseurs GMT, 7380
Lower Foods, Inc., 7611
M J Barleyhoppers Sports Bar, 7677
Marathon Enterprises Inc, 7895
Mendocino Brewing Co Inc, 8153
Mishawaka Brewing Company, 8374
Moonlite Bar-B-Q Inn, 8528
Northampton Brewing Company, 9141
Nutfield Brewing Company, 9228
Oland Breweries, 9396
Orwasher's Bakery, 9575
Pike Brewing Co, 10052
Plumrose USA, 10124
Red Brick Brewing Company, 10602
River Market Brewing Company, 10769
Rock Bottom Restaurant & Brewery, 10810
Rohrbach Brewing Co, 10844
Saranac Brewery, 11218
Schlafly Tap Room, 11291
Sea Dog Brewing Company, 11340
Seven Barrel Brewery, 11470
Sierra Nevada Taproom & Rstrnt, 11592
Snake River Brewing Company, 11749
Southern California Brewing Company, 11846
St Arnold Brewing Co, 11992
Stawnichy Holdings, 12063
Stoudt Brewing Co, 12153
Sweet Water Brewing Co, 12419
Trafalgar Brewing Company, 12919
Triumph Brewing Co, 12990
Vienna Meat Products, 13401
Wellington Brewery, 13643
Yakima Craft Brewing Company, 13982

Israeli/Jewish

Alvarado Street Bakery, 397
Atlanta Bread Co., 758
Aunt Kathy's Homestyle Products, 804
Bagelworks, 937
Best Provision Co Inc, 1271
Boca Bagelworks, 1525
Breadworks, 1682
Brooklyn Bagel Company, 1743
City Foods Inc, 2708
Erba Food Products, 4104
Felix Roma & Son Inc, 4326
Fish Brothers, 4436
Flaum Appetizing, 4478
Gabila's Knishes, 4853
Gold Pure Food Products Co. Inc., 5105
Harlan Bakeries, 5590
Homarus Inc, 5924
Mancini Packing Co, 7832
Manischewitz Co, 7848
Milmar Food Group, 8324
Morabito Baking Co Inc, 8536
Old Fashioned Kitchen Inc, 9412
Orwasher's Bakery, 9575
Otis Spunkmeyer, 9591
Ottenberg's Bakers, 9595
Petrofsky's Bakery Products, 9988
Positively 3rd St Bakery, 10212
Rockland Bakery, 10816
Royal Vista Marketing Inc, 10951
Sarabeth's Office, 11216
Ultimate Bagel, 13138
Weiss Homemade Kosher Bakery, 13632
Wenner Bakery, 13653
Western Bagel Baking Corp, 13677

Italian

A Zerega's Sons Inc, 46
A.C. LaRocco Pizza, 63
Agrusa, 223
Al Dente Pasta Co, 247
Al Gelato Bornay, 248
Alati-Caserta Desserts, 275
Alberta Cheese Company, 280
Alfonso Gourmet Pasta, 298
Alfredo Aiello Italian Food, 303
American Italian Pasta Company, 465
Amoroso's Baking Co, 508
Angy's Food Products Inc, 570
Antoni Ravioli Co, 598
Armanino Foods of Distinction, 680
Atlantic Seasonings, 778
Atwood Cheese Company, 787
Aunt Kathy's Homestyle Products, 804
Authentic Marotti Biscotti, 822
Award Baking Intl, 846
Baker Cheese Factory Inc, 962
Baumer Foods Inc, 1087
BelGioioso Cheese Inc., 1174
Berkshire Mountain Bakery, 1239
Bernardi Italian Foods Company, 1245
Biagio's Banquets, 1305
Biazzo Dairy Products Inc, 1308
Biscoti Di Suzy, 1395
Biscotti & Co., 1397
BJ's Restaurants Inc., 897
Brunnett Dairy Co-Op, 1801
Bruno Specialty Foods, 1802
Buona Vita Inc, 1854
Burke Corp, 1861
Bylada Foods, 1896
Calise & Sons Bakery Inc, 2086
Canadian Fish Exporters, 2122
Cando Pasta, 2129
Cannoli Factory, 2139
Cappola Foods, 2170
Carando Gourmet Frozen Foods, 2193
Carla's Pasta, 2215
Casa Di Lisio Products Inc, 2269
Casa Visco, 2274
Catch Up Logistics, 2312
Cedarlane Foods, 2355
Chef-A-Roni Fancy Foods, 2503
Chelten House Products, 2509
Cherchies, 2514
Chicago Avenue Pizza, 2542
Chicago Pastry, 2547
Chisesi Brothers Meat Packing, 2581
Choice of Vermont, 2631
Ciao Bella Gelato Company, 2669
Cifelli & Sons Inc, 2676
Ciro Foods, 2690
Citterio USA, 2701
Clyde's Italian & German Sausage, 2792
Codinos Food Inc, 2831
Coffee Brothers Inc, 2839
Colonna Brothers Inc, 2887
Colors Gourmet Pizza, 2901
Cookie Factory, 2983
Cookies United, 2989
Cosmo Food Products, 3048
Country Smoked Meats, 3088
Creative Foodworks Inc, 3137
Crofton & Sons Inc, 3177
Cuizina Food Company, 3230
Dabruzzi's Italian Foods, 3325
Dairy Maid Ravioli Mfg Co, 3341
De Iorio's Foods Inc, 3427
Del Monte Foods Inc, 3478
Delgrosso Foods Inc., 3494
Delicious Desserts, 3498
DiGregorio Food Products, 3567
Dol Cice' Gelato Company, 3649
E.D. Smith Foods Ltd, 3844
European Egg Noodle Manufacturing, 4153
F & A Dairy Products Inc, 4195
Fabbri Sausage Mfg Co, 4213
Far West Meats, 4259
Ferrara Bakery & Cafe, 4344
Fiori Bruna Pasta Products, 4410
Fiorucci Foods USA Inc, 4411
Florence Macaroni Manufacturing, 4511
Florentyna's Fresh Pasta Factory, 4513
Floron Food Services, 4524
Fontanini Italian Meats, 4550
Food City USA, 4555
Forte Stromboli Company, 4603
Frank Wardynski & Sons Inc, 4657
Fresh Pasta Delights, 4720
G Debbas Chocolatier, 4815
Garden Complements Inc, 4891
Gardner's Gourmet, 4901
Gaspar's Linguica Co Inc, 4918
Gelati Celesti, 4933
Genarom International, 4943
Giovanni Food Co Inc, 5029
Good Old Dad Food Products, 5168
Gouvea's & Purity Foods Inc, 5219
Grande Cheese Company, 5258
Great Lakes Cheese Company, Inc., 5315
Gumpert's Canada, 5444
Hagerty Foods, 5498
Hanover Foods Corp, 5555
Harvest-Pac Products, 5637
Hirzel Canning Co & Farms, 5893
Home Market Foods Inc., 5929
Home Run Inn Frozen Foods, 5931
Homestead Fine Foods, 5944
Hormel Foods Corp., 6000
Hot Wachula's, 6018
HP Hood LLC, 5486
Icco Cheese Co, 6126
Il Gelato, 6144
Il Giardino Del Dolce Inc, 6145
IMAC, 6117
International Cheese Company, 6251
International Home Foods, 6267
Italian Gourmet Foods Canada, 6320

Ethnic Food Index / Japanese

Itarca, 6323
Ito Cariani Sausage Company, 6326
Ivanhoe Cheese Inc, 6328
John Volpi & Co, 6560
Jones Dairy Farm, 6587
Joseph's Gourmet Pasta, 6605
Kajun Kettle Foods, 6687
Kerry Foodservice, 6806
Kraft Heinz Co., 6977
L & S Packing Co, 7022
La Brea Bakery Inc, 7078
La Nova Wings, 7097
La Piccolina, 7100
La Romagnola, 7104
La Tempesta, 7111
Lakeview Banquit Cheese, 7166
Landolfi's Food Products, 7204
Larosa Bakery Inc, 7223
Leonetti's Frozen Food, 7367
Leprino Foods Co., 7369
Loghouse Foods, 7511
Losurdo Creamery, 7558
Louisa Food Products Inc, 7577
Lucia's Pizza Co, 7625
Lucy's Foods, 7635
M & CP FARMS, 7673
Macabee Foods, 7724
Mamma Lina Ravioli Company, 7824
Mancini Packing Co, 7832
Mancuso Cheese Co, 7833
Mangia Inc., 7842
Marathon Cheese Corp, 7894
Mardi Gras, 7902
Marsan Foods, 7954
Marzipan Specialties Inc, 7988
McCain Foods Ltd., 8054
Mertz Sausage Co, 8186
Mexi-Frost Specialties Company, 8207
MI-AL. Corp, 7701
Miceli Dairy Products Co, 8222
Michael Granese & Company, 8226
Midwest Food, 8266
Millflow Spice Corp., 8314
Miracapo Pizza, 8367
Molinaro's Fine Italian Foods Ltd., 8457
Morabito Baking Co Inc, 8536
Morrison Lamothe, 8560
Mrs Auld's Gourmet Foods Inc, 8625
Mrs. Leeper's Pasta, 8642
Musco Family Olive Co, 8692
Naleway Foods, 8743
Napa Valley Kitchens, 8764
Nardone Brothers, 8770
Nation Pizza & Foods, 8781
Nation Wide Canning Ltd., 8782
Nature's Legacy Inc., 8886
Nicola Pizza, 9045
North American Enterprises, 9119
Nuovo Pasta Productions LTD, 9221
Nustef Foods, 9225
OB Macaroni Company, 9297
Old Mansion Inc, 9419
Olde Tyme Mercantile, 9439
On-Cor Frozen Foods, 9482
Orleans Packing Co, 9569
Paisley Farms Inc, 9712
Pamela's Products, 9730
Papa Leone Food Enterprises, 9752
Paradise Tomato Kitchens, 9767
Park Cheese Company Inc, 9780
Parma Sausage Products, 9788
Parmx, 9792
Pasta Del Mondo, 9808
Pasta Factory, 9809
Pasta Quistini, 9815
Pastene Co LTD, 9819
Pastorelli Food Products, 9821
Peaceworks, 9863
Pecoraro Dairy Products, 9885
Pede Brothers Italian Food, 9887
Piemonte Bakery Co, 10045
Pierino Frozen Foods, 10047
Pine River Cheese & Butter Company, 10064
Pino's Pasta Veloce, 10068
Pinocchio Italian Ice Cream Company, 10069
Pocino Foods, 10136
Pollio Dairy Products, 10155
Porinos Gourmet Food, 10194
Primo Foods, 10302
Progresso Quality Foods, 10337

Putney Pasta, 10402
Quality Ingredients, 10436
R Torre & Co, 10485
Ragozzino Foods Inc, 10533
Ravioli Store, 10575
Red Gold Inc., 10608
Rhodes International Inc, 10698
Rich Products Corp, 10714, 10715
Rio Syrup Co, 10747
Rising Sun Farms, 10759
Riverview Foods, 10776
Riviera Ravioli Company, 10778
Roma Packing Company, 10854
Ron Son Foods Inc, 10860
Rosati Italian Water Ice, 10878
Rosmarino Foods/R.Z. Humbert Company, 10900
Royal Ice Cream Co, 10936
Royale Brands, 10953
S.W. Meat & Provision Company, 11030
Sahagian & Associates, 11083
San Francisco Bay Coffee Company, 11141
Sangudo Custom Meat Packers, 11179
Sardinha's Sausage, 11224
Savino's Italian Ices, 11252
Savoia Foods, 11253
Schiff Food Products Co Inc, 11284
Schneider's Dairy Inc, 11301
Sculli Brothers, 11336
Seviroli Foods, 11481
Siena Foods, 11588
Sierra Cheese Mfg Co, 11589
Sini Fulvi U.S.A., 11668
Sobaya, 11773
SOUPerior Bean & Spice Company, 11050
Specialty Food America Inc., 11899
Spicetec Flavors & Seasonings, 11930
Spruce Foods, 11980
Star Ravioli Mfg Co, 12037
Stawnichy Holdings, 12063
Stello Foods Inc, 12078
Sterling Foods LLC, 12086
Streit Carl & Son Co, 12166
Sun Orchard Inc, 12240
Sun-Re Cheese Co, 12257
Sunnyrose Cheese, 12288
Sunset Farm Foods Inc, 12300
Superbrand Dairies, 12326
Supreme Dairy Farms Co, 12350
Swiss American Inc, 12437
Swiss-American Sausage Company, 12444
Taj Gourmet Foods, 12499
Taste It Presents Inc, 12540
Teeny Foods Inc, 12603
Teti Bakery, 12640
TexaFrance, 12647
Texas Crumb & Food Products, 12652
Thiel Cheese & Ingredients, 12752
Three Lakes Winery, 12783
Tip Top Canning Co, 12820
Tirawisu, 12824
TNT Crust, 12480
Tomasso Corporation, 12860
Tonex, 12868
Treasure Foods, 12936
Tuscan Bakery, 13077
Ultimate Biscotti, 13139
Upstate Niagara Co-Op Inc., 13218
Vella Cheese Co, 13320
Ventre Packing Company, 13326
Victoria Fine Foods, 13388
Wenner Bakery, 13653
West Coast Products, 13661
WillowOak Farms, 13832
Wisconsin Milk Mktng Board Inc, 13877
Wornick Company, 13951
Yohay Baking Co, 14013

Japanese

Ajinomoto Frozen Foods USA, Inc., 238
Azuma Foods Intl Inc USA, 857
Baycliff Co Inc, 1105
Beaverton Foods Inc, 1141
Bunge North America Inc., 1849
Chelten House Products, 2509
Concord Farms, 2942
Dixie USA, 3633
Eden Foods Inc, 3940
Edward & Sons Trading Co, 3956
Favorite Foods, 4311
Glacier Fish Company, 5041

Gold Pure Food Products Co. Inc., 5105
Hardscrabble Enterprises, 5583
Hawaii Candy Inc, 5653
House Foods America Corp, 6021
Island Spring Inc, 6309
JD Sweid Foods, 6394
Kapaa Poi Factory, 6704
Lawry's Foods, 7257
Mando Inc, 7838
Marukai Market, 7975
Miyako Oriental Foods Inc, 8412
Morinaga Nutritional Foods, Inc., 8546
Nanka Seimen Company, 8754
Ohta Wafer Factory, 9380
Pearson's Homestyle, 9879
Peter Pan Seafoods Inc., 9980
Premier Pacific Seafoods Inc, 10250
San-J International Inc, 11157
Senba USA, 11431
Shining Ocean Inc, 11559
Sno-Pac Foods Inc, 11758
St John's Botanicals, 11997
Sun Chlorella USA, 12228
T. Marzetti Company, 12467
Takara Sake USA Inc, 12500
Wan Hua Foods, 13560
WhiteWave Foods, 13734
Yamasho Inc, 13988

Korean

Alternative Health & Herbs, 393
Atkins Ginseng Farms, 754
Dong Kee Company, 3681
Eckroat Seed Company, 3921
Erba Food Products, 4104
House Foods America Corp, 6021
International Specialty Supply, 6273
Island Spring Inc, 6309
Jonathan's Sprouts, 6585
Kapaa Poi Factory, 6704
Lee's Food Products, 7298
Madys Company, 7758
Maine Coast Sea Vegetables, 7788
Mando Inc, 7838
Michigan Sugar Company, 8251
Morinaga Nutritional Foods, Inc., 8546
Nu Naturals Inc, 9201
Penn Herb Co, 9918
Prince of Peace, 10307
San Diego Soy Dairy, 11138
Sessions Co Inc, 11464
Shepherd Farms Inc, 11547
Sovena USA Inc, 11875
St John's Botanicals, 11997
Sunrise Markets, 12298
Tofu Shop Specialty Foods Inc, 12841
Tofutti Brands Inc, 12843
Triple Leaf Tea Inc, 12980
Twenty-First Century Foods, 13088
Twin Oaks Community, 13095
Victoria Fine Foods, 13388
Vitasoy USA, 13473
Western Sugar Cooperative, 13685
World Ginseng Ctr Inc, 13937
Yellow Emperor Inc, 13998

Kosher

Advanced Ingredients, Inc., 190
Al Gelato Bornay, 248
Alaska Smokehouse, 270
All American Foods Inc, 317
Allied Wine Corporation, 346
Alvarado Street Bakery, 397
American Pasien Co, 477
Art CoCo Chocolate Company, 707
Aunt Gussie Cookies & Crackers, 801
Bake Crafters Food Company, 950
BakeMark USA, 955
Ball Park Franks, 992
Ballas Egg Products Corp, 995
Beatrice Bakery Co, 1134
Bernie's Foods, 1251
Biazzo Dairy Products Inc, 1308
Blue Mountain Enterprise Inc, 1488
Bluechip Group, 1506
Butterball Farms, 1882
Byrne Dairy, Inc., 1902
Cache Creek Foods LLC, 1976
Cajun Creole Products Inc, 2021
Calise & Sons Bakery Inc, 2086

Capay Canyon Ranch, 2152
Carmi Flavor & Fragrance Company, 2223
Carole's Cheesecake Company, 2232
Chewys Rugulach, 2538
Chocolate By Design Inc, 2597
Chris Candies Inc, 2641
Ciro Foods, 2690
Coffee Masters, 2848
Cooke Aguaculture, 2981
Cookies United, 2989
Country Fresh Farms, 3074
Cricklewood Soyfoods, 3163
Crown Prince Inc, 3194
Dakota Brands Intl, 3353
Dakota Gourmet, 3354
David's Cookies, 3399
De Iorio's Foods Inc, 3427
Delano Growers Grape Products, 3489
Diehl Food Ingredients, 3593
Dipasa USA Inc, 3615
Durey-Libby Edible Nuts, 3808
East Coast Fresh Cuts Inc, 3879
Ed Roller Inc, 3931
Eda's Sugar Free, 3934
Empress Chocolate Company, 4058
F & S Produce Co Inc, 4196
First District Association, 4424
Foothills Creamery, 4578
Foremost Farms USA, 4591
Franklin Foods, 4665
French Meadow Bakery & Cafe, 4702
Garlic Valley Farms Inc, 4908
Gibbons Bee Farm, 5001
Gimbals Fine Candies, 5017
GKI Foods, 4834
Global Food Industries, 5063
Golden Fluff Popcorn Co, 5123
Golding Farms Foods, 5146
Gorant Chocolatier, 5192
Great Northern Products Inc, 5325
Great Western Juice Co, 5334
Haliburton International Inc, 5519
Harbar LLC, 5573
Harvest Valley Bakery Inc, 5636
Henningsen Foods Inc, 5769
Hialeah Products Co, 5828
Homestead Mills, 5946
Honey Acres, 5953
Hoopeston Foods Inc, 5987
I Rice & Co Inc, 6105
Ivanhoe Cheese Inc, 6328
Jeremiah's Pick Coffee Co, 6497
Jonathan Lord Cheesecakes, 6584
Just Born Inc, 6641
Kangaroo Brands, 6701
Kargher Corp, 6708
Kasilof Fish Company, 6721
Kayco, 6743
Kedem, 6746
Keller's Creamery, 6760
Kerry, Inc, 6808
King Nut Co, 6870
Knappen Milling Co, 6917
La Vigne Enterprises, 7116
LaCrosse Milling Company, 7118
Lake Champlain Chocolates, 7148
Lallemand American Yeast, 7173
Leighton's Honey Inc, 7329
Leo's Bakery & Deli, 7358
Louisiana Rice Mill, 7585
Lukas Confections, 7643
Main Street Gourmet, 7785
Mandarin Soy Sauce Inc, 7836
Martin Farms, 7966
Melchers Flavors of America, 8142
Mendocino Mustard, 8154
Merrill's Blueberry Farms, 8181
Mex America Foods LLC, 8206
Mincing Overseas Spice Company, 8341
Mother Murphy's, 8576
Mrs Clark's Foods, 8627
Mrs. Leeper's Pasta, 8642
Mushroom Co, 8693
Musicon Deer Farm, 8697
My Grandma's Coffee Cake, 8708
Myron's Fine Foods, Inc., 8715
N D Labs, 8719
National Fruit Flavor Co Inc, 8795
New Earth, 8967
New Era Canning Company, 8973
Northland Juices, 9167
Northumberland Dairy, 9170

Ethnic Food Index / Latin American

Northwest Pea & Bean Co, 9179
Northwestern Foods, 9184
Now & Zen, 9196
Nu-World Amaranth Inc, 9205
Oregon Chai, 9525
Oregon Freeze Dry, Inc., 9529
Organic Planet, 9553
Orwasher's Bakery, 9575
Otis Spunkmeyer, 9590
Ottawa Valley Grain Products, 9594
Pacific Spice Co, 9695
Partners Coffee LLC, 9798
Pecoraro Dairy Products, 9885
Pellman Foods Inc, 9906
Perfections by Allan, 9955
Poiret International, 10146
Porkie Company of Wisconsin, 10196
Primo Water Corporation, 10303
Protica Inc, 10350
Queensboro Farm Products, 10456
R L Schreiber Inc, 10481
Ranaldi Bros. Frozen Food Products, 10552
Regal Crown Foods Inc, 10638
Rogers' Chocolates Ltd, 10840
Rowena, 10919
Royal Wine Corp, 10952
Run-A-Ton Group Inc, 10981
Rv Industries, 11001
Santa Barbara Pistachio Co, 11184
Saputo Cheese USA Inc., 11209
Schwan's Food Service Inc., 11317
Scott's Auburn Mills, 11327
Seven Keys Co Of Florida, 11473
Sheryl's Chocolate Creations, 11554
Sierra Cheese Mfg Co, 11589
Siljans Crispy Cup Company, 11608
Snyder's of Hanover, 11769
Sonne, 11802
Spicetec Flavors & Seasonings, 11930
Star Kay White Inc, 12036
Steel's Gourmet Foods, Ltd., 12068
Sterling Extract Co Inc, 12085
Stewart's Private Blend Foods, 12110
Summit Lake Vineyards, 12227
Sunnyland Mills, 12287
Templar Food Products, 12612
Thiel Cheese & Ingredients, 12752
Thomas Canning/Maidstone, 12762
Timber Crest Farms, 12809
Top Hat Co Inc, 12881
Valley Lahvosh, 13256
Van Drunen Farms, 13270
Ventre Packing Company, 13326
Victor Preserving Company, 13385
Victoria Fine Foods, 13388
VIP Foods, 13240
Viterra, Inc, 13475
Wachusset Potato Chip Co Inc, 13523
Wawona Frozen Foods Inc, 13598
White Rock Products Corp, 13728
WILD Flavors (Canada), 13514
Wisconsin Cheeseman, 13874
Woolwich Dairy, 13927
World's Finest Chocolate Inc, 13948
Yohay Baking Co, 14013
Z Specialty Food, LLC, 14034

Latin American

Erba Food Products, 4104
Felbro Food Products, 4324
Fortitude Brands LLC, 4607
Goya Foods Inc., 5223
HealthBest, 5689
Mardi Gras, 7902
McDaniel Fruit, 8065
Prime Produce, 10295
Schiff Food Products Co Inc, 11284
T.W. Garner Food Company, 12473

Lebanese

Toom Dips, 12879

Mediterranean

Choice of Vermont, 2631
Mad Will's Food Company, 7737
Papa Leone Food Enterprises, 9752
Salonika Imports Inc, 11112
Shenk's Foods, 11546

Mexican

Abuelita Mexican Foods, 130
Alamo Tamale Corporation, 259
Algood Food Co, 305
Alimentaire Whyte's Inc, 307
Allied Old English Inc, 345
Alvarado Street Bakery, 397
Amigos Canning Company, 501
Anita's Mexican Foods Corporation, 573
Ariza Cheese Co, 668
Arizona Cowboy, 671
Art's Tamales, 709
Ashman Manufacturing & Distributing Company, 731
Atlantic Seasonings, 778
Avo-King Internatl, 841
Azteca Foods Inc, 855
Baja Foods LLC, 947
Bartush Schnitzius Foods Co, 1064
BBQ Bunch, 887
Bear Creek Country Kitchens, 1126
Bien Padre Foods Inc, 1316
Big B Barbecue, 1324
Blue Pacific Flavors & Fragrances, 1490
Border Foods, 1577
Brooks Tropicals Inc, 1757
Brown-Forman Corp, 1784
Bueno Foods, 1835
Burke Corp, 1861
C J Vitner Co, 1920
C W Resources Inc, 1925
Cacique, 1977
California Fruit and Tomato Kitchens, 2065
Camino Real Foods Inc, 2111
Carmelita Provisions Company, 2221
Casa Visco, 2274
Cedarlane Foods, 2355
Chelten House Products, 2509
Chicago Avenue Pizza, 2542
Choice of Vermont, 2631
Circle R Ranch, 2686
City Foods Inc, 2708
Colorado Salsa Company, 2898
Comanche Tortilla Factory, 2914
Cookies Food Products, 2988
Creative Foodworks Inc, 3137
Cyclone Enterprises Inc, 3284
Dave's Gourmet, 3393
Dean Distributors, Inc., 3441
Del Monte Foods Inc., 3478
Delgrosso Foods Inc, 3494
Dillman Farm Inc, 3601
Dipasa USA Inc, 3615
Diversified Avocado Products, 3622
Dolores Canning Co Inc, 3658
Dorina So-Good Inc, 3695
Double B Foods Inc, 3701
E.D. Smith Foods Ltd, 3844
EDCO Food Products Inc, 3849
El Charro Mexican Food Ind, 3978
El Milagro, 3982
El Rancho Tortilla, 3988
El Rey Cooked Meats, 3989
El Toro Food Products, 3991
Elena's Food Specialties, 4006
Famous Chili Inc, 4243
Father Sam's Bakery, 4306
Fernandez Chili Co, 4339
Fiesta Gourmet of Tejas, 4375
Figaro Company, 4381
Fischer & Wieser Spec Foods, 4432
Food Products Corporation, 4566
Fountain Valley Foods, 4623
Franklin Foods, 4665
Ful-Flav-R Foods, 4784
Garden Complements Inc, 4891
Gedney Foods Co, 4928
Genarom International, 4943
George Chiala Farms Inc, 4963
GNS Spices, 4841
Gold Pure Food Products Co. Inc., 5105
Golden Specialty Foods Inc, 5133
Golding Farms Foods, 5146
Goldwater's Food's Of Arizona, 5149
Goya Foods Inc., 5223
Grande Tortilla Factory, 5261
Great American Appetizers, 5294
Groeb Farms, 5396
Guiltless Gourmet, 5426
Hagerty Foods, 5498
Harbar LLC, 5573
Havoc Maker Products, 5652
Heluva Good Cheese, 5757
Herlocher Foods, 5805
Herr Foods Inc., 5815
Highwood Distillers, 5861
Hirzel Canning Co & Farms, 5893
Hormel Foods Corp., 6000
Hot Wachula's, 6018
Hume Specialties, 6069
Imus Ranch Foods, 6170
Indel Food Products Inc, 6177
Joe Hutson Foods, 6536
Juanita's Foods, 6619
Kajun Kettle Foods, 6687
Kelly Foods, 6769
King's Command Foods Inc, 6873
Kokopelli's Kitchen, 6942
Kozlowski Farms, 6974
La Buena Mexican Foods Products, 7079
La Chiquita Tortilla Manufacturing, 7081
LA Mexicana Tortilla Factory, 7052
LA Mexicana Tortilleria, 7053
LA Reina Inc, 7059
LA Torilla Factory, 7063
LA Vencedora Products Inc, 7064
Laredo Tortilleria & Mexican, 7219
Las Cruces Brand Products, 7231
Las Cruces Foods, 7232
Lawry's Foods, 7257
Leona's Restaurante, 7362
Li'l Guy Foods, 7407
Lone Star Bakery, 7520
Los Altos Food Products, 7546
Luna's Tortillas, 7648
Mad Will's Food Company, 7737
MAK Enterprises, 7694
Mancini Packing Co, 7832
Mangia Inc., 7842
Manhattan Food Brands, LLC, 7845
Manuel's Mexican-American Fine Foods, 7858
Manuel's Odessa Tortilla, 7859
Mari's Candy, 7904
Marie Brizard Wines & Spirits, 7913
Marquez Brothers International, 7949
Martins Famous Pastry Shoppe, 7972
Matador Processors, 8001
McDaniel Fruit, 8065
Meat-O-Mat Corp, 8114
Mertz Sausage Co, 8186
Mex America Foods LLC, 8206
Mexi-Frost Specialties Company, 8207
Mexican Accent, 8208
Mi Ranchito Foods, 8215
Miguel's Stowe Away, 8275
Mild Bill's Spices, 8291
Milnot Company, 8327
Mission Foodservice, 8387
Monterrey Products, 8507
Morgan Foods Inc, 8542
Morse's Sauerkraut, 8564
Mr Jay's Tamales & Chili, 8620
Mrs Auld's Gourmet Foods Inc, 8625
Natures Ingrown Foods Inc, 8898
New Canaan Farms, 8962
O'Garvey Sauces, 9290
Ocean Spray International, 9355
Olde Tyme Mercantile, 9439
Original Chili Bowl, 9561
Orleans Packing Co, 9569
Ottenberg's Bakers, 9595
Ozuna Food Products Corporation, 9626
Pacific Choice Brands, 9672
Paisley Farms Inc, 9712
Palmieri Food Products, 9728
Paradise Products Corporation, 9766
Penguin Frozen Foods Inc, 9912
Pepe's Inc, 9933
Pepe's Mexican Restaurant, 9934
Pepper Creek Farms, 9935
Perez Food Products, 9948
Picklesmith Inc, 10035
Pocino Foods, 10136
Puebla Foods Inc, 10363
Quality Sausage Company, 10442
Queen International Foods, 10453
R & S Mexican Food, 10476
R.W. Garcia, 10500
Ramona's Mexican Foods, 10548
Ready Foods Inc, 10585
Red Gold Inc., 10608
RENFRO Foods Inc, 10508
Riba Foods, 10701
Rio Valley Canning Co, 10749
Robbie's Natural Products, 10785
Romero's Food Products Inc, 10859
Rudolph's Specialty Bakery, 10968
Rudy's Tortillas, 10969
Ruiz Flour Tortillas, 10975
Ruiz Food Products Inc., 10976
Sabra Dipping Company,LL, 11065
Sam's Leon Mexican Food, 11126
San Antonio Farms, 11135
Sanitary Tortilla Manufacturing Company, 11181
Santa Barbara Olive Company, 11183
Santa Cruz Chili & Spice, 11190
Schiff Food Products Co Inc, 11284
Selecto Sausage Co, 11420
Severance Foods Inc, 11477
Shallowford Farms Popcorn, Inc., 11503
Soloman Baking Company, 11790
Spanish Gardens Food Manufacturing, 11887
St. Croix Beer Company, 12004
Stello Foods Inc, 12078
Sun Harvest Foods Inc, 12234
Sunny Avocado, 12280
Supreme Frozen Products, 12351
Sweet Earth Foods, 12396
T.W. Garner Food Company, 12473
Taqueria El Milagro, 12532
Terrell's Potato Chip Co, 12631
Texas Heat, 12653
Timber Crest Farms, 12809
Tolteca Foodservice, 12845
Tom Tom Tamale & Bakery Co, 12852
Torn & Glasser, 12893
Tyson Foods Inc., 13109
Uncle Fred's Fine Foods, 13155
UTZ Quality Foods Inc., 13129
Valley Grain Products, 13255
Van Oriental Food Inc, 13276
Ventre Packing Company, 13326
Victoria Fine Foods, 13388
WACO Beef & Pork Processors, 13509
Walker Foods, 13541
Westbrae Natural Foods, 13672
Wing Nien Food, 13855
Wyandot Inc, 13964

Middle Eastern

Abraham's Natural Foods, 128
Aladdin Bakers, 256
Alta Dena Certified Dairy LLC, 387
Aunt Kathy's Homestyle Products, 804
Balsu, 997
Byblos Bakery, 1894
Caltex Foods, 2096
Choice of Vermont, 2631
Dipasa USA Inc, 3615
East Wind Inc, 3887
Ener-G Foods, 4062
Fancy Lebanese Bakery, 4246
Fantis Foods Inc, 4257
Father Sam's Bakery, 4306
Fillo Factory, The, 4388
Franklin Foods, 4665
Heritage Foods USA, 5798
Hye Cuisine, 6099
Imperial Foods, Inc., 6160
JD Sweid Foods, 6394
Kalustyan, 6696
Lifeway, 7423
Marantha Natural Foods, 7892
Pearl Coffee Co, 9873
Queensboro Farm Products, 10456
Quong Hop & Company, 10472
Royal Vista Marketing Inc, 10951
San Marzano Imports, 11155
Santa Barbara Pistachio Co, 11184
Setton International Foods, 11468
Solo Foods, 11788
Sunnyland Mills, 12287
Tarazi Specialty Foods, 12535
Torrefazione Barzula & Import, 12896
Tribe Mediterranean, 12965
Victoria Fine Foods, 13388
Whole Herb Co, 13746

Ethnic Food Index / Moroccan

Moroccan
CHS Inc., 1948
Ellison Milling Company, 4025
North Dakota Mill & Elevator Assn., 9132
Orleans Packing Co, 9569

Polish
Aunt Kathy's Homestyle Products, 804
Babci's Specialty Foods, 908
Big City Reds, 1328
Boesl Packing Co, 1536
Bradshaw's Food Products, 1650
Country Smoked Meats, 3088
Far West Meats, 4259
Foell Packing Company, 4539
Frank Wardynski & Sons Inc, 4657
Gaspar's Linguica Co Inc, 4918
Gold Pure Food Products Co. Inc., 5105
Heritage Foods USA, 5798
Home Market Foods Inc., 5929
Hot Springs Packing Co Inc, 6017
Hot Wachula's, 6018
Laurent's Meat Market, 7249
Leo G. Fraboni Sausage Company, 7356
Locustdale Meat Packing, 7504
Martin Rosols, 7968
Millie's Pierogi, 8316
Milling Sausage Inc, 8318
Mucke's Meat Products, 8665
Multiflex Company, 8677
Naleway Foods, 8743
Norpaco Inc, 9113
Old Fashioned Kitchen Inc, 9412
Olympia International, 9464
Roma Packing Company, 10854
S.W. Meat & Provision Company, 11030
Sardinha's Sausage, 11224
Schiff Food Products Co Inc, 11284
Silver Star Meats Inc, 11627
Smith Packing Regional Meat, 11728
Smith Provision Co Inc, 11729
Smolich Bros. Home Made Sausage, 11740
Stanley Provision Company, 12032
Sunset Farm Foods Inc, 12300
Victor Ostrowski & Son, 13383
Victoria Fine Foods, 13388

Portuguese
Bradshaw's Food Products, 1650
Canadian Fish Exporters, 2122
Central Meat Market, 2380
Foell Packing Company, 4539
Gaspar's Linguica Co Inc, 4918
Gouvea's & Purity Foods Inc, 5219
Michael's Provision Co, 8232
Nature's Legacy Inc., 8886
New England Muffin Co Inc, 8970
San Joaquin Figs Inc, 11149
Sardinha's Sausage, 11224
Sini Fulvi U.S.A., 11668
Swiss-American Sausage Company, 12444

Puerto Rican
Bacardi Canada, Inc., 913
Banana Distributing Company, 1004
Buffalo Trace Distillery, 1839
Corby Distilleries, 3024
Country Smoked Meats, 3088
Crofton & Sons Inc, 3177
Destileria Serralles Inc, 3545
Dona Yiya Foods, 3676
Goya Foods Inc., 5223
Highwood Distillers, 5861

Hiram Walker & Sons, 5892
Hood River Distillers Inc, 5981
Manuel's Odessa Tortilla, 7859
Marie Brizard Wines & Spirits, 7913
Paradise Inc, 9763
Tantos Foods International, 12527
Trigo Corporation, 12970

Romanian
Aimonetto and Sons, 234
Bob Gordon & Associates, 1517
Home Market Foods Inc., 5929
Olympia International, 9464
Pendery's, 9911
Schiff Food Products Co Inc, 11284
Victoria Fine Foods, 13388

Russian-Ukrainian
Aimonetto and Sons, 234
Alimentaire Whyte's Inc, 307
Alta Dena Certified Dairy LLC, 387
Astro Dairy Products, 745
Aunt Kathy's Homestyle Products, 804
Bacardi Canada, Inc., 913
Bartush Schnitzius Foods Co, 1064
Cascadian Farm Inc, 2286
Cedarvale Food Products, 2357
Corby Distilleries, 3024
Destileria Serralles Inc, 3545
Elgin Dairy Foods, 4008
Emkay Trading Corporation, 4046
Ener-G Foods, 4062
Erba Food Products, 4104
Faribault Foods, Inc., 4267
Farmdale Creamery Inc, 4275
Fishhawk Fisheries, 4450
Fremont Authentic Brands, 4694
Gold Pure Food Products Co. Inc., 5105
Heaven Hill Distilleries Inc., 5720
Highwood Distillers, 5861
Hiram Walker & Sons, 5892
Hirzel Canning Co & Farms, 5893
Hood River Distillers Inc, 5981
Horizon Organic Dairy, 5996
HP Hood LLC, 5486
Hunter Farms - High Point Division, 6085
Jessie's Ilwaco Fish Company, 6508
Junuis Food Products, 6637
Kaiser Pickles, 6686
Kalustyan, 6696
Kelchner's Horseradish, 6758
Kruger Foods, 6993
Lakeside Packing Company, 7164
Lifeway, 7423
Lounsbury Foods, 7594
M.A. Hatt & Sons, 7686
Manischewitz Co, 7848
Marie Brizard Wines & Spirits, 7913
Marva Maid Dairy, 7978
Morehouse Foods Inc, 8539
Morrison Lamothe, 8560
New Harvest Foods, 8980
New Hope Mills Mfg Inc, 8982
Oakhurst Dairy, 9325
Old Fashioned Kitchen Inc, 9412
Olympia International, 9464
Paisley Farms Inc, 9712
Palmieri Food Products, 9728
Pleasant View Dairy, 10113
Queensboro Farm Products, 10455, 10456
R&A Imports, 10487
Red Pelican Food Products, 10614
Rego Smoked Fish Company, 10651
Roos Foods, 10869

Rosenberger's Dairies, 10894
Sazerac Company, Inc., 11264
Schiff Food Products Co Inc, 11284
Schneider's Dairy Inc, 11301
Schneider-Valley Farms Inc, 11302
Setton International Foods, 11468
Silver Spring Foods, 11625
Sisler's Ice & Ice Cream, 11675
Springfield Creamery Inc, 11971
Stawnichy Holdings, 12063
Sterling Caviar LLC, 12083
Strub Pickles, 12175
Thor-Shackel Horseradish Company, 12775
Tribe Mediterranean, 12965
Trigo Corporation, 12970
Umpqua Dairy, 13149
United Pickles, 13196
Valley Lahvosh, 13256
Victoria Fine Foods, 13388
Viking Distillery, 13406
Vitamilk Dairy, 13468
Woeber Mustard Mfg Co, 13894

Scandinavian
Alimentaire Whyte's Inc, 307
Bella Coola Fisheries, 1187
Bob Gordon & Associates, 1517
Calmar Bakery, 2094
Erba Food Products, 4104
Euroam Importers Inc, 4147
Fish Brothers, 4436
Flora Inc, 4509
Koppers Chocolate, 6961
Lefse House, 7308
Penguin Frozen Foods Inc, 9912
Schiff Food Products Co Inc, 11284
Sunnyrose Cheese, 12288
Svenhard's Swedish Bakery Inc, 12375
Victoria Fine Foods, 13388

Spanish
Aryzta, 721
Cacique, 1977
California Fruit and Tomato Kitchens, 2065
Canadian Fish Exporters, 2122
Cibao Meat Products Inc, 2670
Conrad Rice Mill Inc, 2956
Country Smoked Meats, 3088
Crofton & Sons Inc, 3177
Dufflet Pastries, 3782
Ecom Manufacturing Corporation, 3926
Elore Enterprises Inc, 4037
Erba Food Products, 4104
Goya Foods Inc., 5223
Great Northern Products Inc, 5325
KOZY Shack Enterprises Inc, 6676
L & S Packing Co, 7022
Manuel's Odessa Tortilla, 7859
Meat-O-Mat Corp, 8114
Olde Tyme Mercantile, 9439
Orleans Packing Co, 9569
Plaza de Espana Gourmet, 10110
Pompeian Inc, 10161
Raffield Fisheries Inc, 10530
Roos Foods, 10869
Seabrook Brothers & Sons, 11365
Sini Fulvi U.S.A., 11668
Victoria Fine Foods, 13388
Woodlake Ranch, 13919

Swiss
Atlantic Pork & Provisions, 773
Bellville Meat Market, 1204
C F Burger Creamery Co, 1915

Faber Foods and Aeronautics, 4214
Gaiser's European Style, 4861
Guggisberg Cheese, 5420
Heluva Good Cheese, 5757
Holmes Cheese Co, 5915
Houser Meats, 6031
Indian Valley Meats, 6191
Ivanhoe Cheese Inc, 6328
Kolb-Lena Bresse Bleu Inc, 6945
Los Altos Food Products, 7546
Marathon Cheese Corp, 7894
Maytag Dairy Farms Inc, 8043
Middlefield Cheese House, 8263
Mt Capra Products, 8652
Mucke's Meat Products, 8665
New England Natural Bakers, 8971
Paris Pastry, 9776
Penn Cheese, 9914
Quality Ingredients, 10436
Rabbit Barn, 10521
Ragersville Swiss Cheese, 10531
Reilly Dairy & Food Company, 10655
Saag's Products LLC, 11059
Spruce Foods, 11980
Steiner Cheese, 12073
Wenger Spring Brook Cheese Inc, 13650
Yogi® Tea, 14011

Thai
Cinnabar Specialty Foods Inc, 2681
Commodities Marketing Inc, 2923
Ethnic Gourmet Foods, 4138
Lang Pharma Nutrition Inc, 7210
Mo Hotta Mo Betta, 8433
Nielsen Citrus Products Inc, 9049
North Bay Produce Inc, 9126
Pastene Co LTD, 9819
Pearson's Homestyle, 9879
Santa Cruz Chili & Spice, 11190
Setton International Foods, 11468
Taj Gourmet Foods, 12499
Toddy Products Inc, 12833
Torn & Glasser, 12893
Victoria Fine Foods, 13388

Turkish
San Marzano Imports, 11155

West Indian
Bacardi Canada, Inc., 913
Banana Distributing Company, 1004
Benson's Gourmet Seasonings, 1222
Buffalo Trace Distillery, 1839
California-Antilles Trading, 2083
Caribbean Food Delights Inc, 2209
Catskill Mountain Specialties, 2323
Cinnabar Specialty Foods Inc, 2681
Corby Distilleries, 3024
Destileria Serralles Inc, 3545
Erba Food Products, 4104
Highwood Distillers, 5861
Hiram Walker & Sons, 5892
Hood River Distillers Inc, 5981
Kutztown Bologna Company, 7010
Marie Brizard Wines & Spirits, 7913
Mexi-Frost Specialties Company, 8207
Royal Caribbean Bakery, 10924
Royal Home Bakery, 10935
Schiff Food Products Co Inc, 11284
Tantos Foods International, 12527
Trigo Corporation, 12970
Uncle Fred's Fine Foods, 13155
Victoria Fine Foods, 13388

Geographic Index / Alabama

Alabama

A.C. Legg, 64
Adams Foods & Milling, 166
Alabama Gulf Seafood, 254
Amazing Fruit Products, 419
American Wholesale Grocery, 490
Andalusia Distributing Co Inc, 541
Barber Dairies, 1021
Barney Pork House, 1048
Bayou Crab, 1108
Berson Peanuts, 1256
Billy's Seafood Inc, 1356
Blalock Seafood & Specialty, 1435
Boja's Foods Inc, 1545
Bon Secour Fisheries Inc, 1550
Braswell's Winery, 1668
Brooks Peanut Co, 1756
Bryant Vineyard, 1807
CanAmera Foods, 2120
Capt Collier Seafood, 2180
Carrington Foods Co Inc, 2261
Chester's International, LLC, 2533
Chicken Salad Chick, 2556
Conecuh Sausage Co, 2944
Consolidated Sea Products, 2963
Dean Sausage Co Inc, 3443
DIP Seafood Mudbugs, 3312
El Brands, 3977
Elba Custom Meats, 3994
Ensemble Beverages, 4077
Fast Fixing Foods, 4300
Five Ponds Farm, 4457
Flowers Baking Co, 4526, 4528
Fresh Seafood Distrib, 4723
George's Candy Shop Inc, 4969
Golden Eagle Syrup, 5119
Golden Flake Snack Foods, 5122
Graham Fisheries, 5240
Great Western Co LLC, 5333
Gulf City Marine Supply, 5431
Gulf Pecan Company, 5437
Gulf Stream Crab Company, 5441
Harbison Wholesale Meats, 5574
Hartselle Frozen Foods, 5623
Harvard Seafood Company, 5627
Harvest Select, 5633
Hilltop Meat Co, 5877
J & B Seafood, 6335
J & L Seafood, 6342
Jerrell Packaging, 6498
Johnson Sea Products Inc, 6568
Jubilee Foods, 6622
Kelley Foods, 6762
Lartigue Seafood, 7230
Leroy Hill Coffee Co Inc, 7372
Lindsay Farms, 7444
Loafin' Around, 7496
Marshall Durbin Companies, 7955
Marx Brothers Inc, 7980
Miller Johnson Seafood, 8309
Mobile Bay Seafood, 8434
Mobile Processing, 8435
Mrs Stratton's Salads Inc, 8633
N.B.J. Enterprises, 8720
Naji's Pita Gourmet Restaurant, 8735
Nantze Springs Inc, 8760
Peco Foods Inc., 9883
Piknik Products Company, 10054
Piper & Leaf, 10082
Pollman's Bake Shop, 10156
Pond Pure Catfish, 10164
Priester's Pecans, 10281
Quillin Produce Co, 10463
R.L. Zeigler Company, 10497
Red Diamond Coffee & Tea, 10606
Rod Golden Hatchery Inc, 10829
Royal Cup Coffee, 10928
Royal Lagoon Seafood Inc, 10937
S.T. Jerrell Company, 11029
Sandco International, 11166
Scripture Candy, 11335
Sea Lyons, 11345
Sea Pearl Seafood, 11347
Sea-Fresh Seafood Market, 11357
Segall Nathan Co Inc, 11411
Selma Good Company, 11423
Selwoods Farm Hunting Preserve, 11425
Sessions Co Inc, 11464
Sewell's Seafood & Fish Market, 11483
Shashy's Bakery & Fine Foods, 11523
Southern Fish & Oyster Company, 11851
SRA Foods, 11053
Stanley's Best Seafood, 12033
Star Seafood, 12039
Starich, 12043
Stewarts Seafood, 12113
Sunfresh Beverages Inc., 12275
Superbrand Dairies, 12326
Superior Pecans, 12342
Sweet Sue Kitchens, 12416
T'Lish Dressings and Marinades, 12466
Taziki's Cafe, 12580
Tucker Pecan Co, 13047
Tusitala, 13081
Val's Seafood, 13246
W.L. Petrey Wholesale Inc., 13503
Wallace Fisheries, 13548
Waterfront Seafood, 13587
Webbpak Inc, 13613
Whaley Pecan Co Inc, 13702
Whitfield Foods Inc, 13740
Wright Brand Oysters, 13957

Alaska

Alaska Aquafarms, 260
Alaska Bounty Seafoods & Smokery, 261
Alaska Herb & Tea Co, 263
Alaska Jacks, 264
Alaska Ocean Trading, 265
Alaska Pacific Seafoods, 266
Alaska Pasta Co, 267
Alaska Sausage & Seafood, 268
Alaska Seafood Co, 269
Alaskan Brewing Company, 271
Alaskan Gourmet Seafoods, 272
Alaskan Smoked Salmon & Seafood, 274
Alyeska Seafoods, 400
Annette Island Packing Company, 587
Aquatech, 625
Atka Pride Seafoods Inc, 752
Aurora Alaska Premium Smoked Salmon & Seafood, 810
C & J Tender Meat Co, 1912
Cafe Del Mundo, 1991
Cameron Birch Syrup & Confections, 2108
Canoe Lagoon Oyster Company, 2141
Cook Inlet Processing, 2976
Dear North, 3445
Deep Creek Custom Packing, 3464
Dragnet Fisheries, 3743
E.C. Phillips & Son, 3843
Ed's Kasilof Seafoods, 3933
Haines Packing Company, 5508
Heritage Coffee Co & Cafe, 5794
Horst Seafood, 6004
Indian Valley Meats, 6191
Interior Alaska Fish Processors, 6243
International Seafoods - Alaska, 6270
Island Seafoods, 6306
J&R Fisheries, 6370
J.R. Fish Company, 6383
Kachemak Bay Seafood, 6682
Kaladi Brothers, 6689
Kodiak Salmon Packers, 6933
Kwikpak Fisheries, 7013
Miss Scarlett's Flowers, 8381
Northern Keta Caviar, 9152
Northern Meats, 9154
Offshore Systems Inc, 9372
Pelican Seafoods, 9904
R&J Seafoods, 10489
Royal Pacific Fisheries, 10942
Sahalee of Alaska, 11084
Salamatof Seafoods, 11098
Sales Associates Of Alaska, 11104
Salmon River Smokehouse, 11111
Santa's Smokehouse, 11200
Sappore Coffee Co Of Alaska, 11207
Sealaska Corp, 11380
Shawmut Fishing Company, 11527
Taku Smokehouse, 12503
Teddy's Tasty Meats, 12599
Tenth & M Seafoods, 12618
Trident Seafoods Corp, 12969

Alberta

Alberta Cheese Company, 280
Alley Kat Brewing Co, Ltd, 339
Baier's Sausage & Meats, 940
Baker Boys, 960
Big Chief Meat Snacks Inc, 1327
Big Rock Brewery, 1340
Billingsgate Fish Company, 1355
Bob's Custom Cuts, 1518
Bouma Meats, 1622
Bouvry Exports Calgary, 1628
Bow Valley Brewing Company, 1630
Bowness Bakery, 1633
Buns & Roses Organic Wholegrain Bakery, 1853
Byblos Bakery, 1894
Calco of Calgary, 2040
Calgary Italian Bakery, 2045
Calmar Bakery, 2094
Camrose Packers, 2118
Capital Packers Inc, 2162
Carrie's Chocolates, 2259
Centennial Food Corporation, 2367
Chocolaterie Bernard Callebaut, 2614
Clover Leaf Cheese, 2780
Coca-Cola Bottling Company UNITED, Inc., 2813
CTC Manufacturing, 1964
Cupper's Coffee Company, 3255
Daniel's Bagel & Baguette Corporation, 3373
Decadent Desserts, 3455
Delta Food Products, 3513
Dow AgroSciences Canada, 3716
Drader Manufacturing Industries, 3742
Edmonton Potato Growers, 3950
Eiserman Meats, 3976
Ellison Milling Company, 4025
Engel's Bakeries, 4069
European Egg Noodle Manufacturing, 4153
Farmers Meat Market, 4282
Floron Food Services, 4524
Foothills Creamery, 4578
Fratello Coffee Roasters, 4674
Glamorgan Bakery, 5045
Gonard Foods, 5151
Gouw Quality Onions, 5220
Henderson's Gardens, 5764
Highwood Distillers, 5861
Humeniuk's Meat Cutting, 6070
Hung's Noodle House, 6079
Italian Gourmet Foods Canada, 6320
J.P. Sunrise Bakery, 6382
Kinnikinnick Foods, 6884
Kuhlmann's Market Gardens & Greenhouses, 6999
Labatt Breweries Alberta, 7120
Lakeview Bakery, 7165
Lefse House, 7308
Longview Meat & Merchandise Ltd, 7535
MacEwan's Meats, 7720
MacKay's Cochrane Ice Cream, 7722
Mandarin Noodle Manufacturing Company, 7835
McLane's Meats, 8080
Meatco Sales Ltd., 8115
Meatland Packers, 8118
Mediterranean Pita Bakery, 8123
Norac Technologies, 9103
Nossack Fine Meats, 9187
Olivier's Candies, 9455
Onoway Custom Packers, 9497
Paradis Honey, 9761
Parmx, 9792
Pasta Mill, 9812
Pearson's Berry Farm, 9878
Pearson's Homestyle, 9879
Pinocchio Italian Ice Cream Company, 10069
Prairie Mushrooms, 10236
Prime Ostrich International, 10292
Provost Packers, 10358
Red Deer Lake Meat Processing, 10605
Red Hat Cooperative, 10609
Riddles' Sweet Impressions, 10736
Rocky Mountain Coffee Roasters, 10820
Rocky Mountain Meats, 10822
Rogers Sugar Inc., 10839
Rolling Pin Bakery, 10849
Sangudo Custom Meat Packers, 11179
Saxby Foods, 11260
Shrums Sausage & Meats, 11577
Siljans Crispy Cup Company, 11608
Simmons Hot Gourmet Products Corp., 11640
Something Special Deli-Foods, 11798
Stawnichy Holdings, 12063
Sun Sun Food Products, 12247
Sunnyrose Cheese, 12288
Sunterra Meats, 12314
Superior Mushroom Farms, 12336
Tiger Mushroom Farm, 12801
Tofield Packers Ltd, 12839
Vantage Foods, 13295
Vauxhall Foods, 13303
Vermilion Packers Ltd, 13342
Victoria Fancy Sausage, 13387
Westbrook Trading Company, 13674
Western Beef Jerky, 13678
Wings Foods of Alberta Ltd, 13861
Wow! Factor Desserts, 13954

Arizona

Almond Brothers, 355
APS BioGroup, 99
Arbuckle Coffee Roasters, 633
Arizona Cowboy, 671
Arizona Natural Products, 672
Arizona Nutritional Supplements, 673
Arizona Pepper Products, 674
Arizona Pistachio Company, 675
Arizona Sunland Foods, 676
Arizona Vineyards, 677
Armistead Citrus Company, 684
Avalon Gourmet, 828
Bakon Yeast, 981
Bar-S Foods Co, 1017
Bard Valley Medjool Date Growers, 1028
Barone Foods, 1051
Beaver Street Brewery, 1139
Bee Seasonal, 1160
Betsy's Cheese Straws, 1278
Biotec A Z Laboratories, 1380
Brickerlabs.Com, 1703
C C Pollen, 1914
C. Gould Seafoods, 1931
Cheri's Desert Harvest, 2515
China Mist Brands, 2570
Christopher Joseph Brewing Company, 2653
Cinnabar Specialty Foods Inc, 2681
Coffee Reserve, 2855
Crockett Honey, 3173
Daily Nutrition, 3329
Diazteca Inc, 3585
DNX Foods, 3316
Don Jose Foods, 3670
Fairytale Brownies, 4230
Fiesta Canning Co, 4373
Flagstaff Brewing Co, 4466
Flat Tire Bike Shop, 4475
Flavor Right Foods Group, 4483
Flavorbank Company, 4487
Food Products Corporation, 4566
Gadsden Coffee/Caffe, 4857
Gentle Ben's Brewing Co, 4959
Grande Tortilla Factory, 5261
Green Valley Pecan Company, 5367
Gum Technology Corporation, 5442
Halfpops Inc, 5518
Healing Solutions, 5677
Heartbreaking Dawns Artisan Foods, 5703
Hobe Laboratories Inc, 5897
Holsum Bakery Inc, 5917
Homestyle Bread Bakery, 5948
Honso USA, 5978
Hosford & Wood Fresh Seafood Providers, 6008
Illy Espresso of the Americas, 6147
Ivy Foods, 6331
JC's Midnite Salsa, 6392
JoJo's Chocolate, 6526
Klein's Kosher Pickles, 6908
Kokopelli's Kitchen, 6942
L.H. Rodriguez Wholesale Seafood, 7038
La Buena Mexican Foods Products, 7079
LA Canasta Mexican Foods, 7042
Leaves Pure Teas, 7287
Lee's Ice Cream, 7299
Lehi Valley Trading Company, 7319
Lifestar Millennium, 7421
Love You Foods, 7601
M&L Ventures, 7641
Mama Rose's Gourmet Foods, 7818
Marlyn Nutraceuticals, 7947
Meat & Fish Fellas, 8111
Meyer's Bakeries, 8212
Mi Ranchito Foods, 8215
Mikey's, 8283
Mission Foods, 8383

1317

Geographic Index / Arkansas

Nanci's Frozen Yogurt, 8749
North American Enterprises, 9119
Nutri Base, 9245
Oak Creek Brewing Company, 9310
Oats Overnight, 9336
Omega Produce Company, 9478
Paradise Valley Vineyards, 9768
Peanut Patch, 9867
Phoenician Herbals, 10020
Poore Brothers, 10173
PR Bar, 9661
Prescott Brewing Co, 10261
Prime Cut Meat & Seafood Company, 10289
Prolume, 10341
R & S Mexican Food, 10476
R T Foods Inc, 10484
Red Steer Meats, 10622
Rene Produce Dist, 10672
RiceBran Technologies, 10709
Rocky Point Shrimp Association, 10825
Rousseau Farming Co, 10914
Royal Pacific Coffee Co, 10941
Royal Products, 10945
S.W. Meat & Provision Company, 11030
Safeway Milk Plant, 11074
Saguaro Food Products, 11080
San Dominique Winery, 11139
Santa Cruz Chili & Spice, 11190
Shamrock Foods Co, 11504, 11507
Sonoita Vineyards, 11803
Southwest Specialty Food, 11873
Spinato's Fine Foods, 11935
Sprouts Farmers Market Inc., 11979
Sweetleaf Co, 12429, 12430
Tessenderlo Kerley Inc, 12637
Treehouse Farms, 12944
True Nopal Cactus Water, 13033
Tucson Tamale Company, 13048
Union Seafoods, 13172
Unique Ingredients LLC, 13177
United Dairymen of Arizona, 13187
Upper Crust Bakery USA, 13215
Urban Oven, 13225
Vity Meat & Provisions Company, 13476
Wholesome Family Farms, 13752
Willcox Meat Packing House, 13808
Wisdom Natural Brands-Uani, 13883
World Nutrition, Inc., 13940

Arkansas

Bio-Tech Pharmacal Inc, 1370
Bright Harvest Sweet Potato Co, 1713
Broadaway Ham Co, 1727
Bryant Preserving Company, 1806
C & C Packing Co, 1907
Coach Sposato's Bar-B-Que, 2794
Cormier Rice Milling Co Inc, 3033
Cowie Wine Cellars & Vineyards, 3102
Crunch-A-Mame, 3200
Crystal Lake Farms, 3213
Delta Catfish Products, 3512
Diamond Water Bottling Fclty, 3578
Famous Chili Inc, 4243
Fasweet Co, 4302
Fischer Honey Company, 4433
Flying Burrito Co, 4533
George's Inc, 4970
Good Old Days Foods, 5169
Hillbilly Smokehouse, 5868
Hog Haus Brewing Company, 5903
Hot Springs Packing Co Inc, 6017
House of Webster, 6029
J & M Foods Inc, 6343
Jimmy Dean Foods, 6520
John Garner Meats, 6552
Kruse Meat Products, 6996
Land O'Frost Inc, 7196
Lemke Wholesale, 7335
Little Portion Bakery, 7470
Lone Pine Enterprise Inc, 7519
McKnight Milling Company, 8079
Mid-South Fish Company, 8259
Moonlight Mixes LLC, 8527
Mountain Valley Spring Company, 8605
Mt Bethel Winery, 8651
My Brother's Salsa, 8704
Oh Baby Foods, Inc., 9374
Ok Industries, 9389
Ozark Empire, 9621
Pepper Source LTD, 9939
Pepper Source, Rogers, 9940

Pioneer Foods Industries, 10074
Post Familie Vineyards, 10214
Pride of Dixie Syrup Company, 10280
Producers Rice Mill Inc., 10328
Rice Hull Specialty Products, 10707
Riceland Foods Inc., 10710
SFP Food Products, 11040
Simmons Foods Inc, 11639
Sims Wholesale, 11661
Southern Brown Rice, 11845
Specialty Rice Inc, 11908
Tyson Foods Inc., 13109, 13110
Vino's Brew Pub, 13428
Walker's Seafood, 13543
War Eagle Mill, 13566
Wicked Mix, 13760
Wiederkehr Wine Cellars Inc, 13769
Woody's Bar-B-Q Sauce Company, 13926

British Columbia

Abbotsford Growers Ltd., 112
Alpha Health, 375
Aquatec Seafoods Ltd., 624
Asti Holdings Ltd, 742
Avafina Organics, 827
Babe's Honey Farm, 911
BakeMark Ingredients Canada, 954
Bella Coola Fisheries, 1187
Bevco Sales International Inc., 1292
Big Mountain Foods, 1336
Blundell Seafoods, 1512
Bradley Technologies Canada Inc., 1649
Brockmann's Chocolates, 1733
Brookside Foods, 1760
Butter Baked Goods, 1879
Calkins & Burke, 2089
Daiya Foods, 3351
Dan-D Foods Ltd, 3368
Daniel Le Chocolat Belge, 3372
DeeBee's Organics, 3462
Delta Pacific Seafoods, 3514
Ding Hau Food Co, Ltd, 3608
Dollar Food Manufacturing, 3657
E-Fish-Ent Fish Company, 3840
Ethical Bean Coffee, 4135
Everland Foods, 4169
Everland Parks, 4170
Favorite Foods, 4311
Fentimans North America, 4332
FIFO Innovations, 4206
Fine Choice Foods, 4393
Foley's Chocolates & Candies, 4542
FreeYumm, 4680
French Creek Seafood, 4697
Freybe Gourmet Foods Ltd, 4729
Garden Protein International, 4893
GLG Life Tech Corporation, 4836, 4837
Global Gardens Group Inc., 5064
Golden Valley Foods Ltd., 5138
Great Glacier Salmon, 5309
Grimm's Fine Food, 5391
Hagensborg Chocolates LTD., 5497
Happy Planet Foods, 5571
Healthco Canada Enterprises, 5690
Heritage Salmon Company, 5801
Hippie Snacks, 5891
Imperial Salmon House, 6162
Island Farms Dairies Cooperative
  Association, 6299
Island Scallops, 6304
J.S. McMillan Fisheries, 6387
JD Sweid Foods, 6394
Kapow Now!, 6706
Kicking Horse Coffee, 6834
Lentia Enterprises Ltd., 7354
Lesley Stowe Fine Foods, 7391
Mac's Oysters, 7718
Mario's Gelati, 7932
Money's Mushrooms, 8477
Monkey Media, 8480
Mrs. Willman's Baking, 8649
National Importers, 8799
Naturally Homegrown, 8855
Nature's Herbs, 8882
New Generation Foods, 8974
Nicola Valley Apiaries, 9046
Nonna Pia's Gourmet Sauces, 9091
North American Reishi/Nammex, 9120
North Peace Apiaries, 9135
Nutri-Nation, 9249
Oceanfood Sales, 9360

Okanagan Spring Brewery, 9391
One Degree Organic Foods, 9488
Pacific Seafoods International, 9693
Pacific Western Brewing Company, 9701
Paradise Island Foods, 9764
Promolux Lighting, 10344
Quality Bakery, 10426
Quality Foods, 10435
Rene Rey Chocolates Ltd, 10673
Rogers Sugar Inc., 10838
Rogers' Chocolates Ltd, 10840
Russell Breweries, Inc., 10989
Secret Tea Garden, 11403
Service Packing Company, 11461
Shafer-Haggart, 11495
SmartSweets, 11715
Snowcrest Packer, 11766
Sugarplum Desserts, 12209
Summerland Sweets, 12224
Sun-Rype Products, 12259
Sunrise Markets, 12298
Tin Whistle Brewing Co, 12814
Top Tier Foods Inc., 12883
Tropical Link Canada Ltd., 13006
Trumps Food Interest, 13040
Valley Bakery, 13252
Vancouver Island Brewing Company, 13288
Vista D'Oro Farms, 13452
Walcan Seafood, 13537
Whistler Brewing Company, 13710, 13711
Zazubean, 14046

California

18 Rabbits Inc., 5
24 Mantra Organic, 8
24Vegan, 9
360 Nutrition, 15
4505 Meats LLC, 18
479 Degrees, 19
4th & Heart, 22
51 Fifty Enterprises, 25
731 North Beach LLC, 26
99 Ranch Market, 31
A Dozen Cousins, 35
A Perfect Pear, 40
A Plus Label, 41
A Tavola Together, 44
A-1 Eastern-Homemade Pickle Co, 53
A. Nonini Winery, 57
A. Rafanelli Winery, 58
A.C. Calderoni, 60
Abbot's Butcher, 111
ABC Tea House, 72
Acacia Vineyard, 132
Acai Roots, 136
Acme Bread Co, 150
Acqua Blox LLC, 154
Acta Health Products, 156
Action Labs, 157
Adams & Brooks Inc, 163
Adams Olive Ranch, 167
Adams Vegetable Oils Inc, 169
AddGarlic!, 170
Adelaida Cellars Inc, 172
Adler Fels Winery, 177
Adobe Creek Packing Co Inc, 180
Adobe Springs, 181
Adrienne's Gourmet Foods, 183
Agave Dream, 203
AgStandard Smoked Almonds, 202
Agusa, 225
Ahlgren Vineyard, 229
Aidells Sausage Co, 232
Aiya America Inc, 236
Ajinomoto Foods North America, Inc., 237
Ajinomoto Frozen Foods USA, Inc., 238
Ak Mak Bakeries, 241
Alcove Chocolate, 282
AleSmith Brewing Company, 286
Alfer Laboratories, 297
Alfred Louie Inc, 301
Aliotti Wholesale Fish Company, 313
All Goode Organics, 320
Alldran Brothers, 328
Allegria Italian Bakers, 331
Allylix Inc, 350
ALO Drink, 88
ALO Drinks, 89
Alpen Cellars, 369
Alpine Meats, 380
Alta Dena Certified Dairy LLC, 387

Alta Dena Heartland Farms, 388
Alta Vineyard Cellar, 390
Altamura Winery, 391
Alter Eco, 392
Alto Rey Food Corp, 394
Alvarado Street Bakery, 397
Amador Foothill Winery, 403
Amara Organic Baby Food, 415
AmByth Estate, 401
Amcan Beverages Inc, 427
Amella, 430
America's Classic Foods, 437
American Chalkis Intl. Food Corp., 445
American Copak Corporation, 448
American Food Ingredients Inc, 455
American Fruits & Flavors, 458
American Natural & Organic, 473
American Nuts Inc., 475
American Tuna, 487
American Vegetable Oils, 488
Americolor Corp, 494
AmeriGift, 434
AMF Pharma, 94
Amira Nature Foods Ltd., 502
Amizetta Vineyards, 505
Amoretti, 507
Amphora International, 509
Amsnack, 515
Amy & Brian Naturals, 519
Amy's Kitchen Inc, 522
Anabol Naturals, 526
Anchor Brewing Company, 531
Ancient Organics, 536
Ancient Peaks Winery, 537
Andean Naturals LLC, 542
Andersen's Pea Soup, 543
Anderson Seafood, 548
Anderson Valley Brewing Co, 549
Anderson's Conn Valley Vineyards, 550
Andre-Boudin Bakeries, 553
Andrew & Williamson Sales Co, 554
Anette's Chocolate & Ice Cream, 561
Angelo & Franco U.S.A., 565
Anita's Mexican Foods Corporation, 573
Annabelle Candy Co Inc, 583
Annapolis Winery, 586
Annie Chun's, 589
Annie's Homegrown, 591
Annie's Naturals, 592
Antelope Valley Winery, 593
Anton Caratan & Son, 597
AOI Matcha, 96
AOI Tea Company, 97
Apac Chemical Corporation, 600
Arcadia Biosciences, 634
Arctic Zero, 647
Arena & Sons, 653
Argania Butter, 654
Argee Corp, 655
Ariel Vineyards, 663
Aries Prepared Beef, 664
Ariza Cheese Co, 668
Arizmendi Bakery, 669
Armanino Foods of Distinction, 680
Arnabal International, Inc., 685
Arnel's Originals, Inc, 686
Arns Winery, 691
Aroma Vera, 695
Aroma-Life, 696
Arrowood Winery, 706
Artek USA, 711
Artesa Vineyards & Winery, 712
Aryzta, 721
Aspen Mulling Company Inc., 736
ASV Wines, 104
Athens Baking Company, 749
Atlantic Chemicals Trading, 766
Atlas Peak Vineyards, 781
Au Bon Climat Winery, 788
AuNutra Industries Inc, 791
Avery Dennison Corporation, 839
Avo-King Internatl, 841
Avri Co Inc, 845
AVRON Resources Inc, 105
Axiom Foods, Inc., 850
Ayara Products, 852
Azuma Foods Intl Inc USA, 857
B R Cohn Winery & Olive Oil Co, 869
B. Nutty, 880
B.M. Lawrence & Company, 883
Baba Foods, 907
Babcock Winery & Vineyards, 909

1318

Geographic Index / California

Babe Farms Inc, 910
Back to the Roots, 920
Bagai Tea Company, 932
Bagel Factory, 933
Baileyana Winery, 942
Baily Vineyard & Winery, 944
BakeMark USA, 956
Bakeology, 958
Baker Commodities Inc, 963
Bakers of Paris, 974
Balboa Dessert Co Inc, 986
Baldwin-Minkler Farms, 990
Ballantine Produce Company, 993
Barca Wine Cellars, 1026
Bargetto Winery, 1033
Bari Olive Oil Co, 1036
Barnana, 1044
Barney Butter, 1047
Baron Vineyards, 1050
Barsotti Family Juice Co., 1058
Basic American Foods, 1069
Basque French Bakery, 1076
Bautista Family Organic Date, 1088
Bavarian Specialty Foods, LLC, 1092
Bay Cities Produce Co Inc, 1095
Bay Hawk Ales, 1097
Bay Pac Beverages, 1100
Baywood Cellars, 1112
BCFoods, 893
BDS Natural, 895
Bea & B Foods, 1116
Bear Naked, Inc., 1130
Beaucanon Estate Wines, 1135
Beaujolais Panforte, 1136
Beaulieu Vineyard, 1137
Becker Foods, 1146
Beckmann's Old World Bakery, 1148
Beckmen Vineyards, 1149
Bee International, 1158
Bell-Carter Foods Inc, 1185
Bella Chi-Cha Products, 1186
Bella Sun Luci, 1190
Bella Viva Orchards, 1192
Bellerose Vineyard, 1197
Bellucci, 1203
Bellwether Farms, 1205
Belmont Brewing Co, 1208
Benson's Gourmet Seasonings, 1222
Benziger Family Winery, 1225
Berberian Nut Company, 1228
Berkeley Farms, 1234
Bernard & Sons, 1242
Bernardo Winery, 1246
Bernardus Winery Tasting Rm, 1247
Berri Pro, 1253
Berryessa Gap Tasting Room, 1255
Beta Pure Foods, 1273
Beth's Fine Desserts, 1275
Bette's Oceanview Diner, 1280
Better Beverages Inc, 1283
Better Than Coffee, 1287
Beyond Meat, 1299
Bgreen Food, 1300
Bhu Foods, 1302
Bi Nutraceuticals, 1304
Bianchi Winery, 1306
Bien Padre Foods Inc, 1316
Big Poppa Smokers, 1338
Big Train Inc, 1347
Bio-Hydration Research Lab, 1367
Bionutritional Research Group, 1377
Birkholm's Solvang Bakery, 1392
Biscomerica Corporation, 1394
Biscoti Di Suzy, 1395
Bison Brewing Company, 1401
Bitchin' Sauce, 1406
BJ's Restaurants Inc., 897
Black Garlic, 1418
Black Market Gelato, 1421
Black Ranch Organic Grains, 1424
Black Sheep Vintners, 1426
Blansh International, 1437
Bloomfield Bakers, 1458
Blue California Co, 1466
Blue Diamond Growers, 1471
Blue Evolution, 1473
Blue Monkey, 1485
Blue Pacific Flavors & Fragrances, 1490
Blue Sky Beverage Company, 1498
Blue Willow Tea Co, 1501
Bobalu Nuts, 1520
Boboli Intl. Inc., 1524

Bodega Chocolates, 1529
Boeger Winery, 1534
Boggiatto Produce Inc, 1538
Boghosian Raisin Packing Co, 1539
Bogle Vineyards Inc, 1541
Boisset Family Estates, 1543
Bolt House Farms-Shipping Dept, 1548
Bonafide Provisions, 1552
Bonert's Pies Inc, 1556
Bongiovi Brand Pasta Sauces, 1558
Bonk Breaker, 1559
Bonterra Vineyard, 1567
Bordoni Vineyards, 1579
Bornt & Sons Inc, 1583
Borra Vineyards, 1584
Boskovich Farms Inc, 1588
Bossen, 1590
Botanical Bakery, LLC, 1602
Botanical Products, 1603
Bouchaine Vineyards, 1608
Boulder Creek Brewing Company, 1615
Bozzano Olive Ranch, 1643
Bragg Live Food Products Inc, 1652
Brander Vineyard, 1657
Brandt Farms Inc, 1662
Braren Pauli Winery, 1664
Breaktime Snacks, 1683
Brekki, 1689
Briceland Vineyards, 1701
Bridge Brands Chocolate, 1705
Bridgford Foods Corp, 1709
Broadleaf Venison USA Inc, 1730
Bronco Wine Co, 1738
Brother Bru Bru's, 1762
Brother's Trading LLC, 1763
Brothers Desserts, 1766
Brothers International Desserts, 1767
Brownie Baker Inc, 1785
Brucia Plant Extracts, 1797
Brutocao Cellars, 1804
Bubbies Fine Foods, 1811
Bubbles Baking Co, 1813
Bubbles of San Francisco, 1814
Buchanan Hollow Nut Co, 1816
Buddha Teas, 1826
Buehler Vineyards, 1833
Buena Vista Historic Tstng Rm, 1834
Buff Bake, 1836
Buffalo Bill Brewing Company, 1837
Bumble Bee, 1844
Burnett & Son, 1865
Busseto Foods, 1875
Butterfly Creek Winery, 1886
Buttonwood Farm Winery & Vineyard, 1888
Byington Vineyard & Winery, 1895
Byron Vineyard & Winery, 1906
C & F Foods Inc, 1909
C & H Sugar Co Inc, 1911
C&J Trading, 1926
C.C. Graber Company, 1933
C2O Pure Coconut Water, 1939
Cabo Chips, 1970
Cache Cellars, 1975
Cache Creek Foods LLC, 1976
Cacique, 1977
CactuLife, LLC, 1979
Cafe Altura, 1987
Cafe Fanny, 1994
Cafe Moto, 1999
Cafe Sark's Gourmet Coffee, 2000
Cafe Tequila, 2003
Caffe D'Oro, 2008
Caffe D'Vita, 2009
Caffe Trieste, 2013
Cain Vineyard & Winery, 2015
Caito Fisheries Inc, 2016
Cakebread Cellars, 2025
Cal Harvest Marketing Inc, 2026
Cal India Foods Inc, 2027
Cal Ranch, 2028
Cal-Grown Nut Company, 2029
Cal-Java International Inc, 2030
Calafia Cellars, 2034
Calavo Growers, 2037
Calbee America Inc, 2038
Calera Wine Co, 2044
Cali'flour Foods, 2047
Calif Snack Foods, 2050
Calif Watercress Inc, 2051
Califia Farms, 2052
California Almond Packers, 2053

California Balsamic Inc, 2054
California Blending Co, 2055
California Cereal Products, 2056
California Citrus Producers, 2057
California Coast Naturals, 2058
California Custom Foods, 2059
California Custom Fruits, 2060
California Dairies Inc., 2061
California Fruit, 2062
California Fruit & Nut, 2063
California Fruit and Tomato Kitchens, 2065
California Fruit Processors, 2064
California Garden Products, 2066
California Garlic Co, 2067
California Independent Almond Growers, 2068
California Juice Co., 2069
California Lavash, 2070
California Natural Products, 2071
California Nuggets Inc, 2072
California Oils Corp, 2073
California Olive Growers, 2074
California Olive Oil Council, 2075
California Olive Ranch, 2076
California Packing Company, 2077
California Shellfish Company, 2078
California Smart Foods, 2079
California Walnut Co, 2080
California Wholesale Nut, 2081
California Wild Rice Growers, 2082
California-Antilles Trading, 2083
Calio Groves, 2085
Calivirgin Olive Oils, 2088
Callaway Vineyards & Winery, 2091
Calpro Ingredients, 2095
Caltex Foods, 2096
Cambria Winery, 2101
Cambridge Food, 2103
Camino Real Foods Inc, 2111
Campagana Winery, 2112
Cap Candy, 2148
Caparone Winery LLC, 2151
Capay Canyon Ranch, 2152
Capo Drinks, 2169
Caporale Winery, 2167
Cappuccine, 2171
Capriccio, 2174
Capricorn Coffees Inc, 2175
Cardinale Winery, 2201
Caribbean Coffee Co, 2207
Carmela's Gourmet, 2220
Carmelita Provisions Company, 2221
Carmenet Winery, 2222
Carmi Flavor & Fragrance Company, 2223
Carneros Creek Winery, 2225
Carob Tree, 2228
Carol Hall's Hot Pepper Jelly, 2229
Carol's Country Cuisine, 2231
Carrousel Cellars, 2263
Carve Nutrition, 2266
Casa Nuestra Winery & Vineyard, 2271
Casa Sanchez Foods, 2272
Casablanca Market, 2277
Cattaneo Brothers Inc, 2324
Cattle Boyz Foods, 2325
Caulipower, 2328
Cave Shake, 2329
Caveman Foods, 2330
Caymus Vineyards, 2339
Cebro Frozen Food, 2342
Cecchetti Sebastiani Cellar, 2343
Cedar Mountain Winery, 2351
Cedarlane Foods, 2355
Cedarlane Natural Foods Toc, 2356
Cellucon Inc, 2363
Central California Raisin Packing Co, Inc., 2375
Central Coast Seafood, 2376
Central Meat & Provision, 2379
Ceres Fruit Juices, 2392
Certi Fresh Foods Inc, 2394
Certi-Fresh Foods, Inc, 2395
Chacewater Winery and Olive Mill, 2398
Chai Diaries, 2400
Chalk Hill Estate Winery, 2403
Challenge Dairy Products, Inc., 2404
Chalone Vineyard, 2405
Chang Food Company, 2417
Channing Rudd Cellars, 2420
Chaparral Gardens, 2421
Chappellet Winery, 2423
Charles B. Mitchell Vineyards, 2428

Charles Chocolates, 2429
Charles Krug Winery, 2432
Charles Spinetta Winery, 2435
Charlie's Pride, 2441
Charlotte's Confections, 2444
Charlton Natural Foods, Inc., 2446
Chase Brothers Dairy, 2450
Chateau Boswell Winery, 2454
Chateau Chevre Winery, 2455
Chateau Diana Winery, 2456
Chateau Julien Winery, 2459
Chateau Montelena Winery, 2461
Chateau Potelle Winery, 2463
Chateau Souverain, 2465
Chateau St Jean Winery, 2466
Chatom Vineyards Inc, 2469
Chatz Roasting Co, 2472
Chaucer Consumer Solutions, 2473
Cheesecake Factory Inc., 2485
Cheesecake Momma, 2486
Chef America, 2488
Chef Merito Inc, 2490
Cherry Moon Farms, 2522
Chewys Rugulach, 2538
Chicken Of The Sea, 2555
Chico Nut Company, 2557
Chico Pops, 2558
Childlife, 2563
Chimere Winery, 2569
Chino Meat Provision Corporation, 2574
Chino Valley Dairy, 2575
Chino Valley Ranchers, 2576
Choclatique, 2588
Chocoholics Divine Desserts, 2591
Chocolates a La Carte, 2619
ChocoME US LLC, 2590
Choctal, 2626
Chooljian Bros Packing Co, 2634
Chosen Foods, Inc., 2636
Chouinard Vineyards & Winery, 2637
CHR Foods, 1947
Christine Woods Winery, 2650
Christopher Creek Winery, 2652
Christopher Ranch LLC, 2655
Chuao Chocolatier, 2658
Chudabeef Jerky Co., 2660
Cibaria International, 2671
Cielo Foods, 2674
Cienega Valley Winery/DeRose, 2675
Cinnabar Winery, 2682
City Bean, 2704
CJ America, 1952
CJ Foods, 1953
CJ Omni, 1954
Claiborne & Churchill Vintners, 2713
Clara Foods, 2715
Clarmil Manufacturing Corp, 2721
Classic Foods, 2728
Clayton Coffee & Tea, 2734
Cleanfish Inc, 2736
Clear Products Inc., 2739
Clearly Kombucha, 2743
Clemmy's, 2751
Clif Bar & Co, 2756
Cliff Lede Vineyards, 2757
Cline Cellars, 2759
Clorox Company, 2766
Clos Du Bois Winery, 2767
Clos Du Lac Cellars, 2768
Clos Du Val Co LTD, 2769
Clos Pegase Winery, 2770
Cloud Nine, 2772
Cloud Top, 2773
Cloudstone Vineyards, 2775
Clougherty Packing LLC, 2776
Clover Sonoma, 2781
Clover Stornetta Farms Inc, 2782
CMS Fine Foods, 1958
Coach's Oats, 2795
Coast Packing Co, 2796
Coastal Cocktails, 2799
Cocoa Parlor, 2823
CocoaPlanet Inc., 2824
Coconut Beach, 2828
Coffee Brothers Inc, 2839
Coffee Globe LLC, 2845
Coffee Works, 2860
Cold Fusion Foods, 2868
Coldani Olive Ranch LLC, 2871
Colin Ingram, 2878
Colombo Bakery, 2884
Color Garden, 2890

1319

Geographic Index / California

ColorMaker, Inc., 2892
Colors Gourmet Pizza, 2901
Columbus Salame, 2912
Commissariat Imports, 2922
Comvita USA, 2933
Concannon Vineyard, 2941
Concord Farms, 2942
Conrotto A. Winery, 2957
Continental Yogurt, 2974
Cook Natural Products, 2977
Cook's Gourmet Foods, 2978
Cook's Pantry, 2979
Coolhaus, 2995
Coon Creek Winery, 2997
Copper Hills Fruit Sales, 3006
Corazonas Foods, Inc, 3012
Corbin Foods-Edibowls, 3013
Corbion, 3021
Corning Olive Oil Company, 3038
Corona College Heights, 3039
Corrin Produce Sales, 3040
Cosentino Winery, 3046
Costa Macaroni Manufacturing, 3051
Cottonwood Canyon Vineyard, 3057
Country Archer Jerky Co., 3063
Couture Farms, 3093
Cowboy Caviar, 3098
Cowgirl Creamery, 3101
Craft Distillers, 3108
Crain Ranch, 3110
Crain Walnut Shelling, Inc., 3111
Crave Natural Foods, 3118
Crazy Go Nuts, 3122
Creagri Inc, 3127
Creation Nation, 3132
Creative Spices, 3140
Crescini Wines, 3154
Crest International Corporation, 3156
Cribari Vineyard Inc, 3161
Critelli Olive Oil, 3169
Criveller California Corp, 3171
Cronin Vineyards, 3179
Crooked Vine/Stony Ridge Wnry, 3181
Crop One, 3183
Crown Packing Company, 3193
Crown Prince Inc, 3194
Crown Processing Company, 3195
Crown Valley Food Service, 3197
Crunchies Natural Food Company, 3201
Crush Foods Service, 3205
Crusoe Seafood LLC, 3206
Crustacean Foods, 3207
Crystal Creamery, 3210
Crystal Geyser Water Co., 3212
Crystal Noodle, 3215
Crystal Star Herbal Nutrition, 3221
Cucina & Amore, 3223
Cuisine Perel, 3228
Culinary Farms Inc, 3234
Culinary Revolution, 3237
Cup 4 Cup LLC, 3251, 3252
Custom Coffee Plan, 3267
Custom Produce Sales, 3274
Cuvaison Winery, 3280
CVC4Health, 1967
Cybele's Free To Eat, 3282
Cygnet Cellars, 3285
Cypress Grove, 3286
D'Arrigo Brothers Company of California, 3301
D'Oni Enterprises, 3303
Daily Crave, The, 3327
Dairy King Milk Farms/Foodservice, 3339
DairyAmerica, 3345
Dalla Valle Vineyards, 3361
Dandelion Chocolate, 3370
Dang Foods, 3371
Dardimans California, 3382
Dave's Gourmet, 3393
Dave's Gourmet Albacore, 3394
David Rio, 3398
Davis Bread & Desserts, 3405
Davis Bynum Winery, 3406
Day-Lee Foods, Inc., 3416
Daymar Select Fine Coffees, 3420
De Souza's, 3432
Dean Distributors, Inc., 3441
Deanna's Gluten Free Baking Co., 3444
Deaver Vineyards, 3447
Del Mar Food Products Corp, 3477
Del Monte Foods Inc., 3478
Del Rey Packing, 3480

Del Rio Nut Company, 3481
Delano Growers Grape Products, 3489
Delicato Family Vineyards, 3497
Deloach Vineyards, 3509
Delorimier Winery, 3510
Delta Packing, 3515
DeLuscious Cookies, 3438
Deluxe Delight, 3517
Dempsey's Restaurant & Brewery, 3519
Denatale Vineyards, 3521
Derco Foods Intl, 3530
Desert Farms Inc, 3535
Desert King International, 3536
Desert Valley Date, 3538
Designer Protein, 3540
Desserts On Us Inc, 3543
Devlin Wine Cellars, 3551
Diamond Creek Vineyards, 3573
Diamond Foods, 3575
Diamond of California, 3579
Diane's Sweet Heat, 3583
DiBella Baking Company, 3566
Diedrich Coffee, 3591
Dippy Foods, 3617
Discovery Foods, 3618
Diversified Avocado Products, 3622
Divine Delights, 3625
Divine Organics, 3627
Dobake, 3639
Doctor's Best Inc, 3642
Dogswell LLC, 3645
Dole Food Company, Inc., 3654
Dolores Canning Co Inc, 3658
Dolphin Natural Chocolates, 3659
Domaine Chandon, 3661
Domaine St George Winery, 3662
Don Bugito, 3668
Don Sebastiani & Sons, 3672
Donatoni Winery, 3679
Dong Us I, 3683
Donnelly Fine Chocolates, 3685
Donsuemor Madeleines, 3686
Donut Farm, 3687
Double Date Packing, 3702
Double Rainbow Gourmet Ice Cream, 3706
Dough-To-Go, 3709
Dowd & Rogers, 3718
Dr. McDougall's Right Foods, 3733
Dr. Smoothie Brands, 3739
Dr. Tima Natural Products, 3740
Draco Natural Products Inc, 3741
Dragunara Imports, 3744
Drakes Brewing Co, 3746
Dream Foods Intl, 3751
DreamTime, Inc, 3754
Dreyer Sonoma, 3759
Dreyer's Grand Ice Cream Inc., 3760
Driftwood Dairy, 3764
Driscoll Strawberry Assoc Inc, 3765
Driscoll's, 3766
Dry Creek Vineyard, 3771
Duckhorn Vineyards, 3779
Duncan Peak Vineyards, 3793
Dunn Vineyards, 3804
Dutch Henry Winery, 3816
Duverger, 3823
Dwayne Keith Brooks Company, 3825
E & J Gallo Winery, 3834, 3835
E Waldo Ward & Son Marmalades, 3838
E.F. Lane & Son, 3845
Earnest Eats, 3866
Earth & Vine Provisions Inc, 3867
Earth Circle Organics, 3869
Earth Island, 3870
Earth Science, 3871
Earth Song Whole Foods, 3872
Earth Source Organics, 3873, 3874
Earthbound Farm, 3875
Earthrise Nutritionals, 3876
East Side Winery/Oak Ridge Vineyards, 3886
Eastrise Trading Corp., 3895
Eat My Waffles, 3901
EatPastry LLC, 3907
Eberle Winery, 3912
Eckert Cold Storage, 3918
Eckhart Corporation, 3919
Eckhart Seed Company, 3920
Eco-Planet Cookies, 3924
Ed Oliveira Winery, 3930
Eden Creamery, 3939
Edgewood Estate Winery, 3946

Edison Grainery, 3947
Edmunds St. John, 3951
Edna Valley Vineyard, 3952
Edner Corporation, 3953
Edoughble, 3955
Edward & Sons Trading Co, 3956
EFFi Foods, 3851
Egg Roll Fantasy, 3967
Eggology, 3969
Eidon, 3973
EIWA America Inc., 3852
El Grano De Oro, 3979
El Molino Winery, 3983
El Toro Brew Pub, 3990
El Toro Food Products, 3991
Elaine's Toffee Co., 3992
Elemental Superfood, 4003
Elena's Food Specialties, 4006
Elliston Vineyards, 4026
En Garde Health Products, Inc., 4059
Energen Products Inc, 4063
Enjoy Foods International, 4071
Enray, Inc, 4074
Enz Vineyards, 4084
Enzo Olive Oil Co., 4085
Enzyme Innovation, 4089
EOS Estate Winery, 3857
Equator Coffees & Teas, 4101
ERBL, 3858
Erick Schat's Bakery, 4106
Escalon Premier Brand, 4111
Esco Foods Inc, 4113
Espro Manufacturing, 4117
Essential Flavors & Fragrances, 4122
Essential Living Foods, 4123
Esterlina Vineyard & Winery, 4128
Etchandy Farms, 4130
Eternal Water, 4131
Ethical Naturals, 4136
Etna Brewing Co, 4139
Euro Chocolate Fountain, 4145
European Style Bakery, 4155
Evensen Vineyards, 4161
Evergood Fine Foods, 4166
Everson Spice Co, 4171
Evolve, 4178
Expro Manufacturing, 4188
Extreme Creations, 4192
F. Gavina & Sons, 4202
Fabio Imports, 4215
Fabrique Delices, 4216
Fairwinds Gourmet Coffee, 4229
Fall River Wild Rice, 4235
Family Food Company, 4240
Family Tree Farms, 4242
Fantasy Cookie Company, 4254
Far Niente Winery, 4258
Far West Meats, 4259
Far West Rice Inc, 4260
Farallon Fisheries Co, 4261
Farella-Park Vineyards, 4265
Farm 2 Market, 4269
Farm Fresh to You, 4271
Farmdale Creamery Inc, 4275
Farmgate Cheese LLC, 4287
Farmhouse Culture, 4288
Farmstead At Long Meadow Ranch, 4293
Fashion Snackz, 4299
Fayter Farms Produce, 4315
Felbro Food Products, 4324
Fenchem Inc, 4327
Fenestra Winery, 4329
Fermenting Fairy, 4338
Ferrara Winery, 4346
Ferrari-Carano, 4347
Fess Parker Winery, 4353
Fetzer Vineyards, 4355
Ficklin Vineyards Winery, 4358
Ficks & Co., 4359
Field Stone Winery, 4365
Fieldbrook Valley Winery, 4370
Fiesta Mexican Foods, 4376
Fife Vineyards, 4377
Fig Garden Packing Inc, 4379
Figamajigs, 4380
Figuerola Laboratories, 4383
Fiji Water Co LLC, 4384
Fillmore Piru Citrus, 4387
Filsinger Vineyards & Winery, 4389
Fine Dried Foods Intl, 4394
Fiore Di Pasta, 4408
Firestone Vineyard, 4419

Fish Brothers, 4436
Fish Hopper, 4438
Fish King, 4439
Fisher Vineyards, 4445
FitPro USA, 4453
Fitzpatrick Winery & Lodge, 4455
FiveStar Gourmet Foods, 4461
Flamous Brands, 4470
Flanigan Farms, 4472
Flavor House, Inc., 4481
Flavor Producers, 4482
Flavors and Color, 4491
Fleischmann's Vinegar Co Inc, 4499
Flora Springs Winery, 4510
Florentyna's Fresh Pasta Factory, 4513
Flower Essence Svc, 4525
Flurowater, Inc., 4531
Flying Embers, 4535
Fmali Herb, 4537
Foley Estates Vineyard, 4541
Folie ... Deux Winery, 4544
Follmer Development, Inc, 4546
Follow Your Heart, 4547
Fontazzi/Metrovox Snacks, 4551
Food & Vine Inc., 4553
Food for Life Baking, 4570
Food Mill, 4564
Foodstirs, 4576
Foppiano Vineyards, 4579
Forager Project, 4581
Forever Green Food Inc., 4592
Forman Vineyard, 4597
Formosa Enterprises Inc, 4598
Fortino Winery, 4606
Fortuna Cellars, 4610
Fortune Cookie Factory, 4612
Forty Second Street Bagel Cafe, 4615
Fosselman's Ice Cream Co, 4617
Foster Farms Inc., 4621
Four Barrel Coffee, 4624
Four Sigmatic, 4628
Fowler Packing Co, 4633
Fox's Fine Foods, 4642
Foxen Foxen 7200, 4643
Fran's Healthy Helpings, 4647
Franciscan Estate, 4649
Frank & Dean's Cocktail Mixes, 4651
Frank Family Vineyards, 4653
Frank-Lin Distributors, 4658
Franklin's Cheese, 4667
Frankly Natural Bakers, 4668
Franzia Winery, 4670
Fratelli Perata, 4673
Frazier Nut Farms Inc, 4675
Freed, Teller & Freed, 4681
Freemark Abbey Winery, 4688
Freixenet USA Inc, 4693
French Patisserie, 4703
French's Coffee, 4705
Fresh Express, Inc., 4709
Fresh Juice Delivery, 4714
Fresh Origins, 4718
Fresh Start Bakeries, 4724
Frey Vineyards, 4728
Frick Winery, 4730
Frieda's Inc, 4733
Frisco Baking Co Inc, 4738
Frisinger Cellars, 4739
Frog's Leap Winery, 4745
Frozfruit Corporation, 4757
Fruigees, 4759
Fruit Fillings Inc, 4763
Fruit Growers Supply Company, 4764
Frutech International Corp, 4774
FrutStix, 4772
Fruvemex, 4775
Fudge Fatale, 4780
Ful-Flav-R Foods, 4784
Fullbloom Baking Co, 4787
Fusion Gourmet, 4804
Fusion Jerky, 4805
G Debbas Chocolatier, 4815
G M P Laboratories Of Amer Inc, 4817
Gainey Vineyard, 4860
Galante Vineyards, 4862
Galasso's Bakery, 4864
Galaxy Desserts, 4866
Galland's Institutional Food, 4871
Galleano Winery, 4872
Garcoa Laboratories Inc, 4888
Gardein, 4889
Gardner's Gourmet, 4901

Geographic Index / California

Garlic Co, 4906
Garlic Festival Foods, 4907
Garlic Valley Farms Inc, 4908
Garuda International, 4914
Gary Farrell Vineyards-Winery, 4915
Gaslamp Co Popcorn, 4917
Gayle's Sweet N' Sassy Foods, 4925
Gaytan Foods Inc, 4926
GB Ratto International Grocery, 4825
GC Farms, 4826
GCI Nutrients, 4827
Gedney Foods Co, 4928
GeeFree, 4929
Gelateria Naia, 4932
Gelati Celesti, 4933
Gelsinger Food Products, 4939
Gemsa Oils, 4942
Gene Belk Briners, 4945
Genisoy, 4954
Genius Juice, 4956
Genki USA, 4957
George Chiala Farms Inc, 4963
George Noroian, 4966
Georis Winery, 4980
Gertrude & Bronner's Magic Alpsnack, 4988
Geyser Peak Winery, 4992
Ghirardelli Chocolate Co, 4994
Gil's Gourmet Gallery, 5007
Gill's Onions LLC, 5010
Gimbals Fine Candies, 5017
Gimme Health Foods, 5019
Ginco International, 5020
Ginger People, The, 5021
Ginger Shots, 5022
Girard's Food Service Dressings, 5032
Giuliano's Specialty Foods, 5035
Giumarra Companies, 5036
Giusto's Specialty Foods Inc, 5037
Gl Mezzetta Inc, 5039
Glendora Quiche Company, 5053
Glenoaks Food Inc, 5056
Global Bakeries Inc, 5059
Gloria Ferrer Champagne, 5069
Gloria Jean's Gourmet Coffees, 5070
Glossop's Syrup, 5074
Gluten Free Foods Mfg., 5080
GMB Specialty Foods, 4839
GNS Spices, 4841
Go Raw, 5087
Gold Coast Bakeries, 5097
Gold Coast Baking Co Inc, 5098
Gold Coast Ingredients, 5099
Gold Mine Natural Food Company, 5104
Golden Eagle Olive Products, 5118
Golden Island Jerky Co., 5126
Golden Specialty Foods Inc, 5133
Golden State Foods Corp, 5134
Golden State Herbs, 5135
Golden Valley Dairy Products, 5137
Golden West Food Group, 5141
Golden West Fruit Company, 5142
Golden West Specialty Foods, 5143
Goldilocks USA, 5145
Goldthread, 5148
Good Citizens, 5153
Good Culture, 5154
Good Fortunes & Edible Art, 5160
Good! Snacks, 5176
GoodBites Snacks, 5179
Goosecross Cellars Inc, 5189
Gordon Biersch Brewery Restaurant, 5193
Gourmet Foods Inc, 5204
Gourmet Treats, 5213
Gourmet's Fresh Pasta, 5216
Gourmet's Secret, 5217
Govadinas Fitness Foods, 5221
Grace & I, 5225
Grace Baking Company, 5226
Grainaissance, 5248
Grains of Health LLC, 5250
Grandpa Po's Nutra Nuts, 5268
Granite Springs Winery, 5273
Grapevine Trading Company, 5280
Green Beans Coffee Co Inc, 5345
Geyser Foods Corp., 5349
Green Gorilla, 5352
Green Grown Products Inc, 5353
Green Options, 5358
Green Spot Packaging, 5362
Green-Go Cactus Water, 5368
Greenberg Cheese Co, 5369
Greenfield Wine Company, 5373
Greenwave Foods, 5376
Greenwood Ridge Vineyards, 5380
Grimaud Farms-California Inc, 5390
Grimmway Farms, 5393
Groth Vineyards & Winery, 5401
Groundwork Coffee Co., 5404
GU Energy Labs, 4850
Guapo Spices Company, 5415
Guayaki, 5416
Guenoc & Langtry Estate, 5417
Guerra Nut Shelling Co Inc, 5418
Guglielmo Winery, 5421
Guido's International Foods, 5423
Guilliams Winery, 5425
Guittard Chocolate Co, 5428
Gundlach-Bundschu Winery, 5445
GURU Organic Energy, 4851
GuruNanda, 5449
Gustus Vitae Condiments LLC, 5452
Gutsii, 5454
H Coturri & Sons Winery, 5464
H.K. Canning, 5479
H2rOse, LLC, 5480
Hadley's Date Gardens, 5494
Hafner Vineyard, 5496
Hagerty Foods, 5498
Hahn Family Wines, 5499
Haig's Delicacies, 5501
Hak's, 5510
Hakuna Banana, 5511
Half Moon Fruit & Produce Company, 5517
Haliburton International Inc, 5519
Hallcrest Vineyards, 5524
Handley Cellars, 5546
Hangzhou Sanhe USA Inc., 5549
Hannah Max Baking, 5554
Hanzell Vineyards, 5561
Harbor Winery, 5579
Harmless Harvest, 5594
Harmony Cellars, 5597
Harold L King & Co Inc, 5601
Harris Farms Inc, 5609
Harris Moran Seed Co, 5610
Harris Ranch Beef Co, 5611
Harrison Napa Valley, 5614
Hart Winery, 5618
Hartford Family Winery, 5619
Harvest Food Products Co Inc, 5630
Has Beans Coffee & Tea Co, 5639
Health Concerns, 5680
Health Plus, 5682
Health Valley Company, 5684
Health-Ade LLC, 5688
HealthBest, 5689
Healthee, 5691
Healthy Times Baby Food, 5700
Hearthy Foods, 5706
Heck Cellars, 5725
Hecker Pass Winery, 5726
Heidi's Salsa, 5730
Heinke Family Farm, 5732
Heirloom Organic Gardens, 5737
Heitz Wine Cellars, 5739
Helados Mexico, 5741
Helena View/Johnston Vineyard, 5743
Heller Estates, 5747
Helms Bakery, 5751
Hemp2o, 5761
Henry Hill & Co, 5774
Herb Tea Company, 5780
Herbal Products & Development, 5786
Herbal Water, Inc., 5788
Hero Nutritionals, 5812
Hess Collection, 5820
Hiball, Inc., 5829
HiBix Corporation, 5827
Hidden Mountain Ranch Winery, 5835
Hidden Villa Ranch, 5837
Hikari Miso Intl., 5862
Hilmar Cheese Company, 5878
Hilmar Ingredients, 5879
Hint Mint, 5886
Hint Water, 5887
HMC Farms, 5485
Hnina Gourmet, 5895
Hodo, 5899
Holland American International Specialties, 5908
Hol, Mol,, 5923
Homegrown Naturals, 5936
Homegrown Organic Farms, 5937
Homemade Harvey, 5939
Homestead Fine Foods, 5944
Homestead Ravioli Company, 5947
Homewood Winery, 5950
Honey Run Winery, 5962
Hong Tou Noodle Company, 5972
Honig Vineyard and Winery, 5976
Hop Kiln Winery, 5989
Horizon Snack Foods, 5998
Hot Licks, 6015
Houdini Inc, 6019
House Foods America Corp, 6021
House of Tsang, 6028
HP Schmid, 5487
Hsin Tung Yang Foods Inc, 6039
HSR Associates Inc, 5488
Hubble, 6043
Hubert's Lemonade, 6045
Hughson Nut Inc, 6061
Humbly Hemp, 6063
Humboldt Bay Coffee Co., 6064
Humboldt Brews LLC, 6065
Humboldt Chocolate, 6066
Humboldt Creamery, 6067
Humphry Slocombe, 6078
Hungry Sultan, 6080
Hunter Food Inc, 6086
Huppen Bakery, 6087
Husch Vineyards & Winery, 6089
Huy Fong Foods Inc, 6092
HV Food Products Co, 5489
Hybco USA, 6093
Hybread, 6094
Hyde & Hyde Inc, 6095
Hye Cuisine, 6099
Hye Quality Bakery, 6100
I'm Different Snacks, 6106
ICONIC Protein, 6110
Idaho Frank Association Inc, 6135
II Sisters, 6115
Imagine Chocolate, 6150
Imlak'esh Organics, 6153
Immordl, 6155
Imperial Nougat Co, 6161
Impossible Foods, 6165
Imuraya USA, 6169
Incredible Cheesecake, 6175
Indian Rock Vineyards, 6189
Indian Springs Vineyards, 6190
Inglenook, 6203
Ingomar Packing Co, 6206
Ingredient Specialties, 6209
Initiative Foods, 6213
Inka Crops, 6214
Inked Organics, 6215
Inland Empire Foods, 6217
Inn Foods Inc, 6221
Innovative Beverage Concepts, 6227
Inter Health Nutraceuticals, 6236
International Delicacies Inc, 6255
International Tea Importers, 6275
Iron Horse Vineyards, 6289
Ironstone Vineyards, 6290
Irwin Naturals, 6292
Island of the Moon Apiaries, 6312
Island Snacks, 6307
Isodiol, 6313
Issimo Food Group, 6314
It's It Ice Cream Co, 6315
Itarca, 6323
Itella Foods, 6324
Ithaca Craft Hummus, 6325
Ito Cariani Sausage Company, 6326
Iveta Gourmet Inc, 6329
Ivy Cottage Scone Mixes, 6330
J & J Wall Bakery Co, 6339
J & M Wholesale Meat Inc, 6344
J Deluca Fish Co Inc, 6348
J Filippi Winery, 6350
J G Noble Cheese Company, 6351
J Lohr Vineyards & Wines, 6357
J. Fritz Winery, 6372
J. Stonestreet & Sons Vineyard, 6375
J.T. Pappy's Sauce, 6388
Jade Leaf Matcha, 6432
Jaguluna Herbal Products, 6436
Jamae Natural Foods, 6442
James Frasinetti & Sons, 6446
Japan Gold USA, 6453
Jardine Ranch, 6457
Jarrow Industries Inc, 6458
Jasmine Vineyards, Inc., 6460
Jason & Son Specialty Foods, 6461
Java Beans and Joe Coffee, 6465
Javalution Coffee Company, 6469
Javo Beverage Co., Inc., 6471
Jayone Foods Inc, 6475
JC's Pie Pops, 6393
Jecky's Best, 6478
Jeff's Garden, 6481
Jelly Belly Candy Co., 6485
Jensen Meat Company, 6492
JER Creative Food Concepts, Inc., 6396
Jer's Chocolates, 6495
Jeremiah's Pick Coffee Co, 6497
Jess Jones Vineyard, 6506
Jessie's Ilwaco Fish Company, 6508
Jewel Date Co, 6511
Jilz Gluten Free, 6516
Jimtown Store, 6522
JMAC Trading, Inc., 6404
Jo Mar Laboratories, 6524
Jo's Candies, 6525
Jodar Vineyard & Winery, 6527
Jody Maroni's Sausage Kingdom, 6529
John Kelly Chocolates, 6556
Johnson's Alexander Valley Wines, 6569
Johnston Farms, 6576
Joj, Bar, 6580
Jon Donaire Desserts, 6583
Joseph Farms, 6600
Joseph Phelps Vineyards, 6603
Joseph Swan Vineyards, 6604
Josuma Coffee Co, 6611
Joullian Vineyards, 6612
JSL Foods, 6409
Juanita's Foods, 6619
Judicial Flavors, 6624
Juice Mart, 6626
Juicy Whip Inc, 6628
Julian Bakery, 6629
Just Cook Foods, 6642
Just Date Syrup, 6643
Just Delicious Gourmet Foods, 6644
Just Desserts, 6645
JUST Inc, 6411
Just Jan's Inc., 6646
Just Off Melrose, 6647
Just Tomatoes, 6649
Justin Vineyards & Winery LLC, 6651
K L Keller Imports, 6658
K.B. Hall Ranch, 6663
Kagome USA Inc, 6684
Kalifornia Keto, 6692
Kalin Cellars, 6693
Kameda USA Inc., 6697
Kana Organics, 6700
Karine & Jeff, 6709
Karl Strauss Brewing Co, 6711
Karma Nuts, 6716
Karoun Dairies Inc, 6719
Kashi Company, 6720
Kasira, 6722
Kate's Vineyard, 6726
Kathryn Kennedy Winery, 6729
Kathy's Gourmet Specialties, 6730
Katy's Smokehouse, 6733
Keenan Farms, 6749
Kelly Gourmet Foods Inc, 6770
Kelson Creek Winery, 6775
Kendall Frozen Fruits, Inc., 6781
Kendall-Jackson, 6782
Kendon Candies Inc, 6783
Kenko International, 6785
Kenwood Vineyards, 6798
KERN Ridge Growers LLC, 6670
Kerri Kreations, 6805
KeVita, 6745
Keystone Coffee Co, 6829
Kids Kookie Company, 6836
KidsLuv, 6837
Kidsmania, 6838
KiiTO, Inc., 6840
Kill Sauce, 6844
Kilwons Foods, 6846
Kimball Enterprise International, 6849
Kinder's BBQ, 6853
King Floyd's, 6864
King Henry's Inc, 6866
King Oscar, 6870
King's Hawaiian Holding Co Inc., 6874
Kings Canyon, 6877
Kings Seafood Co, 6879
Kingsburg Orchards, 6880

1321

Geographic Index / California

Kirigin Cellars, 6888
Kirin Brewery, 6889
Kiss My Keto, 6891
Kistler Vineyards, 6892
Kite Hill, 6898
Kiwa, 6903
Knudsen Candy, 6926
Koda Farms, 6931
KODA Farms Inc, 6673
KOE Organic Kombucha, 6674
Koia, 6941
KonaRed Corp., 6954
Kor Shots, 6963
Korea Ginseng Corp., 6965
Koryo Winery Company, 6968
Kozlowski Farms, 6974
KP USA Trading, 6677
Kraus & Co, 6980
KRAVE Jerky, 6678
Krave Pure Food, 6981
Kruger Foods, 6993
Kruse & Son, 6995
KT's Kitchens, 6679
Kuju Coffee, 7000
Kuli Kuli, Inc., 7002
Kunde Estate Winery, 7003
Kusha Inc., 7007
Kwangdong USA, 7011
Kween Foods, 7012
L. A. Smoking & Curing Company, 7034
L.A. Libations, 7036
LA Bou Bakery & Cafe, 7039
LA Boulangerie, 7040
La Brea Bakery Inc, 7078
LA Chapalita Inc, 7043
LA Colonial, 7045
La Cookie, 7083
LA Costa Coffee Roasting Co, 7046
LA Jota Vineyard Co, 7048
LA Lifestyle Nutritional Products, 7049
La Pasta, Inc., 7099
LA Patisserie Bakery, 7056
LA Paz Products Inc, 7057
LA Reina Inc, 7059
LA Rocca Vineyards & Winery, 7060
La Rochelle Winery, 7103
La Selva Beach Spice, 7106
La Spiga D'Oro Fresh Pasta Co, 7108
LA Tapatia Tortilleria Inc, 7062
La Tempesta, 7111
LA Torilla Factory, 7063
La Tortilla Factory, 7112
La Tourangelle, 7113
LA Vencedora Products Inc, 7064
La Vigne Enterprises, 7116
LA Wholesale Produce Market, 7066
Lacey Milling Company, 7125
Laetitia Vineyard & Winery, 7133
Lafaza Foods, 7135
Lafollette Vineyard & Winery, 7138
Lagorio Enterprises, 7142
Laguna Beach Brewing Company, 7143
Lahaha Tea Co, 7144
Lahtt Sauce, 7145
Lake Sonoma Winery, 7154
Lallemand/American Yeast, 7176
Lambert Bridge Winery, 7181
Lamitech West, 7183
LaMonde Wild Flavors, 7119
Landmark Vineyards, 7203
Langer Juice Co Inc, 7213
Latcham Vineyards, 7238
Laura Chenel's Chevre, 7243
Laura's French Baking Co, 7245
Laurel Glen Vineyard, 7247
Lava Cap Winery, 7251
Lavash Corp, 7252
Lazy Creek Vineyards, 7262
Le Caramel, 7265
Le Chef Bakery, 7266
Le Grand Confectionary, 7271
Le Vigne Winery, 7276
Leaf Cuisine, 7280
Leaner Creamer, 7284
Lee Andersons, 7294
Lee Kum Kee USA Inc, 7296
Leeward Winery, 7306
Legendary Foods, 7316
Lehr Brothers, 7323
Leiner Health Products, 7331
Lemon & Vine, 7337
Lemur International, 7342

Lenny & Larry's, 7350
Lewis Cellars, 7403
Liberty Vegetable Oil Co, 7411
LifeAID, 7416
Lifeline Food Company, Inc., 7419
LifeTime, 7418
Lincourt Vineyards, 7438
Linda's Gourmet Latkes, 7439
Lindner Bison, 7443
Lindsay's Teas, 7445
Lingle Brothers Coffee, 7448
Lion Raisins Inc, 7451
Lisa's Organics, 7457
Little Red Dot Kitchen, 7471
Live A Little Gourmet Foods, 7479
Live Gourmet, 7480
Live Oaks Winery, 7482
Livermore Valley Cellars, 7484
Living Intentions, 7487
Livingston Farmers Assn, 7489
Livingston Moffett Winery, 7490
Lockwood Vineyards, 7503
Lodi Nut Company, 7506
Lolonis Winery, 7514
Long Vineyards, 7527
Longreen Corp., 7534
LonoLife, 7536
Loriva Culinary Oils, 7545
Los Altos Food Products, 7546
Los Angeles Nut House Brands, 7548
Los Gatos Brewing Company, 7551
Los Gatos Tomato Products, 7552
Los Pericos Food Products, 7553
Lost Coast Brewery, 7554
Lost Coast Roast, 7555
Lotsa Pasta, 7559
Lotus Bakery, 7561
Lotus Foods, 7563
Louis M Martini Winery, 7573
Lovebiotics LLC, 7604
Lucas Winery, 7621
Lucerne Foods, 7622
Lucero Olive Oil Mfr, 7623, 7624
Lucich Santos Farms, 7626
Lucini Italia Company, 7629
Lucky You, 7634
Ludfords, 7637
Luke's Organic, 7644
Lumen, 7646
Lundberg Family Farms, 7650
Luxor California Exports Corp., 7656
Lve & Raymond Vineyards, 7659
Lyons Magnus, 7669
M & CP FARMS, 7673
M&H Erickson Ranch, 7679
M. Marion & Company, 7685
Maat Nutritionals, 7711
Mackie International, Inc., 7732
Mad River Farm Kitchen, 7735
Mad Will's Food Company, 7737
Madera Enterprises Inc, 7747
Madonna Estate Winery, 7753
Madrona Vineyards, 7757
Madys Company, 7758
Maggiora Baking Co, 7763
Magic Gumball Intl, 7764
Magna Foods Corporation, 7769
Magnolia Citrus Assn, 7774
Maisie Jane's California Sunshine, 7793
Majestic Coffee & Tea Inc, 7795
Maju Superfoods, 7797
MAK Enterprises, 7694
Makana Beverages Inc., 7798
Malabar Formulas, 7802
Mallard's Food Products, 7806
Mama Rap's & Winery, 7817
Mamie's Pies, 7822
Mamma Chia, 7823
Mamma Lina Ravioli Company, 7824
Manassero Farms, 7828
Mangia Inc., 7842
Manhattan Beach Brewing Company, 7844
Mann Packing Co, 7853
Mansmith's Barbeque, 7856
Manzana Products Co., 7860
Maple Leaf Consumer Foods, 7873
Maplegrove Foods, 7884
Marantha Natural Foods, 7892
Marathon Packing Corp, 7896
Marcel et Henri Charcuterie Francaise, 7898
Mariani Nut Co, 7910

Mariani Packing Co., 7911
Marich Confectionery, 7912
Marie Brizard Wines & Spirits, 7913
Marie Callender's, 7914
Marie Callender's Gourmet Products/Goldrush Products, 7915
Marie's Quality Foods, 7917
Marietta Cellars, 7920
Marimar Torres Estates, 7922
Marin Brewing Co, 7923
Marin Food Specialties, 7924
Marin French Cheese Co, 7925
Marin Kombucha, 7926
Mark West Wines, 7938
Markham Vineyards, 7941
Marquez Brothers International, 7949
Marquis, 7950
Marroquin Organic Intl., 7951
Marsa Specialty Products, 7953
Martha Olson's Great Foo, 7960
Martin & Weyrich Winery, 7962
Martin Ray Winery, 7967
Martino's Bakery, 7971
Maruchan Inc, 7974
Marukai Market, 7975
Marukan Vinegar USA Inc., 7976
Marukome USA Inc., 7977
Mary Ann's Baking Co Inc, 7981
Mary's Gone Crackers, 7983
Masala Chai Company, 7989
Masienda, 7990
Mastantuono Winery, 7996
Master Mix, 7998
Matanzas Creek Winery, 8003
Mathews Packing, 8006
Matilija Water Company, 8007
Matrix Health Products, 8009
Matson Vineyards, 8011
Maurice Carrie Winery, 8023
Maverick Brands, LLC, 8025
Maxin Marketing Corporation, 8029
Maxine's Heavenly, 8030
Mayacamas Fine Foods, 8034
Mayacamas Vineyards & Winery, 8035
Mayway Corp, 8044
Mazzocco Vineyards, 8048
McAnally Enterprises, 8052
McConnell's Fine Ice Cream, 8059
McConnell's Fine Ice Creams, 8060
McCoy Matt Frontier International, 8063
McDaniel Fruit, 8065
McDowell Valley Vineyards & Cellars, 8066
McEvoy Ranch, 8068
Mcfadden Farm, 8092
McHenry Vineyard, 8071
Medterra CBD, 8126
Megatoys Inc, 8131
Mele-Koi Farms, 8143
Mellace Family Brands, 8147
Meluka Honey, 8149
Memphis Meats, 8152
Mendocino Brewing Co Inc, 8153
Mendocino Mustard, 8154
Menghini Winery, 8157
Mercado Latino, 8161
Mercer Foods, 8162
Mercer Processing, 8163
Meridian Vineyards, 8172
Merryvale Vineyards, 8185
Mesa Salsa, 8187
Metagenics, Inc., 8193
Metro Mint, 8196
Metzer Farms, 8203
Meyenberg Goat Milk, 8210
Mi Rancho, 8216
Michael David Winery, 8224
Michel de France, 8234
Michel-Schlumberger Wine Est, 8238
Mid Valley Nut Co, 8255
Mighty Leaf Tea, 8272
Mighty Soy Inc, 8273
Mikawaya LLC, 8277
Mike's Mighty Good, 8281
Milat Vineyards Winery, 8290
Mill Creek Vineyards, 8301
Milliaire Winery, 8315
Milone Brothers Coffee Co, 8328
Min Tong Herbs, 8339
Minsley, Inc., 8361
Miracle Noodle, 8368
Miss Jones Baking Co., 8379
Miss Meringue, 8380

Mission Foods Corp., 8386
Mission Valley Foods, 8390
Mister Pickle's Inc, 8396
Mister Spear, 8398
Miyako Oriental Foods Inc, 8412
Miyoko's Kitchen, 8413
Mizkan Americas Inc, 8428, 8429, 8431
Moceri South Western, 8436
MODe Sports Nutrition, 7705
Modern Gourmet Foods, 8441
Modern Oats, 8444
Modern Pop, 8447
Modern Table, 8449
Modesto WholeSoy, 8451
Monaco Baking Company, 8469
Mondial Foods Company, 8475
Monster Beverage Corp., 8485
Montchevre-Betin, Inc, 8497
Monte Vista Farming Co, 8499
Monterey Fish Company, 8504
Monterey Mushrooms Inc, 8505
Monterey Vineyard, 8506
Montevina Winery, 8509
Monticello Vineyards-Corley, 8511
Moon Dance Baking, 8520
Moonlight Brewing Company, 8524
Moonlight, 8525
Moorhead & Company, 8534
Morehouse Foods Inc, 8539
Morgan Winery, 8544
Morinaga Nutritional Foods, Inc., 8546
Morningstar Foods, 8552
Morris National, 8558
Morton & Bassett Spices, 8568
Mosby Winery, 8570
Moss Creek Winery, 8572
Mother Nature's Goodies, 8577
Motherland International Inc, 8584
Mount Palomar Winery, 8592
Mountain Organic Foods, 8598
Mountain View Fruit Sales, 8607
Mountanos Family Coffee & Tea Co., 8611
Moutanos Brothers Coffee Company, 8612
Mr Espresso, 8619
Mr Jay's Tamales & Chili, 8620
Mrs. Denson's Cookie Company, 8635
Mrs. Malibu Foods, 8643
Mrs. May's Naturals, 8644
Mt Eden Vineyards, 8654
Mt. Konocti Growers, 8660
Muffin Revolution, 8667
Mulligan Sales, 8673
Munkijo, 8681
Muqui Coffee Company, 8685
Murphy Goode Estate Winery, 8688
Musco Family Olive Co, 8692
MUSH Foods, 7708
My/Mo Mochi Ice Cream, 8711
Mylk Labs, 8714
Naked Infusions LLC, 8740
Naked Juice Company, 8741
Nalle Winery, 8744
Nana Mae's Organics, 8747
Nana's Cookie Co., 8748
Nancy's Specialty Foods, 8753
Nanka Seimen Company, 8754
Napa Barrel Care, 8761
Napa Cellars, 8762
Napa Valley Kitchens, 8764
Napa Wine Company, 8765
Naraghi Group, 8768
Natierra, 8780
National Raisin Co., 8802
Native Kjalii Foods, 8811
Native State Foods, 8813
Natra US, 8814
Natren Inc, 8816
Natur Sweeteners, Inc., 8818
Naturade Inc, 8819
Natural Choice Distribution, 8823
Natural Food Mill, 8831
Natural Food Supplements Inc, 8833
Natural Food World, 8834
Natural Formulas, 8836
Natural Group, 8838
Natural Intentions, Inc., 8841
Natural Oils International, 8843
Natural Rush, 8847
Natural Value, 8850
Naturalife Laboratories, 8852
Naturally Clean Eats, 8853
Nature Kist Snacks, 8860

1322

Geographic Index / California

Nature Quality, 8863
Nature's Guru, 8879
Nature's Hilights, 8883
Naturel, 8897
Natures Sungrown Foods Inc, 8898
Naughty Noah's, 8900
Navarro Vineyards, 8903
Navitas Naturals, 8905
Ne-Mo's Bakery Inc, 8910
Nellson Candies Inc, 8929
Nellson Nutraceutical LLC, 8930
Nelly's Organics, 8931
Neo North America Inc., 8935
Neptune Foods, 8938
Nestle USA Inc, 8945
Neto's Market & Grill, 8946
Nevada City Brewing, 8952
Nevada City Winery, 8953
Nevada County Wine Guild, 8954
New Barn Organics, 8958
New Century Snacks, 8963
New Direction Foods, 8966
New Horizon Foods, 8986
New Jamaican Gold, 8988
New Organics, 8993
Newly Weds Foods Inc, 9017
Newmarket Foods, 9019
Newport Flavours & Fragrances, 9021
Newport Ingredients, 9022
Newport Meat Co North, 9023
Newton Vineyard, 9026
Nicasio Vineyards, 9034
Nichelini Family Winery Inc, 9037
Nichols Farms, 9039
Nick Sciabica & Sons, 9040
Nickabood's Inc, 9042
Nicola International, 9044
Niebaum-Coppola Estate Winery, 9048
Nielsen Citrus Products Inc, 9049
Niman Ranch, 9057
Ninth Avenue Foods, 9062
Nissin Foods USA Co Inc, 9068
Niutang Chemical, Inc., 9073
NOKA, 8723
Nona Lim, 9089
Noosh Brands, 9096
Noour Inc., 9098
Nora Snacks, 9101
Nordman of California, 9107
North American Blueberry Council, 9116
North Coast Farms, 9128
North Coast Processing, 9129
North West Pharmanaturals Inc, 9139
Northridge Laboratories, 9168
Norwalk Dairy, 9186
Nouveau Foods, 9194
Nui Foods, 9215
Nulaid Foods Inc, 9216
Numi Organic Tea, 9217
Numo Broth, 9218
Nunes Co Inc, 9219
Nunes Farms Marketing, 9220
Nutiva, 9229
Nutra Nuts, 9234
Nutralliance, 9241
Nutranique Labs, 9242
NutRaw Foods, 9227
Nutribiotic, 9251
Nutrilabs, 9253
Nutritech Corporation, 9258
Nutritional Specialties, 9265
Nuts About You, 9272
Nuttzo, 9276
NuZee, Inc., 9211
O Olive Oil, 9282
O'Donnell Formulas Inc, 9287
Oak Hill Farm, 9316
Oak Ridge Winery LLC, 9321
Oakhurst Industries, 9326
Oakland Bean Cleaning & Storage, 9327
Oasis Breads, 9330
Obester Winery, 9340
Ocean King International, 9350
Ocean Mist Farms, 9351
Ocean's Halo, 9359
Ogeki Sake USA Inc, 9373
Oh Yes! Foods, 9375
OHi Food, 9300
Oilseeds International LTD, 9383, 9384
Ojai Cook, 9385
Ojai Cook LLC, 9386
Ojai Vineyard, 9387

Ola Loa, 9394
Olam Spices, 9395
Old Country Bakery, 9400
Old Country Meat & Sausage Company, 9402
Old Creek Ranch Winery, 9405
Old Fashioned Natural Products, 9413
Old Sacramento Popcorn Company, 9425
Olde Tyme Mercantile, 9439
Olive Growers Council, 9446
Olive Oil Source, 9448
Olivina. LLC, 9456
OLLI Salumeria Americana, 9302
Om Mushrooms, 9471
Omega Pure, 9480
OMG! Superfoods, 9303
Once Upon a Farm, 9486
One Culture Foods, 9487
One Vineyard and Winery, 9491
One World Enterprises, 9492
Oogolow Enterprises, 9502
Optima Wine Cellars, 9507
Optimal Nutrients, 9509
Opus One, 9511
Orange Bakery, 9512
Orange Bang Inc, 9513
Orange Cove-Sanger Citrus, 9515
Ore-Cal Corp, 9522
Orfila Vineyards, 9540
Organic Germinal, 9543
Organic Girl Produce, 9544
Organic Gourmet, 9545
Organic Milling, 9548
Organic Pastures, 9552
Organic Planet, 9553
Organic RealBar, 9554
Organic Wine Co Inc, 9555
Organics Unlimited, 9557
Oriental Foods, 9558
Orientex Foods, 9559
Original Chili Bowl, 9561
Osso Good, LLC, 9586
Otafuku Foods, 9589
Otsuka America Foods Inc, 9592
Outer Aisle, 9606
Outstanding Foods, 9607
Overhill Farms Inc, 9614
Ozuna Food Products Corporation, 9626
PDEQ, 9627
P & M Staiger Vineyard, 9630
P & T Flannery Seafood Inc, 9633
P C Teas Co, 9634
P G Molinari & Sons, 9635
P R Farms Inc, 9636
Pacheco Ranch Winery, 9667
Pacific American Fish Co Inc, 9668
Pacific Beach Peanut Butter, 9669
Pacific Cheese Co, 9671
Pacific Choice Brands, 9672
Pacific Coast Brewing, 9673
Pacific Coast Producers, 9675
Pacific Echo Cellars, 9677
Pacific Ethanol Inc., 9678
Pacific Farms, 9679
Pacific Fruit Processors, 9682
Pacific Gourmet Seafood, 9685
Pacific Grain & Foods, 9686
Pacific Hop Exchange Brewing Company, 9688
Pacific Ocean Produce, 9690
Pacific Soybean & Grain, 9694
Pacific Spice Co, 9695
Pacific Sun Olive Oil, 9697
Pacific Trellis, 9698
Pacifica Culinaria, 9702
Paddack Enterprises, 9706
Page Mill Winery, 9708
Pahlmeyer Winery, 9709
Palermo Bakery, 9718
Pamela's Products, 9730
Pandol Brothers Inc, 9737
Panoche Creek Packing, 9744
Panorama Meats, 9747
Papa Leone Food Enterprises, 9752
Pappy Meat Company, 9757
Paraiso Vineyards, 9770
Parducci Wine Cellars, 9774
Paris Pastry, 9776
Parmela Creamery, 9790
Parrish's Cake Decorating, 9794
Pasolivo Willow Creek Olive Ranch, 9803
Passetti's Pride, 9806

Passport Food Group, 9807
Pasta Prima, 9814
Pasta Sonoma, 9817
Pastori Winery, 9822
Patagonia Provisions, 9826
Patricia Quintana, 9832
Patterson Frozen Foods, 9839
Patterson Vegetable Company, 9840
Patti's Plum Puddings, 9841
Pavel's Yogurt, 9851
Peaberry's Coffee & Tea, 9857
Peace Village Organic Foods, 9860
Pearl Crop, 9874
Peas of Mind, 9880
Pedrizzetti Winery, 9889
Pedroncelli J Winery, 9890
Peerless Coffee & Tea, 9895
Peet's Coffee, 9896
Peju Province Winery, 9899
Peking Noodle Co Inc, 9902
Pellegrini Wine Co, 9905
Penguin Natural Food Inc, 9913
Penta Water, 9931
People's Sausage Co, 9932
Pepe's Mexican Restaurant, 9934
Pepper Mill Imports, 9937
Perfect Addition, 9949
Perfect Bite Co, 9950
Perfect Puree of Napa Valley, 9953
Perfect Snacks, 9954
Performance Labs, 9957
Pernicious Pickling, 9963
Perricone Juices, 9966
Perry Creek Winery, 9968
Petaluma Poultry, 9974
Peter Michael Winery, 9979
Peter Rabbit Farms, 9981
Petit Pot, 9986
PGP International, 9652
Pharmavite LLC, 9998
Phat Fudge, 10000
Philip Togni Vineyard, 10008
Phivida Organics, 10018
Piedra Creek Winery, 10044
Pine Ridge Vineyards, 10063
Pioneer Marketing International, 10078
Pitbull Energy Products, 10090
Piveg, Inc., 10093
Plaidberry Company, 10096
Plam Vineyards & Winery, 10101
Pleasant Grove Farms, 10111
Plenty, 10117
Plum Organics, 10123
Plus CBD Oil, 10125
Plus Pharma, 10126
Plush Puffs Marshmallows, 10127
Pocino Foods, 10136
Poco Dolce, 10137
Point Reyes Farmstead Cheese Co., 10144
Point Saint George Fisheries, 10145
Pokonobe Industries, 10150
Polarica USA, Inc., 10153
Polly's Gourmet Coffee, 10157
POM Wonderful LLC, 9658
Pommeraie Winery, 10159
Pop & Bottle Inc., 10174
Popchips, 10178
Popcorn Connection, 10179
Popcornopolis LLC, 10183
Popkoff's, 10184
Popsalot, 10193
Porter Creek Vineyards, 10201
Power Crunch, 10223
Prager Winery & Port Works, 10228
Precision Blends, 10241
Premier Meat Co, 10248
Premier Organics, 10249
Premier Protein, 10251
Presto Avoset Group, 10267
Preston Vineyards & Winery, 10270
Prima® Wawona, 10285
Primal Essence, 10286
Primal Kitchen, 10287
Primal Nutrition, 10288
Prime Produce, 10295
Prime Smoked Meats Inc, 10296
Primex International Trading, 10299
Primitive Feast, 10300
Primo Foods, 10302
Prince of Peace, 10307
Principe Foods USA, 10308
Private Harvest, 10311

Private Spring Water, 10313
Pro Form Labs, 10314
Proacec USA, 10319
Producers Dairy Foods Inc, 10326
Project 7, 10339
Protein Research, 10349
Protient, 10352
Psycho Donuts, 10360
Pulmuone Foods USA Inc., 10365
Pure Flo Water Co, 10370
Pure Planet, 10380
Pure Sales, 10381
PureForm CBD, 10387
Purity Organic, 10398
Puroast Coffee Co Inc, 10400
Pyrenees French Bakery, 10406
QST Ingredients, 10414
Quady Winery, 10415
Quail Ridge Cellars & Vineyards, 10416
Quality Candy Company, 10428
Quality Naturally Foods, 10440
Quality Nut Co, 10441
Quantum Energy Squares, 10446
Queen International Foods, 10453
Queensway Foods Company, 10457
Quetzal Internet Cafe, 10459
Quinoa Corporation, 10467
Quivira Vineyards & Winery, 10471
Quong Hop & Company, 10472
R Torre & Co, 10485
R&A Imports, 10487
R.H. Phillips, 10494
R.W. Garcia, 10500
Rabbit Barn, 10521
Rabbit Ridge Winery, 10523
Radanovich Vineyards & Winery, 10528
Rainbow Light Nutritional Systems, 10537
Rainbow Seafood Market, 10539
Ramona's Mexican Foods, 10548
Ramos Orchards, 10549
Rancho De Philo Winery, 10554
Rancho Sierra, 10555
Rancho Sisquoc Winery, 10556
Randal Optimal Nutrients, 10558
Randall Foods Inc, 10560
Randy's Donuts, 10563
Rapazzini Winery, 10567
Ravenswood Winery, 10573
RawFusion, 10578
Ready Pac Foods Inc, 10586
Real Coconut Co. Inc., The, 10588
REBBL, 10505
Red Chamber Co, 10603
Red Hot Foods, 10611
Red White & Brew, 10624
Redwood Hill Farm, 10633
REED'S Inc, 10507
Reed's, Inc., 10635
Reeve Wines, 10636
Reiter Affiliated Companies, 10662
Renaissance Vineyard & Winery, 10668
Renwood Winery, 10676
Republic of Tea, 10677
Republica Del Cacao LLC, 10678
Restaurant Lulu Gourmet Products, 10684
Retzlaff Vineyards, 10688
Revel, Gelato, 10691
Revive Kombucha, 10692
Rhodes Bean & Supply Co-Op, 10697
Rice Company, 10704
Rice Innovations, 10708
Ricex Company, 10713
Richard Bagdasarian Inc, 10717
Richard L. Graeser Winery, 10720
Richardson Vineyards, 10726
Rick's Chips, 10732
Ridge Vineyards Inc, 10737
Righetti Specialties Inc, 10741
Rio Naturals, 10746
Ripple, 10753
Rise Bar, 10756
Rising Dough Bakery, 10758
Risvold's Inc., 10760
Ritchie Creek Vineyard, 10763
Ritual Coffee Roasters, 10765
River Run Vintners, 10771
Road's End Organics, 10780
Robert Keenan Winery, 10790
Robert Mondavi Winery, 10791
Robert Mueller Cellars, 10792
Robert Pecota Winery, 10793
Robert Sinskey Vineyards Inc, 10795

Geographic Index / California

Roberts Ferry Nut Co, 10799
Roche Caneros Estate Winery, 10807
Rock-N-Roll Gourmet, 10812
Rocket Fizz, 10814
Rockview Farms, 10818
Rodney Strong Vineyards, 10833
Roman Sausage Company, 10856
Rombauer Vineyards, 10858
Romero's Food Products Inc, 10859
Rosa Brothers Milk Co Inc, 10872
Rose Frozen Shrimp, 10883
Rosenblum Cellars, 10895
Rosetti's Fine Foods Biscotti, 10897
Roseville Corporation, 10898
Rotteveel Orchards, 10909
Roudon-Smith Vineyards, 10910
Round Hill Vineyards, 10912
Royal Caviar Inc, 10925
Royal Foods Inc, 10931
Royal Hawaiian Orchards LP, 10934
Royal Madera Vineyards, 10938
Royal Medjool Date Gardens, 10939
Royal Palate Foods, 10943
Royal Vista Marketing Inc, 10951
Rpac LLC, 10955
RPM Total Vitality, 10516
Rudd Winery, 10963
Ruiz Flour Tortillas, 10975
Ruiz Food Products Inc., 10976
Rumiano Cheese Co., 10979
Rumiano Cheese Factory, 10980
Russell & Kohne Inc, 10988
Rustic Bakery Inc., 10995
Rutherford Hill Winery, 10999
RW Garcia, 10518
S & E Organic Farms Inc, 11009
S&B International Corporation, 11021
Saag's Products LLC, 11059
Sabor Mexicano, 11063
Sabra Dipping Company,LL, 11065
Sacramento Baking Co, 11067
Sacramento Cookie Factory, 11068
Saddleback Cellars, 11069
Safe Catch, 11071
Safeway Inc., 11073
Sagely Naturals, 11079
Sahara Natural Foods, 11087
Saintsbury, 11092
Salamandre Wine Cellars, 11097
Salty Girl Seafood, 11118
Salute Sante! Food & Wine, 11121
Sambazon, 11128
Sampac Enterprises, 11131
San Anselmo's Cookies & Biscotti, 11134
San Diego Soy Dairy, 11138
San Francisco Bay Coffee, 11140
San Francisco Bay Coffee Company, 11141
San Francisco Fine Bakery, 11142
San Francisco French Bread, 11143
San Francisco Popcorn Works, 11144
San Francisco Salt, 11145
San Francisco Spice Co., 11146
San Franola Granola, 11147
San Joaquin Figs Inc, 11149
San Joaquin Vly Concentrates, 11150
San Jose Apartments, 11151
Sanford Winery, 11178
SANGARIA USA, 11032
Santa Barbara Bar, 11182
Santa Barbara Olive Company, 11183
Santa Barbara Pistachio Co, 11184
Santa Barbara Roasting Co, 11185
Santa Barbara Salsa, 11186
Santa Barbara Salsa/California Creative, 11187
Santa Barbara Winery, 11188
Santa Clara Inc, 11189
Santa Cruz Mountain Brewing, 11191
Santa Cruz Mountain Vineyard, 11192
Santa Monica Seafood Co., 11198
Santa Ynez Wine Corp, 11199
Sante Specialty Foods, 11202
Santini Foods, 11203, 11204
Sarah's Vineyard, 11217
Saticoy Foods Corp, 11234
Satiety Winery & Cafe, 11235
Saucilito Canyon Vineyard, 11240
Sausal Winery, 11245
Savannah Chanelle Vineyards, 11248
Scharffen Berger Chocolate Maker, 11278
Schat's Dutch Bakeries, 11279
Schramsberg Vineyards, 11307

Schug Carneros Estate Winery, 11309
Sconza Candy Co, 11320
Sea Farm & Farm Fresh Importing Company, 11341
Sea Ridge Winery, 11348
Sea Snack Foods Inc, 11352
Sea Stars Goat Cheese, 11353
Sea Veggies, 11354
Seabreeze Fish, 11364
Seafood Dimensions Intl, 11368
Seapoint Farms, 11382
Season Harvest Foods, 11385
Seavey Vineyard, 11394
Sebastiani Vineyards, 11398
Sedona Baking Company, 11405
See Smell Taste, 11406
See's Candies, 11407
Seeds of Change, 11409
Seghesio Family Vineyards, 11413
Select Harvest USA, 11417
Select Supplements Inc, 11419
Semifreddi's Bakery, 11426
Seminis Vegetable Seeds Inc, 11427
Sempio Foods, 11429
Senba USA, 11431
Sencha Naturals, 11432
Senomyx Inc, 11436
Senor Felix's Gourmet Mexican, 11437
Sensible Foods LLC, 11441
Sequoia Brewing Co, 11448
Sequoia Grove, 11449
Sequoia Specialty Cheese Company, 11450
Serengeti Tea Co, 11454
Serv-Rite Meat Co Inc, 11459
Setton Farms, 11467
Setton Pistachio, 11469
Seven Seas Seafoods, 11475
Seville Olive Company, 11480
Shafer Vineyards, 11494
Shaklee Corp, 11501
Shamrock Foods Co, 11508
Shanley Farms, 11516
Shelton's Poultry Inc, 11542
Shenandoah Vineyards, 11545
Sherrill Orchards, 11551
Shields Date Garden, 11555
Shine Foods Inc, 11558
Shoei Foods USA Inc, 11567
Sierra Cheese Mfg Co, 11589
Sierra Nevada Cheese Co., 11591
Sierra Nevada Taproom & Rstrnt, 11592
Sierra Vista Winery, 11593
Signorello Vineyards, 11604
Sigona's, 11605
Silva Farms, 11610
Silvateam USA, 11613
Silver Fox Vineyards, 11618
Silver Mountain Vineyards, 11621
Silver Oak, 11622
Silverado Vineyards Inc, 11632
Simi Winery, 11637
Simon Levi Cellars, 11642
Simpatica, 11644
Simply Gourmet Confections, 11652
Simply Scruptious Confections, 11656
Simply Shari's Gluten Free, 11657
Sinbad Sweets, 11663
Siren Snacks, 11673
Sjaak's Organic Chocolates, 11682
Skipping Stone Productions, 11690
Sky Vineyards, 11695
Slingshot Foods, 11707
Slo Roasted Coffee, 11708
Smashmallow, 11717
Smith Vineyard & Winery, 11730
Smith-Madrone Vineyards & Winery, 11732
Smothers Brothers Tasting Room, 11741
Snack Works/Metrovox Snacks, 11745
Snackerz, 11747
SnackMasters, LLC, 11746
Snak King Corp, 11748
Snapdragon Foods, 11750
Snow Monkey, 11762
Sobon Estate, 11774
Soft Cell Technology, 11778
Solana Beach Baking Company, 11781
Solana Gold Organics, 11782
Solazyme Inc, 11783
Solis Winery, 11786
Sonoma Creamery, 11804
Sonoma Gourmet, 11806
Sonoma Seafoods, 11807

Sonoma Syrup Co. Inc., 11808
Sonoma Wine Services, 11809
Sonoma-Cutrer Vineyards, 11810
Sorrenti Family Farms, 11818
Souperb LLC, 11821
Source Naturals, 11824
South Ceasar Dressing Company, 11829
South Shores Seafood, 11833
South Valley Farms, 11835
Southern California Brewing Company, 11846
Sowden Brothers Farm, 11877
Soy Vay Enterprises, 11878
Soylent, 11882
Sparrow Lane, 11890
SPI West Port, Inc, 11052
Spice & Spice, 11915
Spice King Corporation, 11920
Spice Of Life Co, 11923
Spicely, 11928
Splendid Specialties, 11940
Sportabs International, 11947
Sportsmens Seafoods, 11952
Spottswoode, 11954
Spring Mountain Vineyard, 11966
Sprout House, 11977
Spruce Foods, 11980
Squab Producers of California, 11985
Squair Food Company, 11986
Square-H Brands Inc, 11988
St Francis Winery & Vineyards, 11995
St. Amour Inc/French Cookies, 12002
St. Stan's Brewing Company, 12013
Staff Of Life Natural Foods, 12017
Stags' Leap Winery, 12019
Stanislaus Food Prod, 12030
Star Anise Foods, 12034
Star Fine Foods, 12035
Star Route Farms, 12038
Starport Foods, 12047
Starwest Botanicals Inc, 12051
Stauber Performance Ingrdients, 12059
Stearns Wharf Vintners, 12066
Steltzner Vineyards, 12079
Sterling Caviar LLC, 12083, 12084
Sterling Vineyards, 12087
Steve Mendez, 12092
Stevenot Winery, 12099
Stiebs, 12119
Stinking Rose, The, 12121
Stone Brewing, 12129
Stonegate, 12125
Stoneridge Winery, 12138
Stony Hill Vineyard, 12143
Stonybrook Mountain Winery, 12144
StoreHouse Foods, 12149
Storrs Winery, 12150
Story Winery, 12151
Straus Family Creamery, 12160
Streblow Vineyards, 12165
Stremick's Heritage Foods, 12168
Stretch Island Fruit, 12169
Stryker Sonoma, 12177
Sudwerk Privatbrauerei Hubsch, 12191
Sugar Bowl Bakery, 12195
Sugar Flowers Plus, 12199
Sugar Foods Corp, 12200
Suja Juice, 12213
Sukhi's Gourmet Indian Food, 12215
Sullivan Vineyards, 12217
Summerfield Foods, 12223
Summit Lake Vineyards, 12227
Sun Chlorella USA, 12228
Sun Empire Foods, 12229
Sun Harvest Foods Inc, 12234
Sun Pacific, 12242
Sun Ray International, 12243
Sun Rich Fresh Foods USA Inc, 12244
Sun Tropics Inc, 12248
Sun Valley Packing, 12250
Sun Valley Raisins Inc, 12251
Sun West, 12252
Sun West Foods, 12253
Sun World Intl LLC, 12254
Sun-Maid Growers of California, 12256
Sunchef Farms, 12266
Sundia Corp, 12271
SunFed Ranch, 12261
Sunfood, 12274
Sunny Avocado, 12280
Sunnyland Mills, 12287
Sunridge Farms, 12295

Sunridge Farms Inc, 12296
Sunrise Growers, 12297
Sunrise Winery, 12299
Sunset Specialty Foods, 12301
Sunstone Vineyards & Winery, 12312
Sunsweet Growers Inc., 12313
SunWest Foods, Inc., 12262
SunWest Organics, 12263
Sup Herb Farms, 12317
Super Stores Industries, 12323
Superior Farms, 12333
Superior Foods, 12334
Superior Quality Foods, 12343
SupHerb Farms, 12318
Suprema Specialties, 12347
Supreme Artisan Foods, 12348
Sure-Fresh Produce Inc, 12354
Sutter Buttes Olive Oil, 12367
Sutter Foods LLC, 12368
Sutter Home Winery, 12369
Svenhard's Swedish Bakery Inc, 12375
Swanson Vineyards & Winery, 12378
Sweet Blessings, 12389
Sweet Earth Foods, 12396
Sweet Lady Jane, 12403
Sweet Life Enterprises, 12405
Sweet Peas Floral Design, 12410
Sweet Pillar, 12411
Sweet Traders, 12418
Sweetaly, 12424
Sweetstacks LLC, 12431
Sweety Novelty, 12434
Swiss Dairy, 12439
Swiss-American Sausage Company, 12444
Sycamore Vineyards, 12449
Symphony Foods, 12453
T Hasegawa USA Inc, 12461
T M Duche Nut Co, 12462
Tabco Enterprises, 12486
Table De France, 12487
Tadin Herb & Tea Co, 12490
Taft Street Winery, 12492
Tahitian Gold, 12495
Takara Sake USA Inc, 12500
Takeiya USA, 12502
Talbott Teas, 12505
Talbott Vineyards, 12506
Talenti Gelato e Sorbetto, 12507
Talley Farms, 12513
Talley Vineyards, 12514
Tampico Spice Co, 12522
Tanimura Antle Inc, 12525
Tapatio Hot Sauce, 12531
Tarazi Specialty Foods, 12535, 12536
Tartine Bakery, 12538
Taste of Nature Inc., 12547
Tasty Brand Inc, 12552
Tastybaby, 12558
Taylor Farms, 12566
Taylor Farms Pacific, 12567
TCHO Ventures, 12476
Tea Room, 12586
Tea-n-Crumpets, 12587
Teasdale Quality Foods Inc, 12590
Techno Food Ingredients Co., Ltd, 12593
Techno USA, 12594
Teeccino, 12601
Teixeira Farms, Inc., 12606
Tejon Ranch Co, 12607
Terrace At J Vineyards, 12627
Test Laboratories Inc, 12638
Thackrey & Co, 12661
Thanksgiving Coffee Co, 12663
That's It Nutrition, 12665
Thatcher's Gourmet Specialties, 12666
The Art of Broth, LLC, 12669
The Boisset Collection, 12672
The Coffee Bean & Tea Leaf, 12677
The Coromega Company, 12679
The Food Collective, 12684
The Good Bean, 12685
The Long Life Beverage Company, 12704
The Meeker Vineyard, 12709
The Rubin Family of Wines, 12726
The Wine RayZyn Company, 12746
Thinkthin, LLC, 12754
This Bar Saves Lives, LLC, 12757
Thomas Fogarty Winery, 12764
Thomas Kruse Winery, 12767
Thornton Winery, 12777
Thoughtful Food, 12779
Three Jerks Jerky, 12782

Geographic Index / Colorado

Three Trees Almondmilk, 12787
Three Twins Ice Cream, 12788
Timber Crest Farms, 12809
Tiny Hero Foods, 12818
Tirawisu, 12824
Tkc Vineyards, 12827
Todd's, 12831
TODDS Enterprises Inc, 12481
Toe-Food Chocolates and Candy, 12836
Toffee Boutique, 12837
Tofu Shop Specialty Foods Inc, 12841
Tokunaga Farms, 12844
Tom & Dave's Coffee, 12846
Tommy Tang's Thai Seasonings, 12862
Too Good Gourmet, 12878
Topolos at Russian River Vine, 12887
Torani, 12889
Torn & Glasser, 12893
Torn Ranch, 12894
Trader Vic's Food Products, 12912
Tradin Organics USA, 12916
Traditional Baking Inc, 12917
Traditional Medicinals Inc, 12918
Traina Foods Inc, 12922
Transpacific Foods Inc, 12929
Trattore Farms, 12933
Treasury Wine Estates, 12937
Treat Ice Cream Co, 12938
Trefethen Family Vineyards, 12946
Trentadue Winery, 12950
Tri-Boro Fruit Co, 12956
Tri-Counties Packing Company, 12957
Tribali Foods, 12963
Trinity Fruit Sale Co, 12974
Triple H Food Processors Inc, 12978
Triple Leaf Tea Inc, 12980
Triple Rock Brewing Co Brkly, 12981
Tripper Inc, 12987
Tropical Preserving Co Inc, 13009
Troppers, 13013
TruBrain, 13023
Truchard Vineyards, 13027
Truckee River Winery, 13028
True Jerky, 13032
True Organic Product Inc, 13034
True Story Foods, 13035
TruVibe Organics, 13025
Tsar Nicoulai Caviar LLC, 13042
Tu Me Beverage Company, 13043
Tudal Winery, 13049
Tufts Ranch, 13050
Tulocay Cemetery, 13054
Turlock Fruit Co, 13067
Turveda, 13076
Twenty Rows, 13087
Two Chefs on a Roll, 13098
TyRy Inc, 13105
Ultimate Bagel, 13138
Ultimate Nut & Candy Company, 13142
Ultra Enterprises, 13146
Uncle Lee's Tea Inc, 13156
Uncommon Grounds Coffee, 13160
Unified Food Ingredients, 13166
Union, 13170
Unique Vitality Products, 13179
United Foods USA, 13189
United Meat Company, 13194
United With Earth, 13203
Upper Crust Biscotti, 13216
Uptime Energy, Inc., 13219
Urban Foods LLC, 13223
V Sattui Winery, 13236
Vacaville Fruit Co, 13244
Valhrona, 13251
Valley Fig Growers, 13254
Valley Grain Products, 13255
Valley Lahvosh, 13256
Valley Meat Company, 13257
Valley of the Moon Winery, 13267
Valley Sun Products Inc, 13261
Valley Tea & Coffee, 13262
Valley View Packing Co, 13265
Van Der Heyden Vineyards, 13269
Van's International Foods, 13283
Vance's Foods, 13286
Varni Brothers/7-Up Bottling, 13300
Vege USA, 13310
Vege-Cool, 13311
Veggie Grill, 13314
Vegi-Deli, 13316
Vella Cheese Co, 13320
Venice Baking Co, 13324

Ventana Vineyards Winery, 13325
Ventura Coastal LLC, 13327
Ventura Foods LLC, 13328
Veronica Foods Inc, 13365
Verve Coffee Roasters, 13367
Vessey & Co Inc, 13369
Viader Vineyards & Winery, 13373
Viano Vineyards, 13374
Viansa Winery, 13375
Vichy Springs Mineral Water, 13378
Vickey's Vittles, 13379
Victor Packing, 13384
Victoria's Catered Traditions, 13390
Vie-Del Co, 13397
Vienna Beef LTD, 13399
Villa Barone, 13411
Villa Helena/Arger-Martucci Winery, 13412
Villa Mt. Eden Winery, 13414
Vincent Arroyo Winery, 13420
Vincent B Zaninovich & Sons, 13421
Vine Village Day, 13426
Vinquiry Wine Analysis, 13430
Vintage Wine Estates, 13434
Viola's Gourmet Goodies, 13436
VIP Sales Company, 13241
Virgin Raw Foods LLC, 13440
Visalia Citrus Packing Group, 13448
Visalia Produce Sales, 13449
Vision Pack Brands, 13450
Vit-Best Nutrition, 13453
Vitamer Laboratories, 13467
Vitaminerals, 13469
Vitarich Ice Cream, 13471
Vitatech Nutritional Sciences, 13474
Vive Organic, 13478
Vixen Kitchen, 13483
Vogue Cuisine Foods, 13487
Von Strasser, 13492
Wah Yet Group, 13531
Wai Lana Snacks, 13532
Wakunaga Of America Co LTD, 13536
Walker Foods, 13541
Walsh's Coffee Roasters, 13554
Washington State Juice, 13583
Wawona Frozen Foods Inc, 13598
WCC Honey Marketing, 13511
Wedemeyer's Bakery, 13619
Wei-Chuan USA Inc, 13625
Weibel Vineyards, 13626
Well-Pict Inc, 13640
Wellington Foods, 13644
Wendysue & Tobey's, 13649
Wente Family Estates, 13654
Wermuth Winery, 13657
West Coast Products, 13661
West Coast Specialty Coffee, 13663
West Pak Avocado Inc, 13666
Westar Nutrition Corporation, 13670
Westco-BakeMark, 13675
Western Bagel Baking Corp, 13677
Western Pacific Oils, Inc., 13683
Western Pacific Produce, 13684
Western Syrup Company, 13686
Westwood Winery, 13696
Whaler Vineyard, 13701
Whitcraft Winery, 13713
White Oak Vineyards & Winery, 13725
White Oaks Frozen Foods, 13726
White Rock Vineyards, 13729
Whitehall Lane Winery, 13736
Whitford Cellars, 13741
Whole Herb Co, 13746
Whole Life Nutritional Supplements, 13747
Wholesome Bakery, 13750
Wilbur Packing Company, 13773
Wild Hog Vineyard, 13780
Wild Horse Winery & Vineyards, 13781
Wild Planet Foods, 13783
Wild Poppy, 13784
Wild Rice Exchange, 13785
Wildhurst Vineyards, 13793
Wileman Brothers & Elliott Inc, 13800
Will-Pak Foods, 13805
William Bounds, 13809
William Grant & Sons, 13811
William Harrison Winery LLC, 13812, 13813
William Hill Estate Winery, 13814
Williams Selyem Winery, 13821
Winchell's Donut House, 13839
Winchester Cheese Company, 13840

Windsor Confections, 13845
Windwalker Vineyards & Winery, 13846
Wine Country Chef LLC, 13848
Wine Country Kitchens, 13849
Wine Country Pasta, 13850
Wine Group, 13851
Wing Nien Food, 13855
Wing Sing Chong Company, 13857
Wishnev Wine Management, 13887
Wisteria Candy Cottage, 13888
Wolf Canyon Foods, 13897
Wolfgang Puck Food Company, 13900
Wonderful Pistachios & Almonds, 13907
Wooden Valley Winery, 13916
Woodlake Ranch, 13919
Woodside Vineyards, 13921
World Citrus West, 13932
World Ginseng Ctr Inc, 13937
World Organics Corporation, 13943
Worldwide Specialties In, 13950
Wrawp, 13955
Yamamotoyama of America, 13985
Yamasa Fish Cake Co, 13987
Yaya's, 13995
Yayin Corporation, 13996
Yerba Santa Goat Dairy, 14001
Yergat Packing Co, 14002
Yogavive, 14010
Yogurtland Franchising Inc, 14012
Yokohl Packing Co, 14014
York Mountain Winery, 14018
Yum Yum Donut Shops Inc, 14030
Z Foods Inc., 14033
Z Specialty Food, LLC, 14034
Z&S Distributing, 14035
Zaca Mesa Winery, 14038
Zacky Farms, 14041
Zayante Vineyards, 14044
Zazi Baking Company, 14045
Zd Wines, 14047
Zego Foods, 14049
Zevia, 14061
Zhena's Gypsy Tea, 14062
Zoe's Meats, 14069

Colorado

10 Strawberry Street, 2
34-Degrees, 13
8th Wonder, 30
A2 Milk Company, 69
Agfinity Inc, 204
Agripac, 216
All American Seasonings, 318
Allegro Coffee Co, 332
Alpine Start Foods, 382
Alvalle, 396
Ancient Harvest, 534
Annabella, 582
Applewood Seed & Garden Group, 617
Ardent Mills Corp, 648
Arrowhead Mills, 705
Atkins Nutritionals Inc., 755
Aurora Organic Dairy, 812
Avery Brewing Company, 838
B.B. Bean, Coffee, 881
Banquet Schusters Bakery, 1010
Banzos, 1013
Bearitos, 1133
Bespoke Provisions, 1259
Bhakti, 1301
Birch Benders, 1382
Black River Caviar, 1425
Blue Moose of Boulder, 1487
Bluepoint Bakery, 1509
Bobo's Oat Bars, 1523
Boulder Beer, 1611
Boulder Canyon Natural Foods, 1613
Boulder Cookie, 1614
Boulder Granola, 1616
Boulder Homemade Inc, 1617
Boulder Organic Foods, 1618
Boulder Sausage Co, 1619
Boulder Vegans, 1620
Bountiful Larder LLC, 1624
Boyer's Coffee, 1639
Breckenridge Brewery, 1687
Bremner Biscuit Company, 1690
Brewers Association, 1695
Bristol Brewing Co, 1720
Brush Locker, 1803
Bubba's Fine Foods, 1810

Burrito Kitchens, 1869
Buywell Coffee, 1890
Cable Car Beverage Corporation, 1969
Cafe Cartago, 1989
Callaway Packing Inc, 2090
Canon Potato Company, 2143
Canyon Bakehouse LLC, 2146
Cappello's, 2168
Carlson Vineyards Winery, 2217
Castle Rock Meats, 2303
Chef Soraya, 2497
Chocolate Soup, 2610
Chocolove, 2623
Clark Spring Water Co, 2718
Clyde's Italian & German Sausage, 2792
Cocomels by JJ's Sweets, 2826
Coffee Bean, 2834
Colorado Cellars, 2893
Colorado Hemp Honey, 2894
Colorado Mountain Jams & Jellies, 2895
Colorado Nut Co, 2896
Colorado Popcorn Co, 2897
Colorado Salsa Company, 2898
Colorado Spice Co, 2899
Colorado Sweet Gold, 2900
Columbine Confections LLC, 2910
Continental Sausage, 2972
Cotswold Cottage Foods, 3054
Culinaire, 3232
Cusa Tea, 3263
Dakota, 3352
Danone North America, 3379
Dazbog Coffee Co, 3422
Decadence Cheese Cakes, 3454
Denomega Pure Health, 3526
Don't Go Nuts, 3675
Durango Brewing Co, 3807
Earth Balance, 3868
EcoNatural Solutions, 3925
Eldorado Artesian Springs Inc, 3996
ELP Inc, 3854
Empact Bars, 4050
Enstrom Candies, Inc., 4079
Epicurean Butter, 4094
Ethan's, 4132
Ethnic Gourmet Foods, 4138
Evo Hemp, 4174
Evol Foods, 4175
Faber Foods and Aeronautics, 4214
Farm & Oven Snacks, 4268
Fatworks, 4310
Fernandez Chili Co, 4339
Ferncreek Confections LLC, 4341
FlapJacked, 4473
Food City USA, 4555
Food Should Taste Good, 4568
Foodie Fuel, 4573
Fountain Valley Foods, 4623
Free2b Foods, 4679
Front Range Snacks Inc, 4749
Froozer, 4754
Fuzziwig's Candy Factory, 4810
Garden of the Gods Gourmet, 4899
Generous Coffee, 4949
Golden City Brewery, 5117
Good Karma Foods, 5166
Good Spread, 5172
GoodBelly Probiotics, 5178
Grandcestors, 5257
Grande River Vineyards, 5260
Grass Run Farms, 5281
Great Divide Brewing Co, 5304
Great Western Tortilla, 5336
Grower Shipper Potato Company, 5409
Hain Celestial Group Inc, 5506
Hall Grain Company, 5522
Hammond's Candies, 5535
Healthy Skoop, 5699
Heavenly Hemp Foods, 5721
Heavenly Organics, LLC, 5722
Hendricks Apiaries, 5766
Hickory Baked Ham Co, 5832
High Country Elevators Inc, 5841
High Rise Coffee Roasters, 5848
High Valley Farm, 5851
Home Style Bakery Of Grand Junction, 5932
Homestead Meats, 5945
Honey Bear Fruit Basket, 5954
Honey Stinger, 5963
Hope Foods, 5991
Horizon Organic Dairy, 5996
Imagine Foods, 6151

1325

Geographic Index / Connecticut

IZZE Beverage, 6124
Jack's Bean Co LLC, 6418
Jackfruit Company, The, 6420
Jackson's Honest, 6423
JBS USA LLC, 6391
Jerry's Nut House, 6500
Josh & John's Ice Cream, 6608
Joy's Specialty Foods, 6615
Just Bare, 6640
Just Panela, 6648
Justin's Nut Butter, 6652
Ka-POP!, 6680
Kalot Superfood, 6694
Kim and Jake's, 6848
Know Brainer, 6925
LA Mar's Donuts, 7050
Larabar, 7218
Left Hand Brewing Co, 7309, 7310
Leprino Foods Co., 7369
Leroux Creek, 7371
Lily's Sweets, 7431
Lima Grain Cereal Seeds LLC, 7433
Lombardi Brothers Meat Packers, 7515
Louis Swiss Pastry, 7576
Love Grown Foods, 7598
Love The Wild, 7600
Lowell-Paul Dairy, 7610
Lucile's, 7627
Made In Nature, 7742
Madhava Natural Sweeteners, 7748
Meals-In-A-Minute, 8110
Meridian Trading Co., 8171
Merlinos, 8177
Mesquite Organic Beef LLC, 8188
Michelle Chocolatiers, 8242
Mont Blanc Gourmet, 8487
Mountain Sun Pubs & Breweries, 8602
Mrs. Fields Original Cookies, 8638
My Favorite Jerky, 8707
Natural Balance, 8820
Natural Habitats USA, 8839
Nature's Love, 8887
NestFresh, 8942
New Age Beverages, 8955
New Belgium Brewing Co, 8959
New Hope Natural Media, 8983
Nita Crisp Crackers LLC, 9070
No Cow, 9075
Noosa Yoghurt, 9095
Northern Feed & Bean Company, 9150
Now & Zen, 9196
Nspired Natural Foods, 9198
NuLeaf Naturals, 9208
Odell Brewing Co, 9366
Olomomo Nut Company, 9458
Oogie's Snack LLC, 9501
Organic India USA, 9546
Oskar Blues Brewery, 9582
Pappardelle's Inc, 9756
Patsy's Candy, 9836
Perky Jerky, 9960
Phamous Phloyd's Barbecue, 9996
Picaflor, 10030
Pikes Peak Vineyards, 10053
Pilgrim's Pride Corp., 10056
Plum Creek Winery, 10122
Pressery, 10264
Promised Land Dairy, 10342
Purely Elizabeth, 10389
Quinn Snacks, 10466
Raquelitas Tortillas, 10569
RE Botanicals, 10504
Ready Foods Inc, 10585
Rejuvila, 10665
Rock Bottom Restaurant & Brewery, 10810
Rocky Mountain Chocolate Factory, 10819
Rocky Mountain Natural Meats, 10823
Rodelle Inc, 10831
Royal Crest Dairy, 10927
Rudi's Organic Bakery, 10965
Sage V Foods, 11078
Salba Smart Natural Prod LLC, 11099
San Luis Valley Hemp Co., 11153
Sandbar Trading Corp, 11165
Scooty's Wholesome Foods, 11321
Sejoyia Foods, 11415
Sensible Portions, 11442
Seth Ellis Chocolatier, 11465
Shamrock Foods Co, 11506
Shariann's Organics, 11518
Sierra Madre Coffee, 11590
Silver State Foods Inc, 11628

Skratch Labs, 11692
Smirk's, 11721
Smith & Truslow, 11724
Snikiddy, LLC, 11754
Soloman Baking Company, 11790, 11791
Spitz USA, 11939
Stassen North America, 12054
Steven Roberts Originals, 12098
Stokes Canning Company, 12127
Sweet & Saucy Inc, 12386
Sweetwood Cattle Co, 12433
Taj Gourmet Foods, 12499
Talbott Farms, 12504
Temptee Specialty Foods, 12613
Teton Waters Ranch LLC, 12644
Thanasi Foods LLC, 12662
The Great Western Tortilla Co., 12688
The Honest Stand, 12691
The Naked Edge, LLC, 12711
The Tea Spot, Inc., 12738
Third Street Inc, 12755
Timber Peaks Gourmet, 12811
To Market To Market, 12828
Trinidad Benham Corporation, 12973
Turtle Island Herbs, 13075
Two Leaves & A Bud Inc, 13103
Two Moms In The Raw, 13104
Udi's Gluten-Free Foods, 13132
Udi's Granola, 13133
United Marketing Exchange, 13193
Village Roaster, 13415
Wallaby Yogurt Co, 13546
Wally Biscotti, 13552
Walnut Acres, 13553
Westbrae Natural Foods, 13673
Western Sugar Cooperative, 13685
WhiteWave Foods, 13734
Whitewave Foods Company, 13738
Wild Zora Foods, 13790
Wilde Brands, 13792
Yai's Thai, 13980
Zoelsmann's Bakery & Deli, 14070

Connecticut

Adolf's Meats & Sausage Kitchen, 182
Al's Beverage Company, 252
Aleias Gluten Free Foods, 288
Amalgamated Produce, 406
American Halal Company, 459
American Lecithin Company, 468
Andre Prost Inc, 551
Anmar Nutrition, 578
Archie Moore's, 640
Arista Industries Inc, 666
Ariston Specialties, 667
Arturo's Spinella's Bakery, 717
Asarasi, 723
Athletic Brewing Co., 751
Aurora Products, 814
Bakery on Main, 977
Balticshop.Com LLC, 998
Baretta Provision, 1032
Bedoukian Research Inc, 1154
BetaStatin Nutritional Rsearch, 1274
Bigelow Tea, 1350
Binding Brauerei USA, 1361
BioTech Corporation, 1374
Bishop Farms Winery, 1400
Blue Jay Orchards, 1481
Boehringer Ingelheim Corp, 1535
Brooklyn Baking Company, 1744
Brown Dog Fancy, 1776
Bruce Coffee Svc Plan USA, 1792
Buck's Spumoni Company, 1818
C W Resources Inc, 1925
Calabro Cheese Corp, 2033
Capa Di Roma Inc, 2149
Carla's Pasta, 2215
Castle Beverages Inc, 2300
Cell-Nique, 2361
Centerchem, Inc., 2370
Champion Beverages, 2410
Chas Boggini Co., 2448
Chef Silvio's of Wooster Street, 2496
Chevalier Chocolates, 2537
Chocopologie By Knipschildt, 2625
Coastal Seafoods, 2804
Colchester Bakery, 2865
Colchester Foods, 2866
Cosmo Food Products, 3048
Country Pure Foods Inc, 3084

Crompton Corporation, 3178
Crystal Rock LLC, 3217
Daybreak Coffee Roasters, 3417
De Met's Candy Co, 3430
Deep River Snacks, 3466
Dere Street, 3531
Desserts by David Glass, 3544
Di Fiore Pasta Co, 3563
Diageo North America Inc, 3570
Digrazia Vineyards, 3597
Elm City Cheese Co Inc, 4031
Elmwood Pastry Shop, 4036
Farmtrue, 4294
Forte Gelato, 4602
Foster Family Farm, 4619
Gelato Giuliana, 4936
Gotliebs Guacamole, 5196
Gourmet Conveniences Ltd, 5202
Gourmet Products, 5211
Gracious Gourmet, 5230
Grote & Weigel Inc, 5400
Guida's Dairy, 5422
Guinness Import Co, 5427
Haight Brown Vineyard, 5502
Havoc Maker Products, 5652
Heartline Foods, 5717
HerbaSway Laboratories, 5784
Holly's Oatmeal Inc, 5914
Hopkins Inn Of Lake Waramaug, 5992
Hopkins Vineyard, 5993
Hosmer Mountain Bottling Co, 6009
Hummel Brothers Inc, 6072
I-Health Inc, 6107
Imus Ranch Foods, 6170
Inter-Continental Imports Company, 6238
Jovial Foods, 6613
Kathie's Kitchen, 6728
Kupris Home Bakery, 7004
Late July Snacks, 7239
Lecoq Cuisine Corp, 7293
Leon's Bakery, 7359
Lesserevil Brand Snack Co, 7393, 7394
Lewis Laboratories International Ltd., 7404
Light Rock Beverage Company, 7425
Little's Cuisine, 7476
Liuzzi Angeloni Cheese, 7477
Lombardi's Bakery, 7516
Louis Dreyfus Company LLC, 7570
Love'n Herbs, 7602
Lupi-Marchigiano Bakery, 7651
Lynard Company, 7660
Mama Del's Macacroni, 7812
Mantrose-Haeuser Co Inc, 7857
Maple Hill Farms, 7868
Martin Rosols, 7968
Matthew's Bakery, 8013
Matthews 1812 House, 8014
Micalizzi Italian Ice, 8221
Monini North America, 8479
Moo Chocolate/Organic Children's Chocolate LLC, 8517
Mountain High Organics, 8596
Mozzicato De Pasquale Bakery, 8617
Mt Claire Beverages, 8653
Mucke's Meat Products, 8665
Munk Pack, 8680
Munson's Chocolates, 8683
Mystic Coffee Roasters, 8716
Nardi Breads, 8769
Nature Most Laboratories, 8861
Nature's Bandits, 8868
Nature's First Inc, 8876
New England Country Bakers, 8968
Newman's Own, 9018
Nodine's Smokehouse Inc, 9082
Norpaco Inc, 9113
Nuovo Pasta Productions LTD, 9221
Nutmeg Vineyard, 9230
Oasis Coffee Co Inc, 9331
Olive Oil Factor, 9447
Omar Coffee Co, 9475
Original American Beverage Company, 9560
OSF Flavors Inc, 9308
Palmieri Food Products, 9728
Pan De Oro Tortilla Chip Co, 9733
Passage Foods LLC, 9805
Penotti USA, 9929
Pepperidge Farm Inc., 9942
Peter's Mustards, 9982
Pez Candy Inc, 9991
Pharmco Aaper, 9999

Preferred Brands Inc, 10242
R.L. Albert & Son, 10496
Ragozzino Foods Inc, 10533
RISE Brewing Co., 10512
Rose Hill Distributors, 10884
Royal Ice Cream Co, 10936
Sabatino Truffles USA, 11060
Saffron Road, 11075
Sardinia Cheese, 11225
Sarum Tea Company, 11232
Severance Foods Inc, 11477
Simply Auri, 11649
Simpson & Vail, 11659
Sipp, 11670
SoBe Beverages, 11772
SpecialTeas, 11893
St Clair Ice Cream Co, 11994
Stanley Provision Company, 12032
Statewide Meats & Poultry, 12058
Stonington Vineyards, 12142
Sundial Herb Garden, 12272
Sunshine Dairy, 12303
Superior Bakery Inc, 12328
Superseedz, 12346
Sweet Mavens, LLC, 12407
Switch Beverage, 12447
Target Flavors Inc, 12537
Tearrific Ice Cream, 12589
The Bites Company, 12671
Thermice Company, 12750
Tipiak Inc, 12822
Torie & Howard LLC, 12890
TresOmega, 13075
Triple Springs Spring Water Co, 12982
Ultimate Nutrition, 13143
Vanco Trading Inc, 13287
Victoria Amory & Co LLC, 13386
Virgil's Root Beer, 13439
Vocatura Bakery Inc, 13484
VOD Gourmet, 13243
W.J. Stearns & Sons/Mountain Dairy, 13502
Watson Inc, 13591, 13592
White Oak Farm and Table, 13722
Willoughby's Coffee & Tea, 13829
Wink Frozen Desserts, 13862
World Herbs Gourmet, 13939

Delaware

Allen Harim Foods LLC, 336
Amalfitano's Italian Bakery, 405
Corteva Agriscience, 3044
Dogfish Head Craft Brewery, 3644
Easy Lift Equipment Co Inc, 3898
Ella's Kitchen, 4016
G. Banis Company, 4819
Govatos Chocolates, 5222
J G Townsend Jr & Co, 6352
Kirby Holloway Provision Co, 6887
Lew-Mark Baking Company, 7400
Lewes Dairy Inc, 7401
M-CAP Technologies, 7683
Mountaire Corporation, 8610
Natural By Nature, 8822
Nicola Pizza, 9045
Peppers, 9944
Quality Kitchen Corporation, 10438
Rondo Specialty Foods LTD, 10863
Roos Foods, 10869
Sunshine Nut Company, 12310
Superior Nutrition Corporation, 12339
T.S. Smith & Sons, 12472
The Real Co, 12723
UNOI Grainmill, 13118

District of Columbia

American Palm Oil, 476
Baked & Wired, 957
Blue Circle Foods, 1469
Catania Bakery, 2308
CMA Global Partners/German Foods LLC, 1957
Divine Chocolate, 3624
Dolci Gelati, 3651
Everything Yogurt, 4173
Halifax Group, 5520
Independent Bakers Association, 6179
John I. Haas, 6554
Mason Dixie Biscuit Co., 7992
Misfit Juicery, 8373
New Harvest Foods, 8980

Olde Heurich Brewing Company, 9437
Soupergirl, 11822
Soyfoods of America, 11881
Swapples, 12380
Wagshal's Imports, 13530
Watusee Foods, 13593
Widow's Mite Vinegar Company, 13768

Florida

Advanced Aquaculture Systems, 185
Agro Foods, Inc., 218
AgroCepia, 219
Agumm, 224
Akicorp, 245
Al-Rite Fruits & Syrups Co, 253
Alca Trading Co., 281
Alessi Bakery, 289
Alfonso Gourmet Pasta, 298
Alimentos Finisterre, 308
Alive & Well Olives, 314
All Wrapped Up, 324
Almased USA, 354
Amanida USA Corp, 411
American Fine Food Corporation, 453
Ammerland America, 506
Anastasia Confections Inc, 529
Ancient Nutrition, 535
Anco Foods, 538
Aqua Clara Bottling & Distribution, 620
ARA Food Corp, 100
Arcor USA, 643
Argo Century, Inc., 656
Aromatech USA, 698
Arrowhead Beef, 704
Arteasans Beverages LLC, 710
ASC Seafood Inc, 102
Atlantis Pak USA Inc, 780
Austrade, 820
Baby's Coffee, 912
Bacardi USA Inc, 914
Bad Frog Brewery Co, 925
Badia Spices Inc., 930
BakeryCorp, 978
Balsu, 997
Bang & Soderlund Inc, 1007
Barnie's Coffee and Tea, 1049
Base Culture, 1068
Bauducco Foods Inc., 1085
Bavaria Corp International, 1089
BBS Bodacious BBQ Company, 890
Beaver Street Fisheries, 1140
Ben-Bud Growers Inc., 1216
Beneficial Blends, 1218
Berke-Blake Fancy Foods, Inc., 1233
Better Bagel Bakery, 1281
Bijol & Spices Inc, 1351
Bilgore's Groves, 1352
Blanver USA, 1439
Blue Star Food Products, 1500
Boar's Head, 1514
Boca Bagelworks, 1525
Boca Bons East, 1526
Bottom Line Foods, 1606
Brateka Enterprises, 1669
Brisk Coffee Co, 1718
Brooks Tropicals Inc, 1757
Brownie Brittle, LLC, 1786
Burke Brands, 1859
Bush Brothers Provision Co, 1873
Buzzn Bee Farms, 1893
Byrnes Packing Shed, 1905
C P Vegetable Oil, 1922
C&P Additives, 1927
Cachafaz US, 1974
Cafe Bustelo, 1988
Cafe Descafeinado de Chiapas, 1992
Calamondin Cafe, 2035
Captain Foods, Inc., 2185
Caracolillo Coffee Mills, 2192
Carmine's Bakery, 2224
Carolina Products, 2248
Carolina Summit Mountain Spring Water, 2249
Casino Bakery, 2292
Casual Gourmet Foods, 2305
Cawy Bottling Co, 2338
Cedar Key Aquaculture Farms, 2349
Celebrity Cheesecake, 2359
Celebrity Tea, LLC, 2360
Celsius, 2364
Champion Nutrition Inc, 2411

Cheesecake Etc Desserts, 2484
Chef's Cut: Real Jerky, 2500
Chefwise, 2504
Chiquita Brands LLC., 2580
Chocolates By Mr Roberts, 2616
Choice of Vermont, 2631
Chomps, 2632
Citrop Inc, 2696
Citrosuco North America Inc, 2697
Citrus International, 2698
Citrus Service, 2699
Clayton's Crab Co, 2735
Coastal Promotions, Inc., 2801
Coco Lopez Inc, 2820
Coffee Millers & Roasters, 2851
Coffee Millers & Roasting, 2852
Colonial Coffee Roasters Inc, 2885
Conoley Citrus Packers Inc, 2955
Cordoba Foods LLC, 3025
Country Pure Foods Inc, 3086
Crofton & Sons Inc, 3177
Crystal Springs Bottled Water, 3219
Crystal Springs Water Company, 3220
Cusano's Baking Company, 3265
Cutrale Citrus Juices, 3278
Cutting Edge Beverages, 3279
Cypress Point Creamery, 3287
Cyrils Bakery, 3288
D-Liteful Baking Company, 3304
Daabon Organic USA, Inc., 3324
Dairy-Mix Inc, 3344
Darifair Foods, 3386
Dark Dog, 3388
Davis Food Company, 3407
De Bruyn Produce Company, 3424
Deca & Otto Farms, 3453
Deconna Ice Cream, 3461
Del Monte Fresh Produce Inc., 3479
Delaviuda USA Inc, 3490
Delicae Gourmet, 3496
Dick Garber Company, 3587
Dimond Tager Company Products, 3605
Dixie Egg Co, 3630
DNE World Fruit Sales, 3314
Dockside Market, 3640
Dominex, 3664
Domino Specialty Ingredients, 3666
Don Hilario Estate Coffee, 3669
Douglas Machines Corp, 3711
Dried Ingredients, LLC., 3762
Droga Chocolates, 3767
DS Services of America, 3319
Duda Farm Fresh Foods Inc, 3781
Dulce de Leche Delcampo Products, 3788
Dundee Citrus Growers Assn, 3796
Dundee Groves, 3797
Dutch Packing Co., Inc., 3818
Duval Bakery Products, 3822
Eden Vineyards Winery, 3943
Ella's Flats, 4015
Elore Enterprises Inc, 4037
Energy Foods Intl., 4067
Esper Products DeLuxe, 4115
Essential Products of America, 4125
European Coffee, 4152
Evans Properties, 4159
Everglades Foods, 4165
Evergreen Sweeteners, Inc, 4168
Fantasy Chocolates, 4253
Father's Table Inc, 4308
Fiori Bruna Pasta Products, 4410
Fire Fruits International, 4412
First Roasters of Central Florida, 4429
Flavors from Florida, 4492
Flex Pack USA, 4504
Florida Brewery, 4514
Florida Caribbean Distillers, 4515
Florida Citrus, 4516
Florida Crystals Corporation, 4517
Florida Food Products Inc, 4518
Florida Key West, 4520
Florida Natural Flavors, 4521
Florida Veal Processors, 4522
Florida's Natural Growers, 4523
Fortitude Brands LLC, 4607
Franco's Cocktail Mixes, 4650
Frank Brunckhorst Company, 4652
Frostproof Sunkist Groves, 4755
Fruit of the Boot, 4767
Functional Products LLC, 4797
G A Food Svc Inc, 4813
Gaea North America LLC, 4858

Gama Products, 4877
Gator Hammock Corp, 4921
Gene's Citrus Ranch, 4946
Geneva Food Products, 4952
Gift Basket Supply World, 5006
Gilda Industries Inc, 5008
Ginny Bakes, 5026
Gold Sweet Company, 5109
Goldcoast Salads, 5112
Golden 100, 5113
Golden Edibles LLC, 5120
Golden River Fruit Company, 5132
GoldFoods, 5110
Gourm, Mist, 5218
Green Roads CBD, 5360
Green Source Organics, 5361
Green Turtle Cannery & Seafood, 5364
GS Gelato & Desserts Inc, 4846
Gulf Shrimp, Inc., 5439
H & H Products Co, 5460
Habby Habanero's Food Products, 5491
Haines City Citrus Growers, 5507
Hale Indian River Groves, 5513
Half Moon Bay Trading Co, 5516
Hamersmith, Inc., 5531
Hand Made Lollies, 5545
Happy & Healthy Products Inc, 5562
Happy Egg Dealers, 5566
Havana's Limited, 5648
Health & Nutrition Systems International, 5678
Heinz Portion Control, 5735
Heller Brothers Packing Corp, 5746
Herbal Science LLC, 5787
Hialeah Products Co, 5828
Hillandale, 5866
Hillcrest Orchard, 5869
Hillsboro Coffee Company, 5873
Hobarama Corporation, 5896
Hogtowne B-B-Q Sauce Company, 5905
Home Roast Coffee, 5930
Hot Wachula's, 6018
Howjax, 6036
Hunt Brothers Cooperative, 6081
I Heart Olive Oil, 6103
Ice Cream Club Inc, 6129
Indian River Select® LLC, 6188
Inlet Salmon, 6220
Innocent Chocolate, 6224
Interfood Ingredients, 6241
International Chemical Corp, 6252
International Food Packers Corporation, 6259
International Fruit Marketing, 6263
Island Spice, 6300
Italian Rose Garlic Products, 6322
J J Gandy's Pies Inc, 6355
J J Produce, 6356
J. Matassini & Sons Fish Company, 6373
J.A.M.B. Low Carb Distributor, 6376
J.G. British Imports, 6378
Jada Foods LLC, 6431
Java Cabana, 6466
Jaxon's Ice Cream Parlor, 6472
Jean Niel Inc, 6477
Jodie's Kitchen, 6528
Jodyana Corporation, 6531
Joe Hutson Foods, 6536
Joe Patti's Seafood Co, 6538
Joey's Home Bakery-Gluten Free, 6543
Kastner's Pastry Shop & Grocery, 6724
Kava King, 6740
Kelapo, 6756
Kennesaw Fruit & Juice, 6788
Kentwood Springs, 6797
Key Largo Fisheries, 6824
Key West Key Lime Pie Co, 6825
Keys Fisheries Market & Marina, 6827
Kitchens Seafood, 6896
Kiwi Kiss, 6904
KMC Citrus Enterprises Inc, 6672
Kopali Organics, 6959
La Bonita Ole Inc, 7076
La Romagnola, 7104
LA Segunda Bakery, 7061
LaCroix, 7117
Lakeridge Winery & Vineyards, 7158
Lakewood Juice Co., 7169
Lakewood Juice Company, 7170
Las Olas Confections, 7233
Le Chic French Bakery, 7267
Le Macaron, 7272

Le Roy Ren,, 7274
Leighton's Honey Inc, 7329
Lekithos, 7333
Lender's Bagels, 7345
Leroy Smith Inc, 7373
Let Them Eat Cake, 7395
Life Extension Foundation, 7412
Lifem Spice Ingredients, 7420
Lionel Hitchen Essitional Oils, 7452
Lombardi's Seafood, 7517
Lombardi's Seafood Inc, 7518
Lorina, Inc., 7543
Lou Pizzo Produce, 7565
Louis Dreyfus Company Citrus Inc, 7569
Luban International, 7616
Lucky Nutrition, 7631
M & B Products Inc, 7672
Mac Knight Smoke House Inc, 7714
Mada'n Kosher Foods, 7738
Mancini Packing Co, 7832
Marina Foods, 7927
Mario Camancho Foods, 7931
Marjon Specialty Foods Inc, 7937
Martin Coffee Co, 7965
Mason Jar Cookie Company, 7993
Matouk International USA Inc, 8008
Maxim's Import Corporation, 8028
McArthur Dairy LLC, 8053
Melitta USA Inc, 8146
Mercon Coffee Group.ÿ, 8166
Mermaid Spice Corporation, 8178
Merrill Seafood Center, 8180
Metabolic Nutrition, 8191
Metrohm USA, 8197
Miami Beef Co, 8218
Miami Crab Corporation, 8219
Miami Purveyors Inc, 8220
MIC Foods, 7702
Michael's Gourmet Coffee, 8230
Mid-Eastern Molasses Company, 8257
Miracle Tree, 8369
Miramar Fruit Trading Company, 8370
Miramar Pickles & Food Products, 8371
Mission Foodservice, 8387
Mix-A-Lota Stuff LLC, 8407
Mixallogy, 8408
Mixon Fruit Farms Inc, 8411
Mizkan Americas Inc, 8419
Mom's Famous, 8463
Monin Inc., 8478
Moon's Seafood Company, 8523
Morrison Meat Packers, 8561
Mountain Valley Poultry, 8603
Murvest, 8691
N A P Engineering, 8718
Napoli Pasta Manufacturers, 8767
Natalie's Orchid Island Juice Co., 8777
National Beverage Corporation, 8784
Natural Exotic Tropicals, 8827
Natural Fruit Corp, 8837
Natural Ice Fruits, 8840
Naturally Delicious Inc, 8854
Nature's Products Inc, 8891
Naylor Association Solutions, 8907
New York Bakeries Inc, 9003
New York Intl Bread Co, 9006
New York Pizza, 9007
Nostalgic Specialty Foods, 9188
Nutraplex, 9243
Nutri-Cell, 9248
NutriFusion, 9250
Nutty Bavarian, 9274
O'Donnell-Usen, 9288
Offshore Seafood Co, 9371
Oil & Olives Company, 9381
Olde Estate, 9436
Orange Peel Enterprises, 9516
Orchard Pond, 9520
Orchid Island Juice Co, 9521
Organic Amazon, 9541
Organic Liaison, LLC, 9547
Ormand Peugeog Corporation, 9571
Osceola Farms Sugar Warehouse, 9578
Ouhlala Gourmet, 9599
Our Cookie, 9601
Paca Foods Inc, 9665
Pacari Organic Chocolate, 9666
Pacific Collier Fresh Company, 9676
Packaged Products Division, 9704
Palm Beach Foods, 9720
Palmetto Canning, 9726
Paradise Inc, 9763

Geographic Index / Georgia

Paradise Products Corporation, 9766
Parny Gourmet, 9793
Peace River Citrus Products, 9859
Pelican Bay Ltd., 9903
Penn Dutch Meat & Seafood Market, 9915, 9916, 9917
Perky's Pizza, 9961
Pioneer Growers, 10076
Plaza de Espana Gourmet, 10110
Point Group, 10141
Poiret International, 10146
Poison Pepper Company, 10147
Poppin Popcorn, 10190
Powerful Foods, 10226
Powers Baking Company, 10227
Premier Juices, 10246
Prestige Proteins, 10265
Prestige Technology, 10266
Pride Enterprises Glades, 10279
Prima Foods International, 10283
Productos Del Plata, 10329
Protano's Bakery, 10348
Publix Super Market, 10362
Pure Source LLC, 10382
Pyure Brands, 10407
Quality Seafood, 10443
Queen of America, 10454
Quirch Foods, 10470
R L Schreiber Inc, 10481
Raffield Fisheries Inc, 10530
Ragold Confections, 10532
Red Smith Foods Inc, 10620
Refresco Beverages US Inc., 10637
Register Meat Co, 10649
Reilly Dairy & Food Company, 10655
Reva Foods, 10690
Rich's Ice Cream Co Inc, 10716
Ricos Candy Snack & Bakery, 10735
Rigoni Di Asiago, 10742
Ripensa A/S, 10751
Rivella USA, 10767
Roland Seafood Co, 10847
Ronzoni, 10866
Rosmarino Foods/R.Z. Humbert Company, 10900
Routin America, 10917
Rowland Coffee Roasters Inc., 10920
Ruskin Redneck Trading Company, 10986
Saint Armands Baking Company, 11090
Sam Mills USA, 11125
San Bernardo Ice Cream, 11137
Sandors Bakeries, 11171
Sapore della Vita, 11205
Savannah Cinnamon & Cookie Company, 11249
Savino's Italian Ices, 11252
Seajoy, 11378
Seald Sweet, 11381
SeaSpecialties, 11361
Seitenbacher America LLC, 11414
Selma's Cookies, 11424
Serious Foodie, 11455
Seven Keys Co Of Florida, 11473
Shaw's Southern Belle Frozen, Inc., 11526
Sheila G Brands LLC, 11534
Sheila Gs Brownie Brittle Co, 11535
Signature Brands LLC, 11599
Silver Springs Citrus Inc, 11626
Silver Tray Cookies, 11631
Singleton Seafood, 11666
Singleton Seafood Company, 11667
Skinners' Dairy, 11687
Skinny Mixes LLC, 11688
Smart Baking Co., 11712
Smuggler's Kitchen, 11742
Sneaky Chef Foods, The, 11752
Sopralco, 11816
South Beach Coffee Company, 11826
Southeast Dairy Processors Inc, 11836
Southeastern Fisheries Assn, 11837
Southeastern Grocers, 11838
Southern Gardens Citrus, 11853
Sparkletts, 11889
Specialty Coffee Roasters, 11897
Spice Lab, 11921
Spice World Inc, 11926
Spices of Life Gourmet Coffee, 11929
St Armands Baking Co, 11991
St. Clair Industries, 12003
Stevens Tropical Plantation, 12103
Stone Crabs Inc, 12130

Sugar Cane Growers Co-Op of Florida, 12196
Sugar Sugar, 12204
Suity Confections Co, 12211
Sun Groves Inc, 12233
Sun Olive Oil Company, 12237
Sun Orchard INC, 12239
Sun Orchard Inc, 12240
Sunshine Food Sales, 12307
Super Nutrition Life Extension, 12320
Superbrand Dairies, 12327
Suram Trading Corporation, 12353
Surgital America, 12358
Sweet Endings Inc, 12397
Swiss Chalet Fine Foods, 12438
SYFO Beverage Company of Florida, 11057
T G Lee Dairy, 12460
Tampa Bay Fisheries Inc, 12519
Tampa Maid Foods Inc, 12520
Tata Tea, 12559
Tea Needs Inc, 12585
Terrapin Ridge, 12629
The Pantry Club, 12713
The Stephan Company, 12733
Thirs-Tea Corp, 12756
Tiger Meat & Provisions, 12800
Tigo+, 12802
Todhunter Foods, 12834, 12835
Transnational Foods, 12928
Treatt USA Inc, 12940
Triton Seafood Co, 12989
Tropical Acai LLC, 12994
Tropical Blossom Honey Co, 12995
Tropical Commodities, 12997
Tropical Foods, 13003
Tropical Nut & Fruit Co, 13007
Tuscan Eat/Perdinci, 13079
Twinlab Corporation, 13097
Two Guys Spice Company, 13102
Uncle Matt's Organic, 13157
United Juice Companies of America, 13192
Universal Beverages Inc, 13205, 13206
Urgasa, 13226
US Sugar Company, 13125
Vaxa International, 13304
Velda Farms, 13319
Verlasso, 13341
Vigo Importing Co, 13404
Vintage Italia, 13432
Vitarich Laboratories, 13472
VitaThinQ Inc., 13458
Wainwright Dairy, 13534
Webb's Candy, 13612
Whetstone Candy Company, 13707
Whetstone Chocolates, 13708
Whitney & Sons Seafood, 13743
Williams & Bennett, 13816
Winmix/Natural Care Products, 13863
Winn-Dixie Stores, 13864
Winter Park Farm, 13870
Wish Farms, 13886
World's Greatest Ice Cream, 13949
Y Not Foods, 13973
Yo Mama's Foods, 14006
Zephyr Hills, 14055
Zephyrhills Bottled Water Company, 14056
Zitos Specialty Foods, 14068
Zotter Chocolates, 14072

Georgia

AFF International, 79
AGRO Merchants Grp NA, 82
AHD International, LLC, 84
Alba Foods, Inc, 276
Almark Foods, 352
Amazing Herbs Nutraceuticals, 420
Amelia Bay, 429
American Blanching Company, 441
American Egg Products Inc, 452
Arboris LLC, 631
Arel Group Wine & Spirits Inc, 652
Aroma Ridge, 694
Arylessence Inc, 720
Atlanta Bread Co., 758
Atlanta Burning Bush, 759
Atlanta Coffee Roasters, 761
Atlanta Fish Market, 762
Atlantic Meat Company, 770
Aunt Fannie's Bakery, 800
B. Lloyd's Pecans, 879
Back Bay Trading, 917

Backyard Safari Co, 922
Bake City, 949
Bama Fish Atlanta, 1001
Bell Plantation, 1183
Bella Cucina, 1188
Benton's Seafood Ctr, 1223
Beverage House Inc, 1296
Bhuja Snacks, 1303
Big Island Seafood, LLC, 1334
Blackberry Patch, 1430
Blakely Freezer Locker, 1434
Bland Farms INC, 1436
Blue Ridge Poultry, 1495
Bodacious Foods, 1528
Boutique Seafood Brokers, 1627
Bradley Creek Seafood, 1648
Brown Foods, 1778
Buckhead Beef, 1820
Buckhead Gourmet, 1821
Butter Krust Baking Company, 1881
Byrd Cookie, 1897
C&S Wholesale Meat Company, 1928
Cajun Seafood Enterprises, 2024
Camilla Pecan Company, 2110
Candy Mountain Sweets & Treats, 2135
Cavender Castle Winery, 2331
Chestnut Mountain Winery, 2536
Chick-Fil-A Inc., 2552
Chong Mei Trading, 2633
Chops Snacks, 2635
City Cafe & Bakery, 2706
City Market, 2709
Claxton Bakery Inc, 2732
Coca-Cola Co., 2814
Corbion, 3020
Costas Pasta, 3053
Country Home Bakers, 3078
CP Kelco, 1962
Crazy Jerrys Inc Kahuna-Sauces, 3123
Crickle Company, 3162
Criders Poultry, 3164
Crown Candy Corp, 3189
Culinary Masters Corporation, 3236
Deerland Probiotics & Enzymes, 3471
Dessert Innovations Inc, 3541
Dexpa, 3556
Diamond Crystal Brands Inc, 3574
Diaz Foods, 3584
Dick Garber Company, 3586
Dillon Candy Co, 3602
Dogwood Brewing Company, 3646
Dr Pete's, 3726
Dr. Pete's, 3736
Dr. Pete's/J.C. Specialty Foods, 3737
Dreaming Cow, 3755
Dumbee Gourmet Foods, 3791
Eastside Seafood, 3897
Eat Real Snacks USA, 3902
Ellsworth Foods, 4029
Enterprise Foods, 4081
Epi De France Bakery, 4091
European Bakers, 4151
Federation-Southern Cprtvs, 4319
Field Coffee, 4363
Fieldale Farms, 4368
First Oriental Market, 4427
Fish King Processors, 4440
Flanders, 4471
Flowers Foods Inc., 4529
Food Masters, 4562
Fox Vineyards & Winery, 4641
Fresh Frozen Foods, 4710
Georgia Fruitcake Co, 4974
Georgia Grinders, 4975
Georgia Seafood Wholesale, 4977
Georgia Spice Company, 4978
Georgia Wines Inc, 4979
German Bakery at Village Corner, 4986
Glenn Sales Company, 5054
Golden Harvest Pecans, 5125
Golden Peanut and Tree Nuts, 5130
Goldstar Brands LLC, 5147
Great American Cookie Company, 5296
Greenwood Ice Cream Co, 5379
GSB & Assoc, 4848
Habersham Vineyards & Winery, 5492
Hafner USA, 5495
Halperns' Purveyors of Steak & Seafood, 5527
Hardy Farms, 5584
Harlow House Company, 5593
Harpers Seafood Market, 5603

Hazel Creek Orchards, 5670
HC Brill Company, 5482
Heidi's Gourmet Desserts, 5729
Hemp Fusion, 5758
High Road Craft Ice Cream, Inc., 5849
Holt's Bakery Inc, 5918
Home Delivery Food Service, 5926
Honest Tea Inc, 5952
Honey Bee Company, 5955
Hong Kong Supermarket, 5971
Hongar Farms Gourmet Foods, 5973
Imaex Trading Company, 6149
Inland Seafood Inc, 6219
International Farmers Market, 6257
International Service Group, 6272
Ira Higdon Grocery Company, 6286
J & G Poultry & Seafood, 6336
Jim Foley Company, 6517
Johnny Harris Famous Barbecue Sauce, 6562
Kelly's Candies, 6772
Kendrick Gourmet Products, 6784
Kill Cliff, 6843
King & Prince Seafood, 6854
King & Prince Seafood Corp, 6855
King of Pops Inc, 6872
L&M Evans, 7032
La Chiquita Tortilla Manufacturing, 7081
La Piccolina, 7100
Lane Southern Orchards, 7207
Larry J. Williams Company, 7225
Lavoi Corporation, 7254
Lipsey Mountain Spring Water, 7455
Lord's Sausage & Country Ham, 7541
Los Amigo Tortilla Mfg Co, 7547
Lucky Seafood Corporation, 7632
Lynn Springs Water LLC, 7666
Maggie Lyon Chocolatiers, 7761
Malibu Beach Beverage, 7804
Mar-Jac Poultry Inc., 7889
Mar-Key Foods, 7890
McCleskey Mills, 8057
Mclemores Abbattoir Inc, 8098
Me At Corral, 8102
Meridian Beverage Company, 8169
Merritt Pecan Co, 8184
Metafoods LLC, 8192
Millen Fish, 8306
Miller Brothers Packing Company, 8308
Minas Purely Divine, 8340
Minute Maid Company, 8365
Mirasco, 8372
Mo Hotta Mo Betta, 8433
Modern Day Masala, LLC, 8440
Modern Packaging, 8445
Monarch Beverage Company, 8470
Mrs. Smiths Bakeries, 8647
Naturalmond Almond Butter, 8858
Nature's Kitchen, 8885
Nepco Egg Of Ga, 8936
New Ocean, 8992
Ocean Union Company, 9357
Oh, Sugar! LLC, 9376
Otis Spunkmeyer, 9591
Parker Fish Company, 9782
Partners Coffee LLC, 9798
Pasta Mami, 9811
Paulsen Foods, 9849
Peeler's Jersey Farms, 9893
Pett Spice Products Inc, 9990
Phillips Seafood, 10014
Pickled Pink, 10033
Pippin Snack Pecans, 10084
Poteet Seafood Co, 10216
Prayon Inc., 10239
Pretzelmaker, 10273
Prime Pak Foods Inc, 10293
Printpack Inc., 10310
Purely Pecans, 10390
R & R Seafood, 10475
Red Brick Brewing Company, 10602
Red V Foods, 10623
RFS Limited, 10510
Richmond Baking Co, 10731
Roadrunner Seafood Inc, 10781
Robbins Packing Company, 10786
Roger Wood Foods Inc, 10835
Rose Hill Seafood, 10885
Ross-Smith Pecan Company, 10902
Roy Dick Company, 10921
Russo's Seafood, 10994
Rv Industries, 11001

Geographic Index / Hawaii

Ryals Bakery, 11002
S.A.S. Foods, 11026
Salwa Foods, 11123
SAPNA Foods, 11033
Savannah Bee Co., 11247
Schermer Pecan Co, 11282
Scott's Candy, 11328
SeaPak Shrimp, 11359
Service Foods, 11460
Seydel Co, 11485
Shore Trading Co, 11572
Sister's Gourmet, 11677, 11678
Sisters' Gourmet, 11679
Smith & Sons Seafood, 11723
Smoak's Bakery & Catering Service, 11734
Soteria, 11820
South Georgia Pecan Co, 11831
Southeastern Mills Inc, 11839
Southern Art Company, LLC, 11840
Southern Beverage Packers Inc, 11844
Southern Culture Foods, 11848
Southern Ice Cream Specialties, 11856
Southern Roasted Nuts, 11863
Southern Shellfish, 11866
St. Simons Seafood, 12012
Stewart Candies, 12108
Stone Mountain Pecan Co, 12133
Stripling's General Store, 12170
Sun State Beverage, 12245
Sunny South Pecan Company, 12284
Sunnyland Farms, 12286
Sunset Farm Foods Inc, 12300
Sutherland's Foodservice, 12366
Suzanna's Kitchen, 12371
Sweet Grass Dairy, 12400
Sweet Water Brewing Co, 12419
Tara Foods, 12533
Taylor Orchards, 12570
Terra Botanica Products, 12620
Tetley USA, 12643
Thermo Pac LLC, 12751
Thomas Packing Company, 12769
Thompson Seafood, 12771
Thrive Farmers, 12790
Tip Top Poultry Inc, 12821
Tolteca Foodservice, 12845
Tracy Luckey Pecans, 12909
Tropical Foods, 12998, 13000
Tropical Nut Fruit & Bulk Cndy, 13008
Turkey Creeks Snacks Inc, 13063
Universal Poultry Company, 13210
Valentine Enterprises Inc, 13249
Verdant Kitchen, 13333
Vidalia Brands Inc, 13393
Vidalia Sweets Brand, 13394
Viking Distillery, 13406
Viking Trading, 13408
W.O. Sasser, 13504
W.T.I., 13508
Waken Meat Co, 13535
Walker Meats, 13542
Waltkoch Limited, 13558
Wayfield Foods, 13602
Wayne Farms LLC., 13607
Whitaker & Assoc Architects, 13712
White Oak Pastures, 13724
Williams Institutional Foods, 13819
WK Eckerd & Sons, 13515
Woodsmoke Provisions, 13922
Y&W Shellfish, 13976
Yaupon Tea, 13994
Zartic Inc, 14043

Hawaii

50th State Poultry Processors, 24
Aala Meat Market Inc, 107
Aloha Distillers, 362
Aloha Poi Factory Inc, 364
Aloha Shoyu Co LTD, 365
Aloha Tofu Factory Inc, 366
Amano Fish Cake Factory, 414
American Hawaiian Soy Company, 460
Angelo Pietro Honolulu, 566
Bay View Farm, 1104
Big Island Candies Inc, 1333
Bubbies Homemade Ice Cream, 1812
Captain Cook Coffee Company, 2184
Chic Naturals, 2540
Choyce Produce, 2638
Cyanotech Corp, 3281
D&M Seafood, 3300
Dean & De Luca Inc, 3440
Diamond Bakery Co LTD, 3571
Dow Distribution, 3717
Ed & Don's Of Hawaii Inc, 3927
Eskimo Candy Inc, 4114
Fish Express, 4437
Fishland Market, 4451
Flavors of Hawaii Inc, 4493
Food Factory, 4557
Fresh Island Fish, 4713
Furukawa Potato Chip Factory, 4803
Garden & Valley Isle Seafood, 4890
Gouvea's & Purity Foods Inc, 5219
GREEN Energy, 4844
Greenwell Farms Inc, 5377
H & W Foods, 5461
Harpo's, 5605
Hawaii Candy Inc, 5653
Hawaii Coffee Company, 5654
Hawaii International Seafood, 5655
Hawaii Star Bakery, 5656
Hawaiian Bagel, 5657
Hawaiian Host Inc, 5658
Hawaiian Isles Kona Coffee Co, 5659
Hawaiian King Candies, 5660
Hawaiian Natural Water Company, 5661
Hawaiian Sun Products, 5662
Hibiscus Aloha Corporation, 5830
Higa Food Service, 5838
Hilo Fish Company, 5880
Home Maid Bakery, 5927
Honolulu Fish Company, 5977
Inny's Wholesale, 6229
Island Princess, 6303
Iwamoto Natto Factory, 6332
Kapaa Bakery, 6703
Kapaa Poi Factory, 6704
Kauai Coffee Co Inc, 6735
Kauai Kookie, 6736
Kauai Organic Farms, 6737
Kauai Producers, 6738
Koala Moa, 6927
Koha Food, 6937
Koloa Rum Corp, 6947
Kona Brewing, 6949
Kona Coffee Council, 6950
Kona Cold Lobsters, 6951
Kona Fish Co Inc, 6952
Kona Premium Coffee Company, 6953
Kulana Foods LTD, 7001
Kyong Hae Kim Company, 7016
Love's Bakery, 7603
Mac Farms Of Hawaii Inc, 7713
Maebo Noodle Factory Inc, 7760
Malie Kai Hawaiian Chocolates, 7805
Maui Bagel, 8017
Maui Coffee Roasters Wholesale, 8018
Maui Gold Pineapple Company, 8019
Maui Potato Chip Factory, 8020
Maui Soda & Ice Works, 8021
Maui Wine, 8022
Meadow Gold, 8105
Medeiros Farms, 8120
Menehune Mac, 8155
Mid-Pacific Hawaii Fishery, 8258
Miko Meat, 8285
Modern Macaroni Co LTD, 8443
Monarch Seafoods Inc, 8471
Mt. View Bakery, 8663
Nagasako Fish, 8732
National Food Co LTD, 8789
Nips Potato Chips, 9063
Nisshodo Candy Store, 9067
Noh Foods Of Hawaii, 9085
Norpac Fisheries Inc, 9112
Nutrex Hawaii Inc, 9244
Ohana Seafood, LLC, 9377
Ohta Wafer Factory, 9380
Oils Of Aloha, 9382
Okahara Saimin Factory LTD, 9390
Okuhara Foods Inc, 9393
Ono Cones of Hawaii LLC, 9496
Oversea Fishery & Investment, 9617
P&E Foods, 9637
Pacific Poultry Company, 9691
Pacsea Corporation, 9705
POP Fishing & Marine, 9659
Puueo Poi Shop, 10403
Rare Hawaiian Honey Company, 10570
Redondo's LLC, 10632
Roselani Tropics Ice Cream, 10891
Salty Wahine Gourmet Hawaiian Sea Salt, 11120
Seafood Connection, 11367
Seafood Hawaii Inc, 11370
St-Germain Bakery, 12001
Standard Bakery Inc, 12026
Sugai Kona Coffee, 12192
Sun Noodle, 12235
Surfing Goat Dairy, 12357
T.J. Kraft, 12470
Tamashiro Market Inc, 12518
Tropic Fish Hawaii LLC, 12993
U Okada & Co LTD, 13111
United Fishing Agency LTD, 13188
Upcountry Fisheries, 13214
VIP Food Svc, 13239
Volcano Island Honey Company, 13488
Wainani Kai Seafood, 13533
Wharton Seafood Sales, 13703
Yick Lung Company, 14003
Ying Leong Look Funn Factory, 14004
Young's Noodle Factory Inc, 14028
Zippy's Inc, 14067

Idaho

505 Southwestern, 23
Ace Development, 142
Alta Health Products, 389
Amalgamated Sugar Company, 407
Appleton Produce Company, 615
Aqua Vie Beverage Corporation, 621
B & D Foods, 863
Bateman Products, 1082
BioSynergy, 1373
Blue Lakes Trout Farm, 1482
Camas Prairie Winery, 2100
Casa Valdez Inc, 2273
Circle Valley Produce LLC, 2688
Clear Springs Foods Inc., 2740
Cocolalla Winery, 2825
Cowgirl Chocolates, 3100
Crossings Winery, 3186
CTI Foods, 1965
Dickinson Frozen Foods, 3588
Eddy's Bakery, 3935
Eragrain, 4102
Extravogonzo Gourmet Foods, 4191
Farr Candy Company, 4297
Fish Breeders of Idaho, 4435
Fresca Mexican Foods LLC, 4707
GEM Berry Products, 4828
Gem Berry Products, 4940
Gem Meat Packing Co, 4941
George F Brocke & Sons, 4965
Glanbia Nutritionals, 5046
Golden Valley Natural, 5139
Grand Teton Brewing Co, 5255
Great American Appetizers, 5294
Green Garden Food Products, 5350
Hegy's South Hills Vineyard & Winery, 5728
Hells Canyon Winery, 5749
Henggeler Packing Company, 5767
Hickey Foods, 5831
Homemade By Dorothy Boise, 5938
Hydroblend Limited, 6098
Idaho Candy Co, 6134
Idaho Milk Products, 6136
Idaho Pacific Holdings Inc, 6137
Idaho Supreme Potatoes Inc, 6138
Idaho Trout Company, 6139
Idahoan Foods LLC, 6140
Independent Meat Co, 6181
Irresistible Cookie Jar, 6291
J C Watson Co, 6347
J. R. Simplot Co., 6374
Killer Creamery, 6845
Kingston Fresh, 6882
Lamb Weston Holdings Inc., 7179
Larsen Farms, 7229
Life Force Specialty Foods, 7413
Litehouse Foods, 7461, 7462
M J Barleyhoppers Sports Bar, 7677
Magic Valley Growers, 7767
Magic Valley Quality Milk, 7768
Namaste Foods, 8745
Nature's Earthly Choice, 8874
Nhs Labs Inc, 9030
Nonpareil Farms, 9093
NPC Dehydrators, 8727
Peak Foods, 9864
Pizzey's Milling & Baking Company, 10095
Prosperity Organic Foods, 10347
Rollingstone Chevre, 10851
Rose Creek Vineyards, 10882
Sawtooth Winery, 11259
Sea Pac Of Idaho Inc, 11346
Shamrock Foods Co, 11505
Silver Creek Distillers, 11614
Silver Creek Farms, 11615
Simplot Food Group, 11647
Smoke House, 11736
Sno Shack Inc, 11755
Stacey's Famous Foods, 12014
Ste Chapelle Winery, 12064
Sun Glo Of Idaho, 12231
Sun Valley Mustard, 12249
Symms Fruit Ranch Inc, 12451
Teff Co, 12605
Tram Bar LLC, 12923
Weiser River Packing, 13630
West Pac, 13665
White Cloud Coffee, 13716

Illinois

A La Carte, 39
Abbott Laboratories, 114
ACH Food Co Inc, 73
AJ's Lena Maid Meats Inc, 85
Ajinomoto Heartland Inc, 239
Al Gelato Bornay, 248
Alef Sausage Inc, 287
Alfred L. Wolff, Inc., 300
Allfresh Food Products, 340
Alpine Valley Water, 384
Alto Vineyards & Winery, 395
Amafruits, 404
Amano Enzyme USA Company, Ltd, 413
Ambootia Tea Estate, 424
American Licorice, 469
Amity Packing Co Inc, 503
Amy's Candy Bar, 521
Amylu Foods, 523
Andrews Caramel Apples, 557
Anmar Foods, 577
Archer Daniels Midland Company, 637, 638
Argo Tea, 658
Arlen S Gould & Assoc, 679
Aroma Coffee Company, 692
Arro Corp, 702
Art CoCo Chocolate Company, 707
Art's Tamales, 709
Arway Confections Inc, 719
Ashland Sausage Co, 728
Aurora Packing Co Inc, 813
Avanti Foods Co, 831
Avatar Corp, 833
Axium Foods, 851
Azteca Foods Inc, 855
Baja Foods LLC, 947
BakeMark USA, 955
Bakery Essentials Inc, 976
Baldwin Richardson Foods, 988
Ball Park Franks, 992
Barilla USA, 1037
Barry Callebaut USA, 1056
Batory Foods, 1083
Baxters Vineyards & Winery, 1093
Bays English Muffin Corporation, 1111
Bazaar Inc, 1113
Beam Suntory, 1120
Bear Stewart Corp, 1131
Beer Nuts Co Store-Plant, 1168
Bel Brands USA, 1172
Bell Flavors & Fragrances, 1179
Bell Marketing Inc, 1181
Berghoff Brewery, 1231
Bernard Food Industries Inc, 1244
Berner Food & Beverage LLC, 1249
Berry Processing, 1254
Best Chicago Meat, 1262
Beverage Flavors Intl, 1295
Biagio's Banquets, 1305
Bidwell Candies, 1313
Big Apple Bagels, 1323
Big Fork Brands, 1332
Big Shoulders Coffee, 1342
BioVittoria USA, 1375
Birdie Pak Products, 1386
Black Forest Organic, 1417
Blommer Chocolate Co, 1455
Bob Gordon & Associates, 1517

Geographic Index / Illinois

Boetje Foods Inc, 1537
Bon Ton Products, 1551
Branding Iron, 1658
Brolite Products Inc, 1735
Brookema Company, 1741
Brown Packing Company, 1779
Brown Produce Company, 1780
Bryan Foods, 1805
Buedel Food Products, 1832
Bunge Loders Croklaan, 1848
Burt Lewis Ingredients, 1870
C J Vitner Co, 1920
CA Fortune & Company, 1940
Caldic USA Inc, 2041
Calihan Pork Processors Inc, 2084
Capri Sun, 2173
Captain Alex Seafoods, 2182
Caputo Cheese, 2191
Carl Buddig & Co., 2212
Carousel Candies, 2253
Casper Foodservice Company, 2293
Char Crust, 2424
Chateau Food Products Inc, 2457
Chateau Ra-Ha, 2464
Cheese Merchants of America, 2481
Chester Dairy Co, 2529
Chicago Avenue Pizza, 2542
Chicago Coffee Roastery, 2543
Chicago Food Market, 2544
Chicago Gourmet Steaks, 2545
Chicago Meat Authority Inc, 2546
Chicago Pastry, 2547
Chicago Premier Meats, 2548
Chicago Steaks, 2549
Chicago Vegan Foods, 2550
Chihon Biotechnology Co., Ltd., 2562
Chocolate Fantasies, 2603
Churny Company, 2668
Cipriani's Spaghetti & Sauce Company, 2684
Citrico, 2694
City Foods Inc, 2708
Classic Tea, 2729
Clearwater Coffee Company, 2744
Cloverhill Bakery-Vend Corporation, 2784
Clown Global Brands, 2788
Clyde's Delicious Donuts, 2791
Coastal Seafood Partners, 2802
Coffee Masters, 2848
Coffee Up, 2859
Columbus Vegetable Oils, 2913
Community Bakeries, 2925
Conagra Brands Inc, 2939
Conagra Foodservice, 2940
Confectionately Yours LTD, 2947
Consumers Packing Co, 2965
Consumers Vinegar & Spice Co, 2966
Continental Carbonic Products, 2968
Conway Import Co Inc, 2975
Cookie Kingdom, 2984
Cookie Specialties Inc, 2985
Cool Mountain Beverages Inc, 2994
Cora Italian Specialties, 3009
Corbion, 3018
Corfu Foods Inc, 3028, 3029
Cornfields Inc, 3037
Cosco International, 3045
Cosgrove Distributors Inc, 3047
Country Bob's Inc, 3064
Country Village Meats Inc, 3089
Coupla Guys Foods, 3091
Crawford Sausage Co Inc, 3121
Creative Cotton, 3133
Creme Unlimited, 3145
Crescent Foods, 3152
Crest Foods Inc, 3155
Cugino's Gourmet Foods, 3226
Culligan International Co, 3238
Culligan International Company, 3239
Cupid Candies, 3253
Custom Confections & More, 3268
Custom Culinary Inc., 3269
CVP Systems Inc, 1968
Czimer's Game & Seafoods, 3291
D Seafood, 3297
Dairy Management Inc, 3342
Damron Corp, 3366
Danish Maid Butter Co, 3376
Das Foods, 3391
Davidson's Safest Choice Eggs, 3401
Davis Street Fish Market, 3409
Deerfield Bakery, 3470

Delicious Frookie, 3499
Delicious Frookie Company, 3500
Di Cola's Seafood, 3562
Diamond Seafood, 3577
Diana's Specialty Foods, 3581
DiMario Foods, 3568
Dinkel's Bakery Inc, 3609
Dixon's Fisheries, 3634
DMH Ingredients Inc, 3313
Don's Dock Seafood Market, 3673
Dong Kee Company, 3681
Doodles Cookies, 3689
Door County Fish Market, 3690
Dorina So-Good Inc, 3695
Double Good, 3703
Doumak Inc, 3713
Dreymiller & KRAY Inc, 3761
Dutch Farms Inc, 3813
East Balt Commissary Inc, 3878
Eastern Seafood Co, 3892
Ebro Foods, 3914
Ed Miniat Inc, 3928, 3929
Eden Processing, 3942
Edgar A Weber & Co, 3945
Edlong Corporation, 3948
Egg Cream America Inc, 3964
Eickman's Processing Co, 3972
El Milagro, 3982
Elgin Dairy Foods, 4008
Eli's Cheesecake, 4010
Elmwood Locker Svc, 4035
Enjoy Life Foods, 4072
Erie Foods Intl Inc, 4107
Essen Nutrition Corp, 4118
Ettlinger Corp, 4140
Eureka Locker Inc, 4142
Evans Food Group LTD, 4158
Excalibur Seasoning, 4182
F&Y Enterprises, 4201
Fabbri Sausage Mfg Co, 4213
Fairlife, 4224
Family Sweets Candy Company, 4241
Fantazzmo Fun Stuff, 4255
Fare Foods Corp, 4264
Farmington Foods Inc, 4289
FBC Industries, 4204
FDI Inc, 4205
Ferrara Candy Co Inc, 4345
Finer Foods Inc, 4400
Fizzle Flat Farm, L.L.C., 4463
Flaherty Inc, 4467
FLAT Tech Inc., 4207
Flavorchem Corp, 4488
Flix Candy, 4507
Florence Macaroni Manufacturing, 4511
Florida Fruit Juices, 4519
Focus Foodservice, 4538
Foell Packing Company, 4539
Fona International, 4548
Fontanini Italian Meats, 4550
Fonterra Co-operative Group Limited, 4552
Forkless Gourmet Inc, 4596
Fortella Fortune Cookies, 4604
Fox Deluxe Inc, 4634
Frank Korinek & Co, 4654
Frank Pagano Company, 4656
Fratelli Mantova, 4672
Freeze-Dry Ingredients, 4691
Frontera Foods, 4751
Frontier Soups, 4753
Futureceuticals Inc, 4808
Galena Canning Co, 4868
Galena Cellars Winery, 4869
Garden Row Foods, 4894, 4895
Garon Foods, 4910
Garrett Popcorn Shops, 4911
Gateway Food Products Co, 4920
Gaucho Foods, 4922
Gelnex Gelatins, 4938
Georgia Nut Co, 4976
Gilster-Mary Lee Corp, 5015
Glunz Family Winery & Cellars, 5079
Goat Partners Intl., 5091
Gold Standard Baking Inc, 5106
Gold Star Seafoods, 5107
Gonnella Baking Company, 5152
Goose Island Beer Co, 5188
Gopicnic Inc, 5191
GPI USA LLC., 4843
Graham Chemical Corporation, 5239
Grant Park Packing, 5278
Great American Seafood Company, 5300

Great Expectations Confectionery Gourmet Foods, 5307
Grecian Delight Foods Inc, 5341
Green Bay Cheese, 5343
Greenwood Associates, 5378
Griffith Foods Inc., 5388
GTC Nutrition, 4849
Gust John Foods & Products, 5451
H B Taylor Co, 5462
Halsted Packing House, 5528
Hamilos Bros Inspected Meat, 5532
Hanmi Inc, 5552
Hansen Packing Co, 5559
Harry London Candies Inc, 5616
Harvest Valley Bakery Inc, 5636
Hathaway Coffee Co Inc, 5644
Havi Food Services Worldwide, 5651
Healthmate Products, 5692
Healthy Grain Foods LLC, 5696
Hearthside Food Solutions, 5704
Heinkel's Packing Co, 5733
Henry Broch & Co, 5770
Henry J's Meat Specialties, 5775
Hodgson Mill Inc, 5898
Holton Food Products, 5919
Home Run Inn Frozen Foods, 5931
Homer's Ice Cream, 5940
Hometown Bagel Inc, 5949
Honey Wafer Baking Co, 5964
Hong Kong Noodle Company, 5970
Houser Meats, 6031
Humphrey's Market, 6077
Hunt-Wesson Foods, 6084
Husman Snack Food Company, 6091
I Heart Keenwah, 6102
Il Giardino Del Dolce Inc, 6145
Indiana Sugars, 6194
Ineeka Inc, 6199
Ingredion Inc., 6211
Inko's Tea, 6216
Innova Flavors, 6226
International Casings Group, 6250
International Foodservice Manufacturers' Association, 6262
International Meat Co, 6268
International Seafoods of Chicago, 6271
Inviting Foods, 6282
Isaacson & Stein Fish Company, 6293
Italia Foods, 6316
Iya Foods LLC, 6333
J R Carlson Laboratories Inc, 6364
J&M Food Products Co, 6369
J.R. Poultry, 6384
J.R.'s Seafood, 6386
Jamaica John Inc, 6443
Jel Sert, 6483
Jemm Wholesale Meat Company, 6486
Jewel Bakery, 6510
JiMMY! Bars, 6512
John B. Sanfilippo & Son, 6548
John Hofmeister & Son Inc, 6553
Jones Packing Co, 6588
Jubelt Variety Bakeries, 6620
Juice Tyme, Inc., 6627
Junuis Food Products, 6637
Kalena, 6691
Kamish Food Products, 6698
Karlin Foods, 6713
Kelly Corned Beef Co, 6767
Kelly Flour Company, 6768
Kelly-Eisenberg Gourmet Deli Products, 6773
Kennedy Gourmet, 6787
Kernel Fabyan's Gourmet Popcorn, 6801
Kernel Seasons LLC, 6802
Kerry Sweet Ingredients, 6807
Key Colony Red Parrot Juice, 6822
Kiki's Gluten-Free, 6841
Kim & Scott's Gourmet Pretzels, 6847
King Food Service, 6865
Kitchen Cooked Inc, 6893
Koch Foods Inc, 6930
Kolb-Lena Bresse Bleu Inc, 6945
Korte Meat Processors Inc, 6967
Kosto Food Products Co, 6971
Kraft Heinz Co., 6977
Kronos, 6992
L & L Packing Co, 7018
L & M Slaughterhouse, 7021
L. Craelius & Company, 7035
La Choy, 7082
LA Mexicana Tortilleria, 7053

La Preferida, Inc., 7101
Lagomarcino's Confectionery, 7141
Lallemand American Yeast, 7173
Lambent Technologies, 7180
Land O'Frost Inc., 7197
Land-O-Sun Dairies Inc, 7199
Lawrence Foods Inc, 7256
Lea & Perrins, 7277
Life Spice & Ingredients LLC, 7415
Lifeway, 7423
Lifewise Ingredients, 7424
Lillie's Q, 7429
Limitless, 7436
Lipid Nutrition, 7454
Little Miss Muffin, 7469
Lobster Gram, 7498
Loffredo Produce, 7508
Long Grove Confectionary, 7524
Louis Sherry Premium Chocolate and Tins, 7575
Lovin Oven Cakery, 7605
Lucas Meyer, 7619
Ludwig Dairy Product, 7640
Lynfred Winery Inc, 7664
Magrabar Chemical Corp, 7778
Mah Chena Company, 7779
Mama Tish's Italian Specialties, 7820
Mancuso Cheese Co, 7833
Maplehurst Farms, 7887
Marconi Italian Specialty Foods, 7900
Mardale Specialty Foods, 7901
Mari's Candy, 7904
Market Fisheries, 7939
Market Square Food Co., 7940
Massel USA, 7994
Master Brew, 7997
Matt's Cookies, 8012
Mazzetta Company, 8047
McCain Foods USA Inc., 8055
Mead Johnson Nutrition, 8103
Meadowvale Inc, 8109
Medlee Foods, 8125
Mei Shun Tofu Products Company, 8134
Mel-O-Cream Donuts Intl, 8139, 8140
Merisant, 8173
Metropolitan Sausage Manufacturing Company, 8201
Mezza, 8213
Michele Foods, 8239
Michelle's RawFoodz, 8243
Midwest Food, 8266
Midwest Frozen Foods, Inc., 8268
Milano Bakery Inc, 8288
Milkadamia, 8297
Miller's Meat Market, 8312
Millrose Restaurant, 8319
Milnot Company, 8326
Miracapo Pizza, 8367
Mizkan Americas Inc, 8415
Mj Kellner Co, 8432
Molson Coors Beverage Company, 8459
Molson Coors North America, 8460
Mona Lisa Foods, 8468
Morreale John R Inc, 8555
Morton Salt Inc., 8569
Moweaqua Packing Plant, 8614
Mrs Fisher's Potato Chips, 8628
Mrs Prindables, 8631
MSRF, Inc., 7706
Mullens Dressing, 8671
Muller-Pinehurst Dairy, 8672
Mullins Food Products, 8675
My Own Meals Inc, 8709
N.Y.K. Line (North America), 8721
Nakano Foods, 8738
Nanocor, 8755
Napa Hills, 8763
Nation Pizza & Foods, 8781
Natural Enrichment Industries, 8826
Nature's Apothecary, 8866
Nedlog Company, 8919
Nesbitt Processing, 8939
Nest Eggs, 8941
Neuman Bakery Specialties, 8950
New City Packing Company, 8965
New Packing Company, 8997
Newly Weds Foods Inc, 9016
Nexcel Natural Ingredients, 9028
Nicole's Divine Crackers, 9047
Nielsen-Massey Vanillas Inc, 9050
Noon Hour Food Products Inc, 9094

Geographic Index / Indiana

Northern Dairy, 9146
Northwest Meat Company, 9175
NOW Foods, 8725
Nu-World Amaranth Inc, 9205
Nu-World Foods, 9206
NutraSweet Company, 9236
Nutrilicious Natural Bakery, 9254
Oak State Products Inc, 9323
Oakland Noodle Co, 9328
Oberweis Dairy Inc, 9339
Oceans Prome Distributi ng, 9362
Octavia Tea LLC, 9365
Old Colony Baking Co Inc, 9399
Old Tyme Mill Company, 9429
Old Wisconsin Food Products, 9431
Ole Salty's Potato Chips, 9441
Olympia International, 9464
On-Cor Frozen Foods Redi-Serve, 9483
Optimal Automatics, 9508
Optimum Nutrition, 9510
Oven Fresh Baking Company, 9610
P & S Food & Liquor, 9631
Paisano Food Products, 9711
Paleo Prime Foods, 9716
Papy's Foods Inc, 9759
Parker House Sausage Co, 9784
Pasta Factory, 9809
Pastorelli Food Products, 9821
Path of Life, 9827
Pease's Candy, 9881
Peer Foods Group Inc, 9894
Penguin Frozen Foods Inc, 9912
Pepe's Inc, 9933
Petersen Ice Cream Company, 9983
Pfanstiehl Inc, 9992
Phyter Foods, 10025
Pie Piper Products, 10040
Piemonte Bakery Co, 10045
Pilot Meat & Sea Food Company, 10060
Pioneer Live Shrimp, 10077
Plochman Inc, 10119
Plocky's Fine Snacks, 10120
Pluester Quality Meat Co, 10121
Plumrose USA, 10124
PMP Fermentation Products, 9656
Polka Home Style Sausage, 10154
Popcorner, 10182
Poppie's Dough, 10187
Poppilu, 10189
Prairie City Bakery, 10232
Prairie Farms Dairy Inc., 10233
Premium Ingredients International US, LLC, 10258
Primrose Candy Co, 10305
Prinova, 10309
Profood International, 10334
Prommus Brands, 10343
Psyllium Labs, 10361
Pure's Food Specialties, 10384
PureCircle USA, 10386
Quaker Oats Company, 10419
Quality Croutons, 10430
Quality Fisheries, 10432
Quality Food Products Inc, 10434
Quality Snack Foods Inc, 10444
Quorn Foods, 10473
R.J. Corr Naturals, 10495
Raber Packing Co, 10524
Real Sausage Co, 10592
Red Hot Chicago, 10610
Regal Health Food, 10640
Registry Steak & Seafood, 10650
Reid Foods, 10654
Reimann Food Classics, 10658
Rice Foods, 10705
Robinson's No 1 Ribs, 10804
Roland Machinery, 10846
Roma Bakeries, 10853
Romanian Kosher Sausage Co, 10857
Roquette America Inc., 10871
Rosa's Horchata, LLC, 10875
Rose Packing Co Inc, 10886
Roses Ravioli, 10896
Royal Foods & Flavor, 10930
Rubino's Seafood Company, 10959
Rude Custom Butchering, 10964
Rumi Spice, 10978
RXBAR, 10519
Rymer Foods, 11006
Rymer Seafood, 11007
S & L Produce Inc, 11010
Sahagian & Associates, 11083

Salad Oils Intl Corp, 11096
Salmans & Assoc, 11109
Sampco, 11132
Sapp Birch Water, 11206
Saputo Cheese USA Inc., 11209
Sara Lee Foodservice, 11213
Saratoga Food Specialties, 11220
Sassafras Enterprises Inc, 11233
Sausages by Amy, 11244
Savoia Foods, 11253
Schafer Fisheries Inc, 11275
Schulze & Burch Biscuit Co, 11311
Seafood Merchants LTD, 11372
Seafood Plus Corporation, 11374
Seafood Specialties, 11377
Sedlock Farm, 11404
Seger Egg Corporation, 11412
Seneca Foods Corp, 11433
Sensient Flavors and Fragrances, 11443
Sentry Seasonings, 11446
Sethness Caramel Color, 11466
Shepherd Farms Inc, 11547
Siemer Milling Co, 11587
Signature Fruit, 11601
Silesia Flavors, 11607
Silva International, 11611
Silverland Bakery, 11634
Simple Mills, 11646
Sisler's Ice & Ice Cream, 11675
Skinny Souping, 11689
Slim Jim, 11706
Smiling Fox Pepper Company, 11719
Smolich Bros. Home Made Sausage, 11740
Solo Foods, 11788
SoluBlend Technologies LLC, 11792
Sommers Organic, 11801
Soynut Butter Co, 11884
Specialty Ingredients, 11904
Speco Inc, 11909
Spectrum Foods Inc, 11910
Spiceland, 11927
Square One Organics, 11987
St Charles Trading Inc, 11993
Stampede Meat, Inc., 12023
Stan-Mark Food Products Inc, 12024
State Fish Distributors, 12055
Steckel Produce, 12067
Stefani Premium Foods, 12070
Stepan Co., 12081
Sterling Extract Co Inc, 12085
Stewart's Private Blend Foods, 12110
Stock Yards Packing Company, 12125
Storck U.S.A., 12148
Strube Celery & Vegetable Co, 12176
Stuart Hale Co, 12179
SuckerPunch Gourmet, 12186
Sulpice Chocolate, 12218
Superior Nut & Candy, 12337
Superior Ocean Produce, 12340
Supreme Frozen Products, 12351, 12352
Suter Co Inc, 12365
Swagger Foods Corp, 12377
Sweet Baby Ray's, 12388
Sweet Mountain Magic, 12409
Sweetener Supply Corp, 12426
Swiss Food Products, 12440
Switzer's Inc, 12448
Synergy Flavors Inc, 12456
Synthite USA Inc., 12458
Tallgrass Beef Company, 12515
Tampico Beverages Inc, 12521
Taqueria El Milagro, 12532
Tate & Lyle PLC, 12561
Taylor Precision Products, 12571
Taylor's Mexican Chili Co Inc, 12575
Teelee Popcorn, 12602
Terlato Kitchen, 12619
Terri Lynn Inc, 12623
TH Foods, Inc., 12477
The Bruss Company, 12674
The Cookie Dough Cafe, 12678
The Eli's Cheesecake Company, 12683
The Lovely Candy Company LLC, 12705
The Safe + Fair Food Company, 12727
Think Jerky, 12753
Tiesta Tea, 12799
Tom Ringhausen Orchards, 12850
Tom Tom Tamale & Bakery Co, 12852
Tomer Kosher Foods, 12861
Tone Products Inc, 12866
Tootsie Roll Industries Inc., 12880
Top Hat Co Inc, 12881

Topco Associates LLC, 12885
Torkelson Cheese Co, 12892
TreeHouse Foods, Inc., 12943
Trenton Processing Ctr, 12952
Tropicana Products Inc., 13012
Troy Foods Inc, 13017
Turano Baking, 13060, 13061
UBF Food Solutions, 13115
Uncle Dougie's, 13154
Unica, 13165
Union Fisheries Corp, 13171
Uniquely Together, 13180
Upton's Naturals, 13220
Urban Accents, 13222
US Ingredients, 13123
Us Spice Mill Inc, 13228
V & V Supremo, 13233
Valley Meats, 13258
Van de Kamps, 13282
Van Drunen Farms, 13270
Van Leer Chocolate Corporation, 13274
Van Waters & Roger, 13281
Van-Lang Food Products, 13284
Vanee Foods Co, 13290
Varco Brothers, 13296
Vegetable Juices Inc, 13312
VegGuide.org, 13305
Veritas Chocolatier, 13339
Vienna Beef LTD, 13400
Vincent Formusa Company, 13422
Viobin USA, 13435
Vita Food Products Inc, 13454
Vital Proteins LLC, 13462
Vitamins, 13470
Vosges Haut-Chocolat, 13495
Vyse Gelatin Co, 13498
Wabash Seafood Co, 13518
Wagner Excello Food Products, 13526
Wagner Seafood, 13528
Water Concepts, 13585
Watershed Foods, 13590
Waugh Foods Inc, 13594
Weber Flavors, 13614
Wenda America Inc, 13648
Wenger Spring Brook Cheese Inc, 13650
Westdale Foods Company, 13676
White Fence Farm, 13718
White Stokes International, 13730
White-Stokes Company, 13733
Whitey's Ice Cream Inc, 13739
Wichita Packing Co Inc, 13757
Wildlife Cookies Co, 13794
Windy City Organics, 13847
Wing Seafood Company, 13856
Wisconsin Wilderness Food Products, 13882
World's Finest Chocolate Inc, 13948
Wrench Mints, 13956
Wrigley, 13960
Wurth Dairy, 13963
Xena International, 13968
Y & T Packing Co, 13972
Y.M.C. Corp., 13977
Yamasho Inc, 13988
Ying's Kitchen, 14005
Z-Trim Holdings, Inc, 14036
Zabiha Halal Meat Processors, 14037
Zebra Technologies Corporation, 14048
Zelda's Sweet Shoppe, 14051
Zemas Madhouse Foods Inc., 14052

Indiana

Abbott's Candy Shop, 115
AccuTemp, 138
Agricor Inc, 214
Al Pete Meats, 249
Albanese Confectionery Group, 278
Alpha Baking Company, 374
American Beverage Marketers, 439
AmeriQual Foods, 435
Archibald Frozen Desserts, 639
Atkins Elegant Desserts, 753
Aunt Millie's Bakeries, 807
B & B Food Distributors Inc, 858
Baird Dairy LLC, 946
BBQ'n Fools Catering, LLC, 889
Best Chocolate In Town, 1263
Big B Barbecue, 1324
Black Jewell Popcorn, 1420
Bloomington Brewing Co, 1460
Bnutty, 1513
Bonnie Baking Company, 1561

Bonnie Doon LLC, 1562
Brook Locker Plant, 1739
Brown County Winery, 1773
Bunny Bread, 1852
Butler Winery, 1878
Butterfield Foods, 1884
C & G Salsa, 1910
Cadillac Coffee Co, 1984
Capriole Inc, 2177
Captain Bob's Jet Fuel, 2183
Carbon's Golden Malted, 2197
Chester Inc Information, 2530
Choco Finesse, LLC, 2589
Clabber Girl Corporation, 2711
Claeys Candy Inc, 2712
Clover Blossom Honey, 2777
Collins Cavier Co, 2882
Compton Dairy, 2931
Copper Moon Coffee LLC, 3007
Creighton Brothers, 3142
Crystal Lake LLC, 3214
Culture Systems Inc, 3242
Culver Duck Farms Inc, 3244
DairyChem Inc., 3346
Debrand Chocolatier, 3452
Dewig Brothers Packing Company, 3555
Dillman Farm Inc, 3601
Donaldson's Finer Chocolates, 3678
Dugdale Beef Company, 3784
Easley Winery, 3877
Egg Innovations, 3965
Ellison Bakery, Inc., 4024
Empire Tea Svc, 4055
Endangered Species Chocolate, 4060
Epogee, 4095
Farbest Foods Inc, 4262
Farm Boy Food Svc, 4270
Finest Call, 4401
Foods Alive, 4574
Ghyslain Chocolatier, 4995
Glover's Ice Cream Inc, 5075
Golden Malted, 5128
Grabill Country Meats, 5224
Graham Cheese Corporation, 5238
Greenfield Mills, 5371
Harlan Bakeries, 5590
Heartland Sweeteners, 5715
Henry Davis Company, 5771
Heyerly Bakery, 5823
Homestead Dairy, 5943
Hoople Country Kitchen Inc, 5988
Hubers Orchard Winery-Vineyards, 6044
Hulman & Co, 6062
Indiana Botanic Gardens Inc, 6192
Instant Products of America, 6232
Integrative Flavors, 6234
International Bakers Services, Inc., 6247
IOM Grain, 6121
Key III Candies, 6823
Kingly Heirs, 6876
Kingsbury Country Market, 6881
Kyger Bakery Products, 7014
Ladoga Frozen Food & Retail, 7130
Lafayette Brewing Co, 7134
Laredo Tortilleria & Mexican, 7219
Lebermuth Company, 7290, 7291
Lengerich Meats Inc, 7348
Lewis Bakeries Inc, 7402
Little Crow Foods, 7465
Lowery's Home Made Candies, 7612
Ludwig Fish & Produce Company, 7641
Lyoferm & Vivolac Cultures, 7668
M.A. Johnson Frozen Foods, 7687
Manley Meats Inc, 7852
Maple Leaf Farms, 7874
Maplehurst Bakeries LLC, 7886
Marion-Kay Spice Co, 7934
Mcfarling Foods Inc, 8093
Melchers Flavors of America, 8142
Meridian Foods New Inc, 8170
Merkley & Sons Packing Co Inc, 8174
Middlebury Cheese Company, 8262
Midwest Seafood, 8270
Milroy Canning Company, 8331
Mishawaka Brewing Company, 8374
Mishler Packing Co, 8375
Morgan Foods Inc, 8542
Munsee Meats, 8682
Myers Frozen Food Provisions, 8713
Napoleon Locker, 8766
National Foods, 8791
National Wine & Spirits, 8807

1331

Geographic Index / Iowa

New Business Corp, 8961
New Harmony Coffee & Tea Co., 8979
New Horizons Baking Co, 8987
Nk Hurst Co Inc, 9074
Nutritional Research Associates, 9264
O'Neil's Distributors, 9293
Oliver Winery, 9452
Ossian Smoked Meats, 9585
Park 100 Foods Inc, 9778
Pierceton Foods Inc, 10046
Plainfield Winery & Tasting Rm, 10097
Pleasant View Dairy, 10113
Plyley's Candy, 10128
Popcorn Popper, 10180
Prairie Mills Products LLC, 10235
Pretzels Inc, 10274
Puritan/ATZ Ice Cream, 10391
R D Laney Family Honey Co, 10478
Ralph Sechler & Son Inc, 10545
Ramsey Popcorn Co Inc, 10551
RC Bottling Company, 10503
Red Gold Inc., 10608
Richard Green Company, 10719
Richmond Baking Co, 10730
Rose Acre Farms, 10879
Rose Acre Farms Inc, 10880
Royal Center Locker Plant, 10926
Royal Food Products, 10929
S A L T Sisters, 11014
Schimpffs Confectionery LLC, 11288
Sechler's Fine Pickles, 11400
Sells Best, 11422
Serenade Foods, 11451
Shirley Foods, 11565
Snowbear Frozen Custard, 11765
South Bend Chocolate Co, 11828
Southern Heritage Coffee Company, 11855
Squire Boone Village, 11989
Superior Seafood & Meat Company, 12345
Swiss Way Cheese, 12443
Swissland Milk, 12446
Tell City Pretzel Company, 12609
The Valpo Velvet Shoppe, 12741
Tom Farms, 12849
Tri-State Dairy, 12958
Triple XXX Root Beer Co., 12984
Troyer Foods Inc, 13019
United Pies Of Elkhart Inc, 13197
Verdure Sciences, 13336
Villa Milan Vineyard, 13413
Vivolac Cultures Corporation, 13480
Wabash Heritage Mfg LLC, 13517
Wabash Valley Farms, 13519
Wabash Valley Produce Inc, 13520
Wayne Dairy Products Inc, 13604
Weaver Brothers, 13609
Weaver Popcorn Co Inc, 13611
Westport Locker LLC, 13692
Wick's Pies Inc, 13758
Winterbrook Beverage Group, 13872
Wright's Ice Cream Co, 13959
Zachary Confections Inc, 14039

Iowa

Ackerman Winery, 149
ACP, Inc., 74
All Juice Food & Beverage, 321
All-States Quality Foods, 325
Allied Blending & Ingredients, 342
Amana Meat Shop & Smoke House, 409
American Cheesemen, 446
American Pop Corn Co, 478
Anderson Erickson Dairy, 546
APC Inc, 98
Apotheca Inc, 606
B & R Quality Meats Inc, 867
Betty Jane Homemade Candy, 1290
Birdsall Ice Cream Company, 1387
Boyd's Sausage Co, 1637
Brandmeyer Popcorn Co, 1660
Breads from Anna, 1681
Burke Corp, 1861
Caremoli USA, 2203
Carriage House Foods, 2258
Cedar Valley Fish Market, 2353
Chebe Bread Products, 2478
Chocolaterie Stam, 2615
Community Orchards, 2928
Con Agra Snack Foods, 2935
Cookies Food Products, 2988
D & D Foods Inc, 3292

Devansoy Farms, 3548
DuPont Pioneer, 3774, 3775
Dutchland Frozen Foods, 3820
Embria Health Sciences, 4040
Energenetics International, 4064
Energique, 4065
Essentia Protein Solutions, 4119
Farmer's Hen House, 4278
Foreign Candy Company, 4589
Frontier Co-op, 4752
Galassi Foods, 4863
Gelita North America, 4937
Grain Processing Corp, 5246
Great Midwest Seafood Company, 5321
Harker's Distribution, 5589
Harvest Innovations, 5631
Health & Wholeness Store, 5679
Heartland Strawberry Farm, 5714
Heinz Quality Chef Foods Inc, 5736
Hollman Foods, 5910
J & L Grain Processing, 6341
J M Swank Co, 6359
Joelle's Choice Specialty Foods LLC, 6541
Kemin Industries Inc, 6777
Kent Precision Foods Group Inc, 6792
Kitt's Meat Processing, 6900
LA Quercia LLC, 7058
Lampost Meats, 7187
Landlocked Seafoods, 7202
Lee Seed Co, 7297
Liguria Foods Inc, 7428
Little Amana Winery, 7463
Matthiesen's Deer & Custom, 8015
Maytag Dairy Farms Inc, 8043
Michael's Cookies, 8228
MicroSoy Corporation, 8252
Midamar, 8260
Milani, 8287
Millstream Brewing Co, 8323
Mohn's Fisheries, 8454
Mrs Clark's Foods, 8627
Natural Food Holdings, 8830
Natural Products Inc, 8845
Noble Popcorn, 9080
Oak Street Manufacturing, 9324
Old Wine Cellar, 9430
Oskaloosa Food Products, 9581
P.A. Braunger Institutional Foods, 9642
Palmer Candy Co, 9722
Phyto-Technologies, 10026
Potter Siding Creamery Company, 10220
Rembrandt Foods, 10667
Royale Brands, 10953
Sandstone Winery, 11173
Schillinger Genetics Inc, 11286
Schleswig Specialty Meats, 11292
Shakespeare's, 11500
Sioux Honey Assn., 11669
SKW Nature Products, 11045
Snappy Popcorn, 11751
Solnuts, 11787
Sparboe Foods Corp, 11888
Sterzing Food Co, 12088
Stock Popcorn Ind Inc, 12124
Stoller Fisheries, 12128
Tiny But Mighty Popcorn, 12817
Todd's, 12830
Tri-State Logistics Inc, 12960
Triland Foods Inc, 12971
Triple K Manufacturing Company, Inc., 12979
Twin County Dairy, 13092
Vanmark Equipment, 13293
Varied Industries Corp, 13299
W & G Marketing Company, 13499
Wapsie Creamery, 13564
Wapsie Produce, 13565
Waterfront Seafood Market, 13588
Webster City Custom Meats Inc, 13615
Wells Enterprises Inc, 13645
West Liberty Foods LLC, 13664

Kansas

Advanced Food Services, 188
American Ingredients Co, 463
AnaCon Foods Company, 525
Anderson Erickson Dairy, 547
Art's Mexican Products, 708
Barkman Honey, 1040
BBQ Shack, 888
Bee Harmony Honey, 1157

Best Harvest Bakeries, 1268
Bettah Buttah, LLC, 1279
Bowser Meat Processing, 1634
Browniepops LLC, 1788
Cargill Protein, 2206
Carol Lee Donuts, 2230
CBC Foods, 1943
Central Soyfoods, 2383
Cereal Food Processors Inc, 2389, 2390
Cereal Ingredients, Inc., 2391
Clay Center Locker Plant, 2733
Compass Minerals, 2930
Corbion, 3014
Culver Fish Farm, 3245
Custom Foods Inc, 3271
Dairy Farmers Of America, 3335
Dold Foods, 3652
Donut Whole, 3688
DuPont Nutrition & Biosciences, 3773
Duis Meat Processing, 3786
Ehresman Packaging Co, 3971
El Perico Charro, 3986
Fanestil Packing Company, 4249
Fine Foods Of America Inc, 4396
Finkemeier Bakery, 4404
Grandma Hoerner's Inc, 5265
Guy's Food, 5456
Heartland Food Products, 5710
Heartland Mills Shipping, 5713
Helmuth Country Bakery Inc, 5753
Highland Dairies, 5852
Hilary's Eat Well, 5864
Holton Meat Processing, 5920
Jackson Meat, 6422
Kan-Pak, 6699
KC Innovations Inc, 6668
La Superior Food Products, 7109
Leams, 7283
Lost Trail Root Beer, 7557
Louisburg Cider Mill, 7578
Manildra Milling Corporation, 7847
Marwood Sales, Inc, 7979
MGP Ingredients Inc, 7700
Mid Kansas Co-Op Assn, 8254
New Grass Bison, 8977
North American Water Group, 9121
Nu Life Market, 9200
Old World Spices Inc, 9434
Original Juan, 9565
Pantry Shelf/Mixxm, 9750
Pickle Cottage, 10032
Pines International, 10067
Rabbit Creek, 10522
Research Products Co, 10680
Riffel's Coffee Company, 10740
Rita's Italian Ice, 10761
Rolling Pin Bakery, 10850
Rufus Teague, 10972
Safely Delicious, 11072
Salvy Sousa Dealer Locator, 11122
Sambol Meat Company, 11130
Seaboard Foods, 11363
Sifers Valomilk Candy Co, 11595
SimplyFUEL, LLC, 11658
Spanish Gardens Food Manufacturing, 11887
Spring Hill Meat Market, 11962
Stafford County Flour Mills Company, 12018
Tall Grass Toffee Co, 12511
Twin Valley Developmental Services, 13096
Velvet Creme Popcorn Co, 13321
Wagner Gourmet Foods, 13527
Wichita Fish Co, 13756
Wilke International Inc, 13802
YB Meats of Wichita, 13978

Kentucky

AAK, 70
Adam Matthews Inc, 161
ADM Wild Flavors & Specialty, 77
Algood Food Co, 305
Alltech Inc, 348
Ameri Candy, 431
Ananda Hemp, 528
Applecreek Speciality Foods, 612
Bartons Fine Foods, 1063
Bel Cheese USA, 1173
Bernheim Distilling Company, 1250
Beverly International, 1297
Big Russ Beer Cheese, 1341

Blanton's, 1438
Blend Pak Inc, 1443
Blendex Co, 1445
Bloomfield Farms, 1459
Blue Grass Quality Meat, 1475
Bluegrass Brewing Company, 1507
Bluegrass Dairy & Food, 1508
Boone's Butcher Shop, 1570
Booneway Farms, 1571
Borders Sporting Goods, 1578
Bourbon Barrel Foods, 1626
Bravard Vineyards & Winery, 1672
Broad Run Vineyards, 1726
Broadbent B & B Food Products, 1728
Brown Thompson & Sons, 1781
Brown-Forman Corp, 1784
Buffalo Trace Distillery, 1839
Candyrific, 2136
Castellini Group, 2298
Chambord, 2407
Clarendon Flavor Engineering, 2716
Clem's Seafood & Specialties, 2747
Club Chef LLC, 2789
Country Oven Bakery, 3082
Critchfield Meats Inc, 3168
Cumberland Gap Provision Company, 3248
Custom Food Solutions LLC, 3270
D D Williamson & Co Inc, 3294
DDW: The Color House, 3308
Dippin' Dots LLC, 3616
Dixie Dew Prods Co, 3629
Double B Distributors, 3700
Dryden Provision Co Inc, 3772
Dundee Candy Shop, 3795
East Kentucky Foods, 3882
F B Purnell Sausage Co Inc, 4197
Father's Country Hams, 4307
Feed The Party, 4321
Finchville Farms Country Ham, 4390
Fish Market Inc, 4441, 4442
Fox Hollow, 4635
Glier's Meats Inc, 5058
Harper's Country Hams, 5602
Harvest Manor Farms, 5632
Heaven Hill Distilleries Inc., 5720
Heltzman Bakery, 5756
Heringer Meats Inc, 5792
Heritage Fancy Foods Marketing, 5796
Horton Fruit Co Inc, 6005
Immu Dyne Inc, 6157
J.W. Haywood & Sons Dairy, 6389
John Conti Coffee Co, 6550
Kentucky Beer Cheese, 6795
Kentucky Bourbon, 6796
Kern Meat Distributing, 6800
King Fish Restaurants, 6863
Latonia Bakery, 7241
Lexington Coffee & Tea, 7406
Louise's, 7579
Louisville Dairy, 7593
Luv Yu Bakery, 7653
Lyons Magnus, 7670
Maker's Mark Distillery Inc, 7801
Mattingly Foods Of Louisville, 8016
Mitchell Foods, 8403
Mizkan Americas Inc, 8421, 8430
Moonlite Bar-B-Q Inn, 8528
Muth's Candy Store, 8700
Najla's Specialty Foods Inc, 8737
Nestle USA, 8944
Old Kentucky Hams, 9417
Old Rip Van Winkle Distillery, 9424
Owensboro Grain Co, 9618
Papas Chris A & Son Co, 9753
Paradise Tomato Kitchens, 9767
Perfetti Van Melle USA Inc, 9956
Plehn's Bakery Inc, 10115
Pots de Creme, 10219
Premiere Seafood, 10254
Premium Brands, 10255
Preston Farms Popcorn, 10268
Rebecca-Ruth Candy Factory, 10596
Reiter Dairy, 10663
Riverview Foods, 10776
Robertson's Country Meat Hams, 10801
Robinson Distributing Co, 10803
Rooibee Red Tea, 10868
Ruth Hunt Candy Co, 10998
Sargent and Greenleaf, 11226
Scott Hams, 11326
Scott's Auburn Mills, 11327
Shuckman's Fish Co & Smokery, 11578

Geographic Index / Louisiana

Southern Delight Gourmet Foods, 11849
Specialty Food America Inc, 11899
Specialty Foods Group Inc, 11902
Spreda Group, 11957
Suncrest Farms, 12268
Sutton Honey Farms, 12370
The Kroger Co., 12699
Tova Industries LLC, 12906
Triangle Seafood, 12962
Vegan Metal Fabricators Co, 13307
Weisenberger Mills, 13629
Wild Aseptics, LLC, 13775
Winchester Farms Dairy, 13841

Louisiana

Abita Brewing Co, 125
Acadian Fine Foods, 133
Acadian Ostrich Ranch, 134
Alma Plantation, 351
Alois J Binder Bakery, 367
Ameripure Processing Co, 495
Anglo American Trading, 568
Ashland Plantation Gourmet, 727
Aunt Sally's Praline Shops, 808
Autin's Cajun Cookery, 823
B & C Riverside, 862
Bailey's Basin Seafood, 941
Baker Maid Products, Inc., 964
Baking Leidenheimer, 979
Barataria Spice Company, 1019
Basin Crawfish Processors, 1073
Baumer Foods Inc, 1087
Bayou Food Distributors, 1109
Bayou Land Seafood, 1110
Big Easy Foods, 1330
Blue Runner Foods Inc, 1497
Bodin Foods, 1531
Boquet's Oyster House, 1574
Boscoli Foods Inc, 1587
Boston Direct Lobsters, 1595
Boudreaux's Foods, 1610
Brennan Snacks Manufacturing, 1691
Brown's Dairy, 1782
Bruce Foods Corporation, 1794
C S Steen Syrup Mill Inc, 1924
Cafe Du Monde Coffee Stand, 1993
Cajun Boy's Louisiana Products, 2018
Cajun Brands, 2019
Cajun Crawfish Distributors, 2020
Cajun Creole Products Inc, 2021
Cajun Fry Co Inc, 2022
Cajun Original Foods Inc, 2023
Calhoun Bend Mill, 2046
Camellia Beans, 2105
Cameron Seafood Processors, 2109
Carnival Brands Mfg, 2226
Caro Foods, 2227
Catfish Wholesale, 2316
Cheese Straws & More, 2482
Chef Hans' Gourmet Foods, 2489
Chef Paul Prudhomme's Magic Seasonings Blends, 2491
China Pharmaceutical Enterprises, 2571
Chisesi Brothers Meat Packing, 2581
Chris Hansen Seafood, 2642
CJ's Seafood, 1955
Coastal Seafood Processors, 2803
Coffee Roasters Of New Orleans, 2857
Coffee Roasters of New Orleans, 2858
Colibri Pepper Company, 2877
Comeaux's, 2918
Community Coffee Co., 2926
Conrad Rice Mill Inc, 2956
COnut Butter, 1961
Cora Texas Mfg Co Inc, 3010
Cotton Baking Company, 3056
Creole Delicacies Gourmet Shop, 3147
Creole Fermentation Indu, 3148
Daybrook Fisheries, 3419
De Boles Nutritional Foods, 3423
Diversified Foods & Seasonings, 3623
Dixie Rice, 3631
Doerle Food Svc LLC, 3643
Dong Phuong Oriental Bakery, 3682
Drusilla Seafood, 3770
Dubois Seafood, 3777
Elmer Chocolate®, 4032
Elmers Fine Foods Inc, 4033
Errol's Cajun Foods, 4109
Eschete's Seafood, 4112
Evans Creole Candy, 4157

Falcon Rice Mill Inc, 4232
Farmers Rice Milling Co, 4284
Farmers Seafood Co Wholesale, 4285
French Market Coffee, 4700
French Market Foods, 4701
French Quarter Seafood, 4704
G & J Land & Marine Food Distr, 4812
Gambino's Bakeries Inc, 4879
Gambino's Bakery, 4880
Garber Farms, 4886
Global Preservatives, 5067
Griffin's Seafood, 5387
Guidry's Catfish Inc, 5424
Gulf Atlantic Freezers, 5429
Gulf Crown Seafood Co, 5432
Gulf Food Products Co Inc, 5433
Gulf Marine, 5434
Hanley's Foods Inc., 5551
Haring Catfish, 5588
Harlon's LA Fish, 5592
Harvest Time Seafood Inc, 5635
Haydel's Bakery, 5668
Hi Seas, 5825
Higgins Seafood, 5839
Hightower's Packing, 5860
HongryHawg of Louisiana, 5974
Hue's Seafood, 6058
Indian Ridge Shrimp Co, 6187
J Bernard Seafood, 6346
Jack Miller's Food Products, 6417
Jelks Coffee Roasters, 6484
JFG Coffee, 6399
Johnson's Wholesale Meats, 6572
K.S.M. Seafood Corporation, 6664
Kajun Kettle Foods, 6687
Kate Latter Candy Company, 6725
Keller's Bakery, 6759
Kleinpeter Farms Dairy LLC, 6909
L H Hayward & Co, 7027
La Caboose Specialties, 7080
Lady Gale Seafood, 7132
Lafitte Frozen Foods Corp, 7136
Lafleur Dairy Products,, 7137
Lafourche Sugar LLC, 7139
Lake Charles Poultry, 7149
Landry's Pepper Co, 7206
Laurent's Meat Market, 7249
Leblanc Seafood, 7292
Leidenheimer Baking Co, 7326
Lejeune's Bakery Inc, 7332
Loretta's Authentic Pralines, 7542
Louisiana Fish Fry Products, 7580
Louisiana Gourmet Enterprises, 7581
Louisiana Oyster Processors, 7582
Louisiana Packing Company, 7583
Louisiana Pride Seafood, 7584
Louisiana Rice Mill, 7585
Louisiana Seafood Exchange, 7586, 7588
Louisiana Seafood Promotion & Marketing Board, 7589
Louisiana Seafoods, 7590
Louisiana Sugar Cane Co-Op Inc, 7591
Louisiana Sugar Cane Cooperative, 7592
M.A. Patout & Son LTD, 7688
Magic Seasoning Blends, 7766
Manchac Seafood Market, 7830
Manda Fine Meats Inc, 7834
Martin Brothers Seafood Co, 7964
Maurice French Pastries, 8024
McIlhenny Company, 8072
Melba's Old School Po Boys, 8141
Merlin Candies, 8175
Mizkan Americas Inc, 8424
Music Mountain Water Company, 8696
Natchitoches Crawfish Company, 8779
National Fruit Flavor Co Inc, 8795
National Meat & Provision Company, 8800
New Orleans Fish House II LLC, 8994
New Orleans Food Co-op, 8995
New Orleans Gulf Seafood, 8996
Oak Grove Smoke House Inc, 9315
Ocean Pride Seafood, 9353
Ocean Select Seafood, 9354
Ouachita Lumber Co, 9598
P & J Oyster Co, 9628
P&L Seafood of Venice, 9639
Panola Pepper Co, 9745
Paul Piazza & Son Inc, 9843
Pepper Source Inc, 9938
Pepperland Farms, 9943
Perino's Inc, 9959
Piazza's Seafood World LLC, 10029

PJ's Coffee & Tea, 9653
Plantation Pecan & Gift Company, 10105
Poche's Smokehouse, 10135
Pon Food Corp, 10162
Pontchartrain Blue Crab, 10167
Prairie Cajun Wholesale, 10231
Procell Polymers, 10321
Raceland Raw Sugar Corporation, 10525
Reggie Balls Cajun Foods, 10646
Reily Foods Company, 10657
REX Pure Foods, 10509
Robin & Cohn Seafood Distributors, 10802
Royal Resources, 10946
S&D Bait Company, 11022
Savoie Industries, 11254
Savoie's Sausage and Food Products, 11255
Sazerac Co Inc, 11263
Sazerac Company, Inc., 11264
Seafood International, 11371
Seafood Packaging Inc, 11373
Sharkco's, 11519
Simon Hubig Company, 11641
Sirocco Enterprises Inc, 11674
Slap Ya Mama Cajun Seasoning, 11699
Sno Wizard Inc, 11756
Snowizard Extracts, 11767
SONOCO, 11047
Southern Bar-B-Que, 11842
Southern Belle Sandwich Company, 11843
Southern Shell Fish Company, 11865
Southern Snow, 11867
St Mary Sugar Co-Op, 12000
St. James Sugar Cooperative, 12006
Stimo-O-Stam, Ltd., 12120
Sucre, 12187, 12188
Sugar Plum LLC, 12203
Superior Seafood, 12344
Swerve Sweetener, 12436
T&T Seafood, 12465
Thompson Packers, 12770
Three Rivers Fish Company, 12785
Tideland Seafood Company, 12797
Tomorrow Enterprise, 12864
Tony Chachere's Creole Foods, 12869
Tony's Seafood LTD, 12875
Trappey's Fine Foods Inc, 12930
Tuna Fresh, 13058
Turnbull Bakeries, 13068
Valentine Chemicals, 13248
Vince's Seafoods, 13419
Vincent Piazza Jr & Sons, 13423
Wayne Estay Shrimp Company, 13606
Westway Trading Corporation, 13695
Wilsons Oysters, 13836
Wright Enrichment Inc, 13958

Maine

4Pure, 21
A.C. Inc., 61
Allen's Blueberry Freezer Inc, 337
Annabelle Lee, 584
Appledore Cove LLC, 613
Arnold Farm Sugarhouse, 688
Atlantic Laboratories Inc, 769
Atlantic Salmon of Maine, 774
Atlantic Seafood Direct, 777
B.C. Fisheries, 882
Badger Island Shell-Fish & Lobster, 929
Ballard Custom Meats, 994
Bar Harbor Brewing Company, 1015
Bar Harbor Foods, 1016
Barefoot Contessa Pantry, 1030
Barnes Ice Cream Company, 1046
Bay Haven Lobster Pound, 1096
Bayley's Lobster Pound, 1107
BBS Lobster Co, 891
Beal's Lobster Pier, 1119
Benbow's Coffee Roasters, 1217
Bickford Daniel Lobster Company, 1311
Bitter Love, 1410
Bixby & Co., LLC, 1414
Bold Coast Smokehouse, 1546
Boothbay Lobster Wharf, 1573
Bouchard Family Farm, 1609
Boyton Shellfish, 1642
Burnham & Morrill Co, 1867
C.B.S. Lobster Company, 1932
C.E. Fish Company, 1934
Calendar Islands Maine Lobster LLC, 2043
Can Am Seafood, 2119
Cantrell's Seafood, 2145

Carrabassett Coffee Roasters, 2257
Charlie Beigg's Sauce Company, 2438
Cheating Gourmet, 2477
Cherryfield Foods, 2524
Coastside Lobster Company, 2806
Cobscook Bay Seafood, 2809
Common Folk Farm, 2924
Connors Aquaculture, 2954
Cook-In-The-Kitchen, 2980
Corea Lobster Cooperative, 3027
Cozy Harbor Seafood Inc, 3103
Cranberry Isles Fisherman's, 3113
Custom House Seafoods, 3272
Dl Geary Brewing, 3637
Dole Pond Maple Products, 3655
Doug Hardy Company, 3708
Down East Specialty Products/Cape Bald Packers, 3719
Downeast Candies, 3720
Ducktrap River Of Maine, 3780
Dunham's Lobster Pot, 3801
Elliott Seafood Company, 4022
Falla Imports, 4236
Fiddlers Green Farm, 4362
Finestkind Fish Market, 4402
Fishermens Net, 4449
French & Brawn Marketplace, 4696
Fresh Market Pasta Company, 4716
Fresh Pack Seafood, 4719
Fresh Samantha, 4722
Friendship International, 4735
FW Thurston, 4211
G M Allen & Son Inc, 4816
Gay's Wild Maine Blueberries, 4924
Gelato Fiasco, 4934
Getchell Brothers Inc, 4991
Gifford's Ice Cream, 5004
Gilmore's Seafoods, 5014
Gouldsboro Enterprises, 5198
Graffam Brothers, 5234
GrandyOats, 5271
Hamilton Marine, 5533
Hancock Gourmet Lobster Co, 5543
Harbor Fish Market, 5575
Harmon's Original Clam Cakes, 5595
Haven's Candies, 5649
Heritage Salmon, 5800
Herring Brothers Meats, 5817
Houlton Farms Dairy, 6020
ISF Trading, 6123
Island Lobster, 6300
Island Seafood, 6305
J P's Shellfish Co, 6363
John J. Nissen Baking Company, 6555
Joseph Kirschner & Company, 6602
K Horton Specialty Foods, 6657
Kennebec Fruit Company, 6786
Kent's Wharf, 6794
Len Libby Chocolatier-Maine, 7343
Lepage Bakeries, 7368
Little River Lobster Company, 7474
Livermore Falls Baking Company, 7483
LLJ's Sea Products, 7071
Look Lobster Co, 7537
Lusty Lobster, 7652
Machias Bay Seafood, 7728
Maine Coast Nordic, 7787
Maine Coast Sea Vegetables, 7788
Maine Lobster Outlet, 7789
Maine Mahogony Shellfish, 7790
Maine Seaweed Company, 7791
Maine Wild Blueberry Company, 7792
Maple's Organics, 7882
Marika's Kitchen, 7921
Marine MacHines, 7928
Mclaughlin Seafood, 8097
Merrill's Blueberry Farms, 8181
Mill Cove Lobster Pound, 8300
Mizkan Americas Inc, 8416
Morse's Sauerkraut, 8564
Mother's Mountain Pantry, 8582
Nancy's Shellfish, 8752
New Harbor Fisherman's Cooperative, 8978
Newmeadows Lobster Inc, 9020
NibMor, 9033
North Atlantic Inc, 9122
North Atlantic Products, 9123
North Atlantic Seafood, 9124
O'Hara Corp, 9291
Oak Island Seafood Company, 9317
Oakhurst Dairy, 9325
Ocean Approved, 9343

Geographic Index / Manitoba

Ocean Harvest, 9349
Ocean's Balance, 9358
Oceanledge Seafoods, 9361
P.J. Merrill Seafood Inc, 9645
P.M. Innis Lobster Company, 9646
P.T. Fish, 9647
Pastor Chuck Orchards, 9820
Pemaquid Seafood, 9907
Pemberton's Foods Inc, 9908
Penobscot Mccrum LLC, 9928
Pine Point Seafood, 10062
Pineland Farms, 10066
Port Lobster Co Inc, 10199
Portland Shellfish Company, 10205
Portland Specialty Seafoods, 10206
Power of 3, 10224
Raye's Mustard, 10581
Raye's Old Fashioned Gourmet Mustard, 10582
Redd Superfood Energy Bars, 10626
Rehemond Farm Inc, 10653
Reilly's Sea Products, 10656
Resource Trading Company, 10682
Rier Smoked Salmon, 10739
Royal Rose Syrups, LLC, 10948
S & M Fisheries Inc, 11012
Salt River Lobster Inc, 11115
Sausage Kitchen, 11243
Scandia Seafood Company, 11267
Schlotterbeck & Foss Company, 11294
Sea Dog Brewing Company, 11340
Sea Horse Wharf, 11344
Seafare Market Wholesale, 11366
Seafood Express, 11369
Sealand Lobster Corporation, 11379
Seaview Lobster Co, 11395
Shaker Museum, 11498
Shaner's Family Restaurant, 11512
Shipyard Brewing Co, 11561, 11562
Smiling Hill Farm, 11720
Sorrento Lobster, 11819
Sow's Ear Winery, 11876
Spinney Creek Shellfish, 11938
Spruce Mountain Blueberries, 11982
Stanchfield Farms, 12025
State Of Maine Cheese Co, 12057
Stonewall Kitchen, 12139
Stonington Lobster Co-Op, 12141
Sullivan Harbor Farm, 12216
Sunshine Seafood, 12311
T.B. Seafood, 12468
Taylor Lobster Co, 12568
Theriault's Abattoir Inc, 12749
Thomas Lobster Co, 12768
Todd's Salsa, 12832
Trenton Bridge Lobster Pound, 12951
Uncle Andy's Cafe, 13152
Vinalhaven Fishermens Co-op, 13418
W.A. Beans & Sons, 13501
W.S. Wells & Sons, 13506
Wallace Plant Company, 13550
Walsh's Seafood, 13555
West Bay Fishing, 13659
West Brothers Lobster, 13660
Wicked Whoopies, 13761
Wild Blueberries, 13777
Winter Harbor Co-Op Inc, 13869
Wolverton Seafood, 13904
World Harbors, 13938
Young's Lobster Pound, 14027

Manitoba

Arctic Beverages, 644
Arctic Glacier, 645
Besco Grain Ltd, 1258
Best Cooking Pulses, Inc., 1264
Floating Leaf Fine Foods, 4508
Fort Garry Brewing Company, 4601
Freshwater Fish Market, 4727
Hemp Oil Canada, 5759
Legumex Walker, Inc., 7317
MFI Food Canada, 7698
Naleway Foods, 8743
Richardson International, 10725
Scott-Bathgate, 11331
Shape Foods, 11517
Souris Valley Processors, 11825

Maryland

Analyticon Discovery LLC, 527

Ann's House of Nuts, Inc., 580
Annapolis Produce & Restaurant, 585
Aromi d'Italia, 700
Aufschnitt Meats, 793
Avenue Gourmet, 837
Baily Tea USA Inc, 943
Baltimore Brewing Company, 999
Baltimore Coffee & Tea Co Inc, 1000
Barcelona Nut Co, 1027
Basignani Winery, 1072
Bay Hundred Seafood Inc, 1098
Beverage Capital Corporation, 1294
BGS Jourdan & Sons, 896
Big Al's Seafood, 1322
Bill's Seafood, 1354
Binkert's Meat Products, 1363
Boesl Packing Co, 1536
Boordy Vineyards Inc, 1572
Bradye P. Todd & Son, 1651
Brassica Protection Products, 1667
Brook Meadow Meats, 1740
Byrd's Seafood, 1900
Capital Produce II Inc, 2163
Caribbean Products, 2210
Catoctin Vineyards, 2319
Century Blends LLC, 2386
Char-Wil Canning Company, 2425
Charles H. Parks & Company, 2431
Chempacific Corp, 2510
Chesapeake Bay Crab Cakes & More, 2527
Chesapeake Spice Company, 2528
Chester River Clam Co, 2531
Chester W. Howeth & Brother, 2532
Chestertown Natural Foods, 2535
Chincoteague Seafood Co Inc, 2572
Clear Mountain Coffee Company, 2738
Clement's Pastry Shops Inc, 2749
Clipper City Brewing, 2763
Cloverland/Green Spring Dairy, 2786
Cohen's Original Tasty Coddie, 2863
Corine's Cuisine, 3031
Crab Quarters, 3104
Crea Fill Fibers Corp, 3126
Cushner Seafoods Inc, 3266
Dairy Maid Dairy LLC, 3340
Denzer's Food Products, 3527
Doctor Dread's Jerk, 3641
Dorchester Crab Co, 3694
Dutterer's Home Food Service, 3821
E L K Run Vineyards, 3837
Eagle Coffee Co Inc, 3860
East Coast Fresh Cuts Inc, 3879
Eastern Shore Tea, 3893
Elite Spice Inc, 4012
EMD Sales Inc, 3856
Faidley Seafood, 4217
Fibred, 4357
Fiore Winery, 4409
Fisher's Popcorn, 4446
Flying Dog Brewery, 4534
Frank Mattes & Sons Reliable Seafood, 4655
Fuchs North America, 4778
G Cefalu & Brother Inc, 4814
Galvinell Meat Co Inc, 4876
Georgetown Bagelry, 4971
Giant Food, 4999
Goetze's Candy Co, 5096
Gold Crust Baking Co Inc, 5100
Golden Eye Seafood, 5121
Goll's Bakery, 5150
Great Gourmet Inc, 5310
H R Nicholson Co, 5467
H&S Bakery, 5471
H.Gass Seafood, 5478
Handy International Inc, 5547
Harbor Spice, 5577
Haribo of America, 5587
Harris Crab House, 5608
Huck's Seafood, 6046
Impromtu Gourmet, 6166
Indiana Grain Company, 6193
IOE Atlanta, 6120
Ise America Inc, 6295
J M Clayton Co, 6358
J W Treuth & Sons, 6367
Jason Pharmaceuticals, 6462
Joe Corbis' Wholesale Pizza, 6534
John N Wright Jr Inc, 6558
KOOL Ice & Seafood Co, 6675
LA Pasta Inc, 7055
Lawry's Foods, 7257

Leeward Resources, 7305
Lefty Spices, 7311
Loew Vineyards, 7507
Log 5 Corporation, 7509
Louis J Rheb Candy Co, 7572
M&L Gourmet Ice Cream, 7680
Mama Vida's Inc, 7821
Manger Packing Corp, 7841
Martin Seafood Company, 7969
MarySue.com, 7984
Mayorga Coffee, 8041
McCormick & Company, 8061
Mccutcheon Apple Products, 8091
McNasby's Seafood Market, 8081
Meatcrafters, 8116
Meredith & Meredith, 8167
Metompkin Bay Oyster Company, Inc, 8195
Mid-Atlantic Foods Inc, 8256
Mister Fish Inc., 8395
Moore's Candies, 8532
Mt. Olympus Specialty Foods, 8661
Mushroom Co, 8693
Naron Mary Sue Candies, 8771
Natural Products, 8824
Northeast Foods Inc, 9142
Orinoco Coffee & Tea, 9567
Ottenberg's Bakers, 9595
Paris Foods Corporation, 9775
Parker Flavors Inc, 9783
Paul Schafer Meat Products, 9844
Perdue Farms Inc., 9946
Perfections by Allan, 9955
Perlarom Technology, 9962
Pfefferkorn's Coffee Inc, 9993
Phillips Foods, 10012
Pompeian Inc, 10161
Potomac Farms Dairy Inc, 10218
Price Seafood, 10276
Ravico USA, 10574
Reutter Candy & Chocolates, 10689
Rio Trading Company, 10748
Rippons Seafood, 10755
Ruark & Ashton, 10956
Ruger LLC, 10973
Saval Foods Corp, 11246
Sea Watch Intl, 11356
SEW Friel, 11039
Shuff's Meat Market, 11579
Sibu Sura Chocolates, LLC, 11581
St John's Botanicals, 11997
Sudlersville Frozen Food Locker, 12190
Sweetcraft Candies, 12425
Tessemae's All Natural, 12636
Thymly Products Inc, 12795
TIC Gums, 12478
Tony Vitrano Company, 12871
Tropical Foods, 13004
Tulkoff's Food Products Inc, 13052
Uncle Ralph's Cookies, 13158
Uptown Bakers, 13221
Vanns Spices LTD, 13294
Velatis, 13318
Victor Ostrowski & Son, 13383
W.T. Ruark & Company, 13507
Waverly Crabs, 13596
Wilkins Rogers Inc, 13803
Wockenfuss Candy Co, 13893
Woodfield Fish & Oyster Company, 13917
Zest Tea LLC, 14059

Massachusetts

88 Acres, 29
A Gift Basket by Carmela, 36
Acushnet Fish Corporation, 159
Agri-Mark Inc, 211
Alfredo Aiello Italian Food, 303
Alive and Radiant, 315
Alpine Butcher, 377
Alpine Pure USA, 381
American Food Products Inc, 456
American Nut & Chocolate Co, 474
Amstell Holding, 516
Angy's Food Products Inc, 570
Aralia Olive Oils, 626
Armeno Coffee Roasters LTD, 683
Ashley Food Co Inc, 730
Atlantic Sea Pride, 775
Atlantic Seacove Inc, 776
B&M Fisheries, 876
Babci's Specialty Foods, 908
Bacci Chocolate Design, 915

Bake N Joy Foods, 951
Bari & Gail, 1035
Barrington Coffee Roasting, 1054
Barrows Tea Company, 1055
Baskin-Robbins LLC, 1075
Bay Shore Chowders & Bisques, 1101
Bay State Milling Co., 1102
Bear Meadow Farm, 1129
Bella Ravioli, 1189
Berkshire Bark Inc, 1236
Berkshire Brewing Co Inc, 1237
Berkshire Mountain Bakery, 1239
Bernadette Baking Company, 1241
Biena Foods, 1317
Bittersweet Herb Farm, 1412
Blessed Herbs, 1448
Bliss Brothers Dairy, Inc., 1451
Bloomsberry LLC, 1461
Blossom Water, LLC, 1463
Blount Fine Foods, 1464
Blue Gold Mussels, 1474
Blue Harvest Foods, 1478
Blue Hills Spring Water Company, 1480
BlueWater Seafoods, 1502
BN Soda, 901
Bogland, 1540
Bonnie's Jams, 1564
Boston America Corporation, 1591
Boston Beer Co Inc., 1592
Boston Chowda, 1593
Boston Coffee Cake, 1594
Boston Fruit Slice & Confectionery Corporation, 1596
Boston Seafarms, 1597
Boston's Best Coffee Roasters, 1601
Bountiful Pantry, 1625
Boyajian LLC, 1635
Bradshaw's Food Products, 1650
Brighams, 1711
Brookfield Farm, 1742
Bruegger's Bagels, 1798
Budi Products LLC, 1830
Buzzards Bay Trading Company, 1892
C'est Gourmet, 1930
Cambridge Brands Inc, 2102
Cambridge Packing Company, 2104
Canadian Fish Exporters, 2122
Canarino, 2127
Cape Ann Seafood, 2154
Cape Cod Coffee Roasters, 2155
Cape Cod Potato Chips, 2156
Cape Cod Provisions, 2157
Cape Cod Specialty Foods, 2158
Cape Cod Sweets, LLC, 2159
Capone Foods, 2166
Capt Joe & Sons Inc, 2181
Carando Gourmet Frozen Foods, 2193
Caravan Company, 2195
Carolyn's Gourmet, 2251
Castle Hill Lobster, 2302
Catania Hospitality Group, 2309
Catania Oils, 2310
Cathay Foods Corporation, 2317
Cedar's Mediterranean Foods, 2354
Central Bakery, 2373
Channel Fish Processing, 2419
Channel Fish Processing Co Inc, 2418
Chappaqua Crunch, 2422
Charles H Baldwin & Sons, 2430
Cherrybrook Kitchen, 2523
Chex Finer Foods Inc, 2539
Chicama Vineyards, 2551
Chicopee Provision Co Inc, 2559
Chinese Spaghetti Factory, 2573
Chmura's Bakery, 2584
Chris' Farm Stand, 2643
Christie's, 2647
Cinnamon Bakery, 2683
Cisco Brewers, 2691
Clear-Vu Industries, 2741
Coastal Classics, 2798
Coastal Goods, 2800
Cold Brew EvyTea, 2867
Colony Foods, 2889
Concord Foods, LLC, 2943
Coutts Specialty Foods Inc, 3092
Cream Crock Distributors, 3128
Creative Seasonings, 3138
Crescent Ridge Dairy, 3153
Crocetti's Oakdale Packing Co, 3172
Crowley Beverage Corporation, 3187
Curaleaf, 3256

Cutone Specialty Foods, 3277
Czepiel Millers Dairy, 3290
Dahlicious, 3326
Dancing Deer Baking Company, 3369
Deborah's Kitchen Inc., 3450
Decas Cranberry Sales Inc, 3456
Delftree Corp, 3493
Dimitria Delights Baking Co, 3603
Dole & Bailey Inc, 3653
Dom's Sausage Co Inc, 3660
Doves and Figs LLC, 3715
Downeast Cider House, 3721
Dunkin' Brands Inc., 3803
Durkee-Mower, 3810
Dutch Kitchen Bake Shop & Deli, 3817
Duxbury Mussel & Seafood Corporation, 3824
Eat Your Coffee, 3904
Edelweiss Patisserie, 3938
Effies Homemade, 3963
Eldorado Seafood Inc, 3998
Equal Exchange Inc, 4096, 4097
Eurobubblies, 4148
Evy Tea, 4179
F B Washburn Candy Corp, 4198
F W Bryce Inc, 4200
Fairfield Farm Kitchens, 4222
Falafel Republic, 4231
Fancypants Bakery, 4248
Fantini Baking Co Inc, 4256
Farmwise LLC, 4295
Fastachi, 4301
Feeding the Turkeys, Inc., 4322
Fleet Fisheries Inc, 4497
Fliinko, 4505
FNI Group LLC, 4208
Fortune Seas, 4613
Garelick Farms, 4903
Gaspar's Linguica Co Inc, 4918
GH Bent Company, 4832
Gifford's Ice Cream & Candy Co, 5005
Gillians Foods, 5011
Gilly's Hot Vanilla, 5013
Ginseng Up Corp, 5027
Global Organics, 5066
Gold Medal Bakery Inc, 5103
Golden Cannoli, 5116
Good Food Made Simple, 5158
Good Harbor Fillet Company, 5162
Good Wives, 5174
Gorton's Inc., 5194
Gould's Maple Sugarhouse, 5197
Grace Tea Co, 5228
Great Hill Dairy Inc, 5313
Green Mountain Chocolate Inc, 5354
Greenhills Irish Bakery, 5374
Greg's Lobster Company, 5381
Grillo's Pickles, 5389
Handy Pax, 5548
Hans Kissle Co, 5557
Happy Goat, 5568
Harbar LLC, 5573
Harbor Sweets, 5578
Harmony Bay Coffee, 5596
Harpoon Brewery, 5606
Harvest Direct, 5629
Health from the Sun, 5686
Healthy Life Brands LLC, 5697
Hebert Candies, 5724
Heluva Good Cheese, 5757
Herrell's Ice Cream, 5816
HimalaSalt, 5881
Himalayan Chef, 5882
Hingham Shellfish, 5885
Hoff's Bakery, 5900
Home Market Food Inc, 5928
Home Market Foods Inc., 5929
Homer's Wharf Seafood Company, 5941
Honey Dew Donuts, 5958
Hook Line and Savor, 5985
Hot Mama's Foods, 6016
Howard Foods Inc, 6034
HP Hood LLC, 5486
Ian's Natural Food, 6125
Immaculate Baking Company, 6154
Incredible Foods, 6176
Indigo Coffee Roasters, 6197
Inn Maid Food, 6222
International Brownie, 6248
Ipswich Ale Brewery, 6283
Ipswich Maritime Product Company, 6284
Ipswich Shellfish Co Inc, 6285

J Moniz Co Inc, 6360
J Turner Seafood, 6366
Ja-Ca Seafood Products, 6413
Jasper Wyman & Son, 6464
Java Sun Coffee Roasters, 6467
Jedwards International Inc, 6480
John B. Wright Fish Company, 6549
Johnson's Food Products, 6570
Jonathan's Sprouts, 6585
Joseph's Gourmet Pasta, 6605
Jungbunzlauer Inc, 6634
Kayem Foods, 6744
Ken's Foods Inc, 6779
Kettle Cuisine, 6815
Keurig, Inc, 6819
Klara's Gourmet Cookies, 6906
Kyler's Catch Seafood Market, 7015
Lark Fine Foods, 7220
Laronga Bakery, 7222
Laurel Hill Foods, 7248
Leavitt Corp., The, 7288
Lemate Of New England Inc, 7334
Lenox-Martell Inc, 7352
Leo's Bakery, 7357
Levant Mediterranean Snack Foods LLC, 7398
Lightlife, 7427
Lisbon Sausage Co Inc, 7459
Lisbon Seafood Co, 7460
Longmeadow Building Dept, 7532
Lora Brody Products Inc, 7540
Lyndell's Bakery, 7662
M & M Label Co, 7674
M & S Tomato Repacking Co Inc, 7675
M S Walker Inc, 7678
Maloney Seafood Corporation, 7807
Mama Rosie's Ravioli, 7819
Mange, 7840
Maria and Ricardo's, 7908
Mariner Seafood LLC, 7930
McCrea's Candies, 8064
Mccreas Candies, 8089
Mellos North End Mfr, 8148
Melville Candy Corp, 8150
Menemsha Fish Market, 8156
Merrimack Valley Apiaries, 8182
Michael's Provision Co, 8232
Millie's Pierogi, 8316
Mini Pops Inc, 8350
Minus the Moo, 8364
Mixerz All Natural Cocktail Mixers, 8409
Mom's Food Company, 8464
Monsoon Kitchens, 8484
Montione's Biscotti & Baked Goods, 8512
Mortillaro Lobster Company, 8566
Motto, 8587
Multigrains Bread Co, 8678
Murdock Farm Dairy, 8687
My Grandma's Coffee Cake, 8708
Myron's Fine Foods, Inc., 8715
Nantucket Pasta Company, Inc., 8757
Nantucket Tea Traders, 8758
Nantucket Vineyard, 8759
Nashoba Valley Winery, 8773
Nasoya Foods, 8775
National Fish & Seafood Inc, 8787
National Fish & Seafood Inc, 8786
Natural Feast Corporation, 8828
Nature's Godfather, 8878
Near East Food Products, 8913
Necco, 8917
New England Cranberry, 8969
New England Muffin Co Inc, 8970
New England Natural Bakers, 8971
New England Tea & Coffee Co, 8972
New Salem Tea-Bread Company, 8998
Nordic Group Inc, 9106
Northampton Brewing Company, 9141
Northern Ocean Marine, 9156
Northern Wind Inc, 9165
Nothing But The Fruit, 9190
Ocean Cliff Corp, 9345
Ocean Crest Seafoods, 9346
Ocean Spray International, 9355
OCG Cacao, 9298
OK International Group, 9301
Old Neighborhood, 9422
Olde Tyme Food Corporation, 9438
Olivio Premium Products, 9457
One Source, 9490
Orleans Packing Co, 9569
Our Best Foods, 9600

P.J. Markos Seafood Company, 9644
Panorama Foods Inc., 9746
Paper City Brewery, 9754
Paradise Fruits NA, 9762
Pastene Co LTD, 9819
Paul Stevens Lobster, 9845
Peace Mountain Natural Beverages, 9858
Peggy Lawton Kitchens, 9898
Pekarski Sausage, 9901
Philip R's Frozen Desserts, 10007
Phillip's Candy House, 10009
Piantedosi Baking Co Inc, 10028
Pioneer Dairy, 10073
Pioneer Nutritional Formula, 10079
Pittsfield Rye Bakery, 10092
Planet Oat, 10102
Plantation Products Inc, 10106
Plenus Group Inc, 10118
Plymouth Colony Winery, 10132
Plymouth Lollipop Company, 10133
Pokanoket Ostrich Farm, 10149
Polar Beverages Inc., 10151
Pony Boy Ice Cream, 10171
Powell & Mahoney Ltd., 10222
Praim Co, 10229
Prifti Candy Company, 10282
Prova, 10354
Pure7 Chocolate, 10385
Q's Nuts, 10411
Quinzani Bakery, 10469
R M Lawton Cranberries Inc, 10483
Rachael's Smoked Fish, 10526
Radlo Foods, 10529
Rainbow Seafoods, 10540
Raw Bite, 10576
Regal Crown Foods Inc, 10638
Regco, 10642
Regenie's Crunchy Pi, 10643
Richard's Gourmet Coffee, 10721
Richardson's Ice Cream, 10727
Richelieu Foods Inc, 10728
Rockport Lobster Co, 10817
Root Cellar Preserves, 10870
Royal Atlantic Seafood, 10922
Royal Harvest Foods Inc, 10933
S S Lobster LTD, 11017
Salem Oil & Grease Company, 11101
Salem Old Fashioned Candies, 11102
Sand Springs, 11164
Saratoga Salad Dressing, 11222
Sardinha's Sausage, 11224
Sauces N' Love, 11239
Sea Best Corporation, 11338
Sea Gold Seafood Products Inc, 11343
Sea View Fillet Company, 11355
Seafood Services, 11376
Seaway Company, 11397
Shekou Chemicals, 11538
Shelburne Falls Coffee Roaster, 11539
Shire City Herbals, 11563
Shonna's Gourmet Goodies, 11569
Siegel Egg Co, 11586
Silver Sweet Candies, 11630
Simpson Spring Co, 11660
SJR Foods, 11043
Smoke & Fire Natural Food, 11735
Snow's Ice Cream Co Inc, 11763
Something Natural LLC, 11797
South County Creamery, 11830
Specialty Products, 11907
Spence & Company, 11912
Spindrift Beverage, 11936
Spring Hill Pure Water, 11963
St. Ours & Company, 12011
Stacy's Pita Chip Co, 12015
Stark Candy Company, 12044
State Garden Inc., 12056
Stavis Seafoods, 12062
Stellar Pasta Company, 12077
Steve Connolly Seafood Co Inc, 12091
Steve's Doughnut Shop, 12094
Stirrings, 12123
Stop & Shop Manufacturing, 12146
Strawbury Hill Grand Delights, 12163
Sudbury Soups and Salads, 12189
Sunshine International Foods, 12309
Super Snooty Sea Food Corporation, 12322
Superior Baking Co, 12329
Superior Cake Products, 12331
Superior Nut Company, 12338
Sustainable Sourcing, 12364
Suzhou-Chem Inc, 12374

Table Talk Pies Inc, 12488
Taza Chocolate, 12579
Tea Forte, 12584
Tempest Fisheries LTD, 12611
The Pillsbury Company, 12717
Tichon Sea Food Corp, 12796
Toucan Chocolates, 12902
Trappistine Quality Candy, 12932
Tri-Sum Potato Chip Company, 12961
Tribe Mediterranean, 12965
Trio's Original Italian Pasta Co., 12976
Tripoli Bakery Inc, 12986
Tru Chocolate, 13020
Truth Bar LLC, 13041
Twenty-First Century Foods, 13088
Two Friends Chocolates, 13101
ULDO USA, 13117
United Citrus, 13184
UnReal Brands, 13151
Venus Wafers Inc, 13330
Verde Farms, LLC, 13335
Veronica's Treats, 13366
Via Della Chiesa Vineyards, 13372
Victoria Gourmet Inc, 13389
Viking Seafoods Inc, 13407
Vision Seafood Partners, 13451
Vitasoy USA, 13473
Vivra Chocolate, 13482
Wachusett Brewing Co, 13522
Wachusett Potato Chip Co Inc, 13523
Waltham Beef Company, 13557
Warner-Lambert Confections, 13571
Waterfield Farms, 13586
Weetabix Food Co., 13621
Welch Foods Inc, 13634
Welch Foods Inc, 13635
Welch's Global Ingredients Group, 13636
Westfield Farm, 13687
Westport Rivers Vineyard, 13693
Widoffs Modern Bakery, 13767
Williams Candy Company, 13818
Willow Tree Poultry Farm Inc, 13831
Winfrey Fudge & Candy, 13853
Wing It Inc, 13854
Wing-Time, 13859
Wohrles Foods, 13896
Yankee Specialty Foods, 13992
Ye Olde Pepper Co, 13997
Yeomen Seafoods Inc, 13999

Michigan

Abbott's Meat Inc, 116
Absopure Water Company, 129
Achatz Handmade Pie Co, 148
Adkin & Son Associated Food Products, 176
Al Dente Pasta Co, 247
AM Todd Co, 91
American Soy Products Inc, 482
American Spoon Foods Inc, 485
Apple Valley Market, 611
Applewood Orchards Inc, 616
April Hill Inc, 619
Arbor Springs Water Co, 630
Arbre Farms Inc, 632
Aseltine Cider Company, 724
Atwater Block Brewing Company, 785
Avalon International Breads, 829
Awrey Bakeries, 847
Behm Blueberry Farms, 1171
Bell's Brewery Inc, 1184
Belleharvest Sales Inc, 1196
Ben B. Schwartz & Sons, 1213
Bessinger Pickle Co, 1261
Best Express Foods Inc, 1266
Better Made Snack Foods, 1286
Beverage America, 1293
Big Bucks Brewery & Steakhouse, 1326
Big Dipper Dough Co., 1329
Blueberry Store, 1503
Boskydel Vineyard, 1589
Bradford Co, 1646
Burnette Foods, 1866
Butterball Farms, 1882
C F Burger Creamery Co, 1915
C Roy & Sons Processing, 1923
Cafe Moak, 1998
Carson City Pickle Company, 2264
Cateraid Inc, 2314
Cattleman Meat & Produce, 2326
Cedar Lake Foods, 2350

Geographic Index / Minnesota

Chartreuse Organic Tea, 2447
Chateau Grand Traverse Winery, 2458
Cheeze Kurls, 2487
Chef Shells Catering & Roadside Cafe, 2495
Chef Zachary's Gourmet Blended Spices, 2499
Chef's Pride Gifts LLC, 2501
Chelsea Milling Co., 2508
Cherry Central Cooperative, Inc., 2518
Cherry Hut, 2520
City Farm/Rocky Peanut Company, 2707
Coastlog Industries, 2805
Coffee Barrel, 2833
Coffee Beanery LTD, 2838
Coffee Express Roasting Co, 2844
Cole's Quality Foods, 2873
Collaborative Advantage Marketing, 2879
Coloma Frozen Foods Inc, 2883
Cooper Street Cookies, 3001
Cooperative Elevator Co, 3003
Country Fresh, 3073
Country Home Creations Inc, 3079
Crane's Pie Pantry Restaurant, 3116
Creme Curls, 3143
Dairy Fresh Foods Inc, 3336
Dawn Food Products, Inc, 3412
Dearborn Sausage Co Inc, 3446
Detroit Chili Co, 3547
Dorothy Dawson Food Products, 3696
Drier's Meats, 3763
Dutch Girl Donut Co, 3814
E&H Packing Company, 3839
Eastside Deli Supply, 3896
Eden Foods Inc, 3940
Eden Organic Pasta Company, 3941
Elena's, 4005
Ethel's Baking Co., 4134
Everfresh Beverages, 4163
Farmers Cooperative Grain Co, 4280
Faygo Beverages Inc, 4314
Fenn Valley Vineyards, 4330, 4331
Ferris Organic Farms, 4350
Flamm Pickle & Packing, 4469
Flatout Inc, 4477
Food City Pickle Company, 4554
Food For Thought Inc, 4559
Forbes Co, 4585
Four Percent Company, 4626
Freeland Bean & Grain Co, 4686
Freestone Pickle Co, 4689
Fresh Roasted Almond Company, 4721
Fruit Acres Farm Market and U-Pick, 4760
Fruit Belt Canning Inc, 4761
Fry Krisp Food Products, 4777
Fudge Farms, 4779
Functional Foods, 4795
Garden Fresh Gourmet, 4892
Germack Pistachio Co, 4985
Gielow Pickles Inc, 5003
Giovanni's Appetizing Food Co, 5030
GKI Foods, 4834
GLCC Co, 4835
Gluten Free Sensations, 5082
Golden Brown Bakery Inc, 5115
Good Harbor Vineyards & Winery, 5163
Good Stuff Cacao, 5173
Graceland Fruit Inc, 5229
Graminex, 5251
Gray & Company, 5288
Great Lakes Foods, 5317
Great Lakes Packing Co, 5318
Great Lakes Tea & Spice, 5319
Great Lakes Wine & Spirits, 5320
Greenfield Noodle & Spec Co, 5372
Groeb Farms, 5396
Happy Hive, 5570
Hausbeck Pickle Co, 5645
Home Bakery, 5925
Home Style Foods Inc, 5933
Honee Bear Canning, 5951
House of Flavors Inc, 6023
Hudsonville Ice Cream, 6057
Inbalance Health, 6173
Independent Dairy Inc, 6180
International Noodle Co, 6269
Inverness Dairy, 6281
J Rettenmaier USA LP, 6365
J.N. Bech, 6381
Jack Brown Produce, 6415
JaynRoss Creations LLC, 6474
Jessica's Natural Foods, 6507
Jogue, 6544

Jonny Almond Nut Co, 6591
Kalamazoo Creamery, 6690
Kalsec, 6695
Kay Foods Co, 6741
Keebler Company, 6747
Kellogg Co., 6766
Kent Quality Foods Inc, 6793
King Brewing Company, 6859
King Milling Co Inc, 6869
Knappen Milling Co, 6917
Koegel Meats Inc, 6934
Koeze Company, 6935
Kowalski Sausage Co, 6973
Krupka's Blueberries, 6994
Kubisch Sausage Mfg Co, 6997
L Mawby Vineyards, 7029
Laska Stuff, 7235
Leaf Jerky, 7281
Leelanau Cellars, 7303
Leelanau Fruit Co, 7304
Lemon Creek Winery, 7338
Leonard Fountain Specialties, 7363
Lesley Elizabeth Inc, 7390
LorAnn Oils, 7539
Lotte USA Inc, 7560
Lubbers Family Farm, 7617
Ludwick's Frozen Donuts, 7639
MacKinlay Teas, 7723
Magnum Custom Roastery, 7777
Maple Acres Inc, 7863
Mason County Fruit Packers Cooperative, 7991
McClure's Pickles LLC, 8058
Meelunie America, 8128
Meijer Inc, 8137
Metropolitan Baking Co, 8199
Michaelene's Gourmet Granola, 8233
Michigan Celery Cooperative, 8245
Michigan Dairy LLC, 8246
Michigan Desserts, 8247
Michigan Farm Cheese Dairy, 8248
Michigan Freeze Pack, 8249
Michigan Milk Producers Assn, 8250
Michigan Sugar Company, 8251
Midas Foods Intl, 8261
Midwest Blueberry Farms, 8265
Miljoco Corp, 8294
Mindo Chocolate Makers, 8343
Mizkan Americas Inc, 8422
Mrs. Dog's Products, 8636
Mucci Food Products LTD, 8664
Mucky Duck Mustard Company, 8666
National Flavors, 8788
Naturally Nutty, 8856
Nature's Legacy Inc., 8886
Nature's Select Inc, 8893
New Era Canning Company, 8973
New Holland Brewing Co, 8981
Newby Teas, 9013
North Bay Produce Inc, 9126
Northern Falls, 9148
Northville Winery & Brewing Co, 9171
Nutra Food Ingredients, LLC, 9233
Ocena Wineary & Vineyards, 9364
Old Europe Cheese Inc, 9410
Old Orchard Brands, LLC, 9423
Oliver Packaging & Equipment Co., 9451
Paramount Coffee, 9772
Parmenter's Northville Cider Mill, 9791
Parthenon Food Products, 9795
Paw Paw Grape Juice Company, 9853
Penn Street Bakery, 9920
Perrigo Nutritionals LLC, 9967
Peterson & Sons Winery, 9984
Peterson Farms Inc, 9985
Pierino Frozen Foods, 10047
Pioneer Snacks, 10081
Pita Products, 10089
Pizza Products, 10094
Pontiac Coffee Break, 10169
Premier Malt Products Inc, 10247
Produce Buyers Company, 10322
Purity Foods Inc, 10396
Quality Dairy Co, 10431
Quigley Industries Inc, 10461
Rainbow Valley Frozen Yogurt, 10541
Red Pelican Food Products, 10614
Request Foods Inc, 10679
Rib Rack, 10700
Richards Natural Foods, 10723
Robert & James Brands, 10788
Rocky Top Farms, 10828

Ross Fine Candies, 10901
Rothbury Farms, 10907
Ryke's Bakery, 11005
Saad Wholesale Meats, 11058
Safie Specialty Foods, 11076
Sanders Candy Inc, 11167
Sanders Meat Packing Inc, 11168
Savory Foods, 11257
Schuil Coffee Co, 11310
Seven Lakes Vineyard & Winery, 11474
Shafer Lake Fruit Inc, 11493
Sharon Mill Winery, 11520
Shoreline Fruit, 11574
Short's Brewing Co, 11575
Sill Farm Market, 11609
Silver Spring Foods, 11625
Singer Extract Laboratory, 11664
Smeltzer Orchard Co, 11718
Smith Meat Packing, 11727
Spaulding & Assoc, 11892
Spiech Farms Fruit & Floral, 11932
St Julian Winery, 11998
St Laurent Brothers, 11999
Star of the West Milling Co., 12041
Stroh Brewery, 12171
Stroh's Beer, 12172
Tabor Hill Winery & Restaurant, 12489
The Dow Chemical Company, 12682
Tholstrup Cheese, 12759
Topor's Pickle & Food Svc Inc, 12888
Triple D Orchards Inc, 12977
Truan's Candies, 13026
True Blue Farms, 13031
Turri's Italian Foods, 13072
UBC Food Distributors, 13114
Uncle Ray's Potato Chips, 13159
Universal Formulas, 13207
Vestergaard Farms, 13370
Vollwerth & Baroni Companies, 13489
Warner Vineyards, 13570
West Thomas Partners, LLC, 13669
Weyand's Fishery, 13699
Wiards Orchards Inc, 13754
Williams-R J, 13822, 13823
Winter Sausage Manufacturing Company, 13871
Worthington Foods, 13952
Wysong Corp, 13967
Zoup! Fresh Soup Co LLC, 14073

Minnesota

Abdallah Candies & Gifts, 119
Acatris USA, 137
Advanced Ingredients, Inc., 190
Agricore United, 215
Alakef Coffee Roasters Inc, 257
Alexis Bailly Vineyard, 296
All American Foods Inc, 317
Amaranth Resources, 416
American Crystal Sugar Co., 449
American Importing Co., 462
American Specialty Confections, 483
Amport Foods, 511
Anderson Custom Processing, 544
Angie's Artisan Treats LLC, 567
Annie's Frozen Yogurt, 590
Asian Foods Inc, 734
Associated Milk Producers Inc., 740
August Schell Brewing Co, 796
Aveka Inc, 835
Award Baking Intl, 846
Baldinger Baking Co, 987
Barbara's Bakery, 1020
Barrel O' Fun Snack Foods, 1052
Bellisio Foods, 1200
Bernatello's Foods, 1248
Bevsource, 1298
Big Watt Coffee, 1349
BioAmber, 1371
Bioenergy Life Science, 1376
Biothera, 1381
Bliss Gourmet Foods, 1452
Bobby D'S, 1521
Bongard's Creameries, 1557
Border Foods, 1577
Braham Food Locker Service, 1653
Branding Iron Meats, 1659
Brown's Ice Cream Co, 1783
Browns' Ice Cream Company, 1790
Bt. McElrath Chocolatier, 1809
Buffalo Wild Wings, 1840

C&T Refinery, 1929
Canadian Harvest-U.S.A., 2123
Canelake's Candy, 2137
Captain Ken's Foods Inc, 2186
Cargill Inc., 2204
Cargill Kitchen Solutions Inc., 2205
Caribou Coffee Co Inc, 2211
Caves Of Faribault/SwissValley, 2334
CB Beverage Corporation, 1941
Chip Steak & Provision Co, 2577
Chisholm Bakery, 2582
Christmas Point Wild Rice Co, 2651
CHS Inc., 1948
Clara Foods, 2714
Coffee Bean & Tea Leaf, 2835
Coffee Grounds, 2846
Cold Spring Bakery Inc, 2870
Country Choice Organic, 3066
Crookston Bean, 3182
Crystal Farms Dairy Company, 3211
Curly's Foods Inc, 3258
Dalian Xinfeng International Industry & Trade Co., 3360
Davisco Foods International, 3410
Daybreak Foods Inc, 3418
Deerwood Rice & Grain Procng, 3473
Dennison Meat Locker, 3524
Denny's 5th Avenue Bakery, 3525
Domata Living Flour, 3663
Dr. In The Kitchen, 3731
E A Sween Co, 3836
Edwards Baking Company, 3959
Ellsworth Locker, 4030
Equal Exchange Inc, 4099
European Roasterie, 4154
Everfresh Food Corporation, 4164
Fairmont Foods Of Minnesota, 4225
Fannie May Fine Chocolate, 4250
Faribault Foods, Inc., 4267
Farmers Produce, 4283
First District Association, 4424
Five Star Food Base Company, 4458
Flackers, 4465
Florence Pasta & Cheese, 4512
Fountain Shakes/MS Foods, 4622
French Meadow Bakery & Cafe, 4702
Funkychunky Inc., 4800
G.E.F. Gourmet Foods Inc, 4821
Gartner Studios Inc, 4913
General Mills, 4947
Glacial Ridge Foods, 5040
Golden Walnut Specialty Foods, 5140
GoodMark Foods, 5180
Grain Belt, 5241
Grain Millers Inc, 5243
Grand Metropolitan, 5253
Grandpa Ittel's Meats Inc, 5267
Gray Duck, 5289
Great Northern Baking Company, 5322
Gregory's Foods, Inc., 5382
Grey Owl Foods, 5385
Gurley's Foods, 5448
Happy's Potato Chip Co, 5572
Hastings Co-Op Creamery-Dairy, 5640
Hawkins Inc, 5665
Heart Foods Company, 5701
Herman's Bakery, 5807
Highland Family Farms, 5853
Homestead Mills, 5946
Hoopeston Foods Inc, 5987
Hope Creamery, 5990
Hormel Foods Corp., 6000
In Harvest Inc, 6171
Indian Foods Company, Inc., 6185
Intermountain Canola Cargill, 6245
Iris Brands, 6288
Italian Bakery of Virginia, 6317
Jager Foods, 6433
Jennie-O Turkey Store, 6488
Jenny's Country Kitchen, 6490
Jerabek's New Bohemian Coffee House, 6496
Joia All Natural Soda, 6579
JonnyPops, 6592
Jordahl Meats, 6594
Jordan's Meats & Deli, 6595
Just Truffles, 6650
K'ul Chocolate, 6660
K-Mama Sauce, 6662
Kakookies, 6688
Karlsburger Foods Inc, 6714
Kateri Foods, 6727

Geographic Index / Mississippi

Kay's Naturals, Inc., 6742
KAYS Processing LLC, 6667
Kemps LLC, 6778
Kenny's Candy & Confections, 6789
Ketters Meat Market & Locker Plant, 6812
Klein Foods, Inc, 6907
Knight Seed Company, 6919
Konetzko's Meat Market, 6955
KOZY Shack Enterprises Inc, 6676
Kramarczuk's Sausage Co, 6978
Krenik's Meat Processing, 6984
La Victoria Foods, 7115
Lakeside Foods Inc., 7160
Lamex Foods Inc., 7182
Land O'Lakes Inc, 7198
Le Sueur Cheese Co, 7275
Leech Lake Wild Rice, 7301, 7302
Lehmann Farms, 7321
Leo G. Fraboni Sausage Company, 7356
Living Farms, 7485
Log House Foods, 7510
Loghouse Foods, 7511
Lorissa's Kitchen, 7544
Maddy & Maize, 7741
Madison Foods, 7750
Make It Simple, 7799
Manitoba Harvest Hemp, 7850
Manitok Food & Gifts, 7851
Maple Island, 7870
Meyer Brothers Dairy, 8211
Michael Foods, Inc., 8225
Midwest Nut Co, 8269
Milk Specialties Global, 8295
Mille Lacs Wild Rice Corp, 8305
Minnesota Dehydrated Veg Inc, 8355
Minnesota Hemp Farms, 8356
Minnestalgia Foods LLC, 8357, 8358
Morey's Seafood Intl LLC, 8541
Mountain High Yogurt, 8597
Natural Way Mills Inc, 8851
Nectar Island, 8918
Nelson Ice Cream, 8933
New Horizon Farms, 8985
Nikola's Foods, 9056
Nomi Snacks, 9087
North Aire Market, Inc., 9114
Northern Flair Foods, 9151
Northern Vineyards Winery, 9163
Northwestern Foods, 9184
Nu-Tek Food Science, 9203
Nutricepts, 9252
Old Dutch Foods LTD, 9408
Old Home Foods Inc, 9415
Olsen Fish Co, 9459
Olson Locker, 9461
Pan-O-Gold Baking Co., 9736
Paragon Fruits, 9769
Parker Farm, 9781
Parkers Farm, 9786
Particle Control, 9796
Pearson Candy Co, 9877
Pekarna Meat Market, 9900
Pete & Joy's Bakery, 9975
Phillips Beverage Company, 10010
Pierz Cooperative Association, 10050
Pillsbury, 10059
Plainview Milk Products, 10099
Polypro International Inc, 10158
Positively 3rd St Bakery, 10212
Post Consumer Brands, 10213
Protient, 10351
Quali Tech Inc, 10422
Quality Ingredients, 10436
R Four Meats, 10479
R.D. Offutt Farms, 10492
Rahr Malting Co, 10535
Ramsen Inc, 10550
Randy's Frozen Meats, 10564
Red Baron, 10601
River Hills Harvest, 10768
Robert's Bakery, 10796
Rochester Cheese, 10809
Rosemark Bakery, 10892
Rosen's Diversified Inc., 10893
Rygmyr Foods, 11004
S T Specialty Foods Inc, 11019
S&P Marketing, Inc., 11024
Salad Girl Inc, 11095
Scenic Valley Winery, 11271
Schaefers Market, 11273, 11274
Schumacher Wholesale Meats, 11312
Schwan's Company, 11316
Schwan's Food Service Inc, 11317
Secret Garden, 11402
Seven Sundays, LLC, 11476
SIGCO Sun Products, 11041
Slathars Smokehouse, 11701
Small Planet Foods, 11711
Sno-Pac Foods Inc, 11758
Southern Minnesota Beet Sugar Cooperative, 11857
SoyLife Division, 11879
Splendid Spreads, 11941
St. Croix Beer Company, 12004
Stickney Hill Dairy Inc, 12116
Summit Brewing Company, 12225
Sun-Rise, 12258
Sunny Fresh Foods, 12283
Sunrich LLC, 12294
Super Mom's LLC, 12319
Swany White Flour Mills LTD, 12379
Sweet Harvest Foods, 12401
Taiyo International Inc., 12498
Terra Ingredients, 12622
Terra Ingredients LLC, 12623
Terra's, 12626
The Amazing Chickpea, 12667
Thompson's Fine Foods, 12772
Thornton Foods Company, 12776
Tony Downs Foods, 12870
Tony's Pizza, 12874
Toom Dips, 12879
Totino's, 12901
Turkey Store, 13066
Twin City Bagels, 13090
Uas Laboratories, 13130
US Distilled Products Co, 13120
Vegetarian Traveler, 13313
Vogel Popcorn, 13485
Way Better Snacks, 13600
Waymouth Farms Inc, 13603
Wessanan, 13658
WholeMe, 13749
Widman's Candy Shop, 13764
Wildly Organic, 13796
Willmar Cookie & Nut Company, 13827
Windmill Candies, 13843
World's Best Donuts, 13947
Wuollet Bakery, 13962
Zuccaro Produce, 14074

Mississippi

Acharice Specialties, 147
Almarla Vineyards & Winery, 353
America's Catch, 436
Attala Development Corporation, 784
Biloxi Freezing Processing Inc., 1357
Blendco Inc, 1444
Bryant's Meat Inc., 1808
C F Gollott & Son Seafood, 1916
Cal-Maine Foods Inc., 2031
Central Snacks, 2382
Choctaw Maid Farms, 2627
Consolidated Catfish Co LLC, 2961
Corsair Pepper Sauce, 3041
DeBeukelaer Cookie Co, 3433
DeBeukelaer Corp, 3434
Del's Seaway Shrimp & Oyster Company, 3484
Delta Pride Catfish, 3516
Dutch Ann Foods Company, 3811
Enslin & Son Packing Company, 4078
Flathau's Fine Foods, 4476
Fournier R & Sons Seafood, 4631
Golden Gulf Coast Packing Co, 5124
Gulf Central Seafood, 5430
Gulf Pride Enterprises, 5438
Gulf States Canners Inc, 5440
Happy Acres Packing Company, 5563
Indianola Pecan House Inc, 6195
Jubilations, 6621
Kershenstine Beef Jerky, 6809
Longleaf Plantation, 7531
Louisiana Seafood Exchange, 7587
Mississippi Cheese Straw, 8391
Natchez Pecan Shelling Company, 8778
Ocean Springs Seafood, 9356
Old South Winery, 9426
Primos Northgate, 10304
Rices Potato Chips, 10711
Sanderson Farms, 11169
Seymour & Sons Seafoods Inc, 11486
Shasta Beverages Inc, 11524
Shemper Seafood Co, 11543
Smith's Bakery, 11731
Taste of Gourmet, 12546
The Shed Saucery, 12729
Ubons Sauce LLC, 13131
Winona Packing Company, 13867

Missouri

A Taste of the Kingdom, 43
AB InBev, 71
Adam Puchta Winery, 162
Aileen Quirk & Sons Inc, 233
Alewel's Country Meats, 290
American Botanicals, 442
American Culinary Garden, 450
American Dehydrated Foods, Inc., 451
American Italian Pasta Company, 465
American Micronutrients, 471
Americhicken, 493
Andre's Confiserie Suisse, 552
Andy's Seasoning, 560
Anheuser-Busch, 571
Arcobasso Foods Inc, 642
Askinosie Chocolate, 735
Augusta Winery, 797
Aurora Frozen Foods Division, 811
Backer's Potato Chip Company, 921
BBQ Bunch, 887
Bias Vineyards & Winery, 1307
Bissinger's Handcrafted Chocolatier, 1404
Bissinger's Handcrafted Chocolatier, 1405
Blumenhof Vineyards-Winery, 1511
Boulevard Brewing, 1621
Boyle Meat Company, 1641
Bristle Ridge Vineyards, 1719
Bunge, 1846
Bunge North America Inc., 1849
Burgers' Smokehouse, 1858
Byrd's Pecans, 1899
Castor River Farms, 2304
Centennial Farms, 2366
Center Locker Svc, 2369
Central Dairy, 2378
Champs Chicken, 2449
Chase & Poe Candy Co, 2449
Chauvin Coffee Corporation, 2475
Chocolate Chocolate Chocolate, 2600
Chunco Foods Inc, 2664
Circle B Ranch, 2685
Cloud's Meat Processing, 2774
Corbion, 3016
D F Ingredients Inc, 3295
Dairiconcepts, 3333
Dairy House, 3338
Date Lady Inc., 3392
Deerland Probiotics & Enzymes, 3472
Deko International Company, 3476
Diggs Packing Company, 3596
DiGregorio Food Products, 3567
East Wind Inc, 3887
Edmond's Chile Co, 3949
Edwards Mill, 3960
El Rey Cooked Meats, 3989
Fancy Farms Popcorn, 4245
Fantasia, 4251
Fayes Bakery Products, 4313
Fazio's Bakery, 4316
Ferrigno Vineyards & Wine, 4349
Ficon, 4360
Fine Foods Intl, 4395
Flavors of the Heartland, 4494
Fleischmann's Yeast, 4500
Fort, Products, 4616
French's Flavor Ingredients, 4706
Frick's Quality Meats, 4731
Garden Complements Inc, 4891
Gaston Dupre, 4919
Gibbons Bee Farm, 5001
Gladstone Food Products Company, 5044
Gloria Winery & Vineyard, 5071
Good For You America, 5159
Grandpops Lollipops, 5269
Green Dirt Farm, 5347
Gus' Pretzel Shop, 5450
Gwinn's Foods, 5458
Hammons Black Walnuts, 5536
Hammons Products Co, 5537
Hard-E Foods, 5582
Harlin Fruit Co, 5591
Heartland Farms Dairy & Food Products, LLC, 5708
Heartland Ingredients LLC, 5712
Heffy's BBQ Co., 5727
Hermannhof Vineyards, 5810
Highlandville Packing, 5859
Hiland Dairy Foods Co, 5863
Hostess Brands, 6013
Ice Cream Specialties Inc, 6130
ICL Performance Products, 6109
India's Rasoi, 6183
Indias House, 6196
Ingredient Innovations, 6208
Inland Products, 6218
International Dehydrated Foods, 6254
International Food Products, 6260
J & J Processing, 6337
Jasper Products Corp, 6463
John Volpi & Co, 6560
Jost Chemical, 6610
Keller's Creamery, 6760
Lasco Foods Inc, 7234
Les Bourgeois Vineyards, 7378
Li'l Guy Foods, 7407
Little Hills Winery, 7467
Lochhead Mfg. Co., 7501
Louis Maull Co, 7574
Louisa Food Products Inc, 7577
Lucia's Pizza Co, 7625
Luxco Inc, 7655
Luyties Pharmacal Company, 7658
Madrinas Coffee, 7755
Main Squeeze, 7784
Maria & Son, 7907
McCormick Distilling Co, 8062
McKaskle Family Farm, 8075
Meramec Vineyards, 8159
Merb's Candies, 8160
Merci Spring Water, 8165
Missouri Wine & Gift, 8392
Mizkan Americas Inc, 8414
Montelle Winery, 8502
Morningland Dairy Cheese Company, 8550
Mound City Shelled Nut Inc, 8588
Mr Dell Foods, 8618
Mrs. Leeper's Pasta, 8642
Mt Pleasant Winery, 8658
My Daddy's Cheesecake, 8706
Naked Bacon, 8739
National Beef Packing Co LLC, 8783
National Foods, 8792
National Harvest, 8798
National Vinegar Co, 8806
Nikken Foods, 9053
Norm's Farms, 9111
Northwoods Candy Emporium, 9185
Nutraceutics Corp, 9240
Osage Pecan Co, 9576
Ott Food Products Co, 9593
Panera Bread, 9740
PAR-Way Tryson Co, 9648
Paradise Locker Inc., 9765
Particle Dynamics, 9797
Patric Chocolate, 9831
Peaceful Bend Winery, 9861
Perez Food Products, 9948
Personal Edge Nutrition, 9970
Petrofsky's Bakery Products, 9988
Popcorn World, 10181
Premium Water, 10260
Quelle Quiche, 10458
Rainforest Company, 10542
Real Food Marketing, 10590
Red Monkey Foods, 10613
Rethemeyer Coffee Company, 10687
Ribus Inc., 10703
Riega, 10738
Rinehart Meat Processing, 10744
Rio Syrup Co, 10747
River Market Brewing Company, 10769
River Town Foods Corp, 10772
Roasterie Inc, 10783
Robller Vineyard Winery, 10805
Rocket Products Company, 10815
Roha USA LTD, 10843
Ronnoco Coffee Co, 10864
Rothman's Food Inc, 10908
Russell Stover Candies Inc., 10991
Sainte Genevieve Winery, 11091
Schlafly Tap Room, 11291
Schnuck Markets, Inc., 11303
Shepherdsfield Bakery, 11548
Sommer's Food Products, 11800
Southern Farms Fish Processors, 11850

1337

Geographic Index / Montana

Sporting Colors LLC, 11948
St. James Winery, 12007
Stone Hill Winery, 12131
Stonie's Sausage Shop, 12140
Story's Popcorn Company, 12152
Straub's, 12159
Sugar Creek Winery, 12198
Super Smokers Bar-B-Que, 12321
Swiss American Inc, 12437
Taylor's Sausage Co, 12577
Ted Drewes Frozen Custard, 12597
Triumph Foods, LLC, 12991
Tropical Illusions, 13005
Troverco, 13016
True Beverages, 13030
Uhlmann Co, 13135
US Wellness Meats, 13126
USA Beverage, 13127
Vivienne Dressings, 13479
Volpi Foods, 13490
Wickers Food Products Inc, 13762
Woods Smoked Meats Inc, 13920
Zarda Bar-B-Q & Catering Company, 14042
Zerna Packing, 14057

Montana

Alpine Touch Spices, 383
Bequet Confections, 1226
Big Sky Brewing Co, 1344
Blue Marble Biomaterials, 1483
Country Foods, 3072
Cream Of The West, 3130
Eva Gates Homemade Preserves, 4156
Great Grains Milling Company, 5311
Great Harvest Bread Co, 5312
Great Northern Brewing Co, 5323
Hearthstone Whole Grain Bakery, 5705
Hi Country Snack Foods, 5824
Huckleberry Patch, 6047
King Cupboard, 6861
L & M Lockers, 7020
Lang Creek Brewery, 7209
Milky Whey Inc, 8299
Mission Mountain Winery, 8388
Montana Coffee Traders, 8488
Montana Flour & Grains, 8489
Montana Mex, 8490
Montana Monster Munchies, 8491
Montana Mountain Smoked Fish, 8492
Montana Ranch Brand, 8494
Montana Specialty Mills LLC, 8495
Montana Tea & Spice Trading, 8496
Nutritional Labs Intl, 9263
Park Avenue Bakery, 9779
Pasta Montana, 9813
Rocky Mountain Packing Company, 10824
The Chalet Market, 12675
Timeless Seeds, 12812
Viki's Montana Classics, 13405
Wheat Montana Farms Inc, 13705

Nebraska

A Hill of Beans Coffee Roasters, 37
AG Processing Inc, 81
American Laboratories, 467
Ankle Deep Foods, 576
Baker's Candies Factory Store, 966
Beatrice Bakery Co, 1134
Big City Reds, 1328
Certified Piedmontese Beef, 2396
Coffee Culture-A House, 2841
Coldwater Fish Farms, 2872
Corbion, 3019
D I Mfg LLC, 3296
Fairbury Food Products, 4220
Fortress Systems LLC, 4609
Four Star Beef, 4630
Fremont Beef Co, 4695
Gibbon Packing, 5000
Grain Place Foods Inc, 5244
Grandma Beth's Cookies, 5262
Great Plains Beef LLC, 5327
Greater Omaha Packing Co Inc., 5338
Hastings Meat Supply, 5641
Heartland Gourmet LLC, 5711
Henneshen Foods Inc, 5769
J F O'Neill & Packing Co, 6349
James Skinner Company, 6448
JM All Purpose Seasoning, 6403
Kangaroo Brands, 6701

Kelley Bean Co Inc, 6761
Mi Mama's Tortilla Factory Inc, 8214
Misty's Restaurant & Lounge, 8400
Morrison Farms, 8559
Nebraska Bean, 8915
Nebraska Beef Council, 8916
Norfolk Hatchery, 9108
NSG Transport Inc, 8728
Olson Livestock & Seed, 9460
Omaha Meat Processors, 9472
Pear's Coffee, 9872
Platte Valley Creamery, 10107
Preferred Popcorn, 10244
R.E. Meyer Company, 10493
Roberts Seed, 10800
Roman Packing Company, 10855
Roode Packing Company, 10867
Rotella's Italian Bakery Inc., 10905
Sam's Leon Mexican Food, 11126
Seed Enterprises Inc, 11408
Skylark Meats, 11696
Spicetec Flavors & Seasonings, 11930
Sunnyside Farms, 12289
Sweet Corn Products Co, 12394
Taste Traditions Inc, 12543
Tasty Toppings Inc, 12557
Tecumseh Poultry, LLC, 12596
Trinidad Benham Company, 12972
Vic's Corn Popper, 13377
Wanda's Nature Farm, 13562
West Point Dairy Products, 13668
Westin Foods, 13689
Wildcat Produce, 13791

Nevada

Alpen Sierra Coffee Company, 370
Anderson Dairy Inc, 545
Apex Marketing Group, 603
Basic Food Flavors, 1070
Candy Bouquet of Elko, 2131
Coral LLC, 3011
Damon Industries, 3365
Davidson's Organics, 3400
Dolisos America, 3656
Ethel M Chocolates, 4133
Ex Drinks, 4181
French Gourmet Inc, 4699
Fresh Ideas, 4712
Fun City Popcorn, 4792
Granello Bakery, 5272
Great Spice Company, 5330
Hard Eight Nutrition LLC, 5581
HempNut, 5762
High Quality Organics, 5846
Julie Anne's, 6631
Kimmie Candy Company, 6851
King 888 Company, 6856
Klaire Laboratories, 6905
Lakeview Cheese, 7167
Model Dairy LLC, 8438
Mrs Auld's Gourmet Foods Inc, 8625
Nature's Bakery, 8867
Nevada Baking Company, 8951
Odell's, 9367
Pahrump Valley Winery, 9710
Peri & Sons Farms, 9958
Pure Ground Ingredients, 10375
Pure Life Organic Foods, 10378
Real Aloe Company, 10587
S P Enterprises, 11016
Sahara Coffee, 11085
Sanborn Sourdough Bakery, 11160
Sophia's Sauce Works, 11815
SP Enterprises, Inc., 11051
Sunshine Fresh, 12308
Sweeney's Gourmet Coffee Roast, 12383
Tortillas Inc, 12899
Umpqua Oats, 13150
Vitality Life Choice, 13465

New Brunswick

Botsford Fisheries, 1604
Caraquet Ice Company, 2194
Cavendish Farms, 2332
Cooke Aguaculture, 2981
Covered Bridge Potato Chip Company, 3096
Crosby Molasses Company, 3185
Dairytown Products Ltd, 3349
Duguay Fish Packers, 3785
Eastern Sea Products, 3891

Empire Spice Mills, 4054
Ferme Ostreicole Dugas, 4337
Fresh Hemp Foods, 4711
G.E. Barbour, 4820
Ganong Bros Ltd, 4884, 4885
Gaudet & Ouellette, 4923
H&K Packers Company, 5470
Helshiron Fisheries, 5754
Lakeport Brewing Corporation, 7157
Leslie Leger & Sons, 7392
Maple Leaf Foods, 7875
Mariner Neptune Fish & Seafood Company, 7929
McCain Produce Inc., 8056
McGraw Seafood, 8070
MG Fisheries, 7699
Mills Seafood Ltd., 8322
Misty Islands Seafoods, 8399
Moosehead Breweries Ltd., 8535
North Taste Flavourings, 9138
Northumberland Dairy, 9170
Oven Head Salmon Smokers, 9611
Produits Belle Baie, 10332
Skedaddle Maple, 11683
Springhill Farms, 11973
Tasty Seeds Ltd, 12554
Tundra Wild Rice, 13059
Une-Viandi, 13161
Wong Wing, 13908

New Hampshire

American Flatbread, 454
Artist Coffee, 716
Barn Stream Natural Foods, 1043
Ben's Sugar Shack, 1215
Blake's All Natural Foods, 1433
British Aisles, LTD., 1722
Brown Cow Farm, 1774
Budd Foods, 1824
Byrne & Carlson, 1901
Chatila's, 2468
Chocolatier, 2622
Coca-Cola Beverages Northeast, 2811
Dorothy Timberlake Candies, 3697
Echo Farms Puddings, 3915
Fiesta Candy Company, 4372
Homefree LLC, 5935
J. Crow Company, 6371
Jacques Pastries, 6429
Jubilee Gourmet Creations, 6623
Kura Nutrition, 7005
L A Burdick Chocolate, 7024
Lindt & Sprungli USA, 7446
Mc Lure's Honey & Maple Prod, 8050
MegaFood, 8130
NAR, 8722
No Pudge! Foods, 9077
North Country Smokehouse, 9131
Noyes, P J, 9197
Nutfield Brewing Company, 9228
Original Gourmet Food Co, 9563
Oven Poppers, 9612
Pete and Gerry's Organic Eggs, 9976
Port City Pretzels, 10198
Portsmouth Chowder Co, 10209
Putney House Trading LLC, 10401
Rustic Crust Inc, 10996
Seven Barrel Brewery, 11470
Smuttynose Brewing Co, 11743
Spring Ledge Farm Stand, 11965
St. Julien Macaroons, 12008
Stickney & Poor Company, 12115
Stonyfield Organic, 12145
Suss Sweets, 12363
Tahana Confections LLC, 12494
Three Acre Kitchen, 12780
Van Otis Chocolates, 13277
White Oak Farms Inc, 13723

New Jersey

814 Americas Inc, 28
A Zerega's Sons Inc, 46
A&H Products, Inc, 52
Aak USA Inc, 106
Abimco USA, Inc., 123
Abraham's Natural Foods, 128
Abunda Life, 131
Acetifico Marcello Denigris, 146
Advanced Food Systems, 189
Adventist Book & Food, 193

AeroFarms, 195
Agrusa, 223
Akay USA LLC, 242
Aker BioMarine Antarctic US, LLC., 243
Al & John's Glen Rock Ham, 246
Al Richard's Chocolates, 250
Alba Vineyard & Winery, 277
Alexian P*ft*,s, 295
Allen Flavors Inc, 335
Allied Old English Inc, 345
Alya Foods, 399
Amalthea Cellars Farm Winery, 408
AMCO Proteins, 92
Ameri-Suisse Group, 433
American Instants Inc, 464
American Key Food Products Inc, 466
American Pasien Co, 477
Amoroso's Baking Co, 508
Amwell Valley Vineyard, 518
Animal Pak, 572
Anthony & Sons Italian Bakery, 594
Antonio Mozzarella Factory, 599
Apple Flavor & Fragrance USA, 610
Applegate Farms, 614
Archon Vitamin Corp, 641
Arctic Ice Cream Co, 646
Arnhem Group, 687
Aroma Coffee Roasters Inc, 693
Aromor Flavors & Fragrances, 701
Asiamerica Ingredients, 733
Astor Chocolate Corp, 743
Atlantic Blueberry, 764
Atlantic Capes Fisheries, 765
Atlantic Pak, 768
Au'some Candies, 790
Augustin's Waffles, 798
Aunt Gussie Cookies & Crackers, 801
Aunt Kitty's Foods Inc, 805
Automatic Rolls Of New Jersey, 824
Avebe America Inc., 834
Axelsson & Johnson Fish Company, 849
B & B Poultry Co, 860
B & G Foods, Inc., 864
B-Tea Beverage, LLC, 878
Baker's Coconut, 967
Bakers Best Snack Food Corp., 972
Bakto Flavors, 982
Balic Winery, 991
Barbero Bakery, Inc., 1024
BASF Corp., 886
Baycliff Co Inc, 1105
Bede Inc, 1151
Belcolade, 1175
Belmar Spring Water, 1207
Belmont Chemicals, 1209
Beneo Inc, 1219
Bergen Marzipan & Chocolate, 1229
Best Foods, 1267
Best Provision Co Inc, 1271
Biazzo Dairy Products Inc, 1308
Bierig Brothers Inc, 1319
Bifulco Four Seasons, 1321
Bindi North America, 1360
Bio-Foods, 1366
Bio-Nutritional Products, 1369
Birdseye Food, 1389
Bittersweet Pastries, 1413
BK Specialty Foods, 899
Black Prince Distillery Inc, 1423
Blair's Sauces & Snacks, 1431
Blissfully Better, 1453
Blossom Farm Products, 1462
Bono USA, 1566
Bosco Products Inc, 1586
Boston Tea Company, 1600
Boulder Brands, Inc., 1612
Boylan Bottling Company, 1640
Brand Aromatics Inc, 1655
Brazilian Home Collection, 1674
Buona Vita Inc, 1854
Burger Maker Inc, 1857
Bylada Foods, 1896
C & E Canners Inc, 1908
C.W. Brown Foods, Inc., 1938
Caesar's Pasta, 1986
Campbell Soup Co., 2116
Candy Central, 2132
Capalbo's Fruit Baskets, 2150
Capco Enterprises, 2153
Captiva Limited Inc, 2190
CarbRite Diet, 2196
Carrington Tea Co., 2262

Geographic Index / New Jersey

Cary Randall's Sauces & Dressings, 2267
Casani Candy Company, 2279
Catelli Brothers Inc, 2313
Catherych, 2318
Cento Fine Foods, 2372
Champignon North America Inc, 2409
Chelten House Products, 2509
Chris's Cookies, 2644
Christie-Brown, 2648
Church & Dwight Co., Inc., 2666
Ciao Bella Gelato Company, 2669
Cibo Vita, 2672
CideRoad, LLC, 2673
Cifelli & Sons Inc, 2676
Cinderella Cheese Cake Co, 2680
Citromax Flavors Inc, 2695
CK Living LLC, 1956
Clio Snacks, 2762
Clofine Dairy Products Inc, 2764
CNS Confectionery Products, 1959
Coco International, 2819
Coco Polo, 2821
Coffee Associates, 2832
Coffee Roasters Inc, 2856
Colavita USA, 2864
Colonna Brothers Inc, 2887
Commodities Marketing Inc, 2923
Confoco USA, Inc., 2948
ConSup North America, 2937
Conte's Pasta Co., 2967
Continental Seasoning, 2973
Corbion, 3015, 3017
Corim Industries Inc, 3030
Corsetti's Pasta Products, 3042
Cosmopolitan Foods, 3049
Craby's Fish Market, 3105
Creative Flavors & Specialties LLP, 3134
Crestmont Enterprises, 3158
Crillon Importers LTD, 3165
Crispy Green Inc., 3166
Criterion Chocolates Inc, 3170
Croda Inc, 3174
Crystal & Vigor Beverages, 3209
Crystal Temptations, 3222
Cuisine International, 3227
Culture Republick, 3241
Cumberland Dairy, 3247
Curry King Corporation, 3260
D'Artagnan, 3302
Dale & Thomas Popcorn, 3357
Daregal, 3385
David Bradley Chocolatier, 3396
David's Cookies, 3399
De Nigris, 3431
Debel Food Products, 3449
Debragga & Spitler, 3451
Deep Foods Inc, 3465
DeMedici Imports, 3439
Deosen USA, 3528
Diamond Blueberry Inc, 3572
Diana Naturals, 3580
Djerdan Burek Corp, 3636
Donna & Company, 3684
Dr Praeger's Sensible Foods, 3727
Dr. Schar USA, 3738
Dream Confectioners LTD, 3750
DSM Food Specialties, 3321
Durey-Libby Edible Nuts, 3808
E.W. Bowker Company, 3846
Eastern Brewing Corporation, 3888
Eastern Fish Company, 3889
Eastern Tea Corp, 3894
Eatem Foods Co, 3908
EatKeenwa, Inc., 3906
Edward Johnson's Salsa, 3957
Eight O'Clock Coffee Company, 3974
El Jay Poultry Corporation, 3980
Elan Vanilla Co, 3993
Elegant Desserts, 4000
Elements Truffles, 4004
Ellio's Pizza, 4020
Entenmann's, 4080
Euro Source Gourmet, 4146
Excellentia Intl., 4184
Explore Cuisine, 4187
Extracts and Ingredients Ltd, 4190
F & S Produce Co Inc, 4196
Fa Lu Cioli, 4212
Fantis Foods Inc, 4257
Farbest-Tallman Foods Corp, 4263
Farmland Dairies, 4290
Farmland Fresh Dairies, 4291

FatBoy's Cookie Company, 4305
Federal Pretzel Baking Company, 4318
Ferrero USA Inc, 4348
Ferris, Stahl-Meyer, 4351
Filippo Berio Brand, 4386
Fillo Factory, The, 4388
Fine Foods Trading Company, 4397
Finlandia Cheese, 4405
Finlay Extracts & Ingredients USA, Inc., 4406
Firmenich Inc., 4420
First Food International, 4426
Fizzy Lizzy, 4464
Flavor & Fragrance Specialties, 4479
Flavor Dynamics Two, 4480
Flavorganics, 4489
FlavorHealth, 4486
Food Ingredient Solutions, 4560
Food of Our Own Design, 4571
Food Sciences Corp, 4567
Foreign Domestic Chemicals, 4590
Fossil Farms, 4618
Four Sisters Winery, 4629
Fralinger's, 4645
Franklin Farms, 4664
Fratelli Beretta USA, 4671
Freedman's Bakery, 4683
Freekehlicious, 4685
French Feast Inc., 4698
FrieslandCampina Ingredients North America, Inc., 4736
Frisson Normand, 4740
From the Ground Up, 4747
Fuji Health Science/Inc, 4782
Fun Foods, 4794
Functional Foods, 4796
Funnibonz LLC, 4801
Fuzz East Coast, 4809
Gaiser's European Style, 4861
Galaxy Dairy Products, 4865
Gel Spice Co LLC, 4931
Genarom International, 4943
GFA Brands Inc, 4831
Gharana Foods, 4993
Giambri's Quality Sweets Inc, 4998
Giulia Speciality Food, 5034
Givaudan Fragrances Corp, 5038
Glatech Productions LLC, 5047
GoAvo, 5088
Golden Fluff Popcorn Co, 5123
Golden Platter Foods, 5131
Good Earth Company, 5155
Good Humor-Breyers Ice Cream, 5165
Goodie Girl, 5184
Gourmet Kitchen, Inc., 5207
Goya Foods Inc., 5223
Grasso Foods Inc, 5283
Gratify Gluten Free, 5284
Great Garlic Foods, 5308
Green Turtle Bay Vitamin Company, 5363
Greene Brothers Specialty Coffee Roaster, 5370
Grow Co, 5407
Growing Roots Foods, 5411
GS-AFI, 4847
Guiltless Gourmet, 5426
Gumix International Inc, 5443
Guttenplan's Frozen Dough, 5455
Guylian USA Inc., 5457
H. Reisman Corporation, 5475
H.B. Trading, 5477
Halmoni's Divine Marinade, 5526
Happy Herberts Food Co Inc, 5569
Harris Tea Company, 5612
Hartog Rahal Foods, 5622
Health is Wealth Foods, 5687
Helm New York Chemical Corp, 5750
Herb's Seafood, 5781
Herbalist & Alchemist Inc, 5789
HerbNZest LLC, 5783
Heritage's Dairy Stores, 5804
High Grade Beverage, 5843
Hillard Bloom Packing Co Inc, 5867
Hillside Candy Co, 5874
Holistic Products Corporation, 5907
Honickman Affiliates, 5975
Hosemen & Roche Vitamins & Fine Chemicals, 6007
House of Herbs LLC, 6024
IFC Solutions, 6111
ILHWA American Corporation, 6116
Innophos Holdings Inc., 6225

International Coconut Corp, 6253
International Foodcraft Corp, 6261
International Home Foods, 6267
International Spice, 6274
International Trade Impact Inc, 6276
International Vitamin Corporation, 6278
International Foods, 6279
Italian Connection, 6318
Italian Peoples Bakery Inc, 6321
J & J Snack Foods Corp, 6338
J & K Ingrediants, 6340
Jack & Jill Ice Cream, 6414
James Candy Company, 6445
Jarchem Industries, 6455
Jersey Fruit Co-Op, 6501
Jersey Italian Gravy, 6502
JF Braun & Sons Inc., 6398
Jiaherb, 6513
Jimmys Cookies, 6521
JJ Martin Group, 6400
JK Sucralose, 6402
Joe Tea and Joe Chips, 6539
Joey's Fine Foods, 6542
Johanna Foods Inc., 6545
John W Macy's Cheesesticks Inc, 6561
Joseph J. White, 6601
Joyfuls, 6617
JVM Sales Corp., 6412
Kaffe Magnum Opus, 6683
Kaplan & Zubrin, 6705
Karmalize.Me, 6717
Kayco, 6743
Kedem, 6746
Keto Foods, 6811
Kingchem, 6875
Kobricks Coffee Company, 6928
Kohinoor Foods, 6939
Kolatin Real Kosher Gelatin, 6944
Kollar Cookies, 6946
Konto's Foods, 6956
Kopper's Chocolate, 6960
Koppers Chocolate, 6961
L & M Bakery, 7019
LA Monica Fine Foods, 7054
La Vans Coffee Company, 7114
Lacas Coffee Co Inc, 7124
Laird & Company, 7146
Lanaetex Products Incorporated, 7188
Landolfi's Food Products, 7204
Larosa Bakery Inc, 7223, 7224
Lassonde Pappas & Company, Inc., 7236
Latta USA, 7242
Lazzaroni USA, 7263
Lebanon Cheese Co, 7289
Lenson Coffee & Tea Company, 7353
LFI Inc, 7069
Limpert Bros Inc, 7437
Linda's Lollies Company, 7440
Lioni Latticini Inc, 7453
Losurdo Creamery, 7558
Lucille's Own Make Candies, 7628
Lund's Fisheries, 7649
Macrie Brothers, 7733
Madison Park Foods, 7751
Madrange, 7754
MAFCO Worldwide, 7693
Malt Diastase Co, 7808, 7809
Mamma Says, 7826
Mando Inc, 7838
Manhattan Bagel Company, 7843
Manhattan Food Brands, LLC, 7845
Manischewitz Co, 7848
Marathon Enterprises Inc, 7895
Mardi Gras, 7902
Marlow Candy & Nut Co, 7945
Martin Bauer Group, 7963
McNeil Specialty Products Company, 8083
Medallion Industries International Inc, 8119
Mediterranean Snack Food Co, 8124
MetaBall, 8190
Metropolitan Gourmet, 8200
Mid Atlantic Vegetable Shortening Company, 8253
Mikaela's Simply Divine, 8276
Mincing Overseas Spice Company, 8341
Mint Savor, 8362
Mira International Foods, 8366
Mishrun, 8376
Modena Fine Foods Inc, 8439
Mondelez International, 8474
Morning Star Foods, 8548
Morre-Tec Ind Inc, 8554

Mortgage Apple Cake, 8565
Mr. Green Tea Ice Cream, 8622
Mrs Mazzula Food Products Inc, 8630
Muirhead of Ringoes, NJ, Inc., 8670
Multiflex Company, 8677
Mushroom Wisdom, Inc, 8695
MySuperfoods Company, 8712
Nabisco, 8729
National Starch Food Innovation, 8804
Natural Flavors, 8829
Naturally Scientific, 8857
Naturex Inc, 8899
Nema Food Distribution, 8934
New Nissi Corp., 8991
New Wave Cuisine, 9000
Nexira, 9029
Niche Import Co, 9035
Niche W&S, 9036
Nichem Co, 9038
Nirwana Foods, 9065
Nitta Casings Inc, 9071
No Whey Foods, 9078
North American Beverage Co, 9115
North American Coffees, 9118
Northeastern Products Company, 9144
Northern Valley Baking Co, 9162
Nothin' But Foods, 9189
Nu Products Co Inc, 9202
Nutrisport Pharmacal, 9257
Nutro Laboratories, 9267
Oasis Food Co, 9332
Old Fashioned Kitchen Inc, 9412
Old Monmouth Candies, 9421
OMGhee, 9304
Osem USA Inc, 9579
Otto's Naturals, 9597
Oven Arts, 9609
OWYN, 9309
Ozone Confectioners & Bakers Supplies, 9625
Pan American Coffee Co, 9732
Panos Brands, 9748
Pat LaFrieda Meat Purveyors, 9824
Patriot Pickel Inc, 9834
Paulaur Corp, 9847
Penta Manufacturing Company, 9930
Perfect Life Nutrition, 9952
Perona Farms, 9965
Pharmachem Laboratories, 9997
PLT Health Solutions Inc, 9654
Pocas International, 10134
Point Lobster Co, 10143
Pomodoro Fresca Foods, 10160
Pondini Imports, 10166
POPTime, 9660
Portuguese Baking Company, 10210
Premium Chocolatiers LLC, 10256
Prime Ingredients Inc, 10291
Pro-Source Performance Prods, 10317
Progresso Quality Foods, 10337
Promotion in Motion Companies, 10345
Puebla Foods Inc, 10363
Pure Batch, 10367
Pure Dark, 10368
Pure Indian, 10376
Pure Inventions LLC, 10377
QBI, 10413
Quality Instant Teas, 10437
R C Fine Foods Inc, 10477
RAB Food Group, 10501
RAJB Hog Foods Inc, 10502
Randazzo's Honest To Goodness Sauces, 10561
Rapunzel Pure Organics, 10568
Real Kosher Sausage Company, 10591
Real Torino, 10593
Reckitt Benckiser LLC, 10598
Redondo Iglesias USA, 10631
Reggie's Roast, 10647
Reheis Co, 10652
Renault Winery, 10670
Rich Products Corp, 10715
Rico Foods Inc, 10734
Robertet Flavors, 10797
Rokeach Food Corp, 10845
Ron Son Foods Inc, 10860
Roseland Manufacturing, 10890
Royal Palm Popcorn Company, 10944
Royal Wine Corp, 10952
Ruggiero Seafood, 10974
Run-A-Ton Group Inc, 10981
Russo Farms, 10993

1339

Geographic Index / New Mexico

RW Delights, 10517
Rye Fresh, 11003
Sabinsa Corp, 11061
Salad Depot, 11094
San Marzano Imports, 11155
Savoury Systems Inc, 11258
Schiff Food Products Co Inc, 11284
Schiff Nutrition International, 11285
Schuman Cheese, 11313
Scott Adams Foods, 11324
Scotty Wotty's Creamy Cheesecake, 11332
Sea Breeze Fruit Flavors, 11339
Seabrook Brothers & Sons, 11365
Season Brand, 11384
Seatrade Corporation, 11387
Sensus America Inc, 11445
Seppic Inc, 11447
Serv-Agen Corporation, 11458
Severino Pasta Mfg Co Inc, 11478
Shaanxi Jiahe Phytochem Co., Ltd., 11489
Shabazz Fruit Cola Company, 11490
Shaker Country Meadowsweets, 11497
Shanghai Freemen, 11514
Shelley's, 11541
Sherwood Brands, 11552
Silver Palate Kitchens, 11623
Simit + Smith, 11638
Sini Fulvi U.S.A., 11668
SLT Group, 11046
Smarties, 11716
Snack Factory, 11744
SnowBird Corporation, 11764
Sole Grano LLC, 11784
Solgar Vitamin & Herbal, 11785
Soluble Products Company, 11793
Somerset Syrup & Concessions, 11796
SoyTex, 11880
Specialities Importers & Distributers, 11894
Spice Chain, 11916
Spice Time Foods, 11925
Spicy Sense, 11931
Sprout Nutrition, 11978
Star Ravioli Mfg Co, 12037
Star Snacks, 12040
Steve's PaleoGoods, 12097
Strassburger Steaks, 12156
Streit Carl & Son Co, 12166
Summit Hill Flavors, 12226
Sun Grove Foods Inc, 12232
Sun Noodle New Jersey, 12236
Sunco & Frenchie, 12267
Sunnyside Vegetable Packing, 12292
Suzanne's Specialties, 12372
Sweet Water Seafood, 12420
Sylvan Farms Winery, 12450
Symrise Inc., 12454
Synergy Plus, 12457
Tabatchinick Fine Foods, 12485
Takasago International Corp, 12501
Tamarind Tree, 12517
Tamuzza Vineyards, 12523
Taste It Presents Inc, 12540
Tavalon Tea, 12564
Taylor Provisions Company, 12572
Tea Beyond, 12583
Teawolf LLC, 12591
Templar Food Products, 12612
Testamints Sales-Distribution, 12639
Tetley Tea, 12641
Tetley USA, 12642
That's How We Roll, LLC, 12664
The Jersey Tomato Company, 12695
The Little Kernel, 12701
The Power of Fruit, 12720
The Soulfull Project, 12731
Thumann Inc., 12791
Tofutti Brands Inc, 12843
Tomasello Winery, 12859
Tonex, 12868
Toufayan Bakeries, 12905
Tree Ripe Products, 12941
Tribeca Oven, 12966
Triumph Brewing Co, 12990
Tropical Cheese, 12996
Tru-Blu Cooperative Associates, 13022
True World Foods LLC, 13036
Trumark, 13039
Tuscan Dairy Farms, 13078
Twin Hens, 13093
Ugo Di Lullo & Son, 13134
Ultimate Foods, 13140
Ultimate Gourmet, 13141

Ungars Food, 13162
Ungerer & Co, 13163
Unilever Food Solutions, 13168
Unilever US, 13169
Universal Nutrition, 13209
Universal Preservachem Inc, 13211
Van Dyke Ice Cream, 13271
Van Peenans Dairy, 13278
Varda Chocolatier, 13297
VCPB Transportation, 13238
Veggie Land, 13315
Vintage Plantations Cho colates, 13433
Violet Packing Holdings LLC, 13437
Vita-Pure Inc, 13457
WaffleWaffle, 13525
Walden Farms, 13538, 13539
WBM International, 13510
Wechsler Coffee Corporation, 13617
Welsh Farms, 13646, 13647
Wet Planet Beverage, 13697
White Camel Foods Group, 13714
White Toque, 13731
Wholly Wholesome, 13753
Wild Leaf Active Tea, 13782
Woodstock Farms Manufacturing, 13923
World Confections Inc, 13933
World Of Coffee, 13942
World of Spices, 13946
World Spice, 13944
Yamate Chocolatier, 13989
Yoo-Hoo Chocolate Beverage Company, 14016
Yvonne's Gourmet Sensations, 14032

New Mexico

Assets Grille & Southwest Brewing Company, 738
Avalon Organic Coffees, 830
Balagna Winery Company, 983
Binns Vineyards & Winery, 1364
Bite Size Bakery, 1408
Black Mesa Winery, 1422
Black Shield, 1427
Bueno Foods, 1835
Cannon's Sweets Hots, 2140
Casados Farms, 2278
Cervantes Food Products Inc, 2397
Chimayo To Go / Cibolo Junction, 2568
Chocolate Maven, 2605
Chocolate Smith, 2609
CO YO, 1960
Comfort Foods, 2919
Creamland Dairies Inc, 3131
Deneen Foods, 3522
Eagle Rock Food Co, 3864
El Charro Mexican Food Ind, 3978
Food Processor of New Mexico, 4565
Gallup Sales Company, 4875
Gruet Winery, 5413
Hatch Chile Company, 5642
Herbs Etc, 5791
Jillipepper, 6515
Joseph's Lite Cookies, 6606
LA Chiripada Winery, 7044
LA Vina Winery, 7065
Las Cruces Foods, 7232
Leona's Restaurante, 7362
Los Chileros, 7550
Mac's Meats Inc, 7717
Madison Vineyard, 7752
Maywood International Sales, 8045
Mizkan Americas Inc, 8426, 8427
Mountain States Pecan, 8600
Native Scents, 8812
Nature's Dairy, 8873
New Mexico Green Chile Company, 8990
North of the Border, 9140
Payne Packing Co, 9855
Pecos Valley Spice Company, 9886
Ponderosa Valley Vineyard, 10165
Prairie Thyme LTD, 10237
Rezolex LLC, 10695
Sandia Shadows Vineyard & Winery, 11170
Santa Fe Brewing Co, 11194
Santa Fe Seasons, 11195
Santa Fe Vineyards, 11196
Schadel's Bakery, 11272
Senor Murphy Candymaker, 11438
Senor Pinos de Santa Fe, 11439
Shamrock Foods Co, 11509
Southwest Cheese Company, 11871

Southwest Spirit, 11874
Stahmann Farms, 12021
Sunland Inc/Peanut Better, 12278
Taos Brewing Company, 12529
Taos Mesa Brewing Co, 12530
Texas Reds Steak House, 12654
Tularosa Vineyards, 13051
Victor Allen Coffee Company, 13381
Vitality Works, 13466
Warden Peanut Company, 13568
Windmill Water Inc, 13844
Woodie Pie Company, 13918
Young Pecan, 14022

New York

1000 Islands River Rat Cheese, 3
21st Century Snack Foods, 7
3 Water, 12
3PM Bites, 16
3V Company, 17
4C Foods Corp, 20
A&B American Style, LLC, 50
A.Vogel USA, 67
Abe's Vegan Muffins, 120
Abel & Schafer Inc, 121
Abkit Camocare Nature Works, 127
Accurate Ingredients Inc, 139
Ace Farm USA Inc, 143
Acesur North America, 145
Acme Smoked Fish Corporation, 151
Adair Vineyards, 160
ADH Health Products Inc, 75
Adirondack Beverages Inc, 174
Adirondack Maple Farms, 175
Advanced Bio Development, 186
AEP Colloids, 78
Afieneur, 198
Afineur, 199
Agger Fish Corp, 205
Agrexco USA, 209
Agri-Dairy Products, 210
Agro Farma Inc., 217
Ah Dor Kosher Fish Corporation, 227
Ai Vy Springrolls, Llc, 231
Al Safa Halal, 251
Aladdin Bakers, 256
Alexander International (USA), 292
Alexia Foods, 294
Alkinco, 316
All Round Foods Bakery Prod, 322
All Seasonings Ingredients Inc, 323
Alle Processing Corp, 329
Allen's Pickle Works, 338
Allied Food Products, 344
Allied Wine Corporation, 346
ALOHA, 90
Alpina, 376
Alvita, 398
Amazing Candy Craft Company, 418
Amberg Wine Cellars, 422
Ambrosi Cheese USA, 425
Ambrosial Granola, 426
Amcan Industries, 428
American Almond Products Co, 438
American Biosciences, 440
American Classic Ice Cream Company, 447
American Health, 461
American Mint, 472
American Tartaric Products, 486
American Vintage Wine Biscuits, 489
Americana Vineyards & Winery, 492
Amerol Chemical Corporation, 496
Amest Food, 499
Amrita Health Foods, 513
Amrita Snacks, 514
Anchor Frozen Foods, 532
Angel's Bakeries, 562
Angelic Gourmet Inc, 564
Angry Orchard Cider Company, LLC, 569
Anita's Yogurt, 574
Anthony Road Wine Co, 595
Antoni Ravioli Co, 598
Apple & Eve LLC, 608
Apple Acres, 609
Applewood Winery, 618
Arbor Hill Grapery & Winery, 628
Arbor Mist Winery, 629
Arcadian Estate Winery, 636
Ardith Mae Farmstead Goat Cheese, 649
Argo Fine Foods, 657
Armenia Coffee Corporation, 682

Arnold's Meat Food Products, 690
Aromachem, 697
Artuso Pastry, 718
Asiago PDO & Speck Alto Adige PGI, 732
Astral Extracts, 744
At Last Naturals Inc, 746
Athena Oil Inc, 748
Atlantic Pork & Provisions, 773
Atlantic Veal & Lamb Inc, 779
Atwater Foods, 786
August Kitchen, 795
Aunt Heddy's Bakery, 802
Aunt Jenny's Sauces/Melba Foods, 803
Austrian Trade Commission, 821
B & R Classics LLC, 866
B&D Food Corporation, 872
B&K Coffee, 874
Bad Seed Cider Company, LLC, 926
Bagel Guys, 934
Bagel Lites, 935
Bagels By Bell, 936
Bagelworks, 937
Bagley's, 938
Baker's Dozen & Cafe, 968
Balance Bar Company, 984
Balanced Health Products, 985
Baldwin Vineyards, 989
Banfi Vintners, 1006
Banner Candy Manufacturing Company, 1008
Bantam Bagels, 1011
Barber's Farm Distillery LLC, 1023
Barkeater Chocolates, 1038
Barkthins Snacking Chocolate, 1041
Barrie House Gourmet Coffee, 1053
Bartlett Dairy & Food Service, 1060
Bartolini Ice Cream, 1062
Baruvi Fresh LLC, 1065
Basketfull, 1074
Batampte Pickle Prods Inc, 1079
Batavia Wine Cellars, 1080
Battistoni Italian Spec Meats, 1084
Bauer's Mustard, 1086
Bavarian Nut Co, 1091
Baycliff Company, 1106
BCGA Concept Corporation, 894
Bean Buddies, 1122
Bedell Northfork LLC, 1152
Bedemco Inc, 1153
Bee Raw Honey, 1159
Beech-Nut Nutrition Corp, 1161
Beekman 1802, 1166
Belgian Boys, 1176
Bella-Napoli Italian Bakery, 1193
Bellocq, 1201
Benmarl Wine Co, 1220
Bernie's Foods, 1251
Best Ever Bakery, 1265
Bidwell Vineyard, 1314
Bien Cuit, 1315
Bilinski Sausage Mfg Co, 1353
Bio-Botanica Inc, 1365
Birkett Mills, 1391
Biscotti & Co., 1397
Bison Foods, 1402
Bitsy's Brainfood, 1409
Black Bear Farm Winery, 1415
Black Hound New York, 1419
Blk Enterprises, 1454
Blue Hill Yogurt, 1479
Blue Point Brewing Co, 1492
Blue Ridge Tea & Herb Co, 1496
Bobbysue's Nuts LLC, 1522
Bodek Kosher Produce Inc, 1530
Body Breakthrough Inc, 1532
Bodyonics Limited, 1533
BOLD Organics, 902
Borgattis Ravioli, 1580
Bou Brands, 1607
Bowery Farming Inc., 1631
BP Gourmet, 903
Brad's Organic, 1644
Brad's Taste of New York, 1645
BRAMI Snacks, 904
Brands Within Reach, 1661
Braun Seafood Co, 1671
Bread Alone Bakery, 1678
Bread Box Cafe, 1679
Brewery Ommegang, 1697
Brewla Inc., 1698
BrightFarms, 1714
Brimstone Hill Vineyard, 1716

Geographic Index / New York

BRINS, 905
Bristol-Myers Squibb Co., 1721
Broken Bow Brewery, 1734
Brooklyn Bagel Company, 1743
Brooklyn Bean Roastery, 1745
Brooklyn Biltong, 1746
Brooklyn Brew Shop, 1747
Brooklyn Brewery, 1748
Brooklyn Brine Co LLC, 1749
Brooklyn Cider House, 1750
Brooklyn Cookie Company, 1751
Brooklyn Cured LLC, 1752
Brooklyn Delhi, 1753
Brooklyn Whatever LLC, 1754
Brotherhood Winery, 1764
Brothers All Natural, 1765
Brothers International Food Corporation, 1768
Browns Brewing Co, 1789
Bruce Baking Company, 1791
Bruce Cost Ginger Ale, 1793
Bruno Specialty Foods, 1802
Buddy Fruits, 1827
Bull and Barrel Brewpub, 1841
Bully Hill Vineyards, 1843
Bunker Foods Corp., 1850
Buonitalia, 1855
Burch Farms, 1856
Byrne Dairy, Inc., 1902
C Howard Co, 1918
Cacao Prieto, 1973
Cafe Grumpy, 1995
Cafe La Semeuse, 1997
Cafe Spice, 2002
Cahoon Farms, 2014
Caleb Haley & Co LLC, 2042
Calico Cottage, 2048
Calistoga Food Company, 2087
Calvisius Caviar, 2099
Camellia General Provision Co, 2106
Campari, 2114
Cannoli Factory, 2139
Canton Noodle Corporation, 2144
Capri Bagel & Pizza Corporation, 2172
Capsule Works, 2179
Captain Lawrence Brewing Co, 2187
Care Foods International, 2202
Caribbean Food Delights Inc, 2209
Carousel Cakes, 2252
Casa Di Lisio Products Inc, 2269
Casa Larga Vineyards, 2270
Casa Visco, 2274
Casablanca Foods LLC, 2276
Cascade Mountain Winery, 2284
Castella Imports Inc, 2297
Castello di Borghese Vineyard, 2299
Catskill Brewery, 2321
Catskill Distilling Company, 2322
Catskill Mountain Specialties, 2323
Cayuga Pure Organics, 2340
Cayuga Ridge Estate Winery, 2341
Centflor Manufacturing Co, 2371
Cham Cold Brew Tea, 2406
Champlain Valley Milling Corp, 2413
Charissa, 2427
Charlie Palmer Group, 2439
Charlito's Cocina, 2443
Chateau LA Fayette Reneau, 2460
Chazy Orchards, 2476
Cheese Factory, 2480
Chelsea Flower Market, 2507
Cheribundi, 2516
Chip'n Dipped Cookie Co, 2578
Chloe's Fruit, 2583
Chobani, Inc., 2585
ChocAlive, 2586
Chocolat Michel Cluizel, 2595
Chocolat Moderne, LLC., 2596
Chocolate By Design Inc, 2597, 2598
Chocolate Delivery Systems Inc, 2602
Chocolate Works, 2613
Chocomize, 2624
Chozen Ice Cream, 2639
Christopher Norman Chocolates, 2654
Cibao Meat Products Inc, 2670
Circus Man Ice Cream Corporation, 2689
Cisse Trading Co, 2692
Citrus and Allied Essences, 2700
City Bakery, 2702
City Saucery, 2710
Clarke J F Corp, 2719
Classic Commissary, 2723

Classic Cookings, LLC, 2725
Classic Flavors & Fragrances, 2727
Clemson Bros. Brewery, 2752
Clinton St Baking Co, 2760
Clinton Vineyards Inc, 2761
Coach Farm Enterprises, 2793
Cobraz Brazilian Coffee, 2808
Cocktail Crate, 2817
Cocktail Kits 2 Go LLC, 2818
Codinos Food Inc, 2831
Coffee Holding Co Inc, 2847
Cohen's Bakery, 2862
Comax Flavors, 2916
Community Mill & Bean, 2927
Comte Cheese Association, 2932
Coney Island Classics, 2945
Continental Grain Company, 2970
Cookie Factory, 2983
Cookies United, 2989
Cool Brands International, 2993
Cooper Lake Farm LLC, 2999
Cooperstown Cookie Company, 3004
Cornell Beverages Inc, 3036
Corso's Cookies, 3043
Coulter Giufre & Co Inc, 3060
Country Life, 3080
Couturier Na Inc, 3095
Cracked Candy LLC, 3106
Crazy Mary's, 3124
Creative Food Ingredients, 3136
Crepini, 3149
Crepini & The Crepe Team, 3150
Crescent Duck Farm, 3151
Crop Pharms, LLC, 3184
Crown Maple Syrup, 3191
Crown Regal Wine Cellars, 3196
Crumbs Bake Shop, 3199
Crusty Bakery Inc, 3208
Cucina Antica Foods Corp, 3224
Cudlin's Meat Market, 3225
Culture, 3240
Curtice Burns Foods, 3261
D Steengrafe Co Inc, 3298
Daily Soup, 3330
Dairy Group, 3337
Dairy Maid Ravioli Mfg Co, 3341
Dallis Brothers, 3362
Damascus Bakery, 3363
Damiani Wine Cellars LLC, 3364
Danisco-Cultor, 3375
David Mosner Meat Products, 3397
Dawes Hill Honey Company, 3411
Day Spring Enterprises, 3415
De Iorio's Foods Inc, 3427
De Iorios Frozen Dough Co Inc, 3428
Deep Valley, 3467
Dehydrates Inc, 3474
Delancey Dessert Company, 3488
Delectable Gourmet LLC, 3492
Delicious Desserts, 3498
DeLima Coffee, 3437
Den's Hot Dogs, 3520
Denning's Point Distillery, LLC, 3523
Detoxwater, 3546
DF Mavens, 3309
Di Camillo Baking Co, 3561
Dina's Organic Chocolate, 3607
Dino's Sausage & Meat Co Inc, 3611
Dipaolo Baking Co Inc, 3614
Divvies, 3628
Do Anything Foods, 3638
DO, Cookie Dough Confections, 3317
Dolce Nonna, 3650
Doral International, 3693
Double Play Foods, 3704
Dr Konstantin Frank's Vinifera, 3724
Dr. Paul Lohmann Inc., 3735
Dream Pretzels, 3752
Dresden Stollen Co USA, 3756
DSM Fortitech Premixes, 3322
Dufour Pastry Kitchens Inc, 3783
Dulcette Technologies, 3789
Dutch Cheese Makers Corp, 3812
Dylan's Candy Bar, 3827
Dyna Tabs LLC, 3828
Dynamic Health Laboratories Inc., 3831
Eagle Crest Vineyards LLC, 3861
Eagle Seafood Producers, 3865
Eat It Corporation, 3900
Eating Evolved, 3909
Ed Roller Inc, 3931
Edom Labs Inc, 3954

EFCO Products Inc, 3850
Efco Products Inc, 3962
Egg Low Farms, 3966
El Paso Winery, 3985
Eldorado Coffee Distributors, 3997
Eleanor's Best LLC, 3999
Element Snacks, 4002
Eleni's Cookies, 4007
Eli's Bread Inc, 4009
Ellie's Country Delights, 4019
Elmhurst Milked, 4034
Elwood International Inc, 4038
Emerling International Foods, 4044
Emkay Trading Corporation, 4046
Emmy's Organics, 4049
Empire Coffee Company, 4051
Empire Mayonnaise Company, LLC., 4053
Empress Chocolate Company, 4058
Endico Potatoes Inc, 4061
Energy Brands/Haute Source, 4066
Enlightened, 4073
Enrico's/Ventre Packing, 4076
Enzyme Development Corporation, 4087
Erba Food Products, 4104
Ericas Rugelach & Baking Co, 4105
Escalade Limited, 4110
Ethnic Edibles, 4137
Euro Cafe, 4144
Eve Sales Corp, 4160
Exo Inc., 4186
FAGE USA Dairy Ind Inc, 4203
Fairchester Snacks Corp, 4221
Falcone's Cookie Land LTD, 4233
Fallwood Corp, 4237
Fama Sales Co, 4238
Famous Specialties Co, 4244
Fat Snax, 4303
Father Sam's Bakery, 4306
Fatty Sundays, 4309
Fawen, 4312
Fee Brothers, 4320
Feel Good Foods, 4323
Felix Roma & Son Inc, 4326
Ferolito Vultaggio & Sons, 4342
Ferrara Bakery & Cafe, 4344
Field Trip Jerky, 4366
Fieldbrook Foods Corp., 4369
Fig Food Co., 4378
Filfil Foods LLC, 4385
Finding Home Farms, 4391
Fine & Raw Chocolate, 4392
Finger Lakes Coffee Roasters, 4403
First Spice Mixing Co Inc, 4430
Five Acre Farms, 4456
Flat Cracker Inc., 4474
Flaum Appetizing, 4478
Flavormatic Industries, 4490
Fleischer's Bagels, 4498
Fleurchem Inc, 4503
Floyd, 4530
Food Matters Again, 4563
FoodMatch Inc, 4572
Fora Foods, 4580
Ford Gum & Mach Co Inc, 4586
Fork & Goode, 4595
Formost Friedman Company, 4599
Forto Coffee, 4608
Four Chimneys Farm Winery Trust, 4625
Fowler Farms, 4632
Fox N Hare Brewing Co., 4639
Fox Run Vineyards, 4640
Frank Wardynski & Sons Inc, 4657
Frederick Wildman & Sons LTD, 4677
Freeda Vitamins Inc, 4682
Freeman Industries, 4687
Freeze-Dry Foods Inc, 4690
Fresh Bellies, 4708
Friendship Dairies LLC, 4734
Frontenac Point Vineyard, 4750
Fruit Bliss, 4762
Fruitcrown Products Corp, 4769
Fuji Vegetable Oil Inc, 4783
Fulton Fish Market, 4789
Futurebiotics LLC, 4807
G Scaccianoce & Co, 4818
Gabila's Knishes, 4853
GAF Seelig Inc, 4824
Generation Tea, 4948
Genesee Brewing Company, 4950
George W Saulpaugh & Son, 4968
Georgetown Cupcake, 4972
GH Ford Tea Company, 4833

Gia Michaels Confections Inc, 4996
Gillies Coffee, 5012
Gimme Coffee, 5018
Giovanni Food Co Inc, 5029
Glazier Packing Co, 5048
Glennys, 5055
Glenora Wine Cellars, 5057
GLK Foods, LLC, 4838
Global Beverage Company, 5060
Global Health Laboratories, 5065
Globus Coffee LLC, 5068
Glow Gluten Free, 5076
GNT USA, 4842
Godiva Chocolatier, 5092
Gold Pure Food Products Co. Inc., 5105
Gold Star Smoked Fish Inc, 5108
Good Groceries, 5161
Good-O-Beverages Inc, 5177
Gourmet Basics, 5201
Gourmet Croissant, 5203
Gourmet Ghee, 5205
Gourmet Nut, 5210
Gourmet Sorbet Corporation, 5212
Grace Foods International, 5227
Grady's Cold Brew, 5231
Graft Cider, 5235
Grainful, 5249
Grandma Browns Beans Inc, 5263
Gravity Ciders, Inc., 5286
Gravymaster, Inc, 5287
Great American Barbecue Company, 5295
Great American Dessert Co, 5297
Greyston Bakery Inc, 5386
Grossingers Home Bakery, 5399
Growers Cooperative Juice Co, 5410
Grown-up Soda, 5412
GWB Foods Corporation, 4852
H Fox & Co Inc, 5465
H&S Edible Products Corporation, 5472
H. Interdonati, 5474
Hahn's Old Fashioned Cake Co, 5500
Hain Celestial Group Inc, 5505
Hale and Hearty Soups, 5514
Hampton Chutney Company, 5540
Hanan Products Co, 5542
Hansen Caviar Company, 5558
Happy Family, 5567
Harbor Seafood, 5576
Harford Glen Water, 5585
Harney & Sons Tea Co., 5599
Harvest Bakery, 5628
Haven's Kitchen Sauces, 5650
Hawthorne Valley Farm, 5666
Hayashibara International Inc., 5667
Haydenergy Health, 5669
Hazlitt 1852 Vineyards, 5673
Healing Home Foods, 5676
Health Garden USA, 5681
Health Products Corp, 5683
Healthy Food Brands LLC, 5694
Healthy N Fit International, 5698
Heartland Brewery, 5707
Hearttea Inc., 5718
Heavenscent Edibles, 5723
Heintz & Weber Co, 5734
Hella Cocktail, 5745
Hena Inc, 5763
Hendon & David, 5765
Heritage Foods USA, 5798
Hermann J. Wiemer Vineyard, 5808
Heron Hill Winery, 5814
Heterochemical Corp, 5821
HH Dobbins Inc, 5484
High Ridge Foods LLC, 5847
Hippeas, 5890
Hofmann Sausage Co Inc, 5902
Holey Moses Cheesecake, 5906
Hollow Road Farms, 5911
Homarus Inc, 5924
Hood Sterile Division, 5983
Hornell Brewing Company, 6001
Horseshoe Brand, 6003
House of Spices, 6026
Hu Kitchen, 6041
Hudson River Foods, 6049
Hudson Valley Brewery, 6050
Hudson Valley Farmhouse Cider, 6051
Hudson Valley Foie Gras, 6052
Hudson Valley Fruit Juice, 6053
Hudson Valley Homestead, 6054
Hudson Valley Hops, 6055
Hudson Valley Malt, 6056

1341

Geographic Index / New York

Hummustir, 6075
Hunt Country Vineyards, 6083
Hurd Orchards, 6088
Hyde Park Brewing Company, 6097
Icco Cheese Co, 6126
Icelandic Milk and Skyr Corporation, 6131
Icelandic Provisions, 6132
Ideal Dairy Farms, 6141
Ideal Snacks Corp, 6143
IFM, 6112
Il Gelato, 6144
Illy caffe, 6148
Imani Chimani Chocolate, 6152
Imperial Foods, Inc., 6160
In The Raw, 6172
Ingenuity Beverages, 6201
Intense Milk, 6235
Interfrost, 6242
International Casein Corporation, 6249
International Flavors & Fragrances Inc., 6258
International Glatt Kosher, 6265
International Harvest Inc, 6266
IQ Juice, 6122
Isadore A. Rapasadi & Son, 6294
Ito En USA Inc, 6327
J B & Son LTD, 6345
J H Verbridge & Son Inc, 6354
J.B. Peel Coffee Roasters, 6377
Jacquet Bakery, 6430
Jake's Grillin, 6439
Jane Bakes, 6450
Janowski's Hamburgers Inc, 6452
Java-Gourmet/Keuka Lake Coffee Roaster, 6468
Jeryl's Jems, 6504
Jets Le Frois Corp, 6509
Jianlibao America, 6514
Jin+Ja, 6523
JNB Foods, LLC, 6407
Joel Harvey Distributing, 6540
John A Vassilaros & Son Inc, 6547
Johnson Estate Winery, 6565
Johnston's Winery Inc, 6578
Jomart Chocolates, 6582
Jonathan Lord Cheesecakes, 6584
Joray Candy, 6593
Josephine's Feast, 6607
Joyva Corp, 6618
Julian's Recipe, 6630
Junior's Cheesecake, 6635
Juno Chef's, 6636
Just Bagels, 6639
Kaari Foods, 6681
Kalustyan, 6696
KARI-Out Co, 6665
Karl Ehmer, 6710
KAS Spirits, 6666
Katrina's Tartufo, 6732
Keegan Ales, 6748
Keep Healthy, 6750
Keep Moving Inc., 6751
Kelsen, Inc., 6774
Kemach Food Products, 6776
Kidfresh, 6835
Kind Snacks, 6852
Kitchen Table, 6895
Kith Treats, 6899
Knapp Vineyards, 6916
Knese Enterprise, 6918
Kobu Beverages, LLC,, 6929
Kola, 6943
Koppert Cress USA, 6962
Kosher French Baguettes, 6969
Kossar's Bagels & Bialys, 6970
Kreher Family Farms, 6982
Krinos Foods, 6986
Kusmi Tea, 7008
Kutiks Honey Farm, 7009
Kyowa Hakko, 7017
L & S Packing Co, 7022, 7023
La Cure Gourmande USA, 7087
La Esquina Food Products, 7088
La Flor Spices, 7090
La Flor Spices Company, 7091
La Newyorkina, 7096
La Nova Wings, 7097
La Regina di San Marzano USA, 7102
La Rosa Azzurra, 7105
Lactalis American Group Inc, 7126
Lactalis Ingredients Inc, 7127
Lakeshore Winery, 7159

Lakewood Vineyards Inc, 7171
Lallemand/American Yeast, 7175
Lam's Food Inc, 7177
Lamoreaux Landing Wine Cellars, 7186
Lanco, 7195
Landies Candies Co, 7200
Larkin Cold Storage, 7221
Larry's Vineyards & Winery, 7228
Latitude, LTD, 7240
Laura Paige Candy Company, 7244
Laurie & Sons, 7250
Lavazza Premium Coffees, 7253
LAVVA, 7067
Le Frois Foods Corporation, 7269
Le Pique-Nique, 7273
Leader Candies, 7279
Lee Kum Kee, 7295
Legacy Juice Works, 7313
Legally Addictive Foods, 7314
Leidenfrost Vineyards, 7325
Lemon-X Corporation, 7339
LemonKind, 7340
Lenny's Bee Productions, 7351
Leo's Bakery & Deli, 7358
Les Palais Des Thes, 7384
Les Trois Petits Cochons, 7386
Levain, 7397
LiDestri Food & Drink, 7408
Life Plus Style Gourmet, 7414
LifeIce, 7417
Linden Cookies Inc, 7442
Little Bird, 7464
Little Duck Organics, 7466
Little Red Kitchen, 7472
Loacker USA, 7495
Local Roots Farms, 7500
Lockcoffee, 7502
Lola Granola Bar Corporation, 7512
Long Island Cauliflower Assn, 7525
Lou-Retta's Custom Chocolates, 7566
Love Quiches Desserts, 7599
LSK Smoked Turkey Products, 7072
Lucas Vineyards & Winery, 7620
Lumar Lobster, 7645
M.H. Greenebaum, 7691
Macabee Foods, 7724
Macaron Paris LLC, 7725
Madani Halal, 7739
Madecasse, 7745
Madelaine Chocolate Company, 7746
Magnanini Farm Winery, 7770
Magnificent Muffin, 7772
Magnolia Bakery, 7773
Majestic Foods, 7796
Mama O's Premium Kimchi, 7816
Mamma Lombardi's All Natural Sauces, 7825
Mandarin Soy Sauce Inc, 7836
Manhattan Special Bottling, 7846
Manischewitz Wine Co., 7849
Maple Hill Creamery, 7867
Maplehill Creamery, 7885
Mapleland Farm, 7888
Mari's New York, 7905
MarieBelle, 7918
Marjie's Plantain Foods, Inc., 7936
Marnap Industries, 7948
Marshall Ingredients, 7956
Martens Fresh, 7959
Martin Farms, 7966
Marubeni America Corp., 7973
MatchaBar, 8004
Materne North America, 8005
Maxwell House & Post, 8031
Maya Kaimal, 8033
Mayakaimal Fine Indian Foods, 8036
Mayer Bros, 8037
Mayer's Cider Mill, 8038
Mccadam Cheese Co Inc, 8085
Mccullagh Coffee Roasters, 8090
McDuffies Bakery, 8067
Mcgregor Vineyard Winery, 8095
Meadowbrook Farm, 8106
Meat & Supply Co, 8112
Meat-O-Mat Corp, 8114
Meating Place, 8117
Meditalia, 8121
Mediterranean Gyro Products, 8122
Megpies, 8132
Mercer's Dairy, 8164
Merritt Estate Winery Inc, 8183
Metropolitan Tea Company, 8202

Metzger Specialty Brands, 8205
Mexi-Frost Specialties Company, 8207
MI-AL. Corp, 7701
Michel et Augustin, 8235
Michel's Magnifique, 8237
Mike's Hot Honey, 8280
Milan Provision Co, 8286
Milano's Of New York City, 8289
Milea Estate Vineyard, 8292
MilkBoy Swiss Chocolate, 8296
Millbrook Vineyards, 8303
Miller's Cheese Corp, 8310
Millflow Spice Corp., 8314
Milligan & Higgins, 8317
Milmar Food Group, 8324
Milos, 8329
Milton A. Klein Company, 8333
Miss Tea Brooklyn Inc, 8382
Mister Cookie Face, 8394
Mister Snacks Inc, 8397
Mitch Chocolate, 8401
Mitchel Dairies, 8402
Mitsubishi Chemical Holdings, 8405
Mitsubishi Intl. Corp., 8406
Mizkan Americas Inc, 8417, 8418
MKE Enterprises LTD, 7703
MO Air International, 7704
Modern Italian Bakery of West Babylon, 8442
Modern Tea Packers, 8450
Moet Hennessy USA, 8452
Mogen David Wine Corp, 8453
Mom N' Pops Inc, 8461
Monks' Specialty Bakery, 8481
Monte Cristo Trading, 8498
Moon Rabbit Foods, 8521
Morris J Golombeck Inc, 8556
Morris Kitchen, 8557
Mother Earth Enterprises, 8575
Mother-In-Law's Kimchi, 8583
Mountain States Rosen, 8601
Mountainside Farms Inc, 8609
Mr. Mak's, 8623
Mt. Olympus Specialty Foods, 8662
MUD, 7707
Murray's Chickens, 8690
Musicon Deer Farm, 8697
My Brother Bobby's Salsa, 8703
My Cup of Cake™, 8705
My Sweet, 8710
N D Labs, 8719
Nagase America Corp., 8733
Nahmias et Fils, 8734
Najila's, 8736
Nassau Candy Distributors, 8776
National Foods, 8793
National Grape Co-Op, 8797
Natrium Products Inc, 8817
Natural Earth Products, 8825
Natural Nectar, 8842
Natural Sins, 8848
Nature's Best Inc, 8869, 8870
Nature's Bounty Co., 8871
Nature's Plus, 8890
Nature's Provision Company, 8892
NeuRoast, 8948
New Hope Mills Mfg Inc, 8982
New Land Vineyard, 8989
New York Apple Sales Inc, 9002
New York Bottling Co Inc, 9004
New York Pretzel, 9008
New York Ravioli, 9009
Newburgh Brewing Company, 9012
Niagara Chocolates, 9031
Niagara Foods, 9032
Nirvana Natural Spring Water, 9064
Nobletree Coffee, 9081
Nog Incorporated, 9084
Nomolas Corp, 9088
Nora's Candy Shop, 9102
Norimoor Lic, 9110
North American Breweries Inc., 9117
North Country Natural Spring Water, 9130
North River Roasters, 9136
North Shore Bottling Co, 9137
Northern Farmhouse Pasta LLC, 9149
Northern Orchard Co Inc, 9157
Northern Packing Company, 9158
Northern Soy Inc, 9160
Northland Juices, 9167
Northside Bakery, 9169
Ntc Marketing, 9199

Nutrisciences Labs, 9255
Nutrition 21 Inc, 9259
Nuts + Nuts, 9270
Nysco Products Inc, 9278
O-At-Ka Milk Prods Co-Op Inc., 9296
Oatly, 9335
Oatworks, 9337
Oc Lugo Co Inc, 9342
Oceanside Knish Factory, 9363
Old Chatham Sheepherding Co, 9398
Old Dutch Mustard Company, 9409
Olivia's Kitchen, 9454
Once Again Nut Butter, 9485
Opa! Originals, 9505
Orange County Distillery, 9514
Organic Gemini, 9542
Organic Nectars LLC, 9549
Organic Olive Juice, 9550
Original Herkimer Cheese, 9564
Orto Foods, 9574
Orwasher's Bakery, 9575
Otis Spunkmeyer, 9590
Owl's Brew, 9619
P.D.I Cone-Dutch Treat, 9643
Paesana Products, 9707
Palmer Vineyards Inc, 9724
Paramount Caviar, 9771
Parkside Candy Co, 9787
Pascal Coffee, 9800
Pasta Del Mondo, 9808
Patsy's Brands, 9835
Patsy's Italian Restaurant, 9837
Paumanok Vineyards, 9850
Pavero Cold Storage, 9852
Pawelski Farm, 9854
Pazdar Winery, 9856
PB Leiner USA, 9649
Peaceworks, 9863
Peanut Butter & Co., 9865
Pearl River Pastry & Chocolate, 9875
Peconic Bay Winery, 9884
Pecoraro Dairy Products, 9885
Pede Brothers Italian Food, 9887
Penny Lick Ice Cream Company, 9927
PepsiCo., 9945
Pereg Gourmet Spices, 9947
Perfect Foods Inc, 9951
Pernod Ricard USA, 9964
Perry's Ice Cream Co Inc, 9969
Pestano Products, 9972
Pestos with Panache, 9973
Pfeil & Holding Inc, 9994
Pfizer, 9995
Phin & Phebes, 10016
Phoenix Agro-Industrial Corporation, 10021
Phoenix Laboratories, 10023
Pidy Gourmet Pastry Shells, 10039
Pilgrim Foods, 10055
Pindar Vineyards, 10061
Pino's Pasta Veloce, 10068
Pipsnacks, 10085
Plaza House Coffee, 10108
Plaza Sweets Bakery, 10109
Pleasant Valley Wine Co, 10112
Plymouth Beef Co., 10130
Pollio Dairy Products, 10155
Ponti USA, 10168
Portier Fine Foods, 10203
Porto Rico Importing, 10208
Prime Food Processing Corp, 10290
Private Label Foods, 10312
Pro Portion Food, 10316
ProFormance Foods, 10318
Prohibition Distillery, LLC, 10338
Proper-Chem, 10346
Pure Extracts Inc, 10369
Purity Ice Cream Co, 10397
Purity Products, 10399
Q Bell Foods, 10408
Q Drinks, 10409
Q Mixers, 10410
Quaker Bonnet, 10417
Quaker Sugar Company, 10421
Quality Snacks, 10445
Queen Ann Ravioli & Macaroni, 10448
Queensboro Farm Products, 10455, 10456
R.W. Frookies, 10499
Raaka Chocolate, 10520
Rainbow Pops, 10538
Ralph's Famous Italian Ices, 10546
Ranieri Fine Foods, 10565
Rao's Specialty Foods Inc, 10566

Ratners Retail Foods, 10571
Ravioli Store, 10575
Raw Rev, 10577
Rawmantic Chocolate, 10579
Raymond-Hadley Corporation, 10583
Real Cookies, 10589
Rebound, 10597
Regatta Craft Mixers, 10641
Rego Smoked Fish Company, 10651
Remarkable Liquids, 10666
Restaurant Data, 10683
Restaurant Systems International, 10685
RFi Ingredients, 10511
Rich Products Corp, 10714
Richardson Brands Co, 10724
Rick's Picks, 10733
Rip Van, 10750
Ripple Brand Collective, 10754
River Road Coffee, 10770
Riviera Ravioli Company, 10778
Rob Salamida Co Inc, 10784
Roberian Vineyards, 10787
Rockland Bakery, 10816
Rohrbach Brewing Co, 10844
Rolet Food Products Company, 10848
Roma & Ray's Italian Bakery, 10852
Ronny Brook Farm Dairy, 10865
Rosa Mexicano, 10874
Rose Randolph Cookies, LLC, 10887
Rosebrand Corp, 10888
Rosebud Creamery, 10889
Rosina Food Holdings Inc, 10899
Royal Baltic LTD, 10923
Royal Caribbean Bakery, 10924
Royal Gourmet Caviar, 10932
Royal Seafood Inc, 10949
Rubashkin, 10957
Ruby Rockets, 10961
Rule Breaker, 10977
Russ & Daughters, 10987
Russian Chef, 10992
S S Steiner Inc, 11018
S.L. Kaye Company, 11028
SADKHIN Complex, 11031
Sahadi Fine Foods Inc, 11081
Sahadi Importing Company, 11082
Sahlen's, 11088
Sally Sherman, 11108
Salsa God, 11113
Salt of the Earth Bakery, 11116
Salty Road, 11119
San-Ei Gen FFI, 11156
Sanarak Paper & Popcorn Supplies, 11159
Sapporo USA, Inc., 11208
Sara Snacker Cookie Company, 11215
Sarabeth's Office, 11216
Saranac Brewery, 11218
Sarant International Cmmdts, 11219
Saratoga Peanut Butter Company, 11221
Saratoga Spring Water Co, 11223
Satin Fine Foods, 11236
Sau-Sea Foods, 11238
Saveur Food Group, 11251
SBK Preserves, 11035
SBS Americas, 11036
Scala-Wisell International Inc., 11265
Scally's Imperial Importing Company Inc, 11266
Schaller & Weber Inc, 11276
Schisa Brothers, 11290
Schloss Doepken Winery, 11293
Screamin' Onionz, 11334
Seaberghs Frozen Foods, 11362
Seaside Ice Cream, 11383
Seneca Foods Corp, 11434
Seneca Juice, 11435
Serendipitea, 11452
Serro Foods LLC, 11457
Sesinco Foods, 11463
Setton International Foods, 11468
Seviroli Foods, 11481
Seviroli Foods, 11482
Sexy Pop LLC, 11484
Sfoglini Pasta Shop, 11488
Sheffa Foods, 11533
Sheryl's Chocolate Creations, 11554
Siggi's Dairy, 11596
Signature Beverage, 11598
Signore Winery, 11603
Silver Spoon, 11624
Simple Foods, 11645
Simply Divine, 11651

Simply Gum, 11653
Sir Kensington's, 11671
Sir Real Foods, 11672
Six Mile Creek Vineyard, 11681
SlantShack Jerky, 11698
Small Axe Peppers, 11709
Smith Packing Regional Meat, 11728
Snow Beverages, 11760
Solvaira Specialties, 11794
Soozy's Grain-Free, 11811
Sophia Foods, 11814
South Beach Novelties & Confectionery, 11827
Sovena USA Inc, 11875
Spaten North America Inc, 11891
Specialty Food Association, 11900
Specialty Food Magazine, 11901
Spelt Right Foods, LLC, 11911
Spice House International Specialties, 11918
Spoonable, 11946
Sprinkles Cupcakes, 11975
Sprout Creek Farm, 11976
Stanley Orchards Sales, Inc., 12031
Star Kay White Inc, 12036
Stauffer's, 12061
Sterling Candy, Inc., 12082
Steve & Andy's Organics, 12090
Steve's Authentic Key Lime Pies, 12093
Steve's Ice Cream, Craft Collective, 12095
Steve's Mom, 12096
Stevens Creative Enterprises, Inc., 12100
Stewart's Beverages, 12109
Stewart's Shops Corp, 12111
Stone's Home Made Candy Shop, 12135
Stoutridge Vineyard, 12154
Strauss Bakery, 12161
Streit's, 12167
Strong Roots, 12173
Stuart & CO, 12178
Sugar & Plumm, 12193
Sugar Foods Corp, 12201
Sundance Industries, 12269
Sunray Food Products Corporation, 12293
Suntory International, 12315
Sunup Green Coffee, 12316
SuperEats, 12324
Supreme Chocolatier, 12349
Sure-Good Food Distributors, 12355
Susie's Smart Cookie, 12360
Suzanne's Sweets, 12373
Swatt Baking Co, 12381
Swedish Hill Vineyard & Winery, 12382
Sweet & Sara, 12385
Sweet Additions, 12387
Sweet Breath, 12390
Sweet Fortunes of America, 12398
Sweet Loren's, 12406
Sweet Sams Baking Corp, 12412
Sweet'N Low, 12422
Sweeteners Plus Inc, 12427
SweetWorks Inc, 12423
Swerseys Chocolate, 12435
Swisser Sweet Maple, 12445
Syracuse Casing Co, 12459
T Sterling Assoc, 12464
Taste Wine Co, 12545
Tasty Mix Quality Foods, 12553
Tate's Bake Shop, 12562
Taylor Wine Company, 12574
Teapigs, 12588
Technology Flavors & Fragrances, 12595
Ted Shear Assoc Inc, 12598
Tee Pee Olives, Inc., 12600
Ten Ren Tea & Ginseng Co Inc, 12614
Tenayo, 12615
Terra Flavors & Fragrances, 12621
Terra Origin, Inc., 12624
Terrell's Potato Chip Co, 12631
The Ardent Homesteader, 12668
The Brooklyn Salsa Co LLC, 12673
The Chili Lab, 12676
The Daphne Baking Company, LLC, 12681
The Hampton Popcorn Company, 12689
The Humphrey Co, 12692
The Jam Stand, 12694
The Junket Folks, 12696
The Konery, 12698
The Lobster Place, 12702
The Lollipop Tree, Inc, 12703
The Matzo Project, 12708
The Murphs Famous Inc., 12710
The Poseidon Group, 12719

The Really Great Food Company, 12724
The Roscoe NY Beer Company, Inc., 12725
The Saucey Sauce CompanyInc., 12728
The Sprout House, 12732
The Truffleist, 12740
The Veri Soda Company, 12743
The Vine, 12744
The Worlds Best Cheese, 12747
Thorpe Vineyard, 12778
Three Meadows Spirits LLC, 12784
Tierra Farm, 12798
Tio Gazpacho, 12819
TMI Trading Co, 12479
Tom Cat Bakery Inc, 12848
Too Cool Chix, 12877
Torre Products Co Inc, 12895
TOST Beverages LLC, 12482
Trade Marcs Group, 12910
Tradeshare Corporation, 12913
Trans-Packers Svc Corp, 12926
Transamerica Wine Corporation, 12927
Travel Chocolate, 12934
Treo Brands, 12953
Tristao Trading, 12988
Tropical Valley Foods, 13011
Troy Pork Store, 13018
Tumbador Chocolate, 13056
Tumericalive Healing Enterprise, 13057
Tuthilltown Spirits, 13082
Tuv-Taam Corp, 13084
Twenty First Century Snacks, 13086
Twenty-Two Desserts, 13089
Twin Marquis, 13094
Two Chicks and a Ladle, 13100
Ultra Dairy, 13145
Ultra Seal, 13147
Umanoff & Parsons, 13148
Union Square Wines & Spirits, 13173
United Apple Sales, 13181
United Pickles, 13196
Unna Bakery, 13212
Up Mountain Switchel, 13213
Upstate Farms, 13217
Upstate Niagara Co-Op Inc., 13218
US Chocolate Corp, 13119
V & E Kohnstamm Inc, 13232
V L Foods, 13235
Valley View Cheese Co Inc, 13264
Van Leeuwen, 13275
Vanlab Corporation, 13292
Varet Street Market, 13298
Vegan Rob's, 13308
Ventre Packing Company, 13326
Venture Vineyards, 13329
Verday, 13334
Vetter Vineyards Winery, 13371
Victor Preserving Company, 13385
Victoria Fine Foods, 13388
Vida Blend, 13392
Vigneri Chocolate Inc., 13403
Vikis Foods, 13409
Viktoria's Gourmet Foods, LLC, 13410
Vincent's Food Corporation, 13424
VIP Foods, 13240
Virginia Dare Extract Co, 13444
Vitakem Neutraceutical Inc, 13459
Vitalicious, 13464
Wagner Vineyards, 13529
Walkers Shortbread, 13544
Wandering Bear Coffee, 13563
Warbucks Seafood, 13567
Warwick Valley Winery & Distillery, 13578
Watermark Innovation, 13589
We Rub You, 13608
Wegmans Food Markets Inc., 13624
Weiss Homemade Kosher Bakery, 13632
Well Dressed Food Company, 13639
Wenner Bakery, 13653
West Park Wine Cellars, 13667
Westbrae Natural Foods, 13672
Western New York Syrup Corporation, 13682
Westtown Brew Works, 13694
Whipped Pastry Boutique, 13709
White Cap Fish Market, 13715
White Coffee Corporation, 13717
White Label Yerba Mate Soda, 13721
White Rock Products Corp, 13728
Whitecliff Vineyard & Winery, 13735
Whitney Foods Inc, 13744
Whole Earth Bakery, 13745
Whole in the Wall, 13748

Widmers Wine Cellars, 13766
Wild Thymes Farm Inc, 13788
Wilkinson-Spitz, 13804
William E. Martin & Sons Company, 13810
William Poll Inc, 13815
Willmark Sales Company, 13828
Wixson Honey Inc, 13891
Wolfson Casing Corp, 13902
Wonder Natural Foods Corp, 13905
Wonton Food, 13909
Woodbury Vineyards, 13915
World Casing Corp, 13930
World Cheese Inc, 13931
World Famous Buffalo Wing Sauce, 13935
World Of Chantilly, 13941
Wunder Creamery, 13961
Yancey's Fancy, 13991
Yohay Baking Co, 14013
Yonkers Brewing Company LLC, 14015
Yorktown Baking Company, 14019
Zachys Wine, 14040
Zenobia Co, 14053
Zesty Z: The Za'atar Company, 14060
Zweigle's Inc, 14078

Newfoundland and Labrador

Barry Group, 1057
Breakwater Fisheries, 1684
Central Dairies, 2377
Daley Brothers ltd., 3359
Dark Tickle Company, 3389
Dorset Fisheries, 3698
Fogo Island Cooperative Society, 4540
H.B. Dawe, 5476
Indian Bay Frozen Foods, 6184
International Enterprises, 6256
Labatt Breweries Newfoundland, 7121
Luxury Crab, 7657
Newfound Resources, 9015
Notre Dame Bakery, 9191
Notre Dame Seafoods Inc., 9192
P. Janes & Sons, 9641
Purity Factories, 10394
Sweet Sensations, 12413

North Carolina

350 Cheese Straws, 14
A Southern Season, 42
Adventure Foods, 194
Alamance Foods, 258
Alli & Rose, 341
American Quality Foods, 479
American Skin LLC, 481
Andrews Brewing Co, 556
Arcadia Dairy Farms Inc, 635
Atkinson Milling Co., 757
Atlantic Natural Foods, 772
Atlantic Seasonings, 778
Avoca, 843
B & B Pecan Processors, 859
B & J Seafood, 865
B&H Foods, 873
Bahama Specialty Foods, 939
Bakkavor USA, 980
Banner Pharmacaps, 1009
Barber Foods, 1022
Bartlett Milling Co., 1061
Beamon Brothers, 1121
Bertie County Peanuts, 1257
Bestco Inc, 1272
Big Boss Baking Co, 1325
Big Spoon Roasters, 1345
Biltmore Estate Wine Company, 1358
Bissett Produce Company, 1403
Blackbear Coffee Company, 1429
Blue Mountain Enterprise Inc, 1488
Bon Courage Gourmet, 1549
Bone Suckin' Sauce, 1555
British American Tea & Coffee, 1723
Buchi Kombucha, 1817
Butterball LLC, 1883
Butterfields, 1885
C.J. Distributing, 1936
Cardi Foods, 2199
Carolina Atlantic Seafood Enterprises, 2233
Carolina Beverage Corp, 2234
Carolina Blueberry Co-Op Assn, 2235
Carolina Brewery, 2236
Carolina Classics Catfish Inc, 2237
Carolina Cookie Co, 2238

Geographic Index / North Dakota

Carolina Cracker, 2239
Carolina Fine Snacks, 2240
Carolina Foods Inc, 2242
Carolina Innovative Food Ingredients, Inc., 2244
Carolina Packers Inc, 2245
Carolina Pride Products, 2247
Carolina Treet, 2250
Case Farms, 2287
Cates Addis Company, 2315
CBP Resources, 1944
Celtic Sea Salt, 2365
Chandler Foods Inc, 2416
Chocolate Moon, 2606
City Bakery Cafe, 2703
Clariant, 2717
Cloister Honey LLC, 2765
Coca-Cola Bottling Co. Consolidated, 2812
Coffee Mill Roastery, 2849
Coleman Natural, 2875
Copak Solutions, 3005
Counter Culture Coffee, 3061
Craven Crab Company, 3119
Creative Snacks Co LLC, 3139
Cultures for Health, 3243
Curtis Packing Co, 3262
Daprano & Company, 3381
Delizza, 3505
Dewey's Bakery, 3553
Dillard's Bar-B-Q Sauce, 3600
Divine Foods, 3626
Dixie Trail Farms, 3632
Drakes Fresh Pasta Co, 3747
Dunbar Foods Corp, 3792
Duplin Wine Cellars, 3805
EJZ Foods, 3853
Emmy's Candy from Belgium, 4048
Europa Sports Products, 4150
Fancy's Candy's, 4247
Farm Pak Products Inc, 4272
Flavor Sciences Inc, 4484
Ford's Gourmet Foods, 4587, 4588
Forge Mountain Foods, 4593
Franklin Baking Co., 4662
Franklin Baking Company, 4663
Freirich Foods, 4692
Fuji Foods Corp, 4781
Fulcher's Point Pride Seafood, 4785
Fuzzy's Wholesale Bar-B-Q, 4811
Gaia Herbs Inc, 4859
Garland Truffles, Inc., 4905
Germanton Winery, 4987
Glean, LLC, 5049
Godwin Produce Co, 5094
Golding Farms Foods, 5146
Good Health Natural Foods, 5164
Good Rub, 5171
Great Eastern Sun Trading Co, 5306
Green Mountain Gringo, 5357
Hampton Farms, 5541
Harold Food Company, 5600
Harvest Time Foods, 5634
Horizon Cellars Winery, 5995
Horner International, 6002
Hospitality Mints LLC, 6010
House of Raeford Farms Inc., 6025
House-Autry Mills Inc, 6030
Hunter Farms - High Point Division, 6085
Improved Nature, 6168
Ingles Markets, 6204
Italian Foods Corporation, 6319
J P Green Milling Co, 6362
Jimbo's Jumbos Inc, 6519
Johnson Brothers Produce Company, 6564
Johnson, Nash & Sons Farms, 6573
Johnston County Hams, 6575
Joseph D Teachey Jr Produce Co, 6599
Joyce Farms, 6616
Kerala Curry, 6799
Kerr Jellies, 6804
Kettle Brand, 6814
Krispy Kreme Doughnuts Inc, 6988
Lakeside Mills, 7163
Lance Private Brands, 7194
Larry's Beans, 7226
Larry's Sausage Corporation, 7227
Le Bleu Corp, 7264
Lewis Sausage Corporation, 7405
Lindy's Homemade Italian Ice, 7447
Lisa Shively's Kitchen Helpers, LLC, 7456
Lowcountry Produce, 7607
Lowland Seafood, 7614

M/S Smears, 7692
Mac's Farms Sausage Co Inc, 7716
Made Rite Foods, 7743
Maola Milk & Ice Cream Co, 7862
MATI Energy, 7697
Maxwell's Gourmet Food, 8032
Maysville Milling Company, 8042
Meadowbrook Meat Company, 8107
Mimi's Mountain Mixes, 8337
Miss Jenny's Pickles, 8378
Mitchum Potato Chips, 8404
Mooresville Ice Cream Co, 8533
Moravian Cookies Shop, 8537
Morgan Mill, 8543
Mother Murphy's, 8576
Mountain City Coffee Roasters, 8593
Mountain Valley Spring Water, 8606
Mt Olive Pickle Co, 8657
Nash Produce, 8772
Neese Country Sausage Inc, 8921
Nello's Sauce, 8928
Nitta Gelatin NA, 9072
No Evil Foods, 9076
Novozymes North America Inc, 9195
NPC Dehydrators, 8726
Old London Foods, 9418
Oliva Verde USA, 9444
On The Verandah, 9481
ONE Brands, 9306
Outta the Park Eats, 9608
Pamlico Packing Company, 9731
Peanut Processors Inc, 9869
Peanut Roaster, 9870
Pender Packing Co Inc, 9910
PET Dairy, 9651
Piedmont Candy Co, 10042
Poppies International, 10188
Poppy Hand-Crafted Popcorn, 10192
Poseidon Enterprises, 10211
Postum, 10215
PowerBar, 10225
Primo Water Corporation, 10303
Qualicaps Inc, 10424
Quality Crab Co Inc, 10429
Ragsdale-Overton Food Traditions, 10534
Randolph Packing Co, 10562
REDCLAY Gourmet, 10506
Renwood Mills, 10675
RJ Balson and Sons Inc, 10513
Royce C. Bone Farms, 10954
S & D Coffee Inc, 11008
Salem Baking Company, 11100
San Marco Coffee, Inc., 11154
Sanford Milling Co Inc, 11177
Sara Lee Frozen Bakery, 11214
Sarliz LLC, 11229
Scott Farms Inc, 11325
Scott's Sauce Co Inc, 11329
Sea Safari, 11349
Selina Naturally, 11421
Severn Peanut Co, 11479
Shallowford Farms Popcorn, Inc., 11503
Simply Delicious, 11650
Slawsa, 11703
Smoked Turkey Inc, 11737
Snyder's of Hanover, 11769
Snyder's-Lance Inc., 11770
Source Food Technology, 11823
Southern Peanut Co Inc, 11860
Southern Season, 11864
Spencer Packing Company, 11913
Spring Acres Sales Company, 11958
Stefano Foods, 12071
Stella D'oro, 12074
Stevens Sausage Co, 12102
Stockton Graham & Co, 12126
Sun States, 12246
Sunburst Foods, 12264
Sunburst Trout Farms, 12265
T.L. Herring & Company, 12471
T.W. Garner Food Company, 12473, 12474
Tastebuds Popcorn, 12548
The King's Kitchen, 12697
Thomas Brothers Country Ham, 12761
Thomas Gourmet Foods, 12765
Tom's Foods, 12853
Tom's Snacks Company, 12854
Tony's Ice Cream Co, 12873
Tradewinds Coffee Company, 12915
Treats Island Fisheries, 12939
Tropical Foods, 12999
Tull Hill Farms Inc, 13053

Ultimate Salsa, 13144
Unique Foods, 13176
Van Hees Gmbh, 13273
Vaughn Rue Produce, 13301
Videri Chocolate Factory, 13395
Villar Vintners of Valdese, 13416
Vintage Bee Inc., 13431
Wayco Ham Co, 13601
Wayne E Bailey Produce Co Inc, 13605
Westbend Vinyards, 13671
Wicked Crisps, 13759
Williams Pork, 13820
Wizards Cauldron, LTD, 13892

North Dakota

Aaland Potato Company, 108
AGT Foods USA, 83
Amberland Foods, 423
Anchor Ingredients, 533
Associated Potato Growers, 741
Ax Water, 848
Baker Boy Bake Shop Inc, 959
Buxton Foods, 1889
Cando Pasta, 2129
Carlisle Cereal Company, 2216
Cass-Clay Creamery, 2295
Charlie's Country Sausage, 2440
CHS Sunflower, 1949
CHS Sunprairie, 1950
Cloverdale Foods, 2783
Crystal Potato Seed Co, 3216
Dakota Brands Intl, 3353
Dakota Gourmet, 3354
Dakota Specialty Milling, Inc., 3355
Ed's Honey Co, 3932
Firebird Artisan Mills, 4413
Food First, 4558
Healthy Food Ingredients, 5695
Heartland Flax, 5709
Lone Wolf Farms, 7522
Minn-Dak Farmers Co-Op, 8351
Minn-Dak Growers LTD, 8352
Minn-Dak Yeast Co Inc, 8353
Monsanto Co, 8483
North Dakota Mill & Elevator Assn., 9132
O C Schulz & Sons, 9281
Osowski Farms, 9584
Premium Gold Flax Products & Processing, 10257
Pride Dairies, 10278
Quality Meats & Seafood, 10439
Red River Commodities Inc, 10616
Rubys Apiaries, 10962
Sonne, 11802
Specialty Commodities Inc, 11898
Sperry Apiaries, 11914
SunButter, 12260
United Pulse Trading Inc, 13199
Winger Cheese, 13860
Woodworth Honey & Bee Co, 13925

Nova Scotia

A&C Quinlin Fisheries, 51
Acadian Seaplants, 135
Adams Fisheries Ltd, 165
AgraWest Foods, 207
Baker's Point Fisheries, 969
Birch Street Seafoods, 1383
Blue Harbour Cheese, 1477
C.L. Deveau & Son, 1937
Captain Little Seafood, 2188
Casey Fisheries, 2290
Ceilidh Fisherman's Cooperative, 2358
Chases Lobster Pound, 2451
Cherbogue Fisheries, 2513
Christy Wild Blueberry Farms, 2657
Clearwater Fine Foods, 2745
Comeau's Seafoods, 2917
D Waybret & Sons Fisher ies, 3299
Davis Strait Fisheries, 3408
DB Kenney Fisheries, 3307
Emery Smith Fisheries Limited, 4045
Fancy Lebanese Bakery, 4246
Fireside Kitchen, 4417
Fisherman's Market International, 4447
Garrison Brewing, 4912
Granville Gates & Sons, 5279
H&H Fisheries Limited, 5469
Harbour Lobster Ltd, 5580
High Liner Foods Inc., 5844

Highland Fisheries, 5855
Howard Turner & Son, 6035
I. Deveau Fisheries LTD, 6108
IMO Foods, 6119
Innovative Fishery Products, 6228
Inshore Fisheries, 6231
Intervest Trading Company Inc., 6280
Island Marine Products, 6301
James L. Mood Fisheries, 6447
Johns Cove Fisheries, 6563
K&N Fisheries, 6659
Kings Processing, 6878
La Have Seafoods, 7092
Leo G. Atkinson Fisheries, 7355
M.A. Hatt & Sons, 7686
Newell Lobsters, 9014
North Bay Fisherman's Cooperative, 9125
Northwest Fisheries, 9173
Ocean Pride Fisheries, 9352
Oland Breweries, 9396
Oxford Frozen Foods, 9620
Scotian Gold, 11322
Webster Farms, 13616

Ohio

1-2-3 Gluten Free, 1
80 Acres Farms, 27
A To Z Portion Control Meats, 45
Abitec Corp, 126
Acme Steak & Seafood, 152
ADJR Inc, 76
Advance Pierre Foods, 184
Aglamesis Bros Ice Cream, 206
Agrana Fruit US Inc, 208
Agvest, 226
ALDI, 87
Alfred Nickles Bakery Inc, 302
Alpine Cheese Company, 378
Amanda Hills Spring Water, 410
AME Nutrition, 93
Anthony Thomas Candy Co, 596
Arizona Beverage Company, 670
Aspire, 737
Athens Foods Inc, 750
Avitae, 840
Ballas Egg Products Corp, 995
Ballreich's Potato Chips, 996
Basic Grain Products, 1071
Beck Flavors, 1143
Beckman & Gast Co, 1147
Belleville Brothers Packing, 1199
Belton Foods Inc, 1211
Ben Heggy's Candy Co, 1214
Berardi's Fresh Roast, 1227
Berghausen E Cheml Co, 1230
Berlin Natural Bakery, 1240
Bickford Flavors, 1312
Biery Cheese Co, 1320
Blue Chip Cookies, 1468
Blue Ribbon Meats, 1494
Boston Stoker, 1599
Bowman & Landes Turkeys, 1632
Breitenbach Wine Cellars, 1688
Brewster Dairy Inc, 1699
Brix Chocolates, 1725
Brookside Foods, 1759
Brownie Points Inc, 1787
Buccia Vineyard, 1815
Budenheim USA, Inc., 1829
Bunker Hill Cheese Co Inc, 1851
Busken Bakery, 1874
C J Dannemiller Co, 1919
C Nelson Mfg Co, 1921
Cajohn's Fiery Foods Co, 2017
Cameo Confections, 2040
Campbell's Quality Cuts, 2117
Canal Fulton Provision, 2126
Candy Flowers, 2134
Caprine Estates, 2176
Carl Rittberger Sr Inc, 2213
Casa di Carfagna, 2275
Case Farms Ohio Division, 2288
Cavens Meats, 2333
Chalet Debonne Vineyards, 2402
Charles Rockel & Son, 2434
Cheryl's Cookies, 2526
Chill Pop, 2567
Chocolate Street of Hartville, 2611
Cincinnati Preserving Co, 2679
Classic Delight Inc, 2726
Cleveland Kraut, 2753

Geographic Index / Oklahoma

Cleveland Syrup Corporation, 2754
Cloverland Dairy, 2785
Clovervale Farms, 2787
Clutter Farms, 2790
Cognis, 2861
Columbus Brewing Co, 2911
Con Agra Foods Inc, 2934
Conn's Potato Chips, 2952
Consolidated Biscuit Company, 2960
Consumer Guild Foods Inc, 2964
Cooper Farms Cooked Meats, 2998
Costa Deano's Gourmet Foods, 3050
CostaDeano's Enterprises, 3052
Couch's Country Style Sausages, 3058
Country Pure Foods Inc, 3083, 3085
Country Smoked Meats, 3088
Cowboy Food & Drink, 3099
Crazy Richard's, 3125
Creative Flavors Inc, 3135
Crestar Crusts, 3157
Crooked River Brewing Company, 3180
Curley's Custom Meats, 3257
Davis Bakery & Delicatessen, 3404
Dayton Nut Specialties, 3421
Decko Products Inc, 3460
Deer Creek Honey Farms LTD, 3468
Dei Fratelli, 3475
Delia's Food Co, 3495
Delphos Poultry Products, 3511
Diehl Food Ingredients, 3593
Dismat Corporation, 3619
Distillata, 3621
DNO Inc, 3315
Dohar Meats Inc, 3647
Donald E Hunter Meats, 3677
Doscher's Candies Co., 3699
Douwe Egberts, 3714
Duma Meats Inc, 3790
DyStar Hilton Davis/DyStar Foam Control, 3826
Eagle Brand, 3859
Eagle Family Foods, 3862
Eagle Ice Cream Company, 3863
East Dayton Meat & Poultry, 3880
Edelmann Provision Company, 3937
Ellenbee-Leggett Co Inc, 4017
Emerald Hilton Davis LLC, 4041
Emerald Performance Materials, 4043
English Bay Batter Us Inc, 4070
Equal Exchange Inc, 4100
Esther Price Candies & Gifts, 4129
Ezzo Sausage Company, 4194
Fairmont Snacks Group, 4226
Faroh Candies, 4296
Ferrante Winery & Ristorante, 4343
Firelands Winery, 4416
Five Star Foodies, 4459
Flavor Systems Intl., 4485
Folgers Coffee Co, 4543
Food Ingredient Specialties, 4561
Forbes Chocolate BP, 4584
Foxtail Foods, 4644
Fremont Authentic Brands, 4694
Fresh Mark Inc., 4715
Freshwater Farms Of Ohio, 4726
Frog Ranch Foods, 4744
Frozen Specialties Inc, 4756
Fry Foods Inc, 4776
G.H. Cretors, 4822
Ganeden, Inc, 4883
Garden of Flavor LLC, 4898
Gardner Pie Co, 4900
Genisoy, 4955
Gentile Brothers Company, 4958
Gerber's Poultry Inc, 4983
Gia Russa, 4997
Glory Foods, 5072
Gorant Chocolatier, 5192
Graeter's Mfg. Co., 5232
Grand River Cellars, 5254
Great Lakes Brewing Co., 5314
Great Lakes Cheese Company, Inc., 5315
Great Western Juice Co, 5334
Grimm's Locker Service, 5392
Grippo Foods, 5395
Groovy Candies, 5398
Grounds For Thought, 5402
Guggisberg Cheese, 5420
H Nagel & Son Co, 5466
Hall Brothers Meats, 5521
Harpersfield Vineyard, 5604
Hartville Kitchen, 5625

Hartville Locker Service, 5626
Heartland Vinyards, 5716
Heineman Winery, 5731
Herb Society Of America, 5779
Herman Falter Packing Co, 5806
Hermann Pickle Co, 5809
Herold's Salads, 5813
Hickory Farms, 5833
Hickory Harvest Foods, 5834
Hillson Nut Co, 5876
Hirzel Canning Co & Farms, 5893
Hirzel Canning Co., 5894
Holmes Cheese Co, 5915
Honey Hut, 5959
Honeybaked Ham, 5966
Humphrey Co, 6076
Ice Cream Bowl, 6128
Ingredia Inc, 6207
Instantwhip Foods Inc, 6233
Inter-American Products, 6237
Island Aseptics, 6297
Island Delights, Inc., 6298
J.M. Smucker Co., 6380
Jacob & Sons Wholesale Meats, 6424
Jacob's Meats Inc, 6426
Jagger Cone Co Inc, 6434
Jain Americas Inc, 6437
Jeni's Splendid Ice Creams, 6487
Jenny's Old Fashioned, 6491
JES Foods, 6397
Joe Bertman Foods, 6532
Johlin Century Winery, 6546
Johnson's Real Ice Cream, 6571
Jones Potato Chip Co, 6589
Joseph Adams Corp, 6597
JTM Food Group, 6410
Kahiki Foods Inc, 6685
Kaiser Pickles, 6686
Kantner Group, 6702
Karn Meats, 6718
Katies Korner Inc, 6731
Kelble Brothers Inc, 6757
Kelley's Island Wine Company, 6763
Kerry Foodservice, 6806
Keynes Brothers Inc, 6826
Kilgus Meats, 6842
King Kold Meats, 6868
King Nut Co, 6870
Klingshirn Winery, 6911
Klosterman Baking Co., 6915
Knott's Berry Farms, 6921
Krema Nut Co, 6983
La Crema Coffee Company, 7085
Lake Erie Frozen Foods Co, 7152
Lakeview Farms, 7168
Lancaster Colony Corporation, 7189
Lax & Mandel Bakery, 7258
Lehmann Mills Inc, 7322
Light Vision Confections, 7426
Lubrizol Corp, 7618
Lucy's Sweet Surrender, 7636
Ludo LLC, 7638
M & B Fruit Juice Co, 7671
Mackenzie Creamery, 7731
Mad Chef Enterprise, 7734
Magic Ice Products, 7765
Magnetic Springs, 7771
Main Street Gourmet, 7785
Malcolm Meats Co, 7803
Mancan Wine, 7829
Mane Inc., 7839
Maramor Chocolates, 7891
Maries Candies, 7919
Markko Vineyard, 7942
Marshall's Biscuit Company, 7957
Marshallville Packing Co, 7958
Marzetti, 7986
Marzetti Foodservice, 7987
Mc Glaughlin Oil Co, 8049
McIntosh's Ohio Valley Wines, 8073
McJak Candy Company LLC, 8074
Mehaffies Pies, 8133
Meier's Wine Cellars Inc, 8135, 8136
Mennel Milling Company, 8158
Metzger Popcorn Co, 8204
Miceli Dairy Products Co, 8222
Michael's Finer Meats/Seafoods, 8229
Middlefield Cheese House, 8263
Midwest Foodservice News, 8267
Mikesell's Potato Chip Company, 8282
Milnot Company, 8327
Milos Whole World Gourmet, 8330

Minerva Cheese Factory, 8344
Minerva Dairy Inc, 8345
Minnehaha Spring Water Company, 8354
Mixes by Danielle, 8410
Mom's Gourmet, LLC, 8465
Mon Ami Restaurant, 8467
Moore Organics, 8531
More Than Gourmet, 8538
Moretti's Poultry, 8540
Morningstar Farms, 8551
Mrs. Miller's Homemade Noodles, 8646
Mushroom Harvest, 8694
Nantong Acetic Acid Chemical Co., Ltd., 8756
Natural Foods Inc, 8835
Nature's Nutrition, 8888
New Bakery Company of Ohio, 8956
New York Frozen Foods Inc, 9005
Norben Co, 9104
O'Brian Brothers Food, 9284
O'Danny Boy Ice Cream, 9286
O'Neal's Fresh Frozen Pizza Crust, 9292
Oasis Mediterranean Cuisine, 9333
Ohio Association Of Meat, 9378
Ohio Mushroom Company, 9379
Old Firehouse Winery, 9414
Old Mill Winery, 9420
Old Time Candy Co, 9428
Old World Bakery, 9433
Olympia Candies, 9463
OMYA, Inc., 9305
Original Tony Packo's, 9566
Orlando Baking Co, 9568
Paisley Farms Inc, 9712
Pappy's Sassafras Tea, 9758
Paramount Distillers, 9773
Pearl Coffee Co, 9873
Pearl Valley Cheese Inc, 9876
Peter Cremer North America, 9978
Phillips Syrup Corp, 10015
Pierre's French Ice Cream Inc, 10049
Pioneer Packing Co, 10080
Piper Meat Processing, 10083
Piqua Pizza Supply Co Inc, 10086
PMC Specialties Group Inc, 9655
Queen City Coffee Company, 10451
Queen City Sausage & Provision, 10452
R & D Sausage Co, 10474
R&J Farms, 10488
Ragersville Swiss Cheese, 10531
Rainbow Hills Vineyards, 10536
Randall Food Products, 10559
Ray's Sausage Co, 10580
Reiter Dairy LLC, 10664
Richards Maple Products, 10722
Riverdale Fine Foods, 10773
Robert Rothschild Farm, 10794
Roberto A Cheese Factory, 10798
Rossi Pasta LTD, 10903
Rudolph Foods Co, 10966
Runk Candy Company, 10983
Sandridge Food Corp, 11172
Sandusky Filling & Brittle, 11175
SASIB Biscuits and Snacks Division, 11034
Schiavone's Casa Mia, 11283
Schmidt Bros Inc, 11296
Schobert's Cottage Cheese Corporation, 11304
Schwebel Baking Co., 11318
Sebastiano's, 11399
Select Origins, 11418
Seminole Foods, 11428
Seven Hills Coffee Co, 11471
Shaker Valley Foods, 11499
Shearer's Foods Inc, 11531
Shirer Brothers Meats, 11564
Shreve Meats Processing, 11576
Shur-Good Biscuit Co., 11580
Sidari's Italian Foods, 11582
Sky Haven Farm, 11693
Skyline Chili Inc, 11697
Smith Dairy, 11725
Sofo Foods, 11777
Sonoma Flatbreads, 11805
Spangler Candy Co, 11885
Spring Grove Foods, 11961
Springdale Ice Cream & Bev, 11970
Stehlin & Sons Company, 12072
Steiner Cheese, 12073
Steuk's Country Market &Winery, 12089
Strasburg Provision, 12155
Sugar Creek, 12197

SugarCreek, 12205
Summer Garden Food Manufacturing, 12220
Sunny Delight Beverage Company, 12281
Superior Dairy, 12332
Sweet Designs Chocolatier Inc, 12395
T. Marzetti Company, 12467
Tamarack Farms Dairy, 12516
Tank's Meats Inc, 12526
Taste Weavers, 12544
Tastee Apple, 12549
Tayse Meats, 12578
Temo Candy, 12610
The Invisible Chef, 12693
The Procter & Gamble Company, 12721
The Toasted Oat Bakehouse, 12739
Tiller Foods Company, 12806
Tip Top Canning Co, 12820
Toft Dairy Inc, 12840
Tommy's Jerky Outlet, 12863
Trappist Preserves, 12931
Treier Popcorn Farms, 12948
Tri State Beef Co, 12955
Tri-State Ingredients, 12959
Trophy Nut Co, 12992
Tucker Packing Co, 13046
Turk Brothers Custom Meats Inc, 13062
Ultima Health Products Inc., 13137
United Canning Corporation, 13183
United Dairy Farmers Inc., 13185
United Dairy Inc., 13186
United Provision Meat Company, 13198
Van Roy Coffee Co, 13279
Vegy Vida, 13317
Velvet Ice Cream Co Inc, 13322
Verhoff Alfalfa Mill Inc, 13337
Veryfine Products Inc, 13368
Vinoklet Winery, 13429
Vitale Poultry Company, 13463
Wallingford Coffee Co Inc, 13551
Warren & Son Meat Processing, 13575
Wedding Cake Studio, 13618
Weiss Noodle Company, 13633
Weldon Ice Cream Co, 13638
Werling & Sons Slaughterhouse, 13656
Winans Chocolates & Coffees, 13838
Woeber Mustard Mfg Co, 13894
Wolf Creek Winery, 13898
Wolfies Roasted Nut Co, 13901
Wornick Company, 13951
Worthmore Food Products Co, 13953
Wyandot Inc, 13964
Wyandotte Winery LLC, 13965
Y Z Enterprises Inc, 13974, 13975
Yost Candy Co Inc, 14021
Young's Jersey Dairy, 14026
Zone Perfect Nutrition Company, 14071

Oklahoma

Allied Custom Gypsum Company, 343
B S & B Safety Systems LLC, 870
B-S Foods Company, 877
Bama Foods LTD, 1002
Bama Frozen Dough, 1003
Beck's Waffles of Oklahoma, 1145
Bedre Fine Chocolate, 1155
Bella Vista Farm, 1191
Bishop Brothers, 1399
Braum's Inc, 1670
Carolina Food Company, 2241
Cedar Hill Seasonings, 2348
Chef's Requested Foods, 2502
Cimarron Cellars, 2677
Clements Foods Co, 2750
Cocina De Mino, 2816
Cookshack, 2991
Corn Popper, 3034
Cusack Meats, 3264
Diane's Signature Products, 3582
Eckroat Seed Company, 3921
Eureka Water Co, 4143
Field's Pies, 4367
Fizz-O Water Co, 4462
Food Concentrate Corporation, 4556
Head Country, 5675
IMAC, 6117
KiZE Concepts, 6832
Landreth Wild Rice, 7205
Leonard Mountain Inc, 7364
Lopez Foods, 7538
Matador Processors, 8001

1345

Geographic Index / Ontario

Montello Inc, 8503
National Steak & Poultry, 8805
Neighbors Coffee, 8923
Nonni's Foods LLC, 9092
Oklahoma City Meat Co Inc, 9392
Pepper Creek Farms, 9935
Producers Cooperative Oil Mill, 10325
Ralph's Packing Co, 10547
Schwab Meat Co, 11315
Shawnee Milling Co, 11529, 11530
Shooting Star Farms, 11570
Southern Okie, 11858
Three Springs Farm, 12786
TRC Corp, 12483
White's Meat Processing, 13732
Wynnewood Pecan Company, 13966

Ontario

3 Gyros Inc, 10
A Couple of Squares, Inc, 34
A&A Marine & Drydock Company, 49
A.W. Jantzi & Sons, 68
Ace Bakery, 141
Alexander Gourmet Beverages, 291
Algonquin Tea, 304
Alliston Creamery, 347
Amsterdam Brewing Company, 517
Andrew Peller Limited, 555
Annette's Donuts Ltd., 588
Arla Foods Inc, 678
Astro Dairy Products, 745
Atkins Ginseng Farms, 754
Atwood Cheese Company, 787
B&A Bakery, 871
Bacardi Canada, Inc., 913
Bakerhaus Veit Limited, 971
Bartek Ingredients, Inc., 1059
Beetroot Delights, 1170
Belly Treats, Inc., 1206
Bennett's Apples & Cider, 1221
Big Sky Brands, 1343
BioExx Specialty Proteins, 1372
Bonduelle North America, 1553
Bonnie & Don Flavours Inc., 1560
Bos Smoked Fish Inc, 1585
Bottle Green Drinks Company, 1605
Brick Brewery, 1702
Broadhead Brewing Co, 1729
Brum's Dairy, 1799
Bunge Canada, 1847
Burn Brae Farms, 1864
Cadbury Adams, 1980
Cadbury Beverages Canada, 1981
Campbell Company of Canada, 2115
Canada Bread Co, Ltd, 2121
Canadian Mist Distillers, 2124
Canaf Foods International, 2125
Cangel, 2138
Capolla Food Inc, 2165
Cappola Foods, 2170
Cardinal Meat Specialists, 2200
Carmadhy's Foods, 2219
Carole's Cheesecake Company, 2232
Cedarvale Food Products, 2357
Centreside Dairy, 2384
Cericola Farms, 2393
Chasquis Natural Foods, 2452
Chateau des Charmes Wines, 2467
Cherry Lane Frozen Fruits, 2521
Chicago 58 Food Products, 2541
Chickapea, 2553
Chocolate Signatures LP, 2608
Chudleigh's, 2661
Clarkson Scottish Bakery, 2720
Clearly Canadian Beverage Corporation, 2742
Coby's Cookies, 2810
Cocomira Confections, 2827
Coffee Mill Roasting Company, 2850
Colonial Cookies, Ltd, 2886
Commercial Bakeries, 2920
Conagra Brands Canada, 2938
Corbion, 3022
Corby Distilleries, 3024
Creemore Springs Brewery, 3141
Crofter's Food, 3176
Crystal Springs, 3218
Dainty Confections, 3332
Dare Foods Incorporated, 3384
Del's Pastry, 3483
Derlea Foods, 3532

Diageo Canada Inc., 3569
Dimpflmeier Bakery, 3606
Dr. Oetker Canada Ltd., 3734
Dufflet Pastries, 3782
E.D. Smith Foods Ltd, 3844
Ecom Manufacturing Corporation, 3926
El Peto Products, 3987
Elco Fine Foods, 3995
Embassy Flavours Ltd., 4039
Essiac Canada International, 4126
Evergreen Juices Inc., 4167
Everspring Farms, 4172
Exeter Produce, 4185
Feature Foods, 4317
Ferroclad Fishery, 4352
Fiera Foods, 4371
Fiesta Farms, 4374
Flavouressence Products, 4495
Food Source Company, 4569
Fru-V, 4758
Fruit of the Land Products, 4768
Future Bakery & Cafe, 4806
G.S. Dunn Limited, 4823
Gabriella's Kitchen, 4854
Gelato Fresco, 4935
Global Botanical, 5061
Global Egg Corporation, 5062
GoBio!, 5089
Good Food For Good, 5156
Good Old Dad Food Products, 5168
Gourmantra Foods, 5199
Grain Process Enterprises Ltd., 5245
Grain-Free JK Gourmet, Inc., 5247
Grandview Farms, 5270
Granny's Best Strawberry Products, 5276
Granowska's, 5277
Greaves Jams & Marmalades, 5339
GS Dunn & Company, 4845
Gumpert's Canada, 5444
H&A Health Products, Inc, 5468
Halal Fine Foods, 5512
Harvest-Pac Products, 5637
Hela Spice Company, 5740
Henry H. Misner Ltd., 5773
Herbal Magic, 5785
Hiram Walker & Sons, 5892
Hogtown Brewing Company, 5904
Hollandia Bakeries Limited, 5909
Horizon Poultry, 5997
Howson Mills, 6037
Inca Gold Organics, 6174
Inniskilin Wines, 6223
Inovata Foods, 6230
Intercorp Excelle Foods, 6240
International Cheese Company, 6251
Ivanhoe Cheese Inc, 6328
J.R. Short Canadian Mills, 6385
Jakeman's Maple Products, 6440
Jamieson Laboratories, 6449
Janes Family Foods, 6451
Jay Shah Foods, 6473
Karma Candy, 6715
Kasseler Food Products Inc., 6723
KD Canners Inc, 6669
Kellogg Canada Inc., 6765
Kerr Brothers, 6803
Kii Naturals Inc, 6839
King Cole Ducks Limited, 6860
Kingsville Fisherman's Company, 6883
Kittling Ridge Estate Wines & Spirits, 6901
Knight's Appleden Fruit LTD, 6920
Konzelmann Estate Winery, 6957
Kraft Heinz Canada, 6976
Kurtz Orchards Farms, 7006
L&M Bakers Supply Company, 7031
Labatt Brewery London, 7122
Labatt Brewing Company, 7123
Lake City Foods, 7150
Lakeside Packing Company, 7164
Lanthier Bakery, 7215
Lee's Food Products, 7298
LEF McLean Brothers International, 7068
Lenchner Bakery, 7344
Lennox Farm, 7349
Lilydale Foods, 7432
Lougheed Fisheries, 7567
Lounsbury Foods, 7594
Love Good Fats, 7597
Lynch Foods, 7661
MacGregors Meat & Seafood, 7721
Magnotta Winery Corporation, 7776
Mama Amy's Quality Foods, 7811

Maple Leaf Foods International, 7876
Marie F, 7916
Marsan Foods, 7954
Martha's Garden, 7961
McCain Foods Ltd., 8054
Mememe Inc, 8151
Mexican Corn Products, 8209
Michelle's RawFoodz, 8244
Mike's Beverage Company, 8279
Mimac Glaze, 8336
Minor Fisheries, 8359
Molinaro's Fine Italian Foods Ltd., 8457
Montebello Packaging, 8501
Morrison Lamothe, 8560
Mortimer's Fine Foods, 8567
Mother Parker's Tea & Coffee, 8578
Mother Raw, 8579
Mrs. McGarrigle's Fine Foods, 8645
Nacan Products, 8730
Nation Wide Canning Ltd., 8782
Nature's Habit Brand. Inc., 8880
Nealanders Food Ingredients, 8912
Nona Vegan Foods, 9090
Nor-Cliff Farms, 9099
Norfood Cherry Growers, 9109
Northern Breweries, 9145
Nourishtea, 9193
Nu-Way Potato Products, 9204
NuPasta, 9210
Nustef Products, 9225
Nuts For Cheese, 9273
O'Doughs, 9289
Oakrun Farm Bakery, 9329
Ocean Food Co. Ltd., 9347
Old Credit Brewing Co. Ltd., 9404
Omega Foods, 9476
Ontario Foods, 9498
Ontario Pork, 9499
Original Foods, 9562
Ottawa Valley Grain Products, 9594
Oven Ready Products, 9613
Ozery Bakery, 9623
Ozery Bakery Inc, 9624
P&H Milling Group, 9638
Parmalat Canada, 9789
Pasta International, 9810
Pasta Quistini, 9815
Patty Palace Foods, 9842
Pauline's Pastries, 9848
Penauta Products, 9909
Petra International, 9987
Phipps Desserts, 10017
Picard Peanuts, 10031
Piller Sausages & Delicatessens, 10057
Piller's Fine Foods, 10058
Pine River Cheese & Butter Company, 10064
Pinty's Premium Foods, 10071
Pintys Delicious Foods, 10072
POG, 9657
President's Choice, 10262
Prime Pastries, 10294
Primo Foods, 10301
Puratos Canada, 10366
Pure Foods Meat, 10373
Quaker Oats Company, 10420
Rallis Whole Foods, 10544
Rector Foods, 10599
Reinhart Foods, 10659
Riverside Natural Foods, 10774
Royal Home Bakery, 10935
Royal Touch Foods, 10950
Rubicon Food Products, 10958
Rudolph's Specialty Bakery, 10968
Sable & Rosenfeld Foods, 11062
Santa Maria Foods, 11197
Saxon Chocolates, 11261
SC Enterprises, 11037
Schneider Foods, 11298, 11299, 11300
Seenergy Foods, 11410
Select Food Products, 11416
Shady Maple Farm, 11492
Shah Trading Company, 11496
Shashi Foods, 11522
Shaw Baking Company, 11525
Siena Foods, 11588
Silani Sweet Cheese, 11606
Skjodt-Barrett Foods, 11691
Sleeman Breweries, Ltd., 11704
Snyder Foods, 11768
Sofina Foods Inc, 11776
Sprague Foods, 11955

Springbank Cheese Company, 11968
Sprucewood Handmade Cookie Company, 11983
St. Jacobs Candy Co., 12005
St. Lawrence Starch, 12009
StoneHammer Brewing, 12136
Storck Canada, 12147
Strathroy Foods, 12157
Strub Pickles, 12175
Summer Fresh, 12219
Sun Opta Inc., 12238
Sun Pac Foods, 12241
Sun-Brite Canning, 12255
Sweet Gallery Exclusive Pastry, 12399
Tantos Foods International, 12527
Tasty Selections, 12555
Tatangelo's Wholesale Fruit & Vegetables, 12560
Tea Aura, 12582
Teti Bakery, 12640
The Pur Company, 12722
Thomas Canning/Maidstone, 12762
ThreeWorks Snacks, 12789
Torrefazione Barzula & Import, 12896
Touche Bakery, 12903, 12904
Trafalgar Brewing Company, 12919
Triple-C, 12985
Tropical Treets, 13010
Truffle Treasures, 13037
U.S. Range, 13113
UFL Foods, 13116
Unilever Canada, 13167
United Canadian Malt, 13182
Universal Impex Corporation, 13208
Vicky's Artisan Bakery, 13380
Vienna Meat Products, 13401
Vincor Canada, 13425
VLR Food Corporation, 13242
Voortman Bakery, 13494
Weetabix Canada, 13620
Weil's Food Processing, 13627
Wellington Brewery, 13643
Western Creamery, 13680
Weston Foods, 13691
WG Thompson & Sons, 13513
Wiberg Corporation, 13755
WILD Flavors (Canada), 13514
Wildly Delicious, 13795
Windcrest Meat Packers, 13842
Wing's Food Products, 13858
Woolwich Dairy, 13927
YoFiit, 14007
Yoplait, 14017
Young Winfield, 14024
Zeroodle, 14058

Oregon

A Cajun Life®, LLC, 33
A to Z Wineworks, 48
Adelsheim Vineyard, 173
Ahara Ghee, 228
Airlie Winery, 235
Allann Brothers Coffee Roasters, 327
Aloha From Oregon, 363
Alpenrose Dairy, 373
Alpine Vineyards, 385
Alternative Health & Herbs, 393
Amity Vineyards, 504
Ankeny Lake Wild Rice, 575
AquaCuisine, 622
Argyle Winery, 659
Arico Natural Foods, 661
Arise & Shine Herbal Products, 665
Ashland Vineyards & Winery, 729
Associated Fruit Company, 739
Autumn Wind Vineyard, 826
AvoLov, 842
Bandon Bay Fisheries, 1005
Barhyte Specialty Foods Inc, 1034
Bay Oceans Sea Foods, 1099
Be-Bop Biscotti, 1115
Bean Forge, 1123
Bear Creek Winery, 1128
Beaverton Foods Inc, 1141
Bell Foods International, 1180
Bells Foods International, 1202
Bethel Heights Vineyard, 1276
Betty Lou's, 1291
Big Tree Farms, 1348
Bite Fuel, 1407
Boardman Foods Inc, 1515

Geographic Index / Pennsylvania

Bob's Red Mill Natural Foods, 1519
Boyd's Coffee Co, 1636
Brandborg Cellars, 1656
Brazi Bites, 1673
Brew Dr. Kombucha, 1694
Bridgetown Coffee, 1706
Bridgeview Vineyards Winery, 1707
Bridgewell Resources LLC, 1708
Bright Greens, 1712
Brittle Kittle, 1724
Broadley Vineyards, 1731
Brucepac, 1796
Buckmaster Coffee Co, 1823
Butler Foods LLC, 1877
Calapooia Brewing Co, 2036
Campagna Distinct Flavor, 2113
Candy Basket Inc, 2130
Carlton Farms, 2218
Cary's of Oregon, 2268
Cascade Clear Water, 2281
Cascade Specialties, Inc., 2285
Champoeg Wine Cellars Inc, 2414
Charlton Charters, 2445
Chateau Anne Marie, 2453
Chaucer Foods, Inc. USA, 2474
Chella's Dutch Delicacies, 2506
Christine & Rob's Inc, 2649
Chuck's Seafoods, 2659
Clear Creek Distillery, 2737
Coconut Bliss, 2829
Coffee Bean Intl, 2836
Coffee People, 2853
ColorKitchen, 2891
Coltsfoot/Golden Eagle Herb, 2904
Columbia Empire Farms Inc, 2905
Columbia Phyto Technology, 2907
Confection Art Inc, 2946
Cooper Mountain Vineyards, 3000
Craft Brew Alliance, 3107
Cranberry Sweets Co, 3114
Crater Meat Co Inc, 3117
Cristom Vineyards, 3167
Cuneo Cellars, 3250
DAGOBA Organic Chocolate, 3306
Dannon Yo Cream, 3378
Dave's Killer Bread, 3395
Debbie D's Jerky & Sausage, 3448
Decker Farms Inc, 3458
Deschutes Brewery, 3533
Desserts Of Distinction, 3542
Di Lusso & Be Bop Baskote LLC, 3564
Diamond Fruit Growers, 3576
Duck Pond Cellars, 3778
Dundee Brandied Fruit Co, 3794
Dundee Wine Company, 3798
Dynic USA Corp, 3833
Eberhard Creamery, 3911
Echo Spring Dairy, 3917
Eclectic Institute, 3923
Elk Cove Vineyards, 4013
Entner-Stuart Premium Syrups, 4083
Eola Hills Wine Cellars, 4090
Equal Exchange Inc, 4098
Erath Vineyards Winery, 4103
Euphoria Chocolate Company, 4141
Ever Fresh Fruit Co, 4162
Eweberry Farms, 4180
Eyrie Vineyards, 4193
F C C, 4199
Fenton & Lee Chocolatiers, 4333
Fishhawk Fisheries, 4450
Fishpeople, 4452
Flynn Vineyards Winery, 4536
Foris Vineyards, 4594
Fort Boise Produce Company, 4600
Franz Bakery Outlet Store, 4669
From Oregon, 4746
Fruithill Inc, 4770
Fruition Northwest LLC, 4771
Full Sail Brewing Co, 4786
Fuller Foods, 4788
Fulton Provision Co, 4790
Garden Valley Corp, 4897
Gerard & Dominique Seafoods, 4981
Girardet Wine Cellar, 5033
GloryBee, 5073
Grand Central Bakery, 5252
Great American Smokehouse & Seafood Company, 5301
Great Earth Chemical, 5305
Great Recipes, 5328
Green Valley Foods, 5366

Grow-Pac, 5408
Hair Of The Dog Brewing, 5509
Hallmark Fisheries, 5525
Hanna's Honey, 5553
Happy Campers, 5564
Harry & David, 5615
Hazelnut Growers Of Oregon, 5671
Hazy Grove Nuts, 5674
Henry Estate Winery, 5772
Herb Pharm, 5778
Herbs America, 5790
Highland Laboratories, 5856
Hillcrest Vineyards, 5870
Honey Mama's, 5960
Honeywood Winery, 5969
Hood River Coffee Co, 5980
Hood River Distillers Inc, 5981
Hood River Vineyards and Winery, 5982
Humm Kombucha, 6071
Improper Goods, 6167
Jacobsen's Salt Co., 6427
Jacobsmuhlen's Meats, 6428
Jaguar Yerba Company, 6435
Jensen's Bread and Bakeries, 6493
Jerusalem House, 6503
Judy's Cream Caramels, 6625
K & F Select Fine Coffees, 6654
KERR Concentrates Inc, 6671
Kettle Foods Inc, 6816
King Estate Winery, 6862
Kittridge & Fredrickson LTD, 6902
Kombucha Wonder Drink, 6948
Kramer Vineyards, 6979
Kristin Hill Winery, 6990
Kroger Bakery, 6991
Kubla Khan Food Company, 6998
Laird Superfood, 7147
Lange Estate Winery & Vineyard, 7212
Laurel Foods, 7246
Liberty Natural Products Inc, 7409
Lisanatti Foods, 7458
LivBar, 7466
Living Harvest Foods, 7486
Longbottom Coffee & Tea Inc, 7529
Longford-Hamilton Company, 7530
Lucky Foods, 7630
Luhr Jensen & Sons Inc, 7642
Luna & Larry's Coconut Bliss, 7647
Mama Lil's Peppers, 7813
McKinlay Vineyards, 8078
Mctavish Shortbread, 8100
Meduri Farms, 8127
Michele's Chocolate Truffles, 8240
Monastery Mustard, 8472
Moonstruck Chocolate Co, 8530
Morii Foods, Inc., 8545
Mountain Rose Herbs, 8599
Mrs. Lauralicious, 8641
Muirhead Canning Co, 8669
Murakami Farms, 8686
Nancy's Probiotic Foods, 8751
Naumes, Inc., 8901
Nehalem Bay Winery, 8922
Nestelle's, Inc., 8943
New Earth, 8967
New Season Foods Inc, 8999
Nicky USA Inc, 9043
NORPAC Foods Inc, 8724
Northwest Chocolate Factory, 9172
Northwest Hazelnut Company, 9174
Northwest Wild Products, 9180
Nu Naturals Inc, 9201
NuNaturals, 9209
Nutri Fruit, 9246
Nyssa-Nampa Beet Growers, 9279
Oak Grove Orchards Winery, 9314
Oak Knoll Winery, 9319
Olympia Provisions, 9466
Olympic Provisions Northwest, 9470
Ontario Produce Company, 9500
Orchard Heights Winery, 9519
Oregon Bark, 9524
Oregon Chai, 9525
Oregon Cherry Growers Inc, 9526, 9527
Oregon Freeze Dry, Inc., 9529
Oregon Fruit Products Co, 9530
Oregon Harvest, 9531
Oregon Hill Farms, 9532
Oregon Potato Co, 9534
Oregon Pride, 9536

Oregon Raspberry & Blackberry Commission, 9537
Oregon Seafoods, 9538
Oregon Spice Co Inc, 9539
Organic Partners Intl., 9551
Organically Grown Co, 9556
Ota Tofu, 9588
Our Lady of Guadalupe Trappist Abbey, 9603
Pacific Coast Fruit Co, 9674
Pacific Foods of Oregon, 9681
Pacific Standard Distributors, 9696
Pacific Westcoast Foods, 9700
Panther Creek Cellars, 9749
Paradigm Foodworks Inc, 9760
Phillips Candies, 10011
Pickled Planet, 10034
Pierre's French Bakery, 10048
Pok Pok Som, 10148
Ponzi Vineyards, 10172
Portland Creamery, 10204
Portlandia Foods, 10207
Powder Pure, 10221
Pyramid Juice Company, 10405
Rainsweet Inc, 10543
Raven Creamery Company, 10572
Red Duck Foods, 10607
Red Plate Foods, 10615
Redhawk Vineyard & Winery, 10628
Redhook Brewery, 10629
Reser's Fine Foods Inc, 10681
Reter Fruit, 10686
Rising Sun Farms, 10759
Rodda Coffee Company, 10830
Rogue Ales Brewery, 10841
Rogue Creamery, 10842
Rose City Pepperheads, 10881
Ruth Ashbrook Bakery, 10997
Sagawa's Savory Sauces, 11077
Sakeone Corp, 11093
Sattwa Chai, 11237
Scenic Fruit Co, 11270
Serendipity Cellars, 11453
Shallon Winery, 11502
Shanghai Co, 11513
Silvan Ridge Winery, 11612
Singing Dog Vanilla, 11665
Sister River Foods, 11676
Sivetz Coffee, 11680
Smith Frozen Foods Inc, 11726
So Delicious Dairy Free, 11771
Sokol Blosser Winery, 11780
Spangler Vineyards, 11886
Sportsmen's Cannery, 11950
Sportsmen's Cannery & Smokehouse, 11951
Springfield Creamery Inc, 11971
Springhill Cellars, 11972
St Innocent Winery, 11996
Stahlbush Island Farms Inc, 12020
Starr & Brown, 12048
Stash Tea Co, 12053
Steviva Ingredients, 12107
Strebin Farms, 12164
Stumptown Coffee Roasters Inc, 12181
Sunshine Dairy Foods Inc, 12304
SuperFat, 12325
Tall Talk Dairy, 12512
Teeny Foods Inc, 12603
The Tao of Tea, 12737
The Water Kefir People, 12745
Thoma Vineyards, 12760
Thyme Garden Herb Co, 12794
Tillamook Country Smoker, 12803
Tillamook County Creamery Association, 12804
Tillamook Meat Inc, 12805
Tofurky, 12842
Tony's Chocolonely, 12872
Topaz Farm, 12884
Townsend Farms Inc, 12907
Trailblazer Foods, 12921
Truitt Bros Inc, 13038
Tualatin Estate Vineyards, 13044
Turtle Island Foods, 13073, 13074
Tuscan Bakery, 13077
Tyee Wine Cellars, 13106
Ultimate Biscotti, 13139
Umpqua Dairy, 13149
Union Wine Co, 13174
Valhalla Winery, 13250
Valley View Winery, 13266
Voget Meats Inc, 13486

Voodoo Doughnut, 13493
Vtopian Artisan Cheeses, 13496
Wasson Brothers Winery, 13584
West Coast Seafood Processors Association, 13662
Westnut, 13690
Wicklund Farms, 13763
Wildtime Foods, 13797
Wilhelm Foods, 13801
Willamette Valley Pie Co, 13806
Willamette Valley Walnuts, 13807
Willow Foods, 13830
Witness Tree Vineyard LTD, 13889
Wolferman's, 13899
World Cup Coffee & Tea, 13934
Yamasa Corp USA, 13986
Yamhill Valley Vineyards, 13990
Yellow Emperor Inc, 13998
Yerba Prima, 14000
Yogi® Tea, 14011
Yoshida Food Products Co, 14020

Pennsylvania

3 Springs Water Co, 11
A-Treat Bottling Co, 54
A.C. Kissling Company, 62
Abbott & Cobb Inc, 113
Across Foods, LLC, 155
Adams County Winery, 164
Advanced Food Products LLC, 187
Ajiri Tea Company, 240
Alacer Corp, 255
Albert's Meats, 279
Alderfer Inc, 285
Alexandra & Nicolay Chocolate Company, 293
Alfred & Sam's Italian Bakery, 299
Allegro Winery & Vineyards, 334
Alouette Cheese USA, 368
American Specialty Foods, 484
Ames Company, Inc, 497
Andrews Dried Beef Company, 558
Ann Hemyng Candy Inc, 579
Arnold Foods Company, 689
Artisan Confections, 714
Asher's Chocolates, 725
ASK Foods Inc, 103
Ateeco Inc, 747
Avon Heights Mushrooms, 844
Bachman Company, 916
Bake Rite Rolls Inc, 952
Bakery Barn Inc, 975
Barker System Bakery, 1039
Basciani Foods Inc, 1066
Bassett's, 1078
Bazzini Holdings LLC, 1114
BBU Bakeries, 892
Beck's Ice Cream, 1144
Bell & Evans, 1178
Belletieri Company, 1198
Benzel's Pretzel Bakery, 1224
Berks Packing Company, Inc., 1235
Berkshire Dairy, 1238
Bernardi Italian Foods Company, 1245
Better Baked Foods Inc, 1282
Bickel's Potato Chip Company, 1309
Bickel's Snack Foods Inc, 1310
Bimbo Bakeries USA Inc., 1359
Bird-In-Hand Farms Inc, 1385
Blommer Chocolate Co, 1456
Blue Mountain Vineyards, 1489
Blue Ribbon Farm Dairy Fresh, 1493
Blume Honey Water, 1510
Bonnie's Ice Cream, 1563
Bookbinder Specialties LLC, 1569
Boyer Candy Co Inc, 1638
Brandt Mills, 1663
Brass Ladle Products, 1665
Brenntag North America, 1692
Breslow Deli Products, 1693
Brewers Outlet-Chestnut Hill, 1696
Bridenbaugh Orchards, 1704
Brookmere Wine & Vineyard, 1755
Buckeye Foods, 1819
Buckingham Valley Vineyards, 1822
Buds Kitchen, 1831
Buffalo Bills Premium Snacks, 1838
Bumbleberry Farms LLC, 1845
Byrnes & Kiefer Co, 1903
Byrnes & Kiefer Company, 1904
Caffe D'Amore Gourmet Beverages, 2007

1347

Geographic Index / Pennsylvania

Candy Cottage Company, 2133
Carborator Rental Svc, 2198
Carl Venezia Fresh Meats, 2214
Castle Cheese, 2301
Catawissa Bottling Co, 2311
Catch Up Logistics, 2312
Catoris Candies Inc, 2320
Cawston Press, 2337
Cellone Bakery Inc, 2362
Chaddsford Winery, 2399
Charles Poultry Company, 2433
Charlie's Specialties Inc, 2442
Chef Salt, 2493
Chef Tim Foods, LLC, 2498
Cherchies, 2514
Cherry Hill Orchards, 2519
Chester-Jensen Co., Inc., 2534
Chocolate Creations, 2601
Chocolate Studio, 2612
Chris Candies Inc, 2641
Ciro Foods, 2690
Citterio USA, 2701
Clemens Family Corporation, 2748
Clover Farms Dairy Co Inc, 2778
Clover Hill Vineyards & Winery, 2779
College Coffee Roaster, 2880
Colteryahn Dairy, 2902
Company of a Philadelphia Gentleman, 2929
Con Yeager Spice Co, 2936
Conneaut Cellars Winery LLC, 2953
Conroy Foods, 2958
Cooke Tavern LTD, 2982
Country Butcher Shop, 3065
Country Clubs Famous Desserts, 3068
Country Cupboard, 3069
Country Fresh Mushroom Co, 3077
County Gourmet Foods, LLC, 3090
Cramer's Bakery, 3112
Creuzebergers Meats, 3159
Cricklewood Soyfoods, 3163
Crown Holdings, Inc., 3190
Crum Creek Mils, 3198
Cupoladua Oven, 3254
Dannon Company, 3377
Davis & Davis Gourmet Foods, 3403
DeLallo Foods, 3435
DeLallo Italian Foods, 3436
Delallo's Italian Store, 3487
Delaware Valley Fish Co, 3491
DelGrosso Foods, 3485, 3486
Delgrosso Foods Inc, 3494
Devault Foods, 3549
Devine Foods, 3550
DG Yuengling & Son, Inc., 3310
Dhidow Enterprises, 3558
Di Alfredo Foods, 3559
Di Bruno Bros, 3560
Dieffenbach's Potato Chips, 3592
Dietz & Watson Inc., 3595
Dol Cice' Gelato Company, 3649
Don's Food Products, 3674
Dutch Gold Honey Inc, 3815
E.W. Knauss & Son, 3847
East Indies Coffee & Tea Co, 3881
Eat This, 3903
Eberly Poultry, Inc., 3913
Eclat Chocolate, 3922
Eda's Sugar Free, 3934
Eden's Market, 3944
Edward Marc Brands, 3958
Edy's Grand Ice Cream, 3961
Eggland's Best Eggs, 3968
Egypt Star Bakery Inc, 3970
Ellis Coffee Co, 4023
EMD Performance Materials, 3855
Empire Kosher Foods, 4052
Enrico Biscotti Co, 4075
Erivan Dairy, 4108
Fairview Dairy Inc, 4227
Fairview Swiss Cheese, 4228
Farrell Baking Company, 4298
Fine Line Seafood, 4398
Firth Maple Products, 4431
Fisher Honey Co, 4443
Fitzkee's Candies Inc, 4454
Five Star Home Foods, Inc., 4460
Fleur De Lait Foods, 4502
Forte Stromboli Company, 4603
Fortunes International Teas, 4614
Four Seasons Produce Inc, 4627
Fox Iv Technologies, 4636
Fox Meadow Farm, 4637

Frankford Candy & Chocolate Co, 4659
Franklin Hill Vineyards, 4666
Fresh Tofu Inc, 4725
Fried Provisions Company, 4732
Froehlich Alex Packing Co, 4742
Furmano's Foods, 4802
Galliker Dairy Co, 4873
Garden Spot Distributors, 4896
Gardners Candies Inc, 4902
Gene & Boots Candies Inc, 4944
George E De Lallo Co Inc, 4964
Gerhart Coffee Co, 4984
Gertrude Hawk Chocolates, 4989
Giorgio Foods, 5028
Glen Summit Springs Water Company, 5051
Godshall's Quality Meats, 5093
Goen Technologies Inc, 5095
Goldenberg's Peanut Chews, 5144
Good Food Inc, 5157
Gourmet House, 5206
Gourmet's Finest, 5215
Great American Popcorn Works of Pennsylvania, 5299
Great Valley Mills, 5331
Greater Knead, The, 5337
Gress Enterprises, 5383
Groff's Meats, 5397
Grouse Hunt Farm Inc, 5406
Guers Dairy, 5419
Gutheinz Meats Inc, 5453
Haagen-Dazs, 5490
Hammond Pretzel Bakery Inc, 5534
Hanks Beverage Co, 5550
Hanover Foods Corp, 5555
Hanover Potato Products Inc, 5556
Harner Farms, 5598
Harrisburg Dairies Inc, 5613
Harting's Bakery, 5620
Hartley's Potato Chip Co, 5621
Hatfield Quality Meats, 5643
Hazle Park Quality Meats, 5672
Healthy Beverage LLC, 5693
Helen's Pure Foods, 5742
Heritage Wine Cellars, 5803
Herlocher Foods, 5805
Herr Foods Inc., 5815
Hershey Co., 5818
Hershey Creamery Co, 5819
Honey Butter Products Co, 5957
Hoss-S, 6011
I Rice & Co Inc, 6105
Ingleby Farms, 6202
Ingretec, 6212
Irene's Bakery & Gourmet, 6287
Island Sweetwater Beverage Company, 6310
Jaindl Farms, 6438
Jamaican Gourmet Coffee Company, 6444
Jaquelina's, 6454
Jennies Gluten-Free Bakery, 6489
Jesben, 6505
Joe Clark Fund Raising Candies, 6533
John Copes Food Products, 6551
John Koller & Son Inc, 6557
John Paton Inc, 6559
Jones Brewing Company, 6586
Josh Early Candies, 6609
Joy Cone Co, 6614
JR Laboratories, 6408
Julius Sturgis Pretzel Bakery, 6633
Just Born Inc, 6641
Jyoti Cuisine India, 6653
K & K Gourmet Meats Inc, 6655
Kargher Corp, 6708
Kelchner's Horseradish, 6758
Kervan USA, 6810
Keystone Pretzel Bakery, 6830
Kime's Cider Mill, 6850
Kloss Manufacturing Co Inc, 6914
Knouse Foods Co-Op Inc., 6923
Kutztown Bologna Company, 7010
L C Good Candy Company, 7025
L F Lambert Spawn Co, 7026
L K Bowman, 7028
Lamagna Cheese Co, 7178
Lamonaca Bakery, 7185
Lancaster County Winery LTD, 7190
Lancaster Fine Foods, 7191, 7192
Lancaster Packing Company, 7193
Landis Peanut Butter, 7201
Lang's Chocolates, 7211
Le Donne Brothers Bakery, 7268

Leatex Chemical Co, 7285
Lehigh Valley Dairy Farms, 7320
Leiby's Premium Ice Cream, 7324
Leidy's, 7327
Lengacher's Cheese House, 7347
Leona Meat Plant, 7361
Leonetti's Frozen Food, 7367
Leraysville Cheese Factory, 7370
Lerro Candy Company, 7374
Letterman Enterprises Inc., 7396
Lion Brewery Inc, 7450
Lloyd's, 7494
Loc Maria Biscuits, 7499
Locustdale Meat Packing, 7504
Longacres Modern Dairy Inc, 7528
Longo's Bakery Inc, 7533
Love Beets, 7595
Lucy's Foods, 7635
Lukas Confections, 7643
M Buono Beef Co, 7676
M.E. Franks Inc., 7689
Mac's Donut Shop, 7715
Mack's Bill Ice Cream, 7729
Mack's Homemade Ice Cream, 7730
Mahantongo Game Farm, 7780
Mahoning Swiss Cheese Cooperative, 7782
Maid-Rite Steak Company, 7783
Maple Donuts, 7864
Maple Donuts Inc, 7865
Marburger Farm Dairy, 7897
Marcho Farms Inc, 7899
Martin's Potato Chips, 7970
Martins Famous Pastry Shoppe, 7972
Matangos Candies, 8002
Mavuno Harvest, 8026
McNeil Nutritionals, 8082
Meadow Brook Dairy Co, 8104
Meadows Country Products, 8108
Metropolitan Bakery, 8198
Mex America Foods LLC, 8206
Mia Products, 8217
Michael Granese & Company, 8226
Michael Mootz Candies, 8227
Michel's Bakery, 8236
Michele's Family Bakery, 8241
Middleswarth Potato Chips, 8264
Miesse Candies, 8271
Miller's Mustard LLC, 8313
Morabito Baking Co Inc, 8536
MorningStar Coffee Company, 8549
Moyer Packing Co., 8615
Mrs Baird's, 8626
Mrs. Fly's Bakery, 8639
Mrs. Ts Pierogies, 8648
Mt Nittany Vineyard & Winery, 8656
Mung Dynasty, 8679
My Boy's Baking LLC, 8702
Nardone Brothers, 8770
National Pretzel Company, 8801
Natural Food Source, 8832
Nature Soy Inc, 8864
Naylor Candies Inc, 8908
Naylor Wine Cellars Inc, 8909
Neat Foods, 8914
Neilly's Foods, 8925
Neshaminy Valley Natural Foods, 8940
Network Food Brokers, 8947
Neuchatel Chocolatier, 8949
New Hope Winery, 8984
New World Pasta Co, 9001
Newtown Foods USA Inc, 9027
Nimeks Organics, 9059
Nissley Vineyards & Winery, 9069
NuGo Nutrition, 9207
Nurture, 9222
Nuts About Granola, 9271
O'Boyle's Ice Cream Company, 9283
O'Neill Coffee Co, 9294
Oak Spring Winery, 9322
Old Country Packers, 9403
One Potato Two Potato, 9489
Ore-Ida Foods, 9523
Ottens Flavors, 9596
P & S Ravioli Co, 9632
Palmyra Bologna Co Inc, 9729
Panhandle Food Sales, 9742
Parma Sausage Products, 9788
Pasqualichio Brothers Inc, 9804
Pati-Petite Cookies Inc, 9828
Pellman Foods Inc, 9906
Penn Cheese, 9914
Penn Herb Co, 9918

Penn Shore Winery Vineyards, 9919
Pennfield Farms, 9922
Pennsylvania Brewing Company, 9923
Pennsylvania Dutch: Birch Beer, 9924
Pennsylvania Macaroni Company, 9925
Pennsylvania Renaissance Faire, 9926
Pepper Island Beach, 9936
Philadelphia Baking Company, 10003
Philadelphia Candies Inc, 10004
Philadelphia Cheese Steak, 10005
Philadelphia Macaroni Co, 10006
Phillips Gourmet Inc, 10013
Pittsburgh Brewing Co, 10091
Plainville Farms, 10100
Plantation Candies, 10104
Pocono Cheesecake Factory, 10138
Pocono Mountain Bottling Company, 10139
Pocono Spring Company, 10140
Polar Water Company, 10152
Poppers Supply Company, 10186
Preferred Meal Systems Inc, 10243
Premier Smoked Fish Company, 10252
Presque Isle Wine Cellars, 10263
Pretzel Pete, 10272
Protica Inc, 10350
Protos Inc, 10353
Pulakos 926 Chocolate, 10364
Pure Gourmet, 10374
Purity Candy Co, 10392
Q.E. Tea, 10412
Quaker Maid Meats, 10418
R.M. Palmer Co., 10498
Reading Coffee Roasters, 10584
Red Lion Spicy Foods Company, 10612
Red Rose Trading Company, 10619
Regennas Candy Shop, 10644
Reinhold Ice Cream Company, 10660
Reist Popcorn Co, 10661
Rendulic Meat Packing Corp, 10671
Revonah Pretzel LLC, 10693
Ribble Production, 10702
Rice Fruit Co, 10706
Ritchey's Dairy, 10762
Rivard Popcorn Products, 10766
RM Heagy Foods, 10514
Rocca's Italian Foods Inc, 10806
Rocky Ridge Maple, 10826
Rosa Food Products, 10873
Rosalind Candy Castle Inc, 10876
Rosati Italian Water Ice, 10878
Rosenberger's Dairies, 10894
Ruffner's, 10971
Rutter's Dairy, 11000
S B Global Foods Inc, 11015
S Zitner Co, 11020
S.D. Mushrooms, 11027
Salonika Imports Inc, 11112
Sand Castle Winery, 11162
Sand Hill Berries, 11163
Sandt's Honey Co, 11174
Sandy Candy, 11176
Sanitary Bakery, 11180
Santanna Banana Company, 11201
Sarris Candies Inc, 11230
Sauder's Eggs, 11241
Savor Street, 11256
Scandinavian Formulas Inc, 11268
Scandinavian Laboratories, 11269
Schaller's Bakery Inc, 11277
Schneider's Dairy Inc, 11301
Schneider-Valley Farms Inc, 11302
Sculli Brothers, 11336
SD Watersboten, 11038
Sechrist Brothers, 11401
Senape's Bakery Inc, 11430
Sensational Sweets, 11440
Shane Candy Co, 11511
Shank's Extracts Inc, 11515
Sheinman Provision Co, 11537
Shenk's Foods, 11546
Sherm Edwards Candies, 11550
Shiloh Farms, 11556
Silver Star Meats Inc, 11627
SKW Nature Products, 11044
Slate Quarry Winery, 11700
Smart Juice, 11714
Smith Provision Co Inc, 11729
Society Hill Snacks, 11775
Sommer Maid Creamery Inc, 11799
Sorbee Intl., 11817
South Mill, 11832
Southside Seafood Inc, 11870

1348

Geographic Index / Prince Edward Island

Specialty Bakers, 11895
Specialty Minerals Inc, 11906
Spilke's Baking Company, 11934
Spohrers Bakeries, 11943
Spring Glen Fresh Foods, 11960
Spring Street Bake Shop, 11967
Stangl's Bakery, 12029
Starkist Co, 12046
Starr Hill Winery & Vineyard, 12049
Stauffer Biscuit Co, 12060
Steak-Umm Company, 12065
Steel's Gourmet Foods, Ltd., 12068
Stello Foods Inc, 12078
Stevenson-Cooper Inc, 12104
Stichler Products Inc, 12114
Stoudt Brewing Co, 12153
Straub Brewery Inc, 12158
Stutz Candy Company, 12183
Sugar Plum, 12202
Sugarright, 12210
Sun-Re Cheese Co, 12257
Sunny Dell Foods Inc, 12282
Superior Pasta Co, 12341
Susquehanna Valley Winery, 12362
Sweet Christine's Bakery, 12392
Sweet Jubilee Gourmet, 12402
Sweet Megan Baking Company, 12408
Sweet Street Desserts, 12415
SWELL Philadelphia Chewing Gum Corporation, 11056
Swiss Premium Dairy Inc, 12442
Taif Inc, 12496
Tait Farm Foods, 12497
Tastepoint, 12550
Tasty Baking Company, 12551
Tatra Herb Co, 12563
TBJ Gourmet, 12475
Terranettis Italian Bakery, 12628
The Bauman Family, 12670
The Healthy Beverage Company, 12690
The Lancaster Food Company, 12700
The Stroopie, 12734
The Sunshine Tomato Company, 12735
Three Bakers Gluten Free Bakery, 12781
Tillie's Gourmet, 12807
Titusville Dairy Products Co, 12826
Tom Sturgis Pretzels Inc, 12851
Tomanetti Food Products, 12856, 12857
Tomanetti Food Products Inc, 12855
Tonya's Gluten-Free Kitchen, 12876
Torreo Coffee Company, 12898
Trickling Springs Creamery, 12967
Trotter Soft Pretzels, 13014
Turkey Hill Dairy Inc, 13064
Turner Dairy Farms Inc, 13071
Tuscarora Organic Growers Cooperative, 13080
Two Chefs on a Roll, 13099
Uncle Charley's Sausage, 13153
Unique Pretzel Bakery, Inc., 13178
US Durum Products LTD, 13121
US Mills, 13124
UTZ Quality Foods Inc., 13129
Valdez Food Inc, 13247
Valley Farms LLC, 13253
Vallos Baking Co, 13268
Vanilla Corp Of America LLC, 13291
Vegan Treats, 13309
Vink & Beri, 13427
Vynecrest Winery, 13497
Warrell Corp, 13572, 13573, 13574
Wawa Inc, 13597
Weaver Nut Co. Inc., 13610
Wege of Hanover, 13623
Wege Pretzel Company, 13622
WEIS Markets Inc., 13512
Weiss Brothers Smoke House, 13631
Wenger's Bakery, 13651
Wenzel's Bakery, 13655
Wilbur Chocolate Candy, 13771, 13772
Wild Fruitz Beverages, 13778
Willie's Smoke House LLC, 13826
Wilson Candy Co, 13834
Wise Foods Inc, 13884
World Flavors Inc, 13936
Young's Bakery, 14025
Zeigler's, 14050
Zentis Sweet Ovations, 14054
Zink & Triest Company, 14066

Prince Edward Island

Atlantic Aqua Farms, 763
Atlantic Fish Specialties, 767
Atlantic Mussel Growers Corporation, 771
Belle River Enterprises, 1195
Burleigh Brothers Seafoods, 1862
Case Side Holdings Company, 2289
Johnston's Home Style Products, 6577
L&C Fisheries, 7030
Lobster 4 Dinner, 7497
North Lake Fish Cooperative, 9133
PEI Mussel King, 9650
Spruce Lane Investments, 11981

Puerto Rico

AJM Meat Packing, 86
Borinquen Biscuit Corporation, 1581
Cabo Rojo Enterprises, 1971
Cafe Yaucono/Jimenez & Fernandez, 2004
Destileria Serralles Inc, 3545
Dona Yiya Foods, 3676
Empresa La Famosa, 4056
Empresas La Famosa, 4057
Eurocaribe Packing Company, 4149
Fernando C Pujals & Bros, 4340
Pan Pepin, 9734
Rovira Biscuit Corporation, 10918
Sucesores de Pedro Cortes, 12185
Suiza Dairy Corporation, 12212
Trigo Corporation, 12970

Quebec

1642, 4
A. Lassonde Inc., 56
Abattoir A. Trahan Company, 109
Abattoir Aliments Asta Inc., 110
Agrocan, 220
Agropur, 222
Alati-Caserta Desserts, 275
Alimentaire Whyte's Inc, 307
Aliments Fontaine Sant, Inc, 309
Aliments Jolibec, Inc, 310
Aliments Prince SEC, 311
Aliments Trigone, 312
Alleghany's Fish Farm, 330
Arome Fleurs & Fruits, 699
Atoka Cranberries, Inc., 782
Atrium Biotech, 783
Au Printemps Gourmet, 789
Bacon America, 923
BakeMark Canada, 953
Bernard & Sons Maple Products, 1243
Bio-K + International Inc., 1368
Bleuet Nordic, 1450
Boissons Miami Pomor, 1544
Borden Canada, 1575
Brasserie Brasel Brewery, 1666
Brom Food Group, 1736
Brome Lake Ducks Ltd, 1737
Buddha Brands, 1825
Bull's Head, 1842
Cadbury Trebor Allan, 1982
Carriere Foods Inc, 2260
Charcuterie LaTour Eiffel, 2426
Chocolat Belge Heyez, 2593
Chocolat Jean Talon, 2594
Citadelle Maple Syrup Producers' Cooperative, 2693
Clic International Inc, 2755
Clos Saint-Denis, 2771
Cordon Bleu International, 3026
Cream Hill Estates, 3129
Crevettes Du Nord, 3160
Culinar Canada, 3233
Delicious Without Gluten, 3503
Dion Herbs & Spices, 3613
E. Gagnon & Fils, 3841
Enterprises Pates et Croutes, 4082
Exceldor Cooperative, 4183
Farmers Cooperative Dairy, 4279
FODY Food Co., 4209
France Delices, 4648
Froma-Dar, 4748
Fruit d'Or, 4766
Fumoir Grizzly, 4791
Gadoua Bakery, 4856
Gesco ENR, 4990
Gingras Vinegar, 5024
Glutino, 5085
Golden Town Apple Products, 5136
Gourmedas Inc, 5200
Gourmet du Village, 5214
Gourmet Mondiale, 5209
Grandma Emily, 5264
Great Northern Maple Products, 5324
Groupe Paul Masson, 5405
H Cantin, 5463
J.M. Schneider, 6379
Jazz Fine Foods, 6476
JE Bergeron & Sons, 6395
K+S Windsor Salt Ltd., 6661
Kefiplant, 6753
Koukla Delights, 6972
Krispy Kernels, 6987
L.B. Maple Treat, 7037
La Brasserie McAuslan Brewing, 7077
La Ferme Martinette, 7089
La Maison Le Grand, 7093
La Societe, 7107
Lallemand, 7172
Lallemand Inc, 7174
Lantic Sugar, 7216
Lapierre Maple Farms, 7217
Le Grand, 7270
Leahy Orchards, 7282
Lef Bleuges Marinor, 7307
Les Aliments Livabec Foods, 7375
Les Aliments Ramico Foods, 7376
Les Brasseurs Du Nord, 7379
Les Brasseurs GMT, 7380
Les Chocolats Vadeboncoeur Inc., 7381
Les Industries Bernard et Fils, 7382
Les Mouts De P.O.M., 7383
Les Salaisons Brochu, 7385
Les Viandes du Breton, 7387
Les Viandes or Fil, 7388
Levesque, 7399
LYNQ, 7074
Lyo-San, 7667
Macco Organiques, 7726
Maison Riviera, 7794
Maple Leaf Bakery, 7871
Maple Leaf Meats, 7877
Maple Leaf Pork, 7878
Maple Products, 7879
Mignardise, 8274
Mondiv/Division of Lassonde Inc, 8476
Monster Cone, 8486
Montreal Chop Suey Company, 8514
Mosti Mondiale/Gourmet Mondiale, 8574
Movie Breads Food, 8613
Multi Marques, 8676
MXO Global, 7709
Natrel, 8815
Nature's Touch, 8895
Naya, 8906
Nutri-Bake Inc, 9247
Nutrisoya Foods, 9256
O'Sole Mio, 9295
Office General des Eaux Minerales, 9370
Olymel, 9462
Paklab Products, 9713
Palme d'Or, 9721
Pascobel Inc, 9802
Patience Fruit & Co., 9829
Patisserie Wawel, 9830
PatsyPie, 9838
Pied-Mont/Dora, 10041
Prana, 10238
Produits Alimentaire, 10330, 10331
Produits Ronald, 10333
Prolimer Foods, 10340
Qualifresh Michel St. Arneault, 10425
QualiGourmet, 10423
Rito Mints, 10764
Rogers Sugar Inc, 10837
Rougie Foie Gras, 10911
Saputo Dairy Division (Canada), 11210
Saputo Inc., 11211
Scotsburn Ice Cream Co., 11323
Sherbrooke OEM Ltd, 11549
Sinai Gourmet, 11662
Sobaya, 11773
St. Maurice Laurent, 12010
Sunlike Juice, 12279
Thyme & Truffles Hors d'Oeuvres, 12793
Tomasso Corporation, 12860
Turkey Hill Sugarbush, 13065
Tutti Gourmet, 13083
Unibroue/Unibrew, 13164
Van Eeghen International Inc, 13272
Viau Foods, 13376
Wild Thyme Cottage Products, 13787
Your Bar Factory, 14029
Yum Yum Potato Chips, 14031
Zinda Products, 14065

Rhode Island

A B Munroe Dairy Inc, 32
Bedrock Farm Certified Organic Medicinal Herbs, 1156
Belgravia Imports, 1177
Bess Eaton, 1260
Blue Marble Brands, 1484
Calise & Sons Bakery Inc, 2086
Central Meat Market, 2380
Chef-A-Roni Fancy Foods, 2503
Coffee Exchange, 2843
Comanzo & Company Specialty Bakers, 2915
Daniele Inc, 3374
Del's Lemonade & Refreshments, 3482
Downeast Coffee Roasters, 3722
Drum Rock Specialty Co Inc, 3769
Eastern Food Industries Inc, 3890
Fantastic World Foods, 4252
Finlays, 4407
Galaxy Nutritional Foods Inc, 4867
Galilean Seafood Inc, 4870
Girard Spring Water, 5031
Glee Gum, 5050
Grays Ice Cream, 5291
Great Northern Products Inc, 5325
Hauser Chocolates, 5646
Homestead Baking Co, 5942
Korbs Baking Company, 6964
Lang Pharma Nutrition Inc, 7210
Lemmes Company, 7336
Little Rhody Brand Frankfurts, 7473
Mills Coffee Roasting Co, 8321
Modern Pod Co., 8446
Mrs. Kavanagh's English Muffins, 8640
Newport Vineyards & Winery, 9024
Nuts 'N More, 9269
Pastry Chef, 9823
Peeled Snacks, 9892
Point Judith Fisherman's Company, 10142
Porinos Gourmet Food, 10194
Providence Cheese, 10355
Quality Food Company, 10433
R I Provision Co, 10480
Ranaldi Bros. Frozen Food Products, 10552
Roma Packing Company, 10854
Saugy Inc., 11242
Scialo Brothers Bakery, 11319
Sea Fresh USA Inc, 11342
Sherwood Brands of Rhode Island Inc, 11553
Silver Lake Sausage Shop, 11619
Supreme Dairy Farms Co, 12350
Sweenors Chocolates, 12384
Tase-Rite Co, 12539
Vega Food Industries Inc, 13306
Vienna Bakery, 13398
Virginia & Spanish Peanut Co, 13441
Warwick Ice Cream, 13577
Westfield Foods, 13688
Wildtree, 13798
Winsor SB Dairy, 13868
Wise Mouth, 13885

Saskatchewan

Aunt Kathy's Homestyle Products, 804
Avena Foods Ltd., 836
Bioriginal Food and Science Corp, 1378
Farmer Direct Organic, 4277
FarmGro Organic Foods, 4273
Great Western Brewing Company, 5332
Hemp Production Services, 5760
InfraReady Products Ltd., 6200
NutraSun, 9235
Prairie Berries Inc., 10230
Prairie Malt, 10234
Thomson Meats, 12773
Viterra, Inc, 13475

South Carolina

Adluh Flour, 178
American Bottling & Beverage, 443
Amick Farms LLC, 500
Beacon Drive Inn, 1118
Bittermilk LLC, 1411

1349

Geographic Index / South Dakota

Blenheim Bottling Company, 1447
Callie's Charleston Biscuits, 2092
Carolina Ingredients Inc, 2243
Carolina Pride Foods, 2246
Caughman's Meat Plant, 2327
Charleston Tea Plantation, 2437
Cheraw Packing Plant, 2512
Cruse Vineyards, 3204
Dare Foods, 3383
Devro Inc, 3552
Gentry's Poultry, 4960
Global Food Industries, 5063
Golden Kernel Pecan Co, 5127
Greenjoy, 5375
Grey Ghost Bakery, 5384
Happy Cow Creamery, 5565
Hartsville Oil Mill, 5624
Harvin Choice Meats, 5638
Heritage Short Bread, 5802
Highland Farm Foods, 5854
Holly Hill Locker Company, 5913
Holy Smoke LLC, 5922
Immaculate Consumption, 6155
Know Allergies, 6924
Ladson Homemade Pasta Company, 7131
Lee's Sausage Co, 7300
Limehouse Produce Co, 7434
Livingston's Bulls Bay Seafood, 7491
Long Food Industries, 7523
Low Country Produce, 7606
Lowcountry Shellfish Inc, 7608
Mama Mary's, 7815
Manchester Farms, 7831
Mccall Farms, 8086
Mcclancy Seasonings Co, 8088
Milky Way Jersey Farm Inc, 8298
Mingo Bay Beverages, 8346
Mingo River Pecan Company, 8347
Mod Squad Martha, 8437
Montmorenci Vineyards, 8513
Mother Shucker's Original Cocktail Sauce, 8580
Mustard Seed, 8698
Navas Instruments, 8904
Ninety Six Canning Company, 9061
Nutty Goodness, 9275
Ojeda USA, 9388
Olde Colony Bakery, 9435
Orangeburg Pecan Co, 9517
Palmetto Brewing Co, 9725
Palmetto Pigeon Plant, 9727
Piggie Park Enterprises, 10051
Pontiac Foods, 10170
Port Royal Seafood, 10200
R.C. McEntire & Company, 10491
SeaPerfect Atlantic Farms, 11360
Slather Brand Foods LLC, 11702
SOPAKCO Foods, 11048
Sopakco Foods, 11812
SOPAKCO Packaging, 11049
Sopako Foods, 11813
Southern Baking, 11841
Southern Twist Cocktail, 11869
Specialty Foods South LLC, 11903
Strossner's Bakery & Cafe, 12174
Sunnydale Meats Inc, 12285
Sweetery, 12428
Taylor's Poultry Place, 12576
Terressentia Corp., 12632
The New Primal, 12712
Titan Farms, 12825
Vaughn-Russell Candy Kitchen, 13302
Walter P Rawl & Sons Inc, 13556
Wood Brothers Inc, 13912
Young Pecan, Inc., 14023

South Dakota

Adee Honey Farm, 171
Advanced Sunflower, 192
Artesian Honey Producers, 713
Beef Products Inc., 1163
Cimpl Meats, 2678
Dakota Style, 3356
Dimock Dairy Products, 3604
Folklore Foods, 4545
Hanson Thompson Honey Farms, 5560
Honey World, 5965
Mutchler's Dakota Gold Mustard, 8699
Native American Herbal Tea, 8809
Native American Natural Foods, 8810
Nor-Tech Dairy Advisors, 9100

Red's All Natural, 10625
Schiltz Foods Inc, 11287
Stengel Seed & Grain Co, 12080
Timber Lake Cheese Company, 12810
Triple U Enterprises, 12983
Valley Queen Cheese Factory, 13260
Wall Meat Processing, 13545
Wenk Foods Inc, 13652
Western Buffalo Company, 13679

Tennessee

Adams USA Inc., 168
Allegro Fine Foods Inc, 333
American Mercantile Corp, 470
American Yeast, 491
Ardmore Cheese Company, 650
Aunt Lizzie's Inc, 806
Aussie Crunch, 815
Bainbridge Festive Foods, 945
Bake Crafters Food Company, 950
Beachaven Vineyards & Winery, 1117
Beer Bakers Inc., 1167
BKW Seasonings, 900
Blendtopia, 1446
Blue Planet Foods, 1491
Brimhall Foods, 1715
Brock Seed Company, 1732
BTS Company/Hail Caesar Dressings, 906
Capitol Foods, 2164
CBS Food Products Corporation, 1945
Century Agricultural Products LLC, 2385
Chattanooga Bakery Inc, 2470
Chattem Chemicals Inc, 2471
Choice Food Distributors LLC, 2628
Choice Food Group Inc, 2629
Christie Cookie, 2646
Clifty Farm Country Meats, 2758
Colts Chocolates, 2903
Corky's Ribs & BBQ, 3032
Country Delite Farms LLC, 3070
Country Fresh Food & Confections, Inc., 3075
Cumberland Creamery, 3246
Custom-Pak Meats, 3275
Delmonaco Winery & Vineyards, 3508
Dino-Meat Company, 3612
Double-Cola Company, 3707
Drake Bakeries, 3745
DuPont Tate & Lyle BioProducts Company, LLC., 3776
FarmSoy Company, 4274
Fineberg Packing Company, 4399
Fortenberry Mini-Storage, 4605
Franklin Baker Company, 4661
George A Dickel & Company, 4961
Gold Dollar Products, 5102
Goodson Brothers Coffee, 5187
Gourmet Market, 5208
Grain Craft, 5242
Great Atlantic Trading Company, 5302
Hari Om Farms, 5586
Heritage Farms Dairy, 5797
Heritage Health Food, 5799
Highland Manor Winery, 5857
House of Thaller Inc, 6027
Ingredients Corp Of America, 6210
International Specialty Supply, 6273
Jack Daniel Distillery, 6416
Jakes Brothers Country Meats, 6441
Kelley's Katch Caviar, 6764
Kelly Foods, 6769
Klinke Brothers Ice Cream Co, 6912
Knotts Fine Foods, 6922
Lay Packing Company, 7260
Living Raw, 7488
M. Licht & Son, 7684
Made-Rite Sandwich Co, 7744
Magnolia Meats, 7775
Marlow Wine Cellars, 7946
Marzipan Specialties Inc, 7988
Mayfield Dairy Farms LLC, 8039
Mayfield Farms and Nursery, 8040
Mccartney Produce Co, 8087
McKee Foods Corp., 8076, 8077
Mcredmond Brothers, 8099
Miller's Country Hams, 8311
Mizkan Americas Inc, 8420
Monogram Food Solutions, 8482
Monticello Canning Company, 8510
Moody Dunbar Inc, 8519
Mrs Grissom's Salads Inc, 8629

Mrs Sullivan's Pies, 8634
Natural Spring Water Company, 8849
Nutritional Counselors of America, 9262
Odom's Tennessee Pride Sausage Company, 9368
Ole Smoky Candy Kitchen, 9442
Olive & Sinclair Chocolate Co, 9445
Orlinda Milling Company, 9570
Orr Mountain Winery, 9572
Pasta Shoppe, 9816
Phytotherapy Research Laboratory, 10027
Pickwick Catfish Farm, 10036
Pictsweet Co, 10038
Porky's Gourmet Foods, 10197
Purity Dairies LLC, 10393
Rancho's, 10557
Rocky Top Country Store, 10827
Rus Dun Farms Inc, 10985
S & M Communion Bread Co, 11011
Sally Lane's Candy Farm, 11107
Savannah Food Co, 11250
Seaver's Bakery, 11393
Shenandoah Mills, 11544
Skim Delux Mendenhall Laboratories, 11685
Southern Cotton Oil Co, 11847
Southern Popcorn Company, 11861
Standard Functional Foods Grp, 12027
Stevison Ham Co, 12105
Sun Garden Sprouts, 12230
Taste Maker Foods, 12541
Tennessee Bun Company, 12616
Tennessee Valley Packing Co, 12617
Trail's Best Snacks, 12920
Travis Meats Inc, 12935
Tropical Foods, 13002
Turnbull Cone Baking Company, 13069
USA Laboratories Inc, 13128
Vietti Foods Co Inc, 13402
W.R. Delozier Sausage Company, 13505
Wampler's Farm Sausage Company, 13559
Wilson's Fantastic Candy, 13835
Wonton Food, 13910

Texas

21st Century Products, Inc., 6
Abimar Foods Inc, 122
Acornseekers Inc, 153
Active Organics, 158
Advanced Spice & Trading, 191
Affiliated Rice Milling, 196
Afia Foods, 197
Ahmad Tea, 230
Alamo Tamale Corporation, 259
All American Snacks, 319
Aloe Commodities International, 357
Aloe Farms Inc, 358
Aloe Laboratories, 359
Aloe'Ha Drink Products, 360
Ameri-Kal Inc, 432
Amigos Canning Company, 501
Amplify Snack Brands, 510
Amy Food Inc, 520
Ana's Salsa, 524
Andalucia Nuts, 540
Apani Southwest, 601
Apecka Peppered Pickles, 602
Aphrodite Divine Confections, 604
Apiterra, 605
AquaTec Development, 623
Atkinson Candy Co, 756
August Foods LTD, 794
Aunt Aggie De's Pralines, 799
Austin Slow Burn, 817
Austin Special Foods Company, 818
Austinuts, 819
Authentic Marotti Biscotti, 822
Avary Farms, 832
Azar Nut Co, 854
Azteca Milling, 856
B.W.J.W. Inc., 885
Baker's Ribs No 2, 970
Banana Distributing Company, 1004
Bartush Schnitzius Foods Co, 1064
Bay Valley Foods, 1103
Beanitos, 1125
Bear Creek Smokehouse Inc, 1127
Bearded Brothers, 1132
Beaumont Rice Mills, 1138
Beetnik Foods, LLC, 1169
Bell Mountain Vineyards, 1182

Bellville Meat Market, 1204
Best Maid Products, Inc., 1270
Better Bites Bakery, 1284
Better Living Products, 1285
Big Fatty's Flaming Foods, 1331
Big Red Bottling, 1339
Big Steer, 1346
Black's Barbecue, 1428
Blazzin Pickle Company, 1442
Blue Bell Creameries LP, 1465
Blue Green Organics, 1476
Bluebonnet Meat Company, 1505
Bolner's Fiesta Spices, 1547
Borden Dairy, 1576
Bradley 3 Ranch, 1647
Brazos Legends, 1675
Brazos Valley Cheese, 1676
Briannas Fine Salad Dressings, 1700
Brookshire Grocery Company, 1758
Brothers Sauces, 1769
Broughton Foods LLC, 1770
Burleson Honey, 1863
Burton Meat Processing, 1871
C H Guenther & Son Inc, 1917
Caddo Packing Co, 1983
Cafe Society Coffee Company, 2001
Cal-Tex Citrus Juice LP, 2032
Calidad Foods, 2049
Calvert's, 2098
Candelari's Specialty Sausage, 2128
Canyon Specialty Foods, 2147
Caprock Winery Inc, 2178
Carta Blanca, 2265
Caviness Beef Packers LTD, 2335, 2336
Cece's Veggie Co., 2344
Chameleon Cold Brew, 2408
Charles Walker North America, 2436
Chef Philippe LLC, 2492
Cherith Valley Gardens, 2517
Chickasaw Trading Company, 2554
Chili - Mex, 2564
Chili Dude, 2565
Chill & Moore, 2566
CHO America, 1946
Chocolate Chix, 2599
Chocolates by Mark, 2620
Chocolates El Rey, Inc, 2617
Chocolates Turin, 2618
Chungs Gourmet Foods, 2665
Circle R Ranch, 2686
Classic Confectionery, 2724
Classy Delites, 2730
Claudia B Chocolates, 2731
Coffee Process, 2854
Colgin Co, 2876
Collin Street Bakery, 2881
Columbia Packing Co Inc, 2906
Comanche Tortilla Factory, 2914
Conscious Choice Foods, 2959
Consolidated Mills Inc, 2962
Continental Coffee Products Company, 2969
Cookies By Design Inc, 2987
Cool, 2992
Copper Tank Brewing Company, 3008
Country Estate Pecans, 3071
Country Fresh Inc, 3076
Country Pure Foods Inc, 3087
Crafty Counter, 3109
Creative Foodworks Inc, 3137
Creme D'Lite, 3144
Crunchy Rollers, 3203
Culina, 3231
Culinary Institute Lenotre, 3235
Custom Ingredients Inc, 3273
Cyclone Enterprises Inc, 3284
Czech Stop Grocery & Deli, 3289
Daily Greens LLC, 3328
DairyPure, 3347
Daisy Brand, 3350
Darling Ingredients Inc., 3390
De Coty Coffee Co, 3425
Dean Foods Co., 3442
Decker Food Company, 3459
Deen Meat & Cooked Foods, 3463
Delicious Valley Frozen Foods, 3502
Desert Pepper Trading Co, 3537
Dewied International Inc, 3554
DGZ Chocolate, 3311
Di Mare Fresh Inc, 3565
Dickson's Pure Honey, 3589
Dipasa USA Inc, 3615
Dixie USA, 3633

Geographic Index / Texas

Don Alfonso Foods, 3667
Don Lee Farms, 3671
Double B Foods Inc, 3701
Dr Pepper Snapple Group, 3725
Droubi's Imports, 3768
Durham Ellis Pecan Co, 3809
Dynamic Foods, 3830
East Poultry Co, 3884
Eat Zi's Market & Bakery, 3905
Eilenberger Bakeries, 3975
El Matador Foods, 3981
El Paso Meat Co, 3984
El Rancho Tortilla, 3988
Elegant Edibles, 4001
Epic Provisions, 4092
Epic Source Food, 4093
Evolution Salt Co., 4177
Exquisita Tortillas Inc, 4189
Fall Creek Vineyards, 4234
Farmer Brothers Company, 4276
Farmers Dairies, 4281
Fiesta Gourmet of Tejas, 4375
Figaro Foods, 4381
Figueroa Brothers, 4382
First Food Co, 4425
First Original Texas Chili Company, 4428
Fischer & Wieser Spec Foods, 4432
Fisherman's Reef Shrimp Company, 4448
Flowers Baking Co, 4527
FOND Bone Broth, 4210
Fool Proof Gourmet Products, 4577
Fredericksburg Herb Farm, 4678
Fresh Pasta Delights, 4720
Frio Foods, 4737
Frito-Lay Inc., 4741
Gambrinus Co, 4881
Gandy's Dairies LLC, 4882
Garelick Farms, 4904
Garman Routing Systems Inc, 4909
Gary's Frozen Foods, 4916
Genesis Today, 4951
Genghis Grill Franchise Concepts, 4953
Glacier Foods, 5042
Gladder's Gourmet Cookies, 5043
Glen's Packing Co, 5052
Gluck Brands, 5077
Gluten Free Nation, 5081
GNS Foods, 4840
GoldRush Mustard, 5111
Goldwater's Food's Of Arizona, 5149
Goodart Candy Inc, 5182
Goodheart Brand Specialty Food, 5183
GoodPop, 5181
Gopal's Healthfoods, 5190
Great American Foods Commissary, 5298
Green & Black's Organic Chocolate, 5342
Green Valley Food Corp, 5365
Grumpe's Specialties, 5414
Gulf Marine & Industrial Supplies Inc, 5435
Gulf Packing Company, 5436
H & B Packing Co, 5459
H-E-B Grocery Co. LP, 5473
Haby's Alsatian Bakery, 5493
Hail Merry, 5503
Haile Resources, 5504
Ham I Am, 5529
Hamms Custom Meats, 5538
Hausman Foods LLC, 5647
Hell On The Red Inc, 5744
Helthe Brands, 5755
Heritage Family Specialty Foods Inc, 5795
Hernan, 5811
Heyday Beverage Co., 5822
High Brew Coffee, 5840
Hillmans Shrimp & Oyster, 5872
Holmes Foods, 5916
Holy Kombucha, 5921
HomePlate Peanut Butter, 5934
Honey Blossom, 5956
Honeydrop Beverages, 5967
House of Coffee Beans, 6022
Houston Calco, Inc, 6032
Houston Tea & Beverage, 6033
Hoyt's Honey Farm, 6038
Hughes Springs Frozen Food Center, 6059
Hughson Meat Company, 6060
Humco Holding Group Inc, 6068
Hummingbird Kitchens, 6074
Huse's Country Meats, 6090
Hygeia Dairy Company, 6101
Illes Seasonings & Flavors, 6146
IMAG Organics, 6118

Imperial Sensus, 6163
Imperial Sugar Company, 6164
Indel Food Products Inc, 6177
Intermex Products USA LTD, 6244
International Trading Company, 6277
J & B Sausage Co Inc, 6334
Jackson Brothers Food Locker, 6421
Jardine Foods, 6456
Javed & Sons, 6470
JBS Packing Inc, 6390
JJ's Tamales & Barbacoa, 6401
Julie's Real, 6632
Jus-Made, 6638
Katysweet Confectioners Inc., 6734
Kaurina's, LLC, 6739
Keeter's Meat Company, 6752
Kegg's Candies, 6754
Kent Foods Inc, 6791
Kettle & Fire, 6813
Keurig Dr Pepper, 6818
Kevala, 6820
Kevton Gourmet Tea, 6821
Kiolbassa Provision Co, 6885
Kitchen Pride Mushrooms Farm, 6894
Kitchun Grainfree Food, 6897
Kohana Coffee, 6938
LA Buena Vida Vineyards, 7041
La Cookie, 7084
LA Mexicana Tortilla Factory, 7052
La Tang Cuisine Manufacturing, 7110
Lad's Smokehouse Catering, 7129
Lago Tortillas International, 7140
Lammes Candies, 7184
Lane's Dairy, 7208
Lantana Hummus, 7214
Las Cruces Brand Products, 7231
Lawler Foods LTD, 7255
Laxson Co, 7259
Leigh Olivers, 7328
Leon's Texas Cuisine, 7360
Lily of the Desert, 7430
Limited Edition, 7435
Live Love Pop, 7481
LIVE Soda, 7070
Llano Estacado Winery, 7493
Lola Savannah, 7513
Lone Star Bakery, 7520
Lone Star Consolidated Foods Inc., 7521
Lotus Manufacturing Company, 7564
Love Creek Orchards, 7596
Lowell Farms, 7609
Lt Blender's Frozen Concoctions, 7615
Luna's Tortillas, 7648
LWC Brands Inc., 7073
Mac's Snacks, 7719
Maher Marketing Services, 7781
MALK Organics, 7696
Mammoth Creameries, 7827
Manuel's Odessa Tortilla, 7859
Margarita Man, 7903
MariGold Foods, 7906
Mary of Puddin Hill, 7982
Mazelle's Cheesecakes Concoctions Creations, 8046
Me & the Bees Lemonade, 8101
Meat Center, 8113
Meli's Monster Cookies, 8145
Mertz Sausage Co, 8186
Messina Hof Winery & Resort, 8189
Michael Angelo's Inc, 8223
Michael's Naturopathic Prgms, 8231
Mild Bill's Spices, 8291
Miles of Chocolate, 8293
Milwhite Inc, 8335
Mims Meat Company, 8338
MindFull, Inc., 8342
Minh Food, 8348
Minh Food Corporation, 8349
Minsa Corp, 8360
Mission Foods Corp., 8384, 8385
Mission Pharmacal Company, 8389
Mizkan Americas Inc, 8425
Moledina Commodities, 8456
Molli, 8458
Mom's Bakery, 8462
Monterrey Products, 8507, 8508
Mooala, 8518
Moon Shot Energy, 8522
Moonlight Gourmet, 8526
Moonshine Sweet Tea, 8529
Morrison Milling Co, 8563
Mother Teresa's, 8581

Mott's, 8585
Mott's LLP, 8586
Mount Franklin Foods, 8589
Mozzarella Co, 8616
Mrs Annie's Peanut Patch, 8624
Mrs Rios Corn Products, 8632
Mt Franklin Foods, 8655
NadaMoo, 8731
Nature Nate's, 8862
Nature's Candy, 8872
Nature's Finest Products, 8875
Navarro Pecan Co, 8902
Nell Baking Company, 8927
New Braunfels Smokehouse, 8960
New Canaan Farms, 8962
Newton Candy Company, 9025
Night Hawk Frozen Foods Inc, 9052
Nueces Canyon Range, 9213
Nurture Ranch, 9223
Nutraceutical International, 9239
Nutrition Supply Corp, 9261
Nuts & Stems, 9268
O'Garvey Sauces, 9290
Oak Farm's Dairy, 9311
Oak Farms, 9312
Odwalla, 9369
Oley Distributing Company, 9443
Oliveo LLC, 9449
Onnit Labs, 9495
Oorganik, 9504
Opa's Smoked Meats, 9506
Out of a Flower, 9604
Ozarka Drinking Water, 9622
Pabst Brewing Company, 9664
Pacific Gold Marketing, 9683
Paciugo Distribution, 9703
Palacios & Sons, 9714
Paleo Ranch, 9717
Pangburn Candy Company, 9741
Panhandle Milling, 9743
Papa Dean's Popcorn, 9751
Papes Pecan House, 9755
Parker Products, 9785
Pecan Deluxe Candy Co, 9882
Pederson's Natural Farms, 9888
Pendery's, 9911
Pete's Brewing Company, 9977
Pheasant Ridge Winery, 10001
Phoenicia Patisserie, 10019
Phoenix Foods, 10022
Picklesmith Inc, 10035
Picnik, 10037
Pioneer Frozen Foods, 10075
Pita Pal, 10088
Plains Dairy Products, 10098
Precise Food Ingredients, 10240
Premier Beverages, 10245
Price's Creameries, 10277
Primera Meat Service, 10298
Producers Cooperative, 10324
Provitas LLC, 10357
Pure Milk & Ice Cream Company, 10379
PYCO Industries Inc, 9663
Quality Bakery Products, 10427
Quality Sausage Company, 10442
Quintessential Chocolates, 10468
R Weaver Apiaries, 10486
Ranch Oak Farm, 10553
Red Creek Marinade Company, 10604
Reddy Ice, 10627
Reed Lang Farms, 10634
Regal Food Service, 10639
Renfro Foods, 10674
RENFRO Foods Inc, 10508
Rhythm Superfoods, 10699
Riba Foods, 10701
Ricetec, 10712
Richard E. Colgin Company, 10718
Richland Beverage Association, 10729
Rio Grande Valley Sugar Growers, 10745
Rio Valley Canning Co, 10749
Riviana Foods Inc., 10777
Ron's Home Style Foods, 10861
RoRo's Baking Company, 10779
Round Rock Honey Co, LLC, 10913
Rudolph's Market & Sausage, 10967
Rudy's Tortillas, 10969
Russell E. Womack, Inc., 10990
S&N Food Company, 11023
Sabra Blue & White Food Products, 11064
Sabra-Go Mediterranean, 11066
Sadler's Smokehouse, 11070

Sales USA, 11105
Sam KANE Beef Processors Inc, 11124
Sambets Cajun Deli, 11129
San Angelo Packing, 11133
San Antonio Packing Co, 11136
Sanchez Distributors, 11161
Sanitary Tortilla Manufacturing Company, 11181
Santa Elena Coffee Company, 11193
Schepps Dairy, 11281
Schlotzsky's, 11295
Schoppaul Hill Winery atIvanhoe, 11306
Seawater Food & Beverage, 11396
Selecto Sausage Co, 11420
Serranos Salsa, 11456
Sesaco Corp, 11462
Shamrock Slaughter Plant, 11510
Shedd Food Products, 11532
Shell Ridge Jalapeno Project, 11540
Shine Companies, 11557
Shipley Do-Nut Franchise Co, 11560
Sieco USA Corporation, 11585
Siete Family Foods, 11594
Silver Streak Bass Co, 11629
Silverleaf International Corp, 11635
Simply 7 Snacks, 11658
Skimpy Cocktails LLC, 11686
Smart Flour Foods, LLC, 11713
Smokey Denmark Sausage Co, 11739
Somebody's Mother's Chocolate, 11795
South Texas Spice Co LTD, 11834
Southern Gold Honey Co, 11854
Southern Style Nuts, 11868
Southwest Foods, 11872
Soylent Brand, 11883
Spoetzl Brewery, 11942
Spring Kitchen, 11964
Squirrel Brand Company, 11990
St Arnold Brewing Co, 11992
Stallings Head Cheese Co, 12022
Standard Meat Co LP, 12028
Sterling Foods LLC, 12086
Stevita Naturals, 12106
Sticky Toffee Pudding Company, 12118
Stubb's Legendary BBQ, 12180
Sunday House Foods, 12270
Surlean Foods, 12359
Susie's South Forty Confection, 12361
Sweet Leaf Tea Company, 12404
Sweet Shop USA, 12414
Sweetwater Spice Company, 12432
T.J. Blackburn Syrup Works, 12469
Talk O'Texas Brands Inc, 12509
Tanzamaji USA, 12528
Taste Teasers, 12542
Tasty Tomato, 12556
Taylor Meat Co, 12569
Tekita House Foods, 12608
Terra Sol Chile Company, 12625
Tex-Mex Cold Storage, 12645
Tex-Mex Gourmet, 12646
TexaFrance, 12647
Texas Chili Co, 12649
Texas Coffee Co, 12650
Texas Coffee Traders Inc, 12651
Texas Crumb & Food Products, 12652
Texas Heat, 12653
Texas Sausage Co, 12655
Texas Spice Co, 12656
Texas Tamale Co, 12657
Texas Tito's, 12658
Texas Toffee, 12659
Texas Traditions Gourmet, 12660
The Great San Saba River Pecan Company, 12687
The Pickle Juice Company, 12716
The Sola Company, 12730
Thomas Kemper Soda Company, 12766
Thunderbird Real Food Bar, 12792
Tin Star Foods, 12813
Tipp Distributors Inc, 12823
Toddy Products Inc, 12833
Toffee Co, 12838
Topo Chico Mineral Water, 12886
Tradewinds, 12914
Trans Pecos Foods, 12924
Treesweet Products, 12945
Trinity Spice, 12975
Tropical Foods, 13001
Truco Enterprises, 13029
TruMoo, 13024
Twang Partners LTD, 13085

1351

Geographic Index / Utah

Tyler Candy Co LLC, 13107
Tyler Packing Co, 13108
Uncle Fred's Fine Foods, 13155
United Intertrade Corporation, 13190
United Intratrade, 13191
United Salt Corp, 13200
United Supermarkets, 13201
Universal Beef Products, 13204
Uvalde Meat Processing, 13231
Val Verde Winery, 13245
Van Oriental Food Inc, 13276
Van Tone Creative, 13280
Vending Nut Co, 13323
Vilore Foods Co Inc, 13417
Vital Farms, 13461
Wackym's Kitchen, 13524
WACO Beef & Pork Processors, 13509
Warner Candy, 13569
Warren Laboratories LLC, 13576
Wella Bar, 13641
What's Brewing, 13704
Wholesome!, 13751
Wildway, 13799
Wimberley Valley Winery, 13837
Wine-A-Rita, 13852
Winning Solutions Inc, 13865
Wonderful Citrus, 13906
Wonton Food, 13911
World Art Foods, 13929
World of Chia, 13945
Ximena's Latin Flavors, 13969
Xochitl, 13970
Xooz Gear, 13971
Ya-Hoo Baking Co, 13979
Yarmer Boys Catfish International, 13993
Yoakum Packing Co, 14008
Zummo Meat Co, 14075
Zuni Foods, 14076

Utah

AFI-FlashGril'd Steak, 80
Amano Artisan Chocolate, 412
AMT Labs Inc, 95
Asael Farr & Sons Co, 722
Bear Creek Country Kitchens, 1126
Beehive Cheese, 1165
BetterBody Foods & Nutrition LLC, 1289
Big J Milling Co, 1335
Blue Chip Baker, 1467
Bluebird Restaurant, 1504
Bluechip Group, 1506
Bohemian Brewery, 1542
Brown Dairy Inc, 1775
Caffe Ibis Gallery Deli, 2011
Calcium Springs Water Company, 2039
Casper's Ice Cream, 2294
Central Milling Co, 2381
Cereal Food Processors, 2388
Chef Shamy Gourmet, 2494
Chipper Snax, 2579
Christopher's Herb Shop, 2656
Circle V Meats, 2687
Cocoa Metro, 2822
Cookie Tree Bakeries, 2986
Cornabys, 3035
Country Fresh Farms, 3074
Creminelli Fine Meats, 3146
Cummings Studio Chocolates, 3249
Cutie Pie Corp, 3276
Dailys Premium Meats, 3331
Dale T Smith & Sons Inc, 3358
Deseret Dairy Products, 3534
Designed Nutritional Products, 3539
Dr. Christopher's Herbal Supplements, 3729
Dunford Bakers, 3799
Dynamic Confections, 3829
Dynapro International, 3832
Eat Dutch Waffles, LLC, 3899
Essential Nutrients Inc, 4124
Fendall Ice Cream Company, 4328
Gilt Edge Flour Mills, 5016
Gluten-Free Heaven, 5083
Gossner Foods Inc., 5195
Green Earth Orchards, 5348
Heart to Heart Foods, 5702
High Country Gourmet, 5842
Honeyville Grain Inc, 5968
Horlacher Meats, 5999
Indulgent Foods, 6198
Intermountain Specialty Food Group, 6246
J Morgan's Confections, 6361

JMH International, 6405
Jolly Llama, 6581
Kara Chocolates, 6707
Kencraft, Inc., 6780
Kodiak Cakes, 6932
Lakeview Banquit Cheese, 7166
Lehi Mills, 7318
Lower Foods, Inc., 7611
Lucky Spoon Bakery LLC, 7633
Madyson's Marshmallows, 7759
Mama Maria's Tortillas, 7814
Manuel's Mexican-American Fine Foods, 7858
Maxfield Candy, 8027
McFarland Foods, 8069
Mega Pro Intl, 8129
Montana Naturals, 8493
Moroni Feed Company, 8553
Morrison Meat Pies, 8562
Mrs. Field's Hot Cocoas, 8637
Muir Copper Canyon Farms, 8668
Nature's Fusions, 8877
Nature's Hollow, 8891
Nature's Sunshine Products Company, 8894
Neal's Chocolates, 8911
Norbest, LLC, 9105
Northern Utah Manufacturing, 9161
Nush Foods, 9224
Nutraceutical International, 9237, 9238
Oscar's Wholesale Meats, 9577
Pacific Chai, 9670
Palmer Meat Packing Co, 9723
Parish Chemical Company, 9777
Paul's Candy Factory, 9846
Plentiful Pantry, 10116
Pop Art Snacks, 10175
Pop Zero, 10177
Premium Meat Co, 10259
Pro Pac Labs, 10315
Probar, 10320
Realsalt, 10594
Redmond Minerals Inc, 10630
Rhodes International Inc, 10698
Rocky Mountain Honey Company, 10821
Salt Lake Macaroni & Noodle Company, 11114
Schirf Brewing Company, 11289
Sheila's Select Gourmet Recipe, 11536
Shirley J Ventures, LLC, 11566
Slide Ridge LLC, 11705
Snelgrove Ice Cream Company, 11753
Snow Dairy Inc, 11761
Sportsman's Paradise Whites Ranch, 11949
Springville Meat & Cold Storage, 11974
Startupcandy Co, 12050
Stone Meat Processor, 12132
Superior Meat Co, 12335
Sweet Candy Company, 12391
Synergy, 12455
Taffy Town Inc, 12491
Talisman Foods, 12508
Terrell Meats, 12630
Thor Inc, 12774
Trace Minerals Research, 12908
Treasure Foods, 12936
Tru Fru, LLC, 13021
Uinta Brewing Co, 13136
United Noodle Manufacturing Company, 13195
Utah Coffee Roasters, 13229
V Chocolates, 13234
Wasatch Meats Inc, 13579

Vermont

Anna's Oatcakes, 581
Bascom Family Farms Inc, 1067
Ben & Jerry's Homemade Inc, 1212
Big Picture Farm LLC, 1337
Birnn Chocolates of Vermont, 1393
Blake Hill Preserves, 1432
Blue Moon Foods, 1486
Bove's of Vermont, 1629
Bread & Chocolate Inc, 1677
Brown & Jenkins Trading Company, 1772
Brown Family Farm, 1777
Butternut Mountain Farm, 1887
Cabot Creamery Co-Op, 1972
Cafe Chilku, 1990
Casually Gourmet, 2306
Catamount Specialties of Vermont, 2307
Champlain Valley Apiaries, 2412

Cobb Hill Cheese, 2807
Coffee Enterprises, 2842
Cold Hollow Cider Mill, 2869
Coombs Family Farm, 2996
Cottage Street Pasta, 3055
Couture's Maple Shop/B & B, 3094
Crowley Cheese Inc, 3188
D & D Sugarwoods Farm, 3293
Dell'Amore Enterprises, 3506
Drew's Organics, 3758
Farms For City Kids Foundation, Inc., 4292
Fat Toad Farm, 4304
Flamin' Red's Woodfired, 4468
Foodscience Corp, 4575
Fortunate Cookie, 4611
Fox Meadow Farm of Vermont, 4638
Franklin Foods, 4665
Frog City Cheese, 4743
Gingro Corp, 5025
Grafton Village Cheese Co LLC, 5236
Grand View Winery, 5256
Granny Blossom Specialty Foods, 5274
Great Circles, 5303
Green Mountain Cidery, 5355
Green Mountain Creamery, 5356
Green River Chocolates, 5359
Gringo Jack's, 5394
Halladay's Harvest Barn, 5523
Harrington's of Vermont, 5607
Harry's Cafe, 5617
Herb Bee's Products, 5776
Herb Patch of Vermont, 5777
Hidden Springs Maple, 5836
High Mowing Organic Seeds, 5845
Highland Sugarworks, 5858
Hillside Lane Farm, 5875
Hood Home Service, 5979
Hume Specialties, 6069
Jasmine & Bread, 6459
Jed's Maple Products, 6479
King Arthur Flour, 6857
Koffee Kup Bakery, 6936
Lake Champlain Chocolates, 7148
Leonardo's of Vermont, LLC, 7365
Liz Lovely Inc, 7492
Long Trail Brewing Co Inc, 7526
Madhouse Munchies, 7749
Maple Grove Farms Of Vermont, 7866
Maplebrook Farm, 7883
Mckenzie Country Classic's, 8096
Metarom Corporation, 8194
Miguel's Stowe Away, 8275
Miss Ginny's Orginal Vermont Pickle Works, 8377
Monument Farms Dairy, 8515, 8516
Mount Mansfield Maple Products, 8590
Mountain Fire Foods, 8595
Mountainbrook of Vermont, 8608
Nature Zen USA, 8865
New Chapter, 8964
Northeast Kingdom Mustard Company, 9143
Oak Knoll Dairy, Inc., 9318
Old Cavendish Products, 9397
Olivia's Croutons, 9453
ORB Weaver Farm, 9307
Outback Kitchens LLC, 9605
Phenomenal Fudge Inc, 10002
Plymouth Artisan Cheese, 10129
Poppa's Granola, 10185
Pork Shop of Vermont, 10195
Porter's Pick-A-Dilly, 10202
Potlicker Kitchen, 10217
Putney Pasta, 10402
Rhino Foods Inc, 10696
Roger's Recipe, 10836
Runamok Maple, 10982
Saint Albans Cooperative Creamery, 11089
Sargent's Bear Necessities, 11227
Shoreline Chocolates, 11573
Side Hill Farm, 11583
Sidehill Farm, 11584
Small Batch Organics, 11710
Smith & Salmon, 11722
Stella Foods, 12075
Sugar Bob's Smoked Maple Syrup, 12194
Sugarbush Farm, 12206
Sugarman of Vermont, 12208
Summer In Vermont Jams, 12221
Sunja's Oriental Foods, 12277
Taftsville Country Store, 12493
Teeny Tiny Spice Company of Vermont LLC, 12604

The Maple Guild, 12706
The Mapled Nut Co., 12707
Thomas Dairy, 12763
Tom & Sally's Handmade Chocolates, 12847
Tonewood Maple, 12867
Urban Moonshine, 13224
VerMints Inc., 13331
Vermont Bread Co, 13343
Vermont Chocolatiers, 13344
Vermont Coffee Co, 13345
Vermont Confectionery, 13346
Vermont Country Naturals, 13347
Vermont Creamery, 13348, 13349
Vermont Food Experience, 13350
Vermont Harvest Spec Food LLC, 13351
Vermont Liberty Tea, 13352
Vermont Made Richard's Sauces, 13353
Vermont Natural Co, 13354
Vermont Nut Free Chocolates, 13355
Vermont Pretzel & Cookie Co., 13356
Vermont Signature Sauces, 13357
Vermont Smoke and Cure, 13358
Vermont Specialty Food Association, 13359
Vermont Sweetwater Bottling Co, 13360
Vermont Tea & Trading Co Inc, 13361
Vermont Tortilla Company, 13362
Vermont Village, 13363
Wild Hibiscus Flower Company, 13779

Virginia

A. Smith Bowman Distillery, 59
A.L. Duck Jr Inc, 65
Abingdon Vineyard & Winery, 124
Abuelita Mexican Foods, 130
Afton Mountain Vineyards Inc, 200
Alicita-Salsa, 306
Alpenglow Beverage Company, 372
Amrhein's Wine Cellars, 512
Andros Foods North America, 559
Ariake USA Inc, 660
Ashland Milling, 726
Ashman Manufacturing & Distributing Company, 731
Autumn Hill Vineyards/Blue Ridge Wine, 825
Ayoba-Yo, 853
B & B Produce, 861
B G Smith & Sons Oyster Co, 868
Barboursville Vineyards, 1025
Belmont Peanuts-Southampton, 1210
Birdsong Corp., 1390
Biscotti Goddess, 1398
Blue Crab Bay, 1470
Bone Doctors' BBQ, LLC, 1554
Bonumose LLC, 1568
Boston Spice & Tea Company, 1598
Breadworks, 1682
Breaux Vineyards, 1686
Brookview Farms, 1761
Burnley Vineyards, 1868
Byrd Mill Co, 1898
C C Conway Seafoods, 1913
C.F. Sauer Co., 1935
Cafe Kreyol, 1996
Callis Seafood, 2093
Capital City Processors, 2161
Caribbean Cookie Company, 2208
Casey's Seafood Inc, 2291
Cassandra's Gourmet Classics/Island Treasures Gourmet, 2296
Chateau Morrisette Winery, 2462
Christensen Ridge Winery, 2645
Coffee Bean of Leesburg, 2837
Coffee Butler Service, 2840
Cookiezen, LLC, 2990
Cooper Vineyards, 3002
Countertop Productions, 3062
Cowart Seafood Corp, 3097
Craveright, 3120
Cuisine Solutions Inc, 3229
De Maria's Seafood, 3429
Deer Park Spring Water Co, 3469
Dinner Bell Meat Product, 3610
Dizzy Pig BBQ Co, 3635
Dominion Wine Cellars, 3665
Double Premium Confections, 3705
Douknie Winery, 3712
Dr. Lucy's LLC, 3732
DreamPak LLC, 3753
E. H. Gourmet, 3842

Geographic Index / Washington

Famarco Limited, 4239
Farfelu Vineyards, 4266
Feridies, 4334, 4335
Festive Foods, 4354
Fiorucci Foods USA Inc, 4411
Firehook Bakery & Coffeehouse, 4415
First Colony Coffee & Tea Company, 4422
First Colony Winery, 4423
Flippin-Seaman Inc, 4506
Forbes Candies, 4583
Garber Ice Cream Co Inc, 4887
Gearharts Fine Chocolates, 4927
George A Jeffreys & Company, 4962
George Robberecht Seafood, 4967
Georgetown Farm, 4973
Gerber Products Co, 4982
Gingerhaus, LLC, 5023
Golden Moon Tea, 5129
Graham & Rollins Inc, 5237
Granny Roddy's LLC, 5275
Graves Mountain Lodge Inc., 5285
Grayson Naturla Farms, 5293
Gunther's Gourmet, 5447
Hampton Associates & Sons, 5539
Hancock Peanut Company, 5544
Health Warrior, 5685
Hearty Naturals, 5719
Helms Candy Co., Inc, 5752
Heritage Books & Gifts, 5793
Hill Top Berry Farm & Winery, 5865
Holly Camp Springs Inc, 5912
Horton Vineyards, 6006
Hubbard Peanut Co Inc, 6042
Hudson Henry Baking Co., 6048
Hunt Country Foods Inc, 6082
Ingleside Vineyards, 6205
Interbake Foods, 6239
Island Treasures Gourmet, 6311
Jefferson Vineyards, 6482
Jerry Brothers Industries Inc, 6499
Jody's Gourmet Popcorn, 6530
K & S Cakes, 6656
Kettle Master, 6817
Keyser Brothers, 6828
Kornfections, 6966
L'Esprit De Campagne, 7033
La Abra Farm & Winery, 7075
Lake Packing Co Inc, 7153
Layman Distributing, 7261
Legend Brewing Co, 7315
Lendy's Cafe Raw Bar, 7346
Little River Seafood Inc, 7475
M&M Food Distributors/Oriental Pride, 7682
M.E. Swing Company, 7690
Mad Scientist Nuts, 7736
Manns Sausage Company, 7855
Marion's Smart Delights, 7933
Mars Inc., 7952
Marva Maid Dairy, 7978
Maryland & Virginia Milk Producers Cooperative, 7985
Massimo Zanetti Beverage USA, 7995
Meredyth Vineyard, 8168
Milton's Local, 8334
Montebello Kitchens, 8500
Mountain Cove Vineyards, 8594
Murray Cider Co Inc, 8689
Naked Mountain Winery Vineyard, 8742
Nancy's Candy, 8750
National Fruit Product Co Inc, 8796
National Wooden Pallet & Container Association, 8808
Neptune Fisheries, 8937
Nina's Gourmet Dip, 9060
Northern Neck, 9155
Oasis Winery, 9334
Obis One, 9341
Old Dominion Peanut Corp, 9406
Old Dominion Spice Company, 9407
Old House Vineyards, 9416
Old Mansion Inc, 9419
Oliver Egg Products, 9450
Omega Protein, 9479
Our Farms To You, LLC, 9602
Pasta Valente, 9818
Peanut Corporation of America, 9866
Peanut Patch Gift Shop, 9868
Peanut Shop, 9871
Peg's Salt, 9897
Pennacook Peppers, 9921
Pervida, 9971

Piedmont Vineyards & Winery, 10043
Plant Based Foods, 10103
Pond Brothers Peanut Company, 10163
Prince Michel, 10306
Producers Peanut Company, 10327
Pruden Packing Company, 10359
Purely American, 10388
Quibell Spring Water Beverage, 10460
R M Felts' Packing Co, 10482
Rebec Vineyards, 10595
Red River Foods Inc, 10617
Red Rocker Candy, 10618
Reginald's Homemade LLC, 10648
Roanoke Apple Products, 10782
Rockbridge Vineyard, 10813
Rodgers' Puddings, 10832
Rostov's Coffee & Tea Co, 10904
Route 11 Potato Chips, 10916
Rowena, 10919
Royal Oak Peanuts, 10940
S. Wallace Edward & Sons, 11025
Sahara Date Company, 11086
Samadi Sweets Cafe, 11127
San-J International Inc, 11157, 11158
Sara Lee Coffee & Tea, 11212
Sharp Rock Farm B & B, 11521
Shawnee Canning Co, 11528
Shore Seafood Distr, 11571
Simply Panache, 11655
Sky Valley Foods, 11694
Smithfield Foods Inc., 11733
Smokehouse Winery, 11738
Soho Beverages, 11779
Solo Worldwide Enterprises, 11789
Southern Flavoring Co, 11852
Southern Packing Corp, 11859
Spice Hunter Inc 11919
Spice Rack Chocolates, 11924
Spotted Tavern Winery & Dodd's Cider Mill, 11953
Stone Mountain Vineyards, 12134
Summerfield Farm Products, 12222
Sunergia Soyfoods, 12273
Sunnyside Farms LLC, 12290
Sunnyside Organics Seedlings, 12291
Sweet City Supply, 12393
Sweet Whispers, 12421
T O Williams Inc, 12463
Tabard Farm Potato Chips, 12484
Tanglewood Farms, 12524
Tarara Winery, 12534
Terry Brothers, Inc, 12634
Texas Beach, 12648
The Crispery, 12680
The Peanut Butter Shop of Williamsburg, 12714
The Perfect Pita, 12715
The Swiss Bakery, 12736
The Van Cleve Seafood Company, 12742
Tincture Distillers, 12815
To Your Health Sprouted Flour Co., Inc., 12829
Toms Moms Foods, LLC, 12865
Twin Oaks Community, 13095
V.W. Joyner & Company, 13237
Valley Milk Products, 13259
Veramar Vineyard, 13332
Veritas Vineyard, 13340
Vie De France Yamazaki Inc, 13396
Virginia Artesian Bottling Company, 13442
Virginia Chutney Company, 13443
Virginia Diner Inc, 13445
Virginia Trout Co, 13447
W. Forrest Haywood Seafood Company, 13500
Walden Foods, 13540
Wallace Edwards & Sons, 13547
Wanchese Fish Co Inc, 13561
White Hall Vineyards, 13719
White House Foods, 13720
White Packing Company, 13727
Whitley Peanut Factory Inc, 13742
Wild Bill's Foods, 13776
Williams Candy Co, 13817
Williamsburg Chocolatier, 13824
Williamsburg Winery LTD, 13825
Willowcroft Farm Vineyards, 13833
WillowOak Farms, 13832
Wintergreen Winery, 13873
Woodbine, 13914
Yoder Dairies, 14009

Washington

A J's Edible Arts, 38
A.C. LaRocco Pizza, 63
Agri-Pack, 212
AgriNorthwest, 213
Aimonetto and Sons, 234
Alaska General Seafoods, 262
Alaska Smokehouse, 270
Alaskan Leader Fisheries, 273
Alden's Organic, 283
Alder Springs Smoked Salmon, 284
Allan Bros. Inc., 326
Aloecorp, Inc., 361
Alpine Coffee Roasters, 379
Amavi Cellars, 417
American Canadian Fisheries, 444
American Seafoods, 480
Ames International Inc, 498
Appetizers And, Inc., 607
Arbor Crest Wine Cellars, 627
Ariel Natural Foods, 662
Arrowac Fisheries, 703
Auburn Dairy Products Inc, 792
Austin Chase Coffee, 816
Baker Candy Company, 961
Baker Produce, 965
Bakers Breakfast Cookie, 973
Barlean's Fisheries, 1042
Barnes & Watson Fine Teas, 1045
Batdorf & Bronson, 1081
Bavarian Meat Products, 1090
Bay Baby Produce, 1094
Beecher's Handmade Cheese, 1162
Bering Sea Fisheries, 1232
Bingo Salsa, LLC, 1362
Biscottea, 1396
Blau Oyster Co Inc, 1441
Blue Dog Bakery, 1472
Bornstein Seafoods, 1582
Boundary Fish Company, 1623
Bread Dip Company, 1680
Breakwater Seafoods & Chowder, 1685
Briney Sea Delicaseas, 1717
Brown & Haley, 1771
Caffe Appassionato Coffee, 2005
Caffe Darte, 2010
Caffe Luca Coffee Roaste, 2012
Canoe Ridge Vineyard, 2142
Captain's Choice, 2189
Cascade Coffee, 2282
Cascade Fresh, 2283
Cascadian Farm Inc, 2286
CB's Nuts, 1942
Centennial Mills, 2368
Central Bean Co, 2374
CheeseLand, 2483
Chelan Fresh Marketing, 2505
Chief Wenatchee, 2560
Chocolat, 2592
Chocolati Handmade Chocolates, 2621
Choice Organic Teas, 2630
Chukar Cherries, 2663
Coast Seafoods Company, 2797
Columbia Valley Farms Inc., 2908
Columbia Winery, 2909
Commercial Creamery Co, 2921
Congdon Orchards Inc., 2949
Conifer Foods, 2950
Conifer Specialties Inc, 2951
Continental Mills Inc, 2971
Cougar Mountain Baking Co, 3059
Crane & Crane Inc, 3115
Crown Pacific Fine Foods, 3192
Cuizina Food Company, 3230
Darigold, 3387
Davinci Gourmet LTD, 3402
Demitri's Bloody Mary Seasonings, 3518
Dilettante Chocolates, 3598
Dillanos Coffee Roasters, 3599
Distant Lands Coffee Roaster, 3620
Dohler-Milne Aseptics LLC, 3648
Douglas Cross Enterprises, 3710
Dr. Cookie, 3730
Draper Valley Farms, 3749
Dressel Collins Fish Company, 3757
DRY Soda Co., 3318
Dungeness Development Associates, 3800
Dunham's Meats, 3802
East Point Seafood Company, 3883
Elki Coporation, 4014
Ellenos, 4018

Elliott Bay Baking Co., 4021
Emerald Kalama Chemical, LLC, 4042
Ener-G Foods, 4062
Enfield Farms Inc, 4068
Espresso Vivace, 4116
Essentia Water, 4120
Essential Baking Co, The, 4121
Esteem Products, 4127
Euroam Importers Inc, 4147
Evolution Fresh, 4176
Fair Scones, 4219
Fairhaven Cooperative Flour Mill, 4223
Felix Custom Smoking, 4325
Fidalgo Bay Roasting Co, 4361
Field Roast, 4364
Firefly Fandango, 4414
Firestone Pacific Foods Co, 4418
Fischer Meats, 4434
Flax4Life, 4496
Fletcher's Fine Foods, 4501
Flora Inc, 4509
Flying Bird Botanicals LLC, 4532
Foster Fams, 4620
Fran's Chocolates, 4646
Fresh Nature Foods, 4717
Fungi Perfecti, 4798
Fungus Among Us, 4799
GEM Cultures, 4829
Glacier Fish Company, 5041
Glutenfreeda Foods Inc, 5084
Gold Digger Cellars, 5101
Golden Alaska Seafoods LLC, 5114
Good PLANeT Foods, 5170
Graysmarsh Berry Farm, 5292
Great Pacific Seafoods, 5326
Great Western Malting Co, 5335
Grounds for Change, 5403
Hale's Brewery, 5515
Hama Hama Oyster® Company, 5530
HerbCo International, 5782
HFI Foods, 5483
Hi-Country Foods Corporation, 5826
High Tide Seafoods Inc, 5850
Hinzerling Winery, 5888
Honey Ridge Farms, 5961
Hoodsport Winery, 5984
Hops Extract Corporation of America, 5994
Hot Cakes-Molten Chocolate, 6014
Humming Hemp, 6073
Hyde Candy Company, 6096
I P Callison & Sons, 6104
Ice Chips Candy, 6127
Icicle Seafoods Inc, 6133
Ideal Distributing Company, 6142
IFive Brands, 6113
Indena USA Inc, 6178
Independent Packers Corporation, 6182
International Glace, 6264
Isernio Sausage Company, 6296
Island Spring Inc, 6309
J&D's Foods, 6368
Jack's Paleo Kitchen, 6419
Jensen's Old Fashioned Smokehouse, 6494
Johnson Foods, Inc., 6566
Johnson Foods, Inc. - Cannery Plant, 6567
Jones Soda Company, 6590
Josef Aaron Syrup Company, 6596
Kasilof Fish Company, 6721
Khatsa & Company, 6831
Kibun Foods, 6833
King's Command Foods Inc, 6873
Kiona Vineyards Winery, 6886
Kiska Farms, 6890
Kookaburra, 6958
LA Mexicana Tortilla, 7051
La Panzanella, 7098
Latah Creek Wine Cellar, 7237
Leavenworth Coffee Roast, 7286
Lemoncocco, 7341
Leonetti Cellar, 7366
Les Boulangers Associes Inc, 7377
Liberty Orchards Co Inc, 7410
Little I, 7468
Los Angeles Smoking & Curing Company, 7549
Lost Mountain Winery, 7556
Lowery's Premium Roast Gourmet Coffee, 7613
Luvo Inc., 7654
Lynden Meat Co, 7663
Maberry & Maberry Berry Associates, 7712
Madrona Specialty Foods LLC, 7756

Geographic Index / West Virginia

Maritime Pacific Brewing Co, 7935
Marley Orchards Corporation, 7944
Matson Fruit Co, 8010
Mc Steven's Coca Factory Store, 8051
McSteven's, 8084
Merlino Italian Baking Company, 8176
Mike & Jean's Berry Farm, 8278
Mills Brothers Intl, 8320
Milne Fruit Products Inc, 8325
Minterbrook Oyster Co, 8363
Mountain Valley Products Inc, 8604
Mr. C's, 8621
Mt Baker Vineyards, 8650
Mt Capra Products, 8652
Muntons Ingredients, 8684
Mutual Fish Co, 8701
MYNTZ!, 7710
Mystic Lake Dairy, 8717
National Fish & Oyster, 8785
National Food Corporation, 8790
National Frozen Foods Corp, 8794
National Sign Corporation, 8803
Natural Quick Foods, 8846
Nature Cure Northwest, 8859
Nature's Path Foods, 8889
Neil Jones Food Company, 8924
Nelson Crab Inc, 8932
NewGem Products, 9010
Nisbet Oyster Company, 9066
Noel Corp, 9083
North Pacific Seafoods Inc, 9134
Northern Discovery Seafoods, 9147
Northern Lights Brewing Company, 9153
Northern Products Corporation, 9159
Northwest Natural Foods, 9176
Northwest Naturals LLC, 9177
Northwest Packing Co, 9178
Northwest Pea & Bean Co, 9179
Nuchief Sales Inc, 9212
Nut Factory, 9226
Nutpods, 9232
Nuun Active Hydration, 9277
O'Brines Pickling, 9285
Oberto Brands, 9338
Ocean Beauty Seafoods Inc, 9344
Ocean Fresh Seafoods, 9348
OH Chocolate, 9299
Olympia Oyster Co, 9465
Olympic Cellars, 9467
Olympic Coffee & Roasting, 9468
Olympic Foods, 9469
Omega Nutrition, 9477
Onalaska Brewing, 9484
Oneonta Starr Ranch Growers, 9493, 9494
Orca Bay Foods, 9518
Oregon Ice Cream Co., 9533
Oregon Potato Co, 9535
Ostrom Mushrooms, 9587
Overlake Foods, 9615
Oversea Casing Co, 9616
P & L Poultry, 9629
P-Bee Products, 9640
Pacific Foods, 9680
Pacific Gold Snacks, 9684
Pacific Harvest Products, 9687
Pacific Nutritional, 9689
Pacific Salmon Company, 9692
Pacific Valley Foods Inc, 9699
Pan's Mushroom Jerky, 9735
Pandol Brothers Inc, 9738
Partners: A Tasteful Choice, 9799
Peppered Palette, 9941
Peter Pan Seafoods Inc., 9980
Petschl's Quality Meats, 9989
Phranil Foods, 10024
Pike Brewing Co, 10052
Pita King Bakery, 10087
Pop Gourmet LLC, 10176
Premier Pacific Seafoods Inc, 10250
Premiere Packing Company, 10253
Preston Premium Wines, 10269
Pretzel Perfection, 10271
Price Co, 10275
Producer Marketing Overlake, 10323
Pure Foods, 10372
Pyramid Alehouse-Seattle, 10404
Queen Anne Coffee Roaster, 10449
Quilceda Creek Vintners, 10462
Quillisascut Cheese Co, 10464
Quinault Pride, 10465
Rill Specialty Foods, 10743
Robbie's Natural Products, 10785

Roche Fruit LLC, 10808
Rock Point Oyster Company, 10811
Rosanna Imports Warehouse, 10877
Royal Ridge Fruits, 10947
S A Carlson Inc, 11013
Salishan Vineyards, 11106
Salmolux Inc, 11110
SaltWorks, 11117
San Gennaro Foods Inc, 11148
San Juan Coffee Roasting Co, 11152
Schenk Packing Co Inc, 11280
Sea Bear Smokehouse, 11337
Sea Salt Superstore, 11350, 11351
SeaBear Wild Salmon, 11358
Seafood Producers Co-Op, 11375
Seatech Corporation, 11386
Seattle Bar Company, 11388
Seattle Chocolates, 11389
Seattle Gourmet Foods, 11390
Seattle Seasonings, 11391
Seattle's Best Coffee, 11392
Seven Hills Winery, 11472
Sfoglia Fine Pastas & Gourmet, 11487
Shady Grove Orchards, 11491
Shining Ocean Inc, 11559
Shonan USA Inc, 11568
Signature Seafoods Inc, 11602
Silver Fern Chemical Inc, 11617
Silver Lining Seafood, 11620
Silverbow Honey Company, 11633
Skillet Street Food, 11684
Sno-Co Berry Pak, 11757
Snokist Growers, 11759
SOUPerior Bean & Spice Company, 11050
Southern Pride Catfish Company, 11862
Spice O' Life, 11922
Spinelli Coffee Company, 11937
Spokandy, 11944
Spokane Seed Co, 11945
Stadelman Fruit LLC, 12016
Starbucks, 12042
Starkel Poultry, 12045
Stasero International, 12052
STE Michelle Wine Estates, 11054
Stewarts Market, 12112
Sticky Fingers Bakeries, 12117
Stirling Foods, 12122
Suji's Korean Cuisine, 12214
Sunfresh Foods, 12276
Superior Bean & Spice Company, 12330
Svzusa Inc, 12376
Sweet Swiss Confections Inc, 12417
Symons Frozen Foods, 12452
Talking Rain Beverage Co, 12510
Taylor Shellfish Farms, 12573
Tazo Tea, 12581
Theo Chocolate, 12748
Tim's Cascade Snacks, 12808
Top Pot Doughnuts, 12882
Torrefazione Italia, 12897
Totally Chocolate, 12900
Trans-Ocean Products Inc, 12925
Tree Top Inc, 12942
Trident Seafoods Corp, 12968
Trout Lake Farm, 13015
Tucker Cellars, 13045
Turner & Pease Company, 13070
Twin City Foods Inc., 13091
Unique Beverage Company, 13175
Ursula's Island Farms Company, 13227
Valley View Blueberries, 13263
Vana Life Foods, 13285
Victrola Coffee Roasters, 13391
Vital Choice, 13460
Vitamilk Dairy, 13468
Viva Tierra, 13477
Wabi Fishing Company, 13521
Wallace Grain & Pea Company, 13549
Wan Hua Foods, 13560
Washington Fruit & Produce Company, 13580
Washington Potato Company, 13581
Washington Rhubarb Grower Assn, 13582
Wax Orchards, 13599
Weinberg Foods, 13628
Wellesse, 13642
Western Meat Co, 13681
Wiegardt Brothers, 13770
Wilcox Farms, 13774
Wild Things Snacks, 13786
Woodward Canyon, 13924
Worden, 13928

WSU Creamery, 13516
Yakima Chief-Hopunion LLC, 13981
Yakima Craft Brewing Company, 13982
Yakima Fresh, 13983
Yakima River Winery, 13984

West Virginia

A.T. Gift Company, 66
Blue Smoke Salsa, 1499
Buzz Food Svc, 1891
Country Club Bakery, 3067
De Fluri's Fine Chocolate, 3426
Dr. B's Beverages, LLC, 3728
Dutchess Bakery, 3819
Fisher Ridge Wine Co Inc, 4444
Gunnoe Farms Sausage & Salad, 5446
H3O, 5481
Hardscrabble Enterprises, 5583
Joe Fazio's Famous Italian, 6535
Maggie's Salsa, 7762
Mister Bee Potato Chips Co, 8393
Monastery Fruitcake, 8473
Robert F Pliska & Company Winery, 10789
Spring Creek Natural Foods, 11959
Sunshine Farm & Garden, 12305
Surface Banana Company, 12356
SVB Food & Beverage Company, 11055
Tebay Dairy Company, 12592
Thistledew Farm, 12758
Tomaro's Bakery, 12858
Tumai Water, 13055
United Valley Bell Dairy, 13202
Virginia Honey Company, 13446
Wheeling Coffee & Spice Co, 13706
Ziegenfelder Ice Cream Co, 14063

Wisconsin

A. Gagliano Co Inc, 55
Abbyland Foods Inc, 118
Accurex, 140
Agropur, 221
AgSource Milk Analysis Laboratory, 201
Alluserv, 349
Almost Nuts, 356
Alsum Farms & Produce, 386
American Foods Group LLC, 457
AmTech Ingredients, 402
Anchor Appetizer Group, 530
Ancora Coffee Roasters, 539
Angelic Bakehouse, 563
ARCO Coffee, 101
Armbrust Meats, 681
Auroma International Inc, 809
B&M Enterprises, 875
Back to Basics, 918
Badger Best Pizzas, 927
Badger Gourmet Ham, 928
Baensch Food Products Co, 931
Bakalars Sausage Co, 948
Baker Cheese Factory Inc, 962
Baptista's Bakery, 1014
Baraboo Candy Co LLC, 1018
Bass Lake Cheese Factory, 1077
Becky's Blissful Bakery, 1150
Beehive Botanicals, 1164
BelGioioso Cheese Inc., 1174
Belle Plaine Cheese Factory, 1194
Berres Brothers Coffee, 1252
Best Maid Cookie Co, 1269
Better Than Foods USA, 1288
Bieri's Jackson Cheese, 1318
Biospringer, 1379
Birchwood Foods Inc, 1384
Birdseye Dairy-Morning Glory, 1388
Black Bear Fruits, 1416
Blaser's USA, Inc., 1440
Bletsoe's Cheese Inc, 1449
Boca Foods Company, 1527
Brakebush Brothers, 1654
Briess Malt & Ingredients Co., 1710
Brunkow Cheese Of Wisconsin, 1800
Brunnett Dairy Co-Op, 1801
Buddy Squirrel LLC, 1828
Burke Candy Ingredients Inc, 1860
Butter Buds Food Ingredients, 1880
Cady Cheese Factory, 1985
Caffe D'Amore, 2006
Calumet Diversified Meats Company, 2097
Capital Brewery & Beer Garden, 2160

Carr Cheese Factory/GileCheese Company, 2254
Carr Valley Cheese, 2255
Carr Valley Cheese Company, 2256
Cascade Cheese Co, 2280
Cedar Creek Winery, 2345
Cedar Crest Specialties, 2346
Cedar Grove Cheese Inc, 2347
Cedar Valley Cheese Store, 2352
Century Foods Intl LLC, 2387
Chalet Cheese Co-Op, 2401
Cheddar Box Cheese House, 2479
Cher-Make Sausage Co, 2511
Chieftain Wild Rice, 2561
Chocolate House, 2604
Chocolate Shoppe Ice Cream Co, 2607
Chr Hansen Inc, 2640
Churny Company, 2667
City Brewing Company, 2705
Clasen Quality Chocolate, 2722
Clem Becker Meats, 2746
Colectivo Coffee, 2874
Colony Brands Inc, 2888
Country Maid Inc, 3081
Croft's Crackers, 3175
CROPP Cooperative, 1963
CTL Foods, 1966
Curran's Cheese Plant Inc, 3259
Cybros, 3283
D2 Ingredients, LP., 3305
Dabruzzi's Italian Foods, 3325
Dairy Connection Inc, 3334
Dairy State Foods Inc, 3343
Dairyfood USA Inc, 3348
Dan Carter, 3367
Dawn's Foods, 3413
Day Foods Company, 3414
Decatur Dairy, 3457
Delicious Popcorn, 3501
Dellaco Classic Confections, 3507
Deppeler Cheese Factory, 3529
Didion Milling Inc, 3590
Door County Potato Chips, 3691
Door Peninsula Winery, 3692
Drangle Foods, 3748
Dupont Cheese, 3806
DWC Specialities, 3323
East Shore Specialty Foods, 3885
Eau Galle Cheese Factory Shop, 3910
Echo Lake Foods, Inc., 3916
EDCO Food Products Inc, 3849
Edelman Meats Inc, 3936
Ellsworth Cooperative Creamery, 4028
Emmi Roth USA, 4047
Enzymatic Therapy Inc, 4086
Enzyme Formulations, Inc, 4088
F & A Dairy Products Inc, 4195
Fair Oaks Farms LLC, 4218
Fiberstar, 4356
First Choice Ingredients, 4421
Fontana Flavors Inc, 4549
Foran Spice Inc, 4582
Foremost Farms USA, 4591
Frankfort Cheese, 4660
Fred Usinger Inc, 4676
Fruit Ranch Inc, 4765
Fun Factory, 4793
Gad Cheese Retail Store, 4855
Galloway Co, 4874
Gamay Flavors, 4878
Gehl Foods, Inc., 4930
Gibbsville Cheese Company, 5002
Gile Cheese Store, 5009
Glucona America, 5078
GoMacro, 5090
Graf Creamery Co, 5233
Grande Cheese Company, 5258
Grande Custom Ingredients Group, 5259
Grassland Dairy Products Inc, 5282
Gray's Brewing Co, 5290
Great Lakes Cheese Company, 5316
Great River Organic Milling, 5329
Grebe's Bakery, 5340
Green Bay Packaging Inc., 5344
Green County Foods, 5346
Green Gold Group LLC, 5351
Hawkhaven Greenhouse International, 5663
Hawkins Inc, 5664
Heise Wausau Farms, 5738
Henning Cheese Factory, 5768
Hillestad Pharmaceuticals, 5871
Himalayan Heritage, 5883

Geographic Index / Wyoming

Hoff's United Food, 5901
Honey Acres, 5953
Hooks Cheese Co, 5986
Hsu's Ginseng Enterprises Inc, 6040
Impact Confections, 6158
Imperial Flavors Beverage Co, 6159
Indian Hollow Farms, 6186
Island Oasis Frozen Cocktail, 6302
J G Van Holten & Son Inc, 6353
Jacob Leinenkugel Brewing Co, 6425
Jim's Cheese Pantry, 6518
JMS Specialty Foods, 6406
Johnsonville Sausage LLC, 6574
Jones Dairy Farm, 6587
Joseph Campione Inc, 6598
Kehr's candies, 6755
Kenosha Beef International LTD, 6790
Kerry, Inc, 6808
King B Meat Snacks, 6858
King Juice Co, 6867
Klement Sausage Co Inc, 6910
Klondike Cheese Factory, 6913
Kohler Original Recipe Chocolates, 6940
Kraemer Wisconsin Cheese LTD, 6975
Krier Foods, 6985
Kristian Regale, 6989
La Crosse Milling Company, 7086
LA Grander Hillside Dairy Inc, 7047
LaCrosse Milling Company, 7118
Lactalis USA Inc, 7128
Lake Country Foods Inc, 7151
Lake States Yeast, 7155
Lakefront Brewery Inc, 7156
Lakeside Foods Inc., 7161, 7162
Leach Farms Inc, 7278
Legacy Bakehouse, 7312
Leinenkugel's, 7330
Lesaffre Yeast Corporation, 7389
Linden Cheese Factory, 7441
Link Snacks Inc., 7449
Lodi Canning Co, 7505
Lotus Brands, 7562
Louie's Finer Meats, 7568
Lynn Dairy Inc, 7665
Macfarlane Pheasants, 7727
Main Street Ingredients, 7786
MAK Wood Inc, 7695
Malteurop North America, 7810
Manderfield's Home Bakery, 7837
Mannhardt Inc, 7854
Maple Hollow, 7869
Maple Leaf Cheesemakers, 7872
Maple Ridge Farms, 7880
Maple Valley Cooperative, 7881
Marathon Cheese, 7893
Marathon Cheese Corp, 7894
Marks Meat, 7943
Masters Gallery Foods Inc, 7999

Masterson Co Inc, 8000
Meister Cheese Company, 8138
Meleddy Cherry Plant, 8144
Mexican Accent, 8208
Mill Haven Foods LLC, 8302
Mille Lacs Gourmet Foods, 8304
Miller Baking, 8307
Milling Sausage Inc, 8318
Milsolv Corporation, 8332
Mizkan Americas Inc, 8423
Modern Products Inc, 8448
Momence Packing Company, 8466
Morning Glory Dairy, 8547
Mossholder's Farm Cheese Factory, 8573
Mt Sterling Co-Op Creamery, 8659
Mullins Cheese Inc, 8674
Nan Sea Enterprises of Wisconsin, 8746
Nasonville Dairy, 8774
Natural Ovens Bakery Inc, 8844
Nature's Way, 8896
Neenah Springs, 8920
New Glarus Bakery & Tea Room, 8975
New Glarus Brewing CompaNy, 8976
Newburg Corners Cheese Factory, 9011
Nick's Sticks, 9041
Niemuth's Steak & Chop Shop, 9051
Nikki's Coconut Butter, 9054
Nikki's Cookies, 9055
Nolechek Meats Inc, 9086
North Bay Trading Co, 9127
Northern WIS Produce Co, 9164
Northland Cranberries, 9166
Northwestern Coffee Mills, 9181, 9182
Northwestern Extract, 9183
Nueske's Applewood Smoked Meat, 9214
Nutorious LLC, 9231
O & H Danish Bakery Inc, 9280
Oak Grove Dairy, 9313
Old Country Cheese, 9401
Old Fashioned Foods, 9411
Old Tavern Food Products Inc, 9427
Old Wisconsin Sausage Inc, 9432
Olds Products Co, 9440
Omanhene Cocoa Bean Co, 9474
Ortho-Molecular Products Inc, 9573
Oshkosh Cold Storage, 9580
Oskri Corporation, 9583
Palermo's Pizza, 9719
Park Cheese Company Inc, 9780
Patrick Cudahy LLC, 9833
Pine River Pre-Pack Inc, 10065
Pinter's Packing Plant, 10070
Pleasoning Gourmet Seasonings, 10114
Plymouth Cheese Counter, 10131
Poppingfun Inc, 10191
Porkie Company of Wisconsin, 10196
Prima Kase, 10284
Primer Foods Corporation, 10297

Progenix Corporation, 10335
Progressive Flavors, 10336
Provimi Foods, 10356
PS Seasoning & Spices, 9662
Pure Food Ingredients, 10371
Pure Sweet Honey Farms Inc, 10383
Purity Farms, 10395
R&R Homestead Kitchen, 10490
Racine Danish, 10527
Red Arrow Products Co LLC, 10600
Red Star Yeast, 10621
Regez Cheese & Paper Supply, 10645
Renard's Cheese, 10669
Reynolds Sugar Bush, 10694
Ripon Pickle Co Inc, 10752
Rishi Tea, 10757
Roelli Cheese Co, 10834
Ron's Wisconsin Cheese LLC, 10862
Roth Cheese USA, 10906
Rousselot Inc, 10915
RP's Pasta Company, 10515
Ruef's Meat Market, 10970
Rural Route 1 Popcorn Co, 10984
Salemville Cheese, 11103
San Antonio Farms, 11135
Sargento Foods Inc, 11228
Sartori Co, 11231
Saxon Creamery, 11262
Schneider Cheese, 11297
Schoep's Ice Cream, 11305
Schreiber Foods Inc., 11308
Schuster Marketing Corporation, 11314
Scott's of Wisconsin, 11330
Scray's Cheese, 11333
Sensient Technologies Corp, 11444
Silver Creek Specialty Meats, 11616
Silverston Fisheries, 11636
Simon's Specialty Cheese, 11643
Simply Incredible Foods, 11654
SJH Enterprises, 11042
Specialty Cheese Co Inc, 11896
Specialty Meats & Gourmet, 11905
Spice Galleon, 11917
Spike Seasoning Magic, 11933
Sprecher Brewing Co, 11956
Springdale Cheese Factory, 11969
Spurgeon Vineyards & Winery, 11984
Steep & Brew, 12069
Stella Reedsburg, 12076
Stevens Point Brewery, 12101
Strauss Brands International, 12162
Sturm Foods Inc, 12182
Subco Foods Inc, 12184
Sunshine Burger & Spec Food Co, 12302
Sunshine Farms, 12306
Swiss Heritage Cheese Inc, 12441
Taylor Cheese Corp, 12565
Thiel Cheese & Ingredients, 12752

Thor-Shackel Horseradish Company, 12775
Three Lakes Winery, 12783
TNT Crust, 12480
Torke Coffee Co, 12891
Trade Winds Pizza, 12911
Trega Foods, 12947
Tremblay's Sweet Shop, 12949
Tribe 9 Foods, 12964
U Roast Em Inc, 13112
US Foods & Pharmaceuticals Inc, 13122
Utzy, Inc., 13230
Vande Walle's Candies Inc, 13289
Verifine Dairy, 13338
Vern's Cheese, 13364
Victor Allen's Coffee and Tea, 13382
Vita Plus Corp, 13455
Von Stiehl Winery, 13491
Wausau Paper Corp., 13595
Welcome Dairy Inc, 13637
Wetherby Cranberry Company, 13698
Weyauwega Star Dairy, 13700
Whitehall Specialties Inc, 13737
Widmer's Cheese Cellars Inc, 13765
Winona Foods, 13866
Wisconsin Cheeseman, 13874
Wisconsin Dairyland Fudge Company, 13875
Wisconsin Farmers Union, 13876
Wisconsin Milk Mktng Board Inc, 13877
Wisconsin Packaging Corp, 13878
Wisconsin Specialty Protein, 13879
Wisconsin Spice Inc, 13880
Wisconsin Whey International, 13881
Wixon Inc., 13890
Wohlt Cheese Corp, 13895
Wollersheim Winery, 13903
Wood Sugarbush, 13913
Zimmerman Cheese Inc, 14064
Zurheide Ice Cream Company, 14077

Wyoming

Admiral Beverage Corp, 179
Chugwater Chili, 2662
Donells Candies, 3680
GF Harvest, 4830
Grandma Pat's Products, 5266
Kelly Packing Company, 6771
Lifestyle Health Guide, 7422
Merrill Meat Co, 8179
Mosher Products Inc, 8571
Nutrition Center Inc, 9260
Nutriwest, 9266
Pat's Meat Discounter, 9825
Queen Bee Gardens, 10450
Riverton Packing, 10775
Snake River Brewing Company, 11749
Wild West Spices, 13789

Parent Company Index

Numeric

1-800-Flowers
  Cheryl's Cookies, 2526
1-800-Flowers.com
  Wolferman's, 13899
321 Capital Partners LLC
  Canyon Specialty Foods, 2147
40ParkLake, LLC
  Carolyn's Gourmet, 2251

A

A. Lassonde
  Produits Ronald, 10333
A. Lassonde, Inc
  Golden Town Apple Products, 5136
A.L. Copeland
  Diversified Foods & Seasonings, 3623
A.M. Gilardi & Sons
  Con Agra Foods Inc, 2934
A/S Beverage Marketing
  Island Sweetwater Beverage Company, 6310
AAK AB
  Aak USA Inc, 106
AAK USA Inc.
  AAK, 70
AB InBev
  Labatt Brewing Company, 7123
Abbott Laboratories
  Abbott Laboratories, 114
  Zone Perfect Nutrition Company, 14071
Abel & Schafer Group
  Abel & Schafer Inc, 121
ABF Ingredients
  Abitec Corp, 126
Abitec Corporation
  Roland Machinery, 10846
Adams Milling Company
  Adams Foods & Milling, 166
Adams Wine Group
  Adler Fels Winery, 177
ADFAC
  IMAC, 6117
Advance Pierre Foods
  Barber Foods, 1022
AEI
  Pino's Pasta Veloce, 10068
AGP
  AG Processing Inc, 81
AGRI Industries
  Mrs Clark's Foods, 8627
Agri Pack
  Agri-Pack, 212
Agri-Mark
  Cabot Creamery Co-Op, 1972
Agri-Mark Inc
  Mccadam Cheese Co Inc, 8085
Agricore United Int'l.
  Agricore United, 215
Agrilink Foods
  Tim's Cascade Snacks, 12892
Agro Aceitunera SA
  Agro Foods, Inc., 218
Agroindustrias Deandar
  Indel Food Products Inc, 6179
Agropur
  Agropur, 221
  Main Street Ingredients, 7786
  Sunnyrose Cheese, 12288
Agropur Cooperative
  Scotsbrun Ice Cream Co., 11323
Agropur Dairy Co-Operative
  Northumberland Dairy, 9170
Agropur MSI, LLC
  Agropur, 222
Agspring LLC
  Firebird Artisan Mills, 4413
AGT Food & Ingredients
  AGT Foods USA, 83
Agvest
  Niagara Foods, 9032
Ahuramazda
  Chewys Rugulach, 2538
Ajinomoto Co., Inc.
  Ajinomoto Foods North America, Inc., 237
  Ajinomoto Frozen Foods USA, Inc., 238
  Ajinomoto Heartland Inc, 239

Ajinomoto Foods
  Bernardi Italian Foods Company, 1245
Ajinomoto Windsor
  Original Chili Bowl, 9561
Akay Group
  Akay USA LLC, 242
Albertsons
  Safeway Inc., 11073
Aleutian Pribilof Island Community Development Association
  Atka Pride Seafoods Inc, 752
Alfred L. Wolff GmbH
  Alfred L. Wolff, Inc., 300
Algilani Food Import & Export
  Treasure Foods, 12936
Ali Group
  ACP, Inc., 74
All American Foods
  All American Foods Inc, 317
Alle Processing
  Alle Processing Corp, 329
Allen Foods
  Lasco Foods Inc, 7234
Allied Lyons
  Corby Distilleries, 3024
Aloe Farms, Inc.
  Aloe Laboratories, 359
Alouette Cheese USA
  Kolb-Lena Bresse Bleu Inc, 6945
Alpine Confections
  Kencraft, Inc., 6780
  Maxfield Candy, 8027
Amana Society Corporation
  Amana Meat Shop & Smoke House, 409
Amanida
  Amanida USA Corp, 411
Amano Enzyme
  Amano Enzyme USA Company, Ltd, 413
AMC Chemicals
  Premium Ingredients International US, LLC, 10258
AMCOL International Corp.
  Nanocor, 8755
American Capital Strategies
  Bear Creek Country Kitchens, 1126
American Foods Group
  King's Command Foods Inc, 6873
American Natural & Organic Spices
  Spicely, 11928
AmeriFoods
  Uncle Ray's Potato Chips, 13159
AmeriQual Group LLC
  Thermo Pac LLC, 12751
Anabolic
  Vitamer Laboratories, 13467
Anchor Food Products
  Trans Pecos Foods, 12924
Andros Group
  Andros Foods North America, 559
Angel Camacho S.A.
  Mario Camancho Foods, 7931
Angostura International
  World Harbors, 13938
Another Roadside Attraction
  Snow's Ice Cream Co Inc, 11763
Applewood Seed & Garden Group
  Applewood Seed & Garden Group, 617
Arbor Investments
  Concord Foods, LLC, 2943
Arca Continental
  Wise Foods Inc, 13884
Archer Daniels Midland
  Golden Peanut and Tree Nuts, 5130
Archer Daniels Midland Company
  ADM Wild Flavors & Specialty, 77
  Centennial Mills, 2368
  Southern Cotton Oil Co, 11847
  Specialty Commodities Inc, 11898
  Western New York Syrup Corporation, 13682
Archibald Candy Corporation
  Fannie May Fine Chocolate, 4250
Archie Moore's Bar & Restaurant
  Archie Moore's, 640
Archway Cookies
  Lew-Mark Baking Company, 7400
Arctic Glacier
  Arctic Glacier, 645
Ariake Japan Co., Ltd.
  Ariake USA Inc, 660
Arizona Canning Company, LLC
  Faribault Foods, Inc., 4267

Arkopharma
  Health from the Sun, 5686
Arlon Group
  Wholesome!, 13751
Armenia Coffee Corporation
  Silver Spoon, 11624
Aryzta AG
  La Brea Bakery Inc, 7078
  Otis Spunkmeyer, 9590
ASR Group
  C & H Sugar Co Inc, 1911
Assets Brewing Company
  Assets Grille & Southwest Brewing Company, 738
Associated Micro Breweries
  Karl Strauss Brewing Co, 6711
Assured Natural
  Alpha Health, 375
Atalanta
  Royal Vista Marketing Inc, 10951
Atlantis Pak
  Atlantis Pak USA Inc, 780
Auvergne Farms
  Jakeman's Maple Products, 6440
Avebe
  Glucona America, 5078
AVEBE Group
  Avebe America Inc., 834
Avon Food Company
  Christie's, 2647
Azeta Brands
  Madys Company, 7758

B

B&G Foods
  Burnham & Morrill Co, 1867
  Mama Mary's, 7815
  Maple Grove Farms Of Vermont, 7866
  Trappey's Fine Foods Inc, 12930
B&G Foods, Inc.
  Old London Foods, 9418
B&H Foods
  B&H Foods, 873
B&K International
  Famarco Limited, 4239
B-S Foods Company
  B-S Foods Company, 877
B.V. Solnut
  Solnuts, 11787
Bacardi International
  Bacardi USA Inc, 914
Bacardi Limited
  Bacardi Canada, Inc., 913
Bakkavor
  Two Chefs on a Roll, 13098, 13099
Bakkavor Group
  Bakkavor USA, 980
Bakon Yeast
  Bakon Yeast, 981
Bama Companies
  Bama Frozen Dough, 1003
Barry Callebaut
  Mona Lisa Foods, 8468
Barshop Enterprises
  Banana Distributing Company, 1004
Bartlett & Company
  Bartlett Milling Co., 1061
Barton Brands
  Viking Distillery, 13406
BASF SE
  BASF Corp., 886
Baum International, Inc
  Dyna Tabs LLC, 3828
Bay Beyond, Inc.
  Blue Crab Bay, 1470
Bay Valley Foods, LLC
  San Antonio Farms, 11135
Beam Suntory Inc.
  Maker's Mark Distillery Inc, 7801
Bear Creek Corporation
  Harry & David, 5615
Bearden Sandwich Company
  Southern Belle Sandwich Company, 11843
Beaumont Select Corporation
  Mrs. Willman's Baking, 8649
Beavers Holdings
  Best Chicago Meat, 1262
Bel Brands USA
  Bel Cheese USA, 1173

Belcolade NV/SA
  Belcolade, 1175
Belding Fruit Storage
  Belleharvest Sales Inc, 1196
Bell Farms
  Bells Foods International, 1202
Belletieri Company
  Reser's Fine Foods Inc, 10681
Beneo GmbH
  Beneo Inc, 1219
Beringer Wine Estates
  Chateau St Jean Winery, 2466
Berj, Inc.
  Whole Herb Co, 13746
Berkeley Coffee and Tea
  Uncommon Grounds Coffee, 13160
Bill Macks Homemade Ice Cream
  Mack's Homemade Ice Cream, 7730
Bimbo Bakeries USA
  Entenmann's, 4080
  Mrs Baird's, 8626
Bioforce USA
  A.Vogel USA, 67
Birds Eye Foods
  Husman Snack Food Company, 6091
Biscuits Bouvard
  Pidy Gourmet Pastry Shells, 10039
BJ's Restaurants Inc
  BJ's Restaurants Inc., 897
Blanver
  Blanver USA, 1439
Blue Diamond Growers
  Mac Farms Of Hawaii Inc, 7713
Blue Mountain Enterprises
  Blue Mountain Enterprise Inc, 1488
Bluebonnet Company
  Goodheart Brand Specialty Food, 5183
Boar's Head
  Frank Brunckhorst Company, 4652
Bon Bons Associates
  H Cantin, 5463
Borden
  Lafleur Dairy Products,, 7137
  Mountain High Yogurt, 8597
Bose Corporation
  Les Viandes du Breton, 7387
Boulder Brands
  Earth Balance, 3868
Brad Barry Company
  Caffe D'Oro, 2008
  Caffe D'Vita, 2009
Brand Castle
  Sisters' Gourmet, 11679
Branding Iron Holding Company
  Branding Iron Meats, 1659
Breckenridge Brewery
  Breckenridge Brewery, 1687
Brenntag AG
  Brenntag North America, 1692
Brewers Outlet
  Brewers Outlet-Chestnut Hill, 1696
Bridgewell Resources
  Bridgewell Resources LLC, 1708
Bright Food (Group) Co., Ltd
  Weetabix Food Co., 13621
Brookside Foods
  Brookside Foods, 1760
Brown-Forman
  Chambord, 2407
Brown-Forman Corporation
  Canadian Mist Distillers, 2124
  Jack Daniel Distillery, 6416
Buffalo Rock Company
  Sunfresh Beverages Inc., 12275
Bunge Limited
  Bunge North America Inc., 1849
Bunker Foods
  Bunker Foods Corp., 1850
Burnbrae Farm
  Burn Brae Farms, 1864
Burns Philp Foods
  Fleischmann's Vinegar Co Inc, 4499
Byrnes Kitchen Company
  Charlie's Specialties Inc, 2442

C

C.A.L. Marketing
  Alli & Rose, 341
C.F. Sauer Company
  C&T Refinery, 1929

1357

Parent Company Index

Spice Hunter Inc, 11919
C.H Guenther & Son, Inc.
  Pioneer Frozen Foods, 10075
Cadbury Schweppes
  Cadbury Adams, 1980
  Cadbury Beverages Canada, 1981
Cadbury Schweppes PLC
  Cadbury Trebor Allan, 1982
  Mott's LLP, 8586
Cal-Maine Foods, Inc.
  American Egg Products Inc, 452
Caldic
  Caldic USA Inc, 2041
California Autism Foundation
  Windsor Confections, 13845
California Creative Foods
  Santa Barbara Salsa, 11186
California Shellfish
  Hallmark Fisheries, 5525
  West Coast Seafood Processors Association, 13662
Calson Industries
  Mr. C's, 8621
  Stasero International, 12052
Caltex Trading
  Caltex Foods, 2096
Campari
  Campari, 2114
Campbell Soup
  Godiva Chocolatier, 5092
  Pepperidge Farm Inc., 9942
Campbell Soup Co
  Bolt House Farms-Shipping Dept, 1548
Campbell Soup Company
  Snyder's-Lance Inc., 11770
Canada Bread
  Multi Marques, 8676
Canandaigua Wine Company
  Batavia Wine Cellars, 1080
  Simi Winery, 11637
  Ste Chapelle Winery, 12064
  Taylor Wine Company, 12574
  Viki's Montana Classics, 13405
  Widmers Wine Cellars, 13766
Candy Tree Company
  CTC Manufacturing, 1964
Cape Bald Packers
  Down East Specialty Products/Cape Bald Packers, 3719
Carando Gourmet
  Carando Gourmet Frozen Foods, 2193
Cargill Foods
  Intermountain Canola Cargill, 6245
  St. Lawrence Starch, 12009
  Sunny Fresh Foods, 12283
  Wilbur Chocolate Candy, 13771
Cargill Inc.
  Cargill Kitchen Solutions Inc., 2205
  Cargill Protein, 2206
Cargill Incorporated
  Wilbur Chocolate Candy, 13772
Cargill, Incorporated
  Prairie Malt, 10234
Carl Buddig & Company
  Old Wisconsin Food Products, 9431
Carolina By-Products Company
  CBP Resources, 1944
Casa Visco Finer Food
  Casa Visco, 2274
Cascade Specialties, Inc.
  White Oaks Frozen Foods, 13726
Case Farms
  Case Farms Ohio Division, 2288
Castellini Company
  Club Chef LLC, 2789
Cathay International
  ABC Tea House, 72
Catterton Management Company
  Ferrara Candy Co Inc, 4345
Cavendish Farms Corporation
  Cavendish Farms, 2332
CCMP Capital Advisors LLC
  Jamieson Laboratories, 6449
Cedar Crest Specialties
  Cedar Crest Specialties, 2346
Centennial Specialty Food
  Stokes Canning Company, 12127
Cereal Food Processors
  Cereal Food Processors, 2388
Cerveceria Costa Rica S.A.
  Genesee Brewing Company, 4950

Cesare Fiorucci
  Fiorucci Foods USA Inc, 4411
CFC Inc.
  Columbus Vegetable Oils, 2913
CH Guenther & Son
  Morrison Milling Co, 8563
Chalone Wine Group
  Acacia Vineyard, 132
  Canoe Ridge Vineyard, 2142
  Carmenet Winery, 2222
  Chalone Vineyard, 2405
Charles Poultry Live Broker
  Charles Poultry Company, 2433
Charoen Pokphand Foods
  Bellisio Foods, 1200
Charter Baking Co.
  Rudi's Organic Bakery, 10965
Chaucer Foods Ltd
  Chaucer Foods, Inc. USA, 2474
Cheerwine & Diet Cheerwine
  Carolina Beverage Corp, 2234
Cheese Factory
  Cheese Factory, 2480
Cheiljedang
  CJ America, 1952
Chemische Fabrik Budenheim KG
  Budenheim USA, Inc., 1829
Chenoceaux, Inc
  Portier Fine Foods, 10203
Chesapeake Fine Food Group
  Chesapeake Bay Crab Cakes & More, 2527
Chiquita Brands International, Inc
  Fresh Express, Inc., 4709
Chooljian Brothers Packing Company
  Chooljian Bros Packing Co, 2634
CHS Inc
  Ventura Foods LLC, 13328
CHS, Inc.
  CHS Sunflower, 1949
Cincinnati Preserving Company
  Cincinnati Preserving Co, 2679
Cisco Brewers
  Nantucket Vineyard, 8759
Citadelle
  Maple Products, 7879
Citrico International
  Citrico, 2694
Citrosuco
  Citrosuco North America Inc, 2697
Citrus World
  Haines City Citrus Growers, 5507
City Meat
  Barone Foods, 1051
Clack-Steel
  Steel's Gourmet Foods, Ltd., 12068
Clean Foods
  Cafe Altura, 1987
Cleary Canadian Beverage Company
  Cascade Clear Water, 2281
Clemens Family Coporation
  Wild Bill's Foods, 13776
Clemens Food Group
  Hatfield Quality Meats, 5643
Cliffstar
  Carolina Products, 2248
Clorox Company
  HV Food Products Co, 5489
Clover Capital Partners LLC
  Main Street Gourmet, 7785
Coast Seafoods Company
  Coast Seafoods Company, 2797
Coastal Enterprises
  Misty Islands Seafoods, 8399
Coastal Sun Belt
  East Coast Fresh Cuts Inc, 3879
Cobi Foods
  Interfrost, 6242
Coca-Cola Co.
  Fairlife, 4224
Coca-Cola Company
  Minute Maid Company, 8365
Coffee Associates
  Coffee Associates, 2832
Coleman Natural
  Petaluma Poultry, 9974
Colony Brands, Inc.
  Colony Brands Inc, 2888
Columbus Gourmet
  Kendrick Gourmet Products, 6784
Conagra Brands
  Conagra Brands Canada, 2938

Conagra Foodservice, 2940
  J M Swank Co, 6359
Conagra Brands, Inc.
  Birdseye Food, 1389
ConAgra Foods
  Alexia Foods, 294
  Con Agra Snack Foods, 2935
  Decker Food Company, 3459
  GoodMark Foods, 5180
  Hunt-Wesson Foods, 6084
  International Home Foods, 6267
  Jack's Bean Co LLC, 6418
  La Choy, 7082
  O'Donnell-Usen, 9288
  Singleton Seafood, 11666
  Slim Jim, 11706
  Vogel Popcorn, 13485
ConAgra Refrigerated Prepared Foods
  Butterball LLC, 1883
  National Foods, 8791, 8792, 8793
Consac Industries
  The Long Life Beverage Company, 12704
Consolation Brand
  Frisinger Cellars, 4739
Consolidated Biscuit Co. Ltd.
  Consolidated Biscuit Company, 2960
Consolidated Mills
  Consolidated Mills Inc, 2962
Consolidated Service Distributors, Inc
  Candy Central, 2132
Constellation Brand, Inc.
  Ravenswood Winery, 10573
Constellation Brands
  Manischewitz Wine Co., 7849
Continental Grain Company
  Wayne Farms LLC., 13607
Cooke Inc.
  Omega Protein, 9479
CoolBrands International
  Cool Brands International, 2993
Coop Laitiere Artois Flandre
  Ingredia Inc, 6207
Cooperative Agricultural Producers
  Northwest Pea & Bean Co, 9179
Corbion
  Corbion, 3014
Corn Poppers
  Corn Popper, 3034
Corteva Agriscience
  Corteva Agriscience, 3044
  DuPont Pioneer, 3775
Corticella USA Organic Farms
  Santini Foods, 11204
Costa Deano's Enterprises
  Costa Deano's Gourmet Foods, 3050
Coulton Associates
  Fool Proof Gourmet Products, 4577
Country Home Bakers
  Sanders Candy Inc, 11167
Country Pure Foods
  Cal-Tex Citrus Juice LP, 2032
Cousin Foods
  Paisano Food Products, 9711
Covalda
  Jewel Date Co, 6511
Cowart Seafood
  Lake Packing Co Inc, 7153
Craft Brew Alliance
  Redhook Brewery, 10629
CraftWorks Restaurants & Breweries
  Rock Bottom Restaurant & Brewery, 10810
Cremer
  Peter Cremer North America, 9978
Crimson Wine Group
  Seghesio Family Vineyards, 11413
Croda International P/C
  Croda Inc, 3174
CSM Bakery Solutions
  Westco-BakeMark, 13675
CSM Bakery Supplies North America
  BakeMark Canada, 953
CTI Foods Holding Co., LLC
  CTI Foods, 1965
Culinar Canada
  Culinar Canada, 3233
Culligan Water Technologies
  Culligan International Co, 3238
Cumberland Packing Corp.
  Sweet'N Low, 12422

Curtice Burns
  Curtice Burns Foods, 3261
Cutrale-Safra
  Chiquita Brands LLC., 2580
Cyanotech Corporation
  Cyanotech Corp, 3281
  Nutrex Hawaii Inc, 9244

D

D. Beccaris
  M & CP FARMS, 7673
Daabon Organic
  Daabon Organic USA, Inc., 3324
DaeKyung Oil and Transportation Co.
  Tri State Beef Co, 12955
Dairy Commodities Corporation
  Greenberg Cheese Co, 5369
Dairy Farmers of America
  Dairy Maid Dairy LLC, 3340
  Keller's Creamery, 6760
  Kemps LLC, 6778
  Morning Glory Dairy, 8547
Dairy Farmers of America, Inc.
  Berkshire Dairy, 1238
Daniels Enterprises
  Wanchese Fish Co Inc, 13561
Danish Koffie Connection
  Mokk-a, 8455
Dannone
  Dannon Company, 3377
Dare Foods
  Bremner Biscuit Company, 1690
Dargis Land & Cattle
  Bob's Custom Cuts, 1518
Darigold
  Echo Spring Dairy, 3917
Darling Ingredients
  Rousselot Inc, 10915
Das Brot
  Texas Crumb & Food Products, 12652
DaSilva-Klanko
  Love'n Herbs, 7602
David Rio San Francisco
  David Rio, 3398
David Scott Industries
  A La Carte, 39
Davisco Foods International, Inc.
  Le Sueur Cheese Co, 7275
DCCA
  Golden Valley Dairy Products, 5137
Dean Distributors
  Dean Distributors, Inc., 3441
Dean Foods
  Alta Dena Certified Dairy LLC, 387
  Alta Dena Heartland Farms, 388
  Barber Dairies, 1021
  Broughton Foods LLC, 1770
  Lehigh Valley Dairy Farms, 7320
  Mayfield Dairy Farms LLC, 8039
  Meadow Gold, 8105
  Schepps Dairy, 11281
  Swiss Premium Dairy Inc, 12442
  Velda Farms, 13319
Dean Foods Company
  Berkeley Farms, 1234
  Country Fresh, 3073
  Creamland Dairies Inc, 3131
  DairyPure, 3347
  Gandy's Dairies LLC, 4882
  Louisville Dairy, 7593
  Maplehurst Farms, 7887
  McArthur Dairy LLC, 8053
  Meadow Brook Dairy Co, 8104
  Morning Star Foods, 8548
  Northern Dairy, 9146
  PET Dairy, 9651
  Price's Creameries, 10277
  Purity Dairies LLC, 10393
  Reiter Dairy LLC, 10664
  T G Lee Dairy, 12460
  Tri-State Dairy, 12958
  TruMoo, 13024
  Verifine Dairy, 13338
DeBoles Nutritional Foods
  De Boles Nutritional Foods, 3423
Deepsouth Packing Company
  Southern Shell Fish Company, 11865
Del Monte Foods
  Starkist Co, 12046

1358

Parent Company Index

Del Monte Pacific, Ltd.
Del Monte Foods Inc., 3478
Del Sol Food Company Inc.
Briannas Fine Salad Dressings, 1700
Delicious Frookie Company
Delicious Frookie Company, 3500
Delta Pride Catfish
Delta Pride Catfish, 3516
Dewey's Bakery
Salem Baking Company, 11100
Diageo Chateau & Estate Wines
Sterling Vineyards, 12087
Diageo Chateau & Estate Wines Co.
Beaulieu Vineyard, 1137
Diageo United Distillers and Vinters
Grand Metropolitan, 5253
Haagen-Dazs, 5490
Diana Naturals
Diana Naturals, 3580
Dick Garber Company
Dick Garber Company, 3586, 3587
Diedrich Coffee
Coffee People, 2853
Gloria Jean's Gourmet Coffees, 5070
Diehl
Diehl Food Ingredients, 3593
Dillon Corporation
Jaxon's Ice Cream Parlor, 6472
Direct Access Network
Vaxa International, 13304
Distinguished Vineyards & Wine Partners
Argyle Winery, 659
Doddoli Hermanos Group
Avo-King Internatl, 841
Domino Foods Inc
Domino Specialty Ingredients, 3666
Don Pepino Company
Violet Packing Holdings LLC, 13437
DOW Chemical Company
Dow AgroSciences Canada, 3716
Dr Pepper Snapple Group
Big Red Bottling, 1339
Dr. Pepper Snapple Group
Mott's, 8585
Dr. Pepper/7-UP Bottling Companies
Varni Brothers/7-Up Bottling, 13300
Dried Ingredients GmbH
Dried Ingredients, LLC., 3762
Droubi's Bakery & Delicatessen
Droubi's Imports, 3768
DS Services
Crystal Springs Water Company, 3220
DS Services of America
Hinckley Springs Bottled Water, 5884
Mount Olympus Waters, 8591
Sparkletts, 11889
DS Services of America Inc.
Crystal Springs Bottled Water, 3219
Ds Waters Holdings, LLC
Kentwood Springs, 6797
DSM
DSM Fortitech Premixes, 3322
I-Health Inc, 6107
DUDA
Duda Farm Fresh Foods Inc, 3781
Dunkin' Brands, Inc.
Baskin-Robbins LLC, 1075
Duntreath Farm
Pots de Creme, 10219
DuPont
DuPont Nutrition & Biosciences, 3773
DuPont Pioneer, 3774
DuPont Chemical
M-CAP Technologies, 7683
Personal Edge Nutrition, 9970
Durrset Amigos
Amigos Canning Company, 501
Dutch Gold Honey
Mc Lure's Honey & Maple Prod, 8050
Dynic Corporation
Dynic USA Corp, 3833
DyStar Group
DyStar Hilton Davis/DyStar Foam Control, 3826

E

E & J Gallo Winery
E & J Gallo Winery, 3835
E&J Gallo
Chateau Souverain, 2465
E&J Gallo Winery
Edna Valley Vineyard, 3952
Louis M Martini Winery, 7573
Talbott Vineyards, 12506
Terrace At J Vineyards, 12627
William Hill Estate Winery, 13814
E.A. Sween Company
E A Sween Co, 3836
E.W. Knauss & Sons
Andrews Dried Beef Company, 558
Eagle Family Foods Group LLC
Milnot Company, 8327
Earth Commodities
Green Grown Products Inc, 5353
Earth Power
Phyto-Technologies, 10026
EarthCorp Foundation
Innocent Chocolate, 6224
East Coast Olive Corporation
California Olive Oil Council, 2075
East Wind Community
East Wind Inc, 3887
Ebro Foods, S.A.
Riviana Foods Inc., 10777
Ed Miniat
Ed Miniat Inc, 3929
Eden Foods
Eden Organic Pasta Company, 3941
Meridian Foods New Inc, 8170
Sobaya, 11773
Eden Manufacturing Company
Lake City Foods, 7150
Edner Corporation
Edner Corporation, 3953
Edward & Sons Trading Company, Inc.
Road's End Organics, 10780
Eisenberg Sausage Company
Kelly Corned Beef Co, 6767
Ekstrom Enterprises
Silver Streak Bass Co, 11629
Elan
Flavorganics, 4489
Elcat
Chattem Chemicals Inc, 2471
Elmhurst Dairy
Mountainside Farms Inc, 8609
EMAC International
Golden Walnut Specialty Foods, 5140
Emerald Performance Materials
Emerald Kalama Chemical, LLC, 4042
Encore Frozen Foods
On-Cor Frozen Foods Redi-Serve, 9483
English Bay Batter
English Bay Batter Us Inc, 4070
Engro Foods Canada Ltd.
Al Safa Halal, 251
Equitythink Holdings, LLC
Charlie Beigg's Sauce Company, 2438
Erie Foods International Inc
Erie Foods Intl Inc, 4107
Ernex Corporation
Empress Chocolate Company, 4058
Essential Pharmaceutical
Tabco Enterprises, 12486
Essiac Canada International
Essiac Canada International, 4126
Essity
Wausau Paper Corp., 13595
Euro Am Imports
Euroam Importers Inc, 4147
EuroVita Corp.
3 Water, 12
Evans Food Products
Mac's Snacks, 7719
Evans Gourmet Foods, LLC
Kentucky Beer Cheese, 6795
Excelso
Field Coffee, 4363

F

F&Y Enterprises
F&Y Enterprises, 4201
F. Korbel & Brothers
Heck Cellars, 5725
Fairbury Food
Fairbury Food Products, 4220
Fairfield Gourmet Foods Corp.
David's Cookies, 3399
Fairfield Gourmet Foods Corporation
Bittersweet Pastries, 1413
Fairview Dairy
Fairview Dairy Inc, 4227
Fairview Swiss Cheese
John Koller & Son Inc, 6557
Fannie May
Harry London Candies Inc, 5616
Farm Management Company
South Valley Farms, 11835
Farmer Boys Catfish International
Fisherman's Reef Shrimp Company, 4448
Farmer Bros Co
Boyd's Coffee Co, 1636
Farmer Brothers Company
Coffee Bean Intl, 2836
Farmers Co-op Dairy
Central Dairies, 2377
Farmers Investment Company
Green Valley Pecan Company, 5367
Fch Enterprises, Inc.
Hawaiian Bagel, 5657
FDP USA
Nutranique Labs, 9242
Felknor International
Popcorn Popper, 10180
Fermers Investment
Country Estate Pecans, 3071
Ferrara Candy Company
Black Forest Organic, 1417
Ferrero, SPA
Ferrero USA Inc, 4348
Fiesta Gourmet del Sol
Fiesta Gourmet of Tejas, 4375
FIGGINS FAMILY WINE ESTATES
Leonetti Cellar, 7366
Finlays
Finlay Extracts & Ingredients USA, Inc., 4406
Fisherman Wharf Foods
Nickabood's Inc, 9042
Flagstone Foods
American Importing Co., 462
Flavorchem Corp.
Marnap Industries, 7948
Fletcher's Fine Foods
Fletcher's Fine Foods, 4501
Grimm's Fine Food, 5391
Florida Bottling
Lakewood Juice Co., 7169
Florida Crystals
Osceola Farms Sugar Warehouse, 9578
Florida Family Trust
Lakewood Juice Company, 7170
Florida Ice & Farm Co.
North American Breweries Inc., 9117
Florida Natural Flavors
Florida Natural Flavors, 4521
Florida's Natural Growers'
World Citrus West, 13932
Flowers Baking Company
European Bakers, 4151
Flowers Baking Co, 4526, 4528
Flowers Foods
Franklin Baking Co., 4662
Tasty Baking Company, 12551
Flowers Industries
Aunt Fannie's Bakery, 800
Flowers Baking Co, 4527
Foley Family Wines, Inc
Firestone Vineyard, 4419
Folly Estates
Lincourt Vineyards, 7438
Food Corporation of America
Allfresh Food Products, 340
Food Network
Clown Global Brands, 2788
FoodBrands America
TNT Crust, 12480
Foodonics International
Dixie Egg Co, 3630
FoodScience Corporation
Foodscience Corp, 4575
Fort Pitt Brand Meats
Fried Provisions Company, 4732
Foster Dairy Farms
Humboldt Creamery, 6067
Freixenet America
Gloria Ferrer Champagne, 5069
Freixenet SA
Freixenet USA Inc, 4693
Fresh Start Food Corp.
Golden Valley Foods Ltd., 5138
Frutech International Corporation
Frutech International Corp, 4774
FSB Global Holdings, Inc.
Fresh Start Bakeries, 4724
FSI Nutrition
Fortress Systems LLC, 4609
Fuji Foods Corporation
Fuji Foods Corp, 4781
Fung Nin Fine Foods
Calco of Calgary, 2040
Funk Enterprises
Carson City Pickle Company, 2264
Fuso Chemical Company
PMP Fermentation Products, 9656

G

Gambino's
Gambino's Bakery, 4880
Gambrinus Company
Spice Time Foods, 11925
Spoetzl Brewery, 11942
Garden Row Foods
Garden Row Foods, 4894
Garfield Weston Foundation
Fleischmann's Yeast, 4500
Gator Hammock
Gator Hammock Corp, 4921
General Mills
Pillsbury, 10059
Progresso Quality Foods, 10337
Small Planet Foods, 11711
Yoplait, 14017
General Mills Inc
The Pillsbury Company, 12717
Genisoy
Genisoy, 4955
George Chiala Farms, Inc.
GC Farms, 4826
George Weston Ltd.
Ace Bakery, 141
Gadoua Bakery, 4856
Interbake Foods, 6239
Maplehurst Bakeries LLC, 7886
Weston Foods, 13691
GI Manager L.P
Duckhorn Vineyards, 3779
GI Manager L.P.
Far Niente Winery, 4258
Gillespie & Associates
Pro Form Labs, 10314
Giovanni Food Company Inc.
Ventre Packing Company, 13326
Giroux's Poultry Farm
Chazy Orchards, 2476
Giuseppe Citterio Spa
Citterio USA, 2701
Givaudan
Spicetec Flavors & Seasonings, 11930
Glanbia Nutritionals
Pizzey's Milling & Baking Company, 10095
Watson Inc, 13592
Glanbia Plc
Glanbia Nutritionals, 5046
Glatech Productions
Kolatin Real Kosher Gelatin, 6944
Glazier Foods
Mims Meat Company, 8338
Glencore plc
Viterra, Inc, 13475
GNS Foods
Pacific Gold Marketing, 9683
Golden Cheese Company of California
Calpro Ingredients, 2095
Golden State Vintners
Edgewood Estate Winery, 3946
Gorton's
Specialty Products, 11907
Gortons USA
BlueWater Seafoods, 1502
Gourmet Mixes
Demitri's Bloody Mary Seasonings, 3518
Granada Foods Corporation
Sunday House Foods, 12270
Grand Metropolitan
Diageo Canada Inc., 3569
Grande Cheese Company
Grande Custom Ingredients Group, 5259
Grandma's Pasta Products
Food City USA, 4555

1359

Parent Company Index

Granum Inc
  Choice Organic Teas, 2630
Graves Mountain Lodge
  Graves Mountain Lodge Inc., 5285
Great Atlantic Trading Company
  Great Atlantic Trading Company, 5302
Great Lakes Cheese Company, Inc.
  Great Lakes Cheese Company, 5316
Green Mountain Coffee
  Diedrich Coffee, 3591
Green Valley Packing
  Albert's Meats, 279
GreenField
  Pharmco Aaper, 9999
Griffith Laboratories
  Innova Flavors, 6226
Griffith Laboratories, Inc.
  Custom Culinary Inc., 3269
Groneweg Group
  FDI Inc, 4205
Groupe Grimaud
  Grimaud Farms-California Inc, 5390
Groupe Lactalis
  Lactalis American Group Inc, 7126
Groupe Limagrain
  Harris Moran Seed Co, 5610
Groupo LALA/LALA National Dairy Group
  Farmland Dairies, 4290
Gruma Corporation
  Azteca Milling, 856
  Mission Foods, 8383
  Mission Foods Corp., 8384, 8385, 8386
Grupo Bimbo
  Bimbo Bakeries USA Inc., 1359
  Canada Bread Co, Ltd, 2121
Grupo Empresarial Nutresa
  Abimar Foods Inc, 122
Guiness PLC
  George A Dickel & Company, 4961
  Guinness Import Co, 5427
Gulf City Seafood
  Gulf City Marine Supply, 5431

H

H.J. Heinz Company
  Lea & Perrins, 7277
  Ore-Ida Foods, 9523
H.M. International
  Quality Sausage Company, 10442
HACO
  Girard's Food Service Dressings, 5032
Hailwood
  Chase Brothers Dairy, 2450
Hain Celestial
  Ella's Kitchen, 4016
Hain Celestial Group
  A2 Milk Company, 69
  Ethnic Gourmet Foods, 4138
  Imagine Foods, 6151
Hain Food Group
  Arrowhead Mills, 705
Hampton Farms
  Olde Tyme Food Corporation, 9438
Hanover Foods
  John Copes Food Products, 6551
Hanover Foods Corp
  Aunt Kitty's Foods Inc, 805
  Hanover Potato Products Inc, 5556
Hanover Foods Corporation
  Bickel's Snack Foods Inc, 1310
  L K Bowman, 7028
  Spring Glen Fresh Foods, 11960
Harris Farms, Inc.
  Harris Ranch Beef Co, 5611
Harris Freeman Enterprise
  Harris Tea Company, 5612
Harris Teeter
  Hunter Farms - High Point Division, 6085
Harrison Gypsum
  Allied Custom Gypsum Company, 343
Hartog Rahal Foods
  Hartog Rahal Foods, 5622
Hasbro
  Cap Candy, 2148
Health Addict Inc
  Fru-V, 4758
HealthRite
  Montana Naturals, 8493

Hearthside Food Solutions
  Oak State Products Inc, 9323
Heineman Beverage
  Heineman Winery, 5731
Heinz
  Yoshida Food Products Co, 14020
Heinz Canada
  Intercorp Excelle Foods, 6240
Heinz USA
  Escalon Premier Brand, 4111
  Heinz Quality Chef Foods Inc, 5736
Heller Brothers
  Pacific Collier Fresh Company, 9676
Heller Seasonings
  Newly Weds Foods Inc, 9017
Helm AG
  Helm New York Chemical Corp, 5750
Herbert Brothers Entertainment Inc
  Badger Island Shell-Fish & Lobster, 929
Hero Group
  Beech-Nut Nutrition Corp, 1161
Hi Quality Packing
  United Marketing Exchange, 13193
Hickory Baked Food
  Hickory Baked Ham Co, 5832
Hikari Miso Co., Ltd.
  Hikari Miso Intl., 5862
Hilltop Farm Forestry Group
  Skedaddle Maple, 11683
Hiram Walker-Allied Domeq.
  Callaway Vineyards & Winery, 2091
Hirzel Canning
  Hirzel Canning Co., 5894
Hoffman-La Roche
  Hosemen & Roche Vitamins & Fine Chemicals, 6007
Hollymead Capital
  Tomanetti Food Products, 12857
Hood Foods
  Hood Home Service, 5979
  Hood Sterile Division, 5983
Hormel Foods Corporation
  Century Foods Intl LLC, 2387
  Dold Foods, 3652
  Fontanini Italian Meats, 4550
  Jennie-O Turkey Store, 6488
Hormel Foods International Corporation
  House of Tsang, 6028
Horner International
  Horner International, 6002
Hostess
  Cloverhill Bakery-Vend Corporation, 2784
Houlihan's Culinary Traditions
  Elena's, 4005
House Foods Corporation
  House Foods America Corp, 6021
Hudson Industries Corporation
  Milligan & Higgins, 8317
Huna Totem Corperation
  Dear North, 3445
Hung Kee Holdings Company
  Hung's Noodle House, 6079
Hunstinger Farms, Inc.
  Silver Spring Foods, 11625
Hygeia Dairy Company
  Hygeia Dairy Company, 6101

I

I.L.A.S.
  Old Europe Cheese Inc, 9410
IBC
  San Francisco French Bread, 11143
IBIS
  Busseto Foods, 1875
  Magna Foods Corporation, 7769
ICB Holdings, LLC
  Pittsburgh Brewing Co, 10091
ICL
  BK Giulini Corporation, 898
ICL Holdings
  ICL Performance Products, 6109
Idaho Pacific Corporation
  AgraWest Foods, 207
Ideal Macaroni Company
  Weiss Noodle Company, 13633
IMO Foods
  IMO Foods, 6119
Impact Restaurants
  M J Barleyhoppers Sports Bar, 7677

Indena S.p.A.
  Indena USA Inc, 6178
India's Rasoa
  Indias House, 6196
Indomex Foods
  Petra International, 9987
Industrializadora Integral Del Agave, SA DeCV
  Naturel, 8897
Ingram Farms
  Rod Golden Hatchery Inc, 10829
Ingredion Incorporated
  National Starch Food Innovation, 8804
Inlet Salmon
  Inlet Salmon, 6220
Instantwhip Foods
  Auburn Dairy Products Inc, 792
  Ohio Association Of Meat, 9378
Interfood Holding
  Interfood Ingredients, 6241
Interior Alaska Fish Processors
  Santa's Smokehouse, 11200
International Commissary Corporation
  Marie Callender's Gourmet Products/Goldrush Products, 7915
International Flavors & Fragrances
  KERR Concentrates Inc, 6671
International Flavors & Frangrances Inc.
  Tastepoint, 12550
International Flavors-Fragrances
  Frutarom Meer Corporation, 4773
International Food Trade
  Christy Wild Blueberry Farms, 2657
International Specialty Supply
  International Specialty Supply, 6273
International Whey Technics
  Varied Industries Corp, 13299
Interstate Foods
  Paramount Coffee, 9772
Intrepid Food Holdings
  Health Valley Company, 5684
Inventure Foods Inc
  Poore Brothers, 10173
Iowa Turkey Growers Cooperative
  West Liberty Foods LLC, 13664
Ipswich Shellfish Company, Inc.
  Lowcountry Shellfish Inc, 7608
Island Enterprises
  Uncle Fred's Fine Foods, 13155
Island Pacific Brewing Company
  Vancouver Island Brewing Company, 13288
Italian Peoples Bakery
  Italian Peoples Bakery Inc, 6321

J

J&J Snack Foods
  Country Home Bakers, 3078
J&J Snack Foods Company
  Bakers Best Snack Food Corp., 972
  Mia Products, 8217
  Trotter Soft Pretzels, 13014
J-R Ouimet
  Cordon Bleu International, 3026
J. Lohr Vineyards & Wines
  Ariel Vineyards, 663
J. Rettenmaier & Sohne GmbH & Co KG
  J Rettenmaier USA LP, 6365
J.M Smucker Company
  Folgers Coffee Co, 4543
J.M. Huber Company
  CP Kelco, 1962
J.M. Schneider
  Bacon America, 923
  Capolla Food Inc, 2165
  Horizon Poultry, 5997
  J.M. Schneider, 6379
  Royal Touch Foods, 10950
  Schneider Foods, 11299, 11300
J.M. Smucker Company
  JMS Specialty Foods, 6406
  Knott's Berry Farms, 6921
J.R. Short Milling Company
  J.R. Short Canadian Mills, 6385
J.R. Simplot Company
  Simplot Food Group, 11647
J.S. McMillan
  J.S. McMillan Fisheries, 6387
JAB Holding Company
  Caribou Coffee Co Inc, 2211

  Krispy Kreme Doughnuts Inc, 6988
  Peet's Coffee, 9896
JAIN
  Cascade Specialties, Inc., 2285
Japan Sangaria Beverage Company
  SANGARIA USA, 11032
JBR Gourmet Foods
  Fairwinds Gourmet Coffee, 4229
  San Francisco Bay Coffee Company, 11141
JBS S.A.
  JBS USA LLC, 6391
  Pilgrim's Pride Corp., 10056
JBS USA
  Moyer Packing Co., 8615
  Plumrose USA, 10124
JBS USA, LLC.
  Four Star Beef, 4630
Jean Niel
  Jean Niel Inc, 6477
Jean's Garden Greats
  Adventure Foods, 194
Jed's Maple Products
  Northeast Kingdom Mustard Company, 9143
Jim Pattison Group
  Alaska General Seafoods, 262
Jo Mar Labs
  Jo Mar Laboratories, 6524
Joe Hutson Foods
  Joe Hutson Foods, 6536
Joel
  Quigley Industries Inc, 10461
Jogue Inc.
  Golden 100, 5113
John B. Sanfilippo & Son
  Sunshine Nut Company, 12310
John Koller and Son, Inc
  Fairview Swiss Cheese, 4228
John Morrell/Smithfield Foods
  Curly's Foods Inc, 3258
Johnson & Johnson
  McNeil Nutritionals, 8082
  McNeil Specialty Products Company, 8083
Johnson Development Group
  Imperial Sensus, 6163
Johnson Foods, Inc.
  Johnson Foods, Inc. - Cannery Plant, 6567
Jones Products International
  Crystal Star Herbal Nutrition, 3221
JR Wood
  Glacier Foods, 5042
Jungbunzlauer Suisse AG
  Jungbunzlauer Inc, 6634
Just Born, Inc.
  Goldenberg's Peanut Chews, 5144
JW Childs Associates
  NutraSweet Company, 9236

K

K+S
  K+S Windsor Salt Ltd., 6661
K+S AG
  Morton Salt Inc., 8569
Kake Tribal Corporation
  Pelican Seafoods, 9904
Kalamazoo Holdings
  Kalsec, 6695
Kanan Enterprises
  King Nut Co, 6870
Kayco
  Kedem, 6746
KayCo
  Royal Wine Corp, 10952
KDK Enterprises
  Bite Size Bakery, 1408
Kek Industries
  Klaire Laboratories, 6905
Kellogg Company
  Bear Naked, Inc., 1130
  Kashi Company, 6720
  Keebler Company, 6747
  Kellogg Canada Inc., 6765
  Leaf Jerky, 7281
  Morningstar Farms, 8551
  Worthington Foods, 13952
Kemmons Wilson Companies
  Wilson's Fantastic Candy, 13835

Parent Company Index

Kemps LLC
Cass-Clay Creamery, 2295
Ken's Foods
Sweet Baby Ray's, 12388
Kendall-Jackson Wine
Kendall-Jackson, 6782
Kenny B's Cookie
Award Baking Intl, 846
Kent Corporation
Grain Processing Corp, 5246
Kent Precision Foods Group Inc, 6792
Kent Precision Foods Group
Milani, 8287
Kerry
Caffe D'Amore Gourmet Beverages, 2007
Kerry Food Services
Island Oasis Frozen Cocktail, 6302
Kerry Group Plc
Kerry, Inc, 6808
Kerry Inc.
Kerry Sweet Ingredients, 6807
Keurig Dr Pepper
Dr Pepper Snapple Group, 3725
Kezele Corporation
Ruth Hunt Candy Co, 10998
King Ranch
Young Pecan, Inc., 14023
Kirin Brewery Company, Ltd.
Coca-Cola Beverages Northeast, 2811
KKR
Nature's Bounty Co., 8871
Kofkoff Egg Farm
Colchester Egg Farm, 2866
Koninklijke DSM N.V.
DSM Food Specialties, 3321
Korbel Champagne
Kenwood Vineyards, 6798
Kovar Companies
Glendora Quiche Company, 5053
Kraft Foods
Baker's Coconut, 967
Boca Foods Company, 1527
Capri Sun, 2173
Churny Company, 2667, 2668
Maxwell House & Post, 8031
Nabisco, 8729
Kroger Company
Country Oven Bakery, 3082
Heritage Farms Dairy, 5797
Inter-American Products, 6237
Michigan Dairy LLC, 8246
Southern Ice Cream Specialties, 11856
Tamarack Farms Dairy, 12516
Tara Foods, 12533
The Kroger Co., 12699
Winchester Farms Dairy, 13841
Kruger Gmbh & Company
Instant Products of America, 6232
KV Pharmaceutical
Particle Dynamics, 9797
Kyowa Hakko Kogyo Company
Kyowa Hakko, 7017

L

La Reina
Anita's Mexican Foods Corporation, 573
Queen International Foods, 10453
Labatt Breweries
Oland Breweries, 9396
Labatt Brewing Company
Labatt Breweries Alberta, 7120
Labatt Breweries Newfoundland, 7121
Labatt Brewery London, 7122
Mike's Beverage Company, 8279
Lacas Coffee Company
Dallis Brothers, 3362
Lactalis
Parmalat Canada, 9789
Siggi's Dairy, 11597
Lactalis American Group, Inc.
Lactalis Ingredients Inc, 7127
Lactalis USA Inc, 7128
LaFamille des Grands Vins
Boisset Family Estates, 1543
Lakeside Foods
Lakeside Foods Inc., 7162
Lakeside Mills
Lakeside Mills, 7163

Lallemand, Inc.
Lallemand American Yeast, 7173
Lallemand/American Yeast, 7175, 7176
Lamex Foods
Lamex Foods Inc., 7182
Lance, Inc.
Tom's Snacks Company, 12854
Land O'Lakes
Bongard's Creameries, 1557
Protient, 10351
Lantic, Inc.
L.B. Maple Treat, 7037
Lassonde Industries
Old Orchard Brands, LLC, 9423
Lassonde Industries, Inc.
A. Lassonde Inc., 56
Lassonde Pappas & Company, Inc., 7236
Lauridsen Group
APC Inc, 98
Essentia Protein Solutions, 4119
Lay Packing Company
Lay Packing Company, 7260
LDI
Wege Pretzel Company, 13622
Leadway International, Inc.
Bossen, 1590
Lechner's
Lenchner Bakery, 7344
Lee Kum Kee Company
Lee Kum Kee, 7295
Lehmann Farms
Lehmann Farms, 7321
Lesaffre Group
Lesaffre Yeast Corporation, 7389
Libert, Natural Foods Inc.
Western Creamery, 13680
LiDestri Food & Beverage
Zeigler's, 14050
Lindt & Sprungli
Russell Stover Candies Inc., 10991
Loboratorio Opoterapico Argentino
Fallwood Corp, 4237
Lobster Trap Wholesale Seafood Dealers
BBS Lobster Co, 891
Lofredo Fresh Produce
Loffredo Produce, 7508
Lonza Group Ltd.
Inter Health Nutraceuticals, 6236
Louis Dreyfus Company B.V.
Louis Dreyfus Company LLC, 7570
Louis Dreyfus Holding BV
Imperial Sugar Company, 6164
Lounsbury Foods
Cedarvale Food Products, 2357
LycoRed Company
H. Reisman Corporation, 5475

M

M&M Food Products
Flaum Appetizing, 4478
M.A. Patout & Son
Raceland Raw Sugar Corporation, 10525
Mada'n Corporation
Mada'n Kosher Foods, 7738
Made Rite Foods
Made Rite Foods, 7743
Magnotta Winery Corporation
Kittling Ridge Estate Wines & Spirits, 6901
Majans
Bhuja Snacks, 1303
Malteurop
Malteurop North America, 7810
Manildra Group
Manildra Milling Corporation, 7847
Manola Company
Luyties Pharmacal Company, 7658
Mansmith Enterprises
Mansmith's Barbeque, 7856
Maola Milk & Ice Cream Company
Maola Milk & Ice Cream Co, 7862
Maple Donuts LLC
Maple Donuts, 7864
Maple Leaf Foods
Lightlife, 7427
Maple Leaf Consumer Foods, 7873
Maple Leaf Meats, 7877
Maple Leaf Pork, 7878
Serenade Foods, 11451

Maple Leaf Foods Inc
Grace Baking Company, 5226
Maplehurst Bakeries
Petrofsky's Bakery Products, 9988
Margarine Thibault
JE Bergeron & Sons, 6395
Marie Brizard Wines & Spirits USA
Marie Brizard Wines & Spirits, 7913
Marquez Brothers International
Marquez Brothers International, 7949
Mars
Ethel M Chocolates, 4133
Mars, Inc.
Seeds of Change, 11409
Mars, Incorporated
Wrigley, 13960
Marubeni Corporation
Marubeni America Corp., 7973
Maruha Capital Investment, Inc.
Peter Pan Seafoods Inc., 9980
Maruha Corporation
Trans-Ocean Products Inc, 12925
Maruha Nichiro Corporation
Alyeska Seafoods, 400
Marukai Corporation
Marukai Market, 7975
Marukan Vinegar Co, Ltd
Marukan Vinegar USA Inc., 7976
Maryland & Virginia Milk Producers Coop Assoc, Inc.
Marva Maid Dairy, 7978
Maryland & Virginia Producers Cooperative Association, Inc.
Maola Milk & Ice Cream Co., 7861
MAS Sales
Pasta Factory, 9809
Massimo Zanetti Beverage
Chock Full O'Nuts, 2587
Matosantos Commercial Corp.
Eurocaribe Packing Company, 4149
Mattingly Foods
Mattingly Foods Of Louisville, 8016
Mayer's Cider Mill
Mayer's Cider Mill, 8038
McCain Foods Limited
McCain Foods USA Inc., 8055
McCain Foods Ltd.
McCain Produce Inc., 8056
Wong Wing, 13908
McCain Foods USA
Charcuterie LaTour Eiffel, 2426
McCain Foods USA/H.J. Heinz Company
Anchor Appetizer Group, 530
McCormick & Co.
Doyon, 3723
McCormick & Company
Lawry's Foods, 7257
Signature Brands LLC, 11599
McCormick & Company Inc
Sup Herb Farms, 12317
McKee Foods
Drake Bakeries, 3745
McKee Foods Corporation
Blue Planet Foods, 1491
McKenzie River Partners
Great Northern Brewing Co, 5323
McShares
Research Products Co, 10680
McShares, Inc.
Viobin USA, 13435
Med Opportunity Partners
Pfanstiehl Inc, 9992
Medifast Inc.
Jason Pharmaceuticals, 6462
Meduri Farms
Meduri Farms, 8127
Meherrin Agriculture
Severn Peanut Co, 11479
Meherrin Chemical
Hampton Farms, 5541
Meiji Co., Ltd.
Stauffer Biscuit Co, 12060
Mejores Alimentos de Costa Rica/Alina Foods C.A.
Tantos Foods International, 12527
Mel-O-Cream Donuts International
Mel-O-Cream Donuts Intl, 8140
Merck KgaA Darmstadt
EMD Performance Materials, 3855
Metarom Canada
Metarom Corporation, 8194

Metz Group
Colombo Bakery, 2884
Meyer Holdings
R.E. Meyer Company, 10493
Meyer Honey Company
Rocky Mountain Honey Company, 10821
Meyers Bakeries
Meyer's Bakeries, 8212
MGH Holdings Corporation
Specialty Coffee Roasters, 11897
Michael Foods, Inc.
MFI Food Canada, 7698
Michigan Blueberry Growers Association
Blueberry Store, 1503
Midas Foods India
Michigan Desserts, 8247
MiDAS Foods International
Midas Foods Intl, 8261
Miller Brewing Company
Pete's Brewing Company, 9977
Milnot Company
Milnot Company, 8326
Mincing Trading Corporation
Mincing Overseas Spice Company, 8341
Mindful Foods
Soozy's Grain-Free, 11811
Minerals Technologies Inc
Specialty Minerals Inc, 11906
Minn-Dak Farmers Cooperative
Minn-Dak Yeast Co Inc, 8353
Misono Food
Buonitalia, 1855
Mitsubishi
California Oils Corp, 2073
Mitsubishi Chemical Coorporation
Mitsubishi Chemical Holdings, 8405
Mitsubishi International
Kirin Brewery, 6889
Mitsui & Co.
MO Air International, 7704
MKD Distributing
Snelgrove Ice Cream Company, 11753
MNI Group
Holistic Products Corporation, 5907
Modern Products
Spike Seasoning Magic, 11933
Molkerei Ammerland eG
Ammerland America, 506
Molson Coors Beverage Company
Molson Coors North America, 8460
Molson Coors Brewing Company
Jacob Leinenkugel Brewing Co, 6425
Monkey Media Software
Monkey Media, 8480
Monogram Foods
Trail's Best Snacks, 12920
Monsanto
Schillinger Genetics Inc, 11286
Monster Beverage Corporation
American Fruits & Flavors, 458
Montana Coffee Traders
Texas Coffee Traders Inc, 12651
Moody Dunbar, Inc.
Dunbar Foods Corp, 3792
Saticoy Foods Corp, 11234
Morey's Seafood International
Morey's Seafood Intl LLC, 8541
Morinaga Milk Company
Morinaga Nutritional Foods, Inc., 8546
Morre-Tec Industries, Inc
Extracts and Ingredients Ltd, 4190
Morris National Canada
Morris National, 8558
Morse Company
Fasweet Co, 4302
Morven Partners
LA Wholesale Produce Market, 7066
Motherland International
Motherland International Inc, 8584
Mountain High Organics, Inc.
TresOmega, 12954
Mountain Valley Spring Company
Carolina Summit Mountain Spring Water, 2249
Mountain Valley Water
Diamond Water Bottling Fclty, 3578
Mountanos Family Coffee & Tea Co.
Java Beans and Joe Coffee, 6465
Lindsay's Teas, 7445
Mrs. Fields' Original Cookies
Great American Cookie Company, 5296

1361

Parent Company Index

Mrs. Smiths Bakeries
  Mrs. Smiths Bakeries, 8647
MS Foods
  Fountain Shakes/MS Foods, 4622
Muggenburg Pflanzliche Rohstoffe GmbH & Co.
  Functional Products LLC, 4797
Muntons Malt
  Muntons Ingredients, 8684
Mycal Corporation
  MicroSoy Corporation, 8252

N

Nabisco
  Primo Foods, 10302
National Beverage Company
  Faygo Beverages Inc, 4314
  Shasta Beverages Inc, 11524
National Beverages Corporation
  Everfresh Beverages, 4163
National Dairy Council
  Dairy Management Inc, 3342
National Grape Cooperative
  Welch Foods Inc., 13635
National Starch & Chemical Company
  Nacan Products, 8730
Natra S.A.
  Natra US, 8814
Natrel
  Natrel, 8815
Natural Organics
  Nature's Plus, 8890
Nature's Best
  HealthBest, 5689
Nature's Way Holding Co.
  Enzymatic Therapy Inc, 4086
Naturex
  Brucia Plant Extracts, 1797
Naturex, France Avignon Headquarters
  Naturex Inc, 8899
NBTY
  Solgar Vitamin & Herbal, 11785
Nealanders International
  Nealanders Food Ingredients, 8912
Nestle
  Gerber Products Co, 4982
Nestle S.A.
  Nestle USA Inc, 8945
Nestle USA
  Food Ingredient Specialties, 4561
Nestl,
  Natural Bliss, 8821
Nestl, USA
  Dreyer's Grand Ice Cream Inc., 3760
Nestl, Waters North America
  Zephyr Hills, 14055
New World Pasta
  New World Pasta Co, 9001
New York Bakeries
  New York Bakeries Inc, 9003
New York Coffee & Bagels
  Manhattan Bagel Company, 7843
Newly Weds Foods
  UFL Foods, 13116
Niche Import Company
  Niche W&S, 9036
Nikkens Foods Company
  Nikken Foods, 9053
Nippon Meat Packers
  Day-Lee Foods, Inc., 3416
Nippon Suisan Kaisha
  Gorton's Inc., 5194
Nippon Suisan Kaisha, Ltd.
  King & Prince Seafood Corp, 6855
Nissan Foods
  Camino Real Foods Inc, 2111
Nissin Foods USA Company
  Nissin Foods USA Co Inc, 9068
Nitta Gelatin
  Nitta Gelatin NA, 9072
Norbest, LLC
  Moroni Feed Company, 8553
Nordic Enterprises
  Maine Coast Nordic, 7787
Nordic Group ASA
  Nordic Group Inc, 9106
North American World Trade Group
  Great Earth Chemical, 5305
North East Foods
  Philadelphia Baking Company, 10003

North Pacific Seafoods
  Alaska Pacific Seafoods, 266
Northeast Foods
  Automatic Rolls Of New Jersey, 824
  Bake Rite Rolls Inc, 952
Northern Breweries
  Northern Breweries, 9145
Northwest Packing
  Northwest Packing Co, 9178
Novozymes
  Novozymes North America Inc, 9195
NSpired Natural Foods
  Loriva Culinary Oils, 7545
Nueces Canyon Ranch
  Nueces Canyon Range, 9213
NVK Realty
  Calio Groves, 2085

O

Obem Foods, Inc
  Cheesecake Etc Desserts, 2484
Oberto Sausage Co.
  Pacific Gold Snacks, 9684
Obester Winery
  L. A. Smoking & Curing Company, 7034
Ocean Beauty
  Los Angeles Smoking & Curing Company, 7549
Ocean Spray Cranberries
  Milne Fruit Products Inc, 8325
Oceana Group
  Daybrook Fisheries, 3419
Ohare Enterprises
  VerMints Inc., 13331
OK Industries
  Ok Industries, 9389
Olam International
  Olam Spices, 9395
Old Dutch Foods
  Happy's Potato Chip Co, 5572
Olds Products Company
  Olds Products Co, 9440
Omega Protein
  Omega Pure, 9480
Omstead Foods
  Snowcrest Packer, 11766
Once Again Nut Butter
  Dawes Hill Honey Company, 3411
One Up
  Ginseng Up Corp, 5027
One World Enterprises
  Bloomington Brewing Co, 1460
Oregon Potato
  Washington Potato Company, 13581
Original Alan's Cubana
  Hogtowne B-B-Q Sauce Company, 5905
Oritz Corporation
  Ed & Don's Of Hawaii Inc, 3927
Ortho Molecular Products
  Ortho-Molecular Products Inc, 9573
Osem USA, Inc.
  Gratify Gluten Free, 5284
OSI Group
  Nation Pizza & Foods, 8781
OSI Industries, LLC
  Amick Farms LLC, 500
Otis Spunkmeyer
  Otis Spunkmeyer, 9591
Otsuka America, Inc.
  Ridge Vineyards Inc, 10737
Overlake Farms
  Producer Marketing Overlake, 10323
Owatonna Canning Company
  Midwest Food, 8266
  Seneca Foods Corp, 11433
Oxford Frozen Foods
  Cherryfield Foods, 2524
  Maine Wild Blueberry Company, 7792
Ozarka Houston Water Company
  Ozarka Drinking Water, 9622

P

P&J Lisac Associates
  Lisanatti Foods, 7458
Pabst
  Stroh Brewery, 12171
Pabst Brewing Company
  Stroh's Beer, 12172

Pacific Valley Foods
  Pacific Valley Foods Inc, 9699
Pantheryx, Inc.
  APS BioGroup, 99
Paradise Valley Foods
  Don Jose Foods, 3670
Paramount Distillers
  Firelands Winery, 4416
Parker Development, Inc
  Scott Adams Foods, 11324
Parmalat Bakery Group North America
  Colonial Cookies, Ltd, 2886
  Shur-Good Biscuit Co., 11580
Parmalat Canada
  Astro Dairy Products, 745
  Karoun Dairies Inc, 6719
Parmenter's Northville Cider Mill
  Northville Winery & Brewing Co, 9171
Parrish & Heimbecker
  Ellison Milling Company, 4025
Party Sweets
  Hospitality Mints LLC, 6010
Pastry Chef
  Pastry Chef, 9823
Patriot Pickles
  Kaplan & Zubrin, 6705
Pazdar Beverage Company
  Pazdar Winery, 9856
PeaceWorks
  Meditalia, 8121
Peak Rock Capital of Austin
  Diamond Crystal Brands Inc, 3574
Peanut Processors
  Southern Peanut Co Inc, 11860
Peeler's Jersey Farms
  Peeler's Jersey Farms, 9893
Pegasus Corp
  Optimal Nutrients, 9509
Pennfield Corporation
  Pennfield Farms, 9922
Penta International Corporation
  Penta Manufacturing Company, 9930
Pepsi Company
  Admiral Beverage Corp, 179
PepsiCo
  Frito-Lay Inc., 4741
Pepsico
  Naked Juice Company, 8741
PepsiCo
  Quaker Oats Company, 10419
Pepsico
  SoBe Beverages, 11772
PepsiCo
  Tropicana Products Inc., 13012
PepsiCo Canada
  Quaker Oats Company, 10420
PepsiCo North America
  Honickman Affiliates, 5975
Perdue Farms
  Natural Food Holdings, 8830
Performance Food Group Company
  Caro Foods, 2227
Perk-Up Inc.
  KARI-Out Co, 6665
Perkins
  Foxtail Foods, 4644
Pernod Ricard
  Hiram Walker & Sons, 5892
Pernod Ricard SA
  Pernod Ricard USA, 9964
Perrier Group of America
  Zephyrhills Bottled Water Company, 14056
Petroferm
  Lambent Technologies, 7180
Pfizer
  Pfizer, 9995
Pharmavite Corporation
  Pharmavite LLC, 9998
Philip Morris Companies
  Shipyard Brewing Co, 11562
Phillips Mushroom Farms
  Phillips Gourmet Inc, 10013
Pictsweet
  Pictsweet Co, 10038
Pillsbury Food Service
  Continental Mills Inc, 2971
Pilsner Group
  La Cookie, 7083
Piterra Farms
  Robert F Pliska & Company Winery, 10789

Plaza De Espana Gourmet Foods
  Plaza de Espana Gourmet, 10110
PMC Global, Inc.
  Gedney Foods Co, 4928
  PMC Specialties Group Inc, 9655
Pokka Corporation
  Amcan Beverages Inc, 427
Polar Corporation
  Adirondack Beverages Inc, 174
Post Holdings
  Post Consumer Brands, 10213
Post Holdings Inc
  PowerBar, 10225
Post Holdings, Inc.
  Bob Evans Farms Inc., 1516
  Weetabix Canada, 13620
Prairie Farms Dairy
  Ice Cream Specialties Inc, 6130
  Muller-Pinehurst Dairy, 8672
  Rochester Cheese, 10809
Prayon
  Prayon Inc., 10239
Premium Brands
  Oberto Brands, 9338
President Baking Company
  GWB Foods Corporation, 4852
Presteve Foods Limited
  Ferroclad Fishery, 4352
Pride of Italy
  Day Foods Company, 3414
Private Harvest
  Private Harvest, 10311
Producer Marketing Group
  Overlake Foods, 9615
Productos Frugo S.A. de C.V.
  Sun Harvest Foods Inc, 12234
Progressive Companies
  Stoller Fisheries, 12128
Prova SAS
  Prova, 10354
Providential Foods Corporation
  Battistoni Italian Spec Meats, 1084
Provincial Investments
  Notre Dame Seafoods Inc., 9192
Pulmuone Co., Ltd.
  Pulmuone Foods USA Inc, 10365
Puratos NV
  Puratos Canada, 10366
Pure Diets Intl. Ltd.
  Pure Life Organic Foods, 10378
Pure Milk Company
  Pure Milk & Ice Cream Company, 10379
PureCircle Limited
  PureCircle USA, 10386

Q

Quality Boneless Beef Company
  Quality Meats & Seafood, 10439
Quality Candy Shoppes
  Buddy Squirrel LLC, 1828

R

R&D Technical Center-Gamay Flavors
  Gamay Flavors, 4878
R.W. Bakers Co
  Lavoi Corporation, 7254
R.W. Garcia Company
  R.W. Garcia, 10500
Radeberger Gruppe GmbH
  Binding Brauerei USA, 1361
Randan Corporation
  Garlic Festival Foods, 4907
Rapid Snack
  Your Bar Factory, 14029
Reckitt Benckiser
  Mead Johnson Nutrition, 8103
Reckitt Benckiser LLC
  French's Flavor Ingredients, 4706
Red Smith of Florida, Inc.
  Red Smith Foods Inc, 10620
Redmond Inc.
  Realsalt, 10594
Reed Food Technology
  Taste Maker Foods, 12541
Reed's Ginger Brew
  Virgil's Root Beer, 13439
Regal Extract Company
  Millflow Spice Corp., 8314

Parent Company Index

Reily Foods Company
French Market Coffee, 4700
JFG Coffee, 6399
Reinhart Vinegars
Reinhart Foods, 10659
Renaissance Foods
Quelle Quiche, 10458
Rhinelander Paper Company
Lake States Yeast, 7155
Rice Belt Warehouse
Affiliated Rice Milling, 196
Rich Products Corp.
Jon Donaire Desserts, 6583
Rich Products Corporation
Rich Products Corp, 10714, 10715
Richardson Brands
Gravymaster, Inc., 5287
Richelieu Foods Inc.
Crestar Crusts, 3157
Richland Corporation
Richland Beverage Association, 10729
Ripplewood Holdings
Shaklee Corp, 11501
Riser Foods
Eagle Ice Cream Company, 3863
Riviana Foods
Gourmet House, 5206
Riviana Foods Inc.
Ronzoni, 10866
Robertet SA
Robertet Flavors, 10797
Robinson's #1 Ribs Restaurants
Robinson's No 1 Ribs, 10804
Roche Fruit
Roche Fruit LLC, 10808
ROHA Dyechem Pvt. Ltd.
Roha USA LTD, 10843
Roll International Corporation
Fiji Water Co LLC, 4384
Roquette Freres
Roquette America Inc., 10871
Rosa Foods Inc.
Soylent, 11882
Rose Acre Farms
Nepco Egg Of Ga, 8936
Rose Acre Farms, 10879
Rosen's Diversified
Skylark Meats, 11696
Rosen's Diversified, Inc.
American Foods Group LLC, 457
Routin SA
Routin America, 10917
Royal Caribbean Bakery
Caribbean Food Delights Inc, 2209
Royal FrieslandCampina
FrieslandCampina Ingredients North America, Inc., 4736
Royal Pacific Foods
Ginger People, The, 5021
Royal Schouten Group
Acatris USA, 137
Rudolf Wild GmbH & Co. KG
Wild Aseptics, LLC, 13775
Rudolph Foods
Gaslamp Co Popcorn, 4917
Rumiano Cheese Company
Rumiano Cheese Factory, 10980
RV Industries
Rv Industries, 11001

S

S&S Seafood
Bandon Bay Fisheries, 1005
S. S. Steiner, Inc.
Hops Extract Corporation of America, 5994
SA Products Company
Dwayne Keith Brooks Company, 3825
SABATINO ITALIA SRL
Sabatino Truffles USA, 11060
Safeway Stores
Safeway Milk Plant, 11074
Saint Louis Brewery
Schlafly Tap Room, 11291
Sam Mills Srl.
Sam Mills USA, 11125
Samark SA
Promolux Lighting, 10344
San Jirushi Corporation
San-J International Inc, 11157

San-El Gen FFI
San-Ei Gen FFI, 11156
Sapporo
Unibroue/Unibrew, 13164
Sapporo Holdings
Anchor Brewing Company, 531
Sapporo Holdings Limited
Sleeman Breweries, Ltd., 11704
Saputo
Woolwich Dairy, 13927
Saputo Cheese USA
Green Bay Cheese, 5343
Saputo Dairy Foods USA, LLC
Friendship Dairies LLC, 4734
Saputo, Inc.
Saputo Cheese USA Inc., 11209
Saputo Dairy Division (Canada), 11210
Sara Lee Corporation
Sweet Sue Kitchens, 12416
Sarabeth's Kitchen
Sarabeth's Office, 11216
SBK Preserves, 11035
Saratoga Beverage
Fresh Juice Delivery, 4714
Sarcom Inc
AEP Colloids, 78
Sattwa Chai
Sattwa Chai, 11237
Schneider's Dairy
Maple Leaf Foods, 7875
Schneider-Valley Farms Inc, 11302
Schratter Foods Inc
Anco Foods, 538
Schwabe North America
Nature's Way, 8896
Schwan's
Edwards Baking Company, 3959
Schwan's Company
Schwan's Food Service Inc., 11317
Tony's Pizza, 12874
Schwann's Sales
Florence Pasta & Cheese, 4512
Minh Food, 8348
Minh Food Corporation, 8349
Red Baron, 10601
Scott's Barbecue
Scott's Sauce Co Inc, 11329
Sea Safari
Sea Safari, 11349
Sea Specialties Company
Purity Products, 10399
Seaboard Corporation
Seaboard Foods, 11363
Seaboard Foods
Dailys Premium Meats, 3331
Seafood Restaurant
Drusilla Seafood, 3770
SeaSpecialties
Premier Smoked Fish Company, 10252
Seattle Gourmet Foods
Merlino Italian Baking Company, 8176
SECO & Golden 100
International Fruit Marketing, 6263
See's Candies
See's Candies, 11407
Seeman Brewing & Malting Company
Okanagan Spring Brewery, 9391
Seminis Vegetable Seeds
Seminis Vegetable Seeds Inc, 11427
Senba Foods Company
Senba USA, 11431
Sensient Technologies Corporation
Sensient Flavors and Fragrances, 11443
Sensus
Sensus America Inc, 11445
Seppic
Seppic Inc, 11447
Setton International Foods, Inc.
Setton Pistachio, 11469
Seydel Company
Seydel Co, 11485
Shamrock Foods Co
Shamrock Foods Company
Shamrock Foods Co, 11505, 11506, 11507, 11508, 11509
Shawnee Milling Company
Shawnee Milling Co, 11530
Shearer's Foods
Barrel O' Fun Snack Foods, 1052
Sherwood Brands
Sherwood Brands of Rhode Island Inc, 11553

Shionogi
Qualicaps Inc, 10424
SIAP Marketing Company
Grey Owl Foods, 5385
SIAS MPA
Agrana Fruit US Inc, 208
Signature Brands
Pepe's Mexican Restaurant, 9934
Sills Farms
Pleasant Grove Farms, 10111
Silvateam
Silvateam USA, 11613
Silvestri Sweets, Inc.
Art CoCo Chocolate Company, 707
Sini Fulvi
Sini Fulvi U.S.A., 11668
Siroper/E. Meurens SA
Poiret International, 10146
SKW
SKW Nature Products, 11044
Sloan Acquisition Corporation
Li'l Guy Foods, 7407
Small Planet Foods
Cascadian Farm Inc, 2286
SMG
Liguria Foods Inc, 7428
Smith Dairy
Wayne Dairy Products Inc, 13604
Smithfield Companies
Pruden Packing Company, 10359
V.W. Joyner & Company, 13237
Smithfield Foods
Clougherty Packing LLC, 2776
Cumberland Gap Provision Company, 3248
Patrick Cudahy LLC, 9833
Smithfield Foods, Inc.
Stefano Foods, 12071
Snak King
C J Vitner Co, 1920
Snake River Sugar Company
Amalgamated Sugar Company, 407
Snyder's Lance
Cape Cod Potato Chips, 2156
Snyder's-Lance Inc.
Baptista's Bakery, 1014
Snyders-Lance Inc.
Tom's Foods, 12853
Sobel-Holland
Banner Pharmacaps, 1009
Societa' Per Azioni Lucchese Olii E Vini
Filippo Berio Brand, 4386
Sofina Foods Incorporated
Lilydale Foods, 7432
Sokol and Company
Solo Foods, 11788
Solvent Interntional
Soylent Brand, 11883
Sonne
Dakota Gourmet, 3354
Sonoma Brands
Smashmallow, 11717
Sontory Water Group
Polar Water Company, 10152
Sopacko
SOPAKCO Packaging, 11049
Sopako Foods
Sopako Foods, 11813
Sophia's Sauce Works
Sophia's Sauce Works, 11815
Sopralco
Sopralco, 11816
Southeastern Grocers
Winn-Dixie Stores, 13864
Southeastern Mills, Inc.
Superior Quality Foods, 12343
Southern Flavoring
Southern Flavoring Co, 11852
Space Enterprises
World of Chia, 13945
Sparta Foods
Food Products Corporation, 4566
Spaten-Franziskaner-Brau
Spaten North America Inc, 11891
Specialty Enzymes and Biochemicals Company
Cal India Foods Inc, 2027
Spero Group
Tumai Water, 13055
SPI West Port, Inc.
ALO Drink, 88

Spices of Life Gourmet Coffee
Coffee Millers & Roasters, 2851
St. Francis River Farming
Fancy Farms Popcorn, 4245
Stella Foods
Stella Foods, 12075
Stella Reedsburg, 12076
Stevco Inc.
Lucich Santos Farms, 7626
Stimson Lane
Villa Mt. Eden Winery, 13414
Stolt Sea Farm Group
Sterling Caviar LLC, 12083
Stop & Shop Supermarket Company
Stop & Shop Manufacturing, 12146
Strauss Holdings LTD
Sabra-Go Mediterranean, 11066
Stremicks Heritage Foods, LLC
Jasper Products Corp, 6463
Sucocitrico Cutrale Ltda.
Cutrale Citrus Juices, 3278
Sugar Foods Corporation
Sugar Foods Corp, 12200
Suiza Dairy Group
Brown's Dairy, 1782
Garelick Farms, 4904
Model Dairy LLC, 8438
Oak Farms, 9312
Swiss Dairy, 12439
Suiza Foods
Cumberland Creamery, 3246
Garelick Farms, 4903
Land-O-Sun Dairies Inc, 7199
Reiter Dairy, 10663
Suiza Dairy Corporation, 12212
Summer Garden Foods
Gia Russa, 4997
Sun Orchard, Inc.
Sun Orchard INC, 12239
Suncoast Bakeries
Saint Armands Baking Company, 11090
Sunny Delight Beverage Company
Veryfine Products Inc, 13368
SunOpta
Beta Pure Foods, 1273
Sunset Trails
Circle R Ranch, 2686
Suntory
Suntory International, 12315
Suntory Holdings
Beam Suntory, 1120
Superior Coffee & Foods
Wechsler Coffee Corporation, 13617
SVZ Industrial Products B.V.
Svzusa Inc, 12376
Sweet Leaf Tea
Tradewinds, 12914
SweetWorks Confections LLC
Oak Leaf Confections, 9320
SweetWorks, Inc.
Niagara Chocolates, 9031
Swire
Finlays, 4407
Swiss Colony
Green County Foods, 5346
Symrise AG
Symrise Inc., 12454
SYSCO
Asian Foods Inc, 734
Sysco
Fulton Provision Co, 4790
Newport Meat Co North, 9023
Systems Bio-Industries
Zentis Sweet Ovations, 14054

T

T. Hasegawa Company
T Hasegawa USA Inc, 12461
T. Marzetti
Marshall's Biscuit Company, 7957
T. Marzetti Company
Marzetti, 7986
New York Frozen Foods Inc, 9005
T.A. Ocean Odyssey
Bradye P. Todd & Son, 1651
T.W. Garner Food Company
T.W. Garner Food Company, 12474
Tabard Corporation
Tabard Farm Potato Chips, 12484

1363

Parent Company Index

Takara Group
    Takara Sake USA Inc, 12500
Tall Tree Foods
    Klement Sausage Co Inc, 6910
Tallmadge Brothers
    Hillard Bloom Packing Co Inc, 5867
Tamanda Holdings USA Inc.
    Bestco Inc, 1272
Tata Coffee Limited
    Eight O'Clock Coffee Company, 3974
Tata Tea Ltd
    Tetley Tea, 12641
Taylor Fresh Foods
    Taylor Farms Pacific, 12567
Technical Food Sales Inc
    Tri-State Ingredients, 12959
Techno Food Ingredients Co., Ltd.
    Techno USA, 12594
Temo's
    Temo Candy, 12610
Ten Ren Tea Company
    Uncle Lee's Tea Inc, 13156
Tessenderlo Group
    PB Leiner USA, 9649
Tetley Tea
    Tetley USA, 12642, 12643
Tetley USA
    Rowland Coffee Roasters Inc., 10920
Texas United Corporation
    United Salt Corp, 13200
TFS
    Tommy's Jerky Outlet, 12863
Thai Union Group
    Chicken Of The Sea, 2555
The Carlyle Group, L P
    Balance Bar Company, 984
The Church of Jesus Christ of Latter-day Saints
    Deseret Dairy Products, 3534
The Coca-Cola Company
    Honest Tea Inc, 5952
    Monster Beverage Corp., 8485
The Dannon Company
    Dannon Yo Cream, 3378
The Ellsworth Cooperative Creamery
    Blaser's USA, Inc., 1440
The Hain Celestial Group, Inc.
    Westbrae Natural Foods, 13672
The Jim Pattison Group
    Montebello Packaging, 8501
The Kraft Heinz Company
    Heinz Portion Control, 5735
    Kraft Heinz Canada, 6976
The Lipod Group
    American Lecithin Company, 468
The Manischewitz Company
    Guiltless Gourmet, 5426
The Powell Group
    Farmers Rice Milling Co, 4284
The Vermont Maple Syrup Company
    Butternut Mountain Farm, 1887
The Virginia Food Group
    Old Dominion Peanut Corp, 9406
The Wine Group
    Mogen David Wine Corp, 8453
The Wonderful Company
    POM Wonderful LLC, 9658
Threshold Enterprises
    Source Naturals, 11824
Todhunter International
    Todhunter Foods, 12834, 12835
Tomanetti Foods
    Tomanetti Food Products Inc, 12855
Tootsie Roll Industries
    Cambridge Brands Inc, 2102
Torreo Coffee & Tea Company
    Torreo Coffee Company, 12898
Tova Industries
    New Horizon Foods, 8986
Toyo Suisan Kaisha
    Maruchan Inc, 7974
Tradin Organic
    Tradin Organics USA, 12916
Treasury Wine Estates
    Meridian Vineyards, 8172
    Stags' Leap Winery, 12019

Treatt PLC
    Treatt USA Inc, 12940
Tree Top
    Northwest Naturals LLC, 9177
    Seneca Juice, 11435
TreeHouse Foods
    Sturm Foods Inc, 12182
TreeHouse Foods, Inc.
    Bay Valley Foods, 1103
    Harvest Manor Farms, 5632
    S T Specialty Foods Inc, 11019
TreeHouse Private Brands, Inc.
    American Italian Pasta Company, 465
Tregar
    Laredo Tortilleria & Mexican, 7219
Treier Family Farms
    Treier Popcorn Farms, 12948
Tri-Valley Growers
    Signature Fruit, 11601
Triarc Companies
    Stewart's Beverages, 12109
Tribal Councils Investment Group of Manitoba Ltd.
    Arctic Beverages, 644
Trident Seafoods
    Kasilof Fish Company, 6721
Tropical
    Tropical Foods, 12998
Tropical General Investment (TGI) Group
    Vink & Beri, 13427
Turnbull Bakeries
    Turnbull Cone Baking Company, 13069
Tuscan/Lehigh Valley Dairies
    Ultra Dairy, 13145
TW Garner Food Company
    Green Mountain Gringo, 5357
Twin Laboratories
    Nature's Herbs, 8882
Twinlab
    Alvita, 398
Twinlab Consolidation Corporation
    Nutrisciences Labs, 9255
Twinlab Corporation
    PR Bar, 9661
TyRy, Inc,
    TyRy Inc, 13105
Tyson Foods
    Advance Pierre Foods, 184
    Ball Park Franks, 992
    Mallard's Food Products, 7806
    Philadelphia Cheese Steak, 10005
    The Bruss Company, 12674
Tyson Foods Inc.
    Sara Lee Frozen Bakery, 11214
Tyson Foods, Inc.
    Jimmy Dean Foods, 6520

U

Ubbelea Farms
    Great Lakes Foods, 5317
Unaka Corporation
    SOPAKCO Foods, 11048
Unified Brands
    A la Cart, 47
Unilever
    Best Foods, 1267
    Good Humor-Breyers Ice Cream, 5165
    Talenti Gelato e Sorbetto, 12507
    Tazo Tea, 12581
    UBF Food Solutions, 13115
Unilever N.V. & Unilever plc
    Unilever US, 13169
Unilever US
    Growing Roots Foods, 5411
    Unilever Canada, 13167
Unilever USA
    Shedd Food Products, 11532
    Unilever Food Solutions, 13168
Unisea Foods
    Fish King Processors, 4440
United Apple Sales Inc.
    HH Dobbins Inc, 5484
United Nation of Islam
    UNOI Grainmill, 13118

United Natural Foods
    Woodstock Farms Manufacturing, 13923
Universal Beverages Holding Corporation
    Universal Beverages Inc, 13205
Universal Nutrition
    Animal Pak, 572
    CarbRite Diet, 2196
Upper Lakes Foods
    Brown's Ice Cream Co, 1783
Upstate Niagara Cooperative Inc
    Valley Farms LLC, 13253
Upstate Niagara Cooperative Inc.
    Bison Foods, 1402
    Intense Milk, 6235
    Upstate Farms, 13217
US Enterprise Corporation
    Wing Nien Food, 13855
US Sugar Corporation
    Southern Gardens Citrus, 11853
USA Laboratories
    USA Laboratories Inc, 13128
Utmost Brands
    Grown-up Soda, 5412

V

V & V Supremo Foods
    V & V Supremo, 13233
V Formusa Company
    Marconi Italian Specialty Foods, 7900
Valio International USA
    Finlandia Cheese, 4405
Valpo Velvet Ice Cream Company
    The Valpo Velvet Shoppe, 12741
Van de Kamps
    Van de Kamps, 13282
VAN HEES GmbH
    Van Hees Gmbh, 13273
Venison America
    Specialty Meats & Gourmet, 11905
Vermont Country Maple Mixes
    Vermont Country Naturals, 13347
Vienna Manufacturing Company
    Pie Piper Products, 10040
Violi Foods
    Butterfield Foods, 1884
Visalia Citrus Packing Group
    Visalia Citrus Packing Group, 13448
Vita Food Products
    Virginia Honey Company, 13446
Volk Corporation
    Forbes Co, 4585
VPS Companies, Inc.
    Inn Foods Inc, 6221

W

Wagner Gourmet Foods
    Wagner Gourmet Foods, 13527
Wakunaga Pharmaceutical
    Wakunaga Of America Co LTD, 13536
Walden Foods Inc.
    Walden Foods, 13540
Walkers Shortbread
    Walkers Shortbread, 13544
Walking S Farms
    Lampost Meats, 7187
Warner Vineyards
    Paw Paw Grape Juice Company, 9853
Welch's Food
    Welch's Global Ingredients Group, 13636
Welsh Farms
    Welsh Farms, 13647
Wendy's International
    New Bakery Company of Ohio, 8956
Western Refining Inc.
    Super Mom's LLC, 12319
Western Syrup Company
    Western Syrup Company, 13686
Westfish International
    Barry Group, 1057
Westin Foods
    Great American Appetizers, 5294
Weston Foods
    Rubschlager Baking Corp, 10960

WH Group Limited
    Smithfield Foods Inc., 11733
WhiteWave
    Wallaby Yogurt Co, 13546
Whitlock Packaging Corporation
    Cutting Edge Beverages, 3279
Whole Foods Market
    Allegro Coffee Co, 332
Wilco Farm Stores
    Westnut, 13690
WILD Flavors
    WILD Flavors (Canada), 13514
Wild Flavours
    AM Todd Co, 91
Wild Foods
    Baensch Food Products Co, 931
Wild Thyme Naturals
    Banzos, 1013
Willamette Valley Vineyards
    Tualatin Estate Vineyards, 13044
Windham Foundation
    Grafton Village Cheese Co LLC, 5236
Wine Group
    Concannon Vineyard, 2941
Wing's Food Products
    Wing's Food Products, 13858
Winn Dixie
    Superbrand Dairies, 12326, 12327
Wisconsin Cheeseman
    Scott's Candy, 11328
Wisener Minnow Hatchery Inc.
    Haring Catfish, 5588
Wizard's Cauldron
    Wizards Cauldron, LTD, 13892
Woerner Holdings, L.P.
    Canon Potato Company, 2143
Wonderful Packing LLC
    DNE World Fruit Sales, 3314
Worksource Enterprises
    Breadworks, 1682
WorldPantry.com Inc.
    Prairie Thyme LTD, 10237

X

Xiamen Kingdomway Group Co.
    Vit-Best Nutrition, 13453

Y

Yamasa Corporation
    Yamasa Corp USA, 13986
Yellowstone Brands
    Chungs Gourmet Foods, 2665
Yergat Packing Company
    Yergat Packing Co, 14002
Yogi Tea
    Yogi® Tea, 14011
Yoo-Hoo Chocolate Beverage
    Yoo-Hoo Chocolate Beverage Company, 14016
Yorkshire Foods
    Treehouse Farms, 12944
Young Pecan Company
    Young Pecan, 14022
YSK International Corporation
    Sun Chlorella USA, 12228

Z

Z Capital Partners
    Mrs. Fields Original Cookies, 8638
Zenobia Company
    Sunray Food Products Corporation, 12293
Zeta Wize LLC Company
    Better Living Products, 1285
Zhucheng Haotian Pharm Co.
    Shanghai Freemen, 11514
Zook Molasses Company
    Good Food Inc, 5157
Zwanenberg Food Group BV
    Vietti Foods Co Inc, 13402

2020 Title List

Visit www.GreyHouse.com for Product Information, Table of Contents, and Sample Pages.

Opinions Throughout History
- Opinions Throughout History: Drug Use & Abuse
- Opinions Throughout History: Gender: Roles & Rights
- Opinions Throughout History: Globalization
- Opinions Throughout History: Guns in America
- Opinions Throughout History: Immigration
- Opinions Throughout History: National Security vs. Civil & Privacy Rights
- Opinions Throughout History: Presidential Authority
- Opinions Throughout History: Robotics & Artificial Intelligence
- Opinions Throughout History: Social Media Issues
- Opinions Throughout History: The Death Penalty
- Opinions Throughout History: The Environment
- Opinions Throughout History: Voters' Rights

This is Who We Were
- This is Who We Were: Colonial America (1492-1775)
- This is Who We Were: 1880-1899
- This is Who We Were: In the 1900s
- This is Who We Were: In the 1910s
- This is Who We Were: In the 1920s
- This is Who We Were: A Companion to the 1940 Census
- This is Who We Were: In the 1940s (1940-1949)
- This is Who We Were: In the 1950s
- This is Who We Were: In the 1960s
- This is Who We Were: In the 1970s
- This is Who We Were: In the 1980s
- This is Who We Were: In the 1990s
- This is Who We Were: In the 2000s
- This is Who We Were: In the 2010s

Working Americans
- Working Americans, 1880-2011 - Vol. 1 The Working Class
- Working Americans, 1880-1999 - Vol. 2: The Middle Class
- Working Americans, 1880-1999 - Vol. 3: The Upper Class
- Working Americans, 1880-1999 - Vol. 4: Children
- Working Americans, 1880-2015 - Vol. 5: At War
- Working Americans, 1880-2015 - Vol. 6: Working Women
- Working Americans, 1880-2016 - Vol. 7: Social Movements
- Working Americans, 1880-2017 - Vol. 8: Immigrants
- Working Americans, 1770-1869 - Vol. 9: From the Revolutionary War to the Civil War
- Working Americans, 1880-2009 - Vol. 10: Sports & Recreation
- Working Americans, 1880-2009 - Vol. 11: Inventors & Entrepreneurs
- Working Americans, 1880-2011 - Vol. 12: Our History Through Music
- Working Americans, 1880-2011 - Vol. 13: Education & Educators
- Working Americans, 1880-2016 - Vol. 14: African Americans
- Working Americans, 1880-2018: Vol. 15: Politics & Politicians
- Working Americans, 1880-2020: Vol. 16: Farming & Ranching

Education
- Complete Learning Disabilities Resource Guide
- Educators Resource Guide
- The Comparative Guide to Elem. & Secondary Schools
- Charter School Movement
- Special Education: A Reference Book for Policy & Curriculum Development

General Reference
- African Biographical Dictionary
- American Environmental Leaders
- America's College Museums
- Constitutional Amendments
- Encyclopedia of African-American Writing
- Encyclopedia of Historical Warrior Peoples & Modern Fighting Groups
- Encyclopedia of Invasions & Conquests
- Encyclopedia of Prisoners of War & Internment
- Encyclopedia of Religion & the Law in America
- Encyclopedia of Rural America
- Encyclopedia of the Continental Congresses
- Encyclopedia of the United States Cabinet
- Encyclopedia of War Journalism
- The Environmental Debate
- The Evolution Wars: A Guide to the Debates
- Financial Literacy Starter Kit
- From Suffrage to the Senate
- The Gun Debate: An Encyclopedia of Gun Rights & Gun Control in the US
- History of Canada
- Human Rights and the United States
- Political Corruption in America
- Privacy Rights in the Digital Age
- Religious Right and American Politics
- Speakers of the House of Representatives
- The Value of a Dollar 1600-1865 Colonial to Civil War
- The Value of a Dollar 1860-2019
- US Land & Natural Resources Policy
- World Cultural Leaders of the 20th Century

Business Information
- Business Information Resources
- The Complete Broadcasting Industry Guide: Television, Radio, Cable & Streaming
- Directory of Mail Order Catalogs
- Environmental Resource Handbook
- Food & Beverage Market Place
- The Grey House Homeland Security Resources
- The Grey House Performing Arts Industry Guide
- Guide to Healthcare Group Purchasing Organizations
- Guide to U.S. HMOs and PPOs
- Guide to Venture Capital & Private Equity Firms
- Hudson's Washington News Media Contacts Guide
- New York State Directory
- Sports Market Place

Consumer Health
- Comparative Guide to American Hospitals
- Complete Mental Health Resource Guide
- Complete Resource Guide for Pediatric Disorders
- Complete Resource Guide for People with Chronic Illness
- Complete Resource Guide for People with Disabilities
- Dementia Handbook & Resource Guide
- Older Americans Information Resource

Grey House Publishing | Salem Press | H.W. Wilson | 4919 Route, 22 PO Box 56, Amenia NY 12501-0056

2020 Title List

Visit www.GreyHouse.com for Product Information, Table of Contents, and Sample Pages.

Statistics & Demographics
America's Top-Rated Cities
America's Top-Rated Smaller Cities
Ancestry & Ethnicity in America
The Comparative Guide to American Suburbs
The Hispanic Databook
Profiles of America
Profiles of California
Profiles of Connecticut & Rhode Island
Profiles of Florida
Profiles of Illinois
Profiles of Indiana
Profiles of Massachusetts
Profiles of Michigan
Profiles of New Jersey
Profiles of New York
Profiles of North Carolina & South Carolina
Profiles of Ohio
Profiles of Pennsylvania
Profiles of Texas
Profiles of Virginia
Profiles of Wisconsin
Weather America

Canadian Resources
Canadian Almanac & Directory
Canadian Environmental Update
Associations Canada
Financial Services Canada
Libraries Canada
Canadian Parliamentary Guide
Canadian Venture Capital & Private Equity Firms
Health Guide Canada
Major Canadian Cities: Compared & Ranked, First Edition
Canadian Who's Who
Cannabis Canada
Financial Post Directory of Directors
FP Survey: Industrials
FP Survey: Mines & Energy
FP Survey: Predecessor & Defunct
FP Bonds: Corporate
FP Bonds: Government
FP Equities: Preferreds & Derivatives
Careers & Employment Canada

Weiss Financial Ratings
Financial Literacy Basics
Financial Literacy: How to Become an Investor
Financial Literacy: Planning for the Future
Weiss Ratings Consumer Guides
Weiss Ratings Guide to Banks
Weiss Ratings Guide to Credit Unions
Weiss Ratings Guide to Health Insurers
Weiss Ratings Guide to Life & Annuity Insurers
Weiss Ratings Guide to Property & Casualty Insurers
Weiss Ratings Investment Research Guide to Bond & Money Market Mutual Funds
Weiss Ratings Investment Research Guide to Exchange-Traded Funds
Weiss Ratings Investment Research Guide to Stock Mutual Funds
Weiss Ratings Investment Research Guide to Stocks

Books in Print Series
American Book Publishing Record® Annual
American Book Publishing Record® Monthly
Books In Print®
Books In Print® Supplement
Books Out Loud™
Bowker's Complete Video Directory™
Children's Books In Print®
El-Hi Textbooks & Serials In Print®
Forthcoming Books®
Law Books & Serials In Print™
Medical & Health Care Books In Print™
Publishers, Distributors & Wholesalers of the US™
Subject Guide to Books In Print®
Subject Guide to Children's Books In Print®

Grey House Publishing | Salem Press | H.W. Wilson | 4919 Route, 22 PO Box 56, Amenia NY 12501-0056

SALEM PRESS

2020 Title List

Visit www.SalemPress.com for Product Information, Table of Contents, and Sample Pages.

Critical Insights

- Critical Insights: A Midsummer Night's Dream
- Critical Insights: A Portrait of the Artist as a Young Man
- Critical Insights: A Streetcar Named Desire
- Critical Insights: Abraham Lincoln
- Critical Insights: Absalom, Absalom!
- Critical Insights: Adventures of Huckleberry Finn
- Critical Insights: Aeneid
- Critical Insights: Albert Camus
- Critical Insights: Alice Munro
- Critical Insights: Alice Walker
- Critical Insights: All Quiet on the Western Front
- Critical Insights: American Creative Non-Fiction
- Critical Insights: American Multicultural Identity
- Critical Insights: American Road Literature
- Critical Insights: American Short Story
- Critical Insights: American Sports Fiction
- Critical Insights: American Writers in Exile
- Critical Insights: Ancient Greek Literature
- Critical Insights: Animal Farm
- Critical Insights: Arthur Miller
- Critical Insights: Barbara Kingsolver
- Critical Insights: Beloved
- Critical Insights: Benjamin Franklin
- Critical Insights: Billy Budd, Sailor
- Critical Insights: Brave New World
- Critical Insights: Censored & Banned Literature
- Critical Insights: Charles Dickens
- Critical Insights: Civil Rights Literature, Past & Present
- Critical Insights: Coming of Age
- Critical Insights: Conspiracies
- Critical Insights: Contemporary Canadian Fiction
- Critical Insights: Contemporary Immigrant Short Fiction
- Critical Insights: Contemporary Latin American Fiction
- Critical Insights: Contemporary Speculative Fiction
- Critical Insights: Cormac McCarthy
- Critical Insights: Crime and Detective Fiction
- Critical Insights: Crisis of Faith
- Critical Insights: Cultural Encounters
- Critical Insights: David Foster Wallace
- Critical Insights: Death of a Salesman
- Critical Insights: Dracula
- Critical Insights: Dystopia
- Critical Insights: Edith Wharton
- Critical Insights: Emily Dickinson
- Critical Insights: Ernest Hemingway
- Critical Insights: Eugene O'Neill
- Critical Insights: F. Scott Fitzgerald
- Critical Insights: Fahrenheit 451
- Critical Insights: Family
- Critical Insights: Feminism
- Critical Insights: Flannery O'Connor
- Critical Insights: Flash Fiction
- Critical Insights: Frederick Douglass
- Critical Insights: Gabriel Garcia Marquez
- Critical Insights: Gender, Sex and Sexuality
- Critical Insights: Geoffrey Chaucer
- Critical Insights: George Eliot
- Critical Insights: George Orwell
- Critical Insights: Good & Evil
- Critical Insights: Great Expectations
- Critical Insights: Greed
- Critical Insights: Gustave Flaubert
- Critical Insights: Gwendolyn Brooks
- Critical Insights: Hamlet
- Critical Insights: Harlan Ellison
- Critical Insights: Harlem Renaissance
- Critical Insights: Harry Potter Series
- Critical Insights: Heart of Darkness
- Critical Insights: Henry James
- Critical Insights: Herman Melville
- Critical Insights: Historical Fiction
- Critical Insights: Holocaust Literature
- Critical Insights: Horton Foote
- Critical Insights: I Know Why the Caged Bird Sings
- Critical Insights: In Cold Blood
- Critical Insights: Inequality
- Critical Insights: Invisible Man
- Critical Insights: Isaac Asimov
- Critical Insights: Isabel Allende
- Critical Insights: Jack London
- Critical Insights: James Baldwin
- Critical Insights: James Joyce
- Critical Insights: James McBride
- Critical Insights: Jane Austen
- Critical Insights: Jane Eyre
- Critical Insights: John Cheever
- Critical Insights: John Steinbeck
- Critical Insights: John Updike
- Critical Insights: Joseph Conrad
- Critical Insights: King Lear
- Critical Insights: Kurt Vonnegut
- Critical Insights: Langston Hughes
- Critical Insights: Leo Tolstoy
- Critical Insights: LGBTQ Literature
- Critical Insights: Life of Pi
- Critical Insights: Lillian Hellman
- Critical Insights: Literature of Protest
- Critical Insights: Little Women
- Critical Insights: Lolita
- Critical Insights: Lord of the Flies
- Critical Insights: Louisa May Alcott
- Critical Insights: Louise Erdrich
- Critical Insights: Macbeth
- Critical Insights: Magical Realism
- Critical Insights: Malcolm X
- Critical Insights: Margaret Atwood
- Critical Insights: Mario Vargas Llosa
- Critical Insights: Mark Twain
- Critical Insights: Martin Luther King, Jr.
- Critical Insights: Mary Shelley
- Critical Insights: Maya Angelou
- Critical Insights: Midnight's Children
- Critical Insights: Midwestern Literature
- Critical Insights: Moby-Dick
- Critical Insights: Modern Japanese Literature
- Critical Insights: Mrs. Dalloway
- Critical Insights: Nathaniel Hawthorne
- Critical Insights: Nature & the Environment
- Critical Insights: Neil Gaiman
- Critical Insights: Nineteen Eighty-Four
- Critical Insights: Of Mice and Men
- Critical Insights: One Flew Over the Cuckoo's Nest
- Critical Insights: One Hundred Years of Solitude
- Critical Insights: Oscar Wilde
- Critical Insights: Paradise Lost
- Critical Insights: Paranoia, Fear & Alienation
- Critical Insights: Philip Roth
- Critical Insights: Political Fiction
- Critical Insights: Post-Colonial Literature
- Critical Insights: Pride and Prejudice
- Critical Insights: Pulp Fiction of the '20s and '30s
- Critical Insights: Ray Bradbury
- Critical Insights: Raymond Carver
- Critical Insights: Rebellion
- Critical Insights: Richard Wright
- Critical Insights: Robert A. Heinlein
- Critical Insights: Robert Frost
- Critical Insights: Roberto Bolano
- Critical Insights: Romeo and Juliet
- Critical Insights: Russia's Golden Age
- Critical Insights: Salman Rushdie
- Critical Insights: Satire
- Critical Insights: Saul Bellow
- Critical Insights: Sherman Alexie
- Critical Insights: Short Fiction of Flannery O'Connor
- Critical Insights: Slaughterhouse-Five
- Critical Insights: Social Justice and American Literature
- Critical Insights: Southern Gothic Literature
- Critical Insights: Southwestern Literature
- Critical Insights: Stephen King
- Critical Insights: Survival
- Critical Insights: Sylvia Plath
- Critical Insights: T. S. Eliot

Grey House Publishing | Salem Press | H.W. Wilson | 4919 Route, 22 PO Box 56, Amenia NY 12501-0056

SALEM PRESS

2020 Title List

Visit www.SalemPress.com for Product Information, Table of Contents, and Sample Pages.

Critical Insights (continued)
Critical Insights: Technology & Humanity
Critical Insights: Tennessee Williams
Critical Insights: The American Comic Book
Critical Insights: The American Dream
Critical Insights: The American Thriller
Critical Insights: The Awakening
Critical Insights: The Bell Jar
Critical Insights: The Canterbury Tales
Critical Insights: The Catcher in the Rye
Critical Insights: The Crucible
Critical Insights: The Diary of a Young Girl
Critical Insights: The Fantastic
Critical Insights: The Grapes of Wrath
Critical Insights: The Graphic Novel
Critical Insights: The Great Gatsby
Critical Insights: The Handmaid's Tale
Critical Insights: The Hero's Quest
Critical Insights: The Hobbit
Critical Insights: The House on Mango Street
Critical Insights: The Hunger Games Trilogy
Critical Insights: The Immigrant Experience
Critical Insights: The Inferno
Critical Insights: The Joy Luck Club
Critical Insights: The Kite Runner
Critical Insights: The Metamorphosis
Critical insights: The Odyssey
Critical Insights: The Outsiders
Critical Insights: The Pearl
Critical Insights: The Poetry of Baudelaire
Critical Insights: The Poetry of Edgar Allan Poe
Critical Insights: The Red Badge of Courage
Critical Insights: The Scarlet Letter
Critical Insights: The Slave Narrative
Critical Insights: The Sound and the Fury
Critical Insights: The Sun Also Rises
Critical Insights: The Tales of Edgar Allan Poe
Critical Insights: The Woman Warrior
Critical Insights: Things Fall Apart
Critical Insights: Thomas Jefferson
Critical Insights: Tim O'Brien
Critical Insights: To Kill a Mockingbird
Critical Insights: Toni Morrison
Critical Insights: Violence in Literature
Critical Insights: Virginia Woolf & 20th Century Women Writers
Critical Insights: Walt Whitman
Critical Insights: War
Critical Insights: War and Peace
Critical Insights: Willa Cather
Critical Insights: William Faulkner
Critical Insights: Zora Neale Hurston
Critical Insights: Film - Alfred Hitchcock
Critical Insights: Film - Bonnie & Clyde
Critical Insights: Film - Casablanca
Critical Insights: Film - Stanley Kubrick

Literature
Critical Approaches to Literature: Feminist
Critical Approaches to Literature: Moral
Critical Approaches to Literature: Multicultural
Critical Approaches to Literature: Psychological
Critical Survey of American Literature
Critical Survey of Drama
Critical Survey of Graphic Novels: Heroes & Superheroes
Critical Survey of Graphic Novels: History, Theme, and Technique
Critical Survey of Graphic Novels: Independents and Underground Classics
Critical Survey of Graphic Novels: Manga
Critical Survey of Long Fiction
Critical Survey of Mystery and Detective Fiction
Critical Survey of Mythology & Folklore: Gods & Goddesses
Critical Survey of Mythology & Folklore: Heroes and Heroines
Critical Survey of Mythology & Folklore: Love, Sexuality, and Desire
Critical Survey of Mythology & Folklore: World Mythology
Critical Survey of Poetry
Critical Survey of Science Fiction & Fantasy Literature
Critical Survey of Shakespeare's Plays
Critical Survey of Shakespeare's Sonnets
Critical Survey of Short Fiction
Critical Survey of World Literature
Critical Survey of Young Adult Literature
Cyclopedia of Literary Characters
Cyclopedia of Literary Places
Introduction to Literary Context: American Poetry of the 20th Century
Introduction to Literary Context: American Post-Modernist Novels
Introduction to Literary Context: American Short Fiction
Introduction to Literary Context: English Literature
Introduction to Literary Context: Plays
Introduction to Literary Context: World Literature
Magill's Literary Annual
Masterplots
Masterplots, 2010-2018 Supplement
Notable African American Writers
Notable American Women Writers
Novels into Film: Adaptations & Interpretation
Recommended Reading: 600 Classics Reviewed

The Decades
The Sixties in America
The Fifties in America
The Seventies in America
The Eighties in America
The Nineties in America
The Forties in America
The Thirties in America
The Twenties in America
The 2000s in America
The 1910s in America

Grey House Publishing | Salem Press | H.W. Wilson | 4919 Route, 22 PO Box 56, Amenia NY 12501-0056

SALEM PRESS
2020 Title List

Visit www.SalemPress.com for Product Information, Table of Contents, and Sample Pages.

Defining Documents in American History
Defining Documents: American West
Defining Documents: Business Ethics
Defining Documents: Capital Punishment
Defining Documents: Civil Rights
Defining Documents: Civil War
Defining Documents: Dissent & Protest
Defining Documents: Drug Policy
Defining Documents: Environment & Conservation
Defining Documents: Espionage & Intrigue
Defining Documents: Exploration and Colonial America
Defining Documents: Immigration & Immigrant Communities
Defining Documents: LGBTQ+
Defining Documents: Manifest Destiny and the New Nation
Defining Documents: Mental Health
Defining Documents: Native Americans
Defining Documents: Political Campaigns, Candidates & Discourse
Defining Documents: Postwar 1940s
Defining Documents: Prison Reform
Defining Documents: Secrets, Leaks & Scandals
Defining Documents: Slavery
Defining Documents: Supreme Court Decisions
Defining Documents: The 1900s
Defining Documents: The 1910s
Defining Documents: The 1920s
Defining Documents: The 1930s
Defining Documents: The 1950s
Defining Documents: The 1960s
Defining Documents: The 1970s
Defining Documents: The American Revolution
Defining Documents: The Cold War
Defining Documents: The Emergence of Modern America
Defining Documents: The Free Press
Defining Documents: The Gun Debate
Defining Documents: The Legacy of 9/11
Defining Documents: Reconstruction Era
Defining Documents: Vietnam War
Defining Documents: U.S. Involvement in the Middle East
Defining Documents: World War I
Defining Documents: World War II

Defining Documents in World History
Defining Documents: Asia
Defining Documents: Nationalism & Populism
Defining Documents: Renaissance & Early Modern Era
Defining Documents: The 17th Century
Defining Documents: The 18th Century
Defining Documents: The 19th Century
Defining Documents: The 20th Century (1900-1950)
Defining Documents: The Ancient World
Defining Documents: The Middle Ages
Defining Documents: The Middle East
Defining Documents: Women's Rights

Great Events from History
Great Events from History: The Ancient World
Great Events from History: The Middle Ages
Great Events from History: The Renaissance & Early Modern Era
Great Events from History: The 17th Century
Great Events from History: The 18th Century
Great Events from History: The 19th Century
Great Events from History: The 20th Century, 1901-1940
Great Events from History: The 20th Century, 1941-1970
Great Events from History: The 20th Century, 1971-2000
Great Events from History: Modern Scandals
Great Events from History: African American History
Great Events from History: The 21st Century, 2000-2016
Great Events from History: LGBTQ Events
Great Events from History: Human Rights

Great Lives from History
Computer Technology Innovators
Fashion Innovators
Great Athletes
Great Athletes of the Twenty-First Century
Great Lives from History: African Americans
Great Lives from History: American Heroes
Great Lives from History: American Women
Great Lives from History: Asian and Pacific Islander Americans
Great Lives from History: Inventors & Inventions
Great Lives from History: Jewish Americans
Great Lives from History: Latinos
Great Lives from History: Scientists and Science
Great Lives from History: The 17th Century
Great Lives from History: The 18th Century
Great Lives from History: The 19th Century
Great Lives from History: The 20th Century
Great Lives from History: The 21st Century, 2000-2017
Great Lives from History: The Ancient World
Great Lives from History: The Incredibly Wealthy
Great Lives from History: The Middle Ages
Great Lives from History: The Renaissance & Early Modern Era
Human Rights Innovators
Internet Innovators
Music Innovators
Musicians and Composers of the 20th Century
World Political Innovators

History & Government
American First Ladies
American Presidents
Civil Rights Movements: Past & Present
The 50 States
The Ancient World: Extraordinary People in Extraordinary Societies
The Bill of Rights
The Criminal Justice System
The U.S. Supreme Court

Grey House Publishing | Salem Press | H.W. Wilson | 4919 Route, 22 PO Box 56, Amenia NY 12501-0056

SALEM PRESS

2020 Title List

Visit www.SalemPress.com for Product Information, Table of Contents, and Sample Pages.

Social Sciences
- Countries, Peoples and Cultures
- Countries: Their Wars & Conflicts: A World Survey
- Education Today: Issues, Policies & Practices
- Encyclopedia of American Immigration
- Ethics: Questions & Morality of Human Actions
- Issues in U.S. Immigration
- Principles of Sociology: Group Relationships & Behavior
- Principles of Sociology: Personal Relationships & Behavior
- Principles of Sociology: Societal Issues & Behavior
- Racial & Ethnic Relations in America
- World Geography

Science
- Ancient Creatures
- Applied Science
- Applied Science: Engineering & Mathematics
- Applied Science: Science & Medicine
- Applied Science: Technology
- Biomes and Ecosystems
- Earth Science: Earth Materials and Resources
- Earth Science: Earth's Surface and History
- Earth Science: Earth's Weather, Water and Atmosphere
- Earth Science: Physics and Chemistry of the Earth
- Encyclopedia of Climate Change
- Encyclopedia of Energy
- Encyclopedia of Environmental Issues
- Encyclopedia of Global Resources
- Encyclopedia of Mathematics and Society
- Forensic Science
- Notable Natural Disasters
- The Solar System
- USA in Space

Principles of Science
- Principles of Anatomy
- Principles of Astronomy
- Principles of Biology
- Principles of Biotechnology
- Principles of Botany
- Principles of Chemistry
- Principles of Climatology
- Principles of Communications Technology
- Principles of Computer Science
- Principles of Ecology
- Principles of Mathematics
- Principles of Modern Agriculture
- Principles of Pharmacology
- Principles of Physical Science
- Principles of Physics
- Principles of Programming & Coding
- Principles of Robotics & Artificial Intelligence
- Principles of Scientific Research
- Principles of Sustainability
- Principles of Zoology

Health
- Addictions, Substance Abuse & Alcoholism
- Adolescent Health & Wellness
- Aging
- Cancer
- Community & Family Health Issues
- Complementary & Alternative Medicine
- Genetics and Inherited Conditions
- Infectious Diseases and Conditions
- Magill's Medical Guide
- Nutrition
- Principles of Health: Anxiety & Stress
- Principles of Health: Diabetes
- Principles of Health: Obesity
- Principles of Health: Pain Management
- Psychology & Behavioral Health
- Women's Health

Careers
- Careers in Building Construction
- Careers in Business
- Careers in Chemistry
- Careers in Communications & Media
- Careers in Education & Training
- Careers in Environment & Conservation
- Careers in Financial Services
- Careers in Gaming
- Careers in Green Energy
- Careers in Healthcare
- Careers in Hospitality & Tourism
- Careers in Human Services
- Careers in Information Technology
- Careers in Law, Criminal Justice & Emergency Services
- Careers in Manufacturing & Production
- Careers in Nursing
- Careers in Physics
- Careers in Protective Services
- Careers in Psychology & Behavioral Health
- Careers in Public Administration
- Careers in Sales, Insurance & Real Estate
- Careers in Science & Engineering
- Careers in Social Media
- Careers in Sports & Fitness
- Careers in Sports Medicine & Training
- Careers in Technical Services & Equipment Repair
- Careers in the Arts: Fine, Performing & Visual
- Careers in Transportation
- Careers in Writing & Editing
- Careers Outdoors
- Careers Overseas
- Careers Working with Infants & Children

Business
- Principles of Business: Accounting
- Principles of Business: Economics
- Principles of Business: Entrepreneurship
- Principles of Business: Finance
- Principles of Business: Globalization
- Principles of Business: Leadership
- Principles of Business: Management
- Principles of Business: Marketing

Grey House Publishing | Salem Press | H.W. Wilson | 4919 Route, 22 PO Box 56, Amenia NY 12501-0056

2020 Title List

Visit www.HWWilsonInPrint.com for Product Information, Table of Contents, and Sample Pages.

The Reference Shelf
Affordable Housing
Aging in America
Alternative Facts, Post-Truth and the Information War
American Military Presence Overseas
Arab Spring
Artificial Intelligence
Business of Food, The
Campaign Trends & Election Law
Conspiracy Theories
Democracy Evolving
Dinosaurs
Embracing New Paradigms in Education
Faith & Science
Families - Traditional & New Structures
Future of U.S. Economic Relations: Mexico, Cuba, & Venezuela
Global Climate Change
Graphic Novels and Comic Books
Guns in America
Hate Crimes
Immigration
Immigration in the United States
Internet Abuses & Privacy Rights
Internet Law
Internet Safety
LGBTQ in the 21st Century
Marijuana Reform
National Debate Topic 2014/2015: The Ocean
National Debate Topic 2015/2016: Surveillance
National Debate Topic 2016/2017: US/China Relations
National Debate Topic 2017/2018: Education Reform
National Debate Topic 2018/2019: Immigration
National Debate Topic 2019/2020: Arms Sales
National Debate Topic 2020/2021: Criminal Justice Reform
New Frontiers in Space
The News and its Future
Paranormal, The
Politics of the Oceans
Pollution
Prescription Drug Abuse
Propaganda and Misinformation
Racial Tension in a Postracial Age
Reality Television
Representative American Speeches, Annual Edition
Rethinking Work
Revisiting Gender
Robotics
Russia
Social Networking
Social Services for the Poor
Space Exploration and Development
Sports in America
The American Dream
The Brain
The Digital Age
The South China Sea Conflict
The Supreme Court
The Transformation of American Cities
The Two Koreas
U.S. Infrastructure
Whistleblowers

Core Collections
Children's Core Collection
Fiction Core Collection
Graphic Novels Core Collection
Middle & Junior High School Core
Public Library Core Collection: Nonfiction
Senior High Core Collection
Young Adult Fiction Core Collection

Current Biography
Current Biography Cumulative Index 1946-2017
Current Biography Monthly Magazine
Current Biography Yearbook

Readers' Guide to Periodical Literature
Abridged Readers' Guide to Periodical Literature
Readers' Guide to Periodical Literature

Indexes
Index to Legal Periodicals & Books
Short Story Index
Book Review Digest

Sears List
Sears List of Subject Headings
Sears: Lista de Encabezamientos de Materia

History
Speeches of the American Presidents
American Reformers
American Game Changers: Invention, Innovation & Transformation

Facts About Series
Facts About American Immigration
Facts About China
Facts About the 20th Century
Facts About the Presidents
Facts About the World's Languages

Nobel Prize Winners
Nobel Prize Winners: 1901-1986
Nobel Prize Winners: 1987-1991
Nobel Prize Winners: 1992-1996
Nobel Prize Winners: 1997-2001
Nobel Prize Winners: 2002-2018

Famous First Facts
Famous First Facts
Famous First Facts About American Politics
Famous First Facts About Sports
Famous First Facts About the Environment
Famous First Facts: International Edition

American Book of Days
The American Book of Days
The International Book of Days

Grey House Publishing | Salem Press | H.W. Wilson | 4919 Route, 22 PO Box 56, Amenia NY 12501-0056